W9-BGX-944

Vietnam Stories

VIETNAM
Stories

A Judge's Memoir

COLONEL JACK CROUCHET
U.S. Army Retired

UNIVERSITY PRESS OF COLORADO

Published by the University Press of Colorado
P.O. Box 849
Niwot, Colorado 80544
(303) 530-5337

Printed in the United States of America.

The University Press of Colorado is a cooperative publishing enterprise supported, in part, by Adams State College, Colorado State University, Fort Lewis College, Mesa State College, Metropolitan State College of Denver, University of Colorado, University of Northern Colorado, University of Southern Colorado, and Western State College of Colorado.

The paper used in this publication meets the minimum requirements of the American National Standard for Information Sciences—Permanence of Paper for Printed Library Materials. ANSI Z39.48-1984.

Library of Congress Cataloging-in-Publication Data

Crouchet, Jack, 1923–
Vietnam stories: a judge's memoir / Jack Crouchet.
p. cm.
ISBN 0-87081-453-2 (casebound: alk. paper)
1. Trials (Military offenses) — United States. 2. United States — Armed Forces — Vietnam. I. Title.
KF7641.C76 1997
343.73'0143 —dc21 97-15887
CIP

10 9 8 7 6 5 4 3 2 1

This book is lovingly dedicated to:
My wife Sonja
My son Michael
My daughter Carolyn
and
The memory of my brother George

Contents

Preface

Poor Horseface! I often think of him when washing my face. He remains seared in my memory as a legacy from Vietnam. No one knew his real name. His fellow countrymen, who were torturing him, and the Americans, who had captured him in an open field, simply called him Horseface, laughing when they did. He was tied to the ground as his captors placed a soaking towel over his face to prevent breathing. He squirmed, kicked, and sometimes broke the ropes that bound him.

"Wave a finger if you decide to tell us where your comrades are!" the interrogators advised. But his fingers never waved, although his whole body shook with terror. When it appeared that he was about to suffocate, they removed the towel, drenched it again in a pail of water, and placed it over his face. Several wet towels and less than a gallon of water drowned the victim. A pathetic ending to one who might have been only a landless peasant! No one protested or shed a tear. No funeral or proper burial for Horseface! Descendants would never pay homage to his remains as they would to other ancestors. His body was rolled into a ditch and dirt was spread over the corpse to keep it out of sight and to prevent the stench from later offending his inquisitors.

Meanwhile, on the spacious roof garden of the Rex Hotel in Saigon, a Filipino band blared away as American men and women danced and dined on steaks inspected by army veterinarians, served by uniformed Vietnamese waiters. Others swam in the adjoining pool or sat in lounge chairs observing the skyline, lit by flares dropped from helicopters, and listened to the distant rumble of bombs and mortar shells. From the top of the Rex, their war was not unpleasant.

Simultaneously, young Americans in cold, wet forests listened for the rustle of Viet Cong or North Vietnamese soldiers. Some were wounded, some were dying, others had just died. All the living were afraid. Across the mountains, deltas, and plains of Vietnam, American soldiers were on patrol, engaged in firefights or sleeping in bunkers or hammocks hoping to remain alive until morning. Nineteen-year-olds were longing for their mothers or sweethearts, praying to live until they could be together again.

I was somewhere between all of those places. My job as a military judge took me to every location where commanders ordered trials by general courts-martial. It was in those proceedings that I learned of the torture of the "Horsefaces" and other offenses committed by soldiers and officers in Vietnam. It is not pleasant to be reminded of those horrors, but they were an inevitable result of the engagements of more than half a million American troops in Vietnam. To think that no crimes would be committed there is as unrealistic as to expect that large cities in the United States would be free of criminal activity.

While living at the Rex Hotel, I enjoyed the amenities available to Americans in Saigon. I also had the opportunity to observe the contrast between United States and Vietnamese citizens, especially the million refugees forced into the city, longing to return to little plots of land where they had worked and their ancestors had died for centuries.

There were three United States Army military judges in Vietnam, all living in Saigon but constantly traveling around the country, when I was stationed there from July 1968 to July 1969. We worked long hours, more often than not into the night. Being a judge wasn't as difficult as assignment to a combat unit, but we were in combat zones four or five days each week. We had our share of sleeping in bunkers, running to shelters during mortar attacks, and flying in helicopters and small planes over hostile territory. But, when we returned to Saigon and our comfortable rooms, we also had the pleasant opportunity to experience the culture of the city as well as meeting reporters, newscasters, movie stars, sports celebrities, and visiting firemen from Washington.

The duties of a military judge are similar to the duties of any judge in a criminal case in the United States with unlimited jurisdiction. He rules on objections, motions, and other matters of law as well as instructs the members of the court on their duties prior to findings and, if necessary, sentence. The court members' duties are similar to those of jurors in civilian criminal cases.

The official title of the prosecutor is trial counsel, but he is frequently referred to as prosecutor. The person being tried is the accused, but frequently is also called the defendant. The staff judge advocate is the legal adviser to the commanding general who orders the general court-martial, but does not participate in the trial itself. During the trial, the members of the court (jury) are frequently addressed, or referred to, as "the court": for example, "the court will disregard the last statement of the witness."

Because of the nature of my assignment in Vietnam, much of what I have written in this memoir naturally concerns crimes and courts-martial. These subjects, however, are only a portion of my experience there. Other matters that I have observed, as well as my opinions of prevailing American attitudes, are also included. All references pertaining to conditions and titles are those that existed during 1968–1969.

All of the trials in which military judges in Vietnam participated were general courts-martial. Special courts-martial and summary courts-martial, with which I was not involved, were used for lesser offenses. Neither of those types of courts had the authority to administer a punitive discharge or impose confinement at hard labor in excess of six months. Additionally, certain commanders had the authority to impose nonjudicial punishment for minor offenses, which never resulted in confinement at hard labor or discharge from the service.

Except for the chapter "Love's Labor Lost," all of the cases described or referred to are based upon cases actually tried in Vietnam during the period of my tour there. Liberties have been taken in a few of the cases by changing the names of persons whose mention might cause embarrassment so many years later. "Love's Labor Lost" is a story based upon many different events that I witnessed or heard about, none of which resulted in a court-martial.

This memoir is not a scholarly report with statistical accuracy, but is written with the purpose of presenting to readers an interesting overview of the cases tried, and sharing with them my own unique experiences. For example, "Silent Night" is compiled from four different cases over which I presided. "Riot at the LBJ," although written as one chapter, is in fact based upon the testimony of about thirty witnesses I heard in six different cases resulting from the same incident. The quotation from the Court of Review at the beginning of "Rape and Murder at the Americal" is verbatim. The testimony of witnesses in that chapter is quoted from several records of trial. The accounts of "I Want a Body Count," as well as the facts reported in other cases, are based upon evidence introduced during those trials. Organizations, when mentioned, are accurately stated.

The war in Vietnam, which lasted longer than any other American military experience and was fought against a determined and indigenous enemy, was so different from all of our subsequent military involvements that comparison with them for military justice purposes is impracticable. In Vietnam, ground troops were officially restricted to fighting within the confines of South Vietnam (except for the brief excursion into Cambodia in 1970), although the enemy retreated into Laos, Cambodia, and North Vietnam at any time. Body count and kill ratio were considered to be measures of success or failure. Most soldiers were draftees as opposed to later military operations with all-volunteer forces.

In 1969, after I returned from Vietnam, important changes in military law were made by both the president and Congress.

The accused, for example, was provided the option of being tried by military judge alone, a choice not available while I was in Vietnam. At the same time, although our duties did not change, the title of law officer, as we were officially designated in Vietnam, was changed to military judge, a term that had been in common usage for many years. For convenience, and because the duties were the same, I have used the term military judge throughout this memoir. We were usually addressed as such.

Other changes to the Uniform Code of Military Justice and the *Manual for Courts-Martial* have been made over the years, including the renaming of what were previously known as the Court of Military Review and the Court of Military Appeals. The terms used in this memoir are those that existed during the time when I was in Vietnam.

The literature of our Vietnam experience is voluminous. There are hundreds of histories, novels, memoirs, and criticisms in existence, in addition to the thousands of short stories and articles that appear in anthologies, magazines, journals, and military publications. In my opinion, the best account describing events that eventually led to a court-martial and the court-martial itself is Daniel Lang's *Casualties of War*, which first appeared in the *New Yorker*. There are several excellent books, in addition to official reports and investigations, describing the My Lai massacre, which occurred in March 1968. Twelve members of the unit responsible for that incident were tried, but only one conviction resulted, that of Lieutenant William L. Calley. Recommended books describing that event are the earlier works of Seymour Hersh and the more recent *Four Hours in My Lai* by Michael Bilton and Kevin Sim.

Twenty years after I left Vietnam, Colonel William S. Fulton Jr., Clerk of Court at the United States Army Judiciary in Falls Church, Virginia, assisted me in obtaining over six thousand pages of material from records in cases over which I presided in Vietnam and almost as many pages of other courts-martial tried during the same period but in which I did not participate. It is the memories recalled from reading and copying those records that form the core of the cases described in this book.

I am especially indebted to retired Colonels Richard Arkow, Darrell Peck, John Webb, and Herbert Green, who reminisced with me about certain cases and circumstances that made the cases tried long ago come to life again for me. I would like also to thank Professor Myrek Land of the University of Nevada–Reno who first encouraged me to write these stories, and to Dr. Stephen Leonard, chairman of the History Department of Metropolitan State College in Denver, for encouraging me to continue writing.

Jack Crouchet

The Parable of the Old Man and the Young[1]

So Abram rose, and clave the wood, and went,
And took the fire with him, and a knife.
And they sojourned both of them together,
Isaac the first-born spake and said, My Father,
Behold the preparations, fire and iron,
But where the lamb for this burnt-offering?
Then Abram bound the youth with belts and straps,
And builded parapets and trenches there,
And stretched forth the knife to slay his son.
When lo! an angel called him out of heaven,
Saying, Lay not thy hand upon the lad,
Neither do anything to him. Behold,
A ram, caught in a thicket by its horns;
Offer the Ram of Pride instead of him.
But the old man would not so, but slew his son,
And half the seed of Europe, one by one.

Wilfred Owen
Killed in action on November 4, 1918

---

1. From the collected poems of Wilfred Owen, edited by John Stallworthy. Acknowledgment is made to New Directions Publishing Corporation; the Executor of the Estate of Harold Owen; and Chatto and Windows, Ltd.

Vietnam Stories

CHAPTER ONE

Departure

I was on a Braniff jet that lumbered down the runway of San Francisco International Airport and climbed into the sky heading for Vietnam on the morning of July 8, 1968. As the plane leveled off, a stewardess told the 160 officers on board to make themselves comfortable, it would be a long trip. What a way to go to a dirty war! I thought to myself, as each of us was given a pair of blue-and-white knitted booties. "It's going to be first class all the way," she said, "so leave your troubles behind!"

I had left my family and friends behind and, as far as I could tell, my troubles lay ahead — first class or not. Yet, strangely enough, there were no evident signs of depression among the passengers. The farewells were finished — we had said our goodbyes.

The chartered civilian plane offered every amenity I would have expected if our destination had been Washington. Hostesses, stereo sets, hot food, and movies. There was scarcely time to test the reclining seats before a stewardess offered free drinks. Nothing lacking in the way of creature comforts. But I was in no mood for roasted peanuts and hot towels, and wanted only to escape by sleeping and keeping to myself.

I don't recall who my seat companions were on that long flight to Saigon. I ate the meals served and briefly got off the plane in Honolulu, but mostly I slept and dreamed about the life I left behind.

I had spent one week in Saigon eight years before. I stopped there on a flight between Korea, where I had just completed a tour of duty, and Switzerland, where my family was waiting. My intention was to meet a friend on a diplomatic mission to Vietnam, but I was informed at the American embassy that he had not yet arrived. To my chagrin, I learned that transportation to Europe would not be available until the following week when an embassy flight would be stopping on its way from California to Spain through the Far East.

Ton Son Nhut Airport in Saigon was relatively quiet in 1960. We were met at planeside by Vietnamese hostesses in colorful *au dais*, the national women's dress consisting of a fitted bodice, loose-fitting pajama-like trousers, covered front and back with rectangular silk pieces, reaching almost to the ground and blowing aimlessly in the wind. They spoke with delicate voices and charming accents, explaining what was expected from us during our stay in Vietnam. Do not use the black market, be careful of the drinking water, watch out for terrorists. At that time, there were about one thousand Americans in the country, mostly acting as advisers to the South Vietnamese army. A few had been killed, mostly in the provinces. In Saigon, President Ngo Dinh Diem, America's surrogate, seemed to be firmly in control.

Among the people who deplaned, a young army dentist from California, Captain Len Steinberg, and I were the only two on unofficial visits. Others were reporting for assignments or returning from duty elsewhere. Len and I were told that we would be provided transportation to a United States billet where we would be allowed to stay for the duration of our visit.

I was fascinated with Saigon from the moment I arrived. Riding to our assigned quarters, I was impressed by being in a city the world was reading about, yet everything seemed normal: farmers in rice paddies, large hotels, painted villas surrounded by walls covered with flowers, French restaurants, modern shops, and an exciting atmosphere. The streets were crowded with virtually all modes of transportation, motorized and otherwise. Citroën taxis and pedicabs, or *cyclo pousses* as they were called in Saigon, were everywhere. It was the people, though, who captured my attention more than the environs. Mode of dress and tools often indicated profession or trade. I especially remember the women carrying bamboo poles across the back of their shoulders with dangling ropes at each end holding pans stacked one on top of the other, filled with a variety of cooked Vietnamese food ready for consumption. I looked forward with great anticipation to exploring the city.

Len and I were taken to the Five Oceans Hotel in Cholon, the Chinese section of the city. It was a typical army transient facility that offered nothing exceptional in the way of physical comforts, but was quite suitable for our needs. From our windows, we observed a nightly ritual that added atmosphere to the environment. About midnight, farmers began arriving in an empty parking lot to set up little stalls, stocking them with vegetables, dry goods, and trinkets that they transported on bicycles or little carts. By 2 a.m., the first customers arrived, and buying continued for a few hours. The noise from the market was not disturbing, but rather soothing. After awakening in the morning about seven o'clock, I would see only the empty parking lot. The farmers had vanished into the villages and the townspeople into their homes.

My friend and I learned quickly that our transportation problems could be solved easily by hiring a pedicab for the entire day and as late into the night as we wished. Chao Tan, the Chinese man who operated the vehicle running his with his bare feet, soon became our friend and waited each morning for us to leave the hotel. He was quite willing to transport us to whatever destination we desired, and some that we did not.

One evening, we allowed Chao Tan to take us to a sophisticated night club in Cholon where we were accosted at the entrance by a dozen or so Vietnamese and Chinese hostesses, in single-line formation, dressed in their finest national costumes. We expressed no interest in attaching ourselves to any of the girls, but our desires had no effect on what was about to happen. A waiter led us, and two hostesses followed, to a table in a room with a band the size of Woody Herman's Thundering Herd. We were not so naive as to believe that the hostesses would sit with us for the pleasure of our company, but after a short discussion, Len and I decided that the experience would be worth the expense. Within minutes, one of the girls stood up and said as she departed: "Please excuse me, I have to see the boss!"

The hostess returned thirty minutes later and the conversation among the four of us resumed. Five minutes later, the second girl stood up and said: "Excuse me please, I have to see the boss!"

"Why do you girls always have to visit the boss?" Len asked.

"Oh, he is very important, and he is very strict!" was the reply, and the remaining hostess began to talk rapidly in an attempt to keep our interest high.

The charade of one girl leaving and the other returning occurred again shortly after the second hostess returned. Len then took a turn at excusing himself and returned a minute later quite beside himself.

"These girls are working two tables!"

"Oh no, no, no, sir, we never do that!" said our lone companion.

"Oh yes!" replied my friend, "I saw the other girl at another table with two Americans."

"Oh, they are only very good friends. She only tells them hello!" was her reply.

"Hello, my ass! She's holding hands with both of them. Let's get out of here!"

I tried to calm Len down but failed to do so before the manager appeared, asking what the problem was. Not wanting to remain in the club or participate in a dispute, I settled hastily with the manager, even though Len refused to share the costs. The girls were in a rage as they returned to the end of the line outside the large room where they would have the longest wait for new customers.

We found Chao Tan asleep in his vehicle. "Take us to Saigon!" I said.

"Aha, Saigon number one! I will show you around! We go to the Rue Catinat!" he replied, and off we went into the balmy night through the streets of Cholon and Saigon. The driver took us by the presidential palace where Diem and his family were ensconced. Len and I talked about the fortuitous circumstances that put us physically so close to people we had read so much about. Chao Tan next took us to the great French cathedral in the center of Saigon and past the Continental Palace and Caravelle hotels down the Rue Catinat. Although Diem's sister-in-law, Madame Nhu, had closed the dance halls and night clubs along the famous street, there was still entertainment to be found. Just sitting in an outdoor cafe drinking beer in the warm evening air, watching the parade of exotic people and beautiful women in flowing au dais was more exciting to us than a night club would have been. This was the street of novels and history. Graham Green would have felt at home!

We sat at an outside table of a restaurant on the Rue Catinat until it closed, and started back to our hotel in the open cab well past midnight. Along the main street that joined the cities, we observed a large tent with people inside. I ordered the driver to stop and walked into the tent past dozens of motorcycles and bicycles. There were hundreds of men, all looking at me, the only Caucasian there. A fiery, patriotic speech in progress came to a halt, but I was not harmed or bothered. My act was more foolish than brave. It contrasted with my action the next day when I merely wanted to cross a small bridge into another part of Cholon, but graciously accepted the advice of a Vietnamese policeman who advised me not to do so.

Colonel Paul Durbin, a judge advocate officer whom I had previously known, was stationed in Vietnam and living in Saigon at the time of my visit there. When I called, he extended an invitation to visit his office and offered to act as a guide to the city.

Len and I went to the United States compound, located between Cholon and Saigon, where Colonel Durbin's office was located. As we casually spent a few minutes observing some Vietnamese concessionaires within the enclosure, Lieutenant General Samuel T. Williams, who commanded all the American forces in Vietnam, walked out of the headquarters building. When his eyes lighted on the two of us, he came to an abrupt halt. It was quite unsettling to be stared down by a three-star general. The Vietnamese had not bothered us as we walked along their streets, but now I was concerned that we might be ordered to leave the country, or at least be restricted to our hotel, by a fellow American. Without changing his focus, the general whispered something to his aide who came quickly to check our identifications. He reported back to the general who then continued his march, not letting us out of his line of sight, until he reached the gate to the compound. I thought he might be suggesting that we had no business in Saigon and should take the next flight out of town.

Colonel Durbin had invited the judge advocate general of the South Vietnamese Army to meet me in his office, for no reason other than the latter was once in the United States and had expressed an interest in meeting American lawyers. By coincidence, I had previously met the general when he was visiting the Pentagon and I had been assigned as his escort while touring the building and viewing a training film. We had a delightful visit that flattered me because his French was superior to mine, and he really seemed to remember me from the Pentagon.

After the visit, Len excused himself and Colonel Durbin took me to the beautiful home where he and his family lived, together with servants, on the Rue Pasteur. On the following day, we had lunch at the Cercle Sportif, which had been the gathering place of the French upper class before World War II and during the first Indo-Chinese war. It was then frequented by Americans, high-ranking Vietnamese officers and politicians, and some of the remaining French civilians who made Saigon their home. At the Cercle Sportif, sitting beside the swimming pool sipping a *citron presse,* I saw a bikini bathing suit for the first time. After lunch, we toured the Saigon golf course, the spacious Phu Tho race track, the temples and gardens surrounding the zoo, a few pagodas, and the beautiful tree-lined boulevards on which the opera house, cathedral, presidential palace, and grand hotels were located.

On the plane from San Francisco eight years later, drifting in and out of sleep, these pleasant memories of my former visit to Vietnam haunted me. I wondered idly how much Saigon and my own life would be changed.

CHAPTER TWO

Arrival in Saigon

A half hour before landing at Ton Son Nhut on July 10, the pilot announced that we were approaching Vietnam. Beneath us were golden beaches on either side merging into lush green mountains and forests that, under other circumstances, might have been a garden spot of the world. How could this beautiful land and sea, which appeared so peaceful from above, contain such misery below? My eyes riveted on the landscape until we landed in Saigon.

What a contrast from 1960! Ton Son Nhut had been transformed into the busiest airport in the world. Military and civilian planes of all descriptions in the air and on the ground; helicopters like birds in the sky; military people everywhere. There was nothing romantic about landing this time. No pretty girls in au dais to meet us. We grabbed our luggage without ceremony and entered the terminal for a brief processing. That done, I felt lost among soldiers from several nations and Vietnamese civilians, some rich with servants and others carrying all their worldly possessions in rags or cardboard boxes.

I found my way to a military phone. I contacted the judge advocate office of the Military Assistance Command Vietnam (MACV), a joint command for all American armed forces, from which military judges received logistical support, including offices. The sergeant major promised to dispatch a vehicle for me immediately.

While waiting for transportation, I witnessed the first of a thousand little scenarios one did not read about, but were endemic to Vietnam. A group of Korean officers, their country's finest, were also waiting for transportation. Surrounding us were beggars, some with babies, all poorly dressed, and some with apparent diseases. I gave a few small coins to one family, but the Korean officers abused them by speaking harshly and pushing them aside. The irony of foreigners acting superior to victims in their native land struck me as particularly cruel. The beggars, however, did not react adversely to the insults, but submitted passively to their apparent fate in life.

Within minutes, I was pleasantly surprised to see a jeep coming toward me driven by an old friend, Lieutenant Colonel Joseph Ammerman. Joe was an army lawyer assigned to MACV, with whom I had previously served in Europe. We greeted each other warmly but could have no serious discussion because of the noise from planes, people, and traffic. In less than ten minutes, however, we were at MACV headquarters, which was on the periphery of Ton Son Nhut.

"My God, Joe, this looks like a little Pentagon!" I said.

"It is," he replied. "Come in."

The one-story air-conditioned building, newly built by the United States government, spread over several acres of land, afforded welcome relief from the heat and noise of the outside world. The personnel in the judge advocate office consisted of approximately twenty United States military personnel and ten Vietnamese civilians. The separate office for the military judges displayed the names of Colonel Paul Tobin and Lieutenant Colonel Richard Snyder. After introductions all around, Joe took me to the judges' office, which was equipped with three large desks and chairs, many books, and several phones, but was devoid of human beings.

"Where are Paul and Dick?" I asked, referring to the other judges in Vietnam.

Joe sat down in one of the leather chairs to make himself comfortable before replying: "They're both out of the country."

"Where?"

"Well, Paul went to Korea, Japan, and Okinawa. This is unusual, because judges ordinarily try cases only in Vietnam and Okinawa. Dick went to Japan on leave and is not scheduled to try any cases after his return since he'll be here only a few days."

"When is Paul coming back?" I asked.

"I don't know. I see he's blocked out on the calendar for about ten days or so. He has no cases scheduled after his return, whenever that might be."

I looked at the three large homemade charts on the wall to which he pointed. They represented the months of June, July, and August, 1968. Each chart contained thirty-five spaces, five rows of seven blocks over which the days of a specific month were entered on an acetate covering. In addition, the names of the judges and places where cases had been tried or were scheduled to be tried were entered with different-colored grease pencils. Paul used black; Dick, yellow. Since Dick was leaving soon, only the word "goodbye" was written in yellow after the date of his scheduled return from Japan. The black line indicated approximately where Paul was at the moment.

"For heaven's sake, who's trying cases in Vietnam now?" I asked Joe.

"That's the problem! All the jurisdictions have been calling for judges and there was no one here. The sergeant major has been recording all messages, though. I thought you'd want to see those!" he said, pointing to a stack of notes on the desk that was assigned to me. " And, by the way, I hate to tell you this, but I've authorized the setting of a case for you in Long Binh tomorrow. The people there are in a panic because half their witnesses are due to return to the United States in a few days. I thought you would understand."

"Great!" I said "Where is Long Binh?"

"No sweat," he replied. "It's about twenty-five miles north of here but we've got transportation all set up. I'll take you to Hotel 3, the helicopter pad at Ton Son Nhut. A helicopter will be waiting, and you'll be met in Long Binh by someone from the judge advocate office in USARV, which is an acronym for United States Army Vietnam, the army element of MACV. Now, why don't you read your messages? We have a couple of hours before leaving for the Rex Hotel, where Paul said you could use his room. Do what you have to and I'll get some of my own work done."

When Joe left the office, I read through the messages, all requests for judges. Before answering any of them, I chose a red grease pencil and added my name to the legend below the chart, indicating that I would henceforth be accounted for with the color red on the acetate. I wrote "Long Binh" and my name in the block over July 11. I took a couple of steps back and looked at the calendar with a touch of pride. I was already scheduled for a case in Vietnam and had not yet sat in the chair I was to occupy for one year.

After that small accomplishment, I began to answer the messages, and before Joe returned at six-thirty, I had notes and a red line running through the rest of July and part of August. I had the dubious pleasure of looking forward to trips to Camp Evans, which was near the Demilitarized Zone; Pleiku; Lai Kai; and three to Long Binh, where several different jurisdictions were located.

The ride from MACV to the Rex Hotel, where Joe and the judges lived, was an experience that made me regret my decision not to retire from the army when I had an opportunity to do so. The uncontrolled traffic had increased exponentially since my first visit to Saigon. Joe drove the office sedan and did not hesitate to claim the right of way, whether he had it or not. Who was to know who had the right of way! I mused, with traffic streaming in all directions. Not unexpectedly, we were jolted by an impact with another vehicle which I heard but did not see.

"You had better stop, Joe. We've been in an accident!"

He looked at me and shrugged his shoulders. "I'd never find the son of a bitch who hit me!"

"But maybe you hit him!" I replied.

"Be reasonable, man, this isn't the United States. The people here don't know how to drive!"

I could only speculate as to who "the people" were, since there were hundreds of vehicles being driven by people of different nationalities.

This was no longer the beautiful Saigon that I had known. The shade trees were poisoned by carbon monoxide; the bougainvillea and hibiscus, which had given color to the city, had disappeared. Wire fencing surrounded the tables of sidewalk cafes to protect patrons against "zappers." Soldiers stood guard in strategic places along the road. But downtown Saigon was familiar to me, both from my previous visit and pictures in current newspapers and magazines.

Within the mass of humanity in the city, I was surprised to see a large number of Caucasians on the streets. I first thought that they were French civilians who had remained behind after the loss of their own war. Joe advised me, however, that the numbers of civilians associated with the armed forces, including Department of Defense personnel, business people, and laborers from many countries, were staggering.

After passing the Continental Palace Hotel, which I recognized immediately, we turned right, off Tu Do Street, which had been the Rue Catinat during my prior visit, on to Le Loi, which was the main artery between Saigon and Cholon. On the left side of the first block was Lan Son Park, once beautifully landscaped with flowers and shrubs, but now the site of a gigantic statue of two Vietnamese soldiers in a crouched position. On the right side of the first block was a conglomeration of five-story buildings contiguous to one another. Within the buildings, which occupied an entire square block, were stores, bars, cafes, shops of many descriptions, and apartments on the upper level, some occupied by American civilians. A maze of alleys ran through the buildings at street level, and elevators located near the entrances provided passage to the upper floors.

On the right side of the second block of Le Loi was another park, across which people walked in all directions. The first building on the right side of the third block was the seven-story Rex Hotel, crowned by a roof garden, clearly visible.

The creaky Rex elevator chugged its way to the fifth floor where the judges' rooms were located. Paul's room was quite large, located on the inside of the building, having no view other than structures within the square block in which the Rex was located. It was furnished with a single bed, a shower, a writing table, several chairs, and a divan, which I considered to be luxurious surroundings. I felt a sense of excitement to be in Vietnam, but perhaps that feeling resulted from the fact that I felt secure in the room that I occupied.

At about eight o'clock, Joe came to pick me up for dinner. We walked to the roof. On the right side of the top of the staircase, there was an officers' open mess, which was more than adequate for wartime conditions. But there were better things than that. "Let's eat in the steakhouse tonight," Joe suggested.

"Whatever," I replied.

We turned left and entered the roof garden with tables in the center, a bandstand in one corner, and a long bar along the inside wall. Joe told me that Joey Bishop, Martha Ray, Georgie Jessel and other "walking through Vietnam" celebrities were frequently seen here. The bar and its surroundings, however, was not the pièce de résistance. Through the wall beyond the bar was a door leading to a room that contained pleasant surprises. In the center was an open grill with burning charcoal next to a table of the finest steaks I had ever seen. Surrounding the grill and steaks were tables with tablecloths where people were eating and drinking. We had to pay to eat here, but that was an expense worth the price. The steakhouse on top of the Rex was the place where war correspondents in Saigon and important official United States visitors came to dinner. Some of the diners in our presence were recognizable from the television news back home. There were many fine restaurants in Saigon, but the top of the Rex was the favorite for those authorized to be there. Here was beef inspected by the United States Army Veterinary Corps, at a very reasonable price.

After dinner, Joe and I walked a few yards to the rooftop swimming pool, which was surrounded by lounge chairs. Waiters attended people enjoying drinks in the evening air, observing flares dropped from helicopters all around and over the center of the city. Near the railing on the roof by the side of the pool, we talked about our past and future lives.

When I looked directly below us, my sense of serenity evaporated. There were people on the street with outstretched hands, begging from every American or foreigner passing by. These people were some of the tens of thousands who overflowed from the tents and tin shanties that surrounded Saigon. They were victims of the war, displaced from their villages, hungry and poor. What we left on our plates would have fed many of them. I regretted having eaten.

"What about those people, Joe? Who is responsible for them?"

"They are just a handful of refugees, many from the Tet Offensive in January and February," he replied. "There are two million people in Saigon, a city not big enough for half that number. I'm not smart enough to say where the responsibility lies. Perhaps you will get used to the sight."

Suddenly, from somewhere in the vicinity, we heard a burst of rifle fire. Military training caused us to drop to the concrete floor. From the floor, between the pillars of the railing, I looked down again at the people below, still begging. They did not seek refuge from the rifle fire. To them, perhaps, danger was a necessary risk to survival.

CHAPTER THREE

Surprises

On the morning following my introduction to the Rex, Joe drove me to Hotel 3. Eight hundred helicopters took off and landed there each day. Even at seven in the morning, they were coming in and departing like flies on a dunghill. But the operation was efficient. I merely announced my presence to the radio operator on duty and proceeded to the VIP lounge, where I waited until the helicopter designated to take me to Long Binh was ready for departure.

My first helicopter flight from Saigon seemed surreal. The crew consisted of a pilot, copilot, and two soldiers manning machine guns mounted near the spaces where the doors had been. From the air, Saigon was still unbelievably beautiful. An astonishing number of architecturally diverse buildings, villas, pagodas, churches, parks, and swimming pools with clear green water were visible. Forests and rice paddies with sporadic evidence of earth and trees torn apart by bombs and artillery fire were never out of sight. All around us were the ubiquitous helicopters and airplanes. I was still in awe when we landed at Long Binh fifteen minutes later. An officer from USARV was waiting and drove me to the courtroom.

USARV headquarters was in a compound consisting of several long buildings, connected in a U-shape, equally as impressive as the ones at MACV. They were made of concrete and glass, two stories high, completely air conditioned. A news magazine had recently reported a story about the construction of a sixty-thousand-dollar flagpole with concrete base to complement the existing structures.

The courtroom in Long Binh was as accommodating as any I had used in the United States and far superior to anything I would see elsewhere in Vietnam. Five feet from the back wall was a long table reaching from one side of the room to the other, behind which were nine leather chairs. This area, for use by the court members, could only be entered from a deliberation room in the rear. The judge's bench and leather chair rested on an elevated platform. Furniture for the prosecutor, defense counsel, accused, and court reporter was new, and there was a railing separating the court area from the spectators.

The prosecutor handed me the necessary docket papers. Happily for me, the case was a simple one and disposed of in a few hours, with time out for lunch. All during the trial, members of the court stared curiously at me. The prosecutor later suggested the probable reason; I was the only person in the courtroom (or possibly in Long Binh) not dressed in combat gear. I had not yet had time to secure the proper clothing.

The case ended at three o'clock in the afternoon, affording time to hustle back to Saigon to unwind from my Trans-Pacific flight. But departing from Long Binh was not as well organized as leaving Saigon. I was brought to the helicopter pad by the prosecutor, who assured me that sooner or later there would be transportation back to Saigon. Indeed, I was there but a moment when I noticed a helicopter with its engines revving up, a sign of hope. Within minutes, a staff car arrived flying a flag with two stars, indicating that a major general was the passenger. I recognized him immediately as the commanding general of a major command. More interesting than that was the fact that I had known him as a brigadier general in Stuttgart, Germany, and had written his will. During the period when we were client and lawyer, he was most cordial, serving coffee and even offering a drink over our legal discussions. Yet, after alighting from his car in Long Binh, he passed me without a glance, and walked quickly to his waiting chopper. Not wanting to appear obviously in need of a ride, I tried to appear nonchalant, as if I were waiting for my own transportation. Immediately after entering the chopper, the general's aide, a prim and proper lieutenant colonel, tapped me on the shoulder and asked courteously: "Are you going to MACV, colonel?"

"Yes, I am," I answered, with a look of hope on my face.

"You may join us in the general's chopper, if you wish."

Of course, I was delighted. "Thank you very much, sir!" I said as I entered, passing in front of the passenger already seated near the door.

The general did not acknowledge my remark, nor my existence, for that matter, but only looked straight ahead with steely blue eyes. Perhaps he grunted but I could not hear because of the engine noise. I fastened my seat belt and we were off on a trip as exciting for me as the one earlier in the day. No words were spoken nor glances exchanged. I could not help but ponder the odds of a crash killing both client and lawyer in which the former did not recognize the latter. Surprise at the probate hearing! I thought. When we arrived at MACV, which had its own landing pad, I exited the helicopter with my briefcase and once more thanked the general. Again, no audible response. Perhaps a grunt.

I began my walk to the headquarters building, passing a parked sedan flying a two-star flag, obviously waiting for the main passenger. As I was walking, the general's car stopped beside me. The aide opened the door on his side, courteously offering me a ride in the front seat, which I gladly accepted. I thanked the general again, but received only a grunt in response. We rode the remaining distance to the main entrance of the building in silence. Upon arrival there, I once again thanked my benefactor. Again, he did not respond, but his aide smiled and said, "You are welcome, Colonel. Have a nice day!"

When I returned to my office, there was a note on the desk from Colonel Red Benoit saying that he and I were invited to General William Westmoreland's house that night. Red was an air force officer assigned to the MACV office whom I had met the previous day. I could hardly contain myself with the thought of such an exalted invitation, and rushed over to Red's office. "Don't be too thrilled, Jack. You are not going to meet General Westmoreland. We're going to see Colonel Harvey."

Colonel Hank Harvey was the MACV judge advocate, a personal friend and former classmate of General Westmoreland. He shared the general's house on Tran Quy Cap near the Cercle Sportif. I think that Red was more excited than I, because he was carefully plotting the route through Saigon to insure arrival at the general's house on time. Red was not sure whether we were being invited for a drink or for dinner, but he assumed it was for dinner. We would play it by ear.

The residence in which General Westmoreland and Colonel Harvey lived was surrounded by a large wall. Vietnamese servants and guards lived within the compound. The large white residence reminded me of an antebellum mansion in the old South. On arrival, we were met at the door by Colonel Harvey, who graciously escorted us into a small sitting room with several overstuffed chairs and a divan.

In addition to the area we occupied, there were living and dining rooms that were air conditioned and separated from the remainder of the downstairs by a large glass partition. A stairway led to a second floor where the occupants lived. At that particular time, General Westmoreland was in the United States awaiting reassignment as chief of staff of the army and would soon be replaced by General Creighton Abrams, who would move into less imposing quarters closer to MACV headquarters.

I surveyed as much of the setting as possible, trying not to be obvious while doing so. This must have been the house of Emperor Bao Dai, I thought, or some other princely official, or perhaps the home of a French governor. I noted that Vietnamese houseboys were fussing around the dining room table set for four:

crystal, china, silver, fresh tablecloth with matching napkins, flowers, the whole bit. I felt uncomfortable in the uniform that I had been working and traveling in all day.

Colonel Harvey mixed drinks as we made small talk, which included a toast to my arrival in Vietnam. The conversation was progressing pleasantly enough when two American men in neatly pressed sport shirts and trousers descended the stairs. After introductions, we knew that one was a colonel in the office of Public Affairs at MACV and the other was a Doctor Somebody, a civilian adviser to General Westmoreland. They poured themselves drinks and joined the conversation. The doctor spoke of his day, but not to Red and me, whom he completely ignored. The colonel joined in the general conversation and, although he did not ignore Red and me, he expressed no real interest in either of us. It did not take long for me to be convinced that our invitation for a visit did not include dinner. I finished my drink quickly.

"Well, Colonel Harvey, this has been delightful, but we must be leaving," I said as I stood up.

"What's your hurry, Jack? There's no need for us to leave now," replied Red, who apparently had not noted the dinner setting for four.

"Of course not. Keep your seats and have another drink!" That was Colonel Harvey speaking, a true gentleman, whose response brought discomfort to his housemates.

While we were passing time with the type of conversation that can be terminated at a moment's notice, there were rumblings in the distance. The glass partition shook quite noticeably. I thought perhaps there was a small earthquake somewhere until the civilian commented, with a smile on his face: "The 52s are out tonight!"

"B–52s?" I asked, rather stupidly.

The civilian stared at me, rattling the ice in his glass, but the others nodded politely. The insipid conversation continued.

Good God in Heaven! I thought. People a few miles from here are being torn to bits as we are sitting in splendor, ignoring the passing of life and destruction of property.

When I stood up a second time, Red joined me as we excused ourselves. No objections were made as we prepared to make our departure. Colonel Harvey was escorting us out when the doorbell rang. All three of the residents walked quickly to the door to welcome their expected guest who proved to be the major general who had favored me with a ride to Saigon in his helicopter a few hours earlier. They happily exchanged greetings and handshakes, but Red and I received only a perfunctory nod and a grunt.

Red and I ate that night in the open mess on top of the Rex without much conversation, watching a bat zooming back and forth between the rafters under the roof. It was little consolation to know that General Westmoreland himself had stayed at the Rex when he first reported for duty in Saigon.

CHAPTER FOUR

Pleiku

My first two cases in Vietnam requiring travel by plane were scheduled for the Fourth Infantry Division at Camp Enari, near Pleiku in the Central Highlands. I took it upon myself to arrange transportation and was directed to report to the military terminal for in-country travel at Ton Son Nhut. I did so at the appointed time, carrying a large briefcase filled with law books and a small suitcase for personal items, wearing a steel helmet, flak jacket, and a .45-caliber pistol with holster, in addition to normal combat gear.

The inside of the military terminal consisted of a long row of wooden desks with various designations crudely written on cardboard attached to the appropriate reporting places. To my chagrin, the line from the desk marked "Pleiku" extended outside the building. There was no place for waiting inside the terminal, nor protection from the sun outside. Servicemen were lying on the grass shielding their eyes from the sun with towels, handkerchiefs, or other suitable items from their duffel bags.

Upon arrival at the Pleiku desk, I was given a slip of paper with numbers and letters printed by hand in ink that constituted my boarding pass. I joined others on the grass outside, used my helmet as a pillow, and tried to shield myself from the sun with arms across my eyes. Paul Tobin had written to his mother that "This is the only place in the world where judicial robes consist of bulletproof vests and steel helmets." I could have added that helmets were also useful to rest one's head.

Shortly before departure, we were each given a box lunch consisting of a peanut butter sandwich, a chocolate bar, and an apple. We were told that there were drinking water and paper cups inside the aircraft.

I had been told at MACV that there were usually two or three spaces in the cockpit where pilots could invite passengers, and I should hope to be so lucky. The first thing that came to my attention upon entering the C–140 was two young women in the cockpit with the pilots. Pretty intelligent young men, I thought to myself, making the same decision I would have made. I think there is something romantic about young pilots flying in a combat zone with beautiful ladies in the cockpit. These women, we were informed over the loudspeaker, were with a USO entertainment group traveling to Pleiku.

The passengers, other than those in the cockpit, were seated on long canvas seats either along the inside body of the aircraft, or in rows set up in conventional seating arrangements. As we leveled off, I carefully surveyed all of the passengers, most of whom were young soldiers newly arrived in Vietnam, identifiable by new clothing and boots, going to uncertain destinations.

During the middle part of 1968, there were over two hundred American soldiers killed in Vietnam each week and more than triple that amount wounded during the same period. Statistically, some of these young men on board, whose average age I presumed to be about nineteen, would be among the casualties of the Fourth Infantry Division, a unit that had already participated in many engagements with the enemy, including the recent Tet Offensive. It was constantly fighting, attempting to rid the highlands of Viet Cong and North Vietnamese regular army forces. As I looked into each of their faces, I pondered whether this one or that one would be later counted among the expected casualties.

There was no horseplay or loud talking among the soldiers, but neither, to my surprise, was there an obvious sense of great apprehension. I was twice the age of most of the passengers and pilots, and felt a sense of relief because I was not expected to go into combat. Perhaps it was better that they could not know the future.

I was happy to arrive in Pleiku where the wet season had not yet ended and the temperature was rather mild. The contrast from Saigon was most welcome. Unlike the soldiers with whom I traveled, who were huddled into formations and marched off to waiting trucks, I was met at planeside by Lieutenant Colonel Darrell Peck, the division staff judge advocate, who was waiting for me in the office jeep. He would take me from the airfield to Camp Enari.

As we drove through Pleiku, I remembered it was here that an incident took place which precipitated the first great escalation of the Vietnam War. On February 7, 1965, Viet Cong forces attacked the airfield on which I had just landed, killing 9 Americans and wounding 128 others. Several helicopters were simultaneously destroyed. In retaliation, President Lyndon Johnson launched Operation Rolling Thunder, which authorized the bombing of North Vietnam and rained destruction on that country until November 1968, almost without interruption. I was curious then, as I am today, about the code name of the operation, apparently taken from a Christian hymn. The term "thunder" was frequently used in scripture to describe God's awesome presence and power.

Montagnard children from the Jarai tribe in the surrounding mountains played and begged for cigarettes or candy along the route through the city. They seemed happy, even with ragged clothes and dirty faces. For hundreds of years, their ancestors had survived invasions and occupations by people foreign to their culture, including their own Vietnamese countrymen. Living with occupiers was a way of life for the Montagnards. They tolerated and worked well with Americans, who in turn employed some of them who were not suited for military duties to perform menial tasks at Camp Enari. Colonel Peck told me affectionately about an elderly mamasan who cleaned the legal office but continued to remove papers and scrub his desk with dirty water in defiance of his repeated protests.

A row of empty little shacks along the route to Camp Enari with names such as Luscious Louise, Tender Touch Massage, Washing Done, Paris Bar, and Trucks Washed provided amusement to me as well as entertainment for the children, who ran in and out as if the buildings had been constructed especially for them as a playground. These shanties, whose names reflected the ingenuity of their previous owners, were shut down for business by order of an American general who had determined that they were detrimental to the morale of his troops.

In the center of Pleiku, we passed a Catholic church where, judging by the number of persons standing about and departing, services had just concluded. The scene, like so many others in Vietnam, seemed incongruous to me. Praying for peace in the midst of war. The church looked quite similar to those in small Louisiana towns where the French had also once exercised their influence. I had forgotten the day was Sunday. One day was like another in Vietnam.

The courtroom in Pleiku was more satisfactory than all the others I used in Vietnam, except for the one in Long Binh. An important factor was the climate, cool enough so that windows could often be kept closed, thus eliminating outside noises. The room was located in the rear of a long wooden building, which also contained the offices of the staff judge advocate, and could be entered through the back door.

I enjoyed going to Pleiku, which I did on three separate occasions, each for several days. At Camp Enari, I was assigned quarters in a three-bedroom trailer equipped with sitting room and bathroom. Two other trailers, for use by the commanding general and other high ranking officials, were nearby. Together, they formed a separate little compound. A guest register in my trailer recorded the names of important persons who had used these quarters before me, including the military historian General

S.L.A. Marshall, several prominent media personalities, and a couple of movie stars.

I was automatically included in the membership of the general's mess at the Fourth Infantry Division. The building, separate from other messes, was partitioned to make facilities for a lounge where members and guests gathered for drinks before and movies after dinner. In the dining area, the commanding general sat at the head of a large round table with his chief of staff, one or two other members of his command, and invited guests. On one occasion, Bernard Weinraub of the *New York Times* and I were both so favored at the same time. The experience of hearing the division's leaders discuss their daily combat activities was exciting. More often than not, I skipped the after-dinner movie and returned to the legal office for visits with personnel assigned there. They were a cheerful group, writing letters, playing games, reading, or just lounging around. A young court reporter was especially adept at making bargains with whomever such bargains were made to obtain the best steaks outside of Saigon. When he was successful, there was a barbecue behind the courtroom, and on those occasions I did not go to the general's mess. Frequently, I played Scrabble with a captain who, without fail, outscored me by a close margin. He was not good enough, however, to convince me that he was doing his best.

Between the courtroom and the commanding general's compound was a small garden, kept meticulously neat and green with grass and other growing things by a Montagnard man who possessed a grin that never seemed to disappear. He squatted there with a pair of scissors and a knife cutting grass or puttering around the bushes and flowers. I looked forward to seeing him every day. He tended a crippled man or boy, probably his blood brother, who never left his side. Whenever one moved, so did the other.

The gardener carried the crippled person on his shoulders to work in the morning and home at night. They lunched together and shared conversation, punctuated by laughter, through the day. I was intrigued by these two people with practically no earthly possessions, one disabled, unable to move distances, and the other with a limited capability to make a living, both always seemingly happy! A man who probably had never been taught that it was one's duty to care for his brother, was doing so, sharing life, not as a duty or responsibility, but out of love and an instinctive feeling that all men are brothers. There was so much we could have learned from them. Even the children I had seen in Pleiku shared among themselves whatever possessions they acquired.

The first case at Camp Enari was not a difficult one, but rather typical of the hundreds I had tried in the past and was to try in the future in Vietnam. Private Rodney Spivey was charged with one specification of disobeying Captain Pat Gossard, his commanding officer, and one specification of unlawfully possessing ten grams of marijuana.

On the morning of the first alleged offense, Captain Gossard ordered Spivey to get his gear together and hop on a truck that was leaving on a combat mission. Spivey told Gossard that he had misplaced his rifle and Gossard replied that he would get another one for him. Spivey testified that he took Gossard's words to mean that he would obtain the rifle immediately, so he stood by waiting and watched as the truck departed for combat without him.

On the morning of the second alleged offense, Spivey was apprehended by Sergeant Claude Zimmer in a part of the city of Pleiku that was off-limits to American troops. As a routine part of the apprehension, Zimmer advised Spivey of his legal rights and performed a search of his clothing. A plastic bag containing ten grams of marijuana was found in Spivey's combat trousers. There was no dispute as to these facts. During the trial, Spivey denied knowledge of the presence of the prohibited substance, and testified in part as follows:

Q: (By the defense counsel) What do you have to say with regard to the marijuana?

A: (By the accused Spivey) I didn't even know I had that on me.

Q: Where had you been?

A: In a bar that never closes.

Q: Now, how long were you there?

A: I was there all night. About a day altogether.

Q: Can you account for how the marijuana might have gotten into your trousers?

A: Yes, I can. There was a *boysan* down there . . .

Q: This what?

A: This boysan . . . And he said, "I'll souvenir you something," and I guess that was it.

Q: You didn't know it was there?

A: No, I didn't.

Spivey explained that "a boysan is a young Vietnamese. He was not a real good friend. He worked around the house . . . On the day before I left, the boysan said 'I'll souvenir you something.' The boysan must have given me the marijuana but I did not see him give it to me. The Vietnamese like me. I guess the Vietnamese say they 'souvenir' you when they give you something. I guess that was it."

After findings of guilty, the prosecutor presented evidence that Spivey had been previously convicted for being disrespectful toward a superior officer and failing to obey a lawful order. He was sentenced to be dishonorably discharged from the army and to be confined at hard labor for four years.

That sentence, however, was by no means final. Like all other general courts-martial, the findings and sentence were subject to several reviews and appeals at which time they were subject to be greatly reduced or disapproved altogether.

CHAPTER FIVE

McNamara's Boys

The second case I tried in Pleiku provided my first experience with a soldier whose level of intelligence was officially considered below normal, but had nevertheless been subject to the draft. In 1966, the Department of Defense had launched Project 100,000 or POHT as it was referred to in official reports, which lowered the standards for entry into military service. POHT was, in reality, an effort to increase the diminishing number of acceptable draftees and enlistees at a time when the need for men was increasing and, at the same time, avoiding the political pratfalls of making it more difficult for college students and other privileged categories to avoid the draft.

As announced at its creation, the POHT program had altruistic motives. The project would be an opportunity over the years to rescue hundreds of thousands of economically deprived young men by providing them with the opportunity to enter the armed forces. Moreover, according to the same official sources, the project would assist young men in becoming more responsible citizens as they served their country and when they returned to civilian life.

POHT soldiers were sometimes called "McNamara's boys" or, more cynically, "McNamara's morons" because it was allegedly

Secretary of Defense Robert McNamara's idea to create the program. They had the dubious distinction of being the only service members whose limited intelligence was broadcast by the numerals 67, which preceded the rest of their serial numbers. Thus, the fact that they were officially considered intellectually inferior was known to their commanding officers and company clerks as soon as they reported for duty. Pejorative terms used to describe POHT members were undeserved. Many served with distinction, struggling through the swamps and jungles of Vietnam along with their fellow soldiers, often better. Many were decorated for valor. Others gave their lives.

Studies after the war conducted by the General Accounting Office concluded that the program as a whole was successful, but other independent studies concluded that POHT soldiers were more likely than others to desert and be court-martialed for other crimes. In my own experience, I feel that every POHT soldier who was tried by general court-martial should not have been accepted into the armed forces.

Private Roy House was charged with murder. He was drafted into the army in 1967 after the requirement of a minimum score of thirty on the Armed Forces Quotient Test had been lowered to ten. After nine months of mediocre service in Vietnam, House shot and killed a fellow soldier. The crime could only have happened because of an unfortunate combination of circumstances: House's low intelligence and low regard for himself, the availability of weapons, the heat of the night, and the intensity of a war atmosphere.

The events that resulted in Private House's court-martial occurred when units of the 1st Battalion, 12th Infantry, were located in a forward fire support base outside Plei Djerang in early June, 1968. House was engaging in conversation and drinking beer with Private First Class John Kelly and Private First Class Bob Anka when a mortar shell, fired by the enemy, landed in the midst of the fire support base, forcing most of the soldiers into bunkers. A few minutes later, conversation among the three soldiers resumed outside the bunkers, peaceably at first. House did not drink as much as his comrades. He had, in fact, given most of his ration of beer to Kelly and Anka.

For no discernible reason, an argument developed between House and Kelly. Kelly grabbed House by the collar, but released him and proceeded to his bunker, followed by Anka. House fired six rounds in Kelly's direction, killing Anka almost immediately. Kelly was not hit. After the shooting, House casually walked away and obeyed instructions to lay down his weapon.

In a pretrial statement made to criminal investigators, Kelly swore:

> Me and Bob (Anka) had our three cans of beer . . . we went near Junior's (House's) bunker to fool around and he had three cans of beer so me and Bob drank them . . . an explosion came and everybody ran to the bunker except me and Junior. I jumped behind the wheel of the howitzer and loaded my M–16 and so did he and when everything settled down, I unloaded mine and he didn't. Me and Junior got in an argument and I grabbed him . . . I was just playing with him . . . He jerked and I let him loose and he grabbed his M–16, which was still loaded, and I told him to go ahead and shoot because I thought he was just playing around . . . I was just bullshitting him!

At trial, Kelly repeated under oath substantially what he had said in his pretrial statement, but elaborated:

> I grabbed House . . . on the shirt collar . . . and I was about to let loose on him and he jerked loose and grabbed his weapon . . . I started walking toward him. I thought he was just joking around. Then he told me to come on and that he wanted me to take another step and I knew that he was pretty serious. I told him I was just playing with him. I told him just forget about the whole thing . . . it was just a joke . . . I turned around and I started walking toward my bunker . . . Anka had been following me to the bunker . . . I heard about five or six rounds go off . . . I turned around and looked behind me and Anka was laying there. He had been hit.

Private First Class Jimmy Winn, a member of the unit who was filling sandbags, testified that he saw House with the rifle and heard him say, "Don't fuck with me!" Winn was frightened by what he saw and heard, and returned to his bunker, where he heard six shots fired from the direction where House was standing. Then, "I heard Bob cry out 'I'm hit!' . . . Bob was lying on he ground, sir. He had about three holes in him that I seen."

Corporal Louis Waibel testified:

> Well . . . we were working on the ammunition bunker. We heard somebody yelling. I looked over and saw somebody shooting. I thought gooks were coming through the perimeter. House was coming toward us after the shooting . . . He seemed scared when I halted him. He seemed confused. He gave me no problems . . . I couldn't say if he appeared to know where he was. I halted him . . . and put him on the ground. He was confused. He was docile.

All witnesses agreed that House did not make any effort to conceal himself or to run away after the incident.

House testified in his own behalf, swearing that:

> After a few beers and good conversation with Anka and Kelly, Kelly approached me for no reason and said, 'I'm going to beat your ass' he says, just like that. And, I said, 'Man, why do you want to beat my ass, I haven't done nothing to you . . . I don't want to fight you' and he grabbed me. I tried to remain calm but Kelly said that he will put a bullet right between my head and then . . . the only thing I know . . . all that I can recall is that he grabbed his weapon or something . . . and the next thing I remember I was over . . . I was over there . . . and somebody threw me down on the ground . . . I do not remember firing my weapon.

A psychiatrist brought in by the defense counsel testified:

> House's intelligence placed him in the mentally subnormal population. He has an emotionally unstable personality manifested by poorly controlled angry outbursts. His angry feelings overwhelm him. House was concealing, consciously or unconsciously, the true

nature of his act because he cannot make sense out of what he did. Further, he lacks insight into his own intellectual dullness.

House's judgment, the psychiatrist added:

> . . . seems defective on the basis of his being unable to integrate complex, threatening social situations into meaningful behavior patterns . . . his general intellect seems uniformly dull and he is unable to make very simple abstractions. He cannot calculate how much change he would receive after purchasing something that costs less than a dollar but paying with a dollar . . . he has experienced a lifelong pattern of being a scapegoat and inferior because of his gullibility, general dullness and speech impediment.

The psychiatrist concluded, however, that:

> . . . although House's defective intelligence and emotional instability are important factors in the alleged crime, he is able to distinguish right from wrong, and adhere to the right, and therefore could be held responsible for the offense, if the court so found.

The members of the court found the accused guilty as charged. The defense counsel then introduced evidence that confirmed that House was one of the unfortunate soldiers included within statistics which indicate that the disadvantaged and minorities were disproportionately represented among those required to serve in Vietnam. As a youth, House suffered from living in poverty on the outskirts of a small city and was subjected to the whims of an alcoholic father who was a poor provider. House repeated two grades and was never capable of graduating from high school. His only employment consisted of odd jobs. He was unemployed at the time he was drafted. He had always had a speech impediment.

The court sentenced House to be discharged from the army with a dishonorable discharge and to be confined at hard labor for ten years. I do not know the final disposition of House's case, but it is my experience with similar cases that the Court of

Military Review in Washington would order additional psychiatric examinations, and would substantially reduce the sentences, or even reverse the convictions.

After the trial, I spoke a few words to House, who showed little emotion or understanding of what had transpired. His stuttered sentences and lack of understanding convinced me that he should never have been allowed into military service, even though technically qualified under the revised standards.

As I was proceeding to my quarters after the trial, I conveyed my thoughts about the case to the commanding general of the division, whom I encountered by chance politely speaking to the two Montagnard men who came daily to tend the little compound. The general replied that there were also POHT soldiers who did a creditable job. I did not disagree with that statement but did not pursue discussion of the subject. I continued to my quarters, where I packed and inquired about the next available flight to Saigon.

CHAPTER SIX

Cholon and the Lucky Hotel

After returning to Saigon from my first trip to Pleiku, I began a search for suitable quarters. I wanted to stay at the Rex, where the judges who preceded me had lived, and where Paul was living when he was in town. I was, however, assigned to the Lucky in Cholon, which I was assured would be quite suitable as it had been recently constructed. As much as I hated the task, I packed my belongings and departed from Paul's room in the Rex.

The driver who was assisting me in the move drove to a hotel in Cholon that looked very impressive. It was large and sturdy. On the inside were a reception area, dining room, and elevator. All things considered, the place appeared quite comfortable. To my chagrin, however, I was informed by the desk clerk that this was not the Lucky, but rather the Hong Kong.

I expressed my confusion but was assured that I was in the right place. The only entrance to the Lucky was through the Hong Kong, an established hotel. The clerk assigned me to the tenth floor of the Lucky, above which was only a flat roof.

I was disappointed many times during the few minutes it took to travel from the lobby of the Hong Kong to the top of the Lucky. I discovered that my new hotel was an upward extension of a building contiguous to the Hong Kong, and it had recently been built of what appeared to be cinder blocks. It rose straight into the sky and was seemingly unsupported by any solid construction above the main hotel's sixth floor. The elevator in the Hong Kong worked, but, of course, could rise no higher than the hotel itself. It was therefore necessary to walk across the roof of the Hong Kong and into the Lucky, which had neither lobby nor elevator.

With the help of my escort, I climbed the stairs to the top of the Lucky, dragging luggage I had brought from the United States and all the military equipment that I had been issued in Vietnam. There was absolutely nothing in my assigned room other than two single army cots with bedding. No closets, telephone, toilet, shower, table, or other amenity. The floor was concrete. Living here would mean that I could neither make nor receive phone calls without walking down the stairs of the Lucky, crossing the roof of the Hong Kong, and taking the elevator to the lobby on the bottom floor. I was totally depressed, and decided to make an effort to get something more convenient.

The driver and I returned to the billeting office, where I pleaded for something, anything, at the Rex, but the officer in charge was adamant in his refusal. There was nothing to be had, he said, because a group of officers from Thailand were due to arrive soon and would require all the available spaces. He did, however, tell me that there was an opening at the Brinks, which was just a block or so away from the Rex, and I was welcome to take a look at what was available there. The Brinks was the hotel that had been attacked by Viet Cong terrorists on Christmas Eve in 1964, leaving two American officers dead and about sixty injured.

The driver took me to the Brinks. The quarters offered to me there were a portion of a small living area in a two-bedroom suite. The bedrooms were already occupied. Within the living room, where I would be sleeping on a small cot against one of the walls, were a television, a multispeaker stereo system, and a conversation area consisting of three chairs and a coffee table in the center of the room. I decided to return to the billeting office.

After much cajoling, the billeting officer offered to put me on a waiting list for the Rex, giving in to my plea that it was necessary to be near a telephone and other judges. But he could not promise how long it would be, if ever, before the transfer could be made. So I returned to Cholon and made the long haul once more to the top of the Lucky. I could not unpack because of the lack of closets or furniture, so I opened my suitcases and conveniently arranged their contents according to my needs.

I lived in my new quarters about five weeks, but the actual number of nights I spent there was less, because when Paul or any other friend at the Rex left town, I moved temporarily into his room. Furthermore, I spent about four nights out of every week trying cases in other parts of the country.

Life at the Lucky was an unforgettable experience. Living on the top floor as I did allowed me to step directly outside and to the roof for fresh air. This I did every evening I spent there. From the roof, I could clearly see the Cha Tam church in Cholon about two blocks away where President Nho Dinh Diem and his brother had been captured and then assassinated on November 3, 1963, just three weeks before President John F. Kennedy was killed. Wherever I happened to be in Vietnam, I reenacted in my mind events of historical significance that occurred there, and every time I looked at that little church, I thought of Diem. I did not know then about the United States' participation in his overthrow, but I did know that his death was historically significant and responsible for the series of seven unstable governments in South Vietnam that followed his execution.

At the top of the Lucky, the residents of the upper floors usually gathered in the open air to watch the sunset and discuss the war as we listened to mortar fire going out of and coming into Saigon. The sky was brightened throughout the night by flares dropped from helicopters. When B–52s dropped their bombs in nearby areas, the Lucky was shaken and I worried that, like the walls of Jericho, the building would come tumbling down. My bed moved almost from one side of the room to the other.

Several officers at the Lucky formed a singing group and gathered frequently on the roof. Asked to join, I had to refuse because God did not favor me with a voice capable of harmonizing. Still, listening to them provided background music as I contemplated the war around me.

Whenever I slept at the Lucky, I woke up in the mornings about five-thirty, dressed as fast as I could in order to shorten my stay there, had breakfast in the officers' mess at the Hong Kong, and caught a military bus for the trip to my office, wearing a steel helmet and side arms. The bus, with windows and entrance protected by steel bars and meshed wire, passed through the main section of Cholon, affording a fascinating glimpse of life into that part of the city. There were Chinese car repair stations, food stores, dentists' and doctors' offices, shops for making jewelry, drug stores, and other businesses of varied descriptions.

People were at work in front of their shops or homes, taking advantage of the early morning air while hammering, cooking, sewing, or doing whatever else was necessary to their professions or lives. Others crowded the streets eating, squatting, reading newspapers, or just awaiting the passage of another day. In the parks, which were plentiful and beautiful, but filled with refugees, elderly gentlemen shadowboxed in total concentration, oblivious to everything and everyone around them.

Riding through Cholon on the bus, one could not help but observe that this was a city in the midst of war trying to survive in its own ethnicity. Newspapers and signs everywhere were written in Chinese characters. Before the war, Cholon was the more prosperous part of Saigon. In addition to legitimate industry, it also had the reputation of a city of iniquity with the largest whorehouses and gambling dens in Asia. Warlords had their own armies and lived in palaces connected to each other and to Saigon by a maze of alleys and underground tunnels. Chinese workers on the docks of Saigon, wracking their bodies under bales of rice and other commodities, returned to their hovels in Cholon at night to gamble away the few piasters they had earned during the day. Others sought relief from their misery in the opium dens that proliferated in the city.

After leaving Cholon, we passed the Phu Tho Saigon race track, which had been scarred by thousands of bullets. On television, I had seen some of them put there during the Tet Offensive earlier in the year when fighting raged in the area. I remembered the same beautiful track I had visited eight years previously with Colonel Durbin. Refugees now swarmed around and inside the area. Hundreds of rickety shacks were thrown together with scraps of wood and tin, but I could see no evidence of sanitary facilities or other amenities. Needless to say, the horses were not running.

CHAPTER SEVEN

The Man Who Would Be President

On the morning of July 26, while still officially living at the Lucky, but staying temporarily in a friend's room at the Rex, I phoned my office and received the good news that the case assigned to me that afternoon in Dong Tam had been canceled. I decided to use my free day to attend the trial of a Vietnamese civilian who had been receiving much publicity in the media.

Truong Dinh Dzu was a fifty-one-year-old Saigon lawyer who had run for the presidency of South Vietnam in September 1967 as a peace candidate, but was defeated in the election by Nguyen Van Thieu. In his campaign, Dzu announced that he favored a meeting with the National Liberation Front, the political arm of the Viet Cong and other anti-Diem factions, as a step toward ending the war. As the peace candidate, he had achieved attention in the world press. After the election, which was observed and declared to be fair by United States congressmen, President Thieu ordered Dzu's detention on charges of "action harmful to the anti-communist spirit of the people and the army." Since the beginning of 1968, the South Vietnamese government had been threatening to bring charges against Dzu for his campaign activities and, during the summer, it was announced that a trial would take place on Friday, July 26.

The United States government was much embarrassed about Dzu's trial because the election had been proclaimed one of President Thieu's promised reforms and a landmark for the evolution of democracy in Vietnam. Dzu had not advocated the overthrow of the Diem government, but only made a suggestion that the United States itself later concurred in by negotiating with agents of the National Liberation Front in Paris. No matter, President Thieu was determined to throw his opponent into prison.

About eight-thirty in the morning, I walked leisurely through the streets of the city to the courtroom, located in a depressing building surrounded by a large concrete wall on the banks of the Saigon River. The charges were based entirely on an interview made during the election campaign with members of the British Broadcasting Corporation and United Press International. Now, Dzu was being tried for making statements that, by Western standards, and probably even by normal South Vietnamese standards, were not treasonable.

There were few people in the courtroom, but it was surrounded by armed policemen and South Vietnamese soldiers. There were also guards within the courtroom, where Dzu's wife, son, and daughter were seated in the front row. Dzu's wife, to my surprise, was dressed in modern western style and wore what appeared to be expensive jewelry. Personally, I thought that, under the circumstances, it would have been more appropriate to wear clothes that conformed more to Vietnamese culture. A number of reporters whom I recognized on sight, a representative from the United States Embassy, and a few other spectators were scattered throughout the room. I sat next to Bernard Weinraub of the *New York Times* and Peter Kann of the *Wall Street Journal*.

Dzu was brought into the courtroom under tight security shortly before the trial and allowed to speak briefly with his family. He was accompanied by a lawyer. When the court of five young military officers entered, we all stood.

The entire trial lasted two hours. I could not understand the proceedings but there was much shouting between Dzu's lawyer and the president of the court, a South Vietnamese major. After the reading of required legal documents and much argument, the court recessed, presumably to deliberate. When they returned, Dzu was sentenced to five years' imprisonment. There was more shouting, but the court members ignored the pleas of Dzu, his family, and his counsel, and calmly walked out of the room through the door behind the panel.

As he was dragged from the courtroom by a dozen or so military police with M–16 rifles furnished by the United States to the ARVN (Army of the Republic of Vietnam) for combat action, Dzu shouted a few words to his family. He was then thrown into the bed of a truck and hauled away to prison crying, "I am not guilty!" in English, leaving his wife and children in tears. After the trial, I saw the daughter, a young lady, dressed in a mini skirt, standing alone near a wall outside the building, weeping.

The Vietnamese government announced that, because of the nature of the charges, Dzu would not be able to appeal his sentence. Rumors abounded that he would be confined to Con Son island. The infamous prison there was the home of the so-called Tiger Cages, where several persons occupied a single cell with no windows. Guards paced on cat-walks from which food and water were thrown to prisoners below. Sanitary problems were obnoxious; the cages were disinfected from above. The prison was built by the French when the island was known as Poulo Condore, and used to incarcerate the most troublesome of their political enemies.

After the trial, Weinraub and Kann invited me to join them and a couple of other reporters for lunch. On the casual walk away from the courtroom, we stopped briefly at the Majestic Hotel, where two young American women joined the reporters. I do not recall whether they were also reporters, or merely visitors to Saigon, but they seemed quite at ease in their surroundings. We continued our walk together from the hotel to the Restaurant Le Castel on Tu Do Street. The chef there was well known to the habituès of the establishment, a meeting place for reporters and important civilians.

Within a short time, I felt comfortable as a member of the group and realized that I was not leaving behind all the comforts of home when I departed for Vietnam. There was a well-stocked long mahogany bar just beyond the entrance to the restaurant. The dining room, with piped-in stereophonic music, was decorated in simple but elegant taste. We all sat together in a large booth. I was intrigued by the circumstances in which I found myself less than a month away from home, where relatives and friends were concerned for my safety and comfort. Peter Arnett, already a Pulitzer Prize winner for his reporting in Vietnam, stopped by for a few minutes to chat with his friends.

Our meal began leisurely with vichyssoise, progressing to a rabbit ragout with Côte d'Azur salad, and concluded with fresh fruit and cheese. Intermittently, we were served orange sorbet, and afterwards, espresso coffee. At two-thirty, I regretfully made excuses in order to return to my office. The reporters insisted that I be the guest of their newspapers. Vietnam would never again be this delightful, I thought.

CHAPTER EIGHT

Fire at the Rex

After lunch with the reporters and friends at Le Castel, I walked to the Rex where military phones were available. I called the office for messages and received the sad news from the Red Cross that my father-in-law in Switzerland had passed away. There was nothing I could do other than walk over to the Vietnamese Telephone and Telegraph office to send messages of condolence to my wife and her family. Afterwards, I took a lonely stroll along Nguyen Hue, the Street of Flowers. It made no sense to return to my office. I continued at a slow pace back to the hotel for a solitary meal in the open mess.

I went directly to my borrowed room after dinner and wrote several letters to the family, explaining why it was not possible to leave Vietnam for Switzerland. Then, unable to focus on written material, I mused absent-mindedly, recalling the many happy days when I was stationed in Germany and went to the Swiss mountains on holiday with my family. Before midnight, I drifted off to sleep.

At about four o'clock the following morning, I was awakened by a woman's voice calling to her friend in the room adjoining mine. "Wake up, Mildred! There's a fire in the hotel!" she shouted, banging on Mildred's door.

Nothing in the world starts the adrenaline flowing faster than the knowledge that one is in danger of being engulfed in flames! I rushed out of the door, looked down from the balcony, and saw fire rising from the office on the bottom floor where reporters attended the Five O'Clock Follies, or, more respectfully put, received daily afternoon official briefings. I rushed back into the room, grabbed my trousers and wallet, not bothering with shirt or shoes, and walked to the stairway. Fortunately, the Rex was one of the better-constructed buildings in Saigon, with concrete stairs, and it did not seem that we were in imminent danger. I walked more or less calmly down the stairs, immediately behind Mildred and the woman who had awakened her. There was no panic, even as others joined us, and it appeared that everyone in the building had received word of the fire in time to exit without harm.

The occupants of the Rex, in all states of dress and undress, gathered in the open park adjacent to the entrance of the building. No Vietnamese civilians were in sight. The fire department arrived almost as quickly as residents evacuated the hotel. There was no evidence of fire on the outside, but smoke was emerging from many windows. An effort was made to account for the occupants of the building by calling roll from a roster acquired at the downstairs clerk's desk. Most people whose names were called responded, but not everyone was present, some being away in the field, others on leave, and yet others at unknown places.

When Red Benoit's name was called, there was no answer. I could see quite clearly that a light burned in his room on the second floor, and I was concerned about him. I knew that he was not away from Saigon, so I searched the crowd and made inquiries, but without success. I then took it upon myself to approach the fire marshall, an American sergeant, to report that I knew the person who occupied the room on the second floor where a light was burning, but he had not answered roll.

Without hesitation, the fire marshall ordered two of his men to break into Red's room to search for occupants. Complying with orders, they ran into the building with pickaxes and smoke masks. They broke into Red's room, pushed open the windows, and shouted down to their chief that no one was present there. At that point, Red came from nowhere in a fit of anger ready to strangle the fire marshall.

"Get those fucking weenies out of my room!" he screamed.

"Sir, please, I'm doing my duty!" replied the fire marshall.

"I said get those damned weenies out of my room!" Red shouted again. "I've got a thousand dollars' worth of new stereo equipment in there and I don't want anyone in that room!"

"Sir, please, we're shorthanded already! Let us do our job!" pleaded the sergeant.

"You can see there's no damned fire in that room! And the door was locked, so they must have torn it down. I have no more security!"

"Sir, please, please! Let us do our job!"

At this moment, Joe Ammerman approached Red, asking him to back away from the firemen, and Red did so. I watched them as they returned to the office sedan parked nearby, where they had taken refuge upon leaving the building, accounting for the fact that Red did not answer the roll.

Sheepishly, I walked over to the vehicle and entered the empty front seat. Red was still cursing the "weenies" who had destroyed his door. "Red, I'm sorry, but I'm responsible for the firemen entering your room. You didn't answer the roll call and your light was on, so I thought there was a possibility you were in trouble. I'm very sorry," I said.

Gentleman that he was, Red did not reproach me, although he was still unhappy. He knew that his room could not be immediately secured, and his new stereo equipment had probably been ruined by smoke and possibly water.

With the fire extinguished, we tried to re-enter the building, but smoke was still seeping through the entrance. The fire marshall informed us that no one would be allowed inside until a thorough inspection of the building had been made, which would probably take twenty-four hours.

As dawn was breaking, a military jeep with a large-caliber machine gun mounted on its body came to escort us to the Brinks Hotel two blocks away. We were a ragtag bunch, marching down the streets of Saigon in the dawn's early light, some without shoes, others without shirts and yet others without even undershirts. Fortunately for some of the residents, they had acquaintances in the Brinks or other nearby quarters who were able to furnish them with additional garb, but most of us had to remain only in the clothing with which we had escaped the fire.

I ate breakfast on the roof of the Brinks dressed only in the underclothes in which I had been sleeping and combat trousers. Five other occupants of the Rex, including one woman, all wearing assorted clothing, shared the table. After breakfast, I was invited by an acquaintance to spend the remainder of the waiting period in the room of his friend, who lived nearby but was out of the city at the moment. After a few frustrating hours there, I took the liberty of borrowing a pair of ill-fitting boots and a shirt from the absentee occupant, leaving a note that I would return them as soon as possible.

Outside the building, I hired a Vietnamese cab to take me to the Lucky in Cholon, where I supplemented my clothing. I was unable to shave, though, because my toilet articles were still at the Rex.

When I returned to MACV, where Red and Joe had preceded me, I was not surprised to find a dozen or so messages, inasmuch as I had not been to the office for almost two days. I answered all of the calls. As usual, they concerned future trial dates.

While waiting for a bus to the Lucky that evening, I was delighted to hear from Red that all was clear at the Rex and we could return there. I had the most restful night of my tour in Saigon.

Ten months later, shortly before returning to the United States, I purchased a copy of an English-language Vietnamese newspaper that young boys and girls were forever hawking near the Rex. On page one was the picture of a woman who looked vaguely familiar. In a moment, I recognized her as the person who awakened Mildred in the room next to the one I was occupying on the night of the fire. She was, of course, also responsible for awakening me, a fact for which I am eternally grateful. Beneath her picture, the headline stated that she was being awarded a medal for heroic action. The article explained how, on the night of the fire, she went, without concern for her own safety, to an upper floor of the Rex Hotel for the purpose of saving the life of her friend, and then proceeded calmly down the stairs of the building, giving inspiration and courage for others to follow in an orderly manner.

CHAPTER NINE

Camp Evans

In August 1968 the First Cavalry Division (Air Mobile) was located in the bleakest place I have ever been. Not a single tree or growing thing was evident when I landed there on a hastily constructed runway in late summer. Everything in sight, mostly tents and a few prefabricated huts, had been erected by American soldiers. In March 1968, the First Cav, as it was affectionately called, had moved in to relieve the besieged marines at Khe Sanh. When their presence at Khe Sanh was no longer required, they had moved forty miles east in the middle of nowhere to a place they named Camp Evans. The site was in Quang Tri Province, and they were as close to the Demilitarized Zone as any major unit.

An escort from the legal office greeted me at the runway upon arrival, and together we walked to the office. There were a few vehicles in sight, but Camp Evans was so compact that vehicles were not needed for transportation within the immediate area. Amidst a sea of tents, we arrived at one with a wooden floor, screen siding, and the familiar judge advocate insignia designating it as the legal office. This was it. Just one tent, the kind ordinarily used to sleep eight persons. There were a few steel desks and chairs inside the tent, but no area of privacy for lawyers to speak to clients or judges to work. A new 19.4 cubic foot General Electric refrigerator stood among stacks of papers, books, and legal documents covered with sand and held in place with stones or other heavy objects. I dared not ask how the refrigerator found its way to this remote area, but was informed with pride that its main purpose was to keep beer cool and purloined steaks refrigerated.

I was told to use any desk that I found temporarily vacant and not worry about the person to whom it was assigned. Rather than compete for desk space, I unloaded my flak jacket, steel helmet, pistol, and law books in an empty corner. I planned to return after supper to prepare for the anticipated trial on the following day. Perhaps things would be less hectic later.

A few men without shirts were wielding picks, shovels, and hammers adjacent to the legal tent. They were seriously at work on the latest project of the judge advocate personnel. There, standing on a wooden platform partially completed, with his shirt off and wearing shorts, was Major Earle Lassiter, executive officer and guiding light behind the project. He informed me that they were building a sun deck above an existing bunker which was being enlarged. My God, I thought, the last thing in the world needed here is a sun deck! But Earle advised me that the personnel of his office often sunned themselves; besides, it was his policy that no member of the office would remain idle during daylight hours. Morale lagged when work diminished, he explained, and improved when the men were working on a constructive project. Better to lie in the sun than complain about the heat! All members of the office were well-tanned, and morale was as good as in other areas in spite of the lack of such ordinary basics as a shady refuge, movies, or a recreation room.

I congratulated the workers on their initiative and was invited to further inspect their accomplishment. The men were enlarging the bunker by digging to make it four feet deep and twelve yards square. The platform on which they were working was being built on posts eighteen inches above the hole in the ground. Two deck chairs were already in place on the completed portion of the deck, and four army cots, covered with plastic, were inside the bunker.

Two innocuous-looking soldiers were dozing on the deck chairs, one apparently a guard with an M–16 rifle across his lap and the other apparently his charge. No one seemed concerned. There was no place to escape and, with nothing to keep them busy or no place to keep them comfortable, the attitude seemed to be "Well, what the hell!"

After supper, I joined members of the legal staff in the office tent. We had a couple of beers, played cards, and talked about the home folks. Before a third beer, I retreated to the corner where I had previously laid my possessions to prepare the next day's case, which was alleged as premeditated murder.

We did not sleep that night in the bunker under the sun deck, which was reserved for the accused and his guard, but rather in two very simple tents with dirt floors, lighted by a small naked electric light bulb. We were prepared to dive into the bunker if necessary at the first sound of enemy fire, but fortunately we were spared that experience during the night I was there.

The courtroom was a tent near the helicopter pad, about two hundred yards from the office. Nothing resembling a witness room or deliberation room was anywhere in sight. The prosecutor informed me that we would have the use of a trench normally used as a community bunker. The courtroom contained nothing more than a couple of tables joined together for the court members, card tables for me and the reporter, two small wooden tables for counsel and the accused, and steel folding chairs behind each of the tables. The trench was to be used by court members while legal matters were being discussed inside the courtroom, by other parties to the trial when the court members were deliberating inside, and by witnesses while waiting to testify. The accused, counsel, court reporter, guard, spectators, and I would all be sharing the trench simultaneously. The situation was almost intolerable. No tree to furnish shade, no place for the accused to be with his counsel, not even a rest room.

Private Eugene Hill, the accused in the case, charged not only with murder, but with the unlawful use of marijuana, looked pathetic as he entered the courtroom. In addition to his other woes, he had apparently not slept the previous evening. His hair was disheveled, his clothes were in disarray, and he was confused about finding his assigned seat. My thoughts were briefly drawn to a family gathering back home to celebrate my mother's seventieth birthday. Well, I thought, this is war, and the trial, as well as the war, will go on. The parties took their assigned places. I waited until the noise of the helicopters diminished, although they were never totally silent, and called the court to order.

The evidence was shocking in that it revealed so unnecessary a crime. Having nothing to do on a Sunday, Private Hill and a friend spent the afternoon at the Nevada Bar in An Khe. While there, Hill consumed a few beers and some double shots of scotch. They returned together to base camp about six o'clock because Hill was assigned to guard duty that evening. After supper, he shared a marijuana cigarette with two soldiers before reporting for duty.

Private Hill assumed his duties as guard in a building near the entrance to camp at seven o'clock. While on guard, he spent most of his time sitting down, sometimes dozing, and sometimes talking to Private Philip McQueen. While thinking about nothing in particular, Hill was accosted by a friend and fellow soldier, Private Hal Cooper who, in a playful manner, "poked" the accused in the midsection of his body. Aroused from his lethargy, Hill chambered a round in his M–16.

Private McQueen, a witness for the prosecution, testified that after Cooper playfully assaulted the accused, Hill said: "I'll lay a clip on you!" before loading his weapon. McQueen thought all this was horseplay because Hill and Cooper were close friends. Cooper, however, did not take Hill's words and actions lightly and quickly ran from the scene. McQueen continued:

> I took a step away from Hill and then Cooper said, "Say man, what's the matter? What have I done?" Hill came down with the

> M–16 like a bayonet thrust with his right hand pulling the bolt to the rear and letting it fly forward. This told me only one thing."
>
> Cooper started to run down the hill toward the guard house, still saying, "What did I do? What did I do?" and "What's wrong? What's wrong?" All this time, I was backing up, letting things take their course and getting out of the man's way . . . Hill was pointing his weapon in the direction of Cooper.

When the prosecutor asked McQueen what happened next, the witness answered: "I started whistling. I turned around, and got away from the action."

Other witnesses for the prosecution testified that Cooper ran into the room of a friend, frantically crying that the guard was after him with a weapon. Even before finishing his complaint, Hill entered the room, pointed the rifle at Cooper and said, "Now I got you!" Cooper tried to run from the room but accidentally bumped into Hill's rifle causing him to fall off balance in the doorway and drop into the hall. Hill followed Cooper, who grabbed the rifle, but Hill was able to force the barrel to Cooper's head and fire it, killing him immediately. When subdued, Hill fell to his knees and cried, "God, help me! What did I do?"

Hill's testimony was somewhat, but not altogether, inconsistent. He testified that:

> When Cooper poked me in the back, I jokingly told him I'd put a clip on him. I then chambered a round as part of the joke, but just as I did so, was notified that my tour of duty as a guard was completed. While walking slowly to the guard house, I saw Cooper in a barracks and wanted to play around with him again. I went into the room and said "I got you now!" and we struggled . . .
>
> He lunged and grabbed the weapon with both hands. The barrel of my weapon, in Cooper's hands, was just below his chin . . . and that's when it went off . . . I dropped the weapon, sir . . . a witness came over and I told him, "Blow my brains out for what I did!"

Evidence introduced for the defense indicated that Hill had been a good soldier, was not known to lose his temper, and had been a good friend of Cooper. When asked why he joined the army, he testified that he was married, had four children, and, "I was destitute at the time, I couldn't find any work."

Hill was convicted of unpremeditated murder and wrongful use of marijuana. He was sentenced by the court to be dishonorably discharged and to serve fifteen years' imprisonment. As he left the courtroom with his counsel and guards, Hill was the picture of dejection. He looked as if the end of the world had arrived for him, and it probably had. If he had not been able to support his family before he came into the army, there was little possibility that he would be able to do so, either from prison or after release, with the stigma of a bad discharge.

I had nothing more to do with Hill's case, except authenticate the record of trial, but years later while going through his court-martial papers, I learned that the term of his confinement had been greatly reduced and he was released from prison. I also saw a copy of the telegram notifying Cooper's parents that their son died in line of duty while stationed near An Khe, Republic of Vietnam. I remembered him sadly when I saw his name on the Vietnam Veterans' Memorial in Washington.

CHAPTER TEN

Defiant Child

One of the most exciting places in Saigon-Cholon was the great marketplace on the main thoroughfare from one city to the other. I drove by there on several occasions and entered it once. The traffic in the area seemed never to relax during daylight hours. It was here that, in a fleeting glance on one rather routine day, an enigmatic picture was etched in my memory that remains vivid to this day and will always haunt me.

The entire population of Saigon and Cholon seemed to enter into and exit from the hundred doors of the great market. There were myriads of little stalls within, where Chinese and Vietnamese peasants, farmers, artists, and craftsmen plied their trades or sold their wares. Housewives, houseboys, servants, mandarins, monks, cooks, and chefs spent a part of every day at the market. This was the heartbeat of the city, without which it could not survive. It was a fascinating place in which a sightseeing American could easily become lost.

Across the marketplace, I paused to avoid the relentless traffic. Standing and waiting there, I saw two women who had apparently emerged from the building. A dialogue totally consumed their attention. The younger, about seventeen, looked angelic and appeared fragile but determined. She wore a simple cotton sleeveless dress, not particularly clean, and sandals without socks. She held a small paper bag against her breast.

The older woman was perhaps thirty-five but looked older, weary from life and war. She was dressed in the white blouse and loose black pants that was the dress of almost every working adult Vietnamese female in the city. Her hair was disarrayed, and her eyes passively expressed an acceptance of all the misfortunes life had bestowed upon her. She carried nothing, but spoke continuously, using gestures, frequently staring at the bag in the girl's hands.

Tears streamed from the girl's eyes as she listened and tried to speak. Her eyes pleaded as she occasionally looked into the little bag. The older woman appeared also to concentrate upon the bag, but it seemed of no importance to her. She spoke animatedly, pointing frequently to the girl and her precious possession and to some place in the distance beyond the traffic. She was upset, but made no claim to the bag. The girl was resisting, but I could not determine why. Whatever words she may have spoken had no effect on the older person. Every brief attempt by the girl to speak seemed to bring remonstrance from her elder. Yet, in spite of the dispute, there appeared to be an inexplicable bond between the two. Perhaps they were mother and daughter, or sisters. All part of the enigma.

Vehicles of all description were passing by. Large trucks, small taxis, military vehicles, mopeds, and motorcycles were making so much noise that I could hear only the combined drone of all those machines. Thousands of people, concerned with their own problems, entered the market and departed with vegetables, meat, geese, chickens, pigs, paintings, and bags of all sizes. There were men and women, young and old, Hindu and Muslim, Chinese and Vietnamese, American and Eurasian, poor and rich attending the great market during the brief moment of my scenario. They passed without noticing the two women, whose conversation did not attract a single eye, except mine from a distance. Neither the crowd nor the noise, nor the war, nor heaven nor earth distracted these women from each other. Their conversation was too important, too involved, too emotional, to be a mere sales dispute. The emotion was transmitted through the crowds, through the noise and through the traffic to me. It was total.

The older woman finally made a gesture to indicate that the conversation had terminated. She turned her back to the girl and returned into the marketplace. There was no forgiveness, no agreement. Just a shrug of the shoulder, one more point with the finger, and departure. The young girl watched her vanish into the crowd, looked intensely after her, attempted to hold back more tears, and stood for a brief moment transfixed. She then looked at the bag in her hands and gently placed it on the ground. After standing up briefly, she had a second thought, bent down again and with a gentle touch of the hand, but in a mark of studied defiance, pushed over her little bag, emptying its treasure upon the ground. Then, ever so gently, but still defiantly, with tears streaming down her cheeks, she walked deliberately into the stream of oncoming vehicles.

Several people were attracted to the scene where the dispute had taken place, but only for a few seconds. That was all the time it took to dispose of what had been the young girl's bag of green beans.

CHAPTER ELEVEN

Riot at the LBJ

On the first day of September, during the noon recess of a case in Long Binh, Colonel John Douglass approached me asking whether I would like to take a ride to observe the stockade remains. "Stockade remains?" I asked incredulously. He answered in the affirmative and added that he was surprised that I had not heard about the riot on the preceding evening. Assuming that, if indeed there was a riot, courts-martial might result and I would be assigned to one or more cases, I refused.

The fact that there was a riot in the Long Binh Stockade (more commonly referred to as LBJ, or, Long Binh Jail) did not come as a surprise to me. Over seven hundred prisoners were crowded into a compound built but not suited for five hundred inmates. The overcrowding, combined with summer heat, lack of creature comforts, and harshness of discipline made the situation, in fact, a riot about to happen. The incident received wide publicity throughout the United States.

Twelve general courts-martial resulted from the LBJ riot, in which one person was killed, several were injured, and half the stockade burned. Of the six cases to which I was assigned, one resulted in acquittal and five resulted in convictions with sentences ranging from two to five years.

Much of the same evidence was introduced in each case, and was fairly summarized in the case of Private Richard Fallows. He was charged with riot, manslaughter, and conspiracy to overthrow lawful authority. Captain Clinton Paul Pappas was the trial counsel, or prosecutor; Captain Nancy Fields, the defense counsel; and I, the military judge. After almost two days of testimony, the prosecution rested and the defense counsel asked for an out-of-court hearing, which I granted. The following ensued:

Judge: Defense Counsel, what is the purpose of this out-of-court hearing?

DC (Defense Counsel): Sir, the defense moves for a finding of not guilty. We have heard lots of evidence about a group of men carrying torches, swinging bunk adapters normally used for supporting upper bunks, entering administrative areas of the stockade, releasing maximum security prisoners from the Big Max, assaulting guards and killing one prisoner. The only evidence against the accused, Private Fallows, however, is that two guards saw him in a crowd that was rioting, having a bunk adapter in his hand. There is absolutely nothing to show that he intended to use the adapter in an unlawful manner, or, for that matter, that he ever held it upright. There is no evidence to indicate that he railed against authority. I suggest there is nothing more than the fact that he was caught up in an event in which he was not involved. That's all, your honor.

TC (Trial Counsel): Your honor, Fallows was indeed a part of the crowd that was raining destruction on the stockade. Consider this, there were numerous prisoners not participating in the disturbance and indeed, running away from those raising havoc with authority. Many prisoners had, in fact, assembled at the front gate showing their intent not to get involved in the riot. Private Fallows had a choice to make and he made the wrong one. There is indeed evidence to show that Fallows remained with the crowd and picked up a bunk adapter, which is sufficient to proceed with the trial at this time.

Judge: The motion is denied. The case will proceed. This out-of-court hearing is terminated. Trial counsel, call the court.

TC: Yes, sir. (Trial Counsel enters the deliberation room and returns a moment later with the court members, three officers, and four enlisted persons.)

Judge: The court will come to order. Captain Fields, you may proceed with the case for the defense.

DC: Thank you, your honor. The defense waives an opening statement to the jury and calls the defendant, Private Fallows, as a witness. (Fallows approaches the trial counsel and raises his right hand to be sworn.)

TC: Do you swear to tell the truth, the whole truth, and nothing but the truth?

D (Defendant): Yes, sir.

DC: Now, Private Fallows, try to relax. The court is interested in everything you have to say, so speak slowly and loudly as you can. First of all, you were confined to the Long Binh Stockade on the night of August 31st, 1968, is that correct?

D: Yes, ma'am.

DC: Please tell us just what happened that night.

D: Well, I was just laying on my bunk trying to sleep when my friend Paul and a few prisoners came to my tent with a bunch of rolled up papers burning at the end. Paul came in the tent and said that the brothers were going to get revenge against the chucks for all the shit we've been taking. I told Paul I didn't want to get involved in any of that mess. I had just gotten out of maximum confinement in the Big Max, which was a living hell, and didn't want any more trouble. Well, there were eight white dudes sleeping in the tent with me and they all ran away and I was left alone and I didn't know what was going on so I went with Paul and a few of the other prisoners who were with him.

DC: Where did you go?

D: I did not know where we were going or what was going on. I was just afraid to be left alone, so I joined the brothers and only did so to protect myself. I did not want any trouble. Well, when I got out of the tent, I could see a bunch of guards lined up with rifles about fifty yards away from us and I could hear sirens coming toward the stockade and I was real scared.

DC: Did you pick up a bunk adapter?

D: Yes, ma'am, but I never wanted to use it. In fact, I never did use it. I just held it in case I needed to defend myself. For all I knew, maybe some Viet Congs were attacking the stockade. Everything was confusion.

DC: How did it all end?

D: Finally, a battalion of soldiers arrived to assist the guards. The stockade commander told all the prisoners near the gate to go outside and sit on the grass across the street. They left us brothers inside while the fire brigade was putting out the fires. When the fires were out, they locked us inside and we stayed there for two days. They threw C-rations over the fence and that's all we had to eat.

DC: Private Fallows, why were you in the stockade?

D: For selling grass, ma'am.

DC: How long had you been in the stockade?

D: Seven weeks, the last one in maximum confinement.

DC: Tell us about that.

TC: I object, your honor. Being in maximum confinement before the disturbance has nothing to do with this case.

DC: It does indeed, your honor. It bears upon the state of Private Fallows' mind. The conditions in the Big Max, as it was called, were enough to drive anyone to lose his ability to think rationally.

TC: I object again, your honor, defense counsel is testifying.

Judge: All right, Captain Fields, let the witness do the testifying, but I will overrule the prosecution's objection. You may continue with your examination.

DC: Thank you, your honor. Now, Private Fallows, tell us about maximum confinement.

D: Well, as you said, everybody called it the Big Max. There were these big conex containers, big steel boxes they used to ship things to Vietnam, and the stockade was using them for punishment. There is only one little hole in each side for light and air, and I guess it gets about one hundred and forty degrees in there during the daytime.

DC: Why were you in the Big Max?

D: For smoking grass.

DC: How were you treated while living in a big steel container?

D: Terrible, ma'am. There was no seasoning in our food. We only got out twice a day to go to the bathroom and exercise for half an hour. The guards, especially the chucks, were real nasty. I was in there for seven days.

DC: And how long had you been out of Big Max on the night of the riot?

D: Just three days.

DC: Now, just once more, Private Fallows. Did you intend to hit anyone with that bunk adapter, or join in a riot, or do anything to overthrow lawful authority in any way?

D: No, ma'am.

DC: Or do anything at all that was unlawful?

D: No. When Paul came to my bunk and everybody left, I was alone in the tent with him, and I was scared, so I just joined the group outside. I didn't know what was going to happen. I didn't plan anything.

DC: OK. Now, I'd like for you to tell the court something about your life. Where were you born?

D: Selma, Alabama.

DC: How long did you go to school?

D: About seven years, ma'am, but I never did finish anything.

DC: Are you married?

D: Yes, ma'am, and I have two kids.

DC: Does your family have any means of support other than your army allotment?

D: No, that's all they have.

DC: How long have you been in Vietnam?

D: Five months, ma'am. I spent two months of that time fighting the Viet Cong with the First Division.

DC: Do you know who the Viet Cong are?

D: Not exactly. All I know is they are communists and bad people.

DC: Do you know what a communist is?

D: No, ma'am

DC: Did you know where Vietnam was before you entered the army?

D: Well, everybody was talking about it. But I did not know where it was.

DC: Do you know where it is now?

D: No, ma'am. I just know it's where I am now and far away from home.

DC: Speaking of home, did you ever have a job there?

D: Not exactly. I just did little odds and ends. I swept floors and pumped gas, but that's about all.

DC: (To the military judge.) Your honor, the defense and the prosecution will now offer a stipulation of fact as follows: Private Fallows volunteered for the army under the Project 100,000 program, which lowered the standards for entry into military service. Before that program was in effect, he could not have qualified for service because of his low IQ and his lack of education.

Judge: Private Fallows, do you understand the stipulation?

D: Yes, sir.

Judge: Very well. The stipulation is accepted and the court members may consider the facts stated therein as evidence in this case.

DC: Why did you volunteer for the army, Private Fallows?

D: Well, ma'am. I wasn't making any money to speak of in civilian life and my wife was never feeling well. She washed a few clothes for other people now and then, but her mother had to take care of the kids most of the time. We just couldn't live decent, so I volunteered for the army.

DC: Thank you, Private Fallows, that is all.

Judge: Trial counsel, do you wish to cross examine?

TC: Yes, sir. Private Fallows, no one forced you to come into the army, is that right?

D: Yes, sir.

TC: You went through basic training, right?

D: Yes sir, but I was recycled, and it took a long time.

TC: But you did finish, and were sent to Vietnam, is that correct?

D: Yes, sir

TC: What have you been doing since coming to Vietnam?

D: Like I said, I was in the field fighting the Viet Cong for two months, and the rest of the time, I just hung around.

TC: You just hung around. You also went to the village pretty often to buy grass for your buddies, is that right?

D: Just a couple of times.

TC: And you were court-martialed and sent to the stockade, is that right?

D: Yes, sir.

TC: And in the stockade, you did not behave very well. You smoked a lot of grass in there, did you not?

D: Everybody smoked grass. I smoked some.

TC: And it was only after the second time you were caught that you were sent to the Big Max, is that right?

D: Yes, sir.

TC: Now tell me, on the night of the riot, no one forced you to join that group burning buildings and assaulting guards, is that right?

D: No one forced me, but there was no place to go.

TC: Why didn't you run away with the white dudes in your tent?

D: It just wasn't the thing to do.

TC: Why didn't you run to the front gate where most of the prisoners, including some brothers, had gathered?

D: I can't say. I guess I thought we would eventually get there.

TC: Now you were in the group that entered the administrative building and the kitchen to set them on fire, is that right?

D: I never went into those buildings.

TC: But you stood outside watching.

D: Just watching.

TC: You were with the group that attacked and killed one of the prisoners, is that right?

D: I didn't see that. I didn't even see anyone get hit. They only told me later that someone was killed.

TC: Now, Private Fallows, there were at least two large groups of prisoners. Why did you stay with the group that was raising hell and making most of the noise?

D: It was just natural, sir. I didn't hit anybody. I didn't set anything on fire. I didn't let any of the prisoners out of the Big Max. I was just there.

TC: But you did pick up a bunk adapter. What were you going to do with that?

D: I don't know, sir. Everything was happening so fast.

TC: When your friend Paul came to your tent, he had a burning torch made out of rolled up newspapers, did he not?

D: Yes sir.

TC: And there were a few brothers outside the tent waiting, is that not also right?

D: They weren't waiting. They were just there. I don't know what they were doing.

TC: Private Fallows, let me try to sum things up. Correct me if I make any mistakes. Your friend Paul came to your tent with a flaming torch and asked you to join him. Eight of your tent mates got scared and ran away, but you joined Paul's group, some of whom were yelling "Kill the chucks!" You picked up a bedpost. You watched while members of the group entered and set fire to the administrative building and the kitchen. You were in the group when someone killed another prisoner, although you say you did not see or know about this. Is all of this correct?

D: Yes, sir.

TC: Why didn't you leave the group?

D: Well, sir, them guards in the stockade were fuckin' with me for so long I figured there was nothing in the world I could do to save myself.

TC: Thank you. I have no further questions.

After arguments by the trial and defense counsels, I instructed the members of the court on the law of the case and their responsibility to make findings of guilt or innocence. I advised them that the accused's family background, his lack of education and all other matters which may have influenced his behavior must be considered. One of the requirements of the case was that the accused actually intended to override lawful authority. Did he have that specific intent? Did he have even the ability to form that specific intent?

Fallow's case was the fourth of the alleged rioters in which I participated. In my opinion, he was no worse, and probably less involved, than the others. Although technically he was guilty of some offense by remaining in the group that participated in the disturbances, I believed that he had not personally performed any of the acts of destruction or homicide that had occurred. But that was for the court to determine.

In less than an hour, the court members returned from the deliberation room and the president announced:

"Private Fallows, it is my duty as president of this court to inform you that the court, in closed session, by secret written ballot, two thirds of the members concurring, finds you: Of all specifications and charges: Guilty."

The defense then had an opportunity to present matters in extenuation and mitigation. Fallows testified in his own behalf, repeating substantially what he told the court before findings, adding a few details about the poverty of his family and the health of his children. He continued:

"I tried to join the army a long time ago but the recruiting sergeant said I was not qualified because I did not have an education. A year later, that same sergeant came to my house and told me that the rules had changed. He wanted me to enlist and promised me a lot of good things. I could even get an allotment of money for my family. So I joined the army and was sent to the infantry. Look where I am now!"

The defense counsel offered the following statement in the accused's behalf:

"The system that allows a person as unqualified as Fallows to join the army and be sent to Vietnam is unjust. Moreover, there is an inherent inequity in placing men like Fallows closest to harm's way without an understanding of what other options are open to them.

"In his lifetime, Fallows did not have good advice from any person who really cared about him or could have given him an opportunity to improve himself. Finally, I beg you to consider all of the unfortunate circumstances of the accused's life and to be lenient in your sentence. The army should bear some responsibility for recruiting young men who are totally unqualified to perform the tasks of a soldier."

I then had the responsibility of advising the court members with respect to the appropriateness of a sentence. In the three cases involving the riot in which I had already participated, the courts had imposed sentences of dishonorable discharge, total forfeitures of pay and allowances and confinement at hard labor. Two years confinement in one case, three years in another and five years in the third. In all of those cases, the accused had been seen, as a minimum, lifting bunk adapters or other dangerous objects, and shouting obscene epithets. Paul, the prisoner who had appeared at Fallow's tent and encouraged him and others to join the riot, was considered to be the ringleader. He had received a sentence including confinement at hard labor for ten years in a case tried by my fellow judge, Lieutenant Colonel Wayne Alley, who had come to Vietnam as a replacement for Dick Snyder. I could not advise the court members of those other sentences or that, in my opinion, the accused was the least guilty of all the prisoners charged with crimes. One soldier yet to be tried had been seen actually throwing a fireball into the chapel, and another not yet tried had committed an assault that resulted in the death of another prisoner.

After advising the court of the maximum sentence that could be imposed in Fallow's case, and giving a few other standard instructions, the members retired to the deliberation room to consider punishment.

As the court departed, the defense counsel spoke for a while to the accused, then joined a few of the spectators in the rear of the courtroom smoking cigarettes. Fallows returned to the defense table seeming not to comprehend what had happened. From the bench, I looked at him, totally dejected and alone. I decided to approach Fallows, stepped down and joined him at the defense table. He did not seem to resent my intrusion on his presence but said nothing until I spoke.

"Private Fallows," I said, "whatever happens will not be pleasant but I promise that I will try to help you. Do you have any brothers or sisters?"

"A brother and a sister," he answered, "but they're not much help."

"What about your father?"

"He lives in Detroit somewhere. I only saw him once or twice when he came to visit his relatives and dropped by to see my mama. He didn't talk much to me."

"Do you know if he ever gave money to your mother?"

"I don't know."

"Private Fallows, you don't have to answer this, and I really don't have any business asking, but just for my information, have you ever in your life been happy?"

"Not real happy. A couple of times my cousins came around when some people brought Thanksgiving stuff and we were laughing and horsing around. My wife and mama were feeling good. but, it didn't happen often."

After a long, awkward silence, the members returned to the courtroom and all participants resumed our proper places. Fallows reported to the president, who announced:

"Private Fallows, this court, voting by secret written ballot, two thirds of the members concurring, sentences you: To be dishonorably discharged from the service, to forfeit all pay and allowances and to be confined at hard labor for eight years."

Fallows was stunned. With gentle prodding, his counsel led him back to the defense table where both sat in absolute silence. After a pause, he asked to speak to me.

"What about money? What does forfeit mean?" he asked. "How will my family eat? Will they still get an allotment?"

I hesitated, but could only be honest.

"They will for a time," I answered, "but one day the money will stop."

He looked directly into my eyes, his lips quivering and tears rolling down his cheeks.

"Can your brother help you?" I asked.

"I don't think so," he mumbled. "Mama says he got a pretty good job after his discharge from the army, but I never saw him. I think he went to meet our daddy in Detroit."

Neither of us could think of any other thing to say. There was nothing in the world I could envision in Fallow's future that might be considered encouraging. He was going to jail, he was losing money, and he would eventually be sent into the world with a punitive discharge.

The general who convened the court in Fallow's case reduced the confinement at hard labor to five years, but otherwise approved the findings and sentence. I knew from experience that the reduction of confinement would not be very meaningful, so I took an unusual approach in an attempt to help Fallows.

For the first time since becoming a military judge, I wrote a letter to the Court of Military Review in Washington on behalf of a soldier in whose case I had participated. I emphasized that Fallows entered the army as a Project 100,000 soldier, and, although many of the men recruited under that program made considerable contributions to the armed forces, Fallows was one who did not have the ability to do so. He could barely read or write. Of the two hundred or so prisoners who participated in the riot, Fallows had the misfortune of being one of twelve recognized by guards who would be able to identify him in court.

Most important, I wrote to the court, Private Fallows would never have been involved if others had not encouraged him. He was a follower, not a leader. The evidence in all the cases already tried indicated that some prisoners were planning the riot at least three days before it occurred, and Fallows was never implicated in the plotting. Although he had indeed used marijuana in the stockade, so did at least fifty percent of the other prisoners. Serving more time in prison would be useless. Going into the world with a dishonorable discharge diminished all chances of his future success. I asked the court of review to seriously consider reducing the sentence.

Several months after leaving Vietnam and reporting to my new duty station in Munich, Germany, I received the appellate decision in Fallow's case. It was very short. The findings of guilty were approved in their entirety. I was pleasantly surprised, however, to read that the court acknowledged receiving a letter from the military judge who participated in the appellant's case, recommending clemency. The court then reduced Fallow's confinement to that which had already been served and changed the dishonorable to a bad conduct discharge.

Thus Fallows had returned into the world he left, not better or wiser, but under more distressing circumstances than when he volunteered for the army almost three years before.

CHAPTER TWELVE

Rape and Murder at the Americal

In the appellate decision of the case of *United States v. Captain Robert Cole,* one member of the Court of Review, referring to the evidence of record, quoted General Douglas MacArthur's words when he confirmed the death sentence of Japanese General Tomoyuki Yamashita, as being "shamefully applicable here":

> Rarely has so cruel and wanton a record been spread to public gaze. Revolting as this may be in itself, it pales before the sinister and far reaching implication thereby attached to the profession of arms. The soldier, be he friend or foe, is charged with the protection of the weak and unarmed. It is the very essence and reason of his being . . . This officer . . . has failed utterly his soldier's faith. The transactions resulting therefrom as revealed by the trial are a blot upon the military profession, a stain upon civilization, and constitute a memory of shame and dishonor that can never be forgotten.

The facts that gave rise to Captain Cole's case occurred in a place known as Dragon Valley in the District of Tam Ky, not far from My Lai, scene of the massacre that bears the name of that village. On the rainy afternoon of June 2, 1968, Cole was commanding officer of Company B, 1st Battalion, 52nd Infantry, 198th Infantry Brigade, 23rd Infantry Division (Americal), which was involved in a combat mission sweeping through several small villages. As the men of the First Platoon of that unit were marching in staggered formation, Sergeant Warren Butcher, a highly regarded squad leader, was shot and killed by enemy fire while voluntarily acting as point man. His body was carried away by helicopter, but the men of the platoon continued the mission and captured several enemy suspects in one of the villages.

The circumstances which led to the trial of Captain Cole and four others concerned only three of the captured detainees: two Oriental females, both presumed to be medical personnel affiliated with either the Viet Cong or the North Vietnamese Army, and one Vietnamese man presumed at the time of his capture to be sympathetic to the Viet Cong. The females were clearly distinguishable from each other by every witness who later gave sworn statements or testified at the trials. One, known as Que, thought to be about seventeen years old, was identified as the taller and older of the two. The other, known as Yen, presumed to be about fourteen years old, was repeatedly referred to as the smaller, or younger nurse. One witness thought that these women were "unusually better looking than the ordinary Vietnamese female." The male, who later testified in one of the trials, was identified as a local villager named He Nhai, but was referred to by witnesses during the investigation and at the trial as The Old Gook. He had no known connection with the enemy.

When the members of Company B and the detainees reached the area where they were to spend the night, the two nurses and He Nhai were taken to a place set aside for interrogations near the helicopter landing zone. The other detainees were tied to trees, or escaped. Sometime during the questioning, two Vietnamese interrogators, one named Phan and the other Lun, apparently obtained some hearsay evidence that the younger nurse had knowledge of a small hidden cache, consisting of one or more small-arms weapons.

During the interrogation of the nurses and He Nhai, which lasted about an hour, they were beaten with sticks, hands, and knees. Several members of Company B, including the executive officer, Lieutenant Steven Sales, observed the questioning and physical abuses. The commanding officer, Captain Cole, stopped by, but there was no direct evidence of record that he observed the beatings. Sergeant Alvin Muller of the First Platoon not only observed, but participated in the interrogation and ripped open the girls' blouses. When Phan hit the detainees, causing them to fall backwards, Muller caught them and shoved them back to Phan, who continued the assaults. During the interrogation, Sales said that the girls would be shot the next day.

When interrogation of the three suspects was completed, He Nhai was tied to a tree and Captain Cole gave Muller permission to take the girls to the area designated as a bivouac for the First Platoon. Word of that fact soon spread among the troops. Within minutes, rumors were rife throughout the entire company that the girls would be raped by members of the First Platoon in retaliation for the killing of Sergeant Butcher. Muller led the nurses, with their clothes torn and breasts exposed, to the area where members of his platoon had already begun to prepare for the night.

Corporal Ralph Clayton, a grenadier in the unit, met Muller and the nurses on their arrival at the First Platoon area. An agreement was made that Muller would take Que and Clayton could have Yen. Two or three soldiers standing by agreed that they would take Yen when Clayton was finished with her.

As Que stood by, Muller borrowed Clayton's poncho liner, joined it with his own and fashioned a place for himself and Que to spend the night. It was not yet dark, but the weather was misty, the ground was wet, and overall conditions of the area were miserable. Muller immediately had sexual relations with Que against her will, then departed temporarily.

Corporal Clayton took Yen a short distance away from the meeting place with Muller and forcibly had sexual intercourse with her. He then left her unguarded, knowing there were soldiers waiting for her, walked over to a nearby foxhole, sat on its edge, and, within minutes, observed the girl he had just raped performing oral sodomy upon Specialist John Fulton and Specialist Carroll Burroughs. His (Clayton's) testimony:

"Fulton had the girl perform oral sodomy on him. He forced the girl to perform oral sodomy. He took a knife and held it behind the girl's head, and used profane language describing what she should do."

The prosecutor asked: "Did anything else happen that night?"

Clayton continued:

"Yes, sir, it did . . . when Specialist Fulton got through with the girl, Specialist Burroughs tried to have intercourse with Yen but he said the girl was too small. As he got off, the girl leaned up so nobody else would get on her . . . When she got up . . . Burroughs already had his penis out, and when she moved her head, he held her head and forced her to commit sodomy . . .

"Fulton advised Burroughs to use a knife, it was better that way, but Burroughs did not take Fulton's advice. A third soldier, waiting in line, then forced Yen to commit the same act upon him."

The records do not clearly establish what happened to Yen the rest of that night, but when Clayton last saw her, she was with two other members of his platoon in a foxhole. Evidence did establish that, at a minimum, two soldiers had intercourse with Yen against her will later that night and enough noise emanated from the First Platoon area to warrant a warning about observing night discipline. Sounds of a girl crying were heard throughout the night.

Although not firmly established, there was evidence that at least one and probably two soldiers had intercourse with Que between the time Muller first had intercourse with her and the time he returned to his prepared sleeping area about nine o'clock.

Clayton joined Sergeant Muller and Que in Muller's makeshift bed and went to sleep, with Que between the two soldiers.

During the night, Que began to cry, toss, and turn. Muller ordered her, in Vietnamese, to be silent and announced to Clayton that he was "going to get him some more of that," whereupon he pulled the poncho liner completely off of Clayton, covered himself, and proceeded to have intercourse with Que, once again against her will. When the act was completed, Clayton had intercourse with Que without her consent. Her reaction during the act was "just like a log. She did not make a move."

Clayton awoke the next morning to find blood on his person, his clothing and the bedding. His poncho liner was so stained that he threw it away. Que herself was covered with blood on the lower part of her torso and appeared to be in a state of shock. Muller told Clayton that the girls would be shot.

Early in the morning of June 3, before breakfast but during daylight, events occurred in the First Platoon area that were still not perfectly clear after the interrogation of more than one hundred witnesses by criminal investigators. Nevertheless, certain events of that fateful morning are without dispute.

When Clayton removed himself from Muller's makeshift bed, he noticed a "bunch of people" standing around laughing about something. Closer inspection revealed that Corporal Dave Bellow was having sexual intercourse with Yen. Testimony established that she was "out, unconscious, with her legs in the air over the guy's shoulders." While Bellow was laughing and having intercourse with Yen, she was, according to Clayton, "limp as a wet rag. It was more like torture than sex."

In addition to members of Company B, wandering soldiers from a contiguous unit watched Bellow's activities for a period of at least forty minutes. Sergeant Paul Boxer from Company A testified that he "sat on the ground and cleaned my weapon and watched what was going on." He further testified that the bystanders ". . . were making noise, like a bunch of GIs together, having a bullshit session . . . I would say Bellow was not having sexual relations . . . he was more like torturing her . . . she was about like a dishrag when you throw it against the wall."

When Bellow had finished with Yen, he stood up and walked over to Que, who was huddled in a foxhole weeping. He grabbed her by the hair, looked into her eyes, and announced to the bystanders that he did not think he would take her.

When Que removed herself from the foxhole after Bellow's abusive behavior, Sergeant Ralph Porter saw that she was in pain, clutching her stomach, moaning. In his written statement, he swore:

"Her stomach was very distended looking, and swelled out . . . I pulled her pants down to look at her stomach. And it was swelled out like she was pregnant or something, really all distended and distorted. I pressed on it to see if it was hurting up there internal, they told me she had been raped. I used the flash suppresser of my rifle when I was pressing up against her. I just didn't want to touch her with my hands. She was just sloppy looking and had blood on her."

Sergeant Porter regarded himself as sympathetic to the girl, even though he refused to touch her with his hands, except to pull down her pants. He also swore that he had seen both girls beaten for a period of about forty-five minutes the night before, that he saw Muller assist in the beatings, and saw Lieutenant Sales witnessing the interrogations and beatings. During the morning, he tried to remonstrate with Muller as the soldiers were watching Bellow and Yen, but Muller merely replied that the girls had already been raped between ten and twenty times each. Porter replied:

"I hope they . . . all catch the clap!"

And Muller responded:

". . . that is impossible because the girls were both virgins."

During most of the time the young women were being sexually abused, Captain Cole was at his command post, about a hundred meters away. There was no evidence that he actually witnessed the misconduct, although it was common knowledge, even among members of the adjoining company, what was going on.

Lieutenant Sales was in the area when the assaults were taking place during the morning. At about ten o'clock, when Yen and Que were both lying on straw mats, exhausted, Sales ordered Muller to "bring the girls and The Old Gook" to the command post.

The procession of Muller, He Nhai, and the bleeding girls with their breasts exposed was witnessed by several persons. They halted about six feet from the command post, where Cole was sitting. At the command post, a decision was made by Sales and Cole to take the girls and He Nhai to the landing zone about forty meters away. Sales and Burroughs accompanied Muller and the Vietnamese to the landing zone, which could be seen from the command post if one looked carefully.

Captain Cole remained in the command post during the entire episode that followed, but there was no direct evidence that he witnessed what was happening at the landing zone, although his radio operator, sitting beside him, did.

When the group of soldiers and detainees reached the landing zone, there were about twenty persons awaiting them, including both American soldiers and Vietnamese detainees. Sales announced that a decision had been made to execute the younger girl. He asked Phan, the interpreter, to kill Yen but Phan refused. Someone from the crowd suggested that The Old Gook shoot the girl. Sales agreed.

Although He Nhai knew nothing about shooting a rifle, Sergeant Robert Ivy handed him an M–16 with one bullet in the chamber. Ivy then put his own M–16 to the back of He Nhai's neck to insure that he would not turn against his captors. At this point, Sales requested and was granted permission from Cole to report to nearby American units that there would be a brief period of test firing. The report was duly made by one of Cole's aides and all Americans in the area took necessary safety precautions.

He Nhai fired the M–16 in Yen's direction; the single bullet tore off a portion of her neck and chin, but did not kill her. Lieutenant Sales approached the wounded girl, gasping and bleeding on the ground, and with his own M–16, completed the execution. A witness to the act stated:

"The first round made her head jump . . . The second round hit her head . . . It spread her brain matter all over the ground in the area."

Two soldiers dragged Yen's body away to a nearby road, where bodies of two Vietnamese casualties from the previous day also lay. Corporal Ted Baxter, the radio operator who was with Cole in the command post when the shots were fired, went immediately to the landing zone. He returned in minutes and reported to the Captain: "The girl has been shot by the gook."

After the shooting, Sales also returned to the command post, where, in bloodstained clothes, he exchanged glances with Cole, and after a pause, reported: "The gook shot the girl with an AK 47."

Captain Cole did not report the incident to headquarters, even after he saw Yen's body by the side of the road. He did, however, tell a corporal to keep Que in the unit for a while. This was done, although all of the other detainees were either released or taken to an intelligence gathering unit for further questioning. One sympathetic soldier brought food to Que for a few days and furnished her with a blanket, sleeping space, and other small necessities.

On the day after the execution, Cole's battalion commander came to the area where he noticed Yen's body, as well as those of the other dead Vietnamese, and demanded an explanation. Cole answered that they were suspected Viet Cong who were shot by other Vietnamese the previous day. Cole did not report the non-battle death or other atrocities in his organization as he was required to do pursuant to MACV regulations.

Four days after the incident, Company B's medic thought that Que could not "make it anymore" as she was sick and still bleeding. Because of a misunderstanding and without the consent of Captain Cole, he arranged for her to be transferred to the rear area for medical attention. A soldier testified that when Que was put on a helicopter to be transported to the rear, Cole saw her and remarked: "If she's taken back to Military Intelligence for interrogation, and she tells what happened in the field, we'll all swing for it!" At least one soldier had already made the remark that Que should not be sent back to G-2 because Cole would be hanged if she were.

Specialist Ralph Porter provided most of the information concerning the last days of Que among the American forces. After the events of June 2 and 3, he told Captain Cole, his commanding officer, that he was fed up with what he had heard and seen, and that he was not going to fight the war in such circumstances. Cole told Porter to catch the next chopper and, if he could find a job in the rear, Cole would release him from Company B. Porter departed the next day, June 4.

Porter remained at a place called LZ Bayonet for about eight days, and was successful in finding a position with the 11th Infantry Brigade, another unit of the Americal Division, effective June 10. On June 6, he reported the incidents of June 2 and 3 to a chaplain who, in accordance with Porter's wishes, promised not to make a further report, at least until he had spoken to Captain Cole.

On the morning of June 10, just before the scheduled departure for his new assignment, Porter went to the mail room at LZ Bayonet, but it was locked, which was unusual. When he met the mail clerk a short distance away from the mail room, the latter explained that he placed the wrong lock on the door by mistake the evening before, but he would get Porter's mail for him before his departure. A few minutes later, still concerned about his mail, Porter returned to the mail room and noticed a side door partially opened. In his statement to the criminal investigators, he swore:

"I stuck my head in the door and the supply sergeant was in the mail room. There was also a Vietnamese girl in the mail room with her back to me and the sergeant pushed me, acting very strange and telling me that the mail clerk would be back to get my mail for me."

On June 11, Porter chanced upon Specialist Ray Hornung, who had been in Dragon Valley on June 2 and 3 and had also, by chance, been infused into the 11th Infantry Brigade with Porter. Porter continued his statement:

"Hornung asked me if I had seen the North Vietnamese nurse in the supply room at LZ Bayonet and I began to piece together why the mail room was locked and why the supply sergeant had acted so strange. Hornung told me they couldn't take the North Vietnamese nurse to S–2 because Cole would hang if she were interrogated."

On June 12, Porter made a return visit to the mail room at LZ Bayonet and noticed a cot in the small room where no one usually slept; the room was empty although it had "that lived-in look." He was directed to get his mail from the adjoining supply room rather that the mail room. Porter asked the supply clerk: "Hey, what did you do with the dink?" To which the clerk replied: "We took her home."

"All the way to Tam Ky?" Porter asked. Stammering, the clerk replied: "I don't know, I just work here."

Porter then made a second trip to the chaplain's office, which led to the official report of the incidents of June 2 and 3. Records introduced at the trials reflected only that Que disappeared into a hostile area and was unable to be located for investigation or trial.

Lieutenant Sales was originally charged with premeditated murder, but psychiatrists determined that he was mentally incompetent to stand trial, and he was returned to the United States for treatment. No disciplinary action was taken against him.

Captain Cole was charged with failing to report a non-battle death of a female detainee who was killed while in custody of his unit, and failing to enforce safeguards to protect female detainees in the custody of his unit. He was convicted of violating a lawful general regulation, which was framed in the words of the Geneva Convention pertaining to the protection of civilians in time of war.

After findings were entered, the defense counsel introduced evidence to the effect that Cole was twenty-seven years old, had graduated from a prominent American university, and that all members of his family were successful in their own professions.

Records reflected that he had earned Parachutist and Ranger ratings, as well as the Combat Infantryman's Badge. He had come to Vietnam with Company B in October 1967, had much combat experience, and on the day before the alleged offenses, he returned from R&R in Hawaii. The court sentenced Cole to be reprimanded and to pay a fine of $2,500.

Sergeant Muller was tried for two offenses of raping Que, once on the evening of June 2 and once during the early morning hours of June 3. He was convicted only of the latter offense. After findings of guilty, upon questioning by the Defense Counsel, Muller testified:

"I just feel like my whole life has gone down the drain . . . Sergeant Butcher got killed, and I guess everybody like Lieutenant Sales [who had been found mentally incompetent], everybody was in a state of shock . . . I didn't care if I got killed or not . . . Well, the witnesses against me committed a crime as bad as mine or worse . . . They're going back to their families . . .

"I want to go home worse than I ever wanted to go home before . . . I just wanted to live. Now, I don't know. What's there to live for? . . . I didn't give a damn if . . . the VC killed me. I just wanted to get back on them a little bit. For all the trouble they've caused me, for all the guys I've seen die."

Muller then testified that he had been in Vietnam for eight months and had been on many long-range combat patrols, some when his buddies were killed. On the afternoon of June 2, his friend and leader, Sergeant Butcher, was killed before his very eyes and he couldn't believe it. His testimony continued: "I guess in a way I wish it would have been me instead of him, Butcher. I knew his girlfriend. He would have been married when he got home. I seen Sergeant Butcher get hit. I couldn't believe he was dead."

Muller was sentenced to be confined at hard labor for a period of two years but the time was later reduced to one year.

Ten days after Muller's conviction, Specialist Fulton was brought to trial on charges of committing sodomy with Yen, and assaulting Yen with a knife, with intent to commit sodomy. He was convicted only of the sodomy charge. He explained to the court his feelings in the following words:

"I'm sorry; might as well say that I let myself down. We walked into an ambush, Sergeant Butcher was killed.

"He [Butcher] quit school when he was in the eighth grade to help his parents. He was just great. You could drop him from a chopper; you could go anywhere with him . . . you just wouldn't think twice about doing anything [for him]."

Fulton then explained how upset the entire First Platoon was about Butcher's death and continued:

". . . our company commander gave us the detainees, and not an order given to rape them or anything, but gave them to us to secure for the night. Everybody was upset, one thing led to another . . .

"I, doing such a crime, I just can't see it. Like just animals, there is no cause for doing it even though we were upset. Come to find out after the detainees were interrogated by our interpreter, they knew the ambush was set up there. They let us walk into it; wouldn't say anything. I could have shot them right there. When you see people like Butcher get shot down, excuse me, their guts blown all over, you want to go out and get revenge. Maybe you don't, but I do."

At this point, Fulton broke down in tears and was given time to compose himself. There was no cross examination. He was sentenced to be confined at hard labor for one year.

Specialist Bellow was charged with the rape of Yen. At the end of the prosecution's case, the defense counsel argued that the prosecution failed to show that Yen did not consent to the act, and the only act proven by the government was intercourse with Yen, which was no crime. Based upon those arguments, he made a motion for finding of not guilty. The military judge granted the motion. Bellow was free without having to put on a case.

Specialist Burroughs was charged with sodomy but was found not guilty.

Specialist Porter was granted immunity from prosecution in exchange for his testimony against those who were tried.

Charges against others allegedly involved in the offenses were dropped after the acquittal in Burrough's case and the favorable ruling on the motion in Bellow's case.

No member of Company B was separated from the service as a result of acts committed against He Nhai, Que, and Yen.

CHAPTER THIRTEEN

The Animal Fair

Lieutenant Colonel Bob Jones loved animals. In fact, Bob himself was gentle as a puppy but sharp as any lawyer in Vietnam. He was the staff judge advocate of II Field Force, which was located not far from Long Binh. A collection of dog memorabilia decorated his office. A calendar on the wall guaranteed Bob pictures of different poodles each month. A shelf on another wall displayed little toy dogs he had collected and brought to Vietnam. And his desk was smothered with plastic, ceramic, china, and glass dogs of all pedigrees.

On the first occasion when I was assigned to hear a case at Plantation, Bob surprised me by calling in advance to say that he would himself pick me up at the Lucky Hotel and bring me to the site of the trial. I was happy with this arrangement because, previously, I had traveled away from Saigon only by plane or by helicopter.

When Bob arrived on the scheduled morning, we met in the lobby of the Hong Kong Hotel. As we walked out of the door, I spotted his jeep immediately because, as in some other legal offices, the legend "Here come de Judge!" was painted on the panel below the windshield. Inside the jeep were the driver in his assigned place and Bob's sergeant major sitting in the rear seat, cuddling a fluffy little dog with black spots on its body in places were there should have been hair. Unknown to Bob, the spots had been painted with a chemical by the vendor in order to sell the dog at a higher price with the explanation that this was a rare breed, indeed, found only in Vietnam.

It became immediately apparent to me that the reason Bob wanted to come to Saigon was to buy a dog to substitute for the poodle he had left behind in the United States. The animal he purchased was a friendly little thing and the occupants of the jeep vied for the privilege of holding "de Judge," as the dog had already been named. They offered me the opportunity to take a turn, but I declined with the explanation that "de Judge" had not had a rabies shot. "No matter," they replied, "he's just a puppy!"

Within a few days, two incidents happened that changed the course of events in the legal office of the II Field Forces. First, men who loved the animal built a little doghouse for their mascot surrounded by little sandbags as protection against mortar fire, and put a sign that identified it as being the home of "de Judge." No one could deny that that was the cutest thing at Plantation.

Secondly, "de Judge" expired of rabies. Although this was a shock to all men of the unit, some of them refused to take the series of painful rabies shots recommended by the medics. Most, however, considered the advice wise. So, on several occasions during trials, the court was required to recess in order for one of the court officers or the court reporter to report for his rabies shot. Happily, those who refused to take the shots had not been tainted by "de Judge."

I had not refused to touch Bob's little dog because of a dislike for animals, but rather because of an experience at our office in MACV headquarters. Sergeant Al Dugas was determined to have a squirrel for a pet and went down to the animal market in Saigon to purchase one. The one he selected, however, did not appreciate the gesture of its prospective new owner and bit Dugas, who then refused to buy that or any other squirrel.

When Sergeant Dugas returned to the office, he related the story of the squirrel that bites, pleased that he had discovered the bad habits of his intended pet before purchasing it. He was not pleased, though, when another sergeant advised him that he should indeed have purchased the squirrel in order for the medics to determine whether the animal was diseased. Frantically, Dugas rushed back to the market and made a firm offer to purchase the animal. Sadly, the vendor informed him that he could not keep any pet that bites, and he therefore threw the squirrel into the river. Sergeant Dugas underwent the series of rabies shots.

The incidents of the dog and the squirrel aroused my interest in the animal market. I persuaded Sergeant Dugas to give me a tour of the place when I next had an opportunity to take a few hours off. It came shortly after I received the happy news that a small room at the Rex Hotel was available and mine. I accepted without either thinking about the offer or looking at the room, and arranged to take the following Sunday off, when I would spend the morning moving to my new quarters and the afternoon visiting the animal market. Dugas came to the Rex Hotel in the early afternoon and we began our excursion.

The market was located along the Saigon River, just a few blocks from my new home. We walked there to find something quite unlike anything I had ever seen. The vendors sat in their allotted spaces on the crowded sidewalks selling virtually every kind of animal to be found in Vietnam smaller than a tiger.

Snake peddlers kept most of their wares in baskets, but at least four or five wrapped the reptiles around an arm or leg, or even their entire bodies. An Indian merchant kept a cobra in a hypnotic trance by playing a flute.

Dog vendors had canines of all descriptions and sizes tied on leashes to an overhead wire. Some were fat, but most were thin and mangy except for the puppies, which were easier to sell. Several of the dogs were chemically painted with spots or small circles to give them an exotic look. All seemed to be barking at the same time. The dogs offered for sale as pets were separate from those sold as food.

Small-animal dealers were grouped together. Their wares, intended mostly for sale as pets, included an amazing variety of rodents and other species of animals that I could not identify and whose names I did not learn. Most were confined to old bamboo or screen cages that apparently had been in use for many years. We saw several varieties of monkeys, some tied on ropes and jumping all about, others in cages. Cats, like dogs, were sometimes burned with spots and circles to increase their value.

Continuing down the street, we came to that part of the market where live animals intended to be used exclusively for food, such as goats and pigs, were sold. Chicken sellers were doing a brisk business and seemed to have the easiest time disposing of their wares.

The market sold more than animals. There were special foods available for exotic animal consumption, and others for human consumption thought to have special therapeutic value. Reputed aphrodisiacs made from horns, ears, eyes, or other parts of specified animals were also available.

The animal vendors were interspersed with ordinary country fair–type booths, hawkers selling trinkets or their own handcrafted specialties. The market did not seem to attract any particular category of person. There were male and female, healthy and lame, old and young, all seemingly enjoying themselves. Many of the little ones carried balloons; others attempted to play with the more friendly monkeys, dogs, and cats. None were afraid, and apparently rabies was not a cause to hinder any of the children or adults from taking their pleasure on a sunny Sunday afternoon.

CHAPTER FOURTEEN

Kathy

I first met Kathy at the steakhouse on the roof of the Rex one evening after returning from a trip to Lai Khe. She was having dinner with a captain from Long Binh with whom I had associated frequently in court. He invited me to join them and I did. Kathy was an attractive woman, about thirty-three, I presumed, although she appeared younger. She had short hair, a perfect complexion, a round face with large brown eyes. Her most remarkable features, however, were her constant smile and her ability to listen. People looked at her constantly.

Kathy was a toucher. Her hands seemed always in motion as she gently touched the arm or the hand or the shoulder of the person to whom she was speaking. On the occasion of our meeting, we shook hands and later during the meal she frequently touched my arm or hand to emphasize a point as she spoke. At the same time, she held the hand of the young captain. She was a secretary for the United States Agency for International Development (USAID), one of many American agencies in Vietnam. After dinner, Kathy invited me to join her and her friend for a drink in her apartment.

Kathy lived in that conglomeration of buildings across from the Rex that bordered on the two parks. We walked along Le Loi

Street and turned left on Tu Do Street for fifty yards or so, where we stopped in front of an entrance directly across from the Continental Palace Hotel. We paused before entering when Kathy pointed to a wizened, crooked man crossing the street toward us on his hands and feet under his body as fast as a young boy can run.

The man, whom I had seen several times, had a special place in his heart for Kathy. When he reached us, he looked up and gave her a great, almost toothless grin. It was apparent that he was happy to see her. His legs were frozen in right angles at the knees, with his bare feet flat against the pavement. His back was parallel to the sidewalk, supported at times by one or both arms, but he forced his head in an upright position. Kathy bent down, gently touched his face, smiled at him, and dropped a few piasters into the calloused hand lifted towards her. His smile broadened. The captain and I added a few coins before proceeding inside the entrance to the elevator, which took us up to Kathy's apartment floor.

There was a small kitchen to the left as one entered Kathy's apartment. Directly forward was a dining-living room combination about forty feet long and fifteen feet wide. It was completely furnished, including pictures on the wall, plants, and curtains. To the left, beyond the kitchen, was the door to her bedroom, in which there were a king-size bed, tables, lamps, and other bedroom furniture. A door from her bedroom led to the bathroom, complete with bidet and a combination bath and shower. It was all air-conditioned. "Do members of President Thieu's cabinet have such apartments?" I asked, half joking.

"Oh, this is nothing!" replied Kathy. "There are a dozen apartments in this building alone that are much nicer than mine, with outside views. My boss and a roommate who works for the United States government share a villa you wouldn't believe."

"Do you work for the head of USAID?" I asked.

"Far from it. My boss only handles one section of the agency. And, he has a gardener and a housekeeper to keep the house, which is surrounded by a large wall."

"Where does the big boss live?" I asked.

"You wouldn't believe that, either. I think some famous French general lived there. The last time I visited, a combo entertained and I danced with Ambassador Bunker."

Now it was becoming clear to me that the government was taking very good care of its civilian employees. Kathy had a good selection of liquor and beer, but she herself did not drink except in restaurants with meals. We sat in comfortable chairs and spoke of inconsequential matters with background music provided by the Armed Forces Network.

I was disappointed when I noted the clock on Kathy's wall indicated that the eleven o'clock curfew was fast approaching. I could get to the Rex in a couple of minutes, but there was no way the captain could return to Long Binh in that amount of time. For a moment, I toyed with the idea of inviting him to my room, where I had a folding cot, but quickly realized that the idea might not appeal to him. I stood up, thanked them both for a lovely evening, and excused myself. The captain did not seem concerned about curfew.

As time went by, I saw Kathy frequently, mostly in the company of one or more men, some of whom I knew, and at other times in the company of one or more women. People seemed to gravitate to her.

There was no consistency to Kathy's dress. Frequently she wore miniskirts; at other times, slacks or dresses of various lengths. Once she wore an au dai that she had purchased as a souvenir. She was always smiling, never outwardly depressed. She ate frequently at the open mess or the steakhouse at the Rex, and used the swimming pool there.

One evening in late November, Colonel Tom Edwards and I were sharing a meal in the open mess when Kathy and a woman friend joined us. I had, as the months passed, developed a friendship with Tom, whose room was next to mine and with whom I frequently shared the evening meal. He was about my age, very proper in all respects, and, by army standards, an intellectual. He was in his element when speaking of Herodotus, Tacitus, or

Thucydides and the ancient civilizations about which they wrote. He did most of the talking when we were together but I encouraged him to do so because it was a learning experience I enjoyed. I think Tom enjoyed having someone willing to listen to him.

The conversation with the women at the meal was pleasant, Kathy being her usual ebullient self, and Tom more restrained in his historical orations. Before dessert, Kathy's friend excused herself, leaving only the three of us at the table. We lingered a while, until Kathy asked us to escort her to her apartment. I excused myself because I had work to do and an early flight the next morning. Tom was a bit embarrassed but felt comfortable enough with Kathy by this time to walk home with her. I bid them both good night.

When I returned from Cu Chi the following evening, I showered, changed into comfortable clothes, and went to the open mess. Before I reached the end of the serving line, Tom, who was already in the room, came quickly to me saying that it was very important we talk alone. He excused himself from his former companions and went over to an empty table for two, reserving a place for me.

"What's up, Tom?" I asked when I arrived at the table. "You look a bit troubled."

"Sit down, and listen carefully," he replied. "You won't believe what I have to say."

"Try me!" I offered.

"Well, last night after you left, I escorted Kathy home as she requested. But it didn't end there."

What I am about to hear is not possible, I thought.

"So what happened?"

"Jack, you know I'm no Lothario. I'm forty-five years old and have never had an affair during my married life. I have a son at West Point and a daughter at Bennington. I was president of the PTA at the American High School in Ludwigsburg, Germany. I was . . . "

"I know these things, Tom. What happened?"

"Well, she invited me up to see her apartment and I accepted. You know I looked upon her as a friend . . . "

"Yes, I know you did." At this point I began to suspect Tom more than I did Kathy.

"Really, I did. When she offered me a drink, I accepted a Coke but only to be polite. Then, we sat down to watch a TV program and before I was aware of the time, it was past curfew."

"Please continue. I'm sure you haven't finished."

"Not nearly. She said quite calmly that I'd have to spend the night in her apartment. She went about rummaging for sheets and things to make up the divan in the living room for or me. I was trapped, really. But Kathy had no designs on me. She insisted that I use the bathroom before she got ready for bed. My wife would never believe this."

"I presume you then said good night and went to sleep," I said.

"Not I, but she did. I couldn't help thinking that there was only an unlocked door between the living room and her bedroom. I twisted and turned and got up to walk around. I took milk from the refrigerator. Not only was sleep impossible, but I couldn't even sit down comfortably. Finally, I had to go to the bathroom, passing through her bedroom. I didn't know whether to dress or go in my underwear, but decided to take a chance."

"Did she wake up?"

"Not at that time, but she did when I put on the light in the bathroom. Then, when I left the bathroom she startled me by putting on her bedroom light, asking what was the matter. She really was understanding, what with me stuttering in my shorts, she could see how uncomfortable I was. 'Look,' she said, 'you're all uptight. I know you're married and I'm really not interested in sex if that's what you have on your mind, or if that's what you think I have on my mind. It's three o'clock in the morning. Come in my bed and I'll give you a Seconal and we'll both get some sleep.' Now, how in hell do you think I could calm myself in her bed when I couldn't do so in the living room?"

"Don't stop now," I said. "There must be more!"

"I can't understand how or why, but I took her suggestion."

"You went into her bed and she gave you a Seconal?"

"Yes, but it didn't do much good. I kept turning and twisting."

"Until daybreak?"

"No. Then, I think she got a little irritated. She gave me another Seconal and that did it. When I woke up, she was gone; there was daylight all over, and I missed the bus to work this morning."

"That's some story!" I said. "But, it's over now and nothing happened, so you shouldn't be concerned. Your conscience is clear."

"Would you believe the story of an older man being invited into a younger woman's bed and nothing happened?"

"Probably not. At least, if that's all I heard."

"Do you think I'm going to tell any part of what happened to any person?"

"Look, really. No one is going to hear about it. Kathy certainly won't think twice about what happened. You've had an emotional experience. That's all it was. It's passed. The whole PTA in Ludwigsburg would believe you if they heard the whole story."

He did not appreciate my attempt at humor. He sat a while longer, still disturbed. Then, he stood up without finishing his meal, complaining that he was tired and had to go to bed.

A few nights later, I saw Kathy sitting alone in the open mess and joined her for dinner. She was happy and gregarious as usual. I hoped that she would bring up the subject of Tom spending the night at her apartment, but it was apparent that that had been an event of little consequence to her. I knew what an emotional experience it had been for Tom but curiosity prevailed over propriety, causing me to pursue the matter.

"I'm sorry I couldn't escort you home the other night with Tom," I said. "I hope everything was all right."

"Oh sure!" she answered. "He was very nice. If I'd have known how uptight he was, though, I'd have sent him home before curfew."

"I'm sorry you were inconvenienced."

"I wasn't really, except that he kept me from getting a good night's sleep. I'll say this for him. He's the only guy who ever slept in my apartment without trying to make a pass at me. He was so concerned about his wife. Actually, I left before he woke up and I haven't seen him since. I'd like to, because he is quite nice."

"You will, sooner or later," I replied. "He eats here most of the time. I think he's away now because I knocked on his door tonight and he wasn't in."

"Well, I wish more men were like him."

"I think tonight is the first time I've seen you alone," I said, changing the subject.

"I won't be for long. I'm waiting for a friend who will meet me here after dinner. I met her at a party last night and she doesn't have a place to live. Right now, she's sharing a small room with an older American woman and it's not a satisfactory arrangement."

"Is she going to move in with you?"

"No way!" Kathy responded quickly. "But I know an American civilian who says he works for an oil company and has a villa all to himself. I think he'll let her stay there. I called him today and we're going to see him about nine. Why don't you come with us? I'd feel safer walking home with someone in uniform, anyhow."

I hope it'll be before curfew, I thought, then responded: "Sure, I'll go along. Kathy, you have more friends than anyone I know. You're almost never alone. Do you ever get lonesome?" I asked.

"You bet I do," she answered. "I can't stand to be alone."

"But you always seem to be happy."

"That's how you see me. I always try to be in the company of others, even in my apartment. Before curfew, that is."

"You have so many friends."

"I know a lot of people, but I don't really have many friends. Almost every man I meet wants to go to bed, except your friend

Tom, of course. About three weeks ago, I met a doctor who was here on a fact-finding mission of some kind, and he was no exception. I like people, I really do, and I like to be with them, but the men who visit me all try to use the curfew as an excuse to stay at my place overnight. Sometimes I let them, but I insist they sleep on the divan in the living room."

"Haven't you made any serious attachments since you've been here?" I asked.

"No, and that's a pity. I'd marry tomorrow if the right man came along. But, the men here are either married already or looking for a good time. A lot of married ones are looking for good times, too, I might add."

"I've always had the impression you were quite content. I've seen you with men who were married and men who were not married."

"I don't mind being with married men, as long as we're having fun. I see nothing wrong with that. Of course, I'd prefer to be with single men, but here in Vietnam, it seems they have no desire to get serious."

I pondered a moment about the line of demarcation between having fun and having a good time.

"I guess I know about as many men as anyone around here," she continued, "I have friends in the army, navy, air force and Marines. And even civilians, as you'll find out tonight. One day I'll get marred to a man younger than me. I don't count my years chronologically."

"Vietnam is hardly the place to find a suitable man according to your specifications. If you do want to marry, it might be a good idea not to exclude older men."

"Listen!" she said. "There's something wrong with any man older than me who has never been married. I'm thirty-five, you know."

Perhaps she had a point, but I gave her my advice for what it was worth. "Be practical, Kathy. Don't exclude a whole category of men."

"I'm not conceited, really I'm not, but I do look young. I could have dates with young guys every night. They're all over the place."

"I know they are, and I'm sure they'd like to go out with you, but from what you've said, they're not interested in marriage. Things may not be different in the real world." Since she seemed to have a pretty thick skin, I decided to push on just a little further.

"By the way, what ever happened to you and the captain from Long Binh who was with you the night we met? I still see him occasionally, but never the two of you together."

"Oh, him! He was just like all the others, even worse. He can't be trusted. We had dinner together several times before I met you. We were pretty close, but I also told him I wouldn't go to bed with him or anyone else until I knew they were serious. I'm a perfectly proud Catholic. He didn't believe me."

"What do you mean?"

"Remember that night you just mentioned? You came up to my place with us. I knew he couldn't return to Long Binh so I let him stay in my apartment. We talked a long time after you left; then I fixed a place for him to sleep on the divan. Well, he sat down and was reading a magazine when I went to the bathroom to get ready for bed. When I came out, he was in my bed leering at me, and I knew what his interests were, even though I had forewarned him. We had a fight and I haven't seen him since."

Before I could indicate a reaction, I noticed an attractive young woman standing in front of our table smiling at us. Kathy seemed happy to see her friend and introduced me to Dianne, who sat down to join us for coffee and dessert.

From the ensuing conversation, I understood that Dianne had gone to Hong Kong to meet a boyfriend on leave from Vietnam, but things hadn't worked out very well. Not wanting to return immediately to the United States, she took a part-time job in Hong Kong at a hotel doing business with Americans. The pay there, however, was not sufficient to support her, so, at the suggestion of another American on leave from Vietnam, she decided to come to Saigon to look for work with the American forces. She had no luck up to that time, and was still looking around. Meanwhile, she needed a place to live and Kathy seemed to be her guardian angel.

I do not remember the name of the man whose home Kathy took us to, but he lived about a mile from the center of town. The residential area was the finest in the city, previously reserved for French and then American families. To get there, we walked past the Continental Palace Hotel and several official buildings surrounded by barbed wire and guarded by Vietnamese soldiers.

Kathy's friend lived in a white stucco house surrounded by a concrete wall except for an iron gate at the driveway. We rang a bell at the gate and, at the sound of a buzzer set off from within, we were admitted into the premises. The yard was large enough for trees, a sizable lawn, servant's quarters, and a bed of flowers.

The two-story house was approximately nineteen hundred square feet. The furniture was sparse, but adequate for a single person. We did not go upstairs but were told that it consisted of three small bedrooms and one bath. The house and furnishings had been provided to the occupant by his company and he apparently had no particular desire to make them more attractive.

Our host was polite, but not exceptionally so. My impression was that he thought Dianne much too young to have as a house mate, especially since she was unemployed. He served drinks and snacks, but showed no enthusiasm about the proposed living arrangement. We left the house at ten-thirty, the parties having come to no agreement, which both Kathy and Dianne interpreted as a negative reaction.

The walk back to Kathy's apartment was exciting. At that time, the curfew started at eleven o'clock, and would begin in about thirty minutes. Traffic was minimal and there was a strange silence in contrast to daylight hours, with the exception of an occasional mortar blast in the distance. As we passed along the guarded buildings, the Vietnamese soldiers armed with M–16 rifles stood up and shouted, "Numbah One!" when they saw the two women. No hassles, no problems. In the middle of Saigon, whose datelines filled the papers back home with reports of agony, assassinations, and mortar attacks, we witnessed only peace and quite except for the happy shouts of indigenous soldiers.

We arrived at Kathy's apartment with sufficient time remaining for Dianne and me to return to our respective hotels before curfew.

CHAPTER FIFTEEN

Lai Khe

Big Red One, as the First Infantry Division was commonly known, had fought bitterly in and around Saigon during the 1968 Tet Offensive and other major campaigns. It's mission was partially to defend the approaches to Saigon and the border regions between Vietnam and Cambodia. While continuing to fight Viet Cong and North Vietnamese army forces, the division also participated in pacification activities and training South Vietnamese Army (ARVN) forces. The division headquarters was located at Lai Khe, about thirty miles west of Saigon on what had previously been part of a French rubber plantation. The only remnants of colonial days were a run-down mansion and a broken-down swimming pool.

The garrison at Lai Khe was on alert status during my first visit there. Mortar shells from enemy forces struck the compound almost nightly and frequently during daylight hours. The men of the staff judge advocate section had constructed a bunker next to their office sophisticated enough to accommodate eight sleeping persons during the night. There were two raised wooden platforms against each of the walls for the lucky few who turned in early, but others slept on the ground, usually in sleeping bags.

Inasmuch as the bunker was only seven feet wide, four feet deep and ten feet long, the operation of extricating oneself from a sleeping bag, trying to avoid others sharing the bunker, and negotiating the ladder to the outside in the dark was a delicate operation. There was also the problem of undressing and finding a place to lay one's clothing.

I was invited to spend my first night at Lai Khe in the judge advocate bunker. Because of the obstacles involved, I slept with my clothes on and made no effort to leave the bunker until daylight.

On the morning after my first night in the bunker, I asked several members of the legal staff if they had known anyone sleeping above ground at Lai Khe who had been hit during the nighttime mortar attacks. To my surprise, no one knew of any such casualty. Then and there, I made a decision to forgo the safety of the bunker. On subsequent nights, I joined those brave souls from the office who shared a tent as their quarters and spent the nights on a simple cot above the ground.

My first case at the Big Red One was typical of incidents that happened hundreds of times in Vietnam, as well as other places where troops were stationed. The court-martial could have been avoided, in my opinion, with mature initial guidance and perhaps a mild punishment. A frustrated soldier, perhaps exhausted from combat or under the influence of alcohol, released his emotions in one brief moment of passion by throwing caution to the winds and offering violence to anyone who tried to control his actions or happened to be in the vicinity when the offenses occurred.

The incident began when the soldier refused to comply with the orders of his sergeant to get out of bed. The sergeant was quite willing to forgive the initial disobedience, but after a second refusal by the accused, the sergeant called in his platoon leader to repeat the order. Another refusal, and the platoon leader called in the company commander. Another order given and another refusal to obey. While all three were still present, in addition to a few spectators who happened by, the accused, in a fit of passion, leaped out of bed, grabbed a chair and threw it in the direction of all parties present. As a result, he was charged with disobeying three orders, as well as offering acts of violence to the spectators.

The soldier was sentenced to one year's confinement at hard labor, but no discharge. The staff judge advocate later told me that after three months, the soldier returned to duty.

The second case involved typical military-type offenses that might be expected in a combat zone. The accused was charged with three specifications of desertion. As generally understood, desertion requires proof that the accused departed from his unit with intent never to return. There is, however, another type of desertion, which is absence from one's place of duty, no matter how long, with intent to avoid hazardous duty. In this case, the accused had, on three separate occasions, gone away from his unit after having been assigned to night combat patrols, but returned shortly after the patrols had departed. This case was more serious than the first because it involved three separate incidents of misbehavior. The accused was convicted of all offenses charged and sentenced to five years confinement at hard labor in addition to a dishonorable discharge.

The third trial involved the type of case that sometimes occurred in Vietnam because of unfortunate prevailing circumstances and attitudes under wartime conditions. On the evening of July 29, Miss Than Thi Hong, a nurse employed in Company C, 1st Medical Battalion, sought additional employment at the local noncommissioned officers' club. She was immediately put to work and, at closing time on the same evening, was told to count the money in the cash register. After completing her chores, the sergeant in charge of the club arranged with Corporal Robert Horan, who had a three-quarter-ton truck at his disposal, to escort Miss Hong to Lai Khe Plaza, a central location in the village.

Several American witnesses testified for the prosecution about events preceding and following the alleged offenses before Miss Hong took the witness stand. The evidence tended to show that she entered Horan's vehicle about 10:30 p.m.; that she appealed for help to Americans on duty at a small outpost about

1:30 a.m. the following morning; and that she again reported two alleged incidents of attempted rape at the break of dawn.

Miss Hong was called to give evidence at the trial. I was doubtful whether she should testify in English or in Vietnamese, using an interpreter. I preferred that she testify in English because, while reviewing the pretrial papers, I noted that her English, although faulty, was superior to that of the 1st Infantry Division's interpreter, with whom I had previously spoken.

As Miss Hong entered the courtroom, she was accompanied by the interpreter. Before anyone else spoke, I gave her an opportunity to demonstrate her ability to speak English. I asked a few simple questions, including her name, place of employment, and residence. Although she answered in fractured sentences, she was, in my opinion, capable of conveying her thoughts. I advised her that she should make an effort to testify in English, but if, during her testimony, she did not understand a question or was unable to express her thoughts, she should request an interpreter. Somewhat to his surprise, I directed the prosecutor to proceed without an interpreter. He apparently had never spoken to the witness in English.

After being sworn, Miss Hong answered the first few questions without hesitation but began to falter when the prosecutor used words such as "accused" and "court-martial." When those and other relatively difficult words were explained to her, however, she seemed quite capable of understanding them. I was fully aware of the importance of her testimony because the outcome of the case would largely depend upon her credibility.

In my opinion, her own words in English would express her thoughts better than if funneled through an interpreter. Miss Hong testified in part as follows:

Q: (by the prosecutor): Miss Hong, where do you work?

A: (by Miss Hong): I work for Charlie Med. I am a nurse.

Q: Please explain what you mean by "Charlie Med."

A: Company C, 1st Medical Battalion.

Q: When the NCO Club closed on the evening of July 29, please tell us what happened.

A: Sir, when club closed about 9:45, I must stay in the club and count money and after I count money, I hear the club manager tell me, "You go home. You have a ride now."

Q: Did you get into a truck?

A: Yes, I did.

Q: And who was driving the truck?

A: Horan.

Her testimony was given in halting sentences, but graphic detail. She sobbed sporadically, but continued:

Q: Please continue.

A: When I get in truck, this GI he take me and go for ten minutes, and he stopped, and he told me, "truck has broke" and he forced his hand under my legs. I say, "No, I don't want to do that". . . he hold my neck, I try get out, I fall on right side, it is very difficult to tell this story, he try take off my pants first . . . and this road have many water and wet and I guess we get fight, I don't know. He take me and he go over to tree . . . he force his hand on my mouth, he force me to lie down and he try take off my pants. About twenty minutes later he take down my pants but not all the way and he lie over my body, on my belly I feel his body. He try fuck with me . . . he say he love me and I say "If you love me, you don't do that, because I am not whore and also I am not your animal." And I hit him . . . I try and go away. I run on the road and then he force me back, he say he will kill me if I run, and I . . . Sir, I forget my story.

After a few calming words, a drink of water, and a few moments of silence, she continued:

> And I talk with him. "I can't stay in the woods all this night. If you love me, tonight if you want to, I stay with you." He take me back to the truck. He take me to the motor pool and I call loud, but nobody hear me . . . he take me to a small room, he close door and take off my pants because they are easy for him to take off. He try same as in the woods. I called and nobody came and I am very sad, but I try something. I force my finger in my mouth and I make vomit and he don't let me out. He say "We fuck first, and then you

> go," and I say "I must go now, please, and you let me out" . . . he force me to lie down on bed. And I say, "Now I want to go bath and I am very dirty, my stomach very hurt now. If you don't take me, I don't know where to go. If you keep me, I smell very bad."

At this point, Miss Hong began to cry uncontrollably. I permitted a recess to allow her to compose herself. When we reconvened, she was able to continue her testimony:

A: Oh, I forgot. Inside, he say if I want to go out, I must take off all my clothes first. And I take off my clothes and put them in my bag. And I hold my bag and I go out. He not see my bag because I hide it close to my stomach. I run away, but I fall down in hole same as bunker, and I wet all my clothes.

Miss Hong further testified that she left the hole, put on her wet clothes, went over to a small unit where men were on guard and asked them to phone the military police. One member, acting as a medic, cleaned her arm and neck but told her she could not stay there because she might be a Viet Cong or a whore. Again she asked that the MPs be called but was told that there was no phone. The medic said he was sorry but she could not stay with the soldiers because they would get in trouble. Miss Hong then went out into the night, sat down by some trees, and waited until daylight when she reported the incident again to a different American unit.

On cross-examination, Miss Hong admitted that, when Horan told her to take off all her clothes if she wanted to go outside to the bathroom, she herself removed her blouse. Horan started to go out with her, but she managed to run away with her clothes hidden in her purse, and he could not catch her. When defense counsel asked if Horan ever made love to her, the response was that he tried but she was able to prevent him from having intercourse. She explained that, in nursing school, she learned that if a woman stops breathing, a man could not penetrate her, so she tried that as long as she could. Then she crossed her legs. She was more or less able to achieve success in defending herself against being raped because Horan appeared to be drunk.

She smelled beer and whiskey on his breath. That completed her testimony.

Several witnesses called by the prosecutor confirmed Miss Hong's testimony with respect to complaints and her physical condition following the alleged offenses. The sergeant in charge of the unit to which she reported at daybreak testified that Hong was in a state of emotional distress; her clothes were wet and disheveled; she had apparently been crying a lot because her eyes were red; her hair was messed up; and her neck and left arm were bruised. The prosecutor then rested his case.

The case for the defense was based solely upon the testimony of Corporal Horan. In the initial stages of questioning, the defense counsel elicited testimony that Horan had attended school only for a period of eight years and that his intelligence quotient placed him in the lowest mental category possible to be accepted into the army at the time he enlisted.

Concerning the alleged offenses, Horan testified that between five and nine o'clock in the evening of the incident, he went in and out of the noncommissioned officers' club several times and had about six or eight beers. Just before closing time, he informed the club manager that he had transportation that could be used to take the girls home, if there was such a need. There was, in the case of Miss Hong, who was working late, and the club manager accepted his offer. The record of trial reflects Horan's additional testimony as follows:

> Miss Hong got in the truck and I drove on. She was sitting in the middle of the passenger's seat. I stopped and I asked, well, I sat there and talked for a few minutes and then I asked her, I said, "You make love?" and she said, "No." And, I believe that I kissed her a couple of times. I'm not sure, but then I asked her, I said, "Let's go out there and make out," and I believe she said, "No." I can't say for sure. Anyway, I got out of my side and went around and opened the door and got her by the hand and led her out to the woods . . . And put my arm around her and kissed her a couple of times, and then the next thing I knew, we were on the ground. It was sort of damp. It really wasn't muddy but it was dirty enough out there . . .

It was rough, a lot of weeds and all, a lot of thorns. And, I told her, I said, "Come on. Let's make love," and she says, "No, carry me back to Charlie Med." I said, "then you make love?" and she said "Yes, if we go back." I says, "I have a place in the motor pool. We'll go down there," and she says, "Okay." So we got back and I did not drive her to Charlie Med but to the motor pool.

Well, in my room at the motor pool, we were both sitting down on the bed and I said, "Make love?" and she said "No." I said, "Come on, let's do it?" and she says, "No." And then she asked me if I had any water. I told her, "Let's make love, and then I'll give you some water," and she said, "No." And by that time she acted like she had vomited or something. Then she asked me if she could go outside to use the bathroom, and I said, "Yes, just go outside by the grease rack in the woods there." Anyway, she never did return and I walked outside and looked around for her, but I didn't see her. So I returned to my room and went to sleep.

On further examination, Horan denied ever having taken off either his or Miss Hong's clothes, ever having demanded Hong take off her own clothes, and ever having attempted to have intercourse with Hong against her will.

When the prosecution and defense concluded the presentations of their cases, I instructed the members of the court on their responsibilities with respect to findings. I spoke at length about the issue of credibility. The members of the court had the awful responsibility of making that determination. A finding of guilty would adversely affect Horan for the rest of his life. An acquittal would mean that they were not totally satisfied with Miss Hong's testimony. Whatever the findings, someone would be hurt.

The court members found Horan guilty as charged. They were then informed that Horan had been twice punished for minor disciplinary infractions within his unit. He was sentenced to be dishonorably discharged from the army and to be imprisoned for five years.

I have thought about Horan's case on many occasions during the years following his trial. I have never changed my opinion that his conviction was warranted, but I feel that Horan was not altogether lying. Perhaps he was shading the truth a bit, but not intending to deceive. Perhaps, with his limited intelligence, he did not believe that he was committing criminal offenses on the night of the incidents. There was nothing wrong in asking a girl to make love, he may have thought, and a mere negative response would not necessarily constitute a refusal. Horan may have reasoned to himself that he was innocent because Miss Hong did tell him, after the incident in the woods, that she had no alternative other than to spend the night with him.

At the time of Horan's trial, I regretted, as I do now, that the standards for acceptance of young men into the army were as low as they were during the Vietnam War. If men were indeed needed, the practical approach might have been to call up reserve and National Guard units, to make the draft equally applicable to all young men, and to tighten draft legislation. But no president or Congress was about to make those politically dangerous decisions.

After the trial, I read a letter Horan wrote to the commanding general pleading his innocence. Simple words, such as "rape" and "guilty" were misspelled. He was of the opinion that he had been convicted of the offense of rape, rather than attempted rape. Corporal Horan's letter assumed that, as an American man, he should be believed rather than a Vietnamese woman. I had previously observed a situation where a total disregard for the dignity of Vietnamese women had been expressed. During a training session for personnel bound for Vietnam that I attended at Fort Bliss, Texas, a sergeant lectured to us in graphic detail how to search Viet Cong if we had the opportunity. It included delving into all orifices of the body. Furthermore, he wanted us to know that, if he were present and there were women to be searched, he would be the one to do it. Many of the officers and soldiers laughed, accepting the obscenity of the remark as ordinary conversation about matters taken for granted. Perhaps Horan had been taught certain things in basic training that led him to believe that Vietnamese women were subject to his desires.

A sad note from Lai Khe

Major General Keith L. Ware, commanding general of the 1st Infantry Division, and seven other occupants in his helicopter were killed when his aircraft was shot down near the Cambodian border on September 13. The tail section close to the tail rotor of the helicopter was penetrated by a number of .51-caliber rounds fired by the enemy.

The body of the helicopter began to rotate causing the pilot to lose control. It crashed and burned. The division G–4, Lieutenant Colonel Hank Oliver, who shared a trailer with the staff judge advocate, and whom I had visited on several occasions, was in the aircraft. Ten days before the tragedy, on September 3, I had been in Lai Khe and spoke at length to both General Ware and Colonel Oliver.

General Ware was a quiet, dignified gentleman, fifty-two years old, who worked himself up to his position through the ranks. During World War II, he had been awarded the Congressional Medal of Honor for valor. Away from home, lonesome like everyone else, he adopted a dog named Rex who failed to meet the requirements of the K-Nine Corps but not the affection of the general who kept him by his side at all times. They died together.

General Ware was buried at Arlington National Cemetery shortly after his death. The president of the United States attended his funeral.

CHAPTER SIXTEEN

Election 1968

I did not vote in 1968. Sitting with about ten members from the legal office in Dong Tam, huddled around a small black-and-white television, we watched and listened to the presidential election results. Some of the group supported former vice president Richard Nixon, thinking that he might succeed in his promise to end the war with honor. Others felt that the Peace Conference in Paris would have a better chance of success with the election of Vice President Hubert Humphrey. President Lyndon Johnson, a lame-duck president, had little influence in Paris, but perhaps Humphrey, if elected to the high office, would be more effective. Personally, I did not favor either. I was a skeptic. In my opinion, there was no way to end the war with honor, regardless of who won the election.

I began to doubt the possibility of success in Vietnam during 1967 when the number of United States troops there was growing exponentially with no evidence we were winning the war or approaching a peaceful settlement. Early in 1968, with those doubts growing, I was called out of a courtroom at Fort Polk, Louisiana, and told that I was being considered for an assignment to Vietnam; unless someone else volunteered for the position, I would have no choice.

I could have resisted going to Vietnam. I was eligible for retirement; was stationed in Texas, where I had previously made my home; and was a member of the state bar. I had good prospects for employment and was still young enough to begin a second career. I seriously considered retirement.

During the period of my doubts about accepting an assignment to Vietnam, the United States Marines were besieged at Khe Sanh and the Viet Cong achieved a psychological, if not a military, victory in the Tet Offensive. I watched the fighting on television nightly, witnessed General Loan executing a suspected Viet Cong soldier without trial, and heard prominent newscasters questioning the wisdom of America's presence in Vietnam.

More disturbing than all the headlines and graphic pictures, though, were the changing attitudes of some of the president's closest advisors. Secretary of Defense Robert McNamara, an architect of the war, disappointed the president by his actions, which reflected a feeling that there could be no victory in the war. He was replaced by Clark Clifford, once an advocate of our policies in Vietnam and an adviser to all Democratic presidents since World War II. He, too, grew disenchanted with the possibility of success, and could no longer encourage Johnson to continue his aggressive policies. Wise men from the past were called on to advise and comfort the president, but they could not agree on what their leader should be told except that his policies were untenable.

In the years preceding 1968, there had been much dissent in the United States. Martin Luther King, Jr., was vociferous in his denunciation of the Vietnam War; civil strife and protest marches were increasing; Dr. Benjamin Spock and Rev. William Sloan Coffin, Jr., were indicted for conspiracy to counsel young men to violate the draft laws. In late 1967, Democratic Senator Eugene McCarthy announced he would be a candidate for president in the following year, advocating a negotiated settlement of the war.

Some of us in the military, who had taken an oath to defend our country, and did so when called upon, were beginning to question the wisdom of its Vietnam policies. Sadly, some officers in the United States, who accepted their roles without question, were misinformed about daily occurrences in Vietnam. I heard a Lieutenant Colonel at Fort Bliss, Texas, express surprise to learn that Rolling Thunder, the operation that authorized the constant bombing of North Vietnam, was still in effect in February, 1968.

I called Washington to let my superiors know that I would accept orders to Vietnam, no need to look for a volunteer substitute. I cannot, even now, be certain whether it was a sense of patriotism, duty, or curiosity that compelled me to do so. The army had been my profession for twenty years; I felt that I could not refuse even what I interpreted to be a request. On the other hand, I am sometimes troubled by the thought that my motive might have been curiosity. The opportunity to observe Vietnam firsthand was attractive because my job as a senior military judge would take me to all sections of the country, from the Demilitarized Zone to the Mekong Delta. I would be able to witness for myself the experience of Vietnam.

In March, Senator McCarthy made an impressive showing in the New Hampshire presidential primaries. Robert Kennedy entered the same race soon thereafter as a peace candidate. President Johnson, in effect, acknowledged that he could not lead the country to victory when he announced on March 31 that he would not be a candidate for re-election. In the same month, Richard Nixon, out of office, pledged that a new administration would "end the war" in Vietnam. War protests and peace marches increased. It appeared to me that the average American's assessment of the war was beginning to change.

Those were my thoughts even before the 1968 campaign began. Disturbances since March had added to my apprehension. Martin Luther King, Jr., and Robert Kennedy were murdered; the riots in Chicago during the Democratic Convention were unprecedented for such an occasion; the number of troops in Vietnam increased by ten thousand but the Joint Chiefs of Staff had requested an additional two hundred and five thousand. Young men were fleeing to Canada or seeking legal methods of avoiding the draft.

The campaign did not change my mind. Richard Nixon, as vice president during the Eisenhower years, had certainly concurred in the momentous decisions concerning Indochina in 1954 and thereafter. It was President Eisenhower's decision to replace the French after their defeat at Dien Bien Phu and subsequent departure; to establish, in fact, the nation of South Vietnam; to support Ngo Dinh Diem as the miracle man of Asia; and to send American advisers and treasure to build up the South Vietnamese army.

Nixon believed in the war's necessity. Out of office, in the early 1960s, he did not hesitate to express his opinion that the war in Vietnam must be won, or that the Communist Chinese must be prevented from entering Vietnam by whatever means necessary.

During the campaign, it was widely believed that Nixon had a secret plan to end the war, and he did not discourage that belief. He spoke constantly of ending the war "with honor," but did not explain how that could be done. Perhaps he reasoned that his campaign oratory would have the same effect on the voters as Eisenhower's promise to visit Korea and end the war there if he was elected in 1953.

I did not believe that there would be peace with honor. It was unrealistic to think that Ho Chi Minh could be bombed into submission or that he would accept even an offer of mutual withdrawal of fighting forces from South Vietnam without a promise from the United States to withhold all support to the South Vietnamese government.

Nixon had always advised negotiating from strength. With over half a million American servicemen and women in Vietnam, in addition to a navy and air force second to none in the world, how much more could we be strengthened there? Did he anticipate incursions into Laos, Cambodia, and North Vietnam? Or the use of nuclear weapons? If so, those were not viable alternatives, in my opinion.

Vice President Hubert Humphrey was an unknown insofar as the Vietnam War was concerned. I could only make assumptions.

Although he promised the president not to stray from the path set by him, I assumed that his true liberal feelings would prevail, and, if elected, he would act in accord with his party's original platform to end the war quickly. I could not anticipate how his feelings, whatever they might be, could be translated into extraction of our forces while simultaneously preserving the integrity of the South Vietnamese government.

Convinced that neither party could end the war without being humiliated in the process, I explained to my colleagues in Dong Tam why I had not voted. They did not seem to care. There was neither a mood of elation nor depression when Humphrey conceded. Now what would happen? I wondered. Will Nixon's "secret plan" work? Would we have peace with honor? I did not think so because I did not think anyone could achieve the impossible. But, I said a prayer that somehow, in some impossible-to-predict way, peace would come to the United States and to Vietnam.

CHAPTER SEVENTEEN

Silent Night

Johnny Abadie was a smart cookie. He knew all the answers. Never at a loss for words, he commented about everything in his company. The platoon leader was pretty stupid; he should never had been allowed into Officer Candidate School from which he had graduated only a few months before coming to Vietnam; the commanding officer was not much better; the chow was bad and the first sergeant had his favorites. Johnny spoke louder than any of his fellow soldiers, but he was not offensive, except when discussing officers. He did have a way to get the things he wanted of his fellow soldiers, especially marijuana, and he wasn't bashful about using it or passing it around to his friends.

Johnny had graduated from high school in New York City and boasted to his friends that he played football, basketball, and baseball, and was a general all-around big man on campus. The girls loved him and he loved the girls. He began smoking cigarettes when he was twelve but he had the will power to quit during sporting seasons. When army recruiters came to his school, he volunteered immediately, saying he wasn't afraid of any Viet Cong. He was not unpopular among most of the soldiers, but his officers hated him. Although he managed to avoid serious trouble, he did receive company punishments twice for being late at formations. His record as a combat soldier was as good as anyone's in the unit.

Something happened one day, however, that reversed the tide for Johnny. He purchased a few ounces of marijuana from an outsider and sold some of it to three of his buddies. His offense was reported to the commanding officer, and Johnny was threatened with a court-martial. "Not for me," Johnny confided to his buddies, "they will have to catch me first!" With those words, he departed from his company without permission.

Frustration and the threat of a court-martial were not the only causes of Johnny's departure, although they provided the turning point that pushed him to the decision he made. Johnny was in love. He knew that Kim Hoa, whom he called Kim, would give him the refuge he needed in Saigon.

Kim was not an ordinary girl like those who worked in bars and had formed liaisons with some of Johnny's buddies, but a pharmacist in one of Saigon's largest Western-style drugstores on Tu Do Street. She had come to Johnny's attention on his first trip to Saigon where he had been officially dispatched to pick up supplies. He unofficially extended that trip, however, to visit a pharmacy for the purpose of purchasing what his fellow G.I.s referred to as "beetle juice," a drug that was legal on the Vietnamese market, but forbidden to American soldiers by the Uniform Code of Military Justice.

Johnny was entranced when he first saw Kim, delicate and beautiful, with face and body perfectly sculpted. Her long black hair fell gracefully past her shoulders to her waist. She weighed less than a hundred pounds, but her smile reflected the charm of a Renaissance painting. She spoke English with a fractured but engaging accent. Her au dai flowed gracefully as she moved about. Johnny tried with all his skills and talent to arrange a later meeting, but had no success.

On his second visit to the drugstore, Johnny detected in Kim's attitude what he assumed to be a slight interest in his presence. He followed his instincts, and persuaded her to take a short walk with him. Without touching, they strolled leisurely up and down tree-lined Duy Tan Boulevard to and from Notre Dame Cathedral in the center of the city.

From that day, Johnny thought and dreamed only of Kim. He sneaked away from his unit near Long Binh as often as he could to share Cokes with her on the terrace of the Continental Palace Hotel, which was across the street from Kim's pharmacy.

Within eight weeks after their first meeting, Johnny and Kim were living together in a small room near the large market between Saigon and Cholon, although Kim had never before shared her life with a lover. She was aware that her parents had long ago promised her to a young man in their village, but after three years at the university in Saigon and one year as a pharmacist in a large city, there was little chance that Kim would return home to live.

When Kim insisted that Johnny meet her parents, he managed to get a four-day pass from the first sergeant, convincing him that he deserved a break at the rest and recuperation (R&R) center in Vunc Tau. Indeed, at that time, Johnny had not even taken his authorized week of R&R, after having been in the country for six months. On the way to Vunc Tau, it was nothing at all for Johnny to make a detour to Saigon. From Saigon, he and Kim took a regular Vietnamese bus to Phuoc Vin and from there walked to the village where Kim was born and her family lived.

Kim's parents were not pleased with the idea of their daughter bringing home an American soldier, but they reluctantly consented. They were pleasantly surprised, however, when they met Johnny, who was able to gain their friendship with his congeniality and thoughtfulness for bringing gifts to them and their children. He was respectful at all times and gained favor with the children by teaching them how to play American games. He seemed at ease coping with Vietnamese customs, and enjoyed the food they served. The visit ended with all-around good feelings.

As the weeks progressed following the home visit, Johnny and Kim's love grew deeper and they promised each other that one day they would be married. That was the situation when

Johnny was threatened with a court-martial and departed from his unit.

When Kim saw Johnny at the door of their room with a full duffle bag, she surmised that something was wrong. She welcomed him, however, and when he promised that they would never again be separated, Kim suggested that they be married in her village. The thought of marriage had occurred previously to Johnny, but he had been hesitant to ask because of the possibility of rejection and moreover, there was not a chance in the world that permission to marry would be given to him by any United States official. But now that he was free of military restraints, Johnny eagerly accepted Kim's proposal, encouraging her to arrange a date in the village as soon as possible. She gained her parents' consent and a marriage date was settled with the proper officials.

On the afternoon before the wedding, the couple again went to Kim's village via the local bus. Upon arrival before dusk, most of the villagers (but probably not the young man who continued to hope that one day Kim would be his own bride) were waiting excitedly near the community well, gossiping and playing children's games. Some escorted the couple to Kim's parents' house where a wonderful smell radiated, a sign of preparations for the feast that was to follow the wedding. Kim's mother and her friends had spent a week cooking delicate Vietnamese meat and vegetable dishes as well as traditional sweets. Kim's father and some friends were outside watching a whole pig being roasted over a smoldering fire.

On the evening of their arrival, after a modest meal including rice wine, the entire family and Johnny visited the concrete structure (in the form of a woman's womb) on the outskirts of the village where Kim's ancestors had been buried for centuries. This was a custom more common during the Tet holidays than at weddings, but Johnny himself requested the visitation since he had never before had the opportunity to do so. Later that evening, one of Kim's relatives brought Johnny to his house, where he spent the night.

A traditional Vietnamese marriage is not a simple matter. There are customary notifications, promises, and preparations to be made by the families, first at the time of engagement and later in preparation for the marriage. Kim's parents agreed to forgo all but the essential parts of a wedding, including the acceptance of Johnny's traditional offer of money to compensate them for the education of their daughter.

On the morning of the wedding, Johnny dressed in fashionable shirt and trousers, his latest acquisitions from the Cholon Post Exchange, which he had carefully chosen for this special day. Then, again accompanied by his host, he went to Kim's home where dozens of relatives, friends, village officials, and several Buddhist monks in saffron robes were already assembled. The house was festively decorated with candles in the shape of dragons, Chinese lanterns, red roses, yellow mums, and small lilac flowers.

In all his dreams, Johnny was not prepared for the beauty of his bride, radiant in a completely white au dai, embroidered with likenesses of traditional village flowers. Together with Kim, he was taken to the family shrine where pictures of recent ancestors were honored. Reverently, they joined hands, said silent prayers begging for future blessing, and then turned to bow in respect to Kim's parents.

During the ceremony that followed, performed by the village chief, Johnny respectfully responded to instructions concerning the expected responses of a bridegroom. The villagers who attended were impressed with Johnny's attentiveness to his bride throughout the day, which was spent in feasting and celebrating, accompanied by traditional wedding and popular music. Late in the evening, after the last of the guests departed, Johnny and Kim retired to a small room especially prepared for them in the parents' home. Early the next day, a farmer gave the couple a ride in his hay wagon to Phuoc Vin, whence they took the old bus back to Saigon and a new life.

The first few weeks of marriage were the happiest time of Johnny's life: no money worries; a beautiful, tender, and compliant wife who loved him; a nice enough place to live; and best of all, no one to give him orders. He did not regret his decisions to leave the army and marry Kim. They awoke before dawn each morning and embraced each other until the silence of the night was shattered by the curfew's end, indicating the beginning of a new day. They went to market early in the morning to purchase supplies for the evening meal. Then, as Kim dressed for work and carefully brushed her hair, Johnny looked at her lovingly, wishing there would never be another day in his life without her.

During the day when Kim was at work, Johnny joined a group of American deserters living in the area. They were all young men, barely old enough to vote but living by their wits as outlaws in a war-torn country. They taught Johnny how to obtain illegal ration books to use in the Cholon PX. Radios, television sets, tape recorders, and cameras purchased there would bring enormous profits on the black market.

Johnny was not ashamed of his unlawful transactions. He rationalized that the United States government sent provisions to Vietnam for the Americans, and the bottom line for the Americans was to fight a war. He had already participated in more than his share of combat. His conclusion, therefore, was that other American personnel and their allies, including civilians, who had the freedom to use the PX but had never seen combat, were less deserving of its luxuries than he was.

When not engaged in illegal activities, Johnny and his newfound friends played card games and spent endless hours in idle conversations. Unlike his companions, who drifted along under the influence of drugs, Johnny did not even smoke marijuana, an old army habit. There was no pleasure for him greater than dreaming of Kim and anticipating her return from work. He used some of his time making their little room more comfortable. He bought a large mirror for Kim, a nicer wash-basin than had been furnished with the room, more mellow tapes for his new recorder, and a few inexpensive paintings to hang on the walls. Every evening when Kim returned, Johnny had a gift for her. A doll, a handkerchief, perfume, or any little thing to let her know that he loved her very much. Although his friends cavorted about at night spending money on fancy food and good times, not once did Johnny and Kim leave their own little piece of the city.

Johnny watched in silence as Kim cooked the evening meal. Her lithe body shunted about quietly as a kitten. Sometimes, they did not speak, but took pleasure only in being alone in each other's presence. After dinner, when traffic died down because of the curfew and all was quiet except for the distant rumblings of mortar shells, they embraced and made love in the stillness of the night.

Early one morning, less than a month after their marriage, the little world of Johnny and Kim was shattered. They were awakened by a bullhorn from a vehicle announcing that the location of several American deserters in the area was known to the military and Vietnamese police. The booming voice demanded that all illegal residents come outside to surrender. Preferring to accept the risks of not complying, Johnny hid under the bed but within half an hour, the door to his room was torn apart. When he looked up, American and Vietnamese police in uniforms were staring down at him. Johnny attempted unsuccessfully to resist, but was forced out of the room as Kim cried aloud, powerless to interfere. He was then unceremoniously carted off to the holding stockade in Saigon where he remained until the next day when armed guards from his unit picked him up. Johnny's commanding officer immediately confined him to the Long Binh Stockade, where he was held pending further action.

Court-martial charges were prepared against Johnny alleging that he sold marijuana to his fellow soldiers; deserted the United States Army; stole a .45-caliber pistol that was in his possession when he left his post; and resisted arrest on the morning he was apprehended. The pretrial Article 32 investigating officer recommended that Johnny be tried by a general court-martial on all the charges. The commanding general of the 1st Infantry Division at Lai Khe concurred, and ordered that the case be referred to a general court-martial to be convened on December 24th at Di An.

On the morning of Christmas Eve, 1968, I was taken by helicopter to Di An to preside over the court-martial of Private John M. Abadie. I was met at the helicopter pad by a legal officer who escorted me to the place of trial. All these years later, today it seems incredible that a simple canvas structure could serve as a suitable courtroom. Like many other venues of trial in Vietnam, it was nothing more than a tent originally intended for other purposes, with side flaps rolled up, and a few chairs and tables arranged to make it resemble a place where a trial could take place. We called it a courtroom.

As we approached the courtroom, Johnny was the first person to come to my attention, a fact made obvious by two armed guards who accompanied him. More interesting, however, was the young Vietnamese woman, well groomed, weeping, and holding his hand. All officers of the court had taken their assigned seats before my arrival, at which time the defense counsel motioned Private Abadie and his guards to enter and take their assigned places. The prosecutor informed the witnesses that they must remain outside, or take shelter from the sun in a nearby legal office until they were summoned.

The presentation of evidence to the court consisted of testimony by three members from Private Abadie's unit who testified to the sale of marijuana before Johnny left his unit without authority; the company clerk who proffered the necessary documents to show that Abadie departed and returned on the dates alleged; the first sergeant who testified that the pistol assigned to the accused was missing since the date of his absence; and two military policemen who assisted in apprehending him in Saigon. Johnny testified only that he intended to return to the army one day, and that he intended to return the pistol. The defense counsel offered nothing else in his behalf on the merits of the case. The court found him guilty of everything of which he had been charged and then, about seven in the evening, recessed for dinner, to reconvene an hour later.

In extenuation and mitigation, Johnny swore that he had never been in trouble in civilian life; that he performed his combat duties well, having gone on eight long-range patrols, each lasting more than two days; that he had done nothing in his company that might be considered serious misconduct before his departure. He begged the court to be lenient, especially since he was now happily married and convinced that he could be a good soldier. One of the members of the court, who appeared a bit cynical to me, asked whether Johnny knew he was not legally married, and furthermore, how could he perform combat duties efficiently in the future if he had to be concerned about a woman in Saigon whom he presumed to be his wife.

When Kim Hoa took the witness stand to testify in Johnny's behalf, at about nine-thirty, the entire compound was relatively quiet. Christmas music, dedicated by the Armed Forces Network to homesick Americans, drifted into the courtroom from almost every radio in Di An. Kim looked delicate and fragile as a porcelain doll, even though she had spent the long day in and out of the sun. She described how she had met Johnny at the pharmacy; how their acquaintance had grown into deep affection; and how affection progressed to love and marriage. Even her parents, who were devout Buddhists, respected Johnny for his good manners and the example he gave to the villagers. Most of the members of the court seemed impressed by Kim's background and behavior, but the one who had earlier appeared unsympathetic wanted to know why she had been living with the accused even before she could even presume they were legally married. She simply said that they were in love. Kim pleaded for the members to be lenient as possible with her husband because of her absolute certainty that one day they would be reunited and she wanted that day to arrive as soon as possible. When she completed her testimony, crying softly, the prosecutor touched her gently, pointing to the exit. I felt that even he was a bit sympathetic, but he nevertheless asked for a severe sentence appropriate to the seriousness of Private Abadie's offenses. The court then recessed to determine what sentence would be imposed.

During the deliberations on sentence by the members of the court, I sat alone in the grass on an incline overlooking the courtroom. There were lights in many of the tents on the compound. Cigarettes burning like fireflies indicated that some people were walking about. Johnny and Kim were sitting not more than twenty yards from me, their hands tightly clasped, with guards permissive enough to allow an occasional show of deeper affection. As sentimental as I wished to be about my own absence from home, I could not dismiss thoughts about the future of the accused and his wife. From experience, I knew that Johnny would be sent to prison, leaving Kim alone with her memories in Saigon. Since the marriage had not been sanctioned by American officials, it was doubtful she would be able to immigrate to the United States any time soon, if at all. Yet, I assumed that, in her innocence, Kim was trying to console her husband with thoughts of being together in the near future. Although I knew this could not be, I believed that Johnny had become a more mature person because of his recent experiences.

When the court reconvened, the president announced that Private Abadie was sentenced to be dishonorably discharged from the army and to be confined at hard labor for five years. Johnny had apparently been prepared by his defense counsel because he remained stoic, but Kim's tears reflected emotions that could not be contained.

After adjournment, the court members, spectators, and witnesses departed from the area. At my suggestion, Johnny and Kim remained alone in the lighted courtroom for a few minutes, discreetly observed by the guards outside. When the couple returned to the guards, they embraced, crying softly, until interrupted by an officer who had accompanied Kim from Saigon that morning and was to return her there in a military sedan that was not bound by the curfew rules. Johnny was handcuffed and taken to a waiting jeep that would return him to prison and Kim was led to the sedan that would bring her to an empty room. Their eyes focused on each other until it was impossible to communicate further. The vehicles drove away in different directions as music from the Armed Forces Network concluded its Christmas eve program with the prayerful "Silent Night."

CHAPTER EIGHTEEN

A Hometown Boy

Private Ben Rasteau had a reputation among members of his unit as a loner with no record of misconduct. On the afternoon of the alleged offenses, he had been assigned as a guard in the defense of his company's perimeter. With three other members of his unit, he sat in a bunker, silently separated from the others, who played cards, spoke of home, and drank beer.

Without warning or reason, Rasteau picked up his M–16 and sprayed the bunker with rifle fire, killing all three of his comrades. He then went out into the open where he continued to shoot indiscriminately until he himself was shot in self-defense by his first sergeant. Those were the facts and there were a dozen witnesses to prove them. For the defense, there was only the report of a psychiatrist who believed that, at the time of the alleged offenses, the accused was not capable of forming a specific intent to kill, although he did know right from wrong.

While reviewing a report of the case in the courtroom at Dong Tam early on a Sunday morning, I was distracted by the arrival of a jeep containing the first participants of the drama that was about to unfold. In addition to the driver, there were two armed guards escorting Rasteau whose chest, hips, and entire left leg were enveloped in a white cast. The accused, with great difficulty, and the guards dismounted from the jeep, entered the courtroom, looked around, and departed almost immediately after seeing me. For a while, I watched from my bench, thinking that I had never seen a more innocuous-looking defendant. The three stood outside, probably sharing the same thoughts, but hardly speaking. I decided to join them.

The guards were relieved when they saw me approach. Members of Rasteau's unit, they knew him at least casually, and seemed uncomfortable guarding their fellow soldier. There was no mood of hostility among them. They shared cigarettes and matches, seemingly aware of each other's unpleasant situation.

Rasteau smiled ruefully when I introduced myself, but did not speak in response. I commented upon his obvious physical discomfort and told him that he might remain seated throughout the proceedings. When I asked about his hometown, his reply startled me.

"Lafayette, Louisiana, sir."

Lafayette, the heart of Cajun country, is my own hometown. My reaction to his reply apparently conveyed this information to him. We had spent our youths in the same environment. The thought that we had experienced other Sunday mornings in the same surroundings, although twenty-five years apart and in another world, provided a spirit of kinship between us. He looked into my eyes and spoke with emotion as he talked about the long walks he had taken in woods that I had loved as a child. We fished in the same bayous and spent weekends in the same scout campgrounds. I had seen his father on numerous occasions in the department store where he had worked for thirty years. Rasteau spoke of familiar playing fields, schools, and churches. He sadly mentioned the hospital where his mother died and the cemetery in which she was buried. Before he was drafted, Rasteau worked in a service station where I had often purchased gas. Perhaps I had seen him there while on leave from the army. The landmarks of the cathedral, the courthouse, and the college were as important to us as the familiar mountains and ancestors' tombs were to the Vietnamese.

Although there was a separation in time between us in Lafayette and in job assignments in Vietnam, we nevertheless felt an attachment to each other because of common bonds. He did not attempt to speak of his alleged crimes or other matters between judge and accused that must be left outside the courtroom. The level of his voice remained constant although he knew that after the trial there was nothing but hospitals and probably prisons to look forward to. I knew that I would be returning to an air-conditioned room in Saigon and looking forward to a reunion with my family in Hawaii in a few weeks.

As we stood there looking into the distant fields and mountains, I realized how fortunate I had been. Twenty-five years before, when I was Rasteau's age, there was another war in which I had participated. It was easier then; we knew who the enemy was. Pearl Harbor had been attacked and the Germans had declared war. The issues were clearly drawn. Even near the battlefield, spirit was generally high. We wrote letters to our girlfriends back home who were proud to hear from the boys overseas, listened to the patriotic songs of George M. Cohan and Irving Berlin, took pleasure in trying to devise methods of keeping cool our daily ration of two bottles of beer. No drugs to speak of then. No doubts about our cause. No dissidents calling the president a killer. No one back home suggesting that we were wasting our lives. It was all so different in Vietnam.

Finally, the other participants in the trial began to arrive. The prosecutor, with a sheaf of papers in his hand, called me aside to ask routine questions about seating arrangements and recess times. He tried to steer me away from the court members and the witnesses. Having no privacy, the defense counsel sought out a corner of the courtroom to converse with the accused until time for trial.

I quietly walked over to the judge's bench, avoiding contact with members of the court. A shuffling of feet and the voice of the prosecutor made me aware that the participants were seeking out their assigned seats. Somehow, my mind was not on the pending proceedings. Maybe it was the thought of Sunday morning in

Lafayette, or was it the thought of Sunday morning in Dong Tam? Church bells there, mortar fire here. The prosecutor cleared his throat:

"Your honor, we are ready to proceed."

I looked around quickly, checked the seating of the court members and other participants. I checked Rasteau once more to insure that he was as comfortable as possible under the circumstances, then looked at the president of the court for the first time and finally said:

"The court will come to order!"

CHAPTER NINETEEN

Farmers

Flying in a helicopter over land ravaged by war is never a routine experience. As the experience repeated itself, however, the noise of the engines tended to lull me into a state of unconsciousness, especially in the early morning hours.

Flying to Dong Tam on a Sunday morning in March, I was the sole passenger in a small OH–6 Cayuse helicopter when the pilot nonchalantly disturbed my reverie. He pointed to a much larger UH–1 Huey which had been hit by enemy fire and was rapidly descending in our general direction. There were other helicopters of various sizes and capabilities within our range of vision going about the business of waging war, but we were nearest to the falling craft. "Colonel," the pilot said, "we're going down to assist the chopper that's been hit. Grab that M–16 rifle behind you, just in case."

Strange that this should be happening to me, probably the only officer in Vietnam who, except for one occasion on a rifle range in Korea, had never fired an M–16.

The stricken aircraft landed in a rice paddy without apparent injury to any of its occupants. We hovered nearby for a few moments until the arrival of several larger and better-equipped helicopters. The members of the downed craft indicated that our help was not needed and expressed thanks with a thumbs up sign. I replaced the M–16 on the back panel with a sigh of relief, but before we were on course again, I observed a simple pastoral scene that jolted me into a new perspective of the conflict in which I was participating.

Not fifty yards from where the stricken Huey had alighted, a group of about fifty Vietnamese farmers, bent over with faces to the ground, were working in the fields, apparently oblivious to the circumstances surrounding them. The rhythm of their bobbing heads and hands, and their short steps forward, were not interrupted by the fortuitous circumstances of war. They did not seem even to communicate verbally among themselves. Not one had attempted to offer assistance to the occupants of the damaged craft. They had, it seemed to me, become detached from the war, over which they had no control.

My first reaction was disbelief and anger. How could these people remain indifferent to the misfortunes of a friendly helicopter crew? Was it worth fighting to assist people who were not willing to help in their own defense? The behavior of these workers probably reflected the behavior of most Vietnamese farmers in similar circumstances. I could not offer myself a satisfactory explanation. If I could not understand the behavior of these farmers, who were the heart and core of the Vietnamese people, how then could I understand the rationale for our presence in Vietnam?

As I thought about the farmers, my anger began to fade. There had been few rewards for them in the past, and they could anticipate even fewer in the future. The toil of planting and harvesting rice in the midst of a war offered little satisfaction. A peaceful night's rest near the graves of their ancestors offered the greatest consolation for a hard day's labor. These farmers had only recently witnessed the alien influences of French, Japanese, Vietminh, Americans, and one or more of the religious sects having their own private armies, which were endemic to the area surrounding Saigon. Elected and unelected governments had imposed repression upon them. Their lives, they must have reasoned, could not possibly be improved by assisting foreign visitors. How could Americans who came by day, even from the sky in strange machines, offer more than brown-skinned political agents who visited them by night?

The farmers knew that the Americans would not react adversely to their lack of assistance, but more importantly they knew that the Viet Cong would retaliate if they did assist the Americans. Perhaps there were Viet Cong working with them in the fields. So, there was nothing to be gained and much to be lost by interrupting their labors. They continued to work, therefore, hoping only that a long day's journey of toil might dissolve into an evening of peace.

By the time we landed in Dong Tam, I began to comprehend why the farmers offered no assistance to the endangered soldiers. The answer to a more fundamental question, however, continued to disturb me. If the farmers refused to help us, why should we help defend them against people we presumed to be their enemies? Was it possible they preferred a way of life alien to that which we offered? I could not be comfortable with these questions, so I put them aside to be resolved another day. That day has not arrived.

CHAPTER TWENTY

I Want a Body Count

On the afternoon of November 22, 1968, near the village of Phu Loc, not far from the ancient Vietnamese imperial city of Hue, trouble was anticipated in an area where members of A Company, 2nd Battalion, 505th Infantry, 3rd Brigade, 82nd Airborne Division were on a tactical mission. The company officers were attending a meeting atop a small hill overlooking the surrounding woods when Sergeant Benjamin Martinez, a member of the organization, interrupted to say that four Vietnamese men had been observed walking down a trail from the village toward the hill. One of them appeared to be carrying a pack on his back.

All of the officers stood up to observe the moving group. Captain Calvin Karpov, the Commanding Officer, ordered his Forward Officer, Captain Clint Roberts, to plot artillery targets, but to hold fire for the moment. When the Vietnamese men disappeared into the woods, the meeting resumed.

A few minutes later, the meeting was interrupted a second time when Sergeant Martinez reported that apparently the same four Vietnamese men had been observed again, this time walking toward the village, none apparently carrying anything on his back. Captain Karpov, suspicious of what might be happening, ordered Captain Roberts to plot artillery targets again, where the group had last been seen and ordered another of his officers, Lieutenant Ralph Thompson, to pursue the men. The captain remained in his position on the hill, as did Captain Roberts. There, they could observe Thompson who, together with a radio operator, Corporal Herbert Stall, and a medic, Corporal Rob Rigsby, began to pursue the Vietnamese men.

The evidence as to what happened thereafter, as it appeared in the pretrial investigation, was not entirely consistent, but certain facts were incontrovertible. A member of Thompson's group spotted the Vietnamese men, fired, and hit one of them in his left hand. The wounded man dropped behind some bushes, but came into the open a short while later with his hands raised, one of them bleeding. He approached within ten meters of Lieutenant Thompson. Meanwhile, the radio operator, who had lagged behind talking to Captain Karpov on the hill, approached Thompson, saying that "Sixer" had ordered him to kill the Vietnamese man. "Sixer," as everyone knew, was the radio call signal for Karpov. Thompson took the radio from Stall and reported to his commanding officer that the prisoner was wounded, unarmed, in the process of surrendering, and, apparently had some kind of identification. Karpov replied:

"Dammit, I don't care about prisoners. I want a body count!"

Lieutenant Thompson would not shoot and told his radio operator not to shoot. Stall disregarded the order and discharged a burst of automatic fire from his M–16, killing the Vietnamese man instantly.

When Thompson advised Captain Karpov that he had his body count, he was told to bury the corpse as well as he could. Thompson returned to the unit with the dead man's possessions, which did not include a weapon, but did include South Vietnamese identification.

Captain Roberts, who had been ordered to direct mortar fire in the direction of the Vietnamese men, stood near Karpov on the hill, and substantiated all of the radio conversations between

Karpov and members of Thompson's group. He also heard the shots from Stall's rifle that killed the wounded man.

Approximately thirty minutes after the incident with Thompson's group, Karpov received a radio call from another member of his company who was on patrol in the area saying that a second prisoner had been captured. Karpov directed Sergeant John Bowles, one of his noncommissioned officers, to check the man out. When Bowles asked what to do if the man had identification, Karpov replied: "Are you shitting me?"

When Bowles reached the captured man, whose hands were tied behind his back, he pushed him to his knees and reported this fact to his commanding officer. In reply, Karpov stated: "He's a gook or a dink, and you know what to do with him!"

The prisoner, while kneeling with his hands tied, was summarily executed by Bowles. The rope that bound the hands of the deceased was removed and his body rolled into a ditch. This prisoner was also unarmed and had South Vietnamese identification.

No one reported the incidents to higher headquarters immediately except for the body count. Captain Roberts and Lieutenant Thompson, however, were bothered by the events and sought counsel from a chaplain who advised them to report the matter to their superiors at battalion level. An investigation was conducted, resulting in two charges of premeditated murder against Karpov and one charge of premeditated murder against Stall, the radio operator. Bowles, who killed the second Vietnamese man, drowned three days after the incident before charges against him could be investigated. When I was appointed military judge on the cases, only charges against Karpov and Stall were pending.

At Captain Karpov's trial, Lieutenant Thompson testified that he countermanded Karpov's order. He insisted that Stall not shoot the Vietnamese man. Captain Roberts testified that, while standing on the hill, he heard all of the radio conversations between Karpov and members of Thompson's group, and personally witnessed the second execution.

Some of the personnel from Karpov's unit testified for the prosecution that A Company had a reputation for not taking prisoners; others, however, testifying for the defense, had never heard even a rumor of such a reputation in the company.

With respect to the first killing, the medic, Corporal Rigsby, testified that Thompson told him to check out the man with the bleeding hand who was trying to surrender but, in attempting to obey, he slipped into a gully and dropped his weapon. Almost simultaneously, he heard a voice shouting "Watch out, Doc!" and a burst of rifle fire coming from Stall's weapon. The Vietnamese man fell dead at his feet.

Thompson testified that, after seeing the wounded and unarmed man coming toward him, but before the shooting, he called "Sixer" to report these facts but was rebuffed with: "I don't want any prisoners. Shoot him!" Thompson made a request to spare the man's life, but the captain replied: "I don't care about prisoners. I want a body count! I want that man shot!" Disregarding the captain's request, Thompson would not shoot, and ordered Stall not to shoot the wounded man, who was making an attempt to reach in his back pocket, apparently in an attempt to obtain identification.

After the shooting, Thompson demanded of the radio operator: "Why the hell did you have to shoot a defenseless man?"

Stall replied: "'Sixer' said we had to kill him!"

In explaining his action during the trial, Stall testified that when Rigsby slipped, the Vietnamese man made a suspicious move as if to grab the medic's weapon. He, therefore, opened fire to protect his buddy.

Captain Roberts testified that he quite clearly heard "Sixer" give an order to kill the second man. Roberts then picked up a pair of binoculars and witnessed the shooting of the Vietnamese man, who was kneeling with his hands tied behind his back, making an effort to reach for something in his back pocket.

In his defense, Karpov testified that he never said a word about either killing, but rather only told his subordinates to "pursue the situation." He admitted that Thompson did tell him something to the effect that "you have a body count!" but was shocked by that report. He further testified that Thompson was not a very good platoon leader, but one who had to be "chewed out" every day.

Two men from the company testified that they thought Thompson had a funny attitude toward combat because he did not like to kill people. Another testified that Roberts was "OK" but was not a disciplined officer.

Captain Karpov's brigade commander, a brigadier general, and his battalion commander, a lieutenant colonel, testified that the accused was one of the best company commanders they had ever served with. Several enlisted men from the company, especially those peripherally involved in the incidents, echoed the praises of their commanding officer. Karpov had previously served a tour in Vietnam and had been awarded several medals.

It did not take long for the members of the court to make up their minds. In less than thirty minutes, Karpov was found not guilty. Charges against Stall were dropped as a consequence of his commanding officer's acquittal.

I have no personal knowledge of what happened immediately after the trial. I did not see Captain Karpov again after he fled the courtroom, shielding his face from photographers representing the news media. I was informed by authoritative sources, however, that within his unit, there was great rejoicing at Karpov's acquittal. The defense counsel informed me later that, while celebrating the victory with a party in A Company, the participants were wearing buttons which read: "WINE WOMEN AND BODY COUNT." Hardly able to believe this, I asked him to secure evidence for me, and he did. Among my files, I still have the button, a story of the case as reported by the *Overseas Weekly,* and an article from *Time* magazine quoting the words about body count spoken at the trial.

Three years after the trial of Captain Karpov, while attending a meeting of judge advocate officers in Berchtsgaden, Germany, I was in the audience when a new Department of Defense movie on the Law of War was previewed. The scenario unfolded on a hill overlooking a battlefield, obviously in Vietnam, on which a captain stood giving orders over his field phone: "I don't want any prisoners, dammit! I want a body count!" This was portrayed as an example of an officer disregarding the Law of War. That's not the way the court saw it.

CHAPTER TWENTY-ONE

Sergeant Mika's Headaches

Sergeant Michael Mika was the most sophisticated member of the MACV judge advocate office: tall, smart, handsome, neat, and polite. Hollywood could not have improved his image. He spent free daytime hours visiting the monuments of Saigon and improving his knowledge of Vietnamese culture. Mika was courteous to everyone, military and civilian, regardless of rank. He was admired by everyone who knew him. In short, Mika was as perfect a soldier and gentleman as could be expected. But, Mika had a problem. He had headaches.

It was impossible to avoid knowing about Mika's headaches. His only fault, if it was a fault, was letting people know about them. When they first began, he went to the dispensary at MACV but the medicine prescribed there did no good; he then went to a personal friend who was a doctor in Dong Tam but received no help there; he tried the United States Army Medical Dispensary in downtown Saigon, but again no relief; finally, Joe Ammerman made arrangements for Mika to be admitted to the 3rd Field Hospital near Saigon for tests. He returned to the office three days later still complaining of headaches.

A few days after his return from the hospital, Le Kim Hoa, a young secretary in the office, suggested to Sergeant Mika that he visit a Chinese doctor in Saigon. He ridiculed the idea saying that if American doctors with all their sophisticated paraphernalia could not help him, how could a Chinese doctor unaware of modern technology assist him? Hoa patiently explained that her mother, who once had headaches as bad as Mika's, was cured by their doctor; her father, who had arthritis so bad he could hardly bend his arms, was cured; and she herself, who many times had high fevers, was cured by the same Chinese doctor. "What can you lose? You tried everything else!" she pleaded. Mika was persuaded to try again. He agreed to see Hoa's doctor provided she make all the arrangements and accompany him as his interpreter.

Late one afternoon, I returned from Hotel 3 to the office where I found Sergeant Mika sitting alone at his desk holding a piece of paper that appeared to be torn from a brown paper bag, with Chinese characters inscribed on it. He told me that he had visited Hoa's doctor and was holding a prescription given to him. He would be going to a Chinese drugstore the next morning to have it filled. "This is the end!" he remarked. "I never thought I'd see the day!" Having nothing scheduled the next day, I asked if I could accompany him and he agreed.

Mika met me at the Rex the following morning and we walked to a large Chinese drug store on Nguyen Van Sam, just a few blocks from the hotel. It was crowded and Mika's first inclination was to return to MACV. I encouraged him to stay, promising that I would remain with him. We took our places at the end of the long, snakelike line.

Behind a long counter were two druggists, and behind them a giant desk with at least two hundred drawers, each with labels in Chinese characters. The drawers contained herbs, chemicals, spices, ground-up parts of animals, roots from trees, and whatever else might be called for as ingredients in prescriptions written by Chinese doctors.

Each customer presented to the druggist a piece of ordinary wrapping paper, similar to Mika's, on which Chinese characters were inscribed. Without even a glance, the druggist reached into the drawers behind him with one hand, removed pinches of the prescribed substances, and placed them into the prescription paper resting on the counter under his hand. He wrapped the ingredients into the same paper, weighed the bundle, and exchanged it for a few piasters. It took less than two minutes to fill a prescription, although the ingredients might come from a dozen different drawers. When we arrived at the counter, the druggist followed exactly the same procedure, not for a moment acknowledging that we were the only Americans in his presence, except to write the amount of money we owed. It wasn't much at all.

The most distinguishing feature between the Chinese drugstore and other stores in Saigon was the lack of argument and limited conversation between seller and buyer. The price requested was promptly paid without question, and the transaction was completed without written evidence that it had taken place.

Leaving the drugstore, Mika expressed the opinion that "There must be something to this Chinese medicine, seeing so many apparently satisfied customers!" I think that fact alone made him feel a little better. Certainly, he was satisfied because he suggested that we go for lunch at the International House on Nguyen Hue, the Street of Flowers, where he was a member. Mika was the only person I knew who belonged to the exclusive club, but that did not surprise me, knowing his love for fine food.

The International House was a combination club-restaurant, restricted to persons associated with the American forces and their allies. The initiation fee and monthly dues excluded the ordinary soldier or officer, but Mika was a well-heeled customer. He had no family to support or other obligations. He once told me that, in all his life, he did not pay a penny in interest to anyone.

I was surprised to find such luxury in Saigon. The entrance foyer led to an elegant waiting room, and the dining room beyond was comparable to that of a fine restaurant in a large American city. Brunch was being served, buffet style, and a string quartet provided background music. Waiters in uniform served coffee and drinks. For a moment, I forgot about the masses of hungry people surrounding the building and the war surrounding the city. The contrast between affluent customers dining in the club and troops serving in the field did not seem to be a matter of concern to members. Sergeant Mika mixed the prescribed portion of medicine he received from the Chinese drugstore with a bit of water and swallowed it without blinking. We then proceeded to the line for brunch.

Mika was feeling so much better after brunch that he suggested we not return to the office, but visit a couple of places he had not yet seen in Saigon. We began to stroll aimlessly until we reached a Hindu temple that I recognized immediately from my visit in 1960. A man with a twelve-foot snake writhing around his body stood near the entrance. We joined the small audience that had gathered around him for a moment but Sergeant Mika said he had seen a lot of this type of thing before and preferred to see the inside of the temple. We walked slowly within its enclosure, looking at the pictures of Hindu saints. There was no one inside to explain the meaning of the things we saw. That was the only time I had ever seen Mika at a loss for words to explain something.

From the Hindu environment, we walked to the An Quang pagoda, which I found more interesting because the monks, in saffron robes, were quite willing to chat with us. Several of them spoke excellent English. It was from this very place that the elderly Buddhist monk, Thich Quang Duc, had come to have himself immolated in the center of Saigon in 1963, a highly publicized act that caused much of the Western world to become more concerned with our presence in Vietnam. It was also from this temple and others like it that so much political opposition to past and then present governments had been directed. But our quiet conversation with the monks was more philosophical than political. They did not hide their sympathy for the refugees who, at that very moment, were sleeping, or resting, underneath the outside staircases and around the temple.

From the temple, we took one of the ubiquitous little blue-and-white Renault taxis, which roamed the city like bumper cars at a county fair, to the gardens that bordered on the zoo. We rested on a bench for awhile admiring buildings in the style of ancient pagodas and monuments. They were much as I had remembered them, but sorely in need of repair. A short walk through the zoo convinced us that the animals that remained there were in need of nourishment.

As the leisurely and pleasant day came to an end, I noticed that Mika seemed to be feeling very well. I did not ask about his headaches, afraid to remind him of them, and hoping that they had been permanently relieved.

CHAPTER TWENTY-TWO

Love's Labor Lost

First Sergeant Robert Allen was nearing the end of his third Vietnam tour in the latter part of 1968, hoping that his request for extension would be approved. He was one of the army's most respected first sergeants: handsome and tall, with the voice and military bearing of a soldier who could easily be recognized as a person of authority.

On his first tour in Vietnam, before the influx of American soldiers in 1965, there was time enough for members of the army to spend leisurely hours on the sandy beaches and visit the bars of Nha Trang, where Sergeant Allen was stationed. It was there in the New Saigon Bar that soldiers, including Allen, spent lazy afternoons, drinking beer and playing childish bar games with the working girls. From the time of his first visit to the bar, Allen played the games with Nguyen Thoa Thuc, his favorite companion, whom he called Tam for convenience. She was the daughter of a village official not far away and worked to help support her brothers and sisters. She lived in Nha Trang, however, close to the bar and returned to her village one day each week.

As time went by, Sergeant Allen, thirty-seven years old and never married, fell deeply in love with Tam. He persuaded her to quit working at the bar to take a job that he arranged for her at the Quartermaster Storage Depot in Nha Trang. She began as a general helper but was promoted quickly to filing clerk as her English and typing skills improved. Allen continued to visit Tam at the depot, and frequently drove her home in the evenings.

Sergeant Allen wanted desperately to take Tam as his wife, but the army forbade solders to marry indigenous women. Tam, through her father, could probably have arranged a Vietnamese wedding, but Allen, model soldier for seventeen years, refused to violate the military code. He wanted, however, to have Tam as his common-law wife, and perhaps, when the world was at peace, be legally married and bring her to the United States. Allen's love was reciprocated, and Tam agreed to the arrangement, with the reluctant consent of her parents.

During the Tet holidays of 1965, Allen and Tam, alone in a small Buddhist temple, vowed that they would be faithful to each other until the end of their lives. It did not matter to them that neither the United States nor Vietnam recognized the marriage. They moved into a small apartment and thereafter referred to each other as husband and wife, even to their acquaintances.

After serving eighteen months in Nha Trang, Allen was ordered back to the United States. Six months later, he volunteered successfully for a second tour in Vietnam and was assigned to the 25th Infantry Division in Cu Chi. By the time of his arrival there, Tam had become proficient in her job at the depot in Nha Trang and received praise from her superiors. The chief of staff of the 25th Infantry Division, encouraged by the recommendations of Sergeant Allen, arranged to have Tam transferred as a clerk to that headquarters. Allen and Tam lived together in Cu Chi for a year, after which time he returned again to the United States. Allen did not request a second overseas extension because the unexpected illness of his mother required his presence at home.

While stationed in Nha Trang earlier, Sergeant Allen's military qualities had impressed a young colonel who, since that time, had become a general. In 1968, he was assigned to USARV headquarters in Long Binh. The general arranged for Allen to be transferred from Fort Benning, Georgia, to Long Binh, where he began his third Vietnam tour. The general was also influential in having Tam transferred within the military structure from Cu Chi to Long Binh. Together again, with their combined income, Allen and Tam were able to rent a small house in a village not far from Long Binh.

Long Binh had the largest concentration of American troops in Vietnam, assigned to three division-size units and numerous smaller ones. It was not unexpected, therefore, that Sergeant Allen would meet numerous senior noncommissioned officers with whom he was already acquainted. He frequently had lunch with some of them at the Chinese restaurant or one of the many mess halls on post. Allen invited the best of those friends to attend a regular Friday night poker game at his home. Among those poker players was Master Sergeant Will Morris, an acquaintance of many years.

As the weeks passed, Morris became an even closer friend of both Allen and his wife, visiting them frequently, even on nights when there was no poker game. The men drank beer, and sometimes, when Morris became inebriated, he remained the entire night. He was a trustworthy friend.

When Sergeant Allen's mother died suddenly in June, 1968, he was given two weeks leave to attend her funeral. Sometime during the second week of Allen's absence, Sergeant Morris visited the noncommissioned officers club where he began to drink heavily. At about nine-thirty, he decided to visit Allen's Vietnamese wife. Although Tam was able to detect the odor of alcohol on his breath, she invited him inside, thinking that perhaps he had news of her husband. Morris asked Tam for a drink and she shared one beer with him.

When Tam suggested that Morris leave because she was tired, Morris approached her in an unusually friendly manner by placing his arm around her waist. Tam resisted but Morris persisted. His intentions became more apparent as he tried to loosen Tam's blouse. She begged him to desist, but to no avail. Morris continued his aggressive behavior and succeeded in removing Tam's blouse completely. She screamed, an act which enraged him to further violence. He threw her to the floor, removed her trousers and demanded that she have intercourse with him.

Tam's terrified screams, as Morris continued to assault her, brought neighbors, including two United States enlisted men and the lone village policeman, to her rescue. All together, they were able to restrain Morris. Another neighbor contacted the military police at Long Binh, who answered the call immediately. They arrested Morris, duly noting in their report that Morris had apparently been drinking, had to be forcibly restrained from committing even more violent acts, and was angry and shouting that Tam was a whore who should have acquiesced in his wishes. They brought Morris to his company commander, who assumed responsibility for him until he sobered up.

At the end of his leave, Sergeant Allen was met at Ton Son Nhut airport by his company commander, who thought it best that he personally inform Allen of the assault upon his Vietnamese wife. The captain then drove the sergeant immediately to his home, where Tam was waiting. Allen was shocked to see his wife's condition and to find her so distraught that she was unable to speak coherently. She had not returned to work since the assault because of bruises about her face and body. He treated her with compassion and sympathy, consoling her by promising to remain by her side no matter what further indignities she might be subjected to. Allen told his wife, and he sincerely meant it, that he would have killed Morris then and there if it were in his power to do so.

After Tam had regained her composure, knowing that her husband would not forsake her, Allen went to the Engineer Command where Sergeant Morris worked. His first priority was to find out what, if any, disciplinary action had been taken against his wife's attacker. He was infuriated, therefore, upon arrival at the Engineer Command, to see Morris performing his usual duties in the command headquarters, apparently unconcerned that anything unusual had occurred.

Allen restrained himself for the moment but went directly to Morris' company commander, demanding an immediate explanation for what he considered to be an injustice. The captain explained that he handled the matter himself by reprimanding Morris for his behavior and contemplated no further action, considering Morris's many years of exemplary service to the United States. Allen informed the captain that the action he took was, in his opinion, totally inappropriate and that he was taking the matter directly to the inspector general of the Engineer Command.

In less than thirty minutes, Allen was in the presence of the inspector general, informing him that an injustice had been done to his wife. He insisted that Morris be treated no differently than if he had sexually assaulted an American Red Cross female worker. Allen had enough experience with military justice to know that proof of the crime was easily available through the testimony of his wife and the witnesses who had come to her rescue, including the nurse from the village who tended her on the night of the incident. If no one else would prefer charges, Allen said, he himself would prepare and sign the charge sheet and force an official Article 32 pretrial investigation.

The inspector general knew that, considering Allen's good standing in the community, his complaints could not be dismissed lightly. He, therefore, ordered an investigation by members of his own office, which ultimately resulted in the preferral of charges against Morris alleging assault with intent to commit rape upon Nguyen Thoa Thuc. The commanding general decided that the charges would be tried by General Court Martial.

Sergeant Morris knew most of the senior noncommissioned officers in each of the three legal offices at Long Binh, and sought their advice. They agreed that Morris could do no better than seek the services of Captain Samuel Arkow, who was regarded as the best defense counsel in the area. He was thorough, tough, smart, and never overlooked the slightest possibility of a defense, or matter favorable to his client in mitigation. He fought in court with the tenacity of the best counsel in the United States.

Captain Arkow accepted Sergeant Morris's case. His first demand of Morris was to obtain the names of as many persons as he could who, at any time, present or past, knew Sergeant Allen's Vietnamese wife.

A break for the defense came when Morris located a sergeant who knew Tam in 1964 when she worked at the New Saigon Bar in Nha Trang. He had seen her a few times on the compound at Long Binh but had never spoken to her there. When Arkow questioned him, the witness reported that not only he, but two other soldiers he knew in Nha Trang at the time, had spent the night at least once with Tam before she obtained employment with the United States Army. This information would allow the defense counsel to question Tam about her past life, the matter being pertinent to her credibility.

When the case was brought to trial, Sergeant Allen sat alone in the rear of the courtroom, listening intently to the proceedings. When Tam testified under gentle questioning by the prosecutor, every word she spoke increased her husband's compassion for her and hatred of Morris. Tam explained the circumstances under which she allowed Morris to enter her home while her husband was away; then she described the attack upon her person and her resistance to the assault in even greater detail than she had ever spoken to her husband.

Sergeant Allen was aware of the humiliation that his wife was experiencing and shared her deep sense of embarrassment. He looked at Morris sitting at the defense table with even more contempt in his heart. When Tam completed her testimony for the prosecution, Captain Arkow began his cross-examination.

Defense Counsel (DC): Now, Miss Thuc, you testified that on the night in question, Sergeant Morris attacked you against your will.

Tam: Yes, sir.

DC: You knew Morris quite well, did you not?

Tam: Yes, sir.

DC: And on other occasions when he visited your home, you kissed him, did you not?

Tam: I did not really kiss him, but we said goodbye in a friendly manner.

DC: Did you kiss him on the lips?

Tam: No, sir.

DC: What about New Year's Eve when you were all drinking together?

Tam: Well, maybe on that one occasion.

DC: Did you enjoy his kiss?

Tam: I don't remember.

DC: Well, you did kiss him on the lips. Do you not think this might have made Sergeant Morris feel that his advances were welcome?

Tam: Only that brief time on New Year's Eve.

DC: And you continued to see him afterwards, even until your husband left for the United States?

Tam: Yes, sir, but my husband was always there.

Sergeant Allen was now beginning to feel an intense dislike for the defense counsel as well as Morris. Captain Arkow became even more aggressive on the issue of consent.

DC: Miss Thuc, do you know Sergeant Paul Meany?

Tam: I do not recall the name.

DC: Do you know any servicemen whom you met before you met Sergeant Allen?

Tam: I'm sure I met some.

DC: You met some. Could it be that you met them while you were working at the New Saigon Bar in Nha Trang?

Tam: It is possible.

The anger building up in Sergeant Allen was now obvious to Captain Arkow, but he continued the pursuit.

DC: If I provided you with the name of one of them, would you remember?

Tam: I don't think so.

DC: Did you at any time take any of the soldiers you met at the bar in Nha Trang to your home?

Tam: That was a long time ago.

DC: A long time ago, yes, but do you remember whether you did?

Tam: Maybe one or two.

DC: Could it have been eight or ten?

Tam: I don't think so.

DC: But it was at least three or four, was it not?

Tam: It could be.

DC: And Paul Meany could have been one of them?

Tam: I don't remember.

Sergeant Allen was now enraged with his Vietnamese wife as well as the defense counsel and the accused.

DC: Now, Miss Thuc, I do not mean to embarrass you, but I do want to be specific, because it is very important to the defense of this case. Did you at any time sleep with a soldier other than Sergeant Allen in Nha Trang?

Tam: Yes, sir.

DC: Would I be correct in assuming that you slept with at least three or four.

Tam: Yes, sir.

Tam had assured Allen on several occasions that her employment at the New Saigon Bar was only to help support her family. Unable now to contain the anger against his wife, Sergeant Allen quickly and silently departed from the courtroom. After Tam was temporarily excused as a witness, she could not locate her husband; nor could she leave the area as she had been excused subject to recall.

The case continued with presentation of testimony by witnesses who came to Tam's assistance on the night of the assault, including the nurse who cared for her and the military police. Morris testified that he had assumed Tam was consenting to his advances and did not resist beyond making mere expressions of disapproval. The court, dismissing the protestations of the accused, but believing the testimony of Tam and the other prosecution's witnesses, found Morris guilty and sentenced him to be dishonorably discharged from the army.

That evening, when Tam returned to her home, all of her husband's possessions were missing. He had departed without even a message. She was unable to contact him at his unit and, to her surprise, she was informed that Sergeant Allen had withdrawn his request for an extension of duty in Vietnam.

CHAPTER TWENTY-THREE

Tragedy in White

On January 3, 1969, I received a call from Colonel Tom Reece, telling me that he would arrange ground transportation for my trip on January 10, from Saigon to Long Binh, where I was to be the judge on a premeditated murder case. I was pleased by the travel arrangements because it was more convenient to be picked up at my hotel and delivered to the courtroom in one vehicle than having to schedule my own transportation by military taxi, helicopter, and pickup at destination. I looked forward to the pleasure of having a relatively late and leisurely breakfast for a change.

The promised army sedan arrived at the appointed time and place. Colonel Reece had not informed me, however, that the vehicle would also pick up witnesses for the trial. After leaving the Rex, the driver proceeded to the San Francisco Bar on Tu Do Street, where three Vietnamese hostesses, dressed in colorful national dress, and one Vietnamese man were also waiting for transportation to the trial. I would have preferred not to be closely associated with witnesses, but it was too late to avoid the arrangements with which I had been confronted.

I moved from the rear to the front seat of the sedan and the four prospective witnesses piled into the back seat, chattering excitedly as they did so. The driver then, again to my surprise, proceeded to a hospital where a Vietnamese doctor, who had also been summoned as a witness, was waiting for the military vehicle. I slid into the middle of the front seat and, with the doctor on my right, we proceeded to Long Binh. The little French I spoke restricted conversation with the doctor, who had been educated in France, to the simplest pleasantries. I could not speak Vietnamese.

When we arrived at the building in which the courtroom was located, counsel for the prosecution and defense were peering from the windows, quite amused at the combination of passengers in an official army sedan. I allowed the witnesses, accompanied by the American driver, a few minutes to precede me to the courtroom.

Corporal Eugene Casey was charged that day with the murder of Miss Huyng Le Anh at the San Francisco Bar on Tu Do Street in Saigon on October 20, 1968. The alleged murder was no mystery. Its circumstances did not require the resolution of complicated facts or issues. The case, however, did generate much interest in the English and Vietnam press because it dealt not only with the lifestyles of soldiers who had deserted their units and lived on the fringes of the underworld, but also the famed hostesses of Tu Do Street, who did not differentiate among customers, so long as they were financially solvent.

When Casey departed from his unit without permission and arrived in Cholon on October 6, he moved into the Han Lan Hotel where other AWOL soldiers, some of them acquaintances, lived. While free from military control, Casey led a life of luxury, eating in good restaurants, traveling in borrowed automobiles, meeting women, using drugs, and visiting other absentees from the army. Frequently, he walked about Saigon and Cholon in his military uniform carrying his issued M–16 rifle to mingle inconspicuously with other soldiers. He made illegal purchases in the commissary, PXs, and army liquor stores. He consorted with Filipino and Chinese persons of questionable character.

Casey spent most of the day on October 20 in the hotel drinking with friends, but took leave of them at about four-thirty in the afternoon to visit another absentee soldier, Private Ron Howard. They spent thirty minutes together, during which time Casey consumed two Immenoctal tablets, a barbiturate normally recommended for sleeping disorders and available without prescription in any Western-style drug store in Saigon. It was common knowledge that two of the pills, taken together in the dosage Casey consumed, would make almost any person begin to hallucinate.

When I observed Casey for the first time, standing outside the courtroom with his guard, I was impressed only by the fact that he looked so ordinary. He was tall, neat, nice looking, wore black horned rimmed glasses, and outwardly expressed no sense of emotion. He acknowledged no one and seemed disinterested in his surroundings. I knew from a review of the pretrial papers that his parents had separated when he was quite young and he remained with his father, who showed no interest in the boy except for providing the bare necessities of life. He had grown up as an adequate high school student but without any recorded achievements, or infractions with the law. During the trial, he was courteous when addressed, but otherwise remained silent, even during recesses. I did not see him in conversation with anyone, including his attorney.

Private Ralph Primera, a former resident of the Han Lan Hotel, was the first witness called by the prosecutor. He was wearing one combat boot and one slipper as he entered the courtroom. Primera testified that, after drinking with Casey most of the day on October 20, they met some friends, including a Filipino who owned a car. The group ate at a restaurant and then proceeded to the Mekong, Suzie Wong, and San Francisco bars on Tu Do Street, arriving at the last one about nine thirty. Casey sat in the first empty booth accompanied by a hostess, and his friends scattered about.

The San Francisco was one of many bars on Tu Do, a street famed in novels and history, when it was formerly known as Rue

Catinat. It was only a few blocks long but known to everyone who lived in or visited Saigon because of its fame for bars, night clubs, dance halls, good restaurants, and cheap hotels. In addition to a bar, the San Francisco had about a dozen tables and booths where the hostesses brought their clients. For themselves, the customers ordered whiskey or beer, and for the ladies, champagne, the latter being nothing more than a nonalcoholic mixture commonly referred to as "Saigon tea." The customers were aware that the champagne was tea but accepted that fact as the price of companionship.

Upon arrival at the San Francisco, Casey and his friends were greeted with enthusiasm by the hostesses. All the men appeared happy, were joking, and sat in separate booths. They bought Saigon tea for the hostesses. At about ten forty-five, Primera heard a commotion from the booth adjoining his. When he looked in that direction, Casey was "cocking that little three-inch .22-caliber Astra pistol which he borrowed from the Filipino." The prosecutor continued his examination.

Q: Could you hear it cock?

A: Yes.

Q: Could you see the pistol?

A: No. It was covered by his hand.

Q: What did he do then?

A: He turned and shot the girl. He just turned and pointed it and I think she said "you shoot me," or something.

Q: And what happened then?

A: He shot her again.

Q: How far away was his pistol from the girl?

A: About three feet, three or four feet.

Q: How many times did he shoot her, do you know?

A: I believe about three times, maybe four. He shot her once from a sitting position and the rest from a standing position.

When asked about wearing a slipper, Primera explained that one of the bullets fired from Casey's weapon at the San Francisco hit and damaged his little toe. He did not seek medical attention.

The first Vietnamese witness, Miss Nguyen Thi Nghai, testified through an interpreter that, while sitting at the bar with a customer, the people in Casey's party were joking around. She saw Miss Anh, who was sitting with Casey, return to the bar three times for drinks. Miss Anh then told her that Casey asked her to go out with him, and she agreed but only as a ploy to get him to buy another drink. Casey bought that third drink but when Anh asked for yet another, Casey asked whether she was playing him for a sucker. He then shot Anh four or five times. "Why you shoot me?" Miss Anh cried as she reeled backwards into Miss Nghai's arms.

The second Vietnamese witness, Miss Lam Thi Lan, who was also a hostess at the bar on the night of the shooting, insisted on testifying in English. She was able to embellish on the testimony given my Miss Nghai. Lan was helping her mother who was in charge of the bar when she noticed Casey immediately upon his entry into the bar. He looked "like very nice." The prosecutor continued:

Q: Did anything unusual happen after Casey sat down with Miss Anh?

A: He act very good. Good mood.

Q: How long did Miss Anh sit with this man?

A: About half hour.

Q: What happened then?

A: They talking and laughing. Nothing look like angry.

After half an hour, Miss Lan said that Anh took money from Casey, went to the bar for more drinks, returned to Casey's booth, and again sat down with him. A few minutes later, Anh returned to the bar and told Lan that Casey was a "cheap Charlie" because he would not buy her another drink. She nevertheless returned to his booth. Lan continued:

A: She not sit down. Then I saw him pull the gun and shot Miss Anh. And he shot one shot. Then Miss Anh said: "Why you shot me?" the man stood up. "I shoot you, you know."

Q: Then what did he do?

A: This time, he shot more shots, then he run, go outside.

Q: Did he appear drunk to you?

A: No. He not drunk. He can walk, he can run very good. He no argue. No nothing. Acting very sober. I know sober and drunk.

Doctor Tran Dai Quay, with whom I had shared the front seat of a military sedan earlier in the morning, was called as the next witness and presented us with problems we did not anticipate. He insisted on testifying in French because that was the language of his medical school. There was no French-English interpreter in Long Binh, but there was an old employee who had worked for the French as a Vietnamese-French interpreter.

The language problem was partially solved by allowing the doctor to testify in French and having his testimony translated into Vietnamese by the old French employee. The appointed court interpreter then picked up the testimony, translating it from Vietnamese into English. This was a terrible problem, created by the double translations, the use of medical terms, and the fact that the defense counsel, who had studied French in high school, kept objecting to the way the doctor's French came out at the end of the line in English. Each objection was exhaustingly resolved with the use of French, Vietnamese, and English medical and ordinary dictionaries.

The gist of Doctor Quay's testimony was that several bullets entered Miss Anh's body and one was imbedded in the surface of her skin but fell out when he removed her clothing. He did not attempt removal of the others due to severe internal bleeding. Miss Anh died at five minutes after midnight on the morning of October 21. In Doctor Quay's opinion, death was the result of internal bleeding caused by the cutting of arteries and veins within her body.

The bartender, Huynh Than, who was Miss Anh's uncle, testified that after hearing the first shot, he looked up and saw Casey shooting his niece with a small gun. He did not count but he heard "many more shots" and Casey did not appear to be drunk while firing. After the shooting, Than "took care" of Anh but did not give her first aid because he did not think she was bleeding very much. He and the hostesses were weeping and kneeling beside his niece, not knowing what to do. He later accompanied Anh in the ambulance that took her to the hospital and remained with her until the end. He was not allowed in the room where Anh was being treated, but through the door, he could hear her crying, saying repeatedly that her life was about to end.

Foster Boyd, an American engineer was sitting on a stool at the bar when he heard a noise that sounded like a firecracker. He turned to see Casey fire a few shots at a girl "wearing a white dress" from a small pistol that was almost entirely concealed by his hand. Boyd did not see what he considered to be blood on Anh's dress but only a few red spots that appeared to be a part of the fabric.

Immediately after Casey ran out of the bar, three American patrons followed. They attracted the attention of a United States Military Police patrol consisting of Sergeant Joe Mazarek, Sergeant Donald Hansen, and the driver of the jeep in which they were riding. Sergeant Mazarek ordered the driver to stop, jumped out of the jeep, and ran into the San Francisco to investigate the disturbance. Sergeant Hansen ordered the jeep driver to follow some Vietnamese policemen who were running down Tu Do Street blowing whistles at a taxi. The jeep pulled alongside the taxi, forcing it to stop. Hansen dismounted from his vehicle and opened the rear door of the taxi. Inside, he saw Casey wearing sunglasses, with a small pistol in his hand. Casey pointed the weapon in the direction of the military policeman, but Hansen grabbed the pistol, which he suspected was only a toy. He apprehended Casey and returned him to the San Francisco, where he was immediately identified.

Sergeants Mazarek and Hansen both observed Miss Anh lying on the floor, with the long folds of her white au dai spread out beside her body, and a few red spots in the area of her abdomen. Hansen radioed for an ambulance, which arrived about thirty-five minutes after Miss Anh had been shot. She was taken to a Vietnamese hospital eight blocks away.

As it's final witness, the prosecution called Private Robert LeBlanc, who had previously known Casey from the Long Binh Stockade and was being held in the Saigon detention cell for his own transgressions on the night of the shooting. When he saw Casey being admitted, his first question was: "What did you do this time?" The record of trial contains the following dialogue:

Q: What did Casey say?

A: He told me that he shot a broad. I asked him why. He told me that she was hanging over him, wanting him to spend money on Saigon tea. She just kept hanging on him driving him crazy, I guess. I don't know.

Q: Did he tell you what he shot her with?

A: He said it was a small Astra .22.

Q: Did he tell you how many times he shot her?

A: Four, he thought. He said he pushed her back, and she came at him again. He said he pulled out the gun and shot her.

The defense counsel, in his opening statement, admitted that Casey shot Anh but argued that, because of alcohol and drugs, it was impossible for him to form a specific intent to kill, an essential element of the offense of premeditated murder. The defense counsel also contended that the cause of death was negligence of others in not caring for such a frail person as Miss Anh. Specifically, the delay in taking her to the hospital and the lack of sophistication of the Vietnamese doctor were independent intervening causes that negated Casey's responsibility for the death. I thought these latter statements were specious but did not hinder the defense from proceeding.

Captain Herbert Hall, a United States Army medical doctor, testified that if Miss Anh had been treated within ten or fifteen minutes after the shooting with methods frequently used on the battlefield, there would have been an excellent chance that she could have been brought out of shock. Thereafter, the chances would have been excellent for the performance of a successful operation to stop the hemorrhaging, thus saving the life of the patient. The doctor also made the observation that, since the weapon used had such a low velocity projective, it was unlikely that the bullets would have killed a person stronger or heavier than Miss Anh, who weighed barely eighty pounds, or even killed Anh herself, if she had been more than six yards away.

Casey chose to testify on his own behalf. He admitted everything other witnesses had said about the time spent at the hotel on the day of the incident, the fact that he consumed two Immenoctal tablets at Ron Howard's rented home, and, upon further questioning, replied:

> We departed in a car belonging to a Filipino who worked in Saigon. We ate at the My Canh floating restaurant in Saigon and continued to drink there. By the time we reached the San Francisco Bar, I was in a pretty intoxicated state, even though I was still in control of my senses. A girl was sitting down alongside of me and I bought her three or four Saigon teas. I asked her if she would come with me, and she said yes. I told her not to ask for any more drinks, but she went and asked me for another. I pulled out a gun from under my shirt. I pointed the weapon at her. I thought I was just playing around. Next thing I knew, that weapon went off and she was clutching her stomach and I just sat there. Somebody started yelling, "Get up and run to the car!" I stood up and went for the door. I fired twice more. I ran down the street with the weapon in my hand, got in a taxi and told the driver to take me to Cholon.
>
> I saw a jeep pulling up, and a door of the taxi was pulled open. The military policeman took the gun out of my hand. The only intention I had in the bar was scaring her a little bit for asking me to buy her that other drink, the last drink.

In answer to the prosecutor's question on cross-examination concerning the weapon, Casey responded: "Well, sir, I borrowed it from a Filipino worker that I had known in Saigon. I considered it necessary to carry a weapon around there."

The court found Casey guilty of unpremeditated murder and sentenced him to be dishonorably discharged from the army and to be confined at hard labor for thirty years.

A few days after Casey's trial, two young army lawyers from Nha Trang were visiting Saigon and asked me to accompany them on a stroll in the city. As we walked down Tu Do Street, I pointed out the San Francisco, scene of the then notorious case of Private Casey. All three of us peeked into the bar with hands clasped to our faces against the window for a better view of the inside. Miss Nghai and Miss Lan saw us and recognized me. Both, deserting their customers, ran outside, jumped up and down like children, saying in broken English how happy they were that justice had been done. My friends and I were invited in as guests of the house, but I declined for all of us because of my association with the case. My friends were quite disappointed.

The girls then became serious as Miss Lan explained what happened two days after Miss Anh's death. All employees of the bar contributed to the purchase of a new white au dai in which their friend would be buried. The bar was closed for an afternoon during which they spent the time beside the body of Miss Anh. Lan was in tears when she concluded by saying that Miss Anh looked just like she did five minutes before her murder, dressed all in white with no red spots on her dress.

The case of Private Casey was duly reported in the *Overseas Weekly*, a paper designed and published for United States troops abroad. The story concluded:

> Saigon's English-language papers played the murder up as a jealous lover's spat when they reported the shooting at the San Francisco. "Bullshit," said Miss Nhgai in her cute, original English when an OW reporter asked her about it. "Miss Anh never see boy before in her life."

CHAPTER TWENTY-FOUR

Dinner at Le Castel

Events impossible to foresee frequently happened during my tour in Vietnam. One that I recall with delight occurred on an evening when I was dining alone in the open mess at the Rex with no particular problems. I was startled to see a woman's figure in a gold lamé pantsuit standing before me. Looking up, I saw that it was Kathy, smiling as usual, her short hair messed up a bit, and her large brown eyes staring down at me.

"Hi! May I sit down?"

"Of course!" I replied.

"I've been stood up!" she said, "or maybe the guy had to go off to bomb a village or something. I don't know. Maybe he had another date."

"Probably not," I said. "Well, you're here now. Have dinner and I'll sit with you."

"I wouldn't go through the mess line dressed like this for a million dollars. Take me to Le Castel and I'll pay for dinner."

"I'd be happy to, but I've finished dinner!"

"You can have a glass of wine or something. I've gone to all the trouble of getting dressed and everyone here is staring at me. I'd really appreciate the favor."

"I'm dressed in fatigues, but I guess that's all right."

"As long as we have money, they don't care."

I was a little embarrassed about escorting Kathy because of the combat gear and hat I was wearing. For some odd reason, judges took it upon themselves to look different from other officers in Saigon by wearing hats that looked like World War II fatigue caps. Extended borders ran about two inches entirely around the center and fell over our ears and eyes. Although practical for rainy weather, they looked horrible.

People everywhere stared at Kathy, dressed as she was. It was not unusual to see Vietnamese women, just as attractive and in clothing perhaps even more stunning, but an American woman in a gold lamé pants' suit was something hardly to be expected in Saigon. Everyone seemed to admire her, and if there was one thing Kathy enjoyed, it was being admired.

The attention Kathy received on Tu Do Street was mild compared to that which she received when we entered Le Castel. The long bar near the entrance was crowded with people whom I assumed were civilian contractors, war correspondents, investigators for congressional committees, or those other characters whose presence I always noticed but whose duties I could never determine. It is safe to say that they were among the most affluent in the city because Le Castel was not inexpensive, even for those who changed American Military Payment Certificates (MPCs, or scrip) into piasters on the black market, which I assumed many, if not all, of the patrons did. In deference to the circumstances, I removed my funny hat and soaked up the ambiance, which gave me the courage to give a smug look toward the men sitting at the bar.

A uniformed waiter led us to a booth, rather than sitting us at an open table. Perhaps it was because he wanted to keep the sight of my fatigues away from his more prosperous patrons. I ordered a bottle of wine for both of us and dinner for Kathy. She wanted everything, from soup to dessert with sorbet in between.

While waiting for service, we chatted about nothing in particular. Kathy never inquired about my family except to ask whether she was younger than my wife. There was soft music in the background, mostly from American musicals. But when an Irish tenor crooned "Danny Boy" in a melancholy voice, she stopped speaking and stared into space with eyes wide open and a faint smile on her face. Memories, I thought. Probably some past love.

"I used to have an Irish boyfriend named Danny," she said softly. "We were both quite young and I think that was the only time in my life I was ever really in love, or I thought I was in love. That was over a dozen years ago, when I was nineteen. Danny is probably married now with a house full of kids. But he was beautiful."

"Why didn't you marry him?" I asked.

"He was a medical student and wasn't ready, he said. I was living in St. Louis near the medical school on Grand Avenue, and he was living nearby in a small apartment with other students. We saw each other, at least for a little while, almost every day. At first we were just good friends, and maybe, as far as he was concerned, that's all we ever were. But I fell in love with him. One weekend he asked me to go away with him to Chicago, which was probably as far away as he could afford to go. My parents would have disowned me if they knew the reason I left, so I didn't tell them. Just disappeared for a couple of days. They never forgave me for that."

"What happened while you were away?" Why not ask, I thought, she brought up the subject.

"Well, I know this sounds crazy and a lot of people around here wouldn't believe me, but we didn't make love. At least, not really. We slept in the same room, though. Well, that's the way it was. We walked along Michigan Boulevard, sat in parks and ate in cheap diners during the day, but it was the nights that were so beautiful. It was the nicest weekend of my life."

Tears came to her eyes. Considering the fortune this dinner was going to cost, I was hoping for more than tears and an old love story. Fortunately, the waiter returned with the appetizer and Kathy returned to her outwardly happy self. I continued to sip wine as the meal progressed. People passing by continued to look at her. I was not ordinarily the subject of civilians' envy.

When the waiter brought the bill, I looked at the amount in disbelief. He must have multiplied instead of added, I thought. The moment of truth arrived for me when I remembered that I did not have enough Vietnamese money even to pay the gratuity, because I seldom used it except for things like taxis and newspapers. The waiter would gladly have taken MPCs but, even if I had enough, I would not have made the offer. I had previously rendered several opinions in cases involving illegal money transactions. Not to worry, though! True to her word, Kathy was good for the bill. From her purse, she removed a great roll of piasters, which caused me to believe for a moment that she, too, might have gotten them from someplace other than the finance office. But that was impossible! No, I convinced myself, she just legally exchanged about three hundred American dollars for piasters in case of an emergency such as this.

With the bill and gratuity paid by Kathy, we exited Le Castel, receiving the same reaction from patrons as we did when we entered. Outside, we began a slow walk to Kathy's apartment across from the Continental Palace Hotel. She enjoyed every step of the way. When we arrived, she invited me in. I checked my watch. Half hour to curfew. It wasn't difficult to figure that, allowing five minutes to walk from her place to mine, I'd have twenty-five minutes to spare, so I accepted.

I did not sit down immediately after entering the apartment and am sure that I looked as awkward as my friend Tom must have looked a few months earlier. Kathy asked me to wait a minute while she changed into something comfortable. When she returned, she was wearing a cotton robe. Her shoes and large earrings had been removed.

"Would you like a drink?" she asked with ease and without hesitation, and I am sure with no intent other than to prolong the evening until curfew.

I thanked her but declined. I could not believe that I was alone with a single woman in her apartment and she wasn't even wearing shoes. Or earrings. I walked over to the large window that faced other apartments across the way. Rain began to fall and adrenaline began to flow.

"Don't worry about curfew!" Kathy said, "You can sleep here on the couch and we can talk a while longer."

Think now, I said to myself, you can make it through the night. Well, maybe I could, but I knew it wouldn't be easy and I had a flight scheduled early the next morning.

Kathy stood in her robe smiling, holding a bottle of Triple Sec. "I don't drink except wine with dinner, but you are welcome to this," she said. I compromised my original refusal by agreeing to a quick nightcap. She walked over to the couch with a soft drink and sat down, asking me to do the same.

I did as she requested and Kathy made no effort to come closer, but her eyes alone gave me a better reason to attempt an assault upon her than those in half the cases I heard in court. One gulp emptied my drink. Ten minutes to curfew.

"Let's watch television." Kathy said. "Bobbie will be on in a few minutes with the weather." Bobbie was Kathy's friend who worked as a secretary but did the nightly weather report on the Armed Forces Network. She always wore a miniskirt and finished her bit before the camera with: "Here's wishing you all good things, weatherwise, and, of course, otherwise."

We watched Bobbie, and I was not sure how to interpret the "otherwise" on this particular night. When she finished, though, the late night show began. I took a deep breath.

"This looks pretty good. I'm in the mood for a good movie!" Kathy said.

I did not think that I'd like this particular movie even if I were capable of sitting through it, but the curfew hour had passed. I threw caution to the winds and said: "Well, let's watch."

As the movie progressed, and I do not remember a thing about it, Kathy watched intently, often making comments while sipping from her glass of nonalcoholic whatever. I agreed with all her remarks.

Thirty minutes past curfew. I could wrestle no more with the situation. I'll risk the curfew, I said to myself. When I announced my decision, Kathy did not object but escorted me to the door.

I dashed down the stairs, walked quickly through the maze of shops on the bottom floor, and ran through the rain across the park to the Rex. The armed officer at the door, with clipboard and pencil in hand, stopped me, demanding identification. I complied. He looked at me rather smugly but let me pass without including me in his report of curfew violators.

CHAPTER TWENTY-FIVE

The Bloody Trail

Chu Lai is located forty miles south of Da Nang on a promontory overlooking the South China Sea. In peacetime, it is a virtual paradise. During the Vietnam War, it was headquarters of the Americal Division, and the site where all its general courts-martial were tried. Division personnel were spread out in areas surrounded by the enemy in many villages. They fought in marshy coastal lowlands, in jungles, and on mountain slopes. They fought in the provinces of Quang Tri and Quang Ngai and other areas where the Viet Cong and North Vietnamese army had taken a stronghold. It was difficult to distinguish friend from foe. When they met the enemy in combat, they fought with valor and were victorious. When they doubted who the enemy was, they were perplexed. Many Americal soldiers were killed or injured by unexpected foes.

The desire to liquidate their opponents led members of the division to suspect almost every Vietnamese person in villages of doubtful loyalty. These suspicions led to a hatred (by many soldiers and officers) of every Vietnamese man, woman, and child in areas that were considered to be enemy-infested.

I spent a week trying cases in Chu Lai during the early part of 1969. It was during the Tet season and the enemy was engaged in a second Tet Offensive, although not as serious as the year before. Mortar fire poured into the headquarters compound at unexpected times. Harassment and interdictment of the enemy by division artillery increased the noise level substantially throughout the area.

There were compensations, however, for being in Chu Lai, even though it was the busiest week of my tour of duty in Vietnam. During the noon hour, Lieutenant Colonel Barney Brannen and I jogged on the sandy beach below the headquarters, substituting a bar of candy for the noon meal, before returning to work. When there was an occasional break in the trial schedule, a driver from the legal office took me to the beach for an hour or so of quiet relaxation. In rare evenings when court was not in session, I sat in the general's mess overlooking the China Sea, reading or watching a movie.

The attitude with respect to Vietnamese people in the villages of Quang Nai Province was reflected in the case of Ralph Pilger, a member of a scout dog unit. On two successive days, the dog handlers and their charges had assisted in the sweep of several villages, seeking enemy arms and personnel. But rain on the following morning made it impracticable to use the animals. The handlers were sitting around the command post, chatting with several young Vietnamese boys, when Pilger asked Private Richard Russell to accompany him to a nearby village about five hundred meters away at the end of a trail. Russell refused.

The village Pilger entered was not unusual, consisting of many thatched huts, a small market, and a pagoda. Women of all ages and older men were milling about; children were playing; and three mature younger males, one dressed in the uniform of the Vietnamese Popular Forces and armed with a carbine, were walking among the people.

Thirty minutes after Pilger departed, his fellow dog handlers, who had remained behind, heard two shots from a carbine that they assumed came from the village. A three-minute pause followed, and then many more shots from an M–16, the type of weapon issued to each of the handlers. Before the group could decide what action to take, Pilger came running into the campsite holding a carbine and web belt over his head shouting, "I got a dink up there and there is two more if you want to go get them." A few seconds later, he told Sergeant Pascal Giesler that "I shot a gook, that son of a bitch had shot at me."

With everyone in a state of excitement, Pilger led Lieutenant Samuel Ender, his officer in charge, Sergeant Giesel and Private Russell to the spot on the trail between the command post and the village where the last shots had been fired. A member of the Vietnamese Popular Forces was lying face down, his clothes drenched in a pool of blood. Someone said he thought the person moved. Pilger emptied his automatic weapon into the body, killing him instantly, if he was not already dead. Those facts were undisputed.

Miss Dao Thi Van testified that she observed Pilger in the village near the pagoda. She swore that he approached Than Manh, a member of the Popular Forces, removed his web belt and his carbine, and led Manh out to the trail near the village that led to the command post. Before leading the victim from the village, Pilger fired two shots from Manh's carbine to scare away the children who had gathered around to witness the excitement. A few minutes later, Miss Van heard "a long firing" from the trail. Several villagers corroborated her testimony.

Criminal investigators testified that, on the day following the shooting, Pilger made a statement saying that he went down the trail only to the edge of the village. When walking back to camp, he saw three men behind him, so he started to run. He heard two shots from a carbine, one passing near his eyes and the other near his feet. Then, "I jumped off the trail into some bushes. I waited a minute and the Popular Forces guy ran towards me. I jumped out of the bushes when he was right in front of me and I shot him in self-defense. When I shot him the first time, he spun and I shot him again. He spun more and I must have used a whole clip on him because I just kept shooting. I went to him, took his weapon and gear and ran back to the CP area."

At the trial, Private Russell testified that "Pilger told me that the dink fired at him twice, then he jumped into the brush. He kept on indicating that the dink had fired the two shots first." Russel added that there was no blood on the web belt or carbine that Pilger was carrying when he returned, screaming, to the place where his friends were.

Lieutenant Enders testified Pilger told him that he shot a "dink." He also denied entering the village but was walking toward the village when the "dink" began shooting at him. Later, when Pilger led Enders and two others to the man who had been shot, Pilger began shooting the man again and "the shock of Pilger's weapon firing into the dead or wounded man deafened me. There was a whole lot of mud and dirt flying from the bullets hitting the ground. I saw the dust and dirt going up around the body. The man was definitely dead after that firing."

Investigators from battalion headquarters arrived several hours after the incident to investigate the killing. They searched the area where the man was killed and found nineteen M–16 empty rounds, but could find no carbine or other shells anywhere near the scene where Pilger said the Popular Forces man shot at him. Criminal investigators at the trial, using sketches, testified that they found two carbine casings in the village where Miss Van said she had seen the accused fire a weapon.

Pilger testified in court that he was sorry he could not reconcile all of the statements made during the trial, but the "dink" did shoot at him twice and he jumped into the bushes. When the "gook" passed him, he shot. He could not explain why he shot so many times in the first instance, or why he shot so many times again when he and the others found the man lying in a pool of blood. He swore that he removed the web gear after the man was shot, and not before, inside the village, as Miss Van had testified. He could not explain why the web gear was free from all traces of blood after the shooting.

During Pilger's trial, and especially after supper when darkness had fallen, the noise from mortar fire, both coming into and going out of the area, was deafening. I asked the members of the court whether they would like a recess until the noise abated, or perhaps even until the following morning, but they expressed a desire to continue. One member commented, with a wink towards me, that "We hear this all the time!"

The members of the court deliberated approximately forty-five minutes before returning to announce findings of not guilty. While sitting quietly at the judge's bench after the verdict was announced, not wishing to communicate with anyone, I observed the president of the court walk over to Pilger, put his arm around his shoulder, and say, "Son, you don't let anything like this happen again, because you will never get another chance." Actually, that was another chance for Pilger, because he had been court-martialled twice before. It was not permissible to give this information to the court before findings.

I was totally exhausted after the trial. I departed from the courtroom alone and walked to my quarters thinking of nothing more than a beer and a good night's sleep. Entering my quarters, however, I encountered a delightful surprise. Sitting in the living room of the trailer was a good friend whom I had known in Germany several years before, but had not seen since, and a second person, who looked vaguely familiar, drinking beer together. My friend and I had a hearty reunion, and the stranger introduced himself as Troy Donohue, whom I then recognized. The three of us had a few beers before retiring after midnight.

Early the next morning, we experienced a close encounter with death. An enemy rocket exploded about three meters from our quarters, sending shrapnel through the side of the trailer. My friend and I ran in a couched position to a nearby bunker. I presume Donohue took cover under his bed because he did not follow us, and was still alive when we returned.

CHAPTER TWENTY-SIX

America's Fighting Man

Circumstances of war frequently present occasions in which unsophisticated soldiers are not prepared to cope. Young men who are willing to give their lives for their country, and prove it every day, are placed in situations they are not sufficiently mature to manage. Unplanned crimes occur, therefore, because fighting men are faced with opportunities and temptations to commit offenses.

One of the tragedies of Vietnam was that soldiers who were actually facing the enemy, or were called upon to face the enemy, rather than the eighty-seven percent of troops who supported them, were the ones most often confronted with such opportunities. They succumbed to circumstances that they did not anticipate and now bear the stigma of undesirable discharges that remain part of their lives. Some of the crimes committed took place in the presence of other American soldiers and officers who could have prevented the abuses, but did not. The trial of Corporal Walter Bills, a member of a sister company in the same battalion as the dog handler, Private Ralph Pilger, provided evidence that was typical of this combination of circumstances which led to his court-martial.

At six-thirty on the evening of October 28, 1968, a squad led by Corporal Matt Stahl departed from its company headquarters near Landing Zone Zebra not far from Chu Lai for the purpose of setting up a night ambush close to a nearby village. Nothing of consequence happened before midnight, but early in the morning of the following day, rain began to fall. Stahl took his squad, consisting of himself, Corporal Bills, and five other men to a thatched hut that was empty except for a wooden bunk. The men did not sleep but kept watch, as was their duty.

At dawn, when they were about to return to their company headquarters, the men observed Huynh Thi Chan, an older Vietnamese civilian, about a hundred yards in the distance sitting in a tree looking at them. Stahl, Bills, and Private First Class Ron Darby walked over to Mr. Chan. A group of Vietnamese civilians, including Chan's fourteen-year-old daughter, Huyng Tri Thi, also walked over to Chan, and the two groups converged. Without hesitation or word of explanation, the three soldiers forcibly removed Miss Thi from her father's presence and dragged her into the empty hut where the soldiers had spent the early morning hours. Stahl ordered the other four men of his squad to "keep a watch" on the civilians.

Without much discussion among the three men inside the hut, Stahl undressed the girl who was clothed only in a simple Vietnamese peasant's blouse and pants. Stahl had intercourse with Miss Thi against her will, followed by Bills who committed the same offense. While one was having intercourse, the other held Miss Thi's legs apart. The third soldier, Darby, did not touch her inside the hut. He occasionally looked outside to insure that the civilians, who were being restrained by the other men in the squad, were kept away from the hut.

Stahl, Bills, and Darby were all tried by general court-martial, but I was only involved in the case of Corporal Bills. Although he pleaded guilty to the offense of raping a girl under the age of sixteen, thus admitting all the elements of the offense, the prosecutor chose to present the live testimony of the victim and her father to the court. The papers accompanying the file, including statements from all seven soldiers in Stahl's squad, clearly reflected that members of the squad did nothing to prevent what occurred inside the hut.

Miss Thi testified before the court, as she had previously sworn to investigators, that she was much afraid of the soldiers; that her parents were physically abused when they tried to prevent her removal from their presence; that she was badly bruised by the two soldiers; and that she did not consent to be touched by them at any time.

Mr. Chan testified in substantially the same manner as his daughter with respect to the events outside the thatched hut, and added that when his daughter came out of the hut, she looked exhausted, cried very much, bled profusely, and fell unconscious. Tears came to his eyes when he added that his daughter was only fourteen years old.

During the pretrial investigation, when Stahl was asked, "Why did you rape the girl?" he replied, "Because of hate for the Vietnamese people." When Bills was asked the same question, he replied, "I guess I needed sex." When Kirby was asked, "Why didn't you have sexual relations with the girl?" his response was, "Because these Vietnamese girls don't turn me on."

In extenuation and mitigation, Bills's defense counsel made an effort to explain his client's action to the court members, not as an excuse for the crime, but as a matter to be considered in imposing a lighter sentence. He argued:

> What do they do with these young men over here; eighteen, nineteen, and twenty years old? They have got sex on their minds, they're young. We bring them over here in Vietnam and they make all the villages off limits, so you can't go into them. Gentlemen, these young men get out in the field and do these things because they are no longer what they were in civilian life.

Witnesses who testified in Bills's behalf were unanimous in their praise for him. Officers and noncommissioned officers agreed that he was an outstanding combat soldier who continually volunteered for difficult missions into enemy areas and invariably reserved for himself the position of point man when doing so. His humor helped maintain a high state of morale in his unit even under the most miserable circumstances. He had been assigned combat duties almost from the day of his arrival in the Americal seven months previously and had continued to perform such duties until the day before his trial. He had not even requested the R&R to which he was entitled.

Corporal Bills was sentenced to be dishonorably discharged from the army and to be confined at hard labor for two years.

In an affidavit submitted to the convening authority after the trial, Bills's company commander described him as an example of "America's fighting man." Morale dropped considerably within the company when Bills was taken away to prison after the trial.

I do not have a solution to avoid the tragedy of Corporal Bills and others like him, but I do believe that there is much from his case that should be learned by those responsible for sending young men off to war. More training, better leadership at home and in the field, but most of all, a little more time for the young men to mature. In World War II, the average soldier was twenty-six years old; in Vietnam, nineteen. If there is need for a draft, it should be equally applicable to all men. The burden should not fall upon the disadvantaged and those who are not sophisticated enough to know how to escape being made a part of the military.

CHAPTER TWENTY-SEVEN

It's Prestige, Not Sex

The cases of Private Pilger and Corporal Bills convinced me that it is impossible to predict how a group of soldiers will react to a given situation in a combat zone when there is no combat. The third case in which I was involved at the Americal Division in February 1969 reinforced that conviction. Lieutenant Donald Pitt and a segment of his platoon were involved in a situation for which there was no prepared script and most of them acted in a manner totally out of character with their true selves.

On the morning of September 16, 1968, Lieutenant Pitt and his men marched into the hamlet of Binh Giang, which consisted of a few thatched huts and a bunker. Seeking a suitable place to establish a temporary command post, Pitt chose one of the huts in which several Vietnamese women, old men, and children, all members of an extended family, were congregated. Accompanied by four of his men, Pitt entered the hut. For a few minutes, only expressions of cordiality were exchanged between the two groups. One American soldier performed an act of mercy by giving medicine to, and playing a children's game with, a sick, retarded child.

One of the men in Pitt's group who did not enter the hut was Private First Class Ted Olsen, a twenty-three-year-old soldier who frequently talked about sex, but had never had sexual intercourse. These personal matters were common knowledge in the platoon and Olsen was frequently ridiculed because of lack of such experience at his age.

While things were still peaceful in the hut, Than Thi Liu, a twelve-year-old, sixty-five-pound, four-and-a-half-foot girl, who had been out gathering grass for her buffalo, returned to the hamlet to find the hut where she lived filled with American soldiers and some of her Vietnamese relatives. When Pitt saw Liu, he called Olsen, telling him to enter the hut. When the latter complied, Pitt pointed to Liu and said: "Look at that girl, look at her long hair, she is beautiful and is probably a virgin. You always wanted a young girl. Take her!"

Corporal Steve Seth, a soldier who had entered the hut with Pitt, approached Liu's mother and said: "Why don't you let babysan make boom boom to this GI?" The mother, although unable to understand English, sensed the threat and threw herself upon Olsen. Other soldiers separated them and forced the woman out of her own home.

The incident with Liu and her mother caused much screaming, pushing, and shoving between the races in the hut. Pitt gave the order to his men to eject all the Vietnamese people, except the little girl, from the dwelling. Olsen picked up Liu in his arms and brought her to the village bunker, where he put her down near the entrance and then shoved her inside. Liu's mother, pleading and crying, watched from a distance with other relatives who had also been forced out of the hut.

Olsen testified at the trial that Pitt followed him and Liu into the bunker, and when he hesitated about touching the child, Pitt told him again: "You always wanted a young girl, take her!" Then, Olsen continued, "Lieutenant Pitt reached over and removed the girl's pants from her body, and then just sat there. I told him to get out. He left the bunker."

Olsen slapped Liu, who was crying, and told her to shut up. "I was thinking only of my prestige, not about sex," Olsen testified. "You might say that I wanted to save face, maybe. I wanted to show them that I could do it. I had been teased for a long time. But, when I had the girl in the bunker, I thought, no. I could not. But, when Lieutenant Pitt pulled the girl's pants down, maybe then I was aroused. Lieutenant Pitt encouraged me to have my first sexual encounter. I was being pressured by the platoon. It was a constant pressure, indescribable."

Liu testified that, inside the bunker, Olsen held her down even though she cried and pleaded that she was too young. She swore he lay on top of her and put something in her body which caused her to bleed. "I had big pain in my stomach. I feel very hurt," she testified.

Five minutes after Olsen and Liu entered the bunker, Pitt stooped down near the entrance to ask, "How are you doing?" "Not so good!" replied Olsen, as he emerged alone from the bunker and proceeded to a water barrel, where he washed his bloody hands. Pitt suddenly felt remorse for his behavior and ordered one of his men to retrieve Liu from the bunker. A soldier went inside and dragged her out by the hands and feet. Liu, crying aloud and bleeding profusely, ran to her mother, who carried her into the family hut.

When one of the soldiers who had seen Liu being physically removed from the bunker was asked whether he did not think it strange to see a little girl being dragged out of the ground, he replied that he did not, because ". . . when we check a bunker, we always send in a kid, so if there is something in the bunker, like a grenade or something, it will blow him up first." I thought this soldier was exhibiting a sense of braggadocio, thinking somehow it would help in the trial of his platoon leader.

The entire group of soldiers left the village shortly after the incident in the bunker. While walking away, Olsen asked a friend if he was angry. "No," replied his companion, "but next time get someone who is bigger and older." Olsen was serious and apparently ashamed of what he had done when he replied, "Yes, I'll never do anything like that again!"

On the morning after the incident, Liu and her mother walked four hours to an American base camp five miles away, seeking medical assistance. Liu was attended by American medical personnel for three days, with her mother at her side. The doctor who took care of her verified that she had been sexually abused but could not determine if she had been raped. When released, Liu could walk without assistance but not climb, even up to a bed or into a jeep.

Lieutenant Pitt was charged with encouraging Private First Class Olsen to sexually abuse a girl under the age of sixteen, thereby being a principal to the crime, and with committing a lewd act on the same girl by removing her pants. He denied both allegations. Two thirds of the court members apparently did not believe beyond a reasonable doubt that Pitt had done the acts alleged, because he was found not guilty. Although Pitt was acquitted, the evidence in the trial revealed a sordid story of American servicemen committing offenses that would never have occurred except for the unfortunate circumstances of being placed in situations in which they had the opportunity to act in a manner inconsistent with their normal behavior. Olsen was later tried and convicted of committing an indecent assault upon a minor. The behavior of Lieutenant Pitt and most of his men reflected adversely upon their honor and the honor of every American fighting man.

CHAPTER TWENTY-EIGHT

Mississippi Lawyer

I was alone in my quarters at the Rex Hotel one evening in February when I received a call from Red Benoit inviting me to his room. He said that he was entertaining a civilian lawyer from Mississippi who had arrived that afternoon and would like me to meet him.

The lawyer was portly, middle-aged, and wore a sharkskin suit with silk tie. He seemed very friendly but loquacious and on the pompous side. Arrangements had been made for him to fly to Dong Tam the following morning, where he was to represent an army client. I got the impression from Red's facial expression that it was about time for me to take a turn at entertaining the gentleman inasmuch as they had already eaten together in the steakhouse and Red wasn't talking very much. In fact, within a few moments of my arrival, Red wasn't talking at all but thumbing through papers on his desk.

"Is it possible to go walking in this city?" the lawyer asked.

I informed him that it was, and offered to escort him. It was not for the honor of the exercise but rather to relieve Red from his obvious boredom in return for the many favors he had done for me and, in a small way, to repay him for causing the firemen to break into his room.

"By golly!" the lawyer said as we left the hotel and walked across the park. "Here I am in the middle of a war and walking around like I was back home in Mississippi. Wait till I get back to tell my friends!"

We were still in the shadow of the Rex, not yet across the park, when the lawyer stopped to light a cigar. He offered one to me from a neat row on the inside pocket of his sharkskin coat, but I declined. As he was lighting up, a Vietnamese man, appearing to be a refugee dressed only in short pants and a ragged shirt, approached us holding a naked baby. There was a fixed half grin on his face, transcending an expression of hopelessness as he stood there, slightly stooping, extending his hand towards us. The lawyer stared at the couple for a moment, neither in a friendly nor unfriendly manner.

"That your baby, boy?" he asked, clouds of cigar smoke engulfing the man, the child, and me. Not having an inkling of what the lawyer said, the Vietnamese man made a gallant effort to broaden the stagnant smile on his face.

"Well, here, I'll help you out!" said the southern gentleman as he put a few coins into the ragged man's hand. The man had no more power within him to broaden his smile but he somehow dipped his body in the form of a crude curtsy as an expression of thanks.

"I like to help poor folk," the lawyer informed me as we resumed our walk towards Le Loi and Tu Do Streets. "In fact, that's why I'm here."

"How is that?" I asked.

"Well, that boy they're trying tomorrow! His case got a lot of publicity back home and I offered to defend him free. That's why I'm here!"

"I'm sure he'll appreciate it."

"Yeah, I know he will. His mama used to work for me. She was a good nigger."

As we walked along Tu Do Street, the lawyer peered into the windows of almost every bar, staring at the hostesses. "There's some right pretty girls in there," he said, "and they're wearing mighty pretty costumes, too!" referring to their au dais.

At each bar and at the sight of more hostesses, the lawyer began to use expressions which indicated to me that he would like to get closer to the action. Finally, he said, "Damn, I wish it was safe to go in there but you can image headlines back home: MISSISSIPPI LAWYER MURDERED IN SAIGON WHORE HOUSE."

"Those aren't whore houses," I explained, "and, if you'd like to stand the expense of buying a couple of drinks for yourself and a hostess, we can visit one."

"Let's do it!" he said excitedly.

I took the lawyer to a little bar situated among the shops and stores within the maze of buildings near the park across from the Rex. It was an out of the way, quiet place off the beaten path, unknown to people who were just walking up and down the more popular Tu Do Street. I had visited the bar on previous occasions when friends came to Saigon from the field for one reason or another and wanted to visit a "notorious" Saigon bar with hostesses. It was the safest and quietest place I could find and was appropriately named the Shangri-La.

One of the hostesses at the Shangri-La was a person who never ceased to fascinate me. She sat on a couch, writing constantly in a ledger when she was not otherwise occupied. As customers entered, she made no effort to approach them unless the other hostesses were busy. She had a soulful face, a perfect complexion, jet black hair reaching below her shoulders, and wore the traditional au dai. She always appeared to be sad. Her eyes stared but never smiled. One night I approached her and asked what she was writing and why she was so preoccupied with the project. She did not seem hesitant to speak as I bought her a couple of Saigon teas, and she told me her story.

The hostess did not expect to live long, although she did not know why and was apparently in good health. She had a daughter born of an American father from whom she had not heard since her baby's birth. She was writing everything she did so that one day her daughter would know about her. Nothing was unimportant. She described her work, her dresses, her customers, her ex-lover, the girl's father, everything. She'd lost count of the number of books she had filled but they were all at her home in a safe place. She worked every night.

As we entered the little bar, the lawyer could not keep his eyes on a single girl but threw furtive glances from one to the other. He was too excited to make a quick choice. When he finally settled on one who appeared to be the youngest and friendliest, the three of us sat around a small table. The hostess who wrote made no effort to stand up when we entered, or make a play for either of us although she did smile ever so slightly as a sign of recognition when she saw me.

"How old are you?" was the first question from the bench.

"Me twenty-two," replied the girl smiling with her eyes, lips, and whole body. The lawyer was enthralled.

Much small talk passed among the three of us, most of which was totally incomprehensible to the hostess, who nevertheless held the lawyer's hand and snuggled up to him, a little closer with each new order of Saigon tea. The lawyer started to perspire and began to jabber nonsense. He didn't know what to do. It was getting late, he had to get up early the following morning, there was a curfew, but most importantly, he was very scared.

"I guess we'd better leave!" he finally exploded after making the momentous decision. He stood up, smiling broadly. The hostess held onto his arm and he slipped her an American greenback that pleased her enough to offer him a kiss on the cheek.

As we left the bar and headed towards the Rex, my new acquaintance was ecstatic. "Did you see that? Did you see that?" he said emotionally. "That girl really liked me! By golly, she even kissed me. Holy hell, what if my wife ever found out?"

And then he leaned over toward me as if to share some deep, dark military secret. "And you know what else?" he said quietly, but animatedly: "I pinched her on the ass and she didn't even mind."

TWENTY-NINE

Travel

I am not afraid to fly in helicopters, although my palms begin to sweat in airplanes at the first sign of turbulence. I have no explanation for this gift of feeling safe in a sometimes unsafe situation except that in Vietnam, disregarding existing facts and evidence of which I was aware, I convinced myself that helicopters could always descend by auto-rotation. It made traveling a lot easier because I was a passenger in helicopters several times a week.

From Saigon, traveling by helicopter was the most practical way to reach Dong Tam, Cu Chi, Lai Khe, Phuoc Vihn, and several other smaller places within the Saigon perimeter. Although I made frequent trips to Long Binh and its environs by helicopter, I also traveled there by staff car, jeep, bus, or an occasional civilian vehicle. On longer trips, airplanes were the only feasible way to travel.

I do not know how many helicopter pads and landing zones there were in Vietnam but surely there were hundreds. Some were equipped with sophisticated paraphernalia; others were mere clearings in forests or swamps. The largest of all heliports was Hotel 3, whose appellation was a mystery to me. Others reflected a more personal touch. In combat areas, they usually bore the names of females or instruments of war, such as Landing

Zone Dottie or Charlotte or Bayonet. Hotel 3 was different. It was a superpad, the busiest in Vietnam, located in a corner of the world's busiest airfield on the outskirts of Saigon. Choppers landed there and took off like dragonflies, usually remaining only a few minutes. I was picked up and returned there dozens of times.

It seemed a miracle of the electronic age that the right chopper usually picked up or deposited the right person or cargo. In the case of departing individuals, we merely gave our names to the radio control operator and waited for our designated carriers. Through the windows and within the VIP lounge of Hotel 3, one was able to witness a microcosm of events taking place throughout Vietnam. There were always high-ranking officers waiting to return to their stations from whatever duty or folly had brought them to Saigon. Media people were usually present, which was not surprising inasmuch as they had easy access to military transportation. I once waited with and shared a helicopter with a young woman reporter going out for stories wearing a sleeveless blouse, miniskirt, and sandals, carrying only camera and writing pad. When I inquired about her luggage, she informed me that it would be no problem returning to Saigon by nightfall. She had always been successful. On other occasions, I saw administration officials from Washington, Pulitzer Prize winners, congressmen, senators, movie stars, professional ball players, and civilian lawyers. None of these people seemed unhappy to me. They were well fed, well paid, had interesting jobs, and the risk for them was not really great. Of course, there were also the grunts who didn't look happy going out to combat zones to replace other grunts.

Flying away from Hotel 3 was never boring. Helicopter pilots were required to remain close to the ground for a few minutes, out of the flight pattern of planes using Ton Son Nhut. That experience, in itself, was harrowing enough, but on one occasion, I was with two young pilots who took pleasure not only in shearing treetops but flying even lower between the trees. They scattered fowl to the wind, forced farmers to dive for cover, virtually touched cattle, and threatened their passenger with a heart attack. I thought perhaps these pilots were exploding with excitement after having landed at a firebase amidst a shower of mortar fire an hour or so before. They also knew that later in the day they might be required to risk their lives evacuating wounded and dying fellow Americans from combat areas. I sympathized with the Vietnamese farmers and repressed the anger within myself because I could not reproach the conduct of these young men.

On two occasions, helicopter pilots gave me opportunities to observe historic places that I would not otherwise have seen. The first was flying away from Camp Evans in August 1968. The pilot made a detour to offer me an aerial view of the ruins of Khe Sanh, where the embattled marines had been making national headlines in the earlier part of the year. Khe Sanh was then silent. The second opportunity occurred when a pilot taking me from Camp Eagle to Da Nang made a detour to allow me to see the great Citadel of Hue, laying in ruins but still beautiful after the extended battle fought there during the Tet Offensive.

Returning to Saigon by helicopter did not usually present a problem. I merely stood at a landing zone and waited for the next chopper to Saigon, or a place closer to Saigon. Occasionally, that closer location was without radio or phone communications. When transportation did not arrive before dark, I reported to the nearest military unit for aid and comfort, and waited there until the following day.

Sometimes I had the good fortune after a trial to discover that a helicopter was already scheduled for a flight to Saigon with room for an additional passenger. Often it was for the convenience of a high-ranking officer. More often than not, the officer gave me a private tour of the area over which we were flying. He pointed out firebases, locations of previous and present engagements, areas decimated by B–52s, and cheerfully bantered all the way to Saigon.

Frequently, a chopper ride was sad and depressing. One or more soldiers, recently killed, had been wrapped in green plastic bags and placed on the floor between the two stationary rows of canvas seats. On these flights, there was little banter among the passengers. Our attention was riveted to the plastic bags. Was one perhaps a young soldier who was away from home for the first time? A man with a wife and children? It was impossible to know, but I never for a moment forgot that my own position was relatively free from danger and before me were bodies of fellow Americans who had left their native land never to return. Had they been killed by the enemy? An avoidable accident, perhaps? Sometimes, I thought it best not to know.

Although I had convinced myself (for psychological reasons) that I would not be involved in an accident, the fact that they did occur was painfully brought home to me when I was peripherally involved in an incident that resulted in the death of an officer. A young psychiatrist who had testified in a case but had not yet been excused came to me during a recess requesting permission to depart before completion of the trial. He was scheduled on a flight from Saigon to Hawaii the following day that would take him to his waiting wife. I granted him permission to depart immediately. He was killed in a crash before reaching Saigon.

The return to Hotel 3 always provided a sense of relief, even though the ever present guns mounted on helicopter doorways and the military installations below were a continual reminder that Saigon was a city at war. For me, it was another mission accomplished and a few days sooner to completing my Vietnam tour. I appreciated, but felt uneasy about, the contrast between my own relatively comfortable lifestyle and that of the people who lived in the myriad little houses covered by tin roofs contiguous to each other on the river banks.

The passengers who exited from helicopters when they touched ground at Hotel 3 reflected different moods of the war. There were those coming in for the last time, having completed a tour of combat, bearing grimaces of persons who could not become detached from memories. Some were deliriously happy on their way to R&R, who quickly departed, afraid to miss connections to Hawaii, Singapore, Bangkok, Hong Kong, Sydney, Kuala Lampur, Manila, or Taiwan. High-ranking officers and others with automobiles awaiting their arrival displayed a suave, sophisticated attitude. There were also the wounded and sick coming in for treatment, prisoners under guard on their way to the Long Binh Stockade, and others, including civilians, traveling for reasons unknown to me. It all became routine, except when the long green plastic bags were removed and loaded on those dreadful trucks destined for the mortuary.

On trips to faraway locations, I usually traveled in the comfort of a U–21 eight-passenger turbojet plane. They were the property of a military airplane company in Long Binh, but controlled by the VIP section at MACV. The planes were dispatched to Ton Son Nhut early each morning to pick up and transport persons on official business to distant places within Vietnam. A simple phone call on the evening before departure was all that was usually required. Planes arrived on schedule with reserved seats. I traveled thousands of miles in these aircraft to Cam Rahn Bay, Pleiku, Nha Trang, Chu Lai, Da Nang, and other points north.

On return flights to Saigon from distant places, there was no easy access to transportation. I accepted anything available. There were usually no waiting rooms or regularly scheduled flights. Some of the better-equipped planes passing through had pressurized cabins and canvas seats; smaller planes, like the Caribou C–7, had no pressurized cabins; some had no seats whatsoever.

In Pleiku, while waiting for a flight, I saw a Caribou scheduled to transport Vietnamese elders, women, and children away from their homes, probably flying for the first time in their lives. All were seated on the floor, holding canvas straps that substituted for safety belts. They appeared to be in panic even before liftoff. Later, I read that, before landing, the wheels of that aircraft were jammed and the pilot prepared for a crash landing. The crewmaster, however, was successful in lowering the wheels manually, but only after chopping away with an ax at an area from which he could work. After a safe landing, the passengers raced for the exit, understandably swearing never to fly again. An experience such as that aggravated the tragedy of the passengers who were being forced to unknown destinations with no information about their future.

The most embarrassing and exasperating experience I had while waiting for air transportation occurred at Cam Rahn Bay after returning from a short trip to Singapore. Although I could have waited five days in Singapore for a regularly scheduled flight to Saigon, I chose to take my chances by accepting an earlier flight to Cam Rahn Bay, thinking that there would be no problem getting from there to Saigon. Most of the passengers on that flight were returning from R&R.

Upon landing at Cam Rahn Bay, I was delighted to learn that a flight to Saigon was about to depart, with space enough for passengers. Not with me on it, however. There were regulations to be followed and I was no exception. All returnees from Singapore were ordered to board buses and be taken to an area distant from the terminal. We were then herded into the largest restroom I have ever seen, with dozens of lavatories.

A sergeant entered the cavernous room and issued to everyone little packets with special soap powder and paper towels. He then proceeded to give a stern lecture on the horrors of venereal disease. He explained what precautions had to be taken, and how to use the contents of the little packets, although, he said, it was probably too late to do any good. Following the lecture, many of those who deplaned began the procedure of using the lavatories and packets, scrubbing their bodies furiously. Many, including myself, made use of neither the packets nor the gratuitous information issued to us. The exercise, however, caused many of us to miss connections to our destinations. I returned to the terminal and waited on the concrete floor until midnight when the next scheduled plane departed for Saigon. It was a joy to be "home" again even during pouring rain in the middle of the night.

CHAPTER THIRTY

Distractions

All courtrooms in Vietnam were different. Although some were simple tents also used for other purposes, improvements were made as time went by. Floors and sturdy supports were usually added. There were also makeshift structures, and buildings already in place in which a room was converted into a place of trial. When a tent was used, it was necessary to raise the side flaps because of the intense heat, day and night. During rainstorms, the flaps were dropped causing an almost unbearable combination of humidity and heat.

Improved courtrooms reflected the ingenuity of personnel in the legal offices. Often during trial, I was distracted by looking at wooden floors constructed of unmatched pieces of wood. Markings on what were crates originally destined for certain people or places were clearly visible. I assumed that smaller parts were the remains of what had been intended for, and should have been used as, pallets for storage of critical materials. In World War II, we obtained such necessities by "moonlight requisition," and I presume the troops were doing the same in Vietnam. Some courtrooms, built without engineer specifications, consisted of whatever materials were available for uprights and siding, with corrugated tin roofs.

The tables and benches never matched. Large boxes, fragile card tables, and steel desks were used as working tables. Folding chairs were the only kind available. The exception, of course, was in Long Binh where the courtroom was perfect. Generally, it was better to avoid an enclosed room with an individual air conditioner. High temperatures were easier to cope with than refrigerated air filtered through machines drowning out the sounds of voices.

The most common distraction during trials was noise. We were almost never free from the sounds of helicopters taking off or landing; of trucks and other war machines passing by; of occasional gunfire and mortar explosions; and most irritating of all, the sound of artillery constantly firing harassment and interdictment rounds into Free Fire Zones.

The problem of noise was partially solved by the ingenuity of Wayne Alley. While on a trip to Okinawa, he discovered the wireless microphone, then a novelty in Vietnam, which could be used with an FM radio to amplify sound. Thereafter, when rainstorms or other outside disturbances made hearing difficult, I positioned my FM radio close to the members of the court, and was able to speak in normal tones into the little microphone without wires. A simple solution to a disturbing problem!

The most irritating minor disturbance was peeping into the courtrooms by off-duty personnel, a totally unnecessary act because chairs were always provided for spectators. I think that peeping through canvas or siding was as irresistible to passers-by as peeping through canvas at a carnival sideshow or fence at a ball game.

In the latter part of January, it was nearly midnight in Dong Tam when the lawyers and I were participating in a lengthy session on legal matters after the members of the court had been dismissed for the evening. We were meeting on the second floor of a structure consisting of two floors and a roof supported by pilings. One crude stairway, more like a ladder on the outside of the structure, provided the only normal access to and from the second floor.

The hearing was being held during a period of almost complete stillness when a mortar shell exploded with a thunderous clap just above our heads. The court reporter removed the mask that formed a part of his recording device, screaming "That's incoming, sir!" and departed the hearing by jumping from the second floor to begin his rush to the nearest bunker. The other participants ran to the exit near the stairway, with me in the rear saying only one word, "Recess!"

We returned to the courtroom a few minutes later to find a part of the roof blasted away. Before anyone else spoke, I entered the word "Recess" for the record, followed by an explanation of what had taken place.

The headquarters of the 101st Airborne Division (Airmobile), known as the "Screaming Eagles," was located at a place called Camp Eagle north of Da Nang and close to the ancient capital of Hue when I was assigned to a case there. Units of that division had served with distinction throughout Vietnam since 1965, and remained until nearly the end of the United States' involvement there.

In the middle of an afternoon, the case at Camp Eagle was progressing slowly with only the usual minor distractions. Suddenly, without warning, loudspeakers sounded off with marches of John Philip Souza, making it impossible to hear anything but the music. I recessed the court. Then, having nothing better to do, I went outside to observe whatever celebration would be taking place.

Remnants of several companies marched by in formation. When the soldiers were in place in front of the division headquarters, members of the staff entered the temporary parade ground. Walking next to the commanding general was a lieutenant colonel who was apparently to be the honoree at the ceremony. When all participants were in proper formation, the music stopped.

Voices from the loudspeakers began to recite the accomplishments of the young lieutenant colonel who had finished his tour of duty in Vietnam and was being recognized with a parade at which he was to be decorated. His achievements were recited in detail and then the medals were presented. First, the Distinguished Service Cross, followed by a Silver Star with oak-leaf cluster, Bronze Star with V for valor and six oak-leaf clusters, two Purple Hearts, three Air Medals, and several other medals that were almost routinely given to personnel who had served honorably in Vietnam. In addition, there was a packet of medals from the Vietnamese government frequently given to officers and enlisted persons who had served with the ARVN forces.

The citations convinced me that this particular officer deserved every medal awarded to him. I feel today, however, that the plethora of medals awarded, especially Air Medals to nonflyers and Purple Hearts to some who were only slightly injured in noncombat situations, diminished the meaning of the awards to those who truly deserved them.

After leaving Camp Eagle, I flew to Lai Khe where a court-martial was again disrupted during a rather routine case. A crowd had gathered about fifty yards away and seemed to be growing as it moved towards the headquarters building. Not only did the commotion disturb the proceedings but curiosity overcame my composure, so I called a recess and joined the crowd.

In the center of the group, standing taller than everyone else, was a regimental commander holding the arm of a wiry little Vietnamese man wearing very little clothing. I was informed that the Vietnamese was a captured Viet Cong being brought to intelligence for interrogation. South Vietnamese and American soldiers armed with M–16 rifles and hand grenades were guarding the little man. I presumed they were his captors.

I have often wondered about the function of that alleged Viet Cong. Perhaps he was responsible for killing American soldiers, or blowing up American helicopters, or perhaps a simple soldier awaiting an opportunity to strike a blow for his cause. Or, just by the slightest coincidence, he may have been a simple rice farmer with no allegiances.

A more severe disturbance occurred at a different place when rapid rifle fire was heard just outside the division compound. I recessed the court and walked a hundred yards or so where I was told that several Viet Cong soldiers had been sighted by guards on the perimeter, and a firefight ensued. Reinforcements from within the compound provided immediate relief and the enemy was quickly subdued. A few minutes later, rifle fire was detected from a house in a nearby village. Division artillery quickly silenced the presumed attack on the installation by destroying the house from which the fire came. Several civilians were killed.

That evening, a Vietnamese woman came to the base camp with heart-wrenching cries complaining that several members of her extended family had been killed in the attack during the afternoon. She received little sympathy.

"Was it necessary to respond with artillery fire into a house within the village?" I asked a division staff officer during cocktail hour at the general's mess.

"Of course it was! People like you are not combat-oriented and do not understand these things," he replied blandly. Then, for emphasis, "We have authority under the Rules of Engagement to use whatever firepower is necessary to silence the enemy."

Colonel George S. Patton III, the Commanding Officer of the 11th Armored Cavalry Regiment, was the senior member appointed to a court at Plantation on which I was the military judge. As such, he was president of the court, whose functions included such duties as announcing findings and sentence, but his vote was no more important than any other member's. As a matter of courtesy, however, he was consulted as to the time for convening the court. For this particular trial, all members and officers of the court were present at the prescribed time. But the accused, who had been confined to the Long Binh Stockade and had no control of his whereabouts, was not present.

Colonel Patton, who had a reputation not unlike his father's, was standing with other court members outside the courtroom about thirty yards from the legal office where I was waiting. Twenty minutes past trial time, Colonel Patton demanded in a loud voice, "What's going on here? Doesn't anyone know there's a war going on?" I sent word that the delay was unavoidable.

When the accused and his guards finally appeared, all participants except the court members entered the courtroom to arrange ourselves properly for the proceedings. When the members were called into the courtroom, Colonel Patton was the first to enter. He gave no impression of being anything but compliant with the rules of military legal procedure. He did not even complain about having to lay aside his pistol.

The defense counsel, when exercising his right to a preemptory challenge, stood up and courteously but firmly announced: "The defense respectfully challenges Colonel Patton!"

A few years later I met General Patton, who since the trial at Plantation had been promoted, in the officers' mess in Nuremberg, Germany. We discussed the case in Vietnam on which we had both been assigned. After thinking a while, he told me: "You know, that defense counsel should never have challenged me. I am the best friend a GI ever had!"

On New Year's Eve, Lieutenant Colonel Hugh Clausen and I were awaiting 1969 in his trailer at Lai Khe, reminiscing about years we spent together in prior assignments. At the stroke of midnight, artillery and rifle fire led us to believe that either Viet Cong or North Vietnamese troops were taking this opportunity to break through the defense perimeter. We took cover in the nearest bunker, but soon realized that what we heard was "friendly" fire being expended by American soldiers on duty ringing in the New Year with the hope, no doubt, that this would be their last in Vietnam.

CHAPTER THIRTY-ONE

Friends

One of the compensations for traveling to combat areas was the opportunity to meet so many lawyers assigned to the legal offices throughout Vietnam. They advised their superiors, gave legal assistance to civilian and military personnel, settled claims, and helped troubled soldiers in and out of combat. It was especially pleasant to work with younger counsel who prosecuted and defended the cases to which I was assigned.

Occasionally, while watching television or reading newspapers, I recognize the names of many Vietnam veteran lawyers whom I knew and who have since become prominent. Some have written books referring to cases in which we both participated; many have become judges; some law professors; several promoted to generals; and a few prosecutors and defense counsel have achieved national attention. Wayne Alley, with whom I spent many delightful hours in Saigon, became, in turn, a general, dean of the University of Oklahoma Law School, and is currently a United States District Court judge in Oklahoma.

There was one captain from the Americal division, however, who made more than a fleeting appearance on the national scene during the Watergate period. I do not remember Captain Donald Segretti from Chu Lai, but he did participate in several of the cases tried while I was there and I am sure that we shared meals and otherwise passed time together when court was not in session. He did not stand out among, above, or below the others. I do, however, remember him quite well from a trip we later took together to Cam Ranh Bay, the largest protected natural harbor in South Vietnam.

Captain Segretti was the appointed defense counsel and I was the appointed military judge on two cases scheduled for trial at Cam Ranh Bay early in 1969. The cases were convened by the commanding general of the Engineer Command in Long Binh, but since the incidents occurred in Cam Ranh Bay and the witnesses lived there, the trials were held at that location. Captain Segretti and I traveled by helicopter from Long Binh and were met at our destination by Captain Juan Figuero, the senior judge advocate there. Acting as a representative of his commanding general, Figuero took great pains to make our stay interesting, instructive, and comfortable. He guided us immediately on a tour of the base, which had previously been used by French and Japanese naval forces but was being developed into an even larger seaport by the Americans. He then brought us to our assigned quarters, a new house trailer that we had to ourselves.

Both of the cases tried at the Cam Rahn Bay were guilty pleas, which meant that each could be disposed of in three or four hours. Furthermore, they were tried on successive mornings, leaving us much free time to ourselves. The prosecutor was a lawyer from Captain Figuero's office who returned to his duties immediately upon completion of each of the cases. Segretti and I visited the Post Exchange, spent an afternoon on the beach, and took a boat tour around the harbor.

On one memorable evening, Figuero took us to the officers' club overlooking the South China Sea. A rock-and-roll group called The Surferers was playing music unfamiliar to me but appropriate to the taste of a younger generation, represented by most of the persons there. (It was only recently, when reading letters written from Vietnam, that I learned the correct name of the musical group. I had, for many years, been under the impression that it was the Beach Boys.) The few women present, special services workers and female members of the armed forces, had little time to themselves, with pressures for dancing partners being made by the men who greatly outnumbered them. The audience was a happy one and most of the patrons gyrated to the music, even those without partners.

During an intermission, someone told members of the band that a judge was in the audience. One of them, feeling happy, joined us, treating me as his best friend. He told me that the group was renting a villa in Saigon, surrounded by a very large wall, and I should visit them when I had an opportunity, it was perfectly safe. For what? I thought. The young man wrote his Saigon address for me on a napkin in a clear, bold hand. When the music resumed, my mood mellowed, perhaps due to the flattering visit by the musician. I began to enjoy the party and, when it ended, I invited The Surferers to join me and Captain Segretti at our quarters. They accepted, and we continued to celebrate there, but in a more subdued atmosphere. (My meeting with The Surferers was nothing compared to Wayne's having dined with Gypsy Rose Lee and Pat O'Brien.)

I probably would have forgotten Segretti's name had it not been for the notoriety that came to him later. Even after I read about him, I did not recall the evening at Cam Ranh Bay as being particularly remarkable. A couple of years ago, however, at a dull gathering, I related the incident as part of a rather mundane conversation. A friend of mine thought it was a remarkable story. "Jack," he said, "you were boozing it up with Donald Segretti and a rock-and-roll band on a moonlit night at Cam Ranh Bay in the midst of a war? It's surreal." When he put it that way, I thought that perhaps it was, but Cam Ranh Bay was a pretty safe place to be. President Johnson himself had visited there two years before.

CHAPTER THIRTY-TWO

Billy Bates

Billy Bates was a patriotic young man, the son of a patriotic father who, himself, had already served a tour of combat duty in Vietnam. Billy volunteered for the army when he was seventeen years old. After training in the United States, he had performed very well in Vietnam during five tortuous months there, until the night before his nineteenth birthday.

Billy was a member of the First Cavalry Division when its headquarters was stationed in Phuoc Vinh. It was there that I went for his trial in March 1969. Upon arrival at the headquarters compound, I introduced myself to the newly assigned staff judge advocate, Lieutenant Colonel Ben Stanley, whom I had never met. He was polite in a strictly formal manner, giving me the impression that he thought he should be able to handle his own disciplinary problems without the assistance of a military judge. Within a few minutes after our introduction, he excused himself, indicating that it was time to meet with other staff officers before dinner at the general's mess.

After my own dinner with two friends from the division, I returned to the legal office to review the file in the case of Corporal William P. Bates. The evidence indicated that on the evening of February 22, 1969, Bates had been ordered by his company commander to participate in a night reconnaissance mission. He refused by saying that he was afraid and would not obey the order. The order was repeated and Bates again refused to comply. The commander warned Billy that he must obey or face charges of cowardly conduct, and repeated the order a third time. Bates began to cry and refused again. On the following day, Bates apologized to his company commander, saying that he could not understand his previous night's behavior and begged to return to combat. "Too late!" was the reply, "I gave you three chances. I can't tolerate your kind of behavior in the presence of other troops." The file included four letters from superior noncommissioned officers who were pleased with Bates's performance of duties as a soldier, especially in combat.

Corporal Bates's case upset me because I knew for a fact that most commanding officers in Vietnam would have gladly accepted his apparently sincere offer to return to combat. Not only would they have a soldier proven in battle and ready to fight again, but they would be relieved of the ordeal of having to prepare for a trial.

After reading the file, I walked over to Colonel Stanley's quarters to discuss the matter with him. I told him that, in my opinion, Bates should be given another chance and that, all things considered, he did not deserve a general court-martial.

"Listen, judge!" Stanley said icily, "This case has already been referred for trial by the commanding general and there is nothing I can do."

"Look!" I replied, "This is certainly your business and I can't interfere or do anything to stop this trial, but you know as well as I do that if you approach the general as his legal adviser, even at this late hour, he'll give you a hearing. Tell him again that Bates wants to go into combat, that he is barely nineteen years old, and that you have reconsidered your original opinion. Tell him that other noncommissioned officers have come forward to say that they want him back in the unit, which happens to be true. In my judgment, he will listen to you."

Stanley became perturbed by my remarks and said that nothing in the world would cause him to approach the general at this hour with such a proposition. Moreover, he would not himself reconsider his original decision. The soldier was a coward and deserved to be severely punished.

At the time prescribed on the following morning, all parties to the trial assumed our proper places. I looked at Bates and he responded with a nervous grin. In my opinion, the defense counsel had given him bad advice by convincing him to plead guilty, a fact that I knew in advance. I called the court to order, and, at the proper time, asked the accused: "How do you plead?"

"Guilty, sir," was the reply.

At that point, it was necessary to excuse the members of the court so that I could question Bates as to his understanding of the plea. Privately, I hoped that he would say something inconsistent so that I would have a basis to reject his plea. Legally, the court members could sentence Bates to life imprisonment, but the commanding general had agreed to disapprove any confinement in excess of four years. I thought the defense counsel could have, and the court would have done better.

"Corporal Bates," I asked, "do you know what it means to plead guilty?"

"Yes, sir."

"Do you know that by pleading guilty you are admitting that you willfully refused to obey your company commander?"

"Yes, sir."

"You don't have to plead guilty, Corporal Bates. You may plead not guilty and then the prosecutor would have to prove that you specifically intended not to go on that reconnaissance mission."

"I understand that, sir."

"On February 26th of this year, did you in fact receive an order from your commanding officer to go on a mission in combat?"

"Yes, sir."

"Did you obey that order?"

"No, sir."

"Why not?"

"Because I was scared."

"Tell me, Corporal Bates, and think about this very carefully. Why were you scared?"

"Well, sir, it's hard to say. I thought I had just about enough of combat at that time, and maybe I got especially scared because I had approval to go to Hong Kong three days later. Something told me I just couldn't make it one more time. It was the night before my nineteenth birthday."

"Did anything in particular make you scared?" I asked, hoping for some response that would have prevented his ability to form a specific intent, which was a required element of the offense of willful disobedience.

"Nothing in particular, sir."

"Do you know that your plea would admit that you specifically intended to disobey your commanding officer? Think about that. Was there something on your mind that may have made you confused?"

"Just what I said."

The defense counsel had him well prepared, I thought. But I would not give up so easily.

"You tell me what intent means. Use your own words."

"Well, that I did not want to go into combat that night. That I would not do what was ordered because I was scared."

"Were you nervous at the time? Were you perhaps not feeling well, or even had a headache or a cold?"

"No, sir, just what I said."

"Now, if I accept your plea, do you realize that, without further ado, you will be found guilty? The members of the court could then sentence you to a dishonorable discharge, forfeitures of all pay and allowances, and confinement at hard labor for life?"

I thought that might scare him, but he knew, pursuant to his agreement to plead guilty, the convening authority would not approve any amount of confinement in excess of four years.

"I understand all of that, sir."

I had no choice but to accept the plea. The court members were recalled to the courtroom (tent) and, after informing the court that I had accepted the accused's guilty plea, the defense had an opportunity to present matters in extenuation and mitigation.

The platoon sergeant who had been with Bates since his arrival in Vietnam testified that they had been out together on a few long-range reconnaissance missions. Bates had been reliable, uncomplaining, and faithful to the missions. He had participated bravely in at least three firefights with the Viet Cong or soldiers from the North Vietnamese Regular Army.

Corporal Bates's first sergeant testified that he knew the accused since his arrival in the company five or six months ago; that he was a good soldier; never a troublemaker; and although he was not a born leader, fitted in well with the members of his unit. There had been no disciplinary problems prior to February 22 when he witnessed the incident between the accused and his company commander. He "felt sorry" for Bates and did not feel that prison would serve any purpose. He would be happy to have Bates back, serving in his company.

Corporal Bates took the witness stand to testify in his own behalf. He merely talked about his childhood, schooling, and military experience. He did not go into details of the case or the nature of the combat he had participated in. I thought that the defense counsel should have prepared the accused for a better presentation.

The defense counsel then made what I considered to be a rather lethargic statement on the accused's behalf. He repeated what Bates and the sergeants had already made known to the court, and added a request for mercy. He made no impassioned plea as I had heard in almost every other case in Vietnam. I had a feeling that the defense counsel thought he had already done as much as he could by obtaining an agreement from the convening authority to approve no more than four years confinement in the case, which was a lot less than life imprisonment.

After advising the court of the maximum authorized sentence and other routine instructions about voting, we adjourned. Everyone except the members left the courtroom and wandered about outside to await the sentence of the court.

As the court deliberated, I saw Bates standing under a tree with one of the sergeants who had testified in his behalf, neither of them speaking. I walked over to him and made a casual introduction and some small talk. The nervous grin remained. He spoke only when I asked about his family.

"My father would kill me if he saw me now," Bates replied. "He was in Korea and a master sergeant here in Vietnam as an adviser in 1963. He has a wall full of medals and citations. He wanted me to volunteer for the army and Vietnam even before I graduated from high school. I did that. I think he wanted me to be a hero like he was."

"Well," I answered, "from your record, I'd say you did very well in Vietnam; probably saw a lot more enemy action here than he did."

"I sure did try to be a good soldier, for my father's sake," he replied. "I killed some gooks one night on a mission and got shot at a lot. I was even helpful in saving the lives of two guys in my platoon who were hit by Charlie. The platoon sergeant put me in for a medal before all this mess happened."

"Where is your father now?" I asked.

"He is still in the army at Fort Bragg."

"Would you like me to write a letter to him?"

"No, sir. I don't know what to do. I don't want him to find out about this court-martial. But I don't know how to keep it from him."

I told Bates that I had asked the staff judge advocate to try to have the case dismissed before it went to trial, but to no avail. I added that, in my opinion, he deserved a break. I could not offer him much consolation except to inform him that his case was subject to automatic appeal and there was a good chance for reduction of the sentence, even below four years confinement, if the convening authority approved that much.

"Thank you, sir," he replied sadly. The nervous grin remained on his face indicating to me that he was not consoled by my attempted words of encouragement. He was convinced he was doomed to be thrown out of the army and serve a long time in prison.

I was upset by the entire proceedings against Bates. I knew that almost any other commander in Vietnam would gladly have accepted his apology and offer to return to combat, if for no other reason than to avoid the paperwork of preparing for a trial. Disobedience of orders under existing pressures was not an unusual occurrence, but intelligent commanders and sergeants, more often than not, diplomatically handled the situation when the offender had a good record, apologized for his conduct, and offered to return to combat.

The prosecutor and defense counsel were sitting under a nearby tree as I was speaking to Bates. When my conversation with him ended, I approached the defense counsel and asked to speak to him alone. He stood up and we moved out of hearing of all others in the vicinity.

"Captain," I asked politely, "how long have you been in Vietnam?"

"Three weeks, sir. This is only my second case here."

"How long were you in the army before coming to Vietnam?"

"Ever since my graduation from law school a little over a year ago."

"What did you do in the army before coming to Vietnam?"

"Well, first I went to the basic course at the Judge Advocate General's School in Charlottesville for three months and then spent about eight months at Fort Carson trying and defending cases, as well as giving legal assistance. I volunteered to come to Vietnam as a career move."

"Captain, may I offer you a suggestion?" I asked.

"Of course."

"First of all," I said, "remember that this is a personal matter and has nothing to do with your performance of duty or career plans. You speak very well, have a good education, and I know that you are a good lawyer."

"Thank you, sir."

"It's about the case we're all involved in now," I said. "Look at Bates over there, standing alone, without even a guard. That's unusual and reflects a certain amount of trust by his superiors, don't you think?"

"Yes, sir."

"I've tried many cases in Vietnam and this is only the second time I've seen an accused at trial without a guard. What I would suggest is that you take a personal interest in the appellate process of this case. I am convinced you can get the sentence of this court, whatever it may be, reduced. You probably won't have much luck at the division here, but write a brief to the Court of Review in Washington, and, if necessary, to the United States Court of Military Appeals. Emphasize everything you already know about the case and talk to Bates to find out more about his life and especially his service in Vietnam. Nothing in the world will be gained by his imprisonment or discharge, as you yourself implied in court. Personally, I feel that he should not be punished at all. Argue that the sentence, whatever it might be, is inappropriate. Would you be willing to do that?"

Looking at the accused still standing under a tree alone, the defense counsel answered: "Sir, I will do all that. I will even ask for a conference with the commanding general here before he takes action on the case."

"Thank you," I replied, "and remember, this is just a suggestion."

The accused was sentenced to be discharged from the army with a bad conduct discharge and to be confined at hard labor for four years, the exact amount stated in the pretrial agreement.

The defense counsel visited the commanding general, requesting that he approve an amount of confinement even less than four years, but without success. He then wrote a brief to the Court of Military Review in Washington where the case would be reviewed from a different perspective, away from combat. The court affirmed the findings of the case but no part of the sentence. Bates was therefore restored to duty without further confinement after the court's action.

I don't know what happened to Bates since the Court of Military Review restored him to duty and I did not have contact with him at all after our conversation under the tree at Phuoc Vinh. I do know, however, that because of my suggestion to his counsel, he was not discharged from the army for refusing to fight one evening in Vietnam. I sincerely believe that whatever service he performed after the Court of Review's decision was pleasing to his father. I also feel that the young defense counsel, who was then about twenty-three, may have learned a lesson that will benefit him throughout the career he was so interested in.

Several years ago, while visiting the Pentagon, I passed the office of Colonel Ben Stanley. He had just returned from lunch at the Pentagon Officer's Athletic Club and was sitting with his feet on the desk, eating popcorn. I recognized only his name and knew that he would not remember me, but I dropped in to chat awhile and introduce myself.

"Do you remember that nineteen-year-old combat veteran who refused to fight one night and was sentenced in Phuoc Vinh to four years confinement?" I asked.

"No," he replied, "but it was tough to teach some of those little bastards how to fight."

CHAPTER THIRTY-THREE

Bearcat

Specialist Fourth Class Mark Saunders loved the area surrounding the village of An Loi and the American installation there, Camp Martin Cox, more commonly referred to as Bearcat. In late 1965, Saunders enlisted in the army, passing all required examinations, physical and mental, although he had only a ninth-grade education. He volunteered for Vietnam and was assigned to a unit in Bearcat during most of 1966. While there, and later during his second tour, he was adept at telling stories, usually casting himself as hero. He told acquaintances that he was a champion boxer with the local YMCA midgets, participated in gang fights, argued with his minister, and accomplished other feats of perceived importance. He was not a bit shy about shading the truth. Those who knew him thought he was a grandstander, and did not want to be his close friend. Most, in fact, considered him a bore. When assigned to Bearcat, he managed to rise to the rank of specialist fourth class, but his request for an extension there was denied.

Saunders did manage to return to Vietnam with help from his congressman (he said) in the early part of 1968 and, as luck would have it, was assigned as a tire repairman to the 169th Engineer Battalion at Long Binh, which was close enough to

Bearcat for him to visit there frequently. After returning from such visits, he told acquaintances that he had been visiting old friends in An Loi and roaming forests that he was familiar with, eating wild fruit, and observing nature.

Almost everyone in Saunders's unit knew that he had a dangerous knife. He told them that it had been discarded by the mess hall before he fashioned it to his own needs. He also owned its leather scabbard, which he had made at the hobby shop. His favorite pastime after duty hours was working on his knife, sharpening it and forming the top six wooden inches to fit the palm of his right hand. The finished knife was fifteen inches long with a broad nine-inch blade. He knew that the possession of knives with blades longer than five inches was forbidden by MACV regulations. When Saunders went off on his journeys around Bearcat, he took both his assigned M–14 rifle and his knife, the latter inside its scabbard, attached to his web belt.

On June 4, 1968, Saunders visited An Loi as was his custom on nonworking days, in possession of both his rifle and knife. He approached a group of elderly gentlemen, including Mr. Nguyen Van Ky, tied the latter's hands behind his back, and forced him at gunpoint into the tall elephant grass outside the village. When they parted, Mr. Ky was still tied and either dead or in the process of dying from three stab wounds, one in the middle of his heart.

The criminal investigation department at Bearcat began an intense search for the person last seen with Ky. Descriptions of the suspect were provided by Ky's friends who were with him at the time of his capture in An Loi. Weeks passed with no success. Then, unexpectedly on July 2, Saunders walked into the Military Police Station at Bearcat to report a Korean civilian who had irritated him by driving erratically. He seemed self-assured and proud when he entered the station to make his report of a vehicle violation.

The military policeman on duty casually took note of the wooden handle protruding from Saunders' scabbard, but was unconcerned until he recognized features of the person described in an all points bulletin, who was wanted on suspicion of murder. The MP called Mr. Alfred Paul, a criminal investigator, who took Saunders into his office for questioning.

After complying with the requirements of military and civilian law with respect to confessions and statements, Saunders agreed to talk. For three hours he denied all knowledge of Ky's death, but after the investigator confiscated Saunders' illegal knife, he began to cry and changed his story. He admitted lying before and said that he was now ready to tell the truth.

Yes, Saunders said, he was in An Loi on the afternoon of June 4, but that was not the first time. He was also there on May 20 looking for a girlfriend from the old days, but could not find her. After failing to find the girl or other old friends, he decided to walk in the woods to watch animals, eat fruit, and observe nature. While in the woods, he stumbled into an area where several friendly Thai soldiers on duty at a guard post "were attacked by five Viet Cong guerrillas." Saunders hid in the tall grass but was seen by one of the Viet Cong, who looked him squarely in the eye and fired at him, too, but missed. He did not return the fire.

On June 4, the date of Mr. Ky's death, Saunders continued in his statement to Mr. Paul, he was again in An Loi looking for old friends. While walking around, he noticed a group of Vietnamese men, casually talking, each in possession of hand tools. He immediately recognized one of them as "the Viet Cong who fired at me" a couple of weeks earlier. He instinctively approached the group, wrote the letters *MP* in the palm of his hand and demanded identification from the man he said he recognized. The man complied. But even with proper identification, Saunders was still convinced that he was the one who had fired at him. Therefore, he felt it was his duty as an American soldier to arrest the Viet Cong and take him to the authorities at Bearcat. He tied the man's hands behind his back with a string from his pocket he always carried when going into woods or forests. Then, using his M–14 as an enforcer, he ordered the man to follow his commands. In order to avoid the stares and contemptuous comments of the villagers, Saunders decided not to go directly to Bearcat but take the man there on a path with which he was familiar, through the woods with tall elephant grass.

While walking through the forest, Saunders continued, they came upon a log used as a bridge to cross a mudhole. The VC crossed without difficulty, but he himself slipped and his rifle fell into the mud. The VC, with hands still tied, ran away. Saunders got up without his rifle, chased his prisoner until he caught him and they both fell to the ground. Ky got up first and jumped on him, so he removed his knife from the scabbard and held it upright. Ky threw himself upon Saunders, again apparently not seeing the knife, and it went to his stomach. Despite the wound, Ky continued to jump, and twice more the weapon entered his body. The VC fell on his back, gurgling and making funny noises. Without knowing whether Ky was alive or dead, Saunders left the scene.

"Why didn't you report this incident when it happened?" Mr. Paul wanted to know.

"What good would it have done?" Saunders answered. "I knew someone would find him eventually."

Mr. Paul arranged for Saunders to be placed in custody until he could be returned to his unit. If there was some doubt about the homicide, there was none about the illegal weapon.

At the pretrial investigation, the Vietnamese men who were with Ky on June 4 identified the accused. Four soldiers who lived in the same tent with Saunders gave accounts of his general behavior and of conversations with him about the events of June 4. Each had seen the knife and witnessed the attention that the accused had given to its care. Two had observed Saunders carving the handle. It was general knowledge in the unit that Saunders repeatedly talked about his visits to Bearcat and An Loi and jaunts into woods and forests in that area. One testified that Saunders had told him that on his days off, he liked going into the woods to eat coconuts and bananas, so he needed a very strong knife.

When the trial date arrived in late September, Saunders pleaded not guilty to the charge of unpremeditated murder but guilty to possession of an illegal weapon.

Mr. Ngau Van Thieu was called as the first witness. He testified that he and Mr. Ky were both laborers who spent most of their time pulling weeds and moving rocks, working at the home of a wealthy Vietnamese. On June 4, after work, he and Ky were standing with two friends in the village square at An Loi talking, when they were approached by the accused. Saunders wrote the letters *MP* on the palm of his hand and demanded to see Ky's identification. He complied. Then, for no stated reason, the American tied Ky's hands behind his back with a thick rope that had been hanging from his web belt, and forced Ky into the nearby forest by holding a rifle to his back. Thieu ran to look for Ky's daughter and when he found her, both went into the woods to look for Ky. They found him about twenty minutes later, bleeding profusely and apparently dead. Thieu's testimony as to Ky's apprehension was corroborated by the second Vietnamese witness, Ngo Van Quan, who was one of those accosted but not forced away by the accused.

Private Louis Smith, a member of the accused's unit, testified that he saw Saunders on the night of June 4 when he returned to the tent they shared. Smith asked about something that appeared to be blood on his clothing, and Saunders told him that, fearing for his life, he killed "one of a group of 'cowboys' who jumped him" in An Loi. Smith did not believe Saunders, he told the court, because it was common knowledge that Saunders was a bullshitter. He did, however, notice Saunders cleaning what appeared to be blood from his knife later that same evening.

Corporal Jack Morris, another tentmate, testified that sometime around June 10, Saunders told him that he had killed a monkey a few days before. Morris didn't care whether or not Saunders had killed a monkey, and didn't bother to question him further; he knew the accused told so many wild stories.

Private First Class Lonnie Vasquez, the person who shared the bunk closest to the accused, testified that he had often seen

Saunders filing his knife in the evenings. As he did so, he talked continuously to whomever would listen. On one occasion, Saunders told him that he used a knife to kill turkeys, bears, and deer in Virginia. On another occasion, in early June, Saunders told him that when he was last in An Loi, he went for the purpose of visiting a short-time house. As Saunders was leaving, a papasan jumped on him and beat him with a stick. He then stabbed the papasan in self-defense and ran away. Vasquez did not know whether to believe the story and did not pursue the matter because the accused was well known for his tall tales.

The trial counsel then read the following stipulation:

> The prosecution and defense, with the consent of the accused, stipulate that the following facts are true: First, Mr. Nguyen Van Ky died on June 4, 1968. Second, the accused had no authority to apprehend any civilian in Vietnam. Third, when Mr. Ky's daughter found her father bleeding in the woods on the day he died, she fainted and had to be carried back into the village. She remained unstable since that time and is not physically able to appear in court today as a witness.

Mr. Paul, the criminal investigator who interrogated Saunders on July 2, testified that he properly explained to the accused his rights under the Fifth Amendment to the United States Constitution and appropriate United States Supreme Court decisions. The statement was introduced into evidence without objection. Mr. Paul then testified that he was quite surprised when he learned that Saunders boldly walked into the MP station, especially since an all-points bulletin had been issued and American and Vietnamese police had been searching for the person who killed Mr. Ky for over three weeks.

The defense counsel began the presentation of his case by stipulating, with the consent of the trial counsel, that Specialist Saunders had been committed to a correctional institute for a year by his parents when he was twelve years old and had received psychiatric treatment during that entire time.

Saunders chose to testify in his own behalf. He began by stating that he was a nature lover and had always liked walking in the woods and forests. On his previous assignment to Bearcat, he had taken dozens of pictures of trees, plants, elephant grass, and animals as well as people and buildings in An Loi. He developed the habit at that time of walking around neighboring villages and forests and was therefore thrilled to be assigned on his second tour in Vietnam to Long Binh. He could easily hitch rides from one place to the other.

Saunders acknowledged that he had previously made several inconsistent and exaggerated statements. He explained that he was always nervous when speaking to superior officers, especially Mr. Paul, who had informed him that he was suspected of murder. He only began to talk about the incident because he could not control his crying. As for statements to his tentmates, he was just "shooting the breeze."

During his testimony, Saunders swore that he was in An Loi on June 4 and had gone there to visit a girlfriend whom he had known during his previous tour of duty at Bearcat. Since she was not home, he walked around the village he loved so much when he saw the man he recognized as a VC who, during a firefight a couple of weeks before, had shot at him. He was positive the man was a Viet Cong guerrilla. This was an opportunity to do something really courageous for his country, since he did not otherwise have such an opportunity, working as he did in the tire shop at Long Binh.

Saunders further testified that he tied the Viet Cong's hands behind his back, but only with string he casually removed from a hammock at the home of his former girlfriend. His intention was to take the prisoner to the proper authorities at Bearcat as an enemy of the people. From past wanderings, he knew a path to the compound through the woods. He treated the VC with great respect by walking twenty paces behind him and holding his rifle on his shoulder as if he was going coon hunting.

The accused continued his testimony by saying that, while walking, he and the VC came across a shallow wet spot in the woods that had to be crossed by walking over a log. The VC crossed without mishap, but he himself felt wobbly on the log and fell into the mud. The prisoner ran away, so he got out of the mud to chase him, leaving his rifle behind. When he caught up with Ky, they both fell to the ground. The VC was quicker than he was, and jumped up and down on his body. He explained graphically:

> He jumped on my face. I couldn't see and then he kicked me in the nuts three or four times. He was like a wild animal on top of me, kicking me in the groin. My temples got to hurting real bad and I couldn't bear the pain. I was getting weak when I remembered I had my knife with me. I pulled it out of the scabbard and lunged forward four or five times knowing that this man had to be stopped or he would have killed me. He fell to the ground. It took about fifteen minutes until I could get my strength back. I could hardly see. I ran away. It was really self-defense, sirs.

On cross-examination, when the trial counsel asked why he liked the area around Bearcat so much, and carried a knife when he went there, the accused responded, "I liked my days off. I liked going down in the woods, eating coconuts and bananas, and I needed a knife, but yet I needed a hatchet for breaking coconuts, so I fashioned me a knife heavy enough to do the job of both ax and knife."

The prosecution and defense made vigorous arguments, the prosecution emphasizing that the accused admitted stabbing the victim and was never consistent in explaining why he did so. There was neither reason nor authority for taking the man into custody. What Saunders did was a deliberate, unauthorized act, even if done in the heat of passion. His action was unwarranted and he was guilty as charged. Moreover, if he indeed thought he was doing a courageous act for his country and was without criminal responsibility, he should have reported the incident immediately to the authorities at Bearcat.

The defense counsel was almost tearful when he spoke of the evidence the accused presented in court. Saunders had fallen to the ground and was being attacked viciously. He was blinded, in pain, and fearful for his life. He was indeed unable to save his life other than acting as he did. The action he took was the only way out of a bad situation.

The court found the accused not guilty of the homicide charge, but guilty of carrying an illegal weapon, as they were required to do because of the plea. He was sentenced to confinement at hard labor for nine months but was not discharged from the army.

I was disappointed with the court's verdict, although I could not express that disappointment. It was my belief that Saunders was not speaking the truth when explaining the events of June 4, and that he was guilty of murder. He testified with a boastful attitude and showed no remorse for Mr. Ky's death. I was convinced that if the victim had been a United States citizen, Saunders would have been found guilty as charged.

The case of Specialist Saunders was reported by a member of the Associated Press, who filed the story shortly after the sentence was announced. My family in Louisiana read about it the very next day. Indeed, the Vietnam War was one in which the American public was living, at least vicariously, close to the action.

CHAPTER THIRTY-FOUR

Lawyers, Clients, and Culture

There were approximately one hundred United States Army lawyers in Vietnam at any one time during 1968–1969. Each of the thirteen headquarters that exercised general court-martial jurisdiction had a staff judge advocate with full compliment of assistants to perform legal duties within the command. These duties included preparation of and participation in trials, supervision of all disciplinary matters, giving legal assistance, adjudicating claims, settling foreign claims by Vietnamese civilians and their government, and other legal matters impossible to anticipate. Smaller organizations such as the Port Command in Saigon also had legal departments with fewer lawyers.

In order to become an army lawyer commissioned as a captain in the Judge Advocate General's Corps, it was necessary to have graduated from an accredited law school in the United States and to have been admitted to practice before the highest court of a state within the United States. Acceptance in the corps was not a routine matter, inasmuch as there were more applicants than available positions. Most army lawyers in Vietnam were of a rank higher than captain and had served in the army for as much as twenty years, many of them in Korea and World War II. Some had extensive practice in civilian life.

Military judges were selected on the basis of merit and past service. In Vietnam, Lieutenant Colonel Alley, with twelve years service, including time as an instructor at the Judge Advocate General's School in Charlottesville, Virginia, had served the least amount of time. Colonel Tobin, the oldest and most experienced, had served in almost every position available to a judge advocate officer during the previous twenty-one years. I had been a civilian and army lawyer for eighteen years.

A military lawyer was assigned to represent a soldier or officer as soon as he became a suspect, but the accused could request any other military counsel who was reasonably available to represent him free of charge, as well as hire civilian counsel if he so desired. It was unfortunate that some servicemen and their families distrusted military lawyers in Vietnam as counsel. The United States Court of Military Appeals carefully monitored the trial of cases and had pioneered the rules that led to the United States Supreme Court decision in *Miranda v. Arizona.*

Civilian lawyers from the United States frequently came to Vietnam for the purpose of defending servicemen. My experience was that those lawyers offered no more, and sometimes less, to the defendant than military lawyers who were already in Vietnam, and had expended much time in the preparation of the cases. They often traveled great distances to interview clients confined in the Long Binh Stockade and other witnesses scattered about the country. Moreover, the army lawyers in Vietnam, having no family or other home to return to, often spent evenings working for their clients. Preliminary work on an accused's behalf had usually been accomplished before civilian counsel arrived.

Every amenity available to a military lawyer was offered to a civilian lawyer who came from the United States to defend a client. He was met in Saigon by military personnel, furnished necessary transportation and quarters, and escorted in military aircraft to the place of trial.

In December, a civilian lawyer named Roger Rogers, who had come to Vietnam to act as defense counsel in a particular case, was quartered in the Rex Hotel, where I was living. I had not met him, but others had made arrangements for us to share ground and air transportation to Dong Tam on the date of trial.

I met Mr. Rogers by chance at breakfast on the roof of the hotel, shortly before departure. He mentioned to me that he was taking the case at great expense to himself only because he was a friend of the accused's father, with whom he played golf regularly. He was gregarious and obviously enjoying the experience of being in Vietnam. On the way to the helicopter pad at Ton Son Nhut, he spoke without pause, commenting about the people, the horrendous traffic, and whatever else he observed, especially the presidential palace and the sight near the Notre Dame Cathedral where a Buddhist monk had immolated himself in 1963.

Most aircraft used to transport passengers to places not far from the Saigon area were UH–1 Huey helicopters that carried as many as eight passengers. The chopper waiting for us, however, was a much smaller Cayuse, an egg-shaped aircraft capable of carrying only four persons, including the pilot. The pilot and front passenger were relatively comfortable, but the rear space, resembling the shape of the smaller portion of an egg, was a tight squeeze for two people. Since helicopters in Vietnam were not equipped with doors, one or both passengers in the rear of a Cayuse usually found it more comfortable to keep one leg on the outside of the aircraft.

When Mr. Rogers saw the little chopper, surrounded by dozens of large warships, he blanched, assuming that I would be sitting next to the pilot. He made no objection but became absolutely silent, losing his composure and enthusiasm for the adventure. Seeing his distress, I said to him, "Mr. Rogers, I am about to do a great favor for you."

"How's that?" he remarked without a smile.

"You may ride in the large seat beside the pilot," I said, whereupon his ebullient mood returned. I mention this small and seemingly inconsequential incident only to reflect our concern for the safety and comfort of visiting civilian lawyers.

Mr. Rogers met his client for the first time shortly after our arrival in Dong Tam, two hours before the trial was scheduled to begin. He was offered, but did not accept, the opportunity to have additional time to talk to his client and further prepare the case. He had, as was customary, been previously furnished with all the allied papers in the case.

The accused in Mr. Rogers's case was charged with premeditated murder and there were many important issues of law and fact that had to be decided during trial. The accused and a fellow soldier, both on guard duty, had become involved in a heated dispute over an insignificant matter. Each threatened the other, but the accused fired his weapon at and killed his companion, who had drawn a switch-blade knife from his pocket. There were issues of premeditation, intoxication, self-defense, and lesser included offenses to be decided during the period of trial. Both the prosecutor and military defense counsel were thoroughly prepared.

Except for introducing himself, Mr. Rogers did not address either the court members or me during the trial, although he frequently whispered comments to his cocounsel. The accused was acquitted. In my opinion, it was the convincing closing argument of military defense counsel that tipped the balance in favor of the accused.

After his return to the United States, Mr. Rogers wrote gracious letters to me and others connected with the case, thanking us for the assistance we had given him. In his letter to me, he mentioned that he was scheduled to address students from the state university law school on the subject of military justice, with particular emphasis on his experience in Vietnam.

General courts-martial, even when tried under adverse conditions in Vietnam, were conducted according to standards equal, if not superior to, trials in civilian courts in the United States. Common law rules of evidence and strict rules of procedure required by the *Manual for Courts-Martial* were applied. Witnesses requested by the defense were called from wherever they might be, including combat; some were held over in Vietnam beyond their scheduled dates to rotate home; others were returned from the United States.

The trial of a general court-martial was recorded verbatim and the accused furnished a copy of the transcript. The record was reviewed by the commander who convened the court and later by the Court of Military Review in Washington, where counsel was also provided for the accused. Finally, appeal was available to the United States Court of Military Appeals, which consisted of three civilian judges appointed by the president, and comparable to a United States Circuit Court of Appeals.

The conditions under which the United States entered and fought the war in Vietnam were factors in the behavior of the American forces. Young soldiers could hardly be expected to understand a culture that the architects of the war did not understand. Those men with keen and analytical minds did not believe that our armed forces, possessing such great planes, tanks, and other implements of war, could possibly lose to a group of people who used pieces of old rubber tires as shoes to fight in the jungle. Neither Washington officials nor good soldiers could understand that the Vietnamese people fought foreign invaders and even civil wars to preserve their culture for over two thousand years.

In 1954, the last of the foreign invaders, the French, learned that they could not destroy the will of the Vietnamese people and departed in disgrace. The United States then attempted to do what the French could not do. The ordinary soldier did not understand that he was participating in a futile effort to preserve what was euphemistically known as the doctrine of containment.

Soldiers in Vietnam referred to the United States as the real world. To them, it was a world where things were as they should be. Vietnam was indeed a different world. In 1964, the entire Congress of the United States, with the exception of two senators, gave its approval, in the Gulf of Tonkin Resolution, for the president to act freely in determining who the enemy was and how the enemy could be destroyed. The president was exercising that prerogative.

In the months between November 1963 and July 1965, the political and military leadership in Saigon was in shambles, but we took it upon ourselves to solve their problems. The number of

American fighting men rose exponentially until it exceeded one-half million in 1968, when over two hundred young men were being killed every week. The people in the United States were becoming agitated, but Congress continued to furnish the president with the funding required to continue the killing. The administration depended upon the fighting men to do that.

Although there were crimes committed in Vietnam by American servicemen, they were few in number compared to crimes committed in cities the size of Denver or Seattle where the number of citizens was similar to the number of servicemen in Vietnam. Moreover, most of the crimes committed in Vietnam were of a military nature.

About twelve percent of the servicemen sent to Vietnam actually participated in combat. Those who did matured quickly and fought bravely, even beyond expectations. Wherever the enemy was encountered face to face, the Americans prevailed. During the eight years of severe fighting, young soldiers fought through cities, villages, jungles, mountains, and deltas, never certain what enemy forces might be lurking in the vicinity. It is remarkable that they accomplished so much at such tender ages. About 58,000 made the supreme sacrifice while fighting, mostly without complaint. It should be a source of great pride to loved ones to know that the soldiers in combat consistently risked their lives without question to care for their wounded or endangered comrades. Helicopter pilots did not hesitate to fly to the rescue of the wounded or stranded, regardless of the danger that accompanied their missions.

United States servicemen have traditionally been among the most likable and generous of soldiers anywhere. They played with children on the streets of the cities and in the villages. They gave out candy and chewing gum and taught kids how to throw a baseball. In Vietnam, the American servicemen visited orphanages, donated to charities, and showed other kindnesses to people less fortunate than themselves. They liked and joked with the people who worked in their offices and hooches. Boysan and mamasan were the friendliest of people. Sad to say, however, too many friendships were not based upon equality of status but rather upon a superior-inferior relationship.

It was not uncommon, even by witnesses testifying in court, to refer to Vietnamese people as gooks, dinks, slopes or other obnoxious names. The word "gook" was so common that it was used to refer even to those who worked happily and playfully for and with Americans. When the word "gook" was used, even the most sensitive of Americans in the vicinity did not blink at the use of the pejorative term.

In addition to a feeling of superiority, there was a feeling of privilege, not only by Americans stationed in Vietnam but many who came to visit, under whatever pretext that might be. Kathy told me that an aide to a United States senator, after taking her to dinner, sexually assaulted her in the hallway of the building in which she lived and then attempted to forcibly enter her apartment. When she saw him the next day in the officer's mess, he showed no remorse and casually joined her, uninvited, for breakfast.

Perhaps a reason for failure to communicate more sympathetically with Vietnamese people was the sometimes difficult task of distinguishing friend from foe. They looked alike, spoke the same language, ate the same food, and were of the same cultural background. Unfortunately, the word "enemy" has a connotation of evil and fear, and sometimes innocent Vietnamese civilians were treated as enemies with unnecessary and overzealous caution.

United States servicemen in Vietnam were well clothed, regularly paid, provided with transportation to and from exotic locations for R&R, given the best medical attention any soldiers ever had, and often furnished with more ammunition than needed. Usually, those not in combat were entertained by movies, swam in beaches and canvas swimming pools, worked regular hours, visited cities, and were armed wherever they went. Because of the status attributed to him, the feeling of authority perhaps accompanied the serviceman in uniform, and contributed to a prevailing feeling of superiority.

I have read references to use of the term "mere gook" in pub-hed works as well as having heard it myself on several occa-ns. The phrase was understood to mean that the mistreatment even the negligent killing of a Vietnamese citizen was regarded th less concern than if the victim had been American. In the e where a sergeant shot his carbine into a group of Vietnamese civilians merely to clear the way for quick passage of his truck, a civilian was killed but the sergeant was acquitted. In Cam Rahn Bay, after the acquittal of a soldier who negligently killed three Vietnamese civilians while driving his jeep around a corner at high speed, the defense counsel casually mentioned to me later that the result of trial was application of the "mere gook" rule.

In the chapters "I Want a Body Count" and "Bearcat," included in this memoir, I have suggested that I felt at the time of trial, as I do now, that the acquittals resulted only because the victims were Vietnamese. Light sentences or acquittals for this reason alone, however, did not always result. In the case described in "Tragedy in White," the court was obviously distressed by the behavior of the accused and had no sympathy for him whatsoever.

United States personnel in Vietnam, both military and civilian, contributed much to illegal activities that were apparent in most of the large cities. Prostitution flourished, encouraged by the American dollar. Black-market goods intended for the Post and Base Exchanges could only have been obtained with the cooperation of Americans. Wayne Alley tried a case in which an American civilian assigned to the Exchange System attempted to divert $25,000 worth of batteries in his custody to an agent of the underground. MPCs were issued as payment to United States Armed Forces personnel and those accompanying the armed forces, because the use of United States currency was prohibited by regulation in an attempt to keep dollars off the black market. MPCs were freely accepted on the black market, however, and exchanged for Vietnamese money. On the day the color of MPCs was changed, in an effort to prevent misuse of the scrip, an American civilian lawyer in Saigon, not a part of the United States

Armed Forces, came to MACV in an attempt to exchange over $3,000 in MPCs that he had acquired illegally.

The Vietnamese people recognized the fact that sometimes justice did not prevail when they were the victims. In a village near Pleiku, a soldier shot and killed a farmer whom he "suspected of being a VC." The soldier was charged with but acquitted of manslaughter. When a colonel tried to go into the village on the following day to offer a "sympathetic" payment to the family of the deceased, the angry villagers banded together to prevent the colonel's helicopter from landing.

On my last day in Vietnam, a vehicle dispatched by the motor pool, and driven by an armed soldier, came for me at the Rex shortly after lunch. While driving down Cong Ly Boulevard on the way to the processing center at Ton Son Nhut, we came upon an empty pedicab, but there appeared to be a body beneath a sheet at its base. There was no activity at the scene other than the presence of a few onlookers. Our first concern was that an American had been assaulted by a "zapper," which occasionally happened. We stopped, and the driver rushed to the scene, raised the sheet, replaced it hurriedly and returned to the jeep. "Thank God it's a gook!" he exclaimed, as we prepared to continue our journey.

CHAPTER THIRTY-FIVE

A Week in Dong Tam

My predecessor, Dick Snyder, had advised me that I would not like Dong Tam. The place was frequently attacked by rockets; there was not much to do, no place to relax, and the heat was unbelievable. "Avoid the place if you can," he cautioned, "it's the pits."

Dick was wrong. My first visit to Dong Tam for six days was like a vacation. I arrived there on a Sunday evening, having come directly from Cu Chi, where I had been in court until noon. I had more freedom in Dong Tam than I dared hope for, and enjoyed it all except the first few minutes. The helicopter in which I was being transported experienced difficulties before landing and we descended by auto-rotation. That was certainly better than crashing, but a frightening experience nonetheless.

Dong Tam was one dusty square mile of tents and other temporary structures, surrounded by green rice paddies. American ingenuity had created the compound by dredging dirt from the Mekong Delta and using it to build a compound for the Ninth Infantry Division Headquarters, three feet higher than the surrounding marshy areas. Vietnamese peasants watched in awe as the work progressed and said that only Americans could turn a rice paddy into a desert.

Lieutenant Colonel John Webb met me at the helicopter pad. He allowed a few moments for me to recuperate from the experience of landing without a working engine. Then, apologetically, he advised me that the case scheduled for the following day was canceled, although others for the remainder of the week remained on target. It would be impracticable to make a round trip to Saigon in the time available, so I would just have to entertain myself on the following free day. Then he took me to my assigned quarters, an air-conditioned trailer mounted on the bed of a truck with no working parts. Inside was a steel cot, a lavatory, and a card table with lamp.

Colonel Webb should never have apologized. I was delighted to be alone for a change, with this wonderful gift: a day of splendid air-conditioned solitude, no phones to answer, no cases to authenticate, and no office traffic.

After refreshing myself and putting away my luggage, I went with John to the general's mess. I was told that the Vietnamese cook's daily round to local markets was responsible for making this the best eating place in Vietnam. Lobster, other delicacies from the sea, and fresh vegetables cooked to perfection were the norm rather than the exception. After dinner, I retired early to enjoy some of the reading material I always carried for just such an emergency. There was no incoming mortar fire that night.

Monday was my first completely free day since arriving in Vietnam. After breakfast, I picked up a well-thumbed copy of John Updike's *Couples* from the office and returned to my quarters, an experience so luxurious that I skipped lunch. That evening I went again to the general's mess. Unexpectedly, after dinner, excitement was provided that I could never have anticipated.

A troupe of USO entertainers was visiting Dong Tam and invited to the general's mess for dinner before their scheduled performance. Young female troupers from the group sat on each side of the commanding general as a special treat because it was his birthday. At the request of the officers, one of them presented him with a surprise gift, a small wooden elephant with the division crest embedded on its side. The general wanted to express his appreciation by kissing the young lady on her cheek but she bolted like a spooked horse. I wrote home what a shame that was, but the boss took it with gracious humor and was not offended.

The unplanned entertainment of the evening, however, came a little later. One of the other members of the troop, Ellen Brugger, had been sitting next to the Protestant chaplain, Captain Charles Gross, who was, by inclination and training, also a herpetologist. Ellen was fascinated with his stories about the care and feeding of his reticulated python, Henrietta, which Chaplain Gross kept in a footlocker at the far end of his room. Acquired in Vietnam, Henrietta was nurtured until she grew from six feet and twenty pounds to eight feet and forty pounds under the chaplain's care.

Each week, Chaplain Gross purchased a small live duck from the local village market as food for Henrietta. He tied the fowl's legs together and placed it in the python's path. A sad ending for the victim, but the duckling was already doomed at the market by whomever purchased it for food. Feeding Henrietta in this manner was the only way to satisfy her nutritional needs because, from her enclosure, she was not able to otherwise forage for food. Before the feeding, a group of curious officers and enlisted men usually gathered to witness the event. Henrietta coiled and crushed her quarry, opened her mouth, and took the offering whole.

Miss Brugger, who was dressed in a miniskirt in preparation for her performance later in the evening, became so engrossed with the chaplain's stories that she begged for and received permission from the general to allow Henrietta to be brought into the mess. When the chaplain arrived a few minutes later with the python around his shoulders and torso, Ellen was enthralled. "Could the snake be wrapped around my body?" she asked. The chaplain was dubious but consented.

Gently, very gently, Chaplain Gross wrapped Henrietta around Ellen's body. This done, he stood back to admire his accomplishment with a wide grin. The officers applauded. One who had a camera could not resist commemorating the event for posterity. Without warning, the photographer set off a flash with the snap of his shutter. Henrietta panicked and excreted on poor Miss Brugger. Worse, she began to constrict her grip on the lady. Now it was the chaplain who panicked and, I'm sure, prayed harder there in the mess than he did in the chapel on Sunday. Carefully, he cajoled and, thankfully, was successful in coaxing Henrietta to loosen her grip. He was able to transfer the snake to his own body and promptly removed her from the mess, presumably to her restraining area.

Whether the footlocker in Chaplain Gross's room was really effective enough to restrain Henrietta was a subject of much debate. There were, among the officers, both pro- and anti-Henrietta factions. On one occasion, she escaped from her confinement and writhed under a partition into a room occupied by the Catholic chaplain, who promptly fainted dead away when he saw Henrietta.

When I appeared at the legal office after breakfast on Tuesday morning, I was informed that the accused and his counsel had proposed a plea of guilty, which had been accepted only a few minutes before by the commanding general. The case was over before lunch. I could hardly believe that I would have another afternoon with no scheduled work. After lunch, once again I retreated to my trailer to finish the Updike epic. Later, I joined the officers again for dinner, and retired early.

That evening before midnight, I was awakened by the sound of incoming mortar fire and ran to my assigned bunker. Inside, I recognized an acquaintance from my last duty station in El Paso. He was seated on a wooden bench with only a towel around his waist, his head lowered in his hands. He did not look up when I entered, even after calling his name. He was repeatedly mumbling "Damned communists! Damned communists!" and a few other choice epithets about those who were responsible for his misery. When he departed a few minutes later, he did not take notice of me or the deaf division psychiatrist who entered after I did. My former acquaintance apparently did not appreciate being awakened from a deep sleep by the damned communists.

On the day following the mortar attack, to my surprise, there was a repetition of the previous day's event when the accused decided to enter a plea of guilty. A few hours in court and it was all over. But I still could not return to Saigon because cases were scheduled Thursday and Friday. Subconsciously, I was happy but a sense of guilt tugged at my conscience. I did not feel that I deserved another free afternoon in an air-conditioned trailer. I selected another novel to occupy my time.

After returning to the trailer in the early afternoon, I fell asleep before beginning to read, but was awakened by a rapping at the door. It was an officer from the judge advocate section who wanted to ask a favor. Would I be willing to speak to a sergeant who had appeared at the office, seemingly desperate, asking to discuss a serious matter with a lawyer? Since I had no duties on three consecutive afternoons, he thought that I would not mind taking on this task. I was happy to oblige. A few minutes later, the sergeant appeared at my quarters and we introduced ourselves.

Sergeant First Class Robert Graves was clean-cut, polite, and looked more like a stockbroker than a soldier. We seated ourselves across from one another. It was obvious that he was deeply troubled.

"Sir," he began, "I have a problem and it does not concern military matters."

"I'll be happy to help you in any way that I can," I responded. He told me the following story:

"Well, sir, I've only been in Vietnam a short time and really would like to complete my obligation here, but I received news from the Red Cross that makes it very difficult, if not impossible. I can't sleep or concentrate and must talk to someone who can help me."

"Tell me whatever you like, Sergeant. I'm here to listen and we'll see what, if anything, can be done."

"Colonel, I met my wife last January in Tacoma when I was stationed at Fort Lewis. She was a teller in a bank and we met through mutual friends. We began dating immediately and I had never experienced the feeling of love with anyone like I did with her. I knew right away that the feeling was mutual and I began to see or call her every day.

"One evening about four weeks after we met, I went to her apartment and saw immediately that she had been crying. She continued to sob when I asked what was bothering her. She suggested that we have something to drink and did not speak again until we sat down for coffee.

" 'I have something to tell you,' she said.

"I told her that she need not be concerned about anything she had to tell me. 'I'm pregnant!' she said.

"Of course I was taken by surprise, but my feelings for her were unchanged. I only wanted to know how she felt about me under the circumstances; I asked whether there was another man who was important to her.

" 'No, no, really,' she replied, 'I can't excuse myself for doing what I did. There's no use trying. The man who is the father means nothing to me now and never did. He hasn't even called in five weeks, and I haven't thought of him until today.'

"We talked a long while and decided that we should spend a few days thinking about our lives. We would continue to see each other. As for myself, I did not doubt that I loved her.

"I thought seriously about marriage for the first time in my life. I knew I could be happy with Susan. I was twenty-nine and far enough along in my career to know that I could, and would, be happy to support a small family. I made up my mind that I would ask her to marry me. It was not out of pity, or any altruistic motive. I was willing to claim someone else's child as my own.

"When I proposed to her later, she was not altogether surprised. I think she suspected I would. By that time, we could anticipate each other's thoughts. She didn't give me an answer immediately, but promised to think about it. When I saw her again two days later, she was prepared to respond to my proposal.

" 'I want to marry you, Bob, but I can't ask that you mortgage your future for my sake. I think I will accept your proposal, but only after the baby is born and we have had more time to think about our futures.'

"Her reply did not satisfy me. I wanted to marry her, especially before the baby was born. We took a long walk along the Puget Sound near Fort Lewis, then returned to her apartment for a talk late into the night.

"We reached a compromise that did not satisfy me but was absolutely the only way she would consent to an immediate marriage. I would have to go away until after the baby was born. Meanwhile, she would arrange for its adoption. She wanted only my children, but she cared enough for the one she was carrying to insure that it would be adopted by someone she knew welcomed the responsibility. She could not be persuaded to consent to my wishes.

"I volunteered to come to Vietnam and we were married a few days later in a chapel at Fort Lewis. The happiest weeks of my life were spent while waiting to be shipped here. During the past three months we have corresponded daily. I couldn't bear it in Dong Tam without her letters. She never complained and wrote mostly about plans for our future.

"Susan arranged for the adoption through a Catholic organization in Seattle. She accepted the character reports on the family who would be responsible for her child. She was satisfied and looked forward to our life together, as I did. Even being in Vietnam did not detract from my happiness.

"Until last night!"

"What happened last night?" I asked.

"I received a communication from the Red Cross. The baby was born. Susan was well but the child has a defective heart and the prospective parents backed out of the agreement to take the baby. My wife is on the verge of a nervous breakdown. She had to leave the hospital but the little girl is still there."

"What are your feelings about all this?" I asked.

"I have not changed my mind. I want Susan and I want the baby. I sent a message to her via the MARS station here today. What I want now is for you or someone to arrange an emergency leave so that I can explain my feelings to her in person. I want both her and the baby."

I was not in a position to grant the leave, but Colonel Webb took on that responsibility, willingly and successfully. Sergeant Graves was out of Dong Tam on his way to the United States the following day. This soldier, I thought, deserved a medal for something that had nothing to do with combat.

When I arrived at the judge advocate office on the morning following Sergeant Graves's visit, the prosecutor told me that, for the third consecutive day, an accused decided to plead guilty. Another free afternoon loomed in Dong Tam. I could not depart for Saigon until completion of the case set for the following day, which I was assured would be a long one.

That Thursday afternoon, free from legal work, I had an opportunity to visit a section of the Ninth Division's area of operations, and a little more of the Mekong Delta. The area had long been infiltrated by enemies of the established government, first the Vietminh and then the Viet Cong. Additionally, the area was home to the Hoa Hao religious sect, which had its own army and was very protective of their enclave.

Colonel Webb had previously scheduled visits to some of the division's subordinate units and offered to take me with him. I accepted. We visited the artificial harbor at Dong Tam where a part of the Riverine Assault Force was operating. An entire brigade of the Ninth Division was occupying navy barges and ships, substituting for marines who had earlier been called north to defend the fortress of Khe Sanh. The river barges had 105-mm guns mounted fore and aft, with ammunition stored under the hulls. Navy ships were a little farther away in the Mekong River. We visited two firebases on small islands, using Air Cushion Vehicles, an experimental-type boat, for transportation.

When the official visits were completed, I asked John to take me to the city of My Tho, which had been in the war news frequently, harassed alternately by one or the other of the occupying forces. It was also historically significant as the capital city of Dinh Tung Province. At first he declined, but later said, "Keep your helmet on, your head low, and I'll see how fast this jeep can go." We took the trip and returned without incident, not much worse for a bone-jarring and dust-flying ride.

The entire day on Friday was spent in court, excluding time-out during the noon hour. As in the three previous days at Dong Tam, I had lunch with a dermatologist from Walter Reed Hospital who was doing research on the effect of Mekong Delta terrain on the feet of American soldiers. We had become friendly, having in common the fact that we were both visitors to the division. During a lull in our conversation, I thought it would be an opportune time to ease my mind about a personal matter. For years, I had had a small red spot on my face that did not really bother me except sometimes when shaving.

"Colonel," I asked, "no big deal, but what is this spot on my face?"

He looked carefully and replied: "Nothing to worry about. Just a little cancer."

"Cancer?" I said, horrified.

"Well, if it makes you fell better, don't call it cancer. Just know that it's a basal cell carcinoma. And if that still sounds serious to you, drop by the first-aid station after your case this afternoon and I'll remove it."

I was presented with a dilemma. If it was nothing to worry about, should I not wait until I returned to the United States where I could have the carcinoma removed in a fully equipped military hospital; or should I relieve all concern about cancer, or carcinoma, or whatever, by having it removed in the aid station down the street?

"I'll be there," I said, "probably."

A few hours later, after completion of the case being tried, I walked to the medical aid station where the colonel was sitting in a steel chair looking at slides and files.

"So you decided to come?" he asked. "Just lie down on that gurney behind the sheets there and I'll be with you in a minute."

There was dust on most of the papers and furniture in the station, but the small enclosure where I lay on the gurney looked clean and contained sterilizing equipment. Besides, I trusted the doctor. I trusted all the doctors I met in Vietnam, having seen their remarkable work in a dozen different locations.

I was not asked to remove my shirt, or boots, or anything other than my steel helmet. The colonel cleaned my face with alcohol and a newly opened piece of gauze. There was no assistant. He administered a local anesthetic before removing the carcinoma. The doctor and I then chatted about twenty minutes before he decided that I could get up, and we would go to dinner together. I looked in a mirror and was surprised to see a hole in my face much larger than I expected. There was no bandage and the only instruction I received was to keep my face clean, which I thought was superfluous advice. I bear a scar to this day as a memento of that small operation after work and before dinner on my last evening that week in Dong Tam.

On Saturday, after a case that lasted only through the morning, I returned to Saigon. Everyone in the MACV legal office stared at me in surprise and wanted to know what in the world happened to my face in Dong Tam.

"Nothing much," I replied. "Only a little cancer operation."

CHAPTER THIRTY-SIX

Hi Si

I was not assigned to any case in Vietnam involving the use or sale of hard drugs prohibited by army regulations, but other judges presided over ten such cases during my tour. I was, of course, aware that such drugs were readily available, some legally purchased in Vietnamese drugstores. Serious problems with these substances were more common in the years after President Nixon was elected on the assumption that he had a plan to end the war. The diminishing number of troops in Vietnam was obvious to those who remained. Soldiers saw their comrades leave, knowing that an end to the American presence was approaching. Morale was weakening. No one wanted to be the last to die in Vietnam.

In my opinion, company commanders did a creditable job of adjusting to the changing mores of the time concerning the use and sale of less-powerful drugs. Good soldiers who were first-time users were rarely punished. Small sales to friends for private use were handled by company punishment or special courts-martial that had no jurisdiction to impose a discharge from the army.

Personnel charged with possession, use, or sale of small amounts of marijuana did appear in general courts-martial frequently, but only in conjunction with more serious offenses.

I was the military judge in two cases involving possession of marijuana only. The first occurred near Di An when Corporal Steven Phares attempted to return to his base, apparently stoned, after a night in a nearby village. Without attempting to conceal evidence, he carried a large clear plastic bag containing a green leafy substance, clearly visible to anyone who saw him. The guard at the entrance to the firebase confiscated the bag and its contents. Phares protested that he came from a free country that was fighting the communists and had a right to possess whatever was legally his. The substance in the bag was later confirmed to be thirty-three ounces of marijuana, a fact readily admitted by Phares the following day. After a short trial, Phares was sentenced to serve four months confinement in the Long Binh Stockade. That case was much simpler and less interesting than that of Private First Class Simon Bordes.

Simon Bordes was not a particularly good soldier. He was a supply clerk in the 576th Ordinance Company in Long Binh, but never ambitious enough to advance above the rank of Private First Class. He was a bit lazy and smoked pot occasionally, but clever enough to keep out of serious mischief. His intelligence was limited. Singapore was not in his vocabulary until a buddy advised him to go there on R&R. When his tour of duty in Vietnam was completed, he was leaving without any evidence of misbehavior, but no evidence of particularly good service, either.

On the date of his scheduled departure, Bordes was given probably the only favor any officer had offered to him in Vietnam. The company commander allowed his personal jeep to be used for Bordes's transportation to the processing center at Ton Son Nhut. Everything seemed to be in order at the end of that supposedly last journey when he thanked the driver and told him goodbye.

Before processing began, all departees were required to pass through a large unattended room in the center of which were two large barrels painted yellow. At the door was a sign informing those leaving the country that the barrels could be used for voluntary disposal of any unwanted materials. The conspicuous absence of guards inferentially informed those departing that this was a convenient place to dispose of unauthorized weapons, drugs, pornography or any other material forbidden by regulations. Bordes walked through the room with a duffel bag and two large plastic dolls, one under each arm, without making a deposit.

After passing the yellow barrels, Bordes stopped in the next room for the first step of his processing, which consisted of a routine observation and possible questioning by two military policemen. Their eyes focused on the cheap dolls and Bordes was immediately under scrutiny. The MPs had seen hundreds of persons pass before them and were quite knowledgeable about sizing up persons suspected of misconduct. Without talking, they looked at Bordes and the dolls for half a minute before one of them observed a green leafy substance fall gently to the ground from a fractured part of one of the plastic dolls. He was not so naive as not to suspect that the substance he observed was prohibited by regulation.

"Look, buddy, why don't you go back into the room you just came through?" he asked nonchalantly, being neither polite nor impolite.

"Why should I?" answered Bordes.

"Please make my day easier and return to the room," the MP pleaded.

"I didn't do anything illegal. I don't have anything to hide. I don't want to go back there," Bordes replied.

The MP took a little field kit for testing drugs, used it on the fallen substance, and became convinced that Bordes was carrying a lot of marijuana.

"Look, friend, there are over two hundred people waiting to come through this line, and I'd like to see every one of them get on a Freedom Bird tonight. I'm not accusing you of anything, but please go back right now. I will not ask you again," the MP pleaded, now a bit irritated.

"I went through that room once and I'm not going through it again!" was the final reply.

"Okay, let's have the dolls. I saw enough and have enough evidence to prevent you from proceeding to the rest of the processing routine."

Bordes gave up the dolls without argument and was ordered to sit down to await the officer of the day. After reading the provisional test results, the officer confiscated the dolls and ordered Bordes to be placed in temporary custody where he remained until the following morning when he was returned unceremoniously to his unit. Charges of illegal possession of forty-six ounces of a controlled substance were preferred and investigated. Four weeks later, after all pretrial formalities were properly completed, Bordes appeared for his trial by general court-martial in the courtroom at Long Binh. I was the appointed military judge.

The trial counsel called the two MPs who had first become suspicious of Bordes and the plastic dolls, and a crime laboratory technician who testified that the substance removed from the dolls was indeed marijuana. The defense counsel did not contest any of the evidence. I surmised that Bordes would deny knowledge of the forbidden substance, and indeed that was the case, as reflected in the following testimony:

Defense Counsel (DC): Now, Private Bordes, you heard all of the evidence. What do you have to say?

Accused (A): Yes, sir, I heard the evidence, but I did not know anything was inside those dolls.

DC: What were you going to do with those dolls?

A: Bring them to my little sister.

DC: Are you a good soldier?

A: Yes, sir. I've never been in any kind of a court in my life before and as long as I've been in the army, I never even had company punishment.

DC: I have no further questions.

The trail counsel (TC) cross-examined:

TC: Now, Private Bordes, you say that you have been a good soldier, is that right?

A: Yes, sir.

TC: Have you been given any decorations since you've been here in Vietnam?

A: Everybody gets ribbons, sir.

TC: I mean something special, like the Bronze Star, or the Soldier's Medal, or even the Good Conduct Medal?

A: No, sir.

TC: Were you given a letter of commendation from your commanding officer or anyone else before you were scheduled to depart?

A: No, sir.

TC: Okay. Well now, let's talk about the case. Where did you get those dolls?

A: From a man in a Vietnamese bar, sir.

TC: Did you know this man?

A: Not really, sir. I just met him when I spent the night in the house there.

TC: Why did he give you those dolls?

A: He asked me if I had any little sisters, and I said yes, so he gave them to me.

TC: Where is this Vietnamese bar located?

A: In some little village not far from Long Binh.

TC: Can you be more specific? What is the name of this little village?

A: I don't know, sir. I couldn't even find it if I went looking.

TC: Well then, this man. Did you spend some time with him?

A: Yes, sir, we had a couple of beers and smoked a little pot.

TC: Did you learn what his name is?

Bordes thought a while, then answered.

A: Yes, sir. It was Hi.

TC: Was that his first or last name?

A: His first name, I think.

TC: Well, what was his last name?

Bordes thought again for a moment, then answered hesitatingly.

A: Si.

TC: So your testimony is that you were with this man named Hi Si drinking beer and smoking pot in a house of good times, and, out of the goodness of his heart, he gave you two large plastic dolls?

A: That's exactly what happened, sir.

TC: Is there any way in the world you could tell us where we could find Hi Si, or anyone who might know him, so that we might make an effort to get him into this court to testify?

A: No, sir.

TC: Was Hi Si a Vietnamese?

A: I don't know, sir.

TC: Was he an American?

A: I don't think so, he couldn't speak English very well. He looked like he could be a Vietnamese, or Cambodian, or something.

TC: Did you put anything into those dolls after the man gave them to you?

A: No, sir.

TC: Did they seem to be a bit heavy for two plastic dolls?

A: I don't think so.

TC: I have no further questions.

The defense counsel had no redirect examination. He did, however, make a motion that Hi Si be subpoenaed as a witness.

"Well, defense counsel," I asked, "can you give us any indication where this man might be found, or even the spelling of his name?"

"I have no idea, sir. I think the burden is on the government to produce Mr. Hi Si."

I denied the motion, adding, "I do not think the evidence warrants me to order United States Army authorities to conduct a search for Mr. Hi Si, who might be a Vietnamese and probably lives somewhere in Vietnam or maybe Cambodia."

The defense rested. The prosecution had nothing further. I instructed the court, and Bordes was found guilty about fifteen minutes later. I was not surprised about the conviction, but was surprised at the speed in which the verdict was reached.

After a passionate plea by the defense counsel, emphasizing the accused's lack of prior convictions or punishment, the court sentenced Bordes to be discharged from the army with a bad conduct discharge and to serve six months confinement at hard labor.

Upon completion of the case which, like many others, was being reported by the *Overseas Weekly*, the prosecutor held the two dolls high above his head smiling broadly for the camera. He loved the publicity.

It was my impression that during all of the proceedings, the trial counsel was more amused than serious. I did not hold him in high regard. He continually joked during the recesses of this and other cases. My view of him was apparently shared by his superiors because they approved a three-week drop from his scheduled rotation date to the United States, which was an action almost unheard-of. His request was based upon an invitation he received to become a duke in New Orleans at a supposedly important Mardi Gras function.

Four months later, I received the decision of the Court of Military Review in Bordes's case. The only issue raised on appeal by the appellate defense counsel was that I made an error prejudicial to the accused by refusing to issue a subpoena "for Mr. Hi Si, located somewhere in Vietnam or Cambodia." The issue was not favorably acted upon, but the court disapproved the bad conduct discharge, and approved only so much of the confinement as had already been served. Bordes, by that time, was probably home again ready to start life anew as a seasoned Vietnam veteran with an honorable discharge.

CHAPTER THIRTY-SEVEN

Plantation

Plantation was the name of a compound twenty-three miles north of Saigon located within the Long Binh area. It was headquarters of II (pronounced "two") Field Force, airlifted to Vietnam in March 1966 to provide combat assistance to the South Vietnamese army. Its mission was also to control United States military operations on the approaches to Saigon. II Field Force was a corps-level headquarters and exercised general court-martial jurisdiction over several large military units.

On the occasion of an assignment to a case at Plantation, Colonel Bob Jones emphasized that it was imperative for me to be there on the evening of January 27, 1969. The case to be tried was scheduled for 7:00 A.M. the following morning, an unusual hour to begin a case, but necessary because witnesses were scheduled to depart Vietnam on the evening of that day.

On January 27, I returned to Hotel 3 from Cu Chi about seven in the evening, which normally would be too late to board a helicopter as a passenger. Without returning to my room or office, I contacted Colonel Jones and advised him of my predicament. I heard him order Warrant Officer Bill Heaton to get me to Plantation without delay, even if he had to come for me by jeep with armed guards. Warrant officers in the army are the people to depend upon when an assignment requires extraordinary effort. Mr. Heaton was no exception. He had friends within the headquarters.

Twenty minutes after my call to Colonel Jones, while I was still at Hotel 3, a helicopter appeared. Prominently displayed in the rear seat closest to the right-hand exit were three large stars. Mr. Heaton was sitting next to the pilot, giddy as a child and proud of his accomplishment. He took a picture of me with the seat of stars before returning to Plantation. There were neither door gunners nor copilot, because the urgent demand for transportation did not allow time to secure the personnel. Mr. Heaton was not so happy, however, when we landed at Plantation to find the commanding general's aide and two senior officers waiting, demanding an explanation of how in hell a warrant officer managed to acquire use of a three-star general's chopper. I walked away, and did not find out how Mr. Heaton managed to extricate himself from the crisis, but he was in the office the next morning, although not on the night of my delivery to Plantation.

The case to be tried was one in which two soldiers, Privates William Sellers and Sandy Pollock, were charged with unpremeditated murder. These two young men, each nineteen years old, had been dispatched on November 28 from Headquarters Battery, 5th Battalion, 42nd Artillery, to obtain parachutes at Bien Hoi. On the road there, they had the misfortune of running over a particularly sharp stone, puncturing one of the tires. Sellers and Pollock were not born to fix flat tires. They pulled up to one of those ubiquitous little buildings on the roadsides of Vietnam where one could have trucks or tanks washed, tires changed, buy beer, chat with hostesses, and probably get private entertainment upon request.

When a Vietnamese worker began to change the tire, Sellers and Pollock each bought two bottles of beer and strolled over to a small stream behind the store. They sat down to relax and drink peacefully when Pollock decided to test his rifle by shooting several rounds into the stream. Caught up in the excitement of the firing, Pollock placed a new magazine into his weapon. Sellers did the same with his. They were going to do some shooting, they told each other.

"Are there any VC in the area?" Sellers asked a young girl passing by. She replied in the negative.

Across the stream about eighty yards from where the soldiers were standing, six Vietnamese men were cutting wood in an old rubber plantation that belonged to the village. Together, the soldiers, ignoring the men cutting wood, fired about seventy rounds into the trees, expending all of their ammunition. A bullet struck Nguyen Van Hang. He fell to the ground, and was picked up by his son, who was also cutting wood. When they arrived at a little bridge crossing the stream, a village doctor pronounced Mr. Hang dead.

After the firing, but before learning about the stricken man, Sellers and Pollock returned to the nondescript building to order another beer. A few minutes later, a man who witnessed the shooting ran into the building, hysterically shouting that a person had been shot and killed. Sellers nonchalantly answered that only VC were in the woods, and he could not see them, anyway.

"No VC," said the hysterical man, "and he lay down." A summons went out to the village police. They, in turn, called the Military Police, who took the soldiers into custody.

A perfunctory investigation revealed that Mr. Hang had been shot in the stomach and killed by a single bullet fired by either Sellers or Pollock. Although apparently dead, Hang was placed solemnly on a wooden cart and brought to the local hospital. There was much wailing and cursing of Americans as the little hand-drawn wagon rolled down the street to its destination.

The trial that resulted was ready to proceed as scheduled in the early morning of January 27, when all parties were present. The court members were assembled in the deliberation room, and I was in the legal office across the street when the prosecutor, Major Herbert Green, came to inform me that everyone was ready to proceed. As I entered the courtroom, I accidentally kicked over one of two M–16 rifles that were propped against the side of the inside wall. I said nothing until I reached the judge's bench.

"Major Green!" I intoned seriously. "What are those weapons doing in the courtroom?"

"They belong to the accused, sir. The company commander sent the men over this morning with their weapons, which they apparently always carry."

I paused a moment. The courtroom was silent except for the noise of the air conditioner. "Major Green!" I said with all the composure I could muster. "Get those weapons out of here!"

"Yes, sir!" Green replied as he hurried to the rear of the courtroom and disappeared with the weapons. Upon his return, I asked: "Major Green, how is it possible, first of all, that two soldiers charged with murder are allowed to be carrying weapons and, secondly, to bring them into a courtroom?"

"I don't know, sir. Well, they're not charged with premeditated murder. I don't think their company commander considered them dangerous."

There was no way for me to respond to that kind of logic. I shook my head, and told Green to call the members of the court from the deliberation room.

The case proceeded as expected, the Vietnamese witnesses testifying to the actions of the accused and the untimely death of the victim. Mr. Hang's son brought a stunned silence to the trial when, after his testimony, he solemnly pleaded:

"I make here the request to the United States government to pay for my father's funeral."

When the prosecution rested, both accused admitted firing their weapons but denied seeing anyone near the trees into which they were shooting. They were found not guilty of unpremeditated murder but guilty of negligent homicide, which required only a finding of simple negligence. Each was sentenced to nine months confinement at hard labor and limited forfeitures of pay but no discharge.

After the review was completed by the staff judge advocate, he recommended to the commanding general that since there was no discharge imposed upon either of the accused and two months had passed since their imprisonment, the remainder of the sentence be remitted. The general agreed and the two accused were returned to their unit.

Two years after the trial, I was military judge on a case in Nuremberg, Germany, in which an accused was charged with maiming. He had thrown a live hand grenade out of a window toward his first sergeant, who was walking alone outside the building, causing permanent damage to the intended victim. "Fragging" is the term for throwing a fragmentation grenade at a person, usually a superior, to dispose of that person without leaving evidence of the person who committed the crime. Such offenses were rather common in Vietnam in late 1969 and thereafter, but I had no prior experience with such a case.

William Sellers was the name of the accused in the Nuremberg case. I did not recognize the name, nor the accused himself, during the first part of his trial. After he was found guilty, the prosecutor introduced a record of previous convictions that included an earlier one for negligent homicide in Vietnam.

When Sellers took the witness stand to present matters in extenuation and mitigation, he talked about his life back home, which was more or less normal, although he had never finished high school. His father had been gainfully employed by the City of New York, and he got along with his siblings. He lived in one of a group of homes that had common walls but separate closed-in back yards. When he finished testifying, nothing was brought out, in my opinion, that might evoke sympathy from the court. The trial counsel did not examine him. Out of curiosity because we were in Vietnam at the same time and also hoping to bring out something appropriate that might bear upon his apparently unsympathetic attitude toward human beings, I decided to ask a few questions.

"I note that you were tried by court-martial in Vietnam, is that correct?"

"Yes, sir, for unpremeditated murder, and you were the judge."

I gasped — and then remembered the Sellers and Pollock case.

"Are you sure you were convicted of unpremeditated murder? Your record of prior convictions says negligent homicide, and there is quite a difference."

"Well, sir, I was charged with murder, but you or somebody else in that courtroom knocked it down."

"OK. Now tell the court whether there was anything at all in your childhood that caused you to become bitter about anyone?"

"No, sir. People didn't like me a lot but I didn't like them either, except some special friends."

"Did you have any hobbies?"

"Well, yes, sir, I had one. Three turtles appeared in our back yard one day and I took care of them all the time I was in high school."

I had no further questions. In his argument for leniency, the defense counsel commented upon routine matters, such as youth, service in Vietnam, lack of a good education, but nothing really that seemed to gain sympathy from the members of the court. In frustration, feeling that he was getting nowhere, the defense counsel concluded: "After all, anyone who cares for three turtles during his high school years can't be all bad!"

I wanted to cite the defense counsel for contempt!

The court sentenced Sellers to be dishonorably discharged from the army and to be confined at hard labor for fifteen years. There was little chance he would ever see the day when he would be convicted again by court-martial.

CHAPTER THIRTY-EIGHT

Ears and a Finger, Too

There is a postcard of a beautiful beach in my office. Children are pictured selling balloons and playing in the water. Along the nearby boulevard, colorful hotels and palm trees are visible. Visitors ask whether the scene is from Hawaii or the Caribbean. "No," I tell them, "that is a postcard from Nha Trang, in Vietnam, on the coast of the South China Sea."

Nha Trang was the site of Headquarters, I Field Force, which controlled American operations in the central highlands of Vietnam and along a large part of the China Sea coast. It was a pleasure to go there because I was regularly assigned to a room in one of the hotels near the beach, which was within walking distance to the staff judge advocate office, the courtroom, and the mess hall.

Lieutenant Colonel Ralph Hammack, the staff judge advocate, was a gracious host. Sometimes, when there was a break during a trial, we sat on the beach to escape the heat and catch the gentle sea breezes, whiling away time without thoughts of war or work. Sometimes we ate at a run-down French restaurant where the cook prepared fresh fish and lobster with taste, loving care, and superior skill. Colonel Hammack made his jeep available to me in order to visit nearby installations where I had friends.

Late in April 1969, I was at I Field Force to participate in a case, which involved mutilation of a corpse and two serious assaults. Stories of soldiers desecrating enemy bodies were not uncommon, but except for the incident in which a cameraman for a national news network paid a soldier to cut the ear off a dead Vietnamese, I was not personally aware of any such incident. I heard stories, of course, but thought then, as I do now, that they were exaggerated.

The case to which I was assigned in Nha Trang was my first experience with that type of conduct. After killing a Vietnamese man, Private First Class Herbert Stoss cut off his ears and a finger, and grievously assaulted a second Vietnamese man.

On the afternoon of January 9, 1969, members of a platoon assigned to C Company, 1st Battalion of the 173rd Airborne Brigade, were on a minesweeping mission four kilometers from their company's Forward Operating Base (FOB). One of the tracks (armored personnel carriers) overheated and they could not proceed. It was a break for those who did not have to work on the broken vehicle.

Second Lieutenant John Jones, the platoon leader, was a recent graduate of Officer Candidate School and had been in Vietnam about four months. Neither he nor Private Stoss had yet reached his twenty-second birthday. Jones was considered to be an immature officer by his superiors, and even more so by the sergeants under his command. Although Jones was intellectually superior, having graduated from college, Stoss was by far more aggressive and charismatic.

The ubiquitous Vietnamese "Coke girls" who seemed to be wherever a group of American soldiers gathered for whatever purpose, were also present near the breakdown, selling Cokes, beer, souvenirs, and themselves. All of the men bought beer. Lieutenant Jones went to a nearby "boom boom" shack with one of the girls, told the men to make themselves happy, and disappeared into the tiny building, which consisted of one small room. A soldier took one of the girls down into his track, while two friends watched from above. The others took the beer they had purchased, sat down in the shade of a tree, and began to speak without paying much attention to one another. The beer and the heat contributed to making this an idle conversation.

Sergeant Alfred Mano, the platoon sergeant, was the center of the group in the shade. Private Stoss and four of Mano's subordinates were the other participants in the conversation. Stoss began to speak of the bravery of his best friend, who had departed that morning for Manila on R&R.

"You're not a man like your friend! You cannot kill or hurt anybody! You're just a baby," Sergeant Mano said to Stoss.

"Hell, I've only been here a couple of months! What can I do to prove that I'm a man?"

Although Stoss was inexperienced, he was not afraid of work, always pulled his share of duties without complaint, and had many friends. Lacking in formal education, he nevertheless freely asserted himself, but he was seldom offensive. He was especially respectful to his superiors, even Lieutenant Jones.

"Well," said Mano, "you could bring back some gook ears next time you shoot one! That would be proof of your courage and ability to stand up under fire."

Private Stoss had been in the army less than a year. He was drafted in December 1967; went through basic and advanced infantry training with no problem in six months; and, after a short leave home, was sent to Vietnam in July. He was several years younger than his platoon sergeant.

There was no doubt that Mano spoke to Stoss about "brining back gook ears." One of the witnesses to the conversation said that the sergeant did not sound serious. Others, including Stoss, said that Mano did not appear to be joking. Mano said he was just teasing.

After tending to the overheated track, the platoon returned to the company's FOB. Their only duty before supper was to chase away other "Coke girls" who had somehow managed to infiltrate the company's perimeter. During supper, each soldier was furnished one can of beer. Several, including Stoss, had already drank several that had been purchased from the girls.

Shortly before sunset, the battalion intelligence officer directed the C Company commander by radio to set up a listening post near a small creek just south of the hamlet of Dien Tieu, about four kilometers south of the FOB. It was known that Viet Cong soldiers came down from the mountains into the surrounding villages and hamlets at night.

Dien Tieu hamlet, however, was considered secure. It was surrounded by barbed wire, and a few of its inhabitants were members of the Vietnamese Popular Forces, who presumably were able to protect everyone within the compound, including a few refugees. The battalion intelligence officer was specific in stating that there was no reason to enter the hamlet.

Lieutenant Jones was chosen to lead the small patrol scheduled to begin an hour and a half before midnight. Stoss volunteered for the mission. A medic, Corporal Bill Rhodes, a radio operator, and three other soldiers were chosen to complete the detail. Instructions were repeated to bypass the hamlet, as quietly as possible.

At 2230 hours, the patrol set out, following a ditch line that passed close to, but did not enter, Dien Tieu. When the soldiers approached the hamlet, the members heard laughter and dogs barking from within.

Private Stoss was ready to prove he was a man. He told Lieutenant Jones that suspicious noises were heard in the hamlet and requested permission to enter. Jones told the radio operator to check with the command track back in the FOB. He received a negative reply. When the patrol arrived closer to the entrance of the hamlet, Stoss once again tried to persuade Lieutenant Jones that there were suspicious noises inside and it was his duty to investigate, overriding the prior refusal for permission. While Jones was pondering an answer, Stoss decided on his own to enter the hamlet.

Inside the village, a group of Vietnamese men were seated, talking and laughing on the outside of a hooch. When they saw Stoss approaching with a weapon pointed in their direction, most retreated inside, but one of them, Do Phat, began to run.

Stoss shouted "Dung lai!" which he understood to mean "stop." The man did not stop. Stoss fired a burst of automatic fire at the man's feet, but Phat continued to run. Another burst above the man's head did not have the desired result. Then, four bullets of a third burst of fire entered Do Phat's body, causing him to fall to the ground. Stoss bent down, heard the victim breathing heavily, grabbed Phat by the collar and dragged him to the village entrance, where other members of the patrol had gathered after hearing the three bursts of fire. The medic, Corporal Rhodes, took Phat's pulse and announced that he was breathing and still alive. According to all of the witnesses, Stoss struck Phat on the head with the butt of his rifle, causing breathing to stop. Rhodes checked his pulse again, and pronounced Phat dead.

Two of the inhabitants of the hamlet tried to go to Phat's assistance, but Stoss forced them to lie face down on the ground. He was acting as if he were leading the mission. He demanded identification from Dan Dinh Xuan, one of the men who had come to assist Phat. The man moved upward and handed Stoss a piece of paper. Not satisfied, Stoss said that he was not interested in laundry lists, and struck Xuan with the barrel of his rifle, rendering him unconscious. Rhodes checked Xuan and found that he was "fairly well cut, pretty good, pretty deep."

While Rhodes was administering first aid to the injured man, Stoss became angry and shouted that he should not help a gook because "the gook would not help you if the tables were turned." Another soldier standing by ridiculed Rhodes for helping Xuan. Lieutenant Jones looked on awkwardly and walked away, lacking the courage to intervene. He told the radio operator to report that his platoon had just killed a Viet Cong. A report was made by radio that "one VC was killed."

Stoss asked Rhodes, who was administering first aid to Xuan, for a knife. He denied having one, suspecting that Stoss was preparing to make good on a threat he made earlier to "get some gook ears." Stoss angrily ran to the nearest hooch and returned with a curved knife similar to those used by Vietnamese who work in the fields, making a boast that he "was going to cut off the gook's ears."

The medic turned his head and the other soldiers walked away. Rhodes heard noises "like a dull knife cutting flesh." When he turned to protest, he saw that Mr. Phat's ears had been cut off.

"Are you satisfied?" the medic asked Stoss, who was now acting "like a wild man." "No," was the reply, "I still want a finger."

Corporal Rhodes swore that he "heard the same cutting sound, and then a bone snapped."

When Rhodes once again reprimanded Stoss, the latter said "Here, you want a finger?" and threw it and the knife at him. Lieutenant Jones returned to the scene as the knife was thrown, observed what happened, and gathered together the men of the patrol. He ordered everyone to head back to the company area, saying nothing about the killing or the brutality, except that there would be hell to pay if the company commander found out about the ears and finger. The mission to secure a listening post was abandoned.

When the patrol returned to the company, Stoss went directly to Sergeant Mano and handed him a green handkerchief with something wrapped inside. Mano unfolded the handkerchief and two bloody ears fell to the ground. The sergeant was benumbed and told Stoss to get rid of the ears, but did not reprimand him. Stoss asked Mano if he was now a man and the sergeant, shaken, meekly replied, "Yes, I guess so."

"All right then, you can't call me a baby anymore, you have to call me a man!" Stoss admonished.

Stoss was not charged with killing Do Phat, but assaulting him by striking him on the head, and mutilating his corpse by cutting off both ears and one finger. He was also charged with assaulting Xuan with intent to commit grievous bodily harm. The convening authority apparently believed that Stoss was justified as a soldier in shooting Phat, who was running away from a lawful apprehension.

At the trial, Stoss admitted the three firings and killing Do Phat. He denied every other piece of inculpatory evidence that was presented against him. He specifically denied cutting off Do

Phat's ears and finger, hitting him with his rifle butt, and assaulting Xuan with his rifle barrel. He said he did not throw a finger or knife at Corporal Rhodes, but possibly he did "throw a rock because I always kept a bunch of rocks in my pocket."

I had a rather unique problem in formatting instructions for the members of the court. There was the matter of close timing with respect to the assault and death of Do Phat. If he was dead at the time Stoss allegedly hit him on the head, there could be no assault. If Phat were alive when the ears and finger were severed, there could be no mutilation of a corpse.

The trial counsel argued quite graphically that "by the time the ears and finger were removed, Do Phat, yes, was dead. But at the time that the blow was struck, although dying, Do Phat was alive gasping, wheezing, gurgling, or whatever." Rhodes had indeed testified that Phat was alive when Stoss struck him, but dead when the mutilation took place. All this within a period of minutes, and Rhodes was by no means an expert.

The defense counsel asked the court to believe the accused's testimony. He introduced evidence by stipulation that former employers in the United States praised Stoss highly and would believe him under oath, and that his mother said he was always a good boy, working four years at the same factory to help support the family and was polite to everyone. Sergeants in the accused's company testified they would like to have him back in the unit because of his willingness to work hard.

The court members, according to their verdict, did not believe that Phat was alive when Stoss struck him, or perhaps that Stoss did not strike Phat at all, because they found him guilty only of mutilating the corpse. They also convicted him of committing an assault upon Xuan. I personally believe that it was a compromise verdict, the jury unable to decide the time factor. The court members sentenced the accused to be dishonorably discharged from the army and to be confined at hard labor for one year.

I did not understand then, and I do not understand now, why Private First Class Stoss was not charged with homicide. In my opinion, the evidence I heard was sufficient to prefer a charge of murder against him, and the court members should have been allowed to determine whether the killing was justified.

CHAPTER THIRTY-NINE

DEROS

DEROS. Date Eligible to Return from Overseas. Mine arrived on July 9, 1969. I was up at five in the morning to allow time for a hundred little details that remained before reporting to the processing center in the early afternoon. At the open mess for breakfast, I was pleasantly surprised to find Kathy ahead of me because we had not visited in several weeks. A good way to start the day that ended my tour. We sat together for my last meal at the Rex.

"I've been looking for you these last few days," she said. "I wanted to invite you to a barge party on the river today."

"Sorry, I can't make it, but my day has arrived," I replied.

"It's a pity you can't come!" she said, "It'll be great fun. It's being given by the civilian we visited that evening we were looking for a place for Dianne. All kinds of people will be there. From the embassy, from USAID, two congressmen, and lots of important civilians who have villas."

"Where did your friend get the barge?" I asked.

"I don't know, but I'm sure it's legal. He's very careful about things like that. I'm really sorry you can't come. There will be lots of good food and you would enjoy meeting new people!"

"By the way," I asked, "what ever happened at the picnic you invited me to attend on Con Son Island a few weeks ago?"

"It was great!" she replied. "My pilot friend managed to get hold of a cute little plane, a U–21, I think, and we had a great time. A couple of us bought all the goodies from the commissary and we cooked outside. We spent the whole day at a beautiful beach. And, I want you to know that we did not see those horrible Tiger Cages you told me about."

"Well, I didn't think you would. Beautiful beaches are not the sight for anyone in cages. Besides, they're in a prison which is pretty well secluded."

"Anyway, it was gorgeous, and there was no hint of anyone being tortured there."

Sometimes it's not so difficult to separate appearance from reality, I thought.

Kathy had been afraid of nothing (except, perhaps, being alone) and she enjoyed the excitement of living in Saigon. She was there during the 1968 Tet Offensive and was excited by every minute of it. From her apartment, she could hear the shootings, the mortar shells, and all the uproar. She went outside to get a better view of the action. She walked to the United States Embassy where she watched General William Westmoreland and Ambassador Ellsworth Bunker peering over bodies of Viet Cong soldiers who had been killed while attempting to occupy the building. She never refused a trip that promised excitement. She had been to dozens of places outside Vietnam, including the R&R destinations of Kuala Lampur, Hong Kong, and Manila. She always had friends, especially civilian reporters and pilots who were willing to take her along on noncombat missions.

After reminiscing for an hour or so about her eighteen months and my twelve months in Vietnam, we shook hands and said goodbye. She was off to the barge party before I reached the stairs to return to my room.

After processing in the afternoon, I had dinner with others whose DEROS had arrived. We were then bussed to the waiting room at Ton Son Nhut, where our flight was scheduled to depart in a couple of hours. I sat on a long, hard bench experiencing for the last time the smell of combat uniforms and the sight of young new arrivals who could not know their destinations. I thought about the thousands of United States servicemen and women who had entered Vietnam since my arrival there, but had not lived to experience this, the ecstasy of having reached the day on which they would be returning home.

The dispirited Vietnamese beggars milling around the airport were no different than those who were there a year before. It saddened me to think that, insofar as they were concerned, nothing had improved. I fell into a slight depression trying to make sense of the war, especially since my arrival in Saigon.

My experiences in Vietnam did not change my perspective of the war. How could I, or any one, determine whether we were winning, losing, or making progress? Vietnam was not a war about which the nation could become excited. There was no capture of great cities like Paris or Berlin or stories of General Patton racing to Trier in World War II, or General MacArthur landing at Inchon during the Korean War.

It was nonetheless necessary for those responsible for the continuation of the war to justify to the American people that our efforts were not in vain. This was unfortunately done by announcing that we were killing more of the enemy than the number of losses we were suffering. The particular phrases used were "body count" and "kill ratio." To aggravate the situation, everyone seemed to know that the body count was exaggerated to our advantage. I sat several times in briefings where battalion and higher commanders were reporting the day's results of casualties within their commands. I had never experienced a situation where the kill ratio did not favor the United States.

The terms "body count" and "kill ratio" were bandied about uncritically in combat and in the media. If it were necessary to announce the somber news that one hundred American servicemen had been killed in a particular action, could we take comfort because the announcement also included the fact that nine hundred of the enemy had been killed on the same day?

After the sweep across a village, or destruction of Viet Cong and North Vietnamese soldiers by bombs, bullets, and napalm from the air, we counted the enemy dead. The count sometimes included old men, women, and probably children. We assumed victory in terms of body count. Geography was not the method of determining success, mortality rates were.

Victories that gained territory usually proved ephemeral. In 1967, the United States deployed thirty-two thousand troops using intensive bombing and chemical warfare, including napalm, to clear a 125-square-mile area known as the "Iron Triangle," destroying the village of Ben Suc in the process. The enemy retreated into Cambodia, but returned to use the same land as a staging area for the 1968 Tet Offensive.

A few weeks before my departure from Vietnam, the United States Army and Air Force spent ten days capturing Ap Bia Mountain, better known as Hamburger Hill because of the carnage in that small space. Heavy artillery, napalm, B–52 strikes, and fierce hand-to-hand combat bought that victory at a cost of sixty American lives and over three hundred other casualties. Two weeks later, the enemy returned to the mountain without opposition.

Vietnam made heroes and offered opportunities to turn theories into experience. The majority of regular combat arms officers in Vietnam volunteered for combat duty. Many had to wait their turn for six months in a noncombat position, after which they were given a command of their own. The idea was to gain experience and prepare for the next war.

Many who had proved themselves in combat spoke of their experience with bravado. "I was shot down from helicopters three times and survived," a colonel said to me. Another boasted of sweeping through four villages in two weeks with only three fatalities. Ninety-seven "enemy" killed.

When not in combat, or scheduled for combat, the officers and enlisted persons were not having an unpleasant experience, except for incoming mortar fire. Every division and higher headquarters had a general's mess where the food was excellent.

Often, there were hors d'oeuvres, steaks, fine desserts, and stereophonic music. At some locations, officers enjoyed volleyball or other sports before retiring for showers, cocktails, and dinner. Post exchanges, swimming pools, guaranteed R&Rs, USO shows, and showers were generally available to everyone not in combat. Payroll deadlines were seldom missed and, for those who survived, a guaranteed return to the United States in one year.

When President Nixon was inaugurated, and immediately thereafter, the situation did not improve; protests increased, women marched on Washington, clerics accused the United States of war crimes, students participated in sit-ins, professors advised young men how to avoid military service. Combat operations in Vietnam continued; there was no progress at the Paris Peace negotiations; Vietnamese Vice President Nguyen Cao Ky hinted that perhaps he would talk peace with the National Liberation Front; refugees were still flooding into the cities as their homes and villages were destroyed.

During March, in a supposedly secret operation, President Nixon authorized the bombing of Cambodia, thus extending the war into a neutral country. Two months later, the *New York Times* revealed "the secret bombings." Personnel of the administration, including National Security Adviser Henry Kissinger, became obsessed with trying to prevent leaking secret information. It was interesting to consider that anyone could think the bombing of a neutral country by B–52 stratafortress jet bombers, dropping tons of bombs with each sortie, would be kept secret. There were almost eight hundred media reporters in Vietnam. Once, while the "secret bombings" were taking place, I stood with friends outside the courtroom in Cu Chi listening to bombs falling into the Cambodian countryside. In May, over three thousand tons of bombs were dropped by B–52s alone on areas near the Cambodian-Vietnam border.

In April, Secretary of State William Rogers told the Senate Foreign Relations Committee that "We are not seeking a military victory, nor do we want an escalation." This statement was difficult to comprehend. Few favored an escalation, but it seemed incongruous to say we were not seeking a military victory when, at the same time, the number of United States forces reached its peak at 543,000 and the war had been extended into a neutral country.

A few weeks before my departure, *Life* magazine published individual pictures of 242 American soldiers who had been killed during one week in Vietnam early in May. I think that those pictures of young men happily posing in new military uniforms, sports coats, high school graduation caps and gowns, brought home to me, more than anything I had observed, graphic evidence of what had been occurring in Vietnam and the war in which I was participating. If my views on the war had not been clear when I arrived in Vietnam, they had been defined before the date of my departure.

So many people had advised our past presidents of the futility of our presence in Vietnam. In addition to senators, members of Congress, and ordinary Americans doubting our stated cause, President Charles de Gaulle of France, whose country had experienced the agony of defeat in Indochina, and General Douglas MacArthur, who had almost a lifetime of experience in the Far East, had warned President Kennedy that our goal in Vietnam was unattainable. The greatest tragedy to me, however, was that I could conceive of no solution for victory without giving up on the South Vietnamese people whom we had recruited to our cause.

While occupied with these depressing thoughts and staring at nothing in particular, I saw a smiling face. Kathy had entered the terminal, escorted by a young marine officer. I gave up my space on the hard bench and walked over to them.

"I came to tell you goodbye again," Kathy said. "And to tell you that the party you missed today was not worth going to. The barge leaked, there was no protection from the sun, and the people were mostly stuck up."

"Did you go to the party, too?" I asked the young marine.

"No," he answered, "I'm just one of Kathy's pals she can always depend upon, and she needed a ride here to tell you good-bye."

Kathy's smile faded, and she looked sad. Her feelings were not for me in particular, I thought, but rather a reflection of bidding one more farewell to one of her many friends who merited perhaps a short note in her diary. Impulsively, she embraced me briefly and whispered "God bless you" before turning around and departing without another glance. Thus ended my tour of duty in Vietnam.

DUDEN-TASCHENBÜCHER

Praxisnahe Helfer zu vielen Themen
Herausgegeben vom Wissenschaftlichen Rat der DUDEN-Redaktion: Prof. Dr. Dr. h. c. Günther Drosdowski · Dr. Wolfgang Müller · Dr. Werner Scholze-Stubenrecht · Dr. Matthias Wermke

Band 1: Komma, Punkt und alle anderen Satzzeichen
Sie finden in diesem Taschenbuch Antwort auf alle Fragen, die im Bereich der deutschen Zeichensetzung auftreten können. 165 Seiten.

Band 2: Wie sagt man noch?
Hier ist der Ratgeber, wenn Ihnen gerade das passende Wort nicht einfällt oder wenn Sie sich im Ausdruck nicht wiederholen wollen. 219 Seiten.

Band 3: Die Regeln der deutschen Rechtschreibung
Dieses Buch stellt die Regeln zum richtigen Schreiben der Wörter und Namen sowie die Regeln zum richtigen Gebrauch der Satzzeichen dar. 188 Seiten.

Band 4: Lexikon der Vornamen
Mehr als 3000 weibliche und männliche Vornamen enthält dieses Taschenbuch. Sie erfahren, aus welcher Sprache ein Name stammt, was er bedeutet und welche Persönlichkeiten ihn getragen haben. 239 Seiten.

Band 6: Wann schreibt man groß, wann schreibt man klein?
Jeder weiß, dass die Groß- und Kleinschreibung eines der schwierigsten Kapitel der deutschen Rechtschreibung ist. Dieses Taschenbuch bietet mit rund 8200 Artikeln eine schnelle Hilfe für die tägliche Schreibpraxis. 252 Seiten.

Band 7: Wie schreibt man gutes Deutsch?
Dieser Band stellt die vielfältigen sprachlichen Ausdrucksmöglichkeiten dar. Ein unentbehrlicher Ratgeber für alle, die sich um einen guten Stil bemühen. 163 Seiten.

Band 8: Wie sagt man in Österreich?
Das Buch bringt eine Fülle an Informationen über alle sprachlichen Eigenheiten, durch die sich die deutsche Sprache in Österreich von dem in Deutschland üblichen Sprachgebrauch unterscheidet. 252 Seiten.

Band 9: Wie gebraucht man Fremdwörter richtig?
Mit 4000 Stichwörtern und über 30000 Anwendungsbeispielen ist dieses Taschenbuch eine praktische Stilfibel des Fremdwortes. 368 Seiten.

Band 10: Wie sagt der Arzt?
Dieses Buch gibt die volkstümlichen Bezeichnungen zu rund 9000 medizinischen Fachwörtern an und erleichtert damit die Verständigung zwischen Arzt und Patient. 176 Seiten.

Band 11: Wörterbuch der Abkürzungen
Dieses Wörterbuch enthält rund 38000 nationale und internationale Abkürzungen aus allen Bereichen. 288 Seiten.

Band 13: mahlen oder malen?
Gleich klingende Wörter, die verschieden geschrieben werden, gehören zu den schwierigsten Problemen der deutschen Rechtschreibung. Dieses Buch bietet eine umfassende Sammlung solcher Zweifelsfälle. 191 Seiten.

Band 14: Fehlerfreies Deutsch
Zahlreiche Fragen zur Grammatik werden im DUDEN-Taschenbuch „Fehlerfreies Deutsch“ in leicht lesbarer, oft humorvoller Darstellung beantwortet. 204 Seiten.

Band 15: Wie sagt man anderswo?
Dieses Buch will all jenen helfen, die mit den landschaftlichen Unterschieden in Wort- und Sprachgebrauch konfrontiert werden. 190 Seiten.

Band 17: Leicht verwechselbare Wörter
Der Band enthält Gruppen von Wörtern, die aufgrund ihrer lautlichen Ähnlichkeit leicht verwechselt werden. 334 Seiten.

Band 21: Wie verfaßt man wissenschaftliche Arbeiten?
Dieses Buch behandelt ausführlich und mit vielen praktischen Beispielen die formalen und organisatorischen Probleme des wissenschaftlichen Arbeitens. 216 Seiten.

Band 22: Wie sagt man in der Schweiz?
In rund 4000 Artikeln gibt dieses Wörterbuch Auskunft über die Besonderheiten der deutschen Sprache in der Schweiz. 380 Seiten.

Band 23: Wörter und Gegenwörter
Gegensatzpaare der deutschen Sprache.
Die verschiedensten Wortpaare, weitere Sprachnuancen und verwandte Begriffe. 267 Seiten.

Band 24: Jiddisches Wörterbuch
Mit Hinweisen zur Schreibung, Grammatik und Aussprache. Die 8000 wichtigsten Begriffe des Jiddischen von A bis Z. 204 Seiten.

Band 25: Geographische Namen in Deutschland
In über 1200 Artikeln werden 1700 Ortsnamen, Ländernamen, Fluss- und Gebirgsnamen erklärt und die Entstehungsgeschichte der verschiedensten geographischen Namen erläutert. 288 Seiten.

Band 26: Die Neuregelung der deutschen Rechtschreibung
Eine Einführung in die neue Rechtschreibung mit dem ausführlich erläuterten und kommentierten amtlichen Regeltext. 320 Seiten.

DUDENVERLAG
Mannheim · Leipzig · Wien · Zürich

DUDEN

Band 1

Der Duden in 12 Bänden

Das Standardwerk zur deutschen Sprache

Herausgegeben vom Wissenschaftlichen Rat
der Dudenredaktion:
Prof. Dr. Dr. h. c. Günther Drosdowski,
Dr. Wolfgang Müller,
Dr. Werner Scholze-Stubenrecht,
Dr. Matthias Wermke

1. Rechtschreibung
2. Stilwörterbuch
3. Bildwörterbuch
4. Grammatik
5. Fremdwörterbuch
6. Aussprachewörterbuch
7. Herkunftswörterbuch
8. Sinn- und sachverwandte Wörter
9. Richtiges und gutes Deutsch
10. Bedeutungswörterbuch
11. Redewendungen und sprichwörtliche Redensarten
12. Zitate und Aussprüche

DUDEN

Rechtschreibung

der deutschen Sprache

21., völlig neu bearbeitete und erweiterte Auflage

Herausgegeben von der Dudenredaktion

Auf der Grundlage der neuen amtlichen Rechtschreibregeln

DUDEN BAND 1

DUDENVERLAG

Mannheim · Leipzig · Wien · Zürich

Redaktionelle Bearbeitung:
Dr. Werner Scholze-Stubenrecht und Dr. Matthias Wermke
in Zusammenarbeit mit Prof. Dr. Dr. h. c. Günther Drosdowski
und unter Mitwirkung weiterer Mitarbeiter der Dudenredaktion
in Mannheim und Leipzig sowie des österreichischen und
schweizerischen Dudenausschusses

Telefonische und schriftliche Anfragen beantwortet die
Sprachberatungsstelle der Dudenredaktion,
Postfach 10 03 11, 68003 Mannheim, Telefon (06 21) 3 90 14 26
(Montag bis Freitag von 9 bis 12 Uhr).

Die Deutsche Bibliothek – CIP-Einheitsaufnahme
Der **Duden:** in 12 Bänden; das Standardwerk zur deutschen Sprache /
hrsg. vom Wissenschaftlichen Rat der Dudenredaktion: Günther Drosdowski ... –
Mannheim; Leipzig; Wien; Zürich: Dudenverl.
Früher u.d.T.: Der große Duden
NE: Drosdowski, Günther [Hrsg.]
Bd. 1. Duden, Rechtschreibung der deutschen Sprache. –
21., völlig neu bearb. und erw. Aufl. / hrsg. von der Dudenredaktion
auf der Grundlage der neuen amtlichen Rechtschreibregeln. – 1996
Duden, Rechtschreibung der deutschen Sprache /
[red. Bearb.: Werner Scholze-Stubenrecht und Matthias Wermke
in Zusammenarbeit mit Günther Drosdowski und unter Mitw. weiterer Mitarb.
der Dudenredaktion in Mannheim und in Leipzig sowie des österreichischen
und schweizerischen Dudenausschusses]. –
21., völlig neu bearb. und erw. Aufl. / hrsg. von der
Dudenredaktion auf der Grundlage der neuen Rechtschreibregeln. –
Mannheim; Leipzig; Wien; Zürich: Dudenverl., 1996
(Der Duden; Bd. 1)
ISBN 3-411-04011-4
NE: Scholze-Stubenrecht, Werner [Red.]; Rechtschreibung der deutschen Sprache

Satz: Bibliographisches Institut & F. A. Brockhaus AG (DIACOS Siemens)
Druck: Klambt-Druck GmbH, Speyer
Einband: Graphische Betriebe Langenscheidt, Berchtesgaden
Printed in Germany
ISBN 3-411-04011-4

Vorwort

Im Juli 1996 wurde in Wien von den zuständigen Stellen der deutschsprachigen Länder eine zwischenstaatliche Erklärung über die Neuregelung der deutschen Rechtschreibung unterzeichnet. Damit kann das bisher geltende amtliche Regelwerk von 1901 durch eine Neufassung ersetzt werden. Stichtag für die Einführung der neuen Regeln ist der 1. August 1998. Mit der neuen Rechtschreibung wird das Schreiben erleichtert, ohne dass dadurch das vertraute Schriftbild unserer Sprache wesentlich verändert würde. Dass dieses Ziel der Neuregelung erreicht wurde, zeigt dieses Vorwort. Es ist bereits nach den neuen Regeln abgefasst.

Der Hauptgrund für die Schwierigkeiten mit dem richtigen Schreiben liegt darin, dass sich die Verschriftung der Sprache über einen langen Zeitraum hinweg entwickelt hat, in dem es keine allgemein verbindlichen Regeln gab. So haben sich Schreibweisen herausgebildet, die sich nachträglich nicht mehr in ein einfaches System einordnen lassen. Auch künftig werden wir »lehren« und »leeren« oder »Seite« und »Saite« unterscheiden müssen und »das richtige Schreiben« nicht mit »das Richtige schreiben« verwechseln dürfen.

Die Neuregelung hat zwei Schwerpunkte gesetzt. Sie hat einerseits Ausnahmen zu bestimmten Grundmustern und Grundregeln abgebaut und andererseits in Bereichen wie Silbentrennung und Kommasetzung den Schreibenden zusätzliche Freiräume für eigene Entscheidungen eingeräumt. So wird in Zukunft »Rad fahren« (und nicht mehr »radfahren«) ebenso wie »Auto fahren« und »Ski fahren« geschrieben werden und »in Bezug auf« (statt »in bezug auf«) ebenso wie »mit Bezug auf«. Ob in den Sätzen »Sie fährt nach Leipzig, und er fährt nach Wien« und »Alle haben sich sehr bemüht, eine bessere Lösung zu finden« das nach der alten Regelung vorgeschriebene Komma weiterhin gesetzt wird oder nicht, das entscheiden die Schreibenden künftig selbst. Auch bei den Wortschreibungen wird es eine Reihe von Veränderungen geben. Dies betrifft unter anderem Wörter desselben Wortstammes, die einander angeglichen werden (statt »plazieren« schreibt man zukünftig »platzieren« wegen »Platz«). Zu einigen wenigen Fremdwörtern wird es eingedeutschte Varianten geben (z. B. »Delfin« neben »Delphin«).

So sinnvoll derartige Freiräume unter bestimmten Gesichtspunkten sein können, so sehr bergen sie die Gefahr in sich, die Einheitsschreibung auszuhöhlen. Die Durchsetzung und Bewahrung einer einheitlichen Schreibung im Deutschen hat der Duden seit jeher als seine Hauptaufgabe betrachtet. Die Einheitsschreibung fördert die schriftliche Verständigung, verhindert Missverständnisse und Fehler bei der Entschlüsselung – auch der maschinellen – schriftlicher Nachrichten. Sie erhöht die Lesegeschwindigkeit und erleichtert das Textverstehen. Nicht zuletzt dient sie dem ganzen grafischen Gewerbe, und das nicht nur bei der Ausbildung und Schulung von Redakteuren, Setzern und Korrektoren. Deshalb ist es das Ziel der vorliegenden Neuauflage des Rechtschreibdudens, das amtliche Regelwerk im Hinblick auf klare Entscheidungen auszulegen, die der Zielsetzung der Neuregelung gerecht werden und dem Benutzer dabei doch verlässliche Schreibungen vorgeben. So geschieht dies etwa bei den Angaben zur Worttrennung, wo nicht alle Möglichkeiten im Wörterverzeichnis gezeigt werden, sondern nur diejenigen, die einer sinnvollen Auslegung des Regelwerks entsprechen. Verweise deuten auf weitere Möglichkeiten hin.

Die Neufassung der Richtlinien im Rechtschreibduden basiert auf dem neuen amtlichen Regelwerk. Die Richtlinien verzichten – gemäß der Dudentradition – auf die Erläuterung von Teilbereichen, die zwar für die Rechtschreibtheoretiker wichtig, für den Schreiber im alltäglichen Umgang mit der Rechtschreibung aber wenig nutzbringend sind. So bleiben einige – weniger wichtige – Ausführungen zur Wiedergabe bestimmter Laute durch bestimmte Schriftzeichen (Laut-Buchstaben-Beziehungen) ausgeklammert. Hier beschränkt sich der Duden meist auf eine rote Markierung der neuen Schreibungen im Wörterverzeichnis. Gegebenenfalls wird von der alten auf die neue Schreibung verwiesen, wenn, wie z.B. bei »Quäntchen«, zu erwarten ist, dass die Benutzer noch nach der alten Schreibung (»Quentchen«) im Wörterbuch suchen. Beibehalten wurde die alphabetische Anordnung des Richtlinienteils, der insgesamt gestrafft wurde. Sie hat sich in der Praxis bewährt, weil sie für viele Benutzer einen leichteren Zugang zu den einzelnen Regeln ermöglicht als eine systematische Darstellung.

Für alle, die auch mit dem amtlichen Regelwerk arbeiten möchten, ist dieses in einem Anhang abgedruckt. Verweise leiten von den Duden-Richtlinien zu den entsprechenden Paragraphen des offiziellen Textes. Um die Benutzbarkeit des Dudens nicht einzuschränken, wurde auf den Abdruck des amtlichen Wörterverzeichnisses verzichtet. Die darin aufgelisteten Wörter sind im Duden enthalten.

Mit der vorliegenden Neuauflage des Rechtschreibdudens verfolgt die Dudenredaktion das Ziel, auch die neue deutsche Rechtschreibung für die Allgemeinheit durchschaubar darzustellen, damit sie von jedermann im Alltag leicht gehandhabt werden kann. Sie stellt sich so ausdrücklich in den Dienst der neuen Rechtschreibung in der Absicht, diese schnellstmöglich durchzusetzen. Selbstverständlich wurden auch bei dieser Neuauflage alle Stichworteinträge überprüft und – wo nötig – überarbeitet. Zahlreiche Neubildungen und Entlehnungen aus anderen Sprachen wie zum Beispiel »Datenautobahn«, »Extremsport«, »Cyberspace« und »Peanuts« wurden ins Wörterverzeichnis aufgenommen.

Die Dudenredaktion dankt allen, die zur Fertigstellung dieses Bandes beigetragen haben, insbesondere aber den Mitgliedern des schweizerischen und des österreichischen Dudenausschusses.

Mannheim, im Juli 1996 Die Dudenredaktion

Inhalt

Hinweise für die Wörterbuchbenutzung

I. Zeichen von besonderer Bedeutung

. Ein untergesetzter Punkt kennzeichnet die kurze betonte Silbe, z. B. Referent.

_ Ein untergesetzter Strich kennzeichnet die lange betonte Silbe, z. B. Fassade.

| Der senkrechte Strich dient zur Angabe der Silbentrennung, z. B. Mor|ta|del|la, mü|he|voll.

® Das Zeichen ® macht als Markenzeichen geschützte Wörter (Bezeichnungen, Namen) kenntlich. Sollte dieses Zeichen einmal fehlen, so ist das keine Gewähr dafür, dass das Wort als Handelsname frei verwendet werden darf.

- Der waagerechte Strich vertritt das unveränderte Stichwort bei den Beugungsangaben und auch häufig (um Platz zu sparen) bei den Beispielen für den Gebrauch des Stichworts, z. B. Brett, das; -[e]s, -er; oder: abwracken; ein Schiff -.

... Drei Punkte stehen bei Auslassung von Teilen eines Wortes, z. B. Eindruck, der; -[e]s, ...drücke; oder: Anabolikum, das; -s, ...ka.

‿ Der Bogen steht innerhalb einer Zusammensetzung, um anzuzeigen, dass der vor ihm stehende Wortteil bei den folgenden Wörtern an Stelle der drei Punkte zu setzen ist, z. B. Augen‿arzt, ...aufschlag.

[ ] Die eckigen Klammern schließen Aussprachebezeichnungen, Zusätze zu Erklärungen in runden Klammern und beliebige Auslassungen (Buchstaben und Silben, wie z. B. in abschnitt[s]weise, Wissbegier[de]) ein.

( ) Die runden Klammern schließen Erklärungen und Hinweise zum heutigen Sprachgebrauch ein, z. B. orakeln (in dunklen Andeutungen sprechen). Sie enthalten außerdem stilistische Bewertungen und Angaben zur räumlichen und zeitlichen Verbreitung des Stichwortes, ferner Verweise auf die Richtlinien zur Rechtschreibung, Zeichensetzung und Formenlehre. Auch grammatische Angaben bei Zusammensetzungen innerhalb von Wortgruppen werden von runden Klammern eingeschlossen, z. B. Regierungs‿antritt, ...bank (*Plur.* ...bänke).

⟨ ⟩ Die Winkelklammern schließen Angaben zur Herkunft des Stichwortes ein, z. B. paradieren ⟨franz.⟩.

R Die Abschnitte der Richtlinien zur Rechtschreibung, Zeichensetzung und Formenlehre sind zur besseren Übersicht mit Nummern versehen, auf die im Wörterverzeichnis mit einem Pfeil verwiesen wird, z. B. ↑R 71. Der Punkt ● kennzeichnet hier einen besonders wichtigen Zusatz zu der voranstehenden Grundregel.

II. Auswahl der Stichwörter

Der Duden erfasst den für die Allgemeinheit bedeutsamen Wortschatz der deutschen Sprache. Er enthält Erbwörter, Lehnwörter und Fremdwörter der Hochsprache, auch umgangssprachliche Ausdrücke und landschaftlich verbreitetes Wortgut, ferner Wörter aus Fachsprachen, aus Gruppen- und Sondersprachen, z. B. der Medizin oder Chemie, der Jagd oder des Sports. Für die Auswahl waren hauptsächlich rechtschreibliche und grammatische Gründe maßgebend. Aus dem Fehlen eines Wortes darf also nicht geschlossen werden, dass es nicht gebräuchlich oder nicht korrekt ist.[1]

III. Anordnung und Behandlung der Stichwörter

1. Allgemeines

a) Die Stichwörter sind **halbfett** gedruckt.

b) Die rote Farbe kennzeichnet rechtschreibliche Änderungen gegenüber früheren Dudenauflagen. Jedes Stichwort, das nach der Rechtschreibreform anders zu schreiben ist als bisher, wird in der neuen Schreibung rot hervorgehoben; ebenso erscheinen zahlreiche Verweise auf entsprechende Stellen im Abschnitt „Richtlinien zur Rechtschreibung, Zeichensetzung und Formenlehre" (vor allem zu neuen Schreibvarianten) in Rot. Dort macht die rote Farbe Neuregelungen in Text und Beispiel deutlich. Außerdem werden die neuen Trennstellen bei st und ck rot markiert.

c) Die neuen Regeln zur Silbentrennung (Worttrennung) lassen – besonders bei Fremdwörtern – häufig mehrere unterschiedliche Trennmöglichkeiten zu. Der Duden gibt in diesen Fällen bei den Stichwörtern nur die Variante an, die von der Dudenredaktion als die jeweils sinnvollere angesehen wird. Handelt es sich dabei um eine neue Trennung und ist die alte Trennung auch weiterhin zulässig, so erscheint ein (roter) R-Verweis.

Beispiel: **Chi|rur|gie** (↑R 132)

(Aus Platzgründen erhalten Zusammensetzungen wie Neurochirurgie oder Unfallchirurgie keinen entsprechenden Verweis. Folgen mehrere gleichartige Fälle innerhalb einer Reihe von Wörtern einer Wortfamilie unmittelbar aufeinander, so steht der Verweis nur beim ersten Stichwort.)

d) Die Anordnung der Stichwörter ist alphabetisch.
Die Umlaute ä, ö, ü, äu werden wie die nicht umgelauteten Vokale (Selbstlaute) a, o, u, au behandelt. Die Schreibungen ae, oe, ue (in Namen) werden nach ad usw. eingeordnet. Der Buchstabe ß wird wie ss eingeordnet. Bei gleich lautenden Wörtern steht das Wort mit ß vor dem mit ss.

Beispiele:			
	harken	Godthåb	Mäßchen
	Härlein	Goes	Maße
	Harlekin	Goethe	Masse
	Harm	Gof	Massegläubiger

e) Stichwörter, die sprachlich (etymologisch) verwandt sind, werden in der Regel in Wortgruppen („Nestern") zusammengefasst, soweit die alphabetische Ordnung das zulässt.

f) Gleich geschriebene Stichwörter werden durch hochgestellte Zahlen (Indizes) unterschieden, z. B. ^{1}Elf (Naturgeist); ^{2}Elf (Zahl).

[1] Wer in diesem Band ein Fremdwort vermisst oder wer sich umfassend über die Bedeutungen eines Wortes unterrichten will, schlage im Duden-Fremdwörterbuch oder Duden-Universalwörterbuch nach.

2. Verben (Tätigkeitswörter, Zeitwörter)

a) Bei den schwachen Verben werden im Allgemeinen keine Formen angegeben, da sie regelmäßig im Präteritum (erste Vergangenheit) auf -te und im Partizip II (2. Mittelwort) auf -t ausgehen.
Bei den starken und unregelmäßigen Verben werden in der Regel folgende Formen angegeben: die 2. Person Singular (Einzahl) im Indikativ des Präteritums (Wirklichkeitsform der ersten Vergangenheit), die [umgelautete] 2. Person Singular im Konjunktiv des Präteritums (Möglichkeitsform der ersten Vergangenheit), das Partizip II (2. Mittelwort), der Singular des Imperativs (Befehlsform). Andere Besonderheiten werden nach Bedarf angegeben.

Beispiel: biegen; du bogst; du bögest; gebogen; bieg[e]!

Bei den Verben, deren Stammvokal e (ä, ö) zu i wechselt, und bei Verben, die Umlaut haben, werden ferner angegeben: 2. u. 3. Person Singular im Indikativ des Präsens (Wirklichkeitsform der Gegenwart).

Beispiele: (e/i-Wechsel:) geben; *du gibst, er gibt;* du gabst; du gäbest; gegeben; *gib!*
(mit Umlaut:) fallen; *du fällst, er fällt;* du fielst; du fielest; gefallen; fall[e]!

Bei zusammengesetzten oder mit einer Vorsilbe gebildeten Verben werden die oben genannten Formen nicht aufgeführt. Alle grammatischen Hinweise sind also beim einfachen Verb nachzuschlagen, z. B. vorziehen bei ziehen, behandeln bei handeln, abgrenzen bei grenzen.

b) Bei den Verben, deren Stamm mit einem s-Laut oder Zischlaut endet (s, ß, sch, z, tz), wird die 2. Person Singular im Indikativ des Präsens (Wirklichkeitsform der Gegenwart) angegeben, weil -e- oder -es- der Endung gewöhnlich ausfällt.

Beispiele: zischen; du zischst; lesen; du liest; sitzen; du sitzt

Bei den starken Verben, deren Stamm mit -ß endet, steht wegen des Wechsels von ss und ß zusätzlich die 1. Person Singular im Indikativ des Präteritums (Wirklichkeitsform der ersten Vergangenheit).

Beispiel: beißen; du beißt; *ich biss;* du bissest

3. Substantive (Hauptwörter)

a) Bei einfachen Substantiven sind mit Ausnahme der Fälle unter b der Artikel (das Geschlechtswort), der Genitiv Singular (Wesfall der Einzahl) und, soweit gebräuchlich, der Nominativ Plural (Werfall der Mehrzahl) angeführt.

Beispiel: Knabe, der; -n, -n (das bedeutet: der Knabe, des Knaben, die Knaben)

Substantive, die nur im Plural (Mehrzahl) vorkommen, werden durch ein nachgestelltes *Plur.* gekennzeichnet.

Beispiel: Ferien *Plur.*

b) Die Angabe des Artikels und der Beugung fehlt gewöhnlich bei abgeleiteten Substantiven, die mit folgenden Silben gebildet sind:

-chen:	Mädchen	das; -s, -	**-keit:**	Ähnlichkeit	die; -, -en
-lein:	Brüderlein	das; -s, -	**-ling:**	Jüngling	der; -s, -e
-ei:	Bäckerei	die; -, -en	**-schaft:**	Landschaft	die; -, -en
-er:	Lehrer	der; -s, -	**-tum:**	Besitztum	das; -s, ...tümer
-heit:	Keckheit	die; -, -en	**-ung:**	Prüfung	die; -, -en
-in:	Lehrerin	die; -, -nen			

Ausnahmen: Bei Ableitungen, die in Artikel und Beugung von diesen Beispielen abweichen, sind die grammatischen Angaben hinzugefügt, z. B. bei all denen, die keinen Plural bilden, wie: Besorgtheit, die; - oder: Christentum, das; -s.

c) Bei zusammengesetzten Substantiven und bei Substantiven, die zu zusammengesetzten Verben oder zu solchen mit Vorsilbe gebildet sind, fehlen im Allgemeinen Artikel und Beugungsendungen. In diesen Fällen ist beim Grundwort oder bei dem zum einfachen Verb gebildeten Substantiv nachzusehen.

Beispiele: Eisenbahn bei Bahn, Fruchtsaft bei Saft; Abschluss (Bildung zu abschließen) und Verschluss (Bildung zu verschließen) bei Schluss (Bildung zu schließen)

Artikel und Endungen werden dann angegeben, wenn sie sich von denen des Grundwortes unterscheiden, wenn von zwei Bildungsmöglichkeiten nur eine zutrifft oder wenn keine augenfällige (inhaltliche) Verbindung zwischen den vom einfachen und vom nicht einfachen Verb abgeleiteten Substantiven besteht.

Beispiele: Stand, der; -[e]s, Stände, *aber:* Ehestand, der; -[e]s (kein Plural); Teil, der *od.* das; *aber:* Vorteil, der; Sage, die; -, -n; ebenso: Absage, die; -, -n

4. **Adjektive** (Eigenschaftswörter)

Bei Adjektiven sind vor allem Besonderheiten und Schwankungen in der Bildung der Steigerungsformen vermerkt.

Beispiele: alt, älter, älteste; glatt, glatter, *auch* glätter, glatteste, *auch* glätteste

IV. Herkunft der Wörter

Die Herkunft der Fremdwörter und einiger jüngerer Lehnwörter wird in knapper Form in Winkelklammern angegeben; meist wird die gebende Sprache, nicht die Ursprungssprache genannt. In einigen Fällen werden die Ursprungssprache und die vermittelnde Sprache, verbunden durch einen Bindestrich, angegeben.

Beispiel: Bombast ⟨pers.-engl.⟩

Steht eine Sprachbezeichnung in runden Klammern, so heißt das, dass auch diese Sprache die gebende Sprache gewesen sein kann.

Beispiel: Bronze ⟨ital.(-franz.)⟩

Durch das Semikolon (Strichpunkt) zwischen den Herkunftsangaben wird deutlich gemacht, dass es sich beim Stichwort um eine Zusammensetzung aus Wörtern oder Wortteilen der angegebenen Sprachen handelt.

Beispiel: bipolar ⟨lat.; griech.⟩

Die wörtliche Bedeutung eines Wortes wird gelegentlich in Anführungszeichen an die Herkunftsangabe angeschlossen.

Beispiel: Wodka ⟨russ., „Wässerchen"⟩

V. Erklärungen

Der Duden ist kein Bedeutungswörterbuch; er enthält daher keine ausführlichen Bedeutungsangaben. Nur wo es für das Verständnis eines Wortes erforderlich ist, werden kurze Hinweise zur Bedeutung gegeben, etwa bei schwierigen Fremdwörtern, Fachtermini, umgangssprachlichen, landschaftlichen und veralteten Ausdrücken. Solche Erklärungen stehen in runden Klammern. Zusätze, die nicht notwendig zu den Erklärungen gehören, stehen innerhalb der runden Klammern in eckigen Klammern.

Beispiel: Akteur (Handelnder; [Schau]spieler), Tonsillektomie (operative Entfernung der Gaumenmandeln), Rabatz (*ugs. für* lärmendes Treiben, Unruhe, Krach), Karfiol (*südd., österr. für* Blumenkohl), Gleisner (*veraltet für* Heuchler)

VI. Aussprache

Aussprachebezeichnungen stehen in eckigen Klammern hinter Fremdwörtern und einigen deutschen Wörtern, deren Aussprache von der sonst üblichen abweicht. Die verwendete Lautschrift fußt auf den Aussprachebezeichnungen der Association Phonétique Internationale (Internationale Phonetische Vereinigung), ist aber den Zwecken des Dudens angepasst.

Die übliche Aussprache wurde nicht angegeben bei

c	[k]	vor a, o, u (*wie in* Café)
c	[t͜s]	vor e, i, ä, ae [ɛ(:)], ö, œ [ø(:)] *od.* [œ], ü, ue [y(:)], y (*wie in* Celsius)
i	[i̯]	vor Vokal in Fremdwörtern (*wie in* Union)
sp	[ʃp]	im Stammsilbenanlaut deutscher und im Wortanlaut eingedeutschter Wörter (*wie in* Spiel, Spedition)
sp	[sp]	im Wortinlaut (*wie in* Knospe, Prospekt)
st	[ʃt]	im Stammsilbenanlaut deutscher und im Wortanlaut eingedeutschter Wörter (*wie in* Bestand, Strapaze)
st	[st]	im Wortin- und -auslaut (*wie in* Fenster, Ast, Existenz)
ti	[t͜si̯]	vor Vokal in Fremdwörtern (*wie in* Aktion, Patient)
v	[f]	vor Vokal im Anlaut (*wie in* Vater)

Zeichen der Lautschrift, Beispiele und Umschreibung

[a]	Butler [ˈbat...]
[a:]	Master [ˈma:s...]
[ã]	Centime [sãˈti:m]
[ã:]	Franc [frã:]
[a͜i]	live [la͜if]
[a͜u]	Browning [ˈbra͜u...]
[ç]	Bronchien [...çi̯ən]
[d͜ʒ]	Gin [d͜ʒin]
[e]	Regie [reˈʒi:]
[e:]	Shake [ʃe:k]
[ɛ]	Handikap [ˈhɛndikɛp]
[ɛ:]	fair [fɛ:r]
[ɛ̃]	Impromptu [ɛ̃prɔ̃ˈty:]
[ɛ̃:]	Timbre [ˈtɛ̃:brə]
[ɛi]	Van-Dyck-Braun [vanˈdɛik...]
[ə]	Bulgarien [...i̯ən]
[i]	Citoyen [sito̯aˈjɛ̃:]
[i:]	Creek [kri:k]
[i̯]	Linie [...i̯ə]
[ŋ]	Bon [bɔŋ]
[o]	Logis [loˈʒi:]
[o:]	Plateau [...ˈto:]
[ɔ]	Hobby [ˈhɔbi]
[ɔ:]	Baseball [ˈbe:sbɔ:l]
[ɔ̃]	Bonmot [bɔ̃ˈmo:]
[ɔ̃:]	Chanson [ʃãˈsɔ̃:]
[ø]	pasteurisieren [...tøri...]
[ø:]	Friseuse [...ˈzø:zə]
[œ]	Feuilleton [fœjəˈtõ:]
[œ:]	Girl [gœ:(r)l]
[œ̃]	Dunkerque [dœ̃ˈkɛrk]
[œ̃:]	Verdun [vɛrˈdœ̃:]
[o̯a]	chamois [ʃaˈmo̯a]
[ɔ͜y]	Boykott [bɔ͜y...]
[(r)]	Girl [gœ:(r)l]
[s]	City [ˈsiti]
[ʃ]	Charme [ʃarm]
[t͜s]	Luzie [ˈlu:t͜si:]
[t͜ʃ]	Match [mɛt͜ʃ]
[u]	Routine [ru...]
[u:]	Route [ˈru:...]
[u̯]	Linguist [...ˈgu̯ist]
[v]	Violine [v...]
[w]	Whisky [ˈwiski]
[x]	Achill [aˈxil]
[y]	Budget [byˈdʒe:]
[y:]	Avenue [avəˈny:]
[y̆]	Habitué [(h)abiˈty̆e:]
[z]	Bulldozer [...do:zər]
[ʒ]	Genie [ʒe...]
[θ]	Thriller [ˈθrilə(r)]
[ð]	on the rocks [ɔn ðə ˈrɔks]

Ein Doppelpunkt nach dem Vokal bezeichnet dessen Länge, z. B. Plateau [...ˈto:]. Lautbezeichnungen in runden Klammern bedeuten, dass der betreffende Laut reduziert gesprochen wird, z. B. Girl [gœ:(r)l]. Der Hauptakzent [ˈ] steht vor der betonten Silbe,

z. B. Catenaccio [kateˈnatʃo]. Ein kleiner senkrechter Strich zwischen Vokalen gibt an, dass sie getrennt zu sprechen sind; z. B. Annuität [...u|i...].
Die beim ersten Stichwort stehende Ausspracheangabe ist im Allgemeinen für alle nachfolgenden Wortformen eines Stichwortartikels oder einer Wortgruppe gültig, sofern diese nicht eine neue Angabe erfordern.

VII. Im Wörterverzeichnis verwendete Abkürzungen

Abkürzungen, bei denen nur die Nachsilbe -isch zu ergänzen ist, sind nicht aufgeführt, z. B. ägypt. = ägyptisch. Die Nachsilbe -lich wird ...l. abgekürzt, z. B. ähnl. = ähnlich.

Abk. Abkürzung
afrik. afrikanisch
Akk. Akkusativ (Wenfall)
allg. allgemein
altdt. altdeutsch
alttest. alttestamentlich
amerik. amerikanisch
Amtsspr. Amtssprache
angels. angelsächsisch
Anm. Anmerkung
Anthropol. Anthropologie
aram. aramäisch
Archit. Architektur
astron. astronomisch
Astron. Astronomie
A. T. Altes Testament
Ausspr. Aussprache
austr. australisch

Bankw. Bankwesen
Bauw. Bauwesen
Bed. Bedeutung
Bergmannsspr. Bergmannssprache
Berufsbez. Berufsbezeichnung
bes. besonders
Bez. Bezeichnung
bild. Kunst bildende Kunst
Biol. Biologie
Bot. Botanik
bras. brasil[ian]isch
bret. bretonisch
Buchw. Buchwesen
byzant. byzantinisch

chin. chinesisch

d. dies
Dat. Dativ (Wemfall)
Druckerspr. Druckersprache
Druckw. Druckwesen
dt. deutsch

ehem. ehemals, ehemalig
Eigenn. Eigenname
eigtl. eigentlich
Eisenb. Eisenbahnwesen
eskim. eskimoisch
etw. etwas
europ. europäisch
ev. evangelisch

fachspr. fachsprachlich
fam. familiär
Familienn. Familienname
Fernspr. Fernsprechwesen
Finanzw. Finanzwesen
Fliegerspr. Fliegersprache
Flugw. Flugwesen
Forstw. Forstwirtschaft
fotogr. fotografisch
Fotogr. Fotografie
franz. französisch

Gastron. Gastronomie
Gaunerspr. Gaunersprache
gebr. gebräuchlich
geh. gehoben
gen. genannt
Gen. Genitiv (Wesfall)
Geogr. Geographie
Geol. Geologie
germ. germanisch
Ggs. Gegensatz

Handw. Handwerk
hebr. hebräisch
hist. historisch
Hochschulw. Hochschulwesen
Hptst. Hauptstadt
Hüttenw. Hüttenwesen

idg. indogermanisch
ital. italienisch

Jägerspr. Jägersprache
jap. japanisch
Jh. Jahrhundert
jmd. jemand
jmdm. jemandem
jmdn. jemanden
jmds. jemandes
Jugendspr. Jugendsprache

kath. katholisch
Kaufmannsspr. Kaufmannssprache
Kinderspr. Kindersprache
Konj. Konjunktion (Bindewort)
Kunstw. Kunstwissenschaft
Kurzw. Kurzwort

l. linker, linke, linkes
landsch. landschaftlich

landw.	landwirtschaftlich
Landw.	Landwirtschaft
lat.	lateinisch
lit.	litauisch
Literaturw.	Literaturwissenschaft
m.	männlich
MA.	Mittelalter
Math.	Mathematik
mdal.	mundartlich
med.	medizinisch
Med.	Medizin
Meteor.	Meteorologie
mexik.	mexikanisch
milit.	militärisch
Milit.	Militärwesen
mitteld.	mitteldeutsch
mittelhochd.	mittelhochdeutsch
mlat.	mittellateinisch
mong.	mongolisch
Münzw.	Münzwesen
Mythol.	Mythologie
nationalsoz.	nationalsozialistisch
neutest.	neutestamentlich
ngriech.	neugriechisch
niederl.	niederländisch
nlat.	neulateinisch
Nom.	Nominativ (Werfall)
nordamerik.	nordamerikanisch
nordd.	norddeutsch
nordgerm.	nordgermanisch
norw.	norwegisch
N. T.	Neues Testament
o. Ä.	oder Ähnliches
od.	oder
offz.	offiziell
ökum.	ökumenisch (nach den Loccumer Richtlinien von 1971)
Ortsn.	Ortsname
ostd.	ostdeutsch
österr.	österreichisch
Österr.	Österreich
ostmitteld.	ostmitteldeutsch
Päd.	Pädagogik
palästin.	palästinensisch
Pharm.	Pharmazie
philos.	philosophisch
Philos.	Philosophie
Physiol.	Physiologie
Plur.	Plural (Mehrzahl)
port.	portugiesisch
Postw.	Postwesen
Präp.	Präposition (Verhältniswort)
Psych.	Psychologie
r.	rechter, rechte, rechtes
Rechtsspr.	Rechtssprache
Rechtsw.	Rechtswesen
Rel.	Religion[swissenschaft]
Rhet.	Rhetorik
Rundf.	Rundfunk
sanskr.	sanskritisch
scherzh.	scherzhaft
Schülerspr.	Schülersprache
Schulw.	Schulwesen
schweiz.	schweizerisch
Seemannsspr.	Seemannssprache
Seew.	Seewesen
Sing.	Singular (Einzahl)
singhal.	singhalesisch
skand.	skandinavisch
Soldatenspr.	Soldatensprache
Soziol.	Soziologie
Sportspr.	Sportsprache
Sprachw.	Sprachwissenschaft
Stilk.	Stilkunde
stud.	studentisch
Studentenspr.	Studentensprache
südd.	süddeutsch
südwestd.	südwestdeutsch
svw.	so viel wie
Textilw.	Textilwesen
Theol.	Theologie
Tiermed.	Tiermedizin
Trenn.	Trennung
turkotat.	turkotatarisch
u.	und
u. a.	und andere
u. Ä.	und Ähnliches
übertr.	übertragen
ugs.	umgangssprachlich
ung.	ungarisch
urspr.	ursprünglich
Verkehrsw.	Verkehrswesen
Versicherungsw.	Versicherungswesen
vgl. [d.]	vergleiche [dort]
Völkerk.	Völkerkunde
Vorn.	Vorname
w.	weiblich
Werbespr.	Werbesprache
westmitteld.	westmitteldeutsch
Wirtsch.	Wirtschaft
Zahnmed.	Zahnmedizin
Zollw.	Zollwesen
Zool.	Zoologie
Zus.	Zusammensetzung

Richtlinien zur Rechtschreibung, Zeichensetzung und Formenlehre in alphabetischer Reihenfolge

Die folgenden Richtlinien beruhen auf den amtlichen Regeln für die Rechtschreibung und Zeichensetzung. Sie enthalten darüber hinaus einige weiterführende Hinweise für das Schreiben und für den Buch- und Zeitungsdruck, zum Beispiel zur Abschnittsgliederung, zur Wort- und Formenlehre und zur Schreibung und Beugung von Namen.

Um ein schnelles Auffinden der gewünschten Informationen zu ermöglichen, werden die Regeln und Hinweise unter alphabetisch geordneten Suchbegriffen wie „Apostroph", „Bindestrich", „Datum", „Fremdwörter" oder „Groß- und Kleinschreibung" angeführt.

Die Regeln und Hinweise wurden für diese Auflage in der Darstellung gestrafft und einige frühere Einzelregelungen wurden unter übergeordneten Gesichtspunkten zusammengefasst, um die Benutzbarkeit des Richtlinienteils zu verbessern. Beibehalten wurde das Prinzip, die eine oder andere Regel an mehreren Stellen anzuführen, sodass man zum Beispiel bei einem Problem mit der Groß- und Kleinschreibung in Straßennamen sowohl unter „Groß- und Kleinschreibung" als auch unter „Straßennamen" nachschlagen kann und an beiden Stellen sofort die Problemlösung findet.

Wer sich rasch über die Änderungen informieren möchte, die durch die Rechtschreibreform in den Dudenrichtlinien nötig wurden, wird durch die rot hervorgehobenen Textstellen und Beispiele auf alle Neuregelungen hingewiesen.

Für alle diejenigen, die sich für den genauen Wortlaut der zugrunde liegenden amtlichen Regeln interessieren, wurden an geeigneten Stellen Verweise auf die Paragraphen und Unterabschnitte des Regelwerks eingearbeitet, das auf den Seiten 861 bis 910 abgedruckt ist. Wo solche Verweise fehlen, handelt es sich meist um zusätzliche Empfehlungen und Erläuterungen der Dudenredaktion oder um Bereiche, die nicht zur Rechtschreibung im engeren Sinne gehören.

Abkürzungen

Schreibung der Abkürzungen

R 1 Nach bestimmten Abkürzungen steht ein **Punkt** ‹§ 101›.

Dr. (für: Doktor)
z. B. (für: zum Beispiel)
Weißenburg i. Bay. (für: Weißenburg in Bayern)
Abk.-Verz. (für: Abkürzungsverzeichnis)
Tsd. (für: Tausend)
Pfd. (für: Pfund)
a. D. (für: außer Dienst)
i. V. (für: in Vertretung)
ppa. (für: per procura)

• Steht eine Abkürzung mit Punkt am Satzende, dann ist der Abkürzungspunkt zugleich Schlusspunkt des Satzes ‹§ 103›.

Er verwendet gern Zitate von Goethe, Schiller u. a.
Ihr Vater ist Regierungsrat a. D.

• Keinen Punkt setzt man dagegen bei so genannten Initialwörtern und Kürzeln ‹§102 (2)›.

BGB (gesprochen: be-ge-be, für: Bürgerliches Gesetzbuch)
TÜV (gesprochen: tüf, für: Technischer Überwachungs-Verein)
Na (gesprochen: en-a, für: Natrium)

● Ebenfalls ohne Punkt schreibt man national oder international festgelegte Abkürzungen der metrischen Maße und Gewichte, der Einheiten in Naturwissenschaft und Technik, der Himmelsrichtungen und der meisten Währungseinheiten ‹§ 102 (1)›.

m (für: Meter)
g (für: Gramm)
NO (für: Nordost[en])
DM (für: Deutsche Mark)

● Auch bei fachsprachlichen Abkürzungen vor allem von längeren Zusammensetzungen und Wortgruppen steht im Allgemeinen kein Punkt ‹§ 102 E_1›.

RücklVO (für: Rücklagenverordnung)
LadschlG (für: Ladenschlussgesetz)
BStMdI (für: Bayerisches Staatsministerium des Innern)

In manchen Fällen gibt es Doppelformen ‹§ 102 E_2›.

Co, Co. (gesprochen: ko, für: Compagnie, Kompanie)
AG, A. G. (gesprochen a-ge, für: Atomgewicht)

● Steht am Satzende eine Abkürzung, die an sich ohne Punkt geschrieben wird, dann muss trotzdem der Schlusspunkt gesetzt werden.

Diese Bestimmung finden Sie im BGB.

Beugung der Abkürzungen

R 2 Bei Abkürzungen, die im vollen Wortlaut gesprochen werden, wird die **Beugungsendung im Schriftbild** meist nicht wiedergegeben.

lfd. J. (= laufenden Jahres)
d. M. (= dieses Monats)
im Ndl. (= im Niederländischen)
des Jh., auch: *Jh.s* (= des Jahrhunderts)

Wenn man die Beugungsendungen wiedergeben will, z. B. um Missverständnisse zu vermeiden, gilt Folgendes:
Endet eine Abkürzung mit dem letzten Buchstaben des abgekürzten Wortes, so wird die Beugungsendung unmittelbar angehängt.

die Bde. (= die Bände)

Bei Namen ist es üblich, die Endung nach dem Abkürzungspunkt zu setzen.

B.s Reden (= Bismarcks Reden)

Gelegentlich wird der Plural durch Buchstabenverdoppelung ausgedrückt.

Jgg. (= Jahrgänge)
ff. (= folgende [Seiten])

● Abkürzungen, die auch als solche gesprochen werden, bleiben im Singular oft ohne Beugungsendung.

des Pkw (auch: *des Pkws*)
des EKG (auch: *des EKGs*)

Im Plural ist die Beugung häufiger, besonders bei den weiblichen Abkürzungen, weil bei ihnen der Artikel im Singular und Plural gleich lautet.

die Lkws, neben: *die Lkw* (weil im Singular: der Lkw)
die GmbHs, selten: *die GmbH* (weil der Singular gleich lautet: die GmbH)

Weitere Hinweise: ↑Apostroph (R 15, 17 u. 18), ↑Bindestrich (R 26), ↑Groß- und Kleinschreibung (R 59 u. 60) und in den Abschnitten ↑Maschinenschreiben (S. 75) und ↑Schriftsatz (S. 65).

Abschnittsgliederung

R 3 Bei der Abschnittsgliederung **mit Ziffern**[1] steht zwischen den Zahlen ein Punkt.

Nach der jeweils letzten Zahl wird kein Punkt gesetzt.

1 Punkt
2 Komma
2.1 Komma zwischen Satzteilen
2.1.1 Komma bei Aufzählungen
2.1.2 Komma bei Einschüben
2.2 Komma zwischen Sätzen

In dieser Form werden die Abschnittsnummern auch im fortlaufenden Text angeführt.

Es gilt das unter 1.1.4.3 Gesagte.

Vgl. hierzu auch die Abschnitte 1.4.3 und 1.4.4.

[1] Vgl. Normblatt DIN 1421, Gliederung und Benummerung von Texten; Abschnitte, Absätze, Aufzählungen.

R 4 Bei der Abschnittsgliederung **mit Ziffern und Buchstaben** steht der Punkt nach römischen und arabischen Zahlen und nach Großbuchstaben.

Kleinbuchstaben dagegen erhalten gewöhnlich eine Klammer.

I. Groß- und Kleinschreibung
A. Großschreibung
1. Satzanfänge
2. Nach Doppelpunkt
a) Groß schreibt man ...
b) Groß schreibt man ...

Werden solche Abschnittskennzeichen im fortlaufenden Text angeführt, dann sollten Punkt oder Klammer entfallen.

Wie schon in Kapitel I erwähnt, ist die unter 3 a genannte Ansicht überholt.

Adjektiv (Eigenschaftswort)

Zur Deklination (Beugung) des Adjektivs und des Partizips

Für jedes Adjektiv oder Partizip, das als Beifügung (Attribut) verwendet wird, gibt es eine starke und eine schwache Deklination. Wird das Adjektiv oder Partizip stark gebeugt, so hat es dieselben Endungen wie der gebeugte bestimmte Artikel; die schwache Deklination ist gekennzeichnet durch die Endung -en im Genitiv (Wesfall) und Dativ (Wemfall) Singular und in allen Formen des Plurals. Entsprechendes gilt für substantivierte Adjektive und Partizipien.

R 5 Das Adjektiv oder Partizip wird **stark gebeugt,** wenn es allein vor einem Substantiv steht oder wenn der unbestimmte Artikel, ein Pronomen (Fürwort) oder ein Zahlwort ohne starke Endung vorangeht.

guter Wein, gute Fahrt, gutes Wetter; mit rotem Kopf, mit roter Nase, mit rotem Gesicht; ein (mein, dein, sein, unser[1]*, euer*[1]*, ihr, kein) an das Amt gerichtetes Schreiben; viel (wenig) frisches Gemüse; es sind anständige Menschen, die Hilfe anständiger Menschen*

Auch substantivierte Adjektive und Partizipien werden stark gebeugt, wenn sie allein stehen oder wenn der unbestimmte Artikel, ein Pronomen oder ein Zahlwort ohne starke Endung vorangeht.

ein Jüngerer, mein Lieber, viel Neues, mit Gebratenem, Unglaubliches ist geschehen, das hat auch sein Gutes, drei Geschädigte, du Ärmster

● Das Adjektiv oder Partizip wird aber schwach gebeugt nach den Personalpronomen „wir“ und „ihr“ und (schwankend) nach „mir“ und „dir“.

wir netten Leute, ihr lieben Kinder, wir Armen!

weiblich: *mir/dir armen* (selten: *armer*) *Frau; mir Armen* (selten: *Armer*)
männlich: *mir/dir jungem* (auch: *jungen*) *Mann; mir Unglücklichem* (auch: *Unglücklichen*)

Nur schwach wird heute im Genitiv vor männlichen und sächlichen Substantiven gebeugt.

frohen Sinnes, reinen Gemütes

R 6 Das Adjektiv oder Partizip wird **schwach gebeugt,** wenn der bestimmte Artikel, ein Pronomen (Fürwort) oder ein Zahlwort mit starker Endung vorangeht.

der (dieser, jener, jeder, mancher) gute Freund, des (dieses, jenes, meines, unseres, keines) kleinen Hauses, in dem (einem, meinem, unserem, euerem) geliehenen Auto, die (meine, unsere, keine) wohlhabenden Verwandten

Dasselbe gilt für substantivierte Adjektive und Partizipien.

die Guten, unsere Bekannten, dieser Vermisste, die Arbeit zweier Angestellten (seltener: *Angestellter*)

Nach „zweier“ und „dreier“ (Genitiv von „zwei“ und „drei“) wird jedoch das Adjektiv oder Partizip heute meist stark gebeugt, wenn es nicht substantiviert ist.

die Spielsachen dreier kleiner (seltener: *kleinen*) *Kinder*

[1] Das -er in „unser“ und „euer“ gehört zum Wortstamm und ist daher keine Beugungsendung.

> **R 7** Mehrere Adjektive oder Partizipien, die vor einem Substantiv stehen, werden **parallel,** d. h. in gleicher Weise, **gebeugt.**

der tiefe, breite Graben
ein tiefer, breiter Graben
nach langem, schwerem Leiden
der Wert hoher künstlerischer Leistungen
mit gutem französischem Rotwein

Im Dativ Singular wird bei Adjektiven, die vor einem männlichen oder sächlichen Substantiv stehen, das zweite Adjektiv gelegentlich auch schwach gebeugt.

auf schwarzem hölzernem (auch: *hölzernen*) *Sockel; mit dunklem bayrischem* (auch: *bayrischen*) *Bier*

Entsprechendes gilt, wenn substantivierte Adjektive oder Partizipien eine adjektivische Beifügung bei sich haben. Jedoch überwiegt im Dativ Singular die schwache Beugung des Substantivs.

der gute Bekannte; ein guter Bekannter; mit überraschendem Neuen (auch: *Neuem*)

Die Deklination des Adjektivs oder Partizips nach unbestimmten Pronomen und Zahlwörtern ist schwankend; vgl. deshalb das Wörterverzeichnis, z. B. unter „all“, „solch“, „folgend“.

Weitere Hinweise: ↑Bindestrich (R 27), ↑Getrennt- und Zusammenschreibung (R 39 f. u. 43), ↑Groß- und Kleinschreibung (R 47 u. 55 ff.), ↑Namen (R 93 f., 96 u. 105 f.).

Adresse (Anschrift)

↑Hinweise für das Maschinenschreiben (S. 75)

Adverb (Umstandswort)

↑Getrennt- und Zusammenschreibung (R 38 f. u. 41), ↑Groß- und Kleinschreibung (R 49)

Akkusativ (Wenfall)

↑Substantiv (R 126)

Aneinanderreihungen

↑Bindestrich (R 28), ↑Getrennt- und Zusammenschreibung (R 44)

Anführungszeichen (Gänsefüßchen)

> **R 8** Anführungszeichen stehen vor und hinter einer **wörtlich wiedergegebenen Äußerung** (direkten Rede) ‹§ 89 (1)›.

Sokrates sagte: „Ich weiß, dass ich nichts weiß.“

Dies gilt auch für wörtlich wiedergegebene Gedanken und wörtlich angeführte Textstellen (Zitate) aus Büchern, Schriftstücken, Briefen u. a. ‹§ 89 (2)›.

„Wenn nur schon alles vorüber wäre“, dachte Petra.
Sie schreibt in ihren Memoiren: „Nie werde ich den Tag vergessen, an dem der erste Zeppelin über der Stadt schwebte.“

Wird eine angeführte direkte Rede oder ein Zitat unterbrochen, so werden die einzelnen Teile in Anführungszeichen gesetzt.

„Wir sollten nach Hause gehen“, meinte er. „Hier ist jede Diskussion zwecklos.“
„Der Mensch“, so heißt es in diesem Buch, „ist ein Gemeinschaftswesen.“

> **R 9** Anführungszeichen stehen vor und hinter **zitierten Überschriften, Titeln von Büchern, Filmen, Gedichten, Namen von Zeitungen** u. Ä. ‹§ 94 (1)›.

„Der Biberpelz“ ist eine Komödie von Gerhart Hauptmann. Dieser Artikel stand in der Wochenzeitung „Die Zeit“.

● Der zu einem Titel gehörende Artikel kann mit in die Anführungszeichen gesetzt werden, wenn der volle Titel unverändert bleibt.

Wir mussten „Das Lied von der Glocke“ (oder: *das „Lied von der Glocke“*) *auswendig lernen.*

Ändert sich der Artikel durch die Deklination, dann bleibt er außerhalb der Anführungszeichen.

Es war ein Zitat aus dem „Lied von der Glocke“. Sie arbeitet in der Redaktion der „Zeit“.

Weglassen kann man die Anführungszeichen, wenn eindeutig erkennbar ist, dass ein Titel, eine Gedichtüberschrift o. Ä. vorliegt.

Goethes Faust wurde schon mehrfach verfilmt.

R 10 Anführungszeichen dienen zur **Hervorhebung** einzelner Wortteile, Wörter oder Textteile (z. B. Sprichwörter, Fachwörter) ‹§ 94 (2, 3)›.

Das Wort „fälisch" ist in Anlehnung an West„falen" gebildet. Viele verwenden den Begriff „Sozialethik", ohne sich darunter etwas vorstellen zu können. Das Sprichwort „Geteiltes Leid ist halbes Leid" tröstet nicht immer. Mit einem lauten „Mir reichts" verließ sie den Raum. Mit den Worten „Mehr sein als scheinen" hat Schlieffen Moltke charakterisiert.

Gelegentlich stehen Anführungszeichen auch zur ironischen Hervorhebung ‹§ 94 (4)›.
Er hat „nur" 2 Millionen auf dem Konto. Dieser „treue Freund" verriet ihn als Erster.

R 11 Eine **Anführung innerhalb einer Anführung** wird durch halbe Anführungszeichen deutlich gemacht ‹§ 95›.

„Gehen wir doch ins Kino, heute läuft ‚Der Untergang des Römischen Reiches'", schlug sie vor. Er schreibt in seinem Brief: „Ich kann euch nur empfehlen, den ‚Fänger im Roggen' selbst einmal zu lesen."

R 12 Treffen **Punkt, Frage- oder Ausrufezeichen mit Anführungszeichen** zusammen, so stehen sie vor dem Schlusszeichen, wenn sie zur wörtlich wiedergegebenen Äußerung oder angeführten Textstelle gehören ‹§ 90›.

Wenn nach der wörtlichen Rede oder nach der angeführten Textstelle der übergeordnete Satz folgt oder weitergeführt wird, setzt man ein Komma nach dem schließenden Anführungszeichen ‹§ 93›.

„Wie geht es dir?", sprach er ihn an. Sie fragte: „Weshalb darf ich das nicht?", und schaute mich wütend an. „Bleib sofort stehen!", brüllte er. Als er mich fragte: „Weshalb darf ich das nicht?", war ich sehr verlegen.

Beendet die wörtliche Rede oder die angeführte Textstelle den übergeordneten Satz, dann steht kein Punkt mehr nach dem Schlusszeichen ‹§ 92›.

Er erwiderte: „Das muss jeder selbst entscheiden." Er schrie: „Pass auf!" Sie fragte: „Bist du bereit?"

In allen anderen Fällen stehen Punkt, Frage- und Ausrufezeichen nach dem Schlusszeichen.

Ich habe erst die „Buddenbrooks" gelesen und dann den „Zauberberg". Wer kennt das Theaterstück „Der Stellvertreter"? Kennst du den Roman „Quo vadis?"? Ich brauche dringend den Text der Oper „Figaros Hochzeit"! Lass doch dieses ewige „Ich will nicht!"!

● Ein eingeschobener Satz wird in Kommas eingeschlossen ‹§ 93›.

„Morgen früh", versprach sie, „komme ich zurück."

Vor dem Komma verliert der angeführte Satz seinen Schlusspunkt ‹§ 92›.

„Das weiß ich nicht", antwortete sie. „Wenn du erwachsen bist, wirst du das verstehen", sagte Großvater.

Weitere Hinweise: ↑Groß- und Kleinschreibung (R 59), ↑Richtlinien für den Schriftsatz (S. 65).

Anmerkungszeichen

↑Richtlinien für den Schriftsatz (S. 66)

Anrede

↑Ausrufezeichen (R 21), ↑Groß- und Kleinschreibung (R 52 f.), ↑Komma (R 65)

Anschrift

↑Hinweise für das Maschinenschreiben (S. 75)

Apostroph (Auslassungszeichen)

Der Apostroph deutet an, dass Laute oder Buchstaben, die gewöhnlich gesprochen oder geschrieben werden, ausgelassen worden sind.

R 13 Der Apostroph kennzeichnet **Wörter mit Auslassungen,** wenn die verkürzten Wortformen sonst schwer lesbar oder missverständlich wären ‹§ 96 (2)›.

Diese Formen treten oft in dichterischen Texten auf.

Dass aber der Wein von Ewigkeit sei, daran zweifl' ich nicht ...
Schlaf nun selig und süß, schau im Traum 's Paradies.
Das Wasser rauscht', das Wasser schwoll ...

Die verkürzten Formen sind auch am Satzanfang klein zu schreiben.

's (Es) *ist unglaublich!*

Kein Apostroph steht im Allgemeinen bei Adjektiven und unbestimmten Pronomen, die ungebeugt bleiben.

gut Wetter, solch Glück, manch lieber Freund, ein einzig Wort

• Es steht in der Regel auch kein Apostroph bei Verschmelzungen aus Präposition (Verhältniswort) und Artikel, die allgemein gebräuchlich sind.

Präposition + das:
ans, aufs, durchs, fürs, hinters, ins, übers, ums, unters, vors

Präposition + dem:
am, beim, hinterm, überm, unterm, vorm, zum

Präposition + den:
hintern, übern, untern, vorn

Präposition + der:
zur

Bei umgangssprachlichen und mundartlichen Verschmelzungen kann zur Verdeutlichung ein Apostroph gesetzt werden ‹§ 97›.

Er sitzt auf'm (auf dem) *Tisch. Wir gehen in'n* (in den) *Zirkus.*

• Es steht kein Apostroph für das ausgelassene Schluss-e bei Substantiven und bestimmten Verbformen.

Der Wahn ist kurz, die Reu ist lang.
Das hör ich gern. Ich lass das nicht zu. Ich stoß ihn weg. Ich werd kommen. Behüt dich Gott! Könnt ich das nur erreichen!
bleib!, geh!, trink!, lass!, leg den Mantel ab!, führ den Hund aus!

Es steht auch kein Apostroph bei den kürzeren Formen einiger Substantive, Adjektive und Adverbien, die als gleichberechtigte Nebenformen gelten und (auch in der Standardsprache) allgemein üblich sind.

Bursch neben *Bursche, Hirt* neben *Hirte, blöd, bös, fad, gern, heut, leis, öd, trüb* neben *blöde* usw.

• Ein Apostroph kann bei der schriftlichen Wiedergabe gesprochener Sprache zur Verdeutlichung gesetzt werden ‹§ 97›.

So 'n (ein) *Blödsinn! Wissen S'* (Sie) *schon?*

Im Gegensatz zu „'nauf", „'naus" usw. (statt „hinauf", „hinaus" usw.) werden die mit -r anlautenden Kürzungen heute im Allgemeinen ohne Apostroph geschrieben.

Runter vom Balkon! Reich mir mal das Buch rüber! Er ließ ihn rauswerfen. Was für ein Reinfall!

R 14 Der Apostroph wird gelegentlich gebraucht, um die Grundform eines Namens **vor der Adjektivendung -sch** zu verdeutlichen ‹§ 97 E›.

die Grimm'schen Märchen (aber: *die grimmschen Märchen*)

Vgl. auch R 17 u. R 94.

R 15 Der Apostroph steht bei Wörtern mit **längeren Auslassungen im Wortinneren** ‹§ 96 (3)›.

Lu'hafen (= Ludwigshafen [am Rhein])
D'dorf (= Düsseldorf)
Ku'damm (= Kurfürstendamm)

R 16 Kein Apostroph steht, wenn ein **unbetontes -e- im Wortinnern** ausfällt und die kürzere Form des Wortes (auch in der Standardsprache) allgemein gebräuchlich ist.

ich wechsle (wechsele), *du tratst* (tratest), *auf verlornem* (verlorenem) *Posten, Abrieglung* (Abriegelung), *Wandrer* (Wanderer), *Englein* (Engelein), *wacklig* (wackelig), *wässrig* (wässerig), *edle* (edele) *Menschen, finstre* (finstere) *Gestalten, trockner* (trockener) *Boden, unsre* (unsere) *Verfassung*

Dies gilt auch für einige Wörter und Namensformen mundartlicher Herkunft.

Brettl, Dirndl, Hansl, Rosl

Bei ungebräuchlichen Auslassungen dagegen gilt R 13.

g'nug (genug), *Bau'r* (Bauer)

R 17 Der Apostroph steht zur Kennzeichnung des Genitivs (Wesfalls) von artikellos gebrauchten **Namen, die auf s, ss, ß, tz, z, x enden** ⟨§ 96 (1)⟩.

Hans Sachs' Gedichte, Aristoteles' Schriften, Le Mans' Umgebung, Grass' Blechtrommel, Voß' Übersetzung, Ringelnatz' Gedichte, Marx' Philosophie, das Leben Johannes' des Täufers

● Kein Apostroph steht in der Regel vor dem Genitiv-s von Namen, auch nicht, wenn sie abgekürzt werden.

Brechts Dramen (B.s Dramen), Bismarcks Politik, Hamburgs Hafen, Heidis Briefe

Gelegentlich wird in solchen Fällen ein Apostroph gesetzt, um die Grundform eines Namens zu verdeutlichen ⟨§ 97 E⟩.

Andrea's Blumenecke

R 18 Kein Apostroph steht bei **Abkürzungen** in der Genitiv- oder Pluralform auf -s.

des Lkws, die MGs, die GmbHs

Vgl. hierzu R 2.

Apposition (Beisatz)

↑Komma (R 67 f.)

Attribut (Beifügung)

↑Komma (R 67)

Aufforderungssatz

↑Ausrufezeichen (R 20), ↑Punkt (R 111)

Aufzählungen

↑Doppelpunkt (R 30), ↑Komma (R 63)

Auslassung von Buchstaben

↑Apostroph (R 13 ff.)

Auslassungspunkte

R 19 Drei Auslassungspunkte zeigen an, dass **in einem Wort, Satz oder Text Teile ausgelassen worden sind** ⟨§ 99⟩.

Leck mich am ...! Ihr verdammten Schwei... Der Horcher an der Wand ...

Er gab mit lauter Stimme den Takt an: „Eins – zwei, eins – zwei ..." „Das Straßenverkehrsaufkommen hat sich durch den mit der zunehmenden Industrieproduktion angestiegenen Güterverkehr ... stark erhöht."

Beim Abbruch einer Rede kann an Stelle der Auslassungspunkte auch ein Gedankenstrich stehen (vgl. R 36).

● Stehen Auslassungspunkte am Satzende, dann entfällt der Schlusspunkt ⟨§ 100⟩.

Ich würde es dir sagen, wenn ...

Frage- und Ausrufezeichen werden jedoch gesetzt.

Ist er denn noch ...? Dass dich der ...!

Weiteres: ↑Hinweise für den Schriftsatz (S. 66).

Auslassungssatz

↑Komma (R 81)

Auslassungszeichen

↑Apostroph

Ausrufewort (Interjektion)

↑Ausrufezeichen (R 20), ↑Groß- und Kleinschreibung (R 49), ↑Komma (R 66)

Ausrufezeichen

R 20 Das Ausrufezeichen steht nach **Ausrufen und Ausrufesätzen,** nach **Aufforderungs- bzw. Befehlssätzen** und nach **Wunschsätzen** ⟨§ 69⟩.

Oh! Schade! Welch ein Glück! Das ist herrlich! Umwelt in Gefahr! (Schlagzeile) *„Pfui!", rief sie entrüstet.*
Halt den Mund! Verlassen Sie sofort den Raum, wenn Sie sich nicht anständig benehmen können! Hätte er doch besser aufgepasst! Rauchen verboten! Einfahrt frei halten!

Dies gilt im Allgemeinen auch bei Grußformeln und Glückwünschen.

Guten Tag! Prosit Neujahr!

Folgen mehrere Ausrufewörter (Interjektionen) aufeinander, dann steht das Ausrufezeichen in der Regel erst hinter dem letzten Ausrufewort ⟨§ 69 E_1⟩.

Na, na, na! „Nein, nein!", rief er.

Liegt aber auf jedem Ausrufewort ein besonderer Nachdruck, dann steht hinter jedem ein Ausrufezeichen.

„Na! Na! Passen Sie doch auf!“ Nein! Nein! Und noch einmal: Nein!

● Ein Ausrufewort, das eng zu dem folgenden Satz gehört, wird nicht durch ein Ausrufezeichen abgetrennt. Man setzt in der Regel ein Komma oder auch gar kein Satzzeichen. (Vgl. R 66.)

Au, das tut weh! He, was machen Sie da? Ach lassen wir das. Ei was soll ich tun?

● Es steht auch kein Ausrufezeichen nach Aufforderungs- und Wunschsätzen, die ohne Nachdruck gesprochen werden oder von einem Aussage- oder Fragesatz abhängig sind.

Servieren Sie jetzt bitte den Nachtisch. Er befahl ihm, er solle sich auf den Boden legen. Hast du ihm gesagt, er solle kommen?

Nach Ausrufesätzen, die die Form einer Frage haben, kann ein Ausrufezeichen gesetzt werden.

Wie lange soll ich denn noch warten!

R 21 Das Ausrufezeichen steht in der Regel nach der herausgehobenen **Anrede** ⟨§ 69 E_2 (2)⟩.

Herr Präsident! Meine sehr geehrten Damen und Herren!

Auch nach der einleitenden Anrede in Briefen und in anderen Schriftstücken kann ein Ausrufezeichen gesetzt werden ⟨§ 69 E_3⟩.

Sehr geehrte Frau Schmidt!
Gestern erhielt ich die Nachricht ...

(Heute ist hier das Komma üblich, vgl. R 65.)

Kein Ausrufezeichen steht am Briefschluss hinter Wendungen wie „Hochachtungsvoll“ oder „Mit herzlichem Gruß“.

... wünschen wir Ihnen viel Erfolg.

Mit freundlichen Grüßen
Ihr Arbeitsamt

R 22 Nach **Angaben, die man bezweifelt oder hervorheben will,** steht gelegentlich ein eingeklammertes Ausrufezeichen.

Nach Zeugenaussagen hatte der Angeklagte 24 (!) Schnäpse getrunken, bevor er sich ans Steuer setzte. Alle drei Einbrecher arbeiteten früher als Schweißer (!) und galten als tüchtige Fachleute.

Weitere Hinweise: ↑ Anführungszeichen (R 12), ↑ Klammern (R 61).

Befehlssatz
↑ Ausrufezeichen (R 20)

Beifügung (Attribut)
↑ Komma (R 67)

Beisatz (Apposition)
↑ Komma (R 67 f.)

Beistrich
↑ Komma

Beugung (Deklination)
↑ Adjektiv (R 5 ff.), ↑ Maß-, Mengen- und Münzbezeichnungen (R 90), ↑ Namen (R 98 ff.), ↑ Substantiv (R 124 ff.)

Binde-s
↑ Fugen-s

Bindestrich
Bindestrich zur Ergänzung: R 23
Bindestrich zur Hervorhebung: R 24–27
Bindestrich zur Aneinanderreihung: R 28

Bindestrich zur Ergänzung (Ergänzungs[binde]strich)

R 23 Wird in zusammengesetzten oder abgeleiteten Wörtern ein **gemeinsamer Bestandteil eingespart,** so wird als Ergänzungszeichen ein Bindestrich (Ergänzungsstrich) gesetzt ⟨§ 98 (1, 2)⟩.

Feld- und Gartenfrüchte, Ein- und Ausgang, Rechtschreibreform-Befürworter und -Kritiker, Lederherstellung und -vertrieb, Balkon-, Garten- und Campingmöbel, Geld- und andere Sorgen; saft- und kraft-

los; bergauf und -ab, ein- bis zweimal, 1- bis 2-mal, drei- oder mehrfach; herbeirufen und -winken, ab- und zunehmen (abnehmen und zunehmen), aber: *ab und zu nehmen* (gelegentlich nehmen)

Eine getrennt geschriebene Fügung darf hierbei keinen Bindestrich (Ergänzungsstrich) erhalten.

öffentliche und Privatmittel, aber: *Privat- und öffentliche Mittel*

● Zwei Bindestriche (Ergänzungsstriche) stehen, wenn eine doppelte Einsparung vorliegt ‹§ 98 (3)›.

Warenein- und -ausgang (für: Wareneingang und Warenausgang), *Textilgroß- und -einzelhandel*

Bindestrich zur Hervorhebung

R 24 **Zusammengesetzte Wörter** werden gewöhnlich ohne Bindestrich geschrieben.

Windschutzscheibe, Oberstudiendirektor, Lohnsteuerzahlung, splitterfasernackt, Rotwild, ichbezogen, Jawort, Jazzmusiker, Farbmonitor, Nildelta, moskaufreundlich, Dieselmotor, nasskalt, Sollbestand

Das gilt auch für Wörter aus dem Englischen.

Happyend, Cornedbeef, Software

● Zur Hervorhebung einzelner Bestandteile von Zusammensetzungen kann ein Bindestrich gesetzt werden ‹§ 45 (1)›.

Ich-Sucht (neben: *Ichsucht*); *Soll-Stärke* (neben: *Sollstärke*); *die Hoch-Zeit der Renaissance; etwas be-greifen*

Vgl. auch R 33.

● Einen Bindestrich kann man in unübersichtlichen Zusammensetzungen setzen ‹§ 45 (2)›.

Unübersichtlich ist eine Zusammensetzung zum Beispiel dann, wenn nicht deutlich ist, wo die Haupttrennfuge liegen soll. Diese wird dann durch den Bindestrich festgelegt.

Quecksilberdampf-Lampe
(neben: *Quecksilberdampflampe*)
Umsatzsteuer-Tabelle
(neben: *Umsatzsteuertabelle*)
Leichtathletik-Länderkampf
(neben: *Leichtathletikländerkampf*)

● Einen Bindestrich kann man auch setzen, wenn Missverständnisse auftreten können ‹§ 45 (3)›.

Druck-Erzeugnis (Erzeugnis einer Druckerei)
oder: *Drucker-Zeugnis* (Zeugnis eines Druckers)

● Ein Bindestrich kann auch beim Zusammentreffen von drei gleichen Buchstaben in Zusammensetzungen gesetzt werden ‹§ 45 (4)›.

Kaffee-Ersatz (neben: *Kaffeeersatz*), *Tee-Ernte* (neben: *Teeernte*), *Hawaii-Insel* (neben: *Hawaiiinsel*); *Schiff-Fahrt* (neben: *Schifffahrt*), *Auspuff-Flamme* (neben: *Auspuffflamme*), *Schnee-erhellt* (neben: *schneeerhellt*), *See-erfahren* (neben: *seeerfahren*)

Vgl. auch R 45.

R 25 Ein Bindestrich steht in Zusammensetzungen mit einzelnen **Buchstaben, Ziffern und Formelzeichen** ‹§ 40 (1, 3)›.

i-Punkt, A-Dur, a-Moll, O-Beine, x-beliebig, T-Shirt, Dehnungs-h, Super-G, Fugen-s; n-Eck, γ-Strahlen; 3-Tonner, 8-Zylinder, 5-mal, 100-prozentig, 17-jährig, die 17-Jährige

Vor Nachsilben steht nur dann ein Bindestrich, wenn sie mit einem Einzelbuchstaben verbunden werden ‹§ 41›.

n-fach, n-tel, die x-te Wurzel

Aber: *3fach, der 68er, 32stel, 5%ig*

Vgl. auch R 44.

R 26 Ein Bindestrich steht in Zusammensetzungen mit **Abkürzungen** ‹§ 40 (2)›.

Kfz-Papiere, UKW-Sender, VIP-Lounge, Lungen-Tbc, ABC-Staaten, US-amerikanisch, km-Zahl, Tbc-krank, Rh-Faktor

Ein Bindestrich steht auch bei abgekürzten Zusammensetzungen.

Masch.-Schr. (= Maschine[n]schreiben)
Ausk.-Büro (= Auskunftsbüro)
Reg.-Rat (= Regierungsrat)
Abt.-Leiter (= Abteilungsleiter)
röm.-kath. (= römisch-katholisch)

• Kein Bindestrich steht aber bei Zusammensetzungen mit Kurzformen und bei Ableitungen von Abkürzungen ‹§ 40 (2) E›.

Bushaltestelle, Lokführer
FKKler

R 27 In **Zusammensetzungen aus gleichrangigen Adjektiven** kann ein Bindestrich gesetzt werden ‹§ 45›.

eine süß-saure (neben: *süßsaure) Soße*

Bei längeren Zusammensetzungen ist der Bindestrich einer Zusammenschreibung vorzuziehen.

ein heiter-verspielter Roman, die südost-nordwestliche Richtung, die griechisch-orthodoxe Kirche, geistig-kulturelle Strömungen

Vgl. hierzu auch R 106.

• Kein Bindestrich steht jedoch, wenn das erste Wort verstärkende Funktion hat oder das zweite näher bestimmt.

ein bitterböser Brief, nasskaltes Wetter

• Auch zusammengesetzte Farbbezeichnungen werden in der Regel ohne Bindestrich geschrieben.

ein blaugelbes Emblem, ein schwarzweiß verzierter Rand, ein Foto in Schwarzweiß

Bei unübersichtlichen Zusammensetzungen können Bindestriche gesetzt werden.

die blauweißrote (auch: *blau-weiß-rote*) *Fahne*

Die Schreibung ist in diesen Fällen unabhängig von der Bedeutung der Farbbezeichnung.
Endet die erste Farbbezeichnung auf -lich, wird jedoch nach R 40 getrennt geschrieben.

grünlich blau, gelblich rot

Bindestrich zur Aneinanderreihung

R 28 In einer **Aneinanderreihung** werden alle Wörter durch Bindestriche verbunden (durchgekoppelt). Als Aneinanderreihungen gelten Zusammensetzungen aus Wortgruppen wie in den folgenden Beispielen ‹§ 44›.

September-Oktober-Heft, Magen-Darm-Katarrh, Nord-Süd-Dialog, Ritter-und-Räuber-Romane, Frage-und-Antwort-Spiel, Mund-zu-Mund-Beatmung, Do-it-yourself-Bewegung, Make-up, Go-in, Go-go-Girl, In-dubio-pro-reo-Grundsatz, Links-rechts-Kombination, Schlaf-wach-Rhythmus, Sankt-Josefs-Kirche, Georg-Büchner-Preis, Dortmund-Ems-Kanal, das Entweder-oder, Chrom-Molybdän-legiert, das Als-ob, das Sowohl-als-auch

Bindestriche stehen auch, wenn ein einzelner Buchstabe oder eine Abkürzung an Stelle eines Wortes steht.

A-Dur-Tonleiter, Vitamin-C-haltig, ABC-Waffen-frei, E.-T.-A.-Hoffmann-Straße; aber: *[DIN-]A4-Blatt* (Buchstabe und Zahl bilden eine Einheit); *Côte-d'Azur-Reise, Giro-d'Italia-Gewinner*

Bindestriche stehen auch, wenn das Grundwort mehrteilig ist.

Vertrags-Status-quo

Mit Bindestrichen durchgekoppelt wird ferner, wenn das Bestimmungs- oder Grundwort einer Zusammensetzung selbst bereits einen oder mehrere Bindestriche enthält.

Make-up-Empfehlungen
Management-Buy-out

• Auch bei mehrteiligen substantivierten Infinitiven (substantivierten Grundformen) werden alle Wörter durch Bindestriche verbunden ‹§ 43›.

das An-den-Haaren-Herbeiziehen, das Ins-Blaue-Fahren, das In-den-April-Schicken, zum Aus-der-Haut-Fahren

Aber bei einfachen Zusammensetzungen ‹§ 43 E›:

das Sichausweinen, das Motorradfahren, das Menschsein, das Infragestellen

• Auch Aneinanderreihungen mit Zahlen und Ziffern werden durch Bindestriche verbunden. Als Aneinanderreihungen gelten auch Zusammensetzungen mit Bruchzahlen.

80-Pfennig-Briefmarke, $^{3}/_{4}$-Liter-Flasche, 2-kg-Dose, 70-kW-Motor, 400-m-Lauf, 4 × 100-m-Staffel, Formel-3-Rennwagen, 1.-Klasse-Kabine, 4- bis 5-Zimmer-Wohnung, 3:1(2:0)-Sieg

Aber (bei in Worten geschriebenen Zahlen):

Dreiviertelliterflasche
Sechzigpfennigmarke

Weiter Hinweise: ↑Groß- und Kleinschreibung (R 51), ↑Namen (R 92, R 95–97, R 105 f.).

Bindewort (Konjunktion)

↑Groß- und Kleinschreibung (R 49), ↑Komma (R 69 ff.)

„bis"-Zeichen

↑Richtlinien für den Schriftsatz (S. 72)

bitte

↑Komma (R 81)

Brief

↑Ausrufezeichen (R 21), ↑Groß- und Kleinschreibung (R 52), ↑Komma (R 65), ↑Punkt (R 113), ↑Hinweise für das Maschinenschreiben (S. 75)

Buchtitel

↑Anführungszeichen (R 9), ↑Groß- und Kleinschreibung (R 54), ↑Namen (R 109), ↑Punkt (R 113)

c im Fremdwort

↑Fremdwörter (R 33)

Dativ (Wemfall)

↑Substantiv (R 124)

Datum

R 29 Der Monatstag kann bei einer Datumsangabe als Glied einer **Aufzählung** aufgefasst werden. Dann steht kein Komma hinter dem Monatsnamen. Er kann auch als **nachgestellter Beisatz** (Apposition) angesehen werden; in diesem Fall steht ein Komma hinter dem Monatsnamen. Beide Formen sind korrekt ‹§ 77 (3)›.

Die Familie kommt Montag, den 5. September an.
Die Familie kommt Montag, den 5. September, an.

- Steht bei einer Datumsangabe der Wochentag im Dativ (Wemfall) mit „am", wird der nachfolgende Monatstag gewöhnlich als nachgestellter Beisatz (Apposition) aufgefasst. Er steht dann ebenfalls im Dativ mit Komma hinter dem Monatsnamen.

Die Familie kommt am Montag, dem 5. September, an.

Auch in diesen Fällen kann das schließende Komma entfallen. Steht der Monatstag als selbstständige Zeitangabe im Akkusativ (Wenfall), entfällt das zweite Komma ebenfalls.

Die Familie kommt am Montag, dem 5. September an.
Die Familie kommt am Montag, den 5. September an.

- Steht bei einer Datumsangabe der Wochentag ohne „am", dann steht der Monatstag im Akkusativ (Wenfall).

Wir haben heute Sonntag, den 31. März.
Die Spiele beginnen nächsten Samstag, den 17. Juli.

Weitere Hinweise: ↑Komma (R 68), ↑Punkt (R 113), ↑Hinweise für das Maschinenschreiben (S. 76).

Deklination (Beugung)

↑Adjektiv (R 5 ff.), ↑Maß-, Mengen- und Währungsbezeichnungen (R 90), ↑Namen (R 98 ff.), ↑Substantiv (R 124 ff.)

Doppellaut (Diphthong)

↑Silbentrennung (R 131)

Doppelpunkt

R 30 Der Doppelpunkt steht vor **angekündigten wörtlich wiedergegebenen Äußerungen** (vor direkter Rede) ‹§ 81 (1)›.

Friedrich der Große sagte: „Ich bin der erste Diener meines Staates."

Dies gilt auch für wörtlich wiedergegebene Gedanken.

Eva dachte: „Wenn nur schon alles vorüber wäre!"

● Auch vor angekündigten Sätzen oder Satzstücken steht ein Doppelpunkt ‹§ 81 (2)›.

Das Sprichwort heißt: Der Apfel fällt nicht weit vom Stamm.
Diagnose: chronische Bronchitis.

Ebenso bei bestimmten Angaben in Formularen o. Ä.

Familienstand: verheiratet
Deutsch: gut
Heinrich von Kleist: Der zerbrochene Krug

● Auch vor angekündigten Aufzählungen steht ein Doppelpunkt ‹§ 81 (2)›.

Folgende Teile werden nachgeliefert: gebogene Rohre, Muffen, Verbindungsschläuche, Schlauchklemmen und Dichtungen.

● Der Doppelpunkt steht auch häufig vor Sätzen, die das Vorangegangene zusammenfassen oder daraus eine Folgerung ziehen ‹§ 81 (3)›.

Der Wald, die Felder, der See: All das gehörte früher einem einzigen Mann.
Du arbeitest bis spät in die Nacht, rauchst eine Zigarette nach der anderen, gehst kaum noch an die frische Luft: Du machst dich kaputt, mein Lieber!

Weitere Hinweise: ↑Groß- und Kleinschreibung (R 59).

Eigennamen
↑Namen

Eigenschaftswort
↑Adjektiv

Einzelbuchstaben
↑Bindestrich (R 25), ↑Groß- und Kleinschreibung (R 60)

Erdkundliche Namen
↑Namen (R 101 ff.)

Ergänzungs[binde]strich
↑Bindestrich (R 23)

Familien- und Personennamen
↑Namen (R 91 ff.)

Farben
↑Bindestrich (R 27), ↑Groß- und Kleinschreibung (R 47)

Fax- und Telefonnummern
↑Richtlinien für den Schriftsatz (S. 68)

Firmennamen
↑Namen (R 110)

Fragesatz
↑Fragezeichen (R 31), ↑Punkt (R 111)

Fragezeichen

R 31 Das Fragezeichen steht nach einem **direkten Fragesatz** und nach einzelnen **Fragewörtern** ‹§ 70›.

Wo wohnst du? Wie heißt du? Wie spät ist es und wie komme ich zum Bahnhof? „Weshalb darf ich das nicht?“, fragte er. Woher soll ich wissen, dass er krank ist? Dürfen wir Sie darauf hinweisen, dass die Frist morgen abläuft? Auf die Frage „Wem?“ steht der Dativ, auf die Frage „Wen?“ der Akkusativ.
Wie? Warum? Wohin?

Das Fragezeichen kann auch frei stehende Zeilen (z. B. Überschriften) als Frage kennzeichnen.

Keine Lösung in Sicht?
Wo warst du, Adam?
Hilfe für hungernde Kinder?

● Kein Fragezeichen steht nach indirekten Fragesätzen, die von einem Aussage-, Aufforderungs- bzw. Befehlssatz oder Wunschsatz abhängen.

Sie fragte, wann sie kommen solle. Sag mir, woher du das Geld hast!

Kein Fragezeichen steht nach Ausrufesätzen, die die Form einer Frage haben.

Was erlauben Sie sich!

Wird ein Fragewort nicht besonders hervorgehoben, dann setzt man ein Komma dahinter. Das Fragezeichen steht dann erst am Satzende.

Was, du bist umgezogen?
Wie denn, wo denn, was denn?

R 32 Ein eingeklammertes Fragezeichen steht gelegentlich nach **Angaben, die man bezweifelt.**

Das Mädchen behauptet, das Geld gefunden (?) zu haben.

Weitere Hinweise: ↑Anführungszeichen (R 12), ↑Groß- und Kleinschreibung (R 59), ↑Klammern (R 61).

Fremdwörter

R 33 Häufig gebrauchte Fremdwörter, vor allem solche, die keine dem Deutschen fremden Laute enthalten, können sich nach und nach der deutschen Schreibweise angleichen.

In diesen Fällen sind oft sowohl die eingedeutschten als auch die nicht eingedeutschten Schreibweisen korrekt ‹§ 20 (2), § 32 (2)›. Man sollte aber innerhalb eines Textes auf eine einheitliche Schreibung achten.

Delfin neben: *Delphin*
Exposee neben: *Exposé*
Frisör neben: *Friseur*
Grafit neben: *Graphit*
Jogurt neben: *Joghurt*
Panter neben: *Panther*

In einigen Fällen wird die eingedeutschte Schreibung bereits als die vorzuziehende Form angesehen.

Getto (auch: *Ghetto*)
Grafik (auch: *Graphik*)
differenziell (auch: *differentiell*)

• Vor allem die Wortbestandteile „phon", „phot" und „graph" werden in allgemein gebräuchlichen Wörtern häufig zu „fon", „fot" und „graf".

Mikrofon (auch: *Mikrophon*)
Fotograf (auch: *Photograph*)
Telefon (nur noch eingedeutscht)
Saxofon neben: *Saxophon*
Geografie neben: *Geographie*

Nur in wenigen Fällen wird das aus dem Griechischen stammende „rh" zu „r".

Katarr neben: *Katarrh*
Myrre neben: *Myrrhe*

• Fremdwörter, die [noch] nicht angeglichen sind, werden in der fremden Schreibweise geschrieben. Dies gilt besonders für Wörter des bildungssprachlichen und des fachspezifischen Wortschatzes.

Milieu, Jalousie, Jeans, Moiré, Computer, Breakdance, Macho; Metapher, Philosophie, polysynthetisch

• Ob c in einem Fremdwort im Zuge der Eindeutschung k oder z wird, hängt von seiner ursprünglichen Aussprache ab. Es wird in der Regel zu k vor a, o, u und vor Konsonanten (Mitlauten). Es wird zu z vor e, i, y, ä und ö.

Kopie für: *Copie*
Spektrum für: *Spectrum*
Penizillin für: *Penicillin*
Zäsur für: *Cäsur*
Zentrum für: *Centrum*
Akkusativ für: *Accusativ*

Azetat fachspr.: *Acetat*
Kalzium fachspr.: *Calcium*

• Bei fremdsprachlichen Zusammensetzungen und Wortgruppen (besonders aus dem Englischen) gelten die folgenden Empfehlungen:

Reine „Zitatwörter", die entweder sehr fachsprachlich sind oder kulturelle Einrichtungen, Sachverhalte, Ereignisse u. a. des Herkunftslandes bezeichnen, werden unverändert übernommen. Sind sie im Deutschen weniger gebräuchlich, sollte man sie mit Anführungszeichen oder anderer Schriftart kenntlich machen.

Carnegie Hall, High Church, Grand Old Lady, New Deal
Wir wurden zu einem „business lunch" eingeladen.
Sie schreibt einen Aufsatz über den „nouveau roman".
Es ist ein für die englische detective novel *typisches Handlungsmuster.*

Für gebräuchlichere Wörter und Wortgruppen gelten im Prinzip die deutschen Regeln für Groß- und Kleinschreibung, Getrennt- und Zusammenschreibung sowie Schreibung mit Bindestrich. (Fachsprachliche Schreibweisen können hiervon abweichen.)

Substantive werden großgeschrieben:
Sie mixte sich einen Drink.
Er bestellte sich einen Digestif.

Bei mehrteiligen Substantiven wird das erste Wort großgeschrieben. Das gilt auch für substantivische Bestandteile im Innern mehrteiliger Fügungen ‹§ 55 (3)›:

Sie aßen ein Cordon bleu.
Es blieb alles beim Status quo.
Hier haben wir das Corpus Delicti

Zusammensetzungen werden zusammengeschrieben:

Cocktailparty, Swimmingpool

Ist der erste Bestandteil ein Adjektiv oder Partizip, ist auch Getrenntschreibung möglich ‹§ 37 (1) E_1›:

Hotline, auch: *Hot Line; Coldcream,* auch: *Cold Cream; Standingovations,* auch: *Standing Ovations*

Besteht die Zusammensetzung aus Substantiven (oder Substantivierungen), kann (zur Verdeutlichung) ein Bindestrich gesetzt werden (vgl. R 24):

Swimming-Pool, Desktop-Publishing

Bei Aneinanderreihungen wird mit Bindestrich[en] geschrieben (vgl. R 28):

Go-go-Girl, Walkie-Talkie, Sit-in

Zusammensetzungen aus Fremdwörtern und deutschen Wörtern werden entsprechend behandelt:

Computerfachmann, Abend-Make-up

Weitere Hinweise: ↑Groß- und Kleinschreibung (R 51), ↑Worttrennung (R 130 u. 132).

Fugenzeichen

> **R 34** Fugenzeichen wie -e-, -s-, -n-, -es- oder -en- kennzeichnen die Verbindungsstelle bestimmter Zusammensetzungen.

Hundehütte, Mauseloch, Liebesdienst, Glückstag, Sonnenschein, Tannenbaum, Grabesstille, Schwanenhals, Hahnenkampf

Häufig handelt es sich um eine Beugungsendung, die in die Zusammensetzung eingegangen ist. Viele Zusammensetzungen sind jedoch in Anlehnung an bereits bestehende Muster gebildet worden. (So ist z. B. die Bischofskonferenz nicht die Konferenz eines Bischofs, sondern mehrerer Bischöfe.) Im Zweifelsfall orientiere man sich an Beispielen mit dem gleichen Bestimmungswort im Wörterverzeichnis.

In einigen Fällen stehen Zusammensetzungen mit und ohne Fugenzeichen oder mit unterschiedlichen Fugenzeichen nebeneinander.

Buchstütze	neben: *Bücherstütze*
Speisekarte	neben: *Speisenkarte*
Erbschaftssteuer	behördlich: *Erbschaftsteuer*
Rinderbraten	landschaftlich: *Rindsbraten*
Mondschein	gehoben: *Mondenschein*

● In einigen Fällen kennzeichnet das Fugenzeichen einen Bedeutungsunterschied.

Wassernot (Wassermangel), *Wassersnot* (Überschwemmungskatastrophe); *Landmann* (Bauer), *Landsmann* (jmd., der aus dem gleichen Lande stammt)

Fürwort (Pronomen)

↑Groß- und Kleinschreibung (R 48 u. 52 f.)

Fußnotenzeichen

↑Richtlinien für den Schriftsatz (S. 67)

Gänsefüßchen

↑Anführungszeichen

Gebäudenamen

↑Namen (R 110)

Gedankenstrich

> **R 35** Der Gedankenstrich steht vor und nach **eingeschobenen Satzstücken und Sätzen,** die das Gesagte erläutern oder ergänzen ‹§ 84 (3)›.

Dieses Bild – es ist das letzte und bekannteste der Künstlerin – wurde vor einigen Jahren nach Amerika verkauft.

● Hinter dem zweiten Gedankenstrich steht ein Komma, wenn es auch ohne das eingeschobene Satzstück oder den eingeschobenen Satz stehen müsste ‹§ 85›.

Sie wundern sich – so schreiben Sie –, dass ich nur selten von mir hören lasse.
Er verschweigt – leider! –, wen er mit seinem Vorwurf gemeint hat.

Schließt der eingeschobene Satz mit einem Nebensatz, einer nachgestellten genaueren Bestimmung o. Ä., dann steht am Ende des Einschubs kein Komma, weil der Gedankenstrich bereits die Trennung vom Hauptsatz übernimmt.

Philipp verließ – im Gegensatz zu seinem Vater, der 40 weite Reisen unternommen hatte – Spanien nicht mehr.

Ausrufe- und Fragezeichen bei einem eingeschobenen Satzstück oder Satz stehen vor dem zweiten Gedankenstrich.

Er behauptete – und das in aller Öffentlichkeit! –, ich hätte ihm sein Geld gestohlen.
Unsere kleine Absprache – Sie erinnern sich doch noch? – sollte besser unter uns bleiben.

Der Doppelpunkt dagegen steht nach einem eingeschobenen Satz hinter dem zweiten Gedankenstrich.

Verächtlich rief er ihm zu – er wandte kaum den Kopf dabei –: „Was willst du hier?"

R 36 Innerhalb eines Satzes kennzeichnet der Gedankenstrich eine **längere Pause.**

Dies gilt besonders zwischen Ankündigungs- und Ausführungskommando, zur Vorbereitung auf etwas Unerwartetes oder zur Erhöhung der Spannung, bei Abbruch der Rede und beim Verschweigen eines Gedankenabschlusses ⟨§ 82⟩. (Vgl. hierzu auch R 19.)

Rumpf vorwärts beugen – beugt!
Plötzlich – ein gellender Aufschrei!
„Sei still, du –!", schrie er ihn an.

Zwischen Sätzen kann der Gedankenstrich den Wechsel des Themas oder des Sprechers anzeigen ⟨§ 83⟩.

Wir sprachen in der letzten Sitzung über das Problem der Getreideversorgung. – Hat übrigens jemand inzwischen Herrn Müller gesehen?
„Mein Sohn, was birgst du so bang dein Gesicht?" – „Siehst, Vater, du den Erlkönig nicht?"

Der Gedankenstrich kann auch gesetzt werden, um die Aufmerksamkeit auf das Folgende zu lenken und dieses als bemerkenswert oder wichtig anzukündigen ⟨§ 82⟩.

Hier hilft nur noch eins – sofort operieren.
Der Wald, die Felder, der See – all das gehörte früher einem einzigen Mann.

Genitiv (Wesfall)

↑Apostroph (R 17), ↑Substantiv (R 124 u. 128)

Geographische Namen

↑Namen (R 101 ff.)

Getrennt- und Zusammenschreibung

R 37 Verbindungen mit einem Verb als zweitem Bestandteil, bei denen die Reihenfolge der Bestandteile in allen gebeugten Formen unverändert bleibt **(untrennbare Zusammensetzungen),** werden zusammengeschrieben ⟨§ 33⟩.

schlussfolgern, ich schlussfolgere, ich habe geschlussfolgert
frohlocken, ich frohlocke, ich habe frohlockt
widersprechen, ich widerspreche, ich habe widersprochen

R 38 **Verbindungen mit einem Verb,** bei denen die Reihenfolge der Bestandteile je nach der Stellung im Satz wechselt **(trennbare** bzw. **unfeste Zusammensetzungen),** werden nur im Infinitiv, in den beiden Partizipien sowie bei Endstellung im Nebensatz zusammengeschrieben ⟨§ 34⟩.

auffallen, eine auffallende Ähnlichkeit, er war ihr aufgefallen, um aufzufallen, ... weil es auffällt

Aber: *ich falle auf; auf fällt, dass ...*

fehlschlagen, der Plan ist fehlgeschlagen, ohne fehlzuschlagen, ... wenn alles fehlschlägt

Aber: *der Plan schlug fehl, fehl schlug auch der Plan ...*

• Von den Zusammensetzungen aus Adverb oder Pronominaladverb und Verb sind die Fälle zu unterscheiden, in denen ein selbstständiges Adverb oder Pronominaladverb mit einem Verb eine Wortgruppe bildet ⟨§ 34 E_1⟩.

Er soll dableiben (nicht weggehen).

Aber: *Er soll da bleiben, wo er hingehört.*

Wir sind noch einmal davongekommen.

Aber: *Die Flecken sind davon gekommen, dass ...*

Sie wird sich einer starken Opposition gegenübersehen.

Aber: *Das Haus, das Sie gegenüber sehen können ...*

Meist hilft in diesen Fällen die unterschiedliche Betonung bei der Unterscheidung zwischen Zusammensetzung (das Adverb trägt den Hauptton) und Wortgruppe (Adverb und Verb sind annähernd gleich betont).

● Bei den Adverbien „dahinter", „darin", „darüber", „darunter", „davor" gilt generell Getrenntschreibung, bei den umgangssprachlichen Kurzformen „drin", „drüber", „drauf", „drunter" jedoch auch Zusammenschreibung.

Lies mal, was darunter steht.
Lies mal, was druntersteht.
Lies mal, was drunter geschrieben steht.

Vgl. zu Einzelfällen das Wörterverzeichnis.

R 39 Für **Verbindungen mit einem Verb** als zweitem Bestandteil gilt in den im Folgenden beschriebenen Fällen **Getrenntschreibung.**

● Verbindungen mit dem Verb „sein" werden immer getrennt geschrieben ‹§ 35›.

da sein, da gewesen, dabei sein, hinüber sein

(Aber bei Substantivierung: *das Dasein, die Dabeigewesenen*)

● Ist der erste Bestandteil ein mit „-einander" oder „-wärts" gebildetes Adverb, wird immer getrennt geschrieben ‹§ 34 E_3 (2)›.

aufeinander prallen, miteinander spielen, abwärts gehen, rückwärts fahren

● Zusammengesetzte Adverbien wie die folgenden werden immer getrennt vom Verb geschrieben ‹§ 34 E_3 (2)›:

abhanden, anheim, beiseite, fürlieb, überhand, vonstatten, vorlieb, zugute, zuhanden, zunichte, zupass, zustatten, zuteil

Die Schlüssel waren ihm abhanden gekommen.

Wir müssen mit den Resten vorlieb nehmen
Ihre Hoffnungen wurden zunichte gemacht.

Vgl. auch R 38.

● Ist der erste Bestandteil eine Ableitung auf „-ig", „-isch" oder „-lich", wird immer getrennt geschrieben ‹§ 34 E_3 (3)›.

heilig sprechen, müßig gehen, ruhig bleiben, logisch denken, deutlich machen, heimlich tun

● Ist der erste Bestandteil ein Partizip, wird immer getrennt geschrieben ‹§ 34 E_3 (4)›.

rasend werden, gefangen nehmen, getrennt schreiben, verloren gehen

● Ist der erste Bestandteil ein Substantiv, das eindeutig als solches gebraucht wird, schreibt man getrennt.

Angst haben, Auto fahren, Rad fahren, Eis laufen, Schlittschuh laufen

(Aber: *schlafwandeln, teilnehmen* usw.)

● Ist der erste Bestandteil ein Verb, wird immer getrennt geschrieben ‹§ 34 E_3 (6)›.

spazieren gehen, stehen lassen, kommen lassen, sitzen bleiben, kennen lernen, schreiben lernen

● Ist der erste Bestandteil ein Adjektiv, das gesteigert oder erweitert werden kann, schreibt man getrennt ‹§ 34 E_3 (3)›.

Der Abschied ist uns leicht gefallen (wegen: leichter gefallen).

Einen Stoff [leuchtend] blau färben.

Getrennt schreibt man alle eindeutigen Wortgruppen wie „schwanger werden", „huckepack nehmen", „klein beigeben".

● In Zweifelsfällen, die nicht eindeutig zu klären sind, ist Getrennt- oder Zusammenschreibung zulässig ‹§ 34 E_4›.

R 40 Für **Verbindungen mit einem Adjektiv oder Partizip als zweitem Bestandteil** sind die folgenden Fälle zu unterscheiden.

● Man schreibt zusammen, wenn gegenüber einer entsprechenden gebräuchlichen Wortgruppe z.B. eine Präposition (ein Verhältniswort) oder ein Artikel eingespart wird ‹§ 36 (1)›.

mondbeschienen (= vom Mond beschienen), *sagenumwoben* (= von Sagen umwoben), *herzerquickend* (= das Herz erquickend), *meterhoch* (= einen/mehrere Meter hoch)

● Man schreibt dagegen getrennt, wenn der erste Bestandteil erweitert ist oder wenn bei Zusammenschreibung gegenüber der Wortgruppe kein Artikel und keine Präposition eingespart werden kann.

der Schnee lag drei Meter hoch
die Eisen verarbeitende Industrie
eine Aufsehen erregende Enthüllung

Zu unterscheiden sind Fälle wie:

eine großen Gewinn bringende Investition
eine äußerst gewinnbringende Investition
eine Furcht einflößende Gestalt
eine noch furchteinflößendere Gestalt

● Man schreibt zusammen, wenn ein zusammengeschriebenes Verb zugrunde liegt ‹§ 36 (3)›.

schlafwandelnd (wegen: schlafwandeln)
irregeleitet (wegen: irreleiten)

● Man schreibt dagegen getrennt, wenn eine getrennt geschriebene Wortgruppe zugrunde liegt ‹§ 36 E_1 (1.2)›.

die wild lebenden Tiere (wegen: wild leben)
allein stehend (wegen: allein stehen)
verloren gegangen (wegen: verloren gehen)

● Die Verbindung aus adjektivischem Partizip und Adjektiv wird getrennt geschrieben ‹§ 36 E_1 (3)›.

ein blendend weißes Kleid
kochend heißes Wasser
gestochen scharfe Fotos

● Man schreibt ebenfalls getrennt, wenn der erste Bestandteil eine Ableitung auf „-ig“, „-isch“ oder „-lich“ ist ‹§ 36 E_1 (2)›. (Eine Ausnahme bildet das Wort „richtiggehend“ in der Bedeutung „durchaus so zu nennend“.)

riesig groß, verführerisch leicht, grünlich gelb

Vgl. auch R 27.

● Man schreibt getrennt, wenn der erste Bestandteil gesteigert oder erweitert werden kann ‹§ 36 E_1 (4)›.

eine schwer verständliche Sprache

● Man schreibt zusammen, wenn der erste Bestandteil bedeutungsverstärkende oder bedeutungsmindernde Funktion hat ‹§ 36 (5)›.

bitterkalt, brandgefährlich, halbamtlich, ganzleinen, dunkelrot, hellrot, superklug

● In Zweifelsfällen, die nicht eindeutig zu klären sind, ist Getrennt- oder Zusammenschreibung zulässig ‹§ 36 E_2›.

nicht öffentlich, auch: *nichtöffentlich*
weit reichende (weiter reichende) *Befugnisse*, auch: *weitreichende* (weitreichendere) *Befugnisse*
eine wohl tuende Massage (eine Massage, die wohl tut), auch: *eine wohltuende* (wohltuendere) *Massage*

R 41 Man schreibt ein verblasstes **Substantiv mit einer Präposition (einem Verhältniswort)** zusammen, wenn die Fügung zu einer neuen Präposition oder einem Adverb geworden ist ‹§ 39›.

Wenn man die Fügung als Wortgruppe verstanden wissen will, kann man häufig auch getrennt schreiben.

(Vgl. im Einzelnen das Wörterverzeichnis.)

anstelle (auch: *an Stelle*)
aufgrund (auch: *auf Grund*)
infrage (auch: *in Frage*) *[stellen, kommen]*
zugrunde (auch: *zu Grunde*) *[gehen]*
aufseiten (auch: *auf Seiten*)

Nur zusammen schreibt man z. B.:

anstatt, inmitten, zuliebe

Nur getrennt schreibt man dagegen z. B.:

zu Ende, zu Fuß, unter der Hand

R 42 **Ableitungen auf -er von geographischen Namen** schreibt man zusammen, wenn sie Personen bezeichnen ‹§ 37 (3)›.

Schweizergarde (päpstliche Garde, die aus Schweizern besteht), *Römerbrief* (Brief an die Römer), *Danaergeschenk* (Geschenk der Danaer)

● Man schreibt solche Ableitungen getrennt, wenn sie die geographische Lage bezeichnen ‹§ 38›.

Walliser Alpen (die Alpen im Wallis), *Glatzer Neiße* (die von Glatz kommende Neiße), *Köln-Bonner Flughafen*

Besonders in Österreich und in der Schweiz wird in solchen Fällen oft zusammengeschrieben.

Böhmerwald, Wienerwald, Bielersee

Es gibt geographische Namen, die auf -er enden und keine Ableitungen der oben genannten Art sind. Diese Namen werden zusammengeschrieben ‹§ 37 (3)›.

Glocknergruppe, Brennerpass

> **R 43 Straßennamen** werden zusammengeschrieben, wenn sie aus einem ungebeugten Adjektiv und einem Grundwort zusammengesetzt sind ‹§ 37 (4)›.

Altmarkt, Neumarkt, Hochstraße

Getrennt schreibt man dagegen, wenn das Adjektiv gebeugt ist.

Große Bleiche, Langer Graben, Breite Gasse, Neue Kräme

● Getrennt schreibt man auch bei Ableitungen von Orts- und Ländernamen auf -er ‹§ 38›.

Münchener Straße

> **R 44** In Buchstaben geschriebene **Zahlen** unter einer Million werden zusammengeschrieben ‹§ 36 (6)›.

neunzehnhundertachtundneunzig,
dreiundzwanzigtausend,
tausendsechsundsechzig

● Ableitungen und Zusammensetzungen, die eine Zahl enthalten, werden zusammengeschrieben ‹§ 37 (1)›.

achtfach, achtmal, Achtpfünder, die Achtziger

Wird die Zahl in Ziffern geschrieben, setzt man bei Zusammensetzungen einen Bindestrich ‹§ 40 (3)›.

8-mal, 8-Pfünder, 8-silbig

Aber bei Ableitungen ‹§ 41 E›:

8fach, 17tel, 80er, 32stel

Bei Zusammensetzungen mit Ableitungen ‹§ 42›:

in den 90er-Jahren (auch: *90er Jahren*) *auf ein 1000stel-Gramm genau*

Bei Aneinanderreihungen werden Bindestriche gesetzt ‹§ 44›.

400-m-Lauf, 2-kg-Dose

● Getrennt schreibt man Angaben für Zahlen über eine Million ‹§ 36 (6)›.

zwei Millionen dreitausendvierhundertneunzehn, siebzehn Milliarden

In Ableitungen und Zusammensetzungen werden auch diese Zahlen zusammengeschrieben ‹§ 36 (6)›.

der einmilliardste Teil, das Dreimillionenfache

Groß- und Kleinschreibung

Großschreibung bedeutet Verwendung von großen Anfangsbuchstaben. Großbuchstaben erscheinen im Wortinnern in der Regel nur bei Abkürzungen, in Zusammensetzungen mit Bindestrich und bei genereller Schreibung in Großbuchstaben. Im Gegensatz zu anderen Sprachen ist im heutigen Deutsch die Großschreibung nicht nur auf Namen und Satzanfänge beschränkt. Es ergeben sich gelegentlich Schwierigkeiten, die auch durch ausführliche Richtlinien nicht völlig behoben werden können. In Zweifelsfällen schlage man im Wörterverzeichnis nach.

Schreibung der Substantive und ehemaligen Substantive R 45 f.
Substantivischer Gebrauch anderer Wortarten R 47–51
Anredepronomen (Anredefürwörter) R 52 f.
Titel und Namen R 54–58
Satzanfang R 59
Einzelbuchstaben und Abkürzungen R 60

Schreibung der Substantive und ehemaligen Substantive

> **R 45 Substantive** werden großgeschrieben ‹§ 55›.

Erde, Kindheit, Aktion, Verständnis, Verwandtschaft, Reichtum, Verantwortung, Genie, Rhythmus, Computer

Das gilt auch für Namen wie „Berlin", „Helmut", „Mozart" u. a.

Die Großschreibung der Substantive bleibt in der Regel auch in Zusammensetzungen mit Bindestrich erhalten ‹§ 55 (2)›.

Moskau-freundlich, Fett-triefend

Vgl. auch R 96 u. 105.

● Großgeschrieben werden auch die Bezeichnungen von Tageszeiten nach den Adverbien „vorgestern", „gestern", „heute", „morgen" und „übermorgen" ‹§ 55 (6)›.

vorgestern Abend, gestern Vormittag, heute Morgen (aber: *heute früh*), *morgen Nachmittag, übermorgen Mittag*

Vgl. aber R 46.

R 46 Aus Substantiven entstandene Wörter anderer Wortarten werden kleingeschrieben ‹§ 56 (1, 3, 4 u. 5)›.

Adverbien:
kreuz und quer, anfangs, rings, teils, mitten, morgens, abends, sonntags, willens, rechtens

Präpositionen (Verhältniswörter) und Teile von präpositionalen Fügungen:

dank, kraft, laut, statt, trotz, angesichts, namens, seitens, um ... willen

Unbestimmte Pronomen (Fürwörter) und Zahlwörter:

ein bisschen (= ein wenig)
ein paar (= einige),
aber: *ein Paar* (= zwei zusammengehörende) *Schuhe*

Bestimmte (mit „sein", „bleiben" oder „werden" verbundene) Adjektive:

Mir ist angst. Aber: *Ich habe Angst.*
Uns wurde angst und bange. Aber: *Er hat keine Bange.*
Sie ist mir gram. Aber: *Ihr Gram war groß.*
Ich bin es leid. Aber: *Es tut mir Leid.*
Du bist schuld daran. Aber: *Sie gibt ihm die Schuld daran.*

Weitere Hinweise zur Schreibung von Substantiven in festen Verbindungen mit Verben: ↑Getrennt- und Zusammenschreibung (R 37 ff.).

Substantivischer Gebrauch anderer Wortarten

R 47 Substantivisch gebrauchte **Adjektive und Partizipien** werden großgeschrieben ‹§ 57 (1)›.

das Gute, die Abgeordnete, das Nachstehende, das Schaurig-Schöne, Gutes und Böses, Altes und Neues; und Ähnliches (Abk.: *u. Ä.*); *wir haben Folgendes/das Folgende geplant; das in Kraft Getretene; das dem Schüler Bekannte; das überschaubar Gewordene; die zuletzt Genannte* (auch: *Zuletztgenannte*); *die Rat Suchenden* (auch: *Ratsuchenden*); *das dort zu Findende; Stoffe in Blau und Gelb; er ist bei Rot über die Kreuzung gefahren.*

Adjektive und Partizipien werden vor allem dann großgeschrieben, wenn sie mit Wörtern wie „allerlei", „alles", „etwas", „genug", „nichts", „viel", „wenig" in Verbindung stehen.

allerlei Schönes, alles Gewollte, etwas Wichtiges, etwas derart Banales, nichts Besonderes, wenig Angenehmes

● Großgeschrieben werden auch substantivierte Adjektive und Partizipien in festen Wortgruppen.

Es ist das Beste, wenn wir jetzt gehen. Sie hat sich nicht das Geringste vorzuwerfen. im Argen liegen, zum Guten wenden, auf dem Trockenen sitzen, im Dunkeln tappen, im Trüben fischen, auf dem Laufenden sein, ins Schwarze treffen, aufs Ganze gehen, das Weite suchen, aus dem Vollen schöpfen, zum Besten geben

● Auch nichtdeklinierte Adjektive in Paarformeln zur Bezeichnung von Personen werden großgeschrieben.

Wir bieten ein Programm für Jung und Alt
Vor dem Gesetz sind Arm und Reich gleich.
Gleich und Gleich gesellt sich gern.

● Adjektive und Partizipien, die durch einen Artikel der Form nach substantiviert sind, werden kleingeschrieben, wenn sie Beifügung (Attribut) zu einem vorangehenden oder nachgestellten Substantiv sind ‹§ 58 (1)›.

Sie war die aufmerksamste und klügste meiner Zuhörerinnen.
Mir gefallen alle Krawatten sehr gut. Besonders mag ich die gestreiften.

● Auch Superlative mit „am", nach denen man mit „wie?" fragen kann und bei denen „am" nicht in „an dem" auflösbar ist, werden kleingeschrieben ‹§ 58 (2)›.

Diese Regel ist am leichtesten zu lernen. Etwas zu essen brauchen wir am nötigsten.

Aber: *Es fehlt uns am* (= an dem) *Nötigsten.*

In festen adverbialen Wendungen aus „aufs" oder „auf das" und Superlativ, nach denen man mit „wie?" fragen kann, kann das Adjektiv groß- oder kleingeschrieben werden ‹§ 58 E_1›.

Er erschrak aufs Äußerste/aufs äußerste.

In festen adverbialen Wendungen aus Präposition und artikellosem Adjektiv wird dieses jedoch kleingeschrieben ‹§ 58 (3)›.

Die Schaulustigen wollten alles von nahem sehen. Wir hätten ohne weiteres ein Darlehen bekommen. Die Schule bleibt bis auf weiteres geschlossen.

R 48 Substantivisch gebrauchte **Pronomen (Fürwörter) und Zahlwörter** werden großgeschrieben ‹§ 57 (3, 4)›.

die Acht, sie hatte vier Einsen im Zeugnis, ein Dritter, jeder Dritte, sie war Dritte im Weitsprung, die verhängnisvolle Dreizehn, ein Achtel, ein Zweites möchte ich noch erwähnen; das vertraute Du, ein gewisser Jemand

● Sonst werden Pronomen und Zahlwörter in der Regel kleingeschrieben, in vielen Fällen auch dann, wenn sie mit einem Artikel oder Pronomen gebraucht werden oder mit den Wörtern allerlei, alles, etwas, genug, nichts, viel, wenig u. Ä. in Verbindung stehen ‹§ 58 (4, 5, 6)›.

du, ihr, man, jemand, niemand, derselbe, einer, keiner, jeder, zwei, beide; das wenigste, ein jeder, die beiden, die ersten drei, ein achtel Liter, der eine, der andere

allerlei anderes, etwas anderes, alle drei, alle beide

Die anderen wissen auch nicht Bescheid. Die wahren Hintergründe waren nur wenigen bekannt. Es gab viele, die nicht mitmachen wollten. Sie hat alles vergessen. Was manche sich so alles einbilden!

Wenn hervorgehoben werden soll, dass ein Zahladjektiv wie „viel", „wenig", „eine", „andere" nicht als ein unbestimmtes Zahlwort zu verstehen ist, kann großgeschrieben werden ‹§ 58 E_4›.

Auf der Suche nach dem Anderen (= nach einer neuen, unbekannten Welt) *sein.*
Das Lob der Vielen (= der breiten Masse) *war ihr nicht wichtig.*

● In Verbindung mit dem bestimmten Artikel o. Ä. können Possessivpronomen (besitzanzeigende Fürwörter) auch großgeschrieben werden ‹§ 58 E_3›.

Jedem das seine/Seine. Wir haben das unsere/Unsere zur Finanzierung des Projekts geleistet.

● Kardinalzahlen unter einer Million werden kleingeschrieben ‹§ 58 (6)›.

Alle vier waren jünger als zwanzig. Es hatten sich an die fünfzig gemeldet. Sie kam erst gegen zwölf. Der Redner ist schon über achtzig.

Werden mit „hundert", „tausend" oder „Dutzend" unbestimmte, nicht in Ziffern schreibbare Mengen angegeben, können diese groß- oder kleingeschrieben werden ‹§ 58 E_5›.

Es gab Dutzende/dutzende von Reklamationen. Mehrere Dutzend/dutzend Leute standen vor dem Tor. Auf dem Platz drängten sich Hunderte/hunderte von Menschen. Viele Hundert/hundert kamen dabei ums Leben. Es gab viele Tausende/tausende von Freiwilligen. Einige Tausend/tausend kleiner Vögel verdunkelten die Sonne.

R 49 Substantivisch gebrauchte **Adverbien, Präpositionen (Verhältniswörter), Konjunktionen (Bindewörter) und Interjektionen (Ausrufewörter)** werden großgeschrieben ‹§ 57 (5)›.

das Drum und Dran, das Auf und Nieder, das Wenn und Aber, das Weh und Ach, das Ja und Nein, nach vielem Hin und Her, im Voraus

Bei mehrteiligen substantivierten Konjunktionen, die mit einem Bindestrich verbunden werden, wird nur das erste Wort großgeschrieben ⟨§ 57 E_4⟩.

das Entweder-oder, das Als-ob

R 50 Substantivisch gebrauchte **Infinitive (Grundformen)** werden großgeschrieben ⟨§ 57 (2)⟩.

das Ringen, das Lesen, das Schreiben, [das] Verlegen von Rohren, im Sitzen und Liegen, zum Verwechseln ähnlich, lautes Schnarchen.

Wortgruppen werden bei Substantivierung entweder zusammengeschrieben oder mit Bindestrichen durchgekoppelt (vgl. R 28).

das Zustandekommen, das Geradesitzen, das Sichausweinen, beim (landsch.: *am*) *Kuchenbacken sein, für Hobeln und Einsetzen [der Türen], das In-den-Tag-hinein-Leben, das Für-sich-haben-Wollen*

Infinitive ohne Artikel, Präposition oder nähere Bestimmung können als Substantiv oder als Verb aufgefasst werden, also sowohl groß- als auch kleingeschrieben werden ⟨§ 57 E_3⟩.

..., weil Geben seliger denn Nehmen ist. Oder: *..., weil geben seliger denn nehmen ist.*
Er übte mit den Kindern Kopfrechnen. Oder: *Er übte mit den Kindern kopfrechnen.*

R 51 In substantivischen **Aneinanderreihungen** wird das erste Wort auch dann großgeschrieben, wenn es kein Substantiv ist ⟨§ 57 (2)⟩.

Pro-Kopf-Verbrauch, Ad-hoc-Arbeitsgruppe, das Auf-der-faulen-Haut-Liegen

Vgl. hierzu auch R 28.

● Bei gebräuchlichen fremdsprachigen Wortgruppen, die für einen substantivischen Begriff stehen, schreibt man in deutschen Texten das erste Wort groß ⟨§ 55 (3)⟩.

Das ist eine Conditio sine qua non.

Vgl. R 33.

Anredepronomen (Anredefürwort)

R 52 Die **Anredepronomen „du“ und „ihr“** sowie die entsprechenden Possessivpronomen (besitzanzeigende Fürwörter) „dein“ und „euer“ werden generell kleingeschrieben ⟨§ 66⟩.

Dies gilt auch für Briefe, Widmungen, Fragebogen, schriftliche Mitteilungen u. Ä.

Liebe Silke,
ich hoffe, dass es dir und euch allen gut geht und dass du deine Ferien an der See angenehm verlebst ...

Die Erde möge dir leicht sein.

Dieses Buch sei dir als Dank für treue Freundschaft gewidmet.

Immerhin hast du dir Mühe gegeben, deshalb: noch ausreichend.

Liebe Freunde! Ich habe euch heute zusammengerufen ...

Lies die Sätze langsam vor. Wo machst du eine Pause?

R 53 Die **Höflichkeitsanrede „Sie“** und das entsprechende Possessivpronomen (besitzanzeigende Fürwort) „Ihr“ sowie die zugehörigen flektierten Formen werden immer großgeschrieben ⟨§ 65⟩.

Haben Sie alles besorgen können? Er sagte damals: „Das kann ich Ihnen nicht versprechen.“ Wie geht es Ihren Kindern? Ich bin nur Ihretwegen gekommen.

● Das rückbezügliche Pronomen „sich“ wird dagegen immer kleingeschrieben ⟨§ 66⟩.

Bei diesen Zahlen müssen Sie sich geirrt haben.

Auch in festgelegten Höflichkeitsanreden und Titeln wird das Pronomen großgeschrieben ⟨§ 65 E_2⟩.

Haben Eure Exzellenz noch einen Wunsch?

Veraltet ist die Anrede in der 3. Person Singular ⟨§ 65 E_1⟩.

Schweig Er! Höre Sie mir gut zu!

Titel und Namen

R 54 Das erste Wort eines **Buch-, Film- oder Zeitschriftentitels,** einer **Überschrift** o. Ä. wird großgeschrieben ‹§ 53 (1)›.

Der Artikel stand in der Neuen Rundschau. Er hat in dem Film „Ich bin ein Elefant, Madame" die Hauptrolle gespielt. Der Aufsatz hat die Überschrift „Mein schönstes Ferienerlebnis".

Vgl. auch R 9.

R 55 Das erste Wort eines **Straßennamens oder Gebäudenamens** wird großgeschrieben, ebenso alle zum Namen gehörenden Adjektive und Zahlwörter ‹§ 60 (2.2, 3.2)›.

In der Mittleren Holdergasse, An den Drei Pfählen, Lange Gasse; Zur Alten Post, aber: *Gasthaus zur Alten Post*

R 56 Alle zu einem **mehrteiligen Namen** gehörenden Adjektive, Partizipien, Pronomen (Fürwörter) und Zahlwörter werden großgeschrieben ‹§ 60›.

Klein Dora, Friedrich der Große, der Große Kurfürst, der Alte Fritz, die Ewige Stadt (Rom), *der Große Bär* (Sternbild), *die Medizinische Klinik des Städtischen Krankenhauses Wiesbaden*

Nicht am Anfang des Namens stehende Adjektive werden gelegentlich auch kleingeschrieben ‹§ 60 E_2›.

Gesellschaft für deutsche Sprache

- Es gibt Wortverbindungen, die keine Namen sind, obwohl sie häufig als Namen angesehen werden. Hier werden die Adjektive kleingeschrieben ‹§ 63›.

italienischer Salat, künstliche Intelligenz, westfälischer Schinken, blauer Montag, neues Jahr, der grüne Punkt

Vor allem in der Botanik und in der Zoologie werden die Adjektive in fachsprachlichen Bezeichnungen bestimmter Klassifizierungseinheiten (z. B. von Arten, Unterarten oder Rassen) großgeschrieben ‹§ 64 (2)›.

die Weiße Lilie (Lilium candidum), *die Gefleckte Hyäne* (Crocuta crocuta)

- Daneben gibt es substantivische Wortgruppen, die keine Namen sind, in denen das Adjektiv dennoch großgeschrieben wird. Hierzu gehören Titel, Amtsbezeichnungen, Kalendertage, historische Ereignisse oder Epochen ‹§ 64 (1, 3, 4)›.

Erste Vorsitzende (als Titel, sonst: *erste Vorsitzende*), *Regierender Bürgermeister* (als Titel, sonst: *regierender Bürgermeister*), *Seine Eminenz, der Westfälische Friede, Heiliger Abend, Weißer Sonntag, das Elisabethanische Zeitalter*

R 57 Als Teile von **geographischen Namen** werden Adjektive und Partizipien großgeschrieben ‹§ 60 (2)›.

das Rote Meer, der Große Ozean, der Atlantische Ozean, die Holsteinische Schweiz

Das gilt auch für inoffizielle Namen ‹§ 60 (5)›.

Schwarzer Kontinent, Naher Osten

Die von geographischen Namen abgeleiteten Wörter auf -er schreibt man immer groß ‹§ 61›.

das Ulmer Münster, eine Kölner Firma, die Schweizer Industrie

- Die von geographischen Namen abgeleiteten Adjektive auf -isch werden kleingeschrieben, wenn sie nicht Teil eines Eigennamens sind ‹§ 62›.

chinesische Seide, böhmische Dörfer

Aber: *der Atlantische Ozean*

R 58 Von **Personennamen** abgeleitete Adjektive werden in der Regel kleingeschrieben ‹§ 62›.

platonische Schriften, platonische Liebe, die heineschen Reisebilder, die heinesche Ironie, die darwinsche/darwinistische Evolutionstheorie, kafkaeske Gestalten, eulenspiegelhaftes Treiben, vorlutherische Bibelübersetzungen

Aber als Teil eines Namens: *die Cansteinsche Bibelanstalt*

Vgl. auch R 94.

Satzanfang

R 59 Groß schreibt man das **erste Wort eines Ganzsatzes** ‹§ 54›.

Wir fangen um 9 Uhr an. Was hast du gesagt? Manche tragen schon Wintermäntel. Wenn das Wetter so bleibt, fahren wir morgen ins Grüne. Schön hat er das gesagt! De Gaulle starb am 9. November 1970.

Dies gilt auch für Abkürzungen.

Vgl. hierzu § 110 StVO.

• Klein schreibt man, wenn am Satzanfang ein Apostroph steht ‹§ 54 (6)›.

's ist unglaublich!
'ne Menge Geld ist das!

• Auch das erste Wort einer direkten Rede oder eines Ganzsatzes (selbstständigen Satzes) nach einem Doppelpunkt schreibt man groß ‹§ 54 (1, 2)›.

Er rief mir zu: „Es ist alles in Ordnung!" Gebrauchsanweisung: Man nehme alle 2 Stunden eine Tablette. Das Haus, die Wirtschaftsgebäude, die Scheune und die Stallungen: Alles war den Flammen zum Opfer gefallen.

• Klein schreibt man dagegen, wenn man die Ausführungen nach dem Doppelpunkt nicht als Ganzsatz auffasst. Das kann z. B. bei einer Aufzählung, bei speziellen Angaben oder Erklärungen der Fall sein.

Er hat alles verspielt: sein Haus, seine Jacht, seine Pferde. Richtig muss es heißen: bei weniger als 5 %. 1 000 DM, in Worten: eintausend DM. Rechnen: sehr gut. Familienstand: verheiratet.

• Großschreibung gilt auch für das erste Wort eines angeführten selbstständigen Satzes.

Mit seinem ständigen „Das mag ich nicht!" ging er uns allen auf die Nerven.

• Innerhalb eines Ganzsatzes wird nach Anführungen, die mit einem Fragezeichen oder Ausrufezeichen enden, kleingeschrieben ‹§ 54 (3)›.

„Wohin gehst du?", fragte er. „Grüß dich, altes Haus!", rief er über die Straße. Sie schrie: „Niemals!", und schlug die Tür zu.

• Auch bei in Gedankenstriche oder Klammern eingeschlossenen eingeschobenen Sätzen wird das erste Wort – wenn es kein Substantiv o. Ä. ist – kleingeschrieben ‹§ 54 (4)›. (Vgl. R 35 u. 61.)

Einzelbuchstaben und Abkürzungen

R 60 Substantivisch gebrauchte **Einzelbuchstaben** schreibt man im Allgemeinen groß.

das A und O; ein X für ein U vormachen

Meint man aber den Kleinbuchstaben, wie er im Schriftbild vorkommt, dann schreibt man klein.

der Punkt auf dem i; das n in Land; das Dehnungs-h; das Fugen-s

Die Groß- und Kleinschreibung von Abkürzungen und Zeichen ändert sich in Zusammensetzungen und Ableitungen nicht ‹§ 55 (1, 2)›.

Tbc-krank, US-amerikanisch, das n-Eck

Grundform (Infinitiv)

↑Getrennt- und Zusammenschreibung (R 38), ↑Groß- und Kleinschreibung (R 50), ↑Komma (R 75)

Hauptwort

↑Substantiv

Infinitiv (Grundform)

↑Getrennt- und Zusammenschreibung (R 38), ↑Groß- und Kleinschreibung (R 50), ↑Komma (R 75)

Interjektion (Ausrufe-, Empfindungswort)

↑Ausrufezeichen (R 20), ↑Groß- und Kleinschreibung (R 49), ↑Komma (R 66)

Klammern

R 61 In Klammern stehen **erklärende Zusätze** ‹§ 86 (3)›.

Frankfurt (Oder)
Grille (Insekt) – Grille (Laune)
Als Hauptwerk Matthias Grünewalds gelten die Gemälde des Isenheimer Altars. (Der Zeitpunkt ihrer Vollendung ist umstritten. Einige nehmen 1511 an, andere 1515.)

In Nachschlagewerken werden bei kürzeren Zusätzen oft auch eckige Klammern statt der allgemein üblichen runden Klammern verwendet.

● Bei eingeschobenen Sätzen können Klammern anstelle von Kommas oder Gedankenstrichen gesetzt werden ‹§ 86 (1)›.

In seiner Vergangenheit (nur wenige kannten ihn noch von früher) gab es manchen dunklen Punkt.

● Andere Satzzeichen stehen nach der schließenden Klammer, wenn sie auch ohne den eingeklammerten Zusatz stehen müssten ‹§ 88›.

Sie wohnen in Ilsenburg (Harz). Sie wundern sich (so schreiben Sie), dass ich so wenig von mir hören lasse.

Ausrufe- und Fragezeichen stehen vor der schließenden Klammer, wenn sie zum eingeklammerten Zusatz gehören ‹§ 88›.

Der Antrag ist vollständig ausgefüllt (bitte deutlich schreiben!) an die Bank zurückzusenden. Es gab damals (erinnern Sie sich noch?) eine furchtbare Aufregung.

Der Schlusspunkt steht nur dann vor der schließenden Klammer, wenn ein ganzer Satz eingeklammert ist, der nicht an den vorhergehenden Satz angeschlossen ist ‹§ 88›.

Dies halte ich für das wichtigste Ergebnis meiner Ausführungen. (Die entsprechenden Belege finden sich auf Seite 25.)
Aber: *Mit der Produktion der neuen Modelle wurde bereits begonnen (im Einzelnen werden wir noch darüber berichten).*

● Erläuterungen zu einem bereits eingeklammerten Zusatz werden häufig in eckige Klammern gesetzt.

Mit dem Wort Bankrott (vom italienischen „banca rotta“ [zusammengebrochene Bank]) bezeichnet man die Zahlungsunfähigkeit.

Auch bei eigenen Zusätzen in zitierten Texten oder bei Ergänzungen in nicht lesbaren oder zerstörten Texten werden oft eckige Klammern verwendet.

In ihrem Tagebuch heißt es: „Ich habe das große Ereignis [gemeint ist die Verleihung des Friedenspreises] ganz aus der Nähe miterlebt und war sehr beeindruckt.“

R 62 Buchstaben, Wortteile oder Wörter können in Klammern eingeschlossen werden, um Verkürzungen, Zusammenfassungen, Alternativen o. Ä. zu kennzeichnen.

Mitarbeiter(in) (als Kurzform für: Mitarbeiterin oder Mitarbeiter)
Lehrer(innen) (als Kurzform für: Lehrerinnen und/oder Lehrer)
Kolleg(inn)en (als Kurzform für: Kolleginnen und/oder Kollegen)

Vgl. auch R 115.

Bei weglassbaren Buchstaben, Wortteilen oder Wörtern werden meist eckige Klammern verwendet.

Kopp[e]lung, gern[e], acht[und]einhalb, sieb[en]tens, Besucher mit [schulpflichtigen] Kindern

Kleinschreibung

↑ Groß- und Kleinschreibung

Komma (Beistrich)

Das Komma zwischen Satzteilen R 63 bis 72
Das Komma bei Partizipial- und Infinitivgruppen R 73–75
Das Komma zwischen Sätzen R 76–81
Das Komma vor „und“ oder „oder“ (Zusammenfassung) R 82–87
Das Komma beim Zusammentreffen einer Konjunktion (eines Bindewortes) mit einem Adverb, Partizip u. a. R 88

Das Komma zwischen Satzteilen

Das Komma dient der Gliederung des Satzes. Es steht vor allem bei Aufzählungen, herausgehobenen Satzteilen sowie Einschüben und Zusätzen aller Art. Es steht jedoch in der Regel nicht zwischen Satzgliedern, auch wenn diese durch Beifügungen sehr umfangreich sind.

R 63 Das Komma steht bei **Aufzählungen** zwischen gleichrangigen Wörtern und Wortgruppen, wenn sie nicht durch „und" oder „oder" verbunden sind ⟨§ 71, 72⟩.

Feuer, Wasser, Luft und Erde.

• Kein Komma steht am Schluss einer Aufzählung, wenn der Satz weitergeht.

Er sägte, hobelte, hämmerte die ganze Nacht. Es war ein süßes, klebriges, kaum genießbares Getränk. Sie ist viel, viel schöner.

• Kein Komma steht zwischen nicht gleichrangigen Adjektiven ⟨§ 71 E_1⟩.

ein Glas dunkles bayrisches Bier („bayrisches Bier" wird hier als Einheit angesehen, die durch „dunkles" näher bestimmt ist)
Sehr geehrte gnädige Frau!
Er machte bedeutende, lehrreiche physikalische Versuche.

Gelegentlich hängt es vom Sinn des Satzes ab, ob Gleichrangigkeit vorliegt oder nicht.

die höher liegenden unbewaldeten Hänge (ohne Komma, weil es auch tiefer liegende unbewaldete Hänge gibt)
die höher liegenden, unbewaldeten Hänge (mit Komma, weil die tiefer liegenden bewaldet sind)

Davon zu unterscheiden sind Fälle, in denen ein Adjektiv durch eine Wortgruppe näher bestimmt wird.

Das Buch enthält viele farbige, [und zwar] mit der Hand kolorierte Holzschnitte

Vgl. auch R 67.

• Mehrteilige Wohnungsangaben werden durch Komma gegliedert ⟨§ 77 (3)⟩.

Renate Meier, Dresden, Wilhelmstr. 24, I. Stock, links
Peter Schmidt, Landgraf-Georg-Straße 4, Darmstadt

Die mehrteilige Wohnungsangabe kann als Aufzählung oder als Fügung mit Beisatz (Apposition; vgl. R 67) aufgefasst werden; deshalb ist das Komma nach dem letzten Bestandteil (bei weitergeführtem Text) freigestellt.

Frau Anke Meyer, Heidelberg, Hauptstraße 15[,] hat den ersten Preis gewonnen. Herr Schmitt ist von Bonn, Königstraße 20[,] nach Mannheim-Feudenheim, Eberbacher Platz 14[,] umgezogen.

• Mehrteilige Angaben von Stellen aus Büchern, Zeitschriften o. Ä. werden in der Regel durch Komma gegliedert ⟨§ 77 (3)⟩. Auch hier ist das Komma nach der letzten Angabe freigestellt.

Man findet diese Regel im Duden, Rechtschreibung, S. 43, R 63. Der Artikel ist im „Spiegel", Heft 48, 1994, S. 25 f.[,] erschienen.

Bei Hinweisen auf Gesetze, Verordnungen usw. setzt man kein Komma.

§ 6 Abs. 2 Satz 2 der Personalverordnung

• Mehrere vorangestellte Namen und Titel werden nicht durch Komma getrennt ⟨§ 77 E_2⟩.

Hans Albert Schulze (aber: *Schulze, Hans Albert*)
Direktor Professor Dr. Max Müller
Seine Heiligkeit Papst Johannes Paul II.

In der Regel steht auch kein Komma bei „geb.", „verh.", „verw." usw.

Martha Schneider geb. Kühn

Der Geburtsname o. Ä. kann aber auch als nachgetragener Zusatz aufgefasst werden und wird dann in Kommas eingeschlossen.

Herr Dr. Karl Schneider und seine Frau Martha[,] geb. Kühn[,] werden hiermit gebeten ...

R 64 Das Komma steht nach **herausgehobenen Satzteilen,** die durch ein Pronomen (Fürwort) oder Adverb erneut aufgenommen werden ⟨§ 77 (5)⟩.

Deinen Vater, den habe ich gut gekannt. In diesem Krankenhaus, da haben sie mir die Mandeln herausgenommen.

R 65 Das Komma trennt die **Anrede** vom übrigen Satz ⟨§ 79 (1)⟩.

Kinder, hört doch mal zu! Haben Sie meinen Brief bekommen, Herr Müller? Das, mein Lieber, kannst du nicht von mir verlangen. Hallo, Tina, wie geht es dir?

Nach der Anrede am Anfang eines Briefes wird heute gewöhnlich ein Komma gesetzt (vgl. R 21). Das erste Wort des Brieftextes wird dann kleingeschrieben (wenn es nicht als Substantiv, höfliche Anrede o. Ä. generell großzuschreiben ist) ‹§ 69 E_3›.

Sehr geehrter Herr Schmidt,
gestern erhielt ich ...

In der Schweiz kann dieses Komma entfallen; der Brieftext beginnt dann mit Großschreibung des ersten Wortes.

Sehr geehrter Herr Schmidt
Gestern erhielt ich ...

R 66 Das Komma trennt die **Interjektion (das Ausrufe-, Empfindungswort)** vom Satz ‹§ 79 (2)›.

Ach, das ist schade! Au, du tust mir weh!

Dies gilt auch für die bekräftigende Bejahung und Verneinung ‹§ 79 (3)›.

Ja, daran ist nicht zu zweifeln. Nein, das sollte er nicht sagen.

Kein Komma steht, wenn die Interjektion o. Ä. nicht hervorgehoben werden soll ‹§ 79 (2, 3)›.

Ach lass mich doch in Ruhe! Ja wenn er nur käme! Seine ach so große Vergesslichkeit ...

R 67 Das Komma trennt den **nachgestellten Beisatz (die Apposition), nachgestellte Erläuterungen** sowie **nachgestellte Adjektive und Partizipien** ab ‹§ 77 (2)›.

Wird der Satz nach solchen Beisätzen, Erläuterungen usw. weitergeführt, so werden sie in Kommas eingeschlossen.

Das Auto, Massenverkehrsmittel und Statussymbol zugleich, bestimmt immer mehr das Gesicht unserer Städte. Johannes Gutenberg, der Erfinder der Buchdruckerkunst, wurde in Mainz geboren.

Folgt der Name dem Beisatz, können die Kommas entfallen ‹§ 77 E_1›.

Der Erfinder der Buchdruckerkunst[,] Johannes Gutenberg[,] wurde in Mainz geboren.

● Kein Komma steht, wenn der Beisatz zum Namen gehört ‹§ 77 E_2›.

Heinrich der Löwe wurde im Dom zu Braunschweig begraben. Das ist ein Gemälde von Hans Holbein dem Jüngeren.

Gelegentlich entscheidet allein das Komma, ob eine Aufzählung oder ein Beisatz vorliegt. In diesen Fällen kann also das Komma den Sinn eines Satzes verändern.

Gertrud, meine Schwester, und ich wohnen im selben Haus (Beisatz; 2 Personen).
Gertrud, meine Schwester und ich wohnen im selben Haus (Aufzählung; 3 Personen).

● Nachgestellte Erläuterungen werden häufig durch Wörter und Wortgruppen wie „und zwar“, „nämlich“, „z. B.“, „insbesondere“ eingeleitet ‹§ 77 (4)›.

Das Schiff verkehrt wöchentlich einmal, und zwar sonntags. Wir müssen etwas unternehmen, und das bald. Bei unserer nächsten Sitzung, das ist am Donnerstag, werde ich diese Angelegenheit zur Sprache bringen. Mit einem Scheck über 2 000,- DM, in Worten: zweitausend Deutsche Mark, hat er die Rechnung bezahlt. Es gibt vier Jahreszeiten, nämlich Frühling, Sommer, Herbst und Winter.

Wird eine adjektivische Beifügung (ein Attribut) durch eine unmittelbar folgende zweite Beifügung näher bestimmt, dann setzt man kein schließendes Komma.

Ausländische, insbesondere holländische Firmen traten als Bewerber auf. Das Buch enthält viele farbige, und zwar mit der Hand kolorierte Holzschnitte.

Das schließende Komma steht auch dann nicht, wenn ein Teil des Prädikats (der Satzaussage) näher bestimmt und die zugehörige Personalform des Verbs nur einmal gesetzt wird.

Er wurde erst wieder ruhiger, als er sein Herz ausgeschüttet, d. h. alles erzählt hatte.

● Gelegentlich werden nachgestellte Beisätze oder nachgestellte genauere Bestimmungen nicht als Einschübe gewertet, die den Satz unterbrechen, sondern wie ein Satzglied behandelt und nicht durch Komma abgetrennt. Die Entscheidung liegt in diesen Fällen bei den Schreibenden ‹§ 78 (1, 4)›.

Alle bis auf Hannelore wollen mitfahren. Oder: *Alle, bis auf Hannelore, wollen mitfahren.*

Der Angeklagte Max Müller erschien nicht zur Verhandlung.
Oder: *Der Angeklagte, Max Müller, erschien nicht zur Verhandlung.*

● Wie nachgestellte Adjektive und Partizipien werden auch entsprechende Partizipialgruppen und andere Wortgruppen behandelt ‹§ 77 (7)›.

Er schaut zum Fenster hinaus, müde und gelangweilt. Sie erzählte allerlei Geschichten, erlebte und erfundene. Der November, kalt und nass, löste eine heftige Grippewelle aus. Dein Wintermantel, der blaue, muss in die Reinigung.
Kabeljau, gedünstet
Wir, nicht wenig erschrocken, rannten aus dem Zimmer. Neben ihm saß seine Freundin, den Kopf im Nacken, und hörte der Unterhaltung zu.

Vgl. auch R 74.

Das Komma steht aber nicht, wenn in bestimmten festen Fügungen oder dichterischen Wendungen ein allein stehendes Adjektiv nachgestellt ist ‹§ 77 E_3›.

Aal blau
Karl Meyer junior
Bei einem Wirte wundermild ...

R 68 Mehrteilige **Datums- und Zeitangaben** werden durch Komma gegliedert ‹§ 77 (3)›.

Berlin, den 1. 8. 1998
Mannheim, im Juni 1996

Die mehrteilige Datums- und Zeitangabe kann als Aufzählung oder als Fügung mit Beisatz (Apposition; vgl. R 67) aufgefasst werden; deshalb ist das Komma nach dem letzten Bestandteil (bei weitergeführtem Text) freigestellt.

Mittwoch, den 25. Juli, [um] 20 Uhr[,] findet die Sitzung statt.
Sie kommt Montag, [den] 5. September[,] an.
Sie kommt am Montag, dem 5. September[,] an.

Steht der Wochentag im Dativ und der Monatstag im Akkusativ, liegt kein Beisatz vor; hier steht kein schließendes Komma.

Sie kommt am Montag, den 5. September an.

R 69 Das Komma steht zwischen Satzteilen, die durch **anreihende Konjunktionen (Bindewörter)**[1] in der Art einer Aufzählung verbunden sind ‹§ 72›.

Dies gilt vor allem bei:

bald – bald
einerseits – and[e]rerseits
einesteils – ander[e]nteils
je – desto
ob – ob
teils – teils
nicht nur – sondern auch
halb – halb

Die Kinder spielen teils auf der Straße, teils im Garten. Er ist nicht nur ein guter Schüler, sondern auch ein guter Sportler. Wir waren halb erschrocken, halb erleichtert. Die Investition ist einerseits mit hohen Gewinnchancen, andererseits mit hohem Risiko verbunden.

● Kein Komma steht vor den anreihenden Konjunktionen, die eng zusammengehörige Satzteile verbinden.

Hierzu gehören:

und
sowie
wie
sowohl – als auch
weder – noch

Der prunkvolle Becher war innen wie außen vergoldet. Ich weiß weder seinen Nachnamen noch seinen Vornamen. Der Vorfall war sowohl ihm als auch seiner Frau sehr peinlich. Sie stiegen ins Auto und fuhren nach Hause.

Vor „und“ steht bei Aufzählungen auch dann kein Komma, wenn ein Nebensatz folgt ‹§ 74 E_2›.

Die Mutter kaufte der Tochter einen Koffer, einen Mantel, ein Kleid und was sie sonst noch für die Reise brauchte.

Wird der übergeordnete Satz nach dem Nebensatz weitergeführt, dann setzt man am Ende des Nebensatzes ein Komma.

Die Mutter hatte der Tochter einen Koffer, einen Mantel, ein Kleid und was sie sonst noch für die Reise brauchte, gekauft.

[1] *Als Konjunktionen werden hier der Einfachheit halber auch die einem Satzteil vorangestellten Adverbien (z. B. teils – teils) bezeichnet.*

R 70 Kein Komma steht vor den **ausschließenden Konjunktionen (Bindewörtern),** wenn sie nur Satzteile verbinden ‹§ 72 (2)›.

Hierzu gehören:

oder
beziehungsweise (bzw.)
respektive (resp.)
entweder – oder

Heute oder morgen will sie dich besuchen. Du musst dich entweder für uns oder gegen uns entscheiden.

R 71 Das Komma steht vor den **entgegensetzenden Konjunktionen (Bindewörtern)** ‹§ 72 E_2›.

Hierzu gehören vor allem:

aber
allein
[je]doch
vielmehr
sondern

arm, aber glücklich; nicht schön, doch sehr nützlich
Das war kein Pkw, sondern ein größerer Lieferwagen.

R 72 Kein Komma steht vor den **vergleichenden Konjunktionen (Bindewörtern)** „als", „wie" und „denn", wenn sie nur Satzteile verbinden ‹§ 74 E_3›.

Es ging besser als erwartet. Die neuen Geräte gingen weg wie warme Semmeln. Mehr denn je kommt es heute darauf an, gediegenes Fachwissen zu besitzen.

● Das Komma steht dagegen bei Vergleichssätzen.

Es ging besser, als wir erwartet hatten. Komm so schnell, wie du kannst (aber: *Komm, so schnell du kannst*). *Wir haben mehr Stühle als nötig sind.*

Bei den mit „wie" einem Substantiv nachgestellten näheren Erläuterungen können Kommas gesetzt werden ‹§ 78 (2)›.

Die Auslagen[,] wie Post- und Fernsprechgebühren, Eintrittsgelder, Fahrtkosten u. dgl.[,] ersetzen wir Ihnen.

Das Komma bei Partizipial- und Infinitivgruppen (Mittelwort- und Grundformgruppen)

R 73 **Partizipien** ohne nähere Bestimmung und **Infinitive** ohne „zu" stehen in der Regel ohne Komma.

Lachend kam sie auf mich zu. Gelangweilt sah er zum Fenster hinaus. Schreiend und johlend durchstreiften sie die Straßen. Du kannst mir bei der Arbeit helfen.

Vgl. aber R 67.

R 74 Die **Partizipialgruppe** kann man durch Komma abtrennen, um die Gliederung des Satzes deutlich zu machen oder um Missverständnisse auszuschließen ‹§ 76›.

Aus vollem Halse lachend[,] kam er auf mich zu. Er sank[,] zu Tode getroffen[,] zu Boden. Seinem Vorschlag entsprechend[,] ist das Haus verkauft worden. Ihre Wohnung betreffend[,] möchte ich Ihnen folgenden Vorschlag machen. Das sind[,] grob gerechnet[,] 20 % der Einnahmen. Das ist[,] logisch betrachtet[,] nicht in Ordnung.

● Einige Wortgruppen sind den Partizipialgruppen gleichzustellen, weil man sie durch „habend", „seiend", „werdend", „geworden" ergänzen kann.

Seit mehreren Jahren kränklich[,] hatte er sich in ein Sanatorium zurückgezogen.

R 75 Den **erweiterten Infinitiv** mit „zu" (die Infinitivgruppe, Grundformgruppe) kann man durch Komma abtrennen, um die Gliederung des Satzes deutlich zu machen oder um Missverständnisse auszuschließen ‹§ 76›.

Etwas Schlimmeres[,] als seine Kinder zu enttäuschen[,] konnte ihm nicht passieren.
Wir versuchten[,] die Torte mit Sahne zu verzieren.
Wir empfehlen[,] ihm nichts zu sagen.
Wir empfehlen ihm[,] nichts zu sagen.

Ein Komma ist aber nicht sinnvoll:

● wenn der erweiterte Infinitiv mit dem Hauptsatz verschränkt ist oder wenn er innerhalb der verbalen Klammer steht;

Diesen Vorgang wollen wir zu erklären ver-

suchen. (Hauptsatz: „wir wollen versuchen"; Infinitivgruppe: „diesen Vorgang zu erklären".)
Wir hatten den Betrag zu überweisen beschlossen. (Verbale Klammer: „hatten ... beschlossen"; Infinitivgruppe: „den Betrag zu überweisen".)

• wenn ein Glied des erweiterten Infinitivs an den Anfang des Satzes tritt und der Hauptsatz dadurch von dem erweiterten Infinitiv eingeschlossen wird;

Diesen Betrag bitten wir auf unser Konto zu überweisen. (Hauptsatz: „wir bitten".)

• wenn der erweiterte Infinitiv auf Hilfsverben oder auf die Verben „brauchen", „pflegen", „scheinen" folgt.

Die Spur war deutlich zu sehen. Sie haben nichts zu verlieren. Sie pflegt abends ein Glas Wein zu trinken. Du scheinst heute schlecht gelaunt zu sein.

• Zielt ein hinweisendes Wort (oder eine hinweisende Wortgruppe) auf die Infinitivgruppe, dann müssen Kommas gesetzt werden ‹§ 77 (5)›.

Zu tanzen, das ist ihre größte Freude. Erinnere mich daran, den Mülleimer auszuleeren. Ihre Absicht ist es, im nächsten Jahr nach Mallorca zu fahren. Und dieser Gedanke, einfach alles aufzugeben, ließ ihn nicht mehr los.

• Das gilt auch für eingeschobene erläuternde Infinitivgruppen.
Wir, ohne einen Moment zu zögern, hatten sofort zugestimmt.

Das Komma zwischen Sätzen

Das Komma zwischen Sätzen hat in erster Linie die Aufgabe, den Nebensatz von seinem Hauptsatz und von anderen Nebensätzen zu trennen. Darüber hinaus trennt das Komma aber auch selbstständige Sätze anstelle des Punktes oder des Semikolons, wenn diese Sätze in enger gedanklicher Verbindung aneinander gereiht sind.

R 76 Das Komma trennt **nebengeordnete gleichrangige Sätze** ‹§ 71 (1)›.

Die Musik wird leiser, der Vorhang hebt sich, das Spiel beginnt.

• Es steht aber in der Regel kein Komma, wenn solche Sätze durch eine der folgenden Konjunktionen (eines der folgenden Bindewörter) verbunden sind ‹§ 72 (1)›:
und
oder
beziehungsweise
weder – noch
entweder – oder
Er grübelte und er grübelte. Er lief oder er fuhr. Tue recht und scheue niemand! Seien Sie bitte so nett und geben Sie mir das Buch. Wir werden vorausgehen und die Älteren werden langsam nachkommen. Sie machten es sich bequem, die Kerzen wurden angezündet und der Gastgeber versorgte sie mit Getränken.

Man kann in diesen Fällen ein Komma setzen, um die Gliederung der Satzverbindung deutlich zu machen ‹§ 73›.
Wir stiegen in den Bus[,] und die Kinder weinten, weil sie gern noch geblieben wären. Er schimpfte auf die Regierung[,] und sein Publikum, das auf seiner Seite war, applaudierte.
Vgl. auch R 79.

R 77 Das Komma steht vor und nach dem **eingeschobenen Satz** ‹§ 77 (1)›.

Eines Tages, es war mitten im Winter, stand ein Reh in unserem Garten.
Vgl. auch R 35 u. R 61.

R 78 Das Komma steht zwischen **Haupt- und Nebensatz (Gliedsatz)** ‹§ 74›.

Der Nebensatz kann Vordersatz, Zwischensatz oder Nachsatz sein. Der Zwischensatz wird in Kommas eingeschlossen.
Wenn es möglich ist, erledigen wir den Auftrag sofort. Was er sagt, stimmt nicht. „Ich kenne Sie nicht", antwortete er. Hunde, die bellen, beißen nicht. Es freut mich sehr, dass du wieder gesund bist. Ich weiß, er ist unschuldig. Er fragt, mit welchem Zug du kommst. Sie rief: „Du hast mir gerade noch gefehlt!", als ich hereinkam.

R 79 Das Komma trennt **Nebensätze (Gliedsätze) gleichen Grades** ‹§ 71 (1)›.

Wenn das wahr ist, wenn du ihn wirklich nicht gesehen hast, dann brauchst du dir keine Vorwürfe zu machen. Er kannte niemanden, der ihm geholfen hätte, an den er sich hätte wenden können.

● Es steht aber in der Regel kein Komma, wenn sie durch eine der folgenden Konjunktionen (Bindewörter) verbunden sind ‹§ 72 (1)›:
und
oder
beziehungsweise

Sie sagte, sie wisse Bescheid und der Vorgang sei ihr völlig klar. Wir erwarten, dass er die Ware liefert oder dass er das Geld zurückzahlt.

Man kann in diesen Fällen ein Komma setzen, wenn man die Gliederung des Satzgefüges deutlich machen möchte ‹§ 73›.

Sie fragte mich, ob ich mitfahren wolle[,] und ob sie mich abholen könne, sobald sie gefrühstückt habe.

R 80 Das Komma trennt **Nebensätze (Gliedsätze) verschiedenen Grades** ‹§ 74›.

Er war zu klug, als dass er in die Falle gegangen wäre, die man ihm gestellt hatte.

R 81 Für das Komma in **Auslassungssätzen** gelten dieselben Richtlinien wie bei vollständigen Sätzen.

Vielleicht, dass er noch eintrifft. (Vielleicht geschieht es, dass ...)
Ich weiß nicht, was anfangen. (..., was ich anfangen soll.)
Ehre verloren, alles verloren. (Wenn die Ehre verloren ist, ist alles verloren.)

Unvollständige Nebensätze, die mit „wie“ oder „wenn“ u. a. eingeleitet sind, stehen oft ohne Komma; sie sind formelhaft geworden und wirken wie eine einfache Umstandsangabe. Es ist aber nicht falsch, in diesen Fällen Kommas zu setzen ‹§ 75›.

Er ging wie immer (= gewohntermaßen) *nach dem Essen spazieren.*
Wir wollen die Angelegenheit wenn möglich (= möglichst) *heute noch erledigen.*
Ihre Darlegungen endeten wie folgt (= folgendermaßen): ...

● Das Wort „bitte“ steht als bloße Höflichkeitsformel meist ohne Komma ‹§ 79 (3)›.

Bitte gehen Sie voran. Geben Sie mir bitte das Buch.

Bei besonderer Betonung kann es aber auch durch Komma abgetrennt bzw. in Kommas eingeschlossen werden.

Bitte, kommen Sie einmal zu mir! Geben Sie mir, bitte, noch etwas Zeit.

Das Komma vor „und“ oder „oder“ (Zusammenfassung)

R 82 Das Komma steht, wenn ein **Zwischensatz** oder ein **Beisatz** (eine **Apposition**) vorausgeht ‹§ 72 E_1›.

Wir glauben, dass wir richtig gehandelt haben, und werden diesen Weg weitergehen. Mein Onkel, ein großer Tierfreund, und seine vierzehn Katzen leben jetzt in einer alten Mühle.

Als Zwischensatz gilt auch ein eingeschobener erweiterter Infinitiv, wenn die Gliederung des Satzes deutlich gemacht werden soll. (Vgl. R 75.)

Wir hoffen, Ihre Bedenken hiermit zerstreut zu haben, und grüßen Sie ...

R 83 Das Komma steht, wenn eine **nachgestellte genauere Bestimmung** von „und zwar“ oder „und das“ eingeleitet wird ‹§ 77 (4)›.

Ich werde kommen, und zwar bald. Er gab nicht nach, und das mit Recht.

R 84 Das Komma kann gesetzt werden, wenn „und“ oder „oder“ ein Satzgefüge anschließt, das mit einem **Nebensatz** oder einem **erweiterten Infinitiv** beginnt ‹§ 76›.

Hier wird durch das Komma die Überschaubarkeit des Satzgefüges verbessert.

Ich habe ihn oft besucht, und wenn er in guter Stimmung war, saßen wir bis spät in die Nacht zusammen. Es waren schlechte Zeiten, und um zu überleben, nahm man es mit vielen Dingen nicht so genau.

> **R 85** Es steht im Allgemeinen kein Komma, wenn „und" oder „oder" **selbstständige gleichrangige Sätze** oder **gleichrangige Nebensätze (Gliedsätze)** verbindet ‹§ 72 (1)›.

Es wurde immer kälter und der Südwind türmte Wolken um die Gipfel.
Weil sie die Schwäche ihres Sohnes für den Alkohol kannte und damit er nicht wieder entgleisen sollte, schickte sie ihn schon früh nach Hause.

Man kann aber ein Komma setzen, um die Gliederung des Satzgefüges deutlich zu machen ‹§ 73›. (Vgl. R 76 u. 79.)

> **R 86** Es steht kein Komma, wenn „und" oder „oder" **gleichrangige Wortgruppen** verbindet.

Sie öffnete die Tür und ging in den Garten. Ich gehe morgen ins Theater oder besuche ein Konzert.

> **R 87** Es steht kein Komma vor „und" oder „oder" in **Aufzählungen gleichrangiger Wörter** ‹§ 72 (2)›.

Sie zogen Tomaten, Gurken, Weißkohl und Wirsing in ihrem Kleingarten.

Das gilt auch, wenn ein Nebensatz Teil der Aufzählung ist ‹§ 74 E_2›.

Sie lachte über ihn wegen seiner großen Füße und weil er vor Aufregung stotterte.

Das Komma beim Zusammentreffen einer Konjunktion (eines Bindewortes) mit einem Adverb, Partizip u. a.

Bei bestimmten Fügungen, in denen eine Konjunktion mit einem Adverb, Partizip u. a. zusammentrifft (z. B. „vorausgesetzt, dass"; „auch wenn"), sind besondere Richtlinien für die Kommasetzung innerhalb der Fügung zu beachten.

> **R 88** Werden die Teile der Fügung nicht als Einheit angesehen, dann kann zwischen den Teilen, d. h. **vor der eigentlichen Konjunktion, ein [zusätzliches] Komma** gesetzt werden ‹§ 74 E_1 (2)›.

Hierzu gehören Fügungen wie:
abgesehen davon[,] dass
angenommen[,] dass
ausgenommen[,] dass/wenn
es sei denn[,] dass
gesetzt den Fall[,] dass
vorausgesetzt[,] dass
besonders[,] wenn
geschweige[,] dass (aber: geschweige denn, dass)
im Fall[,] dass/im Falle[,] dass
insofern/insoweit[,] als
je nachdem[,] ob/wie
namentlich[,] wenn
umso eher/mehr/weniger[,] als
ungeachtet[,] dass (aber: ungeachtet dessen, dass)
vor allem[,] wenn/weil

Angenommen[,] dass morgen gutes Wetter ist, wohin wollen wir fahren? Ich komme, es sei denn[,] dass ich im Büro aufgehalten werde. Ich mag ihn gern, ausgenommen[,] wenn er schlechter Laune ist.

● Wird die Fügung als Einheit angesehen, dann steht vor der eigentlichen Konjunktion gewöhnlich kein Komma ‹§ 74 E_1 (1)›.

Hierzu gehören Fügungen wie:
als dass
als ob
[an]statt dass
aber wenn
wie wenn

Der Plan ist viel zu umständlich, als dass wir ihn ausführen könnten. Anstatt dass der Direktor kam, erschien nur sein Stellvertreter. Er tut, als ob er nicht bis drei zählen könnte.

● Gelegentlich kann der Gebrauch des Kommas verdeutlichen, welche Wörter als Einleitung des Nebensatzes verstanden werden ‹§ 74 E_1 (3)›.

Sie freut sich, auch wenn du ihr nur eine Postkarte schreibst.
Sie freut sich auch, wenn du ihr nur eine Postkarte schreibst.

Weitere Hinweise: ↑Anführungszeichen (R 12), ↑Gedankenstrich (R 36), ↑Klammern (R 61), ↑Zahlen (R 134 f.).

Konjunktion (Bindewort)

↑Groß- und Kleinschreibung (R 49), ↑Komma (R 69–72, 76, 79 u. 88)

Konsonant (Mitlaut)

↑Worttrennung (R 129 f.)

Korrekturvorschriften

↑S. 79.

Ländernamen

↑Namen (R 101 ff.)

Laut-Buchstaben-Zuordnungen

Für die Schreibung des Deutschen verwenden wir eine Buchstabenschrift, in der Sprachlaute und Buchstaben einander zugeordnet sind. Rechtschreibliche Schwierigkeiten ergeben sich vor allem dort, wo gleiche Laute durch unterschiedliche Buchstaben wiedergegeben werden.

> **R 89** Die richtige Schreibung eines Wortes kann häufig aus der Schreibung sprachgeschichtlich (gelegentlich auch nur inhaltlich) verwandter Wörter abgeleitet werden ⟨Regelabschnitt A, Vorbemerkung (2.2)⟩.

Gewähr (Garantie), aber: *Gewehr* (zu: Wehr, wehrhaft)
Rechen (Harke), aber: *sich rächen* (zu: Rache)
Bändel (zu: Band)
Karamell (wegen: Karamelle)
nummerieren (wegen: Nummer)

● Einige nur selten vorkommende alte Laut-Buchstaben-Zuordnungen wurden an häufigere vergleichbare Festlegungen angeglichen.

Känguru (früher: Känguruh, jetzt wie Kakadu, Gnu, Emu)
rau (früher: rauh, jetzt wie blau, schlau, genau)
Zierrat (früher: Zierat, jetzt wie Verrat, Vorrat)

Maß-, Mengen- und Währungsbezeichnungen

> **R 90** Folgt auf eine **stark gebeugte Maß- oder Mengenangabe** ein starkes männliches oder sächliches Substantiv, ohne dass durch ein Begleitwort der Fall deutlich wird, dann bleibt im Genitiv (Wesfall) Singular entweder die Angabe oder das davon abhängende Substantiv ungebeugt.

eines Glas Wassers oder: *eines Glases Wasser*
eines Pfund Fleisches oder: *eines Pfundes Fleisch*

● Geht aber dem Gezählten oder Gemessenen ein Adjektiv voran, dann werden in der Regel sowohl die Maß- oder Mengenangabe als auch das Gezählte oder Gemessene gebeugt.

der Preis eines Pfundes gekochten Schinkens

In den anderen Beugungsfällen steht das Gezählte oder Gemessene im gleichen Fall wie die Maß- oder Mengenangabe.

fünf Sack feinstes Mehl; mit einem Tropfen [warmem] Öl; von einem Sack [schlechten] Nüssen; ein Glas guter Wein

Nur selten wird hier der Genitiv gewählt, der im Allgemeinen als gehoben (oder gespreizt) empfunden wird.

ein Glas guten Weines

● In Verbindung mit Zahlwörtern bleiben Maß-, Mengen- und Währungsbezeichnungen im Plural meist ungebeugt.

10 Fass, 2 Dutzend, 3 Zoll, 2 Fuß, 7 Paar, 9 Sack, 30 Pfennig, 10 Schilling, 342 Dollar, zwanzig Grad Kälte, zehn Schritt, 5 Karton (auch: *Kartons*) *Seife*

Fremde Bezeichnungen werden jedoch häufig gebeugt, bei manchen schwankt der Gebrauch.

4 Peseten (Singular: *Peseta*), *100 Lei* (Singular: *Leu*), *500 Lire* (Singular: *Lira*), *100 Centesimi* (Singular: *Centesimo*); *10 Inch* oder *Inches, 5 Yard* oder *Yards*

Weibliche Bezeichnungen, die auf -e ausgehen, werden immer gebeugt.

zwanzig norwegische Kronen, zwei Flaschen Wein, drei Tassen Kaffee, drei Tonnen, 2 Kannen Wasser, drei Dosen Milch

Ohne vorangehenden Artikel wird im Allgemeinen die gebeugte Form gebraucht, wenn das Gemessene nicht folgt.

im Abstand von 50 Metern, ein Gewicht von zwei Zentnern

Folgt aber das Gemessene oder Gezählte, dann wird meist die ungebeugte Form gebraucht.

Die Steckdose ist in 90 Zentimeter Höhe angebracht. Ein Schwein von 3 Zentner Lebendgewicht.

● Die Bezeichnungen werden immer gebeugt, wenn das betreffende Substantiv den konkreten, einzeln gezählten Gegenstand o. Ä. bezeichnet.

er trank 2 Glas, aber: *er zerbrach zwei Gläser; er hatte 30 Schuss Munition,* aber: *es fielen zwei Schüsse*

Mehrzahl (Plural)

↑Maß-, Mengen- und Währungsbezeichnungen (R 90), ↑Namen (R 99), ↑Substantiv (R 124 ff.)

Mengenangaben

↑Maß-, Mengen- und Währungsbezeichnungen

Mitlaut (Konsonant)

↑Worttrennung (R 129 f.)

Mittelwort (Partizip)

↑Adjektiv (R 5 ff.), ↑Getrennt- und Zusammenschreibung (R 40), ↑Groß- und Kleinschreibung (R 47), ↑Komma (R 73 f.)

Namen

Familiennamen, Vornamen, historische Personennamen R 91–100
Geographische (erdkundliche) Namen R 101–107
Sonstige Namen R 108–110
(Straßennamen werden gesondert unter diesem Stichwort behandelt; vgl. R 122 f.)

Familiennamen, Vornamen, historische Personennamen

R 91 Die **Schreibung der Familiennamen** unterliegt nicht den allgemeinen Richtlinien der Rechtschreibung. Für sie gilt die standesamtlich jeweils festgelegte Schreibung.

Bismarck, Goethe, Liszt

R 92 Für die **Schreibung der Vornamen** gelten im Allgemeinen die heutigen Rechtschreibregeln.

Bei einer Reihe von Vornamen sind unterschiedliche Schreibweisen üblich.

Claus neben: *Klaus; Clara* neben: *Klara; Ralph* neben: *Ralf; Günther* neben: *Günter*

Fremde Vornamen werden in der fremden Schreibweise geschrieben.

Jean, Christa, Dorothea, Marcel

● Zwei Vornamen stehen gewöhnlich unverbunden nebeneinander.

Johann Wolfgang, Johanna Katharina

Einige Vornamen werden als feste Paare (Doppelnamen) empfunden und deshalb mit Bindestrich oder sogar in einem Wort geschrieben.

Karl-Heinz, Karlheinz neben: *Karl Heinz*

R 93 Zu einem **mehrteiligen Personennamen** gehörende Adjektive, Partizipien, Pronomen (Fürwörter) und Zahlwörter werden großgeschrieben ‹§ 60 (1)›.

Katharina die Große, Albrecht der Entartete, der Alte Fritz, der Große Kurfürst, Klein Erna, Heinrich der Achte, Unsere Liebe Frau (Maria, Mutter Jesu)

R 94 Von Personennamen **abgeleitete Adjektive** auf -(i)sch werden im Allgemeinen kleingeschrieben ‹§ 62›.

platonische Schriften, platonische Liebe; die heineschen Reisebilder, eine heinesche Ironie; die mozartschen Kompositionen.

Diese Formen werden großgeschrieben, wenn die Grundform des Personennamens durch einen Apostroph verdeutlicht wird.

die Darwin'sche Evolutionstheorie; die Goethe'schen Dramen

Großgeschrieben wird auch, wenn die Fügung als Ganzes ein Eigenname ist (vgl. R 56).

die Meyersche Verlagsbuchhandlung; der Halleysche Komet

● Klein schreibt man auch die von Personennamen abgeleiteten Adjektive auf -istisch, -esk und -haft und die Zusammensetzungen mit vor-, nach- u. Ä.

darwinistische Auffassungen, kafkaeske Gestalten, eulenspiegelhaftes Treiben, vorlutherische Bibelübersetzungen

R 95 Bildet ein **Familien- oder Personenname zusammen mit einem Substantiv** eine geläufige Bezeichnung, so schreibt man zusammen ‹§ 37 (3)›.

Dieselmotor, Kneippkur, Röntgenstrahlen, Thomasmehl, Achillesferse, Bachkantate

● Einen Bindestrich kann man setzen, wenn der Name hervorgehoben werden soll oder wenn dem Namen ein zusammengesetztes Grundwort folgt ‹§ 51›.

Schiller-Theater, Paracelsus-Ausgabe; Mozart-Konzertabend, Beethoven-Festhalle

● Bindestriche setzt man, wenn die Bestimmung zum Grundwort aus mehreren oder aus mehrteiligen Namen besteht ‹§ 50›.

Richard-Wagner-Festspiele, Max-Planck-Gesellschaft, Goethe-und-Schiller-Denkmal, Johann-Sebastian-Bach-Gymnasium, Van-Allen-Gürtel, Sankt-Marien-Kirche (St.-Marien-Kirche), aber: *Marienkirche*

Es steht ein Bindestrich, wenn Vor- und Familienname umgestellt sind und der Artikel vorangeht,

der Huber-Franz, die Hofer-Marie

wenn der Name als Grundwort steht

Möbel-Müller, Bier-Meier

und wenn ein Doppelname vorliegt ‹§ 46 (1)›.

Müller-Frankenfeld

R 96 Zusammensetzungen von **einteiligen Namen mit einem Adjektiv** werden im Allgemeinen zusammengeschrieben.

goethefreundlich, lutherfeindlich

Um den Eigennamen hervorzuheben, kann man solche Zusammensetzungen auch mit Bindestrich schreiben ‹§ 51›.

Richelieu-freundlich, Napoleon-treu

Bei mehrteiligen Namen dagegen schreibt man die Verbindung immer mit Bindestrich ‹§ 50›.

de-Gaulle-treu, Fidel-Castro-freundlich

● Von mehrteiligen Namen abgeleitete Adjektive werden mit Bindestrich geschrieben ‹§ 49›.

die heinrich-mannschen Romane
auch: *die Heinrich-Mann'schen Romane*
die von-bülowschen Zeichnungen
auch: *die von-Bülow'schen Zeichnungen*

R 97 Zusammensetzungen aus einem **Substantiv und einem Vornamen** schreibt man in der Regel zusammen ‹§ 47›.

Wurzelsepp, Schützenliesel, Suppenkaspar

Wird aber eine Berufsbezeichnung mit einem Vornamen zusammengesetzt, so steht ein Bindestrich ‹§ 46 (1)›.

Bäcker-Anna, Schuster-Franz

R 98 Stehen Familien-, Personen- und Vornamen **ohne Artikel oder Pronomen (Fürwort)** im Genitiv (Wesfall), so erhalten sie in der Regel das Genitiv-s.

Goethes, Beethovens, Siegfrieds, Hildegards, Kaiser Karls des Großen

Bei Familiennamen mit von, van, de, ten usw. wird heute gewöhnlich der Familienname gebeugt. Der Vorname wird nur dann gebeugt, wenn der Familienname – besonders bei historischen Namen – als Ortsname erkennbar ist und das übergeordnete Substantiv vorangeht.

Johann Wolfgang von Goethes Werke
Wolfram von Eschenbachs Lieder
aber: *die Lieder Wolframs von Eschenbach*

● Gehen die Familien-, Personen- und Vornamen auf s, ss, ß, x, z, tz aus, dann gibt es folgende Möglichkeiten, den Genitiv zu bilden oder zu umschreiben:

durch Voranstellung des Artikels oder Pronomens mit oder ohne Gattungsnamen,
des Tacitus, des Geschichtsschreibers Tacitus; unseres Paracelsus, unseres großen Gelehrten Paracelsus

durch ein vorgesetztes „von",
die Schriften von Paracelsus; die „Elektra" von Strauss

durch einen Apostroph (vgl. R 17),
Demosthenes' Reden, Paracelsus' Schriften, Ringelnatz' Gedichte

durch die Endung -ens (veraltet).

Horaz, Horazens; Götz, Götzens

● Stehen Familien-, Personen- und Vornamen mit Artikel oder Pronomen (Fürwort) im Genitiv (Wesfall), so bleiben sie ungebeugt.

des Lohengrin, des Anton Meier, eines Schiller; des Kaisers Karl, die Krönung der Königin Elisabeth, die Reise unseres Onkels Paul

Ist ein männlicher Personenname völlig zu einem Gattungsnamen geworden, dann erhält er in der Regel wie ein gewöhnliches Substantiv die Genitivendung -s.

des Dobermanns, des Zeppelins

R 99 Der **Plural der Familiennamen** wird meist mit -s gebildet.

Buddenbrooks, die Rothschilds, die Barrings; Meiers besuchen Müllers

Gelegentlich bleiben die Familiennamen ohne Beugungsendung, besonders wenn sie auf -en, -er, -el ausgehen.

die beiden Schlegel

R 100 Steht vor dem Namen **ein Titel, eine Berufs- oder Verwandtschaftsbezeichnung o. Ä. ohne Artikel oder Pronomen (Fürwort),** dann wird im Allgemeinen nur der Name [und der Beiname] gebeugt.

Professor Lehmanns Sprechstunde, Kaiser Karls des Großen Krönung, Personalchefin Krauses Rede, Tante Dagmars Brief

● Bei Formulierungen mit Artikel oder Pronomen wird nur der Titel usw. gebeugt.

des Herrn Müller, des Professors Lehmann, die Reise unseres Onkels Karl

● Stehen vor dem Namen mehrere mit dem Artikel verbundene Titel, dann wird meist nur der erste Titel gebeugt.

die Sprechstunde des Geheimrats Professor Dr. Lehmann

Ist der erste Titel „Herr", dann wird meist auch der folgende Titel gebeugt.

die Akte des Herrn Finanzrats Heller

● Der Titel „Herr" wird in Verbindung mit einem Namen immer gebeugt.

Herrn Müllers Brief ist eingetroffen. Das müssen Sie Herrn Müller sagen. Würden Sie bitte Herrn Müller rufen?

● Der Titel „Doktor" („Dr.") bleibt, da er als Teil des Namens gilt, immer ungebeugt.

das Gesuch des Dr. Meier

Für die Beugung der Titel in Anschriften gelten dieselben Richtlinien, auch dann, wenn die Präposition (das Verhältniswort) wegfällt.

Herrn A. Müller
[An] Herrn Regierungspräsidenten Müller
Herrn Ersten Bürgermeister Dr. Meier

Geographische (erdkundliche) Namen

R 101 Die **Schreibung der deutschen geographischen Namen** folgt im Allgemeinen dem heutigen Schreibgebrauch.

Freudental, Freiburg im Breisgau, Zell

In vielen Fällen ist jedoch an alten Schreibweisen festgehalten worden.

Frankenthal, Freyburg/Unstrut, Celle

Fremde geographische Namen werden gewöhnlich in der fremden Schreibweise geschrieben.

Toulouse, Marseille, Rio de Janeiro, Reykjavik

Einige fremde geographische Namen sind eingedeutscht.

Kalifornien (für: California)
Kanada (für: Canada)
Rom (für: Roma)

R 102 Zu einem geographischen Namen gehörende **Adjektive und Partizipien** werden großgeschrieben ‹§ 60 (2)›.

die Hohe Tatra, der Kleine Belt, das Schwarze Meer, der Bayerische Wald

Das gilt auch für inoffizielle Namen ‹§ 60 (5)›.

Ferner Osten, Neue Welt (Amerika)

R 103 Die von geographischen Namen **abgeleiteten Wörter auf -er** schreibt man immer groß ‹§ 61›.

der Hamburger Hafen, ein Frankfurter Sportverein, ein Schwarzwälder Rauchschinken

R 104 Die von geographischen Namen abgeleiteten **Adjektive auf -isch** werden kleingeschrieben, wenn sie nicht Teil eines Eigennamens sind ⟨§ 62⟩.

indischer Tee, italienischer Salat
aber: *die Holsteinische Schweiz*

R 105 **Zusammensetzungen** aus einem Grundwort und einem einfachen oder zusammengesetzten geographischen Namen schreibt man im Allgemeinen zusammen ⟨§ 37 (3)⟩.

Nildelta, Rheinfall, Manilahanf, Großglocknermassiv; moskaufreundlich

Das gilt auch für Zusammensetzungen mit ungebeugten Adjektiven oder Bezeichnungen für Himmelsrichtungen.

Großbritannien, Kleinasien, Mittelfranken, Hinterindien, Oberammergau, Niederlahnstein, Untertürkheim
Ostindien, Südafrika, Norddeutschland

Bei unübersichtlichen Zusammensetzungen (vor allem bei zusammengesetztem Grundwort) kann man einen Bindestrich setzen ⟨§ 45 (2)⟩.

Mosel-Winzergenossenschaft

Ein Bindestrich kann auch gesetzt werden, um den Namen besonders hervorzuheben ⟨§ 51⟩.

Jalta-Abkommen; Moskau-freundlich

Ein Bindestrich steht häufig bei nichtamtlichen Zusätzen ⟨§ 46 (2)⟩.

Alt-Wien, Groß-London, Alt-Heidelberg

Dieser Bindestrich bleibt auch bei Ableitungen erhalten ⟨§ 48⟩.

alt-heidelbergisch; Alt-Wiener Theater

Die behördliche Schreibung der Ortsnamen schwankt ⟨§ 46 E_2⟩.

Neuruppin, Groß Räschen, Klein-Auheim

Endet das ungebeugte Adjektiv auf -isch und ist es eine Ableitung von einem Orts-, Völker- oder Ländernamen, so setzt man meist einen Bindestrich.

Spanisch-Guinea, Britisch-Kolumbien

Auch hier gibt es Abweichungen bei behördlich festgelegten Schreibungen.

Schwäbisch Gmünd, Bayrischzell

● Bindestriche setzt man, wenn die Bestimmung zum Grundwort aus mehreren oder mehrteiligen Namen besteht ⟨§ 50⟩.

Dortmund-Ems-Kanal, Saar-Nahe-Bergland; Rio-de-la-Plata-Bucht, Sankt-Gotthard-Tunnel, König-Christian-IX.-Land

Dies gilt auch für Abkürzungen.

St.-Lorenz-Strom, USA-freundlich

Ableitungen von mehrteiligen Namen erhalten in der Regel ebenfalls den Bindestrich ⟨§ 49⟩; enden sie auf -er, dann können sie auch ohne Bindestrich geschrieben werden ⟨§ 49 E⟩.

Sri-Lanker/Sri Lanker, sri-lankisch

● Ableitungen auf -er von geographischen Namen schreibt man zusammen, wenn sie Personen bezeichnen ⟨§ 37 (3)⟩.

Schweizergarde, Römerbrief

Man schreibt solche Ableitungen getrennt, wenn sie die geographische Lage bezeichnen ⟨§ 38⟩.

Walliser Alpen, Köln-Bonner Flughafen

Besonders in Österreich und in der Schweiz wird in solchen Fällen oft zusammengeschrieben.

Bregenzerwald, Bielersee

Es gibt geographische Namen, die auf -er enden und keine Ableitungen der oben genannten Art sind. Diese Namen werden zusammengeschrieben.

Glocknergruppe, Brennerpass

● Die Wörter „Sankt“ und „Bad“ stehen vor geographischen Namen meist ohne Bindestrich und getrennt ⟨§ 46 E_2⟩.

Sankt Blasien (St. Blasien), Sankt Gotthard (St. Gotthard); Bad Elster, Bad Kissingen, Bad Kreuznach; Stuttgart-Bad Cannstatt

Ableitungen auf -er können mit oder ohne Bindestrich geschrieben werden ⟨§ 49 E⟩.

Sankt-Galler/Sankt Galler (aber nur: *sankt-gallisch*); *Bad-Kreuznacher/Bad Kreuznacher Salinen*

R 106 Man setzt einen Bindestrich, wenn **ein geographischer Name aus zwei geographischen Namen zusammengesetzt** ist ‹§ 46 (2)›.

Berlin-Schöneberg, München-Schwabing, Hamburg-Altona, Leipzig-Grünau; Rheinland-Pfalz, Mecklenburg-Vorpommern, Nordrhein-Westfalen

Bei Ableitungen bleibt dieser Bindestrich erhalten.

Schleswig-Holsteiner, schleswig-holsteinisch

Wenn bei Ortsnamen nähere Bestimmungen nachgestellt sind, so kann man einen Bindestrich setzen.

Frankfurt Stadt/Frankfurt-Stadt; Wiesbaden Süd/Wiesbaden-Süd

• Geographische Bezeichnungen, die aus Verbindungen gleichrangiger Adjektive bestehen, kann man zusammenschreiben oder mit Bindestrich ‹§ 45 (2)›.

die Entwicklung des deutschamerikanischen (auch: *deutsch-amerikanischen*) *Schiffsverkehrs; die deutschschweizerischen* (auch: *deutsch-schweizerischen*) *Beziehungen*

Verbindungen nicht gleichrangiger Adjektive werden dagegen nur zusammengeschrieben.

die deutschamerikanische Literatur (Literatur der Deutschamerikaner), *die schweizerdeutsche Mundart*

Nur zusammen schreibt man auch, wenn der erste Bestandteil nicht selbstständig gebraucht wird.

afroamerikanisch, galloromanisch

Endet das erste Adjektiv auf -isch, darf nach R 40 nicht zusammengeschrieben werden.

ein englisch-deutsches Projekt

R 107 Sächliche geographische Namen ohne Artikel bilden den **Genitiv (Wesfall) mit -s.**

die Kirchen Kölns, Deutschlands Geschichte, die Staaten Europas

Männliche oder sächliche geographische Namen mit Artikel erhalten im Genitiv meist ein -s. Das -s wird jedoch, besonders bei fremden Namen, häufig schon weggelassen.

des Brockens, des Rheins

Aber: *des heutigen Europa[s], des Mississippi[s], des Sudan[s]*

• Geographische Namen auf s, ss, ß, x, z, tz bilden den Genitiv wie Familien- und Personennamen, die in gleicher Weise enden (vgl. R 98).

Weißenfels' Einwohner, die Einwohner von Weißenfels, der Schuhstadt Weißenfels

Sonstige Namen

R 108 Zu einem **mehrteiligen Namen** gehörende Adjektive, Partizipien und Zahlwörter werden großgeschrieben ‹§ 60 (3)›.

der Kleine Bär, die Hängenden Gärten der Semiramis, Institut für Angewandte Geodäsie, Römisch-Germanisches Museum

Bei Namen von Gaststätten o. Ä. schreibt man auch das erste Wort des Namens groß.

Zur Neuen Post, In der Alten Schmiede

Adjektive, die nicht am Anfang des mehrteiligen Namens stehen, werden in einigen Fällen auch kleingeschrieben ‹§ 60 E_2›.

Institut für deutsche Sprache

• Es gibt Wortverbindungen, die keine Namen sind, obwohl sie häufig als Namen angesehen werden. Hier werden die Adjektive kleingeschrieben ‹§ 63›. (Im Zweifelsfall schlage man im Wörterverzeichnis nach.)

schwarzer Tee, der blaue Brief, das olympische Feuer, neues Jahr

Vor allem in der Botanik und in der Zoologie werden die Adjektive in Verbindungen dieser Art oft großgeschrieben, weil man Benennungen aus der wissenschaftlichen Systematik von den allgemeinen Gattungsbezeichnungen abheben will ‹§ 64 (2)›.

Schwarzer Holunder (Sambucus nigra), *Kleines Sumpfhuhn* (Porzana parva)

Vgl. R 56.

R 109 Das **erste Wort** eines Buch-, Film- oder Zeitschriftentitels, einer Überschrift o. Ä. wird großgeschrieben ⟨§ 53⟩.

Er war Mitarbeiter der Neuen Rheinischen Zeitung. Wir haben den Film „Der Tod in Venedig" zweimal gesehen.

R 110 Titel von Büchern, Zeitungen usw. **werden gebeugt,** auch wenn sie in Anführungszeichen stehen.

die neue Auflage des Dudens, die Redaktion der „Frankfurter Allgemeinen Zeitung", aus Wagners „Meistersingern"

Dies gilt auch für Firmen-, Gebäude- und Straßennamen o. Ä.

der Senat der Freien Hansestadt Bremen, das Verwaltungsgebäude der Vereinigten Stahlwerke, die Leistungen des Rheinisch-Westfälischen Elektrizitätswerkes, er wohnt in der Oberen Riedstraße

Will man einen solchen Titel oder Firmennamen unverändert wiedergeben, dann sollte er mit einem entsprechenden Substantiv umschrieben werden.

aus der Zeitschrift „Die Kunst des Orients", aus Wagners Oper „Die Meistersinger", im Hotel „Europäischer Hof"

Dies gilt insbesondere für Titel, die mit einem Possessivpronomen (besitzanzeigenden Fürwort) beginnen.

Max Müller liest aus dem Buch „Mein Leben".

Nominativ (Werfall)
↑Substantiv (R 124 ff.)

Ordinalzahl (Ordnungszahl)
↑Punkt (R 112)

Ortsangabe
↑Komma (R 63)

Ortsnamen
↑Namen (R 101 ff.)

Parenthese
↑Klammern

Partizip (Mittelwort)
↑Adjektiv (R 5 ff.), ↑Getrennt- und Zusammenschreibung (R 40), ↑Groß- und Kleinschreibung (R 47), ↑Komma (R 73 f.)

Personennamen
↑Namen (R 91 ff.)

Plural (Mehrzahl)
↑Maß-, Mengen- und Währungsbezeichnungen (R 90), ↑Namen (R 99), ↑Substantiv (R 124 ff.)

Präposition (Verhältniswort)
↑Getrennt- und Zusammenschreibung (R 41), ↑Groß- und Kleinschreibung (R 49)

Pronomen (Fürwort)
↑Groß- und Kleinschreibung (R 48 u. 52 f.)

Punkt

R 111 Der Punkt steht nach einem abgeschlossenen **Aussagesatz** ⟨§ 67⟩.

Es wird Frühling. Wir freuen uns. Wenn du willst, kannst du mitkommen.

Das gilt auch für Frage-, Aufforderungs- und Wunschsätze, die von einem Aussagesatz abhängig sind oder ohne Nachdruck gesprochen werden ⟨§ 67 E_2⟩.

Sie fragte ihn, wann er kommen wolle. Er rief ihm zu, er solle sich nicht fürchten. Er wünschte, alles wäre vorbei. Bitte geben Sie mir das Buch. Vgl. Seite 25 seiner letzten Veröffentlichung.

● Der Punkt steht nicht nach einem Aussagesatz, der als Satzglied oder Beifügung (Attribut) am Anfang oder innerhalb eines anderen Satzes steht ⟨§ 92⟩.

„Aller Anfang ist schwer" ist ein tröstlicher Spruch. Das Sprichwort „Eigener Herd ist Goldes wert" gilt nicht für jeden.

R 112 Der Punkt steht nach Zahlen, um sie als **Ordnungszahlen** zu kennzeichnen ⟨§ 104⟩.

Sonntag, den 15. April
Friedrich II., König von Preußen

Steht eine Ordnungszahl am Satzende, so wird kein zusätzlicher Satzschlusspunkt gesetzt.

Katharina von Aragonien war die erste Frau Heinrichs VIII.

> **R 113** Der Punkt steht nicht nach **Überschriften, Buch- und Zeitungstiteln** und anderen vom übrigen Text deutlich abgehobenen Zeilen ‹§ 68 (1)›.

Der Frieden ist gesichert
Nach den schwierigen Verhandlungen zwischen den Vertragspartnern ...

Religion: gut
Deutsch: mangelhaft
Mathematik: sehr gut

● Der Punkt steht auch nicht nach der Jahreszahl bei selbstständigen Datumsangaben, nach der Anschrift in Briefen und auf Umschlägen sowie nach Grußformeln und Unterschriften unter Briefen und anderen Schriftstücken ‹§ 68 (3)›.

Mannheim, den 1. 4. 1999
Frankfurt, am 28. 8. 49

Herrn
K. Meier
Rüdesheimer Straße 29
65197 Wiesbaden

Mit herzlichem Gruß
Ihr Peter Müller

Mit freundlichen Grüßen
die Schüler der Klasse 9b

Weitere Hinweise: ↑Abkürzungen (R 1), ↑Abschnittsgliederung (R 3 f.), ↑Anführungszeichen (R 12), ↑Klammern (R 61), ↑Zahlen und Ziffern (R 134 f.) sowie in den Hinweisen für das Maschinenschreiben (S. 77).

Schrägstrich

> **R 114** Der Schrägstrich kann zur Angabe von Größen- oder Zahlenverhältnissen **im Sinne von „je“** gebraucht werden ‹§ 106 (3)›.

durchschnittlich 60 km/h
100 Ew./km² (= 100 Einwohner je Quadratkilometer)

Vor allem in nichtmathematischen Texten wird der Schrägstrich häufig als Bruchstrich verwendet.

Das Guthaben wurde mit 3½% verzinst.

> **R 115** Der Schrägstrich kann zur [zusammenfassenden] **Angabe mehrerer Möglichkeiten** gebraucht werden ‹§ 106 (1)›.

Ich/Wir überweise[n] von meinem/unserem Konto ...
für Männer und/oder Frauen
behandelnde Ärzte/Ärztinnen
die Kolleginnen/Kollegen vom Betriebsrat
unsere Mitarbeiter/-innen

Gelegentlich wird der Ergänzungsstrich weggelassen:

ausgezeichnete Sportler/innen

Vgl. auch R 62.

> **R 116** Der Schrägstrich verbindet **Namen verschiedener Personen** o. Ä. ‹§ 106 (1)›.

Becker/Stich erreichten durch einen 3:1-Erfolg das Endspiel.
In dieser Bootsklasse siegte die Renngemeinschaft Ratzeburg/Kiel.

Bei Parteinamen kann der Schrägstrich Fraktionsgemeinschaften o. Ä. kennzeichnen.

Die Pressekonferenz der CDU/CSU wurde mit Spannung erwartet.

> **R 117** Der Schrägstrich kennzeichnet die Zusammenfassung zweier **aufeinander folgender Jahreszahlen, Monatsnamen** o. Ä. ‹§ 106 (1)›.

1870/71, im Wintersemester 96/97, der Beitrag für März/April

> **R 118** Der Schrägstrich dient zur Gliederung von **Akten- oder Diktatzeichen** o. Ä ‹§ 106 (2)›.

M/III/47
Dr. Dr/Ko
Rechn.-Nr. 195/95

Schriftsatz

↑Richtlinien für den Schriftsatz S. 65.

Selbstlaut (Vokal)

↑Worttrennung (R 129), ↑Zusammentreffen von drei gleichen Buchstaben (R 136)

Semikolon (Strichpunkt)

R 119 Das Semikolon kann zwischen gleichrangigen Sätzen oder Wortgruppen stehen, wo der Punkt zu stark, das Komma zu schwach trennen würde ⟨§ 80⟩.

Die Stellung der Werbeabteilung im Organisationsplan ist in den einzelnen Unternehmen verschieden; sie richtet sich nach den Anforderungen, die an die Werbung gestellt werden.

Er denkt immer nur an sich selbst; er trachtet nur danach, andere zu übervorteilen; er kann sich nicht in die Gemeinschaft einfügen: Ein solcher Mensch kann von uns keine Hilfe erwarten.

Unser Proviant bestand aus gedörrtem Fleisch, Speck und Rauchschinken; Ei- und Milchpulver; Reis, Nudeln und Grieß.

Silbentrennung

↑Worttrennung

ss und ß

R 120 Man schreibt **ß** für den (in allen Beugungsformen) stimmlosen s-Laut nach langem Vokal (Selbstlaut) oder nach Doppellaut (Diphthong), wenn im Wortstamm kein weiterer Konsonant folgt ⟨§ 25⟩.

Blöße, Maße, Maß, grüßen, grüßte, Gruß; außer, reißen, es reißt, Fleiß, Preußen (Ausnahmen: *aus, heraus* usw.)

Aber: *Haus* [stimmhaftes s in Häuser], *Gras* [stimmhaftes s in Gräser], *sauste* [stimmhaftes s in sausen]; *meistens* [folgender Konsonant im Wortstamm]

● Man schreibt ss für den stimmlosen s-Laut nach kurzem Vokal (auch im Auslaut der Wortstämme) ⟨§ 2⟩.

Masse, Missetat, missachten, hassen, ihr hasst, Fluss, Flüsse, essen, du isst, iss!, Kongress, wässrig, dass (Konjunktion)

Ausnahmen: *das* (Pronomen, Artikel), *was, des, wes*

● Nur mit s werden jedoch die Bildungen auf „-nis" und bestimmte Fremdwörter geschrieben, obwohl der Plural mit Doppel-s gebildet wird ⟨§ 5⟩.

Zeugnis (trotz: Zeugnisse), *Geheimnis* (trotz: Geheimnisse), *Bus* (trotz: Busse), *Atlas* (trotz: Atlasse)

R 121 Fehlt das **ß** auf der Tastatur einer Schreibmaschine oder eines Computers, kann man dafür **ss** schreiben.

In der Schweiz kann das ß generell durch ss ersetzt werden ⟨§ 25 E_2⟩. (Vgl. R 130.)

● Auch bei der Verwendung von Großbuchstaben steht SS für ß ⟨§ 25 E_3⟩.

Das gilt besonders für Überschriften, Buchtitel, Plakate u. Ä.

STRASSE, AUSSEN, FUSSBALL

In Dokumenten wird bei Namen aus Gründen der Eindeutigkeit auch ß verwendet.

HEINZ GROßE

● Treffen drei s zusammen, kann man zur besseren Lesbarkeit einen Bindestrich setzen ⟨§ 45 (4)⟩.

Bassstimme, auch: *Bass-Stimme*
Flussschiffer, auch: *Fluss-Schiffer*
VERSCHLUSSSACHE,
auch *VERSCHLUSS-SACHE*

Vgl. auch R 136.

Straßennamen

R 122 Das **erste Wort** eines Straßennamens wird großgeschrieben, ebenso alle zum Namen gehörenden Adjektive und Zahlwörter ⟨§ 60 (2.2)⟩.

Im Trutz, Am Alten Lindenbaum, Kleine Bockenheimer Straße, An den Drei Tannen

R 123 Straßennamen, die aus einem **einfachen oder zusammengesetzten Substantiv** (auch Namen) oder aus einem **ungebeugten Adjektiv** und einem für Straßennamen typischen Grundwort bestehen, werden in der Regel zusammengeschrieben ⟨§ 37 (4)⟩.

Brunnenweg, Bahnhofstraße, Rathausgasse, Bismarckring, Beethovenplatz, Augustaanlage, Römerstraße, Dammtor, Wittelsbacherallee, Becksweg, Marienwerderstraße, Drusweilerweg, Herderstraße

Altmarkt, Neumarkt, Hochstraße

● Getrennt schreibt man dagegen, wenn der erste Bestandteil ein gebeugtes Adjektiv ist.

Große Bleiche, Langer Graben, Neue Kräme, Französische Straße

Getrennt schreibt man auch bei Ableitungen auf -er von Orts- und Ländernamen ‹§ 38›.

Münchener Straße, Am Saarbrücker Tor, Schweizer Platz, Kalk-Deutzer Straße

Bei Ortsnamen, Völker- oder Familiennamen auf -er wird jedoch nach R 123 zusammengeschrieben.

Drusweilerweg, Römerplatz, Herderstraße

● Bindestriche setzt man, wenn die Bestimmung zum Grundwort aus mehreren Wörtern besteht ‹§ 50›.

Albrecht-Dürer-Allee, Kaiser-Friedrich-Ring, Van-Dyck-Straße, Ernst-Ludwig-Kirchner-Straße, E.-T.-A.-Hoffmann-Straße, Professor-Sauerbruch-Straße, Berliner-Tor-Platz, Bad-Kissingen-Straße, Sankt-Blasien-Straße, Am St.-Georgs-Kirchhof, Bürgermeister-Dr.-Meier-Platz, Von-Repkow-Platz

● Beispiele für die Zusammenfassung von getrennt geschriebenen und nicht getrennt geschriebenen Straßennamen ‹§ 98›:

Ecke [der] Ansbacher und Motzstraße, Ecke [der] Motz- und Ansbacher Straße
Ecke [der] Schiersteiner und Wolfram-von-Eschenbach-Straße, Ecke [der] Wolfram-von-Eschenbach- und Schiersteiner Straße

Strichpunkt

↑Semikolon

Substantiv (Hauptwort)

Man unterscheidet drei Arten der Deklination (Beugung) des Substantivs: die starke (R 124 f.), die schwache (R 126 f.) und die gemischte (R 128) Deklination.

R 124 Die **stark gebeugten männlichen und sächlichen** Substantive bilden den Genitiv (Wesfall) Singular mit -es oder -s; der Nominativ (Werfall) Plural endet auf -e, -er oder -s, er kann auch endungslos sein oder Umlaut haben.

des Überflusses, des Glases
des Wagens, des Papiers
die Reflexe, die Schafe
die Geister, die Bretter
die Uhus, die Autos
die Lehrer, die Gitter
die Gärten, die Klöster

● Der Dativ (Wemfall) Singular starker männlicher und sächlicher Substantive wird heute gewöhnlich ohne -e gebildet.

dem Bau, im Heu, dem Frühling, dem Ausflug, dem Schicksal; im Senat, mit dem Tabak

● In festen Wendungen, Titeln oder in gehobener Sprache kommt das Dativ-e noch vor.

in diesem Sinne, dem Manne kann geholfen werden; „Vom Winde verweht"

R 125 Die **stark gebeugten weiblichen** Substantive sind im Singular endungslos; der Nominativ (Werfall) Plural endet auf -e oder -s, er kann auch endungslos sein und Umlaut haben.

die Trübsale, die Muttis, die Kräfte, die Töchter

R 126 Die **schwach gebeugten männlichen** Substantive enden in allen Formen mit Ausnahme des Nominativs (Werfalls) Singular auf -en oder -n.

des Menschen, dem Hasen, den Boten, die Studenten

● Die Endung -en bzw. -n darf im Dativ (Wemfall) und Akkusativ (Wenfall) Singular im Allgemeinen nicht weggelassen werden.

Der Professor prüfte den Kandidaten (nicht: den Kandidat).
Er begrüßte den Fabrikanten (nicht: den Fabrikant).
Die Ärztin gab dem Patienten (nicht: dem Patient) *eine Spritze.*

Er sandte ihn als Boten (nicht: als Bote). *Dir als Juristen* (nicht: als Jurist) *legt man die Frage vor.*

Nur in folgenden Fällen ist die endungslose Form richtig: wenn das Substantiv ohne Artikel oder Beifügung (Attribut) nach einer Präposition (einem Verhältniswort) steht oder wenn allein stehende Substantive durch „und" verbunden sind.

eine Seele von Mensch
ein Forstmeister mit Assistent
Die neue Regelung betrifft Patient und Arzt gleichermaßen.

In Anschriften sind beide Formen möglich.

[An] Herrn Präsidenten (auch: *Präsident*) *Karl Müller*

R 127 Die **schwach gebeugten weiblichen** Substantive sind im Singular endungslos, im Plural enden sie auf -en oder -n.

die Frauen, die Gaben, die Kammern

R 128 Die **gemischt gebeugten männlichen und sächlichen** Substantive werden im Singular stark gebeugt (der Genitiv endet auf -es oder -s) und im Plural schwach (der Nominativ endet auf -en oder -n).

des Staates, die Staaten
des Sees, die Seen
des Doktors, die Doktoren

Superlativ

↑Groß- und Kleinschreibung (R 47)

Tätigkeitswort (Verb)

↑Apostroph (R 13 u. 16), ↑Getrennt- und Zusammenschreibung (R 37 ff.), ↑Groß- und Kleinschreibung (R 50)

Telefonnummern

↑Richtlinien für den Schriftsatz (S. 68)

Titel oder sonstige Namen

↑Anführungszeichen (R 9), ↑Groß- und Kleinschreibung (R 54 ff.), ↑Namen (R 91–110)

Transkriptions- und Transliterationssysteme

↑S. 85

Trennung

↑Worttrennung

Überschriften

↑Namen (R 109), ↑Punkt (R 113)

Verb (Tätigkeitswort, Zeitwort)

↑Apostroph (R 13 u. 16), ↑Getrennt- und Zusammenschreibung (R 37 ff.), ↑Groß- und Kleinschreibung (R 50)

Vokal (Selbstlaut)

↑Worttrennung (R 129), ↑Zusammentreffen von drei gleichen Buchstaben (R 136)

Vornamen

↑Namen (R 92 u. 98)

Währungsbezeichnungen

↑Maß-, Mengen- und Währungsbezeichnungen

Wemfall (Dativ)

↑Substantiv (R 124 u. 126)

Wenfall (Akkusativ)

↑Substantiv (R 126)

Werfall (Nominativ)

↑Substantiv (R 124 ff.)

Wesfall (Genitiv)

↑Substantiv (R 124, 126 u. 128)

Worttrennung (Silbentrennung)

Wörter können am Ende einer Zeile mit einem Trennungsstrich getrennt werden, wenn der Platz für das ganze Wort nicht ausreicht. Der Trennungsstrich entfällt, wenn am Zeilenende ein Bindestrich steht.

R 129 Mehrsilbige **einfache und abgeleitete Wörter** trennt man so, wie es sich beim langsamen Sprechen von selbst ergibt, also nach Sprechsilben ‹§ 107›.

Freun-de, Män-ner, Mül-ler, Mül-le-rin, for-dern, wei-ter, Or-gel, kal-kig, Bes-se-rung, Brau-e-rei
Bal-kon, Bal-ko-ne, Fis-kus, Ho-tel, Pla-net, Kon-ti-nent, Re-mi-nis-zenz, Na-ti-on, Na-ti-o-nen, El-lip-se, po-e-tisch, In-di-vi-du-a-list
Ber-lin, El-ba, Tür-kei, Gu-a-te-ma-la

• Ein einzelner Konsonant (Mitlaut) kommt in diesen Fällen auf die folgende Zeile; von mehreren Konsonanten kommt der letzte auf die folgende Zeile ⟨§ 108⟩.

tre-ten, nä-hen, Ru-der, rei-ßen, bo-xen; Ko-kon, Na-ta-li-tät; Kre-ta, Chi-na
An-ker, Fin-ger, war-ten, Fül-lun-gen, Rit-ter, Was-ser, Knos-pen, kämp-fen, Ach-sel, steck-ten, Kat-zen, Städ-ter, Drechs-ler, dunk-le, gest-rig, an-de-re, and-re, neh-men, Bess-rung, Kas-ten (vgl. R 130); *Ar-sen, Hip-pie, Kas-ko, Pek-tin; Un-garn, Hes-sen, At-lan-tik*

Nachsilben, die mit einem Vokal (Selbstlaut) beginnen, nehmen bei der Trennung den vorangehenden Konsonanten zu sich.

Schaffne-rin, Freun-din, Bäcke-rei, Be-steue-rung, Lüf-tung, heu-tig, kin-disch, ta-gen

• Auch ein einzelner Vokal am Wortanfang kann abgetrennt werden.

A-der, E-ber, I-gel, o-der, U-hu, ä-sen, Ö-dem, ü-bel

Die Abtrennung eines einzelnen Vokals am Wortende ist nicht sinnvoll.

R 130 Die **Konsonantenverbindungen ch, ck und sch, in Fremdwörtern auch ph, rh, sh und th** bezeichnen einfache Laute und bleiben ungetrennt ⟨§ 109⟩.

Bü-cher, Zu-cker, ba-cken, Fla-sche, Ma-chete, Pro-phet, Myr-rhe, Bu-shel, ka-tho-lisch, Zwi-ckau

• In Fremdwörtern können die folgenden Buchstabengruppen ungetrennt bleiben ⟨§ 110⟩:

bl, pl, fl, gl, cl, kl, phl; br, pr, dr, tr, fr, vr, gr, cr, kr, phr, str, thr; gn, kn

Pub-li-kum, auch: *Pu-bli-kum, fle-xib-ler,* auch: *fle-xi-bler, Dip-lom,* auch: *Di-plom, Per-sif-la-ge,* auch: *Per-si-fla-ge, Reg-le-ment,* auch: *Re-gle-ment, Bouc-lé,* auch: *Bou-clé, Zyk-lus,* auch: *Zy-klus, Typh-li-tis,* auch: *Ty-phli-tis; Feb-ru-ar,* auch: *Fe-bru-ar, Lep-ra,* auch: *Le-pra, Hyd-rant,* auch: *Hy-drant, neut-ral,* auch: *neu-tral, Chiff-re,* auch: *Chif-fre, Liv-ree,* auch: *Li-vree, In-teg-ral,* auch: *In-te-gral, Suc-re,* auch: *Su-cre, Sak-ra-ment,* auch: *Sa-kra-ment, Neph-ri-tis,* auch: *Ne-phri-tis, In-dust-rie,* auch: *In-dus-trie* oder *In-du-strie, Arth-ri-tis,* auch: *Ar-thri-tis; Mag-net,* auch: *Ma-gnet, pyk-nisch,* auch: *py-knisch; Ok-la-ho-ma,* auch: *O-kla-ho-ma, Ab-ra-ham,* auch: *A-bra-ham*

Stehen die Buchstabengruppen **dsch** oder **tsch** für Einzelbuchstaben aus fremden Sprachen (z. B. für engl. j oder russ. ч), so sollten sie ebenfalls ungetrennt bleiben dürfen:

Fid-schi, auch: *Fi-dschi, Tschet-sche-ne,* auch: *Tsche-tsche-ne*

• Steht **ss** als Ersatz für **ß** (z. B. bei einer Schreibmaschine ohne ß), dann wird zwischen den beiden s getrennt ⟨§ 108⟩.

Grüs-se (für: Grü-ße), *heis-sen* (für: hei-ßen)

• Das frühere Verbot der Trennung von **st** gilt nicht mehr.

las-ten, Wes-ten, sechs-te, er brems-te, des Diens-tes, Akus-tik, Hys-te-rie

R 131 Die Diphthonge (Doppellaute) **ai, au, äu, ei, eu, oi** [gesprochen: ɔy] dürfen nur zusammen abgetrennt werden.

Kai-ser, Trau-ung, Räu-ber, ei-nig, Eu-le, Broi-ler

Der französische Diphthong **oi** [gesprochen o̯a, bei folgendem n: o̯ɛ̃] bleibt besser ebenfalls ungetrennt.

Toi-let-te, Poin-te

• Die stummen Dehnungsbuchstaben e und i werden nicht abgetrennt.

Wie-se
Coes-feld (gesprochen ['ko:s...])
Trois-dorf (gesprochen ['tro:s...])

Das gilt auch für das w in der Namenendung -ow.

Tel-tow-er Rübchen (gesprochen ['tɛlto:ər])

● Mit Rücksicht auf die Lesbarkeit des Textes bleiben die folgenden Wörter besser ungetrennt:

Feen, knien, [auf] Knien, Seen

> **R 132** **Zusammengesetzte Wörter** und Wörter mit einer Vorsilbe werden nach ihren Bestandteilen getrennt ⟨§ 111⟩.

Kleider-schrank, Hosen-träger, Diens-tag, ge-schwungen, be-treten, Be-treuung, Vergnügen

Dasselbe gilt auch für Fremdwörter und geographische Namen.

in-adäquat, Des-interesse, Trans-aktion, kapital-intensiv; Neu-strelitz, Wilmers-dorf

● Wird ein Wort nicht mehr als Zusammensetzung erkannt oder empfunden, so ist auch die Trennung nach Sprechsilben korrekt ⟨§ 112⟩.

wa-rum, auch: *war-um, da-rauf,* auch: *dar-auf, ei-nander,* auch: *ein-ander, Pä-da-go-ge,* auch: *Päd-ago-ge, He-li-kop-ter,* auch: *He-li-ko-pter, in-te-res-sant,* auch: *in-ter-es-sant, Mai-nau,* auch: *Main-au*

Trennungen, die zwar den Vorschriften entsprechen, aber den Leseablauf stören, sollte man vermeiden ⟨§ 111 E_2⟩.

Spar-gelder, aber nicht: Spargel-der
be-stehende, aber nicht: beste-hende
be-inhalten, aber nicht: bein-halten
Gehör-nerven, aber nicht: Gehörner-ven
Deo-spray, aber nicht: De-ospray
Feier-abend, aber nicht: Feiera-bend
ein-üben, aber nicht: einü-ben

> **R 133** Treten in einem deutschen Text einzelne **fremdsprachige Wörter,** Wortgruppen oder kurze Sätze auf, dann trennt man nach den deutschen Regeln ab.

Co-ming man, Swin-ging Lon-don

Die Trennungsregeln fremder Sprachen sollten nur bei längeren Zitaten, d. h. bei fortlaufendem fremdsprachigem Text, angewandt werden.

com-ing, swing-ing

Wunschsatz

↑ Ausrufezeichen (R 20), ↑ Punkt (R 111)

Zahlen und Ziffern

Hinweise zur Schreibung der Zahlen in Buchstaben und als Bestandteile von Ableitungen und Zusammensetzungen finden sich in den Abschnitten Bindestrich (R 25 und 28), Getrennt- und Zusammenschreibung (R 44), Groß- und Kleinschreibung (R 48).

> **R 134** Ganze Zahlen aus **mehr als drei Ziffern** werden von der Endziffer aus in dreistellige Gruppen zerlegt.

3 417 379 DM *25 000 kg* *4 150*

Man gliedert hierbei durch Zwischenraum, nicht durch Komma.
Eine Gliederung durch Punkt ist möglich, kann aber zu Verwechslungen führen, da z. B. im Englischen der Punkt die Dezimalstelle angibt.

10.000.000 kW

Bei Zahlen, die eine Nummer darstellen, sind auch andere Gruppierungen als die Dreiergliederung möglich.

Tel. 70 96 14
Kundennummer 2 1534 5677

Vgl. auch S. 68.

> **R 135** **Dezimalstellen** werden von den ganzen Zahlen durch ein Komma getrennt.

52,36 m
8,745 032 kg
1 244,552 12

Auch nach dem Komma ist eine Gliederung in Dreiergruppen durch Zwischenraum (nicht durch Punkt oder Komma!) möglich.

Entsprechend wird bei der Angabe von Geldbeträgen in DM die Pfennigzahl durch ein Komma abgetrennt.

3,45 DM, auch (besonders in Aufstellungen und im Zahlungsverkehr): *DM 3,45*

Bei vollen Markbeträgen können die Dezimalstellen zusätzlich angedeutet werden.

5 DM
oder: *5,00 DM*
oder: *5,– DM*

In der Schweiz steht zwischen Franken- und Rappenzahl gewöhnlich ein Punkt.

Fr. 4.20

Will man eine Spanne zwischen zwei Geldbeträgen angeben, so achte man auf Eindeutigkeit.
10-25 000 DM (wenn die erste Zahl 10 DM bezeichnet)
10 000-25 000 DM (wenn die erste Zahl 10 000 DM bezeichnet)

● Bei Zeitangaben wird die Zahl der Minuten von der Zahl der Stunden nicht durch ein Komma, sondern durch einen Punkt oder Doppelpunkt oder durch Hochstellung abgehoben, da es sich hier nicht um Dezimalstellen handelt.

6.30 [Uhr]
6:30 [Uhr]
6^{30} [Uhr]

Zeitwort (Verb)

↑Apostroph (R 13 u. 16), ↑Getrennt- und Zusammenschreibung (R 37 ff.), ↑Groß- und Kleinschreibung (R 50)

Ziffern

↑Zahlen und Ziffern

Zusammentreffen von drei gleichen Buchstaben

R 136 Treffen bei Zusammensetzungen **drei gleiche Buchstaben** zusammen, darf keiner von ihnen wegfallen.

Kaffeeersatz, schneeerhellt, Auspuffflamme, Schifffahrt, Pappplakat, Brennnessel, Balletttruppe, Kongressstadt, fetttriefend

● Eine Ausnahme bilden die Wörter „dennoch“, „Drittel“ und „Mittag“.

● Zur besseren Lesbarkeit kann ein Bindestrich gesetzt werden ‹§ 45 (4)›.

Kammmacher, auch: *Kamm-Macher*
Zooorchester, auch: *Zoo-Orchester*
stickstofffrei, auch: *Stickstoff-frei*

Zusammen- und Getrenntschreibung

↑Getrennt- und Zusammenschreibung

Richtlinien für den Schriftsatz

Bei der Herstellung gedruckter Texte sind die folgenden Richtlinien zu beachten. Moderne Textverarbeitungsprogramme nähern sich im hier behandelten Bereich den Möglichkeiten von Satzsystemen immer mehr an, sodass für sie heute dieselben Maßstäbe gelten können. Sofern sie diese nicht erfüllen, gelten die allgemeinen Regeln für das Maschinenschreiben (↑Hinweise für das Maschinenschreiben). Um eine problemlose Umwandlung elektronisch gespeicherter Texte in Schriftsatz zu gewährleisten, sollte schon die Texterfassung in Absprache mit der Druckerei erfolgen.

Einzelheiten, die im Folgenden nicht erfasst sind, und sachlich begründete Abweichungen sollten – als Anleitung für Korrektoren und Setzer – in einer besonderen Satzanweisung für das betreffende Werk eindeutig festgelegt werden.

Abkürzungen

Vgl. hierzu auch R 1 f. u. R 26.

a) Am Satzanfang

Abkürzungen, die für mehr als ein Wort stehen, werden am Satzanfang in der Regel ausgesetzt.

nicht: *Z. B. hat ...*
M. a. W. ...
sondern: *Zum Beispiel hat ...*
Mit anderen Worten ...

b) S., Bd., Nr., Anm.

Abkürzungen wie S., Bd., Nr., Anm. sollen nur verwendet werden, wenn ihnen kein Artikel und keine Zahl vorangeht.

S. 5, Bd. 8, Nr. 4, Anm. B
aber:
die Seite 5, der Band 8, die Nummer 4, die Anmerkung B
5. Seite, 8. Band, 4. Nummer.

c) Mehrgliedrige Abkürzungen

Bei mehrgliedrigen Abkürzungen wird zwischen den einzelnen Gliedern nach dem Punkt ein kleinerer Zwischenraum gesetzt.

z. B., u. v. a. m., i. V., u. dgl. m.

Die Trennung mehrgliedriger Abkürzungen ist zu vermeiden.

nicht: *Die Hütte liegt 2 800 m ü.*
d. M.
sondern: *Die Hütte liegt 2 800 m*
ü. d. M.

Auch abgekürzte Maß- und Währungseinheiten sollen nach Möglichkeit nicht von den dazugehörigen Zahlen getrennt werden.

nicht: *Wir bestellten für rund 590*
DM Gardinenstoff.
sondern: *Wir bestellten für rund*
590 DM Gardinenstoff.

Vgl. auch ↑Festabstände.

Anführungszeichen

Im deutschen Schriftsatz werden vornehmlich die Anführungszeichen „...“ und »...« sowie ihre einfachen Formen ‚...‘ und ›...‹ angewendet. Man setzt sie ohne Zwischenraum vor und nach den eingeschlossenen Textabschnitten, Wörtern u. a.

In anderen Sprachen finden sich: “...”, ‘...’, «...», ‹...›, ”...”, „...”, »...».

„Ja“, sagte er.
Sie rief: »Ich komme!«

Die französische Form «...» ist im Deutschen weniger gebräuchlich; in der Schweiz hat sie sich für den Antiquasatz eingebürgert.

Bei einzelnen aus fremden Sprachen angeführten Wörtern und Wendungen setzt man die Anführungszeichen wie im deutschen Text.

Der „guardia" ist mit unserem Schutzmann zu vergleichen.

Wird ein ganzer Satz oder Absatz aus einer fremden Sprache angeführt, dann verwendet man die in dieser Sprache üblichen Anführungszeichen.

Ein englisches Sprichwort lautet: "Early to bed and early to rise makes a man healthy, wealthy, and wise."
Cavours letzte Worte waren: «Frate, frate! Libera chiesa in libero stato!»
Vgl. auch R 8 ff.

Anmerkungszeichen

↑ Fußnoten- und Anmerkungszeichen

Antiqua im Fraktursatz

a) Wörter aus Fremdsprachen
Fremdsprachige Wörter und Wortgruppen, die nicht durch Schreibung, Beugung oder Lautung als eingedeutscht erscheinen, sind im Fraktursatz in Antiqua zu setzen.

en avant, en vogue, all right, in praxi, in petto, a conto, dolce far niente; Agent provocateur, Tempi passati, Agnus Dei; last, not least

Dies gilt besonders für die italienischen Fachausdrücke in der Musik.

andante, adagio, moderato, vivace usw.

Man setzt aber solche fremdsprachigen Wörter in Fraktur, wenn sie in Schreibung, Beugung oder Lautung eingedeutscht sind oder mit einem deutschen Wort zusammengesetzt werden.

Er spielte ein Adagio (nicht: adagio).

Die Firma leistete eine Akontozahlung (nicht: A-conto-Zahlung).

Auch fremdsprachige Personennamen und geographische Namen werden im Fraktursatz in Fraktur gesetzt.

Michelangelo Buonarroti war ein berühmter Künstler. Cherbourg ist eine Stadt an der Kanalküste.

b) Bindestriche im gemischten Satz
Treffen bei zusammengesetzten Wörtern Teile in verschiedener Schriftart aufeinander, dann ist der Bindestrich aus der Textschrift zu setzen.

Das sinkende Schiff sandte SOS-Rufe.

Innerhalb der gleichen Schriftart darf aber ein Bindestrich anderer Art nicht stehen.

Die Tänze des Staatstheater-Corps-de-ballet wurden begeistert aufgenommen.

Apostroph

Dem Apostroph am Wortanfang geht im Allgemeinen der regelmäßige Wortzwischenraum voran.

aber 's kam anders
so 'n Mann

Vgl. auch R 13 ff.

Auslassungspunkte

Um eine Auslassung in einem Text zu kennzeichnen, setzt man drei Punkte. Vor und nach den Auslassungspunkten wird jeweils ein Wortzwischenraum gesetzt, wenn sie für ein selbstständiges Wort oder mehrere Wörter stehen. Bei Auslassung eines Wortteils werden sie unmittelbar an den Rest des Wortes angeschlossen.

Keiner der genannten Paragraphen ... ist im vorliegenden Fall anzuwenden.
Sie glaubten in Sicherheit zu sein, doch plötzlich ...
Mit „Para..." beginnt das gesuchte Wort.

Am Satzende wird kein zusätzlicher Schlusspunkt gesetzt. Satzzeichen werden ohne Zwischenraum angeschlossen.

Bitte wiederholen Sie den Abschnitt nach „Wir möchten uns erlauben ..."

Bindestrich

Der Bindestrich entspricht typographisch dem Trennstrich der jeweiligen Schrift.
Vgl. auch R 23–28.

„bis"

↑Strich für „gegen" und „bis"

Datum

(Vgl. auch S. 76).

Bei Datumsangaben in Ziffern setzt man einen Punkt nach den Zahlen für Tag und Monat. Die Jahresangabe steht ohne Punkt.

Mannheim, den 1. 9. 1995
am 10. 5. 08 geboren

Zwischen Tag und Monat wird ein kleinerer Zwischenraum, vor dem Jahr ein normaler Wortabstand gesetzt. Erfolgt die Jahresangabe nur zweistellig, ist auch davor ein kleiner Zwischenraum zu setzen. Vgl. auch ↑Festabstände.

Zur Zusammenfassung von aufeinander folgenden oder aus der Geschichte geläufigen Jahreszahlen verwendet man den Schrägstrich.
Vgl. auch R 117.

1995/96
1914/18

Et-Zeichen (&)

Das Et-Zeichen & ist gleichbedeutend mit „u.", darf aber nur bei Firmenbezeichnungen angewendet werden.

Voß & Co.
Meyer & Neumann

In allen anderen Fällen darf nur „u." als Abkürzung für „und" gesetzt werden.

Kosten für Verpflegung u. Unterbringung
Erscheinungstermin für Bd. I u. II

Festabstände

Festabstände, d.h. nicht variable, meist kleinere Zwischenräume zwischen Zeichen, dienen der Ästhetik und Lesbarkeit von Texten. Sie verbinden Zusammengehörendes oder gliedern Unübersichtliches. Ihre Eingabe lässt sich – heute auch am Personalcomputer – mit einer Trennungssperre verbinden, sodass die auf diese Weise verbundenen Zeichen beim Schriftsatz nicht auseinander gerissen werden können. Sie werden z. B. verwendet bei Abkürzungen, beim Datum, bei der Gliederung von Nummern, bei Paragraphzeichen, Prozent- und Promillezeichen, Rechenzeichen und Zahlen.

Formeln

Mathematische, physikalische und chemische Formeln sollten nach Möglichkeit eingerückt und freigestellt werden, z. B.

$$CH_2 = CHCl$$

Ihre Trennung ist zu vermeiden. Ist dies nicht möglich, dürfen sie nur am Gleichheitszeichen (oder einem ähnlichen Zeichen wie $\equiv$, $\approx$, $\leq$ oder $\sim$), wenn nötig auch an einem Rechenzeichen gebrochen werden.

Fußnoten- und Anmerkungszeichen

Als Fußnoten- und Anmerkungszeichen sind hochgestellte Ziffern ohne Klammer den anderen Möglichkeiten wie Sterne, Kreuze oder Ziffern mit Klammern vorzuziehen.

Die verschiedenen Holzsorten[1] werden mit Spezialklebern[2] verarbeitet und später längere Zeit[3] getrocknet.

[1]Zum Beispiel Fichte, Eiche, Buche.
[2]Vorwiegend Zweikomponentenkleber.
[3]Etwa 4 bis 6 Wochen.

Treffen Fußnotenziffern mit Satzzeichen zusammen, gilt folgende Grundregel: Wenn sich die Fußnote auf den ganzen Satz bezieht, steht die Ziffer nach dem schließenden Satzzeichen; wenn die Fußnote sich nur auf das unmittelbar vorangehende Wort oder eine unmittelbar vorangehende Wortgruppe bezieht, steht die Ziffer vor dem schließenden Satzzeichen.

In dem Tagungsbericht heißt es, der Vortrag behandele „einige neue Gesichtspunkte der Heraldik".[1]

[1]Ein ergänzendes Referat wurde von Dr. Meyer gehalten.
(Anmerkung zu dem ganzen Satz.)

In dem Tagungsbericht heißt es, der Vortrag behandele „einige neue Gesichtspunkte der Heraldik"[1].

[1]Tagungsbericht S. 12.
(Stellenangabe für das Zitat.)

In dem Tagungsbericht heißt es, der Vortrag behandele „einige neue Gesichtspunkte der Heraldik[1]".

[1]Wappenkunde.
(Erklärung zu dem einzelnen Wort.)

Gedankenstrich

Der Gedankenstrich ist länger als der Bindestrich und in der Regel kürzer als das Minuszeichen. Gesetzt wird er mit vorausgehendem und folgendem Wortabstand. Er soll nach Möglichkeit nicht am Zeilenanfang stehen.

Diese Straße – sie ist jetzt gesperrt – war einmal eine Hauptverkehrsader.

Vgl. R 55–59, ↑Streckenstrich, ↑Strich bei Währungsangaben, ↑Strich für „gegen" und „bis".

„gegen"

↑Strich für „gegen" und „bis"

Genealogische Zeichen

Familiengeschichtliche Zeichen können in entsprechenden Texten zur Raumersparnis verwendet werden.

** = geboren (geb.), (*) = außerehelich geboren, †* = tot geboren, *† = am Tag der Geburt gestorben, ⁓ = getauft (get.), ○ = verlobt (verl.), ⚭ = verheiratet (verh.), ⚮ = geschieden (gesch.), ⚯ = außereheliche Verbindung, † = gestorben (gest.), ⚔ = gefallen (gef.), ▭ = begraben (begr.), ⚱ = eingeäschert*

Gliederung von Nummern

Telefonnummern, Telefaxnummern und **Postfachnummern** werden, von der letzten Ziffer ausgehend, in Zweiergruppen durch einen kleinen Zwischenraum gegliedert.

14 28
1 14 23
17 09 14

In der Schweiz werden bei siebenstelligen Telefonnummern die ersten drei Ziffern zusammengefasst.

922 71 31

Die **Ortsnetzkennzahl** wird für sich ebenso gegliedert und in runde Klammern gesetzt.

(0 62 81) 4 91

In der Schweiz wird sie nicht gegliedert.

(064) 24 79 39

Kontonummern bestehen aus maximal zehn Ziffern. Sie können von der Endziffer aus jeweils in Dreiergruppen gegliedert werden.

8 582 404
1 843 462 527

Häufig erfolgt keine Gliederung durch Zwischenraum.

8582404
1843462527

Bankleitzahlen bestehen aus acht Ziffern. Sie werden, von links nach rechts in zwei Dreiergruppen und eine Zweiergruppe gegliedert.

670 409 20

Die **ISBN** (Internationale Standardbuchnummer) besteht aus Landes-, Verlags-, Artikelnummer und Reihenschlüssel. Diese vier Angaben werden durch Divis (Bindestrich) oder Zwischenraum voneinander getrennt.

ISBN 3-411-00911-X
ISBN 3-7610-9301-2
ISBN 3 406 06780 8

Postleitzahlen werden nicht gegliedert.

68167 Mannheim

Vgl. auch ↑Festabstände, ↑Zahlen.

Gradzeichen

Bei Temperaturangaben ist zwischen der Zahl und dem Gradzeichen ein Zwischenraum zu setzen; der Kennbuchstabe der

Temperaturskala folgt ohne weiteren Zwischenraum.

– 3 °C
+ 17 °C

Bei anderen Gradangaben wird das Gradzeichen ohne Zwischenraum an die Zahl angeschlossen.

ein Winkel von 30°
50° nördlicher Breite

Hervorhebung von Eigennamen

↑ Schriftauszeichnung

Klammern

↑ Zusätze in Wortverbindungen

Ligaturen

Ligaturen fassen Buchstaben zu einem Zeichen zusammen. Sie dienen der besseren Lesbarkeit. Anzahl und Art der Ligaturen sind nicht festgelegt. Soweit sie verwendet werden, muss dies innerhalb eines Druckwerkes einheitlich geschehen. Gebräuchlich sind (bei Verwendung von Antiqua-Schriften):

ff, fi, fl, zum Teil auch ***ft, ch, ck***

Die Ligatur wird gesetzt, wenn die Buchstaben im Wortstamm zusammengehören.

*scha**ff**en, scha**ff**t, er**fi**nden, P**fiff**, ab**fl**auen, Leidenscha**ft**, he**ft**ig*

K e i n e Ligatur steht zwischen Wortstamm und Endung (Ausnahme: ***fi***).

ich schaufle, ich kaufte, höflich; aber: *strei**fi**g, a**ffi**g*

K e i n e Ligatur steht in der Wortfuge von Zusammensetzungen.

Schaffell, Kaufleute, Schilfinsel

In Zweifelsfällen setzt man die Ligatur entsprechend der Gliederung des Wortes nach Sprechsilben.

*Rohsto**ff**frage, Schi**ff**fahrt, kni**ff**lig, scha**ff**ten*

Schließt eine Abkürzung mit zwei Buchstaben, die eine Ligatur bilden können, dann wird diese angewendet.

Aufl. (aber: *Auflage*), ***gefl.*** (aber: *gefällig, gefälligst*)

Fremdsprachige Ligaturen wie Œ, œ, Æ, æ werden heute als ein Zeichen betrachtet.

Im Fraktursatz werden die nachstehenden Ligaturen gebraucht. (Die Ligatur ß gilt als e i n Buchstabe.)

ch, ck, ff, fi, fl, ft, ll, sch, si, ss, st, tz

Für die Anwendung dieser Ligaturen gilt das oben Gesagte. Wird die Schrift gesperrt, werden ch, ck und tz nicht mitgesperrt. Die Ligaturen fi und si werden wie Antiqua-***fi*** behandelt.

Namen

↑ Schriftauszeichnung (b)

Nummerngliederung

↑ Gliederung von Nummern

Paragraphzeichen

Steht das Wort „Paragraph“ in Verbindung mit einer nachgestellten Zahl, dann setzt man unter Verwendung eines kleineren, festen Zwischenraums das Zeichen §.

§ 9
§ 17 ff.
der § 17

Zwei Paragraphzeichen (§§) kennzeichnen den Plural.

§§ 10 bis 15, §§ 10–15
die §§ 10 bis 15, die §§ 10–15

Ohne Zahlenangabe wird das Wort „Paragraph“ ausgesetzt.

Der Paragraph wurde geändert.

Vgl. auch ↑ Festabstände, ↑ Zahlen.

Prozent- und Promillezeichen

Vor dem Prozent- und dem Promillezeichen ist ein kleinerer, fester Zwischenraum zu setzen.

25 %
0,8 ‰

Der Zwischenraum entfällt bei Ableitungen.

eine 25%ige Umsatzsteigerung

Rechenzeichen

Rechenzeichen werden zwischen den Zahlen mit kleinerem Zwischenraum gesetzt.

$6+2=8$
$6-2=4$
$6 \cdot 2=12;\ 6\times 2=12$
$6:2=3$

Vorzeichen werden aber ohne Zwischenraum (kompress) gesetzt.

$-2a$
$+15$

Vgl. auch ↑Formeln.

Satzzeichen in der Hervorhebung

↑Schriftauszeichnung (c)

Schriftauszeichnung

Die wichtigsten Schriftauszeichnungen sind: halbfette, kursive, gesperrte Schrift, Versalien, Kapitälchen.

a) Sperren
Die Satzzeichen werden im Allgemeinen mit gesperrt.

W a r u m ?
D a r u m !

Dies gilt in der Regel nicht für den Punkt und die Anführungszeichen. Auch Zahlen werden nicht gesperrt.

D e r T a g e s a u s s t o ß b e t r ä g t 10 000 S t ü c k .

b) Hervorhebung von Eigennamen
Bei der Hervorhebung von Eigennamen wird das Genitiv-s stets mit hervorgehoben.

M e y e r s Lexikon, *Meyers* Lexikon, **Meyers** Lexikon, MEYERS Lexikon

Die Ableitungssilbe -sche usw. wird dagegen aus der Grundschrift gesetzt.

der v i r c h o w sche Versuch, der *virchow*sche Versuch, der **virchow**sche Versuch, der VIRCHOWsche Versuch

c) Satzzeichen und Klammern
Die Satzzeichen und Klammern werden – auch am Ende eines ausgezeichneten Textteils – in der Regel in der Auszeichnungsschrift gesetzt.

flaggen: *die Fahne[n] hissen:* wir flaggen heute.

Ausnahmen aus ästhetischen Gründen sind möglich.

Vieraugen[fische] **Vieraugen[fische**]

Wird ein gemischt gesetzter Textteil von Klammern eingeschlossen, so werden im Allgemeinen beide Klammern aus der Grundschrift gesetzt.

Überwiegt die gerade Schrift in der Klammer, so werden Klammern gerade gesetzt.

(xxx *xxx* xxx); (*xx* xxxxxx *xx*);

Beginnt oder endet ein Text unterschiedlich mit kursivem oder gerade stehendem Text, so sind beide Klammern gerade zu setzen.

(*xxx* xxx xxx); (xxx xxx *xxx*);

Ist kursiver Text eingeklammert, so sind die Klammern kursiv zu setzen; nachfolgende Satzzeichen können kursiv oder gerade gesetzt werden.

xxx *(xxxxx);* xxx *(xxxxx)*?

Divis, Gedankenstrich und das Gleichheitszeichen in Verbindung mit halbfetter oder fetter Schrift werden immer halbfett bzw. fett gesetzt.

S-Laute im Fraktursatz

Das s der Antiqua wird in der Fraktur (sog. deutsche Schrift) durch ſ oder s wiedergegeben. Für ss steht ſſ, für ß steht ß. Dabei sind die nachstehenden Richtlinien zu beachten.

a) Das lange ſ
Für Antiqua-s im Anlaut einer Silbe steht langes ſ.

ſagen, ſehen, ſieben, ſezieren, Heldenſage, Höhenſonne; Erbſe, Rätſel, wachſen, kleckſen; leſen, Roſe, Baſis, Friſeur, Muſeum; Mikroſkop; Manuſkript, Proſzenium

Das gilt auch dann, wenn ein sonst im Silbenanlaut stehender s-Laut durch den Ausfall eines unbetonten e in den Auslaut gerät.

auserleſne (für: auserleſene), ich preiſ (für: ich preiſe), Verwechſlung (für: Verwechſelung); Wechſler (zu: wechſeln)

In Zusammensetzungen mit trans-, deren zweiter Bestandteil mit einem s beginnt, ist das s von trans (trans-) meist ausgefallen. Hier steht also ſ.

tranſpirieren, tranſzendent, Tranſkription (aber: transſibiriſch, Transſubſtantiation)

Dies gilt vereinzelt auch, wenn der zweite Bestandteil mit einem Vokal beginnt.

Tranſit, tranſitiv (aber: Transaktion, Trans-uran)

In polnischen Namen wird der Laut [*sch*] durch ſz (nicht ß oder sz) wiedergegeben; das ſ steht auch in der Endung -ſki (nicht: -ski).

Lukaſzewſki

Das lange ſ steht in den Buchstabenverbindungen ſch, ſp, ſt.

ſchaden, Fiſch, maſchinell; Knoſpe, Weſpe, Veſper; geſtern, Herbſt, Optimiſt, er lieſt

Kein ſ steht aber, wenn in Zusammensetzungen s+ch, s+p und s+t zusammentreffen.

Zirkusschef, Lackmuspapier, Dispens, transparent, Dienstag, Preisträger

b) Das Schluß-s
Für Antiqua-s im Auslaut einer Silbe steht Schluss-s.

dies, Gans, Maske, Muskel, Riesling, Klausner, bösartig, Desinfektion, ich las, aus, als, bis; Dienstag, Donnerstag, Ordnungsliebe, Häschen; Kindes, Vaters, welches; Gleichnis, Kürbis, Globus, Atlas, Kirmes; Kubismus, Arabeske, Ischias, Schleswig

Dasselbe gilt für -sk in bestimmten Fremdwörtern.

brüsk, grotesk, Obelisk

In skandinavischen Personennamen, die auf -ſen oder -ſon enden, ist der vorangehende S-Laut mit Schluss-s zu setzen.

Gulbransſen, Jonasſon

c) Das ſſ
Für Doppel-s der Antiqua steht ſſ.

Maſſe, Miſſetat, Flüſſe, Diſſertation, Aſſeſſor, Gleichniſſe, ich laſſ

Kein ſſ steht aber, wenn in Zusammensetzungen s+s zusammentreffen.

Ausſatz, desſelben, Reisſuppe, transſilvaniſch

Sperren

↑ Schriftauszeichnung

ss/ß

a) In deutschsprachigem Satz
Nur wenn in einer Schrift kein ß vorhanden ist, darf – als Notbehelf – dafür ss gesetzt werden. Manuskripte ohne ß müssen im Normalfall den Regeln gemäß mit ß abgesetzt werden. In der Schweiz wird das ß in der Regel nicht verwendet.

Reissbrett (für: *Reißbrett*), *Masse* (für: *Maße*)

Stößt für ß verwendetes ss innerhalb eines Wortes mit s zusammen, dann werden drei s gesetzt.

Fusssohle, Reissschiene, massstabgerecht

Will man nur Großbuchstaben verwenden, so wird das ß durch SS ersetzt.

STRASSE, MASSE (für: *Maße*)
Vgl. auch R 183 ff.

b) In fremdsprachigem Satz
Wird ein deutsches Wort mit ß latinisiert oder erscheint ein deutscher Name mit ß in fremdsprachigem Satz, dann bleibt das ß erhalten.

Weißenburg – der Codex Weißenburgensis
Monsieur Aßmann était à Paris.

Streckenstrich

Bei Streckenangaben setzt man den Gedankenstrich als Streckenstrich.
Strich und Ortsbezeichnungen werden dabei ohne Zwischenraum miteinander verbunden, d. h. kompress gesetzt.

Hamburg–Berlin
Köln–München

Vgl. ↑ Gedankenstrich.

Strich bei Währungsangaben

Der Gedankenstrich kann bei glatten Währungsbeträgen statt der Ziffern hinter dem Komma stehen.

25,– DM, neben *25,00 DM* oder *25 DM*

Vgl. ↑ Gedankenstrich.

Strich für „gegen" und „bis"

Als Zeichen für „gegen" und „bis" findet der Gedankenstrich Verwendung. Für „gegen" (z. B. in Sportberichten) wird er mit Zwischenraum gesetzt.

Schalke 04 – Eintracht Frankfurt 3 : 3
Fernandez/Zwerewa – Novotna/Sanchez 2 : 0

Für „bis" wird er ohne Zwischenraum (kompress) gesetzt.

Das Buch darf 10–12 Mark kosten.
Sprechstunde 8–11, 14–16 Uhr
1991–94

Bei Hausnummern kann auch der Schrägstrich stehen.

Burgstraße 14–16
Burgstraße 14/16

Das „bis"-Zeichen sollte nicht mit anderen Strichen zusammentreffen.

nicht: *vier- – fünfmal*
sondern: *vier- bis fünfmal*

Am Zeilenende oder -anfang ist statt des Striches das Wort „bis" auszusetzen, ebenso in der Verbindung „von ... bis".

Uhrzeit

Für die Uhrzeit sind im deutschsprachigen Raum verschiedene Schreibweisen mit Ziffern üblich:

Es ist 9 Uhr, 17.30 Uhr, 0.12 Uhr
Das Spiel beginnt um 19^{30} Uhr.

Bei zusätzlicher Angabe von Sekunden:
14.31.52 Uhr, 00.25.35 Uhr
Vgl. auch S. 78.

Unterführungszeichen

Das Unterführungszeichen wird im Schriftsatz unter die Mitte des zu unterführenden Wortes gesetzt. Die Unterführung gilt auch für Bindestrich und Komma. Zahlen dürfen nicht unterführt werden.

Hamburg-Altona
„ Finkenwerder
„ Fuhlsbüttel
„ Blankenese

1 Regal, 50 × 80 cm mit Rückwand
1 „ 50 × 80 cm ohne „

Ist mehr als ein Wort zu unterführen, so wird das Unterführungszeichen auch dann unter jedes einzelne Wort gesetzt, wenn die Wörter nebeneinander stehend ein Ganzes bilden.

Unterlauterbach b. Treuen
„ „ „

In der Schweiz wird als Unterführungszeichen das schließende Anführungszeichen der Schweizer Form (») verwendet.

Basel-Stadt
» Land

Zahlen

Zahlen mit mehr als drei Stellen links oder rechts des Kommas werden unter Verwendung eines kleineren Zwischenraums vom Komma ausgehend in 3-stellige Gruppen gegliedert.

7 162 354,53 DM
0,372 18 g

Bei 4-stelligen Zahlen hat sich neben der Schreibung mit Zwischenraum auch die ohne eingebürgert.

5 340 neben *5340*

Jahreszahlen, Seiten- und Paragraphenangaben sind nicht zu gliedern.

Die Zahlen vor Zeichen und Abkürzungen von Maßen, Gewichten, Geldsorten usw. sind in Ziffern zu setzen.

21,5 kg
6 DM
14 ½ cm

Besteht die Ziffer vor einer Einheit oder die Einheit aus nur einem Zeichen, ist ein kleinerer Zwischenraum zu setzen. Die Trennung von Ziffer und Einheit sollte vermieden werden.

Setzt man solche Bezeichnungen aus, dann kann die Zahl in Ziffern oder in Buchstaben gesetzt werden.

2 Mark
oder: *zwei Mark*
(nicht: *zwei DM*)

Bei Ableitungen mit Zahlen wird kein Zwischenraum hinter die Zahl gesetzt.

5%ig, ein 32stel, eine 70er-Bildröhre

Vgl. auch ↑Datum, ↑Festabstände, ↑Gliederung von Nummern, ↑Rechenzeichen, ↑Uhrzeit.

Zeichen

↑Et-Zeichen, ↑Genealogische Zeichen, ↑Gradzeichen, ↑Paragraphzeichen, ↑Prozent- und Promillezeichen, ↑Rechenzeichen

Ziffern

↑Gliederung von Nummern, ↑Uhrzeit, ↑Zahlen

Zusätze in Wortverbindungen

Erklärende Zusätze innerhalb von Wortverbindungen werden in Klammern gesetzt (vgl. dazu R 62).

Gemeinde(amts)vorsteher (= Gemeindevorsteher oder Gemeindeamtsvorsteher), aber: *Gemeinde-(Amts-)Vorsteher (= Gemeindevorsteher oder Amtsvorsteher); Privat-(Haus-)Briefkasten, Magen-(und Darm-)Beschwerden, Ostende-Belgrad-(Tauern-)Express,* aber ohne Klammer: *Fuhr- u. a. Kosten*

In Wörterverzeichnissen werden Erklärungen oft mit Hilfe von eckigen Klammern zusammengezogen.

[Gewebe]streifen (= *Gewebestreifen* und auch: *Streifen*)

Hinweise für das Maschinenschreiben

Die folgenden Hinweise beschränken sich auf die in der Praxis am häufigsten auftretenden Probleme. (Vgl. auch die Richtlinien für den Schriftsatz, S. 65–73).

Abkürzungen

Nach Abkürzungen folgt ein Leerschritt.

```
... desgl. ein Paar
Strümpfe ...
```

```
Sie können das Programm auf
UKW empfangen.
```

Das gilt auch für mehrere aufeinander folgende Wörter, die jeweils mit einem Punkt abgekürzt sind.

```
... z. B. ein Zeppelin ...
... Hüte, Schirme, Taschen
u. a. m.
```

Anrede und Gruß in Briefen

Anrede und Gruß werden vom übrigen Brieftext durch jeweils eine Leerzeile abgesetzt.

```
Sehr geehrter Herr Schmidt,

gestern erhielten wir Ihre
Nachricht vom ... Wir würden
uns freuen, Sie bald hier be-
grüßen zu können.

Mit freundlichen Grüßen
Kraftwerk AG
```

Anschrift

Anschriften auf Postsendungen werden durch Leerzeilen gegliedert[1].
Man unterteilt hierbei wie folgt:

[Art der Sendung];

[Firmen]name;
Postfach oder Straße und Hausnummer [Wohnungsnummer];

Postleitzahl, Bestimmungsort

Die Postleitzahl wird fünfstellig geschrieben und nicht ausgerückt, der Bestimmungsort nicht unterstrichen. Die Länderkennzeichnungen A-, CH-, D- usw. sollen beim Schriftverkehr innerhalb des jeweiligen Landes nicht verwendet werden. Bei Postsendungen ins Ausland empfiehlt die Deutsche Post, Bestimmungsort (und Bestimmungsland) in Großbuchstaben zu schreiben.

```
Einschreiben
Bibliographisches Institut &
F. A. Brockhaus AG
Dudenstraße 6

68167 Mannheim
```

```
Herrn
Helmut Schildmann
Jenaer Str. 18

99425 Weimar
```

```
Frau
Wilhelmine Baeren
Münsterplatz 8

CH-3000 BERN
```

Am Zeilenende stehen keine Satzzeichen; eine Ausnahme bilden Abkürzungspunkte sowie die zu Kennwörtern o. Ä. gehörenden Anführungs-, Ausrufe- oder Fragezeichen.

```
Herrn Major a. D.
Dr. Kurt Meier
Postfach 90 10 98

60450 Frankfurt
```

```
Reisebüro Bauer
Kennwort "Ferienlotterie"
Postfach 70 96 14

A-1121 WIEN
```

[1] In der Schweiz wird jedoch empfohlen, auf die Leerzeile über dem Bestimmungsort zu verzichten.

Ausrufezeichen

↑Punkt ...

Bindestrich

Als Ergänzungsstrich steht der Bindestrich unmittelbar vor oder nach dem zu ergänzenden Wortteil.

Büro- und Reiseschreibmaschine

Eisengewinnung und -verarbeitung

Bei der Kopplung oder Aneinanderreihung gibt es zwischen den verbundenen Wörtern oder Schriftzeichen und dem Bindestrich ebenfalls keine Leerschritte.

Hals-Nasen-Ohren-Arzt,

St.-Martins-Kirche,

C-Dur-Tonleiter,

Berlin-Schöneberg,

Hawaii-Insel, UKW-Sender

Darüber hinaus findet der Bindestrich Verwendung als Trennstrich bei der Silbentrennung, als Gedankenstrich, als Rechenzeichen und als Strich für Strecken, „bis" und „gegen".

Datum

Das nur in Zahlen angegebene Datum wird im Allgemeinen ohne Leerschritte durch Punkte gegliedert. Tag und Monat sollten jeweils zweistellig angegeben werden. Die im deutschsprachigen Raum übliche Reihenfolge ist: Tag, Monat, Jahr.

24.08.1998

24.08.98

Nach DIN 5008 soll (nach internationaler Norm) durch Mittestrich gegliedert werden; die Reihenfolge ist dann: Jahr, Monat, Tag.

1998-08-24

98-08-24

Schreibt man den Monatsnamen in Buchstaben, so schlägt man zwischen den Angaben je einen Leerschritt an.

24. August 1998

24. Aug. 98

Doppelpunkt

↑Punkt ...

Einheitenzeichen

Einheitenzeichen werden mit einem Leerschritt hinter der Ziffer geschrieben.

Höchstgewicht: 2 kg

ein Luftdruck von 998 hPa

Einrücken

↑Hervorhebungen

Fehlende Zeichen

Auf der Schreibmaschinentastatur fehlende Zeichen können in einigen Fällen durch Kombinationen anderer Zeichen ersetzt werden:
Die Umlaute ä, ö, ü kann man als ae, oe, ue schreiben. Das ß kann durch ss wiedergegeben werden.

südlich – suedlich

SÜDLICH – SUEDLICH

mäßig – maessig

Fußsohle – Fusssohle

Die Ziffern 0 und 1 können durch das große O und das kleine l ersetzt werden.

110 – llO

Fragezeichen

↑Punkt ...

Gradzeichen

Als Gradzeichen verwendet man das hochgestellte kleine o. Bei Winkelgraden wird es unmittelbar an die Zahl angehängt.

ein Winkel von 30°

Bei Temperaturgraden ist (vor allem in fachsprachlichem Text) nach der Zahl ein Leerschritt anzuschlagen; das Gradzeichen steht dann unmittelbar vor der Temperatureinheit.

eine Temperatur von 30 °C
Nachttemperaturen um –3 °C

Grußformel

↑Anrede und Gruß in Briefen

Hervorhebungen

Hervorhebungen sind möglich durch Einrücken, Zentrieren, Anführungszeichen, Unterstreichen, Sperren, Großbuchstaben, fette und kursive Schrift und Wechsel der Schriftart.
Beim Unterstreichen werden Satz- und Anführungszeichen mit unterstrichen.

`Wir werden auf alle Fälle kommen.`

`Vorsicht, Glas!`

Beim Sperren werden vor und nach der Sperrung je 3 Leerschritte angeschlagen. Bis auf Punkt und Anführungszeichen werden Satzzeichen, Bindestrich und Trennstrich mitgesperrt. Zahlen werden grundsätzlich nicht gesperrt.

`Diese Übungen finden immer nur   m o n t a g s   statt.`

Hochgestellte Zahlen

Hochzahlen und Fußnotenziffern werden ohne Leerschritt angeschlossen.

eine Entfernung von 10^8 Lichtjahren

ein Gewicht von 10^{-6} Gramm

Nach einer anderen Quelle[4)] hat es diesen Mann nie gegeben.

Klammern

Klammern schreibt man ohne Leerschritt vor und nach den Textabschnitten, Wörtern, Wortteilen oder Zeichen, die von ihnen eingeschlossen werden.

`Das neue Serum (es wurde erst vor kurzem entwickelt) hat sich sehr gut bewährt.`

`Der Grundbetrag (12 DM) wird angerechnet.`

`Lehrer(in) für Deutsch gesucht.`

Komma

↑Punkt ...

Paragraphzeichen

Das Paragraphzeichen wird nur in Verbindung mit darauf folgenden Zahlen gebraucht. Es ist durch einen Leerschritt von der zugehörigen Zahl getrennt.

`Wegen eines Verstoßes gegen § 21 StVO werden Sie ...`

Prozentzeichen

Das Prozentzeichen ist durch einen Leerschritt von der zugehörigen Zahl zu trennen.

`Bei Barzahlung 3 1/2 % Rabatt.`

`Der Verlust beträgt 8 %.`

Der Leerschritt entfällt bei Ableitungen.

`eine 10%ige Erhöhung`

Punkt, Komma, Semikolon, Doppelpunkt, Frage- und Ausrufezeichen

Die Satzzeichen Punkt, Komma, Semikolon, Doppelpunkt, Fragezeichen und Ausrufezeichen werden ohne Leerschritt an das vorangehende Wort oder Schriftzeichen angehängt. Das nächste Wort folgt nach einem Leerschritt.

`Wir haben noch Zeit.`

`Gestern, heute und morgen.`

`Es muss heißen: Hippologie.`

`Wie muss es heißen? Hör doch zu!`

`Am Mittwoch reise ich ab; mein Vertreter kommt nicht vor Freitag.`

Rechenzeichen

Die Rechenzeichen

+, −, · oder ×, :, =

werden mit vorausgehendem und folgendem Leerschritt geschrieben, + und − als Vorzeichen ohne folgenden Leerschritt.

Schrägstrich

Vor und nach dem Schrägstrich wird im Allgemeinen kein Leerschritt angeschlagen. Der Schrägstrich kann als Bruchstrich verwendet werden; er steht außerdem bei Diktat- und Aktenzeichen sowie bei zusammengefassten Jahreszahlen.

```
2/3, 3 1/4 % Zinsen
Aktenzeichen c/XII/14
Ihr Zeichen: Dr/Ls
Er begann sein Studium im Win-
tersemester 1994/95.
```

Semikolon

↑Punkt ...

Silbentrennung

Zur Silbentrennung wird der Bindestrich ohne Leerschritt an die Silbe angehängt.

```
                    ... Vergiss-
meinnicht ...
```

Sperren

↑Hervorhebungen

ss/ß

↑Fehlende Zeichen

Strich für Strecken, „bis" und „gegen"

Als Zeichen für Strecken, „bis" und „gegen" wird der Bindestrich mit einem Leerschritt vor und nach den Angaben verwendet.

```
ICE Frankfurt – Kassel
10 – 20 DM
Borussia Dortmund – VfB Stutt-
gart
```

Uhrzeit

Stunden, Minuten und gegebenenfalls Sekunden werden meist mit Punkten gegliedert. Ziffern und Punkte werden ohne Leerschritt geschrieben.

```
7.00 Uhr,       16.45 Uhr,
0.23 Uhr,       23.14.37 Uhr
```

Nach DIN 5008 soll mit dem Doppelpunkt gegliedert werden; jede Zeiteinheit ist dann zweistellig anzugeben.

```
07:00 Uhr
23:14:37 Uhr
```

Umlaut

↑Fehlende Zeichen

Unterführungen

Unterführungszeichen stehen jeweils unter dem ersten Buchstaben des zu unterführenden Wortes.

```
Duden, Band 2, Stilwörterbuch
"      "    5, Fremdwörterbuch
"      "    7, Herkunftswör-
               terbuch
```

Zahlen dürfen nicht unterführt werden.

```
1 Hängeschrank mit Befestigung
1 Regalteil     "      "
1 "             ohne Rückwand
1 "             " Zwischenboden
```

Ein übergeordnetes Stichwort, das in Aufstellungen wiederholt wird, kann durch den Bindestrich ersetzt werden. Er steht unter dem ersten Buchstaben des Stichwortes.

```
Nachschlagewerke; deutsche und
fremdsprachige Wörterbücher
-; naturwissenschaftliche und
technische Fachbücher
-; allgemeine Enzyklopädien
-; Atlanten
```

Unterstreichen

↑Hervorhebungen

Zahlen

Zahlen können durch Verwendung des Leerschritts gegliedert werden.

↑Hochgestellte Zahlen

Korrekturvorschriften

I. Hauptregeln

Jedes eingezeichnete Korrekturzeichen ist auf dem Rand zu wiederholen. Die erforderliche Änderung ist rechts neben das wiederholte Korrekturzeichen zu ~~zeichn~~en, sofern dieses nicht (wie ⌐, ⌐) für sich selbst spricht. schreib

Korrekturzeichen müssen den Korrekturstellen schnell und eindeutig zugeordnet werden können. Darum ist es bei großer Fehlerdichte wichtig, verschiedene, frei zu wählende Korrekturzeichen – gegebenenfalls auch in verschiedenen Farben – zu benutzen.

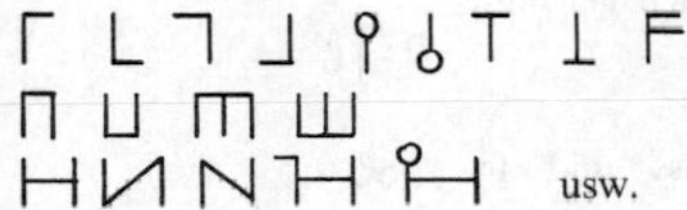

usw.

II. Wichtigste Korrekturzeichen

1. **Andere Schrift** für Wörter oder Zeilen wird verlangt, indem man die betreffende Stelle unterstreicht und auf dem Rand die gewünschte Schriftart (fett, kursiv usw.) oder den gewünschten Schriftgrad (Korpus, Borgis, Petit usw.) oder beides (fette Petit, Borgis kursiv usw.) vermerkt. Gewünschte Kursivschrift wird oft nur durch eine Wellenlinie unter dem Wort und auf dem Rand bezeichnet.

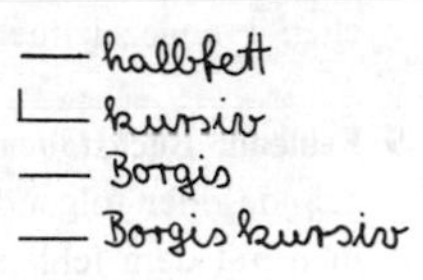

2. **Beschädigte Buchstaben** werden durchgestrichen und auf dem Rand einmal unterstrichen. R

3. **Fälschlich aus anderen Schriften gesetzte Buchstaben (Zwiebelfische)** werden durchgestrichen und auf dem Rand zweimal unterstrichen. R m

4. Um **verschmutzte Buchstaben** und **zu stark erscheinende Stellen** wird eine Linie gezogen. Dieses Zeichen wird auf dem Rand wiederholt.

5. **Falsche Buchstaben** oder **Wörter** sowie **auf dem Kopf stehende Buchstaben** ▯ **(Fliegenköpfe)** werden durchgestrichen und auf dem Rond durch die richtigen ersetzt. Dies gilt auch für quer stehende und umgedrehte Buchstaben.

   Kammen in einer Zeile mehrere Fehler vor, dann erhalten sie ihrer Reihenfolge nach verschiedene Zeichen. Für ein und denselben falschen Buchstaben wird aber nur ein Korrekturzeichen verwendet, das am Rand mehrfach vor den richtigen Buchstaben gesetzt wird.

6. **Ligaturen** (zusammengegossene Buchstaben) werden verlangt, indem man die fälschlich einzeln nebeneinander gesetzten Buchstaben durchstreicht und auf dem Rand mit einem Bogen darunter wiederholt, z. B. Schiff.

   Fälschlich gesetzte Ligaturen werden durchgestrichen, auf dem Rand wiederholt und durch einen Strich getrennt, z. B. Auflage.

7. **Falsche Trennungen** werden am Zeilenschluss und folgenden Zeilenanfang angezeichnet.

8. Wird nach **Streichung eines Bindestrichs** oder **Buchstabens** die Schreibung der verbleibenden Teile zweifelhaft, dann wird außer dem Tilgungszeichen die Zusammenschreibung durch einen Doppelbogen, die Getrenntschreibung durch das Zeichen ⌊ angezeichnet, z. B. blendend weiß.

9. **Fehlende Buchstaben** werden angezeichnet, indem der vorangehnde oder folgende uchstabe durchgestrichen und zusammen mit dem fehlenden wiederholt wird. Es kann auch das ganze Wrt oder die Silbe durchgestichen und auf dem Rand berichtigt werden.

10. **Fehlende Wörter (Leichen)** werden in der Lücke durch Winkelzeichen ⌈ gemacht und auf dem Rand angegeben.
    Bei größeren Auslassungen wird auf die Manuskriptseite verwiesen. Die Stelle ist auf der Manuskriptseite zu kennzeichnen.

    Diese Presse bestand aus ⌈ befestigt war.

Randzeichen: ◯ ◯ | a | s ⌈ h | o | e | i | a | ff | f | l | ol | g | g ◯ ⌈ g ◯ | g ⌉ | he | Bu | Wort | stri | ⌈ kenntlich | ⌈ s. Ms. S. 85

11. **Überflüssige Buchstaben** oder **Wörter** werden durchgestrichen unntd auf auf dem Rand durch ꝺ (für: deleatur, d. h. „es werde getilgt") angezeichnet. | ꝺ ⊢⊣ ꝺ

12. **Fehlende** oder **überflüssige** ,Satzzeichen werden wie fehlende oder überflüssige Buchstaben angezeichnet ꝺ t.

13. **Verstellte Buchstaben** werden durchgestirchen und auf dem Rand in der richtigen Reihenfolge angegeben. tr
Verstellte Wörter durch werden das Umstellungszeichen gekennzeichnet.
Die Wörter werden bei größeren Umstellungen beziffert. d B 1–7
Verstellte Zahlen sind immer ganz durchzustreichen und in der richtigen Ziffernfolge auf den Rand zu schreiben, z. B. 1684. ⊢⊣ 1864.

14. **Für unleserliche** oder **zweifelhafte Manuskriptstellen,** die noch nicht blockiert sind, sowie für noch **zu ergänzenden Text** wird vom Korrektor eine Blockade verlangt, z. B.
Hyladen sind Insekten mit unbeweglichem Prothorax (s. S. ...).

15. **Sperrung** oder **Aufhebung einer Sperrung** wird wie beim Verlangen einer anderen Schrift (vgl. S. 79, 1) durch Unterstreichung gekennzeichnet. nicht sperren / sperren

16. **Fehlender Wortzwischenraum**wird mit ⌊ bezeichnet. **Zu weiter Zwischenraum** wird durch ⊤, zu enger Zwischenraum durch ⊥ angezeichnet. Soll ⊤ ein **Zwischenraum ganz wegfallen,** so wird dies durch zwei Bogen ohne Strich ange deutet.

17. **Spieße,** d. h. im Satz mitgedruckter Ausschluss, Durchschuss oder ebensolche Quadrate, werden unterstrichen und auf dem Rand durch ⧺ angezeigt. ⧺

18. **Nicht Linie haltende Stellen** werden durch über und unter der Zeile gezogene parallele Striche angezeichnet.
Fehlender Durchschuss wird durch einen zwischen die Zeilen gezogenen Strich mit nach außen offenem Bogen angezeichnet.
Zu großer Durchschuss wird durch einen zwischen die Zeilen gezogenen Strich mit einem nach innen offenen Bogen angezeichnet.

19. Ein **Absatz** wird durch das Zeichen ⌐ im Text und auf dem Rand verlangt:

Die ältesten Drucke sind so gleichmäßig schön ausgeführt, dass sie die schönste Handschrift übertreffen. Die älteste Druckerpresse scheint von der, die uns Jost Amman im Jahre 1568 im Bilde vorführt, nicht wesentlich verschieden gewesen zu sein.

20. Das Anhängen eines Absatzes verlangt man durch eine den Ausgang mit dem folgenden Text verbindende Linie:

Die Presse bestand aus zwei Säulen, die durch ein Gesims verbunden waren.
In halber Manneshöhe war auf einem verschiebbaren Karren die Druckform befestigt.

21. Zu tilgender Einzug erhält am linken Rand das Zeichen ⊢, am rechten Rand das Zeichen ⊣, z. B.

Die Buchdruckerpresse ist eine Maschine, deren kunstvollen ⊢ Mechanismus nur der begreift, der selbst daran gearbeitet hat.

22. Fehlender Einzug wird durch ⊏ möglichst genau bezeichnet, z. B. (wenn der Einzug um ein Geviert verlangt wird):

... über das Ende des 14. Jahrhunderts hinaus führt keine Art des Metalldruckes.
Der Holzschnitt kommt in Druckwerken ebenfalls nicht vor dem 14. Jahrhundert vor.

23. Aus Versehen falsch Korrigiertes wird rückgängig gemacht, indem man die Korrektur ~~auf~~ dem Rand durchstreicht und Punkte unter die fälschlich korrigierte Stelle setzt.

24. Mit Randvermerken wird auf eine umfangreiche Korrektur hingewiesen, die rechts neben dem Text zu viel Platz einnehmen würde.

siehe oben
siehe unten
siehe Anlage

25. Der **auf Mitte zu setzende Punkt,** z. B. der Multiplikationspunkt bei mathematischem Satz, wird mit nebenstehendem Zeichen angegeben.

26. Verstellte Zeilen werden mit waagerechten Randstrichen versehen und in der richtigen Reihenfolge nummeriert, z. B.

Sah ein Knab' ein Röslein stehn, —— 1
lief er schnell, es nah zu sehn, —— 4
war so jung und morgenschön, —— 3
Röslein auf der Heiden, —— 2
sah's mit vielen Freuden. —— 5
Goethe —— 6

27. Bei der Korrektur ist auf **zu häufige Trennungen** hinzuweisen, die die Setzerei nach Möglichkeit durch Umsetzen verringern sollte. Bei langen Zeilen sollten nicht mehr als 3, bei kurzen (z. B. im Wörterbuch oder Lexikon) nicht mehr als 5 Trennungen aufeinander folgen.

mmmmmmmmm-
mmmmmmmmm-
mmmmmmmmm-
mmmmmmmmm-
mmmmmmmmm-
mmmmmmmmm-

6 Trennungen

28. Bei der Korrektur sollten auch **sinnentstellende** und **unschöne Trennungen** aufgelöst werden, um einen mühelosen Lesefluss zu gewährleisten. Zu diesem Zweck darf im Flattersatz das Zeichen ⌐ verwendet werden (vgl. 19.), im Blocksatz sind die umzustellenden Zeichen zu umkreisen und mit einer Schleife zu versetzen.

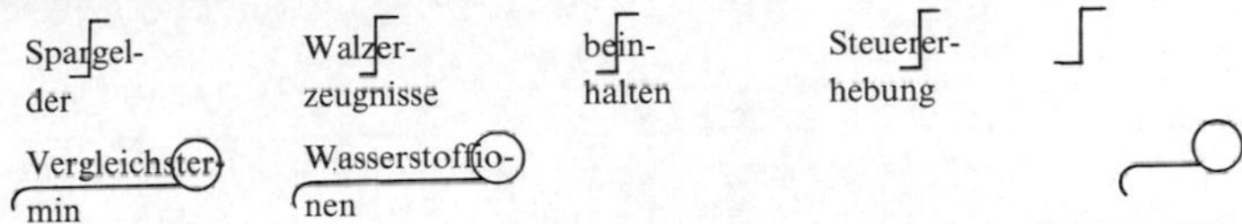

III. Regional übliche Korrekturzeichen

In den neuen Bundesländern werden neben den Zeichen der DIN-Norm häufig auch Korrekturzeichen verwendet, die bis 1990 in der DDR nach dem Standard TGL 0-16511 gültig waren. Dies gilt vor allem für die folgenden Fälle:

1. Mit dem Zeichen _ _ _ werden zu sperrende Wörter oder Wortteile unterstrichen. Das Zeichen wird auf dem Rand wiederholt.

_ _ _ _

2. Einfügungen in Form eines Wortes oder mehrerer Wörter werden durch eins der Zeichen √ √ √ √ √ kenntlich gemacht; der fehlende Textteil wird neben das auf √ Rand wiederholte Zeichen geschrieben.

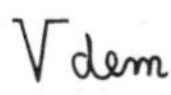

3. Soll ein Wortteil, ein Wort oder eine Gruppe von Wörtern in eine andere Zeile gestellt werden, so wird der umzustellende Text mit einem Pfeil umrandet und an die gewünschte Stelle geführt.

4. Sollen Zeilen oder ganze Abschnitte umgestellt werden,
mit einer Klammer, von der aus ein Pfeil zur richtigen Stelle
so erfasst man sie seitlich (in der Regel am linken Satzrand)
führt.

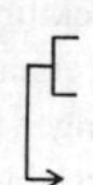

5. Als Exponenten oder Indizes zu setzende Ziffern werden wie folgt gekennzeichnet: Exponent 1. Ordnung mit dem Zeichen ∨, Exponent 2. Ordnung mit dem Zeichen ⩔ (das Zeichen wird unter die Ziffer oder unter den Buchstaben gesetzt):

exn (e^{x^n})

Index 1. Ordnung mit dem Zeichen ∧, Index 2. Ordnung mit dem Zeichen ⩓ (das Zeichen wird über die Ziffer oder über den Buchstaben gesetzt):

H2O, yn3 (H_2O, y_{n_3})

Transkriptions- und Transliterationssysteme

Bei der Tabelle für das Griechische wurde aus Gründen der Übersichtlichkeit auf die Großbuchstaben verzichtet.

Klassisch-griechisches Transkriptions- und Transliterationssystem

I[1]	II[2]	III[3]	IV[4]
α	a	a	a
β	b	b	b
γ	g	g	g
γγ	ng	gg	gg
γκ	nk	gk	gk
γξ	nx	gx	gx
γχ	nch	gh	gch
δ	d	d	d
ε	e	e	e
ζ	z	z	z
η	e	ē	ē
θ	th	th	th
ι	i	i	i
κ	k	k	k
λ	l	l	l
μ	m	m	m
ν	n	n	n
ξ	x	x	x

I[1]	II[2]	III[3]	IV[4]
ο	o	o	o
π	p	p	p
ϱ	r	r	r
σ, ς	s	s	s
τ	t	t	t
υ[5]	y	u	y
φ	ph	f	ph
χ	ch	h	ch
ψ	ps	ps	ps
ω	o	ō	ō
’[6]			
‘[7]	h	'	h
´[8]		´	´
`[8]		`	`
~[8]		~	~
ͺ, ι[9]		j	.
¨[8]		¨	¨

[1] I = Griechische Buchstaben (Minuskeln) und diakritische Zeichen.
[2] II = Transkription (*ts.*).
[3] III = ISO-Transliteration (*ISO-tl.*).
[4] IV = Klassische Transliteration (*kl. tl.*).
[5] αυ, ευ = *ts., kl. tl.* au, eu; ηυ = *ts.* eu, *kl. tl.* ēu; ου = *ts.* u, *kl. tl.* ou; ωυ = *ts.* ou, *kl. tl.* ōu.
[6] Nicht wiedergegeben.
[7] a) h, ' steht vor [Doppel]vokalbuchstabe; z. B. ὁ = *ts., kl. tl.* ho, *ISO-tl.* 'o; οἱ = *ts., kl. tl.* hoi, *ISO-tl.* 'oi. b) ῥ = r.
[8] In *ts.* nicht wiedergegeben.
[9] In *ts.* nicht wiedergegeben; in *ISO-tl.* j nachgesetzt, z. B. ῳ = ōj, Ωι = Ōj; in *kl. tl.* Punkt untergesetzt, z. B. ῳ = ọ̄, Ωι = Ọ̄.

Russisches Transkriptions- und Transliterationssystem

Russischer Buchstabe[1]		Tran-skription	Trans-literation	Russischer Buchstabe[1]		Tran-skription	Trans-literation
А	а	a	a	П	п	p	p
Б	б	b	b	Р	р	r	r
В	в	w	v	С	с	s[11, 12]	s
Г	г	g[2]	g	Т	т	t	t
Д	д	d	d	У	у	u	u
Е	е	e[3]	e	Ф	ф	f	f
Е[4]	е[4]	jo[5]	e	Х	х	ch	h[13]
Ё	ё	jo[5]	ë	Ц	ц	z	c
Ж	ж	sch[6]	ž	Ч	ч	tsch	č
З	з	s	z	Ш	ш	sch	š
И	и	i[7]	i	Щ	щ	schtsch	ŝ (šč)[14]
Й	й	i[8, 9]	j	Ъ	ъ	[15]	"[16]
К	к	k[10]	k	Ы	ы	y	y
Л	л	l	l	Ь	ь	[17]	'[18]
М	м	m	m	Э	э	e	ė
Н	н	n	n	Ю	ю	ju	û (ju)[19]
О	о	o	o	Я	я	ja	â (ja)[20]

[1] Russische Vokalbuchstaben sind: а, е, ё, и, о, у, ы, ю, э, я.
[2] In den Genitivendungen -его und -ого wird г mit w wiedergegeben.
[3] е = je am Wortanfang, nach russischem Vokalbuchstaben, nach ъ und nach ь.
[4] Wenn im Russischen für Е, е auch Ё, ё geschrieben werden kann.
[5] е, ё = o nach ж, ч, ш, щ.
[6] ж kann auch mit sh wiedergegeben werden, um den Unterschied zwischen dem stimmhaft zu sprechenden russischen ж und dem stimmlos zu sprechenden russischen ш deutlich zu machen.
[7] и = ji nach ь.
[8] й wird nach и und nach ы nicht wiedergegeben.
[9] й = i am Wortende sowie zwischen russischem Vokalbuchstaben und russischem Konsonantenbuchstaben.
[10] кс = x in allen Fällen.
[11] кс = x in allen Fällen.
[12] с = ss zwischen russischen Vokalbuchstaben; с = ß nach russischem Vokalbuchstaben vor russischem x.
[13] х = ch in der deutschen Bibliothekstransliteration.
[14] Die in Klammern angegebenen Transliterationsformen können noch angewendet werden, wenn eine Umstellung auf die Transliterationsformen mit nur einem Buchstaben und diakritischem Zeichen mit unvertretbar hohem Aufwand verbunden wäre.
[15] ъ wird nicht wiedergegeben; vgl. aber Fußnote 3.
[16] ъ = ″ oder " in der ISO-Transliteration; in der deutschen Bibliothekstransliteration mit Bindestrich wiedergegeben.
[17] ь = j vor o; ь wird sonst nicht wiedergegeben, vgl. aber Fußnote 3 und 7.
[18] ь = ′ oder ' in der ISO-Transliteration.
[19] vgl. 14. [20] vgl. 14.

Das griechische Alphabet

Buchstabe	Name	Buchstabe	Name	Buchstabe	Name	Buchstabe	Name
A, α	Alpha	H, η	Eta	N, ν	Ny	T, τ	Tau
B, β	Beta	$\Theta, \theta (\vartheta)$	Theta	Ξ, ξ	Xi	Y, υ	Ypsilon
Γ, γ	Gamma	I, ι	Jota	O, o	Omikron	Φ, φ	Phi
Δ, δ	Delta	K, κ	Kappa	Π, π	Pi	X, χ	Chi
E, ε	Epsilon	Λ, λ	Lambda	P, ϱ	Rho	Ψ, ψ	Psi
Z, ζ	Zeta	M, μ	My	$\Sigma, \sigma, \varsigma$	Sigma	Ω, ω	Omega

Vergleichende Gegenüberstellung alter und neuer Schreibungen

Die folgende Liste umfasst die wichtigsten Neuschreibungen; sie erhebt keinen Anspruch auf Vollständigkeit. Zur Verdeutlichung sind die Stichwörter gelegentlich in einen typischen Kontext eingebettet; *die Liste ersetzt aber nicht die ausführliche Darstellung im anschließenden Wörterverzeichnis, das auch zeigt, was in Zukunft unverändert bleibt.* Neue Schreibvarianten, die künftig als bevorzugte Schreibungen gelten sollen, sind mit einem * gekennzeichnet. Zu allen Fragen der Worttrennung (Silbentrennung) vgl. im Kapitel *Richtlinien zur Rechtschreibung, Zeichensetzung und Formenlehre* die Randziffern 129–133.

alt	**neu**
A	
[gestern, heute, morgen] abend	[gestern, heute, morgen] Abend
Ablaß	Ablass
absein	ab sein
Abszeß	Abszess
abwärtsgehen	abwärts gehen
in acht nehmen; außer acht lassen	in Acht nehmen; außer Acht lassen
der/die achte, den/die ich sehe	der/die Achte, den/die ich sehe
achtgeben; achthaben	Acht geben; Acht haben
8jährig; der/die 8jährige	8-jährig; der/die 8-Jährige
8mal	8-mal
über Achtzig; Mitte [der] Achtzig	über achtzig; Mitte [der] achtzig
ackerbautreibende Völker	Ackerbau treibende Völker
Aderlaß	Aderlass
Adreßbuch	Adressbuch
afro-amerikanisch	afroamerikanisch
Afro-Look	Afrolook
After-shave	Aftershave
ich habe ähnliches erlebt; und/oder ähnliches (u. ä./o. ä.)	ich habe Ähnliches erlebt; und/oder Ähnliches (u. Ä./o. Ä.)
alleinerziehend; alleinseligmachend; alleinstehend	allein erziehend; allein selig machend; allein stehend
im allgemeinen	im Allgemeinen
allgemeingültig; allgemeinverständlich	allgemein gültig; allgemein verständlich
allzuoft; allzusehr; allzuviel	allzu oft; allzu sehr; allzu viel
Alpdruck	*auch:* Albdruck
Alptraum	*auch:* Albtraum
als daß	als dass
für alt und jung	für Alt und Jung
er ist immer der alte geblieben	er ist immer der Alte geblieben
alles beim alten lassen	alles beim Alten lassen
Alter ego	Alter Ego
Amboß	Amboss

alt	neu
andersdenkend; andersgeartet	anders denkend; anders geartet
aneinandergeraten; aneinandergrenzen	aneinander geraten; aneinander grenzen
aneinanderreihen	aneinander reihen
angepaßt	angepasst
Anglo-Amerikaner	Angloamerikaner
jmdm. angst machen	jmdm. Angst machen
anheimfallen; anheimstellen	anheim fallen; anheim stellen
Anlaß	Anlass
anläßlich	anlässlich
ansein	an sein
im argen liegen	im Argen liegen
bei arm und reich	bei Arm und Reich
As	Ass
aufeinanderfolgen; aufeinandertreffen	aufeinander folgen; aufeinander treffen
aufgerauht	aufgeraut
aufrauhen	aufrauen
ein aufsehenerregendes Ereignis	ein Aufsehen erregendes Ereignis
aufsein	auf sein
auf seiten	aufseiten, *auch:* auf Seiten
der aufsichtführende Lehrer	der Aufsicht führende Lehrer
aufwärtsgehen	aufwärts gehen
aufwendig	*auch:* aufwändig
auseinandergehen; auseinanderhalten	auseinander gehen; auseinander halten
auseinanderreißen; auseinandersetzen	auseinander reißen; auseinander setzen
aussein	aus sein
außerstande	*auch:* außer Stande
B	
Ballettänzerin	Balletttänzerin, *auch:* Ballett-Tänzerin
Ballokal	Ballokal, *auch:* Ball-Lokal
jmdm. [angst und] bange machen	jmdm. [Angst und] Bange machen
Baroneß	Baroness
baß erstaunt	bass erstaunt
Baß; Baßsänger;	Bass; Basssänger, *auch:* Bass-Sänger
behende; Behendigkeit	behände; Behändigkeit
beieinandersitzen	beieinander sitzen
beifallheischend	Beifall heischend
beisammensein	beisammen sein
belemmert	belämmert
jeder beliebige	jeder Beliebige
Bendel	Bändel
ich will im besonderen erwähnen ...	ich will im Besonderen erwähnen ...
bessergehen	besser gehen
es ist das beste, wenn ...	es ist das Beste, wenn ...
aufs beste geregelt sein	*auch:* aufs Beste geregelt sein
zum besten geben/haben/halten	zum Besten geben/haben/halten
das erste beste	das erste Beste
bestehenbleiben	bestehen bleiben
Bestelliste	Bestellliste, *auch:* Bestell-Liste
um ein beträchtliches höher	um ein Beträchtliches höher

alt	**neu**
in betreff	in Betreff
Bettuch *[zu: Bett]*	Betttuch, *auch:* Bett-Tuch
bewußt	bewusst
in bezug auf	in Bezug auf
bezuschußt	bezuschusst
Bibliographie	*auch:* Bibliografie
Biß	Biss
bißchen	bisschen
Blackout	*auch:* Black-out*
blankpoliert	blank poliert
blaß	blass
Bläßhuhn/Bleßhuhn	Blässhuhn/Blesshuhn
bläßlich	blässlich
der blaue Planet *[die Erde]*	der Blaue Planet
blaugestreift	blau gestreift
bläulichgrün	bläulich grün
bleibenlassen	bleiben lassen
blondgefärbt	blond gefärbt
Bonbonniere	*auch:* Bonboniere
im bösen wie im guten	im Bösen wie im Guten
Boß	Boss
Bouclé	*auch:* Buklee
braungebrannt	braun gebrannt
des langen und breiten	des Langen und Breiten
breitgefächert	breit gefächert
Brennessel	Brennnessel, *auch:* Brenn-Nessel
brütendheiß	brütend heiß
buntschillernd	bunt schillernd
C	
Centre Court	Centrecourt, *auch:* Centre-Court
Choreographie	*auch:* Choreografie
Cleverneß	Cleverness
Comeback	*auch:* Come-back*
Common sense	Commonsense, *auch:* Common Sense
Corned beef	Cornedbeef, *auch:* Corned Beef
Corpus delicti	Corpus Delicti
Countdown	*auch:* Count-down*
D	
dabeisein	dabei sein
dahinterkommen	dahinter kommen
daraufffolgend	darauf folgend
dasein	da sein
daß	dass
datenverarbeitend	Daten verarbeitend
Dekolleté	*auch:* Dekolletee
Delikateßgurke	Delikatessgurke
Delphin	*auch:* Delfin
wir haben derartiges nicht bemerkt	wir haben Derartiges nicht bemerkt

alt	neu
dessenungeachtet	dessen ungeachtet
des weiteren	des Weiteren
auf deutsch	auf Deutsch
das d'Hondtsche System	das d'hondtsche System, *auch:* das d'Hondt'sche System
diät leben	Diät leben
dichtgedrängt	dicht gedrängt
Differential	*auch:* Differenzial*
Diktaphon	*auch:* Diktafon
dortbleiben	dort bleiben
draufsein	drauf sein
Dreß	Dress
drinsein	drin sein
jeder dritte, der mitwollte	jeder Dritte, der mitwollte
die dritte Welt	die Dritte Welt
drückendheiß	drückend heiß
Du *[in Briefen]*	du
im dunkeln tappen/bleiben	im Dunkeln tappen/bleiben
dünnbesiedelt	dünn besiedelt
durcheinanderbringen; durcheinandergeraten	durcheinander bringen; durcheinander geraten
E	
ebensogut; ebensosehr	ebenso gut; ebenso sehr
an Eides Statt	an Eides statt
sein eigen nennen	sein Eigen nennen
sich zu eigen machen	sich zu Eigen machen
einbleuen	einbläuen
aufs eindringlichste warnen	*auch:* aufs Eindringlichste warnen
das einfachste ist, wenn ...	das Einfachste ist, wenn ...
einiggehen	einig gehen
Einlaß	Einlass
einwärtsgebogen	einwärts gebogen
der/die/das einzelne kann ...	der/die/das Einzelne kann ...
jeder einzelne von uns	jeder Einzelne von uns
bis ins einzelne geregelt	bis ins Einzelne geregelt
der/die/das einzige wäre ...	der/die/das Einzige wäre ...
kein einziger war gekommen	kein Einziger war gekommen
er als einziger/sie als einzige hatte ...	er als Einziger/sie als Einzige hatte ...
die eisenverarbeitende Industrie	die Eisen verarbeitende Industrie
eislaufen	Eis laufen
Eisschnellauf	Eisschnelllauf
engbedruckt	eng bedruckt
nicht im entferntesten beabsichtigen	nicht im Entferntesten beabsichtigen
die erdölexportierenden Länder	die Erdöl exportierenden Länder
erholungsuchende Großstädter	Erholung suchende Großstädter
Erlaß	Erlass
ernstgemeint	ernst gemeint
ernstzunehmend	ernst zu nehmend

alt	**neu**
nicht den erstbesten nehmen	nicht den Erstbesten nehmen
der erste, der gekommen ist	der Erste, der gekommen ist
das reicht fürs erste	das reicht fürs Erste
zum ersten, zum zweiten, zum dritten	zum Ersten, zum Zweiten, zum Dritten
die Erste Hilfe	die erste Hilfe
das erstemal; zum erstenmal	das erste Mal; zum ersten Mal
Erstkläßler	Erstklässler
eßbar	essbar
essentiell	*auch:* essenziell*
Eßlöffel	Esslöffel
Existentialismus	*auch:* Existenzialismus*
existentiell	*auch:* existenziell*
Exposé	*auch:* Exposee
expreß	express
Exzeß	Exzess
F	
fahrenlassen	fahren lassen
Fairneß	Fairness
Fair play	Fairplay, *auch:* Fair Play
fallenlassen	fallen lassen
Fallout	*auch:* Fall-out*
Faß	Fass
faßbar	fassbar
du faßt	du fasst
Fast food	Fastfood, *auch:* Fast Food
feingemahlen	fein gemahlen
fernliegen	fern liegen
fertigbringen; fertigstellen	fertig bringen; fertig stellen
festangestellt	fest angestellt
festumrissen	fest umrissen
fettgedruckt	fett gedruckt
Fitneß	Fitness
fleischfressende Pflanzen	Fleisch fressende Pflanzen
das Bier floß in Strömen	das Bier floss in Strömen
flötengehen	flöten gehen
Fluß	Fluss
flüssigmachen	flüssig machen
Flußsand	Flusssand, *auch:* Fluss-Sand
Flußschiffahrt	Flussschifffahrt, *auch:* Fluss-Schifffahrt
die Haare fönen	die Haare föhnen
folgendes ist zu beachten	Folgendes ist zu beachten
wie im folgenden erläutert	wie im Folgenden erläutert
Free Jazz	*auch:* Freejazz
Freßgier	Fressgier
frischgebacken	frisch gebacken
fritieren	frittieren
frühverstorben	früh verstorben
Full-time-Job	Fulltimejob, *auch:* Full-Time-Job

alt	**neu**
funkensprühend	Funken sprühend
fürbaß	fürbass
fürliebnehmen	fürlieb nehmen
Fußballänderspiel	Fußballländerspiel, *auch:* Fußball-Länderspiel
G	
im ganzen gesehen	im Ganzen gesehen
im großen und ganzen	im Großen und Ganzen
Gäßchen	Gässchen
gefangenhalten; gefangennehmen	gefangen halten; gefangen nehmen
gefaßt	gefasst
gefirnißt	gefirnisst
es ist das gegebene, schnell zu handeln	es ist das Gegebene, schnell zu handeln
gegeneinanderstoßen	gegeneinander stoßen
von allen gehaßt	von allen gehasst
geheimhalten	geheim halten
gehenlassen	gehen lassen
Gelaß	Gelass
gutgelaunt	gut gelaunt
Gemse	Gämse
wir haben gemußt	wir haben gemusst
die Wunde hat genäßt	die Wunde hat genässt
genaugenommen	genau genommen
genausogut; genausowenig	genauso gut; genauso wenig
sie genoß den Sonnenschein	sie genoss den Sonnenschein
Genuß	Genuss
genüßlich	genüsslich
genußsüchtig	genusssüchtig
Geographie	*auch:* Geografie
es hat gut gepaßt	es hat gut gepasst
wir haben gepraßt	wir haben geprasst
frisch gepreßter Saft	frisch gepresster Saft
geradestellen	gerade stellen
es geht ihn nicht das geringste an	es geht ihn nicht das Geringste an
nicht im geringsten stören	nicht im Geringsten stören
geringschätzen	gering schätzen
Geschirreiniger	Geschirrreiniger, *auch:* Geschirr-Reiniger
Geschoß	Geschoss *[in Österreich weiterhin mit ß]*
gestern abend/morgen/nacht	gestern Abend/Morgen/Nacht
alle waren gestreßt	alle waren gestresst
getrenntlebend	getrennt lebend
Gewinnummer	Gewinnnummer, *auch:* Gewinn-Nummer
gewiß	gewiss
ich habe es gewußt	ich habe es gewusst
glattgehen; glatthobeln	glatt gehen; glatt hobeln
das gleiche tun	das Gleiche tun
aufs gleiche hinauskommen	aufs Gleiche hinauskommen

alt	**neu**
gleichlautend	gleich lautend
Glimmstengel	Glimmstängel
die Goetheschen Dramen	die goetheschen Dramen, *auch:* die Goethe'schen Dramen
Graphit	*auch:* Grafit
Graphologie	*auch:* Grafologie
gräßlich	grässlich
Greuel	Gräuel
greulich	gräulich
grobgemahlen	grob gemahlen
ein Programm für groß und klein	ein Programm für Groß und Klein
im großen und ganzen	im Großen und Ganzen
groß schreiben *[mit großem Anfangsbuchstaben]*	großschreiben
Guß	Guss
es im guten versuchen	es im Guten versuchen
gutaussehend	gut aussehend
gutgehen	gut gehen
gutgelaunt; gutgemeint	gut gelaunt; gut gemeint
guttun	gut tun
gutunterrichtet	gut unterrichtet
H	
haftenbleiben	haften bleiben
haltmachen	Halt machen
Hämorrhoide	*auch:* Hämorride
Handout	*auch:* Hand-out*
händchenhaltend	Händchen haltend
hängenbleiben; hängenlassen	hängen bleiben; hängen lassen
Happy-End	Happyend, *auch:* Happy End
Hard cover	Hardcover, *auch:* Hard Cover
hartgekocht	hart gekocht
Haß	Hass
häßlich	hässlich
du haßt	du hasst
nach Hause	*in Österreich und der Schweiz auch:* nachhause
zu Hause	*in Österreich und der Schweiz auch:* zuhause
haushalten	*auch:* Haus halten
heiligsprechen	heilig sprechen
heimlichtun	heimlich tun
heißgeliebt	heiß geliebt
helleuchtend	hell leuchtend
hellicht	helllicht
hersein	her sein
heute abend/mittag/nacht	heute Abend/Mittag/Nacht
hierbleiben; hierlassen	hier bleiben; hier lassen
hiersein	hier sein
hierzulande	*auch:* hier zu Lande

alt	neu
High-Society	Highsociety, *auch:* High Society
hilfesuchend	Hilfe suchend
es wurde etwas hineingeheimnißt	es wurde etwas hineingeheimnisst
hintereinanderschalten	hintereinander schalten
er hißt die Flagge	er hisst die Flagge
hofhalten	Hof halten
die Hohe Schule	die hohe Schule
hohnlachen	*auch:* Hohn lachen
Hosteß	Hostess
Hot dog	Hotdog, *auch:* Hot Dog
Hungers sterben	hungers sterben
I	
auch Ihr seid herzlich eingeladen *[in Briefen]*	auch ihr seid herzlich eingeladen
im allgemeinen	im Allgemeinen
im besonderen	im Besonderen
Imbiß	Imbiss
Imbißstand	Imbissstand, *auch:* Imbiss-Stand
im einzelnen	im Einzelnen
im nachhinein	im Nachhinein
imstande	*auch:* im Stande
im übrigen	im Übrigen
im voraus	im Voraus
im vorhinein	im Vorhinein
in betreff	in Betreff
in bezug auf	in Bezug auf
ineinanderfließen	ineinander fließen
in Frage stellen/kommen	*auch:* infrage stellen/kommen
instand halten/setzen	*auch:* in Stand halten/setzen
irgend etwas; irgend jemand	irgendetwas; irgendjemand
I-Tüpfelchen	i-Tüpfelchen
J	
ja sagen	*auch:* Ja sagen*
2jährig, 3jährig, 4jährig ...	2-jährig, 3-jährig, 4-jährig ...
ein 2jähriger, 3jähriger, 4jähriger kann das noch nicht verstehen	ein 2-Jähriger, 3-Jähriger, 4-Jähriger kann das noch nicht verstehen
jedesmal	jedes Mal
Job-sharing	Jobsharing
Joghurt	*auch:* Jogurt
Joint-venture	Jointventure, *auch:* Joint Venture
Jumbo-Jet	Jumbojet
für jung und alt	für Jung und Alt
K	
Kaffee-Ersatz	*auch:* Kaffeeersatz
kaltlächelnd	kalt lächelnd
Kammuschel	Kammmuschel, *auch:* Kamm-Muschel
Känguruh	Känguru

alt	neu
Karamel	Karamell
karamelisieren	karamellisieren
Kartographie	*auch:* Kartografie
Kaßler	Kassler
Katarrh	*auch:* Katarr
kegelschieben	Kegel schieben
kennenlernen	kennen lernen
Kennummer	Kennnummer, *auch:* Kenn-Nummer
keß	kess
Ketchup	*auch:* Ketschup*
an Kindes Statt	an Kindes statt
Kißchen	Kisschen
sich über etwas im klaren sein	sich über etwas im Klaren sein
klarsehen; klarwerden	klar sehen; klar werden
klebenbleiben	kleben bleiben
Klee-Einsaat	*auch:* Kleeeinsaat
bis ins kleinste geregelt	bis ins Kleinste geregelt
ein Staat im kleinen	ein Staat im Kleinen
ein Programm für groß und klein	ein Programm für Groß und Klein
kleingedruckt	klein gedruckt
kleinschneiden	klein schneiden
klein schreiben *[mit kleinem Anfangsbuchstaben]*	kleinschreiben
Klemmappe	Klemmmappe, *auch:* Klemm-Mappe
es wäre das klügste, wenn ...	es wäre das Klügste, wenn ...
Knockout	*auch:* Knock-out*
kochendheiß	kochend heiß
Kolophonium	*auch:* Kolofonium
Koloß	Koloss
Kommiß	Kommiss
Kommißstiefel	Kommissstiefel, *auch:* Kommiss-Stiefel
Kommuniqué	*auch:* Kommunikee
Kompaß	Kompass
kompreß	kompress
Kompromiß	Kompromiss
Komteß	Komtess
Kongreß	Kongress
Kongreßstadt	Kongressstadt, *auch:* Kongress-Stadt
Kontrollampe	Kontrolllampe, *auch:* Kontroll-Lampe
kopfstehen	Kopf stehen
krank schreiben	krankschreiben
kraß	krass
krebserregende Substanzen	Krebs erregende Substanzen
Kreppapier	Krepppapier, *auch:* Krepp-Papier
die kriegführenden Parteien	die Krieg führenden Parteien
kroß	kross
krummnehmen	krumm nehmen
Kunststoffolie	Kunststofffolie, *auch:* Kunststoff-Folie
Küraß	Kürass
den kürzeren ziehen	den Kürzeren ziehen

alt	neu
kürzertreten	kürzer treten
kurzgebraten	kurz gebraten
kurzhalten	kurz halten
kurztreten	kurz treten
Kuß	Kuss
Küßchen	Küsschen
du/er/sie küßt	du/er/sie küsst
L	
Lamé	*auch:* Lamee
etwas des langen und breiten erklären	etwas des Langen und Breiten erklären
langgestreckt	lang gestreckt
länglichrund	länglich rund
langstengelig	langstängelig
läßlich	lässlich
du läßt	du lässt
zu Lasten	*auch:* zulasten
laubtragende Bäume	Laub tragende Bäume
auf dem laufenden sein	auf dem Laufenden sein
laufenlassen	laufen lassen
Layout	*auch:* Lay-out*
leerstehend	leer stehend
leichtfallen; leichtmachen	leicht fallen; leicht machen
leichtverderblich; leichtverständlich	leicht verderblich; leicht verständlich
jmdm. leid tun	jmdm. Leid tun
der letzte, der gekommen ist	der Letzte, der gekommen ist
als letzter fertig sein	als Letzter fertig sein
das letzte, was sie tun würde	das Letzte, was sie tun würde
letzteres trifft zu	Letzteres trifft zu
zum letztenmal	zum letzten Mal
Lichtmeß	Lichtmess
liebhaben	lieb haben
liegenbleiben; liegenlassen	liegen bleiben; liegen lassen
Löß	*auch:* Löss *[bei Aussprache mit kurzem ö]*
M	
2mal, 3mal, 4mal ...	2-mal, 3-mal, 4-mal ...
Malaise	*auch:* Maläse
maschineschreiben	Maschine schreiben
maßhalten	Maß halten
Megaphon	*auch:* Megafon
wir haben das menschenmögliche getan	wir haben das Menschenmögliche getan
Mesner	*auch:* Messner
meßbar	messbar
Meßdiener	Messdiener
Meßinstrument	Messinstrument
Metallegierung	Metalllegierung, *auch:* Metall-Legierung

alt	**neu**
die metallverarbeitende Industrie	die Metall verarbeitende Industrie
Midlife-crisis	Midlifecrisis, *auch:* Midlife-Crisis
millionenmal	Millionen Mal
nicht im mindesten	nicht im Mindesten
mißachten	missachten
Mißbildung	Missbildung
mißbilligen	missbilligen
Mißbrauch; Mißerfolg; Mißernte	Missbrauch; Misserfolg; Missernte
mißfallen	missfallen
Mißgeburt	Missgeburt
mißglücken	missglücken
mißgünstig	missgünstig
Mißklang	Missklang
Mißkredit	Misskredit
mißlich	misslich
mißlingen	misslingen
mißmutig	missmutig
mißraten	missraten
Mißstand	Missstand
Mißtrauen	Misstrauen
mißtrauisch	misstrauisch
Mißverständnis	Missverständnis
mit Hilfe	*auch:* mithilfe
[gestern, heute, morgen] mittag	[gestern, heute, morgen] Mittag
wir sprachen über alles mögliche	wir sprachen über alles Mögliche
sein möglichstes tun	sein Möglichstes tun
Mop	Mopp
morgen abend, mittag, nacht	morgen Abend, Mittag, Nacht
[gestern, heute] morgen	[gestern, heute] Morgen
ich muß	ich muss
du mußt	du musst
müßiggehen	müßig gehen
Myrrhe	*auch:* Myrre
N	
nach Hause	*in Österreich und der Schweiz auch:* nachhause
im nachhinein	im Nachhinein
Nachlaß	Nachlass
[gestern, heute, morgen] nachmittag	[gestern, heute, morgen] Nachmittag
der nächste, bitte!	der Nächste, bitte!
als nächstes wollen wir ...	als Nächstes wollen wir ...
[gestern, heute, morgen] nacht	[gestern, heute, morgen] Nacht
naheliegen	nahe liegen
naheliegend	nahe liegend
etwas des näheren erläutern	etwas des Näheren erläutern
näherliegen	näher liegen
nahestehen	nahe stehen
nahestehend	nahe stehend
Narziß	Narziss

alt	neu
narzißtisch	narzisstisch
naß	nass
Naßschnee	Nassschnee, *auch:* Nass-Schnee
nebeneinanderstellen	nebeneinander stellen
Necessaire	*auch:* Nessessär
Negligé	*auch:* Negligee
es aufs neue versuchen	es aufs Neue versuchen
auf ein neues!	auf ein Neues!
neueröffnet	neu eröffnet
nichtssagend	nichts sagend
die notleidende Bevölkerung	die Not leidende Bevölkerung
in Null Komma nichts	in null Komma nichts
das Thermometer steht auf Null	das Thermometer steht auf null
Nullösung	Nulllösung, *auch:* Null-Lösung
numerieren	nummerieren
Numerierung	Nummerierung
Nuß	Nuss
Nüßchen	Nüsschen
Nußschale	Nussschale, *auch:* Nuss-Schale
O	
obenerwähnt; obenstehend	oben erwähnt; oben stehend
offenbleiben; offenlassen; offenstehen	offen bleiben; offen lassen; offen stehen
des öfteren	des Öfteren
Orthographie	*auch:* Orthografie
P	
Panther	*auch:* Panter
Pappmaché	*auch:* Pappmaschee
parallellaufend	parallel laufend
parallelschalten	parallel schalten
Parnaß	Parnass
Paß	Pass
passé	*auch:* passee
Paßstraße	Passstraße, *auch:* Pass-Straße
es paßt	es passt
Platitüde	Plattitüde, *auch:* Platitude
Playback	*auch:* Play-back*
plazieren	platzieren
pleite gehen	Pleite gehen
Pornographie	*auch:* Pornografie
Portemonnaie	*auch:* Portmonee
Potemkinsche Dörfer	potemkinsche Dörfer, *auch:* Potemkin'sche Dörfer
potentiell	*auch:* potenziell*
er praßt	er prasst
Preßluftbohrer	Pressluftbohrer
Preßspan	Pressspan, *auch:* Press-Span
du preßt	du presst
privatversichert	privat versichert

alt	neu
probefahren	Probe fahren
Progreß	Progress
Prozeß	Prozess
Q	
Quadrophonie	*auch:* Quadrofonie
Quentchen	Quäntchen
Quickstep	Quickstepp
R	
radfahren; radschlagen	Rad fahren; Rad schlagen
zu Rande kommen	*auch:* zurande kommen
ich raßle mit den Ketten	ich rassle mit den Ketten
zu Rate ziehen	*auch:* zurate ziehen
rauh	rau
Rauhfasertapete	Raufasertapete
Rauhhaardackel	Rauhaardackel
Rauhreif	Raureif
recht haben/behalten/bekommen	Recht haben/behalten/bekommen
jmdm. recht geben	jmdm. Recht geben
Rechtens sein	rechtens sein
Regreß	Regress
regreßpflichtig	regresspflichtig
das ist genau das richtige für mich	das ist genau das Richtige für mich
richtigstellen	richtig stellen
Riß	Riss
Roheit	Rohheit
Rolladen	Rollladen, *auch:* Roll-Laden
Rommé	*auch:* Rommee
Roß	Ross
Rößl	Rössl
der rote Planet *[Mars]*	der Rote Planet
rotgestreift	rot gestreift
rötlichbraun	rötlich braun
rückwärtsgewandt	rückwärts gewandt
ruhenlassen	ruhen lassen
ruhigstellen	ruhig stellen
Rußland	Russland
S	
sauberhalten; saubermachen	sauber halten; sauber machen
sausenlassen	sausen lassen
Saxophon	*auch:* Saxofon
sein Schäfchen ins trockene bringen	sein Schäfchen ins Trockene bringen
Schalloch	Schallloch, *auch:* Schall-Loch
schätzenlernen	schätzen lernen
Schiffahrt	Schifffahrt, *auch:* Schiff-Fahrt
schlechtgehen	schlecht gehen
schlechtgelaunt	schlecht gelaunt
das schlimmste ist, daß ...	das Schlimmste ist, dass ...

alt	**neu**
Schloß	Schloss
Schlößchen	Schlösschen
Schluß	Schluss
Schlußstrich	Schlussstrich, *auch:* Schluss-Strich
sie schmiß mit Steinen	sie schmiss mit Steinen
Schmiß	Schmiss
Schmuckblattelegramm	Schmuckblatttelegramm, *auch:* Schmuckblatt-Telegramm
schmutziggrau	schmutzig grau
Schneewächte	Schneewechte
schnellebig	schnelllebig
Schnepper	*auch:* Schnäpper
schneppern	*auch:* schnäppern
schneuzen	schnäuzen
er schoß	er schoss
Schoß *[einer Pflanze]*	Schoss
Schrittempo	Schritttempo, *auch:* Schritt-Tempo
an etwas schuld haben	an etwas Schuld haben
sich etwas zuschulden kommen lassen	*auch:* sich etwas zu Schulden kommen lassen
Schuß	Schuss
schußlig	schusslig
aus schwarz weiß machen	aus Schwarz Weiß machen
Schwarze Magie	schwarze Magie
schwarzrotgolden	*auch:* schwarz-rot-golden
schwerfallen; schwernehmen; schwertun	schwer fallen; schwer nehmen; schwer tun
schwerverständlich	schwer verständlich
Schwimmeister	Schwimmmeister, *auch:* Schwimm-Meister
Science-fiction	Sciencefiction, *auch:* Science-Fiction
seinlassen	sein lassen
Seismograph	*auch:* Seismograf
auf seiten	aufseiten, *auch:* auf Seiten
von seiten	vonseiten, *auch:* von Seiten
selbständig	*auch:* selbstständig
selbsternannt; selbstgebacken; selbstgemacht	selbst ernannt; selbst gebacken; selbst gemacht
seligsprechen	selig sprechen
Séparée	*auch:* Separee
sequentiell	*auch:* sequenziell*
seßhaft	sesshaft
Showbusineß	Showbusiness
Showdown	*auch:* Show-down*
Shrimp	*auch:* Schrimp
das sicherste ist, wenn ...	das Sicherste ist, wenn ...
siedendheiß	siedend heiß
sitzenbleiben; sitzenlassen	sitzen bleiben; sitzen lassen
so daß	sodass, *auch:* so dass
alles sonstige besprechen wir morgen	alles Sonstige besprechen wir morgen

alt	**neu**
Soufflé	*auch:* Soufflee
soviel du willst	so viel du willst
soviel wie	so viel wie
es ist soweit	es ist so weit
soweit wie möglich	so weit wie möglich
ich kann das sowenig wie du	ich kann das so wenig wie du
Spaghetti	*auch:* Spagetti
spazierenfahren; spazierengehen	spazieren fahren; spazieren gehen
Sperriegel	Sperrriegel, *auch:* Sperr-Riegel
Spliß	Spliss
du splißt	du splisst
es sproß neues Grün	es spross neues Grün
Sproß	Spross
Sprößling	Sprössling
staatenbildende Insekten	Staaten bildende Insekten
Stallaterne	Stalllaterne, *auch:* Stall-Laterne
steckenbleiben; steckenlassen	stecken bleiben; stecken lassen
stehenbleiben; stehenlassen	stehen bleiben; stehen lassen
Stengel	Stängel
Step	Stepp
Steptanz	Stepptanz
Stereophonie	*auch:* Stereofonie
Stewardeß	Stewardess
etwas im stillen vorbereiten	etwas im Stillen vorbereiten
Stilleben	Stillleben, *auch:* Still-Leben
stillegen	stilllegen
Stoffetzen	Stofffetzen, *auch:* Stoff-Fetzen
Stop	Stopp
Straß	Strass
strenggenommen	streng genommen
strengnehmen	streng nehmen
Streß	Stress
der Lärm streßt	der Lärm stresst
Streßsituation	Stresssituation, *auch:* Stress-Situation
Stuß	Stuss
substantiell	*auch:* substanziell*
T	
tabula rasa machen	Tabula rasa machen
zutage treten	*auch:* zu Tage treten
2tägig, 3tägig, 4tägig ...	2-tägig, 3-tägig, 4-tägig ...
Täßchen	Tässchen
T-bone-Steak	T-Bone-Steak
Telephon	Telefon
Thunfisch	*auch:* Tunfisch
Tie-Break	*auch:* Tiebreak
tiefbewegt; tiefempfunden	tief bewegt; tief empfunden
Tip	Tipp
Tolpatsch	Tollpatsch
tolpatschig	tollpatschig

alt	**neu**
Topographie	*auch:* Topografie
totgeboren	tot geboren
Trekking	*auch:* Trecking
treuergeben	treu ergeben
auf dem trockenen sitzen	auf dem Trockenen sitzen
sein Schäfchen ins trockene bringen	sein Schäfchen ins Trockene bringen
Troß	Tross
im trüben fischen	im Trüben fischen
Truchseß	Truchsess
Typographie	*auch:* Typografie
U	
übelnehmen	übel nehmen
übelriechend	übel riechend
übereinanderlegen	übereinander legen
überhandnehmen	überhand nehmen
überschwenglich	überschwänglich
ein übriges tun	ein Übriges tun
im übrigen wissen wir doch alle ...	im Übrigen wissen wir doch alle ...
alles übrige später	alles Übrige später
die übrigen kommen nach	die Übrigen kommen nach
übrigbehalten; übrigbleiben; übriglassen	übrig behalten; übrig bleiben; übrig lassen
Ultima ratio	Ultima Ratio
die Liste umfaßt alles Wichtige	die Liste umfasst alles Wichtige
umsein	um sein
um so [mehr, größer, weniger ...]	umso [mehr, größer, weniger ...]
sich ins unabsehbare ausweiten	sich ins Unabsehbare ausweiten
Anzeige gegen Unbekannt	Anzeige gegen unbekannt
und ähnliches (u. ä.)	und Ähnliches (u. Ä.)
unerläßlich	unerlässlich
unermeßlich	unermesslich
im unklaren bleiben	im Unklaren bleiben
im unklaren lassen	im Unklaren lassen
unpäßlich	unpässlich
unrecht haben/behalten/bekommen	Unrecht haben/behalten/bekommen
unselbständig	*auch:* unselbstständig
untenerwähnt	unten erwähnt
untenstehend	unten stehend
unterderhand	unter der Hand
untereinanderstehen	untereinander stehen
V	
va banque spielen	*auch:* Vabanque spielen
Varieté	*auch:* Varietee
veranlaßt	veranlasst
verblaßt	verblasst
verbleuen	verbläuen
im verborgenen blühen	im Verborgenen blühen
das verdroß uns	das verdross uns

alt	**neu**
Verdruß	Verdruss
du verfaßt	du verfasst
vergeßlich	vergesslich
Vergißmeinnicht	Vergissmeinnicht
du vergißt	du vergisst
verhaßt	verhasst
auf jmdn. ist Verlaß	auf jmdn. ist Verlass
verläßlich	verlässlich
verlorengehen	verloren gehen
vermißt	vermisst
er hat den Zug verpaßt	er hat den Zug verpasst
das Geld wurde verpraßt	das Geld wurde verprasst
verschiedenes war noch unklar	Verschiedenes war noch unklar
Verschlußsache	Verschlusssache, *auch:* Verschluss-Sache
verselbständigen	*auch:* verselbstständigen
Vibraphon	*auch:* Vibrafon
viel zuviel	viel zu viel
viel zuwenig	viel zu wenig
vielbefahren; vielgelesen	viel befahren; viel gelesen
aus dem vollen schöpfen	aus dem Vollen schöpfen
voneinandergehen	voneinander gehen
von seiten	vonseiten, *auch:* von Seiten
im voraus	im Voraus
im vorhinein	im Vorhinein
das vorige gilt auch ...	das Vorige gilt auch ...
vorliebnehmen	vorlieb nehmen
[gestern, heute, morgen] vormittag	[gestern, heute, morgen] Vormittag
vorwärtsgehen; vorwärtskommen	vorwärts gehen; vorwärts kommen
W	
ein wachestehender Soldat	ein Wache stehender Soldat
Wächte	Wechte
Waggon	*auch:* Wagon
Walkie-talkie	Walkie-Talkie
Walroß	Walross
wäßrig	wässrig
weichgekocht	weich gekocht
aus schwarz weiß machen	aus Schwarz Weiß machen
weißgekleidet	weiß gekleidet
des weiteren wurde gesagt ...	des Weiteren wurde gesagt ...
weitreichend	weit reichend
weitverbreitet	weit verbreitet
es besteht im wesentlichen aus ...	es besteht im Wesentlichen aus ...
Wetturnen	Wettturnen, *auch:* Wett-Turnen
wieviel	wie viel
wißbegierig	wissbegierig
ihr wißt	ihr wisst
du wußtest	du wusstest
wir wüßten gern ...	wir wüssten gern ...

alt	neu
Wollappen	Wolllappen, *auch:* Woll-Lappen
als ob er wunder was getan hätte	als ob er Wunder was getan hätte
sich wundliegen	sich wund liegen
Z	
Zäheit	Zähheit
eine Zeitlang	eine Zeit lang
Zellstoffabrik	Zellstofffabrik, *auch:* Zellstoff-Fabrik
Zierat	Zierrat
zueinanderfinden	zueinander finden
sich zufriedengeben	sich zufrieden geben
zufriedenstellen	zufrieden stellen
zugrunde gehen/legen/liegen	*auch:* zu Grunde gehen/legen/liegen
zugrundeliegend	zugrunde liegend, *auch:* zu Grunde liegend
zugrunde richten	*auch:* zu Grunde richten
zugunsten	*auch:* zu Gunsten
zu Hause	*in Österreich und der Schweiz auch:* zuhause
bei uns zulande	bei uns zu Lande
zulasten	*auch:* zu Lasten
jmdm. etwas zuleide tun	*auch:* jmdm. etwas zu Leide tun
zumute sein	*auch:* zu Mute sein
sich etwas zunutze machen	*auch:* sich etwas zu Nutze machen
jmdm. zupaß kommen	jmdm. zupass kommen
zu Rande kommen	*auch:* zurande kommen
jmdn. zu Rate ziehen	*auch:* jmdn. zurate ziehen
zur Zeit *[derzeit]*	zurzeit
zusammensein	zusammen sein
zuschanden werden	*auch:* zu Schanden werden
sich etwas zuschulden kommen lassen	*auch:* sich etwas zu Schulden kommen lassen
zusein	zu sein
zustande bringen	*auch:* zu Stande bringen
zustande kommen	*auch:* zu Stande kommen
zutage fördern	*auch:* zu Tage fördern
zutage treten	*auch:* zu Tage treten
zuungunsten	*auch:* zu Ungunsten
zuviel	zu viel
zuwege bringen	*auch:* zu Wege bringen
zuwenig	zu wenig
das Zweite Gesicht	das zweite Gesicht
er hat wie kein zweiter gearbeitet	er hat wie kein Zweiter gearbeitet
jeder zweite war krank	jeder Zweite war krank

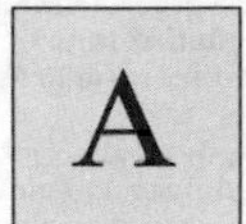

A (Buchstabe); das A; des A, die A, *aber* das a in Land (↑R 60); der Buchstabe A, a; von A bis Z (*ugs. für* alles, von Anfang bis Ende); das A und [das] O (der Anfang und das Ende, das Wesentliche [nach dem ersten und letzten Buchstaben des griech. Alphabets]); a-Laut (↑R 25)
Ä (Buchstabe; Umlaut); das Ä; des Ä, die Ä, *aber* das ä in Bäcker (↑R 60); der Buchstabe Ä, ä
a = [1]Ar; Atto...
a, A, das; -, - (Tonbezeichnung); **a** (*Zeichen für* a-Moll); in a; **A** (*Zeichen für* A-Dur); in A
A = Ampere; Autobahn; Austral
Å = Ångström
A, α = Alpha
à [a] ‹franz.› (*bes. Kaufmannsspr.* zu [je]); 3 Stück à 20 Mark, *dafür besser:* ... zu [je] 20 Mark
a. = am (*bei Ortsnamen,* z. B. Frickenhausen a. Main); *vgl.* a. d.
a. = alt (*schweiz.; vor Amtsbezeichnungen,* z. B. a. Bundesrat)
a., A. = anno, Anno
a. a. = ad acta
Aa, das; - (*Kinderspr.* Kot); - machen
AA = Auswärtiges Amt; Anonyme Alkoholiker
Aa|chen (Stadt in Nordrhein-Westfalen); **Aa|che|ner** (↑R 103)
Aal, der; -[e]s, -e; *aber* Älchen *(vgl. d.)*; **aa|len,** sich (*ugs. für* behaglich ausgestreckt sich ausruhen); **aal|glatt**
Aall [o:l] (norw. Philosoph)
Aal|tier|chen (ein Fadenwurm)
a. a. O. = am angeführten Ort; *auch* am angegebenen Ort
Aar, der; -[e]s, -e (*geh. für* Adler)
Aa|rau (↑R 132; Hptst. des Kantons Aargau); **Aa|re,** die; - (schweiz. Fluss); **Aar|gau,** der; -s (schweiz. Kanton); **Aar|gau|er** (↑R 103); **aar|gau|isch**
Aa|ron (bibl. m. Eigenn.)
Aas, das; -es, *Plur.* (*für* Tierleichen:) -e *u.* (*als* Schimpfwort:) Äser; **Aas|blu|me** (Pflanze, deren Blütengeruch Aasfliegen anzieht); **aa|sen** (*ugs. für* verschwenderisch umgehen); du aast, er aas|te mit den Vorräten; **Aas|gei|er; aa|sig** (ekelhaft; gemein); **Aast,** das; -es, Äs|ter (landsch. Schimpfwort)
A. B. = Augsburger Bekenntnis
ạb; *Adverb:* ab sein *(ugs.)*; ab und zu, *landsch.* ab und an (von Zeit zu Zeit); von ... ab (*ugs. für* von ... an); ab und zu (gelegentlich) nehmen; *aber* (↑R 23): ab- und zunehmen (abnehmen und zunehmen); *Präp. mit Dat.:* ab Bremen, ab [unserem] Werk; ab erstem März; *bei Zeitangaben, Mengenangaben o. Ä. auch mit Akk.:* ab ersten März, ab vierzehn Jahre[n], ab 50 Exemplare[n]
ab... (*in Zus. mit Verben,* z. B. abschreiben, du schreibst ab, abgeschrieben, abzuschreiben)
A|ba, die; -, -s ‹arab.› (weiter, kragenloser Mantel der Araber)
A|ba|kus, der; -, - ‹griech.› (Rechen- od. Spielbrett der Antike; *Archit.* Säulendeckplatte)
A|bä|lard [...'lart, *auch* 'abɛ...] (franz. Philosoph)
ạb|än|der|lich; ạb|än|dern; Ạb|än|de|rung; Ạb|än|de|rungs|vor|schlag
A|ban|don [abã'dɔ̃:], der; -s, -s ‹franz.› (*Rechtsspr.* Abtretung, Preisgabe von Rechten od. Sachen); **a|ban|don|nie|ren** [abãdɔni:...]
ạb|ar|bei|ten; Ạb|ar|bei|tung
Ạb|art; ạb|ar|ten (*selten für* von der Art abweichen); **ạb|ar|tig; Ạb|ar|tig|keit; Ạb|ar|tung**
A|ba|sie, die; -, ...ien ‹griech.› (*Med.* Unfähigkeit zu gehen)
ạb|as|ten, sich (*ugs. für* sich abplagen)
ạb|äs|ten; einen Baum -
A|ba|te, der; -[n], *Plur.* ...ti *od.* ...ten ‹ital.› (*kath. Kirche* Titel der Weltgeistlichen in Italien)
A|ba|ton ['a(:)batɔn], das; -s, ...ta ‹griech.› (*Rel.* das Allerheiligste, der Altarraum in den Kirchen des orthodoxen Ritus)
Abb. = Abbildung
Ạb|ba ‹aram. „Vater!"› (neutest. Anrede Gottes im Gebet)
ạb|ba|cken
Ab|ba|si|de, der; -n, -n; ↑R 126 (Angehöriger eines aus Bagdad stammenden Kalifengeschlechtes)
Ạb|bau, der; -[e]s, *Plur.* (*Bergmannsspr. für* Abbaustellen:) -e *u.* (*landsch. für* abseits gelegene Anwesen, einzelne Gehöfte:) -ten; **ạb|bau|bar; ạb|bau|en; Ạb|bau‿feld** *(Bergmannsspr.)*, **...ge|rech|tig|keit** *(Rechtsspr.)*, **...recht; ạb|bau|wür|dig**
Ạb|be (dt. Physiker)
Ab|bé [a'be:], der; -s, -s ‹franz.› (*kath. Kirche* Titel der niederen Weltgeistlichen in Frankreich)
ạb|bei|ßen
ạb|bei|zen; Ạb|beiz|mit|tel, das
ạb|be|kom|men
ạb|be|ru|fen; Ạb|be|ru|fung
ạb|be|stel|len; Ạb|be|stel|lung
ạb|beu|teln (*südd., österr. für* abschütteln)
Ab|be|vil|li|en [abəvi'liẽ:], das; -[s] ‹nach der Stadt Abbeville in Nordfrankreich› (Kultur der frühesten Altsteinzeit)
ạb|be|zah|len; Ạb|be|zah|lung
ạb|bie|gen; Ạb|bie|ge|spur; Ạb|bie|gung
Ạb|bild; ạb|bil|den; Ạb|bil|dung (*Abk.* Abb.)
ạb|bim|sen (*ugs. für* abschreiben)
ạb|bin|den; Ạb|bin|dung
Ạb|bit|te; - leisten, tun; **ạb|bit|ten**
ạb|bla|sen
ạb|blas|sen
ạb|blät|tern
ạb|blen|den; Ạb|blend|licht *Plur.* ...lichter; **Ạb|blen|dung**
ạb|blit|zen; jmdn. - lassen *(ugs.)*
ạb|blo|cken (*Sportspr.* abwehren)
Ạb|brand (*Hüttenw.* Röstrückstand; Metallschwund durch Oxidation und Verflüchtigung beim Schmelzen); **Ạb|brand|ler, Ạb-**

bränd|ler (*österr. ugs. für* durch Brand Geschädigter)
ab|brau|sen
ab|bre|chen
ab|brem|sen; Ab|brem|sung
ab|bren|nen
Ab|bre|vi|a|ti|on [...v...], die; -, -en ⟨lat.⟩, **Ab|bre|vi|a|tur,** die; -, -en (Abkürzung); **ab|bre|vi|ie|ren**
ab|brin|gen; jmdn. von etwas -
ab|brö|ckeln; Ab|brö|cke|lung, Ab|bröck|lung; ab|bro|cken (*südd., österr. für* abpflücken)
Ab|bruch, der; -[e]s, ...brüche; einer Sache [keinen] - tun; **Ab|bruch‿ar|bei|ten** *(Plur.),* **...fir|ma, ...ge|neh|mi|gung, ...haus; ab|bruch|reif**
ab|brü|hen; *vgl.* abgebrüht
ab|bu|chen; Ab|bu|chung
ab|bum|meln (*ugs. für* [Überstunden] durch Freistunden ausgleichen)
ab|bürs|ten
Abc, A|be|ce, das; -, -; **Abc-Buch,** A|be|ce|buch (Fibel); **Abc-Code,** der; -s (internationaler Telegrammschlüssel); **ABC-Flug;** ↑R 26 ⟨engl.; dt.⟩ (verbilligter Flug mit einem Linienflugzeug)
ab|che|cken [...tʃɛk(ə)n] (*ugs. für* überprüfen)
abc|lich, a|be|ce|lich; **Abc-Schüt|ze,** A|be|ce|schüt|ze; **ABC-Staa|ten** *Plur.;* ↑R 26 (Argentinien, Brasilien und Chile); **ABC-Waf|fen** *Plur.;* ↑R 26 (atomare, biologische u. chemische Waffen); **ABC-Waf|fen-frei**
ab|da|chen; Ab|da|chung
Ab|dampf *(Technik);* **ab|damp|fen** (Dampf abgeben; als Dampf abgeschieden werden; *ugs. für* abfahren); **ab|dämp|fen** ([in seiner Wirkung] mildern); **Ab|dampf|wär|me** *(Technik)*
ab|dan|ken; Ab|dan|kung (*schweiz. auch für* Trauerfeier)
ab|de|cken; Ab|de|cker (jmd., der Tierkadaver beseitigt); **Ab|de|cke|rei; Ab|deck|plat|te; Ab|de|ckung**
Ab|de|ra (altgriech. Stadt); **Ab|de|rit,** der; -en, -en (Bewohner von Abdera; *übertr. für* einfältiger Mensch, Schildbürger)
ab|dich|ten; Ab|dich|tung
Ab|di|ka|ti|on, die; -, -en ⟨lat.⟩ (*veraltet für* Abdankung)
ab|ding|bar (*Rechtsspr.* durch freie Vereinbarung ersetzbar)
ab|di|zie|ren ⟨lat.⟩ (*veraltet für* abdanken)
Ab|do|men, das; -s, *Plur.* - *u.* ...mina ⟨lat.⟩ (*Med.* Unterleib, Bauch; *Zool.* Hinterleib der Gliederfüßer); **ab|do|mi|nal**
ab|dor|ren; abgedorrte Zweige
ab|drän|gen; jmdn. -
ab|dre|hen
Ab|drift, die; -, -en (*Seemannsspr., Fliegerspr.* durch Wind od. Strömung hervorgerufene Kursabweichung); **ab|drif|ten**
ab|dros|seln; Ab|dros|se|lung, Ab|dross|lung
Ab|druck, der; -[e]s, *Plur.* (in Gips u. a.:) ...drücke *u.* (*für* Drucksachen:) ...drucke; **ab|dru|cken;** ein Buch -; **ab|drü|cken;** das Gewehr -
abds. = abends
ab|du|cken *(Boxen)*
Ab|duk|ti|on, die; -, -en ⟨lat.⟩ (*Med.* das Bewegen von Körperteilen von der Körperachse weg, z. B. das Heben des Armes); **Ab|duk|tor,** der; -s, ...oren (eine Abduktion bewirkender Muskel, Abziehmuskel); **ab|du|zie|ren**
ab|eb|ben
A|be|ce *vgl.* Abc; **A|be|ce|buch** *vgl.* Abc-Buch; **a|be|ce|lich,** *vgl.* abclich; **A|be|ce|schüt|ze** *vgl.* Abc-Schütze
A|bee [*auch* ˈabe], der *u.* das; -s, -s (*landsch. für* [1]Abort)
ab|ei|sen (*österr. für* abtauen)
A|bel (bibl. m. Eigenn.)
A|bel|mo|schus [*auch* ˈa:b(ə)l...], der; -, -se ⟨arab.⟩ (eine Tropenpflanze)
A|bend, der; -s, -e; des, eines Abends; gegen Abend; den Abend über; es ist, wird Abend; am Abend; diesen Abend; zu Abend essen; Guten (*auch:* guten) Abend sagen; [bis, von] gestern, heute, morgen Abend (↑R 45). *Kleinschreibung:* abends (*Abk.* abds.); von früh bis abends; von morgens bis abends; abends spät, *aber* spätabends; [um] 8 Uhr abends, abends [um] 8 Uhr; dienstagabends, *auch* dienstags abends; *vgl.* Dienstagabend; **A|bend‿brot, ...däm|me|rung; a|ben|de|lang,** *aber* drei *od.* mehrere Abende lang; **A|bend‿es|sen, ...frie|de[n]** (der; ...dens); **a|bend|fül|lend; A|bend‿gym|na|si|um, ...kas|se, ...kleid, ...kurs, ...kur|sus; A|bend|land,** das; -[e]s; **A|bend|län|der,** der; **a|bend|län|disch; a|bend|lich; A|bend|mahl** *Plur.* ...mahle; **A|bend|mahls|kelch; A|bend-Make-up; A|bend‿pro|gramm, ...rot** *od.* **...rö|te; a|bends** (*Abk.* abds.); ↑R 46; *vgl.* Abend *u.* Dienstag; **A|bend‿schu|le, ...stern, ...ver|kauf, ...zei|tung**
A|ben|teu|er, das; -s, -; **A|ben|teu|er|film; A|ben|teu|e|rin,** A|ben|teu|re|rin, die; -, -nen; **a|ben|teu|er|lich; A|ben|teu|er|lust,** die; -; **a|ben|teu|er|lus|tig; a|ben|teu|ern;** ich ...ere (↑R 16); geabenteuert; **A|ben|teu|er‿spiel|platz, ...ur|laub; A|ben|teu|rer; A|ben|teu|re|rin,** A|ben|teu|e|rin, die; -, -nen; **A|ben|teu|rer|na|tur**
a|ber; *Konj.:* er sah sie, aber (jedoch) er hörte sie nicht. *Adverb in Fügungen wie* aber und abermals (wieder und wiederum); *in Verbindung mit* hundert *und* tausend (↑R 48): aberhundert[e], *auch* Aberhundert[e] Sterne; abertausend[e], *auch* Abertausend[e] kleiner Vögel; die Lichter aberhunderter, *auch* Aberhunderter von Laternen; der Jubel abertausender, *auch* Abertausender von Menschen; tausend- und abertausendmal; (↑R 49:) **A|ber,** das; -s, -; es ist ein Aber dabei; viele Wenn und Aber vorbringen
A|ber|glau|be, *seltener* **A|ber|glau|ben; a|ber|gläu|big** (*veraltet für* abergläubisch); **a|ber|gläu|bisch;**
a|ber|hun|dert; *vgl.* aber
ab|er|ken|nen; ich erkenne ab, *selten* ich aberkenne; ich erkannte ab, *selten* ich aberkannte; **Ab|er|ken|nung**
a|ber|ma|lig; a|ber|mals
Ab|er|ra|ti|on, die; -, -en ⟨lat.⟩ (*Optik, Astron., Biol.* Abweichung)
A|ber|see *vgl.* Sankt-Wolfgang-See
a|ber|tau|send; *vgl.* aber; **A|ber|witz,** der; -es (*geh. für* völliger Unsinn); **a|ber|wit|zig** *(geh.)*
ab|es|sen
A|bes|si|ni|en [...iən] (*ältere Bez. für* Äthiopien); **A|bes|si|ni|er; a|bes|si|nisch**
ABF = Arbeiter-und-Bauern-Fakultät
Abf. = Abfahrt
ab|fa|ckeln (*Technik* überflüssige Gase durch Abbrennen beseitigen)
ab|fä|deln; Bohnen -
ab|fah|ren; Ab|fahrt (*Abk.* Abf.); **Ab|fahrt[s]‿be|fehl, ...gleis; Ab|fahrts‿lauf, ...ren|nen; Ab|fahrt[s]|si|gnal; Ab|fahrts|stre|cke; Ab|fahrt[s]‿tag, ...zei|chen, ...zeit**
Ab|fall, der; **Ab|fall‿auf|be|rei|tung, ...ei|mer; ab|fal|len; ab|fäl|lig;** - beurteilen; **Ab|fall‿pro|dukt, ...quo|te, ...wirt|schaft**
ab|fäl|schen *(Sportspr.);* den Ball [zur Ecke] -
ab|fan|gen; Ab|fang‿jä|ger (ein Jagdflugzeug), **...sa|tel|lit**

ạb|fär|ben

ạb|fa|sen (*fachspr. für* abkanten)

ạb|fas|sen (verfassen; *ugs. für* abfangen); **Ạb|fas|sung**

ạb|fau|len

ạb|fe|dern; Ạb|fe|de|rung

ạb|fe|gen

ạb|fei|ern

ạb|fei|len

ạb|fer|ti|gen; Ạb|fer|ti|gung; Ạb|fer|ti|gungs‿dienst, ...schal|ter

ạb|feu|ern

ạb|fie|ren (*Seemannsspr.* an einem Tau herunterlassen); das Rettungsboot -

ạb|fin|den; Ạb|fin|dung; Ạb|fin|dungs‿er|klä|rung, ...sum|me

ạb|fi|schen

ạb|fla|chen; sich -; **Ạb|fla|chung**

ạb|flau|en (schwächer werden)

ạb|flie|gen

ạb|flie|ßen

Ạb|flug; Ạb|flug‿ge|schwin|dig|keit, ...tag, ...zeit

Ạb|fluss; Ạb|fluss‿hahn, ...rohr

Ạb|fol|ge

ạb|for|dern

ạb|fo|to|gra|fie|ren

ạb|fra|gen *(auch Postw., EDV);* jmdn. *od.* jmdm. etwas -

ạb|fres|sen

ạb|fret|ten, sich (*österr. ugs. für* sich abmühen)

ạb|frie|ren

ạb|frot|tie|ren

ạb|füh|len

Ạb|fuhr, die; -, -en; **ạb|füh|ren; Ạb|führ|mit|tel,** das; **Ạb|füh|rung**

ạb|fül|len; Ạb|fül|lung

ạb|füt|tern; Ạb|füt|te|rung

Abg. = Abgeordnete

Ạb|ga|be (*für* Steuer usw. *meist Plur.*); **ạb|ga|ben‿frei, ...pflich|tig; Ạb|ga|be‿preis** (*vgl.* [2]Preis), **...soll** (*vgl.* [2]Soll), **...ter|min**

Ạb|gang, der; **Ạb|gän|ger** (*Amtsspr.* von der Schule Abgehender); **ạb|gän|gig; Ạb|gän|gig|keits|an|zei|ge** (*österr. für* Vermisstenmeldung); **Ạb|gangs|zeug|nis**

Ạb|gas (bei Verbrennungsvorgängen entweichendes Gas); **ạb|gas|arm; Ạb|gas|ent|gif|tung; ạb|gas|frei; Ạb|gas‿ka|ta|ly|sa|tor, ...rei|ni|ger, ...son|der|un|ter|su|chung** (*früher* Abgasuntersuchung für bestimmte Fahrzeuge; *Abk.* ASU), **...un|ter|su|chung** (Kraftfahrzeuguntersuchung, bei der der Kohlenmonoxidgehalt im Abgas bei Leerlauf des Motors gemessen wird; *Abk.* AU)

ABGB = Allgemeines Bürgerliches Gesetzbuch (für Österreich)

ạb|ge|ar|bei|tet

ạb|ge|ben

ạb|ge|blasst

ạb|ge|brannt; (*ugs. auch für* ohne Geldmittel; *österr. auch für* von der Sonne gebräunt); **Ạb|ge|brann|te,** der *u.* die; -n, -n (↑R 5 ff.)

ạb|ge|brüht (*ugs. für* [sittlich] abgestumpft, unempfindlich); **Ạb|ge|brüht|heit,** die; -

ạb|ge|dro|schen; -e (*ugs. für* [zu] oft gebrauchte) Redensart; **Ạb|ge|dro|schen|heit,** die; -

ạb|ge|feimt (durchtrieben); **Ạb|ge|feimt|heit**

ạb|ge|fuckt [...fakt]; ‹dt.; engl.› (*derb für* in üblem Zustand, heruntergekommen)

ạb|ge|grif|fen

ạb|ge|hackt

ạb|ge|han|gen

ạb|ge|härmt

ạb|ge|här|tet

ạb|ge|hen

ạb|ge|hetzt

ạb|ge|kämpft

ạb|ge|kar|tet *(ugs.);* -e Sache

ạb|ge|klärt; Ạb|ge|klärt|heit *Plur. selten*

ạb|ge|la|gert

Ạb|geld (*selten für* Disagio)

ạb|ge|lebt

ạb|ge|le|dert (*landsch. für* abgenutzt, abgerissen); eine -e Hose

ạb|ge|le|gen

ạb|ge|lei|ert; -e (*ugs. für* [zu] oft gebrauchte, platte) Worte

ạb|gel|ten; Ạb|gel|tung

ạb|ge|macht *(ugs.);* -e Sache

ạb|ge|ma|gert

ạb|ge|mer|gelt (erschöpft; abgemagert); *vgl.* abmergeln

ạb|ge|mes|sen

ạb|ge|neigt; Ạb|ge|neigt|heit, die; -

ạb|ge|nutzt

ạb|ge|ord|net; Ạb|ge|ord|ne|te, der *u.* die; -n, -n; ↑R 5 ff. (*Abk.* Abg.); **Ạb|ge|ord|ne|ten|haus**

ạb|ge|plat|tet

ạb|ge|rech|net

ạb|ge|ris|sen; -e Kleider

ạb|ge|run|det

ạb|ge|sagt; ein -er (*geh. für* erklärter) Feind des Nikotins

Ạb|ge|sand|te, der *u.* die; -n, -n (↑R 5 ff.)

Ạb|ge|sang (*Verslehre* abschließender Strophenteil)

ạb|ge|schabt

ạb|ge|schie|den (*geh. für* einsam [gelegen]; verstorben); **Ạb|ge|schie|de|ne,** der *u.* die; -n, -n; ↑R 5 ff. *(geh.);* **Ạb|ge|schie|den|heit,** die; -

ạb|ge|schlafft (*ugs. für* müde, erschöpft); *vgl.* abschlaffen

ạb|ge|schla|gen; Ạb|ge|schla|gen|heit, die; - (*landsch., schweiz. für* Erschöpfung)

ạb|ge|schlos|sen; abgeschlossenes Intervall *(Math.)*

ạb|ge|schmackt; -e (platte) Worte; **Ạb|ge|schmackt|heit**

ạb|ge|se|hen; abgesehen von ...; abgesehen davon[,] dass (↑R 88)

ạb|ge|son|dert

ạb|ge|spannt

ạb|ge|spielt

ạb|ge|stan|den

ạb|ge|stor|ben

ạb|ge|sto|ßen

ạb|ge|stuft

ạb|ge|stumpft; Ạb|ge|stumpft|heit, die; -

ạb|ge|ta|kelt (*ugs. auch für* heruntergekommen, ausgedient); *vgl.* abtakeln

ạb|ge|tan; -e (erledigte) Sache; *vgl.* abtun

ạb|ge|tra|gen

ạb|ge|wetzt

ạb|ge|win|nen; jmdm. etwas -

ạb|ge|wo|gen; Ạb|ge|wo|gen|heit, die; -

ạb|ge|wöh|nen; ich werde es mir *od.* ihm -; **Ạb|ge|wöh|nung,** die;

ạb|ge|zehrt

ạb|ge|zir|kelt

ạb|ge|zo|gen; -er (*geh. für* abstrakter) Begriff; *vgl.* abziehen

ạb|gie|ßen

Ạb|glanz

ạb|glei|chen (*fachspr. für* abstimmen, gleichmachen)

ạb|glei|ten

ạb|glit|schen *(ugs.)*

Ạb|gott, der; -[e]s, Abgötter; **Ab|göt|te|rei; Ạb|göt|tin; ạb|göt|tisch; Ạb|gott|schlan|ge**

ạb|gra|ben; jmdm. das Wasser -

ạb|gra|sen (*ugs. auch für* absuchen)

ạb|gra|ten; ein Werkstück -

ạb|grät|schen; vom Barren -

ạb|grei|fen

ạb|gren|zen; Ạb|gren|zung

Ạb|grund; ạb|grün|dig; ab|grund|tief

ạb|gu|cken *(ugs.);* [von *od.* bei] jmdm. etwas -

Ạb|guss

Abh. = Abhandlung

ạb|ha|ben *(ugs.);* ..., dass er seine Brille abhat; er soll sein[en] Teil abhaben

ạb|ha|cken

ạb|hä|keln

ạb|ha|ken

ạb|half|tern (*ugs. auch für* entlassen); **Ạb|half|te|rung**

ạb|hal|ten; Ạb|hal|tung

ạb|han|deln; ein Thema -

ab|han|den; *nur in* abhanden kommen (verloren gehen); **Ab-han|den|kom|men**
Ab|hand|lung (*Abk.* Abh.)
Ab|hang; **[1]ab|hän|gen,** *mdal. u. schweiz.* ab|han|gen; das hing von ihm ab, hat von ihm abgehangen; *vgl.* [1]hängen; **[2]ab|hän|gen;** er hängte das Bild ab, hat es abgehängt; *vgl.* [2]hängen; **ab|hän|gig;** -e (indirekte) Rede *(Sprachw.);* **Ab|hän|gig|keit; Ab|hän|gig-keits|ver|hält|nis**
ab|här|men, sich
ab|här|ten; Ab|här|tung, die; -
ab|hau|en (*ugs. auch für* davonlaufen); ich hieb den Ast ab; wir hauten ab
ab|he|ben
ab|he|bern (*fachspr. für* eine Flüssigkeit mit einem Heber entnehmen); ich hebere ab (↑R 16)
ab|hef|ten
ab|hei|len; Ab|hei|lung
ab|hel|fen; einem Mangel -
ab|het|zen; sich -
ab|heu|ern; jmdn. -; er hat abgeheuert
Ab|hil|fe
Ab|hit|ze *vgl.* Abwärme
ab|hold; jmdm., einer Sache abhold sein
ab|ho|len; Ab|ho|ler; Ab|ho|lung
ab|hol|zen; Ab|hol|zung
ab|hor|chen
ab|hö|ren; jmdn. *od.* jmdm. etwas -; **Ab|hör‿ge|rät, ...wan|ze** *(ugs.)*
ab|hun|gern
ab|hus|ten
A|bi, das; -s, -s *Plur. selten* (*Kurzw. für* Abitur)
A|bid|jan [...ˈdʒa:n] (Stadt der [2]Elfenbeinküste)
A|bi|o|ge|ne|se, A|bi|o|ge|ne|sis [*auch* ...ˈge:...], die; - ⟨griech.⟩ (Entstehung von Lebewesen aus unbelebter Materie)
ab|ir|ren
ab|iso|lie|ren (↑R 132); **Ab|iso-lier|zan|ge**
A|bi|tur (↑R 132), das; -s, -e *Plur. selten* ⟨lat.⟩ (Reifeprüfung); **A|bi-tu|ri|ent,** der; -en, -en; ↑R 126 (Reifeprüfling); **A|bi|tu|ri|en-ten|prü|fung; A|bi|tu|ri|en|tin**
ab|ja|gen
Ab|ju|di|ka|ti|on, die; -, -en ⟨lat.⟩ (*veraltet für* Aberkennung); **ab-ju|di|zie|ren** *(veraltet)*
Abk. = Abkürzung
ab|käm|men
ab|kan|ten; ein Brett, Blech -
ab|kan|zeln (*ugs. für* scharf tadeln); ich kanz[e]le ab (↑R 16); **Ab|kan|ze|lung, Ab|kanz|lung** *(ugs.)*
ab|ka|pi|teln (*ugs. für* schelten)
ab|kap|seln; ich kaps[e]le ab (↑R 16); **Ab|kap|se|lung, Ab-kaps|lung**
ab|kas|sie|ren
Ab|kauf *(regional);* **ab|kau|fen**
Ab|kehr, die; -; **ab|keh|ren**
ab|kip|pen
ab|klap|pern (*ugs. für* suchend, fragend ablaufen)
ab|klä|ren; Ab|klä|rung
Ab|klatsch; ab|klat|schen
ab|kle|ben
ab|klem|men
ab|klin|gen; Ab|kling‿kon|stan-te *(Physik),* **...zeit**
ab|klop|fen
ab|knab|bern
ab|knal|len (*ugs. für* niederschießen)
ab|knap|pen (*landsch. für* abknapsen); **ab|knap|sen;** jmdm. etwas - (*ugs. für* wegnehmen)
ab|kni|cken; abknickende Vorfahrt *(Verkehrsw.)*
ab|knöp|fen; jmdm. Geld - (*ugs. für* abnehmen)
ab|ko|chen
ab|kom|man|die|ren
Ab|kom|me, der; -n, -n; ↑R 126 (*geh. für* Nachkomme); **ab|kom-men; Ab|kom|men,** das; -s, -; **Ab|kom|men|schaft,** die; - *(veraltet);* **ab|kömm|lich; Ab|kömm-ling** (*auch für* Derivat *[Chemie]*)
ab|kön|nen (*nordd. ugs. für* aushalten, vertragen); du weißt doch, dass ich das nicht abkann
ab|kon|ter|fei|en (*veraltet für* abmalen, abzeichnen)
ab|kop|peln; Ab|kop|pe|lung, Ab|kopp|lung
ab|kra|gen (*Bauw.* abschrägen)
ab|krat|zen (*derb auch für* sterben)
ab|krie|gen *(ugs.)*
ab|küh|len; sich -; **Ab|küh|lung**
ab|kün|di|gen (von der Kanzel verkünden); **Ab|kün|di|gung**
Ab|kunft, die; -
ab|kup|fern (*ugs. für* abschreiben)
ab|kür|zen; Ab|kür|zung (*Abk.* Abk.); **Ab|kür|zungs|spra|che,** die; -, -n *Plur. selten* (*Kurzw.* Aküsprache); **Ab|kür|zungs‿ver-zeich|nis, ...zei|chen**
ab|la|chen (*ugs. für* ausgiebig, herzhaft lachen)
ab|la|den; *vgl.* [1]laden; **Ab|la|de-platz; Ab|la|der; Ab|la|dung**
Ab|la|ge (*schweiz. auch für* Annahme-, Zweigstelle); **ab|la|gern; Ab|la|ge|rung**
ab|lan|dig (*Seemannsspr.* vom Lande her wehend od. strömend)
Ab|lass, der; -es, Ablässe *(kath. Kirche);* **Ab|lass|brief; ab|las-sen**
Ab|la|ti|on, die; -, -en ⟨lat.⟩ (*fachspr. für* Abschmelzung [von Schnee u. Eis]; *Geol.* Abtragung des Bodens; *Med.* Wegnahme; Ablösung, bes. der Netzhaut); **Ab|la|tiv,** der; -s, -e [...və] (*Sprachw.* Kasus in idg. Sprachen); **Ab|la|ti|vus ab|so|lu|tus** [...v... -], der; - -, ...vi ...ti (*Sprachw.* eine bestimmte Konstruktion in der lat. Sprache)
Ab|lauf; ab|lau|fen; Ab|lauf|rin-ne
ab|lau|gen
Ab|laut (*Sprachw.* gesetzmäßiger Vokalwechsel in der Stammsilbe von Wortformen und etymologisch verwandten Wörtern, z. B. „singen, sang, gesungen"); **ab-lau|ten** (Ablaut haben); **ab|läu-ten** (zur Abfahrt läuten)
Ab|le|ben, das; -s (*geh. für* Tod)
ab|le|cken
ab|le|dern (*ugs. für* mit einem Leder trocken wischen u. blank putzen; *landsch. für* verprügeln); *vgl.* abgeledert
ab|le|gen; Ab|le|ger (Pflanzentrieb; *ugs. scherzh. für* Sohn)
ab|leh|nen; einen Vorschlag -; **Ab|leh|nung**
ab|leis|ten; Ab|leis|tung
ab|lei|ten; Ab|lei|tung (*auch Sprachw.* Bildung eines Wortes durch Lautveränderung [Ablaut] oder durch das Anfügen von Nachsilben, z. B. „Trank" von „trinken", „königlich" von „König"); **Ab|lei|tungs|sil|be**
ab|len|ken; Ab|len|kung; Ab|len-kungs|ma|nö|ver
ab|le|sen; Ab|le|ser
ab|leug|nen
ab|lich|ten; Ab|lich|tung
ab|lie|fern; Ab|lie|fe|rung; Ab|lie-fe|rungs|soll; *vgl.* [2]Soll
ab|lie|gen (*landsch. auch für* durch Lagern gut, reif werden); weit -
ab|lis|ten; jmdm. etwas -
ab|lo|cken
ab|loh|nen *(veraltend);* jmdn. - (bezahlen [u. entlassen])
ab|lö|schen
Ab|lö|se, die; -, -n (*ugs. für* Ablösesumme); **ab|lö|sen; Ab|lö|se-sum|me; Ab|lö|sung; Ab|lö-sungs|sum|me**
ab|luch|sen *(ugs.);* jmdm. etwas -
Ab|luft, die; - (*Technik* verbrauchte, abgeleitete Luft)
ABM = Arbeitsbeschaffungsmaßnahme; ABM-Stelle (↑R 26)
ab|ma|chen; *vgl.* abgemacht; **Ab-ma|chung**
ab|ma|gern; Ab|ma|ge|rung; Ab-ma|ge|rungs|kur
ab|mah|nen; Ab|mah|nung

ab|ma|len; ein Bild -
Ab|marsch, der; **ab|mar|schie|ren**
ab|meh|ren (*schweiz. für* abstimmen durch Handerheben)
ab|mei|ern; jmdn. - (*früher für* jmdm. den Meierhof, das Pachtgut, den Erbhof entziehen); ich meiere ab (↑R 16); **Ab|mei|e|rung**
ab|mel|den; Ab|mel|dung
Ab|melk|wirt|schaft (Rinderhaltung nur zur Milchgewinnung)
ab|mer|geln, sich (*ugs. für* sich abmühen); ich merg[e]le mich ab (↑R 16); *vgl.* abgemergelt
ab|mes|sen; Ab|mes|sung
ab|mon|tie|ren
ab|mü|den *(geh.);* sich -
ab|mü|hen, sich -
ab|murk|sen (*ugs. für* umbringen)
ab|mus|tern (*Seemannsspr.* entlassen; den Dienst aufgeben); **Ab|mus|te|rung**
ab|na|beln; ich nab[e]le ab (↑R 16)
ab|na|gen
ab|nä|hen; Ab|nä|her
Ab|nah|me, die; -, -n *Plur. selten;* **ab|neh|men;** *vgl.* ab; **Ab|neh|mer; Ab|neh|mer|land** *Plur.* ...länder
Ab|nei|gung
ab|nib|beln (*landsch. derb für* sterben); ich nibb[e]le ab (↑R 16)
ab|norm (vom Normalen abweichend, regelwidrig; krankhaft); **ab|nor|mal** (*bes. österr., schweiz. für* nicht normal, ungewöhnlich); **Ab|nor|mi|tät,** die; -, -en
ab|nö|ti|gen; jmdm. etwas -
ab|nut|zen, *bes. südd., österr.* **ab|nüt|zen; Ab|nut|zung,** *bes. südd., österr.* **Ab|nüt|zung; Ab|nut|zungs|ge|bühr**
A|bo, das; -s, -s (*Kurzw. für* Abonnement)
A-Bom|be; ↑R 25 (Atombombe)
A|bon|ne|ment [...ˈmaŋ *od.* ...ˈmã:, *schweiz.* ...ˈmɛnt *od.* abɔnˈmã:], das; -s, *Plur.* -s *u.* (bei deutscher Aussprache:) -e ⟨franz.⟩ (Dauerbezug von Zeitungen u. Ä.; Dauermiete für Theater u. Ä.); **A|bon|ne|ment[s]‿kar|te** (Anrechtskarte), **...preis** (*vgl.* ²Preis), **...vor|stel|lung; A|bon|nent,** der; -en, -en; ↑R 126 (Inhaber eines Abonnements); **A|bon|nen|tin; a|bon|nie|ren;** auf etwas abonniert sein
ab|ord|nen; Ab|ord|nung
Ab|o|ri|gi|nes [apˈoˈri:gine:s *od.* əbəˈridʒini:z] *Plur.* ⟨lat.-engl.⟩ (Ureinwohner [Australiens])
[1]**A|bort** [*schweiz. nur* ˈabɔrt] (↑R 132), der; -[e]s, -e (Toilette)
[2]**A|bort** (↑R 132), der; -s, -e ⟨lat.⟩ (*Med.* Fehlgeburt); **a|bor|tie|ren; A|bor|ti|on,** die; -, -en (Abtreibung); **a|bor|tiv** (abtreibend)
ab o|vo [- ˈo:vo] ⟨lat.⟩ (von Anfang an)
ab|pa|cken
ab|pas|sen
ab|pau|sen; eine Zeichnung -
ab|per|len
ab|pfei|fen *(Sportspr.);* **Ab|pfiff**
ab|pflü|cken
ab|pin|nen (*ugs. für* abschreiben)
ab|pla|gen, sich
ab|plat|ten; Ab|plat|tung
Ab|prall, der; -[e]s, -e *Plur. selten;* **ab|pral|len;** von etwas -; **Ab|pral|ler** *(Sportspr.)*
ab|pres|sen
Ab|pro|dukt (*fachspr.* Abfall, Müll; Abfallprodukt)
ab|prot|zen (*Milit.; derb auch für* seine Notdurft verrichten)
Ab|putz ([Ver]putz); **ab|put|zen**
ab|quä|len, sich
ab|qua|li|fi|zie|ren
ab|ra|ckern, sich *(ugs.)*
A|bra|ham (↑R 130; bibl. m. Eigenn.); **A|bra|ham a San[c]|ta Cla|ra** (dt. Prediger)
ab|rah|men; Milch -
A|bra|ka|da|bra [*auch* ˈa:brakaˈda:...] (↑R 130), das; -s (Zauberwort; [sinnloses] Gerede)
A|bra|sax (↑R 130); *vgl.* Abraxas
ab|ra|sie|ren
Ab|ra|si|on, die; -, -en ⟨lat.⟩ (*Geol.* Abtragung der Küste durch die Brandung)
ab|ra|ten; jmdm. von etwas -
Ab|raum, der; -[e]s (*Bergmannsspr.* Deckschicht über Lagerstätten; *landsch. für* Abfall); **ab|räu|men; Ab|raum‿hal|de, ...salz** *(Bergmannsspr.)*
A|bra|xas, A|bra|sax (↑R 130; Zauberwort)
ab|re|a|gie|ren; sich -
ab|re|beln (*österr. für* [Beeren] einzeln abpflücken)
ab|rech|nen; Ab|rech|nung; Ab|rech|nungs|ter|min
Ab|re|de; etwas in - stellen
ab|re|gen, sich *(ugs.)*
ab|reg|nen
ab|rei|ben; Ab|rei|bung
Ab|rei|se *Plur. selten;* **ab|rei|sen**
Ab|reiß|block; *vgl.* Block; **ab|rei|ßen;** *vgl.* abgerissen; **Ab|reiß|ka|len|der**
ab|rei|ten
ab|rich|ten; Ab|rich|ter (Dresseur); **Ab|rich|tung**
Ab|rieb, der; -[e]s, *Plur.* (*Technik für* abgeriebene Teilchen:) -e; **ab|rieb|fest; Ab|rieb|fes|tig|keit**
ab|rie|geln; Ab|rie|ge|lung, Ab|rieg|lung
ab|rin|gen; jmdm. etwas -
Ab|riss, der; -es, -e
ab|rol|len
ab|rü|cken
Ab|ruf *Plur. selten;* auf -; **ab|ruf|be|reit;** sich - halten; **ab|ru|fen**
ab|run|den; eine Zahl [nach unten, *seltener* oben] -; **Ab|run|dung**
ab|rup|fen
ab|rupt ⟨lat.⟩ (abgebrochen, zusammenhanglos, plötzlich)
ab|rüs|ten; Ab|rüs|tung; ab|rüs|tungs|fä|hig; Ab|rüs|tungs|kon|fe|renz
ab|rut|schen
Ab|ruz|zen (↑R 130) *Plur.* (Gebiet im südl. Mittelitalien; *auch für* Abruzzischer Apennin); **Ab|ruz|zi|sche A|pen|nin,** der; -n -s (Teil des Apennins)
ABS = Antiblockiersystem
Abs. = Absatz; Absender
ab|sa|cken (*ugs. für* [ab]sinken)
Ab|sa|ge, die; -, -n; **ab|sa|gen**
ab|sä|gen
ab|sah|nen (die Sahne abschöpfen; *ugs. für* sich das Beste, Wertvollste aneignen)
Ab|sa|lom, *ökum.* Ab|scha|lom (bibl. m. Eigenn.)
Ab|sam (österr. Ort)
Ab|satz, der; -es, Absätze (*Abk.* Abs.); **Ab|satz‿flau|te, ...ge|biet, ...kick** *(Fußball),* **...trick** *(Fußball);* **ab|satz|wei|se**
ab|sau|fen *(ugs.)*
ab|sau|gen
ab|scha|ben
ab|schaf|fen; *vgl.* [1]schaffen; **Ab|schaf|fung**
Ab|scha|lom *vgl.* Absalom
ab|schal|ten; Ab|schal|tung
ab|schat|ten; ab|schat|tie|ren; Ab|schat|tie|rung; Ab|schat|tung
ab|schät|zen; ab|schät|zig
Ab|schaum, der; -[e]s
ab|schei|den; *vgl.* abgeschieden; **Ab|schei|der** *(Technik, Chemie)*
ab|sche|ren; den Bart -; *vgl.* [1]scheren
Ab|scheu, der; -[e]s, *seltener* die; -; (↑R 40:) [großen] Abscheu erregend, *aber* äußerst abscheuerregend; **ab|scheu|lich; Ab|scheu|lich|keit**
ab|schi|cken
Ab|schie|be|haft, die; -; **ab|schie|ben**
Ab|schied, der; -[e]s, -e *Plur. selten;* **Ab|schieds‿be|such, ...brief, ...fei|er, ...schmerz, ...stun|de, ...sze|ne**
ab|schie|ßen
ab|schil|fern *(landsch.);* **Ab|schil|fe|rung** (Abschuppung)
ab|schin|den, sich *(ugs.)*

Ab|schirm|dienst; ab|schir|men; Ab|schir|mung
ab|schir|ren; die Pferde -
ab|schlach|ten; Ab|schlach|tung
ab|schlaf|fen (*ugs. für* schlaff machen, werden)
Ab|schlag; auf -; **ab|schla|gen; ab|schlä|gig** *(Amtsspr.);* jmdn. *od.* etwas - bescheiden ([jmdm.] etwas nicht genehmigen); **ab|schläg|lich** *(veraltet);* -e Zahlung; **Ab|schlags|zah|lung**
ab|schläm|men (Bodenteilchen wegspülen u. als Schlamm absetzen)
ab|schlei|fen
Ab|schlepp|dienst; ab|schlep|pen; Ab|schlepp|seil
ab|schlie|ßen; Ab|schlie|ßung; Ab|schluss; Ab|schluss‿exa|men (↑R 132), **...fei|er, ...prü|fung, ...trai|ning**
ab|schmal|zen (*österr. für* abschmälzen); **ab|schmäl|zen** (*Kochk.* mit gebräunter Butter übergießen)
ab|schme|cken
ab|schmel|zen; das Eis schmilzt ab; *vgl.* [1,2]schmelzen
ab|schmet|tern *(ugs.)*
ab|schmie|ren; Ab|schmier|fett
ab|schmin|ken
ab|schmir|geln
Abschn. = Abschnitt
ab|schnal|len
ab|schnei|den; Ab|schnitt (*Abk.* Abschn.); **Ab|schnitts|be|voll|mäch|tig|te,** der; -n, -n; ↑R 5 ff. (ehem. in der DDR für ein bestimmtes [Wohn]gebiet zuständiger Volkspolizist; *Abk.* ABV); **ab|schnitt[s]|wei|se**
Ab|schnit|zel, das; -s, - (*südd., österr. für* abgeschnittenes [Fleisch-, Papier]stückchen)
ab|schnü|ren; Ab|schnü|rung
ab|schöp|fen; Ab|schöp|fung
ab|schot|ten; Ab|schot|tung
ab|schrä|gen
ab|schram|men (*derb auch für* sterben)
ab|schrau|ben
ab|schre|cken; *vgl.* [2]schrecken; **ab|schre|ckend; Ab|schre|ckung; Ab|schre|ckungs|stra|fe**
ab|schrei|ben; Ab|schrei|bung; ab|schrei|bungs|fä|hig; Ab|schrift; ab|schrift|lich *(Amtsspr.)*
Ab|schrot, der; -[e]s, -e (meißelförmiger Ambosseinsatz); **ab|schro|ten** (Metallteile auf dem Abschrot abschlagen)
ab|schrub|ben *(ugs.)*
ab|schuf|ten, sich (*ugs. für* sich abarbeiten)
ab|schup|pen; Ab|schup|pung
ab|schür|fen; Ab|schür|fung
Ab|schuss; ab|schüs|sig; Ab|schuss‿lis|te, ...ram|pe
ab|schüt|teln; Ab|schüt|te|lung
ab|schüt|ten
Ab|schütt|lung
ab|schwä|chen; Ab|schwä|chung
ab|schwei|fen; Ab|schwei|fung
ab|schwel|len; *vgl.* [1]schwellen
ab|schwem|men
ab|schwin|gen
ab|schwir|ren (*ugs. auch für* weggehen)
ab|schwö|ren
Ab|schwung
ab|seg|nen (*ugs. für* genehmigen)
ab|seh|bar; in absehbarer Zeit; **ab|se|hen;** *vgl.* abgesehen
ab|sei|fen
ab|sei|len; sich -
ab sein *vgl.* ab
ab|seit, Ab|seit (*österr. Sportspr. neben* abseits, Abseits)
[1]**Ab|sei|te,** die; -, -n (*landsch. für* Nebenraum, -bau)
[2]**Ab|sei|te** (Stoffrückseite); **Ab|sei|ten|stoff** (*für* [1]Reversible); **ab|sei|tig; Ab|sei|tig|keit; ab|seits;** *Präp. mit Gen.:* abseits des Weges; *Adverb:* abseits stehen, sein; die abseits stehenden Kinder; **Ab|seits,** das; -, - *(Sportspr.);* Abseits pfeifen; **Ab|seits‿fal|le, ...stel|lung, ...tor** (das; -[e]s, -e)
Ab|sence [apˈsã:s] die; -, -n [...sən] ‹franz.› (*Med.* kurzzeitige Bewusstseinstrübung, bes. bei Epilepsie)
ab|sen|den; Ab|sen|der (*Abk.* Abs.); **Ab|sen|dung**
ab|sen|ken; Ab|sen|ker (vorjähriger Trieb, der zur Vermehrung der Pflanze in die Erde gelegt wird); **Ab|sen|kung**
ab|sent ‹lat.› (*veraltet für* abwesend); **ab|sen|tie|ren,** sich (*veraltend für* sich entfernen); **Ab|senz,** die; -, -en (*österr., schweiz., sonst veraltend für* Abwesenheit, Fehlen; *Med. auch svw.* Absence)
ab|ser|beln (*schweiz. für* dahinsiechen, langsam absterben); ich serb[e]le ab (↑R 16)
ab|ser|vie|ren (*ugs. auch für* seines Einflusses berauben)
ab|setz|bar; ab|set|zen; sich -; **Ab|set|zung**
ab|si|chern; sich -
Ab|sicht, die; -, -en; **ab|sicht|lich** [*österr. u. schweiz. nur so, sonst bei besonderem Nachdruck auch* ...ˈziçt...]; **Ab|sicht|lich|keit; Ab|sichts|er|klä|rung; ab|sichts‿los, ...voll**
Ab|sin|gen, das; -s; unter Absingen (*nicht:* unter Absingung)
ab|sin|ken
Ab|sinth, der; -[e]s, -e ‹griech.› (Wermutbranntwein)
ab|sit|zen
ab|so|lut ‹lat.› (völlig; ganz und gar; uneingeschränkt); absoluter Nullpunkt *(Physik);* absoluter Ablativ, Nominativ, Superlativ (*Sprachw.; vgl.* Elativ); **Ab|so|lut|heit,** die; -; **Ab|so|lu|ti|on,** die; -, -en (Los-, Freisprechung, bes. Sündenvergebung); **Ab|so|lu|tis|mus,** der; - (uneingeschränkte Herrschaft eines Monarchen, Willkürherrschaft); **Ab|so|lu|tist,** der; -en, -en; ↑R 126 (*veraltet für* Anhänger des Absolutismus); **ab|so|lu|tis|tisch; Ab|so|lu|to|ri|um,** das; -s, ...ien [...i̯ən] (*österr. für* Bestätigung über ein abgeschlossenes Hochschulstudium); **Ab|sol|vent** [...v...], der; -en, -en; ↑R 126 (Schulabgänger mit Abschlussprüfung); **Ab|sol|ven|tin; ab|sol|vie|ren** (erledigen, ableisten; [eine Schule] durchlaufen; *Rel.* Absolution erteilen); **Ab|sol|vie|rung,** die; -
ab|son|der|lich; Ab|son|der|lich|keit; ab|son|dern; sich -; **Ab|son|de|rung**
Ab|sor|bens, das; -, *Plur.* ...benzien [...i̯ən] *u.* ...bentia ‹lat.› (*Technik* der bei der Absorption aufnehmende Stoff); **Ab|sor|ber,** der; -s, - ‹engl.› (Vorrichtung zur Absorption von Gasen, Strahlen)
ab|sor|bie|ren ‹lat.› (aufsaugen; [gänzlich] beanspruchen); **Ab|sorp|ti|on,** die; -, -en; **Ab|sorp|ti|ons|spek|trum; ab|sorp|tiv** (zur Absorption fähig)
ab|spal|ten; Ab|spal|tung
ab|spa|nen, [1]**ab|spä|nen** (*Technik* ein metallisches Werkstück durch Abtrennung von Spänen formen)
[2]**ab|spä|nen** (*landsch. für* entwöhnen)
ab|span|nen; Ab|spann|mast, der *(Elektrotechnik);* **Ab|span|nung,** die; -
ab|spa|ren, sich; du hast es dir vom Munde abgespart
ab|spe|cken (*ugs. für* [gezielt] abnehmen)
ab|spei|chern *(EDV)*
ab|spei|sen
ab|spens|tig; jmdm. jmdn. *od.* etwas abspenstig machen
ab|sper|ren; Ab|sperr‿hahn, ...ket|te, ...kom|man|do, ...mau|er; Ab|sper|rung
ab|spie|geln; Ab|spie|ge|lung, Ab|spieg|lung
Ab|spiel, das; -[e]s *(Sport);* **ab|spie|len**

ab|split|tern; Ab|split|te|rung
Ab|spra|che (Vereinbarung); **ab|spra|che|ge|mäß; ab|spre|chen**
ab|sprin|gen; Ab|sprung; Ab|sprung|ha|fen *(Militär)*
ab|spu|len; ein Tonband -
ab|spü|len; Geschirr -
ab|stam|men; Ab|stam|mung
Ab|stand; von etwas - nehmen (etwas nicht tun); **Ab|stand|hal|ter** (am Fahrrad); **ab|stän|dig;** -er (*Forstw.* dürrer, absterbender) Baum; **Ab|stands|sum|me**
ab|stat|ten; jmdm. einen Besuch - *(geh.);* **Ab|stat|tung**
ab|stau|ben (*ugs. auch für* unbemerkt mitnehmen; *Sportspr.* ein Tor mühelos erzielen); **ab|stäu|ben** (*landsch. für* abstauben); **Ab|stau|ber; Ab|stau|ber|tor**
ab|ste|chen; Ab|ste|cher; einen - machen
ab|ste|cken *vgl.* [2]stecken
ab|ste|hen
ab|stei|fen *(fachspr.);* **Ab|stei|fung**
Ab|stei|ge, die; -, -n *(ugs. abwertend);* **ab|stei|gen; Ab|stei|ge|quar|tier,** *österr.* **Ab|steig|quar|tier; Ab|stei|ger** *(Sportspr.)*
Ab|stell|bahn|hof; ab|stel|len; Ab|stell‿gleis, ...kam|mer, ...raum; Ab|stel|lung
ab|stem|peln; Ab|stem|pe|lung, Ab|stemp|lung
ab|step|pen
ab|ster|ben
Ab|stich
Ab|stieg, der; -[e]s, -e; **ab|stiegs|ge|fähr|det** *(Sportspr.)*
ab|stil|len
ab|stim|men; Ab|stimm‿kreis *(fachspr.),* **...schär|fe** (die; -; *fachspr.*); **Ab|stim|mung; Ab|stim|mungs|er|geb|nis**
abs|ti|nent ‹lat.› (enthaltsam, alkohol. Getränke meidend); **Abs|ti|nent,** der; -en, -en; ↑R 126 (*schweiz., sonst veraltet für* Abstinenzler); **Abs|ti|nenz,** die; -; **Abs|ti|nenz|ler** (enthaltsam lebender Mensch, bes. in Bezug auf Alkohol); **Abs|ti|nenz|tag** (*kath. Kirche* Tag, an dem die Gläubigen kein Fleisch essen dürfen)
ab|stop|pen
Ab|stoß; ab|sto|ßen; ab|sto|ßend; Ab|sto|ßung
ab|stot|tern (*ugs. für* in Raten bezahlen)
Abs|tract ['ɛpstrɛkt], der; -s, -s ‹lat.-engl.› (kurze Inhaltsangabe eines Artikels od. Buches)
ab|stra|fen; Ab|stra|fung
abs|tra|hie|ren ‹lat.› (verallgemeinern)
ab|strah|len; Ab|strah|lung
abs|trakt ‹lat.› (begrifflich, nur gedacht); abstrakte (vom Gegenständlichen absehende) Kunst; **Abs|trakt|heit; Abs|trak|ti|on,** die; -, -en; **Abs|trak|tum,** das; -s, ...ta (*Philos.* allgemeiner Begriff; *Sprachw.* Substantiv, das etwas Nichtgegenständliches benennt, z. B. „Liebe")
ab|stram|peln, sich *(ugs.)*
ab|strän|gen ([ein Zugtier] abspannen)
ab|strei|chen; Ab|strei|cher
ab|strei|fen; Ab|strei|fer
ab|strei|ten
Ab|strich
abs|trus ‹lat.› (verworren, schwer verständlich)
ab|stu|fen; Ab|stu|fung
ab|stump|fen; Ab|stump|fung
Ab|sturz; ab|stür|zen
ab|stüt|zen; sich -
Ab|sud [*auch* ...'zu:t], der; -[e]s, -e (*veraltet für* durch Abkochen gewonnene Flüssigkeit)
ab|surd ‹lat.› (sinnwidrig, sinnlos); *vgl.* ad absurdum; -es Drama (eine moderne Dramenform); **Ab|sur|di|tät,** die; -, -en
Abs|zess, der, *österr. ugs. auch* das; -es, -e ‹lat.› (*Med.* eitrige Geschwulst)
Abs|zis|se, die; -, -n ‹lat.› (*Math.* auf der Abszissenachse abgetragene erste Koordinate eines Punktes); **Abs|zis|sen|ach|se**
Abt, der; -[e]s, Äbte (Kloster-, Stiftsvorsteher)
Abt. = Abteilung
ab|ta|keln; ein Schiff - (das Takelwerk entfernen, außer Dienst stellen); *vgl.* abgetakelt; **Ab|ta|ke|lung, Ab|tak|lung**
ab|tan|zen (*ugs. für* weggehen; ausdauernd tanzen)
ab|tas|ten; Ab|tas|tung
ab|tau|en; einen Kühlschrank -
Ab|tausch; ab|tau|schen
Ab|tei (Kloster, dem ein Abt od. eine Äbtissin vorsteht)
Ab|teil [*ugs. auch, schweiz. nur* 'ap...], das; -[e]s, -e; **ab|tei|len;** [1]**Ab|tei|lung,** die; - (Abtrennung); [2]**Ab|tei|lung** [*österr., schweiz.* 'ap...] (abgeteilter Raum; Teil eines Unternehmens, einer Behörde o. Ä.; *Abk.* Abt.); **Ab|tei|lungs|lei|ter,** der
ab|teu|fen *(Bergmannsspr.);* einen Schacht - (senkrecht nach unten bauen)
ab|tip|pen *(ugs.)*
Äb|tis|sin (Kloster-, Stiftsvorsteherin)
Abt.-Lei|ter = Abteilungsleiter (↑R 26)
ab|tö|nen; Ab|tö|nung
ab|tö|ten; Ab|tö|tung
Ab|trag, der; -[e]s, Abträge; jmdm. *od.* einer Sache Abtrag tun (*geh. für* schaden); **ab|tra|gen; ab|träg|lich** (schädlich); jmdm. *od.* einer Sache - sein *(geh.);* **Ab|träg|lich|keit; Ab|tra|gung**
ab|trai|nie|ren [...trɛ... *od.* ...tre...]; zwei Kilo -
Ab|trans|port; ab|trans|por|tie|ren
ab|trei|ben; Ab|trei|bung; Ab|trei|bungs‿pa|ra|graph (§ 218 des Strafgesetzbuches), **...recht, ...ver|such**
ab|trenn|bar; ab|tren|nen; Ab|tren|nung
ab|tre|ten; Ab|tre|ter; Ab|tre|tung
Ab|trieb, der; -[e]s, -e (das Abtreiben des Viehs von der Weide; *Forstw.* Abholzung; *österr. auch für* Rührteig)
Ab|trift usw. *vgl.* Abdrift usw.
ab|trin|ken
Ab|tritt (*veraltend, noch landsch. auch für* [1]Abort)
ab|trock|nen
ab|trop|fen
ab|trot|zen; jmdm. etw. -
ab|trump|fen (*ugs. auch für* scharf zurechtweisen, abweisen)
ab|trün|nig; Ab|trün|nig|keit, die; -
Abts‿stab, ...wür|de
ab|tun; etw. als Scherz -
ab|tup|fen
Abt|wahl
A|bu [*auch* 'abu] ‹arab., „Vater"› (Bestandteil von Eigenn.); **A|bu Dha|bi** [- 'da:bi] (Scheichtum der Vereinigten Arabischen Emirate; dessen Hauptstadt); **a|bu-dha|bisch**
a|bun|dant (↑R 132) ‹lat.› (*bes. fachspr. für* häufig [vorkommend]); **A|bun|danz,** die; - ([große] Häufigkeit)
ab und zu *vgl.* ab
ab ur|be con|di|ta ‹lat., „seit Gründung der Stadt" [Rom]› (altröm. Zeitrechnung, beginnend mit 753 v. Chr.; *Abk.* a. u. c.)
ab|ur|tei|len; Ab|ur|tei|lung
Ab|usus (↑R 132), der; -, - ‹lat.› (*Med.* Missbrauch [z. B. von Arznei- od. Genussmitteln])
ABV = Abschnittsbevollmächtigter
Ab|ver|kauf (*österr. auch für* Ausverkauf); **ab|ver|kau|fen** *(österr.)*
ab|ver|lan|gen
ab|vie|ren [...f...] (*fachspr. für* vierkantig zuschneiden); **Ab|vie|rung**
ab|wä|gen; du wägst ab; du wägtest, wogst ab; abgewogen, abgewägt; **Ab|wä|gung**

Ab|wahl; ab|wäh|len
ab|wäl|len *(Gastron.)*
ab|wäl|zen
ab|wan|deln; Ab|wan|de|lung, Ab|wand|lung
ab|wan|dern; Ab|wan|de|rung
Ab|wär|me (*Technik* nicht genutzte Wärmeenergie)
Ab|wart, der; -s, -e (*schweiz. für* Hausmeister, -wart); **ab|war|ten; Ab|war|tin** (*schweiz.*)
ab|wärts; abwärts gehen (nach unten gehen; *auch für* schlechter werden); er ist diesen Weg abwärts gegangen; es ist mit ihm abwärts gegangen; **Ab|wärts|trend**
[1]**Ab|wasch,** der; -[e]s (Geschirrspülen; schmutziges Geschirr); [2]**Ab|wasch,** die; -, -en (*landsch. für* Abwaschbecken); **ab|wasch|bar; ab|wa|schen; Ab|wa|schung; Ab|wasch|was|ser** *Plur.* ...wässer
Ab|was|ser *Plur.* ...wässer; **Ab|was|ser|auf|be|rei|tung**
ab|wech|seln; sich -; **ab|wech|selnd; Ab|wech|se|lung, Ab|wechs|lung; ab|wechs|lungs‿los, ...reich**
Ab|weg *meist Plur.*; **ab|we|gig; Ab|we|gig|keit**
Ab|wehr, die; -; **ab|weh|ren; Ab|wehr‿ge|schütz, ...kampf, ...re|ak|ti|on, ...spie|ler** *(Sportspr.)*
[1]**ab|wei|chen;** ein Etikett abweichen; *vgl.* [1]weichen
[2]**ab|wei|chen;** vom Kurs abweichen; *vgl.* [2]weichen; **Ab|weich|ler** (jmd., der von der polit. Linie einer [kommunist.] Partei abweicht); **Ab|wei|chung**
ab|wei|den
ab|wei|sen; Ab|wei|ser (Prellstein); **Ab|wei|sung**
ab|wend|bar; ab|wen|den; ich wandte *od.* wendete mich ab, habe mich abgewandt *od.* abgewendet; er wandte *od.* wendete den Blick ab, hat den Blick abgewandt *od.* abgewendet; *aber nur* er hat das Unheil abgewendet; **ab|wen|dig** (*veraltend für* abspenstig, abgeneigt); **Ab|wen|dung,** die; -
ab|wer|ben; Ab|wer|ber; Ab|wer|bung
ab|wer|fen
ab|wer|ten; Ab|wer|tung
ab|we|send; Ab|we|sen|de, der *u.* die; -n, -n (↑R 5 ff.); **Ab|we|sen|heit,** die; -, -en *Plur. selten*
ab|wet|tern; einen Sturm - (*Seemannsspr.* auf See überstehen); einen Schacht - (*Bergmannsspr.* abdichten)
ab|wet|zen
ab|wich|sen; sich einen - (*derb für* onanieren)
ab|wi|ckeln; Ab|wi|cke|lung, Ab|wick|lung
ab|wie|geln (beschwichtigen); **Ab|wie|ge|lung, Ab|wieg|lung**
ab|wie|gen; *vgl.* [2]wiegen
ab|wim|meln (*ugs. für* [mit Ausflüchten] abweisen)
Ab|wind (*fachspr. für* absteigender Luftstrom)
ab|win|ken
ab|wirt|schaf|ten; abgewirtschaftet
ab|wi|schen
ab|woh|nen
ab|wra|cken; ein Schiff - (verschrotten); **Ab|wrack|fir|ma**
Ab|wurf; Ab|wurf|vor|rich|tung
ab|wür|gen
a|bys|sisch ‹griech.› (aus der Tiefe der Erde stammend; zum Tiefseebereich gehörend; abgrundtief); **A|bys|sus,** der; - (*veraltet für* Tiefe der Erde, Abgrund)
ab|zah|len; ab|zäh|len; Ab|zähl|reim; Ab|zah|lung; Ab|zah|lungs|ge|schäft
ab|zap|fen; Ab|zap|fung
ab|zap|peln, sich
ab|zäu|men
ab|zäu|nen; Ab|zäu|nung
Ab|zeh|rung (Abmagerung)
Ab|zei|chen; ab|zeich|nen; sich -
Ab|zieh|bild; ab|zie|hen; *vgl.* abgezogen; **Ab|zie|her**
ab|zie|len; auf etw. -
ab|zir|keln; Ab|zir|ke|lung, Ab|zirk|lung, die; -
ab|zi|schen (*ugs. für* sich rasch entfernen)
ab|zo|cken (*ugs. für* jmdn. [auf betrügerische Art] um sein Geld bringen)
Ab|zug; ab|züg|lich *(Kaufmannsspr.); Präp. mit Gen.:* abzüglich des gewährten Rabatts; *ein allein stehendes, stark gebeugtes Substantiv steht im Sing. ungebeugt:* abzüglich Rabatt; **ab|zugs‿fä|hig, ...frei; Ab|zugs‿ka|nal, ...schacht**
ab|zup|fen
ab|zwa|cken (*ugs. für* entziehen)
ab|zwe|cken *(selten);* auf eine Sache -
Ab|zweig (*Amtsspr.* Abzweigung); **Ab|zweig|do|se; ab|zwei|gen; Ab|zweig|stel|le; Ab|zwei|gung**
Ac = *chem. Zeichen für* Actinium
a c. = a conto
à c. = à condition
A|ca|dé|mie fran|çaise [akade.mi frã'sɛ:z], die; - - ‹franz.› (Akademie für franz. Sprache und Literatur)
a cap|pel|la ‹ital.› (*Musik* ohne Begleitung von Instrumenten); **A-cap|pel|la-Chor** (↑R 28)
acc. c. inf. = accusativus cum infinitivo; *vgl.* Akkusativ
ac|cel. = accelerando; **ac|ce|le|ran|do** [at͡ʃele...] ‹ital.› (*Musik* schneller werdend)
Ac|cent ai|gu [ak.sã:tɛ'gy:], der; - -, -s -s [ak.sã:zɛ'gy:] (*Sprachw.* Akut; *Zeichen* ´, z. B. é); **Ac|cent cir|con|flexe** [ak.sã:sirkɔ̃'flɛks], der; - -, -s -s [ak.sã:sirkɔ̃'flɛks] (*Sprachw.* Zirkumflex; *Zeichen* ˆ, z. B. â); **Ac|cent grave** [ak.sã:'gra:v], der; - -, -s -s [ak.sã:'gra:v] (*Sprachw.* Gravis; *Zeichen* `, z. B. è)
Ac|ces|soire [aksɛ'so̤a:r], das; -s, -s *meist Plur.* ‹franz.› (modisches Zubehör, z. B. Gürtel, Schmuck)
Ac|cra ['akra] (Hauptstadt von Ghana)
Ac|cro|cha|ge [akrɔ'ʃa:ʒə], die; -, -n ‹franz.› (Ausstellung einer Privatgalerie)
ACE = Auto Club Europa
A|ce|tat [at͡se...] (↑R 33), das; -s, -e ‹lat.› (*Chemie* Salz der Essigsäure; Chemiefaser); **A|ce|tat|sei|de; A|ce|ton,** das; -s (ein Lösungsmittel); **A|ce|ty|len,** das; -s (gasförmiger Kohlenwasserstoff); **A|ce|ty|len|gas**
ach!; ach so!; ach ja!; ach je!; (↑R 49:) **Ach,** das; -s, -[s]; mit Ach und Krach; mit Ach und Weh; Ach und Weh schreien
A|chä|er (Angehöriger eines altgriech. Stammes); **A|cha|ia** [...ja, *auch* a'xaja] (griech. Landschaft)
A|chä|me|ni|de, der; -n, -n; ↑R 126 (Angehöriger einer altpers. Dynastie)
A|chä|ne, die; -, -n ‹griech.› (*Bot.* Schließfrucht)
A|chat, der; -[e]s, -e ‹griech.› (ein Schmuckstein); **a|cha|ten**
A|cha|ti|us, A|chaz (m. Vorn.)
A|che [*auch* 'a:xə] die; - (Bestandteil von Flussnamen); Tiroler -
a|cheln ‹jidd.› (*landsch. für* essen)
A|chen|see, der; -s (See in Tirol)
A|che|ron, der; -[s] (Unterweltsfluss der griech. Sage)
A|cheu|lé|en [aʃøle'ɛ̃:], das; -[s] ‹nach dem Fundort Saint-Acheul in Nordfrankreich› (Kultur der älteren Altsteinzeit)
A|chill, A|chil|les (Held der griech. Sage); **A|chil|le|is,** die; - (Heldengesang über Achill); **A|chil|les‿fer|se** (↑R 95; verwundbare Stelle), **...seh|ne** (sehniges Ende des Wadenmuskels am Fersenbein); **A|chil|leus** [a'xi... *od.* ...'lɔys]; *vgl.* Achill
A|chim (m. Vorn.)
Ach|laut (↑R 24)
Ach|med (m. Vorn.)

a. Chr. [n.] = ante Christum [natum]

A|chro|ma|sie [akro...], die; -, ...ien ‹griech.› (*Physik* Brechung der Lichtstrahlen ohne Zerlegung in Farben); **A|chro|mat**, der; -[e]s, -e (Linsensystem, das Lichtstrahlen nicht in Farben zerlegt); **a|chro|ma|tisch** [*österr.* 'a...] (Achromasie aufweisend); **A|chro|ma|tis|mus** [*österr.* 'a...], der; -, ...men (Achromasie); **A|chro|ma|top|sie** (↑R 132), die; -, ...ien (*Med.* Farbenblindheit)

Achs|bruch *vgl.* Achsenbruch; **Achs|druck** *Plur.* ...drücke; **Ach|se**, die; -, -n

Ach|sel, die; -, -n; **Ach|sel‿griff**, **...höh|le**, **...klap|pe**; **ach|sel|stän|dig** (*Bot.* in der Blattachsel stehend); **Ach|sel|zu|cken**, das; -s; **ach|sel|zu|ckend**

Ach|sen|bruch, *auch* Achs|bruch, der; **ach|sig** (*für* axial); **...ach|sig** (z. B. einachsig); **Ach|sig|keit** (*für* Axialität); **Achs|ki|lo|me|ter** (Maßeinheit bei der Eisenbahn); **Achs‿la|ger** (*Plur.* ...lager), **...last**; **achs|recht** (*für* axial); **Achs|schen|kel|bol|zen** (*Kfz-Technik*)

acht; wir sind [unser] acht; eine Familie von achten *(ugs.)*; wir sind zu acht; die ersten, letzten acht; acht und eins macht, ist (*nicht:* machen, sind) neun; die Zahlen von acht bis zwölf; acht Millionen; acht mal zwei (8 mal 2); acht zu vier (8 : 4); er ist über acht [Jahre]; ein Kind von acht [bis zehn] Jahren; es ist acht [Uhr]; um acht [Uhr]; es schlägt eben acht; ein Viertel auf, vor acht; halb acht; Punkt, Schlag acht; im Jahre acht; die Linie acht; das macht acht fünfzig (*ugs. für* 8,50 DM); er sprang acht zweiundzwanzig (*ugs. für* 8,22 m); *vgl.* [1]Acht [Ziffer, Zahl]; *Ableitungen und Zusammensetzungen:* achtens; achtel *(vgl. d.)*; das Achtel *(vgl. d.)*; der Achter *(vgl. d.)*; acht[und]einhalb; achtundzwanzig; achtmillionste; achterlei; achtfach (8fach); achtjährig (8-jährig; *vgl. d.*); achtmal (8-mal; *vgl. d.*); Achtmetersprung (8-Meter-Sprung; ↑R 28); [1]**Acht**, die; -, -en (Ziffer, Zahl); die Zahl, Ziffer Acht; eine Acht schreiben; eine arabische, römische Acht; eine Acht fahren *(Eislauf)*; mit der Acht (*ugs. für* [Straßenbahn]linie 8) fahren

[2]**Acht**, die; - (*veraltet für* Aufmerksamkeit; Fürsorge); [auf jmdn., etwas] Acht geben, haben; gib gut Acht auf dich!; habt Acht!; sich in Acht nehmen; etwas [ganz] außer Acht lassen; außer aller Acht lassen; das Außer-Acht-Lassen (↑R 28 *u.* 50)

[3]**Acht**, die; - (*früher für* Ächtung); in Acht und Bann tun

Acht|ach|ser (*mit Ziffer* 8-Achser)

acht‿ar|mig, **...bän|dig**

acht|bar; **Acht|bar|keit**, die; -

ach|te; das achte Kapitel, das achte Gebot; der achte Mai, am achten Januar; *aber* der Achte, den ich treffe; sie wurde Achte im Weitsprung; jeder Achte; der Achte, am Achten [des Monats]; Heinrich der Achte; **Acht|eck**; **acht|eckig** (↑R 132); **acht|ein|halb**, acht|und|ein|halb

ach|tel; ein achtel Zentner, drei achtel Liter, *aber* (Maß): ein Achtelliter; **Ach|tel**, das, *schweiz. meist* der; -s, -; ein, das Achtel vom Zentner; ein Achtel Rotwein; drei Achtel des Ganzen, *aber* im Dreiachteltakt (*mit Ziffern* im 3/8-Takt; ↑R 28); **Ach|tel‿fi|na|le** *(Sportspr.)*, **...li|ter** (*vgl.* achtel), **...los**, **...no|te**

ach|ten

äch|ten

Acht|en|der (ein Hirsch mit acht Geweihenden); **ach|tens**; **Ach|ter** (Ziffer 8; Form einer 8; ein Boot für acht Ruderer)

ach|ter|aus (*Seemannsspr.* nach hinten)

Ach|ter|bahn; [auf, mit der] Achterbahn fahren

Ach|ter|deck (Hinterdeck); **ach|ter|las|tig** (*Seemannsspr.* achtern tiefer liegend als vorn)

ach|ter|lei

ach|ter|lich (*Seemannsspr.* von hinten kommend); **ach|tern** (*Seemannsspr.* hinten); nach -

Ach|ter|pa|ckung (*mit Ziffer* 8er-Packung); **Ach|ter|ren|nen** *(Rudersport)*

Ach|ter|ste|ven *(Seemannsspr.)*

acht|fach; **Acht|fa|che** (*mit Ziffer* 8fache), das; -n (↑R 5 ff.); [um] ein Achtfaches; um das Achtfache; **acht‿fal|tig** (acht Falten habend), **...fäl|tig** (*veraltet für* achtfach); **Acht|flach**, das; -[e]s, -e, **Acht|fläch|ner** (*für* Oktaeder); **Acht|fü|ßer** (*für* Oktopode)

Acht ge|ben, ha|ben *vgl.* [2]Acht

acht|hun|dert; **acht|jäh|rig** (*mit Ziffer* 8-jährig); **Acht|jäh|ri|ge**, (*mit Ziffer* 8-Jährige), der *u.* die; -n, -n (↑R 5 ff.); **Acht|kampf** *(Sportspr.)*

acht|kan|tig

acht|los; **Acht|lo|sig|keit**

acht|mal, *mit Ziffer* 8-mal; *bei besonderer Betonung auch* acht Mal; *aber* acht mal zwei (*mit Ziffern* 8 mal 2) ist (*nicht:* sind) sechzehn; achtmal so groß wie (*seltener* als) ...; acht- bis neunmal (↑R 23); *vgl.* bis; **acht|ma|lig**; **acht Mil|li|o|nen Mal**, **acht Mil|li|o|nen Ma|le**; *vgl.* [1]Mal; **acht|mil|li|ons|te**

acht|sam; **Acht|sam|keit**, die; -

acht‿sei|tig, **...spän|nig**, **...stö|ckig**

Acht|stun|den|tag; **acht|tau|send**; **Acht|tau|sen|der** ([über] 8 000 m hoher Berg); **Acht|ton|ner** (*mit Ziffer* 8-Tonner; ↑R 44); **Acht|uhr|zug** (*mit Ziffer* 8-Uhr-Zug; ↑R 28); **acht[|und]|ein|halb**; **Acht|und|sech|zi|ger**, der; -s, - (aktiver Teilnehmer an der Studentenrevolte Ende der Sechzigerjahre); **acht|und|zwan|zig**

Ach|tung, die; -; eine Achtung gebietende Persönlichkeit (↑R 40)

Äch|tung

Ach|tungs‿ap|plaus, **...be|zei|gung**, **...er|folg**; **Ach|tung|stel|lung**, die; - (*schweiz. milit. für* Strammstehen); **ach|tungs|voll**

acht|zehn; *vgl.* acht; im Jahre achtzehn; **Acht|zehn|en|der** (ein Hirsch mit achtzehn Geweihenden); **acht|zehn|hun|dert**; **acht|zehn|jäh|rig**; *vgl.* achtjährig

acht|zig; er ist, wird achtzig [Jahre alt]; mit achtzig [Jahren]; im Jahre achtzig; der Mensch über achtzig [Jahre]; Mitte achtzig; in die achtzig kommen; mit achtzig [Sachen] (*ugs. für* mit achtzig Stundenkilometern) fahren; Tempo achtzig; auf achtzig bringen (*ugs. für* wütend machen); *vgl.* acht, achtziger; **Acht|zig**, die; -, -en (Zahl); *vgl.* [1]Acht

acht|zi|ger (*mit Ziffern* 80er); achtziger Jahrgang (aus dem Jahre achtzig [eines Jahrhunderts]); die Achtzigerjahre, *auch* achtziger Jahre [des vorigen Jahrhunderts] (*mit Ziffern* 80er-Jahre, *auch* 80er Jahre); in den Achtzigerjahren, *auch* achtziger Jahren (über achtzig Jahre alt) war er noch rüstig; in den Achtzigern (über achtzig Jahre alt) sein; Mitte der Achtziger; **Acht|zi|ger** (jmd., der [über] 80 Jahre ist; Wein aus dem Jahre achtzig [eines Jahrhunderts]; *österr. auch für* 80. Geburtstag); **Acht|zi|ge|rin**; **Acht|zi|ger|jah|re** [*auch* 'axtsigər'ja:rə] *Plur.*; *vgl.* achtziger; **acht|zig|fach**; *vgl.* achtfach; **acht|zig‿jäh|rig** (*vgl.* achtjährig), **...mal**; **acht|zigs|te** (*Großschreibung:* er feiert seinen Achtzigsten

[= 80. Geburtstag]; *vgl.* achte); **acht|zigs|tel;** *vgl.* achtel; **Acht|zigs|tel,** das, *schweiz. meist* der; -s, -; *vgl.* Achtel
acht|zöl|lig, *auch* ...zol|lig; **Acht|zy|lin|der** (*ugs. für* Achtzylindermotor od. damit ausgerüstetes Kraftfahrzeug); **Acht|zy|lin|der|mo|tor; acht|zy|lind|rig**
äch|zen; du ächzt
a. c. i. = accusativus cum infinitivo; *vgl.* Akkusativ
A|ci|di|tät [atsi...], die; - ‹lat.› (*Chemie* Säuregrad einer Flüssigkeit); **A|ci|do|se,** die; -, -n (*Med.* krankhafte Vermehrung des Säuregehaltes im Blut)
A|cker, der; -s, Äcker; 30 - Land (↑R 90 f.); **A|cker|bau,** der; -[e]s; Ackerbau treiben; die [noch] Ackerbau treibenden Bewohner; **A|cker|bau|er,** der; *Gen.* -n, *seltener* -s, *Plur.* -n (*veraltet für* Landwirt) *u.* -s, - *meist Plur.* (Bebauer von Äckern); **Ä|cker|chen; A|cker|flä|che; A|cker|mann** *vgl.* Ackersmann; **A|cker|men|nig,** O|der|men|nig, der; -[e]s, -e (eine Heilpflanze); **a|ckern;** ich ...ere (↑R 16); **A|cker|nah|rung,** die; - (*Landw.* Ackerfläche, die zum Unterhalt einer Familie ausreicht); **A|cker[s]|mann** *Plur.* ...leute *u.* ...männer *(veraltet)*
Ack|ja, der; -[s], -s ‹schwed.› (lappischer Schlitten in Bootsform; *auch für* Rettungsschlitten)
AC-Me|tho|de = Assessmentcentermethode
à con|di|ti|on [akõdi'siõ:] ‹franz.› (*Kaufmannsspr.* mit Rückgaberecht; *Abk.* à c.)
a con|to ‹ital.› (*Bankw.* auf [laufende] Rechnung von ...; *Abk.* a c.); *vgl.* Akontozahlung
A|cre ['e:kər], der; -s, -s ‹engl.› (Flächenmaß); 7 - Land (↑R 90 f.)
Ac|ro|le|in (↑R 130) *vgl.* Akrolein
Ac|ryl (↑R 130), das; -s ‹griech.› (eine Chemiefaser); **Ac|ryl|säu|re** (stechend riechende Säure [Ausgangsstoff vieler Kunstharze])
ACS = Automobil-Club der Schweiz
Ac|ti|ni|um, das; -s ‹griech.› (chem. Element; *Zeichen* Ac)
Ac|tion ['ɛkʃ(ə)n], die; - ‹engl.› (spannende [Film]handlung; lebhafter Betrieb); **Ac|tion|pain|ting** ['ɛkʃ(ə)npe:ntiŋ] (↑R 33), das; - (moderne Richtung in der amerik. abstrakten Malerei)
a d. = a dato
a. d. = an der (*bei Ortsnamen,* z. B. Bad Neustadt a. d. Saale)
a. D. = außer Dienst
A. D. = Anno Domini

A|da (w. Vorn.)
A|da|bei, der; -s, -s (*österr. ugs. für* jmd., der überall dabei sein will)
ad ab|sur|dum ‹lat.›; ad absurdum führen (das Widersinnige nachweisen)
ADAC = Allgemeiner Deutscher Automobil-Club
ad ac|ta ‹lat., „zu den Akten"›; (*Abk.* a. a.); ad acta legen (als erledigt betrachten)
a|da|gio [a'da:dʒo] ‹ital.› (*Musik* langsam, ruhig); **A|da|gio,** das; -s, -s
A|dal|bert, A|del|bert (m. Vorn.); **A|dal|ber|ta,** A|del|ber|ta (w. Vorn.)
A|dam (m. Vorn.); *vgl.* [1]Riese; **A|da|mit,** der; -en, -en; ↑R 126 (Angehöriger einer bestimmten Sekte); **a|da|mi|tisch; A|dams‿ap|fel, ...kos|tüm**
A|dap|ta|ti|on (↑R 132), die; -, *Plur.* (*für* Umarbeitung eines literarischen Werkes:) -en ‹lat.› (*Physiol.* Anpassungsvermögen [bes. des Auges gegenüber Lichtreizen]; *Biol.* Anpassung an die Umwelt; *österr. auch für* Anpassung eines Hauses o. Ä. an einen bes. Zweck); **A|dap|ter,** der; -s, - ‹engl.› (*Technik* Verbindungsstück [zum Anschluss von Zusatzgeräten]); **a|dap|tie|ren** ‹lat.› (anpassen *[Biol. u. Physiol.]*; ein literarisches Werk für Film u. Funk umarbeiten; *österr. auch für* eine Wohnung, ein Haus o. Ä. herrichten); **A|dap|tie|rung; A|dap|ti|on,** die; -, -en; *vgl.* Adaptation; **a|dap|tiv** *(fachspr.)*
a|dä|quat (↑R 132) ‹lat.› (angemessen); **A|dä|quat|heit,** die; -
a da|to ‹lat.› (vom Tage der Ausstellung [an]; *Abk.* a d.)
ADB = Allgemeine Deutsche Biographie
ad ca|len|das grae|cas [- - 'grɛ:kas] ‹lat.› (niemals)
Ad|den|dum, das; -s, ...da *meist Plur.* ‹lat.› (*veraltet für* Zusatz, Nachtrag); **ad|die|ren** (zusammenzählen); **Ad|dier|ma|schi|ne**
Ad|dis A|be|ba [- 'a(:)..., *auch* - a'be:ba] (Hptst. Äthiopiens)
Ad|di|ti|on, die; -, -en ‹lat.› (Zusammenzählung); **ad|di|ti|o|nal** (*fachspr. für* zusätzlich); **Ad|di|ti|ons|wort,** *Plur.* ...wörter (*svw.* Kopulativum); **ad|di|tiv** (*fachspr. für* hinzufügend, auf Addition beruhend); **Ad|di|tiv,** das; -s, -e [...və] ‹engl.› (*fachspr. für* Zusatz, der einen chem. Stoff verbessert)
ad|di|zie|ren ‹lat.› (zuerkennen)
Ad|duk|ti|on, die; -, -en ‹lat.› (*Med.* das Bewegen von Körperteilen zur Körperachse hin); **Ad|duk|tor,** der; -s, ...oren (eine Adduktion bewirkender Muskel)
a|de! *(veraltend, noch landsch.);* **A|de,** das; -s, -s; Ade, *auch* ade sagen
A|de|bar, der; -s, -e (*bes. nordd. für* Storch)
[1]**A|del,** der; -s
[2]**A|del,** *auch* O|del, der; -s (*bes. bayr. u. österr. für* Mistjauche)
[1]**A|de|laide** ['ɛdəlit *od.* ...lid] (Hptst. von Südaustralien)
[2]**A|de|la|i|de** (w. Vorn.); **A|del|bert,** A|dal|bert (m. Vorn.); **A|del|ber|ta,** A|dal|ber|ta (w. Vorn.)
A|de|le (w. Vorn.)
A|del|gund, A|del|gun|de (w. Vorn.); **A|del|heid** (w. Vorn.); **a|de|lig,** ad|lig; **a|deln;** ich ...[e]le (↑R 16); **A|dels‿brief, ...prä|di|kat; A|de|lung**
A|den (Hafenstadt in Jemen)
A|de|nau|er (erster dt. Bundeskanzler)
A|de|nom, das; -s, -e ‹griech.› (*Med.* Drüsengeschwulst); **a|de|no|ma|tös**
A|dept (↑R 132), der; -en, -en (↑R 126) ‹lat.› (*früher für* [als Schüler] in eine Geheimlehre Eingeweihter)
A|der, die; -, -n; **Ä|der|chen; a|de|rig,** ad|rig; **ä|de|rig,** äd|rig; **A|der|lass,** der; -es, ...läs|se; **Ä|de|rung**
à deux mains [a dø 'mɛ̃(:)] ‹franz.› (*Klavierspiel* mit zwei Händen)
ADFC = Allgemeiner Deutscher Fahrrad-Club
Ad|go, die; - (Allgemeine Deutsche Gebührenordnung für Ärzte)
ad|hä|rent; ad|hä|rie|ren ‹lat.› (*veraltet für* anhaften; anhängen); **Ad|hä|si|on,** die; -, -en (*fachspr. für* Aneinanderhaften von Stoffen od. Körpern); **Ad|hä|si|ons|ver|schluss** (*Postw.* mit einer Haftschicht versehener Verschluss); **ad|hä|siv** (anhaftend)
ad hoc [*auch* - ho:k] ‹lat.› ([eigens] zu diesem [Zweck]; aus dem Augenblick heraus [entstanden]); **Ad-hoc-Bil|dung**
a|di|a|ba|tisch ‹griech.› (*Physik, Meteor.* ohne Wärmeaustausch)
A|di|a|pho|ra *Plur.* ‹griech.› (*Philos., Theol.* sittlich neutrale Werte)
a|di|eu! [a'diø:] ‹franz.› (*veraltend, noch landsch. für* lebe [lebt] wohl!); **A|di|eu,** das; -s, -s (Lebewohl); jmdm. Adieu, *auch* adieu sagen
A|di|ge ['a:didʒe] (*ital. Name für* Etsch); *vgl.* Alto Adige

Ä|dil, der; *Gen.* -s *u.* -en, *Plur.* -en; ↑R 126 (altröm. Beamter)
ad in|fi|ni|tum, in in|fi|ni|tum ‹lat.› (ohne Ende, unaufhörlich)
Ad|jek|tiv, das; -s, -e [...ve] ‹lat.› (*Sprachw.* Eigenschaftswort, z. B. „schön"); **ad|jek|ti|visch** [...v...]
Ad|ju|di|ka|ti|on, die; -, -en ‹lat.› (richterl. Zuerkennung); **ad|ju|di|zie|ren**
Ad|junkt, der; -en, -en (↑R 126) ‹lat.› (*veraltet für* [Amts]gehilfe; österr. u. schweiz. Beamtentitel)
ad|jus|tie|ren ‹lat.› (*Technik* [Werkstücke] zurichten; eichen; fein einstellen; *österr. auch für* ausrüsten, dienstmäßig kleiden); **Ad|jus|tie|rung** (*Technik* genaue Einstellung; *österr. auch für* Uniform)
Ad|ju|tant, der; -en, -en (↑R 126) ‹lat.› (beigeordneter Offizier); **Ad|ju|tan|tur,** die; -, -en (Amt, Dienststelle des Adjutanten); **Ad|ju|tum,** das; -s, ...ten (*österr. für* erste, vorläufige Entlohnung)
ad l. = ad libitum
Ad|la|tus, der; -, ...ten ‹lat.› (Gehilfe; Helfer)
Ad|ler, der; -s, -; **Ad|ler|blick**
ad lib. = ad libitum
ad li|bi|tum ‹lat.› (nach Belieben; *Abk.* ad l., ad lib., a. l.)
ad|lig, a|de|lig; **Ad|li|ge,** der *u.* die; -n, -n (↑R 5 ff.)
ad ma|io|rem De|i glo|ri|am; *meist für* omnia ad maiorem Dei gloriam ‹lat., „[alles] zur größeren Ehre Gottes"› (Wahlspruch der Jesuiten)
Ad|mi|nist|ra|ti|on (↑R 130), die; -, -en ‹lat.› (das Verwalten; Verwaltung[sbehörde]); **ad|mi|nist|ra|tiv** (zur Verwaltung gehörend); **Ad|mi|nist|ra|tor,** der; -s, ...oren (Verwalter); **ad|mi|nist|rie|ren**
ad|mi|ra|bel ‹lat.› (*veraltet für* bewundernswert); ...ab|le (↑R 130) Schriften
Ad|mi|ral, der; -s, *Plur.* -e, *seltener* ...äle ‹franz.› (Marineoffizier im Generalsrang; ein Schmetterling); **Ad|mi|ra|li|tät,** die; -, -en; **Ad|mi|ra|li|täts|in|seln** *Plur.* (Inselgruppe in der Südsee); **Ad|mi|rals|rang; Ad|mi|ral|stab** (oberster Führungsstab einer Kriegsmarine)
ADN = Allgemeiner Deutscher Nachrichtendienst *(ehemals in der DDR)*
Ad|nex, der; -es, -e ‹lat.› (*veraltet für* Anhang)
ad no|tam ‹lat.›; ad notam nehmen (*veraltet für* zur Kenntnis nehmen)
ad o|cu|los ‹lat., „vor Augen"›; ad oculos demonstrieren (*veraltet für* vorzeigen; klar darlegen)
A|do|les|zenz, die; - ‹lat.› (spätere Abschnitt des Jugendalters)
A|dolf (m. Vorn.)
A|do|nai ‹hebr., „mein Herr"› (alttest. Name Gottes)
[1]**A|do|nis** (schöner Jüngling der griech. Sage); [2]**A|do|nis,** der; -, -se (schöner Jüngling, Mann); **a|do|nisch** (schön wie Adonis); -er Vers (antiker griech. Vers)
a|dop|tie|ren (↑R 132) ‹lat.› (als Kind annehmen); **A|dop|ti|on,** die; -, -en; **A|dop|tiv‿el|tern, ...kind**
a|do|ra|bel (↑R 132) ‹lat.› (*veraltet für* anbetungswürdig); ...ab|le (↑R 130) Heilige; **A|do|ra|ti|on,** die; -, -en (*veraltet für* Anbetung; Huldigung); **a|do|rie|ren** (*veraltet für* anbeten, verehren)
Adr. = Adresse
ad rem ‹lat.› (zur Sache [gehörend])
Ad|re|ma ® (↑R 130), die; -, -s ‹Kurzwort für eine Adressiermaschine›; **ad|re|mie|ren** (mit einer Adrema beschriften)
Ad|re|na|lin, das; -s ‹nlat.› (*Med.* ein Hormon des Nebennierenmarks)
Ad|res|sant (↑R 130), der; -en, -en; ↑R 126 ‹lat.› (Absender); **Ad|res|sat,** der; -en, -en; ↑R 126 (Empfänger; [bei Wechseln:] Bezogener); **Ad|ress|buch; Ad|res|se,** die; -, -n (*Abk.* Adr.); **Ad|res|sen|ver|zeich|nis; ad|res|sie|ren; Ad|res|sier|ma|schi|ne**
ad|rett (↑R 130) ‹franz.› (nett, hübsch, ordentlich, sauber)
A|dria (↑R 130), die; - (Adriatisches Meer); **A|dri|an** (m. Vorn.); *vgl.* Hadrian; **Ad|ri|a|na, Ad|ri|a|ne** (w. Vorn.); **Ad|ri|a|ti|sche Meer,** das; -n -[e]s
ad|rig, a|de|rig; **äd|rig,** ä|de|rig
Ad|rio (↑R 130), das; -s, -s (*schweiz. für* im Netz eines Schweinebauchfells eingenähte Bratwurstmasse aus Kalb- od. Schweinefleisch)
ad|sor|bie|ren ‹lat.› (*fachspr. für* [Gase od. gelöste Stoffe an der Oberfläche fester Körper] anlagern); **Ad|sorp|ti|on,** die; -, -en; **ad|sorp|tiv** (zur Adsorption fähig)
Ad|strin|gens [...st...], das; -, *Plur.* ...genzien [...i̯ən], *auch* ...gentia ‹lat.› (*Med.* zusammenziehendes, Blutungen stillendes Mittel); **ad|strin|gie|ren**
A|du|lar, der; -s, -e (ein Feldspat [Schmuckstein])
A-Dur [*auch* 'a:'du:r], das; - (Tonart; *Zeichen* A); **A-Dur-Ton|lei|ter** (↑R 28)
ad us. = ad usum
ad u|sum ‹lat.› („zum Gebrauch"; *Abk.* ad us.); **ad u|sum Del|phi|ni** (für Schüler bestimmt)
Ad|van|tage [əd'va:ntidʒ], der; -s, -s ‹engl.› (*Sportspr.* der erste gewonnene Punkt nach dem Einstand beim Tennis)
Ad|vent [...v..., *österr. u. schweiz. auch* ...f...], der; -[e]s, -e *Plur. selten* ‹lat., „Ankunft"› (Zeit vor Weihnachten); **Ad|ven|tist,** der; -en, -en (↑R 126) ‹engl.› (Angehöriger einer christl. Glaubensgemeinschaft); **Ad|vent‿ka|len|der** *(österr.)*, **...kranz** *(österr.)*; **Ad|vents‿ka|len|der, ...kranz; Ad|vent|sonn|tag** *(österr.)*; **Ad|vents‿sonn|tag, ...zeit; Ad|vent|zeit** *(österr.)*
Ad|verb [...v...], das; -s, -ien [...i̯ən] ‹lat.› (*Sprachw.* Umstandswort, z. B. „dort"); **ad|ver|bi|al;** -e Bestimmung; **Ad|ver|bi|al,** das; -s, -e (Umstandsbestimmung); **Ad|ver|bi|al‿be|stim|mung, ...satz; ad|ver|bi|ell** (*seltener für* adverbial)
ad|ver|sa|tiv [...v...] ‹lat.› (gegensätzlich, entgegensetzend); -e Konjunktion (*Sprachw.* entgegensetzendes Bindewort, z. B. „aber")
Ad|vo|ca|tus De|i [...v...], der; - -, ...ti - ‹lat.› (Geistlicher, der im kath. kirchl. Prozess für eine Heilig- od. Seligsprechung eintritt); **Ad|vo|ca|tus Di|a|bo|li,** der; - -, ...ti - (Geistlicher, der im kath. kirchl. Prozess Gründe gegen die Heilig- od. Seligsprechung vorbringt; *übertr. für* jmd., der bewusst Gegenargumente in eine Diskussion einbringt); **Ad|vo|kat,** der; -en, -en; ↑R 126 (*landsch. u. schweiz., sonst veraltet für* [Rechts]anwalt); **Ad|vo|ka|tur,** die; -, -en (*veraltet für* Anwaltschaft; Büro eines Anwalts); **Ad|vo|ka|tur|bü|ro** *(schweiz.)*; **Ad|vo|ka|turs|kanz|lei** *(österr. veraltend)*
AdW = Akademie der Wissenschaften
AE = Ångström[einheit]; astronomische Einheit
Aech|mea [ɛç...], die; -, ...meen ‹griech.› (eine Zimmerpflanze)
a|e|ro... [aero... *od.* ɛro...] ‹griech.› (luft...); **A|e|ro...** (Luft...); **a|e|rob** (*Biol.* Sauerstoff zum Leben brauchend); **Ae|ro|bic** [ɛ'ro:bik], das; -s, *meist ohne Artikel* ‹engl.-amerik.› (Fitnesstraining mit tänzeri-

schen u. gymnast. Übungen); **A|e|ro|bi|er** [a|e'ro:biər *od.* ε...] ‹griech.› (*Biol.* Organismus, der nur mit Luftsauerstoff leben kann); **A|e|ro|bi|ont** [a|e... *od.* ε...], der; -en, -en; ↑R 126 (*svw.* Aerobier); **A|e|ro|dy|na|mik** (*Physik* Lehre von der Bewegung gasförmiger Körper); **a|e|ro|dy|na|misch; A|e|ro|flot** [a|e...], die; - ‹griech.; russ.› (russ. Luftfahrtgesellschaft); **A|e|ro|gramm** [a|e... *od.* ε...], das; -s, -e (Luftpostleichtbrief); **A|e|ro|lith** [a|e... *od.* ...'lit], der; *Gen.* -en *u.* -s, *Plur.* -e[n] (↑R 126) ‹griech.› (*veraltet für* Meteorstein); **A|e|ro|lo|gie,** die; - (Wissenschaft von der Erforschung der höheren Luftschichten); **A|e|ro|me|cha|nik,** die; - (*Physik* Lehre von dem Gleichgewicht und der Bewegung der Gase); **A|e|ro|me|di|zin** (Teilgebiet der Medizin, das sich mit den physischen Einwirkungen der Luftfahrt auf den Organismus befasst); **A|e|ro|me|ter,** das; -s, - (Gerät zum Bestimmen des Luftgewichtes, der Luftdichte); **A|e|ro|nau|tik,** die; - (*veraltet für* Luftfahrt); **A|e|ro|plan,** der; -[e]s, -e ‹griech.; lat.› (*veraltet für* Flugzeug); **A|e|ro|sa|lon** [a|e:...], der; -s, -s ‹griech.; franz.› (Luftfahrtausstellung); **A|e|ro|sol** [a|e... *od.* ε...], das; -s, -e ‹griech.; lat.› (feinste Verteilung fester oder flüssiger Stoffe in Gas [z. B. Rauch od. Nebel]); **A|e|ro|sta|tik** ‹griech.› (*Physik* Lehre von den Gleichgewichtszuständen bei Gasen); **a|e|ro|sta|tisch; A|e|ro|tel,** das; -s, -s (Flughafenhotel)

AF = Air France

AFC = automatic frequency control [ɔ:tə'mεtik 'fri:kwənsi kən'tro:l] ‹engl.› (automatische Scharfeinstellung bei Rundfunkgeräten)

Af|fä|re, die; -, -n ‹franz.› (Angelegenheit; unangenehmer, peinlicher Vorfall; Streitsache; *veraltet für* Verhältnis, Liebschaft)

Äff|chen; Af|fe, der; -n, -n (↑R 126)

Af|fekt, der; -[e]s, -e ‹lat.› (Gemütsbewegung, stärkere Erregung); **Af|fek|ta|ti|on,** die; - (*selten für* Getue, Ziererei); **Af|fekt|hand|lung; af|fek|tiert** (geziert, gekünstelt); **Af|fek|tiert|heit; Af|fek|ti|on,** die; -, -en (*Med.* Befall eines Organs mit Krankheitserregern; *veraltet für* Wohlwollen); **af|fek|tiv** (gefühlsbetont); **Af|fek|ti|vi|tät** [...v...], die; -; **Af|fekt|stau** (*Psych.*)

äf|fen (*veraltend für* nachahmen; narren); **Af|fen|art; af|fen|ar|tig; Af|fen|brot|baum** (eine afrik. Baumart); *vgl.* Baobab; **af|fen|geil** (*ugs. für* großartig, toll); **Af|fen‿hit|ze** (*ugs.*), **...lie|be** (die; -), **...schan|de** (*ugs.*), **...the|a|ter** (das; -s; *ugs.*), **...zahn** (der; -s; *ugs.*), **...zeck** (der; -s; *ugs.*); **Äf|fer** (*veraltet für* äffende Person); **Af|fe|rei** (*ugs. abwertend für* eitles Gebaren); **Äf|fe|rei** (*veraltet für* Irreführung)

Af|fi|che [a'fi(:)ʃ(ə)], die; -, -n ‹franz.› (*schweiz., sonst selten für* Anschlag[zettel], Aushang); **af|fi|chie|ren** [afi'ʃi:...]

Af|fi|da|vit [...vit], das; -s, -s ‹lat.› (eidesstattl. Versicherung)

af|fig (*ugs. abwertend für* eitel); **Af|fig|keit** (*ugs. abwertend*)

Af|fi|li|a|ti|on, die; -, -en ‹lat.› (Wechsel der Loge eines Freimaurers; Tochtergesellschaft)

af|fin ‹lat.›; -e Geometrie

Äf|fin, die; -, -nen

af|fi|nie|ren ‹franz.› (*Chemie* läutern; scheiden [z. B. Edelmetalle])

Af|fi|ni|tät, die; -, -en ‹lat.› (Verwandtschaft; Ähnlichkeit; *Chemie* Neigung von Atomen od. Atomgruppen, sich zu verbinden)

Af|fir|ma|ti|on, die; -, -en ‹lat.› (Bejahung, Zustimmung); **af|fir|ma|tiv** (bejahend, zustimmend); **af|fir|mie|ren** (bejahen, bekräftigen)

äf|fisch

Af|fix, das; -es, -e ‹lat.› (*Sprachw.* an den Wortstamm angefügte Vor- od. Nachsilbe); *vgl.* Präfix *u.* Suffix

af|fi|zie|ren ‹lat.› (*Med.* reizen; krankhaft verändern)

Af|fo|dill, As|pho|dill, der; -s, -e ‹griech.› (ein Liliengewächs)

Af|fri|ka|ta, Af|fri|ka|te, die; -, ...ten ‹lat.› (*Sprachw.* Verschlusslaut mit folgendem Reibelaut, z. B. pf)

Af|front [a'frɔ̃:, *auch* a'frɔnt], der; -s, *Plur.* -s *u.* (*bei deutscher Aussprache:*) -e ‹franz.› (Schmähung; Beleidigung)

Af|gha|ne [...'ga:...], der; -n, -n; ↑R 126 (Angehöriger eines vorderasiat. Volkes; *auch* eine Hunderasse); **Af|gha|ni,** der; -[s], -[s] (afghan. Währungseinheit); **af|gha|nisch;** *vgl.* Paschtu; **Af|gha|nis|tan** (↑R 132); Staat in Vorderasien)

AFL ['e:εf'εl] = American Federation of Labor [ə'mεrikən fεdə're:ʃ(ə)n əv 'le:bər] (amerik. Gewerkschaftsverband)

Af|la|to|xin (↑R 130), das; -s, -e ‹lat.› (Giftstoff in Schimmelpilzen)

AFN ['e:εf'εn] = American Forces Network [ə'mεrikən 'fɔ:(r)siz 'nεtwœ:(r)k] (Rundfunkanstalt der außerhalb der USA stationierten amerik. Streitkräfte)

à fonds per|du [a fɔ̃(:) pεr'dy:] ‹franz.› (auf Verlustkonto; [Zahlung] ohne Aussicht auf Gegenleistung od. Rückerhalt)

AFP = Agence France-Presse

Af|ra (↑R 130; w. Vorn.)

a fres|co ‹ital.› (auf den noch feuchten Verputz [gemalt])

Af|ri|ka ['a(:)f...] (↑R 130); **Af|ri|kaan|der,** Af|ri|kan|der (*selten für* weißer Südafrikaner mit Afrikaans als Muttersprache); **af|ri|kaans;** die -e Sprache; **Af|ri|kaans,** das; - (Sprache der Buren); **Af|ri|ka|na** *Plur.* (Werke über Afrika); **Af|ri|kan|der** *vgl.* Afrikaander; **Af|ri|ka|ner; Af|ri|ka|ne|rin; af|ri|ka|nisch; Af|ri|ka|nist,** der; -en, -en; ↑R 126 (Wissenschaftler auf dem Gebiet der Afrikanistik); **Af|ri|ka|nis|tik,** die; - (wissenschaftl. Erforschung der Geschichte, Sprachen u. Kulturen Afrikas); **Af|ro|ame|ri|ka|ner** ['a(:)f...] (Amerikaner schwarzafrikanischer Abstammung); **af|ro|ame|ri|ka|nisch** (↑R 132; die Afroamerikaner betreffend; *auch für* Afrika und Amerika betreffend); -e Beziehungen, Musik; **af|ro|asi|a|tisch** (↑R 132); **Af|ro|look** [...luk], der; -s ‹engl.› (Frisur, bei der das Haar in stark gekrausten, dichten Locken nach allen Seiten absteht)

Af|ter, der; -s, -; **Af|ter‿le|der** (*österr. für* Hinterleder des Schuhes), **...mie|ter** (*veraltet für* Untermieter); **...sau|sen** (das; -; *derb für* Angst)

Af|ter|shave ['a:ftərʃe:v], das; -[s], -s (*kurz für* Aftershavelotion); **Af|ter|shave|lo|tion,** *auch* **Af|ter-Shave-Lo|tion** ['a:ftərʃe:v-lo:ʃən] (↑R 24), die; -, -s ‹engl.› (Rasierwasser zum Gebrauch nach der Rasur)

Ag = Argentum (*chem. Zeichen für* Silber)

a. G. = auf Gegenseitigkeit; (*beim Theater*) als Gast

AG = Aktiengesellschaft, Amtsgericht, Arbeitsgemeinschaft

A|ga, der; -s, -s ‹türk.› (früherer türk. Titel)

Ä|ga|di|sche In|seln *Plur.* (Inselgruppe westl. von Sizilien)

Ä|gä|is, die; - (Ägäisches Meer); **Ä|gä|i|sche Meer,** das; -n -[e]s (↑R 102)

A|ga Khan [- ka:n], der; - -s, - -e ‹türk.› (Oberhaupt eines Zweiges der Ismailiten)
A|ga|mem|non (sagenhafter König von Mykenä)
A|ga|pe, die; - ‹griech.› (schenkende [Nächsten]liebe)
A|gar-A|gar, der *od.* das; -s ‹malai.› (Gallerte aus ostasiat. Algen)
A|ga|the (w. Vorn.); **A|ga|thon** [*auch* 'a...] (m. Eigenn.)
A|ga|ve [...və] die; -, -n ‹griech.› ([sub]trop. Pflanze)
A|gen|ce France-Presse [a'ʒã:s frãs 'prɛs], die; - - ‹franz.› (Name einer franz. Nachrichtenagentur; *Abk.* AFP)
A|gen|da, die; -, ...den ‹lat.› (Merkbuch; Liste von Gesprächspunkten); **A|gen|de,** die; -, -n (*ev. Kirche* Gottesdienstordnung); **A|gen|den** *Plur.* (*österr. für* Obliegenheiten, Aufgaben)
A|gens, das; -, Agenzien [...i̯ən] ‹lat.› (*Philos.* tätiges Wesen od. Prinzip; *Med.* wirkendes Mittel; *Sprachw.* Träger eines im Verb genannten aktiven Verhaltens); **A|gent,** der; -en, -en; ↑R 126 (Spion; Vermittler von Engagements; *veraltet für* Geschäftsvermittler, Vertreter); **A|gen|ten‿ring, ...tä|tig|keit; A|gen|tie** [...'tsi:], die; -, ...tien ‹ital.› (*österr. für* Geschäftsstelle der Donau-Dampfschifffahrtsgesellschaft); **a|gen|tie|ren** (*österr. für* Kunden werben); **A|gen|tin** ‹lat.›; **A|gent pro|vo|ca|teur** [a,ʒã: provoka'tø:r], der; - -, -s -s [a,ʒã: ...'tø:r] ‹franz.› (Lockspitzel); **A|gen|tur,** die; -, -en ‹lat.› (Geschäfts[neben]stelle, Vertretung); **A|gen|zi|en** [...i̯ən] (*Plur. von* Agens)
A|ge|si|la|os, A|ge|si|la|us (König von Sparta)
Ag|fa ® (*Bez. für* fotogr. Erzeugnisse); **Ag|fa|co|lor** ® (Farbfilme, Farbfilmverfahren)
Ag|glo|me|rat, das; -[e]s, -e ‹lat.› (*fachspr. für* Anhäufung; *Geol.* Ablagerung loser Gesteinsbruchstücke); **Ag|glo|me|ra|ti|on,** die; -, -en (*fachspr. für* Anhäufung; Zusammenballung; Ballungsraum); **ag|glo|me|rie|ren**
Ag|glu|ti|na|ti|on, die; -, -en ‹lat.› (*Med.* Verklebung, Verklumpung; *Sprachw.* Anfügung von Bildungselementen an das unverändert bleibende Wort); **ag|glu|ti|nie|ren;** -de Sprachen
Ag|gre|gat, das; -[e]s, -e ‹lat.› (Maschinensatz; aus mehreren Gliedern bestehender mathematischer Ausdruck); **Ag|gre|ga|ti|on,** die; -, -en (*Chemie* Zusammenlagerung [von Molekülen]); **Ag|gre|gat|zu|stand** (*Chemie, Physik* Erscheinungsform eines Stoffes)
Ag|gres|si|on, die; -, -en ‹lat.› (Angriff[sverhalten], Überfall); **Ag|gres|si|ons‿krieg, ...trieb; ag|gres|siv** (angriffslustig); **Ag|gres|si|vi|tät** [...v...], die; -, -en; **Ag|gres|sor,** der; -s, ...oren (Angreifer)
Ä|gid, Ä|gi|di|us (m. Vorn.); **Ä|gi|de,** die; - ‹griech.› (Schutz, Obhut); unter der - von ...
a|gie|ren ‹lat.› (handeln; *Theater* als Schauspieler auftreten)
a|gil ‹lat.› (flink, wendig, beweglich); **A|gi|li|tät,** die; -
Ä|gi|na (griech. Insel; Stadt); **Ä|gi|ne|te,** der; -n, -n; (↑R 126; Bewohner von Ägina); **Ä|gi|ne|ten** *Plur.* (Giebelfiguren des Tempels von Ägina)
A|gio ['a:dʒo, *auch* 'a:ʒi̯o], das; -s, *Plur.* -s *u.* Agien ['a:dʒən, *auch* 'a:ʒi̯ən] ‹ital.› (*Wirtsch.* Aufgeld; z. B. Betrag, um den der Preis eines Wertpapiers über dem Nennwert liegt); **A|gi|o|ta|ge** [aʒio'ta:ʒə, *österr.* ...'ta:ʒ], die; -, -n [...'ta:ʒ(ə)n] ‹franz.› (Ausnutzung von Kursschwankungen an der Börse); **A|gi|o|teur** [aʒi̯o'tø:r], der; -s, -e (Börsenmakler); **a|gi|o|tie|ren** [aʒi̯o...]
Ä|gir (*nord. Mythol.* Meerriese)
Ä|gis, die; - (Schild des Zeus und der Athene)
A|gi|ta|ti|on, die; -, -en ‹lat.› (politische Hetze; intensive politische Aufklärungs-, Werbetätigkeit); **A|gi|ta|tor,** der; -s, ...oren (jmd., der Agitation betreibt); **a|gi|ta|to|risch; a|gi|tie|ren; A|git|prop,** die; - (*Kurzw. aus* Agitation und Propaganda); **A|git|prop|the|a|ter** (Laientheater der Arbeiterbewegung in den 20er Jahren)
Ag|la|ia [...ja] (↑R 130) ‹„Glanz“› (eine der drei griech. Göttinnen der Anmut, der Chariten; w. Vorn.)
Ag|nat (↑R 130), der; -en, -en (↑R 126) ‹lat.› (Blutsverwandte[r] der männl. Linie); **ag|na|tisch**
Ag|nes (↑R 130; w. Vorn.)
Ag|ni (↑R 130; ind. Gott des Feuers)
Ag|no|sie (↑R 132), die; -, ...i̯en ‹griech.› (*Med.* Störung des Erkennens; *Philos.* Nichtwissen); **Ag|nos|ti|ker** (Verfechter des Agnostizismus); **Ag|nos|ti|zis|mus,** der; - (philos. Lehre, die das übersinnliche Sein für unerkennbar hält)
ag|nos|zie|ren ‹lat.› (*veraltet für* anerkennen); einen Toten - (*österr. Amtsspr.* identifizieren)
Ag|nus De|i (↑R 130), das; - -, - - ‹lat., „Lamm Gottes“› (Bezeichnung Christi *[nur Sing.]*; Gebet; geweihtes Wachstäfelchen)
A|go|gik, die; - ‹griech.› (*Musik* Lehre von der individuellen Gestaltung des Tempos); **a|go|gisch**
à go|go [a go'go:] ‹franz.› (*ugs. für* in Hülle u. Fülle, nach Belieben)
A|gon, der; -s, -e ‹griech.› (Wettkampf der alten Griechen; Streitgespräch als Teil der att. Komödie); **a|go|nal** (kämpferisch); **A|go|nie,** die; -, ...i̯en (Todeskampf); **A|go|nist,** der; -en, -en (↑R 126; Teilnehmer an einem Agon)
[1]**A|go|ra,** die; -, Agoren ‹griech.› (Markt u. auch die dort stattfindende Volksversammlung im alten Griechenland)
[2]**A|go|ra,** die; -, Agorot ‹hebr.› (israel. Währungseinheit)
A|go|ra|pho|bie, die; -, ...i̯en ‹griech.› (Platzangst beim Überqueren freier Plätze)
Ag|raf|fe (↑R 130), die; -, -n ‹franz.› (Schmuckspange; *Bauw.* klammerförmige Rundbogenverzierung; *Med.* Wundklammer; *schweiz. auch für* Krampe)
Ag|ram (↑R 130; *früherer dt. Name von* Zagreb)
A|gra|phie die; -, ...i̯en ‹griech.› (*Med.* Verlust des Schreibvermögens)
Ag|rar|be|völ|ke|rung (↑R 130); **Ag|ra|ri|er** [...i̯ər] ‹lat.› (Großgrundbesitzer, Landwirt); **ag|ra|risch; Ag|rar‿land, ...po|li|tik; ag|rar|po|li|tisch; Ag|rar‿pro|dukt, ...re|form, ...staat, ...tech|nik**
Ag|ree|ment [ə'gri:...] (↑R 130), das; -s, -s ‹engl.› (*Politik* formlose Übereinkunft im zwischenstaatl. Verkehr); *vgl.* Gentleman's Agreement; **Ag|ré|ment** [agre'mã:] das; -s, -s ‹franz.› (*Politik* Zustimmung zur Ernennung eines diplomat. Vertreters); **Ag|ré|ments** [agre'mã:s] *Plur.* (*Musik* Verzierungen)
Ag|ri|co|la, Georgius (↑R 130; dt. Naturforscher)
Ag|ri|kul|tur (↑R 130) ‹lat.› (Ackerbau, Landwirtschaft); **Ag|ri|kul|tur|che|mie**
Ag|rip|pa (↑R 130; röm. m. Eigenn.); **Ag|rip|pi|na** (röm. w. Eigenn.)
Ag|ro|nom (↑R 130), der; -en, -en (↑R 126) ‹griech.› (wissenschaftlich ausgebildeter Landwirt); **Ag|ro|no|mie,** die; - (Ackerbaukun-

de, Landwirtschaftswissenschaft); **ag|ro|no|misch; Ag|ro|tech|nik** (Landwirtschaftstechnik)

Ä|gy|p|ten; Ä|gyp|ter; ä|gyp|tisch; eine ägyptische (tiefe) Finsternis; *vgl.* deutsch; **Ä|gyp|tisch,** das; -[s] (Sprache); *vgl.* Deutsch; **Ä|gyp|ti|sche,** das; -n; *vgl.* Deutsche, das; **Ä|gyp|to|lo|ge,** der; -n, -n; ↑R 126 (Wissenschaftler auf dem Gebiet der Ägyptologie); **Ä|gyp|to|lo|gie,** die; - (wissenschaftl. Erforschung des ägypt. Altertums); **Ä|gyp|to|lo|gin; ä|gyp|to|lo|gisch**

A. H. = Alter Herr (einer student. Verbindung)

Ah = Amperestunde

ah!; ah so!; ah was!; **Ah,** das; -s, -s; ein lautes Ah ertönte; **äh!** [*auch* ɛ]; **a|ha!** [*od.* aˈha:]; **A|ha-Er|leb|nis;** ↑R 24 *(Psych.)*

A|has|ver [...ˈve:r *od.* aˈhas...], der; -s, *Plur.* -s *u.* -e, *auch* **A|has|ve|rus,** der; -, -se *Plur. selten* ⟨hebr.-lat.⟩ (ruhelos Umherirrender; der Ewige Jude); **a|has|ve|risch**

ahd. = althochdeutsch

a|his|to|risch (nicht historisch)

Ahl|beck, See|bad (Stadt auf Usedom)

Ah|le, die; -, -n (nadelartiges Werkzeug); *vgl.* Pfriem

Ah|ming, die; -, *Plur.* -e *u.* -s (*Seemannsspr.* Tiefgangsmarke)

Ahn, der; *Gen.* -[e]s *u.* -en, *Plur.* -en; ↑R 126 (Stammvater, Vorfahr)

ahn|den (*geh. für* strafen; rächen); **Ahn|dung**

[1]**Ah|ne,** der; -n, -n; ↑R 126 (*geh. Nebenform von* Ahn); [2]**Ah|ne,** die; -, -n (Stammmutter, Vorfahrin)

äh|neln; ich ...[e]le (↑R 16)

ah|nen

Ah|nen‿gal|le|rie, ...kult, ...rei|he, ...ta|fel; Ahn‿frau *(geh. veraltend),* **...herr** *(geh. veraltend)*

ähn|lich; zwei ähnliche Bilder; sich, jmdm. ähnlich sehen; (↑R 47:) das Ähnliche und das Verschiedene; Ähnliches und Verschiedenes; etwas, viel, nichts Ähnliches; oder Ähnliche[s]; *Abk.* o. Ä.; Hüte, Mützen o. Ä., *aber* Hüte, Mützen o. ä. Kopfbedeckungen; ich habe Ähnliches erlebt; es ging um Abgaben und Ähnliches; und Ähnliche[s]; *Abk.* u. Ä.); und dem Ähnliche[s]; *Abk.* u. d. Ä.); **Ähn|lich|keit**

Ah|nung; ah|nungs|los; Ah|nungs|lo|sig|keit, die; -; **ah|nungs|voll**

a|hoi! [aˈhɔy] (*Seemannsspr.* Anruf [eines Schiffes]); Boot ahoi!

A|horn, der; -s, -e (ein Laubbaum)

Ahr, die; - (l. Nebenfluss des Rheins)

Äh|re, die; -, -n; **Äh|ren|le|se; ...äh|rig** (z. B. kurzährig)

A|hu|ra Mas|dah [- ˈmasda] (Gestalt der iran. Religion); *vgl.* Ormuzd

AHV = Alters- und Hinterlassenenversicherung (Schweiz)

Ai, das; -s, -s ⟨indian.⟩ (ein Dreifingerfaultier)

Ai|chin|ger (österr. Schriftstellerin)

A|i|da (Titelgestalt der gleichnamigen Oper von Verdi)

Aide [ɛ(:)d], der; -n, -n (↑R 126) ⟨franz.⟩ (Mitspieler, Partner bes. im Whist); **Aide-mé|moire** [ɛ:dmeˈmo̯a:r], das; -, -[s] (*Politik* Niederschrift von mündl. getroffenen Vereinbarungen)

Aids [e:ds], das; - *meist ohne Artikel* ⟨*aus* engl. acquired immune deficiency syndrome = erworbenes Immunschwächesyndrom⟩ (eine gefährliche Infektionskrankheit); **aids|krank; Aids‿kran|ke, ...test** (*für* HIV-Test)

Aig|ret|te [ɛˈgrɛt(ə)] (↑R 130), die; -, -n ⟨franz.⟩ (Federschmuck; büschelförmiges Gebilde)

Ai|ki|do, das; -[s] ⟨jap.⟩ (jap. Form der Selbstverteidigung)

Ai|nu, der; -[s], -[s] (Ureinwohner der jap. Inseln u. Südsachalins)

[1]**Air** [ɛ:(r)], das; -s, -s *Plur. selten* ⟨franz.⟩ (Aussehen, Haltung; Fluidum); [2]**Air,** das; -s -s (alte Form der Vokal- od. Instrumentalmusik, z. B. in der Suite)

Air|bag [ˈɛ:(r)bɛk], der; -s, -s ⟨engl.⟩ (Luftkissen im Auto, das sich bei einem Aufprall automatisch vor dem Armaturenbrett aufbläst); **Air|bus** [ˈɛ:(r)...] (ein Großraumflugzeug für Kurz- und Mittelstrecken); **Air|con|di|tio|ner** [...kənˌdiʃ(ə)nər], der; -s, -, **Air|con|di|tio|ning** [...kənˌdiʃ(ə)niŋ] (↑R 24), das; -s, -s (Klimaanlage)

Aire|dale|ter|ri|er [ˈɛ:(r)de:lˌtɛri̯ər] ⟨engl.⟩ (eine Hunderasse)

Air France [ɛrˈfrã:s], die; - - (franz. Luftfahrtges.; *Abk.* AF)

Air|port [ˈɛ:(r)...], der; -s, -s ⟨engl.⟩ (Flughafen)

a|is, A|is, das; -, - (Tonbezeichnung)

Ais|chy|los *vgl.* Äschylus

Ai|tel (*südd., österr. für* [1]Döbel [ein Fisch])

A|ja, die; -, -s ⟨ital.⟩ (*veraltet für* Erzieherin [fürstlicher Kinder])

A|ja|tol|lah, der; -[s], -s ⟨pers.⟩ (schiit. Ehrentitel)

A|jax (griech. Sagengestalt)

[1]**à jour** [a ˈʒu:r] ⟨franz., „bis zum [heutigen] Tag"⟩; à jour sein (auf dem Laufenden sein); [2]**à jour** ⟨franz., *zu* jour „Fenster", eigtl. = durchbrochen⟩ (*Bauw.* frei gegen den Raum stehend [von Bauteilen]; durchbrochen [von Geweben]); à jour gefasst (nur am Rande gefasst [von Edelsteinen]); **A|jour|ar|beit; a|jou|rie|ren** (*österr. für* Ajourarbeit machen)

AK = Armeekorps

A|ka|de|mie, die; -, ...ien ⟨griech.⟩ (wissenschaftliche Gesellschaft; [Fach]hochschule; *österr. auch für* literar. od. musik. Veranstaltung); **A|ka|de|mi|ker** (Person mit Hochschulausbildung); **A|ka|de|mi|ke|rin; a|ka|de|misch;** das -e Viertel

A|kan|thit [*auch* ...ˈtit], der; -s ⟨griech.⟩ (ein Mineral); **A|kan|thus,** der; -, - (stachliges Staudengewächs); **A|kan|thus|blatt**

A|ka|ro|id|harz ⟨griech.; dt.⟩ (ein Baumharz)

a|ka|ta|lek|tisch ⟨griech.⟩ (*Verslehre* unverkürzt)

A|ka|tho|lik, der; -en, -en (↑R 126) ⟨griech.⟩ (nicht katholischer Christ); **a|ka|tho|lisch**

A|ka|zie [...i̯ə], die; -, -n ⟨griech.⟩ (trop. Laubbaum od. Strauch)

A|ke|lei, die; -, -en ⟨mlat.⟩ (eine Zier- u. Wiesenpflanze)

A|ki, das; -[s], -[s] (*Kurzw. für* Aktualitätenkino)

Akk. = Akkusativ

Ak|kad (ehemalige Stadt in Babylonien); **ak|ka|disch;** *vgl.* deutsch; **Ak|ka|disch,** das; -[s] (Sprache); *vgl.* Deutsch; **Ak|ka|di|sche,** das; -n; *vgl.* Deutsche, das

Ak|kla|ma|ti|on, die; -, -en ⟨lat.⟩ (*geh. für* Zuruf; Beifall); **ak|kla|mie|ren** *(geh.)*

Ak|kli|ma|ti|sa|ti|on, die; -, -en ⟨lat.⟩ (Anpassung an veränderte Klima-, Umwelt- od. Lebensbedingungen); **ak|kli|ma|ti|sie|ren;** sich -; **Ak|kli|ma|ti|sie|rung** *vgl.* Akklimatisation

Ak|ko|la|de, die; -, -n ⟨franz.⟩ (feierliche Umarmung beim Ritterschlag u. a.; *Druckw.* Klammer ⟺)

ak|kom|mo|da|bel ⟨franz.⟩; ...able (↑R 130; *fachspr. für* anpassungsfähige) Organe; **Ak|kom|mo|da|ti|on,** die; -, -en (*fachspr. für* Anpassung); **Ak|kom|mo|da|ti|ons|fä|hig|keit; ak|kom|mo|die|ren**

Ak|kom|pag|ne|ment [akɔmpanjəˈmã:] (↑R 130), das; -s, -s

⟨franz.⟩ (*Musik* Begleitung); **ak|kom|pa|gnie|ren** [...'nji:...]

Ak|kord, der; -[e]s, -e ⟨lat.⟩ (*Musik* Zusammenklang; *Wirtsch.* Bezahlung nach Stückzahl; Übereinkommen); **Ak|kord_ar|beit, ...ar|bei|ter; Ak|kor|de|on,** das; -s, -s; **Ak|kor|de|o|nist,** der; -en, -en; (↑R 126; Akkordeonspieler); **ak|kor|die|ren** (vereinbaren)

ak|kre|di|tie|ren ⟨*Politik* franz., *Bankw.* ital.⟩ (*Politik* beglaubigen; bevollmächtigen; *Bankw.* Kredit einräumen, verschaffen); jmdn. bei einer Bank für einen Betrag -; **Ak|kre|di|tie|rung; Ak|kre|di|tiv,** das; -s, -e [...və] ⟨franz.⟩ (*Politik* Beglaubigungsschreiben eines Botschafters; *Bankw.* Handelsklausel, Kreditbrief)

Ak|ku, der; -s, -s (*Kurzw. für* Akkumulator); **Ak|ku|hal|ter** *(Kfz-Technik)*

Ak|kul|tu|ra|ti|on, die; -, -en ⟨lat.⟩ (kultureller Anpassungsprozess); **ak|kul|tu|rie|ren**

Ak|ku|mu|lat, das; -[e]s, -e ⟨lat.⟩ (*Geol.* Anhäufung von Gesteinstrümmern); **Ak|ku|mu|la|ti|on,** die; -, -en (Anhäufung); **Ak|ku|mu|la|tor,** der; -s, ...oren (ein Stromspeicher; ein Druckwasserbehälter; *Kurzw.* Akku); **ak|ku|mu|lie|ren** (anhäufen; sammeln, speichern)

ak|ku|rat ⟨lat.⟩ (sorgfältig, ordentlich; *landsch. für* genau); **Ak|ku|ra|tes|se,** die; - ⟨franz.⟩

Ak|ku|sa|tiv, der; -s, -e [...və] ⟨lat.⟩ (*Sprachw.* Wenfall, 4. Fall; *Abk.* Akk.); Akkusativ mit Infinitiv, *lat.* accusativus cum infinitivo [...v... - ...vo] (eine bestimmte grammatische Konstruktion; *Abk.* acc. c. inf. *od.* a. c. i.); **Ak|ku|sa|tiv|ob|jekt**

Ak|me, die; - ⟨griech.⟩ (*Med.* Höhepunkt [einer Krankheit])

Ak|ne, die; -, -n ⟨griech.⟩ (*Med.* Hautausschlag)

A|ko|luth (*selten für* Akolyth); **A|ko|lyth,** der; *Gen.* -en (↑R 126) *u.* -s, *Plur.* -en ⟨griech.⟩ (Laie, der während der Messe bestimmte Dienste am Altar verrichtet; *früher* kath. Kleriker im 4. Grad der niederen Weihen)

A|kon|to, das; -s, *Plur.* ...ten *u.* -s ⟨ital.⟩ (*österr. für* Anzahlung); **A|kon|to|zah|lung** (*Bankw.* Abschlagszahlung); *vgl.* a conto

AKP = Afrika, Karibik und pazifischer Raum; **AKP-Staa|ten** [a:ka:'pe:...] *Plur.* (mit den EU-Staaten assoziierte Entwicklungsländer aus Afrika, der Karibik und dem Pazifik)

ak|qui|rie|ren [akvi...] ⟨lat.⟩ (als Akquisiteur tätig sein; *veraltet für* erwerben); **Ak|qui|si|teur** [...'tø:r], der; -s, -e ⟨franz.⟩ (Kunden-, Anzeigenwerber); **Ak|qui|si|teu|rin** [...'tø:rin]; **Ak|qui|si|ti|on,** die; -, -en (Anschaffung; *Wirtsch.* Kundenwerbung); **Ak|qui|si|tor,** der; -s, ...oren (*österr. für* Akquisiteur); **ak|qui|si|to|risch**

Ak|ri|bie (↑R 130), die; - ⟨griech.⟩ (höchste Genauigkeit; Sorgfalt); **ak|ri|bisch**

Ak|ro|bat (↑R 130), der; -en, -en (↑R 126) ⟨griech.⟩; **Ak|ro|ba|tik,** die; - (große körperliche Gewandtheit, Körperbeherrschung); **Ak|ro|ba|tin; ak|ro|ba|tisch**

Ak|ro|le|in (↑R 130), das; -s ⟨griech.; lat.⟩ (eine chem. Verbindung)

Ak|ro|nym (↑R 130), das; -s, -e (aus den Anfangsbuchstaben mehrerer Wörter gebildetes Wort, z. B. „Aids“); **Ak|ro|po|lis,** die; -, ...polen (altgriech. Stadtburg [von Athen]); **Ak|ros|ti|chon** [...ç...], das; -s, *Plur.* ...chen *u.*...cha (die Anfangsbuchstaben, -silben oder -wörter der Verszeilen eines Gedichtes, die ein Wort oder einen Satz ergeben); **Ak|ro|ter,** der; -s, -e *u.* **Ak|ro|te|ri|on,** das; -s, ...ien [...iən] (*Archit.* Giebelverzierung); **Ak|ro|ze|pha|le,** der *u.* die; -n, -n; (↑R 126; *Med.* Hoch-, Spitzkopf); **Ak|ro|ze|pha|lie,** die; -, ...ien *(Med.)*

Ak|ryl (↑R 130) *vgl.* Acryl

äks! (*ugs. für* pfui!)

Akt, der; -[e]s, -e ⟨lat.⟩ (Abschnitt, Aufzug eines Theaterstückes; Handlung, Vorgang; künstler. Darstellung des nackten Körpers); *vgl.* Akte

Ak|tant, der; -en, -en (↑R 126) ⟨franz.⟩ (*Sprachw.* abhängiges Satzglied)

Ak|te, die; -, -n, *auch* Akt, der; -[e]s, *Plur.* -e, *österr.* -en ⟨lat.⟩; zu den -n (erledigt; *Abk.* z. d. A.); **Ak|tei** (Aktensammlung); **ak|ten|kun|dig; Ak|ten|la|ge;** nach - *(Amtsspr.);* **Ak|ten_schrank, ...ta|sche, ...zei|chen** (*Abk.* AZ *od.* Az.); **Ak|teur** [ak'tø:r], der; -s, -e ⟨franz.⟩ (Handelnder; [Schau]spieler); **Ak|teu|rin** [...'tø:rin]; **Ak|tie** [...iə], die; -, -n ⟨niederl.⟩ (Anteil[schein]); **Ak|ti|en_ge|sell|schaft** (*Abk.* AG), **...in|ha|ber** (*svw.* Aktionär), **...ka|pi|tal, ...pa|ket**

Ak|ti|nie [...iə], die; -, -n ⟨griech.⟩ (*Zool.* eine sechsstrahlige Koralle); **ak|ti|nisch** (*Physik* radioaktiv; *Med.* durch Strahlung hervorgerufen, z. B. von Krankheiten); **Ak|ti|ni|um** *vgl.* Actinium; **Ak|ti|no|me|ter,** das; -s, - (*Meteor.* Strahlungsmesser); **ak|ti|no|morph** (*Biol.* strahlenförmig)

Ak|ti|on, die; -, -en ⟨lat.⟩ (Unternehmung; Handlung; *schweiz. auch für* Sonderangebot); eine konzertierte -

Ak|ti|o|när, der; -s, -e ⟨franz.⟩ (Besitzer von Aktien); **Ak|ti|o|nä|rin; Ak|ti|o|närs|ver|samm|lung**

Ak|ti|o|nis|mus, der; - ⟨lat.⟩ (Bestreben, das Bewusstsein der Menschen od. bestehende Zustände durch [provozierende, künstlerische] Aktionen zu verändern; übertriebener Tätigkeitsdrang); **Ak|ti|o|nist,** der; -en, -en (↑R 126; Verfechter des Aktionismus); **ak|ti|o|nis|tisch**

Ak|ti|ons_art (*Sprachw.* Geschehensweise beim Verb, z. B. perfektiv: „verblühen“), **...ko|mi|tee, ...preis, ...ra|di|us** (Wirkungsbereich, Reichweite; Fahr-, Flugbereich), **...tag, ...wo|che**

Ak|ti|um (griech. Landzunge)

ak|tiv [*auch* 'ak...] ⟨lat.⟩ (tätig; wirksam; im Dienst stehend; *seltener für* aktivisch); aktive [...və] Bestechung; aktive Bilanz; aktives Wahlrecht; **[1]Ak|tiv,** das; -s, -e [...və] *Plur. selten* (*Sprachw.* Tatform, Tätigkeitsform); **[2]Ak|tiv,** das; -s, *Plur.* -s, *seltener* -e [...və] (*regional für* Gruppe von Personen, die gemeinsam an der Lösung bestimmter Aufgaben arbeiten); **Ak|ti|va** [...va], Ak|ti|ven [...vən] *Plur.* (Summe der Vermögenswerte eines Unternehmens); **Ak|tiv|bür|ger** (*schweiz. für* Bürger im Besitz des Stimm- u. Wahlrechts); **Ak|ti|ven** *vgl.* Aktiva; **Ak|tiv|for|de|rung** (*Kaufmannsspr.* ausstehende Forderung); **ak|ti|vie|ren** [...v...] (in Tätigkeit setzen; [die Wirkung] verstärken; Vermögensteile in die Bilanz einsetzen); **ak|ti|visch** ⟨lat.⟩ (*Sprachw.* das Aktiv betreffend, in der Tatform stehend); **Ak|ti|vis|mus,** der; - (Tätigkeitsdrang; zielstrebiges Handeln); **Ak|ti|vist,** der; -en, -en; (↑R 126; zielbewusst Handelnder; *ehemals in der DDR* jmd., der für vorbildliche Leistungen ausgezeichnet wurde); **ak|ti|vis|tisch; Ak|ti|vi|tas,** die; -, (*Studentenspr.* Gesamtheit der zur aktiven Beteiligung in einer studentischen Verbindung Verpflichteten); **Ak|ti|vi|tät,** die; -, -en (Tätigkeit[sdrang]; Wirksamkeit); **Ak|tiv_koh|le** (staubfeiner, poröser Kohlenstoff), **...le|gi|ti|ma|ti|on** (*Rechtsspr.* im Zivilprozess die Rechtszuständigkeit auf der Klägerseite); **Ak|tiv-_pos|ten, ...sal|do** (Einnahmeüberschuss), **...ver|mö|gen** (wirkliches Vermögen)

Ak|tri|ce [ak'tri:sə], die; -, -n ‹franz.› (*veraltend für* Schauspielerin)

ak|tu|a|li|sie|ren ‹lat.› (aktuell machen); **Ak|tu|a|li|sie|rung; Ak|tu|a|li|tät,** die; -, -en (Gegenwartsbezogenheit; Bedeutsamkeit für die unmittelbare Gegenwart); **Ak|tu|a|li|tä|ten|ki|no** (*Kurzw.* Aki)

Ak|tu|ar, der; -s, -e (*veraltet für* Gerichtsschreiber; *schweiz. auch für* Schriftführer)

ak|tu|ell ‹franz.› (im augenblickl. Interesse liegend, zeitgemäß)

A|ku|pres|sur, die; -, -en ‹lat.› (Heilbehandlung durch leichten Druck und kreisende Bewegung der Fingerkuppen); **a|ku|punk|tie|ren; A|ku|punk|tur,** die; -, -en (Heilbehandlung durch Einstechen von Nadeln an bestimmten Körperpunkten)

A|kü|spra|che, die; -, -n *Plur. selten* (*kurz für* Abkürzungssprache)

A|kus|tik, die; - ‹griech.› (Lehre vom Schall, von den Tönen; Klangwirkung); **a|kus|tisch**

a|kut ‹lat.›; -es (dringendes) Problem; -e (unvermittelt auftretende, heftig verlaufende) Krankheit; **A|kut,** der; -[e]s, -e (*Phon.* ein Betonungszeichen: ´, z. B. é); **A|kut-kran|ken|haus** (für intensive u. möglichst kurze Behandlung)

AKW = Atomkraftwerk; **AKW-Geg|ner** (↑R 26)

Ak|ze|le|ra|ti|on, die; -, -en ‹lat.› (*Physik* Beschleunigung); **Ak|ze|le|ra|tor,** der; -s, ...oren (Beschleuniger); **ak|ze|le|rie|ren**

Ak|zent, der; -[e]s, -e ‹lat.› (Betonung[szeichen]; Tonfall, Aussprache; Nachdruck); **Ak|zent|buch|sta|be; ak|zent_frei, ...los; Ak|zen|tu|a|ti|on,** die; -, -en (Betonung); **ak|zen|tu|ie|ren; Ak|zen|tu|ie|rung; Ak|zent|wech|sel**

Ak|zept, das; -[e]s, -e ‹lat.› (*Bankw.* Annahmeerklärung des Bezogenen auf einem Wechsel; der akzeptierte Wechsel selbst); **ak|zep|ta|bel** (annehmbar); ...able (↑R 130) Bedingungen; **Ak|zep|ta|bi|li|tät,** die; -; **Ak|zep|tant,** der; -en, -en; (↑R 126; *Bankw.* der zur Bezahlung des Wechsels Verpflichtete; Bezogener); **Ak|zep|tanz,** die; - (*bes. Werbespr.* Bereitschaft, etwas [ein Produkt] anzunehmen); **Ak|zep|ta|ti|on,** die; -, -en (Annahme); **ak|zep|tie|ren** (annehmen); **Ak|zep|tie|rung; Ak|zep|tor,** der; -s, ...oren (*Bankw.* Empfänger)

Ak|zes|si|on, die; -, -en ‹lat.› (Zugang; Erwerb; Beitritt [zu einem Staatsvertrag]); **Ak|zes|so|ri|e|tät** [...i|e...], die; -, -en (*Rechtsw.* Abhängigkeit des Nebenrechtes von dem zugehörigen Hauptrecht); **ak|zes|so|risch** (hinzutretend; nebensächlich)

Ak|zi|dens, das; -, *Plur.* ...denzien [...i̯ən] *u.* ...dentia ‹lat.› (das Zufällige, was einer Sache nicht wesenhaft zukommt); **ak|zi|den|tell, ak|zi|den|ti|ell** (zufällig; unwesentlich); **Ak|zi|denz,** die; -, -en *meist Plur.* (Druckarbeit, die nicht zum Buch-, Zeitungs- u. Zeitschriftendruck gehört [z. B. Formulare]); **Ak|zi|denz_druck** (*Plur.* ...drucke), **...set|zer**

Ak|zi|se, die; -, -n ‹franz.› (*früher für* Verbrauchssteuer; Zoll)

Al = *chem. Zeichen für* Aluminium

AL = Alternative Liste

Al. = Alinea

a. l. = ad libitum

ä. L. = ältere[r] Linie *(Genealogie)*

à la ‹franz.› (im Stil, nach Art von)

Ala. = Alabama

al|laaf! (Karnevalsruf); Kölle -!

à la baisse [ala'bɛ:s] ‹franz.› (*Börsenw.* auf Fallen der Kurse [spekulieren])

A|la|ba|ma (Staat in den USA; *Abk.* Ala.)

A|la|bas|ter, der; -s, - *Plur. selten* ‹griech.› (eine Gipsart); **a|la|bas|tern** (aus od. wie Alabaster)

à la bonne heure! [alabɔ'nœ:r] ‹franz.› (so ist es recht!)

à la carte [ala'kart] ‹franz.› (nach der Speisekarte)

A|la|din (m. Eigenn.; Gestalt aus „1001 Nacht")

à la hausse [ala'o:s] ‹franz.› (*Börsenw.* auf Steigen der Kurse [spekulieren])

à la longue [ala'lɔ̃:g] (auf längere Zeit)

à la mode [ala'mɔd] ‹franz.› (nach der neuesten Mode); **A|la|mo|de-_li|te|ra|tur** (die; -), **...zeit** (die; -)

A|land, der; -[e]s, -e (ein Fisch)

Å|land|in|seln ['o:lant...] *Plur.* (finn. Inselgruppe in der Ostsee)

A|la|ne, der; -n, -n (↑R 126; Angehöriger eines alten, urspr. iran. Nomadenvolkes)

A|lant, der; -[e]s, -e (eine Heilpflanze)

A|la|rich (König der Westgoten)

A|larm, der; -[e]s, -e ‹ital.› (Notsignal; Warnung bei Gefahr); **A|larm|an|la|ge; a|larm|be|reit; A|larm_be|reit|schaft, ...ge|rät; a|lar|mie|ren** (zu Hilfe rufen; warnen; aufschrecken); **A|larm-_sig|nal, ...stu|fe, ...zu|stand**

Alas. = Alaska

A|las|ka (nordamerik. Halbinsel; Staat der USA; *Abk.* Alas.)

à la sui|te [a la 'svi:t(ə)] ‹franz.› (*Milit. veraltet* im Gefolge [von])

A|laun, der; -s, -e ‹lat.› (*Chemie* ein Salz); **a|lau|ni|sie|ren** (mit Alaun behandeln); **A|laun|stein**

a-Laut (↑R 25)

¹Alb, der; -[e]s, -en *meist Plur.* (unterird. Naturgeist; *auch für* gespenstisches Wesen; Albdrücken); *vgl. aber* ²Alp

²Alb, die; - (Gebirge); Schwäbische, Fränkische Alb (↑R 102)

Al|ban, Al|ba|nus (m. Vorn.)

Al|ba|ner; Al|ba|ne|rin; Al|ba|ni|en [...i̯ən] (Balkanstaat); **al|ba|nisch** *vgl.* deutsch; **Al|ba|nisch,** das; -[s] (Sprache); *vgl.* Deutsch; **Al|ba|ni|sche,** das; -n; *vgl.* Deutsche, das

Al|ba|nus *vgl.* Alban

Al|bat|ros (↑R 130), der; -, -se ‹angloind.-niederl.› (ein Sturmvogel)

Alb|druck, *auch* Alp|druck, der; -[e]s, ...drücke, **Alb|drü|cken,** *auch* Alp|drü|cken, das; -s

Al|be, die; -, -n ‹lat.› (weißes liturg. Gewand)

Al|be|rei

Al|be|rich (den Nibelungenhort bewachender Zwerg)

¹al|bern; ich ...ere (↑R 16); **²al|bern; Al|bern|heit**

Al|bert (m. Vorn.); **¹Al|ber|ta** [*auch* engl. ɛl'bœ:(r)tə] (kanad. Provinz); **²Al|ber|ta** [al'bɛrta], Al|ber|ti|ne (w. Vorn.); **Al|ber|ti|na,** die; - (Sammlung grafischer Kunst in Wien); **al|ber|ti|ni|sche Li|nie,** die; -n - (sächsische Linie der Wettiner); **Al|ber|ti|num,** das; -s (Museum in Dresden)

Al|bi|gen|ser, der; -s, - (Angehöriger einer mittelalterl. häretischen Gruppe in Südfrankreich)

Al|bin, Al|bi|nus (m. Vorn.)

Al|bi|nis|mus, der; - ‹lat.› (Unfähigkeit, Farbstoffe in Haut, Haaren u. Augen zu bilden); **Al|bi|no,** der; -s, -s ‹span.› (Mensch, Tier od. Pflanze mit fehlender Farbstoffbildung); **al|bi|no|tisch**

Al|bi|nus *vgl.* Albin

Al|bi|on ‹kelt.-lat.› (*alter dichterischer Name für* England)

Al|bo|in, Al|bu|in (langobard. König)

Alb|recht (↑R 132; m. Vorn.)

Alb|traum, *auch* Alp|traum
Al|bu|in *vgl.* Alboin
Al|bu|la, die; - (Fluss in der Schweiz); **Al|bu|la|pass,** der; -es
Al|bum, das; -s, ...ben ‹lat.› (Gedenk-, Sammelbuch); **Al|bu|men,** das; -s (*Med., Biol.* Eiweiß); **Al|bu|min,** das; -s, -e *meist Plur.* (ein Eiweißstoff); **al|bu|mi|nös** (eiweißhaltig); **Al|bu|min|u|rie,** die; -, ...ien ‹lat.; griech.› (*Med.* Ausscheidung von Eiweiß im Harn);
Al|bus, der; -, -se (Weißpfennig, alte dt. Münze)
al|cä|isch [...ts...] *vgl.* alkäisch
Al|can|ta|ra ®, das; -[s] ‹Kunstwort› (Veloursledermimitat)
Al|cä|us [...ts...] *vgl.* Alkäus
Al|ces|te [...ts...] *vgl.* Alkeste
Al|che|mie, die; - ‹arab.› (Chemie des MA.s; vermeintl. Goldmacherkunst; Schwarzkunst); **Al|che|mist,** der; -en, -en; (↑R 126; die Alchemie Ausübender); **al|che|mis|tisch**
Äl|chen (kleiner Aal; *Zool.* Fadenwurm)
Al|chi|mie usw. *vgl.* Alchemie usw.
Al|ci|bi|a|des [...ts...] *vgl.* Alkibiades
Al|cy|o|ne [...ts... *od.* al'tsy:one:] usw. *vgl.* Alkyone usw.
Al|de|ba|ran [*auch* ...'ba:...], der; -s ‹arab.› (ein Stern)
Al|de|hyd, der; -s, -e (*Chemie* eine organ. Verbindung)
Al|der|man ['ɔ:ldə(r)mən], der; -s, ...men ‹engl.› (Ratsherr, Vorsteher in angels. Ländern)
[1]**Al|di|ne,** die; -, -n (Druckwerk des venezian. Druckers Aldus Manutius); [2]**Al|di|ne,** die; - (*Druckw.* halbfette Antiqua)
Ale [e:l], das; -s ‹engl.› (engl. Bier)
a|lea iac|ta est [- 'jakta -] ‹lat., „der Würfel ist geworfen"› (die Entscheidung ist gefallen)
A|le|a|to|rik, die; - ‹lat.› (*Musik* moderner Kompositionsstil, bei dem der Gestaltung des Musikstücks durch den Interpreten ein breiter Spielraum gelassen wird); **a|le|a|to|risch** (vom Zufall abhängig)
A|lek|to (eine der drei Erinnyen)
A|le|man|ne, der; -n, -n (↑R 126; Angehöriger eines germ. Volksstammes); **a|le|man|nisch** *vgl.* deutsch; **A|le|man|nisch,** das; -[s] (dt. Mundart); *vgl.* Deutsch; **A|le|man|ni|sche,** das; -n; *vgl.* Deutsche, das
A|lep|po|kie|fer ‹nach der syr. Stadt Aleppo› (Kiefernart des Mittelmeerraumes)
a|lert ‹ital.› (*landsch. für* munter, flink)
A|leu|ron [*od.* 'a(:)lɔy...], das; -s ‹griech.› (*Biol.* Reserveeiweiß der Pflanzen)
A|le|u|ten [ale'u...] *Plur.* (Inseln zwischen Beringmeer und Pazifischem Ozean)
A|lex (m. Vorn.); **A|le|xan|der** (↑R 132; m. Vorn.); **A|le|xan|der Lu|cas,** die; - -, - - (eine Birnensorte); **A|le|xan|dra** (↑R 130 *u.* 132; w. Vorn.); **A|le|xan|dria** [*auch* ...'dri:a], **A|le|xan|dri|en** [...iən] (ägypt. Stadt); **A|le|xand|ri|ne** (w. Vorn.); **A|le|xand|ri|ner** (Bewohner von Alexandria [↑R 103]; ein Versmaß); **a|le|xand|ri|nisch**
A|le|xi|a|ner, der; -s, - ‹griech.› (Angehöriger einer Laienbruderschaft)
A|le|xie, die; - ‹griech.› (*Med.* Leseunfähigkeit bei erhaltenem Sehvermögen)
A|le|xin, das; -s, -e *meist Plur.* ‹griech.› (*Biochemie* ein Abwehrstoff gegen Bakterien)
Al|fa|gras ‹arab.; dt.› (Grasart, die als Rohstoff zur Papierfabrikation verwendet wird)
Al|fons (m. Vorn.)
Alf|red (↑R 132; m. Vorn.)
al fres|co (*häufig für* a fresco)
Alf|ried (↑R 132; m. Vorn.)
Al|gar|ve [...və], die u. der; - (südlichste Provinz Portugals)
Al|ge, die; -, -n ‹lat.› (eine blütenlose Wasserpflanze)
Al|geb|ra [*österr.* al'ge:...] (↑R 130), die; -, *Plur.* (*für* algebraische Strukturen:) ...ebren ‹arab.› (Lehre von den math. Gleichungen); **al|geb|ra|isch;** algebraische Gleichungen
Al|ge|nib, der; -s ‹arab.› (ein Stern)
Al|ge|ri|en (Staat in Nordafrika); **Al|ge|ri|er; Al|ge|ri|e|rin; al|ge|risch; Al|gier** ['alʒi:r, *schweiz.* 'algi:r] (Hptst. Algeriens)
Al|gol [*auch* 'al...], der; -s ‹arab.› (ein Stern)
ALGOL, das; -[s] ‹Kunstwort aus engl. **al**gorithmic **l**anguage› (eine Programmiersprache)
Al|go|lo|ge, der; -n, -n (↑R 126) ‹lat.; griech.› (Algenforscher); **Al|go|lo|gie,** die; - (Algenkunde)
Al|gon|kin, das; -[s] (eine indian. Sprachfamilie in Nordamerika); **Al|gon|ki|um,** das; -s (*ältere Bez. für* Proterozoikum)
al|go|rith|misch ‹arab.› (*Math.*); **Al|go|rith|mus,** der; -, ...men (nach einem bestimmten Schema ablaufender Rechenvorgang)
Al|gra|phie, die; -, ...ien; (↑R 33) ‹lat.; griech.› (Flachdruckverfahren u. danach hergestelltes Kunstblatt)
Al|hamb|ra (↑R 130), die; - ‹arab.› (Palast bei Granada)
A|li [*auch* 'ali, a'li:] (m. Vorn.)
a|li|as ‹lat.› (anders; sonst, auch ... genannt [z. B. Meyer alias Neumann]); **A|li|bi,** das; -s, -s ([Nachweis der] Abwesenheit [vom Tatort des Verbrechens]; Ausrede, Rechtfertigung); **A|li|bi‿be|weis, ...frau** (*abwertend* Frau, die in einer Firma, einem Gremium o. Ä. [in gehobener Position] arbeitet und als Beweis für die Verwirklichung der Chancengleichheit herhalten muss)
A|li|ce [a'li:sə, *österr.* a'li:s] (w. Vorn.)
A|li|e|na|ti|on [ali̯e...], die; -, -en ‹lat.› (*veraltet für* Entfremdung; Verkauf); **a|li|e|nie|ren** (*veraltet für* entfremden; verkaufen)
A|lig|ne|ment [alinjə'mã:] (↑R 130), das; -s, -s ‹franz.› ([Abstecken einer] Richtlinie); **a|lig|nie|ren** [ali'nji:...]
A|li|men|ta|ti|on, die; -, -en ‹lat.› (Lebensunterhalt); **A|li|men|te** *Plur.* (Unterhaltsbeiträge, bes. für nichteheliche Kinder); **a|li|men|tie|ren** (mit Geldmitteln unterstützen, unterhalten)
A|li|nea, das; -s, -s ‹lat.› (*veraltet für* [mit Absatz beginnende] neue Druckzeile; *Abk.* Al.)
a|li|pha|tisch ‹griech.› (*Chemie*); -e Verbindungen (Verbindungen mit offenen Kohlenstoffketten in der Strukturformel)
a|li|quant ‹lat.› (*Math.* mit Rest teilend); **a|li|quot** [*od.* ...'kvɔ:t] (*Math.* ohne Rest teilend)
Al|ita|lia (↑R 132), die; - ‹ital.› (italien. Luftfahrtgesellschaft)
A|li|za|rin, das; -s ‹arab.› (ein [Pflanzen]farbstoff)
Alk, der; *Gen.* -[e]s *od.* -en, *Plur.* -e[n] (↑R 126) ‹nord.› (ein arkt. Meeresvogel)
Al|kai|os *vgl.* Alkäus; **al|kä|isch** (nach Alkäus benannt)
Al|kal|de, der; -n, -n (↑R 126) ‹span.› (span. Bürgermeister, Dorfrichter)
Al|ka|li [*auch* 'al...], das; -s, ...alien [...iən] *meist Plur.* ‹arab.› (*Chemie* eine stark basische Verbindung); **Al|ka|li|me|tal|le** *Plur.* (Gruppe einwertiger Basen bildender Metalle); **al|ka|lisch** (basisch; laugenhaft); **Al|ka|lo|id,** das; -[e]s, -e ‹arab.; griech.› (eine in Pflanzen vorkommende giftige Stickstoffverbindung)
Al|kä|us (griech. Dichter)
Al|ka|zar [...zar *od.* ...(t)sar, *österr.*

...'za(:)r], der; -s, ...zare ‹arab.-span.› (Burg, Schloss, Palast [in Spanien])

Al|ke, Alk|je (w. Vorn.)

Al|kes|te (w. Gestalt der griech. Mythol.)

Al|ki|bi|a|des (griech. Staatsmann)

Alk|je, Al|ke (w. Vorn.)

Alk|man [*auch* 'alk...] (griech. Dichter); **alk|ma|nisch;** -er Vers

Alk|me|ne (Gattin des Amphitryon, Mutter des Herakles)

Al|ko|hol [*auch* ...'ho:l], der; -s, -e ‹arab.› (eine organ. Verbindung; Äthylalkohol, Bestandteil der alkohol. Getränke); **al|ko|hol‿ab|hän|gig, ...arm, ...frei; Al|ko|ho|li|ka** *Plur.* (alkohol. Getränke); **Al|ko|ho|li|ker; Al|ko|ho|li|ke|rin; al|ko|ho|lisch;** -e Getränke; **al|ko|ho|li|sie|ren** (mit Alkohol versetzen; *scherzh. für* unter Alkohol setzen); **al|ko|ho|li|siert** (betrunken); **Al|ko|ho|li|sie|rung; Al|ko|ho|lis|mus,** der; -; **al|ko|hol|krank; Al|ko|hol‿miss|brauch** (der; -[e]s), **...spie|gel, ...sün|der, ...ver|gif|tung**

Al|kor [*od.* 'al...], der; -s ‹arab.› (ein Stern)

Al|ko|ven [...vən, *auch* 'al...], der; -s, - ‹arab.› (Nebenraum; Bettnische)

Al|ku|in (angels. Gelehrter)

Al|kyl, das; -s, -e ‹arab.; griech.› (*Chemie* einwertiger Kohlenwasserstoffrest); **al|ky|lie|ren** (eine Alkylgruppe einführen)

¹Al|ky|o|ne [*od.* al'ky:one:] (Tochter des Äolus); **²Al|ky|o|ne,** die; - (ein Stern); **al|ky|o|nisch** (*geh. für* friedlich, windstill)

all; alle, alles; all der Schmerz; mit all[er] seiner Habe; all das Schöne; in, vor, bei allem; bei, in, mit, nach, trotz, von, zu allem dem *od.* all[e]dem, all[em] diesem; dem allen (*häufiger für* dem allem), diesem allen (*auch* diesem allem); unter allem Guten; aller erwiesene Respekt; allen Übels (*meist für* alles Übels); etwas allen Ernstes behaupten; das Bild allen (*auch* alles) geistigen Lebens; trotz aller vorherigen Planung; aller guten Dinge sind drei; diese alle; all[e] diese; alle beide; alle, die geladen waren; sie kamen alle; sie alle (*als Anrede* Sie alle); er opferte sich für alle; ich grüße euch alle; alle ehrlichen Menschen; all[e] die Fehler; bei, mit all[e] diesem; alle neun[e] (beim Kegeln); alle (*landsch.* aller) nase[n]lang, naslang *(ugs.);* alle Anwesenden; alle (*ugs. für* zu Ende, aufgebraucht) sein, werden; alles und jedes; alles oder nichts; das, dies[es], was, wer alles; all[es] das, dies[es]; alles, was; für, um alles; alles in allem; alles andere; *aber* mein Ein und [mein] Alles; (↑R 47:) alles Gute, die Summe alles Guten; (*vgl.* beliebig, möglich, übrig); *Zusammenschreibung:* allemal *(vgl. d.), aber* ein für alle Mal[e]; all[e]zeit; allesamt; allenfalls; allenthalben; allerart *(vgl. d.);* allerdings; allerhand *(vgl. d.);* allerlei *(vgl. d.);* allerorten, allerorts; all[er]seits; allerwärts; alle[r]wege *(vgl. d.);* alltags *(vgl. d.);* allwöchentlich; allzu *(vgl. d.)*

All, das; -s (Weltall)

all|abend|lich (↑R 132); **all|abends** (↑R 132; *geh.*)

al|la bre|ve [- ...və] ‹ital.› (*Musik* im $^1/_2$- statt $^1/_4$-Takt); **Al|la-bre|ve-Takt** (↑R 28)

Al|lah ‹arab.› (*bes. islam. Rel.* Gott)

al|la mar|cia [- 'martʃa] ‹ital.› (*Musik* marschmäßig)

al|la po|lac|ca [- po'laka] ‹ital.› (*Musik* in der Art der Polonaise)

Al|lasch, der; -[e]s, -e (ein Kümmellikör)

al|la te|des|ca ‹ital.› (*Musik* in der Art eines deutschen Tanzes)

al|la tur|ca ‹ital.› (*Musik* in der Art der türkischen Musik)

al|la zin|ga|re|se [- ts...] ‹ital.› (*Musik* in der Art der Zigeunermusik)

all|be|kannt

all|da *(veraltend)*

all|dem, al|le|dem; bei all[e]dem; *aber* sie sagte nichts von all dem, was sie wusste

all|die|weil, die|weil *(veraltet)*

al|le *vgl.* all

al|le|dem, all|dem; bei all[e]dem

Al|lee, die; -, Alleen ‹franz.› (von hohen Bäumen dicht gesäumte Straße); *Schreibung in Straßennamen:* ↑R 123

Al|le|ghe|nies ['ɛligɛnis *od.* ...niz] *Plur.* (*svw.* Alleghenygebirge); **Al|le|ghe|ny|ge|bir|ge** ['ɛligɛni...], das; -s (nordamerik. Gebirge)

Al|le|go|rie, die; -, ...ien ‹griech.› (Sinnbild; Gleichnis); **al|le|go|risch; al|le|go|ri|sie|ren** (versinnbildlichen)

al|leg|ret|to (↑R 130) ‹ital.› (*Musik* mäßig schnell, mäßig lebhaft); **Al|leg|ret|to,** das; -s, *Plur.* -s *u.* ...tti; **al|leg|ro** (*Musik* lebhaft); **Al|leg|ro,** das; -s, *Plur.* -s *u.* ...gri

al|lein; allein sein, stehen, bleiben, erziehen; jmdn. allein lassen; von allein[e] *(ugs.);* ich stehe allein; allein gestanden; eine allein erziehende Mutter; die allein selig machende Kirche *(bes. kath. Kirche);* eine allein stehende Frau; die allein Erziehenden, *auch* Alleinerziehenden; die allein Stehenden, *auch* Alleinstehenden; **al|lei|ne** (*ugs. für* allein); **Al|lein|er|be; al|lein er|zie|hend** *vgl.* allein; **Al|lein|er|zie|hen|de,** der *u.* die; -n, -n (↑R 5 ff.); *vgl.* allein; **Al|lein‿flug, ...gang** (der), **...gän|ger**

All|ein|heit, die; - *(Philos.)*

Al|lein‿herr|schaft, ...herr|scher; al|lei|nig; Al|lein|in|ha|ber; Al|lein|sein, das; -s; **al|lein se|lig ma|chend** *vgl.* allein; **al|lein ste|hen** *vgl.* allein; **al|lein ste|hend** *vgl.* allein; **Al|lein|ste|hen|de,** der *u.* die; -n, -n (↑R 5 ff.); *vgl.* allein; **Al|lein‿un|ter|hal|ter, ...ver|die|ner, ...ver|tre|tung, ...ver|trieb**

al|lel ‹griech.› *(Biol.);* -e Gene; **Al|lel,** das; -s, -e *meist Plur.* (eines von zwei einander entsprechenden Genen in homologen Chromosomen)

al|le|lu|ja! usw. *vgl.* halleluja! usw.

al|le|mal (*ugs. für* natürlich, in jedem Fall); das kann sie allemal besser; *aber:* ein für alle Mal, ein für alle Male

Al|le|man|de [al(ə)'mã:də], die; -, -n ‹franz.› (alter dt. Tanz)

al|len|falls; *vgl.* Fall, der; **al|lent|hal|ben**

Al|ler, die; - (Nebenfluss der Weser)

al|ler|al|ler|letz|te

al|ler|art (allerlei); allerart Dinge, *aber* Dinge aller Art

Al|ler|bar|mer, der; -s (Christus)

al|ler|bes|te; das kann sie am allerbesten; *aber* (↑R 47:) es ist das Allerbeste, dass ...

al|ler|christ|lichs|te; Al|ler|christ|lichs|te Ma|jes|tät, die; -n - (*früher* Titel der franz. Könige)

al|ler|dings

al|ler|durch|lauch|tigs|te; Al|ler|durch|lauch|tigs|ter ... (*früher* Anrede an einen Kaiser)

al|ler|en|den (*veraltend* überall)

al|ler|ers|te

al|ler|frü|hes|tens

Al|ler|gen (↑R 132), das; -s, -e *meist Plur.* ‹griech.› (*Med.* Stoff, der eine Allergie hervorrufen kann); **Al|ler|gie,** die; -, ...ien (Überempfindlichkeit); **al|ler|gie|ge|tes|tet; Al|ler|gi|ker; al|ler|gisch; Al|ler|go|lo|ge,** der; -n, -n (↑R126; Wissenschaftler auf dem Gebiet der Allergologie); **Al|ler|go|lo|gie,** die; - (wissenschaftliche Erforschung der Allergien); **Al|ler|go|lo|gin; al|ler|go|lo|gisch**

al|ler|hand *(ugs.);* allerhand Neues (↑R 47); allerhand Streiche; er weiß allerhand (viel); das ist ja allerhand

Al|ler|hei|li|gen, das; - (kath. Fest zu Ehren aller Heiligen); **Al|ler|hei|li|gen|fest; al|ler|hei|ligs|te;** die -n Güter; **Al|ler|hei|ligs|te,** das; -n (↑R 5 ff.)

al|ler|höchs|te; allerhöchstens; auf das, aufs Allerhöchste, *auch* auf das, aufs allerhöchste (↑R 47)

Al|ler|ka|tho|lischs|te Ma|jes|tät, die; -n - (Titel der span. Könige)

al|ler|lei; allerlei Wichtiges (↑R 47); **Al|ler|lei,** das; -s, -s; Leipziger Allerlei (Mischgemüse)

al|ler|letz|te; *vgl.* letzte

al|ler|liebst; Al|ler|liebs|te, der *u.* die; -n, -n (↑R 5 ff.)

Al|ler|manns|har|nisch (Pflanze)

al|ler|meis|te; *vgl.* zuallermeist

al|ler|nächs|te; al|ler|neu|es|te, al|ler|neus|te; (↑R 47:) das Allerneu[e]ste

al|ler|nö|tigs|te; (↑R 47:) das Allernötigste

al|ler|or|ten *(veraltend),* **al|ler|orts** *(geh.)*

Al|ler|see|len, das; - (kath. Gedächtnistag für die Verstorbenen); **Al|ler|see|len|tag**

al|ler|seits, all|seits

al|ler|spä|tes|te; al|ler|spä|tes|tens

al|ler|wärts

al|le[r]|we|ge, al|ler|we|gen, al|ler|wegs (*veraltet für* überall, immer)

al|ler|weil *vgl.* allweil

Al|ler|welts‿kerl, ...mit|tel (das), **...wort** (*Plur.* ...wörter)

al|ler|we|nigs|te; (↑R 48:) das allerwenigste, was ...; am allerwenigsten; allerwenigstens

Al|ler|wer|tes|te, der; -n, -n; ↑R 5 ff. (*ugs. scherzh. für* Gesäß)

al|les *vgl.* all

al|le|samt *(ugs.)*

Al|les‿bes|ser|wis|ser *(ugs.),* **...bren|ner** (Ofen), **...fres|ser, ...kle|ber**

al|le|we|ge *vgl.* alle[r]wege

al|le|weil *vgl.* allweil

al|lez! [a'le:] ‹franz., „geht!"› (vorwärts!)

al|le|zeit, all|zeit (*veraltend, noch landsch. für* immer)

all|fäl|lig [*österr.* ...'fɛl...] (*österr., schweiz. für* etwaig, allenfalls [vorkommend], eventuell); **All|fäl|li|ge,** das; -n (*österr.* letzter Punkt einer Tagesordnung)

All|gäu, das; -s (ein Alpengebiet); **All|gäu|er** (↑R 103); **all|gäu|isch**

All|ge|gen|wart; all|ge|gen|wär|tig

all|ge|mein; die allgemeine Schul-, Wehrpflicht; allgemeine Geschäfts-, Versicherungsbedingungen; die allgemein bildenden Schulen; die allgemein gültigen Ausführungen; allgemein verständliche Texte; (↑R 47:) im Allgemeinen (gewöhnlich; *Abk.* i. Allg.); er bewegt sich stets nur im Allgemeinen (beachtet nicht das Besondere); (↑R 108:) Allgemeine Deutsche Biographie (*Abk.* ADB), Allgemeiner Deutscher Automobil-Club (*Abk.* ADAC), Allgemeiner Deutscher Nachrichtendienst (*ehemals in der DDR; Abk.* ADN), Allgemeiner Studentenausschuss (*Abk.* AStA), Allgemeines Bürgerliches Gesetzbuch (in Österreich geltend; *Abk.* ABGB); **All|ge|mein‿arzt, ...be|fin|den** (das; -s); **all|ge|mein bil|dend** *vgl.* allgemein; **All|ge|mein|bil|dung,** die; -; **all|ge|mein gül|tig** *vgl.* allgemein; **All|ge|mein‿gül|tig|keit** (die; -), **...gut; All|ge|mein|heit,** die; -; **All|ge|mein‿me|di|zin** (die; -), **...me|di|zi|ner, ...platz** (abgegriffene Redensart); **all|ge|mein ver|ständ|lich** *vgl.* allgemein; **All|ge|mein‿wis|sen, ...wohl, ...zu|stand** (der; -[e]s)

All|ge|walt, die; - *(geh.);* **all|ge|wal|tig** *(geh.)*

All|heil|mit|tel, das

All|heit, die; - *(Philos.)*

Al|li|anz, die; -, -en ‹franz.› ([Staaten]bündnis); die Heilige -

Al|li|ga|tor, der; -s, ...oren ‹lat.› (eine Panzerechse)

al|li|ie|ren, sich ‹franz.› (sich verbünden); **Al|li|ier|te,** der *u.* die; -n, -n (↑R 5 ff.)

Al|li|te|ra|ti|on, die; -, -en ‹lat.› (*Verslehre* Anlaut-, Stabreim); **al|li|te|rie|rend** (stabreimend)

all|jähr|lich

all|lie|bend (↑R 136; *geh.*)

All|macht, die; - *(geh.);* **all|mäch|tig; All|mäch|ti|ge,** der; -n (Gott); Allmächtiger!

all|mäh|lich

All|meind, All|mend, die; -, -en (*schweiz. svw.* Allmende); **All|men|de,** die; -, -n (*früher für* gemeinsam genutztes Gemeindegut); **All|mend|recht**

all|mo|nat|lich

all|mor|gend|lich

All|mut|ter, die; - *(geh.);* - Natur

all|nächt|lich

al|loch|thon [...x'to:n] (↑R 132) ‹griech.› (*Geol.* an anderer Stelle entstanden)

Al|lod, das; -[e]s, -e (*MA.* dem Lehensträger persönlich gehörender Grund und Boden); **al|lo|di|al** ‹germ.-mlat.› (zum Allod gehörend)

Al|lo|ga|mie, die; -, ...ien ‹griech.› (*Bot.* Fremdbestäubung)

Al|lo|ku|ti|on, die; -, -en ‹lat.› (feierliche [päpstliche] Ansprache [an die Kardinäle])

Al|lon|ge [a'lɔ̃:ʒə], die; -, -n ‹franz.› (*Wirtsch.* Verlängerungsstreifen [bei Wechseln]); **Al|lon|ge|pe|rü|cke** (langlockige Perücke des 17. u. 18. Jh.s)

Al|lo|path, der; -en, -en (↑R 126) ‹griech.› (Anhänger der Allopathie); **Al|lo|pa|thie,** die; - (ein Heilverfahren der Schulmedizin); **al|lo|pa|thisch**

Al|lot|ria (↑R 130) *Plur., heute meist* das; -[s] ‹griech.› (Unfug)

All|par|tei|en|re|gie|rung

All|rad|an|trieb

all right! ['ɔ:l 'rait] ‹engl.› (richtig!, in Ordnung!)

All|roun|der ['ɔ:l'raundə(r)], der; -s, - *u.* **All|round|man** ['ɔ:l'raundmən], der; -s, ...men [...mən] ‹engl.› (jmd., der in vielen Bereichen Bescheid weiß); **All|round|sport|ler** ['ɔ:l'raund...] (Sportler, der viele Sportarten beherrscht)

all|sei|tig; All|sei|tig|keit; all|seits, al|ler|seits

All-Star-Band ['ɔ:l'sta:(r)bɛnt], die; -, -s ‹engl.› (Jazzband, die aus berühmten Spielern besteht)

All|strom|ge|rät (für Gleich- u. Wechselstrom)

all|stünd|lich

All|tag *Plur. selten;* **all|täg|lich** [*auch* 'altɛ:k... (= alltags) *u.* al'tɛ:k... (= üblich, gewöhnlich)]; **All|täg|lich|keit; all|tags** (↑R 46), *aber* des Alltags; alltags wie feiertags; **All|tags‿an|zug, ...be|schäf|ti|gung, ...kleid, ...sor|gen** *(Plur.),* **...spra|che** (die; -), **...trott**

all|über|all (↑R 132; *geh.*)

all|um|fas|send

Al|lü|re, die; -, -n *meist Plur.* ‹franz.› (*meist abwertend für* eigenwilliges Benehmen, Gehabe)

al|lu|vi|al [...v...] ‹lat.› (*Geol.* angeschwemmt, abgelagert); **Al|lu|vi|on,** die; -, -en (angeschwemmtes Land); **Al|lu|vi|um,** das; -s (*ältere Bez. für* Holozän)

All|va|ter, der; -s (*Bez. für* Gott)

all|ver|ehrt

all|weil, al|le[r]|weil (*bes. österr. ugs. für* immer)

All|wet|ter|klei|dung

all|wis|send; Doktor Allwissend

(Märchengestalt); **All|wis|sen|heit,** die; -
all|wö|chent|lich
all|zeit, al|le|zeit (*veraltend, noch landsch. für* immer)
all|zu; allzu bald, allzu oft, allzu sehr, allzu selten usw. *immer getrennt, aber* **all|zu|mal** (*veraltet für* alle zusammen; immer)
All|zweck|tuch *Plur.* ...tücher
Alm, die; -, -en (Bergweide)
Al|ma (w. Vorn.)
Al|ma-A|ta (Hptst. Kasachstans)
Al|ma Ma|ter (↑R 33), die; - - ‹lat.› (*geh. für* Universität, Hochschule)
Al|ma|nach, der; -s, -e ‹niederl.› (Kalender, Jahrbuch)
Al|man|din, der; -s, -e (Abart des [1]Granats)
al|men (*österr. für* Vieh auf der Alm halten); **Al|men|rausch,** Alm|rausch, der; -[e]s (Alpenrose); **Al|mer** (*österr. neben* Senner); **Al|me|rin,** die; -, -nen
Al|mo|sen, das; -s, - ‹griech.› (kleine Gabe, geringes Entgelt); **Al|mo|sen|emp|fän|ger; Al|mo|se|nier,** der; -s, -e (geistl. Würdenträger)
Alm|rausch *vgl.* Almenrausch; **Alm|ro|se** (*südd., österr. neben* Alpenrose)
Al|mut (w. Vorn.)
A|loe ['a:loe:], die; -, -n ['a:loən] ‹griech.› (eine Zier- und Heilpflanze)
a|lo|gisch ‹griech.› (nicht logisch)
A|lo|is ['a:loi(:)s], A|lo|i|si|us [*landsch. auch* a'lɔy...] (m. Vorn.); **A|lo|i|sia** [*landsch. auch* a'lɔy...] (w. Vorn.)
[1]Alp *frühere Schreibung für* [1]Alb
[2]Alp, Al|pe, die; -, ...pen (*landsch., bes. schweiz. für* Alm)
[1]Al|pa|ka, das; -s, -s ‹indian.-span.› (südamerik. Lamaart); **[2]Al|pa|ka,** das *u.* (*für* Gewebeart:) der; -s (Wolle vom Alpaka; Reißwolle); **[3]Al|pa|ka** (*als* ®*:* Alpacca), das; -s (Neusilber)
al pa|ri ‹ital.› (*Bankw.* zum Nennwert [einer Aktie]); vgl. pari
Alp|druck, *auch* Alb|druck, der; -[e]s, ...drücke; **Alp|drü|cken,** *auch* Alb|drü|cken, das; -s
Al|pe *vgl.* [2]Alp; **al|pen** (*schweiz. für* Vieh auf einer [2]Alp halten); **Al|pen** *Plur.* (Gebirge); **Al|pen|glöck|chen, ...glü|hen** (das; -s), **...jä|ger, ...ro|se, ...veil|chen; Al|pen|vor|land**
Al|pha, das; -[s], -s (griech. Buchstabe: *A, α*); das - und [das] Omega (*geh. für* der Anfang und das Ende)
Al|pha|bet, das; -[e]s, -e (Abc); **al|pha|be|tisch; al|pha|be|ti|sie|ren** (*auch für* Analphabeten lesen und schreiben lehren)
Al|pha Cen|tau|ri [- tsen...], der; - - (hellster Stern im Sternbild Zentaur)
al|pha|me|risch, al|pha|nu|me|risch ‹griech.; lat.› (*EDV* Buchstaben und Ziffern enthaltend)
Al|phard, der; - ‹arab.› (ein Stern)
Al|pha|strah|len, ***α*-Strah|len** *Plur.;* ↑R 25 (*Physik* beim Zerfall von Atomkernen bestimmter radioaktiver Elemente auftretende Strahlen)
Al|phei|os *vgl.* Alpheus; **Al|phe|us,** der; - (peloponnes. Fluss)
Alp|horn *Plur.* ...hörner
al|pin ‹lat.› (die Alpen, das Hochgebirge betreffend od. darin vorkommend); alpine Kombination (Skisport); **Al|pi|na|ri|um,** das; -s, ...ien [...iən] (Naturwildpark im Hochgebirge); **Al|pi|ni** *Plur.* ‹ital.› (ital. Alpenjäger); **Al|pi|nis|mus,** der; - ‹lat.› (sportl. Bergsteigen); **Al|pi|nist,** der; -en, -en; ↑R 126 (sportl. Bergsteiger im Hochgebirge); **Al|pi|nis|tik,** die; - (*svw.* Alpinismus); **Al|pi|num,** das; -s, ...nen (Alpenpflanzenanlage); **Älp|ler** (Alpenbewohner); **älp|le|risch**
Alp|traum, *auch* Alb|traum
Al|raun, der; -[e]s, -e *vgl.* Alraune; **Al|rau|ne,** die; -, -n (menschenähnlich aussehende Zauberwurzel; Zauberwesen)
al s. = al segno
als; als ob; sie ist klüger als ihr Freund, *aber (bei Gleichheit):* sie ist so klug wie ihre Freundin; (↑R 72:) er ist größer als Ludwig; Ilse ist größer, als ihre Mutter im gleichen Alter war; ich konnte nichts Besseres tun[,] als nach Hause zu gehen (↑R 75); **als|bald** [*schweiz.* 'als...]; **als|bal|dig** [*schweiz.* 'als...]; **als|dann** [*schweiz.* 'als...]; **als dass** (↑R 88)
al seg|no [- 'sɛnjo] (↑R 130) ‹ital.› (*Musik* bis zum Zeichen [bei Wiederholung eines Tonstückes]; *Abk.* al s.)
al|so
Als-ob, das; -; **Als-ob-Phi|lo|so|phie** (↑R 28)
Als|ter, die; - (r. Nebenfluss der unteren Elbe); **Als|ter|was|ser** *Plur.* ...wässer; (*landsch. für* Getränk aus Bier und Limonade)
alt; älter, älteste; alte Sprachen; die alten Bundesländer; alter Mann (*auch Bergmannsspr. für* abgebaute Teile der Grube); alten Stils (Zeitrechnung; *Abk.* a. St.). *Großschreibung:* (↑R 47:) etwas Altes; der Alte (Greis), die Alte (Greisin); er ist immer der Alte (derselbe); wir bleiben die Alten (dieselben); es beim Alten lassen; Altes und Neues; eine Mischung aus Alt und Neu; aus Alt mach Neu; Alte und Junge; der Konflikt zwischen Alt und Jung (den Generationen); ein Fest für Alt und Jung (jedermann); die Alten (alte Leute, Völker); der Älteste (Kirchenälteste); die Ältesten (der Gemeinde); mein Ältester (ältester Sohn), *aber* er ist der älteste meiner Söhne. *Schreibung in Namen und namenähnlichen Verbindungen:* (↑R 108:) der Ältere (*Abk.* d. Ä.; als Ergänzung bei Eigenn.); der Alte Fritz; Alter Herr (*Studentenspr. für* Vater *u. für* Altmitglied einer student. Verbindung; *Abk.* A. H.); das Alte Testament (*Abk.* A. T.); die Alte Welt (Europa, Asien u. Afrika im Gegensatz zu Amerika)
Alt, der; -s, -e ‹lat.› (tiefe Frauen- od. Knabenstimme; Sängerin mit dieser Stimme)
Alt... (z. B. Altbundespräsident; in der Schweiz gewöhnlich so geschrieben: alt Bundesrat)
Al|tai, der; -[s] (Gebirge in Zentralasien)
Al|ta|ir *vgl.* Atair
al|ta|isch; -e Sprachen
Al|ta|mi|ra (Höhle in Spanien mit altsteinzeitlichen Malereien)
Alt|am|mann [*auch* alt'am...] (*schweiz.*)
Al|tan, der; -[e]s, -e ‹ital.› (Balkon; Söller)
Alt|an|la|ge, die; -, -n (*Technik*)
Al|tar, der; -[e]s, ...täre ‹lat.›; **Al|tar|bild; Al|ta|rist,** der; -en, -en; ↑R 126 (kath. Priester, der nur die Messe liest); **Al|tar[s]|sak|ra|ment,** das; -[e]s
alt|ba|cken; -es Brot
Alt|bau, der; -[e]s, -ten; **Alt|bau|sub|stanz** (*Plur. selten*), **...woh|nung**
alt|be|kannt
Alt-Ber|lin (↑R 105)
alt|be|währt
Alt|bier (obergäriges, meist dunkles Bier)
Alt|bun|des|kanz|ler; Alt|bun|des|prä|si|dent; Alt|bun|des|trai|ner
alt|deutsch; -e Weinstube
Alt|dorf (Hauptort des Kantons Uri)
Alt|dor|fer (dt. Maler)
Al|te, der *u.* die; -n, -n; ↑R 5 ff. (*ugs. für* Vater u. Mutter, Ehemann u. -frau, Chef u. Chefin)
alt|ehr|wür|dig (*geh.*)

alt|ein|ge|ses|sen
Alt|ei|sen, das; -s
Al|te Land, das; -n -[e]s (Teil der Elbmarschen)
Al|te|na (Stadt im Sauerland); **Al|te|na|er** (↑R 103); **al|te|na|isch**
alt|eng|lisch
Al|ten‿heim, **...hil|fe** (die; -), **...pfle|ger**, **...teil** (das)
Al|ter, das; -s, -; eine Frau mittleren Alters, *aber* (↑R 46:) seit alters *(geh.)*, von alters her *(geh.)*
Al|te|ra|ti|on, die; -, -en ‹lat.› (*Musik* chromatische Veränderung eines Akkordtones; *Med.* krankhafte Veränderung)
Äl|ter|chen
Al|ter Ego [*auch* - 'ɛgo], das; - - ‹lat.› (zweites, anderes Ich; vertrauter Freund)
al|te|rie|ren ‹franz.›; sich - (sich aufregen)
al|tern; ich ...ere (↑R 16); vgl. Alterung; **Al|tern**, das; -s
Al|ter|nanz, die; -, -en ‹lat.› (Wechsel zwischen Dingen, Vorgängen); **al|ter|na|tiv** (wahlweise; zwischen zwei Möglichkeiten die Wahl lassend; eine andere Lebensweise vertretend, für als menschen- und umweltfreundlicher angesehene Formen des [Zusammen]lebens eintretend); -e Wählervereinigungen; **Al|ter|na|tiv|be|we|gung**; **¹Al|ter|na|ti|ve** [...və], die; -, -n (Entscheidung zwischen zwei [oder mehr] Möglichkeiten; Möglichkeit des Wählens zwischen zwei [oder mehreren] Dingen; eine von zwei oder mehr Möglichkeiten); **²Al|ter|na|ti|ve** [...və], der *u.* die; -n, -n; ↑R 5 ff. (jmd., der einer Alternativbewegung angehört); **Al|ter|na|tiv‿ener|gie** (↑R 132), **...kul|tur**, **...pro|gramm**; **al|ter|nie|ren** ([ab]wechseln); **al|ter|nie|rend**; -e Blattstellung *(Bot.)*; -e Reihe *(Math.)*
Al|terns‿for|schung (die; -; *für* Gerontologie), **...vor|gang**
alt|er|probt
al|ters *vgl.* Alter; **al|ters|be|dingt**; **Al|ters|be|schwer|den** *Plur.*; **al|ters|ge|recht**; -e Wohnung; **Al|ters‿gren|ze**, **...grup|pe**, **...heil|kun|de** (die; -; *für* Geriatrie), **...heim**, **...jahr** (*schweiz. für* Lebensjahr), **...py|ra|mi|de** (graph. Darstellung des Altersaufbaus einer Bevölkerung in Form einer Pyramide); **Al|ters‿ren|te**, **...ru|he|geld**; **al|ters|schwach**; **Al|ters|schwä|che**, die; -; **Al|ters|sich|tig|keit**, die; -; **Al|ters‿starr|sinn**, **...ver|si|che|rung**, **...ver|sor|gung**, **...werk**

Al|ter|tum, das; -s; das klassische -; **Al|ter|tü|me|lei**; **al|ter|tü|meln** (Stil u. Wesen des Altertums nachahmen); ich ...[e]le (↑R 16); **Al|ter|tü|mer** *Plur.* (Gegenstände aus dem Altertum); **al|ter|tüm|lich**; **Al|ter|tüm|lich|keit**, die; -; **Al|ter|tums‿for|scher**, **...for|schung** (die; -), **...kun|de** (die; -; *für* Archäologie), **...wis|sen|schaft**
Al|te|rung (*auch für* Reifung; Veränderung durch Altern)
Äl|tes|te, der *u.* die; -n, -n; ↑R 5 ff. (in einer Kirchengemeinde u. a.); **Äl|tes|ten‿rat**, **...recht** (*für* Seniorat)
alt|frän|kisch (*veraltend für* altmodisch)
alt|ge|dient
Alt|gei|ge (Bratsche)
Alt|ge|sel|le
alt|ge|wohnt
Alt|glas, das; -es; **Alt|glas|be|häl|ter**
Alt|gold
Alt|grad *vgl.* Grad
alt|grie|chisch
Alt|händ|ler (*veraltend für* Altwarenhändler)
Al|thee, die; -, -n ‹griech.› (Eibisch)
Alt-Hei|del|berg (↑R 105)
alt|her|ge|bracht; **alt|her|kömm|lich**
Alt|her|ren|mann|schaft *(Sport)*; **Alt|her|ren|schaft** *(Studentenspr.)*
alt|hoch|deutsch (*Abk.* ahd.); *vgl.* deutsch; **Alt|hoch|deutsch**, das; -[s] (Sprache); *vgl.* Deutsch; **Alt|hoch|deut|sche**, das; -n; *vgl.* Deutsche, das
Al|tist, der; -en, -en (↑R 126) ‹lat.› (Knabe mit Altstimme); **Al|tis|tin**
Alt|jahr|abend, **Alt|jahrs|abend** [*auch* ...'ja:r(s)...] (↑R 132; *landsch., schweiz. für* Silvesterabend); **Alt|jahrs|tag** (*österr., schweiz. für* Silvester)
alt|jüng|fer|lich
Alt|kanz|ler
Alt|ka|tho|lik[1]; **alt|ka|tho|lisch**[1]; **Alt|ka|tho|li|zis|mus**[1]
alt|klug; ...kluger, ...klugste (↑R 27)
Alt|last *meist Plur.* (stillgelegte Müllkippen; Halden mit umweltgefährdenden Produktionsrückständen u. Ä., *auch übertr. für* ungelöste Probleme aus der Vergangenheit)

[1] *Die Kirchengemeinschaft selbst verwendet den Bindestrich:* Alt-Katholik, alt-katholisch, Alt-Katholizismus.

ält|lich
Alt|mark, die; - (Landschaft westl. der Elbe)
Alt|ma|te|ri|al
Alt|meis|ter (*urspr.* Vorsteher einer Innung; [als Vorbild geltender] altbewährter Meister in einem Fachgebiet)
Alt|me|tall
alt|mo|disch
alt|nor|disch; *vgl.* deutsch; **Alt|nor|disch**, das; -[s] (älteste nordgermanische Sprachstufe); *vgl.* Deutsch; **Alt|nor|di|sche**, das; -n; *vgl.* Deutsche, das
Al|to A|di|ge [- 'a:didʒe] (*ital. Name für* Südtirol)
Alt|öl
Al|to|na (Stadtteil von Hamburg); **Al|to|na|er** (↑R 103); **al|to|na|isch**
Alt|pa|pier, das; -s; **Alt|pa|pier‿be|häl|ter**, **...samm|lung**
Alt|par|tei|en *Plur.*
Alt|phi|lo|lo|ge; **Alt|phi|lo|lo|gie** (klassische Philologie); **Alt|phi|lo|lo|gin**; **alt|phi|lo|lo|gisch**
alt|rö|misch
alt|ro|sa
Al|tru|is|mus (↑R 130), der; - ‹lat.› (Selbstlosigkeit); **Al|tru|ist**, der; -en, -en (↑R 126); **al|tru|is|tisch** (selbstlos)
Alt|sitz (*veraltet für* Altenteil)
alt|sprach|lich; -er Zweig
Alt|stadt|sa|nie|rung
Alt|stein|zeit, die; - (*für* Paläolithikum)
Alt|stim|me
Alt|stoff *meist Plur.*; **Alt|stoff|samm|lung**
alt|tes|ta|men|ta|risch; **Alt|tes|ta|ment|ler** (Erforscher des A. T.); **alt|tes|ta|ment|lich**
Alt|tier (*Jägerspr.* Muttertier beim Rot- u. Damwild)
alt|über|lie|fert (↑R 132)
alt|vä|te|risch (altmodisch); **alt|vä|ter|lich** (ehrwürdig)
alt|ver|traut
Alt|vor|dern *Plur.* (*veraltend für* Vorfahren)
Alt|wa|ren *Plur.*; **Alt|wa|ren|händ|ler**
Alt|was|ser, das; -s, ...wasser (ehemaliger Flussarm mit stehendem Wasser)
Alt|wei|ber‿fas[t]|nacht (*bes. landsch. für* letzter Donnerstag vor Aschermittwoch), **...ge|schwätz** *(ugs.)*, **...som|mer** (warme Nachsommertage; vom Wind getragene Spinnweben)
Alt-Wien (↑R 105); **alt-wie|ne|risch**
¹Al|lu *(ugs.)* = Arbeitslosenunterstützung

^{2}**A|lu,** das; -s (*ugs. Kurzwort für* Aluminium); **A|lu|fo|lie** (*kurz für* Aluminiumfolie); **A|lu|mi|nat,** das; -[e]s, -e ‹lat.› (*Chemie* Salz der Aluminiumsäure); **a|lu|mi|nie|ren** (Metallteile mit Aluminium überziehen); **A|lu|mi|nit** [*auch* ...'nit], der; -s (ein Mineral); **A|lu|mi|ni|um,** das; -s (chem. Element, Leichtmetall; *Zeichen* Al); **A|lu|mi|ni|um‿fo|lie, ...sul|fat**

A|lum|nat, das; -[e]s, -e ‹lat.› (Schülerheim; *österr. für* Einrichtung zur Ausbildung von Geistlichen); **A|lum|ne,** der; -n, -n (↑R 126) *u.* **A|lum|nus,** der; -, ...nen (Alumnatszögling)

Al|ve|o|lar [...v...], der; -s, -e ‹lat.› (*Sprachw.* am Gaumen unmittelbar hinter den Zähnen gebildeter Laut, z. B. d); **Al|ve|o|le,** die; -, -n (*Med.* Zahnmulde im Kiefer; Lungenbläschen)

Al|weg|bahn ‹Kurzw. nach dem Schweden Axel Leonard Wenner-Gren› (Einschienenbahn)

Al|win (m. Vorn.); **Al|wi|ne** (w. Vorn.)

Alz|hei|mer|krank|heit (↑R 95), die; - ‹nach dem dt. Neurologen Alzheimer› (mit fast völligem Gedächtnisverlust verbundene Gehirnkrankheit)

Am = *chem. Zeichen für* Americium

am; ↑R 13 (an dem; *Abk.* a. [*bei Ortsnamen, z. B.* Ludwigshafen a. Rhein]; *vgl.* an); am Sonntag, dem (*od.* den) 27. März (↑R 29)

a. m. = ante meridiem; ante mortem

A|ma|de|us (m. Vorn.)

A|ma|ler, A|me|lun|gen *Plur.* (ostgot. Königsgeschlecht)

A|mal|gam, das; -s, -e ‹mlat.› (Quecksilberlegierung); **a|mal|ga|mie|ren** (mit Quecksilber legieren; Gold und Silber mit Quecksilber aus Erzen gewinnen)

A|ma|lia, A|ma|lie [...iə] (w. Vorn.)

A|man|da (w. Vorn.); **A|man|dus** (m. Vorn.)

am an|ge|führ|ten, *auch* **an|ge|ge|be|nen Ort** (*Abk.* a. a. O.)

^{1}**A|ma|rant,** der; -s, -e ‹griech.› (eine Zierpflanze); ^{2}**A|ma|rant,** der, *auch* das; -s (ein Farbstoff); **a|ma|ran|ten** (dunkelrot); **a|ma|rant|rot**

A|ma|rel|le, die; -, -n ‹lat.› (eine Sauerkirschensorte)

A|ma|ret|to, der; -s, ...tti ‹ital.› (ein Mandellikör)

A|ma|ryl, der; -s, -e ‹griech.› (künstl. Saphir); **A|ma|ryl|lis,** die; -, ...llen (eine Zierpflanze)

A|ma|teur [...'tø:r], der; -s, -e ‹franz.› (jmd., der Kunst, Sport usw. als Liebhaber ausübt; Nichtfachmann); **A|ma|teur‿film, ...fo|to|graf, ...sport, ...sta|tus**

^{1}**A|ma|ti** (ital. Meister des Geigenbaus); ^{2}**A|ma|ti,** die; -, -s (von der Geigenbauerfamilie Amati hergestellte Geige)

A|ma|zo|nas, der; - (südamerik. Strom); **A|ma|zo|ne,** die; -, -n (Angehörige eines krieger. Frauenvolkes der griech. Sage; *auch für* Turnierreiterin); **A|ma|zo|nen|sprin|gen,** das; -s, - *(Reitsport)*

Am|bas|sa|deur [...'dø:r], der; -s, -e (*veraltet für* Botschafter)

Am|be, die; -, -n ‹lat.› (*Math.* Verbindung zweier Größen in der Kombinationsrechnung)

Am|ber, der; -s, -[n] *u.* **Amb|ra** (↑R 130), die; -, -s ‹arab.› (Ausscheidung des Pottwals; Duftstoff)

Am|bi|ance [ãbiãs], die; - ‹franz.› (*schweiz. für* Umgebung, Atmosphäre)

Am|bi|en|te, das; - ‹ital.› (Umwelt, Atmosphäre)

am|big, am|bi|gue [...guə] ‹lat.› (*fachspr. für* mehrdeutig); **Am|bi|gu|i|tät,** die; -, -en; **Am|bi|ti|on,** die; -, -en (Ehrgeiz); **am|bi|ti|o|niert** (ehrgeizig, strebsam); **am|bi|ti|ös** (ehrgeizig)

am|bi|va|lent [...v...] ‹lat.› (*fachspr. für* doppelwertig; zwiespältig); **Am|bi|va|lenz,** die; -, -en (Doppelwertigkeit)

^{1}**Am|bo,** der; -s, *Plur.* -s *u.* ...ben ‹lat.› (*österr. für* Doppeltreffer beim Lotto)

^{2}**Am|bo,** der; -s, -s, **Am|bon,** der; -s, ...bonen (erhöhtes Lesepult in christl. Kirchen)

Am|boss, der; -es, -e

Amb|ra *vgl.* Amber

Amb|ro|sia (↑R 130), die; - ‹griech.› (Götterspeise in der griech. Sage)

amb|ro|si|a|nisch (↑R 94 *u.* 130) ‹zu Ambrosius›; ambrosianische Hymnen *(kath. Kirche)*

amb|ro|sisch (↑R 130) ‹griech.› (*geh., veraltend für* himmlisch)

Amb|ro|si|us (↑R 130; Kirchenlehrer)

am|bu|lant ‹lat.› (wandernd; *Med.* nicht stationär); ambulantes Gewerbe (Wandergewerbe); ambulante Behandlung; **Am|bu|lanz,** die; -, -en (bewegliches Lazarett; Krankentransportwagen; Abteilung einer Klinik für ambulante Behandlung); **am|bu|la|to|risch;** -e Behandlung; **Am|bu|la|to|ri|um,** das; -s, ...ien [...iən] (Raum, Abteilung, medizin. Einrichtung für ambulante Behandlung)

A|mei|se, die; -, -n; **A|mei|sen‿bär, ...hau|fen, ...säu|re** (die; -)

A|me|lia, A|me|lie [...li(:), *auch* ame'li: *u.* a'me:liə] (w. Vorn.)

A|me|li|o|ra|ti|on, die; -, -en ‹lat.› (Verbesserung [bes. des Ackerbodens]); **a|me|li|o|rie|ren**

A|me|lun|gen *vgl.* Amaler

a|men ‹hebr.›; in Ewigkeit, amen!

A|men, das; -s, - *Plur. selten* (feierliche Bekräftigung); zu allem Ja und Amen (*auch* ja und amen) sagen *(ugs.)*

A|men|de|ment [amã:d(ə)'mã:], das; -s, -s ‹franz.› (Zusatz-, Abänderungsantrag zu Gesetzen); **a|men|die|ren** [amɛn...]

A|men|ho|tep, A|me|no|phis (ägypt. Königsname)

A|me|nor|rhö[1], **A|me|nor|rhöe** [...'rø:], die; -, ...rrhöen ‹griech.› (*Med.* Ausbleiben der Menstruation); **a|me|nor|rho|isch**

A|me|ri|ci|um, das; -s ‹*nach* Amerika› (chem. Element, Transuran; *Zeichen* Am)

A|me|ri|ka; A|me|ri|ka|deut|sche, der *u.* die; **A|me|ri|ka|ner; a|me|ri|ka|nisch;** *vgl.* deutsch; **a|me|ri|ka|ni|sie|ren; A|me|ri|ka|ni|sie|rung; A|me|ri|ka|nis|mus,** der; -, ...men (sprachliche Besonderheit im amerik. Englisch; Entlehnung aus dem Amerikanischen); **A|me|ri|ka|nist,** der; -en, -en (↑R 126); **A|me|ri|ka|nis|tik,** die; - (Erforschung der Geschichte, Sprache u. Kultur Amerikas); **A|me|ri|ka|nis|tin**

A|me|thyst, der; -[e]s, -e ‹griech.› (ein Schmuckstein); **a|me|thys|ten** (amethystfarben)

A|met|rie (↑R 130), die; -, ...ien ‹griech.› (Ungleichmäßigkeit; Missverhältnis); **a|met|risch**

Am|ha|ra *Plur.* (hamit. Volk in Äthiopien); **am|ha|risch;** *vgl.* deutsch; **Am|ha|risch,** das; -[s] (Sprache); *vgl.* Deutsch

A|mi, der; -s, -s (*Kurzw. für* Amerikaner)

A|mi|ant, der; -s, -e ‹griech.› (ein Mineral)

A|mi|go, der; -s, -s ‹span., „Freund“› (*ugs. für* Geschäftsmann als Freund und Gönner eines Politikers)

A|min, das; -s, -e (*Chemie* organ. Stickstoffverbindung); **A|mi|no|säu|re,** die; - (Eiweißbaustein)

A|mi|to|se, die; - ‹griech.› (*Biol.* einfache Zellkernteilung)

---

[1] *Vgl. die Anmerkung zu* Diarrhö, Diarrhöe.

Am|man (Hptst. Jordaniens)
Am|mann, der; -[e]s, ...männer *(schweiz.); vgl.* Gemeinde-, Landammann
Am|me, die; -, -n; **Am|men|märchen**
¹Am|mer, die; -, -n, *fachspr. auch* der; -s, -n (ein Singvogel)
²Am|mer, *im Unterlauf* Am|per, die; - (Isarzufluss)
Am|mon (altägypt. Gott); Jupiter -
Am|mo|ni|ak [*od.* 'a..., *österr.* a'mo:...], das; -s ‹ägypt.› (*Chemie* stechend riechende, gasförmige Verbindung von Stickstoff u. Wasserstoff)
Am|mo|nit [*auch* ...'nit], der; -en, -en (↑R 126) ‹ägypt.› (Ammonshorn)
Am|mo|ni|ter, der; -s, - ‹ägypt.› (Angehöriger eines alttest. Nachbarvolks der Israeliten)
Am|mo|ni|um, das; -s ‹ägypt.› (*Chemie* aus Stickstoff u. Wasserstoff bestehende Atomgruppe)
Am|mons|horn, das; -[e]s, ...hörner ‹ägypt.; dt.› (Versteinerung)
Am|ne|sie (↑R 132), die; -, ...ien ‹griech.› (*Med.* Gedächtnisschwund); **Am|nes|tie,** die; -, ...ien (Begnadigung, Straferlass); **am|nes|tie|ren; Am|nes|ty In|ter|na|tio|nal** ['ɛmnisti intə(r)'nɛʃ(ə)nəl] ‹engl.› (internationale Organisation zum Schutz der Menschenrechte)
A|mö|be, die; -, -n ‹griech.› (*Zool.* ein Einzeller); **a|mö|bo|id** (amöbenartig)
A|mok [*auch* a'mɔk], der; -s ‹malai.›; Amok laufen (mit einer Waffe umherlaufen und blindwütig töten); **A|mok‿fah|rer, ...lau|fen** (das; -s), **...läu|fer, ...schüt|ze**
a-Moll [*auch* 'a:'mɔl], das; - (Tonart; *Zeichen* a); **a-Moll-Ton|lei|ter** (↑R 28)
A|mor (röm. Liebesgott)
a|mo|ra|lisch ‹lat.› (sich über die Moral hinwegsetzend); **A|mo|ra|lis|mus,** der; - (gleichgültige od. feindl. Einstellung gegenüber der geltenden Moral); **A|mo|ra|li|tät,** die; - (amoralische Lebenshaltung)
A|mo|ret|te, die; -, -n, ‹franz.› (*bild. Kunst* Figur eines geflügelten Liebesgottes)
a|morph ‹griech.› (ungeformt, gestaltlos); **A|mor|phie,** die; -, ...ien ‹griech.› (*Physik* formloser Zustand [eines Stoffes])
a|mor|ti|sa|bel ‹franz.› (tilgbar); ...ab|le (↑R 130) Anleihen; **A|mor|ti|sa|ti|on,** die; -, -en ‹lat.› ([allmähliche] Tilgung; Abschreibung, Abtragung [einer Schuld]); **a|mor|ti|sier|bar; a|mor|ti|sie|ren**
A|mos (bibl. Prophet)
A|mou|ren [a'mu:rən] *Plur.* ‹franz.› (*veraltend für* Liebschaften, Liebesabenteuer); **a|mou|rös** [amu...] (Liebes...; verliebt)
Am|pel, die; -, -n (Hängelampe; Hängevase; Verkehrssignal); **Am|pel|ko|a|li|ti|on** ‹nach den Parteifarben Rot, Gelb, Grün› (Koalition aus SPD, FDP und Grünen)
Am|per *vgl.* ²Ammer
Am|pere [am'pɛ:r], das; -[s], - ‹nach dem franz. Physiker Ampère› (Einheit der elektr. Stromstärke; *Zeichen* A); **Am|pere‿me|ter** (das; -s, -; Strommesser), **...se|kun|de** (Einheit der Elektrizitätsmenge; *Zeichen* As), **...stun|de** (Einheit der Elektrizitätsmenge; *Zeichen* Ah)
Am|pex|ver|fah|ren (*Fernsehtechnik* Verfahren zur Bildaufzeichnung)
Amp|fer, der; -s, - (eine Pflanze)
Am|phe|ta|min (↑R 132), das; -s, -e (als Weckamin gebrauchte chemische Verbindung)
Am|phi|bie [...iə], die; -, -n *meist Plur.* ‹griech.› (sowohl im Wasser als auch auf dem Land lebendes Wirbeltier, Lurch); **Am|phi|bi|en‿fahr|zeug** (Land-Wasser-Fahrzeug), **...pan|zer; am|phi|bisch**
Am|phi|bo|lie, die; -, ...ien (*Stilk., Philos.* Mehrdeutigkeit; Doppelsinn); **am|phi|bo|lisch**
Am|phi|go|nie, die; - ‹griech.› (*Biol.* zweigeschlechtige Fortpflanzung)
Am|phik|ty|o|ne (↑R 132), der; -n, -n (↑R 126) ‹griech.› (Mitglied einer Amphiktyonie); **Am|phik|ty|o|nie,** die; -, ...ien (kultisch-polit. Verband altgriech. Nachbarstaaten od. -stämme)
Am|phi|o|le ®, die; -, -n (*Med.* Kombination aus Ampulle und Injektionsspritze)
Am|phi|the|a|ter ‹griech.› (elliptisches, meist dachloses Theatergebäude mit stufenweise aufsteigenden Sitzen); **am|phi|the|at|ra|lisch**
Am|phit|ri|te [...tə *od.* ...te:] (↑R 130; griech. Meeresgöttin)
Am|phit|ry|on (↑R 130; sagenhafter König von Tiryns, Gemahl der Alkmene)
Am|pho|ra, Am|pho|re, die; -, ...oren ‹griech.› (zweihenkliges Gefäß der Antike)
am|pho|ter ‹griech., „zwitterhaft"› (*Chemie* sich teils als Säure, teils als Base verhaltend)
Amp|li|fi|ka|ti|on (↑R 130), die; -, -en ‹lat.› (*fachspr. für* Erweiterung; kunstvolle Ausweitung einer Aussage); **amp|li|fi|zie|ren; Amp|li|tu|de,** die; -, -n (*Physik* Schwingungsweite, Ausschlag)
Am|pul|le, die; -, -n ‹griech.› (Glasröhrchen [bes. mit sterilen Lösungen zum Einspritzen])
Am|pu|ta|ti|on, die; -, -en ‹lat.› (operative Abtrennung eines Körperteils); **am|pu|tie|ren**
Am|rum (Nordseeinsel)
Am|sel, die; -, -n
Ams|ter|dam [*auch* 'am...] (Hptst. der Niederlande); **Ams|ter|da|mer** (↑R 103)
Amt, das; -[e]s, Ämter; von Amts wegen; ein - bekleiden; **Ämt|chen; am|ten** *(schweiz., sonst veraltet);* **Äm|ter‿häu|fung, ...pat|ro|na|ge; Amt|frau; am|tie|ren; amt|lich; Amt|mann** *Plur.* ...männer *u.* ...leute; **Amt|män|nin; amts|ärzt|lich; Amts‿deutsch, ...ent|he|bung, ...ge|heim|nis, ...ge|richt** (*Abk.* AG), **...ge|richts|rat** (*Plur.* ...räte); **amts|hal|ber; amts|han|deln** *(österr.);* ich amtshandle; amtsgehandelt; **Amts‿hand|lung, ...hil|fe, ...kap|pel** (das; -s, -n; *österr. ugs. für* engstirniger Beamter), **...kir|che, ...mie|ne; amts|mü|de; Amts‿per|son, ...rich|ter, ...schim|mel** (der; -s; *ugs.*), **...spra|che, ...vor|stand, ...weg**
A|mu|lett, das; -[e]s, -e ‹lat.› (Gegenstand, dem Unheil abwehrende Kraft zugeschrieben wird)
A|mund|sen (norw. Polarforscher)
A|mur [*od.* a'mu:r], der; -[s] (asiat. Fluss)
a|mü|sant ‹franz.› (unterhaltend; vergnüglich); **A|mü|se|ment** [amyz(ə)'maŋ *od.* ...'mã:], das; -s, -s; **A|mü|sier|be|trieb; a|mü|sie|ren;** sich -
a|mu|sisch ‹griech.› (ohne Kunstverständnis)
A|myg|da|lin, das; -s ‹griech.› (Geschmacksstoff in bitteren Mandeln u. Ä.)
an (*Abk.* a.; *bei Ortsnamen, die durch weibl. Flussnamen bezeichnet sind, nur:* a. d., *z. B.* Bad Neustadt a. d. Saale); *Präp. mit Dat. und Akk.:* an dem Zaun stehen, *aber* an den Zaun stellen; es ist nicht an dem; an [und für] sich (eigentlich, im Grunde); am (an dem; *vgl.* am); ans (an das; *vgl.* ans); *Adverb:* Gemeinden von an

[die] 1 000 Einwohnern; ab und an (*landsch. für* ab und zu); an sein (*ugs. für* angeschaltet sein)

an... (*in Zus. mit Verben,* z. B. anbinden, du bindest an, angebunden, anzubinden)

...a|na, ...i|a|na *Plur.* ‹lat.› (z. B. Afrikana; *vgl. d.*)

A|na|bap|tis|mus, der; - ‹griech.› (Wiedertäuferlehre); **A|na|bap|tist,** der; -en, -en; ↑R 126 (Wiedertäufer)

a|na|bol ‹griech.›; -e Medikamente; **A|na|bo|li|kum,** das; -s, ...ka *meist Plur.* ‹griech.-lat.› (*Med.* muskelbildendes Präparat)

A|na|cho|ret [...ç... *od.* ...x..., *auch* ...k...], der; -en, -en (↑R 126) ‹griech.› (frühchristl. Einsiedler, Klausner); **A|na|cho|re|ten|tum,** das; -s; **a|na|cho|re|tisch**

A|na|chro|nis|mus [...k...], der; -, ...men ‹griech.› (falsche zeitliche Einordnung; veraltete, überholte Einrichtung); **a|na|chro|nis|tisch**

A|na|dy|o|me|ne [...dy'o:mene: *od.* ...dyo'me(:)ne: *od.* ...'me:nə] ‹griech., „die [aus dem Meer] Aufgetauchte"› (Beiname der griech. Göttin Aphrodite)

an|ae|rob (↑R 132) ‹griech.› (*Biol.* ohne Sauerstoff lebend)

A|na|gly|phen|bril|le ‹griech.; dt.› (für das Betrachten von dreidimensionalen Bildern od. Filmen)

A|na|gramm, das; -s, -e ‹griech.› (durch Umstellung von Buchstaben od. Silben eines Wortes entstandenes neues Wort; Buchstabenrätsel)

A|na|ko|luth (↑R 132), das, *auch* der; -s, -e ‹griech.› (*Sprachw.* Satzbruch); **a|na|ko|lu|thisch**

A|na|kon|da, die; -, -s (eine Riesenschlange)

A|na|kre|on (altgriech. Lyriker); **A|na|kre|on|ti|ker** (Nachahmer der Dichtweise Anakreons); **a|na|kre|on|tisch**

a|nal ‹lat.› (*Med.* den After betreffend)

A|na|lek|ten *Plur.* ‹griech.› (gesammelte Aufsätze, Auszüge)

A|na|lep|ti|kum, das; -s, ...ka ‹griech.› (*Med.* anregendes Mittel); **a|na|lep|tisch**

A|nal|ero|tik (↑R 132) ‹lat.; griech.› (*Psych.* [frühkindliches] sexuelles Lustempfinden im Bereich des Afters); **A|nal|fis|sur** *(Med.)*

An|al|ge|sie, An|al|gie, die; -, ...ien ‹griech.› (*Med.* Schmerzlosigkeit); **An|al|ge|ti|kum,** das; -s, ...ka (Schmerzen stillendes Mittel); **An|al|gie** *vgl.* Analgesie

a|na|log ‹griech.› (ähnlich; entsprechend); analog [zu] diesem Fall; **A|na|lo|gie,** die; -, ...ien; **A|na|lo|gie|bil|dung; A|na|lo|gon** [*auch* a'na...], das; -s, ...ga (ähnlicher Fall); **A|na|log‿rech|ner** (eine Rechenanlage), **...uhr** (Uhr mit Zeigern)

An|al|pha|bet [*od.* 'an...], der; -en, -en (↑R 126) ‹griech.› (jmd., der nicht lesen und schreiben gelernt hat); **An|al|pha|be|ten|tum,** das; -s; **An|al|pha|be|tin**

A|nal|ver|kehr ‹lat.; dt.› (Variante des Geschlechtsverkehrs)

A|na|ly|sand, der; -en, -en (↑R 126) ‹griech.› (*Psychoanalyse* die zu analysierende Person); **A|na|ly|se,** die; -, -n (Zergliederung, Untersuchung); **A|na|ly|sen|waa|ge** (chem. Waage); **a|na|ly|sie|ren; A|na|ly|sis,** die; - (Gebiet der Mathematik, in dem mit Grenzwerten u. veränderlichen Größen gearbeitet wird; Voruntersuchung beim Lösen geometr. Aufgaben); **A|na|lyst,** der; -en, -en; ↑R 126 (Fachmann, der das Geschehen an der Börse beobachtet und analysiert); **A|na|ly|tik,** die; - (Kunst od. Lehre der Analyse); **A|na|ly|ti|ker; a|na|ly|tisch;** -e Geometrie

A|nä|mie (↑R 132), die; -, ...ien ‹griech.› (*Med.* Blutarmut); **a|nä|misch**

A|nam|ne|se (↑R 132), die; -, -n ‹griech.› (*Med.* Vorgeschichte einer Krankheit); **a|nam|nes|tisch,** *auch* **a|nam|ne|tisch**

A|na|nas, die; -, *Plur.* - *u.* -se ‹indian.-span.› (trop. Frucht)

A|na|ni|as, *ökum.* Ha|na|ni|as (bibl. m. Eigenn.)

A|nan|kas|mus (↑R 132), der; -, ...men ‹griech.› (*Psych.* krankhafter Zwang zu bestimmten Handlungen)

A|na|päst, der; -[e]s, -e ‹griech.› (ein Versfuß); **a|na|päs|tisch**

A|na|pha|se, die; -, -n ‹griech.› (*Biol.* dritte Phase der indirekten Zellkernteilung)

A|na|pher, die; -, -n *u.* **A|na|pho|ra,** die; -, ...rä ‹griech.› (*Rhet.* Wiederholung des Anfangswortes [in aufeinander folgenden Sätzen], z. B.: mit all meinen Gedanken, mit all meinen Wünschen ...); **a|na|pho|risch** (die Anapher betreffend; *Sprachw.* rückweisend)

a|na|phy|lak|tisch ‹griech.› *(Med.);* -er Schock; **A|na|phy|la|xie,** die; -, ...ien (schockartige allergische Reaktion)

A|nar|chie (↑R 132), die; -, ...ien ‹griech.› ([Zustand der] Herrschafts-, Gesetzlosigkeit; Chaos in polit., wirtschaftl. o. ä. Hinsicht); **a|nar|chisch; A|nar|chis|mus,** der; - (Lehre, die sich gegen jede Autorität richtet u. für unbeschränkte Freiheit des Individuums eintritt); **A|nar|chist,** der; -en, -en; ↑R 126; **a|nar|chis|tisch; A|nar|cho,** der; -[s], -[s] (*ugs. für* jmd., der sich gegen die bürgerliche Gesellschaft mit [gewaltsamen] Aktionen auflehnt); **A|nar|cho|sze|ne**

A|nas|ta|sia (w. Vorn.); **A|nas|ta|si|us** (m. Vorn.)

An|äs|the|sie, die; -, ...ien ‹griech.› (*Med.* Schmerzunempfindlichkeit; Schmerzbetäubung); **an|äs|the|sie|ren,** an|äs|the|ti|sie|ren; **An|äs|the|sist,** der; -en, -en; ↑R 126 (Narkosefacharzt); **An|äs|the|sis|tin; An|äs|the|ti|kum,** das; -s, ...ka (Schmerzen stillendes Mittel); **an|äs|the|tisch; an|äs|the|ti|sie|ren,** an|äs|the|sie|ren

An|as|tig|mat (↑R 132), der; -en, -en, *auch* das; -s, -e ‹griech.› (*Fotogr.* ein Objektiv); **an|as|tig|ma|tisch** (unverzerrt)

A|nas|to|mo|se (↑R 132), die; -, -n ‹griech.› (*Med.* Verbindung, z. B. zwischen Blut- od. Lymphgefäßen)

A|na|them, das; -s, -e *u.* **A|na|the|ma,** das; -s, ...themata ‹griech.› (*Rel.* Verfluchung, Kirchenbann); **a|na|the|ma|ti|sie|ren**

a|na|ti|o|nal ‹lat.› (gleichgültig gegenüber der Nation, der man angehört)

A|na|tol (m. Vorn.); **A|na|to|li|en** [...iən] (asiat. Teil der Türkei); **a|na|to|lisch**

A|na|tom, der; -en, -en (↑R 126) ‹griech.› (*Med.* Lehrer der Anatomie); **A|na|to|mie,** die; -, ...ien (Lehre von Form u. Körperbau der [menschl.] Lebewesen; anatomisches Institut); **a|na|to|mie|ren** (sezieren); **a|na|to|misch**

A|na|xa|go|ras (altgriech. Philosoph)

an|ba|cken

an|bah|nen; An|bah|nung

an|ban|deln (*südd., österr. für* anbändeln); **an|bän|deln** *(ugs.);* ich bänd[e]le an (↑R 16); **An|bän|de|lung, An|bänd|lung** *(ugs.)*

An|bau, der; -[e]s, *Plur.* (*für* Gebäudeteile:) -ten; **an|bau|en; an|bau|fä|hig; An|bau‿flä|che, ...mö|bel**

An|be|ginn *(geh.);* seit -, von - [an]

an|be|hal|ten *(ugs.)*

an|bei [*auch* 'an...] *(Amtsspr.)*

an|bei|ßen; (↑R 50:) zum Anbeißen (*ugs. für* reizend anzusehen)
an|[be|]lan|gen; was mich an[be]langt, so ...
an|bel|len
an|be|que|men, sich (*veraltend für* sich anpassen)
an|be|rau|men; ich beraum[t]e an, *selten* ich anberaum[t]e; anberaumt; anzuberaumen; **An|be|rau|mung**
an|be|ten
An|be|tracht; *nur in* in Anbetracht dessen, dass ...
an|be|tref|fen; *nur in* was mich anbetrifft, so ...
An|be|tung
an|bie|dern, sich *(abwertend);* ich biedere mich an (↑R 16); **An|bie|de|rung** *(abwertend)*
an|bie|ten; An|bie|ter
an|bin|den; angebunden *(vgl. d.)*
An|biss
an|blaf|fen (*ugs. für* anbellen; zurechtweisen)
an|bla|sen
An|blick; an|bli|cken
an|blin|ken
an|boh|ren
An|bot, das; -[e]s, -e (*österr. neben* Angebot)
an|bras|sen (*Seemannsspr.* die Rahen in Längsrichtung bringen)
an|bra|ten; das Fleisch -
an|bräu|nen
an|bre|chen; der Tag bricht an *(geh.)*
an|bren|nen
an|brin|gen; etwas am Haus[e] -
An|bruch, der; -[e]s, *Plur. (Bergmannsspr.)* ...brüche (*geh. für* Beginn; *Bergmannsspr.* bloßgelegter Erzgang)
an|brül|len
an|brum|men
an|brü|ten
ANC = African National Congress [ˈɛfrikən ˈnɛʃ(ə)nəl ˈkɔŋgrɛs] ‹engl.› (Afrikanischer Nationalkongress [südafrikan. Partei])
An|cho|vis [anˈʃo:vis] *vgl.* Anschovis
An|ci|en|ni|tät [ãsiɛniˈtɛ:t], die; - ‹franz.› (*veraltet für* [Reihenfolge nach dem] Dienstalter); **An|ci|en|ni|täts|prin|zip; An|ci|en Ré|gime** [ã.siɛ̃: reˈʒi:m], das; - - (Zeit des franz. Absolutismus [vor der Franz. Revolution])
An|dacht, die; -, *Plur.* (*für* Gebetsstunden:) -en; **an|däch|tig; An|dachts|übung** (↑R 132); **an|dachts|voll** *(geh.)*
An|da|lu|si|en [...iən] (span. Landschaft); **An|da|lu|si|er** [...iər]; **an|da|lu|sisch; An|da|lu|sit** [*auch* ...ˈzit], der; -s, -e (ein Mineral)
An|da|ma|nen *Plur.* (Inselkette im nordöstl. Indischen Ozean)
an|dan|te ‹ital., „gehend"› (*Musik* mäßig langsam); **An|dan|te,** das; -[s], -s (mäßig langsames Tonstück); **an|dan|ti|no** (etwas beschleunigter als andante); **An|dan|ti|no,** das; -s *Plur.* -s *u.* ...ni (kürzeres Musikstück im Andante- od. Andantinotempo)
an|dau|en (*Med.* anfangen zu verdauen)
an|dau|ern; an|dau|ernd
An|dau|ung, die; - ‹*zu* andauen›
An|den *Plur.* (südamerik. Gebirge); *vgl.* Kordilleren
An|den|ken, das; -s, *Plur.* (*für* Erinnerungsgegenstände:) -
an|de|re, and|re; *(nach* ↑R 48 *im Allgemeinen kleingeschrieben:)* der, die, das and[e]re, *aber* die Suche nach dem Anderen (nach einer neuen Welt); der Dialog mit dem Anderen (dem Gegenüber; *Philos.*); eine, keine, jeder, alles and[e]re; die, keine, alle and[e]ren, andern; ein, kein and[e]rer; ein, kein, etwas, allerlei, nichts and[e]res; der eine, der and[e]re; und and[e]re, und and[e]res (*Abk.* u. a.); und and[e]re mehr, und and[e]res mehr (*Abk.* u. a. m.); von etwas and[e]rem, anderm sprechen; unter and[e]rem, anderm (*Abk.* u. a.); zum einen ..., zum anderen ...; eines and[e]ren, andern belehren; sich eines and[e]ren, andern besinnen; ich bin and[e]ren, andern Sinnes; and[e]res gedrucktes Material; and[e]re ähnliche Fälle; andere Gute; ein andermal, *aber* ein and[e]res Mal; das and[e]re Mal; ein um das and[e]re Mal; ein und das and[e]re Mal; *vgl.* anders; **an|de|ren|falls**[1]; *vgl.* Fall, der; **an|de|ren|orts**[1], **an|der|orts**[1] *(geh.);* **an|de|ren|tags**[1]; **an|de|ren|teils**[1], einesteils ..., -; **an|de|rer|seits,** an|der|seits, and|rer|seits; einerseits ..., -; **An|der|ge|schwis|ter|kind** [*auch* andərgəˈʃvi...] (*landsch. für* Verwandte, deren Großväter oder Großmütter Geschwister sind); **An|der|kon|to** (Treuhandkonto); **an|der|lei; an|der|mal;** ein andermal, *aber* ein and[e]res Mal
An|der|matt (schweiz. Ortsn.)
än|dern; ich ...ere (↑R 16)
an|dern|falls usw. *vgl.* anderenfalls usw.; **an|der|orts** *(geh.),* an|de|ren|orts, an|dern|orts
an|ders; jemand, niemand, wer anders (*bes. südd., österr. auch* and[e]rer); mit jemand, niemand anders (*bes. südd., österr. auch* and[e]rem, anderm) reden; ich sehe jemand, niemand anders (*bes. südd., österr. auch* and[e]ren, andern); irgendwo anders (irgendwo sonst), wo anders? (wo sonst?; *vgl. aber* woanders); anders als ... (*nicht:* anders wie ...); *vgl.* andere; anders sein, anders denken[d], anders geartet, lautend; (↑R 47:) die anders Denkenden, *auch* Andersdenkenden; **an|ders|ar|tig; An|ders|ar|tig|keit,** die; -
An|dersch (dt. Schriftsteller)
an|ders den|kend *vgl.* anders; **An|ders|den|ken|de,** der *u.* die; -n, -n (↑R 5 ff.); *vgl.* anders
an|der|seits, an|de|rer|seits, and|rer|seits
An|der|sen (dän. Dichter)
an|ders|far|big; an|ders ge|ar|tet *vgl.* anders; **An|ders|ge|sinn|te,** der *u.* die; -n, -n (↑R 5 ff.); **An|ders|gläu|bi|ge,** der *u.* die; -n, -n (↑R 5 ff.); **an|ders|he|rum; an|ders lau|tend** *vgl.* anders; **an|ders|rum; An|ders|sein; an|ders|spra|chig; an|ders|wie; an|ders|wo; an|ders|wo|her; an|ders|wo|hin**
an|dert|halb; in anderthalb Stunden; anderthalb Pfund; **an|dert|halb|fach; An|dert|halb|fa|che,** das; -n; *vgl.* Achtfache; **an|dert|halb|mal;** anderthalbmal so groß wie (*seltener* als) ...
Än|de|rung; Än|de|rungs|kün|di|gung *(Betriebsrecht)*
an|der|wär|tig; an|der|wärts; an|der|weit, an|der|wei|tig
an|deu|ten; An|deu|tung; an|deu|tungs|wei|se
an|dich|ten; jmdm. etwas -
an|di|cken
an|die|nen (*Kaufmannsspr.* [Waren] anbieten); **An|die|nung,** die; - *(Kaufmannsspr., Versicherungsw.);* **An|die|nungs|pflicht,** die; - *(Versicherungsw.)*
an|din (die Anden betreffend)
an|dis|ku|tie|ren
an|do|cken ‹dt.; engl.› (ein Raumfahrzeug an das andere koppeln)
An|dor|ra (Staat in den Pyrenäen); **An|dor|ra|ner; An|dor|ra|ne|rin; an|dor|ra|nisch**
An|drang, der; -[e]s; **an|drän|gen**
and|re *vgl.* andere
And|ré [anˈdre:, *franz.* ãˈdre:] (↑R 130; m. Vorn.); **And|rea** (w. Vorn.); **And|re|as** (m. Vorn.); **And|re|as‿kreuz, ...or|den** (ehem. höchster russ. Orden)
an|dre|hen; jmdm. etwas - (*ugs. für* jmdm. etwas Minderwertiges aufschwatzen)

[1] *Auch* an|dern|...

an|rer|seits, an|de|rer|seits, an|der|seits
An|dres (↑R 130; dt. Schriftsteller)
and|ro|gyn (↑R 130) ‹griech.› (*Biol.* männliche und weibliche Merkmale vereinigend; zwittrig); **And|ro|gy|nie,** die; -
an|dro|hen; An|dro|hung
And|ro|i|de (↑R 130), der; -n, -n (↑R 5 ff.) ‹griech.› (künstlicher Mensch, menschenähnliche Maschine)
And|ro|lo|ge (↑R 130), der; -n, -n ‹griech.› (*Med.* Facharzt für Andrologie); **And|ro|lo|gie,** die; - (Männerheilkunde); **and|ro|lo|gisch**
And|ro|ma|che [...xe:] (↑R 130; griech. Sagengestalt, Frau Hektors)
[1]**And|ro|me|da** (↑R 130; weibl. griech. Sagengestalt); [2]**And|ro|me|da,** die; - (ein Sternbild)
An|druck, der; -[e]s, -e (*Druckw.* Probe-, Prüfdruck); **an|dru|cken**
an|du|deln; sich einen - (*ugs.* sich betrinken); ich dud[e]le mir einen an (↑R 16)
Ä|ne|as (Held der griech.-röm. Sage)
an|ecken (↑R 132; an etwas anstoßen; *ugs. auch für* [bei jmdm.] Anstoß erregen)
an|ei|fern (*südd., österr. für* anspornen); **An|ei|fe|rung**
an|eig|nen, sich; ich eigne mir Kenntnisse an; **An|eig|nung**
an|ei|nan|der (↑R 132); *immer getrennt:* aneinander denken; sie haben aneinander gedacht; aneinander fügen; er hat die Teile aneinander gefügt; [im Streit] aneinander geraten; aneinander grenzen, legen, reihen usw.
Ä|ne|is, die; - (eine Dichtung Vergils)
A|nek|döt|chen (↑R 132); **A|nek|do|te,** die; -, -n ‹griech.› (kurze, jmdn. [humorvoll] charakterisierende Geschichte); **a|nek|do|ten|haft; a|nek|do|tisch**
an|ekeln (↑R 132); du ekelst mich an
A|ne|mo|graph, der; -en, -en (↑R 126) ‹griech.› (*Meteor.* selbst schreibender Windmesser); **A|ne|mo|me|ter,** das; -s, - (Windmesser); **A|ne|mo|ne,** die; -, -n (Windröschen)
an|emp|feh|len (dringend raten); ich empfehle (empfahl) an *u.* ich anempfehle (anempfahl); anempfohlen; anzuempfehlen
An|er|be, der; -n, -n (*Rechtsspr.* bäuerlicher Alleinerbe, Hoferbe); **An|er|ben‿fol|ge, ...recht**
an|er|bie|ten, sich; ich erbiete mich an; anerboten; anzuerbieten; *vgl.* bieten; **An|er|bie|ten,** das; -s, -; **An|er|bie|tung**
an|er|kann|ter|ma|ßen; an|er|ken|nen; ich erkenne (erkannte) an, *seltener* ich anerkenne (anerkannte); anerkannt; anzuerkennen; *vgl.* kennen; **an|er|ken|nens|wert; An|er|kennt|nis,** das; -ses, -se *(Rechtsspr.), sonst:* die; -, -se; **An|er|ken|nung; An|er|ken|nungs|schrei|ben**
A|ne|ro|id, das; -[e]s, -e ‹griech.› *u.* **A|ne|ro|id|ba|ro|me|ter** (*Meteor.* Gerät zum Anzeigen des Luftdrucks)
an|es|sen; ich habe mir einen Bauch angegessen; ich habe mich angegessen (*österr. ugs. für* bin satt)
A|neu|rys|ma (↑R 132), das; -s, ...men ‹griech.› (*Med.* Erweiterung der Schlagader)
an|fa|chen *(geh.)*
an|fah|ren (*auch für* heftig anreden); **An|fahrt; An|fahrts|weg**
An|fall, der; **an|fal|len; an|fäl|lig; An|fäl|lig|keit** *Plur. selten*
An|fang, der; -[e]s, ...fänge; *vgl.* anfangs; im Anfang; von Anfang an; zu Anfang; Anfang Januar; **an|fan|gen; An|fän|ger; An|fän|ge|rin; An|fän|ger|kurs; an|fäng|lich; an|fangs** (↑R 46); **An|fangs‿buch|sta|be, ...er|folg, ...ge|halt** (das), **...sta|di|um**
an|fas|sen; *vgl.* fassen
an|fau|chen
an|fau|len
an|fa|xen (ein Fax zuschicken)
an|fecht|bar; An|fecht|bar|keit, die; -; **an|fech|ten;** das ficht mich nicht an; **An|fech|tung**
an|fein|den; An|fein|dung
an|fer|ti|gen; An|fer|ti|gung
an|feuch|ten; An|feuch|ter
an|feu|ern; An|feu|e|rung
an|fi|xen (*ugs.* jmdn. zum Einnehmen von Drogen animieren)
an|flan|schen *(Technik)*
an|fle|hen; An|fle|hung
an|flie|gen; An|flug
an|for|dern; An|for|de|rung
An|fra|ge; die kleine oder große - [im Parlament]; **an|fra|gen;** bei jmdm. -, *schweiz.* jmdn. -
an|freun|den, sich; **An|freun|dung**
an|fü|gen; An|fü|gung
An|fuhr, die; -, -en; **an|füh|ren; An|füh|rer; An|füh|rung; An|füh|rungs‿strich, ...zei|chen**
an|fun|ken (durch Funkspruch)
an|fut|tern, sich *(ugs.);* du futterst dir einen Bauch an
An|ga|be (*auch [nur Sing.] ugs. für* Prahlerei, Übertreibung)
an|gän|gig (erlaubt; zulässig)
An|ga|ra [*od.* ...'ra], die; - (Fluss in Mittelsibirien)
an|geb|bar; an|ge|ben; An|ge|ber *(ugs.);* **An|ge|be|rei** *(ugs.);* **an|ge|be|risch** *(ugs.)*
An|ge|be|te|te, der *u.* die; -n, -n (↑R 5 ff.)
An|ge|bin|de, das; -s, - (*geh. für* Geschenk)
an|geb|lich
an|ge|bo|ren
An|ge|bot; An|ge|bots|lü|cke
an|ge|bracht
an|ge|bro|chen; eine Flasche ist -
an|ge|bun|den; kurz angebunden (*ugs. für* abweisend) sein
an|ge|dei|hen; *nur in* jmdm. etwas angedeihen lassen
An|ge|den|ken, das; -s (*veraltet für* Andenken, Souvenir; *geh. für* Erinnerung, Gedenken)
an|ge|führt; am angeführten Ort (*Abk.* a. a. O.)
an|ge|ge|ben; am angegebenen Ort (*Abk.* a. a. O.)
an|ge|gos|sen; wie angegossen sitzen (*ugs. für* genau passen)
an|ge|graut; -e Schläfen
an|ge|grif|fen (*auch für* geschwächt); **An|ge|grif|fen|heit,** die; -
an|ge|hei|ra|tet
an|ge|hei|tert (leicht betrunken)
an|ge|hen; das geht nicht an; es geht mich [nichts] an; jmdn. um etwas angehen (bitten); **an|ge|hend** (künftig)
an|ge|hö|ren; einem Volk[e] -; **an|ge|hö|rig; An|ge|hö|ri|ge,** der *u.* die; -n, -n (↑R 5 ff.); **An|ge|hö|rig|keit,** die; -
an|ge|jahrt
Angekl. = Angeklagte[r]
An|ge|klag|te, der *u.* die; -n, -n; ↑R 5 ff. (*Abk.* Angekl.)
an|ge|knackst *(ugs.)*
an|ge|krän|kelt
An|gel, die; -, -n
An|ge|la [*österr.* aŋ'ge:la, *ital.* 'andʒela] (w. Vorn.)
an|ge|le|gen; ich lasse mir etwas - sein; **An|ge|le|gen|heit; an|ge|le|gent|lich;** auf das, aufs Angelegentlichste *od.* auf das, aufs angelegentlichste (↑R 47)
An|gel|ha|ken
[1]**An|ge|li|ka** (w. Vorn.); [2]**An|ge|li|ka,** die; -, *Plur.* ...ken *u.* -s (Engelwurz)
An|ge|li|na [andʒe'li:na] (w. Vorn.)
an|geln; ich ...[e]le (↑R 16)
An|geln *Plur.* (germ. Volksstamm)
An|ge|lo ['andʒelo] (m. Vorn.)
an|ge|lo|ben (*geh. für* zusagen, versprechen; *österr. für* feierlich vereidigen); **An|ge|lo|bung**

An|gel₋punkt, ...ru|te
An|gel|sach|se, der; -n, -n (Angehöriger eines germ. Volksstammes); **an|gel|säch|sisch;** *vgl.* deutsch; **An|gel|säch|sisch,** das; -[s] (Sprache); *vgl.* Deutsch; **An|gel|säch|si|sche,** das; -n; *vgl.* Deutsche, das
An|gel|schein
An|ge|lus, der, *auch* das; -, - ‹lat.› (kath. Gebet; Glockenzeichen); **An|ge|lus|läu|ten,** das; -s
an|ge|mes|sen; An|ge|mes|sen|heit, die; -
an|ge|nä|hert
an|ge|nehm; etwas Angenehmes erleben
an|ge|nom|men; angenommen, dass ... (↑R 88)
an|ge|passt; An|ge|passt|heit, die; -
An|ger, der; -s, -; **An|ger|dorf**
an|ge|regt
an|ge|säu|selt (*ugs. für* leicht betrunken)
an|ge|schla|gen (*ugs. für* erschöpft; beschädigt)
an|ge|schmutzt (leicht schmutzig)
An|ge|schul|dig|te, der *u.* die; -n, -n (↑R 5 ff.)
an|ge|se|hen (geachtet)
An|ge|sicht *Plur.* Angesichter *u.* Angesichte *(geh.);* **an|ge|sichts** (↑R 46); *Präp. mit Gen.:* - des Todes
an|ge|spannt
an|ge|stammt
An|ge|stell|te, der *u.* die; -n, -n (↑R 5 ff.); **An|ge|stell|ten|ver|si|che|rung; An|ge|stell|ten|ver|si|che|rungs|ge|setz** (*Abk.* AVG)
an|ge|stie|felt; angestiefelt kommen *(ugs.)*
an|ge|strengt; An|ge|strengt|heit, die; -
an|ge|tan
an|ge|trun|ken (leicht betrunken)
an|ge|wandt; -e Kunst; -e Mathematik, Physik; *vgl.* anwenden
an|ge|wie|sen; auf eine Person oder eine Sache - sein
an|ge|wöh|nen; ich gewöhne mir etwas an; **An|ge|wohn|heit; An|ge|wöh|nung**
an|ge|wur|zelt; wie - stehen bleiben
An|gi|na, die; -, ...nen ‹lat.› (*Med.* Mandelentzündung); **An|gi|na pec|to|ris,** die; - - (Herzkrampf)
An|gi|om, das; -s, -e ‹griech.› (*Med.* Gefäßgeschwulst); **An|gi|o|sper|men** *Plur.* (*Bot.* bedecktsamige Blütenpflanzen)
An|kor (Ruinenstadt in Kambodscha)
Ang|lai|se [ãˈglɛːzə] (↑R 130), die; -, -n ‹franz.› („englischer" Tanz)
an|glei|chen; An|glei|chung
Ang|ler
an|glie|dern; An|glie|de|rung
ang|li|ka|nisch (↑R 130) ‹mlat.›; -e Kirche (engl. Staatskirche); **Ang|li|ka|nis|mus,** der; - (Lehre u. Wesen[sform] der engl. Staatskirche); **ang|li|sie|ren** (englische Sitten u. Gebräuche einführen; englisieren); **Ang|list,** der; -en, -en (Wissenschaftler auf dem Gebiet der Anglistik); **Ang|lis|tik,** die; - (engl. Sprach- u. Literaturwissenschaft); **Ang|lis|tin; Ang|li|zis|mus,** der; -, ...men (engl. Spracheigentümlichkeit in einer anderen Sprache); **Ang|lo|ame|ri|ka|ner** (↑R 130 *u.* 132; aus England stammender Amerikaner; *auch* Sammelname für Engländer u. Amerikaner); **ang|lo|fran|zö|sisch** [*auch* ˈaŋglo...]; **Ang|lo|ka|na|di|er;** *vgl.* Angloamerikaner; **Ang|lo|ma|ne,** der; -n, -n (↑R 126) ‹lat; griech.› (jmd., der alles Englische in übertriebener Weise schätzt); **Ang|lo|ma|nie,** die; -; **ang|lo|nor|man|nisch; ang|lo|phil** (englandfreundlich); **Ang|lo|phi|lie,** die; -; **ang|lo|phob** (englandfeindlich); **Ang|lo|pho|bie,** die; -; **ang|lo|phon** (englischsprachig)
An|go|la (Staat in Afrika); **An|go|la|ner; An|go|la|ne|rin; an|go|la|nisch**
An|go|ra₋ka|nin|chen, ...kat|ze, ...wol|le ‹*nach* Angora, dem früheren Namen von Ankara›
An|gos|tu|ra ®, der; -s, -s ‹span.› (ein Bitterlikör)
an|grei|fen; *vgl.* angegriffen; **An|grei|fer**
an|gren|zen; An|gren|zer; An|gren|zung
An|griff, der; -[e]s, -e; in - nehmen; **an|grif|fig** (*schweiz. für* draufgängerisch, zupackend); **An|griffs₋drit|tel** *(Eishockey),* **...geist, ...krieg, ...lust; an|griffs|lus|tig; An|griffs₋spie|ler** *(Sportspr.),* **...waf|fe; an|griffs|wei|se**
Angst, die; -, Ängste; in Angst, in [tausend] Ängsten sein; Angst haben; jmdm. Angst [und Bange] machen; *aber* (↑R 46): mir ist, wird angst [und bange]; **ängs|ten,** sich (*nur noch geh. für* sich ängstigen); **angst₋er|füllt, ...frei; Angst|ge|fühl; Angst|geg|ner** (*Sportspr.* Gegner, der einem nicht liegt, den man fürchtet); **Angst|ha|se** *(ugs.);* **ängs|ti|gen; Ängs|ti|gung; ängst|lich; Ängst|lich|keit,** die; -; **Angst₋neu|ro|se** (*Med., Psych.* krankhaftes Angstgefühl), **...par|tie** *(Sportspr.),* **...psy|cho|se** *(Med., Psych.),* **...röh|re** (*scherzh. für* Zylinder)
Ångst|röm [ˈɔŋ... *od.* ˈaŋ...] (↑R 130), das; -[s] (veraltende Einheit der Licht- u. Röntgenwellenlänge; *Zeichen* Å)
Angst₋ruf, ...schweiß; angst|voll
an|gu|lar ‹lat.› (zu einem Winkel gehörend, Winkel...)
an|gur|ten; sich -
Anh. = Anhang
an|ha|ben *(ugs.);* ..., dass er nichts anhat, angehabt hat; er kann mir nichts -
an|hä|keln (hinzuhäkeln)
an|ha|ken
[1]An|halt (ehem. Land des Deutschen Reichs); **[2]An|halt** (Anhaltspunkt); **an|hal|ten; an|hal|tend; [1]An|hal|ter** *vgl.* Anhaltiner; **[2]An|hal|ter** *(ugs.);* per - fahren (*ugs.* Fahrzeuge anhalten, um mitgenommen zu werden); **An|hal|ti|ner** *od.* An|hal|ter ‹*zu* [1]Anhalt›; **an|hal|tisch** ([1]Anhalt betreffend); **An|halts|punkt**
an|hand *Präp. mit Gen.:* anhand des Buches; anhand von Unterlagen; *vgl.* Hand
An|hang, der; -[e]s, Anhänge (*Abk.* Anh.); **[1]an|hän|gen;** er hing einer Sekte an; *vgl.* [1]hängen; **[2]an|hän|gen;** er hängte den Zettel [an die Tür] an; *vgl.* [2]hängen; **An|hän|ger; An|hän|ger|schaft; an|hän|gig** (*Rechtsspr.* beim Gericht zur Entscheidung liegend); eine Klage - machen (Klage erheben); **an|häng|lich** (treu); **An|häng|lich|keit,** die; -; **An|häng|sel,** das; -s, -; **an|hangs|wei|se**
an|hau|chen
an|hau|en (*ugs. auch für* formlos ansprechen, um etwas bitten); wir hauten das Mädchen an
an|häu|fen; An|häu|fung
an|he|ben (*auch geh. für* anfangen); er hob, *veraltet* hub an zu singen, zu sprechen usw.; **An|he|bung**
an|hef|ten; etwas am Hut *od.* an den Hut anheften
an|heim *(geh.); nur in den Fügungen* anheim fallen (zufallen, zum Opfer fallen); anheim geben (anvertrauen, überlassen); anheim stellen (überlassen)
an|hei|meln; es heimelt mich an
an|heim fal|len, ge|ben, stel|len *vgl.* anheim
an|hei|schig; *nur in* sich anheischig machen (*geh. für* sich verpflichten, sich anbieten)

an|hei|zen
an|herr|schen; jmdn. -
an|heu|ern; jmdn. -; auf einem Schiff -
An|hieb; *nur in* auf Anhieb (sofort)
an|him|meln *(ugs.)*
an|hin; bis - (*schweiz.* bis jetzt)
An|hö|he
an|hö|ren; **An|hö|rung**
An|hyd|rid (↑R 130), das; -s, -e ⟨griech.⟩ (*Chemie* durch Wasserentzug entstandene Verbindung); **An|hyd|rit** [*auch* ...'drit], der; -s, -e (wasserfreier Gips)
än|ig|ma|tisch ⟨griech.⟩ (*selten für* rätselhaft)
A|ni|lin, das; -s ⟨arab.-port.⟩ (Ausgangsstoff für Farben u. Heilmittel); **A|ni|lin‿far|be, ...le|der, ...rot**
a|ni|ma|lisch ⟨lat.⟩ (tierisch; tierhaft; triebhaft); **A|ni|ma|lis|mus**, der; - (religiöse Verehrung von Tieren); **A|ni|ma|teur** [...'tø:r], der; -s, -e ⟨franz.⟩ (Spielleiter in einem Freizeitzentrum); **A|ni|ma|ti|on**, die; -, -en ⟨lat.⟩ (organisierte Sport- u. Freizeitaktivitäten für Urlauber; Belebung, Bewegung der Figuren im Trickfilm); **a|ni|ma|to** ⟨ital.⟩ (*Musik* beseelt, belebt); **a|ni|mie|ren** ⟨franz.⟩ (beleben, anregen, ermuntern); **A|ni|mier‿knei|pe** *(ugs.)*, **...mäd|chen** *(ugs.)*; **A|ni|mis|mus**, der; -, ...men ⟨lat.⟩ (Lehre von der Beseeltheit aller Dinge); **A|ni|mo**, das; -s ⟨ital.⟩ (*österr. für* Schwung, Lust; Vorliebe); **A|ni|mo|si|tät**, die; -, -en ⟨lat.⟩ (Feindseligkeit); **A|ni|mus**, der; - ⟨„Seele"⟩ (*scherzh. für* Ahnung)
An|ion (↑R 132), das; -s, -en ⟨griech.⟩ (*Physik* negativ geladenes elektrisches Teilchen)
A|nis [*od.* 'a:nis, *österr. u. schweiz. nur so*], der; -es, -e ⟨griech.⟩ (eine Gewürz- u. Heilpflanze); **A|nis|bo|gen** *od.* **...schar|te** (*österr.* eine Gebäckart); **A|ni|sette** [...'zɛt], der; -s, -s ⟨franz.⟩ (Anislikör)
A|ni|ta (w. Vorn.)
An|ja (w. Vorn.)
An|jou [ã'ʒu:] (altfranz. Grafschaft; Fürstengeschlecht)
Ank. = Ankunft
An|ka|ra (Hptst. der Türkei)
An|ka|the|te, die; -, -n *(Geom.)*
An|kauf; An- und Verkauf (↑R 23); **an|kau|fen**; **An|kaufs‿etat** (↑R 132), **...recht**
[1]**An|ke** (w. Vorn.)
[2]**An|ke**, der; -n, -n; ↑R 126 (ein Fisch)
An|ken, der; -s (*schweiz. mdal. für* Butter)
An|ker, der; -s, -; vor - gehen, liegen; **An|ker‿bo|je, ...ket|te**; **an|kern**; ich ...ere (↑R 16); **An|ker‿platz, ...spill, ...tau** (das; -[e]s, -e), **...win|de**
an|ket|ten
an|kläf|fen *(ugs.)*
An|kla|ge; **An|kla|ge|bank** *Plur.* ...bänke; **an|kla|gen**; **An|klä|ger**; **An|kla|ge|schrift**
Ank|lam (Stadt an der Peene)
an|klam|mern; sich -
An|klang; - finden
an|kle|ben
An|klei|de|ka|bi|ne; **an|klei|den**; sich -; **An|klei|de|raum**
an|kli|cken
an|klin|gen
an|klop|fen
an|knab|bern
an|knack|sen (*ugs. für* leicht anbrechen; schädigen); meine Gesundheit ist angeknackst
an|knip|sen; das Licht - *(ugs.)*
an|knüp|fen; **An|knüp|fung**; **An|knüp|fungs|punkt**
an|ko|chen
an|koh|len; jmdn. - (*ugs. für* zum Spaß belügen)
an|kom|men; mich (*veraltet* mir) kommt ein Ekel an; es kommt mir nicht darauf an; **An|kömm|ling**
an|kön|nen (*ugs. für* sich gegen jmdn. durchsetzen können); er kann gegen ihn nicht an
an|kop|peln
an|kör|nen (*Handw.* zu bohrende Löcher mit dem Körner markieren)
an|kot|zen *(derb)*; jmdn. - (anwidern)
an|kral|len; sich an das *od.* am Gitter -
an|krat|zen; sich - (*ugs. für* sich einschmeicheln)
an|krei|den; jmdm. etwas - (*ugs. für* zur Last legen)
An|kreis *(Geometrie)*
an|kreu|zen
an|kün|den, *älter u. schweiz. für* **an|kün|di|gen**; **An|kün|di|gung**
An|kunft, die; -, Ankünfte *Plur. selten* (*Abk.* Ank.); **An|kunfts‿stem|pel, ...zeit**
an|kur|beln; **An|kur|be|lung, An|kurb|lung**
An|ky|lo|se, die; -, -n ⟨griech.⟩ (*Med.* Gelenkversteifung)
an|lä|cheln; **an|la|chen**
An|la|ge; etwas als *od.* in der - übersenden; **An|la|ge|be|ra|ter** *(Wirtsch.)*; **An|la|gen|fi|nan|zie|rung**; **An|la|ge|pa|pier**
an|la|gern *(Chemie)*; **An|la|ge|rung**
An|la|ge|ver|mö|gen
an|lan|den; etwas, jmdn. - (an Land bringen); irgendwo - (anlegen); das Ufer landet an (*Geol.* verbreitert sich durch Sandansammlung); **An|lan|dung**
an|lan|gen *vgl.* an[be]langen
An|lass, der; -es, ...lässe; Anlass geben, nehmen; **an|las|sen**; **An|las|ser** *(Technik)*; **an|läss|lich** *(Amtsspr.)*; *Präp. mit Gen.*: anlässlich des Festes
an|las|ten (zur Last legen)
An|lauf; **an|lau|fen**; **An|lauf‿ge|schwin|dig|keit, ...stel|le, ...zeit**
An|laut; **an|lau|ten** (mit einem bestimmten Laut beginnen); **an|läu|ten**; jmdn., *südd. auch, schweiz. nur* jmdm. - (jmdn. telefonisch anrufen)
an|le|gen; **An|le|ge|platz**; **An|le|ger** (jmd., der Kapital anlegt; *Druckw.* Papiereinführer); **An|le|ge|rin**; **An|le|ge|stel|le**
an|leh|nen; ich lehne mich an die Wand an; **An|leh|nung**; **an|leh|nungs|be|dürf|tig**
An|leh|re (*schweiz. für* Anlernzeit, Kurzausbildung)
an|lei|ern (*ugs. für* ankurbeln); ein Hilfsprogramm -
An|lei|he; **An|lei|he|ab|lö|sung**; **An|lei|he|pa|pier**
an|lei|men
an|lei|nen; den Hund -
an|lei|ten; **An|lei|tung**
An|lern|be|ruf; **an|ler|nen**; jmdn. -; das habe ich mir angelernt *(ugs.)*; **An|lern|ling**; **An|lern|zeit**
an|le|sen
an|lie|fern; **An|lie|fe|rung**
an|lie|gen; eng am Körper -; *vgl.* angelegen; **An|lie|gen**, das; -s, - (Wunsch); **an|lie|gend** *(Kaufmannsspr.)*; - (anbei, hiermit) der Bericht; **An|lie|ger** (Anwohner); **An|lie|ger‿staat** (*Plur.* ...staaten), **...ver|kehr**
an|lie|ken (*Seemannsspr.* das Liek an einem Segel befestigen)
an|lo|cken
an|lö|ten
an|lü|gen
an|lu|ven [...f...] (*Seemannsspr.* Winkel zwischen Kurs u. Windrichtung verkleinern)
Anm. = Anmerkung
An|ma|che, die; - *(ugs.)*; **an|mä|che|lig** (*schweiz. mdal. für* reizend, attraktiv); **an|ma|chen** (*ugs. auch für* ansprechen; belästigen) jmdn. -
an|mah|nen
an|ma|len
An|marsch, der; **An|marsch|weg**
an|ma|ßen, sich; du maßt dir etwas an; **an|ma|ßend**; **An|ma|ßung**
an|me|ckern *(ugs.)*

an|mei|ern (*ugs. für* anführen, betrügen)

An|mel|de|for|mu|lar; an|melden; An|mel|de|pflicht; an|mel|de|pflich|tig; An|mel|dung

an|men|gen *(landsch.);* Mehl [mit Sauerteig] - (anrühren)

an|mer|ken; ich ließ mir nichts -; **An|mer|kung** (*Abk.* Anm.)

an|mes|sen; jmdm. etwas -

an|mie|ten; An|mie|tung

an|mon|tie|ren

an|mot|zen (*ugs. für* nörgelnd belästigen); jmdn. -

an|mus|tern (*Seemannsspr.* anwerben; den Dienst aufnehmen); **An|mus|te|rung**

An|mut, die; -; **an|mu|ten;** es mutet mich komisch an; **an|mu|tig; an|mut[s]|voll; An|mu|tung** (*Psych.* emotionale Wirkung von Wahrnehmungen usw. auf den Erlebenden)

[1]**An|na** (w. Vorn.); Anna selbdritt (Anna, Maria u. das Jesuskind)

[2]**An|na,** der; -[s], -[s] ‹Hindi› (frühere Münzeinheit in Indien; $^1/_{16}$ Rupie)

An|na|bel|la (w. Vorn.)

an|na|deln (*österr. für* mit einer Stecknadel befestigen); ich nad[e]le an (↑R 16)

an|na|geln

an|nä|hen

an|nä|hern; sich -; **an|nä|hernd;** - gleich groß; **An|nä|he|rung; An|nä|he|rungs|ver|such; an|nä|he|rungs|wei|se**

An|nah|me, die; -, -n; **An|nah|me₋er|klä|rung, ...stel|le, ...ver|merk, ...ver|wei|ge|rung**

An|na|len *Plur.* ‹lat.› ([geschichtliche] Jahrbücher)

An|na|pur|na, der; -[s] (Gebirgsmassiv im Himalaja)

An|na|ten *Plur.* ‹lat.› (finanzielle Abgaben an die päpstl. Kurie im MA.)

Änn|chen (w. Vorn.); **An|ne, Än|ne** (*für* Anna); **An|ne|do|re; An|ne|gret; An|ne|heid** *u.* **An|ne|hei|de;** ↑R 92 (w. Vorn.)

an|nehm|bar; an|neh|men; *vgl.* angenommen; **an|nehm|lich** *(veraltet);* **An|nehm|lich|keit**

an|nek|tie|ren ‹lat.› (sich [gewaltsam] aneignen)

An|ne|li (w. Vorn.); **An|ne|lie|se; An|ne|lo|re; An|ne|ma|rie; An|ne|ro|se;** ↑R 92 (w. Vorn.)

An|net|te (w. Vorn.)

An|nex, der; -es, -e ‹lat.› (Zubehör; Anhängsel); **An|ne|xi|on,** die; -, -en ([gewaltsame] Aneignung); **An|ne|xi|o|nis|mus,** der; - (Bestrebungen, eine Annexion herbeizuführen)

An|ni, Än|ni (w. Vorn.)

An|ni|ver|sar [...v...], das; -s, -e ‹lat.› *u.* **An|ni|ver|sa|ri|um,** das; -s, ...ien [...iən] *meist Plur.* (*kath. Kirche* jährlich wiederkehrende Gedächtnisfeier für einen Toten)

an|no, ‹lat.› (*veraltet für* im Jahre; *Abk.* a.); anno elf; anno dazumal; anno Tobak (*ugs. für* in alter Zeit); anno Domini, *in älteren Dokumenten o. Ä.:* Anno Domini (im Jahre des Herrn; *Abk.* A. D.)

An|non|ce [aˈnɔŋsə *od.* aˈnõːsə, *österr.* aˈnõːs], die; -, -n [...s(ə)n] ‹franz.› (Zeitungsanzeige); **An|non|cen|ex|pe|di|ti|on** (Anzeigenvermittlung); **An|non|ceu|se** [...ˈsøːzə], die; -, -n (Angestellte im Gaststättengewerbe); **an|non|cie|ren** [...ˈsiː...]

An|no|ne, die; -, -n ‹indian.› (trop. Baum mit essbaren Früchten)

An|no|ta|ti|on, die; -, -en *meist Plur.* ‹lat.› (*veraltet für* Aufzeichnung, Vermerk; *Buchw.* kurze Charakterisierung eines Buches)

an|nu|ell ‹franz.› (*Bot.* einjährig); **An|nu|i|tät** [...u|i...], die; -, -en ‹lat.› (jährliche Zahlung zur Tilgung einer Schuld)

an|nul|lie|ren ‹lat.› (für ungültig erklären); **An|nul|lie|rung**

An|nun|zi|a|ten|or|den (ehem. höchster ital. Orden)

A|no|de (↑R 132), die; -, -n ‹griech.› (*Physik* positive Elektrode, Pluspol)

an|öden (↑R 132; *ugs. für* langweilen)

A|no|den₋bat|te|rie (↑R 132; *Physik*), **...span|nung, ...strah|len** *(Plur.)*

a|no|mal [*od.* ...ˈmaːl] (↑R 132) ‹griech.› (unregelmäßig, regelwidrig); **A|no|ma|lie,** die; -, ...ien

A|no|mie, die; -, -n ‹griech.› (*Soziol.* Zustand, in dem die Stabilität der sozialen Beziehungen gestört ist)

a|no|nym (↑R 132) ‹griech.› (ohne Nennung des Namens, ungenannt); ein -er Anrufer, *aber* (↑R 56): Anonyme Alkoholiker; **a|no|ny|mi|sie|ren; A|no|ny|mi|tät,** die; - (Namenlosigkeit); **A|no|ny|mus,** der; -, *Plur.* ...mi *u.* ...nymen (Ungenannter)

A|no|phe|les (↑R 132), die; -, - ‹griech.› (*Zool.* Malariamücke)

A|no|rak, der; -s, -s ‹eskim.› (Windbluse mit Kapuze)

an|ord|nen; An|ord|nung (*Abk.* AO)

an|or|ga|nisch ‹griech.› (unbelebt); -e Chemie, Natur

a|nor|mal ‹mlat.› (regelwidrig, ungewöhnlich, krankhaft)

A|nor|thit [*auch* ...ˈtit] (↑R 132), der; -s ‹griech.› (ein Mineral)

A|nouilh [aˈnuj] (franz. Dramatiker)

an|pa|cken

an|pad|deln; An|pad|deln, das; -s (jährl. Beginn des Paddelsports)

an|pas|sen; sich -; **An|pas|sung,** die; -, -en *Plur. selten;* **an|pas|sungs|fä|hig**

an|pei|len

an|pfei|fen (*ugs. auch für* heftig tadeln); **An|pfiff**

an|pflan|zen; An|pflan|zung

an|pflau|men (*ugs. für* necken, verspotten); **An|pflau|me|rei**

an|pi|cken (*österr. ugs. für* ankleben)

an|pin|keln *(ugs.)*

an|pin|nen (*ugs. für* mit Pinnen befestigen)

an|pir|schen; sich - (*ugs. für* sich heranschleichen)

an|pö|beln (*ugs. abwertend* in ungebührlicher Weise belästigen)

An|prall, der; -[e]s; **an|pral|len**

an|pran|gern (öffentl. tadeln); ich prangere an (↑R 16); **An|pran|ge|rung**

an|prei|en *(Seemannsspr.);* ein anderes Schiff - (anrufen)

an|prei|sen; An|prei|sung

An|pro|be; an|pro|bie|ren

an|pum|pen *(ugs.);* jmdn. - (sich von jmdm. Geld leihen)

an|quas|seln (*ugs. für* ungeniert ansprechen)

an|quat|schen (*ugs. für* ungeniert ansprechen)

an|rai|nen (angrenzen); **An|rai|ner** (*Rechtsspr., bes. österr. für* Anlieger, Grenznachbar); **An|rai|ner|staat**

an|ran|zen (*ugs. für* scharf tadeln); du ranzt an; **An|ran|zer** *(ugs.)*

an|ra|ten; An|ra|ten, das; -s; auf -

an|rau|chen; die Zigarre -

an|rau|en; angeraut

an|raun|zen (*ugs. für* scharf zurechtweisen)

an|rech|nen; das rechne ich dir hoch an; **An|rech|nung;** *(Amtsspr.:)* in - bringen, *dafür besser:* anrechnen

An|recht; An|rechts|kar|te

An|re|de; An|re|de₋fall (der; *für* Vokativ), **...für|wort** (z. B. du, Sie); **an|re|den;** jmdn. mit Sie, du -

an|re|gen; an|re|gend; An|re|gung; An|re|gungs|mit|tel, das

an|rei|chern; ich reichere an (↑R 16); **An|rei|che|rung**

an|rei|hen; an|rei|hend (*für* kopulativ)

An|rei|se; an|rei|sen; An|rei|se|tag

ạn|rei|ßen; Ạn|rei|ßer (Vorzeichner; aufdringlicher Kundenwerber); **ạn|rei|ße|risch** (aufdringlich; marktschreierisch)
Ạn|reiz; ạn|rei|zen
ạn|rem|peln *(ugs.);* **Ạn|rem|pe|lung, Ạn|remp|lung** *(ugs.)*
ạn|ren|nen
Ạn|rich|te, die; -, -n; **ạn|rich|ten; Ạn|rich|te|tisch**
Ạn|riss, der; -es, -e (*Technik* Vorzeichnung; *Sport* kräftiges Durchziehen zu Beginn eines Ruderschlages)
ạn|rü|chig; Ạn|rü|chig|keit, die; -
ạn|ru|cken (mit einem Ruck anfahren); **ạn|rü|cken** ([in einer Formation] näher kommen)
ạn|ru|dern; Ạn|ru|dern, das; -s (jährl. Beginn des Rudersports)
Ạn|ruf; Ạn|ruf|be|ant|wor|ter; ạn|ru|fen; Ạn|ru|fer; Ạn|ru|fung
ạn|rüh|ren
ạns; ↑R 13 (an das); bis ans Ende
ạn|sä|en; Weizen -
Ạn|sa|ge, die; -, -n; **Ạn|sa|ge|dienst; ạn|sa|gen**
ạn|sä|gen
Ạn|sa|ger (*kurz für* Fernseh- od. Rundfunkansager); **Ạn|sa|ge|rin**
ạn|sa|men (*Forstw.* sich durch herabfallende Samen entwickeln)
ạn|sam|meln; Ạn|samm|lung
ạn|säs|sig; Ạn|säs|sig|keit, die; -
Ạn|satz; Ạn|satz‿punkt, ...rohr *(Med.),* **...stück; ạn|satz|wei|se**
ạn|sau|fen *(derb);* ich saufe mir einen an (betrinke mich)
ạn|sau|gen
ạn|säu|seln; ich säusele mir einen an (*ugs. für* betrinke mich leicht)
Ạns|bach (Stadt in Mittelfranken)
Ạn|schaf|fe, die; - (*ugs.; auch für* Prostitution); **ạn|schaf|fen** (*bayr., österr. auch für* anordnen); *vgl.* [1]schaffen; **Ạn|schaf|fung; Ạn|schaf|fungs|kos|ten** *Plur.*
ạn|schäf|ten; Pflanzen - (veredeln)
ạn|schal|ten
ạn|schau|en; ạn|schau|lich; Ạn|schau|lich|keit, die; -; **Ạn|schau|ung; Ạn|schau|ungs‿ma|te|ri|al, ...un|ter|richt**
Ạn|schein, der; -[e]s; allem, dem - nach; **ạn|schei|nend;** *vgl.* scheinbar
ạn|schei|ßen (*derb für* heftig tadeln)
ạn|schi|cken, sich
ạn|schie|ben
ạn|schie|ßen
ạn|schim|meln
ạn|schir|ren; ein Pferd -
Ạn|schiss, der; -es, -e (*derb für* heftiger Tadel)
Ạn|schlag; ạn|schla|gen; das Essen schlägt an; er hat angeschlagen (*südd., österr. für* das Fass angestochen, angezapft); **Ạn|schlä|ger** *(Bergmannsspr.);* **ạn|schlä|gig** (*landsch. für* schlau, geschickt); **Ạn|schlag|säu|le**
ạn|schlei|chen; sich -
[1]ạn|schlei|fen; sie hat das Messer angeschliffen (ein wenig scharf geschliffen); *vgl.* [1]schleifen; **[2]ạn|schlei|fen;** er hat den Sack angeschleift (*ugs. für* schleifend herangezogen); *vgl.* [2]schleifen
ạn|schlep|pen
ạn|schlie|ßen; ạn|schlie|ßend;
Ạn|schluss; Ạn|schluss|ka|bel; Ạn|schluss|stre|cke (↑R 136); **Ạn|schluss|tref|fer** *(Sport)*
ạn|schmei|cheln, sich
ạn|schmie|gen; sich an jmdn. -; **ạn|schmieg|sam; Ạn|schmieg|sam|keit,** die; -
ạn|schmie|ren (*ugs. auch für* betrügen)
ạn|schmut|zen; angeschmutzt
ạn|schnal|len; sich -; **Ạn|schnall|pflicht,** die; -
ạn|schnau|zen (*ugs. für* grob tadeln); **Ạn|schnau|zer** *(ugs.)*
ạn|schnei|den; Ạn|schnitt
Ạn|schop|pung (*Med.* vermehrte Ansammlung von Blut in den Kapillaren)
An|scho̲|vis [...vis], die; -, - ‹griech.› ([gesalzene] kleine Sardelle)
ạn|schrau|ben
ạn|schrei|ben; Ạn|schrei|ben
ạn|schrei|en
Ạn|schrift
ạn|schul|di|gen; Ạn|schul|di|gung
Ạn|schuss *(Jägerspr.)*
ạn|schwär|zen (*ugs. auch für* verleumden)
ạn|schwei|ßen
[1]ạn|schwel|len; der Strom schwillt an, war angeschwollen; *vgl.* [1]schwellen; **[2]ạn|schwel|len;** der Regen hat die Flüsse angeschwellt; *vgl.* [2]schwellen; **Ạn|schwel|lung**
ạn|schwem|men; Ạn|schwem|mung
ạn|schwin|deln *(ugs.);* jmdn. -
ạn|schwit|zen (in heißem Fett gelb werden lassen)
Ạn|schwung *(Sportspr.)*
ạn|se|geln; Ạn|se|geln, das; -s (jährl. Beginn des Segel[flug]sports)
ạn|se|hen; ich sehe mir etw. an; *vgl.* angesehen; **Ạn|se|hen,** das; -s; ohne - der Person (ganz gleich, um wen es sich handelt); **ạn|se|hens|wert; ạn|sehn|lich; Ạn|sehn|lich|keit,** die; -
ạn|sei|len; sich -
ạn sein *vgl.* an
Ạn|selm (m. Vorn.); *vgl.* Anshelm; **An|se̲l|ma** (w. Vorn.)
ạn|set|zen; am oberen Ende -; einen Saum an den *od.* am Rock -
Ạns|gar (m. Vorn.); **Ạns|helm** (m. Vorn.)
[1]an si̱ch (eigentlich); **[2]ạn sịch;** etw. an sich haben, bringen
Ạn|sicht, die; -, -en; meiner Ansicht nach (*Abk.* m. A. n.); **ạn|sich|tig;** *mit Gen.:* des Gebirges ansichtig werden *(geh.);* **Ạn|sichts‿kar|te, ...sa|che, ...sen|dung**
ạn|sie|deln; sich -; **Ạn|sie|de|lung; Ạn|sied|ler; Ạn|sied|le|rin; Ạn|sied|lung** *vgl.* Ansiedelung
Ạn|sin|nen, das; -s, -; ein - an jmdn. stellen
Ạn|sitz (*Jägerspr.; österr. auch für* repräsentativer Wohnsitz)
an|so̲nst (*schweiz., österr. für* anderenfalls); **an|so̲ns|ten** (*ugs. für* im Übrigen, anderenfalls)
ạn|span|nen; Ạn|span|nung
ạn|spa|ren
ạn|spei|en *(geh.)*
Ạn|spiel, das; -[e]s *(Sportspr.);* **ạn|spiel|bar; ạn|spie|len; Ạn|spie|lung** (versteckter Hinweis)
ạn|spin|nen; etw. spinnt sich an
ạn|spit|zen (*ugs. auch für* antreiben); **Ạn|spit|zer**
Ạn|sporn, der; -[e]s; **ạn|spor|nen; Ạn|spor|nung**
Ạn|spra|che; ạn|sprech|bar; ạn|spre|chen; auf etw. - (reagieren); **ạn|spre|chend;** am -sten (↑R 47); **Ạn|sprech|part|ner**
ạn|sprin|gen
ạn|sprit|zen
Ạn|spruch; etwas in - nehmen; **ạn|spruchs|los; Ạn|spruchs|lo|sig|keit,** die; -; **ạn|spruchs|voll**
Ạn|sprung
ạn|spu|cken
ạn|spü|len; Ạn|spü|lung
ạn|sta|cheln
Ạn|stalt, die; -, -en; keine -en zu etw. machen (nicht beginnen [wollen]); **Ạn|stalts‿er|zie|hung, ...lei|ter** (der)
Ạn|stand, der; -s, ...stände; keinen Anstand an dem Vorhaben nehmen (*geh. für* keine Bedenken haben); auf dem Anstand stehen *(Jägerspr.);* **ạn|stän|dig; Ạn|stän|dig|keit,** die; -; **ạn|stands‿hal|ber, ...los; Ạn|stands‿re|gel, ...wau|wau** *(ugs.)*
ạn|stän|kern *(ugs.);* gegen etw., jmdn. -
ạn|star|ren
an|stạtt; *vgl.* statt; anstatt dass (↑R 88)

an|stau|ben
an|stau|en
an|stau|nen
an|ste|chen; ein Fass - (anzapfen)
an|ste|cken; *vgl.* ²stecken; **an|ste|ckend; An|steck|na|del; An|ste|ckung** *Plur. selten;* **An|ste|ckungs|ge|fahr**
an|ste|hen (*auch Bergmannsspr.* hervortreten, zutage liegen); ich stehe nicht an (habe keine Bedenken); anstehendes (*Geol.* zutage liegendes) Gestein; auf jmdn. - (*österr. für* angewiesen sein)
an|stei|gen
an|stel|le, *auch* **an Stel|le** (↑R 41); *Präp. mit Gen.:* anstelle, *auch* an Stelle des Vaters, von Worten; *aber* an die Stelle des Vaters ist der Vormund getreten
an|stel|len; sich -; **An|stel|le|rei; an|stel|lig** (geschickt); **An|stel|lig|keit,** die; -; **An|stel|lung; An|stel|lungs|ver|trag**
an|steu|ern
An|stich (eines Fasses [Bier])
An|stieg, der; -[e]s, -e
an|stie|ren
an|stif|ten; An|stif|ter; An|stif|te|rin; An|stif|tung
an|stim|men; ein Lied -
An|stoß; - nehmen an etwas; **an|sto|ßen; An|stö|ßer** (*schweiz. für* Anlieger, Anrainer); **an|stö|ßig; An|stö|ßig|keit**
an|strah|len; An|strah|lung
an|strän|gen; ein Pferd - (anschirren)
an|stre|ben; an|stre|bens|wert
an|strei|chen; An|strei|cher
an|stren|gen; sich - (sehr bemühen); einen Prozess -; **an|stren|gend; An|stren|gung**
An|strich
an|stü|cken
An|sturm, der; -[e]s; **an|stür|men**
an|su|chen; um etwas - (*Amtsspr.* um etwas bitten); **An|su|chen,** das; -s, - (förmliche Bitte; Gesuch); auf -; **An|su|cher**
An|ta|go|nis|mus (↑R 132), der; -, ...men ‹griech.› (Widerstreit; Gegensatz); **An|ta|go|nist,** der; -en, -en; ↑R 126 (Gegner); **an|ta|go|nis|tisch**
an|tail|lie|ren [...ta(l)ji:...] (*Schneiderei* mit leichter Taille versehen); leicht antailliert
An|ta|na|na|ri|vo [...vo] (Hptst. von Madagaskar)
an|tan|zen (*ugs. für* kommen)
An|ta|res, der; - ‹griech.› (ein Stern)
Ant|ark|ti|ka (antarktischer Kontinent); **Ant|ark|tis,** die; - ‹griech.› (Gebiet um den Südpol); **ant|ark|tisch**
an|tas|ten
an|tau|chen (*österr. ugs. für* anschieben; sich mehr anstrengen)
an|tau|en
An|tä|us (Gestalt der griech. Sage)
an|täu|schen *(Sport)*
An|te, die; -, -n ‹lat.› (*Archit.* viereckiger Wandpfeiler)
an|te Chris|tum [na|tum] ‹lat.› (*veraltet für* vor Christi Geburt, vor Christus; *Abk.* a. Chr. [n.])
an|te|da|tie|ren ‹lat.› (*veraltet für* [ein Schreiben] vorausdatieren od. zurückdatieren)
An|teil, der; -[e]s, -e; - haben, nehmen; **an|tei|lig; An|teil|nah|me,** die; -; **An|teil|schein; An|teils|eig|ner** (Inhaber eines Anteilscheins); **an|teil[s]|mä|ßig**
an|te me|ri|di|em ‹lat.› (vormittags; *Abk.* a. m.)
an|te mor|tem ‹lat.› (*Med.* kurz vor dem Tode; *Abk.* a. m.)
An|ten|ne, die; -, -n ‹lat.› (Vorrichtung zum Senden od. Empfangen elektromagnet. Wellen; Fühler der Gliedertiere); **An|ten|nen‿an|la|ge, ...mast, ...wald** *(ugs.)*
An|ten|tem|pel ‹lat.› (altgriech. Tempel mit Anten)
An|te|pen|di|um, das; -s, ...ien [...i̯ən] ‹lat.› (Verkleidung des Altarunterbaus)
An|the|mi|on, das; -s, ...ien [...i̯ən] ‹griech.› (*Archit.* [altgriech.] Schmuckfries); **An|the|re,** die; -, -n (*Bot.* Staubbeutel der Blütenpflanzen); **An|tho|lo|gie,** die; -, ...ien ([Gedicht]sammlung; Auswahl); **an|tho|lo|gisch** (ausgewählt)
Anth|ra|cen, *auch* **Anth|ra|zen** (↑R 130), das; -s, -e ‹griech.› (aus Steinkohlenteer gewonnene chem. Verbindung); **anth|ra|zit** [*auch* ...'tsit] (schwarzgrau); **Anth|ra|zit,** der; -s, -e *Plur. selten* (hochwertige, glänzende Steinkohle); **anth|ra|zit‿far|ben** *od.* **...far|big**
anth|ro|po|gen (↑R 130) ‹griech.› (durch den Menschen beeinflusst, verursacht); -e Faktoren; **Anth|ro|po|ge|nie,** die; - ([Lehre von der] Entstehung des Menschen); **anth|ro|po|id** (menschenähnlich); **Anth|ro|po|i|den** *Plur.* (Menschenaffen); **Anth|ro|po|lo|ge,** der; -n, -n; ↑R 126 (Wissenschaftler auf dem Gebiet der Anthropologie); **Anth|ro|po|lo|gie,** die; - (Wissenschaft vom Menschen u. seiner Entwicklung); **Anth|ro|po|lo|gin; anth|ro|po|lo|gisch; anth|ro|po|morph** (menschenähnlich); **anth|ro|po|mor|phisch** (die menschliche Gestalt betreffend); **Anth|ro|po|mor|phis|mus,** der; -, ...men (Vermenschlichung [des Göttlichen]); **Anth|ro|po|pha|ge,** der; -n, -n; ↑R 126 (*fachspr. für* Kannibale); **Anth|ro|po|pho|bie,** die; - (*Psych.* Menschenscheu); **Anth|ro|po|soph,** der; -en, -en; ↑R 126 (Vertreter der Anthroposophie); **Anth|ro|po|so|phie,** die; - (Lehre, nach der der Mensch aufgrund höherer seel. Fähigkeiten übersinnl. Erkenntnisse erlangen kann); **anth|ro|po|so|phisch; anth|ro|po|zent|risch;** (den Menschen in den Mittelpunkt stellend)
An|thu|rie [...i̯ə], die; -, -n ‹griech.› (Flamingoblume, eine Zierpflanze)
an|ti... ‹griech.› (gegen...); **An|ti...** (Gegen...)
An|ti-AKW-De|monst|ra|ti|on [...a:ka:'ve:...] (↑R 28)
An|ti|al|ko|ho|li|ker[1] ‹griech.; arab.› (Alkoholgegner)
an|ti|ame|ri|ka|nisch[1] (↑R 132; gegen die USA gerichtet)
An|ti|apart|heid|be|we|gung (↑R 132)
an|ti|au|to|ri|tär[1] ‹griech.; lat.› (autoritäre Normen ablehnend)
An|ti|ba|by|pil|le [...'be:bi(:)...] ‹griech.; engl.; lat.› (ein hormonales Empfängnisverhütungsmittel)
an|ti|bak|te|ri|ell[1] ‹griech.› (gegen Bakterien wirkend)
An|ti|bi|o|ti|kum, das; -s, ...ka ‹griech.› (*Med.* biologischer Wirkstoff gegen Krankheitserreger); **an|ti|bi|o|tisch**
An|ti|blo|ckier|sys|tem ‹griech.; franz.; griech.› (*Abk.* ABS)
an|ti|chamb|rie|ren [...ʃam'bri:...] (↑R 130) ‹franz.› (*veraltet* im Vorzimmer warten; katzbuckeln, dienern)
An|ti|christ [...krist], der; -[s] (*Rel.* der Widerchrist, Teufel) *u.* der; -en, -en (↑R 126) ‹griech.› (Gegner des Christentums); **an|ti|christ|lich**
an|ti|de|mo|kra|tisch[1] ‹griech.›
An|ti|de|pres|si|vum [...vum], das; -s ...va [...va] *meist Plur.* ‹griech.; lat.› (*Med.* Mittel gegen Depressionen)
An|ti|di|a|be|ti|kum, das; -s, ...ka ‹griech.› (*Med.* Medikament gegen Diabetes)
An|ti|dot, das; -[e]s, -e *u.* **An|ti|do|ton,** das; -s, ...ta ‹griech.› (*Med.* Gegengift)

---
[1] [*auch* 'anti...]

An|ti|dum|ping|ge|setz [anti'dam...] ‹griech.; engl.; dt.› (*Wirtsch.* Verbot des Dumpings)
An|ti|fa|schis|mus[1] ‹griech.; ital.› (Gegnerschaft gegen Faschismus und Nationalsozialismus); **An|ti|fa|schist**[1], der; -en, -en (↑R 126); **an|ti|fa|schis|tisch**[1]
An|ti|fou|ling ['ɛntifaulıŋ, *auch* 'anti...], das; -s ‹griech.; engl.› (Anstrich für den unter Wasser befindlichen Teil des Schiffes, der Bewuchs verhindert)
An|ti|gen, das; -s, -e ‹griech.› (*Med., Biol.* artfremder Eiweißstoff, der im Körper die Bildung von Abwehrstoffen gegen sich selbst bewirkt)
An|ti|go|ne [...ne:] (griech. Sagengestalt, Tochter des Ödipus)
An|ti|gu|a|ner; an|ti|gu|a|nisch; An|ti|gua und Bar|bu|da (Inselstaat in der Karibik)
An|ti|haft|be|schich|tung
An|ti|held ‹griech.; dt.› (inaktive od. negative Hauptfigur in der Literatur)
an|ti|im|pe|ri|a|lis|tisch[1] (gegen den Imperialismus gerichtet)
an|tik ‹lat.› (altertümlich; dem klass. Altertum angehörend); [1]**An|ti|ke**, die; - (das klass. Altertum u. seine Kultur); [2]**An|ti|ke**, die; -, -n *meist Plur.* (antikes Kunstwerk); **An|ti|ken|samm|lung; an|ti|kisch** (der [1]Antike nachstrebend); **an|ti|ki|sie|ren** (nach der Art der [1]Antike gestalten; die [1]Antike nachahmen)
an|ti|kle|ri|kal[1] ‹griech.› (kirchenfeindlich); **An|ti|kle|ri|ka|lis|mus**[1]
An|ti|kli|max, die; -, -e *Plur. selten* ‹griech.› (*Rhet., Stilk.* Übergang vom stärkeren zum schwächeren Ausdruck)
an|ti|kli|nal ‹griech.› (*Geol.* sattelförmig)
An|ti|klopf|mit|tel, das; -s, - (Zusatz zu Vergaserkraftstoffen)
An|ti|kom|mu|nis|mus[1] ‹griech.; lat.›; **an|ti|kom|mu|nis|tisch**[1]
an|ti|kon|zep|ti|o|nell[1] ‹griech.; lat.› (*Med.* die Empfängnis verhütend)
An|ti|kör|per *Plur.* ‹griech.; dt.› (*Med.* Abwehrstoffe im Blut gegen artfremde Eiweiße)
An|ti|kri|tik[1] [*auch* ...'tik] ‹griech.› (Erwiderung auf eine Kritik)
An|til|len *Plur.* (Inselgruppe in der Karibik)
An|ti|lo|pe, die; -, -n ‹franz.› (ein Huftier)
An|ti|ma|chi|a|vell [...makia'vɛl], der; -s ‹griech.; ital.› (Schrift Friedrichs d. Gr. gegen Machiavelli)
An|ti|ma|te|rie[1] ‹griech.; lat.› (*Kernphysik* aus Antiteilchen aufgebaute Materie)
An|ti|mi|li|ta|ris|mus[1], der; - ‹griech.; lat.› (Ablehnung militärischer Gesinnung u. Rüstung); **an|ti|mi|li|ta|ris|tisch**[1]
An|ti|mon [*österr.* 'anti...], das; -s ‹arab.› (chem. Element, Metall; *Zeichen* Sb [*vgl.* Stibium])
an|ti|mo|nar|chisch[1] ‹griech.› (monarchiefeindlich)
An|ti|neu|ral|gi|kum (↑R 132), das; -s, ...ka ‹griech.› (*Med.* Schmerzen stillendes Mittel)
An|ti|no|mie, die; -, ...ien ‹griech.› (Widerspruch eines Satzes in sich oder zweier gültiger Sätze)
An|ti|no|us (schöner griech. Jüngling an Hadrians Hof)
an|ti|o|che|nisch [...'xe:...]; **An|ti|o|chia** [*auch* ...'xi:a] (altsyr. Stadt); **An|ti|o|chi|en** (mittelalterl. Patriarchat in Kleinasien); **An|ti|o|chi|er; An|ti|o|chos, An|ti|o|chus** (m. Eigenname)
An|ti|pa|thie, die; -, ...ien ‹griech.› (Abneigung; Widerwille); **an|ti|pa|thisch**
An|ti|phon, die; -, -en ‹griech.› (liturg. Wechselgesang); **An|ti|pho|na|le**, das; -s, ...lien [...iən] *u.* **An|ti|pho|nar**, das; -s, -ien [...iən] (Sammlung von Antiphonen)
An|ti|po|de, der; -n, -n (↑R 126) ‹griech.› (*Geogr.* auf dem gegenüberliegenden Punkt der Erde wohnender Mensch; *übertr. für* Gegner)
an|tip|pen
An|ti|py|re|ti|kum, das; -s, ...ka ‹griech.› (*Med.* fiebersenkendes Mittel)
An|ti|qua, die; - ‹lat.› (*Druckw.* Lateinschrift); **An|ti|quar**, der; -s, -e (jmd., der mit alten Büchern handelt; Antiquitätenhändler); **An|ti|qua|ri|at**, das; -[e]s, -e (Geschäft, in dem alte Bücher ge- u. verkauft werden; *nur Sing.:* Handel mit alten Büchern); **an|ti|qua|risch; An|ti|qua|schrift** *(Druckw.)*; **an|ti|quiert;** (veraltet; altertümlich); **An|ti|quiert|heit** *Plur selten;* **An|ti|qui|tät**, die; -, -en *meist Plur.* (altertümliches Kunstwerk, Möbel u. a.); **An|ti|qui|tä|ten‿han|del, ...händ|ler, ...samm|ler**
An|ti|ra|ke|te; An|ti|ra|ke|ten|ra|ke|te
An|ti|rau|cher|kam|pag|ne
An|ti|se|mit, der; -en, -en; ↑R 126 (Gegner des Judentums, Feind der Juden); **an|ti|se|mi|tisch; An|ti|se|mi|tis|mus**, der; -
An|ti|sep|sis, An|ti|sep|tik, die; - ‹griech.› (*Med.* Vernichtung von Krankheitskeimen [bes. in Wunden]); **An|ti|sep|ti|kum**, das; -s, ...ka (keimtötendes Mittel; **an|ti|sep|tisch**
An|ti|se|rum[1], das; -s, *Plur.* ...ren *u.* ...ra ‹griech.; lat.› (*Med.* Heilserum mit Antikörpern)
An|ti|spas|mo|di|kum, das; -s, ...ka ‹griech.› (*Med.* krampflösendes Mittel); **an|ti|spas|tisch** (*Med. für* krampflösend)
an|ti|sta|tisch ‹griech.› (elektrostatische Aufladung aufhebend)
An|tis|tes (↑R 132), der; -, ...stites ‹lat.› (*kath. Kirche* Ehrentitel für Bischof u. Abt)
An|ti|stro|phe[1] ‹griech.› (Chorlied im antiken griech. Drama)
An|ti|teil|chen (*Kernphysik* zu einem Elementarteilchen komplementäres Teilchen mit entgegengesetzter elektrischer Ladung)
An|ti|ter|ror|ein|heit
An|ti|the|se[1] ‹griech.› (entgegengesetzte Behauptung); **An|ti|the|tik**, die; - *(Philos.)*; **an|ti|the|tisch**
An|ti|to|xin[1], das; -s, -e ‹griech.› (*Med.* Gegengift); **an|ti|to|xisch**[1]
An|ti|tran|spi|rant (↑R 132), das; -s, *Plur.* -e *u.* -s ‹griech.; lat.› (schweißhemmendes Mittel)
An|ti|zi|pa|ti|on, die; -, -en ‹lat.› (Vorwegnahme; Vorgriff); **an|ti|zi|pie|ren**
an|ti|zyk|lisch[1] [*auch* ...'tsyk...] (*Wirtsch.* einem Konjunkturzustand entgegenwirkend); **An|ti|zyk|lo|ne**[1] (*Meteor.* Hochdruckgebiet)
Ant|je (w. Vorn.)
Antl|litz, das; -es, -e *(geh.)*
An|toi|net|te [antoa'nɛt(ə), *auch* ãtoa'nɛt(ə)] (w. Vorn.); **An|ton** (m. Vorn.)
an|tö|nen (*schweiz. für* andeuten)
An|to|nia, An|to|nie [...iə] (w. Vorn.); **An|to|ni|us** (röm. m. Eigenn.; Heiliger)
an|to|nym (↑R 132) ‹griech.› (*Sprachw.* von entgegengesetzter Bedeutung); **An|to|nym**, das; -s, -e (*Sprachw.* Gegen[satz]wort, Wort mit entgegengesetzter Bedeutung, z. B. „gesund – krank"); **an|to|ny|misch** *vgl.* antonym
an|tör|nen (*ugs. für* in einen Rausch versetzen)
An|trag, der; -[e]s, ...träge; einen - auf etwas stellen; auf, *österr. auch* über - von ...; **an|tra|gen; An-**

[1] [*auch* 'anti...]

trags|for|mu|lar; an|trags|ge|mäß; An|trag|stel|ler; An|trag|stel|le|rin

an|trai|nie|ren

an|trau|en; angetraut

an|tref|fen

an|trei|ben; An|trei|ber

an|tren|zen; sich - (*österr. ugs. für* sich bekleckern)

an|tre|ten

An|trieb; An|triebs‿kraft, ...schei|be, ...sys|tem, ...wel|le

an|trin|ken; sich - (*österr. ugs. für* sich betrinken); ich trinke mir einen an (*ugs.*)

An|tritt, der; -[e]s; **An|tritts‿be|such, ...re|de**

an|trock|nen

an|tun; jmdm. etwas -; ich tue mir das nicht an; (*österr. ugs. auch für* sich über etwas [grundlos] aufregen)

[1]**an|tur|nen** (*ugs. für* herbeieilen)

[2]**an|tur|nen** [ˈantœ(r)nən] ‹dt.; engl.› *vgl.* antörnen

Antw. = Antwort

Ant|wer|pen (belg. Hafenstadt)

Ant|wort, die; -, -en (*Abk.* Antw.); um [*od.* Um] - wird gebeten (*Abk.* u. [*od.* U.] A. w. g.); **ant|wor|ten; ant|wort|lich;** - Ihres Briefes (*Amtsspr.* auf Ihren Brief); **Ant|wort|schein** (*Postw.*)

an und für sich [*auch* - - ˈfy:r -]

An|u|rie, die; -, ...ien ‹griech.› (*Med.* Versagen der Harnausscheidung)

A|nus, der; -, Ani ‹lat.› (*Med.* After); **A|nus prae|ter** [- ˈprɛ:...], der; - -, Ani - (*Med.* künstlicher Darmausgang)

an|ver|trau|en; jmdm. einen Brief -; sich jmdm. -; ich vertrau[t]e an, *seltener* ich anvertrau[t]e; anvertraut; anzuvertrauen

an|ver|wan|deln (*geh.*); sich etwas - (zu eigen machen); du verwandelst dir ihre Meinung an, *seltener* du anverwandelst dir ...; **An|ver|wand|lung** (*geh.*)

An|ver|wand|te, der *u.* die; -n, -n (↑R 5 ff.)

an|vi|sie|ren

Anw. = Anweisung

an|wach|sen

an|wäh|len (*Fernsprechwesen*)

An|walt, der; -[e]s, ...wälte; **An|wäl|tin; An|walt|schaft,** die; -, -en *Plur. selten;* **An|walts|kam|mer**

an|wan|deln; An|wan|de|lung, *häufiger* **An|wand|lung**

an|wär|men

An|wär|ter; An|wart|schaft, die; -, -en *Plur. selten*

an|wei|sen; Geld -; *vgl.* angewiesen; **An|wei|sung** (*Abk.* Anw.)

an|wend|bar; An|wend|bar|keit, die; -; **an|wen|den;** ich wandte *od.* wendete die Regel an, habe angewandt *od.* angewendet; die angewandte *od.* angewendete Regel; *vgl.* angewandt; **An|wen|der; An|wen|dung; an|wen|dungs|be|zo|gen**

an|wer|ben; An|wer|bung

an|wer|fen

An|wert, der; -[e]s (*bayr., österr. für* Wertschätzung)

An|we|sen (Grundstück [mit Wohnhaus, Stall usw.]); **an|we|send; An|we|sen|de,** der *u.* die; -n, -n (↑R 5 ff.); **An|we|sen|heit,** die; -; **An|we|sen|heits|lis|te**

an|wi|dern; es widert mich an

an|win|keln

An|woh|ner; An|woh|ner|schaft, die; -

An|wuchs (*Forstw.*)

An|wurf

an|wur|zeln; *vgl.* angewurzelt

An|zahl, die; -; eine Anzahl gute[r] Freunde; **an|zah|len; an|zäh|len; An|zah|lung; An|zah|lungs|sum|me**

an|zap|fen; An|zap|fung

An|zei|chen

an|zeich|nen

An|zei|ge, die; -, -n; **an|zei|gen; An|zei|ge[n]|blatt; An|zei|gen|teil; An|zei|ge|pflicht; an|zei|ge|pflich|tig;** -e Krankheit; **An|zei|ger; An|zei|ge|ta|fel**

An|zen|gru|ber (österr. Schriftsteller)

An|zet|te|ler, An|zett|ler; **an|zet|teln** (*ugs.*); **An|zet|te|lung, An|zett|lung**

an|zie|hen; sich -; **an|zie|hend** (reizvoll); **An|zie|hung; An|zie|hungs|kraft**

an|zie|len (zum Ziel haben)

an|zi|schen

[1]**An|zucht,** die; -, ...züchte (*Bergmannsspr.* Abwassergraben)

[2]**An|zucht,** die; - (Aufzucht junger Pflanzen [und Tiere]); **An|zucht|gar|ten**

An|zug, der; -[e]s, ...züge (*schweiz. auch für* [Bett]bezug, Überzug; *schweiz. [Basel] auch* Antrag [im Parlament]); es ist Gefahr im -; **an|züg|lich; An|züg|lich|keit; An|zugs|kraft; An|zug|stoff; An|zugs|ver|mö|gen**

an|zün|den; An|zün|der

an|zwe|cken

an|zwei|feln; An|zwei|fe|lung, An|zweif|lung

an|zwit|schern; sich einen - (*ugs. für* sich betrinken); ich zwitschere mir einen an

AO = Abgabenordnung; Anordnung

ao., a. o. [Prof.] = außerordentlich[er Professor]

AOK = Allgemeine Ortskrankenkasse

Äo|li|en (antike Landschaft an der Nordwestküste von Kleinasien); **Äo|li|er;** [1]**äo|lisch** ‹*zu* Äolien›; Äolische Inseln; *vgl.* Liparische Inseln; [2]**äo|lisch** ‹*zu* Äolus› (durch Windeinwirkung entstanden); **Äo|ls|har|fe** (Windharfe); **Äo|lus** (griech. Windgott)

Äon, der; -s, -en *meist Plur.* ‹griech.› (Zeitraum, Weltalter; Ewigkeit); **äo|nen|lang**

A|o|rist, der; -[e]s, -e ‹griech.› (*Sprachw.* eine Zeitform, bes. im Griechischen)

A|or|ta, die; -, ...ten ‹griech.› (*Med.* Hauptschlagader); **A|or|ten|klap|pe**

AP [e:ˈpi:] = Associated Press

APA = Austria Presse Agentur (*so die von den Richtlinien der Rechtschreibung abweichende Schreibung*)

A|pa|che [aˈpatʃə, *auch* aˈpaxə], der; -n, -n; ↑R 126 (Angehöriger eines Indianerstammes; [*nur* ...x...:] *veraltend für* Verbrecher, Zuhälter [in Paris])

A|pa|na|ge [apaˈna:ʒə, *österr.* ...ˈna:ʒ], die; -, -n [...ˈna:ʒ(ə)n] ‹franz.› (regelmäßige finanzielle Zuwendung)

a|part; ‹franz.› (geschmackvoll, reizvoll); etwas Apartes (↑R 47);

A|part|be|stel|lung (*Buchhandel* Einzelbestellung [eines Heftes oder Bandes aus einer Reihe]);

A|part|heid, die; - ‹afrikaans› (*früher* Rassentrennung zwischen Weißen und Farbigen in der Republik Südafrika); **A|part|heid|po|li|tik; A|part|ment** [aˈpartmɛnt, *engl.* əˈpa:(r)tmənt], das; -s, -s ‹engl.› (kleinere Wohnung); *vgl.* Appartement; **A|part|ment|haus**

A|pa|thie, die; -, ...ien *Plur. selten* ‹griech.› (Teilnahmslosigkeit); **a|pa|thisch**

A|pa|tit [*auch* ...ˈtit], der; -s, -e ‹griech.› (ein Mineral)

A|pa|to|sau|rus, der; -, ...rier [...iər] ‹griech.› (ausgestorbene Riesenechse)

A|pel|les (altgriech. Maler)

A|pen|nin, der; -s, *auch* **A|pen|ni|nen** *Plur.* (Gebirge in Italien); **A|pen|ni|nen|halb|in|sel,** die; -; **a|pen|ni|nisch,** *aber* (↑R 102): die Apenninische Halbinsel

a|per (*südd., schweiz., österr. für* schneefrei); -e Wiesen

A|per|çu [apɛrˈsy:], das; -s, -s ‹franz.› (geistreiche Bemerkung)

A|pe|ri|tif, der; -s, *Plur.* -s, *auch* -e ‹franz.› (appetitanregendes alkohol. Getränk)

a|pern ‹*zu* aper› (*südd., schweiz., österr. für* schneefrei werden); es apert (taut)

A|pé|ro [*franz.* ape'ro:], der; -s, -s ‹franz.› (*bes. schweiz., Kurzform von* Aperitif)

A|per|tur, die; -, -en ‹lat.› (*Optik* Maß für die Fähigkeit eines Systems, sehr feine Details abzubilden; *Med.* Öffnung, Eingang eines Organs)

A|pex, der; -, Apizes [...tse:s] ‹lat.› (*Astron.* Zielpunkt der Bewegung eines Gestirns; *Sprachw.* Zeichen zur Bezeichnung langer Vokale, z. B. â, á)

Ap|fel, der; -s, Äpfel; **Ap|fel|baum; Äp|fel|chen; ap|fel|för|mig; Ap|fel‿ge|lee, ...kraut** (das; -[e]s; *landsch.* Sirup), **...most, ...mus; äp|feln;** das Pferd musste -; **Ap|fel‿saft, ...schim|mel** (*vgl.* [2]Schimmel); **Ap|fel|si|ne,** die; -, -n; **Ap|fel|si|nen|scha|le; Ap|fel‿stru|del, ...wein, ...wick|ler** (ein Kleinschmetterling)

A|phä|re|se, A|phä|re|sis (↑R 132), die; -, ...resen ‹griech.› (*Sprachw.* Wegfall eines Lautes od. einer Silbe am Wortanfang, z. B. 's *für* „es")

A|pha|sie, die; -, ...ien ‹griech.› (*Philos.* Urteilsenthaltung; *Med.* Verlust des Sprechvermögens)

A|phel (↑R 132), das; -s, -e ‹griech.› (*Astron.* Punkt der größten Sonnenferne eines Planeten od. Kometen; *Ggs.* Perihel)

A|phe|land|ra (↑R 132), die; -, ...dren ‹griech.› (*Bot.* eine Pflanzengattung; z. T. beliebte Zierpflanzen)

A|phon|ge|trie|be ‹griech.; dt.› (geräuscharmes Schaltgetriebe)

A|pho|ris|mus, der; -, ...men ‹griech.› (geistreicher, knapp formulierter Gedanke); **A|pho|ris|ti|ker; a|pho|ris|tisch**

Aph|ro|di|si|a|kum (↑R 130), das; -s, ...ka ‹griech.› (*Med.* den Geschlechtstrieb anregendes Mittel); **aph|ro|di|sisch** (auf Aphrodite bezüglich; den Geschlechtstrieb steigernd); **Aph|ro|di|te** (griech. Göttin der Liebe); **aph|ro|di|tisch** (auf Aphrodite bezüglich)

Aph|the ['aftə], die; -, -n *meist Plur.* ‹griech.› (*Med.* kleines Geschwür der Mundschleimhaut); **Aph|then|seu|che** (*Tiermed.* Maul- u. Klauenseuche)

A|pia (Hptst. von Samoa)

a|pi|kal ‹lat.› (den Apex betreffend)

A|pis, der; - (heiliger Stier der alten Ägypter); **A|pis|stier**

A|pi|zes (*Plur. von* Apex)

apl. = außerplanmäßig

Ap|la|nat (↑R 130) der; -en, -en, *auch* das; -s, -e ‹griech.› (*Optik* Linsensystem, durch das die Aberration korrigiert wird); **ap|la|na|tisch**

Ap|lomb [a'plɔ̃:] (↑R 130), der; -s ‹franz.› (Sicherheit im Auftreten, Nachdruck; Abfangen einer Bewegung im Balletttanz)

APO, *auch* **A|po,** die; - (außerparlamentarische Opposition)

A|po|chro|mat [...k...], der; -en, -en, *auch* das; -s, -e ‹griech.› (*Optik* Linsensystem, das Farbfehler korrigiert); **a|po|chro|ma|tisch**

a|po|dik|tisch; ‹griech.› (keinen Widerspruch duldend)

A|po|gä|um, das; -s, ...äen ‹griech.› (*Astron.* Punkt der größten Erdferne des Mondes od. eines Satelliten; *Ggs.* Perigäum)

A|po|ka|lyp|se, die; -, -n ‹griech.› (*Rel.* Schrift über das Weltende, bes. die Offenbarung des Johannes; Unheil, Grauen); **a|po|ka|lyp|tisch;** die apokalyptischen Reiter

A|po|ko|pe [...pe], die; -, ...kopen ‹griech.› (*Sprachw.* Abfall eines Lautes od. einer Silbe am Wortende, z. B. „hatt" *für* „hatte"); **a|po|ko|pie|ren**

a|po|kryph ‹griech.› (unecht); **A|po|kryph,** das; -s, -en *meist Plur.* ‹griech.› (*Rel.* nicht anerkannte Schrift [der Bibel])

A|pol|da (Stadt in Thüringen)

a|po|li|tisch ‹griech.› (unpolitisch)

A|poll (*geh. für* [1,2]Apollo); **A|pol|li|na|ris** (Heiliger); **a|pol|li|nisch** (in der Art Apollos; harmonisch, ausgeglichen, maßvoll); **[1]A|pol|lo** (griech.-röm. Gott [der Dichtkunst]); **[2]A|pol|lo,** der; -s, -s (schöner [junger] Mann); **[3]A|pol|lo** (amerik. Raumfahrtprogramm, das die Landung bemannter Raumfahrzeuge auf dem Mond zum Ziel hatte); **A|pol|lo|fal|ter** (ein Schmetterling); **A|pol|lon** *vgl.* [1]Apollo; **A|pol|lo|nia** (w. Vorn.); **A|pol|lo|ni|us** (m. Vorn.); **A|pol|lo-Raum|schiff** (*vgl.* [3]Apollo)

A|po|lo|get, der; -en, -en (↑R 126) ‹griech.› ([nachdrücklicher] Verfechter, Verteidiger); **A|po|lo|ge|tik,** die; -, -en (*bes. Theol.* Verteidigung, Rechtfertigung [der christl. Lehren]); **a|po|lo|ge|tisch; A|po|lo|gie,** die; -, ...ien (*geh. für* Verteidigung; Verteidigungsrede, -schrift)

A|poph|theg|ma [apo'ftɛgma] (↑R 132), das; -s, *Plur.* ...men *u.* ...mata ‹griech.› ([witziger] Aus-, Sinnspruch)

A|po|phy|se, die; -, -n ‹griech.› (*Med.* Knochenfortsatz)

A|pop|lek|ti|ker (↑R 130) ‹griech.› (*Med.* zu Schlaganfällen Neigender; an den Folgen eines Schlaganfalls Leidender); **a|pop|lek|tisch; A|pop|le|xie,** die; -, ...ien (Schlaganfall)

A|po|rie, die; -, ...ien ‹griech.› (*Philos.* Unmöglichkeit, eine philos. Frage zu lösen)

A|pos|ta|sie (↑R 132), die; -, ...ien ‹griech.› (*Rel.* Abfall [vom Glauben]); **A|pos|tat,** der; -en, -en; ↑R 126 (Abtrünniger)

A|pos|tel (↑R 132), der; -s, - ‹griech.›; **A|pos|tel‿brief** (im N. T.), **...ge|schich|te**

a pos|te|ri|o|ri ‹lat.› (*Philos.* aus der Wahrnehmung gewonnen, aus Erfahrung; *geh. für* nachträglich); **A|pos|te|ri|o|ri,** das; -, -; (Erfahrungssatz); **a|pos|te|ri|o|risch** (erfahrungsgemäß)

A|po|stilb, das; -s, - ‹griech.› (veraltete photometr. Einheit der Leuchtdichte; *Zeichen* asb)

A|pos|to|lat, das, *Theol. auch* der; -[e]s, -e ‹griech.› (Apostelamt); **A|pos|to|li|kum,** das; -s (*Theol.* Apostolisches Glaubensbekenntnis); **a|pos|to|lisch** (nach Art der Apostel; von den Aposteln ausgehend); die -e Sukzession; die -en Väter; den -en Segen erteilen; *aber* (↑R 108): das Apostolische Glaubensbekenntnis, die Apostolische Majestät; der Apostolische Delegat, Nuntius, Stuhl

A|po|stroph [*schweiz.* 'apo...], der; -s, -e ‹griech.› (Auslassungszeichen, z. B. in „wen'ge"); **A|po|stro|phe** [*auch* a'pɔstrofe:], die; -, ...ophen (*Rhet.* feierliche Anrede); **a|po|stro|phie|ren** (anreden; nachdrücklich bezeichnen); jmdn. als Ignoranten -; **A|po|stro|phie|rung**

A|po|the|ke, die; -, -n ‹griech.›; **A|po|the|ken|hel|fe|rin; a|po|the|ken|pflich|tig; A|po|the|ker; A|po|the|ker|ge|wicht** (*vgl.* [2]Gewicht); **A|po|the|ke|rin; A|po|the|ker|waa|ge**

A|po|the|o|se, die; -, -n ‹griech.› (Vergöttlichung; Verklärung; *Theater* wirkungsvolles Schlussbild)

a|po|tro|pä|isch ‹griech.-nlat.› (*geh. für* Unheil abwehrend)

Ap|pa|la|chen *Plur.* (nordamerik. Gebirge)

Ap|pa|rat, der; -[e]s, -e ‹lat.› (größeres Gerät, Vorrichtung technischer Art); **Ap|pa|ra|te‿bau** (der; -[e]s), **...me|di|zin** (die; -; med. Versorgung mit [übermäßigem] Einsatz technischer Apparate); **ap|pa|ra|tiv** (den Apparat[ebau] betreffend); apparative Diagnostik; **Ap|pa|rat|schik,** der; -s, -s ‹russ.› (*abwertend* Funktionär im Staats- u. Parteiapparat stalinistisch geprägter Staaten, der Weisungen und Maßnahmen bürokratisch durchzusetzen sucht); **Ap|pa|ra|tur,** die; -, -en (Gesamtanlage von Apparaten)

Ap|par|te|ment [apart(ə)'maŋ *od.* ...'mã:, *schweiz.* ...'mɛnt], das; -s, *Plur.* -s, *schweiz.* -e ‹franz.› (Zimmerflucht in einem Hotel); *vgl.* Apartment

Ap|pas|si|o|na|ta, die; - ‹ital.› (eine Klaviersonate von Beethoven)

Ap|peal [ə'pi:l], der; -s ‹engl.› (Anziehungskraft, Ausstrahlung)

Ap|pease|ment [ə'pi:zmənt], das; -s ‹engl.› (nachgiebige Haltung, Beschwichtigungspolitik)

Ap|pell, der; -s, -e ‹franz.› (Aufruf; Mahnruf; *Milit.* Antreten zum Befehlsempfang usw.); **Ap|pel|la|ti|on,** die; -, -en (*schweiz., sonst veraltet für* Berufung); **Ap|pel|la|ti|ons|ge|richt; Ap|pel|la|tiv,** das; -s, -e [...və] (*Sprachw.* Gattungsname; Wort, das eine Gattung gleich gearteter Dinge od. Wesen u. zugleich jedes einzelne Wesen od. Ding dieser Gattung bezeichnet, z. B. „Mensch"); **ap|pel|lie|ren** (sich mahnend, beschwörend an jmdn. wenden; *veraltet für* Berufung einlegen); **Ap|pell|platz**

Ap|pen|dix, der; *Gen.* -, *auch* -es, *Plur.* ...dizes, *auch* -e (Anhängsel) *u.* die; -, ...dices [...tse:s], *alltagssprachlich auch* der; -, ...dizes [...tse:s] ‹lat.› (*Med.* Wurmfortsatz des Blinddarms); **Ap|pen|di|zi|tis,** die; -, ...itiden (*Med.* Entzündung der Appendix)

Ap|pen|zell (Kanton der Schweiz [Halbkantone Appenzell Außerrhoden u. Appenzell Innerrhoden]; Hauptort von Innerrhoden); **Ap|pen|zel|ler** (↑R 103); **ap|pen|zel|lisch**

Ap|per|zep|ti|on, die; -, -en ‹lat.› (*Psych.* bewusste Wahrnehmung); **ap|per|zi|pie|ren** (bewusst wahrnehmen)

Ap|pe|tenz, die; -, -en ‹lat.› (*Biol.* Trieb); **Ap|pe|tenz|ver|hal|ten; Ap|pe|tit,** der; -[e]s, -e; **ap|pe|tit|an|re|gend;** *aber* (↑R 40): den Appetit anregend; **Ap|pe|tit|hap|pen, ...hem|mer** (*svw.* Appetitzügler); **ap|pe|tit|lich; ap|pe|tit|los; Ap|pe|tit|lo|sig|keit,** die; -; **Ap|pe|tit|züg|ler** (den Appetit zügelndes Mittel); **Ap|pe|ti|zer** ['ɛpitaizə(r)], der; -s, - ‹lat.-engl.› (appetitanregendes Mittel)

ap|plau|die|ren ‹lat.› (Beifall klatschen); jmdm. -; **Ap|plaus,** der; -es, -e *Plur. selten* (Beifall)

Ap|pli|ka|ti|on, die; -, -en ‹lat.› (Anwendung; *Med.* Verabreichung [von Arzneimitteln]; aufgenähte Verzierung); **ap|pli|ka|tiv; ap|pli|zie|ren**

ap|port! ‹franz.› (*Befehl an den Hund* bring es her!); **Ap|port,** der; -s, -e (Herbeibringen); **ap|por|tie|ren**

Ap|po|si|ti|on, die; -, -en ‹lat.› (*Sprachw.* substantivische Beifügung, meist im gleichen Fall wie das Bezugswort, z. B. Konrad Adenauer, „der erste deutsche Bundeskanzler", regierte ...); **ap|po|si|ti|o|nell**

Ap|pre|teur [...'tø:r], der; -s, -e ‹franz.› (*Textilind.* Zurichter, Ausrüster [von Geweben]); **ap|pre|tie|ren** ([Gewebe] zurichten, ausrüsten); **Ap|pre|tur,** die; -, -en ‹lat.› ([Gewebe]zurichtung, -veredelung)

Ap|proach [ə'pro:tʃ], der; -[e]s, -s ‹engl.› (*Wissensch.* Art der Annäherung an ein Problem; *Werbespr.* besonders wirkungsvolle Werbezeile; *Flugw.* Landeanflug)

Ap|pro|ba|ti|on, die; -, -en ‹lat.› (staatl. Zulassung als Arzt od. Apotheker); **ap|pro|bie|ren;** approbierter Arzt

Ap|pro|xi|ma|ti|on, die; -, -en ‹lat.› (*bes. Math.* Annäherung); **ap|pro|xi|ma|tiv** (annähernd)

Apr. = April

Ap|rès-Ski [aprɛ'ʃi:] (↑R 130), das; - ‹franz.; norw.› (bequeme [modische] Kleidung, die man nach dem Skilaufen trägt; Vergnügung nach dem Skilaufen); **Ap|rès-Ski-Klei|dung** (↑R 28)

Ap|ri|ko|se (↑R 130), die; -, -n ‹lat.›; **Ap|ri|ko|sen‿kon|fi|tü|re, ...mar|me|la|de**

Ap|ril (↑R 130), der; -[s], -e ‹lat.› (vierter Monat im Jahr, Ostermond, Wandelmonat; *Abk.* Apr.); **Ap|ril‿scherz, ...tag, ...wet|ter**

a pri|ma vis|ta [- - v...] ‹ital.› (ohne vorherige Kenntnis)

a pri|o|ri ‹lat.› (*bes. Philos.* von der Wahrnehmung unabhängig, aus Vernunftgründen; von vornherein); **A|pri|o|ri,** das; -, - (*Philos.* Vernunftsatz); **a|pri|o|risch** (allein durch Denken gewonnen; aus Vernunftgründen [erschlossen]); **A|pri|o|ris|mus,** der; - (philos. Lehre, die eine von der Erfahrung unabhängige Erkenntnis annimmt)

ap|ro|pos [apro'po:] (↑R 130) ‹franz.› (nebenbei bemerkt)

Ap|si|de, die; -, -n ‹griech.› (*Astron.* Punkt der kleinsten od. größten Entfernung eines Planeten von dem Gestirn, das er umläuft; *auch für* Apsis); **Ap|sis,** die; -, ...siden ‹griech.› (*Archit.* halbrunde, auch vieleckige Altarnische; [halbrunde] Nische im Zelt für Gepäck u. a.)

ap|tie|ren ‹lat.› (*Philatelie* [einen Stempel] so ändern, dass eine weitere Benutzung möglich ist)

A|pu|li|en [...iən] (Region in Italien)

A|qua des|til|la|ta, das; - - ‹lat.› (destilliertes Wasser); **A|quä|dukt,** der, *auch* das; -[e]s, -e (über eine Brücke geführte antike Wasserleitung); **A|qua|kul|tur** (Bewirtschaftung des Meeres, z. B. durch Muschelkulturen); **A|qua|ma|rin,** der; -s, -e (ein Edelstein); **A|qua|naut,** der; -en, -en; ↑R 126 (Unterwasserforscher); **A|qua|pla|ning** [*selten auch* ...'ple:niŋ], das; -[s] ‹lat.; engl.› (Wasserglätte; das Rutschen der Reifen eines Kraftfahrzeugs auf aufgestautem Wasser bei regennasser Straße); **A|qua|rell,** das; -s, -e ‹ital. (-franz.)› (mit Wasserfarben gemaltes Bild); in Aquarell (Wasserfarben) malen; **A|qua|rell|far|be; a|qua|rel|lie|ren** (in Wasserfarben malen); **A|qua|ri|a|ner** ‹lat.› (Aquarienliebhaber); **A|qua|ri|en|glas** [...iən...] *Plur.* ...gläser; **A|qua|ris|tik,** die; - (sachgerechtes Halten und Züchten von Wassertieren u. -pflanzen); **A|qua|ri|um,** das; -s, ...ien [...iən] (Behälter zur Pflege und Züchtung von Wassertieren und -pflanzen; Gebäude für diese Zwecke); **A|qua|tel,** das; -s, -s ‹lat.; franz.› (Hotel, das statt Zimmern Hausboote vermietet); **A|qua|tin|ta,** die; -, ...ten ‹ital.› (ein Kupferstichverfahren *[nur Sing.];* nach diesem Verfahren hergestellte Grafik); **a|qua|tisch** ‹lat.› (dem Wasser angehörend); -e Fauna

Ä|qua|tor, der; -s ‹lat.› (größter Breitenkreis der Erde); **ä|qua|to|ri|al** (in der Nähe des Äquators befindlich); **Ä|qua|to|ri|al|gui|nea** [...gi...] (Staat in Afrika); **Ä|qua|tor|tau|fe**

A|qua|vit [...'vi:t, *auch* ...'vit], der; -s, -e ‹lat.› (ein mit Kümmel aromatisierter Branntwein)
ä|qui|dis|tant ‹lat.› (*Math.* gleich weit voneinander entfernt)
Ä|qui|lib|rist (↑R 130), der; -en, -en (↑R 126) ‹franz.› (Gleichgewichtskünstler, bes. Seiltänzer); **ä|qui|nok|ti|al** ‹lat.› (*fachspr.* das Äquinoktium betreffend); **Ä|qui-nok|ti|al|stür|me** *Plur.*; **Ä|qui-nok|ti|um,** das; -s, ...ien [...i̯ən] (Tagundnachtgleiche)
A|qui|ta|ni|en [...i̯ən] (hist. Landschaft in Südwestfrankreich)
ä|qui|va|lent [...v...] ‹lat.› (gleichwertig); **Ä|qui|va|lent,** das; -[e]s, -e (Gegenwert; Ausgleich); **Ä|qui|va|lenz,** die; -, -en (Gleichwertigkeit); **ä|qui|vok** (mehrdeutig, doppelsinnig)
[1]**Ar,** das, *österr. nur so, auch* der; -s, -e ‹lat.› (ein Flächenmaß; *Zeichen* a); drei - (↑R 90)
[2]**Ar** = *chem. Zeichen für* Argon
A|ra, A|ra|ra, der; -s, -s ‹indian.› (trop. Langschwanzpapagei)
Ä|ra, die; -, Ären *Plur. selten* ‹lat.› (Zeitalter, Epoche)
A|ra|bel|la (w. Vorn.)
A|ra|ber [*auch* 'ara..., *österr. u. schweiz. auch* a'ra:...], der; -s, -; **A|ra|bes|ke,** die; -, -n ‹franz.› (*bild. Kunst* stilisiertes Rankenornament); **A|ra|bi|en** [...i̯ən]; **a|ra-bisch;** (↑R 104:) arabisches Vollblut; arabische Ziffern, *aber* (↑R 108): Arabische Republik Ägypten; Arabisches Meer; Arabische Liga; *vgl.* deutsch; **A|ra-bisch,** das; -[s] (eine Sprache); *vgl.* Deutsch; **A|ra|bi|sche,** das; -n; *vgl.* Deutsche, das; **a|ra|bi-sie|ren; A|ra|bist,** der; -en, -en; ↑R 126 (Wissenschaftler auf dem Gebiet der Arabistik); **A|ra|bis-tik,** die; - (Erforschung der arabischen Sprache u. Literatur)
A|rach|ni|den, A|rach|no|i|den *Plur.* ‹griech.› (*Zool.* Spinnentiere); **A|rach|no|lo|ge,** der; -n, -n; ↑R 126 (Wissenschaftler auf dem Gebiet der Arachnologie); **A|rach|no|lo|gie,** die; - (Wissenschaft von den Spinnentieren)
A|ra|gón [...'gɔn] (*span. Schreibung für* Aragonien); **A|ra|go|ne-se,** der; -n, -n (*auch für* Aragonier); **A|ra|go|ni|en** [...i̯ən] (hist. Provinz in Spanien); **A|ra|go|ni-er; a|ra|go|nisch; A|ra|go|nit** [*auch* ...'nit], der; -s (ein Mineral)
A|ra|lie [...i̯ə], die; -, -n (Pflanzengattung; Zierpflanze)
A|ral|see, der; -s (abflussloser See in Mittelasien)
A|ra|mäa ‹*aram.*, „Hochland"› (alter Name für Syrien); **A|ra-mä|er,** der; -s, - (Angehöriger eines westsemit. Nomadenvolkes); **a|ra|mä|isch;** *vgl.* deutsch; **A|ra|mä|isch,** das; -[s] (eine Sprache); *vgl.* Deutsch; **A|ra-mä|i|sche,** das; -n; *vgl.* Deutsche, das
A|ran|ju|ez [a'ranxu̯ɛs, *span.* araŋ-'xu̯eθ] (span. Stadt)
A|ran|zi|ni *Plur.* ‹pers.-ital.› (*bes. österr. für* überzuckerte od. schokoladenüberzogene gekochte Orangenschalen)
Ä|rar, das; -s, -e ‹lat.› (Staatsvermögen; *österr. für* Fiskus)
A|ra|ra *vgl.* Ara
A|ra|rat ['a(:)...], der; -[s] (höchster Berg der Türkei)
ä|ra|risch ‹lat.› (zum Ärar gehörend; staatlich)
A|rau|ka|ner (chilen. u. argentin. Indianer); **A|rau|ka|rie** [...i̯ə], die; -, -en (Zimmertanne)
A|raz|zo, der; -s, ...zzi ‹ital., nach der frz. Stadt Arras› (gewirkter Bildteppich)
Ar|beit, die; -, -en; Arbeit suchende Menschen; die Arbeit Suchenden, *auch* Arbeitsuchenden; **ar-bei|ten; Ar|bei|ter; Ar|bei|ter-_be|we|gung, ...dich|ter, ...füh-rer; Ar|bei|te|rin; Ar|bei|ter-_klas|se, ...par|tei, ...pries|ter** (kath. Priester, der unter denselben Bedingungen wie die Arbeiter lebt); **Ar|bei|ter|schaft,** die; -; **Ar|bei|ter-und-Bau|ern-Fa|kul-tät** (Bildungseinrichtung in der ehem. DDR; *Abk.* ABF); **Ar|bei-ter|un|fall|ver|si|che|rungs|ge-setz** (↑R 46); **Ar|beit_ge|ber, ...ge|ber|ver|band, ...neh|mer, ...neh|me|rin; ar|beit|sam; Ar-beits_amt, ...be|schaf|fung, ...be|schaf|fungs|maß|nah|me** (*Abk.* ABM), **...be|such** *(Politik)*, **...di|rek|tor, ...es|sen** *(bes. Politik)*; **ar|beits|fä|hig; Ar|beits_fä-hig|keit** (die; -), **...feld, ...gang** (der), **...ge|mein|schaft, ...ge-richt, ...haus, ...hy|gi|e|ne; ar-beits|in|ten|siv; Ar|beits_ka-me|rad, ...kampf, ...kli|ma, ...kraft** (die), **...la|ger, ...lohn; ar-beits|los; Ar|beits|lo|se,** der *u.* die; -n, -n (↑R 5 ff.); **Ar|beits|lo-sen_geld, ...hil|fe** (die; -), **...quo-te, ...un|ter|stüt|zung, ...ver|si-che|rung** (die; -); **Ar|beits|lo-sig|keit,** die; -; **Ar|beits_markt, ...mi|nis|te|ri|um, ...mo|ral, ...platz, ...recht, ...stät|te; ar-beits|su|chend,** Ar|beit suchend; *vgl.* Arbeit; **Ar|beit[s]|su-chen|de,** der *u.* die; -n, -n (↑R 5 ff.); *vgl.* Arbeit; **Ar|beits-tag; ar|beits_täg|lich, ...tei|lig; Ar|beits_tei|lung, ...un|ter|richt** (method. Prinzip der Unterrichtsgestaltung), **...ver|hält|nis, ...ver-mitt|lung; ar|beits|wil|lig; Ar-beits|wil|li|ge,** der *u.* die; -n, -n (↑R 5 ff.); **Ar|beits_zeit, ...zeit-ver|kür|zung, ...zim|mer**
Ar|bit|ra|ge [...'tra:ʒə, *österr.* ...'tra:ʒ] (↑R 130), die; -, -n [...'tra:ʒ(ə)n] ‹franz.› (Schiedsgerichtsvereinbarung im Handelsrecht; [Ausnutzen der] Kursunterschiede an verschiedenen Börsen); **ar|bit|rär** (nach Ermessen, willkürlich); **Ar|bit|ra|ti|on,** die; -, -en (Schiedswesen für Streitigkeiten an der Börse)
ARBÖ = Auto-, Motor- und Radfahrerbund Österreichs
Ar|bo|re|tum, das; -s, ...ten ‹lat.› (*Bot.* Pflanzung verschiedener Bäume zu Studienzwecken)
Ar|bu|se, die; -, -n ‹pers.-russ.› (Wassermelone)
arc = Arkus
Arc de Tri|omphe ['arkdətri'ɔ̃:f], der; - - - (Triumphbogen in Paris)
Ar|cha|i|kum, Ar|chä|i|kum, das; -s ‹griech.› (*Geol.* ältestes Zeitalter der Erdgeschichte); **ar|cha|isch** (aus sehr früher Zeit [stammend], altertümlich); **ar|chä|isch** (das Archäikum betreffend); **ar|cha|i-sie|ren** (archaische Formen verwenden; altertümeln); **Ar|cha|is-mus,** der; -, ...men (altertümliche Ausdrucksform, veraltetes Wort); **ar|cha|is|tisch**
Ar|chan|gelsk [*od.* ...x...] (russ. Stadt)
Ar|chä|o|lo|ge, der; -n, -n (↑R 126) ‹griech.› (Wissenschaftler auf dem Gebiet der Archäologie, Altertumsforscher); **Ar|chä-o|lo|gie,** die; - (Altertumskunde, -wissenschaft); **Ar|chä|o|lo|gin; ar|chä|o|lo|gisch; Ar|chä|op|te-ryx** (↑R 132), der *od.* die; -, *Plur.* -e *u.* ...teryges [...ge:s]; (Urvogel)
Ar|che, die; -, -n ‹lat.› (schiffähnlicher Kasten); - Noah
Ar|che|typ [*auch* 'ar...], der; -s, -en *u.* **Ar|che|ty|pus,** der; -, ...pen ‹griech.› (Urbild, Urform; älteste erreichbare Gestalt [einer Schrift]); **ar|che|ty|pisch** [*auch* 'ar...] (dem Urbild, der Urform entsprechend)
Ar|chi|bald (m. Vorn.)
Ar|chi|di|a|kon ‹griech.› (Titel von Geistlichen [der anglikanischen Kirche]); **Ar|chi|mand|rit** (↑R 130), der; -en, -en; ↑R 126 (*Ostkirche* Klostervorsteher; Ehrentitel für verdiente Priester)
Ar|chi|me|des (altgriech. Mathe-

matiker); **ar|chi|me|disch;** archimedisches Prinzip; archimedischer Punkt (Angelpunkt); archimedische Spirale (↑R 94)

Ar|chi|pel, der; -s, -e ‹griech.-ital.› (Inselmeer, -gruppe); **Ar|chi|tekt,** der; -en, -en (↑R 126) ‹griech.›; **Ar|chi|tek|ten|bü|ro; Ar|chi|tek|to|nik,** die; -, -en (Wissenschaft der Baukunst *[nur Sing.]*; Bauart; planmäßiger Aufbau); **ar|chi|tek|to|nisch** (baulich; baukünstlerisch); **Ar|chi|tek|tur,** die; -, -en (Baukunst; Baustil); **Ar|chi|trav** (↑R 132), der; -s, -e [...və] (*Archit.* auf Säulen ruhender Tragbalken)

Ar|chiv, das; -s, -e [...və] (Akten-, Urkundensammlung; Titel wissenschaftlicher Zeitschriften); **Ar|chi|va|le** [...v...], das; -s, ...lien [...li̯ən] *meist Plur.* (Aktenstück [aus einem Archiv]); **ar|chi|va|lisch** (urkundlich); **Ar|chi|var,** der; -s, -e (Archivbeamter); **Ar|chi|va|rin; Ar|chiv|bild; ar|chi|vie|ren** (in ein Archiv aufnehmen); **Ar|chi|vie|rung**

Ar|chon, der; -s, Archonten ‹griech.›, **Ar|chont,** der; -en, -en; ↑R 126 (höchster Beamter im alten Athen)

Ar|cus *vgl.* Arkus

ARD = Arbeitsgemeinschaft der öffentlich-rechtlichen Rundfunkanstalten der Bundesrepublik Deutschland

Ar|da|bil, Ar|de|bil, der; -[s], -s (iran. Teppich)

Ar|den|nen *Plur.* (Gebirge); **Ar|den|ner Wald,** der; - -[e]s (*früher für* Ardennen)

Ar|dey [ˈardai̯], der; -s (gebirgiger Teil des Sauerlandes)

A|re, die; -, -n (*schweiz. für* [1]Ar); **A|re|al,** das; -s, -e ([Boden]fläche, Gelände)

A|re|ka|nuss ‹Malayalam-port.; dt.› (Frucht der Arekapalme; Betelnuss)

Ä|ren (*Plur. von* Ära)

A|re|na, die; -, ...nen ‹lat.› ([sandbestreuter] Kampfplatz; Sportplatz; Manege im Zirkus; *österr. veraltend auch* Sommerbühne)

A|re|o|pag, der; -s ‹griech.› (Gerichtshof im alten Athen)

A|res (griech. Kriegsgott)

A|rez|zo (ital. Stadt)

arg; ärger, ärgste; ein arger Bösewicht, *aber* der Arge *(vgl. d.);* im Argen liegen; zum Ärgsten kommen; vor dem Ärgsten bewahren; das Ärgste verhüten; nichts Arges denken; **Arg,** das; -s *(geh.);* ohne Arg; kein Arg an einer Sache finden; **Ar|ge,** der; -n (Teufel)

Ar|gen|ti|ni|en [...i̯ən] (südamerik. Staat); **Ar|gen|ti|ni|er** [...i̯ər]; **Ar|gen|ti|ni|e|rin** [...i̯ə...]; **ar|gen|ti|nisch;** argentinische Literatur, *aber* (↑R 102): die Argentinische Republik; **Ar|gen|tit** [*auch* ...ˈtit], der; -s (Silberglanz; Silbersulfid); **Ar|gen|tum,** das; -[s] (*lat. Bez. für* Silber; *Zeichen* Ag)

Är|ger, der; -s; **är|ger|lich; är|gern;** ich ...ere (↑R 16); sich über etwas -; **Är|ger|nis,** das; ...nisses, ...nisse; **Arg|list,** die; -; **arg|lis|tig; arg|los; Arg|lo|sig|keit,** die; -

Ar|go, die; - ‹griech.› (Name des Schiffes der Argonauten; ein Sternbild)

Ar|go|lis (griech. Landschaft)

Ar|gon [*auch* arˈgo:n], das; -s ‹griech.› (chem. Element, Edelgas; *Zeichen* Ar)

Ar|go|naut, der; -en, -en (↑R 126) ‹griech.› (Held der griech. Sage; ein Tintenfisch)

Ar|gon|nen *Plur.* (franz. Gebirge)

Ar|got [arˈgo:], das *od.* der; -s, -s ‹franz.› (franz. Gaunersprache [im MA.]; Jargon bestimmter sozialer Gruppen)

Ar|gu|ment, das; -[e]s, -e ‹lat.› (Beweis[mittel, -grund]); **Ar|gu|men|ta|ti|on,** die; -, -en (Beweisführung); **ar|gu|men|ta|tiv** (mit Argumenten); **ar|gu|men|tie|ren**

[1]**Ar|gus** (Riese der griech. Sage); [2]**Ar|gus,** der; -, -se (scharf beobachtender Wächter); **Ar|gus|au|gen** *Plur.;* ↑R 95 (scharfe, wachsame Augen); **ar|gus|äu|gig**

Arg|wohn, der; -[e]s *(geh.);* **arg|wöh|nen** *(geh.);* ich argwöhne; geargwöhnt; zu -; **arg|wöh|nisch**

A|rhyth|mie *vgl.* Arrhythmie

A|ri|ad|ne (griech. weibliche Sagengestalt); **A|ri|ad|ne|fa|den,** der; -s (↑R 95)

A|ri|a|ne (w. Vorn.; Name einer europ. Trägerrakete)

A|ri|a|ner (*Rel.* Anhänger des Arianismus); **a|ri|a|nisch;** der Arianische Streit (↑R 56); **A|ri|a|nis|mus,** der; - (Lehre des Arius, wonach Christus mit Gott nicht wesenseins, sondern nur wesensähnlich sei)

a|rid ‹lat.› (*Geogr.* trocken; wüstenhaft); **A|ri|di|tät,** die; -

A|rie [...i̯ə], die; -, -n ‹ital.› (Sologesangsstück mit Instrumentalbegleitung)

[1]**A|ri|el** [...i̯ɛl, *auch* ...i̯e:l] ‹hebr.› (alter Name Jerusalems; Name eines Engels; Luftgeist in Shakespeares „Sturm"); [2]**A|ri|el,** der; -s (Uranusmond)

A|ri|er [...i̯ər], der; -s, - ‹sanskr.› (Angehöriger eines der frühgeschichtl. Völker mit idg. Sprache; *nationalsoz.* Nichtjude, Angehöriger der sog. nordischen Rasse)

A|ri|es [...i̯ɛs], der; - ‹lat., „Widder"› (ein Sternbild)

A|ri|ma|thia, *ökum.* A|ri|ma|täa (altpalästin. Ort)

A|ri|on (altgriech. Sänger)

a|ri|o|so ‹ital.› (*Musik* liedmäßig [vorgetragen]); **A|ri|o|so,** das; -s, *Plur.* -s *u.* ...si (liedhaftes Gesangs- od. Instrumentalstück)

A|ri|ost, A|ri|os|to (ital. Dichter)

A|ri|o|vist [...v...] (Heerkönig der Sweben)

a|risch ‹*zu* Arier›; **a|ri|sie|ren** (*nationalsoz.* in arischen Besitz überführen)

A|ris|ti|des (athen. Staatsmann)

A|ris|to|krat, der; -en, -en (↑R 126) ‹griech.› (Angehöriger des Adels; vornehmer Mensch); **A|ris|to|kra|tie,** die; -, ...ien; **a|ris|to|kra|tisch**

A|ris|to|pha|nes (altgriech. Lustspieldichter); **a|ris|to|pha|nisch;** die aristophanische Komödie (↑R 94)

A|ris|to|te|les (altgriech. Philosoph); Aristoteles' Schriften (↑R 98); **A|ris|to|te|li|ker** (Anhänger der Lehre des Aristoteles); **a|ris|to|te|lisch;** die aristotelische Logik (↑R 94)

A|rith|me|tik, die; - ‹griech.› (Zahlenlehre, Rechnen mit Zahlen); **A|rith|me|ti|ker; a|rith|me|tisch** (auf die Arithmetik bezüglich); arithmetisches Mittel (Durchschnittswert); **A|rith|mo|griph,** der; -en, -en; ↑R 126 (Zahlenrätsel)

A|ri|us (alexandrin. Presbyter)

Ariz. = Arizona

A|ri|zo|na (Staat in den USA; *Abk.* Ariz.)

Ark. = Arkansas

Ar|ka|de, die; -, -n ‹franz.› (*Archit.* Bogen auf zwei Pfeilern od. Säulen); **Ar|ka|den** *Plur.* (Bogenreihe)

Ar|ka|di|en [...i̯ən] (griech. Landschaft); **Ar|ka|di|er** [...i̯ər]; **ar|ka|disch;** -e Poesie (Hirten- u. Schäferdichtung)

Ar|kan|sas (Staat in den USA; *Abk.* Ark.)

Ar|ka|num, das; -s, ...na ‹lat.› (Geheimnis; Geheimmittel)

Ar|ke|bu|se, die; -, -n ‹niederl., „Hakenbüchse"› (Gewehr im 15./16. Jh.); **Ar|ke|bu|sier,** der; -s, -e (Soldat mit Arkebuse)

Ar|ko|na (Kap auf Rügen)

Ar|ko|se, die; - ‹franz.› (*Geol.* feldspatreicher Sandstein)

Ark|ti|ker, der; -s, - ‹griech.› (Bewohner der Arktis); **Ark|tis,** die; - (Gebiet um den Nordpol); **ark|tisch; Ark|tur, Ark|tu|rus,** der; - (ein Stern)

Ar|kus, *auch* Ar|cus, der; -, - ['arku:s] ‹lat.› (*Math.* Kreisbogen eines Winkels; *Zeichen* arc)

Arl|berg, der; -[e]s (Alpenpass); **Arl|berg|bahn,** die; -

Ar|les [arl] (franz. Stadt am Rhonedelta)

arm; ärmer, ärmste; arme Ritter (eine Süßspeise); die armen Kinder; *aber* wir Armen (↑R 5); [bei] Arm und Reich (*veraltet für* [bei] jedermann); ein Konflikt zwischen Arm und Reich; Arme und Reiche, bei Armen und Reichen, der Arme *(vgl. d.)* und der Reiche

Arm, der; -[e]s, -e; ein Arm voll Reisig

Ar|ma|da, die; -, *Plur.* ...den *u.* -s ‹span.› ([mächtige] Kriegsflotte)

Ar|mag|nac [arman'jak] (↑R 130), der; -[s], -s ‹franz.› (franz. Weinbrand)

arm|am|pu|tiert; ein -er Mann

Ar|ma|tur, die; -, -en ‹lat.›; **Ar|ma|tu|ren|brett**

Arm|band, das; *Plur.* ...bänder; **Arm|band|uhr; Arm‿beu|ge, ...bin|de, ...blatt** (Einlage gegen Achselschweiß)

Arm|brust, die; -, *Plur.* ...brüste, *auch* -e

Ärm|chen; arm|dick; ein armdicker Ast, *aber* einen Arm dick

Ar|me, der *u.* die; -n, -n (↑R 5 ff.)

Ar|mee, die; -, ...meen ‹franz.› (Heer; Heeresabteilung); **Ar|mee|ein|heit** (↑R 136); **Ar|mee|korps** (*Abk.* AK)

Är|mel, der; -s, -

Ar|me|leu|te‿es|sen, ...ge|ruch *(abwertend),* **...vier|tel**

...är|me|lig, ...ärm|lig (z. B. kurzärm[e]lig); **Är|mel|ka|nal,** der; -s; **Är|mel|län|ge; är|mel|los**

Ar|men‿haus *(veraltet),* **...häus|ler**

Ar|me|ni|en (Staat in Vorderasien); **Ar|me|ni|er; ar|me|nisch**

Ar|men‿pfle|ger *(veraltet),* **...recht** (das; -[e]s); **Ar|men|sün|der|glo|cke,** die; -, -n (*österr. für* Armesünderglocke); **Ar|men|vier|tel**

Ar|mes|län|ge; auf - an jmdn. herankommen; um - voraus sein

Ar|me|sün|der, der; des Armesünders, die Armesünder; *bei Beugung des Adjektivs Getrenntschreibung:* des armen Sünders, die armen Sünder, ein armer Sünder; **Ar|me|sün|der|glo|cke,** die

ar|mie|ren ‹lat.› (*Technik* ausrüsten, bestücken, bewehren); **Ar|mie|rung; Ar|mie|rungs|ei|sen**

...ar|mig (z. B. langarmig)

Ar|min (m. Vorn.); **Ar|mi|ni|us** (Cheruskerfürst)

arm|lang; ein armlanger Stiel, *aber* einen Arm lang; **Arm‿län|ge, ...leh|ne; Arm|leuch|ter** (*auch* Schimpfwort)

ärm|lich; Ärm|lich|keit, die; -

...ärm|lig *vgl.* ...ärmelig; **Ärm|ling** (Ärmel zum Überstreifen); **Arm|mus|kel**

Ar|mo|ri|ka (*kelt. Bez. für* die Bretagne); **ar|mo|ri|ka|nisch,** *aber* (↑R 102): das Armorikanische Gebirge *(Geol.)*

Arm|reif, der; -[e]s, -e

arm|se|lig; Arm|se|lig|keit, die; -

[1]**Arm|strong** ['a:(r)mstrɔŋ], Louis ['lu:i] (amerik. Jazzmusiker); [2]**Arm|strong,** Neil [ni:l] (amerik. Astronaut, der als erster Mensch den Mond betrat)

Arm|sün|der|glo|cke, die; -, -n; *auch* Ar|me|sün|der|glo|cke, *österr.* Ar|men|sün|der|glo|cke

Ar|mu|re [ar'my:rə], **Ar|mü|re,** die; -, -n ‹franz.› (klein gemustertes [Kunst]seidengewebe)

Ar|mut, die; -; **Ar|muts‿flücht|ling** *(Soziol.),* **...zeug|nis**

Arm voll *vgl.* Arm

Arndt (dt. Dichter)

Ar|ni|ka, die; -, -s ‹griech.› (eine Heilpflanze); **Ar|ni|ka|tink|tur**

Ar|nim (märk. Adelsgeschlecht)

[1]**Ar|no,** der; -[s] (ital. Fluss)

[2]**Ar|no** (m. Vorn.); **Ar|nold** (m. Vorn.); **Ar|nulf** (m. Vorn.)

A|rom, das; -s, -e ‹griech.› (*geh. für* Aroma); **A|ro|ma,** das; -s, *Plur.* ...men, -s *u. älter* -ta; **a|ro|ma|tisch;** -e Verbindungen *(Chemie);* **a|ro|ma|ti|sie|ren** (mit Aroma versehen)

A|ron|stab ‹griech.; dt.› (eine Pflanze)

A|ro|sa (Ort in Graubünden); **A|ro|ser** (↑R 103)

Ar|pad (erster Herzog der Ungarn); **Ar|pa|de,** der; -n, -n; ↑R 126 (Angehöriger eines ung. Fürstengeschlechtes)

Ar|peg|gia|tur [arpɛdʒa...], die; -, -en ‹ital.› (*Musik* Reihe gebrochener Akkorde); **ar|peg|gie|ren** [arpɛ'dʒi:...] (nach Harfenart spielen); **ar|peg|gio** [ar'pɛdʒo] (nach Harfenart); **Ar|peg|gio,** das; -s, *Plur.* -s *u.* ...ggien [...dʒiən]

Ar|rak, der; -s, *Plur.* -e *u.* -s ‹arab.› (Branntwein aus Reis od. Melasse)

Ar|ran|ge|ment [araŋʒə'maŋ *od.* arãʒə'mã:], das; -s, -s ‹franz.› (Anordnung; Übereinkunft; Einrichtung eines Musikstücks); **Ar|ran|geur** [araŋ'ʒø:r *od.* arã'ʒø:r], der; -s, -e (jmd., der etwas arrangiert; jmd., der ein Musikstück einrichtet, einen Schlager instrumentiert); **ar|ran|gie|ren** [araŋ'ʒi:... *od.* arã'ʒi:...]; **Ar|ran|gier|pro|be** (*Theater* Stellprobe)

Ar|ras (franz. Stadt)

Ar|rest, der; -[e]s, -e ‹lat.› (Beschlagnahme; Haft; *veraltet für* Nachsitzen); **Ar|res|tant,** der; -en, -en; ↑R 126 (*veraltend für* Häftling); **Ar|rest|zel|le; ar|re|tie|ren** (*Technik* anhalten; sperren; *veraltet für* verhaften); **Ar|re|tie|rung** (Sperrvorrichtung)

Ar|rhe|ni|us (schwed. Chemiker u. Physiker)

Ar|rhyth|mie, die; -, ...ien ‹griech.› (Unregelmäßigkeit in einer sonst rhythm. Bewegung; *Med.* Unregelmäßigkeit des Herzschlags); **ar|rhyth|misch** [*od.* a'ryt...]

Ar|ri|val [ə'raivəl], das; -s, -s ‹engl.› (Ankunft [Hinweis auf Flughäfen]); **ar|ri|vie|ren** [ari'vi:...] ‹franz.› (in der Karriere vorwärts kommen); **ar|ri|viert** (anerkannt, erfolgreich); **Ar|ri|vier|te,** der *u.* die; -n, -n; ↑R 5 ff. (anerkannte[r] Künstler[in]; Emporkömmling)

ar|ro|gant ‹lat.› (anmaßend); **Ar|ro|ganz,** die; -

ar|ron|die|ren [*od.* arõ'di:...] ‹franz.›; Grundbesitz - (abrunden, zusammenlegen); **Ar|ron|die|rung; Ar|ron|dis|se|ment** [arõdis(ə)'mã:], das; -s, -s (Unterabteilung eines franz. Departements; Bezirk)

Ar|row|root ['ɛroru:t], das; -s ‹engl., „Pfeilwurz"› (ein Stärkemehl)

Ar|sa|ki|de, der; -n, -n; ↑R 126 (Angehöriger eines pers. u. armen. Herrschergeschlechtes)

Arsch, der; -[e]s, Ärsche *(derb);* **Arsch‿ba|cke** *(derb),* **...gei|ge** *(derb),* **...krie|cher** (*derb für* übertrieben schmeichlerischer Mensch), **...le|der** *(Bergmannsspr.),* **...loch** *(derb),* **...pau|ker** (*derb für* Lehrer), **...wisch** (*derb für* wertloses Schriftstück)

Ar|sen, das; -s ‹griech.› (chem. Element; *Zeichen* As)

Ar|se|nal, das; -s, -e ‹arab.-ital.› (Geräte-, Waffenlager)

ar|se|nig ‹griech.› (arsenikhaltig); **Ar|se|nik,** das; -s (*Chemie* giftige Arsenverbindung); **ar|se|nik|hal|tig; Ar|sen‿kies** (ein Mineral), **...ver|gif|tung**

Ar|sis, die; -, Arsen ‹griech.› (*Verslehre* Hebung)

Art, die; -, -en; ein Mann [von] der Art (solcher Art), *aber* er hat mich derart (so) beleidigt, dass ...; *vgl.* allerart

Art. = Artikel

Art|an|ga|be (*Sprachw.* Umstandsangabe der Art u. Weise)

Art dé|co [arde'ko], der *u.* das; - - ‹franz.› (Kunst[gewerbe]stil der Jahre 1920–40)

Art|di|rec|tor ['a:(r)tdi'rɛktə(r)], der; -s, -s ‹engl.› (künstlerischer Leiter des Lay-outs in einer Werbeagentur)

Ar|te|fakt, das; -[e]s, -e ‹lat.› (*Archäol.* von Menschen geformter vorgeschichtlicher Gegenstand; *geh. für* Kunstwerk)

art|ei|gen (*Biol.* einer bestimmten Art entsprechend, eigen)

Ar|tel, das; -s, -s ‹russ., „Gemeinschaft"› ([Arbeiter]genossenschaft im alten Russland u. in der sowjet. Kollektivwirtschaft)

Ar|te|mis (griech. Göttin der Jagd)

ar|ten; nach jmdm. -; **Ar|ten‿reich|tum** (der; -s), **...schutz** (der; -es); **art|er|hal|tend**

Ar|te|rie [...i̯ə], die; -, -n ‹griech.› (*Med.* Schlagader); **ar|te|ri|ell**; arterielles Blut; **Ar|te|ri|en|ver|kal|kung** [...i̯ən...]; **Ar|te|ri|i|tis**, die; -, ...iitiden (Arterienentzündung); **Ar|te|ri|o|skle|ro|se** (Arterienverkalkung); **ar|te|ri|o|skle|ro|tisch**

ar|te|sisch ‹*zu* Artois›; artesischer Brunnen (Brunnen, dessen Wasser durch Überdruck des Grundwassers selbsttätig aufsteigt)

art|fremd *(Biol.)*; -es Gewebe; **Art|ge|nos|se**; **art|ge|recht**

Arth|ral|gie (↑R 132), die; -, ...ien ‹griech.› (*Med.* Gelenkschmerz, Gliederreißen); **Arth|ri|ti|ker** (an Arthritis Leidender); **Arth|ri|tis**, die; -, ...itiden (Gelenkentzündung); **arth|ri|tisch**; **Arth|ro|po|den**, *Plur.* (*Zool.* Gliederfüßer); **Arth|ro|se**, die; -, -n (*Med.* chron. Gelenkerkrankung)

Ar|thur *vgl.* Artur

ar|ti|fi|zi|ell ‹franz.› (künstlich)

ar|tig (gesittet; folgsam); **...ar|tig** (z. B. gleichartig); **Ar|tig|keit**

Ar|ti|kel [*auch* ar'ti...], der; -s, - ‹lat.› (Geschlechtswort; Abschnitt eines Gesetzes u. Ä. [*Abk.* Art.]; Ware; Aufsatz); **Ar|ti|kel|se|rie**; **ar|ti|ku|lar** (*Med.* zum Gelenk gehörend); **Ar|ti|ku|la|ti|on**, die; -, -en (*Sprachw.* Lautbildung; [deutliche] Aussprache); **ar|ti|ku|la|to|risch**; **ar|ti|ku|lie|ren** (deutlich aussprechen; zum Ausdruck bringen)

Ar|til|le|rie [*auch* 'ar...], die; -, ...i̯en ‹franz.›; **Ar|til|le|rist** [*auch* 'ar...], der; -en, -en (↑R 126); **ar|til|le|ris|tisch**

Ar|ti|scho|cke, die; -, -n ‹ital.› (eine Zier- u. Gemüsepflanze); **Ar|ti|scho|cken|bo|den**

Ar|tist, der; -en, -en (↑R 126) ‹franz.›; **Ar|tis|tik**, die; - (Kunst der Artisten); **Ar|tis|tin**; **ar|tis|tisch**

Art nou|veau [arnu'vo], der *u.* das, - - ‹franz.› (*Bez. für* Jugendstil in England u. Frankreich)

Ar|tois [ar'to̯a], das; - (hist. Provinz in Nordfrankreich)

Ar|to|thek, die; -, -en ‹lat.; griech.› (Galerie, die Bilder od. Plastiken ausleiht)

Ar|tur (m. Vorn.); **Ar|tus** (sagenhafter walis. König); **Ar|tus|hof**, der; -[e]s

art|ver|wandt; **Art|wort** *Plur.* ...wörter (*für* Adjektiv)

Ar|ve ['arvə, *schweiz.* 'arfə], die; -, -n (Zirbelkiefer)

Arz|nei; **Arz|nei|kun|de**, die; -; **arz|nei|lich**; **Arz|nei|mit|tel**, das; **Arz|nei|mit|tel|leh|re**; **Arzt**, der; -es, Ärzte; **Ärz|te|kam|mer**; **Ärz|te|schaft**, die; -; **Arzt|hel|fe|rin**; **Ärz|tin**; **ärzt|lich**; **Arzt‿rech|nung**, **...ro|man**

[1]**as**, [1]**As**, das; -, - (Tonbezeichnung); [2]**as** (*Zeichen für* as-Moll); in as; [2]**As** (*Zeichen für* As-Dur); in As

[3]**As**, der; Asses, Asse ‹lat.› (altröm. Gewichts- und Münzeinheit)

[4]**As** = *chem. Zeichen für* Arsen

[5]**As** *frühere Schreibung für* Ass

A-Sai|te (z. B. bei der Geige)

asb = Apostilb

As|best, der; -[e]s, -e ‹griech.› (feuerfeste mineralische Faser); **As|bes|to|se**, die; -, -n (*Med.* durch Asbeststaub hervorgerufene Lungenerkrankung); **As|best|plat|te**

Asch, der; -[e]s, Äsche (*ostmitteld. für* Napf, [tiefe] Schüssel)

[1]**A|schan|ti**, der; -, - (Angehöriger eines Volksstammes in Ghana); [2]**A|schan|ti**, die; -, - (*österr. für* Erdnuss); **A|schan|ti|nuss**

Asch|be|cher *vgl.* Aschenbecher; **asch‿bleich**, **...blond**; **A|sche**, die; -, *Plur. (Technik:)* -n

Ä|sche, die; -, -n (ein Fisch)

A|sche|ge|halt, der; **a|schen|arm**; **A|schen|bahn**; **A|schen|be|cher**, Asch|be|cher; **A|schen|brö|del**, das; -s, *Plur.* (*für* jmd., der ein unscheinbares Leben führt:) - (eine Märchengestalt); **A|schen|gru|be**; **a|schen|hal|tig**; **A|schen|put|tel**, das; -s, - *vgl.* Aschenbrödel; **A|scher** (*ugs. für* Aschenbecher); **Ä|scher** (*Gerberei* Aschen- und Kalklauge); **A|scher|mitt|woch** (Mittwoch nach Fastnacht); **asch‿fahl**, **...far|ben** *od.* **...far|big**; **asch‿grau**, *aber* (↑R 47): bis ins Aschgraue (bis zum Überdruss); **a|schig**

Asch|ke|na|sim [...zi:m *od.* ...'zi:m] *Plur.* ‹hebr.› (*Bez. für* die ost- u. mitteleuropäischen Juden); **asch|ke|na|sisch**

Asch|ku|chen (*ostmitteld. für* Napfkuchen)

Asch|mo|dai *vgl.* [1]Asmodi

Asch|ram, der; -s, -s ‹sanskr.› (Zentrum für Meditation in Indien)

äschy|le|isch; **Äs|chy|lus** [*od.* 'ɛ:...] (altgriech. Tragiker)

As|co|na (schweiz. Ort am Lago Maggiore)

As|cor|bin|säu|re *vgl.* Askorbinsäure

As|cot ['ɛskət] (Dorf in der Nähe von London, berühmter Austragungsort für Pferderennen)

As-Dur [*auch* 'as'du:r], das; - (Tonart; *Zeichen* As); **As-Dur-Ton|lei|ter** (↑R 28)

A|se, der; -n, -n *meist Plur.*; ↑R 126 (germ. Gottheit)

ASEAN ['e:siən], die; - ‹*Kurzw. aus* Association of South East Asian Nations› (Vereinigung südostasiat. Staaten zur Förderung von Frieden und Wohlstand); **ASEAN-Staa|ten** *Plur.*

ä|sen; das Rotwild äst (weidet)

A|sep|sis, die; - ‹griech.› (*Med.* Keimfreiheit); **a|sep|tisch**

A|ser (*südd. für* Jagdtasche)

Ä|ser; *vgl.* Aas

A|ser|baid|schan, **A|ser|beid|schan** (↑R 130; Landschaft u. Provinz im nordwestl. Iran; Staat am Kaspischen Meer); **A|ser|baid|scha|ner**, **A|ser|beid|scha|ner**; **a|ser|baid|scha|nisch**, **a|ser|beid|scha|nisch**

a|se|xu|al [*od.* ...'a:l], **a|se|xu|ell** [*od.* ...'ɛl] ‹griech.; lat.› (geschlechtslos)

As|gard (*germ. Mythol.* Sitz der Asen)

A|si|at, der; -en, -en (↑R 126) ‹lat.›; **A|si|a|tin**; **a|si|a|tisch**; (↑R 104:) -e Grippe; **A|si|en**

As|ka|ni|er [...i̯ər], der; -s, - (Angehöriger eines alten dt. Fürstengeschlechtes)

As|ka|ri, der; -s, -s ‹arab.› (eingeborener Soldat im ehemaligen Deutsch-Ostafrika)

As|ka|ris, die; -, ...i̯den *meist Plur.* ‹griech.› (*Med., Zool.* Spulwurm)

As|ke|se, die; - ‹griech.› (enthaltsame Lebensweise); **As|ket,** der; -en, -en; ↑R 126 (enthaltsam lebender Mensch); **As|ke|tik** *vgl.* Aszetik; **as|ke|tisch**

Ask|le|pi|os, Ask|le|pi|us (↑R 130) *vgl.* Äskulap

As|kor|bin|säu|re, *chem. fachspr.* As|cor|bin|säu|re (↑R 132; Vitamin C)

Äs|ku|lap [*auch* 'ɛs...] (griech.-röm. Gott der Heilkunde); **Äs|ku|lap‿schlan|ge, ...stab**

As|ma|ra (Hptst. von Eritrea)

¹As|mo|di, *ökum.* Asch|mo|dai ‹aram.› (ein Dämon im A. T. u. im jüd. Volksglauben); **²As|mo|di** (dt. Dramatiker)

as-Moll [*auch* 'as'mɔl], das; - (Tonart; *Zeichen* as); **as-Moll-Ton|lei|ter** (↑R 28)

As|mus (m. Vorn.)

Ä|sop (altgriech. Fabeldichter); **ä|so|pisch** (*auch veraltend für* witzig); **Ä|so|pus** *vgl.* Äsop

A|sow|sche Meer ['a:sɔf..., *auch* a'sɔf... -], das; -n -[e]s (Teil des Schwarzen Meeres)

a|so|zi|al ‹griech.; lat.› (unfähig zum Leben in der Gemeinschaft; am Rand der Gesellschaft lebend); **A|so|zi|a|le,** der *u.* die (↑R 5 ff.); **A|so|zi|a|li|tät,** die; -

As|pa|ra|gin, das; -s ‹griech.› (chem. Verbindung); **As|pa|ra|gus** [*auch* as'pa... *u.* ...'ra:gus], der; - (Zierspargel)

As|pa|sia (Geliebte [und später Frau] des Perikles)

As|pekt (↑R 132), der; -[e]s, -e ‹lat.› (Ansicht, Gesichtspunkt; *Sprachw.* [den slaw. Sprachen eigentümliche] grammat. Kategorie, die die subjektive Sicht u. Auffassung des Geschehens durch den Sprecher ausdrückt; *Astron.* bestimmte Stellung der Planeten zueinander)

As|per|gill (↑R 132), das; -s, -e ‹lat.› (*kath. Kirche* Weihwasserwedel); **As|per|si|on,** die; -, -en ‹lat.› (Besprengung mit Weihwasser)

As|phalt [*auch* 'as...], der; -[e]s, -e ‹griech.›; **as|phal|tie|ren; as|phal|tisch; As|phalt‿lack, ...stra|ße**

As|pho|dill *vgl.* Affodill

As|pik [*landsch. auch* as'pik *u.* 'aspik], der, *auch* das; -s, -e ‹franz.› (Gallert aus Gelatine od. Kalbsknochen)

As|pi|rant (↑R 132), der; -en, -en (↑R 126) ‹lat.› (Bewerber; Anwärter; *schweiz. auch für* Offiziersschüler); **As|pi|ran|tur,** die; -, -en (*selten* Institution zur Ausbildung des wissenschaftlichen Nachwuchses); **As|pi|ra|ta,** die; -, *Plur.* ...ten *u.* ...tä (*Sprachw.* behauchter Verschlusslaut, z. B. griech. ϑ); **As|pi|ra|teur** [...'tø:r], der; -s, -e ‹franz.› (Maschine zum Vorreinigen des Getreides); **As|pi|ra|ti|on,** die; -, -en ‹lat.› (*veraltet für* Bestrebung *[meist Plur.]; Sprachw.* [Aussprache mit] Behauchung; *Med.* Ansaugung); **As|pi|ra|tor,** der; -s, ...oren (Luft-, Gasansauger); **as|pi|ra|to|risch** (*Sprachw.* mit Behauchung gesprochen); **as|pi|rie|ren** (*Sprachw.* mit Behauchung aussprechen; *österr. auch für* sich um etwas bewerben)

As|pi|rin ® (↑R 132), das; -s (ein Schmerzmittel); **As|pi|rin|tab|let|te**

Ass, das; -es, -e ‹franz.› (Eins [auf Karten]; das od. der Beste [z. B. im Sport]; *Tennis* für den Gegner unerreichbarer Aufschlagball); *österr. ugs. auch für* Abszess

Ass. = Assessor

As|sa|gai, der; -s, -e ‹berberisch› (Wurfspeer der Bantus)

As|sam (Bundesstaat der Republik Indien)

as|sa|nie|ren ‹franz.› (*österr.* Grundstücke, Wohngebiete o. Ä. aus hygienischen, sozialen o. a. Gründen verbessern); **As|sa|nie|rung** *(österr.)*

As|sas|si|ne, der; -n, -n (↑R 126) ‹arab.-ital.› (Angehöriger einer moslem. religiösen Gemeinschaft; *veraltet für* Meuchelmörder)

As|saut [a'so:], das; -s, -s ‹franz.› (Übungsform des Fechtens)

As|se|ku|ranz, die; -, -en ‹lat.› (*veraltet für* Versicherung, Versicherungsgesellschaft)

As|sel, die; -, -n (ein Krebstier)

As|sem|bla|ge [asã'bla:ʒə] (↑R 130), die; -, -n ‹franz.› (*Kunst* Hochrelief; Kombination verschiedener Objekte); **As|sem|bler** [ə'sɛm..., *auch* a'sɛm...], der; -s, - ‹engl.› (*EDV* eine Programmiersprache; Übersetzungsprogramm)

As|ser|ti|on die; -, -en ‹lat.› (*Philos.* bestimmte Behauptung); **as|ser|to|risch** (behauptend)

As|ser|vat [...v...], das; -[e]s, -e ‹lat.› (*Rechtsw.* amtlich aufbewahrte Sache); **As|ser|va|ten|kam|mer**

As|sess|ment|cen|ter|me|tho|de [ə'sɛsmɔntsɛntə(r)...] (↑R 24), die; - ‹engl.› (ein Einstufungstest; *Abk.:* AC-Methode)

As|ses|sor, der; -s, ...oren ‹lat.› (Anwärter der höheren Beamtenlaufbahn nach der zweiten Staatsprüfung; *Abk.* Ass.); **as|ses|so|ral; As|ses|so|rin; as|ses|so|risch**

As|si|bi|la|ti|on die; -, -en ‹lat.› (*Sprachw.* Aussprache eines Verschlusslautes in Verbindung mit einem Zischlaut, z. B. z = ts in „Zahn"; Verwandlung eines Verschlusslautes in einen Zischlaut, z. B. niederdeutsch „Water" = hochdeutsch „Wasser"); **as|si|bi|lie|ren; As|si|bi|lie|rung**

As|si|et|te, die; -, -n ‹franz.› (flacher Behälter aus Aluminiumfolie)

As|si|mi|la|ti|on, die; -, -en ‹lat.› *vgl.* Assimilierung; **as|si|mi|lie|ren;** sich - (anpassen); **As|si|mi|lie|rung** (Angleichung; *Sprachw.* Angleichung eines Mitlautes an einen anderen, z. B. das m in „Lamm" aus mittelhochd. „lamb")

As|si|sen *Plur.* ‹lat.› (Schwurgericht in der Schweiz u. in Frankreich)

As|si|si (mittelital. Stadt)

As|sist [ə'sist], der; -s, -s ‹engl.› (*Eishockey, Basketball* Zuspiel, das zum Tor od. Korb führt); **As|sis|tent,** der; -en, -en (↑R 126) ‹lat.› (Gehilfe, Mitarbeiter [an Hochschulen]); **As|sis|ten|tin; As|sis|tenz,** die; -, -en (Beistand); **As|sis|tenz‿arzt, ...pro|fes|sor, ...trai|ner; as|sis|tie|ren** (beistehen, mitwirken)

As|so|ci|a|ted Press [ə'so:ʃie:tid -], die; - - ‹engl.› (US-amerik. Nachrichtenbüro; *Abk.* AP)

As|so|cié [aso'sie:], der; -s, -s ‹franz.› (*veraltet für* Teilhaber)

As|so|lu|ta, die; -, -s ‹ital.› (weibl. Spitzenstar in Ballett u. Oper)

As|so|nanz, die; -, -en ‹lat.› (*Verslehre* Gleichklang nur der Vokale am Versende, z. B. „haben"; „klagen")

as|sor|tie|ren ‹franz.› (nach Warenarten ordnen und vervollständigen); **As|sor|ti|ment,** das; -[e]s, -e (*veraltet für* Lager; Auswahl, Sortiment)

As|so|zi|a|ti|on, die; -, -en ‹lat.› (Vereinigung; *Psych.* Vorstellungsverknüpfung); **as|so|zi|a|tiv** (durch Vorstellungsverknüpfung bewirkt); **as|so|zi|ie|ren** ‹franz.› (verknüpfen); sich - (sich [genossenschaftlich] zusammenschließen); assoziierte Staaten; **As|so|zi|ie|rung**

ASSR = Autonome Sozialistische Sowjetrepublik (bis 1991)

As|su|an [*od.* 'as...] (oberägypt.

Stadt); **As|su|an|stau|damm,** der; -[e]s (↑R 105)
As|sump|ti|o|nist, der; -en, -en; ↑R 126 (Angehöriger einer kath. Ordensgemeinschaft); **As|sum|ti|on,** die; -, -en (Mariä Himmelfahrt *[nur Sing.]*; deren bildliche Darstellung)
As|sy|rer; As|sy|ri|en [...i̯ən] (altes Reich in Mesopotamien); **As|sy|ri|er** [...i̯ər]; *vgl.* Assyrer; **As|sy|ri|o|lo|ge,** der; -n, -n; ↑R 126 (Wissenschaftler auf dem Gebiet der Assyriologie); **As|sy|ri|o|lo|gie,** die; - (Erforschung der assyrisch-babylon. Kultur u. Sprache; *auch für* Keilschriftforschung); **as|sy|risch**
Ast, der; -[e]s, Äste
a. St. = alten Stils (Zeitrechnung)
As|ta (w. Vorn.)
AStA ['asta], der; -[s], *Plur.* -[s], *auch* ASten = Allgemeiner Studentenausschuss
As|tar|te (altsemit. Liebes- u. Fruchtbarkeitsgöttin)
As|tat, As|ta|tin (↑R 132), das; -s ‹griech.› (chem. Element; *Zeichen* At); **as|ta|tisch** (*Physik* gegen den Einfluss elektr. od. magnet. Felder geschützt)
Äst|chen; as|ten (*ugs. für* sich abmühen); **äs|ten** (Äste treiben)
As|ter, die; -, -n ‹griech.› (eine Gartenblume); **As|te|ris|kus,** der; -, ...ken (*Druckw.* Sternchen; *Zeichen* *); **As|tern|art; As|te|ro|id,** der; -en, -en; ↑R 126 (Planetoid)
ast|frei; -es Holz; **Ast|ga|bel**
As|the|nie (↑R 132), die; -, ...i̯en ‹griech.› (*Med.* allgemeine Körperschwäche); **As|the|ni|ker** (schmaler, schmächtiger Mensch); **as|the|nisch**
Äs|thet, der; -en, -en; ↑R 126 ([überfeinert empfindender] Freund des Schönen); **Äs|the|tik,** die; -, -en *Plur. selten* (Wissenschaft von den Gesetzen der Kunst, bes. vom Schönen; das Schöne, Schönheit); **Äs|the|ti|ker** (Vertreter od. Lehrer der Ästhetik); **äs|the|tisch** (*auch für* überfeinert); **äs|the|ti|sie|ren** ([einseitig] nach den Gesetzen des Schönen urteilen *od.* gestalten); **Äs|the|ti|zis|mus,** der; - (das Ästhetische betonende Haltung)
Asth|ma, das; -s ‹griech.› (anfallsweise auftretende Atemnot); **Asth|ma|an|fall; Asth|ma|ti|ker; asth|ma|tisch**
[1]**As|ti** (ital. Stadt); [2]**As|ti,** der; -[s], - (Wein [von [1]Asti]); - spumante (ital. Schaumwein)
as|tig|ma|tisch (↑R 132) ‹griech.› (*Optik* Punkte strichförmig verzerrend); **As|tig|ma|tis|mus,** der; - (*Med.* Stabsichtigkeit; *Optik* Abbildungsfehler von Linsen)
äs|ti|mie|ren ‹franz.› (*veraltend für* schätzen, würdigen)
Ast|loch
[1]**Ast|ra|chan** [...xa(:)n] (↑R 130; russ. Stadt); [2]**Ast|ra|chan,** der; -s, -s (eine Lammfellart); **Ast|ra|chan|ka|vi|ar** (↑R 105)
ast|ral (↑R 130) ‹griech.› (die Gestirne betreffend; Stern...); **Ast|ral|leib** (*Okkultismus* dem irdischen Leib innewohnender ätherischer Leib)
ast|rein (*ugs. auch für* völlig in Ordnung, sehr schön)
Ast|rid (↑R 132; w. Vorn.)
Ast|ro|graph (↑R 130), der; -en, -en (↑R 126) ‹griech.› (Vorrichtung zur fotograf. Aufnahme von Gestirnen, zum Zeichnen von Sternkarten); **Ast|ro|gra|phie,** die; -, ...i̯en (Sternbeschreibung); **Ast|ro|la|bi|um,** das; -s, ...ien [...i̯ən] (altes astron. Instrument); **Ast|ro|lo|ge,** der; -n, -n; ↑R 126 (Sterndeuter); **Ast|ro|lo|gie,** die; - (Sterndeutung); **Ast|ro|lo|gin; ast|ro|lo|gisch; Ast|ro|naut,** der; -en, -en; ↑R 126 (Weltraumfahrer); **Ast|ro|nau|tik,** die; - (Wissenschaft von der Raumfahrt, *auch* die Raumfahrt selbst); **Ast|ro|nau|tin; ast|ro|nau|tisch; Ast|ro|nom,** der; -en, -en; ↑R 126 (Stern-, Himmelsforscher); **Ast|ro|no|mie,** die; - (wissenschaftl. Stern-, Himmelskunde); **Ast|ro|no|min; ast|ro|no|misch; Ast|ro|phy|sik** [*auch* ...'zi(:)k] (Teilgebiet der Astronomie); **ast|ro|phy|si|ka|lisch**
Äs|tu|ar, das; -s, *Plur.* -e *u.* ...rien [...i̯ən] ‹lat.› (*fachspr. für* trichterförmige Flussmündung)
As|tu|ri|en (hist. Provinz in Spanien); **As|tu|ri|er; as|tu|risch**
Ast|werk, das; -[e]s
ASU = Abgassonderuntersuchung
A|sun|ci|ón [asun'si̯ɔn, *span.* asun'θi̯ɔn] (Hptst. von Paraguay)
Ä|sung ‹*zu* äsen›
A|syl, das; -s, -e ‹griech.› (Zufluchtsort); **A|sy|lant,** der; -en, -en; ↑R 126 (Bewerber um Asylrecht); **A|sy|lan|tin; A|syl‿an|trag, ...be|wer|ber, ...recht** (das; -[e]s)
A|sym|met|rie [*od.* ...me'tri:] (↑R 130), die; -, ...i̯en ‹griech.› (Mangel an Symmetrie); **a|sym|met|risch** [*od.* ...'me:...]
A|symp|to|te (↑R 132), die; -, -n ‹griech.› (*Math.* Gerade, der sich eine ins Unendliche verlaufende Kurve beliebig nähert, ohne sie zu erreichen); **a|symp|to|tisch**
a|syn|chron [...k... *od.* ...'kro:n] ‹griech.› (nicht gleichzeitig)
a|syn|de|tisch [*od.* ...'de...] ‹griech.› (*Sprachw.* nicht durch Konjunktion verbunden); **A|syn|de|ton,** das; -s, ...ta (*Sprachw.* Wort- od. Satzreihe, deren Glieder nicht durch Konjunktionen verbunden sind, z. B. „alles rennet, rettet, flüchtet")
As|zen|dent (↑R 132), der; -en, -en (↑R 126) ‹lat.› (*Genealogie* Vorfahr; Verwandter in aufsteigender Linie; *Astron.* Aufgangspunkt eines Gestirns); **As|zen|denz,** die; - (Verwandtschaft in aufsteigender Linie; Aufgang eines Gestirns); **as|zen|die|ren** (*Astron.* [von Gestirnen] aufsteigen)
As|ze|se usw. *vgl.* Askese usw.; **As|ze|tik,** die; - (*kath. Kirche* Lehre vom Streben nach christlicher Vollkommenheit)
at *(veraltet)* = technische Atmosphäre
At = chem. Zeichen für Astat
A. T. = Altes Testament
A|ta|ir, der; -s ‹arab.› (ein Stern im Sternbild Adler)
A|ta|man, der; -s, -e ‹russ.› (frei gewählter Stammes- u. militär. Führer der Kosaken)
A|ta|ra|xie, die; - ‹griech.› (Unerschütterlichkeit, Seelenruhe [in der griech. Philosophie])
A|ta|vis|mus [...v...], der; -, ...men ‹lat.› (*Biol.* Wiederauftreten von Merkmalen od. Verhaltensweisen aus einem früheren entwicklungsgeschichtlichen Stadium); **a|ta|vis|tisch**
A|te (griech. Göttin des Unheils)
A|te|li|er [atə'li̯e:], das; -s, -s ‹franz.› (Werkstatt eines Künstlers, Fotografen o. Ä.; Gebäude für Filmaufnahmen); **A|te|li|er‿auf|nah|me, ...fens|ter, ...fest, ...woh|nung**
A|tem, der; -s; - holen; außer - sein; **a|tem|be|rau|bend; A|tem|be|schwer|den** *Plur.*; **A|tem|ho|len,** das; -s; **a|tem|los; A|tem‿not** (die; -), **...pau|se**
a tem|po ‹ital.› (*ugs. für* schnell, sofort; *Musik* im Anfangstempo)
a|tem|rau|bend; A|tem‿übung (↑R 132), **...we|ge** *(Plur.)*, **...zug**
Ä|than, *chem. fachspr. auch* E|than, das; -s ‹griech.› (gasförmiger Kohlenwasserstoff)
A|tha|na|sia ‹griech., „die Unsterbliche"› (w. Vorn.); **a|tha|na|si|a|nisch** *(Rel.)*; das Athana-

sianische Glaubensbekenntnis (↑R 56); **A|tha|na|sie,** die; - (*Rel.* Unsterblichkeit); **A|tha|na|si|us** (Kirchenlehrer)

Ä|tha|nol, *chem. fachspr. auch* E|tha|nol, das; -s ‹griech.› (*Chemie* eine organ. Verbindung; Weingeist)

A|the|is|mus, der; - ‹griech.› (Weltanschauung, die die Existenz eines Gottes leugnet); **A|the|ist,** der; -en, -en (↑R 126); **a|the|is|tisch**

A|then (Hptst. Griechenlands); **A|the|nä|um,** das; -s, ...äen (Tempel der Göttin Athene); **A|the|ne** (griech. Göttin der Weisheit); **A|the|ner** (↑R 103); **a|the|nisch**

¹Ä|ther, der; -s ‹griech.› (feiner Urstoff in der griech. Philosophie; *geh. für* Himmel); **²Ä|ther,** *chem. fachspr. auch* E|ther, der; -s, - (chem. Verbindung; Betäubungs-, Lösungsmittel); **ä|the|risch** (ätherartig; himmlisch; zart); -e Öle; **ä|the|ri|sie|ren** (mit ²Äther behandeln)

a|ther|man ‹griech.› (*Physik* für Wärmestrahlen undurchlässig)

Ä|thi|o|pi|en ‹griech.› (Staat in Ostafrika); **Ä|thi|o|pi|er; ä|thi|o|pisch**

Ath|let, der; -en, -en (↑R 126) ‹griech.› (kräftig gebauter, muskulöser Mann; Wettkämpfer im Sport); **Ath|le|tik,** die; -; *bes. in* Leichtathletik, Schwerathletik; **Ath|le|ti|ker** (Mensch von athletischer Konstitution); **Ath|le|tin; ath|le|tisch;** -er Körperbau; -e Übungen

A|thos, der; - (Berg auf der nordgriech. Halbinsel Chalkidike)

Ä|thyl, *chem. fachspr. auch* E|thyl, das; -s ‹griech.› (Atomgruppe zahlreicher chem. Verbindungen); **Ä|thyl|al|ko|hol,** der; -s *vgl.* Äthanol; **Ä|thy|len,** *chem. fachspr. auch* E|thy|len, das; -s (im Leuchtgas enthaltener ungesättigter Kohlenwasserstoff)

Ä|ti|o|lo|gie, die; - ‹griech.› (Lehre von den Ursachen, bes. der Krankheiten); **ä|ti|o|lo|gisch** (ursächlich, begründend)

At|lant, der; -en, -en (↑R 126) ‹griech.› (*Bauw.* Gebälkträger in Form einer Männerfigur); *vgl.* ²Atlas; **At|lan|tik,** der; -s (Atlantischer Ozean); **At|lan|tik|char|ta,** die; - (1941 abgeschlossene Vereinbarung zwischen Großbritannien u. den USA über die Kriegs- u. Nachkriegspolitik); **At|lan|tik|pakt** (NATO); **At|lan|tis** (sagenhaftes, im Meer versunkenes Inselreich); **at|lan|tisch;** *aber* (↑R 102): der Atlantische Ozean; **¹At|las** (griech. Sagengestalt); **²At|las,** der; *Gen.* - *u.* ...lasses, *Plur.* ...lasse *u.* ...lanten (*selten für* Atlant); **³At|las,** der; - (Gebirge in Nordwestafrika); **⁴At|las,** der; *Gen.* - *u.* ...lasses, *Plur.* ...lasse *u.* ...lanten ([als Buch gebundene] Sammlung geographischer Karten; Bildtafelwerk); **⁵At|las,** der; *Gen.* - *u.* ...lasses (*Med.* erster Halswirbel)

⁶At|las, der; *Gen.* - *u.* ...lasses, *Plur.* ...lasse ‹arab.› (ein Seidengewebe); **at|las|sen** (aus ⁶Atlas)

atm *(veraltet)* = physikal. Atmosphäre

at|men; ...at|mig (z. B. kurzatmig)

At|mo|sphä|re, die; -, -n ‹griech.› (Lufthülle; *als Druckeinheit früher für* Pascal; *nur Sing.:* Stimmung, Milieu, Umwelt); **At|mo|sphä|ren|über|druck** (↑R 132) *Plur.* ...drücke; (*Zeichen [veraltet]* atü); **At|mo|sphä|ri|li|en** [...i̯ən] *Plur.* (Bestandteile der Luft); **at|mo|sphä|risch**

AT-Mo|tor = Austauschmotor

At|mung, die; -; **at|mungs|ak|tiv** *(Werbespr);* **At|mungs|or|gan** *meist Plur.*

Ät|na [*od.* 'ɛtna], der; -[s] (Vulkan auf Sizilien)

Ä|to|li|en [...i̯ən] (altgriech. Landschaft; Gebiet im westl. Griechenland); **Ä|to|li|er** [...i̯ər], der; -s, - (Angehöriger eines altgriech. Stammes); **ä|to|lisch**

A|toll, das; -s, -e ‹drawid.› (ringförmige Koralleninsel)

A|tom, das; -s, -e ‹griech.› (kleinste Einheit eines chem. Elements); **A|tom|an|griff; a|to|mar** (das Atom, die Kernenergie, die Atomwaffen betreffend; mit Atomwaffen [versehen]); **a|tom|be|trie|ben; A|tom|bom|be** (*kurz* A-Bombe); **A|tom|bom|ben|ver|such; A|tom‿ener|gie** (↑R 132; die; -), **...geg|ner, ...gewicht; A|to|mi|seur** [...'zø:r], der; -s, -e (Zerstäuber); **a|to|mi|sie|ren** (in Atome auflösen; völlig zerstören); **A|to|mi|sie|rung; A|to|mis|mus,** der; - (Weltanschauung, die alle Vorgänge in der Natur auf Atome und ihre Bewegungen zurückführt); **A|to|mist,** der; -en, -en; ↑R 126 (Anhänger des Atomismus); **a|to|mis|tisch; A|to|mi|um,** das; -s (Bauwerk in Brüssel); **A|tom‿kern, ...kraft** (die; -), **...kraft|werk** (*Abk.* AKW), **...krieg, ...macht** (Staat, der über Atomwaffen verfügt), **...mei|ler, ...mi|ne, ...müll, ...phy|sik, ...ra|ke|te, ...re|ak|tor, ...spreng|kopf, ...stopp, ...strom, ...tech|nik, ...test; A|tom|test|stopp|ab|kom|men; A|tom-U-Boot** (↑R 28); **A|tom|waf|fe** *meist Plur.;* **a|tom|waf|fen|frei;** -e Zone; **A|tom|waf|fen|sperr|ver|trag,** der; -[e]s; **A|tom‿wirt|schaft, ...zeit|al|ter** (das; -s), **...zer|trüm|me|rung** (*früher für* Kernspaltung)

a|to|nal ‹griech.› (*Musik* an keine Tonart gebunden); -e Musik; **A|to|na|li|tät,** die; -

A|to|nie, die; -, ...ien ‹griech.› (*Med.* Muskelerschlaffung); **a|to|nisch**

A|tout [a'tu:], das, *auch* der; -s, -s ‹franz.› (Trumpf im Kartenspiel)

a|to|xisch [*auch* a'tɔ...] ‹griech.› (*fachspr. für* ungiftig)

At|reus ['a:trɔys] (↑R 130; griech. Sagengestalt)

At|ri|um (↑R 130), das; -s, ...ien [...i̯ən] ‹lat.› (nach oben offener [Haupt]raum des altröm. Hauses; *Archit.* Innenhof)

A|tro|phie, die; -, ...ien ‹griech.› (*Med.* Schwund von Organen, Geweben, Zellen); **a|tro|phisch**

At|ro|pin (↑R 130), das; -s ‹griech.› (Gift der Tollkirsche)

At|ro|pos (↑R 130; eine der drei Parzen)

ätsch! *(ugs.)*

At|ta|ché [...'ʃe:], der; -s, -s ‹franz.› (Anwärter des diplomatischen Dienstes; einer Auslandsvertretung zugeteilter Berater); **at|ta|chie|ren** [...'ʃi...] (*veraltet für* zuteilen); **At|ta|cke,** die; -, -n ([Reiter]angriff; *Med.* Anfall); **at|ta|ckie|ren** (angreifen)

At|ten|tat [*auch* ...'ta:t], das; -[e]s, -e ‹franz.› ([Mord]anschlag); **At|ten|tä|ter** [*auch* ...'tɛ:...], der; -s, -

At|ter|see, der; -s (österr. See)

At|test, das; -[e]s, -e ‹lat.› (ärztl. Bescheinigung; Gutachten; Zeugnis); **At|tes|ta|ti|on,** die; -, -en ‹lat.› (*ehem. in der DDR* Qualifikationsbescheinigung ohne Prüfungsnachweis); **at|tes|tie|ren**

Ät|ti, der; -s (*südwestd. u. schweiz. mdal. für* Vater)

¹At|ti|ka (griech. Halbinsel)

²At|ti|ka, die; -, ...ken ‹griech.-lat.› ([Skulpturen tragender] Aufsatz über dem Hauptgesims eines Bauwerks); **At|ti|ka|woh|nung** (*schweiz. für* Penthouse)

¹At|ti|la (Hunnenkönig); *vgl.* Etzel; **²At|ti|la,** die; -, -s (mit Schnüren besetzte Husarenjacke)

at|tisch (aus ¹Attika)

At|ti|tü|de, die; -, -n ‹franz.› (Hal-

tung; [innere] Einstellung; *Ballett* eine [Schluss]figur)
At|ti|zis|mus, der; -, ...men ⟨griech.⟩ (an klassischen Vorbildern orientierter Sprachstil im antiken Griechenland); **At|ti|zist,** der; -en, -en; ↑R 126 (Anhänger des Attizismus); **at|ti|zis|tisch**
Att|nang-Puch|heim (österr. Ort)
At|to... ⟨skand.⟩ (ein Trillionstel einer Einheit, z. B. Attofarad = 10^{-18} Farad; *Zeichen* a)
At|trak|ti|on, die; -, -en ⟨lat.⟩ (etwas, was große Anziehungskraft hat); **at|trak|tiv** (anziehend); **At|trak|ti|vi|tät** [...v...], die; - (Anziehungskraft)
At|trap|pe, die; -, -n ⟨franz.⟩ ([täuschend ähnliche] Nachbildung; Schau-, Blindpackung)
at|tri|bu|ie|ren ⟨lat.⟩ (als Attribut beifügen); **At|tri|but,** das; -[e]s, -e (charakteristische Eigenschaft; *Sprachw.* Beifügung); **at|tri|bu|tiv** [*od.* 'a...] (beifügend); **At|tri|but|satz**
a|tü *(veraltet)* = Atmosphärenüberdruck
a|ty|pisch (nicht typisch)
Ätz|al|ka|li|en *Plur.* (stark ätzende Hydroxide der Alkalimetalle); **Ätz|druck** *Plur.* ...drucke
At|zel, die; -, -n (*landsch. für* Elster)
at|zen (*Jägerspr.* [Greifvögel] füttern); du atzt; **ät|zen** (mit Säure, Lauge o. Ä. bearbeiten); du ätzt; **ät|zend** (*ugs. auch für* sehr schlecht); **Ätz|flüs|sig|keit; At|zung** (*Jägerspr.* Fütterung, Nahrung [der jungen Greifvögel]); **Ät|zung** *(Druckw.)*
au!; au Backe!; auweh!
Au = Aurum (*chem. Zeichen für* Gold)
Au, *österr. nur so, od.* **Aue,** die; -, Auen (*landsch. od. geh. für* flaches Wiesengelände)
AU = Abgasuntersuchung
AUA = Austrian Airlines (österr. Luftverkehrsgesellschaft)
au|ber|gi|ne [obɛr'ʒi:nə] ⟨arab.-franz.⟩ (rötlich violett); **Au|ber|gi|ne,** die; -, -n (Pflanze mit gurkenähnlichen [violetten] Früchten; Eierpflanze)
a. u. c. = ab urbe condita
auch; wenn auch; auch wenn (↑R 88)
Auck|land ['ɔ:klənt *od.* ...lənd] (Hafenstadt in Neuseeland)
au con|traire [o kɔ̃'trɛ:r] (↑R 130) ⟨franz.⟩ (im Gegenteil)
Au|di ® (Kraftfahrzeuge)
au|di|a|tur et al|te|ra pars ⟨lat.⟩ (röm. Rechtsgrundsatz: auch die Gegenpartei soll angehört werden); **Au|di|enz,** die; -, -en (feierl. Empfang; Zulassung zu einer Unterredung); **Au|di|max,** das; - (*stud. Kurzw. für* Auditorium maximum); **Au|di|on,** das; -s, *Plur.* -s *u.* ...onen (*Elektrotechnik* Schaltung in Rundfunkempfängern zur Verstärkung der hörbaren Schwingungen); **Au|di|o|vi|si|on,** die; - (audiovisuelle Technik; Information durch Wort und Bild); **au|di|o|vi|su|ell** (zugleich hör- u. sichtbar, Hören u. Sehen ansprechend); -er Unterricht; **au|di|tiv** ⟨lat.⟩ (*Med.* das Hören betreffend; *Psych.* vorwiegend mit Gehörsinn begabt); **Au|di|tor,** der; -s, ...oren (Beamter der röm. Kurie, Richter im kanonischen Recht; *österr. früher, schweiz.* öffentl. Ankläger bei einem Militärgericht); **Au|di|to|ri|um,** das; -s, ...ien [...iən] (ein Hörsaal [der Hochschule]; Zuhörerschaft); **Au|di|to|ri|um ma|xi|mum,** das; - - (größter Hörsaal einer Hochschule; *stud. Kurzw.* Audimax)
Aud|rey ['ɔ:dri] (↑R 130; w. Vorn.)
Aue *vgl.* Au; **Au|en|land|schaft; Au|en|wald, Au|wald**
Au|er|hahn
Au|er|licht, das; -[e]s ⟨nach dem Erfinder⟩ (ein Gasglühlicht)
Au|er|och|se
Au|er|stedt (Dorf in Thüringen)
auf; *Präp. mit Dat. u. Akk.:* auf dem Tisch liegen, *aber* auf den Tisch legen; aufgrund, *auch* auf Grund (*vgl.* Grund); aufs Neue *od.* aufs neue (*vgl.* neu); auf das, aufs Beste *od.* auf das, aufs beste (*vgl.* beste); aufseiten, *auch* auf Seiten; auf einmal; aufs Mal (*schweiz. svw.* auf einmal); auf seine Aufforderung hin; *Adverb:* auf und ab *(vgl. d.), seltener* auf und nieder; auf und davon *(vgl. d.);* auf sein (*ugs. für* geöffnet sein; nicht mehr im Bett sein). *Großschreibung* (↑R 49): das Auf und Nieder, das Auf und Ab
auf... (*in Zus. mit Verben,* z. B. aufführen, du führst auf, aufgeführt, aufzuführen)
auf|ad|die|ren
auf|ar|bei|ten; Auf|ar|bei|tung
auf|at|men
auf|ba|cken
auf|bag|gern
auf|bah|ren; Auf|bah|rung
auf|bam|meln (*ugs. für* aufhängen)
auf|bän|ken; einen Steinblock - (auf zwei Haublöcke legen)
Auf|bau, der; -[e]s, *Plur.* (*für* Gebäude-, Schiffsteil:) -ten; **Auf|bau|ar|beit, ...dar|le|hen; auf|bau|en;** eine Theorie auf einer Annahme -; jmdn. - (an jmds. Aufstieg arbeiten)
auf|bau|meln (*ugs. für* aufhängen)
auf|bau|men (*Jägerspr.* sich auf einem Baum niederlassen [vom Federwild]; auf einen Baum klettern [von Luchs, Marder u. a.])
auf|bäu|men, sich
auf|bau|schen (*auch für* übertreiben)
Auf|bau|schu|le; Auf|bau|spie|ler *(Sport)*
Auf|bau|ten *vgl.* Aufbau
Auf|bau|trai|ning *(Sport)*
auf|be|geh|ren
auf|be|hal|ten; den Hut -
auf|bei|ßen
auf|be|kom|men; Aufgaben -
auf|be|rei|ten; Auf|be|rei|tung
auf|bes|sern; Auf|bes|se|rung, *selten* **Auf|bess|rung**
auf|bet|ten (*landsch. für* das Bett machen; *auch für* im Bett höher legen); einen Kranken -; **Auf|bet|tung**
auf|be|wah|ren; Auf|be|wah|rung; Auf|be|wah|rungs|ort, der; -[e]s, -e
auf|bie|gen
auf|bie|ten; Auf|bie|tung, die; -; unter Aufbietung aller Kräfte
auf|bin|den; jmdm. etwas - (*ugs. für* weismachen)
auf|blä|hen; *vgl.* aufgebläht; **Auf|blä|hung**
auf|blas|bar; auf|bla|sen; *vgl.* aufgeblasen
auf|blät|tern
auf|blei|ben
auf|blen|den
auf|bli|cken
auf|blin|ken
auf|blit|zen
auf|blo|cken; ein Bild -
auf|blü|hen
auf|bo|cken
auf|boh|ren
auf|bra|ten
auf|brau|chen
auf|brau|sen; auf|brau|send
auf|bre|chen (*Jägerspr. auch für* ausweiden)
auf|bren|nen
auf|brin|gen (*auch für* kapern); *vgl.* aufgebracht; **Auf|brin|gung,** die; -
auf|bri|sen ⟨*zu* Brise⟩ (an Stärke zunehmen [vom Wind])
auf|bro|deln; Nebel brodelt auf
Auf|bruch, der; -[e]s, ...brüche (*Jägerspr. auch für* Eingeweide des erlegten Wildes; *Bergmannsspr.* senkrechter Blindschacht); **Auf|bruch[s]|stim|mung,** die; -
auf|brü|hen
auf|brül|len

auf|brum|men (*ugs. für* auferlegen); eine Strafe -
Auf|bü|gel|mus|ter; auf|bü|geln
auf|bür|den *(geh.);* **Auf|bür|dung**
auf|däm|mern
auf|damp|fen
auf|dämp|fen
auf dass (*veraltend für* damit)
auf|de|cken; Auf|de|ckung
auf|don|nern, sich (*ugs. für* sich auffällig kleiden u. schminken)
auf|drän|geln, sich *(ugs.);* ich dräng[e]le mich auf; **auf|drängen;** jmdm. etwas -; sich jmdm. -
auf|dre|hen (*südd., österr. auch für* einschalten; zu schimpfen anfangen, wütend werden)
auf|dring|lich; Auf|dring|lich|keit
auf|dröh|nen; Beifall dröhnte auf
auf|drö|seln (*landsch. für* [etwas Verheddertes, Wolle o. Ä. mühsam] aufdrehen)
Auf|druck, der; -[e]s, -e; **auf|drucken**
auf|drü|cken
auf|ei|nan|der (↑R 132); *immer getrennt:* aufeinander achten, auffahren, warten; aufeinander beißen, folgen, legen usw.; mit aufeinander gebissenen Zähnen; die Bücher waren aufeinander gestapelt; um nicht aufeinander zu prallen; **Auf|ei|nan|der|fol|ge,** die; -; **auf|ei|nan|der fol|gen, legen, sit|zen, tref|fen** usw. *vgl.* aufeinander
auf|en|tern; *vgl.* entern
Auf|ent|halt, der; -[e]s, -e; **Auf|ent|hal|ter** (*schweiz. für* jmd., der an einem Ort nur vorübergehend seinen Wohnsitz hat); **Auf|ent|halts‿be|schrän|kung, ...dau|er, ...ge|neh|mi|gung, ...ort** (*der;* -[e]s, -e), **...raum**
auf|er|le|gen; ich erlege ihm etwas auf, *seltener* ich auferlege; auferlegt; aufzuerlegen
auf|er|ste|hen; *üblich sind nur ungetrennte Formen,* z. B. wenn er auferstünde, er ist auferstanden; **Auf|er|ste|hung,** die; - *(Rel.)*
auf|er|we|cken; *vgl.* auferstehen; **Auf|er|we|ckung**
auf|es|sen
auf|fä|chern; Auf|fä|che|rung
auf|fä|deln; Auf|fä|de|lung, Auf|fäd|lung
auf|fah|ren; Auf|fahrt, die; -, -en (*nur Sing.: südd. u. schweiz. auch für* Christi Himmelfahrt); **Auf|fahrt|ram|pe; Auf|fahrts|stra|ße; Auf|fahr|un|fall**
auf|fal|len; damit es nicht auffällt; *aber* auf fällt, dass ... (↑R 37); **auf|fal|lend; auf|fäl|lig; Auf|fäl|lig|keit**
Auf|fang|be|cken; auf|fan|gen; Auf|fang‿la|ger, ...stel|le, ...vor|rich|tung
auf|fas|sen; Auf|fas|sung; Auf|fas|sungs‿ga|be, ...sa|che *(ugs.)*
auf|fe|gen (*bes. nordd. für* zusammenfegen u. aufnehmen)
auf|fin|den; Auf|fin|dung
auf|fi|schen
auf|fla|ckern
auf|flam|men
auf|flat|tern
auf|flie|gen (*ugs. auch für* ein jähes Ende nehmen)
auf|for|dern; Auf|for|de|rung; Auf|for|de|rungs|satz
auf|fors|ten (Wald [wieder] anpflanzen); **Auf|fors|tung**
auf|fres|sen
auf|fri|schen; der Wind frischt auf; **Auf|fri|schung**
auf|führ|bar; Auf|führ|bar|keit, die; -; **auf|füh|ren; Auf|füh|rung; Auf|füh|rungs|recht**
auf|fül|len; Auf|fül|lung
auf|fut|tern (*ugs. für* aufessen)
Auf|ga|be
auf|ga|beln (*ugs. auch für* zufällig treffen und mitnehmen)
Auf|ga|ben‿be|reich (der), **...heft, ...stel|lung; Auf|ga|be|stem|pel**
auf|ga|gen [...gɛg(ə)n] (mit Gags versehen, ausstatten)
Auf|ga|lopp (*Reiten* Probegalopp an den Schiedsrichtern vorbei zum Start)
Auf|gang, der; **Auf|gangs|punkt** *(Astron.)*
auf|ge|ben
auf|ge|bläht (*auch abwertend für* großtuerisch)
auf|ge|bla|sen; ein -er (*ugs. für* eingebildeter) Kerl; **Auf|ge|bla|sen|heit,** die; - *(ugs.)*
Auf|ge|bot; Auf|ge|bots|schein
auf|ge|bracht (*auch für* erregt, erzürnt)
auf|ge|don|nert; *vgl.* aufdonnern
auf|ge|dreht (*ugs. für* angeregt)
auf|ge|dun|sen
auf|ge|hen; es geht mir auf (es wird mir klar)
auf|gei|en (*Seemannsspr.* Segel mit Geitauen zusammenholen)
auf|geil|en *(derb);* sich -
auf|ge|klärt; Auf|ge|klärt|heit, die; -
auf|ge|knöpft (*ugs. auch für* mitteilsam)
auf|ge|kratzt; in -er (*ugs. für* froher) Stimmung sein
Auf|geld (*für* Agio)
auf|ge|legt (*auch für* zu etwas bereit, gelaunt; *österr. ugs. auch für* klar, offensichtlich); zum Spazierengehen - sein; ein -er Blödsinn *(österr.)*
auf|ge|passt!
auf|ge|räumt (*auch für* heiter); in aufgeräumter Stimmung sein; **Auf|ge|räumt|heit,** die; -
auf|ge|raut
auf|ge|regt; Auf|ge|regt|heit, die; -, -en
Auf|ge|sang (*Verslehre* erster Teil der Strophe beim Meistersang)
auf|ge|schlos|sen; - (mitteilsam) sein; **Auf|ge|schlos|sen|heit,** die; -
auf|ge|schmis|sen; - (*ugs. für* hilflos) sein
auf|ge|schos|sen; hoch -
auf|ge|schwemmt
auf|ge|ta|kelt (*ugs. für* auffällig, geschmacklos gekleidet)
auf|ge|wärmt
auf|ge|weckt; ein -er (kluger) Junge; **Auf|ge|weckt|heit,** die; -
auf|ge|wor|fen; ein -er Mund
auf|gie|ßen
auf|glei|sen (*Technik* auf Gleise setzen); du gleist auf; er gleis|te auf; **Auf|glei|sung**
auf|glei|ten (*Meteor.* sich [gleitend] über etwas schieben [von Luftmassen])
auf|glie|dern; Auf|glie|de|rung
auf|glim|men
auf|glü|hen
auf|gra|ben; Auf|gra|bung
auf|grät|schen; auf den Barren -
auf|grei|fen
auf|grund, *auch* **auf Grund;** *Präp. mit Gen.:* aufgrund, *auch* auf Grund des Wetters
Auf|guss; Auf|guss‿beu|tel ...tier|chen (*für* Infusorium)
auf|ha|ben *(ugs.);* ..., dass er einen Hut aufhat; er wird einen Hut -; für die Schule viel -; ein Laden, der mittags aufhat (geöffnet ist)
auf|ha|cken; den Boden -
auf|ha|ken (einen Hakenverschluss lösen)
auf|hal|sen (*ugs. für* aufbürden)
auf|hal|ten; Auf|hal|tung
auf|hän|gen; sich -; *vgl.* ²hängen; **Auf|hän|ger; Auf|hän|ge|vor|rich|tung; Auf|hän|gung**
auf|hau|en *(ugs.)*
auf|häu|fen
auf|he|ben; Auf|he|ben, das; -s; [ein] großes -, viel -[s] von dem Buch machen; **Auf|he|bung,** die; -
auf|hei|tern; ich heitere auf (↑R 16); **Auf|hei|te|rung**
auf|hei|zen; Auf|hei|zung
auf|hel|fen
auf|hel|len; Auf|hel|ler; optischer - *(Chemie);* **Auf|hel|lung**
auf|het|zen; Auf|het|zung
auf|heu|len
auf|hol|en; Auf|hol|jagd

auf|hor|chen; die Nachricht ließ -
auf|hö|ren
auf|hu|cken (*ugs. für* auf den Rücken nehmen)
auf|ja|gen
auf|jauch|zen
auf|jau|len
Auf|kauf; auf|kau|fen; Auf|käu|fer
auf|keh|ren (*bes. südd. für* zusammenkehren u. aufnehmen)
auf|kei|men
auf|klapp|bar; auf|klap|pen
auf|kla|ren (klar werden, sich aufklären [vom Wetter]; *Seemannsspr.* aufräumen); es klart auf; **auf|klä|ren** (Klarheit in etwas Ungeklärtes bringen; belehren); der Himmel klärt sich auf (wird klar); **Auf|klä|rer; auf|klä|re|risch; Auf|klä|rung; Auf|klä|rungs‿flug|zeug, ...kam|pag|ne**
auf|klat|schen
auf|klau|ben (*südd., österr. für* aufheben)
auf|kle|ben; Auf|kle|ber
auf|klin|gen
auf|klin|ken
auf|kna|cken
auf|knöp|fen; *vgl.* aufgeknöpft
auf|kno|ten
auf|knüp|fen; Auf|knüp|fung
auf|ko|chen (*südd., österr. auch für* einen bes. Anlass reichlich kochen)
auf|kom|men; Auf|kom|men, das; -s, - (Summe der [Steuer]einnahmen)
auf|krat|zen; *vgl.* aufgekratzt
auf|krei|schen
auf|krem|peln
auf|kreu|zen *(ugs.)*
auf|krie|gen *(ugs.)*
auf|kün|den (*älter für* aufkündigen); **auf|kün|di|gen; Auf|kün|di|gung**
Aufl. = Auflage
auf|la|chen
auf|la|den; *vgl.* [1]laden; **Auf‿la|de|platz, ...la|der**
Auf|la|ge (*Abk.* Aufl.); **Auf|la|ge[n]|hö|he; auf|la|gen|stark**
Auf|la|ger *(Bauw.)*
auf|lan|dig (*Seemannsspr.* auf das Land zu wehend od. strömend)
auf|las|sen (aufsteigen lassen; *Bergmannsspr.* [eine Grube] stilllegen; *Rechtsspr.* [Grundeigentum] übertragen; *bes. südd., österr. für* stilllegen, schließen, aufgeben; *ugs. für* geöffnet lassen); **auf|läs|sig** (*Bergmannsspr.* außer Betrieb); **Auf|las|sung**
auf|las|ten (*für* aufbürden)
auf|lau|ern; jmdm. -
Auf|lauf (Ansammlung; überbackene [Mehl]speise); **Auf|lauf|brem|se; auf|lau|fen** (anwachsen [von Schulden]; *Seemannsspr.* auf Grund geraten); **Auf|lauf|form**
auf|le|ben
auf|le|cken
Auf|le|ge|mat|rat|ze; auf|le|gen; *vgl.* aufgelegt; **Auf|le|ger**
auf|leh|nen, sich; **Auf|leh|nung**
auf|le|sen
auf|leuch|ten
auf|lich|ten; Auf|lich|tung
Auf|lie|fe|rer; auf|lie|fern; Auf|lie|fe|rung
auf|lie|gen (offen ausgelegt sein); sich - (sich wund liegen); **Auf|lie|ge|zeit** (Ruhezeit der Schiffe)
auf|lis|ten; Auf|lis|tung
auf|lo|ckern; Auf|lo|cke|rung
auf|lo|dern
auf|lö|sen; Auf|lö|sung; Auf|lö|sungs‿er|schei|nung, ...pro|zess, ...zei|chen *(Musik)*
auf|lüp|fisch (*schweiz. für* rebellisch, aufrührerisch)
auf|lut|schen *(ugs.);* den Bonbon -
auf|lu|ven [...f...] (*Seemannsspr.* den Winkel zwischen Kurs und Windrichtung verkleinern)
aufm, *auch* **auf'm** ↑R 13 (*ugs. für* auf dem, auf einem)
auf|ma|chen; auf- und zumachen; sich - (sich auf den Weg machen); **Auf|ma|cher** (wirkungsvoller Titel; eingängige Schlagzeile); **Auf|ma|chung**
auf|ma|len
Auf|marsch, der; **Auf|marsch|ge|län|de; auf|mar|schie|ren**
Auf|maß *(Bauw.)*
auf|mei|ßeln
auf|mer|ken; auf|merk|sam; jmdn. auf etwas - machen; **Auf|merk|sam|keit**
auf|mes|sen *(Bauw.)*
auf|mi|schen (*ugs. auch für* verprügeln)
auf|mö|beln (*ugs. für* aufmuntern; erneuern); ich möb[e]le auf (↑R 16)
auf|mon|tie|ren
auf|mot|zen (*ugs. für* effektvoller gestalten, zurechtmachen)
auf|mu|cken *(ugs.)*
auf|mun|tern; ich muntere auf (↑R 16); **Auf|mun|te|rung**
auf|müp|fig (*landsch. für* aufsässig, trotzig); **Auf|müp|fig|keit**
auf|mut|zen (*landsch. für* Vorwürfe machen); jmdm. seine Fehler -
aufn, *auch* **auf'n** ↑R 13 (*ugs. für* auf den, auf einen)
auf|nä|hen; Auf|nä|her
Auf|nah|me, die; -, -n; **Auf|nah|me|be|din|gung** *meist Plur.;* **auf|nah|me|fä|hig; Auf|nah|me‿fä|hig|keit, ...ge|bühr, ...lei|ter** (der; *Film*), **...prü|fung, ...tech|nik; auf|nahms|fä|hig** *(österr.);* **Auf|nahms|prü|fung** *(österr.);*
auf|neh|men; Auf|neh|mer (*landsch. für* Scheuerlappen)
äuf|nen (*schweiz. für* [Güter, Bestände, Fonds] vermehren)
auf|nes|teln
auf|nö|ti|gen; jmdm. etw. -
Äuf|nung, die; - *(schweiz.)*
auf|okt|roy|ie|ren [...ɔktroa'ji:...] (↑R 130; aufdrängen, aufzwingen)
auf|op|fern; sich [für jmdn. *od.* etwas] -; **Auf|op|fe|rung** *Plur. selten;* **auf|op|fe|rungs|voll**
auf|pa|cken
auf|päp|peln *(ugs.);* ein Kind -
auf|pas|sen; Auf|pas|ser
auf|peit|schen
auf|pel|zen (*österr. für* aufbürden)
auf|pep|pen (*ugs.* einer Sache Pep, Schwung geben)
auf|pflan|zen
auf|pfrop|fen
auf|pi|cken (*österr. ugs. auch für* aufkleben)
auf|plat|zen
auf|plus|tern; sich -
auf|po|lie|ren
auf|pols|tern
auf|pop|pen (*ugs. für* nach Art der Popkunst aufmachen)
auf|prä|gen
Auf|prall, der; -[e]s, -e *Plur. selten;* **auf|pral|len**
Auf|preis (Mehrpreis); *vgl.* [2]Preis
auf|pro|bie|ren
auf|pul|vern
auf|pum|pen
auf|pus|ten
auf|put|schen; Auf|putsch|mit|tel, das
auf|put|zen; sich -
auf|quel|len; *vgl.* [1]quellen
auf|raf|fen; sich -
auf|ra|gen
auf|rap|peln, sich (*ugs. für* sich aufraffen)
auf|rau|en
auf|räu|feln (*landsch. für* [Gestricktes] wieder auflösen); ich räuf[e]le auf (↑R 16)
auf|räu|men; *vgl.* aufgeräumt; **Auf‿räu|mer, ...räu|mung; Auf|räu|mungs|ar|bei|ten** *Plur.*
auf|rech|nen; Auf|rech|nung
auf|recht; aufrecht halten, sitzen, stehen, stellen; er kann sich nicht aufrecht halten; aufrecht gehalten; aufrecht zu halten; **auf|recht|er|hal|ten** (weiterhin bestehen lassen, nicht aufgeben); einen Anspruch aufrechterhalten; **Auf|recht|er|hal|tung,** die; -
auf|re|gen; sich -; **auf|re|gend; Auf|re|gung**

auf|rei|ben; sich -; **auf|rei|bend**
auf|rei|hen; sich -
auf|rei|ßen (*auch für* im Überblick darstellen; *ugs. auch für* mit jmdm. eine [sexuelle] Beziehung anzuknüpfen versuchen)
auf|rei|ten (*auch Zool.* [von bestimmten Säugetieren] begatten)
auf|rei|zen; auf|rei|zend
auf|rib|beln (*landsch. für* aufräufeln)
Auf|rich|te, die; -, -n (*schweiz. für* Richtfest); **auf|rich|ten;** sich -; **auf|rich|tig; Auf|rich|tig|keit,** die; -; **Auf|rich|tung,** die; -
Auf|riss (Bauzeichnung)
auf|rol|len; Auf|rol|lung, die; -
auf|rü|cken
Auf|ruf; auf|ru|fen
Auf|ruhr, der; -[e]s, -e *Plur. selten;* **auf|rüh|ren; Auf|rüh|rer; auf|rüh|re|risch**
auf|run|den ([Zahlen] nach oben runden); **Auf|run|dung**
auf|rüs|ten; Auf|rüs|tung
auf|rüt|teln; Auf|rüt|te|lung, Auf|rütt|lung
aufs; ↑R 13 (auf das); *vgl.* auf
auf|sa|gen; Auf|sa|gung (*geh. auch für* Kündigung)
auf|sam|meln
auf|säs|sig; Auf|säs|sig|keit, die; -
Auf|satz; Auf|satz|the|ma
auf|sau|gen
auf|schal|ten (*Fernspr.* eine Verbindung zu einem besetzten Anschluss herstellen); **Auf|schal|tung**
auf|schär|fen (*Jägerspr.* [den Balg] aufschneiden)
auf|schau|en
auf|schau|keln
auf|schäu|men
auf|schei|nen (*österr. für* erscheinen, auftreten, vorkommen)
auf|scheu|chen
auf|scheu|ern; ich habe mir die Knie aufgescheuert
auf|schich|ten; Auf|schich|tung
auf|schie|ben; Auf|schie|bung
auf|schie|ßen
Auf|schlag; auf|schla|gen; Auf|schlä|ger; Auf|schlag‿feh|ler, ...ver|lust (*Tennis*), **...zün|der**
auf|schläm|men
auf|schlie|ßen; *vgl.* aufgeschlossen; **Auf|schlie|ßung,** die; -
auf|schlit|zen
auf|schluch|zen
Auf|schluss; auf|schlüs|seln; Daten -; **Auf|schlüs|se|lung, Auf|schlüss|lung; auf|schluss|reich**
auf|schmei|ßen (*österr. ugs. für* bloßstellen); *vgl.* aufgeschmissen
auf|schnap|pen
auf|schnei|den (*ugs. auch für* prahlen); **Auf|schnei|der; Auf|schnei|de|rei; auf|schnei|derisch; Auf|schnitt,** der; -[e]s
auf|schnü|ren
auf|schrau|ben
¹auf|schre|cken; sie schrak *od.* schreckte auf; sie war aufgeschreckt; *vgl.* ¹schrecken; **²auf|schre|cken;** ich schreckte ihn auf; sie hatte ihn aufgeschreckt; *vgl.* ²schrecken
Auf|schrei
auf|schrei|ben; ich schreibe mir etwas auf
auf|schrei|en
Auf|schrift
Auf|schub
auf|schür|fen
auf|schüt|teln; das Kopfkissen -
auf|schüt|ten; Auf|schüt|tung
auf|schwat|zen, *landsch.* **auf|schwät|zen**
auf|schwei|ßen
¹auf|schwel|len; der Leib schwoll auf, ist aufgeschwollen; *vgl.* ¹schwellen; **²auf|schwel|len;** der Exkurs schwellte das Buch auf, hat das Buch aufgeschwellt; *vgl.* ²schwellen; **Auf|schwel|lung**
auf|schwem|men; Auf|schwem|mung
auf|schwin|gen, sich; **Auf|schwung**
auf|se|hen; zu jmdm. - (jmdn. bewundern); **Auf|se|hen,** das; -s; Aufsehen erregen; ein Aufsehen erregendes Ereignis (↑R 40); **Auf|se|her; Auf|se|he|rin**
auf sein *vgl.* auf
auf|sei|ten, *auch* **auf Sei|ten;** *Präp. mit Gen.:* aufseiten, *auch* auf Seiten der Regierung
auf|set|zen; Auf|set|zer (*bes. Fußball, Handball*)
auf|seuf|zen
Auf|sicht, die; -, -en; der Aufsicht führende Lehrer; (↑R 47:) der Aufsicht Führende, *auch* Aufsichtführende; **Auf|sichts‿be|am|te, ...be|hör|de; auf|sicht[s]|los; Auf|sichts‿pflicht, ...rat** (*Plur.* ...räte); **Auf|sichts|rats‿sit|zung, ...vor|sit|zen|de**
auf|sit|zen; jmdn. aufsitzen lassen (*auch für* jmdn. im Stich lassen); jmdm. aufsitzen (auf jmdn. hereinfallen); **Auf|sit|zer** (*österr. für* Reinfall)
auf|spal|ten; Auf|spal|tung
auf|span|nen
auf|spa|ren; ich spare mir etwas auf; **Auf|spa|rung**
auf|spei|chern; Auf|spei|che|rung
auf|sper|ren
auf|spie|len; sich -
auf|spie|ßen
auf|split|tern; Auf|split|te|rung
auf|spray|en [...ʃpre:ən *od.* ...sp...]
auf|spren|gen; einen Tresor -
auf|sprie|ßen
auf|sprin|gen
auf|sprit|zen
auf|sprü|hen
Auf|sprung
auf|spu|len; ein Tonband -
auf|spü|len; Sand -
auf|spü|ren; Auf|spü|rung
auf|sta|cheln; Auf|sta|che|lung, Auf|stach|lung
auf|stamp|fen
Auf|stand; auf|stän|dern (*Technik* auf Ständern errichten); ich ständere auf (↑R 16); **Auf|stän|de|rung; auf|stän|disch; Auf|stän|di|sche,** der *u.* die; -n, -n (↑R 5 ff.); **Auf|stands|ver|such**
auf|sta|peln; Auf|sta|pe|lung, Auf|stap|lung
Auf|stau (*Technik, Wasserbau*)
auf|stäu|ben
auf|stau|en
auf|ste|chen
auf|ste|cken; *vgl.* ²stecken
auf|ste|hen
auf|stei|gen (*österr. auch für* in die nächste Klasse kommen, versetzt werden); **Auf|stei|ger**
auf|stel|len; Auf|stel|lung
auf|stem|men (mit dem Stemmeisen öffnen); sich -
auf|step|pen
Auf|stieg, der; -[e]s, -e; **Auf|stiegs‿mög|lich|keit, ...spiel** (*Sport*)
auf|stö|bern
auf|sto|cken ([um ein Stockwerk] erhöhen); **Auf|sto|ckung**
auf|stöh|nen
auf|stöp|seln (*ugs.*); eine Flasche -
auf|stö|ren; jmdn. -
auf|sto|ßen; mir stößt etwas auf
auf|stre|ben; auf|stre|bend
auf|strei|chen; Auf|strich
Auf|strom, der; -[e]s (*Technik* aufsteigender Luftstrom)
auf|stu|fen (höher einstufen); **Auf|stu|fung**
auf|stül|pen
auf|stüt|zen
auf|su|chen
auf|sum|men, auf|sum|mie|ren (*EDV* Werte addieren od. subtrahieren)
auf|ta|keln (*Seemannsspr.* mit Takelwerk ausrüsten); sich - (*ugs. für* sich sehr auffällig kleiden und schminken); *vgl.* aufgetakelt; **Auf|ta|ke|lung, Auf|tak|lung**
Auf|takt, der; -[e]s, -e
auf|tan|ken; ein Auto auftanken; das Flugzeug tankt auf
auf|tau|chen
auf|tau|en

auf|tei|len; Auf|tei|lung
auf|tip|pen; den Ball kurz -
auf|ti|schen ([Speisen] auftragen; *ugs. für* vorbringen)
auf|top|pen (*Seemannsspr.* die Rahen in senkrechter Richtung bewegen)
Auf|trag, der; -[e]s, ...träge; im -[e] (*Abk.* i. A. *od.* I. A.; *vgl. d.*); **auf|tra|gen; Auf|trag‿ge|ber, ...neh|mer; Auf|trags‿ar|beit, ...be|stand, ...be|stä|ti|gung, ...buch; auf|trags|ge|mäß; Auf|trags‿la|ge** *(Wirtsch.),* **...pols|ter** (*Wirtsch.* Vorrat an Aufträgen), **...rück|gang; Auf|trag[s]|wal|ze** *(Druckw.)*
auf|tref|fen
auf|trei|ben
auf|tren|nen
auf|tre|ten; Auf|tre|ten, das; -s
Auf|trieb; Auf|triebs|kraft
Auf|tritt; Auf|tritts|ver|bot
auf|trump|fen
auf|tun; sich -
auf|tup|fen; Wassertropfen [mit einem Tuch] -
auf|tür|men; sich -
auf und ab; auf und ab gehen (ohne bestimmtes Ziel), *aber* (*in Zus.;* ↑R 23): auf- und absteigen (aufsteigen und absteigen); **Auf und Ab,** das; - -[s]; **Auf|und|ab|ge|hen,** das; -s; ein Platz zum Aufundabgehen, *aber* (↑R 23 *u.* R 50): das Auf- und Absteigen (Aufsteigen und Absteigen)
auf und da|von; sich auf und davon machen *(ugs.);* zum Auf-und-davon-Laufen sein (↑R 28)
auf|wa|chen
auf|wach|sen
auf|wal|len; Auf|wal|lung
auf|wäl|ti|gen (*Bergmannsspr.; vgl.* gewältigen)
Auf|wand, der; -[e]s; **auf|wän|dig,** *auch:* auf|wen|dig; **Auf|wands|ent|schä|di|gung**
auf|wär|men; Auf|wär|mung
Auf|war|te|frau; auf|war|ten; mit Sekt - *(geh.)*
auf|wärts; auf- und abwärts; aufwärts gehen (nach oben gehen; *auch für* besser werden), aufwärts fahren usw.; sie ist den Fluss aufwärts gegangen; mit ihrer Gesundheit ist es aufwärts gegangen; **Auf|wärts‿ent|wick|lung, ...ha|ken** *(Boxen),* **...trend**
Auf|war|tung
Auf|wasch, der; -[e]s (Geschirrspülen; schmutziges Geschirr); **auf|wa|schen; Auf|wasch|was|ser** (*Plur.* ...wässer)
auf|we|cken; *vgl.* aufgeweckt
auf|wei|chen; *vgl.* [1]weichen; **Auf|wei|chung**
Auf|weis, der; -es, -e; **auf|wei|sen**
auf|wen|den; ich wandte *od.* wendete viel Zeit auf, habe aufgewandt *od.* aufgewendet; aufgewandte *od.* aufgewendete Zeit; **auf|wen|dig,** *auch* auf|wän|dig; **Auf|wen|dung**
auf|wer|fen; sich zum Richter -
auf|wer|ten; Auf|wer|tung
auf|wi|ckeln; Auf|wi|cke|lung, Auf|wick|lung
Auf|wie|ge|lei *(abwertend);* **auf|wie|geln; Auf|wie|ge|lung**
auf|wie|gen
Auf|wieg|ler; auf|wieg|le|risch; Auf|wieg|lung *vgl.* Aufwiegelung
Auf|wind (*Meteor.* aufsteigender Luftstrom)
auf|wir|beln
auf|wi|schen; Auf|wisch|lap|pen
auf|wöl|ben
auf|wöl|ken
Auf|wuchs *(Forstw.)*
auf|wüh|len
Auf|wurf
auf|zah|len (*südd., österr. für* dazuzahlen); **auf|zäh|len; Auf|zah|lung** (*schweiz. auch für* Aufpreis); **Auf|zäh|lung**
auf|zäu|men; das Pferd am *od.* beim Schwanz - (*ugs. für* etwas verkehrt beginnen)
auf|zeh|ren
auf|zeich|nen; Auf|zeich|nung
auf|zei|gen (dartun, darlegen)
auf Zeit (*Abk.* a. Z.)
auf|zie|hen; Auf|zucht; auf|züch|ten
auf|zu|cken
Auf|zug; Auf|zug|füh|rer; Auf|zug[s]|schacht
auf|zün|geln *(geh.)*
auf|zwin|gen; jmdm. etwas -
auf|zwir|beln; die Bartenden -
Aug. = August (Monat)
Aug|ap|fel; Au|ge, das; -s, -n; - um -; **Äu|gel|chen; äu|geln** (*veraltet für* [verstohlen] blicken; *auch für* okulieren); ich ...[e]le (↑R 16); **äu|gen** ([angespannt] blicken); **Au|gen‿arzt, ...auf|schlag, ...bank** (*Plur.* ...banken; *Med.*), **...blick**[1]; **au|gen|blick|lich**[1]; **au|gen|blicks**[1] (*veraltend für* sofort, sogleich); **Au|gen|blicks‿idee**[1] (↑R 132), **...sa|che; Au|gen|braue; Au|gen|brau|en|stift; Au|gen‿de|ckel, ...di|ag|no|se, au|gen|fäl|lig; Au|gen‿far|be, ...glas** (*veraltend; vgl.* [1]Glas), **...heil|kun|de, ...kli|nik, ...krank|heit, ...licht** (das; -[e]s), **...lid; Au|gen-Make-up; Au|gen‿maß** (das), **...merk** (das; -[e]s), **...op|ti|ker, ...pul|ver** (das; -s; *ugs. für* sehr kleine Schrift), **...rin|ge** (*Plur.;* Schatten unter den Augen), **...schat|ten** *(Plur.),* **...schein** (der; -[e]s); **au|gen|schein|lich** [*auch* ...ˈʃain...]; **Au|gen‿stern** (*ugs. für* das Liebste), **...trost** (eine Heilpflanze), **...wei|de** (die; -), **...win|kel, ...wi|sche|rei, ...zahn** (oberer Eckzahn), **...zeu|ge; Au|gen|zeu|gen|be|richt; Au|gen|zwin|kern,** das; -s; **au|gen|zwin|kernd**
Au|gi|as (Gestalt der griech. Sage); **Au|gi|as|stall** [*auch* ˈaugi-as...] (*übertr. auch für* korrupte Verhältnisse)
...äu|gig (z. B. braunäugig)
Au|git [*auch* ...ˈgit], der; -s, -e ‹griech.› (ein Mineral)
Äug|lein
Aug|ment, das; -s, -e ‹lat.› (*Sprachw.* Vorsilbe des Verbstammes zur Bezeichnung der Vergangenheit, bes. im Sanskrit u. im Griechischen); **Aug|men|ta|ti|on,** die; -, -en (*Musik* Vergrößerung der Notenwerte)
au gra|tin [o graˈtɛ̃] ‹franz.› (*Gastron.* mit einer Kruste überbacken)
Augs|burg (Stadt am Lech); **Augs|bur|ger** (↑R 103); - Bekenntnis (*Abk. [österr.]* A. B.); **augs|bur|gisch,** *aber* (↑R 108): die Augsburgische Konfession
Aug‿spross *od.* **...spros|se** (*Jägerspr.* unterste Sprosse am Hirschgeweih)
Au|gur, der; *Gen.* -s *u.* ...uren, *Plur.* ...uren; ↑R 126 ‹lat., „Vogelschauer"› (Priester im alten Rom; Wahrsager); **Au|gu|ren|lä|cheln,** das; -s (wissendes Lächeln der Eingeweihten)
[1]**Au|gust,** der; *Gen.* -[e]s *u.* -, *Plur.* -e ‹lat.› (achter Monat im Jahr, Ernting, Erntemonat; *Abk.* Aug.); [2]**Au|gust** (m. Vorn.); der dumme - (Clown); **Au|gus|ta, Au|gus|te** (w. Vorn.); **au|gus|te|isch** (↑R 94); das Augusteische Zeitalter (Zeitalter des Kaisers Augustus); *aber* ein augusteisches (der Kunst und Literatur günstiges) Zeitalter; [1]**Au|gus|tin** (m. Vorn.); [2]**Au|gus|tin** *vgl.* Augustinus; **Au|gus|ti|ne** (w. Vorn.); **Au|gus|ti|ner,** der; -s, - (Angehöriger eines kath. Ordens); **Au|gus|ti|nus,** Au|gus|tin (Heiliger, Kirchenlehrer); **Au|gus|tus** (Beiname des röm. Kaisers Oktavian)
Auk|ti|on, die; -, -en ‹lat.› (Versteigerung); **Auk|ti|o|na|tor,** der; -s, ...oren (Versteigerer); **auk|ti|o|nie|ren**
Au|la, die; -, *Plur.* ...len *u.* -s ‹lat.›

[1] [*auch* ...ˈblik(...)]

(Fest-, Versammlungssaal in [Hoch]schulen)
Au|le, die; -, -n (*landsch. derb für* Auswurf)
Au|los, der; -, ...oi ‹griech.› (ein antikes griech. Musikinstrument)
au na|tu|rel [o naty'rɛl] ‹franz.› (*Gastron.* ohne künstlichen Zusatz [bei Speisen, Getränken])
au pair [o 'pɛ:r] ‹franz.› (ohne Bezahlung, nur gegen Unterkunft u. Verpflegung); **Au|pair|mäd|chen,** *auch* **Au-pair-Mäd|chen** (↑R 28)
AU-Pla|ket|te
Au|ra, die; -, Auren *od.* Aurae ‹lat.› (besondere Ausstrahlung; *Med.* Unbehagen vor epileptischen Anfällen)
Au|ra|min, das; -s ‹nlat.› (gelber Farbstoff)
Au|rar *vgl.* Eyrir
Au|re|lia, Au|re|lie [...iə] (w. Vorn.); **Au|re|li|an** (röm. Kaiser); **Au|re|lie** *vgl.* Aurelia; **Au|re|li|us** (altröm. Geschlechtername)
Au|re|o|le, die; -, -n ‹lat.› (Heiligenschein; Hof [um Sonne und Mond])
Au|rig|na|ci|en [orinja'si̯ɛ̃:] (↑R 130), das; -[s] ‹nach der franz. Stadt Aurignac› (eine Kulturstufe der jüngeren Altsteinzeit); **Au|rig|nac|mensch** [ori'njak...] (Mensch des Aurignacien)
Au|ri|kel [*auch* au'ri...], die; -, -n ‹lat.› (eine Primelart); **au|ri|ku|lar** (*Med.* die Ohren betreffend)
Au|ri|pig|ment, das; -[e]s ‹lat.› (ein Mineral, Rauschgelb)
[1]Au|ro|ra (röm. Göttin der Morgenröte); **[2]Au|ro|ra,** die; -, -s (ein Schmetterling; Lichterscheinung in der oberen Atmosphäre); **Au|ro|ra|fal|ter**
Au|rum, das; -[s] ‹lat.› (*lat. Bez. für* Gold; *Zeichen* Au)
aus; *Präp. mit Dat.:* aus dem Hause; aus aller Herren Länder[n]; *Adverb:* aus sein (*ugs. für* zu Ende, erloschen, ausgeschaltet sein); auf etwas aus sein (*ugs. für* erpicht sein); aus und ein gehen (verkehren), *aber* (*in Zus.;* ↑R 23): aus- und eingehende (ausgehende und eingehende) Waren; weder aus noch ein wissen; **Aus,** das; -, - (*Sportspr.* Raum außerhalb des Spielfeldes)
aus... (*in Zus. mit Verben,* z. B. ausbeuten, du beutest aus, ausgebeutet, auszubeuten)
aus|agie|ren (↑R 132; *Psych.*)
aus|apern (↑R 132; *südd., österr., schweiz. für* schneefrei werden)
aus|ar|bei|ten; sich -; **Aus|ar|bei|tung**
aus|ar|ten; Aus|ar|tung
aus|äs|ten; Obstbäume -
aus|at|men; Aus|at|mung
aus|ba|cken
aus|ba|den; etwas - müssen *(ugs.)*
aus|bag|gern
aus|ba|ken (*Seew.* mit Baken versehen)
aus|ba|lan|cie|ren
aus|bal|do|wern ‹dt.; jidd.› (*ugs. für* auskundschaften)
Aus|ball *(Sportspr.)*
Aus|bau, der; -[e]s, *Plur.* (*für* Gebäudeteile, abseits gelegene Anwesen:) ...bauten
aus|bau|chen; Aus|bau|chung
aus|bau|en; aus|bau|fä|hig; Aus|bau|woh|nung
aus|be|din|gen, sich; *vgl.* [2]bedingen; ich bedinge mir etwas aus
aus|bei|nen (*landsch. für* Knochen aus dem Fleisch lösen)
aus|bei|ßen; ich beiße mir die Zähne aus
aus|bes|sern; Aus|bes|se|rung; aus|bes|se|rungs|be|dürf|tig
aus|beu|len
Aus|beu|te, die; -, -n
aus|beu|teln (*bes. österr. für* ausschütteln)
aus|beu|ten; Aus|beu|ter; Aus|beu|te|rei, die; -; **aus|beu|te|risch; Aus|beu|ter|klas|se,** die; - *(marxist. Theorie);* **Aus|beu|tung**
aus|be|zah|len
aus|bie|gen
aus|bie|ten (feilbieten); **Aus|bie|tung** (Aufforderung zum Bieten bei Versteigerungen)
aus|bil|den; Aus|bil|den|de, der *u.* die; -n, -n (↑R 5 ff.); **Aus|bil|der; Aus|bild|ner** (*österr. u. schweiz.);* **Aus|bil|dung; Aus|bil|dungs‿bei|hil|fe, ...för|de|rungs|ge|setz, ...ver|trag**
aus|bit|ten; ich bitte mir etwas aus
aus|bla|sen; Aus|blä|ser (ausgebranntes, nicht auseinander gesprengtes Artilleriegeschoss)
aus|blei|ben
[1]aus|blei|chen (bleich machen); du bleichtest aus; ausgebleicht; *vgl.* [1]bleichen; **[2]aus|blei|chen** (bleich werden); es blich aus; ausgeblichen (*auch schon* ausgebleicht); *vgl.* [2]bleichen
aus|blen|den
Aus|blick; aus|bli|cken
aus|blü|hen (*fachspr. auch für* durch Verdunstung an die Oberfläche treten und eine Verkrustung entstehen lassen [von bestimmten Salzen]); **Aus|blü|hung**
aus|blu|ten
aus|bo|gen; ausgebogte Zacken
aus|boh|ren
aus|bo|jen (*Seew.* ein Fahrwasser mit Seezeichen versehen); er bojet aus, hat ausgebojet
aus|bom|ben; *vgl.* Ausgebombte
aus|boo|ten (*ugs. auch für* entmachten, entlassen)
aus|bor|gen; ich borge mir ein Buch von ihm aus
aus|bra|ten; Speck -
aus|bre|chen; Aus|bre|cher
aus|brei|ten; Aus|brei|tung, die; -
aus|brem|sen *(Rennsport)*
aus|bren|nen
aus|brin|gen; einen Trinkspruch -
Aus|bruch, der; -[e]s, ...brüche (*auch für* Wein besonderer Güte); **Aus|bruchs|ver|such**
aus|brü|hen; die Teekanne -
aus|brü|ten
aus|bu|chen (*Kaufmannsspr.* aus dem Rechnungsbuch streichen); *vgl.* ausgebucht
aus|buch|ten; Aus|buch|tung
aus|bud|deln *(ugs.)*
aus|bü|geln (*ugs. auch für* bereinigen)
aus|bu|hen (*ugs.* durch Buhrufe sein Missfallen ausdrücken)
Aus|bund, der; -[e]s; **aus|bün|dig** (*veraltet für* außerordentlich, sehr)
aus|bür|gern; ich bürgere aus (↑R 16); **Aus|bür|ge|rung**
aus|bürs|ten
aus|bü|xen (*landsch. für* weglaufen); du büxt aus
aus|che|cken [...tʃɛkən] ‹dt.; engl.› *(Flugw.)*
Ausch|witz (im 2. Weltkrieg Konzentrationslager der Nationalsozialisten in Polen)
Aus|dau|er; aus|dau|ernd
aus|deh|nen; sich -; **Aus|deh|nung; Aus|deh|nungs|ko|ef|fi|zi|ent**
aus|dei|chen (Landflächen durch Zurückverlegung des Deichs preisgeben)
aus|den|ken; ich denke mir etwas aus
aus|deu|ten (*für* interpretieren)
aus|die|nen; *vgl.* ausgedient
aus|dif|fe|ren|zie|ren; sich -
aus|dis|ku|tie|ren
aus|do|cken (*Schiffbau* aus dem Dock holen)
aus|dor|ren; aus|dör|ren
aus|dre|hen
Aus|druck, der; -[e]s, *Plur.* ...drücke *u. (Druckw.:)* ...drucke; **aus|dru|cken** ([ein Buch] fertig drucken); **aus|drü|cken;** sich -; **aus|drück|lich** [*auch* ...'dryk...]; **Aus|drucks|kunst,** die; - (*auch für* Expressionismus); **aus|drucks|los; Aus|drucks|lo|sig|keit,** die; -; **Aus|drucks|mit|tel** *meist Plur.;*

aus|drucks⌣stark, ...voll; Aus|drucks|wei|se
Aus|drusch, der; -[e]s, -e (Ertrag des Dreschens)
aus|dün|nen; Obstbäume -; **Aus|dün|nung**
aus|duns|ten, *häufiger* **aus|düns|ten; Aus|duns|tung,** *häufiger* **Aus|düns|tung**
aus|ei|nan|der (↑R 132); *in Verbindung mit Verben immer getrennt:* auseinander sein; auseinander biegen, dividieren, fallen, laufen, ziehen usw.; als Freunde auseinander gehen; wir haben uns noch mit diesem Thema auseinander zu setzen; der Lehrer will die Schüler auseinander setzen; jmdm. etwas auseinander klamüsern, posamentieren (*landsch. für* erklären); **Aus|ei|nan|der|ent|wick|lung; aus|ei|nan|der fal|len, hal|ten, le|ben** usw. *vgl.* auseinander; **Aus|ei|nan|der|set|zung; aus|ei|nan|der sprin|gen, sprit|zen** usw. *vgl.* auseinander
aus|er|ko|ren (*geh. für* auserwählt)
aus|er|le|sen
aus|er|se|hen
aus|er|wäh|len; aus|er|wählt; Aus|er|wähl|te, der *u.* die; -n, -n (↑R 5 ff.); **Aus|er|wäh|lung**
aus|fä|chern
aus|fä|deln, sich (*Verkehrsw.*)
aus|fahr|bar; aus|fah|ren; aus|fah|rend (heftig); **Aus|fahr|⌣gleis, ...sig|nal** (*Eisenb.*); **Aus|fahrt; Aus|fahrt[s]⌣er|laub|nis, ...gleis** (*vgl.* Ausfahrgleis); **Aus|fahrts|schild,** das; **Aus|fahrt[s]|sig|nal;** *vgl.* Ausfahrsignal; **Aus|fahrt[s]|stra|ße**
Aus|fall, der; **aus|fal|len;** *vgl.* ausgefallen; **aus|fäl|len** (*Chemie* gelöste Stoffe in Form von Kristallen, Flocken o. Ä. ausscheiden; *schweiz. für* verhängen [eine Strafe usw.]); **aus|fal|lend** *od.* **aus|fäl|lig** (beleidigend); **Aus|fall[s]|⌣er|schei|nung** (*Med.*), **...tor** (das); **Aus|fall|stra|ße; Aus|fäl|lung** (*Chemie*); **Aus|fall|zeit**
aus|falt|bar; aus|fal|ten
aus|fech|ten; einen Streit -
aus|fe|gen (*landsch.*); **Aus|fe|ger** (*landsch.*)
aus|fei|len
aus|fer|ti|gen; Aus|fer|ti|gung
aus|fet|ten; die Backform -
aus|fil|tern
aus|fin|dig; ausfindig machen; **Aus|fin|dig|ma|chen,** das; -s
aus|fit|ten ([ein Schiff] mit seemännischem Zubehör ausrüsten)
aus|flag|gen (mit Flaggen kennzeichnen lassen)
aus|flie|gen
aus|flie|ßen
aus|flip|pen (*ugs. für* sich der Realität durch Drogenkonsum entziehen; sich außerhalb der gesellschaftlichen Norm stellen; außer sich geraten); ausgeflippt sein
aus|flo|cken (Flocken bilden)
Aus|flucht, die; -, ...flüchte *meist Plur.*
Aus|flug; Aus|flüg|ler; Aus|flugs|⌣ort (der; -[e]s, -e), **...schiff, ...ver|kehr, ...ziel**
Aus|fluss
aus|fol|gen (*bes. österr. für* übergeben, aushändigen); **Aus|fol|gung** (*bes. österr.*)
aus|for|men
aus|for|mu|lie|ren
Aus|for|mung
aus|for|schen (*österr. auch für* ausfindig machen); **Aus|for|schung** (*österr. auch für* [polizeiliche] Ermittlung)
aus|fra|gen; Aus|fra|ge|rei (*ugs. abwertend*)
aus|fran|sen; *vgl.* ausgefranst
aus|fres|sen; etwas ausgefressen (*ugs. für* verbrochen) haben
aus|fu|gen; eine Mauer -
Aus|fuhr, die; -, -en; **aus|führ|bar; Aus|führ|bar|keit,** die; -; **aus|füh|ren; Aus|füh|rer** (*für* Exporteur); **Aus|fuhr|land** *Plur.* ...länder (*Wirtsch.*); **aus|führ|lich**[1]; Ausführlicheres in meinem nächsten Brief (↑R 47); **Aus|führ|lich|keit**[1], die; -; **Aus|fuhr|prä|mie; Aus|füh|rung; Aus|füh|rungs|be|stim|mung; Aus|fuhr|ver|bot**
aus|fül|len; Aus|fül|lung
aus|füt|tern
Ausg. = Ausgabe
Aus|ga|be (*Abk. für* Drucke Ausg.); **Aus|ga|be[n]|buch; Aus|ga|ben|po|li|tik; Aus|ga|be|⌣stel|le, ...ter|min**
Aus|gang; aus|gangs (*Amtsspr.;* ↑R 46); *Präp. mit Gen.:* ausgangs des Tunnels; **Aus|gangs|⌣ba|sis, ...la|ge, ...punkt, ...sper|re, ...spra|che** (*Sprachw.*), **...stel|lung**
aus|gä|ren (fertig gären)
aus|ga|sen; Aus|ga|sung
aus|ge|ben; Geld -
Aus|ge|beu|te|te, der *u.* die; -n, -n (↑R 5 ff.)
aus|ge|bil|det
aus|ge|bleicht; *vgl.* [1]ausbleichen; **aus|ge|bli|chen;** *vgl.* [2]ausbleichen
Aus|ge|bomb|te, der *u.* die; -n, -n (↑R 5 ff.)

[1] [*auch* ...'fy:r...]

aus|ge|bucht (voll besetzt, ohne freie Plätze); ein -es Flugzeug
aus|ge|bufft (*ugs. für* raffiniert)
Aus|ge|burt (*geh. abwertend*)
aus|ge|dehnt
aus|ge|dient; ausgedient haben
Aus|ge|din|ge, das; -s, - (*landsch. für* Altenteil); **Aus|ge|din|ger**
aus|ge|dorrt; aus|ge|dörrt
aus|ge|fal|len (*auch für* ungewöhnlich); ausgefallene Ideen
aus|ge|feilt
aus|ge|feimt (*landsch. für* abgefeimt)
aus|ge|flippt (*ugs.*); *vgl.* ausflippen
aus|ge|franst; eine -e Hose
aus|ge|fuchst (*ugs. für* durchtrieben)
aus|ge|gli|chen; ein -er Mensch; **Aus|ge|gli|chen|heit,** die; -
Aus|geh|an|zug; aus|ge|hen; es geht sich aus (*österr. für* es reicht, passt); **Aus|ge|her** (*landsch. für* Bote, Laufbursche)
aus|ge|hun|gert (sehr hungrig)
Aus|geh|uni|form (↑R 132; *Milit.*)
Aus|geh|ver|bot
aus|ge|klü|gelt
aus|ge|kocht (*ugs. auch für* durchtrieben)
aus|ge|las|sen (*auch für* übermütig); **Aus|ge|las|sen|heit** *Plur. selten*
aus|ge|las|tet
aus|ge|latscht (*ugs.*)
aus|ge|laugt; ausgelaugte Böden
aus|ge|lei|ert
aus|ge|lernt; ein ausgelernter Schlosser; **Aus|ge|lern|te,** der *u.* die; -n, -n (↑R 5 ff.)
aus|ge|lit|ten; ausgelitten haben
aus|ge|macht (feststehend); ein ausgemachter (*ugs. für* großer) Schwindel
aus|ge|mer|gelt
aus|ge|mu|gelt (*österr. ugs.*); -e (stark ausgefahrene) Skipisten
aus|ge|nom|men; alle waren zugegen, er ausgenommen (*od.* ausgenommen er); ich erinnere mich aller Vorgänge, ausgenommen dieses einen (*od.* diesen einen ausgenommen); der Tadel galt allen, ausgenommen ihm (*od.* ihn ausgenommen); ausgenommen[,] dass/wenn (↑R 88)
aus|ge|picht (*ugs. für* gerissen)
aus|ge|po|wert (*ugs.*); *vgl.* auspowern
aus|ge|prägt; eine -e Vorliebe; **Aus|ge|prägt|heit,** die; -
aus|ge|pumpt (*ugs. für* erschöpft)
aus|ge|rech|net (eben, gerade)
aus|ge|schamt (*landsch. für* unverschämt)
aus|ge|schla|fen (*ugs. auch für* gewitzt)

aus|ge|schlos|sen
aus|ge|schnit|ten; ein -es Kleid
aus|ge|sorgt; - haben
aus|ge|spielt; - haben
aus|ge|spro|chen (entschieden, sehr groß); eine -e Abneigung; **aus|ge|spro|che|ner|ma|ßen**
aus|ge|stal|ten; eine Feier -; **Aus|ge|stal|tung**
aus|ge|stellt; ein -er (nach unten erweiterter) Rock
aus|ge|steu|ert; Aus|ge|steu|er|te, der *u.* die; -n, -n (↑R 5 ff.)
aus|ge|sucht ([aus]erlesen; ausgesprochen)
aus|ge|wach|sen (voll ausgereift)
aus|ge|wo|gen (sorgfältig abgestimmt, harmonisch); **Aus|ge|wo|gen|heit,** die; -
aus|ge|zehrt
aus|ge|zeich|net; -e Leistungen
aus|gie|big (reichlich); **Aus|gie|big|keit,** die; -
aus|gie|ßen; Aus|gie|ßer; Aus|gie|ßung *Plur. selten*
Aus|gleich, der; -[e]s, -e; **aus|gleich|bar; aus|glei|chen;** *vgl.* ausgeglichen; **Aus|gleichs‿ab|ga|be, ...amt, ...fonds, ...ge|trie|be** (*für* Differenzial), **...sport, ...tref|fer**
aus|glei|ten
aus|glie|dern; Aus|glie|de|rung
aus|glit|schen (*landsch. für* ausrutschen)
aus|glü|hen (z. B. einen Draht)
aus|gra|ben; Aus‿grä|ber; ...gra|bung; ...gra|bungs|stät|te
aus|grei|fen
aus|gren|zen; Aus|gren|zung
aus|grün|den (*Wirtsch.* einen Teil eines Betriebes getrennt als selbstständiges Unternehmen weiterführen); **Aus|grün|dung**
Aus|guck, der; -[e]s, -e; **aus|gu|cken; Aus|guck|pos|ten**
Aus|guss
aus|ha|ben *(ugs.);* ..., dass er den Mantel aushat; das Buch aushaben; um 12 Uhr Schule aushaben
aus|ha|cken; Unkraut -
aus|ha|ken (*ugs. auch für* zornig werden)
aus|hal|ten; (↑R 50:) es ist nicht zum Aushalten
aus|han|deln
aus|hän|di|gen; Aus|hän|di|gung
Aus|hang; Aus|hän|ge|bo|gen *(Druckw.);* **aus|han|gen** (*älter u. mdal. für* [1]aushängen); [1]**aus|hän|gen;** die Verordnung hat ausgehangen; *vgl.* [1]hängen; [2]**aus|hän|gen;** ich habe die Tür ausgehängt; *vgl.* [2]hängen; **Aus|hän|ger** (*svw.* Aushängebogen); **Aus|hän|ge|schild,** das
aus|har|ren
aus|här|ten *(Technik);* **Aus|här|tung**
aus|hau|chen *(geh.);* sein Leben -
aus|hau|en
aus|häu|sig (*landsch. für* außer Hauses; selten zu Haus); **Aus|häu|sig|keit,** die; -
aus|he|ben (herausheben; zum Heeresdienst einberufen; *österr. auch für* [einen Briefkasten] leeren); **Aus|he|ber** (Griff beim Ringen); **aus|he|bern** (mit einem Heber herausnehmen; *Med.* bes. den Magen zu Untersuchungszwecken entleeren); ich hebere aus (↑R 16); **Aus|he|be|rung; Aus|he|bung** (*österr. auch für* Leerung des Briefkastens)
aus|he|cken (*ugs. für* mit List ersinnen)
aus|hei|len; Aus|hei|lung
aus|hel|fen; Aus|hel|fer; Aus|hil|fe; Aus|hilfs‿ar|beit, ...kell|ner, ...koch, ...kraft (die), **...stel|lung; aus|hilfs|wei|se**
aus|höh|len; Aus|höh|lung
aus|ho|len
aus|hol|zen; Aus|hol|zung
aus|hor|chen; Aus|hor|cher
aus|hors|ten (*Jägerspr.* junge Greifvögel aus dem Horst nehmen)
Aus|hub, der; -[e]s, Aushube *Plur. selten*
aus|hun|gern; *vgl.* ausgehungert
aus|hus|ten; sich -
aus|ixen (↑R 132; *ugs. für* [durch Übertippen] mit dem Buchstaben x ungültig machen); du ixt aus
aus|jä|ten
aus|kal|ku|lie|ren
aus|käm|men; Aus|käm|mung
aus|ke|geln (*landsch. auch für* ausrenken)
aus|keh|len; Aus|keh|lung (das Anbringen einer Hohlkehle)
aus|keh|ren; Aus|keh|richt, der; -s *(veraltet, noch landsch.)*
aus|kei|len; ein Pferd keilt aus (schlägt aus); eine Gesteinsschicht keilt aus (läuft nach einer Seite hin keilförmig aus)
aus|kei|men; Aus|kei|mung
aus|ken|nen, sich
aus|ker|ben; Aus|ker|bung
aus|ker|nen; Aus|ker|nung, die; -
aus|kip|pen
aus|kla|gen *(Rechtsspr.);* **Aus|kla|gung**
aus|klam|mern; Aus|klam|me|rung
aus|kla|mü|sern (*ugs. für* austüfteln)
Aus|klang
aus|klapp|bar; aus|klap|pen
aus|kla|rie|ren (Schiff und Güter vor der Ausfahrt verzollen)
aus|klau|ben (*landsch. für* mit den Fingern [mühsam] auslesen)
aus|klei|den; sich -; **Aus|klei|dung**
aus|klin|gen
aus|klin|ken; ein Seil -; ich klinke mich aus der Sitzung aus
aus|klop|fen; Aus|klop|fer
aus|klü|geln; Aus|klü|ge|lung, Aus|klüg|lung
aus|knei|fen (*ugs. für* feige u. heimlich weglaufen)
aus|knip|sen *(ugs.);* das Licht -
aus|kno|beln *(ugs.)*
aus|kno|cken [...nɔkən] ‹engl.› (*Boxen* durch K. o. besiegen)
aus|knöpf|bar; aus|knöp|fen
aus|ko|chen; *vgl.* ausgekocht
aus|kof|fern (*Straßenbau* eine vertiefte Fläche für den Unterbau schaffen); ich koffere aus (↑R 16); **Aus|kof|fe|rung**
aus|kol|ken (*Geol.* auswaschen); **Aus|kol|kung**
aus|kom|men; Aus|kom|men, das; -s; **aus|kömm|lich**
aus|kop|peln
aus|kos|ten
aus|kot|zen *(derb);* sich -
aus|kra|gen (*Bauw.* herausragen [lassen]); **Aus|kra|gung**
aus|kra|men *(ugs.)*
aus|krat|zen
aus|krie|chen
aus|krie|gen *(ugs.)*
aus|kris|tal|li|sie|ren; sich -; **Aus|kris|tal|li|sie|rung**
aus|ku|geln
aus|küh|len; Aus|küh|lung
Aus|kul|tant, der; -en, -en (↑R 126) ‹lat.› (*Rechtsspr. veraltet für* Beisitzer ohne Stimmrecht); **Aus|kul|ta|ti|on,** die; -, -en (*Med.* das Abhorchen); **aus|kul|ta|to|risch** (*Med.* durch Abhorchen); **aus|kul|tie|ren** (*Med.* abhorchen)
aus|kund|schaf|ten
Aus|kunft, die; -, ...künfte; **Aus|kunf|tei; Aus|kunfts‿be|am|te, ...bü|ro, ...stel|le**
aus|kup|peln
aus|ku|rie|ren
aus|la|chen
Aus|lad, der; -s (*schweiz. für* das Ausladen [von Gütern]); [1]**aus|la|den;** Waren -; *vgl.* [1]laden; [2]**aus|la|den;** jmdn. -; *vgl.* [2]laden; **aus|la|dend** (weit ausgreifend); **Aus|la|de|ram|pe; Aus|la|dung**
Aus|la|ge
aus|la|gern; Aus|la|ge|rung
Aus|land, das; -[e]s; **Aus|län|der; Aus|län|der|be|auf|trag|te; aus|län|der|feind|lich; Aus|län|der|feind|lich|keit; Aus|län|de|rin; aus|län|disch; Aus|lands‿ab|satz, ...auf|ent|halt, ...be-**

zie|hun|gen *(Plur.)*; **Aus|land-schwei|zer; aus|lands|deutsch; Aus|lands-deut|sche** (der *u.* die; ↑R 5 ff.), **...ge|schäft, ...ge-spräch, ...kor|res|pon|dent, ...kun|de** (die; -), **...rei|se, ...schutz|brief, ...sen|dung, ...tour|nee, ...ver|tre|tung**
aus|lan|gen (*landsch. für* zum Schlag ausholen; ausreichen); **Aus|lan|gen,** das; -s; das - finden (*österr. für* auskommen)
Aus|lass, der; -es, ...lässe; **aus-las|sen** (*österr. auch für* frei-, loslassen); sich [über jmdn. *od.* etw.] -; *vgl.* ausgelassen; **Aus|las|sung; Aus|las|sungs-punk|te** *(Plur.)*, **...satz** (*für* Ellipse), **...zei|chen** (*für* Apostroph); **Aus|lass|ven|til** (beim Viertaktverbrennungsmotor)
aus|las|ten; Aus|las|tung
aus|lat|schen *(ugs.)*; die Schuhe -
Aus|lauf; Aus|lauf|bahn *(Skisport)*; **aus|lau|fen;** ausgelaufene Farbe; **Aus|läu|fer; Aus|lauf-mo|dell** *(Kaufmannsspr.)*
aus|lau|gen
Aus|laut; aus|lau|ten; auf „n" -
aus|läu|ten
aus|le|ben; sich -
aus|le|cken
aus|lee|ren; Aus|lee|rung
aus|le|gen; Aus|le|ger; Aus|le-ger-boot, ...brü|cke; Aus|le|ge-wa|re, die; - (Teppichmaterial zum Auslegen von Fußböden); **Aus|le|gung**
aus|lei|ern *(ugs.)*
Aus|lei|he; aus|lei|hen; ich leihe mir bei ihm ein Buch aus; **Aus-lei|hung**
aus|lei|ten; Aus|lei|tung
aus|ler|nen; *vgl.* ausgelernt
Aus|le|se; aus|le|sen; Aus|le|se-pro|zess
aus|leuch|ten; Aus|leuch|tung
aus|lich|ten; Obstbäume -
aus|lie|fern; Aus|lie|fe|rung
aus|lie|gen
Aus|li|nie *(Sport)*
aus|lo|ben (*Rechtsspr.* als Belohnung aussetzen); **Aus|lo|bung**
aus|löf|feln; die Suppe -
aus|lo|gie|ren [...ʒiː...] (anderswo einquartieren)
aus|lös|bar
[1]**aus|lö|schen;** er löschte das Licht aus, hat es ausgelöscht; *vgl.* [1]löschen; [2]**aus|lö|schen** *(veraltet)*; das Licht losch (*auch* löschte) aus, ist ausgelöscht; *vgl.* [2]löschen
aus|lo|sen
aus|lö|sen; Aus|lö|ser
Aus|lo|sung (durch das Los getroffene [Aus]wahl)
Aus|lö|sung (pauschale Entschädigung für Reisekosten; Loskaufen [eines Gefangenen])
aus|lo|ten
Aus|lucht, die; -, -en (*Archit.* Vorbau an Häusern; Quergiebel einer Kirche)
aus|lüf|ten
Aus|lug, der; -[e]s, -e (*veraltet für* Ausguck); **aus|lu|gen** *(veraltet)*
aus|lut|schen
ausm, *auch* **aus'm** ↑R 13 (*ugs. für* aus dem, aus einem)
aus|ma|chen; *vgl.* ausgemacht
aus|mah|len; Aus|mah|lung, die; - (z. B. des Kornes)
aus|ma|len; Aus|ma|lung (z. B. des Bildes)
aus|ma|növ|rie|ren
aus|mar|chen (*schweiz. für* seine Rechte, Interessen abgrenzen; sich auseinandersetzen); **Aus-mar|chung** *(schweiz.)*
aus|mä|ren, sich (*bes. ostmitteld. für* trödeln; *auch* zu trödeln aufhören)
Aus|maß, das
aus|mau|ern; Aus|mau|e|rung
aus|mei|ßeln
aus|mer|geln; ich mergele aus (↑R 16); **Aus|mer|ge|lung, Aus-merg|lung**
aus|mer|zen (radikal beseitigen); du merzt aus; **Aus|mer|zung**
aus|mes|sen; Aus|mes|sung
aus|mie|ten *(Landw.)*; Kartoffeln -; **Aus|mie|tung**
aus|mis|ten
aus|mit|teln (*veraltend für* ermitteln); ich mitt[e]le aus (↑R 16); **Aus|mit|te|lung,** Aus|mitt|lung; **aus|mit|tig, au|ßer|mit|tig** (*Technik* außerhalb des Mittelpunktes)
aus|mon|tie|ren; Aus|mon|tie-rung
aus|mu|geln (*österr. ugs. für* [eine Skipiste] ausfahren, uneben machen)
aus|mün|den
aus|mün|zen; Aus|mün|zung (Münzprägung)
aus|mus|tern; Aus|mus|te|rung
Aus|nah|me, die; -, -n (*österr. auch für* Altenteil); **Aus|nah|me-ath|let** *(Sport)*, **...be|stim-mung, ...er|schei|nung, ...fall** (der), **...ge|neh|mi|gung, ...zu-stand; Aus|nahms|fall** *(österr.)*; **aus|nahms-los, ...wei|se; Aus-nahms|zu|stand** *(österr.)*; **aus-neh|men;** sich gut ausnehmen (gut wirken); *vgl.* ausgenommen; **aus|neh|mend** (sehr); **Aus|neh-mer** (*österr. für* Bauer, der auf dem Altenteil lebt)
aus|nüch|tern; Aus|nüch|te-rung; Aus|nüch|te|rungs|zel|le
aus|nut|zen *od.* **aus|nüt|zen,** *südd., österr. u. schweiz. meist so;* **Aus|nut|zung** *od.* **Aus|nüt|zung,** *südd., österr. u. schweiz. meist so*
aus|pa|cken
aus|par|ken
aus|peit|schen; Aus|peit|schung
aus|pen|deln (*Boxen* mit dem Oberkörper seitlich od. nach hinten ausweichen); **Aus|pend|ler** (Person, die außerhalb ihres Wohnortes arbeitet)
aus|pen|nen (*ugs. für* ausschlafen)
aus|pfäh|len (einzäunen; *Bergmannsspr.* mit Pfählen Gesteinsmassen abstützen)
aus|pfei|fen
aus|pflan|zen
aus|pflü|cken
Aus|pi|zi|um (↑R 132), das; -s, ...ien [...i̯ən] *meist Plur.* ‹lat.› (*geh. für* Vorbedeutung; Aussichten); unter jemandes Auspizien (unter jmds. Schirmherrschaft, Oberhoheit)
aus|plau|dern
aus|plau|schen *(österr.)*
aus|plün|dern; Aus|plün|de|rung
aus|pols|tern; Aus|pols|te|rung
aus|po|sau|nen (*ugs. für* überall erzählen)
aus|po|wern ‹dt.; franz.› (*ugs. abwertend für* bis zur Verelendung ausbeuten); ich powere aus (↑R 16); **Aus|po|we|rung**
aus|prä|gen; *vgl.* ausgeprägt; **Aus|prä|gung**
aus|prei|sen (Waren mit einem Preis versehen)
aus|pres|sen
aus|pro|bie|ren
Aus|puff, der; -[e]s, -e; **Aus|puff-an|la|ge; Aus|puff|flam|me** (↑R 136); **Aus|puff|topf**
aus|pum|pen; *vgl.* ausgepumpt
aus|punk|ten (*Boxen* nach Punkten besiegen)
aus|pus|ten
aus|put|zen; Aus|put|zer
aus|quar|tie|ren; Aus|quar|tie-rung
aus|quat|schen *(ugs.)*; sich -
aus|quet|schen
aus|ra|deln, aus|rä|deln (mit einem Rädchen ausschneiden, übertragen); ich ...[e]le aus (↑R 16)
aus|ra|die|ren
aus|ran|gie|ren [...ʒiː...] (*ugs. für* aussondern; ausscheiden)
aus|ra|sie|ren
aus|ras|ten (*ugs. auch für* zornig werden; *südd., österr. für* ausruhen)
aus|rau|ben; aus|räu|bern
aus|räu|chern
aus|rau|fen; ich könnte mir [vor Wut] die Haare ausraufen

aus|räu|men; Aus|räu|mung
aus|rech|nen; Aus|rech|nung
aus|re|cken
Aus|re|de; aus|re|den
aus|reg|nen, sich
aus|rei|ben (*österr. auch für* scheuern); die Küche -; **Aus|reib|tuch** (*österr. für* Scheuertuch)
aus|rei|chen; aus|rei|chend; er hat mit [der Note] „ausreichend" bestanden; er hat nur ein [knappes] Ausreichend bekommen (↑R 47)
aus|rei|fen; Aus|rei|fung, die; -
Aus|rei|se; Aus|rei|se~er|laub|nis, ...ge|neh|mi|gung; aus|rei|sen; Aus|rei|se|sper|re; aus|rei|se|wil|lig
aus|rei|ßen; Aus|rei|ßer
aus|rei|ten
aus|rei|zen; die Karten -
aus|ren|ken; du hast dir den Arm ausgerenkt; **Aus|ren|kung**
aus|rich|ten; etwas ausrichten; **Aus|rich|ter; Aus|rich|tung**
aus|rin|gen (*landsch. für* auswringen)
aus|rin|nen
aus|rip|pen (von den Rippen lösen); Tabakblätter -
Aus|ritt
aus|ro|den; Aus|ro|dung
aus|rol|len
aus|rot|ten; Aus|rot|tung
aus|rü|cken (*ugs. auch für* fliehen)
Aus|ruf; aus|ru|fen; Aus|ru|fer; Aus|ru|fe~satz, ...wort (*für* Interjektion; *Plur.* ...wörter), **...zei|chen; Aus|ru|fung; Aus|ru|fungs|zei|chen** (*selten*); **Aus|ruf|zei|chen** (*österr. u. schweiz.*)
aus|ru|hen; sich -
aus|rup|fen
aus|rüs|ten; Aus|rüs|ter; Aus|rüs|tung; Aus|rüs|tungs~ge|gen|stand, ...stück
aus|rut|schen; Aus|rut|scher
Aus|saat; aus|sä|en
Aus|sa|ge, die; -, -n; **Aus|sa|ge|kraft,** die; -; **aus|sa|gen**
aus|sä|gen
Aus|sa|ge~satz, ...wei|se (die; *Sprachw. für* Modus), **...wert**
Aus|satz, der; -es (eine Krankheit); **aus|sät|zig; Aus|sät|zi|ge,** der *u.* die; -n, -n (↑R 5 ff.)
aus|sau|fen
aus|sau|gen
Aussch. = Ausschuss
aus|scha|ben; Aus|scha|bung
aus|schach|ten; Aus|schach|tung
aus|scha|len (*Bauw.* Verschalung entfernen; verschalen)
aus|schä|len
aus|schal|men; Bäume - (*Forstw.* durch Kerben kennzeichnen)
aus|schal|ten; Aus|schal|ter; Aus|schal|tung
Aus|scha|lung (*Bauw.*)
Aus|schank
aus|schar|ren
Aus|schau, die; -; - halten; **aus|schau|en** (*südd., österr. auch für* aussehen)
aus|schau|feln
aus|schäu|men
Aus|scheid, der; -[e]s, -e (*regional für* Ausscheidungskampf); **aus|schei|den; Aus|schei|dung; Aus|schei|dungs~kampf, ...run|de, ...spiel**
aus|schei|ßen (*derb*); sich - (*auch für* sich aussprechen)
aus|schel|ten
aus|schen|ken (Bier, Wein usw.)
aus|sche|ren (die Linie, Spur verlassen [von Fahrzeugen]); scherte aus; ausgeschert
aus|schi|cken
aus|schie|ßen (*Druckw.*); **Aus|schieß|plat|te** (*Druckw.*)
aus|schif|fen; Aus|schif|fung
aus|schil|dern (mit Schildern markieren); **Aus|schil|de|rung**
aus|schimp|fen
aus|schir|ren
aus|schlach|ten (*ugs. auch für* noch brauchbare Teile aus etwas ausbauen; bedenkenlos für sich ausnutzen); **Aus|schlach|te|rei; Aus|schlach|tung**
aus|schla|fen; sich -; *vgl.* ausgeschlafen
Aus|schlag; aus|schla|gen; aus|schlag|ge|bend
aus|schläm|men (Schlamm aus etwas entfernen)
aus|schle|cken
aus|schlei|men; sich - (*ugs. für* sich aussprechen)
aus|schlie|ßen; *vgl.* ausgeschlossen; **aus|schlie|ßend; aus|schließ|lich**[1]; *Präp. mit Gen.:* ausschließlich der Verpackung; *ein allein stehendes, stark gebeugtes Substantiv steht im Sing. ungebeugt:* ausschließlich Porto; *Dat., wenn bei Pluralformen der Gen. nicht erkennbar ist:* ausschließlich Getränken; **Aus|schließ|lich|keit**[1], die; -; **Aus|schlie|ßung**
aus|schlip|fen (*schweiz. für* ausrutschen)
Aus|schlupf; aus|schlüp|fen
aus|schlür|fen
Aus|schluss
aus|schmie|ren (*ugs. auch für* übertölpeln)
aus|schmü|cken; den Saal -; **Aus|schmü|ckung**
aus|schnau|ben

[1] [*od.* ...ʃli:s..., *auch* 'aus'ʃli:s...]

aus|schnei|den; Aus|schnitt
aus|schnüf|feln
aus|schöp|fen; Aus|schöp|fung, die; -
aus|schop|pen (*österr. ugs. für* ausstopfen)
aus|schrei|ben; Aus|schrei|bung
aus|schrei|en; Aus|schrei|er
aus|schrei|ten; Aus|schrei|tung *meist Plur.*
aus|schro|ten (*österr. für* [Fleisch] zerlegen, ausschlachten)
aus|schu|len (aus der Schule nehmen); **Aus|schu|lung**
Aus|schuss (*Abk. für* „Kommission": Aussch.); **Aus|schuss~mit|glied, ...quo|te, ...sit|zung, ...wa|re**
aus|schüt|teln
aus|schüt|ten; Aus|schüt|tung
aus|schwär|men
aus|schwe|feln
aus|schwei|fen; aus|schwei|fend; Aus|schwei|fung
aus|schwei|gen, sich
aus|schwem|men; Sand -; **Aus|schwem|mung**
aus|schwen|ken
aus|schwin|gen; Aus|schwin|get, der; -s (*schweiz.* Endkampf im Schwingen)
aus|schwit|zen; Aus|schwit|zung
Aus|see, Bad (Solbad in der Steiermark); **Aus|se|er** (↑R 103); **Aus|se|er Land** (↑R 105; Gebiet in der Steiermark)
aus|seg|nen (einem Verstorbenen den letzten Segen erteilen); **Aus|seg|nung**
aus|se|hen; Aus|se|hen, das; -s
aus sein *vgl.* aus
au|ßen; von außen [her]; nach innen und außen; nach außen [hin]; Farbe für außen und innen; außen vor lassen (*nordd. für* unberücksichtigt lassen); er spielt außen (augenblickliche Position eines Spielers), *aber vgl.* Außen; außen liegen usw.; die außen liegenden Kabinen; außen gelegen; **Au|ßen,** der; -, - (*Sportspr.* Außenspieler); er spielt Außen (als Außenspieler), *aber vgl.* außen; **Au|ßen~als|ter, ...an|ten|ne, ...ar|bei|ten** (*Plur.*), **...auf|nah|me** (*meist Plur.*), **...bahn** (*Sport*), **...be|zirk, ...bor|der** ([Boot mit] Außenbordmotor); **Au|ßen|bord|mo|tor; au|ßen|bords** (außerhalb des Schiffes)
aus|sen|den
Au|ßen|dienst; Au|ßen|dienst|ler; au|ßen|dienst|lich
Aus|sen|dung (*österr. auch für* schriftliche Verlautbarung, Pressemitteilung)

Au|ßen‿el|be, ...han|del (der; -s), **...han|dels|po|li|tik** (die; -), **...kur|ve; au|ßen lie|gend** *vgl.* außen; **Au|ßen‿mi|nis|ter, ...mi|nis|te|ri|um, ...po|li|tik** (die; -); **au|ßen|po|li|tisch; Au|ßen‿rist** (*bes. Fußball* äußere Seite des Fußrückens), **...sei|te; Au|ßen|sei|ter; Au|ßen|sei|te|rin; Au|ßen‿spie|gel, ...stän|de** (*Plur.;* ausstehende Forderungen), **...ste|hen|de** (der *u.* die; -n, -n; ↑R 5 ff. *u.* 47), **...stel|le, ...stür|mer, ...tem|pe|ra|tur, ...trep|pe, ...tür, ...ver|tei|di|ger, ...wand, ...welt** (die; -), **...wirt|schaft** (die; -)

au|ßer; *Konj.:* außer dass/wenn/wo; wir fahren in die Ferien, außer [wenn] es regnet (↑R 88); niemand kann diese Schrift lesen außer er selbst; *Präp. mit Dat.:* niemand kann es lesen außer ihm selbst; außer [dem] Haus[e]; außer allem Zweifel; außer Dienst (*Abk.* a. D.); außer Rand und Band; ich bin außer mir (empört); außerstande, *auch* außer Stande sein; sich außerstande, *auch* außer Stande sehen; außerstand, *auch* außer Stand setzen; außer [aller] Acht lassen; *mit Akk. (bei Verben der Bewegung):* außer allen Zweifel setzen; ich gerate außer mich (*od.* mir) vor Freude; *mit Gen. nur in* außer Landes gehen, sein; **Au|ßer|acht|las|sung,** die; -; **au|ßer‿amt|lich, ...be|ruf|lich; au|ßer dass** (↑R 88); **au|ßer|dem** [*auch* ...'de:m]; **au|ßer|dienst|lich; äu|ße|re;** (↑R 102:) die Äußere Mongolei; **Äu|ße|re,** das; ...r[e]n (↑R 5 ff.); im Äußer[e]n; sein -s; ein erschreckendes Äußere[s]; Minister des -n; **au|ßer‿ehe|lich** (↑R 132), **...eu|ro|pä|isch, ...ge|richt|lich, ...ge|wöhn|lich; au|ßer|halb;** außerhalb von München; *als Präp. mit Gen.:* außerhalb des Lagers; außerhalb Münchens; **au|ßer|ir|disch; Au|ßer|kraft|set|zung; äu|ßer|lich; Äu|ßer|lich|keit**

äu|ßerln *nur im Infinitiv gebr. (österr. ugs.);* seinen Hund äußerln (auf die Straße) führen; äußerln gehen

au|ßer|mit|tig *vgl.* ausmittig

äu|ßern; ich ...ere (↑R 16); sich -

au|ßer|or|dent|lich [*auch* 'ausər-or...]; -er [Professor] (*Abk.* ao., a. o. [Prof.]); **au|ßer|orts** (*schweiz. für* außerhalb einer Ortschaft); **au|ßer|par|la|men|ta|risch;** die -e Opposition (*Abk.* APO, *auch* Apo); **au|ßer|plan|mä|ßig** (*Abk.* apl.)

Au|ßer|rho|den (*kurz für* Appenzell Außerrhoden)

au|ßer|schu|lisch

äu|ßerst; mit äußerster Konzentration, *aber* (↑R 47): das Äußerste befürchten; 20 Mark sind *od.* ist das Äußerste; das Äußerste, was ...; auf das, aufs Äußerste (auf die schlimmsten Dinge) gefasst sein; auf das, aufs Äußerste, *auch* auf das, aufs äußerste erschrocken sein; es zum Äußersten kommen lassen; bis zum Äußersten gehen

au|ßer|stand [*auch* 'ausər...], *auch* **au|ßer Stand** *vgl.* außer; **au|ßer|stan|de,** *auch* **au|ßer Stan|de** *vgl.* außer

äu|ßers|ten|falls; *vgl.* Fall, der

au|ßer|tour|lich [...'tu:r...] (*österr. für* außer der Reihe)

Äu|ße|rung

au|ßer wenn/wo (↑R 88)

aus|set|zen; Aus|set|zung

Aus|sicht, die; -, -en; **aus|sichts|los; Aus|sichts|lo|sig|keit,** die; -; **Aus|sichts|punkt; aus|sichts|reich; Aus|sichts|turm; aus|sichts|voll; Aus|sichts|wa|gen**

aus|sie|ben

aus|sie|deln; Aus|sie|de|lung; Aus|sied|ler; Aus|sied|ler|hof; Aus|sied|lung

aus|sit|zen (*ugs. auch für* in der Hoffnung, dass sich etwas von allein erledigt, untätig bleiben)

aus|söh|nen; sich -; **Aus|söh|nung**

aus|son|dern; Aus|son|de|rung

aus|sor|gen; ausgesorgt haben

aus|sor|tie|ren

aus|spä|hen

Aus|spann, der; -[e]s, -e (*früher* Wirtshaus mit Stall); **aus|span|nen** (*ugs. auch für* abspenstig machen); **Aus|span|nung**

aus|spa|ren; Aus|spa|rung

aus|spei|en

aus|sper|ren; Aus|sper|rung

aus|spie|len; Aus|spie|lung

aus|spin|nen

aus|spi|o|nie|ren

Aus|spra|che; Aus|spra|che‿an|ga|be, ...be|zeich|nung, ...wör|ter|buch; aus|sprech|bar; aus|spre|chen; sich -; *vgl.* ausgesprochen

aus|spren|gen; ein Gerücht -

aus|sprit|zen; Aus|sprit|zung

Aus|spruch

aus|spu|cken

aus|spü|len; Aus|spü|lung

aus|staf|fie|ren (ausstatten); **Aus|staf|fie|rung**

Aus|stand, der; -[e]s (*schweiz. auch für* vorübergehendes Ausscheiden aus einem Gremium); in den Ausstand treten (streiken); **aus|stän|dig** (*südd., österr. für* ausstehend); **Aus|ständ|ler** (Streikender)

aus|stan|zen

aus|stat|ten; Aus|stat|tung; Aus|stat|tungs‿film, ...stück

aus|ste|chen

aus|ste|cken

aus|ste|hen; jmdn. nicht - können

aus|stei|fen *(Bauw.);* **Aus|stei|fung**

aus|stei|gen; Aus|stei|ger (jmd., der seinen Beruf, seine gesellschaftlichen Bindungen o. Ä. plötzlich aufgibt)

aus|stei|nen; Pflaumen -

aus|stel|len; Aus|stel|ler; Aus|stell|fens|ter *(Kfz);* **Aus|stel|lung; Aus|stel|lungs‿flä|che, ...ge|län|de, ...hal|le, ...ka|ta|log, ...pa|vil|lon, ...raum, ...stand, ...stück**

Aus|ster|be|etat (↑R 132); *in Wendungen wie* auf dem - stehen (*ugs.* zu Ende gehen, keine Bedeutung mehr haben), auf den - setzen (*ugs.* langsam ausschalten, kalt stellen); **aus|ster|ben**

Aus|steu|er, die; -, -n *Plur. selten;* **aus|steu|ern; Aus|steu|e|rung**

Aus|stich (das Beste [vom Wein]; *schweiz. Sportspr. auch für* Entscheidungskampf)

Aus|stieg, der; -[e]s, -e; **Aus|stieg|lu|ke**

aus|stop|fen; Aus|stop|fung

Aus|stoß, der; -es, Ausstöße *Plur. selten* (z. B. von Bier); **aus|sto|ßen;** jmdn. -; **Aus|sto|ßung**

aus|strah|len; Aus|strah|lung

aus|stre|cken

aus|strei|chen

aus|streu|en; Gerüchte -

Aus|strich *(Med.)*

aus|strö|men

aus|stül|pen; Aus|stül|pung

aus|su|chen; ich suche mir etw. aus; *vgl.* ausgesucht

aus|sü|ßen (zu Süßwasser werden)

aus|tan|zen (*bes. Fußball* den Gegner geschickt und spektakulär umspielen)

aus|ta|pe|zie|ren

aus|ta|rie|ren (ins Gleichgewicht bringen; *österr. auch* [auf der Waage] das Leergewicht feststellen)

Aus|tausch, der; -[e]s; **aus|tausch|bar; Aus|tausch|bar|keit,** die; -; **aus|tau|schen; Aus|tausch‿mo|tor** ([als neuwertig geltender] Ersatzmotor), **...schü|ler, ...stoff** (künstlicher Roh- u. Werkstoff); **aus|tausch|wei|se**

aus|tei|len; Aus|tei|lung

Aus|te|nit [*auch* ...'nit], der; -s, -e

⟨nach dem engl. Forscher Roberts-Austen⟩ (ein Eisenmischkristall, Gammaeisen)
Aus|ter, die; -, -n ⟨niederl.⟩ (essbare Meeresmuschel)
Aus|te|ri|ty [ɔsˈteriti], die; - ⟨engl.⟩ (*engl. Bez. für* Strenge; wirtschaftl. Einschränkung)
Aus|ter|litz (Schlachtort bei Brünn)
Aus|tern‿bank (*Plur.* ...bänke), **...fi|scher** (Watvogel), **...zucht**
aus|tes|ten
aus|til|gen
aus|to|ben; sich -
aus|ton|nen (*Seew.* ausbojen)
Aus|trag, der; -[e]s (*südd. u. österr. auch für* Altenteil); zum - kommen *(Amtsspr.)*; **aus|tra|gen; Aus|trä|ger** (Person, die etwas austrägt); **Aus|träg|ler** (*südd. u. österr. für* Bauer, der auf dem Altenteil lebt); **Aus|tra|gung; Aus|tra|gungs‿mo|dus, ...ort**
aus|trai|niert (völlig trainiert)
Aust|ral (↑R 130), der; -[s], -e ⟨span.⟩ (argentin. Währungseinheit; *Abk.* A); 30 - (↑R 90)
aust|ra|lid (↑R 130) ⟨lat.⟩ (*Anthropol.* Rassenmerkmale der Australiden zeigend); -er Zweig; **Aust|ra|li|de,** der *u.* die; -n, -n (↑R 5 ff.); **Aust|ra|li|en; Aust|ra|li|er; aust|ra|lisch,** *aber* (↑R 108): die Australischen Alpen; **aust|ra|lo|id** (*Anthropol.* den Australiden ähnliche Rassenmerkmale zeigend); **Aust|ra|lo|i|de,** der *u.* die; -n, -n (↑R 5 ff.)
aus|träu|men; ausgeträumt
aus|trei|ben; Aus|trei|bung
aus|tre|ten
Aust|ria (↑R 130; *lat. Form von* Österreich); **Aust|ri|a|zis|mus,** der; -, ...men ⟨lat.⟩ (österr. Sprachvariante)
aus|trick|sen *(auch Sportspr.)*
aus|trin|ken
Aus|tritt; Aus|tritts|er|klä|rung
aust|ro|asi|a|tisch (↑R 130 *u.* 132); -e Sprachen
aus|trock|nen; Aus|trock|nung, die; -
Aust|ro‿fa|schis|mus (↑R 130; [*auch* ˈaustro...] österr. Sonderform des Faschismus [1933 bis 1938]), **...mar|xis|mus** ([*auch* ˈaustro...] österr. Sonderform des Marxismus)
aus|trom|pe|ten *vgl.* ausposaunen
Aust|ro|pop (↑R 130; österr. Popmusik)
aus|tru|deln (*landsch. für* auswürfeln)
aus|tüf|teln; Aus|tüf|te|lung, Aus|tüft|lung
aus|tun; sich austun können (*ugs. für* sich ungehemmt betätigen können)
aus|tup|fen; eine Wunde -
aus|üben; (↑R 132); **Aus|übung,** die; -
aus|ufern (↑R 132; über die Ufer treten; das Maß überschreiten)
Aus|ver|kauf; aus|ver|kau|fen; aus|ver|kauft
aus|ver|schämt (*landsch. für* dreist, unverschämt)
aus|wach|sen; (↑R 50:) es ist zum Auswachsen (*ugs. für* zum Verzweifeln); *vgl.* ausgewachsen
aus|wä|gen (*fachspr. für* das Gewicht feststellen, vergleichen)
Aus|wahl; aus|wäh|len; Aus|wahl‿mann|schaft, ...mög|lich|keit, ...spie|ler, ...wet|te (Wette, bei der Fußballspiele mit der höchsten Gesamttorzahl vorausgesagt werden müssen)
aus|wal|len (*schweiz., auch bayr. für* [Teig] ausrollen)
aus|wal|zen
Aus|wan|de|rer; Aus|wan|de|rer|schiff; aus|wan|dern; Aus|wan|de|rung; Aus|wan|de|rungs|wel|le
aus|wär|tig; auswärtiger Dienst, *aber* (↑R 108): das Auswärtige Amt (*Abk.* AA); Minister des Auswärtigen (↑R 47); **aus|wärts;** nach, von auswärts kommen; nach auswärts gehen; auswärts (nicht zu Hause) essen; auswärts gehen, laufen (mit auswärts gerichteten Füßen); **Aus|wärts|spiel**
aus|wa|schen; Aus|wa|schung
Aus|wech|sel|bank (*Plur.* ...bänke); **aus|wech|sel|bar; aus|wech|seln; Aus|wech|se|lung, Aus|wechs|lung**
Aus|weg; aus|weg|los; Aus|weg|lo|sig|keit, die; -
Aus|wei|che; aus|wei|chen; *vgl.* [2]weichen; **aus|wei|chend; Aus|weich‿ma|nö|ver, ...mög|lich|keit, ...stel|le**
aus|wei|den (*Jägerspr.* Eingeweide entfernen [bei Wild usw.])
aus|wei|nen; sich -
Aus|weis, der; -es, -e; **aus|wei|sen;** sich -; **Aus|weis|kon|trol|le; aus|weis|lich** (*Amtsspr.* wie aus ... zu erkennen ist); *Präp. mit Gen.*: - der Akten; **Aus|weis|pa|pier** *meist Plur.*
aus|wei|ßen (z. B. einen Stall)
Aus|wei|sung
aus|wei|ten; Aus|wei|tung
aus|wel|len; Teig -
aus|wen|dig; - lernen, wissen; **Aus|wen|dig|ler|nen,** das; -s
aus|wer|fen; Aus|wer|fer *(Technik)*
aus|wer|keln; das Türschloss ist ausgewerkelt (*österr. ugs. für* ausgeleiert, stark abgenutzt)
aus|wer|ten; Aus|wer|tung
aus|wet|zen; eine Scharte -
aus|wi|ckeln
aus|wie|gen; *vgl.* ausgewogen
aus|win|den (*landsch. u. schweiz. für* auswringen)
aus|win|tern (durch Frost Schaden leiden); die Saat ist ausgewintert; **Aus|win|te|rung,** die; -
aus|wir|ken, sich; **Aus|wir|kung**
aus|wi|schen; jmdm. eins - (*ugs. für* schaden)
aus|wit|tern (verwittern; an die Oberfläche treten lassen)
aus|wrin|gen; Wäsche -
Aus|wuchs, der; -es, ...wüchse
aus|wuch|ten *(bes. Kfz-Technik)*; die Reifen -; **Aus|wuch|tung**
Aus|wurf; Aus|würf|ling (*Geol.* von einem Vulkan ausgeworfenes Magma- od. Gesteinsbruchstück); **Aus|wurf[s]|mas|se** *(Geol.)*
aus|zah|len; das zahlt sich nicht aus (*ugs. für* das lohnt sich nicht); **aus|zäh|len; Aus|zah|lung; Aus|zäh|lung**
aus|zan|ken (*landsch. für* ausschimpfen)
aus|zeh|ren; Aus|zeh|rung, die; - (Kräfteverfall; *auch veraltet für* Schwindsucht)
aus|zeich|nen; sich -; **Aus|zeich|nung; Aus|zeich|nungs|pflicht**
Aus|zeit (*Sportspr.* [einer Mannschaft zustehende] Spielunterbrechung)
aus|zieh|bar; aus|zie|hen; sich -; **Aus|zieh|tisch**
aus|zir|keln
aus|zi|schen (durch Zischen sein Missfallen kundtun)
Aus|zu|bil|den|de, der *u.* die; -n, -n (↑R 5 ff.); *Kurzw.* Azubi
Aus|zug (*südd. auch für* Altenteil; *schweiz. auch* erste Altersklasse der Wehrpflichtigen); **Aus|züg|ler** (*landsch. für* Bauer, der auf dem Altenteil lebt); **Aus|zug|mehl** *vgl.* Auszugsmehl; **Aus|zugs|bau|er** (*österr. für* Bauer, der auf dem Altenteil lebt); **Aus|zug[s]|mehl** (feines, kleiefreies Weizenmehl); **aus|zugs|wei|se**
aus|zup|fen
au|tark (↑R 132) ⟨griech.⟩ (sich selbst genügend; wirtschaftlich unabhängig vom Ausland); **Au|tar|kie,** die; -, ...ien (wirtschaftliche Unabhängigkeit vom Ausland)
Au|then|tie, die; - ⟨griech.⟩ (*svw.* Authentizität); **au|then|ti|fi|zie|ren** ⟨griech.; lat.⟩ (die Echtheit be-

zeugen; beglaubigen); **au|then|tisch** ‹griech.› (im Wortlaut verbürgt; echt); **au|then|ti|sie|ren** (*geh. für* glaubwürdig, rechtsgültig machen); **Au|then|ti|zi|tät,** die; - (Echtheit; Rechtsgültigkeit)
Au|tis|mus, der; - ‹griech.› (*Med.* [krankhafte] Ichbezogenheit, Kontaktunfähigkeit); **au|tis|tisch**
Au|to, das; -s, -s ‹griech.› (*kurz für* Automobil); (↑R 39:) Auto fahren; ich bin Auto gefahren
au|to... ‹griech.› (selbst...); **Au|to...** (Selbst...)
Au|to‿at|las, ...bahn (*Zeichen* A, z. B. A 14); **au|to|bahn|ar|tig; Au|to|bahn‿auf|fahrt, ...aus|fahrt, ...drei|eck, ...ein|fahrt, ...ge|bühr, ...kreuz, ...maut** *(österr.)*, **...rast|stät|te, ...vig|net|te, ...zu|brin|ger**
Au|to|bi|o|gra|phie (↑R 33), die; -, ...ien ‹griech.› (literar. Darstellung des eigenen Lebens); **au|to|bi|o|gra|phisch** (↑R 33)
Au|to|bom|be
Au|to|bus, der; ...busses, ...busse ‹griech.; lat.›; *vgl. auch* Bus
Au|to|car, der; -s, -s ‹franz.› (*schweiz. für* [Reise]omnibus)
au|toch|thon [...x'to:n] (↑R 132) ‹griech.› (an Ort und Stelle [entstanden]; eingesessen); **Au|toch|tho|ne,** der *u.* die; -n, -n (↑R 5 ff.; Ureinwohner[in], Eingeborene[r])
Au|to|coat [...ko:t], der; -s, -s (kurzer Mantel für den Autofahrer)
Au|to|cross, *auch* **Au|to-Cross,** das; -, -e (Geländeprüfung für Autosportler)
Au|to|da|fé [...da'fe:], das; -s, -s ‹port.› (Ketzergericht u. -verbrennung)
Au|to|di|dakt, der; -en, -en (↑R 126) ‹griech.› (jmd., der sich sein Wissen durch Selbstunterricht angeeignet hat); **au|to|di|dak|tisch**
Au|to|drom, das; -s, -e ‹griech.-franz.› (ringförmige Straßenanlage für Renn- u. Testfahrten; *österr.* [Fahrbahn für] Skooter)
Au|to|ero|tik (↑R 132), die; - (*svw.* Narzissmus, Masturbation); **au|to|ero|tisch**
Au|to‿fäh|re, ...fah|ren (das; -s; ↑R 50; *aber* Auto fahren), **...fah|rer, ...fah|re|rin, ...fahrt**
Au|to|fo|kus (*Fotogr.* Einrichtung zur automatischen Einstellung der Bildschärfe bei Kameras etc.)
au|to|frei; -er Sonntag; **Au|to‿fried|hof** *(ugs.)*, **...gas** (Gasgemisch als Treibstoff für Kraftfahrzeuge)
au|to|gen ‹griech.› (ursprünglich; selbsttätig); -es Schweißen *(Technik)*; -es Training (*Med.* eine Methode der Selbstentspannung)
Au|to|gramm, das; -s, -e ‹griech.› (eigenhändig geschriebener Name); **Au|to|gramm|jä|ger; Au|to|graph,** das; -s, *Plur.* -e *od.* -en (eigenhändig geschriebenes Schriftstück einer bedeutenden Persönlichkeit); **Au|to|gra|phie,** die; -, ...ien (*Druckw.* Umdruckverfahren)
Au|to‿hil|fe, ...hof (Einrichtung des Güterfernverkehrs)
Au|to|hyp|no|se ‹griech.› (Selbsthypnose)
Au|to‿in|dust|rie, ...kar|te, ...ki|no (Freilichtkino, in dem man Filme vom Auto aus betrachtet)
Au|to|klav, der; -s, -en [...vən] ‹griech.; lat.› (Gefäß zum Erhitzen unter Druck)
Au|to‿kna|cker, ...ko|lon|ne, ...kor|so
Au|to|krat, der; -en, -en (↑R 126) ‹griech.› (Alleinherrscher; selbstherrlicher Mensch); **Au|to|kra|tie,** die; -, ...ien (unumschränkte [Allein]herrschaft); **au|to|kra|tisch**
Au|to|ly|se, die; - ‹griech.› (*Med.* Abbau von Körpereiweiß ohne Mitwirkung von Bakterien)
Au|to‿mar|der (*ugs.; svw.* Autoknacker), **...mar|ke**
Au|to|mat, der; -en, -en (↑R 126) ‹griech.›; **Au|to|ma|ten‿kna|cker, ...res|tau|rant; Au|to|ma|tik,** die; -, -en (Vorrichtung, die einen techn. Vorgang steuert u. regelt); **Au|to|ma|tik|ge|trie|be; Au|to|ma|ti|on,** die; - ‹engl.› (vollautomatische Fabrikation); **au|to|ma|tisch** ‹griech.› (selbsttätig; selbst regelnd; unwillkürlich; zwangsläufig); **au|to|ma|ti|sie|ren** (auf vollautomatische Fabrikation umstellen); **Au|to|ma|ti|sie|rung; Au|to|ma|tis|mus,** der; -, ...men (sich selbst steuernder, unbewusster Ablauf)
Au|to|me|cha|ni|ker; Au|to|mi|nu|te (Strecke, die ein Auto in einer Minute fährt); zehn -n entfernt; **Au|to|mo|bil,** das; -s, -e ‹griech.; lat.›; **Au|to|mo|bil‿aus|stel|lung, ...bau** (der; -[e]s), **...in|dust|rie; Au|to|mo|bi|list,** der; -en, -en; ↑R 126 (*bes. schweiz. für* Autofahrer); **Au|to|mo|bil|klub,** *aber* Allgemeiner Deutscher Automobil-Club (*Abk.* ADAC); Automobilclub von Deutschland (*Abk.* AvD)
au|to|nom ‹griech.› (selbstständig, unabhängig); **Au|to|no|me,** der *u.* die; -n, -n (↑R 5 ff.); **Au|to|no|mie,** die; -, ...ien (Selbstständigkeit, Unabhängigkeit)
Au|to‿num|mer, ...öl
Au|to|pi|lot (automatische Steuerung von Flugzeugen u. Ä.)
Au|to|plas|tik (*Med.* Verpflanzung körpereigenen Gewebes)
Au|top|sie (↑R 132), die; -, ...ien ‹griech.› (Prüfung durch Augenschein; *Med.* Leichenöffnung)
Au|tor, der; -s, ...oren ‹lat.› (Verfasser); dem, den Autor
Au|to‿ra|dio, ...rei|fen, ...rei|se|zug
Au|to|ren‿grup|pe, ...kol|lek|tiv *(bes. ehemals in der DDR)*, **...kor|rek|tur** (*selten für* Autorkorrektur), **...le|sung**
Au|to‿ren|nen, ...re|pa|ra|tur
Au|to|re|verse [...rivœ:(r)s], das; - ‹engl.› (Umschaltautomatik bei Kassettenrecordern)
Au|to|rin ‹lat.›; **Au|to|ri|sa|ti|on,** die;-, -en (Ermächtigung, Vollmacht); **au|to|ri|sie|ren; au|to|ri|siert** ([einzig] berechtigt; ermächtigt); **au|to|ri|tär** (unbedingten Gehorsam fordernd; diktatorisch); ein -er Lehrer; -es Regime; **Au|to|ri|tät,** die; -, -en (Einfluss u. Ansehen; bedeutender Vertreter seines Faches; maßgebende Institution); **au|to|ri|ta|tiv** (sich auf echte Autorität stützend, maßgebend); **au|to|ri|täts|gläu|big; Au|tor|kor|rek|tur; Au|tor|re|fe|rat** (Referat des Autors über sein Werk); **Au|tor|schaft,** die; -
Au|to‿schlan|ge, ...schlos|ser, ...schlüs|sel, ...ser|vice, ...skoo|ter, ...stopp (*vgl.* Anhalter), **...strich** (*ugs. für* Prostitution an Autostraßen)
Au|to|sug|ges|ti|on [*od.* ...'tio:n], die; -, -en ‹griech.; lat.› (Selbstbeeinflussung)
Au|to|te|le|fon
Au|to|to|xin (*Med.* Eigengift)
au|to|troph ‹griech.› (*Biol.* sich von anorganischen Stoffen ernährend)
Au|to|ty|pie, die; -, ...ien ‹griech.› (*Druckw.* netzartige Bildätzung für Buchdruck; Netz-, Rasterätzung)
Au|to‿un|fall, ...ver|kehr, ...ver|leih, ...werk|statt
Au|to|zoom [...zu:m] (*Fotogr.* automatische Abstimmung von Brennweite und Entfernungseinstellung bei einer Filmkamera)
autsch!
Au|ver|gne [o'vɛrnjə] (↑R 130), die; - (Region in Frankreich)
Au|wald, Au|en|wald
au|weh!; au|wei!; au|weia!

Au|xin, das; -s, -e ‹griech.› (*Bot.* Pflanzenwuchsstoff)

a v. = a vista

A|val [a'val], der, *seltener* das; -s, -e ‹franz.› (*Bankw.* Wechselbürgschaft); **a|va|lie|ren** ([Wechsel] als Bürge unterschreiben)

A|van|ce [a'vã:sə *od.* a'vaŋsə], die; -, -n ‹franz.› (*veraltet für* Vorteil; Geldvorschuss); jmdm. Avancen machen (jmdm. entgegenkommen, um ihn für sich zu gewinnen); **A|van|ce|ment** [avãsə'mã:, *österr.* avãs'mã:], das; -s, -s (*veraltet für* Beförderung); **a|van|cie|ren** [avaŋ'si:... *od.* avã'si:...] (befördert werden); **A|vant|gar|de** [a'vã... *od.* a'vaŋ...], die; -, -n ‹franz.› (die Vorkämpfer für eine Idee); **A|vant|gar|dis|mus,** der; -; **A|vant|gar|dist,** der; -en, -en (↑R 126); **A|vant|gar|dis|tin;** **a|vant|gar|dis|tisch**

a|van|ti! [...v...] ‹ital.› (*ugs. für* vorwärts!)

AvD = Automobilclub von Deutschland

A|ve [...v...], das; -[s], -[s] ‹lat.› (*kurz für* Ave-Maria); **A|ve-Ma|ria,** das; -[s], -[s] („Gegrüßet seist du, Maria!") (kath. Gebet); **A|ve-Ma|ria-Läu|ten,** das; -s (↑R 28)

A|ven|tin [...v...], der; -s (Hügel in Rom); **A|ven|ti|ni|sche Hü|gel,** der; -n -s

A|ven|tiu|re [avɛn'ty:rə], die; -, -n ‹franz.› (mittelhochd. Rittererzählung); *als Personifikation* Frau Aventiure

A|ven|tu|rin [...v...], der; -s, -e ‹lat.-franz.› (goldflimmriger Quarzstein); **A|ven|tu|rin|glas**

A|ve|nue [avə'ny:], die; -, ...uen [...'ny:ən] (Prachtstraße)

A|ver|ro|es [a'vɛroɛs] (arab. Philosoph u. Theologe im MA.)

A|vers [a'vɛrs, *österr.* a'vɛr], der; -es, -e ‹franz.› (*Münzw.* Vorderseite [einer Münze]); **A|ver|si|on,** die; -, -en ‹lat.› (Abneigung, Widerwille)

AVG = Angestelltenversicherungsgesetz

A|vi|a|ri|um [...v...], das; -s, ...ien [...iən] ‹lat.› (großes Vogelhaus)

A|vig|non ['avinjɔŋ, *franz.* avi'njɔ̃:] (↑R 130; franz. Stadt)

A|vis [a'vi:], der *od.* das; - [a'vi:(s)], - [a'vi:s]; *auch* [a'vi:s], der *od.* das; -es, -e ‹franz.› (*Wirtsch.* Nachricht, Anzeige); **a|vi|sie|ren** (ankündigen; *schweiz. auch für* benachrichtigen); **¹A|vi|so,** der; -s, -s ‹span.› (*früher* kleines, schnelles Kriegsschiff); **²A|vi|so,** das; -s, -s ‹ital.› (*österr. für* Avis)

a vis|ta [a 'vista] ‹ital.› (*Bankw.* bei Vorlage zahlbar; *Abk.* a v.); *vgl.* a prima vista; **A|vis|ta|wech|sel** (Sichtwechsel)

A|vi|ta|mi|no|se [...v...] (↑R 132), die; -, -n ‹lat.› (*Med.* durch Vitaminmangel hervorgerufene Krankheit)

a|vi|vie|ren [...v...] ‹franz.› (*Färberei* Gewebe nachbehandeln, ihnen mehr Glanz verleihen)

A|vo|ca|do [...v...], die; -, -s ‹indian.-span.› (birnenförmige Frucht eines südamerik. Baumes)

A|vo|gad|ro [...v...] (↑R 130; ital. Physiker u. Chemiker)

A|vus [...v...], die; - (*Kurzw. für* Automobil-Verkehrs- und -Übungsstraße [frühere Autorennstrecke in Berlin, heute Teil der Stadtautobahn])

AWACS (= Airborne early warning and control system ['ɛ:(r)bɔ(r)n 'œ:(r)li 'wɔ:(r)niŋ ənd kən'tro:l 'sistəm]; Frühwarnsystem der NATO)

A|wa|re, der; -n, -n; ↑R 126 (Angehöriger eines untergegangenen türk.-mongol. Steppennomadenvolkes); **a|wa|risch**

A|wes|ta, das; - ‹pers.› (heilige Schriften der Parsen); **a|wes|tisch;** -e Sprache

¹A|xel (m. Vorn.); **²A|xel,** der; -s, - (*kurz für* Axel-Paulsen-Sprung); doppelter Axel; **A|xel-Paul|sen-Sprung;** ↑R 95 (nach dem norw. Eiskunstläufer Axel Paulsen benannter Kürsprung)

A|xen|stra|ße, die; - (in der Schweiz)

a|xi|al ‹lat.› (in der Achsenrichtung; längs der Achse); **A|xi|a|li|tät,** die; -, -en; (Achsigkeit); **A|xi|al|ver|schie|bung**

a|xil|lar ‹lat.› (*Bot.* achselständig, winkelständig); **A|xil|lar|knos|pe** (Knospe in der Blattachsel)

A|xi|om, das; -s, -e ‹griech.› (keines Beweises bedürfender Grundsatz); **A|xi|o|ma|tik,** die; -; (Lehre von den Axiomen); **a|xi|o|ma|tisch;** -es System; **a|xi|o|ma|ti|sie|ren**

Ax|mins|ter|tep|pich ['ɛks...] ‹nach dem engl. Ort›; ↑R 105

A|xo|lotl, der; -s, - ‹aztekisch› (mexik. Schwanzlurch)

A|xon, das; -s, *Plur.* Axone *u.* Axonen (*Biol.* zentraler Strang einer Nervenfaser)

Axt, die; -, Äxte; **Axt|helm** (Axtstiel); *vgl.* ²Helm; **Axt|hieb**

A|ya|tol|lah [aja...] *vgl.* Ajatollah

AZ, Az. = Aktenzeichen

a. Z. = auf Zeit

A|za|lee, *auch* **A|za|lie** [...iə], die; -, -n ‹griech.› (eine Zierpflanze aus der Familie der Heidekrautgewächse)

A|ze|tat usw. *vgl.* Acetat usw.

A|zid, das; -[e]s, -e ‹griech.› (*Chemie* Salz der Stickstoffwasserstoffsäure); **A|zi|di|tät** *vgl.* Acidität; **A|zi|do|se** *vgl.* Acidose

A|zi|mut, das, *auch* der; -s, -e ‹arab.› (*Astron.* eine bestimmte Winkelgröße)

A|zo|farb|stoff ‹griech.; dt.› (*Chemie* Farbstoff aus der Gruppe der Teerfarbstoffe); **A|zo|i|kum,** das; -s ‹griech.› (*Geol.* erdgeschichtl. Urzeit ohne Spuren organ. Lebens); **a|zo|isch** (*Geol.* keine Lebewesen enthaltend); **A|zo|o|sper|mie** [atsoospɛr...], die; -, ...ien (*Biol., Med.* Fehlen reifer Samenzellen in der Samenflüssigkeit)

A|zo|ren *Plur.* (Inselgruppe im Atlantischen Ozean)

Az|te|ke, der; -n, -n; ↑R 126 (Angehöriger eines Indianerstammes in Mexiko); **Az|te|ken|reich,** das; -[e]s

A|zu|bi, der; -s, -s *u.* die; -, -s (*ugs. für* Auszubildende[r])

A|zu|le|jos [atsu'lɛxɔs] *Plur.* ‹span.› (bunte, bes. blaue Wandkacheln)

A|zur, der; -s ‹pers.› (*geh. für* Himmelsblau); **a|zur|blau; A|zu|ree|li|ni|en** *Plur.* (waagerechtes, meist wellenförmiges Linienband auf Vordrucken [z. B. auf Schecks]); **a|zu|riert** (mit Azureelinien versehen); **A|zu|rit** [*auch* ...'rit], der; -s (ein dunkelblaues Mineral); **a|zurn** (himmelblau)

a|zyk|lisch ‹griech.› (*Chemie* nicht ringförmig geschlossen; *Med.* zeitlich unregelmäßig; *Bot. bei Blüten* spiralig gebaut)

Az|zur|ri, Az|zur|ris *Plur.* ‹ital., „die Blauen"› (*Bez. für* ital. Sportmannschaften)

B (Buchstabe); das B; des B, die B, *aber* das b in Abend (↑R 60); der Buchstabe B, b

b, B, das; -, - (Tonbezeichnung); **b** (*Zeichen für* b-Moll); in b; **B** (*Zeichen für* B-Dur); in B

B = *Zeichen für* Bel; Bundesstraße
B = *chem. Zeichen für* Bor
B *(auf dt. Kurszetteln)* = Brief (d. h., das Wertpapier wurde zum angegebenen Preis angeboten)
B, β = Beta
b. = bei[m]
B. = Bachelor
Ba = *chem. Zeichen für* Barium
BA [bi'e:] = British Airways ['britiʃ 'ɛ:(r)we:s] (brit. Luftverkehrsgesellschaft)
Baal ‹hebr.› (semit. Wetter- und Himmelsgott); **Baal|bek** (Stadt im Libanon); **Baals|dienst,** der; -[e]s
Baar, die; - (Gebiet zwischen dem Schwarzwald u. der Schwäbischen Alb)
Baas, der; -es, -e ‹niederl.› *(nordd., bes. Seemannsspr.* Herr, Meister, Aufseher)
ba|ba, bä|bä *(Kinderspr.);* das ist - !
bab|beln *(landsch. für* schwatzen); ich ...[e]le (↑R 16)
Ba|bel *vgl.* Babylon
Ba|ben|ber|ger, der; -s, - (Angehöriger eines Fürstengeschlechtes)
Ba|bet|te (w. Vorn.)
Ba|bu|sche, Pam|pu|sche [...u(:)ʃə], die; -, -n *meist Plur.* ‹pers.› *(landsch., bes. ostmitteld. für* Stoffpantoffel)
Ba|by ['be:bi], das; -s, -s ‹engl.› (Säugling, Kleinkind); **Ba|by|jahr** (für Mütter ein zusätzlich anzurechnendes Rentenversicherungsjahr für jedes Kind; einjähriger Mutterschaftsurlaub)
Ba|by|lon, Ba|bel (Ruinenstadt am Euphrat); **Ba|by|lo|ni|en** [...i̯ən] (antiker Name für das Land zwischen Euphrat u. Tigris); **Ba|by|lo|ni|er** [...i̯ər]; **ba|by|lo|nisch;** babylonische Kunst; ein babylonisches Sprachengewirr; *aber* (↑R 108): die Babylonische Gefangenschaft; der Babylonische Turm
Ba|by|nah|rung ['be:bi...]; **ba|by|sit|ten** *nur im Infinitiv gebräuchlich (ugs.);* **Ba|by|sit|ter,** der; -s, - ‹engl.› (jmd., der Kleinkinder bei Abwesenheit der Eltern beaufsichtigt); **Ba|by|speck; Ba|by|zel|le** (kleine, längliche Batterie)
Bac|cha|nal [baxa..., *österr. auch* baka...], das; -s, *Plur.* -e *u.* -ien [...i̯ən] ‹griech.› (altröm. Bacchusfest; wüstes Trinkgelage); **Bac|chant,** der; -en, -en; ↑R 126 *(geh. für* weinseliger Trinker); **Bac|chan|tin; bac|chan|tisch** (trunken; ausgelassen); **bac|chisch** (nach Art des Bacchus); **Bac|chi|us** (antiker Versfuß); **Bac|chus** (griech.-röm. Gott des Weines); **Bac|chus|fest** (↑R 95)
[1]**Bach,** der; -[e]s, Bäche
[2]**Bach,** Johann Sebastian (dt. Komponist)
bach|ab *(schweiz.);* - gehen (zunichte werden); - schicken (verwerfen, ablehnen)
Ba|che, die; -, -n *(Jägerspr.* w. Wildschwein)
Ba|che|lor ['bɛtʃələ(r)], der; -[s], -s ‹engl.› (niedrigster akadem. Grad in England, den USA u. anderen englischsprachigen Ländern; *Abk.* B.; *vgl.* Bakkalaureus)
Bach|fo|rel|le; Bäch|lein; Bach|stel|ze
Bach-Wer|ke-Ver|zeich|nis (↑R 95)
back *(nordd. u. Seemannsspr.* zurück)
[1]**Back,** die; -, -en *(Seemannsspr.* [Ess]schüssel; Esstisch; Tischgemeinschaft; Aufbau auf dem Vordeck)
[2]**Back** [bɛk], der; -s, -s ‹engl.› *(schweiz. u. österr. für* Verteidiger [beim Fußball etc.])
Back|blech
Back|bord, das; -[e]s, -e (linke Schiffsseite [von hinten gesehen]); **back|bord[s]**
Bäck|chen; Ba|cke, die; -, -n, *landsch.* **Ba|cken,** der; -s, -
ba|cken (Brot usw.); du bäckst *od.* backst; er bäckt *od.* backt; du backtest *(älter* buk[e]st); du backtest *(älter* bükest); gebacken; back[e]!; *Beugung in der Bed. von* „kleben" *(vgl.* „festbacken"): der Schnee backt, backte, hat gebackt
Ba|cken|bart; Ba|cken|zahn
Bä|cker; Bä|cke|rei *(österr. auch für* süßes Kleingebäck); **Bä|cke|rin; Bä|cker˯jun|ge, ...la|den; Bä|cker[s]|frau**
Back|fisch *(veraltend auch für* junges Mädchen)
Back|gam|mon [bɛk'gɛmən], das; -[s] ‹engl.› (dem Tricktrack ähnliches Würfelspiel)
Back|ground ['bɛkgraunt], der; -s, -s ‹engl.› (Hintergrund; *übertr. für* [Lebens]erfahrung); **Back|ground|mu|si|ker**
Back|hen|del, das; -s, -n *(österr. für* paniertes Hähnchen); **Back|hen|del|sta|ti|on** *(österr.)*
...ba|ckig, ...bä|ckig (z. B. rotbackig, rotbäckig)
Back|list ['bɛk...], die; -, -s ‹engl.› (Liste lieferbarer Bücher)
Back˯obst, ...ofen (↑R 132), **...papier**
Back|pfei|fe *(landsch. für* Ohrfeige); **back|pfei|fen** *(landsch.);* er backpfeifte ihn, hat ihn gebackpfeift; **Back|pfei|fen|ge|sicht** *(ugs.)*
Back˯pflau|me, ...pul|ver, ...rohr *(österr. für* Backofen), **...röh|re**
Back|schaft *(Seemannsspr.* Tischgemeinschaft); **Back|stag** [...st...] (den Mast von hinten haltendes [Draht]seil)
Back|stein; Back|stein|bau *Plur.* ...bauten
Back|wa|re *meist Plur.*
[1]**Ba|con** ['be:k(ə)n], der; -s ‹engl.› (Frühstücksspeck)
[2]**Ba|con** ['be:k(ə)n] (engl. Philosoph)
Bad, das; -[e]s, Bäder; Bad Ems, Bad Homburg v. d. H., Stuttgart-Bad Cannstatt (↑R 105); **Bad...** *(südd., österr., schweiz. in Zusammensetzungen neben* Bade..., z. B. Badanstalt)
Bad Aus|see *vgl.* Aussee
Bad Bram|bach *vgl.* Brambach
Ba|de˯an|stalt, ...an|zug, ...arzt, ...ho|se, ...kap|pe, ...man|tel, ...mat|te, ...meis|ter, ...müt|ze;
ba|den; baden gehen *(ugs. auch für* keinen Erfolg haben, scheitern)
Ba|den (Teil des Bundeslandes Baden-Württemberg); **Ba|den-Ba|den** (Badeort im nördl. Schwarzwald); **Ba|de|ner,** *auch* **Ba|den|ser** (↑R 103); **Ba|den-Würt|tem|berg** (↑R 106); **Ba|den-Würt|tem|ber|ger** (↑R 103); **ba|den-würt|tem|ber|gisch**
Ba|de|ort, der; -[e]s, -e
Ba|der *(veraltet für* Barbier; Heilgehilfe)
Ba|de˯sai|son, ...salz, ...tuch, ...wan|ne, ...zeit, ...zim|mer
Bad|gas|tein (österr. Badeort)
ba|disch; ↑R 108 (aus Baden)
Bad Ischl *vgl.* Ischl
Bad|min|ton ['bɛdmintən], das; - ‹nach dem Landsitz des Herzogs von Beaufort in England› (Federballspiel)
Bad Oeyn|hau|sen *vgl.* Oeynhausen
Bad Pyr|mont *vgl.* Pyrmont
Bad Ra|gaz *vgl.* Ragaz
Bad Wö|ris|ho|fen *vgl.* Wörishofen
Bae|de|ker ® ['bɛ:...], der; -[s], - (ein Reisehandbuch)
Ba|fel, der; -s, - ‹jidd.› *(ugs. für* Ausschussware; *nur Sing.:* Geschwätz)
baff *(ugs. für* verblüfft); - sein
BAföG, *auch* **Ba|fög,** das; -[s] (= Bundesausbildungsförderungsgesetz; *auch für* Geldzahlungen nach diesem Gesetz)
Ba|ga|ge [ba'ga:ʒə, *österr.* ba'ga:ʒ], die; -, -n [ba'ga:ʒ(ə)n] *Plur. selten*

⟨franz.⟩ (*veraltet für* Gepäck; *ugs. für* Gesindel)
Ba|ga̱s|se, die; -, -n ⟨franz.⟩ (Pressrückstand bei der Rohrzuckergewinnung)
Ba|ga|te̱l|le, die; -, -n ⟨franz.⟩ (unbedeutende Kleinigkeit; kleines, leichtes Musikstück); **ba|ga|tel|li|sie̱|ren** (als unbedeutende Kleinigkeit behandeln); **Ba|ga|te̱ll‿sa|che, ...scha|den**
Ba̱g|dad (Hptst. des Iraks); **Ba̱g|da|der**
Ba̱g|ger, der; -s, - (Baumaschine zum Abtragen von Erdreich od. Geröll); **Ba̱g|ge|rer; Ba̱g|ger|füh|rer; ba̱g|gern;** ich ...ere (↑R 16); **Ba̱g|ger‿prahm, ...see**
Bag|no [ˈbanjo] (↑R 130), das; -s, *Plur.* -s *u.* ...gni ⟨ital.⟩ (*früher für* Straflager [in Italien und Frankreich])
Ba|guette [baˈgɛt], die; -, -n, *auch* das; -s, -s ⟨franz.⟩ (franz. Stangenweißbrot)
bah!, pa̱h! (Ausruf der Geringschätzung)
bäh! (Ausruf der Schadenfreude)
Ba|hai, der; -, -[s] ⟨pers.⟩ (Anhänger des Bahaismus); **Ba|ha|i̱s|mus,** der; - (aus dem Islam hervorgegangene Religion)
Ba|ha̱|ma|er, *auch* Ba|ha̱|mer; **Ba|ha̱|ma|in|seln,** Ba|ha̱|mas *Plur.* (Inselstaat im Atlantischen Ozean); **ba|ha̱|ma|isch,** *auch* ba|ha̱|misch; **Ba|ha̱|mas** *vgl.* Bahamainseln; **Ba|ha̱|mer** usw. *vgl.* Bahamaer usw.
bä|hen (*südd., österr., schweiz.* [Brot] leicht rösten)
Ba̱hn, die; -, -en; ich breche mir Bahn; eine sich Bahn brechende Entwicklung; *vgl. aber* bahnbrechend; **ba̱hn|amt|lich; ba̱hn|bre|chend;** eine bahnbrechende Erfindung; *vgl. aber* Bahn; **Ba̱hn|bre|cher; Ba̱hn|bus** (*Kurzw. für* Bahnomnibus); **ba̱hn|ei|gen; ba̱h|nen;** ich bahne mir einen Weg; **ba̱h|nen|wei|se; Ba̱hn|hof** (*Abk.* Bf., Bhf.); **Ba̱hn|hof|buf|fet** *(schweiz.);* **Ba̱hn|hofs|buch‿hand|lung, ...buf|fet** *od.* **...büf|fet** *(österr.),* **...hal|le, ...mis|si|on, ...vor|stand** (*österr. für* Bahnhofsvorsteher), **...vor|ste|her; Ba̱hn|hof|vor|stand** (*schweiz. für* Bahnhofsvorsteher); **ba̱hn|la|gernd; Ba̱hn‿li|nie, ...schran|ke, ...steig; Ba̱hn|steig‿kan|te, ...kar|te; Ba̱hn‿über|gang** (↑R 132), **...wär|ter**
Ba|hö̱l, der; -s (*österr. ugs. für* großer Lärm, Tumult)
Bah|ra̱in, Bah|re̱in [*auch* bax...] (Inselgruppe u. Scheichtum im Persischen Golf); **Bah|ra̱i|ner,** Bah|re̱i|ner (↑R 103); **bah|ra̱i|nisch,** bah|re̱i|nisch
Ba̱h|re, die; -, -n
Bah|re̱in usw. *vgl.* Bahrain usw.
Ba̱hr|tuch *Plur.* ...tücher
Ba̱ht, der; -, - (Währungseinheit in Thailand)
Bä̱|hung (Heilbehandlung mit warmen Umschlägen oder Dämpfen)
Ba̱i, die; -, -en ⟨niederl.⟩ (Bucht)
Ba̱i|er (*Sprachw.* Sprecher der bayerischen Mundart)
Ba̱i|kal, der; -[s] (*kurz für* Baikalsee); **Bai|kal-A|mu̱r-Ma|gist|ra|le,** die; - (Eisenbahnstrecke in Sibirien); **Ba̱i|kal|see,** der; -s (See in Südsibirien)
Bai|ko|nu̱r (russ. Raumfahrtzentrum)
Bai|ri|ki (Hptst. von Kiribati)
ba̱i|risch (*Sprachw.* die bayerische Mundart betreffend)
Bai|ser [bɛˈzeː], das; -s, -s ⟨franz.⟩ (Schaumgebäck)
Bais|se [ˈbɛːsə], die; -, -n ⟨franz.⟩ ([starkes] Fallen der Börsenkurse od. Preise); **Bais|si|er** [bɛˈsi̯eː], der; -s, -s (auf Baisse Spekulierender)
Ba|ja|de̱|re, die; -, -n ⟨franz.⟩ (ind. [Tempel]tänzerin)
Ba|ja̱z|zo, der; -s, -s ⟨ital.⟩ (Possenreißer; *auch* Titel einer Oper von Leoncavallo)
Ba|jo|ne̱tt, das; -[e]s, -e ⟨nach der Stadt Bayonne in Südfrankreich⟩ (Seitengewehr); **ba|jo|net|tie̱|ren** (mit dem Bajonett fechten); **Ba|jo|ne̱tt|ver|schluss** (*Technik* [leicht lösbare] Verbindung von rohrförmigen Teilen)
Ba|ju|wa̱|re, der; -n, -n; ↑R 126 (*veraltet, noch scherzh. für* [2]Bayer); **ba|ju|wa̱|risch**
Ba̱|ke, die; -, -n (festes Orientierungszeichen für Seefahrt, Luftfahrt, Straßenverkehr; Vorsignal auf Bahnstrecken)
Ba|ke|li̱t ®, das; -s ⟨nach dem belg. Chemiker Baekeland⟩ (ein Kunststoff)
Ba̱|ken|ton|ne (ein Seezeichen)
Bak|ka|lau|re|a̱t, das; -[e]s, -e ⟨lat.⟩ (unterster akadem. Grad [in England u. Nordamerika]; Abschluss der höheren Schule [in Frankreich]); **Bak|ka|la̱u|re|us,** der; -, ...rei [...re|i(ː)] (Inhaber des Bakkalaureats)
Ba̱k|ka|rat [*od.* ...ˈra], das; -s ⟨franz.⟩ (ein Kartenglücksspiel)
Ba̱k|ken, der; -[s], - ⟨norw.⟩ (*Skisport* Sprungschanze)
Ba̱k|schisch, das; -[(e)s], -e ⟨pers.⟩ (Almosen; Trinkgeld)
Bak|te|ri|ä|mie̱, die; -, ...i̱en ⟨griech.⟩ (Überschwemmung des Blutes mit Bakterien); **Bak|te̱|rie** [...i̯ə], die; -, -n *meist Plur.* (einzelliges Kleinstlebewesen, Spaltpilz); **bak|te|ri|e̱ll** (durch Bakterien hervorgerufen, die Bakterien betreffend); **bak|te̱|ri|en|be|stän|dig** (widerstandsfähig gegenüber Bakterien); **Bak|te̱|ri|en|trä|ger** *(Med.);* **Bak|te|ri|o|lo̱|ge,** der; -n, -n (↑R 126; Wissenschaftler auf dem Gebiet der Bakteriologie); **Bak|te|ri|o|lo|gie̱,** die; - (Lehre von den Bakterien); **bak|te|ri|o|lo̱|gisch;** -e Fleischuntersuchung; **Bak|te|ri|o|ly̱|se,** die; -, -n (Auflösung, Zerstörung von Bakterien); **Bak|te|ri|o|pha̱|ge,** der; -n, -n (↑R 126; Kleinstlebewesen, das Bakterien vernichtet); **Bak|te|ri|o̱|se,** die; -, -n (durch Bakterien verursachte Pflanzenkrankheit); **Bak|te̱|ri|um,** das; -s, ...ien [...i̯ən] (*veraltet für* Bakterie); **bak|te|ri|zi̱d** (*Med.* keimtötend); **Bak|te|ri|zi̱d,** das; -s, -e (keimtötendes Mittel)
Ba̱kt|ri|en (↑R 130; altpers. Landschaft)
Ba̱|ku [*od.* baˈkuː] (Hptst. von Aserbaidschan)
Ba|la|la̱i|ka, die; -, *Plur.* -s *u.* ...ken ⟨russ.⟩ (russ. Saiteninstrument)
Ba|lan|ce [baˈlaŋsə *od.* baˈlãːs(ə)], die; -, -n [...s(ə)n] ⟨franz.⟩ (Gleichgewicht); **Ba|lan|ce|akt; Ba|lan|ci̱er|bal|ken; ba|lan|ci̱e|ren** [balaŋˈsiː..., *auch* balãˈsiː...] (das Gleichgewicht halten, ausgleichen); **Ba|lan|ci̱er|stan|ge**
Ba̱|la|ta [*auch* baˈlaːta], die; - ⟨indian.-span.⟩ (kautschukähnliches Naturerzeugnis)
Ba̱|la|ton [*ung.* ˈbɔlɔtɔn], der; -[s] ⟨ung.⟩ (ung. Name für den Plattensee)
bal|bie̱|ren (*landsch. veraltet für* rasieren); jmdn. über den Löffel balbieren [*auch* barbieren] (*ugs. für* betrügen)
Bal|bo̱a, der; -[s], -[s] ⟨nach dem gleichnamigen span. Entdecker⟩ (Münzeinheit in Panama)
ba̱ld; *Steigerung* eher, am ehesten; möglichst bald; so bald wie (als) möglich
Ba̱l|da|chin [*österr. auch* ...ˈxiːn], der; -s, -e ⟨nach der Stadt Baldacco, d. h. Bagdad⟩ (Trag-, Betthimmel); **bal|da|chin|ar|tig**
Bä̱l|de; *nur in* in Bälde (*Amtsspr. für* bald); **ba̱l|dig; ba̱ld|mö̱g|lichst** (*dafür besser* möglichst bald)
bal|do̱|wern (*ugs. für* nachforschen)

Baldr, Bal|dur (*nord. Mythol.* Lichtgott)
Bald|ri|an (↑R 130), der; -s, -e (eine Heilpflanze); **Bald|ri|an₋tee, ...tink|tur, ...trop|fen** *(Plur.)*
Bal|du|in (m. Vorn.)
Bal|dung, Hans, *genannt* Grien (dt. Maler)
Bal|dur (m. Vorn.; *auch für* Baldr)
Ba|le|a|ren *Plur.* (Inselgruppe im westl. Mittelmeer)
Ba|les|ter, der; -s, - ‹lat.› *(früher für* Armbrust, mit der Kugeln abgeschossen werden können)
¹**Balg,** der; -[e]s, Bälge (Tierhaut; Luftsack; ausgestopfter Körper einer Puppe; *auch für* Balgen);
²**Balg** der *od.* das; -[e]s, Bälger *(ugs. für* unartiges Kind)
Bal|ge, die; -, -n *(nordd. für* Waschfass; Wasserlauf im Watt)
bal|gen, sich *(ugs. für* raufen); **Bal|gen,** der; -s, - (ausziehbares Verbindungsteil zwischen Objektiv u. Gehäuse beim Fotoapparat); **Bal|gen|ka|me|ra; Bal|ge|rei** *(ugs.)*; **Balg|ge|schwulst**
Ba|li (westlichste der Kleinen Sundainseln); **Ba|li|ne|se,** der; -n, -n (↑R 126); **ba|li|ne|sisch**
Bal|kan, der; -s (Gebirge; *auch für* Balkanhalbinsel); **Bal|kan|halb|in|sel** (↑R 105); **bal|ka|nisch; bal|ka|ni|sie|ren** (ein Land staatlich so zersplittern wie die Staaten der Balkanhalbinsel vor dem 1. Weltkrieg); **Bal|ka|ni|sie|rung,** die; -; **Bal|ka|nis|tik,** die; - *(svw.* Balkanologie); **Bal|kan|krieg; Bal|ka|no|lo|ge,** der; -n, -n; ↑R 126 (Wissenschaftler auf dem Gebiet der Balkanologie); **Bal|ka|no|lo|gie,** die; - (wissenschaftl. Erforschung der Balkansprachen u. -literaturen)
Bälk|chen; Bal|ken, der; -s, -; **Bal|ken₋de|cke, ...kon|struk|ti|on, ...kopf, ...schrö|ter** (Zwerghirschkäfer), **...waa|ge; Bal|kon** [bal'kɔŋ, *auch, südd., österr. u. schweiz. nur* ...'ko:n], der; -s, *Plur.* -s *u. (bei nicht nasalierter Ausspr.:)* -e ‹franz.›; **Bal|kon₋mö|bel, ...pflan|ze**
¹**Ball,** der; -[e]s, Bälle (kugelförmiges Spielzeug, Sportgerät); Ball spielen (↑R 39), *aber* das Ballspielen (↑R 50)
²**Ball,** der; -[e]s, Bälle ‹franz.› (Tanzfest); **Ball|abend** (↑R 132)
Ball|ab|ga|be *(Sportspr.)*
Bal|la|de, die; -, -n ‹griech.› (episch-dramatisches Gedicht); **bal|la|den|haft,** bal|la|desk; -e Erzählung; **Bal|la|den|stoff**
Ball|an|nah|me *(Sportspr.)*
Bal|last [*auch, österr. u. schweiz. nur* ba'last], der; -[e]s, -e *Plur. selten* (tote Last; Bürde); **Bal|last|stof|fe** *Plur.* (Nahrungsbestandteile, die der Körper nicht verwertet)
Bal|la|watsch *vgl.* Pallawatsch
Ball|be|hand|lung *(Sportspr.)*
Bäll|chen
Bal|lei ‹lat.› ([Ritter]ordensbezirk)
Bal|lei|sen, Bal|len|ei|sen (Werkzeug); **bal|len; Bal|len,** der; -s, -
Bal|len|stedt (Stadt am Harz)
Bal|le|rei *(ugs. für* sinnloses, lautes Schießen)
Bal|le|ri|na, *selten* **Bal|le|ri|ne,** die; -, ...nen ‹ital.› (Balletttänzerin)
Bal|ler|mann, der; -s, ...männer *(scherzh. für* Revolver); **bal|lern** *(ugs. für* knallen, schießen); ich ...ere (↑R 16)
Bal|le|ron, der; -s, -s ‹franz.› *(schweiz.* eine dicke Aufschnittwurst)
bal|les|tern; ↑R 16 *(österr. ugs. für* Fußball spielen)
Bal|lett, das; -[e]s, -e ‹ital.› (Bühnentanz[gruppe]; Ballettmusik); **Bal|let|teu|se** [...'tø:zə], die; -, -n Balletttänzerin); **Bal|lett₋korps** (Theatertanzgruppe), **...meis|ter, ...mu|sik; Bal|lett|tän|zer** (↑R 136); **Bal|lett|tän|ze|rin** (↑R 136); **Bal|lett|the|a|ter** (↑R 136); **Bal|lett|trup|pe** (↑R 136)
Ball₋füh|rung *(Sportspr.)*, **...ge|fühl** (das; -[e]s; *Sportspr.*)
ball|hor|ni|sie|ren *vgl.* verballhornen
bal|lig (ballförmig, gerundet); ballig drehen *(Mechanik)*
Bal|lis|te, die; -, -n ‹griech.› (antikes Wurfgeschütz); **Bal|lis|tik,** die; - (Lehre von der Bewegung geschleuderter od. geschossener Körper); **Bal|lis|ti|ker; bal|lis|tisch;** ballistische Kurve (Flugbahn); ballistisches Pendel (Stoßpendel)
Ball|jun|ge (Junge, der beim Tennis die Bälle aufsammelt)
Ball|kleid, Ball|lo|kal (↑R 136); **Ball|nacht**
Bal|lon [ba'lɔŋ, *auch, südd., österr. u. schweiz. nur,* ...'lo:n], der; -s, *Plur.* -s *u. (bei nicht nasalierter Ausspr.:)* -e ‹franz.› (mit Gas gefüllter Ball; Korbflasche; Glaskolben; Luftfahrzeug); **Bal|lo|nett** [balo'nɛt], das; -[e]s, *Plur.* -e *u.* -s (Luftkammer im Innern von Fesselballons und Luftschiffen); **Bal|lon₋fah|rer, ...kleid, ...müt|ze, ...rei|fen, ...sper|re; Bal|lot** [ba'lo:], das; -s, -s (kleiner Warenballen); **Bal|lo|ta|de** [balo'ta:də], die; -, -n (Sprung des Pferdes bei der hohen Schule); **Bal|lo|ta|ge** [...'ta:ʒə], die; -, -n [...'ta:ʒ(ə)n] (geheime Abstimmung mit weißen od. schwarzen Kugeln); **bal|lo|tie|ren**
Ball|spiel, Ball|spie|len, das; -s, *aber* (↑R 39): Ball spielen; **Ball|tech|nik** *(Sportspr.)*
Bal|lung; Bal|lungs₋ge|biet, ...raum
Ball|wech|sel *(Sportspr.)*
Bal|ly|hoo ['bɛlihu, *auch* ...'hu:], das; - ‹engl.› (Reklamerummel)
Bal|mung (Name von Siegfrieds Schwert)
Bal|ne|o|gra|phie, die; -, ...ien ‹griech.› (Bäderbeschreibung); **Bal|ne|o|lo|gie,** die; -; (Bäderkunde); **Bal|ne|o|the|ra|pie,** die; - (Heilung durch Bäder)
Bal pa|ré [bal pa're:], der; - -, -s -s [bal pa're:] ‹franz.› *(geh. veraltet für* festlicher Ball)
Bal|sa, das; - ‹span.› (sehr leichte Holzart); **Bal|sa|holz**
Bal|sam, der; -s, ...same *Plur. selten* ‹hebr.› (Gemisch von Harzen mit ätherischen Ölen, bes. als Linderungsmittel; *geh. auch für* Linderung, Labsal); **bal|sa|mie|ren** (einsalben); **Bal|sa|mie|rung; Bal|sa|mi|ne,** die; -, -n (eine Zierpflanze); **bal|sa|misch** (würzig; lindernd)
Bal|te, der; -n, -n; ↑R 126 (Angehöriger der balt. Sprachfamilie; [früherer deutscher] Bewohner des Baltikums); **Bal|ten|land**
Bal|tha|sar (m. Vorn.)
Bal|ti|kum, das; -s (das Gebiet der Staaten Estland, Lettland und Litauen)
Bal|ti|more ['baltimo:r] (Stadt in den USA)
bal|tisch, *aber* (↑R 102): der Baltische Höhenrücken; **bal|to|sla|wisch**
Ba|lu|ba, der; -[s], -[s]; *vgl.* Luba
Ba|lus|ter, der; -s, - ‹franz.› *(Archit.* kleine Säule als Geländerstütze); **Ba|lus|ter|säu|le; Ba|lust|ra|de** (↑R 130), die; -, -n (Brüstung, Geländer)
Balz, die; -, -en (Paarungsspiel und Paarungszeit bestimmter Vögel)
Bal|zac [bal'sak] (franz. Schriftsteller)
bal|zen (werben [von bestimmten Vögeln]); **Balz₋ruf, ...zeit**
BAM, die; - (= Baikal-Amur-Magistrale)
Ba|ma|ko [*auch* ba'mako] (Hptst. von Mali)
Bam|berg (Stadt an der Regnitz); **Bam|ber|ger** (↑R 103); - Reiter (bekanntes Standbild im Bamberger Dom); **bam|ber|gisch**
Bam|bi, der; -s, -s (Filmpreis);

Bam|bi|no, der; -s, *Plur.* ...ni, *ugs.* -s ⟨ital.⟩ (*ugs. für* kleines Kind, kleiner Junge)
Bam|bu|le, die; -, -n ⟨franz.⟩ (*Gaunerspr.* Krawall protestierender Häftlinge od. Heiminsassen)
Bam|bus, der; *Gen.* - *u.* ...busses, *Plur.* ...busse ⟨malai.⟩ (trop. baumartige Graspflanze); **Bam|bus‿hüt|te, ...rohr**
Ba|mi|go|reng, das; -[s], -s ⟨malai.⟩ (indones. Nudelgericht)
Bam|mel, der; -s (*ugs. für* Angst); **bam|meln** (*ugs. für* baumeln); ich bamm[e]le (↑R 16)
Bam|per|letsch, Pam|per|letsch, der; -[en], -[en] ⟨ital.⟩ (*österr. ugs. für* kleines Kind)
[1]**Ban,** der; -s, -e *u.* Ba|nus, der; -, - (früherer ung. u. kroat. Gebietsvorsteher)
[2]**Ban,** der; -[s], Bani ⟨rumän.⟩ (rumän. Münzeinheit); 50 - (↑R 90)
ba|nal ⟨franz.⟩ (alltäglich, fade, flach); **Ba|na|li|tät,** die; -, -en
Ba|na|ne, die; -, -n ⟨afrik.-port.⟩; **Ba|na|nen‿flan|ke** (*Fußball*), **...re|pub|lik** (*abwertend*), **...split** (das; -s, -s; Banane mit Eis u. Schlagsahne), **...ste|cker** (*Elektrotechnik*)
Ba|nat, das; -[e]s (Gebiet zwischen Donau, Theiß u. Maros); **Ba|na|ter** (↑R 103)
Ba|nau|se, der; -n, -n (↑R 126) ⟨griech.⟩ (unkultivierter Mensch; Spießbürger); **Ba|nau|sen|tum,** das; -s; **ba|nau|sisch**
[1]**Band,** der; -[e]s, Bände (Buch; *Abk. Sing.:* Bd., *Plur.:* Bde.); [2]**Band,** das; -[e]s, -e *meist Plur.* (*geh. für* Bindung; Fessel); außer Rand und Band; [3]**Band,** das; -[e]s, Bänder ([Gewebe]streifen; Gelenkband); auf Band spielen, sprechen; am laufenden Band
[4]**Band** [bɛnt], die; -, -s ⟨engl.⟩ (Gruppe von Musikern, bes. Tanzkapelle, Jazz- u. Rockband)
Ban|da|ge [...ˈda:ʒə, *österr.* ...ˈda:ʒ], die; -, -n [...ˈda:ʒ(ə)n] ⟨franz.⟩ (Stütz- od. Schutzverband); **ban|da|gie|ren** [...daˈʒi:...] (mit Bandagen versehen); **Ban|da|gist** [...daˈʒist], der; -en, -en; ↑R 126 (Hersteller von Bandagen u. Heilbinden)
Ban|dar Se|ri Be|ga|wan (Hptst. von Brunei)
Band|brei|te; Bänd|chen
[1]**Ban|de,** die; -, -n (Einfassung, z. B. Billardbande)
[2]**Ban|de,** die; -, -n ⟨franz.⟩ (organisierte Gruppe von Verbrechern; *abwertend od. scherzh. für* Gruppe von Jugendlichen)
Band|ei|sen; Ban|del, das; -s, - (*bayr., österr.*), **Bän|del,** der (*schweiz. nur so*) *od.* das; -s, - ([schmales] Band, Schnur)
Ban|den|spekt|rum (*Physik*)
Ban|den|wer|bung (Werbung auf der Einfassung von Spielflächen u. -feldern)
Ban|de|ril|la [...ˈrilja], die; -, -s ⟨span.⟩ (mit Bändern geschmückter Spieß, den der Banderillero dem Stier in den Nacken stößt); **Ban|de|ril|le|ro** [...riˈlje:ro], der; -s, -s (Stierkämpfer, der den Stier mit den Banderillas reizt)
bän|dern; ich ...ere (↑R 16)
Ban|de|ro|le, die; -, -n ⟨franz.⟩ (Verschlussband [mit Steuervermerk]); **Ban|de|ro|len|steu|er,** die (Verbrauchssteuer auf verpackte Konsumgüter); **ban|de|ro|lie|ren** (mit Banderole[n] versehen; versteuern)
Bän|der|riss, der; -es, -e (*Med.* Riss in den [3]Bändern); **Bän|der|ton,** der; -[e]s, ...tone (*Geol.*); **Bän|de|rung; Bän|der|zer|rung** (*Med.*); **Band‿för|de|rer, ...ge|ne|ra|tor, ...ge|schwin|dig|keit**
...bän|dig (z. B. vielbändig)
bän|di|gen; Bän|di|ger
Ban|dit [*auch* ...ˈdit], der; -en, -en (↑R 126) ⟨ital.⟩ ([Straßen]räuber); **Ban|di|ten|we|sen**
Band|ke|ra|mik, die; - (älteste steinzeitliche Kultur Mitteleuropas)
Band|lea|der [ˈbɛntli:də(r)], der; -s, - ⟨engl.⟩ (Leiter einer Jazz- od. Rockgruppe)
Band‿maß (das), **...nu|del** (*meist Plur.*)
Ban|do|ne|on, Ban|do|ni|on, das; -s, -s ⟨nach dem dt. Erfinder Band⟩ (ein Musikinstrument); **Ban|do|ne|o|nist,** der; -en, -en; ↑R 126 (Bandoneonspieler)
Band|sä|ge; Band|schei|be (*Med.*); **Band|schei|ben|scha|den** (*Med.*); **Bänd|sel,** das; -s, - (*Seemannsspr.* dünnes Tau)
Ban|dung (Stadt in Westjava); **Ban|dung|kon|fe|renz** (↑R 105)
Band|wurm; Band|wurm|be|fall
bang, ban|ge; banger *u.* bänger; am bangsten *u.* am bängsten (↑R 47); mir ist angst und bang[e] (↑R 46); *aber* (↑R 50): jemandem Angst und Bange machen; das Bangemachen; Bangemachen (*auch* Bange machen) gilt nicht
Ban|ga|le, Ben|ga|le, der; -n, -n; ↑R 126 (Einwohner von Bangladesch); **ban|ga|lisch,** ben|ga|lisch
Bang|büx *od.* **Bang|bü|xe** *od.* **Bang|bu|xe,** die; -, ...xen (*nordd. scherzh. für* Angsthase); **ban|ge** *vgl.* bang; **Ban|ge,** die; - (*landsch. für* Angst); *vgl.* bang; **ban|gen; Ban|gig|keit,** die; -
Bang|ka (eine Sundainsel)
Bang|kok (Hptst. von Thailand)
Bang|krank|heit, die; -n - (↑R 95) ⟨nach dem dän. Tierarzt B. Bang⟩ (auf Menschen übertragbare Rinderkrankheit)
Bang|la|desch, Bang|la|desh [...ˈdɛʃ] (Staat am Golf von Bengalen); **Bang|la|de|scher,** Bang|la|de|sher; **bang|la|de|schisch,** bang|la|de|shisch
bäng|lich; Bang|nis, die; -, -se
Ban|gui [bãˈgi:] (Hptst. der Zentralafrikanischen Republik)
Ba|ni (*Plur. von* [2]Ban)
Ban|jo [*auch* ˈbɛndʒo], das; -s, -s ⟨amerik.⟩ (ein Musikinstrument)
Ban|jul (Hptst. von Gambia)
[1]**Bank,** die; -, Bänke (Sitzgelegenheit); [2]**Bank,** die; -, -en ⟨ital. (-franz.)⟩ (Kreditanstalt)
Ban|ka *vgl.* Bangka
Bank‿ak|zept (ein auf eine [2]Bank gezogener Wechsel), **...au|to|mat**
Ban|ka|zinn ⟨*zu* Bangka⟩
Bank‿be|am|te, ...be|am|tin, ...buch; Bänk|chen; Bank|ei|sen (gelochtes Flacheisen an Tür- u. Fensterrahmen)
Bän|kel‿lied, ...sang, ...sän|ger; bän|kel|sän|ge|risch
Ban|ker [*auch* ˈbɛŋkər] ⟨engl.⟩ (*ugs. für* Bankier, Bankfachmann); **ban|ke|rott** usw. *vgl.* bankrott usw.
Ban|kert, der; -s, -e (*veraltend, abwertend für* uneheliches Kind)
[1]**Ban|kett,** das; -[e]s, -e ⟨ital.⟩ (Festmahl); [2]**Ban|kett,** das; -[e]s, -e, *auch* **Ban|ket|te,** die; -, -n ⟨franz.⟩ ([unfester] Randstreifen neben einer Straße)
Bank|fach, das; -s, *Plur.* (*nur für* Schließfach:) ...fächer (Spezialgebiet des Bankkaufmanns; Schließfach in einer [2]Bank); **bank|fä|hig;** -er Wechsel; **Bank‿fei|er|tag, ...ge|heim|nis, ...gut|ha|ben, ...hal|ter** (Spielleiter bei Glücksspielen); **Ban|ki|er** [baŋˈkie:], der; -s, -s ⟨franz.⟩ (Inhaber eines Bankhauses); **Bank‿kauf|frau, ...kauf|mann, ...kon|to; Bank|leit|zahl** (*Abk.* BLZ); **Bänk|ler** (*schweiz. svw.* Banker); **Bank‿no|te, ...raub, ...räu|ber**
bank|rott ⟨ital.⟩ (zahlungsunfähig; *auch übertr. für* am Ende, erledigt); bankrott sein, werden; **Bank|rott,** der; -[e]s, -e; Bankrott machen; Bankrott gehen (↑R 39); **Bank|rott|er|klä|rung; Bank|rot|teur** [...ˈtø:r], der; -s, -e (Person, die Bankrott macht); **bank|rot|tie|ren**

Bank‿über|fall (↑R 132), **...ver|bin|dung, ...we|sen** (das; -s)
Bann, der; -[e]s, -e (Ausschluss [aus einer Gemeinschaft]; *geh. für* beherrschender Einfluss, magische Wirkung); **Bann‿bruch** (der; *Rechtsw.*), **...bul|le** (die; *kath. Kirche*); **ban|nen**
Ban|ner, das; -s, - (Fahne); **Ban|ner|trä|ger**
Bann‿fluch (im MA.), **...gut** *(Rechtsw.)*
ban|nig (*nordd. ugs. für* sehr)
Bann‿kreis, ...mei|le, ...strahl, ...wald (Schutzwald gegen Lawinen), **...wa|re, ...wart** (*schweiz. für* Flur- und Waldhüter)
Ban|se, die; -, -n, *auch* der, -s, -e (*mitteld. u. nordd. für* Lagerraum in einer Scheune); **ban|sen,** *auch* ban|seln; Getreide, Holz - (*mitteld. u. nordd. für* aufladen, aufschichten); du banst
Ban|sin, See|bad (auf Usedom)
Ban|tam (Ort auf Java); **Ban|tam|ge|wicht** (Körpergewichtsklasse in der Schwerathletik); **Ban|tam|huhn** (Zwerghuhn)
Ban|tu, der; -[s], -[s] (Angehöriger einer Sprach- u. Völkergruppe in Afrika); **Ban|tu|spra|che**
Ba|nus *vgl.* [1]Ban
Ba|o|bab, der; -s, -s ‹afrik.› (Affenbrotbaum)
Ba|pho|met, der; -[e]s ‹arab.› ([angebl.] Götzenbild der Tempelherren)
Bap|tis|mus, der; - ‹griech.› (Lehre evangel. Freikirchen, die nur die Erwachsenentaufe zulässt); **[1]Bap|tist** (m. Vorn.); **[2]Bap|tist,** der; -en, -en; ↑R 126 (Anhänger des Baptismus); **Bap|tis|te|ri|um,** das; -s, ...ien [...iən] (Taufbecken; Taufkirche, -kapelle)
[1]bar = [1]Bar
[2]bar (bloß); aller Ehre[n] bar; bares Geld, *aber* Bargeld; bar zahlen; in bar; gegen bar; barer Unsinn
...bar (z. B. lesbar, offenbar)
[1]Bar, das; -s, -s ‹griech.› (veraltende Maßeinheit des [Luft]druckes; *Zeichen* bar; *Meteor. nur* b); 5 -
[2]Bar, die; -, -s ‹engl.› (kleines [Nacht]lokal; Schanktisch)
[3]Bar, der; -[e]s, -e (ein Meistersingerlied)
[1]Bär, der; -en, -en ↑R 126; (ein Raubtier); (↑R 108:) der Große, der Kleine - (Sternbilder); **[2]Bär,** der; -s, *Plur.* -en, *fachspr.* -e (Maschinenhammer); *vgl.* Rammbär
Ba|rab|bas (bibl. Gestalt)
Ba|ra|ber, der; -s, - ‹ital.› (*österr. ugs. für* Bauarbeiter); **ba|ra|bern** (*österr. ugs. für* schwer arbeiten)
Ba|ra|cke, die; -, -n ‹franz.› (leichtes, meist eingeschossiges Behelfshaus); **Ba|ra|cken|la|ger,** das; -s, -; **Ba|rack|ler** (*ugs. für* Barackenbewohner)
Ba|ratt, der; -[e]s ‹ital.› (*Kaufmannsspr.* Austausch von Waren); **ba|rat|tie|ren**
Bar|ba|di|er [...iər] (Bewohner von Barbados); **bar|ba|disch; Bar|ba|dos** (Inselstaat im Osten der Kleinen Antillen)
Bar|bar, der; -en, -en (↑R 126) ‹griech.› (*urspr.* Nichtgrieche; *jetzt* roher, ungesitteter, wilder Mensch); **Bar|ba|ra** (w. Vorn.); **Bar|ba|ra|zweig; Bar|ba|rei** (Rohheit); **bar|ba|risch** (roh); **Bar|ba|ris|mus,** der; -, ...men (grober sprachlicher Fehler)
Bar|ba|ros|sa ‹„Rotbart"› (Beiname des Kaisers Friedrich I.)
Bar|be, die; -, -n ‹lat.› (ein Karpfenfisch; *früher* Spitzenband an Frauenhauben)
Bar|be|cue ['ba:(r)bikju:], das; -[s], -s ‹engl.› (Gartenfest mit Spießbraten)
bär|bei|ßig (grimmig; verdrießlich); **Bär|bei|ßig|keit,** die; -
Bär|bel (w. Vorn.)
Bar|bier, der; -s, -e ‹franz.› (*veraltet für* Herrenfriseur); **bar|bie|ren** (*veraltet für* rasieren); *vgl. auch* balbieren
Bar|bi|tu|rat, das; -s, -e ‹Kunstw.› (*Pharm.* Schlaf- u. Beruhigungsmittel); **Bar|bi|tur|säu|re** (chem. Substanz mit narkotischer Wirkung)
bar|bu|sig (busenfrei)
Bar|ce|lo|na [...ts..., *span.* ...θ...] (Hptst. Kataloniens)
Bar|chent, der; -s, -e ‹arab.› (Baumwollflanell)
Bar|da|me
[1]Bar|de, die; -, -n ‹arab.-franz.› (Speckscheibe auf gebratenem magerem Fleisch)
[2]Bar|de, der; -n, -n (↑R 126) ‹kelt.-franz.› ([altkelt.] Sänger u. Dichter; *abwertend für* lyr. Dichter)
bar|die|ren (mit [1]Barden umwickeln)
Bar|diet, das; -[e]s, -e ‹germ.-lat.› *u.* Bar|di|tus, der; -, - (Schlachtgeschrei der Germanen vor dem Kampf); **bar|disch** ‹*zu* [2]Barde›; **Bar|di|tus** *vgl.* Bardiet
Bar|do|wick [...'vi:k, *auch* 'bar...] (Ort in Niedersachsen)
Bä|ren‿dienst (*ugs. für* schlechter Dienst), **...dreck** (*südd., österr. ugs. für* Lakritze), **...fang** (der; -[e]s; Honiglikör), **...fell, ...haut, ...hun|ger** (*ugs. für* großer Hunger); **Bä|ren|klau,** die; - *od.* der; -s (ein Doldengewächs); **bä|ren|mä|ßig; Bä|ren|na|tur** (bes. kräftiger, körperlich unempfindlicher Mensch); **bä|ren|ru|hig** (*ugs. für* sehr ruhig); **bä|ren|stark** (*ugs. für* sehr stark; *auch für* hervorragend); **Bä|ren|trau|be** (eine Heilpflanze); **Bä|ren|trau|ben|blät|ter|tee**
Ba|rents|see, die; - ‹nach dem niederl. Seefahrer W. Barents› (Teil des Nordpolarmeeres)
Bä|ren|zu|cker (*österr. neben* Bärendreck)
Ba|rett, das; -[e]s, *Plur.* -e, *selten* -s ‹lat.› (flache, randlose Kopfbedeckung, auch als Teil einer Amtstracht)
Bar|frei|ma|chung *(Postw.)*
Bar|frost (*landsch. für* Frost ohne Schnee)
bar|fuß; - gehen; **Bar|fuß|arzt** ([in der Volksrepublik China] jmd., der medizin. Grundkenntnisse hat und auf dem Land einfachere Krankheiten behandelt); **Bar|fü|ßer,** der; -s, - (*kath. Kirche* Angehöriger eines Ordens, dessen Mitglieder ursprünglich barfuß gingen); **bar|fü|ßig; Bar|füß|ler** (*svw.* Barfüßer)
Bar|geld, das; -[e]s; **bar|geld|los;** -er Zahlungsverkehr; **Bar|ge|schäft**
bar|haupt *(geh.)*; **bar|häup|tig** *(geh.)*
Bar|ho|cker
Ba|ri (Stadt in Apulien)
Ba|ri|bal, der; -s, -s (nordamerik. Schwarzbär)
bä|rig (*landsch. für* bärenhaft, stark; *ugs. für* gewaltig, toll)
ba|risch ‹griech.› (*Meteor.* den Luftdruck betreffend)
Ba|ri|ton ['ba(:)ritɔn], der; -s, -e [...to:nə] ‹ital.› (Männerstimme zwischen Tenor u. Bass; *auch* Sänger mit dieser Stimme); **ba|ri|to|nal; Ba|ri|to|nist,** der; -en, -en; ↑R 126 (Baritonsänger)
Ba|ri|um, das; -s ‹griech.› (chem. Element, Metall; *Zeichen* Ba)
Bark, die; -, -en ‹niederl.› (ein Segelschiff); **Bar|ka|ro|le,** die; -, -n ‹ital.› (Gondellied); **Bar|kas|se,** die; -, -n ‹niederl.› (Motorboot; größtes Beiboot auf Kriegsschiffen)
Bar|kauf
Bar|ke, die; -, -n (kleines Boot)
Bar|kee|per [...ki:pə(r)], der; -s, - ‹engl.› (Inhaber od. Schankkellner einer [2]Bar)
Bar|lach (dt. Bildhauer, Grafiker u. Dichter)
Bär|lapp, der; -s, -e (moosähnliche Sporenpflanze)

Bar|mann, der; -[e]s, ...männer (*svw.* Barkeeper)
Barm|bek (Stadtteil von Hamburg)
Bär|me, die; - (*nordd. für* Hefe)
bar|men (*nord- u. ostd. abwertend für* klagen, jammern)
Bar|men (Stadtteil von Wuppertal); **Bar|mer** (↑R 103)
barm|her|zig (*geh.*) ein barmherziger Mensch, *aber* (↑R 108): Barmherzige Brüder, Barmherzige Schwestern (religiöse Genossenschaften für Krankenpflege); **Barm|her|zig|keit**, die; - (*geh.*)
Bar|mi|xer (Getränkemischer in einer [2]Bar)
Bar|na|bas (ein urchristl. Missionar); **Bar|na|bit**, der; -en, -en; ↑R 126 (Angehöriger eines kath. Männerordens)
Bar|nim, der; -s (Landsch. nordöstl. von Berlin)
ba|rock ‹franz.› (im Stil des Barocks; verschnörkelt, überladen); **Ba|rock**, das *od.* der; *Gen.* -s, *fachspr. auch* - ([Kunst]stil des 17. u. 18. Jh.s); **Ba|rock₋bau** (*Plur.* ...bauten), **...kir|che**, **...kunst**, **...per|le** (unregelmäßig geformte Perle), **...stil** (der; -[e]s), **...zeit** (die; -)
Ba|ro|graph, der; -en, -en (↑R 126) ‹griech.› (*Meteor.* Gerät zur Registrierung des Luftdrucks); **Ba|ro|me|ter**, das, *österr. u. schweiz. auch* der; -s, - (Luftdruckmesser); **Ba|ro|me|ter|stand; ba|ro|me|trisch;** -e Höhenformel (*Physik*)
Ba|ron, der; -s, -e ‹franz.› (*svw.* Freiherr); **Ba|ro|ness**, die; -, -en, *häufiger* **Ba|ro|nes|se**, die; -, -n (*svw.* Freifräulein); **Ba|ro|net** ['ba... *od.* 'bɛronɛt, *engl.* 'bɛrənit], der; -s, -s ‹engl.› (engl. Adelstitel); **Ba|ro|nie**, die; -, ...ien ‹franz.› (Besitz eines Barons; Freiherrnwürde); **Ba|ro|nin** (*svw.* Freifrau); **ba|ro|ni|sie|ren** (in den Freiherrnstand erheben)
Bar|ra|ku|da, der; -s, -s ‹span.› (Pfeilhecht, ein Raubfisch)
Bar|ras, der; - (*Soldatenspr.* Heerwesen; Militär)
Bar|re, die; -, -n ‹franz.› (*Bauw.* Schranke aus waagerechten Stangen; *Geol.* Sand-, Schlammbank)
Bar|rel ['bɛrəl], das; -s, -s ‹engl., „Fass, Tonne"› (in Großbritannien u. in den USA verwendetes Hohlmaß unterschiedl. Größe); drei Barrel[s] Weizen (↑R 90)
bar|ren (*Pferdesport* [ein Springpferd] durch Schlagen mit einer Stange an die Beine dazu bringen, einen Abwurf zu vermeiden);
[1]**Bar|ren**, das; -s ‹*zu* barren›;
[2]**Bar|ren**, der; -s, - (Turngerät; Handelsform der Edelmetalle; *südd., österr. auch für* Futtertrog)
Bar|ri|e|re, die; -, -n ‹franz.› (Schranke; Sperre); **Bar|ri|ka|de** ([Straßen]sperre, Hindernis)
Bar|ris|ter ['bɛristə(r)], der; -s, - ‹engl.› (Rechtsanwalt bei den englischen Obergerichten)
barsch (unfreundlich, rau)
Barsch, der; -[e]s, -e (ein Raubfisch)
Bar|schaft; Bar|scheck (in bar einzulösender Scheck)
Barsch|heit
Bar|soi [...'zɔy], der; -s, -s ‹russ.› (russ. Windhund)
Bar|sor|ti|ment (Buchhandelsbetrieb zwischen Verlag u. Einzelbuchhandel)
Bart, der; -[e]s, Bärte; **Bärt|chen; Bar|te**, die; -, -n (Hornplatte im Oberkiefer der Bartenwale, Fischbein); **Bar|tel**, die; -, -n *meist Plur.* (bartähnliche Hautanhänge am Maul von Fischen); **Bar|ten|wal; Bar|terl**, das; -s, -n (*bayr. u. österr. für* Kinderlätzchen); **Bart₋flech|te, ...haar**
Bar|thel, Bar|tho|lo|mä|us (m. Vorn.)
Bär|tier|chen (mikroskopisch kleines, wurmförmiges Tier)
bär|tig; Bär|tig|keit, die; -; **bart|los; Bart|lo|sig|keit**, die; -
Bar|tók ['bartɔk], Béla ['be:la] (ung. Komponist)
Bart₋stop|pel, ...trä|ger, ...wisch (*bayr., österr. für* Handbesen; *vgl.* Borstwisch), **...wuchs**
Ba|ruch (Gestalt im A.T.)
ba|ry... ‹griech.› (schwer...); **Ba|ry...** (Schwer...); **Ba|ry|on**, das; -s, ...onen (*Kernphysik* schweres Elementarteilchen); **Ba|ry|sphä|re**, die; - (*Geol.* Erdkern); **Ba|ryt** [*auch* ...'ryt], der; -[e]s, -e (Schwerspat; chem. Bariumsulfat); **Ba|ry|ton**, das; -s, -e (gambenähnliches Saiteninstrument); **Ba|ryt|pa|pier** [*auch* ba'ryt...] (mit Baryt beschichtetes Papier); **ba|ry|zen|trisch** (auf das Baryzentrum bezüglich); **Ba|ry|zen|trum**, das; -s, *Plur.* ...tra *u.* ...tren (*Physik* Schwerpunkt)
Bar|zah|lung
ba|sal (die Basis betreffend)
Ba|salt, der; -[e]s, -e ‹griech.› (vulkan. Gestein)
Ba|sal|tem|pe|ra|tur (*Med.* morgens gemessene Körpertemperatur bei der Frau zur Feststellung des Eisprungs)
ba|sal|ten, ba|sal|tig, ba|sal|tisch; Ba|salt|tuff, der; -s, -e
Ba|sar, der; -s, -e ‹pers.› (orientalisches Händlerviertel; Verkauf von Waren für wohltätige Zwecke)
Bäs|chen
Basch|ki|re, der; -n, -n; ↑R 126 (Angehöriger eines turkotat. Stammes); **Basch|ki|ri|en** [...iən]; **basch|ki|risch**
Basch|lik, der; -s, -s ‹turkotat.› (kaukas. Wollkapuze)
[1]**Ba|se**, die; -, -n (*veraltet, noch südd. für* Kusine)
[2]**Ba|se**, die; -, -n ‹griech.› (*Chemie* Verbindung, die mit Säuren Salze bildet); *vgl.* Basis
Base|ball ['be:sbɔ:l], der; -s ‹engl.› (amerik. Schlagballspiel)
Ba|se|dow [...do:], der; -s (*kurz für* Basedowkrankheit); **Ba|se|dow|krank|heit**, die; - ‹nach dem Arzt K. v. Basedow› (auf vermehrter Tätigkeit der Schilddrüse beruhende Krankheit)
Ba|sel (schweiz. Stadt am Rhein); **Ba|sel|biet**, das; -s (*svw.* Basel-land); **Ba|sel|bie|ter** (↑R 103); **Ba|se|ler**, Bas|ler (*schweiz. nur so;* ↑R 103); Baseler Friede; **Ba|sel-Land|schaft**, *kurz auch* **Ba|sel|land** (schweiz. Halbkanton); **ba|sel-land|schaft|lich** (↑R 105); **Ba|sel-Stadt** (schweiz. Halbkanton); **ba|sel-städ|tisch** (↑R 105)
Ba|sen (*Plur. von* Base, Basis)
BASIC ['be:sik], das; -[s] ‹engl.› (*Kunstwort aus* beginner's all purpose symbolic instruction code; eine einfache Programmiersprache)
Ba|sic Eng|lish ['be:sik 'iŋliʃ], das; - (Grundenglisch; vereinfachte Form des Englischen)
ba|sie|ren ‹franz.›; etwas basiert auf der Tatsache (beruht auf der, gründet sich auf die Tatsache)
Ba|si|li|a|ner (nach der Regel des hl. Basilius [4. Jh.] lebender Mönch)
Ba|si|li|en|kraut [...iən...], *häufiger* Ba|si|li|kum, das; -s, *Plur.* -s *u.* ...ken ‹griech.-lat.› (eine Gewürzpflanze)
Ba|si|li|ka, die; -, ...ken ‹griech.› (altröm. Markt- od. Gerichtshalle; Kirchenbauform mit überhöhtem Mittelschiff); **ba|si|li|kal; ba|si|li|ken|för|mig**
Ba|si|li|kum *vgl.* Basilienkraut
Ba|si|lisk, der; -en, -en (↑R 126) ‹griech.› (Fabeltier; trop. Echse); **Ba|si|lis|ken|blick** (böser, stechender Blick)
Ba|si|li|us (griech. Kirchenlehrer)
Ba|sis, die; -, Basen ‹griech.› (Grundlage; *Math.* Grundlinie,

-fläche; Grundzahl; *Archit.* Fuß[punkt]; Sockel; Unterbau; Stütz-, Ausgangspunkt; *Politik* Masse des Volkes, der Parteimitglieder o. Ä.); **ba|sisch** (*Chemie* sich wie eine Base verhaltend); basische Farbstoffe, Salze; basischer Stahl; **Ba|sis‿de|mo|kra|tie, ...grup|pe** ([links orientierter] politisch aktiver [Studenten]arbeitskreis); **Ba|sis|kurs** *(Börsenw.)*; **Ba|si|zi|tät,** die; - *(Chemie)*

Bas|ke, der; -n, -n; ↑R 126 (Angehöriger eines Pyrenäenvolkes); **Bas|ken‿land** (das; -[e]s), **...müt|ze**

Bas|ket|ball ⟨engl.⟩

bas|kisch; die -e Sprache, Literatur; *vgl.* deutsch; **Bas|kisch,** das; -[s] (Sprache); *vgl.* Deutsch; **Bas|ki|sche,** das; -n; *vgl.* Deutsche, das

Bas|kü|le, die; -, -n ⟨franz.⟩ (Riegelverschluss für Fenster u. Türen, der zugleich oben u. unten schließt); **Bas|kü|le|ver|schluss**

Bas|ler, *schweiz. nur so,* Ba|se|ler (↑R 103); Basler Leckerli; **bas|le|risch**

Bas|re|li|ef [ˈbare.liɛf] ⟨franz.⟩ (*bild. Kunst* Flachrelief)

bass (*veraltet, noch scherzh. für* sehr); er war bass erstaunt

Bass, der; -es, Bässe ⟨ital.⟩ (tiefe Männerstimme; Sänger; Streichinstrument); **Bass‿arie** (↑R 132), **...ba|ri|ton, ...blä|ser, ...buf|fo**

Bas|se, der; -n, -n; ↑R 126 (*Jägerspr.* [älterer] starker Keiler)

Bas|se|na, die; -, -s ⟨ital.⟩ (*ostösterr. für* Wasserbecken für mehrere Mieter im Flur eines Altbaus)

Bas|set [*franz.* baˈsɛ, *engl.* ˈbɛsit], der; -s, -s (eine Hunderasse)

Basse|terre [basˈtɛ:r] (Hptst. von St. Kitts und Nevis)

Bas|sett|horn *Plur.* ...hörner (Blasinstrument des 18. Jh.s); **Bass|gei|ge**

Bas|sin [baˈsɛŋ *od.* baˈsɛ̃:], das; -s, -s ⟨franz.⟩ (künstliches Wasserbecken)

Bas|sist, der; -en, -en (↑R 126) ⟨ital.⟩ (Basssänger); **Bas|so,** der; -, Bassi *(Musik)*; - con|ti|nuo (Generalbass); - osti|na|to (sich oft wiederholendes Bassthema); **Bass‿sän|ger** (↑R 136), **...schlüs|sel, ...stim|me**

Bast, der; -[e]s, -e (Pflanzenfaser; *Jägerspr.* Haut am Geweih)

bas|ta ⟨ital.⟩ (*ugs. für* genug!); [und] damit basta!

Bas|tard, der; -[e]s, -e ⟨franz.⟩ (*Biol.* Pflanze od. Tier als Ergebnis von Kreuzungen; *veraltend für* uneheliches Kind); **bas|tar|die|ren** (*Biol.* Arten kreuzen); **Bas|tar|die|rung; Bas|tard‿pflan|ze, ...schrift** (Druckschrift, die die Merkmale zweier Schriftarten vermischt)

Bas|te, die; -, -n ⟨franz.⟩ (Trumpfkarte in einigen Kartenspielen)

Bas|tei ⟨ital.⟩ (vorspringender Teil an alten Festungsbauten; *nur Sing.:* Felsgruppe im Elbsandsteingebirge)

Bas|tel|ar|beit; bas|teln; ich ...[e]le (↑R 16)

bas|ten (aus Bast); **bast|far|ben, bast|far|big**

Bas|ti|an (m. Vorn.)

Bas|til|le [basˈti:jə], die; -, -n ⟨franz.⟩ (befestigtes Schloss, bes. das 1789 erstürmte Staatsgefängnis in Paris); **Bas|ti|on,** die; -, -en (Bollwerk)

Bast|ler; Bast|le|rin

Bas|to|na|de, die; -, -n ⟨franz.⟩ (Prügelstrafe, bes. Schläge auf die Fußsohlen)

Ba|su|to, der; -[s], -[s] (Angehöriger eines Bantustammes)

BAT = Bundesangestelltentarif

Bat. = Bataillon

Ba|tail|le [baˈtaljə *od.* baˈta:jə], die; -, -n ⟨franz.⟩ (*veraltet für* Schlacht; Kampf); **Ba|tail|lon** [bataˈljo:n], das; -s, -e (Truppenabteilung; *Abk.* Bat., Btl.); **Ba|tail|lons|kom|man|deur**

Ba|ta|te, die; -, -n ⟨indian.-span.⟩ (trop. Süßkartoffel[pflanze])

Ba|ta|ver [...v...], der; -s, - (Angehöriger eines germ. Stammes); **Ba|ta|via** (*alter Name von* Jakarta); **ba|ta|visch**

Bath|se|ba, *ökum.* Bat|se|ba (bibl. w. Eigenn.)

Ba|thy|scaphe [...ˈska:f], der *u.* das; -[s], - [...fə] ⟨griech.⟩ *u.* **Ba|thy|skaph** [...ˈska:f], der; -en, -en; ↑R 126 (Tiefseetauchgerät); **Ba|thy|sphä|re,** die; - (*Geol.* tiefste Schicht des Weltmeeres)

Ba|tik, der; -s, -en, *auch* die; -, -en ⟨malai.⟩ (aus Südostasien stammendes Textilfärbeverfahren unter Verwendung von Wachs *[nur Sing.]*; derart gemustertes Gewebe); **Ba|tik|druck** *Plur.* ...drucke; **ba|ti|ken;** gebatikt

Ba|tist, der; -[e]s, -e ⟨franz.⟩ (feines Gewebe); **ba|tis|ten** (aus Batist)

Bat|se|ba *vgl.* Bathseba

Batt., Battr. = Batterie (Militär)

Bat|te|rie, die; -, ...ien ⟨franz.⟩ (*Milit.* Einheit der Artillerie [*Abk.* Batt(r).]; *Technik* [aus mehreren Elementen bestehender] Stromspeicher); **bat|te|rie|be|trie|ben; Bat|te|rie|ge|rät**

Battr. *vgl.* Batt.

Bat|zen, der; -s, - (*ugs. für* Klumpen; frühere Münze; *schweiz. mdal. veraltend für* Zehnrappenstück)

Bau, der; -[e]s, -ten (Gebäude) *u.* der; -[e]s, -e (Höhle als Unterschlupf für Tiere; *Bergmannsspr.* Stollen); sich im *od.* in - befinden; **Bau‿ab|schnitt, ...ar|bei|ter, ...art, ...auf|sicht** (die; -); **Bau|auf|sichts|be|hör|de; Bau|bi|o|lo|gie** (Lehre von der Beziehung zwischen dem Menschen und seiner Wohnumwelt), **Bau|block** *Plur.* ...blocks *od.* ...blöcke

Bauch, der; -[e]s, Bäuche; **Bauch‿an|satz, ...bin|de, ...de|cke, ...fell, ...fleisch, ...grim|men** (*veraltend für* Bauchschmerzen), **...höh|le; bau|chig, bäu|chig; Bauch‿knei|fen, ...knei|pen** (das; -s; *landsch. für* Bauchschmerzen), **...la|den, ...lan|dung; Bäuch|lein; bäuch|lings; Bauch‿mus|ku|la|tur, ...na|bel; bauch|re|den** *meist nur im Infinitiv gebr.*; **Bauch‿red|ner, ...schmerz** *(meist Plur.)*, **...spei|chel|drü|se, ...tanz; bauch|tan|zen** *meist nur im Infinitiv gebr.*; **Bau|chung; Bauch|weh,** das; -s (*ugs. für* Bauchschmerzen)

Bau|cis [...tsis] (Frau des Philemon; *vgl. d.*)

Baud [*auch* bo:t], das; -[s], - ⟨nach dem franz. Ingenieur Baudot⟩ (Maßeinheit der Telegrafiergeschwindigkeit)

Bau|de, die; -, -n (*ostmitteld. für* Unterkunftshütte im Gebirge)

Bau|de|laire [bod(ə)ˈlɛ:r] (franz. Dichter)

Bau|denk|mal, das; -[e]s, *Plur.* ...mäler, *geh. auch* ...male

Bau|dou|in [boˈduɛ̃:] (m. Vorn.)

Bau|ele|ment (↑R 132); **bau|en; Bau|ent|wurf**

[1]**Bau|er,** der; -s, - (Be-, Erbauer)

[2]**Bau|er,** der; *Gen.* -n, *selten* -s, *Plur.* -n (Landwirt; eine Schachfigur; eine Spielkarte)

[3]**Bau|er,** das, *auch* der; -s, - (Vogelkäfig)

Bäu|er|chen; [ein] - machen (*ugs. für* aufstoßen); **Bäu|e|rin; bäu|e|risch** (*seltener für* bäurisch); **bäu|er|lich; Bau|ern‿brot, ...bur|sche, ...fän|ger** *(abwertend)*; **Bau|ern|fän|ge|rei** *(abwertend)*; **Bau|ern‿früh|stück** (Bratkartoffeln mit Rührei und Speck), **...gut, ...haus, ...hof, ...krieg, ...le|gen** (das; -s; Einziehen von Bauernhöfen durch den Großgrundbesitzer vom 16. bis zum 18. Jh.); **Bau|er[n]|sa|me**, die; - (*schweiz. svw.* Bauernschaft); **Bau|ern|schaft**, die; - (Gesamtheit der Bauern); **bau|ern|schlau; Bau|ern-schläue, ...stand** (der; -[e]s), **...ster|ben** (das; -s), **...stu|be; Bau|er|sa|me** *vgl.* Bauernsame; **Bau|er|schaft** (*landsch. für* Bauernsiedlung); **Bau|ers|frau** (*svw.* Bäuerin); **Bau|ers-leu|te** *(Plur.)*, **...mann** (der; -[e]s; *veraltet*); **Bäu|ert**, die; -, -en (*schweiz. [Berner Oberland] für* Gemeindefraktion)

Bau|er|war|tungs|land, das; -[e]s (zum Bauen vorgesehenes Land); **bau|fäl|lig; Bau|fäl|lig|keit**, die; -; **Bau-fir|ma, ...flucht** (*vgl.* [1]Flucht), **...füh|rer, ...ge|neh|mi|gung, ...ge|nos|sen|schaft, ...ge|spann** (*schweiz. für* Stangen, die die Ausmaße eines geplanten Gebäudes anzeigen), **...ge|wer|be, ...gru|be**

Bau|haus, das; -es (dt. Hochschule für Gestaltung, an der bekannte Maler und Architekten der zwanziger Jahre arbeiteten)

Bau|herr; Bau|her|ren|mo|dell (Finanzierungsmodell für Bauobjekte, bei dem bestimmte Steuervorteile erzielt werden können); **Bau-her|rin, ...holz, ...hüt|te, ...jahr, ...kas|ten; Bau|kas|ten|sys|tem** *(Technik);* **Bau|klotz**, der; -es, *Plur.* ...klötze, *ugs. auch* ...klötzer; Bauklötze[r] staunen *(ugs.);* **Bau|kos|ten** *Plur.;* **Bau|kos|ten|zu|schuss; Bau-kunst** (die; -), **...land** (das; -[e]s; *auch* eine bad. Landschaft); **bau|lich; Bau|lich|keit** *meist Plur. (Amtsspr.);* **Bau|lü|cke**

Baum, der; -[e]s, Bäume

Bau-ma|schi|ne, ...ma|te|ri|al

Baum|blü|te, die; -; **Bäum|chen**

Bau|mé|grad [bo'me:...] ‹nach dem franz. Chemiker Baumé› (alte Maßeinheit für das spezifische Gewicht von Flüssigkeiten; ↑R 95; *Zeichen* °Bé); 5 °Bé

Bau|meis|ter

bau|meln; ich ...[e]le (↑R 16)

[1]**bau|men** *vgl.* aufbaumen; [2]**bau|men**, [1]**bäu|men** (mit dem Wiesbaum befestigen); [2]**bäu|men;** sich -; **Baum-farn, ...gren|ze** *(Plur. selten);* **baum|kan|tig** ([von Holzbalken] an den Kanten noch die Rinde zeigend); **Baum|ku|chen; baum|lang; Baum|läu|fer** (ein Vogel); **Baum|nuss** (*schweiz. für* Walnuss); **baum|reich; Baum-sche|re, ...schu|le, ...stamm; baum|stark; Baum-strunk, ...stumpf, ...wip|fel, ...wol|le; baum|wol|len; Baum|woll-garn, ...hemd, ...in|dust|rie, ...pi|kee** (der), **...spin|ne|rei**

Baun|zerl, das; -s, -n (*österr. für* längliches Milchbrötchen)

Bau-ord|nung, ...plan (*vgl.* [2]Plan), **...platz, ...po|li|zei; bau|po|li|zei|lich; Bau-rat** (*Plur.* ...räte), **...recht; bau|reif;** ein baureifes Grundstück; **Bau|rei|he**

bäu|risch, *seltener* bäu|e|risch

Bau-ru|i|ne, ...satz

Bausch, der; -[e]s, *Plur.* -e *u.* Bäusche; in Bausch und Bogen (ganz und gar)

Bäu|schel, Päu|schel, der *od.* das; -s, - (*Bergmannsspr.* schwerer Hammer)

bau|schen; du bauschst; sich -; **Bau|schen**, der; -s, - (*österr. neben* Bausch); **bau|schig**

bau|spa|ren *fast nur im Infinitiv gebräuchlich;* bauzusparen; **Bau-spa|rer, ...spar|kas|se, ...spar|ver|trag, ...stein, ...stel|le, ...stil, ...stoff, ...stopp, ...sub|stanz**

Bau|ta|stein ‹altnord.› (Gedenkstein der Wikingerzeit in Skandinavien)

Bau|te, die; -, -n (*schweiz. Amtsspr. für* Bau[werk], Gebäude); **Bau|teil**, der (Gebäudeteil) *od.* das (Bauelement); **Bau|ten** *vgl.* Bau; **Bau|trä|ger**

Baut|zen (Stadt in der Oberlausitz); **Baut|ze|ner** (↑R 103); **bautz|nisch**

Bau-un|ter|neh|mer, ...vor|ha|ben, ...wei|se (*vgl.* [2]Weise), **...werk, ...wer|ker, ...we|sen** (das; -s); **Bau|wich**, der; -[e]s, -e (*Bauw.* Häuserzwischenraum); **bau|wür|dig** (*Bergmannsspr.* abbauwürdig)

Bau|xerl, das; -s, -n (*österr. ugs. für* kleines, herziges Kind)

Bau|xit [*auch* ...'ksit], der; -s, -e ‹nach dem ersten Fundort Les Baux in Südfrankreich› (ein Aluminiummineral)

bauz!

Bau|zaun

Ba|va|ria [...v...], die; - ‹lat.› (Frauengestalt als Sinnbild Bayerns)

Bay|er, der; -n, -n (↑R 126); *vgl.* Baier; **bay|e|risch**, bay|risch, *aber* (↑R 102): der Bayerische Wald; *vgl.* bairisch; **Bay|er|land**, das; -[e]s; **Bay|ern**

Bay|reuth (Stadt am Roten Main)

bay|risch *vgl.* bayerisch

Ba|zar [ba'za:r] *vgl.* Basar

Ba|zi, der; -, - (*bayr., österr. ugs. für* Gauner, Taugenichts)

Ba|zil|len|trä|ger ‹lat.; dt.›; **Ba|zil|lus**, der; -, ...llen ‹lat.› (*Biol., Med.* Sporen bildender Spaltpilz)

BBC [*engl.* bibi'si:], die; - (= British Broadcasting Corporation [brit. Rundfunkgesellschaft])

BBk = Deutsche Bundesbank

BCG = Bazillus Calmette-Guérin ‹nach zwei franz. Tuberkuloseforschern›; **BCG-Schutz|imp|fung** (vorbeugende Tuberkuloseimpfung)

Bd. = Band (Buch); Bde. = Bände

BDA = Bund Deutscher Architekten

BDPh = Bund Deutscher Philatelisten

BDÜ = Bundesverband der Dolmetscher und Übersetzer

B-Dur ['be:du:r, *auch* 'be:'du:r], das; - (Tonart; *Zeichen* B); **B-Dur-Ton|lei|ter** (↑R 28)

Be = *chem. Zeichen für* Beryllium

BE = Broteinheit

Bé = Baumé; *vgl.* Baumégrad

be... (*Vorsilbe von Verben*, z. B. beabsichtigen, du beabsichtigst, beabsichtigt, zu beabsichtigen)

be|ab|sich|ti|gen

be|ach|ten; be|ach|tens|wert; be|acht|lich; Be|ach|tung

Beach|vol|ley|ball ['bi:tʃ...] (auf Sand von Zweiermannschaften gespielte Art des Volleyballs)

be|ackern (↑R 132; [den Acker] bestellen; *ugs. auch für* gründlich bearbeiten)

Bea|gle ['bi:gəl], der; -s, -[s] ‹engl.› (eine Hunderasse)

be|am|peln *(fachspr.)*

Be|am|te, der; -n, -n (↑R 5 ff.); **...an|wär|ter, Be|am|ten-be|lei|di|gung, ...deutsch; Be|am|ten|schaft**, die; -; **Be|am|ten|stand**, der; -[e]s; **Be|am|ten|tum**, das; -s; **Be|am|ten|ver|hält|nis**, das; -ses; **be|am|tet; Be|am|te|te**, der *u.* die; -n, -n (↑R 5 ff.); **Be|am|tin**

be|ängs|ti|gend

be|an|schrif|ten *(Amtsspr.)*

be|an|spru|chen; Be|an|spru|chung

be|an|stan|den, *österr. meist* **be|an|stän|den; Be|an|stan|dung**, *österr. meist* **Be|an|stän|dung**

be|an|tra|gen; du beantragtest; beantragt; **Be|an|tra|gung**

be|ant|wor|ten; Be|ant|wor|tung

be|ar|bei|ten; Be|ar|bei|ter; Be|ar|bei|te|rin; Be|ar|bei|tung

be|arg|wöh|nen *(geh.)*

Beat [bi:t], der; -[s] ‹engl.› (*im Jazz* Schlagrhythmus; betonter Taktteil; *kurz für* Beatmusik)

Be|a|ta, Be|a|te (w. Vorn.)

bea|ten ['bi:t(ə)n] ‹engl.› (*ugs.* Beatmusik spielen; nach Beatmusik tanzen); **Beat|fan** ['bi:tfɛn]

Beat|ge|ne|ra|tion ['bi:tdʒɛnə're:ʃ(ə)n], die; - ‹amerik.› (durch eine radikale Ablehnung alles Bürgerlichen gekennzeichnete amerikan. [Schriftsteller]gruppe der fünfziger Jahre)
Be|a|ti|fi|ka|ti|on, die; -, -en ‹lat.› (*kath. Kirche* Seligsprechung); **be|a|ti|fi|zie|ren**
be|at|men (*Med.* Luft od. Gasgemische in die Atemwege blasen); **Be|at|mung; Be|at|mungs-an|la|ge, ...ge|rät, ...stö|rung**
Beat|mu|sik ['bi:t...], die; - ([Tanz]musik mit betontem Schlagrhythmus)
Beat|nik ['bi:t...], der; -s, -s ‹amerik.› (Vertreter der Beatgeneration)
Be|a|tri|ce [...'tri:sə, *ital.* ...'tri:tʃə, *franz.* ...'tri:s], **Be|a|trix;** (w. Vorn.)
Beat|schup|pen ['bi:t...] *(ugs.)*
Be|a|tus ‹lat.› (m. Vorn.)
Beau [bo:], der; -, -s ‹franz.› (*spöttisch für* schöner Mann)
Beau|fort|ska|la ['bo:fərt...], die; - ‹nach dem engl. Admiral› (Skala für Windstärken; ↑R 95)
be|auf|schla|gen (*Technik* auf etw. auftreffen); der Dampf beaufschlagte das Laufrad; beaufschlagt; **Be|auf|schla|gung**
be|auf|sich|ti|gen; Be|auf|sich|ti|gung
be|auf|tra|gen; du beauftragtest; beauftragt; **Be|auf|trag|te,** der *u.* die; -n, -n (↑R 5 ff.)
be|aug|ap|feln *(landsch. scherzh.);* ich ...[e]le (↑R 16); **be|äu|geln** *(ugs. scherzh.);* ich ...[e]le (↑R 16); beäugelt; **be|äu|gen;** beäugt; **be|au|gen|schei|ni|gen** *(Amtsspr.; auch scherzh.);* der neue Wagen wurde beaugenscheinigt
Beau|jo|lais [boʒɔ'lɛ], der; - [...'lɛ(s)], - [...'lɛ(s)] ‹franz.› (ein franz. Rotwein)
Beau|mar|chais [bomar'ʃɛ] (franz. Schriftsteller)
Beau|té [bo'te:], die; -, -s ‹franz.› (*geh. für* schöne Frau)
Beau|ty|farm ['bju:ti...], die; -, -en ‹engl.› (*svw.* Schönheitsfarm)
Beau|voir, de [bo'voa:r] (franz. Schriftstellerin)
be|bän|dern
be|bar|tet (mit Bart versehen)
be|bau|en; Be|bau|ung
Bé|bé [be:'be:], das; -s, -s ‹franz.› (*schweiz. für* Säugling, Baby)
Be|bel (Mitbegründer der dt. Sozialdemokratischen Partei)
be|ben; Be|ben, das; -s, -
be|bil|dern; ich ...ere (↑R 16); **Be|bil|de|rung**
Be|bop ['bi:bɔp], der; -[s], -s ‹amerik.› (Jazzstil der 40er Jahre *[nur Sing.];* Tanz in diesem Stil)
be|brillt
be|brü|ten
Be|bung *(Musik)*
be|bun|kern ([ein Schiff] mit Brennstoff versehen)
be|buscht; ein -er Hang
Bé|cha|mel|kar|tof|feln [beʃa'mɛl...] ‹nach dem Marquis de Béchamel›; **Bé|cha|mel|so|ße**
Be|cher, der; -s, -; **be|cher|för|mig; be|chern** (*ugs. scherzh. für* tüchtig trinken); ich ...ere (↑R 16); **Be|cher|werk** (*Technik* Fördergerät)
be|cir|cen [bə'tsirtsən] *vgl.* bezirzen
Be|cken, das; -s, -; **Be|cken|bruch,** der *(Med.)*
Be|ckett (ir.-franz. Schriftsteller)
Beck|mann (dt. Maler)
Beck|mes|ser (Gestalt aus Wagners „Meistersingern"; *abwertend* kleinlicher Kritiker); **Beck|mes|se|rei; beck|mes|sern** (kleinlich tadeln, kritteln); ich beckmessere *u.* ...messre (↑R 16); gebeckmessert
Bec|que|rel [bɛkə'rɛl], das; -s, - ‹nach dem franz. Physiker› (Maßeinheit für die Aktivität ionisierender Strahlung; *Zeichen* Bq)
be|da|chen (*Handw.* mit einem Dach versehen)
be|dacht; auf eine Sache bedacht sein; **Be|dacht,** der; -[e]s; mit Bedacht; auf etwas Bedacht nehmen *(Amtsspr.);* **Be|dach|te,** der *u.* die; -n, -n; ↑R 5 ff. (jmd., dem ein Vermächtnis ausgesetzt worden ist); **be|däch|tig; Be|däch|tig|keit,** die; -; **be|dacht|sam; Be|dacht|sam|keit,** die; -
Be|da|chung *(Handw.)*
be|damp|fen (*Technik* durch Verdampfen von Metall mit einer Metallschicht überziehen)
be|dan|ken, sich; sei bedankt! *(südd., österr.)*
Be|darf, der; -[e]s, *Plur. (fachspr.);* -e; nach Bedarf; der Bedarf an, *Kaufmannsspr. auch* in etwas; bei Bedarf; **Be|darfs-am|pel, ...ar|ti|kel, ...de|ckung, ...fall** (der; im -[e]); **be|darfs|ge|recht; Be|darfs-gü|ter** *(Plur.),* **...hal|te|stel|le**
be|dau|er|lich; be|dau|er|li|cher|wei|se; be|dau|ern; ich ...ere (↑R 16); **Be|dau|ern,** das; -s; **be|dau|erns|wert**
Be|de, die; -, -n (Abgabe im MA.)
be|de|cken; be|deckt; -er Himmel; **Be|deckt|sa|mer,** der; -s, - *meist Plur.* (*Bot.* Pflanze, deren Samenanlage im Fruchtknoten eingeschlossen ist; *Ggs.* Nacktsamer); **be|deckt|sa|mig** *(Bot.);* **Be|de|ckung**
be|den|ken; bedacht *(vgl. d.);* sich eines Besser[e]n -; **Be|den|ken,** das; -s, -; **be|den|ken|los; Be|den|ken|lo|sig|keit,** die; -; **be|den|kens|wert; be|denk|lich; Be|denk|lich|keit; Be|denk|zeit**
be|dep|pert (*ugs. für* ratlos, gedrückt); - sein, dreinschauen
be|deu|ten; be|deu|tend; am bedeutendsten; *aber* (↑R 47): das Bedeutendste; etwas Bedeutendes; um ein Bedeutendes zunehmen; **be|deut|sam; Be|deut|sam|keit,** die; -; **Be|deu|tung; Be|deu|tungs-an|ga|be, ...leh|re** (die; -; *Sprachw.*); **be|deu|tungs|los; Be|deu|tungs|lo|sig|keit,** die; -; **Be|deu|tungs|un|ter|schied; be|deu|tungs|voll; Be|deu|tungs-wan|del, ...wör|ter|buch**
be|die|nen; sich eines Kompasses bedienen *(geh.);* jmdn. bedienen (*österr. ugs. auch für* benachteiligen); bedient sein (*ugs. für* von etwas, jmdm. genug haben); **Be|die|ner; Be|die|ne|rin** (*bes. österr. für* Aufwartefrau); **be|diens|tet** (in Dienst stehend); **Be|diens|te|te,** der *u.* die; -n, -n (↑R 5 ff.); **Be|dien|te,** der *u.* die; -n, -n; ↑R 5 ff. (*veraltet für* Diener[in]); **Be|die|nung** (*österr. auch* Stelle als Bedienerin); **Be|die|nungs-an|lei|tung, ...feh|ler, ...geld**
[1]**be|din|gen** (voraussetzen; zur Folge haben); sich gegenseitig -; *vgl.* bedingt; [2]**be|din|gen** (*älter für* ausbedingen); du bedangst; bedungen; der bedungene Lohn; **Be|ding|nis,** das; -ses, -se (*österr. Amtsspr. für* Bedingung); **bedingt** (eingeschränkt, an Bedingungen geknüpft); bedingter Reflex; bedingte Verurteilung (*schweiz. für* Verurteilung mit Bewährungsfrist); **Be|dingt|gut,** das; -[e]s (*für* Kommissionsgut); **Be|dingt|heit,** die; -; **Be|dingt|sen|dung** (*für* Kommissionssendung); **Be|din|gung; Be|din|gungs|form** (*für* Konditional); **be|din|gungs|los; Be|din|gungs|satz** (*für* Konditionalsatz); **be|din|gungs|wei|se**
be|drän|gen; Be|dräng|nis, die; -, -se; **Be|dräng|te,** der *u.* die; -n, -n (↑R 5 ff.); **Be|drän|gung**
be|dripst (*nordd. für* kleinlaut; betrübt)
be|dro|hen; be|droh|lich; Be|droh|lich|keit; Be|dro|hung
be|dru|cken; be|drü|cken; Be-

drụ|cker; **be|drụ̈ckt; Be|drụ̈ckt|heit,** die; -; **Be|drụ|ckung,** die; - (das Bedrucken); **Be|drụ̈|ckung**
Be|du|i|ne, der; -n, -n (↑R 126) ‹arab.› (arab. Nomade)
be|dụn|gen *vgl.* ²bedingen
be|dụ̈n|ken *(veraltet);* es will mich -; **Be|dụ̈n|ken,** das; -s; meines -s (*veraltet für* nach meiner Ansicht)
be|dụ̈r|fen *(geh.); mit Gen.:* des Trostes bedürfen; **Be|dụ̈rf|nis,** das; -ses, -se; **Be|dụ̈rf|nis|an|stalt** *(Amtsspr.);* **be|dụ̈rf|nis|los; be|dụ̈rf|tig;** *mit Gen.:* der Hilfe bedürftig; **Be|dụ̈rf|tig|keit,** die; -
be|du|seln, sich (*ugs. für* sich leicht betrinken); er ist beduselt
Bee|fa|lo [ˈbi:...], der; -[s], -s ‹amerik.› (Kreuzung aus Bison und Hausrind); **Beef|ea|ter** [ˈbi:fi:tə(r)], der; -s, -s ‹engl.› (Angehöriger der königl. Leibwache im Londoner Tower); **Beef|steak** [ˈbi:fste:k], das; -s, -s (Rinds[lenden]stück); deutsches - (↑R 108); **Beef|tea** [ˈbi:fti:], der; -s, -s (Rindfleischbrühe)
be|eh|ren *(geh.);* sich -
be|ei|den (mit einem Eid bekräftigen); **be|ei|di|gen** (*geh. für* beeiden; *österr. für* in Eid nehmen); gerichtlich beeidigter Sachverständiger
be|ei|fern, sich (*selten für* sich eifrig bemühen)
be|ei|len, sich; **Be|ei|lung!** (*ugs. für* bitte schnell!)
be|ein|dru|cken; von etwas beeindruckt sein
be|ein|fluss|bar; Be|ein|fluss|bar|keit, die; -; **be|ein|flus|sen;** du beeinflusst; **Be|ein|flus|sung**
be|ein|träch|ti|gen; Be|ein|träch|ti|gung
be|elen|den (↑R 132; *schweiz. für* nahe gehen; betrüben); es beelendet mich
Beel|ze|bub [*auch* beˈɛl...], der; - ‹hebr.› (Herr der bösen Geister, oberster Teufel im N. T.)
be|ẹn|den; beendet; **be|ẹn|di|gen;** beendigt; **Be|ẹn|di|gung; Be|ẹn|dung**
be|ẹn|gen; Be|ẹngt|heit, die; -; **Be|ẹn|gung**
be|ẹr|ben; jmdn. -; **Be|ẹr|bung**
be|er|den ([Pflanzen] mit Erde versehen); **be|er|di|gen; Be|er|di|gung; Be|er|di|gungs|in|sti|tut**
Bee|re, die; -, -n; **Bee|ren|aus|le|se; bee|ren|för|mig; Bee|ren|obst**
Beet, das; -[e]s, -e
Bee|te *vgl.* Bete
Beet|ho|ven [...ho:fən], Ludwig van (dt. Komponist)

be|fä|hi|gen; ein befähigter Mensch; **Be|fä|hi|gung,** die; -; **Be|fä|hi|gungs|nach|weis**
be|fahr|bar; Be|fahr|bar|keit, die; -; **¹be|fah|ren;** -er (*Jägerspr.* bewohnter) Bau; -e (*Seemannsspr.* im Seedienst erfahrene) Matrosen; **²be|fah|ren;** eine Straße -
Be|fạll, der; -[e]s; **be|fạl|len**
be|fạn|gen (schüchtern; voreingenommen); **Be|fạn|gen|heit,** die; -
be|fạs|sen; befasst; sich mit etwas -; jmdn. mit etwas - *(Amtsspr.)*
be|fẹh|den (*geh. für* bekämpfen); sich -; **Be|fẹh|dung** *(geh.)*
Be|fehl, der; -[e]s, -e; **be|feh|len;** du befiehlst; du befahlst; du befählest, *älter* beföhlest; befohlen; befiehl!; **be|feh|le|risch; be|feh|li|gen; Be|fehls₋aus|ga|be, ...emp|fän|ger, ...form** (*für* Imperativ); **be|fehls|ge|mäß; Be|fehls₋ge|walt** (die; -), **...ha|ber; be|fehls|ha|be|risch; Be|fehls₋not|stand, ...satz, ...ton** (der; -[e]s), **...ver|wei|ge|rung**
be|fein|den; sich -; **Be|fein|dung**
be|fẹs|ti|gen; Be|fẹs|ti|gung; Be|fẹs|ti|gungs|an|la|ge *meist Plur.*
be|feuch|ten; Be|feuch|tung
be|feu|ern (*Seemannsspr. auch für* mit Leuchtfeuern versehen); **Be|feu|e|rung**
Bẹff|chen (Halsbinde mit zwei Leinenstreifen vorn am Halsausschnitt von Amtstrachten, bes. des ev. Geistlichen)
be|fie|dern; ich ...ere (↑R 16)
be|fịn|den; befunden; den Plan für gut usw. -; sich -; **Be|fịn|den,** das; -s; **be|fịnd|lich** (vorhanden); *falsch:* sich -; *richtig:* sich befindend; **Be|fịnd|lich|keit** (seel. Zustand, in dem sich jmd. befindet)
be|fịn|gern (*ugs. für* betasten)
be|fị|schen; einen See -; **Be|fị|schung**
be|flag|gen; Be|flag|gung, die; -
be|flẹ|cken; Be|flẹ|ckung
be|fle|geln (*österr. für* beschimpfen)
be|flei|ßen, sich (*veraltet, selten noch für* sich befleißigen); du befleißt dich; ich befliss mich, du beflissest dich; beflissen *(vgl. d.);* befleiß[e] dich!; **be|flei|ßi|gen,** sich *(geh.); mit Gen.:* sich eines guten Stils -
be|flie|gen; eine Strecke -
be|flịs|sen (eifrig bemüht); um Anerkennung -; **Be|flịs|sen|heit,** die; -; **be|flịs|sent|lich** (*seltener für* geflissentlich)
be|flü|geln *(geh.)*
be|flu|ten (unter Wasser setzen); **Be|flu|tung**

be|fọl|gen; Be|fọl|gung, die; -
be|fọ̈r|der|bar; Be|fọ̈r|de|rer, Be|fọ̈rd|rer; **be|fọ̈r|der|lich** (*schweiz. für* beschleunigt, rasch); **be|fọ̈r|dern; Be|fọ̈r|de|rung; Be|fọ̈r|de|rungs₋be|din|gun|gen, ...kos|ten, ...mit|tel** (das), **...ta|rif; Be|fọ̈rd|rer,** Be|fọ̈r|de|rer
be|fọrs|ten (forstlich bewirtschaften); **be|fọ̈rs|tern;** ↑R 16 (*Forstw.* nicht staatliche Waldungen durch staatliche Forstbeamte verwalten lassen); **Be|fọ̈rs|te|rung,** die; -; **Be|fọrs|tung**
be|frạch|ten; Be|frạch|ter; Be|frạch|tung
be|frạckt (einen Frack tragend)
be|fra|gen; du befragst; du befragtest; befragt; befrag[e]!; (↑R 50:) auf Befragen; **Be|fra|gung**
be|frạnst
be|frei|en; sich -; **Be|frei|er; Be|frei|ung,** die; -; **Be|frei|ungs₋be|we|gung, ...kampf, ...krieg, ...schlag** *(Eishockey)*
be|frẹm|den; es befremdet [mich]; **Be|frẹm|den,** das; -s; **be|frẹm|dend; be|frẹmd|lich; Be|frẹm|dung,** die; -
be|freun|den, sich; **be|freun|det**
be|frie|den (Frieden bringen; *geh. für* einhegen); befriedet; **be|frie|di|gen** (zufrieden stellen); **be|frie|di|gend;** *vgl.* ausreichend; **Be|frie|di|gung,** die; -; **Be|frie|dung,** die;
be|frịs|ten; Be|frịs|tung, die; -
be|frụch|ten; Be|frụch|tung
be|fu|gen; Be|fug|nis, die; -, -se; **be|fugt;** befugt sein
be|füh|len
be|fụm|meln (*ugs. für* betasten, untersuchen)
Be|fund, der; -es, -e (Feststellung); nach Befund; ohne Befund (*Med.; Abk.* o. B.)
be|fürch|ten; Be|fürch|tung
be|für|sor|gen (*österr. Amtsspr. für* betreuen)
be|für|wor|ten; Be|für|wor|ter; Be|für|wor|tung
Bẹg, der; -s, -s (höherer türk. Titel); *vgl.* Bei
be|ga|ben (*geh. für* mit etw. ausstatten); **be|gabt; Be|gab|te,** der *u.* die; -n, -n (↑R 5 ff.); **Be|gab|ten|för|de|rung; Be|ga|bung; Be|ga|bungs|re|ser|ve**
be|gaf|fen *(ugs. abwertend)*
Be|gäng|nis, das; -ses, -se (*veraltet, noch geh. für* feierliche Bestattung)
be|ga|sen *(fachspr.);* du begast; **Be|ga|sung**
be|gat|ten; sich -; **Be|gat|tung**
be|gau|nern (*ugs. für* betrügen)
be|geb|bar; ¹be|ge|ben (*Bankw.*

verkaufen, in Umlauf setzen); einen Wechsel -; ²**be|ge|ben,** sich (irgendwohin gehen; sich ereignen; verzichten); er begibt sich eines Rechtes (er verzichtet darauf); **Be|ge|ben|heit; Be|ge|ber** (*für* Girant [eines Wechsels]); **Be|geb|nis,** das; -ses, -se (*veraltend für* Begebenheit, Ereignis); **Be|ge|bung** *(Bankw.);* die - von Aktien

be|geg|nen; jmdm. -; **Be|geg|nung; Be|geg|nungs|stät|te**

be|geh|bar; Be|geh|bar|keit; be|ge|hen

Be|gehr, das, *auch* der; -s *(veraltet);* **be|geh|ren; Be|geh|ren,** das; -s; **be|geh|rens|wert; be|gehr|lich; Be|gehr|lich|keit**

Be|ge|hung

be|gei|fern (*auch für* beschimpfen); **Be|gei|fe|rung**

be|geis|tern; ich ...ere (↑R 16); sich -; **Be|geis|te|rung,** die; -; **be|geis|te|rungs|fä|hig; Be|geis|te|rungs|sturm;** *vgl.* ¹Sturm

be|gich|ten (*Hüttenw.* Erz in den Schachtofen einbringen); **Be|gich|tung**

Be|gier *(geh.);* **Be|gier|de,** die; -, -n; **be|gie|rig**

be|gie|ßen; Be|gie|ßung

Be|gi|ne, die; -, -n ‹niederl.› (Angehörige einer halbklösterl. Frauenvereinigung)

Be|ginn, der; -[e]s; von - an; zu -; **be|gin|nen;** du begannst; du begännest, *seltener* begönnest; begonnen; beginn[e]!; **Be|gin|nen,** das; -s (Vorhaben)

be|glän|zen *(geh.)*

be|glau|bi|gen; beglaubigte Abschrift; **Be|glau|bi|gung; Be|glau|bi|gungs|schrei|ben**

be|glei|chen; eine Rechnung -; **Be|glei|chung** *Plur. selten*

Be|gleit‿ad|res|se (Begleitschein), **...brief; be|glei|ten** (mitgehen); begleitet; **Be|glei|ter; Be|glei|te|rin; Be|gleit‿er|schei|nung, ...flug|zeug, ...mu|sik, ...pa|pier** *(meist Plur.),* **...per|son, ...schein** *(Zollw.),* **...schrei|ben, ...text, ...um|stand; Be|glei|tung**

Beg|ler|beg, der; -s, -s ‹türk.› (Provinzstatthalter in der alten Türkei)

be|glot|zen (*ugs. für* anstarren)

be|glü|cken; Be|glü|cker; Be|glü|ckung; be|glück|wün|schen; beglückwünscht; **Be|glück|wün|schung**

be|gna|det (hoch begabt); **be|gna|di|gen** (jmdm. seine Strafe erlassen); **Be|gna|di|gung; Be|gna|di|gungs|recht,** das; -[e]s

be|gnü|gen, sich

Be|go|nie [...i̯ə], die; -, -n ‹nach dem Franzosen Michel Bégon› (eine Zierpflanze)

be|gön|nern; ich ...ere (↑R 16)

be|gö|schen (*nordd. für* beschwichtigen); du begöschst

begr. = begraben (*Zeichen* ▭);

be|gra|ben; Be|gräb|nis, das; -ses, -se; **Be|gräb|nis‿fei|er, ...fei|er|lich|keit, ...kos|ten** *(Plur.),* **...stät|te**

be|gra|di|gen ([einen ungeraden Weg od. Wasserlauf] gerade legen, [eine Grenzlinie] ausgleichen); **Be|gra|di|gung**

be|grannt (mit Grannen versehen)

be|grap|schen (*landsch. abwertend für* betasten, anfassen)

be|grei|fen; *vgl.* begriffen; **be|greif|lich; be|greif|li|cher|wei|se**

be|gren|zen; Be|gren|zer (*Technik* bei Erreichen eines Grenzwertes einsetzende Unterbrechervorrichtung); **be|grenzt; Be|grenzt|heit** *Plur. selten;* **Be|gren|zung**

Be|griff, der; -[e]s, -e; im - sein; **be|grif|fen;** diese Tierart ist im Aussterben -; **be|griff|lich;** -es Substantiv (*für* Abstraktum); **Be|griffs‿be|stim|mung, ...bil|dung, ...form** (*für* Kategorie); **be|griffs‿mä|ßig, ...stut|zig, ...stüt|zig** *(österr.);* **Be|griffs|ver|wir|rung**

be|grün|den; be|grün|dend; Be|grün|der; Be|grün|dung; Be|grün|dungs‿an|ga|be (*Sprachw.* Umstandsangabe des Grundes), **...satz** (*für* Kausalsatz), **...wei|se**

be|grü|nen; sich - (grün werden); **Be|grü|nung,** die; -

be|grü|ßen (*schweiz. auch* jmdn., eine Stelle befragen); **be|grü|ßens|wert; Be|grü|ßung; Be|grü|ßungs‿abend** (↑R 132), **...an|spra|che, ...kuss, ...trunk**

be|gu|cken *(ugs.)*

Be|gum [*auch* 'be:gam], die; -, -en ‹angloind.› (Titel ind. Fürstinnen)

be|güns|ti|gen; Be|güns|ti|gung

be|gut|ach|ten; begutachtet; **Be|gut|ach|ter; Be|gut|ach|tung**

be|gü|tert

be|gü|ti|gen; Be|gü|ti|gung

be|haa|ren, sich; **be|haart; Be|haa|rung**

be|hä|big; Be|hä|big|keit, die; -

be|ha|cken (*ugs. auch für* betrügen)

be|haf|ten *(schweiz.);* jmdn. auf od. bei etwas - (jmdn. auf etwas festlegen, beim Wort nehmen); **be|haf|tet;** mit etwas - sein

be|ha|gen; Be|ha|gen, das; -s; **be|hag|lich; Be|hag|lich|keit**

be|hal|ten; Be|häl|ter; Be|hält|nis, das; -ses, -se

be|häm|mern; be|häm|mert (*ugs. für* verrückt)

be|hän|de (↑R 89)

be|han|deln

be|hän|di|gen (*schweiz. Amtsspr. für* an sich nehmen)

Be|hän|dig|keit, die; -

Be|hand|lung; Be|hand|lungs‿kos|ten *(Plur.),* **...pflicht, ...raum, ...stuhl, ...wei|se**

be|hand|schuht

Be|hang, der; -[e]s, Behänge (*Jägerspr. auch* Schlappohren); **be|han|gen;** der Baum ist mit Äpfeln -; **be|hän|gen;** *vgl.* ²hängen; **be|hängt;** eine grün -e Wand

be|har|ken; sich - (*ugs. für* bekämpfen)

be|har|ren; be|harr|lich; Be|harr|lich|keit, die; -; **Be|har|rung; Be|har|rungs|ver|mö|gen**

be|hau|chen; behauchte Laute (*für* Aspiraten); **Be|hau|chung**

be|hau|en; ich behaute den Stein

be|haup|ten; sich -; **be|haup|tet** (*Börse* fest, gleichbleibend); **Be|haup|tung**

be|hau|sen; Be|hau|sung

Be|ha|vi|o|ris|mus [biheviə'ris...], der; - ‹engl.› (amerik. sozialpsychologische Forschungsrichtung); **be|ha|vi|o|ris|tisch**

be|he|ben (beseitigen; *österr. auch für* abheben, abholen, z. B. Geld von der Bank); **Be|he|bung** (Beseitigung; *österr. auch für* Abhebung, Abholung)

be|hei|ma|ten; be|hei|ma|tet; Be|hei|ma|tung, die; -

be|heiz|bar; be|hei|zen; Be|hei|zung, die; -

Be|helf, der; -[e]s, -e; **be|hel|fen,** sich; ich behelfe mich; **Be|helfs|heim; be|helfs|mä|ßig; Be|helfs|un|ter|kunft; be|helfs|wei|se**

be|hel|li|gen (belästigen); **Be|hel|li|gung**

be|helmt

be|hem|det *(selten)*

Be|he|mot[h] [*auch* 'be:...], der; -[e]s, -s ‹hebr., „Riesentier"› (im A. T. Name des Nilpferdes)

be|hen|de *frühere Schreibung für* behände

Be|hen|nuss, Ben|nuss ‹span.; dt.› (ölhaltige Frucht eines afrik. Baumes)

be|her|ber|gen; Be|her|ber|gung

be|herrsch|bar; Be|herrsch|bar|keit, die; -; **be|herr|schen;** sich -; **Be|herr|scher; be|herrscht; Be|herrsch|te,** der *u.* die; -n, -n (↑R 5 ff.); **Be|herrscht|heit,** die; -; **Be|herr|schung**

be|her|zi|gen; be|her|zi|gens|wert; Be|her|zi|gung; be|herzt (entschlossen); **Be|herzt|heit,** die; -
be|he|xen
be|hilf|lich
Be|hind [biˈhaind], das; -s ⟨engl.⟩ (*schweiz. Sportspr.* Raum hinter der Torlinie)
be|hin|dern; be|hin|dert; geistig -; **Be|hin|der|te,** der *u.* die; -n, -n (↑R 5 ff.); die körperlich -n; **Be|hin|der|ten|sport; Be|hin|de|rung; Be|hin|de|rungs|fall,** der; im -[e]
Behm|lot ⟨nach dem dt. Physiker Behm⟩ (Echolot)
be|ho|beln
be|hor|chen (*ugs. für* abhören, belauschen)
Be|hör|de, die; -, -n; **Be|hör|den‿deutsch, ...schrift|ver|kehr, ...spra|che** (*svw.* Behördendeutsch); **be|hörd|lich; be|hörd|li|cher|seits**
be|host (*ugs. für* mit Hosen bekleidet)
Be|huf, der; -[e]s, -e (*Amtsspr. veraltend für* Zweck, Erfordernis); zum -[e]; zu diesem -[e]; **be|hufs** (*Amtsspr. veraltet;* ↑R 46); *Präp. mit Gen.:* - des Verfahrens
be|hum[p]|sen (*ostmitteld. für* übervorteilen, bemogeln)
be|hü|ten; behüt' dich Gott!; **be|hut|sam; Be|hut|sam|keit,** die; -; **Be|hü|tung,** die; -
bei (*Abk.* b.); *Präp. mit Dat.;* beim (*vgl. d.*); bei all[e]dem; bei dem allen (*häufiger für* allem); bei diesem allem (*neben* allen); bei weitem (↑R 47); bei der Hand sein; bei[m] Abgang des Schauspielers; bei aller Bescheidenheit; bei all dem Treiben
Bei, der; -s, *Plur.* -e *u.* -s ⟨türk., „Herr"⟩ (türk. Titel, *oft hinter Namen,* z. B. Ali-Bei); *vgl.* Beg
bei... (*in Zus. mit Verben,* z. B. beidrehen, du drehst bei, beigedreht, beizudrehen)
bei|be|hal|ten; Bei|be|hal|tung, die; -
bei|bie|gen (*ugs. für* jmdm. etw. beibringen; mit diplomatischem Geschick sagen)
Bei|blatt
Bei|boot
bei|brin|gen; jmdm. etwas - (lehren, übermitteln); eine Bescheinigung, Zeugen -; jmdm. eine Wunde -; **Bei|brin|gung,** die; -
Beich|te, die; -, -n; **beich|ten; Beicht|ge|heim|nis; Beich|ti|ger** (*veraltet für* Beichtvater); **Beicht‿kind** (der od. die Beichtende), **...sie|gel** (das; -s; *svw.* Beichtgeheimnis), **...stuhl, ...va|ter** (die Beichte hörender Priester)
beid|ar|mig (*Sportspr.* mit beiden Armen [gleich geschickt]); -es Reißen; -er Stürmer; **beid|bei|nig** (*Sportspr.*); ein -er Absprung; **bei|de;** (↑R 48:) beides; alles beides; beide jungen Leute; alle beide; wir beide (*selten* wir beiden); ihr beide[n]; ihr beiden jungen Leute; sie beide (*als Anrede* Sie beide); die[se] beiden; dies[es] beides; einer von beiden; euer beider Anteilnahme; mit unser beider Hilfe; für uns beide; von beider Leben ist nichts bekannt; man bedarf aller beider; beide Mal, beide Male; **bei|der|lei;** - Geschlecht[e]s; **bei|der|sei|tig; bei|der|seits;** *Präp. mit Gen.:* - des Flusses; **Bei|der|wand,** die; - *od.* das; -[e]s (grobes Gewebe); **beid|fü|ßig** (*Sportspr.* mit beiden Füßen [gleich geschickt]); -er Stürmer; **Beid|hän|der** (jmd., der mit beiden Händen gleich geschickt ist); **beid|hän|dig**
bei|dre|hen (*Seemannsspr.* die Fahrt verlangsamen)
beid|sei|tig; *vgl.* beiderseitig; **beid|seits** (*bes. schweiz. für* zu beiden Seiten); - des Rheins
bei|ein|an|der; *in Verbindung mit Verben immer getrennt:* beieinander sein (*auch ugs. für* gesund sein); beieinander haben, sitzen, stehen usw.
bei|ern (*landsch.* mit dem Klöppel läuten); ich beiere (↑R 16)
beif. = beifolgend
Bei|fah|rer; Bei|fah|rer|sitz
Bei|fall, der; -[e]s; ein Beifall heischender Blick; **bei|fal|len** (*veraltet für* in den Sinn kommen); **Bei|fall hei|schend;** *vgl.* Beifall; **bei|fäl|lig; Bei|fall[s]|klat|schen,** das; -s; **Bei|falls‿kund|ge|bung, ...sturm** (*vgl.* ¹Sturm)
Bei|film
bei|fol|gend (*Amtsspr. veraltend; Abk.* beif.); - (anbei) der Bericht
bei|fü|gen; Bei|fü|gung (*auch für* Attribut)
Bei|fuß, der; -es (eine Gewürz- u. Heilpflanze)
Bei|fut|ter (Zugabe zum gewöhnlichen Futter); *vgl.* ¹Futter
Bei|ga|be (Zugabe)
beige [beːʃ] ⟨franz.⟩ (sandfarben); ein beige (*ugs. auch gebeugt* beiges) Kleid; *vgl.* blau; **¹Beige,** das; -, *Plur.* -, *ugs.* -s
²Bei|ge, die; -, -n (*südd. u. schweiz. für* Stoß, Stapel)
bei|ge|ben (*auch für* sich fügen); klein -
beige|far|ben [ˈbeːʃ...]; eine -e Couch
bei|gen (*südd. u. schweiz. für* [auf]schichten, stapeln)
Bei|ge|ord|ne|te, der *u.* die; -n, -n (↑R 5 ff.)
Bei|ge|schmack, der; -[e]s
bei|ge|sel|len (*geh.*); sich jmdm. -
Beig|net [bɛˈnjeː] (↑R 130), der; -s, -s ⟨franz.⟩ (Schmalzgebackenes mit Füllung, Krapfen)
Bei|heft; bei|hef|ten; beigeheftet
Bei|hil|fe; - beantragen; **bei|hil|fe|fä|hig** (*Amtsspr.*)
Bei|hirsch (*Jägerspr.* im Rudel mitlaufender, in der Brunft vom Platzhirsch verdrängter Hirsch)
Bei|jing [beiˈdjiŋ] *vgl.* Peking
Bei|klang
Bei|koch, der (Hilfskoch); **Bei|kö|chin**
bei|kom|men; ihm ist nicht beizukommen (er ist nicht zu fassen, zu besiegen); mir ist nichts beigekommen (*geh. für* nichts eingefallen)
Bei|kost (zusätzliche Nahrung)
Beil, das; -[e]s, -e
beil. = beiliegend
bei|la|den; *vgl.* ¹laden; **Bei|la|dung** (*auch Rechtsw.*)
Bei|la|ge
Bei|la|ger (*veraltet für* Beischlaf)
bei|läu|fig (*österr. auch für* ungefähr, etwa); **Bei|läu|fig|keit**
bei|le|gen; Bei|le|gung
bei|lei|be; - nicht (auf keinen Fall)
Bei|leid; Bei|leids‿be|zei|gung *od.* **...be|zeu|gung, ...kar|te, ...schrei|ben**
bei|lie|gend (*Abk.* beil.); **Bei|lie|gen|de,** das; -n (↑R 5 ff.)
Beiln|gries (Stadt in der Oberpfalz)
beim; ↑R 13 (bei dem; *Abk.* b.); es beim Alten lassen (↑R 47); (↑R 50:) beim Singen und Spielen
Bei|mann *Plur.* ...männer (*schweiz. veraltend für* Gehilfe, Hilfsarbeiter)
bei|men|gen; Bei|men|gung
bei|mes|sen; Bei|mes|sung
bei|mi|schen; Bei|mi|schung
be|imp|fen
Bein, das; -[e]s, -e
bei|nah, bei|na|he [*beide auch* ...ˈnaː...]; **Bei|na|he|zu|sam|men|stoß** (bes. bei Flugzeugen)
Bei|na|me
bein|am|pu|tiert; ein -er Mann; **Bein|am|pu|tier|te,** der *u.* die (↑R 5 ff.); **Bein|ar|beit** (*Sport*)
Bein|brech, der; -[e]s (Liliengewächs); **Bein|bruch,** der; **bei|nern** (aus Knochen); **Bein|fleisch** (*österr. für* Rindfleisch mit Knochen)

be|in|hal|ten (*Amtsspr.* enthalten); es beinhaltete; beinhaltet
bein|hart (*südd., österr. für* sehr hart); **Bein|haus** (Aufbewahrungsort für ausgegrabene Gebeine auf Friedhöfen); **...bei|nig** (z. B. hochbeinig); **Bein|kleid** (*veraltet für* Hose); **Bein|ling** (Strumpfoberteil; *auch* Hosenbein); **Bein‿pro|the|se, ...ring, ...sche|re** *(Sport),* **...schlag** *(Sport),* **...stumpf; bein|ver|sehrt; Bein|well,** der; -s (eine Heilpflanze); **Bein|zeug** (Beinschutz der Ritterrüstung)
bei|ord|nen; bei|ord|nend (*für* koordinierend); **Bei|ord|nung**
Bei|pack, der; -[e]s (zusätzliches Frachtgut; *Fernmeldetechnik* um den Mittelleiter liegende Leitungen bei Breitbandkabeln); **bei|pa|cken;** beigepackt; **Bei|pack|zet|tel** (einer Ware beiliegender Zettel mit Angaben zur Zusammensetzung und Verwendung)
bei|pflich|ten
Bei|pro|gramm *(Film)*
Bei|rat *Plur.* ...räte
Bei|ried, das; -[e]s *u.* die; - (*österr. für* Rippen-, Rumpfstück)
be|ir|ren; sich nicht - lassen
Bei|rut [*auch* 'bai..., 'be:ru:t] (Hptst. des Libanons); **Bei|ru|ter** (↑R 103)
bei|sam|men; beisammen sein (*auch für* in guter körperl. Verfassung sein; bei Verstand sein); **bei|sam|men‿blei|ben, ...ha|ben; Bei|sam|men|sein,** das; -s; **bei|sam|men‿sit|zen, ...ste|hen**
Bei|sas|se, der; -n, -n; ↑R 126 (Einwohner ohne Bürgerrecht im MA., Häusler)
Bei|satz (*für* Apposition)
bei|schie|ßen (einen [Geld]beitrag leisten)
Bei|schlaf (*geh., Rechtsw.* Geschlechtsverkehr); **bei|schla|fen; Bei|schlä|fer; Bei|schlä|fe|rin**
Bei|schlag, der; -[e]s, Beischläge (*Archit.* erhöhter Vorbau an Häusern)
bei|schla|gen (*Jägerspr.* in das Bellen eines anderen Hundes einstimmen)
Bei|schluss (*österr. für* das Beigeschlossene; Anlage); unter - von ...
Bei|se|gel (zusätzliches Segel)
Bei|sein, das; -s; in seinem -
bei|sei|te (↑R 41); beiseite legen, schaffen, stoßen usw.; **Bei|sei|te|schaf|fung,** die; -; **Bei|sei|te|set|zung** (*svw.* Hintansetzung); **bei|seits** (*südwestd. für* beiseite)
Bei|sel, *auch* Beisl, das; -s, -[n] (*bayr. ugs., österr. für* Kneipe)
bei|set|zen; Bei‿set|zung, ...sit|zer
Beisl *vgl.* Beisel
Bei|spiel, das; -[e]s, -e; zum - (*Abk.* z. B.); **bei|spiel|ge|bend; bei|spiel|haft; bei|spiel|los; Bei|spiel|satz; Bei|spiels|fall,** der; **bei|spiels‿hal|ber, ...wei|se**
bei|sprin|gen (*geh. für* helfen)
Bei|ßel, der; -s, - (*mitteld. für* Beitel, Meißel)
bei|ßen; du beißt; ich biss, du bissest; gebissen; beiß[e]; der Hund beißt ihn (*auch* ihm) ins Bein; sich - ([von Farben] nicht harmonieren); **Bei|ßer** (*österr. auch für* Brecheisen); **Bei|ße|rei; Beiß‿korb, ...ring; beiß|wü|tig; Beiß|zan|ge**
Bei|stand, der; -[e]s, Beistände (*österr. auch für* Trauzeuge); **Bei|stands|pakt; bei|ste|hen**
bei|stel|len (*österr. für* [zusätzlich] zur Verfügung stellen); **Bei|stell|mö|bel; Bei|stel|lung**
Bei|steu|er, die *(bes. südd.);* **bei|steu|ern**
bei|stim|men
Bei|strich (*für* Komma)
Bei|tel, der; -s, - (meißelartiges Werkzeug)
Bei|trag, der; -[e]s, ...träge; **bei|tra|gen;** er hat das Seine, sie hat das Ihre dazu beigetragen; **Bei|trä|ger; Bei|trags‿be|mes|sungs|gren|ze** *(Sozialversicherung),* **...klas|se, ...rück|er|stat|tung, ...satz, ...zah|lung**
bei|trei|ben *(Rechtsw.);* Schulden -; **Bei|trei|bung**
bei|tre|ten; Bei|tritt; Bei|tritts|er|klä|rung
Bei|wa|gen; Bei|wa|gen|fah|rer
Bei|werk, das; -[e]s ([schmückende] Zutat; Unwichtiges)
bei|woh|nen *(geh.);* einem Staatsakt -; einer Frau - (Geschlechtsverkehr mit einer Frau haben); **Bei|woh|nung**
Bei|wort *Plur.* ...wörter (*für* Adjektiv)
Beiz, die; -, -en (*schweiz. mdal. für* Dorfschenke, Wirtshaus)
Bei|zäu|mung *(Pferdesport)*
[1]**Bei|ze,** die; -, -n (chem. Flüssigkeit zum Färben, Gerben u. Ä.)
[2]**Bei|ze,** die; -, -n (Beizjagd)
[3]**Bei|ze,** die; -, -n (*landsch. für* Wirtshaus)
bei|zei|ten (↑R 41)
bei|zen; du beizt
Bei|zer (*landsch.* Besitzer einer [3]Beize)
bei|zie|hen (*bes. südd., österr., schweiz. für* hinzuziehen); **Bei|zie|hung,** die; -
Beiz|jagd
Bei|zung (Behandlung mit [1]Beize)
Beiz|vo|gel (für die Jagd abgerichteter Falke)
be|ja|gen *(Jägerspr.);* **Be|ja|gung**
be|ja|hen
be|jahrt *(geh.)*
Be|ja|hung
be|jam|mern; be|jam|merns|wert
be|ju|beln
be|ka|keln (*nordd. ugs. für* gemeinsam besprechen)
be|kämp|fen; Be|kämp|fung
be|kannt; bekannt sein; bekannt geben; er hat die Verfügung bekannt gegeben; bekannt machen (*auch für* veröffentlichen, öffentlich mitteilen); er soll mich mit ihm bekannt machen; sich mit einer Sache bekannt (vertraut) machen; einen Schriftsteller bekannt machen; das Gesetz wurde bekannt gemacht (veröffentlicht); bekannt werden (*auch für* veröffentlicht werden, in die Öffentlichkeit dringen); ich bin bald mit ihm bekannt geworden; erst jetzt bekannt werdende Absprachen; der Wortlaut ist bekannt geworden; (↑R 47:) jemand Bekanntes; **Be|kann|te,** der *u.* die; -n, -n (↑R 5 ff.); liebe Bekannte; **Be|kann|ten|kreis; be|kann|ter|ma|ßen; Be|kannt|ga|be,** die; -; **be|kannt ge|ben** *vgl.* bekannt; **Be|kannt|heit,** die; -; **Be|kannt|heits|grad,** der; -[e]s; **be|kannt|lich; be|kannt ma|chen** *vgl.* bekannt; **Be|kannt|ma|chung; Be|kannt|schaft; be|kannt wer|den** *vgl.* bekannt
be|kan|ten (mit Kanten versehen); **Be|kan|tung,** die; -
Be|kas|si|ne, die; -, -n ‹franz.› (Sumpfschnepfe)
be|kau|fen, sich (*landsch. für* zu teuer, unüberlegt einkaufen)
be|keh|ren; sich -; **Be|keh|rer; Be|keh|re|rin; Be|kehr|te,** der *u.* die; -n, -n (↑R 5 ff.); **Be|keh|rung**
be|ken|nen; sich -; Bekennende Kirche (Name einer Bewegung in den dt. ev. Kirchen); ↑R 108; **Be|ken|ner‿brief** (*svw.* Bekennerschreiben), **...schrei|ben** (Schreiben, in dem sich jmd. zu einem [politischen] Verbrechen bekennt); **Be|kennt|nis,** das; ...nisses, ...nisse (*österr. auch für* Steuererklärung); **Be|kennt|nis‿buch, ...frei|heit** (die; -), **...kir|che** (Bekennende Kirche); **be|kennt|nis|mä|ßig; Be|kennt|nis|schu|le** (Schule mit Unterricht im Geiste eines religiösen Bekenntnisses)
be|kie|ken (*landsch.* betrachten)

be|kiest; -e Wege
be|kla|gen; sich -; **be|kla|gens|wert; Be|klag|te,** der *u.* die; -n, -n; ↑R 5 ff. (jmd., gegen den eine [Zivil]klage erhoben wird)
be|klat|schen (mit Händeklatschen begrüßen)
be|klau|en (*ugs. für* bestehlen)
be|kle|ben; Be|kle|bung
be|kle|ckern (*ugs. für* beklecksen); sich -; **be|kleck|sen;** sich -; bekleckst
be|klei|den; ein Amt -; **Be|klei|dung; Be|klei|dungs|in|dust|rie**
be|klem|men; beklemmt; **be|klem|mend; Be|klemm|nis,** die; -, -se; **Be|klem|mung; be|klom|men** (ängstlich, bedrückt); **Be|klom|men|heit,** die; -
be|klop|fen
be|kloppt (*ugs. für* blöd)
be|knab|bern
be|knackt (*ugs. für* dumm; unerfreulich)
be|knien; jmdn. - (*ugs. für* jmdn. dringend u. ausdauernd bitten)
be|ko|chen; jmdn. - (*ugs. für* regelmäßig für jmdn. kochen)
be|kö|dern (*Angeln* mit einem Köder versehen)
be|koh|len (*fachspr. für* mit Kohlen versorgen); **Be|koh|lung**
be|kom|men; ich habe es -; es ist mir gut -; **be|kömm|lich;** der Wein ist leicht bekömmlich, ein leicht bekömmliches Essen; **Be|kömm|lich|keit,** die; -
be|kom|pli|men|tie|ren (jmdm. viele Komplimente machen)
be|kös|ti|gen; Be|kös|ti|gung
be|kot|zen *(derb)*
be|kräf|ti|gen; Be|kräf|ti|gung
be|krallt (mit Krallen versehen)
be|krän|zen; Be|krän|zung
be|kreu|zen (mit dem Kreuzzeichen segnen); bekreuzt; **be|kreu|zi|gen,** sich
be|krie|chen
be|krie|gen
be|krit|teln (*abwertend für* bemängeln, [kleinlich] tadeln); **Be|krit|te|lung,** Be|kritt|lung
be|krit|zeln; Wände -
be|krö|nen; Be|krö|nung
be|ku|cken (*nordd. für* begucken)
be|küm|mern; das bekümmert ihn; sich um jmdn. *od.* etwas -; **Be|küm|mer|nis,** die; -, -se *(geh.);* **Be|küm|mert|heit,** die; -; **Be|küm|me|rung,** die; -
be|kun|den *(geh.);* sich -; **Be|kun|dung**
Bel, das; -s, - ‹nach dem amerik. Physiologen A. G. Bell› (eine physikal. Zählungseinheit; *Zeichen* B)
Bé|la ['be:la] (m. Vorn.)
be|lä|cheln; be|la|chen
be|la|den; *vgl.* [1]laden; **Be|la|dung**
Be|lag, der; -[e]s, ...läge
Be|la|ge|rer; be|la|gern; Be|la|ge|rung; Be|la|ge|rungs|zu|stand
Bel|ami, der; -[s], -s ‹franz.› (Frauenliebling)
be|läm|mern (*nordd. für* [mit dauernden Bitten] belästigen); **be|läm|mert** (*ugs. für* betreten, eingeschüchtert; übel)
Be|lang, der; -[e]s, -e; von Belang sein; **be|lan|gen;** was mich belangt (*veraltend für* an[be]langt); jmdn. - (zur Rechenschaft ziehen; verklagen); **be|lang|los; Be|lang|lo|sig|keit; be|lang|reich; Be|lang|sen|dung** (*österr. für* Sendung einer Interessenvertretung in Funk u. Fernsehen); **Be|lan|gung; be|lang|voll**
be|la|rus|sisch [*od.* 'b(i)ɛ...] (weißrussisch)
be|las|sen; Be|las|sung, die; -
be|last|bar; Be|last|bar|keit; be|las|ten; be|las|tend
be|läs|ti|gen; Be|läs|ti|gung
Be|las|tung; Be|las|tungs-EKG; Be|las|tungs‿gren|ze, ...ma|te|ri|al, ...pro|be, ...zeu|ge
be|lau|ben, sich; **Be|lau|bung**
be|lau|ern; Be|lau|e|rung
[1]**Be|lauf,** der; -[e]s (*veraltet für* Betrag; Höhe [der Kosten]); [2]**Be|lauf** (Forstbezirk); **be|lau|fen;** sich -; die Kosten haben sich auf ... belaufen
be|lau|schen
Bel|can|to, *eindeutschend* Bel|kan|to, der; -s ‹ital.› (ital. Gesangsstil)
Bel|chen, der; -s; ↑R 102 (Erhebung im südl. Schwarzwald); Großer -, Elsässer - (Erhebung in den Vogesen)
be|le|ben; be|lebt; Be|lebt|heit; Be|le|bung
be|le|cken
Be|leg, der; -[e]s, -e (Beweis[stück]); zum -[e]; **Be|leg|arzt; be|leg|bar; be|le|gen; Be|leg|exem|plar** (↑R 132); **Be|leg|schaft; Be|leg|schafts‿ak|tie, ...stär|ke; Be|leg|sta|ti|on** (im Krankenhaus); **Be|leg|stück; be|legt; Be|le|gung** *Plur. selten;* **Be|le|gungs|dich|te**
be|leh|nen (*früher* in ein Lehen einsetzen; *schweiz. für* beleihen); **Be|leh|nung**
be|lehr|bar; be|leh|ren; (↑R 48:) eines and[e]ren *od.* andern -, *aber* (↑R 47): eines Besser[e]n *od.* Bessren -; **Be|leh|rung**
be|leibt; Be|leibt|heit, die; -
be|lei|di|gen; Be|lei|di|ger; be|lei|digt; Be|lei|di|gung; Be|lei|di|gungs‿kla|ge, ...pro|zess
be|leih|bar; be|lei|hen; Be|lei|hung
be|lem|mern, be|lem|mert *frühere Schreibungen für* belämmern, belämmert
Be|lem|nit [*auch* ...'nit], der; -en, -en (↑R 126) ‹griech.› (*Geol.* fossiler Schalenteil von Tintenfischen)
be|le|sen (unterrichtet; viel wissend); **Be|le|sen|heit,** die; -
Bel|esp|rit [bɛlɛs'pri:], der; -s, -s ‹franz.› (*veraltet, noch spöttisch für* Schöngeist); **Bel|eta|ge** [bɛle'ta:ʒə] (↑R 132), die; -, -n (*veraltet für* Hauptgeschoss, erster Stock)
be|leuch|ten; Be|leuch|ter; Be|leuch|tung; Be|leuch|tungs‿an|la|ge, ...ef|fekt, ...tech|nik
be|leum|det, be|leu|mun|det; er ist gut, übel -
Bel|fast [*od.* 'bɛl...] (Hptst. von Nordirland)
bel|fern (*ugs. für* bellen; keifend schimpfen); ich ...ere (↑R 16)
Bel|gi|en; Bel|gi|er; Bel|gi|e|rin; bel|gisch
Bel|grad (Hptst. Jugoslawiens und Serbiens); *vgl.* Beograd
Be|li|al, *ökum.* **Be|li|ar,** der; -[s] ‹hebr.› (Teufel im N. T.)
be|lich|ten; Be|lich|tung; Be|lich|tungs‿mes|ser (der), **...zeit**
be|lie|ben (*geh. für* wünschen): es beliebt (gefällt) mir *(oft iron.);* **Be|lie|ben,** das; -s; nach -; es steht in seinem -; **be|lie|big;** x-beliebig (↑R 25); ein beliebiges Beispiel; *aber* (↑R 47): alles Beliebige; etwas Beliebiges; jeder Beliebige; **be|liebt; Be|liebt|heit,** die; -
be|lie|fern; Be|lie|fe|rung, die; -
Be|lin|da (w. Vorn.)
Be|lize [bɛ'li:z] (Staat in Mittelamerika); **Be|li|zer** [bɛ'li:zər]; **be|li|zisch** [bɛ'li:ziʃ]
Bel|kan|to *vgl.* Belcanto
Bel|la (w. Vorn.)
Bel|la|don|na, die; -, ...nnen ‹ital.› (Tollkirsche)
Belle-Al|li|ance [bɛla'liã:s]; die Schlacht bei - (Waterloo)
Belle Époque [bɛle'pɔk], die; - - ‹franz.› (Bez. für die Zeit des gesteigerten Lebensgefühls in Frankreich zu Beginn des 20. Jh.s.)
bel|len; Bel|ler
Bel|let|rist (↑R 130), der; -en, -en (↑R 126) ‹franz.› (Unterhaltungsschriftsteller); **Bel|let|ris|tik,** die; - (Unterhaltungsliteratur); **bel|let|ris|tisch**
[1]**Belle|vue** [bɛl'vy:], die; -, -n [...'vy:ən] ‹franz.› (*veraltet für* Aussichtspunkt); [2]**Belle|vue,** das; -[s], -s (*Bez. für* Schloss, Gaststätte mit schöner Aussicht)

Bel|li|ni (ital. Malerfamilie; ital. Komponist)
Bel|lin|zo|na (Hptst. des Kantons Tessin)
Bel|lo (ein Hundename)
Bel|lo|na (röm. Kriegsgöttin)
Bel|mo|pan (Hptst. von Belize)
be|lo|ben (*veraltet für* belobigen); **be|lo|bi|gen; Be|lo|bi|gung; Be|lo|bi|gungs|schrei|ben; Be|lo|bung** (*veraltet für* Belobigung)
be|loh|nen; Be|loh|nung
be|lo|rus|sisch [*od.* 'b(i)ɛ...] *vgl.* belarussisch
Bel-Pa|e|se, der; -; (ein ital. Weichkäse)
Bel|sa|zar, *ökum.* **Bel|schaz|zar** (babylon. Kronprinz, nach dem A.T. letzter König von Babylon)
Belt, der; -[e]s, -e; ↑R 102 (Meerenge); der Große -, der Kleine -
be|lüf|ten; Be|lüf|tung, die; -
[1]Be|lu|ga, die; -, -s ‹russ.› (Hausen [*vgl. d.*]; Weißwal); **[2]Be|lu|ga,** der; -s (der aus dem Rogen des Hausens bereitete Kaviar)
be|lü|gen
be|lus|ti|gen; sich -; **Be|lus|ti|gung**
Be|lut|sche [*od.* be'lu...], (↑R 130), der; -n, -n; ↑R 126 (Angehöriger eines asiat. Volkes); **be|lut|schisch; Be|lut|schis|tan** (↑R 132; westpakistan. Hochland)
Bel|ve|de|re [...v...], das; -[s], -s ‹ital., „schöne Aussicht"› (Aussichtspunkt; *Bez. für* Schloss, Gaststätte mit schöner Aussicht)
[1]bel|zen (*landsch. für* sich vor der Arbeit drücken); *vgl.* [1]pelzen
[2]bel|zen (*landsch. für* [2]pelzen)
Belz|ni|ckel, der; -s, - (*westmitteld. für* Nikolaus)
Bem. = Bemerkung
be|ma|chen (*ugs. für* besudeln; betrügen); sich - (*ugs. auch für* sich aufregen)
be|mäch|ti|gen, sich (*geh.*); sich des Geldes -; **Be|mäch|ti|gung,** die; -
be|mä|keln (*ugs. für* bemängeln, bekritteln); **Be|mä|ke|lung, Be|mäk|lung**
be|ma|len; Be|ma|lung
be|män|geln; ich ...[e]le (↑R 16); **Be|män|ge|lung, Be|mäng|lung**
be|man|nen; ein Schiff -; **Be|man|nung** (*auch für* Besatzung)
be|män|teln (beschönigen); ich ...[e]le (↑R 16); **Be|män|te|lung, Be|mänt|lung**
be|ma|ßen (*fachspr. für* [eine Zeichnung] mit Maßen versehen); **Be|ma|ßung**
be|mas|ten (mit einem Mast versehen); **Be|mas|tung**
be|mau|sen (*ugs. für* bestehlen)
Bem|bel, der; -s, - (*landsch. für* [Apfelwein]krug; kleine Glocke)
be|meh|len; Be|meh|lung
be|mei|ern (*ugs. für* überlisten); ich ...ere (↑R 16)
be|merk|bar; sich - machen; **be|mer|ken; Be|mer|ken,** das; -s; mit dem -; **be|mer|kens|wert; Be|mer|kung** (*Abk.* Bem.)
be|mes|sen; sich -; die Steuern - sich nach dem Einkommen; **Be|mes|sung**
be|mit|lei|den; Be|mit|lei|dung
be|mit|telt (wohlhabend)
Bemm|chen (*ostmitteld.*); **Bem|me,** die; -, -n ‹slaw.› (*ostmitteld. für* Brotschnitte mit Aufstrich, Belag)
be|mo|geln (*ugs. für* betrügen)
be|moost
be|mü|hen; sich -; er ist um sie bemüht; **be|mü|hend** (*schweiz. für* unerfreulich, peinlich); **Be|mü|hung**
be|mü|ßi|gen (*veraltet für* veranlassen, nötigen); **be|mü|ßigt;** ich sehe mich - (*geh., oft iron.*)
be|mus|tern (*Kaufmannsspr.* mit Warenmustern versehen); einen Katalog -; **Be|mus|te|rung**
be|mut|tern; ich ...ere (↑R 16); **Be|mut|te|rung**
be|mützt
Ben (*bei hebr. u. arab. Eigennamen* Sohn od. Enkel)
be|nach|bart
be|nach|rich|ti|gen; Be|nach|rich|ti|gung
be|nach|tei|li|gen; Be|nach|tei|li|gung
be|na|geln (mit Nägeln versehen); **Be|na|ge|lung**
be|na|gen
Be|nag|lung *vgl.* Benagelung
be|nam|sen (*ugs. u. scherzh. für* benennen); du benamst
be|nannt
be|narbt (mit Narben bedeckt)
Be|na|res (*früherer Name für* Varanasi)
be|näs|sen (*geh.*)
Ben|del *frühere Schreibung für* Bändel
Ben|dix (m. Vorn.)
be|ne ‹lat.› (gut)
be|ne|beln (verwirren, den Verstand trüben); **be|ne|belt** (*ugs. für* [durch Alkohol] geistig verwirrt); **Be|ne|be|lung, Be|neb|lung** *Plur. selten*
be|ne|dei|en ‹lat.› (segnen; selig preisen); du benedeist; du benedeitest; gebenedeit (*auch* benedeit); die Gebenedeite (*vgl. d.*)
Be|ne|dic|tus, das; -, - ‹lat.› (Teil der lat. Liturgie); **Be|ne|dikt, Be|ne|dik|tus** (m. Vorn.); **Be|ne|dik|ta** (w. Vorn.)
Be|ne|dikt|beu|ern (Ort u. Kloster in Bayern)
Be|ne|dik|ten|kraut, das; -[e]s (eine Heilpflanze); **Be|ne|dik|ti|ner** (Mönch des Benediktinerordens; *auch* Likörsorte); **Be|ne|dik|ti|ner|or|den,** der; -s (*Abk.* OSB; *vgl. d.*); **Be|ne|dik|ti|on,** die; -, -en (Segnung, kath. kirchl. Weihe); **Be|ne|dik|tus** *vgl.* Benedikt; **be|ne|di|zie|ren** (segnen, weihen)
Be|ne|fiz, das; -es, -e ‹lat.› (Vorstellung zugunsten eines Künstlers; Ehrenvorstellung); **Be|ne|fi|zi|ar,** der; -s, -e *u.* **Be|ne|fi|zi|at,** der; -en, -en; ↑R 126 (Inhaber eines [kirchl.] Benefiziums); **Be|ne|fi|zi|um,** das; -s, ...ien [...i̯ən] (mit einer Pfründe verbundenes Kirchenamt; mittelalterl. Lehen); **Be|ne|fiz_kon|zert, ...spiel, ...vor|stel|lung**
be|neh|men; sich -; *vgl.* benommen; **Be|neh|men,** das; -s; sich mit jmdm. ins - setzen
be|nei|den; be|nei|dens|wert
Be|ne|lux [*od.* ...'luks] (*Kurzw. für* die seit 1947 in einer Zollunion zusammengefassten Länder **Bel**gique [Belgien], **Ne**derland [Niederlande] u. **Lux**embourg [Luxemburg]); **Be|ne|lux|staa|ten** *Plur.*
be|nen|nen; Be|nen|nung
be|net|zen (*geh.*); **Be|net|zung**
Ben|ga|le, der; -n, -n; ↑R 126 (Einwohner von Bengalen); **Ben|ga|len** (vorderind. Landschaft); **Ben|ga|li,** das; -[s] (Sprache); **ben|ga|lisch;** -es Feuer (Buntfeuer); -e Beleuchtung
Ben|gel, der; -s, *Plur.* -, *ugs.* -s ([ungezogener] Junge; *veraltet, noch landsch. für* Stock, Prügelholz)
be|nie|sen; etwas -
Be|nimm, der; -s (*ugs. für* Betragen, Verhalten)
Be|nin (Staat in Afrika, *früher* Dahome[y]); **Be|ni|ner** (Einwohner von Benin); **be|ni|nisch**
Be|ni|to (m. Vorn.)
[1]Ben|ja|min (m. Vorn.); **[2]Ben|ja|min,** der; -s, -e (Jüngster in einer Gruppe)
Benn (dt. Dichter)
Ben|ne, die; -, -n ‹lat.› (*schweiz. mdal. für* Schubkarren)
Ben|no (m. Vorn.)
Ben|nuss *vgl.* Behennuss
be|nom|men (fast betäubt); **Be|nom|men|heit,** die; -
be|no|ten
be|nö|ti|gen
Be|no|tung

Ben|thal, das; -s ‹griech.› (*Biol.* Bodenregion eines Gewässers); **Ben|thos**, das; - (in der Bodenregion eines Gewässers lebende Tier- und Pflanzenwelt)
be|num|mern; Be|num|me|rung
be|nutz|bar *od.* **be|nütz|bar**[1]; **Be-nutz|bar|keit**, die; -; **be|nut|zen** *od.* **be|nüt|zen**[1]; **Be|nut|zer** *od.* **Be|nüt|zer**[1]; **Be|nut|zer|kreis**; **Be|nut|zung** *od.* **Be|nüt|zung**[1]; **Be|nut|zungs|ge|bühr**
Ben|ve|nu|ta [...v...] (w. Vorn.); **Ben|ve|nu|to** (m. Vorn.)
Benz (dt. Ingenieur)
ben|zen *vgl.* penzen
Ben|zin, das; -s, -e ‹arab.› (Treibstoff; Lösungsmittel); **Ben|zin-hahn, ...ka|nis|ter, ...kut|sche** (*ugs. scherzh. für* Auto), **...preis, ...preis|er|hö|hung, ...tank, ...uhr, ...ver|brauch**; **Ben|zoe** [...tso|e(:)], die; - (ein duftendes ostind. Harz); **Ben|zo|e|harz**; **Ben|zo|e|säu|re** (ein Konservierungsmittel); **Ben|zol**, das; -s, -e (Teerdestillat aus Steinkohle; Lösungsmittel); **Benz|py|ren**, das; -s (*Chemie* ein als Krebs erzeugend geltender Kohlenwasserstoff); **Ben|zyl**, das; -s (*Chemie* Atomgruppe in zahlreichen chem. Verbindungen); **Ben|zyl-al|ko|hol** (*Chemie* aromat. Alkohol; Grundstoff für Parfüme)
Beo, der; -s, -s ‹indones.› (Singvogel aus Indien)
be|obach|ten (↑R 132); **Be-obach|ter**; **Be|obach|ter|sta|tus** (*Völkerrecht*); **Be|obach|tung**; **Be|obach|tungs-ga|be, ...sta|ti-on**
Be|o|grad [*od.* bɛ'ɔ...] (*serbischer Name für* Belgrad)
be|ölen (↑R 132), sich (*Jugendspr.* sich sehr amüsieren)
be|or|dern; ich ...ere (↑R 16)
be|pa|cken
be|pelzt
be|pflan|zen; Be|pflan|zung
be|pflas|tern; Be|pflas|te|rung
be|pin|keln (*ugs.*)
be|pin|seln; Be|pin|se|lung, Be-pins|lung
be|pis|sen (*derb*)
be|pu|dern; Be|pu|de|rung
be|quas|seln (*ugs. für* bereden)
be|quat|schen (*ugs. für* bereden)
be|quem; be|que|men, sich; **be-quem|lich** (*veraltet für* bequem); **Be|quem|lich|keit**
be|ran|ken; Be|ran|kung
Be|rapp, der; -[e]s (*Bauw.* rauer Verputz); [1]**be|rap|pen**
[2]**be|rap|pen** (*ugs. für* bezahlen)

[1] *Südd., österr. u. schweiz. meist so.*

be|ra|ten; beratender Ingenieur; **Be|ra|ter**; **Be|ra|ter|ver|trag** (*Wirtsch.*); **be|rat|schla|gen**; du beratschlagtest; beratschlagt; **Be|rat|schla|gung; Be|ra|tung; Be|ra|tungs-aus|schuss, ...ge-spräch, ...stel|le, ...ver|trag** (*Wirtsch.*)
be|rau|ben; Be|rau|bung
be|rau|schen; sich [an etw.] -; **be-rau|schend; be|rauscht; Be-rauscht|heit**, die; -; **Be|rau-schung**, die, -
Ber|ber, der; -s, - (Angehöriger einer Völkergruppe in Nordafrika; *auch für* Nichtsesshafter); **Ber-be|rei**, die; - (alter Name für die Küstenländer im westl. Nordafrika); **ber|be|risch**
Ber|be|rit|ze, die; -, -n ‹lat.› (Sauerdorn, ein Zierstrauch)
Ber|ber-pferd, ...tep|pich
Ber|ceu|se [bɛr'sø:zə], die; -, -n ‹franz.› (*Musik* Wiegenlied)
Berch|tes|ga|den (Luftkurort in Oberbayern); **Berch|tes|ga|de-ner** (↑R 103); Berchtesgadener Alpen
Berch|told (m. Vorn.); **Berch-tolds|tag** (2. Januar; in der Schweiz vielerorts Feiertag)
be|re|chen|bar; Be|re|chen|bar-keit, die; -; **be|rech|nen; be-rech|nend; Be|rech|nung; Be-rech|nungs|grund|la|ge**
be|rech|ti|gen; be|rech|tigt; Be-rech|tig|te, der *u.* die; -n, -n (↑R 5ff.); **be|rech|tig|ter|wei-se; Be|rech|ti|gung; Be|rech|ti-gungs|schein**
be|re|den; be|red|sam; Be|red-sam|keit, die; -; **be|redt; Be-redt|heit**, die; -; **Be|re|dung**
be|ree|dert (*Seew.* einer Reederei gehörend, von ihr betreut)
be|reg|nen; Be|reg|nung; Be-reg|nungs|an|la|ge
Be|reich, der, *selten* das; -[e]s, -e
be|rei|chern; ich ...ere (↑R 16); sich [an etwas] -; **Be|rei|che-rung; Be|rei|che|rungs-ab-sicht, ...ver|such**
be|rei|fen (mit Reifen versehen); das Auto ist neu bereift
be|reift (mit Reif bedeckt)
Be|rei|fung
be|rei|ni|gen; Be|rei|ni|gung
be|rei|sen; ein Land -; **Be|rei-sung**
be|reit; zu etwas bereit sein; sich bereit erklären, finden; *vgl. aber* bereithaben, bereithalten, bereitlegen usw. (↑R 39); [1]**be|rei|ten** (zubereiten); bereitet
[2]**be|rei|ten** (zureiten); beritten; **Be|rei|ter** (Zureiter)
be|reit|ha|ben; wir werden alles rechtzeitig bereithaben; **be|reit-hal|ten**; ich habe das Geld bereitgehalten; wir werden uns bereithalten; (↑R 23:) bereit- u. zur Verfügung halten, *aber* zur Verfügung u. bereithalten; **be|reit|le-gen**; ich habe das Buch bereitgelegt; **be|reit|lie|gen**; die Bücher werden bereitliegen; **be|reit|ma-chen**; ich habe alles bereitgemacht; ich habe mich bereitgemacht; **be|reits** (schon); **Be|reit-schaft; Be|reit|schafts-arzt, ...dienst, ...po|li|zei; be|reit|ste-hen**; das Essen hat bereitgestanden; **be|reit|stel|len**; ich habe die Kisten bereitgestellt; **Be|reit-stel|lung; Be|rei|tung; be|reit-wil|lig; Be|reit|wil|lig|keit**, die; -
Be|re|ni|ce [...'ni:tsə *od.* ...tʃe] *vgl.* Berenike; **Be|re|ni|ke** (w. Vorn.)
be|ren|nen; das Tor - (*Sportspr.*)
be|ren|ten (*Amtsspr.* eine Rente zusprechen)
Be|re|si|na [*od.* ...'na], die; - (Nebenfluss des Dnjepr)
Bé|ret [berɛ], das; -s, -s (*schweiz. für* Baskenmütze)
be|reu|en
[1]**Berg** (früheres Großherzogtum)
[2]**Berg**, Alban (österr. Komponist)
[3]**Berg**, der; -[e]s, -e; zu -[e] fahren; die Haare stehen einem zu -[e] (*ugs.*); **berg|ab**; - gehen; **berg|ab-wärts; Berg-ahorn** (↑R 132); **...aka|de|mie** (↑R 132)
Ber|ga|mas|ke, der; -n, -n; ↑R 126 (Bewohner von Bergamo); **Ber|ga|mas|ker** (↑R 103); **ber|ga|mas|kisch; Ber|ga|mo** (ital. Stadt)
Ber|ga|mot|te, die; -, -n ‹türk.› (eine Birnensorte; eine Zitrusfrucht); **Ber|ga|mott|öl**
Berg|amt (Aufsichtsbehörde für den Bergbau)
berg|an; bergan gehen; **Berg-ar|bei|ter; berg|auf**; bergauf steigen; **berg|auf|wärts; Berg-bahn, ...bau** (der; -[e]s), **...bau-er** (der; -n, -n), **...be|hör|de, ...be|woh|ner; Ber|ge** *Plur.* (taubes Gestein); **ber|ge|hoch**, berghoch
Ber|ge|lohn (*Seew.*); **ber|gen**; [in] sich -; du birgst; du bargst; du bärgest; geborgen; birg!
Ber|gen|gruen [...gry:n] (dt. Schriftsteller)
Ber|ges|hö|he (*geh.*); **ber|ge|wei-se** (*ugs. für* in großen Mengen); **Berg|fahrt** (Fahrt den Strom, den Berg hinauf; *Ggs.* Talfahrt); **berg|fern; Berg|fex** (leidenschaftl. Bergsteiger); **Berg|fried**, der; -[e]s, -e (Hauptturm auf Burgen; Wehrturm); *vgl. auch* Burg-

fried; **Berg‿füh|rer, ...gip|fel; berg|hoch,** ber|ge|hoch; **Berg‿ho|tel, ...hüt|te; ber|gig**

ber|gisch (zum Lande Berg gehörend), *aber* (↑R 102): das Bergische Land (Gebirgslandschaft zwischen Rhein, Ruhr und Sieg)

Berg|isel (↑R 132), der; - (Berg bei Innsbruck)

Berg‿ket|te, ...kie|fer (die), **...knap|pe** *(veraltet),* **...krank|heit, ...kris|tall** (der; -s, -e; ein Mineral), **...kup|pe; Berg|ler,** der; -s, - (im Bergland Wohnender); **Berg|luft,** die; -; **Berg|mann** *Plur.* ...leute, *seltener* ...männer; **berg|män|nisch; Berg|manns|spra|che; Berg‿mas|siv, ...meis|ter, ...not, ...par|te** (die; -, -n; *Bergmannsspr.* Paradebeil der Bergleute), **...pfad, ...pre|digt** (die; -; *N. T.*); **berg|reich; Berg‿ren|nen** *(Motorsport),* **...ret|tungs|dienst, ...rutsch, ...schä|den** (*Plur.;* durch den Bergbau an der Erdoberfläche hervorgerufene Schäden), **...schi** (*vgl.* ...ski), **...schuh; berg|schüs|sig** (*Bergmannsspr.* reich an taubem Gestein); **Berg|see; berg|seits; Berg|ski,** Berg|schi (bei der Fahrt am Hang der obere Ski); **Berg|spit|ze; berg|stei|gen** *nur im Infinitiv und Partizip II gebräuchlich;* berggestiegen; **Berg‿stei|gen** (das; -s), **...stei|ger; berg|stei|ge|risch; Berg|stra|ße** (am Westrand des Odenwaldes); **Berg|strä|ßer** (↑R 103); - Wein; **Berg‿tod** (der; -[e]s), **...tour; Berg-und-Tal-Bahn,** die; -, -en (↑R 28)

Ber|gung; Ber|gungs|mann|schaft

Berg‿wacht, ...wand, ...wan|de|rung, ...werk; Berg|werks|ab|ga|be

Be|ri|be|ri die; - ⟨singhal.⟩ (auf einem Mangel an Vitamin B_1 beruhende Krankheit)

Be|richt, der; -[e]s, -e; - erstatten; **be|rich|ten;** falsch, gut berichtet sein *(veraltend);* **Be|rich|ter; Be|richt|er|stat|ter; Be|richt|er|stat|tung; be|rich|ti|gen; Be|rich|ti|gung; Be|richts‿heft** (Heft für wöchentl. Arbeitsberichte von Auszubildenden), **...jahr, ...zeit|raum**

be|rie|chen; sich - (*ugs. für* vorsichtig Kontakte herstellen)

be|rie|seln; ich ...[e]le (↑R 16); **Be|rie|se|lung,** Be|ries|lung *Plur. selten;* **Be|rie|se|lungs|an|la|ge**

be|rin|gen ([Vögel u. a.] mit Ringen [am Fuß] versehen)

Be|ring‿meer (*das;* -[e]s; nördlichstes Randmeer des Pazifiks), **...stra|ße** (die; -; ↑R 105)

Be|rin|gung (von Vögeln u. a.)

Be|ritt ([Forst]bezirk; [kleine] Abteilung Reiter); **be|rit|ten**

Ber|ke|li|um, das; -s ⟨nach der Universität Berkeley in den USA⟩ (chem. Element, Transuran; *Zeichen* Bk)

Ber|lin (Hptst. und Land der Bundesrepublik Deutschland); **Ber|li|na|le,** die; -, -n (*Bez. für* die Filmfestspiele in Berlin); **Ber|lin-Char|lot|ten|burg** [- ʃar...]; **Ber|lin-Dah|lem; Ber|li|ner;** ↑R 103 (*auch kurz für* Berliner Pfannkuchen); ein - Kind; - Bär (Wappen von Berlin); **Ber|li|ner Blau,** das; - -s (ein Farbstoff); **ber|li|ne|risch; ber|li|nern** (berlinerisch sprechen); ich ...ere (↑R 16); **ber|li|nisch; Ber|lin-Jo|han|nis|thal; Ber|lin-Kö|pe|nick; Ber|lin-Neu|kölln; Ber|lin-Pan|kow** [...ˈpaŋko:]; **Ber|lin-Prenz|lau|er Berg; Ber|lin-Rei|ni|cken|dorf, Ber|lin-Span|dau; Ber|lin-Steg|litz; Ber|lin-Trep|tow** [...ˈtre:pto:, *auch* ˈtrɛpto:]; **Ber|lin-Wel|ßen|see; Ber|lin-Wil|mers|dorf; Ber|lin-Zeh|len|dorf**

Ber|li|oz [bɛrˈliɔs] (franz. Komponist)

Ber|litz|schu|le ⟨nach dem Gründer⟩ (↑R 95; eine Sprachschule)

Ber|lo|cke, die; -, -n ⟨franz.⟩ (kleiner Schmuck an [Uhr]ketten)

Ber|me, die; -, -n (*Deichbau* Absatz an einer Böschung)

Ber|mu|da|drei|eck, das; -s (Teil des Atlantiks, in dem sich auf bisher nicht befriedigend geklärte Weise Schiffs- und Flugzeugunglücke häufen); **Ber|mu|da|in|seln** *od.* **Ber|mu|das** *Plur.* (Inseln im Atlantik); **Ber|mu|da|shorts** [...ʃo:(r)ts] *Plur.* (fast knielange Shorts od. Badehose)

Bern (Hptst. der Schweiz und des gleichnamigen Kantons)

Ber|na|dette [...ˈdɛt] (w. Vorn.)

Ber|na|dotte [...ˈdɔt] (schwed. Königsgeschlecht)

Ber|na|nos (franz. Schriftsteller)

Ber|nar|di|no, der; -[s] (*ital. Form von* Bernhardin)

Bern|biet, das; -s (*svw.* Kanton Bern)

Bernd, *auch* Bernt (m. Vorn.)

Ber|ner (↑R 103); die Berner Alpen, das Berner Oberland

Bern|hard (m. Vorn.); **Bern|har|de** (w. Vorn.); **Bern|har|din,** der; -s, *auch* Bern|har|din|pass, der; -es (*kurz für* Sankt-Bernhardin-Pass); *vgl.* Bernardino; **Bern|har|di|ne** (w. Vorn.); **Bern|har|di|ner,** der; -s, - (eine Hunderasse); **Bern|har|di|ner|hund**

Bern|hild, Bern|hil|de (w. Vorn.)

Ber|ni|na, der; -s, *auch* die; - (*kurz für* Piz Bernina *bzw. für* Berninagruppe, -massiv); **Ber|ni|na|bahn,** die; -

ber|nisch ⟨*zu* Bern⟩

[1]**Bern|stein** [*auch* ˈbœ:(r)nst...], Leonard (amerik. Komponist u. Dirigent)

[2]**Bern|stein** ([als Schmuckstein verarbeitetes] fossiles Harz); **bern|stei|ne[r]n** (aus Bernstein); **Bern|stein|ket|te**

Bernt *vgl.* Bernd; **Bern|ward** (m. Vorn.); **Bern|wards|kreuz,** das; -es

Be|ro|li|na, die; - (Frauengestalt als Sinnbild Berlins)

Ber|sag|li|e|re [bɛrsalˈje:rə] (↑R 130), der; -[s], ...ri ⟨ital.⟩ (ital. Scharfschütze)

Ber|ser|ker [*od.* ...ˈzɛr...], der; -s, - ⟨altnord.⟩ (wilder Krieger der altnord. Sage; *auch für* blindwütig tobender Mensch); **ber|ser|ker|haft; Ber|ser|ker|wut**

bers|ten; es birst; es barst; geborsten; **Berst|schutz,** der; -es *(Kerntechnik)*

Bert (m. Vorn.)

Ber|ta; ↑R 92 (w. Vorn.); **Bert|hil|de** (w. Vorn.); **Bert|hold** *vgl.* Bertold; **Ber|ti** (w. *od.* m. Vorn.)

Ber|ti|na, Ber|ti|ne (w. Vorn.)

Ber|told, Bert|hold (m. Vorn.)

Bert|ram (m. Vorn.); **Bert|rand** (m. Vorn.)

be|rüch|tigt

be|rü|cken (betören); **be|rü|ckend**

be|rück|sich|ti|gen; Be|rück|sich|ti|gung, die; -

Be|rü|ckung (*geh., selten für* Bezauberung)

Be|ruf, der; -[e]s, -e; **be|ru|fen** (*österr. auch für* Berufung einlegen); sich auf jmdn. *od.* etwas -; **be|ruf|lich; Be|rufs‿an|fän|ger, ...auf|bau|schu|le** (Schulform des zweiten Bildungsweges zur Erlangung der Fachschulreife), **...aus|bil|dung, ...aus|sich|ten** *(Plur.),* **...be|am|te; be|rufs|be|dingt; be|rufs|be|glei|tend;** -e Schulen; **Be|rufs‿be|ra|ter, ...be|ra|tung, ...be|zeich|nung; be|rufs|be|zo|gen; be|rufs|bil|dend;** -e Schulen; **Be|rufs|bil|dungs|werk** (Einrichtung zur Berufsausbildung für behinderte Jugendliche); **Be|rufs|bo|xen,** das; -s; **Be|rufs|eig|nung; be|rufs|er|fah|ren; Be|rufs‿er|fah-**

rung, ...ethos (↑R 132), **...fachschu|le, ...fah|rer, ...feu|erwehr; be|rufs|fremd; Be|rufs_ge|heim|nis, ...ge|nos|senschaft, ...heer, ...klas|se, ...kleidung, ...krank|heit, ...le|ben; berufs_los, ...mä|ßig; Be|rufs_orga|ni|sa|ti|on, ...pä|da|go|gik, ...prak|ti|kum, ...re|vo|lu|ti|onär, ...rich|ter, ...ri|si|ko, ...schule, ...sol|dat, ...spie|ler, ...sportler, ...stand; be|rufs_ständisch, ...tä|tig; Be|rufs|tä|ti|ge,** der *u.* die; -n, -n (↑R 5 ff.); **Berufs_ver|band, ...ver|bot, ...verbre|cher, ...ver|kehr** (der; -[e]s), **...wahl** (die; -), **...wech|sel; Be|ru|fung; Be|ru|fungs_frist** *(Rechtsspr.),* **...in|stanz, ...recht, ...ver|fah|ren**

be|ru|hen; auf einem Irrtum -; die Sache auf sich - lassen; **be|ruhi|gen;** sich -; **Be|ru|hi|gung; Be|ru|hi|gungs_mit|tel** (das), **...sprit|ze**

be|rühmt; be|rühmt-be|rüchtigt; Be|rühmt|heit

be|rüh|ren; sich -; **Be|rüh|rung; Be|rüh|rungs_angst** *(Psych.),* **...li|nie, ...punkt**

be|ru|ßen; berußt sein

Be|ryll, der; -[e]s, -e ‹griech.› (ein Edelstein); **Be|ryl|li|um,** das; -s (chem. Element, Metall; *Zeichen* Be)

bes. = besonders

be|sab|beln (*ugs. für* mit Speichel beschmutzen); sich -; ich ...[e]le (↑R 16)

be|sab|bern (*ugs. für* mit Speichel beschmutzen); sich -; ich ...ere (↑R 16)

be|sä|en

be|sa|gen; das besagt nichts; **besagt** (*Amtsspr. für* erwähnt)

be|sai|ten; besaitet; *vgl.* zartbesaitet

be|sa|men

be|sam|meln (*schweiz. für* sammeln [von Truppen u. Ä.]); ich ...[e]le (↑R 16); sich - (*schweiz. für* sich versammeln); **Be|sammlung** *(schweiz.)*

Be|sa|mung (Befruchtung); künstliche -; **Be|sa|mungs_stati|on, ...zent|rum**

Be|san, der; -s, -e ‹niederl.› (*Seemannsspr.* Segel am hintersten Mast)

be|sänf|ti|gen; Be|sänf|ti|gung

Be|san|mast (*Seemannsspr.* hinterster Mast eines Segelschiffes)

be|sät; mit etwas - (über u. über bedeckt) sein

Be|satz, der; -es, ...sätze; **Be|satzer,** der; -s, - (*ugs. abwertend für* Angehöriger einer Besatzungsmacht); **Be|satz|strei|fen; Besat|zung; Be|sat|zungs_kind, ...kos|ten** *(Plur.),* **...macht, ...soldat, ...zo|ne**

be|sau|fen, sich (*derb für* sich betrinken); besoffen; [1]**Be|säuf|nis,** das; -ses, -se *od.* die; -, -se (*ugs. für* Sauferei, Zechgelage); [2]**Besäuf|nis,** die; - (*ugs. für* Volltrunkenheit)

be|säu|seln, sich (*ugs. für* sich [leicht] betrinken); **be|säu|selt**

be|schä|di|gen; Be|schä|di|gung

be|schaff|bar; [1]**be|schaf|fen** (besorgen); *vgl.* [1]schaffen; [2]**beschaf|fen** (geartet); mit etwas ist es gut, schlecht beschaffen; **Beschaf|fen|heit,** die; -; **Be|schaffung,** die; -; **Be|schaf|fungs|krimi|na|li|tät** (kriminelle Handlungen zur Beschaffung von [Geld für] Drogen)

be|schäf|ti|gen; sich [mit etw.] -; beschäftigt sein; **Be|schäf|tig|te,** der *u.* die; -n, -n (↑R 5 ff.); **Be|schäf|ti|gung; be|schäf|tigungs|los; Be|schäf|ti|gungs_stand** (der; -[e]s), **...the|ra|pie**

be|schä|len (begatten [von Pferden]); **Be|schä|ler** (Zuchthengst)

be|schal|len (starken Schall eindringen lassen; *Technik u. Med.* mit Ultraschall behandeln, untersuchen); **Be|schal|lung**

be|schä|men; be|schä|mend; be|schä|men|der|wei|se; Beschä|mung

be|schat|ten; Be|schat|tung

Be|schau, die; -; **be|schau|en; Be|schau|er; be|schau|lich; Beschau|lich|keit,** die; -

Be|scheid, der; -[e]s, -e; - geben, sagen, tun, wissen; [1]**be|scheiden;** ein -er Mann; [2]**be|scheiden;** beschied; beschieden; ein Gesuch abschlägig - (*Amtsspr.* ablehnen); jmdn. irgendwohin - (*geh. für* kommen lassen); sich - (sich zufrieden geben); **Be|scheiden|heit,** die; -; **be|schei|dentlich** *(geh., veraltend)*

be|schei|nen

be|schei|ni|gen; Be|schei|nigung

be|schei|ßen (*derb für* betrügen); beschissen

be|schen|ken; Be|schenk|te, der *u.* die; -n, -n (↑R 5 ff.)

[1]**be|sche|ren** (beschneiden); beschoren; *vgl.* [1]scheren

[2]**be|sche|ren** (schenken; zuteil werden lassen; *auch für* beschenken); jmdm. [etwas] bescheren; die Kinder wurden [reich] beschert; **Be|sche|rung**

be|scheu|ert (*derb für* dumm, schwer von Begriff)

be|schich|ten *(fachspr.);* **Beschich|tung**

be|schi|cken

be|schi|ckert (*ugs. für* leicht betrunken)

Be|schi|ckung

be|schie|den; das ist ihm beschieden; *vgl.* [2]bescheiden

be|schie|ßen; Be|schie|ßung

be|schil|dern (mit einem [1]Schild versehen); **Be|schil|de|rung**

be|schimp|fen; Be|schimp|fung

be|schir|men; Be|schir|mer; beschirmt (*scherzh. für* mit einem Schirm ausgerüstet)

Be|schiss, der; -es (*derb für* Betrug); **be|schis|sen** (*derb für* sehr schlecht); *vgl.* bescheißen

be|schlab|bern, sich (sich beim Essen beschmutzen)

Be|schlächt, das; -[e]s, -e (hölzerner Uferschutz)

be|schla|fen (überschlafen) ich muss das noch -

Be|schlag, der; -[e]s, Beschläge; mit Beschlag belegen; in Beschlag nehmen, halten; **Be|schläg,** das; -s, -e (*schweiz. für* Beschlag, Metallteile an Türen, Fenstern, Schränken); [1]**be|schla|gen;** gut - (bewandert; kenntnisreich) sein; [2]**be|schla|gen;** Pferde -; die Fenster sind -; die Glasscheibe beschlägt [sich] (läuft an); die Hirschkuh ist - [worden] (*Jägerspr. für* befruchtet, begattet [worden]); **Be|schla|gen|heit,** die; - ‹*zu* [1]beschlagen›; **Beschlag|nah|me,** die; -, -n; **beschlag|nah|men;** beschlagnahmt; **Be|schlag|nah|mung**

be|schlei|chen

be|schleu|ni|gen; Be|schleu|niger; be|schleu|nigt (schnell); **Be|schleu|ni|gung; Be|schleuni|gungs_an|la|ge** *(Kernphysik),* **...ver|mö|gen** (das; -s; *Technik*), **...wert** *(Technik)*

be|schleu|sen (mit Schleusen versehen); einen Fluss -

be|schlie|ßen; Be|schlie|ßer (*veraltend für* Aufseher, Haushälter); **Be|schlie|ße|rin** *(veraltend);* **be|schlos|sen; be|schlos|sener|ma|ßen; Be|schluss; beschluss|fä|hig; Be|schluss|fähig|keit,** die; -; **Be|schluss_fassung, ...or|gan, ...recht**

be|schmei|ßen *(ugs.)*

be|schmie|ren

be|schmut|zen; ich beschmutze mir das Kleid; **Be|schmut|zung**

be|schnei|den; Be|schnei|dung; - Jesu (kath. Fest)

be|schnei|en; beschneite Dächer

be|schnüf|feln (*ugs. auch für* vorsichtig prüfen)

be|schnup|pern
be|schö|ni|gen; Be|schö|ni|gung
be|schot|tern *(fachspr.);* **Be|schot|te|rung**
be|schrän|ken; sich -; **be|schrankt** (*Eisenb.* mit Schranken versehen); -er Bahnübergang; **be|schränkt** (beengt; geistesarm); **Be|schränkt|heit,** die; -; **Be|schrän|kung**
be|schreib|bar; be|schrei|ben; Be|schrei|bung
be|schrei|en; etwas nicht -
be|schrei|ten *(geh.)*
Be|schrieb, der; -s, -e (*schweiz. neben* Beschreibung)
be|schrif|ten; Be|schrif|tung
be|schu|hen; be|schuht
be|schul|di|gen; eines Verbrechens -; **Be|schul|di|ger; Be|schul|dig|te,** der *u.* die; -n, -n (↑R 5 ff.); **Be|schul|di|gung**
be|schu|len (*Amtsspr.* mit [Schulen u.] Schulunterricht versorgen); **Be|schu|lung** *Plur. selten*
be|schum|meln *(ugs.)*
be|schup|pen *vgl.* beschupsen
be|schuppt (mit Schuppen bedeckt)
be|schup|sen (*ugs. für* betrügen)
be|schürzt
Be|schuss, der; -es
be|schüt|zen; Be|schüt|zer
be|schwat|zen, *landsch.* **be|schwät|zen** *(ugs.)*
Be|schwer, die; -, *auch* das; -[e]s (*veraltet für* Anstrengung, Bedrückung); **Be|schwer|de,** die; -, -n; - führen; **Be|schwer|de|buch; be|schwer|de|frei; Be|schwer|de₋frist** *(Rechtsw.),* **...füh|ren|de** (der *u.* die; -n, -n; ↑R 5 ff.), **...füh|rer, ...in|stanz, ...weg** (der; -[e]s; auf dem -); **be|schwe|ren;** sich -; **be|schwer|lich; Be|schwer|lich|keit; Be|schwer|nis,** die; -, -se, *auch* das; -ses, -se; **Be|schwe|rung**
be|schwich|ti|gen; Be|schwich|ti|gung
be|schwin|deln
be|schwin|gen (in Schwung bringen); **be|schwingt; Be|schwingt|heit,** die; -
be|schwipst (*ugs. für* leicht betrunken); **Be|schwips|te,** der *u.* die; -n, -n (↑R 5 ff.)
be|schwö|ren; du beschworst; er beschwor; du beschwörest; beschworen; beschwör[e]!; **Be|schwö|rer; Be|schwö|rung; Be|schwö|rungs|for|mel**
be|see|len (*geh. für* beleben; mit Seele erfüllen); **be|seelt; Be|seelt|heit,** die; -; **Be|see|lung**
be|se|geln; die Meere -; **Be|se|gel|lung,** *seltener* **Be|seg|lung**
be|se|hen
be|sei|ti|gen; Be|sei|ti|gung
be|se|li|gen (*geh. für* glücklich machen); **be|se|ligt** *(geh.);* **Be|se|li|gung** *(geh.)*
Be|sen, der; -s, -; **Be|sen₋bin|der, ...kam|mer, ...ma|cher** (Berufsbez.); **be|sen|rein; Be|sen₋schrank, ...stiel; Be|serl|baum** (*österr. ugs. für* unansehnlicher Baum); **Be|serl|park** (*österr. ugs. für* kleiner Park)
be|ses|sen; von einer Idee -; **Be|ses|se|ne,** der *u.* die; -n, -n (↑R 5 ff.); **Be|ses|sen|heit,** die; -
be|set|zen; besetzt; **Be|setzt|zei|chen** *(Telefon);* **Be|set|zung; Be|set|zungs|lis|te** (Liste der Rollenverteilung für ein Theaterstück)
be|sich|ti|gen; Be|sich|ti|gung
be|sie|deln; Be|sie|de|lung, Be|sied|lung
be|sie|geln; Be|sie|ge|lung
be|sie|gen
Be|sieg|lung *vgl.* Besiegelung
Be|sieg|te, der *u.* die; -n, -n (↑R 5 ff.)
be|sin|gen
be|sin|nen, sich; sich eines and[e]ren, andern besinnen, *aber* (↑R 47): sich eines Besseren, Bessren besinnen; **be|sinn|lich; Be|sinn|lich|keit,** die; -; **Be|sin|nung,** die; -; **Be|sin|nungs|auf|satz; be|sin|nungs|los**
Be|sitz, der; -es; **Be|sitz|an|spruch; be|sitz|an|zei|gend;** -es Fürwort (*für* Possessivpronomen); **Be|sitz₋bür|ger** *(meist abwertend),* **...bür|ger|tum; be|sit|zen; Be|sit|zer; Be|sit|zer|grei|fung; Be|sit|zer₋stolz, ...wech|sel; be|sitz|los; Be|sitz|lo|se,** der *u.* die; -n, -n (↑R 5 ff.); **Be|sitz|lo|sig|keit,** die; -; **Be|sitz|nah|me,** die; -, -n; **Be|sitz|stand; Be|sitz|tum; Be|sit|zung; Be|sitz₋ver|hält|nis|se** *(Plur.),* **...ver|tei|lung, ...wech|sel**
Bes|ki|den *Plur.* (Teil der Karpaten)
be|sof|fen (*derb für* betrunken); **Be|sof|fen|heit,** die; - *(derb)*
be|soh|len; Be|soh|lung
be|sol|den; Be|sol|de|te, der *u.* die; -n, -n (↑R 5 ff.); **Be|sol|dung; Be|sol|dungs₋grup|pe, ...ord|nung, ...recht, ...ta|rif**
be|söm|mern (*Landw.* den Boden nur im Sommer nutzen)
be|son|de|re; zur besonderen Verwendung (*Abk.* z. b. V.); insbesond[e]re; (↑R 47:) das Besond[e]re; etwas, nichts Besond[e]res; im Besonder[e]n, im Besondren; **Be|son|der|heit; be|son|ders** (*Abk.* bes.); besonders[,] wenn (↑R 88)
[1]**be|son|nen** (überlegt, umsichtig)
[2]**be|son|nen;** sich - (von der Sonne bescheinen) lassen
Be|son|nen|heit, die; -
be|sonnt; -e Hänge
be|sor|gen; Be|sorg|nis, die; -, -se; (↑R 40:) Besorgnis erregend, *aber* höchst besorgniserregend; **be|sorgt; Be|sorgt|heit,** die; -; **Be|sor|gung**
be|span|nen; Be|span|nung
be|spei|en (*geh. für* bespucken)
be|spickt (dicht besteckt)
be|spie|geln; Be|spie|ge|lung, Be|spieg|lung
be|spiel|bar; be|spie|len
be|spi|ken [bəˈspaikən] (*fachspr.* mit Spikes versehen)
be|spit|zeln; Be|spit|ze|lung, Be|spitz|lung
be|spöt|teln; be|spot|ten
be|spre|chen; Be|spre|chung
be|spren|gen; mit Wasser -
be|spren|keln
be|sprin|gen (begatten [von Tieren])
be|sprit|zen
be|sprü|hen; Be|sprü|hung
be|spu|cken
Bes|sa|ra|bi|en (Gebiet nordwestl. vom Schwarzen Meer)
Bes|se|mer|bir|ne; ↑R 95 ⟨nach dem engl. Erfinder⟩ (techn. Anlage zur Stahlgewinnung)
bes|ser; es ist besser, wenn ..., *aber* es ist das Bessere, wenn ...; eines Besser[e]n, *auch* Bessren belehren; sich eines Besser[e]n, *auch* Bessren besinnen; eine Wendung zum Besser[e]n, *auch* Bessren; das Bessere ist des Guten Feind; mit den neuen Schuhen wirst du besser gehen; dem Kranken wird es bald besser gehen; besser stellen (in eine bessere finanzielle, wirtschaftliche Lage versetzen); die besser Gestellten, *auch* Bessergestellten; die besser Verdienenden, *auch* Besserverdienenden (↑R 47); du musst immer alles besser wissen!; **Bes|ser|ge|stell|te,** der *u.* die; -n, -n (↑R 5 ff.); *vgl.* besser; **bes|sern;** ich bess[e]re (↑R 16); sich -; **bes|ser stel|len** *vgl.* besser; **Bes|se|rung,** *auch* Bess|rung; **Bes|se|rungs|an|stalt; Bes|ser|ver|die|nen|de,** der *u.* die; -n, -n (↑R 5 ff.); *vgl.* besser; **Bes|ser|wis|ser; Bes|ser|wis|se|rei; bes|ser|wis|se|risch; Bess|rung** *vgl.* Besserung;
Best, das; -s, -e (*bayr., österr. für* ausgesetzter [höchster] Preis, Gewinn); **best...** (z. B. bestgehasst)
be|stal|len (*Amtsspr.* [förmlich] in

ein Amt einsetzen); wohlbestallt; **Be|stal|lung; Be|stal|lungs|ur|kun|de**

Be|stand, der; -[e]s, Bestände; Bestand haben; von Bestand sein; der zehnjährige Bestand (*österr. für* das Bestehen) des Vereins; ein Gut in Bestand (*österr. für* Pacht) haben, nehmen; **be|stan|den** (bewachsen); dicht mit Wald - sein; (*schweiz. auch für* in vorgerücktem Alter:) ein bestandener Mann; **Be|stan|des|auf|nah|me** (*schweiz. svw.* Bestandsaufnahme); **Be|stan|des|ver|trag,** Be|stand|ver|trag (*österr. Amtsspr. für* Pachtvertrag); **be|stän|dig;** das Barometer steht auf „beständig"; **Be|stän|dig|keit,** die; -; **Be|stands|auf|nah|me; Be|stand[s]|ju|bi|lä|um** (*österr. für* Jubiläum des Bestehens); **Be|stand|teil,** der; **Be|stand|ver|trag** *vgl.* Bestandesvertrag

be|stär|ken; Be|stär|kung

be|stä|ti|gen; Be|stä|ti|gung

be|stat|ten; Be|stat|tung; Be|stat|tungs|in|sti|tut

be|stau|ben; bestaubt; sich - (staubig werden); **be|stäu|ben** (*Bot.*); **Be|stäu|bung**

be|stau|nen

best‿aus|ge|rüs|tet, ...be|währt, ...be|zahlt; Best|bie|ter

bes|te; bestens; bestenfalls; das beste [Buch] seiner Bücher; dieser Wein ist der beste; es ist am besten, wenn ...; wir fangen am besten gleich an; *aber* ich halte es für das Beste, wenn ...; er ist der Beste in der Klasse; er hat sein Bestes getan; aus etwas das Beste machen; wir arbeiten aufs, auf das Beste, *auch* beste zusammen; *aber nur* seine Wahl ist auf das, aufs Beste gefallen; mit ihrer Gesundheit steht es nicht zum Besten (nicht gut); etw. zum Besten geben, jmdn. zum Besten haben, halten; es ist nur zu deinem Besten; ich will nicht das erste Beste

be|ste|chen; be|stech|lich; Be|stech|lich|keit, die; -; **Be|ste|chung; Be|ste|chungs‿geld, ...skan|dal, ...sum|me, ...ver|such**

Be|steck, das; -[e]s, *Plur.* -e, *ugs.* -s; **be|ste|cken; Be|steck|kas|ten**

Be|steg, der; -[e]s, -e (*Geol.* tonige Zwischenlage zwischen Gesteinsschichten)

be|ste|hen; auf etwas bestehen; ich bestehe auf meiner (*heute selten* meine) Forderung; die Verbindung soll bestehen bleiben; bestehen lassen (beibehalten); **Be|ste|hen,** das; -s; seit Bestehen der Firma

be|steh|len

be|stei|gen; Be|stei|gung

Be|stell|block *Plur.* ...blocks; **be|stel|len; Be|stel|ler; Be|stell|geld** (*Postw.* Zustellgebühr); **Be|stell|kar|te; Be|stell|lis|te** (↑R 136), die; -, -n; **Be|stell|num|mer; Be|stel|lung**

bes|ten|falls; *vgl.* Fall, der; **bes|tens**

be|sternt; der -e Himmel

be|steu|ern; Be|steu|e|rung

Best|form, die; - (*Sport*)

best‿ge|hasst, ...ge|pflegt

bes|ti|a|lisch ‹lat.› (unmenschlich, grausam); **Bes|ti|a|li|tät,** die; -, -en; (Unmenschlichkeit, grausames Verhalten); **Bes|ti|a|ri|um,** das; -s, ...ien [...iən] (Titel mittelalterlicher Tierbücher)

be|sti|cken; Be|stick|hö|he (*Deichbau*); **Be|sti|ckung**

Bes|tie [...iə], die; -, -n (wildes Tier; Unmensch)

be|stie|felt

be|stimm|bar; be|stim|men; be|stimmt; an bestimmten Tagen; bestimmter Artikel (*Sprachw.*); **Be|stimmt|heit,** die; -; **Be|stim|mung; Be|stim|mungs|bahn|hof; be|stim|mungs|ge|mäß; Be|stim|mungs‿ha|fen, ...ort, ...wort** (*Plur.* ...wörter; *Sprachw.* Wort als Vorderglied einer Zusammensetzung, das das Grundwort [*vgl. d.*] näher bestimmt, z. B. „Schinken" in „Schinkenbrötchen")

best|in|for|miert

be|stirnt; der -e Himmel

Best|leis|tung

Best|mann, der; -[e]s, ...männer (*Seemannsspr.* erfahrener Seemann, der auf Küstenschiffen den Schiffsführer vertritt)

Best|mar|ke (*Sport* Rekord)

best|mög|lich; *falsch:* bestmöglichst

be|sto|cken; Be|sto|ckung (*Bot.* Seitentriebbildung; *Forstw.* Aufforstung)

be|sto|ßen (*fachspr.; schweiz. auch für* [eine Alp] mit Vieh besetzen)

be|stra|fen; Be|stra|fung

be|strah|len; Be|strah|lung; Be|strah|lungs‿do|sis, ...zeit

be|stre|ben, sich; **Be|stre|ben,** das; -s; **be|strebt;** - sein; **Be|stre|bung**

be|strei|chen; Be|strei|chung

be|strei|ken; Be|strei|kung

be|strei|ten; Be|strei|tung

best|re|nom|miert; das bestrenommierte Hotel

be|streu|en; Be|streu|ung

be|stri|cken (bezaubern; für jmdn. stricken); **be|stri|ckend; Be|stri|ckung**

be|strumpft

Best|sel|ler, der; -s, - ‹engl.› (Ware [bes. Buch] mit bes. hohen Verkaufszahlen); **Best|sel|ler‿au|tor, ...lis|te**

be|stü|cken (ausstatten, ausrüsten); **Be|stü|ckung**

be|stuh|len (mit Stühlen ausstatten); **Be|stuh|lung**

be|stür|men; Be|stür|mung

be|stür|zen; be|stür|zend; be|stürzt; - sein; **Be|stürzt|heit,** die; -; **Be|stür|zung,** die; -

be|stusst (*ugs. für* dumm, nicht bei Verstand)

best|vor|be|rei|tet

Best‿wert (*für* Optimum), **...zeit** (*Sport* Rekordzeit), **...zu|stand**

Be|such, der; -[e]s, -e; auf, zu - sein; **be|su|chen; Be|su|cher; Be|su|cher|fre|quenz; Be|su|che|rin; Be|su|cher‿strom, ...zahl; Be|suchs‿er|laub|nis, ...kar|te, ...rit|ze** (*scherzh. für* Spalt zwischen zwei Ehebetten), **...tag, ...zeit, ...zim|mer**

be|su|deln; Be|su|de|lung, Be|sud|lung

Be|ta, das; -[s], -s (griech. Buchstabe: *Β, β*); **Be|ta|blo|cker** (*kurz für* Betarezeptorenblocker)

be|tagt (*geh. für* alt); *vgl.* hochbetagt; **Be|tagt|heit,** die; -

be|ta|keln (*Seemannsspr.* mit Takelwerk versehen; *österr. ugs. für* beschwindeln); **Be|ta|ke|lung, Be|tak|lung**

Be|ta|ni|en *vgl.* Bethanien

be|tan|ken; ein Fahrzeug -; **Be|tan|kung**

Be|ta|re|zep|to|ren|blo|cker *od.* ***β*-Re|zep|to|ren-Blo|cker;** ↑R 28 (Arzneimittel für bestimmte Herzkrankheiten)

be|tas|ten

Be|ta|strah|len, *β*-Strah|len *Plur.* (↑R 25; *Kernphysik*); **Be|ta|strah|ler** (*Med.* Bestrahlungsgerät); **Be|ta|strah|lung** (*Kernphysik*)

Be|tas|tung

be|tä|ti|gen; sich -; **Be|tä|ti|gung; Be|tä|ti|gungs|feld**

Be|tat|ron (↑R 130), das; -s, *Plur.* ...one *od.* -s (*Kernphysik* Elektronenschleuder)

be|tat|schen (*ugs. für* betasten, streicheln)

be|täu|ben; Be|täu|bung; Be|täu|bungs|mit|tel, das

be|tau|en; betaute Wiesen

Be|ta|zer|fall (*Kernphysik*)

Bet‿bank, ...bru|der

Be|te, *landsch. Nebenform* Bee|te, die; -, -n (Wurzelgemüse; Futterpflanze); Rote Bete, *auch* Beete (↑R 56)
Be|tei|geu|ze, der; - ⟨arab.⟩ (ein Stern)
be|tei|len (*österr. für* beschenken; versorgen); **be|tei|li|gen;** sich -; **Be|tei|lig|te,** der *u.* die; -n, -n (↑R 5 ff.); **Be|tei|ligt|sein; Be|tei|li|gung; Be|tei|li|gungs|fi|nan|zie|rung; Be|tei|lung** (*österr. für* Beschenkung, Zuteilung)
Be|tel, der; -s ⟨Malajalam-port.⟩ (Genussmittel aus der Betelnuss); **Be|tel‿kau|er, ...nuss**
be|ten; Be|ter
Be|tes|da *vgl.* Bethesda
be|teu|ern; ich ...ere (↑R 16); **Be|teu|e|rung**
be|tex|ten
Be|tha|ni|en, *ökum.* Be|ta|ni|en [...i̯ən] (bibl. Ortsn.)
Be|thel (Heil- u. Pflegeanstalt bei Bielefeld)
Be|thes|da, *ökum.* Be|tes|da, der; -[s] (ehem. Teich in Jerusalem)
Beth|le|hem, *ökum.* Bet|le|hem (palästin. Stadt); **beth|le|he|mi|tisch;** (↑R 104:) der bethlehemitische Kindermord
Beth|männ|chen ⟨nach der Frankfurter Bankiersfamilie Bethmann⟩ (ein Gebäck aus Marzipan und Mandeln)
Be|ti|se, die; -, -n ⟨franz.⟩ (*geh. für* Dummheit)
be|ti|teln [*auch* ...ti...]
Bet|le|hem *vgl.* Bethlehem
be|töl|peln (übertölpeln); **Be|töl|pe|lung**
Be|ton [be'tɔŋ, *österr.* be'to:n], der; -s, *Plur.* -s, *österr.* -e ⟨franz.⟩ (Baustoff aus einer Mischung von Zement, Wasser, Sand usw.); **Be|ton‿bau** (*Plur.* ...bauten), **...block** (*Plur.* ...blöcke)
be|to|nen
Be|to|nie [...i̯ə], die; -, -n ⟨lat.⟩ (eine Wiesenblume; Heilpflanze)
be|to|nie|ren (*auch übertr. für* festlegen, unveränderlich machen); **Be|to|nie|rung; Be|ton|kopf** (*abwertend für* uneinsichtiger, auf seinen [politischen] Ansichten beharrender Mensch); **Be|ton|misch|ma|schi|ne**
be|ton|nen (*Seemannsspr.* ein Fahrwasser durch Seezeichen [Tonnen usw.] bezeichnen)
be|tont; be|ton|ter|ma|ßen; Be|to|nung
be|tö|ren (*geh.*); **Be|tö|rer; Be|tö|re|rin; Be|tö|rung**
Bet|pult (*kath. Kirche*)
betr. = betreffend, betreffs; **Betr.** = Betreff
Be|tracht, der; *nur noch in Fügungen wie* in Betracht kommen, ziehen; außer Betracht bleiben; **be|trach|ten;** sich -; **Be|trach|ter; Be|trach|te|rin; be|trächt|lich;** eine beträchtliche Summe, *aber* um ein Beträchtliches [höher]; **Be|trach|tung; Be|trach|tungs‿wei|se** (die), **...win|kel**
Be|trag, der; -[e]s, Beträge; **be|tra|gen;** sich -; **Be|tra|gen,** das; -s
be|tram|peln (*ugs.*)
be|trau|en; mit etwas betraut sein
be|trau|ern
be|träu|feln
Be|trau|ung
Be|treff, der; -[e]s, -e (*Amtsspr.; Abk.* Betr.); in dem Betreff (in dieser Beziehung); in Betreff, *aber* betreffs (*vgl. d.*) des Neubaus; **be|tref|fen;** was mich betrifft, so ...; **be|tref|fend** (zuständig; sich auf jmdn., etwas beziehend; *Abk.* betr.); die betreffende Behörde; den Neubau betreffend; **Be|tref|fen|de,** der *u.* die; -n, -n (↑R 5 ff.); **Be|treff|nis,** das; -ses, -se (*schweiz. für* Anteil; Summe, die auf jmdn. entfällt); **be|treffs** (*Amtsspr.; Abk.* betr.; ↑R 46); *Präp. mit Gen.:* betreffs des Neubaus (*besser:* wegen)
be|trei|ben (*schweiz. auch für* jmdn. durch das Betreibungsamt zur Zahlung einer Schuld veranlassen); **Be|trei|ben,** das; -s; auf mein -; **Be|trei|ber; Be|trei|be|rin; Be|trei|bung** (Förderung, das Voranbringen; *schweiz. auch für* Beitreibung)
be|tresst (mit Tressen versehen)
[1]be|tre|ten (verlegen); **[2]be|tre|ten;** einen Raum -; **Be|tre|ten,** das; -s; **Be|tre|ten|heit,** die; -
be|treu|en; Be|treu|er; Be|treu|e|rin; Be|treu|te, der *u.* die; -n, -n (↑R 5 ff.); **Be|treu|ung,** die; -; **Be|treu|ungs|stel|le**
Be|trieb, der; -[e]s, -e; eine Maschine in Betrieb setzen; die Maschine ist in Betrieb (läuft); **be|trieb|lich; be|trieb|sam; Be|trieb|sam|keit,** die; -; **Be|triebs‿an|ge|hö|ri|ge, ...an|lei|tung, ...arzt, ...aus|flug, ...aus|schuss, ...be|ge|hung; be|triebs‿be|reit, ...blind; Be|triebs‿blind|heit, ...di|rek|tor; be|triebs|ei|gen; Be|triebs|er|laub|nis; be|triebs|fä|hig; Be|triebs‿fe|ri|en, ...fest, ...form; be|triebs|fremd; Be|triebs‿frie|den, ...füh|rer, ...ge|heim|nis, ...ge|mein|schaft, ...grö|ße, ...in|ha|ber; be|triebs|in|tern; Be|triebs‿ka|pi|tal, ...kli|ma, ...kos|ten, ...kran|ken|kas|se, ...kü|che, ...lei|ter** (der), **...lei|tung; Be|triebs|nu|del** (*ugs.* jmd., der immer Betrieb zu machen versteht); **Be|triebs‿ob|mann, ...or|ga|ni|sa|ti|on, ...rat** (*Plur.* ...räte), **...rä|tin; Be|triebs|rats‿mit|glied, ...vor|sit|zen|de; Be|triebs‿ru|he, ...schluss** (der; -es), **...schutz; be|triebs|si|cher; Be|triebs‿stät|te** (*amtl. auch* Be|trieb|stät|te), **...stoff, ...stö|rung; Be|triebs|sys|tem** (*EDV*); **be|trieb|stö|rend; Be|triebs‿treue, ...un|fall, ...ver|fas|sung; Be|triebs|ver|fas|sungs|ge|setz; Be|triebs‿wirt, ...wir|tin, ...wirt|schaft; Be|triebs|wirt|schaf|ter** (*schweiz. für* Betriebswirt); **Be|triebs|wirt|schafts|leh|re**
be|trin|ken, sich; betrunken
be|trof|fen; - sein; **Be|trof|fe|ne,** der *u.* die; -n, -n (↑R 5 ff.); **Be|trof|fen|heit,** die; -
be|trü|ben; be|trüb|lich; be|trüb|li|cher|wei|se; Be|trüb|nis, die; -, -se (*geh.*); **be|trübt; Be|trübt|heit,** die; -
Be|trug, der; -[e]s; **be|trü|gen; Be|trü|ger; Be|trü|ge|rei; Be|trü|ge|rin; be|trü|ge|risch**
be|trun|ken; Be|trun|ke|ne, der *u.* die; -n, -n (↑R 5 ff.)
Bet|schwes|ter (*abwertend*)
Bett, das; -[e]s, -en; zu Bett gehen
Bet|tag; *vgl.* Buß- und Bettag
Bett‿bank (*Plur.* ...bänke; *österr.* auch als Bett benutzbare Couch), **...be|zug, ...couch, ...de|cke**
Bet|tel, der; -s (*abwertend für* minderwertiges Zeug, Kram); **bet|tel|arm; Bet|te|lei** (*abwertend*); **Bet|tel‿mann** (*Plur.* ...leute; *veraltet*), **...mönch; bet|teln;** ich ...[e]le (↑R 16); **Bet|tel|stab;** jmdn. an den - bringen (finanziell ruinieren)
bet|ten; sich -; **Bet|ten‿bau** (der; -[e]s), **...ma|chen** (das; -s), **...man|gel** (der; -s); **Bett‿fe|der, ...ge|stell, ...ha|se** (*ugs.*), **...him|mel, ...hup|ferl** (das; -s, -; *landsch. für* Süßigkeiten vor dem Zubettgehen)
Bet|ti, Bet|ti|na, Bet|ti|ne (w. Vorn.)
Bett‿ja|cke, ...kan|te, ...kas|ten, ...la|de (*landsch. für* Bett[stelle]); **bett|lä|ge|rig; Bett‿la|ken, ...lek|tü|re**
Bett|ler; Bett|ler‿stolz, ...zin|ken
Bett‿näs|ser, ...pfan|ne, ...pfos|ten, ...rand; bett|reif (*ugs.*); **Bett‿ru|he, ...schwe|re** (*ugs.*), **...statt** (*Plur.* ...stätten, *schweiz.* ...statten; *landsch. u. schweiz. für* Bett[stelle]), **...stel|le, ...sze|ne** (*Film*); **Bett|tru|he** (↑R 136);

Bett|tuch (↑R 136), das; -[e]s, ...tücher
Bet|tuch; *Plur.* ...tücher (beim jüdischen Gottesdienst)
Bett|um|ran|dung; Bet|tung *(fachspr.);* **Bett‿vor|le|ger, ...wäsche**
Bet|ty (w. Vorn.)
Bett|zeug
be|tucht ‹jidd.› (*ugs. für* vermögend, wohlhabend)
be|tu|lich (in umständlicher Weise freundlich u. geschäftig; gemächlich); **Be|tu|lich|keit,** die; -; **be|tun,** sich (sich umständlich benehmen; sich zieren); betan
be|tup|fen
be|tu|sam (*seltener für* betulich)
be|tü|tern (*nordd. für* umsorgen); sich - (*nordd. ugs. für* sich einen Schwips antrinken); **be|tü|tert** (*nordd. ugs. für* beschwipst)
Beu|che, die; -, -n (*fachspr.* Lauge zum Bleichen von Textilien); **beu|chen** (in Lauge kochen)
beug|bar (*auch für* flektierbar); **Beu|ge,** die; -, -n (Turnübung; *selten für* Biegung); **Beu|ge|haft,** die; **Beu|gel,** das; -s, - (*österr.* ein bogenförmiges Gebäck, Hörnchen); **Beu|ge|mus|kel; beu|gen** (*auch für* flektieren, deklinieren, konjugieren); sich -; **Beu|ger** (Beugemuskel); **beug|sam** *(veraltet);* **Beu|gung** (*auch für* Flexion, Deklination, Konjugation); **Beugungs|en|dung** *(Sprachw.);* **Beugungs-s,** das; -, - (↑R 25; *Sprachw.)*
Beu|le, die; -, -n; **beu|len;** sich -; **Beu|len|pest,** die; -; **beu|lig**
be|un|ru|hi|gen; sich -; **Be|un|ru|hi|gung** *Plur. selten*
be|ur|grun|zen (*ugs. scherzh. für* näher untersuchen)
be|ur|kun|den; Be|ur|kun|dung
be|ur|lau|ben; Be|ur|lau|bung
be|ur|tei|len; Be|ur|tei|ler; Be|ur|tei|lung; Be|ur|tei|lungs|maß|stab
Beu|schel, das; -s, - (*österr. für* Gericht aus Lunge u. Herz)
beut, beutst (*veraltet u. geh. für* bietet, bietest); *vgl.* bieten
[1]**Beu|te,** die; - (Erbeutetes)
[2]**Beu|te,** die; -, -n (*landsch. für* Holzgefäß; *Imkerspr.* Bienenstock)
beu|te|gie|rig; Beu|te|gut
Beu|tel, der; -s, -; **beu|teln;** ich ...[e]le (↑R 16; *südd., österr. für* derb schütteln; sich bauschen); das Kleid beutelt [sich]; **Beu|tel‿rat|te, ...schnei|der** (*ugs. für* Taschendieb; Wucherer), **...tier**
beu|tel|lüs|tern; beu|te|lus|tig
beu|ten; Bienen - (*Imkerspr.* einsetzen); du beutst; er beutet; gebeutet; **Beu|ten|ho|nig**
Beu|te‿recht, ...stück, ...zug
Beut|ler (*Zool.* Beuteltier)
Beut|ner (*Imkerspr.* Bienenzüchter); **Beut|ne|rei,** die; -
beutst; *vgl.* beut
Beuys [bɔys], Joseph (dt. Zeichner u. Aktionist)
be|völ|kern; ich ...ere (↑R 16); **Be|völ|ke|rung; Be|völ|ke|rungs‿dich|te, ...ex|plo|si|on, ...grup|pe, ...kreis, ...po|li|tik, ...schicht, ...schwund, ...sta|tis|tik, ...wis|sen|schaft, ...zahl, ...zu|nah|me**
be|voll|mäch|ti|gen; Be|voll|mäch|tig|te, der *u.* die; -n, -n (↑R 5 ff.); **Be|voll|mäch|ti|gung**
be|vor
be|vor|mun|den; Be|vor|mun|dung
be|vor|ra|ten (mit einem Vorrat ausstatten); **Be|vor|ra|tung,** die; -
be|vor|rech|ten (*älter für* bevorrechtigen); bevorrechtet; **be|vor|rech|ti|gen;** bevorrechtigt; **Be|vor|rech|ti|gung; Be|vor|rech|tung** (*älter für* Bevorrechtigung)
be|vor|schus|sen; du bevorschusst *(Amtsspr.);* **Be|vor|schus|sung**
be|vor|ste|hen
be|vor|tei|len (jmdm. einen Vorteil zuwenden; *veraltet für* übervorteilen); **Be|vor|tei|lung**
be|vor|wor|ten (mit einem Vorwort versehen)
be|vor|zu|gen; Be|vor|zu|gung
be|wa|chen; Be|wa|cher
be|wach|sen
Be|wa|chung
be|waff|nen; Be|waff|ne|te, der *u.* die; -n, -n (↑R 5 ff.); **Be|waff|nung**
be|wah|ren (hüten; aufbewahren); jmdn. vor Schaden -; Gott bewahre uns davor!, *aber* gottbewahre! *(ugs.)*
be|wäh|ren, sich
Be|wah|rer; be|wahr|hei|ten, sich; **Be|wahr|hei|tung**
be|währt; Be|währt|heit, die; -
Be|wah|rung (Schutz; Aufbewahrung)
Be|wäh|rung (Erprobung); **Be|wäh|rungs‿frist** *(Rechtsspr.),* **...hel|fer, ...pro|be, ...zeit**
be|wal|den; be|wal|det; be|wald|rech|ten (*Forstw.* [gefällte Bäume] behauen); **Be|wal|dung**
be|wäl|ti|gen; Be|wäl|ti|gung
be|wan|dert (erfahren; unterrichtet)
be|wandt (*veraltet für* gestaltet, beschaffen); **Be|wandt|nis,** die; -, -se
be|wäs|sern; Be|wäs|se|rung, *selten* Be|wäss|rung; **Be|wäs|se|rungs|sys|tem**
be|weg|bar; [1]**be|we|gen** (Lage ändern); du bewegst; du bewegtest; bewegt; beweg[e]!; sich -;
[2]**be|we|gen** (veranlassen); du bewegst; du bewogst; du bewögest; bewogen; beweg[e]!; **Be|weg|grund; be|weg|lich; Be|weg|lich|keit,** die; -; **be|wegt;** - sein; **Be|wegt|heit,** die; -; **Be|we|gung; Be|we|gungs‿ab|lauf, ...drang, ...frei|heit** (die; -); **be|we|gungs|los; Be|we|gungs‿stu|die, ...the|ra|pie; be|we|gungs|un|fä|hig**
be|weh|ren (*Technik* ausrüsten; *veraltend für* bewaffnen); **Be|weh|rung**
be|wei|ben, sich (*veraltet, noch scherzh. für* sich verheiraten)
be|wei|den *(Landw.)*
be|weih|räu|chern (*auch abwertend für* übertrieben loben); **Be|weih|räu|che|rung**
be|wei|nen
be|wein|kau|fen (*landsch.* einen Kauf durch Weintrinken besiegeln)
Be|wei|nung; - Christi
Be|weis, der; -es, -e; unter Beweis stellen *(Amtsspr.);* **Be|weis‿an|trag** *(Rechtsspr.),* **...auf|nah|me; be|weis|bar; Be|weis|bar|keit,** die; -; **be|wei|sen;** bewiesen; **Be|weis‿er|he|bung, ...füh|rung, ...kraft; be|weis|kräf|tig; Be|weis‿last, ...mit|tel** (das), **...stück**
be|wen|den, *nur in* es bei etw. bewenden lassen; **Be|wen|den,** das; -s; es hat dabei sein Bewenden (es bleibt dabei)
Be|werb, der; -s, -e (*österr. Sportspr. für* Wettbewerb); aus dem - werfen; **Be|werb|chen** *(landsch.); nur in* sich ein - machen (unter Vortäuschung einer Beschäftigung ein bestimmtes Ziel verfolgen); ich mache mir ein -; **be|wer|ben,** sich; sich um eine Stelle -; **Be|wer|ber; Be|wer|be|rin; Be|wer|bung; Be|wer|bungs‿schrei|ben, ...un|ter|la|gen** *(Plur.)*
be|wer|fen; Be|wer|fung
be|werk|stel|li|gen; Be|werk|stel|li|gung
be|wer|ten; Be|wer|tung
Be|wet|te|rung (*Bergmannsspr.* Versorgung der Grubenbaue mit Frischluft)
be|wi|ckeln; Be|wi|cke|lung, Be|wick|lung
be|wil|li|gen; Be|wil|li|gung
be|will|komm|nen; du bewill-

kommnest; bewillkommnet; **Be|will|komm|nung**
be|wim|pert
be|wir|ken; Be|wir|kung
be|wir|ten; be|wirt|schaf|ten; Be|wirt|schaf|tung; Be|wir|tung; Be|wir|tungs|ver|trag
Be|wit|te|rung (Methode der Werkstoffprüfung, bei der Verwitterungsvorgänge simuliert werden)
be|wit|zeln
be|wohn|bar; be|woh|nen; Be|woh|ner; Be|woh|ne|rin; Be|woh|ner|schaft
be|wöl|ken, sich; **be|wölkt;** -er Himmel; **Be|wöl|kung,** die; -; **Be|wöl|kungs‿auf|lo|cke|rung, ...zu|nah|me**
be|wu|chern
Be|wuchs, der; -es
Be|wun|de|rer, Be|wund|rer; **Be|wun|de|rin,** Be|wund|re|rin; **be|wun|dern; be|wun|derns|wert; be|wun|derns|wür|dig; Be|wun|de|rung** *Plur. selten;* **be|wun|de|rungs|wert; be|wun|de|rungs|wür|dig; Be|wund|rer,** Be|wun|de|rer; **Be|wund|re|rin,** Be|wun|de|rin
Be|wurf
be|wur|zeln, sich (Wurzeln bilden)
be|wusst; *mit Gen.:* ich bin mir keines Vergehens bewusst; ich war mir dessen bewusst; sich eines Versäumnisses bewusst werden; er hat den Fehler bewusst (mit Absicht) gemacht; sie hat mir den Zusammenhang bewusst gemacht (klar gemacht); **Be|wusst|heit,** die; -; **be|wusst|los; Be|wusst|lo|sig|keit,** die; -; **be|wusst ma|chen** *vgl.* bewusst; **Be|wusst|ma|chung; Be|wusst|sein,** das; -s; **Be|wusst|seins‿bil|dung** (die; -), **...er|wei|te|rung, ...spal|tung** *(Psych.),* **...trü|bung; Be|wusst|wer|dung,** die, -
Bey *vgl.* Bei
bez., bez, bz = bezahlt
bez. = bezüglich
Bez. = Bezeichnung
Bez., Bz. = Bezirk
be|zah|len; eine gut bezahlte Stellung; **Be|zah|ler; be|zahlt** (*Abk.* bez., bez, bz); sich - machen (lohnen); **Be|zah|lung** *Plur. selten*
be|zähm|bar; be|zäh|men; sich -; **Be|zäh|mung**
be|zau|bern; be|zau|bernd; Be|zau|be|rung
be|zecht (betrunken)
be|zeich|nen; be|zeich|nend; be|zeich|nen|der|wei|se; Be|zeich|nung (*Abk.* Bez.); **Be|zeich|nungs|leh|re,** die; - (*für* Onomasiologie)
be|zei|gen (*geh. für* zu erkennen geben, bekunden); Gunst, Beileid, Ehren -; **Be|zei|gung**
be|zeu|gen (Zeugnis ablegen; bekunden); **Be|zeu|gung**
be|zich|ti|gen; jemanden eines Verbrechens -; **Be|zich|ti|gung**
be|zieh|bar; be|zie|hen; sich auf eine Sache -; **be|zie|hent|lich** (*Amtsspr.* mit Bezug auf); *Präp. mit Gen.:* - des Unfalles; **Be|zie|her; Be|zie|hung;** in - setzen; **Be|zie|hungs|kis|te** (*ugs. für* Beziehung zu einem [Lebens]partner); **Be|zie|hungs|leh|re** (Theorie der Soziologie); **be|zie|hungs|los; Be|zie|hungs|lo|sig|keit,** die; -; **be|zie|hungs|reich; be|zie|hungs|wei|se** (*Abk.* bzw.)
be|zif|fern; ich ...ere (↑R 16); sich - auf; **Be|zif|fe|rung**
Be|zirk, der; -[e]s, -e (*Abk.* Bez. *od.* Bz.); **be|zirk|lich; Be|zirks‿amt, ...ge|richt** *(österr. u. schweiz.),* **...haupt|mann** *(österr.),* **...haupt|mann|schaft** *(österr.),* **...kar|te** *(Verkehrsw.),* **...klas|se** *(Sport),* **...li|ga** *(Sport),* **...rich|ter** *(österr. u. schweiz.),* **...schul|rat** *(österr.),* **...vor|ste|her** *(österr.);* **be|zirks|wei|se**
be|zir|zen ⟨nach der sagenhaften griech. Zauberin Circe⟩ (*ugs. für* verführen, bezaubern)
Be|zo|ar, der; -s, -e ⟨pers.⟩ (in der Volksmedizin verwendeter Magenstein von Wiederkäuern)
Be|zo|ge|ne, der; -n, -n; ↑R 5 ff. (*Bankw.* Adressat u. Akzeptant [eines Wechsels]); **Be|zo|gen|heit**
be|zopft
Be|zug (*österr. auch für* Gehalt; *vgl.* Bezüge); in Bezug auf; mit Bezug auf; auf etwas Bezug haben, nehmen (*dafür besser* sich auf etwas beziehen); Bezug nehmend auf (*dafür besser* mit Bezug auf); **Be|zü|ge** *Plur.* (Einkünfte); **Be|zü|ger** (*schweiz. für* Bezieher); **be|züg|lich;** bezügliches Fürwort (*für* Relativpronomen); *als Präp. mit Gen.* (*Amtsspr.; Abk.* bez.): bezüglich Ihres Briefes; **Be|züg|lich|keit; Be|zug|nah|me,** die; -, -n; **be|zugs|fer|tig; Be|zugs‿per|son, ...punkt, ...quel|le, ...recht; Be|zug[s]‿schein, ...stoff, ...sys|tem**
be|zu|schus|sen *(Amtsspr.);* du bezuschusst; **Be|zu|schus|sung**
be|zwe|cken
be|zwei|feln; Be|zwei|fe|lung, Be|zweif|lung
be|zwing|bar; be|zwin|gen; be|zwin|gend; Be|zwin|ger; Be|zwin|gung, die; -; **be|zwun|gen**
Bf. = Bahnhof; Brief
BfA = Bundesversicherungsanstalt für Angestellte
BFM = Bundesfinanzminister; Bundesfinanzministerium
bfn. = brutto für netto
bfr *vgl.* Franc
Bg. = Bogen (Papier)
BGB = Bürgerliches Gesetzbuch
BGBl. = Bundesgesetzblatt
BGS = Bundesgrenzschutz
[1]**BH** *(österr.)* = Bezirkshauptmannschaft; Bundesheer
[2]**BH** [be'ha:], der; -[s], -[s] (*ugs. für* Büstenhalter)
Bhag|van, Bhag|wan, der; -s, -s ⟨Hindi⟩ (Ehrentitel für religiöse Lehrer des Hinduismus *[nur Sing.];* Träger dieses Ehrentitels)
Bha|rat ['ba:...] (*amtl. Bez. der* Republik Indien)
Bhf. = Bahnhof
Bhu|tan ['bu:...] (Königreich im Himalaja); **Bhu|ta|ner** (Einwohner von Bhutan); **bhu|ta|nisch**
bi (*ugs. für* bisexuell)
Bi = Bismutum (*chem. Zeichen für* Wismut)
bi... ⟨lat.⟩ (zwei...; doppel[t]...); **Bi...** (Zwei...; Doppel[t]...)
Bi|af|ra (↑R 130; Teil von Nigeria)
Bi|a|łys|tok [bia'listɔk, *poln.* ...'wi...] (Stadt in Polen)
Bi|an|ca, Bi|an|ka (w. Vorn.)
Bi|ath|let, der; -en, -en ⟨lat.; griech.⟩; **Bi|ath|lon,** das; -s, -s (Kombination aus Skilanglauf u. Scheibenschießen)
bib|bern (*ugs. für* zittern)
Bi|bel, die; -, -n ⟨griech.⟩; **Bi|bel|druck,** der; -[e]s, -e; **Bi|bel|druck|pa|pier**
Bi|be|les|käs, der; -es, **Bi|be|les|kä|se,** der; -s (*alemannisch für* Quark)
bi|bel|fest; Bi|bel‿kon|kor|danz, ...le|se *(ev. Kirche),* **...re|gal** (kleine Orgel des 16. bis 18. Jh.s), **...spruch, ...stun|de, ...vers, ...wort** (*Plur.* ...worte)
[1]**Bi|ber,** der; -s, - (ein Nagetier; Pelz); [2]**Bi|ber,** der *od.* das; -s (Rohflanell); [3]**Bi|ber,** der; -s, - (*schweiz.* eine Art Lebkuchen)
Bi|be|rach an der Riß (↑R 132; Stadt in Oberschwaben)
Bi|ber|bett|tuch (↑R 136); **Bi|ber|geil,** das; -[e]s (Drüsenabsonderung des Bibers)
Bi|ber|nel|le, die; -, -n (*Nebenform von* Pimpernell)
Bi|ber‿pelz, ...schwanz (*auch* Dachziegelart)
Bi|bi, der; -s, -s (*ugs. für* steifer Hut; Kopfbedeckung)

Bib|li|o|graf, Bib|li|o|gra|fie usw. *eindeutschende Schreibung für* Bibliograph, Bibliographie usw.; **Bib|li|o|graph** (↑R 33 *u.* 130), der; -en, -en (↑R 126) ‹griech.› (Bearbeiter einer Bibliographie); **Bib|li|o|gra|phie** (↑R 33), die; -, ...ien (Bücherkunde; Bücherverzeichnis); **bib|li|o|gra|phie|ren** (↑R 33; den Titel einer Schrift bibliographisch verzeichnen, *auch* genau feststellen); **bib|li|o|gra|phisch** (↑R 33; bücherkundlich), *aber* (↑R 108): das Bibliographische Institut

Bib|li|o|ma|ne (↑R 130), der; -n, -n; ↑R 126 (Büchernarr); **Bib|li|o|ma|nie,** die; - (krankhafte Bücherliebe)

bib|li|o|phil (↑R 130; schöne od. seltene Bücher liebend; für Bücherliebhaber); **Bib|li|o|phi|le,** der *u.* die; -n, -n (Bücherliebhaber[in]); zwei -[n]; **Bib|li|o|phi|lie,** die; - (Liebe zu Büchern)

Bib|li|o|thek (↑R 130), die; -, -en ([wissenschaftliche] Bücherei); Deutsche Bibliothek (in Frankfurt); **Bib|li|o|the|kar,** der; -s, -e (Beamter od. Angestellter in Bibliotheken od. Volksbüchereien); **Bib|li|o|the|ka|rin; bib|li|o|the|ka|risch; Bib|li|o|theks‿saal, ...sig|na|tur, ...we|sen**

bib|lisch (↑R 130); ‹griech.›; eine biblische Geschichte

Bick|bee|re (*nordd. für* Heidelbeere)

Bi|det [bi'de:], das; -s, -s ‹franz.› (längliches Sitzbecken für Spülungen u. Waschungen)

Bi|don [bidõ:], das; -s, -s (*schweiz. für* Kanne, Kanister)

bie|der; Bie|der|keit, die; -; **Bie|der‿mann** (*Plur.* ...männer), **...mei|er** (das; *Gen.* -s, *fachspr. auch* -; [Kunst]stil in der Zeit des Vormärz [1815 bis 1848]); **bie|der|mei|er|lich; Bie|der|mei|er‿stil** (der; -[e]s), **...zeit** (die; -), **...zim|mer; Bie|der|sinn,** der; -[e]s *(geh.)*

bieg|bar; Bie|ge, die; -, -n (*landsch. für* Krümmung); **bie|gen;** du bogst; du bögest; gebogen; bieg[e]!; sich -; (↑R 50:) es geht auf Biegen oder Brechen *(ugs.)*; **bieg|sam; Bieg|sam|keit,** die; -; **Bie|gung**

Biel (BE) (schweiz. Stadt)

Bie|le|feld (Stadt am Teutoburger Wald); **Bie|le|fel|der** (↑R 103)

Bie|ler See, der; - -s; ↑R 105 (in der Schweiz)

Bien, der; -s (*Imkerspr.* Gesamtheit des Bienenvolkes); **Bienchen; Bie|ne,** die; -, -n; **Bie|nen|fleiß; bie|nen|flei|ßig; bie|nen|haft; Bie|nen‿haus, ...ho|nig, ...kö|ni|gin, ...korb, ...schwarm, ...spra|che, ...stich** (*auch* Hefekuchen mit Kremfüllung und Mandelbelag), **...stock** (*Plur.* ...stöcke), **...volk, ...wachs; Bie|nen|wachs|ker|ze; Bie|nen‿zucht, ...züch|ter**

bi|en|nal [biε...] ‹lat.› (zweijährlich; alle zwei Jahre stattfindend); **Bi|en|na|le,** die; -, -n ‹ital.› (zweijährliche Veranstaltung od. Schau, bes. in der bildenden Kunst u. im Film)

Bier, das; -[e]s, -e; (↑R 90:) 5 Liter helles -; 3 [Glas] -; untergäriges, obergäriges -; **Bier‿abend** (↑R 132), **...arsch** (*derb für* breites Gesäß); **Bier|bank|po|li|tik** *(abwertend)*; **Bier‿bass** *(ugs.)*, **...bauch** (*ugs. für* dicker Bauch), **...brau|er, ...de|ckel, ...do|se, ...ei|fer** *(ugs.)*; **bier|ernst** (*ugs. für* übertrieben ernst); **Bier‿ernst** *(ugs.)*, **...fass, ...fla|sche, ...gar|ten, ...glas** (*Plur.* ...gläser), **...kas|ten, ...kel|ler, ...krug, ...lachs** (beim Skat ein Spiel um eine Runde Bier), **...lei|che** (*ugs. scherzh. für* Betrunkener), **...rei|se** *(ugs. scherzh.)*, **...ru|he** (*ugs. für* unerschütterliche Ruhe), **...schin|ken** (eine Wurstsorte), **...sei|del; bier|se|lig** *(scherzh.)*; **Bier‿sie|der** (Berufsbez.), **...stim|me** (*ugs. für* tiefe Stimme), **...ver|lag** (Unternehmen für den Zwischenhandel mit Bier), **...wär|mer, ...wurst, ...zei|tung, ...zelt**

Bie|se, die; -, -n (farbiger Streifen an Uniformen; Ziersäumchen)

Bies|flie|ge (Dasselfliege)

[1]Biest, das; -[e]s, -er (*ugs. für* Tier; Schimpfwort)

[2]Biest, der; -[e]s (Biestmilch)

Bies|te|rei ‹*zu* [1]Biest› (*ugs. abwertend für* Gemeinheit); **bies|tig** (*ugs. für* gemein; unangenehm; sehr [stark]); eine -e Kälte

Biest|milch ‹*zu* [2]Biest› (erste Kuhmilch nach dem Kalben)

bie|ten; du bietest (*selten* bietst); *vgl.* beut; du botst (*geh.* botest); du bötest; geboten; biet[e]!; sich -; **Bie|ter**

Bi|fo|kal|bril|le ‹lat.; dt.› (Brille mit Bifokalgläsern); **Bi|fo|kal|glas** *Plur.* ...gläser (Brillenglas mit Fern- und Nahteil)

Bi|ga, die; -, ...gen ‹lat.› (von zwei Pferden gezogener [Renn]wagen in der Antike)

BIGA, Bi|ga = Bundesamt für Industrie, Gewerbe und Arbeit (in der Schweiz)

Bi|ga|mie, die; -, ...ien ‹lat.; griech.› (Doppelehe); **bi|ga|misch; Bi|ga|mist,** der; -en, -en (↑R 126); **bi|ga|mis|tisch**

Big|band, *auch* **Big Band** [...bεnt] (↑R 33), die; -, -s ‹engl.-amerik.› (großes Jazz- od. Tanzorchester)

Big Ben, der; - - ‹engl.› (Stundenglocke der Uhr im Londoner Parlamentsgebäude; *auch* der Glockenturm)

Big|busi|ness, *auch* **Big Business** [...'biznis] (↑R 33), das; - ‹engl.-amerik.› (Geschäftswelt der Großunternehmer)

bi|gott ‹franz.› (engherzig fromm; scheinheilig; blindgläubig); **Bi|got|te|rie,** die; -, ...ien

Big|point, *auch* **Big Point** (↑R 33), der; -s -s ‹engl.› (*Tennis* [spiel]entscheidender Punkt)

Bi|jou [bi'ʒu:], der *od.* das; -s, -s ‹franz.› (*schweiz. für* Kleinod, Schmuckstück); **Bi|jou|te|rie** [biʒu...], die; -, ...ien ([billiger] Schmuck; *schweiz. auch für* Schmuckwarengeschäft)

Bi|kar|bo|nat, *chem. fachspr.* **Bi|car|bo|nat** ‹lat.› (doppeltkohlensaures Salz)

Bi|ki|ni, der; -s, -s ‹nach dem Südseeatoll› (knapper, zweiteiliger Badeanzug)

bi|kon|kav [*auch* ...'ka:f] ‹lat.› (*Optik* beiderseits hohl)

bi|kon|vex [*auch* ...'vεks] ‹lat.› (*Optik* beiderseits gewölbt)

bi|la|bi|al [*auch* ...'bia:l] ‹lat.› (*Sprachw.* mit beiden Lippen gebildet); **Bi|la|bi|al,** der; -s, -e *u.* **Bi|la|bi|al|laut,** der; -[e]s, -e (mit Ober- u. Unterlippe gebildeter Laut, z. B. p)

Bi|lanz, die; -, -en ‹ital.› (*Wirtsch.* Gegenüberstellung von Vermögen u. Schulden für ein Geschäftsjahr; *übertr. für* Ergebnis); **Bi|lanz|buch|hal|ter; bi|lan|zie|ren** (*Wirtsch.* sich ausgleichen; eine Bilanz abschließen); **Bi|lan|zie|rung; bi|lanz|si|cher;** ein -er Buchhalter; **Bi|lanz|sum|me**

bi|la|te|ral [*od.* ...'ra:l] ‹lat.› (zweiseitig); -e Verträge

Bilch, der; -[e]s, -e ‹slaw.› (ein Nagetier); **Bilch|maus**

Bild, das; -[e]s, -er; im -e sein; **Bild‿ar|chiv, ...aus|schnitt, ...band** (der), **...bei|la|ge, ...be|richt, ...be|richt|er|stat|ter, ...be|schrei|bung; Bild|chen; bil|den;** sich -; die bildenden Künste (↑R 108); **Bil|der‿at|las, ...bo|gen, ...buch; Bil|der|buch‿ehe** (↑R 132; ideale, sehr gute Ehe), **...kar|ri|e|re, ...lan|dung, ...tor** *(Sport)*, **...wet|ter; Bil|der‿chro|nik, ...rah|men, ...rät|sel; bil|der-**

reich; Bil|der₋schrift, ...sturm (der; -[e]s), **...stür|mer; Bil|der-stür|me|rei; Bild₋flä|che, ...fol-ge, ...fre|quenz, ...funk, ...ge-schich|te, ...ge|stal|tung; bild-haft; Bild|haf|tig|keit,** die; -; **Bild|hau|er; Bild|hau|e|rei; Bild|hau|e|rin; bild|hau|e|risch; Bild|hau|er|kunst; bild|hau|ern** *(ugs.);* ich ...ere (↑R 16); gebild-hauert; **bild|hübsch; Bild₋in-halt, ...kon|ser|ve** *(Fernsehjar-gon),* **...kraft** (die; -); **bild|kräf-tig; bild|lich; bild|mä|ßig; Bild-mi|scher** *(Fernsehen);* **Bild|ner; bild|ne|risch; Bild|nis,** das; -ses, -se; **Bild₋plat|te, ...re|por|ta|ge, ...re|por|ter, ...röh|re; bild|sam** *(geh.);* **Bild|sam|keit,** die; - *(geh.);* **Bild₋säu|le, ...schär|fe; Bild|schirm; Bil|dschirm₋le|xi-kon, ...text** *(Abk.* Btx), **...zei-tung; bild|schön; Bild₋stel|le, ...stock** *(Plur.* ...stöcke), **...stö-rung, ...strei|fen; bild|syn-chron;** -er Ton; **Bild₋ta|fel, ...te-le|fon, ...te|le|gra|fie; Bild-Ton-Ka|me|ra** (↑R 28)

Bil|dung; Bil|dungs|an|stalt *(Amtsspr.);* **bil|dungs|be|flis|sen; Bil|dungs₋bür|ger|tum** *(Soziol.),* **...chan|cen** *(Plur.),* **...er|leb|nis; bil|dungs₋fä|hig, ...feind|lich; Bil|dungs₋gang** (der), **...grad, ...lü|cke, ...not|stand, ...po|li|tik, ...pri|vi|leg, ...rei|se; bil|dungs-sprach|lich; Bil|dungs₋stu|fe, ...ur|laub, ...weg**

Bild₋vor|la|ge, ...wer|bung, ...wer|fer *(für* Projektionsappa-rat), **...wör|ter|buch, ...zu|schrift**

Bil|ge, die; -, -n ‹engl.› *(See-mannsspr.* Kielraum, in dem sich das Leckwasser sammelt); **Bil|ge-was|ser,** das; -s

Bil|har|zi|o|se, die; -, -n ‹nach dem dt. Arzt Bilharz› (eine Wurm-krankheit)

bi|lin|gu|al [*auch* 'bi:...] ‹lat.› *(fachspr. für* zwei Sprachen spre-chend; zweisprachig); **bi|lin|gu-isch** [*auch* 'bi:...] (in zwei Spra-chen geschrieben; zweisprachig)

Bi|li|ru|bin, das; -s ‹lat.› *(Med.* Gal-lenfarbstoff)

[1]**Bill,** die; -, -s ‹engl.› (Gesetzent-wurf im engl. Parlament)

[2]**Bill** (m. Vorn.)

Bil|lard ['biljart, *österr.* bi'ja:r], das; -s, *Plur.* -e, *österr.* -s ‹franz.› (Ku-gelspiel; dazugehörender Tisch); **bil|lar|die|ren** (beim Billard in re-gelwidriger Weise stoßen); **Bil-lard|queue** [...kø:] (Billardstock)

Bill|ber|gie [...iə], die; -, -n ‹nach dem schwed. Botaniker Billberg› (eine Zimmerpflanze)

Bil|le|teur [biljɛ'tø:r, *österr.* bijɛ-'tø:r], der; -s, -e *(österr. für* Platz-anweiser; *schweiz. für* Schaffner); **Bil|le|teu|se** [...'tø:zə], die; -, -n; **Bil|lett** [bi'ljɛt, *österr. meist* bi'je:, *auch* bi'lɛt], das; -[e]s, *Plur.* -s *u.* -e *(veraltet für* Zettel, kurzes Brief-chen; *bes. österr. für* Glück-wunschbriefchen; *schweiz. für* Einlasskarte, Fahrkarte)

Bil|li|ar|de, die; -, -n ‹franz.› (10^{15}; tausend Billionen)

bil|lig; das ist nur recht und -; **Bil-lig|an|ge|bot; bil|li|gen; bil|li-ger|ma|ßen; bil|li|ger|wei|se; Bil|lig|keit,** die; -; **Bil|lig|preis; Bil|li|gung,** die; -; **Bil|lig|wa|re**

Bil|li|on, die; -, -en ‹franz.› (10^{12}; eine Million Millionen od. tau-send Milliarden); **bil|li|on[s]|tel;** *vgl.* achtel; **Bil|li|on[s]|tel,** das, *schweiz. meist* der; -s, -; *vgl.* Ach-tel

Bil|lon [bi'ljõ:], der *od.* das; -s ‹franz.› (Silberlegierung mit ho-hem Kupfergehalt [für Münzen])

Bil|sen|kraut, das; -[e]s (ein gifti-ges Kraut)

Bil|wiss, der; -es *(landsch. für* Ko-bold, Zauberer)

bim!; bim, bam!; **Bim|bam,** das; -s; *aber* heiliger Bimbam! *(ugs.)*

Bi|mes|ter, das; -s, - ‹lat.› *(veraltet für* Zeitraum von zwei Monaten)

Bi|me|tall *(Elektrotechnik* zwei miteinander verbundene Streifen aus verschiedenem Metall); **Bi-me|tal|lis|mus,** der; - (Doppel-währung)

Bim|mel, die; -, -n *(ugs. für* Glo-cke); **Bim|mel|bahn** *(ugs.);* **Bim-me|lei,** die; - *(ugs.);* **bim|meln** *(ugs.);* ich ...[e]le (↑R 16)

bim|sen *(ugs. für* schleifen, drillen; angestrengt lernen); du bimst; **Bims|stein**

bi|när, bi|när, bi|na|risch ‹lat.› *(fachspr.* aus zwei Einheiten be-stehend, Zweistoff...)

Bin|de, die; -, -n; **Bin|de|ge|we-be; Bin|de|ge|webs₋ent|zün-dung, ...fa|ser, ...mas|sa|ge, ...schwä|che; Bin|de₋glied, ...haut, ...haut|ent|zün|dung, ...mit|tel** (das); **bin|den;** du bandst (bandest); du bändest; ge-bunden *(vgl. d.);* bind[e]!; sich -; **Bin|der; Bin|de|rei; Bin|de|rin; Bin|de-s,** das; -, - (↑R 25); **Bin-de₋strich, ...wort** *(Plur.* ...wör-ter; *für* Konjunktion); **Bind|fa-den; bin|dig;** -er (schwerer, zä-her) Boden; **Bin|dung**

Bin|ge, Pin|ge, die; -, -n *(Berg-mannsspr.* durch Einsturz alter Grubenbaue entstandene trich-terförmige Vertiefung)

Bin|gel|kraut (ein Gartenunkraut)

Bin|gen (Stadt am Rhein); **Bin|ger** (↑R 103); das - Loch; **bin|ge-risch**

Bin|go ['biŋgo], das; -[s] ‹engl.› (Glücksspiel; eine Art Lotto)

Bin|kel, der; -s, -[n] *(bayr., österr. ugs. für* Bündel)

bin|nen; *Präp. mit Dat.:* binnen ei-nem Jahr *(geh. auch mit Gen.:* binnen eines Jahres); binnen drei Tagen *(auch* binnen dreier Tage); binnen kurzem (↑R 47); binnen Jahr und Tag; **bin|nen|bords** (in-nerhalb des Schiffes); **Bin|nen-₋deut|sche** (der *u.* die; -n, -n), **...eis, ...fi|sche|rei, ...han|del, ...land** *(Plur.* ...länder), **...markt, ...meer, ...schif|fer, ...see** (der)

Bi|no|kel [*auch* bi'nɔk(ə)l], (↑R 132), das; -s, - ‹franz.› *(veral-tet für* Brille, Fernrohr, Mikro-skop für beide Augen); **bi|no|ku-lar** [*auch* 'bi:n...] ‹lat.› (mit beiden Augen, für beide zugleich)

Bi|nom, das; -s, -e ‹lat.; griech.› *(Math.* Summe aus zwei Glie-dern); **Bi|no|mi|al₋ko|ef|fi|zi-ent, ...rei|he; bi|no|misch** *(Math.* zweigliedrig); -er Lehrsatz

Bin|se, die; -, -n; in die -n gehen *(ugs. für* verloren gehen; un-brauchbar werden); **Bin|sen-₋wahr|heit** (allgemein bekannte Wahrheit), **...weis|heit**

bi|o... ‹griech.› (leben[s]...); **Bi|o...** (Leben[s]...); **bi|o|ak|tiv**[1] (biolo-gisch aktiv); ein -es Waschmittel; **Bi|o|che|mie**[1] (Lehre von den chemischen Vorgängen in Lebe-wesen); **Bi|o|che|mi|ker**[1]; **bi|o-che|misch**[1]; **bi|o|dy|na|misch** (nur mit organischer Düngung); **Bi|o|gas** (bei der Zersetzung von Mist o. Ä. entstehendes Gas); **bi-o|gen** *(Biol.* von Lebewesen stam-mend); **Bi|o|ge|ne|se,** die; -, -n (Entwicklung[sgeschichte] der Lebewesen); **bi|o|ge|ne|tisch; Bi|o|ge|o|gra|phie**[1] (↑R 33), die; - (Beschreibung der geogr. Ver-breitung der Lebewesen); **Bi|o-ge|o|zö|no|se,** die; - (Wechselbe-ziehungen zwischen Pflanzen u. Tieren einerseits u. der unbeleb-ten Umwelt andererseits)

Bi|o|graf, Bi|o|gra|fie usw. *ein-deutschende Schreibung für* Bio-graph, Biographie usw.; **Bi|o-graph** (↑R 33), der; -en, -en; ↑R 126 (Verfasser einer Lebens-beschreibung); **Bi|o|gra|phie** (↑R 33), die; -, ...ien (Lebens-beschreibung); **Bi|o|gra|phin** (↑R 33); **bi|o|gra|phisch** (↑R 33)

---

[1] [*auch* 'bi:o...]

Bi|o|ka|ta|ly|sa|tor[1] (die Stoffwechselvorgänge steuernder biolog. Wirkstoff); **Bi|o|kost** (Kost, die nur aus natürlichen, nicht mit chemischen Mitteln behandelten Nahrungsmitteln besteht); **Bi|o|la|den** (Laden, in dem nur chemisch unbehandelte Produkte verkauft werden); **Bi|o|lo|ge,** der; -n, -n (↑R 126); **Bi|o|lo|gie,** die; - (Lehre von der belebten Natur); **Bi|o|lo|gie|un|ter|richt; Bi|o|lo|gin; bi|o|lo|gisch;** biologische Schädlingsbekämpfung, *aber* (↑R 108): Biologische Anstalt Helgoland; **bi|o|lo|gisch-dy|na|misch** (nur mit organischer Düngung [arbeitend]); **Bi|o|ly|se,** die; -, -n (chem. Zersetzung durch lebende Organismen); **bi|o|ly|tisch; Bi|o|mas|se,** die; - (Gesamtheit der lebenden, toten und zersetzten Organismen einschließlich der von ihnen produzierten organischen Substanz an einem Ort); **Bi|o|met|rie, Bi|o|met|rik** (↑R 130), die; - ([Lehre von der] Zählung u. [Körper]messung an Lebewesen); **Bi|o|müll** (organische [Haushalts]abfälle); **Bi|o|nik,** die; - ⟨nach engl.-amerik. bionics, *Kurzw. aus* bio... *u.* electronics⟩ (Wissenschaft, die elektronische Probleme nach dem Vorbild biologischer Funktionen zu lösen versucht); **bi|o|nisch; Bi|o|phy|sik**[1] (Lehre von den physikalischen Vorgängen in u. an Lebewesen; heilkundlich angewandte Physik); **Bi|op|sie,** die; -, -n (*Med.* Untersuchung von Gewebe, das dem lebenden Organismus entnommen ist); **Bi|o|sphä|re**[1] (gesamter irdischer Lebensraum der Pflanzen und Tiere); **Bi|o|tech|nik**[1] (Nutzbarmachung biologischer Vorgänge); **bi|o|tisch** (*fachspr. für* auf Lebewesen, auf Leben bezüglich)

Bi|o|tit [*auch* ...'tit], der; -[e]s, -e ⟨nach dem franz. Physiker Biot⟩ (ein Mineral)

Bi|o|ton|ne ⟨griech.; dt.⟩ (Mülltonne für organische [Haushalts]abfälle); **Bi|o|top,** der *u.* das; -s, -e ⟨griech.⟩ (*Biol.* durch bestimmte Lebewesen od. eine bestimmte Art gekennzeichneter Lebensraum); **Bi|o|typ, Bi|o|ty|pus** (*Biol.* Gruppe von Lebewesen mit gleicher Erbanlage); **Bi|o|zö|no|se,** die; - (Lebensgemeinschaft von Pflanzen u. Tieren); **bio|zö|no|tisch**

bi|po|lar [*od.* ...'la:r] ⟨lat.; griech.⟩ (zweipolig); **Bi|po|la|ri|tät** [*od.* ...'tɛ:t], die; -

Bi|quad|rat ⟨lat.⟩ (*Math.* Quadrat des Quadrats, vierte Potenz); **bi|quad|ra|tisch** [*od.* ...'dra:...]; -e Gleichung (Gleichung vierten Grades)

Bir|cher‿mus *od.* **...mü|es|li** ⟨nach dem Arzt Bircher-Benner⟩; ↑R 95; *vgl.* Müesli *u.* Müsli

Bir|die ['bœ:(r)di], das; -s, -s ⟨engl.⟩ (*Golf* ein Schlag unter Par)

Bi|re|me, die; -, -n ⟨lat., „Zweiruderer"⟩ (antikes Kriegsschiff)

Bi|rett, das; -[e]s, -e ⟨lat.⟩ (Kopfbedeckung des katholischen Geistlichen)

Bir|ger (m. Vorn.)

Bir|git, Bir|git|ta (w. Vorn.)

Bir|ke, die; -, -n (Laubbaum); **bir|ken** (aus Birkenholz); **Bir|ken|wald; Birk‿hahn, ...huhn**

Bir|ma (Staat in Hinterindien; *vgl.* Myanmar); **Bir|ma|ne,** der; -n, -n (↑R 126); **bir|ma|nisch**

Bir|ming|ham ['bœ:(r)miŋəm] (engl. Stadt)

Birn|baum; Bir|ne, die; -, -n; **bir|nen|för|mig, birn|för|mig; Birn|stab** (*Archit.* Stilelement der got. Baukunst)

Bir|te (w. Vorn.)

bis[1]; bis [nach] Berlin; bis hierher; bis wann?; bis jetzt; bis auf weiteres (↑R 47); bis nächsten Montag; bis ans Ende der Welt; bis zu 50%; wir können bis zu vier gebundene Exemplare abgeben („bis zu" *hier ohne Einfluss auf die folgende Beugung, weil adverbial gebraucht*), *aber* Gemeinden bis zu 10 000 Einwohnern („bis zu" *hier Präposition mit Dativ*); vier- bis fünfmal (↑R 23; *mit Ziffern* 4- bis 5-mal); bis und mit (*schweiz.* bis einschließlich); bis und mit achtem August

Bi|sam, der; -s, *Plur.* -e *u.* -s ⟨hebr.⟩ (Moschus *[nur Sing.];* Pelz); **Bi|sam|rat|te**

Bis|ca|ya *vgl.* Biskaya

bi|schen (*mitteld. für* [ein Baby] beruhigend auf dem Arm wiegen); du bischst

Bisch|kek (Hptst. Kirgisiens)

Bi|schof, der; -s, Bischöfe (kirchl. Würdenträger); **Bi|schö|fin,** die; -, -nen; **bi|schöf|lich; Bi|schofs‿hut** (der), **...kon|fe|renz; bi|schofs|li|la; Bi|schofs‿müt|ze, ...sitz, ...stab, ...stuhl**

Bi|se, die; -, -n (*schweiz. für* Nord[ost]wind)

Bi|se|xu|a|li|tät [*auch* ...'tɛ:t] (*Biol.* Doppelgeschlechtigkeit; *Med., Psych.* Nebeneinander von homo- u. heterosexuellen Veranlagungen); **bi|se|xu|ell** [*auch* ...'ɛl] ⟨lat.⟩ (doppelgeschlechtig; sowohl heterosexuell als auch homosexuell)

bis|her (bis jetzt); **bis|he|rig;** der bisherige Außenminister; *aber* das Bisherige; im Bisherigen (im bisher Gesagten, Geschriebenen)

Bis|ka|ya, Bis|ca|ya [*beide* ...'ka:ja], die; - (*kurz für* Golf von Biskaya; Bucht des Atlantiks)

Bis|kot|te, die; -, -n ⟨ital.⟩ (*österr. für* Löffelbiskuit)

Bis|kuit [...'kvi(:)t], das, *auch* der; -[e]s, *Plur.* -s, *auch* -e ⟨franz.⟩ (feines Gebäck aus Eierschaum); **Bis|kuit‿por|zel|lan, ...teig**

bis|lang (bis jetzt)

Bis|marck (Gründer und erster Kanzler des Deutschen Reiches); **Bis|marck‿ar|chi|pel** (der; -s; Inselgruppe nordöstl. von Neuguinea), **...he|ring; bis|mar|ckisch, bis|marcksch** (↑R 94); die bismarck[i]schen Sozialgesetze; ein Politiker von bismarck[i]schem Format

Bis|mark (Stadt in der Altmark)

Bis|mut *vgl.* Wismut; **Bis|mu|tum,** das; -[s] (*lat. Bez. für* Wismut; *Zeichen* Bi)

Bi|son, der; -s, -s (nordamerik. Büffel)

Biss, der; -es, -e

Bis|sau (Hptst. von Guinea-Bissau)

biss|chen (↑R 46); das bisschen; ein bisschen (ein wenig); ein klein bisschen; mit ein bisschen Geduld; **Biss|chen** (kleiner Bissen); **bis|sel,** bisserl (*landsch. für* bisschen); ein - Brot; **Bis|sen,** der; -s, -; **bis|sen|wei|se; bis|serl** *vgl.* bissel; **Biss|gurn,** die; -, - (*bayr., österr. ugs. für* zänkische Frau); **bis|sig; Bis|sig|keit**

Bis|ten, das; -s (Lockruf der Haselhenne)

Bis|ter, der *od.* das; -s ⟨franz.⟩ (braune Wasserfarbe)

Bist|ro [*auch* ...'tro:] (↑R 130), das;

---

[1] [*auch* 'bi:o...]

---

[1] Ein Strich (–) darf, muss aber nicht dafür gesetzt werden, wenn „bis" einen Zwischenwert angibt, z. B.: er hat eine Länge von 6–8 Metern, das Buch darf 3–4 Mark kosten, 4–5fach. Der Strich darf nicht gesetzt werden, wenn „bis" in Verbindung mit „von" eine Erstreckung bezeichnet. Also nicht: die Tagung dauerte vom 5.–9. Mai. Bei verkürzter Wiedergabe ohne „von" kann der Strich jedoch gesetzt werden: Sprechstunde 8–10, 15–17. Am Zeilenanfang od. -ende wird „bis" immer ausgeschrieben.

-s, -s ‹franz.› (kleine Schenke od. Kneipe)

Bis|tum, das; -s, ...tümer (Amtsbezirk eines kath. Bischofs)

bis|wei|len

Bis|wind, der; -[e]s (*schweiz., südbad. neben* Bise)

Bit, das; -[s], -[s] ‹engl.; *Kurzw. aus* binary digit› (*Nachrichtentechnik* Informationseinheit); *Zeichen* bit

Bi|thy|ni|en [...i̯ən] (antike Landschaft in Kleinasien); **Bi|thy|ni|er** [...i̯ər]; **bi|thy|nisch**

Bitt|brief; bit|te; bitte schön!; bitte wenden! (*Abk.* b. w.); geben Sie mir[,] bitte[,] das Buch (↑R 81); du musst Bitte, *auch* bitte sagen; **Bit|te,** die; -, -n; **bit|ten;** du batst (batest); du bätest; gebeten; bitt[e]!; **Bit|ten,** das; -s

bit|ter; bit|ter|bö|se; Bit|te|re, der; ...tter[e]n, ...tter[e]n *u.* Bittre, der; ...ttren, ...ttren; ↑R 5 ff. (bitterer Schnaps); **bit|ter|ernst;** es wird - (sehr ernst); **bit|ter|kalt;** es ist bitterkalt; ein bitterkalter Wintertag; **Bit|ter|keit,** die; -; **Bit|ter|klee; bit|ter|lich; Bit|ter|ling** (Fisch; Pflanze; Pilz); **Bit|ter|man|del|öl,** das; -s; **Bit|ter|nis,** die; -, -se *(geh.)*; **Bit|ter|salz** (Magnesiumsulfat); **bit|ter|süß,** *auch* **bit|ter-süß** (↑R 27); **Bit|ter‿was|ser** (*Plur.* ...wässer; Mineralwasser mit Bittersalzen), **...wurz** *od.* **...wur|zel** (Gelber Enzian)

Bit|te|schön, das; -s; er sagte ein höfliches -; *vgl. aber* bitte; **Bitt‿gang** (der), **...ge|bet, ...ge|such**

Bitt|re *vgl.* Bittere

Bitt‿schrift *(veraltend)*, **...stel|ler; Bitt|tag** (↑R 136; *kath. Kirche*); **bitt|wei|se** *(selten)*

Bi|tu|men, das; -s, *Plur.* -, *auch* ...mina ‹lat.› (teerartige [Abdichtungs- u. Isolier]masse); **bi|tu|mig; bi|tu|mi|nie|ren** (mit Bitumen behandeln); **bi|tu|mi|nös**

[1]**bit|zeln** (*bes. südd. für* prickeln; [vor Kälte] beißend weh tun; *österr. auch für* zornig, gereizt sein); bitzelnder neuer Wein

[2]**bit|zeln** (*mitteld. für* kleine Stückchen abschneiden); ich bitz[e]le (↑R 16)

Bit|zel|was|ser (*bes. südd. für* Sprudelwasser)

bi|va|lent [*auch* 'bi:...] (zweiwertig)

Bi|wak, das; -s, *Plur.* -s *u.* -e ‹nordd.-franz.› (behelfsmäßiges Nachtlager im Freien); **bi|wa|kie|ren**

bi|zarr ‹franz.› (wunderlich; seltsam); **Bi|zar|re|rie,** die; -, ...i̯en

Bi|zeps, der; -[es], -e ‹lat.› (Beugemuskel des Oberarmes)

Bi|zet [bi'ze:] (franz. Komponist)

bi|zyk|lisch, *chem. fachspr.* bi|cyc-lisch [*od.* ...'tsy(:)...] (einen Kohlenstoffdoppelring enthaltend)

Björn (m. Vorn.); **Bjørn|son** ['bjœ:rnsɔn] (norweg. Schriftsteller)

Bk = *chem. Zeichen für* Berkelium

Bl. = Blatt (Papier)

Bla|bla, das; -[s] (*ugs. für* Gerede)

Bla|che (*landsch. u. schweiz. Nebenform von* Blahe)

Blach|feld (*geh. veraltend für* flaches Feld)

Black|box, *auch* **Black Box** ['blɛk...], die; -, -es ‹engl.› (Teil eines kybernetischen Systems; Flugschreiber); **Black-out,** *auch* **Black|out** [blɛk'a̯ut], das *u.* der; -[s], -s (Geistesabwesenheit, Erinnerungslücke; *Theater* plötzliche Verdunkelung am Szenenschluss; *auch* kleiner Sketsch; *Raumfahrt* Unterbrechung des Funkkontakts); **Black|pow|er,** *auch* **Black Pow|er** ['blɛk'pa̯uə(r)], die; - (Bewegung nordamerik. Schwarzer gegen die Rassendiskriminierung)

blad (*österr. ugs. für* dick); **Bla|de,** der *u.* die; -n, -n (↑R 5 ff.)

blaf|fen, bläf|fen (*ugs. für* bellen); **Blaf|fer, Bläf|fer** *(ugs.)*

Blag, das; -s, -en *u.* **Bla|ge,** die; -, -n (*ugs. für* [lästiges] Kind)

Bläh|bauch (aufgeblähter Bauch)

Bla|he, *landsch. auch* Bla|che, *österr.* Pla|che, die; -, -n (Plane, Wagendecke; grobe Leinwand)

blä|hen; sich -; **Blä|hung**

bla|ken (*nordd.* schwelen, rußen)

blä|ken (*ugs. abwertend* schreien)

Bla|ker ‹*zu* blaken› (metallene [Wand]leuchte mit reflektierendem Schild)

bla|kig (*nordd. für* rußend)

bla|ma|bel ‹franz.› (beschämend); ...ab|le (↑R 130) Geschichte; **Bla|ma|ge** [...'ma:ʒə, *österr.* ...'ma:ʒ], die; -, -n [...'ma:ʒ(ə)n] (Schande; Bloßstellung); **bla|mie|ren;** sich -

Blan|ca (w. Vorn.)

blan|chie|ren [blaŋ'ʃi..., *auch* blã-'ʃi:...] ‹franz.› (*Gastron.* abbrühen, überbrühen)

bland ‹lat.› (*Med.* milde, reizlos [von einer Diät]; ruhig verlaufend [von einer Krankheit])

Blan|di|ne (w. Vorn.)

blank (rein, bloß); blanker, blankste; blank machen, reiben, polieren usw., blank (*südd., österr. für* ohne Mantel) gehen; *vgl. aber* blankziehen; die blank polierte Dose; die Dose ist blank poliert; (↑R 102:) der Blanke Hans (*nordd. für* stürmische Nordsee);

Blank [blæŋk], das; -s, -s ‹engl.› (*EDV* [Wort]zwischenraum, Leerstelle); **Blan|ka** (w. Vorn.); **Blän|ke,** die; -, -n (*selten für* kleiner Tümpel); **Blank|eis** ([Gletscher]eis ohne Schnee)

Blan|ke|ne|se (Stadtteil von Hamburg)

Blan|kett, das; -[e]s, -e ‹*zu* blank› (unterschriebenes, noch nicht [vollständig] ausgefülltes Schriftstück); **blan|ko** ‹ital.› (leer, unausgefüllt); **Blan|ko‿scheck, ...voll|macht** (*übertr. für* unbeschränkte Vollmacht); **Blank|vers** ‹engl.› (fünffüßiger Jambenvers); **blank|zie|hen** er hat den Säbel blankgezogen (aus der Scheide)

Bläs|chen; Bla|se, die; -, -n; ein Blasen ziehendes Mittel; **Bla|se|balg** *Plur.* ...bälge; **bla|sen;** du bläst, er bläst; ich blies, du bliesest; geblasen; blas[e]!; **Bla|sen‿bil|dung, ...ent|zün|dung, ...kam|mer** (*Kernphysik* Gerät zum Sichtbarmachen der Bahnspuren ionisierender Teilchen), **...ka|tarrh** (↑R 33), **...ka|the|ter, ...lei|den, ...spie|ge|lung, ...stein, ...tang** (eine Braunalgenart); **Bla|sen zie|hend** *vgl.* Blase; **Blä|ser; Bla|se|rei**

bla|siert ‹franz.› (dünkelhaft-herablassend; hochnäsig); **Bla|siert|heit,** die; -

bla|sig; Blas|in|stru|ment

Bla|si|us (m. Vorn.)

Blas|ka|pel|le; Blas|mu|sik

Bla|son [bla'zɔ̃:], der; -s, -s ‹franz.› (*Heraldik* Wappen[schild]); **bla|so|nie|ren** [...zo...] (Wappen fachgerecht beschreiben); **Bla|so|nie|rung**

Blas|phe|mie, die; -, ...i̯en ‹griech.› (Gotteslästerung); **blas|phe|mie|ren; blas|phe|misch, blas|phe|mis|tisch**

Blas|rohr

blass; -er (*auch* blässer), -este (*auch* blässeste); blass sein; blass werden; **blass|blau; Bläs|se,** die; - (Blassheit); *vgl. aber* Blesse; **blas|sen** (*selten für* blass werden); du blasst; geblasst; **Bläss|huhn,** Bless|huhn; **bläss|lich; blass|ro|sa**

Blas|to|ge|ne|se, die; - ‹griech.› (*Biol.* ungeschlechtliche Entstehung eines Lebewesens); **Blas|tom,** das; -s, -e (*Med.* Geschwulst); **Blas|tu|la,** die; -, ...lae [...lɛ:] (*Biol.* Entwicklungsstadium des Embryos nach der Furchung der Eizelle)

Blatt, das; -[e]s, Blätter (*Jägerspr. auch für* Schulterstück od. Instrument zum Blatten; *Abk.* Bl. [Papier]); 5 - Papier (↑R 90); **blat|ten** (*Jägerspr.* auf einem Blatt [Pflanzenblatt od. Instrument] Rehe anlocken); **Blat|ter** (Instrument zum Blatten); **blät|te|rig,** blätt|rig; **Blät|ter|ma|gen** (Magen der Wiederkäuer); **blät|tern;** ich ...ere (↑R 16)

Blat|tern *Plur.* (*älter für* Pocken); **Blat|ter|nar|be** (*älter für* Pockennarbe); **blat|ter|nar|big** (*älter für* pockennarbig)

Blät|ter‿teig, ...wald (*scherzh. für* Vielzahl von Zeitungen); **blät|ter|wei|se,** blätt|wei|se; **Blät|ter|werk,** Blätt|werk, das; -[e]s; **Blatt‿fe|der, ...gold, ...grün, ...laus; blatt|los; Blatt|pflan|ze; blätt|rig,** blät|te|rig; **Blatt|schuss; Blatt|tang** (↑R 136), der; -[e]s; **Blatt|trieb** (↑R 136); **blatt|wei|se,** blät|ter|wei|se; **Blatt|werk,** Blät|ter|werk, das; -[e]s

blau; -er; -[e]ste; sein blaues Wunder erleben (*ugs. für* staunen); blauer Montag; jmdm. blauen Dunst vormachen *(ugs.);* einen blauen Brief (*ugs. für* Mahnschreiben der Schule an die Eltern; *auch* Kündigungsschreiben) erhalten; unsere blauen Jungs (*ugs. für* Marinesoldaten); die blaue Blume (Sinnbild der Romantik); die blaue Mauritius; blauer Fleck (*ugs. für* Bluterguss); blau sein (*auch ugs. für* betrunken sein); Aal blau; *im Pass o. Ä.:* Augen: blau. *Getrennt- und Zusammenschreibung:* ein blau gestreifter Stoff; etwas blau färben, machen, streichen; *vgl. aber* blaumachen. *Farbbezeichnungen:* blaugrün, blaurot usw. (↑R 27). *Großschreibung:* die Farbe Blau; ins Blaue reden; Fahrt ins Blaue; (↑R 102 *u.* 108:) das Blaue Band des Ozeans; die Blaue Grotte (von Capri); der Blaue Nil; Blauer Eisenhut; der Blaue Engel (Siegel für umweltschonende Produkte); der Blaue Planet (die Erde); der Blaue Reiter (Name einer Künstlergemeinschaft); *vgl. auch* Blau, Blaue; **Blau,** das; -s, *Plur.* -, *ugs.* -s (blaue Farbe); in Blau gekleidet; mit Blau bemalt; Stoffe in Blau; das Blau des Himmels; **blau|äu|gig** (↑R 24); **Blau‿bart** (der; -[e]s, ...bärte; Frauenmörder [im Märchen]), **...ba|salt, ...bee|re** (*ostmitteld. für* Heidelbeere); **blau|blü|tig** (*ugs. für* adlig); **Blau|druck** *Plur.* ...drucke; **Blaue,** das; -n (↑R 47); ins Blaue schießen; das Blaue vom Himmel [herunter]reden; Fahrt ins Blaue; **Bläue,** die; - (Himmel[sblau]); **Blau|ei|sen|erz; blau|en** (*geh. für* blau werden); der Himmel blaut; **bläu|en** (blau machen, färben; *ugs. auch für* schlagen); **Blau‿fel|chen** (ein Fisch), **...fuchs; blau|grau** (↑R 27); **blau|grün** (↑R 27); **Blau|helm,** der; -[e]s, -e (UNO-Soldat); **Blau|ja|cke** (*ugs. für* Matrose); **Blau|kraut,** das; -[e]s; (*landsch. u. österr. für* Rotkohl); **bläu|lich;** bläulich grün, bläulich rot usw. (↑R 40); **Blau|licht** *Plur.* ...lichter; **Blau|ling, Bläu|ling** (ein Schmetterling; Fisch); **blau|ma|chen** (*ugs. für* nicht zur Arbeit, Schule o. Ä. gehen), *aber* blau ma|chen (blau färben); **Blau‿mann** (*Plur.* ...männer; *ugs. für* blauer Monteuranzug), **...mei|se, ...ra|cke** (ein Vogel); **blau|rot** (↑R 27); **Blau‿säu|re** (die; -), **...schim|mel; blau|sti|chig; Blau|strumpf** (*veraltend scherzh. für* intellektuelle Frau); **Blau|weiß|por|zel|lan** (↑R 28)

Bla|zer ['ble:zə(r)], der; -s, - ⟨engl.⟩ (Klubjacke; sportl.-elegante Jacke)

Blech, das; -[e]s, -e; **Blech‿blas|in|stru|ment, ...büch|se, ...do|se; ble|chen** (*ugs. für* zahlen); **ble|chern** (aus Blech); **Blech‿la|wi|ne** (*ugs. für* lange Kolonne dicht aufeinander folgender Autos); **...mu|sik; Blech|ner** (*südd. für* Klempner); **Blech‿sa|lat** (*ugs. für* Autounfall mit Totalschaden), **...schach|tel, ...scha|den, ...sche|re**

ble|cken; die Zähne -

[1]**Blei,** der; -[e]s, -e (*svw.* Brachse) [2]**Blei,** das; -[e]s, -e (chem. Element, Metall; *Zeichen* Pb [*vgl.* Plumbum]; Richtblei; *zollamtlich für* Plombe); [3]**Blei,** der, *auch* das; -[e]s, -e (*ugs. kurz für* Bleistift); **Blei|asche** (↑R 132)

Blei|be, die; -, -n *Plur. selten* (Unterkunft); **blei|ben;** du bliebst; geblieben; bleib[e]!; (↑R 39:) bleiben lassen (*auch für* unterlassen); er hat es bleiben lassen (*seltener* bleiben gelassen); *vgl. auch* hängen, liegen, sitzen, stehen

bleich; Blei|che, die; -, -n; [1]**blei|chen** (bleich machen); du bleichtest; gebleicht; bleich[e]!; die Sonne bleicht das Haar; [2]**blei|chen** (bleich werden); du bleichtest (*veraltet* blichst); gebleicht (*veraltet* geblichen); bleich[e]!; der Teppich bleicht in der Sonne; **Blei|che|rei; Blei|chert,** der; -s, -e (blasser Rotwein); **Bleich‿ge|sicht** (*Plur.* ...gesichter), **...sand** (*Geol.* graublaue Sandschicht), **...sucht** (die; -); **bleich|süch|tig**

blei|en (mit Blei versehen); **blei|ern** (aus Blei); **blei|far|ben; blei|frei;** sein Auto fährt bleifrei (mit bleifreiem Benzin); **Blei|frei,** das; -s *meist ohne Artikel;* Bleifrei (bleifreies Benzin) tanken; **Blei|fuß** *(ugs.);* mit Bleifuß (ständig mit Vollgas) fahren; **Blei|gie|ßen,** das; -s; **Blei|glanz** (ein Mineral); **blei|hal|tig; Blei|kris|tall; blei|schwer; Blei|stift,** der; *vgl. auch* [3]Blei; **Blei|stift‿ab|satz** *(ugs.),* **...spit|zer, ...stum|mel; Blei|weiß** (Bleifarbe)

Blen|de, die; -, -n (*auch* blindes Fenster, Nische; *Optik* lichtabschirmende Scheibe; ein Mineral); **blen|den** (*auch* Bauw. [ver]decken); **Blen|den|au|to|ma|tik** *(Fototechnik);* **blen|dend;** ein blendend weißes Kleid; der Schnee war blendend weiß; **Blen|der; blend|frei; Blend‿gra|na|te, ...la|ter|ne, ...schutz, ...schutz|zaun** *(Verkehrsw.);* **Blen|dung; Blend|werk** *(geh.)*

Bles|se, die; -, -n (weißer Stirnfleck od. -streifen; Tier mit weißem Stirnfleck); *vgl. aber* Blässe; **Bless|huhn** *vgl.* Blässhuhn

bles|sie|ren ⟨franz.⟩ (*veraltet für* verwunden); **Bles|sur,** die; -, -en (*geh. für* Verwundung)

bleu [blø:] ⟨franz.⟩ (blassblau); *vgl. auch* beige; **Bleu,** das; -s, *Plur.* -, *ugs.* -s

Bleu|el, der; -s, - (*veraltet für* Schlägel [zum Wäscheklopfen])

bleu|en *frühere Schreibung für* bläuen

Blick, der; -[e]s, -e; **blick|dicht;** -e Strumpfhosen; **bli|cken; Blick‿fang, ...feld, ...kon|takt; blick|los; Blick‿punkt, ...rich|tung, ...win|kel**

blind; blinder Alarm; blind sein, werden; (↑R 39:) blind fliegen (ohne Sicht, nur mit Instrumenten), blind schreiben (auf der Schreibmaschine), blind spielen *(Schach);* **Blind|darm; Blind|darm|ent|zün|dung; Blin|de,** der *u.* die; -n, -n (↑R 5ff.); **Blin|de|kuh** *ohne Artikel;* - spielen; **Blin|den‿an|stalt, ...füh|rer, ...hund, ...schrift, ...stock; Blin|den|ver|band;** Deutscher -; **blind flie|gen** *vgl.* blind; **Blind‿flie|gen** (das; -s), **...flug, ...gän|ger; Blind|ge|bo|re|ne, Blind|ge|bor|ne,** der *u.* die; -n, -n (↑R 5ff.); **Blind|heit,** die; -; **blind|lings; Blind‿schacht** (*Bergmannsspr.* nicht zu Tage gehender Schacht), **...schlei|che** (die; -, -n); **blind**

schrei|ben *vgl.* blind; **Blind-schreib|ver|fah|ren; blind spie-len** *vgl.* blind; **Blind|spie|ler; blind|wü|tig; Blind|wü|tig|keit,** die; -

blink; - und blank; **blin|ken; Blin-ker; Blin|ke|rei; blin|kern;** ich ...ere (↑R 16); **Blink-feu|er** (Seezeichen), **...leuch|te, ...licht** (*Plur.* ...lichter), **...zei|chen**

blin|zeln; ich ...[e]le (↑R 16)

Blis|ter, der; -s, - ‹engl.› (der Verpackung dienende Kunststofffolie)

Blitz, der; -es, -e; **Blitz-ab|lei|ter, ...ak|ti|on; blitz|ar|tig; blitz-blank,** *ugs. auch* blit|ze|blank; **blitz|blau,** *ugs. auch* blit|ze|blau; **blit|zen** (*ugs. auch für* mit Blitzlicht fotografieren; [mit der Absicht zu provozieren] nackt über belebte Straßen o. Ä. rennen); **Blit|zes|schnel|le,** die; -; **Blitz-ge|rät; blitz|ge|scheit; Blitz-ge-spräch, ...kar|ri|e|re, ...krieg, ...lam|pe** (*Fototechnik*), **...licht** (*Plur.* ...lichter); **Blitz|licht|auf-nah|me; blitz|sau|ber; Blitz-schach, ...schlag; blitz-schnell; Blitz-sieg, ...strahl, ...um|fra|ge, ...wür|fel** (*Fototechnik*)

Bliz|zard ['blizə(r)t], der; -s, -s ‹engl.› (Schneesturm [in Nordamerika])

[1]**Bloch,** der, *auch* das; -[e]s, *Plur.* Blöcher, *österr. meist* Bloche (*südd. u. österr. für* Holzblock, -stamm)

[2]**Bloch** (dt. Philosoph)

blo|chen (*schweiz. für* bohnern); **Blo|cher** (*schweiz. für* Bohner[besen])

Block, der; -[e]s, *Plur.* (*für* Beton-, Eisen-, Fels-, Granit-, Hack-, Holz-, Metall-, Motor-, Stein-, Zylinderblock:) Blöcke *u.* (*für* Abreiß-, Brief-, Buch-, Formular-, Häuser-, Kalender-, Kassen-, Notiz-, Rezept-, Schreib-, Steno[gramm]-, Wohn-, Zeichenblock:) Blocks *od., österr. u. schweiz. nur,* Blöcke; (*für* Macht-, Militär-, Währungs-, Wirtschaftsblock u. a.:) Blöcke, *selten* Blocks; **Blo|cka|de,** die; -, -n ‹franz.› ([See]sperre, Einschließung; *Druckw.* durch Blockieren gekennzeichnete Stelle); **Block-bil-dung, ...buch** (aus einzelnen Holzschnitten geklebtes Buch des 15. Jh.s), **...buch|sta|be; blo-cken** (*südd. auch für* bohnern); **Blo|cker** (*südd. für* Bohnerbesen); **Block|flö|te; Block|haus; blo|ckie|ren** ‹franz.› (einschließen, blocken, [ab]sperren; unterbinden, unterbrechen; *Druckw.* fehlenden Text durch ▮▮ kennzeichnen); **Blo|ckie|rung; blo-ckig** (klotzig); **Block-malz** (Hustenbonbon[s] aus Malzzucker), **...po|li|tik**

Blocks|berg, der; -[e]s (*in der Volkssage für* [2]Brocken)

Block-scho|ko|la|de, ...schrift, ...sig|nal (*Eisenb.*), **...stel|le** (*Eisenb.*), **...stun|de** (*Schulw.* Doppelstunde im Schulunterricht); **Blo|ckung; Block|un|ter|richt** (*Schulw.*); **Block|werk** (*Eisenb.* Kontrollstelle für einen Streckenabschnitt)

blöd, blö|de; blödeste (*veraltet für* schwachsinnig; *ugs. für* dumm); **Blö|del,** der; -s, - (*ugs. abwertend für* dummer Mensch); **Blö|del-bar|de; Blö|de|lei; blö|deln** (*ugs. für* Unsinn reden, albern sein); ich ...[e]le (↑R 16); **Blöd|ham|mel** (*svw.* Blödel); **Blöd|heit** (Dummheit); **Blö|di|an,** der; -[e]s, -e (*svw.* Blödel); **Blö|dig|keit,** die; - (*veraltet für* Schwäche; Schüchternheit); **Blöd|ling** (*svw.* Blödel); **Blöd|mann** *Plur.* ...männer (*svw.* Blödel); **Blöd|sinn,** der; -[e]s (*ugs.*); **blöd|sin|nig** (*svw.* blöd); **Blöd|sin|nig|keit** (*ugs.*)

blö|ken

blond ‹franz.›; blond gefärbtes, blond gelocktes Haar; ihr Haar war blond gefärbt; [1]**Blon|de,** die *u.* der; -n, -n (blonde Frau; blonder Mann); [2]**Blon|de,** die *u.* das; -n, -n (Glas Weißbier, helles Bier); zwei Blonde; ein kühles Blondes (↑R 5 ff.); [3]**Blon|de** [*auch* 'blɔ̃:d(ə)], die; -, -n ['blɔ̃:d(ə)n] (Seidenspitze); **blond ge|lockt** *vgl.* blond; **Blond|haar,** das; -[e]s; **blon|die|ren** (blond färben); **Blon|di|ne,** die; -, -n (blonde Frau); zwei reizende Blondinen; **Blond|kopf; blond|lo|ckig**

[1]**bloß** (nur); [2]**bloß** (entblößt); **Blö-ße,** die; -, -n; **bloß|fü|ßig** (*veraltend*); **bloß-le|gen, ...lie|gen, ...stel|len; Bloß|stel|lung; bloß-stram|peln,** sich

Blou|son [blu'zɔŋ *od.* ...'zɔ̃:], das, *auch* der; -[s], -s ‹franz.› (über Rock od. Hose getragene, an den Hüften eng anliegende Jacke mit Bund)

Blow-up ['blo:ap], das; -s, -s ‹engl.› (fotograf. Vergrößerung)

blub|bern (*nordd. für* glucksen; rasch u. undeutlich sprechen); ich ...ere (↑R 16)

Blü|cher (preuß. Feldmarschall)

Blu|denz (österr. Stadt)

Blue|jeans, *auch* **Blue Jeans** ['blu:dʒi:ns] (↑R 33) *Plur.* ‹amerik.› (blaue [Arbeits]hose aus geköpertem Baumwollgewebe);

Blues [blu:s], der; -, - (*urspr.* Volkslied der nordamerik. Schwarzen; ältere Jazzform; langsamer Tanz im $^4/_4$-Takt)

Bluff [*auch* noch blœf, *österr. auch* blaf], der; -s, -s ‹engl.› (Verblüffung; Täuschung); **bluf|fen**

blü|hen; Blü|het, der; -s (*schweiz. für* [Zeit der] Baumblüte); **Blüm-chen; Blüm|chen|kaf|fee** (*ugs. scherzh. für* dünner Kaffee); **Blu-me,** die; -, -n; **Blu|men-beet, ...bin|der** (Berufsbez.), **...bin|de-rin, ...brett, ...bu|kett, ...draht, ...frau, ...ge|schäft; blu|men|ge-schmückt** (↑R 40); **Blu|men-gruß, ...kas|ten, ...kind, ...kohl, ...ra|bat|te; blu|men|reich; Blu-men-strauß** (*Plur.* ...sträuße), **...topf**

blü|me|rant ‹franz.› (*ugs. für* übel, flau); mir ist ganz -

blu|mig; Blüm|lein

Blun|ze, die; -, -n, *auch* **Blun|zen,** die; -, - (*bayr., österr. ugs. für* Blutwurst); das ist mir Blunzen (völlig gleichgültig)

Blu|se, die; -, -n ‹franz.›

Blü|se, die; -, -n (*Seemannsspr.* Leuchtfeuer)

blu|sig

Blust, der *od.* das; -[e]s (*südd. u. schweiz., sonst veraltet für* Blütezeit, Blühen)

Blut, das; -[e]s, *Plur.* (*Med. fachspr.*) -e; (↑R 40:) ein Blut bildendes Medikament; der Blut saugende Vampir; **Blut-ader** (↑R 132), **...al|ko|hol, ...an-drang;** [1]**blut|arm** (arm an Blut); [2]**blut|arm** (*ugs. für* sehr arm); **Blut-ar|mut, ...bad, ...bahn, ...bank** (*Plur.* ...banken; Sammelstelle für Blutkonserven); **blut-be|schmiert; Blut|bild; Blut bil-dend** *vgl.* Blut; **Blut-bla|se, ...bu|che, ...do|ping** (*Sport* leistungssteigernde Eigenblutinjektion), **...druck** (der; -[e]s); **blut-druck|sen|kend; Blut|durst** (*geh.*); **blut|dürs|tig** (*geh.*)

Blü|te, die; -, -n

Blut-egel (↑R 132), **...ei|weiß; blu|ten**

Blü|ten-blatt, ...ho|nig, ...kelch, ...le|se; blü|ten|los; -e Pflanze; **Blü|ten-stand, ...staub; blü-ten|weiß;** -e Wäsche; **Blü|ten-zweig**

Blu|ter (jmd., der an der Bluterkrankheit leidet); **Blut|er|guss; Blu|ter|krank|heit,** die; - (erbl. Störung der Gerinnungsfähigkeit des Blutes)

Blü|te|zeit

Blut₋farb|stoff, ...fleck, ...ge|fäß, ...ge|rinn|sel; Blut|grup|pe; Blut|grup|pen|un|ter|su|chung; Blut₋hoch|druck, ...hund; blu|tig; ¹...blü|tig (z. B. heißblütig)

²...blü|tig ‹*zu* Blüte› (z. B. langblütig)

blut|jung (*ugs. für* sehr jung); **Blut₋kon|ser|ve** (konserviertes Blut), **...kör|per|chen, ...krebs** (der; -es), **...kreis|lauf, ...la|che; blut|leer** (ohne Blut)

...blüt|ler (z. B. Lippenblütler)

blut|mä|ßig *vgl.* blutsmäßig; **Blut₋oran|ge** (↑R 132), **...pfropf, ...plas|ma, ...plätt|chen, ...pro|be, ...ra|che, ...rausch; blut₋rei|ni|gend** (↑R 40), **...rot; blut|rüns|tig; Blut sau|gend** *vgl.* Blut; **Blut|sau|ger; Bluts₋bru|der, ...brü|der|schaft; Blut|schan|de,** die; -; **blut|schän|de|risch; Blut₋sen|kung, ...se|rum; bluts|mä|ßig** (durch Blutsverwandtschaft bedingt); **Blut₋spen|der, ...spur; blut|stil|lend;** -e Watte (↑R 40); **Bluts|trop|fen; Blut|sturz; bluts|ver|wandt; Bluts₋ver|wand|te, ...ver|wandt|schaft; Blut₋tat, ...trans|fu|si|on; blut₋trie|fend, ...über|strömt** (↑R 132); **Blut|über|tra|gung** (↑R 132); **Blu|tung; blut|un|ter|lau|fen; Blut₋un|ter|su|chung, ...ver|gie|ßen, ...ver|gif|tung, ...ver|lust; blut₋ver|schmiert, ...voll; Blut₋wä|sche, ...was|ser; blut|we|nig** (*ugs. für* sehr wenig); **Blut₋wurst, ...zeu|ge** (*für* Märtyrer), **...zoll** *(geh.)*, **...zu|cker, ...zu|fuhr**

BLZ = Bankleitzahl

B-Ma|tu|ra (*österr.* Beamtenaufstiegsprüfung)

b-Moll ['be:mɔl, *auch* 'be:'mɔl], das; - (Tonart; *Zeichen* b); **b-Moll-Ton|lei|ter** (↑R 28)

BMW ® = Bayerische Motoren Werke AG

BMX-Rad ‹zu engl. bicycle motocross› (kleineres, bes. geländegängiges Fahrrad)

BND = Bundesnachrichtendienst

Bö, *auch* Böe, die; -, Böen (heftiger Windstoß)

Boa, die; -, -s (eine Riesenschlange; Schal aus Pelz oder Federn)

Boat|peo|ple ['bo:t'pi:p(ə)l] *Plur.* ‹engl.› (mit Booten geflohene [vietnamesische] Flüchtlinge)

¹Bob (m. Vorn.)

²Bob, der; -s, -s ‹engl., *Kurzform für* Bobsleigh› (Rennschlitten); **Bob|bahn; bob|ben** (beim Bobfahren durch eine ruckweise Oberkörperbewegung die Fahrt beschleunigen)

Bob|by ['bɔbi], der; -s, -s ‹nach dem Reorganisator der engl. Polizei, Robert („Bobby") Peel› (*engl. ugs. für* Polizist)

¹Bo|ber, der; -s, - (schwimmendes Seezeichen)

²Bo|ber, der; -s (Nebenfluss der Oder)

Bo|bi|ne, die; -, -n ‹franz.› ([Garn]spule in der Baumwollspinnerei; endloser Papierstreifen zur Herstellung von Zigarettenhülsen; *Bergmannsspr.* Wickeltrommel für Flachseile an Fördermaschinen); **Bo|bi|net** [*auch* ...'nɛt], der; -s, -s ‹engl.› (Gewebe; engl. Tüll)

Bob|sleigh ['bɔbsle:], der; -s, -s; *vgl.* ²Bob

Bob|tail [...'te:l], der; -s, -s ‹engl.› (Hunderasse)

Boc|cac|cio [bɔ'katʃo] (ital. Dichter)

Boc|cia ['bɔtʃa], das *od.* die; -, -s ‹ital.› (ital. Kugelspiel)

Boche [bɔʃ], der; -, -s ‹franz.› (franz. Schimpfname für den Deutschen)

Bo|cholt (Stadt im Münsterland)

Bo|chum (Stadt im Ruhrgebiet); **Bo|chu|mer** (↑R 103)

¹Bock, der; -[e]s, Böcke (Ziegen-, Rehbock o. Ä.; Gestell; Turngerät); Bock springen; *aber* das Bockspringen; *(bes. Jugendspr.)* auf etw. Bock (Lust) haben

²Bock, das, *auch* der; -s (*Kurzform für* Bockbier); zwei - **bock|bei|nig**

Bock|bier

Böck|chen; böckeln (*landsch. für* nach ¹Bock riechen); **bo|cken; Bo|ckerl,** das; -s, -n (*österr. ugs. für* Föhrenzapfen); **bo|ckig; Bo|ckig|keit,** die; -; **Bock|kä|fer; Bock|lei|ter,** die

Böck|lin (schweiz. Maler)

Bock|mist (*ugs. für* Blödsinn, Fehler); **Bocks₋beu|tel** (bauchige Flasche; Frankenwein in solcher Flasche), **...dorn** (der; -[e]s; Strauch); **Böck|ser,** der; -s, - (*Winzerspr.* fauliger Geruch u. Geschmack bei jungem Wein); **Bocks|horn** *Plur.* ...hörner; lass dich nicht ins - jagen *(ugs. für* einschüchtern); **Bocks|hörndl,** das; -s, -n (*österr. ugs. für* Frucht des Johannisbrotbaumes); **Bocks|horn|klee,** der; -s (eine Pflanze); **Bock₋sprin|gen** (das; -s; ↑R 50), **...sprung, ...wurst**

Bod|den, der; -s, - (*nordd. für* Strandsee, [Ostsee]bucht)

Bo|de|ga, die; -, -s ‹span.› (span. Weinkeller, -schenke)

Bo|de|gym|nas|tik (↑R 95), die; - (von Rudolf Bode geschaffene Ausdrucksgymnastik)

Bo|del|schwingh (dt. ev. Theologe)

Bo|den, der; -s, Böden; **Bo|den₋ab|wehr** *(Milit.)*, **...be|ar|bei|tung, ...be|lag; Bo|den-Bo|den-Ra|ke|te; Bo|den₋ero|si|on** (↑R 132; *Geol.)*, **...frei|heit** *(Technik)*, **...frost, ...haf|tung** *(Motorsport)*, **...kam|mer, ...le|ger** (Berufsbez.); **bo|den|los;** (↑R 47:) ins Bodenlose fallen; **Bo|den₋ne|bel, ...per|so|nal, ...re|form, ...satz, ...schät|ze** *(Plur.)*

Bo|den|see, der; -s

Bo|den|spe|ku|la|ti|on; bo|den|stän|dig; Bo|den₋sta|ti|on, ...tur|nen, ...va|se, ...wel|le, ...wich|se (*schweiz. für* Bohnerwachs); **bo|di|gen** (*schweiz. für* besiegen); **Bod|me|rei** (Schiffsbeleihung, -verpfändung)

Bo|do (m. Vorn.); *vgl.* Boto

Bo|dy ['bɔdi], der; -s, -s ‹engl.› (*kurz für* Bodysuit); **Bo|dy|buil|der** ['bɔdibildə(r)], der; -s, - (jmd., der Bodybuilding betreibt); **Bo|dy|buil|ding,** das; -[s] (Training[smethode] zur besonderen Ausbildung der Körpermuskulatur); **Bo|dy|check** [...tʃɛk], der; -s, -s (erlaubtes Rempeln des Gegners beim Eishockey); **Bo|dy|guard** [...ga(r)d], der; -s, -s (Leibwächter); **Bo|dy|sto|cking** [...stɔkiŋ], der; -[s], -s *vgl.* Bodysuit; **Bo|dy|suit** [...sju:t], der; -[s], -s (eng anliegende, einteilige Unterkleidung)

Böe *vgl.* Bö

Boe|ing ['bo:iŋ], die; -, -s (amerik. Flugzeugtyp)

Bo|e|thi|us (spätröm. Philosoph)

Bo|fist *vgl.* Bovist

Bo|gen, der; -s, *Plur.* - u. *(bes. südd., österr. u. schweiz.)* Bögen; *Abk.* (für den Bogen Papier:) Bg.; in Bausch und Bogen (ganz und gar); **Bo|gen₋füh|rung** *(Musik)*, **...lam|pe, ...schie|ßen** (das; -s; *Sport*), **...schüt|ze; bo|gig**

Bo|gis|law (m. Vorn.)

Bo|go|tá [...'ta] (Hptst. von Kolumbien)

Bo|heme [bɔ'ɛ:m, *auch* bo'hɛ:m], die; - (unkonventionelles Künstlermilieu); **Bo|he|mi|en** [boe'miɛ̃:, *auch* bohe...], der; -s, -s (Angehöriger der Boheme)

Boh|le, die; -, -n (starkes Brett); **Boh|len|be|lag**

böh|ma|keln (*österr. ugs. für* radebrechen); **Böh|me,** der; -n, -n (↑R 126); **Böh|men; Böh|mer|land,** das; -[e]s; **Böh|mer|wald,** der; -[e]s; ↑R 105 (Gebirge);

Böh|mer|wäld|ler; Böh|min; böh|misch (*auch ugs. für* unverständlich); (↑R 104:) das kommt mir - vor; das sind für mich -e Dörfer, *aber* (↑R 102): Böhmisches Mittelgebirge
Böhn|chen; Boh|ne, die; -, -n;
boh|nen (*landsch. für* bohnern)
Boh|nen‿ein|topf, ...kaf|fee, ...kraut, ...sa|lat, ...stan|ge; Boh|nen|stroh; dumm wie - (*ugs.*)
Boh|ner (*svw.* Bohnerbesen); **Boh|ner|be|sen; boh|nern;** ich ...ere (↑R 16); **Boh|ner|wachs**
boh|ren; Boh|rer; Bohr‿fut|ter (*Technik*), **...ham|mer** (mit Druckluft betriebener Schlagbohrer), **...in|sel, ...loch, ...ma|schi|ne, ...turm; Boh|rung**
bö|ig; -er Wind (in kurzen Stößen wehender Wind)
Boi|ler ['bɔy...], der; -s, - ⟨engl.⟩ (Warmwasserbereiter)
Boi|zen|burg ['bɔy...] (Stadt an der Elbe)
Bo|jar, der; -en, -en (↑R 126) ⟨russ.⟩ (hoher Adliger im alten Russland; adliger Großgrundbesitzer im alten Rumänien)
Bo|je, die; -, -n (*Seemannsspr.* [verankerter] Schwimmkörper als Seezeichen od. zum Festmachen); **Bo|jen|ge|schirr**
Bok|mål ['bo:kmo:l], das; -[s] ⟨norw.⟩ (vom Dänischen beeinflusste norw. Schriftsprache [*vgl.* Riksmål *u.* Nynorsk])
Bol *vgl.* Bolus
Bo|la, die; -, -s ⟨span.⟩ (südamerik. Wurf- und Fangleine); **Bo|le|ro,** der; -s, -s (Tanz; kurze Jacke); **Bo|le|ro|jäck|chen**
Bo|lid, Bo|li|de, der; ...iden, ...iden (schwerer Rennwagen; *Astron.* Meteor)
Bo|li|var [...v...], der; -[s], -[s] (Währungseinheit in Venezuela; *Abk.* Bs); **Bo|li|vi|a|ner,** *auch* Bo|li|vi|er; **bo|li|vi|a|nisch,** *auch* bo|li|visch; **Bo|li|vi|a|no,** der; -[s], -[s] (bolivian. Münzeinheit); **Bo|li|vi|en** (südamerik. Staat); **Bo|li|vi|er** *vgl.* Bolivianer; **bo|li|visch** *vgl.* bolivianisch
böl|ken (*nordd. für* blöken [vom Rind, Schaf], brüllen; aufstoßen)
Böll (dt. Schriftsteller)
Bol|lan|dist, der; -en, -en; ↑R 126 (Mitglied der jesuit. Arbeitsgemeinschaft zur Herausgabe von Heiligenleben)
Bol|le, die; -, -n (*landsch. für* Zwiebel; Loch im Strumpf)
Böl|ler (kleiner Mörser zum Schießen, Feuerwerkskörper); **bol|lern** (*landsch. für* poltern, krachen); **böl|lern;** ich ...ere (↑R 16); **Bol|ler|wa|gen** (*landsch. für* Handwagen)
Bol|let|te, die; -, -n ⟨ital.⟩ (*österr. für* Zoll-, Steuerbescheinigung)
Boll|werk
Bo|log|na [bo'lɔnja] (↑R 130; ital. Stadt); **Bo|log|ne|se** [...'nje:...], der; -n, -n; **Bo|log|ne|ser; bo|log|ne|sisch**
Bo|lo|me|ter, das; -s, - ⟨griech.⟩ (Strahlungsmessgerät)
Bol|sche|wik, der; -en, *Plur.* -i *u.* (abwertend) -en (↑R 126) ⟨russ.⟩ (*histor. Bez. für* Mitglied der kommunistischen Partei Russlands bzw. der Sowjetunion); **bol|sche|wi|sie|ren; Bol|sche|wi|sie|rung; Bol|sche|wis|mus,** der; -; **Bol|sche|wist,** der; -en, -en (↑R 126); **bol|sche|wis|tisch; Bol|schoi|the|a|ter** [...'ʃɔy...] (führende Opern- u. Ballettbühne in Moskau)
Bo|lus, Bol, der; -, ...li ⟨griech.⟩ (Tonerdesilikat; *Med.* Bissen; große Pille)
Bol|za|no (*ital. Name von* Bozen)
bol|zen (*Fußball* derb, systemlos spielen); du bolzt; **Bol|zen,** der; -s, -; **bol|zen|ge|ra|de; Bol|ze|rei; Bolz|platz**
Bom|ba|ge [bɔm'ba:ʒə, *österr.* ...'ba:ʒ], die; -, -n [...'ba:ʒ(ə)n] ⟨franz.⟩ (Biegen des Glases im Ofen; Umbördeln von Blech; Hervorwölbung des Deckels von Konservendosen bei Zersetzung des Inhalts); **Bom|bar|de,** die; -, -n (Steinschleudermaschine des 15. bis 17. Jh.s); **Bom|bar|de|ment** [...'mã:, *österr.* bɔmbard'mã:, *schweiz.* bɔmbardə'mɛnt], das; -s, *Plur.* -s, *schweiz.* -e (Beschießung; Abwurf von Bomben); **bom|bar|die|ren; Bom|bar|dier|kä|fer** (*Zool.*); **Bom|bar|die|rung; Bom|bar|don** [...'dõ:], das; -s, -s (Basstuba)
Bom|bast, der; -[e]s ⟨pers.-engl.⟩ ([Rede]schwulst, Wortschwall); **bom|bas|tisch**
Bom|bay [...be:] (Stadt in Indien)
Bom|be, die; -, -n ⟨franz.⟩ (mit Sprengstoff angefüllter Hohlkörper; *auch ugs.* sehr kräftiger Schuss aufs [Fußball]tor); **bom|ben** (*ugs.*); **Bom|ben‿an|griff, ...an|schlag, ...dro|hung, ...er|folg** (*ugs. für* großer Erfolg); [1]**bom|ben|fest;** ein -er Unterstand; [2]**bom|ben|fest** (*ugs. für* ganz sicher); er behauptet es -; **Bom|ben‿flug|zeug, ...form** (*ugs.*), **...ge|schäft** (*ugs.*), **...krieg, ...schuss** (*Sport*); [1]**bom|ben|si|cher;** ein -er Keller; [2]**bom|ben|si|cher** (*ugs.*); er weiß es -; **Bom|ben‿stim|mung** (*ugs.*), **...tep|pich, ...ter|ror; Bom|ber; Bom|ber‿ja|cke, ...ver|band**
bom|bie|ren ⟨*zu* Bombage⟩ (*fachspr. für* biegen [von Glas, Blech]); **Bom|bie|rung**
bom|big (*ugs. für* hervorragend)
Bom|mel, die; -, -n *u.* der; -s, - (*landsch. für* Quaste)
Bon [bɔŋ], der; -s, -s ⟨franz.⟩ (Gutschein; Kassenzettel)
bo|na fi|de ⟨lat.⟩ (guten Glaubens)
Bo|na|par|te (Familienn. Napoleons); **Bo|na|par|tis|mus,** der; -; **Bo|na|par|tist,** der; -en, -en; ↑R 126 (Anhänger der Familie Bonaparte)
Bo|na|ven|tu|ra [...v...] (Kirchenlehrer)
Bon|bon [bɔŋ'bɔŋ, *auch* bõ'bõ:, *österr. nur so*], der *od.* (*österr. nur*) das; -s, -s ⟨franz.⟩ (Süßigkeit zum Lutschen); **bon|bon|far|ben; Bon|bon|nie|re,** *auch* Bon|bo|nie|re [bɔŋbɔŋ'jɛ:rə, *auch* bõbɔn'jɛ:rə, *österr. nur so*], die; -, -n (gut ausgestattete Pralinenpackung)
Bond, der; -s, -s ⟨engl.⟩ (*engl. Bez. für* Schuldverschreibung mit fester Verzinsung)
bon|gen ⟨franz.⟩ (*ugs. für* einen Kassenbon tippen); ist gebongt (*ugs. für* ist abgemacht, wird erledigt)
Bon|go ['bɔŋgo], das; -[s], -s *od.* die; -, -s *meist Plur.* ⟨span.⟩ (paarweise verwendete [Jazz]trommel mit nur einem Fell)
Bön|ha|se (*nordd. für* Pfuscher; nichtzünftiger Handwerker)
Bon|ho|mie [bɔno'mi:], die; -, ...ien ⟨franz.⟩ (*veraltet für* Gutmütigkeit, Einfalt); **Bon|homme** [bɔ'nɔm], der; -, -s (*veraltet für* gutmütiger, einfältiger Mensch)
Bo|ni|fa|ti|us, Bo|ni|faz [*auch* 'bo:...] (Verkünder des Christentums in Deutschland; m. Vorn.); **Bo|ni|fa|ti|us|brun|nen**
Bo|ni|fi|ka|ti|on, die; -, -en ⟨lat.⟩ (Vergütung, Gutschrift); **bo|ni|fi|zie|ren** (vergüten, gutschreiben); **Bo|ni|tät,** die; -, -en (*Kaufmannsspr.* [guter] Ruf einer Person od. Firma in Bezug auf ihre Zahlungsfähigkeit [*nur Sing.*]; *Forstw., Landw.* Güte, Wert eines Bodens); **bo|ni|tie|ren** ([Grundstück, Boden, Waren] schätzen); **Bo|ni|tie|rung**
Bon|mot [bõ'mo:, *auch* bɔŋ'mo:], das; -s, -s ⟨franz.⟩ (geistreiche Wendung)
Bonn (Stadt am Rhein)
Bon|nard [bɔ'na:r] (franz. Maler)
Bon|ne, die; -, -n ⟨franz.⟩ (*veraltet für* Kindermädchen, Erzieherin)

Bon|ner ‹*zu* Bonn› (↑R 103)
Bon|net [bɔˈneː], das; -s, -s ‹franz.› (Damenhaube des 18. Jh.s)
[1]**Bon|sai,** der; -[s], -s ‹jap.› (japan. Zwergbaum); [2]**Bon|sai,** das; - (Kunst des Ziehens von Zwergbäumen)
Bon|sels (dt. Schriftsteller)
Bont|je, der; -s, -s (*landsch. für* Bonbon)
Bo|nus, der; *Gen.* - *u.* Bonusses, *Plur.* - *u.* Bonusse, *auch* Boni ‹lat.› (Vergütung; Rabatt)
Bon|vi|vant [bõviˈvãː], der; -s, -s ‹franz.› (*veraltend für* Lebemann; *Theater* Fach des Salonhelden)
Bon|ze, der; -n, -n (↑R 126) ‹jap.› ([buddhistischer] Mönch, Priester; *abwertend für* dem Volk entfremdeter höherer Funktionär); **Bon|zen|tum,** das; -s; **Bon|zo|kra|tie,** die; -, ...ien ‹jap.; griech.› (Herrschaft der Bonzen)
Boof|ke, der; -s, -s (*bes. berlin. für* ungebildeter Mensch, Tölpel)
Boo|gie-Woo|gie [ˈbugiˈvugi], der; -[s], -s ‹amerik.› (Jazzart; ein Tanz)
Boom [buːm], der; -s, -s ‹engl.› ([plötzlicher] Wirtschaftsaufschwung, Hausse an der Börse); **boo|men** [ˈbuː...] (*ugs. für* einen Boom erleben)
[1]**Boot,** das; -[e]s, *Plur.* -e, *landsch. auch* Böte; - fahren
[2]**Boot** [buːt], der; -s, -s *meist Plur.* ‹engl.› (bis über den Knöchel reichender [Wildleder]schuh)
Boot|chen (*landsch.*)
Bo|o|tes, der; - ‹griech.› (ein Sternbild)
Bö|o|ti|en [...iən] (altgriech. Landschaft); **Bö|o|ti|er** [...iər]; **bö|o|tisch** (*veraltet auch für* denkfaul, unkultiviert)
Boot|leg|ger [ˈbuːt...], der; -s, - ‹amerik.› (*amerik. Bez. für* Alkoholschmuggler)
Boots‿bau (*Plur.* ...bauten), **...gast** (*Plur.* -en; Matrose im Bootsdienst), **...ha|ken, ...haus, ...län|ge, ...mann** (*Plur.* ...leute); **Boots|manns|maat; Boots‿mo|tor, ...steg; boot[s]|wei|se**
Bor, das; -s ‹pers.› (chem. Element, Nichtmetall; *Zeichen* B)
Bo|ra, die; -, -s ‹ital.› (kalter Adriawind)
Bo|ra|go, der; -s ‹arab.› (Borretsch)
Bo|rat, das; -[e]s, -e ‹pers.› (borsaures Salz); **Bo|rax,** der, *österr. auch* das; *Gen.* - *u.* -es (Borverbindung)
Bor|chardt (dt. Schriftsteller)
Bor|chert (dt. Schriftsteller)
[1]**Bord,** das; -[e]s, -e ([Bücher-, Wand]brett); [2]**Bord,** der; -[e]s, -e ([Schiffs]rand, -deck, -seite; *übertr. auch für* Schiff, Luftfahrzeug); *heute meist in Fügungen wie* an - gehen; Mann über -!; [3]**Bord,** das; -[e]s, -e (*schweiz. für* Rand, [kleiner] Abhang, Böschung); **Bord|buch** (Schiffstagebuch; Fahrtenbuch); **Bord|case** [...keːs], das *u.* der; -, *Plur.* - *u.* -s [...keːsiz] ‹dt.; engl.› (kleiner Koffer [für Flugreisen]); **Bord‿com|pu|ter, ...dienst**
Bör|de, die; -, -n (fruchtbare Ebene); Magdeburger -, Soester -
[1]**Bor|deaux** [bɔrˈdoː] (franz. Stadt); Bordeaux' [...ˈdoːs] Hafen (↑R 107); [2]**Bor|deaux,** der; - [...ˈdoː(s)], *Plur.* (*Sorten:*) - [...ˈdoːs] (ein Wein); **bor|deaux|rot** (weinrot); **Bor|de|lai|ser** [...ˈlɛːzər] (↑R 103); - Brühe (Mittel gegen [Reben]krankheiten); **Bor|de|le|se,** der; -n, -n; ↑R 126 (Einwohner von Bordeaux); **Bor|de|le|sin**
Bor|dell, das; -s, -e (Haus, in dem Prostituierte ihrem Gewerbe nachgehen)
bör|deln (Blech mit einem Rand versehen; umbiegen); ich ...[e]le (↑R 16); **Bör|de|lung**
Bor|de|reau [bɔrdəˈroː], *auch* **Bor|de|ro,** der *od.* das; -s, -s ‹franz.› (*Bankw.* Verzeichnis eingelieferter Wertpapiere); **Bor|der|preis** ‹engl.; dt.› (Preis frei Grenze)
Bord‿funk, ...fun|ker
bor|die|ren ‹franz.› (*fachspr. für* einfassen, besetzen); **Bor|die|rung**
Bord‿ka|me|ra, ...kan|te, ...stein
Bor|dü|re, die; -, -n ‹franz.› (Einfassung, [farbiger] Geweberand, Besatz); **Bor|dü|ren|kleid**
Bord‿waf|fe (*meist Plur.*), **...zei|tung**
bo|re|al ‹griech.› (nördlich); [1]**Bo|re|as** (griech. Gottheit [des Nordwindes]); [2]**Bo|re|as,** der; - (Nordwind im Gebiet des Ägäischen Meeres)
[1]**Borg** (das Borgen); *nur noch in* auf - kaufen
[2]**Borg,** der; -[e]s, -e (bereits als Ferkel kastriertes männliches Schwein)
bor|gen
Bor|ghe|se [...ˈgeːzə] (röm. Adelsgeschlecht)
Bor|gia [ˈbɔrdʒa], der; -s, -s (Angehöriger eines span.-ital. Adelsgeschlechtes)
Bor|gis, die; - ‹franz.› (*Druckw.* ein Schriftgrad)
borg|wei|se (*selten*)
Bo|ris (m. Vorn.)
Bor|ke, die; -, -n (Rinde); **Bor|ken‿kä|fer, ...krepp, ...scho|ko|la|de; bor|kig**
Bor|kum (eine der Ostfriesischen Inseln)
Born, der; -[e]s, -e (*veraltet, noch geh. für* Wasserquelle, Brunnen)
Bör|ne (dt. Schriftsteller)
Bor|neo (größte der Großen Sundainseln)
Born|holm (eine dän. Ostseeinsel)
bor|niert ‹franz.› (unbelehrbar, engstirnig); **Bor|niert|heit**
Bor|retsch, der; -[e]s (ein Küchenkraut)
Bör|ri|es [...iəs] (m. Vorn.)
Bor|ro|mä|i|sche In|seln *Plur.* (↑R 94; im Lago Maggiore); **Bor|ro|mä|us** (m. Eigenn.); **Bor|ro|mä|us|ver|ein**
Bor‿sal|be (die; -; ein Heilmittel), **...säu|re** (die; -)
Borschtsch, der; - ‹russ.› (russ. Kohlsuppe mit Fleisch)
Bör|se, die; -, -n ‹niederl.› (*Wirtsch.* Markt für Wertpapiere u. vertretbare Waren; *veraltend für* Portemonnaie; *Boxen* Einnahme aus einem Wettkampf); **Bör|sen‿be|richt, ...ge|schäft, ...kurs, ...mak|ler, ...spe|ku|lant, ...spe|ku|la|ti|on, ...tipp, ...ver|ein; Bör|si|a|ner** (*ugs. für* Börsenspekulant)
Bors|te, die; -, -n (starkes Haar); **Bors|ten|vieh** (*ugs. scherzh.*); **bors|tig; Bors|tig|keit; Borst|wisch** (*ostmitteld. für* Handfeger; vgl. Bartwisch)
Bor|te, die; -, -n (gemustertes Band als Besatz)
Bo|rus|se, der; -n, -n; ↑R 126 (*scherzh. für* Preuße); **Bo|rus|sia,** die; - (Frauengestalt als Sinnbild Preußens)
Bor|was|ser, das; -s
bös *vgl.* böse; **bös|ar|tig; Bös|ar|tig|keit,** die; -
[1]**Bosch,** Robert (dt. Erfinder); die boschsche Zündkerze (↑R 94)
[2]**Bosch** [*niederl.* bɔs], Hieronymus (niederländ. Maler)
bö|schen (*Eisenb., Straßenbau* abschrägen); **Bö|schung; Bö|schungs|win|kel**
Bos|co [ˈbɔsko], Don (kath. Priester u. Pädagoge)
bö|se, bös; böser, böseste; böser Blick, eine böse Sieben; jenseits von gut und böse; *Großschreibung* (↑R 47): das Gute und das Böse unterscheiden; sich zum Bösen wenden; der Böse (*vgl. d.*); im Bösen auseinander gehen; im Guten wie im Bösen; **Bö|se,** der; -n, -n; ↑R 5 ff. (*auch für* Teufel [*nur Sing.*]); **Bö|se|wicht,** der; -[e]s,

Plur. -er, *auch, österr. nur,* -e; **bos|haft; Bos|haf|tig|keit; Bos|heit**

Bos|kett, das; -s, -e ‹franz.› (Ziergebüsch [bes. in Barockgärten])

Bos|koop, *schweiz. nur so, od.* **Bos|kop,** der; -s, - ‹nach dem niederl. Ort Boskoop› (Apfelsorte)

Bos|ni|ak, der; -en, -en (↑R 126); (südslaw. Moslem in Bosnien und Herzegowina); **Bos|ni|en** (Gebiet im Norden von Bosnien und Herzegowina); **Bos|ni|en und Her|ze|go|wi|na** (Staat in Südosteuropa); **Bos|ni|er**

Bos|nigl, der; -s, -n (*bayr., österr. ugs. für* boshafter Mensch)

bos|nisch

Bos|po|rus, der; - (Meerenge bei Istanbul)

Boss, der; -es, -e ‹amerik.› (Chef; Vorgesetzter)

Bos|sa No|va [- 'no:va], der; - -, - -s ‹port.› (ein Modetanz)

Bo|ßel, der; -s, - *u.* die; -, -n (*nordd. für* Kugel); **bos|se|lie|ren** *vgl.* bossieren; **bo|ßeln** (*nordd. für* mit der [dem] Boßel werfen; den Kloot schießen); ich ...[e]le (↑R 16); **bos|seln** (*ugs. für* kleine Arbeiten [peinlich genau] machen; *auch für* bossieren); ich boss[e]le (↑R 16); **Bos|sen‿qua|der** *(Bauw.),* **...werk** (rau bearbeitetes Mauerwerk); **Bos|sier|ei|sen** (Gerät zum Behauen roher Mauersteine); **bos|sie|ren** (die Rohform einer Figur aus Stein herausschlagen; Mauersteine behauen; *auch* in Ton, Wachs od. Gips modellieren); **Bos|sie|rer; Bos|sier|wachs**

[1]**Bos|ton** ['bɔst(ə)n] (Stadt in England und in den USA); [2]**Bos|ton,** das; -s (ein Kartenspiel); [3]**Bos|ton,** der; -s, -s (ein Tanz)

bös|wil|lig; Bös|wil|lig|keit, die; -

Bot, Bott, das; -[e]s, -e (*schweiz. für* Mitgliederversammlung)

Bo|ta|nik, die; - ‹griech.› (Pflanzenkunde); **Bo|ta|ni|ker; bo|ta|nisch;** botanische Gärten, *aber* (↑R 108): der Botanische Garten in München; **bo|ta|ni|sie|ren** (Pflanzen sammeln); **Bo|ta|ni|sier|trom|mel**

Böt|chen (kleines Boot)

Bo|te, der; -n, -n (↑R 126)

Bo|tel, das; -s, -s ‹*Kurzw. aus* Boot u. Hotel› (als Hotel ausgebautes Schiff)

Bo|ten‿dienst, ...frau, ...gang, ...lohn; Bo|tin

Böt|lein (kleines Boot)

bot|mä|ßig (*geh., veraltet für* untertan); **Bot|mä|ßig|keit,** die; -

Bo|to (m. Vorn.)

Bo|to|ku|de, der; -n, -n; ↑R 126 (bras. Indianer); **bo|to|ku|disch**

Bot|schaft (diplomatische Vertretung); **Bot|schaf|ter; Bot|schaf|ter|ebe|ne** (↑R 132); auf -; **Bot|schaf|te|rin; Bot|schafts‿rat** (*Plur.* ...räte), **...sek|re|tär**

Bot|su|a|na (↑R 132; Staat in Afrika); **Bot|su|a|ner; Bot|su|a|ne|rin; bot|su|a|nisch**

Bots|wa|na (↑R 132) usw. *vgl.* Botsuana usw.

Bott *vgl.* Bot

Bött|cher (Bottichmacher); *vgl. auch* Büttner *u.* Küfer; **Bött|cher|ar|beit; Bött|che|rei; bött|chern;** ich böttch[e]re (↑R 16)

Bot|ten *Plur.* (*landsch. für* Stiefel; große, klobige Schuhe)

Bot|ti|cel|li [...'tʃɛli], Sandro (ital. Maler)

Bot|tich, der; -[e]s, -e

Bot|tle|par|ty ['bɔt(ə)l...], die; -, -s ‹engl.› (Party, zu der die Gäste die Getränke mitbringen)

bott|nisch, *aber* (↑R 102): der Bottnische Meerbusen

Bo|tu|lis|mus, der; - ‹lat.› (*Med.* bakterielle Lebensmittelvergiftung)

[1]**Bouc|lé,** *eindeutschend* Buk|lee [bu'kle:] (↑R 33 *u.* 130), das; -s, -s ‹franz.› (Garn mit Knoten u. Schlingen); [2]**Bouc|lé,** *eindeutschend* Buk|lee, der; -s, -s (Gewebe u. Teppich aus diesem Garn)

Bou|doir [bu'doa:r], das; -s, -s ‹franz.› (*veraltet für* elegantes Zimmer einer Dame)

Bou|gain|vil|lea [bugɛ̃'vilea], die; -, ...leen [...leən] ‹nach dem Comte de Bougainville› (eine Zierpflanze)

Bou|gie [bu'ʒi:], die; -, -s ‹franz.› (*Med.* Dehnsonde); **bou|gie|ren** [bu'ʒi:...] (mit der Dehnsonde untersuchen, erweitern)

Bouil|la|baisse [buja'bɛ:s], die; -, -s [buja'bɛ:s] ‹franz.› (provenzal. Fischsuppe); **Bouil|lon** [bul'jɔŋ, *auch* bul'jõ:, *österr.* bu'jõ:], die; -, -s (Kraft-, Fleischbrühe); **Bouil|lon|wür|fel**

Boule [bu:l], das; -[s], *auch* die; - ‹franz.› (franz. Kugelspiel)

Bou|le|vard [bulə'va:r, *österr.* bul'va:r], der; -s, -s ‹franz.› (breite [Ring]straße); **Bou|le|vard‿pres|se** *(abwertend),* **...the|a|ter, ...zei|tung**

Bou|lez [bu'lɛ:z] (franz. Komponist u. Dirigent)

Bou|log|ner [bu'lɔnjər] (↑R 130 *u.* 103); **Bou|log|ne-sur-Mer** [bu'lɔnjəsyr'mɛ:r] (franz. Stadt)

Bou|quet [bu'ke:], das; -s, -s ‹franz.›; *vgl.* Bukett

Bou|qui|nist [buki'nist], der; -en, -en ‹franz.› ([Straßen]buchhändler in Paris)

Bour|bo|ne [bur...], der; -n, -n; ↑R 126 (Angehöriger eines franz. Herrschergeschlechtes); **bour|bo|nisch**

bour|geois [bur'ʒoa] ‹franz.› (der Bourgeoisie angehörend, entsprechend); -es [bur'ʒoa:zəs] Verhalten; **Bour|geois,** der; -, - (*abwertend für* wohlhabender, selbstzufriedener Bürger); **Bour|geoi|sie** [...ʒoa'zi:], die; -, ...ien ([wohlhabender] Bürgerstand; *marxist.* herrschende Klasse in der kapitalistischen Gesellschaft)

Bour|rée [bu're:], die; -, -s ‹franz.› (ein alter Tanz; Teil der Suite)

Bour|ret|te [bu...], die; -, -n ‹franz.› (Gewebe aus Abfallseide)

Bour|tan|ger Moor ['bu:r... -], das; - -[e]s (teilweise trockengelegtes Moorgebiet westl. der mittleren Ems)

Bou|teille [bu'tɛ:j], die; -, -n [bu'tɛ:jən] ‹franz.› (*veraltet für* Flasche)

Bou|tique [bu'ti:k, *österr.* bu'tik], die; -, *Plur.* -n [...kən], *selten* -s (↑R 33) ‹franz.› (kleiner Laden für [meist exklusive] mod. Neuheiten)

Bou|ton [bu'tõ:], der; -s, -s ‹franz.› (Ohrklips in Knopfform)

Bo|vist ['bo:vist, *auch* bo'vist] *od.* **Bo|fist** [*auch* bo'fist], der; -[e]s, -e (ein Pilz)

Bow|den|zug ['baud(ə)n...], der; -s, ...züge (↑R 95) ‹nach dem engl. Erfinder Bowden› (*Technik* Drahtkabel zur Übertragung von Zugkräften)

Bo|wie|mes|ser ['bo:vi...], das; -s, - (↑R 95) ‹nach dem amerik. Oberst James Bowie› ([nordamerik.] Jagdmesser)

Bow|le ['bo:lə], die; -, -n ‹engl.› (Getränk aus Wein, Zucker u. Früchten; Gefäß für dieses Getränk)

bow|len ['bo:lən] ‹engl.› (*Sport* Bowling spielen)

Bow|len|glas ['bo:lən...] *Plur.* ...gläser

Bow|ling ['bo:liŋ], das; -s, -s ‹engl.› (amerik. Art des Kegelspiels mit 10 Kegeln; engl. Kugelspiel auf glattem Rasen); **Bow|ling|bahn**

Box, die; -, -en ‹engl.› (Pferdestand; Unterstellraum; Montageplatz bei Autorennen; einfache, kastenförmige Kamera)

Box|calf *vgl.* Boxkalf

bo|xen ‹engl.›; du boxt; er boxte ihn (*auch* ihm) in den Magen

Bo|xen|stopp *(Automobilsport)*

Bo|xer, der; -s, - (*bes. südd., österr. auch* Faustschlag; eine Hunderasse); **bo|xe|risch;** -es Können; **Bo|xer‿mo|tor** *(Technik),* **...nase; Box‿hand|schuh, ...hieb**
Box|kalf, Box|calf [*auch* engl. 'bokska:f], das; -s, -s ⟨engl.⟩ (Kalbsleder); **Box|kalf|schuh**
Box‿kampf, ...ring, ...sport
Boy [bɔy], der; -s, -s ⟨engl.⟩ ([Hotel]diener, Bote)
Boy|kott [bɔy...], der; -[e]s, *Plur.* -s, *auch* -e ⟨nach dem geächteten engl. Gutsverwalter Boycott⟩ (politische, wirtschaftliche od. soziale Ächtung; Nichtbeachten); **boy|kot|tie|ren; Boy|kott|maß|nah|me** *meist Plur.*
Boyle-Ma|ri|otte-Ge|setz [ˌbɔyl-ma'riɔt...], das; -es; *vgl.* Mariotte
Boy|scout ['bɔyskaut], der; -[s], -s (*engl. Bez. für* Pfadfinder)
Bo|zen (Stadt in Südtirol); *vgl.* Bolzano; **Boz|ner** (↑R 103)
Bq = Becquerel
Br = *chem. Zeichen für* Brom
BR = Bayerischer Rundfunk
Bra|ban|çonne [brabã'sɔn], die; - ⟨franz.; nach der belg. Provinz Brabant⟩ (belg. Nationalhymne); **Bra|bant** (belg. Provinz); **Bra|ban|ter** (↑R 103); - Spitzen
brab|beln (*ugs. für* undeutlich vor sich hin reden); ich ...[e]le (↑R 16)
brach (unbestellt; unbebaut); brachliegen *(vgl. d.);* **Bra|che,** die; -, -n (Brachfeld); **Bra|chet,** der; -s, -e (*alte Bez. für* Juni); **Brach|feld**
bra|chi|al ⟨griech.⟩ (*Med.* den Arm betreffend; mit roher Körperkraft); **Bra|chi|al|ge|walt,** die; - (rohe, körperliche Gewalt); **Bra|chi|o|sau|rus,** der; -, ...rier [...iər] (eine ausgestorbene Riesenechse)
brach|le|gen; ↑R 38 f. (nicht bebauen; nicht nutzen); **brach|lie|gen;** ↑R 38 f. (unbebaut liegen; nicht genutzt werden); der Acker liegt brach; brachgelegen; brachzuliegen; brachliegende Felder; **Brach‿mo|nat** *od.* **...mond** *vgl.* Brachet
Brach|se, die; -, -n *u.* **Brach|sen,** *schweiz.* **Brachs|men,** der; -s, - (ein Karpfenfisch); *vgl. auch* Brasse *u.* Brassen
Brach|vo|gel (Schnepfenart)
bra|chy... [...x...] ⟨griech.⟩ (kurz...); **Bra|chy...** (Kurz...); **Bra|chy|lo|gie,** die; -, ...ien (*Rhet., Stilk.* Kürze im Ausdruck)
Brack, das; -[e]s, *Plur.* -s *od.* -en (*landsch. für* Tümpel, kleiner See; Brackwasser)
Bra|cke, der; -n, -n (↑R 126), *seltener* die; -, -n (Spürhundrasse)
bra|ckig (schwach salzig u. daher ungenießbar)
Bräckin (*w. Form von* Bracke)
bra|ckisch (aus Brackwasser abgelagert); **Brack|was|ser,** das; -s, ...wasser (Gemisch aus Salz- und Süßwasser)
Brä|gen, der; -s, - (*Nebenform von* Bregen)
Bra|gi (nord. Gott der Dichtkunst)
Brah|ma ⟨sanskr.⟩ (ind. Gott); **Brah|ma|huhn** *vgl.* Brahmaputrahuhn; **Brah|ma|is|mus;** *vgl.* Brahmanismus; **Brah|man,** das; -s (*ind. Rel. u. Philos.* Weltseele); **Brah|ma|ne,** der; -n, -n; ↑R 126 (Angehöriger einer ind. Priesterkaste); **brah|ma|nisch; Brah|ma|nis|mus,** der; - (eine ind. Religion; *auch für* Hinduismus); **Brah|ma|put|ra** [...'pu(:)tra] (↑R 130), der; -[s] (südasiat. Strom); **Brah|ma|put|ra|huhn** (↑R 105), *auch* Brah|ma|huhn; ↑R 95 (eine Hühnerrasse)
Brahms (dt. Komponist)
Braille|schrift ['bra:j...], die; - (↑R 95) ⟨nach dem franz. Erfinder Braille⟩ (Blindenschrift)
Brain|drain ['bre:ndre:n], der; -s ⟨engl.-amerik.⟩ (Abwanderung von Wissenschaftlern [z. B. nach Amerika]); **Brain|stor|ming** ['bre:nstɔ:(r)miŋ], das; -s (*bes. Wirtsch.* gemeinsames Bemühen, [in einer Sitzung] durch spontane Äußerung von Einfällen zur Lösung eines Problems beizutragen); **Brain|trust** ['bre:ntrast], der; -[s], -s ([wirtschaftl.] Beratungsausschuss)
Brak|te|at, der; -en, -en (↑R 126) ⟨lat.⟩ (einseitig geprägte mittelalterl. Münze)
Bram, die; -, -en ⟨niederl.⟩ (*Seemannsspr.* zweitoberste Verlängerung der Masten sowie deren Takelung)
Bra|mar|bas, der; -, -se (Aufschneider, Prahlhans); **bra|mar|ba|sie|ren** (aufschneiden, prahlen)
Bram|bach, Bad (Stadt im südl. Vogtland)
Bram|busch (*nordd. für* Ginster)
Bram|me, die; -, -n (*Walztechnik* Eisenblock); **Bram|men|walz|werk**
Bram|se|gel *(Seemannsspr.)*
bram|sig (*nordd. ugs. für* derb; protzig; prahlerisch)
Bram|sten|ge *vgl.* Bram
Bran|che ['brã:ʃə, *österr.* brã:ʃ], die; -, -n ⟨franz.⟩ (Wirtschafts-, Geschäftszweig; *ugs. für* Fachgebiet); **Bran|che[n]|er|fah|rung; bran|che[n]|fremd; Bran|che[n]|kennt|nis; bran|che[n]‿kun|dig, ...üb|lich; Bran|chen|ver|zeich|nis**
Bran|chi|at, der; -en, -en (↑R 126) ⟨griech.⟩ (mit Kiemen atmender Gliederfüßer); **Bran|chie** [...iə], die; -, -n *meist Plur.* (*Zool.* Kieme)
Brand, der; -[e]s, Brände; in - stecken; **brand|ak|tu|ell; Brand‿an|schlag, ...bin|de, ...bla|se, ...bom|be, ...brief** *(ugs.),* **...di|rek|tor; brand|ei|lig** (*ugs. für* sehr eilig); **bran|deln** (*österr. ugs. für* brenzlig riechen; *auch* viel zahlen müssen); **bran|den**
Bran|den|burg (Stadt an der Havel; dt. Land); **Bran|den|bur|ger** (↑R 103); **bran|den|bur|gisch,** *aber* (↑R 108): die Brandenburgischen Konzerte (von Bach)
Brand‿en|te (ein Vogel), **...fa|ckel, ...grab** *(Archäol.);* **brand|heiß; Brand|herd; bran|dig; Brand‿kas|se, ...le|ger** (*österr. für* Brandstifter), **...le|gung** (*österr. für* Brandstiftung), **...mal** (*Plur.* ...male, *seltener* ...mäler; *geh.*); **brand|mar|ken;** gebrandmarkt; **Brand‿mau|er, ...meis|ter; brand‿neu, ...rot; Brand|sal|be; brand|schat|zen;** du brandschatzt; gebrandschatzt (*früher für* durch Branddrohung erpressen); **Brand‿schat|zung** *(früher),* **...soh|le, ...stif|ter, ...stif|tung, ...teig; Bran|dung; Brand‿ur|sa|che, ...wa|che, ...wun|de; Bran|dy** ['brɛndi], der; -s, -s ⟨engl.⟩ (*engl. Bez. für* Weinbrand); **Brand|zei|chen; Brannt‿kalk** (Ätzkalk), **...wein; Brannt|wei|ner** (*österr. für* [Wirt einer] Branntweinschenke); **Brannt|wein|steu|er,** die
Braque [brak] (franz. Maler)
[1]**Bra|sil,** der; -s, *Plur.* -e *u.* -s ⟨nach Brasilien⟩ (Tabak; Kaffeesorte); [2]**Bra|sil,** die; -, -[s] (Zigarre); **Bra|sil|holz** (↑R 105); **Bra|sí|lia, Bra|si|lia** [*beide* ...'zi:lia] (Hptst. von Brasilien); **Bra|si|li|a|ner; Bra|si|li|a|ne|rin; bra|si|li|a|nisch; Bra|si|li|en** (südamerik. Staat); **Bra|si|li|en|holz** *vgl.* Brasilholz
Brass, der; -es (*ugs. für* Ärger, Wut); - haben; in - kommen
[1]**Bras|se,** die; -, -n *u.* Bras|sen, der; -s, - (*nordd., mitteld. für* Brachse)
[2]**Bras|se,** die; -, -n (*Seemannsspr.* Tau zum Stellen der Segel)
Bras|se|lett, das; -s, -e ⟨franz.⟩ (Armband; *Gaunerspr.* Handschelle)
bras|sen (*Seemannsspr.* die [2]Brassen benutzen); du brasst

Bra|sen *vgl.* [1]Brasse
Brät, das; -s (fein gehacktes [Bratwurst]fleisch); **Brat|ap|fel; brä|teln;** ich ...[e]le (↑R 16); **bra|ten;** du brätst, er brät; du brietst; du brietest; gebraten; brat[e]!; **Bra|ten**, der; -s, -; **Bra|ten₋duft, ...fett, ...rock** (*veraltend scherzh. für* Gehrock), **...saft, ...so|ße; Brä|ter** (*landsch. für* Schmortopf); **brat|fer|tig; Brat₋fisch, ...hähn|chen, ...hen|del** (das; -s, -n; *südd., österr. für* Brathähnchen); **Brat|he|ring**
Bra|tis|la|va [...v...] (↑R 132; Hptst. der Slowakei); *vgl.* Preßburg
Brat|kar|tof|fel *meist Plur.;* **Brat|ling** (gebratener Kloß aus Gemüse, Hülsenfrüchten); **Brät|ling** (Pilz; Fisch); **Brat₋pfan|ne, ...röh|re, ...rost**
Brat|sche, die; -, -n ‹ital.› (ein Streichinstrument); **Brat|scher** (Bratschenspieler); **Brat|schist**, der; -en, -en (↑R 126)
Brat₋spieß, ...spill (*Seemannsspr.* Ankerwinde mit waagerechter Welle), **...wurst**
Bräu, das; -[e]s, *Plur.* -e *u.* -s (*bes. südd. für* Bier; Brauerei); z. B. in Löwenbräu
Brauch, der; -[e]s, Bräuche; in *od.* im - sein; **brauch|bar; Brauch|bar|keit**, die; -; **brau|chen;** du brauchst, er braucht; du brauchtest; du brauchtest (*ugs. auch* bräuchtest); gebraucht; er hat es nicht zu tun brauchen; *vgl. aber* gebrauchen; **Brauch|tum**, das; -s, ...tümer *Plur. selten;* **Brauch|was|ser**, das; -s (Wasser für industrielle Zwecke)
Braue, die; -, -n
brau|en; Brau|er; Brau|e|rei; Brau|e|rin; Brau₋haus, ...meis|ter
braun; eine braun gebrannte Frau; die Sonne hat uns braun gebrannt; *vgl.* blau; **Braun**, das; -s, *Plur.* -, *ugs.* -s (braune Farbe); *vgl.* Blau; **Braun|al|ge; braun|äu|gig; Braun|bär;** [1]**Brau|ne**, der; -n, -n; ↑R 5 ff. (braunes Pferd; *österr. auch für* Kaffee mit Milch); [2]**Brau|ne**, das; -n (↑R 47); **Bräu|ne**, die; - (braune Färbung; *veraltend für* Halsentzündung); **Braun|ei|sen₋erz** (das; -es) *od.* **...stein** (der; -[e]s); [1]**Brau|nel|le**, die; -, -n (ein Singvogel); [2]**Brau|nel|le** *vgl.* Brunelle; **bräu|nen;** braun ge|brannt *vgl.* braun; **Braun₋kehl|chen, ...koh|le; Braun|koh|len₋berg|werk, ...bri|kett; bräun|lich;** bräunlich gelb usw.

Braun|schweig (Stadt im nördl. Vorland des Harzes); **Braun|schwei|ger; braun|schwei|gisch**
Braun|stein, der; -[e]s (ein Mineral); **Bräu|nung; Bräu|nungs|stu|dio**
Braus, der; *nur noch in* in Saus und - (verschwenderisch) leben
Brau|sche, die; -, -n (*landsch. für* Beule, bes. an der Stirn)
Brau|se, die; -, -n; **Brau|se₋bad, ...kopf** (*veraltend für* Hitzkopf); **Brau|se|li|mo|na|de; brau|sen;** du braust; er braus|te; **Brau|sen**, das; -s; **Brau|se|pul|ver**
Bräu|stüb|chen (*südd. für* kleines Gasthaus; Gastraum)
Braut, die; -, Bräute; **Braut₋el|tern** *(Plur.)*, **...füh|rer; Bräu|ti|gam**, der; -s, -e; **Braut₋jung|fer, ...kleid, ...kranz; Braut|leu|te; bräut|lich; Braut₋mut|ter, ...nacht, ...paar; Braut|schau;** auf - gehen; **Braut₋stand** (der; -[e]s), **...va|ter**
brav; ‹franz.› (tüchtig; artig, ordentlich); **Brav|heit**, die; -; **bra|vis|si|mo!** [...v...] ‹ital.› (sehr gut!); **bra|vo!** (gut!); [1]**Bra|vo**, das; -s, -s (Beifallsruf); Bravo, *auch* bravo rufen; [2]**Bra|vo**, der; -s, *Plur.* -s *u.* ...vi (*ital. Bezeichnung für* Meuchelmörder, Räuber); **Bra|vo|ruf; Bra|vour** [...'vu:r], *eindeutschend* Bra|vur (↑R 33), die; - ‹franz.› (Tapferkeit; meisterhafte Technik); **Bra|vour₋arie** (↑R 132), **...leis|tung; bra|vou|rös** (schneidig; meisterhaft); **Bra|vour|stück;** Bra|vur usw. *vgl.* Bravour usw.
Braz|za|ville [braza'vil] (Hptst. der Republik Kongo)
BRD = Bundesrepublik Deutschland
break! [bre:k] ‹engl., „trennt euch"› (Trennkommando des Ringrichters beim Boxkampf); **Break**, der *od.* das; -s, -s (*Sport* unerwarteter Durchbruch; *Tennis* Durchbrechen des gegnerischen Aufschlags; *Jazz* kurzes Zwischensolo); **Break|dance** [...dɛns], der; -[s] ‹amerik.› (tänzerisch-akrobatische Darbietung zu moderner Popmusik); **Break|dan|cer** [...dɛnsə(r)]; **brea|ken** ['bre:kən] ‹*zu* Break› (*Tennis* dem Gegner bei dessen Aufschlag einen Punkt abnehmen; *Funktechnik* über CB-Funk ein Gespräch führen)
Brec|cie ['brɛtʃə] *od.* Brek|zie [...jə], die; -, -n ‹ital.› (*Geol.* aus kantigen Gesteinstrümmern gebildetes u. verkittetes Gestein)

brech|bar; Brech₋boh|ne, ...durch|fall; Bre|che, die; -, -n (*früher für* Gerät zum Zerknicken der Flachsstängel u. a.); **Brech|ei|sen; bre|chen;** du brichst, er bricht; du brachst; du brächest; gebrochen; brich!; sich -; brechend voll; er brach den Stab über ihn (*nicht* ihm); auf Biegen oder Brechen *(ugs.)*; **Bre|cher** (Sturzsee; Grobzerkleinerungsmaschine); **Brech₋mit|tel** (das), **...reiz, ...stan|ge**
Brecht, Bert[olt] (dt. Schriftsteller)
Bre|chung; Bre|chungs|win|kel *(Physik)*
Bre|douil|le [bre'duljə], die; - ‹franz.› (*ugs. für* Verlegenheit, Bedrängnis); in der - sein
Bree|ches ['bri(:)tʃəs] *Plur.* ‹engl.› (Sport-, Reithose)
Bre|gen, der; -s, - (*nordd. für* Gehirn [vom Schlachttier]); *vgl. auch* Brägen; **bre|gen|klü|te|rig** (*nordd. für* melancholisch)
Bre|genz (österr. Stadt; Hptst. des Landes Vorarlberg); **Bre|gen|zer** (↑R 103); **Bre|gen|zer|wald**, der; -[e]s, *auch* **Bre|gen|zer Wald**, der; - -[e]s; ↑R 105 (Bergland)
Brehm (dt. Zoologe)
Brei, der; -[e]s, -e; **brei|ig**
Brein, der; -s (*österr. mdal. für* Hirse, Hirsebrei)
Brei|sach (Stadt am Oberrhein); **Breis|gau**, der, *landsch.* das; -[e]s (südwestdt. Landschaft)
breit; weit und breit; (↑R 47:) des Langen und Breiten (umständlich), des Breiter[e]n darlegen; ein Langes und Breites (viel) sagen; ins Breite fließen; *Schreibung in Verbindung mit Verben und Partizipien* (↑R 39): z. B. man wird die Straße breit, viel breiter machen; sich breit machen (*ugs. für* viel [Platz] in Anspruch nehmen); du hast dich breit gemacht, immer breiter gemacht; breit getretene Schuhe; ein [sehr] breit gefächertes Angebot; die Angebote sind [sehr] breit gefächert; *vgl. aber* breitschlagen, breittreten; **breit|bei|nig; Brei|te**, die; -, -n; nördliche Breite (*Abk.* n. Br.); südliche Breite (*Abk.* s. Br.); in die Breite gehen (*ugs. für* dick werden); **brei|ten;** ein Tuch über den Tisch breiten; **Brei|ten₋ar|beit** (die; -), **...grad** *(Geogr.)*, **...sport, ...wir|kung;** breit ge|fä|chert *vgl.* breit; **Breit|ling** (Fisch); breit ma|chen *vgl.* breit; **breit₋na|sig, ...ran|dig; breit|schla|gen;** ↑R 38 f. (*ugs. für* durch Überredung für etwas gewinnen); er hat mich breitgeschlagen; sich -

lassen; *aber* er hat den Nagel breit geschlagen; **breit₋schul|te|rig, ...schult|rig; Breit₋schwanz** (ein Lammfell), **...sei|te; breit|spu|rig; breit|tre|ten** (*ugs. für* weitschweifig darlegen); ein Thema -; **Breit|wand** (im Kino); **Breit|wand|film**

Brek|zie [...i̯ə] *vgl.* Breccie

Bre|me, die; -, -n (*südd., schweiz. mdal. für* Stechfliege, ²Bremse)

Bre|men (Land und Hafenstadt an der Weser); **Bre|mer** (↑R 103); **Bre|mer|ha|ven** [...fən] (Hafenstadt an der Wesermündung); **bre|misch**

Brems₋ba|cke *(Technik),* **...be|lag, ...berg** *(Bergbau);* **¹Brem|se,** die; -, -n (Hemmvorrichtung)

²Brem|se, die; -, -n (ein Insekt)

brem|seln (*österr. für* kribbeln)

brem|sen; du bremst

Brem|sen₋pla|ge, ...stich

Brem|ser; Brem|ser|häus|chen; Brems₋flüs|sig|keit, ...he|bel, ...klotz, ...licht (*Plur.* ...lichter), **...pe|dal, ...pro|be, ...ra|ke|te, ...spur; Brem|sung; Brems|weg**

brenn|bar; Brenn|bar|keit, die; -; **Brenn|dau|er; Brenn|ele|ment** (↑R 132; *Kernphysik*); **bren|nen;** du branntest; *selten* du brenntest; gebrannt; brenn[e]!; brennend gern *(ugs.);* **¹Bren|ner**

²Bren|ner, der; -s (ein Alpenpass); **Bren|ner|bahn,** die; - (↑R 105)

Bren|ne|rei; Brenn₋glas, ...holz (das; -es), **...ma|te|ri|al; Brenn|nes|sel,** die; -, -n (↑R 136); **Brenn₋punkt, ...sche|re, ...spie|gel, ...spi|ri|tus, ...stab** *(Kernphysik),* **...stoff, ...stoff|fra|ge** (↑R 136), **...wei|te** *(Optik)*

Bren|ta|no (dt. Dichter)

Bren|te, die; -, -n (*schweiz. für* Tragbütte)

bren|zeln (*landsch. für* nach Brand riechen); **brenz|lich** (*landsch. für* brenzlig); **brenz|lig**

Bre|sche, die; -, -n ‹franz.› (*veraltend für* große Lücke)

Bres|lau (*poln.* Wrocław); **Bres|lau|er** (↑R 103)

brest|haft (*veraltet für* mit Gebrechen behaftet)

Bre|tag|ne [breˈtanjə] (↑R 130), die; - (franz. Halbinsel); **Bre|ton** [brə-ˈtõ:], der; -s, -s ([Stroh]hut mit hochgerollter Krempe); **Bre|to|ne** [bre...], der; -n, -n (↑R 126); **Bre|to|nin; bre|to|nisch**

Brett, das; -[e]s, -er; **Bret|tel,** Brettl, das; -s, -[n] *meist Plur.* (*südd., österr. für* kleines Brett; Ski); **Bret|ter|bu|de; bret|tern** (aus Brettern bestehend); **Bret|ter₋wand, ...zaun; bret|tig;** -er Stoff; **Brettl,** das; -s, - (Kleinkunstbühne; *vgl.* Brettel); **Brett₋se|geln** (*veraltend für* Windsurfing), **...spiel**

Bret|zel, die; -, -n (*schweiz. für* ein Waffelgebäck)

Breu|ghel [ˈbrɔ̞ygəl, *niederl.* ˈbrø:xəl] *vgl.* Brueg[h]el

Bre|ve [...v...], das; -s, *Plur.* -n *u.* -s ‹lat.› (päpstl. Erlass in kurz gefasster Form); **Bre|vet** [breˈve:, *franz.* breˈvɛ], das; -s, -s (*früher* Gnadenbrief des franz. Königs; *veraltet für* Schutz-, Verleihungs-, Ernennungsurkunde; *schweiz. für* Prüfungsausweis); **bre|ve|tie|ren** (*schweiz.* ein Brevet erwerben, erteilen); **Bre|vier,** das; -s, -e (Gebetbuch der kath. Geistlichen; Stundengebet)

Bre|zel, die; -, -n, *österr. auch* das; -s, -; **Bre|zen,** die; -, - *(bayr., österr.)*

Bri|and-Kel|logg-Pakt [bri.ã:...], der; -[e]s (↑R 95) ‹nach dem franz. Außenminister A. Briand u. dem nordamerik. Außenminister F. B. Kellogg› (Kriegsächtungspakt von 1928)

Bri|cke, die; -, -n (*landsch. für* Neunauge)

Bri|de, die; -, -n ‹franz.› (*schweiz. für* Kabelschelle)

Bridge [britʃ *od.* bridʒ], das; - ‹engl.› (Kartenspiel); **Bridge|par|tie**

Bridge|town [ˈbridʒtau̯n] (Hptst. von Barbados)

Brief, der; -[e]s, -e *(Abk.* Bf., *auf dt. Kurszetteln* B; *vgl. d.);* **Brief₋adel** (↑R 132), **...be|schwe|rer, ...block** (*vgl.* Block), **...bo|gen, ...bom|be, ...druck|sa|che, ...freund, ...freun|din, ...ge|heim|nis** (das; -ses)

Brie|fing, das; -s, -s ‹engl.-amerik.› (kurze [Lage]besprechung; Informationsgespräch)

Brief₋kar|te, ...kas|ten (*Plur.* ...kästen); **Brief|kas|ten₋fir|ma** (Scheinfirma), **...on|kel, ...tan|te; Brief|kopf; brief|lich; Brief|mar|ke;** (↑R 28:) 80-Pfennig-Briefmarke; 1-DM-Briefmarke; **Brief|mar|ken₋auk|ti|on, ...block** (*vgl.* Block), **...kun|de** (die; -), **...samm|ler; Brief₋öff|ner, ...pa|pier, ...part|ner, ...part|ne|rin, ...por|to, ...ro|man; Brief|schaf|ten** *Plur.;* **Brief₋schrei|ber, ...schrei|be|rin, ...stel|ler** *(veraltend),* **...ta|sche, ...tau|be, ...trä|ger, ...trä|ge|rin, ...um|schlag, ...wahl, ...wech|sel, ...zu|stel|ler**

Brie|kä|se (↑R 105)

Brienz (BE) (schweiz. Ort); -er See (See im Berner Oberland)

Bries, das; -es, -e *u.* **Brie|sel,** das; -s, - (innere Brustdrüse bei Tieren, bes. beim Kalb); **Bries|chen,** *auch* Brös|chen (Gericht aus Briesen des Kalbs)

Bri|ga|de, die; -, -n ‹franz.› (größere Truppenabteilung; *ehemals in der DDR* kleinste Arbeitsgruppe in einem Produktionsbetrieb); **Bri|ga|de₋füh|rer, ...ge|ne|ral, ...lei|ter** (der), **...lei|te|rin; Bri|ga|di|er** [...ˈdi̯e:], der; -s, -s (Befehlshaber einer militär. Brigade) *u.* [...ˈdi̯e:, *auch* ...ˈdi:r], der; -s, *Plur.* -s [...ˈdi̯e:s] *od.* -e [...ˈdi:rə] (*ehemals in der DDR* Leiter einer Arbeitsbrigade); **Bri|ga|die|rin; Bri|gant,** der; -en, -en (↑R 126) ‹ital.› (*früher für* [Straßen]räuber in Italien); **Bri|gan|ti|ne,** die; -, -n (*svw.* Brigg)

Brigg, die; -, -s ‹engl.› (zweimastiges Segelschiff)

Briggs (engl. Mathematiker); (↑R 94:) briggssche Logarithmen; **Briggs-Lo|ga|rith|mus**

Bri|git|ta, Bri|git|te (w. Vorn.)

Bri|kett, das; -s, *Plur.* -s, *selten* -e ‹franz.› (aus kleinen Stücken od. Staub gepresstes [Kohlen]stück); **bri|ket|tie|ren** (zu Briketts formen); **Bri|ket|tie|rung; Bri|kett|trä|ger** (↑R 136)

bri|ko|lie|ren ‹franz.› (*Billard* durch Rückprall [von der Bande] treffen)

bril|lant [brilˈjant] ‹franz.› (glänzend; fein); **¹Bril|lant,** der; -en, -en; ↑R 126 (geschliffener Diamant); **²Bril|lant,** die; - (*Druckw.* ein Schriftgrad); **Bril|lant₋bro|sche, ...feu|er|werk; Bril|lan|tin,** das; -s, -e (*österr. neben* Brillantine); **Bril|lan|ti|ne,** die; -, -n (Haarpomade); **Bril|lant₋kol|li|er, ...na|del, ...ring, ...schliff, ...schmuck; Bril|lanz,** die; - (Glanz, Feinheit)

Bril|le, die; -, -n; **Bril|len₋etui** (↑R 132), **...fut|te|ral, ...ge|stell, ...glas** (*Plur.* ...gläser), **...schlan|ge** (*ugs. scherzh. auch für* Brillenträger[in]), **...trä|ger, ...trä|ge|rin**

bril|lie|ren [briˈlji:..., *auch, österr. nur,* briˈli:...] (glänzen)

Brim|bo|ri|um, das; -s ‹lat.› (*ugs. für* Gerede; Umschweife)

Brim|sen, der; -s, - ‹tschech.› (*österr. für* Schafskäse)

Bri|nell|här|te, die; - ‹nach dem schwed. Ingenieur Brinell›; ↑R 95 (Maß der Härte eines Werkstoffes; *Zeichen* HB)

brin|gen; du brachtest; du brächtest; gebracht; bring[e]!; mit sich bringen; **Brin|ger** (*veraltend für* Überbringer); **Bring|schuld**

(*Rechtsspr.* Schuld, die beim Gläubiger bezahlt werden muss)

Bri|oche [bri'ɔʃ], die; -, -s ‹franz.› (ein Gebäck)

Bri|o|ni|sche In|seln *Plur.* (Inselgruppe vor Istrien)

bri|sant ‹franz.› (sprengend, hochexplosiv; sehr aktuell); **Bri|sanz,** die; -, -en (Sprengkraft; *nur Sing.:* brennende Aktualität)

Bris|bane ['brisbe:n, *auch* 'brizbən] (austr. Stadt)

Bri|se, die; -, -n ‹franz.› (leichter Wind [am Meer])

Bri|so|lett, das; -s, -e *u.* **Bri|so|let|te,** die; -, -n ‹franz.› (gebratenes Kalbfleischklößchen)

[1]**Bris|sa|go** (Ort am Lago Maggiore); [2]**Bris|sa|go,** die; -, -s (*schweiz.* eine Zigarrensorte)

Bris|tol ['brist(ə)l] (engl. Stadt am Avon); **Bris|tol‿ka|nal** (Bucht zwischen Wales u. Cornwall), **...kar|ton** (↑R 105; Zeichenkarton aus mehreren Lagen)

Brit (w. Vorn.)

Bri|tan|ni|a|me|tall, das; -s; ↑R 105 (Zinnlegierung); **Bri|tan|ni|en** [...iən]; **bri|tan|nisch; Bri|te,** der; -n, -n (↑R 126); **Bri|tin; bri|tisch,** *aber* (↑R 108): die Britischen Inseln, das Britische Museum; **Bri|tisch-Hon|du|ras;** *vgl.* Belize; **Bri|tisch-Ko|lum|bi|en** (kanad. Provinz); **Bri|ti|zis|mus,** der; -, ...men (Spracheigentümlichkeit des britischen Englisch)

Britsch|ka, die; -, -s ‹poln.› (*früher für* leichter, offener Reisewagen)

Brit|ta (w. Vorn.)

Brit|ten (engl. Komponist)

Brno ['br(ə)nɔ] (Stadt in Mähren; *vgl.* Brünn)

Broad|way ['brɔ:dwe:], der; -s ‹engl.› (Straße in New York)

Broc|co|li *vgl.* Brokkoli

Broch (österr. Schriftsteller)

Bröck|chen; bröck|chen|wei|se; brö|cke|lig, bröck|lig; **Brö|cke|lig|keit,** Bröck|lig|keit, die; -; **brö|ckeln;** ich ...[e]le (↑R 16); **bro|cken** (einbrocken; *südd. u. österr. auch für* pflücken); [1]**Bro|cken,** der; -s, - (das Abgebrochene)

[2]**Bro|cken,** der; -s (höchster Berg des Harzes)

bro|cken|wei|se

Bro|ckes (dt. Dichter)

bröck|lig, brö|cke|lig; **Bröck|lig|keit** *vgl.* Bröckeligkeit

Brod (österr. Schriftsteller)

bro|deln (dampfend aufsteigen, aufwallen; *österr. ugs. für* Zeit vertrödeln)

Bro|dem, der; -s (*geh. für* Qualm, Dampf, Dunst)

Bro|de|rie, die; -, ...ien ‹franz.› (*veraltet für* Stickerei; Einfassung)

Brod|ler (*österr. ugs. für* jmd., der die Zeit vertrödelt)

Broi|ler ['brɔy...], der; -s, - ‹engl.› (*regional für* Hähnchen zum Grillen); **Broi|ler|mast,** die

Bro|kat, der; -[e]s, -e ‹ital.› (kostbares gemustertes Seidengewebe); **Bro|ka|tell,** der; -s, -e *u.* **Bro|ka|tel|le,** die; -, -n (ein Baumwollgewebe); **bro|ka|ten** *(geh.);* ein -es Kleid

Bro|ker, der; -s, - ‹engl.› (*engl. Bez. für* Börsenmakler)

Brok|ko|li *Plur., auch* der; -s, -s ‹ital.› (Spargelkohl)

Brom, das; -s ‹griech.› (chem. Element, Nichtmetall; *Zeichen* Br)

Brom|bee|re; Brom|beer|strauch

brom|hal|tig; Bro|mid, das; -[e]s, -e ‹griech.› (Salz des Bromwasserstoffs); **Bro|mit** [*auch* ...'mit], das; -s, -e (Bromsilber [ein Mineral]); **Brom‿säu|re** (die; -), **...sil|ber, ...sil|ber|pa|pier**

bron|chi|al ‹griech.›; **Bron|chi|al‿asth|ma, ...ka|tarrh** (↑R 33; Luftröhrenkatarrh); **Bron|chie** [...iə], die; -, -n *meist Plur.* (*Med.* Luftröhrenast); **Bron|chi|tis,** die; -, ...itiden (Bronchialkatarrh)

Bronn, der; -[e]s, -en *u.* **Bron|nen,** der; -s, - (*veraltet für* Brunnen)

Bron|to|sau|rus, der; -, ...rier [...iər] ‹griech.› (eine ausgestorbene Riesenechse)

Bron|ze ['brɔŋsə *od.* 'brɔ̃:sə, *österr.* brɔ̃:s], die; -, -n [...s(ə)n] ‹ital.(-franz.)› (Metallmischung; Kunstgegenstand aus Bronze; *nur Sing.:* Farbe); **bron|ze‿far|ben, ...far|big; Bron|ze‿kunst** (die; -), **...me|dail|le; bron|zen** (aus Bronze); **Bron|ze|zeit,** die; - (vorgeschichtliche Kulturzeit); **bron|ze|zeit|lich; bron|zie|ren** [brɔŋ'si:... *od.* brɔ̃'si:..., *österr. nur so*] (mit Bronze überziehen); **Bron|zit** [*auch* ...'tsit], der; -s (ein Mineral)

Brook|lyn ['bruklin] (Stadtteil von New York)

Bro|säm|chen; Bro|sa|me, die; -, -n *meist Plur.*

brosch. = broschiert; **Bro|sche,** die; -, -n ‹franz.› (Anstecknadel)

Brös|chen *vgl.* Brieschen

bro|schie|ren ‹franz.› (Druckbogen in einen Papierumschlag heften od. leimen); **bro|schiert** (*Abk.* brosch.); [1]**Bro|schur,** die; - (das Heften od. Leimen); [2]**Bro|schur,** die; -, -en (in Papierumschlag geheftete Druckschrift); **Bro|schü|re,** die; -, -n (leicht geheftetes Druckwerk)

Brö|sel, der, *österr.* das; -s, - *meist Plur.* (Krümel, Bröckchen); **brö|se|lig,** brös|lig; **brö|seln** (bröckeln); ich ...[e]le (↑R 16)

Brot, das; -[e]s, -e; **Brot‿auf|strich, ...beu|tel; Bröt|chen; Bröt|chen|ge|ber** (*scherzh. für* Arbeitgeber); **Brot‿ein|heit** (*Med.; Abk.* BE), **...er|werb, ...fab|rik, ...ge|trei|de, ...kas|ten, ...korb, ...kru|me, ...krü|mel, ...laib; brot|los;** -e Künste; **Brot‿ma|schi|ne, ...mes|ser, ...neid, ...preis, ...schei|be, ...schnit|te, ...stu|di|um** (das; -s), **...sup|pe, ...teig, ...zeit** (*landsch. für* Zwischenmahlzeit [am Vormittag])

Brow|ning ['brauniŋ], der; -s, -s ‹nach dem amerik. Erfinder› (eine Schusswaffe)

brr! (*Zuruf an Zugtiere* halt!)

BRT = Bruttoregistertonne

[1]**Bruch,** der; -[e]s, Brüche ['bryçə] (Brechen; Zerbrochenes; Bruchzahl; *ugs. für* Einbruch); zu Bruch gehen; in die Brüche gehen

[2]**Bruch** [*od.* bru:x], der *u.* das; -[e]s, *Plur.* Brüche ['bryçə *od.* 'bry:çə], *landsch.* Brücher (Sumpfland)

Bruch‿band (das; *Plur.* ...bänder; *Med.*), **...bu|de** (*ugs. für* schlechtes, baufälliges Haus); **bruch|fest; Bruch|fes|tig|keit**

bru|chig [*od.* 'bru:...] (sumpfig)

brü|chig (morsch); **Brü|chig|keit,** die; -; **bruch|lan|den** *fast nur im Partizip II gebr.:* bruchgelandet; **Bruch|lan|dung; bruch|los; bruch|rech|nen** *nur im Infinitiv üblich;* **Bruch‿rech|nen** (das; -s), **...rech|nung** (die; -), **...scha|den, ...scho|ko|la|de; bruch|si|cher;** - verpackt; **Bruch‿stein, ...stel|le, ...strich, ...stück; bruch|stück|haft; Bruch‿teil** (der), **...zahl**

Brück|chen; Brü|cke, die; -, -n; *Schreibung in Straßennamen:* ↑R 123; **Brü|cken‿bau** (*Plur.* ...bauten), **...ge|län|der, ...kopf** *(Milit.),* **...pfei|ler, ...zoll** *(früher)*

Bruck|ner (österr. Komponist)

Brü|den, der; -s, - (*Technik* Schwaden, Abdampf); *vgl.* Brodem

Bru|der, der; -s, Brüder; die Brüder Grimm; **Brü|der|chen; Brü|der|ge|mei|ne,** die; -, -n ‹*Kurzform von* Herrnhuter Brüdergemeine› (pietistische Freikirche); **Bru|der‿hand, ...herz** (*veraltend, noch scherzh. für* Bruder, Freund), **...krieg, ...kuss; Brü|der|lein; brü|der|lich; Brü|der|lich|keit,** die; -; **Bru|der Lus|tig,** der; *Gen.* Bruder Lustigs *u.* Bruder[s] Lustig, *Plur.* Brüder Lustig (*veraltend für* leichtlebiger Mensch); **Bru|der|mord; Bru|der|schaft** ([rel.] Vereinigung); **Brü|der|schaft** (brüderliches Verhältnis); - trinken; **Bru|der‿volk, ...zwist**

Brue|g[h]el ['brø:xəl] (fläm. Malerfamilie)

Brüg|ge (belg. Stadt)

Brü|he, die; -, -n; **brü|hen; brüh|heiß; Brüh|kar|tof|feln** *Plur.*

Brühl, der; -[e]s, -e (*veraltet für* sumpfige Wiese)

brüh|warm *(ugs.)*; **Brüh‿wür|fel, ...wurst**

Brüll|af|fe; brül|len; Brül|ler

Bru|maire [bry'mɛ:r], der; -[s], -s ‹franz., „Nebelmonat"› (2. Monat des Kalenders der Franz. Revolution: 22. Okt. bis 20. Nov.)

Brumm‿bär *(ugs.)*, **...bass; brummeln** (*ugs. für* leise brummen; undeutlich sprechen); ich ...[e]le (↑R 16); **brum|men; Brum|mer** *(ugs.)*; **Brum|mi,** der; -s, -s (*ugs. scherzh. für* Lastkraftwagen); **brum|mig; Brum|mig|keit,** die; -; **Brumm‿krei|sel, ...schä|del** *(ugs.)*

Brunch [bran(t)ʃ], der; -[e]s, *Plur.* -[e]s *u.* -e ‹engl.› (das Mittagessen ersetzendes Frühstück)

Bru|nei (Staat auf Borneo); **Bru|nei|er** (↑R 103); **bru|nei|isch**

Bru|nel|le, Brau|nel|le, die; -, -n ‹franz.› (eine Pflanze); **brü|nett** (braunhaarig, -häutig); **Brü|net|te,** die; -, -n (brünette Frau); zwei reizende Brünette[n]

Brunft, die; -, Brünfte (*Jägerspr. svw.* Brunst beim Wild); **brunf|ten; Brunft|hirsch; brunf|tig; Brunft‿schrei, ...zeit**

Brun|hild, Brun|hil|de (dt. Sagengestalt; w. Vorn.)

brü|nie|ren ‹franz.› (*fachspr. für* [Metall] bräunen)

Brunn, der; -[e]s, -en (*veraltet für* Brunnen); *vgl. auch* Born *u.* Bronn

Brünn (*tschech.* Brno)

Brünn|chen

Brün|ne, die; -, -n (Nackenschutz der mittelalterl. Ritterrüstung)

Brun|nen, der; -s, -; *vgl. auch* Brunn, Bronn *u.* Born; **Brun|nen‿fi|gur, ...kres|se** (Salatpflanze), **...ver|gif|ter** (*abwertend für* Verleumder), **...ver|gif|tung**

Brünn|lein *(geh.)*

Bru|no (m. Vorn.)

Brunst, die; -, Brünste (Periode der geschlechtl. Erregung u. Paarungsbereitschaft bei einigen Tieren); *vgl. auch* Brunft; **bruns|ten; bruns|tig; Brunst|zeit**

brun|zen (*landsch. derb* urinieren)

brüsk; -este (barsch; schroff); **brüs|kie|ren** (barsch, schroff behandeln); **Brüs|kie|rung**

Brüs|sel, *niederl.* **Brus|sel** ['brysəl] (Hptst. Belgiens); *vgl.* Bruxelles; **Brüs|se|ler,** *seltener* **Brüss|ler** (↑R 103)

Brust, die; -, Brüste; **Brust‿bein, ...beu|tel, ...bild, ...brei|te; Brüst|chen; brüs|ten,** sich; **Brust|fell; Brust|fell|ent|zün|dung; brust|hoch; Brust|höh|le; ...brüs|tig** (z. B. engbrüstig); **Brust‿kas|ten** (*Plur.* ...kästen), **...kind, ...korb, ...krebs, ...la|ge; brust|schwim|men** *im Allg. nur im Infinitiv gebr.*; **Brust‿schwim|men** (das; -s), **...stim|me, ...ta|sche, ...tee, ...ton** (*Plur.* ...töne), **...um|fang; Brüs|tung; Brust‿war|ze, ...wehr** (die), **...wi|ckel**

brut [bryt] ‹franz.› (*von Schaumweinen* sehr trocken)

Brut, die; -, -en *Plur. selten*

bru|tal ‹lat.› (roh; gefühllos; gewalttätig); **bru|ta|li|sie|ren; Bru|ta|li|sie|rung; Bru|ta|li|tät,** die; -, -en

Brut|ap|pa|rat; brü|ten; brü|tend; -e Hitze; ein brütend heißer Tag; **Brü|ter** (Kernreaktor, der mehr spaltbares Material erzeugt, als er verbraucht); schneller Brüter; **Brut|hit|ze** *(ugs.)*; **bru|tig** (*österr. auch für* brütig); **brü|tig** (zum Brüten bereit); **Brut‿kas|ten, ...ofen** (↑R 132), **...pfle|ge, ...re|ak|tor** (*svw.* Brüter), **...schrank, ...stät|te**

brut|to ‹ital.› (mit Verpackung; ohne Abzug der [Un]kosten; *Abk.* btto.); brutto für netto (*Abk.* bfn.); **Brut|to‿ein|kom|men, ...er|trag** (Rohertrag), **...ge|halt** (das), **...ge|wicht, ...mas|se** (die; -), **...raum|zahl** (*Abk.* BRZ), **...re|gis|ter|ton|ne** (*früher für* Bruttoraumzahl; *Abk.* BRT); **Brut|to|so|zi|al|pro|dukt** *(Wirtsch.)*; **Brut|to|ver|dienst,** der

Bru|tus (röm. Eigenn.)

brut|zeln (*ugs. für* in zischendem Fett braten); ich ...[e]le (↑R 16)

Bru|xelles [bry'sɛl] (*franz. Form von* Brüssel)

Bru|yère|holz [bry'jɛ:r...] ‹franz.; dt.› (Wurzelholz der Baumheide)

Bry|o|lo|gie, die; - ‹griech.› (Mooskunde)

BRZ = Bruttoraumzahl

Bs = Bolivar

BSA = Bund schweizerischer Architekten

BSE = bovine spongiforme Enzephalopathie (Rinderwahnsinn)

bst! *vgl.* pst!

Btl. = Bataillon

btto. = brutto

Bttr. = Batterie *(Militär)*

Btx = Bildschirmtext

Bub, der; -en, -en; ↑R 126 (*südd., österr. u. schweiz. für* Junge); **Büb|chen; Bu|be,** der; -n, -n (*veraltend für* gemeiner, niederträchtiger Mensch; Spielkartenbezeichnung); **bu|ben|haft; Bu|ben‿streich** (*auch veraltend für* übler Streich), **...stück** *(veraltend)*; **Bü|be|rei** *(veraltend)*; **Bu|bi,** der; -s, -s (*Koseform von* Bub); **Bu|bi|kopf** (Damenfrisur); **Bü|bin** *(abwertend)*; **bü|bisch**

Bu|bo, der; -s, ...onen ‹griech.› (*Med.* entzündl. Lymphknotenschwellung in der Leistenbeuge)

Buch, das; -[e]s, Bücher; Buch führen; die Buch führende Geschäftsstelle; zu Buche schlagen

[1]**Bu|cha|ra** (Landschaft u. Stadt in Usbekistan); [2]**Bu|cha|ra,** der; -[s], -s (ein Teppich); **Bu|cha|re,** der; -n, -n (↑R 126)

Buch‿aus|stat|tung, ...be|spre|chung, ...bin|der; Buch|bin|de|rei; Buch|bin|de|rin; buch|bin|dern; ich ...ere (↑R 16); gebuchbindert; **Buch‿block** (*vgl.* Block), **...de|ckel, ...druck** (der; -[e]s), **...dru|cker; Buch|dru|cke|rei; Buch|dru|cker|kunst,** die; -; **Buch|druck|ge|wer|be,** das; -s

Bu|che, die; -, -n; **Buch|ecker** (↑R 132); **Bu|chel,** die; -, -n (*landsch. für* Buchecker)

Bü|chel|chen

[1]**bu|chen** (aus Buchenholz)

[2]**bu|chen** (in ein Rechnungsbuch eintragen; reservieren lassen)

Bu|chen‿holz, ...klo|ben

Bu|chen|land, das; -[e]s (dt. Name der Bukowina); **bu|chen|län|disch**

Bu|chen‿scheit, ...wald

Bü|cher‿bord (das), **...brett; Bü|che|rei;** Deutsche Bücherei (in Leipzig; *Abk.* DB); **Bü|cher|kun|de,** die; -; **bü|cher|kund|lich; Bü|cher‿reff, ...re|gal, ...re|vi|sor** ([Rechnungs]buchprüfer), **...schrank, ...stu|be, ...ver|bren|nung, ...wand, ...wurm** (der; *scherzh.*)

Buch|fink

Buch‿füh|rung, ...ge|mein|schaft, ...ge|wer|be (das; -s), **...hal|ter, ...hal|te|rin; buch|hal|te|risch; Buch‿hal|tung, ...han|del** (*vgl.* [1]Handel), **...händ|ler, ...händ|le|rin; buch|händ|le|risch; Buch‿hand|lung, ...kri|tik, ...kunst** (die; -), **...lauf|kar|te; Büch|lein; Buch‿ma|cher, ...mes|se**

Büch|ner (dt. Dichter)
Buch|prü|fer (Bücherrevisor)
Buchs, der; -es, -e (*svw.* Buchsbaum); **Buchs|baum**
Büchs|chen; Buch|se, die; -, -n (Steckdose; Hohlzylinder als Lager einer Welle, eines Zapfens usw.); **Büch|se**, die; -, -n (zylindrisches [Metall]gefäß mit Deckel; Feuerwaffe); **Büch|sen‿fleisch, ...licht** (das; -[e]s; zum Schießen ausreichende Helligkeit), **...ma|cher, ...milch, ...öff|ner, ...schuss**
Buch|sta|be, der; *Gen.* -ns, *selten* -n, *Plur.* -n; **buch|sta|ben‿getreu, ...gläu|big; Buch|sta|ben‿kom|bi|na|ti|on, ...rät|sel; buch|sta|bie|ren; ...buch|sta|big** (z. B. vierbuchstabig; *mit Ziffer* 4-buchstabig; ↑R 44); **buch|stäb|lich** (genau nach dem Wortlaut); **Buch|stüt|ze**
Bucht, die; -, -en
Buch|tel, die; -, -n ⟨tschech.⟩ (*österr.* ein Hefegebäck)
buch|tig
Buch|ti|tel
Bu|chung; Bu|chungs|ma|schi|ne
Buch‿ver|leih, ...ver|sand
Buch|wei|zen (eine Nutzpflanze); **Buch|wei|zen|mehl**
Buch‿we|sen (das; -s), **...wis|sen** (*abwertend*), **...zel|chen**
Bu|cin|to|ro [butʃin...], der; -s ⟨ital.⟩ (*ital. für* Buzentaur)
Bü|cke, die; -, -n (Turnübung)
[1]**Bu|ckel**, der; -s, -, *auch* die; -, -n (erhabene Metallverzierung [auf Schilden]); [2]**Bu|ckel**, der; -s, - (Höcker, Rücken); **Bu|ckel|flie|ge; bu|cke|lig**, buck|lig; **Bu|ckel|kra|xe**, die; -, -n (*bayr., österr. ugs.* eine Rückentrage); **bu|ckel|kra|xen** (*österr. für* huckepack); - tragen; **bu|ckeln** (*ugs. für* einen Buckel machen; auf dem Buckel tragen; *abwertend für* sich unterwürfig verhalten); ich ...[e]le (↑R 16); **Bu|ckel|rind** (Zebu)
bü|cken, sich; **Bu|ckerl**, das; -s, -n (*österr. ugs. für* Verbeugung)
Bü|cking (*landsch. für* [2]Bückling)
Bu|cking|ham ['bakiŋəm] (engl. Orts- u. Familienn.); **Bu|cking|ham-Pa|last**, der; -[e]s (↑R 95)
buck|lig *vgl.* buckelig; **Buck|li|ge**, der *u.* die; -n, -n (↑R 126)
[1]**Bück|ling** (*scherzh., auch abwertend für* Verbeugung)
[2]**Bück|ling** (geräucherter Hering)
Buck|ram, der; -s ⟨nach der Stadt Buchara⟩ (stark appretiertes Gewebe [für Bucheinbände])
Buck|skin, der; -s, -s ⟨engl.⟩ (gerautes Wollgewebe)

Bu|cu|reș|ti [buku'rɛʃtj] (*rumän. Form von* Bukarest)
Bu|da|pest (Hptst. Ungarns); **Bu|da|pes|ter** (↑R 103)
Büd|chen (kleine Bude)
Bud|del, But|tel, die; -, -n (*ugs. für* Flasche)
Bud|de|lei (*ugs.*); **Bud|del|kas|ten** (*ugs.*); **bud|deln** (*ugs. für* [im Sand] graben); ich ...[e]le (↑R 16)
Bud|del|schiff
Bud|den|brooks (Titel eines Romans von Thomas Mann)
[1]**Bud|dha** ['buda] ⟨sanskr., „der Erwachte, der Erleuchtete"⟩ (Ehrenname des ind. Religionsstifters Siddhartha); [2]**Bud|dha**, der; -s, -s (Abbild, Statue Buddhas); **Bud|dhis|mus**, der; - (Lehre Buddhas); **Bud|dhist**, der; -en, -en (↑R 126); **bud|dhis|tisch**
Budd|leia, Budd|le|ja, die; -, -s ⟨nach dem engl. Botaniker A. Buddle⟩ (ein Gartenzierstrauch)
Bu|de, die; -, -n; **Bu|del**, die; -, -[n] (*bayr. u. österr. ugs. für* Verkaufstisch); **Bu|den|zau|ber** (*ugs. für* ausgelassenes Fest auf der Bude, in der Wohnung)
Bud|get [by'dʒe:], das; -s, -s ⟨franz.⟩ ([Staats]haushaltsplan, Voranschlag); **bud|ge|tär; Bud|get|be|trag; bud|ge|tie|ren** (ein Budget aufstellen)
Bu|di|ke, die; -, -n ⟨franz.⟩ (*ugs. für* kleiner Laden; kleine Kneipe); *vgl. auch* Boutique; **Bu|di|ker** (Besitzer einer Budike)
Büd|ner (*landsch. für* Kleinbauer)
Bu|do, das; -s ⟨jap.⟩ (Sammelbezeichnung für Judo, Karate u. ä. Sportarten); **Bu|do|ka**, der; -[s], -[s] (Budosportler)
Bu|e|nos Ai|res (Hptst. Argentiniens)
Bü|fett, das; -[e]s, *Plur.* -s *u.* -e, *auch (bes. österr., schweiz.)* Buf|fet [by'fe:, *schweiz.* 'byfe], das; -s, -s ⟨franz.⟩ (Anrichte; Geschirrschrank; Theke); kaltes - (zur Selbstbedienung angerichtete kalte Speisen); **Bü|fet|ti|er** [byfɛ'tie:], der; -s, -s ([Bier]ausgeber, Zapfer); **Bü|fett|mam|sell**
Büf|fel, der; -s, - (wild lebende Rinderart); **Büf|fe|lei** (*ugs.*); **Büf|fel|her|de; büf|feln** (*ugs. für* angestrengt lernen); ich ...[e]le (↑R 16)
Buf|fet *vgl.* Büfett
Buf|fo, der; -s, *Plur.* -s *u.* Buffi ⟨ital.⟩ (Sänger komischer Rollen); **buf|fo|nesk** (im Stil eines Buffos)
[1]**Bug**, der; -[e]s, *Plur.* (*für* Schiffsvorderteil:) -e *u.* (*für* Schulterstück [des Pferdes u. des Rindes]:) Büge

[2]**Bug**, der; -s (Fluss in Osteuropa); der Westliche -, der Südliche -
Bü|gel, der; -s, -; **Bü|gel‿au|tomat, ...brett, ...ei|sen, ...fal|te; bü|gel‿fest, ...frei; bü|geln**; ich ...[e]le (↑R 16); **Bü|gel|sä|ge**
Bug|gy ['bagi], der; -s, -s ⟨engl.⟩ (leichter [offener] Wagen; kleines Auto mit offener Karosserie; zusammenklappbarer Kindersportwagen)
Büg|le|rin
bug|sie|ren ⟨niederl.⟩ ([ein Schiff] schleppen, ins Schlepptau nehmen; *ugs. für* mühsam an einen Ort befördern); **Bug|sie|rer** (*Seemannsspr.* Bugsierschiff)
Bug|spriet, das *u.* der; -[e]s, -e (*Seemannsspr.* über den Bug hinausragende Segelstange); **Bug|wel|le**
buh! (Ausruf als Ausdruck des Missfallens); **Buh**, das; -s, -s (*ugs.*); es gab viele -s
Bu|hei, das; -s (*landsch. für* Aufheben); großes - [um etw.] machen
Bü|hel, der; -s, - *u.* Bühl, der; -[e]s, -e (*südd. u. österr. für* Hügel)
bu|hen (*ugs. für* durch Buhrufe sein Missfallen ausdrücken)
Bühl *vgl.* Bühel
[1]**Buh|le**, der; -n, -n; ↑R 126 (*geh. veraltet für* Geliebter); [2]**Buh|le**, die; -, -n (*geh. veraltet für* Geliebte); **buh|len** (*veraltet*); um jmds. Gunst - (*geh.*); **Buh|ler** (*veraltet*); **Buh|le|rei** (*veraltet*); **Buh|le|rin** (*veraltet*); **buh|le|risch** (*veraltet*); **Buhl|schaft** (*veraltet für* Liebesverhältnis)
Buh|mann *Plur.* ...männer (*ugs. für* böser Mann, Schreckgespenst, Prügelknabe)
Buh|ne, die; -, -n (künstlicher Damm zum Uferschutz)
Büh|ne, die; -, -n ([hölzerne] Plattform; Schaubühne; Spielfläche; *südd., schweiz. auch für* Dachboden; *vgl.* Heubühne); **Büh|nen‿ar|bei|ter, ...aus|spra|che, ...be|ar|bei|tung, ...bild, ...bild|ner, ...bild|ne|rin, ...fas|sung, ...ge|stalt, ...haus**
Buh|nen|kopf (äußerstes Ende einer Buhne [*vgl. d.*])
büh|nen|mä|ßig; Büh|nen|mu|sik; büh|nen|reif; Büh|nen|schaf|fen|de, der *u.* die; -n, -n (↑R 5 ff.); **büh|nen|wirk|sam**
Buh|ruf
Bu|hurt, der; -[e]s, -e ⟨franz.⟩ (mittelalterl. Reiterkampfspiel)
Bu|jum|bu|ra [...ʒum... *od.* bujum'bu:ra] (Hptst. von Burundi)
Bu|ka|ni|er [...iər], der; -s, - ⟨engl.⟩ (westind. Seeräuber im 17. Jh.)
Bu|ka|rest (Hptst. Rumäniens);

vgl. București; **Bu|ka|res|ter** (↑R 103)
Bu|kett, das; -[e]s, *Plur.* -s *u.* -e ‹franz.› ([Blumen]strauß; Duft [des Weines])
Buk|lee *vgl.* [1,2]Bouclé
Bu|ko|lik, die; - ‹griech.› (*Literaturw.* Hirtendichtung); **bu|ko|lisch;** -e Dichtung
Bu|ko|wi|na, die; - (Karpatenlandschaft; *vgl.* Buchenland); **Bu|ko|wi|ner; bu|ko|wi|nisch**
bul|bös ‹lat.› (*Med.* zwiebelartig, knollig); -e Schwellung; **Bul|bus,** der; -, *Plur.* ...bi *od., Bot. nur,* ...ben (*Bot.* Zwiebel; *Med.* Augapfel; Anschwellung)
Bu|let|te, die; -, -n ‹franz.› (*landsch. für* Frikadelle)
Bul|ga|re, der; -n, -n (↑R 126); **Bul|ga|ri|en; Bul|ga|rin; bul|ga|risch; Bul|ga|risch,** das; -[s]; *vgl.* Deutsch; **Bul|ga|ri|sche,** das; -n; *vgl.* Deutsche, das
Bu|li|mie, die; - ‹griech.› (*Med.* Ess-Brech-Sucht)
Bulk|car|ri|er ['balkkɛri̯ə(r)], der; -s, - ‹engl.› (Massengutfrachtschiff); **Bulk|la|dung** ['bulk...] (*Seemannsspr.* Schüttgut)
Bull|au|ge (rundes Schiffsfenster)
Bull|dog ®, der; -s, -s ‹engl.› (Zugmaschine); **Bull|dog|ge** (eine Hunderasse); **Bull|do|zer** [...do:zə(r)], der; -s, - (schwere Zugmaschine, Planierraupe)
[1]**Bul|le,** der; -n, -n; ↑R 126 (männl. Rind; männl. Tier verschiedener großer Säugetierarten; *ugs. oft abwertend für* Polizist)
[2]**Bul|le,** die; -, -n ‹lat.› (mittelalterl. Urkunde; feierl. päpstl. Erlass); die Goldene - (↑R 108)
Bul|len|bei|ßer (*svw.* Bulldogge; *ugs. für* unfreundlicher, grober Mensch); **Bul|len|hit|ze** *(ugs.);* **bul|len|stark** *(ugs.)*
bul|le|rig, bull|rig (*landsch. für* polternd, aufbrausend); **bul|lern** *(ugs.);* der Ofen bullert
Bul|le|tin [byl(ə)'tɛ̃:], das; -s, -s ‹franz.› (amtliche Bekanntmachung; Krankenbericht)
Bull|finch [...fintʃ], der; -s, -s ‹engl.› (Hecke als Hindernis beim Pferderennen)
bul|lig
bull|rig *vgl.* bullerig
Bull|ter|ri|er (engl. Hunderasse)
Bul|ly, das; -s, -s ‹engl.› (Anspiel im [Eis]hockey)
Bü|low ['by:lo] (Familienn.)
Bult, der; -s, *Plur.* Bülte *od.* Bulten *u.* **Bül|te,** die; -, -n (*nordd. für* feste, grasbewachsene [Moor]stelle; Hügelchen); **Bult|sack** (*früher für* Seemannsmatratze)
bum!; bum, bum!
Bum|bass, der; -es, -e (*früher* Instrument der Bettelmusikanten)
Bum|boot (kleines Händlerboot zur Versorgung großer Schiffe)
Bum|bum, das; -s (*ugs. für* Gepolter)
Bu|me|rang [*auch* 'bu...], der; -s, *Plur.* -s *od.* -e ‹engl.› (gekrümmtes Wurfholz)
[1]**Bum|mel,** der; -s, - (*ugs. für* Spaziergang); [2]**Bum|mel** *vgl.* Bommel; **Bum|me|lant,** der; -en, -en; ↑R 126 *(ugs.);* **Bum|me|lei** *(ugs.);* **bum|me|lig** *(ugs.);* **Bum|me|lig|keit,** die; - *(ugs.);* **bum|meln;** ich ...[e]le; ↑R 16 *(ugs.);* **Bum|mel‿streik, ...zug** *(scherzh.);* **Bum|merl,** das; -s, -n (*österr. ugs. für* Verlustpunkt beim Kartenspiel); das - (der Gefoppte, Benachteiligte) sein; **bum|mern** (*ugs. für* dröhnend klopfen); ich ...ere (↑R 16); **Bumm|ler** *(ugs.);* **bumm|lig** *(ugs.);* **Bumm|lig|keit,** die; - *(ugs.)*
bums!; Bums, der; -es, -e (*ugs. für* dumpfer Schlag); **bum|sen** (*ugs. für* dröhnend aufschlagen; koitieren); du bumst; **Bums‿lo|kal** (*ugs. für* zweifelhaftes Vergnügungslokal), **...mu|sik** (*ugs. für* laute, dröhnende Musik); **bums|voll** (*ugs. für* sehr voll)
Bu|na ®, der *od.* das; -[s] (synthet. Gummi); **Bu|na|rei|fen**
[1]**Bund,** der; -[e]s, Bünde („das Bindende"; Vereinigung; oberer Rand an Rock od. Hose); der Alte, Neue - (↑R 108); [2]**Bund,** das; -[e]s, -e („das Gebundene"; Gebinde); vier - Stroh (↑R 90)
BUND = Bund für Umwelt und Naturschutz Deutschland
Bun|da, die; -, -s ‹ung.› (Schaffellmantel ung. Bauern)
Bünd|chen; Bün|del, das; -s, -; **Bün|de|lei; bün|deln;** ich ...[e]le (↑R 16); **Bün|den** (*schweiz. Kurzform von* Graubünden); **Bun|des‿amt, ...an|ge|stell|ten|ta|rif** (*Abk.* BAT), **...an|lei|he, ...an|stalt, ...an|walt, ...an|walt|schaft** (die; -), **...aus|bil|dungs|för|de|rungs|ge|setz** (*Abk.* BAföG), **...au|to|bahn, ...bahn, ...bank** (die; -), **...be|hör|de, ...bru|der, ...bür|ger; bun|des|deutsch; Bun|des|deut|sche,** der *u.* die; **Bun|des|ebe|ne** (↑R 132), die; -; auf -; **bun|des|ei|gen; Bun|des‿frau|en|mi|nis|te|rin, ...ge|biet** (das; -[e]s), **...ge|nos|se; bun|des|ge|nös|sisch; Bun|des‿ge|richt, ...ge|richts|hof** (der; -[e]s), **...ge|setz|blatt** (*Abk.* BGBl.), **...grenz|schutz** (der; -es; *Abk.* BGS), **...haupt|stadt, ...haus** (das; -es), **...haus|halt, ...ka|bi|nett, ...kanz|ler, ...kri|mi|nal|amt** (das; -[e]s), **...la|de** *(jüd. Rel.),* **...land** (*Plur.* ...länder), **...li|ga** (Spielklasse im Fußball u. a. in Deutschland; die Erste, Zweite -); **Bun|des|li|gist,** der; -en, -en; **Bun|des‿ma|ri|ne, ...mi|nis|ter, ...mi|nis|te|rin, ...mi|ni|s|te|ri|um, ...nach|rich|ten|dienst** (*Abk.* BND), **...post** (die; -), **...prä|si|dent, ...pres|se|amt, ...rat, ...rech|nungs|hof, ...re|gie|rung; bun|des|re|pub|li|ka|nisch; Bun|des|re|pub|lik Deutsch|land** (*nichtamtl. Abk.* BRD); **Bun|des‿so|zi|al|ge|richt** (das; -[e]s), **...staat** (*Plur.* ...staaten), **...stadt** (die; -; *schweiz. für* Bern als Sitz von Bundesregierung u. -parlament; *auch für* Bonn als ehemalige bundesdeutsche Hauptstadt), **...stra|ße** (*Zeichen* B, *z. B.* B 38); **Bun|des|tag; Bun|des|tags‿ab|ge|ord|ne|te, ...de|bat|te, ...prä|si|dent, ...prä|si|den|tin, ...sit|zung, ...wahl; Bun|des‿trai|ner, ...ver|dienst|kreuz, ...ver|fas|sungs|ge|richt** (das; -[e]s), **...ver|samm|lung** (die; -), **...vor|stand, ...wehr** (die; -); **bun|des|weit; Bund|fal|ten|ho|se; Bund|ho|se; bün|dig** (bindend; *Bauw.* in gleicher Fläche liegend); kurz und bündig; **Bün|dig|keit,** die; -; **bün|disch** (der freien Jugendbewegung angehörend); die -e Jugend; **Bünd|ner** (*schweiz. Kurzform von* Graubündner); **Bünd|ner Fleisch** (↑R 103); **bünd|ne|risch** (*schweiz. Kurzform von* graubündnerisch); **Bünd|nis,** das; -ses, -se; Bündnis 90/Die Grünen (*Kurzform* die Grünen, *auch* Bündnisgrünen); **Bünd|nis‿block** (*vgl.* Block), **...sys|tem, ...treue, ...ver|trag; Bund‿schuh** (Bauernschuh im MA.), **...steg** *(Druckw.),* **...wei|te**
Bun|ga|low ['buŋgalo:], der; -s, -s ‹Hindi-engl.› (eingeschossiges Wohn- od. Sommerhaus mit flachem Dach)
Bun|ge, die; -, -n (kleine Fischreuse aus Netzwerk od. Draht)
Bun|gee|jum|ping ['bandʒidʒampiŋ], das; -s ‹engl.› (Springen aus großer Höhe, wobei der Springer durch ein starkes Gummiseil gesichert ist)
Bun|ker, der; -s, - (Behälter für Massengut [Kohle, Erz]; Betonunterstand; *Golf* Sandloch); **bun|kern** (in den Bunker füllen;

Brennstoff aufnehmen [von Schiffen]); ich ...ere (↑R 16)
Bun|ny ['bani], das; -s, -s ‹engl.› (als Häschen kostümierte Serviererin in bestimmten Klubs)
Bun|sen|bren|ner ‹nach dem Erfinder› (↑R 95)
bunt; bunt bemalen; ein bunter Abend; ein bunt gefiederter Vogel; ein bunt gemischtes Programm; eine bunt gescheckte Katze; bunt schillernde Fische; ein bunt gestreiftes Tuch; in Bunt gekleidet; *vgl. aber* buntscheckig
Bunt‿bart|schlüs|sel, ...druck (*Plur.* ...drucke), **...film, ...fo|to; bunt ge|fie|dert, ge|mischt** *vgl.* bunt; **Bunt|heit,** die; -; **Bunt‿me|tall, ...pa|pier, ...sand|stein** (Gestein; *nur Sing.: Geol.* unterste Stufe der Trias); **bunt|sche|ckig** (↑R 27); **bunt schil|lernd** *vgl.* bunt; **Bunt‿specht, ...stift** (der), **...wä|sche**
Bunz|lau (Stadt in Niederschlesien); **Bunz|lau|er;** - [Stein]gut
Bu|o|nar|ro|ti [*ital.* ...'ro:ti], Michelangelo (ital. Künstler)
Burck|hardt (Historiker)
Bür|de, die; -, -n
Bu|re, der; -n, -n; ↑R 126 (Nachkomme der niederl. u. dt. Ansiedler in Südafrika); **Bu|ren|krieg,** der; -[e]s
Bu|ren|wurst (*ostösterr. für* eine Brühwurst)
Bü|ret|te, die; -, -n ‹franz.› (Messröhre für Flüssigkeiten)
Burg, die; -, -en
Bür|ge, der; -n, -n (↑R 126)
Bur|gel (w. Vorn.)
bür|gen
Bur|gen|land, das; -[e]s (österr. Bundesland); **bur|gen|län|disch**
Bur|ger, der; -s, - (*schweiz. landsch. für* Ortsbürger); **Bür|ger; Bür|ger‿be|geh|ren** (das; -s, -), **...be|we|gung, ...haus; Bür|ge|rin; Bür|ger‿Ini|ti|a|ti|ve** (↑R 132), **...ko|mi|tee, ...krieg; bür|ger|lich;** -e Ehrenrechte; -es Recht, *aber* (↑R 108): das Bürgerliche Gesetzbuch (*Abk.* BGB); **Bür|ger|lich|keit,** die; -; **Bür|ger|meis|ter** [*auch* ...'maj...]; **Bür|ger|meis|te|rei; bür|ger|nah;** -e Politik; **Bür|ger‿nä|he, ...pflicht, ...recht; Bür|ger|recht|ler; Bür|ger|schaft; bür|ger|schaft|lich; Bür|ger‿schreck** (der; -s; Mensch mit provozierendem Verhalten), **...sinn** (*svw.* Gemeinsinn); **Bür|gers|mann** *Plur.* ...leute *(veraltet);* **Bür|ger|steig; Bür|ger|tum,** das; -s; **Burg|fried** *vgl.* Bergfried; **Burg‿frie|de[n], ...gra|ben, ...graf**
Burg|hild, Burg|hil|de (w. Vorn.)
Bür|gin
Burgk|mair (dt. Maler)
Bur|gos (span. Stadt)
Burg|ru|i|ne
Bürg|schaft
Burg|the|a|ter (österr. Nationaltheater in Wien)
Bur|gund (franz. Landschaft und früheres Herzogtum); **Bur|gun|de,** der; -n, -n; ↑R 126 (Angehöriger eines germ. Volksstammes); **Bur|gun|der;** ↑R 103 (Einwohner von Burgund; franz. Weinsorte; *auch für* Burgunde); **Bur|gun|der|wein** (↑R 105); **bur|gun|disch,** *aber* (↑R 102): die Burgundische Pforte
Burg‿ver|lies, ...vogt
bu|risch ‹*zu* Bure›
Bur|ja|te, *auch* **Bur|jä|te,** der; -n, -n; ↑R 126 (Angehöriger eines mongol. Volksstammes); **bur|ja|tisch,** *auch* **bur|jä|tisch**
Burk|hard (m. Vorn.)
Bur|ki|na Fa|so (Staat in Westafrika, früher Obervolta); **Bur|ki|ner; bur|ki|nisch**
bur|lesk ‹franz.› (possenhaft); **Bur|les|ke,** die; -, -n (Posse, Schwank)
Bur|ma (*engl. und schweiz. für* Birma); **Bur|me|se,** der; -n, -n (↑R 126); **bur|me|sisch**
Burns [bœ:(r)ns] (schott. Dichter)
Bur|nus, der; *Gen.* - *u.* -ses, *Plur.* -se ‹arab.› (Beduinenmantel mit Kapuze)
Bü|ro, das; -s, -s ‹franz.›; **Bü|ro‿an|ge|stell|te, ...ar|beit, ...be|darf, ...ge|hil|fe, ...ge|hil|fin, ...ge|mein|schaft, ...haus, ...kauf|frau, ...kauf|mann, ...klam|mer; Bü|ro|krat,** der; -en, -en (↑R 126); **Bü|ro|kra|tie,** die; -, ...ien; **bü|ro|kra|tisch; bü|ro|kra|ti|sie|ren; Bü|ro|kra|ti|sie|rung; Bü|ro|kra|tis|mus,** der; - (*abwertend für* bürokratische Pedanterie); **Bü|ro|kra|ti|us,** der; - (*scherzh.* Personifizierung des Bürokratismus); heiliger -!; **Bü|ro|list,** der; -en, -en (*schweiz. veraltend für* Büroangestellter); **Bü|ro‿ma|te|ri|al, ...mensch** *(ugs.),* **...mö|bel, ...schluss** (der; -es), **...zeit**
Bursch, der; -en, -en; ↑R 126 (*landsch. für* junger Mann; *Studentenspr.* Verbindungsstudent mit allen Rechten); **Bürsch|chen; Bur|sche,** der; -n, -n; ↑R 126 (*Studentenspr. auch für* Bursch); ein toller -; **Bur|schen|schaft; Bur|schen|schaf|ter; bur|schen|schaft|lich; bur|schi|kos** ([betont] ungezwungen; formlos); **Bur|schi|ko|si|tät,** die; -, -en; **Bur|se,** die; -, -n (*früher für* Studentenheim)
Bürst|chen; Bürs|te, die; -, -n; **bürs|ten; Bürs|ten‿ab|zug** (*Druckw.* Probeabzug), **...bin|der, ...[haar|]schnitt**
Bu|run|der *vgl.* Burundier; **Bu|run|di** (Staat in Afrika); **Bu|run|di|er,** Bu|run|der; **bu|run|disch**
Bür|zel, der; -s, - (Schwanz[wurzel], bes. von Vögeln); **Bür|zel|drü|se** *(Zool.)*
Bus, der; Busses, Busse (*Kurzform für* Autobus, Omnibus)
[1]**Busch** (dt. Maler, Zeichner und Dichter); die buschschen Gedichte (↑R 94)
[2]**Busch,** der; -[e]s, Büsche; **Busch|boh|ne; Büsch|chen; Bü|schel,** das; -s, -; **bü|sche|lig,** büsch|lig; **bü|scheln** (*südd. u. schweiz. für* zu einem Büschel, Strauß zusammenbinden); ich ...[e]le (↑R 16); **bü|schel|wei|se; Bu|schen,** der; -s, - (*südd., österr. ugs. für* [Blumen]strauß); **Bu|schen|schank,** *auch* **Bu|schen|schen|ke** (*österr. für* Straußwirtschaft); **Busch|hemd; bu|schig; Busch|klep|per** (*veraltet für* sich in Gebüschen versteckt haltender Dieb); **büsch|lig,** bü|sche|lig; **Busch|mann** *Plur.* ...männer (Angehöriger eines in Südwestafrika lebenden Eingeborenenvolkes); **Busch‿mes|ser** (das), **...werk** (das; -s), **...wind|rös|chen**
Bu|sen, der; -s, -; **bu|sen|frei; Bu|sen‿freund, ...freun|din, ...grap|schen** (das; -s; *ugs.*), **...grap|scher** *(ugs.),* **...star** *(ugs.)*
Bus‿fah|rer, ...hal|te|stel|le
Bu|shel ['buʃ(ə)l], der; -s, -s ‹engl.› (engl.-amerik. Getreidemaß); 6 -[s] (↑R 90)
bu|sig *(ugs.);* eine -e Schönheit
Busi|ness ['biznis], das; - ‹engl.› (Geschäft[sleben])
bus|per (*südwestd. u. schweiz. mdal. für* munter, lebhaft)
Buß|an|dacht *(kath. Kirche)*
Bus|sard, der; -s, -e ‹franz.› (ein Greifvogel)
Bu|ße, die; -, -n (*auch für* Geldstrafe); **bü|ßen** (*schweiz. auch für* jmdn. mit einer Geldstrafe belegen); du büßt; **Bü|ßer; Bü|ßer|hemd; Bü|ße|rin**
Bus|serl, das; -s, -[n] (*bayr., österr. ugs. für* Kuss)
buß|fer|tig *(Rel.);* **Buß|fer|tig|keit,** die; -; **Buß|geld; Buß|geld|be|scheid; Buß|got|tes|dienst** *(kath. Kirche)*
Bus|so|le, die; -, -n ‹ital.› (Magnetkompass)

Bu̲ß‿pre|di|ger, ...sak|ra|ment *(kath. Kirche)*, **...tag; Bu̲ß- und Be̲t|tag**

Bü̲s|te [*od.* 'by:...], die; -, -n; **Büs|ten|hal|ter** (*Abk.* BH)

Bus|ti|er [bys'ti̯e:], das; -s, -s ‹franz.› (miederartig anliegendes, nicht ganz bis zur Taille reichendes Damenunterhemd ohne Ärmel)

Bust|ro|phe|dọn (↑R 130 *u.* 132), das; -s ‹griech.› (Art des Schreibens, bei der die Schrift abwechselnd nach rechts u. nach links läuft [in alten Inschriften])

Bu|su̲|ki, die; -, -s ‹ngriech.› (griech. Lauteninstrument)

Bu|ta|di|e̲n, das; -s (*Chemie* ungesättigter gasförmiger Kohlenwasserstoff); **Bu|ta̲n,** das; -s ‹griech.› (gesättigter gasförmiger Kohlenwasserstoff); **Bu|ta̲n|gas** (Heiz- u. Treibstoff)

bu̲|ten (*nordd. für* draußen, jenseits [der Deiche])

Bu|ti̲|ke *vgl.* Budike, Boutique

But|ja̲|din|gen (Halbinsel zwischen der Unterweser u. dem Jadebusen)

But|ler ['batlə(r)], der; -s, - ‹engl.› (Diener in vornehmen [engl.] Häusern)

Bu|tor [by'tɔ:r] (franz. Schriftsteller)

Bụt|scher *vgl.* Buttje[r]

Bụts|kopf (Schwertwal)

Bụtt, der; -[e]s, -e (*nordd. für* Scholle)

Bụ̈tt, die; -, -en (*landsch. für* fassförmiges Vortragspult für Karnevalsredner); in die - steigen; **Bụt|te,** die; -, -n (*südd. u. österr. für* Bütte); **Bụ̈t|te,** die; -, -n (wannenartiges Gefäß)

Bụt|tel *vgl.* Buddel

Bụ̈t|tel, der; -s, - (*veraltend, noch abwertend für* Ordnungshüter, Polizist)

Bụ̈t|ten, das; -s ‹*zu* Bütte› (Papierart); **Bụ̈t|ten‿pa|pier, ...re|de**

Bụt|ter, die; -; **Bụt|ter‿berg** (*ugs.*), **...bir|ne, ...blu|me, ...brot; Bụt|ter|brot|pa|pier; Bụt|ter|creme,** Bụt|ter|krem; **Bụt|ter|do|se; Bụt|ter|fahrt** (*ugs. für* Schiffsfahrt mit der Möglichkeit, [zollfrei] billig einzukaufen); **Bụt|ter|fass**

But|ter|fly ['batə(r)flai̯], der; -s ‹engl.›, **But|ter|fly|stil,** der; -[e]s (*Schwimmsport* Schmetterlingsstil)

Bụt|ter|ge|bäck; Bụt|ter|ge|ba|cke|ne, das; -n ↑R 5 ff.; **bụt|ter|ge̲lb; bụt|te|rig,** bụtt|rig; **Bụt|ter|kä|se; Bụt|ter|krem,** Bụt|ter|creme; **Bụt|ter‿ku|chen, ...milch; bụt|tern;** ich ...ere (↑R 16); **Bụt|ter|stul|le** (*nordostd.*); **bụt|ter|we̲ich**

Bụtt|je[r], Bụt|scher, der; -s, -s (*nordd. für* Junge, Kind)

Bụ̈tt|ner (*landsch. für* Böttcher)

But|ton ['bat(ə)n], der; -s, -s ‹engl.-amerik.› (runde Ansteckplakette)

bụtt|rig, bụt|te|rig

Bu|ty̲l|al|ko|hol ‹griech.; arab.› (chem. Verbindung); **Bu|ty|ro|me̲|ter,** das; -s, - ‹griech.› (Fettgehaltmesser)

Bụtz, der; -en, -en *vgl.* [1]Butze; **Bụ̈tz|chen** (*rhein. für* Kuss); **[1]Bụt|ze,** der; -n, -n (*landsch. für* Kobold; Knirps); **[2]Bụt|ze,** die; -, -n (*nordd. für* Verschlag, Wandbett); **Bụt|ze|mann** *Plur.* ...männer (*svw.* Kobold, Kinderschreck); **bụ̈t|zen** (*rhein. für* küssen); **Bụt|zen,** der; -s, - (*landsch. für* Kerngehäuse; Verdickung [im Glas]; *Bergmannsspr.* unregelmäßige Mineralanhäufung im Gestein); **Bụt|zen|schei|be** (in der Mitte verdickte [runde] Glasscheibe)

Bụ̈x, die; -, Büxen *u.* **Bụ|xe,** die; -, Buxen (*nordd. für* Hose)

Bux|te|hu̲|de (Stadt südwestl. von Hamburg); *auch in Wendungen wie* aus - (*ugs. scherzh. für* von weit her) sein

Buy-out ['bai̯au̯t] (↑R 28), das; -s, -s (*kurz für* Management-Buy-out)

Bu|zen|ta̲ur, der; -en, -en (↑R 126) ‹griech.› (Untier in der griech. Sage; Prunkschiff der Dogen von Venedig); *vgl.* Bucintoro

BV = [schweizerische] Bundesverfassung

BVG = Berliner Verkehrs-Betriebe (*früher* Berliner Verkehrs-Gesellschaft); Bundesversorgungsgesetz

b. w. = bitte wenden!

BWV = Bach-Werke-Verzeichnis (*vgl. d.*)

bye-bye! ['bai̯'bai̯] ‹engl.› (*ugs. für* auf Wiedersehen!)

By|pass ['bai̯pas], der; -es, ...pässe ‹engl.› (*Med.* Überbrückung eines krankhaft veränderten Abschnittes der Blutgefäße); **By|pass-ope|ra|ti|on** (↑R 132)

By|ron ['bai̯rən] (engl. Dichter)

Bys|sus, der; - ‹griech.› (feines Gewebe des Altertums; *Zool.* Haftfäden mancher Muscheln)

Byte [bai̯t], das; -[s], -[s] ‹engl.› (*EDV* Zusammenfassung von acht Bits)

By|zan|ti̲|ner (Bewohner von Byzanz; *veraltet für* Kriecher, Schmeichler); **by|zan|ti̲|nisch;** -e Zeitrechnung, *aber* (↑R 108): das Byzantinische Reich; **By|zan|ti|nịs|mus,** der; - (*abwertend für* Kriecherei, Schmeichelei); **By|zan|ti|nịst,** der; -en, -en; ↑R 126 (Wissenschaftler auf dem Gebiet der Byzantinistik); **By|zan|ti|nịs|tik,** die; - (Wissenschaft von der byzantinischen Literatur u. Kultur); **By|za̲nz** (*alter Name von* Istanbul)

bz, bez, bez. = bezahlt (*auf Kurszetteln*)

Bz., Bez. = Bezirk

bzw. = beziehungsweise

Vgl. auch **K, Sch** *und* **Z**

C (Buchstabe); das C; des C, die C, *aber* das c in Tacitus (↑R 60)

c = Cent, Centime; Zenti...

c, C, das; -, - (Tonbezeichnung); das hohe C; **c** (*Zeichen für* c-Moll); in c; **C** (*Zeichen für* C-Dur); in C

C = Carboneum (*chem. Zeichen für* Kohlenstoff); Celsius (*fachsprachl.* °C); Coulomb

C (röm. Zahlzeichen) = 100

C. = Cajus; *vgl.* Gajus

Ca = *chem. Zeichen für* Calcium (*vgl.* Kalzium)

ca. = circa; *vgl.* zirka

Ca. = Carcinoma; *vgl.* Karzinom

Cab [kɛb], das; -s, -s ‹engl.› (einspännige engl. Droschke)

Ca|bal|le|ro [kabal'je:ro, *auch* ka-val...], der; -s, -s ‹span.› (Herr; *früher* span. Edelmann, Ritter)

Ca|ban [ka'bã:], der; -s, -s ‹franz.› (kurzer Mantel)

Ca|ba|ret [kaba're:] *vgl.* Kabarett

Ca|bo|chon [kabɔ'ʃɔ̃:], der; -s, -s ‹franz.› (ein gewölbt geschliffener Edelstein)

Ca̲b|rio (↑R 130) *vgl.* Kabrio; **Cab|ri|o|let** [kabrio'le:] *vgl.* Kabriolett

Ca|che|nez [kaʃ(ə)'ne:], das; - [...'ne:(s)], - [...'ne:s] ‹franz.› ([seidenes] Halstuch)

Ca|chet [kaʃɛ], das; -s, -s ‹franz.› (*schweiz., sonst veraltet für* Gepräge; Eigentümlichkeit)

Ca|che|te̲|ro [katʃe...], der; -s, -s

⟨span.⟩ (Stierkämpfer, der dem Stier den Gnadenstoß gibt)
Cä|ci|lia, Cä|ci|lie [...iə] (w. Vorn.); **Cä|ci|li|en-Ver|band** (↑R 95), der; -[e]s (Vereinigung für kath. Kirchenmusik)
CAD = computer-aided design [kɔm'pjutə(r)'e:did di'zain] (*EDV* computerunterstütztes Konstruieren)
Cad|die ['kɛdi], der; -s, -s ⟨engl.⟩ (jmd., der für den Golfspieler die Schlägertasche trägt; ® Einkaufswagen im Supermarkt; zweirädriger Wagen zum Transportieren der Golfschläger)
Ca|dil|lac ® [*franz.* kadi'jak, *engl.* 'kɛdilɛk] (amerik. Kraftfahrzeugmarke)
Cá|diz ['ka:dis] (span. Hafenstadt u. Provinz)
Cad|mi|um *vgl.* Kadmium
Cae|li|us ['tsɛ:...], der; - (Hügel in Rom)
Cae|sar ['tsɛ:...] *vgl.* ¹Cäsar
Cae|si|um ['tsɛ:...] *vgl.* Zäsium
Ca|fard [kafa:r], der; -s ⟨franz.⟩ (*schweiz. für* Unlust, Überdruss)
Ca|fé [ka'fe:], das; -s, -s ⟨franz.⟩ (Kaffeehaus, -stube); *vgl.* Kaffee; **Ca|fé comp|let** [kafe kɔ̃'plɛ] (↑R 130), der; - -, -s -s (*schweiz. für* Kaffee mit Milch, Brötchen, Butter und Marmelade); **Ca|fé crème** [kafe 'krɛ:m], der; - -, -s - (*schweiz. für* Kaffee mit Sahne); **Ca|fe|te|ria**, die; -, *Plur.* -s *u.* ...ien ⟨amerik.-span.⟩ (Café od. Restaurant mit Selbstbedienung); **Ca|fe|ti|er** [...'tie:], der; -s, -s ⟨franz.⟩ (*veraltet für* Kaffeehausbesitzer); **Ca|fe|ti|e|re** [...'tie:rə], die; -, -n (*veraltet für* Kaffeehauswirtin; *auch für* Kaffeekanne)
Cag|li|ost|ro [kal'jɔstro] (↑R 130; ital. Abenteurer)
Ca|is|sa (Göttin des Schachspiels)
Cais|son [kɛ'sɔ̃:], der; -s, -s ⟨franz.⟩ (Senkkasten für Bauarbeiten unter Wasser); **Cais|son|krank|heit**, die; - (*Med.*)
Ca|jus *vgl.* Gajus
cal = Kalorie
Cal., Calif. = California; *vgl.* Kalifornien
Ca|lais [ka'lɛ:] (franz. Stadt)
Ca|la|ma|res *Plur.* ⟨span.⟩ (Gericht aus Tintenfischstückchen)
ca|lan|do ⟨ital.⟩ (*Musik* an Tonstärke u. Tempo gleichzeitig abnehmend)
Ca|lau (Stadt in der Niederlausitz)
Ca|lbe (Saa|le) (Stadt an der unteren Saale); *vgl.* Kalbe (Milde)
Cal|ci... usw. *vgl.* Kalzi... usw.
Cal|de|rón ['kalderɔn, *span.* kalde'rɔn] (span. Dichter)
Ca|lem|bour, Ca|lem|bourg [*beide* kalã'bu:r], der; -s, -s ⟨franz.⟩ (*veraltet für* Wortspiel; Kalauer)
Ca|li|ban ['ka(:)..., *engl.* 'kɛlibɛn] *vgl.* Kaliban
Ca|lif. *vgl.* Cal.; **Ca|li|for|ni|um**, das; -s (stark radioaktives chem. Element, ein Transuran; *Zeichen* Cf)
Ca|li|gu|la (röm. Kaiser)
Ca|lixt, Ca|lix|tus *vgl.* Kalixt[us]
Ca|lla, die; -, -s ⟨griech.⟩ (eine Zierpflanze)
Cal|la|ne|tics ® [kɛlə'netiks] *Plur.* ⟨nach der Amerikanerin Callan Pinckney⟩ (Fitnesstraining, das besonders auf tiefere Muskelschichten wirkt)
Call|boy ['kɔ:lbɔy], der; -s, -s ⟨engl.⟩ (männl. Gegenstück zum Callgirl); **Call|girl** ['kɔ:lgœ:(r)l], das; -s, -s (Prostituierte, die auf telefonischen Anruf hin kommt od. jmdn. empfängt)
Cal|mette [kal'mɛt] (franz. Bakteriologe)
Ca|lu|met *vgl.* Kalumet
Cal|va|dos [...v...], der; -, - ⟨franz.⟩ (ein Apfelbranntwein)
Cal|vin [kal'vi:n, *österr.* 'kal...] (Genfer Reformator); **cal|vi|nisch** usw. *vgl.* kalvinisch usw.
Calw [kalf] (Stadt a. d. Nagold); **Cal|wer** ['kalvər] (↑R 103)
Ca|lyp|so [ka'lipso], der; -[s], -s (Tanz im Rumbarhythmus); *vgl. aber* Kalypso
CAM = computer-aided manufacturing [kɔm'pjutə(r)'e:did mɛnju'fɛktʃəriŋ] (computerunterstütztes Fertigen)
Ca|margue [ka'marg], die; - (südfranz. Landschaft)
Cam|bridge ['ke:mbridʒ] (engl. u. nordamerik. Ortsn.)
Cam|burg (Stadt a. d. Saale)
Cam|cor|der ['kam...], der; -s, - ⟨engl.⟩; *vgl.* Kamerarecorder
Ca|mem|bert ['kaməmbe:r, *auch* kamã'bɛ:r], der; -s, -s ⟨nach dem franz. Ort⟩ (ein Weichkäse mit weißem Schimmelbelag)
Ca|me|ra obs|cu|ra (↑R 132), die; - -, ...rae [...rɛ:] ...rae [...rɛ:] ⟨lat.⟩ (Lochkamera)
Ca|mi|lla (w. Vorn.); **Ca|mi|llo** (m. Vorn.)
Ca|mi|on [kamiɔ̃], der; -s, -s ⟨franz.⟩ (*schweiz. für* Lastkraftwagen); **Ca|mi|on|na|ge** [kamiɔ'na:ʒə], die; - (*schweiz. für* Spedition); **Ca|mi|on|neur** [kamiɔnø:r], der; -s, -e (*schweiz. für* Spediteur)
Ca|mõ|es [ka'mõiʃ] (port. Dichter)
Ca|mor|ra *vgl.* Kamorra
Ca|mouf|la|ge [kamu'fla:ʒə] (↑R 130), die; -, -n ⟨franz.⟩ (*veraltet für* milit. Tarnung; Verbergen); **ca|mouf|lie|ren** (*veraltet*)
Camp [kɛmp], das; -s, -s ⟨engl.⟩ ([Feld-, Gefangenen]lager)
Cam|pag|na [...'panja] (↑R 130), die; - (ital. Landschaft)
Cam|pag|ne *vgl.* Kampagne
Cam|pa|ni|le *vgl.* Kampanile
Cam|pa|ri ®, der; -s, - ⟨ital.⟩ (ein Bitterlikör)
Cam|pe|che|holz [kam'petʃe...] *vgl.* Kampescheholz
cam|pen ['kɛm...] ⟨engl.⟩ (im Zelt od. Wohnwagen leben); **Cam|per; Cam|pe|si|no** [kam...], der; -s, -s ⟨span.⟩ (armer Landarbeiter, Bauer [in Spanien u. Lateinamerika]); **Cam|ping** ['kɛm...], das; -s ⟨engl.⟩ (Leben auf Zeltplätzen im Zelt od. Wohnwagen); **Cam|ping‿an|hän|ger, ...ar|ti|kel, ...aus|rüs|tung, ...beu|tel, ...bus, ...füh|rer, ...platz; Cam|pus** ['kam..., *engl.* 'kɛmpəs], der; -, - ⟨lat.-engl.⟩ (Universitätsgelände, bes. in den USA)
Ca|mus [ka'my:] (franz. Schriftsteller)
Ca|na|da (*engl. Schreibung von* Kanada)
Ca|nail|le *vgl.* Kanaille
Ca|na|let|to (ital. Maler)
Ca|na|pé *vgl.* Kanapee
Ca|nas|ta, das; -s ⟨span.⟩ (ein Kartenspiel)
Ca|na|ve|ral *vgl.* Kap Canaveral
Can|ber|ra ['kɛnbərə] (Hptst. Australiens)
Can|can [kã'kã:], der; -s, -s ⟨franz.⟩ (ein Tanz)
cand. = candidatus; *vgl.* Kandidat
Can|de|la, die; -, - ⟨lat.⟩ (Lichtstärkeeinheit; *Zeichen* cd)
Can|di|da (w. Vorn.); **Can|di|dus** (m. Vorn.)
Ca|net|ti, Elias (deutschsprachiger Schriftsteller)
Can|na, die; -, -s ⟨sumer.-lat.⟩ (eine Zierpflanze)
Can|na|bis, der; - ⟨griech.-lat.⟩ (Hanf; *auch für* Haschisch)
Can|nae *vgl.* Kannä
Can|nel|lo|ni *Plur.* ⟨ital.⟩ (gefüllte Röllchen aus Nudelteig)
Cannes [kan] (Seebad an der Côte d'Azur)
Cann|statt, Bad (↑R 105; Stadtteil von Stuttgart); **Cann|stat|ter** (↑R 103); - Wasen (Volksfest)
Ca|ñon ['kanjɔn, *auch* ka'njo:n], der; -s, -s ⟨span.⟩ (enges, tief eingeschnittenes Tal, bes. im westl. Nordamerika)
Ca|no|pus *vgl.* ²Kanopus
Ca|nos|sa (Ort u. Burg im Nordapennin); *vgl.* Kanossa; **Ca|nos|sa|gang** *vgl.* Kanossagang

Can|stein|sche Bi|bel|an|stalt, die; -n - (↑R 108) ‹nach dem Gründer Frhr. von Canstein›
can|ta|bi|le ‹ital.› (*Musik* gesangartig, ausdrucksvoll); **Can|ta|te** *vgl.* ²Kantate
Can|ter|bu|ry ['kɛntə(r)bəri] (engl. Stadt)
Can|tha|ri|din *vgl.* Kantharidin
Can|to, der; -s, -s ‹ital.› (Gesang); **Can|tus fir|mus,** der; - -, - [...tu:s] ...mi (Hauptmelodie eines mehrstimmigen Chor- od. Instrumentalsatzes)
Ca|pa, die; -, -s ‹span.› (roter Umhang der Stierkämpfer); **Cape** [ke:p], das; -s, -s ‹engl.› (ärmelloser Umhang); **Ca|pe|a|dor** [ka...], der; -s, -es ‹span.› (Stierkämpfer, der den Stier mit der Capa reizt)
Ca|pel|la *vgl.* Kapella
Cap|puc|ci|no [kapu'tʃi:no], der; -[s], -[s] ‹ital.› (Kaffeegetränk)
Cap|re|se (↑R 130), der; -n, -n (Bewohner von Capri); **cap|re|sisch; Ca|pri** (Insel im Golf von Neapel)
Cap|ric|cio [ka'pritʃo] (↑R 130), das; -s, -s ‹ital.› (scherzhaftes, launiges Musikstück); **cap|ric|cio|so** [...'tʃo:so] (*Musik* scherzhaft, launig); **Cap|ri|ce** [ka'pri:sə, *franz.* ka'pris] *vgl.* Kaprice
Cap|ta|tio Be|ne|vo|len|ti|ae [- benevo'lɛntsiɛ], die; - - ‹lat.› (Redewendung, mit der man das Wohlwollen des Publikums zu gewinnen sucht)
Ca|pua (ital. Stadt)
Ca|pu|let|ti *Plur.; vgl.* Montecchi und Capuletti
Ca|put mor|tu|um [- ...tu|um], das; - - ‹lat.› (Eisenrot, rote Malerfarbe; *veraltet für* Wertloses)
Car, der; -s, -s ‹franz.› (*schweiz. kurz für* Autocar)
Ca|ra|bi|ni|e|re *vgl.* Karabiniere
Ca|ra|cas (Hptst. Venezuelas)
ca|ram|ba! ‹span.› (*ugs. für* Donnerwetter!, Teufel!)
Ca|ra|van ['ka(:)ravan *od.* ...'va:n, *auch* 'kɛrəvɛn], der; -s, -s ‹engl.› (kombinierter Personen- u. Lastenwagen; Wohnwagen); **Ca|ra|va|ner; Ca|ra|va|ning,** das; -s (Leben im Wohnwagen)
Car|bid *vgl.* ²Karbid
Car|bo... usw. *vgl.* Karbo... usw.; **Car|bo|ne|um,** das; -s ‹lat.› (*veraltete Bez. für* Kohlenstoff, chem. Element; *Zeichen* C)
Car|bo|run|dum ® *vgl.* Karborund
Car|ci|no|ma *vgl.* Karzinom
Car|di|gan, der; -s, -s ‹engl.› (lange Damenstrickweste)
CARE [kɛ:(r)] (= Cooperative for American Remittances to Europe; eine Hilfsorganisation)
care of ['kɛ:(r) ɔv] ‹engl.› (*in Briefanschriften usw.* wohnhaft bei ...; per Adresse; *Abk.* c/o)
Care|pa|ket; *vgl.* CARE
Car|go *vgl.* Kargo
Ca|ri|na *vgl.* Karina
Ca|ri|o|ca, die; -, -s ‹indian.-port.› (lateinamerik. Tanz)
Ca|ri|tas, die; - (*kurz für* Deutscher Caritasverband); *vgl.* Karitas
Car|los (m. Vorn.)
Car|lyle [ka:(r)'lail] (schott. Schriftsteller u. Historiker)
Car|ma|gno|le [karman'jo:lə] (↑R 130), die; -, -n (*nur Sing.:* franz. Revolutionslied; *auch für* ärmellose Jacke der Jakobiner)
Car|men (w. Vorn.)
Car|nal|lit *vgl.* Karnallit
Car|ne|gie [ka:(r)'nɛgi] (nordamerik. Milliardär); **Car|ne|gie Hall** ['ka:(r)nɛgi .hɔ:l], die; - - (Konzerthalle in New York)
Car|net [de Pas|sa|ges] [kar'nɛ (də pa'sa:ʒə)], das; - - -, -s [kar'nɛ] - - (Zollbescheinigung zur Einfuhr von Kraftfahrzeugen)
Car|not|zet [...tsɛt, *schweiz.* ...tsɛ], das; -s, -s ‹franz. mdal.› (kleine [Keller]schenke [in der französischen Schweiz])
Ca|ro|la *vgl.* Karola
Ca|ros|sa (dt. Schriftsteller)
Ca|ro|tin *vgl.* Karotin
Car|port, der; -s, -s ‹engl.-amerik.› (überdachter Abstellplatz für Autos)
Car|ra|ra (ital. Stadt); **Car|ra|rer; car|ra|risch;** -er Marmor
Car|roll ['kɛrəl], Lewis ['lu:is] (engl. Schriftsteller)
Cars|ten *vgl.* Karsten
Cars|tens (fünfter dt. Bundespräsident)
car|te|si|a|nisch, car|te|sisch *vgl.* kartesianisch, kartesisch; **Car|te|si|us** (*lat. Form von* Descartes)
Car|tha|min *vgl.* Karthamin
Car|toon [kar'tu:n], der *od.* das; -[s], -s ‹engl.› (Karikatur, Witzzeichnung; kurzer Comicstrip); **Car|too|nist,** der; -en, -en; ↑R 126 (Cartoonzeichner); **Car|too|nis|tin**
Ca|ru|so (ital. Sänger)
Ca|sa|blan|ca (Stadt in Marokko)
Ca|sals (span. Cellist)
¹**Ca|sa|no|va** [...va] (ital. Abenteurer, Schriftsteller u. Frauenheld); ²**Ca|sa|no|va,** der; -[s], -s (*ugs. für* Frauenheld, -verführer)
¹**Cä|sar** (röm. Feldherr u. Staatsmann; m. Vorn.); ²**Cä|sar,** der; Cäsaren, Cäsaren; ↑R 126 (Ehrenname der römischen Kaiser); **Cä|sa|ren|wahn; cä|sa|risch** (kaiserlich; selbstherrlich); **Cä|sa|ris|mus,** der; - (unbeschränkte [despotische] Staatsgewalt); **Cä|sa|ro|pa|pis|mus,** der; - (Staatsform, bei der der weltl. Herrscher zugleich geistl. Oberhaupt ist)
cash [kɛʃ] ‹engl.› (*Wirtsch.* bar); **Cash,** das; - (*Wirtsch.* Kasse, Bargeld, Barzahlung); **Cash-and-car|ry-Klau|sel** ['kɛʃənd'kɛri...], die; - (*Überseehandel* Klausel, nach der der Käufer die Ware bar bezahlen u. abholen muss)
Ca|shew|nuss ['kɛʃu...], die; -, ...nüsse ‹port.-engl.; dt.› (trop. Nusssorte)
Cash|flow ['kɛʃflo:], der; -s ‹engl.› (*Wirtsch.* Überschuss nach Abzug aller Unkosten)
Ca|si|mir *vgl.* Kasimir
Cä|si|um *vgl.* Zäsium
Cas|sa|ta, die; -, -s (Speiseeisspezialität)
Cas|si|us (Name eines röm. Staatsmannes)
Cas|tel Gan|dol|fo (ital. Stadt am Albaner See; Sommerresidenz des Papstes)
Cas|tor|be|häl|ter ‹engl.; dt.› (Spezialbehälter für radioaktives Material)
Cast|ries ['ka:stris, *auch* ka:'stri:] (↑R 130; Hptst. von St. Lucia)
Cast|ro, Fidel (↑R 130; kuban. Politiker)
Ca|sus Bel|li, der; - -, - [...zu:s] - ‹lat., „Kriegsfall"› (Grund für einen Konflikt); **Ca|sus ob|li|quus** [- ...kvus], der; - -, - [...zu:s] ...qui (*Sprachw.* abhängiger Fall, z. B. Genitiv, Dativ, Akkusativ); **Ca|sus rec|tus,** der; - -, - [...zu:s] ...ti (*Sprachw.* unabhängiger Fall, Nominativ)
Ca|ta|nia (Stadt auf Sizilien)
Cat|boot ['kɛt...], das; -[e]s, -e ‹engl.; dt.› (kleines Segelboot)
Catch-as-catch-can ['kɛtʃəz'kɛtʃ'kɛn], das; - ‹amerik.› (Freistilringkampf); **cat|chen** ['kɛtʃ(ə)n]; **Cat|cher**
Cat|chup *vgl.* Ketschup
Ca|te|nac|cio [kate'natʃo], der; -[s] ‹ital.› (Verteidigungstechnik im Fußball)
Ca|ter|pil|lar ['kɛtə(r)pilə(r)], der; -s, -[s] ‹engl.› (Raupenschlepper)
Cat|gut ['kɛtgat] *vgl.* Katgut
Ca|ti|li|na (röm. Verschwörer); *vgl.* katilinarisch
Ca|to (röm. Zensor)
Cat|ta|ro (*ital. Name von* Kotor)
Ca|tull, Ca|tul|lus (röm. Dichter)
Cau|dil|lo [kau'diljo], der; -[s], -s ‹span.› (Diktator)

Cau|sa, die; -, ...sae [...zɛ] ‹lat.› (Grund, Ursache, [Streit]sache); **Cause cé|lèb|re** [ˌko:zseˈlɛ:br(ə)] (↑R 130), die; - -, *Plur.* -s -s [ˌko:zseˈlɛ:br(ə)] ‹franz.› (berühmter Rechtsstreit); **Cau|seur** [koˈzø:r], der; -s, -e (*veraltet für* unterhaltsamer Plauderer)
ca|ve ca|nem! [ˈka:və -] ‹lat., „hüte dich vor dem Hund!"› (altröm. Inschrift)
Ca|yenne [kaˈjɛn] (Hptst. von Französisch-Guayana); **Ca|yenne|pfef|fer;** ↑R 105
CB [tse:ˈbe:, *engl.* si:ˈbi:] = Citizen-Band [ˈsitis(ə)nˈbɛnd] ‹engl.-amerik.› (für den privaten Funkverkehr freigegebener Wellenbereich); **CB-Funk**
cbm = Kubikmeter (*früher für* m^3)
cc = carbon copy ‹engl.› (Durchschlag, Kopie)
CC = Corps consulaire
ccm = Kubikzentimeter (*früher für* cm^3)
cd = Candela
Cd = *chem. Zeichen für* Cadmium (*vgl.* Kadmium)
¹**CD** = Corps diplomatique
²**CD,** die; -, -s ‹*zu* engl. compact disc› (*kurz für* CD-Platte; *vgl. d.*); **CD-Lauf|werk** (für CDs od. CD-ROMs); **CD-Plat|te** (Kompaktschallplatte); **CD-Play|er,** der; -s, - (CD-Spieler); **CD-ROM,** die; -, -[s] (Nur-Lese-Speicher auf CD); **CD-Spie|ler** (Plattenspieler für CD-Platten)
CDU = Christlich-Demokratische Union (Deutschlands)
C-Dur [ˈtse:du:r, *auch* ˈtse:ˈdu:r], das; - (Tonart; *Zeichen* C); **C-Dur-Ton|lei|ter** (↑R 28)
Ce = *chem. Zeichen für* Cer
Ce|dil|le [seˈdi:j(ə)], die; -, -n ‹franz.› (Häkchen als Ausspracheze ichen, z. B. bei franz. ç als stimmloses s vor a, o, u)
Ce|le|bes [(t)seˈle:..., *auch* ˈtse:...] (eine der Großen Sundainseln)
Ce|les|ta [tʃe...], die; -, *Plur.* -s *u.* ...sten ‹ital.› (ein Tasteninstrument)
Ce|li|bi|da|che [tʃelibiˈdake] (rumän. Dirigent)
Cel|la [ˈtsɛla], die; -, Cellae [...lɛ] ‹lat.› (Hauptraum im antiken Tempel; *Med.* Zelle)
Cel|le [ˈtsɛlə] (Stadt an der Aller); **Cel|ler** (↑R 103)
Cel|li|ni [tʃɛ...] (ital. Bildhauer)
cel|lisch, *auch* cel|lesch ‹*zu* Celle›
Cel|list [tʃɛ...], der; -en, -en (↑R 126) ‹ital.› (Cellospieler); **Cel|lis|tin; Cel|lo,** das; -s, *Plur.* -s *u.* ...lli (*Kurzform für* Violoncello)
Cel|lo|phan ®, das; -s *u.* **Cel|lo|pha|ne** ®, die; - ‹lat.; griech.› (glasklare Folie); **cel|lo|pha|nie|ren; Cel|lu|loid** *vgl.* Zelluloid; **Cel|lu|lo|se** *vgl.* Zellulose
Cel|si|us ‹nach dem Schweden Anders Celsius› (Gradeinheit auf der Celsiusskala; *Zeichen* C; *fachspr.* °C); 5° C (*fachspr.* 5 °C)
Cem|ba|lo [ˈtʃɛm...], das; -s, *Plur.* -s *u.* ...li ‹ital.› (ein Tasteninstrument)
Ce|no|man [tse...], das; -s ‹nach der röm. Stadt Cenomanum = Le Mans› (*Geol.* Stufe der Kreideformation)
Cent [(t)sɛnt], der; -[s], -[s] ‹engl.› (Münze in den USA, in Kanada usw.; *Abk.* c *u.* ct, *im Plur.* cts; *Zeichen* ¢); 5 - (↑R 90)
Cen|ta|vo [senˈta:vo], der; -[s], -[s] ‹port. *u.* span.› (Münze in Süd- u. Mittelamerika usw.)
Cen|ter [ˈsɛntə(r)], das; -s, - ‹amerik.› (Geschäftszentrum; Großeinkaufsanlage)
Cen|te|si|mo [tʃɛn...], der; -[s], ...mi ‹ital.› (ehem. ital. Münze)
Cen|té|si|mo [sɛnˈte:...], der; -[s], -[s] ‹span.› (Münze in Chile, Panama, Uruguay)
Cen|time [sãˈti:m], der; -s [sãˈti:ms], -s [sãˈti:m(s)] ‹franz.› (belg., franz., luxemburg. usw. Münze; *schweiz. veraltend neben* Rappen; *Abk.* c, ct, *im Plur.* ct[s], *schweiz. nur* Ct., *im Plur.* Cts.)
Cén|ti|mo [ˈsɛn...], der; -[s], -[s] ‹span.› (Münze in Spanien, Mittel- u. Südamerika)
Cen|tre|court, *auch* **Cen|tre-Court** [ˈsɛntə(r)kɔ:(r)t], der; -s, -s ‹engl.› (Hauptplatz großer Tennisanlagen)
Cer, das; -s ‹lat.› (chem. Element, Metall; *Zeichen* Ce)
Cer|be|rus *vgl.* Zerberus
Cer|cle [ˈsɛrk(ə)l], der; -s, -s ‹franz.› (*veraltet für* Empfang [bei Hofe], vornehmer Gesellschaftskreis; *österr. auch für* die ersten Reihen im Theater u. Konzertsaal); - halten; **Cer|cle|sitz** (*österr. für* Sitz im Cercle)
Ce|re|a|li|en *Plur.* ‹lat.› (altröm. Fest zu Ehren der Ceres); *vgl. aber* Zerealie
Ce|re|bel|lum *vgl.* Zerebellum; **Ce|reb|rum** (↑R 130) *vgl.* Zerebrum
Ce|res (röm. Göttin des Ackerbaus)
Ce|re|sin *vgl.* Zeresin
ce|rise [səˈri:z] ‹franz.› (kirschrot); ein cerise Kleid; *vgl. auch* beige; in Cerise (↑R 47)
Cer|to|sa [tʃɛr...], die; -, ...sen ‹ital.› (Kloster der Kartäuser in Italien)
Cer|van|tes [sɛrˈvantɛs, *span.* θɛr...] (span. Dichter)
Cer|ve|lat [sɛrvəla], der; -s, -s ‹franz.› (*schweiz. für* Brühwurst aus Rindfleisch mit Schwarten und Speck); *vgl.* Servela *u.* Zervelatwurst
ces, Ces, das; -, - (Tonbezeichnung); **Ces** (*Zeichen für* Ces-Dur); in Ces; **Ces-Dur** [*auch* ˈtsɛsˈdu:r], das; - (Tonart; *Zeichen* Ces); **Ces-Dur-Ton|lei|ter** (↑R 28)
ce|te|ris pa|ri|bus ‹lat.› (unter [sonst] gleichen Umständen)
ce|te|rum cen|seo ‹lat., „übrigens meine ich"› (als Einleitung einer immer wieder vorgebrachten Forderung od. Ansicht)
Će|vap|či|ci, Će|vap|či|ći [tʃeˈvaptʃitʃi] *Plur.* ‹serbokroat.› (gegrillte Hackfleischröllchen)
Ce|ven|nen [seˈvɛn...] *Plur.* (franz. Gebirge)
Cey|lon [ˈtsailɔn, *österr.* ˈtsei...] (*früherer Name von* Sri Lanka); **Cey|lo|ne|se,** der; -n, -n (↑R 126); **cey|lo|ne|sisch; Cey|lon|tee** (↑R 105)
Cé|zanne [seˈzan] (franz. Maler)
cf = cost and freight [ˈkɔst ənd ˈfre:t] ‹engl.› (*Klausel im Überseehandel* Verladekosten und Fracht im Preis eingeschlossen)
Cf = *chem. Zeichen für* Californium
cf., conf., cfr. = confer!
C-Fal|ter [ˈtse:...]; ↑R 25 (ein Tagfalter)
cfr., cf., conf. = confer!
cg = Zentigramm
CGS-Sys|tem, das; -s (älteres physikal. Maßsystem, das auf den Grundeinheiten Zentimeter [C], Gramm [G] u. Sekunde [S] aufgebaut ist; *vgl.* MKS-System)
CH = Confoederatio Helvetica
Chab|lis [ʃaˈbli:] (↑R 130), der; - [ʃabˈli:(s)], - [ʃabˈli:s] ‹franz.› (franz. Weißwein)
Cha-Cha-Cha [ˈtʃaˈtʃaˈtʃa], der; -[s], -s (ein Tanz)
Cha|co *vgl.* Gran Chaco
Cha|conne [ʃaˈkɔn], die; -, *Plur.* -s *u.* -n [...nən] ‹franz.› *u.* **Ci|a|co|na** [tʃaˈko:na], die; -, -s ‹ital.› (ein Tanz; Instrumentalstück)
Cha|gall [ʃaˈgal] (russ. Maler)
¹**Chag|rin** [ʃaˈgrɛ̃:] (↑R 130), der; -s ‹franz.› (*veraltet für* Gram, Kummer); ²**Chag|rin,** das; -s, -s (Leder mit künstl. Narben); **chag|ri|nie|ren** [ʃagri...] (Leder künstlich mit Narben versehen); **Chag|rin|le|der** [ʃaˈgrɛ̃:...]

Chai|ne [ˈʃɛ:n(ə)], die; -, -n ‹franz.› (*Weberei* Kettfaden)

Chair|man [ˈtʃɛ:(r)mən], der; -, ...men ‹engl.› (*engl. Bez. für* Vorsitzender)

Chai|se [ˈʃɛ:zə], die; -, -n ‹franz.› (*veraltet für* Stuhl, Sessel; *ugs. für* altes Auto); **Chai|se|longue** [ʃɛzəˈlɔŋ], die; -, *Plur.* -n [...ˈlɔŋən] *od.* -s, *ugs. auch* das; -s, -s (gepolsterte Liege mit Kopflehne)

Chal|dä̲a [kal...] (*A. T.* Babylonien); **Chal|dä̲|er** (Angehöriger eines aramäischen Volksstammes); **chal|dä̲|isch**

Cha|let [ʃaˈle:, *auch* ʃaˈlɛ], das; -s, -s ‹franz.› (Sennhütte; Landhaus)

Chal|ki|di|ke [çalˈki:dike:], die; - (nordgriech. Halbinsel)

Chal|ko|che|mi|gra|phi̲e [çalko...] (↑R 33), die; - ‹griech.› (Metallgravierung); **chal|ko|ge̲n** ‹griech.-lat., „Erz bildend"› (*Chemie*); **Chal|ko|ge̲n,** das; -s, -e *meist Plur.* (Element einer chem. Gruppe); **Chal|ko|li̲|thi|kum** [*auch* ...ˈli...], das; -s (*Urgesch.* jungsteinzeitl. Stufe, in der schon Kupferbearbeitung bekannt war)

Chal|len|ger [ˈtʃɛlindʒə(r)], die; - ‹engl., „Herausforderer"› (Name einer amerik. Raumfähre)

Chal|ze|do̲n [kal...], der; -s, -e (ein Mineral)

Cham [ka:m] (Stadt am Regen u. Gemeinde im schweiz. Kanton Zug)

Cha|ma̲|de [ʃa...] *vgl.* Schamade

Cha|mä̲|le|on [ka...], das; -s, -s ‹griech.› (eine Echse; *abwertend für* oft seine Überzeugung wechselnder Mensch); **cha|mä̲|le|on|ar|tig**

Cha|ma|ve [çaˈma:və], der; -n, -n; ↑R 126 (Angehöriger eines germ. Volksstammes)

Cham|ber|lain [ˈtʃe(:)mbə(r)lin] (engl. Familienn.)

Chamb|re sé|pa|rée [ˌʃã:br(ə) sepaˈre:] (↑R 130), das; - -, -s -s [ˌʃã:br(ə) sepaˈre:] ‹franz.› (*veraltet für* kleiner Nebenraum für ungestörte Zusammenkünfte)

Cha|mi̩s|so [ʃa...] (dt. Dichter)

cha|mois [ʃaˈmo̯a] ‹franz.› (gämsfarben, bräunlich gelb); ein chamois Hemd; *vgl. auch* beige; **Chamois,** das; - (chamois Farbe; weiches Gämsen-, Ziegen-, Schafleder); Stoffe in Chamois; **Chamois|le|der**

Cham|pa|gne [ʃãˈpanjə] (↑R 130), die; - (franz. Landschaft); **Champa|gner** [ʃamˈpanjər] (ein Schaumwein); **cham|pa̩g|ner|far|ben, cham|pa̩g|ner|far|big; Cham|pa̩g|ner|wein**

Cham|pi|gnon [ˈʃampinjɔŋ] (↑R 130), der; -s, -s (ein Edelpilz)

Cham|pi|on [ˈtʃɛmpi̯ən, *franz.* ʃãˈpi̯õ:], der; -s, -s ‹engl.› (Meister in einer Sportart); **Cham|pi|o|na̲t** [ʃam...], das; -[e]s, -e ‹franz.› (Meisterschaft in einer Sportart); **Cham|pi|ons League** [ˈtʃɛmpi̯ənz ˈli:g], die; - - ‹engl.› (*Fußball* Austragungsmodus des Europapokals der Landesmeister, bei dem die Viertelfinalgegner durch Punktspiele ermittelt werden)

Champs-É|ly|sées [ʃãzeliˈze:] *Plur.* (eine Hauptstraße in Paris)

Chan [ka:n, *auch* xa:n] usw. *vgl.* Khan usw.

Chan|ce [ˈʃã:s(ə), *auch* ˈʃaŋsə], die; -, -n ‹franz.› (günstige Gelegenheit; *meist Plur.:* Aussichten auf Erfolg)

Chan|cel|lor [ˈtʃa:nsələ(r)], der; -s, -s ‹engl.› (*engl. Bez. für* Kanzler)

Cha̲n|cen|gleich|heit, die; -

Change [tʃe:ndʒ], der; - ‹engl.› *u.* [ʃã:ʒ], die; - ‹franz.› (*engl. u. franz. Bez. für* Tausch, [Geld]wechsel); **chan|geant** [ʃãˈʒã:] ‹franz.› (in mehreren Farben schillernd [von Stoffen]); ein changeant Stoff; *vgl. auch* beige; **Chan|geant,** der; -[s], -s (schillernder Stoff; Edelstein mit schillernder Färbung); **chan|gie|ren** [ʃaŋˈʒi:..., *auch* ʃãˈʒi:...] (schillern [von Stoffen]; *Jägerspr.* die Fährte wechseln [vom Jagdhund])

Chang|ji|ang, Chang Ji|ang [*beide* tʃaŋˈdji̯aŋ] *vgl.* Jangtse

Chan|son [ʃãˈsõ:], das; -s, -s ‹franz.› ([Kabarett]lied); **Chanson|ne̩t|te,** *auch* Chan|so|ne̩t|te [*beide* ʃãsɔˈnɛtə], die; -, -n (Chansonsängerin; kleines Chanson); **Chan|son|ni|er,** *auch* Chan|so|nier [ʃãsɔˈni̯e:], der; -s, -s (Chansonsänger, -dichter); **Chan|son|ni|è|re,** *auch* Chan|so|ni|e|re [ʃãsɔˈni̯e:re], die; -, -n (Chansonsängerin)

Cha|nuk|ka̲ [x...], die; - ‹hebr.› (ein jüd. Fest); **Cha|nuk|ka̲|leuch|ter** (Leuchter, der zur Chanukka angezündet wird)

Cha|os [ˈka:ɔs], das; - ‹griech.› (wüstes Durcheinander, Auflösung aller Ordnung); **Cha̲|os|the|o|rie** (eine mathematisch-physikalische Theorie); **Cha|ot** [kaˈo:t], der; -en, -en (jmd., der [ohne klare politische Linie] die bestehende Gesellschaftsordnung durch Gewaltaktionen zu zerstören versucht; *ugs. für* sprunghafter Mensch, Wirrkopf); **cha|o̲|tisch**

Cha|peau [ʃaˈpo:], der; -s, -s ‹franz.› (*veraltet, noch scherzh. für* Hut); **Cha|peau claque** [ʃapo ˈklak], der; - -, -x -s [ʃapo ˈklak] (Klappzylinder)

Chap|lin [ˈtʃɛp...] (engl. Filmschauspieler, Autor u. Regisseur); **Chap|li|na̲|de** [tʃa...], die; -, -n (komischer Vorgang [wie in Chaplins Filmen]); **chap|li|ne̩sk**

Cha|ra̲|de [ʃa...] *ältere Schreibung für* Scharade

Cha|ra̩k|ter [ka...], der; -s, ...e̲re ‹griech.›; **Cha|ra̩k|ter‿an|la|ge, ...bild, ...bil|dung, ...dar|stel|ler, ...ei|gen|schaft, ...feh|ler; cha|ra̩k|ter|fest; Cha|ra̩k|ter|fes|tig|keit,** die; -; **cha|rak|te|ri|si̲e|ren; Cha|rak|te|ri|si̲e|rung; Cha|rak|te|ri̩s|tik,** die; -, -en (Kennzeichnung; [treffende] Schilderung); **Cha|rak|te|ri̩s|ti|kum,** das; -s, ...ka (kennzeichnendes Merkmal); **cha|rak|te|ri̩s|tisch; cha|rak|te|ri̩s|ti|scher|wei̲|se; Cha|ra̩k|ter‿kopf, ...kun|de** (die; -; *für* Charakterologie); **cha|ra̩k|ter|lich; cha|ra̩k|ter|los; Cha|ra̩k|ter|lo|sig|keit; Cha|rak|te|ro|lo|gi̲e,** die; - (Charakterkunde, Persönlichkeitsforschung); **cha|rak|te|ro|lo̲|gisch; Cha|ra̩k|ter‿rol|le, ...schwä|che, ...stär|ke** (die; -), **...stu|die; cha|ra̩k|ter|voll; Cha|ra̩k|ter|zug**

Char|ge [ˈʃarʒə], die; -, -n ‹franz.› (Amt; Rang; *Militär* Dienstgrad; *Pharm.* eine bestimmte Serie von Arzneimitteln; *Technik* Ladung, Beschickung; *Theater* [stark ausgeprägte] Nebenrolle); **Cha̩r|gen|num|mer** (*Pharm.*); **char|gie|ren** [...ˈʒi:...] (*Technik* beschicken; *Theater* eine Charge spielen); **Char|gi̲er|te,** der; -n, -n; ↑R 5 ff. (Mitglied des Vorstandes einer stud. Verbindung)

Cha|ris [ˈça(:)...], die; -, ...i̲ten *meist Plur.* ‹griech.› (eine der griech. Göttinnen der Anmut [Aglaia, Euphrosyne, Thalia]); **Cha|ris|ma** [ˈça(:)..., *auch* ...ˈrisma], das; -s, *Plur.* ...ri̩smen *u.* ...ri̩smata (besondere Ausstrahlung); **cha|ris|ma̲|tisch; Cha|ri|té** [ʃariˈte:], die; -, -s ‹franz., „[Nächsten]liebe"› (Name von Krankenhäusern); **Cha|ri̲|ten** [ça...] *vgl.* Charis; **Cha|ri̲|tin,** die; -, -nen ‹griech.› (*svw.* Charis)

Cha|ri|va|ri [ʃariˈva:ri], das; -s, -s ‹franz.› (*veraltet für* Durcheinander; Katzenmusik; *bayr. für* [Anhänger für die] Uhrkette)

Char|kow [ˈçarkɔf, *auch* ˈx...] (Stadt in der Ukraine)

Charles [*franz.* ʃarl, *engl.* tʃa:(r)lz] (m. Vorn.)

Charles|ton ['tʃa:(r)lst(ə)n], der; -, -s ‹engl.› (ein Tanz)
Char|ley, Char|lie [*beide* 'tʃa:(r)li] (m. Vorn.)
Char|lot|te [ʃar...] (w. Vorn.); **Char|lot|ten|burg** (Stadtteil Berlins); *vgl.* Berlin
char|mant [ʃar...]; *eindeutschend* schar|mant; ‹franz.›; **Charme** [ʃarm], der; -s, *eindeutschend* Scharm, der; -[e]s (bezauberndes Wesen, Liebenswürdigkeit); **Char|meur** [...'mø:r], der; -s, *Plur.* -s *od.* -e (charmanter Plauderer); **Char|meuse** [...'mø:s], die; - (maschenfeste Wirkware [aus synthet. Fasern])
Cha|ron ['ça:rɔn] (in der griech. Sage Fährmann in der Unterwelt)
Chart [tʃa(r)t], der *od.* das; -s, -s ‹engl.› (grafische Darstellung von Zahlenreihen); *vgl.* Charts
Char|ta ['karta], die; -, -s ‹lat.› ([Verfassungs]urkunde); **Char|te** ['ʃartə], die; -, -n ‹franz.› (wichtige Urkunde im Staats- u. Völkerrecht)
Char|ter ['(t)ʃa(r)...], der; -s, -s ‹engl.› (Freibrief, Urkunde; Frachtvertrag); **Char|te|rer** (Mieter eines Schiffes od. Flugzeugs); **Char|ter‿flug, ...ge|schäft, ...ge|sell|schaft, ...ma|schi|ne; char|tern** (ein Schiff od. Flugzeug mieten); ich ...ere (↑R 16); gechartert
Chart|res ['ʃartrə] (↑R 130; franz. Stadt)
[1]**Chart|reu|se** [ʃar'trø:zə] (↑R 130), die; - ‹franz.› (Hauptkloster des Kartäuserordens); [2]**Chart|reu|se** ®, der; - (Kräuterlikör der Mönche von [1]Chartreuse); [3]**Chart|reu|se,** die; -, -n (Pudding aus Gemüse u. Fleischspeisen)
Charts [tʃa:(r)ts] *Plur.* ‹engl.› (Liste[n] der beliebtesten Schlager)
Cha|ryb|dis [ç...], die; - ‹griech.› (Meeresstrudel in der Straße von Messina); *vgl.* Szylla
Chas|sis [ʃa'si:, *auch* 'ʃasi:], das; - [...si:(s)], - [...s] ‹franz.› (Fahrgestell von Kraftfahrzeugen; Montagerahmen [eines Rundfunkgerätes])
Cha|su|ble [*franz.* ʃa'zyb(ə)l, *engl.* 'tʃɛzub(ə)l], das; -s, -s ‹franz.› (westenähnliches Überkleid)
Cha|teau, *auch* **Châ|teau** [ʃa'to:], das; -s, -s ‹franz.› (*franz. Bez. für* Schloss)
Cha|teau|bri|and [ʃatobri'ã:] ‹nach dem franz. Schriftsteller u. Politiker› (gebratene, dicke Rindslendenschnitte)
Chat|scha|tur|jan [xatʃatu'rjan] (↑R 132; armen. Komponist)
Chat|te [k..., *auch* ç...], der; -n, -n; ↑R 126 (Angehöriger eines westgerm. Volksstammes)
Chau|cer ['tʃɔ:sə(r)] (engl. Dichter)
Chau|deau [ʃo'do:], das; -[s], -s ‹franz.› (Weinschaumsoße)
Chauf|feur [ʃɔ'fø:r], der; -s, -e ‹franz.› (Fahrer); *vgl. auch* Schofför; **chauf|fie|ren** *(veraltend)*
Chau|ke [ç...], der; -n, -n; ↑R 126 (Angehöriger eines westgerm. Volksstammes)
Chaus|see [ʃɔ...], die; -, ...sseen ‹franz.› (*veraltend für* Landstraße); ↑R 123; **Chaus|see‿baum, ...gra|ben**
Chau|vi ['ʃo:vi], der; -s, -s (*ugs. für* Mann, der sich Frauen gegenüber überlegen fühlt, der ein übertriebenes männliches Selbstwertgefühl hat); **Chau|vi|nis|mus** [ʃovi...], der; - ‹franz.› (übersteigerter Nationalismus, Patriotismus; übertriebenes männliches Selbstwertgefühl); **Chau|vi|nist,** der; -en, -en (↑R 126); **chau|vi|nis|tisch**
Chaux-de-Fonds *vgl.* La Chaux-de-Fonds
Che [tʃe:] (*volkstüml. Name von* Guevara)
Cheb [xɛp] (tschech. Stadt in Westböhmen; *vgl.* Eger)
[1]**Check** [ʃɛk] *vgl.* [1]Scheck; [2]**Check** [tʃɛk], der; -s, -s ‹engl.› (*Eishockey* Behinderung, Rempeln); **che|cken** (*Eishockey* behindern, [an]rempeln; *bes. Technik* kontrollieren; *ugs. auch für* begreifen); **Check|lis|te** (Kontrollliste); **Check|point** ['tʃɛkpɔynt], der; -s, -s (Kontrollpunkt an Grenzübergängen)
chee|rio! ['tʃi:rio] ‹engl.› (*ugs. für* auf Wiedersehen!; zum Wohl!)
Cheese|bur|ger ['tʃi:sbœ:(r)ge(r)], der; -s, - ‹engl.› ([2]Hamburger, der zusätzlich eine Scheibe Käse enthält)
Chef [ʃɛf, *österr.* ʃe:f], der; -s, -s ‹franz.›; **Chef|arzt; Chef de Mis|si|on** [ʃɛf də mi'siɔ̃:], der; -[s] - -, -s - - ‹franz.› (Leiter einer [sportl.] Delegation); **Chef‿di|ri|gent, ...eta|ge** (↑R 132); **Che|fin; Chef‿in|ge|ni|eur, ...lek|tor, ...pi|lot, ...re|dak|teur, ...sek|re|tä|rin, ...trai|ner; Chef|vi|si|te** (Visite des Chefarztes)
Chel|lé|en [ʃɛle'ɛ̃:] das; -[s] ‹nach der Stadt Chelles in Nordfrankreich› (*älter für* Abbevillien)
Che|mie [ç..., *südd., österr.* k...], die; - ‹arab.› (Lehre von den Stoffen und ihren Verbindungen); **Che|mie‿ar|bei|ter, ...fa|ser, ...in|ge|ni|eur, ...wer|ker; Che|mi|graph** (↑R 33), der; -en, -en (↑R 126) ‹arab.; griech.› (Hersteller von Druckplatten); **Che|mi|gra|phie** (↑R 33), die; - (fotomechan. Bildreproduktion u. Druckplattenherstellung); **Che|mi|ka|lie** [...iə], die; -, -n; **Che|mi|kant,** der; -en, -en; ↑R 126 (*regional für* Chemiefacharbeiter); **Che|mi|ker; Che|mi|ke|rin**
Che|mi|née ['ʃəmine:], das; -s, -s ‹franz.› (*schweiz. für* offener Kamin in einem Wohnraum)
che|misch [ç..., *südd., österr.* k...] ‹arab.›; -e Reinigung; -es Element; -e Waffen; -e Keule (Tränengasspray); **che|misch-tech|nisch** (↑R 27)
Che|mise [ʃə'mi:z], die; -, -n [...zən] ‹franz.› (*veraltet für* Hemd); **Che|mi|sett,** das; -[e]s, *Plur.* -s *u.* -e *u.* **Che|mi|set|te,** die; -, -n (Hemdbrust; Einsatz an Damenkleidern)
che|mi|sie|ren [ç..., *südd., österr.* k...] ‹arab.; lat.› (die Chemie in anderen Wirtschaftszweigen anwenden); **Che|mis|mus,** der; - (Gesamtheit der chem. Vorgänge, bes. beim Stoffwechsel)
Chem|nitz ['kɛm...] (Stadt und Fluss in Sachsen); **Chem|nit|zer** (↑R 103)
Che|mo|keu|le [ç..., *südd., österr.* k...] ‹arab.; dt.› (chemische Keule); **che|mo|tak|tisch** ‹arab.; griech.› (*Biol.* die Chemotaxis betreffend); **Che|mo|ta|xis,** die; -, ...xen (durch chem. Reizung ausgelöste Orientierungsbewegung niederer Organismen); **Che|mo|tech|ni|ker; Che|mo|the|ra|peu|ti|kum** *meist Plur. (Pharm.);* **che|mo|the|ra|peu|tisch; Che|mo|the|ra|pie** (Heilbehandlung mit Chemotherapeutika)
...chen (z. B. Mädchen, das; -s, -)
Che|nil|le [ʃə'niljə, *auch* ʃə'ni:jə], die; -, -n ‹franz.› (Garn mit seitl. flauschig abstehenden Fasern)
Che|ops [ç..., *südd., österr.* k...] (altägypt. Herrscher); **Che|ops|py|ra|mi|de,** die; - (↑R 95)
Cheque [ʃɛk] *vgl.* [1]Scheck
Cher|bourg [ʃɛr'bu:r] (franz. Stadt)
cher|chez la femme! [ʃɛr'ʃe: la 'fam] ‹franz., „sucht nach der Frau!"› (hinter der Sache steckt bestimmt eine Frau)
Cher|ry|bran|dy ['tʃɛri'brɛndi], der; -s, -s ‹engl.› (feiner Kirschlikör)
Che|rub [ç..., *auch* k...], *ökum.* Kerub, der; -s, *Plur.* -im *u.* -inen ‹hebr.› (das Paradies bewachen-

der Engel); **che|ru|bi|nisch** (engelgleich), *aber* (↑R 108): der Cherubinische Wandersmann (eine Sinnspruchsammlung)
Che|rus|ker [ç...], der; -s, - (Angehöriger eines westgerm. Volksstammes)
Ches|ter [ˈtʃɛstə(r)] (engl. Stadt); **Ches|ter|field** [ˈtʃɛstə(r)fi:lt] (engl. Stadt); **Ches|ter|kä|se** (↑R 105)
che|va|le|resk [ʃəva...] ‹franz.› (ritterlich); **Che|va|li|er** [ʃəvaˈli̯e:], der; -s, -s (franz. Adelstitel); **Che|vau|le|ger** [ʃəvoleˈʒe:], der; -s, -s (*Milit. früher* leichter Reiter)
Che|vi|ot [ˈ(t)ʃɛvi̯ɔt, *auch* ˈʃe:..., *österr.* ˈʃɛ:...], der; -s, -s ‹engl.› (ein Wollstoff)
Chev|reau [ʃəˈvro:, *auch* ˈʃɛvro] (↑R 130), das; -s, -s ‹franz.› (Ziegenleder); **Chev|reau|le|der**
Chev|ron [ʃəˈvrõ:] (↑R 130), der; -s, -s (Gewebe mit Fischgrätenmusterung; franz. Dienstgradabzeichen; *Heraldik* Sparren [nach unten offener Winkel])
Che|wing|gum [ˈtʃu:iŋgam] (↑R 33), der; -[s], -s ‹engl.› (Kaugummi)
Chey|enne [ʃaiˈɛn], der; -, - (Angehöriger eines nordamerik. Indianerstammes)
Chi [çi:], das; -[s], -s (griech. Buchstabe: *X*, *χ*)
Chi|an|ti [k...], der; -[s], -s (ein ital. Rotwein)
Chi|as|mus [çi...], der; -, ...men ‹griech.› (*Sprachw.* Kreuzstellung von Satzgliedern, z. B.: „der Einsatz war groß, gering war der Gewinn")
Chi|as|so [k...] (schweiz. Ortsn.)
chi|as|tisch [çi...] ‹griech.› (*Sprachw.* in der Form des Chiasmus)
chic usw. *vgl.* schick usw. *(gebeugte Formen nur in deutscher Schreibung)*
Chi|ca|go [ʃi...] (Stadt in den USA)
Chi|chi [ʃiˈʃi:], das; -[s] ‹franz.› (Getue, Gehabe; verspielte Accessoires)
Chi|co|rée [ˈʃikore:], *eindeutschend* Schi|ko|ree, (↑R 33), der; -s, *auch* die; - ‹franz.› (ein Gemüse)
Chiem|see [ki:m...], der; -s
Chif|fon [ˈʃifɔŋ, *auch* ʃiˈfõ:, *österr.* ʃiˈfo:n], der; -s, *Plur.* -s, *österr.* -e (feines Gewebe)
Chiff|re [ˈʃifrə, *auch* ˈʃifər] (↑R 130), die; -, -n ‹franz.› (Ziffer; Geheimzeichen; Kennwort); **Chiff|re|schrift** (Geheimschrift); **chiff|rie|ren** [ʃiˈfri:...] (in Geheimschrift abfassen); **Chiff|rier|kunst**, die; -
Chig|non [ʃinˈjõ:] (↑R 130), der; -s, -s ‹franz.› (im Nacken getragener Haarknoten)
Chi|hu|a|hua [tʃiˈu̯au̯a], der; -s, -s ‹span.› (eine Hunderasse)
Chi|ka|go [ʃi...] (*dt. Form von* Chicago)
Chil|bi *vgl.* Kilbi
Chi|le [ˈtʃi:le(:), *österr. u. schweiz. nur so, auch* ˈçi:le(:)] (südamerik. Staat); **Chi|le|ne**, der; -n, -n (↑R 126); **Chi|le|nin; chi|le|nisch; Chi|le|sal|pe|ter** (↑R 105)
Chi|li [ˈtʃi:li], der; -s ‹span.› (ein scharfes Gewürz)
Chi|li|as|mus [ç...], der; - ‹griech.› (Lehre von der Erwartung des Tausendjährigen Reiches Christi); **Chi|li|ast**, der; -en, -en; ↑R 126 (Anhänger des Chiliasmus); **chi|li|as|tisch**
Chi|mä|ra, **[1]Chi|mä|re** [*beide* ç...], die; - ‹griech.› (Ungeheuer der griech. Sage); **[2]Chi|mä|re** usw. *vgl.* Schimäre usw.; **[3]Chi|mä|re**, die, -, -n (*Biol.* auf dem Wege der Mutation od. Pfropfung entstandener Organismus)
Chim|bo|ras|so [tʃim...], der; -[s] (ein südamerik. Berg)
Chi|na [ç..., *südd., österr.* k...]; **Chi|na|kohl**, der; -[e]s
Chi|na|rin|de [ç..., *südd., österr.* k...] (eine chininhaltige Droge)
[1]Chin|chil|la [tʃinˈtʃil(j)a], die; -, -s *od., österr. nur,* das; -s, -s ‹indian.-span.› (Nagetier); **[2]Chin|chil|la**, das; -s, -s (Kaninchenrasse; Fell von [1,2]Chinchilla)
Chi|ne|se [ç..., *südd., österr.* k...], der; -n, -n (↑R 126); **Chi|ne|sin; chi|ne|sisch**, *aber* (↑R 108): die Chinesische Mauer; **Chi|ne|sisch**, das; -[s] (Sprache); *vgl.* Deutsch; **Chi|ne|si|sche**, das; -n; *vgl.* Deutsche, das
Chi|nin [ç..., *südd., österr.* k...], das; -s ‹indian.› (Alkaloid der Chinarinde als Arznei gegen Fieber)
Chi|noi|se|rie [ʃinoazə...], die; -, ...ien ‹franz.› (kunstgewerbl. Arbeit in chin. Stil)
Chintz [tʃ...], der; -[es], -e ‹Hindi› (bedrucktes [Baumwoll]gewebe)
Chip [tʃip], der; -s, -s ‹engl.› (Spielmarke [bei Glücksspielen]; *meist Plur.:* roh in Fett gebackene Kartoffelscheiben; *Elektronik* sehr kleines Halbleiterplättchen mit elektronischen Schaltelementen); **Chip|kar|te** (Plastikkarte mit einem elektronischen Chip, die als Ausweis, Zahlungsmittel o. Ä. verwendet wird)
Chip|pen|dale [ˈ(t)ʃipəndeːl], das; -[s] ‹nach dem engl. Tischler› ([Möbel]stil); **Chip|pen|dale|stil**, der; -[e]s (↑R 95)
Chi|rac [ʃiˈrak] (frz. Staatspräsident)
Chi|rag|ra [ç..., *südd., österr.* k...] (↑R 132), das; -s ‹griech.› (*Med.* Handgicht); **Chi|ro|mant**, der; -en, -en; ↑R 126 (Handliniendeuter); **Chi|ro|man|tie**, die; -; **Chi|ro|prak|tik**, die; - (Einrenken verschobener Wirbelkörper u. Bandscheiben mithilfe der Hände); **Chi|ro|prak|ti|ker**
Chi|rurg (↑R 132), der; -en, -en; (↑R 126; Facharzt für operative Medizin); **Chi|rur|gie**, die; -, ...ien; **Chi|rur|gin; chi|rur|gisch**
Chi|tin [ç..., *südd., österr.* k...], das; -s ‹semit.› (hornähnlicher Stoff im Panzer der Gliederfüßer); **chi|ti|nig; Chi|ton**, der; -s, -e (altgriech. Untergewand)
chlad|ni|sche Klang|fi|gur [kl...-], die; -n -, -n -en (↑R 94) ‹nach dem dt. Physiker Chladni›
Chla|mys [ˈçla:mys, *auch* çlaˈmys], die; -, - ‹griech.› (altgriech. Überwurf für Reiter u. Krieger)
ch-Laut [tse:ˈha:...] (↑R 25)
Chlod|wig [ˈklo:t...] (fränk. König)
Chloe [ˈklo:e] (w. Eigenn.)
Chlor [klo:r], das; -s ‹griech.› (chem. Element; *Zeichen* Cl); **Chlo|ral**, das; -s (*Chemie* eine Chlorverbindung); **chlo|ren** (mit Chlor behandeln; *Chemie* Chlor in eine chem. Verbindung einführen); **chlor|hal|tig; Chlo|rid**, das; -[e]s, -e (*Chemie* eine Chlorverbindung); **chlo|rie|ren** (*svw.* chloren); **chlo|rig; [1]Chlo|rit** [*auch* ...ˈrit], der; -s, -e (ein Mineral); **[2]Chlo|rit** [*auch* ...ˈrit], das; -s, -e (*Chemie* ein Salz); **Chlor|kalk; Chlo|ro|form**, das; -s ‹griech.; lat.› (Betäubungs-, Lösungsmittel); **chlo|ro|for|mie|ren** (mit Chloroform betäuben); **Chlo|ro|phyll**, das; -s ‹griech.› (*Bot.* Blattgrün); **Chlo|rung**
Chlot|hil|de [klo...] *vgl.* Klothilde
Cho|do|wi|ec|ki [kodoˈvi̯ɛtski, *auch* x...] (dt. Kupferstecher)
Choke [tʃo:k], der; -s, -s ‹engl.› (*Kfz-Technik* Luftklappe am Vergaser; Kaltstarthilfe); **Cho|ker**, der; -s, - (*svw.* Choke)
Cho|le|ra [k...], die; - ‹griech.› (*Med.* eine Infektionskrankheit); **Cho|le|ra|epi|de|mie** (↑R 132); **Cho|le|ri|ker** (leicht erregbarer, jähzorniger Mensch); **cho|le|risch** (jähzornig; aufbrausend); **Cho|les|te|rin**, *fachspr.* Cho|les|te|rol [*beide* ç..., *auch* k...], das; -s (eine in tierischen Geweben vor-

kommende organ. Verbindung; Hauptbestandteil der Gallensteine); **Cho|les|te|rin|spie|gel; Cho|les|te|rol** *vgl.* Cholesterin
Cho|mai|ni *vgl.* Khomeini
Cho|pin [ʃɔ'pɛ̃:] (poln. Komponist)
Chop|per [tʃɔpə(r)], der; -s, -[s] ‹engl.› (aus Teilen verschiedener Motorräder gebautes Motorrad)
Chop|su|ey [tʃɔp'su:i], das; -[s], -s ‹chin.-engl.› (Gericht aus Fleisch- od. Fischstückchen mit Gemüse u. anderen Zutaten)
Chor [k...], der; -[e]s, Chöre ‹griech.› ([erhöhter] Kirchenraum mit [Haupt]altar; Gruppe von Sängern; Komposition für Gruppengesang); gemischter -; **Cho|ral,** der; -s, ...räle (Kirchengesang, -lied); **Cho|ral‿buch, ...vor|spiel; Chör|chen**
Chor|da [k...], die; -, ...den ‹griech.-lat.› (*Biol.* knorpeliges Gebilde als Vorstufe der Wirbelsäule); **Chor|dat,** der; -en, -en *u.* **Chor|da|te,** der; -n, -n *od.* **Chor|da|tier,** das; -[e]s, -e, *alle meist im Plur.* (*Zool.* Angehöriger eines Tierstammes, dessen Kennzeichen die Chorda ist)
Cho|rea [k...], die; - ‹griech.› (*Med.* Veitstanz); - Huntington
Cho|re|o|graf, Cho|re|o|gra|fie usw. *eindeutschende Schreibung für* Choreograph, Choreographie usw.; **Cho|re|o|graph** (↑R 33), der; -en, -en; **Cho|re|o|gra|phie** (↑R 33), die; -, ...ien (Gestaltung, Einstudierung eines Balletts); **cho|re|o|gra|phie|ren** (↑R 33); ein Ballett -; **Cho|re|o|gra|phin** (↑R 33)
Cho|reut [ç...], der; -en, -en (↑R 126; altgriech. Chortänzer);
Chor‿ge|bet [k...], **...ge|sang, ...ge|stühl, ...herr** *(kath. Kirche);* **...chö|rig** (z. B. zwei-, dreichörig)
Cho|rin [k...] (Ort u. ehem. Zisterzienserkloster bei Angermünde)
cho|risch [k...] ‹griech.›; **Cho|rist,** der; -en, -en; ↑R 126 ([Berufs]chorsänger); **Cho|ris|tin; Chor|kna|be; Chör|lein** (vieleckiger kleiner Erker an mittelalterl. Wohnbauten); **Chor‿lei|ter** (der), **...re|gent** (*südd. für* Leiter eines kath. Kirchenchors), **...sän|ger, ...sän|ge|rin; Cho|rus,** der; -, -se (Sängerchor; *Jazz* das mehrfach wiederholte u. improvisierte Thema)
Cho|se ['ʃo:zə], *auch* Scho|se, die; -, -n *Plur. selten* ‹franz.› (*ugs. für* Sache, Angelegenheit)
Chow-Chow [(t)ʃau'(t)ʃau], der; -s, -s ‹chin.-engl.› (chin. Spitz)
Chres|to|ma|thie [k...], die; -, ...ien ‹griech.› (Auswahl von Texten bekannter Autoren)
Chri|sam *vgl.* Chrisma; **Chris|ma** [ç...], das; -s *u.* Chri|sam [ç...], das *od.* der; -s ‹griech.› (Salböl der kath. Kirche)
[1]**Christ** [k...] ‹griech.› (*veraltet für* Christus); [2]**Christ,** der; -en, -en; ↑R 126 (Anhänger des Christentums); **Chris|ta** (w. Vorn.); **Christ|baum** (*landsch. für* Weihnachtsbaum); **Christ|de|mo|krat,** der; -en, -en (Anhänger einer christlich-demokratischen Partei); **Christ|de|mo|kra|tin; Chris|tel** (w. Vorn.); **Chris|ten|glau|be[n]; Chris|ten|heit,** die; -; **Chris|ten|leh|re,** die; - (kirchl. Unterweisung der konfirmierten ev. Jugend; *regional für* christl. Religionsunterricht); **Chris|ten|tum,** das; -s; **Chris|ten|ver|fol|gung; Christ|fest** (*veraltet für* Weihnachten); **Chris|ti|an** (m. Vorn.); **Chris|ti|a|ne** (w. Vorn.); **Chris|ti|a|nia** (*früherer Name von* Oslo; *ältere Schreibung von* [1]Kristiania); **chris|ti|a|ni|sie|ren; Chris|ti|a|ni|sie|rung; Chris|tin; Chris|ti|na, Chris|ti|ne** (w. Vorn.); **christ|ka|tho|lisch** (*schweiz. für* altkatholisch); **Christ|kind; Christ|kö|nigs|fest** *(kath. Kirche);* **christ|lich;** -e Seefahrt, *aber* (↑R 108): die Christlich-Demokratische Union [Deutschlands] (*Abk.* CDU), die Christlich-Soziale Union (*Abk.* CSU); **Christ|lich|keit,** die; -; **Christ‿met|te, Christ|mo|nat** *od.* **...mond** (*veraltet für* Dezember); **Chris|to|lo|gie,** die; -, ...ien (*Theol.* Lehre von Christus); **chris|to|lo|gisch; Chris|toph** (m. Vorn.); **Chris|to|pher** (m. Vorn.); **Chris|to|pho|rus** [*auch* ...'tɔ...] (legendärer Märtyrer); **Christ‿ro|se, ...stol|le[n]; Chris|tus** ‹„Gesalbter"› (Jesus Christus); Christi Himmelfahrt; nach Christo *od.* nach Christus (*Abk.* n. Chr.), nach Christi Geburt (*Abk.* n. Chr. G.); vor Christo *od.* vor Christus (*Abk.* v. Chr.), vor Christi Geburt (*Abk.* v. Chr. G.); *vgl.* Jesus Christus; **Chris|tus‿dorn** (der; -s, -e; Zierpflanze), **...kopf, ...mo|no|gramm, ...or|den** (port. geistl. Ritterorden; höchster päpstl. Orden)
Chrom [k...], das; -s ‹griech.› (chem. Element, Metall; *Zeichen* Cr); **Chro|ma|tik,** die; - (*Physik* Farbenlehre; *Musik* Veränderung der Grundtöne um einen Halbton); **chro|ma|tisch** (die Chromatik betreffend; *Musik* in Halbtönen fortschreitend); -e Tonleiter; **Chro|ma|to|phor,** das; -s, -en *meist Plur.* (*Bot.* Farbstoffträger in der Pflanzenzelle; *Zool.* Farbstoffzelle bei Tieren, die den Farbwechsel der Haut ermöglicht); **Chro|mat|ron** (↑R 130), das; -s, *Plur.* ...one, *auch* -s (spezielle Bildröhre für das Farbfernsehen); **chrom|blit|zend; Chrom‿gelb** (eine Farbe), **...grün** (eine Farbe); **Chro|mo|lith** [*auch* ...'lit], der; *Gen.* -s *u.* -en, *Plur.* -e[n]; (↑R 126; unglasiertes, farbig gemustertes Steinzeug); **Chro|mo|li|tho|gra|phie** (Farben[stein]druck); **Chro|mo|som,** das; -s, -en *meist Plur.* (*Biol.* in jedem Zellkern vorhandenes, das Erbgut tragendes, fadenförmiges Gebilde); **chro|mo|so|mal; Chro|mo|so|men‿satz, ...zahl; Chro|mo|sphä|re,** die; - (glühende Gasschicht um die Sonne); **Chrom|rot** (eine Farbe)
Chro|nik [k...], die; -, -en ‹griech.› (Aufzeichnung geschichtl. Ereignisse nach ihrer Zeitfolge; *im Sing. auch für* Chronika); **Chro|ni|ka** *Plur.* (Geschichtsbücher des A. T.); **chro|ni|ka|lisch; Chro|nique scan|da|leuse** [krɔ,nik skãda'lø:z], die; - -, -s -s [...nik ...'lø:z] ‹franz.› (Skandalgeschichten); **chro|nisch** ‹griech.› (*Med.* langsam verlaufend, langwierig; *ugs. für* dauernd); **Chro|nist,** der; -en, -en; ↑R 126 (Verfasser einer Chronik); **Chro|nis|ten|pflicht; Chro|nis|tin; Chro|no|gra|phie,** die; -, ...ien (Geschichtsschreibung nach der zeitl. Abfolge); **chro|no|gra|phisch; Chro|no|lo|gie,** die; -, -n (*nur Sing.:* Wissenschaft von der Zeit[messung]; zeitliche Folge); **chro|no|lo|gisch** (zeitlich geordnet); **Chro|no|me|ter,** das, *ugs. auch* der; -s, - (genau gehende Uhr); **chro|no|me|trisch** (↑R 130)
Chruscht|schow [k...] (↑R 130; sowjet. Politiker)
Chry|san|the|me [k...], die; -, -n ‹griech.› *u.* **Chry|san|the|mum** [*auch* ç...] (↑R 132), das; -s, -[s] (Zierpflanze mit großen strahligen Blüten)
Chry|so|be|ryll [ç...] ‹griech.› (ein Schmuckstein); **Chry|so|lith** [*auch* ...'lit], der; *Gen.* -s *u.* -en, *Plur.* -e[n]; ↑R 126 (ein Mineral); **Chry|so|pras,** der; -es, -e (ein Edelstein)
Chry|sos|to|mus [ç...] (griech. Kirchenlehrer)
chtho|nisch [ç...] ‹griech.› (der Erde angehörend; unterirdisch)

Chur [ku:r] (Hptst. des Kantons Graubünden)
Chur|chill ['tʃœ:(r)tʃil] (engl. Familienn.)
Chur|firs|ten ['ku:r...] *Plur.* (schweiz. Bergkette)
Chut|ney ['tʃatni], das; -[s], -s ‹Hindi-engl.› (Paste aus Früchten und Gewürzen)
Chuz|pe [x...], die; - ‹hebr.-jidd.› (*ugs. abwertend für* Dreistigkeit, Unverschämtheit)
Chy|mo|sin [ç...], das; -s ‹griech.› (*Biol.* Labferment); **Chy|mus,** der; - (*Med.* Speisebrei)
Ci = Curie
CIA [si:ai:'e:] = Central Intelligence Agency ['sɛntrəl in'tɛlidʒ(ə)ns 'e:dʒ(ə)nsi], die *od.* der; - (US-amerik. Geheimdienst)
Cia|co|na *vgl.* Chaconne
ciao! [tʃau] ‹ital.› (*ugs.* [Abschieds]gruß); *vgl.* tschau
¹Ci|ce|ro ['tsi(:)tsəro] (röm. Redner); **²Ci|ce|ro,** die, *schweiz.* der; - (ein Schriftgrad); 3 -; **Ci|ce|ro|ne** [tʃitʃe...], der; -[s], *Plur.* -s *u.* ...ni ‹ital.› (*scherzh. für* geschwätziger Fremdenführer); **Ci|ce|ro|ni|a|ner** [tsitsə...] ‹lat.› (Anhänger der mustergültigen Schreibweise Ciceros); **ci|ce|ro|ni|a|nisch, ci|ce|ro|nisch** (von Cicero; nach der Art des Cicero; mustergültig, stilistisch vollkommen); cicero[nia]nische Beredsamkeit, cicero[nia]nische Schriften
Ci|cis|beo [tʃitʃis...], der; -[s], -s ‹ital.› (Hausfreund)
Cid [sit], der; -[s] ‹„Herr"› (span. Nationalheld)
Cid|re ['si:dr(ə), *auch* 'si:dər], (↑R 130) **Zi|der,** der; -s ‹franz.› (franz. Apfelwein)
Cie. (*schweiz., sonst veraltet für* Co.)
cif [(t)sif] = cost, insurance, freight [kɔst, in'ʃu:r(ə)ns, fre:t] ‹engl.› (*Klausel im Überseehandel* frei von Kosten für Verladung, Versicherung, Fracht)
Cil|li [ts...] (w. Vorn.)
Cin|cin|na|ti [sinsi'nɛti] (Stadt in den USA)
Cin|cin|na|tus [tsintsi...] (röm. Staatsmann)
Ci|ne|ast [s...], der; -en, -en (↑R 126) ‹griech.› (Filmfachmann; Filmfan); **ci|ne|as|tisch**
Ci|ne|cit|tà [tʃinetʃit'ta] ‹ital.› (ital. Filmproduktionszentrum bei Rom)
Ci|ne|ma|scope ® [sinəma'sko:p], das; - ‹engl.› (besonderes Breitwand- u. Raumtonverfahren beim Film); **Ci|ne|ma|thek** [s...], die; -, -en ‹griech.› (*svw.* Kinemathek); **Ci|ne|ra|ma** ®, das; - (besonderes Breitwand- u. Raumtonverfahren)
Cin|que|cen|tist [tʃiŋkvetʃɛn...], der; -en, -en (↑R 126) ‹ital.› (Dichter, Künstler des Cinquecentos); **Cin|que|cen|to,** das; -[s] (Kunst u. Kultur in Italien im 16. Jh.)
CIO [si:ai'o:] = Congress of Industrial Organizations ['kɔŋgrɛs əv in'dastriəl ɔ:(r)gənai'ze:ʃ(ə)nz] (Spitzenverband der amerik. Gewerkschaften)
CIP [tsip] = cataloguing in publishing ['kɛtəlɔgiŋ in 'pabliʃiŋ] (Neuerscheinungs-Sofortdienst der Deutschen Bibliothek)
Ci|pol|lin, Ci|pol|li|no [*beide* tʃ...], der; -s ‹ital.› (Zwiebelmarmor)
cir|ca *vgl.* zirka (*Abk.* ca.)
Cir|ce [tsirtsə], die; -, -n (verführerische Frau; *nur Sing.:* eine Zauberin der griech. Mythologie); *vgl.* becircen
Cir|cu|lus vi|ti|o|sus [ts... v...], der; - -, ...li ...si; (Zirkelschluss; Teufelskreis); **Cir|cus** *vgl.* Zirkus
¹cis, Cis, das; -, - (Tonbezeichnung); **²cis** (*Zeichen für* cis-Moll); in cis; **Cis** (*Zeichen für* Cis-Dur); in Cis; **Cis-Dur** [*auch* 'tsis'du:r], das; - (Tonart; *Zeichen* Cis); **Cis-Dur-Ton|lei|ter** (↑R 28)
Cis|la|weng *vgl.* Zislaweng
cis-Moll [*auch* 'tsis'mɔl], das; - (Tonart; *Zeichen* cis); **cis-Moll-Ton|lei|ter** (↑R 28)
ci|tis|si|me [ts...] ‹lat.› (*veraltet für* sehr eilig); **ci|to** (*veraltet für* eilig)
Ci|to|yen [sitoa'jɛ̃:], der; -s, -s ‹franz.› (*franz. Bez. für* Bürger)
Cit|rat, Cit|rin (↑R 130) *vgl.* Zitrat, Zitrin
Ci|ty ['sɪti], die; -, -s ‹engl.› (Geschäftsviertel in Großstädten; Innenstadt)
Ci|vet [si've:, *auch* si'vɛ], das; -s, -s ‹franz.› (Ragout von Hasen u. anderem Wild)
Ci|vi|tas Dei [ts... -], die; - - ‹lat.› (der kommende [jenseitige] Gottesstaat [nach Augustinus])
cl = Zentiliter
Cl = *chem. Zeichen für* Chlor
c. l. = citato loco [ts... 'lo:ko] ‹lat.› (am angeführten Ort)
Claim [kle:m], das; -[s], -s ‹engl.› (Anspruch, Besitztitel; Anteil an einem Goldgräberunternehmen)
Clair-obs|cur [klɛ:rɔp'sky:r] (↑R 132), das; -s ‹franz.› (Helldunkelmalerei)
Clair|vaux [klɛr'vo:] (ehemalige franz. Abtei)
Clan [kla:n, *engl.* klɛn], der; -s, *Plur.* -e, *bei engl. Ausspr.* -s ‹engl.› ([schott.] Lehns-, Stammesverband; Gruppe von Personen, die jmd. um sich schart)
Claque [klak], die; -, -n ‹franz.› (eine bestellte Gruppe von Claqueuren); **Cla|queur** [kla'kø:r], der; -s, -e (bezahlter Beifallklatscher)
Clau|del [klo'dɛl] (franz. Schriftsteller)
Clau|dia, Clau|di|ne (w. Vorn.); **Clau|dio** (m. Vorn.); **¹Clau|di|us** (röm. Kaiser)
²Clau|di|us, Matthias (dt. Dichter)
Claus *vgl.* Klaus
Clau|se|witz (preuß. General)
Claus|thal-Zel|ler|feld (Stadt im Harz)
Cla|vi|cem|ba|lo [klavi'tʃɛm...], das; -s, *Plur.* -s *u.* ...li ‹ital.› (*älter für* Cembalo; *vgl.* Klavizimbel); **Cla|vi|cu|la** *vgl.* Klavikula
clean [kli:n] ‹engl., „sauber"› (*ugs. für* nicht mehr [drogen]süchtig)
Clea|ring ['kli:riŋ], das; -s, -s ‹engl.› (*Wirtsch.* Verrechnung[sverfahren]); **Clea|ring-ver|kehr,** der; -[e]s
Cle|ma|tis *vgl.* Klematis
Cle|mens (m. Vorn.); **Cle|men|tia** (w. Vorn.); **¹Cle|men|ti|ne** (w. Vorn.)
²Cle|men|ti|ne *vgl.* ²Klementine
Clerk [kla:(r)k], der; -s, -s ‹engl.› (kaufmänn. Angestellter, Verwaltungsbeamter in England u. in den USA)
cle|ver ['klɛvə(r)] ‹engl.› (klug, gewitzt); **Cle|ver|ness,** die; -
Cli|ché *vgl.* Klischee
Clinch [klin(t)ʃ], der; -[e]s ‹engl.› (Umklammerung des Gegners im Boxkampf); mit jmdm. im - liegen (*ugs. für* Streit haben); **clin|chen** (*Boxen*)
Clin|ton ['klintən] (Präsident der USA)
Clip *vgl.* Klipp, Klips, Videoclip
Clip|per ® ‹engl.› (amerik. Langstreckenflugzeug); *vgl. aber* Klipper
Cli|que ['kli(:)ke], die; -, -n (Freundeskreis [junger Leute]; Klüngel); **Cli|quen‿we|sen** (das; -s), **...wirt|schaft** (die; -)
Cli|via [...via], die; -, ...ien [...iən] ‹nach Lady Clive [klaiv]› (eine Zierpflanze); *vgl. auch* Klivie
Clo|chard [klɔ'ʃa:r], der; -[s], -s ‹franz.› (franz. Bez. für Stadt- od. Landstreicher)
Clog, der; -s, -s *meist Plur.* ‹engl.› (mod. Holzpantoffel)
Cloi|son|né [kloazɔ'ne:], das; -s, -s ‹franz.› (Art der Emailmalerei)
Clo|qué [klɔ'ke:], der; -[s], -s ‹franz.› (Krepp mit blasiger Oberfläche)

Cloth [klɔθ], der *od.* das; -[s], -s ‹engl.› (glänzendes Baumwollgewebe)
Clou [klu:], der; -s, -s ‹franz.› (Glanzpunkt; Zugstück)
Clown [klaun], der; -s, -s ‹engl.› (Spaßmacher); **Clow|ne|rie,** die; -, ...ien (Betragen nach Art eines Clowns); **clow|nesk** (nach Art eines Clowns); **Clow|nin**
Club *vgl.* Klub
Clu|ny [kly'ni:] (franz. Stadt; Abtei)
Clus|ter ['klastə(r)], der; -s, - ‹engl.› (*Chemie, Physik* aus vielen Teilen od. Molekülen zusammengesetztes System; *Musik* Klangballung; *Sprachw.* ungeordnete Menge semantischer Merkmale eines Begriffs)
cm = Zentimeter
Cm = *chem. Zeichen für* Curium
cm² = Quadratzentimeter
cm³ = Kubikzentimeter
cmm = Kubikmillimeter (*früher für* mm³)
c-Moll ['tse:mɔl, *auch* 'tse:'mɔl], das; - (Tonart; *Zeichen* c); **c-Moll-Ton|lei|ter** (↑R 28)
cm/s, *früher auch* **cm/sec** = Zentimeter in der Sekunde
c/o = care of
¹Co = Cobaltum (*chem. Zeichen für* Kobalt)
²Co, Co. = Compagnie, Kompanie (↑R 1); *vgl.* Komp. *u.* Cie.
Coach [ko:tʃ], der; -[s], -s ‹engl.› (Sportlehrer; Trainer u. Betreuer eines Sportlers, einer Mannschaft); **coa|chen** ['ko:tʃən] (trainieren, betreuen); **Coa|ching,** das; -[s] (das Coachen, bes. das Betreuen während des Wettkampfs)
Coat [ko:t], der; -[s], -s ‹engl.› (dreiviertellanger Mantel)
Co|balt *vgl.* Kobalt; **Co|bal|tum,** das; -[s] (*lat. Bez. für* Kobalt; *Zeichen* Co)
Cobb|ler (↑R 130), der; -s, -s ‹engl.› (Cocktail mit Fruchtsaft)
COBOL, das; -[s] ‹engl.› (*Kunstwort aus* common business oriented language ['kɔmən 'biznis 'ɔ:riɛntid 'lɛŋgwidʒ]; eine Programmiersprache)
Co|burg (Stadt in Oberfranken); die Veste Coburg
¹Co|ca *vgl.* Koka; **²Co|ca,** das; -[s], -s *od.* die; -, -s (*ugs. kurz für* Coca-Cola); **Co|ca-Co|la** ® [koka'ko:la], das; -[s] *od.* die; - (Erfrischungsgetränk); 5 [Flaschen] -; **Co|ca|in** *vgl.* Kokain
Co|chem (Stadt a. d. Mosel)
Co|che|nil|le [kɔʃə'niljə] *vgl.* Koschenille
Co|chon|ne|rie [kɔʃɔnə'ri:], die; -, ...ien ‹franz.› (*veraltet für* Schweinerei)
Co|cker|spa|ni|el, der; -s, -s ‹engl.› (engl. Jagdhundeart)
Cock|ney ['kɔkni], das; -[s] ‹engl.› (Londoner Mundart)
Cock|pit, das; -s, -s ‹engl.› (Pilotenkabine in [Düsen]flugzeugen; Fahrersitz in einem Rennwagen; vertiefter Sitzraum für die Besatzung von Jachten u. Ä.)
Cock|tail [...te:l], der; -s, -s ‹engl.› (alkohol. Mischgetränk); **Cock|tail‿kleid, ...par|ty, ...schür|ze**
Coc|teau [kɔk'to:] (franz. Dichter)
Co|da *vgl.* Koda
Code *vgl.* Kode; **Code ci|vil** [ko:d si'vil], der; - - (bürgerliches Gesetzbuch in Frankreich)
Co|de|in *vgl.* Kodein
Code Na|po|lé|on [ko:d napɔle'õ:], der; - - (Bez. des Code civil im 1. u. 2. franz. Kaiserreich); **Co|dex** usw. *vgl.* Kodex usw.; **co|die|ren, Co|die|rung** *vgl.* kodieren, Kodierung
Coes|feld ['ko:s...] (Stadt in Nordrhein-Westfalen)
Cœur [kø:r], das; -[s], -[s] ‹franz.› (Herz im Kartenspiel); **Cœur|ass** ['kø:ras, *auch* 'kø:r'as], das; -es, -e
Cof|fe|in *vgl.* Koffein
co|gi|to, er|go sum ‹lat., „ich denke, also bin ich"› (Grundsatz des franz. Philosophen Descartes)
cog|nac ['kɔnjak] (↑R 130; goldbraun); ein cognac Hemd; *vgl. auch* beige; in Cognac (↑R 47); **¹Cog|nac** [kɔn'jak] (franz. Stadt); **²Cog|nac** ® ['kɔnjak], der; -s, -s (franz. Weinbrand); *vgl. aber* Kognak; **cog|nac|far|ben**
Coif|feur [koa'fø:r], der; -s, -e (*schweiz., sonst geh. für* Friseur); **Coif|feu|se** [koa'fø:zə], die; -, -n; **Coif|fure** [koa'fy:r], die; -, -n (*franz. Bez. für* Frisierkunst; *schweiz. auch für* Coiffeursalon)
Co|ir, das; -[s] *od.* die; - ‹engl.› (Faser der Kokosnuss)
Co|i|tus usw. *vgl.* Koitus usw.
Coke ® [ko:k], das; -[s], -s ‹amerik.› (*Kurzw. für* Coca-Cola)
col. = columna (Spalte)
Col., Colo. = Colorado
Co|la, das; -[s], -s *od.* die; -, -s (*ugs. kurz für* Coca-Cola)
Co|la|ni *vgl.* Kolani
Cold|cream ['ko:ldkri:m], die; -, -s ‹engl.› (kühlende Hautcreme)
Co|le|op|ter (↑R 132), der; -s, - ‹griech.› (senkrecht startendes Ringflügelflugzeug)
Cö|les|tin *vgl.* ²Zölestin; **Cö|les|ti|ne** *vgl.* Zölestine; **Cö|les|ti|nus** *vgl.* Zölestinus
Co|lig|ny [kɔlin'ji:] (↑R 130; franz. Hugenottenführer)
Col|la|ge [kɔ'la:ʒə, *österr.* kɔ'la:ʒ], die; -, -n [...'la:ʒ(ə)n] ‹franz.› (*Kunst* aus Papier od. anderem Material geklebtes Bild; *auch für* literar. od. musikal. Komposition aus verschiedenen sprachl. bzw. musikal. Materialien); **col|la|gie|ren** [kɔla'ʒi:...] (aus verschiedenen Materialien zusammensetzen)
Col|lege ['kɔlitʃ, *auch* 'kɔlidʒ], das; -[s], -s ‹engl.› (höhere Schule in England; Eingangsstufe der Universität in den USA); **Col|lège** [kɔ'lɛ:ʒ], das; -[s], -s ‹franz.› (höhere Schule in Frankreich, Belgien u. in der Westschweiz); **Col|le|gi|um mu|si|cum,** das; - -, ...gia ...ca ‹lat.› (freie Vereinigung von Musizierenden, bes. an Universitäten)
Col|li|co ®, der; -s, -s (zusammenlegbare, bahneigene Transportkiste aus Metall); **Col|li|co|kis|te** (↑R 24)
Col|lie, der; -s, -s ‹engl.› (schott. Schäferhund)
Col|li|er *vgl.* Kollier
Col|mar (Stadt im Elsass); **Col|ma|rer** (↑R 103); **col|ma|risch**
Colo., Col. = Colorado
Co|lom|bo (Hptst. von Sri Lanka)
Co|lón [ko'lɔn], der; -[s], -[s] (Münzeinheit von Costa Rica [= 100 Céntimos] u. El Salvador [= 100 Centavos])
Co|lo|nel [*franz.* kɔlɔ'nɛl, *engl.* 'kœ:(r)n(ə)l], der; -s, -s ‹franz. (-engl.)› (*franz. u. engl. Bez. für* Oberst)
Co|lo|ni|a|kü|bel, Ko|lo|ni|a|kübel (*ostösterr. für* Mülltonne)
Co|lor... ['kɔlɔr..., *auch* kɔ'lo:r...] ‹lat.› (*in Zus.* = Farb..., z. B. Colorfilm, Colornegativfilm)
Co|lo|ra|do (Staat in den USA; *Abk.* Col., Colo.); **Co|lo|ra|do|kä|fer** *vgl.* Koloradokäfer
Colt ®, der; -s, -s ‹nach dem amerik. Erfinder› (Revolver); **Colt|ta|sche**
Co|lum|bia *vgl.* D. C.
Com|bine *vgl.* Kombine
Com|bo, die; -, -s (kleines Jazz- od. Tanzmusikensemble)
Come-back, *auch* **Come|back** [kam'bɛk], das; -[s], -s ‹engl.› (erfolgreiches Wiederauftreten eines bekannten Künstlers, Sportlers, Politikers nach längerer Pause)
COMECON, Co|me|con = Council for Mutual Economic Assistance/Aid ['kaunsil fɔ:(r) 'mju:tjuəl ikə'nɔmik ə'sistəns/e:d], der *od.* das; - (*engl. Bez. für* RGW; *vgl. d.*)

Co|me|ni|us (tschech. Theologe u. Pädagoge)
Co|mer See, der; - -s (in Italien)
Co|mes|ti|bles [komɛsti:b(ə)l] *Plur.* ‹franz.› (*schweiz. für* Feinkost, Delikatessen)
Co|mic ['kɔmik], der; -s, -s ‹amerik.› (*kurz für* Comicstrip); **Comic_heft, ...held, ...hel|din; Co|mic|strip** ['kɔmikstrip], der; -s, -s (Bildgeschichte [mit Sprechblasentext])
Co|ming-out [kamiŋ'aut], das; -[s], -s ‹engl.› (öffentliches Sichbekennen zu seiner Homosexualität; das Öffentlichmachen von etwas [als bewusstes Handeln])
Com|me|dia dell'Ar|te, die; - - ‹ital.› (volkstümliche ital. Stegreifkomödie des 16. bis 18. Jh.s)
comme il faut [kɔm il 'fo:] ‹franz.› (wie es sich gehört, musterhaft, vorbildlich)
Com|mon|sense, *auch* **Com|mon Sense** ['kɔmən'sɛns], der; - ‹engl.› (gesunder Menschenverstand)
Com|mon|wealth ['kɔmənwɛlθ], das; - ‹engl.› (*kurz für* British Commonwealth of Nations ['britiʃ - ɔv 'ne:ʃ(ə)nz]; Gemeinschaft der Staaten des ehemaligen brit. Weltreichs)
Com|pact|disc, *auch* **Com|pact Disc** [engl. kəm'pɛktdisk] (↑R 33), die; -, -s ‹engl.› (*Abk.* CD); *vgl.* CD-Platte
Com|pag|nie [kɔmpa'ni:] (↑R 130) *vgl.* Kompanie
Com|pi|ler [kɔm'pailə(r)], der; -s, - ‹engl.› (*EDV* Programm zur Übersetzung einer Programmiersprache in eine andere)
Com|po|sé [kõpo'se:], das; -[s], -s ‹lat.-franz.› (mehrere farblich u. im Muster aufeinander abgestimmte Stoffe); **Com|po|ser** [kɔm'po:zə(r)], der; -s, - ‹engl.› (*Druckw.* halbautomat. Schreibsatzmaschine)
Com|pound|ma|schi|ne [kɔm'paunt...] ‹engl.; franz.› (Verbunddampfmaschine; *Elektrotechnik* Gleichstrommaschine)
Com|pre|te ®, die; -, -n *meist Plur.* (ein Arzneimittel)
Com|pu|ter [...'pju:...], der; -s, - ‹engl.› (programmgesteuerte, elektron. Rechenanlage; Rechner); **Com|pu|ter_ani|ma|ti|on** (↑R 132; durch Computer erzeugte bewegte Bilder), **...bild, ...di|ag|nos|tik, ...ge|ne|ra|ti|on; com|pu|ter_ge|steu|ert, ...ge|stützt; com|pu|te|ri|sie|ren; Com|pu|ter|kri|mi|na|li|tät; com|pu|tern** (mit dem Computer arbeiten, umgehen); **Com|pu|ter_spiel, ...spra|che, ...to|mo|gra|phie** (die; -, -n; *Abk.* CT), **...vi|rus**
Co|nak|ry [kɔna'kri, *auch* ko'na:kri] (↑R 130; Hptst. von [1]Guinea)
con|axi|al (↑R 132) *vgl.* koaxial
con brio ‹ital.› (*Musik* lebhaft, feurig)
Con|cept|art ['kɔnsɛpt..., *auch* kɔn'sɛpt...] (↑R 33), die; - ‹engl.› (moderne Kunstrichtung)
Con|cha *vgl.* Koncha
Con|ci|erge [kõ'siɛrʃ, *auch* kõ'siɛrʒ], der *u.* die; -, -s ‹franz.› (*franz. Bez. für* Pförtner[in])
Con|corde [kõ'kɔrd], die; -, -s [kõ'kɔrd] (brit.-franz. Überschallverkehrsflugzeug)
Con|di|tio si|ne qua non, die; - - - - ‹lat.› (unerlässliche Bedingung)
conf., cf., cfr. = confer!
con|fer! ‹lat.› (vergleiche!; *Abk.* cf., cfr., conf.)
Con|fé|rence [kõfe'rã:s], die; -, -n [...sən] ‹franz.› (Ansage); **Con|fé|ren|ci|er** [kɔnferaŋ'sie:, *auch* kõferã'sie:], der; -s, -s (Sprecher, Ansager); **con|fe|rie|ren** [kɔnfe'ri:...] (*bes. österr. für* als Conférencier sprechen); *vgl.* konferieren
Con|fi|se|rie *vgl.* Konfiserie
Con|foe|de|ra|tio Hel|ve|ti|ca [...fø... ...v...], die; - - ‹lat.› (Schweizerische Eidgenossenschaft; *Abk.* CH)
Conn. = Connecticut; **Con|nec|ti|cut** [kə'nɛtikət] (Staat in den USA; *Abk.* Conn.)
Con|se|cu|tio Tem|po|rum, die; - - ‹lat.› (*Sprachw.* Zeitenfolge in einem zusammengesetzten Satz)
Con|si|li|um Ab|e|un|di, das; - - ‹lat.› (*veraltend für* Aufforderung, eine höhere Schule od. Hochschule zu verlassen)
Con|som|mé [kõsɔ'me:], die; -, -s *od.* das; -s, -s (Fleischbrühe)
con sor|di|no ‹ital.› (*Musik* mit Dämpfer, gedämpft)
Con|stan|tin *vgl.* Konstantin; **Con|stan|ze** *vgl.* Konstanze
Con|sti|tu|ante [kõstity'ã:t], die; -, -s [...ty'ã:t] *u.* Kon|sti|tu|ante, die; -, -n ‹franz.› (grundlegende verfassunggebende [National]versammlung, bes. die der Franz. Revolution von 1789)
Con|tai|ner [kɔn'te:nə(r)], der; -s, - ‹engl.› ([genormter] Großbehälter); **Con|tai|ner_bahn|hof, ...ha|fen, ...schiff, ...ver|kehr**
Con|te|nance [kõtə'nã:s], die; - ‹franz.› (*veraltend für* Haltung)
Con|ti|nuo, der; -s, -s ‹ital.› (Generalbass)
con|tra (↑R 130; *lat. Schreibung von* kontra)
cont|re..., Cont|re... ['kõtrə...] (↑R 130) *vgl.* konter..., Konter...
Con|trol|ler [kɔn'trɔlər, *auch* kən'tro:lə(r)], der; -s, - ‹engl.› (*Wirtsch.* Fachmann für Kostenrechnung u. -planung in einem Betrieb); **Con|trol|ling** [kɔn'tro:liŋ], das; -s ‹engl.› (von der Unternehmensführung ausgeübte Steuerungsfunktion)
Con|vey|er [kɔn've:ə(r)], der; -s, - ‹engl.› (Becherwerk, Förderband)
Cook [kuk] (brit. Entdecker)
cool [ku:l] ‹engl.-amerik.› (*ugs. für* ruhig, überlegen, kaltschnäuzig); **Cool|jazz,** *auch* **Cool Jazz** [...'dʒɛs], der; - (Jazzstil der 50er Jahre)
Cop, der; -s, -s ‹amerik.› (*amerik. ugs. Bez. für* Polizist)
Co|pi|lot *vgl.* Kopilot
Co|py|right ['kɔpirait], das; -s, -s ‹engl.› (Urheberrecht; *Zeichen* ©)
Coq au Vin [kɔk o 'vɛ̃:], das; - - - -s - - ‹franz.› (Hähnchen in Weinsoße)
Co|ra (w. Vorn.)
co|ram pub|li|co ‹lat.› (↑R 130; vor aller Welt; öffentlich)
Cord, Kord, der; -[e]s, *Plur.* -e *u.* -s ‹engl.› (geripptes Gewebe); **Cord|an|zug,** Kord|an|zug
Cor|de|lia, Cor|de|lie [...iə] (w. Vorn.)
Cord|ho|se, Kord|ho|se
[1]**Cór|do|ba** ['kɔr...] (span. Stadt); [2]**Cór|do|ba,** der; -[s], -[s] ‹nach dem span. Forscher› (Währungseinheit in Nicaragua [= 100 Centavos])
Cor|don bleu [kɔrdõ 'blø:], das; - -, -s -s [kɔrdõ 'blø:] ‹franz.› (mit Käse u. gekochtem Schinken gefülltes [Kalbs]schnitzel)
Cord|samt, Kord|samt
Cor|du|la (w. Vorn.)
Core [kɔ:(r)], das; -[s], -s ‹engl.› (*Kernphysik* wichtigster Teil eines Kernreaktors)
Co|rel|li (ital. Komponist)
Co|rin|na (w. Vorn.)
Co|rinth, Lovis ['lo:vis] (dt. Maler)
Cor|nea, die; -, ...neae [...neɛ:] ‹lat.› (*Med.* Hornhaut des Auges)
Cor|ned|beef, *auch* **Cor|ned Beef** ['kɔrnət..., *auch* 'kɔ:(r)ntbi:f], das; - (gepökeltes [Büchsen]rindfleisch); **Cor|ned|beef|büch|se,** *auch* **Cor|ned-Beef-Büch|se**
Cor|neille [kɔr'nɛ:j] (franz. Dramatiker)
Cor|ne|lia, Cor|ne|lie [...iə] (w. Vorn.); **Cor|ne|li|us** (m. Vorn.)
Cor|ner ['kɔ:(r)nə(r)], der; -s, -

‹engl.› (*Börse* planmäßig herbeigeführter Kursanstieg; *Boxen* Ringecke; *österr. u. schweiz. für* Eckball beim Fußballspiel)

Corn|flakes ['kɔrnfle:ks, *auch* 'kɔ:(r)n...] *Plur.* ‹engl.› (geröstete Maisflocken)

Cor|ni|chon [kɔrni'ʃɔ̃:], das; -s, -s (kleine Pfeffergurke)

Corn|wall ['kɔ:(r)nwəl] (Grafschaft in Südwestengland)

Co|ro|na (w. Vorn.); *vgl. auch* ²Korona; **Co|ro|ner** ['kɔrənə(r)], der; -s, -s ‹engl.› (Beamter in England u. in den USA, der ungeklärte Todesfälle untersucht)

Cor|po|ra (*Plur. von* Corpus)

Corps *vgl.* Korps; **Corps con|su|laire** [kɔ:r kɔ̃sy'lɛ:r], das; - -, - -s (Konsularisches Korps; *Abk.* CC); **Corps de Bal|let** [kɔ:r də ba'lɛ], das; - - -, - - - (Ballettgruppe, -korps); **Corps dip|lo|ma|tique** [kɔ:r diploma'tik] (↑R 130), das; - -, - -s (Diplomatisches Korps; *Abk.* CD); **Cor|pus,** das; -, ...pora ‹lat.› *vgl.* ²Korpus; **Cor|pus De|lic|ti,** das; - -, ...pora - ‹lat.› (Gegenstand od. Werkzeug eines Verbrechens; Beweisstück); **Cor|pus Ju|ris,** das; - - (Gesetzbuch, -sammlung)

Cor|reg|gio [kɔ'rɛdʒo] (ital. Maler)

Cor|ri|da [de to|ros], die; - [- -], -s [- -] ‹span.› (Stierkampf)

cor|ri|ger la for|tune [kɔriʒe: la fɔr'ty:n] ‹franz.› (dem Glück nachhelfen; falsch spielen)

Cor|so *vgl.* Korso

Cor|tes *Plur.* ‹span.› (Volksvertretung in Spanien)

Cor|tez, *span.* Cortés ['kɔrtɛs, *span.* kɔr'tes] (span. Eroberer)

Cor|ti|na d'Am|pez|zo (Kurort in den Dolomiten)

cor|ti|sche Or|gan, das; -n -s, -n -e ‹nach dem ital. Arzt Corti› (*Med.* Teil des inneren Ohres)

Cor|ti|son *vgl.* Kortison

Cor|vey ['kɔrvai] (ehem. Benediktinerabtei bei Höxter)

cos = Kosinus

Co|sa Nost|ra (↑R 130), die; - - ‹ital., „unsere Sache"› (amerik. Verbrechersyndikat)

cosec = Kosekans

Co|sì fan tut|te [kɔ'si(:) - -] ‹ital., „so machen's alle [Frauen]"› (Titel einer Oper von Mozart)

Co|si|ma (w. Vorn.); **Co|si|mo** (m. Vorn.)

Cos|ta Bra|va [- ...va], die; - - (Küstengebiet in Nordostspanien)

Cos|ta Ri|ca *vgl.* Kostarica (Staat in Mittelamerika); **Cos|ta-Ri|caner; cos|ta-ri|ca|nisch** (↑R 105)

Cos|wig (dt. Ortsn.)

cot = Kotangens

Côte d'A|zur [kot da'zy:r], die; - - (franz. Riviera); **Côte d'I|voire** [kot 'divoa:r], die; - - (*amtl. Bez. für* ²Elfenbeinküste); **Côte d'Or** [kot 'dɔ:r], die; - - (franz. Landschaft)

CO-Test ‹*zu* CO = Kohlenmonoxid› (Messung des Kohlenmonoxidgehalts in Abgasen)

Co|to|nou [kɔtɔ'nu:] (Regierungssitz von Benin)

Cot|tage ['kɔtitʃ, *auch* 'kɔtidʒ], das; -, -s ‹engl.› (*engl. Bez. für* Landhaus)

Cott|bus (Stadt an der Spree); **Cott|bus|ser,** *auch* Cott|bu|ser (↑R 103)

Cot|ti|sche Al|pen *Plur.* (↑R 102; Teil der Westalpen)

Cot|ton ['kɔt(ə)n], der *od.* das; -s ‹engl.› (*engl. Bez. für* Baumwolle, Kattun); *vgl.* Koton usw.

Cot|ton|ma|schi|ne ['kɔt(ə)n...] ‹nach dem Erfinder› (Wirkmaschine zur Herstellung von Damenstrümpfen)

Cot|ton|öl ['kɔt(ə)n...], das; -s (Öl aus Baumwollsamen)

Cou|ber|tin [kubɛr'tɛ̃:] (Initiator der Olympischen Spiele der Neuzeit)

Couch [kautʃ], die; -, *Plur.* -s, *auch* -en, *schweiz. auch* der; -s, -[e]s ‹engl.› (Liegesofa); **Couch.gar|ni|tur, ...tisch**

Cou|den|ho|ve-Ka|ler|gi [kud(ə)n'ho:vəka'lɛrgi] (Gründer der Paneuropa-Bewegung)

Cou|é|is|mus [kue'is...], der; - ‹nach dem Franzosen Coué› (ein Heilverfahren)

Cou|leur [ku'lø:r], die; -, -s ‹franz.› (*nur Sing.:* bestimmte [Eigen]art, Prägung; Trumpf [im Kartenspiel]; *Studentenspr.* Band u. Mütze einer Verbindung)

Cou|loir [ku'loa:r], der *od.* das; -s, -s ‹franz.› (*Alpinistik* Schlucht, schluchtartige Rinne; *Reiten* ovaler Sprunggarten für Pferde)

Cou|lomb [ku'lɔ̃:, *auch* ku'lɔmp], das; -s, - ‹nach dem franz. Physiker› (Maßeinheit für die Elektrizitätsmenge; *Zeichen* C); 6 - (↑R 90)

Count [kaunt], der; -s, -s ‹engl.› (engl. Titel für einen nichtbritischen Grafen)

Count-down, *auch* **Count|down** ['kaunt'daun], der *u.* das; -[s], -s ‹amerik.› (bis zum [Start]zeitpunkt Null rückwärts schreitende Zeitzählung; die letzten [techn.] Vorbereitungen vor dem Beginn eines Unternehmens)

Coun|ter|part ['kauntə(r)pa(r)t], der; -s, -s ‹engl.› (einem Entwicklungsexperten in der Dritten Welt zugeordnete [heimische] Fachkraft)

Coun|ter|te|nor ['kauntə(r)te.no:r] ‹engl.› (*Musik* Altist)

Coun|tess ['kauntis], die; -, ...tesses [...tisiz] *u.* ...tessen ‹engl.› (Gräfin)

Count|ry|mu|sic ['kantrimju:zik], (↑R 130), die; - ‹amerik.› (Volksmusik [der Südstaaten in den USA]); **Count|ry|song**

Coun|ty ['kaunti], die; -, *Plur.* -s [...ti:s] ‹engl.› (Verwaltungsbezirk in England u. in den USA)

Coup [ku:], der; -s, -s ‹franz.› (Schlag; [Hand]streich); **Coup d'É|tat** [- de'ta], der; - -, -s - [ku -] ‹franz.› (*veraltend für* Staatsstreich)

Coupe [kup], die; -, *Plur.* -s [kup] *od.* -n ['kupən], *auch* der; -s, *Plur.* -s [kup] *od.* -n ['kupən] ‹franz.› (*schweiz. für* Eisbecher)

Cou|pé, *eindeutschend* Ku|pee [ku'pe:], das; -s, -s (Auto mit sportlicher Karosserie; *österr., sonst veraltet für* [Wagen]abteil);

Coup|let [ku'ple:] (↑R 130), das; -s, -s ‹franz.› (scherzhaft-satirisches Lied [für die Kleinkunstbühne])

Cou|pon *vgl.* Kupon

Cour [ku:r], die; - ‹franz.›; *in* jmdm. die Cour machen, schneiden (den Hof machen)

Cou|ra|ge [ku'ra:ʒə, *österr.* ...'ra:ʒ], die; - ‹franz.› (Mut); **cou|ra|giert** [kura'ʒi:rt] (beherzt)

Cour|bet [kur'bɛ] (franz. Maler)

Court [kɔ:(r)t], der; -s, -s ‹engl.› (Tennisplatz)

Cour|ta|ge [kur'ta:ʒə], *eindeutschend auch* Kur|ta|ge, die; -, -n ‹franz.› (Maklergebühr bei Börsengeschäften)

Courths-Mah|ler ['kurts...] (dt. Schriftstellerin)

Cour|toi|sie [kurtoa'zi:], die; -, ...ien ‹franz.› (*veraltend für* feines, ritterliches Benehmen, Höflichkeit)

Cous|cous ['kuskus] *vgl.* ²Kuskus

Cou|sin [ku'zɛ̃:, *auch* ku'zɛŋ], der; -s, -s ‹franz.› (Vetter); **Cou|si|ne** [ku'zi:nə], die; -, -n (¹Base); *vgl. auch* Kusine

Cou|ture [ku'ty:r] *vgl.* Haute Couture; **Cou|tu|ri|er** [kuty'rie:], der; -s, -s ‹franz.› (Modeschöpfer)

Cou|vert [ku'vɛ:r], das; -s, -s usw. *frühere Schreibung für* Kuvert usw.

Co|vent|ry ['kɔvəntri] (↑R 130; engl. Stadt)

Co|ver ['kavə(r)], das; -s, -[s] ‹engl.› (Titelbild; Schallplattenhülle); **Co|ver|coat** ['kavə(r)ko:t], der; -[s], -s ([Mantel aus] Wollstoff); **Co|ver|girl** ['kavə(r)gœ:(r)l], das; -s, -s (auf der Titelseite einer Illustrierten abgebildete junge Frau)
Cow|boy ['kauboy], der; -s, -s ‹engl.› (berittener amerik. Rinderhirt); **Cow|boy|hut**
Cow|per ['kau...], der; -s, -[s] ‹nach dem engl. Erfinder› (*Technik* Winderhitzer bei Hochöfen)
Cox' O|ran|ge ['kɔks o.rã:ʒə], die; - -, - -n, *eindeutschend auch* Cox O|ran|ge, der; - -, - - ‹nach dem engl. Züchter Cox› (eine Apfelsorte)
Co|yo|te *vgl.* Kojote
cr. = currentis
Cr = *chem. Zeichen für* Chrom
Crack [krɛk], der; -s, -s ‹engl.› (*Sport* bes. aussichtsreicher Spitzensportler; gutes Rennpferd; Kokain enthaltendes synthetisches Rauschgift); **Cra|cker** ['krɛkə(r)], der; -s, -[s] *meist Plur.* ‹engl.› (sprödes Kleingebäck)
Cra|nach (dt. Malerfamilie)
Cra|que|lé [krak(ə)'le:], das; -s, -s ‹franz.› (feine Haarrisse in der Glasur von Keramiken, auch auf Glas); *vgl. auch* Krakelee
Crash [krɛʃ], der; -s, -s ‹engl.› (Zusammenstoß; Zusammenbruch); **Crash|test** (Test, mit dem das Unfallverhalten von Kraftfahrzeugen ermittelt wird)
Cras|sus (röm. Staatsmann)
Crawl [krɔ:l], **craw|len** usw. *vgl.* Kraul, kraulen usw.
Cra|yon [krɛ'jõ:] *vgl.* Krayon
Cream [kri:m], die; -, -s (*engl. Bez. für* Creme; Sahne)
Cre|do *vgl.* Kredo
Creek [kri:k], der; -s, -s ‹engl.› ([zeitweise ausgetrockneter] Flusslauf, bes. in Nordamerika u. Australien)
creme [krɛ:m, *auch* kre:m] ‹franz.› (mattgelb); ein creme Kleid; *vgl. auch* beige; in Creme (↑R 47); **Creme,** die; -, *Plur.* -s, *schweiz. u. österr.* -n ['krɛ:mən] ‹franz.› (Salbe zur Hautpflege; Süßspeise; Tortenfüllung; *nur Sing.:* gesellschaftl. Oberschicht); *vgl. auch* Krem; **creme|far|ben** *od.* **...far|big; Crème fraîche** [krɛm 'frɛʃ], die; - -, -s -s [krɛm 'frɛʃ] ‹franz.› (saure Sahne mit hohem Fettgehalt); **cre|men;** die Haut -; **Creme|tor|te; cre|mig,** *auch* kremig
[1]**Crêpe** [krɛp] *vgl.* Krepp; [2]**Crêpe,** *eindeutschend* Krepp, die; -, -s (dünner Eierkuchen); **Crêpe de Chine** ['krɛp də 'ʃi:n], der; - - -, -s - - ['krɛp - -] ‹franz.› (Seidenkrepp in Taftbindung); **Crêpe Georgette** ['krɛp ʒɔr'ʒɛt], der; - -, -s - ['krɛp -] (zartes, durchsichtiges Gewebe aus Kreppgarn); **Crêpe Su|zette** ['krɛp sy'zɛt], die; - -, -s - ['krɛp -] (dünner Eierkuchen, mit Likör flambiert)
cresc. = crescendo; **cre|scen|do** [krɛ'ʃɛndo] ‹ital.› (*Musik* anschwellend; *Abk.* cresc.); **Cre|scen|do,** das; -s, *Plur.* -s *u.* ...di
Cres|cen|tia *vgl.* Kreszentia
Cre|tonne [kre'tɔn], die *od.* der; -, -s ‹franz.› (Baumwollstoff)
Creutz|feldt-Ja|kob-Krank|heit, die; - ‹nach den Neurologen H. G. Creutzfeldt u. A. Jakob› (*Med.* eine Erkrankung des Nervensystems)
Cre|vet|te *vgl.* Krevette
Crew [kru:], die; -, -s ‹engl.› ([Schiffs-, Flugzeug]mannschaft)
c. r. m. = cand. rev. min.; *vgl.* Kandidat
Croi|sé [kroa'ze:], das; -[s], -s ‹franz.› (ein Gewebe in Köperbindung)
Crois|sant [kroa'sã:], das; -[s], -s [...'sã:s] ‹franz.› (Blätterteighörnchen)
Cro|mag|non|ras|se [kroma'njõ:...] (↑R 130), die; - ‹nach dem Fundort› (Menschenrasse der jüngeren Altsteinzeit)
Cro|mar|gan ® (↑R 132), das; -s (rostfreier Chrom-Nickel-Stahl)
Crom|well ['krɔmwəl] (engl. Staatsmann)
Cro|quet|te [kro'kɛtə] *vgl.* Krokette
Cro|quis [kro'ki:] *vgl.* Kroki
cross ‹engl.› (*Tennis* diagonal); den Ball - spielen; **Cross,** der; -, - (*Tennis* diagonal über den Platz geschlagener Ball; *kurz für* Crosscountry); **Cross|count|ry** ['krɔskantri], das; -[s], -s (Querfeldeinwettbewerb)
Crou|pi|er [kru'pie:], der; -s, -s ‹franz.› (Angestellter einer Spielbank); **Crou|pon** [kru'põ:], der; -s, -s (Kern-, Rückenstück einer [gegerbten] Haut)
Croû|ton [kru'tõ:], der; -[s], -s (gerösteter Weißbrotwürfel)
crt. = courant; *vgl.* kurant
Cruise|mis|sile ['kru:zmisail], das; -s, -s ‹engl.-amerik.› (*Milit.* Marschflugkörper)
Crux, *auch* Krux, die; - ‹lat., „Kreuz“› (Last, Kummer)
Cru|zei|ro [kru'ze:ro, *auch* kru'zɛiru], der; -s, -s ‹port.› (Münzeinheit in Brasilien)
Cs = *chem. Zeichen für* Cäsium
Csar|das, Csár|dás ['tʃa(:)rda(:)ʃ], der; -, - ‹ung.› (ungarischer Nationaltanz)
C-Schlüs|sel (*Musik*)
Csi|kós ['tʃi(:)ko:ʃ], der; -, - *eindeutschend auch* Tschi|kosch, der; -[es], -[e] ‹ung.› (ungarischer Pferdehirt)
Cso|kor ['tʃɔ...] (österr. Schriftsteller)
CSU = Christlich-Soziale Union
ct = Centime[s]; Cent[s]
CT = Computertomographie
Ct. = Centime
c. t. = cum tempore
cts = Centimes; Cents
Cu = Cuprum; *chem. Zeichen für* Kupfer
Cu|ba (*span. Schreibung von* Kuba)
cui bo|no? ‹lat., „wem nutzt es?“› (wer hat einen Vorteil?)
Cul de Pa|ris [ky də pa'ri], der; - - -, -s - - [ky] ‹franz.› (um die Jahrhundertwende unter dem Kleid getragenes Gesäßpolster)
Cu|le|mey|er, der; -s, -s ‹nach dem Erfinder› (schwerer Tieflader, auf den ein Eisenbahnwaggon verladen werden kann)
Cul|li|nan ['kalinən], der; -s ‹engl.› (ein großer Diamant)
Cu|ma|rin usw. *vgl.* Kumarin usw.
Cum|ber|land|so|ße ['kambə(r)lənd...], die; - ‹nach der engl. Grafschaft› (pikante Würzsoße)
cum gra|no sa|lis ‹lat., „mit einem Körnchen Salz“› (mit entsprechender Einschränkung)
cum lau|de ‹lat., „mit Lob“› (drittbeste Note der Doktorprüfung)
cum tem|po|re ‹lat.› (mit akadem. Viertel, d. h. [Vorlesungsbeginn] eine Viertelstunde nach der angegebenen Zeit; *Abk.* c. t.)
Cun|ni|lin|gus, der; - ‹lat.› (sexuelle Stimulierung der äußeren weibl. Geschlechtsorgane mit der Zunge); *vgl.* Fellatio
Cup [kap], der; -s, -s ‹engl.› (Pokal; Pokalwettbewerb; Schale des Büstenhalters); **Cup|fi|na|le**
Cu|pi|do (röm. Liebesgott, Amor)
Cup|rum (↑R 130), das; -s (*lat. Bez. für* Kupfer; *Zeichen* Cu)
[1]**Cu|ra|çao** [kyra'sa:o] (Insel im Karibischen Meer); [2]**Cu|ra|çao** ®, der; -[s], -s (ein Likör)
Cu|ra pos|te|ri|or, die; - - ‹lat., „spätere Sorge“› (nicht vorrangig zu klärende Angelegenheit)
Cu|ra|re *vgl.* Kurare
Cur|cu|ma *vgl.* Kurkuma
Cu|ré [ky're:], der; -s, -s ‹franz.› (kath. Pfarrer in Frankreich)

Cu|rie [ky'ri:], das; -, - ‹nach dem franz. Physikerehepaar› (Maßeinheit der Radioaktivität; *Zeichen* Ci); **Cu|ri|um,** das; -s (chem. Element, Transuran; *Zeichen* Cm)
Cur|ling [kœ:(r)liŋ], das; -s (schott. Eisspiel)
cur|ren|tis ‹lat.› (*veraltet für* „[des] laufenden" [Jahres, Monats]; *Abk.* cr.); am 15. cr., *dafür besser* am 15. d. M.; **cur|ri|cu|lar** (*Päd.* das Curriculum betreffend); **Cur|ri|cu|lum,** das; -s, ...la ‹lat.-engl.› (*Päd.* Theorie des Lehr- u. Lernablaufs; Lehrplan, -programm); **Cur|ri|cu|lum Vi|tae** [- 'vi:tɛ:], das; - -, ...la - (Lebenslauf)
Cur|ry ['kœri, *seltener* 'kari], der, *auch* das; -s ‹angloind.› (Gewürzpulver; indisches Gericht); **Cur|ry‿pul|ver** (eine Gewürzmischung), **...wurst**
Cur|sor ['kœ:(r)sə(r)], der; -s, -s ‹engl.› (*EDV* [meist blinkendes] Zeichen auf dem Bildschirm, das anzeigt, an welcher Stelle die nächste Eingabe erscheint)
Cus|tard ['kastə(r)t], der; -, -s ‹engl.› (eine engl. Süßspeise)
Cut [kœt, *auch* kat], der; -s, -s (*kurz für* Cutaway; *Boxen* Riss der Haut; *Golf* Ausscheiden der schlechteren Spieler vor den beiden Schlussrunden); **Cu|ta|way** ['kœtəwe:, *auch* 'ka...] (↑R 132), der; -s, -s ‹engl.› (abgerundet geschnittener Herrenschoßrock)
cut|ten ['katən, *auch* 'kœ...] ‹engl.› (Filmszenen, Tonbandaufnahmen schneiden und zusammenkleben); **Cut|ter** ['katə(r), *auch* 'kœ...], der; -s, - (*Film, Rundf., Fernsehen* Schnittmeister; Gerät zum Zerkleinern von Fleisch); **Cut|te|rin; cut|tern;** ich ...ere (↑R 16); *vgl.* cutten
Cu|vi|er [ky'vie:] (franz. Zoologe)
Cux|ha|ven [...fən] (Hafenstadt a. d. Elbmündung)
CVJM = *früher* Christlicher Verein Junger Männer; *heute in Deutschland:* ... Menschen
CVP = Christlichdemokratische Volkspartei (in der Schweiz)
c_w = Luftwiderstandsbeiwert
cwt, cwt. *vgl.* Hundredweight
c_w-Wert *(Technik)*
Cy|an *vgl.* Zyan
Cy|ber|space ['saibə(r)spe:s] der; -, -s [...siz] ‹engl.› (*EDV* virtueller Raum)
cyc|lisch ['tsy:k..., *auch* 'tsyk...] (↑R 130) *vgl.* zyklisch
Cy|pern usw. *vgl.* Zypern usw.
Cy|re|nai|ka [tsy...], die; - (Landschaft in Nordafrika)
Cy|rus [tsy:...] *vgl.* Kyros

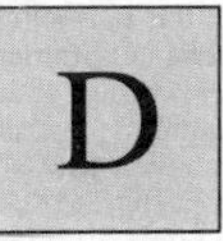

D (Buchstabe); das D; des D, die D, *aber* das d in Bude (↑R 60); der Buchstabe D, d
d = dextrogyr; Denar; Dezi...; Penny, Pence
d, D, das; -, - (Tonbezeichnung); **d** (*Zeichen für* d-Moll); in d; **D** (*Zeichen für* D-Dur); in D
d *[stets in Kursiv zu setzen]* = Durchmesser
₰ = deleatur
D = Deuterium; (iran.) Dinar
D (röm. Zahlzeichen) = 500
Δ, δ = Delta
D. = Decimus
D. *vgl.* Doktor
da; hier und da, da und dort; da (weil) er krank war, konnte er nicht kommen; *immer getrennt:* da sein, weil wir da sind, es ist alles schon da gewesen, noch nie da gewesene Ereignisse (↑R 39), *aber* das Dasein; etwas noch nie da Gewesenes, *auch* Dagewesenes (↑R 47); *vgl.* dableiben, dalassen usw.; dabei, dafür usw.
da = Deka...; Deziar
d. Ä. = der Ältere
DAAD = Deutscher Akademischer Austauschdienst
DAB = Deutsches Arzneibuch
da|be|hal|ten (zurückbehalten, nicht weglassen); sie haben ihn gleich dabehalten
da|bei [*auch* 'da:...]; sie ist sehr schön und dabei (trotzdem) gar nicht eitel; *immer getrennt:* dabei sein, weil sie dabei ist, wir sind dabei gewesen; alle dabei Gewesenen, *auch* Dabeigewesenen (↑R 47); *vgl.* dabeibleiben, dabeisitzen, dabeistehen; **da|bei|blei|ben** (bei einer Tätigkeit bleiben); er hat mit dem Training begonnen, ist aber nicht dabeigeblieben; *aber* wenn er dabei (bei der Behauptung) bleibt; falls es dabei (bei der Verabredung, bei den Gegebenheiten) bleibt; **da|bei|ha|ben** (*ugs. für* bei sich haben; teilnehmen lassen); ..., weil er nichts dabeihatte; sie wollten ihn gern dabeihaben (*vgl.* dabei); **dabei sein** *vgl.* dabei; **da|bei|sit|zen** (sitzend zugegen sein); er hat nur dabeigesessen und kein Wort gesagt; *aber* du kannst dabei (bei dieser Tätigkeit) sitzen (brauchst nicht zu stehen); **da|bei|ste|hen** (stehend zugegen sein); er hat bei dem Gespräch dabeigestanden; *aber* du solltest dabei (bei dieser Tätigkeit) stehen (nicht sitzen)
da|blei|ben (nicht fortgehen); er ist den ganzen Tag dageblieben; *aber* er ist da geblieben, wo er war
da ca|po [- 'ka:po] ‹ital.› (*Musik* noch einmal von Anfang an; *Abk.* d. c.); *vgl.* Dakapo
Dac|ca ['daka] *vgl.* Dhaka
d'ac|cord [da'ko:r] ‹franz.› (*veraltet für* einig; einverstanden)
Dach, das; -[e]s, Dächer; **dach|ar|tig**
Da|chau (↑R 132; Stadt in Bayern; ehem. Konzentrationslager)
Dach‿bo|den, ...de|cker; Dä|chel|chen; Dä|cher|chen *Plur.;* **Dach‿fens|ter, ...first, ...gar|ten, ...gau|be** *od.* **...gau|pe, ...ge|schoss, ...ge|sell|schaft** (Spitzen-, Muttergesellschaft), **...glei|che** (die; -, -n; *österr. svw.* Dachgleichenfeier); **Dach|glei|chen|fei|er** (*österr. für* Richtfest); **Dach‿ha|se** (*ugs. scherzh. für* Katze), **...haut** (*Bauw.* äußerste Schicht der Dachkonstruktion), **...kam|mer, ...lat|te, ...la|wi|ne** (vom Hausdach abrutschende Schneemasse); **Dach‿lu|ke, ...or|ga|ni|sa|ti|on, ...pap|pe, ...pfan|ne, ...rei|ter, ...rin|ne**
Dachs, der; -es, -e; **Dachs|bau** *Plur.* ...baue
Dach|scha|den, der; -s (*ugs. für* geistiger Defekt)
Dächs|chen; Däch|sel, der; -s, - (*Jägerspr.* Dachshund); **Dachs‿fell, ...haar, ...hund; Däch|sin**
Dach|spar|ren
Dachs|pin|sel (Rasierpinsel aus Dachshaar; ein Hutschmuck)
Dach‿stu|be, ...stuhl; Dach|stuhl|brand
Dach|tel, die; -, -n (*landsch. für* Ohrfeige)
Dach‿ter|ras|se, ...trau|fe, ...ver|band, ...woh|nung, ...zie|gel, ...zie|gel|ver|band *(Med.)*
Da|ckel, der; -s, - (Dachshund, Teckel)
Da|da|is|mus, der; - ‹nach franz. kindersprachl. „dada" = Holzpferdchen› (Kunst- u. Literaturrichtung um 1920); **Da|da|ist,** der; -en, -en (↑R 126)
Dä|da|lus (Baumeister u. Erfinder in der griech. Sage)
Dad|dy ['dɛdi], der; -s, -s ‹engl.› (*engl. ugs. Bez. für* Vater)
da|durch [*auch* 'da:...]; dadurch, dass er zu spät kam; dadurch, dass *u.* dadurch, weil (↑R 88)

Daff|ke *(berlin.); nur in* aus - (aus Trotz; nur zum Spaß)
da|für [*auch* 'da:...]; das Auto ist gebraucht, dafür aber billig; dafür sein, dass ...; etwas, nichts dafür können; **da|für|hal|ten** (meinen); da ich dafürhalte, dass ...; *aber* er war der Täter, obwohl niemand ihn dafür hielt; **Da|für|hal|ten,** das; -s; nach meinem -; **da|für kön|nen** *vgl.* dafür; **da|für|ste|hen** (*veraltet für* für etwas bürgen; *österr. für* sich lohnen); es steht [nicht] dafür
dag = Dekagramm
DAG = Deutsche Angestellten-Gewerkschaft
da|ge|gen [*auch* 'da:...]; euere Arbeit war gut, seine dagegen schlecht; dagegen sein; etwas, nichts dagegen haben; *vgl.* dagegenhalten, dagegensetzen, dagegenstellen; **da|ge|gen|hal|ten** (vorhalten, erwidern); sie wird dagegenhalten, das sei zu teuer; *aber* ob die Wandfarbe zu den Fliesen passt, sieht man erst, wenn man eine dagegen hält; **da|ge|gen|set|zen** (entgegensetzen, gegen etwas vorbringen); er hatte nichts dagegenzusetzen; **da|ge|gen|stel|len,** sich (sich widersetzen); die Verwaltung hat sich dagegengestellt; *aber* die Tür bleibt zu, wenn du einen Stuhl dagegen stellst
Dag|mar (w. Vorn.); **Dag|ny** [...ni] (w. Vorn.); **Da|go|bert** (m. Vorn.)
Da|gon (Hauptgott der Philister)
Da|guerre [da'gɛ:r] (Erfinder der Fotografie); **Da|guer|reo|ty|pie** [dagero...], die; - (fotogr. Verfahren mit Metallplatten)
da|ha|ben (*ugs. für* vorrätig haben); mal sehen, was ich dahabe; *aber* da haben wir den Salat!; mal sehen, was ich da habe (was ich da gefunden habe)
da|heim; daheim bleiben, sein, sitzen; von daheim; **Da|heim,** das; -s; **Da|heim|ge|blie|be|ne,** der *u.* die; -n, -n (↑R 5 ff.)
da|her [*auch* 'da:...]; daher (von da) bin ich; daher, dass *u.* daher, weil (↑R 88); **da|her|brin|gen** (*südd., österr. für* herbeibringen); **da|her|flie|gen;** ein Luftballon kam dahergeflogen; **da|her|ge|lau|fen;** ein -er Kerl; **Da|her|ge|lau|fe|ne,** der *u.* die; -n, -n (↑R 5 ff.); **da|her|kom|men;** man sah ihn daherkommen; *aber* es wird daher kommen, dass ...; **da|her|re|den;** dümmlich -
da|hier (*österr., sonst veraltet für* an diesem Ort)
da|hin [*auch* 'da:...]; wie weit ist es bis dahin?; da- und dorthin (↑R 23); dahin (an das bezeichnete Ziel) fahren, gehen, kommen; ein dahin gehender Antrag; er äußerte sich dahin gehend; *vgl.* dahindämmern, dahineilen usw.
da|hi|nab [*auch* 'da:...] (↑R 132); **da|hi|nauf** [*auch* 'da:...]; **da|hi|naus** [*auch* 'da:...]
da|hin|däm|mern; ich dämmere dahin (↑R 16); **da|hin|ei|len** (*geh. für* vergehen); die Jahre sind dahingeeilt (*vgl.* dahin)
da|hi|nein [*auch* 'da:...] (↑R 132)
da|hin|fah|ren (*geh. verhüllend für* sterben); er ist dahingefahren (*vgl.* dahin); **da|hin|fal|len** (*schweiz. für* als erledigt, als überflüssig wegfallen); **da|hin|flie|gen** (*geh. für* vergehen); die Zeit ist dahingeflogen (*vgl.* dahin)
da|hin|ge|gen [*auch* 'da:...]
da|hin|ge|hen (*geh. für* vergehen); wie schnell sind die Tage dahingegangen (*vgl.* dahin); **da|hin|ge|stellt;** dahingestellt bleiben, sein; dahingestellt sein lassen; **da|hin|le|ben; da|hin|plät|schern; da|hin|raf|fen; da|hin|schlep|pen,** sich (sich mühsam fortbewegen; *vgl.* dahin); **da|hin|schwin|den** (*geh. für* sich vermindern, abnehmen); **da|hin|se|geln** (*vgl.* dahin); **da|hin|sie|chen;** elend -; **da|hin|ste|hen** (nicht sicher, noch fraglich sein); **da|hin|ster|ben** (*geh. für* sterben)
da|hin|ten [*auch* 'da:...]; - auf der Heide; **da|hin|ter** [*auch* 'da:...]; *in Verbindung mit Verben getrennt:* sie hat sich dahinter gekniet (*auch ugs. für* sie hat sich dabei angestrengt); er wird sich dahinter klemmen (*auch ugs. für* es mit Nachdruck betreiben); wir werden dahinter kommen (*auch ugs. für* es erkennen, erfahren); was wohl dahinter steckt? (*auch ugs. für* zu bedeuten hat); er hat dahinter gestanden (*auch für* es unterstützt); **da|hin|ter|her;** dahinterher sein (*ugs. für* sich intensiv darum bemühen); **da|hin|ter klem|men, knien, kom|men** usw. *vgl.* dahinter
da|hi|nun|ter [*auch* 'da:...] (↑R 132)
Däh|le, Dälle, die; -, -n (*westschweiz. für* Föhre)
Dah|lie [...i̯ə], die; -, -n ⟨nach dem schwed. Botaniker Dahl⟩ (Zierpflanze); *vgl.* [1]Georgine
Da|ho|me *u.* **Da|ho|mey** [da(h)o'mɛ(:)] (*früher für* Benin)
Dail Ei|reann [da:l 'e:rin], der; - - (das irische Abgeordnetenhaus)
Dai|mo|ni|on, das; -s ⟨griech.⟩ (die warnende innere Stimme [der Gottheit] bei Sokrates)
[1]**Dai|na,** die; -, Dainos ⟨lit.⟩ (lit. Volkslied); [2]**Dai|na,** die; -, -s ⟨lett.⟩ (lett. Volkslied)
Dai|sy ['de:zi] (w. Vorn.)
Da|ka|po, das; -s, -s ⟨ital.⟩ (*Musik* Wiederholung); *vgl.* da capo; **Da|ka|po|arie** (↑R 132)
Da|kar [*franz.* da'ka:r] (Hptst. des Staates Senegal)
Da|ker; Da|ki|en [...i̯ən] (*im Altertum* das Land zwischen Theiß, Donau und Dnjestr); **da|kisch,** *aber* (↑R 108): die Dakischen Kriege
Dak|ka *vgl.* Dhaka
[1]**Da|ko|ta,** der; -[s], -[s] (Angehöriger eines nordamerik. Indianerstammes); [2]**Da|ko|ta** (Staaten in den USA [Nord- u. Süddakota])
dak|ty|lisch ⟨griech.⟩ (*Verslehre* aus Daktylen bestehend [*vgl.* Daktylus]); **Dak|ty|lo,** die; -, -s (*kurz für* Daktylographin); **Dak|ty|lo|gramm,** das; -s, -e (Fingerabdruck); **Dak|ty|lo|gra|phin** (*schweiz. für* Maschinenschreiberin); **Dak|ty|lo|sko|pie,** die; -, ...ien (Fingerabdruckverfahren); **Dak|ty|lus,** der; -, ...ylen (*Verslehre* ein Versfuß)
dal = Dekaliter
Da|lai-La|ma, der; -[s], -s ⟨tibet.⟩ (weltl. Oberhaupt des Lamaismus)
da|las|sen; sie hat uns etwas Geld dagelassen; er lässt mir seine Uhr da; *aber* wenn man das Bild genau da (dort) lässt, wo es sich befindet ...
Dal|be, Dal|ben (*Kurzw. für* Duckdalbe, Duckdalben)
Dal|be|rei (*landsch. veraltend für* Alberei); **dal|be|rig,** dalbrig (*landsch. veraltend für* albern); **dal|bern;** ich ...ere; ↑R 16 (*landsch. veraltend für* sich albern verhalten); **dalb|rig** *vgl.* dalberig
Dä|le *vgl.* Dähle
Da|lí [da'li] (span. Maler)
da|lie|gen (hingestreckt liegen); er hat wie tot dagelegen; *aber* lass es da (dort) liegen, wo es liegt
Da|li|la *vgl.* Delila
Dalk, der; -[e]s, -e (*südd., österr. ugs. für* ungeschickter Mensch); **dal|ken** (*österr. ugs. für* kindisch, dumm reden); **dal|kert** (*österr. ugs. für* dumm, ungeschickt; nichts sagend)
Dal|las ['dɛləs] (Stadt in Texas)
Dal|le, die; -, -n (*landsch. für* Delle)
Dal|les, der; - ⟨hebr.-jidd.⟩ (*landsch. für* Armut; Not)

dal|li! ‹poln.› (*ugs. für* schnell!)
Dal|ma|ti|en [...i̯ən] (Küstenland an der Adria); **Dal|ma|tik, Dal|ma|ti|ka,** die; -, ...ken (liturg. Gewand); **Dal|ma|ti|ner;** ↑R 103 (*auch* Hunderasse; Wein); **dal|ma|ti|nisch, dal|ma|tisch**
Dal|to|nis|mus, der; - ‹nach dem engl. Physiker J. Dalton› (*Med.* angeborene Farbenblindheit)
dam = Dekameter
da|ma|lig; da|mals
Da|mas|kus (Hptst. von Syrien); **Da|mast,** der; -[e]s, -e (ein Gewebe); **da|mast|ar|tig; Da|mast|be|zug; da|mas|ten** (*geh. für* aus Damast); **Da|mas|ze|ner** (↑R 103); - Klinge, Stahl; **da|mas|ze|nisch; da|mas|zie|ren** (Stahl mit flammigen, aderigen Zeichnungen versehen); **Da|mas|zie|rung**
Dam|bock (*Jägerspr. selten für* männl. Damhirsch)
Däm|chen; Da|me, die; -, -n (*ohne Artikel kurz für* Damespiel); **Da|me|brett**
Dä|mel, der; -s, - (*ugs. für* Dummkopf, alberner Kerl)
Da|men‿bart, ...be|glei|tung (die; -), **...be|kannt|schaft, ...be|such, ...bin|de** (*svw.* Monatsbinde), **...dop|pel** (*Sport*), **...ein|zel** (*Sport*), **...fahr|rad, ...fri|seur** (↑R 33), **...fuß|ball, ...ge|sell|schaft; da|men|haft; Da|men‿hut** (der), **...mann|schaft, ...ober|be|klei|dung** (↑R 132), **...re|de, ...sat|tel, ...schnei|der, ...toi|let|te, ...wahl** (beim Tanz); **Da|me‿spiel, ...stein**
Dam|hirsch
da|misch (*bayr.-schwäb., österr. ugs. für* dumm, albern; schwindlig; sehr)
¹**da|mit** [*auch* 'da:...]; [und] damit basta! (*ugs.*); was soll ich damit tun?
²**da|mit;** er sprach langsam, damit es alle verstanden
Däm|lack, der; -s, *Plur.* -e *u.* -s (*ugs. für* Dummkopf)
Dam|le|der; dam|le|dern
däm|lich (*ugs. für* dumm, albern)
Damm, der; -[e]s, Dämme
Dam|mar, das; -s (Harz südostasiat. Bäume); **Dam|ma|ra‿fich|te, ...lack; Dam|mar|harz**
Damm|bruch, der; -[e]s, ...brüche; **däm|men** (*auch für* isolieren)
Däm|mer, der; -s (*geh. für* Dämmerung); **däm|me|rig, dämm|rig; Däm|mer|licht,** das; -[e]s; **däm|mern;** es dämmert; **Däm|mer‿schein** (der; -[e]s; *geh.*), **...schlaf** (der; -[e]s), **...schop|pen, ...stun|de; Däm|me|rung; däm|me|rungs|ak|tiv;** -e Tiere; **Däm|me|rungs|schal|ter** (vom Tageslicht abhängiger Lichtschalter); **Däm|mer|zu|stand; dämm|rig** *vgl.* däm|me|rig
Damm‿riss (*Med.*), **...schnitt** (*Med.*), **...schutz** (*Med.*)
Däm|mung (*auch für* Isolierung)
Dam|num, das; -s, ...na ‹lat.› (*Wirtsch.* Abzug vom Nennwert eines Darlehens)
Da|mok|les (↑R 130; griech. m. Eigenn.); **Da|mok|les|schwert** (↑R 95), das; -[e]s
Dä|mon, der; -s, ...onen ‹griech.›; **dä|mo|nen|haft; Dä|mo|nie,** die; -, ...i̯en; **dä|mo|nisch; dä|mo|ni|sie|ren; Dä|mo|nis|mus,** der; - (Glaube an Dämonen); **Dä|mo|no|lo|gie,** die; -, ...i̯en (Lehre von den Dämonen)
Dampf, der; -[e]s, Dämpfe; **Dampf‿bad, ...bü|gel|ei|sen, ...dom** (*Technik; vgl.* ²Dom), **...druck** (*Plur. meist* ...drücke); **damp|fen;** die Suppe dampft, hat gedampft; **dämp|fen;** ich dämpfe das Gemüse, den Ton, seinen Zorn usw., habe gedämpft; **Damp|fer** (*kurz für* Dampfschiff); **Dämp|fer;** einen - bekommen (*ugs. für* eine Rüge einstecken müssen); jmdm. einen - aufsetzen (*ugs. für* jmds. Überschwang dämpfen); **Damp|fer|fahrt; Dampf|hei|zung; damp|fig** (voll Dampf); **dämp|fig** (kurzatmig [vom Pferd]; *landsch. für* schwül); **Dämp|fig|keit,** die; - (Atembeschwerden bei Pferden); **Dampf‿kes|sel, ...koch|topf, ...lo|ko|mo|ti|ve, ...ma|schi|ne, ...nu|del, ...ra|dio** (*scherzh. für* Radio [im Gegensatz zu den moderneren Medien wie Fernsehen und Video]), **...schiff, ...schiff|fahrt** (↑R 136); **Dämp|fung** (Abschwächung, Milderung); **Dampf|wal|ze**
Dam|wild
Dan, der; -, - ‹jap.› (Rangstufe im Budo)
da|nach [*auch* 'da:...]; sich - richten
Da|nae ['da:nae:, *auch* da'nae:] (Mutter des Perseus); **Da|na|er|ge|schenk** [...naər...]; ↑R 105 (Unheil bringendes Geschenk [der Danaer = Griechen]); **Da|na|i|de,** die; -, -n *meist Plur.* (Tochter des Danaos); **Da|na|i|den‿ar|beit, ...fass; Da|na|os, Da|na|us** (sagenhafter König, Stammvater der Griechen)
Dan|cing ['da:nsiŋ], das; -s, -s ‹engl.› (Tanz[veranstaltung], Tanzlokal)
Dan|dy ['dɛndi], der; -s, -s ‹engl.› (sich übertrieben modisch kleidender Mann); **dan|dy|haft; Dan|dy|is|mus,** der; -; **Dan|dy|tum,** das; -s
Dä|ne, der; -n, -n (↑R 126)
da|ne|ben [*seltener* 'da:...]; daneben (neben dem/den bezeichneten Ort od. Gegenstand) gehen, liegen, stellen usw.; ich will den Stuhl daneben stellen; *vgl. aber* danebenbenehmen, danebengehen usw.; ↑R 38; **da|ne|ben|be|neh|men,** sich (*ugs. für* sich unpassend benehmen); **da|ne|ben|ge|hen** (*ugs. für* misslingen); es ist danebengegangen; ↑R 38; **da|ne|ben|grei|fen** (einen Fehlgriff tun); er hat mit seiner Bemerkung ein wenig danebengegriffen; **da|ne|ben|hau|en** (*ugs. für* aus der Rolle fallen, sich irren); **da|ne|ben|lie|gen** (*ugs. für* sich irren); er hat mit seiner Ansicht danebengelegen; ↑R 38; **da|ne|ben|schie|ßen** (*ugs. für* sich irren); ↑R 38
Da|ne|brog (↑R 130 *u.* 132), der; -s ‹dän.› (dän. Flagge); **Dä|ne|mark; Da|ne|werk,** das; -[e]s (dän. Grenzwall)
da|nie|den (*veraltet, noch geh. für* [hier] unten auf der Erde); **da|nie|der** (*geh.*); **da|nie|der|lie|gen** (↑R 38); die Wirtschaft hat daniedergelegen
Da|ni|el [...i̯e:l, *auch* ...i̯ɛl] (m. Vorn.; bibl. Prophet); **Da|ni|e|la** (w. Vorn.); **Da|ni|elle** [...'i̯ɛl] (w. Vorn.)
Dä|nin; dä|nisch; (↑R 56:) Dänische Dogge; (↑R 57:) der Dänische Wohld (Halbinsel in Schleswig-Holstein); *vgl.* deutsch; **Dä|nisch,** das; -[s] (Sprache); *vgl.* Deutsch; **Dä|ni|sche,** das; -n; *vgl.* Deutsche, das; **dä|ni|sie|ren** (dänisch machen)
dank (↑R 46); *Präp. mit Gen. od. Dat., im Plur. meist mit Gen.:* dank meinem Fleiße; dank eures guten Willens; dank raffinierter Verfahren; **Dank,** der; -[e]s; Gott sei Dank!; vielen, herzlichen, tausend Dank!; hab[t] Dank!; er weiß dir dafür (*auch* dessen) keinen Dank; jmdm. Dank sagen (*vgl.* danksagen), schulden, wissen; mit Dank [zurück]; zu Dank verpflichtet; **Dank|ad|res|se; dank|bar; Dank|bar|keit,** die; -; **dan|ke!;** du musst danke sagen; danke schön!; ich möchte ihm danke schön sagen; er sagte: „Danke schön!“, *vgl. aber* Dankeschön; **dan|ken; dan|kens|wert; dan|kens|wer|ter|wei|se;**

dạnk|er|füllt *(geh.);* **Dạnk|kes|be|zei|gung** (*nicht* ...bezeugung); **Dạn|ke|schön,** das; -s; er sagte ein herzliches Dankeschön, *vgl. aber* danke!; **Dạn|kes-for|mel, ...schuld, ...wor|te** *(Plur.);* **Dạnk|ge|bet**

Dạnk|mar (m. Vorn.); **Dạnk|rad** (m. Vorn.)

dạnk|sa|gen *u.* **Dạnk sa|gen** (↑R 39); du danksagtest *u.* du sagtest Dank; dankgesagt *u.* Dank gesagt; dankzusagen *u.* Dank zu sagen; *aber* ich sage vielen Dank; *vgl.* Dank; **Dạnk|sa|gung; Dạnk|schrei|ben**

Dạnk|ward (m. Vorn.)

dạnn; dann und wann; *vgl.* dannzumal *u.* dazumal

dạn|nen; *nur in* von dannen (*veraltet für* von da weg) gehen, eilen

dạnn|zu|mal (*schweiz. für* dann, in jenem Augenblick)

Danse ma|cab|re [dã:s ma'ka:br(ə)] (↑R 130), der; - -, -s -s [dã:s ma'ka:br(ə)] ‹franz.› (Totentanz)

Dạn|te A|li|ghi|e|ri [- ...'gjɛ:ri] (ital. Dichter)

Dạn|tes, Tạn|tes *Plur.* ‹span.› (*veraltet für* Spielmarken)

dan|tẹsk (nach Art der Schöpfungen Dantes); **dạn|tisch;** Verse von dantischer Schönheit, die dantischen Werke

Dan|ton [dã'tõ:] (franz. Revolutionär)

Dạn|zig (*poln.* Gdańsk); **Dạn|zi|ger** (↑R 103); Danziger Goldwasser (ein Likör)

[1]**Dạph|ne** (w. Vorn.); [2]**Dạph|ne,** die; -, -n ‹griech.› (Seidelbast, ein Zierstrauch); **Dạph|nia, Dạph|nie** [...i̯ə], die; -, ...ien (Wasserfloh)

dar... (*in Zus. mit Verben,* z. B. dartun, du tust dar, dargetan, darzutun)

da|rạn [*auch* 'da:...] (↑R 132), *ugs.* drạn; *vgl.* dran *u. die Zusammensetzungen mit* dran; daran denken, glauben, sein, zweifeln, dass ...; er ist nahe daran gewesen, alles aufzugeben; du wirst gut daran tun, dir das zu merken; *vgl.* darangeben, darangehen usw.; **da|rạn|ge|ben** (*auch geh. für* opfern); sie wollte alles darangeben; **da|rạn|ge|hen;** er ist endlich darangegangen, die Garage aufzuräumen; **da|rạn|hal|ten;** du musst dich schon daranhalten (dich anstrengen, beeilen), wenn du fertig werden willst; *aber* wir müssen uns alle daran (an diese Vorschrift) halten; ↑R 38; **da|rạn|ma|chen** *(ugs.);* er soll einen Zettel, eine Schnur daranmachen; wir werden uns daranmachen (damit beginnen), die Kartoffeln zu schälen; *aber* was kann ich denn daran machen (ändern)?; ↑R 38; **da|rạn|set|zen;** sie hat alles darangesetzt, um ihr Ziel zu erreichen; ↑R 38

da|rauf [*auch* 'da:...] (↑R 132), *ugs.* drauf; *vgl.* drauf *und die Zusammensetzungen mit* drauf; darauf vertrauen, dass ...; darauf (auf das Ziel) losgehen, *aber* drauflosgehen *(vgl. d.)*; darauf folgen; das Schreiben und der darauf folgende Briefwechsel, am darauf folgenden Tag; wenn eine schwarze Zehn ausliegt, kann man eine rote Neun darauf legen; die Bank ist frisch gestrichen, ich würde mich nicht darauf setzen; würdest du zehn Mark darauf setzen, dass das Pferd gewinnt?; *vgl. aber* draufgehen, drauflegen usw.; **da|rauf|hịn** [*auch* 'da:...] (↑R 132; demzufolge, danach, darauf, unter diesem Gesichtspunkt); sein Vermögen wurde daraufhin beschlagnahmt; wir haben alles daraufhin überprüft, ob ...; *aber* darauf hindeuten; alles deutet darauf hin; darauf hinweisen; er hat darauf hingewiesen, dass ...

da|raus [*auch* 'da:...] (↑R 132), *ugs.* draus; sich nichts daraus machen; es wird nichts daraus werden

dar|ben (*geh. für* Not, Hunger leiden)

dar|bie|ten *(geh.);* **Dar|bie|tung; Dar|bie|tungs|kunst**

dar|brin|gen; Dar|brin|gung

Dar|da|nẹl|len *Plur.* (Meerenge zwischen der Ägäis u. dem Marmarameer)

da|rein [*auch* 'da:...] (↑R 132; *geh.), ugs.* drein; **da|rein|fin|den** *(geh.), ugs.* drein|fin|den, sich; er hat sich dareingefunden; **da|rein|mi|schen** *(geh.), ugs.* drein|mischen, sich; du darfst dich nicht überall dareinmischen; ↑R 38; **da|rein|re|den** *(seltener), ugs.* drein|re|den; er hat uns ständig dareingeredet; **da|rein|set|zen** (*geh. für* aufbieten, einsetzen); sie hat ihren Ehrgeiz, ihren Stolz dareingesetzt, als Erste fertig zu sein; ↑R 38

Da|res|sa|lam (↑R 132; frühere Hptst. von Tansania; *vgl.* Dodoma)

Darg, Dạrk, der; -s, -e (*nordd. für* fester Moorgrund, torfartige Schicht)

Dar|ge|bot, das; -[e]s (*Technik* die einer Anlage zur Verfügung stehende [Wasser]menge)

dar|ge|tan; *vgl.* dartun

da|rịn [*auch* 'da:...] (↑R 132), *ugs.* drịn; wir können alle darin (im Wagen) sitzen, *aber* drinsitzen *(vgl. d.);* der Schlüssel bleibt darin (im Schloss) stecken, *aber* drinstecken *(vgl. d.);* **da|rịn|nen** (*geh. für* drinnen)

Da|ri|us (pers. König)

Dạrk *vgl.* Darg

dar|le|gen; Dar|le|gung

Dar|le|hen, *seltener* Dar|lehn, das; -s, -; **Dar|le|hens-kas|se** (*auch* Dar|lehns|kas|se), **...sum|me** (*auch* Dar|lehns|sum|me), **...vertrag** (*auch* Dar|lehns|ver|trag), **...zins** (*auch* Dar|lehns|zins); **Darlehn** usw. *vgl.* Darlehen usw.; **Dar|lei|her** *(Rechtsw.)*

Dar|ling, der; -s, -s ‹engl.› (*svw.* Liebling)

Dạrm, der; -[e]s, Därme; **Dạrm|bak|te|ri|en** *Plur.* (die die Darmflora bildenden Bakterien); **Dạrm-blu|tung, ...bruch** (der), **...ent|lee|rung; Dạrm|flo|ra** (*Plur. selten; Med.* Gesamtheit der im Darm lebenden Bakterien); **Dạrm-in|fek|ti|on, ...ka|nal, ...ka|tarrh** (↑R 33), **...krank|heit, ...krebs, ...pa|ra|sit, ...sai|te, ...spü|lung**

Dạrm|stadt (Stadt in Hessen); **Dạrm|städ|ter** (↑R 103); **dạrm|städ|tisch**

Dạrm-tä|tig|keit, ...träg|heit, ...trakt, ...ver|schlin|gung, ...ver|schluss, ...vi|rus, ...wand, ...wind

dar|nach, dar|ne|ben, dar|nie|der (*älter für* danach usw.)

da|rọb [*auch* 'da:...] (↑R 132), drọb (*veraltet für* deswegen)

Dar|re, die; -, -n (*fachspr. für* Trocken- od. Röstvorrichtung; *auch svw.* Darrsucht)

dar|rei|chen *(geh.);* **Dar|rei|chung** *(geh.)*

dạr|ren (*fachspr. für* dörren, trocknen, rösten); **Dạrr-ge|wicht, ...malz, ...ofen** (↑R 132), **...sucht** (die; -; eine Tierkrankheit); **Dạr|rung**

Darß, der; -es (Halbinsel an der Ostseeküste); -er Ort

dar|stell|bar; dar|stel|len; darstellende Geometrie; **Dar|stel|ler; Dar|stel|le|rin; dar|stel|le|risch; Dar|stel|lung; Dar|stel|lungs-form, ...kunst, ...mit|tel** (das), **...wei|se**

dar|stre|cken (*veraltet für* hinstrecken)

Darts, das; - ‹engl.› (ein Wurfpfeilspiel)

dar|tun (zeigen); dargetan

da|rü|ber [*auch* 'da:...] (↑R 132),

ugs. drü|ber; sie ist darüber sehr böse; darüber hinaus; *in Verbindung mit Verben getrennt:* darüber fallen, fliegen, liegen; sich darüber machen (*ugs. für* mit etwas beginnen); mit der Hand darüber fahren; die Vorwürfe stören uns nicht, weil wir darüber stehen (darüber erhaben sind); *aber in Zusammenschreibung:* drüberfahren, drüberfallen, drüberfliegen usw.; **da|rü|ber hin|aus** (außerdem); es gab darüber hinaus nicht viel Neues; *aber* darüber hinausgehende Informationen; **da|rü|ber ma|chen, ste|hen** *vgl.* darüber

da|rum [*auch* 'da:...] (↑R 132), *ugs.* drum; er lässt darum bitten; darum herum; nicht darum herumkommen; er hat nur darum herumgeredet; **da|rum|kom|men** (nicht bekommen); er ist darumgekommen; *aber* weil er nur darum (aus diesem Grunde) kommt; **da|rum|le|gen** (um etwas legen); sie hat den Verband darumgelegt; **da|rum|ste|hen** (um etwas stehen); sie sah das brennende Auto und die Leute, die darumstanden

da|run|ter [*auch* 'da:...] (↑R 132), *ugs.* drunter; *in Verbindung mit Verben getrennt:* es sollen auch kleine Kinder darunter sein; darunter legen, sitzen, stehen; darunter fallen (*auch für* davon betroffen sein; dem zuzuordnen sein); ihre Schätzungen haben darunter gelegen (waren niedriger); *aber in Zusammenschreibung:* drunterfallen, drunterlegen usw.

Dar|win (engl. Naturforscher); **dar|wi|nisch, dar|winsch,** die darwinische *od.* darwinsche Lehre; **Dar|wi|nis|mus,** der; - (Lehre Darwins); **Dar|wi|nist,** der; -en, -en (↑R 126); **dar|wi|nis|tisch**

das *(Nom. u. Akk.); vgl.* der; alles das, was ich gesagt habe

da sein *vgl.* da; **Da|sein,** das; -s; **Da|seins|angst; da|seins|be|din|gend; Da|seins~be|rech|ti|gung** (die; -), **...form, ...freu|de; da|seins|hung|rig; Da|seins|kampf,** der; -[e]s; **da|seins|mä|ßig** (*für* existenziell); **Da|seins~recht, ...wei|se** (die), **...zweck**

da|selbst (*geh., veraltend für* dort)

Dash [dɛʃ], der; -s, -s ‹engl.› (Spritzer, kleinste Menge [bei der Bereitung eines Cocktails])

das heißt (*Abk.* d. h.); ↑R 67; seine Freunde werden ihn am 27. August, d. h. an seinem Geburtstag, besuchen; wir weisen darauf hin, dass der Teilnehmerkreis gemischt ist, d. h., dass ein Teil bereits gute Fachkenntnisse besitzt

[1]**da|sig** (*österr. mdal. für* hiesig)

[2]**da|sig** (*südd., österr. mdal. für* verwirrt, schüchtern)

das ist (*Abk.* d. i.); ↑R 67

da|sit|zen; wenn ihr so dasitzt ...; *aber* er soll da (dort) sitzen

das|je|ni|ge; *Gen.* desjenigen, *Plur.* diejenigen

dass; so dass *od.* sodass; auf dass *(veraltet);* bis dass *(veraltet);* ich glaube, dass ...; Dasssatz, *auch* dass-Satz

das|sel|be; *Gen.* desselben, *Plur.* dieselben; es ist alles ein und dasselbe

Das|sel~beu|le, ...flie|ge, ...lar|ve

Dass|satz, *auch* **dass-Satz,** (↑R 136)

da|ste|hen; fassungslos, steif dastehen; die Firma hat glänzend dagestanden (war wirtschaftlich gesund); ein einmalig dastehender Fall; *aber* er soll da (dort) stehen (↑R 39)

Da|sy|me|ter, das; -s, - ‹griech.› (Gasdichtemesser)

dat. = datum

Dat. = Dativ

Date [de:t], das; -[s], -s ‹amerik.› (*ugs. für* Verabredung, Treffen);

Da|tei [da...] (Beleg- u. Dokumentensammlung, bes. in der Datenverarbeitung); **Da|ten** (*Plur. von* Datum; Zahlenwerte; Angaben); Daten verarbeitende Maschinen (↑R 40); **Da|ten~au|to|bahn** (*EDV* Einrichtung zur schnellen Übertragung großer Datenmengen [z. B. über das Telefonnetz]), **...bank** (*Plur.* ...banken), **...be|stand, ...er|fas|sung, ...schutz; Da|ten|schutz~be|auf|trag|te** (der *u.* die; ↑R 126), **...ge|setz; Da|ten~trä|ger, ...ty|pis|tin, ...über|tra|gung** (↑R 132); **Da|ten ver|ar|bei|tend** *vgl.* Daten; **Da|ten|ver|ar|bei|tung** (*Abk.* DV); elektronische - (*Abk.* EDV); **Da|ten|ver|ar|bei|tungs|an|la|ge; da|tie|ren** ‹franz.› ([Brief usw.] mit Zeitangabe versehen); einen Brief [auf den 5. Mai] -; die Handschrift datiert (stammt) aus dem 4. Jh.; der Brief datiert (trägt das Datum) vom 1. Oktober; **Da|tie|rung**

Da|tiv, der; -s, -e [...və] ‹lat.› (*Sprachw.* Wemfall, 3. Fall; *Abk.* Dat.); das Dativ-e; **Da|tiv|ob|jekt; Da|ti|vus e|thi|cus** [...v... ...kus], der; - -, ...vi ...ci [...vi ...tsi] *(Sprachw.)*

da|to ‹ital.› (*Kaufmannsspr. veraltet* heute); bis dato (bis heute); **Da|to|wech|sel** (*Bankw.* der auf eine bestimmte Zeit nach dem Ausstellungstag zahlbar gestellte Wechsel)

Dat|scha, die; -, *Plur.* -s *od.* ...schen ‹russ.› (russ. Holzhaus, Wochenendhaus); **Dat|sche,** die; -, -n (*regional für* bebautes Wochenendgrundstück)

Dat|tel, die; -, -n; **Dat|tel~pal|me, ...pflau|me, ...trau|be**

da|tum ‹lat., „gegeben"› (*veraltet für* geschrieben; *Abk.* dat.); **Da|tum,** das; -s, ...ten; *vgl.* Daten; **Da|tums~an|ga|be, ...gren|ze, ...stem|pel**

Dau, Dhau [dau], die; -, -en ‹arab.› (arab. Segelschiff)

Dau|be, die; -, -n (Seitenbrett eines Fasses; hölzernes Zielstück beim Eisschießen)

Dau|bel, die; -, -n (*österr. für* Fischnetz)

Dau|er, die; -, *Plur. fachspr. gelegentlich* -n; **Dau|er~ar|beits|lo|se** (der *u.* die), **...ar|beits|lo|sig|keit, ...auf|trag, ...aus|weis, ...be|las|tung, ...be|schäf|ti|gung, ...bren|ner, ...ein|rich|tung, ...frost, ...gast** (*Plur.* ...gäste), **...ge|schwin|dig|keit; dau|er|haft; Dau|er|haf|tig|keit,** die; -; **Dau|er~kar|te, ...kun|de** (der), **...lauf, ...lut|scher, ...mie|ter;**

[1]**dau|ern;** es dauert nicht lange

[2]**dau|ern** (*geh. für* Leid tun); es dauert mich; mich dauert jeder Pfennig

dau|ernd; Dau|er~par|ker, ...re|gen, ...ritt, ...scha|den, ...schlaf, ...stel|lung, ...test, ...ton (*Plur.* ...töne), **...wel|le, ...wurst, ...zu|stand** *(Plur. selten)*

Däum|chen; Däu|me|lin|chen (eine Märchengestalt); **Dau|men,** der; -s, -; **Dau|men~ab|druck, ...bal|len; dau|men|breit;** ein -er Abstand, *aber* der Abstand ist 2 Daumen breit; **dau|men|dick;** *vgl.* daumenbreit; **Dau|men~lut|scher, ...na|gel, ...re|gis|ter, ...schrau|be**

Dau|mi|er [do'mie:] (franz. Grafiker, Zeichner u. Maler)

Däum|ling (Daumenschutzkappe; *nur Sing.:* eine Märchengestalt)

Dau|ne, die; -, -n (Flaumfeder); **Dau|nen~bett, ...de|cke, ...fe|der, ...kis|sen; dau|nen|weich**

Dau|phin [do'fɛ̃:], der; -s, -s ‹franz.› (*früher* franz. Thronfolger); **Dau|phi|né** [dofi'ne:], die; - (franz. Landschaft)

[1]**Daus;** *in* ei der -! (veralteter Ausruf des Erstaunens)

[2]**Daus,** das; -es, *Plur.* Däuser, *auch* -e ‹lat.› (zwei Augen im Würfelspiel; Ass in der Spielkarte)

Da|vid ['da:fid, *auch* ...v...] (m. Vorn.; bibl. König); **Da|vid[s]-stern** *vgl.* ²Stern
Da|vis|cup ['de:viskap], **Da|vis-po|kal,** der; -s (↑R 95) ⟨nach dem amerik. Stifter⟩ (internationaler Tenniswanderpreis); **Da|vis|po-kal|mann|schaft**
Da|vis|stra|ße ['de:vis...], die; - (↑R 95) ⟨nach dem Entdecker⟩ (Durchfahrt zwischen Grönland u. Nordamerika)
Da|vit ['de:vit], der; -s, -s ⟨engl.⟩ (drehbarer Schiffskran)
da|von [*auch* 'da:...]; er will etwas, viel, nichts davon haben; auf und davon laufen; es ist davon (von der bezeichneten Sache) gekommen, dass ...; es ist nichts davon geblieben; er kann nicht davon lassen; *vgl. aber* davonbleiben, davonkommen, davonlassen usw.; **da|von|blei|ben** (sich entfernt halten, nicht anfassen); er sollte besser davonbleiben (*vgl.* davon); **da|von, dass** (↑R 88); **da|von|ge|hen** (weggehen); sie ist davongegangen (*vgl.* davon); **da|von|kom|men** (glücklich entrinnen); er ist noch einmal davongekommen (*vgl.* davon); **da|von-las|sen;** er soll die Finger davonlassen (sich nicht damit abgeben; *vgl.* davon); **da|von|lau|fen** (weglaufen); wenn sie davonläuft; (↑R 50:) es ist zum Davonlaufen; *aber* auf und davon laufen (*vgl.* davon); **da|von|ma|chen,** sich (*ugs. für* davonlaufen, *auch für* sterben); er hat sich davongemacht (*vgl.* davon); **da|von|steh-len,** sich (sich unbemerkt entfernen); sie hat sich davongestohlen (*vgl.* davon); **da|von|tra|gen** (wegtragen); weil er den Sack davontrug; er hat den Sieg davongetragen (gesiegt; *vgl.* davon)
da|vor [*auch* 'da:...]; ich fürchte mich davor; davor war alles gut; *in Verbindung mit Verben getrennt:* sie soll einen Vorhang davor hängen; du musst einen Riegel davor schieben
Da|vos [da'vo:s] (Kurort in der Schweiz); **Da|vo|ser** (↑R 103)
Da|vy ['de:vi] (engl. Chemiker); **da|vysch** ['de:viʃ] (↑R 94); davysche Lampe
da|wai! ⟨russ.⟩ (los!); dawai, dawai! (los, los!)
Dawes [dɔ:z] (amerik. Finanzmann); **Dawes|plan** ['dɔ:z...], der; -[e]s (↑R 95)
da|wi|der (*veraltet für* dagegen); dawider sein; **da|wi|der|re|den** (*veraltet für* das Gegenteil behaupten); sie hat dawidergeredet

DAX ® = Deutscher Aktienindex (Durchschnittskurs der 30 wichtigsten deutschen Aktien)
Da|zi|en [...i̯ən], **Da|zi|er** [...i̯ər] usw. *vgl.* Dakien, Daker usw.
da|zu [*auch* 'da:...]; dazu bin ich gut; er ist nicht dazu bereit; die Entwicklung wird dazu führen, dass ...; weil viel Mut dazu (zu dieser Sache) gehört; er war nicht dazu gekommen, zu antworten; *vgl. aber* dazubekommen, dazugeben, dazugehören usw.; **da|zu-be|kom|men** (zusätzlich bekommen); sie hat noch zwei Äpfel dazubekommen (*vgl.* dazu); **da|zu-ge|ben** (hinzutun); du musst noch etwas Mehl dazugeben (*vgl.* dazu); **da|zu|ge|hö|ren** (zu jmdm. od. etw. gehören); ich weiß, dass er auch dazugehört (*vgl.* dazu); **da|zu|ge|hö|rig; da-zu|hal|ten,** sich (*landsch. für* sich anstrengen, beeilen); er hat sich nach Kräften dazugehalten (*vgl.* dazu); **da|zu|kom|men** (hinzukommen); sie ist eben dazugekommen (*vgl.* dazu); **da|zu|kön-nen** (*ugs. für* dafür können); **da-zu|le|gen** (zu etwas anderem legen); du kannst deine Tasche dazulegen; **da|zu|ler|nen** (zusätzlich, neu lernen); man kann immer noch [etwas] dazulernen
da|zu|mal; anno dazumal
da|zu|rech|nen (rechnend hinzufügen); er hat den Betrag dazugerechnet (*vgl.* dazu); **da|zu|schau-en** (*österr. für* sich anstrengen); er muss dazuschauen, dass er fertig wird (*vgl.* dazu); **da|zu|schrei-ben** (hinzufügen); er hat einige Zeilen dazugeschrieben; **da|zu-set|zen** (hinzusetzen); sie hat sich am Nachbartisch dazugesetzt; *aber* du musst dich dazu (zu dieser Tätigkeit) setzen; **da|zu|tun** (hinzutun); er hat einen Apfel dazugetan; *aber* was kann ich noch dazu tun? (*vgl.* dazu); **Da|zu|tun,** das (Hilfe, Unterstützung); *noch in* ohne mein Dazutun; **da|zu-ver|die|nen** (zusätzlich verdienen); in den Ferien hat er sich etwas dazuverdient (*vgl.* dazu)
da|zwi|schen [*seltener* 'da:...]; dazwischen hindurchgehen; dazwischen sein; sich genau dazwischen befinden (↑R 38); *vgl.* dazwischenfahren, dazwischenfragen, dazwischengehen usw.; **da|zwi-schen|fah|ren** (sich in etwas einmischen, Ordnung schaffen); du musst mal ordentlich dazwischenfahren (*vgl.* dazwischen); **da|zwi-schen|fra|gen;** er hat ständig dazwischengefragt (*vgl.* dazwischen); **da|zwi|schen|fun|ken** (*ugs. für* sich in etwas einschalten, etwas durchkreuzen); der Chef hat dauernd dazwischengefunkt (*vgl.* dazwischen); **da|zwi|schen-kom|men** (*auch übertr. für* sich in etwas einmischen); er ist dazwischengekommen (*vgl.* dazwischen); **Da|zwi|schen|kunft,** die; -, ...künfte *(veraltet);* **da|zwi-schen|re|den;** er hat ständig dazwischengeredet (*vgl.* dazwischen); **da|zwi|schen|ru|fen;** sie hat ständig dazwischengerufen (*vgl.* dazwischen); **da|zwi|schen-schla|gen** (mit Schlägen in eine Auseinandersetzung o. Ä. eingreifen; *vgl.* dazwischen); **da|zwi-schen|tre|ten** (*auch übertr. für* schlichten, ausgleichen); er ist mutig dazwischengetreten (*vgl.* dazwischen); **Da|zwi|schen|tre-ten,** das; -s
dB = *Zeichen für* Dezibel
DB = Deutsche Bücherei; Deutsche Bundesbahn (bis 1993); Deutsche Bahn (ab 1994)
DBB = Deutscher Beamtenbund
DBD = Demokratische Bauernpartei Deutschlands *(ehem. in der DDR)*
DBGM = Deutsches Bundes-Gebrauchsmuster
DBP = Deutsche Bundespost; Deutsches Bundespatent
d. c. = da capo
D. C. = District of Columbia ['distrikt əv kə'lambi̯ə] (dem Bundeskongress unterstellter Bundesdistrikt der USA um Washington)
d. d. = de dato
Dd. = doctorandus; *vgl.* Doktorand
DDR = Deutsche Demokratische Republik (1949–1990); **DDR-Bür|ger;** die ehemaligen -
DDT ®, das; - ⟨*aus* Dichlordiphenyltrichloräthan⟩ ([heute weitgehend verbotenes] Mittel zur Ungezieferbekämpfung)
D-Dur ['de:du:r, *auch* 'de:'du:r], das; - (Tonart; *Zeichen* D); **D-Dur-Ton|lei|ter** (↑R 28)
Dead|line ['dɛdlain], die; -, -s ⟨engl.⟩ (letzter Termin)
Deal [di:l], der; -s, -s (*ugs. für* Handel, Geschäft); **dea|len** ⟨engl.⟩ (illegal mit Rauschgift handeln); **Dea|ler,** der; -s, - (Rauschgifthändler)
De|ba|kel, das; -s, - ⟨franz.⟩ (Zusammenbruch; Niederlage)
De|bat|te, die; -, -n ⟨franz.⟩ (Diskussion, Erörterung [im Parlament]); **De|bat|ter** ⟨engl.⟩ (*svw.* Debattierer); **De|bat|te|rin; de-bat|tie|ren** ⟨franz.⟩ (erörtern, ver-

handeln); **De|bat|tie|rer** (jmd., der an einer Debatte teilnimmt, der debattiert); **De|bat|tier|klub** *(abwertend)*
de Beau|voir [də bo'vo̤a:r]; *vgl.* Beauvoir, de
De|bet, das; -s, -s ‹lat.› *(Bankw.* die linke Seite, Sollseite eines Kontos)
de|bil ‹lat.› *(Med.* leicht schwachsinnig); **De|bi|li|tät,** die; - *(Med.* leichter Grad der Schwachsinnigkeit)
de|bi|tie|ren ‹lat.› *(Bankw.* jmdn., ein Konto belasten); **De|bi|tor,** der; -s, ...oren *meist Plur.* (Schuldner, der Waren auf Kredit bezogen hat); **De|bi|to|ren|kon|to**
De|bo|ra (bibl. w. Eigenn.); **De|bo|rah,** *auch* De|bo|ra (w. Vorn.)
Deb|re|cen ['dɛbrɛtsɛn] (↑R 130; Stadt in Ungarn); **Deb|re|[c]zin** ['dɛbrɛtsi:n] *(im Dt. gebräuchliche Formen von* Debrecen); **Deb|re|czi|ner,** *auch* **Deb|re|zi|ner,** die; -, - (stark gewürztes Würstchen)
De|bus|sy [dəby'si:] (franz. Komponist)
De|büt [de'by:], das; -s, -s ‹franz.› (erstes Auftreten); **De|bü|tant** [deby...], der; -en, -en; ↑R 126 (erstmalig Auftretender; Anfänger); **De|bü|tan|tin; De|bü|tan|tin|nen|ball; de|bü|tie|ren**
De|ca|me|ro|ne (↑R 132), der, *auch* das; -s ‹ital.› *vgl.* Dekameron
De|cha|nat [dɛça...], De|ka|nat [deka...], das; -[e]s, -e ‹lat.› (Amt od. Sprengel eines Dechanten, Dekans); **De|cha|nei,** De|ka|nei (Wohnung eines Dechanten); **De|chant** [*auch, österr. nur,* 'dɛç...], der; -en, -en; ↑R 126 *u.* Dekan (höherer kath. Geistlicher, Vorsteher eines kath. Kirchenbezirkes u. a.)
De|cher, das *od.* der; -s, - ‹lat.› (früheres deutsches Maß [= 10 Stück] für Felle u. Rauchwaren)
de|chiff|rie|ren [deʃi'fri:...] (↑R 130) ‹franz.› ([Geheimschrift, Nachricht] entschlüsseln); **De|chiff|rie|rung**
Dech|sel, die; -, -n (beilähnliches Werkzeug)
De|ci|mus ['de:tsi...] (röm. m. Vorn.; *Abk.* D.)
Deck, das; -[e]s, *Plur.* -s, *selten* -e; **Deck‿ad|res|se, ...an|schrift, ...auf|bau|ten** *(Plur.),* **...bett, ...blatt; De|cke,** die; -, -n; **De|ckel,** der; -s, -; **De|ckel‿glas** *(Plur.* ...gläser), **...kan|ne, ...krug; de|ckeln** *(ugs. auch für* rügen; [Ausgaben] begrenzen); ich ...[e]le (↑R 16); **de|cken; De|cken‿be|leuch|tung, ...ge|mäl|de, ...kon|struk|ti|on, ...lam|pe, ...ma|le|rei; Deck‿far|be, ...haar, ...hengst, ...man|tel, ...na|me** (der; -ns, -n); **Deck|of|fi|zier** *(Seemannsspr.);* **Deck|plat|te; Deck[s]‿la|dung, ...last, ...plan|ke; De|ckung; De|ckungs|feh|ler** *(Sportspr.);* **de|ckungs|gleich** *(für* kongruent); **De|ckungs‿kar|te** *(Kfz-Versicherung),* **...lü|cke, ...sum|me; Deck‿weiß, ...wort** *(Plur.* ...wörter)
De|co|der *(Elektronik* Datenentschlüssler); **de|co|die|ren** *vgl.* dekodieren
De|col|la|ge [dekɔ'la:ʒə, *österr.* dekɔ'la:ʒ], die; -, -n [...'laʒ(ə)n] ‹franz.› (Kunstwerk, das durch zerstörende Veränderung von Materialien entsteht); **De|col|la|gist** [...la'ʒist], der; -en, -en; ↑R 126 (Künstler, der Decollagen herstellt)
Dé|col|le|té *vgl.* Dekolleté
de|cou|ra|giert [dekura'ʒi:rt] ‹franz.› *(veraltend für* verzagt)
de|cresc. = decrescendo; **de|cre|scen|do** [dekrɛ'ʃɛndo] ‹ital.› *(Musik* abnehmend; *Abk.* decresc.); **De|cre|scen|do,** das; -s, *Plur.* -s *u.* ...di *(Musik)*
de da|to ‹lat.› *(veraltet für* vom Tage der Ausstellung an; *Abk.* d. d.); *vgl.* a dato
De|di|ka|ti|on, die; -, -en ‹lat.› (Widmung; Geschenk); **de|di|zie|ren** (widmen; schenken)
De|duk|ti|on, die; -, -en ‹lat.› *(Philos.* Herleitung des Besonderen aus dem Allgemeinen; Beweis); **de|duk|tiv** [*auch* 'de:...]; **de|du|zier|bar; de|du|zie|ren**
Deern, die; -, -s *(nordd. für* Mädchen)
De|es|ka|la|ti|on [*auch* 'de:...], die; -, -en ‹franz.-engl.› (stufenweise Abschwächung); **de|es|ka|lie|ren** [*auch* 'de:...]
DEFA, die; - (= Deutsche Film-AG)
de fac|to ‹lat.› (tatsächlich [bestehend]); **De-fac|to-An|er|ken|nung** (↑R 28)
De|fä|ka|ti|on, die; -, -en ‹lat.› *(Med.* Stuhlentleerung); **de|fä|kie|ren**
De|fä|tis|mus, *schweiz. meist* Defai|tis|mus [...fɛ...], der; - ‹franz.› (Mut- u. Hoffnungslosigkeit, Neigung zum Aufgeben); **De|fä|tist,** *schweiz. meist* De|fai|tist [...fɛ...], der; -en, -en; ↑R 126 (jmd., der mut- u. hoffnungslos ist und die eigene Sache für aussichtslos hält); **de|fä|tis|tisch,** *schweiz. meist* de|fai|tis|tisch [...fɛ...]
de|fekt ‹lat.› (schadhaft; fehlerhaft); **De|fekt,** der; -[e]s, -e; **de|fek|tiv** [*auch* 'de:...] (mangelhaft); **De|fek|ti|vum** [...vum], das; -s, ...va [...va] *(Sprachw.* nicht an allen grammatischen Möglichkeiten seiner Wortart teilnehmendes Wort, z. B. „Leute" [ohne Singular])
de|fen|siv [*auch* 'de:...] ‹lat.› (verteidigend); **De|fen|si|ve** [...və], die; -, -n *Plur. selten* (Verteidigung, Abwehr); **De|fen|siv‿krieg, ...spiel** *(Sportspr.),* **...spie|ler** *(Sportspr.),* **...stel|lung, ...tak|tik; De|fen|sor,** der; -s, ...oren (Verteidiger, *z. B. in* Fidei Defensor = Verteidiger des Glaubens [Ehrentitel des engl. Königs])
De|fe|reg|gen (↑R 132), das; -s (österr. Alpental); **De|fe|reg|gen|tal**
De|fi|lee [*schweiz.* 'de...], das; -s, *Plur.* -s, *schweiz. nur so, sonst auch* ...leen ‹franz.› ([parademäßiger] Vorbeimarsch); **de|fi|lie|ren** (parademäßig od. feierlich vorbeiziehen)
de|fi|nier|bar; de|fi|nie|ren ‹lat.› ([einen Begriff] erklären, bestimmen); **de|fi|nit** (bestimmt); -e Größen *(Math.* Größen, die immer das gleiche Vorzeichen haben); **De|fi|ni|ti|on,** die; -, -en; - eines Dogmas *(kath. Kirche* unfehlbare Entscheidung darüber); **de|fi|ni|tiv** [*auch* 'de:...] (endgültig, abschließend; ein für allemal); **De|fi|ni|ti|vum** [...vum], das; -s, ...va [...va] (endgültiger Zustand); **de|fi|ni|to|risch** (die Definition betreffend)
De|fi|zi|ent, der; -en, -en (↑R 126) ‹lat.› *(veraltet für* Dienstunfähiger); **De|fi|zit,** das; -s, -e (Fehlbetrag; Mangel); **de|fi|zi|tär**
De|fla|ti|on, die; -, -en ‹lat.› *(Geol.* Abblasung lockeren Gesteins durch Wind; *Wirtsch.* Abnahme des Preisniveaus); **de|fla|ti|o|när, de|fla|ti|o|nis|tisch, de|fla|to|risch** *(Wirtsch.* eine Deflation betreffend, bewirkend)
De|flek|tor, der; -s, ...oren ‹lat.› *(Technik* Saug-, Rauchkappe; *Kerntechnik* Ablenkungselektrode im Zyklotron)
De|flo|ra|ti|on, die; -, -en ‹lat.› (Zerstörung des Jungfernhäutchens beim ersten Geschlechtsverkehr, Entjungferung); **De|flo|ra|ti|ons|an|spruch** *(Rechtsw.* Kranzgeld); **de|flo|rie|ren; De|flo|rie|rung**
De|foe [də'fo:] (engl. Schriftsteller)
De|for|ma|ti|on, die; -, -en (Formänderung; Verunstaltung); **de-**

for|mie|ren; De|for|mie|rung (*svw.* Deformation); **De|for|mi|tät,** die; -, -en (*Med.* Missbildung)
De|frau|dant, der; -en, -en (↑R 126) ‹lat.› (*veraltend für* Betrüger); **De|frau|da|ti|on,** die; -, -en (Unterschlagung, Hinterziehung); **de|frau|die|ren**
De|fros|ter ‹engl.›, **De|fros|ter-an|la|ge** ‹engl.; dt.› (Anlage im Kraftfahrzeug, die das Beschlagen od. Vereisen der Windschutzscheibe verhütet)
def|tig (derb, saftig; tüchtig, sehr); **Def|tig|keit**
De|ga|ge|ment [degaʒəˈmã:], das; -s, -s ‹franz.› (*veraltet für* Zwanglosigkeit; Befreiung [von einer Verbindlichkeit]); **de|ga|gie|ren** [...ˈʒi:...] (*veraltet für* [von einer Verbindlichkeit] befreien)
De|gas [dəˈga] (franz. Maler)
de Gaulle [də ˈgo:l]; *vgl.* Gaulle, de; **De-Gaulle-An|hän|ger** (↑R 95); **de-Gaulle-freund|lich** (↑R 96)
[1]**De|gen,** der; -s, - (*altertüml. für* [junger] Held; Krieger)
[2]**De|gen,** der; -s, - (Stichwaffe)
De|ge|ne|ra|ti|on, die; -, -en (Entartung; Rückbildung); **De|ge|ne|ra|ti|ons|er|schei|nung; de|ge|ne|ra|tiv; de|ge|ne|rie|ren**
De|gen‿fech|ten, ...griff, ...gurt
De|gen|hard (m. Vorn.)
De|gen‿klin|ge, ...korb, ...stoß
De|gout [deˈgu:], der; -s ‹franz.› (*geh. für* Ekel, Widerwille); **de|gou|tant** [deguˈtant] (*geh. für* ekelhaft); **de|gou|tie|ren** (*geh. für* anekeln; ekelhaft finden)
De|gra|da|ti|on, die; -, -en ‹lat.› (Degradierung; Ausstoßung eines kath. Geistlichen aus dem geistl. Stand); **de|gra|die|ren; De|gra|die|rung** (Herabsetzung [im Rang]; Herabwürdigung)
De|gres|si|on, die; -, -en ‹franz.› (*Wirtsch.* relative Kostenabnahme bei steigender Produktionsmenge; *Steuerw.* Abnahme des Steuersatzes bei abnehmendem Einkommen); **de|gres|siv** (abnehmend, sich [stufenweise] vermindernd); degressive Kosten
De|gus|ta|ti|on, die; -, -en ‹lat.› (*bes. schweiz. für* Kostprobe); **de gus|ti|bus non est dis|pu|tan|dum** ‹lat., „über den Geschmack ist nicht zu streiten"›; **de|gus|tie|ren** (*bes. schweiz. für* probieren, kosten); Weine -
dehn|bar; Dehn|bar|keit, die; -; **deh|nen; Dehn‿fä|hig|keit, ...son|de; Deh|nung; Deh|nungs-h,** das; -, - (↑R 25); **Deh|nungs|zei|chen**
De|hors [deˈo:r(s)] *Plur.* ‹franz.› (*veraltend für* äußerer Schein; gesellschaftlicher Anstand); die - wahren
De|hyd|ra|ta|ti|on (↑R 130), die; -, -en ‹lat.; griech.› (*fachspr. für* Trocknung [von Lebensmitteln]); **De|hyd|ra|ti|on** die; -, -en; *vgl.* Dehydrierung; **de|hyd|ra|ti|sie|ren** ([Lebensmitteln] zur Trocknung Wasser entziehen); **de|hyd|rie|ren** ([einer chem. Verbindung] Wasserstoff entziehen); **De|hyd|rie|rung** (Entzug von Wasserstoff)
Dei|bel *vgl.* Deiwel
Deich, der; -[e]s, -e (Damm); **Deich‿bau** (der; -[e]s), **...bruch** (der); **dei|chen; Deich‿fuß, ...graf, ...haupt|mann, ...kro|ne**
[1]**Deich|sel,** die; -, -n (Wagenteil)
[2]**Deich|sel,** die; -, -n (*Nebenform von* Dechsel)
Deich|sel‿bruch (der), **...kreuz**
deich|seln (*ugs. für* [etwas Schwieriges] zustande bringen); ich ...[e]le (↑R 16)
De|i|fi|ka|ti|on, die; -, -en ‹lat.› (Vergottung einer Person od. Sache); **de|i|fi|zie|ren; Dei gra|tia** (von Gottes Gnaden; *Abk.* D. G.)
deik|tisch [*auch* deˈik... (*mit Trennung* de|ik|tisch)] ‹griech.› (hinweisend; auf Beispiele gegründet)
[1]**dein;** *(auch in Briefen kleingeschrieben:)* deine, dein (dein Tisch usw.); Wessen Buch ist das? Ist es dein[e]s?; ein Streit über Mein und Dein; Mein und Dein verwechseln; *vgl. auch* deine; [2]**dein,** dei|ner (*Gen. von* „du"; *geh.*); ich gedenke dein[er]; **dei|ne,** dei|ni|ge; Wessen Garten ist das? Ist es der dein[ig]e?; *aber* grüße die dein[ig]en *od.* die Dein[ig]en (deine Angehörigen); du musst das dein[ig]e *od.* das Dein[ig]e tun; **dei|ner** *vgl.* [2]dein; **dei|ner|seits; dei|nes|glei|chen; dei|nes|teils; dei|net|hal|ben** *(veraltend);* **dei|net|we|gen; dei|net|wil|len;** um -; **dei|ni|ge** *vgl.* deine
De|is|mus, der; - ‹lat.› (Gottesglaube [aus Vernunftgründen]); **De|ist,** der; -en, -en (↑R 126); **de|is|tisch**
Dei|wel, Dei|xel, der; -s (*ugs. für* Teufel); pfui -!
Dé|jà-vu-Er|leb|nis [deʒaˈvy:...] ‹franz.; dt.› (*Psych.* Eindruck, Gegenwärtiges schon einmal „gesehen", erlebt zu haben)
De|jekt, das; -[e]s, -e ‹lat.› (*Med.* Ausgeschiedenes [bes. Kot]); **De|jek|ti|on,** die; -, -en (Ausscheidung)
De|jeu|ner [deʒøˈne:], das; -s, -s ‹franz.› (*geh. für* Frühstücksgedeck; *veraltet für* Frühstück)
de ju|re ‹lat.› (von Rechts wegen); **De-ju|re-An|er|ken|nung** (↑R 28)
De|ka, das; -[s], - ‹griech.› (*österr. Kurzform für* Dekagramm); **de|ka...** (zehn...); **De|ka...** (Zehn...; das Zehnfache einer Einheit, z. B. Dekameter = 10 Meter; *Zeichen* da); **De|kab|rist** (↑R 130), der; -en, -en (↑R 126) ‹griech.-russ.› (Teilnehmer an dem Aufstand im Dezember 1825 in Russland); **De|ka|de,** die; -, -n ‹griech.› (zehn Stück; Zeitraum von zehn Tagen, Wochen, Monaten oder Jahren)
de|ka|dent ‹lat.› (im Verfall begriffen); **De|ka|denz,** die; - ([kultureller] Verfall, Niedergang)
de|ka|disch ‹griech.› (zehnteilig); -er Logarithmus, -es System *(Math.);* **De|ka|e|der,** das; -s, - (Zehnflächner); **De|ka|gramm** [*auch* ˈdɛka...] (10 g; *Zeichen* dag); *vgl.* Deka; **De|ka|li|ter** [*auch* ˈdɛka...] (10 l; *Zeichen* dal)
De|kal|kier|pa|pier ‹lat.; griech.› (für den Druck von Abziehbildern)
De|ka|log, der; -[e]s ‹griech.› (*christl. Rel.* die Zehn Gebote)
De|ka|me|ron (↑R 132), das; -s ‹ital.› (Boccaccios Erzählungen der „zehn Tage"); *vgl.* Decamerone
De|ka|me|ter [*auch* ˈdɛka...] ‹griech.› (10 m; *Zeichen* dam)
De|kan, der; -s, -e ‹lat.› (Vorsteher einer Fakultät; Amtsbezeichnung für Geistliche); *vgl.* Dechant; **De|ka|nat,** das; -[e]s, -e (Amt, Bezirk eines Dekans); *vgl.* Dechanat; **De|ka|nei** (Wohnung eines Dekans); *vgl.* Dechanei; **De|ka|nin**
de|kan|tie|ren ‹franz.› (*bes. Chemie* [eine Flüssigkeit vom Bodensatz] abgießen)
de|ka|pie|ren ‹franz.› (*fachspr. für* [Metalle] abbeizen; entzundern)
De|ka|po|de, der; -n, -n *meist Plur.;* ↑R 126 ‹griech.› (*Zool.* Zehnfußkrebs)
De|kar (↑R 132), das; -s, -e; 3 - (↑R 90) *u. schweiz.* **De|ka|re,** die; -, -n ‹lat.› (10 Ar)
de|kar|tel|lie|ren, de|kar|tel|li|sie|ren ‹franz.› (*Wirtsch.* Kartelle entflechten, auflösen); **De|kar|tel|li|sie|rung**
De|ka|ster, der; -s, *Plur.* -e *u.* -s ‹griech.› (10 Ster = 10 m^3)
De|ka|teur [dekaˈtø:r], der; -s, -e ‹franz.› (*Textilw.* Fachmann, der dekatiert); **de|ka|tie|ren** (bes. Wollstoffe durch Dämpfen

krumpffrei und bügelecht machen); **De|ka|tie|rer** *vgl.* Dekateur; **De|ka|tur,** die; -, -en (Vorgang des Dekatierens)

De|kla|ma|ti|on (↑R 132), die; -, -en ‹lat.› (kunstgerechter Vortrag [einer Dichtung]); **De|kla|ma|tor,** der; -s, ...oren; **de|kla|ma|to|risch; de|kla|mie|ren**

De|kla|ra|ti|on (↑R 132), die; -, -en ‹lat.› ([öffentl.] Erklärung; Steuer-, Zollerklärung; Inhalts-, Wertangabe); **de|kla|ra|tiv;** von rein deklarativem Charakter; **de|kla|ra|to|risch;** deklaratorische Urkunde; **de|kla|rie|ren; De|kla|rie|rung**

de|klas|sie|ren ‹lat.› (herabsetzen; *Sport* [einen Gegner] überlegen besiegen); **De|klas|sie|rung**

de|kli|na|bel ‹lat.› (*Sprachw.* veränderlich, beugbar); ...ab|le (↑R 130) Wörter; **De|kli|na|ti|on,** die; -, -en (*Sprachw.* Beugung der Substantive, Adjektive, Pronomen u. Numeralien; *Geophysik* Abweichung der Richtung einer Magnetnadel von der wahren Nordrichtung; *Astron.* Abweichung, Winkelabstand eines Gestirns vom Himmelsäquator); **De|kli|na|ti|ons|en|dung** *(Sprachw.)*; **De|kli|na|tor,** der; -s, ...oren *u.* **De|kli|na|to|ri|um,** das; -s, ...ien [...iən] (*Geophysik* Gerät zur Bestimmung [zeitlicher Änderungen] der Deklination); **de|kli|nier|bar** (*Sprachw.* beugbar); **de|kli|nie|ren** (*Sprachw.* [Substantive, Adjektive, Pronomen u. Numeralien] beugen)

de|ko|die|ren, *in der Technik meist* de|co|die|ren (eine Nachricht entschlüsseln); **De|ko|die|rung**

De|kokt, das; -[e]s, -e ‹lat.› (*Pharm.* Abkochung, Absud [von Arzneimitteln])

De|kolle|té, *eindeutschend* De|kolle|tee [dekɔl'te:], das; -s, -s ‹franz.› (tiefer [Kleid]ausschnitt); **de|kolle|tie|ren; de|kolle|tiert**

De|ko|lo|ni|sa|ti|on, die; -, -en ‹nlat.› (Entlassung einer Kolonie aus der Abhängigkeit vom Mutterland); **de|ko|lo|ni|sie|ren; De|ko|lo|ni|sie|rung**

de|ko|lo|rie|ren (*fachspr.* entfärben, ausbleichen)

de|kom|po|nie|ren ‹lat.› (zerlegen [in die Grundbestandteile]); **De|kom|po|si|ti|on,** die; -, -en; **de|kom|po|si|to|risch** (*geh. für* zersetzend, zerstörend)

De|kom|pres|si|on, die; -, -en ‹lat.› (*Technik* Druckabfall; Druckentlastung); **de|kom|pri|mie|ren**

De|kon|ta|mi|na|ti|on, die; -, -en ‹nlat.› (Entgiftung; Entseuchung; Beseitigung od. Verringerung radioaktiver Verstrahlung); **de|kon|ta|mi|nie|ren; De|kon|ta|mi|nie|rung**

De|kon|zent|ra|ti|on, die; -, -en ‹nlat.› (Zerstreuung, Zersplitterung); **de|kon|zent|rie|ren**

De|kor, der *od.* das; -s, *Plur.* -s *u.* -e ‹franz.› ([farbige] Verzierung, Ausschmückung, Vergoldung; Muster); **De|ko|ra|teur** [...'tø:r], der; -s, -e; **De|ko|ra|teu|rin** [...'tø:rin]; **De|ko|ra|ti|on,** die; -, -en; **De|ko|ra|ti|ons‿ma|ler, ...pa|pier, ...stoff; de|ko|ra|tiv; de|ko|rie|ren** (ausschmücken, gestalten; mit einem Orden ehren); **De|ko|rie|rung** (*auch für* Auszeichnung mit Orden u. Ä.)

De|kort [de'ko:r, *auch* de'kɔrt], der; -s, *Plur.* -s *u. (bei dt. Ausspr.)* -e ‹franz.› (*Wirtsch.* Zahlungsabzug wegen Mindergewicht, Qualitätsmangel u. Ä.; Preisnachlass); **de|kor|tie|ren**

De|ko|rum, das; -s ‹lat.› (*veraltend für* Anstand, Schicklichkeit); das - wahren

De|ko|stoff (*Kurzform für* Dekorationsstoff)

DEKRA = Deutscher Kraftfahrzeug-Überwachungsverein

De|kre|ment, das; -[e]s, -e ‹lat.› (*Med.* Abklingen einer Krankheit; Verminderung, Verfall)

De|kre|pi|ta|ti|on, die; -, -en (*Chemie* Verpuffen, knisterndes Zerplatzen [von Kristallen beim Erhitzen]); **de|kre|pi|tie|ren**

De|kre|scen|do *vgl.* Decrescendo; **De|kres|zenz,** die; -, -en (*fachspr. für* Abnahme)

Dek|ret (↑R 130), das; -[e]s, -e ‹lat.› (Beschluss; Verordnung; behördliche, richterliche Verfügung); **Dek|re|ta|le,** das; -, ...lien [...iən] *od.* die; -, -n *meist Plur.* ([päpstlicher] Entscheid); **dek|re|tie|ren**

De|ku|ma|ten|land, De|ku|mat|land, das; -[e]s ‹lat.; dt., „Zehntland"› (altröm. Kolonialgebiet zw. Rhein, Main u. Neckar)

de|ku|pie|ren ‹franz.› (ausschneiden, aussägen); **De|ku|pier|sä|ge** (Schweif-, Laubsäge)

De|ku|rie [...iə], die; -, -n ‹lat.› (*bei den Römern urspr.* Abteilung von zehn Mann; *dann allgemein für* Gruppe von Senatoren, Richtern, Rittern); **De|ku|rio,** der; *Gen.* -s *u.* ...onen, *Plur.* ...onen (*urspr.* Vorsteher einer Dekurie; *dann auch* Mitglied des Gemeinderates in altröm. Städten)

De|ku|vert [...'ve:r, *auch* ...'vɛ:r], das; -s, -s ‹franz.› (*Börse* Überschuss der Baissegeschäfte über die Haussegeschäfte); **de|kuv|rie|ren** (↑R 130; *geh. für* entlarven); **De|kuv|rie|rung** *(geh.)*

del. = deleatur; delineavit

Del. = [1]Delaware

De|la|croix [dəla'kroa], Eugène [ø'ʒɛ(:)n] (franz. Maler)

[1]**De|la|ware** ['dɛləwɛ:(r)] (Staat in den USA; *Abk.* Del.); [2]**De|la|wa|re** [dela'va:rə], der; -n, -n; ↑R 126 (Angehöriger eines nordamerik. Indianerstammes)

de|le|a|tur ‹lat., „man streiche"› (*Druckw.* Anweisung zur Streichung; *Abk.* del.; *Zeichen* ₰); **De|le|a|tur,** das; -s, - (*Druckw.* Tilgungszeichen ₰); **De|le|a|tur|zei|chen**

De|le|gat, der; -en, -en (↑R 126) ‹lat.› (Bevollmächtigter); Apostolischer -; **De|le|ga|ti|on,** die; -, -en (Abordnung); **De|le|ga|ti|ons‿lei|ter** (der), **...mit|glied; de|le|gie|ren** (abordnen; auf einen anderen übertragen); **De|le|gier|te,** der *u.* die; -n, -n; ↑R 5 ff. (Abgesandte[r], Mitglied einer Delegation); **De|le|gier|ten‿kon|fe|renz, ...ver|samm|lung; De|le|gie|rung**

de|lek|tie|ren ‹lat.› (*geh. für* ergötzen, erfreuen); sich -

de|le|tär ‹nlat.› (*Med.* tödlich, verderblich)

Del|fin, del|fin|schwim|men usw. *vgl.* Delphin, delphinschwimmen usw.

Delft (niederl. Stadt); **Delf|ter** (↑R 103); Delfter Fayencen

Del|hi ['de:li] (Hptst. der Republik Indien); *vgl.* Neu-Delhi

De|lia (w. Vorn.)

de|li|kat; ‹franz.› (lecker, wohlschmeckend; zart; heikel); **De|li|ka|tes|se,** die; -, -n (Leckerbissen; Feinkost; *nur Sing.*: Zartgefühl); **De|li|ka|tes|sen|ge|schäft, De|li|ka|tess|ge|schäft; De|li|ka|tess|gur|ke; De|li|ka|tess|senf** (↑R 136), **De|li|kat|la|den** (*ehem. in der DDR* Geschäft für hochwertige Lebens- u. Genussmittel)

De|likt, das; -[e]s, -e ‹lat.› (Vergehen; Straftat)

De|li|la (w. Vorn.; bibl. w. Eigenn.)

de|lin., del. = delineavit; **de|li|ne|a|vit** [...vit] ‹lat., „hat [es] gezeichnet"› (unter Bildern; *Abk.* del., delin.)

de|lin|quent ‹lat.› (straffällig, verbrecherisch); **De|lin|quent,** der; -en, -en; ↑R 126 (Übeltäter); **De|lin|quenz,** die; - (*fachspr. für* Straffälligkeit)

de|li|rie|ren ‹lat.› (*Med.* irre sein, irrereden); **De|li|ri|um,** das; -s, ...ien [...iən] (Bewusstseinstrübung mit Sinnestäuschungen u. Wahnideen); **De|li|ri|um tre|mens,** das; - - (Säuferwahnsinn)
de|lisch (von Delos); (↑R 104): das delische Problem (von Apollo den Griechen gestellte Aufgabe, seinen würfelförmigen Altar auf Delos zu verdoppeln), *aber* (↑R 108): der Delische Bund
de|li|zi|ös; ‹franz.› (*geh. für* köstlich); **De|li|zi|us,** der; -, -; *vgl.* Golden Delicious
Del|kre|de|re, das; -, - ‹ital.› (*Wirtsch.* Haftung; Wertberichtigung für voraussichtliche Ausfälle)
Del|le, die; -, -n (*landsch. für* [leichte] Vertiefung; Beule)
de|lo|gie|ren [...'ʒi:...] ‹franz.› (*bes. österr. für* jmdn. zum Auszug aus einer Wohnung veranlassen od. zwingen); **De|lo|gie|rung** (Zwangsräumung)
De|los (Insel im Ägäischen Meer)
Del|phi (altgriech. Orakelstätte)
Del|phin, *auch* Del|fin (↑R 33), der; -s, -e ‹griech.› (ein Zahnwal); **Del|phi|na|ri|um** (↑R 33), das; -s, ...ien [...iən] (Anlage zur Pflege, Züchtung und Dressur von Delphinen); **Del|phi|no|lo|ge** (↑R 33), der; -n, -n (↑R 197; Delphinforscher); **del|phin|schwim|men** (↑R 33; *im Allg. nur im Infinitiv gebr.*); **Del|phin₋schwim|men** (↑R 33; das; -s), **...schwim|mer, ...sprung**
del|phisch; (↑R 104): ein delphisches (doppelsinniges) Orakel; *aber* das Delphische (in Delphi bestehende) Orakel
[1]**Del|ta,** das; -[s], -s (griech. Buchstabe: Δ, δ); [2]**Del|ta,** das; -s, *Plur.* -s *u.* ...ten (fächerförmiges Gebiet im Bereich einer mehrarmigen Flussmündung); **del|ta|för|mig; Del|ta|strah|len, δ-Strah|len** *Plur.* (beim Durchgang radioaktiver Strahlung durch Materie freigesetzte Elektronenstrahlen); **Del|to|id,** das; -[e]s, -e ‹griech.› (Viereck aus zwei gleichschenkligen Dreiecken)
de Luxe [də'lyks] ‹franz.› (aufs Beste ausgestattet, mit allem Luxus); **De-Luxe-Aus|stat|tung**
dem *vgl.* der
De|ma|go|ge (↑R 132), der; -n, -n (↑R 126) ‹griech.› (Volksverführer, -aufwiegler); **De|ma|go|gie,** die; -, ...ien; **De|ma|go|gin, de|ma|go|gisch**
De|mant [*auch* de'mant], der; -[e]s, -e ‹franz.› (*geh. für* Diamant); **de|man|ten** (*geh. für* diamanten); **De|man|to|id,** der; -[e]s, -e ‹griech.› (ein Mineral)
De|mar|che [de'marʃ(ə)], die; -, -n ‹franz.› (diplomatischer Schritt, mündlich vorgetragener diplomatischer Einspruch)
De|mar|ka|ti|on, die; -, -en ‹franz.› (Abgrenzung); **De|mar|ka|ti|ons|li|nie; de|mar|kie|ren; De|mar|kie|rung**
de|mas|kie|ren ‹franz.› (entlarven); sich - (die Maske abnehmen); **De|mas|kie|rung**
De|men (*Plur. von* Demos)
dem|ent|ge|gen (dagegen)
De|men|ti, das; -s, -s ‹lat.› (offizieller Widerruf; Berichtigung)
De|men|tia, die; -, ...tiae [...tsiε:] ‹lat.› (*svw.* Demenz)
de|men|tie|ren ‹lat.› (widerrufen; für unwahr erklären)
dem|ent|spre|chend; er war müde und dementsprechend ungehalten, *aber* eine dem [Gesagten] entsprechende Antwort (↑R 40)
De|menz, die; -, -en ‹lat.› (*Med.* erworbener Schwachsinn)
De|me|rit, der; -en, -en (↑R 126) ‹franz.› (*kath. Kirche* straffällig gewordener Geistlicher)
De|me|ter [*österr. meist* 'de:...] (griech. Göttin des Ackerbaues)
dem|ge|gen|über (↑R 132; anderseits), *aber* dem [Mann] gegenüber saß ...; **dem|ge|mäß**
De|mi|john ['de:midʒɔn], der; -s, -s ‹engl.› (Korbflasche)
de|mi|li|ta|ri|sie|ren (entmilitarisieren); **De|mi|li|ta|ri|sie|rung**
De|mi|mon|de [dəmi'mõ:d(ə)], die; - ‹franz.› („Halbwelt")
de|mi|nu|tiv usw. (*Nebenform von* diminutiv usw.)
de|mi-sec [...'sεk] ‹franz.› (halbtrocken [von Schaumweinen])
De|mis|si|on ‹franz.› (Rücktritt eines Ministers od. einer Regierung); **De|mis|si|o|när,** der; -s, -e (*schweiz. für* Funktionär, der seinen Rücktritt erklärt hat); **de|mis|si|o|nie|ren**
De|mi|urg, der; *Gen.* -en (↑R 126) *u.* -s ‹griech.› (Weltschöpfer, göttlicher Weltbaumeister [bei Platon u. in der Gnosis])
dem|nach; dem|nächst [*auch* ...'nε:çst]
De|mo [*auch* 'dεmo], die; -, -s (*ugs. kurz für* Demonstration)
De|mo|bi|li|sa|ti|on, die; -, -en ‹lat.›; **de|mo|bi|li|sie|ren** (den Kriegszustand beenden); **De|mo|bi|li|sie|rung; De|mo|bil|ma|chung**
De|mo|graph, der; -en, -en (↑R 126) ‹griech.› (jmd., der berufsmäßig Demographie betreibt); **De|mo|gra|phie,** die; -, ...ien (Bevölkerungsstatistik, -wissenschaft); **De|mo|gra|phin; de|mo|gra|phisch**
De|moi|selle [demoa'zεl], die; -, -n [...ən] ‹franz.› (*veraltet für* unverheiratete Frau)
De|mo|krat, der; -en, -en (↑R 126) ‹griech.›; **De|mo|kra|tie,** die; -, ...ien ‹griech., „Volksherrschaft"› (Staatsform, in der die vom Volk gewählten Vertreter die Herrschaft ausüben); mittelbare, parlamentarische, repräsentative, unmittelbare -; **De|mo|kra|tie|ver|ständ|nis; De|mo|kra|tin; de|mo|kra|tisch;** eine demokratische Verfassung, demokratische Wahlen; *aber* (↑R 108): Freie Demokratische Partei (*Abk.* F.D.P.); Partei des Demokratischen Sozialismus (*Abk.* PDS); **de|mo|kra|ti|sie|ren; De|mo|kra|ti|sie|rung**
De|mo|krit (griech. Philosoph); **De|mo|kri|tos** *vgl.* Demokrit
de|mo|lie|ren ‹franz.› (gewaltsam beschädigen); **De|mo|lie|rung**
de|mo|ne|ti|sie|ren ‹franz.› (*Bankw.* [Münzen] aus dem Verkehr ziehen); **De|mo|ne|ti|sie|rung**
De|monst|rant (↑R 130), der; -en, -en (↑R 126) ‹lat.›; **De|monst|ran|tin; De|monst|ra|ti|on,** die; -, -en ([Protest]kundgebung; nachdrückliche Bekundung; Veranschaulichung); **De|monst|ra|ti|ons₋ma|te|ri|al, ...ob|jekt, ...recht, ...ver|bot, ...zug; de|monst|ra|tiv; De|monst|ra|tiv,** das; -s, -e [...və]; *vgl.* Demonstrativpronomen; **De|monst|ra|tiv|pro|no|men;** (*Sprachw.* hinweisendes Fürwort, z. B. „dieser, diese, dieses"); **De|monst|ra|tor,** der; -s, ...oren (Vorführer); **de|monst|rie|ren** (beweisen, vorführen; eine Demonstration veranstalten, daran teilnehmen)
De|mon|ta|ge [demɔn'ta:ʒə, *auch* demɔŋ'ta:ʒə, *österr.* ...'ta:ʒ] ‹franz.› (Abbau, Abbruch [insbes. von Industrieanlagen]); **de|mon|tie|ren; De|mon|tie|rung**
De|mo|ra|li|sa|ti|on, die; -, -en ‹franz.› (Untergrabung der Moral; Entmutigung); **de|mo|ra|li|sie|ren** (jmdm. entmutigen); **De|mo|ra|li|sie|rung**
de mor|tu|is nil ni|si be|ne ‹lat.› („von den Toten [soll man] nur gut [sprechen]")
De|mos, der; -, Demen (*früher* altgriech. Stadtstaat; *heute* in Griechenland kleinster staatl. Verwal-

tungsbezirk); **De|mo|skop** (↑R 132), der; -en, -en (↑R 126) ⟨griech.⟩ (Meinungsforscher); **De|mo|sko|pie,** die; -, ...ien (Meinungsumfrage, Meinungsforschung); **De|mo|sko|pin; de|mo|sko|pisch;** -e Untersuchungen

De|mos|the|nes (altgriech. Redner); **de|mos|the|nisch;** demosthenische Beredsamkeit; die demosthenischen Reden (↑R 58)

de|mo|tisch ⟨griech.⟩ (altägyptisch [in der volkstüml. jüngeren Form]); demotische Schrift; **De|mo|tisch,** das; -[s]; *vgl.* Deutsch; **De|mo|ti|sche,** das; -n; *vgl.* Deutsche, das

De|mo|ti|va|ti|on, die; -, -en ⟨nlat.⟩ (das Demotivieren; das Demotiviertsein); **de|mo|ti|vie|ren** (jmds. Motivation schwächen)

De|mut, die; -; **de|mü|tig; de|mü|ti|gen; De|mü|ti|gung; De|muts‿ge|bär|de, ...hal|tung; de|mut[s]|voll**

dem|zu|fol|ge (demnach); demzufolge ist die Angelegenheit geklärt, *aber* das Vertragswerk, dem zufolge die Staaten sich verpflichten ...

den *vgl.* der

den = Denier

De|nar, der; -s, -e ⟨lat.⟩ (altröm. Münze; merowing.-karoling. Münze, Pfennig [*Abk.* d])

De|na|tu|ra|li|sa|ti|on, die; -, -en ⟨lat.⟩ (Entlassung aus der bisherigen Staatsangehörigkeit); **de|na|tu|ra|li|sie|ren; de|na|tu|rie|ren** (*fachspr. für* ungenießbar machen; vergällen); denaturierter Spiritus; **De|na|tu|rie|rung**

de|na|zi|fi|zie|ren (*svw.* entnazifizieren); **De|na|zi|fi|zie|rung**

Dend|rit [*auch* ...'drit] (↑R 130), der; -en, -en (↑R 126) ⟨griech.⟩ (*Geol.* Gestein mit feiner, verästelter Zeichnung; *Med.* verästelter Protoplasmafortsatz einer Nervenzelle); **dend|ri|tisch** (verzweigt, verästelt); **Dend|ro|lo|gie,** die; - (wissenschaftliche Baumkunde); **Dend|ro|me|ter,** das; -s, - (Baummessgerät)

De|neb, der; -s ⟨arab.⟩ (ein Stern)

de|nen *vgl.* der

Den|gel, der; -s, - (Schneide einer Sense o. Ä.); **Den|gel‿am|boss, ...ham|mer; den|geln** ([eine Sense o. Ä.] durch Hämmern schärfen); ich ...[e]le (↑R 16)

Den|gue|fie|ber ['dɛŋge...], das; -s ⟨span.⟩ (eine trop. Infektionskrankheit)

Deng Xi|ao|ping [- çiau...] (chin. Politiker)

Den Haag *vgl.* Haag, Den

De|ni|er [də'nie:], das; -[s], - ⟨franz.⟩ (Einheit für die Fadenstärke bei Seide u. Chemiefasern; *Abk.* den); *vgl.* Tex

De|nise [də'ni:z] (w. Vorn.)

Denk‿an|satz, ...an|stoß, ...art, ...auf|ga|be; denk|bar; die denkbar günstigsten Bedingungen; **den|ken;** du dachtest; du dächtest; gedacht; denk[e]!; **Den|ken,** das; -s; sein ganzes Denken; **Den|ker; Den|ke|rin; den|ke|risch; Den|ker|stirn; denk|faul; Denk‿feh|ler, ...form, ...hil|fe, ...mal** (*Plur.* ...mäler, *österr. nur so, auch* ...male); **Denk|mal[s]|kun|de,** die; -; **denk|mal[s]|kund|lich; Denk|mal[s]‿pfle|ge, ...pfle|ger; denk|mal[s]|pfle|ge|risch; Denk|mal[s]‿schän|dung, ...schutz; Denk‿mo|dell, ...mus|ter, ...pau|se, ...pro|zess, ...schab|lo|ne, ...schrift, ...sport; Denk|sport|auf|ga|be; Denk|spruch; denks|te!** (*ugs. für* das hast du dir so gedacht!); **Denk‿stein, ...übung** (↑R 132); **Den|kungs|art; Denk‿ver|mö|gen** (das; -s), **...wei|se** (die); **denk|wür|dig; Denk|wür|dig|keit,** die; -, -en; **Denk|zet|tel;** jmdm. einen - geben

denn; es sei denn, dass ...; mehr denn je; man kennt ihn eher als Maler denn als Dichter; **den|noch** (↑R 136); **denn|schon** *vgl.* wennschon

De|no|mi|na|ti|on, die; -, -en ⟨lat.⟩ (*veraltet für* Benennung; *amerik. Bez. für* christliche Glaubensgemeinschaft, Sekte); **De|no|mi|na|tiv,** das; -s, -e [...və] *u.* **De|no|mi|na|ti|vum** [...vum], das; -s, ...va [...va] (*Sprachw.* Ableitung von einem Substantiv od. Adjektiv, z. B. „trösten" von „Trost", „bangen" von „bang")

De|no|ta|ti|on, die; -, -en (*Sprachw.* begriffliche od. Sachbedeutung eines Wortes); **de|no|ta|tiv**

Den|si|me|ter, das; -s, - ⟨lat.; griech.⟩ (Gerät zur Messung des spezifischen Gewichts [vorwiegend von Flüssigkeiten])

den|tal ⟨lat.⟩ (*Med.* die Zähne betreffend; *Sprachw.* mithilfe der Zähne gebildet); **Den|tal,** der; -s, -e *od.* **Den|tal|laut,** der; -[e]s, -e (*Sprachw.* Zahnlaut, an den oberen Schneidezähnen gebildeter Laut, z. B. t); **den|tel|lie|ren** [dãtə'li:...] ⟨franz.⟩ (*Textilw.* auszacken [von Spitzen]); **Den|tin,** das; -s ⟨lat.⟩ (*Med.* Zahnbein; *Biol.* Hartsubstanz der Haischuppen); **Den|tist,** der; -en, -en; ↑R 126 (*früher für* Zahnarzt ohne Hochschulprüfung); **Den|ti|ti|on,** die; -, -en (*Med.* Zahnen; Zahndurchbruch); **Den|to|lo|gie,** die; - ⟨lat.; griech.⟩ (Zahnheilkunde)

De|nu|da|ti|on, die; -, -en ⟨lat.⟩ (*Geol.* Abtragung der Erdoberfläche durch Wasser, Wind u. a.)

De|nun|zi|ant, der; -en, -en (↑R 126) ⟨lat.⟩ (jmd., der einen anderen denunziert); **De|nun|zi|an|ten|tum,** das; -s; **De|nun|zi|a|ti|on,** die; -, -en (Anzeige eines Denunzianten); **de|nun|zi|a|to|risch; de|nun|zie|ren** (aus persönlichen, niedrigen Beweggründen anzeigen; brandmarken)

Den|ver [...vər] (Hptst. des amerik. Bundesstaates Colorado)

Deo, das; -s, -s (*Kurzwort für* Deodorant); **De|o|do|rant,** das; -s, *Plur.* -s, *auch* -e ⟨engl.⟩ (Mittel gegen Körpergeruch); **De|o|do|rant|spray; de|o|do|rie|ren** ([Körper]geruch hemmen)

Deo gra|ti|as! ⟨lat., „Gott sei Dank!"⟩ *(kath. Kirche)*

De|o|rol|ler (ein Deodorantstift); **De|o|spray** (*kurz für* Deodorantspray)

De|par|te|ment [departə'mã:, *österr.* depart'mã:, *schweiz.* departə'mɛnt], das; *Gen.* -s, *schweiz.* -[e]s, *Plur.* -s, *schweiz.* -e ⟨franz.⟩ (Verwaltungsbezirk in Frankreich; Ministerium beim Bund und in einigen Kantonen der Schweiz; *veraltet für* Abteilung, Geschäftsbereich); **De|part|ment** [di'pa:(r)tmənt], das; -s, -s (*engl. Form von* Departement)

De|par|ture [di'pa(r)tʃə(r)], das; -s, -s ⟨engl.⟩ (Abflug [Hinweis auf Flughäfen])

De|pen|dance [depã'dã:s], die; -, -n [...sən] ⟨franz.⟩ (Zweigstelle; Nebengebäude [eines Hotels]); **De|pen|denz,** die; -, -en ⟨lat.⟩ (*Philos., Sprachw.* Abhängigkeit); **De|pen|denz|gram|ma|tik** (Forschungsrichtung der modernen Linguistik)

De|pe|sche, die; -, -n ⟨franz.⟩ (*veraltet für* Telegramm); **de|pe|schie|ren** (*veraltet für* telegrafieren)

De|pi|la|ti|on, die; -, -en ⟨lat.⟩ (*Med.* Enthaarung); **De|pi|la|to|ri|um,** das; -s, ...ien [...iən] (Enthaarungsmittel); **de|pi|lie|ren**

De|place|ment [deplasə'mã:], das; -s, -s ⟨franz.⟩ (*Seew.* Wasserverdrängung eines Schiffes); **de|pla|cie|ren** [depla'(t)si:...] (*veraltet für* verrücken, verdrängen); **de|pla|ciert,** *eindeutschend:* **de|plat|ziert** (unangebracht)

De|po|la|ri|sa|ti|on, die; -, -en ‹lat.› (*Physik* Aufhebung der Polarisation); **de|po|la|ri|sie|ren**
De|po|nat, das; -[e]s, -e ‹lat.› (etwas, was deponiert ist); **De|po|nens**, das; -, *Plur.* ...nentia *u.* ...nenzien [...iən] (*Sprachw.* Verb mit passivischen Formen, aber aktivischer Bedeutung); **De|po|nent**, der; -en, -en; ↑R 126 (jmd., der etw. hinterlegt); **De|po|nie**, die; -, ...ien ‹lat.-franz.› (zentraler Müllabladeplatz); geordnete, wilde -; **de|po|nie|ren** ‹lat.›; **De|po|nie|rung**
De|port [*auch* de'pɔ:r], der; -s, *Plur.* -s, *bei dt. Ausspr.* -e ‹franz.› (*Bankw.* Kursabschlag)
De|por|ta|ti|on, die; -, -en ‹lat.› (zwangsweise Verschickung; Verbannung); **De|por|ta|ti|ons|la|ger; de|por|tie|ren; De|por|tier|te**, der *u.* die; -n, -n (↑R 5 ff.); **De|por|tie|rung**
De|po|si|tar ‹lat.›, **De|po|si|tär** ‹franz.›, der; -s, -e (Verwahrer von Wertgegenständen, -papieren u. a.); **De|po|si|ten** *Plur.* ‹lat.› (*Bankw.* Gelder, die bei einem Kreditinstitut gegen Verzinsung angelegt, aber nicht auf ein Spar- od. Kontokorrentkonto verbucht werden); **De|po|si|ten_bank** (*Plur.* ...banken), **...kas|se; De|po|si|ti|on**, die; -, -en (Hinterlegung; Absetzung eines kath. Geistlichen); **De|po|si|to|ri|um**, das; -s, ...ien [...iən] (Aufbewahrungsort; Hinterlegungsstelle); **De|po|si|tum**, das; -s (das Hinterlegte; hinterlegter Betrag); *vgl.* Depositen
De|pot [de'po:], das; -s, -s ‹franz.› (Aufbewahrungsort; Hinterlegtes; Sammelstelle, Lager; Bodensatz; *Med.* Ablagerung); **De|pot_fund** (*Archäol.* Sammelfund), **...prä|pa|rat** (*Med.*), **...schein** (*Bankw.* Hinterlegungsschein), **...wech|sel** (*Bankw.* als Sicherheit hinterlegter Wechsel)
Depp, der; *Gen.* -en, *auch* -s, *Plur.* -en, *auch* -e (*bes. südd., österr. ugs. für* ungeschickter, einfältiger Mensch); **dep|pert** (*südd., österr. ugs. für* einfältig, dumm)
Dep|ra|va|ti|on [...v...] (↑R 130 *u.* 132), die; -, -en ‹lat.› (Wertminderung im Münzwesen; *Med.* Verschlechterung eines Krankheitszustandes); **dep|ra|vie|ren** (*geh. für* verderben; im Wert mindern [von Münzen])
De|pres|si|on, die; -, -en ‹lat.› (Niedergeschlagenheit; Senkung; wirtschaftlicher Rückgang; *Meteor.* Tief); **de|pres|siv** (gedrückt, niedergeschlagen); **De|pres|si|vi|tät**, die; -
de|pri|mie|ren ‹franz.› (niederdrücken; entmutigen); **de|pri|miert** (entmutigt, niedergeschlagen, schwermütig)
De|pri|va|ti|on [...v...], die; -, -en ‹lat.› (*Psych.* Entzug von Liebe und Zuwendung; Absetzung eines kath. Geistlichen); **de|pri|vie|ren** (*Psych.* [Liebe] entbehren lassen)
De pro|fun|dis, das; - - ‹lat., „Aus der Tiefe [rufe ich, Herr, zu dir]"› (Anfangsworte und Bez. des 130. Psalms nach der Vulgata)
De|pu|tant, der; -en, -en (↑R 126) ‹lat.› (jmd., der auf ein Deputat Anspruch hat); **De|pu|tat**, das; -[e]s, -e (regelmäßige Leistungen in Naturalien als Teil des Lohnes); **De|pu|ta|ti|on**, die; -, -en (Abordnung); **De|pu|tat|lohn; de|pu|tie|ren** (abordnen); **De|pu|tier|te**, der *u.* die; -n, -n (↑R 5 ff.); **De|pu|tier|ten|kam|mer**
der, die (*vgl. d.*), das (*vgl. d.*); des *u.* dessen (*vgl. d.*), dem, den; *Plur.* die, der, deren *u.* derer (*vgl. d.*), den *u.* denen, die
De|ran|ge|ment [derãʒə'mã:], das; -s, -s ‹franz.› (*veraltet für* Störung, Verwirrung); **de|ran|gie|ren** [derã'ʒi:...] (verwirren, durcheinander bringen; *veraltet für* stören); **de|ran|giert** (verwirrt, zerzaust)
der|art (so); *vgl.* Art; **der|ar|tig**; derartige Überlegungen; etwas derartig Schönes; wir haben Derartiges, etwas Derartiges noch nie erlebt (↑R 47)
derb; Derb|heit; derb|kno|chig; derb|ko|misch (↑R 27)
[1]**Der|by** ['da:(r)bi] (engl. Stadt)
[2]**Der|by** ['dɛrbi], das; -[s], -s ‹nach dem 12. Earl of Derby› (Pferderennen); **Der|by|ren|nen**
De|re|gu|lie|rung (Beseitigung von Regeln, Vorschriften o. Ä.)
der|einst, *selten* **der|eins|tig**
de|ren; *Gen. Sing. des zurückweisenden Demonstrativpronomens und des Relativpronomens* die, *Gen. Plur. der zurückweisenden Demonstrativpronomen und der Relativpronomen* der, die, das (*vgl. d.*); mit deren nettem Mann; von deren bester Art; seit deren erstem Hiersein; mit Ausnahme der Mitarbeiter und deren Angehöriger; die Frist, innerhalb deren ...; die Freunde, deren Geschenke du siehst; ich habe deren (z. B. Freunde) nicht viele; *vgl.* derer; **de|rent|hal|ben; de|rent|we|gen; de|rent|wil|len**; um -
de|rer; *Gen. Plur. der vorausweisenden Demonstrativpronomen* der, die, das (derer *ist richtig, sobald dafür* derjenigen *stehen kann*); der Andrang derer, die ...; gedenkt derer, die euer gedenken; das Haus derer von Arnim; *vgl.* deren
der|ge|stalt (so)
der|glei|chen (*Abk.* dgl.); und - [mehr] (*Abk.* u. dgl. [m.])
De|ri|vat [...v...], das; -[e]s, -e ‹lat.› (*Chemie* chem. Verbindung, die aus einer anderen entstanden ist; *Sprachw.* abgeleitetes Wort, z. B. „kräftig" von „Kraft"; *Biol.* aus einer Vorstufe abgeleitetes Organ); **De|ri|va|ti|on**, die; -, -en (*Sprachw.* Ableitung); **de|ri|va|tiv** (durch Ableitung entstanden); **De|ri|va|tiv**, das; -s, -e [...və]; **de|ri|vie|ren**
der|je|ni|ge *Gen.* desjenigen, *Plur.* diejenigen
Derk (m. Vorn.)
der|lei (dergleichen)
Der|ma, das; -s, -ta (*Med.* Haut); **der|mal** (*Med.* die Haut betreffend, an ihr gelegen)
der|mal|einst (*veraltet*); **der|ma|len** [*österr.* ...'ma:...] (*veraltet für* jetzt); **der|ma|lig** [*österr.* ...'ma:...] (*veraltet für* jetzig)
der|ma|ßen (so)
der|ma|tisch *vgl.* dermal; **Der|ma|ti|tis**, die; -, ...itiden ‹griech.› (*Med.* Hautentzündung); **Der|ma|to|lo|ge**, der; -n, -n; ↑R 126 (Hautarzt); **Der|ma|to|lo|gie**, die; - (Lehre von den Hautkrankheiten); **Der|ma|to|lo|gin; Der|ma|to|plas|tik**, die; -, -en (*Med.* operativer Ersatz von kranker od. verletzter Haut durch gesunde); **Der|ma|to|se**, die; -, -n (*Med.* Hautkrankheit); **Der|mo|gra|phie**, die; - *u.* **Der|mo|gra|phis|mus**, der; - (*Med.* Streifen- od. Striemenbildung auf gereizten Hautstellen); **Der|mo|plas|tik**, die; -, -en (Verfahren zur lebensgetreuen Präparation von Tieren; *Med. svw.* Dermatoplastik)
Der|ni|er Cri [dɛrnie 'kri:], der; - -, -s -s [dɛrnie 'kri:] ‹franz., „letzter Schrei"› (neueste Mode)
de|ro (*veraltet für* deren); *in der Anrede* Dero
De|ro|ga|ti|on, die; -, -en ‹lat.› (*Rechtsspr.* Teilaufhebung [eines Gesetzes]); **de|ro|ga|tiv, de|ro|ga|to|risch** ([ein Gesetz] zum Teil aufhebend); **de|ro|gie|ren** ([ein Gesetz] zum Teil aufheben)
De|rou|te [de'ru:t(ə)], die; -, -n ‹franz.› (*Wirtsch.* Kurs-, Preissturz; *veraltet für* wilde Flucht)

de|ro|we|gen (*veraltet); vgl.* dero
Der|rick, der; -s, -s ‹nach einem engl. Henker› (Drehkran); **Der|rick|kran**
der|sel|be *Gen.* desselben, *Plur.* dieselben; ein und derselbe; mit ein[em] und demselben; ein[en] und denselben; es war derselbe Hund; **der|sel|bi|ge** (↑R 48; *veraltet für* derselbe)
der|weil, der|wei|le[n]
Der|wisch, der; -[e]s, -e ‹pers.› (Mitglied eines islamischen religiösen Ordens); **Der|wisch|tanz**
der|zeit (augenblicklich, gegenwärtig; *veraltend für* früher, damals; *Abk.* dz.); **der|zei|tig** (*vgl.* derzeit)
des; *auch ältere Form für* dessen *(vgl. d.);* des (dessen) bin ich sicher; des ungeachtet
des, Des, das; -, - (Tonbezeichnung); **Des** (*Zeichen für* Des-Dur); in Des
des. = designatus
des|ar|mie|ren ‹franz.› (*veraltet für* entwaffnen; *Fechten* dem Gegner die Klinge aus der Hand schlagen)
De|sas|ter, das; -s, - ‹franz.› (schweres Missgeschick; Zusammenbruch)
des|a|vou|ie|ren [...avu...] ‹franz.› (nicht anerkennen, in Abrede stellen; bloßstellen); **Des|a|vou|ie|rung**
Des|cartes [de'kart] (franz. Philosoph)
Des|de|mo|na [*auch* ...'de:...] (Frauengestalt bei Shakespeare)
Des-Dur [*auch* 'dɛs'du:r], das; - (Tonart; *Zeichen* Des); **Des-Dur-Ton|lei|ter** (↑R 28)
de|sen|si|bi|li|sie|ren ‹lat.› (*Med.* unempfindlich machen; *Fotogr.* Filme weniger lichtempfindlich machen); **De|sen|si|bi|li|sie|rung**
De|ser|teur [...'tø:r], der; -s, -e ‹franz.› (Fahnenflüchtiger, Überläufer); **de|ser|tie|ren; De|ser|ti|on,** die; -, -en (Fahnenflucht)
desgl. = desgleichen; **des|glei|chen** (*Abk.* desgl.)
des|halb
de|si|de|ra|bel ‹lat.› (*geh. für* wünschenswert); ...ab|le (↑R 130) Erfolge; **De|si|de|rat,** das; -[e]s, -e *u.* **De|si|de|ra|tum,** das; -s, ...ta (vermisstes u. zur Anschaffung in Bibliotheken vorgeschlagenes Buch; etwas Erwünschtes, Fehlendes)
De|sign [di'zain], das; -s, -s ‹engl.› (Plan, Entwurf, Muster, Modell); **De|sig|na|ti|on** (↑R 130), die; -, -en ‹lat.› (Bestimmung; vorläufige Ernennung); **de|sig|na|tus** (im Voraus ernannt, vorgesehen; *Abk.* des.; z. B. Dr. des.); **De|sig|ner** [di'zainər], der; -s, - ‹engl.› (Formgestalter für Gebrauchs- u. Verbrauchsgüter); **De|sig|ner|dro|ge** ([in Abwandlung einer bekannten Droge] synthetisch hergestelltes, neuartiges Rauschmittel); **De|sig|ne|rin; De|sig|ner|mo|de; de|sig|nie|ren** ‹lat.› (bestimmen, für ein Amt vorsehen)
Des|il|lu|si|on, die; -, -en ‹franz.› (Enttäuschung; Ernüchterung); **des|il|lu|si|o|nie|ren; Des|il|lu|si|o|nie|rung**
Des|in|fek|ti|on, Des|in|fi|zie|rung, die; -, -en ‹lat.› (Vernichtung von Krankheitserregern; Entkeimung); **Des|in|fek|ti|ons-lö|sung, ...mit|tel** (das); **Des|in|fi|zi|ens** [...iəns], das; -, *Plur.* ...zienzien [...iən] *u.* ...zientia (Entkeimungsmittel); **des|in|fi|zie|ren; Des|in|fi|zie|rung** *vgl.* Desinfektion
Des|in|for|ma|ti|on [*auch* 'dɛs...], die; -, -en ‹lat.› (bewusst falsche Information)
Des|in|teg|ra|ti|on, die; -, -en ‹lat.› (Spaltung, Auflösung eines Ganzen in seine Teile); **Des|in|teg|ra|tor,** der; -s, ...oren (eine techn. Apparatur); **des|in|teg|rie|ren**
Des|in|te|res|se, das; -s ‹franz.› (Uninteressiertheit, Gleichgültigkeit); **des|in|te|res|siert**
De|skrip|ti|on, die; -, -en ‹lat.› (Beschreibung); **de|skrip|tiv** (beschreibend); **De|skrip|tor,** der; -s, ...oren (*Buchw., EDV* Kenn-, Schlagwort)
Desk|top|pub|li|shing, *auch* **Desktop-Pub|li|shing** [-'pabliʃiŋ] (↑R 24 *u.* 130), das; -[s] ‹engl.› (*EDV* das Erstellen von Satz und Lay-out eines Textes am Schreibtisch mithilfe der EDV; *Abk.* DTP)
Des|o|do|rant, das; -s, *Plur.* -s, *auch* -e ‹nlat.›; *vgl.* Deodorant; **des|o|do|rie|ren,** des|o|do|ri|sie|ren; *vgl.* deodorieren; **Des|o|do|rie|rung, Des|o|do|ri|sie|rung**
de|so|lat; ‹lat.› (trostlos, traurig)
Des|ord|re [de'zɔrdər] (↑R 130), der; -s, -s ‹franz.› (*veraltet für* Unordnung, Verwirrung)
Des|or|ga|ni|sa|ti|on [*auch* 'dɛs...], die; -, -en ‹franz.› (Auflösung, Zerrüttung, Unordnung); **des|or|ga|ni|sie|ren** [*auch* 'dɛs...]
des|ori|en|tiert [*auch* 'dɛs...] (↑R 132; falsch unterrichtet; verwirrt); **Des|ori|en|tie|rung**
Des|oxi|da|ti|on, *nichtfachspr. auch* Des|oxy|da|ti|on (↑R 132), die; -, -en ‹griech.› (Entzug von Sauerstoff); *vgl.* Oxidation; **des|oxi|die|ren,** *nichtfachspr. auch* des|oxy|die|ren; **Des|oxy|ri|bo|nuk|le|in|säu|re** (Bestandteil des Zellkerns; *Abk.* DNS)
des|pek|tier|lich (↑R 132) ‹lat.› (*geh. für* geringschätzig, abfällig; respektlos)
Des|pe|ra|do [...sp...] (↑R 132), der; -s, -s ‹span.› (zu jeder Verzweiflungstat entschlossener [politischer] Abenteurer; Bandit); **des|pe|rat** ‹lat.› (verzweifelt, hoffnungslos)
Des|pot, der; -en, -en (↑R 126) ‹griech.› (Gewaltherrscher; herrische Person); **Des|po|tie,** die; -, ...ien; **Des|po|tin; des|po|tisch; Des|po|tis|mus,** der; -
Des|sau (Stadt nahe der Mündung der Mulde in die Elbe); **Des|sau|er** (↑R 103); der Alte Dessauer (Leopold I. von Anhalt-Dessau; ↑R 93); **des|sau|isch**
des|sel|ben; *vgl.* der-, dasselbe
des|sen (*Gen. Sing. der [als Vertreter eines Substantivs gebrauchten] Pronomen* der, das); mit dessen neuem Wagen; die Ankunft meines Bruders und dessen Verlobter; dessen ungeachtet; *vgl.* des; indessen, währenddessen *(vgl. d.);* **des|sent|hal|ben; des|sent|we|gen,** des|we|gen; **des|sent|wil|len,** des|wil|len; um -; **des|sen un|ge|ach|tet** [*auch* -ʊngə'axtət]; *vgl.* dessen
Des|sert [dɛ'sɛ:r, *österr. nur so, auch* dɛ'sɛrt, *schweiz.* 'dɛsɛ:r], das; -s, -s ‹franz.› (Nachtisch); **Des|sert-ga|bel, ...löf|fel, ...mes|ser** (das), **...tel|ler, ...wein**
Des|sin [dɛ'sɛ̃:], das; -s, -s ‹franz.› (Zeichnung; Muster); **Des|si|na|teur** [dɛsina'tø:r], der; -s, -e (Musterzeichner [im Textilgewerbe]); **des|si|nie|ren** (*fachspr. für* [Muster] zeichnen); **des|si|niert** (gemustert); **Des|si|nie|rung**
Des|sous [dɛ'su:], das; - [dɛ'su:(s)], - [dɛ'su:s] *meist Plur.* ‹franz.› (Damenunterwäsche)
de|sta|bi|li|sie|ren ‹lat.› (aus dem Gleichgewicht bringen, weniger stabil machen); **De|sta|bi|li|sie|rung**
Des|til|lat (↑R 132), das; -[e]s, -e ‹lat.› (wieder verflüssigter Dampf bei einer Destillation); **Des|til|lat|bren|ner** (Lehrberuf der Industrie); **Des|til|la|teur** [...'tø:r], der; -s, -e ‹franz.› (Branntweinbrenner); **Des|til|la|ti|on,** die; -, -en ‹lat.› (Trennung flüssiger Stoffe durch Verdampfung u. Wieder-

verflüssigung; Branntweinbrennerei); **Des|til|la|ti|ons|gas; Des|til|le,** die; -, -n (*ugs. veraltend für* Branntweinausschank); **Des|til|lier|ap|pa|rat; des|til|lie|ren;** destilliertes Wasser (chemisch reines Wasser); **Des|til|lier-kol|ben, ...ofen** (↑R 132)

Des|ti|na|tar [...st...] (↑R 132) ‹lat.›, **Des|ti|na|tär,** der; -s, -e ‹franz.› (*auf Seefrachtbriefen* Empfänger von Gütern); **Des|ti|na|ti|on,** die; -, -en ‹lat.› (*veraltet für* Bestimmung, Endzweck)

des|to; desto besser, größer, mehr, weniger; *aber* nichtsdestoweniger

de|stru|ie|ren [...st...] ‹lat.› (*selten für* zerstören); **De|struk|ti|on,** die; -, -en (Zerstörung; *Geol.* Abtragung der Erdoberfläche durch Verwitterung); **de|struk|tiv** [*auch* 'de:...] (zersetzend, zerstörend); **De|struk|ti|vi|tät,** die; - (*auch für* destruktive Art)

des un|ge|ach|tet [*auch* - ungəˈaxtət]; *vgl.* des; **des|we|gen,** dessent|we|gen; **des Wei|te|ren;** *vgl.* weiter; **des|wil|len** *vgl.* dessentwillen

des|zen|dent (↑R 132) ‹lat.› (*fachspr. für* nach unten sinkend, absteigend); deszendentes Wasser; **Des|zen|dent,** der; -en, -en; ↑R 126 (Nachkomme, Ab-, Nachkömmling; *Astron.* Gestirn im Untergang; Untergangspunkt); **Des|zen|denz,** die; -, -en (Abstammung; Nachkommenschaft; *Astron.* Untergang eines Gestirns); **Des|zen|denz|the|o|rie,** die; - (Abstammungslehre); **des|zen|die|ren** (*fachspr. für* absteigen, sinken)

De|ta|che|ment [detaʃ(ə)ˈmã:, *schweiz.* ...əˈmɛnt], das; -s, *Plur.* -s, *schweiz.* -e ‹franz.› (*veraltet für* abkommandierte Truppe); [1]**De|ta|cheur** [...ˈʃø:r], der; -s, -e (Maschine zum Lockern des Mehls)

[2]**De|ta|cheur** [...ˈʃø:r], der; -s, -e ‹franz.› (Fachmann für chem. Fleckenentfernung); **De|ta|cheu|se** [...ˈʃø:zə], die; -, -n (w. Detacheur); [1]**de|ta|chie|ren** [...ˈʃi:...] (von Flecken reinigen)

[2]**de|ta|chie|ren** [...ˈʃi:...] ‹franz.› (Mehl auflockern; *veraltet für* abkommandieren, entsenden)

De|tail [deˈtai̯, *auch* deˈta:j], das; -s, -s ‹franz.› (Einzelheit, Einzelteil); *vgl.* en détail; **De|tail|fra|ge; de|tail|ge|treu; De|tail|han|del** ‹*zu* [1]Handel› (*schweiz., sonst veraltet für* Einzelhandel); **De|tail|kennt|nis; de|tail|lie|ren** [detaˈji:...] (im Einzelnen darlegen); **de|tail|liert; De|tail|list** [detai̯ˈlist, *auch* ...ˈjist], der; -en, -en; ↑R 126 (*schweiz. für* Einzelhändler); **de|tail|reich**

De|tek|tei ‹lat.› (Detektivbüro); **De|tek|tiv,** der; -s, -e [...və]; dem, den Detektiv; **De|tek|tiv-bü|ro, ...ge|schich|te; De|tek|ti|vin** [...ˈti:vin]; **de|tek|ti|visch** [...viʃ]; **De|tek|tiv-ka|me|ra** [...f...], **...ro|man; De|tek|tor,** der; -s, ...oren ‹lat.› (*Technik* Hochfrequenzgleichrichter); **De|tek|tor-emp|fän|ger, ...ge|rät**

Dé|tente [deˈtã:t], die; - ‹franz.› (Entspannung zwischen Staaten); **Dé|tente|po|li|tik**

De|ter|gens, das; -, *Plur.* ...gentia *u.* ...genzien [...i̯ən] *meist Plur.* ‹lat.› (*fachspr. für* Wasch-, Reinigungsmittel)

De|te|ri|o|ra|ti|on, die; -, -en ‹lat.› (*Rechtsw.* Wertminderung einer Sache); **de|te|ri|o|rie|ren; De|te|ri|o|rie|rung** *vgl.* Deterioration

De|ter|mi|nan|te, die; -, -n ‹lat.› (Hilfsmittel der Algebra zur Lösung eines Gleichungssystems; bestimmender Faktor); **De|ter|mi|na|ti|on,** die; -, -en (nähere Begriffsbestimmung); **de|ter|mi|na|tiv** (bestimmend, begrenzend, festlegend; entschieden, entschlossen); **de|ter|mi|nie|ren** (bestimmen, begrenzen, festlegen); **De|ter|mi|niert|heit,** die; -; **De|ter|mi|nis|mus,** der; - (Lehre von der Unfreiheit des menschlichen Willens); **De|ter|mi|nist,** der; -en, -en (↑R 126); **de|ter|mi|nis|tisch**

de|tes|ta|bel ‹lat.› (*veraltet für* verabscheuungswürdig); ...ab|le (↑R 130) Ansichten

Det|lef [*auch* ˈdɛt...] (m. Vorn.)

Det|mold (Stadt am Teutoburger Wald)

[1]**De|to|na|ti|on,** die; -, -en ‹lat.› (Knall, Explosion)

[2]**De|to|na|ti|on,** die; -, -en ‹franz.› (*Musik* Unreinheit des Tones)

De|to|na|tor, der; -s, ...oren ‹lat.› (*fachspr. für* Zündmittel); [1]**de|to|nie|ren** (knallen, explodieren)

[2]**de|to|nie|ren** ‹franz.› (*Musik* unrein singen, spielen)

Det|ri|tus (↑R 130), der; - ‹lat.› (*Med.* Zell- u. Gewebstrümmer; *Geol.* zerriebenes Gestein; *Biol.* Schwebe- und Sinkstoffe in den Gewässern)

Det|roit [diˈtrɔy̆t] (↑R 130; Stadt in den USA)

det|to ‹ital.› (*bes. bayr., österr. für* dito)

De|tu|mes|zenz, die; - ‹lat.› (*Med.* Abschwellung [einer Geschwulst])

Deu|bel *vgl.* Deiwel

deucht usw. *vgl.* dünken

Deu|ka|li|on (Gestalt der griech. Sage); die Sintflut des Deukalion

De|us ex Ma|chi|na [- - ...x...], der; - - -, Dei - - [ˈde:i - -] *Plur. selten* ‹lat., „Gott aus der [Theater]maschine"› (unerwarteter Helfer)

Deut, der ‹niederl.› (*veraltet für* kleine Münze); *nur noch in* keinen -, nicht einen - (*ugs. für* gar nicht, gar nichts)

deut|bar; Deu|te|lei (*abwertend für* kleinliche Auslegung); **deu|teln;** ich ...[e]le (↑R 16); **deu|ten; Deu|ter**

Deu|te|ra|go|nist (↑R 132), der; -en, -en (↑R 126) ‹griech.› (zweiter Schauspieler auf der altgriech. Bühne)

Deu|te|ri|um, das; -s ‹griech.› (schwerer Wasserstoff, Wasserstoffisotop; *Zeichen* D); **Deu|te|ron,** das; -s, ...onen (Atomkern des Deuteriums); **Deu|te|ro|no|mi|um,** das; -s (5. Buch Mosis)

...deu|tig (z. B. zweideutig); **Deut|ler; deut|lich;** auf das, aufs Deutlichste *od.* auf das, aufs deutlichste (↑R 47); etwas - machen; **Deut|lich|keit; deut|lich|keits|hal|ber**

deutsch (*Abk.* dt.); **I.** *Kleinschreibung:* **a)** der Redner hat deutsch (nicht englisch) gesprochen; am Nebentisch saß ein (gerade jetzt, bei dieser Gelegenheit) deutsch sprechendes Ehepaar; sich deutsch unterhalten; der Brief ist deutsch (in deutscher Sprache bzw. in deutscher Schreibschrift) geschrieben; deutsch mit jmdm. reden (*auch ugs. für* jmdm. unverblümt die Wahrheit sagen); Staatsangehörigkeit: deutsch (in Formularen u. Ä.); (*vgl. aber* II a *u.* Deutsch); **b)** das deutsche Volk; die deutsche Sprache; die deutschen Meisterschaften [im Eiskunstlauf]; das deutsche Recht; der deutsche Michel; (↑R 108:) Gesellschaft für deutsche Sprache; Institut für deutsche Sprache; *vgl. aber* II b. **II.** *Großschreibung* (↑R 47): **a)** etwas auf Deutsch sagen; der Brief ist in Deutsch abgefasst; eine Zusammenfassung in Deutsch; auf gut Deutsch gesagt; das heißt auf/zu Deutsch ...; *vgl. aber* I a; *vgl. auch* Deutsch; **b)** der Deutsch-Französische Krieg (1870/71) [*aber* ein deutsch-französischer Krieg (irgendeiner)]; Deutscher Akademischer Austauschdienst (*Abk.* DAAD); Deutsche Angestellten-Gewerkschaft (*Abk.* DAG); die Deutsche Bibliothek (in Frankfurt); die Deutsche Bücherei (in Leipzig; *Abk.* DB); die Deutsche Bucht (Teil der Nordsee); der Deutsche Bund (1815–66); der Deutsche Bundestag; Deutsche Bahn (*Abk.* DB); Deutsche Bundesbank (*Abk.* BBk); Deutsche Bundespost *u.* Deutsches Bundespatent (*Abk.* DBP); Deutsche Demokratische Republik (1949–90; *Abk.* DDR); die Deutsche Dogge; der Tag der Deutschen Einheit (3. Oktober); Deutscher Fußball-Bund (*Abk.* DFB); Deutscher Gewerkschaftsbund (*Abk.* DGB); Deutscher Industrie- und Handelstag (*Abk.* DIHT); Verein Deutscher Ingenieure; Deutsches Institut für Normung (*Zeichen* DIN; *vgl. d.*); Deutsche Jugendherberge (*Abk.* DJH); Deutsche Jugendkraft (ein kath. Verband für Sportpflege; *Abk.* DJK); Deutsche Lebens-Rettungs-Gesellschaft (*Abk.* DLRG); Deutsche Mark (*Abk.* DM); der Deutsche Orden; Deutsche Presse-Agentur (*Abk.* dpa); das Deutsche Reich; Deutsches Rotes Kreuz (*Abk.* DRK); der Deutsche Schäferhund; Deutscher Turnerbund (*Abk.* DTB); *vgl.* I b, Deutsch *u.* Deutsche, das; **Deutsch**, das; des Deutsch[s], dem Deutsch (die deutsche Sprache, sofern sie die Sprache eines Einzelnen oder einer bestimmten Gruppe bezeichnet oder sonst näher bestimmt ist; Kenntnis der deutschen Sprache); mein, dein, sein Deutsch ist schlecht; die Aussprache seines Deutsch[s]; das Plattdeutsch Fritz Reuters; das Kanzleideutsch, das Kaufmannsdeutsch, das Schriftdeutsch; er kann, lehrt, lernt, schreibt, spricht, versteht [kein, nicht, gut, schlecht] Deutsch; ein Deutsch sprechender Ausländer (*vgl. aber* deutsch I a); [das ist] gutes Deutsch; er spricht gut[es] Deutsch; er kann kein Wort Deutsch; ein Lehrstuhl für Deutsch; er hat eine Eins in Deutsch (im Fach Deutsch); in heutigem Deutsch *od.* im heutigen Deutsch; *vgl. auch* Deutsche, das *u.* deutsch I a *u.* II a; **Deutsch|ame|ri|ka|ner** [*auch* ...'ka:...]; ↑R 132 *u.* 106 (Amerikaner dt. Abstammung); **deutsch|ame|ri|ka|nisch** (↑R 106); die deutschamerikanische Kultur; der deutschamerikanische Schiffsverkehr; **Deutsch|ar|beit**; eine - schreiben; **deutsch-deutsch**; die -en Beziehungen (*früher* zwischen der Bundesrepublik Deutschland und der DDR); [1]**Deut|sche**, der *u.* die; -n, -n (↑R 5 ff.); ich Deutscher; wir Deutschen (*auch* wir Deutsche); alle Deutschen; alle guten Deutschen; [2]**Deut|sche**, das; des -n, dem -n (die deutsche Sprache überhaupt; in Zusammensetzungen bes. zur Bezeichnung der hist. u. landsch. Teilbereiche der deutschen Sprache); das Deutsche (z. B. im Ggs. zum Französischen); das Althochdeutsche, das Mittelhochdeutsche, das Neuhochdeutsche; die Laute des Deutschen (z. B. im Ggs. zum Englischen); die Formen des Niederdeutschen; im Deutschen (z. B. im Ggs. zum Italienischen); aus dem Deutschen, ins Deutsche übersetzen; *vgl. auch* Deutsch; **Deut|schen‿feind, ...freund, ...hass; deutsch‿feind|lich, ...freund|lich; Deutsch‿herr** (*meist Plur.; svw.* Deutschordensritter), **...kun|de** (die; -); **deutsch|kund|lich;** -er Unterricht; **Deutsch|land;** des vereinigten -[s]; **Deutsch|land‿funk** (in Köln), **...lied** (das; -[e]s; Nationalhymne des Deutschen Reiches [seit 1922], deren dritte Strophe heute die offizielle Hymne Deutschlands ist), **...po|li|tik, ...sen|der** (der; -s; *früher*); **Deutsch|leh|rer; Deutsch|meis|ter** (Landmeister des Deutschen Ordens); **Deutsch|or|dens|rit|ter; Deutsch|rit|ter|or|den,** der; -s; **Deutsch|schweiz,** die; - (*schweiz. für* deutschsprachige Schweiz); **Deutsch|schwei|zer** (Schweizer deutscher Muttersprache); **deutsch|schwei|ze|risch** (↑R 106); die deutschschweizerische Literatur; ein deutschschweizerisches Abkommen; *vgl.* schweizerdeutsch; **deutsch|spra|chig** (die deutsche Sprache sprechend, in ihr abgefasst, vorgetragen); -e Bevölkerung; **deutsch|sprach|lich** (die deutsche Sprache betreffend); -er Unterricht; **Deutsch|spre|chen,** das; -s; **deutsch sprechend, Deutsch spre|chend** *vgl.* deutsch, Deutsch; **deutsch|stäm|mig; Deutsch|tum,** das; -s (deutsche Eigenart); **Deutsch|tü|me|lei** (*abwertend für* aufdringliche Betonung des Deutschtums); **Deutsch|tüm|ler** (*abwertend);* **Deutsch|un|ter|richt,** der; -[e]s **Deu|tung; Deu|tungs|ver|such Deut|zie** [...i̯ə], die; -, -n ‹nach dem Holländer van der Deutz› (ein Zierstrauch)

Deux|pi|èces [døˈpi̯ɛ:s], das; -, - ‹franz.› (zweiteiliges Kleid)

De|val|va|ti|on [devalva...], die; -, -en ‹lat.› (Abwertung einer Währung); **de|val|va|to|risch,** *auch* de|val|va|ti|o|nis|tisch (abwertend); **de|val|vie|ren**

De|vas|ta|ti|on, die; -, -en ‹lat.› (Verwüstung, Zerstörung); **de|vas|tie|ren**

De|ver|ba|tiv [devɛr...], das; -s, -e [...və] *u.* **De|ver|ba|ti|vum** [...vum], das; -s, ...va [...va] ‹lat.› (*Sprachw.* von einem Verb abgeleitetes Substantiv od. Adjektiv, z. B. „Eroberung" von „erobern", „hörig" von „hören")

de|vi|ant [...v...]; ‹lat.› (*fachspr. für* abweichend); **De|vi|a|ti|on,** die; -, -en (Abweichung); **de|vi|ie|ren**

De|vi|se [...v...], die; -, -n ‹franz.› (Wahlspruch); **De|vi|sen** *Plur.* (Zahlungsmittel in ausländ. Währung); **De|vi|sen‿aus|gleich, ...be|stim|mung** *(meist Plur.),* **...be|wirt|schaf|tung, ...brin|ger, ...ge|schäft, ...han|del** (*vgl.* [1]Handel), **...kurs, ...markt, ...re|ser|ve, ...schmug|gel, ...ver|ge|hen, ...ver|kehr**

De|von [...v...], das; -[s] ‹nach einer engl. Grafschaft› (*Geol.* eine Formation des Paläozoikums); **de|vo|nisch**

de|vot [...v...] ‹lat.› (unterwürfig); **De|vo|ti|on,** die; -, -en (Unterwürfigkeit; Andacht); **De|vo|ti|o|na|li|en** [...i̯ən] *Plur.* (*kath. Kirche* der Andacht dienende Gegenstände)

De|wa|na|ga|ri, die; - ‹sanskr.› (ind. Schrift [für das Sanskrit])

Dext|rin (↑R 130), das; -s, -e ‹lat.› ([Klebe]stärke); **dext|ro|gyr** ‹lat.; griech.› (*Chemie* die Ebene polarisierten Lichtes nach rechts drehend; *Zeichen* d); **Dext|ro|kar|die,** die; -, ...i̯en ‹lat.; griech.› (*Med.* anomale rechtsseitige Lage des Herzens); **Dext|ro|se,** die; - (Traubenzucker)

Dez, der; -es, -e (*mdal. für* Kopf)

Dez. = Dezember

De|zem|ber, der; -[s], - ‹lat.› (zwölfter Monat im Jahr; Christmond, Julmond, Wintermonat; *Abk.* Dez.); **De|zem|ber‿abend** (↑R 132), **...tag; De|zem|vir** [...v...], der; *Gen.* -s *u.* -n, *Plur.* -n; ↑R 126 (Mitglied des Dezemvirats); **De|zem|vi|rat,** das; -[e]s, -e (altröm. Zehnmännerkollegium);

De|zen|ni|um, das; -s, ...ien [...i̯ən] (Jahrzehnt)

de|zent ‹lat.› (zurückhaltend, taktvoll, feinfühlig; unaufdringlich)

de|zent|ral [*auch* ˈde:...] ‹nlat.›

(vom Mittelpunkt entfernt); **De|zent|ra|li|sa|ti|on** *u.* De|zent|ra|li|sie|rung, die; -, -en (Auseinanderlegung von Verwaltungen usw.); **de|zent|ra|li|sie|ren; De|zent|ra|li|sie|rung** *vgl.* Dezentralisation

De|zenz, die; - ‹lat.› (*geh. für* Anstand, Zurückhaltung; unauffällige Eleganz)

De|zer|nat, das; -[e]s, -e ‹lat.› (Geschäftsbereich eines Dezernenten; Sachgebiet); **De|zer|nent,** der; -en, -en; ↑R 126 (Sachbearbeiter mit Entscheidungsbefugnis [bei Behörden]; Leiter eines Dezernats)

De|zi... ‹lat.› (Zehntel...; ein Zehntel einer Einheit [z. B. Dezimeter = $^1/_{10}$ Meter]; *Zeichen* d)

De|zi|bel, das; -s, - ($^1/_{10}$ Bel; bes. Maß der relativen Lautstärke; *Zeichen* dB)

de|zi|diert ‹lat.› (entschieden, energisch, bestimmt)

De|zi|gramm ‹lat.; griech.› ($^1/_{10}$ g; *Zeichen* dg); **De|zi|li|ter** ($^1/_{10}$ l; *Zeichen* dl); **de|zi|mal** ‹lat.› (auf die Grundzahl 10 bezogen); **De|zi|mal|bruch,** der (Bruch, dessen Nenner mit [einer Potenz von] 10 gebildet wird); **De|zi|ma|le,** die; -[n], -n (*Math.* eine Ziffer der Ziffernfolge, die rechts vom Komma einer Dezimalzahl steht); **de|zi|ma|li|sie|ren** (auf das Dezimalsystem umstellen); **De|zi|ma|li|sie|rung; De|zi|mal‿klas|si|fi|ka|ti|on** (die; -; *Abk.* DK), **...maß, ...rech|nung, ...stel|le, ...sys|tem** (das; -s), **...waa|ge, ...zahl; De|zi|me,** die; -, -n (*Musik* zehnter Ton vom Grundton an); **De|zi|me|ter** ‹lat.; griech.› ($^1/_{10}$ m; *Zeichen* dm); **de|zi|mie|ren** ‹lat.› (große Verluste beibringen; stark vermindern); **de|zi|miert; De|zi|mie|rung**

de|zi|siv ‹lat.› (entscheidend, bestimmt)

De|zi|ton|ne (100 kg; *Zeichen* dt)

DFB = Deutscher Fußball-Bund

DFF = Deutscher Fernsehfunk; **DFF-Län|der|ket|te** (ehemalige Rundfunkkette in den neuen Bundesländern)

dg = Dezigramm

Dg = Dekagramm

D. G. = Dei gratia

DGB = Deutscher Gewerkschaftsbund

dgl. = dergleichen

d. Gr. = der *od.* die Große

d. h. = das heißt

Dha|ka (Hptst. von Bangladesch)

Dhau *vgl.* Dau

d'hondt|sche Sys|tem, das; -n -s ‹nach dem belgischen Juristen d'Hondt› (ein Berechnungsmodus bei [Parlaments]wahlen)

d. i. = das ist

Di. = Dienstag

Dia, das; -s, -s (*Kurzform für* Diapositiv)

Di|a|bas, der; -es, -e ‹griech.› (ein Ergussgestein)

Di|a|be|tes, der; - ‹griech.› (*Med.* Harnruhr); - mellitus (*Med.* Zuckerkrankheit); **Di|a|be|ti|ker; Di|a|be|ti|ke|rin; di|a|be|tisch**

Di|a|bo|lie, Di|a|bo|lik, die; - ‹griech.› (teuflisches Verhalten); **di|a|bo|lisch** (teuflisch); -es (magisches) Quadrat; **Di|a|bo|lo** das; -s, -s ‹ital.› (ein Geschicklichkeitsspiel); **Di|a|bo|los, Di|a|bo|lus,** der; - ‹griech.› (der Teufel)

di|a|chron [...k...], di|a|chro|nisch ‹griech.› (*Sprachw.* [entwicklungs]geschichtlich); **Di|a|chro|nie,** die; - (*Sprachw.* [Darstellung der] geschichtl. Entwicklung einer Sprache); **di|a|chro|nisch** *vgl.* diachron

Di|a|dem, das; -s, -e ‹griech.› (kostbarer [Stirn]reif)

Di|a|do|che, der; -n, -n (↑R 126) ‹griech.› (mit anderen konkurrierender Nachfolger [Alexanders d. Gr.]); **Di|a|do|chen‿kämp|fe** *(Plur.)*, **...zeit** (die; -)

Di|a|ge|ne|se, die; -, -n ‹griech.› (Veränderung eines Sediments durch Druck u. Temperatur)

Di|ag|no|se (↑R 132), die; -, -n ‹griech.› ([Krankheits]erkennung; *Zool., Bot.* Bestimmung); **Di|ag|no|se‿ver|fah|ren, ...zent|rum; Di|ag|nos|tik,** die; - (*Med.* Fähigkeit und Lehre, Krankheiten usw. zu erkennen); **Di|ag|nos|ti|ker; di|ag|nos|tisch; di|ag|nos|ti|zie|ren**

di|a|go|nal ‹griech.› (schräg laufend); **Di|a|go|nal,** der; -[s], -s (schräg gestreifter Kleiderstoff in Köperbindung); **Di|a|go|na|le,** die; -, -n (Gerade, die zwei nicht benachbarte Ecken eines Vielecks miteinander verbindet); drei Diagonale[n]; **Di|a|go|nal|rei|fen**

Di|a|gramm, das; -s, -e ‹griech.› (zeichnerische Darstellung errechneter Werte in einem Koordinatensystem; Stellungsbild beim Schach)

Di|a|kaus|tik, die; -, -en ‹griech.› (die beim Durchgang von parallelem Licht bei einer Linse entstehende Brennfläche); **di|a|kaus|tisch**

Di|a|kon [*österr.* 'di:...], der; *Gen.* -s *u.* -en (↑R 126), *Plur.* -e[n] ‹griech.› (kath., anglikan. od. orthodoxer Geistlicher, der um einen Weihegrad unter dem Priester steht; karitativ od. seelsorgerisch tätiger Angestellter in ev. Kirchen); *vgl.* Diakonus; **Di|a|ko|nat,** das, *auch* der; -[e]s, -e (Diakonenamt, -wohnung); **Di|a|ko|nie,** die; - ([berufsmäßige] Sozialtätigkeit [Krankenpflege, Gemeindedienst] in der ev. Kirche); **Di|a|ko|nin; di|a|ko|nisch; Di|a|ko|nis|se,** die; -, -n *u.* Di|a|ko|nis|sin, die; -, -nen (ev. Kranken- u. Gemeindeschwester); **Di|a|ko|nis|sen|haus; Di|a|ko|nis|sin** *vgl.* Diakonisse; **Di|a|ko|nus,** der; -, ...kone[n] (*veraltet für* zweiter od. dritter Pfarrer einer ev. Gemeinde, Hilfsgeistlicher)

Di|a|kri|se, Di|a|kri|sis, die; -, ...isen ‹griech.› (*Med.* entscheidende Krise einer Krankheit); **di|a|kri|tisch** [*auch* ...'kri...] (unterscheidend); diakritisches Zeichen *(Sprachw.)*

Di|a|lekt, der; -[e]s, -e ‹griech.› (Mundart); **di|a|lek|tal** (mundartlich); -e Besonderheiten; **Di|a|lekt‿aus|druck, ...dich|tung, ...fär|bung, ...for|schung; di|a|lekt|frei; Di|a|lekt|ge|o|gra|phie; Di|a|lek|tik,** die; - (Erforschung der Wahrheit durch Aufweisung u. Überwindung von Widersprüchen; Gegensätzlichkeit); **Di|a|lek|ti|ker** (jmd., der die dialektische Methode anwendet); **di|a|lek|tisch** (mundartlich; die Dialektik betreffend; *auch für* spitzfindig); dialektische Methode (von den Sophisten ausgebildete Kunst der Gesprächsführung; das Denken in These, Antithese, Synthese [Hegel]); dialektischer Materialismus (marxist. Lehre von den Grundbegriffen der Dialektik u. des Materialismus); dialektische Theologie (eine Richtung der ev. Theologie nach dem 1. Weltkrieg); **Di|a|lek|to|lo|gie,** die; - (Mundartforschung); **di|a|lek|to|lo|gisch**

Di|a|log, der; -[e]s, -e ‹griech.› (Zwiegespräch; Wechselrede); **Di|a|log|be|reit|schaft,** die; -; **di|a|lo|gisch** (in Dialogform); **di|a|lo|gi|sie|ren** (in Dialogform kleiden); **Di|a|log|kunst,** die; -

Di|a|ly|sa|tor, der; -s, ...oren ‹griech.› (*Chemie* Gerät zur Durchführung der Dialyse); **Di|a|ly|se,** die; -, -n (chem. Trennungsmethode; *Med.* Blutwäsche); **Di|a|ly|se‿sta|ti|on, ...zent|rum** (für Nierenkranke); **di|a|ly|sie|ren; di|a|ly|tisch** (auf Dialyse beruhend)

¹Di|a|mant, die; - ‹franz.› (*Druckw.* ein Schriftgrad); **²Di|a|mant,** der; -en, -en (↑R 126); *vgl. auch* Demant; **Di|a|mant|boh|rer; di|a|man|ten;** diamantene Hochzeit (60. Jahrestag der Hochzeit); **Di|a|mant_feld, ...kol|li|er, ...leim** (zum Fassen von Schmucksteinen), **...na|del, ...ring, ...schild|krö|te, ...schlei|fer, ...schliff, ...schmuck, ...staub, ...tin|te** (ein Ätzmittel für Glas)

DIAMAT, Di|a|mat, der; - (= dialektischer Materialismus; *vgl.* dialektisch)

Di|a|me|ter, der; -s, - ‹griech.› (Durchmesser); **di|a|met|ral** (↑R 130; entgegengesetzt [wie die Endpunkte eines Durchmessers]); **di|a|met|risch** (dem Durchmesser entsprechend)

Di|a|na (röm. Göttin der Jagd)

Di|a|pa|son, der; -s, *Plur.* -s *u.* ...one ‹griech.› (Kammerton; Stimmgabel; [*auch* das; -s, -s:] engl. Orgelregister)

di|a|phan ‹griech.› (*Kunstw.* durchscheinend); **Di|a|phan|bild** (durchscheinendes Bild)

Di|a|pho|ra, die; - ‹griech.› (*Rhet.* Betonung des Unterschieds zweier Dinge); **Di|a|pho|re|se,** die; -, -n (*Med.* Schwitzen); **di|a|pho|re|tisch** (schweißtreibend)

Di|a|phrag|ma, das; -s, ...men ‹griech.› (*Chemie* durchlässige Scheidewand; *Med.* Zwerchfell; mechanisches Empfängnisverhütungsmittel)

Di|a|po|si|tiv [*auch* ...'ti:f], das; -s, -e [...ve] ‹griech.; lat.› (durchscheinendes fotografisches Bild; *Kurzform* Dia); **Di|a|pro|jek|tor** (Vorführgerät für Dias)

Di|ä|re|se *u.* **Di|ä|re|sis,** die; -, ...resen ‹griech.› (*Sprachw.* getrennte Aussprache zweier Vokale, z. B. naiv; *Verslehre* Einschnitt im Vers an einem Wortende; *Philos.* Begriffszerlegung; *Med.* Zerreißung eines Gefäßes mit Blutaustritt)

Di|a|ri|um, das; -s, ...ien [...iən] ‹lat.› (Tagebuch; Kladde)

Di|ar|rhö[1], **Di|ar|rhöe** [...'rø:], die; -, ...rrhöen ‹griech.› (*Med.* Durchfall); **di|ar|rhö|isch**

---

[1] In Übereinstimmung mit der Arbeitsgruppe für medizin. Literaturdokumentation in der Deutschen Gesellschaft für Dokumentation und mit führenden Fachverlagen wurde die Form auf -oe zugunsten der Form auf -ö aufgegeben.

Di|a|skop, das; -s, -e ‹griech.› (*veraltend für* Diaprojektor)

Di|as|po|ra (↑R 132), die; - ‹griech.› (*Rel.* Gebiet, in dem die Anhänger einer Konfession in der Minderheit sind; religiöse od. nationale Minderheit); **Di|as|po|ra|ge|mein|de**

Di|as|to|le [...stole:, *auch* ...'sto:lə] (↑R 132), die; -, ...olen (*Med.* mit der Systole rhythmisch abwechselnde Erweiterung des Herzens); **di|as|to|lisch;** -er Blutdruck (*Med.*)

Di|ät, die; -, *Plur. (Arten:)* -en ‹griech.› (Krankenkost; Schonkost; spezielle Ernährungsweise); Diät leben; Diät halten, kochen; jmdn. auf Diät setzen; **Di|ät|as|sis|ten|tin** (*svw.* Diätistin)

Di|ä|ten *Plur.* ‹lat.› (Tagegelder; Aufwandsentschädigung u. a. [bes. von Parlamentariern])

Di|ä|te|tik, die; -, -en ‹griech.› (Ernährungslehre); **Di|ä|te|ti|kum,** das; -s, ...ka (für eine Diät geeignetes Nahrungsmittel); **di|ä|te|tisch** (der Diätetik gemäß); **Di|ät|feh|ler** (*Med.* Fehler in der Ernährungsweise)

Di|a|thek, die; -, -en ‹griech.› (Diapositivsammlung)

di|a|ther|man ‹griech.› (*Med., Meteor.* Wärmestrahlen durchlassend); **Di|a|ther|mie,** die; - (*Med.* Heilverfahren, bei dem Hochfrequenzströme innere Körperabschnitte durchwärmen)

Di|a|the|se, die; -, -n ‹griech.› (*Med.* Veranlagung zu bestimmten Krankheiten)

Di|äthy|len|gly|kol, *chem. fachspr. auch* Di|ethy|len|gly|kol (↑R 132) ‹griech.› (Bestandteil von Frostschutzmitteln u. a.)

di|ä|tisch ‹griech.› (die Ernährung betreffend); **Di|ä|tis|tin** (w. Fachkraft, die bei der Aufstellung von Diätplänen mitwirkt); **Di|ät_koch, ...kost, ...kü|che, ...kur**

Di|a|to|mee, die; -, -n *meist Plur.* ‹griech.› (*Bot.* Kieselalge); **Di|a|to|me|en_er|de** (die; -; *svw.* Kieselgur), **...schlamm** (Ablagerung von Diatomeen)

Di|a|to|nik, die; - ‹griech.› (*Musik* Dur-Moll-Tonsystem; das Fortschreiten in der Tonfolge der 7-stufigen Tonleiter); **di|a|to|nisch** (auf der Diatonik beruhend); die -e Tonleiter

Di|ät|plan

Di|at|ri|be (↑R 130), die; -, -n ‹griech.› (Abhandlung; Streitschrift)

Dib|bel|ma|schi|ne ‹engl.; franz.›; **dib|beln** ‹engl.› (*Landw.* in Reihen mit größeren Abständen säen); ich ...[e]le (↑R 16); *vgl. aber* tippeln

dich *(auch in Briefen kleingeschrieben)*

Di|cho|to|mie [...ç...], die; -, ...ien ‹griech.› (Zweiteilung [in Begriffspaare]; *Bot.* Gabelung); **di|cho|to|misch,** di|cho|tom

Di|chro|is|mus [...k...], der; - ‹griech.› (*Physik* Zweifarbigkeit von Kristallen bei Lichtdurchgang); **di|chro|i|tisch;** -e Spiegel; **di|chro|ma|tisch** (*Optik* zweifarbig); -e Gläser; **Di|chro|skop,** das; -s, -e (besondere Lupe zur Prüfung auf Dichroismus); **di|chro|sko|pisch**

dicht; eine dicht behaarte Brust; dicht bevölkerte Landstriche; die Menschen standen dicht gedrängt; der Verschluss hat dicht gehalten; ein Fass dicht machen; *vgl. aber* dichthalten, dichtmachen; **dicht|auf;** - folgen; **dicht be|haart;** *vgl.* dicht; **dicht be|völ|kert;** *vgl.* dicht; **Dich|te,** die; -, -n *Plur. selten* (*Technik auch für* Verhältnis der Masse zur Raumeinheit); **Dich|te|mes|ser,** der (*für* Densimeter); **¹dich|ten** (dicht machen)

²dich|ten (Verse schreiben); **Dich|ten,** das; -s; (↑R 50:) das Dichten und Trachten der Menschen; **Dich|ter; Dich|te|rin; dich|te|risch;** -e Freiheit; **Dich|ter_kom|po|nist** (Dichter u. Komponist in einer Person), **...kreis, ...le|sung, ...spra|che; Dich|ter|tum,** das; -s; **Dich|ter|wort** *Plur.* ...worte

dicht ge|drängt; *vgl.* dicht; **dicht|hal|ten** (*ugs. für* nichts verraten); sie hat dichtgehalten (↑R 39); *vgl.* dicht; **Dicht|heit,** die; -; **Dich|tig|keit,** die; -

Dicht|kunst, die; -

dicht|ma|chen (*ugs. für* schließen); sie haben die Fabrik dichtgemacht; gegen sechs macht er seinen Laden dicht; *vgl.* dicht

¹Dich|tung (Gedicht)

²Dich|tung (Vorrichtung zum Dichtmachen)

Dich|tungs_art, ...gat|tung

Dich|tungs_mas|se, ...ma|te|ri|al, ...mit|tel (das), **...ring, ...schei|be, ...stoff**

dick; durch dick und dünn (↑R 47); **dick|bau|chig; Dick|darm; Dick|darm|ent|zün|dung; di|cke;** *nur in* jmdn., eine Sache - haben (*ugs. für* jmds., einer Sache überdrüssig sein); **¹Di|cke,** die; -, -n (*nur Sing.:* Dicksein; *[in Verbindung mit Maßangaben]* Abstand von einer Seite zur ande-

ren); Bretter von 2 mm -, von verschiedenen -n; [2]**Di|cke,** der *u.* die; -n, -n (↑R 5 ff.); **di|cken** (zähflüssig machen, werden); Brombeersaft dickt leicht
Di|ckens (engl. Schriftsteller)
Di|cken|wachs|tum (z. B. eines Baumes); **Di|cker|chen; di|cke-tun,** dick|tun; ↑R 37 (*ugs. für* sich wichtig machen); ich tue mich dick[e]; dick[e]getan; dick[e]zutun; **dick|fel|lig** *(ugs. abwertend);* **Dick|fel|lig|keit,** die; - *(ugs. abwertend);* **dick|flüs|sig; Dick-häu|ter; Di|ckicht,** das; -s, -e; **Dick|kopf** *(ugs.);* **dick‿köp|fig** *(ugs.),* **...lei|big; dick|lich; Dick-‿ma|cher** (*ugs. für* sehr kalorienreiches Nahrungsmittel), **...milch, ...schä|del** *(ugs.),* **...schiff** (großes Seeschiff), **...sein** (das; -s); **Dick|te,** die; -, -n (*Druckw.* Buchstabenbreite); **Dick|tu|er; Dick|tu|e|rei; dick-tun** *vgl.* dicketun; **Di|ckung** (*Jägerspr.* Dickicht); **dick|wan|dig; Dick‿wanst** *(ugs. abwertend),* **...wurz** (Runkelrübe)
Di|dak|tik, die; -, -en ‹griech.› (Unterrichtslehre); **Di|dak|ti|ker; Di|dak|ti|ke|rin; di|dak|tisch** (unterrichtskundlich; lehrhaft)
di|del|dum!, di|del|dum|dei!
Di|de|rot [didəˈroː] (franz. Schriftsteller u. Philosoph)
Di|do (sagenhafte Gründerin Karthagos)
die; *Gen.* der *u.* deren *(vgl. d.); Plur. vgl.* der
Dieb, der; -[e]s, -e; **Die|be|rei; Die|bes‿ban|de** (*vgl.* [2]Bande), **...beu|te, ...gut, ...ha|ken** ([2]Dietrich), **...nest; die|bes|si|cher; Die|bes‿tour, ...zug; Die|bin; die|bisch; Diebs|ge|sin|del; Dieb|stahl,** der; -[e]s, ...stähle; **Dieb|stahl|ver|si|che|rung**
Dief|fen|ba|chie [...xi̯ə], die; -, -n ‹nach dem österr. Botaniker Dieffenbach› (eine Zierpflanze mit großen, länglich-runden Blättern)
die|je|ni|ge; *Gen.* derjenigen, *Plur.* diejenigen
Die|le, die; -, -n
Di|elek|tri|kum (↑R 130 *u.* 132), das; -s, ...ka ‹griech.› (elektr. Nichtleiter); **di|elek|trisch; Di-elek|tri|zi|täts|kon|stan|te** (Wert, der die elektr. Eigenschaften eines Stoffes kennzeichnet; *Zeichen ε*)
die|len; Die|len‿bo|den, ...brett, ...lam|pe
Die|me, die; -, -n *u.* **Die|men,** der; -s, - (*nordd. für* [Heu]haufen)
die|nen; Die|ner; Die|ne|rin; die-nern; ich ...ere (↑R 16); **Die-ner|schaft; Die|ner|schar** *vgl.* [1]Schar; **dien|lich; Dienst,** der; -[e]s, -e; zu Diensten stehen; etw. in Dienst stellen (in Betrieb nehmen); außer Dienst (*Abk.* a. D.); der Dienst habende Beamte; die Dienst tuende Ärztin; (↑R 47:) der Diensthabende wurde gerufen; **Dienst|ab|teil**
Diens|tag, der; -[e]s, -e (*Abk.* Di.); ich werde Sie Dienstag aufsuchen; eines Dienstags; des Dienstags, *aber* (↑R 46): dienstags; alle Dienstage, *aber* immer dienstags; [am] Dienstag früh beginnen wir, *aber* am [nächsten] Dienstagabend; *vgl. d.; entsprechend in Verbindung mit* Morgen, morgens usw.; **Diens|tag|abend** [*auch* ˈdiːnstaːkˈaː...] (↑R 132); meine Dienstagabende sind schon alle belegt; er ist für Dienstagabend bestellt; *aber* dienstagabends *od.* dienstags abends spielen wir Skat; am, jeden Dienstagabend; eines schönen Dienstagabends; *vgl.* Dienstag; **diens|tä|gig** *vgl.* ...tägig; **diens|täg|lich** *vgl.* ...täglich; **Diens|tag|nacht** [*auch* ˈdiːnstaːk-ˈnaxt]; *vgl.* Dienstag; **diens|tags** (↑R 46); *vgl.* Dienstag, Dienstagabend; **Diens|tags|ver|an|stal-tung**
Dienst‿al|ter, ...äl|tes|te, ...antritt, ...an|zug, ...auf|fas|sung, ...auf|sicht; Dienst|auf|sichts-be|schwer|de *(Rechtsw.);* **Dienst|aus|weis; dienst|bar; Dienst|bar|keit; dienst|be|flis-sen; Dienst|be|ginn; dienst|be-reit; Dienst‿be|reit|schaft** (die; -), **...bo|te; dienst‿eif|rig, ...fer-tig, ...frei** (- haben, sein); **Dienst-‿ge|ber** (*österr. neben* Arbeitgeber), **...ge|brauch** (nur für den -), **...ge|heim|nis, ...ge|spräch, ...grad; Dienst ha|bend** *vgl.* Dienst; **Dienst|ha|ben|de,** der *u.* die; -n, -n (↑R 5 ff. *u.* 47); **Dienst-‿herr, ...jahr** *(meist Plur.);* **Dienst|leis|tung; Dienst|leis-tungs‿abend** (↑R 132), **...be-trieb, ...ge|sell|schaft** *(Soziol.),* **...ge|wer|be; dienst|lich; Dienst|mäd|chen** (*veraltet für* Hausgehilfin); [1]**Dienst|mann** *Plur.* ...mannen (*früher für* Lehnsmann); [2]**Dienst|mann** *Plur.* ...männer, *österr. u. schweiz. nur so, u.* ...leute (*veraltend für* Gepäckträger); **Dienst‿neh|mer** (*österr. neben* Arbeitnehmer), **...per|so|nal, ...pflicht; dienst-pflich|tig; Dienst|prag|ma|tik,** die; - (*österr. früher für* generelle Norm für das öffentl.-rechtl. Dienstverhältnis); **Dienst|rang; dienst|recht|lich; Dienst‿rei-se, ...sa|che, ...schluss** (der; -es), **...sie|gel, ...stel|le, ...stem-pel; dienst|taug|lich; Dienst tu-end** *vgl.* Dienst; **dienst|un|fä-hig; Dienst|un|fä|hig|keit,** die; -; **dienst|ver|pflich|tet; Dienst-‿vor|schrift, ...waf|fe, ...wa-gen, ...weg; dienst|wid|rig; Dienst‿woh|nung, ...zeit**
Dierk *vgl.* Dirk
dies, dieses (↑R 48); *Gen.* dieses; diesjährig, diesmal, diesseits
Di|es [ˈdiːɛs], der; - (*kurz für* Dies academicus); **Di|es a|ca|de|mi-cus,** der; - - ‹lat.› (vorlesungsfreier Tag an der Universität, an dem eine Feier o. Ä. angesetzt ist); **Di-es a|ter,** der; - - ‹lat., „schwarzer Tag"› (Unglückstag)
dies|be|züg|lich
Die|sel, der; -[s], - ‹nach dem Erfinder› (*kurz für* Dieselkraftstoff; [Auto mit] Dieselmotor)
die|sel|be; *Gen.* derselben; *Plur.* dieselben; ein[e] und -; **die|sel|bi-ge;** ↑R 48 (*veraltet für* dieselbe)
die|sel|elek|trisch (↑R 132); **Die-sel‿kraft|stoff** (*Abk.* DK), **...lo|ko|mo|ti|ve, ...ma|schi|ne, ...mo|tor** (↑R 95); **die|seln** (wie ein Dieselmotor ohne Zündung weiterlaufen [vom Ottomotor]); **Die|sel‿öl, ...trieb|wa-gen** (↑R 95)
die|ser (↑R 48), diese, dieses (dies); *Gen.* dieses, dieser, dieses; *Plur.* diese; dieser selbe [Augenblick]; **die|ser|art** (auf diese Weise; so); *aber* Fälle [von] dieser Art; **die|ser|halb** (*veraltend für* deshalb); **die|ses** *vgl.* dies; **die-ses Jah|res** (*Abk.* d. J.); **die|ses Mo|nats** (*Abk.* d. M.); **dies|falls** *(veraltet)*
die|sig (dunstig, trübe u. feucht); **Die|sig|keit,** die; -
Di|es I|rae [ˈdiːɛs ˈiːrɛ], das; - - ‹lat., „Tag des Zornes"› (Anfang eines Hymnus auf das Weltgericht; Teil des Requiems)
dies|jäh|rig; dies|mal, *aber* dieses Mal, dieses *od.* dies eine, letzte Mal; **dies|ma|lig; dies|sei|tig; Dies|sei|tig|keit,** die; -; **dies-seits;** *Präp. mit Gen.:* - des Flusses; **Dies|seits,** das; -; im -; **Dies-seits|glau|be**
Die|ter, Die|ther; ↑R 92 (m. Vorn.); **Diet|hild, Diet|hil|de** (w. Vorn.)
Di|ethy|len|gly|kol (↑R 132); *vgl.* Diäthylenglykol
Diet|lind, Diet|lin|de (w. Vorn.); **Diet|mar** (m. Vorn.); [1]**Diet|rich** (m. Vorn.); [2]**Diet|rich,** der; -s, -e (Nachschlüssel)

die|weil, all|die|weil *(veraltet)*

Dif|fa|ma|ti|on, die; -, -en ‹lat.› (Verleumdung); **dif|fa|ma|to|risch; Dif|fa|mie,** die; -, ...ien (verleumderische Bosheit; Beschimpfung); **dif|fa|mie|ren; Dif|fa|mie|rung**

dif|fe|rent ‹lat.› (verschieden, ungleich); **dif|fe|ren|ti|al, Dif|fe|ren|ti|al** usw. *vgl.* differenzial, Differenzial usw.; **dif|fe|ren|ti|ell** *vgl.* differenzial; **Dif|fe|renz,** die; -, -en (Unterschied; Unstimmigkeit); **Dif|fe|renz‿be|trag, ...geschäft** (Börsentermingeschäft); **dif|fe|ren|zi|al,** *auch* dif|fe|ren|ti|al (einen Unterschied begründend od. darstellend); **Dif|fe|ren|zi|al,** *auch* Dif|fe|ren|ti|al, das; -s, -e (*Math.* unendlich kleine Differenz; *kurz für* Differenzialgetriebe); **Dif|fe|ren|zi|al‿di|ag|no|se** (*Med.* Unterscheidung ähnlicher Krankheitsbilder), **...ge|o|met|rie** *(Math.)*; **...ge|trie|be** (Ausgleichsgetriebe beim Kraftfahrzeug), **...quo|ti|ent** *(Math.)*, **...rech|nung** *(Math.)*, **...schal|tung** *(Elektrotechnik)*, **...ta|rif** *(Verkehrsw.)*; **Dif|fe|ren|zi|a|ti|on,** *auch* Dif|fe|ren|ti|a|ti|on, die; -, -en (*Math.* Anwendung der Differenzialrechnung; *Geol.* Aufspaltung einer Stammschmelze); **dif|fe|ren|zi|ell,** *auch* dif|fe|ren|ti|ell (*svw.* differenzial); **dif|fe|ren|zie|ren** (trennen; unterscheiden; abstufen; *Math.* die Differenzialrechnung anwenden); **Dif|fe|ren|ziert|heit,** die; - (Unterschiedlichkeit; Abgestuftsein); **Dif|fe|ren|zie|rung** (Abstufung; Auseinanderentwicklung); **dif|fe|rie|ren** (verschieden sein; voneinander abweichen)

dif|fi|zil ‹franz.› (schwierig, kompliziert; schwer zu behandeln)

dif|form ‹lat.› (*Med.* missgestaltet); **Dif|for|mi|tät,** die; -, -en (Missbildung)

Dif|frak|ti|on, die; -, -en ‹lat.› (*Physik* Strahlenbrechung, Beugung des Lichtes)

dif|fun|die|ren ‹lat.› (*fachspr. für* durchdringen; zerstreuen); **diffus** (zerstreut; ungeordnet; verschwommen); -es Licht; **Dif|fu|si|on,** die; -, -en (*Chemie* gegenseitige Durchdringung [von Gasen od. Flüssigkeiten]; *Physik* Zerstreuung; *Bergmannsspr.* Wetteraustausch; *Zuckerherstellung* Auslaugung); **Dif|fu|sor,** der; -s, ...oren (*Technik* Rohrleitungsteil, dessen Querschnitt sich erweitert; *Fot.* transparente, Licht streuende Plastikscheibe zur Erweiterung des Messwinkels bei Lichtmessern)

Di|gam|ma, das; -[s], -s (Buchstabe im ältesten griech. Alphabet; Ϝ)

di|gen ‹griech.› (*Biol.* durch Verschmelzung zweier Zellen gezeugt)

di|ge|rie|ren ‹lat.› (*Chemie* auslaugen, -ziehen; *Med.* verdauen); **Digest** ['daidʒɛst], der *od.* das; -[s], -s ‹engl.› (bes. in den angels. Ländern übliche Art von Zeitschriften, die Auszüge aus Büchern, Zeitschriften u. Ä. bringen); **Di|ges|ten** [di'gɛ...] *Plur.* ‹lat.› (Gesetzessammlung des Kaisers Justinian); **Di|ges|tif** [diʒes'tif], der; -s, -s ‹franz.› (die Verdauung anregendes alkoholisches Getränk); **Di|ges|ti|on** [...g...], die; -, -en ‹lat.› (*Med.* Verdauung; *Chemie* Auslaugen, -ziehen); **di|ges|tiv** (*Med.* Verdauungs...)

Di|git ['didʒit], das; -[s], -s ‹engl.› (Ziffer einer elektron. Anzeige); **di|gi|tal** [digi...] ‹lat.› (*Med.* mit dem Finger; *Technik* in Ziffern dargestellt, ziffernmäßig; *EDV* in Stufen erfolgend); **Di|gi|ta|lis,** die; -, - (Fingerhut, eine Arzneipflanze); **di|gi|ta|li|sie|ren** (*Technik* mit Ziffern darstellen; in ein digitales Signal umwandeln); **Di|gi|tal‿rech|ner, ...tech|nik, ...uhr, ...ver|fah|ren**

Di|glos|sie, die; -, -n ‹griech.› (*Sprachw.* Form der Zweisprachigkeit)

Di|glyph, der; -s, -e ‹griech.› (*Archit.* zweigeschlitzte Platte am Gebälk [ital. Renaissance])

Dig|ni|tar (↑R 130) ‹lat.›, **Dig|ni|tär** ‹franz.›, der; -s, -e (Würdenträger der kath. Kirche); **Dig|ni|tät,** die; -, -en ‹lat.› (kath. kirchl. Würde)

Di|gres|si|on, die; -, -en ‹lat.› (*Astron.* Winkel zwischen dem Meridian u. dem Vertikalkreis, der durch ein polnahes Gestirn geht)

DIHT = Deutscher Industrie- und Handelstag (*vgl.* deutsch)

di|hyb|rid (↑R 130) ‹griech.› (*Biol.* sich in zwei erblichen Merkmalen unterscheidend)

Di|jam|bus, der; -, ...ben ‹griech.› (*Verslehre* Doppeljambus)

Di|ke ['di:kə, *auch* 'di:ke:] (griech. Göttin der Gerechtigkeit, eine der [2]Horen)

di|klin ‹griech.› (*Bot.* eingeschlechtig)

Di|ko|ty|le, Di|ko|ty|le|do|ne, die; -, -n ‹griech.› (*Bot.* zweikeimblättrige Pflanze)

Dik|ta|fon *eindeutschende Schreibung für* Diktaphon; **dik|tan|do** ‹lat.› (*selten für* diktierend, beim Diktieren); **Dik|tant,** der; -en, -en; ↑R 126 (jmd., der diktiert); **Dik|ta|phon** (↑R 33), das; -s, -e ‹lat.; griech.› (Tonbandgerät zum Diktieren); **Dik|tat,** das; -[e]s, -e ‹lat.›; **Dik|ta|tor,** der; -s, ...oren (unumschränkter Machthaber); **dik|ta|to|risch; Dik|ta|tur,** die; -, -en; **dik|tie|ren** (zur Niederschrift vorsprechen; aufzwingen); **Dik|tier|ge|rät; Dik|ti|on,** die; -, -en (Schreibart; Ausdrucksweise); **Dik|ti|o|när,** das *u.* der; -s, -e ‹franz.› (*veraltend für* Wörterbuch); **Dik|tum,** das; -s, ...ta ‹lat., „Gesagtes"› ([bedeutsamer] Ausspruch)

di|la|ta|bel ‹lat.› (dehnbar); ...table (↑R 130) Buchstaben; **Di|la|ta|bi|les** [...le:s] *Plur.* (in die Breite gezogene hebr. Buchstaben); **Di|la|ta|ti|on,** die; -, -en (*Physik* Ausdehnung; *Med.* Erweiterung [von Körperhöhlen])

Di|la|ti|on, die; -, -en ‹lat.› (*Rechtsw.* Aufschub[frist]); **di|la|to|risch** (aufschiebend)

Di|lem|ma, das; -s, *Plur.* -s, *auch* -ta ‹griech.› (Zwangslage; Wahl zwischen zwei [unangenehmen] Dingen)

Di|let|tant, der; -en, -en (↑R 126) ‹ital.› (*geh. für* [Kunst]liebhaber; Nichtfachmann; Stümper); **di|let|tan|ten|haft, di|let|tan|tisch** (unfachmännisch, laienhaft; stümperhaft); **Di|let|tan|tis|mus,** der; - (laienhafte Beschäftigung mit etwas, Liebhaberei; Stümperhaftigkeit); **di|let|tie|ren** (*selten für* sich als Dilettant betätigen)

Di|li|gence [dili'ʒã:s], die; -, -n [...s(ə)n] ‹franz.› (*früher* [Eil]postkutsche)

Dill, der; -s, -e, *bes. österr. auch* **Dil|le,** die; -, -n (eine Gewürzpflanze); **Dil|len|kraut, Dill|kraut** *(österr.)*

Dil|they [...tai] (dt. Philosoph)

di|lu|vi|al [...v...] ‹lat.› (*älter für* pleistozän); **Di|lu|vi|um,** das; -s (*älter für* Pleistozän)

dim. = diminuendo

Dime [daim], der; -s, -s (US-amerik. Münze); 10 - (↑R 90)

Di|men|si|on, die; -, -en ‹lat.› (Ausdehnung; [Aus]maß; Bereich); **di|men|si|o|nal** (die Ausdehnung bestimmend); **di|men|si|o|nie|ren** (abmessen; *Technik* die Maße festlegen)

Di|me|ter, der; -s, - ‹griech.› (*Verslehre* antike Verseinheit aus zwei Füßen)

di|mi|nu|en|do ‹ital.› (*Musik* in der Tonstärke abnehmend; *Abk.* dim.); **Di|mi|nu|en|do,** das; -s, *Plur.* -s *u.* ...di; **di|mi|nu|ie|ren** ‹lat.› (verkleinern, verringern); **Di|mi|nu|ti|on,** die; -, -en (Verkleinerung, Verringerung; *Musik* Verkürzung der Notenwerte; variierende Verzierung); **di|mi|nu|tiv** (*Sprachw.* verkleinernd); **Di|mi|nu|tiv,** das; -s, -e [...və] *u.* Di|mi|nu|ti|vum [...vum], das; -s, ...va [...va] (*Sprachw.* Verkleinerungswort, z. B. „Öfchen"); **Di|mi|nu|tiv|form** [...f...] *(Sprachw.)*; **Di|mi|nu|ti|vum** *vgl.* Diminutiv

di|mit|tie|ren ‹lat.› (*veraltet für* entlassen, verabschieden)

Dim|mer, der; -s, - ‹engl.› (stufenloser Helligkeitsregler)

di|morph ‹griech.› (zweigestaltig, -formig); **Di|mor|phis|mus,** der; -, ...men

DIN ® [di:n] ‹*Abk. für* Deutsche Industrie-Norm(en), *später gedeutet als* Das Ist Norm› (Verbandszeichen des Deutschen Instituts für Normung e. V. [*früher* Deutscher Normenausschuss]); *Schreibweise:* DIN (*mit einer Nummer zur Bezeichnung einer Norm* [z. B. DIN 16511] *u. bei Kopplungen* [z. B. DIN-Norm, DIN-Mitteilungen, DIN-Format]; *vgl. auch* R 28)

Di|na (w. Vorn.; bibl. w. Eigenn.)

Di|nar, der; -[s], -e (Münzeinheit verschiedener Staaten; iran. Münze [100 Dinar = 1 Rial]; *Abk. iran.* D); 6 - (↑R 90)

di|na|risch; -e Rasse (ein Menschentypus, benannt nach dem Dinarischen Gebirge), *aber* (↑R 102): das Dinarische Gebirge (Gebirgssystem im Westen des ehem. Jugoslawien)

Di|ner [di'ne:], das; -s, -s ‹franz.› (*geh. für* [festliches] Abend- od. Mittagessen mit mehreren Gängen)

[1]Ding, das; -[e]s, *Plur.* -e, *ugs.* -er (Sache); guter -e sein

[2]Ding, das; -[e]s, -e (germ. Volks-, Gerichts- u. Heeresversammlung); *vgl. auch* Thing

Din|gel|chen (kleines Ding)

din|gen (*veraltend für* zu Dienstleistungen gegen Entgelt verpflichten; in Dienst nehmen); du dingtest (*selten* dangst, *Konj.* dängest); gedungen (*seltener* gedingt); ding[e]!

Din|ger|chen *Plur.*

ding|fest; *nur in* jmdn. - machen (verhaften)

Din|gi ['diŋgi], das; -s, -s ‹Hindi› (kleines Beiboot)

ding|lich (eine Sache betreffend; gegenständlich); -er Anspruch; **Ding|lich|keit,** die; -

Din|go ['diŋgo], der; -s, -s ‹austr.› (austr. Wildhund)

...dings (z. B. neuerdings); **Dings,** der, die, das; - *u.* **Dings|bums,** der, die, das; - *u.* **[1]Dings|da,** der, die, das; - (*ugs. für* eine unbekannte od. unbenannte Person od. Sache); **[2]Dings|da, Dings|kir|chen** [*auch* ...'kir...] (*ugs. für* einen unbekannten od. unbenannten Ort); **Ding|wort** *Plur.* ...wörter (*für* Substantiv)

di|nie|ren ‹franz.› (*geh. für* [in festlichem Rahmen] essen, speisen); **Di|ning|room** ['dainiŋru(:)m], der; -s, -s ‹engl.› (*engl. Bez. für* Speisezimmer)

Dink, der; -s, -s *meist Plur.* ‹*aus* engl. double income, no kids = doppeltes Einkommen, keine Kinder› (jmd., der in einer Partnerschaft lebt, in der beide Partner einem Beruf nachgehen u. keine Kinder vorhanden sind)

Din|kel, der; -s, - *Plur. selten* (nur noch vereinzelt angebaute Weizenart, Spelt)

Din|ner, das; -s, -[s] ‹engl.› (Hauptmahlzeit in England [abends eingenommen]); **Din|ner|ja|cket** [...dʒɛkit], das; -s, -s (*engl. Bez. für* Smoking[jackett])

Di|no, der; -s, -s (*ugs. kurz für* Dinosaurier); **Di|no|sau|ri|er** [...iər], der; -s, - *u.* **Di|no|sau|rus,** der; -, ...rier [...iər] ‹griech.› (ausgestorbene Riesenechse); **Di|no|the|ri|um,** das; -s, ...ien [...iən] (ausgestorbenes Rüsseltier Europas)

Di|o|de, die; -, -n ‹griech.› (elektron. Bauelement)

Di|o|ge|nes (altgriech. Philosoph)

Di|o|k|le|ti|an (↑R 130; röm. Kaiser); **di|o|k|le|ti|a|nisch;** die diokletianischen Reformen; ↑R 94

Di|o|len ®, das; -[s] (eine synthet. Faser)

Di|on, die; -, -en (*österr. kurz für* Direktion, *selten für* Division)

Di|o|ny|si|en [...iən] *Plur.* ‹griech.› (Dionysosfest); **di|o|ny|sisch;** ↑R 94 (dem Gott Dionysos zugehörend; *auch für* wild begeistert, tobend; rauschend [von Festen]); **Di|o|ny|sos** (griech. Gott des Weines, des Rausches u. der Fruchtbarkeit)

di|o|phan|tisch ‹nach dem altgriech. Mathematiker Diophantos›; -e Gleichung; ↑R 94

Di|op|ter, das; -s, - ‹griech.› (Zielgerät; *Fotogr.* Rahmensucher); **Di|opt|rie** (↑R 130), die; -, ...ien (*Optik* Maßeinheit für den Brechwert von Linsen); *Abk.* dpt, dptr., Dptr.; **di|opt|risch** (das Licht brechend); -es Fernrohr

Di|o|ra|ma, das; -s, ...men ‹griech.› (plastisch wirkendes Schaubild)

Di|o|rit [*auch* ...'rit], der; -s, -e ‹griech.› (ein Tiefengestein)

Di|os|ku|ren *Plur.* ‹griech., „Zeussöhne"› (Kastor u. Pollux; *auch für* unzertrennliche Freunde)

Di|o|ti|ma [*auch* ...'ti:ma] (myth. Priesterin bei Platon; Gestalt bei Hölderlin)

Di|oxid, *nichtfachspr. auch* Di|oxyd [*auch* ...'ksy:t] (↑R 132; Oxid, das zwei Sauerstoffatome enthält); *vgl.* Oxid; **Di|o|xin,** das; -s, -e ‹griech.› (hochgiftige Verbindung von Chlor und Kohlenwasserstoff); **Di|oxyd** *vgl.* Dioxid

Di|ö|ze|san, der; -en, -en (↑R 126) ‹griech.› (Angehöriger einer Diözese); **Di|ö|ze|se,** die; -, -n (Amtsgebiet eines katholischen Bischofs); **Di|ö|zie,** die; - (*Bot.* Zweihäusigkeit); **di|ö|zisch** *(Bot.)*

Dip, der; -s, -s ‹engl.› (Soße zum Eintunken)

Diph|the|rie, die; -, ...ien ‹griech.› (*Med.* eine Infektionskrankheit); **Diph|the|rie_schutz|imp|fung, ...se|rum; diph|the|risch**

Diph|thong (↑R 132), der; -s, -e ‹griech.› (*Sprachw.* Doppellaut, z. B. ei, au; *Ggs.* Monophthong); **diph|thon|gie|ren** (einen Vokal zum Diphthong entwickeln); **Diph|thon|gie|rung; diph|thon|gisch**

dipl. *(schweiz.)* = diplomiert; **Dipl.-Betriebsw.** = Diplombetriebswirt[in]; **Dipl.-Bibl.** = Diplombibliothekar[in]; **Dipl.-Biol.** = Diplombiologe/-biologin; **Dipl.-Chem.** = Diplomchemiker[in]; **Dipl.-Dolm.** = Diplomdolmetscher[in]

Dip|lex|be|trieb (↑R 130) *vgl.* Duplexbetrieb

Dipl.-Hdl. = Diplomhandelslehrer[in]; **Dipl.-Hist.** = Diplomhistoriker[in]; **Dipl.-Holzw.** = Diplomholzwirt[in]; **Dipl.-Ing.** = Diplomingenieur[in]; **Dipl.-Kff[r].** = Diplomkauffrau; **Dipl.-Kfm.** = Diplomkaufmann; **Dipl.-Landw.** = Diplomlandwirt[in]; **Dipl.-Math.** = Diplommathematiker[in]; **Dipl.-Med.** = Diplommediziner[in]; **Dipl.-Met.** = Diplommeteorologe/-meteorologin

Dip|lo|do|kus (↑R 130), der; -, ...ken ‹griech.› (ausgestorbene Riesenechse)

dip|lo|id (↑R 130) ‹griech.› (*Biol.* mit doppeltem Chromosomensatz)

Dipl.-Ök. = Diplomökonom[in]
Dip|lo|kok|kus (↑R 130), der; -, ...kken ‹griech.› (*Med.* Kokkenpaar [Krankheitserreger])
Dip|lom (↑R 130), das; -[e]s, -e ‹griech.› (amtl. Schriftstück; Urkunde; [Ehren]zeugnis; akadem. Grad); **Dip|lo|mand,** der; -en, -en; ↑R 126 (jmd., der sich auf die Diplomprüfung vorbereitet); **Dip|lo|man|din; Dip|lom|ar|beit**
Dip|lo|mat (↑R 130), der; -en, -en; ↑R 126 ‹griech.› (beglaubigter Vertreter eines Landes bei einem fremden Staat); **Dip|lo|ma|ten‿aus|weis, ...kof|fer, ...lauf|bahn, ...pass; Dip|lo|ma|tie,** die; - (Regeln u. Methoden für die Führung außenpolit. Verhandlungen; Gesamtheit der Diplomaten; Geschicktheit im Umgang); **Dip|lo|ma|tik,** die; - (Urkundenlehre); **Dip|lo|ma|ti|ker** (Urkundenforscher u. -kenner); **Dip|lo|ma|tin; dip|lo|ma|tisch** (die Diplomatie u. die Diplomatik betreffend; urkundlich; klug u. geschickt im Umgang); das diplomatische Korps; *vgl. aber* ↑R 56: das Diplomatische Korps in Rom; **Dip|lom‿be|triebs|wirt**[1] (↑R 130; *Abk.* Dipl.-Betriebsw.), **...bib|li|o|the|kar**[1] (*Abk.* Dipl.-Bibl.), **...bi|o|lo|ge**[1] (*Abk.* Dipl.-Biol.), **...che|mi|ker**[1] (*Abk.* Dipl.-Chem.), **...dol|met|scher**[1] (*Abk.* Dipl.-Dolm.), **...han|dels|leh|rer**[1] (*Abk.* Dipl.-Hdl.), **...his|to|ri|ker**[1] (*Abk.* Dipl.-Hist.), **...holz|wirt**[1] (*Abk.* Dipl.-Holzw.); **dip|lo|mie|ren** (ein Diplom erteilen); **Dip|lom‿in|ge|ni|eur**[1] (*Abk.* Dipl.-Ing.), **...kauf|frau**[1] (*Abk.* Dipl.-Kff[r].), **...kauf|mann**[1] (*Plur.* ...leute; *Abk.* Dipl.-Kfm., *österr.* Dkfm.), **...land|wirt**[1] (*Abk.* Dipl.-Landw.), **...ma|the|ma|ti|ker**[1] (*Abk.* Dipl.-Math.), **...me|di|zi|ner**[1] (*Abk.* Dipl.-Med.), **...me|te|o|ro|lo|ge**[1] (*Abk.* Dipl.-Met.), **...öko|nom**[1] (↑R 132; *Abk.* Dipl.-Ök.), **...pä|da|go|ge**[1] (*Abk.* Dipl.-Päd.), **...phy|si|ker**[1] (*Abk.* Dipl.-Phys.), **...psy|cho|lo|ge**[1] (*Abk.* Dipl.-Psych.), **...sport|leh|rer**[1] (*Abk.* Dipl.-Sportl.), **...volks|wirt**[1] (*Abk.* Dipl.-Volksw.), **...wirt|schafts|in|ge|ni|eur**[1] (*Abk.* Dipl.-Wirtsch.-Ing.); **Dipl.-Päd.** = Diplompädagoge/-pädagogin; **Dipl.-Phys.** = Diplomphysiker[in]; **Dipl.-Psych.** = Diplompsychologe/-psychologin; **Dipl.-Sportl.** = Diplomsportlehrer[in]; **Dipl.-Volksw.** = Diplomvolkswirt[in]; **Dipl.-Wirtsch.-Ing.** = Diplomwirtschaftsingenieur[in]
Di|po|die, die; -, ...ien ‹griech.› (*Verslehre* zweiteilige Taktgruppe in einem Vers); **di|po|disch**
Di|pol, der; -s, -e ‹griech.› (*Physik* Anordnung von zwei entgegengesetzt gleichen elektrischen Ladungen); **Di|pol|an|ten|ne**
Dip|pel, der; -s, - (*südd. für* Dübel; *österr. ugs. für* Beule; *vgl.* Tippel); **Dip|pel|baum** (*österr. für* Trag-, Deckenbalken)
¹dip|pen (*landsch. für* eintauchen); **²dip|pen** ‹engl.› (*Seemannsspr.* die Flagge zum Gruß halb niederholen u. wieder hochziehen)
Dip|tam (↑R 132), der; -s ‹griech.› (eine Zierpflanze)
Dip|te|ren (↑R 132) *Plur.* ‹griech.› (*Zool.* zweiflüglige Insekten); **Dip|te|ros,** der; -, ...roi [...rɔy] (Tempel mit doppelter Säulenreihe)
Dip|ty|chon [...çɔn] (↑R 132), das; -s, *Plur.* ...chen *u.* ...cha ‹griech.› (zusammenklappbare Schreibtafel im Altertum; zweiflügeliges Altarbild)
dir (*auch in Briefen kleingeschrieben;* ↑R 5:) dir alten (*selten* alter) Frau; dir jungem (*auch* jungen) Menschen; dir Geliebten (*weibl.; selten* Geliebter); dir Geliebtem (*männl.; neben* Geliebten)
Dir. = Direktor
Di|rec|toire [dirɛk'toa:r], das; -[s] ‹franz.› (französ. [Kunst]stil Ende des 18. Jh.s); **di|rekt** ‹lat.›; -e Rede (*Sprachw.* wörtliche Rede); **Di|rekt|flug; Di|rekt|heit; Di|rek|ti|on,** die; -, -en (Leitung, Verwaltung; Vorstand; *schweiz. auch* kantonales Ministerium); **Di|rek|ti|ons|kraft** (*Physik);* **di|rek|ti|ons|los** (richtungslos); **Di|rek|ti|ons‿sek|re|tä|rin, ...zim|mer; Di|rek|ti|ve** [...və], die; -, -n (Weisung; Verhaltensregel); **Di|rekt|man|dat; Di|rek|tor,** der; -s, ...oren (*Abk.* Dir.); **Di|rek|to|rat,** das; -[e]s, -e; **di|rek|to|ri|al** (dem Direktor zustehend, von ihm herrührend); **Di|rek|to|rin; Di|rek|to|ri|um,** das; -s, ...ien [...iən]; **Di|rek|tor|zim|mer; Di|rek|tri|ce** [...tri:sə, *österr.* ...'tri:s] (↑R 130), die; -, -n ‹franz.› (leitende Angestellte [bes. in der Bekleidungsindustrie]); **Di|rek|trix** (↑R 130), die; - ‹lat.› (*Math.* Leitlinie von Kegelschnitten); **Di|rekt‿sen|dung, ...spiel** *(Sport),* **...über|tra|gung** (↑R 132), **...ver|kauf, ...wer|bung; Di|ret|tis|si|ma,** die; -, -s ‹ital.› (Route, die ohne Umwege zum Berggipfel führt); **Di|rex,** der; -, -e (*Schülerspr.* Direktor)
Dir|ham, *auch* **Dir|hem,** der; -s, -s (Währungs- u. Münzeinheit in arab. Ländern; frühere Gewichtseinheit in islam. Ländern)
Di|ri|gat, das; -[e]s, -e ‹lat.› (das Dirigieren [eines Orchesters]); **Di|ri|gent,** der; -en, -en (↑R 126); **Di|ri|gen|ten‿pult, ...stab; Di|ri|gen|tin; di|ri|gie|ren** ([ein Orchester] leiten; lenken); **Di|ri|gis|mus,** der; - (staatl. Lenkung der Wirtschaft); **di|ri|gis|tisch**
di|ri|mie|ren ‹lat.› (*österr. für* bei Stimmengleichheit entscheiden)
Dirk, Dierk (m. Vorn.)
Dirn, die; -, -en (*bayr., österr. mdal. für* Magd); **Dirndl,** das; -s, -n (*bayr., österr. für* junges Mädchen; Dirndlkleid; *ostösterr. ugs. auch für* [Frucht der] Kornelkirsche); **Dirndl|kleid; Dirndl|strauch** (*ostösterr. ugs. für* Strauch der Kornelkirsche); **Dir|ne,** die; -, -n (Prostituierte; *mdal. für* junges Mädchen)
dis, Dis, das; -, - (Tonbezeichnung); **dis** (*Zeichen für* dis-Moll); in dis
Dis|agio [...'a:dʒo, *auch* ...'a:ʒio] (↑R 132), das; -s, *Plur.* -s *u.* ...gien [...'a:dʒən, *auch* ...'a:ʒjən] ‹ital.› (Abschlag, um den der Kurs von Wertpapieren od. Geldsorten unter dem Nennwert od. der Parität steht)
Disc|jo|ckey *vgl.* Diskjockey; **Disco** *vgl.* Disko
Dis|coun|ter [dis'kauntə(r)], der; -s, - (Besitzer eines Discountgeschäftes); **Dis|count‿ge|schäft, ...la|den, ...preis** (*vgl.* ²Preis)
Dis|co|ve|ry [dis'kavəri], die; - ‹engl., „Entdeckung"› (Name einer amerik. Raumfähre)
Dis|en|gage|ment [disin'ge:dʒmənt], das; -s ‹engl.› (milit. Auseinanderrücken der Machtblöcke)
Di|seur [di'zø:r], der; -s, -e ‹franz.› (Sprecher, Vortragskünstler); **Di|seu|se** [di'zø:zə], die; -, -n
Dis|har|mo|nie [*auch* 'dis...], die; -, ...ien ‹lat.; griech.› (Missklang; Uneinigkeit); **dis|har|mo|nie|ren** [*auch* 'dis...]; **dis|har|mo|nisch** [*auch* 'dis...]
Dis|junk|ti|on, die; -, -en ‹lat.› (Trennung; Sonderung); **dis|junk|tiv** (trennend); -e Konjunktion (*Sprachw.* ausschließendes Bindewort, z. B. „oder")

[1] Heute oft Diplom-Betriebswirt usw.; die weibl. Titel enden (mit Ausnahme von Diplomkauffrau) auf -in.

Dis|kant, der; -s, -e ‹lat.› (*Musik* höchste Stimm- od. Tonlage); **Dis|kant˽schlüs|sel, ...stim|me**
Dis|ken (*Plur. von* Diskus); **Dis|ket|te,** die; -, -n ‹engl.; franz.›; *vgl.* Floppydisk; **Disk|jo|ckey** [...dʒɔke:, *engl.* ...ki], der; -s, -s ‹engl.› (jmd., der Schallplatten präsentiert); **Disk|ka|me|ra** ‹griech.; lat.› (Kamera, bei der die Fotos auf einer runden Scheibe belichtet werden); **Dis|ko,** die; -, -s ‹engl.› (Tanzlokal u. -veranstaltung mit Schallplattenmusik); **Dis|ko|gra|phie** (↑R 33), die; -, ...ien ‹griech.› (Schallplattenverzeichnis); **Dis|ko|mu|sik**
Dis|kont, der; -s, -e ‹ital.› (*Bankw.* Zinsvergütung bei noch nicht fälligen Zahlungen); **Dis|kon|ten** *Plur.* (inländische Wechsel); **Diskont˽er|hö|hung, ...ge|schäft, ...he|rab|set|zung; dis|kon|tie|ren** (eine später fällige Forderung unter Abzug von Zinsen ankaufen)
dis|kon|ti|nu|ier|lich [*auch* 'dis...] ‹lat.› (aussetzend, unterbrochen, zusammenhanglos); **Dis|kon|ti|nu|i|tät** [*auch* 'dis...], die; -, -en
Dis|kont˽satz (*Bankw.* Zinssatz), **...sen|kung, ...spe|sen** (*Plur.;* Wechselspesen)
Dis|kor|danz, die; -, -en ‹lat.› (Uneinigkeit, Missklang; *Geol.* ungleichförmige Lagerung zweier Gesteinsverbände)
Dis|ko|rol|ler [*auch* ...ro:lə(r)], der; -s, - ‹engl.› (Rollschuh [mit Kunststoffrollen]); **Dis|ko|thek,** die; -, -en ‹griech.› (Schallplattensammlung; *auch svw.* Disko); **Dis|ko|the|kar,** der; -s, -e (Verwalter einer Diskothek [beim Rundfunk])
Dis|kre|dit, der; -[e]s ‹lat.› (übler Ruf); **dis|kre|di|tie|ren** (in Verruf bringen); **Dis|kre|di|tie|rung**
dis|kre|pant ‹lat.› (abweichend; widersprüchlich); **Dis|kre|panz,** die; -, -en (Missverhältnis)
dis|kret ‹lat.› (taktvoll, rücksichtsvoll; unauffällig; vertraulich; *Physik, Math.* abgegrenzt, getrennt); -e Nachforschungen; -e Zahlenwerte; **Dis|kre|ti|on,** die; - (Verschwiegenheit, [2]Takt)
Dis|kri|mi|nan|te, die; -, -n ‹lat.› (math. Ausdruck bei Gleichungen zweiten u. höheren Grades); **dis|kri|mi|nie|ren; Dis|kri|mi|nie|rung** (unterschiedliche Behandlung; Herabsetzung)
dis|kur|rie|ren ‹lat.› (*veraltet, aber noch landsch. für* sich eifrig unterhalten; diskutieren); **Dis|kurs,** der; -es, -e ([eifrige] Erörterung; methodisch aufgebaute Abhandlung); **dis|kur|siv** (*Philos.* von Begriff zu Begriff logisch fortschreitend)
Dis|kus, der; *Gen.* - *u.* -ses, *Plur.* ...ken *u.* -se ‹griech.› (Wurfscheibe)
Dis|kus|si|on, die; -, -en ‹lat.› (Erörterung; Aussprache; Meinungsaustausch); **Dis|kus|si|ons˽abend** (↑R 132), **...bei|trag; dis|kus|si|ons|freu|dig; Dis|kus|si|ons˽ge|gen|stand, ...grund|la|ge, ...lei|ter** (der), **...red|ner, ...run|de, ...teil|neh|mer, ...the|ma; dis|kus|si|ons|wür|dig**
Dis|kus˽wer|fen (das; -s), **...wer|fer, ...wurf**
dis|ku|ta|bel ‹lat.› (erwägenswert; strittig); ...ab|le (↑R 130) Fragen; **Dis|ku|tant,** der; -en, -en; ↑R 126 (Diskussionsteilnehmer); **Dis|ku|tan|tin; dis|ku|tier|bar; dis|ku|tie|ren;** [über] etwas -
Dis|lo|ka|ti|on, die; -, -en ‹lat.› (räumliche Verteilung [von Truppen]; *Geol.* Störung der normalen Lagerung von Gesteinsverbänden; *Med.* Verschiebung der Bruchenden); **dis|lo|zie|ren** ([Truppen] räumlich verteilen, verlegen); **Dis|lo|zie|rung**
dis-Moll [*auch* 'dis'mɔl], das; - (Tonart; *Zeichen* dis); **dis-Moll-Ton|lei|ter** (↑R 28)
Dis|ney ['dizni], Walt [wɔ:lt] (amerik. Trickfilmzeichner u. Filmproduzent)
Dis|pa|che [dis'paʃə], die; -, -n ‹franz.› (*Seew.* Schadensberechnung u. -verteilung bei Seeschäden); **Dis|pa|cheur** [...'ʃø:r], der; -s, -e (Seeschadenberechner); **dis|pa|chie|ren** [...'ʃi:...]
dis|pa|rat ‹lat.› (ungleichartig; unvereinbar); **Dis|pa|ri|tät,** die; -, -en (Ungleichheit)
Dis|pat|cher [...'pɛtʃə(r)], der; -s, - ‹engl.› (leitender Angestellter in der Industrie, der den Produktionsablauf überwacht); **Dis|pat|cher|sys|tem**
Dis|pens, der; -es, -e *u. (österr. u. im kath. Kirchenrecht nur)* die; -, -en ‹lat.› (Aufhebung einer Verpflichtung, Befreiung; Ausnahme[bewilligung]); **Dis|pen|saire-be|treu|ung** [...pɛn'sɛ:r..., *auch* ...pã'sɛ:r...] ‹franz.; dt.› (vorbeugende med. Betreuung Gefährdeter); **Dis|pen|sa|ti|on** [...pɛnza...], die; -, -en ‹lat.› (Befreiung); **Dis|pen|sa|to|ri|um,** das; -s, ...ien [...iən] (Arznei-, Apothekerbuch); **Dis|pens|ehe** (↑R 132); **dis|pen|sie|ren** (von einer Vorschrift befreien, freistellen; Arzneien bereiten u. abgeben); **Dis|pen|sie|rung**
dis|per|gie|ren (↑R 132) ‹lat.› (zerstreuen; verbreiten); **dis|pers** (fein verteilt; zerstreut); -e Phase *(Physik);* **Dis|per|si|on,** die; -, -en (feinste Verteilung eines Stoffes in einem anderen; *Physik* Abhängigkeit der Fortpflanzungsgeschwindigkeit einer Wellenbewegung von der Wellenlänge); **Dis|per|si|ons|far|be**
Dis|placed Per|son [dis'ple:st 'pœ:(r)s(ə)n], die; - -, - -s (*Bez. für* Ausländer, der während des 2. Weltkriegs nach Deutschland [zur Arbeit] verschleppt wurde)
Dis|play [...'ple:], das; -s, -s ‹engl.› (optisch wirksames Ausstellen von Waren; aufstellbares Werbungsmaterial; *EDV* optische Datenanzeige); **Dis|play|er,** der; -s, - (Dekorations-, Packungsgestalter); **Dis|play˽funk|ti|on, ...gra|fi|ker** (↑R 33), **...ma|te|ri|al**
Di|spon|de|us, der; -, ...een ‹griech.› (*Verslehre* Doppelspondeus)
Dis|po|nen|de, die; -, -n *meist Plur.* ‹lat.› (bis zum Abrechnungstermin unverkauftes Buch, dessen weitere Lagerung beim Sortimentsbuchhändler der Verleger gestattet); **Dis|po|nent,** der; -en, -en; ↑R 126 (kaufmänn. Angestellter mit besonderen Vollmachten, der einen größeren Unternehmungsbereich leitet); **Dis|po|nen|tin; dis|po|ni|bel** (verfügbar); ...ib|le (↑R 130) Gelder; **Dis|po|ni|bi|li|tät,** die; - (Verfügbarkeit); **dis|po|nie|ren; dis|po|niert** (*auch für* aufgelegt; empfänglich [für Krankheiten]); **Dis|po|si|ti|on,** die; -, -en (Anordnung, Gliederung; Verfügung; Anlage; Empfänglichkeit [für Krankheiten]); zur - (im einstweiligen Ruhestand; *Abk.* z. D.); **dis|po|si|ti|ons|fä|hig** (geschäftsfähig); **Dis|po|si|ti|ons˽fonds, ...gel|der** (*Plur.;* Verfügungsgelder), **...kre|dit** (Überziehungskredit); **dis|po|si|tiv** (anordnend, verfügend; *Rechtsw.* abdingbar; *vgl. d.*); -es Recht
Dis|pro|por|ti|on [*auch* 'dis...], die; -, -en ‹lat.› (Missverhältnis); **dis|pro|por|ti|o|nal** [*auch* 'dis...] (schlecht proportioniert); **Dis|pro|por|ti|o|na|li|tät** [*auch* 'dis...], die; -, -en (*svw.* Disproportion); **dis|pro|por|ti|o|niert** [*auch* 'dis...] (*svw.* disproportional)
Dis|put, der; -[e]s, -e ‹lat.› (Wortwechsel; Streitgespräch); **dis|pu|ta|bel** (strittig); ...ab|le (↑R 130)

Fragen; **Dis|pu|tant,** der; -en, -en; ↑R 126 (Disputierender); **Dis|pu|ta|ti|on,** die; -, -en (gelehrtes Streitgespräch); **dis|pu|tie|ren**

Dis|qua|li|fi|ka|ti|on, die; -, -en; ⟨lat.⟩; **dis|qua|li|fi|zie|ren** (vom sportl. Wettbewerb ausschließen; für untauglich erklären); **Dis|qua|li|fi|zie|rung**

Dis|ra|e|li [*engl.* diz're:li] (brit. Schriftsteller u. Politiker)

Diss. = Dissertation

Dis|sens, der; -es, -e ⟨lat.⟩ (*Rechtsspr.* Meinungsverschiedenheit); **Dis|sen|ter,** der; -s, -s *meist Plur.* ⟨engl.⟩ (sich nicht zur anglikan. Kirche Bekennender); **dis|sen|tie|ren** ⟨lat.⟩ (abweichender Meinung sein)

Dis|ser|tant, der; -en, -en (↑R 126) ⟨lat.⟩ (jmd., der eine Dissertation anfertigt); **Dis|ser|tan|tin; Dis|ser|ta|ti|on,** die; -, -en (wissenschaftl. Abhandlung zur Erlangung der Doktorwürde; *Abk.* Diss.); **dis|ser|tie|ren** (eine Dissertation anfertigen)

Dis|si|dent, der; -en, -en (↑R 126) ⟨lat.⟩ (jmd., der außerhalb einer staatlich anerkannten Religionsgemeinschaft steht; jmd., der von einer offiziellen politischen Meinung abweicht); **Dis|si|den|tin; dis|si|die|ren** (anders denken; [aus der Kirche] austreten)

Dis|si|mi|la|ti|on, die; -, -en ⟨lat.⟩ (*Sprachw.* „Entähnlichung" von Lauten, z. B. Wechsel von t zu k in „Kartoffel" [*aus* „Tartüffel"]; *Naturwiss.* Abbau u. Verbrauch von Nährstoffen unter Energiegewinnung); **dis|si|mi|lie|ren**

Dis|si|mu|la|ti|on, die; -, -en ⟨lat.⟩ (*Med., Psych.* bewusste Verheimlichung einer Krankheit); **dis|si|mu|lie|ren**

Dis|si|pa|ti|on, die; -, -en ⟨lat.⟩ (*Physik* Übergang einer Energieform in Wärmeenergie); **Dis|si|pa|ti|ons|sphä|re,** die; - (*svw.* Exosphäre)

dis|so|lu|bel ⟨lat.⟩ (löslich, auflösbar, zerlegbar); ...ub|le (↑R 130) Mischungen; **Dis|so|lu|ti|on,** die; -, -en (Auflösung, Trennung)

dis|so|nant ⟨lat.⟩ (misstönend); **Dis|so|nanz,** die; -, -en (Missklang; Unstimmigkeit); **dis|so|nie|ren**

Dis|so|zi|a|ti|on, die; -, -en ⟨lat.⟩ (*fachspr. für* Zerfall, Trennung; Auflösung); **dis|so|zi|ie|ren**

Dis|stress, der; -es, -e ⟨griech., engl.⟩ (*Psych., Med.* lang andauernder starker Stress)

dis|tal (↑R 132) ⟨lat.⟩ (*Med.* weiter von der Körpermitte, bei Blutgefäßen weiter vom Herzen entfernt liegend); **Dis|tanz,** die; -, -en (Entfernung; Abstand); **Dis|tanz|ge|schäft** (Verkauf nach Katalog od. Mustern); **dis|tan|zie|ren** ([im Wettkampf] überbieten, hinter sich lassen); sich - (von jmdm. od. etwas abrücken); **dis|tan|ziert** (zurückhaltend); **Dis|tan|zie|rung; Dis|tanz‿re|lais** (*Elektrotechnik*), **...ritt** (Ritt über eine sehr lange Strecke), **...wech|sel** (*Bankw.* Wechsel mit verschiedenem Ausstellungs- u. Zahlungsort)

Dis|tel, die; -, -n; **Dis|tel‿fal|ter** (ein Schmetterling), **...fink** (ein Vogel)

Dis|then (↑R 132), der; -s, -e ⟨griech.⟩ (ein Mineral)

Dis|ti|chon [...çɔn] (↑R 132), das; -s, ...chen ⟨griech.⟩ (*Verslehre* Verspaar aus Hexameter u. Pentameter)

dis|tin|guiert [...stiŋ'gi:rt] (↑R 132) ⟨lat.⟩ (betont vornehm); **Dis|tin|guiert|heit,** die; -; **dis|tinkt** (klar und deutlich [abgegrenzt]); **Dis|tink|ti|on,** die; -, -en (Auszeichnung; [hoher] Rang; *österr. für* Rangabzeichen); **dis|tink|tiv** (unterscheidend)

Dis|tor|si|on, die; -, -en ⟨lat.⟩ (*Optik* Verzerrung, Verzeichnung; *Med.* Verstauchung)

dis|tra|hie|ren ⟨lat.⟩ (*fachspr. für* auseinander ziehen; trennen); **Dis|trak|ti|on,** die; -, -en (*veraltet für* Zerstreuung; *Geol.* Zerrung von Teilen der Erdkruste; *Med.* Behandlung von Knochenbrüchen mit Streckverband)

Dis|tri|bu|ent, der; -en, -en (↑R 126) ⟨lat.⟩ (Verteiler); **dis|tri|bu|ie|ren** (verteilen); **Dis|tri|bu|ti|on,** die; -, -en (Verteilung; Auflösung; *Wirtsch.* Einkommensverteilung, Verteilung von Handelsgütern; *Sprachw.* die Umgebung eines sprachlichen Elements; *Psych.* Verteilung u. Aufspaltung der Aufmerksamkeit); **Dis|tri|bu|ti|ons|for|mel** (Spendeformel beim Abendmahl); **dis|tri|bu|tiv** (verteilend); **Dis|tri|bu|tiv‿ge|setz** (*Math.*), **...zahl** (im Deutschen mit „je" gebildet, z. B. „je acht")

Dist|rikt (↑R 130 *u.* 132), der; -[e]s, -e ⟨lat.⟩ (Bezirk, Bereich); **Dist|rikts|vor|ste|her**

Dis|zip|lin (↑R 130), die; -, -en ⟨lat.⟩ (*nur Sing.:* Zucht, Ordnung; Fach einer Wissenschaft; Teilbereich des Sports); **dis|zip|li|när** (*bes. österr. für* disziplinarisch); **Dis|zip|li|nar‿ge|walt** (Ordnungsgewalt); **dis|zip|li|na|risch,** dis|zip|li|nell (die Disziplin, Dienstordnung betreffend; mit gebotener Strenge); **Dis|zip|li|nar‿maß|nah|me, ...recht** (Teil des Beamtenrechts), **...stra|fe, ...ver|fah|ren, ...ver|ge|hen** (Vergehen im Dienst); **dis|zip|li|nell** *vgl.* disziplinarisch; **dis|zip|li|nie|ren** (zur Ordnung erziehen); **dis|zip|li|niert; Dis|zip|li|niert|heit,** die; -; **dis|zip|lin‿los, ...wid|rig**

Di|tet|ro|de (↑R 130), die; -, -n ⟨griech.⟩ (*Elektrotechnik* Doppelvierpolröhre)

Dith|mar|schen (Gebiet an der Nordseeküste); **Dith|mar|scher** (↑R 103); **dith|mar|sisch**

Di|thy|ram|be, die; -, -n ⟨griech.⟩ *u.* Di|thy|ram|bus, der; -, ...ben (Weihelied [auf Dionysos]; überschwängliches Gedicht); **di|thy|ram|bisch** (begeistert, überschwänglich); **Di|thy|ram|bus** *vgl.* Dithyrambe

di|to ⟨lat.⟩ (dasselbe, ebenso; *Abk.* do. *od.* dto.); *vgl.* detto

Di|tro|chä|us [...x...], der; -, ...äen ⟨griech.⟩ (*Verslehre* Doppeltrochäus)

Dit|te (w. Vorn.)

Dit|to|gra|phie, die; -, ...ien ⟨griech.⟩ (Doppelschreibung von Buchstaben[gruppen])

Di|u|re|se, die; -, -n ⟨griech.⟩ (*Med.* Harnausscheidung); **Di|u|re|ti|kum,** das; -s, ...ka (harntreibendes Mittel); **di|u|re|tisch** (harntreibend)

Di|ur|nal, das; -s, -e ⟨lat.⟩ *u.* **Di|ur|na|le,** das; -, ...lia (Gebetbuch der kath. Geistlichen mit den Tagesgebeten); **Di|ur|num,** das; -s, ...nen (*österr. veraltet für* Tagegeld)

Di|va ['di:va], die; -, *Plur.* -s *u.* ...ven [...vən] ⟨ital., „Göttliche"⟩ (erste Sängerin, gefeierte Schauspielerin)

di|ver|gent [...v...] ⟨lat.⟩ (auseinander gehend; in entgegengesetzter Richtung [ver]laufend); **Di|ver|genz,** die; -, -en (Auseinandergehen; Meinungsverschiedenheit); **di|ver|gie|ren**

di|vers [...v...] ⟨lat.⟩ (verschieden; *bei attributivem Gebrauch im Plur.* mehrere); **Di|ver|sant,** der; -en, -en; ↑R 126 (*im kommunist. Sprachgebrauch* Saboteur); **Di|ver|si|fi|ka|ti|on,** die; -, -en (Abwechslung, Mannigfaltigkeit; *Wirtsch.* Ausweitung des Waren- oder Produktionssortiments eines Unternehmens); **di|ver|si|fi|zie-**

ren; **Di|ver|si|on,** die; -, -en (*veraltet für* Ablenkung; Angriff von der Seite; *im kommunist. Sprachgebrauch* Sabotage durch den Klassenfeind); **Di|ver|ti|kel,** das; -s, - (*Med.* Ausbuchtung an Organen); **Di|ver|ti|men|to,** das; -s, *Plur.* -s *u.* ...ti ‹ital.› (*Musik* heiteres Instrumentalstück; Tanzeinlage; Zwischenspiel); **Di|ver|tis|sement** [...tis(ə)'mã:], das; -s, -s ‹franz.› (Gesangs- od. Balletteinlage der franz. Oper des 17./18. Jh.s; *selten für* Divertimento)

di|vi|de et im|pe|ra ['di:vide: - -] ‹lat., „teile und herrsche!"› (legendäres Prinzip der altrömischen Außenpolitik)

Di|vi|dend [...v...], der; -en, -en (↑R 126) ‹lat.› (*Math.* zu teilende Zahl; Zähler eines Bruchs); **Di|vi|den|de,** die; -, -en (*Wirtsch.* der auf eine Aktie entfallende Gewinnanteil); **Di|vi|den|den‿aus|schüt|tung, ...schein** (Gewinnanteilschein); **di|vi|die|ren** (*Math.* teilen); zehn dividiert durch fünf ist, macht, gibt (*nicht:* sind, machen, geben) zwei

Di|vi|di|vi [divi'di:vi] *Plur.* ‹indian.-span.› (gerbstoffreiche Schoten einer [sub]tropischen Pflanze)

Di|vi|na Com|me|dia [di'vi:na -], die; - - ‹ital.› (Dantes „Göttliche Komödie")

Di|vi|na|ti|on [...v...], die; -, -en ‹lat.› (*selten für* Ahnung; Wahrsagung, Wahrsagekunst); **di|vi|na|to|risch** (vorahnend; seherisch); **Di|vi|ni|tät,** die; - (Göttlichkeit; göttliches Wesen)

Di|vis [...v...], das; -es, -e ‹lat.› (*Druckw.* Trennungs- od. Bindestrich); **Di|vi|si|on,** die; -, -en (*Math.* Teilung; Heeresabteilung); **Di|vi|si|o|när,** der; -s, -e ‹franz.› (*bes. schweiz. für* Befehlshaber einer Division); **Di|vi|si|ons‿kom|man|deur, ...la|zarett, ...stab; Di|vi|sor,** der; -s, ...oren ‹lat.› (*Math.* teilende Zahl; Nenner); **Di|vi|so|ri|um,** das; -s, ...ien [...i̯ən] (*Druckw.* gabelförmige Klammer [zum Halten der Vorlage])

Di|wan, der; -s, -e ‹pers.› (*veraltend für* niedriges Liegesofa; *Literaturw.* [oriental.] Gedichtsammlung; *früher* türk. Staatsrat); [Goethes] „Westöstlicher Diwan"

Dix (dt. Maler)

Di|xie, der; -s (*ugs. Kurzform für* Dixieland); **Di|xie|land** ['diksilɛnd], der; -[s] ‹amerik.› *u.* **Di|xie|land|jazz** (eine nordamerik. Variante des Jazz)

d. J. = dieses Jahres; der Jüngere

Dja|kar|ta [dʒa...] (*ältere Schreibung für* Jakarta)

Djer|ba ['dʒɛrba] (tunes. Insel)

DJH = Deutsche Jugendherberge

Dji|bu|ti [dʒi'bu:ti] *vgl.* Dschibuti

DJK = Deutsche Jugendkraft

DK = Dezimalklassifikation; Dieselkraftstoff

Dkfm. (*österr.*) = Diplomkaufmann

DKP = Deutsche Kommunistische Partei

dkr = dänische Krone (Münze)

dl = Deziliter

DLF = Deutschlandfunk

DLG = Deutsche Landwirtschafts-Gesellschaft

DLRG = Deutsche Lebens-Rettungs-Gesellschaft

dm = Dezimeter

dm² = Quadratdezimeter

dm³ = Kubikdezimeter

DM = Deutsche Mark

d. M. = dieses Monats

d-Moll ['de:mɔl, *auch* 'de:'mɔl], das; - (Tonart; *Zeichen* d); **d-Moll-Ton|lei|ter** (↑R 28)

Dnjepr, der; -[s] (russ. Strom)

Dnjestr, der; -[s] (russ. Strom)

DNS = Desoxyribonukleinsäure

do. = dito

Do. = Donnerstag

d. O. = der *od.* die Obige

Do|bel *vgl.* Tobel

¹Dö|bel, der; -s, - (ein Fisch)

²Dö|bel usw. *vgl.* Dübel usw.

Do|ber|mann, der; -s, ...männer ‹nach dem Züchter› (Hunderasse); **Do|ber|mann|pin|scher**

Döb|lin (dt. Schriftsteller)

Dob|ratsch (↑R 130), der; -[e]s (Gebirge in Kärnten)

Dob|rud|scha (↑R 130 *u.* 132), die; - (Gebiet zwischen Donau u. Schwarzem Meer)

doch; ja doch!; nicht doch!; o dass doch ...!

Docht, der; -[e]s, -e; **Docht|schere**

Dock, das; -s, *Plur.* -s, *selten* -e ‹niederl. *od.* engl.› (Anlage zum Ausbessern von Schiffen)

Do|cke, die; -, -n (Garnmaß; zusammengedrehter Garnstrang; *landsch. für* Puppe); *vgl. aber* Dogge; **¹do|cken** (Garn, Flachs, Tabak bündeln)

²do|cken ‹niederl. *od.* engl.› (ein Schiff ins Dock bringen; im Dock liegen; *auch svw.* andocken); **Docker** (Arbeiter in einem Dock); **Dock|ha|fen;** *vgl.* ¹Hafen; **Docking,** das; -s, -s (Ankoppelung an ein Raumfahrzeug); **Docking|ma|nö|ver**

do|de|ka|disch ‹griech.› (zwölf Einheiten umfassend, duodezimal); **Do|de|ka|e|der,** das; -s, - (von zwölf gleichen, regelmäßigen Fünfecken begrenzter Körper); **Do|de|ka|nes,** der; - ‹„Zwölfinseln"› (Inselgruppe im Ägäischen Meer); **Do|de|ka|pho|nie** (↑R 33), die; - (Zwölftonmusik); **do|de|ka|pho|nisch** (die Dodekaphonie betreffend); **Do|de|ka|pho|nist,** der; -en, -en; ↑R 126 (Komponist od. Anhänger der Zwölftonmusik)

Do|de|rer, Heimito von (österr. Schriftsteller)

Do|do|ma (Hptst. von Tansania)

Do|do|na (Orakelheiligtum des Zeus); **do|do|nä|isch**

Do|ga|res|sa, die; -, ...essen ‹ital.› (Gemahlin des Dogen)

Dog|cart ['dɔgka:(r)t], der; -s, -s ‹engl.› (offener, zweirädriger Einspänner)

Do|ge ['do:ʒə, *ital.* 'do:dʒə], der; -n, -n ‹ital., „Herzog"› (*früher* Titel des Staatsoberhauptes in Venedig u. Genua); **Do|gen‿müt|ze, ...pa|last**

Dog|ge, die; -, -n ‹engl.› (eine Hunderasse); *vgl. aber* Docke

¹Dog|ger, der; -s ‹engl.› (*Geol.* mittlere Juraformation; Brauner Jura)

²Dog|ger, der; -s, - ‹niederl.› (niederl. Fischereifahrzeug); **Dog|ger|bank,** die; - (Untiefe in der Nordsee)

Dög|ling ‹schwed.› (Pott-, Entenwal)

Dog|ma, das; -s, ...men ‹griech.› (Kirchenlehre; [Glaubens]satz; Lehrmeinung); **Dog|ma|tik,** die; -, -en (Glaubenslehre); **Dog|ma|ti|ker** (Glaubenslehrer; *abwertend für* [unkritischer] Verfechter einer Lehrmeinung); **Dog|ma|ti|ke|rin; dog|ma|tisch** (die [Glaubens]lehre betreffend; lehrhaft; streng [an Lehrsätze] gebunden); **dog|ma|ti|sie|ren** (zum Dogma erheben); **Dog|ma|tis|mus,** der; - (*oft abwertend für* [unkritisches] Festhalten an Lehrmeinungen u. Glaubenssätzen); **Dog|men|geschich|te**

Dog|skin, das; -s ‹engl.› (Leder aus kräftigem Schaffell)

Do|ha (Hptst. von Katar)

Doh|le, die; -, -n (ein Rabenvogel)

Doh|ne, die; -, -n (Schlinge zum Vogelfang); **Doh|nen‿steig, ...stieg** (der; -[e]s, -e)

do it your|self! ['du: it ju:(r)'sɛlf] ‹engl., „mach es selbst!"› (Schlagwort für die eigene Ausführung handwerklicher Arbeiten); **Do-it-your|self-Be|we|gung** (↑R 28)

Do|ket, der; -en, -en (↑R 126)

‹griech.› (Anhänger einer Sekte der ersten christl. Jahrhunderte)
dok|tern; ‹lat.› (*ugs. u. scherzh. für* den Arzt spielen); ich ...ere (↑R 16); **Dok|tor,** der; -s, ...oren (höchster akadem. Grad; *ugs. auch für* Arzt; *Abk.* Dr. [*im Plur.* Dres., *wenn mehrere Personen, nicht mehrere Titel einer Person gemeint sind*] *u.* D. [*in* D. theol.]); Ehrendoktor, - ehrenhalber, *auch* Ehren halber (*Abk.* Dr. eh., Dr. e. h. *u.* Dr. E. h.; *vgl.* E. h.), - honoris causa (*Abk.* Dr. h. c.); mehrfacher - (*Abk.* Dr. mult.); mehrfacher - honoris causa (*Abk.* Dr. h. c. mult.); *im Brief:* Sehr geehrter Herr/Sehr geehrte Frau Doktor!, Sehr geehrter Herr/Sehr geehrte Frau Dr. Schmidt!; - der Arzneikunde (*Abk.* Dr. pharm.); - der Bergbauwissenschaften (*Abk.* Dr. rer. mont., *österr.* Dr. mont.); *österr.* - der Bodenkultur (*Abk.* Dr. nat. techn.); - der Forstwissenschaft (*Abk.* Dr. forest.); - der Gartenbauwissenschaften (*Abk.* Dr. rer. hort.); habilitierter - [z. B. der Philosophie] (*Abk.* Dr. [z. B. phil.] habil.); *österr.* - der Handelswissenschaften (*Abk.* Dr. rer. comm.); - der Humanwissenschaften (*Abk.* Dr. sc. hum.); - der Ingenieurwissenschaften (Doktoringenieur, *Abk.* Dr.-Ing.); - der Landwirtschaft (*Abk.* Dr. [sc.] agr.); - der mathematischen Wissenschaften (*Abk.* Dr. sc. math.); - der Medizin (*Abk.* Dr. med.); *österr.* - der gesamten Medizin (*Abk.* Dr. med. univ.); - der Naturwissenschaften (*Abk.* Dr. phil. nat. *od.* Dr. rer. nat. *od.* Dr. sc. nat.); - der Pädagogik (*Abk.* Dr. paed.); - der Philosophie (*Abk.* Dr. phil.); - der Rechtswissenschaft (*Abk.* Dr. jur.); - beider Rechte (*Abk.* Dr. j. u. *od.* Dr. jur. utr.); - der Sozialwissenschaften (*Abk.* Dr. disc. pol.); *österr.* - der Sozial- und Wirtschaftswissenschaften (*Abk.* Dr. rer. soc. oec.); *schweiz.* - der Staatswirtschaftskunde (*Abk.* Dr. rer. camer.); - der Staatswissenschaften (*Abk.* Dr. rer. pol. *od.* Dr. sc. pol. *od.* Dr. oec. publ.); - der technischen Wissenschaften (*Abk.* Dr. rer. techn., Dr. sc[ient]. techn. [*österr.* Dr. techn.]); - der Theologie (*Abk.* Dr. theol.; Ehrenwürde der ev. Theologie, *Abk.* D. *od.* D. theol.); - der Tierheilkunde (*Abk.* Dr. med. vet.); - der Wirtschaftswissenschaft (*Abk.* Dr. oec. *od.* Dr. rer. oec.); - der Zahnheilkunde (*Abk.* Dr. med. dent.); **Dok|to|rand,** der; -en, -en; ↑R 126 (Student, der sich auf die Doktorprüfung vorbereitet; *Abk.* Dd.); **Dok|to|ran|din; Dok|tor|ar|beit; Dok|to|rat,** das; -[e]s, -e (*veraltend für* Doktorwürde); **Dok|tor‿dip|lom, ...exa|men** (↑R 132), **...fra|ge** (sehr schwierige Frage), **...grad, ...hut** (der); **dok|to|rie|ren** (*veraltet für* die Doktorwürde erlangen, an der Doktorschrift arbeiten); **Dok|to|rin** [*auch* 'dɔk...] (*ugs. auch für* Ärztin); **Dok|tor‿in|ge|ni|eur** (*Abk.* Dr.-Ing.), **...prü|fung, ...schrift, ...ti|tel, ...va|ter, ...wür|de; Dokt|rin** (↑R 130), die; -, -en (Lehrsatz; Lehrmeinung); **dokt|ri|när** ‹franz.› (*abwertend für* an einer Lehrmeinung starr festhaltend); **Dokt|ri|när,** der; -s, -e; **Dokt|ri|na|ris|mus,** der; - ‹lat.› (*abwertend für* starres Festhalten an einer Lehrmeinung)
Do|ku|ment, das; -[e]s, -e ‹lat.› (Urkunde; Schriftstück; Beweis); **Do|ku|men|ta|list,** der; -en, -en (↑R 126) *u.* **Do|ku|men|tar,** der; -s, -e (wissenschaftlicher Mitarbeiter in einer Dokumentationsstelle); **Do|ku|men|tar‿auf|nah|me, ...film** (Film, der Ereignisse u. Zustände tatsachengetreu zu schildern sucht); **do|ku|men|ta|risch** (urkundlich; belegbar); **Do|ku|men|ta|rist,** der; -en, -en ([künstler.] Gestalter von Dokumentarfilmen); **Do|ku|men|ta|ti|on,** die; -, -en (Zusammenstellung, Ordnung und Nutzbarmachung von Dokumenten u. Materialien jeder Art); **Do|ku|men|ten|samm|lung; do|ku|men|tie|ren** (beurkunden; beweisen)
Dol|by-Sys|tem ® ‹nach dem amerik. Elektrotechniker› (Verfahren zur Rauschunterdrückung bei Tonbandaufnahmen)
dol|ce ['dɔltʃə] ‹ital.› (*Musik* sanft, lieblich, weich); **dol|ce far ni|en|te** ‹„süß [ist's], nichts zu tun"›; **Dol|ce|far|ni|en|te,** das; - (süßes Nichtstun); **Dol|ce Vi|ta** [- 'vi:ta], das *od.* die; - - ‹„süßes Leben"› (ausschweifendes u. übersättigtes Müßiggängertum)
Dolch, der; -[e]s, -e; **Dolch‿mes|ser** (das), **...spit|ze, ...stich, ...stoß; Dolch|stoß|le|gen|de,** die; -
Dol|de, die; -, -n (schirmähnlicher Blütenstand); **Dol|den|blüt|ler; dol|den|för|mig; Dol|den‿ge|wächs, ...ris|pe; dol|dig**
Do|le, die; -, -n (bedeckter Abzugsgraben; *schweiz. auch für* Sinkkasten)
Do|le|rit [*auch* ...'rit], der; -s, -e ‹griech.› (grobkörnige Basaltart)
Dolf (m. Vorn.)
do|li|cho|ke|phal usw. *vgl.* dolichozephal usw.; **do|li|cho|ze|phal** [...ç...] ‹griech.› (*Med., Biol.* langköpfig); **Do|li|cho|ze|pha|lie,** die; - (Langköpfigkeit)
do|lie|ren *vgl.* dollieren
Do|li|ne, die; -, -n ‹slaw.› (*Geol.* trichterförmige Vertiefung im Karst)
Dol|lar, der; -[s], -s ‹amerik.› (Währungseinheit in den USA, in Kanada, Australien u. a.; *Zeichen* $); 30 - (↑R 90); **Dol|lar|kurs**
Dol|lart, der; -s (Nordseebucht an der Emsmündung)
Dol|lar‿wäh|rung, ...zei|chen
Doll|bord, der; -[e]s, -e (obere Planke auf dem Bootsbord); **Dol|le,** die; -, -n (Vorrichtung zum Halten der Riemen [Ruder]); **Dol|len,** der; -s, - (*fachspr. für* Dübel)
dol|lie|ren, do|lie|ren ‹franz.› (*Gerberei* [Leder] abschleifen)
Doll|punkt (*ugs. für* immer wieder aufgegriffenes Thema, umstrittener Punkt)
Dol|man, der; -s, -e ‹türk.› (Leibrock der alttürk. Tracht; mit Schnüren besetzte Jacke der Husaren; kaftanartiges Frauengewand auf dem Balkan)
Dol|men, der; -s, - ‹breton.-franz.› (prähistorisches Grab aus senkrecht aufgestellten Steinen mit einer steinernen Deckplatte)
Dol|metsch, der; -[e]s, -e ‹türk.-ung.› (*österr., sonst seltener für* Dolmetscher; *meist übertr. für* sich zum Dolmetsch machen); **dol|met|schen;** du dolmetschst; **Dol|met|scher,** der; -s, - (jmd., der [berufsmäßig] mündlich übersetzt); **Dol|met|sche|rin; Dol|met|scher‿in|sti|tut, ...schu|le**
Do|lo|mit [*auch* ...'mit], der; -s, -e ‹nach dem franz. Mineralogen Dolomieu› (ein Mineral; Sedimentgestein); **Do|lo|mi|ten** *Plur.* (Teil der Südalpen)
Do|lo|res (w. Vorn.)
do|los ‹lat.› (*Rechtsspr.* arglistig, mit bösem Vorsatz); -e Täuschung; **Do|lus,** der; - (*Rechtsw.* List; böse Absicht); **Do|lus e|ven|tu|a|lis** [- evɛn...], der; - - (*Rechtsw.* das Inkaufnehmen einer [wenn auch unerwünschten] Folge)
[1]**Dom,** der; -[e]s, -e ‹lat.› (Bischofs-, Hauptkirche); [2]**Dom,** der; -[e]s, -e ‹griech.› (gewölbeartige Decke; gewölbter Aufsatz); [3]**Dom** [*port.* dõ:], der; - ‹port.› (Herr; *in Ver-*

bindung mit Namen ohne Artikel); **Do|ma**, das; -s, ...men ‹griech.› (Kristallfläche, die zwei Kristallachsen schneidet); **Do|mä|ne**, die; -, -n ‹franz.› (Staatsgut, -besitz; besonderes [Arbeits-, Wissens]gebiet); **Do|mä|nen|amt**; **Do|ma|ni|al|be|sitz** (staatlicher Landbesitz); **Dom‿chor** (*vgl.* Chor), **...de|chant**; **Do|mes|tik**, der; -en, -en *meist Plur.*; ↑R 126 (*veraltend für* Dienstbote; *Radsport* jmd., der Hilfsdienste leistet); **Do|mes|ti|ka|ti|on**, die; -, -en ‹lat.› (Umzüchtung wilder Tiere zu Haustieren); **Do|mes|ti|ke**, der; -n, -n; *vgl.* Domestik; **do|mes|ti|zie|ren**; **Dom|frei|heit** (der einem [1]Dom zunächst gelegene Bereich, der im MA. unter der geistl. Gerichtsbarkeit des Domstiftes stand); **Dom|herr**; **Do|mi|na**, die; -, ...nä ‹„Herrin"› (Stiftsvorsteherin; *Jargon* Prostituierte, die sadistische Handlungen vornimmt); **do|mi|nant** (vorherrschend; überlagernd, überdeckend); **Do|mi|nan|te**, die; -, -n (vorherrschendes Merkmal; *Musik* die Quinte vom Grundton aus); **Do|mi|nanz**, die; -, -en (*Vererbungslehre* Vorherrschen bestimmter Merkmale); **Do|mi|ni|ca** (Inselstaat in Mittelamerika); **do|mi|nie|ren** ([vor]herrschen; beherrschen); leuchtende Farben - in der neuen Mode; junge Autoren - die literarische Szene; **Do|mi|nik**, Do|mi|ni|kus (m. Vorn.); **[1]Do|mi|ni|ka|ner**, der; -s, - (Angehöriger des vom hl. Dominikus gegr. Ordens); **[2]Do|mi|ni|ka|ner** (Einwohner der Dominikanischen Republik); **Do|mi|ni|ka|ner‿klos|ter**, **...mönch**, **...orden** (der; -s; *Abk.* O. P. *od.* O. Pr.; *vgl. d.*); **do|mi|ni|ka|nisch**, *aber* (↑R 93): **Do|mi|ni|ka|ni|sche Re|pub|lik**, die; -n - (Staat in Mittelamerika); **Do|mi|ni|kus** *vgl.* Dominik; **Do|mi|ni|on** [do'miniən], das; -s, *Plur.* -s *u.* ...ien [...iən] ‹engl.› (*früher* sich selbst regierender Teil des Commonwealth); **Do|mi|nique** [...'ni:k] (m. *u.* w. Vorn.); **Do|mi|ni|um**, das; -s, *Plur.* -s *u.* ...ien [...iən] ‹lat.› (altröm. Herrschaftsgebiet); **[1]Do|mi|no**, der; -s, -s (Maskenmantel, -kostüm); **[2]Do|mi|no**, das; -s, -s (Spiel); **Do|mi|no‿spiel**, **...stein**; **Do|mi|nus vo|bis|cum!** [- v...] ‹„Der Herr sei mit euch!"› (liturg. Gruß); **Do|mi|zil**, das; -s, -e (Wohnsitz; *Bankw.* Zahlungsort [von Wechseln]); **do|mi|zi|lie|ren** (ansässig sein, wohnen; *Bankw.* [Wechsel] an einem andern Ort als dem Wohnort des Bezogenen zahlbar anweisen); **Do|mi|zil|wech|sel** *(Bankw.)*; **Dom‿ka|pi|tel**, **...ka|pi|tu|lar** (Domherr)

Do|mo|wi|na ['do:..., *auch* 'dɔ...], die; - ‹sorb., „Heimat"› (Organisation der sorb. Minderheit in Deutschland)

Dom|pfaff, der; *Gen.* -en, *auch* -s, *Plur.* -en (ein Singvogel [Gimpel])

Domp|teur [...'tø:r], der; -s, -e ‹franz.› (Tierbändiger); **Dompteur|kunst**; **Domp|teu|se** [...'tø:zə], die; -, -n

Do|m|ra, die; -, *Plur.* -s *u.* ...ren ‹russ.› (russ. Volksinstrument)

Dom|schatz

[1]Don, der; -[s] (russ. Fluss)

[2]Don, der; -[s], -s (*in Verbindung mit Namen ohne Artikel)* ‹span. *u.* ital., „Herr"› (*in Spanien* höfl. Anrede, *w. Form* Doña; *vgl. d.*; *in Italien* Titel der Priester u. bestimmter Adelsfamilien, *w. Form* Donna; *vgl. d.*); **Do|ña** ['dɔnja], die; -, -s ‹span.› (Frau; *in Verbindung mit Namen ohne Artikel*)

Do|nar (germ. Gott); *vgl.* Thor; **Do|na|rit** [*auch* ...'rit], der; -s (ein Sprengstoff)

Do|na|tor, der; -s, ...oren ‹lat.› (*schweiz., sonst veraltet für* Geber, Spender; *Physik, Chemie* Atom od. Molekül, das Elektronen od. Ionen abgibt)

Do|na|tus (m. Vorn.)

Do|nau, die; - (europ. Strom); Donauauen, *auch* die Donau-Auen (↑R 24); **Do|nau-Dampf|schiff|fahrts|ge|sell|schaft**, die; - ; ↑R 24; **Do|nau|mo|nar|chie**, die; - (österreichisch-ungarische Monarchie von 1869-1918); **Do|nau|wörth** (Stadt in Bayern)

Don|bass [*auch* ...'bas], der, *auch* das; - ‹russ.› (*russ. Kurzw. für* Donez-Steinkohlenbecken; Industriegebiet westl. des Donez)

Don Bos|co *vgl.* Bosco

Don Car|los (span. Prinz)

Dö|ner, der; -s, - (*kurz für* Dönerkebab); **Dö|ner|ke|bab**, der; -[s], -s ‹türk.› (Kebab aus an einem senkrecht stehenden Spieß gebratenem Hammelfleisch)

Do|nez [*russ.* da'n(i)ɛts], der; - (r. Nebenfluss des Don)

Dong, der; -[s], -[s] (vietnam. Währungseinheit); 50 - (↑R 90)

Don Gio|van|ni [dɔn dʒɔ'vani] ‹ital.› (Titelgestalt der gleichnamigen Oper von Mozart)

Do|ni|zet|ti (ital. Komponist)

Don|ja, die; -, -s ‹span., „Herrin"› (*scherzh. für* [Dienst]mädchen; *veraltend für* Geliebte); *vgl.* Doña

Don|jon [dõ'ʒõ:], der; -s, -s ‹franz.› (Hauptturm mittelalterl. Burgen in Frankreich)

Don Ju|an [dɔn 'xu̯an], der; - -s, - -s ‹span.› (span. Sagengestalt; Verführer; Frauenheld)

Don|ko|sak *meist Plur.* (Angehöriger eines am Don wohnenden Stammes der Kosaken); **Don|ko|sa|ken|chor**, der; -[e]s

Don|na, die; -, *Plur.* -s *u.* Donnen ‹ital.› (Herrin; *vor Namen ohne Artikel*); *vgl. auch* Madonna

Don|ner, der; -s, -; - und Doria! (*ugs.*; *vgl.* Doria); **Don|ner‿bal|ken** (*ugs. scherzh. für* Latrine), **...büch|se** (*scherzh. für* Feuerwaffe); **Don|ne|rer** (Donnergott); **Don|ner|keil** (Belemnit); **Don|ner|litt|chen!**, **Don|ner|lütt|chen!** (*landsch.* Ausruf des Erstaunens); **don|nern**; ich ...ere; **Don|ner|schlag**; **Don|ners|tag**, der; -[e]s, -e (*Abk.* Do.); *vgl.* Dienstag; **don|ners|tags** (↑R 46); *vgl.* Dienstag; **Don|ner|wet|ter**; - [noch einmal]!

[1]Don Qui|chotte [dɔn ki'ʃɔt] ‹span.› (Romanheld bei Cervantes); **[2]Don Qui|chotte**, der; - -s, - -s (weltfremder Idealist); **Don|qui|chot|te|rie**, die; -, ...ien (Torheit [aus weltfremdem Idealismus]); **Don Qui|jo|te** *u.* **Don Qui|xo|te** [*beide* dɔn ki'xo:tə] *vgl.* Don Quichotte

Dont|ge|schäft ['dõ:...] ‹franz.; dt.› (*Börse* Termingeschäft)

doof (*ugs. für* dumm; einfältig); **Doof|heit**, die; - *(ugs.)*

Dope [do:p], das; -[s] ‹niederl.-engl.› (*ugs. für* Rauschgift, Droge); **do|pen** [*auch* 'do:...] (*Sport* durch [verbotene] Anregungsmittel od. muskelaufbauende Präparate zu Höchstleistungen bringen); gedopt; **Do|ping**, das; -s, -s; **Do|ping|kon|trol|le**

[1]Dop|pel, das; -s, - (zweite Ausfertigung [einer Schrift]; *[Tisch]tennis* Doppelspiel); **[2]Dop|pel**, der; -s, -e (*schweiz. für* Einsatz beim Schützenfest); **Dop|pel...** (z. B. Doppel-a, Doppelgänger); **Dop|pel‿ad|ler**, **...agent** (↑R 132), **...axel** (↑R 132; doppelter [2]Axel), **...bau|er** (der; *Schach*), **...be|las|tung**, **...be|lich|tung** *(Fotogr., Film)*, **...be|steu|e|rung**, **...bett**, **...bock** (das, *auch* der; -s; ein Starkbier); **dop|pel|bö|dig** (hintergründig); **Dop|pel|bö|dig|keit**; **Dop|pel‿brief**, **...buch|sta|be**, **...ci|ce|ro** (ein Schriftgrad), **...de|cker** (ein Flugzeugtyp; *ugs. für* Omnibus mit Oberdeck); **dop|pel|deu|tig**; **Dop|pel|deu-**

tig|keit; **Dop|pel-er|folg, ...feh|ler** (*Sport*), **...fens|ter, ...gän|ger; dop|pel|glei|sig; Dop|pel-haus, ...heft; Dop|pel|heit** *Plur. selten;* **Dop|pel-he|lix** (die; -; *Biol.* Struktur des DNS-Moleküls), **...hoch|zeit, ...kinn, ...klick** (*EDV* zweimaliges Betätigen der Maustaste), **...kno|ten, ...kopf** (der; -[e]s; Kartenspiel), **...laut** (*für* Diphthong), **...le|ben** (das; -s), **...lutz** (doppelter [2]Lutz), **...mo|ral, ...mord; dop|peln;** ich ...[e]le (↑R 16); Schuhe - (*südd. mdal. u. österr. für* Schuhe sohlen); **Dop|pel-na|me, ...nel|son** (doppelter [2]Nelson), **...num|mer** (doppeltes Heft einer Zeitschrift u. Ä.), **...part|ner** (*[Tisch]tennis*), **...pass** (*Fußball*), **...punkt; dop|pel|rei|hig; Dop|pel-ritt|ber|ger** (doppelter Rittberger), **...rol|le, ...sal|chow** (doppelter Salchow); **dop|pel|schlä|fig, dop|pel|schläf|rig;** eine - Couch; **dop|pel|sei|tig;** eine -e Anzeige; **dop|pel|sin|nig; dop|pelt;** doppelte Buchführung; ein doppelt wirkendes Mittel; doppelt gemoppelt (*ugs. für* unnötigerweise zweimal); doppelt so groß, doppelt so viel; er ist doppelt so reich wie (*seltener* als) ich; (↑R 47:) um das, ums Doppelte größer, das Doppelte an Zeit; **dop|pelt|koh|len|sau|er** (*Chemie*) doppeltkohlensaures Natron; **Dop|pel-T-Trä|ger,** der; -s, -; ↑R 28 (von I-förmigem Querschnitt); **Dop|pel|tür; dop|pelt wir|kend** *vgl.* doppelt; **Dop|pe|lung; Dop|pel-ver|die|ner, ...zent|ner** (100 kg; *Zeichen* dz), **...zim|mer; dop|pel|zün|gig** (*abwertend*); **Dop|pel|zün|gig|keit**

Dop|pik, die; - (doppelte Buchführung)

Dopp|ler (*südd. mdal. u. österr. für* erneuerte Schuhsohle)

Dopp|ler|ef|fekt, der; -[e]s (↑R 95) ⟨nach dem österr. Physiker⟩ (ein physikal. Prinzip)

Dopp|lung

Do|ra (w. Vorn.)

Do|ra|de, die; -, -n ⟨franz.⟩ (ein Fisch); **Do|ra|do** *vgl.* Eldorado

Do|rant, der; -[e]s, -e ⟨mlat.⟩ (Zauber abwehrende Pflanze)

Dor|chen (w. Vorn.)

Dor|dog|ne [...ˈdɔnjə] (↑R 130), die; - (Fluss u. Departement in Frankreich)

Dord|recht (↑R 130 *u.* 132; Stadt in den Niederlanden)

Do|reen [doˈri:n] (w. Vorn.)

Do|rer *vgl.* Dorier

Dorf, das; -[e]s, Dörfer; **Dorf-an|ger, ...bach, ...be|woh|ner; Dörf|chen; dör|fisch** (*meist abwertend*); **Dorf|klub** (*regional für* kulturelles Zentrum auf dem Land); **Dörf|ler; dörf|lich; Dorf|lin|de; Dorf|schaft** (*schweiz. für* Dorf, Gesamtheit der Dorfbewohner); **Dorf-schen|ke, ...schö|ne, ...schön|heit, ...schu|le, ...schul|ze** (*veraltet*), **...stra|ße, ...teich, ...trot|tel**

Do|ria (ital. Familienn.); *nur in* Donner und -! (Ausruf)

Do|ri|er [...iər], Do|rer, der; -s, - (Angehöriger eines altgriech. Volksstammes); **[1]Do|ris** (altgriech. Landschaft)

[2]Do|ris (w. Vorn.)

do|risch (auf die Dorier bezüglich; aus [1]Doris); -e Tonart

Do|rit (w. Vorn.)

Dor|mi|to|ri|um, das; -s, ...ien [...iən] ⟨lat.⟩ (Schlafsaal eines Klosters)

Dorn, der; -[e]s, *Plur.* -en, *ugs. auch* Dörner, *in der Technik* -e; **Dorn|busch; Dörn|chen; Dor|nen|he|cke,** Dorn|he|cke; **Dor|nen|kro|ne; dor|nen|reich; Dor|nen|weg** (Leidensweg); **Dorn-fort|satz** (*Med.* nach hinten gerichteter Wirbelfortsatz), **...ge|strüpp, ...he|cke** (*vgl.* Dornenhecke); **Dor|nicht,** das; -s, -e (*veraltet für* Dorngestrüpp); **dor|nig; Dorn|rös|chen** (eine Märchengestalt); **Dorn|rös|chen|schlaf**

Do|ro|thea, Do|ro|thee [ˈdo:..., *auch* ...ˈte:(ə)] (w. Vorn.)

Dor|pat (*estn.* Tartu)

Dör|re, die; -, -n (*landsch. für* Darre [Trocken- od. Röstvorrichtung]); **dor|ren** (*geh. für* dürr werden); **dör|ren** (dürr machen); *vgl.* darren; **Dörr-fleisch, ...ge|mü|se, ...obst, ...ofen** (↑R 132), **...pflau|me**

dor|sal ⟨lat.⟩ (*Med.* den Rücken betreffend, rückseitig); **Dor|sal,** der; -s, -e *od.* **Dor|sal|laut,** der; -[e]s, -e (*Sprachw.* mit dem Zungenrücken gebildeter Laut)

Dorsch, der; -[e]s, -e (junger Kabeljau)

dort; dort drüben; von dort aus; dort behalten; dort bleiben; **dort|her** [*auch* ˈdɔrt...]; von -; **dort|hin** [*auch* ˈdɔrt...] (↑R 23:) da- und dorthin; **dort|hi|nab** [*auch* ˈdɔrt...]; **dort|hi|naus** [*auch* ˈdɔrt...]; bis dorthinaus (*ugs. für* sehr, maßlos); **dor|tig**

Dort|mund (Stadt im Ruhrgebiet); **Dort|mund-Ems-Ka|nal,** der; -[e]s; ↑R 105; **Dort|mun|der** (↑R 103)

dort|sei|tig (*Amtsspr. für* dortig); **dort|seits** (*Amtsspr. für* [von] dort); **dort|selbst** (*veraltend*); **dort|zu|lan|de,** *auch* **dort zu Lande** (↑R 41)

Do|ry|pho|ros, der; - ⟨griech., „Speerträger"⟩ (eine berühmte Statue des griech. Bildhauers Polyklet)

Dos, die; -, Dotes [ˈdo:te:s] ⟨lat.⟩ (*Rechtsspr.* Mitgift)

dos à dos [dozaˈdo:] ⟨franz.⟩ (Rücken an Rücken)

Dös|chen; Do|se, die; -, -n (kleine Büchse; *selten für* Dosis); **Do|sen** (*Plur. von* Dose u. Dosis)

dö|sen (*ugs. für* wachend träumen; halb schlafen; unaufmerksam vor sich hin starren); du döst; er dös|te

Do|sen-bier, ...blech; do|sen|fer|tig; Do|sen-fleisch, ...ge|mü|se, ...milch, ...öff|ner, ...sup|pe, ...wurst

do|sier|bar; do|sie|ren ⟨franz.⟩ (ab-, zumessen); **Do|sie|rung**

dö|sig (*ugs. für* schläfrig; *auch für* stumpfsinnig)

Do|si|me|ter, das ⟨griech.⟩ (Gerät zur Messung der aufgenommenen Menge radioaktiver Strahlen); **Do|si|met|rie** (↑R 130), die; - (Messung der Energiemenge von Strahlen); **Do|sis,** die; -, ...sen (zugemessene [Arznei]gabe, kleine Menge)

Dos|si|er [dɔˈsie:], das, *veraltet* der; -s, -s ⟨franz.⟩ (Aktenheft, -bündel); **dos|sie|ren** (*fachspr. für* abschrägen; böschen); **Dos|sie|rung** (flache Böschung)

Dost, der; -[e]s, -e (eine Gewürzpflanze)

Dos|tal, Nico (österr. Komponist)

Dos|to|jews|ki [...ˈjɛfski] (russ. Schriftsteller)

Do|ta|ti|on, die; -, -en ⟨lat.⟩ (Schenkung; [geldliche] Zuwendung; *veraltet für* Mitgift); **do|tie|ren** (mit einer bestimmten Geldsumme ausstatten; bezahlen); **Do|tie|rung**

Dot|ter, der *u.* das; -s, - (Eigelb); **Dot|ter|blu|me; dot|ter|gelb; Dot|ter|sack** (*Zool.*)

Dou|a|ne [duˈa:n(ə)], die; -, -n ⟨arab.-franz.⟩ (*veraltet für* Zoll, Zollamt); **Dou|a|ni|er** [duaˈnie:], der; -s, -s (*franz. Bez. für* Zollaufseher)

dou|beln [ˈdu:...] ⟨franz.⟩ (↑R 33; *Film* als Double spielen); ich ...[e]le (↑R 16); **Dou|ble** [ˈdu:b(ə)l], das; -s, -s (*Film* Ersatzspieler [ähnlichen Aussehens]); **Doub|lé** [duˈble:] (↑R 130); *vgl.* Dublee; **doub|lie|ren** [duˈbli:...]; *vgl.* dublieren

Doug|las|fich|te [ˈdu(:)...] (↑R 130

u. ↑R 95) *u.* **Doug|la|sie** [du'gla:zi̯ə], die; -, -n *u.* **Doug|las|tan|ne** ['du(:)...] (↑R 95) ‹nach dem schott. Botaniker David Douglas› (schnell wachsender Nadelbaum)
Dou|ro ['doru], der; - (port. Name des Duero)
do̱ ut de̱s ‹lat., „ich gebe, damit du gibst"›
Do|ver ['do:və(r)] (engl. Hafenstadt)
Dow-Jones-In|dex ['dau̯'dʒo:nz'indɛks], der; - ‹nach der amerik. Firma Dow, Jones & Co.› (*Wirtsch.* Aufstellung der errechneten Durchschnittskurse der 30 wichtigsten Aktien in den USA)
down! [dau̯n] ‹engl.› (*Befehl an Hunde* nieder!); down sein (*ugs. für* bedrückt, abgespannt sein)
Dow|ning Street ['dau̯niŋ 'stri:t], die; - - ‹nach dem engl. Diplomaten Sir George Downing› (Straße in London; Amtssitz des Premierministers; *übertr. für* die britische Regierung)
Down|syn|drom ['dau̯n-] (↑R 95; genetisch bedingte, teils schwer wiegende Entwicklungshemmungen und Veränderungen des Erscheinungsbildes eines Menschen)
Do|xa̱|le, das; -s, -s ‹lat.› (*Archit.* Gitter zwischen hohem Chor u. Hauptschiff); **Do|xo|lo|gi̱e,** die; -, ...i̱en ‹griech.› (gottesdienstliche Lobpreisungsformel)
Do|yen [do̱a'jɛ̃:], der; -s, -s ‹franz.› ([Rang]ältester u. Wortführer des diplomatischen Korps)
Doz. = Dozent; **Do|ze̱nt,** der; -en, -en (↑R 126) ‹lat.› (Lehrer [an einer Universität od. Hochschule]; *Abk.* Doz.); **Do|ze̱n|ten|schaft; Do|ze̱n|tin; Do|zen|tu̱r,** die; -, -en; **do|zi̱e̱|ren**
DP = Deutsche Post
dpa = Deutsche Presse-Agentur; **dpa-Mel|dung** (↑R 26)
dpt, dptr., Dptr. = Dioptrie
Dr = Drachme
DR = Deutsche Reichsbahn
Dr. = do̱ctor, Doktor; *vgl. d.*
Dr. ... (z. B. phil.)
d. R. = der Reserve *(Milit.);* des Ruhestandes
Dra̱|che, der; -n, -n; ↑R 126 (ein Fabeltier); **Dra̱|chen,** der; -s, - (Fluggerät; Segelboot; *kurz für* Drachenviereck; *abwertend für* zänkische Frau); **Dra|chen|boot** *(Segeln);* **Dra̱|chen|fels,** der; - (Berg im Siebengebirge); **Dra̱|chen‿flie|gen** (das; -s; *Sport*), **...flie|ger, ...gift, ...klas|se** *(Segeln),* **...saat, ...vier|eck** *(Math.)*
Dra̱ch|me, die; -, -n ‹griech.› (griech. Währungseinheit; *Abk.* Dr; früheres Apothekergewicht)
Dra̱|cu|la (Titelfigur eines Vampirromans)
Dra|gee, *auch* **Dra|gée** [*beide* dra'ʒe:], das; -s, -s ‹franz.› (mit Zucker od. Schokolade überzogene Süßigkeit; Arzneipille); **Dra|geur** [...'ʒø:r], der; -s, -e (jmd., der Dragees herstellt)
Dra̱g|gen, der; -s, - (*Seemannsspr.* mehrarmiger Anker ohne Stock)
dra|gie|ren [...'ʒi:...] ‹franz.› (Dragees herstellen)
Dra̱|go|man, der; -s, -e ‹arab.› (einheim. Dolmetscher, Übersetzer im Nahen Osten)
Dra|go̱n, Dra|gu̱n, der *od.* das; -s ‹arab.› (*seltener für* Estragon)
Dra|go|na̱|de, die; -, -n ‹franz.› (*früher* gewaltsame [durch Dragoner ausgeführte] Maßregel); **Dra|go̱|ner,** der; -s, - (*früher* leichter Reiter; *österr. noch für* Rückenspange am Rock u. am Mantel; *ugs. für* derbe, resolute Frau)
Dr. agr. = do̱ctor agrono̱miae; *vgl.* Doktor
Dra|gu̱n *vgl.* Dragon
dra̱hn (*österr. ugs. für* [nachts] feiern, sich vergnügen); **Dra̱h|rer,** der; -s, - (*österr. ugs. für* Nachtschwärmer)
Dra̱ht, der; -[e]s, Drähte; **Dra̱ht‿be|sen, ...bürs|te; Dra̱ht|chen;** [1]**dra̱h|ten** (*veraltend für* telegrafieren; mit Draht zusammenflechten); [2]**dra̱h|ten** (aus Draht); **Dra̱ht‿esel** (↑R 132; *ugs. scherzh. für* Fahrrad), **...funk** (Verbreitung von Rundfunksendungen über Fernsprecher), **...geflecht, ...git|ter, ...glas; Dra̱ht|haar|fox** (eine Hunderasse); **dra̱ht|haa|rig; dra̱h|tig; ...dräh|tig** (z. B. dreidrähtig); **Dra̱ht‿kom|mo|de** (*ugs. scherzh. für* Klavier), **...korb; Dra̱ht|leh|re** (Werkzeug zur Bestimmung der Drahtdicke); **dra̱ht|los;** -e Telegrafie; **Dra̱ht‿sche|re, ...seil; Dra̱ht|seil‿akt, ...bahn; Dra̱ht‿ver|hau, ...zan|ge, ...zaun, ...zie|her** (*auch für* jmd., der im Verborgenen andere für seine [polit.] Ziele einsetzt)
Drain [drɛ:n, *auch* drɛ̃:], der; -s, -s, *auch* Drä̱n, der; -s, *Plur.* -s *u.* -e ‹franz.› (*Med.* Wundröhrchen; *vgl. auch* Drän); **Drai|na|ge,** *auch* Drä|na|ge [...'na:ʒə, *österr.* ...'naʒ], die; -, -n [...'na:ʒ(ə)n] (*Med.* Ableitung von Wundabsonderungen; *vgl. auch* Dränage); **drai|ni̱e̱|ren,** *auch* drä|ni̱e̱|ren (*Med.; vgl. auch* dränen)
Drai|si̱|ne [drai̯..., *auch, bes. österr.,* drɛ...], die; -, -n ‹nach dem dt. Erfinder Drais› (Vorläufer des Fahrrades; Eisenbahnfahrzeug zur Streckenkontrolle)
Drake [dre:k] (engl. Seefahrer)
Dra̱|ko *vgl.* Drakon; **Dra̱|kon** (altgriech. Gesetzgeber); **dra|ko̱|nisch** (sehr streng)
dra̱ll (derb, stramm); **Dra̱ll,** der; -[e]s, -e *Plur. selten* ([Geschoss]drehung; Windung der Züge in Feuerwaffen; Drehung bei Garn und Zwirn); **Dra̱ll|heit,** die; -
Dra̱|lon ®, das; -[s] (eine synthet. Faser)
Dra̱|ma, das; -s, ...men ‹griech.› (Schauspiel; erregendes od. trauriges Geschehen); **Dra|ma̱|tik,** die; - (dramatische Dichtkunst; erregende Spannung); **Dra|ma̱|ti|ker** (Dramendichter); **dra|ma̱|tisch** (in Dramenform; auf das Drama bezüglich; gesteigert lebhaft; erregend, spannend); -e Musik; **dra|ma|ti|si̱e̱|ren** (als Schauspiel für die Bühne bearbeiten; als besonders aufregend, schlimm darstellen); **Dra|ma|ti|si̱e̱|rung; Dra|ma|tu̱rg,** der; -en, -en; ↑R 126 (literarisch-künstler. Berater bei Theater, Film u. Fernsehen); **Dra|ma|tur|gi̱e,** die; -, ...i̱en (Gestaltung, Bearbeitung eines Dramas; Lehre vom Drama); **Dra|ma|tu̱r|gin; dra|ma|tu̱r|gisch**
dra̱n (*ugs. für* daran); dran sein (*ugs. für* an der Reihe sein); dran glauben müssen (*ugs. für* vom Schicksal ereilt werden); das Drum und Dran (↑R 49)
Drä̱n, der; -s, *Plur.* -s *u.* -e, *auch, bes. schweiz.* Drain [drɛ:n, *schweiz.* drɛ̃:], der; -s, -s ‹franz.› (der Entwässerung dienendes unterirdisches Abzugsrohr; *vgl. auch* Drain); **Drä|na|ge,** *schweiz.* Drai|na|ge [...'na:ʒə, *österr.* ...'na:ʒ], die; -, -n [...'na:ʒ(ə)n] (*schweiz., sonst veraltet für* Dränung; *vgl. auch* Drainage)
dra̱n|blei|ben (*ugs. für* an jmdm., etwas bleiben); am Gegner -
drä̱|nen, *schweiz.* drai|ni̱e̱|ren [drɛ...] ‹*zu* Drän› ([Boden] entwässern; *vgl. auch* drainieren)
Dra̱ng, der; -[e]s, Dränge *Plur. selten*
dra̱n|ge|ben (*ugs. für* darangeben *[vgl. d.]*); **dra̱n|ge|hen** (*ugs. für* darangehen *[vgl. d.]*)
Drän|ge|le̱i; drä̱n|geln; ich ...[e]le (↑R 16); **drä̱n|gen; Drän|ge|re̱i; Dra̱ng|pe|ri|o|de** *(Ballsport);* **Dra̱ng|sal,** die; -, -e, *veraltet* das;

-[e]s, -e *(geh.)*; **drang|sa|lie|ren** (quälen, peinigen); **drang|voll**
dran|hal|ten, sich (*ugs. für* daranhalten, sich *[vgl. d.]*); **dran|hängen** (*ugs. für* zusätzlich Zeit für etwas aufbringen)
drä|nie|ren (*älter für* dränen; *auch für* drainieren)
Drank, der; -[e]s (*nordd. für* Küchenabfälle, Spülwasser, flüssiges Viehfutter); **Drank|fass**
dran|kom|men (*ugs. für* an die Reihe kommen); **dran|krie|gen** *(ugs.)*; jmdn. -
Drank|ton|ne *(nordd.)*
dran|ma|chen *vgl.* daranmachen
Drän‿netz, ...rohr
dran|set|zen (*ugs. für* daransetzen *[vgl. d.]*)
Drän|sys|tem; Drä|nung (Bodenentwässerung durch Dräne)
Dra|pé, *auch* Dra|pee [dra'pe:] (↑R 33), der; -s, -s ‹franz.› (ein Stoff); **Dra|pe|rie,** die; -, ...ien (*veraltend für* Behang; [kunstvoller] Faltenwurf); **dra|pie|ren** ([mit Stoff] behängen, [aus]schmücken; raffen; in Falten legen); **Dra|pie|rung**
drapp, drapp‿far|ben *od.* **...farbig** (*österr. für* sandfarben)
Drasch, der; -s (*landsch. für* lärmende Geschäftigkeit, Hast)
Dras|tik, die; - ‹griech.› (Deutlichkeit, Derbheit); **Dras|ti|kum,** das; -s, ...ka (*Pharm.* starkes Abführmittel); **dras|tisch** (sehr deutlich; derb)
Drau, die; - (Nebenfluss der Donau)
dräu|en (*veraltet für* drohen)
drauf (*ugs. für* darauf); drauf und dran (*ugs. für* nahe daran) sein, etwas zu tun; drauf sein (*ugs. auch für* [gut/schlecht] gelaunt sein); **Drauf|ga|be** (Handgeld beim Vertragsabschluss od. Kaufabschluss; *österr. auch für* Zugabe des Künstlers); **Drauf|gän|ger; drauf|gän|ge|risch; Drauf|gän|ger|tum,** das; -s; **drauf|ge|ben;** jmdm. eins - (*ugs. für* einen Schlag versetzen; zurechtweisen); **drauf|ge|hen** (*ugs. auch für* verbraucht werden, sterben); er geht drauf; ist draufgegangen; *vgl.* darauf; **Drauf|geld** (Draufgabe); **drauf‿ha|ben** (*ugs. für* beherrschen), **...hal|ten** (*ugs. für* etwas zum Ziel nehmen), **...hau|en** *(ugs.)*, **...krie|gen** (eins, etwas -: *ugs. für* getadelt werden; eine Enttäuschung erleben), **...le|gen** (*ugs. für* zusätzlich bezahlen); **drauf|los;** immer -!; **drauf|los‿ge|hen** (er geht drauflos; drauflosgegangen; draufloszugehen; *vgl.* darauf), **...re|den, ...rei|ten, ...schie|ßen, ...schimp|fen, ...wirt|schaf|ten; drauf|ma|chen;** einen - (*ugs. für* ausgiebig feiern); **drauf|sat|teln** (*ugs. für* zusätzlich geben); **drauf|schla|gen** (*ugs. für* auf etwas schlagen; erhöhen, steigern, aufschlagen); **drauf sein** *vgl.* drauf; **Drauf|sicht,** die; - *(Zeichenlehre)*; **drauf|ste|hen** (*ugs. für* darauf zu lesen sein); **drauf|zah|len** (drauflegen; *vgl. d.*)
draus (*ugs. für* daraus)
drau|ßen; die Hunde müssen draußen bleiben
Dra|wi|da [*auch* 'dra:...], der; -[s], -[s] (Angehöriger einer Völkergruppe in Vorderindien); **dra|wi|disch;** -e Sprachen
Draw|ing|room ['drɔ:iŋru(:)m], der; -s, -s ‹engl.› (in England Empfangszimmer)
Dr. disc. pol. = doktor disciplinarum politicarum; *vgl.* Doktor
Dream|team, *auch* **Dream-Team** ['dri:mti:m], das; -s, -s ‹engl.› (*bes. Sport* ideal besetzte Mannschaft)
Drech|sel|lei (*auch für* geschraubte [Schreib]weise); **drech|seln;** ich ...[e]le (↑R 16); **Drechs|ler; Drechs|ler|ar|beit; Drechs|le|rei**
Dreck, der; -[e]s *(ugs.)*; **Dreck‿ar|beit, ...ei|mer** *(ugs.)*, **...fink** (der; *Gen.* -en, *auch* -s, *Plur.* -en; *ugs.*), **...hau|fen** *(ugs.)*; **dre|ckig** *(ugs.)*; **Dreck|kerl** *vgl.* Deckskerl; **Dreck‿nest** (*ugs. abwertend für* Dorf, Kleinstadt), **...pfo|te** (*ugs. für* schmutzige Hand), **...sack** *(derb abwertend)*; **Drecks|ar|beit** *(ugs. abwertend)*; **Dreck|sau** *(derb abwertend)*; **Dreck|schleu|der** (*ugs. für* freches Mundwerk; Fabrikanlage o. Ä., die die Luft stark verschmutzt); **Drecks|kerl** *(derb abwertend)*; **Dreck|spatz** *(ugs.)*
Dred|sche, die; -, -n ‹engl.› (*fachspr. für* Schleppnetz)
Dreesch usw. *vgl.* Driesch usw.
Dr. eh., *auch* **e. h.** *u.* **E. h.** = Ehrendoktor, Doktor Ehren halber; *vgl.* Doktor
Dreh, der; -[e]s, *Plur.* -s *od.* -e (*ugs. für* Einfall, Kunstgriff; *seltener für* Drehung);
Dreh‿ach|se, ...ar|beit (die; -, -en; *meist Plur.; Film*), **...bank** (*Plur.* ...bänke; *älter für* Drehmaschine); **dreh|bar;** -er Sessel; **Dreh‿be|we|gung, ...blei|stift, ...brü|cke, ...buch** (Vorlage für Filmaufnahmen); **Dreh|buch|au|tor; Dreh|büh|ne; Dre|he,** die; - (*landsch. ugs. für* Gegend); in der - kenne ich mich aus; **dre|hen; Dre|her; Dre|he|rei; Dreh‿kran, ...krank|heit** (die; -), **...kreuz, ...ma|schi|ne, ...mo|ment** (das; *Physik*), **...or|gel, ...ort** *(Film)*, **...pau|se** *(Film)*, **...punkt, ...res|tau|rant, ...schei|be, ...schuss** *(Fußball)*; **Dreh|strom** *(Elektrotechnik)*; **Dreh|strom|mo|tor; Dreh‿stuhl, ...tür; Dre|hung; Dreh‿vor|rich|tung, ...wurm, ...zahl** (Anzahl der Umdrehungen in einer Zeiteinheit); **Dreh|zahl|mes|ser,** der
drei, *Gen.* dreier, *Dat.* dreien, drei; zu dreien *od.* zu dritt; herzliche Grüße von uns dreien; die drei sagen, dass ...; *(im Zeugnis:)* Latein: drei Komma fünf (*vgl. aber* Drei); er kann nicht bis drei zählen (*ugs. für* er ist sehr dumm); (↑R 6:) dreier großer, *selten* großen Völker, *aber* dreier Angestellten, *seltener* Angestellter; der Saal war erst drei viertel voll; eine Dreiviertelmillion; es ist drei viertel acht; in einer Dreiviertelstunde, *aber* in drei viertel Stunden (*mit Ziffern* $^3/_4$ Stunden), in drei Viertelstunden; *vgl.* acht *u.* Viertel; **Drei,** die; -, -en; eine Drei würfeln; er schrieb in Latein eine Drei; die Note „Drei“; mit [der Durchschnittsnote] „Drei-Komma-fünf“ bestanden; *vgl.* [1]Acht *u.* Eins; **Drei|ach|ser** (Wagen mit drei Achsen; *mit Ziffer* 3-Achser; ↑R 25); **drei|ach|sig; Drei|ach|tel|takt,** der; -[e]s (*mit Ziffern* $^3/_8$-Takt; ↑R 28); im -; **Drei|an|gel,** der; -s, - (*landsch. für* winkelförmiger Riss im Stoff); **drei‿ar|mig, ...bän|dig, ...bei|nig; Drei|blatt** (Name von Pflanzen); **drei‿blät|te|rig, ...blätt|rig; Drei|bund,** der; -[e]s; **drei|di|men|si|o|nal;** -es Bild, -er Film *od.* (↑R 28:) Drei-D-Bild, Drei-D-Film *od.*, *mit Ziffer:* 3-D-Bild, 3-D-Film; **Drei|eck; drei|eckig** (↑R 132); **Drei|eck|schal|tung** *(Technik)*; **Drei|ecks‿ge|schich|te, ...mes|sung, ...netz; Drei|eck[s]|tuch; drei|ein|halb,** dreiund|ein|halb; **drei|ei|nig;** der -e Gott; **Drei|ei|nig|keit,** die; - *(christl. Rel.)*; **Drei|ei|nig|keits|fest** (erster Sonntag nach Pfingsten); **Drei|er;** *vgl.* Achter; **Drei|er|kom|bi|na|ti|on** *(Sportspr.)*; **drei|er|lei; Drei|er|rei|he; drei|fach; Drei|fa|che,** das; -n; *vgl.* Achtfache; **Drei|fal|tig|keit,** die; - (*svw.* Dreieinigkeit); **Drei|fal|tig|keits|fest** (erster Sonntag nach Pfingsten); **Drei|far|ben|druck** *Plur.* ...drucke; **drei|far-**

big; **Drei|fel|der|wirt|schaft**, die; -; **drei|fenst|rig; Drei|fin|ger|faul|tier** (Ai); **Drei‿fuß, ...ge|stirn; drei|ge|stri|chen** (*Musik*); **Drei|heit**, die; -; **drei|hun|dert; drei|jäh|rig;** *vgl.* achtjährig; **Drei|kai|ser|bünd|nis; Drei|kant**, das *od.* der; -[e]s, -e (↑R 44); **Drei|kan|ter** (Gesteinsform); **drei|kan|tig; Drei|kant|stahl** (*vgl.* [1]Stahl *u.* ↑R 44); **Drei|kä|se|hoch**, der; -s, -[s]; **Drei|klang; Drei|klas|sen|wahl|recht**, das; -[e]s; **Drei|kö|ni|ge** *ohne Artikel* (Dreikönigsfest); an, auf, nach, vor, zu -; **Drei|kö|nigs‿fest** (6. Jan.), **...spiel; Drei|län|der|tref|fen; Drei|ling** (alte Münze; altes Weinmaß); **drei|mäh|dig** (dreischürig); **drei|mal;** (↑R 23:) zwei- bis dreimal (2- bis 3-mal); *vgl.* achtmal; **drei|ma|lig; Drei|mas|ter** (dreimastiges Schiff; *auch für* Dreispitz); **drei|mas|tig; Drei|mei|len|zo|ne; Drei|me|ter|brett** (↑R 28)

drein (*ugs. für* darein); **drein|bli|cken** (in bestimmter Weise blicken); finster -; **drein|fah|ren** (*ugs. für* energisch in eine Angelegenheit eingreifen); **drein|fin|den**, sich (*ugs. für* dareinfinden, sich); **Drein|ga|be** (*landsch. u. schweiz. für* Zugabe); **drein|mi|schen**, sich (*ugs. für* dareinmischen, sich); **drein|re|den** (*ugs. für* dareinreden); **drein|schla|gen** (*ugs. für* in etwas hineinschlagen)

Drei|pass, der; -es, -e (gotisches dreibogiges Maßwerk); **Drei|pfund|brot; Drei|pha|sen|strom** (*svw.* Drehstrom); **Drei|punkt|gurt** (*Verkehrsw.*); **Drei|rad; Drei|raum|woh|nung** (*regional für* Dreizimmerwohnung); **Drei‿ru|de|rer** (antikes Kriegsschiff), **...satz, ...schneuß** (Ornament im got. Maßwerk); **Drei|schritt|re|gel**, die; - (*Handball*); **drei|schü|rig;** -e (drei Ernten liefernde) Wiese; **Drei|se|kun|den|re|gel** (*Handball, Basketball*); **drei‿sil|big, ...spal|tig; Drei‿spän|ner, ...spitz** (*früher* ein dreieckiger Hut), **...sprung; drei|ßig** usw. *vgl.* achtzig usw.; **drei|ßig|jäh|rig;** eine dreißigjährige Frau, *aber* (↑R 108): der Dreißigjährige Krieg; *vgl.* achtjährig

dreist

drei|stel|lig; Drei|ster|ne|ho|tel

Dreist|heit; Dreis|tig|keit

drei‿stim|mig, ...stö|ckig, ...strah|lig; drei|stück|wei|se (↑R 28); **Drei|stu|fen|ra|ke|te; Drei|ta|ge|fie|ber** (subtrop. Infektionskrankheit); **drei|tau|send; Drei|tau|sen|der** ([über] 3000 m hoher Berg); **drei|tei|lig; drei|und|ein|halb**, drei|ein|halb; **drei|und|zwan|zig;** *vgl.* acht; **drei vier|tel** *vgl.* drei *u.* Viertel; **drei|vier|tel|lang** [...'fir...]; **Drei|vier|tel|li|ter|fla|sche** (*mit Ziffern* ¾-Liter-Flasche; ↑R 28); **Drei|vier|tel|mehr|heit** [...'fir...]; **Drei|vier|tel|stun|de; Drei|vier|tel|takt** [...'fir...], der; -[e]s (*Musik; mit Ziffern* ¾-Takt; ↑R 28); im -; **Drei|we|ge|ka|ta|ly|sa|tor** (*Kfz-Technik*); **Drei|zack**, der; -[e]s, -e; **drei|za|ckig; drei|zehn;** die verhängnisvolle Dreizehn (↑R 48); *vgl.* acht; **drei|zehn|hun|dert; Drei|zim|mer|woh|nung** (*mit Ziffer* 3-Zimmer-Wohnung; ↑R 28); **Drei|zü|ger** (mit drei Zügen zu lösende Aufgabe im Problemschach)

Drell, der; -s, -e (*nordd. für* Drillich)

drem|meln (*landsch. für* bittend drängen); ich ...[e]le (↑R 16)

Drem|pel, der; -s, - (Mauer zur Vergrößerung des Dachraumes; Schwelle [im Schleusenbau])

Dres. = doctores; *vgl.* Doktor

Dre|sche, die; - (*ugs. für* Prügel); **dre|schen;** du drischst, er drischt; du droschst, *veraltet* drasch[e]st; du dröschest, *veraltet* dräschest; gedroschen; drisch!; **Dre|scher; Dre|sche|rin; Dresch‿fle|gel, ...gut** (das; -[e]s), **...ma|schi|ne**

Dres|den (Hptst. von Sachsen); **Dres|den-Alt|stadt; Dres|de|ner**, Dresd|ner (↑R 103); **Dres|den-Neu|stadt; Dresd|ner** *vgl.* Dresdener

Dress, der; -[es], -e *österr. auch* die; -, -n *Plur. selten* ⟨engl.⟩ ([Sport]kleidung); **Dres|seur** [...'sø:r], der; -s, -e ⟨franz.⟩ (jmd., der Tiere abrichtet); **Dres|seu|rin** [...'sø:rin]; **dres|sie|ren; Dres|sing**, das; -s, -s ⟨engl.⟩ (Salatsoße; Kräuter- *od.* Gewürzmischung für Füllungen); **Dress|man** [...mən], der; -s, ...men ⟨anglisierend⟩ (männl. Person, die auf Modeschauen Herrenkleidung vorführt); **Dres|sur**, die; -, -en ⟨franz.⟩; **Dres|sur‿akt, ...leis|tung, ...num|mer, ...prü|fung, ...rei|ten** (das; -s)

Drey|fus|af|fä|re ['draifu:s...], die; - (der 1894–1906 gegen den franz. Offizier A. Dreyfus geführte Prozess u. seine Folgen)

Dr. forest. = doctor scientiae rerum forestalium; *vgl.* Doktor

Dr. ... habil. = doctor ... (z.B. philosophiae) habilitatus; *vgl.* Doktor

Dr. h. c. = doctor honoris causa; *vgl.* Doktor; **Dr. h. c. mult.** = doctor honoris causa multiplex; *vgl.* Doktor

drib|beln ⟨engl.⟩ (*Sport* den Ball durch kurze Stöße vortreiben); ich ...[e]le (↑R 16); **Dribb|ling**, das; -s, -s (das Dribbeln)

Driesch, Dreesch, der; -s, -e (*landsch. für* Brache)

Drift, die; -, -en (vom Wind bewirkte Strömung an der Meeresoberfläche; *auch* svw. Abtrift; *vgl.* Trift); **drif|ten** (*Seemannsspr.* treiben); **drif|tig** (treibend)

Drilch, der; -[e]s, -e (*schweiz. für* Drillich)

[1]**Drill**, der; -[e]s, -e (*Nebenform von* Drell)

[2]**Drill**, der; -[e]s (*Milit.* Einübung, harte Ausbildung); **Drill|boh|rer; dril|len** (*Milit.* einüben, hart ausbilden; mit dem Drillbohrer bohren; *Landw.* in Reihen säen)

Dril|lich, der; -s, -e (ein festes Gewebe); **Dril|lich‿an|zug, ...ho|se, ...zeug** (das; -[e]s); **Dril|ling** (*auch für* Jagdgewehr mit drei Läufen)

Drill|ma|schi|ne (*Landw.* Maschine, die in Reihen sät)

drin (*ugs. für* darin); drin sein (*ugs. auch für* möglich sein)

Dr.-Ing. = Doktoringenieur, Doktor der Ingenieurwissenschaften; *vgl.* Doktor

drin|gen; du drang[e]st; du drängest; gedrungen; dring[e]!; **drin|gend;** auf das, aufs Dringendste *od.* auf das, aufs dringendste (↑R 47); **dring|lich; Dring|lich|keit**, die; -; **Dring|lich|keits‿an|fra|ge, ...an|trag**

Drink, der; -[s], -s ⟨engl.⟩ (alkohol. [Misch]getränk)

drin|nen; drin sein *vgl.* drin; **drin|sit|zen** (*ugs. für* in der Patsche sitzen); er hat ganz schön dringesessen; *vgl.* darin; **drin|ste|cken** (*ugs. für* viel Arbeit, Schwierigkeiten haben); er hat bis über die Ohren dringesteckt; *vgl.* darin; **drin|ste|hen** (*ugs. für* in etwas zu lesen sein); *vgl.* darin

Dri|schel, der; -s, - *od.* die; -, -n (*bayr. u. österr. für* [Schlagkolben am] Dreschflegel)

dritt *vgl.* drei; **drit|te;** (↑R 56:) das Dritte Reich; Friedrich der Dritte; der dritte Stand (Bürgerstand); *aber* die Dritte Welt (die Entwicklungsländer); von dreien der Dritte; jeder Dritte; zum Dritten; er ist der Dritte im Bunde; ein Dritter (ein Unbeteiligter); es bleibt noch ein Drittes zu erwähnen; die Dritten (*ugs. für* die dritten Zähne, das künstliche Gebiss);*vgl.* achte *u.* erste; **drit|tel;** *vgl.* achtel; **Drit|tel,** das, *schweiz. meist* der; -s, -; *vgl.* Achtel; **drit|teln** (in drei Teile teilen); ich ...[e]le (↑R 16); **Drit|ten|ab|schla|gen,** das; -s (ein Laufspiel); **drit|tens; Drit|te-Welt-La|den** (Laden, in dem Erzeugnisse der Entwicklungsländer [zu deren Unterstützung] verkauft werden); *vgl.* dritte; **dritt|höchs|te; Dritt|land** *Plur.* ...länder; **dritt|letz|te;** die drittletzte Seite; der, die, das Drittletzte; **Dritt|mit|tel** *Plur.;* etwas aus Drittmitteln finanzieren; **Dritt‿scha|den** *(Rechtsspr.),* **...schuld|ner**

Drive [draif, *engl.* draiv], der; -s, -s ‹engl.› (Schwung; Tendenz, Neigung; Treibschlag beim Golf u. Tennis; *Jazz* treibender Rhythmus); **Drive-in-Res|tau|rant** (Schnellgaststätte für Autofahrer mit Bedienung am Fahrzeug); **Dri|ver** [ˈdraivə(r)], der; -s, - (ein Golfschläger)

Dr. j. u., Dr. jur. utr. = doctor juris utriusque; *vgl.* Doktor

Dr. jur. = doctor juris; *vgl.* Doktor

DRK = Deutsches Rotes Kreuz

Dr. med. = doctor medicinae; *vgl.* Doktor

Dr. med. dent. = doctor medicinae dentariae; *vgl.* Doktor

Dr. med. univ. (in Österr.) = doctor medicinae universae; *vgl.* Doktor

Dr. med. vet. = doctor medicinae veterinariae; *vgl.* Doktor

Dr. mont. (in Österr.) = doctor rerum montanarum; *vgl.* Doktor

Dr. mult. = doctor multiplex; *vgl.* Doktor

Dr. nat. techn. = doctor rerum naturalium technicarum; *vgl.* Doktor

drob *vgl.* darob; **dro|ben** (*geh.; südd. u. österr. für* da oben)

Dr. oec. = doctor oeconomiae; *vgl.* Doktor

Dr. oec. publ. = doctor oeconomiae publicae; *vgl.* Doktor

Dro|ge, die; -, -n ‹franz.› (bes. medizinisch verwendeter tier. od. pflanzl. [Roh]stoff; *auch für* Rauschgift)

drö|ge (*nordd. für* trocken; langweilig)

dro|gen|ab|hän|gig; Dro|gen|ab|hän|gi|ge, der *u.* die; -n, -n (↑R 5 ff.); **Dro|gen‿be|ra|tungs|stel|le, ...ge|schäft, ...kon|sum, ...miss|brauch, ...sucht, ...sze|ne** (die; -; *ugs. für* Rauschgiftmilieu), **...to|te; Dro|ge|rie,** die; -, ...ien; **Dro|ge|rie|markt; Dro|gist,** der; -en, -en (↑R 126); **Dro|gis|tin**

Droh|brief; dro|hen; Droh|ge|bär|de

Drohn, der; -en, -en; ↑R 126 (*fachspr. für* Drohne); **Droh|ne,** die; -, -n (Bienenmännchen)

dröh|nen (*ugs. auch für* Rauschgift nehmen)

Droh|nen‿da|sein, ...schlacht

Dröh|nung (*ugs. für* Rauschgiftdosis; Rauschzustand)

Dro|hung; Droh|wort *Plur.* ...worte

drol|lig; Drol|lig|keit

Dro|me|dar [*auch* ˈdro:...], das; -s, -e ‹griech.› (einhöckeriges Kamel)

Dröm|ling, der; -s (Landschaft im Südwesten der Altmark)

Dron|te, die; -, -n (ein ausgestorbener Vogel)

Dront|heim (norweg. Stadt); *vgl. auch* Trondheim

Drop|kick, der; -s, -s ‹engl.› (*Fußball* Schuss, bei dem der Ball beim Aufprall auf den Boden sofort gespielt wird); **Drop-out** [...aut], der; -[s], -s (jmd., der aus seiner sozialen Gruppe ausgebrochen ist; *Tontechnik* Aussetzen der Schallaufzeichnung)

Drops, der, *auch* das; -, - *meist Plur.* ‹engl.› (Fruchtbonbon)

Drosch|ke, die; -, -n ‹russ.›; **Drosch|ken‿gaul, ...kut|scher**

drö|seln (*landsch. für* [Faden] drehen; trödeln); ich ...[e]le (↑R 16)

¹Dros|sel, die; -, -n (ein Singvogel)

²Dros|sel, die; -, -n (*Jägerspr.* Luftröhre des Wildes; *auch für* Drosselspule); **Dros|sel|bart;** König Drosselbart (eine Märchengestalt); **Dros|sel|klap|pe** *(Technik);* **dros|seln;** ich dross[e]le (↑R 16); **Dros|sel|spu|le** *(Elektrotechnik);* **Dros|se|lung; Dros|sel|ven|til** *(Technik);* **Dross|lung** *vgl.* Drosselung

Drost, der; -es, -e (*nordd. früher* Verwalter einer Drostei); **Dros|te-Hüls|hoff** (dt. Dichterin); **Dros|tei** (*nordd. früher* Verwaltungsbezirk)

Dr. paed. = doctor paedagogiae; *vgl.* Doktor

Dr. pharm. = doctor pharmaciae; *vgl.* Doktor

Dr. phil. = doctor philosophiae; *vgl.* Doktor

Dr. phil. nat. = doctor philosophiae naturalis; *vgl.* Doktor

Dr. rer. camer. = doctor rerum cameralium; *vgl.* Doktor

Dr. rer. comm. (in Österr.) = doctor rerum commercialium; *vgl.* Doktor

Dr. rer. hort. = doctor rerum hortensium; *vgl.* Doktor

Dr. rer. mont. = doctor rerum montanarum; *vgl.* Doktor

Dr. rer. nat. = doctor rerum naturalium; *vgl.* Doktor

Dr. rer. oec. = doctor rerum oeconomicarum; *vgl.* Doktor

Dr. rer. pol. = doctor rerum politicarum; *vgl.* Doktor

Dr. rer. soc. oec. (in Österr.) = doctor rerum socialium oeconomicarumque; *vgl.* Doktor

Dr. rer. techn. = doctor rerum technicarum; *vgl.* Doktor

Dr. sc. agr. = doctor scientiarum agrarium; *vgl.* Doktor

Dr. sc. hum. = doctor scientiarum humanarum; *vgl.* Doktor

Dr. sc[ient]. techn. = doctor scientiarum technicarum; *vgl.* Doktor

Dr. sc. math. = doctor scientiarum mathematicarum; *vgl.* Doktor

Dr. sc. nat. = doctor scientiarum naturalium *od.* doctor scientiae naturalis; *vgl.* Doktor

Dr. sc. pol. = doctor scientiarum politicarum *od.* doctor scientiae politicae; *vgl.* Doktor

Dr. techn. (in Österr.) = doctor rerum technicarum; *vgl.* Doktor

Dr. theol. = doctor theologiae; *vgl.* Doktor

drü|ben (auf der anderen Seite); hüben und drüben; **drü|ber** (*ugs. für* darüber; *vgl. d.);* es geht drunter und drüber; **drü|ber|fah|ren** *(ugs.)*

Druck, der; -[e]s, *Plur. (Technik:)* Drücke, *seltener* -e, *(Druckw.:)* Drucke *u.* (*Textilw.* bedruckte Stoffe:) -s; **Druck‿ab|fall** (der; -[e]s), **...an|stieg** (der; -[e]s), **...aus|gleich** (der; -[e]s), **...bo|gen** (der; -s, -), **...buch|sta|be; Drü|cke|ber|ger; drü|cke|ber|ge|risch; druck|emp|find|lich; dru|cken; drü|cken; drü|ckend;** drückend heißes Wetter; es war drückend heiß; **Dru|cker; Drü|cker; Dru|cke|rei; Drü|cke|rei; Drü|cker|fisch** (ein Aquarienfisch); **Druck|er|laub|nis,** die; -; **Dru|cker‿pres|se, ...schwär|ze, ...spra|che; ¹Druck|er|zeug|nis,** *aber* **²Dru|cker|zeug|nis** (↑R 24); **Druck‿fah|ne, ...feh|ler, ...feh|ler|teu|fel** *(scherzh.);* **druck‿fer|tig, ...fest, ...frisch; Druck‿gra|fik** (↑R 33; *Kunstw.*), **...in|dust|rie, ...ka|bi|ne, ...kes|sel, ...knopf, ...koch|topf, ...le|gung; Druck|luft|brem|se; druck|luft|ge|steu|ert; Druck‿mit|tel** (das), **...mus|ter, ...pa|pier,**

...plat|te, ...punkt; druck|reif; Druck⌣sa|che, ...schrift, ...sei|te; druck|sen (*ugs. für* nicht recht mit der Sprache herauskommen); du druckst; **Druck|se|rei; Druck⌣sor|te** (*österr. für* Formular), **...spal|te, ...stel|le, ...stock** (*Plur.* ...stöcke), **...tas|te, ...ver|band, ...ver|fah|ren, ...wel|le, ...we|sen, ...zy|lin|der**

Dru|de, die; -, -n (Nachtgeist; Zauberin); **Dru|den|fuß** (Zeichen gegen Zauberei; Pentagramm)

Drug|store ['dragstɔ:(r)], der; -s, -s ‹engl.-amerik.› ([in den USA] Verkaufsgeschäft für gängige Bedarfsartikel mit Imbissecke)

Dru|i|de, der; -n, -n; ↑R 126 (kelt. Priester); **dru|i|disch**

drum (*ugs. für* darum); drum herum, *aber* das Drumherum; das Drum und Dran

Drum [dram], die; -, -s ‹engl.› (*engl. Bez. für* Trommel); *vgl.* [1]Drums

Drum|he|rum, das; -s (*ugs.*)

Drum|lin [*engl.* 'dramlin], der; -s, -s ‹kelt.-engl.› (*Geol.* ellipt. Hügel der Grundmoräne)

Drum|mer ['dramə(r)], der; -s, - ‹engl.› (Schlagzeuger in einer [4]Band); **[1]Drums** [drams] *Plur.* (*Bez. für* das Schlagzeug)

[2]Drums [*engl.* drams] *Plur.* ‹kelt.-engl.› (*svw.* Drumlins)

Drum und Dran, das; - - -

drun|ten (da unten); **drun|ter** (*ugs. für* darunter; *vgl. d.*); es geht drunter und drüber; **drun|ter⌣lie|gen** (*ugs.*), **...stel|len** (*ugs.*); **Drun|ter und Drü|ber,** das; - - - (*ugs.*)

Drusch, der; -[e]s, -e (Dreschen; Dreschertrag); **Drusch|ge|mein|schaft** (*ehem. in der DDR*)

Dru|schi|na, die; - ‹russ.› (Gefolgschaft altruss. Fürsten)

[1]Dru|se, die; -, -n (innen mit kristallisierten Mineralien besetzter Hohlraum im Gestein; eine Pferdekrankheit)

[2]Dru|se, der; -n, -n; ↑R 126 (Angehöriger einer kleinasiatisch-syrischen Sekte des Islams)

Drü|se, die; -, -n

Dru|sen *Plur.* (*veraltet, noch landsch. für* Weinhefe, Bodensatz)

Drü|sen⌣funk|ti|on, ...schwel|lung

dru|sig ‹*zu* [1]Druse›

drü|sig (voll Drüsen)

Dru|sin ‹*zu* [2]Druse›; **dru|sisch**

Dru|sus (röm. Beiname)

dry [drai] ‹engl., „trocken"› ([von alkohol. Getränken] herb)

Dry|a|de, die; -, -n *meist Plur.* ‹griech.› (*griech. Mythol.* Baumnymphe)

DSA = Deutscher Sprachatlas

Dsche|bel, der; -[s] ‹arab.› (*in arab. erdkundl. Namen* Gebirge, Berg)

Dschi|bu|ti (Staat u. dessen Hptst. in Nordostafrika)

D-Schicht, die; -; ↑R 25 (*Meteor.* stark ionisierte Luftschicht in der hohen Atmosphäre)

Dschig|ge|tai, der; -s, -s ‹mong.› (wilder Halbesel in Asien)

Dschin|gis Khan (mongol. Eroberer)

Dschinn, der; -s, *Plur.* - *u.* -en ‹arab.› (Dämon, Geist im Volksglauben der Araber)

Dschun|gel, der, *selten* das; -s, - ‹Hindi› (undurchdringlicher tropischer Sumpfwald); **Dschun|gel⌣krieg, ...pfad**

Dschun|ke, die; -, -n ‹chin.-malai.› (chin. Segelschiff)

DSG = Deutsche Schlafwagen- und Speisewagen-Gesellschaft mbH; *vgl.* Mitropa

Dsun|ga|rei, die; - (zentralasiat. Landschaft); **dsun|ga|risch**

dt = Dezitonne

dt. = deutsch

DTB = Deutscher Turnerbund

DTC = Deutscher Touring Automobil Club

dto. = dito

DTP = Desktoppublishing

DTSB = Deutscher Turn- und Sportbund

Dtzd. = Dutzend

du (*auch in Briefen kleingeschrieben*); Leute wie du und ich; **Du,** das; -[s], -[s]; (↑R 47:) das traute Du; jmdm. das Du anbieten; jmdn. mit Du anreden; mit jmdm. auf Du und Du stehen

du|al ‹lat.› (eine Zweiheit bildend); ein duales System, *aber* die Gesellschaft Duales System Deutschland GmbH (↑R 108); **Du|al,** der; -s, -e (*Sprachw.* Zweizahl)

[1]Du|a|la (Hafenstadt in Kamerun); **[2]Du|a|la,** der; -[s], -[s] (Angehöriger eines Bantustammes); **[3]Du|a|la,** das; - (Sprache)

Du|a|lis, der; -, ...le ‹lat.›; *vgl.* Dual; **Du|a|lis|mus,** der; - (Zweiheit; Gegensätzlichkeit); **Du|a|list,** der; -en, -en (↑R 126); **du|a|lis|tisch;** -e Weltanschauung; **Du|a|li|tät,** die; - (Zweiheit; Doppelheit; Vertauschbarkeit); **Du|al|sys|tem,** das; -s (*Math., Soziol.*)

Du|bai (Hafenstadt u. Scheichtum am Persischen Golf)

Dü|bel, der; -s, - (Pflock, Zapfen zum Verankern von Schrauben, Nägeln, Haken u. a.; *Bauw.* Verbindungselement zum Zusammenhalten von Bauteilen); **Dü|bel|mas|se,** die; -; **dü|beln;** ich ...[e]le (↑R 16)

du|bi|os ‹lat.›, *seltener* **du|bi|ös** ‹franz.› (zweifelhaft; unsicher); **Du|bi|o|sen** *Plur.* (*Wirtsch.* unsichere Forderungen); **du|bi|ta|tiv** (Zweifel ausdrückend)

Dub|lee (↑R 130), das; -s, -s ‹franz.› (Metall mit Edelmetallüberzug; Stoß beim Billardspiel); **Dub|lee|gold; Dub|let|te,** die; -, -n; **dub|lie|ren** ([Garn] verdoppeln; Dublee herstellen); **Dub|lier|ma|schi|ne** (*Spinnerei*)

Dub|lin ['dablin] (Hptst. der Republik Irland)

Dub|lo|ne (↑R 130), die; -, -n ‹lat.› (frühere span. Goldmünze); **Dub|lü|re,** die; -, -n ‹franz.› (Unterfutter; Aufschlag an Uniformen; verzierte Innenseite des Buchdeckels)

Dub|rov|nik [...v...] (↑R 130; Hafenstadt in Kroatien)

[1]Du|chesse [dy'ʃɛs], die; -, -n [...s(ə)n] ‹franz.› (*franz. Bez. für* Herzogin); **[2]Du|chesse,** die; - (ein Seidengewebe)

Ducht, die; -, -en (*Seemannsspr.* Sitzbank im Boot)

Duck|dal|be, *seltener* **Dück|dal|be,** die; -, -n *meist Plur., auch* **Duck|dal|ben, Dück|dal|ben,** der; -s, - *meist Plur.* (*Seemannsspr.* in den Hafengrund gerammte Pfahlgruppe [zum Festmachen von Schiffen])

du|cken; sich -; **Du|cker** (Schopfantilope); **Duck|mäu|ser** (*ugs. für* verängstigter, feiger, heuchlerischer Mensch); **duck|mäu|se|risch**

du|del|dum|dei!; Du|de|lei; Du|de|ler, Dud|ler; du|deln; ich ...[e]le (↑R 16); **Du|del|sack** ‹türk.› (ein Blasinstrument); **Du|del|sack|pfei|fer; Dud|ler** *vgl.* Dudeler

Du|ell, das; -s, -e ‹franz.› (Zweikampf); **Du|el|lant,** der; -en, -en (↑R 126); **du|el|lie|ren,** sich

Du|en|ja, die; -, -s ‹span., „Herrin"› (*veraltet für* Erzieherin)

Du|e|ro, der; - ‹span.› (Fluss auf der Pyrenäenhalbinsel); *vgl.* Douro

Du|ett, das; -[e]s, -e ‹ital.› (Musikstück für zwei Singstimmen)

duff (*nordd. für* matt); -es Gold

Düf|fel, der; -s, - ‹nach einem belg. Ort› (ein weiches Gewebe); **Duf|fle|coat** ['daf(ə)lko:t], der; -s, -s ‹engl.› (dreiviertellanger Sportmantel)

Duft, der; -[e]s, Düfte; **Düft|chen**

duf|te ‹jidd.› (*ugs., bes. berlin. für* gut, fein)

duf|ten; duf|tig; Duf|tig|keit, die; -; **Duft‿mar|ke** *(Biol.)*, **...no|te; duft|reich; Duft‿stoff, ...was|ser** (*Plur.* ...wässer), **...wol|ke**

Du|gong, der; -s, *Plur.* -e *u.* -s ‹malai.› (Seekuh der austr. Gewässer u. des Roten Meeres)

Duis|burg ['dy:s...] (Stadt in Nordrhein-Westfalen); **Duis|bur|ger** (↑R 103); - Hafen

du jour [dy'ʒu:r] ‹franz., „vom Tage"›; - - sein (*veraltend für* Tagesdienst haben)

Du|ka|ten, der; -s, - ‹ital.› (frühere Goldmünze); **Du|ka|ten‿esel** (↑R 132; *ugs. für* unerschöpfliche Geldquelle), **...schei|ßer** *(derb)*

Duke [dju:k], der; -s, -s ‹engl.› (*engl. Bez. für* Herzog)

Dü|ker, der; -s, - (Rohrleitung unter einem Deich, Fluss, Weg o. Ä.; *landsch. für* Tauchente)

duk|til ‹lat.› (*Technik* dehn-, verformbar); **Duk|ti|li|tät**, die; -; **Duk|tus**, der; - (charakteristische Art, Linienführung)

dul|den; Dul|der; Dul|der|mie|ne; duld|sam; Duld|sam|keit, die; -; **Dul|dung**

Dult, die; -, -en (*bayr. für* Messe, Jahrmarkt)

Dul|zi|nea, die; -, *Plur.* -een *u.* -s ‹span.; nach der Geliebten des Don Quichotte› (*scherzh. abwertend für* Geliebte, Freundin)

Du|ma, die; -, -s ‹russ.› (Rat der fürstl. Gefolgsleute im alten Russland; russ. Stadtverordnetenversammlung [seit 1870]; russ. Parlament)

Du|mas d. Ä., Du|mas d. J. [*beide* dy'ma - -], (Dumas der Ältere u. der Jüngere: franz. Schriftsteller)

Dum|dum, das; -[s], -[s] ‹nach dem Ort der ersten Herstellung in Indien› (Geschoss mit sprenggeschossartiger Wirkung); **Dum|dum|ge|schoss**; *vgl.* Geschoss

dumm; dümmer, dümmste; -er August (Clown); **Dumm|bar|tel**, der; -s, - (*ugs. für* dummer Mensch); **Dumm|chen** *(ugs.)*; **dumm|dreist; Dum|me|jun|gen|streich**, der; *Gen.* des Dumme[n]jungenstreich[e]s, *Plur.* die Dumme[n]jungenstreiche; ein Dumme[r]jungenstreich; **Dum|men|fang**, der; -[e]s; auf - ausgehen; **Dum|mer|chen** *(ugs.)*; **Dum|mer|jan**, Dumm|ri|an, der; -s, -e (*ugs. für* dummer Kerl); **Dum|merl**, das; -s, -n (*österr. ugs. für* Dummerchen); **Dum|mer|ling** *(ugs.)*; **dum|mer|wei|se; dumm|frech** (↑R 27); **Dumm|heit; Dum|mi|an**, der; -s, -e (*landsch. u. österr. für* Dummerjan); **Dumm|kopf** *(abwertend)*; **dümm|lich; Dümm|ling; Dumm|ri|an** *vgl.* Dummerjan; **dumm|stolz**

Dum|my ['dami], der, *auch* (*für* Attrappe, Probeband:) das; -s, -s ‹engl.› (Puppe für Unfalltests; Attrappe; Probeband zu Werbezwecken)

düm|peln (*Seemannsspr.* leicht schlingern)

Dum|per ['dam..., *auch* 'dum...], der; -s, - ‹engl.› (ein Kippfahrzeug)

dumpf; Dumpf|ba|cke (*ugs. für* törichter, einfältiger Mensch); **Dumpf|heit**, die; -; **dump|fig; Dump|fig|keit**, die; -

Dum|ping ['dam...], das; -s ‹engl.› (*Wirtsch.* Unterbieten der Preise im Ausland); **Dum|ping|preis** (Preis einer Ware, der deutlich unter ihrem Wert liegt)

dun (*nordd. für* betrunken)

Dü|na, die; - (Westliche Dwina; *vgl.* Dwina)

Du|nant [dy'nɑ̃:], Henri, *später* Henry (schweiz. Philanthrop, Gründer des Roten Kreuzes)

Du|ne, die; -, -n (*nordd. für* Daune)

Dü|ne, die; -, -n; **Dü|nen|gras**

Dung, der; -[e]s; **Dung|ab|la|ge; Dün|ge|mit|tel**, das; **dün|gen; Dün|ger**, der; -s, -; **Dün|ger|wirt|schaft**, die; -; **Dung‿gru|be, ...hau|fen; Dün|gung**

dun|kel; ein dunkler, dunklerer Farbton; etwas dunkel färben, lackieren usw.; dunkelblau usw.; (↑R 47:) seine Spuren verloren sich im Dunkeln; im Dunkeln lassen; im Dunkeln ist gut munkeln; im Dunkeln tappen; ein Sprung ins Dunkle; **Dun|kel**, das; -s

Dün|kel, der; -s (*abwertend für* Eingebildetheit, Hochmut)

Dun|kel|ar|rest; dun|kel‿äu|gig, ...blau, ...blond, ...braun|rot (*vgl.* dunkel), **...haa|rig**

dün|kel|haft *(abwertend)*; **Dün|kel|haf|tig|keit**, die; -

dun|kel|häu|tig; Dun|kel|heit; Dun|kel‿kam|mer, ...mann (*Plur.* ...männer); **dun|keln**; es dunkelt; **dun|kel|rot; Dun|kel|zif|fer** (nicht bekannte Anzahl)

dün|ken; mich *od.* mir dünkt, *veraltet* deucht; dünkte, *auch* deuchte; hat gedünkt, *veraltet* gedeucht

Dun|king ['daŋkiŋ], das; -s, -s ‹engl.› (*Basketball* Korbwurf, bei dem die Hände des Werfers oberhalb des Korbrings sind)

Dün|kir|chen, *franz.* Dun|kerque [dœ̃'kɛrk] (franz. Hafenstadt)

dünn; durch dick und dünn; eine dünn besiedelte Gegend; dünn bevölkerte Landstriche; dünn gesät sein (selten, spärlich vorhanden sein; nur schwer zu finden sein); sich dünn machen (*ugs. für* wenig Platz einnehmen); könnt ihr euch ein bisschen dünner machen?; *vgl. aber* dünnmachen; **dünn|bei|nig; dünn be|sie|delt** *vgl.* dünn; **dünn be|völ|kert** *vgl.* dünn; **Dünn|bier; Dünn|brett|boh|rer** (*ugs. für* wenig intelligenter Mensch; jmd., der den Weg des geringsten Widerstandes geht); **Dünn|darm; Dünn|darm|ent|zün|dung; Dünn|druck** *Plur.* ...drucke; **Dünn|druck‿aus|ga|be, ...pa|pier; Dün|ne**, die; -

dun|ne|mals (*landsch. für* damals)

dünn|flüs|sig; dünn|häu|tig (*auch übertr. für* empfindlich, sensibel); **Dünn|heit**, die; -; **dünn|ma|chen**, sich (*ugs. für* weglaufen); er hat sich dünngemacht; *vgl. aber* dünn; **Dünn‿pfiff** (*ugs. für* Durchfall), **...säu|re** (*Chemie* Schwefelsäure als Abfallprodukt); **Dünn|säu|re|ver|klap|pung; Dünn‿schiss** (*derb für* Durchfall), **...schliff, ...schnitt; Dün|nung** (*Jägerspr.* Flanke des Wildes); **dünn|wan|dig**

Dun|sel, der; -s, - (*landsch. für* Dummkopf, Tollpatsch)

Duns Sco|tus [- 'sko:tus] (schott. Philosoph u. Theologe)

Dunst, der; -[e]s, Dünste; **duns|ten** (Dunst verbreiten); **düns|ten** (dunsten; durch Dampf gar machen); **Dunst‿glo|cke, ...hau|be; duns|tig; Dunst|kreis; Dunst|obst**, *österr. nur so, od.* **Dünst|obst; Dunst‿schicht, ...schlei|er, ...wol|ke**

Dü|nung (durch Wind hervorgerufener Seegang)

Duo, das; -s, -s ‹ital.› (Musikstück für zwei Instrumente; *auch für* die zwei Ausführenden)

Du|o|de|num, das; -s, ...na ‹lat.› (*Med.* Zwölffingerdarm)

Du|o|dez, das; -es ‹lat.› (*Buchw.* Zwölftelbogengröße; *Zeichen* 12°); **Du|o|dez...** (*in Zus. übertr.* Begriff des Kleinen, Lächerlichen); **Du|o|dez|fürs|ten|tum; du|o|de|zi|mal** (zwölfteilig); **Du|o|de|zi|mal|sys|tem**, das; -s; **Du|o|de|zi|me**, die; -, -n (der zwölfte Ton der diaton. Tonleiter; Intervall von zwölf diaton. Tonstufen)

dü|pie|ren ‹franz.› (täuschen, überlisten); **Dü|pie|rung**

Du̱p|la (↑R 130; *Plur. von* Duplum); **Du̱p|lex|be|trieb,** *auch* Di̱p|lex|be|trieb ‹lat.; dt.› (Doppelbetrieb); **dup|li̱e̱|ren** ‹lat.› (verdoppeln); **Dup|li̱e̱|rung; Dup|li̱k,** die; -, -en ‹franz.› (*veraltend für* Gegenantwort auf eine Replik); **Dup|li|ka̱t,** das; -[e]s, -e ‹lat.› (Doppel; Ab-, Zweitschrift); **Dup|li|ka|ti|o̱n,** die; -, -en (Verdopplung); **Dup|li|ka|tu̱r,** die; -, -en (*Med.* Verdopplung, Doppelbildung); **dup|li|zi̱e̱|ren** (verdoppeln); **Dup|li|zi|tä̱t,** die; -, -en (Doppelheit; doppeltes Vorkommen, Auftreten; *veraltet für* Zweideutigkeit); **Du̱p|lum,** das; -s, ...la (Duplikat)

Dups, der; -es, -e ‹poln.› (*landsch. veraltend für* Gesäß)

Du̱r, das; - ‹lat.› (*Musik* Tongeschlecht mit großer Terz); A-Dur, A-Dur-Tonleiter (↑R 28); *vgl.* [1]Moll

du|ra̱|bel ‹lat.› (dauerhaft; bleibend); ...ab|le (↑R 130) Ausführung

Du̱r|ak|kord *(Musik)*

Du̱|ra|lu|min ® (↑R 132), das; -s (eine Aluminiumlegierung)

du̱|ra|tiv ‹lat.› (*Sprachw.* verlaufend, dauernd)

dụrch; *Präp. mit Akk.:* durch mich, sie, ihn; durch und durch; die ganze Nacht [hin]durch; der Zug wird schon durch sein (*ugs. für* durchgekommen sein); es muss bald elf Uhr durch sein (*ugs. für* nach elf Uhr sein); bei jmdm. unten durch sein (*ugs. für* jmds. Wohlwollen verscherzt haben); **durch...** *in Verbindung mit Verben:* **a)** *unfeste Zusammensetzungen,* z. B. dụrcharbeiten *(vgl. d.),* dụrchgearbeitet; dụrchdürfen *(vgl. d.);* **b)** *feste Zusammensetzungen,* z. B. durchạrbeiten *(vgl. d.),* durchạrbeitet

dụrch|ackern (R 132; *ugs. für* sorgsam durcharbeiten); sie hat das ganze Buch durchgeackert

dụrch|ar|bei|ten (sorgsam bearbeiten; pausenlos arbeiten); der Teig ist tüchtig durchgearbeitet; er hat die Nacht durchgearbeitet; **durch|ạr|bei|ten** *(selten, meist im Partizip II);* eine durcharbeitete Nacht; **Dụrch|ar|bei|tung**

dụrch|at|men; sie hat tief durchgeatmet

durch|au̱s [*auch* 'durç...]

dụrch|ba|cken; durchgebackenes Brot; **durch|bạ|cken;** mit Rosinen durchbackenes Brot

durch|be̱|ben *(geh.);* von Schauern durchbebt

dụrch|bei|ßen (beißend trennen); sie hat den Faden durchgebissen; sich -; **durch|bei̱|ßen** (beißend durchdringen); der Hund hat ihm beinahe die Kehle durchbissen

dụrch|be|ra|ten; der Plan ist durchberaten

dụrch|bet|teln; er hat sich durchgebettelt [und nichts gearbeitet]; **durch|bẹt|teln;** er hat das Land durchbettelt

dụrch|bie|gen; das Regal hat sich durchgebogen

dụrch|bil|den (vollständig ausbilden); sein Körper ist gut durchgebildet; **Dụrch|bil|dung**

dụrch|bla|sen; der Arzt hat ihm die Ohren durchgeblasen

dụrch|blät|tern, durch|blạ̈t|tern; sie hat das Buch durchgeblättert *od.* durchblättert

dụrch|bläu|en (*ugs. für* durchprügeln); er hat ihn durchgebläut

Dụrch|blick; dụrch|bli|cken (hindurchblicken); sie hat [durch das Fernrohr] durchgeblickt; - lassen (andeuten); sie hat durchblicken lassen, dass ...

durch|blịt|zen; ein Gedanke hat sie durchblitzt

dụrch|blu|ten (Blut durch etwas dringen lassen); die Wunde hat durchgeblutet; **durch|blu̱|ten** (mit Blut versorgen); frisch durchblutete Haut; **Durch|blu̱|tung; Durch|blu̱|tungs|stö|rung**

dụrch|boh|ren; er hat ein Loch durchgebohrt; der Wurm hat sich durchgebohrt; **durch|bo̱h|ren;** eine Kugel hat die Tür durchbohrt; von Blicken durchbohrt; **Durch|bo̱h|rung**

dụrch|bo|xen (*ugs. für* durchsetzen); er hat das Projekt durchgeboxt; sich -

dụrch|bra|ten; das Fleisch war gut durchgebraten

dụrch|brau|sen; der Zug ist durchgebraust; **durch|brau̱|sen;** der Sturm hat das Tal durchbraust

dụrch|bre|chen; er ist [durch das Eis] durchgebrochen; er hat den Stock durchgebrochen; **durch|brẹ|chen;** er hat die Schranken, die Schallmauer durchbrochen; durchbrochene Arbeit (Stickerei, Goldarbeit); **Durch|brẹ|chung**

dụrch|bren|nen (*ugs. auch für* sich heimlich davonmachen); der Faden ist durchgebrannt; der Kassierer ist mit einer großen Summe durchgebrannt; **Dụrch|bren|ner** (*ugs. für* Ausreißer)

dụrch|brin|gen; sie haben die Flüchtlinge glücklich durchgebracht; es war schwer, sich ehrlich durchzubringen; er hat die ganze Erbschaft durchgebracht (vergeudet, verschwendet)

Dụrch|bruch, der; -[e]s, ...brüche

dụrch|bum|meln *(ugs.);* sie haben die ganze Nacht durchgebummelt; **durch|bụm|meln** *(ugs.);* eine durchbummelte Nacht

dụrch|che|cken (vollständig checken; bis zum Zielort abfertigen); wir haben die Liste durchgecheckt

dụrch|den|ken; ich habe die Sache noch einmal durchgedacht; **durch|dẹn|ken;** ein fein durchdachter Plan

dụrch|dis|ku|tie|ren; die Frage ist noch nicht durchdiskutiert

dụrch|drän|gen; sich -; sie hat sich durchgedrängt

dụrch|dre|hen; das Fleisch [durch den Wolf] -; ich bin völlig durchgedreht (*ugs. für* verwirrt)

dụrch|drin|gen; sie ist mit ihrer Ansicht durchgedrungen; **durch|drịn|gen;** sie hat das Urwaldgebiet durchdrungen; sie war von der Idee ganz durchdrungen (erfüllt); **Durch|drịn|gung,** die; -

Dụrch|druck *Plur.* ...drucke (ein Druckverfahren); **dụrch|drucken;** sie haben die ganze Nacht durchgedruckt

dụrch|drü|cken; er hat die Änderung doch noch durchgedrückt (*ugs. für* durchgesetzt)

durch|drụn|gen; von etwas - (erfüllt); *vgl.* durchdringen

dụrch|dür|fen (*ugs. für* hindurchgelangen dürfen); wir haben nicht durchgedurft

dụrch|ei|len; er ist schnell durchgeeilt; **durch|ei̱|len;** er hat den Hof durcheilt

durch|ei|nạn|der (↑R 132); durcheinander sein; etwas durcheinander bringen; alles durcheinander essen und trinken; es war alles durcheinander gegangen; damit nichts durcheinander gerät; sie waren ziellos durcheinander gelaufen; als alle durcheinander redeten; die Schneeflocken wurden durcheinander gewirbelt; **Durch|ei|nạn|der** [*auch* 'durç...], das; -s; **durch|ei|nạn|der brin|gen, gehen, lau|fen** usw. *vgl.* durcheinander; **Durch|ei|nạn|der|lau|fen,** das; -s; **durch|ei|nạn|der re|den, wir|beln** usw. *vgl.* durcheinander

dụrch|es|sen, sich; er hat sich überall durchgegessen

dụrch|exer|zie|ren (↑R 132; *ugs.*); wir haben den Plan durchexerziert

dụrch|fah|ren; ich bin die ganze Nacht durchgefahren; **durch-**

fa̱h|ren; er hat das ganze Land -; ein Schreck durchfuhr sie; **Dụrch|fahrt;** - verboten!; **Dụrch-fahrts‿recht, ...stra|ße**

Dụrch|fall, der; -[e]s, ...fälle; **dụrch|fal|len;** die kleinen Steine sind [durch den Rost] durchgefallen; er ist durchgefallen (*ugs. für* hat die Prüfung nicht bestanden); **durch|fạl|len;** der Stein hat den Raum -

dụrch|fau|len; das Brett ist durchgefault

dụrch|fa|xen (*ugs. für* per Fax senden)

dụrch|fech|ten; er hat den Kampf durchgefochten

dụrch|fe|gen; er hat nur durchgefegt

dụrch|fei|ern; sie haben bis zum Morgen durchgefeiert; **durch|fei̱|ern;** die Nacht wurde durchfeiert

dụrch|fei|len; er hat das Gitter durchgefeilt

durch|feuch|ten; vom Regen durchfeuchtet

dụrch|fil|zen (*ugs. für* genau durchsuchen); die Gefangenen wurden durchgefilzt

dụrch|fin|den; sich -; ich habe mich gut durchgefunden

dụrch|flech|ten; sie hat das Band [durch den Kranz] durchgeflochten; **durch|flẹch|ten;** mit Blumen durchflochten

dụrch|flie|gen; der Stein ist [durch die Fensterscheibe] durchgeflogen; er ist durchgeflogen (*ugs. für* hat die Prüfung nicht bestanden); **durch|flie̱|gen;** das Flugzeug hat die Wolken durchflogen; ich habe das Buch nur durchflogen (rasch gelesen)

dụrch|flie|ßen; das Wasser ist durchgeflossen; **durch|flie̱|ßen;** das Tal wird von einem Bach durchflossen

Dụrch|flug; Dụrch|flugs|recht

Dụrch|fluss

dụrch|flu|ten; das Wasser ist durch den Riss im Deich durchgeflutet; **durch|flu̱|ten;** das Zimmer ist von Licht durchflutet

dụrch|for|men (vollständig formen); die Statue ist durchgeformt; **Dụrch|for|mung**

durch|fọr|schen (forschend durchsuchen); er hat alles durchforscht; **Durch|fọr|schung**

durch|fọrs|ten (den Wald ausholzen; etw. [kritisch] durchsehen); durchforstet; **Durch|fọrs|tung**

dụrch|fra|gen, sich; sie hat sich zum Bahnhof durchgefragt

dụrch|fres|sen; der Rost hat sich durchgefressen; er hat sich bei anderen durchgefressen (*derb für* durchgegessen); **durch|frẹs|sen;** von Lauge -

dụrch|frie|ren; der Teich ist bis auf den Grund durchgefroren; wir waren völlig durchgefroren; **durch|frie̱|ren;** ich bin ganz durchfroren

Dụrch|fuhr, die; -, -en (*Wirtsch.* Transit); **dụrch|führ|bar; Dụrch-führ|bar|keit,** die; -; **dụrch|füh-ren;** er hat die ihm gestellte Aufgabe noch nicht durchgeführt; **Dụrch|fuhr|er|laub|nis; Dụrch-füh|rung; Dụrch|füh|rungs‿be-stim|mung, ...ver|ord|nung, ...vor|schrift; Dụrch|fuhr|ver-bot**

durch|fụr|chen; ein durchfurchtes Gesicht

dụrch|fut|tern, sich (*ugs. für* sich durchessen); er hat sich überall durchgefuttert

dụrch|füt|tern; wir haben das Vieh durchgefüttert

Dụrch|ga|be; die - eines Telegramms

Dụrch|gang; Dụrch|gän|ger; dụrch|gän|gig; Dụrch|gangs-‿arzt, ...bahn|hof, ...la|ger, ...pra|xis, ...sta|di|um, ...sta|ti-on, ...stra|ße, ...ver|kehr (der; -[e]s)

dụrch|ga|ren; das Gemüse ist nicht durchgegart

dụrch|gau|nern, sich (*ugs.*); du hast dich oft durchgegaunert

dụrch|ge|ben; er hat die Meldung durchgegeben

dụrch|ge|dreht (*ugs. für* verwirrt); er ist völlig durchgedreht; *vgl.* durchdrehen

dụrch|ge|hen; ich bin [durch alle Räume] durchgegangen; das Pferd ist durchgegangen; wir sind den Plan Punkt für Punkt durchgegangen; **durch|ge̱|hen** (*veraltet);* ich habe den Wald durchgangen; **dụrch|ge|hend,** *österr.* **dụrch|ge|hends;** das Geschäft ist - geöffnet

durch|geis|tigt

dụrch|ge|stal|ten; das Motiv ist künstlerisch durchgestaltet

dụrch|glie|dern, durch|glie̱|dern (unterteilen); ein gut durchgegliedertes *od.* durchgliedertes Buch; **Dụrch|glie|de|rung** [*auch* ...'gli:...]

dụrch|glü|hen; das Eisen wird durchgeglüht; **durch|glü̱|hen;** von Begeisterung durchglüht

dụrch|grei|fen; sie hat energisch durchgegriffen

dụrch|ha|ben (*ugs. für* hindurchbewegt haben; ganz gelesen, bearbeitet haben); er hat das Buch bald durchgehabt

dụrch|hal|ten (bis zum Ende aushalten); er hat bis zum Schluss durchgehalten; **Dụrch|hal|te‿pa-ro|le, ...ver|mö|gen** (das; -s)

dụrch|hän|gen (*ugs. auch für* müde, abgespannt sein); das Seil hat stark durchgehangen; **Dụrch-hän|ger;** einen - haben (*ugs. für* in schlechter Verfassung sein, abgespannt sein)

Dụrch|hau *vgl.* Durchhieb; **dụrch-hau|en** (*ugs. auch für* durchprügeln); er hieb den Ast mit der Axt durch, hat ihn durchgehauen; er haute den Jungen durch, hat ihn durchgehauen; **durch|ha̱u|en;** er hat den Knoten mit einem Schlag durchhauen; durchhauener Wald

Dụrch|haus (*österr. für* Haus mit einem Durchgang, der zwei Straßen verbindet)

dụrch|he|cheln; Flachs -; die lieben Verwandten wurden durchgehechelt (*ugs. für* es wurde unfreundlich über sie geredet)

dụrch|hei|zen; das Haus ist gut durchgeheizt

dụrch|hel|fen; er hat ihr durchgeholfen

Dụrch|hieb (Schneise, ausgehauener Waldstreifen)

dụrch|hun|gern, sich; ich habe mich durchgehungert

durch|ir|ren; sie hat die Straßen durchirrt

dụrch|ixen (↑R 132; *ugs. für* auf der Schreibmaschine mit dem Buchstaben x ungültig machen); du ixt durch; in dem Text waren einige Wörter durchgeixt

dụrch|ja|gen; der Antrag wurde durchgejagt

dụrch|käm|men; das Haar wurde durchgekämmt; die Polizei hat den Wald durchgekämmt; **durch-kạ̈m|men;** die Polizei durchkämmte den Wald, hat ihn durchkämmt; **Dụrch|käm|mung** [*auch* ...'kɛm...]

dụrch|kämp|fen; er hat sich zum Ausgang durchgekämpft; **durch-kạ̈mp|fen;** sie hat manche Nacht durchkämpft

dụrch|kau|en (*ugs. auch für* eingehend, immer wieder erörtern); das Thema wurde durchgekaut

dụrch|kit|zeln; er wurde gehörig durchgekitzelt

dụrch|klet|tern; sie ist unterm Zaun durchgeklettert; **durch-klẹt|tern;** der Bergsteiger hat den Kamin durchklettert; **Durch-klẹt|te|rung**

dụrch|klin|gen; der Bass hat zu laut durchgeklungen; **durch|klịn-gen;** die Musik hat das ganze Haus durchklungen

durch|kne|ten; sie hat den Teig, die Muskeln gut durchgeknetet
durch|knöp|fen; das Kleid ist durchgeknöpft
durch|kom|men; er ist noch einmal durchgekommen
durch|kom|po|nie|ren (ein Gedicht von Strophe zu Strophe wechselnd vertonen); die Lieder sind durchkomponiert
durch|kön|nen (*ugs. für* hindurchgelangen, vorbeikommen können); wir haben wegen der Absperrungen nicht durchgekonnt
durch|kon|stru|ie|ren; der Motor war gut durchkonstruiert
durch|kos|ten; er hat alle Weine durchgekostet; **durch|kos|ten** (*geh. für* ganz genießen); er hat alle Freuden durchkostet
durch|kreu|zen (kreuzweise durchstreichen); sie hat den Brief durchgekreuzt; **durch|kreu|zen;** man hat ihren Plan durchkreuzt (vereitelt); **Durch|kreu|zung**
durch|krie|chen; er ist unter dem Zaun durchgekrochen; **durch|krie|chen;** er hat das Gestrüpp durchkrochen
durch|la|den; er hatte das Gewehr durchgeladen
durch|län|gen (*Bergmannsspr.* Strecken anlegen); durchgelängt
Durch|lass, der; -es, ...lässe; **durch|las|sen;** sie haben ihn noch durchgelassen; **durch|läs|sig; Durch|läs|sig|keit,** die; -
Durch|laucht [*auch* ...'lauxt], die; -, -en; *vgl.* euer, ihr *u.* sein; **durch|lauch|tig; durch|lauch|tigst;** *in der Anrede u. als Ehrentitel* Durchlauchtigst
Durch|lauf; durch|lau|fen; er ist die ganze Nacht durchgelaufen; das Wasser ist durchgelaufen; **durch|lau|fen;** er hat den Wald -; das Projekt hat viele Stadien -; es durchläuft mich eiskalt; **Durch|lauf|er|hit|zer, Durch|lauf-Was|ser|er|hit|zer;** ↑R 24 (ein Gas- od. Elektrogerät)
durch|la|vie|ren, sich (*ugs. für* sich geschickt durchbringen); er hat sich überall durchlaviert
durch|le|ben; wir haben die Tage froh durchlebt
durch|lei|den; sie hat viel durchlitten
durch|le|sen; ich habe den Brief durchgelesen
durch|leuch|ten; das Licht hat [durch die Vorhänge] durchgeleuchtet; **durch|leuch|ten** (mit Licht, mit Röntgenstrahlen durchdringen); die Brust des Kranken wurde durchleuchtet; **Durch|leuch|tung**
durch|lie|gen, sich (sich wund liegen); die Kranke hat sich durchgelegen
durch|lo|chen; er hat das Papier durchlocht; **durch|lö|chern;** von Kugeln durchlöchert
durch|lot|sen (*ugs. für* geschickt hindurchgeleiten); sie hat uns durchgelotst
durch|lüf|ten (gründlich lüften); er hat zehn Minuten durchgelüftet; **durch|lüf|ten** (von der Luft durchziehen lassen); das Zimmer wurde durchlüftet; **Durch|lüf|ter; Durch|lüf|tung**
durch|lü|gen, sich (*ugs.*); er hat sich frech durchgelogen
durch|ma|chen (*ugs.*); die Familie hat viel durchgemacht
Durch|marsch, der (*ugs. auch für* Durchfall); **durch|mar|schie|ren;** sie sind durchmarschiert
durch|mes|sen (vollständig messen); er hat alle Räume durchgemessen; **durch|mes|sen;** er hat die Strecke laufend -; **Durch|mes|ser,** der (*Zeichen d* [nur kursiv] *od.* ∅)
durch|mi|schen; der Salat ist gut durchgemischt; **durch|mi|schen;** der Kalk ist mit Sand durchmischt
durch|mo|geln, sich (*ugs.*); du hast dich da durchgemogelt
durch|müs|sen (*ugs. für* hindurchgelangen müssen); wir haben hier durchgemusst
durch|mus|tern, durch|mus|tern; er hat sämtliche Waren durchgemustert *od.* durchmustert; **Durch|mus|te|rung** [*auch* ...'mus...]
durch|na|gen, durch|na|gen; die Maus hat den Strick durchgenagt *od.* durchnagt
Durch|nah|me, die; -
durch|näs|sen; sie war völlig durchnässt
durch|neh|men; die Klasse hat den Stoff schon durchgenommen
durch|num|me|rie|ren; die Seiten waren durchnummeriert; **Durch|num|me|rie|rung**
durch|or|ga|ni|sie|ren; es war alles gut durchorganisiert
durch|ör|tern (*Bergmannsspr.* Strecken anlegen); durchörtert
durch|pau|ken (*ugs. auch für* schnell u. unbeirrt durchsetzen); das Gesetz wurde durchgepaukt
durch|pau|sen; er hat die Zeichnung durchgepaust
durch|peit|schen; man hat ihn grausam durchgepeitscht; der Gesetzentwurf wurde im Parlament durchgepeitscht (*ugs. abwertend für* eilig durchgebracht)
durch|prü|fen; wir haben alles noch einmal durchgeprüft
durch|prü|geln; man hat ihn tüchtig durchgeprügelt
durch|pul|sen; von Begeisterung durchpulst
durch|que|ren; sie hat das Land zu Fuß durchquert; **Durch|que|rung**
durch|quet|schen, sich; sie haben sich durchgequetscht
durch|ra|sen; der Zug ist durchgerast; **durch|ra|sen;** der Wagen hat die Stadt durchrast
durch|ras|seln (*ugs. für* eine Prüfung nicht bestehen); er ist durchgerasselt
durch|ra|ti|o|na|li|sie|ren; durchrationalisierte Betriebe
durch|rau|schen (*ugs. für* eine Prüfung nicht bestehen); er ist durchgerauscht
durch|rech|nen; er hat die Aufgabe noch einmal durchgerechnet
durch|reg|nen; es hat durchgeregnet; **durch|reg|nen;** ich bin ganz durchregnet *od.* durchgeregnet
Durch|rei|che, die; -, -n (Öffnung zum Durchreichen von Speisen); **durch|rei|chen;** er hat es ihm durchgereicht
Durch|rei|se; durch|rei|sen; ich bin oft durchgereist; **durch|rei|sen;** er hat das Land durchreist; **Durch|rei|sen|de,** der *u.* die; -n, -n (↑R 5 ff.); **Durch|rei|se|vi|sum**
durch|rei|ßen; sie hat den Brief durchgerissen
durch|rei|ten; sie ist nur durchgeritten; **durch|rei|ten;** sie hat den Parcours durchritten
durch|rie|seln; der Sand ist durchgerieselt; **durch|rie|seln;** von Wonne durchrieselt
durch|rin|gen; er hat sich zu dieser Überzeugung durchgerungen
durch|rol|len; der Ball ist durchgerollt
durch|ros|ten; das Rohr ist ganz durchgerostet
durch|rut|schen (*ugs.*); er ist bei der Prüfung gerade noch durchgerutscht
durch|rüt|teln; der Bus hat uns durchgerüttelt
durchs; ↑R 13 (durch das); durchs Haus
durch|sa|cken; das Flugzeug ist durchgesackt
Durch|sa|ge, die; -, -n; **durch|sa|gen;** der Termin wurde durchgesagt
durch|sä|gen; er hat das Brett durchgesägt
Durch|satz (*fachspr. für* der in einer bestimmten Zeit durch Hochöfen u. Ä. geleitete Stoff)

durch|sau|sen (*ugs. für* eine Prüfung nicht bestehen); er ist durchgesaust
durch|schau|bar; durch|schau|en; er hat [durch das Fernrohr] durchgeschaut; **durch|schau|en;** ich habe ihn durchschaut
durch|schau|ern *(geh.);* von Entsetzen durchschauert
durch|schei|nen; die Sonne hat durchgeschienen; **durch|schei|nen;** vom Tageslicht durchschienen; **durch|schei|nend**
durch|scheu|ern; der Ärmel ist durchgescheuert
durch|schie|ßen; er hat den Ball zwischen den Stangen durchgeschossen; **durch|schie|ßen;** er hat das Blech durchschossen
durch|schim|mern; die Sterne haben durchgeschimmert; **durch|schim|mern;** von Licht durchschimmert
durch|schla|fen; sie hat durchgeschlafen (ohne Unterbrechung); **durch|schla|fen;** er hat die Tage durchschlafen
Durch|schlag (*Bergmannsspr. auch* Treffpunkt zweier Grubenbaue, die aufeinander zulaufen); **durch|schla|gen;** sie hat die Suppe [durch das Sieb] durchgeschlagen; **durch|schla|gen;** die Kugel hat den Panzer durchschlagen; **durch|schla|gend;** ein -er Erfolg; **durch|schlä|gig** *(Bergmannsspr.);* **Durch|schlag|pa|pier; Durch|schlags|kraft,** die; -; **durch|schlags|kräf|tig**
durch|schlän|geln, sich; ich habe mich überall durchgeschlängelt
durch|schlei|chen; er hat sich durchgeschlichen
durch|schlep|pen *(ugs.);* er hat ihn bis zum Abitur, drei Jahre durchgeschleppt
durch|schleu|sen; das Schiff wurde durchgeschleust
Durch|schlupf, der; -[e]s, -e; **durch|schlüp|fen;** er ist durchgeschlüpft
durch|schmo|ren; das Kabel war durchgeschmort
durch|schmug|geln; er hat den Brief durchgeschmuggelt
durch|schnei|den; er hat das Tuch durchgeschnitten; **durch|schnei|den;** die Landschaft ist von Kanälen durchschnitten; **Durch|schnitt;** im -; **durch|schnitt|lich; Durch|schnitts_al|ter, ...bil|dung** (die; -), **...bür|ger, ...ein|kom|men, ...ge|schwin|dig|keit, ...ge|sicht, ...leis|tung, ...mensch, ...schü|ler, ...tem|pe|ra|tur, ...wert**
durch|schnüf|feln, *auch* **durch|schnüf|feln** (*ugs. für* untersuchen); er hat alle Winkel durchgeschnüffelt *od.* durchschnüffelt
durch|schos|sen; ein [mit leeren Seiten] -es Buch; *(Druckw.)* -er Satz
Durch|schrei|be|block *Plur.* ...blocks; **durch|schrei|ben;** er hat diese Rechnung durchgeschrieben; **Durch|schrei|be|ver|fah|ren**
durch|schrei|ten; sie haben den Fluss durchschritten
Durch|schrift
durch|schum|meln, sich *(ugs.);* du hast dich durchgeschummelt
Durch|schuss (*Druckw.* Zeilenzwischenraum); *vgl.* Reglette
durch|schüt|teln; wir wurden im Bus kräftig durchgeschüttelt
durch|schwär|men; eine durchschwärmte Nacht
durch|schwei|fen; sie haben die Gegend durchschweift
durch|schwim|men; er ist unter dem Seil durchgeschwommen; **durch|schwim|men;** er hat den Fluss durchschwommen
durch|schwin|deln, sich; er hat sich frech durchgeschwindelt
durch|schwit|zen; er hat das Hemd durchgeschwitzt
durch|se|geln; das Schiff ist [durch den Kanal] durchgesegelt; **durch|se|geln;** er hat das Meer durchsegelt
durch|se|hen; sie hat die Akten durchgesehen
durch sein *vgl.* durch
durch|setz|bar; durch|set|zen (erreichen); ich habe es durchgesetzt; **durch|set|zen;** das Gestein ist mit Erzen durchsetzt; **Durch|set|zung,** die; -; **Durch|set|zungs|ver|mö|gen,** das; -s
durch|seu|chen; das Gebiet war völlig durchseucht
Durch|sicht; durch|sich|tig; Durch|sich|tig|keit, die; -
durch|si|ckern; die Nachricht ist durchgesickert
durch|sie|ben; sie hat das Mehl durchgesiebt; **durch|sie|ben;** die Tür war von Kugeln durchsiebt
durch|sit|zen; er hat die Hose durchgesessen
durch|spie|len; 90 Minuten voll -; er hat alle Möglichkeiten durchgespielt
durch|spre|chen; sie haben den Plan durchgesprochen
durch|sprin|gen; der Löwe ist [durch den Reifen] durchgesprungen; **durch|sprin|gen;** der Löwe hat [den Reifen] durchsprungen
durch|star|ten; der Pilot hat die Maschine durchgestartet
durch|ste|chen; ich habe [durch das Tuch] durchgestochen; **durch|ste|chen;** der Damm wird durchstochen; **Durch|ste|che|rei** (Täuschung, Betrug)
durch|ste|hen; sie hat viel durchgestanden; er hat den Skisprung durchgestanden
durch|stei|gen; er ist [durch das Fenster] durchgestiegen; da steig ich nicht mehr durch (*ugs. für* das verstehe ich nicht); **durch|stei|gen;** er hat die Gebirgswand durchstiegen; **Durch|stei|gung**
durch|stel|len; sie hat das Gespräch zum Chef durchgestellt
Durch|stich
Durch|stieg
durch|stö|bern; er hat die Papiere durchstöbert
Durch|stoß; durch|sto|ßen; er hat die Stange [durch das Eis] durchgestoßen; **durch|sto|ßen;** er hat das Eis durchstoßen
durch|stre|cken; er hat den Kopf durchgestreckt
durch|strei|chen; das Wort ist durchgestrichen; **durch|strei|chen** *(veraltend);* er hat das Land durchstrichen
durch|strei|fen; er hat das Land durchstreift
durch|strö|men; große Scharen sind durchgeströmt; **durch|strö|men;** das Land wird von Flüssen durchströmt
durch|struk|tu|rie|ren (bis ins Einzelne strukturieren); **Durch|struk|tu|rie|rung**
durch|sty|len [...stai...] ‹dt.; engl.›; durchgestylte Räume
durch|su|chen; sie hat schon das ganze Adressbuch durchgesucht; **durch|su|chen;** alle Koffer wurden durchsucht; **Durch|su|chung; Durch|su|chungs|be|fehl**
durch|tan|ken, sich (*Handball, Fußball* mit kraftvollem Einsatz die Abwehr überwinden); er hat sich durchgetankt
durch|tan|zen; er hat die Nacht durchgetanzt; **durch|tan|zen;** er hat ganze Nächte durchgetanzt
durch|to|ben; ein vom Bürgerkrieg durchtobtes Land
durch|trai|nie|ren; mein Körper ist durchtrainiert
durch|trän|ken; das Papier ist mit Öl durchtränkt
durch|trei|ben; er hat den Nagel durch das Holz durchgetrieben
durch|tren|nen, durch|tren|nen; er hat das Kabel durchgetrennt *od.* durchtrennt
durch|tre|ten; er hat das Gaspedal ganz durchgetreten

durch|trie|ben (gerissen, verschlagen); ein durchtriebener Bursche; **Durch|trie|ben|heit,** die; -
durch|wa|chen; sie hat bis zum Morgen durchgewacht; **durchwa|chen;** ich habe die Nacht durchwacht
durch|wach|sen; [mit Fleisch] -er Speck; [mit Speck, Fett] -es Fleisch; -es (*ugs. für* abwechselnd besseres u. schlechteres) Wetter; die Stimmung ist - (*ugs. für* nicht besonders gut)
durch|wa|gen, sich; ich habe mich durchgewagt
Durch|wahl, die; -; **durch|wäh|len** (beim Telefon); wir haben nach Tokio durchgewählt; **Durch|wahl|num|mer**
durch|wal|ken; das Tuch wurde durchgewalkt; er wurde durchgewalkt (*ugs. für* verprügelt)
durch|wan|dern; er ist ohne Rast durchgewandert; **durch|wan|dern;** er hat das ganze Land durchwandert
durch|wär|men, durch|wär|men; der Tee hat uns durchgewärmt *od.* durchwärmt
durch|wa|schen; sie hat die Strümpfe durchgewaschen
durch|wa|ten; er ist [durch den Bach] durchgewatet; **durch|wa|ten;** er hat den Bach durchwatet
durch|we|ben; der Stoff ist durchgewebt; **durch|we|ben;** mit Goldfäden durchwebt; das Haar war von Silberfäden durchwoben (*geh.*)
durch|weg [*auch* ...'vɛk]; **durchwegs** [*auch* ...'ve:ks] (*österr. u. schweiz. nur so, sonst ugs. neben* durchweg)
durch|wei|chen, durch|wei|chen; ich bin vom Regen ganz durchgeweicht *od.* durchweicht worden; *vgl.* [1]weichen
durch|wet|zen; seine Ärmel waren durchgewetzt
durch|win|den, sich; ich habe mich zwischen den Tischen durchgewunden
durch|win|ken; an der Grenze wurden alle nur durchgewinkt
durch|win|tern; sie hat die Knollen im Keller durchwintert; **Durch|win|te|rung**
durch|wir|ken; der Teig war gut durchgewirkt; **durch|wir|ken;** mit Goldfäden durchwirkt
durch|wit|schen; er ist mir durchgewitscht (*ugs. für* entkommen)
durch|wol|len (*ugs. für* hindurchgelangen wollen); an dieser Stelle haben sie durchgewollt
durch|wüh|len; die Maus hat sich durchgewühlt; er hat den Schrank durchgewühlt; **durch|wüh|len;** die Diebe haben alles durchwühlt
durch|wursch|teln, durch|wursteln, sich (*ugs.);* er hat sich irgendwie durchgewurschtelt *od.* durchgewurstelt
durch|zäh|len; er hat durchgezählt; **Durch|zäh|lung**
durch|ze|chen; er hat die Nacht durchgezecht; **durch|ze|chen;** er hat ganze Nächte durchzecht
durch|zeich|nen; er hat die Skizze durchgezeichnet
durch|zie|hen; ich habe den Faden durchgezogen; **durch|ziehen;** wir haben das Land durchzogen
durch|zit|tern; Freude hat ihn durchzittert
durch|zu|cken; Blitze haben den Himmel durchzuckt
Durch|zug; Durch|züg|ler (*Zool.);* **Durch|zugs|ar|beit** (*Weberei*)
durch|zwän|gen; ich habe mich durchgezwängt
Dur|drei|klang (*Musik*)
Dü|rer (dt. Maler)
dür|fen; du darfst, er darf; du durftest; du dürftest; gedurft; du hast [es] nicht gedurft, *aber* das hättest du nicht tun dürfen
dürf|tig; Dürf|tig|keit, die; -
Du|ro|plast, der; -[e]s, -e *meist Plur.* ‹lat.; griech.› (in Hitze härtbarer, aber nicht schmelzbarer Kunststoff)
dürr
Dur|ra, die; - ‹arab.› (eine Getreidepflanze; Sorgho)
Dür|re, die; -, -n; **Dür|re|ka|tastro|phe**
Dür|ren|matt (schweiz. Dramatiker u. Erzähler)
Dür|re‿pe|ri|o|de, ...schä|den (*Plur.*)
Dürr|fut|ter (Trockenfutter)
Durst, der; -[e]s; **durs|ten** (*geh. für* Durst haben); **dürs|ten** (*geh.);* mich dürstet, ich dürste; **durs|tig; durst‿lö|schend** (↑R 40), **...stillend** (↑R 40); **Durst|stre|cke** (Zeit der Entbehrung)
Dur‿ton|art, ...ton|lei|ter (*Musik*)
Dusch|bad [*auch* 'du:ʃ...]; **Dusche,** die; -, -n ‹franz.›; **Duschecke** (↑R 132); **du|schen;** du duschst; **Dusch‿gel, ...ge|legen|heit, ...ka|bi|ne, ...raum, ...schaum, ...vor|hang**
Dü|se, die; -, -n
Du|sel, der; -s (*ugs. für* unverdientes Glück; *landsch. für* Schwindel, Rausch); **Du|se|lei** (*ugs.);* **duse|lig,** dus|lig, *nordd.* **dü|se|lig** (*ugs.);* **du|seln** (*ugs. für* im Halbschlaf sein); ich ...[e]le (↑R 16)
dü|sen (*ugs. für* sausen); du düst; er düs|te; **Dü|sen‿ag|gre|gat, ...an|trieb, ...flug|zeug, ...jä|ger, ...ma|schi|ne, ...trieb|werk**
dus|lig *vgl.* duselig
Dus|sel, der; -s, - (*ugs. für* Dummkopf)
Düs|sel|dorf (Hptst. von Nordrhein-Westfalen); **Düs|sel|dorfer** (↑R 103)
Dus|se|lei (*ugs.);* **dus|se|lig,** dusslig (*ugs.);* **Dus|se|lig|keit,** Dusslig|keit (*ugs.);* **duss|lig** *vgl.* dusselig; **Duss|lig|keit** *vgl.* Dusseligkeit
Dust, der; -[e]s (*nordd. für* Dunst, Staub)
dus|ter (*landsch. für* düster); **düster;** düst[e]rer, -ste; **Düs|ter,** das; -s (*geh.);* **Düs|ter|heit, Düs|terkeit,** die; -; **düs|tern** (*geh.);* es düstert; **Düs|ter|nis,** die; -, -se
Dutch|man ['datʃmən], der; -s, ...men [...mən] ‹engl.› (Niederländer; von englisch sprechenden Matrosen verwendete Bez. für einen deutschen Seemann)
Dutt, der; -[e]s, *Plur.* -s *od.* -e (*landsch. für* Haarknoten)
Dut|te, die; -, -n (*landsch. für* Zitze)
Du|ty|free|shop, *auch* **Duty-free-Shop** ['dju:ti'fri:ʃɔp] ‹engl.› (Laden, in dem zollfreie Waren verkauft werden)
Dut|zend, das; -s, -e (*Abk.* Dtzd.); 6 Dutzend (↑R 90); *bei Angabe unbestimmter Mengen auch kleingeschrieben:* es gab Dutzende *od.* dutzende von Reklamationen; [einige, viele] Dutzend[e] *od.* dutzend[e] Mal[e]; ein halbes, zwei Dutzend Mal[e]; **dut|zend|fach; Dut|zend|wa|re; dut|zend|weise**
Du|um|vir [...v...], der; *Gen.* -s *u.* -n, *Plur.* -n *meist Plur.* (↑R 126) ‹lat.› (altröm. Beamtentitel); **Duum|vi|rat,** das; -[e]s, -e (Amt der Duumvirn)
Du|vet [dy'vɛ], das; -s, -s ‹franz.› (*schweiz. für* Feder-, Deckbett); **Duve|tine** [dyf'ti:n], der; -s, -s (ein samtartiges Gewebe)
Du|wock, der; -s, -s (*nordd. für* Schachtelhalm)
Duz|bru|der; du|zen; du duzt; **Duz|freund; Duz|fuß;** *nur in* mit jmdm. auf [dem] - stehen
DV = Datenverarbeitung
Dvo|řák ['dvɔrʒa(:)k], Antonín ['antɔni:n] (tschech. Komponist)
DW = Deutsche Welle
dwars (*Seemannsspr.* quer); **Dwars‿li|nie** (in - [nebeneinander] fahren), **...see** (die)
Dweil, der; -s, -e (*Seemannsspr.* schrubberähnlicher Aufwischer)

Dwi|na, die; - (russ. Fluss, Nördliche Dwina; russ.-lett. Fluss, Düna od. Westliche Dwina)
Dy = *chem. Zeichen für* Dysprosium
dy|a|disch ‹griech.› (dem Zweiersystem zugehörend); -es Zahlensystem; **Dy|as,** die; - (*veraltet für* [2]Perm)
Dyck, van [van, *auch* fan 'daik] (flämischer Maler)
dyn = Dyn
Dyn, das; -s ‹griech.› (veraltete Maßeinheit der Kraft, 10^{-5} Newton; *Zeichen* dyn); **Dy|na|mik,** die; - (Lehre von den Kräften; Schwung, Triebkraft); **dy|na|misch** (die Kraft betreffend; voll innerer Kraft; eine Entwicklung aufweisend; Kraft...); -e Belastung; -e Rente; **dy|na|mi|sie|ren** (vorantreiben; an eine Entwicklung anpassen); Renten -; **Dy|na|mi|sie|rung; Dy|na|mis|mus,** der; - (*Philos.* Weltanschauung, die die Wirklichkeit auf Kräfte u. deren Wirkungen zurückführt); **Dy|na|mit** [*auch* ...'mit], das; -s (Sprengstoff); **Dy|na|mit|pat|ro|ne** (↑R 130); **Dy|na|mo** [*auch* 'dy:...], der; -s, -s (*Kurzform für* Dynamomaschine); **Dy|na|mo|ma|schi|ne** (Stromerzeuger); **Dy|na|mo|me|ter,** das; -s, - (Vorrichtung zum Messen von Kräften u. von mechan. Arbeit); **Dy|nast,** der; -en, -en; ↑R 126 (Herrscher; [kleiner] Fürst); **Dy|nas|tie,** die; -, ...ien (Herrschergeschlecht, -haus); **dy|nas|tisch**
dys... ‹griech.› (übel, schlecht, miss...); **Dys...**
Dys|en|te|rie, die; -, ...ien ‹griech.› (*Med.* [1]Ruhr); **dys|en|te|risch** (ruhrartig)
Dys|funk|ti|on, die; -, -en ‹griech.; lat.› (*Med.* gestörte Funktion)
dys|mel ‹griech.› (mit Dysmelie behaftet); **Dys|me|lie,** die; -, ...ien (*Med.* angeborene Missbildung an Gliedmaßen)
Dys|me|nor|rhö[1], **Dys|me|nor|rhöe** [...'rø:], die; -, ...rrhöen ‹griech.› (*Med.* Menstruationsschmerzen)
Dys|pep|sie, die; -, ...ien ‹griech.› (*Med.* Verdauungsbeschwerden); **dys|pep|tisch** (schwer verdaulich; schwer verdauend)
Dys|pnoe [...'pno:e], die; - ‹griech.› (*Med.* Atembeschwerden)
Dys|pro|si|um, das; -s ‹griech.› (chem. Element, Metall; *Zeichen* Dy)
Dys|to|nie, die; -, ...ien ‹griech.› (*Med.* Störung des normalen Spannungszustandes der Muskeln u. Gefäße); vegetative -
dys|troph ‹griech.› (*Med.* die Ernährung störend); **Dys|tro|phie,** die; -, ...ien (*Med.* Ernährungsstörung); **Dys|tro|phi|ker** (jmd., der an Dystrophie leidet)
Dys|u|rie, die; -, ...ien ‹griech.› (*Med.* Harnbeschwerden)
dz = Doppelzentner
dz. = derzeit
D-Zug ['de:...] ‹„Durchgangszug“› (Schnellzug); **D-Zug-ar|tig** (↑R 28); **D-Zug-Wa|gen** (↑R 28)

E

E (Buchstabe); das E; des E, die E, *aber* das e in Berg (↑R 60); der Buchstabe E, e
e, E, das; -, - (Tonbezeichnung); **e** (*Zeichen für* e-Moll); in e; **E** (*Zeichen für* E-Dur); in E
ε = *Zeichen für* Dielektrizitätskonstante
E = *(internationale Wetterkunde)* East [i:st] ‹engl.› *od.* Est [ɛst] ‹franz.› (Ost)
E = Eilzug; Europastraße
E, ε = Epsilon
H, η = Eta
Ea|gle ['i:g(ə)l], das; -s, -s ‹engl., „Adler“› (*Golf* zwei Schläge unter Par)
EAN = europäische Artikelnummerierung (für den Strichkode auf Waren)
[1]**Earl** [œ:(r)l], der; -s, -s ‹engl.› (*engl. Bez. für* Graf); [2]**Earl** (m. Vorn.)
Ea|sy|ri|der ['i:ziraidə(r)] (↑R 33), der; -s, -[s] ‹nach dem amerik. Spielfilm› (Jugendlicher, der ein Motorrad mit hohem, geteiltem Lenker u. einem Sattel mit hoher Rückenlehne fährt)
Eau de Co|lo|gne [o: də ko'lɔnjə, *österr.* ...'lɔn] (↑R 130), das, *seltener* die; - - -, Eaux - - [o: - -] ‹franz.› (Kölnischwasser); **Eau de Par|fum** [o: də par'fœ̃], das; - - -, Eaux - - [o: - -] (Duftwasser, das stärker als Eau de Toilette duftet); **Eau de Toi|lette** [o: də toa'lɛt], das; - - -, Eaux - - [o: - -] (Duftwasser)
Eb|be, die; -, -n; **eb|ben;** es ebbte (die Ebbe kam); **Eb|be|strom** *vgl.* Ebbstrom
Eb|bo (m. Vorn.)
Ebb|strom (Strömung bei Ebbe)
ebd. = ebenda
e|ben; -es (flaches) Land; das ist nun eben (einmal) so; *vgl. aber* ebenso; **E|ben|bild; e|ben|bür|tig; E|ben|bür|tig|keit,** die; -; **e|ben|da** [*auch* ...'da:] (*Abk.* ebd.); **e|ben|da|her** [*auch* ...'da:...]; **e|ben|da|hin** [*auch* ...'da:...]; **e|ben|dann** [*auch* ...'dan]; **e|ben|da|rum** [*auch* ...'da:...]; **e|ben|da|selbst** [*auch* ...'zɛlbst]; **e|ben|der** [*auch* ...'de:r]; **e|ben|der|sel|be** [*auch* ...'zɛlbə]; **e|ben|des|halb** [*auch* ...'dɛs...]; **e|ben|des|we|gen** [*auch* ...'dɛs...]; **e|ben|die|ser** [*auch* ...'di:...]; **e|ben|dort** [*auch* ...'dɔrt]; **e|ben|dort|selbst** [*auch* ...'zɛlbst]; **E|be|ne,** die; -, -n; **e|ben|er|dig; e|ben|falls; E|ben|heit,** die; - (ebene Beschaffenheit)
E|ben|holz ‹ägypt.; dt.›
e|ben|je|ner [*auch* ...'je:...];
E|ben|maß, das; -es; **e|ben|mä|ßig; E|ben|mä|ßig|keit,** die; -
e|ben|so; ebenso wie; ebenso viel, ebenso wenig; er hat zwei Autos, sie hat ebenso viele; wir können ihn ebenso gut auch einladen; wir können ihn ebenso gut leiden wie ihr; das macht sie ebenso schnell wie er; das dauert bei ihr ebenso lange wie bei ihm; ich habe den Film ebenso oft gesehen wie du; wir freuen uns ebenso sehr wie die anderen; **e|ben|solch** [*auch* ...'zɔlç]; **e|ben|sol|cher** [*auch* ...'zɔl...]; **e|ben|so oft, sehr, viel** usw. *vgl.* ebenso
E|ber, der; -s, - (m. Schwein)
E|ber|esche (↑R 132; ein Laubbaum)
E|ber|hard (m. Vorn.)
eb|nen
Eb|ner-E|schen|bach, Marie von (österr. Schriftstellerin)
Eb|nung
E|bo|nit [*auch* ...'nit], das; -s ‹ägypt.› (Hartgummi aus Naturkautschuk)
Eb|ro (↑R 130), der; -[s] (Fluss in Spanien)
EC = Eurocityzug
Ec|ce-Ho|mo [ˌɛktsə...], das; -[s], -[s] ‹lat., „Sehet, welch ein Mensch!“› (Darstellung des dornengekrönten Christus)

---
[1] *Vgl. die Anmerkung zu* „Diarrhö, Diarrhöe“.

E|charpe [e'ʃarp], die; -, -s ‹franz.› (*schweiz. u. fachspr., sonst veraltend für* Schärpe, Schal)
e|chauf|fie|ren [eʃɔ'fi:...], sich (*veraltend für* sich erhitzen; sich aufregen); **e|chauf|fiert**
E|che|ve|ria [ɛtʃe've:ria], die; -, ...ien [...iən] ‹nach dem mexikan. Pflanzenzeichner Echeverría› (ein Dickblattgewächs)
E|chi|nit [...ç..., *auch* ...'nit], der; *Gen.* -s *u.* -en, *Plur.* -e[n] (↑R 126) ‹griech.› (*Geol.* versteinerter Seeigel); **E|chi|no|der|me,** der; -n, -n *meist Plur.;* ↑R 126 (*Zool.* Stachelhäuter); **E|chi|no|kok|kus,** der; -, ...kken (*Med.* Blasenwurm [ein Hundebandwurm] od. dessen Finne); **E|chi|nus,** der; -, - (ein Seeigel; *Archit.* ein Säulenwulst)
¹E|cho (Nymphe des griech. Mythos); **²E|cho,** das; -s, -s ‹griech.› (Widerhall); **e|cho|en** ['ɛçoən]; es echot; geechot; **E|cho|lot; E|cho|lo|tung**
Ech|se, die; -, -n (ein Kriechtier, z. B. Eidechse)
echt; ein echtgoldener, *auch* echt goldener Ring; die Kette ist echtsilbern, *auch* echt silbern
Ech|ter|nach (Stadt in Luxemburg); **Ech|ter|na|cher** (↑R 103); - Springprozession
echt|gol|den *vgl.* echt; **Echt|haar; Echt|haar|pe|rü|cke; Echt|heit,** die; -; **Echt|heits|prü|fung; Echt|sil|ber;** aus -; **echt|sil|bern** *vgl.* echt
Eck, das; -[e]s, *Plur.* -e, *österr.* -en *u.* (*für* Dreieck usw.:) -e (*bes. südd. u. österr. für* Ecke; *sonst fast nur noch in geogr. Namen u. in* Dreieck usw.); das Deutsche Eck
E|ckart, Eck|hart, E|cke|hart (dt. Mystiker, *gen.* Meister -; m. Vorn.)
Eck‿ball *(Sport),* **...bank** (*Plur.* ...bänke)
Eck|bert, Eg|bert (m. Vorn.); **Eck|brecht,** Eg|brecht (m. Vorn.)
Eck|brett; Eck|chen; Eck|da|ten *Plur.* (Richtwerte); **E|cke,** die; -, -n; *vgl.* Eck
E|cke|hard, E|cke|hart (m. Vorn.)
e|cken (*veraltet für* mit Ecken versehen); **E|cken|band** *vgl.* Eggenband; **e|cken|los; E|cken|ste|her** *(ugs. veraltend)*
E|cker, die; -, -n (*svw.* Buchecker, *selten für* Eichel)
E|cker|mann (Vertrauter u. Gehilfe Goethes)
E|ckern *Plur., als Sing. gebraucht* (Farbe im dt. Kartenspiel); - spielen; - sticht
E|ckern|för|de (Hafenstadt in Schleswig-Holstein)

Eck‿fah|ne, ...fens|ter
Eck|hard, Eck|hart (m. Vorn.)
Eck|haus; e|ckig; E|ckig|keit, die; -; **Eck|lohn**
Eck|mann|schrift, die; - (eine Druckschrift des Jugendstils)
Eck‿pfei|ler, ...plat|te, ...satz *(Musik),* **...schrank, ...stein, ...stoß** *(Sport),* **...stück, ...tisch, ...wer|te** *(Plur.),* **...zahn, ...zim|mer, ...zins**
Ec|lair [e'klɛ:r] (↑R 130), das; -s, -s ‹franz.› (ein Gebäck)
E|co|no|mi|ser [i'kɔnəmaizə(r)], der; -s, - ‹engl.› (*Technik* Vorwärmer bei Dampfkesselanlagen); **E|co|no|my|class** [i'kɔnəmikla:s], **E|co|no|my|klas|se** (Tarifklasse im Flugverkehr)
E|cos|sai|se *vgl.* Ekossaise
Ecs|ta|sy ['ɛkstəzi] (↑R 132), die; -, -s ‹engl.› (eine Droge)
E|cu, ECU [*beide* e'ky:], der; -[s], -[s] *u.* die; -, - ‹*Abk. für engl.* European Currency Unit, in Anlehnung an die alte franz. Silbermünze „Écu"› (europ. Währungseinheit); 10 -; *vgl.* EWS
E|cu|a|dor, E|ku|a|dor (südamerik. Staat); **E|cu|a|do|ri|a|ner,** E|ku|a|do|ri|a|ner (↑R 103); **e|cu|a|do|ri|a|nisch,** e|ku|a|do|ri|a|nisch
ed. = edidit ‹lat., „herausgegeben hat es ..."›; ediert; **Ed.** = Edition
E|dam (niederl. Stadt); **¹E|da|mer** (↑R 103); - Käse, *österr.* Edamerkäse; **²E|da|mer,** der; -s, - (ein Käse)
E|da|phon, das; -s ‹griech.› (*Biol.* die in und auf dem Erdboden lebenden Kleinlebewesen)
edd. = ediderunt ‹lat., „herausgegeben haben es ..."›
¹Ed|da, die; - ‹altnord.› (Sammlung altnord. Dichtungen)
²Ed|da (w. Vorn.)
ed|disch ‹*zu* ¹Edda›; -e Lieder
e|del; ein ed|les Pferd; **E|del|bert** (m. Vorn.); **E|del|fäu|le** (*fachspr. für* Überreife von Weintrauben); **E|del‿frau** (*früher für* Adlige), **...fräu|lein** *(früher);* **E|del|gard** (w. Vorn.); **E|del|gas** *(Chemie);* **E|de|ling** (germ. Adliger); **E|del‿kas|ta|nie, ...kitsch** *(iron.),* **...mann** (*Plur.* ...leute; *früher für* Adliger); **e|del|män|nisch; E|del‿mar|der, ...me|tall, ...mut** (der); **e|del|mü|tig; E|del|pilz|kä|se; E|del‿rost** (*für* Patina), **...stahl, ...stein, ...tan|ne; E|del|traud, E|del|trud** (w. Vorn.); **E|del|weiß,** das; -[es], -[e] (eine Gebirgspflanze); **E|del|zwi|cker** (ein elsässischer Weißwein)
E|den, das; -s ‹hebr.› (Paradies im A. T.); der Garten -

E|den|ta|te, der; -n, -n *meist Plur.;* ↑R 126 (*Zool.* zahnarmes Säugetier)
E|der, die; - (Nebenfluss der Fulda)
Ed|gar (m. Vorn.)
e|die|ren ‹lat.› (herausgeben, veröffentlichen; *EDV auch für* editieren); **e|diert** (*Abk.* ed.)
E|dikt, das; -[e]s, -e ‹lat.› (amtl. Erlass [von Kaisern u. Königen])
E|din|burg (*dt. Form von* Edinburgh); **E|din|burgh** ['ɛdinbərə] (Hptst. Schottlands)
E|di|son [*engl.* 'ɛdis(ə)n] (amerik. Erfinder)
E|dith, E|di|tha (w. Vorn.)
e|di|tie|ren ‹engl.› (*EDV* Daten in ein Terminal eingeben, löschen, verändern); **E|di|ti|on,** die; -, -en ‹lat.› (Ausgabe; *Abk.* Ed.); **E|di|tor** [*auch* e'di:...], der; -s, ...oren (Herausgeber); **e|di|to|risch**
Ed|le, der *u.* die; -n, -n (↑R 5 ff.); Edler von ... (Adelstitel)
Ed|mund (m. Vorn.)
E|dom (Land östl. u. südöstl. des Toten Meeres im A. T.); **E|do|mi|ter**
Ed|schmid [*auch* 'ɛt...] (dt. Schriftsteller)
E|du|ard (m. Vorn.)
E|du|ka|ti|on, die; - ‹lat.› (*veraltet für* Erziehung); **E|dukt,** das; -[e]s, -e (*fachspr. für* aus Rohstoffen abgeschiedener Stoff [z. B. Öl])
E-Dur [*auch* 'e:'du:r], das; - (Tonart; *Zeichen* E); **E-Dur-Ton|lei|ter** (↑R 28)
EDV = elektronische Datenverarbeitung; **EDV-Pro|gramm** (↑R 26)
Ed|ward (m. Vorn.); **Ed|win** (m. Vorn.)
Ed|zard (m. Vorn.)
EEG = Elektroenzephalogramm
E|fen|di, der; -s, -s ‹türk.› (*früher* ein türk. Anredetitel)
E|feu, der; -s; **e|feu|be|wach|sen; E|feu|ran|ke**
Eff|eff *(ugs.);* etwas aus dem - (*ugs. für* gründlich) verstehen
Ef|fekt, der; -[e]s, -e ‹lat.› (Wirkung, Erfolg; Ergebnis); **Ef|fek|ten** *Plur.* (Wertpapiere); **Ef|fek|ten‿bank** (*Plur.* ...banken), **...bör|se, ...gi|ro|ver|kehr, ...han|del; Ef|fekt|ha|sche|rei** *(abwertend);* **ef|fek|tiv** (tatsächlich; wirksam; greifbar); -e Leistung (Nutzleistung); **Ef|fek|tiv,** das; -s, -e [...və] (*Sprachw.* Verb des Verwandelns, z. B. „knechten" = „zum Knecht machen"); **Ef|fek|tiv|be|stand** (Istbestand); **Ef|fek|ti|vi|tät** [...v...], die; - (Wirkungskraft); **Ef|fek|tiv|lohn** [...f...]; **ef-**

fek|tu|ie|ren ‹franz.› (*Wirtsch.* einen Auftrag ausführen; eine Zahlung leisten); **ef|fekt|voll** (wirkungsvoll)
ef|fe|mi|niert ‹lat.› (*Med., Psych.* verweiblicht)
Ef|fen|di *vgl.* Efendi
Ef|fet [ɛ'fe:], der, *selten* das; -s, -s ‹franz.› (Drall einer [Billard]kugel, eines Balles); **Ef|fi|cien|cy** [ə'fiʃ(ə)nsi], die; - ‹engl.› (*Wirtsch.* Wirtschaftlichkeit, bestmöglicher Wirkungsgrad)
ef|fi|lie|ren ‹franz.› (die Haare beim Schneiden ausdünnen); **Ef|fi|lier|sche|re**
ef|fi|zi|ent ‹lat.› (wirksam; wirtschaftlich); **Ef|fi|zi|enz,** die; -, -en (Wirksamkeit)
Ef|flo|res|zenz, die; -, -en ‹lat.› (*Med.* Hautblüte [z. B. Pusteln]; *Geol.* Mineralüberzug auf Gesteinen); **ef|flo|res|zie|ren**
Ef|fu|si|on, die; -, -en ‹lat.› (*Geol.* Ausfließen von Lava); **ef|fu|siv** (durch Erguss gebildet); **Ef|fu|siv|ge|stein** (Ergussgestein)
EFTA, die; - ‹engl.; *Kurzwort für* European Free Trade Association [ju(ə)rə'pi:ən 'fri: 'tre:dəso:'sie:ʃ(ə)n]› (Europäische Freihandelsassoziation)
eG, e. G. = eingetragene Genossenschaft; *vgl.* eingetragen
EG = Europäische Gemeinschaft[en] *vgl.* EU
[1]**e|gal** (*ugs. für* gleichgültig); das ist mir -; [2]**e|gal** (*landsch. für* immer [wieder, noch]); er hat - etwas an mir auszusetzen; **e|ga|li|sie|ren** (gleichmachen, ausgleichen); **E|ga|li|sie|rung; e|ga|li|tär** (auf Gleichheit gerichtet); **E|ga|li|ta|ris|mus,** der; -; **E|ga|li|tät,** die; - (*geh. für* Gleichheit); **É|ga|li|té** *vgl.* Liberté
E|gart, die; - (*bayr. u. österr. veraltet für* Grasland); **E|gar|ten|wirt|schaft, E|gart|wirt|schaft,** die; - (Feldgraswirtschaft)
Eg|bert, Eg|brecht (m. Vorn.)
E|gel, der; -s, - (ein Wurm); **E|gel|schne|cke**
E|ger (*tschech.* Cheb); **E|ger|land,** das; -[e]s; **E|ger|län|der** (↑R 103)
E|ger|ling (*landsch. für* Champignon)
[1]**Eg|ge,** die; -, -n (Gewebekante, -leiste); [2]**Eg|ge,** die; -, -n (ein Ackergerät); **eg|gen;** das Feld wird geeggt; **Eg|gen|band** *Plur.* ...bänder (festes Band, das Nähte vor dem Verziehen schützen soll)
Egg|head ['ɛghɛd], der; -[s], -s ‹engl.-amerik., „Eierkopf"› (*in den USA iron. od. abwertende Bez. für* Intellektueller)
E|gil [*auch* 'ɛgil] (nord. Sagengestalt)
E|gi|nald [*auch* 'ɛ...] (m. Vorn.); **E|gin|hard,** Ein|hard (m. Vorn.)
Egk [ɛk] (dt. Komponist)
Eg|li, das; -[s], - (*bes. schweiz. für* Flussbarsch)
eGmbH, *auch* **EGmbH** = eingetragene, *auch* Eingetragene Genossenschaft mit beschränkter Haftpflicht (*dafür jetzt* eG, e. G.; *vgl. d.*)
Eg|mont (Titelgestalt der gleichnamigen Tragödie von Goethe)
eGmuH, *auch* **EGmuH** (↑R 108) = eingetragene, *auch* Eingetragene Genossenschaft mit unbeschränkter Haftpflicht (*dafür jetzt* eG, e. G.; *vgl. d.*)
e|go [*auch* 'ɛgo] ‹lat.› (ich); *vgl.* Alter ego; **E|go,** das; -, -s (*Philos., Psych.* das Ich); **E|go|is|mus,** der; -, ...men (Selbstsucht; *Ggs.* Altruismus); **E|go|ist,** der; -en, -en (↑R 126); **E|go|is|tin; e|go|is|tisch**
E|golf (m. Vorn.)
E|gon (m. Vorn.)
E|go|tis|mus, der; - ‹lat.› (Neigung, sich selbst in den Vordergrund zu stellen); **E|go|tist,** der; -en, -en (↑R 126); **E|go|tis|tin;**
E|go|trip ‹engl.›; auf dem - sein (*ugs. für* sich egozentrisch verhalten); **E|go|zent|rik** (↑R 130), die; - ‹lat.› (Ichbezogenheit); **E|go|zent|ri|ker; E|go|zent|ri|ke|rin; e|go|zent|risch**
eg|re|nie|ren (↑R 130 *u.* 132) ‹franz.› (*fachspr. für* Baumwollfasern von den Samen trennen); **Eg|re|nier|ma|schi|ne**
E|gyp|ti|enne [*fachspr.* egip'tsiɛn, *auch* eʒip'siɛn], die; - ‹franz.› (*Druckw.* eine Antiquaschriftart)
[1]**eh** (*südd., österr. für* sowieso)
[2]**eh!**
eh *vgl.* ehe
eh., e. h. = ehrenhalber
e. h. (*österr.*) = eigenhändig
E. h. = Ehren halber (*frühere Schreibung von* ehrenhalber), *z. B. in* Dr.-Ing. E. h.
e|he; ehe (eh) ich das nicht weiß, ...; (↑R 13:) seit eh und je; *vgl.* eher *u.* eheste
E|he, die; -, -n; **e|he|ähn|lich; E|he|an|bah|nungs|in|sti|tut**
e|he|bal|dig[st] (*österr. für* möglichst bald)
E|he‿be|ra|ter, ...be|ra|te|rin, ...be|ra|tung, ...be|ra|tungs|stel|le, ...bett; e|he|bre|chen *nur im Infinitiv u. Partizip I gebr.; sonst:* er bricht die Ehe, hat die Ehe gebrochen; die Ehe zu brechen (↑R 39); **E|he‿bre|cher, ...bre|che|rin; e|he|bre|che|risch; E|he|bruch,** der
e|he|dem (*geh. für* vormals)
E|he‿dis|pens, ...fä|hig|keit (die; -), **...frau, ...füh|rung, ...gat|te** (*bes. Amtsspr.*), **...gat|tin, ...ge|spons** (*veraltet, noch scherzh.*)
e|he|ges|tern (*veraltet für* vorgestern); gestern und -
E|he‿glück, ...hafen (*scherzh.*), **...hälf|te** (*scherzh.*), **...hin|der|nis, ...hy|gi|e|ne, ...joch** (*ugs. scherzh.*), **...krach** (*ugs.*), **...kre|dit** ([staatlicher] Kredit für junge Ehepaare), **...kri|se, ...le|ben, ...leu|te** (*Plur.*); **e|he|lich;** -es Güterrecht; **e|he|li|chen** (*veraltend*); **E|he|lich|er|klä|rung** (*BGB*); **E|he|lich|keit,** die; - (Abstammung aus rechtsgültiger Ehe); **E|he|lich|keits|er|klä|rung** *svw.* Ehelicherklärung; **e|he|los; E|he|lo|sig|keit,** die; -
e|he|ma|lig; e|he|mals
E|he|mann *Plur.* ...männer; **e|he|männ|lich** (*meist scherzh.*); **E|he‿na|me, ...paar, ...part|ner**
e|her; je eher (früher), je lieber; je eher (früher), desto besser; eher ([viel]mehr) klein [als groß]; er wird es umso eher (lieber) tun, als ...
E|he‿recht (das; -[e]s), **...ring**
e|hern; -es (unveränderliches) Gesetz; ehernes Lohngesetz (*Sozialwissenschaft*), die eherne Schlange (*bibl.*)
E|he‿schei|dung, ...schlie|ßung
e|hest (*österr. für* baldmöglichst)
E|he|stand, der; -[e]s
e|hes|te; bei ehester (nächster) Gelegenheit; mit Ehestem (*Kaufmannsspr.* so früh wie möglich); am ehesten (am leichtesten);
e|hes|tens (frühestens; *österr. für* so schnell wie möglich)
E|he‿streit, ...tra|gö|die, ...verbot, ...ver|mitt|lung, ...ver|sprechen, ...ver|trag, ...weib (*veraltet, noch scherzh.*); **e|he|wid|rig;** -es Verhalten
Ehr|ab|schnei|der; ehr|bar (*geh.*); **Ehr|bar|keit,** die; -; **ehr|be|gie|rig; Ehr‿be|griff, ...be|lei|di|gung** (*vgl.* Ehrenbeleidigung); **Eh|re,** die; -, -n; in, mit Ehren, jmdm. zu Ehren; *vgl.* E. h.; **eh|ren; Eh|ren|amt; eh|ren|amt|lich; Eh|ren‿be|lei|di|gung, ...be|zei|gung,** *seltener* **...be|zeu|gung, ...bür|ger, ...bür|ger|brief, ...dienst, ...dok|tor** (*vgl.* Doktor), **...ein|tritt** (*für* Intervention [bei einem Wechsel]), **...er|klä|rung, ...es|kor|te, ...fä|hig|keit** (die; -; *schweiz. Rechtsspr.*); **Eh|ren|fried** (m. Vorn.); **Eh|ren‿ga|be, ...gar-**

de, ...gast (*Plur.* ...gäste), ...geleit, ...ge|richt; eh|ren|haft; Eh|ren|haf|tig|keit, die; -; eh|ren|hal|ber (*Abk.* eh. *u.* e. h.; *vgl. aber* E. h.); Eh|ren-kar|te, ...ko|dex, ...kom|pa|nie, ...le|gi|on (die; -; franz. Orden), ...mal (*Plur.* ...male *u.* ...mäler), ...mann (*Plur.* ...männer), ...mit|glied, ...na|del, ...name, ...pflicht, ...platz; [1]Eh|ren|preis (Gewinn; *vgl.* [2]Preis); [2]Eh|ren|preis, das *od.* der; -es, - (eine Heilpflanze); Eh|ren-pro|mo|ti|on, ...rat, ...rech|te (*Plur.;* die bürgerlichen -); eh|ren|reich; Eh|ren|ret|tung; eh|ren|rüh|rig; Eh|ren|run|de; Eh|ren|sa|che; das ist für mich eine -; Ehrensache! (*ugs. für* selbstverständlich!); Eh|ren-sa|lut, ...sal|ve; eh|ren|schän|de|risch (*geh.*); Eh|ren-schuld, ...sold, ...spa|lier, ...stra|fe, ...tag, ...tanz, ...ti|tel, ...tor (das; *Sport*); Eh|ren|traud (w. Vorn.); Eh|ren|tri|bü|ne; Eh|ren|trud (w. Vorn.); Eh|ren|ur|kun|de; eh|ren-voll, ...wert; Eh|ren|wort *Plur.* ...worte; eh|ren|wört|lich; Eh|ren|zei|chen; ehr|er|bie|tig (*geh.*); Ehr|er|bie|tig|keit, die; - (*geh.*); Ehr|er|bie|tung, die; -; Ehr|furcht; ein Ehrfurcht gebietendes Schauspiel; ehr|fürch|tig; ehr|furchts-los, ...voll; Ehr-ge|fühl (das; -[e]s), ...geiz; ehr|gei|zig; Ehr|geiz|ling (*abwertend*); ehr|lich; ein -er Makler (redlicher Vermittler) sein; ehr|li|cher|wei|se; Ehr|lich|keit, die; -; ehr|lie|bend; ehr|los; Ehr|lo|sig|keit, die; -; ehr|pus|se|lig (mit einem kleinlichen, spießigen Ehrbegriff); Ehr|pus|se|lig|keit, die; -; ehr|puss|lig usw. *vgl.* ehrpusselig usw.; ehr|sam (*geh. veraltend*); Ehr|sam|keit, die; - (*geh. veraltend*); Ehr|sucht, die; -; ehr|süch|tig; Eh|rung; ehr|ver|ges|sen; Ehr|ver|lust, der; -[e]s (*Rechtsspr.*); Ehr|wür|den (*kath. Kirche [veraltend]* Anrede für Brüder u. Schwestern in geistl. Orden u. Kongregationen); ehr|wür|dig; Ehr|wür|dig|keit, die; -

ei!; ei, ei!; ei machen (*Kinderspr.* streicheln, liebkosen)

Ei, das; -[e]s, -er

...ei (z. B. Bäckerei, die; -, -en)

eia!

Ei|ab|la|ge (*Zool.*)

ei|a|po|peia!, hei|a|po|peia!

Ei|be, die; -, -n (ein Nadelbaum); ei|ben (aus Eibenholz)

Ei|bisch, der; -[e]s, -e (eine Heilpflanze); Ei|bisch|tee, der; -s

Eib|see, der; -s

Eich (dt. Lyriker u. Hörspielautor)

Eich|amt

Eich|baum ([1]Eiche); [1]Ei|che, die; -, -n (ein Baum)

[2]Ei|che, die; -, -n (Eichung; *fachspr.* ein Maischemaß)

Ei|chel, die; -, -n; Ei|chel|hä|her (ein Vogel); Ei|chel|mast, die; Ei|cheln *Plur., als Sing. gebraucht* (Farbe im dt. Kartenspiel); - sticht, - spielen; [1]ei|chen (aus Eichenholz)

[2]ei|chen (das gesetzl. Maß geben; prüfen)

Ei|chen, das; -s, - (kleines Ei)

Ei|chen|baum (*geh. für* [1]Eiche)

Ei|chen|dorff (dt. Dichter)

Ei|chen-hain, ...holz, ...klotz, ...kranz, ...laub, ...tisch, ...wick|ler (ein Schmetterling)

Ei|cher (Eichmeister); Eich|ge|wicht

Eich-hörn|chen, *landsch.* ...kätz|chen *od.* ...kat|ze

Eich-maß (das), ...meis|ter (Beamter beim Eichamt), ...me|ter (das)

Eichs|feld, das; -[e]s (dt. Landschaft); Eichs|fel|der (↑R 103); eichs|fel|disch

Eich|stätt (Stadt am Rand der Fränkischen Alb)

Eich-stem|pel, ...strich; Ei|chung

Eid, der; -[e]s, -e; an Eides statt [erklären]

Ei|dam, der; -[e]s, -e (*veraltet für* Schwiegersohn)

Eid|bruch, der; eid|brü|chig

Ei|dechs|chen; Ei|dech|se, die; -, -n; Ei|dech|sen|le|der, Ei|dechs|le|der

Ei|der, die; - (ein Fluss)

Ei|der|dau|ne ‹isländ.; dt.›; Ei|der-en|te, ...gans

Ei|der|stedt (Halbinsel an der Nordseeküste); Ei|der|sted|ter (↑R 103)

Ei|des-be|leh|rung, ...for|mel; Ei|des|hel|fer, *auch* Eid|hel|fer; Ei|des|leis|tung; ei|des|statt|lich (an Eides statt); -e Versicherung

Ei|de|tik, die; - ‹griech.› (*Psych.* Fähigkeit, früher Geschehenes od. Vorgestelltes anschaulich zu vergegenwärtigen); Ei|de|ti|ker; ei|de|tisch

eidg. = eidgenössisch; Eid|ge|nos|se; Eid|ge|nos|sen|schaft, die; -; Schweizerische Eidgenossenschaft (amtl. Name der Schweiz); eid|ge|nös|sisch (*Abk.* eidg.), *aber* (↑R 108): Eidgenössische Technische Hochschule (*Abk.* ETH); Eid|hel|fer *vgl.* Eideshelfer; eid|lich; eine -e Erklärung

Ei|dot|ter (das Gelbe im Ei); Ei|er-be|cher, ...bri|kett; Ei|er|chen *Plur.;* Ei|er-frau (*ugs.*), ...hand|gra|na|te, ...kopf (*für* Egghead), ...korb, ...ku|chen, ...lau|fen (das; -s), ...li|kör, ...löf|fel, ...mann (*ugs.*); ei|ern (*ugs. für* ungleichmäßig rotieren; wackelnd gehen); das Rad eiert; Ei|er|pe|cken, das; -s (*österr.* ein Osterbrauch); Ei|er-pfann|ku|chen, ...punsch, ...scha|le (*auch, bes. fachspr.* Eischale), ...sche|cke (die; *landsch. für* eine Kuchensorte), ...schnee (*vgl.* Eischnee), ...schwamm (*landsch. für* Pfifferling); Ei|er|speis, die *od.* ...spei|se (Gericht, für das bes. Eier verwendet werden; *österr. für* Rührei); Ei|er-stich (Suppeneinlage aus Ei), ...stock (*Plur.* ...stöcke; *Med.*), ...tanz (*ugs.*), ...uhr, ...wär|mer

Ei|fel, die; - (Teil des westl. Rhein. Schiefergebirges); Ei|fe|ler, Eif|ler (↑R 103)

Ei|fer, der; -s; Ei|fe|rer; ei|fern; ich ...ere (↑R 16); Ei|fer|sucht, die; -, ...süchte *Plur. selten;* Ei|fer|süch|te|lei; ei|fer|süch|tig; Ei|fer|suchts|sze|ne

Eif|fel|turm (in Paris); (↑R 95)

Eif|ler *vgl.* Eifeler

ei|för|mig

eif|rig

Ei|gelb, das; -s, -e (Dotter); 3 - (↑R 90)

ei|gen; eig[e]ne; mein eigen Kind (*geh.*), mein eig[e]ner Sohn; das ist ihr eigen (für sie charakteristisch); eigene Aktien (*Wirtsch.*); etwas Eigenes besitzen; *vgl.* Eigen; Ei|gen, das; -s; mein Eigen (*geh. für* Besitz); etwas sein Eigen nennen; sich etwas zu Eigen machen (aneignen); Ei|gen|art; ei|gen|ar|tig; Ei|gen-ar|tig|keit, ...bau (der; -[e]s), ...be|darf, ...be|richt, ...be|sitz (*BGB*), ...be|sit|zer (*BGB*), ...be|we|gung; Ei|gen|brö|te|lei; Ei|gen|bröt|ler (Sonderling); Ei|gen|bröt|le|rei (*svw.* Eigenbrötelei); ei|gen|bröt|le|risch; Ei|gen|dün|kel (*geh.*); Ei|ge|ne, Eig|ne, das; -n (Eigentum; Eigenart); -s und Fremdes; Ei|gen-fi|nan|zie|rung, ...ge|schwin|dig|keit; ei|gen|ge|setz|lich; Ei|gen-ge|setz|lich|keit, ...ge|wicht; ei|gen|hän|dig (*Abk. österr.* e. h.); Ei|gen|hän|dig|keit, die; -; Ei|gen-heim, ...hei|mer (*ugs.*); Ei|gen|heit; Ei|gen-hil|fe, ...ini|ti|a|ti|ve (↑R 132), ...ka|pi|tal, ...kir|che (*im MA.*), ...le|ben, ...leis|tung, ...lie|be, ...lob; ei|gen|mäch|tig;

ei|gen|mäch|ti|ger|wei|se; Ei|gen‿mäch|tig|keit, ...mar|ke *(Wirtsch.),* **...mit|tel** *(Plur.),* **...na|me, ...nutz** (der; -es); **ei|gen|nüt|zig; Ei|gen|nüt|zig|keit,** die; -; **Ei|gen|pro|duk|ti|on; ei|gens** *(geh.);* **Ei|gen|schaft; Ei|gen|schafts|wort** *Plur.* ...wörter (*für* Adjektiv); **ei|gen|schafts|wört|lich; Ei|gen‿schwin|gung, ...sinn** (der; -[e]s); **ei|gen|sin|nig; Ei|gen|sin|nig|keit; ei|gen|staat|lich; Ei|gen|staat|lich|keit,** die; -; **ei|gen|stän|dig; Ei|gen|stän|dig|keit,** die; -; **Ei|gen|sucht,** die; -; **ei|gen|süch|tig; ei|gent|lich** (*Abk.* eigtl.); **Ei|gent|lich|keit,** die; -; **Ei|gen|tor,** das *(Sport)*

Ei|gen|tum, das; -s, *Plur.* (*für* Wohnungseigentum u. Ä.:) ...tume; **Ei|gen|tü|mer; Ei|gen|tü|me|rin; ei|gen|tüm|lich; Ei|gen|tüm|lich|keit; Ei|gen|tums‿bil|dung, ...de|likt, ...recht, ...streu|ung, ...ver|ge|hen, ...woh|nung**

ei|gen|ver|ant|wort|lich; Ei|gen‿ver|brauch, ...ver|si|che|rung, ...wär|me, ...wech|sel (*für* Solawechsel), **...wer|bung, ...wert** (der; -[e]s); **ei|gen|wer|tig; Ei|gen|wil|le; ei|gen|wil|lig; Ei|gen|wil|lig|keit; ei|gen|wüch|sig** *(selten)*

Ei|ger, der; -s (Bergstock in den Berner Alpen); **Ei|ger|nord|wand,** die; -

Eig|ne *vgl.* Eigene; **eig|nen;** etwas eignet ihm (*geh. für* ist ihm eigen); sich eignen (geeignet sein); **eig|ner, ei|ge|ner** *vgl.* eigen; **Eig|ner** ([Schiffs]eigentümer); **Eig|nung** (Befähigung); **Eig|nungs‿prü|fung, ...test**

eigtl. = eigentlich

...ei|ig (z. B. eineiig)

Ei|ke (m., *seltener* w. Vorn.)

Ei|klar, das; -s, - (*österr. für* Eiweiß)

Ei|ko (m. Vorn.)

Ei|land, das; -[e]s, -e (*geh. für* Insel)

Eil|an|ge|bot

Eil|bert (m. Vorn.)

Eil‿bo|te, ...brief; Ei|le, die; -

Ei|lei|ter, der *(Med.)*

ei|len; eile mit Weile!; **ei|lends; eil|fer|tig; Eil|fer|tig|keit; Eil|gut; Eil|gü|ter|zug**

Eil|hard (m. Vorn.)

ei|lig; (↑R 47:) etwas Eiliges zu besorgen haben; nichts Eiligeres (Wichtigeres) zu tun haben, als ...; **ei|ligst; Eil‿marsch, ...päck|chen, ...schritt, ...sen|dung, ...tem|po, ...trieb|wa|gen, ...zug** (Zeichen E), **...zu|stel|lung**

Ei|mer, der; -s, -; im - sein (*ugs. für* entzwei, verdorben sein); **ei|mer|wei|se**

[1]**ein; I.** *Unbestimmter Artikel (nicht betont; als Beifügung zu einem Subst. od. Pronomen):* es war ein Mann, nicht eine Frau; es war ein Kind und kein Erwachsener. **II.** *Unbestimmtes Pronomen* **1.** *[allein stehend]:* wenn einer (jemand) das nicht versteht, dann soll er darüber nicht reden; da kann einer (*ugs. statt* man) doch völlig verrückt werden; nach den Aussagen eines (jemandes), der dabei war, ...; ein[e]s (etwas) fehlt ihm: Geduld; das tut einem (mir) wirklich Leid; sie sollen einen in Ruhe lassen; sie ist eine von uns, unsereiner; ein[e]s von uns Kindern; *ugs.:* einen (einen Schnaps) heben, eins (ein Lied) singen, gib ihm eins (einen Schlag), jmdm. eins auswischen. **2.** *in [hinweisender] Gegenüberstellung:* vom einen, von einem (von diesem) zum and[e]ren, andern (zu jenem); die einen (diese) [Zuschauer] klatschten, die and[e]ren, andern (jene) [Zuschauer] pfiffen. **III.** *Zahlwort (betont; als Beifügung oder allein stehend):* es war ein Mann, eine Frau, ein Kind (nicht zwei); wenn [nur] einer das erfährt, dann ist der Plan zunichte; einer für alle und alle für einen; der eine, *aber* (↑R 48): der Eine (*Bez. für* Gott); ein[e]s der beiden Pferde, nicht beide; zwei Augen sehen mehr als ein[e]s; in einem fort; unter einem (*österr. für* zugleich); zwei Pfund Wurst in einem [Stück]; in ein[em] und einem halben Jahr; in ein[er] und derselben Straße; ein und dieselbe Sache; es läuft alles auf eins (ein und dasselbe) hinaus; sie ist sein Ein und [sein] Alles; einundzwanzig; einmal; einhalbmal; ein für alle Mal[e]; ein oder mehrmals (*vgl.* Mal); ein bis zwei Tage; *vgl.* eins

[2]**ein;** *Adverb:* nicht ein noch aus wissen (ratlos sein); wer bei dir ein und aus geht (verkehrt), *aber* (*in Zus.;* ↑R 23): ein- und aussteigen (einsteigen und aussteigen);

ein... (*in Zus. mit Verben,* z. B. einbürgern, du bürgerst ein, eingebürgert, einzubürgern)

Ein|achs|an|hän|ger *(Kfz-W.);* **ein|ach|sig**

Ein|ak|ter (Bühnenstück aus nur einem Akt); **ein|ak|tig**

ei|nan|der (↑R 132; *meist geh.*); *vgl.* an-, auf-, aus-, beieinander usw.

ein|ant|wor|ten (*österr. Amtsspr. veraltend für* übergeben); **Ein|ant|wor|tung** *(österr.)*

Ei|nar (m. Vorn.)

ein|ar|bei|ten; Ein|ar|bei|tung

ein|ar|mig

ein|äschern (↑R 132); ich äschere ein (↑R 16); eingeäschert (*Zeichen* ▯); **Ein|äsche|rung; Ein|äsche|rungs|hal|le** (*für* Krematorium)

ein|at|men; Ein|at|mung, die; -

ein|ato|mig (↑R 132; *Chemie, Physik*)

ein|ät|zen

ein|äu|gig; Ein|äu|gi|ge, der *u.* die; -n, -n (↑R 5 ff.)

Ein|back, der; -[e]s, *Plur.* -e *u.* ...bäcke, *ugs. auch* -s (ein Gebäck)

ein|bah|nig; -er Verkehr; **Ein|bahn‿stra|ße, ...ver|kehr**

ein|bal|lie|ren (*veraltet für* in Ballen verpacken); **Ein|bal|lie|rung**

ein|bal|sa|mie|ren; Ein|bal|sa|mie|rung

Ein|band, der; -[e]s, ...bände; **Ein|band|de|cke**

ein|bän|dig

ein|ba|sig, *auch* **ein|ba|sisch** *(Chemie);* -e Säure

Ein|bau, der; -[e]s, *Plur.* (*für* eingebauter Teil:) -ten; **ein|bau|en; ein|bau|fer|tig; Ein|bau|kü|che**

Ein|baum (Boot aus einem ausgehöhlten Baumstamm)

Ein|bau|mö|bel; ein|bau|reif; Ein|bau‿schrank, ...teil (das)

Ein|bee|re (eine Giftpflanze)

ein|be|grif|fen, in|be|grif|fen (*österr. u. schweiz. nur so);* in dem *od.* den Preis [mit] einbegriffen; alle waren beteiligt, er einbegriffen; sie erinnerte sich aller Beteiligten, ihn einbegriffen; der Tadel galt allen, ihn einbegriffen; er zahlte die Zeche, den Wein einbegriffen

ein|be|hal|ten; Ein|be|hal|tung

ein|bei|nig

ein|be|ken|nen (*österr. für* eingestehen); **Ein|be|kennt|nis**

ein|be|rech|nen (*selten für* einkalkulieren)

ein|be|ru|fen; Ein|be|ru|fe|ne, der *u.* die; -n, -n (↑R 5 ff.); **Ein|be|ru|fung; Ein|be|ru|fungs|be|fehl**

ein|be|schlie|ßen *(geh.)*

ein|be|schrie|ben *(Math.);* -er Kreis (Inkreis)

ein|be|stel|len (*Amtsspr.* an einen bestimmten Ort bestellen)

ein|be|to|nie|ren; Ein|be|to|nie|rung

ein|bet|ten; Ein|bet|tung

ein|beu|len

ein|be|zie|hen; Ein|be|zie|hung; unter - von ...

ein|bie|gen; Ein|bie|gung

ein|bil|den, sich; du bildest dir die Geschichte nur ein; **Ein|bil|dung; Ein|bil|dungs|kraft,** die; -
ein|bim|sen (*ugs. für* durch angestrengtes Lernen einprägen)
ein|bin|den; Ein|bin|dung
ein|bla|sen; Ein|blä|ser (*Schülerspr. auch für* Vorsager)
Ein|blatt *(Kunstw.);* **Ein|blatt-druck** *Plur.* ...drucke
ein|bläu|en (blau machen; *auch ugs. für* mit Nachdruck einprägen, einschärfen)
ein|blen|den; sich - *(Rundf., Fernsehen);* **Ein|blen|dung**
ein|bleu|en *frühere Schreibung für die umgangssprachliche Bedeutung von* einbläuen *(vgl. d.)*
Ein|blick
ein|boh|ren; sich -
ein|boo|ten *(Seew.);* Passagiere -
ein|bre|chen; in ein[em] Haus -; **Ein|bre|cher**
Ein|brenn, die; -, -en *(österr.) u.* **Ein|bren|ne,** die; -, -n (*bes. südd. für* Mehlschwitze); **ein|bren|nen; Ein|brenn|la|ckie|rung; Ein-brenn|sup|pe** *(österr.)*
ein|brin|gen; sich -; **ein|bring-lich; Ein|brin|gung**
ein|bro|cken; sich, jmdm. etwas - *(ugs.)*
Ein|bruch, der; -[e]s, ...brüche; **Ein|bruch[s]|dieb|stahl; ein-bruch[s]|si|cher; Ein|bruch-stel|le; Ein|bruch[s]|werk|zeug**
ein|buch|ten (*ugs. für* ins Gefängnis sperren); **Ein|buch|tung**
ein|bud|deln *(ugs.)*
ein|bü|geln; eingebügelte Falten
ein|bun|kern (*ugs. auch für* ins Gefängnis sperren)
ein|bür|gern; Ein|bür|ge|rung
Ein|bu|ße; ein|bü|ßen
ein|che|cken [...tʃɛkən] ‹dt.; engl.› ([am Flughafen] abfertigen; sich abfertigen lassen)
ein|cre|men
ein|däm|men; Ein|däm|mung
ein|damp|fen; Ein|damp|fung
ein|de|cken; sich mit Obst -
Ein|de|cker (ein Flugzeugtyp)
ein|dei|chen; Ein|dei|chung
ein|del|len (*ugs. für* eine Delle in etwas machen)
ein|deu|tig; Ein|deu|tig|keit
ein|deut|schen; du deutschst ein; **Ein|deut|schung**
ein|di|cken
ein|di|men|si|o|nal
ein|do|cken (*Schiffbau* ins Dock transportieren)
ein|do|sen (in Dosen einkochen); du dost ein; sie dos|te ein
ein|dö|sen (*ugs. für* in Halbschlaf fallen; einschlafen)
ein|drän|gen; auf jmdn. -; sich -
ein|dre|hen; sich die Haare -
ein|dre|schen; er hat auf das Pferd eingedroschen
ein|dril|len (*ugs. für* einüben)
ein|drin|gen; ein|dring|lich; auf das, aufs Eindringlichste *od.* auf das, aufs eindringlichste (↑R 47); **Ein|dring|lich|keit,** die; -; **Ein-dring|ling**
Ein|druck, der; -[e]s, ...drücke; **ein|dru|cken; ein|drü|cken; ein-drück|lich** (*bes. schweiz. für* eindrucksvoll); **ein|drucks|voll**
ein|dü|beln (mit einem Dübel befestigen)
ein|du|seln (*ugs. für* in Halbschlaf fallen)
ei|ne; I. *Unbestimmter Artikel: vgl.* [1]ein, I. **II.** *Unbestimmtes Pronomen: vgl.* [1]ein, II. **III.** *Zahlwort: vgl.* [1]ein, III.
ein|eb|nen; Ein|eb|nung
Ein|ehe (↑R 132; *für* Monogamie); **ein|ehig** (*für* monogam)
ein|ei|ig; -e Zwillinge
ein|ein|deu|tig (*fachspr. für* umkehrbar eindeutig); **Ein|ein|deu-tig|keit** *Plur. selten*
ein|ein|halb, ein|und|ein|halb; eineinhalb Tage, *aber* ein und ein halber Tag; ein[und]einhalbmal so viel
Ei|nem, von (österr. Komponist)
ei|nen (*geh. für* einigen)
ein|en|gen; Ein|en|gung
ei|ner; I. *Unbestimmtes Pronomen: vgl.* [1]ein, II. **II.** *Zahlwort: vgl.* [1]ein, III.; **[1]Ei|ner, Ein|ser** (Zahl); **[2]Ei|ner** (einsitziges Sportboot); **Ei|ner|ka|jak; ei|ner|lei; Ei|ner-lei,** das; -s; **ei|ner|seits;** einerseits ... ander[er]seits, andrerseits; **ei|nes; I.** *Unbestimmter Artikel (Gen.): vgl.* [1]ein, I. **II.** *Unbestimmtes Pronomen: vgl.* [1]ein, II. **III.** *Zahlwort: vgl.* [1]ein, III.; **ei|nes-teils;** einesteils ... ander[e]nteils
ein|exer|zie|ren (↑R 132)
ein|fach; einfache Buchführung; einfache Fahrt; am einfachsten; *aber* das Einfachste ist, wenn ...; das Einfachste, was er finden konnte; [sich] etwas Einfaches [wünschen]; **Ein|fa|che,** das; -n (↑R 5 ff.); das - einer Zahl
ein|fä|chern (in Fächer verteilen)
Ein|fach|heit, die; -; der - halber; **ein|fach|heits|hal|ber**
ein|fä|deln; sich - *(Verkehrsw.);* **Ein|fä|de|lung, Ein|fäd|lung**
ein|fah|ren; Ein|fahr‿gleis, ...sig-nal *(Eisenb.);* **Ein|fahrt; Ein-fahrt[s]‿er|laub|nis, ...gleis** (*vgl.* Einfahrgleis), **...sig|nal** (*vgl.* Einfahrsignal)
Ein|fall, der; **ein|fal|len; ein|falls-los; Ein|falls|lo|sig|keit,** die; -;
ein|fall[s]|reich; Ein|fall[s]-‿reich|tum, ...win|kel
Ein|falt, die; -; **ein|fäl|tig; Ein|fäl-tig|keit,** die; -; **Ein|falts|pin|sel** *(abwertend)*
ein|fal|zen *(Buchw.);* **Ein|fal|zung**
Ein|fa|mi|li|en|haus
ein|fan|gen
ein|fär|ben; ein|far|big, *österr.* **ein|fär|big; Ein|fär|bung**
ein|fa|schen (*österr. für* verbinden; *vgl.* Fasche)
ein|fas|sen; Ein|fas|sung
ein|fen|zen ‹dt.; engl.› (einzäunen); du fenzt ein
ein|fet|ten; Ein|fet|tung
ein|filt|rie|ren (*ugs. für* einflößen)
ein|fin|den, sich
ein|flech|ten; Ein|flech|tung
ein|fli|cken
ein|flie|gen; Ein|flie|ger *(Flugw.)*
ein|flie|ßen
ein|flö|ßen; Ein|flö|ßung
Ein|flug
ein|flü|ge|lig, ein|flüg|lig
Ein|flug|schnei|se *(Flugw.)*
Ein|fluss; Ein|fluss|be|reich, der; **Ein|fluss|nah|me,** die; -, -n *Plur. selten;* **ein|fluss|reich**
ein|flüs|tern; Ein|flüs|te|rung
ein|for|dern; Ein|for|de|rung
ein|för|mig; Ein|för|mig|keit
Ein|fran|ken|stück (*mit Ziffer* 1-Franken-Stück; ↑R 28); **Ein-fränk|ler,** der; -s, - (*schweiz. svw.* Einfrankenstück)
ein|fres|sen, sich; der Rost hatte sich tief eingefressen
ein|frie|den, *seltener* **ein|frie|di-gen** (*geh. für* einhegen); **Ein|frie-di|gung,** *häufiger* **Ein|frie|dung**
ein|frie|ren; Ein|frie|rung
ein|fros|ten; Ein|fros|tung
ein|fuch|sen (*ugs. für* gut einarbeiten)
ein|fü|gen; sich -; **Ein|fü|gung**
ein|füh|len, sich; **ein|fühl|sam; Ein|füh|lung,** die; -; **Ein|füh-lungs‿ga|be** (die; -), **...ver|mö-gen** (das; -s)
Ein|fuhr, die; -, -en; **Ein|fuhr|be-schrän|kung; ein|füh|ren; Ein-fuhr‿ha|fen** (*vgl.* [1]Hafen), **...kon-tin|gent, ...land, ...sper|re; Ein-füh|rung; Ein|füh|rungs‿kurs, ...preis** (*vgl.* [2]Preis), **...vor|trag; Ein|fuhr‿ver|bot, ...zoll**
ein|fül|len; Ein|füll|öff|nung
[1]ein|füt|tern (*EDV* in den Computer eingeben)
[2]ein|füt|tern (*Gartenbau* [Pflanzen] tief eingraben)
Ein|ga|be *(auch EDV);* **Ein|ga|be-ge|rät** *(EDV)*
Ein|gang; Ein- und Ausgang (↑R 23); **ein|gän|gig; Ein|gän-gig|keit,** die; -; **ein|gangs**

(*Amtsspr.;* ↑R 46); *Präp. mit Gen.:* eingangs des Briefes; **Ein|gangs-buch, ...da|tum, ...hal|le, ...stem|pel, ...stro|phe, ...tür, ...ver|merk**
ein|ge|äschert (↑R 132; *Zeichen* ◻)
ein|ge|ben
ein|ge|bet|tet; - in die *od.* in der Landschaft
ein|ge|bil|det; - sein
Ein|ge|bin|de (*veraltet für* Patengeschenk)
[1]**ein|ge|bo|ren;** der eingeborene (einzige) Sohn [Gottes]
[2]**ein|ge|bo|ren;** die -e Bevölkerung; **Ein|ge|bo|re|ne,** Ein|ge-bor|ne, der *u.* die; -n, -n (↑R 5 ff.); **Ein|ge|bo|re|nen|spra|che; Ein-ge|bor|ne** *vgl.* Eingeborene
ein|ge|bracht; -es Gut, -e Sachen *(Rechtsspr.);* **Ein|ge|brach|te,** das; -n; ↑R 5 ff. (*veraltet für* Heiratsgut)
Ein|ge|bung
ein|ge|denk *(geh.); mit Gen.:* - des Verdienstes
ein|ge|fal|len; mit -em Gesicht
ein|ge|fleischt; -er Junggeselle
ein|ge|frie|ren
ein|ge|fuchst (*ugs. für* eingearbeitet)
ein|ge|hen; ein|ge|hend; auf das, aufs Eingehendste *od.* auf das, aufs eingehendste (↑R 47)
ein|ge|keilt; in eine[r] Menge -
Ein|ge|mach|te, das; -n (↑R 5 ff.)
ein|ge|mein|den; Ein|ge|mein-dung
ein|ge|nom|men (begeistert); er ist von dem Plan sehr -; **Ein|ge-nom|men|heit,** die; -
ein|ge|rech|net; den Überschuss -
Ein|ge|rich|te, das; -s, - (*fachspr.* innerer Bau eines Türschlosses)
ein|ge|sandt; Ein|ge|sandt, das; -s, -s (*veraltet für* Leserzuschrift)
ein|ge|schlech|tig (*für* diklin)
ein|ge|schlos|sen; - im, *auch* in den Preis
ein|ge|schos|sig (*vgl.* ...geschossig)
ein|ge|schwo|ren; sie ist auf diese Musik -
ein|ge|ses|sen (einheimisch)
Ein|ge|sot|te|ne, das; -n; ↑R 5 ff. (*österr. für* eingemachte Früchte)
ein|ge|spielt; sie sind aufeinander -
ein|ge|sprengt; -es Gold
ein|ge|stan|de|ner|ma|ßen, ein-ge|stand|ner|ma|ßen; Ein|ge-ständ|nis; ein|ge|ste|hen
ein|ge|stri|chen *(Musik);* -e Note
ein|ge|tra|gen; eingetragene Genossenschaft (*Abk.* eG, e. G.), *auch* (↑R 108:) Eingetragene Genossenschaft (*Abk.* EG); eingetragener Verein (*Abk.* e. V.), *auch* (↑R 108:) Eingetragener Verein (*Abk.* E. V.)
Ein|ge|tropf|te, das; -n; ↑R 5 ff. (*österr. für* als Einlage in die Suppe getropfter Teig)
Ein|ge|wei|de, das; -s, - *meist Plur.;* **Ein|ge|wei|de|bruch**
Ein|ge|weih|te, der *u.* die; -n, -n (↑R 5 ff.)
ein|ge|wöh|nen; sich -; **Ein|ge-wöh|nung,** die; -
ein|ge|zo|gen; - (zurückgezogen) leben; **Ein|ge|zo|gen|heit,** die; -
ein|gie|ßen; Ein|gie|ßung
ein|gip|sen; einen Haken -
ein|git|tern
Ein|glas *Plur.* ...gläser (*veraltet für* Monokel)
ein|gla|sen
ein|glei|sen (wieder auf das Gleis bringen); du gleist ein; er gleis|te ein
ein|glei|sig
ein|glie|dern; sich -; **Ein|glie|de-rung**
ein|gra|ben; Ein|gra|bung
ein|gra|vie|ren [...v...]
ein|grei|fen; Ein|greif|trup|pe (Sondereinsatztruppe in militärischen Krisengebieten)
ein|gren|zen; Ein|gren|zung
Ein|griff; Ein|griffs|mög|lich|keit
ein|grü|nen; Ein|grü|nung
ein|grup|pie|ren; Ein|grup|pie-rung
Ein|guss ⟨*zu* eingießen⟩ *(Technik)*
ein|ha|cken; der Sperber hackte auf die Beute ein
ein|ha|ken; den Riemen -; sich bei jmdm. -; er hakte hier ein (*ugs. für* unterbrach das Gespräch)
ein|halb|mal; - so teuer
Ein|halt, der; -[e]s; - gebieten, tun; **ein|hal|ten; Ein|hal|tung**
ein|häm|mern
ein|han|deln
ein|hän|dig
ein|hän|di|gen; Ein|hän|di|gung, die; -
Ein|hand|seg|ler (jmd., der ein Segelboot allein führt)
ein|hän|gen; *vgl.* [2]hängen; **Ein-hän|ge|öse** (↑R 132)
Ein|hard (m. Vorn.)
ein|har|ken (*nordd. für* [Samen, Dünger] mit der Harke unter das Erdreich mischen)
ein|hau|chen *(geh.);* **Ein|hau-chung**
ein|hau|en; er hieb auf den Fliehenden ein; er haute tüchtig ein (*ugs. für* aß tüchtig)
ein|häu|sig (*Bot.* monözisch)
ein|he|ben; einen Betrag - (*bes. südd. für* einziehen); **Ein|he|bung**
ein|hef|ten
ein|he|gen; Ein|he|gung
ein|hei|len *(Med.);* **Ein|hei|lung**
ein|hei|misch; Ein|hei|mi|sche, der *u.* die; -n, -n (↑R 5 ff.)
ein|heim|sen *(ugs.);* du heimst ein
Ein|hei|rat; ein|hei|ra|ten
Ein|heit; Tag der Deutschen - (3. Oktober); **Ein|hei|ten|sys-tem;** das Internationale - (↑R 108); *vgl. auch* SI; **ein|heit-lich; Ein|heit|lich|keit,** die; -; **Ein|heits‿front** (die; -), **...ge-werk|schaft, ...kurz|schrift** (die; -), **...lis|te, ...look, ...par|tei, ...preis** (*vgl.* [2]Preis), **...wert**
ein|hei|zen
ein|hel|fen (vorsagen); jmdm. -
ein|hel|lig; Ein|hel|lig|keit, die; -
ein|hen|ke|lig, ein|henk|lig
ein|hen|keln; ich henk[e]le ein (↑R 16); **ein|henk|lig** *vgl.* einhenkelig
ein|her...; ein|her‿fah|ren, ...ge-hen (er ist einhergefahren, einhergegangen)
Ein|he|ri|er [...i̯ər], der; -s, - (*nord. Mythol.* der gefallene Kämpfer in Walhall)
ein|her|schrei|ten *(geh.)*
ein|hie|ven [...f..., *auch* ...v...]; die Ankerkette - (einziehen)
ein|hö|cke|rig, ein|höck|rig
ein|ho|len; Ein|hol‿netz, ...ta-sche; Ein|ho|lung, die; -
ein|hö|ren, sich
Ein|horn *Plur.* ...hörner (ein Fabeltier)
Ein|hu|fer *(Zool.);* **ein|hu|fig**
ein|hül|len; Ein|hül|lung
ein|hun|dert
ein|hü|ten (*nordd. für* sich in jmds. Abwesenheit um die Wohnung kümmern)
ei|nig; [sich] einig sein, werden; einig gehen (*Kaufmannsspr.* übereinstimmen, *dafür besser* einig sein); **ei|ni|ge;** einige Stunden später; einige Mal, einige Male; einige tausend *od.* Tausend Schüler; von einigen wird behauptet ...; einiges, was; einige (etwas; *oft auch* [sehr] viel) Mühe haben; sie wusste einiges (↑R 48); einiger politischer Sinn; einiges milde (*selten* mildes) Nachsehen; bei einigem guten Willen; einige gute Menschen; die Taten einiger guter (*selten* guten) Menschen; mit einigem Neuen
ein|igeln (↑R 132), sich; ich ig[e]le mich ein (↑R 16); **Ein|ige|lung**
ei|ni|ge Mal *vgl.* einige
ei|ni|gen; Ei|ni|ger; ei|ni|ger|ma-ßen; ei|ni|ges *vgl.* einige; **ei|nig ge|hen** *vgl.* einig; **Ei|nig|keit,** die; -; **Ei|ni|gung; Ei|ni|gungs‿be-**

stre|bung *(meist Plur.),* **...ver|trag, ...werk**

ein|imp|fen; Ein|imp|fung

ein|ja|gen; jmdm. einen Schrecken -

ein|jäh|rig; [1]**Ein|jäh|ri|ge,** der *od.* die; -n, -n (↑R 5 ff.); [2]**Ein|jäh|ri|ge,** das; -n *(veraltend für* mittlere Reife); **Ein|jäh|rig-Frei|wil|li|ge,** der; -n, -n; ↑R 5 ff. (im ehem. deutschen Heer)

ein|jo|chen *(veraltet)*

ein|ka|cheln *(ugs. für* stark heizen)

ein|kal|ku|lie|ren (einplanen)

Ein|kam|mer|sys|tem, das; -s

ein|kamp|fern (mit Kampfer behandeln); ich kampfere ein (↑R 16)

ein|kap|seln; ich kaps[e]le ein (↑R 16); sich -; **Ein|kap|se|lung, Ein|kaps|lung**

Ein|ka|rä|ter (einkarätiger Edelstein); **ein|ka|rä|tig**

ein|kas|sie|ren; Ein|kas|sie|rung

Ein|kauf; ein|kau|fen; Ein|käu|fer; Ein|käu|fe|rin; Ein|kaufs‿ab|tei|lung, ...beu|tel, ...bum|mel, ...cen|ter, ...ge|nos|sen|schaft, ...korb, ...mög|lich|keit, ...netz, ...preis *(vgl.* [2]Preis), **...quel|le, ...ta|sche, ...wa|gen, ...zent|rum**

Ein|kehr, die; - (das Einkehren; *geh. für* innere Sammlung); **ein|keh|ren**

ein|kei|len *meist im Partizip II;* wir waren rundherum eingekeilt

ein|keim|blät|te|rig, ein|keim|blätt|rig *(Bot.);* -e Pflanzen (mit nur einem Keimblatt)

ein|kel|lern; ich kell[e]re ein (↑R 16); **Ein|kel|le|rung; Ein|kel|le|rungs|kar|tof|feln** *Plur.*

ein|ker|ben; Ein|ker|bung

ein|ker|kern *(geh.);* ich kerk[e]re ein (↑R 16); **Ein|ker|ke|rung** *(geh.)*

ein|kes|seln; ich kess[e]le ein (↑R 16); **Ein|kes|se|lung** *(bes. Milit.)*

ein|kip|pen *(ugs. für* eingießen)

ein|kla|gen; einen Rechnungsbetrag -; **Ein|kla|gung**

ein|klam|mern; Ein|klam|me|rung

Ein|klang; mit etwas im *od.* in - stehen

Ein|klas|sen|schu|le; ein|klas|sig; eine -e Schule

ein|kle|ben

ein|klei|den; sich -; **Ein|klei|dung**

ein|klem|men; du hast dir die Finger eingeklemmt; **Ein|klem|mung**

ein|klin|ken

ein|kni|cken; Ein|kni|ckung

ein|knöp|fen; Ein|knöpf|fut|ter; *vgl.* [2]Futter

ein|knüp|peln; auf jmdn. -

ein|ko|chen; Ein|koch|topf

ein|kom|men; um Urlaub, Versetzung - *(Amtsspr.* bitten); **Ein|kom|men,** das; -s, -; **Ein|kom|mens|gren|ze; ein|kom|mens‿los, ...schwach, ...stark; Ein|kom|mens|steu|er,** *fachspr. auch* **Ein|kom|men|steu|er,** die (↑R 34); **Ein|kom|men|steu|er|er|klä|rung; ein|kom|men|steu|er|pflich|tig; Ein|kom|mens‿ver|hält|nis|se** *(Plur.),* **...zu|wachs**

ein|köp|fen *(Fußball* durch einen Kopfball ein Tor erzielen)

Ein|korn, das; -[e]s (Weizenart)

ein|kra|chen *(ugs.)*

ein|krei|sen; Ein|krei|sung; Ein|krei|sungs|po|li|tik, die; -

ein|kre|men *vgl.* eincremen

ein|kreu|zen *(Biol.* durch Kreuzung verändern); **Ein|kreu|zung**

ein|krie|gen *(ugs. für* einholen)

Ein|kris|tall, der *(fachspr. für* einheitlich aufgebauter Kristall)

ein|küh|len (in einer Kühlanlage haltbar machen); **Ein|küh|lung**

Ein|künf|te *Plur.*

ein|kup|peln; langsam -

ein|ku|scheln; sich - *(ugs.)*

Ein|lad, der; -s *(schweiz. svw.* Verladung); [1]**ein|la|den;** Waren -; *vgl.* [1]laden

[2]**ein|la|den;** zum Essen -; *vgl.* [2]laden; **ein|la|dend; Ein|la|dung; Ein|la|dungs‿kar|te, ...schrei|ben**

Ein|la|ge

ein|la|gern; Ein|la|ge|rung

ein|lan|gen *(österr. für* eintreffen)

Ein|lass, der; -es, ...lässe; **ein|las|sen** *(südd. u. österr. auch für* mit Wachs einreiben; lackieren); sich auf etwas -; **Ein|lass|kar|te; ein|läss|lich** *(schweiz. für* gründlich); des Einlässlichsten (↑R 47); **Ein|las|sung** *(Rechtsspr.)*

Ein|lauf; ein|lau|fen; sich -; **Ein|lauf|wet|te** (beim Pferderennen)

ein|läu|ten; den Sonntag -

ein|le|ben, sich

Ein|le|ge|ar|beit; ein|le|gen; Ein|le|ger *(Bankw.);* **Ein|le|ge|rin** *(Bankw.);* **Ein|le|ge|soh|le; Ein|le|gung;** die; -

ein|lei|ten; Ein|lei|te|wort *Plur.* ...wörter *(Sprachw.);* **Ein|lei|tung; Ein|lei|tungs|ka|pi|tel**

ein|len|ken; Ein|len|kung *Plur. selten*

ein|ler|nen

ein|le|sen; sich -

ein|leuch|ten; dieser Grund leuchtet mir ein; **ein|leuch|tend**

Ein|lie|fe|rer; ein|lie|fern; Ein|lie|fe|rung; Ein|lie|fe|rungs‿schein, ...ter|min

ein|lie|gend *od., österr., schweiz. nur,* in|lie|gend *(Kaufmannsspr.);* - (anbei, hiermit) der Bericht; **Ein|lie|ger** (Mieter [bei einem Bauern]); **Ein|lie|ger|woh|nung**

ein|li|nig

ein|lo|chen *(ugs. für* ins Gefängnis sperren; *Golf* den Ball ins Loch spielen)

ein|lo|gie|ren [...ʒi:...]

ein|lös|bar; ein|lö|sen; Ein|lö|se|sum|me; Ein|lö|sung; Ein|lö|sungs|sum|me

ein|lul|len *(ugs.)*

Ein|mach, Ein|ma|che, die; - *(österr. für* Mehlschwitze); **ein|ma|chen; Ein|mach|glas** *Plur.* ...gläser

ein|mäh|dig *(svw.* einschürig; *vgl. d.)*

ein|mah|nen; Ein|mah|nung

ein|mal; auf einmal; noch einmal; nicht einmal; nun einmal; (↑R 23:) ein- bis zweimal *(mit Ziffern* 1- bis 2-mal); *vgl.* mal; **Ein|mal|eins,** das; -; das große -, das kleine -; **Ein|mal|hand|tuch; ein|ma|lig; Ein|ma|lig|keit,** die; -

Ein|mann‿be|trieb, ...ge|sell|schaft *(Wirtsch.* Kapitalgesellschaft, deren Anteile in einer Hand sind)

Ein|mark|stück *(mit Ziffer* 1-Mark-Stück; ↑R 28)

Ein|marsch, der; **ein|mar|schie|ren**

ein|mas|sie|ren

Ein|mas|ter; ein|mas|tig

ein|mau|ern; Ein|mau|e|rung

ein|mei|ßeln

ein|men|gen, sich

Ein|me|ter|brett *(mit Ziffer* 1-Meter-Brett; ↑R 28)

[1]**ein|mie|ten;** sich -; *vgl.* [1]mieten

[2]**ein|mie|ten;** Feldfrüchte -; *vgl.* [2]mieten

Ein|mie|ter *meist Plur. (Zool.* Insekt, das in Nestern anderer Tiere lebt); **Ein|mie|tung**

ein|mi|schen, sich; **Ein|mi|schung**

ein|mo|na|tig; ein -er (einen Monat dauernder) Lehrgang

ein|mon|tie|ren

ein|mo|to|rig; -es Flugzeug

ein|mot|ten

ein|mum|meln *od.* **ein|mum|men** *(ugs. für* warm einhüllen); sich -

ein|mün|den; Ein|mün|dung

ein|mü|tig; Ein|mü|tig|keit, die; -

ein|nach|ten *(schweiz. für* nachten)

ein|nä|hen

Ein|nah|me, die; -, -n; **Ein|nah-**

me⌣aus|fall, ...buch, ...quel|le, ...sei|te, ...soll; Ein|nahms|quel|le *(österr.)*
ein|näs|sen *(bes. Med., Psych.)*; das Kind nässt ein
ein|ne|beln; ich neb[e]le ein (↑R 16); **Ein|ne|be|lung; Ein|neb|lung**
ein|neh|men; ein|neh|mend; Ein|neh|mer *(veraltend)*
ein|ni|cken (*ugs.* [für kurze Zeit] einschlafen)
ein|nis|ten, sich; **Ein|nis|tung** (*für* Nidation)
ein|nor|den; eine Landkarte -
Ein|öde (↑R 132); **Ein|öd|hof**
ein|ölen (↑R 132); sich -
ein|ord|nen; sich links, rechts -; **Ein|ord|nung; Ein|ord|nungs|schwie|rig|kei|ten** *Plur.*
ein|pa|cken; Ein|pa|ckung
ein|par|ken
Ein|par|tei[en]⌣re|gie|rung, ...sys|tem
ein|pas|sen; Ein|pas|sung
ein|pau|ken *(ugs.)*; **Ein|pau|ker**
ein|peit|schen; Ein|peit|scher
ein|pen|deln, sich; **Ein|pend|ler** (Person, die an einem Ort arbeitet, aber nicht dort wohnt)
ein|pen|nen (*ugs. für* einschlafen)
Ein|per|so|nen⌣haus|halt, ...stück *(Theater)*
ein|pfar|ren (einer Pfarrei eingliedern); **Ein|pfar|rung**
Ein|pfen|nig|stück (*vgl.* Einmarkstück)
ein|pfer|chen; Ein|pfer|chung
ein|pflan|zen; Ein|pflan|zung
Ein|pha|sen|strom *(Elektrotechnik)*; **Ein|pha|sen-Wech|sel|strom|sys|tem** (↑R 24); **ein|pha|sig**
ein|pin|seln; Ein|pin|se|lung, Ein|pins|lung
ein|pla|nen; Ein|pla|nung
ein|pö|keln
ein|pol|dern; Ein|pol|de|rung (Eindeichung)
ein|po|lig *(Elektrotechnik)*
ein|prä|gen; sich -; **ein|präg|sam; Ein|präg|sam|keit**, die; -; **Ein|prä|gung**
ein|pras|seln; Fragen prasselten auf sie ein
ein|pres|sen
ein|pro|gram|mie|ren *(EDV)*
ein|pu|dern; du puderst dir das Gesicht ein
ein|pup|pen, sich *(Biol.)*
ein|quar|tie|ren; Ein|quar|tie|rung
ein|rah|men; ein Bild -; **Ein|rah|mung**
ein|ram|men; Pfähle -
ein|ran|gie|ren; Ein|ran|gie|rung
ein|ras|ten
ein|räu|men; jmdm. etwas -; **Ein|räu|mung; Ein|räu|mungs|satz** (*für* Konzessivsatz); **Ein|raum|woh|nung** (*regional für* Einzimmerwohnung)
ein|rech|nen; *vgl.* eingerechnet
Ein|re|de (*Rechtsspr.* Einwand, Einspruch); **ein|re|den**
ein|reg|nen; es hat sich eingeregnet
ein|re|gu|lie|ren; Ein|re|gu|lie|rung
ein|rei|ben; Ein|rei|bung
ein|rei|chen; Ein|rei|chung
ein|rei|hen; sich -; **Ein|rei|her** *(Textilwirtsch.)*; **ein|rei|hig**; -er Anzug; **Ein|rei|hung**
Ein|rei|se; Ein|rei|se⌣er|laub|nis, ...ge|neh|mi|gung; ein|rei|sen; nach Frankreich, in die Schweiz - (wohin?), *aber* er ist in Frankreich (wo?) eingereist; **Ein|rei|se⌣ver|wei|ge|rung, ...vi|sum**
ein|rei|ßen; Ein|reiß|ha|ken
ein|rei|ten
ein|ren|ken; Ein|ren|kung
ein|ren|nen
ein|re|xen (*österr. für* einwecken); du rext ein
ein|rich|ten; sich -; **Ein|rich|ter; Ein|rich|tung; Ein|rich|tungs⌣ge|gen|stand, ...haus, ...stück**
Ein|riss
ein|rit|zen; Ein|rit|zung
ein|rol|len
ein|ros|ten
ein|rü|cken; Ein|rü|ckung
ein|rüh|ren; sich, jmdm. etwas - (*ugs. auch für* Unannehmlichkeiten bereiten)
ein|rüs|ten; ein Haus - (mit einem Gerüst versehen)
eins; I. *Zahlwort* (Zahl 1): eins u. zwei macht, ist (*nicht* machen, sind) drei; er war eins, zwei, drei damit fertig; es ist, schlägt eins (ein Uhr); ein Viertel auf, vor eins; halb eins; gegen eins; das ist eins a [Ia] (*ugs. für* ausgezeichnet); Nummer, Abschnitt, Punkt, Absatz eins; im Jahr[e] eins; *vgl.* drei *u.* [1]ein, III. **II.** (*für* einig, gleich, dasselbe:) eins (einig) sein, werden; in eins setzen (gleichsetzen); es ist mir alles eins (gleichgültig). **III.** *Unbestimmtes Pronomen:* ein[e]s *vgl.* [1]ein, II; **Eins**, die; -, -en; sie hat die Prüfung mit der Note „Eins" bestanden; er würfelt drei Einsen; er hat in Latein eine Eins geschrieben; *vgl.* [1]Acht
Ein|saat *(Landw.)*
ein|sa|cken
ein|sä|en
ein|sa|gen (*landsch. für* vorsagen); **Ein|sa|ger**
ein|sal|ben
ein|sal|zen; eingesalzen, *seltener* eingesalzt; **Ein|sal|zung**
ein|sam; Ein|sam|keit, die; -, -en *Plur. selten;* **Ein|sam|keits|ge|fühl**
ein|sam|meln; Ein|sam|me|lung, Ein|samm|lung *Plur. selten*
ein|sar|gen; Ein|sar|gung
Ein|sat|te|lung, Ein|satt|lung (sattelförmige Vertiefung)
Ein|satz, der; -es, Einsätze; **Ein|satz|be|fehl; ein|satz|be|reit; Ein|satz⌣be|reit|schaft** (die; -), **...dienst; ein|satz⌣fä|hig, ...freu|dig; Ein|satz⌣grup|pe, ...kom|man|do, ...lei|ter** (der), **...mög|lich|keit, ...wa|gen** (nach Bedarf einzusetzender [Straßenbahn]wagen; Spezialfahrzeug der Polizei); **Ein|satz|zen|tra|le**
ein|sau|en (*derb für* [stark] beschmutzen)
ein|säu|ern; Ein|säu|e|rung
ein|sau|gen; Ein|sau|gung
ein|säu|men
ein|schach|teln; Ein|schach|te|lung, Ein|schacht|lung
ein|scha|len (*Bauw.* verschalen); **Ein|scha|ler** (jmd., der einschalt)
ein|schal|ten; sich -; **Ein|schalt⌣he|bel, ...quo|te; Ein|schal|tung**
Ein|scha|lung
ein|schär|fen; jmdm. etw. -
ein|schar|ren
ein|schätz|bar; ein|schät|zen; sich -; **Ein|schät|zung**
ein|schäu|men
ein|schen|ken; Wein -
ein|sche|ren (*Verkehrsw.* sich in den Verband, in die Kolonne einreihen; *Seemannsspr.* Tauwerk durch Halterungen o. Ä. ziehen); scherte ein; eingeschert
Ein|schicht, die; - (*südd., österr. für* Öde, Einsamkeit); **ein|schich|tig** (*südd., österr. für* abseits gelegen, einsam)
ein|schi|cken
ein|schie|ben; Ein|schieb|sel, das; -s, -; **Ein|schie|bung**
Ein|schie|nen|bahn
ein|schie|ßen; sich
ein|schif|fen; sich -; **Ein|schif|fung**
einschl. = einschließlich
ein|schla|fen
ein|schlä|fe|rig *vgl.* einschläfig
ein|schlä|fern; ich schläfere ein (↑R 16); **ein|schlä|fernd; Ein|schlä|fe|rung**
ein|schlä|fig, ein|schläf|rig; -es Bett (für eine Person)
Ein|schlag; ein|schla|gen; ein|schlä|gig (zu etwas gehörend); **Ein|schlag|pa|pier**

ein|schläm|men *(Landw.);* Sträucher - (stark bewässern)
ein|schlei|chen, sich
ein|schlei|fen; das hat sich bei ihr eingeschliffen (ist ihr zur Gewohnheit geworden)
ein|schlep|pen; Ein|schlep|pung
ein|schleu|sen; Ein|schleu|sung
ein|schlie|ßen; ein|schließ|lich (*Abk.* einschl.); *Präp. mit Gen.:* einschließlich des Kaufpreises; *ein allein stehendes, stark gebeugtes Substantiv steht im Sing. ungebeugt:* einschließlich Porto; *mit Dat., wenn bei Pluralformen der Gen. nicht erkennbar ist:* einschließlich Getränken; **Ein|schlie|ßung**
ein|schlum|mern
Ein|schlupf
Ein|schluss
ein|schmei|cheln, sich; sich [bei jmdm.] - wollen; **Ein|schmei|che|lung; Ein|schmeich|ler; Ein|schmeich|lung**
ein|schmei|ßen (*ugs. für* einwerfen)
ein|schmel|zen; Ein|schmel|zung; Ein|schmel|zungs|pro|zess
ein|schmie|ren; sich -
ein|schmug|geln
ein|schnap|pen (*ugs. auch für* gekränkt sein)
ein|schnei|den; ein|schnei|dend; -e Veränderung
ein|schnei|en
Ein|schnitt
ein|schnü|ren; Ein|schnü|rung
ein|schrän|ken; sich -; **Ein|schrän|kung**
ein|schrau|ben
Ein|schreib|brief, Ein|schrei|be|brief; ein|schrei|ben; Ein|schrei|ben, das; -s, - (eingeschriebene Postsendung); etwas per - schicken; **Ein|schrei|be|sen|dung, Ein|schreib|sen|dung; Ein|schrei|bung**
ein|schrei|ten
ein|schrump|fen; Ein|schrump|fung
Ein|schub, der; -[e]s, Einschübe; **Ein|schub‿de|cke** *(Bauw.),* **...tech|nik** (die; -)
ein|schüch|tern; ich schüchtere ein (↑R 16); **Ein|schüch|te|rung; Ein|schüch|te|rungs|ver|such**
ein|schu|len; Ein|schu|lung; Ein|schu|lungs|al|ter, das; -s
ein|schü|rig; -e (nur eine Ernte im Jahr liefernde) Wiese
Ein|schuss; Ein|schuss|stel|le (↑R 136)
ein|schwär|zen (*veraltet auch für* einschmuggeln)
ein|schwe|ben *(Flugw.)*
ein|schwei|ßen
ein|schwen|ken (einen Richtungs- od. Gesinnungswechsel vollziehen)
ein|schwim|men *(Technik)*
ein|schwin|gen
ein|schwö|ren; er ist auf diese Mittel eingeschworen
ein|seg|nen; Ein|seg|nung
ein|seh|bar; ein|se|hen; Ein|se|hen, das; -s; ein - haben
ein|sei|fen (*ugs. auch für* anführen, betrügen)
ein|sei|tig; -es Rechtsgeschäft; **Ein|sei|tig|keit** *Plur. selten*
ein|sen|den; Ein|sen|der; Ein|sen|de|rin; Ein|sen|de‿schluss, ...ter|min; Ein|sen|dung
ein|sen|ken; sich -; **Ein|sen|kung**
Ein|ser *vgl.* Einer
ein|set|zen; Ein|set|zung
Ein|sicht, die; -, -en; in etwas - nehmen; **ein|sich|tig; Ein|sich|tig|keit,** die; -; **Ein|sicht|nah|me,** die; -, -n *(Amtsspr.);* **ein|sichts‿los, ...voll**
ein|si|ckern
Ein|sie|de|glas *Plur.* ...gläser (*südd., österr. für* Einmachglas)
Ein|sie|de|lei; Ein|sie|deln (Abtei u. Wallfahrtsort in der Schweiz)
ein|sie|den (*südd., österr. für* einkochen, einmachen)
Ein|sied|ler; ein|sied|le|risch; Ein|sied|ler|krebs
Ein|sil|ber *vgl.* Einsilbler; **ein|sil|big; Ein|sil|big|keit,** die; -; **Ein|silb|ler,** Ein|sil|ber (einsilbiges Wort)
ein|si|lie|ren (*Landw.* in einem Silo einlagern)
ein|sin|gen; sich -
ein|sin|ken; Ein|sink|tie|fe
ein|sit|zen (*Rechtsspr.* im Gefängnis sitzen)
Ein|sit|zer; ein|sit|zig
ein‿söm|me|rig *od.* **...söm|me|rig;** -e Forellen
ein|sor|tie|ren; Ein|sor|tie|rung, die; -
ein|spal|tig *(Druckw.)*
ein|span|nen
Ein|spän|ner (*österr. auch für* Mokka mit Schlagsahne; einzelnes Frankfurter Würstchen); **ein|spän|nig**
ein|spa|ren; Ein|spar|mög|lich|keit; Ein|spa|rung; Ein|spa|rungs|maß|nah|me *meist Plur.*
ein|spei|cheln; Ein|spei|che|lung
ein|spei|sen (*Technik* zuführen, eingeben)
ein|sper|ren (*ugs. auch für* gefangen setzen)
ein|spie|len; Ein|spiel|er|geb|nis; Ein|spie|lung
ein|spin|nen; sich -
Ein|spon|be|trug (eine Form des Wirtschaftsbetrugs)
Ein|spra|che (*österr., schweiz. für* Einspruch)
ein|spra|chig; Ein|spra|chig|keit, die; -
ein|spre|chen; er hat auf sie eingesprochen
ein|spren|gen; Ein|spreng|sel
ein|sprin|gen
Ein|spritz|dü|se; ein|sprit|zen; Ein|sprit|zer (*ugs. für* Einspritzmotor); **Ein|spritz|mo|tor; Ein|sprit|zung**
Ein|spruch; - erheben; **Ein|spruchs|recht**
ein|sprü|hen
ein|spu|rig
Eins|sein
einst *(geh.);* **Einst,** das; - *(geh.);* das Einst und [das] Jetzt (↑R 49)
ein|stal|len *(Landw.);* Kühe -
ein|stamp|fen; Ein|stamp|fung
Ein|stand, der; -[e]s, Einstände; **Ein|stands|preis**
ein|stan|zen
ein|stau|ben (*österr. auch für* einstäuben); **ein|stäu|ben** (pudern)
ein|ste|chen
Ein|steck|bo|gen *(Druckw.);* **ein|ste|cken;** *vgl.* [2]stecken; **Ein|steck|kamm**
ein|ste|hen (bürgen)
Ein|stei|ge|dieb|stahl; ein|stei|gen; Ein|stei|ger *(ugs.)*
Ein|stein (dt.-amerik. Physiker); **Ein|stei|ni|um,** das; -s ⟨*nach* Einstein⟩ (chem. Element; *Zeichen* Es); **ein|stein|sche Glei|chung,** die; -n - (↑R 94)
ein|stell|bar; ein|stel|len; sich -; **Ein|stell|platz; Ein|stel|lung; Ein|stel|lungs‿be|scheid, ...ge|spräch, ...stopp, ...test**
eins|tens (*veraltet für* einst)
Ein|stich; Ein|stich|stel|le
Ein|stieg, der; -[e]s, -e; **Ein|stiegs|dro|ge** (Droge, deren ständiger Genuss meist zur Einnahme stärkerer Rauschgifte führt)
ein|stie|len (mit Stiel versehen); einen Besen, Hammer -
eins|tig
ein|stim|men; sich -
ein|stim|mig; Ein|stim|mig|keit, die; -
Ein|stim|mung
ein|stip|pen *(landsch.);* das Brot - (eintauchen)
einst|ma|lig; einst|mals *(veraltend)*
ein|stö|ckig
ein|sto|ßen
ein|strah|len; Ein|strah|lung
ein|strei|chen; er strich das Geld ein (*ugs. für* nahm es an sich)

Ein|streu *(Landw.)*; **ein|streu|en**
ein|strö|men
ein|stu|die|ren; Ein|stu|die|rung
ein|stu|fen; ein|stu|fig; Ein|stu|fung
ein|stül|pen; sich -; **Ein|stül|pung**
Ein|stun|den|takt; die Züge verkehren im -
ein|stür|men; alles stürmt auf ihn ein
Ein|sturz *Plur.* ...stürze; **Ein|sturz|be|ben; ein|stür|zen; Ein|sturz|ge|fahr,** die; -
einst|wei|len; einst|wei|lig *(Amtsspr.)*; -e Verfügung
Eins|wer|den, das; -s *(geh.)*; **Eins|wer|dung,** die;
Ein|tags‿fie|ber, ...flie|ge
ein|tan|zen; Ein|tän|zer (in Tanzlokalen angestellter Tanzpartner); **Ein|tän|ze|rin**
ein|tas|ten (über eine Tastatur eingeben)
ein|tä|to|wie|ren
ein|tau|chen
Ein|tausch, der; -[e]s; **ein|tau|schen**
ein|tau|send
ein|ta|xie|ren
ein|tei|gen
ein|tei|len
ein|tei|lig
Ein|tei|lung; Ein|tei|lungs|prin|zip
Ein|tel, das, *schweiz. meist* der; -s, - (*Math.* Ganzes)
ein|tip|pen; den Betrag -
ein|tö|nig; Ein|tö|nig|keit, die; -
Ein|topf
ein|top|fen; eine Pflanze -
Ein|topf|ge|richt
Ein|tracht, die; -; **ein|träch|tig; Ein|träch|tig|keit,** die; -; **ein|träch|tig|lich** *(veraltet)*
Ein|trag, der; -[e]s, ...träge; **ein|tra|gen;** *vgl.* eingetragen; **ein|träg|lich; Ein|träg|lich|keit,** die; -; **Ein|tra|gung**
ein|trai|nie|ren
ein|trän|ken; jmdm. etwas - (*ugs. für* heimzahlen)
ein|träu|feln; Ein|träu|fe|lung, Ein|träuf|lung
ein|tref|fen
ein|treib|bar; ein|trei|ben; Ein|trei|ber; Ein|trei|bung
ein|tre|ten; in ein Zimmer, eine Verhandlung -; auf etwas - (*schweiz. für* auf etwas eingehen, mit der Beratung von etwas beginnen); **ein|tre|ten|den|falls** *(Amtsspr.)*; *vgl.* Fall, der; **Ein|tre|tens|de|bat|te** (*schweiz. für* allg. Aussprache über eine Vorlage im Parlament)
ein|trich|tern (*ugs. für* einflößen; einprägen)
Ein|tritt; Ein|tritts‿geld, ...kar|te, ...preis
ein|trock|nen
ein|tröp|feln; Ein|tröp|fe|lung, Ein|tröpf|lung
ein|trü|ben; sich -; **Ein|trü|bung**
ein|tru|deln (*ugs. für* langsam eintreffen)
ein|tun|ken *(landsch.)*; das Brot - (eintauchen)
ein|tü|rig; ein -er Schrank
ein|tü|ten (in Tüten füllen)
ein|üben (↑R 132); sich -; **Ein|über** (*für* Korrepetitor); **Ein|übung**
ein und aus ge|hen; *vgl.* [2]ein
ein und der|sel|be; *vgl.* derselbe
ein|[und|]ein|halb; ein[und]einhalbmal so viel; **ein|und|zwan|zig**
Ei|nung (*veraltet für* Einigung)
ein|ver|lei|ben; sich -; er verleibt ein, *auch* er einverleibt; einverleibt; einzuverleiben; **Ein|ver|lei|bung**
Ein|ver|nah|me, die; -, -n (*bes. österr., schweiz. für* Verhör); **ein|ver|neh|men** ⟨*zu* Einvernahme⟩; **Ein|ver|neh|men,** das; -s; mit jmdm. in gutem - stehen; sich ins - setzen; **ein|ver|nehm|lich**
ein|ver|stan|den; ein|ver|ständ|lich; Ein|ver|ständ|nis; Ein|ver|ständ|nis|er|klä|rung
Ein|waa|ge, die; - (in Dosen o. Ä. eingewogene Menge; Gewichtsverlust beim Wiegen)
[1]**ein|wach|sen;** ein eingewachsener Zehennagel
[2]**ein|wach|sen** (mit Wachs einreiben)
Ein|wand, der; -[e]s, ...wände
Ein|wan|de|rer; Ein|wan|de|rin; ein|wan|dern; Ein|wan|de|rung; Ein|wan|de|rungs‿be|hör|de, ...land
ein|wand|frei
ein|wärts; einwärts gebogene Gitterstäbe; einwärts gedrehte Locken; einwärts (mit einwärts gerichteten Füßen) gehen, laufen
ein|we|ben
ein|wech|seln; Ein|wech|se|lung, Ein|wechs|lung
ein|we|cken ([in Weckgläsern] einmachen); **Ein|weck|glas** *Plur.* ...gläser
Ein|weg‿fla|sche (Flasche zum einmaligen Gebrauch), **...glas, ...hahn** *(Chemie)*, **...schei|be** (nur einseitig durchsichtige Glasscheibe), **...sprit|ze**
ein|wei|chen; *vgl.* [1]weichen; **Ein|wei|chung**
ein|wei|hen; Ein|wei|hung
ein|wei|sen; jmdn. in ein Amt -; **Ein|wei|ser; Ein|wei|sung**
ein|wen|den; ich wandte *od.* wendete ein, habe eingewandt *od.* eingewendet; **Ein|wen|dung**
ein|wer|fen
ein|wer|tig *(fachspr.)*; **Ein|wer|tig|keit,** die; -
ein|wi|ckeln; Ein|wi|ckel|pa|pier; Ein|wick|lung
ein|wie|gen
ein|wil|li|gen; Ein|wil|li|gung
ein|win|keln; die Arme -
ein|win|ken *(Verkehrsw.)*
ein|win|tern; ich wintere Kartoffeln ein (↑R 16)
ein|wir|ken; Ein|wir|kung; Ein|wir|kungs|mög|lich|keit
ein|woh|nen *(selten)*; **Ein|woh|ner; Ein|woh|ne|rin; Ein|woh|ner|mel|de|amt; Ein|woh|ner|schaft; Ein|woh|ner‿ver|zeich|nis, ...zahl**
ein|wüh|len; sich -
Ein|wurf
ein|wur|zeln; Ein|wur|ze|lung, Ein|wurz|lung
Ein|zahl, die; -, -en *Plur. selten* (*für* Singular)
ein|zah|len; Ein|zah|ler; Ein|zah|lung; Ein|zah|lungs‿be|leg, ...schal|ter, ...schein (*schweiz. für* Zahlkarte)
ein|zäu|nen; Ein|zäu|nung
ein|ze|hig *(Zool.)*
ein|zeich|nen; Ein|zeich|nung
ein|zei|lig
Ein|zel, das; -s, - (*Sportspr.* Einzelspiel); **Ein|zel‿ab|teil, ...ak|ti|on, ...aus|ga|be, ...be|o|bach|tung, ...ding** (*Plur.* ...dinge), **...dis|zi|plin** *(Sportspr.)*, **...er|schei|nung, ...fall** (der), **...gän|ger, ...gän|ge|rin, ...grab, ...haft** (die), **...han|del** (*vgl.* [1]Handel); **Ein|zel|han|dels|ge|schäft; Ein|zel|händ|ler; Ein|zel|heit; Ein|zel‿kämp|fer, ...kind, ...leis|tung**
Ein|zel|ler (*Biol.* einzelliges Lebewesen); **ein|zel|lig**
Ein|zel|mit|glied|schaft
ein|zeln; bitte einzeln eintreten; ein einzelner Baum; jede einzelne Mitarbeiterin; ein einzeln stehendes Haus; *aber* der, die, das Einzelne; ich als Einzelner; jeder Einzelne ist verantwortlich; bis ins Einzelne geregelt; Einzelne werden sich fragen, ob ...; wir wollen nicht zu sehr ins Einzelne gehen; Einzelnes blieb ungeklärt; die Dinge müssen im Einzelnen noch geklärt werden; **Ein|zel‿per|son, ...rei|se, ...rich|ter, ...staat; Ein|zel|ste|hen|de,** der *u.* die; -n, -n (↑R 5 ff.); **Ein|zel‿stück, ...tä|ter, ...teil** (das), **...ver|kauf** (der; -s), **...we|sen, ...zel|le, ...zim|mer**

ein|ze|men|tie|ren
ein|zie|hen; Ein|zieh|schacht (*Bergmannsspr.* Frischluftschacht); **Ein|zie|hung**
ein|zig; wir waren die einzigen Gäste; er ist einzig in seiner Art; eine einzig dastehende Leistung; das ist einzig und allein deine Schuld; *aber* der, die, das Einzige; das Einzige (*nicht* Einzigste) wäre, zu ...; ein Einziger; kein Einziger; er als Einziger, sie als Einzige; Karl ist unser Einziger; **einzig|ar|tig;** (↑R 47:) das Einzigartige ist, dass ...; **Ein|zig|ar|tig|keit; Ein|zig|keit,** die; -
Ein|zim|mer|woh|nung
ein|zu|ckern
Ein|zug; [1]Ein|zü|ger (*schweiz. für* Einnehmer)
[2]Ein|zü|ger (mit einem Zug zu lösende Schachaufgabe)
Ein|zugs‿be|reich, ...er|mäch|ti-gung, ...ge|biet
ein|zwän|gen; Ein|zwän|gung
Ei|pul|ver (Trockenei)
Éi|re ['e:ri, *engl.* 'ɛərə] (*ir. Name von* Irland)
Ei|re|ne (griech. Göttin des Friedens, eine der [2]Horen)
ei|rund; Ei|rund
eis, Eis, das; -, - (Tonbezeichnung)
Eis, das; -es; [drei] Eis essen; Eis laufen, sie ist Eis gelaufen
Ei|sack, der; -s (l. Nebenfluss der Etsch)
Eis‿bahn, ...bär, ...be|cher, ...bein (eine Speise), **...berg, ...beu|tel; Eis|blink,** der; -[e]s, -e (*Meteor.* Widerschein des Polareises am Horizont); **Eis‿block** (*Plur.* ...blöcke), **...blu|me, ...bom|be, ...bre|cher, ...ca|fé** (Lokal; *vgl.* Eiskaffee)
Ei|scha|le *(bes. fachspr.);* **Ei-schnee,** Ei|er|schnee
Eis‿creme (*od.* ...krem), **...de|cke, ...die|le; ei|sen** (mit Eis kühlen, mischen); du eist; ge|eis|te Früchte
Ei|sen, das; -s, - (*nur Sing.:* chem. Element, Metall; *Zeichen* Fe; *vgl.* Ferrum; Gegenstand aus Eisen); die Eisen schaffende, Eisen verarbeitende Industrie
Ei|se|nach (↑R 132; Stadt am Thüringer Wald); **Ei|se|na|cher** (↑R 103)
Ei|sen|bahn; Ei|sen|bah|ner; Ei-sen|bahn‿fahr|plan (↑R 24), **...wa|gen, ...we|sen** (das; -s)
Ei|sen|bart[h] (dt. Wanderarzt); ein Doktor - (*übertr. für* derbe Kuren anwendender Arzt)
Ei|sen|bau *Plur.* ...bauten; **ei|sen-be|schla|gen; Ei|sen‿be|ton, ...blech, ...block** (*Plur.* ...blöcke), **...blü|te** (ein Mineral), **...fres|ser** (*ugs. für* Aufschneider), **...guss; ei|sen|hal|tig; ei|sen|hart**
Ei|sen|how|er [...hauə(r)] (Präsident der USA)
Ei|sen|hut, der (eine Heil- u. Zierpflanze); **Ei|sen‿hüt|te, ...hüt-ten|we|sen** (das; -s), **...in|dust-rie, ...lup|pe** *(Technik),* **...rahm** (der; -[e]s, -e; ein Mineral); **Ei-sen schaf|fend** *vgl.* Eisen; **ei-sen|schüs|sig** (eisenhaltig); **Ei-sen|stadt** (Hptst. des Burgenlandes); **Ei|sen|stan|ge; Ei|sen verar|bei|tend** *vgl.* Eisen; **Ei|sen-wa|ren** *Plur.;* **Ei|sen|wa|ren-hand|lung; Ei|sen|zeit,** die; - (frühgeschichtl. Kulturzeit); **ei-sern;** mit eiserner Faust; ein eiserner Wille; mit eisernem Besen auskehren *(ugs.);* die eiserne Ration; die eiserne Lunge *(Med.);* eiserne Hochzeit (65. Jahrestag der Hochzeit); der eiserne Vorhang (feuersicherer Abschluss der Theaterbühne), *aber* (↑R 56): der Eiserne Vorhang (zwischen Ost u. West in der Zeit des Kalten Krieges); die Eiserne Krone (die lombard. Königskrone); das Eiserne Kreuz (ein Orden); (↑R 102:) das Eiserne Tor (Durchbruchstal der Donau)
Ei|ses|käl|te; Eis‿fach, ...flä|che; eis|frei; dieser Hafen ist -; **Eis-gang; eis|ge|kühlt; eis|glatt; Eis|glät|te; eis|grau; Eis|hei|li-gen** *Plur.* (Maifröste); die -; **Eis-ho|ckey** [...hɔke:]; **Eis|ho|ckey-län|der|spiel** (↑R 24); **ei|sig;** es waren eisig kalte Tage, die Tage waren eisig kalt; **Eis‿jacht** (Schlitten zum Eissegeln), **...kaf-fee** (Kaffee mit Eis und Sahne; *vgl.* Eiscafé); **eis|kalt; Eis‿kas-ten** (*bes. südd., österr. für* Kühlschrank), **...krem** *od.* **...creme, ...kris|tall** *(meist Plur.),* **...kü|bel; Eis|kunst|lauf,** der; -[e]s; **Eis-kunst|läu|fer; Eis|kunst|läu|fe-rin; Eis|lauf,** der; -[e]s; **Eis lau-fen** *vgl.* Eis
Eis|le|ben (Stadt im östl. Harzvorland); **Eis|le|be|ner, Eis|le|ber** (↑R 103)
Eis|män|ner *Plur.* (*bayr., österr. für* Eisheilige); **Eis|meer;** (↑R 102:) das Nördliche, Südliche -; **Eis|mo|nat** *od.* ...mond (*alte Bez. für* Januar), **...pi|ckel**
Ei|sprung (*Med.* Follikelsprung)
Eis|re|vue
Eiß, der; -es, -e *u.* Ei|ße, die; -, -n (*südd. u. schweiz. mdal. für* Blutgeschwür; Eiterbeule)
Eis|schie|ßen, das; -s (*svw.* Eisstockschießen)
Eis|schnell|lauf (↑R 136), der; -[e]s; **Eis|schnell|läu|fer; Eis-schnell|läu|fe|rin**
Eis‿schol|le, ...schrank, ...se-geln (das; -s); **Eis‿spross** *od.* **...spros|se** *(Jägerspr.),* **...sta|di-on, ...stau; Eis|stock** *Plur.* ...stöcke (ein Sportgerät); - schießen, wir schießen -; **Eis|stock-schie|ßen,** das; -s; **Eis‿stoß** (*landsch. für* aufgestautes Eis in Flüssen), **...tanz, ...vo|gel, ...wein, ...wür|fel, ...zap|fen, ...zeit; eis|zeit|lich**
[1]ei|tel; ein eitler Mensch; **[2]ei|tel** (*veraltend für* nur, nichts als); - Sonnenschein; **Ei|tel|keit**
Ei|ter, der; -s; **Ei|ter‿beu|le, ...er-re|ger, ...herd; ei|te|rig,** eit|rig; **ei|tern; Ei|ter|pi|ckel; Ei|te-rung; eit|rig** *vgl.* eiterig
Ei|vis|sa [...v...] (katalanischer Name von Ibiza)
Ei|weiß, das; -es, -e; 2 - (↑R 90); **Ei|weiß‿be|darf, ...ge|halt** (der), **...man|gel** (der); **ei|weiß|reich; Ei|weiß|stoff; Ei|zel|le**
E|ja|ku|lat, das; -[e]s, -e ‹lat.› (*Med.* ausgespritzte Samenflüssigkeit); **E|ja|ku|la|ti|on,** die; -, -en (Samenerguss); **e|ja|ku|lie-ren; E|jek|ti|on,** die; -, -en (*Geol.* Ausschleudern von Magma); **E|jek|tor,** der; -s, ...oren (Auswerfer bei Jagdgewehren; absaugende Strahlpumpe); **e|ji|zie|ren** (*Geol.* ausschleudern)
E|kart [e'ka:r], der; -s, -s ‹franz.› (*Börsenw.* Abstand zwischen Basis- u. Prämienkurs); **[1]E|kar|té** [...'te:], das; -s, -s (*Ballett* Stellung schräg zum Zuschauer)
[2]E|kar|té [...'te:], das; -s, -s ‹franz.› (ein Kartenspiel)
EKD = Evangelische Kirche in Deutschland
e|kel *(geh.);* eine ek|le Angelegenheit; **[1]E|kel,** der; -s; eine Ekel erregende Brühe; es roch Ekel erregend (↑R 40); **[2]E|kel,** das; -s, - (*ugs. für* widerlicher Mensch); **E|kel er|re|gend** *vgl.* [1]Ekel; **e|kel|haft; e|ke|lig,** ek|lig; **e|keln;** es ekelt mich *od.* mir; sich ekeln; ich ek[e]le mich (↑R 16)
E|kel|na|me (Spitz-, Übername)
EKG, Ekg = Elektrokardiogramm
Ek|ke|hard (*scheffelsche Schreibung von* Eckehard)
Ek|kle|sia, die; - ‹griech.-lat.› (*Theol.* christl. Kirche); **Ek|kle|si-as|ti|kus,** der; - (*in der Vulgata* Titel des Buches Jesus Sirach); **Ek|kle|si|o|lo|gie,** die; - (Lehre von der Kirche)
Ek|lat [e'kla(:)] (↑R 130), der; -s, -s ‹franz.› (Aufsehen erregendes Er-

eignis, Skandal); **ek|la|tant** (Aufsehen erregend; offenkundig)
Ek|lek|ti|ker ‹griech., „Auswähler"› (Vertreter des Eklektizismus); **ek|lek|tisch; Ek|lek|ti|zis|mus,** der; - (unschöpferische, unselbstständige, mechan. Vereinigung zusammengetragener Gedanken-, Stilelemente usw.); **ek|lek|ti|zis|tisch**
ek|lig, e|ke|lig
Ek|lip|se, die; -, -n ‹griech.› (Sonnen- od. Mondfinsternis); **Ek|lip|tik,** die; -, -en (scheinbare Sonnenbahn; Erdbahn); **ek|lip|tisch**
Ek|lo|ge, die; -, -n ‹griech.› (altröm. Hirtenlied)
E|ko|no|mi|ser *vgl.* Economiser
E|kos|sai|se [ekɔ'sɛːzə], die; -, -n ‹franz.› (ein Tanz)
Ek|ra|sit (↑R 130 *u.* 132), das; -s ‹franz.› (ein Sprengstoff)
Ek|rü|sei|de (↑R 130 *u.* 132) ‹franz.› (Rohseide)
Eks|ta|se (↑R 132), die; -, -n ‹griech.› ([religiöse] Verzückung; höchste Begeisterung); **Eks|ta|ti|ker; eks|ta|tisch**
Ek|ta|se, Ek|ta|sis, die; -, Ektasen ‹griech.› (*antike Verslehre* Dehnung eines Selbstlautes); **Ek|ta|sie,** die; -, ...ien (*Med.* Erweiterung); **Ek|ta|sis** *vgl.* Ektase
ek|to... ‹griech.› (außen...); **Ek|to...** (Außen...)
Ek|to|derm, das; -s, -e ‹griech.› (*Zool.* äußeres Keimblatt des Embryos); **Ek|to|derm|zel|le**
Ek|to|mie, die; -, ...ien ‹griech.› (*Med.* operative Entfernung)
Ek|to|pa|ra|sit ‹griech.› (*Med.* Schmarotzer der äußeren Haut)
E|ku|a|dor usw. *vgl.* Ecuador usw.
Ek|zem, das; -s, -e ‹griech.› (*Med.* eine Entzündung der Haut)
E|la|bo|rat, das; -[e]s, -e ‹lat.› (schriftl. Ausarbeitung; *meist abwertend für* Machwerk)
E|lan, der; -s ‹franz.› (Schwung; Begeisterung)
E|last, der; -[e]s, -e *meist Plur.* ‹griech.› (elastischer Kunststoff); **E|las|tik,** das; -s, -s *od.* die; -, -en (ein elastisches Gewebe); **E|las|tik|akt** *(Artistik);* **e|las|tisch** (biegsam, dehnbar, aber wieder in die Ausgangsform zurückstrebend; *übertr. für* flexibel); **E|las|ti|zi|tät,** die; - (Federkraft; Spannkraft); **E|las|ti|zi|täts‿gren|ze, ...mo|dul** (der; -s, -n; *Physik, Technik* Messgröße der Elastizität), **...ver|lust; E|las|to|mer,** das; -s, -e *u.* **E|las|to|me|re,** das; -n, -n *meist Plur.;* ↑R 5 ff. ([synthetischer] Kautschuk u. Ä.)
E|la|tiv, der; -s, -e [...və] ‹lat.› (*Sprachw.* absoluter Superlativ [ohne Vergleich], z. B. „beste [= sehr gute] Lage")
El|ba (ital. Mittelmeerinsel)
elb|ab|wärts; elb|auf|wärts; El|be, die; - (ein Strom); **El|be-Lü|beck-Ka|nal,** der; -s (↑R 105); **El|be|sei|ten|ka|nal,** der; -s (↑R 105); **Elb-Flo|renz;** ↑R 106 (*Bez. für* Dresden); **Elb‿kahn, ...mün|dung** (die; -)
El|brus (↑R 130), der; - (höchste Erhebung des Kaukasus)
Elb|sand|stein|ge|bir|ge, das; -s (↑R 105); **Elb‿strand** (der; -[e]s), **...strom** (der; -[e]s)
El|burs, der; - (iran. Gebirge)
Elch, der; -[e]s, -e (Hirschart); **Elch‿bul|le** (der), **...jagd, ...kuh**
El|do|ra|do, Do|ra|do, das; -s, -s ‹span.› (sagenhaftes Goldland in Südamerika; *übertr. für* Paradies)
E|le|a|te, der; -n, -n *meist Plur.;* ↑R 126 (Vertreter einer altgriech. Philosophenschule); **e|le|a|tisch;** -e Schule
E|le|fant, der; -en, -en (↑R 126) ‹griech.›; **E|le|fan|ten‿bul|le** (der), **...fuß** (runder Trittschemel), **...haut** (die; -; wasser- und wischfester Schutzanstrich), **...hoch|zeit** (*ugs. für* Zusammenschluss von mächtigen Unternehmen, Verbänden o. Ä.); **E|le|fan|ten‿kuh, ...ren|nen** (*ugs. für* langwieriger Überholvorgang zwischen Lastwagen), **...run|de** (*salopp für* Fernsehdiskussionsrunde der Parteivorsitzenden nach einer Wahl); **E|le|fan|ti|a|sis,** die; -, ...iasen (*Med.* unförmige Hautverdickung)
e|le|gant ‹franz.›; **E|le|gant** [ele'gãː], der; -s, -s (*veraltet für* sich übertrieben modisch kleidender Mann); **E|le|ganz,** die; -
E|le|gie, die; -, ...ien ‹griech.› (eine Gedichtform; Klagelied); **E|le|gi|en|dich|ter; E|le|gi|ker** (Elegiendichter); **e|le|gisch** (wehmütig); **E|leg|jam|bus** (ein altgriech. Versmaß)
E|lei|son [*auch* e'leizɔn], das; -s, -s ‹griech., „Erbarme dich!"› (Bittformel im gottesdienstl. Gesang); *vgl.* Kyrie eleison
e|lek|tiv ‹lat.› (auswählend); *vgl.* selektiv; **E|lek|to|rat,** das; -[e]s, -e (*früher für* Kurfürstentum, Kurwürde)
E|lek|tra (↑R 130; griech. Sagengestalt)
E|lek|tri|fi|ka|ti|on (↑R 130), die; -, -en ‹griech.› (*schweiz. neben* Elektrifizierung); **e|lek|tri|fi|zie|ren** (auf elektr. Betrieb umstellen); **E|lek|tri|fi|zie|rung**
E|lek|trik (↑R 130), die; - (Gesamtheit einer elektr. Anlage; *ugs. für* Elektrizitätslehre); **E|lek|tri|ker**
e|lek|trisch (↑R 130); -e Eisenbahn; -e Lokomotive (*Abk.* E-Lok); -er Strom; -er Stuhl; -es Feld; -es Klavier; **E|lek|tri|sche,** die; -n, -n (*ugs. veraltet für* elektr. Straßenbahn); vier -[n]
e|lek|tri|sie|ren (↑R 130); **E|lek|tri|sier|ma|schi|ne**
E|lek|tri|zi|tät (↑R 130); die; -; **E|lek|tri|zi|täts|werk** (*Abk.* E-Werk)
E|lek|tro|akus|tik[1] (↑R 130 *u.* 132; Umwandlung von Schall in elektr. Spannung u. umgekehrt); **e|lek|tro|akus|tisch**[1]; **E|lek|tro|au|to; E|lek|tro|che|mie**[1]; **e|lek|tro|che|misch**[1]; -e Spannungsreihe
E|lek|tro|de (↑R 130), die; -, -n (den Stromübergang vermittelnder Leiter)
E|lek|tro|dy|na|mik[1] (↑R 130); **e|lek|tro|dy|na|misch**[1]; **E|lek|tro|en|ze|pha|lo|gramm** (*Med.* Aufzeichnung der Hirnströme; *Abk.* EEG); **E|lek|tro|ge|rät; E|lek|tro|gra|phie,** die; - (*Elektrotechnik, EDV* galvanische Hochätzung); **E|lek|tro‿herd, ...in|dus|trie, ...in|ge|ni|eur, ...in|stal|la|teur; E|lek|tro|kar|di|o|gramm** (*Med.* Aufzeichnung der Aktionsströme des Herzens; *Abk.* EKG, Ekg); **E|lek|tro|kar|re[n]**
E|lek|tro|ly|se (↑R 130), die; -, -n (elektr. Zersetzung chem. Verbindungen); **E|lek|tro|lyt,** der; *Gen.* -s, *selten* -en, *Plur.* -e, *selten* -en (durch Strom zersetzbarer Stoff); **e|lek|tro|ly|tisch;** -e Dissoziation
E|lek|tro|mag|net[1] (↑R 130); **e|lek|tro|mag|ne|tisch**[1]; -es Feld; -e Wellen; **E|lek|tro‿me|cha|ni|ker, ...meis|ter; E|lek|tro|me|ter,** das; -s, -; **E|lek|tro‿mon|teur, ...mo|tor**
[1]**E|lek|tron** [*auch* e'lɛk..., ...'troːn] (↑R 130), das; -s, ...onen (*Kernphysik* negativ geladenes Elementarteilchen); [2]**E|lek|tron** ®, das; -s (eine Magnesiumlegierung); **E|lek|tro|nen‿blitz, ...[ge]hirn, ...mik|ro|skop, ...or|gel, ...rech|ner, ...röh|re, ...schleu|der** (*für* Betatron), **...stoß** (Stoß eines Elektrons auf Atome), **...the|o|rie** (Lehre vom Elektron), **...volt** (*vgl.* Elektronvolt)
E|lek|tro|nik (↑R 130), die; - (Zweig der Elektrotechnik; Gesamtheit der elektron. Bauteile einer Anlage); **E|lek|tro|ni|ker** (Be-

[1] [*auch* e'lɛk...]

rufsbez.); **e|lekt|ro|nisch**; -e Musik; -e Datenverarbeitung (*Abk.* EDV); **E|lekt|ron|volt**, E|lekt|ronen|volt (Energieeinheit der Kernphysik; *Zeichen* eV)
E|lekt|ro|ofen (↑R 130 *u.* 132); **E|lekt|ro|pho|re|se**, die; - (Transport elektr. geladener Teilchen durch elektr. Strom); **E|lekt|ro|phy|sik**[1]; **E|lekt|ro-ra|sie|rer, ...ra|sur, ...schock** (der); **...smog** (elektromagnetische Strahlung, die von elektrischen Leitungen, Geräten, Sendern o. Ä. ausgeht); **E|lekt|ro|sta|tik; e|lekt|ro|sta|tisch; E|lekt|ro-tech|nik**[1] (die; -), **...tech|ni|ker**[1]; **e|lekt|ro|tech|nisch**[1]; **E|lekt|ro|the|ra|pie; E|lekt|ro|to|mie**, die; -, ...ien (*Med.* Operation mit einer elektr. Schneidschlinge)
E|le|ment, das; -[e]s, -e ‹lat.› (Urstoff; Grundbestandteil; chem. Grundstoff; Naturgewalt; ein elektr. Gerät; *meist Plur.: abwertend für* verdächtige, zwielichtige Person; *vgl.* Elemente); er ist, fühlt sich in seinem -; **e|le|men|tar** (grundlegend; naturhaft; einfach; Anfangs...); -e Begriffe; -e Gewalt; **E|le|men|tar-ge|walt** (Naturgewalt), **...schu|le** (Anfänger-, Volksschule), **...teil|chen; E|le|men|te** *Plur.* (Grundbegriffe [einer Wissenschaft])
E|le|mi, das; -s ‹arab.› (trop. Harz); **E|le|mi|öl**, das; -[e]s
E|len, das, *seltener* der; -s, - ‹lit.› (Elch); **E|len|an|ti|lo|pe**
e|lend; ihm war elend [zumute]; **E|lend**, das; -[e]s; **e|len|dig** *(landsch.)*, **e|len|dig|lich** *(geh.)*; **E|lends-ge|stalt, ...quar|tier, ...vier|tel**
E|len|tier (Elen, Elch)
E|le|o|no|re (w. Vorn.)
E|le|phan|ti|a|sis *vgl.* Elefantiasis
E|leu|si|ni|en [...i̯ən] *Plur.* ‹*nach* Eleusis› (Fest mit Prozession zu Ehren der griech. Ackerbaugöttin Demeter); **e|leu|si|nisch**, *aber* (↑R 108): die Eleusinischen Mysterien (Geheimkult im alten Athen); **E|leu|sis** (altgriech. Ort)
E|le|va|ti|on [...v...], die; -, -en ‹lat.› (Erhebung; Emporheben der Hostie u. des Kelches beim kath. Messopfer; *Astron.* Höhe eines Gestirns über dem Horizont); **E|le|va|tor**, der; -s, ...oren (*Technik* Förder-, Hebewerk); **E|le|ve**, der; -n, -n (↑R 126) ‹franz.› (Schauspiel-, Ballettschüler; Land- u. Forstwirt während der prakt. Ausbildung); **E|le|vin**

elf; wir sind zu elfen *od.* zu elft; *vgl.* acht
[1]**Elf**, der; -en, -en; ↑R 126 (m. Naturgeist)
[2]**Elf**, die; -, -en (Zahl; [Fußball]mannschaft); *vgl.* [1]Acht
El|fe, die; -, -n (w. Naturgeist)
Elf|eck; elf|eckig (↑R 132); **elf|ein|halb**, elf|und|ein|halb
El|fen|bein, das; -[e]s, -e *Plur. selten;* **el|fen|bei|nern** (aus Elfenbein); **el|fen|bein|far|ben;** [1]**El|fen|bein|küs|te**, die; - (Küstenstreifen in Westafrika); [2]**El|fen|bein|küs|te**, die; -; *auch ohne Artikel* (Staat in Westafrika; *vgl.* Côte d'Ivoire); **El|fen|bein-schnit|zer, ...turm** (im - [abgekapselt] leben)
el|fen|haft; El|fen|rei|gen
El|fer (*ugs. für* Elfmeter); *vgl.* Achter; **el|fer|lei; El|fer-rat** (beim Karneval), **...wet|te** (beim Fußballtoto); **elf|fach**
El|fi (w. Vorn.)
el|fisch ‹*zu* [1]Elf›
elf|mal; *vgl.* achtmal; **elf|ma|lig; Elf|me|ter**, der; -s, - (Strafstoß beim Fußball); **Elf|me|ter-mar|ke, ...punkt; elf|me|ter|reif;** -e Situationen; **Elf|me|ter-schie|ßen, ...schuss, ...tor**
El|frie|de (w. Vorn.)
elft; *vgl.* elf; **elf|tau|send; elf|te;** der Elfte im Elften (karnevalist. Bezeichnung für den 11. November); *vgl.* achte; **elf|tel;** *vgl.* achtel; **Elf|tel**, das, *schweiz. meist* der; -s, -; *vgl.* Achtel; **elf|tens; elf|[und|]ein|halb**
E|li|as, *ökum.* E|li|ja (Prophet im A. T.)
e|li|die|ren ‹lat.› (*Sprachw.* eine Elision vornehmen); **E|li|die|rung**
E|li|gi|us (ein Heiliger)
E|li|ja *vgl.* Elias
E|li|mi|na|ti|on, die; -, -en ‹lat.› (Beseitigung, Ausscheidung); **e|li|mi|nie|ren; E|li|mi|nie|rung**
E|li|ot [ˈɛljət] (amerik.-engl. Schriftsteller)
E|li|sa (w. Vorn.); [1]**E|li|sa|beth** (w. Vorn.); [2]**E|li|sa|beth**, *ökum.* E|li|sa|bet (bibl. w. Eigenn.); **e|li|sa|be|tha|nisch**, *aber* (↑R 56): das Elisabethanische Zeitalter
E|li|se (w. Vorn.)
E|li|si|on, die; -, -en ‹lat.› (*Sprachw.* Auslassung eines unbetonten Vokals, z. B. des „e" in „Wand[e]rung")
e|li|tär (einer Elite angehörend, auserlesen); **E|li|te** [*österr.* eˈlit], die; -, -n ‹franz.› (Auslese der Besten); **E|li|te|trup|pe** *(Milit.)*
E|li|xier, das; -s, -e ‹griech.› (Heil-, Zaubertrank)

El|ke (w. Vorn.)
El|la (w. Vorn.)
Ell|bo|gen, El|len|bo|gen, der; -s, ...bogen; **Ell|bo|gen|frei|heit**, El|len|bo|gen|frei|heit, die; -
El|le, die; -, -n (ein Unterarmknochen; alte Längeneinheit); drei -n Tuch (↑R 90)
El|len (w. Vorn.)
El|len|bo|gen *vgl.* Ellbogen; **El|len|bo|gen|frei|heit** *vgl.* Ellbogenfreiheit; **El|len|bo|gen|ge|sell|schaft** *(abwertend);* **el|len|lang** *(ugs.)*
El|ler, die; -, -n (*nordd. für* Erle)
El|li (w. Vorn.)
El|lip|se, die; -, -n ‹griech.› (*Sprachw.* Ersparung von Redeteilen, z. B. „[ich] danke schön"; Auslassungssatz; *Math.* Kegelschnitt); **el|lip|sen|för|mig; El|lip|so|id**, das; -[e]s, -e (*Geom.* durch Drehung einer Ellipse entstandener Körper); **el|lip|tisch** (ellipsenförmig; *Sprachw.* unvollständig); **El|lip|ti|zi|tät**, die; - (*Astron.* Abplattung)
El|lok, die; -, -s; *vgl.* E-Lok
Ell|wan|gen (Jagst) (Stadt an der Jagst); **Ell|wan|ger** (↑R 103)
El|ly (w. Vorn.)
Elm, der; -s (Höhenzug südöstl. von Braunschweig)
El|mar, El|mo (m. Vorn.)
Elms|feu|er (elektr. Lichterscheinung); *vgl. auch* Sankt
E|lo|ge [...ʒə], die; -, -n ‹franz.› (Lob, Schmeichelei)
E|lo|him ‹hebr.› (*im A. T.* Gottesbezeichnung)
E-Lok, die; -, -s; ↑R 26 (= elektrische Lokomotive)
E|lon|ga|ti|on, die; -, -en ‹lat.› (*Physik* Ausschlag des Pendels; *Astron.* Winkel zwischen Sonne u. Planeten)
e|lo|quent ‹lat.› (beredt); **E|lo|quenz**, die; -
E|lo|xal ®, das; -s (Schutzschicht auf Aluminium); **e|lo|xie|ren**
El|rit|ze, die; -, -n (ein Karpfenfisch)
Els, El|sa (w. Vorn.)
El Sal|va|dor [- ...v...] (mittelamerik. Staat); *vgl.* Salvadorianer *u.* salvadorianisch
El|sass, das; -[es]; **El|säs|ser** (↑R 103); **El|säs|se|rin; el|säs|sisch; El|sass-Loth|rin|gen; el|sass-loth|rin|gisch**
Els|beth, El|se (w. Vorn.)
El|se|vir *vgl.* Elzevir
El|si (w. Vorn.)
[1]**Els|ter**, die; - (Flussname); die Schwarze -, die Weiße - (↑R 102)
[2]**Els|ter**, die; -, -n (ein Vogel); **Els|tern|nest**

[1] [*auch* eˈlɛk...]

El|ter, das *u.* der; -s, -n (*fachspr. für* ein Elternteil); **el|ter|lich;** -e Gewalt; **El|tern** *Plur.;* **El|tern-abend** (↑R 132), **...ak|tiv** (*ehem. in der DDR* Elternvertretung einer Schulklasse); **El|tern-bei|rat, ...haus, ...lie|be; el|tern|los; El|tern|recht; El|tern|schaft** *Plur. selten;* **El|tern-se|mi|nar, ...teil** (der)

Elt|vil|le am Rhein [ɛlt'vilə, *auch* 'ɛlt...] (Stadt im Rheingau)

El|vi|ra [ɛl'vi:ra] (w. Vorn.)

e|ly|sä|isch *vgl.* e|ly|sisch; **É|ly|sée** [eli...], das; -s ‹franz.› (Palast in Paris); **e|ly|sisch** ‹griech.› (wonnevoll, paradiesisch); -e Gefilde; **E|ly|si|um** [e'ly:...], das; -s ‹griech.› (Aufenthaltsort der Seligen in der griech. Sage)

E|ly|t|ron (↑R 130), das; -s, ...ytren *meist Plur.* ‹griech.› (*Zool.* Deckflügel [der Insekten])

El|ze|vir ['ɛlzəvi:r], die; - ‹nach der niederl. Buchdruckerfamilie Elsevi(e)r› (*Druckw.* eine Antiquadruckschrift); **El|ze|vi|ri|a|na** *Plur.* (Elzevirdrucke)

em. = emeritiert, emeritus (*vgl.* Emerit)

E-Mail ['i:me:l], die; -, -s ‹engl.› (elektronischer Daten- u. Nachrichtenaustausch über Computernetze)

E|mail [e'mai, *auch* e'ma:j, *österr.* e'mail], das; -s, -s *(österr. nur so) u.* E|mail|le [e'maljə, *auch* e'ma:j], die; -, -n ‹franz.› (Schmelzüberzug); **E|mail|far|be; E|mail|le** *vgl.* Email; **E|mail|leur** [ema(l)'jø:r], der; -s, -e (Schmelzarbeiter); **e|mail|lie|ren** [ema(l)'ji:..., *österr.* emai'li:...]; **E|mail|lier|ofen** (↑R 132); **E|mail|ma|le|rei**

E|ma|na|ti|on, die; -, -en ‹lat., „Ausfluss"› (das Ausströmen; Ausstrahlung); **e|ma|nie|ren**

E|ma|nu|el [...e:l, *auch* ...ɛl], Imma|nu|el (m. Vorn.); **E|ma|nu|e|la** (w. Vorn.)

E|man|ze, die; -, -n ‹lat.› (*ugs. abwertend für* emanzipierte, sich für die Emanzipation einsetzende Frau); **E|man|zi|pa|ti|on,** die; -, -en (Befreiung von Abhängigkeit; Gleichstellung); **E|man|zi|pa|ti|ons-be|we|gung, ...stre|ben; e|man|zi|pa|to|risch; e|man|zi|pie|ren;** sich -; **e|man|zi|piert** (unabhängig; frei von überkommenen Vorstellungen); **E|man|zi|pie|rung,** die; -

Em|bal|la|ge [ãba'la:ʒə, *österr.* ...'la:ʒ], die; -, -n [...'la:ʒ(ə)n] ‹franz.› (Verpackung [einer Ware]); **em|bal|lie|ren**

Em|bar|go, das; -s, -s ‹span.› (Zurückhalten od. Beschlagnahme [von Schiffen] im Hafen; Ausfuhrverbot)

Emb|lem [*auch* ã'ble:m] (↑R 130), das; -s, -e ‹franz.› (Kennzeichen, Hoheitszeichen; Sinnbild); **Emb|le|ma|tik,** die; - (sinnbildliche Darstellung; Emblemforschung); **emb|le|ma|tisch** (sinnbildlich)

Em|bo|lie, die; -, ...ien ‹griech.› (*Med.* Verstopfung eines Blutgefäßes); **Em|bo|lus,** der; -, ...li (*Med.* Pfropf, Fremdkörper in der Blutbahn)

Em|bon|point [ãbɔ̃'pɔ̃ɛ:], das *od.* der; -s ‹franz.› (*veraltet für* Wohlbeleibtheit; dicker Bauch)

Emb|ryo (↑R 130 *u.* 132), der, *österr. auch* das; -s, *Plur.* -s *u.* ...onen ‹griech.› (noch nicht geborenes Lebewesen); **Emb|ry|o|lo|gie,** die; - (Lehre von der Entwicklung des Embryos); **emb|ry|o|nal, emb|ry|o|nisch** (im Anfangsstadium der Entwicklung); **Emb|ry|o|trans|fer** (*Biol.* Übertragung u. Einpflanzung von Eizellen, die außerhalb des Körpers befruchtet wurden)

Emd, das; -[e]s (*schweiz. für* Grummet); *vgl.* Öhmd; **em|den** (*schweiz. für* Grummet machen)

Em|den (Hafenstadt an der Emsmündung); **Em|der,** *auch* Em|dener (↑R 103)

Em|det, *der; -s* (*schweiz. für* zweiter Grasschnitt)

E|men|da|ti|on, die; -, -en ‹lat.› (*Literaturw.* Verbesserung, Berichtigung [von Texten]); **e|men|die|ren**

E|me|ren|tia, E|me|renz (w. Vorn.)

E|me|rit, der; -en, -en (↑R 126) ‹lat.› (*kath. Kirche* im Alter dienstunfähig gewordener Geistlicher; *vgl.* em.); **e|me|ri|tie|ren** (in den Ruhestand versetzen); **e|me|ri|tiert** (*Abk.* em.); -er Professor; **E|me|ri|tie|rung; e|me|ri|tus** *vgl.* emeritiert; **E|me|ri|tus,** der; -, ...ti (emeritierter Hochschulprofessor); *vgl.* Emerit

E|me|ti|kum, das; -s, ...ka ‹griech.› (*Pharm.* Brechmittel); **e|me|tisch** (Brechen erregend)

E|mig|rant (↑R 130), der; -en, -en (↑R 126) ‹lat.› (Auswanderer [bes. aus polit. od. religiösen Gründen]); **E|mig|ran|ten|schick|sal; E|mig|ran|tin; E|mig|ra|ti|on,** die; -, -en; **e|mig|rie|ren**

E|mil (m. Vorn.); **E|mi|lia, E|mi|lie** [...iə] (w. Vorn.)

e|mi|nent ‹lat.› (hervorragend; außerordentlich); **E|mi|nenz,** die; -, -en (früherer Titel der Kardinäle); *vgl. auch* euer *u.* [1]sein; *vgl.* grau

E|mir [*auch* e'mi:r], der; -s, -e ‹arab.› (arab. [Fürsten]titel); **E|mi|rat,** das; -[e]s, -e (arab. Fürstentum)

E|mis|sär, der; -s, -e ‹franz.› (Abgesandter mit geheimem Auftrag); **E|mis|si|on,** die; -, -en ‹lat.› (*Physik* Ausstrahlung; *Technik* Abblasen von Gasen, Ruß u. Ä. in die Luft; *Wirtsch.* Ausgabe [von Wertpapieren]; *Med.* Entleerung); **E|mis|si|ons|stopp; E|mit|tent,** der; -en, -en; ↑R 126 (*Bankw.* Ausgeber von Wertpapieren); **E|mit|ter,** der; -s, - ‹engl.› (*Technik* Teil des Transistors); **e|mit|tie|ren** ‹lat.›; Wertpapiere - (ausgeben); Elektronen - (*Physik* aussenden)

Em|ma (w. Vorn.)

Em|ma|us (bibl. Ort)

Emm|chen *meist Plural* (*ugs. scherzh. für* Mark); zehn -

Em|me, die; - (Nebenfluss der Aare); Kleine - (Nebenfluss der Reuß)

Em|men|tal, das; -[e]s (schweiz. Landschaft); **[1]Em|men|ta|ler** (↑R 103); - Käse; **[2]Em|men|ta|ler,** der; -s, - (ein Käse)

Em|mer, der; -s (eine Weizenart)

Em|me|rich (m. Vorn.); **Em|mi** (w. Vorn.); **Em|mo** (m. Vorn.)

e-Moll [*auch* 'e:'mɔl], das; - (Tonart; *Zeichen* e); **e-Moll-Ton|lei|ter** (↑R 28)

E|mo|ti|on, die; -, -en ‹lat.› (Gemütsbewegung, seelische Erregung); **e|mo|ti|o|nal** (gefühlsmäßig; seelisch erregt); **e|mo|ti|o|na|li|sie|ren; E|mo|ti|o|na|li|tät,** die; -; **e|mo|ti|o|nell** *vgl.* emotional; **e|mo|ti|ons-frei, ...ge|la|den** (eine -e Diskussion), **...los**

EMPA, Em|pa = Eidgenössische Materialprüfungs- und Forschungsanstalt

Em|pa|thie, die; - ‹griech.› (*Psych.* Fähigkeit, sich in andere hineinzuversetzen); **em|pa|thisch**

Em|pe|dok|les (↑R 130; altgriech. Philosoph)

Emp|fang, der; -[e]s, ...fänge; **emp|fan|gen;** du empfängst; du empfingst; du empfingest; empfangen; empfang[e]!; **Emp|fän|ger; Emp|fän|ger|ab|schnitt; Emp|fän|ge|rin; emp|fäng|lich; Emp|fäng|lich|keit,** die; -; **Emp|fang|nah|me,** die; - *(Amtsspr.);* **Emp|fäng|nis,** die; -, -se; **emp|fäng|nis|ver|hü|tend;** ein -es Mittel; **Emp|fäng|nis-ver|hü|tung, ...zeit; Emp|fangs|an|ten|ne; emp|fangs|be|rech|tigt;** allein - sein; **Emp|fangs‿be|schei|ni|gung, ...be|stä|ti|gung, ...chef, ...da|me, ...saal, ...sta|ti|on, ...stö|rung, ...zim|mer**

emp|feh|len; du empfiehlst; du empfahlst; du empföhlest, *auch* empfählest; empfohlen; empfiehl!; sich empfehlen; **emp|feh|lens|wert; Emp|feh|lung; Emp|feh|lungs‿brief, ...schrei|ben**

emp|find|bar; emp|fin|den; du empfandst; du empfändest; empfunden; empfind[e]!; **Emp|fin|den,** das; -s; **emp|find|lich; Emp|find|lich|keit; emp|find|sam;** -e Dichtung; **Emp|find|sam|keit,** die; -; **Emp|fin|dung; emp|fin|dungs|los; Emp|fin|dungs|lo|sig|keit,** die; -; **Emp|fin|dungs|wort** *Plur.* ...wörter (*für* Interjektion)

Em|pha|se, die; -, -n ‹griech.› (Nachdruck [im Reden]); **em|pha|tisch** (mit Nachdruck, stark)

Em|phy|sem, das; -s, -e ‹griech.› (*Med.* Luftansammlung im Gewebe)

[1]**Em|pire** [ã'pi:r], das; *Gen.* -s, *fachspr. auch* - ‹franz.› (Kunststil der Zeit Napoleons I.); [2]**Em|pi|re** ['ɛmpai̯ə(r)], das; -[s] ‹engl.› (das frühere britische Weltreich)

Em|pi|rem, das; -s, -e ‹griech.› (Erfahrungstatsache)

Em|pire|stil [ã'pi:r...], der; -[e]s ‹*zu* [1]Empire›

Em|pi|rie, die; - ‹griech.› (Erfahrung, Erfahrungswissen[schaft]); **Em|pi|ri|ker; Em|pi|ri|o|kri|ti|zis|mus** (eine Richtung der Philosophie, die sich allein auf die kritische Erfahrung beruft); **em|pi|risch; Em|pi|ris|mus,** der; - (Lehre, die allein die Erfahrung als Erkenntnisquelle gelten lässt); **Em|pi|rist,** der; -en, -en (↑R 126); **em|pi|ris|tisch**

em|por; em|por... (*in Zus. mit Verben,* z. B. emporkommen, du kamst empor, emporgekommen, emporzukommen); **em|por‿ar|bei|ten** (sich -), **...bli|cken; Em|po|re,** die; -, -n (erhöhter Sitzraum [in Kirchen]); **em|pö|ren;** sich -; **em|pö|rend** (unerhört); **Em|pö|rer** (*geh. für* Rebell); **em|pö|re|risch; em|por|kom|men; Em|por|kömm|ling** *(abwertend);* **em|por‿ra|gen, ...schla|gen, ...stei|gen, ...stre|ben; Em|pö|rung; Em|pö|rungs|schrei**

em|py|re|isch ‹griech.› (lichtstrahlend; himmlisch); **Em|py|re|um,** das; -s (Himmel in der antiken u. scholast. Philosophie)

Ems, die; - (Fluss in Nordwestdeutschland)

[1]**Em|scher,** die; - (r. Nebenfluss des Niederrheins); [2]**Em|scher,** das; -s ‹*nach* [1]Emscher› (eine geolog. Stufe)

Em|ser ‹*nach* Bad Ems› (↑R 103); Emser Depesche; Emser Salz

em|sig; Em|sig|keit, die; -

Ems-Ja|de-Ka|nal, der; -s (↑R 105)

E|mu, der; -s, -s ‹port.› (ein straußenähnl. Laufvogel)

E|mu|la|ti|on, die; -, -en ‹lat.-engl.› (*EDV* Nachahmung der Funktionen eines anderen Computers)

E|mul|ga|tor, der; -s, ...oren ‹lat.› (*Chemie* Stoff, der die Bildung einer Emulsion ermöglicht); **e|mul|gie|ren** (eine Emulsion bilden); **E|mul|sin,** das; -s (Ferment in bitteren Mandeln); **E|mul|si|on,** die; -, -en (feinste Verteilung einer Flüssigkeit in einer anderen, nicht mit ihr mischbaren Flüssigkeit; lichtempfindl. Schicht auf fotogr. Platten, Filmen u. Ä.)

E-Mu|sik, die; -; ↑R 26 (*kurz für* ernste Musik; *Ggs.* U-Musik)

E|na|ki|ter, E|naks|kin|der, E|naks|söh|ne *Plur.* (*im A. T.* sagenhaftes Volk von Riesen)

En|al|la|ge [ɛn'alage, *auch* ɛnala'ge:], die; - ‹griech.› (Versetzung des Attributs, z. B. „mit einem blauen Lächeln seiner Augen" *statt* „mit einem Lächeln seiner blauen Augen")

En|an|them, das; -s, -e ‹griech.› (*Med.* Schleimhautausschlag)

en a|vant! [ãna'vã:] ‹franz.› (vorwärts!)

en bloc [ã 'blɔk] ‹franz.› (im Ganzen); **En-bloc-Ab|stim|mung**

en car|rière [ã ka'riɛ:r] ‹franz.› (in vollem Lauf)

en|co|die|ren *vgl.* enkodieren

En|coun|ter [in'kau̯ntə(r)], das, *auch* der; -s, - ‹engl.› (*Psych.* Gruppentraining zur Steigerung der Empfindungsfähigkeit)

End‿ab|rech|nung, ...aus|schei|dung, ...bahn|hof, ...be|scheid, ...be|trag; End|chen; ein - Schnur; **End‿drei|ßi|ger** (Mann Ende dreißig), **...drei|ßi|ge|rin;**

En|de, das; -s, -n; am Ende; zu Ende sein, bringen, führen, gehen, kommen; das dicke Ende kommt nach *(ugs.);* Ende Januar; letzten Endes; eine Frau Ende dreißig; **End|ef|fekt;** im -; **En|del,** das; -s, - (*bayr., österr. für* Stoffrand); **en|deln** (*bayr., österr. für* Stoffränder einfassen)

En|de|mie, die; -, ...ien ‹griech.› (*Med.* örtlich begrenztes Auftreten einer Infektionskrankheit); **en|de|misch** *(Med., Biol.);* **En|de|mis|mus,** der; - (*Biol.* begrenztes Vorkommen von Tieren u. Pflanzen in einem Bezirk)

en|den; nicht enden wollender Beifall; **...en|der** (z. B. Achtender); **End‿er|folg, ...er|geb|nis**

en dé|tail [ã de'taj, *auch* de'ta:j] ‹franz.› (im Kleinen; einzeln; im Einzelverkauf; *Ggs.* en gros); *vgl.* Detail

End‿fas|sung, ...ge|rät (*EDV* Eingabe- oder Ausgabegerät, z. B. Terminal), **...ge|schwin|dig|keit; end|gül|tig; End|gül|tig|keit; End|hal|te|stel|le; en|di|gen** (*älter für* enden); **En|di|gung** *(veraltet)*

En|di|vie [...vi̯ə], die; -, -n ‹ägypt.› (Salatpflanze); **En|di|vi|en|sa|lat**

End‿kampf, ...kon|so|nant; End|la|ger; end|la|gern *nur im Inf. u. Partizip II gebr.;* **End‿la|ger|stät|te, ...la|ge|rung, ...lauf; End|lein;** ein - Schnur; **end|lich;** eine -e Größe; *aber* (↑R 47): im Endlichen (im endlichen Raum); **End|lich|keit** *Plur. selten;* **end|los;** endloses Band; *aber* (↑R 47): bis ins Endlose; **End|los‿band** (*Plur.* ...bänder), **...for|mu|lar** *(Druckw.);* **End|lo|sig|keit,** die; -; **End|mo|rä|ne**

en|do... ‹griech.› (innen...); **En|do...** (Innen...)

En|do|ga|mie, die; -, ...ien ‹griech.› (*Völkerk.* Heirat innerhalb von Stamm, Kaste usw.)

en|do|gen ‹griech.› (*Bot.* im Innern entstehend; *Med.* von innen kommend); -e Psychosen

En|do|kard, das; -s, -e ‹griech.› (*Med.* Herzinnenhaut); **En|do|kar|di|tis,** die; -, ...itiden (Entzündung der Herzinnenhaut)

En|do|karp, das; -s, -e ‹griech.› (*Bot.* die innerste Schicht der Fruchtwand)

en|do|krin ‹griech.› (*Med.* mit innerer Sekretion); -e Drüsen; **En|do|kri|no|lo|gie,** die; - (Lehre von der inneren Sekretion)

En|do|pro|the|se ‹griech.› (*Med.* künstl. Gelenk od. Knochenersatz zur Einpflanzung in den Körper)

En|dor|phin, das; -s, -e ‹*aus* endo... *u.* Morphin› (*Med., Biol.* körpereigener Eiweißstoff mit schmerzstillender Wirkung)

En|do|skop (↑R 132), das; -s, -e ‹griech.› (*Med.* Instrument zur Untersuchung von Körperhöhlen); **En|do|sko|pie,** die; -, ...ien (Untersuchung mit dem Endoskop)

En|do|thel, das; -s, -e *u.* **En|do-**

the|li|um, das; -s, ...ien [...i̯ən] ‹griech.› (Zellschicht, die Blut- u. Lymphgefäße auskleidet)
en|do|therm ‹griech.› (*Chemie* Wärme bindend, aufnehmend)
End‿pha|se, ...punkt, ...reim, ...re|sul|tat, ...run|de, ...sil|be, ...spiel, ...spurt, ...sta|di|um, ...sta|ti|on, ...stück, ...sum|me; En|dung; en|dungs|los *(Grammatik)*
En|du|ro, die; -, -s ‹engl.› (geländegängiges Motorrad)
End‿ur|sa|che, ...ver|brau|cher, ...vier|zi|ger, ...vo|kal, ...zeit; end|zeit|lich; End‿ziel, ...zif|fer, ...zu|stand, ...zweck
E|ner|ge|tik, die; - ‹griech.› (Lehre von der Energie; *Philos.* Auffassung von der Energie als Grundkraft aller Dinge); **e|ner|ge|tisch; E|ner|gie,** die; -, ...ien (Tatkraft; *Physik* Fähigkeit, Arbeit zu leisten); **e|ner|gie|arm; E|ner|gie|be|darf; e|ner|gie|be|wusst; E|ner|gie|bün|del** (*ugs. für* energiegeladener Mensch); **E|ner|gie‿ein|spa|rung, ...er|spar|nis; e|ner|gie|ge|la|den** (↑R 40); **E|ner|gie‿haus|halt, ...kri|se; e|ner|gie|los; E|ner|gie|lo|sig|keit,** die; -; **E|ner|gie‿po|li|tik, ...quel|le; e|ner|gie|reich; E|ner|gie‿spa|rer, ...spar|pro|gramm, ...trä|ger, ...ver|brauch, ...ver|sor|gung, ...wirt|schaft, ...zu|fuhr; e|ner|gisch**
E|ner|va|ti|on [...v...], die; -, -en ‹lat.› (*Med.* Ausschaltung der Verbindung zwischen Nerv u. dazugehörigem Organ); **e|ner|vie|ren** (entnerven, entkräften)
E|nes|cu, *auch* E|nes|co (rumän. Komponist u. Geigenvirtuose)
en face [ã 'fas] ‹franz.› (von vorn; gegenüber)
en fa|mille [ã fa'mij] ‹franz., „in der Familie"› (*veraltend für* im engsten [Familien]kreis)
En|fant ter|ri|ble [ã.fã tɛ'ri:b(ə)l], das; - -, -s -s [ã.fã tɛ'ri:b(ə)l] ‹franz.› (jmd., der gegen die geltenden [gesellschaftlichen] Regeln verstößt und dadurch seine Umgebung oft schockiert)
eng; ein eng anliegendes Kleid; eng befreundete Familien; ein eng bedrucktes Blatt; ein eng umgrenztes Gebiet; eine mit uns eng verwandte Person; die Bereiche sind auf das, aufs Engste *od.* auf das, aufs engste miteinander verflochten
En|ga|din [*auch*, schweiz. nur, ...'di:n], das; -s (Talschaft des Inns in der Schweiz)
En|ga|ge|ment [ãgaʒ(ə)'mã:], das; -s, -s (Verpflichtung, Bindung; [An]stellung, bes. eines Künstlers; persönlicher Einsatz); **en|ga|gie|ren** [ãga'ʒi:...] (verpflichten, binden); sich - (sich einsetzen); **en|ga|giert; En|ga|giert|heit,** die; -
eng an|lie|gend, be|druckt, be|freun|det usw. *vgl.* eng; **eng|brüs|tig; En|ge,** die; -, -n
En|gel, der; -s, -
En|gel|laut (*für* Frikativ)
En|gel|berg (schweiz. Abtei u. Kurort südl. des Vierwaldstätter Sees)
En|gel|bert (m. Vorn.); **En|gel|ber|ta** (w. Vorn.); **En|gel|brecht** (m. Vorn.)
En|gel|chen, En|gel|lein; en|gel|gleich, en|gels|gleich; **en|gel|haft; En|gel|haf|tig|keit,** die; -
En|gel|hard (m. Vorn.)
En|gel|kopf, En|gels|kopf; **En|gel|ma|cher** (*ugs. verhüllend für* Kurpfuscher, der illegale Abtreibungen vornimmt); **En|gel|ma|che|rin; en|gel|rein** *(geh.);* eine -e Stimme
En|gels (Mitbegründer des Marxismus)
En|gels|burg, die; - (in Rom); **en|gel|schön** *(geh.);* **En|gels‿ge|duld, ...ge|sicht** (*Plur.* ...gesichter); **en|gels|gleich; En|gels‿haar, ...kopf, ...stim|me; En|gel|süß,** das; -es (Farnart); **En|gels|zun|gen** *Plur.; nur in* mit [Menschen- und mit] Engelszungen (so eindringlich wie möglich) reden; **En|gel|wurz** (eine Heilpflanze)
en|gen (*selten für* einengen)
En|ger|ling (Maikäferlarve)
eng|her|zig; Eng|her|zig|keit, die; -; **En|gig|keit,** die; -
Eng|land; Eng|län|der (*auch* Bez. für ein zangenartiges Werkzeug); **Eng|län|de|rin**
Eng|lein
eng|lisch; englischer Trab; ein englischer Garten; englische Broschur (ein Bucheinband); englische Woche *(Fußball);* die englische Krankheit (*veraltet für* Rachitis); *aber* (↑R 108): das Englische Fräulein *(vgl. d.),* der Englische Garten in München; *vgl.* deutsch; **Eng|lisch,** das; -[s] (Sprache); *vgl.* Deutsch; **Eng|li|sche,** das; -n; *vgl.* Deutsche, das; **Eng|li|sche Fräu|lein,** das; -n -s, -n - (Angehörige eines Frauenordens)
Eng|li|sche Gruß, der; -n -es ‹*zu* Engel› (ein Gebet)
Eng|lisch|horn *Plur.* ...hörner (ein Holzblasinstrument); **Eng|lish spo|ken** ['iŋgliʃ 'spo:k(ə)n] ‹engl., [hier wird] „Englisch gesprochen"›; **Eng|lish|waltz** ['iŋgliʃwɔ:ls], der; -, - (langsamer Walzer); **eng|li|sie|ren** ([einem Pferd] die niederziehenden Schweifmuskeln durchschneiden, damit es den Schwanz hoch trägt; anglisieren; *vgl. d.*)
eng|ma|schig
En|go|be [ã'go:bə], die; -, -n ‹franz.› (keram. Überzugsmasse); **en|go|bie|ren**
Eng|pass
En|gramm, das; -s, -e ‹griech.› (*Med., Psych.* bleibende Spur geistiger Eindrücke, Erinnerungsbild)
en gros [ã 'gro:] ‹franz.› (im Großen; *Ggs.* en détail); **En|gros‿han|del** (Großhandel), **...preis; En|gros|sist** (*österr. neben* Grossist)
eng|stir|nig *(abwertend);* **Eng|stir|nig|keit,** die; -; **eng um|grenzt, ver|wandt** *vgl.* eng
en|har|mo|nisch ‹griech.› ([von Tönen] dem Klang nach gleich, in der Bez. verschieden, z. B. cis = des); -e Verwechslung
e|nig|ma|tisch *vgl.* änigmatisch
En|jam|be|ment [ãʒãb(ə)'mã:], das; -s, -s (*Verslehre* Übergreifen eines Satzes auf den nächsten Vers)
en|kaus|tie|ren ‹griech.› (*bild. Kunst* mit flüssigem Wachs verschmolzene Farbe auftragen); **En|kaus|tik,** die; -; **en|kaus|tisch**
¹En|kel, der; -s, - (*landsch. für* Fußknöchel)
²En|kel, der; -s, - (Kindeskind); **En|ke|lin; En|kel‿kind, ...sohn, ...toch|ter**
En|kla|ve [...və], die; -, -n ‹franz.› (ein fremdstaatl. Gebiet im eigenen Staatsgebiet); *vgl.* Exklave
En|kli|se, En|kli|sis, die; -, ...isen ‹griech.› (*Sprachw.* Anlehnung eines unbetonten Wortes an das vorausgehende betonte; *Ggs.* Proklise); **En|kli|ti|kon,** das; -s, *Plur.* ...ka *od.* ...ken (unbetontes Wort, das sich an das vorhergehende betonte anlehnt, z. B. *in ugs.* „kommste" *für* „kommst du"); **en|kli|tisch**
en|ko|die|ren, *fachspr. meist* en|co|die|ren ‹engl.› ([eine Nachricht] verschlüsseln)
En|ko|mi|on, En|ko|mi|um, das; -s, ...ien [...i̯ən] ‹griech.› (Lobrede, -schrift)
en masse [ã 'mas] ‹franz.› (*ugs. für* massenhaft, gehäuft)
en mi|ni|a|ture [ã minia'ty:r] ‹franz.› (in kleinem Maßstab, im Kleinen)

en|net (*schweiz. mdal. für* jenseits), *Präp. mit Dat.;* - dem Gebirge; **en|net|bir|gisch** (*schweiz. für* jenseits der Alpen gelegen); **en|net|rhei|nisch** (*schweiz. für* jenseits des Rheins gelegen)
En|no (m. Vorn.)
[1]**Enns,** die; - (r. Nebenfluss der Donau); [2]**Enns** (Stadt in Oberösterreich); **Enns|tal** (Tal in der Steiermark); **Enns|ta|ler Al|pen**
en|nu|yie|ren [ãny'ji:...] (*veraltet für* langweilen)
e|norm ‹franz.› (außerordentlich; ungeheuer); **E|nor|mi|tät,** die; -
en pas|sant [ã pa'sã:] ‹franz.› (im Vorübergehen; beiläufig)
en pro|fil [ã prɔ'fi(:)l] ‹franz.› (im Profil, von der Seite)
En|quete [ã'kɛ:t], die; -, -n [...tən] ‹franz.› (Untersuchung, Erhebung; *österr. auch für* Arbeitstagung); **En|quete|kom|mis|si|on**
en|ra|giert [ãra'ʒi:rt] ‹franz.› (*veraltet für* leidenschaftlich erregt)
en route [ã 'rut] ‹franz.› (unterwegs)
En|sem|ble [ã'sã:b(ə)l], das; -s, -s ‹franz.› (ein zusammengehörendes Ganzes; Künstlergruppe; mehrteiliges [Damen]kleidungsstück); **En|sem|ble|spiel,** das; -[e]s
En|si|la|ge [ãsi'la:ʒə], Si|la|ge, die; - ‹franz.› (Gärfutter[bereitung])
En|sor (belg. Maler)
en suite [ã 'svit] ‹franz.› (ununterbrochen)
ent... (*Vorsilbe von Verben,* z. B. entführen, du entführst, er hat ihn entführt, zu entführen)
...ent (z. B. Referent, der; -en, -en; ↑R 126)
ent|am|ten (*veraltet für* des Amtes entheben); **Ent|am|tung**
ent|ar|ten; ent|ar|tet; -e Kunst (*Nationalsoz.*); **Ent|ar|tung; Ent|ar|tungs|er|schei|nung**
ent|a|schen (↑R 132); **Ent|a|schung**
En|ta|se, En|ta|sis, die; -, ...asen ‹griech.› (*Archit.* Schwellung des Säulenschaftes)
ent|as|ten, ent|äs|ten (Äste entfernen)
ent|äu|ßern, sich (*geh.*); ich entäußere mich allen Besitzes; **Ent|äu|ße|rung,** die; -
Ent|bal|lung; - von Industriegebieten
ent|beh|ren; ein Buch -; des Trostes -; **ent|behr|lich; Ent|behr|lich|keit,** die; -; **Ent|beh|rung; ent|beh|rungs‿reich, ...voll**
ent|bei|nen (Knochen aus etwas entfernen)
ent|bie|ten (*geh.*); Grüße -
ent|bin|den; Ent|bin|dung; Ent|bin|dungs‿heim, ...pfle|ger (Berufsbez.), **...sta|ti|on**
ent|blät|tern; sich -
ent|blö|den; *nur in* sich nicht entblöden (*geh. für* sich nicht scheuen)
ent|blö|ßen; du entblößt; sich -; **Ent|blö|ßung**
ent|bren|nen (*geh.*)
ent|bü|ro|kra|ti|sie|ren; Ent|bü|ro|kra|ti|sie|rung, die; -
Ent|chen
ent|chlo|ren; Trinkwasser -
ent|de|cken; Ent|de|cker; Ent|de|cker|freu|de; Ent|de|cke|rin; ent|de|cke|risch; Ent|de|ckung; Ent|de|ckungs‿fahrt, ...rei|se, ...rei|sen|de
ent|dröh|nen (*Technik* dröhnende Geräusche dämpfen); eine Maschine -; **Ent|dröh|nung**
ent|dun|keln; ich ...[e]le (↑R 16)
En|te, die; -, -n (*ugs. auch für* falsche [Presse]meldung); ↑R 108: kalte - (ein Getränk)
ent|eh|ren; ent|eh|rend; Ent|eh|rung
ent|eig|nen; Ent|eig|nung
ent|ei|len (*geh.*)
ent|ei|sen (von Eis befreien); du enteist; er ent|eis|te; enteist
ent|ei|se|nen (von Eisen befreien); du enteisenst; enteisent; enteisentes Wasser; **Ent|ei|se|nung**
Ent|ei|sung (Befreiung von Eis)
En|te|le|chie, die; -, ...ien ‹griech.› (*Philos.* im Organismus liegende Kraft zur Entwicklung u. Vollendung der Anlagen); **en|te|le|chisch**
En|ten‿bra|ten, ...ei, ...grüt|ze (die; -; Geflecht von Wasserlinsen), **...kü|ken** (*vgl.* [1]Küken)
En|tente [ã'tã:t], die; -, -n [...tən] ‹franz.› (Bündnis zwischen Staaten); (↑R 108:) die Kleine - (*hist.*); **En|tente cor|di|ale** [- kɔr'djal], die; - - (*Bez. für* das franz.-engl. Bündnis nach 1904)
En|ten‿teich, ...wal
En|ter, das, *auch* der; -s, - (*nordd. für* einjähr. Fohlen, Kalb)
ent|er|ben
En|ter|brü|cke
Ent|er|bung
En|ter|ha|ken
En|te|rich, der; -s, -e (m. Ente)
En|te|ri|tis, die; -, ...itiden ‹griech.› (*Med.* Darmentzündung)
en|tern ‹niederl.› (auf etwas klettern); ein Schiff - (mit Enterhaken festhalten und erobern); ich ...ere (↑R 16)
En|te|ro|kly|se, die; -, -n ‹griech.› (*Med.* Darmspülung); **En|te|ro|skop** (↑R 132), das; -s, -e (*Med.* Endoskop zur Untersuchung des Dickdarms); **En|te|ros|to|mie** (↑R 132), die; -, ...ien (*Med.* Anlegung eines künstl. Afters)
En|ter|tai|ner [...te:nə(r)], der; -s, - ‹engl.› ([berufsmäßiger] Unterhalter); **En|ter|tai|ne|rin**
En|te|rung
ent|fa|chen (*geh.*); **Ent|fa|chung**
ent|fah|ren; ein Fluch entfuhr ihm
ent|fal|len
ent|falt|bar; ent|fal|ten; sich -; **Ent|fal|tung; Ent|fal|tungs|mög|lich|keit**
ent|fär|ben; Ent|fär|ber (Entfärbungsmittel)
ent|fer|nen; sich -; **ent|fernt;** weit [davon] entfernt, das zu tun; nicht im Entferntesten; **Ent|fer|nung;** in einer - von 4 Meter[n] (↑R 90); **Ent|fer|nungs|mes|ser,** der
ent|fes|seln; Ent|fes|se|lung, *seltener* Ent|fess|lung; **Ent|fes|se|lungs|künst|ler; Ent|fess|lung** *vgl.* Entfesselung
ent|fes|ti|gen; Metalle - (weich[er] machen); **Ent|fes|ti|gung**
ent|fet|ten; Ent|fet|tung; Ent|fet|tungs|kur
ent|feuch|ten; Ent|feuch|ter (Gerät, das der Luft Feuchtigkeit entzieht); **Ent|feuch|tung**
ent|flamm|bar; ent|flam|men (*geh.*); **ent|flammt; Ent|flam|mung**
ent|flech|ten; er entflicht (*auch* entflechtet); er entflocht (*auch* entflechtete); entflochten; **Ent|flech|tung**
ent|flie|gen
ent|flie|hen
ent|frem|den; sich -; **Ent|frem|dung**
ent|fris|ten (von einer Befristung lösen); Tarifverträge -
ent|fros|ten; Ent|fros|ter; Ent|fros|tung
ent|füh|ren; Ent|füh|rer; Ent|füh|rung
ent|ga|sen; du entgast; **Ent|ga|sung**
ent|ge|gen; meinem Vorschlag - *od.* - meinem Vorschlag; **ent|ge|gen...** (*in Zus. mit Verben,* z. B. entgegenkommen, du kommst entgegen, entgegengekommen, entgegenzukommen); **ent|ge|gen‿bli|cken, ...brin|gen** (jmdm. Vertrauen -), **...fah|ren, ...ge|hen; ent|ge|gen|ge|setzt;** *aber* das Entgegengesetzte (↑R 47); er ging in die -e Richtung; **ent|ge|gen|ge|setz|ten|falls** (*Amtsspr.*); *vgl.* Fall, der; **ent|ge|gen‿hal|ten, ...kom|men; Ent|ge|gen|kom|men,** das; -s; **ent|ge|gen|kom|mend; ent|ge|gen|kom-**

men|der|wei|se; *aber* in entgegenkommender Weise; **ent|ge|gen⌣lau|fen, ...neh|men, ...se|hen, ...set|zen; ent|ge|gen|set|zend** (*auch für* adversativ); **ent|ge|gen⌣ste|hen, ...stel|len, ...stem|men** (sich), **...tre|ten; ent|geg|nen** (erwidern); **Ent|geg|nung**

ent|ge|hen; ich lasse mir nichts -

ent|geis|tert (sprachlos; verstört)

Ent|gelt, das; -[e]s, -e; gegen, ohne -; **ent|gel|ten** *(geh.);* er lässt mich meine Nachlässigkeit nicht -; **ent|gelt|lich** (gegen Bezahlung); **Ent|gelt[s]|ta|rif**

ent|gif|ten; Ent|gif|tung

ent|glei|sen; du entgleist; er entgleis|te; **Ent|glei|sung**

ent|glei|ten

ent|glo|ri|fi|zie|ren; Ent|glo|ri|fi|zie|rung

ent|got|ten; ent|göt|tern; ich ...ere (↑R 16); **Ent|göt|te|rung; Ent|got|tung**

ent|gra|ten; entgratetes Eisen

ent|grä|ten; entgräteter Fisch

ent|gren|zen (*geh. für* aus der Begrenztheit lösen); **Ent|gren|zung**

ent|haa|ren; Ent|haa|rung; Ent|haa|rungs|mit|tel, das

ent|haf|ten (*selten für* aus der Haft entlassen); **Ent|haf|tung**

ent|hal|ten; sich -; ich enthielt mich der Stimme; **ent|halt|sam; Ent|halt|sam|keit,** die; -; **Ent|hal|tung**

ent|här|ten; Ent|här|tung

ent|haup|ten; Ent|haup|tung

ent|häu|ten; Ent|häu|tung

ent|he|ben *(geh.);* jmdn. seines Amtes -; **Ent|he|bung**

ent|hei|li|gen; Ent|hei|li|gung

ent|hem|men *(Psych.);* **Ent|hemmt|heit,** die; -; **Ent|hem|mung**

ent|hül|len *(geh.);* sich -; **Ent|hül|lung**

ent|hül|sen

ent|hu|ma|ni|sie|ren; Ent|hu|ma|ni|sie|rung

en|thu|si|as|mie|ren ⟨franz.⟩ (begeistern); **En|thu|si|as|mus,** der; - ⟨griech.⟩ (Begeisterung; Leidenschaftlichkeit); **En|thu|si|ast,** der; -en, -en (↑R 126); **En|thu|si|as|tin; en|thu|si|as|tisch**

ent|ide|o|lo|gi|sie|ren (↑R 132; von ideologischen Zielen, Vorurteilen befreien); **Ent|ide|o|lo|gi|sie|rung**

En|ti|tät, die; -, -en ⟨lat.⟩ (*Philos.* Dasein im Unterschied zum Wesen eines Dinges)

ent|jung|fern; Ent|jung|fe|rung

ent|kal|ken; Ent|kal|kung

ent|kei|men; Ent|kei|mung

ent|ker|nen; Früchte -; **Ent|ker|ner; Ent|ker|nung**

ent|klei|den *(geh.);* sich -; **Ent|klei|dung; Ent|klei|dungs|sze|ne** (im Film, Theaterstück)

ent|kno|ten

ent|kof|fe|i|nie|ren entkoffeinierter Kaffee

ent|ko|lo|ni|a|li|sie|ren; Ent|ko|lo|ni|a|li|sie|rung

ent|kom|men; Ent|kom|men, das; -s

ent|kop|peln; Ent|kop|pe|lung, Ent|kopp|lung

ent|kor|ken

ent|kräf|ten; Ent|kräf|tung

ent|kramp|fen; Ent|kramp|fung

ent|krau|ten; den Boden -

ent|kri|mi|na|li|sie|ren; Ent|kri|mi|na|li|sie|rung, die; -

ent|la|den; *vgl.* [1]laden; sich -; **Ent|la|dung**

ent|lang; *bei Nachstellung mit Akk.:* den Wald entlang (*selten Dat.:* dem Wald entlang); *bei Voranstellung mit Dat.:* entlang dem Fluss (*selten Gen.:* entlang des Flusses; *veraltet Akk.:* entlang den Fluss); am Ufer entlang; am, das Ufer entlanglaufen; *vgl.* längs; **ent|lang...** (*in Zus. mit Verben,* z. B. entlanglaufen, du läufst entlang, entlanggelaufen, entlangzulaufen); **ent|lang⌣fah|ren, ...füh|ren, ...ge|hen, ...kom|men, ...lau|fen** (*vgl.* entlang *u.* entlang...)

ent|lar|ven [...f...]; **Ent|lar|vung**

Ent|lass... (*südd. in Zus. für* Entlassungs..., z. B. Entlassfeier); **ent|las|sen; Ent|las|sung; Ent|las|sungs⌣fei|er, ...pa|pie|re** *(Plur.),* **...schein, ...schü|ler**

ent|las|ten; Ent|las|tung; Ent|las|tungs⌣an|griff, ...ma|te|ri|al, ...schlag, ...zeu|ge, ...zug

ent|lau|ben; Ent|lau|bung

ent|lau|fen

ent|lau|sen; Ent|lau|sung; Ent|lau|sungs|schein

Ent|le|buch, das; -s (schweiz. Landschaft)

ent|le|di|gen *(geh.);* sich der Aufgabe -; **Ent|le|di|gung**

ent|lee|ren; Ent|lee|rung

ent|le|gen; Ent|le|gen|heit, die; - *(geh.)*

ent|leh|nen; Ent|leh|nung

ent|lei|ben, sich (*geh. für* sich töten)

ent|lei|hen (für sich leihen); **Ent|lei|her; Ent|lei|hung**

ent|lo|ben, sich; **Ent|lo|bung**

ent|lo|cken

ent|loh|nen, *schweiz.* **ent|löh|nen; Ent|loh|nung,** *schweiz.* **Ent|löh|nung**

ent|lüf|ten; Ent|lüf|ter; Ent|lüf|tung; Ent|lüf|tungs⌣hau|be, ...ven|til

ent|mach|ten; Ent|mach|tung

ent|mag|ne|ti|sie|ren

ent|man|nen; Ent|man|nung

ent|men|schen; ent|mensch|li|chen; ent|menscht

ent|mie|ten (Häuser, Wohnungen nicht mehr vermieten, um sie [in saniertem Zustand] zu verkaufen oder teurer zu vermieten)

ent|mi|li|ta|ri|sie|ren; entmilitarisierte Zone; **Ent|mi|li|ta|ri|sie|rung**

ent|mi|schen *(Chemie, Technik);* **Ent|mi|schung**

ent|mis|ten; Ent|mis|tung

ent|mün|di|gen; Ent|mün|di|gung

ent|mu|ti|gen; Ent|mu|ti|gung

ent|mys|ti|fi|zie|ren (mystische Vorstellungen, die mit etwas verknüpft sind, beseitigen); **Ent|mys|ti|fi|zie|rung**

ent|my|thi|sie|ren *vgl.* entmythologisieren; **Ent|my|thi|sie|rung; ent|my|tho|lo|gi|sie|ren** (mythische od. irrationale Vorstellungen, die mit etwas verknüpft sind, beseitigen); **Ent|my|tho|lo|gi|sie|rung**

Ent|nah|me, die; -, -n

ent|na|ti|o|na|li|sie|ren (ausbürgern; die Verstaatlichung rückgängig machen); **Ent|na|ti|o|na|li|sie|rung**

ent|na|zi|fi|zie|ren; Ent|na|zi|fi|zie|rung

ent|neh|men; [aus] den Worten -

ent|ner|ven [...f...]; **ent|nervt; Ent|ner|vung**

En|to|derm, das; -s, -e ⟨griech.⟩ (*Biol.* inneres Keimblatt des Embryos)

ent|ölen (↑R 132); entölter Kakao

En|to|mo|lo|ge, der; -n, -n (↑R 126) ⟨griech.⟩ (Insektenforscher); **En|to|mo|lo|gie,** die; -; **en|to|mo|lo|gisch**

en|to|pisch ⟨griech.⟩ (*fachspr. für* am Ort befindlich, einheimisch)

ent|op|tisch (↑R 132) ⟨griech.⟩ (*Med.* im Innern des Auges gelegen)

en|to|tisch (↑R 132) ⟨griech.⟩ (*Med.* im Innern des Ohres entstehend)

ent|per|sön|li|chen (das Persönliche bei etwas ausschalten); **Ent|per|sön|li|chung**

ent|pflich|ten (von Amtspflichten entbinden); **Ent|pflich|tung**

ent|po|li|ti|sie|ren; Ent|po|li|ti|sie|rung

ent|pul|pen (*fachspr. für* [Rübenzuckersaft] entfasern)

ent|pup|pen, sich; **Ent|pup|pung**
ent|quel|len *(geh.)*
ent|rah|men; Ent|rah|mer (Maschine, mit der die Milch entrahmt wird); **Ent|rah|mung**
ent|ra|ten (*veraltend für* entbehren); des Brotes [nicht] - können
ent|rät|seln; Ent|rät|se|lung, *seltener* **Ent|räts|lung**
Ent|re|akt [ãtrə'|akt, *auch* ã'trakt] (↑R 130), der; -[e]s, -e ‹franz.› (*Theater* Zwischenakt, Zwischenspiel, Zwischenmusik)
ent|rech|ten; Ent|rech|tung
Ent|re|cote [ãtrə'ko:t] (↑R 130), das; -[s], -s ‹franz.› (Rippenstück vom Rind)
Ent|ree [ã'tre:] (↑R 130), das; -s, -s ‹franz.› (Eintritt[sgeld], Eingang; Vorspeise; Eröffnungsmusik [bei Balletten]); **Ent|ree|tür**
ent|rei|ßen
ent|re nous [ˌãtrə 'nu] (↑R 130) ‹franz., „unter uns"› (*selten für* ungezwungen, vertraulich)
Ent|re|pot [ãtr(ə)'po:] (↑R 130), das; -, -s ‹franz.› (zollfreier Stapelplatz)
ent|rich|ten; Ent|rich|tung
ent|rie|geln; Ent|rie|ge|lung
ent|rin|den; Baumstämme -
ent|rin|gen, sich *(geh.)*; ein Seufzer entrang sich ihm
ent|rin|nen *(geh.)*; **Ent|rin|nen,** das; -s
ent|risch (*bayr., österr. mdal. für* unheimlich, nicht geheuer)
ent|rol|len *(geh.)*; sich -
En|tro|pie, die; -, ...ien ‹griech.› (*Physik* Größe der Thermodynamik; *Informationstheorie* Größe des Nachrichtengehalts einer Zeichenmenge)
ent|ros|ten; Ent|ros|ter (Mittel gegen Rost); **Ent|ros|tung**
ent|rü|cken *(geh.)*; **Ent|rückt|heit; Ent|rü|ckung**
ent|rüm|peln; ich ...[e]le (↑R 16); **Ent|rüm|pe|lung,** *seltener* **Ent|rümp|lung**
ent|ru|ßen; den Ofen -
ent|rüs|ten; sich -; **ent|rüs|tet; Ent|rüs|tung; Ent|rüs|tungs|sturm**
ent|saf|ten; Ent|saf|ter
ent|sa|gen *(geh.)*; dem Vorhaben -; **Ent|sa|gung** *(geh.)*; **ent|sa|gungs|voll**
ent|sah|nen
ent|sal|zen; entsalzt; **Ent|sal|zung**
Ent|satz, der; -es; jmdm. - bringen
ent|säu|ern; Ent|säu|e|rung
ent|schä|di|gen; Ent|schä|di|gung; Ent|schä|di|gungs|sum|me
ent|schär|fen; Ent|schär|fung
Ent|scheid, der; -[e]s, -e; **ent|schei|den;** sich für od. gegen etwas -; **ent|schei|dend; Ent|schei|dung; Ent|schei|dungs-_be|fug|nis, ...fin|dung, ...fra|ge** *(Sprachw.)*, **...frei|heit, ...ge|walt, ...schlacht; ent|schei|dungs|schwer** *(geh.)*; **Ent|schei|dungs|spiel; ent|schie|den;** auf das, aufs Entschiedenste *od.* auf das, aufs entschiedenste; **Ent|schie|den|heit,** die; -
ent|schla|cken; Ent|schla|ckung
ent|schla|fen (*geh., verhüllend für* sterben); **Ent|schla|fe|ne,** der *u.* die; -n, -n (↑R 5 ff.)
ent|schla|gen, sich *(veraltet)*; sich aller Sorgen -
ent|schlam|men; Ent|schlam|mung
ent|schlei|ern *(geh.)*; ich ...ere (↑R 16); **Ent|schlei|e|rung**
ent|schlie|ßen, sich; sie entschloss sich; **Ent|schlie|ßung; ent|schlos|sen; Ent|schlos|sen|heit,** die; -
ent|schlüp|fen
Ent|schluss
ent|schlüs|seln; Ent|schlüs|se|lung, Ent|schlüss|lung
ent|schluss|fä|hig; Ent|schluss-_fä|hig|keit (die; -), **...frei|heit** (die; -), **...freu|dig|keit** (die; -), **...kraft** (die; -); **ent|schluss|los; Ent|schluss|lo|sig|keit,** die; -
Ent|schlüss|lung *vgl.* Entschlüsselung
ent|schrot|ten; Ent|schrot|tung
ent|schuld|bar; Ent|schuld|bar|keit, die; -; **ent|schul|den** (Schulden senken); **ent|schul|di|gen;** sich wegen *od.* für etwas -; **Ent|schul|di|gung; Ent|schul|di|gungs-_brief, ...grund, ...schrei|ben; Ent|schul|dung**
ent|schup|pen
ent|schwe|ben *(geh., oft iron.)*
ent|schwe|feln; Ent|schwe|fe|lung, Ent|schwef|lung
ent|schwei|ßen ([Wolle] von Schweiß und Fett reinigen)
ent|schwin|den *(geh.)*
ent|seelt (*geh. für* tot); **Ent|see|lung,** die; - (*geh. für* das Seelenloswerden); die - der Umwelt
ent|sen|den; Ent|sen|dung
ent|set|zen; sich -; **Ent|set|zen,** das; -s; ein Entsetzen erregender Anblick; **Ent|set|zens|schrei; ent|setz|lich; Ent|setz|lich|keit; ent|setzt**
ent|seu|chen (*fachspr. für* desinfizieren); **Ent|seu|chung**
ent|si|chern; das Gewehr -
ent|sie|geln; Ent|sie|ge|lung, *seltener* **Ent|sieg|lung**
ent|sin|nen, sich; ich habe mich deiner entsonnen; **ent|sinn|li|chen; Ent|sinn|li|chung,** die; -
ent|sitt|li|chen; Ent|sitt|li|chung
ent|sor|gen; Ent|sor|gung (Beseitigung von Müll u. Ä.)
ent|span|nen; sich -; **ent|spannt;** -es Wasser; **Ent|span|nung; Ent|span|nungs-_po|li|tik, ...übung** (↑R 132)
ent|spie|geln; eine Brille -; **Ent|spie|ge|lung, Ent|spieg|lung**
ent|spin|nen, sich
ent|spre|chen; ent|spre|chend; entsprechend seinem Vorschlag *od.* seinem Vorschlag entsprechend; (↑R 47:) Entsprechendes, das Entsprechende gilt für ...; **Ent|spre|chung**
ent|sprie|ßen *(geh.)*
ent|sprin|gen
ent|sta|li|ni|sie|ren; Ent|sta|li|ni|sie|rung, die; -
ent|stam|men
ent|stau|ben; Ent|stau|ber; Ent|stau|bung
ent|ste|hen; Ent|ste|hung; Ent|ste|hungs-_ge|schich|te, ...ort, ...ur|sa|che, ...zeit
ent|stei|gen *(geh.)*
ent|stei|nen; Kirschen -
ent|stel|len (verunstalten); **ent|stellt; Ent|stel|lung**
ent|stem|peln; die Nummernschilder wurden entstempelt
ent|sti|cken (*Chemie* Stickoxide aus Rauchgasen entfernen); **Ent|sti|ckung**
ent|stoff|li|chen
ent|stö|ren; Ent|stö|rung; Ent|stö|rungs-_dienst, ...stel|le
ent|strö|men *(geh.)*
ent|süh|nen *(geh.)*; **Ent|süh|nung**
ent|sump|fen; Ent|sump|fung
ent|ta|bu|ie|ren, ent|ta|bu|i|sie|ren ([einer Sache] den Charakter des Tabus nehmen); **Ent|ta|bu|ie|rung; ent|ta|bu|i|sie|ren** *vgl.* enttabuieren; **Ent|ta|bu|i|sie|rung**
ent|tar|nen; Ent|tar|nung
ent|täu|schen; Ent|täu|schung; ent|täu|schungs|reich
ent|tee|ren; Ent|tee|rung
ent|thro|nen; Ent|thro|nung
ent|trüm|mern; Ent|trüm|me|rung
ent|völ|kern; ich ...ere (↑R 16); **Ent|völ|ke|rung,** die; -
entw. = entweder
ent|wach|sen
ent|waff|nen; Ent|waff|nung
ent|wal|den; Ent|wal|dung
ent|wan|zen; Ent|wan|zung
ent|war|nen; Ent|war|nung
ent|wäs|sern; Ent|wäs|se|rung, Ent|wäss|rung; **Ent|wäs|se|rungs|gra|ben; Ent|wäss|rung** *vgl.* Entwässerung

ent|we|der [*auch* ...'ve:...] (*Abk.* entw.); *nur in* entweder – oder; **Ent|we|der-o|der,** das; -, - (↑R 49)
ent|wei|chen; *vgl.* ²weichen; **Ent|weich|ge|schwin|dig|keit** (*svw.* Fluchtgeschwindigkeit); **Ent|wei|chung**
ent|wei|hen; Ent|wei|hung
ent|wen|den; ich entwendete, habe entwendet; **Ent|wen|dung**
ent|wer|fen; Pläne -; **Ent|wer|fer**
ent|wer|ten; Ent|wer|ter (Automat zur Entwertung von Fahrscheinen); **Ent|wer|tung**
ent|we|sen; ein Gebäude - (*fachspr. für* von Ungeziefer reinigen); **Ent|we|sung**
ent|wi|ckeln; sich -; **Ent|wi|ckelung** *vgl.* Ent|wick|lung; **Ent|wick|ler** *(Fotogr.);* **Ent|wick|lung,** *(veraltet:)* Entwickelung; **Ent|wick|lungs|dienst; ent|wick|lungs|fä|hig; Ent|wick|lungs|ge|schich|te; ent|wick|lungs|ge|schicht|lich; Ent|wick|lungs‿ge|setz, ...grad, ...hel|fer, ...hel|fe|rin; ent|wick|lungs|hem|mend; Ent|wick|lungs‿hil|fe, ...jah|re** *(Plur.),* **...land** (*Plur.* ...länder), **...pro|zess, ...ro|man, ...stö|rung, ...stu|fe, ...zeit**
ent|wid|men (*Amtsspr.* einer bestimmten Benutzung entziehen); einen Weg -; **Ent|wid|mung**
ent|win|den; *vgl.* ¹winden
ent|wirr|bar; ent|wir|ren; sich -; **Ent|wir|rung**
ent|wi|schen (*ugs. für* entkommen)
ent|wöh|nen; Ent|wöh|nung
ent|wöl|ken, sich *(geh.);* **Ent|wöl|kung**
ent|wür|di|gen; Ent|wür|di|gung
Ent|wurf; Ent|wurfs‿ge|schwin|dig|keit (Richtwert im Straßenbau), **...zeich|nung**
ent|wur|men; Ent|wur|mung
ent|wur|zeln; ich ...[e]le (↑R 16); **Ent|wur|ze|lung,** *seltener* **Ent|wurz|lung**
ent|zau|bern; Ent|zau|be|rung
ent|zer|ren; Ent|zer|rer *(Technik);* **Ent|zer|rung**
ent|zie|hen; sich -; **Ent|zie|hung; Ent|zie|hungs‿an|stalt, ...er|schei|nung, ...kur**
ent|zif|fer|bar; Ent|zif|fe|rer; ent|zif|fern; ich ...ere (↑R 16); **Ent|zif|fe|rung**
ent|zü|cken; Ent|zü|cken, das; -s *(geh.);* **ent|zü|ckend; Ent|zü|ckung** *(geh.)*
Ent|zug, der; -[e]s; **Ent|zugs|er|schei|nung**
ent|zünd|bar; ent|zün|den; sich -
ent|zün|dern (*für* dekapieren); ich ...ere (↑R 16)
ent|zünd|lich; ein leicht entzündliches Gemisch; **Ent|zünd|lich|keit,** die; -; **Ent|zün|dung; ent|zün|dungs|hem|mend; Ent|zün|dungs|herd**
ent|zwei; entzwei sein; **ent|zwei...** (*in Zus. mit Verben,* z. B. entzweibrechen, du brichst entzwei, entzweigebrochen, entzweizubrechen); **ent|zwei|bre|chen; ent|zwei|en;** sich -; **ent|zwei‿ge|hen, ...ma|chen** *(ugs.),* **...schnei|den; Ent|zwei|ung**
E|nu|me|ra|ti|on, die; -, -en ‹lat.› (Aufzählung); **e|nu|me|ra|tiv** (aufzählend)
En|ve|lop|pe [ãvəˈlɔp(ə)], die; -, -n ‹franz.› (*Math.* einhüllende Kurve)
En|vi|ron|ment [ɛnˈvai(ə)rənmənt], das; -s, -s ‹amerik.› (*Kunstw.* künstlerisch gestalteter Raum)
en|vi|ron|men|tal [ɛnvirɔn...]; **En|vi|ron|to|lo|gie,** die; - (Umweltforschung)
en vogue [ã ˈvo:k] ‹franz.› (beliebt; modisch; im Schwange)
En|vo|yé [ãvoaˈje:], der; -s, -s ‹franz.› (*franz. für* Gesandter)
Enz, die; - (l. Nebenfluss des Neckars)
En|ze|pha|li|tis, die; -, ...itiden ‹griech.› (*Med.* Gehirnentzündung); **En|ze|pha|lo|gramm,** das; -s, -e (Röntgenbild der Gehirnkammern)
En|zi|an, der; -s, -e (eine Alpenpflanze; ein alkohol. Getränk); 3 [Glas] - (↑R 90); **en|zi|an|blau**
En|zio (m. Vorn.)
En|zyk|li|ka [ɛnˈtsy(:)...] (↑R 130), die; -, ...ken ‹griech.› (päpstl. Rundschreiben); **en|zyk|lisch** (einen Kreis durchlaufend)
En|zyk|lo|pä|die (↑R 130), die; -, ...ien ‹griech.› (ein Nachschlagewerk); **en|zyk|lo|pä|disch** (umfassend); **En|zyk|lo|pä|dist,** der; -en, -en; ↑R 126 (Mitarbeiter an der berühmten franz. „Enzyklopädie")
En|zym, das; -s, -e ‹griech.› (*Biochemie* den Stoffwechsel regulierende Verbindung); **en|zy|ma|tisch; En|zy|mo|lo|gie,** die; - (Lehre von den Enzymen)
eo ip|so ‹lat.› (von selbst; selbstverständlich)
E|o|li|enne [eɔˈliɛn], die; - ‹franz.› (ein [Halb]seidengewebe in Taftbindung)
E|o|lith [*auch* ...ˈlit], der; *Gen.* -s *u.* -en (↑R 126), *Plur.* -e[n] ‹griech.› (vermeintl. vorgeschichtl. Werkzeug); **E|os** (griech. Göttin der Morgenröte)
EOS = erweiterte Oberschule; *vgl.* erweitern
E|o|sin, das; -s ‹griech.› (ein roter Farbstoff); **e|o|si|nie|ren** (mit Eosin färben)
e|o|zän ‹griech.› (*Geol.* das Eozän betreffend); **E|o|zän,** das; -s (zweitälteste Stufe des Tertiärs); **E|o|zo|i|kum,** das; -s (*svw.* Algonkium); **e|o|zo|isch**
ep..., Ep... *vgl.* epi..., Epi...
e|pa|go|gisch (↑R 132) ‹griech.› (*Philos.* zum Allgemeinen führend)
E|pau|lett [epo...], das; -s, -s ‹franz.›, *häufiger* **E|pau|let|te** [epoˈlɛtə], die; -, -n (Schulterstück auf Uniformen)
E|pen (*Plur. von* Epos)
E|pen|the|se, E|pen|the|sis (↑R 132), die; -, ...thesen ‹griech.› (*Sprachw.* Einschaltung von Lauten [zur Ausspracheerleichterung], z. B. „t" in „namentlich")
E|pe|xe|ge|se (↑R 132), die; -, -n ‹griech.› (*Rhet.* hinzugefügte Erklärung, z. B. drunten „im Unterland")
eph..., Eph..., *vgl.* epi..., Epi...
E|phe|be, der; -n, -n (↑R 126) ‹griech.› (*im alten Griechenland Bez. für* den wehrfähigen jungen Mann); **e|phe|bisch**
E|phe|li|den (↑R 132) *Plur.* ‹griech.› (*Med.* Sommersprossen)
e|phe|mer (↑R 132) ‹griech.› (nur einen Tag dauernd; vorübergehend); -e Blüten, Pflanzen; **E|phe|me|ri|de,** die; -, -n (*Astron.* Gestirn[berechnungs]tafel)
E|phe|ser (Bewohner von Ephesus); **E|phe|ser|brief,** der; -[e]s (*N. T.;* ↑R 105); **e|phe|sisch; E|phe|sos** *vgl.* Ephesus; **E|phe|sus** (altgriech. Stadt in Kleinasien)
E|phor, der; -en, -en; ↑R 126 ‹griech.› (einer der fünf höchsten Beamten im alten Sparta); **E|pho|rat,** das; -[e]s, -e (Amt eines Ephoren od. Ephorus); **E|pho|ren|amt; E|pho|rie,** die; -, ...ien ([kirchl.] Aufsichtsbezirk); **E|pho|rus** [*auch* ˈɛ...], der; -, Ephoren (Dekan in der reformierten Kirche; Leiter eines ev. Predigerseminars)
Eph|ra|im (↑R 130; m. Vorn.)
e|pi..., E|pi... *vor Selbstlauten und h* ep..., Ep... (*griech. Vorsilbe* darauf *[örtl. u. zeitl.],* daneben, bei, darüber)
E|pi|de|mie, die; -, ...ien ‹griech.› (Seuche, Massenerkrankung); **E|pi|de|mi|o|lo|ge,** der; -n, -n

(↑R 126); **E|pi|de|mi|o|lo|gie,** die; - (Lehre von den epidemischen Erkrankungen); **e|pi|de|mi|o|lo|gisch;** **e|pi|de|misch** (seuchenartig)

E|pi|der|mis, die; -, ...men ‹griech.› (*Med.* Oberhaut)

E|pi|di|a|skop, das; -s, -e ‹griech.› (Bildwerfer, der als Diaskop und Episkop verwendbar ist)

E|pi|ge|ne|se, die; -, -n ‹griech.› (*Biol.* Entwicklung durch Neubildung; *Geol.* nachträgliche Entstehung eines Flusstals in älteren Ablagerungen); **e|pi|ge|ne|tisch**

e|pi|go|nal (nachahmend, unschöpferisch); **E|pi|go|ne,** der; -n, -n (↑R 126) ‹griech.› (Nachahmer ohne Schöpferkraft); **e|pi|go|nen|haft;** **E|pi|go|nen|tum,** das; -s

E|pi|gramm, das; -s, -e ‹griech.› (Sinn-, Spottgedicht); **E|pi|gram|ma|ti|ker** (Verfasser von Epigrammen); **e|pi|gram|ma|tisch** (kurz, treffend); **E|pi|graph,** das; -s, -e (antike Inschrift); **E|pi|gra|phik,** die; - (Inschriftenkunde); **E|pi|gra|phi|ker** (Inschriftenforscher)

E|pik, die; - ‹griech.› (erzählende Dichtkunst)

E|pi|karp, das; -s, -e ‹griech.› (*Bot.* äußerste Schicht der Fruchtschale)

E|pi|ker ‹*zu* Epik›

E|pik|le|se (↑R 130), die; -, -n ‹griech.› (Anrufung des Heiligen Geistes in der orthodoxen Kirche)

E|pi|kon|dy|li|tis, die; -, ...itiden ‹griech.› (*Med.* Tennisarm)

E|pi|kri|se, die; -, -n ‹griech.› (*Med.* abschließende Beurteilung einer Krankheit)

E|pi|kur (griech. Philosoph); **E|pi|ku|re|er** (Anhänger der Lehre Epikurs; *seit der röm. Zeit für* Genussmensch); **e|pi|ku|re|isch** (*auch für* auf Genuss gerichtet), (↑R 94): epikureische Schriften; **e|pi|ku|risch** *vgl.* epikureisch

E|pi|la|ti|on, die; -, -en ‹lat.› (*Med.* Enthaarung)

E|pi|lep|sie, die; -, ...ien ‹griech.› (Erkrankung mit plötzlich eintretenden Krämpfen u. kurzer Bewusstlosigkeit); **E|pi|lep|ti|ker;** **E|pi|lep|ti|ke|rin;** **e|pi|lep|tisch**

e|pi|lie|ren ‹lat.› (*Med.* enthaaren)

E|pi|log, der; -s, -e ‹griech.› (Nachwort; Nachspiel, Ausklang)

E|pin|glé [epɛ̃'gle:], der; -[s], -s ‹franz.› (Kleider- u. Möbelstoff mit ungleich starken Querrippen)

E|pi|ni|ki|on, das; -s, ...ien [...i̯ən] ‹griech.› (altgriech. Siegeslied)

E|pi|pha|ni|as, das; - ‹*zu* Epiphanie› (Fest der Erscheinung des Herrn; Dreikönigsfest); **E|pi|pha|nie,** die; - ‹griech., „Erscheinung“›; **E|pi|pha|ni|en|fest** (*svw.* Epiphanias)

E|pi|pho|ra [*auch* e'pi...], die; -, ...rä ‹griech.› (*Med.* Tränenfluss; *Rhet., Stilk.* Wiederholung von Wörtern am Ende aufeinander folgender Sätze oder Satzteile)

E|pi|phyl|lum, das; -s, ...llen ‹griech.› (ein Blätterkaktus)

E|pi|phy|se, die; -, -n ‹griech.› (*Med.* Zirbeldrüse; Endstück der Röhrenknochen); **E|pi|phyt,** der; -en, -en; ↑R 126 (*Bot.* Pflanze, die [bei selbstständiger Ernährung] auf anderen Pflanzen wächst)

E|pi|rot, der; -en, -en; ↑R 126 (Bewohner von Epirus); **e|pi|ro|tisch;** **E|pi|rus** (westgriech. Landschaft)

e|pisch ‹griech.› (erzählend; das Epos betreffend); -es Theater

E|pi|skop (↑R 132), das; -s, -e ‹griech.› (Bildwerfer für nicht durchsichtige Bilder [z. B. aus Büchern])

e|pis|ko|pal, *auch* e|pis|ko|pisch (↑R 132) ‹griech.› (bischöflich); **E|pis|ko|pa|lis|mus,** der; - (Auffassung, nach der das Konzil der Bischöfe über dem Papst steht); **E|pis|ko|pa|list,** der; -en, -en; ↑R 126 (Anhänger des Episkopalismus); **E|pis|ko|pal|kir|che;** **E|pis|ko|pat,** das, *Theol.* der; -[e]s, -e (Gesamtheit der Bischöfe [eines Landes]; Bischofswürde); **e|pis|ko|pisch** *vgl.* episkopal; **E|pis|ko|pus,** der; -, ...pi (*lat. Bez. für* Bischof)

E|pi|so|de, die; -, -n ‹griech.› (vorübergehendes, nebensächl. Ereignis); **E|pi|so|den|film;** **e|pi|so|den|haft;** **e|pi|so|disch**

E|pis|tel (↑R 132), die; -, -n ‹griech.› (Apostelbrief; vorgeschriebene gottesdienstl. Lesung; *ugs. für* Brief, Strafpredigt)

E|pis|te|mo|lo|gie (↑R 132), die; - ‹griech.-engl.› (*Philos.* Erkenntnistheorie); **e|pis|te|mo|lo|gisch**

E|pis|tyl (↑R 132), das; -s, -e ‹griech.› (*svw.* Architrav)

E|pi|taph, das; -s, -e ‹griech.› *u.* **E|pi|ta|phi|um,** das; -s, ...ien [...i̯ən] (Grabschrift; Grabmal mit Inschrift)

E|pi|tha|la|mi|on, **E|pi|tha|la|mi|um,** das; -s, ...ien [...i̯ən] ‹griech.› ([antikes] Hochzeitslied)

E|pi|thel, das; -s, -e ‹griech.› *u.* **E|pi|the|li|um,** das; -s, ...ien [...i̯ən] (*Biol.* oberste Zellschicht der Haut); **E|pi|thel|zel|le**

E|pi|the|ton, das; -s, ...ta ‹griech.› (*Sprachw.* Beiwort); **E|pi|the|ton or|nans,** das; - -, ...ta ...antia ‹griech.; lat., „schmückendes“ Beiwort› (typisierendes, immer wiederkehrendes Attribut; z. B. „grüne“ Wiese)

E|pit|rit (↑R 130 *u.* 132), der; -en, -en (↑R 126) ‹griech.› (altgriech. Versfuß)

E|pi|zen|trum ‹griech.› (senkrecht über dem Erdbebenherd liegender Erdoberflächenpunkt)

E|pi|zyk|lo|i|de, die; -, -n ‹griech.› (*Math.* eine geometr. Kurve)

e|po|chal ‹griech.› (für einen [großen] Zeitabschnitt geltend; [sehr] bedeutend); **E|po|che,** die; -, -n (Zeitabschnitt); das Buch hat Epoche gemacht; eine Epoche machende Erfindung (↑R 40); **E|po|chen|un|ter|richt,** der; -[e]s (*Päd.*)

E|po|de (↑R 132), die; -, -n ‹griech.› (eine [antike] Gedichtform)

E|po|pöe [*auch* ...'pø:], die; -, -n [...'pø:(ə)n] ‹griech.› (*veraltet für* Epos); **E|pos,** das; -, Epen (erzählende Versdichtung; Heldengedicht)

Ep|pich, der; -s, -e (*landsch.* Bez. für mehrere Pflanzen, z. B. Efeu)

Ep|rou|vette [epru'vɛt] (↑R 130 *u.* 132), die; -, -n [...tən] ‹franz.› (*österr. für* Proberöhrchen, Reagenzglas)

Ep|si|lon, das; -[s], -s (griech. Buchstabe [kurzes e]: *Ε, ε*)

E|qua|li|zer ['i:kwəlaizə(r)], der; -s, - ‹engl.› (Zusatzgerät an Verstärkern von Hi-Fi-Anlagen zur Klangverbesserung)

E|quil|lib|rist (↑R 130) *ältere Schreibung für* Äquilibrist

E|qui|pa|ge [ek(v)i'pa:ʒə, *österr.* ...'pa:ʒ], die; -, -n [...'pa:ʒ(ə)n] ‹franz.› (*veraltet für* elegante Kutsche; Ausrüstung eines Offiziers);

E|qui|pe [e'ki:p, *auch* e'kip, *schweiz.* e'kipə], die; -, -n [...p(ə)n] ([Reiter]mannschaft); **e|qui|pie|ren** (*veraltet für* ausrüsten); **E|qui|pie|rung**

er; - kommt; **[1]Er;** ↑R 53 (veraltete Anrede an eine Person männl. Geschlechts); höre Er!; jmdn. Er nennen; (↑R 48:) das veraltete Er; **[2]Er,** der; -, -s (*ugs. für* Mensch oder Tier männl. Geschlechts); es ist ein Er; ein Er und eine Sie saßen dort

[3]Er = *chem. Zeichen für* Erbium

er... (*Vorsilbe von Verben,* z. B. erahnen, du erahnst, erahnt, zu erahnen)

...er (z. B. Lehrer, der; -s, -)

er|ach|ten; jmdn. *od.* etwas als *od.* für etwas -; **Er|ach|ten,** das; -s; meinem Erachten nach, meines Erachtens (*Abk.* m. E.); (*falsch:* meines Erachtens nach)
er|ah|nen
er|ar|bei|ten; Er|ar|bei|tung
e|ras|misch (von Erasmus; *auch* in der Weise des Erasmus von Rotterdam), (↑R 94): die erasmische Satire „Lob der Torheit"; **E|ras|mus** (m. Vorn.); **E|ras|mus von Rot|ter|dam** (niederländ. Theologe; Humanist u. Gegner Luthers)
E|ra|to [*auch* 'e:...] (Muse der Lyrik, bes. der Liebesdichtung)
E|ra|tos|the|nes (altgriech. Gelehrter)
er|äu|gen *(meist scherzh.)*
Erb‿adel (↑R 132), **...an|la|ge, ...an|spruch**
er|bar|men; sich -; du erbarmst dich seiner, *seltener* über ihn; er erbarmt mich, *österr. auch* mir (tut mir leid); **Er|bar|men,** das; -s; (↑R 50:) zum Erbarmen; **er|bar|mens|wert; Er|bar|mer,** der; -s *(geh.)*; **er|bärm|lich; Er|bärm|lich|keit,** die; -; **Er|bar|mung** *Plur. selten;* **er|bar|mungs|los; Er|bar|mungs|lo|sig|keit,** die; -; **er|bar|mungs‿voll, ...wür|dig**
er|bau|en; sich an einem Lied -; **Er|bau|er; Er|bau|e|rin; er|bau|lich** *(veraltend);* **Er|bau|lich|keit,** die; - *(veraltend);* **Er|bau|ung; Er|bau|ungs|li|te|ra|tur,** die; -
Erb‿bau|recht, ...be|gräb|nis; erb|be|rech|tigt; Erb‿bild (*für* Genotyp), **...bi|o|lo|gie; erb|bi|o|lo|gisch;** [1]**Er|be,** der; -n, -n (↑R 126); der gesetzliche -; [2]**Er|be,** das; -s; das kulturelle -
er|be|ben
erb|ei|gen (ererbt); **erb|ein|ge|ses|sen** (alteingesessen); **er|ben; Er|ben|ge|mein|schaft**
[1]**er|be|ten** (durch Beten erlangen); erbetete, erbetet
[2]**er|be|ten;** ein -er Gast
er|bet|teln
er|beu|ten; Er|beu|tung
erb|fä|hig; Erb‿fak|tor, ...fall (der; *Rechtsspr.* Todesfall, der jmdn. zum Erben macht), **...feind, ...fol|ge** (die; -); **Erb|fol|ge|krieg; Erb‿fol|ger, ...groß|her|zog, ...gut, ...hof**
er|bie|ten, sich *(geh.);* **Er|bie|ten,** das; -s *(geh.)*
Er|bin
Erb|in|for|ma|ti|on *(Genetik)*
er|bit|ten; jmds. Rat -
er|bit|tern; es erbittert mich; **Er|bit|te|rung,** die; -

Er|bi|um, das; -s (chem. Element, Metall; *Zeichen* Er)
Erb|krank|heit
er|blas|sen (*geh. für* bleich werden); die Baroness erblasste
Erb|las|sen|schaft *(Rechtsw.);* **Erb|las|ser** (der eine Erbschaft Hinterlassende); **Erb|las|se|rin; erb|las|se|risch; Erb|las|sung; Erb|le|hen**
er|blei|chen (bleich werden); du erbleichtest; erbleicht *u.* (*veraltet, im Sinne von* „gestorben":) erblichen; *vgl.* [2]bleichen
Erb‿lei|den, ...lei|he; erb|lich; Erb|lich|keit, die; -
er|bli|cken
er|blin|den; Er|blin|dung
erb|los
er|blü|hen
Erb|mas|se; erb|mä|ßig; Erb|on|kel *(ugs. scherzh.)*
er|bo|sen (erzürnen); du erbost; sein Verhalten erboste mich; sich erbosen; ich habe mich erbost
er|bö|tig (bereit); er ist -, macht sich -, diesen Dienst zu leisten; **Er|bö|tig|keit,** die; -
Erb‿pacht *(früher),* **...päch|ter** *(früher),* **...pfle|ge** (die; -; *für* Eugenik), **...prinz**
er|bre|chen; sich -; **Er|bre|chen,** das; -s; bis zum Erbrechen (*ugs. für* bis zum Überdruss)
Erb|recht
er|brin|gen; den Nachweis -
er|brü|ten (*fachspr. für* ausbrüten)
Erbs|brei *vgl.* Erbsenbrei
Erb|schaft; Erb|schafts|steu|er, Erb|schaft|steu|er, die (↑R 34); **Erb‿schein, ...schlei|cher**
Erb|se, die; -, -n; **Erb|sen|bein** (*Med.* Knochen der Handwurzel); **Erb|sen|brei, Erbs|brei; erb|sen|groß; Erb|sen|stroh,** Erbs|stroh; **Erb|sen|sup|pe; Erbs|stroh** *vgl.* Erbsenstroh
Erb‿stück, ...sün|de *(christl. Rel.)*
Erbs|wurst
Erb|tan|te *(ugs. scherzh.);* **Erb|teil,** das (*BGB* der); **Erb|tei|lung; erb|tüm|lich;** erb- und eigentümlich (↑R 23); **Erb‿ver|trag, ...ver|zicht; Erb|ver|zichts|ver|trag; Erb|we|sen,** das; -s
Erd|ach|se, die; -
er|dacht; eine -e Geschichte
Erd‿al|ka|li|en *(Plur.; Chemie),* **...an|zie|hung** (die; -), **...ap|fel** (*landsch. für* Kartoffel), **...ar|bei|ten** *(Plur.),* **...at|mo|sphä|re**
er|dau|ern (*schweiz. für* [ein Problem] reifen lassen; sich durch Warten verdienen); **Er|dau|e|rung** *(schweiz.)*
Erd‿ball (der; -[e]s), **...be|ben; Erd|be|ben‿herd, ...mes|ser** (der), **...war|te, ...wel|le; Erd|beer|bow|le; Erd|bee|re; Erd|beer|eis; erd|beer‿far|ben** *od.* **...far|big; Erd‿be|schleu|ni|gung** (*Physik* Fallbeschleunigung), **...be|schrei|bung, ...be|stat|tung, ...be|völ|ke|rung** (die; -), **...be|we|gung, ...bir|ne** (*landsch. für* Kartoffel), **...bo|den, ...boh|rer** *(Technik);* **erd|braun; Er|de,** die; -, -n *Plur. selten;* **er|den** (*Elektrotechnik* Verbindung zwischen einem elektr. Gerät und der Erde herstellen); **Er|den‿bür|ger, ...glück**
er|denk|bar; er|den|ken; er|denk|lich; alles -e Gute wünschen
Er|den|le|ben; Er|den|rund, das; -[e]s; **Erd|fall,** der (trichterförmige Senkung von Erdschichten); **erd‿far|ben** *od.* **...far|big, ...fern** (ein -er Planet); **Erd|fer|ne,** die; -
Erdg. = Erdgeschichte; Erdgeschoss
Erd|gas; erd|gas|höf|fig (reiches Erdgasvorkommen versprechend); **erd|ge|bo|ren** (*geh. für* sterblich, irdisch); **Erd|ge|bo|re|ne, Erd|ge|bor|ne,** der *u.* die; -n, -n (↑R 5ff.); **erd|ge|bun|den; Erd‿geist** (*Plur.* ...geister), **...ge|schich|te** (die; -; *Abk.* Erdg.), **...ge|schoss** (*Abk.* Erdg.; *vgl.* Geschoss); **erd|haft; Erd‿höh|le, ...hörn|chen** (ein Nagetier)
er|dich|ten ([als Ausrede] erfinden; sich ausdenken)
er|dig; Erd‿kern (der; -s), **...kreis** (der; -es), **...krus|te, ...ku|gel, ...kun|de** (die; -); **Erd|kund|ler; erd|kund|lich; erd|mag|ne|tisch;** -e Wellen; **Erd|mag|ne|tis|mus**
Erd|männ|chen (Kobold; ein Tier)
erd|nah; ein -er Planet; **Erd‿nä|he** *(Astron.),* **...nuss; Erd|nuss|but|ter; Erd|ober|flä|che** (↑R 132), die; -
Erd|öl; Erdöl fördernde, Erdöl exportierende Länder
er|dol|chen *(geh.);* **Er|dol|chung**
Erd|öl ex|por|tie|rend, för|dernd *vgl.* Erdöl; **erd|öl|höf|fig** (reiches Erdölvorkommen versprechend); **Erd|öl‿pro|duk|ti|on, ...vor|kom|men; Erd‿pech, ...rauch** (eine Pflanze), **...reich** (das; -[e]s)
er|dreis|ten, sich *(geh.)*
Erd|rin|de, die; -
er|dröh|nen
er|dros|seln; Er|dros|se|lung, *seltener* **Er|dross|lung**
er|drü|cken; er|drü|ckend
Er|drusch, der; -[e]s, -e (Ertrag des Dreschens)

Erd₋rutsch, ...sa|tel|lit, ...schicht, ...schlipf (*schweiz. neben* Erdrutsch), **...schluss** *(Elektrotechnik)*, **...schol|le, ...sicht** *(Flugw.)*, **...spal|te, ...stoß, ...strö|me** (*Plur.*; elektr. Ströme in der Erdkruste), **...teil** (der), **...tra|bant**
er|dul|den; Er|dul|dung, die; -
Erd₋um|krei|sung, ...um|run|dung; erd|um|span|nend; Er|dung (das Erden); **Erd₋ver|mes|sung, ...wachs** (*für* Ozokerit), **...wall, ...wär|me, ...zeit|al|ter**
E|re|bos, E|re|bus, der; - ‹griech.› (Unterwelt der griech. Sage)
E|rech|thei|on [*auch* eˈrɛç...] (↑R 132), das; -s (Tempel des Erechtheus in Athen); **E|rech|the|um** *vgl.* Erechtheion; **E|rech|theus** [eˈrɛçtɔys] (griech. Sagengestalt)
er|ei|fern, sich; **Er|ei|fe|rung**
er|eig|nen, sich; **Er|eig|nis,** das; -ses, -se; ein freudiges -; ein großes -; **er|eig|nis₋los, ...reich**
er|ei|len *(geh.)*; das Schicksal ereilte ihn
E|rek (m. Vorn.)
e|rek|til ‹lat.› (*Med.* aufrichtbar, schwellfähig); **E|rek|ti|on,** die; -, -en (Aufrichtung, Anschwellung [des Penis])
E|re|mit [*auch* ...ˈmit], der; -en, -en (↑R 126) ‹griech.› (Einsiedler; Klausner); [1]**E|re|mi|ta|ge** [...ˈtaːʒə, *österr.* ...ˈtaːʒ], die; -, -n [...ˈtaːʒ(ə)n] (abseits gelegene Grotte od. Nachahmung einer Einsiedelei in Parkanlagen des 18. Jh.s); [2]**E|re|mi|ta|ge,** Er|mi|ta|ge, die; - (Kunstsammlung in Sankt Petersburg)
E|ren, Ern, der; -, - (*landsch., bes. südwestd. veraltend für* Hausflur, -gang)
er|er|ben *(veraltet)*; **er|erbt;** -er Besitz
E|re|this|mus, der; - ‹griech.› (*Med., Psych.* krankhafte Gereiztheit)
er|fahr|bar; [1]**er|fah|ren;** etwas Wichtiges -; [2]**er|fah|ren;** -er Mann; **Er|fah|re|ne,** der *u.* die; -n, -n (↑R 5 ff.); **Er|fah|ren|heit,** die; -; **Er|fah|rung; Er|fah|rungs₋aus|tausch, ...be|richt; er|fah|rungs₋ge|mäß, ...mä|ßig; Er|fah|rungs₋schatz, ...tat|sa|che, ...wert, ...wis|sen|schaft** (die; -; *für* Empirie)
er|fass|bar; er|fas|sen; erfasst; **Er|fas|sung**
er|fech|ten; erfochtene Siege
er|fin|den; Er|fin|der; Er|fin|der|geist, der; -[e]s; **Er|fin|de|rin; er|fin|de|risch; er|find|lich;** nicht - (erkennbar, verständlich) sein; **Er|fin|dung; Er|fin|dungs₋ga|be, ...kraft** (die; -); **er|fin|dungs|reich**
er|fle|hen *(geh.)*; erflehte Hilfe
Er|folg, der; -[e]s, -e; alle Maßnahmen, die Erfolg versprechen; Erfolg versprechende Maßnahmen, *aber* höchst erfolgversprechende Maßnahmen (↑R 40); **er|fol|gen; er|folg|ge|krönt** *(geh.)*; **Er|folg|ha|sche|rei,** die; - *(abwertend)*; **er|folg|los; Er|folg|lo|sig|keit,** die; -; **er|folg|reich; Er|folgs₋aus|sicht** *(meist Plur.)*, **...au|tor, ...buch, ...den|ken, ...er|leb|nis, ...kurs** (der; -es); **er|folgs|ori|en|tiert** (↑R 132); **Er|folgs₋prä|mie, ...quo|te, ...rech|nung** *(Wirtsch.)*, **...se|rie; er|folgs|si|cher; Er|folgs₋stück, ...zif|fer, ...zwang; Er|folg ver|spre|chend** *vgl.* Erfolg
er|for|der|lich; er|for|der|li|chen|falls *(Amtsspr.)*; *vgl.* Fall, der; **er|for|dern; Er|for|der|nis,** das; -ses, -se
er|forsch|bar; er|for|schen; Er|for|scher; Er|for|schung
er|fra|gen; Er|fra|gung
er|fre|chen, sich *(veraltend)*
er|freu|en; sich -; **er|freu|lich;** manches Erfreuliche (↑R 47); **er|freu|li|cher|wei|se**
er|frie|ren; Er|frie|rung; Er|frie|rungs|tod
er|fri|schen; sich -; **er|fri|schend;** ein -er Humor; **Er|fri|schung; Er|fri|schungs₋ge|tränk, ...raum, ...stand, ...tuch**
Erft, die; - (l. Nebenfluss des Niederrheins)
er|füh|len *(geh.)*
er|füll|bar; -e Wünsche; **er|fül|len;** sich -; **Er|füllt|heit,** die; -; **Er|fül|lung; Er|fül|lungs|ort** der; -[e]s, -e *(Rechtsw.)*
Er|furt (Hptst. von Thüringen); **Er|fur|ter** (↑R 103); der - Dom
erg = Erg; **Erg,** das; -s, - ‹griech.› (ältere physikal. Energieeinheit; *Zeichen* erg)
erg. = ergänze!; **er|gän|zen;** du ergänzt; ergänze! (*Abk.* erg.); **Er|gän|zung; Er|gän|zungs₋ab|ga|be** (zusätzliche Steuer), **...band** (der; *Abk.* Erg.-Bd.), **...bin|de|strich, ...fra|ge** *(Sprachw.)*, **...satz** (*für* Objektsatz)
er|gat|tern (*ugs. für* sich durch eifriges, geschicktes Bemühen verschaffen); ich ...ere (↑R 16)
er|gau|nern (*ugs. für* sich durch Betrug verschaffen); ich ...ere (↑R 16)
Erg.-Bd. = Ergänzungsband
[1]**er|ge|ben;** die Zählung hat ergeben, dass ...; sich ins Unvermeidliche ergeben; [2]**er|ge|ben;** ergebener Diener; **Er|ge|ben|heit,** die; -; **Er|ge|ben|heits|ad|res|se; er|ge|benst; Er|geb|nis,** das; -ses, -se; **er|geb|nis|los; Er|geb|nis|lo|sig|keit,** die; -; **er|geb|nis|reich; Er|ge|bung** *(geh.)*; **er|ge|bungs|voll** *(geh.)*
er|ge|hen; wie ist es dir ergangen?; sich im Park ergehen (*geh. für* spazieren gehen); sie erging sich in Vermutungen; er hat es über sich ergehen lassen; **Er|ge|hen,** das; -s (Befinden)
er|gie|big; Er|gie|big|keit, die; -
er|gie|ßen; sich -; **Er|gie|ßung**
er|glän|zen *(geh.)*
er|glü|hen *(geh.)*
er|go ‹lat.› (folglich, also)
Er|go|graph, der; -en, -en (↑R 126) ‹griech.› (*Med.* Gerät zur Aufzeichnung der Muskelarbeit); **Er|go|lo|gie,** die; - ([historische] Erforschung der Arbeitsgeräte); **Er|go|me|ter,** das; -s, - (*Med.* Gerät zur Messung der körperl. Leistungsfähigkeit); **Er|go|no|mie, Er|go|no|mik,** die; - (Erforschung der Leistungsmöglichkeiten u. optimalen Arbeitsbedingungen des Menschen); **er|go|no|misch**
Er|gos|te|rin (↑R 132), das; -s (Vorstufe des Vitamins D_2)
Er|go|the|ra|pie, die; -, -n ‹griech.› (Arbeits- und Beschäftigungstherapie)
er|göt|zen *(geh.)*; du ergötzt; sich -; **Er|göt|zen,** das; -s *(geh.)*; **er|götz|lich** *(geh.)*; **Er|göt|zung** *(geh.)*
er|grau|en; ergraut
er|grei|fen; er|grei|fend; Er|grei|fung *Plur. selten*; **er|grif|fen;** er war sehr -; **Er|grif|fen|heit,** die; -; **Er|grif|fen|sein,** das; -s
er|grim|men *(geh.)*
er|gründ|bar; er|grün|den; Er|grün|dung *Plur. selten*
er|grü|nen *(geh.)*; die Natur ergrünt
Er|guss; Er|guss|ge|stein (*für* Effusivgestein)
er|ha|ben; -e (erhöhte) Stellen einer Druckplatte; über allen Zweifel -; **Er|ha|ben|heit**
Er|halt, der; -[e]s (*Amtsspr.* Empfang; Erhaltung, Bewahrung); **er|hal|ten;** etwas frisch erhalten; sich gesund erhalten; erhalten bleiben; **er|hal|tens|wert; Er|hal|ter** (Ernährer); **er|hält|lich; Er|hal|tung,** die; -; **Er|hal|tungs|trieb; er|hal|tungs|wür|dig; Er|hal|tungs|zu|stand**
er|han|deln
er|hän|gen; sich -; *vgl.* [2]hängen;

Er|häng|te, der *u.* die; -n, -n (↑R 5 ff.)
Er|hard (m. Vorn.)
er|här|ten; Er|här|tung
er|ha|schen
er|he|ben; sich -; **er|he|bend** (feierlich); **er|heb|lich; Er|he|bung**
er|hei|ra|ten (durch Heirat erlangen)
er|hei|schen (*geh. für* erfordern)
er|hei|tern; ich ...ere (↑R 16); **Er|hei|te|rung**
[1]**er|hel|len;** sich - (hell, heiter werden); [2]**er|hel|len;** daraus erhellt (wird klar), dass ...; **Er|hel|lung**
er|hit|zen; du erhitzt; sich -; **Er|hit|zer; Er|hit|zung**
er|hof|fen; ich erhoffe mir Vorteile
er|hö|hen; Er|hö|hung; Er|hö|hungs|zei|chen (*Musik* ♯)
er|ho|len, sich; **er|hol|sam; Er|ho|lung,** die; -; Feriengebiete für Erholung suchende Großstädter; (↑R 47:) die Erholung Suchenden, *auch* Erholungsuchenden; **Er|ho|lungs|auf|ent|halt; er|ho|lungs|be|dürf|tig; Er|ho|lungs‿ge|biet, ...heim, ...pau|se, ...rei|se, ...stät|te; Er|ho|lung su|chend;** *vgl.* Erholung; **Er|ho|lung|su|chen|de,** der *u.* die; -n, -n (↑R 5 ff.); *vgl.* Erholung; **Er|ho|lungs‿ur|laub, ...wert, ...zeit, ...zent|rum**
er|hö|ren; Er|hö|rung
E|rich (m. Vorn.)
E|ri|da|nos, [1]**E|ri|da|nus,** der; - ‹griech.› (Fluss der griech. Sage); [2]**E|ri|da|nus,** der; - (ein Sternbild)
E|rie|see [*engl.* 'iəri...], der; -s (in Nordamerika)
e|ri|gi|bel ‹lat.› (*svw.* erektil); **e|ri|gie|ren** (*Med.* sich aufrichten)
E|rik (m. Vorn.)
[1]**E|ri|ka** (w. Vorn.)
[2]**E|ri|ka,** die; -, ...ken ‹griech.› (Heidekraut)
er|in|ner|lich; er|in|nern; ich ...ere (↑R 16); jemanden an etwas erinnnern; sich erinnern; ich erinnere mich an das Ereignis, *geh.* des Ereignisses; **Er|in|ne|rung; Er|in|ne|rungs‿bild, ...fo|to; er|in|ne|rungs|los; Er|in|ne|rungs‿lü|cke, ...mal** (*vgl.* [2]Mal), **...schrei|ben** (*veraltet*); **er|in|ne|rungs|schwer; Er|in|ne|rungs‿stät|te, ...stück, ...ver|mö|gen** (das; -s), **...zei|chen**
E|rin|nye [...nÿə], **E|rin|nys,** die; -, ...yen *meist Plur.* ‹griech.› (griech. Rachegöttin)
E|ris (griech. Göttin der Zwietracht); **E|ris|tik,** die; - ‹griech.› (Kunst u. Technik des Redestreits)
E|rit|rea (↑R 130; Staat in Nordostafrika); **E|rit|re|er; e|rit|re|isch**
E|ri|wan *vgl.* Jerewan
er|ja|gen
er|kal|ten; erkaltet; **er|käl|ten,** sich; erkältet; **Er|kal|tung,** die; -; **Er|käl|tung; Er|käl|tungs‿ge|fahr, ...krank|heit**
er|kämp|fen
er|kau|fen
er|kenn|bar; Er|kenn|bar|keit, die; -; **er|ken|nen;** sich zu erkennen geben; auf eine Freiheitsstrafe erkennen (*Rechtsspr.* als Urteil verkünden); **er|kennt|lich;** sich - zeigen; **Er|kennt|lich|keit;** [1]**Er|kennt|nis,** die; -, -se (Einsicht); [2]**Er|kennt|nis,** das; -ses, -se (*österr., sonst veraltet für* richterl. Urteil); **Er|kennt|nis‿fä|hig|keit** (die; -), **...kri|tik** (*Philos.*); **er|kennt|nis|the|o|re|tisch** (*Philos.*); **Er|kennt|nis|the|o|rie** (*Philos.*); **Er|ken|nung,** die; -; **Er|ken|nungs|dienst; er|ken|nungs|dienst|lich; Er|ken|nungs‿mar|ke, ...me|lo|die, ...zei|chen**
Er|ker, der; -s, -; **Er|ker‿fens|ter, ...zim|mer**
er|kie|sen (*geh. für* [aus]wählen); *meist nur noch im Präteritum und Partizip II gebr.;* ich erkor, du erkorst; erkoren; *vgl.* [2]kiesen
er|klär|bar; Er|klär|bar|keit, die; -; **er|klä|ren;** sich -; **Er|klä|rer; er|klär|lich; er|klär|li|cher|wei|se; er|klärt** (entschieden; offenkundig); ein -er Nichtraucher, der -e Publikumsliebling; **er|klär|ter|wei|se; Er|klä|rung**
er|kleck|lich (*geh. für* beträchtlich; *vgl. d.*)
er|klet|tern; Er|klet|te|rung
er|klim|men (*geh.*); **Er|klim|mung**
er|klin|gen
er|ko|ren *vgl.* erkiesen
er|kran|ken; Er|kran|kung; Er|kran|kungs|fall, der; im -
er|küh|nen, sich
er|kun|den; er|kun|di|gen, sich; **Er|kun|di|gung; Er|kun|dung; Er|kun|dungs‿fahrt, ...flug**
er|küns|teln (*abwertend*); **er|küns|telt**
er|kü|ren; *vgl.* küren
er|la|ben (*veraltet*); sich -
Er|lag, der; -[e]s (*österr. für* Hinterlegung); **Er|lag|schein** (*österr. für* Zahlkarte der Post)
er|lah|men; Er|lah|mung, die; -
er|lan|gen
Er|lan|gen (Stadt a. d. Regnitz); **Er|lan|ger** (↑R 103)
Er|lan|gung, die; - (*Amtsspr.*)
Er|lass, der; -es, *Plur.* -e, *österr.* Erlässe; **er|las|sen; Er|las|sung**
er|lau|ben; sich -; ich erlaube mir zu fragen; **Er|laub|nis,** die; -, ...sse *Plur. selten;* **Er|laub|nis|schein**
er|laucht (*geh.*); **Er|laucht,** die; -, -en (ein Adelstitel); *vgl.* euer, ihr *u.* sein
er|lau|fen; den Ball - (*Sport*)
er|lau|schen (*selten*)
er|läu|tern; ich ...ere (↑R 16); **Er|läu|te|rung; er|läu|te|rungs|wei|se**
Er|le, die; -, -n (ein Laubbaum)
er|le|ben; Er|le|ben, das; -s; **Er|le|bens|fall,** der; -[e]s; im (*Versicherungsw.*); **Er|leb|nis,** das; -ses, -se; **Er|leb|nis‿auf|satz, ...be|richt, ...fä|hig|keit** (die; -; *Psych.*), **...hun|ger; er|leb|nis|hung|rig; er|leb|nis|reich; Er|leb|nis|ro|man; er|lebt;** -e Rede (*Sprachw.*)
er|le|di|gen; er|le|digt (*ugs. für* völlig erschöpft); **Er|le|di|gung**
er|le|gen (*Jägerspr.* [Wild] töten; *bes. österr. auch für* [einen Betrag] zahlen); **Er|le|gung**
er|leich|tern; ich ...ere (↑R 16); sich -; **er|leich|tert; Er|leich|te|rung**
er|lei|den
er|len (aus Erlenholz); **Er|len‿bruch** (*vgl.* [2]Bruch), **...holz**
Er|len|mey|er|kol|ben (↑R 95) ‹nach dem dt. Chemiker R. Erlenmeyer› (*Chemie* kegelförmiger oder bauchiger Glaskolben mit flachem Boden)
er|lern|bar; Er|lern|bar|keit, die; -; **er|ler|nen; Er|ler|nung,** die; -
er|le|sen; ein -es (ausgesuchtes) Gericht; **Er|le|sen|heit,** die; -
er|leuch|ten; Er|leuch|tung
er|lie|gen; (↑R 50:) zum Erliegen kommen
er|lis|ten; Er|lis|tung, die; -
Erl|kö|nig („Elfenkönig") (*nur Sing.:* Sagengestalt; *ugs. für* getarnter Versuchswagen)
er|lo|gen; *vgl.* erlügen
Er|lös, der; -es, -e
er|lö|schen; *vgl.* [2]löschen; **Er|lö|schen,** das; -s
er|lö|sen; erlöst; **Er|lö|ser; Er|lö|ser|bild** (*Rel.*); **er|lö|ser|haft; Er|lö|sung** *Plur. selten*
er|lü|gen; erlogen
er|mäch|ti|gen; Er|mäch|ti|gung
er|mah|nen; Er|mah|nung
er|man|geln (*geh.*); jeglichen Sachverstandes -; **Er|man|ge|lung, Er|mang|lung,** die; -; in - eines Besser[e]n (*geh.*)
er|man|nen, sich (*geh.*); **Er|man|nung,** die; -
er|mä|ßi|gen; Er|mä|ßi|gung
er|mat|ten; Er|mat|tung, die; -
er|mess|bar; er|mes|sen; Er-

mes|sen, das; -s; nach meinem -; **Er|mes|sens‿ent|schei|dung, ...fra|ge, ...frei|heit**
Er|mi|ta|ge *vgl.* ²Eremitage
er|mit|teln; ich ...[e]le (↑R 16); **Er|mitt|ler; Er|mitt|lung; Er|mitt|lungs‿ar|beit, ...be|am|te, ...rich|ter, ...ver|fah|ren**
Erm|land, das; -[e]s (Landschaft im ehem. Ostpreußen)
er|mög|li|chen; Er|mög|li|chung, die; -
er|mor|den; Er|mor|dung
er|müd|bar; Er|müd|bar|keit, die; -; **er|mü|den; Er|mü|dung** *Plur. selten;* **Er|mü|dungs‿er|schei|nung, ...zu|stand**
er|mun|tern; ich ...ere (↑R 16); **Er|mun|te|rung**
er|mu|ti|gen; Er|mu|ti|gung
Ern *vgl.* Eren
Er|na (w. Vorn.)
er|näh|ren; sich -; **Er|näh|rer; Er|näh|re|rin; Er|näh|rung,** die; -; **Er|näh|rungs‿ba|sis, ...bei|hil|fe, ...for|schung** (die; -), **...la|ge, ...leh|re** *(Med.),* **...phy|si|o|lo|gie** *(Med.);* **er|näh|rungs|phy|si|o|lo|gisch** *(Med.);* **Er|näh|rungs‿plan, ...stö|rung** *(Med.)*
er|nen|nen; Er|nen|nung; Er|nen|nungs‿schrei|ben, ...ur|kun|de
Er|nes|ta, Er|nes|ti|ne (w. Vorn.)
er|nes|ti|ni|sche Li|nie (↑R 94), die; -n - (herzogl. Linie der Wettiner)
er|neu|en *(seltener für* erneuern); **Er|neu|er,** *häufiger* **Er|neu|e|rer,** Er|neu|rer; **Er|neu|e|rin; er|neu|ern;** sich -; **Er|neu|e|rung; er|neu|e|rungs|be|dürf|tig; Er|neu|rer** *vgl.* Erneuerer; **er|neut** (nochmals); **Er|neu|ung** *(seltener für* Erneuerung)
er|nied|ri|gen; sich -; **er|nied|ri|gend; Er|nied|ri|gung; Er|nied|ri|gungs|zei|chen** *(Musik* ♭)
ernst; z. B. ernst sein, werden, nehmen; es ist mir [vollkommen] ernst damit; die Lage wird ernst; eine Sache [für] ernst nehmen; ein ernst gemeinter Rat; ein ernst zu nehmender Vorschlag; ein ernst genommener Hinweis; *vgl.* Ernst; **¹Ernst,** der; -es; im Ernst; Ernst machen; Scherz für Ernst nehmen; es ist mir [vollkommener] Ernst damit; es wurde Ernst [aus dem Spiel]; allen Ernstes; **²Ernst** (m. Vorn.); **Ernst|fall,** der; **ernst ge|meint** *vgl.* ernst; **ernst|haft; Ernst|haf|tig|keit,** die; -; **ernst|lich; ernst zu neh|mend** *vgl.* ernst
Ern|te, die; -, -n; **Ern|te‿aus|fäl|le** *(Plur.;* Einbußen bei der Ernte), **...bri|ga|de** *(ehem. in der DDR);* **Ern|te|dank|fest; Ern|te‿ein|satz, ...er|geb|nis, ...fest** (Erntedankfest), **...kranz, ...kro|ne, ...ma|schi|ne, ...mo|nat** *od.* **...mond** *(alte Bez. für* August); **ern|ten; Ern|te‿se|gen** (der; -s; reicher -), **...ver|si|che|rung, ...zeit; Ern|ting,** der; -s, -e *(alte Bez. für* August)
er|nüch|tern; ich ...ere (↑R 16); **Er|nüch|te|rung**
Er|o|be|rer (↑R 132); **Er|o|be|rin; er|o|bern;** ich ...ere (↑R 16); **Er|o|be|rung; Er|o|be|rungs‿drang, ...krieg, ...lust; er|o|be|rungs|lus|tig; Er|o|be|rungs|zug**
e|ro|die|ren ‹lat.› *(Geol.* auswaschen)
er|öff|nen; Er|öff|nung; Er|öff|nungs‿be|schluss *(Rechtsw.),* **...bi|lanz** *(Wirtsch.),* **...re|de, ...vor|stel|lung**
e|ro|gen ‹griech.› *(Med.* geschlechtliche Erregung auslösend); -e Zone
E|ro|i|ca, *auch* **E|ro|i|ka,** die; - ‹griech.› *(kurz für* Sinfonia eroica [Titel der 3. Sinfonie Es-Dur von Beethoven])
er|ör|tern; Er|ör|te|rung
¹E|ros (griech. Gott der Liebe); *vgl.* Eroten; **²E|ros** *[auch* 'ɛrɔs] der; - ‹griech.› (sinnl. Liebe; *Philos.* Drang nach Erkenntnis); philosophischer -; **³E|ros,** der; - (ein Planet); **E|ros|cen|ter** ‹griech.-engl.› *(verhüllend für* Bordell)
E|ro|si|on, die; -, -en ‹lat.› *(Geol.* Erdabtragung durch Wasser, Eis od. Wind); **e|ro|siv**
E|ro|ten *Plur.* ‹griech.› (allegor. Darstellung geflügelter Liebesgötter, meist in Kindergestalt); *vgl.* ¹Eros; **E|ro|tik,** die; - (den geistig-seel. Bereich einbeziehende sinnliche Liebe); **¹E|ro|ti|ka** *(Plur. von* Erotikon); **²E|ro|ti|ka** *Plur.* (sexuell anregende Gegenstände, Mittel o. Ä.); **E|ro|ti|ker** (Verfasser von Liebesliedern u. erotischen Schriften; sinnlicher Mensch); **E|ro|ti|kon,** das; -s, *Plur.* ...ka *od.* ...ken (erotisches Buch); **e|ro|tisch; e|ro|ti|sie|ren; E|ro|ti|sie|rung; E|ro|tis|mus, E|ro|ti|zis|mus,** der; - (Überbetonung des Erotischen); **E|ro|to|ma|nie,** die; - *(Med., Psych.* krankhaftes sexuelles Verlangen)
Er|pel, der; -s, - (Enterich)
er|picht (begierig)
er|press|bar; Er|press|bar|keit, die; -; **er|pres|sen; Er|pres|ser; Er|pres|ser|brief; Er|pres|se|rin; er|pres|se|risch; Er|pres|sung; Er|pres|sungs|ver|such**
er|pro|ben; er|probt; er|prob|ter|wei|se; Er|pro|bung; er|pro|bungs|hal|ber
er|qui|cken *(geh. für* erfrischen); sich -; **er|quick|lich** *(geh.);* **Er|qui|ckung** *(geh.)*
Er|ra|ta *(Plur. von* Erratum)
er|rat|bar; er|ra|ten
er|ra|tisch ‹lat.› *(Geol.* verirrt, zerstreut); -er Block (Findling[sblock]); **Er|ra|tum,** das; -s, ...ta (Versehen, Druckfehler)
er|re|chen|bar; er|rech|nen
er|reg|bar; Er|reg|bar|keit, die; -; **er|re|gen;** sich -; **Er|re|ger; Er|regt|heit,** die; -; **Er|re|gung; Er|re|gungs|zu|stand**
er|reich|bar; Er|reich|bar|keit, die; -; **er|rei|chen; Er|rei|chung,** die; -
er|ret|ten *(geh.);* - von *od.* vor etwas; **Er|ret|ter; Er|ret|tung**
er|rich|ten; Er|rich|tung
er|rin|gen; Er|rin|gung, die; -
er|rö|ten; Er|rö|ten, das; -s
Er|run|gen|schaft
Er|satz, der; -es; **Er|satz‿bank** *(Plur.* ...bänke; *Sport),* **...be|frie|di|gung** *(Psych.),* **...deh|nung** *(Sprachw.),* **...dienst; Er|satz|dienst|leis|ten|de,** der; -n, -n (↑R 126); **er|satz|dienst|pflich|tig; Er|satz|dienst|pflich|ti|ge,** der; -n, -n (↑R 126); **Er|satz|dro|ge; er|satz|ge|schwächt** *(bes. Sport);* **Er|satz‿hand|lung** *(Psych.),* **...in|fi|ni|tiv** *(Sprachw.* Infinitiv an Stelle eines Partizips II nach einem reinen Infinitiv, z. B. er hat ihn kommen „hören" statt „gehört"), **...kas|se; er|satz|los;** - gestrichen; **Er|satz|mann** *Plur.* ...leute, *auch* ...männer; **er|satz|pflich|tig; Er|satz‿rad, ...re|ser|ve** (die; -; *Milit.),* **...spie|ler** *(Sport),* **...teil** (das, *seltener* der); **Er|satz|teil|la|ger; er|satz|wei|se; Er|satz|zeit** *(Versicherungsw.)*
er|sau|fen *(ugs. für* ertrinken); ersoffen; **er|säu|fen** (ertränken); ersäuft
er|schaf|fen; *vgl.* ²schaffen; **Er|schaf|fer** *(geh.; meist für* Gott); **Er|schaf|fung,** die; - *(geh.)*
er|schal|len *(geh.);* es erscholl *od.* erschallte; es erschölle *od.* erschallte; erschollen *od.* erschallt; erschall[e]!
er|schau|dern *(geh.)*
er|schau|en
er|schau|ern *(geh.)*
er|schei|nen; Er|schei|nung; Er|schei|nungs‿bild, ...form, ...jahr, ...ort, ...termin
er|schie|ßen; Er|schie|ßung
er|schim|mern *(geh.)*

er|schlaf|fen; er|schlafft; Er|schlaf|fung, die; -
er|schla|gen
er|schlei|chen (durch List erringen); **Er|schlei|chung**
er|schließ|bar; er|schlie|ßen; sich -; **Er|schlie|ßung**
er|schmel|zen *(Hüttenw.)*
er|schöpf|bar; er|schöp|fen; sich -; **er|schöpft; Er|schöp|fung** *Plur. selten;* **Er|schöp|fungs‿tod, ...zu|stand**
[1]**er|schre|cken;** ich bin darüber erschrocken; *vgl.* [1]schrecken; [2]**er|schre|cken;** sein Aussehen hat mich erschreckt; *vgl.* [2]schrecken; [3]**er|schre|cken,** sich *(ugs.);* ich habe mich sehr erschreckt, erschrocken; **er|schre|ckend; er|schreck|lich** (*veraltet für* erschreckend, schrecklich); **Er|schro|cken|heit,** die; -; **er|schröck|lich** (*scherzh. für* erschrecklich)
er|schüt|tern; er|schüt|ternd; Er|schüt|te|rung
er|schwe|ren; Er|schwer|nis, die; -, -se; **Er|schwer|nis|zu|la|ge** (Zulage bei bes. schwerer od. Schichtarbeit); **Er|schwe|rung**
er|schwin|deln
er|schwing|bar (*svw.* erschwinglich); **er|schwin|gen; er|schwing|lich** (finanziell zu bewältigen); **Er|schwing|lich|keit,** die; -
er|se|hen
er|seh|nen *(geh.);* du ersehnst dir etwas
er|setz|bar; Er|setz|bar|keit, die; -; **er|set|zen; Er|set|zung**
er|sicht|lich
er|sin|nen; er|sinn|lich (*veraltet für* erdenklich)
er|sit|zen; ersessene Rechte; **Er|sit|zung** (*Rechtsw.* Eigentumserwerb durch langjährigen Besitz)
er|sor|gen (*schweiz. für* mit Sorge erwarten)
er|spä|hen *(geh.)*
er|spa|ren; Er|spar|nis, die; -, -se, *österr. auch* das; -ses, -se; **Er|spa|rung,** die; -
er|spie|len; du hast [dir] einen guten Platz erspielt
er|sprie|ßen *(geh.);* **er|sprieß|lich** *(geh.);* **Er|sprieß|lich|keit,** die; -
er|spü|ren *(geh.)*
erst; - recht; - mal (*ugs. für* erst einmal)
er|star|ken; Er|star|kung, die; -
er|star|ren; Er|star|rung, die; -
er|stat|ten; Er|stat|tung
erst|auf|füh|ren *meist nur im Infinitiv u. Partizip II gebr.;* die Oper wurde in Kairo erstaufgeführt; **Erst|auf|füh|rung**
er|stau|nen; Er|stau|nen, das; -s; **er|stau|nens|wert; er|staun|lich; Er|staunt|heit,** die; -
Erst‿aus|ga|be, ...aus|stat|tung, ...beich|te *(kath. Kirche),* **...be|sitz; erst|bes|te;** die erstbeste Gelegenheit, *aber* wir nehmen nicht gleich den Erstbesten, den ersten Besten; **Erst‿be|stei|gung, ...be|zug, ...druck** (*Plur.* ...drucke)
ers|te; erstere *(vgl. d.); Kleinschreibung:* der erste (1.) April; das erste Mal; beim, zum ersten Mal; der erste Rang; erste Geige spielen; erster Geiger; die erste heilige Kommunion; der erste Spatenstich; erster Klasse fahren; Bachstraße 7, erster Stock; die erste Hilfe (bei Unglücksfällen); *Großschreibung* (↑R 48): der Erste, der gekommen ist; als Erster, Erste durchs Ziel gehen; als Erstes tun; fürs Erste; zum Ersten; mein Erstes war, ein Heft zu kaufen (zuerst kaufte ich ...); die Ersten werden die Letzten sein; der Erste des Monats; vom nächsten Ersten an; Otto der Erste (*Abk.* Otto I.); der Erste Weltkrieg; der Erste Staatsanwalt; der Erste Vorsitzende *(als Dienstbez.);* der Erste Schlesische Krieg; der Erste Mai (Feiertag); die Erste Bundesliga; Erstes Deutsches Fernsehen (*für* ARD); *besondere Unterscheidungen:* die ersten beiden (das erste und das zweite Glied, das erste Paar einer Gruppe), *aber* die beiden Ersten (von zwei Gruppen das jeweils erste Glied); *vgl.* achte, erstbeste
er|ste|chen
er|ste|hen; Er|ste|her
Ers|te-Hil|fe-Aus|rüs|tung (↑R 28)
Er|ste|hung
er|steig|bar; Er|steig|bar|keit, die; -; **er|stei|gen; Er|stei|ger**
er|stei|gern; Er|stei|ge|rung
Er|stei|gung
er|stel|len (errichten; aufstellen); **Er|stel|ler; Er|stel|lung**
ers|te Mal; *vgl.* erste; **ers|tens; ers|ter;** *vgl.* erste
er|ster|ben *(geh.)*
ers|te|re; erstere Bedeutung von beiden; (↑R 47:) Erstere *od.* die Erstere kommt nicht in Betracht; Ersteres muss noch geprüft werden; **Ers|te[r]-Klas|se-Ab|teil** (↑R 28); **erst|er|wähnt,** *aber* (↑R 47): der Ersterwähnte; **Erst|ge|bä|ren|de,** die; -n, -n; ↑R 5 ff. *(Med.);* **erst|ge|bo|ren; Erst|ge|bo|re|ne, Erst|ge|bor|ne,** der, die, das; -n, -n (↑R 5 ff.); **Erst|ge|burt; Erst|ge|burts|recht,** das; -[e]s; **erst|ge|nannt,** *aber* (↑R 47): der Erstgenannte; **Erst|hel|fer** (jmd., der einem Unfallopfer als Erster Hilfe leistet); **Erst|hel|fe|rin**
er|sti|cken; Er|sti|ckung, die; -; **Er|sti|ckungs‿an|fall, ...ge|fahr, ...tod**
Erst|kläs|ser (*mitteld. für* Erstklässler); **erst|klas|sig; Erst|klas|sig|keit,** die; -; **Erst|klass|ler** *(landsch., bes. österr.) u.* **Erst|kläss|ler** (*schweiz. u. südd. für* Schüler der ersten Klasse); **Erst|klass|wa|gen** (*schweiz. für* Wagen erster Klasse); **Erst‿kom|mu|ni|kant, ...kom|mu|ni|on** *(kath. Kirche);* **erst|lich** (*veraltet für* erstens); **Erst|ling; Erst|lings‿aus|stat|tung, ...druck** (*Plur.* ...drucke), **...film, ...ro|man, ...stück, ...werk; erst|ma|lig; Erst|ma|lig|keit,** die; -; **erst|mals; Erst|plat|zier|te,** der *u.* die; -n, -n (↑R 5 ff.); *vgl.* platzieren
er|strah|len
erst|ran|gig; Erst|ran|gig|keit, die; -
er|stre|ben *(geh.);* **er|stre|bens|wert**
er|stre|cken, sich; **Er|stre|ckung**
er|strei|ten *(geh.)*
Erst|schlag *(Milit.);* **Erst|schlag|waf|fe; Erst|se|mes|ter; erst|stel|lig;** -e Hypothek; **Erst|stim|me; Erst|tags‿brief, ...stem|pel**
er|stun|ken (*derb für* erdichtet); - und erlogen
er|stür|men; Er|stür|mung
Erst|ver|kaufs|tag; erst|ver|öf|fent|li|chen *nur im Infinitiv u. Partizip II gebr.;* **Erst‿ver|öf|fent|li|chung, ...ver|sor|gung** (erste Hilfe), **...ver|stor|be|ne** (der *u.* die; -n, -n; ↑R 5 ff.), **...wa|gen, ...wäh|ler, ...zu|las|sung**
er|su|chen; Er|su|chen, das; -s, -; auf -
er|tap|pen; sich bei etwas -
er|tei|len; Er|tei|lung
er|tö|nen
er|tö|ten *(geh.);* Begierden -; **Er|tö|tung,** die; -
Er|trag, der; -[e]s, ...träge; **er|trag|bar; er|tra|gen; er|trag|fä|hig,** *auch* er|trags|fä|hig; **Er|trag|fä|hig|keit,** *auch* Er|trags|fä|hig|keit, die; -; **er|träg|lich; Er|träg|lich|keit,** die; -; **er|trag|los; Er|träg|nis,** das; -ses, -se (*seltener für* Ertrag); **er|träg|nis|reich** (*seltener für* ertragreich); **er|trag|reich; Er|trags|aus|sich|ten** *Plur.;* **er|trags|fä|hig** *vgl.* ertragfähig; **Er|trags|fä|hig|keit** *vgl.* Ertragfähigkeit; **Er|trags‿la|ge, ...min-**

de|rung; **er|trags|si|cher; Er|trag[s]‿stei|ge|rung, ...steu|er**

er|trän|ken; ertränkt; **Er|trän|kung**

er|träu|men; ich erträume mir etwas

er|trin|ken; ertrunken; **Er|trin|ken,** das; -s; **Er|trin|ken|de,** der *u.* die; -n, -n (↑R 5 ff.)

er|trot|zen; Er|trot|zung

er|trun|ken; *vgl.* ertrinken; **Er|trun|ke|ne,** der *u.* die; -n, -n (↑R 5 ff.)

er|tüch|ti|gen; Er|tüch|ti|gung, die; -

er|üb|ri|gen; er hat viel erübrigt (gespart); es erübrigt sich (ist überflüssig)[,] zu erwähnen, ...; **Er|üb|ri|gung,** die; -

e|ru|ie|ren ‹lat.› (herausbringen; ermitteln); **E|ru|ie|rung**

e|rup|tie|ren; E|rup|ti|on, die; -, -en ‹lat.› ([vulkan.] Ausbruch); **e|rup|tiv; E|rup|tiv|ge|stein**

Er|ve ['ɛrvə], die; -, -n (eine Hülsenfrucht)

er|wa|chen; Er|wa|chen, das; -s

[1]er|wach|sen; ein erwachsener Mensch; **[2]er|wach|sen;** mir sind Bedenken erwachsen; **Er|wach|se|ne,** der *u.* die; -n, -n (↑R 5 ff.); **Er|wach|se|nen‿bil|dung** (die; -), **...tau|fe; Er|wach|sen|sein,** das; -s

er|wä|gen; du erwägst; du erwogst; du erwögest; erwogen; erwäg[e]!; **er|wä|gens|wert; Er|wä|gung;** in - ziehen

er|wäh|len *(geh.)*; **Er|wähl|te,** der *u.* die; -n, -n (↑R 5 ff.); **Er|wäh|lung**

er|wäh|nen; er|wäh|nens|wert; er|wähn|ter|ma|ßen *(Amtsspr.)*; **Er|wäh|nung**

er|wah|ren (*schweiz. für* als wahr erweisen; das Ergebnis einer Abstimmung od. Wahl amtl. bestätigen); **Er|wah|rung**

er|wan|dern; Er|wan|de|rung

er|wär|men (warm machen); sich - (begeistern) für; **Er|wär|mung**

er|war|ten; Er|war|ten, das; -s; wider -; **Er|war|tung; er|war|tungs|ge|mäß; Er|war|tungs|hal|tung; er|war|tungs|voll**

er|we|cken; Er|we|ckung

er|weh|ren, sich; ich konnte mich seiner kaum -

er|weich|bar; er|wei|chen; ich lasse mich nicht -; *vgl.* [1]weichen; **Er|wei|chung**

Er|weis, der; -es, -e (*veraltend für* Nachweis, Beweis); **er|wei|sen;** sich -; **er|weis|lich** *(veraltet)*; **Er|wei|sung,** die; -

er|wei|tern; die erweiterte Oberschule (*ehem. in der DDR* mit dem Abitur abschließende Schule; *Abk.* EOS); **Er|wei|te|rung; Er|wei|te|rungs|bau** *Plur.* ...bauten

Er|werb, der; -[e]s, -e; **er|wer|ben; Er|wer|ber; Er|wer|be|rin; er|werbs‿be|schränkt, ...fä|hig; Er|werbs|fä|hig|keit,** die; -; **er|werbs|ge|min|dert; Er|werbs|le|ben;** im - stehen; **er|werbs|los; Er|werbs|lo|se,** der *u.* die; -n, -n (↑R 5 ff.); **Er|werbs|lo|sig|keit,** die; -; **Er|werbs‿min|de|rung, ...mög|lich|keit, ...quel|le, ...stre|ben; er|werbs|tä|tig; Er|werbs|tä|ti|ge,** der *u.* die; -n, -n (↑R 5 ff.); **er|werbs|un|fä|hig; Er|werbs|zweig; Er|wer|bung**

er|wi|dern; ich ...ere (↑R 16); **Er|wi|de|rung**

er|wie|sen; er|wie|se|ner|ma|ßen

Er|win (m. Vorn.)

er|wir|ken; Er|wir|kung, die; -

er|wirt|schaf|ten; Gewinn -; **Er|wirt|schaf|tung**

er|wi|schen (*ugs. für* ertappen; fassen, ergreifen); mich hat es erwischt (*ugs. für* ich bin krank, *auch für* ich bin verliebt)

er|wor|ben; -e Rechte

er|wünscht

er|wür|gen; Er|wür|gung

e|ry|man|thisch, *aber* (↑R 108): der Erymanthische Eber; **E|ry|man|thos, E|ry|man|thus,** der; - (Gebirge im Peloponnes)

E|ry|si|pel, das; -s, -e ‹griech.› (*Med.* Wundrose [Hautentzündung]); **E|ry|them,** das; -s, -e (*Med.* Hautrötung)

E|ryth|rä|i|sche Meer (↑R 130), das; -n -[e]s (*altgriech. Name für* das Arabische Meer)

E|ryth|rin (↑R 130), der; -s ‹griech.› (ein Mineral); **E|ryth|ro|zyt,** der; -en, -en *meist Plur.*; ↑R 126 (*Med.* rotes Blutkörperchen)

Erz[1], das; -es, -e

erz... ‹griech.› (*verstärkende Vorsilbe,* z. B. erzböse); **Erz...** (*in Titeln,* z. B. Erzbischof, *u. in Scheltnamen,* z. B. Erzschelm)

Erz|ader[1] (↑R 132)

er|zäh|len; erzählende Dichtung; **er|zäh|lens|wert; Er|zäh|ler; Er|zäh|le|rin; er|zäh|le|risch; Er|zähl|kunst,** die; -; **Er|zäh|lung**

Erz|bau[1], der; -[e]s; **Erz|berg|bau**[1], der; -[e]s

Erz|bi|schof; erz|bi|schöf|lich; Erz|bis|tum; erz|bö|se; Erz|di|ö|ze|se; erz|dumm

er|zei|gen *(geh.)*; sich dankbar -

er|zen[1] (aus Erz)

[1] [*auch* 'ɛrts...]

Erz|en|gel

er|zeu|gen; Er|zeu|ger; Er|zeu|ger‿land, ...preis (*vgl.* [2]Preis); **Er|zeug|nis,** das; -ses, -se; **Er|zeu|gung; Er|zeu|gungs|kos|ten** *Plur.*

erz|faul; Erz‿feind, ...feind|schaft, ...gau|ner

Erz|ge|bir|ge[1], das; -s; **erz|ge|bir|gisch**[1]; **Erz|ge|birg|ler**[1]; **Erz‿ge|win|nung**[1], **...gie|ßer**[1], **...gie|ße|rei**[1]; **erz|hal|tig**[1]

Erz|ha|lun|ke; Erz|her|zog; Erz|her|zo|gin; Erz|her|zog-Thron|fol|ger (↑R 24); **Erz|her|zog|tum**

erz|höf|fig[1] (reiches Erzvorkommen versprechend)

er|zieh|bar; er|zie|hen; Er|zie|her; Er|zie|her|ga|be, die; -; **Er|zie|he|rin; er|zie|he|risch; er|zieh|lich** *(bes. österr.)*; **Er|zie|hung,** die; -; **Er|zie|hungs‿an|stalt, ...bei|hil|fe, ...be|ra|tung; Er|zie|hungs|be|rech|tig|te,** der *u.* die; -n, -n (↑R 5 ff.); **Er|zie|hungs‿geld, ...heim, ...schwie|rig|kei|ten** *(Plur.)*, **...sys|tem, ...ur|laub, ...we|sen, ...wis|sen|schaft**

er|zie|len; Er|zie|lung, die; -

er|zit|tern

erz|kon|ser|va|tiv; Erz|lüg|ner; Erz|lump; Erz|pries|ter; Erz‿schelm, ...spitz|bu|be, ...übel (↑R 132)

er|zür|nen; Er|zür|nung

Erz|va|ter

er|zwin|gen; Er|zwin|gung, die; -; **Er|zwun|ge|ne,** das; -n (↑R 5 ff.); etwas -s; **er|zwun|ge|ner|ma|ßen**

[1]es; es sei denn, dass (↑R 88); (↑R 13): er ists, *auch* ist's; er sprachs, *auch* sprach's; 's ist nicht anders, 's war einmal; (↑R 48:) das unbestimmte Es; **[2]es;** *alter Gen. von* „es", *nur noch in Wendungen wie* ich bin es zufrieden; ich habe *od.* ich bin es satt

[3]es, [1]Es, das; -, - (Tonbezeichnung); **[4]es** (*Zeichen für* es-Moll); in es; **[2]Es** (*Zeichen für* Es-Dur); in Es

[3]Es = Einsteinium

[4]Es, das; -, - *(Psych.)*

ESA, die; - (= European Space Agency [ju(ə)rə'pi:ən 'spe:s 'e:dʒ(ə)nsi]; Europäische Weltraumorganisation)

E|sau (bibl. m. Eigenn.)

Esc = Escudo

Es|cha|to|lo|gie [ɛsça...], die; - ‹griech.› (Lehre vom Endschicksal des einzelnen Menschen u. der Welt); **es|cha|to|lo|gisch**

[1] [*auch* 'ɛrts...]

E|sche, die; -, -n (ein Laubbaum); **e|schen** (aus Eschenholz); **E|schen|holz**

E-Schicht, die; -; ↑R 25 (eine Schicht der Ionosphäre)

Es|co|ri|al, der; -[s] (span. Kloster u. Schloss)

Es|cu|do, der; -[s], -[s] ‹port.› (port. Währungseinheit; *Abk.* Esc)

Es-Dur [*auch* 'ɛs'du:r], das; - (Tonart; *Zeichen* Es); **Es-Dur-Ton|lei|ter** (↑R 28)

E|sel, der; -s, -; **E|sel|chen; E|se|lei; e|sel|haft; E|sel|hengst; E|se|lin; E|sels‿brü|cke** *(ugs.),* **...ohr** *(ugs.),* **...rü|cken; E|sel|stu|te**

es|ka|la|die|ren ‹franz.› *(früher für* mit Sturmleitern erstürmen; *veraltet für* eine Eskaladierwand überwinden); **Es|ka|la|dier|wand** *(veraltet für* Kletterwand);

Es|ka|la|ti|on, die; -, -en ‹franz.-engl.› (stufenweise Steigerung, Verschärfung); **es|ka|lie|ren** ([sich] stufenweise steigern); **Es|ka|lie|rung**

Es|ka|mo|ta|ge [...'ta:ʒə, *österr.* ...'ta:ʒ], die; -, -n [...'ta:ʒ(ə)n] ‹franz.› *(veraltet für* Taschenspielerei); **Es|ka|mo|teur** [...'tø:r], der; -s, -e (Taschenspieler, Zauberkünstler); **es|ka|mo|tie|ren** (wegzaubern)

Es|ka|pa|de, die; -, -n ‹franz.› *(Reiten* Sprung zur Seite; *geh. für* mutwilliger Streich); **Es|ka|pis|mus,** der; - ‹engl.› *(Psych.* vor der Realität ausweichendes Verhalten); **es|ka|pis|tisch**

Es|ka|ri|ol, der; -s ‹lat.› (Winterendivie)

[1]Es|ki|mo, der; -[s], -[s] (Angehöriger eines arkt. Volkes); **[2]Es|ki|mo,** der; -s, -s ‹indian.› (ein Wollstoff); **es|ki|mo|isch; Es|ki|mo|i|sche,** das; -en (Sprache der Eskimos); *vgl.* Deutsche, das

Es|ko|ri|al *vgl.* Escorial

Es|kor|te, die; -, -n ‹franz.› (Geleit, Schutz; Begleitmannschaft); **es|kor|tie|ren; Es|kor|tie|rung**

Es|ku|do *vgl.* Escudo

[1]Es|me|ral|da, die; -, -s ‹span.› (ein span. Tanz); **[2]Es|me|ral|da** (w. Vorn.)

es-Moll [*auch* 'ɛs'mɔl], das; - (Tonart; *Zeichen* es); **es-Moll-Ton|lei|ter** (↑R 28)

E|so|te|rik, die; - ‹griech.› (Geheimlehre); **E|so|te|ri|ker** (in eine Geheimlehre Eingeweihter); **E|so|te|ri|ke|rin; e|so|te|risch** (nur für Eingeweihte, Fachleute u. Ä. verständlich)

Es|pag|no|le [ɛspa'njo:lə] (↑R 130), die; -, -n [...o:len] ‹franz.› (ein spanischer Tanz); **Es|pag|no|let|te|ver|schluss** [...'lɛt...] (Drehstangenverschluss für Fenster)

Es|pan, der; -[e]s, -e *(landsch. für* Viehweide)

Es|par|set|te, die; -, -n ‹franz.› (eine Futterpflanze)

Es|par|to, der; -s ‹span.› (ein Gras); **Es|par|to|gras**

Es|pe, die; -, -n (Zitterpappel); **es|pen** (aus Espenholz); **Es|pen|laub**

Es|pe|ran|tist, der; -en, -en; ↑R 126 (Kenner, Anhänger des Esperanto); **Es|pe|ran|to,** das; -[s] ‹nach dem Pseudonym „Dr. Esperanto" des poln. Erfinders L. Zamenhof› (eine künstl. Weltsprache); **Es|pe|ran|to|lo|ge,** der; -n, -n; ↑R 126 (Erforscher von Sprache u. Literatur des Esperantos); **Es|pe|ran|to|lo|gie,** die; -; **Es|pe|ran|to|lo|gin**

Es|pla|na|de, die; -, -n ‹franz.› (freier Platz)

es|pres|si|vo [...vo] ‹ital.› *(Musik* ausdrucksvoll); **[1]Es|pres|so,** der; -[s], *Plur.* -s *od.* ...ssi (in der Maschine bereitetes, starkes Kaffeegetränk); **[2]Es|pres|so,** das; -[s], -s (kleines Café); **Es|pres|so‿bar** (die), **...ma|schi|ne**

Esp|rit [ɛs'pri:] (↑R 130), der; -s ‹franz.› (Geist, Witz)

Esq. = Esquire

Es|qui|lin, der; -s (Hügel in Rom)

Es|qui|re [is'kwaiə(r)], der; -s, -s ‹engl.› (engl. Höflichkeitstitel, *Abk.* Esq.)

Es|ra (bibl. m. Vorn.)

Es|say ['ɛse:, *auch* ɛ'se:, *österr. nur so*], der *od.* das; -s, -s ‹engl.› (kürzere Abhandlung); **Es|say|ist,** der; -en, -en; ↑R 126 (Verfasser von Essays); **Es|say|is|tin; es|say|is|tisch**

ess|bar; Ess|ba|re, das; -n (↑R 5 ff.); etwas Essbares auftreiben; **Ess|bar|keit,** die; -; **Ess|be|steck**

Es|se, die; -, -n (Schmiedeherd; *bes. ostmitteld. für* Schornstein)

Ess|ecke (↑R 132)

es sei denn, dass (↑R 88)

es|sen; du isst; du aßest; du äßest; gegessen; iss!; zu Mittag essen; selber essen macht fett; **[1]Es|sen,** das; -s, -

[2]Es|sen (Stadt im Ruhrgebiet)

Es|sen|aus|ga|be

es|sen|disch *vgl.* essensch

Es|sen|emp|fang

[1]Es|se|ner *Plur.* ‹hebr.› (eine altjüdische Sekte)

[2]Es|se|ner (↑R 103)

Es|sen‿hol|ler, ...kar|te

Es|sen|keh|rer *(bes. ostmitteld. für* Schornsteinfeger)

Es|sen|mar|ke, Es|sens|mar|ke

es|sensch ‹*zu* [2]Essen›

Es|sens|mar|ke *vgl.* Essenmarke; **Es|sens|zeit**

es|sen|ti|ell *vgl.* essenziell; **Es|senz,** die; -, -en *(nur Sing.:* Wesen, Kern; konzentrierter Auszug); **es|sen|zi|ell** (↑R 33) ‹franz.› *(Philos.* wesentlich; *Biol., Chemie* lebensnotwendig); essenzielle Fettsäuren

Es|ser; Es|se|rei, die; - *(ugs. abwertend);* **Es|se|rin; Ess‿ge|schirr, ...ge|wohn|heit** *(meist Plur.),* **...gier**

Es|sig, der; -s, -e; **Es|sig‿baum, ...es|senz, ...gur|ke, ...mut|ter** (die; -; die sich im Essigfass bildende Bakterienkultur); **es|sig|sau|er** *(Chemie);* essigsaure Tonerde; **Es|sig|säu|re**

Ess|koh|le (eine Steinkohlenart)

Ess‿kul|tur, ...löf|fel; ess|löf|fel|wei|se; Ess|lust, die; -; **ess|lus|tig; Ess‿tisch, ...un|lust, ...wa|ren** *(Plur.),* **...zim|mer**

Es|tab|lish|ment [is'tɛbliʃmənt] (↑R 130), das; -s, -s ‹engl.› (Schicht der Einflussreichen u. Etablierten)

Es|tam|pe [ɛs'tã:p(ə)] (↑R 132), die; -, -n (Abdruck eines Holz-, Kupfer- od. Stahlstichs)

Es|tan|zia (↑R 132), die; -, -s ‹span.› (südamerik. Landgut [mit Viehwirtschaft])

Es|te[1], der; -n, -n; ↑R 126 (Estländer)

[1]Es|ter, der; -s, - *(Chemie* eine organ. Verbindung)

[2]Es|ter *vgl.* [1]Esther

[1]Es|ther, *ökum.* Es|ter (bibl. w. Eigenn.); **[2]Es|ther** (w. Vorn.)

Es|tin[1]; **Est|land**[1]; **Est|län|der**[1]; **est|län|disch**[1]; **est|nisch**[1]; -e Sprache; *vgl.* deutsch; **Est|nisch**[1], das; -[s] (Sprache); *vgl.* Deutsch; **Est|ni|sche**[1], das; -n; *vgl.* Deutsche, das

Es|to|mi|hi ‹lat., „Sei mir [ein starker Fels]!"› (letzter Sonntag vor der Passionszeit)

Est|ra|de (↑R 130 *u.* 132), die; -, -n ‹franz.› *(veraltend für* erhöhter Teil des Fußbodens; Podium; *regional für* volkstüml. künstler. Veranstaltung mit gemischtem Programm [aus Musik, Artistik u. Ä.]); **Est|ra|den|kon|zert** *(regional)*

Est|ra|gon (↑R 130 *u.* 132), der; -s ‹arab.› (eine Gewürzpflanze)

---

[1] [*auch* 'ɛst...]

[1]**Est|re|ma|du|ra** (↑R 130; hist. Provinz in Spanien; port. Landschaft); [2]**Est|re|ma|du|ra,** die; - *u.* **Est|re|ma|du|ra|garn,** das; -[e]s; (↑R 105; ein glattes Baumwollgarn)

Est|rich, der; -s, -e (fugenloser Fußboden; *schweiz. für* Dachboden, -raum)

Es|zett, das; -, - (Buchstabe: „ß“)

et ‹lat.› (und; *Zeichen [in Firmennamen]* &); *vgl.* Et-Zeichen

E|ta, das; -[s], -s (griech. Buchstabe [langes e]: *Η, η*)

e|tab|lie|ren (↑R 130) ‹franz.› (festsetzen; begründen); sich - (sich [als selbstständiger Geschäftsmann] niederlassen; einen sicheren [gesellschaftl.] Platz gewinnen); **E|tab|lier|te,** der *u.* die; -n, -n; ↑R 5 ff. (jmd., der es zu etwas gebracht hat); **E|tab|lie|rung; E|tab|lis|se|ment** [etablis(ə)'mã:, *schweiz.* ...blisə'mɛnt], das; -s, *Plur.* -s, *schweiz.* -e (*geh. für* Betrieb; Niederlassung; [vornehme] Gaststätte; *auch für* [Nacht]lokal, Bordell)

E|ta|ge [e'ta:ʒə, *österr.* e'ta:ʒ], die; -, -n [e'ta:ʒ(ə)n] (Stock[werk], [Ober]geschoss); **E|ta|gen|bett; e|ta|gen|för|mig; E|ta|gen‿hei|zung, ...tür, ...woh|nung; E|ta|ge|re** [...ʒɛ:rə], die; -, -n (drei übereinander angeordnete, mit einem Stab in der Mitte verbundene Schalen für Obst u. Ä.; *veraltend auch für* Gestell für Bücher od. Geschirr)

et al. *vgl.* et alii

et a|lii [- 'a(:)li|i] ‹lat.› (und andere; *Abk.* et al.)

E|ta|lon [...'lɔ̃:], der; -s, -s ‹franz.› (*fachspr. für* Normalmaß, Eichmaß)

E|ta|min, das, *auch, bes. österr.* der; -s ‹franz.› *od.* **E|ta|mi|ne,** die; - (ein Gewebe)

E|tap|pe, die; -, -n ‹franz.› ([Teil]strecke, Abschnitt; Stufe; *Milit.* Versorgungsgebiet hinter der Front); **E|tap|pen‿ha|se** *(Soldatenspr.),* **...hengst** *(Soldatenspr.),* **...sieg** *(Rennsport);* **e|tap|pen|wei|se**

E|tat [e'ta:], der; -s, -s ‹franz.› ([Staats]haushalt[splan]; Geldmittel); **E|tat|auf|stel|lung; e|ta|ti|sie|ren** [etati...] (in den Etat aufnehmen); **E|tat‿jahr** [e'ta:...], **...la|ge; e|tat|mä|ßig** (dem Etat gemäß; eine Planstelle innehabend; *Sport* auf einer Position regelmäßig eingesetzt); **E|tat‿pe|ri|o|de, ...pos|ten, ...re|de, ...über|schrei|tung** (↑R 132)

E|ta|zis|mus, der; - ‹griech.› (Aussprache des griech. Eta [η] wie langes e)

etc. = et cetera; *dafür besser* usw.; **et ce|te|ra** (und so weiter; *Abk.* etc.); **etc. pp.** (*verstärkend für* etc.); *vgl.* pp.

e|te|pe|te|te (*ugs. für* geziert, zimperlich; übertrieben feinfühlig)

E|ter|nit ® [*auch* ...'nit], das *od.* der; -s ‹lat.› (Faserzement); **E|ter|nit|plat|te**

E|te|si|en [...i̯ən] *Plur.* ‹griech.› (passatartige Winde im Mittelmeer); **E|te|si|en|kli|ma,** das; -s (winterfeuchtes, sommertrockenes Mittelmeerklima)

ETH = Eidgenössische Technische Hochschule; ETHL (in Lausanne; *oft auch* EPFL = École Polytechnique Fédérale Lausanne); ETHZ (in Zürich)

E|than *vgl.* Äthan; **E|tha|nol** *vgl.* Äthanol; **E|ther** *vgl.* [2]Äther

E|thik, die; -, -en *Plur. selten* ‹griech.› (Sittenlehre; Gesamtheit der sittlichen und moralischen Grundsätze [einer Gesellschaft]); **E|thi|ker** (Vertreter der Ethik); **e|thisch** (sittlich)

ETHL *vgl.* ETH

Eth|nie, die; -, ...i̯en ‹griech.› (*Völkerk.* Volk, Stamm); **eth|nisch** (die [einheitliche] Kultur- u. Lebensgemeinschaft einer Volksgruppe betreffend); **Eth|no|graf, Eth|no|gra|fie** usw. *eindeutschende Schreibung für* Ethnograph, Ethnographie usw.; **Eth|no|graph** (↑R 33), der; -en, -en; ↑R 126 (Völkerkundler); **Eth|no|gra|phie** (↑R 33), die; -, ...i̯en ([beschreibende] Völkerkunde); **Eth|no|gra|phin** (↑R 33); **eth|no|gra|phisch** (↑R 33); **Eth|no|lo|ge,** der; -n, -n; ↑R 126 (Völkerkundler); **Eth|no|lo|gie,** die; -, ...i̯en (Völkerkunde); **Eth|no|lo|gin; eth|no|lo|gisch; Eth|no|pop** (von der Volksmusik [bes. Afrikas, Asiens od. Südamerikas] beeinflusste Popmusik)

E|tho|lo|gie, die; - ‹griech.› (Wissenschaft vom Verhalten der Tiere u. des Menschen; Verhaltensforschung); **E|thos,** das; - (die sittl.-moral. Gesamthaltung)

E|thyl usw. *vgl.* Äthyl usw.

ETHZ *vgl.* ETH

E|ti|kett, das; -[e]s, *Plur.* -e[n], *auch* -s *u. (schweiz., österr., sonst veraltet)* [1]**E|ti|ket|te,** die; -, -n ‹franz.› (Zettel mit [Preis]aufschrift, Schild[chen]; Auszeichnung [von Waren]); [2]**E|ti|ket|te,** die; -, -n (Gesamtheit der herkömmlichen Umgangsformen; Vorschriften für den förmlichen Umgang); **E|ti|ket|ten|schwin|del** (*ugs. für* irreführende Benennung); **e|ti|ket|tie|ren** (mit einem Etikett versehen); **E|ti|ket|tie|rung**

e|ti|o|lie|ren ‹franz.› (*Bot.* vergeilen)

et|li|che; etliche Tage, Stunden usw. sind vergangen; ich weiß etliches darüber zu erzählen; etlicher politischer Zündstoff; etliche gute Menschen; die Taten etlicher guter, *selten* guten Menschen; etliche Mal, etliche Male

Et|mal, das; -[e]s, -e (*Seemannsspr.* Zeit von Mittag bis Mittag; innerhalb dieses Zeitraums zurückgelegte Strecke)

E|ton ['i:t(ə)n] (engl. Schulstadt)

Et|ru|ri|en [...i̯ən] (↑R 130; altital. Landschaft); **Et|rus|ker** (Einwohner Etruriens); **et|rus|kisch**

Etsch, die; - (Zufluss der Adria); *vgl.* Adige; **Etsch|tal**

Et|ter, der *od.* das; -s, - (*südd. für* bebautes Ortsgebiet)

E|tü|de, die; -, -n ‹franz.› (*Musik* Übungsstück)

E|tui [ɛt'vi:], das; -s, -s ‹franz.› (Behälter, [Schutz]hülle); **E|tui|kleid** (sehr eng geschnittenes Kleid)

et|wa; in etwa (annähernd, ungefähr); **et|wa|ig;** etwaige weitere Kosten; **et|was** (↑R 47 f.:) etwas Auffälliges, Derartiges, Passendes usw., *aber* etwas anderes; *vgl. auch* was; **Et|was,** das; -, -; ein gewisses Etwas; **et|wel|che** *Plur.* (*veraltet für* einige)

E|ty|mo|lo|ge, der; -n, -n (↑R 126) ‹griech.›; **E|ty|mo|lo|gie,** die; -, ...i̯en (*Sprachw.* Ursprung u. Geschichte der Wörter; Forschungsrichtung, die sich damit befasst); **e|ty|mo|lo|gisch; e|ty|mo|lo|gi|sie|ren** (nach Herkunft u. Wortgeschichte untersuchen); **E|ty|mon** [*auch* 'ɛ...], das; -s, ...ma (Wurzel-, Stammwort)

Et-Zei|chen, das; -s, - (Und-Zeichen [in Firmennamen]: &)

Et|zel (*in der dt. Sage* Name des Hunnenkönigs Attila; *vgl. d.*)

Eu = *chem. Zeichen für* Europium

EU = Europäische Union

eu... ‹griech.› (wohl..., gut...); **Eu...** (Wohl..., Gut...)

Eu|bi|o|tik, die; - ‹griech.› (*Med.* Lehre von der gesunden Lebensführung)

Eu|bö|a (griech. Insel); **eu|bö|isch**

euch (↑R 52 f.); *auch in Briefen kleingeschrieben*

Eu|cha|ris|tie [...ç...], die; -, ...i̯en ‹griech.› (*kath. Kirche* Abendmahl, Altarsakrament); **eu|cha|ris|tisch;** eucharistische Taube (ein liturg. Gefäß), *aber* (↑R 108): der Eucharistische Kongress

Eu|dä|mo|nie, die; - ‹griech.› (*Philos.* Glückseligkeit); **Eu|dä|mo|nis|mus**, der; - (Glückseligkeitslehre); **eu|dä|mo|nis|tisch**

[1]**eu|er**, eu[e]|re, eu|er; (↑R 52 f.); *auch in Briefen kleingeschrieben;* euer Tisch, eu[e]rem, euerm Tisch usw.; euer von allen unterschriebener Brief (↑R 5); *vgl.* eu[e]re. *In Titeln: Nom., Akk.:* Euer, Eure (*Abk. für beide* Ew.) Hochwürden usw.; *Gen., Dat.:* Euer, Eurer (*Abk. für beide* Ew.) Hochwürden usw.; [2]**eu|er** (↑R 52 f.); *auch in Briefen kleingeschrieben* (*Gen. von* [2]ihr; *geh.*); euer (*nicht* eurer) sind drei, sind wenige; ich gedenke, ich erinnere mich euer (*nicht* eurer); **eu[e]|re**, *(geh.:)* eu|ri|ge; *Groß- oder Kleinschreibung:* unser Bauplatz ist dicht bei dem eur[ig]en; *aber* grüße die Euern, Euren, Eurigen *od.* die euern, euren, eurigen; ihr müsst das Eu[e]re, Eurige *od.* eu[e]re, eurige tun; **eu|er|seits**, eu|rer|seits; **eu|ers|glei|chen**, eu|res|glei|chen; **eu|ert|hal|ben**, eu|ret|hal|ben *(veraltend);* **eu|ert|we|gen**, eu|ret|we|gen; **eu|ert|wil|len**, eu|ret|wil|len; um euertwillen, um euretwillen

Eu|gen ['ɔyge:n, *auch* ɔy'ge:n] (m. Vorn.); **Eu|ge|nie** [...iə] (w. Vorn.)

Eu|ge|nik, die; - ‹griech.› (*Med.* Erbgesundheitslehre, -forschung, -pflege); **Eu|ge|ni|ker**; **eu|ge|nisch**

Eu|ka|lyp|tus, der; -, *Plur.* ...ten *u.* - ‹griech.› (ein Baum); **Eu|ka|lyp|tus|öl**

Euk|lid (↑R 130; altgriech. Mathematiker); **euk|li|disch** (↑R 94): die euklidische Geometrie; der euklidische Lehrsatz

Eu|la|lia, Eu|la|lie [...iə] (w. Vorn.)

Eu|le, die; -, -n (*nordd. auch für* [Decken]besen); **eu|len|äu|gig**; **Eu|len|flucht**, die; - (*nordd. für* Abenddämmerung); **Eu|len|flug**, der; -[e]s; **eu|len|haft**

Eu|len|spie|gel (Titelgestalt eines dt. Volksbuches); **Eu|len|spie|ge|lei**

Eu|ler (schweiz. Mathematiker)

Eu|mel, der; -s, - (*ugs. für* Dummkopf; Gegenstand, Ding)

Eu|me|ni|de, die; -, -n *meist Plur.* ‹griech.-lat., die „Wohlwollende"› (verhüllender Name der ↑Erinnye)

Eu|no|mia [*auch* ...'mi:a] (griech. Göttin der Gesetzmäßigkeit, eine der [2]Horen)

Eu|nuch, der; -en, -en (↑R 126) ‹griech.› (Kastrat [als Haremswächter]); **Eu|nu|che**, der; -n, -n; *vgl.* Eunuch; **eu|nu|chen|haft;** **Eu|nu|chen|stim|me**

Eu|phe|mia (w. Vorn.)

Eu|phe|mis|mus, der; -, ...men ‹griech.› (beschönigendes, verhüllendes Wort, Hüllwort, z. B. „einschlafen" für „sterben"); **eu|phe|mis|tisch**

Eu|pho|nie, die; -, ...ien ‹griech.› (Wohlklang, -laut); **eu|pho|nisch** (wohlklingend; [von Lauten] des Wohllauts wegen eingeschoben, z. B. „t" in „eigen*t*lich")

Eu|phor|bia, Eu|phor|bie [...iə], die; -, ...ien [...iən] ‹griech.› (*Bot.* ein Wolfsmilchgewächs)

Eu|pho|rie, die; - ‹griech.› (Zustand gesteigerten Hochgefühls); **eu|pho|risch**; **eu|pho|ri|sie|ren** (in Euphorie versetzen)

Euph|rat (↑R 130), der; -[s] (Strom in Vorderasien)

Euph|ro|sy|ne [...nə, *auch* ...ne:] (↑R 130 *u.* 132) ‹griech., „die Frohsinnige"› (eine der drei Chariten)

Eu|phu|is|mus, der; - ‹engl.› (schwülstiger Stil der engl. Barockzeit); **eu|phu|is|tisch**

Eu|ra|si|en [...iən] (Festland von Europa u. Asien); **Eu|ra|si|er**, der; -s, - (Bewohner Eurasiens; Nachkomme eines europ. und eines asiat. Elternteils); **Eu|ra|si|e|rin; eu|ra|sisch; Eu|ra|tom**, die; - (*Kurzw. für* Europäische Atomgemeinschaft)

eu|re, eu|e|re, eu|ri|ge; *vgl.* eu[e]re; **Eu|rer** (*Abk.* Ew.); *vgl.* [1]euer; **eu|[r]er|seits; eu|res|glei|chen**, eu|ers|glei|chen; **eu|ret|hal|ben**, eu|ert|hal|ben *(veraltend);* **eu|ret|we|gen**, eu|ert|we|gen; **eu|ret|wil|len**, eu|ert|wil|len; um -

Eu|rhyth|mie, die; - ‹griech.› (schönes Gleichmaß von Bewegungen; *Med.* Regelmäßigkeit des Pulses)

eu|ri|ge *vgl.* eu[e]re

eu|ri|pi|de|isch (↑R 94): die euripideischen Dramen; **Eu|ri|pi|des** (altgriech. Tragiker)

Eu|ro, der; -[s], -[s] (↑R 90; europ. Währungseinheit); **Eu|ro|cheque**, *internationale Schreibung auf den Formularen* **eu|ro|cheque** [*beide* ...ʃɛk], der; -s, -s ‹*Kurzw. aus* europäisch *u.* franz. chèque› (bei den Banken zahlreicher [europ.] Länder einlösbarer Scheck); **Eu|ro|cheque|kar|te** (↑R 24); **Eu|ro|ci|ty**, der; -s, -s; *kurz für* Eurocityzug; **Eu|ro|ci|ty|zug** (europaweit verkehrender Intercityzug; *Abk.* EC); **Eu|ro‿dol|lars** (*Plur.;* Dollarguthaben in Europa), **...kom|mu|nis|mus** (westeurop. Richtung des Kommunismus), **...kom|mu|nist**, **...norm** (in der EU geltende Norm)

Eu|ro|pa ‹griech.› (*auch* griech. weibl. Sagengestalt); **Eu|ro|pa|cup** *vgl.* Europapokal; **Eu|ro|pä|er**, der; -s, -; **Eu|ro|pä|e|rin; eu|ro|pä|id** (*Anthropol.* Europäern ähnlich); **Eu|ro|pä|i|de**, der *u.* die; -n, -n (↑R 5 ff.); **eu|ro|pä|isch;** der europäische Gedanke; eine europäische Gemeinschaft, *aber* (↑R 108): die Europäische Gemeinschaft (*Abk.* EG); die Europäische Union (*Abk.* EU); das Europäische Parlament; **eu|ro|pä|i|sie|ren; Eu|ro|pä|i|sie|rung; Eu|ro|pa‿meis|ter**, **...meis|ter|schaft**, **...par|la|ment** (das; -[e]s), **...po|kal** (internationale Sporttrophäe, bes. im Fußball), **...rat** (der; -[e]s), **...re|kord**, **...stra|ße** (*Zeichen* E, z. B. E 5), **...uni|on** (↑R 132, die; -); **eu|ro|pid** (*Anthropol.* zu den Europiden gehörend); **Eu|ro|pi|de**, der *u.* die; -n, -n; ↑R 5 ff. (Angehörige[r] der in Europa, Nordafrika und im Westteil Asiens einheimischen Menschenrasse); **Eu|ro|pi|um**, das; -s (chem. Element, Metall; *Zeichen* Eu); **Eu|ro|tun|nel**, der; -s (unter dem Ärmelkanal); **Eu|ro|vi|si|on** ‹*Kurzw. aus* europäisch *u.* Television› (europ. Organisation zur gemeinsamen Veranstaltung von Fernsehsendungen); **Eu|ro|vi|si|ons|sen|dung**

Eu|ry|di|ke [...ke:, *auch* ...ry'di:ke:] (*griech. Mythol.* Gattin des Orpheus)

Eu|ryth|mie, die; - ‹*von R. Steiner gebrauchte Schreibung für* ↑Eurhythmie› (in der Anthroposophie gepflegte Bewegungskunst); **eu|ryth|misch**

eu|ry|top ‹griech.› (*Biol.* weit verbreitet [von Tieren u. Pflanzen])

Eu|se|bi|us (m. Eigenn.); - von Cäsarea (griech. Kirchenschriftsteller)

Eus|tach, Eus|ta|chi|us (↑R 132; m. Vorn.); **eus|ta|chi|sche Röh|re, eus|ta|chi|sche Tu|be**, die; -n -, -n -n ‹nach dem ital. Arzt Eustachi[o]›; (↑R 94; *Med., Biol.* Ohrtrompete); **Eus|ta|chi|us** *vgl.* Eustach

Eu|stress, der; -es, -e ‹griech.; engl.› (*Med., Psych.* anregender, stimulierender Stress)

Eu|ter, das, *landsch. auch* der; -s, -

Eu|ter|pe (Muse der lyr. Poesie u. des lyr. Gesangs)

Eu|tha|na|sie, die; - ‹griech.› (*Med.* Erleichterung des Sterbens [durch Narkotika]; bewusste Herbeiführung des Todes)
Eu|tin (Stadt im Ostholsteinischen Hügelland)
eu|troph ‹griech.› (nährstoffreich); -e Pflanzen (an nährstoffreichen Boden gebundene Pflanzen); **Eu|tro|phie,** die; - (*Med.* guter Ernährungszustand); **Eu|tro|phie|rung** (Zunahme von Nährstoffen in Gewässern, die zu unerwünschtem Wuchern bestimmter Pflanzenarten führt)
eV = Elektronvolt
ev. = evangelisch
Ev. = Evangelium
e. V. = eingetragener Verein; **E. V.** = Eingetragener Verein (*vgl.* eingetragen)
E|va ['e:fa, *auch* 'e:va] (w. Vorn.)
e|va|ku|ie|ren [...v...] ‹lat.› ([ein Gebiet von Bewohnern] räumen; [Bewohner aus einem Gebiet] aussiedeln; *Technik* ein Vakuum herstellen); **E|va|ku|ier|te,** der *u.* die; -n, -n (↑R 5 ff.); **E|va|ku|ie|rung**
E|va|lu|a|ti|on [...v...], die; -, -en ‹lat.› (Bewertung; Beurteilung); **e|va|lu|ie|ren**
E|van|ge|li|ar [...v...], das; -s, *Plur.* -e *u.* -ien [...iən] *u.* **E|van|ge|li|a|ri|um,** das; -s, ...ien [...iən] ‹mlat.› (Evangelienbuch); **E|van|ge|li|en|buch; e|van|ge|li|kal** (die unbedingte Autorität des Evangeliums vertretend); **E|van|ge|li|ka|le,** der *u.* die; -n, -n (↑R 5 ff.); **E|van|ge|li|sa|ti|on,** die; -, -en (Verkündigung des Evangeliums außerhalb des Gottesdienstes); **e|van|ge|lisch** (das Evangelium betreffend; auf dem Evangelium fußend; protestantisch; *Abk.* ev.); die evangelische Kirche, *aber* (↑R 108): die Evangelische Kirche in Deutschland (*Abk.* EKD); der Evangelische Bund; **e|van|ge|lisch-lu|the|risch** [*auch noch* ...lu'te:...] (*Abk.* ev.-luth.); **e|van|ge|lisch-re|for|miert** (*Abk.* ev.-ref.); **e|van|ge|li|sie|ren** ([Außenstehenden] das Evangelium verkünden); **E|van|ge|list,** der; -en, -en; ↑R 126 (Verfasser eines der vier Evangelien; Titel in ev. Freikirchen; Wanderprediger); **E|van|ge|li|um,** das; -s, *Plur.* (*für* die vier ersten Bücher im N. T.:) ...ien [...iən] ‹„gute Botschaft“› (Heilsbotschaft Christi; *Abk.* Ev.)
E|va|po|ra|ti|on [...v...], die; -, -en ‹lat.› (*fachspr. für* Verdunstung); **E|va|po|ra|tor,** der; -s, ...oren (Gerät zur Verdunstung, bes. bei der Süßwassergewinnung aus Meerwasser); **e|va|po|rie|ren** (verdunsten; eindampfen)
E|va|si|on [...v...], die; -, -en ‹lat.› (Massenflucht)
E|vas‿kos|tüm ['e:fas..., *auch* 'e:vas...], **...toch|ter; E|ve|li|ne, E|ve|lyn** (w. Vorn.)
E|vent [...v...], der *od.* das; -s, -s ‹engl.› (Veranstaltung)
E|ven|tu|al... [...v...] ‹lat.› (möglicherweise eintretend, für mögliche Sonderfälle bestimmt); **E|ven|tu|al‿an|trag** (*Rechtsspr.* Neben-, Hilfsantrag), **...fall** (der; im -[e]), **...haus|halt; E|ven|tu|a|li|tät,** die; -, -en; (Möglichkeit, möglicher Fall); **e|ven|tu|a|li|ter** (*veraltet für* eventuell); **e|ven|tu|ell** ‹franz.› (möglicherweise eintretend; gegebenenfalls; *Abk.* evtl.)
E|ve|rest *vgl.* Mount Everest
E|ver|glades ['ɛvə(r)gle:dz] *Plur.* (Sumpfgebiet in Florida)
E|ver|glaze ® ['ɛvə(r)gle:z], das; -, - ‹engl.› (ein [Baumwoll]gewebe); **E|ver|green** [...gri:n], der, *auch* das; -s, -s (populär gebliebener Schlager usw.)
E|ver|teb|rat [...v...], **In|ver|teb|rat** (↑R 130), der; -en, -en; ↑R 126 ‹lat.› (*Zool.* wirbelloses Tier)
E|vi ['e:fi] (w. Vorn.)
e|vi|dent [...v...] ‹lat.› (offenbar; einleuchtend); **E|vi|denz,** die; - (Deutlichkeit, völlige Klarheit); in Evidenz halten (*österr. Amtsspr.* auf dem Laufenden halten, registrieren); **E|vi|denz|bü|ro** (*österr. für* Büro, in dem Personen, Daten registriert werden)
ev.-luth. = evangelisch-lutherisch
E|vo|ka|ti|on [...v...], die; -, -en ‹lat.› (Erweckung von Vorstellungen bei Betrachtung eines Kunstwerkes; *Rechtsspr.* Vorladung eines Beklagten vor ein höheres Gericht); **e|vo|ka|tiv**
E|vo|lu|ti|on [...v...], die; -, -en ‹lat.› ([allmählich fortschreitende] Entwicklung; *Biol.* stammesgeschichtl. Entwicklung der Lebewesen von niederen zu höheren Formen); **e|vo|lu|ti|o|när** (sich stetig weiterentwickelnd); **E|vo|lu|ti|o|nis|mus,** der; - (eine naturphilos. Richtung des 19. Jh.s); **E|vo|lu|ti|ons|the|o|rie,** die; -; **E|vol|ven|te** [evɔl'vɛntə], die; -, -n (eine math. Kurve); **e|vol|vie|ren** (entwickeln, entfalten)
E|vo|ny|mus [e'vo:...], der; - ‹griech.› (ein Zierstrauch, Spindelbaum)
e|vo|zie|ren [evo...] ‹lat.› (hervorrufen; *Rechtsspr.* vorladen)
ev.-ref. = evangelisch-reformiert
evtl. = eventuell
ev|vi|va [ɛ'vi:va] ‹ital., „er, sie, es lebe hoch!“› (ital. Hochruf)
Ew. *vgl.* euer
E|wald (m. Vorn.)
¹E|we, der; -, - (Angehöriger eines westafrik. Volkes); **²E|we,** das; - (Sprache); *vgl.* Deutsch
E|wen|ke, der; -n, -n; ↑R 126 (Angehöriger eines sibir. Volksstammes; Tunguse)
E|wer, der; -s, - (*nordd. für* kleines Küsten[segel]schiff)
E-Werk, das; -[e]s, -e; ↑R 26 (*kurz für* Elektrizitätswerk)
EWG = Europäische Wirtschaftsgemeinschaft
e|wig; auf ewig; für immer und ewig; ein ewiges Einerlei; das ewige Leben; der ewige Frieden; ewiger Schnee; die ewige Seligkeit; das ewige Licht; die Ewige Stadt (Rom); der Ewige Jude (Ahasver); **E|wig|gest|ri|ge,** der *u.* die; -n, -n (↑R 5 ff.); **E|wig|keit; E|wig|keits|sonn|tag** (Totensonntag, letzter Sonntag des ev. Kirchenjahres); **e|wig|lich** (*veraltet für* ewig); **E|wig|weib|li|che,** das; -n (↑R 5 ff.)
Ew. M. = Euer *od.* Eure Majestät
EWS = Europäisches Währungssystem
ex ‹lat.› (*ugs. für* aus; tot); ex trinken
Ex... (ehemalig, z. B. Exminister)
e|xakt (↑R 132) ‹lat.› (genau; sorgfältig; pünktlich); die exakten Wissenschaften (Naturwissenschaften u. Mathematik); **E|xakt|heit,** die; -
E|xal|ta|ti|on (↑R 132), die; -, -en ‹lat.› (Überspanntheit; leidenschaftl. Erregung); **e|xal|tiert; E|xal|tiert|heit**
E|xa|men (↑R 132), das; -s, *Plur.* -, *seltener* ...mina ‹lat.› ([Abschluss]prüfung); **E|xa|mens‿angst, ...ar|beit, ...kan|di|dat, ...not; E|xa|mi|nand,** der; -en, -en; ↑R 126 (Prüfling); **E|xa|mi|na|tor,** der; -s, ...oren (Prüfer); **e|xa|mi|nie|ren** (prüfen)
E|xan|them (↑R 132), das; -s, -e ‹griech.› (*Med.* Hautausschlag)
E|xarch (↑R 132), der; -en, -en (↑R 126) ‹griech.› (byzant. weltl. od. geistl. Statthalter); **E|xar|chat,** das, *auch* der; -[e]s, -e (Amt[szeit] od. Verwaltungsgebiet eines Exarchen)
Ex|ar|ti|ku|la|ti|on, die; -, -en ‹lat.› (*Med.* Abtrennung eines Gliedes im Gelenk)
E|xau|di (↑R 132) ‹lat., „Erhöre!“› (6. Sonntag nach Ostern)

exc., excud. = excudit
ex ca|thed|ra (↑R 130) ‹lat., „vom [Päpstl.] Stuhl"› (aus päpstl. Vollmacht; unfehlbar)
Ex|change [iks'tʃe:ndʒ], die; -, -n [...dʒən] (*Bankw.* Tausch, Kurs)
ex|cud., exc. = excudit
ex|cu|dit ‹lat., „hat es gebildet, verlegt od. gedruckt"› (Vermerk hinter dem Namen des Verlegers [Druckers] bei Kupferstichen; *Abk.* exc. *u.* excud.)
E|xed|ra (↑R 130 *u.* 132), die; -, Exedren ‹griech.› (*Archit.* [halbrunde] Nische)
E|xe|ge|se (↑R 132), die; -, -n ‹griech.› ([Bibel]erklärung; Wissenschaft von der Bibelauslegung); **E|xe|get**, der; -en, -en; ↑R 126 (gelehrter [Bibel]erklärer); **E|xe|ge|tik**, die; - (*veraltet für* Wissenschaft der Bibelauslegung); **e|xe|ge|tisch**
e|xe|ku|tie|ren ‹lat.› (vollstrecken); exekutiert (*österr. für* gepfändet) werden; **E|xe|ku|ti|on**, die; -, -en (Vollstreckung [eines Urteils]; Hinrichtung; *österr. auch für* Pfändung); **e|xe|ku|tiv** (ausführend); **E|xe|ku|ti|ve** [...və], die; -, -n *u.* **E|xe|ku|tiv|gewalt** (vollziehende Gewalt [im Staat]); **E|xe|ku|tor**, der; -s, ...oren (Vollstrecker; *österr. für* Gerichtsvollzieher); **e|xe|ku|to|risch**
E|xem|pel (↑R 132), das; -s, - ‹lat.› ([warnendes] Beispiel; Aufgabe); **E|xem|plar** (↑R 130 *u.* 132), das; -s, -e ([einzelnes] Stück; *Abk.* Expl.); **e|xem|pla|risch** (beispielhaft; warnend, abschreckend); -es Lernen; **E|xem|pli|fi|ka|ti|on**, die; -, -en (Erläuterung durch Beispiele); **e|xem|pli|fi|zie|ren**
e|xemt (↑R 132) ‹lat.› (*Rechtsw.* befreit); **E|xem|ti|on**, die; -, -en ([gesetzliche] Freistellung)
e|xen ‹*zu* lat. ex› (*Schülerspr.* von der Schule weisen)
E|xe|qua|tur, das; -s, ...uren ‹lat., „er vollziehe!"› (Zulassung eines ausländ. Konsuls); **E|xe|qui|en** [...iən] *Plur.* (kath. Totenmesse)
e|xer|zie|ren (↑R 132) ‹lat.› ([von Truppen] üben); **E|xer|zier|platz; E|xer|zi|ti|en** *Plur.* (geistl. Übungen); **E|xer|zi|ti|um**, das; -s, ...ien [...iən] (Übung; Hausarbeit)
Ex|ha|la|ti|on, die; -, -en ‹lat.› (*Med.* Ausatmung; *Geol.* Ausströmen vulkan. Gase u. Dämpfe); **ex|ha|lie|ren**
ex|haus|tiv ‹lat.› (*geh. für* vollständig, erschöpfend); **Ex|haus|tor**, der; -s, ...oren (*Technik* Absauger, Entlüfter)
ex|hi|bie|ren ‹lat.› (zur Schau stellen, vorzeigend darbieten); **Ex|hi|bi|ti|on**, die; -, -en (*Med.* Zurschaustellung); **Ex|hi|bi|ti|o|nis|mus**, der; - (*Med.* krankhafte Neigung zur öffentl. Entblößung der Geschlechtsteile); **Ex|hi|bi|ti|o|nist**, der; -en, -en (↑R 126); **ex|hi|bi|ti|o|nis|tisch**
ex|hu|mie|ren ‹lat.› ([einen Leichnam] wieder ausgraben); **Ex|hu|mie|rung**
E|xil, das; -s, -e ‹lat.› (Verbannung[sort]); **e|xi|liert** (ins Exil geschickt); **E|xil‿li|te|ra|tur, ...po|li|ti|ker, ...re|gie|rung**
e|xi|mie|ren (↑R 132) ‹lat.› (*Rechtsspr.* von einer Verbindlichkeit, bes. von der Gerichtsbarkeit eines anderen Staates, befreien)
e|xis|tent ‹lat.› (wirklich, vorhanden); **e|xis|ten|ti|al, E|xis|ten|ti|a|lis|mus** usw. *vgl.* existenzial, Existenzialismus usw.; **e|xis|ten|ti|ell** *vgl.* existenziell; **E|xis|tenz**, die; -, -en (Dasein; Lebensgrundlage; *abwertend für* Mensch); **E|xis|tenz|angst** (Daseinsangst); **e|xis|tenz|be|dro|hend** (↑R 40); **E|xis|tenz|be|rech|ti|gung**, die; -; **e|xis|tenz|fä|hig; E|xis|tenz|grund|la|ge; e|xis|ten|zi|al** (das [menschl.] Dasein hinsichtlich seines Seinscharakters betreffend); **E|xis|ten|zi|a|lis|mus**, der; - (philosophische Richtung des 20. Jh.s); **E|xis|ten|zi|a|list**, der; -en, -en (↑R 126); **E|xis|ten|zi|a|lis|tin; e|xis|ten|zi|a|lis|tisch; E|xis|ten|zi|al|phi|lo|so|phie** *vgl.* Existenzialismus; **e|xis|ten|zi|ell** ‹franz.› (auf das unmittelbare u. wesenhafte Dasein bezogen; lebenswichtig); **E|xis|tenz‿kampf, ...mi|ni|mum, ...phi|lo|so|phie** (*vgl.* Existenzialismus); **e|xis|tie|ren** (vorhanden sein, bestehen)
E|xi|tus (↑R 132), der; - ‹lat.› (*Med.* Tod)
Ex|kai|ser; Ex|kai|se|rin
Ex|kar|di|na|ti|on, die; -, -en ‹lat.› (*kath. Kirche* Entlassung eines Geistlichen aus seiner Diözese)
Ex|ka|va|ti|on [...v...], die; -, -en ‹lat.› (*Med.* Aushöhlung, Ausbohrung; *fachspr. für* Ausschachtung); **ex|ka|vie|ren**
exkl. = exklusive
Ex|kla|ma|ti|on, die; -, -en ‹lat.› (*veraltet für* Ausruf); **ex|kla|ma|to|risch; ex|kla|mie|ren**
Ex|kla|ve [...və], die; -, -n ‹lat.› (ein eigenstaatl. Gebiet in fremdem Staatsgebiet); *vgl.* Enklave
ex|klu|die|ren ‹lat.› (*veraltet für* ausschließen); **Ex|klu|si|on**, die; -, -en (*veraltet für* Ausschließung); **ex|klu|siv** (nur einem bestimmten Personenkreis zugänglich; sich [gesellschaftl.] absondernd; ausschließlich auf eine Zeitung, einen Sender o.Ä. beschränkt); **ex|klu|si|ve** [...və] (mit Ausschluss von ..., ausschließlich; *Abk.* exkl.); *Präp. mit Gen.:* exklusive aller Versandkosten; *ein allein stehendes, stark gebeugtes Substantiv steht im Sing. ungebeugt:* exklusive Porto; *mit Dativ, wenn der Gen. nicht erkennbar ist:* exklusive Getränken; **Ex|klu|siv|in|ter|view** [...f...]; **Ex|klu|si|vi|tät** [...v...], die; - (Ausschließlichkeit, [gesellschaftl.] Abgeschlossenheit)
Ex|kom|mu|ni|ka|ti|on, die; -, -en ‹lat.› (*kath. Kirche* Ausschluss aus der Kirchengemeinschaft); **ex|kom|mu|ni|zie|ren**
Ex|kö|nig; Ex|kö|ni|gin
Ex|kre|ment, das; -[e]s, -e *meist Plur.* ‹lat.› (Ausscheidungsprodukt, z. B. Kot)
Ex|kret, das; -[e]s, -e ‹lat.› (*Med., Zool.* vom Körper ausgeschiedenes wertloses Stoffwechselprodukt); **Ex|kre|ti|on**, die; -, -en (Ausscheidung von Exkreten); **ex|kre|to|risch** (ausscheidend, absondernd)
Ex|kul|pa|ti|on, die; -, -en ‹lat.› (*Rechtsw.* Rechtfertigung, Entlastung); **ex|kul|pie|ren**; sich -
Ex|kurs, der; -es, -e ‹lat.› (Abschweifung; einer Abhandlung beigefügte kürzere Ausarbeitung; Anhang); **Ex|kur|si|on**, die; -, -en (Lehrfahrt; Streifzug)
Ex|lib|ris (↑R 130), das; -, - ‹lat.› (Bücherzeichen mit dem Namen[szeichen] des Bucheigentümers)
Ex|mat|ri|kel [*auch, österr. nur* ...'trikəl] (↑R 130), die; -, -n ‹lat.› (Bescheinigung über das Verlassen einer Hochschule); **Ex|mat|ri|ku|la|ti|on**, die; -, -en (Streichung aus der Matrikel einer Hochschule); **ex|mat|ri|ku|lie|ren**
Ex|mi|nis|ter; Ex|mi|nis|te|rin
Ex|mis|si|on, die; -, -en ‹lat.› (*Rechtsw.* gerichtl. Ausweisung aus einer Wohnung); **ex|mit|tie|ren; Ex|mit|tie|rung**
E|xo|bi|o|lo|gie, die; - ‹griech.› (Wissenschaft vom außerirdischen Leben); **e|xo|bi|o|lo|gisch**
E|xo|dus (↑R 132), der; - ‹griech., „Auszug"› (das 2. Buch Mosis)
ex of|fi|cio ‹lat.› (*Rechtsspr.* von Amts wegen)
E|xo|ga|mie, die; -, ...ien ‹griech.›

(*Völkerk.* Heirat außerhalb von Stamm, Kaste usw.)

e|xo|gen ‹griech.› (*Bot.* außen entstehend; *Med.* von außen wirkend; *Psych.* umweltbedingt)

E|xo|karp, das; -s, -e ‹griech.› (*Bot.* äußere Schicht der Fruchtwand)

e|xo|krin ‹griech.› (*Med.* nach außen abscheidend); -e Drüsen

E|xo|nym (↑R 132), das; -s, -e ‹griech.› (vom amtlichen Namen abweichende Ortsnamenform, z. B. dt. „Mailand" für ital. „Milano")

e|xor|bi|tant (↑R 132) ‹lat.› (übertrieben; gewaltig)

ex o|ri|en|te lux ‹lat., „aus dem Osten [kommt das] Licht"› (von der Sonne, dann von Christentum u. Kultur)

e|xor|zie|ren, e|xor|zi|sie|ren (↑R 132) ‹griech.› (böse Geister durch Beschwörung austreiben); **E|xor|zis|mus,** der; -, ...men (Beschwörung böser Geister); **E|xor|zist,** der; -en, -en; ↑R 126 (Geisterbeschwörer; *früher* dritter Grad der kath. niederen Weihen)

E|xo|sphä|re, die; - ‹griech.› (oberste Schicht der Erdatmosphäre)

E|xot, der; -en, -en (↑R 126) ‹griech.› (Mensch, Tier, Pflanze aus fernen, meist überseeischen od. tropischen Ländern; *Plur. auch für* überseeische Wertpapiere); **E|xo|ta|ri|um,** das; -s, ...ien [...i̯ən] (Anlage für exotische Tiere)

e|xo|te|risch ‹griech.› (für Außenstehende, allgemein verständlich)

e|xo|therm ‹griech.› (*Physik, Chemie* Wärme abgebend)

E|xo|tik, die; - ‹griech.› (Anziehungskraft, die vom Fremdländischen ausgeht); **E|xo|tin; e|xo|tisch** (fremdländisch, -artig)

Ex|pan|der, der; -s, - ‹engl.› (Trainingsgerät zur Stärkung der Arm- u. Oberkörpermuskulatur); **ex|pan|die|ren** ‹lat.› ([sich] ausdehnen); **ex|pan|si|bel** ‹franz.› (*veraltet für* ausdehnbar); ...ib|le (↑R 130) Stoffe; **Ex|pan|si|on,** die; -, -en ‹lat.› (Ausdehnung; Erweiterung; Ausbreitung [eines Staates]); **ex|pan|si|o|nis|tisch; Ex|pan|si|ons‿be|stre|bun|gen** (*Plur.*), **...ge|schwin|dig|keit, ...kraft** (die; *Physik*), **...po|li|tik; ex|pan|siv** ([sich] ausdehnend); **Ex|pan|siv|kraft,** die (*Physik*)

ex|pat|ri|ie|ren (↑R 130) ‹lat.› (ausbürgern)

Ex|pe|di|ent, der; -en, -en (↑R 126) ‹lat.› (Abfertigungsbeauftragter in der Versandabteilung einer Firma); **Ex|pe|di|en|tin; ex|pe|die|ren** (abfertigen; absenden; befördern); **Ex|pe|dit,** das; -[e]s, -e (*österr. für* Versandabteilung); **Ex|pe|di|ti|on,** die; -, -en (Forschungsreise; Gruppe von Forschungsreisenden; Versand- od. Abfertigungsabteilung); **Ex|pe|di|ti|ons|lei|ter,** der; **Ex|pe|di|tor,** der; -s, ...oren (*seltener, bes. österr., für* Expedient)

Ex|pek|to|rans, das; -, *Plur.* ...ranzien [...i̯ən] *u.* ...rantia *u.* **Ex|pek|to|ran|ti|um,** das; -s, ...tia ‹lat.› (*Pharm.* schleimlösendes [Husten]mittel); **Ex|pek|to|ra|ti|on,** die; -, -en (*veraltet für* Erklärung [von Gefühlen], das Sichaussprechen; *Med.* Auswurf); **ex|pek|to|rie|ren** (*veraltet für* Gefühle aussprechen; *Med.* Schleim aushusten)

ex|pen|siv ‹lat.› (*selten für* kostspielig)

Ex|pe|ri|ment, das; -[e]s, -e ‹lat.› ([wissenschaftlicher] Versuch); **Ex|pe|ri|men|tal...** (auf Experimenten beruhend, z. B. Experimentalphysik); **Ex|pe|ri|men|ta|tor,** der; -s, ...oren; **ex|pe|ri|men|tell** (auf Experimenten beruhend); -e Psychologie; **Ex|pe|ri|men|tier|büh|ne** (Bühne für experimentelles Theater); **ex|pe|ri|men|tie|ren; ex|pe|ri|men|tier|freu|dig; Ex|per|te,** der; -n, -n; ↑R 126 (Sachverständiger, Gutachter); **Ex|per|ten|sys|tem** (*EDV* hoch entwickeltes Programmsystem, das Elemente künstlicher Intelligenz besitzt); **Ex|per|tin; Ex|per|ti|se,** die; -, -n ‹franz.› (Gutachten)

Expl. = Exemplar

Ex|plan|ta|ti|on, die; -, -en ‹lat.› (*Med., Zool.* Entnahme von Zellen od. Gewebe aus dem lebenden Organismus); **ex|plan|tie|ren**

Ex|pli|ka|ti|on, die; -, -en ‹lat.› (*veraltet für* Erklärung, Erläuterung); **ex|pli|zie|ren; ex|pli|zit** (erklärt, ausführlich dargestellt; *Ggs.* implizit); -e Funktion (*Math.*); **ex|pli|zi|te** [...te] (ausdrücklich); etwas - sagen

ex|plo|dier|bar; ex|plo|die|ren ‹lat.› (krachend [zer]bersten; einen Gefühlsausbruch haben)

Ex|ploi|ta|ti|on [...ploata...], die; -, -en ‹franz.› (*veraltet für* Ausbeutung; Nutzbarmachung); **ex|ploi|tie|ren**

Ex|plo|rand, der; -en, -en (↑R 126) ‹lat.› (*fachspr. für* zu Untersuchender; zu Befragender); **Ex|plo|ra|ti|on,** die; -, -en (Untersuchung, Erforschung); **ex|plo|ra|to|risch; Ex|plo|rer** [iks'plɔ:rə(r)], der; -s, - ‹engl., „Erforscher"› (*Bez. für* die ersten amerik. Erdsatelliten); **ex|plo|rie|ren** ‹lat.›

ex|plo|si|bel ‹franz.› (explosionsfähig, -gefährlich); ...ib|le (↑R 130) Stoffe; **Ex|plo|si|on,** die; -, -en ‹lat.›; **ex|plo|si|ons|ar|tig; Ex|plo|si|ons‿ge|fahr, ...herd, ...ka|ta|stro|phe, ...kra|ter** (*Geol.*), **...mo|tor; ex|plo|si|ons|si|cher; ex|plo|siv** (leicht explodierend, explosionsartig); **Ex|plo|siv,** der; -s, -e [...və] *u.* Ex|plo|siv|laut (*Sprachw.* Verschlusslaut, z. B. b, k); **Ex|plo|siv|ge|schoss; Ex|plo|si|vi|tät** [...v...], die; - (explosive Beschaffenheit); **Ex|plo|siv‿kör|per** [...f...], **...laut** (*vgl.* Explosiv), **...stoff**

Ex|po|nat, das; -[e]s, -e ‹russ.› (Ausstellungs-, Museumsstück); **Ex|po|nent,** der; -en, -en (↑R 126) ‹lat.› (Hochzahl, bes. in der Wurzel- u. Potenzrechnung; herausgehobener Vertreter [einer bestimmten Richtung, Politik usw.]); **Ex|po|nen|ti|al‿funk|ti|on** (*Math.*), **...glei|chung** (*Math.*), **...grö|ße, ...röh|re** (*Technik*); **ex|po|nen|ti|ell** (*Math.*); **Ex|po|nen|tin; ex|po|nie|ren** (hervorheben; [einer Gefahr] aussetzen); **ex|po|niert** (gefährdet; [Angriffen] ausgesetzt; herausgehoben)

Ex|port, der; -[e]s, -e ‹engl.› (Ausfuhr); ↑R 23: Ex- u. Import; **ex|port|ab|hän|gig; Ex|port‿ab|hän|gig|keit, ...an|teil, ...ar|ti|kel; Ex|por|ten** *Plur.* (Ausfuhrwaren); **Ex|por|teur** [...'tø:r], der; -s, -e ‹franz.› (Ausfuhrhändler od. -firma); **Ex|port|ge|schäft; ex|por|tie|ren; ex|port|in|ten|siv;** -e Branchen; **Ex|port‿kauf|mann, ...quo|te, ...über|schuss** (↑R 132)

Ex|po|sé, *eindeutschend* **Ex|po|see** [...'ze:] (↑R 33), das; -s, -s ‹franz.› (Denkschrift, Bericht, Darlegung; Zusammenfassung; Plan, Skizze [für ein Drehbuch]); **Ex|po|si|ti|on,** die; -, -en ‹lat.› (Ausstellung, Schau; *Literaturw., Musik* Einleitung, erster Teil; *veraltet für* Darlegung); **Ex|po|si|tur,** die; -, -en (*kath. Kirche* abgegrenzter selbstständiger Seelsorgebezirk einer Pfarrei; *österr. für* auswärtige Geschäftsfiliale, auswärtiger Teil einer Schule); **Ex|po|si|tus,** der; -, ...ti (Geistlicher einer Expositur)

ex|press ‹lat.› (*veraltet, noch ugs. für* eilig, Eil...; *landsch. für* eigens, ausdrücklich, zum Trotz); **Ex|press,** der; -es, -e (*kurz für* Expresszug); per - zustellen; **Ex|press‿bo|te** (*veraltet für* Eilbote), **...gut; Ex|pres|si|on,** die; -, -en (Ausdruck); **Ex|pres|si|o|nis|mus,** der; - (Kunstrichtung im frühen 20. Jh., Ausdruckskunst); **Ex|pres|si|o|nist,** der; -en, -en (↑R 126); **Ex|pres|si|o|nis|tin; ex|pres|si|o|nis|tisch; ex|pres|sis ver|bis** [- v...] (ausdrücklich; mit ausdrücklichen Worten); **ex|pres|siv** (ausdrucksvoll); **Ex|pres|si|vi|tät** [...v...], die; - (Fülle des Ausdrucks, Ausdrucksfähigkeit; *Biol.* Ausprägungsgrad einer Erbanlage); **Ex|press‿rei|ni|gung, ...zug** (*regional für* Schnellzug; *vgl.* Express)

Ex|prop|ri|a|ti|on (↑R 130), die; -, -en ‹lat.› (Enteignung [marxist. Begriff]); **ex|prop|ri|ie|ren**

Ex|pul|si|on, die; -, -en ‹lat.› (*Med.* Austreibung, Abführung); **ex|pul|siv**

ex|qui|sit ‹lat.› (ausgesucht, erlesen); **Ex|qui|sit,** das; -s, -s (*kurz für* Exquisitladen); **Ex|qui|sit|la|den** (*ehem. in der DDR* Geschäft für auserlesene Waren zu hohen Preisen)

Ex|sik|ka|ti|on, die; -, -en ‹lat.› (*Chemie* Austrocknung); **ex|sik|ka|tiv; Ex|sik|ka|tor,** der; -s, ...oren (Gerät zum Austrocknen od. zum trockenen Aufbewahren von Chemikalien)

ex|spek|ta|tiv (*Med.* abwartend [bei Krankheitsbehandlung])

Ex|spi|ra|ti|on, die; - ‹lat.› (*Med.* Ausatmung); **ex|spi|ra|to|risch** (*Med.* auf Exspiration beruhend); -er Akzent (*Sprachw.* Druckakzent); -e Artikulation (*Sprachw.* Lautbildung beim Ausatmen); **ex|spi|rie|ren** (*Med.*)

Ex|stir|pa|ti|on, die; -, -en ‹lat.› (*Med.* völlige Entfernung [eines Organs]); **ex|stir|pie|ren**

Ex|su|dat, das; -[e]s, -e ‹lat.› (*Med.* Ausschwitzung; *Biol.* Absonderung); **Ex|su|da|ti|on,** die; -, -en (Ausschwitzen, Absondern eines Exsudates)

Ex|tem|po|ra|le, das; -s, ...lien [...i̯ən] ‹lat.› (*veraltet für* unvorbereitet anzufertigende [Klassen]arbeit); **Ex|tem|po|re** [...re], das; -s, -s (*Theater* Zusatz, Einlage; Stegreifspiel); **ex tem|po|re** [- ...re] (aus dem Stegreif); **ex|tem|po|rie|ren** (aus dem Stegreif reden, schreiben usw.)

ex|ten|die|ren ‹lat.› (strecken; ausdehnen); **Ex|ten|si|on,** die; -, -en; **Ex|ten|si|tät,** die; - (Ausdehnung; Umfang); **ex|ten|siv** (der Ausdehnung nach; räumlich; nach außen wirkend); -e Wirtschaft (Form der Bodennutzung mit geringem Einsatz von Arbeitskraft u. Kapital); **Ex|ten|sor,** der; -s, ...oren (*Med.* Streckmuskel)

Ex|te|ri|eur [...'ri̯øːr], das; -s, *Plur.* -s *u.* -e ‹franz.› (Äußeres; Außenseite)

ex|tern ‹lat.› (draußen befindlich; auswärtig); **Ex|ter|nat,** das; -[e]s, -e (Lehranstalt, deren Schüler außerhalb der Schule wohnen); **Ex|ter|ne,** der *u.* die; -n, -n; ↑R 5 ff. (nicht im Internat wohnender Schüler bzw. nicht dort wohnende Schülerin; von auswärts zugewiesener Prüfling); **Ex|ter|nist,** der; -en, -en; ↑R 126 (*österr. für* Externer)

Ex|tern|stei|ne *Plur.* (Felsgruppe im Teutoburger Wald)

ex|ter|ri|to|ri|al ‹lat.› (den Landesgesetzen nicht unterworfen); **Ex|ter|ri|to|ri|a|li|tät,** die; - (exterritorialer Status, Charakter)

Ex|tink|ti|on, die; -, -en ‹lat.› (*fachspr. für* Schwächung einer Strahlung)

ext|ra (↑R 130) ‹lat.› (nebenbei, außerdem, besonders, eigens); **Ext|ra,** das; -s, -s ([nicht serienmäßig mitgeliefertes] Zubehör[teil]); **Ext|ra‿aus|ga|be, ...blatt** (Sonderausgabe), **...chor** (zusätzlicher, nur in bestimmten Opern eingesetzter Theaterchor); **ext|ra dry** [- draɪ̯] ‹engl.› (sehr herb); *vgl.* dry; **ext|ra|fein**

ext|ra|ga|lak|tisch (↑R 130) ‹lat.-griech.› (*Astron.* außerhalb der Galaxis gelegen)

ext|ra‿groß, ...hart

ex|tra|hie|ren ‹lat.› (einen Auszug machen; [einen Zahn] ausziehen; auslaugen)

Ext|ra|klas|se (↑R 130); ein Film, Sportler der -

ext|ra|kor|po|ral (↑R 130; *Biol.*, *Med.* außerhalb des Organismus befindlich, geschehend)

Ex|trakt, der, *auch* das; -[e]s, -e ‹lat.› (Auszug [aus Büchern, Stoffen]; Hauptinhalt; Kern); **Ex|trak|ti|on,** die; -, -en (Auszug; Auslaugung; Herausziehen, z. B. eines Zahnes); **ex|trak|tiv** ‹franz.› (ausziehend; auslaugend)

ext|ra|or|di|när (↑R 130) ‹franz.› (*veraltend für* außergewöhnlich, außerordentlich); **Ext|ra|or|di|na|ri|um,** das; -s, ...ien [...i̯ən] ‹lat.› (außerordentl. Haushaltsplan od. Etat); **Ext|ra|or|di|na|ri|us,** der; -, ...ien [...i̯ən] (außerordentl. Professor)

Ext|ra|po|la|ti|on (↑R 130), die; -, -en ‹lat.› (das Extrapolieren); **ext|ra|po|lie|ren** (*Math.*, *Statistik* aus den bisherigen Werten einer Funktion auf weitere schließen)

Ext|ra|post (↑R 130; *früher für* besonders eingesetzter Postwagen)

Ext|ra|sys|to|le (↑R 130), die; -, -n ‹lat.; griech.› (*Med.* vorzeitige Zusammenziehung des Herzens innerhalb der normalen Herzschlagfolge)

ext|ra|ter|rest|risch (↑R 130) ‹lat.› (*Astron.*, *Physik* außerhalb der Erde gelegen)

Ext|ra|tour (↑R 130; *ugs. für* eigenwilliges Verhalten od. Vorgehen)

ext|ra|va|gant [...v..., *auch* 'ɛks...] (↑R 130) ‹franz.› (verstiegen, überspannt); **Ext|ra|va|ganz,** die; -, -en

Ext|ra|ver|si|on, Ext|ro|ver|si|on [*beide* ...v...] (↑R 130), die; -, -en ‹lat.› (Konzentration der eigenen Interessen auf äußere Objekte); **ext|ra|ver|tiert,** ext|ro|ver|tiert (nach außen gerichtet); ein -er Mensch; **Ext|ra|ver|tiert|heit,** die; -

Ext|ra|wurst (↑R 130) (*ugs.*); jmdm. eine - braten; **Ext|ra|zug** (*schweiz. für* Sonderzug)

ext|rem (↑R 130) ‹lat., „äußerst"› (bis an die äußerste Grenze gehend; radikal; krass); **Ext|rem,** das; -s, -e (höchster Grad; äußerster Standpunkt); **Ext|rem|fall,** der; im -; **Ext|re|mis|mus,** der; -, ...men (übersteigert radikale Haltung); **Ext|re|mist,** der; -en, -en (↑R 126); **Ext|re|mis|tin; ext|re|mis|tisch; Ext|re|mi|tät,** die; -, -en (äußerstes Ende); **Ext|re|mi|tä|ten** *Plur.* (Gliedmaßen); **Ext|rem|si|tu|a|ti|on; Ext|rem|sport** (mit höchster körperlicher Beanspruchung od. mit besonderen Gefahren verbundener Sport [z. B. Triathlon mit extrem langen Strecken, Klettern in Steilwänden ohne Hilfsmittel]); **Ext|rem|sport|art**

Ext|ro|ver|si|on (↑R 130) *vgl.* Extraversion; **ext|ro|ver|tiert** *vgl.* extravertiert

Ext|ru|der (↑R 130), der; -s, - ‹engl.› (*Technik* Maschine zum Ausformen thermoplastischer Kunststoffe; Schneckenpresse); **ext|ru|die|ren** (mit dem Extruder formen)

Ex|ul|ze|ra|ti|on, die; -, -en ‹lat.› (*Med.* Geschwürbildung); **ex|ul|ze|rie|ren**

Ex-und-hopp-Fla|sche (*ugs. für* Einwegflasche)

ex u|su ⟨lat., „aus dem Gebrauch heraus"⟩ (aus der Erfahrung, durch Übung)
E|xu|vie [...viə] (↑R 132), die; -, -n ⟨lat.⟩ (abgestreifte tierische Körperhülle [z. B. Schlangenhaut])
ex vo|to [- 'vo:to] ⟨lat., „auf Grund eines Gelübdes"⟩ (Inschrift auf Votivgaben); **Ex|vo|to,** das; -s, *Plur.* -s *od.* ...ten (Weihegabe, Votivbild)
Ex|welt|meis|ter *(Sport)*
Exz. = Exzellenz
Ex|ze|dent, der; -en, -en ⟨lat.⟩ (über die gewählte Versicherungssumme hinausgehender Betrag)
ex|zel|lent ⟨lat.⟩ (hervorragend); **Ex|zel|lenz,** die; -, -en (ein Titel; *Abk.* Exz.); *vgl.* euer; **ex|zel|lie|ren** (hervorragen; glänzen)
Ex|zen|ter, der; -s, - *u.* **Ex|zen|ter|schei|be** ⟨nlat.[; dt.]⟩ (*Technik* exzentrisch angebrachte Steuerungsscheibe); **Ex|zent|rik** (↑R 130), die; - ([mit Groteske verbundene] Artistik; Überspanntheit); **Ex|zent|ri|ker; Ex|zent|ri|ke|rin; ex|zent|risch** (*Math., Astron.* außerhalb des Mittelpunktes liegend; *geh. für* überspannt); **Ex|zent|ri|zi|tät,** die; -, -en (Abweichen, Abstand vom Mittelpunkt; Überspanntheit)
ex|zep|ti|o|nell ⟨franz.⟩ (ausnahmsweise eintretend, außergewöhnlich); **ex|zep|tiv** ⟨lat.⟩ (*veraltet für* ausschließend)
ex|zer|pie|ren ⟨lat.⟩ (ein Exzerpt machen); **Ex|zerpt,** das; -[e]s, -e (schriftl. Auszug aus einem Werk); **Ex|zerp|ti|on,** die; -, -en (das Exzerpieren); **Ex|zerp|tor,** der; -s, ...oren (jmd., der Exzerpte anfertigt)
Ex|zess, der; -es, -e ⟨lat.⟩ (Ausschreitung; Ausschweifung); **ex|zes|siv** (das Maß überschreitend; ausschweifend)
ex|zi|die|ren ⟨lat.⟩ (*Med.* herausschneiden); **Ex|zi|si|on,** die; -, -en (*Med.* Ausschneidung, z. B. einer Geschwulst)
ex|zi|tie|ren ⟨lat.⟩ (*Med.* anregen, beleben)
Eyck, van [van, *auch* fan 'aik] (niederl. Maler)
Eye|li|ner ['ailainər], der; -s, - ⟨engl.⟩ (flüssiges Kosmetikum zum Ziehen des Lidstriches)
Ey|rir ['ai...], der *od.* das; -s, Aurar ⟨isländ.⟩ (isländ. Währungseinheit; 100 Aurar = 1 Krone)
E|ze|chi|el [...çie:l, *auch* ...ɛl] (bibl. Prophet; *bei Luther* Hesekiel)
Ez|zes *Plur.* ⟨hebr.-jidd.⟩ (*österr. ugs. für* Tipps, Ratschläge)

F

F (Buchstabe); das F, des F, die F, *aber* das f in Haft (↑R 60); der Buchstabe F, f
f = Femto...; forte
f, F, das; -, - (Tonbezeichnung); **f** (*Zeichen für* f-Moll); in f; **F** (*Zeichen für* F-Dur); in F
F = Fahrenheit; Farad; *vgl.* Franc
F = *chem. Zeichen für* Fluor
f. = folgende [Seite]; für
Fa. = Firma
Faa|ker See, der; - -s (in Kärnten)
Fa|bel, die; -, -n ⟨franz.⟩ (erdichtete [lehrhafte] Erzählung; Grundhandlung einer Dichtung); **Fa|bel‿buch, ...dich|ter; Fa|be|lei; fa|bel|haft; fa|beln** (Erfundenes erzählen); ich ...[e]le (↑R 16); **Fa|bel‿tier, ...welt, ...we|sen**
Fa|bia (w. Vorn.); **Fa|bi|an** (m. Vorn.); **Fa|bi|er** [...iər], der; -s, - (Angehöriger eines altröm. Geschlechtes); **Fa|bi|o|la** (w. Vorn.); **Fa|bi|us** (Name altröm. Staatsmänner)
Fab|rik[1] (↑R 130), die; -, -en ⟨franz.⟩; **Fab|rik|an|la|ge**[1]; **Fab|ri|kant,** der; -en, -en; (↑R 126; Fabrikbesitzer; Hersteller); **Fab|rik‿ar|beit**[1] (die; -), **...ar|bei|ter; Fab|ri|kat,** das; -[e]s, -e ⟨lat.⟩ (Industrieerzeugnis); **Fab|ri|ka|ti|on,** die; -, -en (fabrikmäßige Herstellung); **Fab|ri|ka|ti|ons‿feh|ler, ...ge|heim|nis, ...me|tho|de, ...pro|zess; Fab|rik‿be|sit|zer**[1], **...ge|bäu|de, ...ge|län|de, ...hal|le, ...mar|ke; fab|rik‿mä|ßig**[1], **...neu; fab|riks..., Fab|riks...** (*österr. für* fabrik..., Fabrik..., z. B. Fabriksarbeiter, Fabriksbesitzer, fabriksneu); **Fab|rik‿schorn|stein**[1], **...si|re|ne; fab|ri|zie|ren** ([fabrikmäßig] herstellen; *ugs. auch für* mühsam anfertigen; anrichten)
Fa|bu|lant, der; -en, -en (↑R 126) ⟨lat.⟩ (Erzähler von phantastisch ausgeschmückten Geschichten; Lügner, Schwätzer); **fa|bu|lie|ren** (phantasievoll erzählen); **Fa|bu|lier|kunst; fa|bu|lös** (phantastisch anmutend)
Fa|cet|te [fa'sɛtə], *eindeutschend* Fas|set|te (↑R 33), die; -, -n ⟨franz.⟩ (eckig geschliffene Fläche von Edelsteinen u. Glaswaren); **Fa|cet|ten‿au|ge** (*Zool.* Netzauge), **...glas** (*Plur.* ...gläser), **...schliff; fa|cet|tie|ren** (mit Facetten versehen)
Fach, das; -[e]s, Fächer
...fach (z. B. vierfach [*mit Ziffer* 4fach; ↑R 44]; *mit Einzelbuchstabe* n-fach)
Fach|ar|bei|ter; Fach|ar|bei|ter|brief; Fach‿arzt, ...ärz|tin; fach|ärzt|lich; Fach‿aus|druck, ...be|griff, ...be|reich, ...bib|li|o|thek, ...buch
...fa|che (z. B. Vierfache, das; -n [*mit Ziffer* 4fache; ↑R 44])
fä|cheln; ich ...[e]le (↑R 16); **fa|chen** (*seltener für* anfachen); **Fä|cher,** der; -s, -; **fä|cher|för|mig; fä|che|rig; fä|chern;** ich ...ere (↑R 16); **Fä|cher|pal|me; Fä|che|rung**
Fach‿frau, ...ge|biet; fach‿ge|mäß, ...ge|recht; Fach‿ge|schäft, ...grup|pe, ...han|del (*vgl.* [1]Handel), **...hoch|schu|le** (*Abk.* FH), **...hoch|schul|rei|fe, ...idi|ot** (↑R 132; *abwertend für* jmd., der nur sein Fachgebiet kennt), **...jar|gon, ...ken|ner, ...kennt|nis, ...kraft** (die), **...kreis** (in -en), **...kun|de** (die); **fach|kun|dig** (Fachkenntnisse habend); **fach|kund|lich** (die Fachkunde betreffend); **Fach‿leh|rer, ...leh|re|rin, ...leu|te** *(Plur.)*; **fach|lich; Fach‿li|te|ra|tur, ...mann** (*Plur.* ...leute, *selten* ...männer); **fach|män|nisch; fach|mä|ßig; Fach‿ober|schu|le** (↑R 132), **...pres|se, ...re|fe|rent, ...rich|tung; Fach|schaft; Fach|schu|le; Fach|sim|pe|lei** *(ugs.)*; **fach|sim|peln** (*ugs. für* [ausgiebige] Fachgespräche führen); ich ...[e]le (↑R 16); gefachsimpelt; zu fachsimpeln; **Fach|spra|che; fach‿sprach|lich, ...über|grei|fend** (↑R 132); **Fach‿ver|käu|fer, ...ver|käu|fe|rin, ...welt** (die; -), **...werk, ...werk|haus, ...wis|sen|schaft, ...wort** (*Plur.* ...wörter), **...wör|ter|buch, ...zeit|schrift**
Fa|ckel, die; -, -n ⟨lat.⟩; **Fa|ckel|licht** *Plur.* ...lichter; **fa|ckeln;** ich ...[e]le (↑R 16); wir wollen nicht lange - (*ugs. für* zögern); **Fa|ckel‿schein** (der; -s), **...trä|ger, ...zug**
Fact [fɛkt], der; -s, -s *meist Plur.* ⟨engl.⟩ (Tatsache[nmaterial]; *vgl.* Fakt); **Fac|to|ring** ['fɛktəriŋ], das; -s (bestimmte Methode der Absatzfinanzierung mit Absicherung des Kreditrisikos)

[1] [*auch* ...'rik(...)]

Fa|cul|tas Do|cen|di, die; - - ‹lat.› (Lehrbefähigung)

fad, fa|de; fad[e]ste ‹franz.› (schlecht gewürzt, schal; langweilig, geistlos)

Fäd|chen

fa|de *vgl.* fad

fä|deln (einfädeln); ich ...[e]le (↑R 16); **Fa|den**, der; -s, *Plur.* Fäden *(u. als Längenmaß:)* -; *(Seemannsspr.:)* 4 Faden tief (↑R 90); **fa|den|dünn; Fa|den-en|de, ...hef|tung** *(Buchbinderei)*, **...kreuz, ...lauf** *(Weberei)*, **...nu|del, ...pilz; fa|den|schei|nig;** -e (nicht sehr glaubhafte) Gründe; **Fa|den-schlag** (der; -[e]s; *schweiz. für* lockere [Heft]naht; Heftfaden; *übertr. für* Vorbereitung), **...wurm, ...zäh|ler** *(Weberei)*

Fad|heit

fä|dig (aus feinen Fäden bestehend); **...fä|dig** (z. B. feinfädig)

Fa|ding [ˈfeːdiŋ], das; -s, -s ‹engl.› (Schwund, An- und Abschwellen der Lautstärke im Rundfunkgerät; *Technik* Nachlassen der Bremswirkung infolge Erhitzung der Bremsen)

fa|di|sie|ren *(österr. ugs. für* langweilen); sich -

Fae|ces [ˈfɛːtseːs] *vgl.* Fäzes

Faf|ner, Faf|nir (nord. Sagengestalt)

Fa|gott, das; -[e]s, -e (ein Holzblasinstrument); **Fa|gott|blä|ser; Fa|got|tist**, der; -en, -en; ↑R 126 (Fagottbläser)

Fä|he, die; -, -n *(Jägerspr.* weibl. Tier bei Fuchs, Marder u. a.)

fä|hig; *mit Gen.* (eines Betruges -) *od. mit* „zu" (zu allem - sein); **...fä|hig** (z. B. begeisterungsfähig, transportfähig); **Fä|hig|keit**

fahl; -es Licht; **Fahl|erz** (Silber- od. Kupfererz mit fahlem Glanz); **fahl|gelb; Fahl|heit**, die; -; **Fahl|le|der**, das; -s *(fachspr. für* Rindsoberleder)

Fähn|chen *(ugs. auch für* billiges Kleid)

fahn|den (polizeilich suchen); **Fahn|der; Fahn|dung; Fahn|dungs-ap|pa|rat, ...buch, ...foto, ...lis|te**

Fah|ne, die; -, -n; **Fah|nen-abzug** *(Druckw.)*, **...eid** *(Milit.)*, **...flucht** (die; -; *vgl.* ²Flucht); **fahnen|flüch|tig; Fah|nen-jun|ker, ...kor|rek|tur** *(Druckw.)*, **...mast** (der), **...schwin|ger, ...stan|ge, ...wei|he; Fähn|lein** *(auch* Truppeneinheit; Formation); **Fähn|rich**, der; -s, -e

Fahr-ab|tei|lung, ...aus|weis (Fahrkarte, -schein; *schweiz. auch für* Führerschein), **...bahn; Fahrbahn-mar|kie|rung, ...ver|en|gung, ...wech|sel; fahr|bar; fahr|be|reit; Fahr|be|reit|schaft**

Fähr|be|trieb

Fahr|damm *(landsch.)*

Fähr|de, die; -, -n *(geh. für* Gefahr)

Fahr|dienst, der; -[e]s *(Eisenb.)*; **Fahr|dienst-lei|ter** (der), **...lei|te|rin; Fahr|draht** (elektr. Oberleitung)

Fäh|re, die; -, -n

fah|ren; du fährst, er fährt; du fuhrst; du führest; gefahren; fahr[e]!; erster, zweiter [Klasse] fahren; Auto fahren; Rad fahren (↑R 39), ich bin Rad gefahren, um Rad zu fahren; spazieren fahren (↑R 39), sie ist spazieren gefahren, um spazieren zu fahren; fahren lassen (↑R 39; *ugs. auch für* nicht mehr festhalten, aufgeben); wir hatten alle Hoffnung fahren lassen, *seltener* fahren gelassen; **fah|rend;** -e Habe *(Rechtsspr.* Fahrnis), -e Leute; **Fah|ren|de**, der; -n, -n; ↑R 5 ff. *(früher für* umherziehender Spielmann, Gaukler)

Fah|ren|heit ‹nach dem dt. Physiker› (Einheit der Grade beim 180-teiligen Thermometer; *Zeichen* F, *fachspr.* °F); 5 °F

fah|ren las|sen *vgl.* fahren; **Fahrens|mann** *Plur.* ...leute *u.* ...männer *(Seemannsspr.)*; **Fah|rer; Fah|re|rei**, die; - *(oft abwertend)*; **Fah|rer-flucht** (die; -), **...haus; Fah|re|rin; fah|re|risch;** -es Können; **Fah|rer|er|laub|nis; Fah|rer|sitz; Fahr|gast** *Plur.* ...gäste; **Fahr|gast|schiff; Fahr-ge|fühl, ...geld, ...ge|le|genheit, ...ge|mein|schaft, ...geschwin|dig|keit, ...ge|stell, ...ha|be** (die; -, -n; *schweiz. für* Fahrnis), **...hau|er** *(Bergmannsspr.)*; **fah|rig** (zerstreut); **Fah|rig|keit**, die; -; **Fahr|kar|te; Fahr|kar|ten-aus|ga|be, ...au|to|mat, ...kon|trol|le, ...schal|ter; Fahr|kom|fort; Fahr|kosten**, Fahrt|kos|ten *Plur.*; **fahr|lässig;** -e Tötung; **Fahr|läs|sig|keit; Fahr-leh|rer, ...leh|re|rin**

Fähr|mann *Plur.* ...männer *u.* ...leute

Fahr|nis, die; -, -se *od.* das; -ses, -se *(Rechtsspr.* fahrende Habe, bewegliches Vermögen)

Fähr|nis, die; -, -se *(geh. für* Gefahr)

Fahr|plan; *vgl.* ²Plan; **fahr|plan|mä|ßig; Fahr-preis** *(vgl.* ²Preis), **...prü|fung; Fahr|rad; Fahr|rad-rei|fen, ...schlüs|sel, ...ständer; Fahr-rin|ne, ...schein; Fahr|schein|heft**

Fähr|schiff

Fahr-schu|le, ...schü|ler, ...si|cher|heit (die; -), **...spur, ...stei|ger** *(Bergmannsspr.)*, **...stil, ...strahl** *(Math., Physik)*, **...stra|ße, ...stuhl, ...stun|de; Fahrt**, die; -, -en; - ins Blaue; **fahr|taug|lich; Fahr|taug|lich|keit; Fahrt|dau|er**

Fähr|te, die; -, -n (Spur)

fahr|tech|nisch

Fahr|ten-buch, ...mes|ser (das), **...schrei|ber** *(amtlich* Fahrtschreiber), **...schwim|mer**

Fähr|ten|su|cher

Fahr|test; Fahrt|kos|ten *vgl.* Fahrkosten; **Fahr|trep|pe** *(fachspr. für* Rolltreppe); **Fahrt-richtung, ...schrei|ber** *(vgl.* Fahrtenschreiber); **fahr|tüch|tig; Fahrtüch|tig|keit; Fahrt-un|ter|brechung, ...wind** (beim Auto u. Ä.); **Fahr-un|tüch|tig|keit, ...ver|bot, ...ver|hal|ten, ...wasser** (das; -s), **...weg, ...wel|le** (die), **...werk, ...wind** (guter Segelwind), **...zeit, ...zeug; Fahrzeug-bau** (der; -[e]s), **...füh|rer, ...hal|ter, ...len|ker, ...park, ...rah|men**

Fai|ble [ˈfɛːb(ə)l], das; -s, -s ‹franz.› (Schwäche; Neigung, Vorliebe); ein - für etwas haben

fair [fɛːr] ‹engl.› (gerecht; anständig; den Regeln entsprechend); das war ein -es Spiel; **Fair|ness** [ˈfɛːr...], die; -; **Fair|play**, *auch* **Fair Play** [ˈfɛːrˈpleː], das; - (ehrenhaftes, anständiges Spiel od. Verhalten [im Sport])

Fait ac|comp|li [fɛːtakɔ̃ˈpliː] (↑R 130), das; - -, -s -s [fɛːzakɔ̃ˈpliː] ‹franz.› (vollendete Tatsache)

fä|kal ‹lat.› *(Med.* kotig); **Fä|kal|dün|ger; Fä|ka|li|en** *Plur.* *(Med.* Kot)

Fa|kir [*österr.* faˈkiːr], der; -s, -e ‹arab.› ([indischer] Büßer, Asket; Zauberkünstler)

Fak|si|mi|le [...leː], das; -s, -s ‹lat., „mache ähnlich!"› (getreue Nachbildung einer Vorlage, z. B. einer alten Handschrift); **Fak|si|mi|le-aus|ga|be, ...druck** *(Plur.* ...drucke); **fak|si|mi|lie|ren**

Fakt, der, *auch* das; -[e]s, *Plur.* -en, *auch* -s *(svw.* Faktum); das ist -; **Fak|ta** *(Plur. von* Faktum); **Fakten|wis|sen**

Fak|ti|on, die; -, -en ‹lat.› *(veraltet für* polit. [bes. aktive od. radikale] Gruppe in einer Partei); **fak|ti|ös** ‹franz.› *(veraltet für* vom Parteigeist beseelt; aufrührerisch)

fak|tisch ‹lat.› (tatsächlich); -es

Vertragsverhältnis *(Rechtsspr.)*; **fak|ti|tiv** [*auch* 'fak...] (bewirkend); **Fak|ti|tiv,** das; -s, -e [...və] (*Sprachw.* Verb des Bewirkens, z. B. „schärfen" = „scharf machen"); **Fak|ti|zi|tät,** die; -, -en (Tatsächlichkeit, Gegebenheit, Wirklichkeit); **Fak|tor,** der; -s, ...oren (bestimmender Grund, Umstand; *Math.* Vervielfältigungszahl; *veraltend für* Werkmeister [in einer Buchdruckerei]); **Fak|to|rei** (*veraltet für* Handelsniederlassung, bes. in Kolonien); **Fak|to|tum,** das; -s, *Plur.* -s *u.* ...ten ‹lat., „tu alles!"› (jmd., der alles besorgt; Mädchen für alles); **Fak|tum,** das; -s, *Plur.* ...ten, *veraltend auch* ...ta ([nachweisbare] Tatsache; Ereignis); *vgl.* Fakt

Fak|tur, die; -, -en ‹ital.› ([Waren]rechnung); **Fak|tu|ra,** die; -, ...ren (*österr. u. schweiz., sonst veraltet für* Faktur); **Fak|tu|ren|buch** *(veraltend)*; **fak|tu|rie|ren** ([Waren] berechnen, Fakturen ausschreiben); **Fak|tu|rier|ma|schi|ne; Fak|tu|rist,** der; -en, -en (↑R 126); **Fak|tu|ris|tin**

Fa|kul|tas, die; -, ...täten ‹lat.› ([Lehr]befähigung); *vgl.* Facultas Docendi; **Fa|kul|tät,** die; -, -en (zusammengehörende Wissenschaftsgebiete umfassende Abteilung einer Hochschule; math. Ausdruck); **fa|kul|ta|tiv** (freigestellt, wahlfrei); -e Fächer

falb; Fal|be, der; -n, -n (graugelbes Pferd mit dunklem Mähnen- u. Schwanzhaar); zwei -n

Fal|bel, die; -, -n ‹franz.› (gekrauster od. gefältelter Kleidbesatz); **fäl|beln** (mit Falbeln versehen); ich ...[e]le (↑R 16)

Fa|ler|ner, der; -s, - (eine Weinsorte); - Wein

Falk (m. Vorn.); **Fal|ke,** der; -n, -n (↑R 126); **Fal|ken‿au|ge, ...bei|ze; Fal|ke|nier,** der; -s, -e (*svw.* Falkner); **Fal|ken|jagd**

Fal|ken|see; Fal|ken|se|er [...ze:ər] (↑R 103 *u.* 105); Falkenseer Forst

Falk|land|in|seln *Plur.* (östl. der Südspitze Südamerikas)

Falk|ner (Falkenabrichter); **Falk|ne|rei** (Jagd mit Falken); **Fal|ko** (m. Vorn.)

[1]**Fall,** der; -[e]s, Fälle (*auch für* Kasus); (↑R 88:) für den Fall, dass ...; gesetzt den -, dass ...; im Fall[e](,) dass ...; von - zu -; zu Fall bringen; erster (1.) Fall; *Klein- u. Zusammenschreibung* (↑R 46): besten-, nötigen-, eintretenden-, gegebenenfalls; allen-, ander[e]n-, jeden-, keinesfalls u. Ä.; [2]**Fall,** das; -[e]s, -en (*Seemannsspr.* ein Tau)

Fal|la|da (dt. Schriftsteller)

Fäll|bad (bei der Chemiefaserherstellung); **Fall‿beil, ...be|schleu|ni|gung** (*Physik; Zeichen g*), ...**brü|cke** *(früher)*; **Fal|le,** die; -, -n; **fal|len;** du fällst, er fällt; du fielst; du fielest; gefallen *(vgl. d.)*; fall[e]!; fallen lassen (↑R 39; *auch für* aufgeben, nicht weiter verfolgen); ich habe den Teller fallen lassen; er hat eine Bemerkung fallen lassen, *seltener* fallen gelassen; die Maske fallen lassen (sein wahres Gesicht zeigen); der fallen gelassene Plan; anheim fallen; *vgl. auch* leicht, schwer; **fäl|len;** du fällst; er fällt; du fälltest; du fälltest; gefällt; fäll[e]!; **fal|len las|sen** *vgl.* fallen; **Fal|len|stel|ler**

Fal|lers|le|ben (Stadt am Mittellandkanal); **Fal|lers|le|be|ner, Fal|lers|le|ber** (↑R 103)

Fall‿ge|schwin|dig|keit *(Physik)*, **...ge|setz** *(Physik)*, **...gru|be** *(Jägerspr.)*, **...hö|he** *(Physik)*

fal|lie|ren ‹ital.› (zahlungsunfähig werden; *schweiz. ugs. für* misslingen); die Firma hat falliert; der Kuchen ist falliert

fäl|lig; ein fälliger, fällig gewordener Wechsel; **Fäl|lig|keit; Fäl|lig|keits|tag**

Fall|li|nie (↑R 136; Linie des größten Gefälles; *Skisport* kürzeste Abfahrt); **Fäll|mit|tel,** das (*Chemie* Mittel zum Ausfällen eines Stoffes); **Fall|obst**

Fall-out, *auch* **Fall|out** [fɔ:l'aut], der; -s, -s ‹engl.› (*Kernphysik* radioaktiver Niederschlag [nach Kernwaffenexplosionen])

Fall|plätt|chen (Metallplättchen an der Schachuhr, das vom Zeiger mitgenommen wird); **Fall|reep** (*Seemannsspr.* äußere Schiffstreppe); **Fall|rohr; Fall|rück|zie|her** *(Fußball)*; **falls;** komme doch[,] falls möglich[,] schon um 17 Uhr (↑R 81); **Fall|schirm; Fall|schirm‿jä|ger** *(Milit.)*, **...sei|de, ...sprin|gen** (das; -s), **...sprin|ger, ...trup|pe; Fall‿strick, ...stu|die** *(Psych., Soziol.)*, **...sucht** (die; -; *veraltet für* Epilepsie); **fall|süch|tig; Fall|tür; Fäl|lung; fall|wei|se** (*österr. für* von Fall zu Fall); **Fall|wind**

Fal|lott, der; -en, -en (↑R 126) ‹franz.› (*österr. für* Gauner)

Fal|sa (*Plur. von* Falsum)

falsch; falsch sein; falsche Zähne; unter falscher Flagge segeln; an die falsche Adresse geraten; falscher Hase (Hackbraten); (↑R 47:) Falsch und Richtig nicht unterscheiden können. *Getrenntschreibung in Verbindung mit Verben:* falsch spielen (*auch für* betrügerisch spielen); die Melodie wurde [völlig] falsch gespielt; er hat beim Skat falsch gespielt; falsch liegen (*auch ugs. für* das Falsche tun, sich irren); er hat mit seiner Schätzung [ganz] falsch gelegen (↑R 39); **Falsch,** der; *nur noch in* es ist kein Falsch an ihm; sie ist ohne Falsch; *vgl. auch* falsch; **Falsch‿aus|sa|ge, ...bu|chung** *(Wirtsch.)*, **...eid** (unwissentl. falsches Schwören); **fäl|schen;** du fälschst; **Fäl|scher; Fäl|sche|rin; Falsch‿fah|rer, ...geld; Falsch|heit,** die; -; **fälsch|lich; fälsch|li|cher|wei|se; falsch lie|gen** *vgl.* falsch; **Falsch‿mel|dung, ...mün|zer, ...mün|ze|rei, ...par|ker; falsch spie|len** *vgl.* falsch; **Falsch|spie|ler; Fäl|schung; fäl|schungs|si|cher**

Fal|sett, das; -[e]s, -e ‹ital.› (*Musik* Kopfstimme); **fal|set|tie|ren; Fal|set|tist,** der; -en, -en (↑R 126); **Fal|sett|stim|me**

Fal|si|fi|kat, das; -[e]s, -e ‹lat.› (Fälschung); **Fal|si|fi|ka|ti|on,** die; -, -en (*veraltet für* Fälschung); **fal|si|fi|zie|ren**

Fals|taff (Gestalt bei Shakespeare)

Fals|ter (dän. Insel)

Fal|sum, das; -s, ...sa ‹lat.› (*veraltet für* Betrug, Fälschung)

Falt|ar|beit; falt|bar; Falt‿blatt, ...boot; Fält|chen; Fal|te, die; -, -n; **fäl|teln;** ich ...[e]le (↑R 16); **fal|ten;** gefaltet; **Fal|ten‿bil|dung, ...ge|bir|ge** *(Geol.)*; **fal|ten|los; fal|ten|reich; Fal|ten‿rock, ...wurf**

Fal|ter, der; -s, - (Schmetterling)

fal|tig (Falten habend)

...fäl|tig (z. B. vielfältig)

Falt‿kar|te, ...kar|ton, ...schach|tel, ...tür; Fal|tung

Falz, der; -es, -e; **Falz|bein** *(Buchbinderei)*; **fal|zen;** du falzt; **Fal|zer; Fal|ze|rin; fal|zig; Fal|zung; Falz|zie|gel**

Fa|ma, die; - ‹lat.› (Ruf; Gerücht)

fa|mi|li|är ‹lat.› (die Familie betreffend; vertraut); **Fa|mi|li|a|ri|tät,** die; -, -en; **Fa|mi|lie** [...i̯ə], die; -, -n; **Fa|mi|li|en‿ähn|lich|keit, ...al|bum, ...an|ge|le|gen|heit, ...an|schluss** (der; -es), **...be|sitz, ...be|trieb, ...bild, ...fei|er, ...fest, ...fla|sche, ...for|schung, ...ge|setz|buch** (das; -[e]s; *ehem. in der DDR; Abk.* FGB), **...grab, ...gruft, ...kreis, ...kun|de** (die; -), **...las|ten|aus|gleich, ...le|ben** (das; -s), **...mi|nis|ter, ...mi|nis-**

te|rin, ...mit|glied, ...na|me, ...ober|haupt (↑R 132), ...packung, ...pla|nung, ...sinn (der; -[e]s), ...stand (der; -[e]s), ...tag, ...va|ter, ...ver|hält|nis|se *(Plur.)*, ...vor|stand, ...wap|pen, ...zu|lage, ...zu|sam|men|füh|rung

fa|mos ‹lat.› *(ugs. für* großartig)

Fa|mu|la, die; -, ...lä *(weibl. Form zu* Famulus); **Fa|mu|la|tur,** die; -, -en ‹lat.› (von Medizinstudenten abzuleistendes Krankenhauspraktikum); **fa|mu|lie|ren; Fa|mu|lus,** der; -, *Plur.* -se *u.* ...li ‹„Diener"› (Medizinstudent im Praktikum)

Fan [fɛn], der; -s, -s ‹engl.› (begeisterter Anhänger)

Fa|nal, das; -s, -e ‹griech.› (Aufmerksamkeit erregendes Zeichen)

Fa|na|ti|ker ‹lat.› (blinder, rücksichtsloser Eiferer); **Fa|na|ti|ke|rin; fa|na|tisch; fa|na|ti|sie|ren** (fanatisch machen; aufhetzen); **Fa|na|tis|mus,** der; -

Fan|be|treu|er ['fɛn...] (Betreuer der Fans eines Sportvereins)

Fan|dan|go [...'daŋgo], der; -s, -s (ein schneller span. Tanz)

Fan|fa|re, die; -, -n ‹franz.› (Trompetensignal; Blasinstrument); **Fan|fa|ren‿blä|ser, ...stoß, ...zug**

Fang, der; -[e]s, Fänge; **Fang‿arm** *(Zool.)*, **...ball** (der; -[e]s), **...ei|sen; fan|gen;** du fängst, er fängt; du fingst; du fingest; gefangen; fang[e]!; **Fan|gen,** das; -s; - spielen; **Fän|ger; Fang|fra|ge; fang|frisch; Fang‿ge|rät, ...gru|be, ...grün|de** *(Plur.)*

fän|gisch *(Jägerspr.* fangbereit [von Fallen]); **Fang‿korb, ...lei|ne, ...mes|ser** (das; *Jägerspr.*), **...netz**

Fan|go ['faŋgo], der; -s ‹ital.› (heilkräftiger Mineralschlamm); **Fan|go‿bad, ...pa|ckung**

Fang‿schnur *(Plur.* ...schnüre; Uniformteil), **...schuss** *(Jägerspr.)*; **fang|si|cher;** ein -er Torwart; **Fang‿spiel, ...stoß** *(Jägerspr.)*, **...vor|rich|tung, ...zahn** *(Jägerspr.)*

Fan|klub ['fɛn...] ‹engl.› (Klub für die Fans eines Filmstars, Sportvereins usw.)

Fan|ni, Fan|ny (w. Vorn.)

Fant, der; -[e]s, -e *(veraltet für* unreifer junger Mensch)

Fan|ta|sia, die; -, -s ‹griech.› (nordafrik. Reiterkampfspiel); **Fan|ta|sie,** die; -, ...ien (Musikstück; *auch für* Phantasie; *vgl. d.*); **fan|ta|sie|be|gabt,** *auch* phan|tasie|be|gabt; **fan|ta|sie|los,** *auch* phan|ta|sie|los; **fan|ta|sie|ren,** *auch* phan|ta|sie|ren; **fan|ta|sie|voll,** *auch* phan|ta|sie|voll; **Fan|tast,** *auch* Phan|tast *(vgl. d.)*; **fan|tas|tisch,** *auch* phantastisch; **Fan|ta|sy** ['fɛntəzi], die; - ‹engl.› (Roman-, Filmgattung, die märchen- u. mythenhafte Traumwelten darstellt); **Fan|ta|sy|ro|man**

Fa|rad, das; -[s], - ‹nach dem engl. Physiker Faraday› (Maßeinheit der elektr. Kapazität; *Zeichen* F); 3 - (↑R 90); **Fa|ra|day|kä|fig** ['farade:..., *auch* 'fɛrədi...] *(Physik* Abschirmung gegen äußere elektrische Felder); **fa|ra|day|sche Ge|set|ze** [...'de:ʃə -] *Plur.* (Grundgesetze der Elektrolyse); **Fa|ra|di|sa|ti|on** [faradi...], die; -, -en (med. Anwendung faradischer Ströme); **fa|ra|disch;** -e Ströme (Induktionsströme); **fa|ra|di|sie|ren**

Farb‿ab|stim|mung, ...auf|nah|me, ...band (das; *Plur.* ...bänder), **...beu|tel, ...be|zeich|nung, ...bild, ...brü|he; Farb|druck** *vgl.* Farbendruck; **Far|be,** die; -, -n; eine blaue -; die - Blau; **farb|echt; Farb‿ef|fekt, ...ei; Fär|be|mit|tel,** das; **...far|ben** *od.* ...farbig (z. B. cremefarben, cremefarbig; beigefarben, beigefarbig); **fär|ben; Far|ben|be|zeich|nung** *vgl.* Farbbezeichnung; **far|ben|blind; Far|ben‿blind|heit** (die; -), **...druck** *(Plur.* ...drucke); **far|ben‿freu|dig, ...froh; Far|ben|kas|ten** *vgl.* Farbkasten; **Far|ben‿leh|re, ...pracht** (die; -); **far|ben|präch|tig; Far|ben|pro|be; Far|ben‿sinn** (der; -[e]s), **...sym|bo|lik; Fär|ber; Fär|ber|baum** (Pflanze); *vgl.* Sumach; **Fär|be|rei; Fär|be|rin; Fär|ber|waid** (Pflanze); **Farb‿fern|se|hen, ...fern|se|her, ...fern|seh|ge|rät, ...film, ...fil|ter, ...fo|to, ...fo|to|gra|fie, ...ge|bung** (die; -; *für* Kolorit), **...holz; far|big,** *österr. auch* **fär|big;** farbig ausgeführt, *aber* (↑R 47): in Farbig ausgeführt; **...far|big,** *österr.* **...fär|big,** z. B. einfarbig, *österr.* einfärbig; *vgl.* ...farben; **Far|bi|ge,** der *u.* die; -n, -n; ↑R 5 ff. (Angehöriger einer nichtweißen Rasse); **Far|big|keit,** die; -; **Farb‿kas|ten, ...kom|bi|na|ti|on, ...kom|po|nen|te, ...kon|trast, ...kör|per** *(für* Pigment); **Farb|leh|re** *vgl.* Farbenlehre; **farb|lich; farb|los; Farb|lo|sig|keit,** die; -; **Farb‿mi|ne, ...mo|ni|tor, ...nu|an|ce, ...pro|be** *(vgl.* Farbenprobe), **...schicht, ...stift, ...stoff, ...ton** *(Plur.* ...töne); **farb|ton|rich|tig** *(für* isochromatisch); **Farb‿tup|fen, ...tup|fer; Fär|bung; Farb|wal|ze** *(Druckw.)*

Far|ce ['farsə, *österr.* fars], die; -, -n [...s(ə)n] ‹franz.› (Posse; Verhöhnung, Karikatur eines Geschehens; *Gastron.* Füllsel); **far|cie|ren** [...'si:...] *(Gastron.* füllen)

Fa|rin, der; -s ‹lat.› (nicht raffinierter, gelblicher Zucker)

Fä|rin|ger *vgl.* ²Färöer

Farm, die; -, -en ‹engl.›; **Far|mer,** der; -s, -; **Far|mers|frau**

Farn, der; -[e]s, -e (eine Sporenpflanze)

Far|ne|se, der; -, - (Angehöriger eines ital. Fürstengeschlechtes); **far|ne|sisch,** *aber* (↑R 94): der Farnesische Stier

Farn‿kraut, ...pflan|ze, ...we|del

¹Fä|rö|er [*auch* fɛ'rø:ər] *Plur.* ‹„Schafinseln"› (dän. Inselgruppe im Nordatlantik); **²Fä|rö|er** *od.* Fä|rin|ger, der; -s, - (Bewohner der ¹Färöer); **fä|rö|isch** [*auch* fɛ'rø:iʃ]

Far|re, der; -n, -n; (↑R 126; *landsch. für* junger Stier); **Fär|se,** die; -, -n (Kuh, die noch nicht gekalbt hat); *vgl. aber* Ferse

Fa|san, der; -[e]s, -e[n]; **Fa|sa|nen‿ge|he|ge, ...zucht; Fa|sa|ne|rie,** die; -, ...ien (Fasanengehege)

Fa|sche, die; -, -n ‹ital.› *(österr. für* Binde); **fa|schen** *(österr. für* mit einer Fasche umwickeln)

fa|schie|ren ‹franz.› *(österr. für* Fleisch durch den Fleischwolf drehen); faschierte Laibchen (Frikadellen); **Fa|schier|ma|schi|ne** *(österr. seltener neben* Fleischmaschine); **Fa|schier|te,** das; -n; ↑R 5 ff. *(österr. für* Hackfleisch)

Fa|schi|ne, die; -, -n ‹franz.› (Reisigbündel zur Sicherung von [Ufer]böschungen o. Ä.); **Fa|schi|nen‿mes|ser** (das; eine Art Seitengewehr), **...wall**

Fa|sching, der; -s, *Plur.* -e *u.* -s; **Fa|schings‿ball, ...diens|tag, ...kos|tüm, ...krap|fen** *(österr.)*, **...prinz, ...prin|zes|sin, ...scherz, ...zeit** (die; -), **...zug**

fa|schi|sie|ren (mit faschistischen Tendenzen durchsetzen); **Fa|schis|mus,** der; - ‹ital.› (antidemokratische, nationalistische Staatsauffassung od. Herrschaftsform); **Fa|schist,** der; -en, -en (↑R 126); **fa|schis|tisch; fa|schis|to|id** (dem Faschismus ähnlich)

Fa|se, die; -, -n (Abschrägung einer Kante)

Fa|sel, der; -s, - (junges Zuchttier); **Fa|sel|eber** (↑R 132)

Fa|se|lei; Fa|se|ler *vgl.* Fasler; **Fa-**

sel|hans, der; -[es], *Plur.* -e *u.* ...hänse; **fa|se|lig; fa|seln** (törichtes Zeug reden); ich ...[e]le (↑R 16)
fa|sen (abkanten); du fast
Fa|ser, die; -, -n; **Fä|ser|chen; fa|se|rig** *vgl.* fasrig; **fa|sern;** das Gewebe, Papier fasert; **fa|ser|nackt** (völlig nackt); **Fa|ser‿pflan|ze, ...plat|te; fa|ser|scho|nend;** ein -es Waschmittel; **Fa|ser|schrei|ber; Fa|se|rung,** die; -
Fa|shion ['fɛʃ(ə)n], die; - ⟨engl.⟩ (Mode; feine Lebensart); **fa|shio|na|ble** ['fɛʃənəbəl] (modisch, fein); ...ab|le (↑R 130) Kleidung
Fas|ler, Fa|se|ler
Fas|nacht (*landsch. u. schweiz. für* Fastnacht)
fas|rig, fa|se|rig; -es Papier
Fass, das; -es, Fässer; zwei Fass Bier (↑R 90)
Fas|sa|de, die; -, -n ⟨franz.⟩ (Vorder-, Schauseite; Ansicht); **Fas|sa|den‿klet|te|rer, ...rei|ni|gung**
fass|bar; Fass|bar|keit, die; -
Fass‿bier, ...bin|der (*südd. u. österr. für* Böttcher); **Fäss|chen; Fass|dau|be**
fas|sen; du fasst; er fasst; du fasstest; gefasst; fasse! *u.* fass!
fäs|ser|wei|se (in Fässern)
Fas|set|te *vgl.* Facette
fass|lich; Fass|lich|keit, die; -
[1]**Fas|son** [fa'sɔŋ, *auch* fa'sõ:, *südd., österr. u. schweiz. meist* fa'so:n], die; -, *Plur.* -s, *österr., schweiz.* -en ⟨franz.⟩ (Form; Muster; Art; Zuschnitt); [2]**Fas|son,** das; -s, -s (Revers); **fas|so|nie|ren** [faso'ni:...]; **Fas|son|schnitt** (ein Haarschnitt)
Fass‿rei|fen, ...spund (↑R 136)
Fas|sung; Fas|sungs|kraft, die; -; **fas|sungs|los; Fas|sungs|lo|sig|keit,** die; -; **Fas|sungs|ver|mö|gen**
Fass|wein; fass|wei|se
fast (beinahe)
Fast|back ['fa:stbɛk], das; -s, -s ⟨engl.⟩ (Fließheck [bei Autos])
Fast|ebe|ne (↑R 132; *Geogr.* nicht ganz ebene Fläche, Rumpffläche)
Fas|tel|abend (↑R 132; *rheinisch für* Fastnacht); **fas|ten;** [1]**Fas|ten,** das; -s; [2]**Fas|ten** *Plur.* (Fasttage); **Fas|ten‿kur, ...mo|nat, ...sonn|tag, ...spei|se, ...zeit**
Fast|food, *auch* **Fast Food** ['fa:stfu:d], *das;* -[s] ⟨engl., „schnelles Essen"⟩ (schnell verzehrbare kleinere Gerichte)
Fast|nacht, die; -; **Fast|nachts‿brauch, ...diens|tag, ...kos|tüm, ...spiel, ...trei|ben** (das; -s), **...zeit** (die; -), **...zug; Fast|tag**
Fas|zes ['fastse:s] *Plur.* ⟨lat.⟩ (Bündel aus Stäben [Ruten] u. einem Beil, Abzeichen der altröm. Liktoren); **Fas|zie** [...iə], die; -, -n (*Med.* sehnenartige Muskelhaut); **Fas|zi|kel,** der; -s, - ([Akten]bündel; Lieferung)
Fas|zi|na|ti|on, die; -, -en ⟨lat.⟩ (fesselnde Wirkung; Anziehungskraft); **fas|zi|nie|ren**
Fa|ta (*Plur. von* Fatum); **fa|tal** ⟨lat.⟩ (verhängnisvoll; unangenehm; peinlich); **fa|ta|ler|wei|se; Fa|ta|lis|mus,** der; - (Glaube an Vorherbestimmung; Schicksalsglaube); **Fa|ta|list,** der; -en, -en (↑R 126); **Fa|ta|lis|tin; fa|ta|lis|tisch; Fa|ta|li|tät,** die; -, -en (Verhängnis, Missgeschick)
Fa|ta Mor|ga|na, die; - -, *Plur.* - ...nen *u.* - -s ⟨ital.⟩ (durch Luftspiegelung verursachte Täuschung)
fa|tie|ren ⟨lat.⟩ (*veraltet für* bekennen; *österr. für* seine Steuererklärung abgeben); **Fa|tie|rung**
Fa|ti|ma (w. Vorn.)
Fa|tum, das; -s, ...ta ⟨lat.⟩ (Schicksal)
Fatz|ke, der; *Gen.* -n (↑R 126) *u.* -s, *Plur.* -n *u.* -s (*ugs. für* eitler Mensch)
fau|chen
faul; fauler (*ugs. für* deckungsloser) Wechsel; fauler Zauber; auf der faulen Haut liegen *(ugs.);* **Faul‿baum** (eine Heilpflanze), **...brut** (die; -; eine Bienenkrankheit); **Fäu|le,** die; -; **fau|len; fau|len|zen;** du faulenzt; **Fau|len|zer; Fau|len|ze|rei; Fau|len|ze|rin; Faul|heit,** die; -; **fau|lig**
Faulk|ner ['fɔ:knər] (amerik. Schriftsteller)
Fäul|nis, die; -; **Fäul|nis|er|re|ger; Faul‿pelz** (*ugs. für* fauler Mensch), **...schlamm** (Bodenschlamm in flachen u. stehenden Gewässern), **...tier**
Faun, der; -[e]s, -e (gehörnter Waldgeist; Faunus; *auch für* lüsterner Mensch); **Fau|na,** die; -, ...nen (Tierwelt [eines Gebietes]); **fau|nisch** ([lüstern] wie ein Faun); **Fau|nus** (röm. Feld- u. Waldgott)
Fau|ré [fo're:] (franz. Komponist)
[1]**Faust** (Gestalt der dt. Dichtung)
[2]**Faust,** die; -, Fäuste; **Faust‿abwehr** *(Sport),* **...ball; Fäust|chen; faust|dick;** er hat es - hinter den Ohren; **Fäus|tel,** der; -s, - (Hammer, Schlägel der Bergleute); **faus|ten** *(Sport);* **Faust|feu|er|waf|fe; faust|groß; Faust‿hand|schuh, ...hieb**
faus|tisch (nach Art u. Wesen des [1]Faust)
Faust‿kampf (*veraltend für* Boxen), **...keil; Fäust|ling** (Fausthandschuh; *Bergmannsspr.* faustgroßer Stein); **Faust‿pfand, ...recht** (das; -[e]s; [gewaltsame] Selbsthilfe), **...re|gel, ...schlag, ...skiz|ze**
faute de mieux [fot də 'mjø:] ⟨franz.⟩ (in Ermangelung eines Besseren; im Notfall)
Fau|teuil [fo'tœ:j], der; -s, -s ⟨franz.⟩ (*österr. u. schweiz., sonst veraltend für* Lehnsessel)
Faut|fracht ⟨franz.; dt.⟩ (*Verkehrsw.* abmachungswidrig nicht genutzter [Schiffs]frachtraum; Summe, die beim Rücktritt vom Frachtvertrag zu zahlen ist)
Fau|vis|mus [fo'vis...], der; - ⟨franz.⟩ (Richtung der franz. Malerei im frühen 20. Jh.); **Fau|vist,** der; -en, -en *meist Plur.* (↑R 126); **fau|vis|tisch**
Faux|pas [fo'pa], der; - [fo'pa(s)], - [fo'pas] ⟨franz., „Fehltritt"⟩ (Taktlosigkeit; Verstoß gegen die Umgangsformen)
Fa|ve|la [fa'vɛla], die; -, -s ⟨port.⟩ (Slum in Südamerika)
fa|vo|ra|bel [...v...] ⟨franz.⟩ (*veraltet für* günstig, geneigt; vorteilhaft); ...ab|le (↑R 130) Werte; **fa|vo|ri|sie|ren** (begünstigen; *Sport* als voraussichtlichen Sieger nennen); **Fa|vo|rit,** der; -en, -en; ↑R 126 (Günstling; Liebling; *Sport* voraussichtlicher Sieger); **Fa|vo|ri|ten|rol|le; Fa|vo|ri|tin** (Geliebte [eines Herrschers]; *Sport* voraussichtliche Siegerin)
Fa|vus ['fa:vus], der; -, *Plur.* ...ven *u.* ...vi ⟨lat.⟩ (*Med.* eine Hautkrankheit; *Zool.* Wachsscheibe im Bienenstock)
Fax, das; -, -[e] (*kurz für* Telefax); **Fax|an|schluss**
Fa|xe, die; -, -n *meist Plur.* (Grimasse; dummer Spaß)
fa|xen (*kurz für* telefaxen)
Fa|xen|ma|cher (Grimassenschneider; Spaßmacher)
Fax|num|mer
Fa|yence [fa'jã:s, *auch* fa'jaŋs], die; -, -n [...sən] ⟨franz.⟩ (feinere Töpferware); **Fa|yence‿krug, ...ofen** (↑R 132), **...tel|ler**
Fa|zen|da [fa'tsɛnda, *auch* fa'zɛnda], die; -, -s ⟨port.⟩ (Farm in Brasilien)
Fä|zes ['fɛ:tse:s] *Plur.* ⟨lat.⟩ (*Med.* Ausscheidungen, Kot)
fa|zi|al ⟨lat.⟩ (*Med.* das Gesicht betreffend; Gesichts...); **Fa|zi|a|lis,** der; - (*Med.* Gesichtsnerv); **Fa|zi|es** ['fa:tsiɛs], die; -, - [...tsie:s] (*Geol.* Merkmal von Sedimentgesteinen)

Fa|zi|li|tät, die; -, -en ‹lat.› (*Wirtsch.* Kreditmöglichkeit)

Fa|zit, das; -s, *Plur.* -e *u.* -s (Ergebnis; Schlussfolgerung)

FBI [ɛfbiˈai] = Federal Bureau of Investigation [ˈfɛdərəl bju(ə)ˈro: əv invɛstiˈge:ʃ(ə)n], der *od.* das; - (Bundeskriminalpolizei der USA)

FC = Fußballclub; Fechtclub; Fanfarencorps

FCKW = Fluorchlorkohlenwasserstoff

FDGB = Freier Deutscher Gewerkschaftsbund *(ehem. in der DDR)*

FDJ = Freie Deutsche Jugend *(ehem. in der DDR);* **FDJler** (↑R 26); **FDJle|rin** (↑R 26)

FDP = Freisinnig-Demokratische Partei (der Schweiz)

FDP, *parteiamtliche Schreibung* **F.D.P.** = Freie Demokratische Partei (Deutschlands)

F-Dur [ˈɛfdu:r, *auch* ˈɛfˈdu:r], das; - (Tonart; *Zeichen* F); **F-Dur-Ton|lei|ter** (↑R 28)

Fe = Ferrum (*chem. Zeichen für* Eisen)

Fea|ture [ˈfi:tʃə(r)], das; -s, -s, *auch* die; -, -s ‹engl.› (aktuell aufgemachter Dokumentarbericht, bes. für Funk od. Fernsehen)

Fe|ber, der; -s, - (*österr. für* Februar); **Febr.** = Februar

feb|ril (↑R 130) ‹lat.› (*Med.* fieberhaft)

Feb|ru|ar (↑R 130), der; -[s], -e ‹lat.› (der zweite Monat des Jahres, Hornung; *Abk.* Febr.)

fec. = fecit

Fech|ser (*Landw.* Schössling, Steckling)

Fecht‿bahn, ...bo|den *(Studentenspr.),* **...bru|der** (*veraltend für* Bettler); **fech|ten;** du fichtst, er ficht; du fochtest; du föchtest; gefochten; ficht!; **Fech|ter; Fech|ter|flan|ke** *(Turnen);* **Fech|te|rin; fech|te|risch; Fecht‿hand|schuh, ...hieb, ...kunst, ...mas|ke, ...meis|ter, ...sport**

fe|cit ‹lat., „hat [es] gemacht"› (*Abk.* fec.); ipse - *(vgl. d.)*

Fe|da|jin, der; -s, - ‹arab.› (arabischer Freischärler; arabischer Untergrundkämpfer)

Fe|der, die; -, -n; **Fe|der‿ball, ...bein** *(Technik),* **...bett, ...blu|me** (eine Kunstblume), **...boa, ...busch, ...fuch|ser** (Pedant); **fe|der|füh|rend; Fe|der‿füh|rung** (die; -), **...ge|wicht** (Körpergewichtsklasse in der Schwerathletik), **...hal|ter; fe|de|rig** *vgl.* fedrig; **Fe|der|kern|mat|rat|ze; Fe|der|kleid; fe|der|leicht; Fe|der|le|sen,** das; -s; *in* nicht viel -[s] (Umstände) machen; **Fe|der|ling** (ein Insekt); **Fe|der‿mäpp|chen, ...mes|ser** (das); **fe|dern;** ich ...ere (↑R 16); **Fe|der‿nel|ke, ...schmuck, ...spiel** (*Jägerspr.* zwei Taubenflügel zum Zurücklocken des Beizvogels), **...stiel** (*österr. für* Federhalter), **...strich; Fe|de|rung; Fe|der‿vieh** (*ugs. für* Geflügel), **...waa|ge; Fe|der|wei|ße,** der; -n, -n; ↑R 5 ff. (gärender Weinmost); **Fe|der‿wild, ...wol|ke, ...zan|ge** (*für* Pinzette), **...zeich|nung**

Fe|dor, Fe|o|dor (m. Vorn.)

fed|rig; Fed|rig|keit, die; -

Fee, die; -, Feen ‹franz.› (eine w. Märchengestalt)

Feed-back, *auch* **Feed|back** [ˈfi:dbɛk], das; -s, -s ‹engl.› (*Kybernetik* Rückmeldung; *Rundf., Fernsehen* Reaktion des Publikums)

Fee|ling [ˈfi:liŋ], das; -s, -s ‹engl.› (Einfühlungsvermögen; Gefühl)

fe|en|haft; Fe|en‿mär|chen, ...rei|gen, ...schloss

Feet [fi:t] (*Plur. von* Foot)

Fe|ge, die; -, -n (Werkzeug zum Getreidereinigen); **Fe|ge|feu|er,** *selten* Feg|feu|er; **fe|gen; Fe|ger; Feg|nest,** das; -[e]s, -e (*schweiz. mdal. für* unruhiger Mensch [bes. Kind]); **feg|nes|ten** *(schweiz. mdal.);* gefegnestet; zu -; **Feg|sel,** das; -s, - (*landsch. für* Kehricht)

Feh, das; -[e]s, -e (russ. Eichhörnchen; Pelzwerk)

Feh|de, die; -, -n (Streit; kriegerische Auseinandersetzung); **Feh|de|hand|schuh**

fehl; fehl am Platz; **Fehl,** der; *nur noch in* ohne Fehl [und Tadel]; **Fehl|an|zei|ge; fehl|bar** (*schweiz. für* [einer Übertretung] schuldig); **Fehl|bar|keit,** die; -; **Fehl|be|die|nung; fehl|be|le|gen** *(Amtsspr.); vgl.* fehlbesetzen; **Fehl|be|le|gung; fehl|be|set|zen;** er besetzt[e] fehl; fehlbesetzt; fehlzubesetzen; **Fehl‿be|set|zung, ...be|stand, ...be|trag, ...deu|tung, ...di|ag|no|se, ...dis|po|si|ti|on, ...ein|schät|zung; feh|len; Fehl‿ent|schei|dung, ...ent|wick|lung; Feh|ler; feh|ler|frei; feh|ler|haft; Feh|ler|haf|tig|keit,** die; -; **feh|ler|los; Feh|ler|lo|sig|keit,** die; -; **Feh|ler‿quel|le, ...zahl; Fehl‿far|be, ...funk|ti|on, ...ge|burt; fehl‿ge|hen, ...grei|fen;** *vgl.* fehlbesetzen; **Fehl‿griff, ...in|for|ma|ti|on, ...in|ter|pre|ta|ti|on; fehl|in|ter|pre|tie|ren;** *vgl.* fehlbesetzen; **Fehl‿in|ves|ti|ti|on, ...kon|struk|ti|on, ...leis|tung; fehl|lei|ten;** *vgl.* fehlbesetzen; **Fehl‿lei|tung, ...mel|dung, ...pass** *(Sport),* **...pla|nung; fehl|schie|ßen;** *vgl.* fehlbesetzen; **Fehl|schlag,** der; -[e]s, ...schläge; **fehl|schla|gen;** *vgl.* fehlbesetzen; **Fehl|schuss; Fehl|sich|tig|keit,** die; - *(Med.);* **Fehl‿sprung** *(Sport),* **...start** *(Sport);* **fehl|tre|ten;** *vgl.* fehlbesetzen; **Fehl‿tritt, ...ur|teil, ...ver|hal|ten, ...zün|dung**

Feh|marn (eine Ostseeinsel); **Feh|marn|belt,** der; -[e]s

Fehn, das; -[e]s, -e ‹niederl.›; *vgl.* Fenn; **Fehn‿ko|lo|nie** (Moorsiedlung), **...kul|tur** (die; -; bes. Art Moorkultur)

Fehr|bel|lin (Stadt in Brandenburg)

Feh|werk, das; -[e]s (Pelzwerk)

fei|en (*geh. für* [durch vermeintliche Zaubermittel] schützen); gefeit (sicher, geschützt)

Fei|er, die; -, -n

Fei|er|abend (↑R 132); **Fei|er|abend|heim** (*regional für* Altenheim); **fei|er|abend|lich**

Fei|e|rei, die; -; **fei|er|lich; Fei|er|lich|keit; fei|ern;** ich ...ere (↑R 16); **Fei|er‿schicht, ...stun|de; Fei|er|tag;** des Feiertags, *aber* (↑R 46): feiertags, sonn- u. feiertags (↑R 23); **fei|er|täg|lich; fei|er|tags;** *vgl.* Feiertag; **Fei|er|tags|stim|mung**

feig, fei|ge

Fei|ge, die; -, -n; **Fei|gen‿baum, ...blatt, ...kak|tus**

Feig|heit, die; -; **feig|her|zig; Feig|her|zig|keit,** die; -; **Feig|ling**

Feig|war|ze (*Med.* eine Hautwucherung)

feil (*veraltend für* verkäuflich); **feil|bie|ten** (↑R 37); er bietet feil; feilgeboten; feilzubieten; **Feil|bie|tung**

Fei|le, die; -, -n; **fei|len; Fei|len|hau|er**

feil|hal|ten; *vgl.* feilbieten

feil|schen; du feilschst

Feil‿span, ...staub

Feim, der; -[e]s, -e *u.* **Fei|me,** die; -, -n *u.* **Fei|men,** der; -s, - (*landsch. für* geschichteter Getreidehaufen; Schober)

fein; sehr fein (*Zeichen* ff); (↑R 40:) fein gemahlenes Mehl; feiner, am feinsten gemahlenes Mehl; das Mehl ist fein gemahlen; fein geädert, geschnitten, geschwungen, gesponnen, gestreift, vermahlen; *vgl.* feinfühlend, feinkörnig usw.; (↑R 39:) sich [ganz] fein machen; das hast du [sehr] fein gemacht!; eine Fläche fein schleifen, *auch (bes. fachspr.)* feinschleifen; (↑R 47:) [das Feinste] vom Feinsten; **Fein‿ab|stim|mung, ...ar|beit, ...bä|cke|rei, ...blech**

Feind, der; -[e]s, -e; jemandes Feind bleiben, sein, werden; jemandem Feind bleiben, sein, werden *(veraltend);* **Feind‿be|rüh|rung, ...ein|wir|kung; Fein|des|hand,** die; -; in - sein, geraten; **Fein|des|land,** das; -[e]s; **Fein|din; feind|lich;** *Schreibung in Zusammensetzungen:* menschenfeindlich, kirchenfeindlich; moskaufeindlich, *auch* Moskau-feindlich (↑R 105); **Feind|lich|keit; Feind|schaft; feind|schaft|lich; feind|se|lig; Feind|se|lig|keit**

Fei|ne, die; - (Feinheit); **fei|nen** (*Hüttenw.* [Metall] veredeln); **Fein|frost|ge|mü|se** (*regional für* tiefgefrorenes Gemüse); **fein|füh|lig; Fein|füh|lig|keit,** die; -; **fein ge|ädert** (↑R 132); *vgl.* fein; **Fein‿ge|bäck, ...ge|fühl** (das; -[e]s), **...ge|halt** (der); **fein ge|mah|len, ge|schnit|ten, ge|schwun|gen** usw. *vgl.* fein; **Fein|ge|wicht; fein|glie|de|rig, fein|glied|rig; Fein|gold; Fein|heit; Fein|ke|ra|mik; fein‿ke|ra|misch, ...kör|nig; Fein‿kör|nig|keit** (die; -), **...kost; fein ma|chen** *vgl.* fein; **fein|ma|schig; Fein‿me|cha|ni|ker, ...mes|sung; fein‿ner|vig, ...po|rig, ...san|dig; fein schlei|fen** *vgl.* fein; **Fein‿schliff, ...schme|cker, ...schnitt, ...sil|ber; fein|sin|nig; Fein|sin|nig|keit,** die; -; **Feins|lieb|chen** (*veraltet für* Geliebte); **Fein|strumpf|ho|se; Feinst|waa|ge; fein ver|mah|len** *vgl.* fein; **Fein|wasch|mit|tel**

feiß (*südwestd. u. schweiz. mdal. für* fett, feist); **feist; Feist,** das; -[e]s (*Jägerspr.* Fett); **Feis|te, Feist|heit,** die; -; **Feist|hirsch** *(Jägerspr.);* **Feis|tig|keit,** die; -

Fei|tel, der; -s, - (*südd., österr. ugs. für* einfaches Taschenmesser)

fei|xen *(ugs.);* du feixt

Fe|bel, der; -s, - ‹ital.› (ein Gewebe)

Fel|ber, der; -s, -, **Fel|ber|baum** (*südd. mdal. für* Weidenbaum)

Fel|chen, der; -s, - (ein Fisch)

Feld, das; -[e]s, -er; elektrisches -; feldein u. feldaus; querfeldein; ins - (in den Krieg) ziehen; (↑R 23:) Feld- u. Gartenfrüchte; **Feld‿ar|beit, ...ar|til|le|rie, ...bett, ...blu|me, ...dienst; feld|ein;** feldein u. feldaus; querfeldein; **Feld‿fla|sche, ...flüch|ter** (Taube), **...flur** (die; -), **...for|schung** *(Soziol., Sprachw.),* **...frucht** *(meist Plur.),* **...got|tes|dienst; feld|grau; Feld‿hand|ball, ...heer, ...herr; Feld|herrn|blick; Feld‿ho|ckey, ...huhn, ...hü|ter; ...fel|dig** (z. B. vierfeldig); **Feld‿jä|ger** *(Milit.),* **...kü|che, ...la|ger, ...mark** (die; [1]Flur), **...mar|schall** (der; -[e]s; *früher*); **feld|marsch|mä|ßig** *(Milit.);* **Feld‿maß** (das), **...maus, ...mes|ser** (der), **...post** *(Milit.),* **...sa|lat; Feld|scher,** der; -s, -e (*veraltet für* Wundarzt; *ehem. in der DDR* milit. Arzthelfer); **Feld‿spat** (ein Mineral), **...spie|ler** *(Sport),* **...stär|ke** *(Physik),* **...ste|cher** (Fernglas), **...stein, ...stuhl, ...the|o|rie** *(Sprachw.),* **...über|le|gen|heit** (↑R 132; *Sport*), **...ver|weis** *(Sport);* **Feld-Wald-und-Wie|sen-...** (*ugs. für* durchschnittlich, Allerwelts...); z. B. Feld-Wald-und-Wiesen-Programm; **Feld|we|bel,** der; -s, -; **Feld‿weg, ...wei|bel** (*schweiz.* ein Unteroffiziersgrad), **...zug**

Felg|auf|schwung (Reckübung); **Fel|ge,** die; -, -n (Radkranz; eine Reckübung); **fel|gen** ([ein Rad] mit einer Felge versehen); **Fel|gen|brem|se; Felg|um|schwung** (eine Reckübung)

Fe|lix (m. Vorn.); **Fe|li|zia** (w. Vorn.); **Fe|li|zi|tas** (w. Vorn.)

Fell, das; -[e]s, -e

Fel|la|che, der; -n, -n (↑R 126) ‹arab.› (Bauer im Vorderen Orient); **Fel|la|chin**

Fel|la|tio, die; -, ...ones ‹lat.› (Herbeiführen der Ejakulation mit Lippen u. Zunge)

Fell|ei|sen, das; -s, - (*veraltet für* Rucksack, Tornister)

Fell|müt|ze

Fel|low ['fɛlo:], der; -s, -s ‹engl.› (Mitglied eines College, einer wissenschaftlichen Gesellschaft)

Fe|lo|nie, die; -, ...ien ‹franz.› (Untreue [gegenüber dem Lehnsherrn im MA.])

[1]**Fels,** der; - (hartes Gestein); auf - stoßen; im - klettern; [2]**Fels,** der; *Gen.* -ens, *älter* -en, *Plur.* -en (*geh. für* Felsen, Felsblock); ein - in der Brandung; **Fels‿bild** *(vorgeschichtl. Kunst),* **...block** (*Plur.* ...blöcke); **Fel|sen,** der; -s, - ([aufragende] Gesteinsmasse, Felsblock); **fel|sen|fest; Fel|sen‿nest, ...riff; Fel|sen|schlucht** usw. *vgl.* Felsschlucht usw.; **fel|sig; Fel|sit** [*auch* ...'zit], der; -s, -e (ein Quarzporphyr); **Fels‿ma|le|rei, ...schlucht, ...spalt, ...spal|te, ...spit|ze, ...stück, ...vor|sprung, ...wand, ...zeich|nung**

Fe|lu|ke, die; -, -n ‹arab.› (Küstenfahrzeug des Mittelmeers)

Fe|me, die; -, -n (heiml. Gericht, Freigericht); **Fe|me|ge|richt**

Fe|mel, Fim|mel, der; -s (*Landw.* Gesamtheit der männl. Hanfpflanzen); **Fe|mel|be|trieb** (Art des Forstbetriebes); **Fe|mel|hanf** *vgl.* Femel

Fe|me|mord; Fem|ge|richt *vgl.* Femegericht

fe|mi|nie|ren ‹lat.› (*Med., Zool.* verweiblichen); **fe|mi|nin** [*auch* ...'ni:n] (weiblich; weibisch); **Fe|mi|ni|num,** das; -s, ...na (*Sprachw.* weibliches Substantiv, z. B. „die Erde“); **Fe|mi|nis|mus,** der; -, ...men (Richtung der Frauenbewegung, die ein neues Selbstverständnis der Frau und die Aufhebung der traditionellen Rollenverteilung anstrebt *[nur Sing.]; Med., Zool.* Ausbildung weibl. Merkmale bei männl. Wesen; Verweiblichung); **Fe|mi|nis|tin** (Vertreterin des Feminismus); **fe|mi|nis|tisch**

Femme fa|tale [fam fa'tal], die; - -, -s -s [fam fa'tal] ‹franz.› (charmante Frau, die durch Extravaganz o. Ä. ihrem Partner zum Verhängnis wird)

Fem|to... ‹skand.› (ein Billiardstel einer Einheit, z. B. Femtofarad = 10^{-15} Farad; *Zeichen* f)

Fench, Fen|nich, der; -[e]s, -e ‹lat.› (Hirseart); **Fen|chel,** der; -s (eine Heil- und Gemüsepflanze); **Fen|chel‿ge|mü|se, ...öl, ...tee**

Fen|dant [fã'dã:], der; -s ‹franz.› (Weißwein aus dem Wallis)

Fen|der, der; -s, - ‹engl.› (Stoßschutz an Schiffen [aus Tauwerk, Reifen o. Ä.])

Fe|nek *vgl.* Fennek

Fenn, das; -[e]s, -e (*nordd. für* Sumpf-, Moorland)

Fen|nek, der; -s, *Plur.* -s *u.* -e ‹arab.› (Wüstenfuchs)

Fen|nich *vgl.* Fench

Fen|no|sar|ma|tia ‹lat.› (*Geol.* europäischer Urkontinent); **fen|no|sar|ma|tisch; Fen|no|skan|dia** (ein Teil von Fennosarmatia); **fen|no|skan|disch**

Fen|rir (Untier der nord. Mythol.); **Fen|ris|wolf,** der; -[e]s (*svw.* Fenrir)

Fens|ter, das; -s, -; **Fens|ter‿bank** (*Plur.* ...bänke), **...brett, ...brief|um|schlag, ...flü|gel, ...glas** (*Plur.* ...gläser), **...griff, ...kreuz, ...la|den** (*Plur.* ...läden, *selten* ...laden), **...lai|bung, ...le|der; fens|terln** (*südd., österr. für* die Geliebte nachts [am od. durchs Fenster] besuchen); ich fensterle, du fensterlst, er fensterlt, hat gefensterlt; **fens|ter|los;**

Fens|ter_ni|sche, ...öff|nung, ...platz, ...put|zer, ...rah|men, ...re|de (großspurige Ansprache, Propagandarede), **...ro|se** (rundes [gotischen] Kirchenfenster), **...schei|be, ...schnal|le** (*österr. für* Fenstergriff), **...sims, ...stock** (*Plur.* ...stöcke); **...fenst|rig** (z. B. zweifenstrig)

Fenz, die; -, -en ‹engl.› (Einfried[ig]ung in Nordamerika)

Fe|o|dor (m. Vorn.); **Fe|o|do|ra** (w. Vorn.)

Fe|ra|li|en [...i̯ən] *Plur.* ‹lat.› (altröm. jährliches Totenfest)

Fer|di|nand (m. Vorn.); **Fer|di|nan|de** (w. Vorn.); **Ferdl** (m. Vorn.)

Fe|renc ['fɛrɛnt͡s] (m. Vorn.)

Fer|ge, der; -n, -n; ↑R 126 (*veraltet für* Fährmann)

ferg|gen (*schweiz. für* abfertigen, fortschaffen); **Ferg|ger** (*schweiz. für* Spediteur)

Fe|ri|al... ‹lat.› (*österr. neben* Ferien..., z. B. Ferialarbeit, Ferialpraxis, Ferialtag); **Fe|ri|en** [...i̯ən] *Plur.* ‹lat.› (zusammenhängende Freizeiten [im Schulleben]; Urlaub); die großen Ferien; **Fe|ri|en_ar|beit, ...be|ginn, ...dorf, ...en|de, ...häus|chen, ...heim, ...job, ...kind, ...kurs, ...la|ger, ...ort** (der; -[e]s, -e), **...pa|ra|dies, ...park, ...rei|se, ...son|der|zug, ...tag, ...woh|nung, ...zeit**

Fer|kel, das; -s, -; **Fer|ke|lei; fer|keln; Fer|kel|zucht**

Fer|man, der; -s, -e ‹pers.› (*früher* in islam. Ländern Erlass des Landesherrn)

Fer|ma|te, die; -, -n ‹ital.› (*Musik* Haltezeichen; *Zeichen* 𝄐)

Fer|ment, das; -s, -e ‹lat.› (*veraltend für* Enzym); **Fer|men|ta|ti|on,** die; -, -en (Gärung); **fer|men|ta|tiv** (durch Ferment hervorgerufen); **Fer|ment|bil|dung; fer|men|tie|ren** (durch Fermentation veredeln)

Fer|mi|um, das; -s ‹nach dem ital. Physiker Fermi› (chem. Element, ein Transuran; *Zeichen* Fm)

fern; ferne Länder; (↑R 39:) fern liegen (*auch für* nicht, kaum in Betracht kommen); fern stehen (*auch für* keine innere Beziehung haben); ferner liegen, stehen; fern liegend; wir wollten uns von allem fern halten, so fern wie möglich halten; *vgl.* fernbleiben, fernsehen usw.; *Präp. mit Dat.* fern dem Heimathaus; *vgl.* ferne. **I.** *Kleinschreibung* (↑R 47): von nah und fern; von fern, von fern her, *vgl. aber* fernher. **II.** *Großschreibung:* **a)** (↑R 108:) der Ferne Osten (*svw.* Ostasien); **b)** (↑R 47:) das Ferne suchen; **fern|ab** *(geh.)*

Fer|nam|buk|holz *vgl.* Pernambukholz

Fern_amt, ...auf|nah|me, ...bahn, ...be|ben, ...be|die|nung; fern|be|heizt; -e Wohnung; **fern|blei|ben** (↑R 37); er bleibt [dem Unterricht] fern, ist ferngeblieben; *vgl. auch* fern; **fer|ne** *(geh.);* von - [her]; **Fer|ne,** die; -, -n; **fer|ner;** er rangiert unter „ferner liefen"; *aber* des Ferner[e]n darlegen (*Amtsspr.;* ↑R 47)

Fer|ner, der; -s, - (*westösterr., bayr. für* Gletscher); *vgl.* Firn

fer|ner|hin [*auch* 'fɛrnər'hin]; **Fern|fah|rer; fern|ge|lenkt; Fern|ge|spräch; fern|ge|steu|ert; Fern|glas** *Plur.* ...gläser; **fern hal|ten** *vgl.* fern; **Fern|hei|zung; fern|her** (*geh. für* aus der Ferne), *aber* von fern her; **fern|hin** *(geh.);* **fern|ko|pie|ren** (über das Fernsprechnetz originalgetreu übertragen); **Fern|ko|pie|rer** (Gerät zum Fernkopieren); **Fern_kurs, ...kur|sus, ...las|ter** (der; *ugs. für* Fernlastzug), **...last|zug, ...lei|he, ...leih|ver|kehr** *(Buchw.),* **...lei|tung; fern|len|ken;** *vgl.* fernbleiben; **Fern_len|kung, ...licht** (*Plur.* ...lichter); **fern lie|gen, fern lie|gend** *vgl.* fern; **Fern|mel|de_amt, ...dienst, ...ge|bühr, ...tech|nik, ...turm, ...we|sen** (das; -s); **fern|münd|lich** (*für* telefonisch); **Fern|ost;** in -; **fern|öst|lich; Fern_pend|ler, ...rohr, ...ruf, ...schrei|ben, ...schrei|ber; Fern|schreib|netz; fern|schrift|lich; Fern|seh_an|sa|ger, ...an|sa|ge|rin, ...an|ten|ne, ...ap|pa|rat, ...bild, ...emp|fang** *(Plur. selten),* **...emp|fän|ger; fern|se|hen; Fern|se|hen,** das; -s; **Fern|se|her** (Fernsehgerät; Fernsehteilnehmer); **Fern|seh_film, ...ge|bühr, ...ge|rät, ...in|ter|view, ...ka|me|ra, ...kom|men|ta|tor, ...leuch|te; fern|seh|mü|de; Fern|seh_pro|gramm, ...re|por|ta|ge, ...re|por|ter, ...schirm, ...sen|der, ...sen|dung, ...se|rie, ...spiel, ...stu|dio, ...teil|neh|mer, ...tru|he, ...turm, ...über|tra|gung** (↑R 132), **...zeit|schrift, ...zu|schau|er; Fern|sicht; fern|sich|tig; Fern|sich|tig|keit,** die; -; **Fern|sprech_amt, ...an|schluss, ...ap|pa|rat, ...auf|trags|dienst; Fern|spre|cher; Fern|sprech_ge|bühr, ...ge|heim|nis** (das; -ses), **...teil|neh|mer, ...ver|zeich|nis, ...zel|le; Fern|spruch; fern ste|hen** *vgl.* fern; **fern|steu|ern;** *vgl.* fernbleiben; **Fern_steu|e|rung, ...stra|ße, ...stu|dent, ...stu|di|um, ...sucht** (die; -); **fern|trau|en;** *nur im Inf. u. Part. II gebr.;* **Fern|trau|ung; Fern_un|ter|richt, ...ver|kehr** (der; -[e]s); **Fern|ver|kehrs|stra|ße; Fern_wär|me, ...weh** (das; -s), **...ziel**

Fer|ra|ra (ital. Stadt)

Fer|ra|ri ® (ital. Automarke)

Fer|rit [*auch* ...'rit], der; -s, -e ‹lat.› (reine Eisenkristalle; *Nachrichtentechnik* ein magnetischer Werkstoff); **Fer|rit|an|ten|ne**

Fer|ro (kleinste der Kanarischen Inseln); *vgl.* Hierro; **Fer|rum,** das; -s ‹lat.› (*lat. Bez. für* Eisen, chem. Element; *Zeichen* Fe)

Fer|se, die; -, -n (*vgl.* [1]Hacke); *vgl. aber* Färse; **Fer|sen|geld;** *nur noch in* - geben (*scherzh. für* fliehen)

fer|tig; *in Verbindung mit Verben immer getrennt* (↑R 39): fertig sein, werden; fertig bringen (vollbringen); ich bringe es fertig, habe es fertig gebracht, habe es fertig zu bringen; fertig bekommen (*ugs. für* fertig bringen); fertig kochen; fertig machen (*ugs. auch für* zermürben; völlig besiegen); fertig stellen (die Herstellung abschließen); **Fer|tig_bau** (*Plur.* ...bauten), **...bau|wei|se; fer|tig be|kom|men, brin|gen** *vgl.* fertig; **fer|ti|gen; Fer|tig_er|zeug|nis, ...ge|richt, ...haus; Fer|tig|keit; Fer|tig|klei|dung** (*für* Konfektion); **fer|tig ko|chen, ma|chen, stel|len** *vgl.* fertig; **Fer|tig_stel|lung, ...teil** (das); **Fer|ti|gung; Fer|ti|gungs_bri|ga|de** *(ehem. in der DDR),* **...kos|ten** *(Plur.),* **...me|tho|de, ...pro|zess, ...stra|ße, ...tech|nik, ...ver|fah|ren; Fer|tig|wa|re**

fer|til ‹lat.› (*Biol., Med.* fruchtbar); **Fer|ti|li|tät,** die; - (Fruchtbarkeit)

fes, [1]Fes, das; -, - (Tonbezeichnung)

[2]Fes, der; -[es], -[e] ‹türk.› (rote Filzkappe)

[3]Fes [fɛ:s] (Stadt in Marokko)

fesch ‹engl.› (*ugs. für* flott, schneidig); **Fe|schak,** der; -s, -s (*österr. ugs. für* fescher Kerl)

[1]Fes|sel, die; -, -n (Teil des Beines)

[2]Fes|sel, die; -, -n (Band, Kette); **Fes|sel|bal|lon; fes|sel|frei**

Fes|sel|ge|lenk

fes|sel|los; fes|seln; ich fessele *u.* fessle (↑R 16); **fes|selnd; Fes|se|lung, Fess|lung**

fest; feste Kosten; fester Wohnsitz; festes Gehalt. **I.** *Schreibung in Verbindung mit den Partizipien*

(↑R 40): die fest geschnürte Schlinge; fester geschnürt; fest angestellt, besoldet, gefügt, umrissen, verwurzelt; fest kochende Kartoffeln; *aber* zum festgesetzten Zeitpunkt. **II.** *Schreibung in Verbindung mit Verben* (↑R 39): fest stehen (festen Stand haben); *aber* feststehen (sicher sein, entschieden sein); eine Schleife [ganz] fest binden; *aber* festbinden (anbinden); die Kuh ist festgebunden; *vgl.* festbeißen, festfahren, festlegen, festnehmen, festschreiben, feststehen usw.

Fest, das; -[e]s, -e; **Fest|akt**

fest an|ge|stellt *vgl.* fest; **Fest|an|ge|stell|te**, der *u.* die; -n, -n (↑R 5 ff.)

Fest_an|spra|che, ...auf|füh|rung

fest|ba|cken (ankleben); der Schnee backt fest, hat festgebackt, festzubacken; *vgl.* fest, II

Fest|ban|kett

fest|bei|ßen, sich (*auch für* sich intensiv u. ausdauernd mit etwas beschäftigen); der Hund hat sich festgebissen; wir haben uns an dem Problem festgebissen; *vgl.* fest, II

Fest_bei|trag, ...be|leuch|tung

fest be|sol|det *vgl.* fest; **Fest|be|sol|de|te**, der *u.* die; -n, -n (↑R 5 ff.); **fest|bin|den** (anbinden); die Kuh ist festgebunden; *vgl.* fest, II; **fest|blei|ben** (nicht nachgeben); er ist in seinem Entschluss festgeblieben; *vgl.* fest, II; **Fest|brenn|stoff**

Fes|te, die; -, -n (*veraltet für* Festung; *geh. für* Himmel); *vgl. auch* Veste

fes|ten (*schweiz., sonst selten für* ein Fest feiern); **Fes|tes|freu|de** *(geh.)*; **Fest|es|sen; Fes|tes|stim|mung** *(geh.)*

fest|fah|ren; sich -; **fest|fres|sen**, sich; der Kolben hat sich festgefressen; *vgl.* fest, II

Fest|freu|de

fest ge|fügt, ge|schnürt *vgl.* fest

Fest_ge|wand, ...got|tes|dienst

fest|ha|ken; sich -

Fest|hal|le

fest|hal|ten; die Aussage wurde [schriftlich] festgehalten; man hat sie zwei Stunden auf der Wache festgehalten, *aber* das Kind [ganz] fest halten; *vgl.* fest, II; **fest|hef|ten;** *vgl.* fest, II; **fes|ti|gen; Fes|ti|ger** (*kurz für* Haarfestiger); **Fes|tig|keit**, die; -; **Fes|tig|keits|leh|re**, die; - *(Technik)*; **Fes|ti|gung**, die; -

Fes|ti|val ['fɛstiv(ə)l, *auch* 'fɛsti-val], das; -s, -s ‹engl.› (Musikfest, Festspiel); **Fes|ti|vi|tät** [...v...], die; -, -en ‹lat.› (*schweiz., sonst nur noch scherzh. für* Festlichkeit)

fest|klam|mern; sich -; *vgl.* fest, II; **fest|kle|ben;** *vgl.* fest, II; **fest|klop|fen** (*ugs. für* festlegen, besiegeln); *vgl.* fest, II; **fest|kno|ten;** *vgl.* fest, II; **fest ko|chend** *vgl.* fest, I

Fest|ko|mi|tee

Fest|kör|per (*Physik* bes. die Kristalle); **Fest|kör|per|phy|sik; Fest|land** *Plur.* ...länder; **fest|län|disch; Fest|land[s]_block** (*Plur.* ...blöcke), **...so|ckel; fest|lau|fen; fest|le|gen** (*auch für* anordnen); sie hat die Hausordnung festgelegt; sich - (sich binden); sie hat sich mit dieser Äußerung festgelegt; *vgl.* fest, II; **Fest|le|gung**

fest|lich; Fest|lich|keit

fest|lie|gen; auf einer Sandbank -; *vgl.* fest, II; **Fest|lohn** (*svw.* Mindestlohn); **Fest|ma|che|bo|je; fest|ma|chen** (*auch für* vereinbaren); *vgl.* fest, II

Fest|mahl

Fest|me|ter (*alte Maßeinheit für* 1 m^3 fester Holzmasse, im Gegensatz zu Raummeter; *Abk.* Fm, fm); **fest|na|geln** (*ugs. auch für* jmdn. auf etwas festlegen); ich nag[e]le fest (↑R 16); ich habe ihn festgenagelt; *vgl.* fest, II; **fest|nä|hen;** *vgl.* fest, II; **Fest|nah|me**, die; -, -n; **fest|neh|men** (verhaften); *vgl.* fest, II; **Fest|of|fer|te** (*Kaufmannsspr.* festes Angebot)

Fes|ton [fɛs'tɔŋ, *auch* ...'tõ:], das; -s, -s ‹franz.› (Blumengewinde, meist als Ornament; Stickerei); **fes|to|nie|ren** [fɛstɔ'ni:...] (mit Festons versehen; Stoffkanten mit Knopflochstich ausarbeiten); **Fes|ton|stich**

Fest_ord|ner, ...pla|ket|te

Fest|plat|te *(EDV)*

Fest|platz

Fest|preis; *vgl.* ²Preis

Fest_pro|gramm, ...re|de, ...red|ner, ...red|ne|rin

fest|ren|nen, sich; *vgl.* festbeißen, sich

Fest|saal

fest|sau|gen, sich; **fest|schnal|len;** *vgl.* fest, II; sich -; **fest|schrei|ben** (durch einen Vertrag o. Ä. vorläufig festlegen); *vgl.* fest, II; **Fest|schrei|bung**

Fest|schrift

fest|set|zen (bestimmen, anordnen; gefangen setzen); er wurde nach dieser Straftat festgesetzt; *vgl.* fest, II; **Fest|set|zung; fest|sit|zen** (*ugs. für* nicht weiterkommen); *vgl.* fest, II

Fest|spiel; Fest|spiel_haus, ...stadt

fest|ste|hen (festgelegt, sicher, gewiss sein); fest steht, dass ... (↑R 38); es hat festgestanden, dass ...; *vgl.* fest, II; **fest|ste|hend** (festgelegt, sicher, gewiss); **fest|stell|bar; Fest|stell|brem|se; fest|stel|len** (ermitteln, [be]merken, nachdrücklich aussprechen); *vgl.* fest, II; **Fest|stell_he|bel, ...tas|te; Fest|stel|lung**

Fest|stie|ge (*österr. für* Prunktreppe); **Fest|stim|mung; Fest|tag;** des Festtags, *aber* (↑R 46): festtags, sonn- und festtags; **fest|täg|lich; fest|tags;** *vgl.* Festtag; **Fest|tags_klei|dung, ...stim|mung**

fest|tre|ten *vgl.* fest, II; **fest um|ris|sen** *vgl.* fest, I

Fest|um|zug

Fes|tung; Fes|tungs_ge|län|de, ...gra|ben, ...wall

Fest_ver|an|stal|tung, ...ver|samm|lung

fest ver|wur|zelt *vgl.* fest, I; **fest|ver|zins|lich;** festverzinsliche Wertpapiere

Fest_vor|stel|lung, ...vor|trag

fest|wach|sen; *vgl.* fest, II

Fest_wie|se, ...wo|che, ...zelt

fest|zie|hen; *vgl.* fest, II

Fest|zug

fe|tal, *auch* fö|tal ‹lat.› (*Med.* zum Fetus gehörend, auf ihn bezüglich)

Fe|te [*auch* 'fɛ:tə], die; -, -n ‹franz.› (*ugs. für* Fest)

Fe|tisch, der; -[e]s, -e ‹franz.› (magischer Gegenstand; Götzenbild); **fe|ti|schi|sie|ren** (zum Fetisch erheben); **Fe|ti|schis|mus**, der; - (Fetischverehrung; krankhaftes Übertragen des Geschlechtstriebes auf Gegenstände); **Fe|ti|schist**, der; -en, -en (↑R 126); **Fe|ti|schis|tin; fe|ti|schis|tisch**

fett; fetter Boden; ein Schwein fett füttern; *Schreibung in Verbindung mit dem Partizip II:* fett gedruckt, fetter, am fettesten gedruckt; **Fett**, das; -[e]s, -e; **Fett|an|satz; fett|arm; Fett_au|ge, ...bauch, ...creme, ...de|pot** *(Med.)*; **Fet|te**, die; - (*geh. für* Fettheit); **fet|ten; fett|fein** *(Druckw.)*; **Fett|fleck** *od.* **...fle|cken; fett|frei; fett füt|tern, fett ge|druckt** *vgl.* fett; **Fett_ge|halt** (der), **...ge|we|be** *(Med.)*; **fett_glän|zend, ...hal|tig; Fett|heit**, die; -; **Fett|hen|ne** (Zierpflanze); **fet|tig; Fet|tig|keit**, die; - (das Fettigsein); **Fett|koh|le** (Steinkohlenart); **Fett|le|be**, die; - (*ugs. für* reichhaltige, üppige Mahlzeit; Wohlleben); - machen (üppig leben); **fett|lei-**

big; Fettleibigkeit, die; -; Fettnäpfchen; bei jmdm. ins - treten (jmds. Unwillen erregen); Fettpolster, ...sack (*derb für* fetter Mensch), ...säule (*Chemie*), ...schicht, ...stift (der), ...sucht (die; -); fetttriefend (↑R 136); Fetttropfen (↑R 136); Fetttusche (↑R 136); Fettwanst (*derb für* fetter Mensch)

Fe|tus, *auch* Fö|tus, der; *Gen.* - *u.* -ses, *Plur.* -se *u.* ...ten ‹lat.› (*Med.* Leibesfrucht vom dritten Monat an)

Fetz|chen; fet|zeln (*landsch. für* in Fetzen zerreißen); ich ...[e]le (↑R 16); **fet|zen;** du fetzt; **Fet|zen**, der; -s, -; **fet|zig** (*ugs. für* toll, mitreißend); **Fetz|lein**

feucht; feucht werden; **Feucht|bi|o|top; Feuch|te**, die; -; **feuch|ten** (*geh.*); **feucht|fröh|lich** (fröhlich beim Zechen); **feucht|heiß; Feuch|tig|keit**, die; -; **Feuch|tig|keits_ge|halt** (der; -[e]s), **...grad, ...mes|ser** (der); **feucht|kalt; Feucht|raum|ar|ma|tur** (*Technik*)

Feucht|wan|ger, Lion (dt. Schriftsteller)

feucht|warm

feu|dal ‹germ.-mlat.› (das Lehnswesen betreffend; Lehns...; *ugs. für* vornehm, großartig; *abwertend für* reaktionär); **Feu|dal_ge|sell|schaft, ...herr|schaft; Feu|da|lis|mus**, der; - (auf dem Lehnswesen beruhende, den Adel privilegierende Gesellschafts- u. Wirtschaftsordnung [im MA.]); **feu|da|lis|tisch; Feu|da|li|tät**, die; - (Lehnsverhältnis im MA.; Vornehmheit); **Feu|dal_staat, ...sys|tem** (das; -s)

Feu|del, der; -s, - (*nordd. für* Scheuerlappen); **feu|deln**

Feu|er, das; -s, -; offenes -; ein Feuer speiender Vulkan; **Feu|er_alarm** (↑R 132), **...an|zün|der, ...ball, ...be|fehl** (*Milit.*), **...be|reit|schaft** (*Milit.*); **feu|er|be|stän|dig; Feu|er_be|stat|tung, ...boh|ne, ...dorn** (Zierstrauch), **...ei|fer; feu|er|fest; Feu|er_fes|tig|keit** (die; -), **...fres|ser, ...ge|fahr** (die; -); **feu|er|ge|fähr|lich; Feu|er_ge|fähr|lich|keit** (die; -), **...ge|fecht, ...ha|ken, ...hal|le** (*österr. neben* Krematorium), **...herd, ...holz** (das; -es); **Feu|er|land** (Südspitze von Südamerika); **Feu|er|län|der**, der; **Feu|er_lei|ter** (die), **...li|lie, ...loch, ...lö|scher; Feu|er|lösch_ge|rät, ...teich, ...zug; Feu|er_mau|er, ...mel|der; feu|ern;** ich ...[e]re (↑R 16); **Feu|er_pau|se** (*Milit.*), **...po|li|zei; feu|er|po|li|zei|lich; Feu|er|pro|be; feu|er|rot; Feu|er|sa|la|man|der; Feu|ers|brunst; Feu|er_scha|den, ...schein, ...schiff, ...schlu|cker, ...schutz; Feu|ers|ge|fahr; feu|er|si|cher; Feu|ers|not**, die; - (*veraltet*); **Feu|er spei|end** *vgl.* Feuer; **Feu|er_sprit|ze, ...stät|te, ...stein, ...stel|le, ...stoß** (*bes. Milit.*), **...stuhl** (*ugs. für* Motorrad), **...tau|fe, ...tod** (*geh.*), **...über|fall** (↑R 132); **Feu|e|rung; Feu|e|rungs|an|la|ge; Feu|er|ver|si|che|rung; feu|er|ver|zinkt; Feu|er_wa|che, ...waf|fe, ...was|ser** (das; -s; *ugs. für* Branntwein), **...wehr; Feu|er|wehr_au|to, ...haus, ...mann** (*Plur.* ...männer *u.* ...leute), **...übung** (↑R 132); **Feu|er|werk; feu|er|wer|ken;** ich feuerwerke; gefeuerwerkt; zu -; **Feu|er|wer|ker; Feu|er|werks|kör|per; Feu|er|zan|ge; Feu|er|zan|gen|bow|le; Feu|er_zei|chen, ...zeug**

Feuil|la|ge [fœ'ja:ʒə], die; -, -n ‹franz.› (geschnitztes, gemaltes usw. Laubwerk); **Feuil|le|ton** [fœjə'tõ:, *auch* 'fœ...], das; -s, -s (literarischer, kultureller oder unterhaltender Teil einer Zeitung; im Plauderton geschriebener Aufsatz); **Feuil|le|to|nist**, der; -en, -en (↑R 126); **feuil|le|to|nis|tisch; Feuil|le|ton_re|dak|teur, ...stil** (der; -[e]s)

feu|rig; -e Kohlen auf jmds. Haupt sammeln (ihn beschämen); **feu|rio!** (alter Feuerruf)

Fex, der; *Gen.* -es, *seltener* -en, *Plur.* -e, *seltener* -en; ↑R 126 (*südd., österr. für* Narr; jmd., der in etwas vernarrt ist)

[1]**Fez** [fe:(t)s] *vgl.* [2]Fes

[2]**Fez**, der; -es ‹franz.› (*ugs. für* Spaß, Vergnügen)

ff = sehr fein; *vgl.* Effeff

ff = fortissimo

ff. = folgende [Seiten]

FF *vgl.* Franc

FGB = Familiengesetzbuch

FH = Fachhochschule

FHD = Frauenhilfsdienst[leistende] (*früher in der Schweiz*)

Fi|a|ker, der; -s, - ‹franz.› (*österr. für* Pferdedroschke; Kutscher)

Fi|a|le, die; -, -n ‹ital.› ([gotisches] Spitztürmchen)

Fi|as|ko, das; -s, -s ‹ital.› (Misserfolg; Zusammenbruch)

fi|at! ‹lat., „es geschehe!"›

Fi|at ® (Kraftfahrzeuge)

[1]**Fi|bel**, die; -, -n ‹griech.› (Abc-Buch; Elementarlehrbuch)

[2]**Fi|bel**, die; -, -n ‹lat.› (frühgeschichtl. Spange oder Nadel)

Fi|ber, die; -, -n ‹lat.› ([Muskel- od. Pflanzen]faser); *vgl. aber* Fieber; **Fib|ril|le** (↑R 130), die; -, -n (*Med.* Einzelfaser des Muskel- u. Nervengewebes); **Fib|rin**, das; -s (Eiweißstoff des Blutes); **Fib|ro|in**, das; -s (Eiweißstoff der Naturseide); **Fib|rom**, das; -s, -e (*Med.* Bindegewebsgeschwulst); **fib|rös** (aus Bindegewebe bestehend)

Fi|bu|la, die; -, *Plur.* Fibuln *u.* (*Med.*) Fibulae [...lɛ] ‹lat.› ([2]Fibel; *Med.* Wadenbein)

[1]**Fiche** [fi:ʃ], die; -, -s ‹franz.› (Spielmarke); [2]**Fi|che** ['fiʃ(ə)], die; -, -n (*schweiz. für* Karteikarte); [3]**Fiche** [fi:ʃ], das *od.* der; -s, -s (Filmkarte mit Mikrokopien)

[1]**Fich|te** (dt. Philosoph)

[2]**Fich|te**, die; -, -n (ein Nadelbaum); **Fich|tel|ge|bir|ge**, das; -s; **fich|ten** (aus Fichtenholz); **Fich|ten_hain, ...holz, ...na|del**

Fi|chu [fi'ʃy:], das; -s, -s ‹franz.› (Schultertuch)

Fick, der; -s, -s (*derb für* Koitus); **fi|cken** (*derb für* koitieren); **fi|cke|rig** (*landsch. für* nervös, unruhig; *derb für* geil); **Fick|fack**, der; -[e]s, -e (*landsch. für* Ausflucht, Vorwand); **fick|fa|cken** (*landsch. für* Ausflüchte suchen); **Fick|fa|cker** (*landsch. für* unzuverlässiger Mensch); **Fick|fa|cke|rei; Fick|müh|le** (*landsch. für* Zwickmühle)

Fi|cus, der; -, ...ci [...tsi] ‹lat.› (ein [Zier]baum)

Fi|de|i|kom|miss [fidei..., *auch* 'fi...], das; -es, -e ‹lat.› (*Rechtsspr.* unveräußerliches u. unteilbares Familienvermögen)

fi|del ‹lat.› (*ugs. für* lustig, heiter)

Fi|del, die; -, -n (der Geige ähnliches Streichinstrument [des Mittelalters]); *vgl.* Fiedel

Fi|del Cast|ro (↑R 130) *vgl.* Castro

Fi|di|bus, der; *Gen.* - *u.* -ses, *Plur.* - *u.* -se (gefalteter Papierstreifen als [Pfeifen]anzünder)

Fid|schi (↑R 130; Inselstaat im Südwestpazifik); **Fid|schi|a|ner; fid|schi|a|nisch; Fid|schi|in|seln** *Plur.*

Fi|duz, das; -es (*ugs. für* Mut); *nur noch in* kein - zu etwas haben

Fie|ber, das; -s, - *Plur. selten* ‹lat.›; *vgl. aber* Fiber; **Fie|ber|an|fall; fie|ber|frei; Fie|ber|frost; fie|ber|haft; Fie|ber|hit|ze; fie|be|rig** *vgl.* fiebrig; **fie|ber|krank; Fie|ber_kur|ve, ...mes|ser** (der; *ugs. für* Fieberthermometer); **fie|bern;** ich ...ere (↑R 16); **Fie|ber_phan|ta|sie** (*meist Plur.*), **...ta|bel|le, ...ther|mo|me|ter, ...traum; fieb|rig**

Fie|del, die; -, -n (*veraltend für* Geige); *vgl.* Fidel; **fie|deln;** ich ...[e]le (↑R 16)
Fie|der, die; -, -n (*veraltet für* kleine Feder); **Fie|der|blatt** (*Bot.* gefiedertes Blatt); **fie|de|rig; fieder|tei|lig; Fie|de|rung**
Fied|ler
fie|pen (*Jägerspr.* [von Rehkitz u. Rehgeiß], *auch* allg. einen leisen, hohen Ton von sich geben)
Fi|e|rant [fiə..., *auch* fie...], der; -en, -en (↑R 126) ‹ital.› (*österr. für* Markthändler)
fie|ren (*Seemannsspr.* [Tau] ablaufen lassen, herablassen)
fies (*ugs. für* ekelhaft, widerwärtig); fieses Gefühl
Fi|es|co, *bei Schiller* **Fi|es|ko** (genues. Verschwörer)
Fies|ling (*ugs. für* widerwärtiger Mensch)
Fi|es|ta, die; -, -s ‹span.› ([span.] Volksfest)
FIFA, Fi|fa, die; - ‹franz.› (*Kurzw. für* Fédération Internationale de Football Association [federaˌsi̯õ: ɛ̃tɛrnasi̯oˌnal də fut'bo:l asɔsiaˌsi̯õ:]; Internationaler Fußballverband)
fif|ty-fif|ty ['fifti'fifti] ‹engl.› (*ugs. für* halbpart)
Fi|ga|ro, der; -s, -s (Lustspiel- u. Opernfigur; *auch* scherzh. für Friseur)
Fight [fait], der; -s, -s ‹engl.› (*Boxen* [draufgängerisch geführter Nah]kampf); **figh|ten** ['faitən] *(Boxen);* **Figh|ter** ['faitə(r)], der; -s, - (*Boxen* Kämpfer)
Figl (österr. Politiker)
Fi|gur, die; -, -en; **Fi|gu|ra;** *in* wie - zeigt (wie klar vor Augen liegt); **fi|gu|ral** (mit Figuren versehen); **Fi|gu|ral|mu|sik** (in der Kirchenmusik des MA.); **Fi|gu|rant,** der; -en, -en; ↑R 126 (*veraltet für* Statist); **Fi|gu|ran|tin; Fi|gu|ra|ti|on,** die; -, -en *u.* Fi|gu|rie|rung (*Musik* Ausschmückung einer Figur od. Melodie); **fi|gu|ra|tiv** (bildlich [darstellend]); **Fi|gür|chen; fi|gu|rie|ren** (in Erscheinung treten, auftreten; *Musik* eine Figur od. Melodie ausschmücken); **fi|gu|riert** (gemustert; *Musik* ausgeschmückt); -es Gewebe; **Fi|gu|rie|rung** *vgl.* Figuration; **...fi|gu|rig** (z. B. kleinfigurig); **Fi|gu|ri|ne,** die; -, -n ‹franz.› (Figürchen; Nebenfigur in Landschaftsgemälden; Kostümzeichnung [für Bühne od. Mode]); **Fi|gür|lein; fi|gür|lich**
Fik|ti|on, die; -, -en ‹lat.› (Erdachtes; falsche Annahme); **fik|ti|o|nal** (auf einer Fiktion beruhend); **fik|tiv** (nur angenommen, erdacht)
Fi|la|ment, das; -s, -e ‹lat.› (*Bot.* Staubfaden der Blüte)
File [fail], das; -s, -s ‹engl.› (*EDV* bestimmte Art von Datei)
Fi|let [fi'le:], das; -s, -s ‹franz.› (Netzstoff; Lenden-, Rückenstück); **Fi|let‿ar|beit, ...de|cke, ...hand|schuh; fi|le|tie|ren** [file'ti:...] (Filets herausschneiden); **Fi|le|tier|ma|schi|ne; Fi|let‿na|del** [fi'le:...], **...spit|ze, ...steak**
Fi|lia hos|pi|ta|lis, die; - -, ...ae ...les ['filiɛ ...le:s] ‹lat.› (*Studentenspr.* Tochter der Wirtsleute); **Fi|li|a|le,** die; -, -n (Zweiggeschäft, -stelle); **Fi|li|a|list,** der; -en, -en (↑R 126; Filialleiter); **Fi|li|al‿kir|che** (Tochterkirche), **...lei|ter** (der); **Fi|li|a|ti|on,** die; -, -en (rechtliche Abstammung; Gliederung des Staatshaushaltsplanes)
Fi|li|bus|ter *vgl.* Flibustier
fi|lie|ren ‹franz.› (Netzwerk knüpfen; *auch für* filetieren); **fi|liert** (netzartig); **Fi|lig|ran** (↑R 130), das; -s, -e ‹ital.› (Goldschmiedearbeit aus feinem Drahtgeflecht); **Fi|lig|ran‿ar|beit, ...glas, ...schmuck**
Fi|li|pi|na, die; -, -s ‹span.› (*weibl. Form zu* Filipino); **Fi|li|pi|no,** der; -s, -s (Bewohner der Philippinen)
Fi|li|us, der; -, ...usse ‹lat.› (*scherzh. für* Sohn)
Fil|lér ['filər, *ung.* 'file:r], der; -[s], - (ung. Münze; 100 Fillér = 1 Forint)
Film, der; -[e]s, -e ‹engl.›; **Film‿ama|teur** (↑R 132), **...ar|chiv, ...ate|li|er** (↑R 132), **...au|tor, ...ball, ...bran|che, ...di|va; Fil|me‿ma|cher, ...ma|che|rin; fil|men; Film‿fan, ...fes|ti|val, ...fest|spie|le** *(Plur.),* **...ge|sell|schaft, ...in|dust|rie; fil|misch; Film‿ka|me|ra, ...kom|po|nist, ...ko|pie; Fil|mo|thek** (↑R 33), die; -, -en ‹engl.; griech.› (*svw.* Kinemathek); **Film‿pla|kat, ...pro|du|zent, ...schau|spie|ler, ...schau|spie|le|rin, ...stadt, ...star** (*Plur.* ...stars), **...stu|dio, ...sze|ne, ...ver|leih, ...vor|füh|rer**
Fi|lou [fi'lu:], der; -s, -s ‹franz.› (*scherzh. für* Betrüger, Spitzbube; Schlaukopf)
Fils, der; -, - ‹arab.› (irak. Münze; 1 000 Fils = 1 Dinar)
Fil|ter, der, *Technik meist* das; -s, - ‹mlat.›; **fil|ter|fein;** - gemahlener Kaffee; **fil|tern;** ich ...ere (↑R 16); **Fil|ter|pa|pier,** Filt|rier|pa|pier (↑R 130); **Fil|ter|tü|te ®; Fil|te|rung; Fil|ter|zi|ga|ret|te; Filt|rat** (↑R 130), das; -[e]s, -e (durch Filtration geklärte Flüssigkeit); **Filt|ra|ti|on,** die; -, -en (Filterung); **filt|rie|ren; Filt|rier|pa|pier** *vgl.* Filterpapier
Filz, der; -es, -e (*ugs. auch für* Geizhals; *österr. auch für* unausgeschmolzenes Fett); **Filz|de|cke; fil|zen** (*ugs. auch für* nach [verbotenen] Gegenständen durchsuchen; schlafen); du filzt; **Filz|hut,** der; **fil|zig; Filz|laus; Fil|zo|kra|tie,** die; -, ...ien ‹dt.; griech.› („verfilzte" Machtverhältnisse); **Filz‿pan|tof|fel, ...schrei|ber, ...stift** (der)
[1]**Fim|mel** (Hanf); *vgl.* Femel
[2]**Fim|mel,** der; -s, - (*ugs. für* übertriebene Vorliebe für etwas; Tick, Spleen)
FINA, Fi|na, die; - ‹franz.› (*Kurzw. für* Fédération Internationale de Natation Amateur [federaˌsi̯õ: ɛ̃tɛrnasi̯oˌnal də nataˌsi̯õ: ama'tø:r]; Internationaler Amateur-Schwimmverband)
fi|nal ‹lat.› (den Schluss bildend; zweckbezeichnend); **Fi|nal,** der; -s, -s ‹franz.› (*schweiz. für* Finale *[Sport]*); **Fi|nal|ab|schluss** (*Wirtsch.* Endabschluss); **Fi|na|le,** das; -s, *Plur.* -, *im Sport auch* Finals ‹franz.› (Schlussteil; *Musik* Schlussstück, -satz; *Sport* Endrunde, Endspiel); **Fi|na|list,** der; -en, -en; ↑R 126 (Endrundenteilnehmer); **Fi|nal‿pro|dukt** (*regional für* End-, Fertigprodukt), **...satz** (*Sprachw.* Umstandssatz der Absicht, Zwecksatz)
Fi|nan|ci|er [finã'sie:] *vgl.* Financier; **Fi|nanz,** die; - ‹franz.› (Geldwesen; Gesamtheit der Geld- und Bankfachleute); *vgl.* Finanzen; **Fi|nanz‿ab|tei|lung, ...amt, ...aus|gleich, ...be|am|te, ...buch|hal|ter, ...buch|hal|tung; Fi|nan|zen** *Plur.* (Geldwesen; Staatsvermögen; Vermögenslage); **Fi|nan|zer** (*österr. ugs. für* Zollbeamter); **Fi|nanz‿ex|per|te, ...ge|ba|ren, ...ge|nie, ...ho|heit** (die; -); **fi|nan|zi|ell; Fi|nan|zi|er** [finan'tsie:], der; -s, -s (kapitalkräftiger Geldgeber); **fi|nan|zier|bar; fi|nan|zie|ren** (mit Geldmitteln ausstatten; geldlich ermöglichen); **Fi|nan|zie|rung; fi|nanz|kräf|tig; Fi|nanz‿kri|se, ...la|ge** (die; -), **...mi|nis|ter, ...plan** (*vgl.* [2]Plan); **fi|nanz‿po|li|tisch, ...schwach, ...stark; Fi|nanz‿ver|wal|tung, ...we|sen** (das; -s), **...wirt|schaft**
Fin|del|kind; fin|den; du fandst; du fändest; gefunden; find[e]!;

ein gefundenes Fressen für jmdn. sein (*ugs. für* jmdm. sehr gelegen kommen); **Fin|der; Fin|der|lohn,** der; -[e]s
Fin de Siè|cle [fɛ̃dˈsjɛkl], das; - - - (durch Verfallserscheinungen in Gesellschaft, Kunst u. Literatur geprägte Zeit des ausgehenden 19. Jh.s)
fin|dig; ein -er Kopf (einfallsreicher Mensch); **Fin|dig|keit,** die; -; **Find|ling; Find|lings|block** *Plur.* ...blöcke; **Fin|dung** *Plur. selten* (das [Heraus]finden)
Fines Herbes [finˈzɛrb] *Plur.* ⟨franz.⟩ (*Gastron.* fein gehackte Kräuter)
Fi|nes|se, die; -, -n ⟨franz.⟩ (Feinheit; Kniff)
Fin|ger, der; -s, -; der kleine -; jmdn. um den kleinen - wickeln *(ugs.);* etwas mit spitzen -n (vorsichtig) anfassen; lange, krumme - machen (*ugs. für* stehlen); **Fin|ger|ab|druck** *Plur.* ...drücke; **fin|ger|breit;** ein fingerbreiter Spalt, *aber* der Spalt ist keinen Finger breit, 3 Finger breit (*vgl. aber* Fingerbreit); **Fin|ger|breit,** der; -, -; einen, ein paar - größer; keinen - nachgeben; **fin|ger|dick;** *vgl.* fingerbreit; **Fin|ger|far|be** (für Kinder); **fin|ger|fer|tig; Fin|ger‿fer|tig|keit** (die; -), **...glied; Fin|ger|ha|keln,** das; -s (alpenländischer Wettkampf); **Fin|ger‿hand|schuh, ...hut** (der); **...fin|ge|rig,** ...fing|rig (z. B. vierfing[e]rig); **Fin|ger|kup|pe** (Fingerspitze); **fin|ger|lang;** *vgl.* fingerbreit; **Fin|ger|ling; fin|gern;** ich ...ere (↑R 16); **Fin|ger‿na|gel, ...ring, ...satz** (*Musik* Fingerverteilung beim Spielen eines Instruments), **...spiel, ...spit|ze; Fin|ger|spit|zen|ge|fühl,** das; -[e]s; **Fin|ger|übung** (↑R 132); **Fin|ger|zeig,** der; -[e]s, -e
fin|gie|ren ⟨lat.⟩ (erdichten; vortäuschen; unterstellen)
...fing|rig *vgl.* ...fingerig
Fi|nis, das; -, - ⟨lat., „Ende"⟩ (*veraltet für* Schlussvermerk in Druckwerken); **Fi|nish** [ˈfiniʃ], das; -s, -s ⟨engl.⟩ (letzter Schliff; Vollendung; *Sport* Endspurt, Endkampf)
Fi|nis|ter|re (nordwestspan. Kap)
fi|nit ⟨lat.⟩ (*Sprachw.* bestimmt, konjugiert); -e Form (Personalform, Form des Verbs, die im Ggs. zur infiniten Form [*vgl.* infinit] nach Person u. Zahl bestimmt ist, z. B. [er] „erwacht" [3. Pers. Sing.])
Fink, der; -en, -en; ↑R 126 (ein Singvogel)
Fin|ken, der; -s, - (*schweiz. mdal. für* warmer Hausschuh)
Fin|ken|schlag, der; -[e]s (das Zwitschern des Finken)
Fin|ken|wer|der (Elbinsel)
Fink|ler, der; -s, - (*veraltet für* Vogelfänger)
Finn-Din|gi [...diŋgi], das; -s, -s ⟨schwed.; Hindi⟩ (kleines Einmann-Sportsegelboot)
[1]**Fin|ne,** die; -, -n (Jugendform bestimmter Bandwürmer; entzündete Pustel); [2]**Fin|ne,** die; -, -n (Rückenflosse von Hai u. Wal; zugespitzte Seite des Hammers)
[3]**Fin|ne,** die; - (Höhenzug in Thüringen)
[4]**Fin|ne,** der; -n, -n; ↑R 126 (Einwohner von Finnland)
fin|nig (von [1]Finnen befallen)
Fin|nin; fin|nisch, *aber* (↑R 102): der Finnische Meerbusen; *vgl.* deutsch; **Fin|nisch,** das; -[s] (Sprache); *vgl.* Deutsch; **Fin|ni|sche,** das; -n; *vgl.* Deutsche, das; **fin|nisch-ug|risch** (↑R 106 *u.* 130); finnisch-ugrische Sprachen, Völker; **Finn|land; Finn|län|der** ([4]Finne mit schwed. Muttersprache); **finn|län|disch;** [1]**Finn|mark,** die; -, - (finn. Währungseinheit; *Abk.* Fmk); [2]**Finn|mark** (norw. Verwaltungsbezirk); **fin|no|ug|risch** (↑R 106 *u.* 130) *vgl.* finnisch-ugrisch; **Fin|no|ug|rist** (↑R 130), der; -en, -en; ↑R 126 (Fachmann für finnisch-ugrische Sprachen); **Fin|no|ug|ris|tik** (↑R 130), die; -
Finn|wal
Fi|now|ka|nal [ˈfi:no:...], der; -s; ↑R 105
fins|ter; es wurde immer finst[e]rer; eine finst[e]re Nacht; finster dreinblicken; im Finstern tappen (*auch für* nicht Bescheid wissen); **Fins|ter|keit,** die; -; **Fins|ter|ling** (grimmig wirkender Mensch); **fins|tern** (*veraltet für* dunkel werden); es finstert; **Fins|ter|nis,** die; -, -se
Fin|te, die; -, -n ⟨ital.⟩ (Vorwand, Täuschung[smanöver]; *Sport* Scheinangriff); **fin|ten|reich**
fin|ze|lig, finz|lig (*landsch. für* überzart, überfein; die Augen [über]anstrengend)
Fi|o|ret|te, die; -, -n *meist Plur.* ⟨ital., „Blümchen"⟩ (*Musik* Gesangsverzierung); **Fi|o|ri|tur,** die; -, -en *meist Plur.* (*svw.* Fiorette)
Fips, der; -es, -e (*landsch. für* kleiner, unscheinbarer Mensch); Meister - (*Spottname für* Schneider); **fip|sig** (*ugs. für* unbedeutend, klein)
Fi|ren|ze (*ital. Form von* Florenz)
Fir|le|fanz, der; -es (*ugs. für* überflüssiges, wertloses Zeug; Unsinn); **Fir|le|fan|ze|rei**
firm ⟨lat.⟩; in etw. firm (erfahren, beschlagen) sein
Fir|ma, die; -, ...men ⟨ital.⟩ (*Abk.* Fa.)
Fir|ma|ment, das; -[e]s ⟨lat.⟩ *(geh.)*
fir|men ⟨lat.⟩ (jmdm. die Firmung erteilen)
Fir|men‿auf|druck, ...buch, ...chef, ...in|ha|ber, ...in|ha|be|rin, ...kopf (*svw.* Firmenaufdruck), **...re|gis|ter, ...schild** (das), **...stem|pel, ...ver|zeich|nis, ...wert** (der; -[e]s), **...zei|chen; fir|mie|ren** (einen bestimmten Geschäfts-, Handelsnamen führen)
Firm|ling ⟨lat.⟩ (der zu Firmende); **Firm‿pa|te, ...pa|tin; Fir|mung** (kath. Sakrament)
firn (*fachspr. für* alt, abgelagert [von Wein]); ein firner Wein; **Firn,** der; -[e]s, *Plur.* -e, *auch* -en (körnig gewordener Altschnee im Hochgebirge; *österr., schweiz. auch für* damit bedeckter Gipfel, Gletscher); **Fir|ne,** die; -, -n (Reife des Weines); **Firn|eis,** das; -es; **Fir|ne|wein; fir|nig**
Fir|nis, der; -ses, -se ⟨franz.⟩ (schnell trocknender Schutzanstrich); **fir|nis|sen;** du firnisst
Firn|schnee
First, der; -[e]s, -e; **First|bal|ken**
first class [ˈfœ:(r)st ˈkla:s] ⟨engl.⟩ (erstklassig, von gehobenem Standard); **First-Class-Ho|tel** ⟨engl.; franz.⟩ (Luxushotel); **First La|dy** [ˈfœ:(r)st ˈle:di], die; - -, - ...dies ⟨engl., „Erste Dame"⟩ (Frau eines Staatsoberhauptes)
First‿pfet|te, ...zie|gel
fis, Fis, das; -, - (Tonbezeichnung); **fis** (*Zeichen für* fis-Moll); in fis; **Fis** (*Zeichen für* Fis-Dur); in Fis
FIS, Fis, die; - ⟨franz.⟩ (*Kurzw. für* Fédération Internationale de Ski [federaˈsjɔ̃: ɛ̃tɛrnasjɔˈnal də ˈski]; Internationaler Skiverband); FIS-Rennen
Fisch, der; -[e]s, -e; faule -e (*ugs. für* Ausreden); kleine -e (*ugs. für* Kleinigkeiten); frische Fische; die Fisch verarbeitende Industrie; **Fisch|ad|ler; fisch|arm; Fisch|au|ge** (*auch* ein fotograf. Objektiv); **fisch|äu|gig; Fisch‿bein** (das; -[e]s), **...be|stand, ...be|steck, ...bla|se; Fisch|bla|sen|stil,** der; -[e]s *(Archit.);* **Fisch|blut; Fisch|bra|te|rei, Fisch|brat|kü|che** (Gaststätte für Fischgerichte); **Fisch‿bröt|chen, ...brut; fi|scheln** (*bes. österr. für* nach Fisch riechen); **fi|schen;** du

fischst; **Fi|schenz,** die; -, -en (*schweiz. für* Fischpacht); **Fi|scher; Fi|scher|boot**
Fi|scher-Dies|kau (dt. Sänger)
Fi|scher|dorf; Fi|sche|rei; Fi|sche|rei˯gren|ze, ...ha|fen, ...we|sen (das; -s); **Fi|sche|rin; Fi|scher˯netz, ...ste|chen** (das; -s; Brauch der Fischer, bei dem diese versuchen, sich gegenseitig mit langen Stangen aus dem Boot zu stoßen)
Fi|scher von Er|lach (österr. Barockbaumeister)
Fisch˯frau, ...ge|richt, ...ge|schäft, ...grä|te; Fisch|grä|ten|mus|ter; Fisch|grün|de *Plur.*; **fi|schig; Fisch˯kal|ter** (*bayr., österr. für* Fischbehälter), **...kon|ser|ve, ...kut|ter, ...la|den, ...laich, ...leim, ...markt, ...maul, ...mehl, ...mes|ser** (das), **...ot|ter** (der), **...rei|her, ...reu|se, ...ro|gen, ...stäb|chen** *(meist Plur.)*, **...sup|pe; Fisch ver|ar|bei|tend** *vgl.* Fisch; **Fisch˯ver|gif|tung, ...zug**
Fis-Dur [*auch* ˈfisˈduːr], das; - (Tonart; *Zeichen* Fis); **Fis-Dur-Ton|lei|ter** (↑R 28)
Fi|sett|holz, das; -es (einen gelben Farbstoff enthaltendes Holz)
Fi|si|ma|ten|ten *Plur.* (*ugs. für* leere Ausflüchte); mach keine -!
fis|ka|lisch (dem Fiskus gehörend; staatlich); **Fis|kus,** der; -, *Plur.* ...ken *u.* -se *Plur. selten* (der Staat als Eigentümer des Staatsvermögens; Staatskasse)
fis-Moll [*auch* ˈfisˈmɔl], das; - (Tonart; *Zeichen* fis); **fis-Moll-Ton|lei|ter** (↑R 28)
Fi|so|le, die; -, -n ‹ital.› (*österr. für* grüne Gartenbohne)
fis|se|lig (*landsch. für* dünn, fein; Geschicklichkeit erfordernd)
fis|sil ‹lat.› (spaltbar); **Fis|si|li|tät,** die; -; **Fis|si|on,** die; -, -en (*Kernphysik* Kernspaltung); **Fis|sur,** die; -, -en (*Med.* Spalte, Riss)
Fis|tel, die; -, -n ‹lat.› (*Med.* krankhafter od. künstlich angelegter röhrenförmiger Kanal, der ein Organ mit der Körperoberfläche od. einem anderen Organ verbindet); **fis|teln** (mit Fistelstimme sprechen, singen); ich ...[e]le (↑R 16); **Fis|tel|stim|me** (Kopfstimme)
fit; fitter, fitteste ‹engl.-amerik.› (in guter [körperlicher] Verfassung; durchtrainiert); sich fit halten; ein fitter Bursche
Fi|tis, der; *Gen.* - *u.* -ses, *Plur.* -se (ein Singvogel)
Fit|ness, die; - ‹engl.-amerik.› (gute körperliche Gesamtverfassung, Bestform); **Fit|ness˯cen|ter, ...test, ...trai|ning**
Fit|sche, die; -, -n (*landsch. für* Tür-, Fensterangel, Scharnier)
Fit|tich, der; -[e]s, -e (*geh. für* Flügel)
Fit|ting, das; -s, -s *meist Plur.* ‹engl.› (Formstück zur Installation von Rohrleitungen)
Fitz, der; -es, -e (*landsch. für* Fadengewirr); **Fitz|boh|ne** (*landsch. für* Schnittbohne); **Fitz|chen** (Kleinigkeit); **Fit|ze,** die; -, -n (*landsch. für* Faden; Garngebinde; geflochtene Rute); **fit|zen** (*landsch. für* sich verwirren; nervös sein); du fitzt
Fi|u|ma|ra, Fi|u|ma|re, die; -, ...re[n] ‹ital.› (*Geogr.* Flusslauf, der nur in regenreicher Zeit Wasser führt); **Fi|u|me** (*ital. Name von* Rijeka)
Five o'clock [ˈfaivəˈklɔk], der; - -, - -s, **Five o'clock tea** [- - ˈtiː], der; - - -, - - -s ‹engl.› (Fünfuhrtee)
fix ‹lat., „fest"› (sicher, stetig, feststehend; *ugs. für* gewandt, schnell); fixe Idee (Zwangsvorstellung; törichte Einbildung); fixer Preis (fester Preis); fixes Gehalt; fixe Kosten; fix und fertig; **Fi|xa|teur** [...ˈtøːr], der; -s, -e ‹franz.› (Zerstäuber für Fixiermittel); **Fi|xa|tiv,** das; -s, -e [...və] ‹lat.› (Fixiermittel für Zeichnungen u. Ä.); **fi|xen** ‹engl.› (*Börsenw.* Leerverkäufe von Wertpapieren tätigen; *ugs. für* sich Drogen spritzen); du fixt; **Fi|xer** (*Börsenw.* Leerverkäufer; Börsenspekulant; *ugs. für* jmd., der sich Drogen spritzt); **fix|fer|tig** (*schweiz. für* fix und fertig); **Fi|xier|bad** *(Fotogr.)*; **fi|xie|ren; Fi|xier|mit|tel,** das; **Fi|xie|rung; Fi|xig|keit,** die; - (*ugs. für* Gewandtheit); **Fix˯kos|ten** (*Plur.;* fixe Kosten), **...punkt** (Festpunkt), **...stern** (scheinbar unbeweglicher Stern; *vgl.* [2]Stern); **Fi|xum,** das; -s, ...xa (festes Entgelt); **Fix|zeit** (Festzeit, während der auch bei gleitender Arbeitszeit alle Arbeitnehmer anwesend sein müssen)
Fjäll ‹schwed.› *od.* **Fjell** ‹norw.›, *ältere Form* Fjeld ‹dän.›, der; -s, -s (baumlose Hochfläche in Skandinavien)
Fjord, der; -[e]s, -e ‹skand.› (schmale Meeresbucht [mit Steilküsten])
FKK = Freikörperkultur; **FKKler;** ↑R 26 *(ugs.)*; **FKK-Strand** (↑R 26)
fl., Fl. = Florin (Gulden)
Fla. = Florida
Flab, die; - (*schweiz. Kurzw. für* Fliegerabwehr); *vgl.* Flak
flach; auf dem flachen Land[e] (außerhalb der Stadt) wohnen; flach atmen; einen Hut flach drücken; **Flach,** das; -[e]s, -e (*Seemannsspr.* Untiefe); **...flach** (z. B. Achtflach, das; -[e]s, -e); **Flach|bau** *Plur.* ...bauten; **flach|brüs|tig; Flach˯dach, ...druck** (*Plur.* ...drucke; *Druckw.*); **Flä|che,** die; -, -n; **Flach|ei|sen** (ein Werkzeug); **Flä|chen˯aus|deh|nung, ...blitz, ...brand; flä|chen|de|ckend; Flä|chen|er|trag; flä|chen|haft; Flä|chen|in|halt; flach|fal|len** (↑R 38 f.; *ugs. für* nicht stattfinden); **Flach|feu|er|ge|schütz; Flach|heit; flä|chig; Flach˯kopf** (*svw.* Dummkopf), **...küs|te, ...land** (*Plur.* ...länder), **...län|der** (der), **...mann** (*ugs. für* Taschenflasche); **...fläch|ner** (z. B. Achtflächner)
Flachs, der; -es (Faserpflanze); **flachs|blond; Flachs|bre|che**
Flach|schuss *(bes. Fußball)*
Flachs|dar|re
Flach|se (*bayr., österr. für* Flechse)
flach|sen (*ugs. für* necken, spotten, scherzen); du flachst; **fläch|sen,** fläch|sern (aus Flachs); **Flach|se|rei; fläch|sern** *vgl.* flächsen; **Flachs˯haar, ...kopf**
Flach|zan|ge
fla|cken (*landsch. für* flackern); **Fla|cker|feu|er; fla|cke|rig,** flack|rig; **fla|ckern**
Fla|den, der; -s, - (flacher Kuchen; breiige Masse; *kurz für* Kuhfladen); **Fla|den|brot**
Fla|der, die; -, -n (Maser, Holzader; bogenförmiger Jahresring in Schnittholz); **Fla|der|holz; fla|de|rig,** flad|rig (gemasert)
fla|dern (*österr. ugs. für* stehlen)
Fla|der|schnitt; Fla|de|rung, die; - (Maserung)
Fläd|le, das; -s, - (*bes. schwäb. für* Streifen aus Eierteig als Suppeneinlage); **Fläd|le|sup|pe**
flad|rig *vgl.* fladerig
Fla|gel|lant, der; -en, -en *meist Plur.;* ↑R 126 ‹lat., „Geißler"› (Angehöriger religiöser Bruderschaften des Mittelalters, die sich zur Sündenvergebung selbst geißelten); **Fla|gel|lan|ten|tum,** das; -s; **Fla|gel|lat,** der; -en, -en *meist Plur.;* ↑R 126 (*Biol.* Geißeltierchen)
Fla|geo|lett [flaʒoˈlɛt], das; -s, *Plur.* -e *u.* -s ‹franz.› (kleinster Typ der Schnabelflöte; flötenähnlicher Ton bei Streichinstrumenten u. Harfen; Flötenregister der Orgel); **Fla|geo|lett|ton** (↑R 136)
Flag|ge, die; -, -n; **flag|gen; Flag-**

gen‿al|pha|bet, ...gruß, ...mast (*vgl.* [1]Mast); **Flagg‿of|fi|zier, ...schiff**

flag|rant (↑R 130) ⟨lat.⟩ (deutlich u. offenkundig); *vgl.* in flagranti

Flair [flɛːr], das; -s ⟨franz.⟩ (Fluidum, Atmosphäre, gewisses Etwas; *bes. schweiz. für* feiner Instinkt, Gespür)

Flak, die; -, *Plur.* -, *auch* -s (*Kurzw. für* Flugzeugabwehrkanone; Flugabwehrartillerie); die leichten und schweren Flak[s]; **Flak|bat|te|rie**

Fla|ke, die; -, -n (*nordd. für* [Holz]geflecht; Netz)

Flak|hel|fer

Fla|kon [...ˈkõː], der *od.* das; -s, -s ⟨franz.⟩ ([Riech]fläschchen)

Flam|beau [flãˈboː], der; -s, -s ⟨franz.⟩ (mehrarmiger Leuchter mit hohem Fuß)

Flam|berg, der; -[e]s, -e (zweihändiges [meist flammenförmiges] Schwert der Landsknechte)

flam|bie|ren ([Speisen] mit Alkohol übergießen u. brennend auftragen; *veraltet für* absengen)

Fla|me, der; -n, -n; ↑R 126 (Angehöriger der Bevölkerung im Westen u. Norden Belgiens u. in den angrenzenden Teilen Frankreichs u. der Niederlande)

Fla|men|co, der; -[s], -s ⟨span.⟩ (andalus. [Tanz]lied; Tanz)

Fla|min, Flä|min

Flä|ming, der; -s (Landrücken in der Mark Brandenburg)

Fla|min|go, der; -s, -s ⟨span.⟩ ([rosafarbener] langbeiniger, großer Wasservogel); **Fla|min|go|blu|me**

flä|misch; *vgl.* deutsch; **Flä|misch,** das; -[s] (Sprache); *vgl.* Deutsch; **Flä|mi|sche,** das; -n; *vgl.* Deutsche, das; **Flam|län|der** *vgl.* Flame

Flämm|chen; Flam|me, die; -, -n; **Flamm|ei|sen** (ein Tischlerwerkzeug); **flam|men; fläm|men** (*Technik* absengen); **Flam|men‿meer, ...tod, ...wer|fer**

Flam|me|ri, der; -[s], -s ⟨engl.⟩ (eine kalte Süßspeise)

Flamm|garn; flam|mig; Flamm|koh|le (mit langer Flamme brennende Steinkohle); **Flämm|lein; Flamm|punkt** (Temperatur, bei der die Dämpfe über einer Flüssigkeit entflammbar sind)

Flan|dern (Gebiet zwischen der Schelde u. der Nordsee); **flandrisch;** die flandrische Küste

Fla|nell, der; -s, -e ⟨franz.⟩ (gerautes Gewebe); **Fla|nell|an|zug; fla|nel|len** (aus Flanell); **Fla|nell‿hemd, ...ho|se**

Fla|neur [flaˈnøːr], der; -s, -e ⟨franz.⟩ (müßig Umherschlendernder); **fla|nie|ren**

Flan|ke, die; -, -n ⟨franz.⟩; **flanken; Flan|ken‿an|griff, ...ball, ...wech|sel**

Flan|kerl, das; -s, -n (*österr. ugs. für* Fussel)

flan|kie|ren ⟨franz.⟩ ([schützend] begleiten)

Flansch, der; -[e]s, -e (Verbindungsansatz an Rohren, Maschinenteilen usw.); **flan|schen** (mit einem Flansch versehen); **Flan|schen|dich|tung; Flansch|ver|bin|dung**

Fla-Pan|zer (Flugabwehrpanzer)

Flap|pe, die; -, -n (*landsch. für* schiefer Mund); eine - ziehen (schmollen)

Flaps, der; -es, -e (*ugs. für* Flegel); **flap|sig** (*ugs.*)

Fla-Ra|ke|te (Flugabwehrrakete)

Fläsch|chen; Fla|sche, die; -, -n (*ugs. auch für* Versager); **Fla|schen‿bier, ...bürs|te, ...gar|ten** (Zierpflanzen in einer Flasche), **...gä|rung** (bei Schaumwein); **fla|schen|grün; Fla|schen‿hals** (*ugs. auch für* Engpass), **...kind, ...öff|ner, ...pfand, ...post, ...zug; Fläsch|lein; Flasch|ner** (*südd. für* Klempner, Spengler)

Fla|ser, die; -, -n (Ader im Gestein); **fla|se|rig, flas|rig**

Flat|sche [ˈfla(ː)tʃə], die; -, -n *u.* **Flat|schen,** der; -s, - (*landsch. für* großes Stück; breiige Masse)

Flat|ter, die; -; *nur in* die - machen (*ugs. für* verschwinden, fliehen); **Flat|ter|geist** *Plur.* ...geister; **flat|ter|haft; Flat|ter|haf|tig|keit,** die; -; **flat|te|rig,** flattrig; **Flat|ter|mann** *Plur.* ...männer (*ugs. für* Unruhe, Nervosität; unruhiger Mensch; *auch für* Brathähnchen); **Flat|ter|mar|ke** (*Druckw.*); **Flat|ter|mi|ne** (*veraltet für* Tretmine); **flat|tern;** ich ...ere (↑R 16); **Flat|ter|satz** (*Druckw.*)

flat|tie|ren ⟨franz.⟩ (*schweiz. für* schmeicheln, gut zureden)

flatt|rig *vgl.* flatterig

Fla|tu|lenz, die; - ⟨lat.⟩ (*Med.* Darmaufblähung); **Fla|tus,** der; -, - [ˈflaːtuːs] (*Med.* Blähung)

flau (*ugs. für* schlecht, übel)

Flau|bert [floˈbɛːr] (franz. Schriftsteller)

Flau|heit, die; -

[1]**Flaum,** der; -[e]s; *vgl.* Flom[en]

[2]**Flaum,** der; -[e]s (weiche Bauchfedern; erster Bartwuchs)

Flau|ma|cher (*svw.* Miesmacher)

Flau|mer, der; -s, - (*schweiz. für* Mopp)

Flaum|fe|der; flau|mig; flaum|weich; *vgl.* pflaumenweich

Flaus, der; -es, -e (*veraltet für* Flausch); **Flausch,** der; -[e]s, -e (weiches Wollgewebe); **flau|schig; Flausch|rock; Flau|se,** die; -, -n *meist Plur.* (*ugs. für* Ausflucht; törichter Einfall)

Flau|te, die; -, -n (Windstille; *übertr. für* Unbelebtheit [z. B. im Geschäftsleben])

Fla|via [...vi̯a] (w. Vorn.); **Fla|vi|er** [...vi̯ər], der; -s, - (Angehöriger eines röm. Kaisergeschlechtes); **Fla|vio** (m. Vorn.); **fla|visch**

Fläz, der; -es, -e (*ugs. für* plumper, roher Mensch, Lümmel); **flä|zen,** sich (*ugs. für* nachlässig sitzen; sich hinlümmeln); du fläzt dich; **flä|zig** (*ugs.*)

Fleb|be, die; -, -n *meist Plur.* (*Gaunerspr.* Ausweispapier)

Flech|se, die; -, -n (Sehne); **flech|sig**

Flech|te, die; -, -n (Pflanze; Hautausschlag; *geh. für* Zopf); **flech|ten;** du flichtst, er flicht; du flochtest; du flöchtest; geflochten; flicht!; **Flech|ter; Flech|te|rin; Flecht|werk,** das; -[e]s

Fleck, der; -[e]s, -e *u.* **Fle|cken,** der; -s, -; der blinde Fleck (im Auge); **Fleck|chen; Fle|cke** *Plur.* (*landsch. für* Kaldaunen); **fle|cken** (Flecke[n] machen, annehmen; *landsch. auch für* vorankommen, z. B. es fleckt); **Fle|cken,** der; -s, - (*svw.* Fleck; größeres Dorf); **Fle|cken|ent|fer|ner; fle|cken|los; Fle|cken|lo|sig|keit,** die; -; **Fleck|ent|fer|ner** *svw.* Fleckenentferner; **Fle|cken|was|ser; Fle|ckerl,** das; -s, -n (*österr. für* quadratisch geschnittenes Nudelteigstück als Suppeneinlage); **Fle|ckerl‿sup|pe** (*österr.*), **...tep|pich** (*südd. u. österr.* Teppich aus Stoffstreifen); **Fleck|fie|ber,** das; -s; **fle|ckig; Fle|ckig|keit,** die; -; **Fleck|lein; Fleck‿ty|phus, ...vieh**

Fled|de|rer; fled|dern (*Gaunerspr.* [Leichen] ausplündern); ich ...ere (↑R 16)

Fle|der‿maus, ...wisch

Fleece [fliːs], das; - ⟨engl.⟩ ([synthetischer] Flausch)

Fleet, das; -[e]s, -e (Kanal in Küstenstädten, bes. in Hamburg)

Fle|gel, der; -s, -; **Fle|ge|lei; fle|gel|haft; Fle|gel|haf|tig|keit; fle|ge|lig; Fle|gel|jah|re** *Plur.*; **fle|geln,** sich; ich ...[e]le mich (↑R 16) aufs Sofa

fle|hen; fle|hent|lich

Fleisch, das; -[e]s; (↑R 40:) Fleisch fressende Pflanzen, Tiere;

der Fleisch gewordene (*veraltend für* personifizierte) Antichrist; **Fleisch‿bank** (*Plur.* ...bänke; *österr. auch für* Fleischerei), **...beschau** (die; -), **...be|schau|er, ...brü|he, ...ein|la|ge, ...ein|waage; Flei|scher; Flei|sche|rei; Flei|scher‿ha|ken, ...in|nung, ...meis|ter, ...mes|ser; flei|schern** (aus Fleisch); **Flei|scheslust; Fleisch|ex|trakt; fleisch|far|ben, fleisch|far|big; Fleisch fres|send** *vgl.* Fleisch; **Fleisch|ge|richt; Fleisch ge|wor|den** *vgl.* Fleisch; **Fleisch‿ha|cker** (*ostösterr. ugs.*), **...hau|er** (*österr. für* Fleischer); **Fleisch|hau|e|rei** (*österr. für* Fleischerei); **flei|schig; Flei|schig|keit,** die; -; **Fleisch‿kä|se** (*landsch.*), **...klopfer, ...klöß|chen, ...kon|ser|ve, ...laib|chen** (das; -s, -) *u.* **...laiberl** (das; -, -n; *österr. für* Frikadelle); **fleisch|lich;** -e Lüste (*geh., veraltet*); **Fleisch|lich|keit,** die; -; **fleisch|los; Fleisch‿ma|schi|ne** (*österr. für* Fleischwolf), **...sa|lat, ...to|ma|te, ...ver|gif|tung, ...vogel** (*schweiz. für* Roulade), **...waren** (*Plur.*), **...wer|dung** (Menschwerdung, Verkörperung), **...wolf** (der), **...wun|de, ...wurst**

Fleiß, der; -es; **Fleiß|ar|beit; fleißig,** *aber* (↑R 108): das Fleißige Lieschen (eine Zierpflanze)

Flei|ver|kehr, der; -[e]s (Flug-Eisenbahn-Güterverkehr)

flek|tier|bar ‹lat.› (*Sprachw.* beugbar); **flek|tie|ren** ([ein Wort] beugen, d. h. deklinieren oder konjugieren); *vgl. auch* Flexion

Fle|ming (dt. Dichter)

flen|nen (*ugs. für* weinen); **Flenne|rei** (*ugs.*)

Flens|burg (Stadt in Schleswig-Holstein)

Fles|serl, das; -s, -n (*österr. mdal.* ein Salz-, Mohngebäck)

flet|schen (die Zähne zeigen); du fletschst

flet|schern ‹nach dem Amerikaner Fletcher› (sorgfältig u. lange kauen); ich ...ere (↑R 16)

Flett, das; -[e]s, -e (Wohn- u. Herdraum im niedersächs. Bauernhaus)

Flett|ner (dt. Maschinenbauer); **Flett|ner|ru|der** (↑R 95; Hilfsruder)

Fletz [*auch* flɛts], das *od.* der; -es, -e (*südd. für* Hausflur)

fleucht; *nur in* alles, was da kreucht und fleucht (kriecht und fliegt = alle Tiere)

Fleur [flœ:r] (w. Vorn.)

Fleu|ron [flœ'rɔ̃:], der; -s, -s ‹franz.› (Blumenornament); **Fleurons** [flœ'rɔ̃:s] *Plur.* (ungesüßte Blätterteigstückchen [zum Garnieren])

Fleu|rop [*auch* 'flø:rɔp], die; - (internationale Blumengeschenkvermittlung)

fle|xi|bel ‹lat.› (biegsam, elastisch; sehr anpassungsfähig; *Sprachw.* beugbar); ...ib|le (↑R 130) Wörter; **fle|xi|bi|li|sie|ren** (flexibel gestalten); **Fle|xi|bi|li|sie|rung; Fle|xi|bi|li|tät,** die; - (Biegsamkeit, Elastizität; Anpassungsfähigkeit); **Fle|xi|on,** die; -, -en (*Med.* Beugung, Abknickung; *Sprachw.* Beugung, d. h. Deklination od. Konjugation); **Fle|xi|ons|en|dung; fle|xi|ons‿fä|hig, ...los; fle|xi|visch** [...vɪʃ] (*Sprachw.* die Beugung betreffend); **Fle|xur,** die; -, -en (*Geol.* Verbiegung)

Fli|bus|ti|er [...i̯ər], der; -s, - ‹niederl.› (Seeräuber des 17. Jh.s)

Flic [flik], der; -s, -s ‹franz.› (*franz. ugs. für* Polizist)

Flick|ar|beit; fli|cken; Fli|cken, der; -s, -; **Fli|cken‿de|cke, ...teppich; Fli|cker; Fli|cke|rei; Fli|cke|rin**

Flick|flack, der; -s, -s ‹franz.› (in schneller Folge geturnter Handstandüberschlag)

Flick‿korb, ...schnei|der (*veraltet*), **...schus|ter** (*veraltet, aber noch ugs. für* Stümper), **...werk** (das; -[e]s)

Flie|boot ‹niederl.› (kleines Fischerboot; *auch für* Beiboot)

Flie|der, der; -s, - (Zierstrauch; *landsch. für* Holunder); **Flieder‿bee|re, ...beer|sup|pe** (*landsch.*), **...blü|te, ...busch; flieder‿far|ben** *od.* **...far|big; Flieder‿strauch, ...tee** (der; -s *landsch.*)

Flie|ge, die; -, -n; **flie|gen;** er fliegt; du flogst (flogest); du flögest; geflogen; flieg[e]!; fliegende Blätter, fliegende Hitze, fliegende Brücke (Fähre), fliegende Untertasse, in fliegender Eile; *aber* Fliegende Fische (*Zool.*); (↑R 108): Fliegende Blätter (frühere humoristische Zeitschrift), der Fliegende Holländer (Sagengestalt, Oper); **Flie|gen‿dreck, ...fänger, ...fens|ter, ...ge|wicht** (Körpergewichtsklasse in der Schwerathletik), **...ge|wicht|ler, ...klappe, ...klat|sche, ...kopf** (*Druckerspr.*), **...pilz, ...schnäp|per** (ein Singvogel); **Flie|ger; Flieger‿ab|wehr, ...alarm** (↑R 132); **Flie|ge|rei,** die; -; **Flie|ger|horst; flie|ge|risch; Flie|ger‿ren|nen** (*Radsport; Pferdesport*), **...sprache**

Flieh|burg (*früher*); **flie|hen;** er flieht; du flohst (flohest); du flöhest; geflohen; flieh[e]!; **flie|hend** (schräg nach hinten verlaufend); eine -e Stirn; **Flieh|kraft** (*für* Zentrifugalkraft); **Flieh|kraft|kupp|lung** (*Technik*)

Flie|se, die; -, -n (Wand- od. Bodenplatte); **flie|sen** (mit Fliesen versehen); du fliest; er flieste; gefliest; **Flie|sen|le|ger**

Fließ, das; -es, -e (*veraltet für* Bach); **Fließ‿ar|beit** (Arbeit am laufenden Band), **...band** (das; *Plur.* ...bänder); **Fließ|band‿arbeit, ...ar|bei|ter, ...ar|bei|te|rin; Fließ|ei** (Vogelei ohne Kalkschale); **flie|ßen;** du fließt, er fließt; ich floss, du flossest; du flössest; geflossen; fließ[e]!; ineinander fließen; ineinander fließende Farben; **Fließ‿heck** (bei Autos; *vgl.* [1]Heck), **...laut** (*Sprachw.; für* Liquida), **...pa|pier** (Löschpapier), **...was|ser** (das; -s; *österr. für* Wasserleitungsanschluss; Zimmer mit -)

Flim|mer, der; -s, -; **Flim|mer‿epi|thel** (↑R 132; *Biol.* mit Wimpern versehene Zellschicht), **...kis|te** (*ugs. für* Fernsehgerät); **flim|mern;** ich ...ere (↑R 16)

flink; Flink|heit, die; -; **flink|züngig**

Flin|serl, das; -s, -n (*österr. ugs. für* Flitter; kleines Gedicht)

Flint, der; -[e]s, -e (*nordd. für* Feuerstein); **Flin|te,** die; -, -n (Jagdgewehr, bes. Schrotgewehr); **Flinten‿ku|gel, ...schuss, ...weib** (*abwertend*); **Flint|glas** *Plur.* ...gläser (sehr reines Glas)

Flinz, der; -es, -e (ein Gestein)

Flip, der; -s, -s ‹engl.› (ein alkohol. Mischgetränk mit Ei); **Flip|chart** [...tʃa:(r)t], das; -s, -s (auf einem Gestell befestigter großer Papierblock); **Flip|flop,** das; -s, -s *u.* **Flip|flop|schal|tung** (elektron. Kippschaltung); **Flip|per,** der; -s, - (Spielautomat); **flip|pern** (am Flipper spielen); **flip|pig** (*ugs. für* kess, flott)

flir|ren (flimmern)

Flirt [flœrt, *auch* flirt], der; -[e]s, -s ‹engl.› (Liebelei; harmloses, kokettes Spiel mit der Liebe); **flirten**

Fli|scherl, das; -s, -n (*österr. ugs. für* Flittchen); **Flitt|chen** (*ugs. für* leichtes Mädchen, Dirne)

Flit|ter, der; -s, -; **Flit|ter‿glanz, ...gold, ...kram; flit|tern** (glänzen); **Flit|ter‿werk** (das; -[e]s), **...wo|chen** (*Plur.*), **...wöch|ner**

Flitz, der; -es, -e (*veraltet für* Pfeil); **Flitz|bo|gen** (*ugs.*); **flit|zen** (*ugs.*

für sausen, eilen); du flitzt; du flitztest; **Flịt|zer** (*ugs. für* kleines, schnelles Fahrzeug)
floa|ten ['flo:...] ‹engl.› (*Wirtsch.* den Wechselkurs freigeben); **Floa|ting,** das; -s
Flo̲|bert|ge|wehr [*auch* flo'bɛ:r...] ‹nach dem franz. Waffenschmied› (↑R 95)
F-Loch, das; -[e]s, F-Löcher; ↑R 25 (an Streichinstrumenten)
Flọ|cke, die; -, -n; **flọ|cken; flọ|cken|för|mig; flọ|cken|wei|se; flọ|ckig; Flọck|sei|de,** die; - (äußere Schicht des Seidenkokons); **Flọ|ckung** (*Chemie*); **Flọ|ckungs|mit|tel,** das
Flö̲|del, der; -s, - (schmaler Doppelstreifen am Rand von Decke u. Boden bei Streichinstrumenten)
Flo̲h, der; -[e]s, Flöhe; **Flo̲h|biss; flö̲|hen; Flo̲h‿markt** (Trödelmarkt), **...zir|kus**
Flo|ka̲|ti, der; -s, -s ‹ngriech.› (Teppich aus langen Wollfäden)
Flo̲m, der; -[e]s *u.* **Flo̲|men,** der; -s (Bauch- u. Nierenfett des Schweines usw.); *vgl.* [1]Flaum
Flọp, der; -s, -s ‹engl.› (Misserfolg; *auch kurz für* Fosburyflop); **flọp|pen** (*ugs. für* ein Flop sein); **Flọp|py|dịsk,** *auch* **Flọp|py Dịsk,** die; -, -s (*EDV* als Datenspeicher dienende [flexible] Magnetplatte)
[1]**Flo̲r,** der; -s, -e *Plur. selten* ‹lat.› (*geh. für* Blüte, Blumenfülle; Gedeihen); [2]**Flo̲r,** der; -s, *Plur.* -e, *selten* Flöre ‹niederl.› (dünnes Gewebe; samtartige Oberfläche eines Gewebes); [1]**Flo̲|ra** (altröm. Göttin; w. Vorn.); [2]**Flo̲|ra,** die; -, Floren ‹lat.› (Pflanzenwelt [eines Gebietes]); **Flo̲r|band,** das; *Plur.* ...bänder; **Flo|re|a̲l,** der; -[s], -s ‹franz., „Blütenmonat"› (8. Monat des Kalenders der Franz. Revolution: 20. April bis 19. Mai); **Flo|ren|tin** (m. Vorn.); **Flo|ren|ti̲|ne** (w. Vorn.)
Flo|ren|ti̲|ner (↑R 103); - Hut; **flo|ren|ti̲|nisch; Flo|rẹnz** (ital. Stadt)
Flo|res|zẹnz, die; -, -en *Plur. selten* ‹lat.› (*Bot.* Blütenstand; Blütezeit)
Flo|rẹtt, das; -[e]s, -e ‹franz.›; **Flo|rẹtt‿fech|ten** (das; -s), **...sei|de** (die; -; Abfallseide)
Flo̲|ri|an (m. Vorn.)
Flo̲|ri|da (Halbinsel u. Staat in den USA; *Abk.* Fla.)
flo|ri̲e̲|ren ‹lat.› (blühen, [geschäftlich] vorankommen; gedeihen); **Flo|ri|le̲|gi|um,** das; -s, ...ien [...i̯ən] (*veraltet für* Anthologie; Sammlung von schmückenden Redewendungen); **Flo|ri̲n,** der; -s, *Plur.* -e *u.* -s (Gulden in den Niederlanden; ehem. engl. Silbermünze; *Abk.* fl. *u.* Fl.); **Flo|rịst,** der; -en, -en; ↑R 126 (Erforscher einer Flora; Blumenbinder); **Flo|rịs|tin; flo|rịs|tisch; Flọs|kel,** die; -, -n ([inhaltsarme] Redensart); **flọs|kel|haft**
Flo̲ß, das; -es, Flöße (Wasserfahrzeug); **flö̲ß|bar; Flọs|se,** die; -, -n; **flö̲|ßen;** du flößt; **Flọs|sen|fü|ßer** (*Zool.*); **Flö̲|ßer; ...flos|ser** (z. B. Bauchflosser); **Flö|ße|rei̲,** die; -; **Flo̲ß‿fahrt, ...gas|se** (*Wasserbau*), **...holz**
Flo|ta|ti|o̲n, die; -, -en ‹engl.› (*Technik* Verfahren zur Aufbereitung von Erzen); **flo|ta|ti̲v**
Flö̲|te, die; -, -n; (↑R 39:) - spielen, *aber* (↑R 50): beim Flötespielen; [1]**flö̲|ten**
[2]**flö̲|ten;** *nur in* flöten gehen (*ugs. für* verloren gehen)
Flö̲|ten‿blä|ser, ...spiel (das; -[e]s), **...ton** (*Plur.* ...töne)
flo|ti̲e̲|ren ‹engl.› (*Technik* Erze durch Flotation aufbereiten)
Flö|tịst, der; -en, -en; ↑R 126 (Flötenbläser); **Flö|tịs|tin**
Flo̲|tow [...to] (dt. Komponist)
flọtt (leicht; rasch, flink; *Seemannsspr.* frei schwimmend, fahrbereit) ein flott gehendes Geschäft, ein flott geschriebenes Buch; flott machen (*ugs. für* sich beeilen; *vgl. aber* flottmachen (↑R 39 *u.* 40); **Flọtt,** das; -[e]s (*nordd. für* Milchrahm); **flọtt|be|kom|men** (fahrbereit machen); **Flọt|te,** die; -, -n; **Flọt|ten‿ab|kom|men, ...ba|sis, ...stütz|punkt; flot|ti̲e̲|ren** (schwimmen; schweben); -de (schwebende, kurzfristige) Schuld; **Flot|til|le** [*österr. nur so, sonst auch* ...'tiljə], die; -, -n ‹span.› (Verband kleiner Kriegsschiffe); **flọtt|ma|chen** (*Seemannsspr.* zum Schwimmen bringen; *ugs. für* fahrbereit machen); *vgl.* flott; **flọtt|wẹg** (*ugs. für* in einem weg; zügig)
Flọtz|maul (der stets feuchte Nasenteil beim Rind)
Flö̲z, das; -es, -e (abbaubare [Kohle]schicht)
Flu|a̲t, das; -[e]s, -e (*Kurzw. für* Fluorosilikat)
Flu̲ch, der; -[e]s, Flüche; **flu̲ch|be|la|den; flu̲|chen; Flu̲|cher**
[1]**Flụcht,** die; -, -en ‹*zu* fliegen› (Fluchtlinie, Richtung, Gerade)
[2]**Flụcht,** die; -, -en ‹*zu* fliehen›; **flụcht|ar|tig; Flụcht|burg** (*svw.* Fliehburg)
flụch|ten (*Bauw.* in eine gerade Linie bringen)
flụ̈ch|ten; sich -; **Flụcht‿fahr|zeug, ...ge|fahr** (die; -), **...ge|schwin|dig|keit** (*Physik* Geschwindigkeit, die nötig ist, um das Gravitationsfeld eines Planeten zu überwinden); **Flụcht|hel|fer**
flụch|tig (*veraltet für* perspektivisch)
flụ̈ch|tig; Flụ̈ch|tig|keit; Flụ̈ch|tig|keits|feh|ler; Flụ̈cht|ling; Flụ̈cht|lings|la|ger
Flụcht‿li|nie, ...punkt
Flụcht|ver|dacht; flụcht|ver|däch|tig; Flụcht‿ver|such, ...wa|gen, ...weg
flu̲ch|wür|dig (*geh.*)
Flüe ['fly:(ə)], Nik[o]laus von (schweiz. Heiliger)
Flu̲g, der; -[e]s, Flüge; die Zeit vergeht im -[e]; **Flu̲g‿ab|wehr, ...asche** (↑R 132), **...bahn, ...ball** (*bes. Tennis*), **...be|glei|ter** (Steward), **...be|glei|te|rin** (Stewardess); **flu̲g|be|reit; Flu̲g‿blatt, ...boot, ...ech|se** (*vgl.* Flugsaurier); **Flü̲|gel,** der; -s, -; **Flü̲|gel‿ad|ju|tant** (*veraltet*), **...al|tar, ...horn; ...flü|ge|lig, ...flüg|lig** (z. B. einflüg[e]lig); **flü̲|gel|lahm; Flü̲|gel|mann** *Plur.* ...männer *u.* ...leute; **flü̲|geln** (*Jägerspr.* in den Flügel schießen); ich ...[e]le (↑R 16); geflügelt (*vgl. d.*); **Flü̲|gel‿ra|ke|te, ...schlag; flü̲|gel|schla|gend; Flü̲|gel‿schrau|be, ...stür|mer** (*Sport*), **...tür; Flu̲g‿funk, ...gast** (*Plur.* ...gäste); **flü̲g|ge; Flu̲g‿ge|sell|schaft, ...ha|fen** (*vgl.* [2]Hafen), **...hö|he, ...hund** (Fledermausart), **...ka|pi|tän, ...ki|lo|me|ter, ...kör|per, ...lärm, ...leh|rer; ...flüg|lig** *vgl.* ...flügelig; **Flu̲g‿li|nie, ...loch, ...lot|se, ...plan** (*vgl.* [2]Plan), **...platz, ...rei|se; flu̲gs** (*veraltend für* schnell, sogleich); ↑R 46; **Flu̲g‿sand, ...sau|ri|er** (*für* Pterosaurier), **...schein, ...schrei|ber** (Gerät), **...schrift, ...schü|ler, ...si|che|rung, ...steig, ...stun|de, ...taug|lich|keit, ...tech|nik, ...tou|ris|tik, ...ver|kehr, ...we|sen** (das; -s), **...zet|tel** (*österr. für* Flugblatt), **...zeug** (das; -[e]s, -e); **Flu̲g|zeug‿ab|sturz, ...ab|wehr|ka|no|ne** (*Kurzw.* Flak); **Flu̲g|zeug‿bau** (der; -[e]s), **...ent|füh|rer, ...ent|füh|rung, ...füh|rer, ...mut|ter|schiff, ...trä|ger**
Flu̲h, die; -, Flühe (*schweiz. für* Fels[wand]); **Flü̲h|vo|gel** (*schweiz. für* [1]Braunelle)
flu|i̲d ‹lat.› (*Chemie* flüssig); **Flu|i̲d** [*auch* flu'i:t], das; -s, *Plur.* -s, *bei Ausspr.* [flu'i:t] -e ‹engl.› (*fachspr. für* flüssiges Mittel, Flüssigkeit); **Flu|i|dum,** das; -s, ...da ‹lat.› (von einer Person od. Sache ausströmende Wirkung)

Flu̲ke, die; -, -n (quer stehende Schwanzflosse der Wale)
Fluk|tu|a|ti|o̲n, die; -, -en ⟨lat.⟩ (Schwanken, Wechsel); **fluk|tu|ie̲|ren**
Flu̯n|der, die; -, -n (ein Fisch)
Flun|ke|rei̲; Flu̯n|ke|rer; Flu̯n|ke|rin; flu̯n|kern (*ugs. für* schwindeln, aufschneiden); ich ...ere (↑R 16)
Flu̯nsch, die; -, -en *u.* der; -[e]s, -e (*ugs. für* [verdrießlich od. zum Weinen] verzogener Mund)
Flu̲or, das; -s ⟨lat.⟩ (chem. Element; Nichtmetall; *Zeichen* F); **Flu|o|res|ze̲nz,** die; - (Aufleuchten unter Strahleneinwirkung); **flu|o|res|zie̲|ren;** fluoreszierender Stoff (Leuchtstoff); **Flu|o|ri̲d,** das; -[e]s, -e (*Chemie* Salz des Fluorwasserstoffs); **flu|o|ri|die̲|ren** *vgl.* fluorieren; **flu|o|rie̲|ren** (mit Fluor anreichern); Trinkwasser -; **Flu|o|ri̲t** [*auch* ...'rit], das; -[e]s, -e (*Chemie* Flussspat); **Flu|o|ro|pho̲r,** der; -s, -e (Fluoreszenzträger); **Flu|o|ro|si|li|ka̲t** (Mittel zur Härtung von Baustoffen); *vgl.* Fluat
[1]**Flu̲r,** die; -, -en (nutzbare Landfläche; Feldflur); [2]**Flu̲r,** der; -[e]s, -e (Gang [mit Türen], Hausflur); **Flu̲r‿be|rei|ni|gung, ...buch** (*für* Kataster), **...för|de|rer** (Fahrzeug), **...gar|de|ro|be, ...hü|ter, ...na|me, ...scha|den, ...schütz** (der), **...um|gang** (*früher* Flurkontrollgang [mit Segnungen])
Flu̲|se, die; -, -n (*landsch. für* Fadenrest, Fussel)
Flu̯ss, der; -es, Flüsse; **fluss|a̯b, fluss|a̯b|wärts; Flu̯ss|arm; fluss|au̲f, fluss|au̲f|wärts; Flu̯ss|bett; Flü̯ss|chen; Flu̯ss‿di|a|gramm** (graph. Darstellung von Arbeitsabläufen), **...fisch, ...gott; flü̯s|sig;** flüssige (verfügbare) Gelder; flüssige Kristalle. *Schreibung in Verbindung mit Verben* (↑R 39): flüssig machen (*auch für* [Geld] verfügbar machen); **Flü̯s|sig‿ei** (das; -[e]s), **...gas; Flü̯s|sig|keit; Flü̯s|sig|keits‿brem|se** (hydraulische Bremse), **...maß** (das), **...men|ge; Flü̯s|sig|kris|tall|an|zei|ge** ([Ziffern]anzeige mithilfe flüssiger Kristalle); **flüs|sig ma|chen** *vgl.* flüssig; **Flu̯ss‿land|schaft, ...lauf; Flüss|lein; Flu̯ss‿mün|dung, ...pferd, ...re|gu|lie|rung; Flu̯ss|sand** (↑R 136); **Flu̯ss|schiff|fahrt** (↑R 136); **Flu̯ss|spat** (↑R 136; ein Mineral; *vgl.* [1]Spat); **Flu̯ss|stahl** (↑R 136; *vgl.* [1]Stahl); **Flu̯ss|ufer** (↑R 132)
Flü̯s|te|rer; flü̯s|tern; ich ...ere (↑R 16); **Flü̯s|ter‿pro|pa|gan|da, ...stim|me, ...ton** (der; -[e]s; im - sprechen), **...tü|te** (*scherzh. für* Sprachrohr), **...witz** (gegen ein totalitäres Regime gerichteter Witz)
Flu̲t, die; -, -en; **flu̲|ten; Flu̲t‿hö|he, ...ka|ta|stro|phe, ...licht** (das; -[e]s)
flu̯t|schen (*ugs. für* gut vorankommen, -gehen); es flutscht
Flu̲t‿war|nung, ...wel|le, ...zeit
flu|vi|a̲l [...v...] ⟨lat.⟩ (*Geol.* von fließendem Wasser verursacht)
Fly|er ['flai̯ə(r)], der; -s, - ⟨engl.⟩ (Vorspinn-, Flügelspinnmaschine; Arbeiter an einer solchen Maschine); **Fly|e|rin; Fly|ing Dutch|man** ['flai̯iŋ 'datʃmən], der; - -, - ...men ⟨engl.⟩ (ein Zweimann-Sportsegelboot); **Fly-over** [flai̯'o:və(r)], der; -s, -s (Straßenüberführung)
Flysch [fliʃ, *schweiz.* fli:ʃ, *österr.* fly:ʃ], das, *österr.* der; -[e]s (ein Gestein)
Fm = Fermium
Fm, fm = Festmeter
FMH = Foederatio Medicorum Helveticorum (Vereinigung schweiz. [Fach]ärzte)
Fmk = Finnmark; *vgl.* Markka
f-Moll ['ɛfmɔl, *auch* 'ɛf'mɔl], das; - (Tonart; *Zeichen* f); **f-Moll-Ton|lei|ter** (↑R 28)
fo̯b = free on board [fri: ɔn 'bɔ:(r)d] ⟨engl., „frei an Bord"⟩; - Hamburg, - deutschen Ausfuhrhafen; **Fo̯b|klau|sel**
Fo̯ck, die; -, -en (Vorsegel; unterstes Rahsegel des Vormastes); **Fo̯ck‿mast** (der), **...ra|he, ...se|gel**
fö|de|ra̲l (föderativ); **Fö|de|ra|li̯s|mus,** der; - ⟨lat.-franz.⟩ ([Streben nach] Selbstständigkeit der einzelnen Länder innerhalb eines Staatsganzen); **Fö|de|ra|li̯st,** der; -en, -en (↑R 126); **fö|de|ra|li̯s|tisch; Fö|de|ra|ti|o̲n,** die; -, -en (loser [Staaten]bund); **fö|de|ra|ti̲v** (bundesmäßig); **Fö|de|ra|ti̲v|staat** *Plur.* ...staaten; **fö|de|rie̲rt** (verbündet)
Fo̯|gosch, der; -[e]s, -e ⟨ung.⟩ (*österr. für* Zander)
fo̲h|len (ein Fohlen zur Welt bringen); **Fo̲h|len,** das; -s, -
Fö̲hn, der; -[e]s, -e (warmer, trockener Fallwind; *auch für* Haartrockner [als ®: Fön]); **fö̲h|nen** (föhnig werden; *auch für* mit dem Föhn trocknen); es föhnt; sie föhnt ihr Haar; **fö̲h|nig;** -es Wetter; **Fö̲hn‿krank|heit, ...wind**
Fö̲hr (eine der Nordfries. Inseln)
Fö̲h|re, die; -, -n (*landsch. für* Kiefer); **fö̲h|ren** (aus Föhrenholz); **Fö̲h|ren|wald**
fo|ka̲l ⟨lat.⟩ (den Fokus betreffend, Brenn...); **Fo|ka̲l|in|fek|ti|o̲n** (*Med.* von einem Streuherd ausgehende Infektion); **Fo̲|kus,** der; -, -se (*Physik* Brennpunkt; *Med.* Krankheitsherd); **fo|kus|sie̲|ren** ([eine Linse] ausrichten; [ein Objektiv] scharf stellen; [Strahlen] bündeln)
fol., Fol. = Folio; Folioblatt
Fo̯l|ge, die; -, -n; Folge leisten; zur Folge haben; für die Folge, in der Folge; demzufolge (*vgl. d.*); infolge; zufolge; infolgedessen; **Fo̯l|ge‿er|schei|nung, ...kos|ten** (*Plur.*), **...las|ten** (*Plur.*); **fo̯l|gen;** er ist mir gefolgt (nachgekommen); er hat mir gefolgt (Gehorsam geleistet); **folgend;** folgende [Seite] (*Abk.* f.); folgende [Seiten] (*Abk.* ff.); folgendes politische Bekenntnis; folgende lange (*seltener* langen) Ausführungen; Folgendes (dieses); das Folgende (dieses; das später Erwähnte, Geschehende; die nachfolgenden Ausführungen); in, mit, aus Folgendem; im Folgenden; alle Folgenden (↑R 47 f.); **fo̯l|gen|der|ge|stalt; fo̯l|gen|der|ma̲|ßen; fo̯l|gen‿reich, ...schwer; Fo̯l|gen|schwe|re,** die; -; **fo̯l|ge|recht** (*veraltend*); **fo̯l|ge|rich|tig; Fo̯l|ge|rich|tig|keit; fo̯l|gern;** ich ...ere (↑R 16); **fo̯l|gernd; Fo̯l|ge|rung; Fo̯l|ge|satz** (*für* Konsekutivsatz); **Fo̯l|ge|scha|den; fo̯l|ge|wid|rig; Fo̯l|ge‿wid|rig|keit, ...zeit; fo̯lg|lich; fo̯lg|sam; Fo̯lg|sam|keit,** die; -
Fo̲|lia (*Plur. von* Folium); **Fo|li|a̲nt,** der; -en, -en (↑R 126) ⟨lat.⟩ (Buch in Folio); **Fo̲|lie** [...i̯ə], die; -, -n (dünnes [Metall]blatt; Prägeblatt; Hintergrund); **Fo̲|li|en|schweiß|ge|rät; fo̲|li|en|ver|packt;** -e Ware
Fo|lies-Ber|gère [fɔlibɛr'ʒɛ:r] *Plur.* ⟨franz.⟩ (Varieté u. Tanzkabarett in Paris)
fo|li|ie̲|ren ⟨lat.⟩ ([Bogenseiten] beziffern; mit einer Folie unterlegen); **Fo̲|lio,** das; -s, *Plur.* Folien [...i̯ən] *u.* -s (*Buchw.* Halbbogengröße [*nur Sing.;* Buchformat; *Abk.* fol., Fol. *od.* 2°]; Blatt im Geschäftsbuch); in -; **Fo̲|li|o‿band** (der), **...blatt** (*Abk.* Fol.), **...for|mat; Fo̲|li|um,** das; -s, *Plur.* Folia *u.* Folien [...i̯ən] (*Bot.* Pflanzenblatt)
Folk [fo:k], der; -s ⟨engl.⟩ (an englischsprachige Volksmusik anknüpfende, [vom [2]Rock beeinflusste] populäre Musik)

Fọl|ke, Fọl|ko (m. Vorn.)
Fọl|ke|ting, das; -s (Bez. für das dän. Parlament)
Folk|lo|re, die; - ⟨engl.⟩ (volkstüml. Überlieferung; Volkskunde; Volksmusik [in der Kunstmusik]); **Folk|lo|rịst,** der; -en, -en (↑R 126); **Folk|lo|rịs|tik,** die; - (Wissenschaft von der Folklore); **Folk|lo|rịs|tin; folk|lo|rịs|tisch**
Fọl|ko *vgl.* Folke
Folk|song ['fo:k...] ⟨engl.⟩ (volkstümliches Lied, volksliedhafter [Protest]song); **Fọlk|wang** (*nord. Mythol.* Palast der Freyja)
Fol|li|kel, der; -s, - ⟨lat.⟩ (*Biol., Med.* Drüsenbläschen; Hülle der reifenden Eizelle im Eierstock); **Fol|li|kel‿hor|mon, ...sprung; fol|li|ku|lar, fol|li|ku|lär** (auf den Follikel bezüglich)
Fọl|ter, die; -, -n; **Fọl|ter|bank** *Plur.* ...bänke; **Fọl|te|rer; Fọl|ter‿in|stru|ment, ...kam|mer; fọl|tern;** ich ...ere (↑R 16); **Fọl|te|rung; Fọl|ter|werk|zeug**
Fon *eindeutschende Schreibung für* Phon
Fön ® *vgl.* Föhn
Fond [fõ:], der; -s, -s ⟨franz.⟩ (Hintergrund; Rücksitz im Wagen; ausgebratener od. -gekochter Fleischsaft)
Fon|dant [fõ'dã:], der, *auch, österr. nur* das; -s, -s ⟨franz.⟩ ([Konfekt aus] Zuckermasse)
Fonds [fõ:], der; - [...(s)], - [...s] ⟨franz.⟩ (Geldmittel, -vorrat, Bestand; *Plur. auch für* Anleihen)
Fon|due [fõ'dy:], das; -s, -s *od.* die; -, -s ⟨franz.⟩ (schweiz. Käsegericht; bei Tisch gegartes Fleischgericht); **Fon|due|ga|bel**
fö|nen *frühere Schreibung für* [die Haare] föhnen
fo|no..., Fo|no... *eindeutschende Schreibungen für* phono..., Phono...
Fon|taine|bleau [fõtɛn'blo:] (Stadt u. Schloss in Frankreich)
Fon|ta|ne (dt. Dichter)
Fon|tä|ne, die; -, -n ⟨franz.⟩ ([Spring]brunnen); **Fon|ta|nẹl|le,** die; -, -n (*Med.* Knochenlücke am Schädel Neugeborener)
Fon|tan|ge [fõ'tã:ʒə], die; -, -n ⟨nach einer franz. Herzogin⟩ (Frauenhaartracht des 17. Jh.s)
Foot [fut], der; -, Feet [fi:t] ⟨engl.⟩ (engl. Längenmaß; *Abk.* ft; *Zeichen* '); **Foot|ball** ['futbɔ:l], der; -[s] (amerik. Mannschaftsspiel)
fọp|pen; Fọp|per; Fop|pe|rei
Fo|ra|mi|ni|fe|re, die; -, -n *meist Plur.* ⟨lat.⟩ (*Biol.* zu den Wurzelfüßern gehörendes Urtierchen)
Force de frappe [fɔrs də 'frap], die; - - ⟨franz.⟩ (Gesamtheit der franz. Atomstreitkräfte); **for|cie|ren** [fɔr'si:...] (erzwingen; verstärken); **for|ciert**
Ford ® (Kraftfahrzeugmarke)
För|de, die; -, -n (*nordd. für* schmale, lange Meeresbucht)
För|der‿band (das; *Plur.* ...bänder), **...be|trieb** (der; -[e]s); **För|de|rer; För|de|rer|kreis** *vgl.* Förderkreis; **För|de|rin; För|der‿kọh|le, ...korb, ...kreis** (eines Museums u. Ä.); **För|der‿kurs, ...land; för|der|lich**
fọr|dern; ich ...ere (↑R 16)
fọ̈r|dern; ich ...ere (↑R 16); **För|der‿preis** (zur Förderung junger Künstler u. Ä.), **...schacht, ...seil, ...stu|fe** (*Schulw.*), **...turm**
Fọr|de|rung
För|de|rung; För|de|rungs|maß|nah|me; För|der|werk (*Technik*)
Fö|re, die; - ⟨skand.⟩ (*Skisport* Gefügigkeit)
Fore|che|cking ['fɔ:(r)tʃɛkiŋ], das; -s, -s ⟨engl.⟩ (*Eishockey* das Stören und Angreifen des Gegners in dessen Verteidigungsdrittel)
Fo|reign Of|fice ['fɔrin 'ɔfis], das; - - (Brit. Außenministerium)
Fo|rẹl|le, die; -, -n (ein Fisch); **Fo|rẹl|len‿teich, ...zucht**
fo|rẹn|sisch ⟨lat.⟩ (gerichtlich)
Fo|rint [*österr.* fɔ'rint], der; -[s], *Plur.* -s, *österr.* Forinte ⟨ung.⟩ (ung. Währungseinheit; *Abk.* Ft); 10 - (↑R 90)
Fọr|ke, die; -, -n (*nordd. für* Heu-, Mistgabel); **fọr|keln** (*Jägerspr.* mit dem Geweih kämpfen)
Fọr|le, die; -, -n (*südd. für* Kiefer); **Fọrl|eu|le** (Schmetterling)
Fọrm, die; -, -en; in - sein; in - von; *vgl.* pro forma; **for|mal** (auf die Form bezüglich; nur der Form nach)
Fọrm|al|de|hyd [*auch* ...'hy:t], der; -s (ein Gas als Desinfektionsmittel)
For|ma|lie [...iə], die; -, -n *meist Plur.* (formale Einzelheit, Äußerlichkeit)
For|ma|lin ®, das; -s (ein Konservierungs-, Desinfektionsmittel)
for|ma|li|sie|ren ⟨franz.⟩ (in [strenge] Form bringen; formal darstellen); **For|ma|lịs|mus,** der; -, ...men ⟨lat.⟩ (Überbetonung der Form, des rein Formalen; formalist. Arbeitsweise); **For|ma|lịst,** der; -en, -en (↑R 126); **For|ma|lịs|tin; for|ma|lịs|tisch; For|ma|li|tät,** die; -, -en (Äußerlichkeit, Formsache; [behördliche] Vorschrift); **for|ma|li|ter** (förmlich); **for|mal‿ju|ris|tisch, ...recht|lich; Fọrm|an|stieg** (*Sportspr.*);
For|mat, das; -[e]s, -e; **For|ma|ti|on,** die; -, -en (Anordnung; Gruppe, Verband; *Geol.* Zeitabschnitt, Folge von Gesteinsschichten); **For|ma|ti|ons‿flug, ...tanz; for|ma|tiv** (auf die Gestaltung bezüglich, gestaltend); **fọrm|bar; Fọrm|bar|keit,** die; -; **fọrm|be|stän|dig; Fọrm|be|stän|dig|keit; Fọrm‿blatt, ...ei|sen; Fọr|mel,** die; -, -n; **For|mel-1-Wa|gen** [...'ains...]; ↑R 28 (ein Rennwagen); **fọr|mel|haft; Fọr|mel|haf|tig|keit,** die; -; **Fọr|mel|kram,** der; -[e]s; **for|mẹll** ⟨franz.⟩ (förmlich, die Formen [peinlich] beachtend; rein äußerlich; zum Schein vorgenommen); **Fọr|mel|spra|che; fọr|men; Fọr|men|leh|re,** die; - (Teil der Sprachlehre u. der Musiklehre); **fọr|men|reich; Fọr|men|reich|tum,** der; -s; **Fọr|men|sinn,** der; -[e]s; **Fọr|mer; For|me|rei; Fọrm‿feh|ler, ...fra|ge, ...ge|bung, ...ge|fühl** (das; -[e]s), **...ge|stal|ter** (*für* Designer), **...ge|stal|tung; fọrm|ge|wandt; Fọrm|ge|wandt|heit,** die; -
for|mi|da|bel ⟨franz.⟩ (*veraltend für* furchtbar; *auch für* großartig); ...ab|le (↑R 130) Erscheinung
for|mie|ren ⟨franz.⟩; sich -; **For|mie|rung; ...för|mig** (z. B. nadelförmig); **Fọrm|kri|se** (*Sportspr.*); **fọ̈rm|lich; Fọ̈rm|lich|keit; fọrm|los; Fọrm|lo|sig|keit;** die; -; **Fọrm‿obst** (Spalierobst[bäume]), **...sa|che, ...sand** (*Gießerei*); **fọrm|schön; Fọrm|schön|heit;** die; -; **Fọrm‿schwan|kung** (*Sportspr.*), **...stren|ge** (die; -), **...tief** (*Sportspr.*); **fọrm|treu; For|mu|lar,** das; -s, -e ⟨lat.⟩; **For|mu|lar|block** (*vgl.* Block); **for|mu|lie|ren** (in eine angemessene sprachliche Form bringen); **For|mu|lie|rung; Fọr|mung; fọrm|voll|en|det**
Fọr|nix, der; -, ...nices [...tse:s] ⟨lat.⟩ (*Med.* Gewölbe eines Organs)
fọrsch ⟨lat.⟩ (schneidig, kühn, selbstbewusst); **Fọr|sche,** die; - (*ugs. für* Nachdruck)
fọr|schen; du forschst; **Fọr|scher; Fọr|scher|geist,** der; -[e]s; **Fọr|sche|rin; fọr|sche|risch; Fọr|schung; Fọr|schungs‿auf|trag, ...be|richt, ...er|geb|nis, ...in|sti|tut, ...la|bor, ...me|tho|de, ...ra|ke|te, ...rei|se, ...rei|sen|de, ...rich|tung, ...schiff, ...se|mes|ter, ...sta|ti|on, ...sti|pen|di|um, ...stu|dent** (*regional*), **...stu|di|um** (*regional*), **...zent|rum, ...zweig**

Forst, der; -[e]s, -e[n]; **Forst|amt; För|ster; Förs|te|rei; Förs|te|rin; Forst‿fre|vel, ...haus; forst|lich; Forst‿mann** (*Plur.* ...männer *u.* ...leute), **...meis|ter, ...rat** (*Plur.* ...räte; *früher*), **...re|vier, ...scha|den, ...schu|le, ...ver|wal|tung, ...we|sen** (das; -s), **...wirt, ...wirt|schaft, ...wis|sen|schaft** (die; -)

For|sy|thie [...'zy:t(s)iə, *österr. u. schweiz.* ...'zi:tsiə], die; -, -n ‹nach dem engl. Botaniker Forsyth› (ein Zierstrauch)

fort; fort sein; fort mit ihm!; und so fort (*Abk.* usf.); in einem fort; weiter fort; immerfort

fort... (*in Zus. mit Verben,* z. B. fortbestehen, du bestehst fort, fortbestanden, fortzubestehen)

Fort [fo:r], das; s, -s ‹franz.› (Festungswerk)

fort|ab; fort|an

Fort|be|stand, der; -[e]s; **fort|be|ste|hen**

fort|be|we|gen; sich -; *vgl.* [1]bewegen; **Fort|be|we|gung**

fort|bil|den; sich -; **Fort|bil|dung**

fort|blei|ben

fort|brin|gen

Fort|dau|er; fort|dau|ern; fort|dau|ernd

for|te ‹ital.› (*Musik* stark, laut; *Abk.* f); **For|te**, das; -s, *Plur.* -s *u.* ...ti

fort|ent|wi|ckeln; sich -; **Fort|ent|wick|lung**

For|te|pi|a|no, das; -s, *Plur.* -s *u.* ...ni ‹ital.› (*alte Bez. für* Pianoforte)

fort|er|ben, sich

fort|fah|ren

Fort|fall, der; -[e]s; in Fortfall kommen *(Amtsspr.)*; **fort|fal|len**

fort|flie|gen

fort|füh|ren; Fort|füh|rung

Fort|gang, der; -[e]s; **fort|ge|hen**

fort|ge|schrit|ten; Fort|ge|schrit|te|ne, der *u.* die; -n, -n (↑R 5 ff.)

fort|ge|setzt

fort|ha|ben; etwas - wollen *(ugs.)*

fort|hin *(veraltend)*

For|ti|fi|ka|ti|on, die; -, -en ‹lat.› (*veraltet für* Befestigungswerk; *nur Sing.:* Befestigungskunst); **for|ti|fi|zie|ren**

For|tis, die; -, ...tes ‹lat.› (*Sprachw.* starker, mit großer Intensität gesprochener Konsonant, z. B. p, t, k; *Ggs.* Lenis; *[vgl. d.]*); **for|tis|si|mo** ‹ital.› (*Musik* sehr stark, sehr laut; *Abk.* ff); **For|tis|si|mo**, das; -s, *Plur.* -s *u.* ...mi

fort|ja|gen

fort|kom|men; Fort|kom|men, das; -

fort|kön|nen

fort|las|sen; Fort|las|sung; unter - des Titels

fort|lau|fen; fort|lau|fend; - nummeriert

fort|le|ben

fort|lo|ben; einen Mitarbeiter -

fort|ma|chen

fort|müs|sen

fort|pflan|zen; sich -; **Fort|pflan|zung**, die; -; **Fort|pflan|zungs‿or|gan, ...trieb**

FORTRAN, das; -s ‹*Kurzwort für* engl. formula translator „Formelübersetzer"› (eine Programmiersprache)

fort|rei|ßen; jmdn. mit sich -

fort|ren|nen

fort|rüh|ren; sich [nicht] -

Fort|satz, der; -es, Fortsätze

fort|schaf|fen; *vgl.* [1]schaffen

fort|sche|ren, sich *(ugs.)*

fort|schi|cken

fort|schrei|ben ([eine Statistik] fortlaufend ergänzen; *Wirtsch.* den Grundstückseinheitswert neu feststellen); **Fort|schrei|bung**

fort|schrei|ten; fort|schrei|tend; Fort|schritt; Fort|schritt|ler; fort|schritt|lich; Fort|schritt|lich|keit, die; -; **fort|schritts|feind|lich; Fort|schritts|glau|be; fort|schritts|gläu|big**

fort|set|zen; Fort|set|zung; Fort|set|zungs|ro|man

fort|steh|len, sich

fort|stre|ben

fort|tra|gen

For|tu|na (röm. Glücksgöttin); **For|tu|nat, For|tu|na|tus** (m. Vorn.); **For|tune** [...'ty:n], *eingedeutscht* **For|tü|ne**, die; - ‹franz.› (Glück, Erfolg); keine - haben

fort|wäh|rend

fort|wer|fen

fort|wol|len

fort|zie|hen

Fo|rum, das; -s, *Plur.* ...ren *u.* ...ra ‹lat.› (altröm. Marktplatz, Gerichtsort; *Plur. nur* ...ren: Öffentlichkeit; öffentliche Diskussion); **Fo|rums|ge|spräch**

For|ward ['fo:rvart, *engl.* 'fɔ:(r)wəd], der; -s, -s ‹engl.› (*schweiz. Sportspr.* Stürmer)

for|za|to *vgl.* sforzato

Fos|bu|ry|flop ['fɔsbəriflɔp] (↑R 95), der; -s, -s ‹nach dem amerik. Leichtathleten› (ein Hochsprungstil *[nur Sing.]*; einzelner Sprung in diesem Stil)

Fo|se, die; -, -n (*derb für* Dirne)

Fo|ße, die; -, -n ‹franz.› (*nordd. für* minderwertige Spielkarte)

fos|sil ‹lat.› (versteinert; vorweltlich); fossile Brennstoffe (z.B. Kohle, Erdöl); fossil befeuerte Kraftwerke; **Fos|sil**, das; -s, -ien [...iən] ([versteinerter] Überrest von Tieren od. Pflanzen)

fö|tal *vgl.* fetal

[1]**Fo|to**[1], das; -s, -s, *schweiz.* die; -, -s (*kurz für* Fotografie); [2]**Fo|to**, der; -s, -s (*ugs. kurz für* Fotoapparat); **Fo|to‿al|bum, ...ama|teur** (↑R 132), **...ap|pa|rat, ...ar|ti|kel, ...ate|li|er** (↑R 132); **Fo|to|che|mie, Fo|to|elekt|ri|zi|tät** usw. *vgl.* Photochemie, Photoelektrizität usw.; **Fo|to|fi|nish** (Zieleinlauf, bei dem der Sieger durch Zielfoto ermittelt wird); **fo|to|gen**, *auch* pho|to|gen (zum Fotografieren od. Filmen geeignet, bildwirksam); **Fo|to|ge|ni|tät**, die; - (Bildwirksamkeit); **Fo|to|graf**, der; -en, -en (↑R 126); **Fo|to|gra|fie**, die; -, ...ien; **fo|to|gra|fie|ren; Fo|to|gra|fik** [*auch* 'fo:...] (fotografisches Verfahren mit gestalterischen Elementen *[nur Sing.]*; gestaltetes Foto); **Fo|to|gra|fin; fo|to|gra|fisch; Fo|to|in|dust|rie; Fo|to|ko|pie** (Lichtbildabzug von Schriften, Dokumenten u. a.); **Fo|to|ko|pier|au|to|mat; fo|to|ko|pie|ren; Fo|to|li|tho|gra|fie** *vgl.* Photolithographie; **Fo|to|met|rie** *vgl.* Photometrie; **Fo|to‿mo|dell, ...mon|ta|ge** (Zusammenstellung verschiedener Bildausschnitte zu einem Gesamtbild), **...re|a|lis|mus** (der; -; moderne Kunstrichtung), **...re|por|ter, ...sa|fa|ri; Fo|to|satz** *vgl.* Photosatz; **Fo|to|syn|the|se** *vgl.* Photosynthese; **Fo|to|thek**, die; -, -en (Lichtbildsammlung); **fo|to|trop**, *auch* pho|to|trop ([von Brillengläsern] sich unter Lichteinwirkung verfärbend); **Fo|to|vol|ta|ik** *vgl.* Photovoltaik; **Fo|to|zeit|schrift; Fo|to|zel|le** *vgl.* Photozelle

Fö|tus *vgl.* Fetus

Fot|ze, die; -, -n (*derb für* weibl. Scham; *bayr. u. österr. ugs. für* Ohrfeige; Maul)

Föt|zel, der; -s, - (*schweiz. für* Lump, Taugenichts)

fot|zen (*bayr. u. österr. ugs. für* ohrfeigen); **Fotz|ho|bel** (*bayr. u. österr. ugs. für* Mundharmonika)

Fou|cault [fu'ko:] (franz. Physiker); **fou|cault|sche Pen|del|ver|such** [fu'ko:ʃə -], der; -n -[e]s

Fou|ché [fu'ʃe:] (franz. Staatsmann)

foul [faul] ‹engl.› (*Sport* regelwidrig); **Foul**, das; -s, -s (Regelverstoß)

Fou|lard [fu'la:r], der, *schweiz.* das;

[1] [*Vgl. auch* photo..., Photo... *u.* R 33]

-s, -s ‹franz.› (leichtes [Kunst]seidengewebe; *schweiz. für* Halstuch aus [Kunst]seide); **Foul|lé** [fu'le:], der; -[s], -s (ein Gewebe)
Foul|elf|me|ter ['faul...], der *(Sport);* **foul|len** ['faulən] ‹engl.› (*Sport* sich regelwidrig verhalten);
Foul|spiel ['faul...], das; -[e]s (regelwidriges Spielen)
Fou|qué [fu'ke:] (dt. Dichter)
Four|gon [fur'gõ:], der; -s, -s (*veraltet für* Packwagen, Vorratswagen; *schweiz. für* Militär-, Postlastauto)
Fou|rier [fu'ri:r], der; -s, -e ‹franz.› (*österr. u. schweiz. für* Furier)
Fox, der; -[es], -e (*Kurzform für* Foxterrier, Foxtrott); **Fox|ter|ri|er** [...iər] ‹engl.› (Hunderasse); **Fox|trott,** der; -[e]s, *Plur.* -e *u.* -s ‹engl.-amerik.› (ein Tanz)
Fo|yer [foa'je:], das; -s, -s ‹franz.› (Wandelhalle [im Theater])
FPÖ = Freiheitliche Partei Österreichs
fr = Franc
Fr = *chem. Zeichen für* Francium
fr. = frei
Fr. = Frau; Freitag; *vgl.* [2]Franken
Fra ‹ital.› (Ordens„bruder"; *meist vor konsonantisch beginnenden Namen,* z. B. Fra Tommaso); *vgl.* Frate
Fracht, die; -, -en; **Fracht_brief, ...damp|fer;** **Frach|ten|aus|schuss,** der; -es *(Wirtsch.);* **Frach|ter** (Frachtschiff); **fracht|frei;** **Fracht_gut, ...raum, ...schiff, ...stück, ...ver|kehr**
Frack, der; -[e]s, *Plur.* Fräcke *u.* -s ‹engl.›; **Frack_hemd, ...ho|se, ...sau|sen** (*nur in* - haben [*ugs. für* Angst haben]), **...wes|te**
Fra Di|a|vo|lo [- di'a:volo] ‹„Bruder Teufel"› (neapolitan. Räuberhauptmann)
Fra|ge, die; -, -n; *vgl.* infrage; **Fra|ge_bo|gen, ...für|wort** (*für* Interrogativpronomen); **fra|gen;** du fragst (*landsch.* frägst); er fragt (*landsch.* frägt); du fragtest (*landsch.* frugst); gefragt; frag[e]!; **Fra|gen_ka|ta|log, ...kom|plex, ...kreis;** **Fra|ger;** **Fra|ge|rei;** **Fra|ge|rin;** **Fra|ge_satz** (*für* Interrogativsatz), **...stel|lung, ...stun|de** (im Parlament); **Fra|ge-und-Ant|wort-Spiel** (↑R 28); **Fra|ge_wort** (*Plur.* ...wörter), **...zei|chen**
fra|gil ‹lat.› (zerbrechlich; zart); **Fra|gi|li|tät,** die; -
frag|lich; **Frag|lich|keit;** **frag|los;** **Frag|lo|sig|keit,** die; -
Frag|ment, das; -[e]s, -e ‹lat.› (Bruchstück; unvollendetes Werk); **frag|men|ta|risch**
Frag|ner, der; -s, - (*bayr. u. österr. veraltet für* Krämer)
frag|wür|dig; **Frag|wür|dig|keit**
frais [frɛ:s] *od., österr. nur,* **fraise** ['frɛ:z] ‹franz.› (erdbeerfarben); mit einem frais[e] Band; *vgl. auch* beige; in Frais[e] (↑R 47)
Frai|sen *Plur.* (*südd., österr. für* Krämpfe [bei kleinen Kindern])
frak|tal ‹lat.-engl.›; -e Geometrie (Geometrie der Fraktale); **Frak|tal,** das; -s, -e (komplexes geometrisches Gebilde [wie es ähnlich auch in der Natur vorkommt]); **Frak|ti|on,** die; -, -en ‹franz.› (organisatorischer Zusammenschluss [im Parlament]; *Chemie* Destillat; *westösterr. für* Teil einer Gemeinde); **frak|ti|o|nell;** **Frak|ti|o|nier|ap|pa|rat** *(Chemie);* **frak|ti|o|nie|ren** (Gemische durch Verdampfung in Destillate zerlegen); fraktionierte Destillation; **Frak|ti|ons_aus|schuss, ...be|schluss, ...dis|zi|plin** (die; -), **...füh|rer, ...mit|glied, ...stär|ke, ...vor|sit|zen|de, ...vor|stand, ...zwang;** **Frak|tur,** die; -, -en ‹lat.› (*Med.* Knochenbruch; *nur Sing.:* dt. Schrift, Bruchschrift); **Frak|tur_satz** (der; -es; *Druckw.*), **...schrift**
Fram|bö|sie, die; -, ...ien ‹franz.› (*Med.* trop. Hautkrankheit)
Frame [fre:m], der; -n ['fre:mən], -n (↑R 126) ‹engl.› (*Technik* Rahmen, Träger in Eisenbahnfahrzeugen)
Franc [frã:], der; -, -s [frã:] ‹franz.› (Währungseinheit; *Abk.* fr, *Plur.* frs); 100 - (↑R 90); franz. Franc (*Abk.* F, FF); belg. Franc (*Abk.* bfr, *Plur.* bfrs); Luxemburger Franc (*Abk.* lfr, *Plur.* lfrs); *vgl.* [2]Franken
Fran|çai|se [frã'sɛ:zə], die; -, -n ‹franz.› (alter franz. Tanz)
France [frã:s], Anatole [...'tɔl] (franz. Schriftsteller); France' Werke (↑R 17)
Fran|ces|ca [fran'tʃɛska] (w. Vorn.); **Fran|ces|co** [...'tʃɛsko] (m. Vorn.)
[1]**Fran|chi|se** [frã'ʃi:zə], die; -, -n ‹franz.› (Betrag der Selbstbeteiligung an der Versicherung; *veraltet für* Freiheit, Freimütigkeit); [2]**Fran|chise** ['frɛntʃais], das; - *u.* **Fran|chi|sing** [...tʃaiziŋ], das; -s ‹franz.-engl.› (*Wirtsch.* Vertrieb aufgrund von Lizenzverträgen)
Fran|ci|um [...tsium], das; -s (chem. Element, Metall; *Zeichen* Fr)
Fran|cke (dt. Theologe u. Pädagoge); **Fran|cke|sche Stif|tun|gen** *Plur.* (↑R 108)
Fran|co, Francisco [...'θisko] (span. General u. Politiker)
frank ‹mlat.-franz.› (frei, offen); frank und frei
Frank (m. Vorn.); **Fran|ka** (w. Vorn.)
Fran|ka|tur, die; -, -en ‹ital.› (das Freimachen von Postsendungen, Porto)
Fran|ke, der; -n, -n; ↑R 126 (Angehöriger eines germanischen Volksstammes; Einwohner von [1]Franken); [1]**Fran|ken** (Land); [2]**Fran|ken,** der; -s, - (schweiz. Währungseinheit; *Abk.* Fr., sFr.; *im dt. Bankwesen* sfr, *Plur.* sfrs); *vgl.* Franc; **Fran|ken|stein** (Gestalt eines Schauerromans); **Fran|ken|wald,** der; -[e]s (Gebirge in Bayern); **Fran|ken|wein**
Frank|furt am Main (Stadt in Hessen); [1]**Frank|fur|ter** (↑R 103); [2]**Frank|fur|ter,** die; -, - *meist Plur.* (Frankfurter Würstchen); **frank|fur|tisch;** **Frank|furt (Oder)** (Stadt in Brandenburg)
fran|kie|ren ‹ital.› *(Postw.);* **Fran|kier|ma|schi|ne**
Frän|kin; **frän|kisch;** (↑R 102): die Fränkische Alb, die Fränkische Schweiz
Frank|lin ['frɛŋklin] (nordamerik. Staatsmann u. Schriftsteller)
fran|ko ‹ital.› (*Kaufmannsspr. veraltend* portofrei [für den Empfänger]); franko nach allen Stationen; franko Basel; franko dort; franko hier
Fran|ko|ka|na|di|er [...iər] (französisch sprechender Bewohner Kanadas); **fran|ko|ka|na|disch;** ↑R 106
fran|ko|phil ‹germ.; griech.› (frankreichfreundlich); **fran|ko|phon** (französischsprachig); die -en Staaten; **Fran|ko|pho|nie,** die; - (Französischsprachigkeit)
Frank|reich
Frank|ti|reur [frãkti'rø:r, *auch* frã...], der; -s, *Plur.* -e, *bei franz. Ausspr.* -s (*früher für* Freischärler)
Fräns|chen; **Fran|se,** die; -, -n; **fran|sen;** der Stoff franst, hat gefranst; **fran|sig;** **Fräns|lein**
Franz (m. Vorn.)
Franz_band (der; Ledereinband mit tiefem Falz), **...brannt|wein** (der; -[e]s), **...brot** (kleines Weißbrot), **...bröt|chen**
Frän|ze (w. Vorn.)
fran|zen (*Motorsport* als Beifahrer dem Fahrer den Verlauf der Strecke angeben); du franzt; **Fran|zer** *(Motorsport)*
Frän|zi, **Fran|zis|ka** (w. Vorn.); **Fran|zis|ka|ner,** der; -s, - (Ange-

höriger des Mönchsordens der Franziskaner); **Fran|zis|ka|ne|rin** (Angehörige des Ordens der Franziskanerinnen); **Fran|zis|ka|ner|or|den,** der; -s (*Abk.* OFM); **fran|zis|ka|nisch; fran|zis|ko|jo|se|phi|nisch** (↑R 106) ‹nach dem österr. Kaiser Franz Joseph›; franziskojosephinische Bauten; *aber* (↑R 108:) das Franziskojosephinische Zeitalter; **Fran|zis|kus** (m. Vorn.); **Fran|zi|um** *vgl.* Francium; **Franz-Jo|seph-Land,** das; -[e]s; ↑R 105 (eine arktische Inselgruppe)

Franz|mann *Plur.* ...männer (*ugs. veraltend für* Franzose); **Fran|zo|se,** der; -n, -n (↑R 126); **fran|zo|sen‿feind|lich, ...freund|lich; fran|zö|sie|ren** (franz. Verhältnissen anpassen; nach franz. Art gestalten); **Fran|zö|sin; fran|zö|sisch;** französische Broschur; die französische Schweiz (der französische Teil der Schweiz), *aber* (↑R 108): die Französische Republik; die Französische Revolution (1789 bis 1794); *vgl.* deutsch; **Fran|zö|sisch,** das; -[s] (Sprache); *vgl.* Deutsch; **Fran|zö|si|sche,** das; -n; *vgl.* Deutsche, das; **fran|zö|si|sie|ren** *vgl.* französieren

frap|pant ‹franz.› (auffallend, überraschend); **[1]Frap|pé** [fra'pe:], *eindeutschend* Frap|pee, der; -s, -s (Stoff mit eingepresstem Muster); **[2]Frap|pé,** *eindeutschend* Frappee, das; -s, -s (mit Eis serviertes alkohol. Getränk); **frap|pie|ren** (überraschen, verblüffen; Wein u. Sekt in Eis kühlen)

Fräs|dorn *Plur.* ...dorne; **Frä|se,** die; -, -n (Maschine zum spanabhebenden Formen); **frä|sen;** du fräst, er fräs|te; **Frä|ser** (Teil an der Fräsmaschine; Berufsbez.); **Fräs|ma|schi|ne**

Fraß, der; -es, -e; **Fraß‿gift, ...spur**

Fra|te ‹ital.› (Ordensbruder; *meist vor vokalisch beginnenden Namen,* z.B. Frate Elia, Frat'Antonio); *vgl.* Fra; **Fra|ter,** der; -s, Fra|tres [...re:s] (↑R 130) ‹lat.› ([Ordens]bruder); **fra|ter|ni|sie|ren** ‹franz.› (sich verbrüdern; vertraut werden); **Fra|ter|ni|tät,** die; -, -en ‹lat.› (Brüderlichkeit; Verbrüderung; kirchl. Bruderschaft); **Fra|ter|ni|té** *vgl.* Liberté; **Fra|tres** (↑R 130; *Plur. von* Frater)

Fratz, der; *Gen.* -es, *österr.* -en, *Plur.* -e, *österr.* -en ‹ital.› (ungezogenes Kind; schelmisches Mädchen); **Frätz|chen; Frat|ze,** die; -, -n (verzerrtes Gesicht; Grimasse); **Frat|zen|ge|sicht; frat|zen|haft**

Frau, die; -, -en (*Abk.* Fr.); **Frau|chen; Frau|en‿ar|beit, ...arzt, ...ärz|tin, ...be|auf|trag|te** (die), **...be|ruf, ...be|we|gung** (die; -), **...buch|la|den, ...ca|fé, ...eis** (ein Mineral), **...eman|zi|pa|ti|on** (↑R 132; die; -), **...feind; frau|en|feind|lich;** eine frauen- und kinderfeindliche (↑R 23) Gesellschaft

Frau|en|feld (Hptst. des Kantons Thurgau)

Frau|en‿film, ...fra|ge, ...ge|fäng|nis, ...grup|pe, ...haar; frau|en|haft; Frau|en‿haus (für Frauen, die von ihren Männern misshandelt werden), **...heil|kun|de** (die; -; *für* Gynäkologie), **...held, ...hilfs|dienst** (der; -es; früher in der Schweiz; *Abk.* FHD); **Frau|en|hilfs|dienst|leis|ten|de,** die; -n, -n; ↑R 5 ff. (*Abk.* FHD); **Frau|en‿ken|ner, ...kleid** (in -ern), **...krank|heit, ...lei|den, ...mann|schaft, ...parkplatz; Frau|en|recht|le|rin; frau|en|recht|le|risch; Frau|en‿schuh** (*auch* eine Orchideenart), **...schutz; Frau|ens‿leu|te** *(veraltet),* **...per|son** *(veraltet);* **Frau|en|tum,** das; -s *(geh.);* **Frau|en‿über|schuss** (↑R 132), **...wahl|recht** (das; -[e]s), **...zeit|schrift, ...zim|mer** *(veraltet);* **Frau|ke** (w. Vorn.); **Fräu|lein,** das; -s, *Plur.* -, *ugs. auch* -s (*als titelähnliche Bez. bzw. Anrede für eine unverheiratete weibliche Person heute allgemein durch „Frau" ersetzt; Abk.* Frl.); die Adresse Fräulein Müllers, des Fräulein Müller, Ihres Fräulein Tochter; Ihr, *veraltet* Ihre Fräulein Braut, Tochter; **frau|lich; Frau|lich|keit,** die; -

Fraun|ho|fer|li|ni|en (↑R 95), **fraun|ho|fer|sche Li|ni|en** *Plur.* ‹nach dem dt. Physiker› (Linien im Sonnenspektrum)

frdl. = freundlich

Freak [fri:k], der; -s, -s ‹amerik.› (jmd., der sich nicht in das normale bürgerliche Leben einfügt; jmd., der sich [in übertriebener Weise] für etwas begeistert)

frech; Frech|dachs (*ugs. scherzh. für* freches Kind); **Frech|heit; Frech|ling**

Fred [fre:t, *auch* frɛt] (m. Vorn.)

Free|clim|bing ['fri:'klaimiŋ] (↑R 33); das; -s ‹engl.› (Bergsteigen ohne Hilfsmittel); **Free|hol|der** ['fri:ho:ldə(r)], der; -s, -s (*früher* lehnsfreier Grundbesitzer in England); **Free|jazz,** *auch* **Free Jazz** ['fri:'dʒɛs] der; - (Spielweise des Modernjazz)

Free|sie [...i̯ə], die; -, -n ‹nach dem Kieler Arzt Freese› (eine Zierpflanze)

Free|town ['fri:ta̯un] (Hptst. von Sierra Leone)

Freeze [fri:z], das; - ‹engl.› (das Einfrieren aller atomaren Rüstung)

Fre|gat|te, die; -, -n ‹franz.› (Kriegsschiff [zum Geleitschutz]; *ugs. auch für* [aufgetakelte] Frau); **Fre|gat|ten|ka|pi|tän; Fre|gatt|vo|gel** (ein großer, an [sub]tropischen Küsten lebender Vogel)

frei (*Abk.* fr.); frei Haus, frei deutschen Ausfuhrhafen, frei deutsche Grenze liefern; frei nach Goethe; frei lebende Tiere; *vgl. auch* freischaffend, freitragend (↑R 40). **I.** *Kleinschreibung:* das Signal steht auf „frei" (↑R 59); der freie Fall; der freie Wille; freie Beweiswürdigung; freie Rücklagen; freie Wahlen; freier Eintritt; freier Journalist; freier Mitarbeiter; freier Schriftsteller; in freier Wildbahn; die freie (nicht staatlich gelenkte) Marktwirtschaft. **II.** *Großschreibung:* **a)** (↑R 47:) das Freie, im Freien, ins Freie; **b)** (↑R 108:) Sender Freies Berlin (*Abk.* SFB); Freie Demokratische Partei (*Abk.* FDP *u. parteiamtlich* F.D.P.); Freie Deutsche Jugend (*ehem. in der DDR; Abk.* FDJ); Freier Architekt (*im Titel, sonst* [er ist ein] freier Architekt); Freie und Hansestadt Hamburg; Freie Hansestadt Bremen, *aber* Frankfurt war lange Zeit eine freie Reichsstadt (*vgl.* I). **III.** *In Verbindung mit Verben* (↑R 37 f.): **a)** *Getrenntschreibung:* frei sein, werden, bleiben; frei (für sich) stehen; ein Gewicht frei halten (*vgl. aber* freihalten); frei (ohne Manuskript) sprechen; frei (ohne Stütze, ohne Leine) laufen; **b)** *Zusammenschreibung:* z. B. freikaufen, freikommen; [jmdn.] freihalten; Gefangene freilassen; sich freischwimmen; jmdn. freisprechen; [jmdm.] freistehen; jmdm. etw. freistellen *(vgl. d.);* **c)** *wenn keine eindeutige Festlegung nach R 39 möglich ist, dann gilt Getrennt- oder Zusammenschreibung*

Frei|a *vgl.* Freyja

Frei‿bad, ...bank (*Plur.* ...bänke); **frei|be|kom|men;** eine Stunde, ein paar Tage freibekommen; *vgl.* frei, III

Frei|berg (Stadt in Sachsen)

frei|be|ruf|lich; Frei|be|trag; Frei|beu|ter (Seeräuber); **Frei|beu|te|rei; frei|beu|te|risch; Frei|bier,** das; -[e]s; **frei blei|ben** *vgl.*

frei, III; **frei|blei|bend** (*Kaufmannsspr.* ohne Verbindlichkeit, ohne Verpflichtung [bei Angeboten]); (↑R 40:) das -e Angebot, das Angebot ist -; **Frei‿bord** (der; Höhe des Schiffskörpers über der Wasserlinie), **...brief**

Frei|burg (Kanton der Schweiz; *franz.* Fribourg); **Frei|burg im Breis|gau** (Stadt in Baden-Württemberg); **Frei|burg im Üecht|land** *od.* **Üecht|land** [- - 'yəxt...] (Hptst. des Kantons Freiburg)

Frei|de|mo|krat (Mitglied der Freien Demokratischen Partei); **Frei|de|mo|kra|tin; frei|de|mo|kra|tisch**

Frei|den|ker; Frei|den|ke|rin; frei|den|ke|risch

Freie, der; -n, -n; ↑R 5 ff. (*früher für* jmd., der Rechtsfähigkeit u. polit. Rechte besitzt)

frei|en (*veraltet für* heiraten; um eine Frau werben); **Frei|er; Frei|ers|fü|ße** *Plur.; nur in* auf -n gehen (*scherzh.*); **Frei|ers|mann** *Plur.* ...leute (*veraltet*)

Frei‿exemp|lar (↑R 132), **...frau, ...fräu|lein, ...ga|be, ...gän|ger** (*Rechtsw.*); **frei|ge|ben;** einen Gefangenen freigeben; es wurden neue Frequenzen für den Funk freigegeben; *vgl.* frei, III *u.* R 39; **frei|ge|big; Frei|ge|big|keit,** die; -; **Frei‿ge|he|ge, ...geist** (*Plur.* ...geister); **Frei|geis|te|rei,** die; -; **frei|geis|tig; Frei|ge|las|se|ne,** der *u.* die; -n, -n (↑R 5 ff.); **Frei‿ge|richt** (*früher* Feme), **...graf** (*früher* Vorsitzender des Freigerichts), **...gren|ze** (*Steuerwesen*), **...gut** (*Zollw.*); **frei|ha|ben;** ein paar Tage freihaben (Urlaub, keinen Dienst haben); *vgl.* frei, III *u.* R 39; **Frei|ha|fen** (*vgl.* [2]Hafen); **frei|hal|ten;** ich werde dich freihalten (für dich bezahlen); die Ausfahrt freihalten (nicht verstellen); *vgl.* frei, III *u.* R 39; **Frei|hand|bü|che|rei** (Bibliothek, in der man die Bücher selbst aus den Regalen entnehmen kann); **Frei|han|del,** der; -s; **Frei|han|dels|zo|ne; frei|hän|dig; Frei|hand|zeich|nen,** das; -s; **Frei|heit; frei|heit|lich; Frei|heits‿be|griff** (*Plur. selten*), **...be|rau|bung, ...drang** (der; -[e]s), **...ent|zug; frei|heits|feind|lich; Frei|heits‿kampf, ...krieg; frei|heits|lie|bend; Frei|heits‿sinn** (der; -[e]s), **...sta|tue, ...stra|fe; frei|he|raus** (↑R 132); etwas freiheraus (offen) sagen; **Frei|herr** (*Abk.* Frhr.); **Frei|herrn|stand,** der; -[e]s; **Frei|in** (Freifräulein); **Frei|kar|te; frei|kau|fen** (durch ein Lösegeld befreien); *vgl.* frei, III; **Frei|kir|che;** eine protestantische -; **Frei|klet|tern,** das; -s (*svw.* Freeclimbing); **frei|kom|men** (loskommen); *vgl.* frei, III; **Frei|kör|per|kul|tur,** die; - (*Abk.* FKK); **Frei|korps** (*früher*); **Frei|la|de|bahn|hof** (*Eisenb.*); **Frei|land** (das; -[e]s); **Frei|land|ge|mü|se; frei|las|sen** (Gefangene freilassen); *vgl.* frei, III; **Frei‿las|sung, ...lauf** (*Technik*); **frei|lau|fen,** sich (*Sport*); *vgl.* frei, III; **frei le|bend** *vgl.* frei; **frei|le|gen** (deckende Schicht entfernen); *vgl.* frei, III *u.* R 39; **Frei‿le|gung, ...lei|tung**

frei|lich

Frei|licht‿büh|ne, ...mu|se|um

Frei|lig|rath (dt. Dichter)

Frei|luft‿kon|zert, ...schu|le; frei|ma|chen; einen Brief freimachen (*Postw.*); ein paar Tage freimachen (Urlaub machen); sich freimachen (Zeit nehmen); den Oberkörper freimachen; *vgl.* frei III u. ↑R 39; **Frei|ma|chung** (*Postw.*); **Frei|mar|ke; Frei|mau|rer; Frei|mau|re|rei,** die; -; **frei|mau|re|risch; Frei|mau|rer|lo|ge; Frei|mund** (m. Vorn.); **Frei|mut; frei|mü|tig; Frei|mü|tig|keit,** die; -; **Frei‿plas|tik, ...platz; frei|pres|sen** (durch Erpressung jmds. Freilassung erzwingen); **Frei|raum; frei|re|li|gi|ös; Frei‿sass, ...sas|se** (*früher*); **frei|schaf|fend;** ein freischaffender Künstler, Architekt; **Frei‿schar** (*vgl.* [1]Schar), **...schär|ler, ...schlag** (*bes. Hockey, Polo*); **frei|schwim|men,** sich (die Schwimmprüfung ablegen); *vgl.* frei, III; **Frei|schwim|mer; frei|set|zen** (aus einer Bindung lösen); Energie, Kräfte freisetzen; *vgl.* frei, III; **Frei|sinn,** der; -[e]s (*veraltet*); **frei|sin|nig** (*veraltet*); **frei|spie|len** (*Sport*); sich, einen Stürmer freispielen; *vgl.* frei, III; **frei|spre|chen** (für nicht schuldig erklären; *Handwerk* zum Gesellen erklären); *vgl.* frei, III; **Frei‿spre|chung, ...spruch, ...staat** (*Plur.* ...staaten), **...statt** *od.* **...stät|te; frei|ste|hen;** das soll dir freistehen (gestattet sein); die Wohnung hat lange freigestanden; *vgl.* frei, III *u.* R 39; **frei|stel|len** (erlauben); jmdm. etwas freistellen; *vgl.* frei, III *u.* R 39; **Frei‿stem|pel** (*Postw.*), **...stemp|ler** (Frankiermaschine); **Frei|stil,** der; -s (*Sport*); **Frei|stil‿rin|gen, ...schwim|men** (das; -s); **Frei|stoß** (beim Fußball); [in]direkter -; **Frei|stun|de**

Frei|tag, der; -[e]s, -e (*Abk.* Fr.); (↑R 108:) der Stille Freitag (Karfreitag); *vgl.* Dienstag; **frei|tags** (↑R 46); *vgl.* Dienstag

Frei|te, die; - (*veraltet für* Brautwerbung); *in* auf die - gehen

Frei‿tisch (*veraltend*), **...tod** (Selbstmord); **frei|tra|gend;** freitragende Brücken, Treppen; **Frei‿trep|pe, ...übung** (↑R 132), **...um|schlag, ...wa|che** (*Seemannsspr.*); **frei|weg** (unbekümmert, ohne Skrupel); **frei wer|den;** *vgl.* frei, III; eine frei werdende Wohnung; das Freiwerden (↑R 50); **Frei|wild; frei|wil|lig;** die freiwillige Feuerwehr, *aber* (↑R 108): die Freiwillige Feuerwehr Nassau; **Frei|wil|li|ge,** der *u.* die; -n, -n (↑R 5 ff.); **Frei|wil|lig|keit,** die; -; **Frei‿wurf** (*bes. Handball, Basketball*), **...zei|chen, ...zeit; Frei|zeit‿an|zug, ...be|schäf|ti|gung, ...ein|rich|tung, ...ge|stal|tung, ...hemd, ...klei|dung, ...kos|tüm, ...park, ...wert, ...zent|rum; frei|zü|gig; Frei|zü|gig|keit,** die; -

fremd; Fremd|ar|bei|ter (*veraltend*); **fremd|ar|tig; Fremd|ar|tig|keit,** die; -; **Fremd|be|stim|mung;** [1]**Frem|de,** der *u.* die; -n, -n (↑R 5 ff.); [2]**Frem|de,** die; - (Ausland); in der -; **Fremd|ein|wir|kung,** die; - (*Verkehrsw.*); **frem|deln** (*landsch.*); ich ...[e]le (↑R 16) *u.* **frem|den** (*schweiz. für* vor Fremden scheu, ängstlich sein); **Frem|den‿bett, ...buch, ...füh|rer, ...heim, ...le|gi|on** (die; -), **...pass, ...po|li|zei, ...sit|zung** (öffentliche Karnevalssitzung), **...ver|kehr** (der; -[e]s), **...zim|mer; fremd|ge|hen** (*ugs. für* untreu sein); **Fremd|heit,** die; - (das Fremdsein); **Fremd‿herr|schaft** (*Plur. selten*), **...ka|pi|tal, ...kör|per; fremd|län|disch; Fremd|ling** (*veraltend*); **Fremd|mit|tel** *Plur.*; **Fremd|spra|che; Fremd|spra|chen‿kor|res|pon|den|tin, ...un|ter|richt; fremd|spra|chig** (eine fremde Sprache sprechend; in einer fremden Sprache geschrieben, gehalten); fremdsprachiger (in einer Fremdsprache gehaltener) Unterricht; fremdsprachiger Druck; **fremd|sprach|lich** (auf eine fremde Sprache bezüglich); fremdsprachlicher (über eine Fremdsprache gehaltener) Unterricht; **fremd|stäm|mig; Fremd|stäm|mig|keit,** die; -; **Fremd‿stoff, ...ver|schul|den** (*Amtsspr.*); **Fremd|wort** *Plur.* ...wörter; **Fremd|wör|ter|buch; fremd|wort‿frei, ...reich**

fre|ne|tisch ‹franz.› (rasend); -er Beifall; *vgl. aber* phrenetisch
fre|quent ‹lat.› (häufig, zahlreich; *Med.* beschleunigt [vom Puls]); **Fre|quen|ta|ti|on,** die; - *(veraltet);* **fre|quen|tie|ren** (*geh. für* häufig besuchen; ein u. aus gehen; verkehren); **Fre|quenz,** die; -, -en (Besucherzahl, Verkehrsdichte; Schwingungszahl, Periodenzahl); **Fre|quenz‿be|reich, ...mes|ser** (der; zur Zählung der Wechselstromperioden)
Fres|ke, die; -, -n ‹franz.› *u.* **Fres|ko,** das; -s, ...ken ‹ital., „frisch"› (Wandmalerei auf feuchtem Kalkputz); *vgl.* a fresco; **Fres|ko|ma|le|rei**
Fres|nel|lin|se [frɛˈnɛl...] (↑R 95) ‹nach dem franz. Physiker› (eine zusammengesetzte Linse)
Fres|sa|li|en [...i̯ən] *Plur.* (*ugs. scherzh. für* Esswaren); **Fres|se,** die; -, -n (*derb für* Mund, Maul); **fres|sen;** du frisst, er frisst; du fraßest; du fräßest; gefressen; friss!; **Fres|sen,** das; -s; **Fresser; Fres|se|rei; Fress‿gier, ...korb** *(ugs.),* **...napf; Fress|paket** *(ugs.);* **Fress|sack** (↑R 136; *ugs. für* gefräßiger Mensch); **Fress|werk|zeu|ge** *(Plur.; Zool.)*
Frett|chen, das; -s, - ‹niederl.› (Iltisart)
fret|ten, sich (*südd., österr. für* sich abmühen)
fret|tie|ren ‹niederl.› (*Jägerspr.* mit dem Frettchen jagen)
Freud (österr. Psychiater u. Neurologe)
Freu|de, die; -, -n; [in] Freud und Leid (↑R 13); **Freu|den‿be|cher** *(geh.),* **...bot|schaft, ...fest, ...feu|er, ...ge|heul, ...haus** (*verhüllend für* Bordell); **freu|de[n]|los** *vgl.* freudlos; **Freu|den|mädchen** (*verhüllend für* Dirne); **freu|den|reich; Freu|den‿ruf, ...sprung, ...tag, ...tanz, ...taumel, ...trä|ne; freu|de|strahlend; freu|de|trun|ken**
Freu|di|a|ner (Schüler, Anhänger Freuds); **Freu|di|a|ne|rin; freu|di|a|nisch**
freu|dig; ein freudiges Ereignis; **Freu|dig|keit,** die; -; **freud|los; Freud|lo|sig|keit,** die; -
freud|sche Fehl|leis|tung *(bes. Psych.)*
freu|en; sich -
Freund, der; -[e]s, -e; jemandes Freund bleiben, sein, werden; gut Freund [mit jmdm.] sein; jmdm. Freund (freundlich gesinnt) sein, bleiben, werden; **Freund|chen** *(meist [scherzh.] drohend als Anrede);* **Freun|des‿kreis, ...treue; Freund-Feind-Den|ken; Freundin; freund|lich** (*Abk.* frdl.); *Schreibung in Zusammensetzungen:* menschenfreundlich, kinderfreundlich; moskaufreundlich, *auch* Moskau-freundlich (↑R 105); **freund|li|cher|wei|se; Freund|lich|keit; freund|nachbar|lich; Freund|schaft; freundschaft|lich; Freund|schafts‿ban|de** *(Plur.),* **...dienst, ...spiel** *(Sport),* **...ver|trag**
fre|vel *(veraltet);* frevler Mut; **Frevel,** der; -s, - (Verstoß, Verbrechen); **fre|vel|haft; Fre|vel|haftig|keit,** die; -; **Fre|vel|mut** *(veraltet);* **fre|veln;** ich ...[e]le (↑R 16); **Fre|vel|tat; fre|vent|lich** *(veraltend);* **Frev|ler; Frev|le|rin; frevle|risch**
Frey, Freyr (*nord. Mythol.* Gott der Fruchtbarkeit u. des Friedens)
Frey|burg/Un|strut (Stadt an der unteren Unstrut)
Frey|ja (*nord. Mythol.* Liebesgöttin)
Frey|tag (dt. Schriftsteller)
Frhr. = Freiherr
Fri|aul *auch mit Artikel* das; -[s] (ital. Landschaft)
Fri|csay [ˈfritʃai̯] (ung. Dirigent)
Fri|de|ri|cus (*lat. Form für* Friedrich); - Rex (König Friedrich [der Große]); **fri|de|ri|zi|a|nisch**
Fri|do|lin (m. Vorn.)
Frie|da (w. Vorn.); **Fried|bert,** Frie|de|bert (m. Vorn.)
Frie|de, der; -ns, -n (*älter, geh. für* Frieden)
Frie|del (m. u. w. Vorn.)
Frie|dell (österr. Schriftsteller)
Frie|de|mann (m. Vorn.)
frie|den (*selten für* einfrieden, befrieden); gefriedet; **Frie|den,** der; -s, -; *vgl.* Friede; **Frie|dens‿bedin|gung, ...be|reit|schaft, ...bewe|gung, ...bruch** (der), **...fahrt** (Amateurradrennen zwischen Prag, Warschau und Berlin), **...for|schung, ...freund, ...ini|ti|a|ti|ve** (↑R 132), **...kon|fe|renz, ...kurs, ...la|ger** (das; -s; *ehemals in der DDR Bez. für* die sozialist. Staaten), **...lie|be, ...no|bel|preis, ...ord|nung, ...pfei|fe, ...pflicht, ...po|li|tik** (die; -), **...rich|ter, ...schluss; Frie|den[s]‿stif|ter, ...stö|rer; Frie|dens‿tau|be, ...ver|hand|lun|gen** *(Plur.),* **...ver|trag, ...zei|chen, ...zeit**
Frie|der (m. Vorn.); **Frie|de|ri|ke** (w. Vorn.)
frie|de|voll *vgl.* friedvoll; **friedfer|tig; Fried|fer|tig|keit,** die; -; **Fried|fisch**
Fried|helm (m. Vorn.)
Fried|hof; Fried|hofs‿gärt|ner, ...gärt|ne|rei, ...ka|pel|le, ...mau|er, ...ru|he
Fried|län|der (Bez. Wallensteins nach dem Herzogtum Friedland; einer aus Wallensteins Mannschaft); **fried|län|disch**
fried|lich; Fried|lich|keit, die; -; **fried‿lie|bend, ...los**
Fried|mann (m. Vorn.)
Frie|do|lin *vgl.* Fridolin; [1]**Fried|rich** (m. Vorn.); Friedrich der Große (↑R 93); [2]**Fried|rich,** Caspar David (dt. Maler)
Fried|rich|ro|da (Stadt am Nordrand des Thüringer Waldes)
Fried|richs|dor, der; -s, -e (alte preuß. Goldmünze); 10 -
Fried|richs|ha|fen (Stadt am Bodensee)
Fried|rich Wil|helm, der; - -s, - -s (*ugs. für* Unterschrift)
fried|sam *(veraltet);* **fried|voll**
frie|meln (*landsch. für* basteln)
frie|ren; du frierst; du frorst; du frörest; gefroren; frier[e]!; ich friere an den Füßen; mich friert an den Füßen (*nicht* an die Füße)
Fries, der; -es, -e ‹franz.› (Gesimsstreifen; ein Gewebe)
Frie|se, der; -n, -n; ↑R 126 (Angehöriger eines germ. Stammes an der Nordseeküste)
Frie|sel, der *od.* das; -s, -n *meist Plur.* (Pustel); **Frie|sel|fie|ber**
Frie|sen|nerz (*scherzh. für* Öljacke, Regencape); **Frie|sin; friesisch; Fries|land; Fries|län|der,** der; **fries|län|disch**
Frigg (*nord. Mythol.* Wodans Gattin); *vgl.* Frija
fri|gid, fri|gi|de ‹lat.› (sexuell nicht erregbar, nicht zum Orgasmus fähig [von Frauen]); **Fri|gi|daire** ® [friʒiˈdɛ:(r), *auch* frigi...], *eindeutschende Schreibung:* **Fri|gi|där,** der; -s, -[s] ‹franz.› (Kühlschrank); **Fri|gi|da|ri|um,** das; -s, ...ien [...i̯ən] ‹lat.› (Abkühlungsraum [in altröm. Bädern]); **fri|gide** *vgl.* frigid; **Fri|gi|di|tät,** die; - (mangelnde sexuelle Erregbarkeit, Unfähigkeit zum Orgasmus [von Frauen])
Fri|ja (*altd. Name für* Frigg)
Fri|ka|del|le, die; -, -n ‹ital.›; **Fri|kan|deau** [...ˈdo:], das; -s, -s ‹franz.› (Teil der [Kalbs]keule); **Fri|kan|del|le,** die; -, -n (Schnitte aus gedämpftem Fleisch; *auch für* Frikadelle); **Fri|kas|see,** das; -s, -s (Gericht aus klein geschnittenem Fleisch); **fri|kas|sie|ren** (zu Frikassee verarbeiten)
fri|ka|tiv ‹lat.› (auf Reibung beruhend); **Fri|ka|tiv,** der; -s, -e [...və] *u.* **Fri|ka|tiv|laut,** der; -[e]s, -e

(*Sprachw.* Reibe-, Engelaut, z. B. f, sch); **Frik|ti|on,** die; -, -en (Reibung); **Frik|ti|ons|kupp|lung** *(Technik);* **frik|ti|ons|los**

Fri|maire [fri'mɛ:r], der; -[s], -s *Plur. selten* ‹franz., „Reifmonat"› (3. Monat des Kalenders der Franz. Revolution: 21. Nov. bis 20. Dez.)

Fris|bee ® ['frisbi], das; -, -s ‹engl.› (Wurfscheibe)

frisch; -este; etwas frisch halten; sich frisch machen; auf frischer Tat ertappen; frisch-fröhlich (↑R 27). *In Verbindung mit dem Partizip II* (↑R 40): frisch gestrichen; das frisch gebackene Brot; ein frisch gebackenes (*scherzh. für* gerade erst getrautes) Ehepaar; *vgl. aber* frischbacken; (↑R 102:) die Frische Nehrung, das Frische Haff

Frisch (schweiz. Erzähler u. Dramatiker)

frisch|auf! (*veraltend* Wanderergruß); **frisch|ba|cken;** ein frischbackenes Brot; **Frisch|blut** (erst vor kurzer Zeit entnommenes Blut); **Fri|sche,** die; -; **Frisch|ei; fri|schen** (*Hüttenw.* Metall herstellen, reinigen; [vom Wildschwein] Junge werfen); du frischst; **frisch-fröh|lich** *vgl.* frisch; **frisch ge|ba|cken** *vgl.* frisch; **Frisch‿ge|mü|se, ...gewicht; Frisch|hal|te|pa|ckung; Frisch‿kä|se, ...kost; Frisch|ling** (junges Wildschwein); **Frischluft; frisch|mel|kend;** *nur in* -e Kuh (Kuh, die gerade gekalbt hat); **Frisch‿milch, ...was|ser** (das; -s; *auch* auf Schiffen mitgeführtes Süßwasser [für Dampfkessel]); **frisch|weg; Frisch|zelle; Frisch|zel|len|the|ra|pie**

Fris|co (*amerik. Abk. für* San Francisco)

Fri|sée|sa|lat [fri'ze:...] ‹franz.; dt.› (Kopfsalat mit kraus gefiederten Blättern)

Fri|seur [fri'zø:r], der; -s, -e ‹*zu* frisieren›; **Fri|seu|rin** [...'zø:rin]; **Fri|seur|sa|lon; Friseu|se** [...'zø:zə], die; -, -n (*älter für* Friseurin); **fri|sie|ren** ‹franz.› (*ugs. auch für* herrichten, [unerlaubt] verändern); sich -; **Fri|sier‿kom|mo|de, ...sa|lon, ...toi|lette, ...um|hang**

Fri|sör usw. (*eindeutschend für* Friseur usw.)

Frist, die; -, -en; **fris|ten; Fris|ten‿lö|sung, ...re|ge|lung** (Regelung für straffreien Schwangerschaftsabbruch in den ersten [drei] Monaten); **frist‿ge|mäß, ...ge|recht; frist|los;** -e Entlassung; **Frist‿über|schrei|tung** (↑R 132), **...wech|sel** (*Kaufmannsspr.* Datowechsel)

Fri|sur, die; -, -en

Fri|teu|se *frühere Schreibung für* Fritteuse

Frit|flie|ge (Getreideschädling)

Frit|hjof (norweg. Held; m. Vorn.); **Frit|hjof[s]|sa|ge,** die; -

fri|tie|ren *frühere Schreibung für* frittieren; **Frit|ta|te,** die; -, -n ‹ital.› (Eierkuchen); **Frit|ta|tensup|pe** (*svw.* Flädlesuppe); **Fritte,** die; -, -n ‹franz.› (Schmelzgemenge; *Plur. ugs. auch für* Pommes frites); **frit|ten** (eine Fritte machen; [von Steinen] sich durch Hitze verändern; *ugs. auch für* frittieren); **Frit|teu|se** [...'tø:zə], die; -, -n (elektr. Gerät zum Frittieren); **frit|tie|ren** ‹franz.›; Fleisch, Kartoffeln - (in schwimmendem Fett braun braten); **Frittü|re,** die; -, -n ‹franz.› (heißes Ausbackfett; die darin gebackene Speise; *auch für* Fritteuse)

Fritz (m. Vorn.); **...frit|ze,** der; -n, -n (↑R 126; *ugs. abwertend,* z. B. Filmfritze, Zeitungsfritze)

fri|vol [...v...] ‹franz.› (leichtfertig; schlüpfrig); **Fri|vo|li|tät,** die; -, -en; **Fri|vo|li|tä|ten|ar|beit** (*veraltet für* Okkiarbeit)

Frl. = Fräulein

Frö|bel (dt. Pädagoge)

froh; frohen Sinnes (↑R 5); die froh[e]sten Menschen; froh gelaunt, froher gelaunt; *vgl. aber* frohgemut; frohes Ereignis, *aber* (↑R 108): die Frohe Botschaft (Evangelium); **Froh|bot|schaft,** die; - (*svw.* Evangelium); **froh gelaunt** *vgl.* froh; **froh|ge|mut;** die frohgemutesten Menschen; **fröhlich; Fröh|lich|keit,** die; -; **frohlo|cken;** er hat frohlockt; **Frohmut** *(geh.);* **froh|mü|tig** *(geh.);* **Froh‿na|tur, ...sinn** (der; -[e]s); **froh|sin|nig** *(selten)*

Frois|sé [froa'se:], der *od.* das; -s, -s ‹franz.› (künstlich geknittertes Gewebe)

Fro|mage de Brie [frɔma:ʒ də 'bri:], der; - - -, -s [frɔma:ʒ] - - ‹franz.› (Briekäse)

fromm; frommer *od.* frömmer, frommste *od.* frömmste; **Fromme,** der; -n (*veraltet für* Ertrag; Nutzen), *noch in* zu Nutz und -n; **Fröm|me|lei,** die; -; **fröm|meln** (sich [übertrieben] fromm zeigen); ich ...[e]le (↑R 16); **frommen** (*veraltend für* nutzen); es frommt ihm nicht; **Fromm|heit,** die; -; **Fröm|mig|keit,** die; -; **Frömm|ler; Frömm|le|rei; Frömm|le|rin; frömm|le|risch**

Fron, die; -, -en (dem Lehnsherrn zu leistende Arbeit); **Fron|ar|beit** (*schweiz. auch für* unbezahlte Gemeinschaftsarbeit für Gemeinde, Verein o. Ä.); **¹Fron|de,** die; -, -n (*veraltet für* Fron)

²Fron|de ['frɔ̃:də], die; -, -n ‹franz.› (regierungsfeindliche Gruppe)

fron|den (*veraltet für* fronen)

Fron|deur [frɔ̃'dø:r], der; -s, -e ‹franz.› (Anhänger der ²Fronde)

Fron|dienst (*früher* Dienst für den Lehnsherrn; *schweiz. svw.* Fronarbeit)

fron|die|ren [frɔ̃'di:...] ‹franz.› (Widerspruch erheben; als Frondeur auftreten)

fro|nen (Frondienste leisten); **frönen** (sich einer Neigung, Leidenschaft o. Ä. hingeben); **Frö|ner** (Arbeiter im Frondienst); **Fronleich|nam,** der; -[e]s *(meist ohne Artikel)* („des Herrn Leib") (kath. Fest); **Fron|leich|nams‿fest, ...pro|zes|si|on**

Front, die; -, -en ‹franz.›; Front machen (sich widersetzen); **Front|ab|schnitt; fron|tal; Frontal‿an|griff, ...zu|sam|menstoß; Front‿an|trieb, ...be|gradi|gung, ...be|richt, ...brei|te, ...dienst, ...ein|satz, ...frau** (*vgl.* Frontmann); **Fron|tis|piz** (↑R 132), das; -es, -e (*Archit.* Giebeldreieck; *Buchw.* Titelblatt [mit Titelbild]); **Front‿kämp|fer, ...lader** (Schleppfahrzeug), **...li|nie; Front|mann** (Musiker, der [als Sänger] in einer Gruppe im Vordergrund agiert); **Front‿mo|tor, ...sol|dat, ...wech|sel** (Gesinnungswandel)

Frosch, der; -[e]s, Frösche; **Frosch‿au|ge, ...biss** (Sumpf- und Wasserpflanze); **Fröschchen; Frosch‿go|scherl** (das; -s, -n; *österr. ugs. für* Löwenmaul; geraffte Borte, bes. an Trachtenkleidern), **...kö|nig** (der; -s; eine Märchengestalt), **...laich; Frösch|lein; Frosch‿mann** (*Plur.* ...männer), **...per|spek|tive, ...schen|kel, ...test** (ein Schwangerschaftstest)

Frost, der; -[e]s, Fröste; **frost|anfäl|lig; Frost‿auf|bruch, ...beule; frös|te|lig,** fröst|lig; **frös|teln;** ich ...[e]le (↑R 16); mich fröstelt; **fros|ten; Fros|ter,** der; -s, - (Tiefkühlteil einer Kühlvorrichtung); **frost|frei; Frost‿ge|fahr** (die; -), **...gren|ze; frost|hart; fros|tig; Fros|tig|keit,** die; -; **frost‿klar, ...klir|rend; fröst|lig,** frös|te|lig; **Frost‿scha|den, ...schutz|mittel** (das), **...span|ner** (ein Schmetterling), **...wet|ter**

Frot|tee, *auch* Frot|té [*beide* ...'te: *(österr. nur so), auch* 'frɔ...], das *od.* der; -[s], -s ‹franz.› ([Kleider]stoff aus gekräuseltem Zwirn; *auch für* Frottiergewebe); **Frot|tee‿hand|tuch, ...kleid, ...stoff, ...tuch** (*vgl.* Frottiertuch); **frot|tie|ren; Frot|tier|tuch** *Plur.* ...tücher

Frot|ze|lei; frot|zeln (*ugs. für* necken, aufziehen); ich ...[e]le (↑R 16)

Frucht, die; -, Früchte; **frucht|bar; Frucht|bar|keit,** die; -; **Frucht‿be|cher** *(auch Bot.),* **...bla|se, ...blatt** (*für* Karpell), **...bo|den, ...bon|bon; frucht|brin|gend;** eine fruchtbringende Tätigkeit; **Frücht|chen** (*ugs. auch für* kleiner Taugenichts); **Früch|te|brot; fruch|ten;** es fruchtet (nutzt) nichts; **Früch|ten|brot** (*österr. für* Früchtebrot); **früch|te|reich** *vgl.* fruchtreich; **Frucht‿fleisch, ...fol|ge** (Anbaufolge der einzelnen Feldfrüchte), **...ge|schmack, ...holz** (fruchttragendes Holz der Obstbäume); **fruch|tig** (z. B. vom Wein); **...fruch|tig** (z. B. einfruchtig); **Frucht|kno|ten** *(Bot.);* **Frücht|lein; frucht|los; Frucht|lo|sig|keit,** die; -; **Frucht‿mark** (das), **...pres|se; frucht|reich,** früch|te|reich; **Frucht‿saft, ...was|ser** (das; -s), **...wech|sel, ...zu|cker**

Fruc|to|se, die; - ‹lat.› (Fruchtzucker)

fru|gal ‹lat.› (mäßig; einfach; bescheiden); **Fru|ga|li|tät,** die; -

früh; früh[e]stens; ein früher Winter; eine frühe Sorte Äpfel; früh verstorben, vollendet; am früh[e]sten; (↑R 47:) zum, mit dem Frühesten; morgens früh (*aber:* frühmorgens); von [morgens] früh bis [abends] spät; morgen früh; [am] Dienstag früh; frühestmöglich *(vgl. d.);* allzu früh; von früh auf; **Früh‿auf|ste|her, ...beet; Früh|chen** (Frühgeborenes); **Früh‿di|ag|no|se** *(Med.),* **...dienst, ...druck** (*Plur.* ...drucke); **Frü|he,** die; -; in der Frühe; in aller Frühe; bis in die Früh; **Früh|ehe** (↑R 132); **frü|her; Früh|er|ken|nung,** die; - *(Med.);* **frü|hes|tens,** früh|s|tens; **frü|hest|mög|lich;** zum -en Termin; **Früh‿ge|burt, ...ge|mü|se, ...ge|schich|te** (die; -); **früh‿ge|schicht|lich, ...go|tisch; Früh|in|va|li|di|tät; Früh|jahr; früh|jahrs; Früh|jahrs‿an|fang, ...be|stel|lung, ...kol|lek|ti|on, ...mü|dig|keit, ...putz; Früh|jahrs-Tag-und|nacht|glei|che; Früh|kar|tof|fel; früh|kind|lich; Früh|ling,** der; -s, -e; **früh|lings** (*selten für* frühjahrs); **Früh|lings‿an|fang, ...fest, ...ge|fühl** (-e haben; *ugs. scherzh. für* sich [im reifen Alter noch einmal] verlieben); **früh|ling[s]|haft; Früh|lings‿mo|nat** *od.* **...mond** (März), **...rol|le** (chin. Vorspeise), **...tag, ...zeit; Früh|met|te; früh|mor|gens;** *vgl.* früh; **früh|neu|hoch|deutsch;** *vgl.* deutsch; **Früh|neu|hoch|deutsch,** das; -[s]; *vgl.* Deutsch; **Früh|neu|hoch|deut|sche,** das; -n; *vgl.* Deutsche, das; **früh|reif; Früh‿reif** (gefrorener Tau), **...rei|fe** (die; -), **...ren|te, ...rent|ner, ...schicht, ...schop|pen, ...som|mer, ...sport, ...sta|di|um, ...start; früh|s|tens** *vgl.* frühestens; **Früh|stück; früh|stü|cken;** gefrühstückt; **Früh|stücks‿brett|chen, ...brot, ...bü|fett, ...ei, ...fern|se|hen** (Fernsehprogramm am frühen Morgen), **...pau|se; früh ver|stor|ben** *vgl.* früh; **früh voll|en|det** *vgl.* früh; **Früh|warn|sys|tem** *(Milit.);* **früh|zei|tig**

Fruk|ti|dor [fryk...], der; -[s], -s ‹franz., „Fruchtmonat"› (12. Monat des Kalenders der Franz. Revolution: 18. Aug. bis 16. Sept.); **Fruk|ti|fi|ka|ti|on,** die; -, -en ‹lat.› (*Bot.* Frucht- bzw. Sporenbildung); **fruk|ti|fi|zie|ren; Fruk|to|se** *vgl.* Fructose

Frust, der; -[e]s (*ugs. für* Frustration); **Frust|ra|ti|on** (↑R 130), die; -, -en ‹lat.› (*Psych.* Enttäuschung durch erzwungenen Verzicht od. Versagung von Befriedigung); **frust|rie|ren** ([eine Erwartung] enttäuschen); frustriert sein; **Frust|rie|rung**

Frut|ti *Plur.* ‹ital.› (Früchte); **Frut|ti di Ma|re** *Plur.* ‹„Meeresfrüchte"› (mit dem Netz gefangene Muscheln, Krebse u. Ä.)

F-Schlüs|sel *(Musik)*

ft = Foot, Feet

Ft = Forint

Fuchs, der; -es, Füchse; **Fuchs|bau** *Plur.* ...baue; **Füchs|chen; fuch|sen;** sich - (*ugs. für* sich ärgern); du fuchst dich; das fuchst ihn; **Fuchs|hatz** *(Jägerspr.)*

Fuch|sie [...i̯ə], die; -, -n ‹nach dem Botaniker Leonhard Fuchs› (eine Zierpflanze)

fuch|sig (fuchsrot; fuchswild)

Fuch|sin, das; -s (roter Farbstoff)

Füch|sin; Fuchs|jagd; Fuchs|lein; Fuchs‿loch, ...pelz; fuchs|rot; Fuchs|schwanz; fuchs|[teu|fels|]wild

Fuch|tel, die; -, -n (*früher* breiter Degen; strenge Zucht; *österr. ugs. für* herrschsüchtige, zänkische Frau); unter jmds. - stehen; **fuch|teln;** ich ...[e]le (↑R 16); **fuch|tig** (*ugs. für* aufgebracht)

fud. = fudit

Fu|der, das; -s, - (Wagenladung, Fuhre; Hohlmaß für Wein); **fu|der|wei|se**

fu|dit ‹lat., „hat [es] gegossen"› (auf künstlerischen Gusswerken; *Abk.* fud.)

Fud|schi|ja|ma [fudʒi...] (↑R 130), der; -s (jap. Vulkan)

Fuff|zehn *(landsch.); meist in* 'ne - machen (Pause machen); **Fuff|zi|ger,** der; -s, - (*landsch. für* Fünfzigpfennigstück); ein falscher - (*ugs. für* unaufrichtiger Mensch)

Fug, der; *in* mit - und Recht

fu|ga|to ‹ital.› (*Musik* fugenartig); **Fu|ga|to,** das; -s, *Plur.* -s *u.* ...ti

[1]**Fu|ge,** die; -, -n (schmaler Zwischenraum; Verbindungsstelle)

[2]**Fu|ge,** die; -, -n ‹lat.-ital.› (kontrapunktisches Musikstück)

fu|gen ([Bau]teile verbinden); **fü|gen;** sich fügen; aneinander fügen; **fu|gen|los; Fu|gen-s,** das; -, - (↑R 25)

Fu|gen|stil, der; -[e]s *(Musik)*

Fu|gen|zei|chen (*Sprachw.* die Fuge einer Zusammensetzung kennzeichnender Laut oder kennzeichnende Silbe, z. B. -es- in „Liebesdienst")

Fug|ger (Augsburger Kaufmannsgeschlecht im 15. und 16. Jh.); **Fug|ge|rei,** die; - (Handelsgesellschaft der Fugger; Stadtteil in Augsburg)

fu|gie|ren (ein musikal. Thema nach Fugenart durchführen)

füg|lich; füg|sam; Füg|sam|keit, die; -; **Fu|gung; Fü|gung**

fühl|bar; Fühl|bar|keit, die; -; **füh|len;** er hat den Schmerz gefühlt, *aber* er hat das Fieber kommen fühlen (*od.* gefühlt); **Füh|ler; Fühl|horn** *Plur.* ...hörner; **fühl|los; Fühl|lo|sig|keit,** die; -; **Füh|lung; Füh|lung|nah|me,** die; -, -n

Fuh|re, die; -, -n

Füh|re, die; -, -n (*Bergsteigen* Route); **füh|ren;** Buch führen; jmdn. spazieren führen; **Füh|rer; Füh|rer‿aus|weis** (*schweiz. amtl. für* Führerschein), **...haus; Füh|re|rin; füh|rer|los; Füh|rer|na|tur; Füh|rer|schaft; Füh|rer‿schein, ...sitz, ...stand; Führ|hand** *(Boxen);* **füh|rig** usw. *vgl.* geführig usw.

Fuhr‿lohn, ...mann (*Plur.* ...männer *u.* ...leute), **...park**

Füh|rung; Füh|rungs‿an|spruch,

...**auf|ga|be**, ...**kraft**, ...**schie|ne** *(Technik)*, ...**spit|ze**, ...**tor** (das; *Sport*), ...**wech|sel**, ...**zeug|nis**
Fuhr‿un|ter|neh|men, ...**un|ter|neh|mer**, ...**werk; fuhr|wer|ken;** ich fuhrwerke; gefuhrwerkt; zu fuhrwerken
Ful|be *Plur.* (westafrik. Volk)
[1]**Ful|da**, die; - (Quellfluss der Weser); [2]**Ful|da** (Stadt a. d. Fulda); **Ful|da|er** (↑R 103); **ful|da|isch, ful|disch**
Ful|gu|rit [*auch* ...'rit], der; -s, -e ‹lat.› (*Geol.* Blitzröhre in Sandboden)
Fül|le, die; -; **fül|len**
Fül|len, das; -s, - (*geh. für* Fohlen)
Fül|ler; Füll‿fe|der, ...**[fe|der|]hal|ter**, ...**horn** (*Plur.* ...hörner); **fül|lig; Füll|ort** (*Bergmannsspr.; Plur.* ...örter); **Füll|sel**, das; -s, -
Full|time|job, *auch* **Full-Time-Job** ['fultaim...] ‹engl.› (Ganztagsbeschäftigung)
Fül|lung; Füll|wort *Plur.* ...wörter
ful|mi|nant ‹lat.› (glänzend, prächtig); **Ful|mi|nanz**, die; -
Fulp|mes (Ort in Tirol)
Fu|ma|ro|le, die; -, -n ‹ital.› (vulkan. Dampfquelle); **Fu|mé** [fy'me:], der; -[s], -s ‹franz.› (Probeabdruck eines Holzschnittes mithilfe feiner Rußfarbe)
Fum|mel, der; -s, - (*ugs. für* billiges Kleid; Fähnchen); **Fum|mel|lei; fum|meln** (*ugs. für* sich [unsachgemäß] an etwas zu schaffen machen); ich ...[e]le (↑R 16)
Fu|na|fu|ti (Hptst. von Tuvalu)
Fund, der; -[e]s, -e
Fun|da|ment, das; -[e]s, -e ‹lat.›; **fun|da|men|tal** (grundlegend; schwer wiegend); **Fun|da|men|ta|lis|mus**, der; -; **Fun|da|men|ta|list**, der; -en, -en (jmd., der [kompromisslos] an seinen [politischen, religiösen] Grundsätzen festhält); **Fun|da|men|ta|lis|tin; Fun|da|men|tal|satz; fun|da|men|tie|ren** (den Grund legen); **Fun|da|ment|wan|ne** *(Bauw.)*
Fund|amt
Fun|da|ti|on, die; -, -en ([kirchliche] Stiftung; *schweiz. für* Fundament[ierung])
Fund‿bü|ro, ...**gru|be**
Fun|di, der; -s, -s (*ugs. für* Fundamentalist [bes. bei den Grünen])
fun|die|ren ‹lat.› ([be]gründen; mit [den nötigen] Mitteln versehen); **fun|diert** ([fest] begründet; *Kaufmannsspr.* durch Grundbesitz gedeckt)
fün|dig (*Bergmannsspr.* ergiebig, reich); fündig werden (entdecken, ausfindig machen; *Bergmannsspr.* auf Lagerstätten stoßen)
Fund‿ort (der; -[e]s, -e), ...**sa|che**, ...**stät|te**, ...**un|ter|schla|gung**
Fun|dus, der; -, - ‹lat.› (Grund u. Boden; Grundlage; Bestand an Kostümen, Kulissen usw.)
Fü|nen (dän. Insel)
Fu|ne|ra|li|en [...iən] *Plur.* ‹lat.› (*veraltet für* [feierliches Gepränge bei einem] Leichenbegängnis)
fünf; die fünf Sinne; wir sind heute zu fünfen *od.* zu fünft; fünf gerade sein lassen (*ugs. für* etwas nicht so genau nehmen); *vgl.* acht, drei; in fünf viertel Stunden *od.* in fünf Viertelstunden; *vgl.* Viertelstunde; **Fünf**, die; -, -en (Zahl); eine Fünf würfeln, schreiben; *vgl.* [1]Acht *u.* Eins; **Fünf|eck; fünf|eckig** (↑R 132); **fünf|ein|halb**, fünf|und|ein|halb; **Fün|fer** (*ugs. auch für* Fünfpfennigstück); *vgl.* Achter; **fün|fer|lei; Fün|fer|rei|he;** in -n; **fünf|fach; Fünf|fa|che**, das; -n; *vgl.* Achtfache; **Fünf|flach**, das; -[e]s, -e, **Fünf|fläch|ner** (*für* Pentaeder); **Fünf|fran|ken|stück** (*mit Ziffer* 5-Franken-Stück; ↑R 28), **Fünf|fränk|ler** *(schweiz.)*; **fünf|hun|dert** (*als röm. Zahlzeichen* D); **Fünf|jahr|plan**, Fünf|jah|res|plan (*mit Ziffer* 5-Jahr[es]-Plan; ↑R 28; für jeweils fünf Jahre aufgestellter Wirtschaftsplan in sozialistischen Ländern); **Fünf|kampf; Fünf|li|ber**, der; -s, - (*schweiz. mdal. für* Fünffrankenstück); **Fünf|ling; fünf|mal;** *vgl.* achtmal; **fünf|ma|lig; Fünf|mark|stück** (*mit Ziffer* 5-Mark-Stück; ↑R 28); **fünf|mark|stück|groß; Fünf|pass**, der; -es, -e (gotisches Maßwerk); **Fünf|pfen|nig|stück; Fünf|pro|zent|klau|sel**, die; - (*mit Ziffer* 5-Prozent-Klausel, ↑R 28; *mit Zeichen* 5 %-Klausel, *vgl.* Prozent *u.* ...prozentig); **fünf|stel|lig; Fünf|strom|land**, das; -[e]s (*für* Pandschab); **fünft** *vgl.* fünf; **Fünf|ta|ge‿fie|ber** (das; -s; Infektionskrankheit), ...**wo|che; fünf|tau|send; fünf|te;** die - Kolonne; *vgl.* achte; **fünf|tel;** *vgl.* achtel; **Fünf|tel**, das, *schweiz. meist* der; -s, -; *vgl.* Achtel; **fünf|tens; Fünf|ton|ner** (*mit Ziffer* 5-Tonner; ↑R 44); **Fünf|uhr|tee; fünf|und|ein|halb**, fünf|ein|halb; **fünf|und|sech|zig|jäh|rig;** *vgl.* achtjährig; **fünf|und|zwan|zig;** *vgl.* acht; **fünf|zehn;** *vgl.* acht *u.* Fuffzehn; **fünf|zehn|hun|dert; fünf|zig** (*als röm. Zahlzeichen* L) usw.; *vgl.* achtzig usw.; **Fünf|zi|ger**, der; -s, - (*ugs. auch für* Fünfzigpfennigstück); *vgl.* Fuffziger; **fünf|zig|jäh|rig;** *vgl.* achtjährig; **Fünf|zig|mark|schein** (*mit Ziffern* 50-Mark-Schein; ↑R 28); **Fünf|zim|mer|woh|nung** (*mit Ziffer* 5-Zimmer-Wohnung)
fun|gi|bel ‹lat.› (einsetzbar, ersetzbar; *Rechtsspr.* vertretbar); ...gible (↑R 130) Sache; **Fun|gi|bi|li|tät**, die; -; **fun|gie|ren** (ein Amt verrichten, verwalten; tätig, wirksam sein)
Fun|gi|zid, das; -[e]s, -e ‹lat.› (Mittel zur Pilzbekämpfung); **Fun|gus**, der; -, ...gi (*Med.* schwammige Geschwulst)
Funk, der; -s (Rundfunk[wesen], drahtlose Telegrafie); **Funk‿ama|teur** (↑R 132), ...**an|la|ge**, ...**aus|stel|lung**, ...**bild; Fünk|chen; Funk|dienst; Fun|ke**, *auch* Fun|ken, der; ...kens, ...ken; eine Funken sprühende Lokomotive; **fun|keln;** ich ...[e]le (↑R 16); **fun|kel|na|gel|neu** *(ugs.)*; **fun|ken** (durch Funk übermitteln); **Fun|ken** *vgl.* Funke; **Fun|ken‿flug**, ...**ma|rie|chen** (Tänzerin im Karneval), ...**re|gen; Fun|ken sprü|hend** *vgl.* Funke; **funk|ent|stö|ren;** ein funkentstörtes Elektrogerät; **Fun|ker; Funk‿ge|rät**, ...**haus**
Fun|kie [...iə], die; -, -n ‹nach dem dt. Apotheker Funck› (eine Zierpflanze)
Funk‿im|puls, ...**kol|leg**, ...**kon|takt; Fünk|lein; Funk‿mess|tech|nik**, ...**pei|lung**, ...**schat|ten**, ...**sprech|ge|rät**, ...**sprech|ver|kehr**, ...**spruch**, ...**sta|ti|on**, ...**stil|le**, ...**stö|rung**, ...**strei|fe**, ...**strei|fen|wa|gen**, ...**ta|xi**, ...**tech|nik** (die; -)
Funk|ti|on, die; -, -en ‹lat.› (Tätigkeit; Aufgabe; Wirkungsweise; *Math.* abhängige Größe); **funk|ti|o|nal** (funktionell); -e Grammatik; **funk|ti|o|na|li|sie|ren; Funk|ti|o|na|lis|mus**, der; - *(Archit., Philos.)*; **Funk|ti|o|na|list**, der; -en, -en (↑R 126); **Funk|ti|o|när**, der; -s, -e ‹franz.›; **funk|ti|o|nell** (auf die Funktion bezüglich; wirksam); -e Erkrankung *(Med.)*; **Funk|ti|o|nen|the|o|rie; funk|ti|o|nie|ren; Funk|ti|ons|ein|heit; funk|ti|ons|fä|hig; Funk|ti|ons|stö|rung; funk|ti|ons|tüch|tig; Funk|ti|ons|verb** (*Sprachw.* Verb, das in verblasster Bedeutung in einer festen Verbindung mit einem Substantiv gebraucht wird, z. B. „[zur Durchführung] bringen")
Funk‿turm, ...**ver|bin|dung**, ...**wa|gen**, ...**wer|bung**, ...**we|sen** (das; -s)

Fu̦n|zel, *selten* Fu̦n|sel, die; -, -n (*ugs. für* schlecht brennende Lampe)

fu̲r (*Abk.* f.); *Präp. mit Akk.* für ihn; ein für allemal; für und wider, *aber* (↑R 49): das Für und [das] Wider; *vgl.* fürs

Fu|ra|ge [fu'ra:ʒə, *österr.* fu'ra:ʒ], die; - ‹franz.› (*Milit.* Lebensmittel; Mundvorrat; Futter); **fu|ra|gie|ren** [...'ʒi:...] (*Milit.* Lebensmittel, Futter empfangen, holen)

für|ba̦ss (*veraltet für* weiter); fürbass schreiten

Fu̲r|bit|te; fu̲r|bit|ten, *nur im Infinitiv gebräuchlich;* fürzubitten; **Fu̲r|bit|ten,** das; -s; **Fu̲r|bit|ter; Fu̲r|bit|te|rin**

Fu̦r|che, die; -, -n; **fu̦r|chen; fu̦r|chig**

Fu̦rcht, die; -; ein Furcht einflößender, erregender (↑R 40) Anblick; **fu̦rcht|bar; Fu̦rcht|bar|keit,** die; -

Fu̲rch|te|gott (m. Vorn.)

Fu̦rcht ein|flö|ßend *vgl.* Furcht; **fu̲rch|ten; fu̲rch|ter|lich; Fu̦rcht er|re|gend** *vgl.* Furcht; **fu̦rcht|los; Fu̦rcht|lo|sig|keit,** die; -; **fu̦rcht|sam; Fu̦rcht|sam|keit,** die; -

Fu̦r|chung

fu̲r|der, fu̲r|der|hin (*veraltet für* von jetzt an, künftig)

für|ei|na̦n|der (↑R 132); *Getrenntschreibung in Verbindung mit Verben:* füreinander einstehen, leben usw.

Fu̲|rie [...i̯ə], die; -, -n ‹lat.› (röm. Rachegöttin; wütende Frau)

Fu|ri̲er, der; -s, -e ‹franz.› (*Milit. veraltet* der für Unterkunft u. Verpflegung sorgende Unteroffizier)

fü̲|rio! (*schweiz. für* feurio!)

fu|ri|o̲s ‹lat.› (*veraltend für* hitzig, leidenschaftlich; mitreißend); **fu|ri|o̲|so** ‹ital.› (*Musik* leidenschaftlich); **Fu|ri|o̲|so,** das; -s, *Plur.* -s *u.* ...si (*Musik*)

Fu̦r|ka, die; - (schweiz. Alpenpass)

für|li̲eb neh|men (*älter für* vorlieb nehmen); ich nehme fürlieb; fürlieb genommen; fürlieb zu nehmen

Fur|ni̲er, das; -s, -e ‹franz.› (dünnes Deckblatt aus wertvollem Holz); **fur|ni̲e|ren; Fur|ni̲er‿holz, ...plat|te; Fur|ni̲e|rung**

Fu̲|ror, der; -s ‹lat.› (Wut); **Fu|ro̲|re,** die; - *od.* das; -s ‹ital.›; *meist in* - machen ([durch Erfolg] Aufsehen erregen); **Fu̲|ror teu|to̲|ni|cus,** der; - - ‹lat., „teutonisches Ungestüm"›

fu̲rs; ↑R 13 (für das); fürs Erste (↑R 48)

Fu̲r|sor|ge, die; - (*früher auch für* Sozialhilfe); **Fu̲r|sor|ge‿amt, ...emp|fän|ger, ...er|zie|hung, ...pflicht; Fu̲r|sor|ger** (Sozialarbeiter); **Fu̲r|sor|ge|rin** (Sozialarbeiterin); **fu̲r|sor|ge|risch** (zum Fürsorgewesen gehörend); **Fu̲r|sor|ge|un|ter|stüt|zung; fu̲r|sorg|lich** (pfleglich, liebevoll); **Fu̲r|sorg|lich|keit,** die; -

Fu̲r|spra|che; Fu̲r|sprech, der; -s, -e (*veraltet für* Fürsprecher, Wortführer; *schweiz. für* Rechtsanwalt); **Fu̲r|spre|cher; Fu̲r|spre|che|rin**

Fu̦rst, der; -en, -en (↑R 126); **Fu̦rst‿abt, ...bi|schof; fu̦rs|ten;** *fast nur noch im Partizip II;* gefürstet; **Fu̦rs|ten‿ge|schlecht, ...haus, ...hof, ...sitz; Fu̦rs|ten|tum; Fu̦rst|e̦rz|bi|schof; Fu̦rs|tin; Fu̦rs|tin|mu̦t|ter,** die; -; **fu̦rst|lich,** *in Titeln* (↑R 108): Fürstlich; **Fu̦rst|lich|keit; Fu̦rst-Pu̦ck|ler-Eis** ‹nach Hermann Fürst von Pückler-Muskau› (Sahneeis in drei Schichten)

Fu̦rt, die; -, -en

Fu̦rth (Nachbarstadt von Nürnberg)

Fu̦rt|wäng|ler (dt. Dirigent)

Fu|ru̦n|kel, der, *auch* das; -s, - ‹lat.› (Geschwür, Eiterbeule); **Fu|run|kul|o̲|se,** die; -, -n

für|wa̲hr (*veraltend*)

Fu̲r|witz, der; -es (*älter für* Vorwitz); **fu̲r|wit|zig** (*älter für* vorwitzig)

Fu̲r|wort *Plur.* ...wörter (*für* Pronomen); **fu̲r|wört|lich**

Fu̦rz, der; -es, Fürze (*derb für* abgehende Blähung); **fu̦r|zen;** du furzt

Fu|sche|le̲i; fu̦|scheln (*landsch. für* rasch hin u. her bewegen; täuschen; pfuschen); ich ...[e]le (↑R 16); **fu̦|schen** (*svw.* fuscheln); du fuschst; **fu̦|schern** (*svw.* fuscheln); ich ...ere (↑R 16)

Fu̲|sel, der; -s, - (*ugs. für* schlechter Branntwein)

fu̲|seln (*landsch. für* hastig u. schlecht arbeiten); ich ...[e]le (↑R 16)

Fu̲|sel|öl

Fü|si|li̲er, der; -s, -e ‹franz.› (*schweiz., sonst veraltet für* Infanterist); **fü|si|li̲e|ren** (standrechtlich erschießen); **Fü|sil|la|de** [fyzi'ja:də], die; -, -n (*veraltet für* standrechtliche Massenerschießung)

Fu|si|o̲n, die; -, -en ‹lat.› (Verschmelzung, Zusammenschluss); **fu|si|o|ni̲e|ren; Fu|si|o|ni̲e|rung; Fu|si|o̲ns|ver|hand|lung**

Fu̲ß, der; -es, Füße; drei Fuß lang (↑R 90); nach Fuß rechnen; zu Fuß gehen; zu Füßen fallen; Fuß fassen; einen Fuß breit, *aber* keinen Fußbreit (*vgl. d.*) weichen; der Weg ist kaum fußbreit; **Fu̲ß‿ab|strei|fer, ...ab|tre|ter, ...ab|wehr** (*Sport*), **...an|gel, ...bad**

Fu̲ß|ball; Fußball spielen (↑R 39), *aber* das Fußballspielen (↑R 50); **Fu̲ß|ball|braut** (*ugs.*); **Fu̲ß|ball|bu̦n|des|trai|ner** (↑R 24); **Fu̲ß|bal|ler; fu̲ß|bal|le|risch; Fu̲ß|ball‿fan, ...feld, ...klub; Fu̲ß|ball|län|der|spiel** (↑R 136); **Fu̲ß|ball‿mann|schaft, ...meis|ter|schaft, ...schuh, ...spiel; Fu̲ß|ball|spie|len,** das; -s, *aber* (↑R 39) Fußball spielen; **Fu̲ß|ball‿spie|ler, ...spie|le|rin, ...sta|di|on, ...ten|nis** (ein Spiel), **...tor, ...to|to, ...trai|ner, ...ver|ein, ...welt|meis|ter|schaft** (*Abk.:* Fußball-WM)

Fu̲ß‿bank (*Plur.* ...bänke), **...bo|den; Fu̲ß|bo|den‿hei|zung, ...le|ger; fu̲ß|breit;** eine fußbreite Rinne; *vgl.* Fuß; **Fu̲ß|breit,** der; -, - (Maß); keinen Fußbreit weichen; keinen Fußbreit Landes hergeben; *vgl.* Fuß; **Fu̲ß|chen**

Fu̦s|sel, die; -, -n, *auch* der; -s, -[n] (Fädchen, Faserstückchen); **fu̦s|se|lig,** fu̦ss|lig; **fu̦s|seln;** der Stoff fusselt

fü̲|ßeln (*landsch. für* mit den Füßen unter dem Tisch Berührung suchen); ich ...[e]le (↑R 16); **fu̲|ßen;** du fußt; auf einem Vertrag -

Fü̦s|sen (Stadt am Lech)

Fu̲ß|en|de

Fu̦s|sen|eg|ger (österr. Schriftstellerin)

...fü|ßer (z. B. Bauchfüßer), ...füßler (z. B. Tausendfüßler); **Fu̲ß|fall,** der; **fu̲ß|fäl|lig; Fu̲ß|feh|ler** (*Hockey, Tennis*); **fu̲ß|frei** (die Füße freilassend); **Fu̲ß|gän|ger; Fu̲ß|gän|ger|am|pel; Fu̲ß|gän|ge|rin; Fu̲ß|gän|ger‿tun|nel, ...über|weg** (↑R 132), **...zo|ne; Fu̲ß|ge|her** (*österr. neben* Fußgänger); **fu̲ß|ge|recht;** -es Schuhwerk; **fu̲ß|hoch;** das Wasser steht -; *vgl.* Fuß; **...fü|ßig** (z. B. vierfüßig); **fu̲ß|kalt;** ein -es Zimmer; **fu̲ß|krank; fu̲ß|lang;** *vgl.* Fuß; **Fu̲ß|lap|pen; fu̲ß|lei|dend; Fü̲ß|lein; ...füß|ler** *vgl.* ...füßer

Fü̲ß|li, Fü̦ss|li (schweiz.-engl. Maler)

fuss|lig, fu̦s|se|lig

Fü̲ß|ling (Fußteil des Strumpfes); **Fu̲ß‿marsch** (der), **...no|te, ...pfad, ...pfle|ge, ...pfle|ger, ...pfle|ge|rin, ...pilz, ...ras|te, ...sack, ...soh|le, ...sol|dat, ...spur; Fu̲ß|[s]tap|fe,** die; -, -n *u.* **Fuß|[s]tap|fen,** der; -s, -; **fuß|tief;** ein fußtiefes Loch; *vgl.* Fuß; **Fuß‿tritt, ...volk, ...wan|de|rung, ...wa|schung, ...weg; fuß|wund**

Fus|ta|ge [...'ta:ʒə, *österr.* ...'ta:ʒ], die; -, -n [...'ta:ʒ(ə)n] ‹franz.› ([Preis für] Leergut)

Fus|ta|nel|la, die; -, ...llen ‹ital.› (kurzer Männerrock der Albaner und Griechen)

Fus|ti *Plur.* ‹ital.› ([Vergütung für] unbrauchbare Bestandteile einer Ware)

Fus|tik|holz ‹arab.; dt.› (einen gelben Farbstoff enthaltendes Holz)

Fu|thark ['fu:θark], das; -s, -e (Runenalphabet)

Fu|ton, der; -s, -s ‹jap.› (jap. Matratze)

futsch, *österr.* pfutsch (*ugs. für* weg, verloren)

[1]**Fut|ter,** das; -s (Nahrung [der Tiere])

[2]**Fut|ter,** das; -s, - (innere Stoffschicht der Oberbekleidung)

Fut|te|ra|ge [...'ra:ʒə, *österr.* ...'ra:ʒ], die; - (*ugs. für* Essen)

Fut|te|ral, das; -s, -e ‹germ.-mlat.› ([Schutz]hülle, Überzug; Behälter)

Fut|ter‿ge|trei|de, ...häus|chen (für Vögel), **...kar|tof|fel, ...krip|pe**

Fut|ter|mau|er (Stützmauer)

Fut|ter|mit|tel, das; **fut|tern** (*ugs. scherzh. für* essen); ich ...ere (↑R 16); [1]**füt|tern;** den Hund -; ich ...ere (↑R 16)

[2]**füt|tern** (Futterstoff einlegen); ich ...ere (↑R 16)

Fut|ter‿neid, ...platz, ...rau|fe, ...rü|be, ...schnei|de|ma|schi|ne *od.* **...schneid|ma|schi|ne**

Fut|ter‿sei|de, ...stoff

Fut|ter|trog; Füt|te|rung

Fu|tur, das; -s, -e *Plur. selten* ‹lat.› (*Sprachw.* Zukunftsform, Zukunft); **fu|tu|risch** (das Futur betreffend, im Futur auftretend); **Fu|tu|ris|mus,** der; - (Kunstrichtung des 20. Jh.s); **Fu|tu|rist,** der; -en, -en; ↑R 126 (Anhänger des Futurismus); **fu|tu|ris|tisch; Fu|tu|ro|lo|ge,** der; -n, -n; ↑R 126 (Zukunftsforscher); **Fu|tu|ro|lo|gie,** die; - (Zukunftsforschung); **fu|tu|ro|lo|gisch; Fu|tu|rum,** das; -s, ...ra (*älter für* Futur); **Fu|tu|rum e|xak|tum** (↑R 132), das; - -, ...ra ...ta (*Sprachw.* vollendete Zukunft, Vorzukunft)

Fu|zel, der; -s, - (*österr. ugs. für* Fussel); **fu|zeln** (*österr. ugs. für* sehr klein schreiben); ich ...[e]le (↑R 16); **Fu|zerl,** das; -s, -n (*svw.* Fuzel)

Fuz|zi, der; -s, -s (*ugs. für* nicht ganz ernst zu nehmender Mensch)

Fuz|zy|lo|gik ['fazi-] ‹engl.-griech.› (*EDV* bei Systemen der künstlichen Intelligenz angewandte Methode der Nachahmung des menschlichen Denkens)

G (Buchstabe); das G; des G, die G, *aber* das g in Lage (↑R 60); der Buchstabe G, g

g = Gramm; *in Österreich auch* Groschen

g = *Zeichen für* Fallbeschleunigung

ᵍ = *früheres Zeichen für* Gon

g, G, das; -, - (Tonbezeichnung); **g** (*Zeichen für* g-Moll); in g; **G** (*Zeichen für* G-Dur); in G

G *(auf dt. Kurszetteln)* = Geld (d. h., das betr. Wertpapier war zum angegebenen Preis gesucht)

G = [2]Gauß; Giga...; Gourde

Γ, γ = Gamma

Ga = *chem. Zeichen für* Gallium

Ga. = Georgia

Gäa (griech. Göttin der Erde)

Ga|bar|dine ['gabardi:n, *auch* ...'di:n], der; -s, *auch* [...'di:nə], die; - ‹franz.› (ein Gewebe); **Ga|bar|dine|man|tel**

Gab|bro (↑R 130), der; -s ‹ital.› (*Geol.* ein Tiefengestein)

Ga|be, die; -, -n; **gä|be** *vgl.* gang

Ga|bel, die; -, -n; **Ga|bel‿bis|sen, ...bock** *(Jägerspr.);* **Gä|bel|chen; Ga|bel‿deich|sel, ...früh|stück, ...hirsch** *(Jägerspr.);* **ga|be|lig,** gab|lig; **ga|beln;** ich ...[e]le (↑R 16)

Ga|bels|ber|ger (Familienn.); die gabelsbergersche Stenographie (↑R 94)

Ga|bel‿schlüs|sel, ...stap|ler; Ga|be|lung, Gab|lung; **Ga|bel|wei|he** (ein Greifvogel)

Ga|ben|tisch

Ga|bi (w. Vorn.)

Gäb|lein; Gab|ler (*Jägerspr.* Gabelbock, -hirsch); **gab|lig,** ga|be|lig; **Gab|lung,** Ga|be|lung

Ga|bo|ro|ne (Hpst. von Botsuana)

Gab|ri|el [...e:l, *auch* ...ɛl] (↑R 130; ein Erzengel; m. Vorn.); **Gab|ri|el|le** (w. Vorn.)

Ga|bun (Staat in Afrika); **Ga|bu|ner; Ga|bu|ne|rin; ga|bu|nisch**

Ga|cke|lei; ga|ckeln (*landsch. für* gackern); ich ...[e]le (↑R 16); **ga|ckern;** ich ...ere (↑R 16); **gack|sen** (*landsch. für* gackern); du gackst; gicksen und gacksen

Gad (bibl. m. Eigenn.)

Ga|den, der; -s, - (*landsch. für* einräumiges Haus; Kammer)

Ga|do|li|ni|um, das; -s ‹nach dem finn. Chemiker Gadolin› (chem. Grundstoff; *Zeichen* Gd)

Gaf|fel, die; -, -n (um den Mast drehbare, schräge Segelstange); **Gaf|fel‿scho|ner, ...se|gel**

gaf|fen; Gaf|fer; Gaf|fe|rei

Gag [gɛk], der; -s, -s ‹engl.-amerik.› (witziger Einfall; überraschende Besonderheit)

Ga|gat, der; -[e]s, -e ‹griech.› (Pechkohle, Jett); **Ga|gat|koh|le**

Ga|ge ['ga:ʒə, *österr.* ga:ʒ], die; -, -n ['ga:ʒ(ə)n] ‹germ.-franz.› (Bezahlung, Gehalt [von Künstlern])

gäh|nen; Gäh|ne|rei, die; -

Gail|lar|de [ga'jardə], die; -, -n ‹franz.› (ein Tanz)

Gains|bo|rough ['ge:nzbərə] (engl. Maler)

Ga|jus (altröm. m. Vorn.; *Abk.* C. [nach der alten Schreibung Cajus])

Ga|la ['ga(:)la], die; - ‹span.› (Kleiderpracht; Festkleid); **Ga|la‿abend** (↑R 132), **...an|zug, ...di|ner, ...emp|fang, ...kon|zert**

ga|lak|tisch ‹griech.› (zur Galaxis gehörend); **Ga|lak|tor|rhö**[1], **Ga|lak|tor|rhöe** [...'rø:], die; -, ...rrhöen (*Med.* Milchfluss nach dem Stillen); **Ga|lak|to|se,** die; -, -n (einfacher Zucker)

ga|la|mä|ßig ['ga(:)la...]

Ga|lan, der; -s, -e ‹span.› (*veraltend für* [vornehm auftretender] Liebhaber); **ga|lant** ‹franz.› (betont höflich, ritterlich; aufmerksam); galante Dichtung (eine literar. Strömung in Europa um 1700); galanter Stil (eine Kompositionsweise des 18. Jh.s in Deutschland); **Ga|lan|te|rie,** die; -, ...ien (Höflichkeit [gegenüber Frauen]); **Ga|lan|te|rie|wa|ren** *Plur.* (*veraltet für* Schmuck-, Kurzwaren); **Ga|lant|homme** [galan'tɔm], der; -s, -s ‹franz.› (*veraltend für* Ehrenmann)

Ga|la|pa|gos|in|seln *Plur.* (zu Ecuador gehörend)

---

[1] *Vgl. die Anmerkung zu* „Diarrhö, Diarrhöe“.

Ga|la|tea (griech. Meernymphe)
Ga|la|ter *Plur.* (griech. Name der Kelten in Kleinasien); **Ga|la|ter|brief,** der; -[e]s; ↑R 105 *(N. T.)*
Ga|la-uni|form (['ga(:)la...]; ↑R 132), **...vor|stel|lung**
Ga|la|xie, die; -, ...xi|en ‹griech.› *(Astron.* großes Sternsystem); **Ga|la|xis,** die; -, ...xi|en (die Milchstraße *[nur Sing.]; selten für* Galaxie)
Gal|ba (röm. Kaiser)
Gä|le, der; -n, -n; ↑R 126 (irisch-schottischer Kelte)
Ga|le|as|se, die; -, -n ‹ital.› (Küstenfrachtsegler; *früher* größere Galeere); **Ga|lee|re,** die; -, -n (Ruderkriegsschiff); **Ga|lee|ren-skla|ve, ...sträf|ling**
Ga|len, Ga|le|nus (altgriech. Arzt); **ga|le|nisch;** galenische Schriften (↑R 94)
Ga|le|o|ne, Ga|li|o|ne, die; -, -n ‹niederl.› (mittelalterl. Segel[kriegs]schiff); **Ga|le|o|te,** Ga|li|o|te, die; -, -n (der Galeasse ähnliches kleineres Küstenfahrzeug)
Ga|le|rie, die; -, ...i|en ‹ital.›; **Ga|le|rist,** der; -en, -en; ↑R 126 (Besitzer, Leiter einer Galerie); **Ga|le|ris|tin**
Gal|gant|wur|zel ‹arab.; dt.› (heilkräftige Wurzel)
Gal|gen, der; -s, -; **Gal|gen-frist, ...hu|mor** (der; -s; *vgl.* [1]Humor), **...strick** *(svw.* Galgenvogel), **...vo|gel** *(ugs. für* Strolch, Taugenichts)
Ga|li|ci|en [...tsiən] (hist. Provinz in Spanien); *vgl. aber* Galizien; **Ga|li|ci|er** [...tsiər]; **ga|li|cisch**
Ga|li|läa (Gebirgsland westl. des Jordans); **Ga|li|lä|er; ga|li|lä|isch,** *aber* (↑R 102): das Galiläische Meer (See Genezareth)
Ga|li|lei (ital. Physiker)
Ga|li|ma|thi|as, der *u.* das; - ‹franz.› *(veraltend für* verworrenes Gerede)
Ga|li|on, das; -s, -s ‹niederl.› (Vorbau am Bug älterer Schiffe); **Ga|li|o|ne** *vgl.* Galeone; **Ga|li|ons|fi|gur; Ga|li|o|te** *vgl.* Galeote
Ga|li|pot [...'po:], der; -s ‹franz.› (ein Fichtenharz)
gä|lisch; -e Sprache (Zweig des Keltischen); *vgl.* deutsch; **Gä|lisch,** das; -[s] (Sprache); *vgl.* Deutsch; **Gä|li|sche,** das; -n; *vgl.* Deutsche, das
Ga|li|zi|en *(früher für* Gebiet nördl. der Karpaten); *vgl. aber* Galicien; **Ga|li|zi|er; ga|li|zisch**
Gall|ap|fel (kugelförmiger Auswuchs an Blättern usw.); [1]**Gal|le,** die; -, -n (Geschwulst [bei Pferden]; Gallapfel)
[2]**Gal|le,** die; -, -n (Sekret der Leber; Gallenblase); **gal|le[n]|bit|ter; Gal|len-bla|se, ...gang** (der), **...ko|lik, ...lei|den, ...stein, ...tee; gal|len|trei|bend; Gal|len|we|ge** *Plur.*
Gal|lert [*auch* ga'lɛrt], das; -[e]s, -e ‹lat.› (durchsichtige, steife Masse aus eingedickten pflanzl. od. tier. Säften); **gal|lert|ar|tig; Gal|ler|te** [*auch* 'ga...], die; -, -n *(svw.* Gallert); **gal|ler|tig** [*auch* 'ga...]; **Gal|lert|mas|se**
Gal|li|en (röm. Name Frankreichs); **Gal|li|er; Gal|li|e|rin**
gal|lig ‹*zu* [2]Galle› (gallebitter; verbittert); -er Humor
gal|li|ka|nisch; -e [kath.] Kirche (in Frankreich vor 1789); **gal|lisch** (aus, von Gallien; Gallien, die Gallier betreffend); **Gal|li|um,** das; -s (chem. Element, Metall; *Zeichen* Ga); **Gal|li|zis|mus,** der; -, ...men *(Sprachw.* franz. Spracheigentümlichkeit in einer nichtfranz. Sprache); **Gal|lo|ma|ne,** der; -n, -n (↑R 126) ‹lat.; griech.› (leidenschaftlicher Bewunderer alles Französischen); **Gal|lo|ma|nie,** die; - (übertriebene Vorliebe für alles Französische)
Gal|lo|ne, die; -, -n ‹engl.› (engl.-amerik. Hohlmaß)
gal|lo|ro|ma|nisch (den roman. Sprachen auf gallischem Boden angehörend, von ihnen abstammend)
Gal|lup|in|sti|tut [*auch* 'gɛləp...], das; -[e]s (↑R 95) ‹nach seinem Gründer George H. Gallup› (amerik. Meinungsforschungsinstitut)
Gal|lus (m. Eigenname)
Gal|lus-säu|re (die; - ‹*zu* [1]Galle›), **...tin|te** (die; -); **Gall|wes|pe**
Gal|mei [*auch* 'gal...], der; -s, -e ‹griech.› (Zinkerz)
Ga|lon [ga'lõ:], der; -s, -s ‹franz.› *u.* **Ga|lo|ne** [ga'lo:nə], die; -, -n ‹ital.› (Borte, Tresse); **ga|lo|nie|ren** (mit Borten, Tressen usw. besetzen)
Ga|lopp, der; -s, *Plur.* -s *u.* -e ‹ital.›; **Ga|lop|per** (Pferd für Galopprennen); **ga|lop|pie|ren;** galoppierende Schwindsucht *(volkstüml. Bez. für* die in kurzer Zeit tödl. verlaufende Form der Lungentuberkulose); **Ga|lopp|ren|nen**
Ga|lo|sche, die; -, -n ‹franz.› *(veraltend für* Überschuh; *ugs. für* ausgetretener Schuh)
Gals|wor|thy ['gɔ:lswœ(r)ði] (engl. Schriftsteller)
galt *(bayr., österr., schweiz. für* [von Kühen] keine Milch gebend; vorübergehend unfruchtbar); *vgl.* [1]gelt; **Galt|vieh** *(bayr., österr., schweiz. für* Jungvieh; Kühe, die keine Milch geben)
Gal|va|ni [...v...] (ital. Naturforscher); **Gal|va|ni|sa|ti|on,** die; - ‹nlat.› *(Med.* therapeutische Anwendung des elektrischen Gleichstromes); **gal|va|nisch;** galvanischer Strom; galvanisches Element; galvanische Verbindung; **Gal|va|ni|seur** [...'zø:r], der; -s, -e ‹franz.› (Facharbeiter für Galvanotechnik); **gal|va|ni|sie|ren** (durch Elektrolyse mit Metall überziehen); **Gal|va|nis|mus,** der; - ‹nlat.› (Lehre vom galvanischen Strom); **Gal|va|no,** das; -s, -s ‹ital.› *(Druckw.* galvanische Abformung eines Druckstockes); **Gal|va|no-kaus|tik** ‹ital.; griech.› *(Med.* Anwendung des Galvanokauters), **...kau|ter** *(Med.* auf galvanischem Wege glühend gemachtes chirurg. Instrument), **...me|ter** (das; -s, -; Strommesser), **...plas|tik** (Verfahren, Gegenstände galvanisch mit Metall zu überziehen, bes. die Herstellung von Galvanos), **...plas|ti|ker** (Berufsbez.); **gal|va|no|plas|tisch; Gal|va|no-skop** (das; -s, -e; ein elektr. Messgerät), **...tech|nik** (die; -; Technik des Galvanisierens), **...ty|pie** (die; -; *früher für* Galvanoplastik)
Ga|man|der, der; -s, - ‹griech.› (eine Pflanze)
Ga|ma|sche, die; -, -n ‹arab.› (eine Leder- od. Stoffbekleidung des Beins); **Ga|ma|schen|dienst** *(veraltend für* kleinlicher, pedantischer [Kasernen]drill)
Gam|be, die; -, -n ‹ital.› (ein Streichinstrument)
Gam|bia (Staat in Afrika); **Gam|bi|er; Gam|bi|e|rin; gam|bisch**
Gam|bist, der; -en, -en (↑R 126) ‹ital.› (Gambenspieler); **Gam|bis|tin**
Gam|bit, das; -s, -s ‹span.› (eine Schachspieleröffnung)
Gam|bri|nus (↑R 130; [sagenhafter] König, angeblicher Erfinder des Bieres)
Game|boy ® ['ge:mbɔy], der; -[s], -s ‹engl.› (ein elektronisches Spielgerät)
Ga|me|lan, das; -s, -s ‹indones.› (Orchester mit einheimischen Instrumenten auf Java u. Bali)
Ga|mel|le, die; -, -n ‹franz.› *(schweiz. für* Koch- u. Essgefäß des Soldaten im Feld)
Game|show ['ge:mʃo:] (↑R 33; Unterhaltungssendung im Fernsehen)

Ga|met, der; -en, -en (↑R 126) ‹griech.› (*Biol.* Geschlechtszelle); **Ga|me|to|phyt**, der; -en, -en; ↑R 126 (*Bot.* die Pflanzengeneration, die sich geschlechtlich fortpflanzt)
Gam|ma, das; -[s], -s (griech. Buchstabe; *Γ, γ*); **Gam|ma|strah|len, γ-Strah|len** *Plur.*; ↑R 25 (radioaktive Strahlen, kurzwellige Röntgenstrahlen)
Gam|mel, der; -s (*ugs. für* wertloses Zeug); **gam|me|lig**, gammlig (*ugs. für* verkommen; verdorben, faulig); **gam|meln** (*ugs. für* verderben [von Nahrungsmitteln]; *auch für* [ohne Ansprüche] in den Tag hinein leben); ich ...[e]le (↑R 16); **Gamm|ler; Gamm|le|rin; Gamm|ler|tum**, das; -s; **gamm|lig** *vgl.* gammelig
Gams, der *od.* die, *Jägerspr. u. landsch.* das; -, -[en] (*bes. Jägerspr. u. landsch. für* Gämse); **Gams|bart, Gäms|bart; Gams|bock, Gäms|bock; Gäm|se** (↑R 89), die; -, -n; *vgl. auch* Gams; **gäms|far|ben** (*für* chamois); **Gäms|jä|ger, ...le|der, ...wild**
Ga|nau|ser (*österr. mdal. für* Gänserich)
Gand, die; -, -en *od.* das; -s, Gänder (*tirol. u. schweiz. für* Schuttfeld, Geröllhalde)
Gan|dhi, Mahatma (ind. Staatsmann)
Ga|neff *vgl.* Ganove
Gan|er|be, der (*früher für* Miterbe); **Gan|erb|schaft**, die; -
gang; *nur noch in* gang und gäbe sein, *landsch. auch* gäng und gäbe sein (allgemein üblich sein);
[1]**Gang**, der; -[e]s, Gänge; im Gang[e] sein; in Gang bringen, halten, setzen, *aber* (↑R 50): das Inganghalten, Ingangsetzen
[2]**Gang** [gɛŋ], die; -, -s ‹engl.-amerik.› ([Verbrecher]bande)
gäng (*landsch. svw.* gang); **Gang|art; gang|bar; Gang|bar|keit**, die; -; **Gän|gel|band**, das; -[e]s, ...bänder; jmdn. am - führen; **Gän|ge|lei; gän|geln** (dauernd bevormunden); ich ...[e]le (↑R 16)
Gan|ges ['gaŋgɛs], der; - (Fluss in Vorderindien)
Gang|ge|stein *(Geol.)*; **gän|gig**; gängige Ware; eine gängige Formulierung; **Gän|gig|keit**, die; -
Gang|li|en|zel|le ['gaŋ(g)liən...] (↑R 130; *Med.* Nervenzelle); **Gang|li|on**, das; -s, ...ien [...iən] ‹griech.› (Nervenknoten; Überbein)
Gan|grän [gaŋ'grɛ:n], die; -, -en, *auch* das; -s, -e ‹griech.› (*Med.* Brand der Gewebe, Knochen); **gan|grä|nes|zie|ren** (brandig werden); **gan|grä|nös** (brandig)
Gang|schal|tung
Gang|spill ‹niederl.› (*Seew.* Ankerwinde)
Gangs|ter ['gɛŋstə(r)], der; -s, - ‹engl.-amerik.› ([organisierter] Schwerverbrecher); **Gangs|ter‿ban|de, ...boss, ...braut, ...me|tho|de; Gangs|ter|tum**
Gang|way ['gɛŋwe:], die; -, -s ‹engl.› (Laufgang zum Besteigen eines Schiffes od. Flugzeuges)
Ga|no|ve [...v...], der; -n, -n (↑R 126) ‹jidd.-hebr.› *u.* Ganeff, der; -[s], *Plur.* -e *u.* -s (*ugs. abwertend für* Gauner, Betrüger); **Ga|no|ven‿eh|re, ...spra|che**
Gans, die; -, Gänse; **Gans|bra|ten** (*südd., österr. für* Gänsebraten); **Gäns|chen; Gän|se‿blüm|chen, ...bra|ten, ...brust, ...fe|der, ...fett** (das; -[e]s), **...füß|chen** (*ugs. für* Anführungsstrich), **...haut** (die; -), **...keu|le, ...kiel, ...klein** (das; -s), **...le|ber, ...marsch** (der; -es); **Gan|ser** (*südd., österr. für* Gänserich); **Gän|se|rich**, der; -s, -e; **Gän|se‿schmalz, ...wein** (der; -[e]s; *scherzh. für* Wasser); **Gans|jung**, das; -s (*südd. für* Gänseklein); **Gans|le|ber** (*österr. für* Gänseleber); **Gäns|lein; Gansl|jun|ge**, das; -n; ↑R 5 ff. (*österr. für* Gänseklein)
Gant, die; -, -en (*schweiz. für* öffentl. Versteigerung)
Gan|ter (*nordd. für* Gänserich)
Ga|ny|med [*auch, österr. nur*, 'ga:...], **Ga|ny|me|des** (Mundschenk des Zeus)
ganz; [in] ganz Europa; ganze Zahlen *(Math.)*; ganz und gar; ganz und gar nicht; etwas wieder ganz machen; die ganzen Leute (*mdal. u. ugs. für* alle Leute); (↑R 47:) ein Ganzes; als Ganzes; das [große] Ganze; ein großes Ganze *od.* Ganzes; aufs Ganze gehen; im Ganzen [gesehen]; im großen Ganzen; im Großen und Ganzen; fürs Ganze; ums Ganze; *Schreibung in Verbindung mit einem Adjektiv:* ganz hell, ganz groß; *aber* (↑R 40): ein ganzleinener, ganzwollener Kleiderstoff, der Kleiderstoff ist ganzleinen, ganzwollen; **Gän|ze**; *nur in Wendungen wie* zur Gänze (ganz, vollständig); in seiner/ihrer Gänze (*geh. für* in seinem/ihrem ganzen Umfang); **ganz|gar** (*Gerberei* fertig gegerbt); ganzgare Häute, *aber* das Fleisch ist noch nicht ganz gar; *vgl.* ganz; **Ganz|glas|tür; Ganz|heit**, die; - (gesamtes Wesen); **ganz|heit|lich; Ganz|heits‿me|di|zin** (die; -), **...me|tho|de, ...the|o|rie; ganz|jäh|rig** (während des ganzen Jahres); **Ganz|le|der|band**, der; **ganz|le|dern** (aus reinem Leder; *vgl.* ganz); **ganz|lei|nen** (aus reinem Leinen; *vgl.* ganz); **Ganz|lei|nen**, das; -s; **Ganz|lei|nen|band**, der; **gänz|lich; ganz‿sei|den** (aus reiner Seide; *vgl.* ganz), **...sei|tig** (eine ganzseitige Anzeige), **...tä|gig** (während des ganzen Tages); **ganz|tags; Ganz|tags|schu|le; Ganz|ton** *Plur.* ...töne; **ganz|wol|len** (aus reiner Wolle; *vgl.* ganz); **Ganz|wort|me|tho|de**, die; - *(Päd.)*
[1]**gar** (fertig gekocht; *südd., österr. ugs. für* zu Ende); das Fleisch ist noch nicht ganz gar, erst halb gar; *vgl. auch* ganzgar; das Fleisch gar kochen; gar gekochtes Fleisch; um das Fleisch gar zu kochen; [2]**gar** (ganz, sehr, sogar; *stets getrennt geschrieben*); ganz und gar, gar kein, gar nicht, gar nichts; gar sehr, gar wohl; du sollst das nicht gar so sehr ernst nehmen
Ga|ra|ge [ga'ra:ʒə, *österr.* ga'ra:ʒ], die; -, -n [ga'ra:ʒ(ə)n] ‹franz.›; **Ga|ra|gen‿ein|fahrt, ...tor, ...wa|gen** (meist in einer Garage geparktes Auto); **ga|ra|gie|ren** (*österr. neben, schweiz. für* [Wagen] einstellen)
Ga|ra|mond [...'mɔ̃:, *fachspr.* 'ga(:)ramɔnt], die; - ‹nach dem franz. Stempelschneider› (eine Antiquadruckschrift)
Ga|rant, der; -en, -en (↑R 126) ‹franz.›; **Ga|ran|tie**, die; -, ...ien (Gewähr; Zusicherung); **Ga|ran|tie|an|spruch; ga|ran|tie|ren; Ga|ran|tie|schein**
Gar|aus, der; *nur in* jmdm. den - machen (jmdn. umbringen)
Gar|be, die; -, -n; **Gar|ben|bin|de|ma|schi|ne; Gar|ben|bund**, das
Gar|bo, Greta (schwed. Filmschauspielerin)
Gär|bot|tich
Gar|cía Lor|ca [gar'θi:a -] (span. Dichter)
Gar|çon [gar'sɔ̃:], der; -s, -s ‹franz.› (*veraltet für* Kellner; Junggeselle); **Gar|çonne** [gar'sɔn], die; -, -n [...nən] (*veraltet für* Junggesellin); **Gar|çon|ni|ère** [garsɔ'niɛ:r], die; -, -n (*österr. für* Einzimmerwohnung)
Gar|da|see, der; -s (in Oberitalien)
Gar|de, die; -, -n ‹franz.› (*Milit.* Elitetruppe); **Gar|de|du|korps**

[gard(ə)dy'ko:r], das; - (*früher für* Leibgarde); **Gar|de₋maß** (das; -es), **...of|fi|zier, ...re|gi|ment**
Gar|de|ro|be, die; -, -n ‹franz.› (Kleidung; Kleiderablage; Ankleideraum im Theater); **Gar|de|ro|ben₋frau, ...ha|ken, ...mar|ke, ...schrank, ...stän|der; Gar|de|ro|bi|er** [...'bie:], der; -s, -s (*Theater* jmd., der den Künstlern beim Ankleiden hilft und für die Pflege der Kostüme zuständig ist); **Gar|de|ro|bi|e|re,** die; -, -n (Garderobenfrau; *Theater vgl.* Garderobier)
gar|dez! [gar'de:] ‹franz.› (bei privaten Schachpartien manchmal verwendeter Hinweis auf die Bedrohung der Dame)
Gar|di|ne, die; -, -n ‹niederl.›; **Gar|di|nen₋pre|digt** (*ugs.*), **...schnur, ...stan|ge**
Gar|dist, der; -en, -en (↑R 126) ‹franz.› (Soldat der Garde)
Ga|re, die; - (*Landw.* günstigster Zustand des Kulturbodens)
ga|ren (gar kochen)
gä|ren; es gor (*auch, bes. in übertr. Bedeutung* gärte); es göre (*auch* gärte); gegoren (*auch* gegärt); gär[e]!
gar ge|kocht *vgl.* [1]gar
Ga|ri|bal|di (ital. Freiheitskämpfer)
gar kein; *vgl.* [2]gar
Gar₋koch (der), **...kü|che** (*veraltet für* Küche in einer einfachen Gaststätte o. Ä.)
Gar|misch-Par|ten|kir|chen (bayr. Fremdenverkehrsort)
Garn, das; -[e]s, -e
Gar|ne|le, die; -, -n (ein Krebstier)
gar|ni *vgl.* Hotel garni
gar nicht; gar nichts; *vgl.* [2]gar
gar|nie|ren ‹franz.› (schmücken, verzieren); **Gar|nie|rung; Gar|ni|son,** die; -, -en (Standort einer [Besatzungs]truppe); **gar|ni|so|nie|ren** (*veraltend für* in der Garnison liegen); **Gar|ni|son[s]|kir|che; Gar|ni|tur,** die; -, -en (Verzierung; Anzahl od. Satz zusammengehöriger Gegenstände)
Garn|knäu|el
Ga|ronne [ga'rɔn], die; - (franz. Fluss)
Ga|rot|te usw. *vgl.* Garrotte usw.; **Gar|rot|te,** die; -, -n ‹span.› (Würgschraube od. Halseisen zum Hinrichten [Erdrosseln]); **gar|rot|tie|ren**
gars|tig; Gars|tig|keit
Gär|stoff
Gärt|chen; gär|teln (*südd. für* Gartenarbeit aus Liebhaberei verrichten); ich ...[e]le (↑R 16); **Gar|ten,** der; -s, Gärten; **Gar|ten₋ar|beit, ...ar|chi|tekt, ...bank** (*Plur.* ...bänke), **...bau** (der; -[e]s); **Gar|ten|bau|aus|stel|lung; Gar|ten₋beet, ...blu|me, ...fest, ...freund, ...frucht, ...ge|rät, ...haus, ...lau|be, ...lo|kal, ...par|ty, ...rot|schwanz** (ein Singvogel), **...schach, ...stadt, ...weg, ...wirt|schaft, ...zaun, ...zwerg; Gärt|lein; Gärt|ner; Gärt|ne|rei; Gärt|ne|rin; Gärt|ne|rin|art;** *nur in* nach - (*Gastron.*); **gärt|ne|risch; gärt|nern;** ich ...ere (↑R 16); **Gärt|ners|frau**
Gä|rung; Gä|rungs|pro|zess
Gar|zeit
Gas, das; -es, -e; Gas geben
Ga|sa; *vgl.* Gaza
Gas₋an|griff, ...an|zün|der, ...ba|de|ofen (↑R 132), **...be|ton** (*Bauw.*)
Ga|sel, Gha|sel [ga...], das; -s, -e ‹arab.› *u.* **Ga|se|le,** Gha|se|le, die; -, -n (eine [oriental.] Gedichtform)
ga|sen; es gast; es gas|te; **Gas₋ex|plo|si|on, ...feu|er|zeug, ...fla|sche; gas|för|mig; Gas₋ge|misch, ...hahn, ...hei|zung, ...herd, ...hül|le; ga|sie|ren** (*Textiltechnik* Garne durch Absengen von Faserenden befreien); **ga|sig; Gas₋ko|cher, ...lei|tung; Gas-Luft-Ge|misch;** ↑R 28; **Gas₋mann, ...mas|ke, ...ofen** (↑R 132), **...öl; Ga|so|me|ter,** der; -s, - ‹franz.› (*veraltend für* großer Gasbehälter); **Gas₋pe|dal, ...pis|to|le, ...rech|nung**
gass|aus, gass|ein (*veraltet*); **Gäss|chen**
Gas|schlauch; Gas[|schmelz]|schwei|ßung (autogene Schweißung)
Gas|se, die; -, -n (enge, schmale Straße; *österr. in bestimmten Verwendungen auch für* Straße, z. B. über die Gasse); *Schreibung in Straßennamen:* ↑R 123; **Gas|sen₋bu|be, ...hau|er** (*ugs. für* allbekanntes Lied), **...jun|ge, ...lied, ...lo|kal** (*österr.*); **gas|sen|sei|tig** (*österr. für* nach der Straße zu gelegen); **Gas|sen₋ver|kauf** (*österr. für* Verkauf über die Straße), **...woh|nung** (*österr.*); **Gas|si;** *nur in* Gassi gehen (*ugs. für* mit dem Hund auf die Straße [Gasse] gehen); **Gäss|lein**
Gast, der; -[e]s, *Plur.* Gäste *u.* (*Seemannsspr. für* bestimmte Matrosen:) -en; zu Gast sein; zu Gast bitten; als Gast (*Abk.* a. G.); **Gast₋ar|bei|ter, ...ar|bei|te|rin, ...do|zent, ...do|zen|tin; Gäs|te₋bett, ...buch, ...hand|tuch, ...haus, ...heim; Gas|te|rei** (*veraltet für* üppiges Gastmahl); **Gäs|te₋toi|let|te, ...zim|mer; gast|frei; Gast₋frei|heit** (die; -), **...freund; gast|freund|lich; Gast₋freund|lich|keit** (die; -), **...freund|schaft** (die; -), **...ge|ber, ...ge|be|rin, ...ge|schenk, ...haus, ...hof, ...hö|rer; gas|tie|ren** (*Theater*); **Gast|land; gast|lich; Gast|lich|keit,** die; -; **Gast₋mahl** (*Plur.* ...mähler *u.* -e; *geh.*), **...mann|schaft** (*Sport*), **...pflan|ze** (*Bot.* Schmarotzer)
Gast|räa (↑R 130), die; -, ...äen ‹griech.› (*Zool.* angenommenes Urdarmtier); **gast|ral** (*Med.* zum Magen gehörend, den Magen betreffend); **Gast|ral|gie,** die; -, ...ien (Magenkrampf)
Gast₋recht, ...red|ner, ...red|ne|rin
gast|risch (↑R 130) ‹griech.› (*Med.* zum Magen gehörend, vom Magen ausgehend); -es Fieber; **Gast|ri|tis,** die; -, ...itiden (Magenschleimhautentzündung)
Gast|rol|le
Gast|ro|nom (↑R 130), der; -en, -en (↑R 126) ‹griech.› (Gastwirt mit besonderen Kenntnissen auf dem Gebiet der Kochkunst u. des Gaststättenwesens); **Gast|ro|no|mie,** die; - (Gaststättengewerbe; feine Kochkunst); **Gast|ro|no|min; gast|ro|no|misch; Gast|ro|po|de,** der; -n, -n *meist Plur.;* ↑R 126 (*Zool.* Schnecke); **Gast|ro|skop,** das; -s, -e (*Med.* ein Gerät zur Untersuchung des Mageninneren); **Gast|ro|sto|mie,** die; -, ...ien (*Med.* Anlegung einer Magenfistel); **Gast|ro|to|mie,** die; -, ...ien (*Med.* Magenschnitt); **Gast|ru|la,** die; - (*Biol.* Entwicklungsstadium vielzelliger Tiere)
Gast₋spiel, ...stät|te; Gast|stät|ten|ge|wer|be, das; -s; **Gast₋stu|be, ...tier** (Schmarotzer), **...vor|le|sung, ...vor|stel|lung, ...vor|trag, ...wirt, ...wirt|schaft, ...wort** (*Plur.* ...wörter; geläufiges Fremdwort), **...zim|mer**
Gas₋ver|gif|tung, ...werk, ...zäh|ler
Gat *vgl.* Gatt; **Gatt,** Gat, das; -[e]s, *Plur.* -en *u.* -s (*Seemannsspr.* Öse, Loch; enger Raum; Schiffsheck)
Gat|te, der; -n, -n (↑R 126); **gat|ten,** sich (*geh. für* sich paaren); **Gat|ten₋lie|be, ...mord, ...wahl**
Gat|ter, das; -s, - (Gitter, [Holz]zaun); **Gat|ter|sä|ge**
gat|tie|ren (verschiedene Eisensorten u. Zusätze für das Gießen von Gusseisen zusammenstellen); **Gat|tin; Gat|tung; Gat|tungs|na|me** (*auch für* Appellativ)

Gau, der, *landsch.* das; -[e]s, -e; **Gäu**, das; -[e]s, -e (*landsch. für* Gau); das Obere -; das Allgäu
GAU, der; -s, -s (= größter anzunehmender Unfall)
Gau|be, Gau|pe, die; -, -n (*Bauw. u. landsch. für* aus einem Dach herausgebautes Fenster)
Gauch, der; -[e]s, *Plur.* -e *u.* Gäuche ‹„Kuckuck"› (*veraltet für* Narr); **Gauch|heil**, der; -[e]s, -e (Zierpflanze u. Ackerunkraut)
Gau|cho [ˈgaut͡ʃo], der; -[s], -s ‹indian.-span.› (südamerik. Viehhirt)
Gau|de|a|mus, das; - ‹lat., „Freuen wir uns!"› (Name [u. Anfang] eines Studentenliedes)
Gau|dee, die; -, -n (*österr. Nebenform von* Gaudi); **Gau|di**, die; -, *österr. nur so, auch* das; -s (*ugs. für* Gaudium)
Gau|dieb (*nordd. veraltet für* Gauner)
Gau|di|um, das; -s ‹lat.› (Freude; Ausgelassenheit; Spaß); **Gau|di|wurm** (*ugs. scherzh. für* Fastnachtszug)
gauf|rie|ren [goˈfriː...] (↑R 130) ‹franz.› (mit dem Gaufrierkalander prägen); **Gauf|rier|ka|lan|der** (Kalander zur Narbung od. Musterung von Papier u. Geweben)
Gau|graf (*früher* Graf, dessen Herrschaftsbereich ein Gau ist)
Gau|guin [goˈgɛ̃ː] (franz. Maler)
Gau|ke|lei; gau|kel|haft; gau|keln (*veraltend*); ich ...[e]le (↑R 16); **Gau|kel-spiel, ...werk** (das; -[e]s); **Gauk|ler; Gauk|le|rei; gauk|ler|haft; Gauk|le|rin; gauk|le|risch; Gauk|ler|trup|pe**
Gaul, der; -[e]s, Gäule; **Gäul|chen**
Gaulle [goːl], **de** (franz. General u. Staatsmann); *vgl.* de-Gaulle-freundlich; **Gaul|lis|mus** [goˈlismus], der; - ‹nach de Gaulle› (politische Bewegung in Frankreich); **Gaul|list** [goˈlist], der; -en, -en; ↑R 126 (Anhänger des Gaullismus)
Gault [gɔːlt], der; -[e]s ‹engl.› (*Geol.* zweitälteste Stufe der Kreide)
Gau|men, der; -s, -; **Gau|men-kit|zel, ...laut** (*für* Guttural), **...se|gel, ...zäpf|chen; gau|mig;** - sprechen
Gau|ner, der; -s, -; **Gau|ner|ban|de; Gau|ne|rei; gau|ner|haft; Gau|ne|rin; gau|ne|risch; gau|nern;** ich ...ere (↑R 16); **Gau|ner|spra|che**
Gau|pe *vgl.* Gaube
Gaur, der; -s, -[s] ‹Hindi› (wild lebendes Rind in Indien)

[1]**Gauß** (dt. Mathematiker); [2]**Gauß**, das; -, - (alte Maßeinheit der magnetischen Induktion; *Zeichen* G); *vgl.* Tesla
Gautsch-brett (Gerät zum Pressen des nassen Papiers), **...brief; Gaut|sche**, die; -, -n (*südd. für* Schaukel); **gaut|schen** (Papier zum Pressen ins Gautschbrett legen; *auch* Lehrlinge nach altem Buchdruckerbrauch unter die Gehilfen aufnehmen; *südwestd. für* schaukeln); du gautschst; **Gautscher; Gautsch|fest**
Ga|vot|te [gaˈvɔt, *österr. nur so, auch* gaˈvɔtə], die; -, -n ‹franz.› (ein alter Tanz)
Ga|wein (Gestalt der Artussage)
Ga|za, *auch* Ga|sa (Stadt im östl. Mittelmeerraum); **Ga|za|strei|fen**, der; -s
Ga|ze [ˈgazə], die; -, -n ‹pers.› (durchsichtiges Gewebe; Verbandmull)
Ga|zel|le, die; -, -n ‹arab.-ital.› (Antilopenart)
Ga|zet|te [*auch* gaˈzɛt(ə)], die; -, -n ‹franz.› (*veraltet, noch abwertend für* Zeitung)
GBl. = Gesetzblatt
Gd = chem. Zeichen für Gadolinium
Gdańsk [gdansk, *poln.* gdaĩsk] (poln. Hafenstadt an der Ostsee; *vgl.* Danzig)
G-Dur [ˈgeːduːr, *auch* ˈgeːˈduːr], das; - (Tonart; *Zeichen* G); **G-Dur-Ton|lei|ter** (↑R 28)
Ge = chem. Zeichen für Germanium
ge... (*Vorsilbe von Verben,* z. B. gehorchen, du gehorchst, gehorcht, zu gehorchen)
Ge|äch|te|te, der *u.* die; -n, -n (↑R 5 ff.)
Ge|äch|ze, das; -s
Ge|äder (↑R 132), das; -s; **geädert;** das Blatt ist schön -
Ge|äf|ter, das; -s, - (*Jägerspr.* die beiden hinteren Zehen beim Schalenwild u. a.)
Ge|al|be|re, das; -s
ge|ar|tet; das Kind ist gut -
Ge|äse (↑R 132), das; -s, - (*Jägerspr.* Äsung; *auch* Maul bei Hirsch und Reh)
Ge|äst, das; -[e]s (Astwerk)
[1]**geb.** = geboren[e], *auch* geborener (*Zeichen* *)
[2]**geb.** = gebunden (bei Büchern)
Ge|bab|bel, das; -s (*landsch. für* Geplapper, dauerndes Reden)
Ge|bäck, das; -[e]s, -e; **Ge|ba|cke|ne**, das; -n (↑R 5 ff.); **Ge|bäck-scha|le**
Ge|bal|ge, das; -s (Prügelei)
Ge|bälk, das; -[e]s, -e *Plur. selten*

Ge|bän|de, das; -s, - (eine mittelalterl. Kopftracht)
Ge|bär|de, die; -, -n; **ge|bär|den**, sich; **Ge|bär|den-spiel** (das; -[e]s), **...spra|che; ge|ba|ren**, sich (*veraltet für* sich gebärden)
ge|bä|ren; du gebärst, sie gebärt (*geh.* gebierst, gebiert); du gebarst; du gebärest; geboren (*vgl. d.*); gebär[e]! (*geh.* gebier!)
Ge|ba|ren, das; -s
Ge|bä|re|rin; Ge|bär-kli|nik (*österr. für* Entbindungsabteilung, -heim), **...mut|ter** (die; -, ...mütter); **Ge|bär|mut|ter|spie|gel**
Ge|ba|rung (Gebaren; *österr. für* Buch-, Geschäftsführung)
ge|bauch|pin|selt (*ugs. für* geehrt, geschmeichelt); **ge|baucht** (bauchig)
Ge|bäu|de, das; -s, -; **Ge|bäu|de-kom|plex, ...teil** (der); **Ge|bäu|lich|keit** *meist Plur.* (*südd., schweiz. für* Baulichkeit)
ge|be|freu|dig
Ge|bein, das; -[e]s, -e
Ge|bel|fer, das; -s (Belfern, Bellen); **Ge|bell**, das; -[e]s; **Ge|bel|le**, das; -s
ge|ben; du gibst, er gibt; du gabst; du gäbest; gegeben (*vgl. d.*); gib!; (↑R 50:) Geben (*auch* geben) ist seliger denn Nehmen (*auch* nehmen)
Ge|ben|de *vgl.* Gebände
Ge|be|ne|dei|te, die; -n ‹*zu* benedeien› (Gottesmutter)
Ge|ber; Ge|be|rin; Ge|ber|lau|ne, die; -; in -; **Ge|ber|spra|che** (*Sprachw.*)
Ge|bet, das; -[e]s, -e; **Ge|bet-buch; Ge|bets-man|tel, ...müh|le, ...ni|sche, ...rie|men, ...tep|pich**
Ge|bet|tel, das; -s
ge|beut (*veraltet für* gebietet); die Stunde -, dass ...
Geb|hard (m. Vorn.)
Ge|biet, das; -[e]s, -e; **ge|bie|ten;** geboten; **ge|bie|tend; Ge|bie|ter; Ge|bie|te|rin; ge|bie|te|risch; ge|biet|lich; Ge|biets-an|spruch, ...er|wei|te|rung, ...ho|heit, ...kör|per|schaft** (*Rechtsw.*), **...kran|ken|kas|se** (*österr.*), **...re|form; ge|biets|wei|se**
Ge|bild|brot (Gebäck besonderer Gestalt zu bestimmten Festtagen); **Ge|bil|de**, das; -s, -; **ge|bil|det; Ge|bil|de|te**, der *u.* die; -n, -n (↑R 5 ff.)
Ge|bim|mel, das; -s
Ge|bin|de, das; -s, -
Ge|bir|ge, das; -s, -; **ge|bir|gig; Ge|bir|gig|keit**, die; -; **Ge|birg|ler; Ge|birgs-bach, ...jä|ger** (*Militär.*), **...kamm, ...ket|te, ...land-**

schaft, ...mas|siv, ...stock (*Plur.* ...stöcke), **...zug**
Ge|biss, das; -es, -e
Ge|blaf|fe, das; -s *(ugs.)*
Ge|bla|se, das; -s (Blasen); **Ge|blä|se,** das; -s, - *(Technik)*
Ge|blö|del, das; -s *(ugs.)*
Ge|blök, das; -[e]s *u.* **Ge|blö|ke,** das; -s
ge|blümt, *österr.* **ge|blumt** (mit Blumen gemustert)
Ge|blüt, das; -[e]s *(geh.)*
ge|bo|gen (gekrümmt); **ge|bogt** (bogenförmig geschnitten); ein -er Kragen
ge|bo|ren (*Abk.* geb.; *Zeichen* *); er ist ein geborener Schmitt; sie ist eine geborene Schulz; Frau Müller geb. Schulz *od.* Frau Müller, geb. Schulz (↑R 63); **Ge|bo|ren|zei|chen**
ge|bor|gen; hier fühle ich mich -; **Ge|bor|gen|heit,** die; -
Ge|bot, das; -[e]s, -e; zu -[e] stehen; das erste, zweite Gebot, *aber* die Zehn Gebote (↑R 54); **Ge|bots|schild** *Plur.* ...schilder *(Verkehrsw.)*
Gebr. = Gebrüder
Ge|bräch, das; -[e]s, -e *u.* **Ge|brä|che,** das; -s, - (*Bergmannsspr.* Gestein, das leicht in Stücke zerfällt; *Jägerspr.* der vom Schwarzwild mit dem Rüssel aufgewühlte Boden)
Ge|brä|me, das; -s, - (*veraltet für* Verbrämung)
ge|brand|markt
ge|brannt; -er Kalk
Ge|bra|te|ne, das; -n (↑R 5 ff.)
Ge|bräu, das; -[e]s, -e
Ge|brauch, der; -[e]s, *Plur.* (*für* Sitte, Verfahrensweise:) Gebräuche; **ge|brau|chen** (benutzen); **ge|bräuch|lich; Ge|bräuch|lich|keit,** die; -; **Ge|brauchs‿an|wei|sung, ...ar|ti|kel; ge|brauchs|fer|tig; Ge|brauchs‿ge|gen|stand, ...gra|fik** (↑R 33), **...gut, ...mu|sik, ...mus|ter, ...wert; Ge|braucht|wa|gen; Ge|braucht|wa|gen|markt**
Ge|braus, das; -es *u.* **Ge|brau|se,** das; -s
Ge|brech, das; -[e]s, -e (*Bergmannsspr.* Gebräch; *Jägerspr.* Rüssel des Schwarzwildes); **Ge|bre|che,** das; -s, - (*Bergmannsspr., Jägerspr.* Gebräch); **ge|bre|chen** (*geh. für* fehlen, mangeln); es gebricht mir an [einer Sache]; **Ge|bre|chen,** das; -s, - (*geh. für* Körperschaden); **ge|brech|lich; Ge|brech|lich|keit,** die; -
Ge|bres|ten, das; -s, - (*schweiz., sonst veraltet für* Gebrechen)
ge|bro|chen; -e Farben, Zahlen
Ge|brö|ckel, das; -s
Ge|bro|del, das; -s
Ge|brü|der *Plur.* (*Abk.* Gebr.)
Ge|brüll, das; -[e]s
Ge|brumm, das; -[e]s *u.* **Ge|brum|me,** das; -s; **Ge|brum|mel,** das; -s
ge|buch|tet; eine -e Küste
Ge|bück, das; -[e]s, -e (*früher für* geflochtene Hecke zum Schutz von Anlagen oder Siedlungen)
Ge|bühr, die; -, -en; nach, über Gebühr; **ge|büh|ren;** etwas gebührt ihm (kommt ihm zu); es gebührt sich nicht, dies zu tun; **ge|büh|rend;** er erhielt die gebührende (entsprechende) Antwort; **ge|büh|ren|der‿ma|ßen, ...wei|se; Ge|büh|ren|ein|zugs|zent|ra|le** (*Abk.* GEZ); **Ge|büh|ren|er|hö|hung; ge|büh|ren|frei; Ge|büh|ren‿frei|heit** (die; -), **...ord|nung; ge|büh|ren|pflich|tig; Ge|büh|ren|vig|net|te** (für die Autobahnbenutzung [in der Schweiz]); **ge|bühr|lich** *(veraltet);* **Ge|bühr|nis,** die; -, -se (*veraltet für* Gebühr, Abgabe)
Ge|bum|se, das; -s *(ugs.)*
Ge|bund, das (*landsch. für* Bund); 4 Gebund Seide; **ge|bun|den** (*Abk. [bei Büchern]* geb.); gebundenes System *(roman. Baukunst);* gebundene Rede (Verse); **Ge|bun|den|heit,** die; -
Ge|burt, die; -, -en; **Ge|bur|ten‿be|schrän|kung, ...häu|fig|keit, ...kon|trol|le, ...re|ge|lung** *od.* **...reg|lung, ...rück|gang; ge|bur|ten‿schwach, ...stark; Ge|bur|ten‿über|schuss** (↑R 132), **...zif|fer; ge|bür|tig; Ge|burts‿adel** (↑R 132), **...an|zei|ge, ...da|tum, ...feh|ler, ...haus, ...hel|fer, ...hel|fe|rin, ...hil|fe** (die; -), **...jahr, ...na|me, ...ort** (der; -[e]s, -e), **...schein, ...tag; Ge|burts|tags‿fei|er, ...ge|schenk, ...kind, ...tor|te; Ge|burts|ur|kun|de**
Ge|büsch, das; -[e]s, -e
ge|chintzt [gəˈtʃɪntst]; eine gechintzte Bluse; *vgl.* Chintz
Geck, der; -en, -en (↑R 126); **Ge|cken|art,** die; -; **ge|cken|haft; Ge|cken|haf|tig|keit,** die; -
Ge|cko, der; -s, *Plur.* -s *u.* ...onen ⟨malai.⟩ (eine trop. Eidechse)
ge|dacht ⟨*von* denken, gedenken⟩; ich habe nicht daran gedacht; ich habe seiner gedacht; **Ge|dach|te,** das; -n (↑R 5 ff.); **Ge|dächt|nis,** das; -ses, -se; **Ge|dächt|nis‿aus|stel|lung, ...fei|er, ...kon|zert, ...pro|to|koll, ...schwä|che, ...schwund** (der; -[e]s), **...stö|rung, ...stüt|ze**
ge|dackt (*Orgelbau* oben verschlossen); -e Pfeife
Ge|dan|ke, *selten* **Ge|dan|ken,** der; ...kens, ...ken; **Ge|dan|ken‿ar|beit, ...aus|tausch, ...blitz, ...flug, ...frei|heit** (die; -), **...gang** (der), **...gut** (das; -[e]s), **...le|sen** (das; -s); **ge|dan|ken|los; Ge|dan|ken|lo|sig|keit; ge|dan|ken‿reich, ...schnell; Ge|dan|ken‿spiel, ...split|ter, ...sprung, ...strich; Ge|dan|ken|über|tra|gung** (↑R 132); **Ge|dan|ken|ver|bin|dung; ge|dan|ken|ver|lo|ren; ge|dan|ken|voll; ge|dank|lich**
Ge|därm, das; -[e]s, -e *u.* **Ge|där|me,** das; -s, -
Ge|deck, das; -[e]s, -e; **ge|deckt**
Ge|deih, der; *nur in* auf Gedeih und Verderb; **ge|dei|hen;** du gedeihst; du gediehst; du gediehest; gediehen; gedeih[e]!; **Ge|dei|hen,** das; -s; **ge|deih|lich** (*geh. für* nützlich, fruchtbar); **Ge|deih|lich|keit,** die; -
Ge|den|ke|mein, das; -s, - (eine Waldblume); **ge|den|ken;** *mit Gen.:* gedenket unser!; **Ge|den|ken,** das; -s; **Ge|denk‿fei|er, ...mar|ke, ...mi|nu|te, ...mün|ze, ...re|de, ...stät|te, ...stun|de, ...ta|fel, ...tag**
ge|deucht *vgl.* dünken
Ge|dicht, das; -[e]s, -e; **Ge|dicht‿in|ter|pre|ta|ti|on, ...samm|lung**
ge|die|gen; -es (reines) Gold; du bist aber -! (*ugs. für* wunderlich); **Ge|die|gen|heit,** die; -
ge|dient; gedienter Soldat
Ge|din|ge, das; -s, - (Akkordlohn im Bergbau); **Ge|din|ge|ar|bei|ter**
Ge|don|ner, das; -s
Ge|döns, das; -es (*landsch. für* Aufheben, Getue); viel - um etwas machen
Ge|drän|ge, das; -s; **Ge|drän|gel,** das; -s *(ugs.);* **ge|drängt; Ge|drängt|heit,** die; -
Ge|dröhn, das; -[e]s *u.* **Ge|dröh|ne,** das; -s
ge|drückt; seine Stimmung ist -
Ge|druck|te, das; -n (↑R 5 ff.)
Ge|drückt|heit, die; -
ge|drun|gen; eine -e (untersetzte) Gestalt; **Ge|drun|gen|heit,** die; -
Ge|du|del, das; -s *(ugs.)*
Ge|duld, die; -; **ge|dul|den,** sich; **ge|dul|dig; Ge|dulds‿ar|beit, ...fa|den** (*nur in* jmdm. reißt der Geduldsfaden), **...pro|be; Ge|duld[s]|spiel**
ge|dun|gen; ein -er Mörder
ge|dun|sen; ein -es Gesicht; **Ge|dun|sen|heit,** die; -

Ge|dụns|te|te, das; -n; ↑R 5 ff. *(österr.)*
ge|eig|net; ge|eig|ne|ten|orts *(Amtsspr. veraltet);* **Ge|eig|net|heit,** die; -
Geest, die; -, -en (hoch gelegenes, trockenes, weniger fruchtbares Land im Küstengebiet); **Geest|land,** das; -[e]s
gef. = gefallen (*Zeichen* ⚔)
Ge|fạch, das; -[e]s, *Plur.* -e *u.* Gefächer (Fach, Lade)
Ge|fahr, die; -, -en; Gefahr laufen; Gefahr bringend (↑R 40); **ge|fähr|den; Ge|fähr|dung**
Ge|fah|re, das; -s (*ugs. für* häufiges [unvorsichtiges, schlechtes] Fahren)
Ge|fah|ren‿be|reich, ...ge|mein|schaft, ...herd, ...mo|ment (das), **...quel|le, ...zo|ne, ...zu|la|ge; ge|fähr|lich;** gefährliche Körperverletzung *(Rechtsspr.);* **Ge|fähr|lich|keit,** die; -; **ge|fahr|los; Ge|fahr|lo|sig|keit,** die; -
Ge|fährt, das; -[e]s, -e (Wagen); **Ge|fähr|te,** der; -n, -n; ↑R 126 (Begleiter); **Ge|fähr|tin**
ge|fahr|voll
Ge|fäl|le, das; -s, -; **Ge|fäl|le|mes|ser,** der *(Geodäsie);* [1]**ge|fạl|len;** es hat mir gefallen; sich etwas gefallen lassen; [2]**ge|fạl|len;** er ist gefallen (*Abk.* gef.; *Zeichen* ⚔); [1]**Ge|fạl|len,** der; -s, -; jmdm. einen Gefallen tun; jmdm. etwas zu Gefallen tun; [2]**Ge|fạl|len,** das; -s; [kein] Gefallen an etwas finden; **Ge|fạl|le|ne,** der *u.* die; -n, -n (↑R 5 ff.); **Ge|fạl|le|nen‿fried|hof, ...ge|denk|fei|er; Ge|fäl|le|stre|cke** *vgl.* Gefällstrecke; **ge|fäl|lig** (*Abk.* gefl.); **Ge|fäl|lig|keit; Ge|fäl|lig|keits|wech|sel** *(Bankw.);* **ge|fäl|ligst** (*Abk.* gefl.); **Ge|fäll|stre|cke; Ge|fạll|sucht,** die; -; **ge|fạll|süch|tig**
Ge|fäl|tel, das; -s (viele kleine Falten)
ge|fạn|gen; gefangen halten, nehmen, setzen; er wurde gefangen gehalten; um ihn gefangen zu nehmen; ↑R 39; **Ge|fạn|ge|ne,** der *u.* die; -n, -n (↑R 5 ff.); **Ge|fạn|ge|nen‿aus|tausch, ...be|frei|ung, ...haus** (*österr. neben* Gefängnis), **...la|ger, ...wär|ter; ge|fạn|gen hal|ten** *vgl.* gefangen; **Ge|fạn|gen|haus** (*österr. amtl. Form für* Gefangenenhaus); **Ge|fạn|gen|nah|me,** die; -; **ge|fạn|gen neh|men** *vgl.* gefangen; **Ge|fạn|gen|schaft,** die; -, -en *Plur. selten;* **ge|fạn|gen set|zen** *vgl.* gefangen; **Ge|fäng|nis,** das; -ses, -se; **Ge|fäng|nis‿auf|se|her, ...stra|fe, ...wär|ter, ...zel|le**

ge|färbt; dunkel gefärbt usw.; *vgl.* blau
Ge|fa|sel, das; -s *(ugs.)*
Ge|fa|ser, das; -s
Ge|fäß, das; -es, -e; **Ge|fäß‿chi|rur|gie** (die; -), **...er|wei|te|rung, ...krank|heit**
ge|fasst; auf alles gefasst sein; **Ge|fasst|heit,** die; -
Ge|fẹcht, das; -[e]s, -e; **ge|fẹchts|be|reit; Ge|fẹchts‿be|reit|schaft** (die; -), **...kopf** (Vorderteil mit Sprengstoff und Zünder bei Raketen o. Ä.); **ge|fẹchts|mä|ßig; Ge|fẹchts‿pau|se, ...stand**
Ge|fe|ge, das; -s, - (*Jägerspr.* vom Geweih abgefegter Bast)
Ge|feil|sche, das; -s
ge|feit (sicher, geschützt); sie ist gegen böse Einflüsse gefeit
Ge|fẹls, das; -es (*veraltet für* Felsen)
ge|fẹns|tert
Ge|fẹr|tig|te, der *u.* die; -n, -n; ↑R 5 ff. (*Kaufmannsspr. veraltet für* Unterzeichnete[r])
Ge|fie|del, das; -s
Ge|fie|der, das; -s, -; **ge|fie|dert;** -e (mit Federn versehene) Pfeile; -es Blatt
Ge|fịl|de, das; -s, - (*geh. für* Gegend; Landschaft)
ge|fịn|gert; -es Blatt
ge|fịn|kelt (*österr. für* schlau, durchtrieben)
Ge|fi|on (nord. Göttin)
ge|fịr|nisst; das Brett ist -
ge|fịtzt (*schweiz. mdal. für* schlau, geschickt)
gefl. = gefällig, gefälligst
Ge|fla|cker, das; -s
ge|flammt; -e Muster
Ge|flạt|ter, das; -s
Ge|flẹcht, das; -[e]s, -e
ge|flẹckt; rot gefleckt usw.; *vgl.* blau
Ge|flen|ne, das; -s (*ugs. für* andauerndes Weinen)
Ge|flịm|mer, das; -s
Ge|flịs|sen|heit, die; -; **ge|flịs|sent|lich**
Ge|flu|che, das; -s
Ge|flu|der, das; -s, - (*Bergmannsspr.* Wasserrinne)
Ge|flü|gel, das; -s; **Ge|flü|gel‿farm, ...sa|lat, ...sche|re; ge|flü|gelt;** geflügeltes Wort (oft angeführtes Zitat); geflügelte Worte
Ge|flun|ker, das; -s *(ugs.)*
Ge|flüs|ter, das; -s
Ge|fọl|ge, das; -s, - *Plur. selten;* im - von ...; **Ge|folg|schaft; Ge|fọlgs|mann** *Plur.* ...männer *u.* ...leute
Gefr. = Gefreite
Ge|fra|ge, das; -s; dein dummes -; **ge|fragt**

ge|frä|ßig; der Kerl ist dumm und -; **Ge|frä|ßig|keit,** die; -
Ge|frei|te, der; -n, -n; ↑R 5 ff. (*Abk.* Gefr.)
Ge|frett *vgl.* Gfrett
ge|freut (*schweiz. mdal. für* erfreulich)
ge|frie|ren; Ge|frier‿fach (im Kühlschrank), **...fleisch, ...ge|mü|se; ge|frier|ge|trock|net; Ge|frier‿ket|te** (die; -; System von Lagerung und Transport tiefgekühlter Lebensmittel), **...punkt, ...schrank, ...schutz|mit|tel, ...trock|nung, ...tru|he, ...ver|fah|ren, ...wa|re**
Ge|frieß *vgl.* Gfrieß
Ge|fro|re|ne, Ge|fror|ne, das; -n; ↑R 5 ff. (*südd., österr. für* [Speise]eis)
Ge|fü|ge, das; -s, -; **ge|fü|gig; Ge|fü|gig|keit,** die; -
Ge|fühl, das; -[e]s, -e; **ge|fühl|lig** (gefühlvoll); **Ge|füh|lig|keit,** die; -; **ge|fühl|los; Ge|fühl|lo|sig|keit; ge|fühls‿arm, ...be|tont; Ge|fühls|du|se|lei** *(ugs.);* **ge|fühls‿du|se|lig, ...dus|lig; ge|fühls|echt; ge|fühls|mä|ßig; Ge|fühls‿mensch, ...re|gung, ...sa|che; ge|fühl|voll**
ge|füh|rig ([vom Schnee] für das Skilaufen günstig); **Ge|füh|rig|keit,** die; - (*für* Före)
Ge|fụm|mel, das; -s *(ugs.)*
Ge|fun|kel, das; -s
ge|fụrcht; eine gefurchte Rinde
ge|fürs|tet; gefürstete Abtei
Ge|ga|cker, das; -s
ge|ge|ben; aus gegebenem Anlass; etw. als gegeben voraussetzen; er nahm das Gegebene gern; es ist das Gegebene, jetzt zu handeln (↑R 47); **ge|ge|be|nen|fạlls** (*Abk.* ggf.); *vgl.* [1]Fall; **Ge|ge|ben|heit**
ge|gen; *Präp. mit Akk.:* er rannte gegen das Tor; *Adverb:* gegen 20 Leute kamen; gegeneinander; gegenüber; *vgl.* gen; **Ge|gen‿ak|ti|on, ...an|ge|bot, ...an|griff, ...an|trag, ...ar|gu|ment, ...be|haup|tung, ...be|such, ...be|weis, ...bu|chung**
Ge|gend, die; -, -en
Ge|gen‿dar|stel|lung *(bes. Zeitungsw.),* **...de|monst|ra|ti|on, ...dienst, ...druck** (der; -[e]s)
ge|gen|ei|nan|der; *in Verbindung mit Verben immer getrennt:* gegeneinander drücken, prallen, pressen, stehen, stellen, stoßen; die Kugeln sind gegeneinander geprallt; ohne gegeneinander zu stoßen
Ge|gen‿fahr|bahn, ...for|de|rung, ...fra|ge, ...füß|ler *(veral-*

tend für Antipode), **...ga|be, ...ge|ra|de** *(Sportspr.),* **...ge|walt** (die; -), **...ge|wicht, ...gift** (das), **...kan|di|dat, ...ka|the|te, ...kla|ge, ...kul|tur, ...kurs; ge|gen|läu|fig; Ge|gen|lei|s|tung; ge|gen|len|ken** (um eine Abweichung von der Fahrtrichtung auszugleichen); **ge|gen|le|sen** (als zweiter zur Kontrolle lesen); **Ge|gen|licht,** das; -[e]s; im -; **Ge|gen|licht|auf|nah|me** *(Fotogr.);* **Ge|gen‿lie|be, ...maß|nah|me, ...mit|tel** (das), **...papst, ...part** (*svw.* Widerpart), **...par|tei, ...pol, ...pro|be, ...re|de, ...re|for|ma|ti|on** (die; -), **...re|gie|rung, ...rich|tung, ...satz; ge|gen|sätz|lich; Ge|gen|sätz|lich|keit; Ge|gen|satz|wort,** Ge|gen|wort *Plur.* ...wörter (*für* Antonym); **Ge|gen‿schlag, ...sei|te; ge|gen|sei|tig; Ge|gen|sei|tig|keit,** die; -; **Ge|gen‿spie|ler, ...spie|le|rin, ...sprech|an|la|ge**

Ge|gen|stand; ge|gen|stän|dig (*Bot.* [von Blättern] gegenüberstehend); **ge|gen|ständ|lich** (sachlich, anschaulich, klar); -es Hauptwort (*für* Konkretum); **Ge|gen|ständ|lich|keit,** die; -; **ge|gen|stands|los** (keiner Berücksichtigung wert); **Ge|gen|stands|lo|sig|keit,** die; -

Ge|gen|stim|me; ge|gen|stim|mig; Ge|gen‿stoß, ...strom; ge|gen‿stro|mig *od.* **...strö|mig; Ge|gen‿strö|mung, ...stück**

Ge|gen|teil, das; -[e]s, -e; im Gegenteil; ins Gegenteil umschlagen; **ge|gen|tei|lig**

Ge|gen‿the|se (*svw.* Antithese), **...tor, ...tref|fer** *(Sport)*

ge|gen|über (↑R 132); *Präp. mit Dat.:* die Schule steht gegenüber dem Rathaus, *auch* dem Rathaus gegenüber; *bei Ortsnamen auch mit* „von": gegenüber von Blankenese. *Schreibung in Verbindung mit Verben* (↑R 38): gegenüber (dort drüben, auf der anderen Seite) stehen zwei Häuser; *vgl. aber* gegenüberliegen, gegenüberstehen usw.; **Ge|gen|über,** das; -s, -; **ge|gen|über‿lie|gen** (die Truppen haben sich gegenübergelegen), **...se|hen** (er wird sich Problemen gegenübersehen), **...sit|zen** (wir wollen uns gegenübersitzen), **...ste|hen** (sie haben sich gegenübergestanden), **...stel|len; Ge|gen|über|stel|lung; ge|gen|über|tre|ten**

Ge|gen‿ver|kehr (der; -[e]s), **...vor|schlag**

Ge|gen|wart, die; -; **ge|gen|wär|tig** [*auch* ...'vɛr...]; (↑R 47:) die hier Gegenwärtigen; **ge|gen|warts|be|zo|gen; Ge|gen|warts|form,** die; - (*für* Präsens); **ge|gen|warts|fremd; Ge|gen|warts|kun|de; ge|gen|warts‿nah** *od.* **...na|he; Ge|gen|warts|spra|che**

Ge|gen‿wehr (die), **...wert, ...wind, ...wir|kung; Ge|gen|wort** *vgl.* Gegensatzwort

ge|gen|zeich|nen ([als zweiter] mitunterschreiben); ich zeichne gegen; gegengezeichnet; gegenzuzeichnen; **Ge|gen|zeich|nung**

Ge|gen‿zeu|ge, ...zug

Ge|gir|re, das; -s

Ge|gli|t|zer, das; -s

Geg|ner; Geg|ne|rin; geg|ne|risch; Geg|ner|schaft, die; -

ge|go|ren; der Saft ist -

gegr. = gegründet

Ge|grin|se, das; -s

Ge|grö|le, das; -s (*ugs. für* Geschrei)

ge|grün|det (*Abk.* gegr.)

Ge|grun|ze, das; -s

geh. = geheftet

Ge|ha|be, das; -s (Ziererei; eigenwilliges Benehmen); **ge|ha|ben,** sich; gehab[e] dich wohl!; **Ge|ha|ben,** das; -s

Ge|hack|te, das; -n; ↑R 5 ff. (Hackfleisch)

Ge|ha|der, das; -s

[1]**Ge|halt,** das, *österr. veraltend auch* der; -[e]s, Gehälter (regelmäßige monatliche Bezahlung); [2]**Ge|halt,** der; -[e]s, -e (Inhalt; Wert); **ge|halt|arm; ge|hal|ten;** die Teilnehmer sind gehalten (verpflichtet) ...; **ge|halt|los; Ge|halt|lo|sig|keit,** die; -; **ge|halt|reich; Ge|halts‿aus|zah|lung, ...emp|fän|ger, ...er|hö|hung, ...kon|to, ...nach|zah|lung, ...stu|fe; Ge|halts|vor|rü|ckung** (*österr. für* Gehaltserhöhung der Beamten); **Ge|halts‿zah|lung, ...zu|la|ge; ge|halt|voll**

Ge|häm|mer, das; -s

Ge|ham|pel, das; -s *(ugs.)*

ge|han|di|kapt [gə'hɛndikɛpt] ⟨engl.⟩ (behindert, benachteiligt)

Ge|hän|ge, das; -s, - (*auch Jägerspr.* Tragriemen für das Jagdhorn, Hirschfängerkoppel)

Ge|häng|te, der *u.* die; -n, -n (↑R 5 ff.); *vgl. auch* Gehenkte

ge|har|nischt; ein -er Reiter; ein -er (scharfer) Protest

ge|häs|sig; Ge|häs|sig|keit

Ge|häu|se, das; -s, -

ge|haut (*österr. ugs. für* durchtrieben)

Geh|bahn; geh|be|hin|dert; Geh|be|hin|der|te, der *u.* die; -n, -n (↑R 5 ff.); **Geh|be|hin|de|rung**

Ge|heck, das; -[e]s, -e (*Jägerspr.* die Jungen vom Raubwild; Brut [bei Entenvögeln])

ge|hef|tet (*Abk.* geh.)

Ge|he|ge, das; -s, -

ge|hei|ligt

ge|heim; ein geheimer Vorbehalt; etwas muss geheim bleiben; etwas geheim halten; wir haben den Plan geheim gehalten; ohne etwas geheim zu halten; [mit etwas] geheim tun; insgeheim; *Großschreibung:* im Geheimen; (↑R 108): [Wirklicher] Geheimer Rat, Geheime Staatspolizei (polit. Polizei im nationalsoz. Reich; *Abk.* Gestapo), Geheimes Staatsarchiv

Ge|heim‿ab|kom|men, ...agent (↑R 132), **...bund** (der); **Ge|heim|bün|de|lei,** die; - *(veraltend);* **Ge|heim‿bünd|ler, ...dienst, ...di|plo|ma|tie, ...do|ku|ment, ...fach; ge|heim hal|ten** *vgl.* geheim; **Ge|heim|hal|tung,** die; -; **Ge|heim‿leh|re, ...mit|tel** (das); **Ge|heim|nis,** das; -ses, -se; **Ge|heim|nis|krä|mer; Ge|heim|nis|krä|me|rei; Ge|heim|nis|trä|ger; Ge|heim|nis|tu|er; Ge|heim|nis|tu|e|rei,** die; -; **ge|heim|nis|tu|e|risch; ge|heim|nis|voll; Ge|heim‿num|mer, ...po|li|zei, ...rat** (*Plur.* ...räte; *vgl.* geheim); **Ge|heim|rats‿ecken** (↑R 132; *Plur.*), **...ti|tel; Ge|heim‿re|zept, ...schrift, ...sen|der, ...spra|che; ge|heim|sprach|lich; Ge|heim|tipp; Ge|heim|tu|er; Ge|heim|tu|e|rei,** die; -; **ge|heim|tu|e|risch; ge|heim tun** *vgl.* geheim; **Ge|heim‿tür, ...waf|fe**

Ge|heiß, das; -es; auf Geheiß des ...; auf sein Geheiß

ge|hemmt; Ge|hemmt|heit, die; -

ge|hen; du gehst; du gingst, er ging; du gingest; gegangen; geh[e]! (*südd., österr.* Ausdruck der Ablehnung, des Unwillens); vor sich gehen; baden gehen, schlafen gehen; sich gehen lassen; jemanden gehen lassen (*auch für* in Ruhe lassen); sie haben ihn gehen lassen, *seltener* gehen gelassen; ↑R 39; *vgl. auch* gut II a; **Ge|hen,** das; -s (Sportart); (↑R 28:) 20-km-Gehen

Ge|henk, das; -[e]s, -e (*selten für* Gehänge)

ge|hen|kelt (mit Henkeln versehen)

Ge|henk|te, der *u.* die; -n, -n; ↑R 5 ff. (durch Erhängen hingerichtete Person); *vgl. auch* Gehängte

ge|hen las|sen *vgl.* gehen

Ge|hen|na, die; - ⟨hebr.⟩ (spätjüd.-neutest. Bez. der Hölle)

Ge|her *(Sport);* **Ge|he|rin**
Ge|hetz|ze, das; -s
ge|heu|er; das ist mir nicht -
Ge|heul, das; -[e]s
Geh|fal|te; Geh-gips (stützender Gipsverband für Bein u. Fuß), **...hil|fe**
Ge|hil|fe, der; -n, -n (↑R 126); **Ge|hil|fen|brief; Ge|hil|fen|schaft** *(schweiz. Rechtsspr. für* Beihilfe); **Ge|hil|fin**
Ge|hirn, das; -[e]s, -e; **Ge|hirn-akro|ba|tik** (die; -; *ugs. scherzh.*), **...chi|rur|gie** (die; -), **...er|schüt|te|rung, ...er|wei|chung** (*für* Paralyse), **...haut** (die; -), **...scha|le, ...schlag, ...schmalz** *(ugs. scherzh.),* **...schwund, ...wä|sche** (Versuch der Umorientierung eines Menschen durch phys. und psych. Druck)
gehl (*landsch. für* gelb); **Gehl|chen** (*landsch. für* Pfifferling, Gelbling)
ge|ho|ben; -er Sprachgebrauch
Ge|höft [*auch* ...'hœft], das; -[e]s, -e
Ge|höh|ne, das; -s
Ge|hölz, das; -es, -e; **Ge|hol|ze,** das; -s (*Sportspr.* rücksichtsloses u. stümperhaftes Spielen)
Ge|hop|se, das; -s
Ge|hör, das; -[e]s; - finden, schenken; **Ge|hör|bil|dung** *(Musik);* **ge|hor|chen;** du musst ihm -; der Not gehorchend; **ge|hö|ren;** das Haus gehört mir; die mir gehörenden Häuser; ich gehöre zur Familie; *südd., österr., schweiz. auch* ihm gehört (gebührt) eine Strafe; **Ge|hör-feh|ler, ...gang** (der); **ge|hör|ge|schä|digt; ge|hö|rig;** er hat -en Respekt; -en Ortes *(Amtsspr.);* **ge|hör|los; Ge|hör|lo|se,** der *u.* die; -n, -n (↑R 5 ff.); **Ge|hör|lo|sen|schu|le; Ge|hör|lo|sig|keit,** die; -
Ge|hörn, das; -[e]s, -e; **ge|hörnt;** -es Wild
ge|hor|sam; Ge|hor|sam, der; -s; **Ge|hor|sam|keit,** die; -; **Ge|hor|sams-pflicht** (die; -), **...ver|wei|ge|rung**
Ge|hör|sinn, der; -[e]s
[1]**Geh|re** *vgl.* Gehrung; [2]**Geh|re,** die; -, -n *u.* **Geh|ren,** der; -s, - (*landsch. für* Zwickel, Einsatz, Schoß); **geh|ren** (*fachspr. für* schräg abschneiden)
Geh|rock
Geh|rung, die; -, -en, *fachspr. auch* Geh|re, die; -, -n (schräger Zuschnitt von Brettern o. Ä., die unter einem [beliebigen] Winkel zusammenstoßen); **Geh|rungs|sä|ge**
Geh|steig
Geht|nicht|mehr; *nur in* bis zum - ([bis] zum Überdruss)
Ge|hu|del, das; -s *(landsch.)*
Ge|hu|pe, das; -s
Ge|hüp|fe, das; -s
Geh-ver|band *(Med.),* **...weg, ...werk** (Teil des Uhrwerkes)
Gei, die; -, -en (*Seemannsspr.* Tau zum Geien); **gei|en** ([Segel] zusammenschnüren)
Gei|er, der; -s, -; **Gei|er|na|se**
Gei|fer, der; -s; **Gei|fe|rer; gei|fern;** ich ...ere (↑R 16)
Gei|ge, die; -, -n; die erste - spielen; **gei|gen; Gei|gen-bau** (der; -[e]s), **...bau|er** (der; -s, -), **...bo|gen, ...hals, ...kas|ten, ...sai|te, ...spie|ler; Gei|ger; Gei|ge|rin**
Gei|ger|zäh|ler ⟨nach dem dt. Physiker⟩; ↑R 95 (Gerät zum Nachweis radioaktiver Strahlen)
geil (*Jugendspr. auch für* großartig, toll); [1]**Gei|le,** die; - (*veraltet für* Geilheit); [2]**Gei|le,** die; -, -n (*Jägerspr.* Hoden); **gei|len; Geil|heit,** die; -
Gei|sa (*Plur. von* Geison)
Gei|sel, die; -, -n; -n stellen; *vgl. aber* Geißel; **Gei|sel-dra|ma, ...gangs|ter, ...haft; Gei|sel|nah|me,** die; -, -n; **Gei|sel|neh|mer**
Gei|ser, der; -s, - (*eindeutschende Schreibung für* Geysir)
Gei|se|rich (König der Wandalen)
Gei|sha ['ge:ʃa], die; -, -s ⟨jap.⟩ (jap. Gesellschafterin)
Gei|son, das; -s, *Plur.* -s *u.* ...sa ⟨griech.⟩ (Kranzgesims des antiken Tempels)
Geiß, die; -, -en (*südd., österr., schweiz. für* Ziege); **Geiß-bart** (der; -[e]s; eine Waldpflanze), **...blatt** (das; -[e]s; ein [Kletter]strauch), **...bock** *(südd., österr., schweiz.)*
Gei|ßel, die; -, -n (*landsch. auch für* Peitsche; *übertr. für* Plage); eine Geißel der Menschheit; *vgl. aber* Geisel; **gei|ßeln;** ich ...[e]le (↑R 16); **Gei|ßel|tier|chen** (*Biol.* ein Einzeller); **Gei|ße|lung,** Geiß|lung
Geiß|fuß, der; -es, ...füße (Werkzeug; zahnärztl. Instrument; *nur Sing.:* ein Wiesenkraut); **Geiß|hirt** *(südd., österr., schweiz.);* **Geiß|lein** (junge Geiß)
Geiß|ler ⟨*zu* geißeln⟩; **Geiß|lung** *vgl.* Geißelung
Geist, der; -[e]s, *Plur.* (*für* Gespenst, kluger Mensch:) -er *u.* (*für* Weingeist usw.:) -e; **geist|bil|dend; Geis|ter-bahn, ...be|schwö|rung, ...er|schei|nung, ...fah|rer** (jmd., der auf der Autobahn auf der falschen Seite fährt); **geis|ter|haft; Geis|ter|hand;** wie von -; **geis|tern;** es geistert; **Geis|ter-se|her, ...stadt** (von den Menschen verlassene Stadt), **...stun|de; geis|tes|ab|we|send; Geis|tes-ab|we|sen|heit** (die; -), **...ar|beit, ...ar|bei|ter, ...blitz, ...ga|ben** *(Plur.),* **...ge|gen|wart; geis|tes|ge|gen|wär|tig; Geis|tes|ge|schich|te,** die; -; **geis|tes|ge|schicht|lich; geis|tes|ge|stört; Geis|tes|ge|stör|te,** der *u.* die; -n, -n (↑R 5 ff.); **Geis|tes-grö|ße, ...hal|tung; geis|tes|krank; Geis|tes|kran|ke,** der *u.* die; -n, -n (↑R 5 ff.); **Geis|tes-krank|heit, ...schwä|che** (die; -), **...stö|rung; geis|tes|ver|wandt; Geis|tes-wis|sen|schaf|ten** *(Plur.),* **...wis|sen|schaft|ler; geis|tes|wis|sen|schaft|lich; Geis|tes|zu|stand,** der; -[e]s; **geist|feind|lich; geis|tig;** geistiges Eigentum; geistig behindert sein; **Geis|tig|keit,** die; -; **geis|tig-see|lisch** (↑R 27); **geist|lich;** geistlicher Beistand, *aber* (↑R 108): Geistlicher Rat *(kath. Kirche);* **Geist|li|che,** der *u.* die; -n, -n (↑R 5 ff.); **Geist|lich|keit,** die; -; **geist|los; geist-reich, ...tö|tend, ...voll**
Gei|tau, das; -[e]s, -e (Tau zum Geien)
Geiz, der; -es, -e (übertriebene Sparsamkeit *[nur Sing.];* die Entwicklung beeinträchtigender Nebentrieb einer Pflanze); **gei|zen;** du geizt; **Geiz|hals** (geiziger Mensch); **gei|zig; Geiz|kra|gen** (*svw.* Geizhals)
Ge|jam|mer, das; -s
Ge|jauch|ze, das; -s
Ge|jau|le, das; -s
Ge|jo|del, das; -s
Ge|joh|le, das; -s
Ge|kalk, das; -[e]s (*Jägerspr.* Ausscheidung [von Greifvögeln])
Ge|kei|fe, das; -s
Ge|ki|cher, das; -s
Ge|kläff, das; -[e]s *u.* **Ge|kläf|fe,** das; -s
Ge|klap|per, das; -s
Ge|klat|sche, das; -s
Ge|klim|per, das; -s
Ge|klin|gel, das; -s
Ge|klirr, das; -[e]s *u.* **Ge|klir|re,** das; -s
Ge|klop|fe, das; -s
Ge|klüft, das; -[e]s, -e *u.* **Ge|klüf|te,** das; -s, - *(geh.)*
Ge|knat|ter, das; -s
ge|knickt (*ugs. auch für* bedrückt, traurig)
Ge|knir|sche, das; -s
Ge|knis|ter, das; -s
ge|knüp|pelt; *nur in* geknüppelt voll (*ugs. für* sehr voll)

ge|konnt; sein Spiel wirkte sehr -; **Ge|konnt|heit**, die; -
ge|kö|pert (in Köperbindung gewebt)
ge|ko|ren; *vgl.* [2]kiesen
ge|körnt *(fachspr.)*; ein -es Werkstück
Ge|kräch|ze, das; -s
Ge|kra|kel, das; -s *(ugs.)*
Ge|krätz, das; -es (*Technik* Metallabfall); **Ge|krat|ze**, das; -s
Ge|kräu|sel, das; -s
Ge|kreisch, das; -[e]s *u.* **Ge|krei|sche**, das; -s
Ge|kreu|zig|te, der; -n, -n (↑R 5 ff.)
Ge|krit|zel, das; -s
ge|kröpft (hakenförmig gebogen)
Ge|krö|se, das; -s, - (Innereien, bes. vom Rind)
ge|küns|telt; ein -es Benehmen
Gel, das; -s, -e *u.* -s (gallertartige Substanz; Gelatine)
Ge|lab|ber, das; -s (*landsch. für* fades Getränk)
Ge|la|ber, das; -s (*ugs. für* seichtes Gerede)
Ge|läch|ter, das; -s, -
ge|lack|mei|ert (*ugs. für* angeführt); **Ge|lack|mei|er|te**, der *u.* die; -n, -n (↑R 5 ff.)
ge|lackt; *vgl.* lacken
ge|la|den; geladen (*ugs. für* zornig, wütend) sein
Ge|la|ge, das; -s, -; **Ge|lä|ger**, das; -s, - (Ablagerung im Weinfass nach der Gärung)
ge|lähmt; **Ge|lähm|te**, der *u.* die; -n, -n (↑R 5 ff.)
ge|lahrt (*veraltet, noch scherzh. für* gelehrt); ein -er Mann
Ge|län|de, das; -s, -; **Ge|län|de⌣fahrt**, **...fahr|zeug**; **ge|län|de|gän|gig**; **Ge|län|de⌣lauf** *(Leichtathletik)*, **...marsch**
Ge|län|der, das; -s, -
Ge|län|de⌣ritt, **...spiel**, **...sport** (der; -[e]s), **...übung** (↑R 132), **...wa|gen**
ge|lan|gen; der Brief gelangte nicht in meine Hände; an jmdn. - (*schweiz. für* an jmdn. herantreten, sich an jmdn. wenden)
ge|lappt; -e Blätter *(Bot.)*
Ge|lär|me, das; -s
Ge|lass, das; -es, -e (*geh. für* Raum)
ge|las|sen; sie steht der Gefahr gelassen gegenüber; **Ge|las|sen|heit**, die; -
Ge|la|ti|ne [ʒe...], die; - ‹franz.› ([Knochen]leim, Gallert); **Ge|la|ti|ne|kap|sel**; **ge|la|ti|nie|ren** (zu Gelatine erstarren; in Gelatine verwandeln); **ge|la|ti|nös** (gelatineartig); -e Masse
Ge|läuf, das; -[e]s, -e (*Jägerspr.* Spuren u. Wechsel des Federwildes; *Sport* Boden einer Pferderennbahn, eines Spielfeldes); **Ge|lau|fe**, das; -s; **ge|läu|fig**; die Bezeichnung ist nicht sehr geläufig; **Ge|läu|fig|keit**, die; -
ge|launt; gut gelaunt; der gut gelaunte Vater; der Vater ist gut gelaunt
Ge|läut, das; -[e]s, -e (Glocken einer Kirche); **Ge|läu|te**, das; -s (anhaltendes Läuten)
gelb; das gelbe Fieber, die gelbe Rasse, das gelbe Trikot (des Spitzenreiters im Radsport), die gelbe Karte *(bes. Fußball)*; Gelbe Rüben (Möhren); (↑R 108): der Gelbe Fluss; die Gelben Engel (des ADAC); *vgl.* blau; **Gelb**, das; -s, *Plur.* -, *ugs.* -s (gelbe Farbe); bei Gelb ist die Kreuzung zu räumen; die Ampel steht auf Gelb; *vgl.* Blau; **gelb|braun**; *vgl.* blau; **Gel|be**, das; -n; **Gelb⌣fie|ber**, **...fil|ter**; **gelb|grün** (↑R 27); **Gelb⌣kör|per|hor|mon** (ein Sexualhormon), **...kreuz** (ein Giftgas); **gelb|lich**; gelblich rot, grün usw. (↑R 27 *u.* 40); **Gelb|licht**, das; -[e]s; **Gelb|ling** (ein Pilz); **Gelb|rand|kä|fer**; **gelb|rot**; **Gelb⌣rü|be** (*südd. für* Möhre), **...schna|bel** (*seltener für* Grünschnabel), **...sucht** (die; -); **gelb|süch|tig**; **Gelb|vei|ge|lein** (*südd. für* Goldlack); **Gelb⌣wurst**, **...wur|zel** (tropisches Ingwergewächs)
Geld, das; -[e]s, -er *(Börse; Abk. auf dt. Kurszetteln* G *[vgl. d.])*; (↑R 23:) Geld- und andere Sorgen; **Geld⌣adel** (↑R 132), **...an|ge|le|gen|heit**, **...an|la|ge**, **...au|to|mat**, **...beu|tel**, **...bom|be**, **...bör|se**, **...brief|trä|ger**, **...bu|ße**, **...ent|wer|tung**
Gel|dern (Stadt im Niederrhein. Tiefland); **Gel|der|ner** (↑R 103)
Gel|des|wert, der; -[e]s; **Geld⌣fra|ge**, **...ge|ber**, **...ge|be|rin**, **...gier**; **geld|gie|rig**; **Geld|hahn**; *meist in* jmdm. den - zudrehen (*ugs. für* jmdm. kein Geld mehr geben); **Geld⌣hei|rat**, **...in|sti|tut**; **geld|lich**, *aber* unentgeltlich; **Geld⌣markt**, **...men|ge**, **...mit|tel** *(Plur.)*, **...quel|le**
geld|risch ‹*zu* Geldern›
Geld⌣sack, **...schein**, **...schnei|de|rei**, **...schrank**, **...schrank|kna|cker**, **...sor|gen** *(Plur.)*, **...sor|te**, **...stra|fe**, **...stück**, **...sum|me**, **...ta|sche**, **...um|tausch**, **...ver|le|gen|heit**; **Geld|wasch|an|la|ge** (*ugs. für* Institution, die [steuerbegünstigte] Spendengelder an eine polit. Partei weiterleitet); **Geld|wä|sche** (*ugs. für* Umtausch von illegal erworbenem Geld in solches von unverdächtiger Herkunft); **Geld|wech|sel**; **geld|wert** *(Finanzw.)*; ein -er Vorteil; **Geld⌣wert** (der; -[e]s), **...we|sen**, **...wirt|schaft** (die; -)
ge|leckt; das Zimmer sieht aus wie - (*ugs. für* sehr sauber)
Ge|lee [ʒə...], das, *auch* der; -s, -s ‹franz.›
Ge|le|ge, das; -s, -
ge|le|gen; das kommt mir sehr gelegen (das kommt zur rechten Zeit); zu gelegener Zeit; **Ge|le|gen|heit**; **Ge|le|gen|heits⌣ar|beit**, **...ar|bei|ter**, **...ge|dicht**, **...kauf**; **ge|le|gent|lich**; *als Präp. mit Gen.:* gelegentlich seines Besuches (*Amtsspr., dafür besser* bei seinem Besuch)
ge|leh|rig; **Ge|leh|rig|keit**, die; -; **ge|lehr|sam**; **Ge|lehr|sam|keit**, die; -; **ge|lehrt**; ein -er Mann; **Ge|lehr|te**, der *u.* die; -n, -n (↑R 5 ff.); **Ge|lehr|ten|streit**; **Ge|lehrt|heit**, die; -
Ge|lei|er, das; -s
Ge|lei|se, das; -s, - (*österr., sonst geh. für* Gleis)
Ge|leit, das; -[e]s, -e; **Ge|lei|te**, das; -s, - *(veraltet)*; **ge|lei|ten**; **Ge|leit⌣schutz** (der; -es), **...wort** (*Plur.* ...worte), **...zug**
ge|lenk (*veraltet für* gelenkig); **Ge|lenk**, das; -[e]s, -e; **Ge|lenk⌣band** (das; *Plur.* ...bänder), **...ent|zün|dung**, **...fahr|zeug**; **ge|len|kig**; **Ge|len|kig|keit**, die; -; **Ge|lenk⌣kap|sel**, **...knor|pel**, **...pfan|ne**, **...rheu|ma|tis|mus**, **...schmie|re**; **Ge|lenks|ent|zün|dung** (*österr. für* Gelenkentzündung); **Ge|lenk|wel|le** (*für* Kardanwelle)
ge|lernt; ein gelernter Maurer
Ge|leucht, das; -[e]s *u.* **Ge|leuch|te**, das; -s (*Bergmannsspr.* Licht, Beleuchtung unter Tage)
Ge|lich|ter, das; -s (*veraltend für* Gesindel)
Ge|lieb|te, der *u.* die; -n, -n (↑R 5 ff.)
ge|lie|fert; - (*ugs.* verloren, ruiniert) sein
ge|lie|ren [ʒe...] ‹franz.› (zu Gelee werden); **Ge|lier⌣mit|tel** (das), **...zu|cker**
ge|lind, **ge|lin|de**; das ist[,] gelinde gesagt[,] sehr übereilt (↑R 74)
ge|lin|gen; es gelang; es gelänge; gelungen; geling[e]!; **Ge|lin|gen**, das; -s
Ge|lis|pel, das; -s
ge|lis|tet; *vgl.* listen
[1]**gell** (hell tönend)
[2]**gell?**, **gel|le?** (*landsch. svw.* [2]gelt?)

gel|len; es gellt; es gellte; gegellt
Geln|hau|sen (Stadt a. d. Kinzig)
ge|lo|ben; jmdm. etwas geloben (versprechen); ich habe es mir gelobt (ernsthaft vorgenommen); (↑R 108:) das Gelobte Land *(bibl.);* **Ge|löb|nis,** das; -ses, -se
Ge|lock, das; -[e]s; **ge|lockt**
ge|löscht; gelöschter Kalk
ge|löst; Ge|löst|heit, die; -
Gel|se, die; -, -n *(österr. für* Stechmücke)
Gel|sen|kir|chen (Stadt im Ruhrgebiet); **Gel|sen|kir|che|ner Barock** *(scherzh. für* neu gefertigte Möbel im traditionellen Stil mit überladenen Verzierungen)
[1]**gelt** *(mitteld. für* unfruchtbar [bes. von Kühen]); *vgl.* galt
[2]**gelt?** *(bes. südd. u. österr. für* nicht wahr?); *vgl. auch* gell?
gel|ten; du giltst, er gilt; du galtst (galtest); du gältest, *auch* göltest; gegolten; *(selten:)* gilt!; gelten lassen; geltend machen; **Gel|tend|ma|chung,** die; - *(Amtsspr.);* **Gel|tung,** die; -; **Gel|tungs‿be|dürf|nis** (das; -ses), **...be|reich** (der), **...dau|er, ...sucht** (die; -)
Ge|lüb|de, das; -s, -
Ge|lum|pe, das; -s *(ugs.)*
Ge|lün|ge, das; -s *(svw.* [1]Geräusch)
ge|lun|gen; eine gut gelungene Aufführung
Ge|lüst, das; -[e]s, -e *u.* **Ge|lüs|te,** das; -s, - *(geh.);* **ge|lüs|ten** *(geh.);* es gelüstet mich; **Ge|lüs|ten,** das; -s *(veraltet);* **ge|lüs|tig** *(landsch. für* begierig)
Gel|ze, die; -, -n *(veraltet, noch landsch. für* verschnittene Sau); **gel|zen** *(veraltet, noch landsch. für* [ein Schwein] verschneiden); du gelzt
GEMA = Gesellschaft für musikal. Aufführungs- u. mechan. Vervielfältigungsrechte
ge|mach; gemach, gemach! (langsam, nichts überstürzen); **Gemach,** das; -[e]s, *Plur.* ...mächer, *veraltet* -e; **ge|mäch|lich** [*auch* gəˈmɛç...]; **Ge|mäch|lich|keit,** die; -
Ge|mächt, das; -[e]s, -e *u.* **Gemäch|te,** das; -s, - *(veraltet für* männliche Geschlechtsteile)
[1]**Ge|mahl,** der; -[e]s, -e; [2]**Ge|mahl,** das; -[e]s, -e *(veraltet für* Gemahlin); **Ge|mah|lin**
ge|mah|nen *(geh. für* erinnern); das gemahnt mich an ...
Ge|mäl|de, das; -s, -; **Ge|mäl|de‿aus|stel|lung, ...ga|le|rie, ...samm|lung**
Ge|mar|chen *Plur. (schweiz. für* Gemarkung); **Ge|mar|kung**
ge|ma|sert; -es Holz
ge|mäß; dem Befehl gemäß *(seltener* gemäß dem Befehl; *nicht:* gemäß des Befehles); gemäß Erlass vom ...; **...ge|mäß** (z. B. zeitgemäß); **Ge|mäß|heit,** die; - (Angemessenheit); **ge|mä|ßigt;** gemäßigte Zone *(Meteor.)*
Ge|mäu|er, das; -s, -
Ge|mau|schel, das; -s *(ugs.)*
Ge|me|cker, das; -s *u.* **Ge|me|ckere,** das; -s *u.* **Ge|meck|re,** das; -s
ge|mein; das gemeine Recht, *aber* (↑R 108): die Gemeine Stubenfliege; **Ge|mein|be|sitz; Gemein|de,** die; -, -n; **Ge|mein|deam|mann** *(schweiz. für* Gemeindevorsteher; Gerichtsvollzieher); **Ge|mein|de‿amt, ...be|am|te; ge|mein|de|ei|gen; Ge|meinde‿gut** (Allmende), **...haus, ...hel|fer** *(ev. Kirche* Diakon), **...kir|chen|rat, ...ord|nung, ...rat** *(Plur.* ...räte), **...rä|tin, ...schwester, ...steu|er** (die); **Ge|mein|deum|la|ge** *meist Plur.;* **ge|meindeutsch; Ge|mein|de‿ver|tretung, ...ver|wal|tung, ...vor|steher, ...wahl, ...zent|rum; gemeind|lich; Ge|mein|ei|gentum; ge|mein‿fass|lich, ...gefähr|lich; Ge|mein‿geist** (der; -[e]s), **...gut** (das; -[e]s); **Gemein|heit; ge|mein|hin; ge|meinig|lich** *(veraltend für* gewöhnlich, im Allgemeinen); **Ge|meinkos|ten** *Plur.* (indirekte Kosten); **Ge|mein|nutz,** der; -es; **gemein|nüt|zig; Ge|mein|platz** *(svw.* Phrase); **ge|mein|sam;** (↑R 108): der Gemeinsame Markt; **Ge|mein|sam|keit; Gemein|schaft; ge|mein|schaftlich; Ge|mein|schafts‿an|tenne, ...ar|beit, ...ge|fühl** (das; -[e]s), **...geist** (der; -[e]s), **...haus, ...kun|de** (die; -; ein Schulfach), **...pra|xis, ...pro|duk|ti|on, ...raum, ...schu|le, ...sen|dung, ...un|ter|neh|men, ...ver|pflegung** (die; -), **...wer|bung; Gemein‿sinn** (der; -[e]s), **...sprache** (allgemeine Sprache); **gemein|sprach|lich**
ge|meint; ein gut gemeinter Vorschlag
ge|mein|ver|ständ|lich; Gemein|werk, das; -[e]s *(schweiz. für* unbezahlte gemeinschaftl. Arbeit für die Gemeinde, eine Genossenschaft u. Ä.); **Ge|mein‿we|sen, ...wirt|schaft** (die; -), **...wohl**
Ge|men|ge, das; -s, -; **Ge|mengsel,** das; -s, -
ge|mes|sen; in -er Haltung; **Gemes|sen|heit,** die; -
Ge|met|zel, das; -s, -
Ge|mi|na|ti|on, die; -, -en ‹lat.› *(Sprachw.* Konsonantenverdoppelung); **ge|mi|nie|ren**
Ge|misch, das; -[e]s, -e; **gemischt;** -es Doppel *(Sport);* **gemischt|spra|chig; Ge|mischtwa|ren|hand|lung; ge|mischtwirt|schaft|lich**
Gem|ma, die; - ‹lat.› (ein Stern);
Gem|me, die; -, -n (Schmuckstein mit eingeschnittenem Bild); **Gem|mo|lo|gie,** die; - (Edelsteinkunde)
Gem|se usw. *frühere Schreibung für* Gämse usw.
Ge|mun|kel, das; -s
Ge|mur|mel, das; -s
Ge|mur|re, das; -s
Ge|mü|se, das; -s, -; Mohrrüben sind ein nahrhaftes Gemüse; Mohrrüben u. Bohnen sind nahrhafte Gemüse; **Ge|mü|se|anbau, Ge|mü|se|bau,** der; -[e]s; **Ge|mü|se‿beet, ...bei|la|ge, ...ein|topf, ...frau** *(ugs.),* **...garten, ...händ|ler, ...la|den, ...mann** *(Plur.* ...männer; *ugs.*), **...pflan|ze, ...saft, ...sup|pe**
ge|mus|tert
Ge|müt, das; -[e]s, -er; zu Gemüte führen; **ge|müt|haft; ge|mütlich; Ge|müt|lich|keit,** die; -; **ge|müts|arm; Ge|müts‿art, ...be|we|gung; ge|müts|krank; Ge|müts‿kran|ke, ...krank|heit, ...la|ge, ...lei|den, ...mensch** *(ugs.),* **...ru|he, ...ver|fas|sung, ...zu|stand; ge|müt|voll**
gen *(veraltend für* in Richtung, nach [*vgl.* gegen]); gen Himmel
Gen, das; -s, -e *meist Plur.* ‹griech.› (Träger der Erbanlage)
gen. = genannt
Gen. = Genitiv; Genosse; Genossenschaft
ge|nannt *(Abk.* gen.)
ge|nant [ʒe...] ‹franz.› *(veraltend für* unangenehm; peinlich)
ge|narbt; -es Leder
ge|nä|schig *(geh. für* naschhaft)
ge|nau; genau[e]stens; etwas genau nehmen; das ist[,] genau genommen[,] (↑R 40 *u.* 74) ein ganz anderer Fall; die Karten werden genau so verteilt, dass jeder Spieler ...; *vgl. aber* genauso; auf das, aufs Genau[e]ste, *auch* genau[e]ste; wir wissen nichts Genaues; etwas des Genaueren erläutern *(veraltend);* **Ge|nau|igkeit,** die; -; **ge|nau|so** (ebenso); genauso viele Freunde; du kannst genauso gut die Bahn nehmen; das dauert genauso lang[e]; das stört mich genauso wenig; *vgl. aber* genau

Gen|bank *Plur.* ...banken
Gen|darm [ʒan..., *auch* ʒã...], der; -en, -en (↑R 126) ⟨franz.⟩ (*österr., sonst veraltet für* Polizist [auf dem Lande]); **Gen|dar|me|rie,** die; -, ...ien
Ge|ne|a|lo|ge, der; -n, -n (↑R 126) ⟨griech.⟩; **Ge|ne|a|lo|gie,** die; -, ...ien (Geschlechterkunde, Familienforschung); **ge|ne|a|lo|gisch**
ge|nehm; jmdm. - sein *(geh.)*; **ge|neh|mi|gen;** **Ge|neh|mi|gung;** **Ge|neh|mi|gungs|pflicht;** **ge|neh|mi|gungs|pflich|tig**
ge|neigt; er ist - zuzustimmen; **Ge|neigt|heit,** die; -
Ge|ne|ra (*Plur. von* Genus)
Ge|ne|ral, der; -s, *Plur.* -e *u.* ...räle ⟨lat.⟩; **Ge|ne|ral˯ab|so|lu|ti|on** *(kath. Kirche),* **...ad|mi|ral, ...agent** (↑R 132; Hauptvertreter), **...am|nes|tie, ...an|griff, ...arzt** *(Milit.)*; **Ge|ne|ra|lat,** das; -[e]s, -e (Generalswürde); **Ge|ne|ral˯bass** *(Musik),* **...beich|te, ...be|voll|mäch|tig|te, ...bun|des|an|walt, ...di|rek|tor; Ge|ne|ral|feld|mar|schall; Ge|ne|ral˯gou|ver|ne|ment, ...gou|ver|neur; Ge|ne|ra|lin; Ge|ne|ral˯in|spek|teur, ...in|ten|dant; Ge|ne|ra|li|sa|ti|on,** die; -, -en (Verallgemeinerung); **ge|ne|ra|li|sie|ren** (verallgemeinern); **Ge|ne|ra|li|sie|rung; Ge|ne|ra|lis|si|mus,** der; -, *Plur.* ...mi *u.* ...musse ⟨ital.⟩ (Oberbefehlshaber); **Ge|ne|ra|list,** der; -en, -en; ↑R 126 (jmd., der nicht auf ein bestimmtes Gebiet festgelegt ist); **Ge|ne|ra|li|tät,** die; -, -en ⟨franz.⟩; **ge|ne|ra|li|ter** ⟨lat.⟩ (*veraltend für* im Allgemeinen; allgemein betrachtet); **Ge|ne|ral˯ka|pi|tel** *(kath. Kirche),* **...klau|sel** *(Rechtsspr.),* **...kom|man|do, ...kon|su|lat, ...leut|nant, ...ma|jor, ...mu|sik|di|rek|tor** (*Abk.* GMD), **...nen|ner, ...oberst** (↑R 132), **...pau|se** *(Musik),* **...pro|be, ...sek|re|tär; Ge|ne|rals|rang; Ge|ne|ral|staa|ten** *Plur.* (das niederländische Parlament); **Ge|ne|ral|staats|an|walt; Ge|ne|ral|stab;** der Große - (↑R 108; *früher*); **Ge|ne|ral|stäb|ler; Ge|ne|ral|stabs|kar|te; Ge|ne|ral|streik; Ge|ne|rals|uni|form** (↑R 132); **ge|ne|ral|über|ho|len** (↑R 132); *nur im Infinitiv u. Partizip II gebr.:* ich lasse den Wagen generalüberholen; der Wagen wurde generalüberholt; **Ge|ne|ral˯über|ho|lung** (↑R 132), **...ver|samm|lung, ...ver|tre|ter, ...vi|kar** (Vertreter des kath. Bischofs, bes. in der Verwaltung)
Ge|ne|ra|ti|on, die; -, -en ⟨lat.⟩ (Glied in der Geschlechterfolge; Gesamtheit der Menschen ungefähr gleicher Altersstufe); Generation X (durch Orientierungslosigkeit, mangelnde Zukunftsaussichten u. a. charakterisierte Gruppe der 20- bis 30-Jährigen); **Ge|ne|ra|ti|o|nen|ver|trag; Ge|ne|ra|ti|ons˯kon|flikt, ...wech|sel; ge|ne|ra|tiv** (erzeugend; *Biol.* die geschlechtl. Fortpflanzung betreffend); generative Zelle; generative Grammatik *(Sprachw.)*; **Ge|ne|ra|tor,** der; -s, ...oren (Maschine, die Strom erzeugt; Apparat zur Gasgewinnung); **ge|ne|rell** ⟨franz.⟩ (allgemein [gültig]); **ge|ne|rie|ren** ⟨lat.⟩ (hervorbringen); **Ge|ne|ri|kum,** das; -s, ...ka (pharmazeut. Präparat mit der gleichen Zusammensetzung wie ein Markenarzneimittel); **ge|ne|risch** (das Geschlecht od. die Gattung betreffend, Gattungs...)
ge|ne|rös [*seltener* ʒe...] ⟨franz.⟩ (groß-, edelmütig; freigebig); **Ge|ne|ro|si|tät,** die; -
Ge|ne|se, die; -, -n ⟨griech.⟩ (Entstehung, Entwicklung)
ge|ne|sen; du genest, er genest; du genasest, er genas; du genäsest; genesen; genese!; **Ge|ne|sen|de,** der *u.* die; -n, -n (↑R 5 ff.)
Ge|ne|sis [*auch* ˈgeː...], die; - ⟨griech.⟩ (Entstehung, Ursprung; [1. Buch Mosis mit der] Schöpfungsgeschichte)
Ge|ne|sung; Ge|ne|sungs˯heim, ...pro|zess, ...ur|laub
Ge|net [ʒəˈnɛ] (franz. Schriftsteller)
Ge|ne|tik, die; - ⟨griech.⟩ (Vererbungslehre); **ge|ne|tisch** (erblich bedingt; die Vererbung betreffend)
Ge|ne|tiv (*veraltend für* Genitiv)
Ge|nève [ʒəˈnɛːv] (*franz. Form von* Genf)
Ge|ne|ver [ʒeˈneːvər, *auch* ge...], der; -s, - (Wacholderbranntwein)
Ge|ne|za|reth *vgl.* See Genezareth
Genf (Kanton u. Stadt in der Schweiz); *vgl.* Genève; **Gen|fer** (↑R 103); Genfer Konvention; **gen|fe|risch; Gen|fer See,** der; - -s
Gen|for|schung
ge|ni|al ⟨lat.⟩ (überaus begabt und schöpferisch; großartig); **ge|ni|a|lisch** (nach Art eines Genies); **Ge|ni|a|li|tät,** die; -
Ge|nick, das; -[e]s, -e; **Ge|nick˯fang** (der; -[e]s, -e *Plur. selten; Jägerspr.*), **...fän|ger** (Wildmesser), **...schuss, ...star|re**
[1]**Ge|nie** [ʒe...], das; -s, -s ⟨franz.⟩ (*nur Sing.:* höchste schöpferische Geisteskraft; höchstbegabter, schöpferischer Mensch); [2]**Ge|nie,** die; - *od.* das; -s *meist nur in Zus.* (*schweiz. für* Pioniertruppe); **Ge|ni|en** [ˈgeː...] (*Plur. von* Genius); **Ge|nie|of|fi|zier** [ʒe...] *(schweiz.)*
ge|nie|ren [ʒe...] ⟨franz.⟩; sich -; **ge|nier|lich** (*ugs. für* peinlich; schüchtern)
ge|nieß|bar; Ge|nieß|bar|keit, die; -; **ge|nie|ßen;** du genießt; ich genoss, du genossest, er genoss; du genössest; genossen; genieß[e]!; **Ge|nie|ßer; Ge|nie|ße|rin; ge|nie|ße|risch**
Ge|nie|streich [ʒe...]; **Ge|nie|trup|pe** *(schweiz.)*
ge|ni|tal ⟨lat.⟩ (die Genitalien betreffend); **Ge|ni|ta|le,** das; -s, ...lien [...i̯ən] *meist Plur.* (Geschlechtsorgan); **Ge|ni|tal|tu|ber|ku|lo|se**
Ge|ni|tiv, der; -s, -e [...və] ⟨lat.⟩ (*Sprachw.* Wesfall, 2. Fall; *Abk.* Gen.); **Ge|ni|tiv|ob|jekt; Ge|ni|us,** der; -, ...ien [...i̯ən] (Schutzgeist im röm. Altertum; *geh. für* [1]Genie); Genius Loci [- ˈloːtsi] (Schutzgeist eines Ortes)
Gen|ma|ni|pu|la|ti|on ⟨griech.; lat.⟩ (Manipulation des Erbgutes); **Gen|mu|ta|ti|on,** die; -, -en (erbliche Veränderung eines Gens)
Gen|ne|sa|ret *vgl.* See Genezareth
Ge|nom, das; -s, -e ⟨griech.⟩ (*Genetik* die im Chromosomensatz vorhandenen Erbanlagen); **Ge|nom|ana|ly|se** (↑R 132)
ge|noppt (mit Noppen versehen)
Ge|nör|gel, das; -s
Ge|nos|se, der; -n, -n (↑R 126; *Abk.* Gen.); **Ge|nos|sen|schaft** (*Abk.* Gen.); *vgl.* EG; **Ge|nos|sen|schaf|ter, Ge|nos|sen|schaft|ler; ge|nos|sen|schaft|lich; Ge|nos|sen|schafts˯bank** (*Plur.* ...banken), **...bau|er** (der; *bes. ehem. in der DDR*); **Ge|nos|sin; Ge|noss|sa|me** (↑R 136), die; -, -n (*schweiz. für* Alp-, Allmendgenossenschaft)
Ge|no|typ, der; -s, -en, **Ge|no|ty|pus,** der; -, ...typen ⟨griech.⟩ (*Biol.* Gesamtheit der Erbfaktoren eines Lebewesens); **ge|no|ty|pisch** (erbmäßig)
Ge|no|ve|va [...ˈfeːfa] (w. Vorn.)
Ge|no|zid, der, *auch* das; -[e]s, *Plur.* -e *u.* -ien [...i̯ən] ⟨griech.; lat.⟩ (Völkermord)
Gen|re [ʒãːrə], das; -s, -s ⟨franz.⟩ (Art, Gattung; Wesen); **Gen|re|bild** (Bild aus dem täglichen Leben); **gen|re|haft** (in der Art der Genremalerei); **Gen|re|ma|le|rei**

[1]Gẹnt (Stadt in Belgien)
[2]Gent [dʒɛnt], der; -s, -s ⟨engl.⟩ ([übertrieben] modisch gekleideter Mann)
Gẹn|tech|nik *Plur. selten* ⟨griech.⟩ (Technik der Erforschung und Manipulation der Gene); **gẹn|tech|nisch; Gẹn|tech|no|lo|gie,** die; -; **gẹn|tech|no|lo|gisch**
gen|til [ʒɛnˈti:l, *auch* ʒã...] ⟨franz.⟩ (*veraltet für* fein, nett, liebenswürdig); **Gen|til|homme** [ʒãtiˈjɔm], der; -s, -s (*veraltet für* Mann von vornehmer Gesinnung); **Gen|tle|man** [ˈdʒɛnt(ə)lmən], der; -s, ...men ⟨engl.⟩ (Mann von Lebensart u. Charakter [mit tadellosen Umgangsformen]); **gẹn|tle|man|like** [...laik] (nach Art eines Gentlemans; höflich); **Gen|tle|man's** *od.* **Gen|tle|men's Agree|ment** [*beide* ˈdʒɛnt(ə)lmənz əˈgri:mənt] (↑R 130), das; - -, - -s (diplomat. Übereinkunft ohne formalen Vertrag; Abkommen auf Treu u. Glauben)
Gẹn|trans|fer ⟨griech.; engl.⟩ (*Genetik* Übertragung fremder Erbanlagen in die befruchtete Eizelle)
Gent|ry [ˈdʒɛntri] (↑R 130), die; - ⟨engl.⟩ (niederer Adel und wohlhabendes Bürgertum in England)
Gẹ|nua (ital. Stadt); **Ge|nu|e|se,** der; -n, -n (↑R 126); **Ge|nu|e|ser** (↑R 103); **ge|nu|e|sisch**
ge|nug; genug u. übergenug; (↑R 47:) genug Gutes, Gutes genug; genug des Guten; von etw. genug haben; genug getan haben; *vgl. aber* genugtun; **Ge|nü|ge,** die; -; - tun, leisten; zur -; **ge|nü|gen;** dies genügt für unsere Zwecke; **ge|nü|gend;** *vgl.* ausreichend; **ge|nug|sam** (*veraltend für* hinreichend); **ge|nüg|sam** (anspruchslos); **Ge|nüg|sam|keit,** die; -; **ge|nug|tun** (*veraltend);* ↑R 37 f.; jmdm. genugtun (Genugtuung gewähren); er hat mir genuggetan; ich kann mir damit nicht genugtun (kann damit nicht aufhören); *aber* ich habe jetzt genug (genügend) getan; **Ge|nug|tu|ung** *Plur. selten*
ge|nu|in ⟨lat.⟩ (echt; *Med.* angeboren, erblich); **Gẹ|nus** [*auch* ˈge:...], das; -, Gẹnera (Gattung, Art; *Sprachw.* grammatisches Geschlecht); *vgl.* in genere
Ge|nụss, der; -es, Genüsse; **ge|nụss|freu|dig; Ge|nụss|gift; ge|nụ̈ss|lich; Ge|nụ̈ss|ling** (*veraltend für* Genussmensch); **Ge|nụss|mit|tel,** das; **ge|nụss|reich; Ge|nụss|sucht** (↑R 136), die; -; **ge|nụss‿süch|tig** (↑R 136), **...voll**

Gẹ|nus Ver|bi [- ˈvɛrbi], das; - -, Genera - ⟨lat.⟩ (*Sprachw.* Verhaltensrichtung des Verbs: Aktiv u. Passiv)
Ge|o|bo|ta|nik[1] ⟨griech.⟩ (Wissenschaft von der geograph. Verbreitung der Pflanzen); **ge|o|bo|ta|nisch**[1]**; Ge|o|che|mie**[1] (Wissenschaft von der chemischen Zusammensetzung der Erde); **ge|o|che|misch**[1]**; Ge|o|dä|sie,** die; - (Vermessungskunde); **Ge|o|dät,** der; -en, -en; ↑R 126 (Fachmann, Wissenschaftler auf dem Gebiet der Geodäsie); **ge|o|dä|tisch; Gẹ|o|drei|eck** ® (transparentes Dreieck zum Ausmessen u. Zeichnen von Winkeln o. Ä.); **Ge|o|ge|nie, Ge|o|go|nie,** die; - (Lehre von der Entstehung der Erde); **Ge|o|graf, Ge|o|gra|fie** usw. *eindeutschende Schreibung für* Geograph, Geographie usw.; **Ge|o|graph** (↑R 33), der; -en, -en (↑R 126); **Ge|o|gra|phie** (↑R 33); die; -; **Ge|o|gra|phin** (↑R 33); **ge|o|gra|phisch** (↑R 33); **Ge|o|lo|ge,** der; -n, -n (↑R 126); **Ge|o|lo|gie,** die; - (Wissenschaft vom Aufbau, von der Entstehung u. Entwicklung der Erde); **Ge|o|lo|gin; ge|o|lo|gisch; Ge|o|man|tie,** die; - (Kunst, aus Linien u. Figuren im Sand wahrzusagen); **Ge|o|me|ter,** der; -s, - (*svw.* Geodät); **Ge|o|met|rie** (↑R 130), die; - (ein Zweig der Mathematik); **ge|o|met|risch;** geometrischer Ort; geometrisches Mittel; **Ge|o|mor|pho|lo|gie**[1], die; - (Lehre von der äußeren Gestalt der Erde u. deren Veränderungen); **Ge|o|phy|sik**[1] (Lehre von den physikal. Eigenschaften des Erdkörpers); **ge|o|phy|si|ka|lisch**[1]; geophysikalische Untersuchungen; **Ge|o‿plas|tik**[1] (die; -; räuml. Darstellung von Teilen der Erdoberfläche), **...po|li|tik**[1] (die; -; Lehre von der Einwirkung geograph. Faktoren auf polit. Vorgänge); **ge|o|po|li|tisch**[1]
ge|ord|net; in geordneten Verhältnissen leben; eine gut geordnete Bibliothek; die Bibliothek ist gut geordnet
Ge|org [*auch* geˈɔrk] (m. Vorn.); **George** [dʒɔ:(r)dʒ] (m. Vorn.); **George|town** [ˈdʒɔ:(r)dʒtaun] (Hptst. von Guyana); **[1]Geor|gette** [ʒɔrˈʒɛt] (w. Vorn.); **[2]Geor|gette,** der; -s (*svw.* Crêpe Georgette); **Geor|gia** [ˈdʒɔ:(r)dʒ(i)ə] (Staat in den USA; *Abk.* Ga.); **Ge|or|gi|en** [...iən] (Staat am Südhang des Kaukasus); **Ge|or|gi|er; Ge|or|gi|e|rin; [1]Ge|or|gi|ne,** die; -, -n ⟨nach dem Petersburger Botaniker Georgi⟩ (*svw.* Dahlie); **[2]Ge|or|gi|ne** (w. Vorn.); **ge|or|gisch;** -e Sprache; **Ge|or|gisch,** das; -[s] (Sprache); *vgl.* Deutsch; **Ge|or|gi|sche,** das; -n; *vgl.* Deutsche, das

[1] [*auch* ˈge:o...]

Ge|o|tek|to|nik[1] ⟨griech.⟩ (Lehre von Entwicklung u. Aufbau der gesamten Erdkruste); **ge|o|tek|to|nisch**[1]; **ge|o|ther|misch**[1] (die Wärmeverhältnisse im Erdkörper betreffend); -e Energie; **ge|o|trop, ge|o|tro|pisch; Ge|o|tro|pis|mus** (*Bot.* Vermögen der Pflanzen, sich in Richtung der Schwerkraft zu orientieren); **Ge|o|wis|sen|schaft; ge|o|zent|risch**[1] (auf die Erde als Mittelpunkt bezogen; auf den Erdmittelpunkt bezogen); **ge|o|zyk|lisch**[1] [*auch* ...ˈtsyk...] (den Umlauf der Erde betreffend)
Ge|päck, das; -[e]s; **Ge|päck‿ab|fer|ti|gung, ...ab|la|ge, ...an|nah|me;** (↑R 23: Gepäckannahme und -ausgabe); **Ge|päck|auf|be|wah|rung; Ge|päck|auf|be|wah|rungs|schein; Ge|päck‿aus|ga|be, ...netz; Ge|päcks...** (*österr. für* Gepäck..., z. B. Gepäcksaufbewahrung, Gepäcksstück, Gepäcksträger); **Ge|päck‿schal|ter, ...schein, ...stück, ...trä|ger, ...wa|gen**
Gẹ|pard, der; -s, -e ⟨franz.⟩ (ein katzenartiges Raubtier)
ge|perlt (mit Perlen versehen); -e Arm- und Beinringe
ge|pfef|fert (*ugs.);* -e Preise
Ge|pfei|fe, das; -s
ge|pflegt; ein gepflegtes Äußere[s]; ein gut gepflegter Rasen; der Rasen ist gut gepflegt; **Ge|pflegt|heit,** die; -; **Ge|pflo|gen|heit** (Gewohnheit)
Ge|pi|de, der; -n, -n; ↑R 126 (Angehöriger eines ostgerm. Volkes)
Ge|pie|pe, das; -s; **Ge|piep|se,** das; -s
Ge|plän|kel, das; -s, -
Ge|plap|per, das; -s
Ge|plärr, das; -[e]s *u.* **Ge|plär|re,** das; -s
Ge|plät|scher, das; -s
Ge|plau|der, das; -s
Ge|po|che, das; -s
Ge|pol|ter, das; -s
Ge|prä|ge, das; -s
Ge|prah|le, das; -s
Ge|prän|ge, das; -s (*geh. für* Prunk, Prachtentfaltung)
Ge|pras|sel, das; -s

[1] [*auch* ˈge:o...]

ge|punk|tet; -er Stoff
Ge|qua|ke, Ge|quä|ke, das; -s
Ge|quas|sel, das; -s *(ugs.)*
Ge|quat|sche, das; -s *(ugs.)*
Ge|quen|gel, das; -s *u.* **Ge|quen|ge|le, Ge|queng|le,** das; -s *(ugs.)*
Ge|quie|ke, das; -s
Ge|quiet|sche, das; -s
Ger, der; -[e]s, -e (germ. Wurfspieß)
Ge|ra (Stadt in Thüringen)
ge|rad...[1] (z. B. geradlinig); **Ge|rad...**[1] (z. B. Geradflügler)
ge|ra|de, *(ugs.:)* gra|de; eine gerade Zahl; fünf gerade sein lassen *(ugs.);* gerade darum; der Weg ist gerade (ändert die Richtung nicht); er wohnt mir gerade (direkt) gegenüber; sie fuhr gerade so langsam, dass ...; *vgl. aber* geradeso; sie kommt gerade (soeben) heraus; *vgl. aber* geradeheraus; *Schreibung in Verbindung mit Verben* (↑R 39): gerade biegen, halten, legen, sitzen, stehen usw.; er hat den Stab wieder [ganz] gerade gebogen; um sich, die Kerze [ganz] gerade zu halten; das Buch [ganz] gerade legen; er soll [ganz] gerade sitzen, stehen; da er gerade sitzt, steht (sich soeben hingesetzt hat, soeben aufgestanden ist); *vgl. aber* geradebiegen, geradestehen; **Ge|ra|de**[1], die; -n, -n (gerade Linie; ein Boxschlag); vier Gerade[n]; **ge|ra|de|aus**[1]; geradeaus blicken, gehen; **ge|ra|de|bie|gen**[1] *(ugs. für* einrenken); *vgl.* gerade; **ge|ra|de hal|ten,** sich; *vgl.* gerade; **ge|ra|de|he|raus**[1] (freimütig, direkt); etwas geradeheraus sagen; **ge|ra|de|hin**[1] (leichtfertig); etwas geradehin versprechen; **ge|ra|de le|gen, ma|chen** *vgl.* gerade; **ge|ra|den|wegs**[1] *vgl.* geradewegs; **ge|ra|de rich|ten** *vgl.* gerade
ge|rä|dert; sich wie gerädert (erschöpft, zerschlagen) fühlen
ge|ra|de sit|zen *vgl.* gerade; **ge|ra|de|so**[1] (ebenso *vgl. d.*); das kann ich geradeso gut wie du; *vgl.* gerade; **ge|ra|de|ste|hen**[1]; für etwas geradestehen (die Folgen auf sich nehmen); *vgl.* gerade; **ge|ra|de stel|len** *vgl.* gerade; **ge|ra|des|wegs**[1] *(schweiz., sonst selten für* geradewegs); **ge|ra|de|wegs**[1], ge|ra|den|wegs[1]; **ge|ra|de|zu**[1] [*auch* ...'tsu:]; das ist geradezu absurd!; er ist immer sehr geradezu *(landsch. für* geradeheraus); **Ge|rad|flüg|ler** *(Zool.* Libelle u. dgl.); **Ge|rad|heit**[1], die; -;

[1] *Ugs. häufig in der verkürzten Form* „grad...“, „Grad...“

ge|rad|li|nig[1]; **Ge|rad|li|nig|keit**[1], die; -; **ge|rad|sin|nig**[1]
Ge|rald, Ge|rold (m. Vorn.); **Ge|ral|di|ne** (w. Vorn.)
ge|ram|melt; *in der Wendung* gerammelt voll *(ugs. für* übervoll)
Ge|ran|gel, das; -s
Ge|ra|nie [...iə], die; -, -n ⟨griech.⟩ *u.* **Ge|ra|ni|um,** das; -s, ...ien [...iən] *(svw.* Pelargonie)
Ge|rank, das; -s *(geh. für* Rankenwerk)
Ge|rant [ʒe...], der; -en, -en ⟨franz.⟩ *(schweiz. für* Geschäftsführer; Herausgeber)
Ge|ra|schel, das; -s
Ge|ras|sel, das; -s
Ge|rät, das; -[e]s, -e; **ge|ra|ten;** es gerät [mir]; geriet; geraten; ich gerate außer mir *(auch* mich) vor Freude; **Ge|rä|te‿schup|pen, ...ste|cker; Ge|rä|te|tur|nen,** das; -s; **Ge|rä|te‿tur|ner, ...wart; Ge|ra|te|wohl** [*auch* gəˈra:...], das; *nur in* aufs - (auf gut Glück); **Ge|rät|schaf|ten** *Plur.*
Ge|rat|ter, das; -s
Ge|rät|tur|nen usw. *vgl.* Geräteturnen usw.
Ge|räu|cher|te, das; -n (↑R 5 ff.)
Ge|rau|fe, das; -s
ge|raum *(geh.);* geraume (längere) Zeit; **Ge|räum|de,** das; -s, - *(Forstw.* abgeholztes Waldstück); **ge|räu|mig; Ge|räu|mig|keit,** die; -; **Ge|räum|te,** das; -s, - *(svw.* Geräumde)
Ge|rau|ne, das; -s
[1]**Ge|räusch,** das; -[e]s *(Jägerspr.* Herz, Lunge, Leber u. Nieren des Schalenwildes, Gelünge)
[2]**Ge|räusch,** das; -[e]s, -e; **ge|räusch|arm; Ge|räusch‿däm|mung, ...dämp|fung; Ge|rau|sche,** das; -s; **ge|räusch|emp|find|lich; Ge|räusch|ku|lis|se; ge|räusch|los; Ge|räusch|lo|sig|keit,** die; -; **Ge|räusch|pe|gel; ge|räusch|voll**
Ge|räus|per, das; -s
ger|ben; Leder -; **Ger|ber**
Ger|be|ra, die; -, -[s] ⟨nach dem dt. Arzt u. Naturforscher T. Gerber⟩ (eine Schnittblume)
Ger|be|rei; Ger|be|rin; Ger|ber|lo|he, die; -, -n
Ger|bert (m. Vorn.)
Gerb‿säu|re, ...stoff; Ger|bung
Gerd (m. Vorn.); **Ger|da** (w. Vorn.)
Ge|re|bel|te, der; -n, -n; ↑R 5 ff. *(österr. für* Wein aus einzeln abgenommenen Beeren); *vgl.* rebeln
ge|recht; jmdm., einer Aufgabe gerecht werden; **Ge|rech|te,** der *u.* die; -n, -n (↑R 5 ff.); **Ge|rech|tig|keit,** die; -; **Ge|rech|tig|keits‿lie|be** (die; -), **...sinn** (der; -[e]s); **Ge|recht|sa|me,** die; -, -n *(Rechtsspr. veraltet für* [Vor]recht)

[1] *Ugs. häufig in der verkürzten Form* „grad...“, „Grad...“

Ge|re|de, das; -s; ins - kommen
ge|re|gelt; -er Arbeit nachgehen
ge|rei|chen *(geh.);* es gereicht mir zur Ehre
Ge|rei|me, das; -s
ge|reizt; Ge|reizt|heit, die; -
Ge|ren|ne, das; -s
ge|reu|en *(veraltend);* es gereut mich
Ger|fal|ke (Jagdfalke)
Ger|hard (m. Vorn.); **Ger|har|de, Ger|har|di|ne** (w. Vorn.)
Ger|hardt, Paul (dt. Dichter)
Ger|hild, Ger|hil|de (w. Vorn.)
Ge|ri|a|ter (↑R 132) ⟨griech.⟩ (Facharzt für Geriatrie); **Ge|ri|at|rie** (↑R 130), die; - *(Med.* Altersheilkunde); **Ge|ri|at|ri|kum,** das; -s, ...ka (Medikament zur Behandlung von Altersbeschwerden); **ge|ri|at|risch**
Ge|richt, das; -[e]s, -e; **ge|richt|lich;** gerichtliche Medizin, Psychologie; **Ge|richts‿arzt, ...as|ses|sor; Ge|richts|bar|keit; Ge|richts‿be|schluss, ...fe|ri|en** *(Plur.),* **...ge|bäu|de, ...herr** *(früher),* **...hof, ...kos|ten** *(Plur.),* **...me|di|zin** (die; -), **...me|di|zi|ner; ge|richts|no|to|risch** *(Rechtsspr.* vom Gericht zur Kenntnis genommen); **Ge|richts‿ort, ...prä|si|dent, ...saal, ...spra|che, ...stand** *(Rechtsspr.),* **...ur|teil, ...ver|fah|ren, ...ver|hand|lung, ...voll|zie|her, ...weg**
ge|rie|ben *(auch ugs. für* schlau); **Ge|rie|ben|heit,** die; -
ge|rie|hen *(landsch. u. fachspr. für* gereiht); *vgl.* reihen
ge|rie|ren, sich ⟨lat.⟩ *(geh. für* sich benehmen, auftreten als ...)
Ge|rie|sel, das; -s
ge|rif|felt
ge|ring; das wird am geringsten (wenigsten) auffallen; (↑R 47:) ein Geringes tun; um ein Geringes erhöhen; es ist nichts Geringes, nichts Geringeres als ...; es geht ihn nicht das Geringste an; er ist auch im Geringsten treu; das Geringste, was er tun kann, ist ...; es stört mich nicht im Geringsten; auch der Geringste hat Anspruch auf ...; kein Geringerer als ...; *Schreibung in Verbindung mit Verben:* gering achten, schätzen; geringer achten, schätzen; ich achte gering; gering geachtet; gering zu achten
ge|rin|gelt; -e Socken

ge|ring|fü|gig; Ge|ring|fü|gig|keit; ge|ring|hal|tig *(Mineral.)*; **ge|ring schät|zen** *vgl.* gering; **ge|ring|schät|zig; Ge|ring|schät|zung,** die; -; **ge|rings|ten|falls;** *vgl.* [1]Fall

ge|rinn|bar; Ge|rinn|bar|keit, die; -; **Ge|rin|ne,** das; -s, -; **ge|rin|nen; Ge|rinn|sel,** das; -s, -; **Ge|rin|nung,** die; -

Ge|rip|pe, das; -s, -; **ge|rippt**

Ge|riss, das; -es *(landsch. für* Wetteifern); **ge|ris|sen** (durchtrieben, schlau); ein -er Bursche; **Ge|ris|sen|heit,** die; -

ge|ritzt; ist - *(ugs. für* ist in Ordnung; wird erledigt)

Ger|lin|de (w. Vorn.)

Germ, der; -[e]s, *österr.* die; - *(bayr., österr. für* Hefe)

Ger|ma|ne, der; -n, -n (↑R 126); **Ger|ma|nen|tum,** das; -s; **Ger|ma|nia,** die; - (Frauengestalt als Sinnbild Deutschlands; *lat. Bez. für* Deutschland); **Ger|ma|ni|en** [...iən] (das zur Römerzeit von den Germanen besiedelte Gebiet); **Ger|ma|nin; ger|ma|nisch;** germanische Kunst, *aber* (↑R 108): Germanisches Nationalmuseum (Nürnberg); **ger|ma|ni|sie|ren** (eindeutschen); **Ger|ma|nis|mus,** der; -, ...men *(Sprachw.* deutsche Spracheigentümlichkeit in einer nichtdeutschen Sprache); **Ger|ma|nist,** der; -en, -en; ↑R 126 (Wissenschaftler auf dem Gebiet der Germanistik); **Ger|ma|nis|tik,** die; - (deutsche [*auch* germanische] Sprach- u. Literaturwissenschaft); **Ger|ma|nis|tin; ger|ma|nis|tisch; Ger|ma|ni|um,** das; -s (chem. Element; Metall; *Zeichen* Ge)

Ger|mar (m. Vorn.)

Ger|mer, der; -s, - (eine Pflanze)

Ger|mi|nal [ʒɛr...], der; -[s], -s ‹franz., „Keimmonat"› (7. Monat des Kalenders der Franz. Revolution: 21. März bis 19. April); **Ger|mi|na|ti|on,** die; -, -en ‹lat.› *(Bot.* Keimungsperiode der Pflanzen)

Ger|mund (m. Vorn.)

gern, ger|ne; lieber, am liebsten; jmdn. gern haben, mögen; etwas gern tun; gar zu gern; allzu gern; ein gern gesehener Gast; er ist gern gesehen; **Ger|ne|groß,** der; -, -e *(ugs. scherzh.)*; **Ger|ne|klug,** der; -, -e *(ugs. scherzh.)*

Ger|not [*auch* 'gɛr...] (m. Vorn.); **Ge|ro** (m. Vorn.)

Ge|rö|chel, das; -s

ge|ro|chen *vgl.* riechen *u.* rächen

Ge|rold *vgl.* Gerald; **Ge|rolf** (m. Vorn.)

Ge|röll, das; -[e]s, -e *u.* **Ge|röl|le,** das; -s, -; **Ge|röll‿hal|de, ...schutt**

Ge|ront, der; -en, -en (↑R 126) ‹griech.› (Mitglied der Gerusia); **Ge|ron|to|lo|ge; Ge|ron|to|lo|gie,** die; - (Alternsforschung)

Ge|rös|te|te [*auch* ...'rœ...] *Plur.* *(südd., österr. für* Bratkartoffeln)

Gersh|win ['gœ:(r)ʃwin] (amerikanischer Komponist)

Gers|te, die; -, *Plur. (Sorten:)* -n; **Gers|tel,** das; -s; -[n] *(österr. für* Graupe); **Gers|tel|sup|pe** *(österr. für* Graupensuppe); **Gers|ten|korn,** das; *Plur.* ...körner *(auch* Vereiterung einer Drüse am Augenlid); **Gers|ten‿saft** (der; -[e]s; *scherzh. für* Bier), **...schrot, ...sup|pe**

Gert (m. Vorn.); **Ger|ta** (w. Vorn.)

Ger|te, die; -, -n; **Ger|tel,** der; -s, - *(schweiz. für* [1]Hippe); **ger|ten|schlank; ger|tig** *(selten)*

Ger|traud, Ger|trau|de, Ger|traut, Ger|trud, Ger|tru|de (w. Vorn.)

Ge|ruch, der; -[e]s, Gerüche; **ge|ruch|frei** *vgl.* geruch[s]frei; **ge|ruch|los; Ge|ruch|lo|sig|keit,** die; -; **Ge|ruchs|be|läs|ti|gung; ge|ruchs|bin|dend; ge|ruch[s]|frei; Ge|ruchs‿or|gan, ...sinn** (der; -[e]s), **...ver|mö|gen** (das; -s), **...ver|schluss** *(für* Trap)

Ge|rücht, das; -[e]s, -e; **Ge|rüch|te|ma|cher**

ge|ruch|til|gend

ge|rücht|wei|se

Ge|ru|fe, das; -s

ge|ru|hen *(veraltend, noch iron. für* sich bereit finden); **ge|ru|hig** *(veraltet für* ruhig)

ge|rührt *vgl.* rühren

ge|ruh|sam; Ge|ruh|sam|keit, die; -

Ge|rum|pel, das; -s *(ugs. für* Rumpeln)

Ge|rüm|pel, das; -s (Unbrauchbares)

Ge|run|di|um, das; -s, ...ien [...iən] ‹lat.› *(Sprachw.* gebeugter Infinitiv des lat. Verbs); **Ge|run|div,** das; -s, -e [...və] *(Sprachw.* Partizip des Passivs des Futurs, z. B. der „zu billigende" Schritt)

Ge|ru|sia, Ge|ru|sie, die; - ‹griech.› (Rat der Alten [in Sparta])

Ge|rüst, das; -[e]s, -e; **Ge|rüst|bau,** der; -[e]s; **Ge|rüst|bau|er; Ge|rüs|ter** *(österr. für* Gerüstarbeiter)

Ge|rüt|tel, das; -s; **ge|rüt|telt;** ein gerüttelt Maß; gerüttelt voll

Ger|va|si|us [...'va:...] (ein Heiliger)

Ger|wig (m. Vorn.); **Ger|win** (m. Vorn.)

ges, Ges, das; -, - (Tonbezeichnung); **Ges** *(Zeichen für* Ges-Dur); in Ges

Ge|sa, Ge|se (w. Vorn.)

Ge|sab|ber, das; -s *(ugs. für* dummes Geschwätz)

Ge|sä|ge, das; -s

Ge|salb|te, der *u.* die; -n, -n (↑R 5 ff.; *Rel.)*

ge|sal|zen; gesalzene Preise; *vgl.* salzen; **Ge|sal|ze|ne,** das; -n (↑R 5 ff.)

ge|sam|melt; -e Aufmerksamkeit

ge|samt; im Gesamten *(veraltend für* insgesamt); **Ge|samt,** das; -s *(selten)*; im -; **Ge|samt‿an|sicht, ...aus|ga|be, ...be|trag; ge|samt|deutsch;** -e Fragen; **Ge|samt|deutsch|land** (↑R 105); **Ge|samt‿ein|druck, ...er|geb|nis; ge|samt|eu|ro|pä|isch; Ge|samt|ge|winn; ge|samt|haft** *(schweiz. u. westösterr. für* [ins]gesamt); **Ge|samt|heit,** die; -; **Ge|samt‿hoch|schu|le, ...in|te|res|se, ...klas|se|ment, ...kom|plex, ...kunst|werk, ...no|te, ...scha|den, ...schuld|ner** *(Rechtsspr.)*, **...schu|le, ...sieg, ...sie|ger, ...sum|me, ...ver|band, ...wer|tung**

Ge|sand|te, der *u.* die; -n, -n (↑R 5 ff.); **Ge|sand|ten|pos|ten; Ge|sand|tin; Ge|sandt|schaft; ge|sandt|schaft|lich; Ge|sandt|schafts|rat** *Plur.* ...räte

Ge|sang, der; -[e]s, Gesänge; **Ge|sang‿buch** *(österr.* Ge|sangs|buch), **...leh|rer, ...leh|re|rin; ge|sang|lich; Ge|sang|schu|le; Ge|sangs|kunst; Ge|sang[s]‿pä|da|go|ge, ...pä|da|go|gin, ...stück, ...stun|de, ...un|ter|richt; Ge|sang|ver|ein,** *österr.* Ge|sangs|ver|ein

Ge|säß, das; -es, -e; **Ge|säß‿fal|te, ...mus|kel, ...ta|sche**

ge|sät|tigt; gesättigte Kohlenwasserstoffe *(Chemie)*

Ge|sätz, das; -es, -e *(Literaturw.* Strophe im Meistergesang); **Ge|sätz|lein** *(südd. für* Abschnitt, Strophe)

Ge|säu|ge, das; -s *(Jägerspr.* Milchdrüsen)

Ge|sau|se, das; -s; **Ge|säu|se,** das; -s (ein Alpental); **Ge|säu|sel,** das; -s

gesch. *(Zeichen* ∞) = geschieden

Ge|schä|dig|te, der *u.* die; -n, -n (↑R 5 ff.)

Ge|schäft, das; -[e]s, -e; geschäftehalber, *aber* dringender Geschäfte halber; **Ge|schäf|te|ma|cher; Ge|schäf|te|ma|che|rei;**

ge|schäf|tig; Ge|schäf|tig|keit, die; -; **Ge|schaftl|hu|ber,** Gschaftl|hu|ber, der; -s, - (*bes. südd., österr.* fast unangenehm betriebsamer, wichtigtuerischer Mensch); **ge|schäft|lich; Ge|schäfts‿ab|schluss, ...auf|ga|be, ...auf|lö|sung, ...be|reich** (der), **...be|richt, ...brief, ...buch, ...er|öff|nung; ge|schäfts|fä|hig** (*Rechtsspr.*); **Ge|schäfts‿frau, ...freund, ...füh|rer, ...füh|re|rin, ...füh|rung, ...ge|ba|ren, ...ge|heim|nis, ...geist** (der; -[e]s), **...in|ha|ber, ...in|ha|be|rin, ...in|te|res|se, ...jahr, ...kos|ten** (*in* auf -); **ge|schäfts|kun|dig; Ge|schäfts‿la|ge, ...le|ben, ...lei|tung, ...mann** (*Plur.* ...leute, *selten* ...männer); **ge|schäfts|mä|ßig; Ge|schäfts‿ord|nung, ...part|ner, ...rei|se; ge|schäfts|schä|di|gend; Ge|schäfts‿schluss, ...sinn** (der; -[e]s), **...sitz, ...stel|le, ...stra|ße, ...stun|den** (*Plur.*), **...trä|ger; ge|schäfts‿tüch|tig, ...un|fä|hig** (*Rechtsspr.*); **Ge|schäfts‿ver|bin|dung, ...ver|kehr, ...vier|tel, ...zei|chen, ...zeit**

Ge|schä|ker, das; -s

ge|scha|mig, gscha|mig, **ge|schä|mig,** gschä|mig (*österr. u. bayr. für* schamhaft)

Ge|schar|re, das; -s

Ge|schau|kel, das; -s

ge|scheckt; ein -es Pferd

ge|sche|hen; es geschieht; es geschah; es geschähe; geschehen; **Ge|sche|hen,** das; -s, -; **Ge|scheh|nis,** das; -ses, -se

Ge|schei|de, das; -s, - (*Jägerspr.* Magen u. Gedärme des Wildes)

Ge|schein, das; -[e]s, -e (*Bot.* Blütenstand der Weinrebe)

ge|scheit; Ge|scheit|heit, die; -, -en

Ge|schenk, das; -[e]s, -e; **Ge|schenk‿ar|ti|kel, ...pa|ckung, ...pa|pier, ...sen|dung; ge|schenk|wei|se**

ge|schert, gschert (*bayr., österr. ugs. für* ungeschlacht, grob, dumm); **Ge|scher|te,** Gscher|te, der; -n, -n; ↑R 5 ff. (*bayr., österr. ugs. für* Tölpel, Landbewohner)

Ge|schich|te, die; -, -n; **Ge|schich|ten|buch** (Buch mit Geschichten [Erzählungen]); **ge|schicht|lich; Ge|schicht|lich|keit,** die; -; **Ge|schichts‿at|las, ...be|wusst|sein, ...buch** (Buch mit Geschichtsdarstellungen), **...fäl|schung, ...for|scher, ...for|schung, ...kennt|nis** (*meist Plur.*), **...klit|te|rung; ge|schichts|los; Ge|schichts‿phi|lo|so|phie, ...schrei|bung** (die; -), **...stu|di|um; ge|schichts|träch|tig; Ge|schichts‿un|ter|richt** (*Plur. selten*), **...werk, ...wis|sen|schaft** (die; -), **...wis|sen|schaft|ler**

Ge|schick, das; -[e]s, *Plur.* (*für* Schicksal:) -e; **Ge|schick|lich|keit,** die; -; **Ge|schick|lich|keits‿prü|fung** (*Motorsport*), **...spiel; ge|schickt;** ein -er Arzt; **Ge|schickt|heit,** die; -

Ge|schie|be, das; -s, -; **Ge|schie|be|mer|gel** (*Geol.*)

ge|schie|den (*Abk.* gesch.; *Zeichen* ⚮); **Ge|schie|de|ne,** der *u.* die; -n, -n (↑R 5 ff.)

Ge|schie|ße, das; -s

Ge|schimp|fe, das; -s

Ge|schirr, das; -[e]s, -e; **Ge|schirr|ma|cher; Ge|schirr|rei|ni|ger** (↑R 136); **Ge|schirr‿schrank, ...spü|ler, ...spül|ma|schi|ne, ...tuch** (*Plur.* ...tücher)

Ge|schiss, das; -es (*derb*); *meist in* Geschiss (ärgerliches Aufheben) [um etw.] machen

Ge|schlab|ber, das; -s (*ugs.*)

ge|schla|gen; eine -e Stunde

ge|schlämmt; -e Kreide

Ge|schlecht, das; -[e]s, -er; das andere -; **Ge|schlech|ter‿buch, ...fol|ge, ...kun|de** (die; -), **...rol|le** (*Soziol.*); **...ge|schlech|tig** (z. B. getrenntgeschlechtig); **ge|schlecht|lich;** -e Fortpflanzung; **Ge|schlecht|lich|keit,** die; -; **Ge|schlechts‿akt, ...ap|pa|rat, ...be|stim|mung; ge|schlechts|krank; Ge|schlechts‿krank|heit, ...le|ben** (das; -s), **...lei|den; ge|schlecht[s]|los; Ge|schlechts‿merk|mal, ...na|me; ge|schlechts|neut|ral; Ge|schlechts|or|gan; ge|schlechts|reif; Ge|schlechts‿rei|fe** (die; -), **...rol|le** (*vgl.* Geschlechterrolle); **ge|schlechts|spe|zi|fisch; Ge|schlechts‿teil** (das, *auch* der), **...trieb** (der; -[e]s), **...um|wand|lung, ...ver|kehr** (der; -[e]s), **...wort** (*Plur.* ...wörter)

Ge|schleck, das; -[e]s *u.* **Ge|schle|cke,** das; -s

Ge|schleif, das; -[e]s *u.* **Ge|schlei|fe,** das; -s (*Jägerspr.* Röhren des Dachsbaus)

Ge|schlep|pe, das; -s (*Jägerspr.* hinterhergezogener Köder)

ge|schlif|fen; Ge|schlif|fen|heit

Ge|schlin|ge, das; -s, - (Herz, Lunge, Leber bei Schlachttieren)

ge|schlos|sen; -e Gesellschaft; **Ge|schlos|sen|heit,** die; -

Ge|schluch|ze, das; -s

Ge|schmack, der; -[e]s, *Plur.* Geschmäcke, *scherzh.* Geschmäcker; nach jmds. Geschmack sein; **ge|schma|ckig** (*österr. für* wohlschmeckend; nett; kitschig); **ge|schmäck|le|risch** (*abwertend*); **ge|schmack|lich; ge|schmack|los;** eine -e Bemerkung; **Ge|schmack|lo|sig|keit; Ge|schmack|sa|che** *vgl.* Geschmackssache; **ge|schmacks|bil|dend; Ge|schmacks‿emp|fin|dung, ...knos|pe** (*meist Plur.*; *Biol., Med.*), **...rich|tung; Ge|schmacks|sa|che,** die; -; *meist in* das ist -; **Ge|schmacks‿sinn** (der; -[e]s), **...stoff, ...test, ...ver|ir|rung, ...ver|stär|ker; ge|schmack|voll**

Ge|schmat|ze, das; -s

Ge|schmau|se, das; -s

Ge|schmei|chel, das; -s

Ge|schmei|de, das; -s, -; **ge|schmei|dig; Ge|schmei|dig|keit,** die; -

Ge|schmeiß, das; -es (Ekel erregendes Ungeziefer; Gesindel; *Jägerspr.* Raubvogelkot)

Ge|schmet|ter, das; -s

Ge|schmier, das; -[e]s *u.* **Ge|schmie|re,** das; -s

Ge|schmor|te, das; -n (↑R 5 ff.)

Ge|schmun|zel, das; -s

Ge|schmu|se, das; -s (*ugs.*)

Ge|schnä|bel, das; -s

Ge|schnat|ter, das; -s

Ge|schnet|zel|te, das; -n (↑R 5 ff.)

ge|schnie|gelt; *meist in* - und gebügelt (*ugs. scherzh.*)

Ge|schnör|kel, das; -s

Ge|schnüf|fel, das; -s

Ge|schöpf, das; -[e]s, -e

Ge|schoss, *südd., österr. auch* Geschoß, das; -es, -e; **Ge|schoss‿bahn, ...ha|gel; ...ge|schos|sig,** *südd., österr. auch* ...ge|scho|ßig (z. B. dreigeschossig, *mit Ziffer* 3-geschossig; ↑R 25)

ge|schraubt (*abwertend*); -er Stil; **Ge|schraubt|heit,** die; -

Ge|schrei, das; -s

Ge|schrei|be, das; -s; **Ge|schreib|sel,** das; -s

Ge|schütz, das; -es, -e; **Ge|schütz‿be|die|nung, ...bet|tung, ...rohr**

Ge|schwa|der, das; -s, - (Verband von Kriegsschiffen od. Kampfflugzeugen)

Ge|schwa|fel, das; -s (*ugs.*)

Ge|schwätz, das; -es; **Ge|schwat|ze,** *landsch.* **Ge|schwät|ze,** das; -s; **ge|schwät|zig; Ge|schwät|zig|keit,** die; -

ge|schweift; -e Tischbeine

ge|schwei|ge [denn] (noch viel weniger); geschweige[,] dass; geschweige denn[,] dass (↑R 88)

ge|schwịnd; (*landsch. für* schnell, rasch, flink); **Ge|schwịn|dig|keit; Ge|schwịn|dig|keits‿be|gren|zung, ...be|schrän|kung, ...kon|trol|le, ...mes|ser** (der), **...über|schrei|tung** (↑R 132); **Ge|schwịnd|schritt;** im - **Ge|schwịrr,** das; -s **Ge|schwị|s|ter,** das; -s, - (*im allg. Sprachgebrauch nur Plur.; Sing. nur fachspr. für* eines der Geschwister [Bruder od. Schwester]); **Ge|schwị|s|ter|kind** (*veraltet, noch landsch. für* Neffe, Nichte); **ge|schwị|s|ter|lich; Ge|schwị|s|ter‿lie|be, ...paar**
ge|schwọl|len; ein -er Stil; *vgl.* [1]schwellen
ge|schwo̱|ren; ein geschworener Feind des Alkohols; **Ge|schwo̱|re|ne,** *österr. amtl. auch* Geschwo̱r|ne, der *u.* die; -n, -n (↑R 5 ff.); **Ge|schwo̱|re|nen|lis|te; Ge|schwo̱r|ne** *vgl.* Geschworene
Ge|schwụlst, die; -, Geschwülste; **ge|schwụlst|ar|tig; Ge|schwụlst|bil|dung**
ge|schwụn|gen; eine -e Linie
Ge|schwü̱r, das; -[e]s, -e; **Ge|schwü̱r|bil|dung; ge|schwü̱|rig**
Gẹs-Dur [*auch* 'gɛs'du:r], das; - (Tonart; *Zeichen* Ges); **Ges-Dur-Ton|lei|ter** (↑R 28)
Ge̱|se, Ge̱|sa (w. Vorn.)
ge|seg|net; gesegnete Mahlzeit!
Ge|se̱ich, das; -s (*landsch. derb für* leeres Geschwätz)
Ge|se̱i|re, das; -s ‹jidd.› (*ugs. für* unnützes Gerede, Gejammere)
Ge|sẹlch|te, das; -n; ↑R 5 ff. (*bayr., österr. für* Rauchfleisch)
Ge|sẹll, der; -en, -en; ↑R 126 (*veraltet*); ein fahrender -; **Ge|sẹl|le,** der; -n, -n (↑R 126); **ge|sẹl|len;** sich -; **Ge|sẹl|len‿brief, ...prü|fung, ...stück; ge|sẹl|lig; Ge|sẹl|lig|keit** *Plur. selten;* **Ge|sẹl|lin; Ge|sẹll|schaft;** Gesellschaft mit beschränkter Haftung (*Abk.* GmbH); **Ge|sẹll|schaf|ter; Ge|sẹll|schaf|te|rin; ge|sẹll|schaft|lich; Ge|sẹll|schafts‿an|zug, ...da|me; ge|sẹll|schafts|fä|hig; Ge|sẹll|schafts‿form, ...in|seln** (*Plur.;* in der Südsee), **...klei|dung, ...kri|tik** (die; -), **...leh|re, ...ord|nung, ...po|li|tik** (die; -); **ge|sẹll|schafts|po|li|tisch; Ge|sẹll|schafts‿rei|se, ...schicht, ...spiel, ...sys|tem, ...tanz, ...wis|sen|schaft** (*meist Plur.*)
Ge|sẹnk, das; -[e]s, -e (*Technik* Hohlform zum Pressen von Werkstücken; *Bergmannsspr.* von oben nach unten hergestellte Verbindung zweier Sohlen)

Ge|sẹtz, das; -es, -e; **Ge|sẹtz‿aus|le|gung, ...blatt** (*Abk.* GBl.), **...buch, ...ent|wurf; Ge|sẹt|zes‿bre|cher, ...ent|wurf** (*schweiz.*), **...hü|ter, ...kraft** (die; -); **Ge|sẹt|zes|samm|lung,** Gesẹtz|samm|lung; **Ge|sẹt|zes‿spra|che, ...text, ...vor|la|ge, ...werk; ge|sẹtz|ge|bend;** gesetzgebende Gewalt; **Ge|sẹtz|ge|ber; ge|sẹtz|ge|be|risch; Ge|sẹtz|ge|bung; ge|sẹtz|lich;** gesetzliche Erbfolge; gesetzliche Krankenversicherung; gesetzliche Zinsen; **Ge|sẹtz|lich|keit,** die; -; **ge|sẹtz|los; Ge|sẹtz|lo|sig|keit; ge|sẹtz|mä|ßig; Ge|sẹtz|mä|ßig|keit; Ge|sẹtz|samm|lung** *vgl.* Gesetzessammlung
ge|sẹtzt; gesetzt[,] dass ...; gesetzt den Fall[,] [dass] ... (↑R 88); **Ge|sẹtzt|heit,** die; -
ge|sẹtz|wid|rig
Ge|se̱uf|ze, das; -s
ges. gesch. = gesetzlich geschützt
[1]**Ge|sịcht,** das; -[e]s, -er; sein - wahren; [2]**Ge|sị̱cht,** das; -[e]s, -e (*für* Vision); **Ge|sịchts‿aus|druck, ...creme, ...er|ker** (*ugs. scherzh. für* Nase), **...far|be, ...feld, ...kreis, ...mas|ke, ...par|tie, ...punkt, ...sinn** (der; -[e]s), **...was|ser** (*Plur.* ...wässer), **...win|kel, ...zug** (*meist Plur.*)
Ge|sịms, das; -es, -e
Ge|sịn|de, das; -s, - (*früher* Gesamtheit der Knechte u. Mägde); **Ge|sịn|del,** das; -s; **Ge|sịn|de|stu|be**
Ge|sịn|ge, das; -s
ge|sịnnt (von einer bestimmten Gesinnung); ein gut gesinnter Mensch; er ist gut gesinnt; *vgl.* gesonnen; **Ge|sịn|nung; Ge|sịn|nungs|ge|nos|se; ge|sịn|nungs|los; Ge|sịn|nungs|lo|sig|keit,** die; -; **Ge|sịn|nungs‿lump** (*ugs.*), **...schnüf|fe|lei, ...tä|ter, ...wan|del**
ge|sịt|tet; Ge|sịt|tung, die; -
Ge|sọcks, das; -[es] (*derb für* Gesindel)
Ge|sọ̈ff, das; -[e]s, -e (*ugs. für* schlechtes Getränk)
ge|sọn|dert; - verpacken
ge|sọn|nen (willens); gesonnen sein[,] etwas zu tun (↑R 75); *vgl.* gesinnt
ge|sọt|ten; Ge|sọt|te|ne, das; -n; ↑R 5 ff. (*landsch. für* Gekochtes)
ge|spạl|ten; eine gespaltene Persönlichkeit; *vgl.* spalten
[1]**Ge|spa̱n,** der; *Gen.* -[e]s *u.* -en (↑R 126), *Plur.* -e[n] (*veraltet für* Mitarbeiter, Helfer; Genosse)

[2]**Ge|spa̱n,** der; -[e]s, -e ‹ung.› (*früher* ung. Verwaltungsbeamter)
Ge|spạ̈n|ge, das; -s (Spangenwerk)
Ge|spạnn, das; -[e]s, -e (Zugtiere; Wagen mit Zugtieren)
ge|spạnnt; Ge|spạnnt|heit, die; -
Ge|spạ̈r|re, das; -s (*Bauw.* ein Paar sich gegenüberliegender Dachsparren)
Ge|spẹnst, das; -[e]s, -er; **Ge|spẹns|ter|chen** *Plur.;* **Ge|spẹns|ter‿furcht, ...glau|be[n]; ge|spẹns|ter|haft; ge|spẹns|tern;** ich ...ere (↑R 16); **Ge|spẹns|ter|stun|de; ge|spẹns|tig, ge|spẹns|tisch**
ge|spẹr|bert (*Jägerspr.* in der Art des Sperbers); -es Gefieder
Ge|spẹr|re, das; -s, - (*Jägerspr.* bei Auer-, Birkwild, Fasan die Jungen [mit Henne]; *Technik* Hemmvorrichtung)
[1]**Ge|spie̱|le,** das; -s (andauerndes Spielen); [2]**Ge|spie̱|le,** der; -n, -n; ↑R 126 (*veraltend für* Spielkamerad); **Ge|spie̱|lin**
Ge|spịnst, das; -[e]s, -e
[1]**Ge|spọns,** der; -es, -e (*veraltet, noch scherzh. für* Bräutigam; Gatte); [2]**Ge|spọns,** das; -es, -e (*veraltet, noch scherzh. für* Braut; Gattin)
ge|spọn|sert *vgl.* sponsern
Ge|spọ̈tt, das; -[e]s; jmdn. zum - machen; **Ge|spọ̈t|tel,** das; -s
Ge|spra̱ch, das; -[e]s, -e; **ge|sprä̱|chig; Ge|sprä̱|chig|keit,** die; -; **ge|spra̱chs|be|reit; Ge|spra̱chs‿form, ...part|ner, ...part|ne|rin, ...stoff, ...teil|neh|mer, ...teil|neh|me|rin, ...the|ma; ge|spra̱chs|wei|se**
ge|spre̱izt; -e (gezierte) Reden; **Ge|spre̱izt|heit,** die; -
Ge|sprẹn|ge, das; -s, - (*Archit.* Aufbau über spätgot. Altären; *Bergmannsspr.* steil aufsteigendes Gebirge)
ge|sprẹn|kelt; ein -es Fell
Ge|sprịtz|te, der; -n, -n; ↑R 5 ff. (*bes. südd., österr. für* Wein mit Sprudel)
Ge|spru̱|del, das; -s
Ge|spü̱r, das; -s
Gẹß|ner, Salomon (schweiz. Dichter u. Maler)
Gẹst, der; -[e]s *od.* die; - (*nordd. für* Hefe)
gest. (*Zeichen* †) = gestorben
Ge|sta̱|de, das; -s, - (*geh. für* Küste, Ufer)
Ges|ta|ge̱n, das; -s, -e ‹lat.› (*Biol.* Schwangerschaftshormon)
Ge|stạlt, die; -, -en; dergestalt (so); **ge|stạlt|bar; ge|stạl|ten; ge|stạl|ten|reich; Ge|stạl|ter;**

Ge|stal|te|rin; ge|stal|te|risch; ge|stalt|haft; ge|stalt|los; Ge|stal|tung; Ge|stal|tungs‿kraft (die; -), **...prin|zip**
Ge|stam|mel, das; -s
Ge|stamp|fe, das; -s
Ge|stän|de, das; -s, - (*Jägerspr.* Füße, bes. der Beizvögel; [2]Horst); **ge|stan|den;** ein -er Mann
ge|stän|dig; Ge|ständ|nis, das; -ses, -se
Ge|stän|ge, das; -s, -
Ge|stank, der; -[e]s
Ge|sta|po = Geheime Staatspolizei (*nationalsoz.*)
ge|stat|ten
Ges|te [*auch* 'ge:...], die; -, -n ‹lat.› (Gebärde)
Ge|steck, das; -[e]s, -e (Blumenarrangement; *bayr., österr. für* Hutschmuck)
ge|ste|hen; gestanden; **Ge|ste|hungs|kos|ten** *Plur.* (*Wirtsch.* Herstellungs-, Selbstkosten)
Ge|stein, das; -[e]s, -e; **Ge|steins‿art, ...block** (*Plur.* ...blöcke), **...boh|rer, ...kun|de** (die; -), **...pro|be, ...schicht**
Ge|stell, das; -[e]s, -e; **Ge|stel|lung** (*Amtsspr.*); **Ge|stel|lungs|be|fehl** (*veraltet für* Einberufungsbefehl)
ge|stelzt; eine -e Sprache
ges|tern; (↑R 45:) gestern Abend, Morgen, Nachmittag, Nacht; gestern früh; bis gestern; die Mode von gestern; zwischen gestern und morgen, *auch substantivisch* (↑R 49): zwischen [dem] Gestern und [dem] Morgen liegt das Heute; vorgestern; ehegestern; **Ges|tern,** das; - (die Vergangenheit)
Ge|sti|chel, das; -s (*ugs.*)
ge|stie|felt; gestiefelt u. gespornt (fertig) sein; *aber* (↑R 108): der Gestiefelte Kater (im Märchen)
ge|stielt; ein -er Besen
Ges|tik [*auch* 'ge:...], die; - ‹lat.› (Gesamtheit der Gesten [als Ausdruck einer inneren Haltung]); **Ges|ti|ku|la|ti|on,** die; -, -en (Gebärde, Gebärdensprache); **ges|ti|ku|lie|ren**
Ge|stimmt|heit (Stimmung)
Ges|ti|ons|be|richt (*österr. Amtsspr. für* Geschäftsbericht)
Ge|stirn, das; -[e]s, -e; **ge|stirnt;** der -e Himmel
ges|tisch [*auch* 'ge:...]
Ge|stö|ber, das; -s, -
ge|sto|chen; eine -e Handschrift
ge|stockt; -e Milch (*südd. u. österr. für* Dickmilch)
Ge|stöhn, das; -[e]s; **Ge|stöh|ne,** das; -s
Ge|stol|per, das; -s
Ge|stör, das; -[e]s, -e (Teil eines Floßes)
ge|stor|ben (*Abk.* gest.; *Zeichen* †)
ge|stört; ein -es Verhältnis zu etwas haben
Ge|stot|ter, das; -s
Ge|stram|pel, das; -s
Ge|sträuch, das; -[e]s, -e
ge|streckt; -er Galopp
ge|streift; rot gestreift (*vgl.* blau)
Ge|strei|te, das; -s
ge|streng (*veraltend*); *aber* (↑R 108): die Gestrengen Herren (Eisheiligen)
Ge|streu, das; -[e]s
Ge|strick, das; -[e]s, -e (Strickware)
gest|rig; mein -er Brief
Ge|ström, das; -[e]s (Strömung); **ge|stromt** (streifig ohne scharfe Abgrenzung); eine -e Katze
Ge|strüpp, das; -[e]s, -e
Ge|stü|be, das; -s (*Hüttenw.* Gemisch von Koksrückstand u. Lehm)
Ge|stü|ber, das; -s, - (*Jägerspr.* Kot des Federwildes)
Ge|stühl, das; -[e]s, -e
Ge|stüm|per, das; -s (*ugs.*)
Ge|stürm, das; -[e]s (*schweiz. mdal. für* aufgeregtes Gerede, Getue)
Ges|tus, der; - ‹lat.› (Gestik, Ausdruck)
Ge|stüt, das; -[e]s, -e; **Ge|stüt‿hengst, ...pferd; Ge|stüts|brand** (Brandzeichen eines Gestütes)
Ge|such, das; -[e]s, -e; **Ge|such|stel|ler** (*Amtsspr., veraltet*)
ge|sucht; eine -e Ausdrucksweise; **Ge|sucht|heit,** die; -
Ge|su|del, das; -s
Ge|summ, das; -[e]s *u.* **Ge|sum|me,** das; -s
Ge|sums, das; -es (*ugs.*)
ge|sund; gesünder, *seltener* gesunder, gesündeste, *seltener* gesundeste; gesund sein, werden, bleiben; jmdn. wieder [ganz] gesund machen (*ugs.*), pflegen; *vgl.* gesundbeten, gesundschreiben, gesundschrumpfen, gesundstoßen; **ge|sund|be|ten** (durch Gebete o. Ä. zu heilen versuchen); **Ge|sund‿be|ten** (das; -s), **...be|ter, ...be|te|rin, ...brun|nen** (etw., was jmdn. gesund macht, in Schwung hält); **Ge|sun|de,** der *u.* die; -n, -n (↑R 5 ff.); **ge|sun|den; Ge|sund|heit,** die; -; **ge|sund|heit|lich; Ge|sund|heits‿amt, ...apos|tel** (↑R 132; *scherzh.*), **...er|zie|hung** (die; -); **ge|sund|heits|hal|ber; Ge|sund|heits|pfle|ge,** die; -; **ge|sund|heits‿schä|di|gend, ...schäd|lich; Ge|sund|heits‿schutz** (der; -es), **...we|sen** (das; -s), **...zeug|nis, ...zu|stand** (der; -[e]s); **ge|sund|schrei|ben;** der Arzt hat sie gesundgeschrieben; **ge|sund|schrump|fen;** sich - (*ugs. für* durch Verkleinerung [eines Betriebes] die rentable Größe erreichen); **ge|sund|sto|ßen,** sich; (*ugs. für* sich bereichern); **Ge|sun|dung,** die; -
get. (*Zeichen* ⁓) = getauft
Ge|tä|fel, das; -s (Tafelwerk, Täfelung); **ge|tä|felt; Ge|tä|fer,** das; -s (*schweiz. für* Getäfel); **ge|tä|fert** (*schweiz. für* getäfelt)
Ge|tän|del, das; -s
ge|tauft (*Abk.* get.; *Zeichen* ⁓)
Ge|tau|mel, das; -s
ge|teilt *vgl.* teilen
Geth|se|ma|ne [...ne:], **Geth|se|ma|ni,** *ökum.* Get|se|ma|ni (Garten am Ölberg bei Jerusalem)
Ge|tier, das; -[e]s
ge|ti|gert (geflammt)
Ge|tön, das; -[e]s; **Ge|tö|ne,** das; -s
Ge|to|se, das; -s; **Ge|tö|se,** das; ...ses
ge|tra|gen; eine -e Redeweise; **Ge|tra|gen|heit,** die; -
Ge|tram|pel, das; -s
Ge|tränk, das; -[e]s, -e; **Ge|trän|ke‿au|to|mat, ...kar|te, ...steu|er** (die)
Ge|trap|pel, das; -s
Ge|tratsch, das; -[e]s *u.* **Ge|trat|sche,** das; -s (*ugs.*)
ge|trau|en, sich; ich getraue mich (*seltener* mir)[,] das zu tun (↑R 75)
Ge|trei|de, das; -s, -; **Ge|trei|de‿an|bau, ...aus|fuhr, ...ein|fuhr, ...ern|te, ...feld, ...müh|le, ...spei|cher**
ge|trennt; getrennt schreiben, getrennt leben, getrennt vorkommen u. a.; ein getrennt lebendes Paar; **ge|trennt|ge|schlech|tig** (*Biol.*); **Ge|trennt|schrei|bung**
ge|treu; getreu seinem Vorsatz; die getreu[e]sten Freunde; **Ge|treue,** der *u.* die; -n, -n (↑R 5 ff.); **ge|treu|lich** (*geh.*)
Ge|trie|be, das; -s, -; **ge|trie|ben;** aus -em Gold; **Ge|trie|be‿öl, ...scha|den**
Ge|tril|ler, das; -s
Ge|trip|pel, das; -s
Ge|trom|mel, das; -s
ge|trost; ge|trös|ten, sich (*geh.*)
Get|se|ma|ni *vgl.* Gethsemane
Get|to, *auch* Ghet|to ['geto], das; -s, -s ‹ital.› (abgesondertes [jüd.] Wohnviertel); **get|to|i|sie|ren,** *auch* ghet|to|i|sie|ren (isolieren)
Ge|tue, das; -s

Ge|tüm|mel, das; -s, -
ge|tüp|felt, ge|tupft; ein -er Stoff
ge|türkt (*ugs. für* vorgetäuscht)
Ge|tu|schel, das; -s
ge|übt; Ge|übt|heit, die; -
Geu|se, der; -n, -n *meist Plur.;* ↑R 126 ‹niederl.› (niederländ. Freiheitskämpfer gegen Spanien)
Ge|vat|ter, der; *Gen.* -s, *älter* -n (↑R 126), *Plur.* -n (*veraltet, noch scherzh. für* Freund, guter Bekannter); **Ge|vat|te|rin** *(veraltet, noch scherzh.);* **Ge|vat|ter|schaft** (*veraltet für* Patenschaft); **Ge|vat|ters|mann** *Plur.* ...leute *(veraltet)*
Ge|viert, das; -[e]s, -e (Viereck, Quadrat); ins Geviert; **ge|vier|teilt; Ge|viert|schein** *(Astron.)*
Ge|wächs, das; -es, -e; **ge|wach|sen;** jmdm., einer Sache - sein; -er Boden; **Ge|wächs|haus**
ge|wachst (mit Wachs behandelt)
Ge|wa|ckel, das; -s *u.* **Ge|wa|cke|le, Ge|wack|le,** das; -s
Ge|waff, das; -[e]s (*Jägerspr.* Eckzähne des Keilers); **Ge|waf|fen,** das; -s (*veraltet für* Gesamtheit der Waffen)
ge|wagt; Ge|wagt|heit
ge|wählt; sich - ausdrücken
ge|wahr; *nur in Wendungen wie* eine[r] Sache gewahr werden; es (*vgl.* [2]es) *u.* dessen gewahr werden
Ge|währ, die; - (Bürgschaft, Sicherheit); ohne Gewähr; *vgl.* gewährleisten
ge|wah|ren (*geh. für* bemerken, erkennen); er gewahrte den Freund
ge|wäh|ren (bewilligen); **Ge|währ|frist; ge|währ|leis|ten** (↑R 39); ich gewährleiste, habe gewährleistet; zu gewährleisten; *aber* ich leiste [dafür] Gewähr, habe [dafür] Gewähr geleistet; um [dafür] Gewähr zu leisten; **Ge|währ|leis|tung**
[1]**Ge|wahr|sam,** der; -s, -e (Haft, Obhut); [2]**Ge|wahr|sam,** das; -s, -e (*veraltet für* Gefängnis)
Ge|währs|mann *Plur.* ...männer *u.* ...leute; **Ge|wäh|rung** *Plur. selten*
ge|walmt ‹*zu* [2]Walm›; -es Dach
Ge|walt, die; -, -en; **Ge|walt‿akt, ...an|dro|hung, ...an|wen|dung, ...be|reit|schaft, ...ein|wir|kung; Ge|wal|ten|tei|lung,** die; -; **ge|walt|frei; Ge|walt‿herr|schaft, ...herr|scher; ge|wal|tig; ge|wäl|ti|gen** (*Bergmannsspr.* wieder zugänglich machen); **Ge|wal|tig|keit,** die; -; **ge|walt|los; Ge|walt|lo|sig|keit,** die; -; **Ge|walt‿marsch** (der), **...maß|nah|me, ...mensch; ge|walt|sam; Ge|walt|sam|keit; Ge|walt‿schuss** *(Sportspr.),* **...streich, ...tat; ge|walt|tä|tig; Ge|walt|tä|tig|keit; Ge|walt‿ver|bre|chen, ...ver|bre|cher, ...ver|herr|li|chung, ...ver|zicht** (der; -[e]s); **Ge|walt|ver|zichts|ab|kom|men**
Ge|wand, das; -[e]s, ...wänder; **Ge|wän|de,** das; -s, - (*Archit.* seitl. Umgrenzung der Fenster und Türen); **ge|wan|den** (*veraltet, noch geh. od. scherzh. für* kleiden); **Ge|wand|haus** (*früher für* Lagerhaus der Tuchhändler); **Ge|wand|haus|or|ches|ter,** das; -s (in Leipzig); **Ge|wand|meis|ter** (*Theater, Film usw.* Leiter der Kostümschneiderei)
ge|wandt; ein -er Tänzer; *vgl.* wenden; **Ge|wandt|heit,** die; -
Ge|wan|dung
Ge|wann, das; -[e]s, -e, *seltener* **Ge|wan|ne,** die; -s, - (*bes. südd.* Ackergrenze, an der der Pflug gewendet wird)
ge|wär|tig; einer Sache gewärtig sein; ich bin es (*vgl.* [2]es) gewärtig; **ge|wär|ti|gen** *(geh.);* zu - (erwarten) haben
Ge|wäsch, das; -[e]s (*ugs. für* [leeres] Gerede)
Ge|wäs|ser, das; -s, -; **Ge|wäs|ser|schutz,** der; -es; **ge|was|sert;** das gewasserte Flugzeug; **ge|wäs|sert;** gewässerte Salzheringe
Ge|we|be, das; -s, -; **Ge|we|be‿bank** (*Plur.* ...banken), **...brei|te, ...leh|re** (die; -; *für* Histologie), **...trans|plan|ta|ti|on, ...ver|än|de|rung; Ge|webs|flüs|sig|keit**
ge|weckt (aufgeweckt)
Ge|wehr, das; -[e]s, -e; **Ge|wehr‿kol|ben, ...lauf**
Ge|weih, das; -[e]s, -e; **Ge|weih|farn;** [1]**ge|weiht** (*Jägerspr.* Geweih tragend)
[2]**ge|weiht** ‹*zu* weihen›
Ge|wen|de, das; -s, - (*veraltet für* Feldstück; *noch landsch. für* Ackergrenze)
Ge|wer|be, das; -s, -; **Ge|wer|be|auf|sicht,** die; -; **Ge|wer|be|auf|sichts|amt; Ge|wer|be‿be|trieb, ...frei|heit** (die; -), **...ge|biet, ...in|spek|tor, ...leh|rer, ...leh|re|rin, ...ord|nung** (die; -; *Abk.* GewO), **...schein, ...schu|le, ...steu|er** (die); **ge|wer|be|trei|bend; Ge|wer|be|trei|ben|de,** der *u.* die; -n, -n (↑R 5 ff.); **Ge|wer|be|zweig; ge|werb|lich;** -er Rechtsschutz; **ge|werbs|mä|ßig**
Ge|werk, das; -[e]s, -e (*regional für* Zweig des Bauhandwerks; *veraltet für* Gewerbe; Zunft); **Ge|wer|ke,** der; -n, -n; ↑R 126 (*veraltet für* Mitglied einer bergrechtlichen Gewerkschaft); **Ge|werk|schaft; Ge|werk|schaf|ter,** Ge|werk|schaft|ler; **Ge|werk|schaf|te|rin,** Ge|werk|schaft|le|rin; **Ge|werk|schaft|ler** usw. *vgl.* Gewerkschafter usw.; **ge|werk|schaft|lich; Ge|werk|schafts‿ap|pa|rat, ...be|we|gung** (die; -), **...boss** *(ugs.),* **...bund** (der; -es, ...bünde *Plur. selten*), **...funk|ti|o|när, ...mit|glied, ...ver|samm|lung, ...vor|sit|zen|de**
Ge|we|se, das; -s, - (*ugs. für* auffallendes Gebaren *[nur Sing.]; nordd. für* Anwesen)
[1]**Ge|wicht,** das; -[e]s, -er (*Jägerspr.* Rehgehörn)
[2]**Ge|wicht,** das; -[e]s, -e; **ge|wich|ten** (Schwerpunkte bei etw. setzen; *Statistik* einen Durchschnittswert unter Berücksichtigung der Häufigkeit vorhandener Einzelwerte bilden); **Ge|wicht|he|ben,** das; -s (Sportart); **Ge|wicht|he|ber; ge|wich|tig; Ge|wich|tig|keit,** die; -; **Ge|wichts‿klas|se** *(Sport),* **...kon|trol|le, ...ver|la|ge|rung, ...ver|lust; Ge|wich|tung**
ge|wieft (*ugs. für* schlau, gerissen)
ge|wiegt (*ugs. für* sehr erfahren; schlau, durchtrieben)
Ge|wie|her, das; -s
ge|willt; *nur in* gewillt (bereit) sein[,] etw. zu tun (↑R 75)
Ge|wim|mel, das; -s
Ge|wim|mer, das; -s
Ge|win|de, das; -s, -; **Ge|win|de‿boh|rer, ...gang, ...schnei|der**
Ge|winn, der; -[e]s, -e; (↑R 40:) großen Gewinn bringende Geschäfte; sein Geld Gewinn bringend, *auch* gewinnbringend anlegen; *aber* eine höchst gewinnbringende Unternehmung; **Ge|winn‿an|teil, ...aus|schüt|tung, ...be|tei|li|gung; Ge|winn brin|gend** *vgl.* Gewinn; **Ge|winn|chan|ce; ge|win|nen;** du gewannst; du gewönnest, *auch* gewännest; gewonnen; gewinn[e]!; **ge|win|nend; Ge|win|ner; Ge|win|ne|rin; Ge|win|ner|stra|ße;** *nur in* auf der - sein *(Sport ugs.);* **Ge|winn|klas|se; Ge|winn|num|mer** (↑R 136); **Ge|winn|quo|te; Ge|winn‿satz** *(Sport),* **...span|ne, ...stre|ben** (das; -s), **...sucht** (die; -); **ge|winn‿süch|tig, ...träch|tig; Ge|winn-und-Ver|lust-Rech|nung** (↑R 28); **Ge|win|nung; Ge|winn|zahl**
Ge|win|sel, das; -s
Ge|winst, der; -[e]s, -e (*veraltet für* Gewinn)

Ge|wirk, das; -[e]s, -e *u.* **Ge|wir|ke,** das; -s, - (aus Maschen bestehender Textilstoff); **ge|wirkt;** -er Stoff

Ge|wirr, das; -[e]s

Ge|wis|per, das; -s

ge|wiss; (↑R 47:) etwas, nichts Gewisses; (↑R 48:) ein gewisses Etwas; ein gewisser Jemand

Ge|wis|sen, das; -s, -; **ge|wis|sen|haft; Ge|wis|sen|haf|tig|keit,** die; -; **ge|wis|sen|los; Ge|wis|sen|lo|sig|keit,** die; -; **Ge|wis|sens|biss** *meist Plur.;* **Ge|wis|sens‿ent|schei|dung, ...er|for|schung, ...fra|ge, ...frei|heit** (die; -), **...grün|de** (*Plur.;* etwas aus -n verweigern), **...kon|flikt, ...wurm** (der; -[e]s; *ugs. scherzh.*)

ge|wis|ser|ma|ßen; Ge|wiss|heit; ge|wiss|lich *(veraltend)*

Ge|wit|ter, das; -s, -; **Ge|wit|ter|front; ge|wit|te|rig** *vgl.* gewittrig; **ge|wit|tern;** es gewittert; **Ge|wit|ter‿nei|gung, ...re|gen; ge|wit|ter|schwül; Ge|wit|ter‿stim|mung** (die; -), **...sturm, ...wand, ...wol|ke; ge|witt|rig,** *selten* ge|wit|te|rig

Ge|wit|zel, das; -s; **ge|wit|zigt** (klug geworden); **ge|witzt** (schlau); **Ge|witzt|heit,** die; -

GewO = Gewerbeordnung

Ge|wo|ge, das; -s

ge|wo|gen (zugetan); er ist mir -; **Ge|wo|gen|heit,** die; -

ge|wöh|nen; sich an etw. *od.* jmdn. gewöhnen; **Ge|wohn|heit; ge|wohn|heits|mä|ßig; Ge|wohn|heits‿mensch** (der; -en, -en), **...recht, ...tier** *(scherzh.),* **...trin|ker, ...ver|bre|cher; ge|wöhn|lich;** für - (meist); **Ge|wöhn|lich|keit,** die; -; **ge|wohnt;** ich bin es gewohnt, bin schwere Arbeit gewohnt; die gewohnte Arbeit; jung gewohnt, alt getan; **ge|wöhnt** (*Partizip II von* gewöhnen); ich habe mich an diese Arbeit gewöhnt; ich bin daran gewöhnt; **Ge|wöh|nung,** die; -

Ge|wöl|be, das; -s, -; **Ge|wöl|be‿bo|gen, ...pfei|ler**

Ge|wölk, das; -[e]s

Ge|wöl|le, das; -s, - (*Jägerspr.* von Greifvögeln herausgewürgter Klumpen unverdaulicher Nahrungsreste)

Ge|wühl, das; -[e]s

ge|wür|felt; -e Stoffe

Ge|würm, das; -[e]s

Ge|würz, das; -es, -e; **Ge|würz|gur|ke; ge|wür|zig** (*selten für* würzig); **Ge|würz‿ku|chen, ...mi|schung, ...nel|ke, ...tra|mi|ner** (eine Rebsorte)

Ge|wu|sel, das; -s *(landsch.)*

Gey|sir ['gai...], der; -s, -e ‹isländ.› (in bestimmten Abständen eine Wasserfontäne ausstoßende heiße Quelle); *vgl.* Geiser

gez. = gezeichnet

GEZ = Gebühreneinzugszentrale

ge|zackt; der Felsgipfel ist -

Ge|zä|he, das; -s, - (*Bergmannsspr.* Werkzeug der Bergleute)

ge|zahnt, ge|zähnt; -es Blatt

Ge|zänk, das; -[e]s; **Ge|zan|ke,** das; -s

Ge|zap|pel, das; -s

ge|zeich|net (*Abk.* gez.)

Ge|zeit, die; -, -en (*im allg. Sprachgebrauch Plur.; Sing. fachspr. für* eine der Gezeiten [Ebbe od. Flut]); **Ge|zei|ten‿kraft|werk, ...ta|fel, ...wech|sel**

Ge|zer|re, das; -s

Ge|ze|ter, das; -s

Ge|zie|fer, das; -s (*veraltend für* Ungeziefer)

ge|zielt; - fragen

ge|zie|men, sich *(veraltend);* es geziemt sich für ihn; **ge|zie|mend;** eine -e Antwort

Ge|zie|re, das; -s; **ge|ziert; Ge|ziert|heit**

Ge|zirp, das; -[e]s, **Ge|zir|pe,** das; -s

Ge|zisch, das; -[e]s, **Ge|zi|sche,** das; -s; **Ge|zi|schel,** das; -s

Ge|zücht, das; -[e]s, -e (*veraltet für* Brut; Gesindel)

Ge|zün|gel, das; -s

Ge|zweig, das; -[e]s

ge|zwirnt; *vgl.* zwirnen

Ge|zwit|scher, das; -s

ge|zwun|ge|ner|ma|ßen; Ge|zwun|gen|heit, die; -

Gfrast, das; -s, -er (*bayr., österr. ugs. für* Fussel; Nichtsnutz)

Gfrett, Ge|frett, das; -s (*südd., österr. ugs. für* Ärger, Plage)

Gfrieß, Ge|frieß, das; -es, -er (*südd., österr. ugs. abwertend für* Gesicht)

GG = Grundgesetz

ggf. = gegebenenfalls

g.g.T., ggT = größter gemeinsamer Teiler *(Math.)*

Gha|na ['ga:...] (Staat in Afrika); **Gha|na|er; Gha|na|e|rin; gha|na|isch**

Gha|sel [ga...], **Gha|se|le** *vgl.* Gasel, Gasele

Ghet|to *vgl.* Getto

Ghi|bel|li|ne *vgl.* Gibelline

Ghost|wri|ter ['go:straitə(r)], der; -s, - ‹engl.› (Autor, der für eine andere Person schreibt und nicht als Verfasser genannt wird)

G.I., GI [dʒi:'ai], der; -[s], -[s] ‹*amerik. Abk. v.* Government Issue ['gavə(r)nmənt 'iʃu] = „Regierungsausgabe" [urspr. für die Ausrüstung der Truppe]› (*ugs. für* amerik. Soldat)

Gi|aur, der; -s, -s ‹pers.› (*im Islam* Nichtmoslem, Ungläubiger)

Gib|bon, der; -s, -s ‹franz.› (ein Affe)

Gi|bel|li|ne, Ghi|bel|li|ne [gi...], der; -n, -n (↑R 126) ‹ital.› (ital. Anhänger der Hohenstaufen im 13. Jh.)

Gib|ral|tar [*auch* ...'ta:r, *österr.* 'gi:...] (↑R 130) ‹arab.› (Halbinsel an der Südspitze Spaniens)

¹Gicht, die; -, -en (*Hüttenw.* oberster Teil des Hochofens)

²Gicht, die; - (eine Stoffwechselkrankheit); **Gicht|bee|re** (*bes. nordd., ostd. für* Schwarze Johannisbeere); **gicht|brü|chig** *(veraltet);* **gich|tig; gich|tisch; Gicht|kno|ten; gicht|krank**

Gi|ckel, der; -s, - (*landsch. für* Hahn)

gi|ckeln, gi|ckern (*landsch. für* kichern, albern lachen)

gicks *(ugs.);* weder - noch gacks sagen; **gick|sen,** kick|sen (*landsch. für* einen [leichten] Schrei ausstoßen; stechen; stoßen); du gickst; gicksen und gacksen

Gide [ʒi(:)d] (franz. Schriftsteller)

Gi|de|on (m. Vorn.; bibl. m. Eigenn.)

¹Gie|bel, der; -s, - (ein Fisch)

²Gie|bel, der; -s, - (senkrechter Dachabschluss); **Gie|bel|fens|ter; gie|be|lig,** gieb|lig; **Gie|bel|wand; gieb|lig** *vgl.* giebelig

Giek|baum (*Seemannsspr.* Rundholz für Gaffelsegel)

Gie|men, das; -s (krankhaftes Atmungsgeräusch)

Gien, das; -s, -e ‹engl.› (*Seemannsspr.* starker Flaschenzug); **Gien|block** *Plur.* ...blöcke

Gien|gen an der Brenz ['giŋən - - -] (Stadt in Baden-Württemberg)

Gie|per, der; -s (*bes. nordd. für* Gier, Appetit); einen - auf etwas haben; **gie|pern;** ich ...ere (↑R 16); nach etwas -; **giep|rig**

Gier, die; -; **¹gie|ren** (gierig sein)

²gie|ren ([von Schiffen, Flugzeugen] seitlich abweichen); **Gier|fäh|re** (Seilfähre)

gie|rig; Gie|rig|keit, die; -

Giersch, der; -[e]s (*landsch. für* Geißfuß [ein Wiesenkraut])

Gieß|bach; gie|ßen; du gießt; ich goss, du gossest; du gössest; gegossen; gieß[e]!

Gie|ßen (Stadt a. d. Lahn)

Gie|ßer; Gie|ße|rei; Gieß‿form, ...harz (das), **...kan|ne; Gieß|kan|nen|prin|zip,** das; -s; *nur in* etwas nach dem - (unterschiedslos, willkürlich) verteilen

[1]**Gift**, das; -[e]s, -e; [2]**Gift**, der; -[e]s (*bes. südd. für* Ärger, Zorn); einen - auf jmdn. haben; **gif|ten** (*ugs. für* gehässig reden); sich - (sich ärgern); das giftet mich; **gift‿fest, ...frei; Gift|gas; giftgrün; gif|tig; Gif|tig|keit**, die; -; **Gift‿mi|scher, ...mi|sche|rin, ...mord, ...müll, ...nu|del** (*ugs. für* boshafter Mensch), **...pflan|ze, ...pilz, ...schlan|ge, ...schrank, ...sta|chel, ...stoff, ...zahn, ...zwerg** (*ugs. für* boshafter Mensch)

[1]**Gig**, das; -s, -s ‹engl.› (leichter Einspänner); [2]**Gig**, die; -, -s, *seltener* das; -s, -s (Sportruderboot; leichtes Beiboot)

[3]**Gig**, der; -s, -s ‹engl.› (Auftritt bei einem Pop- od. Jazzkonzert)

Gi|ga... ‹griech.› (das Milliardenfache einer Einheit, z. B. Gigameter = 10^9 Meter; *Zeichen* G)

Gi|gant, der; -en, -en (↑R 126) ‹griech.› (Riese); **gi|gan|tisch; Gi|gan|tis|mus**, der; - (übersteigerte Größensucht; *Med.* krankhafter Riesenwuchs); **Gi|gan|toma|chie**, die; - (Kampf der Giganten gegen Zeus); **Gi|gan|toma|nie**, die; - (Übertreibungssucht)

Gi|gerl, der, *auch* das; -s, -n (*bes. österr. für* Modegeck); **gi|gerlhaft**

Gig|li ['dʒilji] (↑R 130; ital. Sänger)

Gi|go|lo ['ʒi(:)...], der; -s, -s ‹franz.› (Eintänzer; *ugs. für* Hausfreund, ausgehaltener Mann)

Gi|got [ʒigo], das; -s, -s (*schweiz. für* Hammelkeule)

Gigue [ʒi:k], die; -, -n ['ʒi:gən] (ein alter Tanz)

gil|ben (*geh. für* gelb werden)

Gil|bert (m. Vorn.); **Gil|ber|ta** (w. Vorn.)

Gilb|hard, Gilb|hart, der; -s, -e (*alte Bez. für* Oktober)

Gil|de, die; -, -n (*bes. im MA.* Vereinigung bes. von Handwerkern u. Kaufleuten); **Gil|de‿haus, ...meis|ter; Gil|den|hal|le; Gilden|schaft**

Gi|let [ʒi'le:], das; -s, -s ‹franz.› (*österr. neben, schweiz. für* Weste)

Gil|ga|mesch (sagenhafter babylonischer Herrscher); **Gil|gamesch|epos** (↑R 95 *u.* 132)

Gil|ling, die; -, -s *u.* **Gil|lung**, die; -, -en (*Seemannsspr.* einwärts gebogene Seite des Rahsegels; nach innen gewölbter Teil des Hinterschiffs)

Gim|mick, der, *auch* das; -s, -s ‹engl.› (Werbegag, -geschenk)

Gim|pe, die; -, -n (mit Seide umsponnener Baumwollfaden)

Gim|pel, der; -s, - (ein Singvogel; *ugs. für* einfältiger Mensch)

Gin [dʒin], der; -s, -s ‹engl.› (Wacholderbranntwein); **Gin|fizz** *auch* **Gin-Fizz** ['dʒinfis] (↑R 33), der; -, - (ein Mixgetränk mit Gin)

Gin|gan ['giŋgan] ‹malai.› *u.* Gingham ['giŋəm] ‹engl.›, der; -s, -s (ein Baumwollstoff)

Gin|ger ['dʒindʒə(r)], der; -s, - ‹engl.› (*engl. Bez. für* Ingwer); **Gin|ger|ale** [...'e:l], das; -s (ein Erfrischungsgetränk)

Gink|go ['giŋko], *eindeutschende Schreibung:* **Gin|ko**, der; -s, -s ‹jap.› (ein in Japan u. China heimischer Zierbaum)

Gin|seng [*auch* 'ʒin...], der; -s, -s ‹chin.› (ostasiat. Pflanze mit heilkräftiger Wurzel)

Gins|ter, der; -s, - (ein Strauch)

Gin To|nic ['dʒin-], der; -[s], -s ‹engl.› (Gin mit Tonic)

gio|co|so [dʒo'ko:zo] ‹ital.› (*Musik* heiter, spaßhaft)

Giot|to ['dʒɔto] (ital. Maler)

Gio|van|ni [dʒo'vani] (m. Vorn.)

Gip|fel, der; -s, - (*schweiz. auch für* Hörnchen, Kipfel); **gip|fe|lig**, gipflig; **Gip|fel‿kon|fe|renz, ...kreuz** (Kreuz auf dem Berggipfel); **gip|feln; Gip|fel‿punkt, ...tref|fen; gipf|lig**, gip|fe|lig

Gips, der; -es, -e; **Gips‿ab|druck** (*Plur.* ...abdrücke), **...bein** (*ugs.*), **...büs|te; gip|sen**; du gipst; **Gipser; gip|sern** (aus Gips; gipsartig); **Gips‿fi|gur, ...manschet|te, ...ver|band**

Gi|pü|re, die; -, -n ‹franz.› (Klöppelspitze aus Gimpen)

Gi|raf|fe [*südd., österr.* ʒi...], die; -, -n ‹arab.› (langhalsiges Tier)

Gi|ran|do|la [dʒi...] ‹ital.› *u.* **Giran|do|le** [dʒi...], die; -, ...olen ‹franz.› (Feuergarbe beim Feuerwerk; Armleuchter); **Gi|rant** [ʒi...], der; -en, -en (↑R 126) ‹ital.› (*Bankw.* jmd., der einen Scheck od. einen Wechsel durch Giro auf einen anderen überträgt; Indossant); **Gi|rat**, der; -en, -en (↑R 126) *u.* **Gi|ra|tar**, der; -s, -e (Person, der bei der Übertragung eines Orderpapiers ein Indossament erteilt wurde)

Gi|rau|doux [ʒiro'du:] (franz. Schriftsteller); Giraudoux' [ʒiro'du:s] Werke (↑R 98)

gi|rie|ren ‹ital.› ([einen Wechsel] übertragen)

Girl [gœ:(r)l], das; -s, -s ‹engl.› (*scherzh. für* Mädchen; weibl. Mitglied einer Tanztruppe)

Gir|lan|de, die; -, -n ‹franz.› (Gewinde aus Laub, Blumen, buntem Papier o. Ä.)

Gir|litz, der; -es, -e (ein Singvogel)

Gi|ro ['ʒi:ro], das; -s, *Plur.* -s, *österr. auch* Giri ‹ital.› (Überweisung im bargeldlosen Zahlungsverkehr; Übertragungsvermerk eines Orderpapiers); **Gi|ro|bank** *Plur.* ...banken; **Gi|ro d'I|ta|lia** ['dʒi:ro di'ta:lia], der; - - (in Italien ausgetragenes Etappenrennen für Berufsradsportler); **Gi|ro‿kas|se** ['ʒi:ro...], **...kon|to**

Gi|ronde [ʒi'rɔ̃:d], die; - (Mündungstrichter der Garonne; franz. Departement); **Gi|rondist**, der; -en, -en *meist Plur.*; ↑R 126 (gemäßigter Republikaner der Franz. Revolution)

Gi|ro|ver|kehr ['ʒi:ro...] (bargeldloser Zahlungsverkehr)

gir|ren; die Taube girrt

gis, Gis, das; -, - (Tonbezeichnung); **gis** (*Zeichen für* gis-Moll); in gis

Gis|bert (m. Vorn.); **Gis|ber|ta** (w. Vorn.)

Gis|card d'Es|taing [ʒiskardɛs'tɛ̃:] (franz. Staatsmann)

gi|schen (*veraltet für* gischten); du gischst; **Gischt**, der; -[e]s, -e *u.* die; -, -en *Plur. selten* (Schaum; Sprühwasser, aufschäumende See); **gisch|ten**

Gi|se[h] ['gi:ze] (Stadt in Ägypten)

Gi|se|la [*österr.* gi'ze:la] (w. Vorn.); **Gi|sel|bert** (m. Vorn.); **Gi|selher, Gi|sel|mar** (m. Vorn.)

gis-Moll [*auch* 'gis'mɔl], das; - (Tonart; *Zeichen* gis); **gis-Moll-Ton|lei|ter** (↑R 28)

gis|sen (*Seemannsspr., Fliegerspr.* die Position eines Flugzeugs od. Schiffes schätzen)

Gi|tar|re, die; -, -n ‹span.› (ein Saiteninstrument); **Gi|tar|ren|spieler; Gi|tar|rist**, der; -en, -en (↑R 126); **Gi|tar|ris|tin**

Git|ta, Git|te (w. Vorn.)

Git|ter, das; -s, -; **Git|ter‿bettchen, ...fens|ter; git|tern** (*selten*); ich ...ere (↑R 16); **Git|ter‿netz, ...rost, ...span|nung** (*Elektronik*)

Glace [gla(:)s, *schweiz.* 'glasə], die; -, *Plur.* -s [gla(:)s], *schweiz.* -n ['glasən] ‹franz.› (Zuckerglasur; Gelee aus Fleischsaft; *schweiz.* Speiseeis); **Gla|cé**, *eindeutschende Schreibung* Glacee [gla'se:], der; -[s], -s (ein glänzendes Gewebe); **Gla|cé‿hand|schuh, ...leder; gla|cie|ren** [gla'si:...] (mit Glace überziehen; *veraltet für* zum Gefrieren bringen); **Gla|cis** [gla'si:], das; - [gla'si:(s)], - [gla'si:s] (*Milit.* Erdaufschüttung vor einem Festungsgraben, die keinen toten Winkel entstehen lässt)

Gla|di|a|tor, der; -s, ...oren ‹lat.› (altröm. Schwertkämpfer bei Zirkusspielen); **Gla|di|o|le,** die; -, -n (ein Schwertliliengewächs)

gla|go|li|tisch ‹slaw.›; -es Alphabet (kirchenslaw. Alphabet); **Gla|go|li|za,** die; - (die glagolitische Schrift)

Gla|mour ['glɛmə(r)], der *u.* das; -s ‹engl.› (Glanz, betörende Aufmachung); **Gla|mour|girl** (Reklame-, Filmschönheit)

Glans, die; -, Glandes [...de:s] ‹lat.› (*Med.* Eichel des Penis)

Glanz, der; -es, *Plur. (fachspr.)* -e; **Glanz|bürs|te; glän|zen;** du glänzt; **glän|zend;** glänzend schwarze Haare; seine Augen waren glänzend schwarz; **Glanz‿koh|le** *(Plur. selten),* **...le|der, ...leis|tung, ...licht** (*Plur.* ...lichter); **glanz|los; Glanz‿num|mer, ...pa|pier, ...punkt** (Höhepunkt), **...rol|le, ...stück; glanz|voll; Glanz|zeit**

Glar|ner; ↑R 103 ‹*zu* Glarus›; **Glar|ner Al|pen** *Plur.*; **glar|ne|risch; Gla|rus** (Kanton und Stadt in der Schweiz)

[1]**Glas,** das; -es, Gläser; zwei Glas Bier (↑R 90); ein Glas voll; Glas blasen; [2]**Glas,** das; -es, -en (*Seemannsspr.* halbe Stunde); **glas|ar|tig; Glas‿au|ge, ...bau|stein, ...blä|ser, ...blä|se|rei, ...blä|se|rin; Gläs|chen**

gla|sen (*Seemannsspr.* die halbe Stunde für die Schiffswache schlagen)

Gla|ser; Gla|se|rei; Gla|se|rin; Glä|ser|klang, der; -[e]s *(geh.);* **Gla|ser|meis|ter; glä|sern** (aus Glas, glasartig); **Glas|fa|ser; Glas|fa|ser|ka|bel; Glas|fi|ber|stab** *(Sport)*

Glas|gow ['gla:sgo:] (Stadt in Schottland)

Glas|har|fe; glas|hart; Glas‿haus, ...hüt|te; gla|sie|ren (mit Glasur versehen); **gla|sig; glas|klar; Glas|kopf,** der; -[e]s (Eisenerzart); **Glas|kör|per** (*Med.* gallertiger Teil des Auges); **Glas‿ma|ler, ...ma|le|rei, ...ma|le|rin**

Glas|nost, die; - ‹russ.› ([polit.] Offenheit)

Glas‿nu|del, ...per|le, ...rei|ni|ger, ...röh|re, ...schei|be, ...schrank, ...schüs|sel, ...split|ter, ...sturz (*Plur.* ...stürze; Glasglocke)

Glast, der; -[e]s (*veraltet, noch südd. für* Glanz); **glas|tig**

Glas|tür; Gla|sur, die; -, -en (glasiger Überzug, Schmelz; Zucker-, Schokoladenguss); **Glas|ver|si|che|rung; glas|wei|se; Glas|wol|le**

glatt; glatter, *auch* glätter, glatteste, *auch* glätteste; ein Brett [ganz] glatt hobeln; ich hob[e]le glatt; glatt gehobelt; glatt zu hobeln; glatt kämmen, legen, rühren, streichen usw.; glatt gehen (*ugs. für* ohne Komplikationen ablaufen); ich hoffe, dass alles glatt geht; es ist glatter gegangen, als ich dachte; *vgl. aber* glattmachen, glattstellen; ↑R 39; **Glät|te,** die; -; **Glatt|eis; Glatt|eis‿bil|dung, ...ge|fahr** (die; -); **glät|ten** (*landsch. u. schweiz. auch für* bügeln); **glat|ter|dings; Glät|te|rin** (*schweiz. für* Büglerin); **glatt ge|hen, ho|beln, käm|men** usw. *vgl.* glatt; **glatt|ma|chen** (*ugs. für* bezahlen); *vgl.* glatt; **glatt rüh|ren, schleifen** *vgl.* glatt; **Glätt|stahl** (*landsch. für* Bügeleisen); **glatt|stel|len** (*Kaufmannsspr.* ausgleichen); *vgl.* glatt; **Glatt|stel|lung; glatt strei|chen** *vgl.* glatt; **Glät|tung; glatt|weg; glatt zie|hen** *vgl.* glatt; **glatt|zün|gig; Glatt|zün|gig|keit,** die; -

Glat|ze, die; -, -n; **Glatz|kopf; glatz|köp|fig**

Glau|be, der; -ns, -n *Plur. selten;* jmdm. Glauben schenken; **glau|ben;** er wollte mich glauben machen, dass ...; **Glau|ben,** der; -s, - *Plur. selten* (*seltener für* Glaube); **Glau|bens‿ar|ti|kel, ...be|kennt|nis, ...din|ge** *(Plur.),* **...ei|fer, ...frei|heit, ...ge|mein|schaft, ...krieg, ...leh|re, ...sa|che, ...satz; glau|bens|stark; Glau|bens|streit; glau|bens|voll**

Glau|ber|salz, das; -es (Natriumsulfat)

glaub|haft; Glaub|haf|tig|keit, die; -; **gläu|big; Gläu|bi|ge,** der *u.* die; -n, -n (↑R 5 ff.); **Gläu|bi|ger,** der; -s, - (jmd., der berechtigt ist, von einem Schuldner Geld zu fordern); **Gläu|bi|ge|rin; Gläu|bi|ger|ver|samm|lung; Gläu|big|keit,** die; -; **glaub|lich;** kaum -; **glaub|wür|dig; Glaub|wür|dig|keit,** die; -

Glau|kom, das; -s, -e ‹griech.› (*Med.* grüner Star [Augenkrankheit]); **Glau|ko|nit** [*auch* ...'nit], der; -s, -e (Mineral)

gla|zi|al ‹lat.› (*Geol.* eiszeitlich, die Gletscher betreffend); **Gla|zi|al‿fau|na, ...flo|ra, ...see, ...zeit** (Vereisungszeit); **Gla|zi|o|lo|ge,** der; -n, -n (↑R 126) ‹lat.; griech.›; **Gla|zi|o|lo|gie,** die; - (Eis- u. Gletscherkunde); **gla|zi|o|lo|gisch**

Glei|bo|den ‹russ.; dt.› (*Geol.* feuchter, mineralischer Boden)

gleich; die Sonne ging gleich einem roten Ball unter; der gleiche Hut; die gleiche Jacke; das gleiche Spielzeug; *Großschreibung* (↑R 47): das Gleiche (dasselbe) tun; das Gleiche gilt ...; es kommt aufs Gleiche hinaus; Gleiches mit Gleichem vergelten; es kann uns Gleiches begegnen; ins Gleiche (in Ordnung) bringen; ein Gleiches tun; Gleicher unter Gleichen; Gleich und Gleich gesellt sich gern; *Schreibung in Verbindung mit Adjektiven, Verben und Partizipien* (↑R 39 f.:) gleich alt, groß, gut, lang, schnell, verteilt, wahrscheinlich, weit usw.; zwei gleich große Kinder; die Kinder waren gleich groß; gleich sein, werden; gleich denken, klingen, lauten; gleich denkende Menschen; gleich lautende Wörter; gleich geartete Verhältnisse; ein nicht nur ähnlich, sondern völlig gleich gelagerter Fall; gleich gesinnte Freunde; zwei gleich gestimmte Seelen; die Wörter werden gleich geschrieben; sie sind einander [völlig] gleich geblieben; er soll gleich (sofort) kommen; *vgl.* gleichkommen, gleichmachen, gleichsetzen, gleichstellen usw.; **gleich|al|te|rig, gleich|alt|rig; gleich|ar|tig;** Gleichartiges (↑R 47); **Gleich|ar|tig|keit,** die; -; **gleich|auf;** gleichauf liegen; **gleich|be|deu|tend** (dasselbe bedeutend); **Gleich|be|hand|lung; gleich|be|rech|tigt; Gleich|be|rech|ti|gung,** die; -; **gleich blei|ben** *vgl.* gleich; **gleich den|kend** *vgl.* gleich; **Glei|che,** die; -; etwas in die Gleiche bringen; **glei|chen** (gleich sein); du glichst; geglichen; gleich[e]!; **Glei|chen|fei|er** (*österr. für* Richtfest); **glei|chen|tags** (*schweiz. für* am selben Tage); **glei|cher|ge|stalt** *(veraltet);* **glei|cher|ma|ßen; glei|cher|wei|se; gleich|falls;** *vgl.* Fall, der; **gleich‿far|big, ...för|mig; Gleich|för|mig|keit,** die; -; **gleich ge|ar|tet, gelagert** *vgl.* gleich; **gleich|ge|schlecht|lich; gleich ge|sinnt** *vgl.* gleich; **Gleich|ge|sinn|te,** der *u.* die; -n, -n (↑R 5 ff. *u.* 47); **gleich gestimmt** *vgl.* gleich; **Gleich|ge|wicht,** das; -[e]s, -e; **gleich|ge|wich|tig; Gleich|ge|wichts‿la|ge, ...or|gan, ...sinn, ...stö|rung; gleich|gül|tig; Gleich|gül|tig|keit,** die; -; **Gleich|heit; Gleich|heits‿grund|satz, ...prin|zip, ...zei|chen** (*Zeichen* =); **Gleich|klang; gleich|kom|men;** ↑R 38 f. (entsprechen); das war einer Kampfansage gleichgekommen; *vgl. aber* gleich; **Gleich|lauf,** der; -[e]s *(Technik);* **gleich|lau|fend** (gleichzeitig, parallel); **gleich|läu|fig** *(Technik);* **Gleich|läu|fig|keit,** die; -; **gleich lau|tend** *vgl.* gleich; **gleich|ma|chen;** ↑R 38 f. (angleichen); dem Erdboden gleichmachen; *vgl.* gleich; **Gleich|macher; Gleich|ma|che|rei; gleich|ma|che|risch; Gleich|maß,** das; **gleich|mä|ßig; Gleich|mä|ßig|keit,** die; -; **Gleich|mut,** der; -[e]s, *selten* die; -; **gleich|mü|tig; Gleich|mü|tig|keit,** die; -; **gleich|na|mig; Gleich|na|mig|keit,** die; -; **Gleich|nis,** das; -ses, -se; **gleich|nis|haft; gleich|nis|wei|se; gleich|ran|gig; Gleich|rich|ter** *(Elektrotechnik);* **gleich|sam;** -[,] als ob/wenn (↑R 89); **gleich|schal|ten;** ↑R 38 f. (auf eine einheitliche Linie bringen); *vgl.* gleich; **Gleich|schal|tung; gleich|schen|ke|lig, gleich|schenk|lig; Gleich|schritt,** der; -[e]s; im -; **gleich|se|hen** (ähneln); **gleich sein; gleich|sei|tig; Gleich|sei|tig|keit,** die; -; **gleich|set|zen;** ↑R 38 f.; etwas mit einer Sache gleichsetzen; *vgl.* gleich; **Gleich|set|zung; Gleich|set|zungs⌣ak|ku|sa|tiv** (*Sprachw.* Gleichsetzungsglied neben einem Akkusativobjekt, z. B. er nennt mich „einen Lügner"), **...no|mi|na|tiv** (*Sprachw.* Ergänzung im Nominativ, z. B. er ist „ein Lügner"), **...satz** *(Sprachw.);* **Gleich|stand,** der; -[e]s; **gleich|ste|hen;** ↑R 38 f. (gleich sein); *vgl.* gleich; **gleich|stel|len;** ↑R 38 f. (auf die gleiche Stufe stellen); *vgl.* gleich; **Gleich|stel|lung; gleich|stim|mig; Gleich|strom; Gleich|strom|ma|schi|ne; gleich|tun;** ↑R 38 f. (nacheifern); es jmdm. gleichtun; *vgl.* gleich; **Glei|chung; gleich|viel;** gleichviel[,] ob/wann/wo (↑R 88); gleichviel[,] ob du kommst, *aber* wir haben gleich viel; **gleich wer|den; gleich|wer|tig; Gleich|wer|tig|keit,** die; -; **gleich|wie; gleich|win|ke|lig, gleich|wink|lig; gleich|wohl;** *aber* wir befinden uns alle gleich (in gleicher Weise) wohl; **gleich|zei|tig; Gleich|zei|tig|keit,** die; -; **gleich|zie|hen;** ↑R 38 f. (auf den gleichen Leistungsstand kommen); *vgl.* gleich

Gleis, das; -es, -e; **Gleis⌣an|schluss, ...ar|bei|ter, ...bau** (der; -[e]s), **...bett** (Unterlage aus Schotter für Gleise), **...drei|eck**

Gleis|ner *(veraltet für* Heuchler); **Gleis|ne|rei,** die; -; **gleis|ne|risch**

Glei|ße, die; -, -n *(landsch. für* Hundspetersilie); **glei|ßen** (glänzen, glitzern); du gleißt; du gleißtest; gegleißt; gleiß[e]!

Gleit⌣bahn, ...boot; glei|ten; du glittst; geglitten; gleit[e]!; gleitende Arbeitszeit, Lohnskala; **Glei|ter** *(Flugw.);* **Gleit⌣flä|che, ...flug, ...klau|sel, ...schie|ne, ...schuh, ...schutz** (der; -es); **gleit|si|cher; Gleit|zeit**

Glen|check [ˈglɛntʃɛk], der; -[s], -s ‹engl.› (ein Gewebe; großflächiges Karomuster)

Glet|scher, der; -s, -; **glet|scher|ar|tig; Glet|scher⌣brand, ...feld, ...milch** (die; -; milchig-trübes Schmelzwasser des Gletschers), **...müh|le** (ausgespülter Schacht im Eis oder Fels), **...schliff, ...spal|te, ...sturz, ...tor** (Austrittsstelle des Gletscherbaches), **...zun|ge**

Gle|ve [ˈgle:fə], die; -, -n ‹franz.› (eine mittelalterl. Waffe)

Glib|ber, der; -s *(nordd. für* glitschige Masse); **glib|be|rig**

Glied, das; -[e]s, -er; **Glie|der|fü|ßer** *(für* Arthropoden); **...glie|de|rig, ...glied|rig** (z. B. zweigliederig, zweigliedrig, *mit Ziffer* 2-gliederig, 2-gliedrig; ↑R 44); **Glie|der|kak|tus; glie|der|lahm; glie|dern;** ich ...ere (↑R 16); **Glie|der⌣pup|pe, ...rei|ßen, ...schmerz, ...tier** *(Zool.);* **Glie|de|rung; Glied|ma|ße,** die; -, -n *meist Plur.;* **...glied|rig** *vgl.* ...gliederig; **Glied⌣satz** *(Sprachw.),* **...staat** *(Plur.* ...staaten); **glied|wei|se**

glim|men; es glomm, *auch* glimmte; es glömme, *auch* glimmte; geglommen, *auch* geglimmt; glimm[e]!; **Glim|mer,** der; -s, - (eine Mineralgruppe); **glim|me|rig** *vgl.* glimmrig; **glim|mern; Glim|mer|schie|fer; Glimm|lam|pe; glimm|rig,** glim|me|rig *(veraltend);* **Glimm|stän|gel** *(scherzh. für* Zigarette)

glimpf|lich

Gli|om, das; -s, -e ‹griech.› (*Med.* Geschwulst im Gehirn, Rückenmark od. an der Netzhaut des Auges)

Glis|sa|de, die; -, -n ‹franz.› (Gleitschritt beim Tanzen); **glis|san|do** ‹ital.› (*Musik* gleitend); **Glis|san|do,** das; -s, *Plur.* -s *u.* ...di

Glitsch|bahn; Glit|sche, die; -, -n *(landsch. für* Schlitterbahn); **glit|schen** *(ugs. für* schlittern); du glitschst; **glit|sche|rig, glit|schig, glitsch|rig** *(ugs. für* glatt, rutschig)

Glit|zer, der; -s, -; **glit|ze|rig, glitz|rig; glit|zern**

glo|bal ‹lat.› (auf die ganze Erde bezüglich; umfassend; allgemein); **glo|ba|li|sie|ren** (weltweit ausrichten); **Glo|bal|sum|me; Glo|be|trot|ter,** der; -s, - ‹engl.› (Weltenbummler); **Glo|bin,** das; -s ‹lat.› (*Med., Biol.* Eiweißbestandteil des Hämoglobins); **Glo|bu|lin,** das; -s, -e (Eiweißkörper); **Glo|bus,** der; *Gen.* - *u.* ...busses, *Plur.* ...ben *u. (bereits häufiger)* ...busse ‹lat., „Kugel"› (Nachbildung der Himmelskörper, bes. der Erde)

Glöck|chen; Glo|cke, die; -, -n; **Glo|cken⌣ap|fel, ...blu|me; glo|cken|för|mig; Glo|cken⌣ge|läut** *od.* **...ge|läu|te, ...gie|ßer, ...gie|ße|rei, ...guss, ...hei|de** (die; -; Heidekraut, Erika); **glo|cken|hell; Glo|cken⌣klang, ...läu|ten, ...man|tel, ...rock, ...schlag, ...spiel, ...stuhl, ...ton, ...turm; glo|ckig; Glöck|lein; Glöck|ner**

Glogg|nitz (österr. Stadt)

[1]**Glo|ria,** das; -s *u.* die; - ‹lat.› (*meist iron. für* Ruhm, Ehre); mit Glanz und -; [2]**Glo|ria,** das; -s (Lobgesang in der kath. Messe); **Glo|rie** [...iə], die; -, -n (*geh. für* Ruhm, Glanz; Heiligenschein); **Glo|ri|en|schein; Glo|ri|fi|ka|ti|on,** die; -, -en (Verherrlichung); **glo|ri|fi|zie|ren; Glo|ri|fi|zie|rung; Glo|ri|o|le,** die; -, -n (Heiligenschein); **glo|ri|os** (ruhmvoll); **glor|reich**

glo|sen *(landsch. für* glühen, glimmen); es glos|te

Glos|sar, das; -s, -e ‹griech.› (Sammlung von Glossen; Wörterverzeichnis [mit Erklärungen]); **Glos|sa|tor,** der; -s, ...oren (Verfasser von Glossen); **Glos|se** [*fachspr. auch* ˈglo:sə], die; -, -n (Erläuterung zu einem erklärungsbedürftigen Ausdruck innerhalb eines Textes; spöttische [Rand]bemerkung; [polemischer] Kommentar zu aktuellen Problemen); **glos|sie|ren; Glos|so|la|lie,** die; - ‹griech.› (*Psych.* das Hervorbringen unverständlicher Laute in religiöser Ekstase)

Glot|tal, der; -s, -e ‹griech.› (*Sprachw.* Stimmritzenlaut, Kehlkopflaut); **Glot|tis,** die; -, Glottides [...de:s] (Stimmapparat, Stimmritze); **Glot|tis|schlag**

Glotz|au|ge; glotz|äu|gig; Glot|ze, die; -, -n *(ugs. für* Fernsehgerät); **glot|zen** *(ugs.);* du glotzt; **Glotz|kopf** *(ugs.)*

Glo|xi|nie [...iə], die; -, -n ‹nach dem Arzt Gloxin› (eine Zimmerpflanze)
glub|schen *vgl.* glupschen
gluck!; gluck, gluck!
Gluck (dt. Komponist)
Glück, das; -[e]s, -e *(Plur. selten);* jmdm. Glück wünschen; eine Glück bringende, verheißende Nachricht; **Glück|ab,** das; -s; **Glück ab!** (Fliegergruß); **Glück-auf,** das; -s; er rief ihm ein Glückauf zu; **Glück auf!** (Bergmannsgruß); **Glück brin|gend** *vgl.* Glück
Glu|cke, die; -, -n; **glu|cken** *(ugs. auch für* untätig herumsitzen)
glü|cken
glu|ckern; ich ...ere (↑R 16)
glück|haft
Gluck|hen|ne
glück|lich; glück|li|cher|wei|se; glück|los; Glück|sa|che, die; - *(svw.* Glückssache); **Glücks-‿brin|ger, ...bu|de; glück|se|lig; Glück|se|lig|keit**
gluck|sen; du gluckst
Glücks‿fall (der), **...fee, ...ge|fühl, ...göt|tin, ...kä|fer, ...kind, ...pfen|nig, ...pilz, ...rad, ...rit|ter, ...sa|che** (die; -), **...schwein, ...spiel, ...stern** (der; -s), **...sträh|ne** (die; -), **...tag; glück|strah|lend** (↑R 40); **Glücks‿tref|fer, ...um|stand, ...zahl; Glück|wunsch; Glück|wunsch‿kar|te, ...te|le|gramm; Glück zu!; Glück|zu,** das; -
Glu|co|se *vgl.* Glukose
Glüh|bir|ne; glü|hen; glü|hend; ein glühender Verehrer; ein glühend heißes Eisen; das Eisen ist glühend heiß; **glüh|heiß; Glüh-‿hit|ze** *(vgl.* Gluthitze), **...lam|pe, ...strumpf, ...wein, ...würm|chen**
Glu|ko|se, *chem. fachspr.* Glu|co|se, die; - ‹griech.› (Traubenzucker)
Glum|pert, Klum|pert, das; -s *(österr. ugs. für* wertloses Zeug)
Glum|se, die; - *(landsch. für* Quark)
Glupsch|au|ge *meist Plur.;* **glup|schen** *(nordd. für* mit großen Augen starr blicken); du glupschst
Glut, die; -, -en
Glu|ta|mat (↑R 132), das; -[e]s, -e ‹lat.› (Würzzusatz bei Suppen u. Konserven); **Glu|ta|min|säu|re**
glut|äu|gig *(geh.)*
Glu|ten, das; -s (Kleber)
Glut|hit|ze
Glu|tin, das; -s ‹lat.› (Eiweißstoff)
Gly|ce|rin *vgl.* Glyzerin; **Gly|ce|rol** *vgl.* Glyzerin; **Gly|kä|mie** (↑R 132), die; - ‹griech.› (Zuckergehalt des Blutes); **Gly|ko|gen,** das; -s (tierische Stärke); **Gly|kol,** das; -s, -e (ein Frostschutz- u. Lösungsmittel); **Gly|ko|se,** die; - *(ältere Form für* Glukose); **Gly|ko|sid,** das; -[e]s, -e *(Chemie* eine zuckerhaltige Verbindung); **Gly|kos|u|rie,** die; -, ...ien *(Med.* Zuckerausscheidung im Harn)
Glyp|te, die; -, -n ‹griech.› (geschnittener Stein; Skulptur); **Glyp|tik,** die; - (Steinschneidekunst); **Glyp|to|thek,** die; -, -en (Sammlung von geschnittenen Steinen od. [antiken] Skulpturen)
Gly|san|tin ®, das; -s (ein Frostschutzmittel); **Gly|ze|rin,** *chem. fachspr.* Gly|ce|rin *u.* Gly|ce|rol [*beide* ...ts...], das; -s ‹griech.› (dreiwertiger Alkohol); **Gly|ze|rin|sei|fe; Gly|zi|ne, Gly|zi|nie** [...iə], die; -, -n (ein Kletterstrauch)
G-Man [ˈdʒi:mɛn], der; -[s], G-Men ‹amerik. Kurzw. aus government man = Regierungsmann› (Sonderagent des FBI)
GmbH = Gesellschaft mit beschränkter Haftung; **GmbH-Gesetz**
GMD = Generalmusikdirektor
g-Moll [ˈge:mɔl, *auch* ˈge:ˈmɔl], das; - (Tonart; *Zeichen* g); **g-Moll-Ton|lei|ter** (↑R 28)
Gmünd (österr. Stadt)
Gmun|den (österr. Stadt)
Gna|de, die; -, -n; von Gottes Gnaden; Euer Gnaden *(veraltet; vgl.* [1]euer); **gna|den** *(veraltet für* gnädig sein); *heute nur noch im Konjunktiv Präsens:* gnade dir Gott!; **Gna|den‿akt, ...be|weis, ...brot** (das; -[e]s), **...er|lass, ...frist, ...ge|such, ...hoch|zeit** (siebzigster Hochzeitstag); **gna|den|los; gna|den|reich; Gna|den|stoß; gna|den|voll; Gna|den|weg,** der; -[e]s; **gnä|dig**
Gna|gi, das; -s *(schweiz. für* gepökelte Teile von Kopf, Beinen und Schwanz des Schweines)
Gnatz, der; -es, -e *(landsch. für* üble Laune); **gnat|zen** *(landsch. für* mürrisch, übellaunig sein); du gnatzt; **gnat|zig** *(landsch.)*
Gneis, der; -es, -e (ein Gestein)
Gnei|se|nau (preuß. Generalfeldmarschall)
gnei|ßen *(österr. ugs. für* merken, durchschauen); du gneißt
Gnit|te, Gnit|ze, die; -, -n *(nordd. für* kleine Mücke)
Gnom, der; -en, -en; ↑R 126 (Kobold; Zwerg)
Gno|me, die; -, -n ‹griech.› (lehrhafter [Sinn-, Denk]spruch)
gno|men|haft
Gno|mi|ker ‹griech.› (Verfasser von [Sinn-, Denk]sprüchen); **gno|misch;** -er Dichter (Spruchdichter); **Gno|mon,** der; -s, ...mone (antikes astronom. Instrument [Sonnenuhr]); **Gno|sis,** die; - ([Gottes]erkenntnis; Wissen um göttliche Geheimnisse); **Gnos|tik,** die; - (Lehre der Gnosis); **Gnos|ti|ker; gnos|tisch; Gnos|ti|zis|mus,** der; -
Gnu, das; -s, -s ‹hottentott.› (ein Steppenhuftier)
Go, das; - (ein jap. Brettspiel)
Goa (ind. Bundesstaat)
Goal [go:l], das; -s, -s ‹engl.› *(veraltet, aber noch österr. u. schweiz. für* Tor [beim Fußball]); **Goal|get|ter** *(bes. österr. u. schweiz. für* Torschütze); **Goa|lie,** *auch* Goa|li [ˈgo:li], der; -s, -s *(schweiz. Sportspr.* Torhüter); **Goal‿kee|per** *(bes. österr. u. schweiz. für* Torhüter), **...mann** *(Plur.* ...männer; *bes. österr. u. schweiz. für* Torhüter)
Go|be|lin [gɔbəˈlɛ̃:], der; -s, -s ‹franz.› (Wandteppich mit eingewirkten Bildern)
Go|bi, die; - ‹mong.› (Wüste in Innerasien)
Go|ckel, der; -s, - *(bes. südd. für* Hahn); *vgl. auch* Gickel; **Go|ckel|hahn**
Go|de *(Nebenform von* Gote [Pate]); **Go|del,** Godl, die; -, -n *(südd. u. österr. für* Patin)
Gode|mi|ché [go:tmiˈʃe:], der; -, -s ‹franz.› (künstlich nachgebildeter erigierter Penis)
Go|den, die; -, - *(svw.* Godel)
Go|der, der; -s, - *(österr. ugs. für* Doppelkinn); **Go|derl,** das; -s, -n; jmdm. das - kratzen *(österr. ugs. für* jmdm. schöntun)
Godl *vgl.* Godel
Godt|håb [ˈgɔdhɔ:b] (Hptst. von Grönland)
Goes [gø:s] (dt. Schriftsteller)
Goe|the [ˈgø:...] (dt. Dichter); **Goe|the|a|num,** das; -s (Tagungs- und Aufführungsgebäude in Dornach bei Basel); **Goe|the|band,** der; -[e]s, ...bände (↑R 95); **goe|the|freund|lich** (↑R 96); **Goe|the|haus,** das; -es (↑R 95); **goe|thesch,** goe|thisch; goethesche *od.* goethische Dramen; ihm gelangen Verse von goethescher *od.* goethischer Klarheit (↑R 94); **Goe|the-und-Schil|ler-Denk|mal** (↑R 95); **goe|thisch** *vgl.* goethesch
Gof, der *od.* das; -s, -en *(schweiz. für* [kleines, ungezogenes] Kind)
Gog (König im A.T.); - und Magog

Gogh, van [fan 'gɔx, *auch* fan 'go:k] (niederl. Maler)
Go-go-Girl, das; -s, -s ‹amerik.› (Vortänzerin in Tanzlokalen)
Go|gol ['go:..., *auch* 'gɔ...] (russ. Schriftsteller)
Goi, der; -[s], Gojim [*auch* go'ji:m] ‹hebr.› (jüd. Bez. des Nichtjuden)
Go-in [go:'in], das; -[s], -s ‹engl.› (unbefugtes [gewaltsames] Eindringen demonstrierender Gruppen, meist um eine Diskussion zu erzwingen)
Go|kart ['go:...], der; -[s], -s ‹engl.› (niedriger, unverkleideter kleiner Sportrennwagen)
go|keln (*mitteld. für* mit Feuer spielen); ich ...[e]le (↑R 16); *vgl.* kokeln
Gold, das; -[e]s (chem. Element, Edelmetall; *Zeichen* Au); etwas ist - wert; *vgl.* Aurum; **gold|ähnlich; Gold‿am|mer** (ein Singvogel), **...am|sel** (Pirol), **...bar|ren, ...barsch; gold|blond; Gold‿bro|kat, ...bron|ze; Gold|doub|lé** [...du'ble:], **Gold|dub|lee** (↑R 130); **gol|den;** goldene Hochzeit; goldene Worte; den goldenen Mittelweg einschlagen; goldenes Tor (*Sportspr.* den Sieg entscheidendes Tor); der goldene Schnitt *(Math.)*; das goldene Zeitalter (*vgl.* saturnisch); *Großschreibung* (↑R 102 *u.* 108:) die Goldene Aue (Gebiet zwischen Harz u. Kyffhäuser); das Goldene Buch (einer Stadt); die Goldene Bulle; die Goldene Rose; Goldener Sonntag (*früher* letzter Sonntag vor Weihnachten); die Goldene Stadt (Prag); das Goldene Kalb *(bibl.)*; das Goldene Vlies (*vgl.* Vlies); die Goldenen Zwanziger; **Gol|den De|li|ci|ous** ['go:ld(ə)n di'liʃəs], der; - -, - - ‹engl.› (eine Apfelsorte); **gold‿far|ben, ...far|big; Gold‿fa|san, ...fisch; gold|gelb** (↑R 40); **gold|ge|rän|dert; Gold‿grä|ber, ...gru|be; gold|haa|rig; Gold|hähn|chen** (ein Singvogel); **gold|hal|tig,** *österr.* **gold|häl|tig; Gold‿hams|ter, ...ha|se** (ein Nagetier); **gol|dig; Gold‿jun|ge, ...klum|pen, ...kro|ne, ...küs|te** (die; -; in Westafrika), **...lack** (der; -s; eine Blume), **...le|gie|rung, ...leis|te, ...ma|cher, ...me|dail|le, ...mi|ne, ...mull** (der; -s, -e; ein maulwurfähnlicher Insektenfresser), **...mün|ze**
Gol|do|ni (ital. Dramatiker)
Gold‿pa|pier, ...par|mä|ne (die; -, -n; eine Apfelsorte), **...preis, ...rand, ...rausch, ...re|gen** (ein Strauch, Baum), **...re|ser|ve; gold|rich|tig** *(ugs.)*; **Gold‿ring, ...schmied, ...schmie|din, ...schnitt** *(Buchw.)*, **...stern** (ein Liliengewächs), **...stück, ...waa|ge, ...wäh|rung, ...wert** (der; -[e]s), **...zahn**
Go|lem, der; -s ‹hebr.› (durch Zauber zum Leben erweckte menschl. Tonfigur der jüd. Sage)
¹Golf, der; -[e]s, -e ‹griech.› (größere Meeresbucht); der Persische Golf
²Golf, das; -s ‹schott.-engl.› (ein Rasenspiel); Golf spielen (↑R 39); **gol|fen** (*ugs. für* Golf spielen); **Gol|fer,** der; -s, - (Golfspieler)
Golf‿krieg, ...kri|se
Golf‿platz, ...schlä|ger, ...schuh, ...spiel
Golf|strom, der; -[e]s
Gol|ga|tha, *ökum.* **Gol|go|ta** ‹hebr., „Schädelstätte"› (Hügel vor dem alten Jerusalem)
¹Go|li|ath, *ökum.* Go|li|at (Riese im A.T.); **²Go|li|ath,** der; -s, -s (riesiger Mensch)
Göl|ler, das; -s, - (*schweiz. für* Schulterpasse)
Go|lo (m. Vorn.)
Go|mor|rha, *ökum.* **Go|mor|ra** *vgl.* Sodom
gon = Gon; **Gon,** das; -s, -e ‹griech.› (in der Geodäsie verwendete Einheit für [ebene] Winkel [1 gon = 100. Teil eines rechten Winkels], früher auch Neugrad genannt [*vgl.* Grad]; *Zeichen* gon); 5 Gon (↑R 90)
Go|na|de, die; -, -n ‹griech.› (*Med., Biol.* Keimdrüse)
Go|nag|ra (↑R 130), das; -s ‹griech.› (*Med.* Gicht im Kniegelenk)
Gon|del, die; -, -n ‹ital.› (langes, schmales venezianisches Ruderboot; Korb am Luftballon; Kabine am Luftschiff); **gon|deln** (*ugs. für* [gemächlich] fahren); ich ...[e]le (↑R 16); **Gon|do|lie|re,** der; -, ...ri (Gondelführer)
Gong, der, *selten* das; -s, -s ‹malai.›; **gon|gen;** es gongt; **Gong|schlag**
Go|ni|o|me|ter, das; -s, - ‹griech.› (Winkelmesser); **Go|ni|o|met|rie** (↑R 130), die; - (Winkelmessung)
gön|nen; Gön|ner; gön|ner|haft; Gön|ner|haf|tig|keit, die; -; **Gön|ne|rin; gön|ne|risch** (*selten für* gönnerhaft); **Gön|ner|mie|ne**
Go|no|kok|kus, der; -, ...kken *meist Plur.* ‹griech.› (eine Bakterienart [Trippererreger]); **Go|nor|rhö**[1], **Go|nor|rhöe** [...'rø:], die; -, ...rrhöen (Tripper); **go|nor|rho|isch**

[1] *Vgl. die Anmerkung zu* „Diarrhö, Diarrhöe".

good|bye! [gud'bai] ‹engl., „auf Wiedersehen!"›
Good|will ['gudwil], der; -s ‹engl.› (Ansehen; Wohlwollen, freundliche Gesinnung; Firmen-, Geschäftswert); **Good|will|rei|se**
Gö|pel, der; -s, - (alte Drehvorrichtung zum Antrieb von Arbeitsmaschinen durch im Kreis herumgehende Menschen od. Tiere); **Gö|pel|werk**
Gör, das; -[e]s, -en *u.* Gö|re, die; -, -n (*nordd. für* [kleines] Kind; ungezogenes Mädchen)
Go|ral|le, der; -n, -n (Angehöriger der poln. Bergbevölkerung in den Beskiden u. der Tatra)
Gor|bat|schow [gɔrba'tʃɔf] (↑R 132; sowjet. Staatsmann)
Gor|ding, die; -, -s (*Seemannsspr.* Tau zum Zusammenholen der Segel)
gor|disch; der [berühmte] Gordische Knoten; ein [beliebiger] gordischer (unauflösbarer) Knoten
Gor|don ['gɔ:(r)d(ə)n] (m. Vorn.)
Gö|re *vgl.* Gör
Gor|go, die; -, ...gonen (weibl. Ungeheuer der griech. Sage); **Gor|go|nen|haupt**
Gor|gon|zo|la, der; -s, -s ‹nach dem gleichnamigen ital. Ort› (ein Käse)
Go|ril|la, der; -s, -s ‹afrik.› (größter Menschenaffe; *ugs. für* Leibwächter)
Go|ri|zia (*ital. Form von* Görz)
¹Gor|ki (russ. Schriftsteller); **²Gor|ki** *vgl.* Nischni Nowgorod
Gör|litz (Stadt an der Neiße)
Gör|res (dt. Publizist)
Görz (ital. Stadt); *vgl.* Gorizia
Gösch, die; -, -en ‹niederl.› (*Seemannsspr.* kleine rechteckige Nationalflagge; andersfarbiges Obereck am Flaggenstock)
Go|sche, Gu|sche, die; -, -n (*landsch. für* Mund)
Go|se, die; -, -n (*mitteld. für* obergäriges Bier)
Gos|lar (Stadt am Nordrand des Harzes)
Go-slow [go:'slo:], der *u.* das; -s, -s ‹engl.› (Bummelstreik)
Gos|pel, das *od.* der; -s, -s *u.* **Gos|pel|song** (religiöses Lied der Afroamerikaner)
Gos|po|dar *vgl.* Hospodar; **Gos|po|din,** der; -s, ...da ‹russ., „Herr"› (russ. Anrede)
Gos|se, die; -, -n
Gös|sel, das; -s, -[n] (*nordd. für* Gänseküken)
¹Go|te, der; -n, -n; ↑R 126 (*landsch. für* Pate); **²Go|te,** die; -,

-n (*landsch. für* Patin); *vgl. auch* Gotte *u.* Gode
³Go|te, der; -n, -n; ↑R 126 (Angehöriger eines germ. Volkes)
Gö|te|borg (Hafenstadt an der Südwestküste Schwedens)
¹Go|tha (Stadt im Thüringer Becken); **²Go|tha,** der; - (Adelskalender); **Go|tha|er** (↑R 103); **go|tha|isch**
Go|tik, die; - ‹franz.› (Kunststil vom 12. bis 15. Jh.; Zeit des got. Stils); **go|tisch** (den Goten gemäß; im Stil der Gotik, die Gotik betreffend); **¹Go|tisch,** die; - ‹*zu* Gotik› (eine Schriftart); **²Go|tisch,** das; -[s] ‹*zu* ³Gote› (Sprache); *vgl.* Deutsch; **Go|ti|sche,** das; -n; *vgl.* Deutsche, das; **Got|land** (schwed. Ostseeinsel)
Gott, der; *Gen.* -es, *selten in festen Wendungen* -s (z. B. Gotts Wunder!), *Plur.* Götter; um Gottes willen; in Gottes Namen; Gott sei Dank! Gott befohlen!; weiß Gott!; Gott[,] der Herr[,] hat ...; grüß [dich] Gott!; **gott|ähn|lich; Gott|ähn|lich|keit,** die; -; **gott|be|gna|det; gott|be|wah|re!** *(ugs.), aber* Gott bewahre uns davor!
Got|te, die; -, -n (*schweiz. mdal. für* Patin)
Gott|er|bar|men; *in* zum - (*ugs. für* jämmerlich [schlecht]); **Göt|ter˯bild, ...bo|te, ...däm|me|rung, ...gat|te** *(scherzh.)*; **gott|er|ge|ben; göt|ter|gleich; Göt|ter˯spei|se** (*auch* eine Süßspeise), **...trank; Got|tes˯acker** (↑R 132; *landsch. für* Friedhof), **...an|be|te|rin** (eine Heuschreckenart), **...be|weis, ...dienst, ...furcht; got|tes|fürch|tig; Got|tes˯ga|be, ...ge|richt; Got|tes|gna|de;** es ist eine -, *aber in Titeln:* von Gottes Gnaden König ...; **Got|tes|gna|den|tum,** das; -s; **Got|tes˯haus, ...kind|schaft** (die; -); **got|tes|läs|ter|lich; Got|tes˯läs|te|rung, ...leug|ner, ...lohn** (der; -[e]s), **...mann** (*Plur.* ...männer), **...mut|ter** (die; -), **...sohn** (der; -[e]s), **...ur|teil; Gott|fried** (m. Vorn.); **gott˯ge|fäl|lig, ...ge|wollt, ...gläu|big; ¹Gott|hard** (m. Vorn.); **²Gott|hard,** der; -s (*kurz für* Sankt Gotthard); **Gott|hard|bahn,** die; -; **Gott|heit; ¹Gott|helf** (m. Vorn.)
²Gott|helf (schweiz. Schriftsteller)
Gott|hold (m. Vorn.)
Göt|ti, der; -s, - (*schweiz. mdal. für* Pate)
Göt|tin
Göt|tin|gen (Stadt a. d. Leine); **Göt|tin|ger** (↑R 103)
gött|lich; die göttliche Gnade, *aber* (↑R 108): die Göttliche Komödie (von Dante); **Gött|lich|keit,** die; -; **Gott|lieb** (m. Vorn.); **gott|lob!; Gott|lob** (m. Vorn.); **gott|los; Gott|lo|se,** der *u.* die; -n, -n (↑R 5 ff.); **Gott|lo|sig|keit; Gott|mensch,** der; -en (Christus); **Gott|schalk** (m. Vorn.)
Gott|sched (dt. Gelehrter u. Schriftsteller)
Gott|sei|bei|uns [*auch* ...'zai...], der; - (*verhüllend für* Teufel); **gott|se|lig** *(veraltend)*; **Gott|se|lig|keit,** die; - *(veraltend)*; **gotts˯er|bärm|lich, ...jäm|mer|lich; Gott|su|cher; Gott|va|ter,** der; -s *meist ohne Artikel*; **gott|ver|dammt** *(derb)*; ein -er Feigling; **gott|ver|las|sen; Gott|ver|trau|en; gott|voll; Gott|wald** (m. Vorn.); **Gott|we|sen,** das; -s (Gott); **Götz** (m. Vorn.); **Göt|ze,** der; -n, -n; ↑R 126 (Abgott); **Göt|zen˯al|tar, ...bild, ...die|ner, ...dienst** (der; -es)
Gou|ache [gu'a(:)ʃ], die; -, -n ‹franz.› (Malerei mit Wasserdeckfarben *[nur Sing.]*; Bild in dieser Maltechnik); *vgl.* Guasch
¹Gou|da ['xauda] (niederl. Stadt bei Rotterdam); **²Gou|da** ['gauda], der; -s, -s *u.* **Gou|da|kä|se,** der; -s, - (ein Schnittkäse)
Goud|ron [gu'drɔ̃:] (↑R 130), der, *auch* das; -s ‹arab.-franz.› (wasserdichter Anstrich)
Gou|nod [gu'no:] (franz. Komponist)
Gourde [gurd], der; -, -s [gurd] ‹franz.› (Währungseinheit in Haiti; *Abk.* G; 1 Gourde = 100 Centimes); 10 - (↑R 90)
Gour|mand [gur'mã:], der; -s, -s ‹franz., „Vielfraß"› (Schlemmer); **Gour|man|di|se** [gurmã'di:zə], die; -, -n (Leckerbissen); **Gour|met** [gur'mɛ, *auch* ...'me:], der; -s, -s (Feinschmecker)
gou|tie|ren [gu'ti:...] ‹franz.› (Geschmack an etwas finden)
Gou|ver|nan|te [guvɛr...], die; -, -n ‹franz.› (*veraltet für* Erzieherin); **gou|ver|nan|ten|haft; Gou|ver|ne|ment** [...'mã:], das; -s, -s (Regierung; Verwaltung, Verwaltungsbezirk); **gou|ver|ne|men|tal** [...mã'ta:l] (*schweiz., sonst veraltet für* regierungsfreundlich; Regierungs...); **Gou|ver|neur** [...'nø:r], der; -s, -e (Statthalter)
Go|ya ['go(:)ja] (span. Maler)
GPU, die; - ‹*Abk. aus* russ. Gossudarstwennoje polititscheskoje uprawlenije = staatliche politische Verwaltung› (sowjet. Geheimpolizei bis 1934)
Gr. = Greenwich
Gr.-2° = Großfolio
Gr.-4° = Großquart
Gr.-8° = Großoktav
Grab, das; -[e]s, Gräber
Grab|be (dt. Dichter)
Grab|bei|ga|be
Grab|be|lei; grab|beln (*nordd. für* herumtasten); ich ...[e]le (↑R 16); *vgl. aber* krabbeln; **Grab|bel˯sack** *(ugs.)*, **...tisch** *(ugs.)*
Gräb|chen; Gra|be|land, das; -[e]s (kleingärtnerisch genutztes Brachland; künftiges Bauland); **gra|ben;** du gräbst; du grubst; du grübest; gegraben; grab[e]!; **Graben,** der; -s, Gräben; *Schreibung in Straßennamen:* ↑R 123; **Grä|ber; Grä|ber|feld; Gra|bes˯käl|te, ...kir|che** (in Jerusalem), **...ru|he, ...stil|le, ...stim|me; Grab˯ge|sang, ...ge|wöl|be, ...hü|gel, ...kam|mer; Grab|le|gung; Gräb|lein; Grab˯mal** (*Plur.* ...mäler, *geh.* ...male), **...plat|te, ...re|de, ...schän|dung, ...scheit** (*landsch. für* Spaten)
grab|schen *vgl.* grapschen; **Grab|scher;** der; -s, - *(abwertend)*; *vgl.* Grapscher
Grab˯spruch, ...stät|te, ...stein, ...stel|le, ...stel|le, ...sti|chel (ein Werkzeug); **Gra|bung**
Grac|che ['graxə], der; -n, -n *meist Plur.* (Angehöriger eines altröm. Geschlechtes)
Grace [gre:s] (w. Vorn.)
Gracht, die; -, -en ‹niederl.› (Wassergraben, Kanal[straße] in niederl. Städten)
grad. = graduiert; *vgl.* graduieren
grad..., Grad... (*ugs. für* gerad..., Gerad...)
Grad, der; -[e]s, -e ‹lat.› (Temperatureinheit; Einheit für [ebene] Winkel [1° = 90. Teil eines rechten Winkels], *früher auch* Altgrad *genannt* [*vgl.* Gon]; *Zeichen* °); 3 Grad C (↑R 90) *oder* 3° C (*fachspr. nur* 3 °C); *aber auch* der 30. Grad (*nicht:* 30. °); es ist heute um einige Grad wärmer; ein Winkel von 30°; **Gra|da|ti|on,** die; -, -en (Steigerung, stufenweise Erhöhung; Abstufung); **Grad|bo|gen**
gra|de (*ugs. für* gerade)
Grad|ein|tei|lung; Gra|del, Gradl, der; -s, - (*südd., österr. für* ein Gewebe); **Gra|di|ent,** der; -en, -en (↑R 126) ‹lat.› (*fachspr.* Gefälle od. Anstieg einer Größe auf einer bestimmten Strecke); **Gra|di|en|te,** die; -, -n (von Gradienten gebildete Neigungslinie); **gra|die|ren** (Salzsole konzentrieren; verstärken; in Grade einteilen); **Gra-**

dierlhaus (Salzgewinnungsanlage); **Gra|die|rung** (Verstärkung; Verdunstung); **Gra|dier|werk** (Solerieselanlage [in Kurorten]); **...gra|dig,** *österr. u. schweiz.* **...grä|dig** (z. B. dreigradig, *mit Ziffer* 3-gradig; ↑R 44); **Grä|dig|keit** *(Chemie)*

Gra|ditz (Ort südöstl. von Torgau); **Gra|dit|zer** (↑R 103)

Gradl *vgl.* Gradel

grad|mä|ßig; Grad_mes|ser (der), **...netz; gra|du|al** ‹lat.› (den Rang betreffend); **Gra|du|a|le,** das; -s, ...lien [...i̯ən]; (kurzer Psalmengesang nach der Epistel in der kath. Messe; das die Choralmessgesänge enthaltende Buch); **gra|du|ell** ‹franz.› (grad-, stufenweise); **gra|du|ie|ren** (*Technik* mit genauer Einteilung versehen; einen [akadem.] Grad erteilen); graduierter Ingenieur, *Abk.* Ing. (grad.); **Gra|du|ier|te,** der *u.* die; -n, -n; ↑R 5ff. (jmd., der einen akademischen Grad besitzt); **Gra|du|ie|rung; Grad|un|ter|schied; grad|wei|se**

Grae|cum ['grɛ:...], das; -s ‹griech.› (Prüfung im Altgriechischen)

Graf, der; -en, -en (↑R 126); **Gra|fen_kro|ne, ...ti|tel**

Graf|fel, das; -s (*österr. ugs. für* Gerümpel)

Graf|fi|to, der *u.* das; -[s], ...ti ‹ital.› (in eine Wand eingekratzte Inschrift; *meist Plur.*: Wandkritzelei; auf Mauern, Fassaden o. Ä. gesprühte od. gemalte Parole)

Gra|fie *eindeutschende Schreibung für* Graphie

Gra|fik, *auch* Gra|phik (↑R 33), die; -, -en ‹griech.› (Schaubild, Illustration; *nur Sing.*: Sammelbezeichnung für Holzschnitt, Kupferstich, Lithographie u. Handzeichnung; **Gra|fi|ker** *auch* Gra|phi|ker; **Gra|fi|ke|rin** *auch* Gra|phi|ke|rin

Grä|fin; Grä|fin|wit|we

gra|fisch, *auch* gra|phisch

Gra|fit usw. *vgl.* Graphit usw.

gräf|lich, *im Titel* (↑R 56): Gräflich

Gra|fo|lo|ge usw. *eindeutschende Schreibung für* Graphologe usw.

Graf|schaft

Gra|ham|brot ‹nach dem amerik. Arzt› (↑R 95)

Grain [gre:n], der; -s, -s ‹engl.› (älteres Gewicht); 5 - (↑R 90)

Gra|ji|sche Al|pen (↑R 102) *Plur.* (Teil der Westalpen)

grä|ko|la|tei|nisch; ↑R 106 (griechisch-lateinisch); **Grä|ko|ma|nie,** die; - ‹griech.› ([übertriebene] Vorliebe für altgriech. Kultur)

Gral, der; -s ‹franz.› (Wunder wirkende Schale im höfischen Roman); der Heilige - (↑R 108); **Grals_burg, ...hü|ter, ...rit|ter, ...sa|ge**

gram; jmdm. - sein (↑R 46); **Gram,** der; -[e]s; **grä|meln** (*bes. mitteld., nordd. für* missmutig sein); ich ...[e]le (↑R 16); **grä|men** *(geh.)*; sich -; **gram|er|füllt**

Gram|fär|bung ‹nach dem dän. Arzt H. C. J. Gram›; ↑R 95 (Färbemethode zur Unterscheidung von Bakterien); (↑R 96:) gramnegativ, grampositiv

gram|ge|beugt (↑R 40); **gräm|lich; Gräm|lich|keit,** die; -

Gramm, das; -s, -e ‹griech.› (*Zeichen* g); 2 - (↑R 90); **Gram|ma|tik,** die; -, -en (Sprachlehre); **gram|ma|ti|ka|lisch** (*seltener für* grammatisch); **Gram|ma|ti|ker; Gram|ma|tik|the|o|rie; gram|ma|tisch;** -es Geschlecht (Genus)

Gram|mel, die; -, -n (*bayr., österr. für* Griebe)

...gräm|mig (*schweiz.;* z. B. hundertgrämmig, *mit Ziffern* 100-grämmig); **Gramm|mol, Gramm|mo|le|kül** (↑R 136) ‹griech.; lat.› *u.* **Mol,** das; -s, -e ‹lat.› (*früher für* so viele Gramm einer chemischen Verbindung, wie deren Molekulargewicht angibt); **Gram|mo|phon** ®, *eindeutschende Schreibung:* Gram|mo|fon, das; -s, -e ‹griech.› (Plattenspieler)

gram_ne|ga|tiv, ...po|si|tiv (↑R 96); *vgl.* Gramfärbung

gram|voll

Gran ‹lat.›, *auch* **Grän,** das; -[e]s, -e ‹franz.› (altes Apotheker- und Edelmetallgewicht); 3 - (↑R 90)

Gra|na|da (Hptst. der gleichnamigen span. Provinz)

Gra|na|dil|le *vgl.* Grenadille

[1]**Gra|nat,** der; -[e]s, -e ‹niederl.› (kleines Krebstier, Garnelenart)

[2]**Gra|nat,** der; -[e]s, -e, *österr.* der; -en, -en; ↑R 126 ‹lat.› (ein Edelstein); **Gra|nat|ap|fel** (Frucht einer subtrop. Pflanze); **Gra|na|te,** die; -, -n ‹ital.›; **Gra|nat_schmuck, ...split|ter, ...trich|ter, ...wer|fer** (ein Geschütz)

Gran Ca|na|ria (kanar. Insel)

Gran Cha|co [- 'tʃako], der; - -s (südamerik. Landschaft)

[1]**Grand,** der; -[e]s (*nordd. für* Kies)

[2]**Grand,** der; -[e]s, -e (*bayr. für* Wasserbehälter)

[3]**Grand** [grã:, *auch* graŋ], der; -s, -s ‹franz.› (höchstes Spiel im Skat); **Gran|de,** der; -n, -n (↑R 126) ‹span.› (*früher* Mitglied des Hof-, Hochadels in Spanien)

Gran|del, Grä|ne, die; -, -n (*Jägerspr.* oberer Eckzahn des Rotwildes)

Gran|deur [grã'dø:r], die; - ‹franz.› (Großartigkeit, Größe); **Gran|dez|za,** die; - ‹ital.› (würdevoll-elegantes Benehmen); **Grand|ho|tel** ['grã:...]; **gran|dig** ‹roman.› (*landsch. für* groß, stark); **gran|di|os** ‹ital.› (großartig, überwältigend); **Grand Old La|dy** ['grɛnd 'o:ld 'le:di], die; - - -, *Plur.* - - Ladies ‹engl.› (älteste bedeutende weibliche Persönlichkeit in einem bestimmten Bereich); **Grand Old Man** ['grɛnd 'o:ld 'mɛn], der; - - -, - - Men [- - 'mɛn] (älteste bedeutende männliche Persönlichkeit in einem bestimmten Bereich); **Grand ou|vert** [grã:, *auch* graŋ u'vɛ:r], der; - -[s], - -s [grã:, *auch* graŋ u'vɛ:rs] ‹franz.› (Grand aus der Hand, bei dem der Spieler seine Karten offen hinlegen muss); **Grand Prix** [grã(:) 'pri:], der; - -, - -s [grã(:) -] ‹franz., „großer Preis"›; **Grand|seig|neur** [grãsɛ'njø:r] (↑R 130), der; -s, *Plur.* -s *u.* -e ‹franz.› (vornehmer, weltgewandter Mann); **Grand|slam** ['grɛnd'slɛm], der; -[s], -s, *auch* **Grand Slam,** der; - -[s], - -s ‹engl.› *(Tennis);* **Grand-Tou|ris|me-Ren|nen** [grãtu'rism(ə)...], das; -s, - (Sportwagenrennen)

Grä|ne *vgl.* Grandel

gra|nie|ren ‹lat.› (*fachspr. für* körnig machen); **Gra|nit** [*auch* ...'nit], der; -s, -e ‹ital.› (ein Gestein); **gra|nit|ar|tig; Gra|nit|block** *Plur.* ...blöcke; **gra|ni|ten** (aus Granit); **Gra|nit|qua|der**

Gran|ne, die; -, -n (Ährenborste); **gran|nig**

Gran|ny Smith ['grɛni 'smiθ], der; - -, - - ‹engl.› (eine Apfelsorte)

Grant, der; -s (*bayr., österr. für* Übellaunigkeit; Unmut); **gran|tig; Gran|tig|keit,** die; -

Gra|nu|lat, das; -[e]s, -e ‹lat.› (Substanz in Körnchenform); **Gra|nu|la|ti|on,** die; -, -en (körnige [Oberflächen]struktur; Herstellung, Bildung einer solchen Struktur); **gra|nu|lie|ren; Gra|nu|lit** [*auch* ...'lit], der; -s, -e (ein Gestein); **Gra|nu|lom,** das; -s, -e (*Med.* Granulationsgeschwulst); **gra|nu|lös** (körnig)

Grape|fruit ['gre:pfru:t], die; -, -s ‹engl.› (eine Zitrusfrucht)

[1]**Graph** (↑R 33), der; -en, -en (↑R 126) ‹griech.› (*Math.* grafische Darstellung); [2]**Graph,** das; -s, -e (*Sprachw.* Schriftzeichen); **Gra|phem,** das; -s, -e (*Sprachw.* kleinste bedeutungsunterschei-

dende Einheit der geschriebenen Sprache); **Gra|phie** (↑R 33), die; -, -n (*Sprachw.* Schreibung); **...gra|phie** (↑R 33; ...[be]schreibung, z. B. Geographie); **Gra|phik, Gra|phi|ker, Gra|phi|ke|rin, gra|phisch** *vgl.* Grafik, Grafiker, Grafikerin, grafisch; **Gra|phit,** *eindeutschend* Gra|fit [*auch* ...'fit] (↑R 33), der; -s, -e (ein Mineral); **gra|phit-grau,** *eindeutschend* gra|fit|grau; **Gra|pho|lo|ge** (↑R 33), der; -n, -n (↑R 126); **Gra|pho|lo|gie** (↑R 33), die; - (Lehre von der Deutung der Handschrift als Ausdruck des Charakters); **gra|pho|lo|gisch** (↑R 33); **Gra|pho|sta|tik** (zeichnerische Methode zur Lösung von Aufgaben der Statik); drei - (↑R 90)

Grap|pa, der; -s, -s, *auch* die; -, -s ‹ital.› (ital. Tresterbranntwein)

grap|schen, grab|schen (*ugs. für* schnell nach etwas greifen); du grapschst, grabschst; **Grap-scher,** Grab|scher, der; -s, - (*abwertend für* männliche Person, die eine Frau unsittlich berührt); **grap|sen** (*österr. ugs. für* stehlen); du grapst

Gras, das; -es, Gräser; **Gras-af|fe** (*Schimpfwort für* unreifer Mensch); **gras|ar|tig; Gras-bahn|ren|nen** *(Motorradsport);* **gras|be|wach|sen** (↑R 40); **Gräs|chen; Gras|de|cke; gra-sen;** du grast; er graste; **Gra|ser** (*Jägerspr. für* Zunge von Rot- u. Damwild); **Grä|ser|chen** *Plur.;* **Gras‿flä|che, ...fleck; gras-grün; Gras‿halm, ...hüp|fer; gra|sig; Gras|land,** das; -[e]s; **Gräs|lein; Gras|li|lie; Gras|mü-cke,** die; -, -n (ein Singvogel); **Gras|nar|be**

Graß, *aus grafischen Gründen mit Zustimmung des Autors auch* Grass (dt. Schriftsteller); Graß' Roman (↑R 98)

gras|sie|ren ‹lat.› (sich ausbreiten; wüten [von Seuchen])

gräss|lich; Gräss|lich|keit

Gras‿step|pe, ...strei|fen; gras-über|wach|sen (↑R 132)

Grat, der; -[e]s, -e (Kante; Bergkamm[linie]); **Grä|te,** die; -, -n (Fischgräte); **grä|ten|los**

Gra|ti|an, Gra|ti|a|nus (röm. Kaiser; m. Vorn.); **Gra|ti|as,** das; -, - (Dank[gebet]); **Gra|ti|fi|ka|ti|on,** die; -, -en ([freiwillige] Vergütung, [Sonder]zuwendung)

grä|tig (viele Gräten enthaltend; *ugs. für* reizbar, aufbrausend)

Gra|tin [gra'tɛ̃:], das; -s, -s ‹franz.› (überbackenes Gericht)

Grä|ting, die; -, *Plur.* -e *od.* -s ‹engl.› (*Seemannsspr.* Gitterrost [auf Schiffen])

gra|ti|nie|ren ‹franz.› (mit einer Kruste überbacken)

gra|tis ‹lat.› (unentgeltlich); - und franko; **Gra|tis‿ak|tie, ...pro|be, ...pros|pekt, ...vor|stel|lung**

Grat|leis|te (in der Tischlerei)

Grät|sche, die; -, -n (eine Turnübung); **grät|schen** ([die Beine] seitwärts spreizen); du grätschst; **Grätsch|stel|lung,** die; -

Gra|tu|lant, der; -en, -en (↑R 126) ‹lat.›; **Gra|tu|lan|tin; Gra|tu|la|ti-on,** die; -, -en; **Gra|tu|la|ti|ons-cour** [...ku:r], die; -, -en ‹lat.; franz.› ([feierliche] Beglückwünschung durch viele Gratulanten); **gra|tu|lie|ren;** jmdm. zum Geburtstag gratulieren

Grat|wan|de|rung

Grät|zel, das; -s, -n (*österr. ugs. für* Teil eines Wohngebiets)

grau; grau werden; grau in grau malen; grau gestreift, meliert usw.; (↑R 108:) in grauer Vorzeit; sich keine grauen Haare wachsen lassen (*ugs. für* sich keine Sorgen machen); grauer Markt; grauer Star; eine graue Eminenz (*Bez. für* eine nach außen kaum in Erscheinung tretende, aber einflussreiche [polit.] Persönlichkeit), *aber* (↑R 93): die Graue Eminenz (F. v. Holstein); (↑R 108:) die Grauen Schwestern (kath. Kongregation), die Grauen Panther (Seniorenschutzbund); *vgl.* blau; **Grau,** das; -s, *Plur.* -, *ugs.* -s (graue Farbe); in Grau; *vgl.* Blau; **grau|äu|gig; Grau|bart; grau-bär|tig; grau|blau** (↑R 27); **Grau|brot**

Grau|bün|den (schweiz. Kanton); *vgl.* Bünden; **Grau|bünd|ner** (↑R 103); *vgl.* Bündner; **grau-bünd|ne|risch;** *vgl.* bündnerisch

Grau|chen (Eselchen)

Gräu|el, der; -s, -; **Gräu|el‿mär-chen, ...pro|pa|gan|da, ...tat;**

[1]**grau|en** (Furcht haben); mir, *seltener* mich graut [es] vor dir

[2]**grau|en** (allmählich hell, dunkel werden; dämmern); der Morgen, der Abend graut

Grau|en, das; -s, -; es überkommt ihn ein - (Furcht, Schauder); die - (Schrecken) des Atomkrieges; Grauen erregend, *aber* äußerst grauenerregend (↑R 40); **grau-en|haft; grau|en|voll**

Grau|gans; grau|grün (↑R 27); **grau|haa|rig; Grau|kopf**

grau|len (sich fürchten); es grault mir; ich graule mich; [1]**gräu|lich** ‹zu Grauen›

[2]**gräu|lich,** *auch* grau|lich ‹*zu* grau›; **grau me|liert** *vgl.* grau

Gräup|chen; Grau|pe, die; -, -n *meist Plur.* ([Getreide]korn); **Grau|pel,** die; -, -n *meist Plur.* (Hagelkorn); **grau|peln;** es graupelt; **Grau|pel‿schau|er, ...wet-ter; Grau|pen|sup|pe**

graus (*veraltet für* grausig); -es Morden; **Graus,** der; -es (*veraltet für* Schrecken); o Graus!

grau|sam; Grau|sam|keit

Grau‿schim|mel, ...schlei|er

grau|sen (sich fürchten); mir *od.* mich grauste; sich grausen; **Grau-sen,** das; -s; **grau|sig** (Grauen erregend); **graus|lich** (*bes. österr. für* unangenehm, hässlich)

Grau‿specht, ...spieß|glanz (ein Mineral), **...tier** (Esel), **...wa|cke** (*Geol.* Sandstein), **...werk** (das; -[e]s; Pelzwerk, bes. aus dem grauen Winterpelz russ. Eichhörnchen; Feh), **...zo|ne** (Übergangszone [zwischen Legalität u. Illegalität])

gra|ve [...və] ‹ital.› (*Musik* schwer, wuchtig)

Gra|ven|ha|ge *vgl.* 's-Gravenhage

Gra|ven|stei|ner [...v...] (eine Apfelsorte); ↑R 103

Gra|veur [...'vø:r], der; -s, -e ‹franz.› (Metall-, Steinschneider, Stecher); **Gra|veur|ar|beit** [...'vø:r...] *vgl.* Gravierarbeit; **Gra-veu|rin** [...'vø:rin]

gra|vid [...v...] ‹lat.› (*Med.* schwanger); **Gra|vi|di|tät,** die; -, -en (Schwangerschaft)

Gra|vier|an|stalt [...v...] ‹franz.; dt.›; **Gra|vier|ar|beit,** Gra|veur-ar|beit; **gra|vie|ren** [...v...] ([in Metall, Stein, Glas o. Ä.] [ein]schneiden)

gra|vie|rend [...v...] ‹lat.› (schwer wiegend; belastend)

Gra|vie|rung [...v...]

Gra|vi|me|ter [...v...], das ‹lat.; griech.› (*Physik* Gerät zum Messen der Schwerkraft[änderungen]); **Gra|vi|met|rie** (↑R 130), die; - *(Physik, Chemie);* **gra|vi-met|risch; Gra|vis,** der; -, - ‹lat.› (*Sprachw.* ein Betonungszeichen: ˋ, z. B. è); **Gra|vi|tät,** die; - (*veraltet für* [steife] Würde); **Gra|vi-ta|ti|on,** die; - (Schwerkraft, Anziehungskraft); **Gra|vi|ta|ti|ons-‿feld, ...ge|setz** (das; -es); **gra-vi|tä|tisch** (würdevoll); **gra|vi-tie|ren** ([aufgrund der Gravitation] zu etwas hinstreben)

Gra|vur [...v...], die; -, -en ‹franz.› (Darstellung, Zeichnung auf Metall, Stein, Glas o. Ä.); **Gra|vü|re,** die; -, -n ([Kupfer-, Stahl]stich)

Gray [gre:], das; -[e]s, - ‹nach dem

engl. Physiker⟩ (Maßeinheit der Energiedosis; *Zeichen* Gy)
Graz (Hptst. der Steiermark); **Grazer** (↑R 103)
[1]**Gra|zie** [...iə], die; - ⟨lat.⟩ (Anmut); [2]**Gra|zie,** die; -, -n *meist Plur.* (eine der drei röm. Göttinnen der Anmut; *scherzh. für* anmutige, hübsche junge Frau)
gra|zil ⟨lat.⟩ (schlank, geschmeidig, zierlich); **Gra|zi|li|tät,** die; -
gra|zi|ös ⟨franz.⟩ (anmutig); **gra|zi|o|so** ⟨ital.⟩ (*Musik* anmutig); **Gra|zi|o|so,** das; -s, *Plur.* -s *u.* ...si
grä|zi|sie|ren ⟨griech.⟩ (nach griech. Muster formen; die alten Griechen nachahmen); **Grä|zis|mus,** der; -, ...men (*Sprachw.* altgriech. Spracheigentümlichkeit [in einer nichtgriech. Sprache]); **Grä|zist,** der; -en, -en; ↑R 126 (Kenner, Erforscher des Altgriechischen); **Grä|zis|tik,** die; - (Erforschung des Altgriechischen); **Grä|zis|tin; Grä|zi|tät,** die; - (Wesen der altgriech. Sprache u. Sitte)
Greene [gri:n] (engl. Schriftsteller)
Green|horn ['gri:n...], das; -s, -s ⟨engl.⟩ (Anfänger, Neuling)
Green|peace ['gri:npi:s] ⟨engl.⟩ (internationale Umweltschutzorganisation)
Green|wich ['grinidʒ] (Stadtteil Londons; *Abk.* Gr.); **Green|wi|cher** (↑R 103); - Zeit (westeuropäische Zeit)
Grège [grɛ:ʒ], die; - ⟨franz.⟩ (Naturseidenfaden); **Grège|sei|de**
Gre|gor, Gre|go|ri|us (m. Vorn.); **gre|go|ri|a|nisch;** (↑R 94): der gregorianische Kalender; der gregorianische Choral
Greif, der; *Gen.* -[e]s *u.* -en, *Plur.* -e[n] (Fabeltier [Vogel]; *auch für* Greifvogel)
Greif‿arm, ...bag|ger; greif|bar; grei|fen; du griffst; gegriffen; greif[e]!; um sich greifen; (↑R 50:) zum Greifen nahe; **Grei|fer**
Greifs|wald (Stadt in Vorpommern); **Greifs|wal|der** (↑R 103)
Greif|vo|gel
Greif|zan|ge
grei|nen (*ugs. für* weinen)
greis (*geh. für* sehr alt); **Greis,** der; -es, -e; **Grei|sen|al|ter,** das; -s; **grei|sen|haft; Grei|sen|haf|tig|keit,** die; -; **Grei|sen|stim|me; Grei|sin**
Greiß|ler (*ostösterr. für* Krämer); **Greiß|le|rei**
grell; (↑R 40:) die grell beleuchtete Bühne; grellgelb, grellrot usw.; **Grel|le,** die; -
Gre|mi|um, das; -s, ...ien [...iən] ⟨lat.⟩ (Ausschuss; Körperschaft)

Gre|na|da (Staat im Bereich der Westindischen Inseln)
Gre|na|dier, der; -s, -e ⟨franz.⟩ (Infanterist)
Gre|na|dil|le, die; -, -n ⟨franz.⟩, Gra|na|dil|le, die; -, -n ⟨span.⟩ (Passionsblumenfrucht)
[1]**Gre|na|di|ne,** die; - ⟨franz.⟩ (Saft, Sirup aus Granatäpfeln)
[2]**Gre|na|di|ne,** die; - (ein Gewebe)
Grenz‿aus|gleich, ...bahn|hof, ...baum, ...be|am|te, ...be|fes|ti|gung *(meist Plur.),* **...be|reich, ...be|woh|ner; Gren|ze,** die; -, -n; **gren|zen;** du grenzt; **gren|zen|los;** bis ins Grenzenlose (↑R 47); **Gren|zen|lo|sig|keit,** die; -; **Gren|zer** (*ugs. für* Grenzjäger, -bewohner); **Grenz‿fall** (der), **...fluss, ...for|ma|li|tät** *(meist Plur.),* **...gän|ger, ...ge|biet, ...kon|trol|le, ...land, ...li|nie; grenz|nah;** -e Gebiete; **Grenz‿pos|ten, ...rain, ...schutz** (der; -es), **...si|tu|a|ti|on, ...stadt, ...stein, ...strei|tig|keit** *(meist Plur.),* **...trup|pen** *(Plur.; ehem. in der DDR),* **...über|gang** (↑R 132); **grenz|über|schrei|tend** (↑R 132); -er Verkehr; **Grenz‿über|tritt** (↑R 132), **...ver|kehr, ...ver|let|zung, ...wall, ...wert, ...zwi|schen|fall**
Gret, Gret|chen (w. Vorn.); **Gret|chen|fra|ge; Gre|te, Gre|tel, Gre|ti** (w. Vorn.)
Greu|el usw. *frühere Schreibung für* Gräuel usw.; **greu|lich** *frühere Schreibung für* [1]gräulich
Gre|ven|broich [gre:vən'bro:x] (Stadt in Nordrhein-Westfalen)
Grey|erz ['graiərts] (schweiz. Ortsn.); -er Käse; *vgl.* Gruyères
Grey|hound ['gre:haund], der; -[s], -s ⟨engl.⟩ (bes. für Rennen gezüchteter engl. Windhund; ein amerik. Überlandbus)
Grie|be, die; -, -n (ausgebratener Speckwürfel; *landsch. auch für* Bläschenausschlag am Mund); **Grie|ben‿fett** (das; -[e]s), **...schmalz, ...wurst**
Griebs, der; -es, -e (*landsch. für* Kerngehäuse des Obstes; *mitteld. für* Gurgel)
Grie|che, der; -n, -n (↑R 126); **Grie|chen|land; Grie|chin; grie|chisch;** *vgl.* deutsch; **Grie|chisch,** das; -[s] (Sprache); *vgl.* Deutsch; **Grie|chi|sche,** das; -n; *vgl.* Deutsche, das; **grie|chisch-ka|tho|lisch** (*Abk.* gr.-kath.); **grie|chisch-or|tho|dox; grie|chisch-rö|misch** *(Ringen);* **grie|chisch-u|niert**
Grie|fe, die; -, -n (*mitteld. für* Griebe)

Grieg, Edvard (norw. Komponist)
grie|meln (*westmitteld. für* schadenfroh in sich hineinlachen); ich ...[e]le (↑R 16)
grie|nen (*ugs. für* grinsen)
grie|seln (*nordd. für* erschauern [vor Kälte usw.]); mich grieselt
Gries|gram, der; -[e]s, -e (missmutiger, mürrischer Mensch); **gries|grä|mig,** *seltener* **gries|grä|misch, gries|gräm|lich**
Grieß, der; -es, -e; **Grieß|brei; grie|ßeln** (körnig werden; *auch* rieseln); es grießelt; **grie|ßig;** -es Mehl; **Grie|ßig,** das; -s (Bienenkot); **Grieß‿kloß, ...koch** (*bayr., österr. für* Grießbrei; *vgl.* [2]Koch), **...mehl, ...schmar|ren** (*österr.* Süßspeise aus geröstetem Grieß), **...sup|pe**
Griff, der; -[e]s, -e; **griff|be|reit; Griff|brett**
Grif|fel, der; -s, -
griff|fest (↑R 136); **grif|fig; Grif|fig|keit,** die; -; **griff|los**
Grif|fon [gri'fɔ̃:], der; -s, -s ⟨franz.⟩ (ein Vorstehhund)
Griff|tech|nik *(Ringen)*
Grill, der; -s, -s ⟨engl.⟩ (Bratrost); **Gril|la|de** [gri'ja:də], die; -, -n ⟨franz.⟩ (gegrilltes Stück Fleisch, Fisch o. Ä.)
Gril|le, die; -, -n (ein Insekt; *auch für* sonderbarer Einfall; Laune)
gril|len ⟨engl.⟩ (auf dem Grill braten)
Gril|len|fän|ger (trüben Gedanken nachhängender Mensch); **gril|len|fän|ge|risch; gril|len|haft** (sonderbar; launisch); **Gril|len|haf|tig|keit,** die; -
Gril|let|te [gri'lɛt(ə)], die; -, -n (*regional für* gegrilltes Hacksteak); **Grill‿fest, ...ge|rät, ...ge|richt; gril|lie|ren** [*auch* gri'ji:...] ⟨franz.⟩ (grillen)
gril|lig (*svw.* grillenhaft); **Gril|lig|keit**
Grill|par|zer (österr. Dichter)
Grill‿platz, ...res|tau|rant; Grill|room ['grilru:m], der; -s, -s ⟨engl.⟩ (Grillrestaurant, -stube)
Gri|mas|se, die; -, -n ⟨franz.⟩ (Verzerrung des Gesichts); **gri|mas|sie|ren**
Grim|bart, der; -s (der Dachs in der Tierfabel)
grimm (*veraltet für* zornig); [1]**Grimm,** der; -[e]s *(veraltend)*
[2]**Grimm,** Jacob *u.* Wilhelm (dt. Sprachwissenschaftler); die Brüder Grimm
Grimm|darm (Dickdarmteil)
Grim|mels|hau|sen (dt. Schriftsteller im 17. Jh.)
grim|men (*veraltet für* ärgern)
Grim|men, das; -s ([Bauch]weh)

grim|mig; Grim|mig|keit, die; -

grimmsch; das grimmsche Wörterbuch; die grimmschen Märchen

Grind, der; -[e]s, -e (Schorf; *schweiz. derb für* Kopf; *Jägerspr.* Kopf von Hirsch od. Gämse); **grin|dig; Grind|wal** (eine Delphinart)

Grin|go ['griŋgo], der; -s, -s ‹span.› (*abwertend für* nichtromanischer Fremder in Südamerika)

Grin|sel, das; -s, -[n] (*österr. für* Kimme am Gewehrlauf)

grin|sen; du grinst

Grin|zing (Stadtteil von Wien)

grip|pal *vgl.* grippös; **Grip|pe,** die; -, -n ‹franz.› (eine Infektionskrankheit); **Grip|pe‿an|fall, ...epi|de|mie** (↑R 132), **...vi|rus, ...wel|le; grip|pös,** grip|pal (*Med.* grippeartig)

Grips, der; -es, -e (*ugs. für* Verstand, Auffassungsgabe)

Gri|saille [gri'za:j], die; -, -n [...'za:jən] (schwarzweißer Seidenstoff; Malerei in Grautönen *[nur Sing.]*; in dieser Weise hergestelltes Kunstwerk)

Gri|sel|dis (w. Vorn.)

Gri|set|te, die; -, -n ‹franz.› (*veraltet für* leichtlebiges Mädchen)

Gris|li|bär, *auch* Grizz|ly|bär ‹engl.; dt.› (großer nordamerik. Braunbär)

[1]**Grit,** der; -s, -e ‹engl.› (grober Sand; Sandstein)

[2]**Grit[t]** (w. Vorn.)

Grizz|ly|bär ['grizli...] *vgl.* Grislibär

gr.-kath. = griechisch-katholisch

grob [*auch* grɔp]; gröber, gröbste; grob fahrlässig; Korn grob mahlen; grob gemahlenes Korn; (↑R 47:) jmdn. aufs Gröbste, *auch* gröbste beleidigen; aus dem Gröbsten heraus sein; **Grob|blech; Grö|be,** die; - (Siebrückstand); **grob|fa|se|rig; grob gemah|len** *vgl.* grob; **Grob|heit; Gro|bi|an,** der; -[e]s, -e (grober Mensch); **grob‿kno|chig, ...körnig; gröb|lich** (ziemlich grob; stark; sehr); **grob|ma|schig; Grob|ma|schig|keit,** die; -; **grob|schläch|tig** (von grober Art); **Grob|schläch|tig|keit,** die; -; **Grob‿schmied, ...schnitt**

Gro|den, der; -s, - (*nordd. für* [mit Gras bewachsenes] angeschwemmtes Deichvorland)

Grog, der; -s, -s ‹vielleicht nach dem Spitznamen des engl. Admirals Vernon: „Old Grog"› (heißes alkohol. Getränk); **grog|gy** ['grɔgi] ‹*eigentl.* „vom Grog betrunken"› (*Boxen* schwer angeschlagen; *ugs. auch für* zerschlagen, erschöpft)

Groitzsch [grɔytʃ] (Stadt südl. von Leipzig)

grö|len (*ugs. für* schreien, lärmen); **Grö|le|rei**

Groll, der; -[e]s; **grol|len**

Gro|nin|gen (niederl. Stadt)

Grön|land; Grön|län|der (↑R 103); **Grön|län|de|rin; Grön|land|fah|rer; grön|län|disch; Grön|land|wal**

Groom [gru:m], der; -s, -s ‹engl.› (Reitknecht)

Gro|pi|us (amerik. Architekt dt. Herkunft)

Grop|pe, die; -, -n (ein Fisch)

[1]**Gros** [gro:], das; - [gro:(s)], - [gro:s] ‹franz.› (überwiegender Teil); *vgl.* en gros; [2]**Gros** [grɔs], das; -es, -e ‹niederl.› (12 Dutzend); 2 Gros Nadeln (↑R 90 f.);

Gro|schen, der; -s, - ‹mlat.› (österr. Münze; *Abk.* g [100 Groschen = 1 Schilling]; *ugs. für* dt. Zehnpfennigstück); **Gro|schen‿blatt** (billige, anspruchslose Zeitung), **...grab** (*scherzh. für* Spielautomat, Parkuhr o. Ä.), **...heft, ...ro|man**

groß; größer, größte; (↑R 46:) groß[en]teils, größer[e]nteils, größtenteils. **I.** *Kleinschreibung:* **a)** (↑R 47:) sein Haus war am größten; **b)** (↑R 108:) die großen Ferien; auf große Fahrt gehen; Kapitän auf großer Fahrt *(Seew.)*; die große Anfrage; die große Kreisstadt; das große Einmaleins; das große Latinum; das große Los; die große Pause; die große (vornehme) Welt; auf großem Fuß (*ugs. für* verschwenderisch) leben; etwas an die große Glocke hängen (*ugs. für* überall erzählen); einen großen Bahnhof (*ugs. für* feierlichen Empfang) bekommen; im großen Ganzen. **II.** *Großschreibung:* **a)** (↑R 47:) etwas, nichts, viel, wenig Großes; Groß und Klein (jedermann), Große und Kleine, die Großen und die Kleinen; im Großen und Ganzen; im Großen (en gros) einkaufen; vom Kleinen auf das Große schließen; ein Zug ins Große; im Großen wie im Kleinen treu sein; das Größte (*ugs. für* sehr gut) wäre, wenn ...; ein gutes Fußballspiel ist für ihn das Größte; er ist der Größte (*ugs. für* ist uneingeschränkt anerkannt, ist unübertroffen); **b)** (↑R 93, 102 *u.* 108:) Otto der Große (*Abk.* d. Gr.), *Gen.:* Ottos des Großen; der Große Schweiger (Moltke); der Große Wagen, der Große Bär; die Große Strafkammer; die Große Mauer (in China); der Große Rat (*schweiz.* das Kantonsparlament); der Große Teich (*ugs. für* Atlant. Ozean); der Große Belt. **III.** *Schreibung in Verbindung mit dem Partizip II:* groß gemustert, kariert, gewachsen; ein groß angelegter Plan, der Plan ist groß angelegt; **IV.** *Schreibung in Verbindung mit Verben* (↑R 37 f.): groß sein, werden; ein Wort [ganz] groß/noch größer an die Tafel schreiben; Teamarbeit wird bei uns groß geschrieben (*ugs. für* wichtig genommen); *aber* ein Wort großschreiben (mit großem Anfangsbuchstaben); er muss immer großtun; Kinder großziehen (↑R 38 f.)

Groß‿ab|neh|mer, ...ad|mi|ral, ...ak|ti|o|när, ...alarm (↑R 132); **groß an|ge|legt** *vgl.* groß, III; **groß|ar|tig; Groß|ar|tig|keit,** die; -; **Groß‿auf|nah|me, ...auf|trag, ...bank, ...bau|stel|le; Groß-Ber|lin** (↑R 105); **Groß-Ber|li|ner** (↑R 103); **Groß‿betrieb, ...bour|geoi|sie, ...brand; Groß|bri|tan|ni|en; groß|bri|tan|nisch; Groß|buch|sta|be; groß|bür|ger|lich; Groß|bür|ger|tum; groß|deutsch** (*bes. nationalsoz.*); **Grö|ße,** die; -, -n; Schuhe in - vierzig; **Groß‿einkauf, ...ein|satz, ...el|tern** *(Plur.)*, **...en|kel, ...en|ke|lin; Grö|ßen|ord|nung; gro|ßen|teils,** großteils; **Grö|ßen‿un|ter|schied, ...ver|hält|nis, ...wahn; grö|ßen|wahn|sin|nig; grö|ßer** *vgl.* groß; **Groß|er|eig|nis; grö|ße|ren|teils, grö|ßern|teils; Groß‿fahn|dung, ...fa|mi|lie, ...feu|er; groß‿fi|gu|rig, ...flä|chig; Groß‿flug|zeug, ...fo|lio** (das; -s; *Buchw.; Abk.* Gr.-2°), **...for|mat, ...fürst, ...fürs|tin; Groß|fürs|tin-Mut|ter,** die; -; **Groß|ge|mein|de; groß ge|mus|tert, ge|wach|sen** *vgl.* groß, III; **Groß|glock|ner** [*auch* 'gro:s...], der; -s (ein Berg); **Groß|glock|ner|mas|siv** (↑R 105); **Groß‿grund|be|sit|zer, ...han|del; Groß|han|dels|preis; Groß|händ|ler; groß|her|zig; Groß|her|zig|keit,** die; -; **Groß|her|zog; groß|her|zog|lich,** *im Titel* (↑R 56): Großherzoglich; **Groß|hirn; Groß|hirn|rin|de; Groß‿hun|dert** (ein altes Zählmaß; 120 Stück), **...in|dust|ri|el|le**

Gros|sist, der; -en, -en (↑R 126) ‹franz.› (Großhändler)

groß|jäh|rig (*veraltend für* volljährig); **Groß|jäh|rig|keit,** die; -;

groß|ka|lib|rig; Groß|kampf|tag (*Milit.; auch ugs. für* harter Arbeitstag); **groß ka|riert** *vgl.* groß, III; **Groß|kat|ze** (z. B. Löwe); **Groß|kauf|mann** *Plur.* ...kaufleute; **Groß|kind** (*schweiz. für* Enkelkind); **Groß‿kli|ma, ...knecht** *(früher),* **...kon|zern; Groß|kopfe|te,** *bes. bayr., österr.* **Großkop|fer|te,** der *u.* die; -n, -n; ↑R 5 ff. (*ugs. für* einflussreiche Persönlichkeit); **groß|köp|fig; Groß|kotz,** der; -es, -e (*derb für* Angeber, Protz); **groß|kot|zig; Groß|kot|zig|keit,** die; -; **Großkund|ge|bung; Groß|macht; groß|mäch|tig** (*veraltet für* sehr mächtig; sehr groß); **Großmacht|po|li|tik; Groß|ma|ma; Groß|manns|sucht,** die; -; **groß|manns|süch|tig; Großmarkt; groß|ma|schig; groß‿maß|stä|big,** *häufiger* **...maßstäb|lich; Groß|mast** (*Seemannsspr.* zweiter Mast von vorn); **Groß|maul** (*ugs. für* Angeber); **groß|mäu|lig; Groß|mäu|lig|keit,** die; -; **Groß‿meis|ter, ...mo|gul, ...mut** (die; -); **großmü|tig; Groß|mü|tig|keit,** die; -; **Groß‿mut|ter** (*Plur.* ...mütter), **...nef|fe, ...nich|te; Groß|ok|tav,** das; -s (*Buchw.; Abk.* Gr.-8°); **Groß‿on|kel, ...pa|ckung, ...papa; Groß|quart,** das; -[e]s (*Buchw.; Abk.* Gr.-4°); **Groß|rat** *Plur.* ...räte (Mitglied eines schweiz. Kantonsparlaments); **Groß|raum‿bü|ro, ...flug|zeug; groß|räu|mig; Groß|raum|wagen** (bei der Straßen- od. Eisenbahn); **Groß|rech|ner** *(EDV);* **Groß|rei|ne|ma|chen, Großrein|ma|chen,** das; -s; **Großschiff|fahrts|weg** (↑R 24); **Groß|schnau|ze,** die; -, -n (*ugs. svw.* Großmaul); **groß|schnauzig, groß|schnäu|zig; großschrei|ben;** ↑R 38 f. (mit großem Anfangsbuchstaben schreiben); Substantive großschreiben; *vgl. aber* groß, IV; **Groß|schreibung; Groß|se|gel; groß|spreche|risch; groß|spu|rig; Großspu|rig|keit,** die; -; **Groß‿stadt, ...städ|ter, ...städ|te|rin; groß|städ|tisch; Groß|stadt‿mensch, ...ver|kehr; Großstein|grä|ber|leu|te** *Plur.* (Megalithiker der jüngeren Steinzeit); **Groß‿tan|te, ...tat; größ|te** *vgl.* groß; **Groß|teil,** der; **größ|tenteils; Größt|maß,** das; **größtmög|lich** (*falsch:* größtmöglichst); **Groß|tu|er; Groß|tu|erei,** die; -; **groß|tu|e|risch; großtun** (↑R 38 f.; prahlen); er soll nicht so großtun; **Groß|va|ter; Groß|va|ter|ses|sel; Groß‿veran|stal|tung, ...ver|die|ner, ...vieh, ...we|sir, ...wet|ter|la|ge, ...wild; groß|zie|hen** (↑R 38 f.; aufziehen); **groß|zü|gig; Großzü|gig|keit,** die; -

[1]**Grosz** [grɔs] (dt.-amerik. Maler u. Grafiker)

[2]**Grosz** [grɔʃ], der; -, -e ['grɔʃɛ], *Gen. Plur.* -y ['grɔʃi] ‹dt.-poln.› (Währungseinheit in Polen [100 Groszy = 1 Zloty])

gro|tesk ‹franz.› (wunderlich, grillenhaft; überspannt, verzerrt); **Gro|tesk,** die; - (*Druckw.* eine Schriftgattung); **Gro|tes|ke,** die; -, -n (phantastisch geformte Tier- u. Pflanzenverzierung der Antike u. der Renaissance; phantastische Erzählung); **gro|tes|ker|wei|se; Gro|tesk|tanz**

Grot|te, die; -, -n ‹ital.› ([künstl.] Felsenhöhle); **Grot|ten|bau** *Plur.* ...bauten; **Grot|ten|olm,** der; -[e]s, -e (ein Lurch)

Grot|zen, der; -s, - (*mdal. für* Griebs, Kerngehäuse)

Grou|pie ['gru:pi], das; -s, -s ‹engl.› (weiblicher Fan, der engen Kontakt mit seinem Idol sucht)

Gro|wi|an, der; -[e]s, -e, *auch* die; -, -en (große Windenergieanlage zur Erzeugung von Elektrizität)

grub|ben *vgl.* grubbern; **Grub|ber,** der; -s, - ‹engl.› (ein landw. Gerät); **grub|bern** (mit dem Grubber pflügen); ich ...ere (↑R 16)

Grüb|chen; Gru|be, die; -, -n

Grü|be|lei; grü|beln; ich ...[e]le (↑R 16)

Gru|ben‿ar|bei|ter, ...aus|bau, ...bau (*Plur.* ...baue), **...brand, ...gas, ...lam|pe, ...un|glück**

Grüb|ler; Grüb|le|rin; grüb|lerisch

Gru|de, die; -, -n (Braunkohlenkoks); **Gru|de|koks**

grü|e|zi ['gryətsi] (schweiz. Grußformel)

Gruft, die; -, Grüfte; **Gruf|ti,** der; -s, -s (*Jugendspr.* älterer Mensch)

grum|meln (*landsch. für* ein rollendes od. polterndes Geräusch verursachen; undeutlich sprechen; murren); ich ...[e]le (↑R 16)

Grum|met, das; -s, *österr. nur so, u.* **Grumt,** das; -[e]s (zweites Heu)

grün; I. *Kleinschreibung:* **a)** (↑R 47:) er ist mir nicht grün (*ugs. für* gewogen); **b)** (↑R 108:) am grünen Tisch; der grüne Star; die grüne Grenze; die grüne Minna (*ugs. für* Polizeiauto); die grüne Welle *(Verkehrsw.);* die grüne Hochzeit; die grüne Versicherungskarte; die grüne Hölle (trop. Urwald); die grüne Lunge (Grünflächen) der Großstadt; eine grüne Witwe (Frau, deren Mann tagsüber beruflich abwesend ist und die sich vernachlässigt fühlt); ein grüner (*ugs. für* unerfahrener) Junge; ach du grüne Neune! (*ugs.* Ausruf des Erstaunens). **II.** *Großschreibung:* **a)** (↑R 47:) die Grünen *(vgl. d.);* ins Grüne fahren; *vgl.* Grün; **b)** (↑R 108:) die Grüne Insel (Irland); die Grüne Woche (Berliner Ausstellung); das Grüne Gewölbe (Kunstsammlung in Dresden); *vgl.* blau; **Grün,** das; -s, *Plur.* -, *ugs.* -s (grüne Farbe); das erste Grün; bei Grün darf man die Straße überqueren; die Ampel steht auf, zeigt Grün; in Grün; das ist dasselbe in Grün (*ugs. für* [fast] ganz dasselbe); *vgl.* Blau; **Grün‿al|ge, ...an|la|ge; grün|äugig; grün|blau** (↑R 27)

Grund, der; -[e]s, Gründe; im Grunde; von Grund auf; von Grund aus; aufgrund, *auch* auf Grund [dessen, von]; auf Grund laufen; in [den] Grund bohren; im Grunde genommen; zugrunde, *auch* zu Grunde gehen, legen, liegen, richten; der Grund und Boden *(vgl. d.);* **Grund|ak|kord** *(Musik);* **grund|an|stän|dig; Grund‿an|strich, ...aus|bil|dung, ...aus|stat|tung, ...bedarf, ...be|deu|tung, ...be|dingung, ...be|griff, ...be|sitz, ...besit|zer, ...buch; Grund|buchamt; Grund|deutsch** *(Sprachw.);* **grund|ehr|lich; Grund‿ei|gentum, ...ei|gen|tü|mer, ...eis; Grun|del, Grün|del,** die; -, -n, *auch* der; -s, - (ein Fisch); **gründeln** ([von Enten] Nahrung unter Wasser suchen); **grün|den;** gegründet (*Abk.* gegr.); sich auf eine Tatsache gründen; **Grün|der; Grün|de|rin; Grün|der‿jah|re** *(Plur.),* **...va|ter** *(meist Plur.);* **Grund|er|werb; Grund|erwerbs|steu|er, Grund|er|werbsteu|er,** die (↑R 34); **Grün|derzeit,** die; -; **grund|falsch; Grund‿far|be, ...feh|ler; Grundfes|ten** *Plur.;* in den - erschüttert; **Grund‿form** (*für* Infinitiv), **...frage, ...ge|bühr; Grund|ge|danke; Grund|ge|setz** (Statut); Grundgesetz für die Bundesrepublik Deutschland vom 23. Mai 1949 (*Abk.* GG); **Grund|haltung; grund|häss|lich; Grundhol|de,** der; -n, -n; ↑R 5 ff. (ehem. an Grund und Boden gebundener Höriger); **grun|die|ren** (Grundfarbe auftragen); **Grun|dierung; Grund|kurs; Grund|la-**

ge; **Grund|la|gen|for|schung; grund|le|gend** (↑R 40); **gründ|lich; Gründ|lich|keit,** die; -; **Gründ|ling** (ein Fisch); **Grund|li|nie; Grund|li|ni|en|spiel,** das; -[e]s *(Tennis);* **grund|los; Grund|lo|sig|keit,** die; -; **Grund‿mau|er** *(meist Plur.),* **...mo|rä|ne** *(Geol.),* **...nah|rungs|mit|tel**

Grün|don|ners|tag

Grund‿ord|nung, ...pfei|ler, ...prin|zip, ...recht, ...re|gel, ...ren|te, ...riss, ...satz; Grund|satz‿de|bat|te, ...ent|schei|dung, ...er|klä|rung; grund|sätz|lich; (↑R 47:) im Grundsätzlichen (grundsätzlich) hat sie Recht; er bewegt sich stets nur im Grundsätzlichen; **Grund|satz‿re|de, ...re|fe|rat, ...ur|teil; grund|schlecht; Grund‿schnel|lig|keit** *(Sport),* **...schuld, ...schu|le, ...schü|ler, ...schü|le|rin; grund|so|li|de; grund|stän|dig** (bodenständig; *Bot.* unten am Spross der Pflanze stehend); -e Blätter; **Grund|stein; Grund|stein|le|gung; Grund‿stel|lung, ...steu|er** (die), **...stock** (*Plur.* ...stöcke), **...stoff, ...stre|cke** *(Bergbau),* **...stück; Grund|stücks‿ei|gen|tü|mer, ...ei|gen|tü|me|rin; Grund‿stu|di|um, ...stu|fe** *(für* [2]Positiv), **...ten|denz, ...ton** (*Plur.* ...töne), **...übel** (↑R 132), **...um|satz** (*Med.* Energiebedarf des ruhenden Menschen); **Grund und Bo|den,** der; - - -s; ein Teil meines Grund und Bodens; **Grün|dung; Grün|dungs‿fei|er, ...jahr, ...ka|pi|tal, ...mit|glied, ...ver|samm|lung**

Grün|dün|gung

grund‿ver|kehrt, ...ver|schie|den; Grund|ver|sor|gung; Grund|was|ser, das; -s (*Ggs.* Oberflächenwasser); **Grund|was|ser‿ab|sen|kung** (künstl. Tieferlegen des Grundwasserspiegels), **...spie|gel; Grund‿wehr|dienst, ...wert, ...wort** (*Plur.* ...wörter; *Sprachw.* durch das Bestimmungswort näher bestimmter zweiter Bestandteil einer Zusammensetzung, z. B. „Wagen" in „Speisewagen"); **Grund‿wort|schatz, ...zahl** (*für* Kardinalzahl), **...zins** (*Plur.* ...zinsen), **...zug, ...zu|stand** *(Physik)*

[1]Grü|ne, das; -n; im Grünen lustwandeln; ins Grüne gehen; Fahrt ins Grüne; **[2]Grü|ne** *(Plur.) vgl.* Bündnis; **[3]Grü|ne,** der *u.* die; -n, -n; ↑R 5 (Mitglied der Partei Bündnis 90/Die Grünen); **[4]Grü|ne,** die; - (*veraltet, noch geh. für* grüne Farbe, Grünsein); **grü|nen** (grün werden, sein); **Grü|nen|ab|ge|ord|ne|te** ⟨*zu* [2]Grüne⟩

Grü|ne|wald (dt. Maler)

Grün‿flä|che, ...fut|ter (*vgl.* [1]Futter)

Grunge [grandʒ], der; - ⟨engl.-amerik.⟩ (eine Stilrichtung der Rockmusik; lässige, bewusst unansehnliche Kleidung)

grün|gelb (↑R 27); **Grün‿gür|tel, ...horn** (*Plur.* ...hörner; *selten für* Neuling), **...kern** (der; -[e]s), **...kohl** (der; -[e]s); **Grün|kram|la|den** *(landsch.);* **Grün|land,** das; -[e]s *(Landw.);* **grün|lich;** grünlich gelb (↑R 27); **Grün|li|lie** (eine Zimmerpflanze); **Grün|ling** (*ugs. auch für* unerfahrener, unreifer Mensch); **Grün‿pflan|ze, ...rock** (*scherzh. für* Förster, Jäger); **Grün|rot|blind|heit** *vgl.* Rotgrünblindheit; **Grün‿schna|bel** (*ugs. für* unerfahrener, unreifer, vorlauter Mensch), **...span** (der; -[e]s; grüner Belag auf Kupfer od. Messing), **...specht, ...strei|fen**

grun|zen; du grunzt

Grün‿zeug (das; -[e]s; *ugs.*), **...zo|ne**

Grupp, der; -s, -s ⟨franz.⟩ (Paket aus Geldrollen); **Grüpp|chen; [1]Grup|pe,** die; -, -n

[2]Grup|pe, Grüp|pe, die; -, -n (*landsch. für* [Wasser]graben, Rinne); **grüp|peln** (eine [2]Gruppe ausheben); ich ...[e]le (↑R 16); **grup|pen** (*svw.* grüppeln)

Grup|pen‿abend (↑R 132), **...ar|beit, ...auf|nah|me, ...bild, ...bil|dung, ...dy|na|mik, ...füh|rer, ...füh|re|rin, ...lei|ter** (der), **...lei|te|rin, ...psy|cho|lo|gie, ...rei|se, ...sex, ...sieg** *(Sport),* **...the|ra|pie, ...un|ter|richt, ...ver|si|che|rung; grup|pen|wei|se; Grup|pen|ziel; grup|pie|ren; Grup|pie|rung; Grüpp|lein**

Grus, der; -es, -e („Grieß") (verwittertes Gestein; Kohlenstaub); *vgl. aber* Gruß

Gru|sel‿ef|fekt, ...film, ...ge|schich|te; gru|se|lig, grus|lig (schaurig, unheimlich); **Gru|sel‿ka|bi|nett, ...mär|chen; gru|seln;** ich ...[e]le mich (↑R 16); mir *od.* mich gruselt es; **Gru|si|cal** ['gru:zik(ə)l], das; -s, -s ⟨anglisierende Neubildung nach dem Vorbild von „Musical"⟩ (*scherzh. für* [nach Art eines Musicals aufgemachter] Gruselfilm)

gru|sig ⟨*zu* Grus⟩

Gru|si|ni|en [...iən] (*russ. Name für* Georgien); **gru|si|nisch**

Grus|koh|le, die; - (grobkörniger Kohlenstaub)

grus|lig *vgl.* gruselig

Gruß, der; -es, Grüße; *vgl. aber* Grus; **Gruß|ad|res|se; grü|ßen;** du grüßt; grüß [dich] Gott!; grüß Gott sagen; **Gruß|for|mel; gruß|los; Gruß|wort** *Plur.* ...worte

Grütz|beu|tel (Balggeschwulst [bes. unter der Kopfhaut]); **Grüt|ze,** die; -, -n

Gruy|ère [gry'jɛ:r], der; -s (*franz. Bez. für* Greyerzer Käse, ein Schweizer Hartkäse); **Gruy|ères** [gry'jɛ:r] (Stadt im Kanton Freiburg, *dt.* Greyerz)

Gry|phi|us (dt. Dichter)

Grzi|mek ['gʒimɛk] (dt. Zoologe)

G-Sai|te ['ge:...] *(Musik)*

Gschaftl|hu|ber *vgl.* Geschaftl...

gscha|mig, gschä|mig *vgl.* geschamig, geschämig

gschert *vgl.* geschert; **Gscher|te** *vgl.* Gescherte

G-Schlüs|sel ['ge:...] (Violinschlüssel)

Gschnas, das; -, - (*österr. für* Kostümfest, Ball); **Gschnas|fest**

gschupft (*österr. ugs., schweiz. mdal. für* überspannt, affektiert)

gspa|ßig (*bayr., österr. ugs. für* spaßig, lustig)

Gspu|si, das; -s, -s ⟨ital.⟩ (*südd., österr. ugs. für* Liebschaft; Liebste[r])

GST = Gesellschaft für Sport und Technik (ehem. in der DDR paramilitärische Organisation)

Gstaad (schweiz. Kurort)

Gstan|zel, Gstanzl, das; -s, -n (*bayr., österr. für* Schnaderhüpfl)

Gstät|ten, die; -, - (*ostösterr. für* abschüssige, steinige Wiese)

Gu|a|de|loupe [...'lup] (Insel der Kleinen Antillen; franz. Überseedepartement)

Gu|a|jak|harz, das; -es ⟨indian.; dt.⟩; **Gu|a|jak|holz,** das; -es; **Gu|a|ja|kol,** das; -s (eine als Antiseptikum verwendete Alkoholart)

Gu|a|na|ko, das, *älter* der; -s, -s ⟨indian.⟩ (südamerik. Lama)

Gu|a|no, der; -s ⟨indian.⟩ ([Vogel]dünger); **Gu|a|no|in|seln** *Plur.* (an der Westküste Südamerikas)

Gu|a|ra|ni, der; -, - (Angehöriger eines südamerik. Indianerstammes; Währungseinheit in Paraguay)

Gu|ar|dia ci|vil [- si'vil], die; - - ⟨span.⟩ (span. Gendarmerie); **Gu|ar|di|an** [*österr.* 'gua:r...], der; -s, -e ⟨mlat.⟩ (Oberer [bei Franziskanern u. Kapuzinern])

Gu|asch, die; -, -en (*eindeutschende Schreibung von* Gouache); **Gu|asch|ma|le|rei**

Gu|a|te|ma|la (Staat und Stadt in

Mittelamerika); **Gu|a|te|mal|te|ke,** der; -n, -n; ↑R 126 (Bewohner von Guatemala); **Gu|a|te|mal|te|kin; gu|a|te|mal|te|kisch**

Gu|a|ya|na (Landschaft in Südamerika; *vgl.* Guyana)

gu|cken (*ugs. für* blicken, sehen); *vgl. auch* kucken; **Gu|cker**

Gu|cker|sche|cken *vgl.* Gugerschecken

Guck|fens|ter; Gu|cki, der; -s, -s (*ugs.* Gerät zum Betrachten von Dias; Skatausdruck); **Guck|in|die|luft;** Hans -; **Guck|kas|ten** *(früher);* **Guck|kas|ten|büh|ne; Guck|loch**

Gü|del|mon|tag *od.* **Gü|dis|mon|tag** (*schweiz. für* Rosenmontag)

Gud|run (w. Vorn.)

Gu|du|la (w. Vorn.)

Gu|el|fe [ˈg(u)ɛlfə], der; -n, -n (↑R 126) ‹ital.› (mittelalterl. Anhänger der päpstl. Politik, Gegner der Gibellinen)

Gue|ri|cke [ˈgeː...] (dt. Physiker); guerickesche Halbkugel, guerickesche Leere *(Physik)*

¹Gue|ril|la [geˈril(j)a], die; -, -s ‹span.› (*kurz für* Guerillakrieg); **²Gue|ril|la,** der; -[s], -s *meist Plur.* (Angehöriger einer Einheit, die einen Guerillakrieg führt); **Gue|ril|la|krieg** (von Guerilleros geführter Krieg); **Gue|ril|le|ro** [geriˈljeːro], der; -s, -s (Untergrundkämpfer in Lateinamerika)

Guer|ni|ca [gɛr...] (span. Ort.; berühmtes Gemälde Picassos)

Gue|va|ra [geˈvaːra] (kuban. Politiker u. Guerillaführer); *vgl.* Che

Gu|gel|hopf (*schweiz. für* Gugelhupf); **Gu|gel|hupf,** der; -[e]s, -e (*südd., österr. u. seltener schweiz. für* Napfkuchen)

Gu|ger|sche|cken *od.* Gu|cker|sche|cken *Plur.* (*österr. ugs. für* Sommersprossen)

Güg|gel, der; -s, - (*schweiz. mdal. für* Gockel); **Güg|ge|li** [ˈgykəli], das; -s, - (*schweiz. für* Backhähnchen)

Gui|do [ˈgiːdo, *österr. meist* ˈguːido] (m. Vorn.)

Guil|loche [gi(l)ˈjɔʃ, *österr.* guiˈjɔʃ], die; -, -n ‹franz.› (verschlungene Linienzeichnung; Werkzeug zum Anbringen solcher Linien); **Guil|lo|cheur** [...ˈʃøːr], der; -s, -e (Linienstecher); **guil|lo|chie|ren** (Guillochen stechen)

Guil|lo|ti|ne [gi(l)jo...], die; -, -n ‹nach dem franz. Arzt Guillotin› (Fallbeil); **guil|lo|ti|nie|ren**

¹Gui|nea [gi...] (Staat in Westafrika); **²Gui|nea** [ˈgini], die; -, -s ‹engl.› (*vgl.* Guinee); **Gui|nea-Bis|sau** [gi...] (Staat in Westafrika); **Gui|nee,** die; -, ...een ‹franz.› (ehem. engl. Münze); **Gui|ne|er** (Einwohner von ¹Guinea); **Gui|ne|e|rin; gui|ne|isch** (¹Guinea betreffend)

Gu|lasch [ˈgu(ː)...], das, *österr. u. schweiz. nur so, od.* der; -[e]s, *Plur.* -e, *österr. nur so, u.* -s ‹ung.›; **Gu|lasch‿ka|no|ne** (*scherzh. für* Feldküche), **...sup|pe**

Gul|brans|sen, Trygve (norweg. Schriftsteller)

Gul|brans|son, Olaf (norweg. Zeichner u. Karikaturist)

Gul|den, der; -s, - (niederl. Münzeinheit; *Abk.* hfl [*vgl.* holländisch]); **gül|den** (*geh. für* golden); **gül|disch** (*Bergmannsspr.* goldhaltig); **Gül|disch|sil|ber** (*Bergmannsspr.* goldhaltiges Silber)

Gül|le, die; - (*Landw.* flüssiger Stalldünger; *südwestd. u. schweiz. für* Jauche); **gül|len** *(südwestd. u. schweiz.);* **Gül|len|fass**

Gul|ly, der, *auch* das; -s, -s ‹engl.› (Einlaufschacht für Straßenabwässer)

Gült, Gül|te, die; -, ...ten (*südd. für* Grundstücksertrag; Zins; Grundschuld; *schweiz. für* Art des Grundpfandrechts); **Gült‿brief, ...buch; gül|tig; Gül|tig|keit,** die; -; **Gül|tig|keits|dau|er**

Gu|lyás [ˈgulaʃ], das *od.* der; -, - (*bes. österr. neben* Gulasch)

¹Gum|mi, der *u.* das; -s, -[s] (elastisches Kautschukprodukt); **²Gum|mi,** das; -s, -s (*kurz für* Gummiband); **³Gum|mi,** der; -s, -s (*kurz für* Radiergummi; *ugs. für* Präservativ); **Gum|mi|ad|ler** (*ugs. scherzh. für* [zähes] Brathähnchen); **Gum|mi|ara|bi|kum** (↑R 132), das; -s ‹nlat.› (Klebstoff); **gum|mi|ar|tig; Gum|mi‿ball, ...band** (das; *Plur.* ...bänder), **...bär|chen, ...baum, ...druck** (der; -[e]s); **Gum|mi|elas|ti|kum** (↑R 132), das; -s (Kautschuk); **gum|mie|ren** (mit Gummi[arabikum] bestreichen); **Gum|mi|gutt,** das; -s ‹ägypt.; malai.› (giftiges Harz, Farbe); **Gum|mi‿hand|schuh, ...ho|se, ...knüp|pel, ...lö|sung** (ein Klebstoff), **...man|tel, ...pa|ra|graph** (*ugs. für* Paragraph, der so allgemein formuliert ist, dass er verschiedene Auslegungen zulässt); **Gum|mi‿rei|fen, ...ring, ...schuh, ...schür|ze, ...soh|le, ...stie|fel, ...tier, ...zel|le; Gum|mo|se,** die; -, -n (*Bot.* krankhafter Harzfluss)

Gum|pe, die; -, -n (*Bergmannsspr.* Schlammkasten; *südd. für* Wasseransammlung, Wasserloch, tiefe Stelle in Wasserläufen und Seen)

Gun|del|re|be, die; -, -n *u.* **Gun|der|mann,** der; -[e]s (eine Heilpflanze)

Gun|du|la (w. Vorn.)

Gun|hild (w. Vorn.)

Gun|nar (m. Vorn.)

Gün|sel, der; -s, - (eine Pflanze)

Gunst, die; -; nach Gunst; in Gunst stehen; zu seinen Gunsten, zu seines Freundes Gunsten, *aber* (↑R 41): zugunsten, *auch* zu Gunsten; zuungunsten, *auch* zu Ungunsten der Armen; **Gunst‿be|weis, ...be|zei|gung, ...ge|werb|le|rin** (*scherzh. für* Prostituierte); **güns|tig; güns|ti|gen|falls, güns|tigs|ten|falls;** *vgl.* Fall, der; **Günst|ling; Günst|lings|wirt|schaft,** die; -

Gün|ter, *auch* **Gün|ther;** ↑R 92 (m. Vorn.); **Gun|ther** (dt. Sagengestalt; m. Vorn.); **Gunt|hild, Gunt|hil|de** (w. Vorn.)

Gupf, der; -[e]s, *Plur.* Güpfe, *österr.* -e (*südd., österr. ugs. u. schweiz. mdal. für* Gipfel, Spitze; stumpfer Teil des Eies)

Gup|py, der; -s, -s ‹nach dem engl.-westind. Naturforscher› (ein Aquarienfisch)

Gur, die; - (*Geol.* breiige, erdige Flüssigkeit)

Gur|gel, die; -, -n; **Gur|gel|mit|tel,** das; **gur|geln;** ich ...[e]le (↑R 16); **Gur|gel|was|ser** *Plur.* ...wässer

Gürk|chen; Gur|ke, die; -, -n (*ugs. auch für* [große] Nase; minderwertiger Gegenstand; unfähiger Mensch); **gur|ken** (*ugs. für* fahren); durch die Gegend -; **Gur|ken‿ge|würz, ...glas** (*Plur.* ...gläser), **...ho|bel, ...kraut, ...sa|lat, ...trup|pe** (*ugs. abwertend für* unfähige [Sport]mannschaft)

Gur|kha [...ka], der; -[s], -[s] ‹anglo-ind.› (Angehöriger eines Volkes in Nepal)

Gürk|lein

gur|ren; die Taube gurrt

Gurt, der; -[e]s, *Plur.* -e, *landsch. u. fachspr.* -en; **Gurt|bo|gen** *(Archit.);* **Gur|te,** die; -, -n (*schweiz. für* Sicherheitsgurt); **Gür|tel,** der; -s, -; **Gür|tel‿li|nie, ...rei|fen, ...ro|se** (die; -; eine Krankheit), **...ta|sche, ...tier; gur|ten** (mit einem Gurt anschnallen); **gür|ten; Gurt|ge|sims** *(Archit.);* **Gürt|ler** (Messingschlosser); **Gurt‿muf|fel** (*ugs. für* jmd., der sich im Auto nicht anschnallt), **...straf|fer** (der; -s, -; im Kraftfahrzeug)

Gu|ru, der; -s, -s ‹Hindi› (religiöser Lehrer des Hinduismus)

GUS [*auch* ge|uːˈ|ɛs], die; - (= Gemeinschaft Unabhängiger Staaten [Verbindung unabhängiger Staaten der ehem. Sowjetunion])

Gu|sche *vgl.* Gosche

Guss, der; -es, Güsse; **Guss|eisen,** das; -s; **guss|ei|sern; Guss‿form, ...re|gen, ...stahl** (↑R 136)

güst (*bes. nordd. für* unfruchtbar, nicht Milch gebend [von Tieren])

Gus|tav (m. Vorn.); **Gus|tav A|dolf** (Schwedenkönig); **Gustav-A|dolf-Werk,** das; -[e]s (↑R 95)

Gus|te (w. Vorn.); **Gus|tel** (m. *u.* w. Vorn.)

Güs|ter (ein Karpfenfisch)

Gus|ti (w. Vorn.)

gus|tie|ren ‹ital.› (*svw.* goutieren; *österr. ugs. für* kosten, prüfen); **gus|ti|ös** (*österr. ugs. für* appetitlich); **Gus|to,** der; -s, -s (Appetit; Neigung); **Gus|to|stü|ckerl,** das; -s, -n (*österr. ugs. für* besonders gutes Stück)

gut; besser *(vgl. d.),* beste *(vgl. d.);* einen guten Morgen wünschen; Guten (*auch:* guten) Morgen sagen; ein gut Teil; guten Mutes (↑R 5); gute Sitten; gut und gern; so gut wie; so weit, so gut; es gut sein lassen; ins gute [Heft] schreiben; *vgl. auch* Gut *u.* ausreichend. **I.** *Großschreibung:* **a)** (↑R 47:) jmdm. etwas im Guten sagen; im Guten wie im Bösen (allezeit); Gut und Böse unterscheiden können; jenseits von gut und böse sein; ein Guter; Gutes und Böses; sein Gutes haben; des Guten zu viel tun; vom Guten das Beste; zum Guten lenken, wenden; etwas, nichts, viel, wenig Gutes; alles Gute; **b)** (↑R 93:) der Gute Hirte (Christus); das Kap der Guten Hoffnung. **II.** *Getrennt- u. Zusammenschreibung:* **a)** *in Verbindung mit Verben* (↑R 39): er will gut sein; sie wird es gut haben; es damit gut sein lassen; es wird alles gut werden; sie wird mit ihm gut auskommen; er will gut leben; ich kann in den Schuhen gut gehen; es wird ihr dort gut gehen, vielleicht sogar besser gehen als hier; die Bücher werden gut gehen (sich gut verkaufen); *vgl. aber* gutbringen, guthaben, gutheißen, gutmachen, gutsagen, gutschreiben, gutsprechen. **b)** *in Verbindung mit Adjektiven u. Partizipien* (↑R 40): der gut gelaunte Besucher; die Besucher waren alle gut gelaunt; sie ist heute besser gelaunt; gut aussehend, bezahlt, dotiert, gemeint usw.; **Gut,** das; -[e]s, Güter; all sein Hab und Gut; (↑R 46:) zugute halten, kommen, tun; **gut|ach|ten** *nur im Infinitiv u. Partizip I;* **Gut|ach|ten,** das; -s, -; **Gut|ach|ter; Gut|ach|te|rin; gut|ach|ter|lich; gut|acht|lich; gut|ar|tig; Gut|ar|tig|keit,** die; -; **gut aus|se|hend, bezahlt** *vgl.* gut, II; **gut|brin|gen;** ↑R 37f. (*Kaufmannsspr.* gutschreiben); er hat mir diese Summe gutgebracht; *vgl.* gut, II; **gut|bür|ger|lich;** -e Küche; **[1]Güt|chen;** *nur in* sich an etwas ein - tun (*ugs. für* etwas genießen); **[2]Güt|chen** (kleines Besitztum, kleines Gut); **gut do|tiert** *vgl.* gut, II; **Gut|dün|ken,** das; -s; nach [seinem] -; **Gü|te,** die; -; sich in Güte einigen; **Gut|edel,** der; -s (↑R 132; eine Rebsorte); **Gü|te|klas|se** (einer Ware); **Gu|te|nacht‿gruß, ...kuss, ...lied**

Gu|ten|berg (Erfinder des Buchdrucks mit bewegl. Lettern)

Gu|ten|mor|gen|gruß; Gü|ter‿ab|fer|ti|gung, ...aus|tausch, ...bahn|hof; Gü|ter|fern|verkehr; Gü|ter|ge|mein|schaft; Gü|ter|nah|ver|kehr; Gü|ter‿tren|nung, ...ver|kehr, ...wagen, ...zug; Gü|te‿ver|fah|ren *(Rechtsw.),* **...zei|chen; gut Freund!** (Antwort auf den Ruf: Halt! Wer da?); **gut ge|hen** *vgl.* gut, II; **gut ge|hend, ge|klei|det, ge|launt, ge|meint** usw. *vgl.* gut, II; **Gut|ge|sinn|te,** der *u.* die; -n, -n (↑R 5ff.); **gut|gläu|big; Gut|gläu|big|keit,** die; -; **gut|ha|ben;** ↑R 37f. (*Kaufmannsspr.* zu fordern haben); du hast bei mir noch 10 DM gut; den Betrag hat er noch gutgehabt; *vgl.* gut, II; **Gut|ha|ben,** das; -s, -; **gut Heil!** (alter Turnergruß); **gut|hei|ßen;** ↑R 37 (billigen); gutgeheißen; **Gut|heit,** die; -; **gut|her|zig; Gut|her|zig|keit,** die; -; **gut Holz!** (Keglergruß); **gü|tig; Gut|leut|haus** (*früher für* Heim der Leprakranken; *heute vereinzelt südd. für* Armenhaus); **güt|lich;** etwas gütlich regeln; sich gütlich tun; **gut|ma|chen;** ↑R 37 (in Ordnung bringen; erwerben, Vorteil erringen); er hat etwas gutgemacht; *vgl.* gut, II; **gut|mü|tig; Gut|mü|tig|keit,** die; -; **gut|nach|bar|lich; Gut|punkt** *(Sportspr.);* **gut|sa|gen;** ↑R 38 (bürgen); ich habe für ihn gutgesagt; *vgl.* gut, II; **Guts‿be|sit|zer, ...be|sit|ze|rin; Gut|schein; gut|schrei|ben;** ↑R 38 (anrechnen); er versprach, den Betrag gutzuschreiben; *vgl.* gut, II; **Gut|schrift** (eingetragenes Guthaben); **gut sein** *vgl.* gut, II; **Gut|sel,** das; -s, - (*landsch. für* Bonbon); **Guts‿haus, ...herr, ...her|rin, ...herr|schaft, ...hof; gut si|tu|iert, sit|zend** *vgl.* gut, II

Guts|Muths (Mitbegründer des dt. Turnens)

gut|spre|chen; ↑R 38f. (*veraltet für* bürgen, gutsagen); er hat für mich gutgesprochen; *vgl.* gut, II; **Guts|ver|wal|ter**

Gut|ta|per|cha, die; - *od.* das; -[s] ‹malai.› (kautschukartiger Stoff)

Gut|temp|ler; Gut|temp|ler|or|den, der; -s (den Alkoholgenuss bekämpfender Bund)

Gut|ti|o|le ®, die; -, -n ‹lat.› (Fläschchen, mit dem man Medizin einträufeln kann)

gut tun *vgl.* gut, II

gut|tu|ral ‹lat.› (die Kehle betreffend; Kehl..., kehlig); **Gut|tu|ral,** der; -s, -e *u.* **Gut|tu|ral|laut** (*Sprachw.* Gaumen-, Kehllaut)

gut un|ter|rich|tet *vgl.* gut, II; **gut wer|den** *vgl.* gut, II; **gut|wil|lig; Gut|wil|lig|keit,** die; -

Guy [*franz.* gi, *engl.* gai] (m. Vorn.)

Gu|ya|na (Staat in Südamerika); **Gu|ya|ner; gu|ya|nisch**

Gwirkst, das; -s (*österr. ugs. für* verzwickte Angelegenheit; mühsame Arbeit)

Gy = Gray

Gym|kha|na [...ˈka:na], das; -s, -s ‹angloind.› (ein [sportl.] Geschicklichkeitswettbewerb)

Gym|naest|ra|da [...nɛ...] (↑R 130), die; -, -s ‹griech.; span.› (internationales Turnfest); **Gym|na|si|al‿bil|dung** (die; -), **...leh|rer, ...leh|re|rin, ...pro|fes|sor** (*österr., sonst veraltet für* Lehrer an einem Gymnasium); **Gym|na|si|ast,** der; -en, -en (↑R 126) ‹griech.› (Schüler eines Gymnasiums); **Gym|na|si|as|tin; Gym|na|si|um,** das; -s, ...ien [...iən] (*im Altertum* Schule, Raum für Leibesübungen, Versammlungsraum für Philosophen; *in Deutschland, Österreich u. der Schweiz* eine Form der höheren Schule); **Gym|nas|tik,** die; -; **Gym|nas|ti|ker; Gym|nas|tik|un|ter|richt; Gym|nas|tin** (Lehrerin der Heilgymnastik); **gym|nas|tisch; Gym|no|sper|men** *Plur.* (*Bot.* nacktsamige Pflanzen)

Gy|nä|kei|on, das; -s, ...keien ‹griech.› (Frauengemach des altgriech. Hauses); *vgl.* Gynäzeum; **Gy|nä|ko|lo|ge,** der; -n, -n; ↑R 126 (Frauenarzt); **Gy|nä|ko|lo|gie,** die; - (Frauenheilkunde); **Gy|nä|ko|lo|gin; gy|nä|ko|lo|gisch; Gy|nand|rie** (↑R 130 *u.* 132), die; -, ...ien (*Biol.* Verwach-

sung der männl. u. weibl. Blütenorgane; Scheinzwittrigkeit bei Tieren durch Auftreten von Merkmalen des anderen Geschlechtes); **Gy|nä|ze|um,** das; -s, ...een (*svw.* Gynäkeion; *Bot.* Gesamtheit der weibl. Blütenorgane)
Gy|ros, das; -, - ‹griech.› (griech. Gericht aus am senkrechten Drehspieß gebratenem Fleisch); **Gy|ro|skop** (↑R 132), das; -s, -e (Messgerät zum Nachweis der Achsendrehung der Erde)

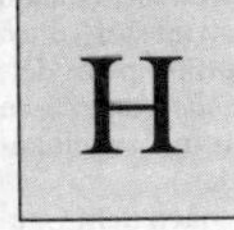

H (Buchstabe); das H; des H, die H, *aber* das h in Bahn (↑R 60); der Buchstabe H, h
h = *Zeichen für* plancksches Wirkungsquantum
h = Hekto...; hora (Stunde); 8 h = 8 Stunden, 8 Uhr; *hochgestellt* 8^h = 8 Uhr
h, H, das; -, - (Tonbezeichnung); **h** (*Zeichen für* h-Moll); in h; **H** (*Zeichen für* H-Dur); in H
H = [2]Henry; Hydrogenium (*chem. Zeichen für* Wasserstoff)
ha! [*auch* ha:]; haha!
ha = Hektar, Hektare
Ha = *chem. Zeichen für* Hahnium
Haag, Den (Residenzstadt der Niederlande); *dt. auch* Haag, der; im Haag; in Den Haag, *auch* in Haag; *vgl.* 's-Gravenhage; **Haager** (↑R 103)
[1]**Haar,** die; -, *auch* Haar|strang, der; -[e]s (Höhenzug in Westfalen)
[2]**Haar,** das; -[e]s, -e; *vgl. aber* Härchen; **Haar‿an|satz, ...aus|fall, ...band** (*Plur.* ...bänder); **Haarbreit;** *nur in* nicht [um] ein -
Haard, die; - (Waldhöhen im Münsterland); *vgl.* Hardt
Haardt, die; - (östl. Teil des Pfälzer Waldes); *vgl.* Hardt
haa|ren; sich -; der Hund hat [sich] gehaart; **Haa|res|brei|te;** *nur in* um -, *aber* um eines Haares Breite; **Haar‿far|be, ...farn; haar|fein; Haar|fes|ti|ger; Haargarn|tep|pich; haar|ge|nau; haa|rig** (*ugs. auch für* heikel); **Haar‿klam|mer, ...kleid** (*geh. für* Fell); **haar|klein;** jmdm. etw. - (in allen Einzelheiten) erzählen; **Haar|kranz**
Haar|lem (niederl. Stadt); **Haarle|mer** (↑R 103)
Haar|ling (eine Lausart); **haarlos; Haar|na|del; Haar|na|delkur|ve; Haar‿pfle|ge, ...pracht, ...riss, ...röhr|chen; haar|scharf; Haar‿schnei|der, ...schnitt, ...schopf, ...spal|ter** (spitzfindiger Mensch); **Haar|spal|te|rei; haar|spal|te|risch; Haar‿spange, ...spit|ze; Haar|spit|zen|katarrh** (↑R 33; *scherzh. für* Kopfschmerzen [nach durchzechter Nacht]); **Haar|spray**
Haar|strang *vgl.* [1]Haar
haar|sträu|bend; Haar‿teil (das), **...trock|ner, ...wasch|mit|tel, ...was|ser** (*Plur.* ...wässer), **...wild** (*Jägerspr.: Sammelbez. für* alle jagdbaren Säugetiere), **...wuchs; Haar|wuchs|mit|tel,** das; **Haar|wur|zel**
Ha|ba|kuk (bibl. Prophet)
Ha|ba|na [a'bana], **La** (*span. Form von* Havanna); **Ha|ba|ne|ra,** die; -, -s (ein kubanischer Tanz)
Ha|be, die; - (*geh.*); *vgl.* Hab und Gut
Ha|be|as|kor|pus|ak|te, die; - ‹lat.› (engl. Staatsgrundgesetz von 1679 zum Schutz der persönlichen Freiheit)
ha|ben; du hast, er hat; du hattest; du hättest; gehabt; hab[e]!; Gott hab ihn selig! (↑R 13); habt acht! (*österr. Kommando für* „still gestanden!"); ich habe auf dem Tisch Blumen stehen (*nicht:* ... zu stehen); **Ha|ben,** das; -s, -; [das] Soll und [das] -; **Ha|be|nichts,** der; *Gen.* - *u.* -es, *Plur.* -e; **Haben‿sei|te** (↑R 24; *für* [2]Kredit), **...zin|sen** (*Plur.*)
Ha|ber, der; -s (*südd., österr. u. schweiz. mdal. neben* Hafer)
Ha|be|rer, der; -s, - (*österr. ugs. für* Verehrer; Kumpan)
Ha|ber|feld|trei|ben, das; -s, - (*früher* volkstüml. Rügegericht in Bayern u. Tirol)
Ha|ber|geiß (*bayr. u. österr. veraltend* eine Spukgestalt)
ha|bern; ich ...ere; ↑R 16 (*österr. ugs. für* essen)
Hab|gier, die; -; **hab|gie|rig; habhaft;** des Diebes - werden (ihn festnehmen)
Ha|bicht, der; -s, -e; **Ha|bichts‿kraut, ...na|se**
ha|bil ‹lat.› (*veraltet für* geschickt, fähig; handlich; passend); **habil.** = habilitatus; *vgl.* Dr. ... habil.; **Ha|bi|li|tand,** der; -en, -en; ↑R 126 (jmd., der zur Habilitation zugelassen wird); **Ha|bi|li|tan|din; Ha|bi|li|ta|ti|on,** die; -, -en (Erwerb der Lehrberechtigung an Hochschulen); **Ha|bi|li|ta|ti|onsschrift; ha|bi|li|tie|ren** (die Lehrberechtigung an Hochschulen erlangen, verleihen)
[1]**Ha|bit** [*österr. u. schweiz. meist* 'ha:...], das, *auch* der; -s, -e ‹franz.› ([Amts]kleidung, [Ordens]tracht; Aufzug); [2]**Ha|bit** ['hɛbit], das, *auch* der; -s, -s ‹engl.› (*Psych.* Gewohnheit, Verhaltensart; *auch* Lernschritt); **Ha|bi|tat,** das; -s, -e ‹lat.› (Wohnplatz, Wohngebiet [einer Tierart]); **habi|tu|a|li|sie|ren** (*Psych.* zur Gewohnheit werden, machen); **Habi|tué** [(h)abi'ty̆e:], der; -s, -s ‹franz.› (*österr., sonst veraltet für* ständiger Besucher, Stammgast); **ha|bi|tu|ell** (gewohnheitsmäßig; ständig); **Ha|bi|tus,** der; - ‹lat.› (Erscheinungsbild [von Menschen, Pflanzen u. Kristallen]; Anlage; Haltung; Körperbau)
hab|lich (*schweiz. für* wohlhabend)
Habs|burg [die; -] (Ort u. Burg im Kanton Aargau); **Habs|bur|ger,** der; -s, - (Angehöriger eines dt. Fürstengeschlechtes); **Habs|burger|mo|nar|chie** (↑R 105), die; -; **habs|bur|gisch**
Hab|schaft (*veraltet für* Habe); **Hab|se|lig|keit,** die; -, -en *meist Plur.* (Besitztum); **Hab|sucht,** die; -; **hab|süch|tig**
Habt|acht|stel|lung (*österr. für* stramme [milit.] Haltung)
Hab und Gut, das; - - -[e]s (↑R 13)
Háček ['ha:tʃɛk], *eingedeutscht* Hat|schek, das; -s, -s ‹tschech.› (Aussprachezeichen bes. in slaw. Sprachen, z. B. č [tʃ] *u.* ž [ʒ])
hach!
Hach|se, *südd.* Ha|xe, die; -, -n (unterer Teil des Beines von Kalb od. Schwein); *vgl.* [2]Hesse
Hack, das; -s (*kurz für* Hackfleisch); **Hack‿bank** (*Plur.* ...bänke), **...bau** (der; -[e]s), **...beil, ...block** (*Plur.* ...blöcke), **...braten, ...brett** (Hackbank für Fleischer; ein Saiteninstrument)
[1]**Ha|cke,** die; -, -n, *seltener* Hacken, der; -s, - (Ferse)
[2]**Ha|cke,** die; -, -n (ein Werkzeug; *österr. svw.* Beil); **Ha|cke|beil** (*svw.* Hackbeil); **ha|cken** (hauen; mit dem Beil spalten); gehacktes Fleisch
Ha|cken *vgl.* [1]Hacke; **Ha|ckentrick** (*Fußball* Spielen des Balls mit der [1]Hacke [zur Täuschung des Gegners])
Ha|cke|pe|ter, der; -s, - (*landsch.*

für angemachtes Hackfleisch); **Ha|cker** (*auch für* jmd., der sich unerlaubt Zugang zu fremden Computersystemen zu verschaffen sucht); **Hä|cker|ling,** der; -s (*veraltend für* Häcksel); **Hack‿fleisch, ...frucht, ...klotz, ...mes|ser** (das), **...ord|nung** (die; -; *Verhaltensforschung*); **Häck|sel,** das *od.* der; -s (Schnittstroh); **Häck|sel|ler, Häcks|ler** (Häckselmaschine); **Hack‿steak, ...stock** (*österr. für* Hackklotz)

¹Ha|der, der; -s, *Plur.* -n *u.* (*für* Scheuertücher:) - (*südd., österr. für* Lumpen; *ostmitteld. für* Scheuertuch)

²Ha|der, der; -s (*geh. für* Zank, Streit); **Ha|de|rer, Had|rer**

Ha|der|lump (*österr. für* liederlicher Mensch, Taugenichts)

ha|dern ⟨*zu* ²Hader⟩ (*geh. für* unzufrieden sein; streiten); ich ...ere (↑R 16)

ha|dern|hal|tig (*fachspr. für* Stoff-, Lumpenreste in der Herstellungsmasse enthaltend); -es Papier

¹Ha|des (griech. Gott der Unterwelt); **²Ha|des,** der; - (Unterwelt)

Had|rer *vgl.* Haderer

Had|ri|an [*od., österr. nur,* 'ha:...] (↑R 130; röm. Kaiser; Papstname); *vgl.* Adrian

Had|schi (↑R 130), der; -s, -s ⟨arab.⟩ (Mekkapilger; *auch für* christl. Jerusalempilger im Orient)

Ha|du|brand (germ. Sagengestalt)

Hae|ckel ['hɛ...] (dt. Naturforscher)

Hae|moc|cult-Test ® [hɛm...] (↑R 132) ⟨griech.; lat.; engl.⟩ (zur Krebsvorsorgeuntersuchung)

¹Ha|fen, der, *auch* das; -s, Häfen (*südd., schweiz., österr. für* Topf); **²Ha|fen,** der; -s, Häfen (Lande-, Ruheplatz); **Hä|fen,** der, *auch* das; -s, - (*österr. für* ¹Hafen; *österr. ugs. für* Gefängnis); **Ha|fen‿amt, ...an|la|gen** (*Plur.*), **...ar|bei|ter, ...ein|fahrt, ...ge|bühr, ...knei|pe, ...kom|man|dant, ...po|li|zei, ...rund|fahrt, ...schen|ke, ...stadt, ...um|schlag, ...vier|tel**

Ha|fer, der; -s, *Plur.* (*Sorten:*) -; *vgl. auch* Haber; **Ha|fer‿brei, ...flo|cken** (*Plur.*), **...grüt|ze**

Ha|ferl, Hä|ferl, das; -s, -n (*österr. ugs. für* Tasse); **Ha|ferl|schuh** (*österr. für* ein Sporthalbschuh)

Ha|fer‿mark (das), **...mehl, ...sack, ...schleim**

Haff, das; -[e]s, *Plur.* -s *od.* -e (durch Nehrungen vom Meer abgetrennte Küstenbucht); ↑R 102: das Frische -, das Kurische -; **Haff|fi|scher** (↑R 136)

Ha|fis (pers. Dichter)

Haf|lin|ger (Pferd einer Gebirgsrasse); **Haf|lin|ger|ge|stüt**

Haf|ner (*schweiz. nur so*), **Häf|ner,** der; -s, - (*südd., österr. für* Töpfer, [Kachel]ofensetzer); **Haf|ne|rei**

Haf|ni|um ['ha(:)f...], das; -s ⟨nlat.⟩ (chem. Element, Metall; *Zeichen* Hf)

...haft (z. B. krankhaft)

¹Haft, die; - (Gewahrsam); **²Haft,** der; -[e]s, -e[n] (*veraltet für* Haken; Spange); **Haft‿an|stalt, ...aus|set|zung; haft|bar; Haft|bar|ma|chung; Haft‿be|din|gun|gen** (*Plur.*), **...be|fehl, ...dau|er; Haf|tel,** der *od.* das, *österr. nur so;* -s, - (*südd., österr. für* Häkchen und Öse); **häf|teln** (*landsch. für* durch ein Haftel schließen); ich ...[e]le (↑R 16); **haf|ten;** haften bleiben; einige haften bleibende Eindrücke; **Haft‿ent|las|sung, ...ent|schä|di|gung, ...er|leich|te|rung; haft|fä|hig; Haft|fä|hig|keit; Häft|ling; Haft|pflicht; haft|pflich|tig; haft|pflicht|ver|si|chert; Haft|pflicht|ver|si|che|rung; Haft‿prü|fungs|ter|min, ...prü|fungs|ver|fah|ren, ...rei|bung** (die; -; *Physik*), **...rei|fen, ...rich|ter, ...scha|le** (*meist Plur.*), **...stra|fe; haft|un|fä|hig; Haft|un|fä|hig|keit; Haf|tung,** die; -; *vgl.* GmbH; **Haft‿un|ter|bre|chung, ...ur|lau|ber, ...ver|scho|nung, ...ze|her** (eine Eidechsenart)

Hag, der; -[e]s, *Plur.* -e, *schweiz.* Häge (*schweiz. für* Hecke, Zaun; *veraltet für* Hecke; umfriedeter Bezirk; Waldgrundstück)

Ha|ga|na, die; - ⟨hebr.⟩ (Vorläufer der israel. Nationalarmee)

Ha|gar (bibl. w. Eigenn.)

Ha|ge|bu|che (*svw.* Hainbuche); **Ha|ge‿but|te** (die; -, -n), **...dorn** (*Plur.* ...dorne; *svw.* Weißdorn)

Ha|gel, der; -s; **ha|gel|dicht; Ha|gel|korn,** das; *Plur.* ...körner; **ha|geln;** es hagelt; **Ha|gel‿scha|den, ...schau|er, ...schlag, ...schlo|ße** (*landsch.*)

Ha|gel|stan|ge (dt. Schriftsteller)

Ha|gel‿wet|ter, ...zu|cker

Ha|gen (m. Vorn.); - von Tronje (Gestalt der Nibelungensage)

ha|ger; Ha|ger|keit, die; -

Ha|ge|stolz, der; -es, -e (*veraltet für* [alter] Junggeselle)

Hag|gai (bibl. Prophet)

Ha|gia So|phia, die; - - ⟨griech.⟩ (Kirche in İstanbul [heute ein Museum]); **Ha|gi|o|graph,** der; -en, -en; ↑R 126 (Verfasser von Heiligenleben); **Ha|gi|o|gra|phen** *Plur.* (dritter Teil der Bücher des A. T.); **Ha|gi|o|gra|phie,** die; -, ...ien (Erforschung u. Beschreibung von Heiligenleben); **Ha|gi|o|lat|rie** (↑R 130), die; -, ...ien (Verehrung der Heiligen)

ha|ha!, ha|ha|ha! [*beide auch* ...'ha]

Hä|her, der; -s, - (ein Rabenvogel)

Hahn, der; *Gen.* -[e]s, *schweiz.* -en, *Plur.* Hähne, *landsch., schweiz. u. fachspr.* (*für* techn. Vorrichtungen:) -en; **Hähn|chen; Hah|nen‿bal|ken** (*Bauw.* oberster Querbalken im Sparrendach), **...fe|der, ...fuß** (der; -es; eine Wiesenblume), **...kamm** (*auch* Zierpflanze; Pilz), **...kampf, ...ruf, ...schrei, ...tritt** (der; -[e]s; Keimscheibe im Hühnerei; ein Stoffmuster; *auch für* Zuckfuß); **Hah|ne|pot,** der, *auch* das; -s, -en, *selten* die; -, -en (*Seemannsspr.* Tau mit auseinander laufenden Enden)

Hah|ni|um, das; -s ⟨nach dem Chemiker Otto Hahn⟩ (chem. Element; *Zeichen* Ha)

Hahn|rei, der; -[e]s, -e (*veraltet für* betrogener Ehemann)

Hai, der; -[e]s, -e ⟨niederl.⟩ (ein Raubfisch)

Hai|fa (Hafenstadt in Israel)

Hai|fisch; Hai|fisch|flos|sen|sup|pe

Hai|kai ['haikai] *u.* **Hai|ku** ['hai...], das; -[s], -s ⟨jap.⟩ (eine japanische Gedichtform)

Hai|mons|kin|der *Plur.* (Helden des karoling. Sagenkreises)

Hain, der; -[e]s, -e (*geh. für* kleiner [lichter] Wald); **Hain‿bu|che** (ein Baum), **...bund** (der; -[e]s; ein dt. Dichterbund)

Hain|lei|te, die; - (Höhenzug in Thüringen)

Hair|sty|list ['hɛ:(r)stailist], der; -en, -en ⟨engl.⟩ (Friseur mit künstlerischem Anspruch)

Ha|i|ti (Staat in Mittelamerika); **Ha|i|ti|a|ner,** *auch* Ha|i|ti|er; **ha|i|ti|a|nisch,** *auch* **ha|i|tisch**

Häk|chen; Hä|kel|ar|beit; Ha|ke|lei (*Sport*); **Hä|ke|lei; Hä|kel|garn; ha|keln** (*Sport*); ich ...[e]le (↑R 16); **hä|keln;** ich ...[e]le (↑R 16); **Hä|kel|na|del; ha|ken; Ha|ken,** der; -s, -; **Ha|ken|büch|se** (*früher* eine Handfeuerwaffe); **ha|ken|för|mig; Ha|ken‿kreuz, ...na|se; ha|kig**

Ha|kim, der; -s, -s ⟨arab.⟩ (Gelehrter, Philosoph, Arzt [im Orient])

Ha|la|li, das; -s, -[s] ⟨franz.⟩ (ein Jagdruf); - blasen

halb; er hat mich wohl nur halb

verstanden; es ist, es schlägt halb eins; alle (*besser:* jede) halbe Stunde; alle halbe[n] Stunden; eine viertel und eine halbe Stunde; eine halbe und eine Dreiviertelstunde; [um] voll und halb jeder Stunde; der Zeiger steht auf halb; ein halbes Brot; ein halb[es] Dutzend; ein halbes Dutzend Mal[e], ein halbes Hundert Mal[e]; drei[und]einhalb Prozent, *aber* drei und ein halbes Prozent; anderthalb; (↑R 48:) ein Halbes, einen Halben bestellen; eine Halbe (*bayr. für* halbe Maß); (↑R 47:) nichts Halbes und nichts Ganzes; *mit Adjektiven zusammengeschrieben, wenn* „halb" *als bedeutungsabschwächender Zusatz aufgefasst wird* (↑R 40): ein halbhoher (nicht sehr hoher) Zaun, halbbittere (nicht sehr bittere) Schokolade; *aber* halb ausgeschlafen, halb fertig, halb leer, halb offen usw.; **Halb|af|fe; halb|amt|lich;** eine -e Nachricht, *aber* etwas geschieht halb amtlich, halb privat; **halb|bat|zig** (*schweiz. für* ungenügend, nicht zu Ende geführt, halbherzig); **Halb|bil|dung,** die; -; **halb|bit|ter; halb blind;** *vgl.* halb; **Halb|blut,** das; -[e]s; **Halb|blü|tige,** der *u.* die; -n, -n; ↑R 5 ff. (Mischling); **Halb|bruder; halb|bür|tig** (nur einen Elternteil gemeinsam habend); **halb|dun|kel; Halb|dun|kel; Halbe,** der, die, das; -n, -n (↑R 5 ff.); **Halb|edel|stein** (↑R 132; *veraltet für* Schmuckstein); **hal|be-halbe;** [mit jmdm.] - machen (*ugs. für* teilen); **...hal|ben** (z. B. meinethalben); **hal|ber;** *Präp. mit Gen.:* der Ehre -; gewisser Umstände -; des [guten] Beispiels -; **...hal|ber** (z. B. beispielshalber, umständehalber); **Halb|fab|rikat; halb|fett;** halbfette Buchstaben, der Name ist halbfett gesetzt *(Druckw.); vgl.* halb; **Halb|fi|na|le** *(Sport);* **Halb|franz,** das; - *(Buchw.);* in - [binden]; **Halb|franz|band,** der (Halblederband); **halb gar;** *vgl.* halb; **halbge|bil|det;** *vgl.* halb; **Halb|ge|bilde|te,** der *u.* die; **Halb|ge|fro|rene,** das; -n; **Halb‿glat|ze, ...gott; Halb|heit; halb|her|zig; Halbher|zig|keit; halb|hoch; hal|bieren; Hal|bie|rung; Halb‿in|sel, ...jahr; Halb|jah|res|kurs,** Halbjahrs|kurs; **halb|jäh|rig** (ein halbes Jahr alt, ein halbes Jahr dauernd); -e Übungszeit; **halb|jährlich** (jedes Halbjahr wiederkehrend, alle halben Jahre); -e Zusammenkunft; **Halb|jahrs|kurs** *vgl.* Halbjahreskurs; **Halb‿kanton** (in der Schweiz), **...kreis, ...ku|gel; halb‿lang, ...laut;** (*vgl.* halb); **Halb|le|der** (ein Bucheinband); **halb leer;** *vgl.* halb; **halblei|nen;** ein halbleinenes Tuch, *aber* ein halb leinenes, halb wollenes Tuch; **Halb|lei|nen; Halb|leinen|band,** der; **Halb|lei|ter,** der (*Elektrotechnik* Stoff, der bei Zimmertemperatur elektrisch leitet u. bei tieferen Temperaturen isoliert); **Halb|lin|ke,** der; -n, -n; ↑R 5 ff. *(Sport);* **halb links;** sich halb links halten; halb links spielen *(Sport); vgl.* halb; **halb|mast** (als Zeichen der Trauer); [Flagge] - hissen; auf - setzen, stehen; **Halb|mes|ser,** der (*für* Radius); **Halb|me|tall** (Element mit teils metallischen, teils nichtmetallischen Eigenschaften); **halbme|ter|dick; halb|mi|li|tä|risch; Halb|mond; halb|mond|för|mig; halb nackt;** *vgl.* halb; **halb offen;** *vgl.* halb; **halb|part;** *meist in* [mit jmdm.] - machen (*ugs. für* teilen); **Halb|pen|si|on,** die; - (Unterkunft mit Frühstück u. einer warmen Mahlzeit); **Halbpreis|abon|ne|ment** (↑R 132), ½-Preis-A|bon|ne|ment (*schweiz. für* Abonnement zum Bezug von Fahrkarten zum halben Preis); **Halb|rech|te,** der; -n, -n; ↑R 5 ff. *(Sport);* **halb rechts;** sich halb rechts halten; halb rechts spielen *(Sport); vgl.* halb; **halb|rund** (halbkreisförmig); **Halb‿rund, ...schat|ten; halb|schläch|tig** (*veraltet für* nicht eindeutig, schwankend); **Halb‿schlaf** (*vgl.* [2]Schlaf), **...schuh; halb|schü|rig** (*veraltet für* minderwertig); **Halb‿schwer|ge|wicht** (Körpergewichtsklasse in verschiedenen Sportarten), **...schwes|ter, ...seide; halb|sei|den;** ein halbseidenes Tuch, *aber* ein halb seidenes, halb wollenes Tuch; **halb|sei|tig; halb|staat|lich;** ein halbstaatlicher Betrieb *(ehem. in der DDR), aber* der Betrieb ist halb staatlich, halb privat; **Halb|star|ke,** der; -n, -n (↑R 5 ff.); **Halb|stie|fel; halbstock** (*Seemannsspr. svw.* halbmast); **halb|stün|dig** (eine halbe Stunde dauernd); **halb|stündlich** (jede halbe Stunde [stattfindend]); **Halb|stür|mer** *(bes. Fußball);* **halb|tags; Halb|tags‿arbeit, ...schu|le; Halb|tax|abonne|ment** (↑R 132; *früher für* Halbpreisabonnement); **Halb‿teil** (das, *auch* der; *selten für* Hälfte), **...ton** (*Plur.* ...töne); **halb tot;** *vgl.* halb; **Halb|to|ta|le** *(Film);* **halb|tro|cken;** ein halbtrockener Wein; *vgl.* halb; **halb ver|hun|gert;** *vgl.* halb; **halb voll;** *vgl.* halb; **halb wach;** *vgl.* halb; **Halb‿wahr|heit, ...wai|se; halbwegs; Halb|welt,** die; -; **Halbwelt|da|me; Halb|wel|ter|gewicht** *(Boxen);* **Halb|werts|zeit** (*Kernphysik* Zeit, nach der die Hälfte einer Anzahl radioaktiver Atome zerfallen ist); **Halb|wissen; Halb|wol|le; halb|wol|len;** ein halbwollenes Tuch, *aber* ein halb wollenes, halb baumwollenes Tuch; **halb|wüch|sig; Halbwüch|si|ge,** der *u.* die; -n, -n (↑R 5 ff.); **Halb|zeit; Halb|zeit‿pau|se, ...pfiff; Halb|zeug** (Halbfabrikat)

Hal|de, die; -, -n

Ha|léř [ˈhalɛːrʃ], der; -, ...ře [...rʒɛ], *Gen. Plur.* ...řů [...rʒuː] (Heller, tschech. u. slowak. Münze; 100 Haléřů = 1 Krone)

Hal|fa|gras *vgl.* Alfagras

Hälf|te, die; -, -n; meine bessere - (*scherzh. für* meine Ehefrau, mein Ehemann); zur -; **hälf|ten** (*svw.* halbieren)

[1]**Half|ter,** der *od.* das; -s, -, *schweiz., sonst veraltet,* die; -, -n (Zaum ohne Gebiss)

[2]**Half|ter,** das; -s, -, *auch* die; -, -n (Pistolentasche)

half|tern (den [1]Halfter anlegen); ich ...ere (↑R 16); **Half|ter|riemen**

hälf|tig; Hälf|tung

Half|vol|ley [ˈhaːf...], der; -s, -s ⟨engl.⟩ (*Tennis* Ball, der im Augenblick des Abprallens vom Boden geschlagen wird)

Hal|ky|o|ne usw. *vgl.* Alkyone usw.

[1]**Hall,** der; -[e]s, -e

[2]**Hall** (Name mehrerer Orte)

Hal|le, die; -, -n

Hall|ef|fekt ([elektronisch erzeugter] Hall, Nachhall)

hal|le|lu|ja! ⟨hebr., „lobet den Herrn!"⟩; **Hal|le|lu|ja,** das; -s, -s (liturg. Freudengesang); das - singen

hal|len (schallen)

Hal|len‿bad, ...fuß|ball (der; -[e]s), **...hand|ball** (der; -[e]s), **...ho|ckey, ...kir|che**

Hal|len|ser (Einwohner von Halle [Saale]); ↑R 103

Hal|len‿sport, ...ten|nis, ...turnier

Hal|ler (Einwohner von [2]Hall u. von Halle [Westf.]); ↑R 103

Hal|ler|tau, *auch* Hol|le|dau [*auch* ˈhɔl...] (↑R 132), die; - (Landschaft in Bayern)

Hal|le (Saa|le) (Stadt an der mitt-

leren Saale); *vgl.* Hallenser; **hallesch** *vgl.* hallisch
Halle (Westf.) (Stadt am Teutoburger Wald); *vgl.* Haller
Halley-Komet ['hale:...], der; -en ‹nach dem engl. Astronomen›, **Halleysche Komet,** der; -n -en
Hallig, die; -, -en (kleinere, bei Sturmflut überflutete Insel im nordfries. Wattenmeer); **Halligen** *Plur.* (eine Inselgruppe im Wattenmeer); **Halligleute** *Plur.*
Hallimasch, der; -[e]s, -e (ein Pilz)
hallisch ‹*zu* Halle [Saale]›
hällisch *vgl.* schwäbisch-hällisch
Halljahr (*A. T.* Feier-, Jubeljahr)
hallo! [*auch* ha'lo:]; - rufen; **Hallo,** das; -s, -s; mit großem -; **Hallodri** (↑R 130), der; -s, -[s] (*bayr. u. österr. für* ausgelassener Mensch)
Hallore, der; -n, -n; ↑R 126 (*früher* Salinenarbeiter in Halle [Saale])
Hallstatt (Ort in Oberösterreich); **Hallstätter See,** der; - -s; **Hallstattzeit,** die; - (ältere Eisenzeit)
Halluzination, die; -, -en ‹lat.› (Sinnestäuschung); **halluzinativ; halluzinieren; Halluzinogen,** das; -s, -e (Medikament, das Halluzinationen hervorruft)
Halm, der; -[e]s, -e
Halma, das; -s ‹griech.› (ein Brettspiel)
Halm‿fliege (ein Getreideschädling), **...frucht** (*meist Plur.*); **...halmig** (z. B. langhalmig)
Halo, der; -[s], *Plur.* -s *od.* ...onen ‹griech.› (*Physik* Hof um eine Lichtquelle; *Med.* Ring um die Augen; Warzenhof)
halo... ‹griech.› (salz...); **Halo...** (Salz...)
Haloeffekt [*auch* 'he:lo:...] (*Psych.* Beeinflussung einer Beurteilung durch bestimmte Vorkenntnisse)
halogen ‹griech.› (*Chemie* Salz bildend); **Halogen,** das; -s, -e (Salz bildendes chem. Element); **Halogenid,** Haloid, das; -[e]s, -e (Metallsalz eines Halogens); **Halogenidsalz,** Haloidsalz; **halogenieren** (Salz bilden); **Halogen‿lampe, ...scheinwerfer; Haloid** *vgl.* Halogenid; **Haloidsalz** *vgl.* Halogenidsalz; **Halophyt,** der; -en, -en; ↑R 126 (*Bot.* auf Salzboden wachsende Pflanze)
[1]**Hals,** Frans (niederl. Maler)
[2]**Hals,** der; -es, Hälse; - über Kopf; Hals- und Beinbruch; **Halsabschneider** (Wucherer); **halsabschneiderisch; Hals‿ausschnitt, ...band** (das; *Plur.* ...bänder), **...berge** (die; -, -n; Teil der mittelalterl. Rüstung); **halsbrecherisch; Halse,** die; -, -n (*Seemannsspr.* ein Wendemanöver); **halsen** (*veraltet für* umarmen; *Seemannsspr.* eine Halse durchführen); du halst; **Halsentzündung; halsfern;** ein -er Kragen; **Halsgericht** (im späten MA. Gericht für schwere Verbrechen); **...halsig** (z. B. langhalsig); **Hals‿kette, ...krause; halsnah;** *vgl.* halsfern; **Hals-Nasen-Ohren-Arzt** (*Abk.* HNO-Arzt); **Halsschlagader** (↑R 132); **Halsschmerz** *meist Plur.*; **halsstarrig; Halsstarrigkeit,** die; -; **Halstuch** *Plur.* ...tücher; **Hals über Kopf** (*ugs.*); **Hals- und Beinbruch!** (*ugs.*); **Halsung** (*Jägerspr.* Hundehalsband); **Hals‿weh, ...weite, ...wirbel**
[1]**halt** (*landsch. u. schweiz. für* eben, wohl, ja, schon)
[2]**halt!;** Halt! Wer da?; *vgl.* Werda; **Halt,** der; -[e]s, *Plur.* -e *u.* -s; [laut] Halt, *auch* halt rufen; Halt finden; Halt machen; ich mache Halt; Halt zu machen; Halt gemacht
haltbar; Haltbarkeit, die; -; **Halte‿bogen** (*Musik*), **...bucht, ...griff, ...gurt, ...linie; halten** (*landsch., bes. österr. auch für* [Kühe] hüten); du hältst, er hält; du hieltst; du hieltest; gehalten; halt[e]!; an sich halten; ich hielt an mich; **Haltepunkt; Halter** (*landsch., bes. österr. auch für* Viehhirt)
Haltere, die; -, -n *meist Plur.* ‹griech.› (*Zool.* umgebildeter Hinterflügel der Zweiflügler)
Halterin
haltern (festmachen, festklemmen); ich ...ere (↑R 16); **Halterung** (Haltevorrichtung)
Halte‿stelle, ...tau, ...verbot (*amtl.* Haltverbot); **Halteverbotsschild; haltig** (*Bergmannsspr.* Erz führend); **...haltig,** *österr.* **...hältig** (z. B. mehlhaltig); **haltlos; Haltlosigkeit,** die; -; **Halt machen** *vgl.* Halt; **Haltmachen,** das; -s; **Haltung; Haltungs‿fehler, ...note** (*Sport*); **Haltverbot** *vgl.* Halteverbot
Halunke, der; -n, -n (↑R 126) ‹tschech.› (*abwertend* Schuft, Spitzbube; *scherzh.* Schlingel); **Halunkenstreich**
Ham (bibl. m. Eigenn.)
Hamamelis, die; - ‹griech.› (Zaubernuss, ein Zierstrauch, eine Heilpflanze)
Hämatin, das; -s ‹griech.› (*Med.* eisenhaltiger Bestandteil des roten Blutfarbstoffs); **Hämatinon,** das; -s (rote Glasmasse [im Altertum sehr beliebt]); **Hämatit** [*auch* ...'tit], der; -s, -e (wichtiges Eisenerz); **Hämatologie,** die; - (Lehre vom Blut u. seinen Krankheiten); **Hämatom,** das; -s, -e (*Med.* Bluterguss); **Hämatozoon,** das; -s, ...zoen *meist Plur.* (*Zool.* im Blut lebender tierischer Parasit); **Hämaturie,** die; -, ...ien (*Med.* Blutharnen)
Hamburg (Land u. Hafenstadt an der unteren Elbe); [1]**Hamburger;** ↑R 103 (Einwohner von Hamburg); [2]**Hamburger** [*engl.* 'hɛmbœ:(r)ge(r)], der; -s, *Plur.* -, *bei engl. Ausspr.* -s (Brötchen mit gebratenem Rinderhackfleisch); **hamburgern** (hamburgisch sprechen); ich ...ere (↑R 16); **hamburgisch**
Häme, die; - (Gehässigkeit)
Hameln (Stadt an der Weser); **Hamelner,** *auch* Hameller (↑R 103); **hamelnsch**
Hamen, der; -s, - (Fangnetz; *landsch. auch für* Kummet)
Hämin, das; -s, -e ‹griech.› (*Chemie* Salz des Hämatins; *vgl. d.*)
hämisch
Hamit *od.* **Hamite,** der; ...ten, ...ten (↑R 126) ‹*zu* Ham› (Angehöriger einer Völkergruppe in Afrika); **hamitisch;** hamitische Sprachen
Hamlet (Dänenprinz der Sage)
Hamm (Stadt an der Lippe)
Hammel, der; -s, *Plur.* - *u.* Hämmel; **Hammelbein;** *meist in* jmdm. die -e lang ziehen (*ugs. für* jmdn. heftig tadeln; drillen); **Hammel‿braten, ...keule, ...sprung** (ein parlamentar. Abstimmungsverfahren)
Hammer, der; -s, Hämmer; **Hammer‿hai, ...klavier;** [1]**Hämmerlein;** [2]**Hämmerlein** *u.* **Hämmerling** (*veraltet für* böser Geist, Teufel); Meister - (Teufel; Henker); **hämmern;** ich ...ere (↑R 16); **Hammer‿schmied, ...werfen** (das; -s; *Sport*), **...werfer, ...zehe** (*Med.*)
Hammondorgel ['hɛmənd...] (↑R 95) ‹nach dem amerik. Erfinder› (elektroakustische Orgel)
Hammurabi (babylon. König)
Hämoglobin, das; -s ‹griech.; lat.› (*Med.* roter Blutfarbstoff; *Zeichen* Hb); **Hämophilie,** die; -, ...ien ‹griech.› (Bluterkrankheit); **Hämorrhagie,** die; -, ...ien (Blutung); **Hämorrhoidalleiden; Hämorrhoide,**

eindeutschend **Hä|mor|ri|de** (↑R 33), die; -, -n *meist Plur.* ‹griech.› ([leicht blutender] Venenknoten des Mastdarms); **Hä|mo|zyt**, der; -en, -en; ↑R 126 (Blutkörperchen)
Ham|pel|mann *Plur.* ...männer; **ham|peln** (zappeln); ich ...[e]le (↑R 16)
Hams|ter, der; -s, - (ein Nagetier); **Hams|ter|ba|cke** *meist Plur.* *(ugs.)*; **Hams|te|rer** (*ugs. für* Mensch, der [gesetzwidrig] Vorräte aufhäuft); **Hams|ter|kauf**; **hams|tern**; ich ...ere (↑R 16)
Ham|sun (norw. Dichter)
Ha|na|ni|as *vgl.* Ananias
Hand, die; -, Hände; Hand anlegen; linker Hand, rechter Hand; letzter Hand; freie Hand haben; von langer Hand [her] (lange) vorbereitet; etwas an, bei, unter der Hand haben; an etwas Hand anlegen; jmdm. an die Hand gehen; *aber* anhand des Buches, anhand von Unterlagen; Hand in Hand arbeiten, die Hand in Hand Arbeitenden, *aber* (↑R 28): das Hand-in-Hand-Arbeiten; etwas unter der Hand regeln; von Hand zu Hand; das ist nicht von der Hand zu weisen (ist möglich); von Hand (mit der Hand) eintragen; zur Hand sein; zu Händen *(vgl. d.)*. *Zur Zusammenschreibung vgl. die folgenden Stichwörter:* allerhand, zuhanden, abhanden, kurzerhand, vorderhand, vorhanden, handhaben; *aber* überhand nehmen. *Bei Maßangaben:* das Regalbrett ist eine Hand breit, *aber (als Maßeinheit):* eine Handbreit *(vgl. d.)* Tuch ansetzen, der Rand ist kaum handbreit; zwei Hände *od.* Hand breit, groß, lang; er hat die eine Hand voll Kirschen, *(auch als Mengenangabe getrennt:)* eine Hand voll Kirschen essen; **Hand|än|de|rung** (*schweiz. für* Besitzerwechsel bei Grundstücken); **Hand|ap|pa|rat**; **Hand|ar|beit**; **hand|ar|bei|ten**; gehandarbeitet; *vgl. aber* handgearbeitet; **Hand|ar|bei|ter**; **Hand|ar|beits|un|ter|richt**; **Hand|auf|he|ben**; eine Abstimmung durch -; **Hand|ball**; Handball spielen (↑R 39), *aber* das Handballspielen (↑R 50); **Hand‿bal|len**, **...bal|ler** (Handballspieler), **...be|sen**, **...be|trieb** (der; -[e]s), **...be|we|gung**, **...brau|se**; **hand|breit**; ein handbreiter Saum, *aber* der Streifen ist eine Hand breit; **Hand|breit**, die; -, -; eine, zwei, keine Handbreit, *aber* ein zwei Hand breiter Streifen; **Hand‿brem|se**, **...buch**; **Händ|chen**; ein Händchen haltendes Paar; **Händ|chen|hal|ten**, das; -s; **Händ|chen hal|tend** *vgl.* Händchen; **Hand|creme**; **Hän|de‿druck** (*Plur.* ...drücke), **...hand|tuch**, **...klat|schen** (das; -s)
[1]**Han|del**, der; -s (Kaufgeschäft); -treiben; ein Handel treibendes Volk; Handels wegen; [2]**Han|del**, der; -s, Händel *meist Plur.* (*veraltend für* Streit); Händel suchen
Hän|del (dt. Komponist)
Han|del-Maz|zet|ti (österr. Schriftstellerin)
[1]**han|deln**; ich ...[e]le (↑R 16); es handelt sich um ...; [2]**han|deln** ['hɛndl̩n] ‹engl.› (handhaben, gebrauchen); **Han|deln**, das; -s; **Han|dels‿ab|kom|men**, **...aka|de|mie** (↑R 132; *österr. für* höhere Handelsschule), **...bank** (*Plur.* ...banken), **...be|zie|hun|gen** *(Plur.)*, **...bi|lanz**, **...brauch**; **han|dels‿ei|nig** *od.* **...eins**; **Han|dels‿em|bar|go**, **...fir|ma**, **...flot|te**, **...ge|richt**; **han|dels|ge|richt|lich**; **Han|dels‿ge|sell|schaft**, **...ge|setz|buch** (*Abk.* HGB), **...ha|fen** (*vgl.* [2]Hafen), **...kam|mer**, **...klas|se**, **...leh|rer**, **...leh|re|rin**, **...mann** (*Plur.* ...leute, *selten* ...männer), **...ma|ri|ne**, **...mar|ke**, **...or|ga|ni|sa|ti|on** (die; -; *ehem. in der DDR; Abk.* HO; *vgl. d.*), **...platz**, **...po|li|tik**; **han|dels|po|li|tisch**; **Han|dels|recht**; **han|dels|recht|lich**; **Han|dels‿re|gis|ter**, **...rei|sen|de**, **...schiff**, **...schu|le**, **...span|ne**, **...stand** (der; -[e]s), **...stra|ße**; **han|dels|üb|lich**; **Hän|del|sucht**, die; - *(veraltend)*; **hän|del|süch|tig**; **Han|dels‿ver|trag**, **...ver|tre|ter**, **...ver|tre|te|rin**, **...ver|tre|tung**, **...vo|lu|men**, **...weg**; **Han|del trei|bend** *vgl.* [1]Handel
Hän|de|rin|gen, das; -s; **hän|de|rin|gend** (↑R 40); **Hän|de|wa|schen**, das; -s; **Hand|fe|ger**; **Hand|fer|tig|keit**; **hand|fest**; **Hand|fes|te** (*früher für* Urkunde); **Hand‿feu|er|lö|scher**, **...feu|er|waf|fe**, **...flä|che**; **hand|ge|ar|bei|tet**; ein -es Möbelstück; *vgl. aber* handarbeiten; **Hand|ge|brauch**, der; -[e]s; zum, für den -; **hand‿ge|bun|den**, **...ge|knüpft**; **Hand‿geld**, **...ge|lenk**; **hand|ge|mein**; - werden; **Hand‿ge|men|ge**, **...ge|päck**; **hand‿ge|schöpft**; **...ge|schrie|ben**, **...ge|strickt**, **...ge|webt**; **Hand|gra|na|te**; **hand|greif|lich**; **Hand|greif|lich|keit**; **Hand|griff**; **hand|groß**; ein -er Flecken; *vgl.* Hand II; **hand|hab|bar**; **Hand|hab|bar|keit**, die; -; **Hand|ha|be**, die; -, -n; **hand|ha|ben**; du handhabst; du handhabtest; gehandhabt; das ist schwer zu handhaben; **Hand|ha|bung**; **Hand|har|mo|ni|ka**
Han|di|cap usw. *vgl.* Handikap usw.
...hän|dig (z. B. zweihändig)
Han|di|kap, *auch* Handicap [*beide* 'hɛndikɛp], das; -s, -s ‹engl.› (Behinderung; *Sport* [Wettkampf mit] Ausgleichsvorgabe); **han|di|ka|pen**, *auch* han|di|ca|pen [*beide* ...kɛpən]; gehandikapt, gehandicapt; **han|di|ka|pie|ren**, *auch* han|di|ca|pie|ren [...kɛ'pi:...] (*schweiz. für* handikapen)
Hand-in-Hand-Ar|bei|ten, das; -s (↑R 28); **Hand-in-Hand-Ge|hen**, das; -s (↑R 28); **hän|disch** (manuell); **Hand|kan|ten|schlag**; **Hand|kä|se** *(landsch.)*
Hand|ke (österr. Schriftsteller)
hand|kehr|um (*schweiz. für* plötzlich, unversehens); **Hand|kehr|um**; *nur in* im - (*schweiz. für* im Handumdrehen); **Hand|kof|fer**; **hand|ko|lo|riert**; **Hand‿kom|mu|ni|on** *(kath. Kirche)*, **...korb**, **...kuss**; **hand|lang**; ein -er Schnitt, *aber* der Schnitt war zwei Hand lang; **Hand|lan|ger**; **Hand|lan|ger|dienst** *meist Plur.*; **Hand|lan|ge|rin**; **hand|lan|gern** *(ugs.)*; ich ...ere (↑R 16); **Hand|lauf** (an Treppengeländern)
Händ|ler; **Händ|le|rin**
Hand|le|se|kunst; **Hand|le|se|rin**; **Hand|le|xi|kon**; **hand|lich**; **Hand|lich|keit**, die; -
Hand|ling ['hɛndlɪŋ], das; -[s] ‹engl.› (Handhabung, Gebrauch)
Hand|lung; **Hand|lungs|ab|lauf**; **Hand|lungs|be|darf**; **Hand|lungs|be|voll|mäch|tig|te**, der *u.* die; -n, -n (↑R 5 ff.); **hand|lungs|fä|hig**; **Hand|lungs‿fä|hig|keit** (die; -), **...frei|heit** (die; -), **...ge|hil|fe**, **...rei|sen|de**, **...spiel|raum**; **hand|lungs|un|fä|hig**; **Hand|lungs‿un|fä|hig|keit** (die; -), **...wei|se** (die)
Hand|ma|le|rei; **Hand|mehr**, das; -s (*schweiz. für* durch Handaufheben festgestellte Mehrheit); **Hand|or|gel** (*schweiz. für* Handharmonika); **hand|or|geln**
Hand-out, *auch* **Hand|out** ['hɛnd|aut] (↑R 33), das; -s, -s ‹engl.› (Informationsunterlage)
Hand‿pferd, **...pres|se**, **...pup|pe**, **...rei|chung**, **...rü|cken**
Hands [hɛnts], das; -, - ‹engl.› (*österr., schweiz. für* Handspiel)
hand|sam (*österr., sonst veraltet für* handlich); **Hand‿schel|le** *(meist Plur.)*, **...schlag**, **...schrei-**

ben, ...schrift (*in der Bedeutung* „altes Schriftstück" *Abk.* Hs., *Plur.* Hss.); **Hand|schrif|ten‿deu|tung** (die; -), **...kun|de** (die; -), **...kun|di|ge; hand|schrift|lich; Hand|schuh;** ein Paar Handschuhe; **Hand|schuh|fach; Hand|set|zer** *(Druckw.)*; **hand|sig|niert** (↑R 130); **Hand‿spie|gel, ...spiel** *(bes. Fußball)*, **...stand, ...stein** (*nordd. für* Ausguss), **...streich, ...ta|sche; Hand|ta|schen‿raub, ...räu|ber; Hand‿tel|ler, ...tuch** (*Plur.* ...tücher); **Hand|tuch|hal|ter; Hand|um|dre|hen,** das; -s; im - (schnell [u. mühelos]); **hand|ver|le|sen** (*auch für* sorgfältig ausgewählt); **Hand voll** *vgl.* Hand; **Hand|wa|gen; hand|warm; Hand|wech|sel** (*veraltend für* Besitzwechsel [bei Grundstücken]); **Hand‿werk, ...wer|ker, ...wer|ke|rin; Hand|wer|ker|stand,** der; -[e]s; **hand|werk|lich; Hand|werks‿be|trieb, ...bur|sche, ...kam|mer, ...mann** (*Plur.* ...leute; *veraltet für* Handwerker), **...meis|ter, ...rol|le** (Verzeichnis der selbstständigen Handwerker), **...zeug** (das; -[e]s); **Hand‿wör|ter|buch, ...wur|zel**

Han|dy ['hændı], das; -s, -s ‹engl.› (handliches schnurloses Funktelefon)

Hand‿zei|chen, ...zeich|nung, ...zet|tel

ha|ne|bü|chen (*veraltend für* unverschämt, unerhört)

Hanf, der; -[e]s (eine Faserpflanze); **han|fen, hän|fen** (aus Hanf); **Hanf|garn; Hänf|ling** (eine Finkenart); **Hanf‿sa|men, ...seil**

Hang, der; -[e]s, Hänge; **hang|ab|wärts**

Han|gar [*auch* ...'ga:r], der; -s, -s ‹germ.-franz.› ([Flugzeug]halle)

Hän|ge‿arsch *(derb)*, **...ba|cken** *(Plur.)*, **...bank** (*Plur.* ...bänke; *Bergbau*); **Hän|ge|bauch; Hän|ge|bauch|schwein; Hän|ge‿bo|den, ...brü|cke, ...bu|sen, ...lam|pe; han|geln** *(Turnen)*; ich ...[e]le (↑R 16); **Hän|ge|mat|te; han|gen** (*schweiz., landsch., sonst veraltet für* [1]hängen); mit Hangen und Bangen; **[1]hän|gen;** du hängst; du hingst; du hingest; gehangen; häng[e]!; die Kleider hängen an der Wand; der Rock hing an der Wand, hat dort gehangen; an einem Nagel hängen bleiben; von dem Gelernten ist wenig hängen geblieben; hängen lassen (vergessen; *ugs. für* [jmdn.] im Stich lassen); (↑R 50:) mit Hängen und Würgen (*ugs. für* mit Müh und Not); hängende Gärten (terrassenförmig angelegte Gärten im Altertum), *aber* (↑R 108): die Hängenden Gärten der Semiramis; **[2]hän|gen;** du hängst; du hängtest; gehängt; häng[e]!; ich hängte den Rock an die Wand, habe ihn an die Wand gehängt; **hän|gen blei|ben** *vgl.* [1]hängen; **Han|gen|de,** das; -n; ↑R 5 ff. (*Bergmannsspr.* Gesteinsschicht über einer Lagerstätte); **hän|gen las|sen** *vgl.* [1]hängen; **Hän|ge|par|tie** (*Schach* vorläufig abgebrochene Partie); **Hän|ger** (eine Mantelform; *auch für* [Fahrzeug]anhänger); **Han|gerl,** das; -s, -n (*österr. ugs. für* Lätzchen; Wischtuch [der Kellner]); **Hän|ge‿schloss, ...schrank; hän|gig** (*fachspr. für* abschüssig; *schweiz. für* schwebend, unerledigt); **Hang‿la|ge, ...täl|ter**

Han|na (w. Vorn.)

Han|ne, Han|ne|lo|re (w. Vorn.); **Han|nes** (m. Vorn.); **Han|ni** (w. Vorn.)

Han|ni|bal (karthag. Feldherr)

Hann. Mün|den [ha'no:fɛrʃ -] (*post- u. bahnamtl. Schreibung von* [Hannoversch] Münden)

Han|no (m. Vorn.)

Han|no|ver [...fər] (Hptst. von Niedersachsen); **Han|no|ve|ra|ner** [...v...] (*auch* eine Pferderasse); **han|no|ve|risch, han|nö|ve|risch, han|no|versch, han|nö|versch** [*alle* ...f...], *aber* (↑R 47): im Hannöverschen

Ha|noi [ha'nɔy] (Hptst. von Vietnam)

Hans (m. Vorn.); Hans' Mütze (↑R 98); Hans im Glück; Hans Taps; *vgl.* Hansdampf, Hansnarr, Hanswurst; (↑R 102:) der Blanke Hans (*nordd. für* die stürmische Nordsee)

Han|sa *vgl.* Hanse usw.

Han|sa|plast ®, das; -[e]s (ein Verbandpflaster)

Häns|chen (*Koseform von* Hans); **Hans|dampf** [*auch* 'hans...], der; -[e]s, -e; - in allen Gassen

Hans|die|ter (m. Vorn.)

Han|se, die; - (mittelalterl. nordd. Kaufmanns- u. Städtebund); **Han|se|at,** der; -en, -en; ↑R 126 (Mitglied der Hanse; Hansestädter); **Han|se|a|ten|geist,** der; -[e]s; **Han|se|a|tin; han|se|a|tisch;** *vgl.* hansisch; **Han|se‿bund** (der; -[e]s), **...kog|ge**

Han|sel, der; -s, -[n] (*landsch. für* unfähiger od. dummer Mensch); **Hän|sel;** - und Gretel (dt. Märchen)

Han|sel|bank *vgl.* Heinzelbank

Hän|se|lei; hän|seln (necken); ich ...[e]le (↑R 16)

Han|se|stadt; han|se|städ|tisch

Han|si (m. *u.* w. Vorn.)

han|sisch (hansestädtisch), *aber* (↑R 108): die Hansische Universität (in Hamburg)

Hans|jo|a|chim [*auch* ...'jo:...], **Hans|jür|gen** (m. Vorn.); **Hans|narr** [*auch* 'hans...]; **Hans Taps;** *vgl.* Taps; **Hans|wurst** [*auch* 'hans...], der; -[e]s, *Plur.* -e, *scherzh. auch* ...würste (derbkomische Figur; dummer Mensch); **Hans|wurs|te|rei; Hans|wurs|ti|a|de,** die; -, -n

Han|tel, die; -, -n (ein Sportgerät); **han|teln;** ich ...[e]le (↑R 16)

han|tie|ren ‹niederl.› (handhaben; umgehen mit ...); **Han|tie|rung**

han|tig (*bayr., österr. für* bitter, scharf; barsch, unwillig)

ha|pe|rig, hap|rig (*nordd. für* stockend); **ha|pern;** es hapert (geht nicht vonstatten; fehlt [an])

hap|lo|id (↑R 130) ‹griech.› (*Biol.* mit einfachem Chromosomensatz)

Häpp|chen; hap|pen (*nordd. für* zubeißen); **Hap|pen,** der; -s, -

Hap|pe|ning ['hɛpənıŋ], das; -s, -s ‹engl.› ([Kunst]veranstaltung, bei der durch Aktionen ein künstlerisches Erlebnis vermittelt werden soll)

hap|pig (*ugs. für* zu stark, übertrieben; *nordd. veraltend für* gierig);

hap|py ['hɛpi] ‹engl.› (*ugs. für* glücklich, zufrieden); sie ist richtig -; **Hap|py|end,** *auch* **Hap|py End** ['hɛpi'ɛnt], das; -[s], -s ‹„glückliches Ende"›

hap|rig *vgl.* haperig

Hap|tik, die; - ‹griech.› (Lehre vom Tastsinn); **hap|tisch** (den Tastsinn betreffend)

har! (*Zuruf an Zugtiere* links!)

Ha|ra|ki|ri, das; -[s], -s ‹jap.› (ritueller Selbstmord durch Bauchaufschneiden [in Japan])

Ha|rald (m. Vorn.)

Ha|ra|re (Hptst. von Simbabwe)

Ha|rass, der; -es, -e ‹franz.› (Lattenkiste [zum Verpacken von Glas od. Porzellan])

Här|chen ‹*zu* Haar›

Hard|co|ver, *auch* **Hard Co|ver** ['ha:(r)d'kavə(r)] (↑R 33), das; -s, -s ‹engl.› (Buch mit festem Einband); **Hard|co|ver|ein|band,** *auch* **Hard-Co|ver-Ein|band**

Har|de, die; -, -n (*früher in Schleswig-Holstein* Verwaltungsbezirk von mehreren Dörfern od. Höfen); **Har|des|vogt** (*früher* Amtsvorsteher einer Harde)

Har|di, Har|dy (m. Vorn.)
Hard|li|ner ['ha:(r)dlainə(r)], der; -s, - ‹engl.› (Vertreter eines harten [politischen] Kurses); **Hard|rock,** *auch* **Hard Rock** ['ha:(r)d...], der; -[s] (laute Rockmusik mit einfachen Harmonien und Rhythmen)
Hardt, die; - (Teil der Schwäb. Alb); *vgl.* Haard *u.* Haardt
Hard|top ['ha:(r)dtɔp], das *od.* der; -s, -s ‹engl.› (abnehmbares, nicht faltbares Verdeck von Kraftwagen, bes. Sportwagen; auch der Wagen selbst); **Hard|ware** ['ha:(r)dwɛ:(r)], die; -, -s ‹engl.› (*EDV* die apparativen Bestandteile der Anlage; *Ggs.* Software)
Har|dy *vgl.* Hardi
Ha|rem, der; -s, -s ‹arab.› (von Frauen bewohnter Teil des islam. Hauses; die Frauen darin)
hä|ren (aus Haar); -es Gewand
Hä|re|sie, die; -, ...ien ‹griech.› (Ketzerei); **Hä|re|ti|ker; Hä|re|ti|ke|rin; hä|re|tisch**
Har|fe, die; -, -n; **har|fen; Har|fe|nist,** der; -en, -en; ↑R 126 (Harfenspieler); **Har|fe|nis|tin; Har|fen‿klang, ...spiel** (das; -[e]s); **Harf|ner** (*veraltet für* Harfenspieler)
Har|ke, die; -, -n (*nordd. für* Rechen); **har|ken** (rechen)
Här|lein ‹*zu* Haar›
Har|le|kin [...ki:n], der; -s, -e ‹franz.› (Hanswurst; Narrengestalt); **Har|le|ki|na|de,** die; -, -n (Hanswursterei); **har|le|ki|nisch**
Harm, der; -[e]s (*veraltend für* Kummer, Leid); **här|men,** sich (*geh. für* sich sorgen); **harm|los; Harm|lo|sig|keit**
Har|mo|nie, die; -, ...ien ‹griech.› (Wohlklang; ausgewogenes Verhältnis; Einklang); **Har|mo|nie|leh|re; har|mo|nie|ren** (gut zusammenklingen, zusammenpassen); **Har|mo|nik,** die; - (Lehre von der Harmonie); **Har|mo|ni|ka,** die; -, *Plur.* -s *u.* ...ken (ein Musikinstrument); **Har|mo|ni|ka|tür** (*svw.* Falttür); **har|mo|nisch;** -e Funktion *(Math.);* **har|mo|ni|sie|ren** (in Einklang bringen); **Har|mo|ni|sie|rung; Har|mo|ni|um,** das; -s, *Plur.* ...ien [...iən] *od.* -s (ein Tasteninstrument)
Harn, der; -[e]s, -e; **Harn‿bla|se, ...drang** (der; -[e]s); **har|nen** *(selten)*
Har|nisch, der; -[e]s, -e ([Brust]panzer); jmdn. in - (in Wut) bringen
Harn‿lei|ter (der), **...röh|re, ...ruhr** (*für* Diabetes), **...säu|re, ...stoff; harn|trei|bend** (↑R 40)
Har|pu|ne, die; -, -n ‹niederl.› (Wurfspeer od. pfeilartiges Geschoss für den [Wal]fischfang); **Har|pu|nier,** der; -s, -e *u.* **Har|pu|nie|rer,** der; -s, - (Harpunenwerfer); **har|pu|nie|ren**
Har|py|ie [...'py:jə], die; -, -n (Sturmdämon in Gestalt eines vogelartigen Mädchens in der griech. Sage; ein Greifvogel)
har|ren (*geh. für* warten)
Har|ri, Har|ro (m. Vorn.); **Har|ry** ['hari, *engl.* 'hɛri] (m. Vorn.)
harsch; Harsch, der; -[e]s (hart gefrorener Schnee); **har|schen** (hart, krustig werden); der Schnee harscht; **har|schig**
Harst, der; -[e]s, -e (*schweiz. für* [Heer]schar, Haufen)
hart; härter, härteste; hart auf hart; -e Währung. *Schreibung in Verbindung mit dem Partizip II:* ein hart gebrannter Stein; hart gefrorener Boden; das hart gewordene Brot; das Brot ist hart geworden; ein hart gekochtes, *(landsch.:)* hart gesottenes Ei; *vgl.* hartgesotten; **Hart|brand|zie|gel; Har|te,** der; -n, -n (*ugs. für* Schnaps); **Här|te,** die; -, -n; **Här|te‿aus|gleich, ...fall** (der), **...fonds, ...grad, ...klau|sel; här|ten; Här|te|pa|ra|graph; Här|ter** *(Chemie);* **Här|te|rei** *(Metallurgie);* **Hart|fa|ser|plat|te; hart ge|brannt** *vgl.* hart; **hart ge|fro|ren** *vgl.* hart; **hart ge|kocht** *vgl.* hart; **Hart|geld,** das; -[e]s; **hart|ge|sot|ten;** ein hartgesottener Sünder, die hartgesottensten Sünder; *vgl.* hart; **Hart|gum|mi,** der *u.* das; **hart|her|zig; Hart|her|zig|keit** *Plur. selten;* **Hart‿heu** (Johanniskraut), **...holz; hart|hö|rig; Hart|hö|rig|keit,** die; -; **Hart|kä|se; hart|köp|fig; Hart|köp|fig|keit,** die; -; **hart|lei|big; Hart|lei|big|keit,** die; -; **Härt|ling** (*Geol.* Erhebung, die aus abgetragenem Gestein aufragt); **hart|lö|ten** *(Technik); nur im Infinitiv u. Partizip II gebr.;* hartgelötet
Hart|mann (m. Vorn.)
hart|mäu|lig (von Pferden); **Hart|mäu|lig|keit,** die; -; **Hart|me|tall**
Hart|mo|nat, Hart|mond (*alte Bez. für* Januar [*auch für* November od. Dezember])
Hart|mut (m. Vorn.)
hart|nä|ckig; Hart|nä|ckig|keit, die; -
Hart|platz *(Sport)*
Hart|rie|gel, der; -s, - (ein Strauch); **hart‿rin|dig, ...scha|lig**
Hart|schier, der; -s, -e ‹ital.› (*früher* Leibwächter [der bayr. Könige])
Hart|spi|ri|tus, der; - (ein Brennstoff); **Har|tung,** der; -s, -e (*alte Bez. für* Januar); **Här|tung; Hart|wei|zen**
Hart|wig (m. Vorn.)
Ha|rus|pex (↑R 132), der; -, *Plur.* -e *u.* ...spizes [...tse:s] ‹lat.› (jmd., der aus den Eingeweiden von Opfertieren wahrsagt [bei den Etruskern od. Römern])
Har|vard|uni|ver|si|tät [...və(r)t...] (↑R 132), die; -; ↑R 95 ‹nach dem Mitbegründer J. Harvard› (in Cambridge [Mass.])
[1]**Harz,** das; -es, -e (zähflüssige, klebrige Absonderung, bes. aus dem Holz von Nadelbäumen)
[2]**Harz,** der; -es (dt. Gebirge)
har|zen (Harz ausscheiden; *schweiz. auch für* schwer, schleppend vonstatten gehen)
[1]**Har|zer** (↑R 103) ‹*zu* [2]Harz›; - Käse; - Roller (Kanarienvogel); [2]**Har|zer,** der; -s, - (eine Käseart)
har|zig (*schweiz. auch für* mühsam, schleppend); **Harz|säu|re**
Ha|sard, das; -s ‹franz.› (*Kurzform für* Hasardspiel); **Ha|sar|deur** [...'dø:r], der; -s, -e (Glücksspieler); **ha|sar|die|ren** (*veraltend für* wagen, aufs Spiel setzen); **Ha|sard|spiel** (Glücksspiel)
Hasch, das; -s (*ugs. für* Haschisch)
Ha|schee, das; -s, -s ‹franz.› (Gericht aus feinem Hackfleisch)
[1]**ha|schen** (fangen); du haschst; sich -
[2]**ha|schen** (*ugs. für* Haschisch rauchen); du haschst
Ha|schen, das; -s; - spielen
[1]**Ha|scher** (*österr. ugs. für* armer, bedauernswerter Mensch)
[2]**Ha|scher** (*ugs. für* Haschischraucher)
Hä|scher (*veraltet für* Büttel; Gerichtsdiener)
Ha|scherl, das; -s, -n (*bayr. u. österr. ugs. für* bedauernswertes Kind, bedauernswerter Mensch)
ha|schie|ren (zu Haschee machen)
Ha|schisch, das, *auch* der; -[s] ‹arab.› (ein Rauschgift)
Hasch|mich, der; *nur in* einen - haben (*ugs. für* nicht recht bei Verstand sein)
Ha|se, der; -n, -n; ↑R 126; (↑R 108:) falscher - (Hackbraten)
[1]**Ha|sel,** der; -s, - (ein Fisch)
[2]**Ha|sel,** die; -, -n (ein Strauch); **Ha|sel‿busch, ...huhn, ...maus, ...nuss; Ha|sel|nuss|strauch** (↑R 136); **Ha|sel‿stau|de, ...wurz** (die; -; eine Pflanze)
Ha|sen‿bra|ten, ...fell, ...fuß (*scherzh. für* überängstlicher Mensch); **ha|sen|fü|ßig** *(ugs.);*

Ha|sen|herz (*svw.* Hasenfuß); **ha|sen|her|zig** *(ugs.);* **Ha|sen‿jun|ge** (das; -n; *österr. für* Hasenklein), **...klein** (das; -s; Gericht aus Innereien, Kopf u. Vorderläufen des Hasen); **Ha|senpa|nier,** das; *nur in* das - ergreifen (*ugs. für* fliehen); **Ha|sen|pfeffer,** der; -s (Hasenklein); **ha|senrein** *(Jägerspr.);* nicht ganz - (verdächtig, nicht einwandfrei); **Hasen|schar|te; Hä|sin**

Has|pe, die; -, -n (Tür- od. Fensterhaken); **Has|pel,** die; -, -n, *seltener* der; -s, - (Garnwinde; Gerbereibottich; Seilwinde); **haspeln;** ich ...[e]le (↑R 16); **Haspen,** der; -s, - (*svw.* Haspe)

Hass, der; -es; **has|sen;** du hasst; gehasst; hasse! *u.* hass!; **hassens|wert; Has|ser; hass|erfüllt** (↑R 40); **häss|lich; Hässlich|keit; Hass‿lie|be, ...ti|ra|de; hass|ver|zerrt**

Hast, die; -; **has|ten; has|tig; Has|tig|keit,** die; -

Hat|schek (↑R 130; *eingedeutschte Schreibung für* Háček)

Hät|sche|lei; Hät|schel|kind; hät|scheln; ich ...[e]le (↑R 16)

hat|schen (*bayr., österr. ugs. für* schlendernd gehen, *auch für* hinken); du hatschst; **Hat|scher,** der; -s, - (*österr. ugs. für* langer Marsch; ausgetretener Schuh)

hat|schi!, hat|zi! [*beide auch* 'ha...]

Hat|trick ['hɛt...], der; -s, -s ⟨engl.⟩ (*Fußball* dreimaliger Torerfolg hintereinander in einer Halbzeit durch denselben Spieler)

Hatz, die; -, -en (*landsch., bes. bayr. für* Eile, Hetze; *Jägerspr.* Hetzjagd mit Hunden)

hat|zi! *vgl.* hatschi!

Hatz|rü|de *(Jägerspr.)*

Hau, der; -[e]s, -e (*veraltet für* Stelle, wo Holz geschlagen wird; *landsch. für* Hieb); *vgl.* ²Haue; **Hau|bank** *Plur.* ...bänke (*landsch. für* Werkbank zum Zurichten von Schieferplatten)

Hau|barg, der; -[e]s, -e (Bauernhaus mit hohem Reetdach, unter dem das Heu gelagert wird)

Hau|bar|keits|al|ter *(Forstw.)*

Häub|chen; Hau|be, die; -, -n; **Hau|ben‿ler|che, ...tau|cher**

Hau|bit|ze, die; -, -n ⟨tschech.⟩ (Flach- u. Steilfeuergeschütz)

Hauch, der; -[e]s, -e; **hauch|dünn; hau|chen; hauch|fein; Hauchlaut** *(Sprachw.);* **hauch|zart**

Hau|de|gen (alter, erprobter Krieger; Draufgänger)

¹Haue, die; -, -n (*südd., österr. u. schweiz. für* ²Hacke); **²Haue,** die; - ⟨*eigtl. Plur. zu* Hau⟩ (*ugs. für* Hiebe); - kriegen; **hau|en;** du haust; du hautest (*für* „mit dem Schwert schlagen“ *und geh.* hiebest); gehauen (*landsch.* gehaut); hau[e]!; sich -; er hat Holz gehauen; er hat ihm (*auch* ihn) ins Gesicht gehauen; **Hau|er** (Bergmann mit abgeschlossener Ausbildung; *österr. svw.* Weinhauer, Winzer; *Jägerspr.* Eckzahn des Keilers); **Häu|er** (*bes. österr. für* Hauer [Bergmann])

Häuf|chen; Hau|fe, der; -ns, -n (*veraltend für* Haufen); **häu|feln;** ich ...[e]le (↑R 16); **Hau|fen,** der; -s, -; (↑R 41:) zuhauf; **häu|fen;** sich -; **Hau|fen|dorf; hau|fenwei|se; Hau|fen|wol|ke**

Hauff (dt. Schriftsteller)

häu|fig; Häu|fig|keit *Plur. selten;* **Häu|fung; Hauf|werk,** Hauwerk, das; -[e]s (*Bergmannsspr.* durch Hauen erhaltenes Roherzeugnis)

Hau|he|chel, die; -, -n (eine Heilpflanze)

Hau|ke (m. Vorn.)

Hau|klotz

Häu|nel, das; -s, -n (*österr. für* kleine ¹Haue)

Haupt, das; -[e]s, Häupter *(geh.);* zu Häupten; **Haupt|al|tar; haupt|amt|lich; Haupt‿an|geklag|te, ...au|gen|merk, ...bahnhof** (*Abk.* Hbf.), **...be|ruf; hauptbe|ruf|lich; Haupt‿be|schäf|tigung, ...be|stand|teil, ...buch, ...dar|stel|ler, ...dar|stel|le|rin, ...ein|gang; Häup|tel,** das; -s, -[n] (*südd., österr. für* Kopf einer Gemüsepflanze, z. B. von Salat); **Häup|tel|sa|lat** (*österr. für* Kopfsalat); **Haup|tes|län|ge;** um -; **Haupt‿fach, ...feld|we|bel, ...figur, ...film, ...ge|bäu|de, ...gericht, ...ge|schäfts|zeit, ...gewicht, ...ge|winn, ...ge|win|ner, ...ge|win|ne|rin, ...haar** (das; -[e]s; *geh.*), **...hahn; Häupt|ling; häupt|lings; Haupt|mahl|zeit; ¹Haupt|mann** *Plur.* ...leute

²Haupt|mann, Gerhart (dt. Dichter)

Haupt‿mie|ter, ...nen|ner, ...person, ...por|tal, ...post, ...postamt, ...pro|be, ...punkt, ...quartier, ...rei|se|zeit, ...rol|le, ...sache; haupt|säch|lich; Haupt‿sai|son, ...satz, ...schlag|ader (↑R 132), **Haupt‿schul|abschluss; Haupt‿schuld, ...schule, ...schwie|rig|keit, ...se|gel, ...stadt** (*Abk.* Hptst.); **hauptstäd|tisch; Haupt‿stra|ße, ...teil** (der), **...the|ma, ...tref|fer; Haupt- und Staats|ak|ti|on** (↑R 23); **Haupt‿ver|ant|wortung, ...ver|die|ner, ...ver|handlung, ...ver|kehrs|stra|ße, ...verkehrs|zeit, ...ver|le|sen** (das; -s; *schweiz. Milit.* Appell vor Ausgang od. Urlaub), **...ver|sammlung, ...ver|wal|tung, ...wert, ...wohn|sitz, ...wort** (*Plur.* ...wörter; *für* Substantiv); **haupt|wörtlich** (*für* substantivisch); **Haupt‿zeu|ge, ...ziel, ...zweck**

hau ruck!, ho ruck!; **Hau|ruck,** das; -s; mit einem kräftigen -

Haus, das; -es, Häuser; Haus halten (*vgl.* haushalten); er hält Haus, hat Haus gehalten; außer [dem] Hause; außer Haus; nach Hause (*auch* Haus); zu Hause; von Hause; von Haus (*auch* Hause) aus; von Haus zu Haus; von zu Hause *(ugs.);* im Hause (*auch* Haus; *Abk.* i. H.); *(österr. u. schweiz. auch:)* zuhause, nachhause; *vgl.* Zuhause

Hau|sa *vgl.* Haussa

Haus‿an|ge|stell|te, ...an|zug, ...apo|the|ke (↑R 132), **...arbeit, ...ar|rest, ...arzt, ...ärz|tin, ...auf|ga|be, ...auf|satz; hausba|cken; Haus‿ball, ...bar, ...bau** (*Plur.* ...bauten), **...beset|zer, ...be|set|ze|rin, ...be|sitzer, ...be|sit|ze|rin, ...be|sor|ger** (*österr. neben* Hausmeister), **...be|woh|ner, ...be|woh|ne|rin, ...boot; Haus|buch** (*ehem. in der DDR* polizeil. Kontrollbuch über Hausbewohner u. deren Besucher); **Haus|bur|sche; Häuschen,** Häus|lein, *landsch. auch* Häu|sel *od.* Häusl, das; -s, -; **Haus‿da|me, ...dra|chen** (*ugs. für* herrschsüchtige Ehefrau od. Hausangestellte), **...durch|suchung** (*bes. österr. u. schweiz. für* Haussuchung); **haus|ei|gen;** -e Sauna; **Haus|ein|gang; Häu|sel** *vgl.* Häuschen; **hau|sen;** du haust; er haus|te

Hau|sen, der; -s, - (ein Fisch); **Hau|sen|bla|se,** die; - (Fischleim)

Hau|ser (*bayr., westösterr. für* Haushälter, Wirtschaftsführer); **Häu|ser‿block** (*vgl.* Block), **...front; Hau|se|rin, Häu|se|rin** (*bayr., westösterr. für* Haushälterin); **Häu|ser‿meer, ...rei|he; Haus‿flur** (der), **...frau; hausfrau|lich; Haus‿freund, ...friedens|bruch** (der; -[e]s), **...gebrauch** (für den - genügen), **...gehil|fin; haus|ge|macht; Hausge|mein|schaft; Haus|halt,** der; -[e]s, -e; **haus|hal|ten;** er haushaltet *(veraltend); vgl. auch* Haus; **Haus‿hal|ter** *od.* **...hälter; Haus|häl|te|rin; haus|häl-**

te|risch (sparsam); **Haus|halt[s]‿aus|gleich, ...aus|schuss, ...buch, ...de|bat|te, ...de|fi|zit, ...fra|ge, ...füh|rung, ...geld, ...ge|rät, ...ge|setz, ...hil|fe, ...jahr, ...kas|se, ...mit|tel** *(Plur.)*, **...plan, ...pla|nung, ...po|li|tik** (die; -), **...pos|ten, ...sum|me, ...tag** *(regional)*; **haus|halts|üb|lich;** in -en Mengen; **Haus|halts|wa|ren,** Haus|halt|wa|ren *Plur.*; **Haus|hal|tung; Haus|hal|tungs‿schu|le, ...vor|stand, ...we|sen** (das; -s); **Haus|halt|wa|ren** *vgl.* Haushaltswaren; **Haus‿herr, ...her|rin; haus|hoch;** haushohe Wellen; **Haus|hof|meis|ter** *(früher)*; **hau|sie|ren** (*veraltend für* Waren von Haus zu Haus anbieten); **Hau|sie|rer; ...häu|sig** (z. B. einhäusig); **haus|in|tern;** eine -e Regelung; **Haus‿ju|rist, ...kat|ze; Häusl** *vgl.* Häuschen; **Haus|leh|rer; Häus|lein** *vgl.* Häuschen; **Häus|ler** (Dorfbewohner, der ein kleines Haus ohne Land besitzt); **Haus|leu|te** *Plur.*; **häus|lich; Häus|lich|keit,** die; -; **Haus|ma|cher‿art** (die; -; nach -), **...wurst; Haus‿macht** (die; -), **...mann** (*Plur.* ...männer)

Haus|man|nit [*auch* ...'nit], der; -s (ein Mineral)

Haus|manns|kost; Haus‿mär|chen, ...mar|ke, ...mei|er (Vorsteher der merowing. Hofhaltung), **...meis|ter, ...mit|tel** (das), **...mu|sik, ...müt|ter|chen, ...num|mer, ...ord|nung, ...putz, ...rat** (der; -[e]s); **Haus|rat|ver|si|che|rung**

[1]**Haus|sa,** *auch* Hau|sa, der; -[s], -[s] (Angehöriger eines afrik. Volkes); [2]**Haus|sa,** *auch* Hau|sa, das; - (Sprache der Haussa)

Haus‿samm|lung, ...schaf; [1]**haus|schlach|ten** *nur im Infinitiv u. im Partizip II gebr.*; hausgeschlachtet; [2]**haus|schlach|ten;** -e Wurst; **Haus‿schlach|tung, ...schlüs|sel, ...schuh, ...schwamm, ...schwein**

Hausse ['ho:s(ə), *auch* o:s], die; -, -n ‹franz.› ([starkes] Steigen der Börsenkurse; allg. Aufschwung der Wirtschaft); **Haus|si|er** [(h)o'si̯e:], der; -s, -s (auf Hausse Spekulierender); **haus|sie|ren** [(h)o:'si:...] (im Kurswert steigen)

Haus‿stand (der; -[e]s), **...stre|cke** *(Sportspr.)*, **...su|chung** (*vgl.* Hausdurchsuchung), **...tier, ...tür, ...ty|rann, ...ur|ne** (ein vorgeschichtl. Tongefäß), **...ver|bot, ...ver|wal|ter, ...ver|wal|te|rin, ...ver|wal|tung, ...wart** (der; -[e]s, -e; *landsch.*), **...war|tin** *(schweiz.)*, **...we|sen** (das; -s), **...wirt, ...wir|tin, ...wirt|schaft; Haus|wirt|schafts‿meis|te|rin, ...pfle|ge|rin** *(regional)*, **...schu|le; Haus‿wurz** (die; -; eine Pflanze), **...zelt, ...zins** (*Plur.* ...zinse; *südd. u. schweiz. für* Miete); **Haus[-zu]-Haus-Ver|kehr;** ↑R 28

Haut, die; -, Häute; (↑R 28:) zum Aus-der-Haut-Fahren; **Haut‿arzt, ...ärz|tin, ...aus|schlag, ...bank** (*Plur.* ...banken; *Med.*); **Haut|creme**

Haute Coif|fure [(h)o:t ko̯a'fy:r], die; - - ‹franz.› (für die Mode tonangebende Friseurkunst [bes. in Paris]); **Haute Cou|ture** [(h)o:t ku'ty:r], die; - - (für die Mode tonangebende Schneiderkunst [bes. in Paris]); **Haute-Cou|ture-Mo|dell** (↑R 28); **Haute|fi|nance** [(h)o:tfi'nã:s], die; - (Hochfinanz); **Haute|lisse** [(h)o:t'lis], die; -, -n [...'lis(ə)n] (Webart mit senkrechten Kettfäden); **Haute|lisse|stuhl**

häu|ten; sich -; **haut|eng**

Haute|vo|lee [(h)o:tvo'le:], die; - ‹franz.› (vornehmste Gesellschaft)

Haut‿far|be, ...fet|zen, ...flüg|ler *(Zool.)*; **haut|freund|lich;** ein -er Stoff

Haut|gout [o'gu:], der; -s ‹franz.› (scharfer Wildgeschmack; *auch übertr. für* Anrüchigkeit)

häu|tig; Haut‿ju|cken (das; -s), **...kli|nik, ...krank|heit, ...krebs; haut|nah; Haut|pfle|ge**

Haut|re|li|ef ['(h)o(:)re.li̯ɛf] ‹franz.› (Hochrelief); **Haut-Sau|ternes** [oso'tɛrn], der; - (ein südwestfranz. Weißwein)

haut|scho|nend; Haut|schrift, die; - (*für* Dermographie); **haut|sym|pa|thisch; Haut|trans|plan|ta|ti|on; Häu|tung; Haut|ver|pflan|zung**

Hau|werk *vgl.* Haufwerk

[1]**Ha|van|na** [...v...] (Hptst. Kubas); *vgl.* Habana; [2]**Ha|van|na,** die; -, -s (Havannazigarre); **Ha|van|na|zi|gar|re** (↑R 105)

Ha|va|rie [...v...], die; -, ...i̯en ‹arab.› (Unfall von Schiffen od. Flugzeugen; schwere Betriebsstörung durch Brand, Explosion u. Ä.; *österr. auch für* Kraftfahrzeugunfall, -schaden); **ha|va|rie|ren; Ha|va|rist,** der; -en, -en; ↑R 126 (*Seew.* havariertes Schiff; dessen Eigentümer)

Ha|vel [...f...], die; - (r. Nebenfluss der Elbe); **Ha|vel|land,** das; -[e]s (↑R 105); **ha|vel|län|disch,** *aber* (↑R 102:) das Havelländische Luch

Ha|ve|lock ['ha:vəlɔk], der; -s, -s ‹nach dem engl. General› (ärmelloser Herrenmantel mit Schulterkragen)

Ha|waii (Hauptinsel der Hawaiiinseln im Pazif. Ozean; Staat der USA; *vgl.* Hawaiiinseln); **Ha|wai|i|a|ner; Ha|waii|gi|tar|re; Ha|waii|in|sel** (↑R 24), die; -, -n (eine der Hawaiiinseln); **Ha|waii|in|seln** (↑R 24) *Plur.* (Inselgruppe im Pazif. Ozean, die den Staat Hawaii *[vgl. d.]* bildet); **ha|wai|isch**

Ha|xe, die; -, -n (*südd. für* Hachse)

Haydn (österr. Komponisten); **haydnsch;** eine haydnsche Sinfonie (↑R 58)

Ha|zi|en|da, die; -, *Plur.* -s, *auch* ...den ‹span.› (südamerik. Farm)

Hb = Hämoglobin

HB = Brinellhärte

H. B. = Helvetisches Bekenntnis

Hbf. = Hauptbahnhof

H-Bom|be ['ha:...]; ↑R 26 ‹nach dem chem. Zeichen H = Wasserstoff› (Wasserstoffbombe)

h. c. = honoris causa

H-Dur ['ha:du:r, *auch* 'ha:'du:r], das; - (Tonart; *Zeichen* H); **H-Dur-Ton|lei|ter** (↑R 28)

he!; he̱da!

He = *chem. Zeichen für* Helium

Head|hun|ter ['hɛd...], der; -s, - ‹engl.› (jmd., der Führungskräfte abwirbt); **Head|line** ['hɛdlai̯n], die; -, -s (*engl. Bez. für* Schlagzeile)

Hea|ring ['hi:riŋ], das; -[s], -s ‹engl.› ([öffentliche] Anhörung)

Hea|vi|side ['hɛvisai̯d] (engl. Physiker); **Hea|vi|side|schicht,** die; -; ↑R 95 (*svw.* Kennelly-Heaviside-Schicht)

Hea|vy|me|tal ['hɛvi'mɛt(ə)l] (↑R 33), das; -[s] ‹engl.› (*svw.* Hardrock)

Heb|am|me, die; -, -n

Heb|bel, Christian Friedrich (dt. Dichter)

He|be (griech. Göttin der Jugend)

He|be‿baum, ...büh|ne, ...fi|gur *(Sport)*

[1]**He|bel,** Johann Peter (dt. [Mundart]dichter)

[2]**He|bel,** der; -s, -; **He|bel‿arm, ...griff; he|beln;** ich ...[e]le (↑R 16); **he|ben;** du hobst, *veraltet* hub[e]st; du höbest, *veraltet* hübest; gehoben; heb[e]!; sich -; **He|be|prahm; He|ber; He|be‿satz** *(Steuerwesen)*, **...schmaus** (Bewirtung beim Richtfest), **...werk**

Heb|rä|er (↑R 130; *bes. im A. T. für* Angehörige des Volkes Israel); **Heb|rä|er|brief,** der; -[e]s; ↑R 105 *(bibl.)*; **Heb|rä|e|rin; Heb|ra|i|cum,** das; -s ‹lat.› (Prüfung über bestimmte Kenntnisse des Hebräischen); **heb|rä|isch;** -e Schrift; *vgl.* deutsch; **Heb|rä|isch,** das; -[s] (Sprache); *vgl.* Deutsch; **Heb|rä|i|sche,** das; -n; *vgl.* Deutsche, das; **Heb|ra|ist,** der; -en, -en; ↑R 126 (Forscher u. Kenner des Hebräischen); **Heb|ra|is|tik,** die; - (wissenschaftl. Erforschung der hebr. Sprache u. Literatur); **Heb|ra|is|tin**

Heb|ri|den (↑R 130) *Plur.* (schott. Inselgruppe); Äußere u. Innere -; die Neuen - (Inselgruppe im Pazifischen Ozean; *jetzt* Vanuatu)

He|bung

He|chel, die; -, -n; (ein landw. Gerät); **He|che|lei** *(ugs. für* boshaftes Gerede); **he|cheln;** ich ...[e]le (↑R 16)

Hecht, der; -[e]s, -e; **hecht|blau; hech|ten** *(ugs. für* einen Hechtsprung machen); **hecht|grau; Hecht₋rol|le** (eine Bodenturnübung), **...sprung; Hecht|suppe;** es zieht wie - *(ugs. für* es zieht sehr)

[1]**Heck,** das; -[e]s, *Plur.* -e *od.* -s (hinterster Teil eines Schiffes, Flugzeugs, Autos); [2]**Heck,** das; -[e]s, -e *(nordd. für* Gattertür; Weide, Koppel); **Heck|an|trieb;** [1]**He|cke,** die; -, -n (Umzäunung aus Sträuchern)

[2]**He|cke,** die; -, -n *(veraltet für* Nistplatz; Paarungs- *od.* Brutzeit; Brut); **he|cken** *(veraltet für* Junge zur Welt bringen [von Vögeln und kleineren Säugetieren])

He|cken₋ro|se, ...sche|re, ...schüt|ze; Heck₋fens|ter, ...flos|se, ...klap|pe; heck|lastig; Heck|la|ter|ne

Heck|meck, der; -s *(ugs. für* Geschwätz; unnötige Umstände)

Heck|mo|tor

Heck|pfen|nig ‹*zu* hecken› *(scherzh. für* Münze, die man nicht ausgibt)

Heck|schei|be

He|cu|ba *vgl.* Hekuba

he|da! *(veraltend)*

Hed|da (w. Vorn.)

[1]**He|de** (w. Vorn.)

[2]**He|de,** die; -, -n *(nordd. für* Werg); **he|den** (aus [2]Hede)

He|de|rich, der; -s, -e (ein Unkraut)

He|di (w. Vorn.)

He|din, Sven (schwed. Asienforscher)

He|do|ni|ker, He|do|nist, der; -en, -en (↑R 126) ‹griech.› (Anhänger des Hedonismus); **He|do|nis|mus,** der; - (philosoph. Lehre, nach der das höchste ethische Prinzip das Streben nach Sinnenlust ist)

Hed|schas (↑R 130; Landschaft in Arabien); **Hed|schas|bahn,** die; -

Hedsch|ra (↑R 130), die; - ‹arab.› (Übersiedlung Mohammeds von Mekka nach Medina; Beginn der islam. Zeitrechnung)

Hed|wig (w. Vorn.)

Heer, das; -[e]s, -e; **Heer|bann** *(früher)*; **Hee|res₋be|richt, ...bestand** *(meist Plur.)*, **...grup|pe, ...lei|tung, ...zug** *(vgl.* Heerzug); **Heer₋füh|rer, ...la|ger, ...schar** *(vgl.* [1]Schar), **...schau, ...stra|ße, ...we|sen** (das; -s); **Heer|zug,** Hee|res|zug

He|fe, die; -, -n; **He|fe₋brot, ...kloß, ...kranz, ...ku|chen, ...stück|chen** (Kleingebäck), **...teig, ...zopf; he|fig**

Hef|ner|ker|ze; ↑R 95 ‹nach dem dt. Elektrotechniker› (frühere Lichtstärkeeinheit; *Zeichen* HK)

Heft, das; -[e]s, -e; **Hef|tel,** das; -s, - *(landsch. für* Häkchen, Spange); **hef|teln** *(landsch.)*; ich ...[e]le (↑R 16); **hef|ten;** geheftet *(Abk.* geh.); die Akten wurden geheftet; **Hef|ter** (Mappe zum Abheften); **Heft|fa|den** *Plur.* ...fäden

hef|tig; Hef|tig|keit

Heft₋klam|mer, ...la|de (Gerät in der Buchbinderei), **...pflas|ter, ...zwe|cke**

He|gau, der; -[e]s (Landschaft am Bodensee)

He|ge, die; - (Pflege u. Schutz des Wildes)

He|gel (dt. Philosoph); **He|ge|li|aner** (Anhänger Hegels); **he|ge|li|a|nisch; he|gelsch;** die hegelsche Philosophie (↑R 94)

He|ge|meis|ter (Forstbeamter)

he|ge|mo|ni|al ‹griech.› (den Herrschaftsbereich [eines Staates] betreffend); **He|ge|mo|ni|al...** (Vorherrschafts...); **He|ge|mo|nie,** die; -, ...ien ([staatliche] Vorherrschaft); **he|ge|mo|nisch**

he|gen; - und pflegen; **He|ger** *(Jägerspr.)*; **He|ge₋ring** (kleinster jagdlicher Bezirk), **...zeit**

Hehl, das, *auch* der; *nur in* kein, *auch* keinen - daraus machen (es nicht verheimlichen); **heh|len; Heh|ler; Heh|le|rei; Heh|le|rin**

hehr *(geh. für* erhaben; heilig)

hei!; Heia, die; -, -[s] *(Kinderspr. für* Bett); **Hei|a|bett; hei|a|popeia!** *vgl.* eiapopeia!; **hei|da!**

[1]**Hei|de,** der; -n, -n; ↑R 126 (Nichtchrist; *auch für* Ungetaufter, Religionsloser)

[2]**Hei|de,** die; -, -n (sandiges, unbebautes Land; *nur Sing.:* Heidekraut)

[3]**Hei|de** (w. Vorn.)

Hei|deg|ger (dt. Philosoph)

Hei|de₋korn (das; -[e]s), **...kraut** (das; -[e]s), **...land** (das; -[e]s); **Hei|del|bee|re; Hei|del|beer|kraut,** das; -[e]s

Hei|del|berg (Stadt am Neckar)

Hei|de|ler|che

Hei|den, der; -s *(ostösterr. für* Buchweizen)

Hei|den... *(ugs. für* groß, sehr viel, z. B. Heidenangst, Heidenarbeit, Heidenlärm, Heidenspaß); **Heiden|chris|ten|tum; hei|den|mäßig** *(ugs. für* sehr, groß)

Hei|den|rös|chen, Hei|de|röschen

Hei|den|tum, das; -s; **Hei|denvolk**

Hei|de|rös|chen *vgl.* Heidenröschen; **Hei|de|ro|se** (w. Vorn.)

hei|di! [*auch* 'haidi] *(nordd. für* lustig!; schnell!); - gehen *(ugs. für* verloren gehen)

Hei|di (w. Vorn.)

Hei|din

Heid|jer (Bewohner der [Lüneburger] Heide)

heid|nisch

Heid|schnu|cke, die; -, -n (eine Schafrasse)

Hei|duck, der; -en, -en (↑R 126) ‹ung.› *(früher* ungarischer [Grenz]soldat)

Hei|er|mann *(ugs. für* Fünfmarkstück)

Hei|ke (w., *seltener* m. Vorn.)

hei|kel (schwierig; *landsch. auch für* wählerisch [beim Essen]); eine heik|le Sache; sei nicht so -!

Hei|ko (m. Vorn.)

heil; Heil, das; -[e]s; Berg Heil!; Ski Heil!; *vgl.* heilbringend; **Heiland,** der; -[e]s, -e *(geh. für* Retter, Erlöser); unser Herr und Heiland [Jesus Christus]; **Heil₋anstalt, ...an|zei|ge** *(Med.* Indikation), **...bad; heil|bar; Heil|barkeit,** die; -; **heil|brin|gend** (↑R 40); die -e Botschaft

Heil|bronn (Stadt am Neckar)

Heil|butt (ein Fisch); **hei|len; Heil₋er|de, ...er|folg; heil|froh; Heil₋gym|nast, ...gym|nas|tik, ...gym|nas|tin; hei|lig** *(Abk.* hl., *für den Plur.* hll.). **I.** *Kleinschreibung:* in heiligem Zorn; mit heiligem Ernst; heilige Einfalt! (Ausruf der Verwunderung); der heilige Paulus, die heilige Theresia; (↑R 108:) das heilige Abendmahl, die heilige Messe, die erste heilige Kommunion, die heilige Taufe, der heilige Krieg;

das heilige Pfingstfest usw. **II.** *Großschreibung* (↑R 108): der Heilige Abend; Heiliger Abend (24. Dez.); die Heilige Allianz; die Heilige Familie; der Heilige Christ; die Heilige Dreifaltigkeit; der Heilige Geist; der Heilige Vater; das Heilige Grab; der Heilige Gral; die Heilige Jungfrau; die Heiligen Drei Könige; Heilige Drei Könige (6. Jan.); das Heilige Land; die Heilige Nacht; der Heilige Rock von Trier; das Heilige Römische Reich Deutscher Nation; die Heilige Schrift; die Heilige Stadt (Jerusalem). **III.** *In Verbindung mit Verben,* z. B. heilig halten (feiern), heilig gehalten, heilig zu halten; heilig sprechen (zum *od.* zur Heiligen erklären), heilig gesprochen, heilig zu sprechen; **Hei|lig|abend** (↑R 132); **Hei|li|ge,** der *u.* die; -n, -n (↑R 5 ff.); **Hei|li|ge|drei|kö|nigs|tag,** Heilige[n]dreikönigstag[e]s, Heilige[n]dreikönigstage; ein Heilige[r]dreikönigstag; **hei|li|gen; Hei|li|gen‿bild, ...fi|gur, ...le|ben, ...schein, ...schrein; Hei|lig|geist|kir|che; hei|lig hal|ten** *vgl.* heilig; **Hei|lig|keit,** die; -; Seine -; ↑R 56 (der Papst); **hei|lig spre|chen** *vgl.* heilig; **Hei|lig|spre|chung; Hei|lig|tum; Hei|li|gung; heil|kli|ma|tisch; Heil|kraft; heil|kräf|tig; Heil|kun|de,** die; -, -n; **heil|kun|dig; Heil|kun|di|ge,** der *u.* die; -n, -n (↑R 5 ff.); **heil|los; Heil|mit|tel,** das; **Heil‿pä|da|go|ge, ...pä|da|go|gin; heil|pä|da|go|gisch; Heil‿pflan|ze, ...prak|ti|ker, ...prak|ti|ke|rin, ...quel|le, ...ruf; heil|sam; Heil|sam|keit,** die; -; **Heils‿ar|mee** (die; -), **...bot|schaft; Heil‿schlaf, ...schlamm, ...se|rum; Heils|leh|re; Hei|lung; Hei|lungs|pro|zess; Heil‿ver|fah|ren, ...wir|kung, ...zweck** (*meist in* zu -en)

heim...; *vgl.* heimbegeben, sich; *vgl.* heimbegleiten usw.; **Heim,** das; -[e]s, -e; **Heim‿abend** (↑R 132), **...ar|beit; Hei|mat,** die; -, -en; **hei|mat|be|rech|tigt; Hei|mat‿dich|ter, ...dich|tung, ...er|de** (die; -), **...fest, ...film, ...for|scher; hei|mat|ge|nös|sig** (*schweiz.* *neben* heimatberechtigt); **Hei|mat‿ha|fen** (*vgl.* [2]Hafen), **...kun|de** (die; -); **hei|mat|kund|lich; Hei|mat‿kunst** (die; -), **...land** (*Plur.* ...länder); **hei|mat|lich; hei|mat|los; Hei|mat|lo|se,** der *u.* die; -n, -n (↑R 5 ff.); **Hei|mat|lo|sig|keit,** die; -; **Hei|mat‿mu|se|um, ...ort** (der; -[e]s, ...orte), **...recht, ...staat** (*Plur.* ...staaten), **...stadt, ...ver|trie|be|ne; heim|be|ge|ben,** sich; du hast dich heimbegeben; **heim|be|glei|ten;** er hat sie heimbegleitet; **heim|brin|gen;** er hat sie heimgebracht; **Heim|chen** (eine Grille); **Heim|com|pu|ter; Heim|dal[l]** (*nord. Mythol.* Wächter der Götter u. ihres Sitzes); **hei|me|lig** (anheimelnd); **Hei|men, Hei|met,** das; -s, - (*schweiz. für* Bauerngut); *vgl.* Heimwesen; **heim|fah|ren;** er ist heimgefahren; **Heim|fahrt; Heim|fall,** der; -[e]s (*Rechtsspr.* das Zurückfallen [eines Gutes] an den Besitzer); **heim|füh|ren;** er hat ihn heimgeführt; **Heim|gang,** der; -[e]s, ...gänge *Plur. selten;* **heim|ge|gan|gen** (*verhüllend für* gestorben); **Heim|ge|gan|ge|ne,** der *u.* die; -n, -n (↑R 5 ff.); **heim|ge|hen;** er ist heimgegangen; **heim|gei|gen** (*svw.* heimleuchten); **heim|ho|len;** er wurde heimgeholt; **hei|misch; Heim|kehr,** die; -; **heim|keh|ren;** er ist heimgekehrt; **Heim‿keh|rer, ...ki|no** (*auch scherzh. für* Fernsehen); **heim|kom|men;** sie ist heimgekommen; **Heim|kunft,** die; -; **Heim‿lei|ter** (der), **...lei|te|rin; heim|leuch|ten;** dem haben sie heimgeleuchtet (*ugs.* ihn derb abgefertigt); **heim|lich;** heimlich tun (geheimnisvoll tun), sie hat sehr heimlich getan; er hat es heimlich getan; **heim|lich|feiß** (*schweiz. mdal. für* einen Besitz, ein Können verheimlichend); **Heim|lich|keit; Heim|lich|tu|er; Heim|lich|tu|e|rei; Heim|lich|tu|e|rin; heim|lich tun** *vgl.* heimlich; **Heim|mann|schaft** (*Sport);* **heim|müs|sen; Heim‿mut|ter** (*Plur.* ...mütter), **...nie|der|la|ge** (*Sport),* **...rei|se; heim|rei|sen;** er ist heimgereist; **Heim‿sieg** (*Sport),* **...spiel** (*Sport),* **...statt, ...stät|te; heim|su|chen;** er wurde von Unglück u. Krankheit schwer heimgesucht; **Heim|su|chung; Heim‿tier** (z. B. Hund, Katze, Meerschweinchen), **...trai|ner** (*für* Hometrainer; Trainer im heimatlichen Verein), **...tü|cke** (hinterlistige Bösartigkeit); **Heim|tü|cker** (heimtückischer Mensch); **heim|tü|ckisch; Heim|volks|hoch|schu|le; Heim|vor|teil,** der; -s (*Sport);* **heim|wärts; Heim‿weg** (der; -[e]s), **...weh** (das; -s); **heim|weh|krank; Heim‿wer|ker** (jmd., der handwerkliche Arbeiten zu Hause selbst macht; Bastler), **...we|sen** (*schweiz. für* Anwesen); **heim|wol|len; heim|zah|len;** jmdm. etwas -; **heim|zu** (*ugs. für* heimwärts)

Hein (m. Vorn.); Freund - (*verhüllend für* der Tod)

Hei|ne (dt. Dichter)

Hei|ne|mann (dritter dt. Bundespräsident)

Hei|ner (m. Vorn.)

hei|nesch; die heineschen Reisebilder (↑R 94)

[1]**Hei|ni** (m. Vorn.); [2]**Hei|ni,** der; -s, -s (*ugs. für* einfältiger Mensch)

hei|nisch *vgl.* heinesch

Hein|rich (m. Vorn.); [1]**Heinz** (m. Vorn.); [2]**Heinz,** der; -en, -en (↑R 126) *u.* [1]**Hein|ze,** der; -n, -n; ↑R 126 (*südd. für* Heureuter; Stiefelknecht); [2]**Hein|ze,** die; -, -n (*schweiz. für* Heureuter); **Hein|zel|bank** *Plur.* ...bänke (*österr. für* eine Art von Werkbank); **Hein|zel|männ|chen** ⟨*zu* [1]Heinz⟩ (hilfreicher Hausgeist)

Hei|rat, die; -, -en; **hei|ra|ten; Hei|rats‿ab|sicht** (*meist Plur.),* **...an|non|ce, ...an|trag, ...an|zei|ge; hei|rats‿fä|hig, ...lus|tig; Hei|rats‿markt, ...schwind|ler, ...ur|kun|de, ...ver|mitt|ler, ...ver|mitt|le|rin**

hei|sa!, hei|ßa!

hei|schen (*geh. für* fordern, verlangen); du heischst

hei|ser; Hei|ser|keit

heiß; -er, -este; am -esten (↑R 47); das Wasser heiß machen; jmdm. die Hölle heiß machen (*ugs. für* jmdm. heftig zusetzen; jmdn. bedrängen); was ich nicht weiß, macht mich nicht heiß; (↑R 108:) ein heißes Eisen (*ugs. für* eine schwierige Angelegenheit); ein heißer (sehnlicher) Wunsch; heißer Draht ([telefon.] Direktverbindung für schnelle Entscheidungen); heiße Höschen (*ugs. für* Hotpants); heißer Ofen (*ugs. für* Sportwagen, schweres Motorrad). *Schreibung in Verbindung mit dem Partizip II:* heiß begehrt; heiß ersehnt; seine heiß ersehnte Ankunft, seine Ankunft wurde heiß ersehnt; ein heiß geliebtes Mädchen; ein heiß umkämpfter Sieg; das ist eine heiß umstrittene Frage, die Frage war lange Zeit heiß umstritten usw.

hei|ßa!, hei|sa!; **hei|ßas|sa!**

heiß be|gehrt *vgl.* heiß; **Heiß|be|hand|lung; heiß|blü|tig**

[1]**hei|ßen** (einen Namen tragen; nennen; befehlen); du heißt; ich hieß, du hießest; geheißen; heiß[e]!; er hat es mich geheißen, *aber* wer hat dich das tun heißen?;

er hat mich kommen heißen, *seltener* geheißen; das heißt (*Abk.* d. h.)

[2]**hei|ßen** (hissen); du heißt; du heißtest; geheißt; heiß[e]!

heiß er|sehnt *vgl.* heiß; **heiß geliebt** *vgl.* heiß; **Heiß|hun|ger; heiß|hung|rig; heiß|lau|fen;** der Motor hat sich heißgelaufen; der Motor ist heißgelaufen; **Heiß-luft‿hei|zung, ...herd; Heiß‿man|gel** (die), **...sporn** (*Plur.* ...sporne; hitziger, draufgängerischer Mensch); **heiß|spor|nig; heiß um|kämpft** *vgl.* heiß; **heiß um|strit|ten** *vgl.* heiß; **Heiß-was|ser‿be|rei|ter, ...spei|cher**

Hei|s|ter, der; -s, - (junger Laubbaum aus Baumschulen)

...heit (z. B. Keckheit, die; -, -en)

hei|ter; heit[e]rer, -ste; **Hei|ter-keit,** die; -; **Hei|ter|keits|er|folg**

Heiz|an|la|ge; heiz|bar; Heiz|de-cke; hei|zen; du heizt; **Hei|zer; Heiz‿gas, ...ge|rät, ...kes|sel, ...kis|sen, ...kör|per, ...kos|ten** (*Plur.*), **...öl, ...pe|ri|o|de, ...plat-te, ...rohr, ...son|ne; Hei|zung; Hei|zungs‿an|la|ge, ...kel|ler, ...mon|teur, ...rohr, ...tank**

He|ka|te [...te: *od.* heˈka:te] (griech. Nacht- u. Unterweltsgöttin)

He|ka|tom|be, die; -, -n (griech.) (einem Unglück zum Opfer gefallene, erschütternd große Zahl von Menschen)

hekt..., hek|to... (griech.) (100); **Hek|tar** [*auch* ...ˈta:r] (↑R 132), das, *auch* der; -s, -e (griech.; lat.) (100 a; *Zeichen* ha); 3 - gutes Land *od.* guten Landes (↑R 90); **Hek|ta|re,** die; -, -n (*schweiz. für* Hektar; *Zeichen* ha); **Hek|tar|er-trag** *meist Plur.*

Hek|tik, die; - (griech.) (fieberhafte Aufregung, nervöses Getriebe); **hek|tisch** (fieberhaft, aufgeregt, sprunghaft); -e Röte; -es Fieber

hek|to... *vgl.* hekt...; **Hek|to...** (das Hundertfache einer Einheit, z. B. Hektoliter = 100 Liter; *Zeichen* h); **Hek|to|graph,** der; -en, -en; ↑R 126 (Vervielfältigungsgerät); **Hek|to|gra|phie,** die; -, ...ien (Vervielfältigung); **hek|to|gra-phie|ren; Hek|to|li|ter** (100 l; *Zeichen* hl); **Hek|to|pas|cal** (100 Pascal; *Zeichen* hPa)

Hek|tor (Held der griech. Sage)

He|ku|ba (w. griech. Sagengestalt)

Hel (nord. Todesgöttin; *auch* Welt der Toten; Unterwelt)

He|lan|ca ®, das; - (hochelastisches Kräuselgarn aus Nylon)

he|lau! (Karnevalsruf)

Held, der; -en, -en (↑R 126); **Hel-den‿brust** (*scherzh.*), **...dar|stel-ler, ...epos** (↑R 132), **...fried|hof; hel|den|haft; Hel|den|mut; hel-den|mü|tig; Hel|den‿tat, ...te-nor, ...tod; Hel|den|tum,** das; -s

Hel|der, der *od.* das; -s, - (*nordd. für* uneingedeichtes Marschland)

Hel|din; hel|disch

He|le|na (w. griech. Sagengestalt; w. Eigenn.); **He|le|ne** (w. Vorn.)

Hel|fe, die; -, -n (Schnur am Webstuhl); **hel|fen;** du hilfst; du halfst; du hülfest, *selten* hälfest; geholfen; hilf!; sie hat ihr beim Nähen geholfen, *aber* sie hat ihr nähen helfen *od.* geholfen; sich zu - wissen; **Hel|fer; Hel|fe|rin; Hel-fers|hel|fer** (Mittäter, Komplize)

Helf|gott (m. Vorn.)

Hel|ga (w. Vorn.); [1]**Hel|ge** (m. u. w. Vorn.)

[2]**Hel|ge,** die; -, -n *u.* [1]**Hel|gen,** der; -s, - (*aus* Helligen) (*Nebenform von* Helling)

[2]**Hel|gen,** der; -s, - (*schweiz. mdal. für* Bild)

Hel|go|land; Hel|go|län|der (↑R 103); **hel|go|län|disch**

He|li|and, der; -s („Heiland") (altsächs. Evangeliendichtung)

He|li|an|thus, der; -, ...then (griech.) (*Bot.* Sonnenblume)

[1]**He|li|kon,** das; -s, -s (griech.) (runde Basstuba)

[2]**He|li|kon,** der; -[s] (Gebirge in Böotien)

He|li|kop|ter (↑R 132), der; -s, - (engl.) (Hubschrauber)

He|li|o... (griech.) (Sonnen...); **He-li|o|dor,** der; -s, -e (ein Edelstein); **He|li|o|graph,** der; -en, -en; ↑R 126 (ein Signalgerät für Blinkzeichen mithilfe des Sonnenlichts); **He|li|o|gra|phie,** die; - (ein Tiefdruckverfahren; Zeichengeben mit dem Heliographen); **he|li|o|gra|phisch; He-li|o|gra|vü|re,** die; -, -n (*nur Sing.:* ein älteres Tiefdruckverfahren; Ergebnis dieses Verfahrens); **He|li|os** (griech. Sonnengott); **He|li|o|skop,** das; -s, -e (Gerät mit Lichtschwächung zur direkten Sonnenbeobachtung); **He-li|os|tat** (↑R 132), der; *Gen.* -[e]s *u.* -en, *Plur.* -en; ↑R 126 (Spiegelvorrichtung, die den Sonnenstrahlen eine gleichbleibende Richtung gibt); **He|li|o|the|ra-pie,** die; - (*Med.* Heilbehandlung mit Sonnenlicht); [1]**He|li|o|trop,** das; -s, -e (eine Zierpflanze; *nur Sing.:* eine Farbe; *früher* Spiegelvorrichtung [in der Geodäsie]); [2]**He|li|o|trop,** der; -s, -e (ein Edelstein); **he|li|o|tro|pisch** (*veraltet für* phototropisch); **he|li|o|zent-risch** (auf die Sonne als Mittelpunkt bezüglich); -es Weltsystem; **He|li|o|zo|on,** das; -s, ...zoen (*Zool.* Sonnentierchen)

He|li|port, der; -s, -s (engl.) (Landeplatz für Hubschrauber); **He|li-ski|ing** [...skiːiŋ], das; -[s] (Abfahrt von einem Berggipfel, zu dem der Skiläufer mit dem Helikopter gebracht worden ist)

He|li|um, das; -s (chem. Element, Edelgas; *Zeichen* He)

He|lix, die; -, ...ices [...tse:s] (griech.-lat.) (*Chemie* spiralige Molekülstruktur)

Hel|ke (w. Vorn.)

hell; hellblau usw.; dieser hell leuchtende Stern; die hell lodernde Flamme; hell strahlend

Hel|la (w. Vorn.)

Hel|las (Griechenland)

hell|auf; hellauf lachen (laut u. fröhlich lachen); *aber* hell auflachen (plötzlich zu lachen anfangen); hellauf begeistert; **hell|äu|gig; hell|blau;** - färben; **hell|blond; hell|dun|kel** (↑R 27); **Hell|dun-kel; Hell-Dun|kel-A|dap|[ta|]ti-on** (*Physiol.* Anpassung des Auges an die Lichtverhältnisse); **Hell|dun|kel|ma|le|rei; hel|le** (*landsch. für* aufgeweckt, gewitzt); [1]**Hel|le,** die; - (Helligkeit); [2]**Hel|le,** das; -n, -n (*ugs. für* [ein Glas] helles Bier); 3 Helle (↑R 90)

Hel|le|bar|de [*schweiz.* ˈhɛ...], die; -, -n (Hieb- u. Stoßwaffe im MA.; Paradewaffe der Schweizergarde im Vatikan); **Hel|le|bar|dier,** der; -s, -e (mit einer Hellebarde Bewaffneter)

Hel|le|gat[t], das; -s, *Plur.* -en *u.* -s ([Vorrats-, Geräte]raum auf Schiffen)

hel|len, sich (*veraltet für* sich erhellen)

Hel|le|ne, der; -n, -n; ↑R 126 (Grieche); **Hel|le|nen|tum,** das; -s; **Hel|le|nin; hel|le|nisch; hel-le|ni|sie|ren** (nach griech. Vorbild gestalten, einrichten); **Hel|le-nis|mus,** der; - (nachklass. griech. Kultur); **Hel|le|nist,** der; -en, -en; ↑R 126 (Gelehrter des nachklass. Griechentums; Forscher u. Kenner des Hellenismus); **Hel|le|nis|tik,** die; - (wissenschaftl. Erforschung der hellenist. Sprache u. Literatur); **hel|le-nis|tisch**

Hel|ler, der; -s, - (ehem. dt. Münze); auf Heller u. Pfennig; ich gebe keinen [roten] Heller dafür; *vgl.* Haléř

Hel|les|pont, der; -[e]s (griech.) (*antike Bez. für* Dardanellen)

Hell|gat[t] *vgl.* Hellegat[t]

hell˙grün, ...haa|rig, ...häu|tig; hell|hö|rig (schalldurchlässig); - (stutzig) werden; jmdn. - machen (jmds. Aufmerksamkeit erregen)
Hel|li|gen (*Plur. von* Helling)
Hel|lig|keit, die; -, *Plur. (fachspr.)* -en; **Hel|lig|keits|reg|ler**
Hel|ling, die; -, *Plur.* -en *u.* Helligen, *auch* der; -s, -e (Schiffsbauplatz); *vgl.* Helge[n]
hell leuch|tend *vgl.* hell; **hell|licht** (↑R 136); es ist -er Tag; **hell|li|la** (↑R 136); ein helllila Kleid; *vgl.* beige; in Helllila (↑R 47); **hell lodernd** *vgl.* hell; **hell|rot; hell|sehen** *nur im Infinitiv gebräuchlich;* **Hell˙se|hen** (das; -s), **...se|her; Hell|se|he|rei; Hell|se|he|rin; hell|se|he|risch; hell|sich|tig** (scharfsinnig; vorausschauend); **Hell|sich|tig|keit,** die; -; **hellwach**
Hell|weg, der; -[e]s (in Westfalen)
[1]**Helm,** der; -[e]s, -e (Kopfschutz; Turmdach)
[2]**Helm,** der; -[e]s, -e (Stiel von Werkzeugen zum Hämmern o. Ä.)
Hel|ma (w. Vorn.)
Helm|busch
Helm|holtz (dt. Physiker)
Hel|mi|ne (w. Vorn.)
Hel|min|the, die; -, -n *meist Plur.* ‹griech.› (*Med.* Eingeweidewurm); **Hel|min|thi|a|sis,** die; -, ...thiasen (*Med.* Wurmkrankheit)
Helm|stedt (Stadt östl. von Braunschweig); **Helm|sted|ter** (↑R 103)
Helm|traud, Helm|traut, Helmtrud (w. Vorn.); **Hel|mut** (m. Vorn.); **Helm|ward** (m. Vorn.)
He|lo|i|se (w. Eigenn.)
He|lot, der; -en, -en, *seltener* **He|lo|te,** der; -n, -n (↑R 126) ‹griech.› ([spartan.] Staatssklave); **He|lo|ten|tum,** das; -s
Hel|sing|fors (*schwed. für* Helsinki); **Hel|sin|ki** (Hptst. Finnlands)
Hel|ve|ti|en [...'ve:tsiən] (*lat. Name für* Schweiz); **Hel|ve|ti|er** (Angehöriger eines kelt. Volkes); **hel|ve|tisch,** *aber* (↑R 108): die Helvetische Republik; das Helvetische Bekenntnis (*Abk.* H. B.); **Hel|ve|tis|mus,** der; -, ...men ‹lat.› (schweizerische Spracheigentümlichkeit)
hem!, hm!; **hem, hem!;** hm, hm!
Hemd, das; -[e]s, -en; **hemd|är|me|lig** *vgl.* hemdsärmelig; **Hemd|blu|se; Hemd|blu|sen|kleid; Hem|den|knopf,** Hemdknopf; **Hem|den|matz** (*ugs. für* Kind, das nur ein Hemdchen anhat); **Hemd|ho|se; Hemd|knopf** *vgl.* Hemdenknopf; **Hemd|kragen; Hemds|är|mel** *meist Plur.;* **hemds|är|me|lig,** *schweiz. auch* hemdärm[e]lig
he|mi... ‹griech.› (halb...); **He|mi...** (Halb...);
He|ming|way [...we:] (amerik. Schriftsteller)
He|mi|ple|gie, die; -, ...ien (*Med.* halbseitige Lähmung); **He|mip|te|re** (↑R 132), die; -, -n *meist Plur.* (*Zool.* Schnabelkerf); **He|mi|sphä|re,** die; -, -n ([Erd- od. Himmels]halbkugel; *Med.* rechte bzw. linke Hälfte des Groß- u. Kleinhirns); **he|mi|sphä|risch; He|mis|ti|chi|on, He|mis|ti|chi|um** (↑R 132), das; -s, ...ien [...iən] (Halbvers in der altgriech. Metrik); **he|mi|zyk|lisch** [*auch* ...'tsyk...] (halbkreisförmig)
Hem|lock|tan|ne *vgl.* Tsuga
hem|men; Hemm|nis, das; -ses, -se; **Hemm˙schuh, ...schwel|le** (*bes. Psych.*), **...stoff** (*Chemie* Substanz, die chem. Reaktionen hemmt); **Hem|mung; hem|mungs|los; Hem|mungs|lo|sig|keit; Hemm|wir|kung**
Hems|ter|huis ['hɛmstərhœis], Frans (niederl. Philosoph)
Hen|de|ka|gon, das; -s, -e ‹griech.› (Elfeck); **Hen|de|ka|syl|la|bus,** der; -, *Plur.* ...syllaben *u.* ...syllabi (elfsilbiger Vers)
Hen|del, das; -s, -n (*südd., österr. für* [junges] Huhn; Brathuhn)
Hen|di|a|dy|oin [...dy'oyn], das; -s ‹griech.›, *seltener* **Hen|di|a|dys,** das; - (*Rhet.* Ausdrucksverstärkung durch Verwendung von zwei sinnverwandten Wörtern, z. B. „bitten und flehen")
Hengst, der; -es, -e
Henk (m. Vorn.)
Hen|kel, der; -s, -; **Hen|kel˙glas** (*Plur.* ...gläser), **...korb, ...krug, ...mann** (*Plur.* ...männer; *ugs. für* Gefäß zum Transport von [warmen] Mahlzeiten); **Hen|kel|topf**
hen|ken (*veraltend für* durch den Strang hinrichten); **Hen|ker; Hen|kers˙beil, ...frist, ...knecht, ...mahl[|zeit]** (letzte Mahlzeit)
Hen|na, die; - *od.* das; -[s] ‹arab.› (rotgelber Farbstoff, der u. a. zum Färben von Haaren verwendet wird); **Hen|na|strauch**
Hen|ne, die; -, -n
Hen|ne|gat[t] (*nordd. für* [1]Koker)
Hen|ne|gau, der; -[e]s (belg. Provinz)
Hen|ni (w. Vorn.)
Hen|nig, [1]**Hen|ning** (m. Vorn.)
[2]**Hen|ning** (der Hahn in der Tierfabel)
Hen|ny (w. Vorn.)
He|no|the|is|mus ‹griech.› (Verehrung einer Gottheit, ohne andere Gottheiten zu leugnen)
Hen|ri [ã'ri:] (m. Vorn.); **Hen|ri|et|te** [hɛn...] (w. Vorn.)
Hen|ri|quat|re [ãri'katr(ə)] (↑R 130), der; -[s] [...'katr(ə)], -s [...'katr(ə)] ‹franz.› (Spitzbart [wie ihn Heinrich IV. von Frankreich trug])
[1]**Hen|ry** ['hɛnri] (m. Vorn.)
[2]**Hen|ry** ['hɛnri], das; -, - ‹nach dem amerik. Physiker› (Einheit der Induktivität; *Zeichen* H)
Hen|ze (dt. Komponist)
he|pa|tisch ‹griech.› (*Med.* zur Leber gehörend); **He|pa|ti|tis,** die; -, ...itiden (Leberentzündung); **He|pa|to|lo|gie,** die; - (Lehre von den Funktionen u. Krankheiten der Leber)
He|phais|tos, *auch* He|phäst, Hephäs|tus (griech. Gott des Feuers u. der Schmiedekunst)
Hep|ta|chord [...'kɔrt], der *od.* das; -[e]s, -e ‹griech.› (*Musik* große Septime); **Hep|ta|gon,** das; -s, -e (Siebeneck); **Hep|ta|me|ron** (↑R 132), das; -s (Novellensammlung, an „sieben Tagen" erzählt, von Margarete von Navarra); **Hep|ta|me|ter,** der; -s, - (siebenfüßiger Vers); **Hep|tan,** das; -s (*Chemie* Kohlenwasserstoff mit sieben Kohlenstoffatomen, Bestandteil von Erdöl, Benzin usw.); **Hep|ta|teuch,** der; -s (die ersten sieben bibl. Bücher); **Hep|to|de** (↑R 132), die; -, -n (*Physik* Elektronenröhre mit sieben Elektroden)
her (Bewegung auf den Sprechenden zu); her zu mir!; her damit!; hin und her; *auch zeitlich:* von früher her; her sein; obwohl es schon drei Jahre her ist, war; hinter jmdm. her sein (*für ugs.* nach jmdm. fahnden; sich um jmdn. bemühen); *vgl.* hin
her... (*in Zus. mit Verben,* z. B. herbringen, du bringst her, hergebracht, herzubringen); *aber* her sein
He|ra, He|re (Gemahlin des Zeus)
he|rab (↑R 132); **he|rab...** (z. B. herablassen; er hat sich herabgelassen); **he|rab|bli|cken; he|rab|fal|len; he|rab|hän|gen;** die Deckenverkleidung hing herab; *vgl.* [1]hängen; **he|rab|las|sen;** sich -; **he|rab|las|send; He|rab|las|sung,** die; -; **he|rab|se|hen;** auf jemanden -; **he|rab|set|zen; He|rab|set|zung; he|rab|wür|di|gen; He|rab|wür|di|gung**
He|rak|les (↑R 130; Halbgott u. Held der griech.-röm. Sage); *vgl.* Herkules; **He|rak|li|de,** der; -n,

-n; ↑R 126 (Nachkomme des Herakles); **He|rak|lit** [*auch* ...'klit] (altgriech. Philosoph)

He|ral|dik, die; - ‹franz.› (Wappenkunde); **He|ral|di|ker** (Wappenforscher); **he|ral|disch**

he|ran (↑R 132), *ugs.* ran (↑R 13); heran sein; sobald er heran ist; **he|ran...** (z. B. heranbringen; er hat es mir herangebracht); *aber* heran sein; **he|ran|ar|bei|ten;** sich; **he|ran|bil|den; He|ran|bil|dung; he|ran|brin|gen** *vgl.* heran...; **he|ran|dür|fen; he|ran|fah|ren;** er ist zu nahe herangefahren; **he|ran|füh|ren; he|ran|ge|hen; he|ran|kom|men; he|ran|kön|nen; he|ran|las|sen; he|ran|ma|chen,** sich (*ugs.* für sich [mit einer bestimmten Absicht] nähern; beginnen); **he|ran|müs|sen; he|ran|rei|chen; he|ran|rei|fen** (allmählich reif werden); **he|ran|rü|cken; he|ran|schaf|fen** *vgl.* [1]schaffen; **he|ran sein** *vgl.* heran; **he|ran|tas|ten,** sich; **he|ran|tra|gen; he|ran|tre|ten; he|ran|wach|sen; He|ran|wach|sen|de,** der *u.* die; -n, -n (↑R 5 ff.); **he|ran|wa|gen,** sich; **he|ran|wol|len; he|ran|zie|hen**

he|rauf (↑R 132), *ugs.* rauf (↑R 13); **he|rauf...** (z. B. heraufziehen; er hat den Eimer heraufgezogen); **he|rauf|be|mü|hen; he|rauf|be|schwö|ren; he|rauf|brin|gen; he|rauf|däm|mern; he|rauf|ho|len; he|rauf|las|sen; he|rauf|set|zen; he|rauf|zie|hen**

he|raus (↑R 132), *ugs.* raus (↑R 13); heraus sein; sobald es heraus war; **he|raus...** (z. B. herausstellen; er hat die Schuhe herausgestellt); *aber* heraus sein; **he|raus|ar|bei|ten; He|raus|ar|bei|tung; he|raus|be|kom|men; he|raus|bil|den,** sich; **He|raus|bil|dung; he|raus|brin|gen; he|raus|dür|fen; he|raus|fah|ren; he|raus|fin|den; He|raus|for|de|rer; He|raus|for|de|rin; he|raus|for|dern;** ich fordere heraus (↑R 16); **he|raus|for|dernd; He|raus|for|de|rung; He|raus|ga|be,** die; -; **he|raus|ge|ben;** ich gebe heraus; *vgl.* herausgegeben; **He|raus|ge|ber** (*Abk.* Hg. *u.* Hrsg.); **He|raus|ge|be|rin; he|raus|ge|ge|ben** (*Abk.* hg. *u.* hrsg.); - von ...; **he|raus|ge|hen;** du musst mehr aus dir - (dich freier, weniger befangen äußern); **he|raus|ha|ben** (*ugs. auch für* etwas begriffen haben; etwas gelöst haben); schnell -, wie das Gerät funktioniert; er hat die Aufgabe heraus; **he|raus|hal|ten,** sich -; [1]**he|raus|hän|gen;** die Fahne hing zum Fenster heraus; *vgl.* [1]hängen; [2]**he|raus|hän|gen;** er hängte die Fahne heraus; *vgl.* [2]hängen; **he|raus|hau|en;** er haute ihn heraus (befreite ihn); **he|raus|he|ben,** sich -; **he|raus|ho|len; he|raus|hö|ren; he|raus|keh|ren;** den Vorgesetzten -; **he|raus|kom|men;** es wird nichts dabei herauskommen *(ugs.);* **he|raus|kön|nen; he|raus|kris|tal|li|sie|ren,** sich -; **he|raus|las|sen; he|raus|ma|chen;** sich - (*ugs. für* sich gut entwickeln); **he|raus|müs|sen; he|raus|neh|men;** sich etwas - (*ugs. für* sich dreisterweise erlauben); **he|raus|pau|ken** (*ugs. für* befreien; retten); **he|raus|plat|zen; he|raus|ra|gen;** eine herausragende Leistung; **he|raus|rei|ßen** (*ugs. auch für* befreien; retten); **he|raus|rü|cken;** mit der Sprache - *(ugs.);* **he|raus|rut|schen; he|raus|schaf|fen** *vgl.* [1]schaffen; **he|raus|schä|len;** sich - (allmählich deutlich, erkennbar werden); **he|raus|schau|en** (*ugs. auch für* als Nutzen, Gewinn erbringen); **he|raus|schi|cken; he|raus|schin|den; he|raus sein** *vgl.* heraus

he|rau|ßen (↑R 132; *bayr., österr. für* hier außen)

he|raus|spie|len (↑R 132); **he|raus|sprin|gen** (*auch für* sich als Gewinn, als Vorteil ergeben); **he|raus|spru|deln; he|raus|stel|len;** *vgl.* heraus...; es hat sich herausgestellt, dass ...; **he|raus|stre|cken; he|raus|strei|chen** (*auch für* hervorheben); **he|raus|tra|gen; he|raus|wach|sen;** sie ist aus dem Kleid herausgewachsen; *aber* seine Sicherheit ist aus den Erfahrungen heraus gewachsen; **he|raus|wa|gen,** sich; **he|raus|win|den,** sich; **he|raus|wirt|schaf|ten; he|raus|wol|len; he|raus|zie|hen**

herb

Her|ba|ri|um, das; -s, ...ien [...i̯ən] ‹lat.› (Sammlung getrockneter Pflanzen)

Her|bart (dt. Philosoph)

Her|be, die; - (*geh. für* Herbheit)

her|bei; her|bei... (z. B. herbeieilen; er ist herbeigeeilt); **her|bei|brin|gen; her|bei|füh|ren; her|bei|las|sen,** sich; **her|bei|lo|cken; her|bei|re|den;** ein Unglück -; **her|bei|ru|fen;** herbeirufen und -winken (↑R 23); **her|bei|schaf|fen** *vgl.* [1]schaffen; **her|bei|schlep|pen; her|bei|seh|nen; her|bei|strö|men; her|bei|wün|schen; her|bei|zi|tie|ren**

her|be|mü|hen; sich -; er hat sich herbemüht; **her|be|or|dern**

Her|ber|ge, die; -, -n; **her|ber|gen** (*veraltet für* Unterkunft finden); du herbergtest; geherbergt; **Her|bergs‿el|tern** *(Plur.),* **...mut|ter, ...va|ter**

Her|bert (m. Vorn.)

Herb|heit, die; -

her|bit|ten; er hat ihn hergebeten

Her|bi|vo|re [...v...], der; -n, -n (↑R 126) ‹lat.› (*Zool.* Pflanzen fressendes Tier); **Her|bi|zid,** das; -[e]s, -e (*Chemie* Unkrautbekämpfungsmittel)

Herb|ling (unreife Frucht aus später Blüte)

her|brin|gen

Herbst, der; -[e]s, -e; **Herbst|an|fang; Herbst|blu|me; herbs|teln,** *österr. nur so, od.* **herbs|ten** (*landsch. auch für* Trauben ernten); es herbste[l]t; **Herbst|fe|ri|en** *Plur.;* **herbst|lich;** herbstlich gelbes Laub; **Herbst|ling** (ein Pilz); **Herbst‿meis|ter, ...meis|ter|schaft** (*bes. Fußball* erster Tabellenplatz nach der Hinrunde), **...mes|se, ...mo|de, ...mo|nat** *od.* **...mond** (*alte Bez. für* September), **...ne|bel, ...son|ne** (die; -), **...sturm, ...tag; Herbst-Tag-und|nacht|glei|che,** die; -, -n (↑R 24); **Herbst|zeit|lo|se,** die; -, -n

herb|süß

Her|cu|la|ne|um, Her|cu|la|num (röm. Ruinenstadt am Vesuv); **her|cu|la|nisch; Her|cu|la|num** *vgl.* Herculaneum

Herd, der; -[e]s, -e

Herd|buch (*Landw.* Zuchtstammbuch); **Her|de,** die; -, -n; **Her|den‿mensch, ...tier, ...trieb** (der; -[e]s); **her|den|wei|se**

Her|der (dt. Philosoph u. Dichter); **her|de|risch, her|dersch;** eine herderische, *auch* herdersche Betrachtungsweise; die herderische, *auch* herdersche Philosophie (↑R 94; Philosophie von Herder)

Herd‿feu|er, ...plat|te

her|dür|fen

he|re|di|tär ‹lat.› (die Erbschaft betreffend; *Biol.* vererbbar, erblich)

he|rein (↑R 132), *ugs.* rein (↑R 13); „Herein!" rufen; **he|rein...** (z. B. hereinbrechen; der Abend ist hereingebrochen); **he|rein|be|kom|men; he|rein|be|mü|hen; he|rein|bre|chen; he|rein|brin|gen; he|rein|dür|fen; he|rein|fah|ren; he|rein|fal|len;** auf etw. - *(ugs.);* **He|rein|ga|be** *(Sport);* **he|rein|ge|ben; He|rein|ge|schmeck|te,** Rein|ge|schmeck|te, der *u.* die; -n,

-n; ↑R 5 ff. (*schwäb. für* Ortsfremde[r], Zugezogene[r]); **he|rein|hol|len; he|rein|kom|men; he|rein|kön|nen; he|rein|las|sen; he|rein|le|gen;** jmdn. - (*ugs. für* anführen, betrügen); **he|rein|müs|sen; he|rein|neh|men; he|rein|plat|zen** (*ugs. für* unerwartet erscheinen); **he|rein|ras|seln** (*ugs. für* hereinfallen; in eine schlimme Situation geraten); **he|rein|ru|fen;** jmdn. -; *vgl. aber* herein; **he|rein|schaf|fen** *vgl.* [1]schaffen; **he|rein|schi|cken; he|rein|schlei|chen,** sich -; **he|rein|schnei|en** (*ugs. für* unvermutet hereinkommen); **he|rein|spa|zie|ren** (*ugs.);* hereinspaziert!; **he|rein|strö|men; he|rein|stür|zen; he|rein|wa|gen,** sich; **he|rein|wol|len**
He|re|ro, der; -[s], -[s] (Angehöriger eines Bantustammes)
her|fah|ren; Her|fahrt; *vgl.* Hin- und Herfahrt (↑R 23)
her|fal|len; über jmdn. -
her|füh|ren
Her|ga|be, die; -
Her|gang, der; -[e]s
her|ge|ben; sich [für *od.* zu etwas] -
her|ge|brach|ter|ma|ßen
her|ge|hen; hinter jmdm. -; hoch - (*ugs. für* laut, toll zugehen)
her|ge|hö|ren
her|ge|lau|fen; Her|ge|lau|fe|ne, der *u.* die; -n, -n (↑R 5 ff.)
her|ha|ben *(ugs.);* wo sie das wohl herhat?
her|hal|ten; er musste dafür - (büßen)
her|ho|len; das ist weit hergeholt (ist kein nahe liegender Gedanke); *aber* diesen Wein haben wir von weither geholt
her|hö|ren; alle mal -!
He|ri|bert (m. Vorn.)
He|ring, der; -s, -e (ein Fisch; Zeltpflock); **He|rings‿fang, ...fass, ...fi|let, ...milch** (die; -), **...ro|gen, ...sa|lat**
he|rin|nen (↑R 132; *bayr. u. österr. für* [hier] drinnen)
He|ris, der; -, - ⟨nach dem iran. Ort⟩ (ein Perserteppich)
He|ri|sau (↑R 132; Hauptort des Halbkantons Appenzell Außerrhoden)
her|ja|gen
her|kom|men; er ist hinter mir hergekommen; *aber* er ist von der Tür her gekommen; **Her|kommen,** das; -s; **her|kömm|lich; her|kömm|li|cher|wei|se**
her|kön|nen
her|krie|gen
[1]**Her|ku|les** (*lat. Form von* Herakles); [2]**Her|ku|les,** der; - (ein Sternbild); [3]**Her|ku|les,** der; -, -se (Mensch von großer Körperkraft); **Her|ku|les|ar|beit; her|ku|lisch** (riesenstark)
Her|kunft, die; -, ...künfte; **Her|kunfts‿an|ga|be, ...ort** (*Plur.* ...orte)
her|lau|fen; hinter jmdm. -
her|lei|hen (*ugs. für* verleihen)
her|lei|ten; sich -
Her|lin|de (w. Vorn.)
Her|ling (*veraltet für* unreife, harte Weintraube)
Her|lit|ze [*auch* ...'lɪtsə], die; -, -n (Kornelkirsche, ein Ziergehölz)
her|ma|chen *(ugs.);* sich über etwas -
Her|mann (m. Vorn.); **Her|manns‿denk|mal** (das; -[e]s), **...schlacht** (die; -)
Her|mann|stadt (*rumän.* Sibiu)
Her|maph|ro|dis|mus (↑R 132) *vgl.* Hermaphroditismus; **Her|maph|ro|dit,** der; -en, -en (↑R 126) ⟨griech.⟩ (*Biol., Med.* Zwitter); **her|maph|ro|di|tisch; Her|maph|ro|di|tis|mus,** der; - (Zwittrigkeit); **Her|me,** die; -, -n (Büstenpfeiler, -säule)
[1]**Her|me|lin,** das; -s, -e (großes Wiesel); [2]**Her|me|lin,** der; -s, -e (ein Pelz); **Her|me|lin|kra|gen**
Her|me|neu|tik, die; - ⟨griech.⟩ (Auslegekunst, Deutung); **her|me|neu|tisch**
Her|mes (griech. Götterbote, Gott des Handels, Totenführer); **Her|mes|bürg|schaft,** die; -, -en (Ausfuhrgarantien der dt. Bundesregierung)
her|me|tisch ⟨griech.⟩ ([luft- u. wasser]dicht)
Her|mi|ne (w. Vorn.)
Her|mi|no|nen *Plur.* (germ. Stammesgruppe); **her|mi|no|nisch**
Her|mi|ta|ge [ɛrmi'ta:ʒə], der; - ⟨franz.⟩ (ein franz. Wein)
Her|mun|du|re, der; -n, -n; ↑R 126 (Angehöriger eines germ. Volksstammes)
her|müs|sen
her|nach (*landsch. für* nachher)
her|neh|men *(ugs.)*
Her|nie [...iə], die; -, -n ⟨lat.⟩ (*Med.* [Eingeweide]bruch; *Biol.* eine Pflanzenkrankheit)
her|nie|der *(geh.);* **her|nie|der...** (z. B. herniedergehen; der Regen ist herniedergegangen)
Her|ni|o|to|mie, die; -, ...ien ⟨lat.; griech.⟩ (*Med.* Bruchoperation)
He|ro (w. Eigenn.); *vgl.* Hero-und-Leander-Sage
He|roa (*Plur. von* Heroon)
he|ro|ben (↑R 132; *bayr., österr. für* hier oben)
He|ro|des (jüd. Königsname)
He|ro|dot [*auch* ...'do:t, *österr.* 'he...] (griech. Geschichtsschreiber)
He|roe, der; -n, -n (↑R 126) ⟨griech.⟩ (Heros); **He|ro|en|kult, He|ro|en|kul|tus** (Heldenverehrung); **He|ro|ik,** die; - (Heldenhaftigkeit); [1]**He|ro|in,** das; -s (ein Rauschgift); [2]**He|ro|in** (Heldin; *auch für* Heroine); **He|ro|i|ne,** die; -, -n (Heldendarstellerin); **he|ro|in|süch|tig; He|ro|in|süch|ti|ge,** der *u.* die; -n, -n (↑R 5 ff.); **he|ro|isch** (heldenmütig, heldisch; erhaben); **he|ro|i|sie|ren** (zum Helden erheben; verherrlichen); **He|ro|is|mus,** der; -
He|rold, der; -[e]s, -e (Verkündiger, Ausrufer [im MA.]); **He|rolds‿amt** (*früher* Wappenamt), **...stab** *(früher)*
He|ron (griech. Mathematiker); **He|rons|ball** (↑R 95); *vgl.* [1]Ball
He|ro|on, das; -s, Heroa ⟨griech.⟩ (Heroentempel); **He|ros,** der; -, ...oen (Held; Halbgott [bes. im alten Griechenland])
He|rost|rat (↑R 130 *u.* 132), der; -en, -en (↑R 126) ⟨nach dem Griechen Herostratos, der den Artemistempel zu Ephesus anzündete, um berühmt zu werden⟩ (Verbrecher aus Ruhmsucht); **He|rost|ra|ten|tum,** das; -s; **he|rost|ra|tisch** (ruhmsüchtig)
He|ro-und-Le|an|der-Sa|ge, die; - (↑R 28)
Her|pes, der; - ⟨griech.⟩ (*Med.* Bläschenausschlag); **Her|pe|to|lo|gie,** die; - (Zweig der Zoologie, der sich mit den Lurchen u. Kriechtieren befasst)
Herr, der; -n, -en (*Abk.* Hr., *Dat. u. Akk.* Hrn.); mein Herr!; meine Herren!; seines Unmutes Herr werden; der Besuch eines Ihrer Herren; Ihres Herrn Vaters; aus aller Herren Länder[n]; Herrn Ersten Staatsanwalt Müller (*vgl.* erste II, a); Herrn Präsident[en] Meyer
Her|rei|se; *vgl.* Hin- und Herreise (↑R 23)
Her|ren‿abend (↑R 132), **...aus|stat|ter, ...be|glei|tung, ...be|kannt|schaft, ...be|klei|dung, ...be|such**
Her|ren|chiem|see [...'ki:m...] (Ort u. Schloss auf der Herreninsel im Chiemsee)
Her|ren‿dop|pel *(Sport),* **...ein|zel** *(Sport),* **...fah|rer, ...fahr|rad, ...haus; her|ren|los; Her|ren‿ma|ga|zin, ...mann|schaft, ...mensch, ...mo|de, ...par|tie,**

...rei|ter, ...sa|lon, ...schnei|der, ...sitz (der; -es), **...toi|let|te; Her|ren|tum** (das; -s); **Her|ren‿witz, ...zim|mer; Herr|gott,** der; -s; **Herr|gotts|frü|he,** die; -; *nur in* in aller -; **Herr|gotts‿schnit|zer** (*südd., österr. für* Holzbildhauer, der bes. Kruzifixe schnitzt), **...win|kel** (*südd., österr. für* Ecke, die mit dem Kruzifix geschmückt ist)

her|rich|ten; etwas - lassen; **Her|rich|tung**

Her|rin; her|risch; herr|je! ⟨*aus* Herr Jesus!⟩, **herr|je|mi|ne!; herr|lich; Herr|lich|keit**

Herrn|hut (Stadt im Lausitzer Bergland); **Herrn|hu|ter** (↑R 103); - Brüdergemeine (*vgl. d.*); **herrn|hu|tisch**

Herr|schaft; herr|schaft|lich; Herr|schafts‿an|spruch, ...be|reich (der), **...form, ...ord|nung, ...struk|tur, ...wis|sen** (als Machtmittel genutztes [anderen nicht zugängliches] Wissen); **herr|schen;** du herrschst; **herr|schend; Herr|scher; Herr|scher‿ge|schlecht, ...haus; Herr|sche|rin; Herrsch|sucht,** die; -; **herrsch|süch|tig**

her|rüh|ren

her|sa|gen; etwas auswendig -

her|schau|en (*ugs.*); da schau her! (*bayr., österr. für* sieh mal an!)

Her|schel (engl. Astronom dt. Herkunft); herschelsches Teleskop (↑R 94)

her|schi|cken

her|schie|ben; etwas vor sich -

her sein *vgl.* her

her|stam|men

her|stel|len; Her|stel|ler; Her|stel|ler|fir|ma; Her|stel|le|rin; Her|stel|lung, die; -; **Her|stel|lungs‿kos|ten** (*Plur.*), **...land**

Her|ta, Her|tha; ↑R 92 (w. Vorn.)

her|trei|ben; Kühe vor sich -

Hertz, das; -, - ⟨nach dem dt. Physiker⟩ (Maßeinheit der Frequenz; *Zeichen* Hz); 440 -

he|rü|ben (↑R 132; *bayr., österr. für* hier auf dieser Seite; diesseits)

he|rü|ber (↑R 132), *ugs.* rü|ber (↑R 13); **he|rü|ber...** (z. B. herüberkommen; herübergekommen); **he|rü|ber|bit|ten; he|rü|ber|brin|gen; he|rü|ber|ho|len; he|rü|ber|kom|men; he|rü|ber|rei|chen; he|rü|ber|win|ken; he|rü|ber|zie|hen**

he|rum (↑R 132), *ugs.* rum (↑R 13); um den Tisch -; herum sein; sobald die Zeit herum war; **he|rum...** (z. B. herumlaufen; er ist herumgelaufen); *aber* herum sein; **he|rum|al|bern** (*ugs.*); **he|rum|är|gern,** sich (*ugs.*); **he|rum|bal|gen,** sich (*ugs.*); **he|rum|deu|teln** (*ugs.*); **he|rum|dok|tern** (*ugs.*); an etwas, jmdm. - (etwas, jmdn. mit dilettantischen Methoden zu heilen versuchen); **he|rum|dre|hen; he|rum|drü|cken,** sich (*ugs.*); **he|rum|druck|sen** (*ugs.*); **he|rum|ex|pe|ri|men|tie|ren** (*ugs.*); **he|rum|füh|ren; he|rum|fuhr|wer|ken** (*ugs. für* heftig u. planlos hantieren); **he|rum|ge|hen; he|rum|geis|tern** (*ugs.*); **he|rum|kom|men;** nicht darum - (*ugs.*); **he|rum|krie|gen** (*ugs. für* umstimmen); **he|rum|lau|fen; he|rum|lie|gen; he|rum|lun|gern** (*ugs.*); ich lungere herum; **he|rum|re|den; he|rum|rei|ßen;** das Steuer -; **he|rum|schar|wen|zeln** (*ugs.*); **he|rum|schla|gen,** sich (*ugs.*); **he|rum sein** *vgl.* herum; **he|rum|sit|zen** (*ugs.*); **he|rum|spre|chen;** etwas spricht sich herum (wird allgemein bekannt); **he|rum|stie|ren** (*österr. für* herumstöbern); **he|rum|stö|bern** (*ugs.*); **he|rum|tol|len; he|rum|trel|ben,** sich (*ugs.*); **He|rum|trei|ber; He|rum|trei|be|rin; he|rum|wer|fen;** das Steuer -

he|run|ten (↑R 132; *bayr., österr. für* hier unten)

he|run|ter (↑R 132), *ugs.* run|ter (↑R 13); herunter sein (*ugs. für* abgearbeitet, elend sein); **he|run|ter...** (z. B. herunterkommen; er ist sofort heruntergekommen); *aber* herunter sein; **he|run|ter|be|kom|men; he|run|ter|bren|nen; he|run|ter|brin|gen; he|run|ter|dür|fen; he|run|ter|fal|len; he|run|ter|ge|hen; he|run|ter|ge|kom|men** (*ugs. für* armselig; verkommen); ein -er Mann; **he|run|ter|hän|gen;** der Vorhang hing herunter; *vgl.* [1]hängen; **he|run|ter|kom|men; he|run|ter|kön|nen; he|run|ter|krem|peln;** die Ärmel -; **he|run|ter|las|sen; he|run|ter|ma|chen** (*ugs. für* abwerten, schlechtmachen; ausschelten); **he|run|ter|müs|sen; he|run|ter|rei|ßen; he|run|ter sein** *vgl.* herunter; **he|run|ter|spie|len** (*ugs. für* nicht so wichtig nehmen); **he|run|ter|wirt|schaf|ten; he|run|ter|wol|len; he|run|ter|zie|hen**

her|vor; her|vor... (z. B. hervorholen; er hat es hervorgeholt); **her|vor|bre|chen; her|vor|brin|gen; her|vor|ge|hen; her|vor|he|ben; her|vor|ho|len; her|vor|keh|ren; her|vor|ra|gen; her|vor|ra|gend; her|vor|ru|fen; her|vor|ste|chen; her|vor|trau|en,** sich; **her|vor|tre|ten; her|vor|tun,** sich; **her|vor|wa|gen,** sich; **her|vor|zau|bern; her|vor|zie|hen**

her|wärts

Her|weg; *vgl.* Hin- und Herweg

Her|wegh (dt. Dichter)

Her|wig (m. Vorn.); **Her|wi|ga** (w. Vorn.)

Herz, das; -ens, *Dat.* -en, *Plur.* -en, (*Med. auch starke Beugung* des Herzes, am Herz, die Herze); von Herzen kommen; zu Herzen gehen, nehmen; mit Herz und Hand (*formelhaft ungebeugt;* ↑R 126); *vgl.* Herze; **herz|al|ler|liebst; Herz‿al|ler|liebs|te, ...an|fall, ...ano|ma|lie** (↑R 132); **Herz|ass** [*auch* 'hɛrt͜s'|as]; **Herz‿asth|ma, ...at|ta|cke; herz|be|klem|mend** (↑R 40); **Herz|beu|tel; Herz|beu|tel|ent|zün|dung; herz|be|we|gend; Herz‿bin|kerl** (das; -s, -n; *österr. ugs. für* Lieblingskind), **...blatt, ...blätt|chen, ...blut; Herz|chen** (*auch für* naive Person); **Herz|chi|rur|gie,** die; -; **Her|ze,** das; -ns, -n (*veraltet für* Herz)

Her|ze|go|wi|na [*auch* ...'vi:na], die; - (südl. Teil von Bosnien und Herzegowina)

Her|ze|leid (*veraltend*); **her|zen** (*geh.*); du herzt; **Her|zens‿an|ge|le|gen|heit, ...angst, ...be|dürf|nis, ...bre|cher, ...bru|der, ...er|gie|ßung** (*veraltet*), **...freund** (*veraltend*); **her|zens|gut; Her|zens‿gü|te, ...lust** (*nur in* nach -), **...sa|che, ...wunsch; herz‿er|freu|end, ...er|fri|schend, ...er|grei|fend, ...er|qui|ckend** (↑R 40), **...er|wei|chend; Herz‿feh|ler, ...flim|mern** (das; -s; *Med.*); **herz|för|mig; Herz‿fre|quenz, ...ge|gend; herz|haft; Herz|haf|tig|keit,** die; -

her|zie|hen; ... so dass ich den Sack hinter mir herzog; er ist, hat über ihn hergezogen (*ugs. für* hat schlecht von ihm gesprochen); *aber* von der Tür her zog es

her|zig; Herz|in|farkt; herz|in|nig (*veraltend*); **herz|in|nig|lich** (*veraltend*); **Herz‿in|suf|fi|zi|enz** (*Med.*), **...kam|mer, ...ka|the|ter** (*Med.*), **...kir|sche, ...klap|pe; Herz|klap|pen|feh|ler; Herz|klop|fen,** das; -s; **herz|krank; Herz|krank|heit; Herz|kranz|ge|fäß; Herz-Kreis|lauf-Er|kran|kung** (↑R 28); **herz|lich;** aufs, auf das Herzlichste, *auch* herzlichste (↑R 47); **Herz|lich|keit; herz|los; Herz|lo|sig|keit; Herz-Lun|gen-Ma|schi|ne** (↑R 28; *Med.*)

Herz|ma|novs|ky-Or|lan|do [...ski...] (österr. Schriftsteller)

Hẹrz‿mas|sa|ge, ...mit|tel (das; *ugs.*), **...mus|kel; Hẹrz|mus|kel-schwä|che; hẹrz|nah**

[1]**Hẹr|zog,** der; -[e]s, *Plur.* ...zöge, *auch* -e

[2]**Hẹr|zog,** Roman (siebter dt. Bundespräsident)

Her|zo|gen|bụsch (niederl. Stadt)

Hẹr|zo|gin; Hẹr|zo|gin|mụt|ter *Plur.* ...mütter; **hẹr|zog|lich,** *im Titel* (↑R 56): Herzoglich; **Hẹr-zogs|wür|de,** die; -; **Hẹr|zog-tum**

Hẹrz|rhyth|mus; Hẹrz|rhyth-mus|stö|rung; Hẹrz‿schlag, ...schmerz *(meist Plur.),* **...schritt|ma|cher, ...schwä|che, ...spen|der, ...spen|de|rin; hẹrz-stär|kend** (↑R 40); **Hẹrz‿stich** *(meist Plur.),* **...still|stand** (der; -[e]s), **...stück, ...tä|tig|keit, ...ton** (*Plur.* ...töne), **...trans-plan|ta|ti|on, ...trop|fen** *(Plur.)*

her|zu *(geh.); aber* [komm] her zu mir!; **her|zu...** (z. B. herzukommen; er ist herzugekommen)

Hẹrz‿ver|pflan|zung, ...ver|sa-gen

her|zy|nisch (*Geol.* von Nordwesten nach Südosten verlaufend), *aber* (↑R 108): der Herzynische Wald (antiker Name der dt. Mittelgebirge)

hẹrz|zer|rei|ßend (↑R 40)

He|se|ki|el [...ki̯e:l, *auch* ...ki̯ɛl] (bibl. Prophet); *vgl.* Ezechiel

He|si|od [*auch* heˈzi̯ɔt] (altgriech. Dichter)

Hes|pe|ri|de, die; -, -n *meist Plur.* (Tochter des Atlas); **Hes|pe|ri-den|äp|fel** *Plur.;* **Hes|pe|ri|en** [...i̯ən] *(im Altertum Bez. für* Land gegen Abend [Italien, Westeuropa]); **Hẹs|pe|ros, Hẹs|pe|rus,** der; - (Abendstern in der griech. Mythol.)

[1]**Hẹs|se** (dt. Dichter)

[2]**Hẹs|se,** die; -, -n (*landsch. für* unterer Teil des Beines von Rind od. Pferd); *vgl.* Hachse

[3]**Hẹs|se,** der; -n, -n; ↑R 126 (Angehöriger eines dt. Volksstammes); **Hẹs|sen; Hẹs|sen-Dạrm-stadt; Hẹs|sen|land,** das; -[e]s; **Hẹs|sen-Nạs|sau; Hẹs|sin; hẹs-sisch,** *aber* (↑R 108): das Hessische Bergland

Hẹs|tia (griech. Göttin des Herdes)

He|tä|re, die; -, -n ‹griech.› ([hochgebildete] Freundin, Geliebte bedeutender Männer in der Antike); **He|tä|rie,** die; -, ...i̯en (eine altgriech. polit. Verbindung)

he|te|ro... ‹griech.› (anders..., fremd...); **He|te|ro...** (Anders..., Fremd...); **he|te|ro|dọx** (anders-, irrgläubig); **He|te|ro|do|xie,** die; -, ...i̯en (*Rel.* Irrlehre); **he|te|ro-gen** (anders geartet, ungleichartig, fremdstoffig); **He|te|ro|ge|ni-tät,** die; -; **he|te|ro|mọrph** (anders-, verschiedengestaltig); **He-te|ro|phyl|lie,** die; - (*Bot.* Verschiedengestaltigkeit der Blätter bei einer Pflanze); **He|te|ro|se-xu|a|li|tät,** die; - (auf das andere Geschlecht gerichtetes Empfinden im Ggs. zur Homosexualität); **he|te|ro|se|xu|ẹll; He|te|ro-sphä|re,** die; - (*Meteor.* der obere Bereich der Atmosphäre); **he|te-ro|trọph** (*Biol.* sich von organ. Stoffen ernährend); **He|te|ro|tro-phie,** die; -; **he|te|rö|zisch** (*svw.* diözisch); **he|te|ro|zy|gọt** (*Biol.* ungleicherbig)

He|thi|ter, *ökum.* He|ti|ter, der; -s, - (Angehöriger eines idg. Kulturvolkes in Kleinasien); **he|thi-tisch,** *ökum.* he|ti|tisch; **He|ti|ter** usw. *vgl.* Hethiter usw.

Hẹt|man, der; -s, *Plur.* -e *od.* -s (Oberhaupt der Kosaken; in Polen [bis 1792] vom König eingesetzter Oberbefehlshaber)

Hẹt|sche|petsch, die; -, - *u.* **Het-scherl,** das; -s, -n (*österr. mdal. für* Hagebutte)

Hẹtt|stedt (Stadt östl. des Harzes)

Hẹtz, die; -, -en *Plur. selten* (*österr. ugs. für* Spaß); aus -; **Hẹt|ze,** die; -, -n; **hẹt|zen;** du hetzt; **Hẹt|zer; Het|ze|rei; Hẹt|ze|rin; hẹt|ze-risch; hẹtz|hal|ber** (*österr. ugs. für* zum Spaß); **Hẹtz‿jagd, ...kam|pa|gne, ...re|de**

Heu, das; -[e]s; **Heu‿bo|den, ...büh|ne** (*schweiz. svw.* Heuboden), **...bün|del**

Heu|che|lei; heu|cheln; ich ...[e]le (↑R 16); **Heuch|ler; Heuch|le-rin; heuch|le|risch; Heuch|ler-mie|ne**

Heu|die|le (*schweiz. für* Heuboden); **heu|en** (*landsch. u. schweiz. für* Heu machen)

heu|er (*südd., österr., schweiz. für* in diesem Jahr)

[1]**Heu|er** (*landsch. u. schweiz. für* Heumacher)

[2]**Heu|er,** die; -, -n (Lohn eines Seemanns; Anmusterungsvertrag); **Heu|er‿baas, ...bü|ro; heu|ern** ([Schiffsleute] einstellen; [ein Schiff] chartern); ich ...ere (↑R 16)

Heu|ern|te; Heu|ert *vgl.* [1]Heuet; [1]**Heu|et,** der; -s, -e (*für* Heumonat); [2]**Heu|et,** der; -s, *südd. auch* die; - (*südd. u. schweiz. für* Heuernte); **Heu‿feim** *od.* **...fei|me** *od.* **...fei|men** (*landsch., bes. nordd. für* Heuhaufen), **...fie|ber** (das; -s), **...ga|bel, ...hüp|fer** (*ugs. für* Heuschrecke)

Heul|bo|je *(Seew.);* **heu|len;** das heulende Elend bekommen; (↑R 50:) Heulen und Zähneklappern; das ist [ja] zum Heulen; **Heu|ler; Heul‿krampf, ...su|se** (Schimpfwort), **...ton**

Heu‿mahd, ...mo|nat *od.* **...mond** (*alte Bez. für* Juli), **...ochs** *od.* **...och|se** (Schimpfwort), **...pferd** (Heuschrecke), **...rei|ter** *(österr.) od.* **...reu|ter** (*südd. für* Gestell zum Heu- u. Kleetrocknen)

heu|re|ka! ‹griech., „ich hab's [gefunden]!"›

Heu|reu|ter *vgl.* Heureiter

heu|rig (*südd., österr., schweiz. für* diesjährig); **Heu|ri|ge,** der; -n, -n; ↑R 5 ff. (*bes. österr. für* junger Wein im ersten Jahr; Lokal für den Ausschank jungen Weins, Straußwirtschaft; *Plur.:* Frühkartoffeln); **Heu|ri|gen‿abend** (↑R 132), **...lo|kal**

Heu|rịs|tik, die; - ‹griech.› (Lehre von den Methoden zur Auffindung neuer wissenschaftl. Erkenntnisse); **heu|rịs|tisch** (erfinderisch; das Auffinden bezweckend); -es Prinzip

Heu‿schnup|fen, ...scho|ber, Heu‿schreck, der; -[e]s, -e (*österr. neben* Heuschrecke); **Heu|schre|cke,** die; -, -n (ein Insekt)

Heuss (erster dt. Bundespräsident); heussche Reden (↑R 14 *u.* 94)

Heu‿sta|del (*südd., österr., schweiz. für* Scheune zum Aufbewahren von Heu), **...stock** (*Plur.* ...stöcke; *schweiz., österr. für* Heuvorrat [auf dem Heuboden])

heu|te, *ugs. auch* heut; (↑R 45:) heute Abend, Mittag, Morgen, Nachmittag, Nacht; *aber* heute früh; die Frau von heute; bis heute; hier und heute; **Heu|te,** das; - (die Gegenwart); das - und das Morgen; **heu|tig;** (↑R 47:) am Heutigen; *nicht gut ist kaufmänn.* mein Heutiges (Schreiben vom selben Tag); **heu|ti|gen|tags** (↑R 46); **heut|zu|ta|ge** (↑R 46)

He|xa|chord [...ˈkɔrt], der *od.* das; -[e]s, -e ‹griech.› (*Musik* Aufeinanderfolge von sechs Tönen der diaton. Tonleiter); **He|xa|e|der,** das; -s, - (Sechsflächner, Würfel); **he|xa|e|drisch** (↑R 130); **He|xa-e|me|ron,** das; -s (Schöpfungswoche außer dem Sabbat); **He-xa|gọn,** das; -s, -e (Sechseck); **he|xa|go|nal; He|xa|grạmm,** das; -s, -e (Figur aus zwei gekreuzten gleichseitigen Dreiecken; Sechsstern); **He|xa|me|ter,** der; -s, - (sechsfüßiger Vers); **he|xa|me|trisch** (↑R 130); **He|xa|teuch,** der; -s (die ersten sechs bibl. Bücher)

He|xe, die; -, -n; **he|xen;** du hext; **He|xen_jagd, ...kes|sel, ...kü|che, ...meis|ter, ...sab|bat, ...schuss, ...tanz, ...ver|bren|nung, ...wahn; He|xer; He|xe|rei**

He|xo|de (↑R 132), die; -, -n ‹griech.› (Elektronenröhre mit sechs Elektroden)

Hey|er|dahl (norw. Forscher)

Heym, Georg (dt. Lyriker)

Hf = *chem. Zeichen für* Hafnium

hfl = Hollands florijn [- 'flo:rɛin] (holländ. Gulden)

Hg = Hydrargyrum (*chem. Zeichen für* Quecksilber)

hg., hrsg. = herausgegeben

Hg., Hrsg. = Herausgeber

HGB = Handelsgesetzbuch

hi!; hi|hi!

Hi|as (m. Vorn.)

Hi|at, der; -s, -e ‹lat.› (*svw.* Hiatus); **Hi|a|tus,** der; -, - (*Sprachw.* Zusammentreffen zweier Vokale im Auslaut des einen u. im Anlaut des folgenden Wortes oder Wortteiles, z. B. „sagte *er*" *od.* „Kooperation"; *Geol.* zeitliche Lücke bei der Ablagerung von Gesteinen; *Med.* Öffnung, Spalt)

Hi|ber|na|kel, das; -s, -[n] *meist Plur.* ‹lat.› (Überwinterungsknospe von Wasserpflanzen); **Hi|ber|na|ti|on,** die; - (*Med.* künstl. „Winterschlaf", Schlafzustand als Ergänzung zur Narkose od. als Heilschlaf)

Hi|ber|nia ‹lat.› (*lat. Name von* Irland)

Hi|bis|kus, der; -, ...ken ‹griech.› (Eibisch)

hick!

hi|ckeln (*landsch. für* hinken, humpeln; auf einem Bein hüpfen); ich ...[e]le (↑R 16)

Hick|hack, der *u.* das; -s, -s (*ugs. für* nutzlose Streiterei; törichtes, zermürbendes Hinundhergerede)

[1]**Hi|cko|ry,** der; -s, -s, *auch* die; -, -s ‹indian.-engl.› (nordamerik. Walnussbaum); [2]**Hi|cko|ry,** das; -s (Holz des [1]Hickorys); **Hi|cko|ry|holz,** das; -es

hick|sen (*landsch. für* Schluckauf haben); du hickst

Hi|dal|go, der; -s, -s ‹span.› (Angehöriger des niederen span. Adels; eine mexikanische Goldmünze)

Hid|den|see (dt. Ostseeinsel); **Hid|den|seer** [...ze:ər] (↑R 103)

hid|ro|tisch (↑R 130) ‹griech.› (*Med.* schweißtreibend)

hie; *nur in Wendungen wie* hie und da; hie Pflicht, hie Neigung

Hieb, der; -[e]s, -e

hie|bei[1] (*südd., österr., sonst veraltet neben* hierbei)

hieb|fest; *nur in* hieb- und stichfest (↑R 23); **Hiebs|art** (*Forstw.* Art des Holzfällens)

hie|durch[1] (*südd., österr., sonst veraltet neben* hierdurch)

Hie|fe (*landsch. für* Hagebutte); **Hie|fen|mark,** das

hie|für[1], **hie|ge|gen**[1], **hie|her**[1], **hie|mit**[1], **hie|nach**[1], **hie|ne|ben**[1] (*südd., österr., sonst veraltet neben* hierfür usw.); **hie|nie|den**[1] (*geh. für* auf d[ies]er Erde)

hier; hier und da; von hier aus; hier oben, unten usw.; hier behalten (zurückbehalten, nicht weglassen); sie hat ihr Buch hier behalten; du sollst hier bleiben (nicht weggehen); du sollst hier (an der bezeichneten Stelle) bleiben; er hat das Buch hier gelassen; er soll das Buch hier (nicht dort) lassen; hier sein (*auch für* zugegen sein); **hier|amts** (*österr. Amtsspr.*); **hie|ran**[2] (↑R 132)

Hie|rar|chie [hi(e)...] (↑R 132), die; -, ...ien ‹griech.› ([pyramidenförmige] Rangfolge, Rangordnung); **hie|rar|chisch; hie|rar|chi|sie|ren; hie|ra|tisch** (priesterlich); -e Schrift (altägypt. Priesterschrift)

hie|rauf[2] (↑R 132); **hie|rauf|hin**[2]; **hie|raus**[2] (↑R 132); **hier be|hal|ten** *vgl.* hier; **hier|bei**[2]; **hier blei|ben** *vgl.* hier; **hier|durch**[2]; **hie|rein**[2] (↑R 132); **hier|für**[1]; **hier|ge|gen**[2]; **hier|her**[2]; hierher gehörend; hierher gehörig; hierher kommen; er ist hierher gekommen; **hier|he|rauf**[2] (↑R 132); **hier|her ge|hö|rend** *vgl.* hierher; **hier|her ge|hö|rig** *vgl.* hierher; **hier|her kom|men** *vgl.* hierher; **hier|he|rum**[2] (↑R 132); **hier|hin**[2]; hierhin laufen; **hier|hin|ter**[2]; **hie|rin**[2] (↑R 132); **hie|rin|nen**[2] (↑R 132; *veraltet*); **hier|lands** (*veraltet für* hierzulande); **hier las|sen** *vgl.* hier; **hier|mit**[2], **hier|nach**[2]; **hier|ne|ben**[2]

[1]**Hi|e|ro|du|le** [hi(e)...], der; -n, -n (↑R 126) ‹griech.› (Tempelsklave des griech. Altertums); [2]**Hi|e|ro|du|le,** die; -, -n (Tempelsklavin); **Hie|ro|gly|phe** [hi:..., *auch* hie...], die; -, -n (Bilderschriftzeichen; *nur Plur.: scherzh. für* schwer entzifferbare Schriftzeichen); **hie|ro|gly|phisch** (in Bilderschrift; rätselhaft); **Hi|e|ro|kra|tie** [hi(e)...], die; -, -n (Priesterherrschaft); **Hi|e|ro|mant,** der; -en, -en; ↑R 126 (aus [Tier]opfern Weissagender); **Hi|e|ro|man|tie,** die; - (Weissagung aus [Tier]opfern); **Hi|e|ro|ny|mus** [*auch* hi(e)'rɔ...] (m. Vorn.; lat. Kirchenvater)

hier|orts[1] (*Amtsspr.*)

Hier|ro ['jɛro] (*span. Form von* Ferro) **hier sein** *vgl.* hier; **Hier|sein,** das; -s; **hier|selbst**[1] (*veraltet*); **hie|rü|ber**[1] (↑R 132); **hie|rum**[1] (↑R 132); **hie[r] und da;** *vgl.* hier; **hie|run|ter**[1] (↑R 132); **hier|von**[1]; **hier|vor**[1]; **hier|wi|der**[1] (*veraltet*); **hier|zu**[1]; **hier|zu|lan|de,** *auch* **hier zu Lan|de** (↑R 41); **hier|zwi|schen**[1]

hie|selbst[2] (*südd., österr., sonst veraltet neben* hierselbst)

hie|sig; -en Ort[e]s; **Hie|si|ge,** der *u.* die; -n, -n (↑R 5 ff.)

hie|ven [...f..., *auch* ...v...] (*Seemannsspr. u. ugs. für* [eine Last] hochziehen; heben)

hie|von[2], **hie|vor**[2], **hie|wi|der**[2], **hie|zu**[2], **hie|zu|lan|de**[2], **hie|zwi|schen**[2] (*südd., österr., sonst veraltet neben* hiervon usw.)

Hi-Fi ['haifi, *auch* 'hai'fai] = Highfidelity; **Hi-Fi-An|la|ge; Hi-Fi-Turm**

Hift|horn *Plur.* ...hörner (Jagdhorn)

high [hai] ‹engl.› (*ugs. für* in gehobener Stimmung [nach dem Genuss von Rauschgift]); **High Church** ['hai'tʃœ:(r)tʃ], die; - ‹engl., Hochkirche› (Richtung der engl. Staatskirche); **High|fi|de|li|ty** ['haifi'dɛliti], die; - ‹engl.› (originalgetreue Wiedergabe bei Schallplatten u. elektroakustischen Geräten); *Abk.* Hi-Fi); **High|life** ['hailaif], das; -[s] ‹engl.› (glanzvolles Leben der begüterten Gesellschaftsschicht); **High|light** ['hailait], das; -[s], -s ‹engl.› (Höhepunkt, Glanzpunkt); **High|ri|ser** ['hairaizə(r)], ‹engl.› (Fahrrad, Moped mit hohem, geteiltem Lenker und Sattel mit Rückenlehne); **High|so|ci|e|ty** ['haisə'saiəti], die; - ‹engl.› (die vornehme Gesellschaft, die große Welt); [1]**High|tech** ['hai'tɛk], der; -[s] ‹engl.› (moderner Stil der Innenarchitektur); [2]**High|tech,** das; -[s], *auch* die; - (*bes. in Zus.* Spitzentechnologie); **High|tech|in|dust|rie** (↑R 24 *u.* 33); **High|way** ['haiwe:], der; -s, -s (*amerik. Bez. für* Fernstraße)

Footnotes (middle column):
[1] [*auch* 'hi:...]
[2] [*auch* 'hi:r...]

Footnotes (right column):
[1] [*auch* 'hi:r...]
[2] [*auch* 'hi:...]

hi|hi!
Hi|ja|cker ['haidʒɛkə(r)], der; -s, - ‹engl.› (Luftpirat)
Hil|da, Hild|burg, Hild|chen, Hil|de (w. Vorn.); **Hil|de|brand** (m. Eigenn.); **Hil|de|brands|lied,** das; -[e]s; **Hil|de|burg,** Hild|burg (w. Vorn.); **Hil|de|fons,** Il|de|fons (m. Vorn.); **Hil|de|gard, Hil|de|gund, Hil|de|gun|de** (w. Vorn.)
Hil|des|heim (Stadt in Niedersachsen)
Hil|fe, die; -, -n; (↑R 108:) die erste Hilfe (bei Verletzungen usw.); Hilfe leisten, suchen; zu Hilfe kommen, eilen; *aber* der Mechaniker, mithilfe dessen (*auch* mit Hilfe dessen *od.* mit dessen Hilfe) er sein Auto reparierte; Hilfe bringend; sich Hilfe suchend umschauen; hilferufend, *aber* um Hilfe rufend; **Hil|fe|er|su|chen; hil|fe|fle|hend** (↑R 40); **Hil|fe‿leis|tung, ...ruf; hil|fe|ru|fend** (↑R 40); **Hil|fe|stel|lung; Hil|fe su|chend** *vgl.* Hilfe; **hilf|los; Hilf|lo|sig|keit,** die; -; **hilf|reich** *(geh.);* **Hilfs‿ak|ti|on, ...ar|bei|ter, ...ar|bei|te|rin; hilfs|be|dürf|tig; Hilfs|be|dürf|tig|keit; hilfs|be|reit; Hilfs‿be|reit|schaft** (die; -), **...kraft** (die), **...leh|rer, ...leh|re|rin, ...lie|fe|rung, ...mit|tel** (das), **...mo|tor, ...or|ga|ni|sa|ti|on, ...po|li|zist, ...po|li|zis|tin, ...pro|gramm, ...quel|le, ...schiff, ...schu|le, ...she|riff, ...verb; hilfs|wei|se; Hilfs|werk; hilfs|wil|lig; Hilfs‿wis|sen|schaft, ...zeit|wort** (*für* Hilfsverb)
Hi|li (*Plur. von* Hilus)
Hil|ke (w. Vorn.)
Hill|bil|ly|mu|sic [...'mju:zik], *eindeutschend auch* Hill|bil|li|mu|sik (↑R 24), die; - (ländliche Musik der nordamerik. Südstaaten)
Hil|le|bil|le, die; -, -n (ein altes hölzernes Signalgerät)
Hil|mar (m. Vorn.)
Hil|traud, Hil|trud (w. Vorn.)
Hi|lus, der; -, Hili ‹lat.› (*Med.* Ein- od. Austrittsstelle der Gefäße, Nerven usw. an einem Organ)
Hi|ma|la|ja [*auch* hima'la:ja], der; -[s] (Gebirge in Asien)
Him|bee|re; him|beer|far|ben, him|beer|far|big; Him|beer‿geist (der; -[e]s; ein Obstschnaps), **...saft** (der; -[e]s)
Him|mel, der; -s, -; um [des] -s willen; **him|mel|an** *(geh.);* **him|mel|angst;** es ist mir -; **Him|mel|bett; him|mel|blau; Him|mel|don|ner|wet|ter!; Him|mel|fahrt** *(christl. Kirche);* **Him|mel|fahrts|kom|man|do** ([Kriegs]auftrag, der das Leben kosten kann; *auch für* die Ausführenden eines solchen Auftrags); **Him|mel|fahrts‿na|se** (*ugs. für* nach oben gebogene Nase), **...tag; Him|mel|herr|gott!; him|mel|hoch; Him|mel|hund** (*ugs. für* Schuft; Teufelskerl); **him|meln;** ich ...[e]le (↑R 16); **Him|mel|reich,** das; -[e]s; **Him|mels‿ach|se** (die; -), **...bahn, ...bo|gen** (der; -s; *geh.*), **...braut** (*für* Nonne); **Him|mel|schlüs|sel,** *seltener* Him|mels|schlüs|sel, der, *auch* das (Schlüsselblume); **him|mel|schrei|end** (↑R 40); **Him|mels‿fes|te** (die; -; *geh.*), **...ge|gend, ...kör|per, ...ku|gel** (die; -), **...lei|ter** (die; -; *A. T.*), **...rich|tung; Him|mels|schlüs|sel** *vgl.* Himmelschlüssel; **Him|mels|strich** (*svw.* Himmelsgegend); **Him|mel[s]|stür|mer; Him|mels‿tür** (die; -; *geh.*), **...zelt** (das; -[e]s; *geh.*); **him|mel|wärts; him|mel|weit; himm|lisch**
hin (Bewegung vom Sprechenden weg); bis zur Mauer hin; über die ganze Welt hin verstreut; vor sich hin brummen usw.; hin und her laufen (ohne bestimmtes Ziel), *aber* (↑R 23): hin- und herlaufen (hin- und wieder zurücklaufen); nach langem Hin und Her; *auch zeitlich:* gegen Abend hin; hin und wieder (zuweilen); hin sein (*ugs. für* völlig kaputt sein; tot sein; hingerissen sein); alles ist hin; weil alles hin ist
hin... (*in Zus. mit Verben,* z. B. hingehen, du gehst hin, hingegangen, hinzugehen); *aber* hin sein
hi|nab (↑R 132); etwas weiter -; **hi|nab...** (z. B. hinabgehen; er ist hinabgegangen); **hi|nab‿fah|ren, ...fal|len, ...rei|ßen, ...sen|ken, ...sin|ken, ...stei|gen, ...stür|zen** (sich -), **...tau|chen, ...zie|hen**
hi|nan (↑R 132; *geh.*); etwas weiter -; **hi|nan...** (z. B. hinangehen; er ist hinangegangen)
hin|ar|bei|ten; auf eine Sache -, *aber* auf seine Mahnungen hin arbeiten
hi|nauf (↑R 132), *ugs.* 'nauf (↑R 13); den Rhein -; **hi|nauf...** (z. B. hinaufsteigen; er ist hinaufgestiegen); **hi|nauf‿bli|cken, ...brin|gen, ...dür|fen, ...füh|ren, ...ge|hen, ...klet|tern, ...kön|nen, ...las|sen, ...müs|sen, ...rei|chen, ...schrau|ben, ...sol|len, ...stei|gen, ...wol|len, ...zie|hen**
hi|naus (↑R 132), *ugs.* 'naus (↑R 13); auf das Meer hinaus; hinaus sein; darüber hinaus sein; **hi|naus...** (z. B. hinausgehen; er ist hinausgegangen); *aber* hinaus sein; **hi|naus‿be|för|dern, ...be|glei|ten, ...beu|gen** (sich), **...bli|cken, ...brin|gen, ...drän|gen** (sich -), **...dür|fen, ...ekeln** (↑R 132; *ugs.*), **...fah|ren, ...fin|den, ...füh|ren, ...ge|hen** (alles darüber Hinausgehende), **...ge|lei|ten, ...grei|fen** (darüber -), **...ka|ta|pul|tie|ren, ...kom|men, ...kom|pli|men|tie|ren, ...kön|nen, ...las|sen, ...lau|fen** (aufs Gleiche -), **...müs|sen, ...po|sau|nen** (*ugs.*), **...schaf|fen** (*vgl.* [1]schaffen), **...schie|ben, ...schmei|ßen** (*ugs.*); **hi|naus sein** *vgl.* hinaus; **hi|naus‿sprin|gen, ...stel|len; Hi|naus|stel|lung** *(Sport);* **hi|naus‿tra|gen, ...trei|ben, ...wach|sen** (z. B. über sich selbst -), **...wa|gen** (sich), **...wer|fen, ...wol|len** (zu hoch -); **Hi|naus|wurf; hi|naus‿zie|hen, ...zö|gern**
hin|be|ge|ben, sich
hin|be|kom|men *(ugs.)*
hin|bie|gen (*ugs. für* in Ordnung bringen)
hin|blät|tern *(ugs.);* Geldscheine -
Hin|blick; *nur in* im, *seltener* in - auf
hin|brin|gen
Hin|de *vgl.* Hindin
Hin|de|mith (dt. Komponist)
hin|der|lich; hin|dern; ich ...ere (↑R 16); **Hin|der|nis,** das; -ses, -se; **Hin|der|nis‿lauf, ...ren|nen; Hin|de|rung; Hin|de|rungs|grund**
hin|deu|ten; alles scheint darauf hinzudeuten, dass ...
Hin|di, das; - (Amtsspr. in Indien)
Hin|din, die; -, -nen, *auch* Hin|de, die; -, -n (*veraltet für* Hirschkuh)
Hin|dos|tan [*auch* ...s'ta(:)n]; *vgl.* Hindustan; **Hin|du,** der; -[s], -[s] (Anhänger des Hinduismus); **Hin|du|is|mus,** der; - (indische Volksreligion); **hin|du|is|tisch; Hin|du|kusch,** der; -[s] (zentralasiat. Hochgebirge)
hin|durch; durch alles -; **hin|durch...** (z. B. hindurchgehen; er ist hindurchgegangen); **hin|durch|müs|sen; hin|durch|zwän|gen;** sich -
hin|dür|fen (*ugs. für* hingehen, hinkommen [o. Ä.] dürfen)
Hin|dus|tan [*auch* ...s'ta(:)n] (*veraltete Bez. für* Indien); **Hin|dus|ta|ni,** das; -[s] (Form des Westhindi); **hin|dus|ta|nisch**
hi|nein (↑R 132), *ugs.* 'nein (↑R 13); **hi|nein...** (z. B. hineingehen; er ist hineingegangen); **hi|nein‿be|ge|ben** (sich), **...be|mü|hen, ...bit|ten, ...brin|gen, ...dür|fen, ...fal|len, ...fin|den** (sich -),

...flüch|ten (sich -); **hi|nein|ge|bo|ren; hi|nein|ge|heim|nis|sen;** du geheimnisst hinein; **hi|nein‿ge|hen, ...ge|ra|ten** (in etwas -), **...grät|schen** *(Fußball),* **...grei|fen, ...in|ter|pre|tie|ren, ...kom|men, ...kom|pli|men|tie|ren, ...kön|nen, ...las|sen, ...müs|sen, ...pas|sen, ...pfu|schen, ...plat|zen** *(ugs.),* **...re|den, ...ren|nen** (in sein Unglück -), **...schaf|fen** (*vgl.* [1]schaffen), **...schau|en, ...schlit|tern** *(ugs.),* **...schüt|ten, ...ste|cken, ...stei|gern** (sich), **...stel|len, ...stop|fen** *(ugs.),* **...tap|pen** *(ugs.),* **...tra|gen, ...tre|ten, ...ver|set|zen** (sich -), **...wa|gen** (sich), **...wol|len, ...zie|hen**

hin|fah|ren; Hin|fahrt; Hin- und Herfahrt, Hin- und Rückfahrt *(vgl. d.)*

hin|fal|len; hin|fäl|lig; Hin|fäl|lig|keit, die; -

hin|fin|den; sich -

hin|flä|zen, sich *(ugs.)*

hin|fle|geln, sich *(ugs.)*

Hin|flug; Hin- und Rückflug *(vgl. d.)*

hin|fort (*geh., veraltend für* in Zukunft)

hin|füh|ren

Hin|ga|be, die; -; **hin|ga|be|fä|hig**

Hin|gang (*geh. für* Tod, Sterben)

hin|ge|ben; sich -; er hat sein Geld hingegeben; *aber* auf sein Verlangen hin geben; **hin|ge|bend; Hin|ge|bung,** die; -; **hin|ge|bungs|voll**

hin|ge|gen

hin|ge|gos|sen *(ugs.);* sie lag wie - auf dem Sofa

hin|ge|hen

hin|ge|hö|ren

hin|ge|ris|sen (begeistert); er war von diesem Spiel hingerissen

hin|ge|zo|gen; sich - fühlen

hin|gu|cken *(ugs.)*

hin|hal|ten; er hat das Buch hingehalten; mit der Rückgabe des Buches hat er sie lange hingehalten; hinhaltend antworten; **Hin|hal|te|tak|tik**

hin|hän|gen; *vgl.* [2]hängen

hin|hau|en *(ugs.);* das haute hin (das traf zu, das war in Ordnung); ich haute mich hin (legte mich schlafen); er haut hin (*landsch. u. österr. für* beeilt sich)

hin|ho|cken; sich -

hin|hor|chen

Hin|ke‿bein *(ugs.),* **...fuß** *(ugs.)*

Hin|kel, das; -s, - (*landsch. für* [junges] Huhn)

Hin|kel|stein (größerer, unbehauener [kultischer] Stein)

hin|ken; gehinkt

hin|knien; sich -

hin|kön|nen *(ugs.)*

hin|krie|gen (*ugs. für* zustande bringen); wir werden das schon -

Hin|kunft, die; -; *nur in* in - (*österr. für* in Zukunft)

hin|lan|gen *(ugs.);* **hin|läng|lich**

hin|le|gen; sich -

hin|ma|chen (*landsch. für* sich beeilen, sich hinbegeben)

hin|müs|sen *(ugs.)*

Hin|nah|me, die; -; **hin|neh|men**

hin|nei|gen; sich -; **Hin|nei|gung**

hin|nen *(veraltet); noch in* von - gehen

hin|rei|chen; hin|rei|chend

Hin|rei|se; Hin- und Herreise *(vgl. d.);* **hin|rei|sen**

hin|rei|ßen; sich - lassen; hin- und hergerissen sein (sich nicht entscheiden können; *scherzh. auch für* begeistert sein); **hin|rei|ßend**

Hin|rich (m. Vorn.)

hin|rich|ten; Hin|rich|tung

Hin|run|de (*Sportspr.; Ggs.* Rückrunde)

hin|sa|gen; das war nur so hingesagt

hin|schau|en

hin|schau|keln (*ugs. für* zustande bringen)

hin|schi|cken

hin|schie|ben

Hin|schied, der; -[e]s (*schweiz. für* Ableben, Tod)

hin|schla|gen; er ist lang hingeschlagen *(ugs.)*

hin|schlep|pen; sich -

hin|schmei|ßen *(ugs.);* sich -

hin|se|hen

hin sein *vgl.* hin

hin|set|zen; sich -

Hin|sicht, die; -, -en; in - auf ...; **hin|sicht|lich** *Präp. mit Gen.:* - des Briefes

hin|sie|chen *(geh.)*

hin|sin|ken *(geh.)*

Hin|spiel (*Sportspr.; Ggs.* Rückspiel)

hin|stel|len; sich -

hin|stre|cken; sich -

hin|streu|en

hin|strö|men

hin|stür|zen

hint|an... (*geh.,* z. B. hintansetzen; er hat seine Wünsche hintangesetzt); **hint|an|hal|ten; Hint|an|hal|tung,** die; -; **hint|an|set|zen; Hint|an|set|zung,** die; -; **hint|an|stel|len; Hint|an|stel|lung,** die; -; unter - aller Wünsche; **hin|ten; hin|ten|an; hin|ten|an|set|zen; hin|ten|drauf** *(ugs.);* **hin|ten|he|rum** (↑R 132); **hin|ten|hin; hin|ten|nach** *(landsch., bes. südd., österr.);* **hin|ten|rum** (*ugs. für* hintenherum)

hin|ten|über (↑R 132); **hin|ten|über...** (z. B. hintenüberfallen; er ist hintenübergefallen); **hin|ten|über‿kip|pen, ...stür|zen**

hin|ter; *Präp. mit Dat. u. Akk.:* hinter dem Zaun stehen, *aber* hinter den Zaun stellen; **hin|ter...** *in Verbindung mit Verben: unfeste Zusammensetzungen,* z. B. hinterbringen *(vgl. d.),* hintergebracht; *feste Zusammensetzungen,* z. B. hinterbringen *(vgl. d.),* hinterbracht

Hin|ter‿ab|sicht, ...ach|se, ...an|sicht, ...aus|gang, ...ba|cke, ...bänk|ler (wenig einflussreicher Parlamentarier [der auf einer der hinteren Bänke sitzt]), **...bein** *(bei Tieren)*

hin|ter|blei|ben; die hinterbliebenen Kinder; **Hin|ter|blie|be|ne,** der *u.* die; -n, -n (↑R 5 ff.); **Hin|ter|blie|be|nen|ren|te**

hin|ter|brin|gen (*ugs. für* nach hinten bringen); er hat das Essen kaum hintergebracht (*ostmitteld. für* hinunterschlucken, essen können); **hin|ter|brin|gen** (heimlich melden); er hat die Nachricht hinterbracht; **Hin|ter|brin|gung**

hin|ter|drein *(veraltend);* er war -; **hin|ter|drein...** (z. B. hinterdreinlaufen; er ist hinterdreingelaufen)

hin|te|re; hinterst *(vgl. d.);* **Hin|te|re,** der; ...ter[e]n, ...ter[e]n (*ugs. für* Gesäß); *vgl. auch* Hintern *u.* Hinterste

hin|ter|ei|nan|der (↑R 132); *in Verbindung mit Verben immer getrennt geschrieben:* hintereinander fahren, gehen, schalten, schreiben; hintereinander hergehen; **Hin|ter|ei|nan|der|schal|tung** *(Elektrotechnik);* **hin|ter|ei|nan|der|weg** (*ugs. für* ohne Pause)

Hin|ter|ein|gang

hin|ter|es|sen (*ostmitteld. für* mit Mühe, *auch* unwillig essen); er hat das Gemüse hintergegessen

hin|ter|fot|zig (*bayr., österr. ugs., sonst derb für* hinterlistig, heimtückisch); **Hin|ter|fot|zig|keit** *(bayr., österr. ugs., sonst derb)*

hin|ter|fra|gen; etwas - (nach den Hintergründen von etwas fragen); hinterfragt

Hin|ter‿front, ...fuß

Hin|ter|gau|men|laut (*für* Velar); **Hin|ter|ge|dan|ke**

hin|ter|ge|hen (*ugs. für* nach hinten gehen); hintergegangen; **hin|ter|ge|hen** (täuschen, betrügen); hintergangen; **Hin|ter|ge|hung**

Hin|ter|glas‿bild, ...ma|le|rei

Hin|ter|grund; hin|ter|grün|dig; Hin|ter|grün|dig|keit; Hin|ter|grund‿in|for|ma|ti|on, ...mu|sik

hin|ter|ha|ken (*ugs. für* einer Sache auf den Grund gehen)
Hin|ter|halt, der; -[e]s, -e; **hin|ter|häl|tig; Hin|ter|häl|tig|keit**
Hin|ter|hand, die; -
Hin|ter|haupt *(Med.);* **Hin|ter|haupt[s]|bein**
Hin|ter|haus
hin|ter|her [*auch* 'hin...]; hinterher (danach) polieren, *aber* hinterherlaufen (nachlaufen); er ist hinterhergelaufen; *aber* hinterher sein *(ugs.);* **hin|ter|her|hin|ken; hin|ter|her|kle|ckern** *(ugs.);* **hin|ter|her sein** *vgl.* hinterher; **hin|ter|her|wer|fen**
Hin|ter|hof
Hin|ter|in|di|en (südöstl. Halbinsel Asiens; ↑R 105)
Hin|ter|kopf
Hin|ter|la|der (eine Feuerwaffe)
Hin|ter|la|ge (*schweiz. für* Hinterlegung, Faustpfand)
Hin|ter|land, das; -[e]s
hin|ter|las|sen (zurücklassen; vererben); er hat etwas -; **Hin|ter|las|se|ne,** der *u.* die; -n, -n; ↑R 5 ff. (*schweiz. für* Hinterbliebene); **Hin|ter|las|sen|schaft; Hin|ter|las|sung,** die; - *(Amtsspr.);* unter - von ...
hin|ter|las|tig
hin|ter|le|gen (als Pfand usw.); **Hin|ter|le|ger; Hin|ter|le|gung**
Hin|ter|leib
Hin|ter|list, die; -; **hin|ter|lis|tig; Hin|ter|lis|tig|keit**
hin|term; ↑R 13 (*ugs. für* hinter dem)
Hin|ter|mann *Plur.* ...männer; **Hin|ter|mann|schaft** *(Sport)*
hin|ter|mau|ern *(Bauw.)*
hin|tern; ↑R 13 (*ugs. für* hinter den)
Hin|tern, der; -s, - (*ugs. für* Gesäß)
Hin|ter|rad; Hin|ter|rad|an|trieb; Hin|ter|rei|fen
Hin|ter|rhein (Quellfluss des Rheins)
hin|ter|rücks
hin|ters; ↑R 13 (*ugs. für* hinter das)
Hin|ter˘sass *od.* **...sas|se,** der; ...sassen, ...sassen (*früher* vom Feudalherrn abhängiger Bauer)
Hin|ter|schin|ken
hin|ter|schlin|gen (*landsch. für* hinunterschlingen); **hin|ter|schlu|cken** (*landsch. für* hinunterschlucken)
Hin|ter|sinn, der; -[e]s (geheime Nebenbedeutung); **hin|ter|sin|nen,** sich (*südd. u. schweiz. für* grübeln, schwermütig werden); du hast dich hintersonnen; **hin|ter|sin|nig;** -er Humor
hin|terst; zuhinterst; der hinterste Mann, *aber* (↑R 47): die Hintersten müssen stehen; **Hin|ters|te,** der; -n, -n (*ugs. für* Gesäß)
Hin|ter˘ste|ven, ...stüb|chen, ...teil (das; Gesäß), **...tref|fen** (*ugs.;* ins - kommen, geraten)
hin|ter|trei|ben (vereiteln); er hat den Plan hintertrieben
Hin|ter|trep|pe; Hin|ter|trep|pen|ro|man
Hin|ter|tup|fin|gen (*ugs. für* abgelegener, unbedeutender Ort)
Hin|ter|tür
Hin|ter|wäld|ler (rückständiger Mensch); **hin|ter|wäld|le|risch**
hin|ter|wärts (*veraltet für* zurück, [nach] hinten)
hin|ter|zie|hen (unterschlagen); er hat die Steuer hinterzogen; **Hin|ter|zie|hung**
hin|tra|gen
hin|trei|ben
hin|tre|ten; vor jmdn. -; **Hin|tritt,** der; -[e]s (*veraltet für* Tod)
hin|tun *(ugs.)*
hi|nü|ber (↑R 132), *ugs.* 'nü|ber (↑R 13); hinüber sein *(ugs.);* **hi|nü|ber...** (z. B. hinübergehen; er ist hinübergegangen); *aber* hinüber sein; **hi|nü|ber˘brin|gen, ...dür|fen, ...fah|ren, ...ge|hen, ...ge|lan|gen, ...kön|nen, ...müs|sen, ...ret|ten, ...schaf|fen** (*vgl.* [1]schaffen), **...schau|en, ...schi|cken, ...schwim|men; hi|nü|ber sein** *vgl.* hinüber; **hi|nü|ber˘spie|len** (ein ins Grünliche hinüberspielendes Blau), **...wech|seln, ...wer|fen, ...win|ken, ...wol|len, ...zie|hen**
hin und her; *vgl.* hin; **Hin und Her,** das; - - -[s]; nach längerem - - -; ein ewiges - - -; **Hin|und|her|fah|ren,** das; -s; *aber* (↑R 23): [das] Hin- und [das] Herfahren; **Hin- und Her|fahrt** (↑R 23); **Hin|und|her|ge|re|de; Hin- und Her|rei|se** (↑R 23); **Hin- und Her|weg** (↑R 23); **Hin- und Rück|fahrt** (↑R 23); **Hin- und Rück|flug** (↑R 23)
hi|nun|ter (↑R 132), *ugs.* 'nun|ter (↑R 13); **hi|nun|ter...** (z. B. hinuntergehen; er ist hinuntergegangen); **hi|nun|ter˘be|för|dern, ...be|glei|ten, ...bli|cken, ...brin|gen, ...ei|len, ...flie|ßen, ...ge|hen, ...kip|pen, ...rei|chen, ...rei|ßen, ...rol|len, ...schlu|cken, ...stür|zen, ...tau|chen, ...wer|fen, ...wür|gen**
hin|wa|gen, sich
hin|wärts
hin|weg; hin|weg... (z. B. hinweggehen; er ist hinweggegangen)
Hin|weg; Hin- und Herweg (↑R 23)
hin|weg˘brin|gen, ...fe|gen, ...ge|hen, ...hel|fen (sie half ihm darüber hinweg), **...kom|men, ...kön|nen, ...raf|fen, ...se|hen, ...set|zen** (sich darüber -), **...stei|gen, ...täu|schen, ...trös|ten**
Hin|weis, der; -es, -e; **hin|wei|sen;** hinweisendes Fürwort (*für* Demonstrativpronomen); **Hin|weis|schild,** das; **Hin|wei|sung**
hin|wen|den; sich -; **Hin|wen|dung**
hin|wer|fen; sich -
hin|wie|der, hin|wie|de|rum (↑R 132; *veraltend*)
Hinz (m. Vorn.); - und Kunz (*ugs. für* jedermann)
hin|zie|hen (*auch für* verzögern); der Wettkampf hat sich lange hingezogen (hat lange gedauert)
hin|zie|len; auf Erfolg -
hin|zu; hin|zu... (z. B. hinzukommen; er ist hinzugekommen, *aber* [↑R 38]: hinzu kommt, dass ...); **hin|zu|dich|ten; hin|zu|fü|gen; Hin|zu|fü|gung; hin|zu˘ge|sel|len** (sich), **...kau|fen, ...kom|men, ...ler|nen, ...rech|nen, ...sprin|gen, ...tre|ten; Hin|zu|tun,** das; -s
Hi|ob, Job, *ökum.* Ijob (bibl. m. Eigenn.); **Hi|obs˘bot|schaft, ...post** (die; -, -en; Unglücksbotschaft)
Hip-Hop, der; -s ‹engl.-amerik.› (eine Richtung der modernen Popmusik)
hipp..., hip|po... ‹griech.› (pferde...); **Hipp...,** Hip|po... (Pferde...); **Hip|parch** (↑R 132), der; -en, -en; ↑R 126 (Befehlshaber der Reiterei bei den alten Griechen); **Hip|pa|ri|on,** das; -s, ...ien [...iən] (fossiles Urpferd)
[1]Hip|pe, die; -, -n (sichelförmiges Messer)
[2]Hip|pe, die; -, -n (*südd. für* eine Art Fladenkuchen)
[3]Hip|pe, die; -, -n (*landsch. für* Ziege)
hipp, hipp, hur|ra!; hipp, hipp, hurra rufen; er rief: „Hipp, hipp, hurra!"; **Hipp|hipp|hur|ra,** das; -s, -s (Hochruf beim [Ruder]sport); er rief ein kräftiges -
Hip|pi|at|rik (↑R 130 *u.* 132), die; - ‹griech.› (Pferdeheilkunde)
Hip|pie ['hipi], der; -s, -s ‹amerik.› (Anhänger einer antibürgerlichen, pazifistischen, naturnahen Lebensform; Blumenkind)
hip|po... *vgl.* hipp...; **Hip|po...** *vgl.* Hipp...; **Hip|po|drom,** der *od., österr. nur,* das; -s, -e ‹griech.› (Reitbahn); **Hip|po|gryph,** der; *Gen.* -s *u.* -en, *Plur.* -e[n]; ↑R 126 (Flügelross der Dichtkunst)

Hip|po|kra|tes (altgriech. Arzt); **Hip|po|kra|ti|ker** (Anhänger des Hippokrates); **hip|po|kra|tisch;** hippokratischer Eid (Hippokrates zugeschriebenes Gelöbnis als Grundlage der ärztlichen Ethik); -es Gesicht (*Med.* Gesichtsausdruck des Sterbenden), die hippokratischen Schriften (↑R 94; Schriften von Hippokrates)

Hip|po|lo|gie, die; - ‹griech.› (wissenschaftl. Pferdekunde); **hip|po|lo|gisch** (die Hippologie betreffend); **Hip|po|lyt, Hip|po|ly|tos, Hip|po|ly|tus** (m. Eigenn.); **Hip|po|po|ta|mus,** der; -, - (Flusspferd); **Hip|pu|rit** [*auch* ...'rit], der; -en, -en; ↑R 126 (fossile Muschel); **Hip|pur|säu|re,** die; - (*Biol., Chemie* eine organ. Säure)

Hi|ra|ga|na, das; -[s] *od.* die; - (eine jap. Silbenschrift)

Hirn, das; -[e]s, -e; **Hirn|an|hangs|drü|se; Hirn|blu|tung; Hirn|er|schüt|te|rung** (*schweiz. neben* Gehirnerschütterung); **hirn|ge|schä|digt; Hirn|ge|spinst; Hirn|haut|ent|zün|dung; Hirn|holz,** das; -es (quer zur Faser geschnittenes Holz mit Jahresringen); **Hir|ni,** der; -s, -s (*ugs. für* törichter Mensch); **hirn|los; Hirn|rin|de; hirn|ris|sig** (*ugs. für* unsinnig, verrückt); **Hirn|scha|le; Hirn|strom|bild; Hirn|tod; hirn|ver|brannt** (*ugs. für* unsinnig, verrückt); **hirn|ver|letzt; Hirn|win|dung**

Hi|ro|hi|to (jap. Kaiser)

Hi|ro|schi|ma [*auch* hi'ro(:)...], *häufig auch* **Hi|ro|shi|ma** [...ʃ...] (jap. Stadt, auf die 1945 die erste Atombombe abgeworfen wurde)

Hirsch, der; -[e]s, -e; **Hirsch‿art, ...fän|ger, ...ge|weih, ...horn** (das; -[e]s), **...kä|fer, ...kalb, ...kuh; hirsch|le|dern**

Hir|se, die; -, *Plur. (Sorten:)* -n; **Hir|se‿brei, ...korn** (*Plur.* ...körner)

Hirt, der; -en, -en (↑R 126), *auch* **Hir|te,** der; -n, -n; **Hir|ten‿amt, ...brief** (bischöfl. Rundschreiben), **...flö|te, ...ge|dicht, ...stab, ...tä|schel** (das; -s, -; eine [Heil]pflanze), **...volk; Hir|tin**

his, His, das; -, - (Tonbezeichnung)

¹His|bol|lah, die; - (Gruppe extremistischer, schiitischer Moslems); **²His|bol|lah,** der; -s, -s (Anhänger der ¹Hisbollah)

His|kia, His|ki|as, *ökum.* **His|ki|ja** (jüd. König)

His|pa|ni|en [his'pa:ni̯ən] (alter Name der Pyrenäenhalbinsel); **his|pa|nisch; his|pa|ni|sie|ren** (spanisch machen); **His|pa|nist; His|pa|nis|tik,** die; - (Wissenschaft von der span. Sprache u. Literatur); **His|pa|nis|tin**

his|sen ([Flagge, Segel] hochziehen); du hisst; du hisstest; gehisst; hisse! *od.* hiss!; *vgl. auch* ²heißen

His|ta|min, das; -s, -e (ein Gewebehormon); **His|to|gramm,** das; -s, -e ‹griech.› (*Statistik* graph. Darstellung von Häufigkeiten in Form von Säulen); **His|to|lo|ge,** der; -n, -n; ↑R 126 (*Med.* Forscher u. Lehrer der Histologie); **His|to|lo|gie,** die; - (Lehre von den Geweben des Körpers); **His|to|lo|gin; his|to|lo|gisch**

His|tör|chen ‹griech.› (Geschichtchen); **His|to|rie** [...i̯ə], die; -, -n (*nur Sing.: veraltend für* [Welt]geschichte; *veraltet für* Bericht, Erzählung); **His|to|ri|en|ma|le|rei; His|to|rik,** die; - (Geschichtsforschung); **His|to|ri|ker** (Geschichtsforscher); **His|to|ri|ke|rin; His|to|ri|o|graph,** der; -en, -en; ↑R 126 (Geschichtsschreiber); **his|to|risch;** -e Grammatik; ein -er (bedeutungsvoller) Augenblick; -es Präsens; **his|to|ri|sie|ren** (das Geschichtliche betonen, anstreben); **His|to|ris|mus,** der; -, ...men (Überbetonung des Geschichtlichen); **his|to|ris|tisch**

Hist|ri|o|ne (↑R 130), der; -n, -n (↑R 126) ‹lat.› (altröm. Schauspieler)

Hit, der; -[s], -s ‹engl.› (*ugs. für* [musikalischer] Verkaufsschlager); **Hit‿lis|te, ...pa|ra|de**

Hit|sche, Hut|sche, Hüt|sche, die; -, -n (*landsch. für* Fußbank; kleiner Schlitten)

Hit|ze, die; -, *Plur. (fachspr.)* -n; ein Hitze abweisendes Material (↑R 40); **hit|ze|be|stän|dig; Hit|ze‿bläs|chen, ...fe|ri|en** *(Plur.);* **hit|ze|frei; Hit|ze|frei,** das; -; Hitzefrei *od.* hitzefrei haben, bekommen; *aber nur groß:* Hitzefrei erteilen; kein Hitzefrei bekommen, haben; **Hit|ze‿pe|ri|o|de, ...schild** (der), **...wel|le; hit|zig; Hitz|kopf; hitz|köp|fig; Hitz‿po|cke** *(meist Plur.),* **...schlag**

HIV [ha:|i:'fau̯], das; -[s], -[s] *Plur. selten* ‹*Abk. aus engl.* human immunodeficiency virus› (ein Aidserreger); **HIV-ne|ga|tiv; HIV-po|si|tiv** (↑R 26)

Hi|wi, der; -s, -s ‹*kurz für* Hilfswilliger› (*ugs. für* Hilfskraft)

Hjal|mar ['jal...] (m. Vorn.)

HK = Hefnerkerze

hl = Hektoliter

hl. = heilig; **hll.** = heilige *Plur*

hm!; hm, hm!

H-Milch ['ha:...] (*kurz für* haltbare Milch)

h-Moll ['ha:mɔl, *auch* 'ha:'mɔl], das; - (Tonart; *Zeichen* h); **h-Moll-Ton|lei|ter,** die; -, -n (↑R 28)

HNO-Arzt = Hals-Nasen-Ohren-Arzt; **HNO-ärzt|lich**

ho!; ho|ho!; ho ruck!

Ho = *chem. Zeichen für* Holmium

HO = Handelsorganisation *(ehem. in der DDR);* HO-Geschäft (↑R 26)

Ho|ang|ho *vgl.* Hwangho

Hob|bes [*engl.* 'hɔbz] (engl. Philosoph)

Hob|bock, der; -s, -s (ein Versandbehälter)

Hob|by, das; -s, -s ‹engl.› (Steckenpferd; Liebhaberei); **Hob|by|gärt|ner; Hob|by|ist,** der; -en, -en (↑R 126); **Hob|by‿kel|ler, ...koch, ...raum**

Ho|bel, der; -s, -; **Ho|bel|bank** *Plur.* ...bänke; **ho|beln;** ich ...[e]le (↑R 16); **Ho|bel|span; Hob|ler**

hoch; höher *(vgl. d.),* höchst *(vgl. d.); vgl.* hohe. *Schreibung in Verbindung mit Verben* (↑R 38 f.): hoch sein; es wird hoch hergehen; hoch/höher springen, fliegen, steigen usw.; jmdn. hoch achten, hoch schätzen; die Preise [sehr] hoch schrauben/höher schrauben; *aber* hochrechnen; sich [zum Direktor] hocharbeiten; [vor Schreck] hochfahren; an der Mauer hochspringen; die Treppe hochsteigen usw. *Schreibung in Verbindung mit einem Adjektiv oder Partizip* (↑R 40): hoch begabt, geehrt, gestellt, stehend; eine sehr hoch begabte Frau; [sehr] hoch gesteckte Ziele; eine höher gestellte Persönlichkeit; *aber* hochanständig, hochbetagt, hochberühmt, hocherfreut, hochfahrend, hochglänzend, hochtrabend usw.; *Großschreibung:* bei Hoch und Niedrig (*veraltet für* bei jedermann)

Hoch, das; -s, -s (Hochruf; *Meteor.* Gebiet hohen Luftdrucks)

hoch ach|ten *vgl.* hoch; **Hoch|ach|tung; hoch|ach|tungs|voll; Hoch|adel** (↑R 132); **hoch‿ak|tu|ell, ...al|pin; Hoch‿al|tar, ...amt; hoch|an|stän|dig; hoch|ar|bei|ten,** sich; *vgl.* hoch

Hoch‿bahn, ...bau (*Plur.* ...bauten); **hoch be|gabt** *vgl.* hoch; **hoch|be|glückt;** *vgl.* hocherfreut; **hoch|bei|nig; hoch|be|kom|men** (↑R 38 f.); *vgl.* hoch; **hoch|be|rühmt;** sie ist -; **hoch be|steu|ert** *vgl.* hoch; **hoch|be|tagt;** er ist -; **Hoch|be|trieb,** der;

-[e]s; es herrscht Hochbetrieb; **hoch be|zahlt** *vgl.* hoch; **hoch|bin|den** (↑R 38 f.); *vgl.* hoch; **Hoch|blü|te,** die; -; **hoch|brin|gen** (↑R 38 f.); *vgl.* hoch; **Hoch|burg; hoch|bu|sig**

hoch|deutsch; auf Hochdeutsch; *vgl.* deutsch; **Hoch|deutsch,** das; -[s] (Sprache); *vgl.* Deutsch; **Hoch|deut|sche,** das; -n; im -n; *vgl.* Deutsche, das; **hoch|die|nen,** sich (↑R 38 f.); *vgl.* hoch; **hoch do|tiert** *vgl.* hoch; **hoch|dre|hen** (↑R 38 f.); den Motor - (auf hohe Drehzahlen bringen); **Hoch|druck,** der; -[e]s, *Plur.* (*für* Erzeugnis im Hochdruckverfahren:) ...drucke; **Hoch|druck‿ge|biet** *(Meteor.),* **...ver|fah|ren**

Hoch|ebe|ne (↑R 132); **hoch emp|find|lich** *vgl.* hoch; **hoch ent|wi|ckelt** *vgl.* hoch; **hoch|er|freut; hoch|ex|plo|siv;** ein -es Gemisch

hoch|fah|ren; er ist aus dem Schlaf hochgefahren; *vgl.* hoch; **hoch|fah|rend;** ein hochfahrender Plan; **hoch|fein; Hoch|fi|nanz,** die; -; **hoch|flie|gen;** ..., dass die Späne hochfliegen; *vgl.* hoch; **hoch|flie|gend;** eine hochfliegende Idee; **Hoch|form,** die; - *(Sportspr.);* in - sein; **Hoch|for|mat; hoch|fre|quent** *(Physik);* **Hoch|fre|quenz; Hoch|fre|quenz|strom; Hoch|fri|sur**

Hoch|ga|ra|ge; hoch|ge|bil|det (↑R 40); **Hoch|ge|bir|ge; hoch|ge|bo|ren** *(veraltet); als Titel* Hochgeboren; *in der Anrede* Eure, Euer Hochgeboren; **hoch geehrt** *vgl.* hoch; **Hoch|ge|fühl; hoch|ge|hen** (↑R 38 f.); *vgl.* hoch; **hoch|ge|lehrt;** eine -e Abhandlung; **hoch|ge|mut** *(geh.);* ein -er Mensch; **Hoch‿ge|nuss, ...ge|richt** *(früher);* **hoch‿ge|schlos|sen, ...ge|spannt; hoch ge|steckt** *vgl.* hoch; **hoch|ge|stellt;** -e Zahlen (Indizes); *aber* hoch gestellte Persönlichkeiten; *vgl.* hoch; **hoch|ge|sto|chen** *(ugs.);* er ist - (eingebildet); **hoch ge|wach|sen** (↑R 40); **hoch‿ge|züch|tet, ...gif|tig; Hoch|glanz; hoch|glän|zend;** -e Seide; **Hoch|glanz|pa|pier; hoch|glanz|po|liert; hoch|gra|dig**

hoch|ha|ckig; -e Schuhe; **hoch|hal|ten** (↑R 38 f.); *vgl.* hoch; **Hoch|haus; hoch|he|ben** (↑R 38 f.); *vgl.* hoch; **Hoch|hei|mer** (ein Wein); **hoch|herr|schaft|lich; hoch|her|zig; Hoch|her|zig|keit,** die; -; **hoch|ho|len** (↑R 38 f.); *vgl.* hoch

Ho Chi Minh [hotʃi'min] (nordvietnames. Politiker); **Ho-Chi-Minh-Pfad,** der; -[e]s (↑R 95); **Ho-Chi-Minh-Stadt** (Stadt in Vietnam [*früher* Saigon])

hoch in|dus|tri|a|li|siert (↑R 40); *vgl.* hoch; **hoch‿in|tel|li|gent, ...in|te|res|sant**

hoch|ja|gen (aufscheuchen, aufjagen; *ugs. auch für* auf hohe Drehzahlen bringen); er hat den Motor hochgejagt; **hoch|ju|beln** *(ugs. für* durch übertriebenes Lob allgemein bekannt machen)

hoch|kant; - stellen; **hoch|kan|tig;** *meist in* jmdn. - rauswerfen *(ugs.);* **hoch|ka|rä|tig; Hoch|kir|che; hoch|klap|pen** (↑R 38 f.); *vgl.* hoch; **hoch|klet|tern** (↑R 38 f.); *vgl.* hoch; **hoch|kom|men** (↑R 38 f.); *vgl.* hoch; **Hoch|kon|junk|tur; hoch|krem|peln** (↑R 38 f.); *vgl.* hoch; **Hoch|kul|tur; hoch|kur|beln** (↑R 38 f.); *vgl.* hoch

Hoch|land *Plur.* ...länder, *auch* ...lande; **Hoch|län|der,** der (*auch für* Schotte); **hoch|län|disch** (*auch für* schottisch); **Hoch|lau|tung,** die; - (*Sprachw.* normierte Aussprache des Deutschen); **hoch|le|ben;** er hat ihn hochleben lassen; er lebe hoch!; **hoch|le|gen** (↑R 38 f.); *vgl.* hoch; **Hoch|leis|tung; Hoch|leis|tungs‿mo|tor, ...sport** (der; -[e]s), **...trai|ning; höch|lich; hoch|löb|lich**

Hoch|meis|ter *(früher);* **hoch‿mo|dern, ...mo|disch, ...mö|gend** *(veraltet),* **...mo|le|ku|lar** (*Chemie* aus Makromolekülen bestehend); **Hoch‿moor, ...mut; hoch|mü|tig; Hoch|mü|tig|keit,** die; -

hoch|nä|sig (*ugs. für* hochmütig); **Hoch|nä|sig|keit,** die; -; **Hoch|ne|bel; hoch|neh|men;** jmdn. - (*ugs. für* übervorteilen; necken, verspotten; verhaften); **hoch|not|pein|lich** (sehr streng); -es Gericht *(früher)*

Hoch|ofen (↑R 132); **hoch|of|fi|zi|ell; Hoch|öf|ner**

hoch|päp|peln *(ugs.);* **Hoch|par|ter|re; hoch|prei|sen;** er hat Gott hochgepriesen; **hoch|prei|sig;** -e Produkte; **hoch|pro|zen|tig**

hoch qua|li|fi|ziert (↑R 40); *vgl.* hoch

hoch|rä|de|rig, hoch|räd|rig; ein -er Wagen; **hoch|ran|gig** (↑R 40); **hoch|rap|peln,** sich *(ugs.);* **hoch|rech|nen** (*Statistik* aus repräsentativen Teilergebnissen [mit dem Computer] das Gesamtergebnis vorausberechnen); **Hoch‿rech|nung, ...re|li|ef, ...rip|pe; hoch|rot; Hoch|ruf**

Hoch|sai|son; hoch schät|zen *vgl.* hoch; **Hoch|schät|zung,** die; -; **Hoch|schau|bahn** (*österr. für* Achterbahn); **hoch|schau|keln** *(ugs.);* sich -; *vgl.* hoch; **hoch|scheu|chen** *vgl.* hoch; **hoch|schie|ben** (↑R 38 f.); *vgl.* hoch; **hoch|schla|gen** (↑R 38 f.); den Kragen hochschlagen; *vgl.* hoch; **Hoch|schrank; hoch|schre|cken;** *vgl.* [1]schrecken; **Hoch|schul|ab|schluss; Hoch‿schu|le, ...schü|ler, ...schü|le|rin; Hoch|schul‿leh|rer, ...leh|re|rin, ...re|form, ...rei|fe; hoch|schul|te|rig, hoch|schult|rig; hoch|schwan|ger; Hoch|see‿an|geln** (das; -s), **...fi|sche|rei, ...jacht; Hoch|seil; Hoch|si|cher|heits|trakt** (besonders ausbruchssicherer Teil bestimmter Strafvollzugsanstalten); **hoch|sin|nig; Hoch‿sitz** *(Jägerspr.),* **...som|mer; hoch|som|mer|lich; Hoch|span|nung; Hoch|span|nungs‿lei|tung, ...mast** (der); **hoch|spie|len;** er hat die Angelegenheit hochgespielt; *vgl.* hoch; **Hoch|spra|che; hoch|sprach|lich; hoch|sprin|gen** (↑R 38 f.); *vgl.* hoch; **Hoch|sprung**

höchst; höchstens; am höchsten; sie war auf das/aufs Höchste, *auch* auf das/aufs höchste erfreut; das höchste der Gefühle; sein Sinn ist auf das/aufs Höchste gerichtet; nach dem Höchsten streben

Hoch|stamm *(Gartenbau);* **hoch|stäm|mig; Hoch|sta|pe|lei; hoch|sta|peln** (etwas vortäuschen); **Hoch|stap|ler; Hoch|stap|le|rin**

Höchst|be|trag; Höchst|bie|ten|de, der *u.* die; -n, -n (↑R 5 ff.); **höchst|der|sel|be** *(veraltet);* höchstdieselben

hoch ste|hend *vgl.* hoch; **hoch|stei|gen** (↑R 38 f.); die Treppe hochsteigen; *vgl.* hoch

höchst|ei|gen *(veraltend);* in höchsteigener Person

hoch|stel|len; die Stühle hochstellen; *vgl.* hoch

höchs|tens; Höchst‿fall (*nur in* im -), **...form, ...ge|schwin|dig|keit, ...gren|ze**

Hoch|stift (*früher* reichsunmittelbarer Territorialbesitz eines Bischofs); **hoch|sti|li|sie|ren** (übertreibend hervorheben); **Hoch|stim|mung,** die; -

Höchst‿leis|tung, ...maß (das); **höchst|mög|lich;** die -e (*falsch:* höchstmöglichste) Leistung;

höchst|per|sön|lich; er ist höchstpersönlich (selbst, in eigener Person) gekommen, *aber* das ist eine höchst (im höchsten Grade, rein) persönliche Ansicht; **Höchst|preis; Hoch|stra|ße; höchst|rich|ter|lich; Höchst⌣satz, ...stand, ...stra|fe, ...stu|fe** (*für* Superlativ); **höchst|wahr|schein|lich;** er hat es höchstwahrscheinlich getan, *aber* es ist höchst (im höchsten Grade) wahrscheinlich, dass ...; **Höchst⌣wert, ...zahl; höchst|zu|läs|sig**

Hoch|tal; hoch tech|ni|siert (↑R 40); *vgl.* hoch; **Hoch⌣tech|no|lo|gie** (*svw.* Spitzentechnologie), **...ton** (*Plur.* ...töne; *Sprachw.*); **hoch|tö|nend; hoch|to|nig** (*Sprachw.* den Hochton tragend); **Hoch|tour; hoch|tou|rig; Hoch|tou|rist,** der; -en, -en; **hoch|tra|bend** (↑R 40)

hoch|ver|dient; hoch|ver|ehrt; *in der Anrede auch* hochverehrtest (↑R 40); **Hoch⌣ver|rat, ...ver|rä|ter; hoch⌣ver|rä|te|risch, ...ver|zins|lich** *(Bankw.)*

Hoch⌣wald, ...was|ser (*Plur.* ...wasser); **hoch|wer|fen** (↑R 38 f.); *vgl.* hoch; **hoch|wer|tig;** -es Metall; **Hoch|wild; hoch|will|kom|men** (↑R 40); **hoch|win|den** (↑R 38 f.); sich -; *vgl.* hoch; **hoch|wir|beln** (↑R 38 f.); *vgl.* hoch; **hoch|wirk|sam;** eine -e Medizin; **hoch|wohl|ge|bo|ren** *(veraltet), als Titel* Hochwohlgeboren; *in der Anrede* Eure, Euer Hochwohlgeboren; **hoch|wohl|löb|lich** *(veraltend);* **hoch|wöl|ben** (↑R 38 f.); sich -; *vgl.* hoch; **Hoch|wür|den** (Anrede für kath. Geistliche); Eure, Euer (*Abk.* Ew.) -; **hoch|wür|dig** *(veraltend);* der -e Herr Pfarrer; **hoch|wür|digst** (Anrede für höhere kath. Geistliche)

Hoch|zahl (*für* Exponent); **¹Hoch|zeit** (Feier der Eheschließung); silberne, goldene -; **²Hoch|zeit** (glänzender Höhepunkt, Hochstand); **Hoch|zei|ter** *(landsch.);* **Hoch|zei|te|rin** *(landsch.);* **hoch|zeit|lich; Hoch|zeits⌣bit|ter** (der; -s, -; *veraltet*), **...fei|er, ...flug** *(Zool.),* **...ge|schenk, ...kleid, ...kut|sche, ...nacht, ...paar, ...rei|se, ...schmaus, ...tag; hoch|zie|hen;** die Strickleiter hochziehen (↑R 38 f.); *vgl.* hoch; **Hoch|ziel; Hoch|zins|po|li|tik** *(Wirtsch., Bankw.)*

Hock, Höck, der; -s, Höcke (*schweiz. mdal. für* geselliges Beisammensein); **Ho|cke,** die; -, -n (auf dem Feld zusammengesetzte Garben; eine Turnübung); **ho|cken;** sich -; **Ho|cken|heim|ring,** der; -[e]s (Autorennstrecke in Nordbaden); **Ho|cker** (Schemel)

Hö|cker, der; -s, - (Buckel)

Ho|cker|grab *(Archäol.)*

hö|cke|rig; Hö|cker|schwan

Ho|ckey [ˈhɔke:, *auch* ˈhɔki], das; -s ⟨engl.⟩ (eine Sportart); **Ho|ckey⌣feld, ...schlä|ger, ...spie|ler, ...spie|le|rin**

Hock|stel|lung

Ho|de, der; -n, -n (↑R 126) *od.* die; -, -n (*selten für* Hoden); **Ho|den,** der; -s, - (männl. Keimdrüse); **Ho|den⌣bruch** (der; -[e]s, ...brüche), **...sack**

Hod|ler (schweiz. Maler)

Ho|do|me|ter, das; -s, - ⟨griech.⟩ (Wegemesser, Schrittzähler)

Hödr, Hö|dur (*nord. Mythol.* der blinde Gott)

Hod|scha (↑R 130), der; -[s], -s ⟨pers.⟩ ([geistl.] Lehrer)

Hö|dur *vgl.* Hödr

Hoek van Hol|land [ˈhuk fan -] (niederl. Hafen- u. Badeort)

Hof, der; -[e]s, Höfe; Hof halten; ich halte Hof, Hof gehalten, Hof zu halten; **Hof|da|me; hof|fä|hig; Hof|fä|hig|keit,** die; -

Hof|fart, die; - (*veraltend für* Dünkel, Hochmut); **hof|fär|tig; Hof|fär|tig|keit**

hof|fen

Hof|fens|ter

hof|fent|lich

...höf|fig (reiches Vorkommen versprechend, z. B. erdölhöffig); **höff|lich** (*Bergmannsspr.* reiche Ausbeute verheißend)

Hoff|mann, E. T. A. (dt. Schriftsteller)

Hoff|mann von Fal|lers|le|ben (dt. Dichter)

Hoff|nung; Hoff|nungs|lauf *(Sport);* **hoff|nungs|los; Hoff|nungs|lo|sig|keit,** die; -; **Hoff|nungs⌣schim|mer** (der; -s), **...strahl** *(Plur. selten),* **...trä|ger, ...trä|ge|rin; hoff|nungs|voll**

Hof|gas|tein, Bad (österr. Ort)

Hof hal|ten *vgl.* Hof; **Hof|hal|tung**

Hof|hund

ho|fie|ren (den Hof machen); jmdn. -

hö|fisch; -e Kunst; **Hof|knicks**

höf|lich; Höf|lich|keit; Höf|lich|keits⌣be|such, ...flos|kel; höf|lich|keits|hal|ber

Höf|ling; Hof|mann *Plur.* ...leute (*veraltet für* Höfling); **hof|män|nisch**

Hof|manns|thal (österr. Dichter)

Hof|mann von Hof|manns|wal|dau (dt. Dichter)

Hof|mar|schall (Inhaber des die gesamte fürstliche Hofhaltung umfassenden Hofamtes)

Hof⌣meis|ter (*veraltet für* Hauslehrer, Erzieher), **...narr, ...rat** (*Plur.* ...räte); **Hof|rei|te,** die; -, -n (*südd. für* bäuerl. Anwesen); **Hof|schran|ze,** die; -, -n, *selten* der; -n, -n (↑R 126) *meist Plur.* (*veraltend für* Höfling); **Hof|staat,** der; -[e]s; **Hof|statt,** die; -, -en (*schweiz. für* [Bauernhaus mit Hof und] Hauswiese, Obstgarten)

Höft, das; -[e]s, -e (*nordd. für* Haupt; Landspitze; Buhne)

Hof⌣tor (das), **...trau|er, ...tür**

hö|gen (*nordd. für* freuen); sich -

HO-Ge|schäft *vgl.* HO

ho|he; *Kleinschreibung* (↑R 108): die hohe Jagd; das hohe C; die hohe Schule *(Reiten);* das hohe Haus (Parlament); auf hoher See. *Großschreibung:* (↑R 102:) die Hohe Tatra; die Hohen Tauern; das Hohe Lied, des Hohen Liedes Salomo[n]s; *vgl.* Hohelied; der Hohe Priester, des Hohen Priesters, ein Hoher Priester; *vgl.* Hohepriester; (↑R 108:) die Hohe Messe in h-Moll (von J. S. Bach);

Hö|he, die; -, -n

Ho|heit (↑R 129); *vgl.* euer, Ew., ihr *u.* sein; **ho|heit|lich; Ho|heits⌣ad|ler, ...akt, ...ge|biet, ...ge|walt, ...ge|wäs|ser** *(meist Plur.),* **...recht; ho|heits|voll; Ho|heits|zei|chen** (sinnbildliches Zeichen der Staatsgewalt, z. B. Flagge, Siegel u. a.)

Ho|he|lied, das; ein Hohelied der Treue singen; *bei Beugung des ersten Bestandteils getrennt geschrieben; vgl.* hohe

hö|hen (*Malerei* bestimmte Stellen hervortreten lassen); weiß gehöht

Hö|hen⌣an|ga|be, ...angst (die; -), **...flug**

Ho|hen|fried|ber|ger, der; -s; der - Marsch

hö|hen|gleich *(Verkehrsw.);* **Hö|hen⌣krank|heit** (die; -), **...kur|ort, ...la|ge, ...leit|werk** *(Flugw.),* **...li|nie** *(Geogr.)*

Ho|hen|lo|he (Teil von Württemberg)

Hö|hen⌣luft (die; -), **...mar|ke, ...mes|ser** (der), **...mes|sung, ...rü|cken, ...ru|der** *(Flugw.),* **...son|ne** (*als* ®: Ultraviolettlampe)

Ho|hen|stau|fe, der; -n, -n; ↑R 126 (Angehöriger eines dt. Fürstengeschlechts); **¹Ho|hen|stau|fen** (Ort am gleichnamigen Berg); **²Ho|hen|stau|fen,** der; -s (Berg vor der Schwäb. Alb); **ho|hen|stau|fisch**

Hö|hen_steu|er (das; *Flugw.*), **...strah|lung** (kosmische Strahlung)
Ho|hen|twiel, der; -s (Bergkegel bei Singen)
Hö|hen_un|ter|schied, ...weg
Ho|hen|zol|ler, der; -n, -n; ↑R 126 (Angehöriger eines dt. Fürstengeschlechts); **ho|hen|zol|le|risch; Ho|hen|zol|lern,** der; -s (Berg vor der Schwäb. Alb); **Ho|hen|zol|lern-Sig|ma|rin|gen**
Hö|hen|zug
Ho|he|pries|ter; des Hohepriesters; *bei Beugung des ersten Bestandteils getrennt geschrieben; vgl.* hohe; **Ho|he|pries|ter|amt,** das; -[e]s, ...ämter; **ho|he|pries|ter|lich**
Hö|he|punkt
hö|her; -e Gewalt; -[e]n Ort[e]s; die höhere Laufbahn; höheres Lehramt; höhere Schule (Oberschule, Gymnasium usw.), *aber* (↑R 56): Höhere Handelsschule in Stuttgart; höher achten; jmdn. höher gruppieren; einen Beamten höher stufen (auf eine höhere Stufe bringen); die Preise höher schrauben; etwas lässt die Herzen höher schlagen; eine höher gestellte Person; seine Ziele höher stecken; **Hö|her|ent|wick|lung; hö|he|rer|seits; hö|her ge|stellt** *vgl.* höher; **hö|her grup|pie|ren** *vgl.* höher; **hö|her|ran|gig; hö|her schrau|ben** *vgl.* höher; **hö|her stu|fen** *vgl.* höher; **Hö|her|stu|fung**
ho|he Schu|le, die; -n -; ↑R 108 (Reitkunst; *übertr. für* Kunstfertigkeit, Gewandtheit); die - - reiten; die - - des Lebens
hohl; hohl|äu|gig; Hohl|block|stein; Höh|le, die; -, -n; **Hohl|ei|sen** (ein Werkzeug); **höh|len; Höh|len_bär, ...be|woh|ner, ...brü|ter, ...for|scher, ...ma|le|rei, ...mensch; Hohl|heit; Hohl_keh|le** (rinnenförmige Vertiefung), **...kopf** (dummer Mensch), **...kör|per, ...ku|gel, ...maß** (das), **...na|del, ...naht, ...raum; Hohl|raum_kon|ser|vie|rung, ...ver|sie|ge|lung** *(Kfz-Technik);* **Hohl|saum; hohl|schlei|fen** *(Technik);* **Hohl_schliff, ...spie|gel; Höh|lung; Hohl|ve|ne; hohl|wan|gig; Hohl_weg, ...zie|gel**
Hohn, der; -[e]s; Hohn lachen, ich lache Hohn; *auch:* hohnlachen, ich hohnlache; Hohn sprechen, das spricht allem Recht Hohn; *auch:* hohnsprechen *(vgl. d.);* **höh|nen; Hohn|ge|läch|ter; höh|nisch; hohn|lä|cheln** (↑R 39); *fast nur im Infinitiv u. im Partizip I gebräuchlich:* hohnlächelnd; *vgl.* Hohn; **hohn|la|chen** (↑R 39); *meist im Infinitiv u. im Partizip I gebräuchlich:* hohnlachend; *vgl.* Hohn; **hohn|spre|chen** (↑R 39); *meist im Infinitiv u. im Partizip I gebräuchlich:* jmdm. hohnsprechen; eine allem Recht hohnsprechende Entscheidung; *vgl.* Hohn
ho|ho!
hoi! [hɔy]
Hö|ker (*veraltet für* Kleinhändler); **Hö|ke|rei; Hö|ke|rin; hö|kern;** ich ...ere (↑R 16); **Hö|ker|weib**
Ho|kus|po|kus, der; - ‹engl.› (Zauberformel der Taschenspieler, Gaukelei; Blendwerk)
Hol|ark|tis, die; - ‹griech.› (*Pflanzen- u. Tiergeographie* Gebiet zwischen Nordpol u. nördlichem Wendekreis); **hol|ark|tisch**
Hol|bein (dt. Maler); **hol|beinsch;** die holbeinsche Madonna (↑R 94)
hold
[1]Hol|da, Hol|le (Gestalt der dt. Mythologie); Frau Holle; **[2]Hol|da** (w. Vorn.)
Hol|der, der; -s, - (*landsch. für* Holunder); **Hol|der|baum**
Höl|der|lin (dt. Dichter)
Hol|ding|ge|sell|schaft [ˈho:l-diŋ...] ‹engl.; dt.› (*Wirtsch.* Gesellschaft, die nicht selbst produziert, aber Aktien anderer Gesellschaften besitzt)
hol|dri|o! [*auch* ...driˈo:] (Freudenruf); **[1]Hol|dri|o,** das; -s, -s; **[2]Hol|dri|o,** der; -[s], -[s] (*veraltet für* leichtlebiger Mensch)
hold|se|lig (*veraltend für* liebreizend); **Hold|se|lig|keit,** die; -
ho|len (abholen); etwas - lassen
Hol|ger (m. Vorn.)
Ho|lis|mus, der; - ‹griech.› (eine philos. Ganzheitslehre)
Holk *vgl.* Hulk
hol|la!
Hol|la|brunn (österr. Stadt)
Hol|land; [1]Hol|län|der (↑R 103); - Käse; der Fliegende - (Oper; *vgl.* fliegen); **[2]Hol|län|der** (Kinderfahrzeug; Holländermühle, *vgl. d.*); **[3]Hol|län|der,** der; -s, - (Käse); **Hol|län|de|rin; Hol|län|der|müh|le** (Zerkleinerungsmaschine für Papier); **hol|län|dern** (*Buchw.* [ein Buch] mit Fäden heften, die im Buchrücken verleimt werden); ich ...ere (↑R 16); **hol|län|disch;** -er Gulden (*Abk.* hfl); **Hol|län|disch,** das; -[s] (Sprache; *vgl.* Niederländisch); *vgl.* Deutsch; **Hol|län|di|sche,** das; -n; *vgl.* Deutsche, das
[1]Hol|le, die; -, -n (Federhaube [bei Vögeln])
[2]Hol|le *vgl.* [1]Holda
Höl|le, die; -, -n
Hol|le|dau (↑R 132); *vgl.* Hallertau
Höl|len... (*ugs. auch für* groß, sehr viel, z. B. Höllenlärm); **Höl|len_brut, ...fahrt, ...hund, ...lärm** *(ugs.),* **...ma|schi|ne, ...spek|ta|kel** (der; -s; *ugs.*), **...stein** (der; -[e]s; ein Ätzmittel)
Hol|ler, der; -s, -, Hol|ler|baum (*südd. u. österr. meist für* Holunder)
Höl|ler, Karl (dt. Komponist)
Hol|ler|baum *vgl.* Holler
hol|le|ri|thie|ren (*Datenverarbeitung* auf Lochkarten bringen); **Hol|le|rith|ma|schi|ne** ‹nach dem dt.-amerik. Erfinder› (Lochkartenmaschine zum Speichern u. Sortieren von Daten)
höl|lisch
Hol|ly|wood [ˈhɔliwud] (US-amerik. Filmstadt); **Hol|ly|wood|schau|kel;** ↑R 105 (breite, frei aufgehängte Sitzbank)
[1]Holm, der; -[e]s, -e (Griffstange des Barrens, Längsstange der Leiter)
[2]Holm, der; -[e]s, -e (*nordd. für* kleine Insel); **Holm|gang,** der (altnord. Zweikampf, der auf einem [2]Holm ausgetragen wurde)
Hol|mi|um, das; -s (chem. Element, Metall; *Zeichen* Ho)
Ho|lo|caust [*auch* ˈhɔlɔkɔ:st], der; -[s], -s ‹griech.-engl.› (Tötung einer großen Zahl von Menschen, bes. der Juden in der Zeit des Nationalsozialismus)
Ho|lo|fer|nes (assyr. Feldherr)
Ho|lo|gramm, das; -s, -e ‹griech.› (*Optik* Speicherbild); **Ho|lo|gra|phie** (↑R 33), die; -, ...ien (besondere Technik zur Bildspeicherung u. -wiedergabe in dreidimensionaler Struktur; Laserfotografie); **ho|lo|gra|phisch** (*Bibliotheksw., Rechtsspr.* [ganz] eigenhändig geschrieben)
ho|lo|kris|tal|lin ‹griech.› (ganz kristallin [von Gesteinen]); **Ho|lo|zän,** das; -s (*Geol.* jüngste Abteilung des Quartärs)
hol|pe|rig; Hol|pe|rig|keit, die; -; **hol|pern;** ich ...ere (↑R 16); **holp|rig; Holp|rig|keit,** die; -
Hols|te, der; -n, -n; ↑R 126 (*altertüml. für* Holsteiner); **Hol|stein** (Teil des Bundeslandes Schleswig-Holstein); **Hol|stei|ner** (*auch für* eine Pferderasse); ↑R 103; **Hol|stei|ne|rin; hol|stei|nisch;** holsteinische Butter, *aber:* die Holsteinische Schweiz
Hols|ter, das; -s, - ‹engl.› (Pistolen-, Revolvertasche)
hol|ter|die|pol|ter! *(ugs.)*

hol|über! (↑R 132; Ruf an den Fährmann)
Ho|lun|der, der; -s, - (ein Strauch; *nur Sing. auch für* Holunderbeeren); Schwarzer Holunder *(fachspr.);* **Ho|lun|der|bee|re**
Holz, das; -es, Hölzer; er siegte mit 643 - (↑R 90; *Kegeln*); Holz verarbeitendes Gewerbe; **Holz‿ap|fel, ...art, ...bein, ...blä|ser, ...blas|in|stru|ment, ...block** (*vgl.* Block), **...bock, ...bo|den; Hölz|chen; Holz|ein|schlag** *(Forstw.);* **hol|zen;** du holzt; **Hol|zer** (*landsch. für* Waldarbeiter; *Sport* roher Spieler [im Fußball]); **Hol|ze|rei** (*ugs. für* Prügelei; *Sport* regelwidriges, rohes Spiel); **höl|zern** (aus Holz); **Holz‿es|sig** (der; -s), **...fäl|ler; holz|frei;** -es Papier; **Holz‿geist** (der; -[e]s; Methylalkohol), **...ge|rüst, ...ha|cker** (*bes. österr. für* Holzfäller), **...ham|mer; Holz|ham|mer|me|tho|de** (plumpe Art und Weise); **Holz|haus; hol|zig; Holz‿kis|te, ...klas|se** (*früher ugs. für* billigste Klasse, bes. in der Bahn), **...klotz, ...knecht** (*veraltet, noch österr. für* Holzfäller), **...koh|le, ...pflock, ...scheit, ...schliff** *(fachspr.);* **holz|schliff|frei** (↑R 136); **Holz‿schnei|der, ...schnitt, ...schnit|zer, ...schuh, ...schutz|mit|tel, ...span, ...sta|pel, ...stoß, ...trep|pe; Hol|zung; Holz ver|ar|bei|tend** *vgl.* Holz; **holz|ver|klei|det; Holz‿weg, ...wol|le** (die; -), **...wurm**
Hom|burg, der; -s, -s (ein steifer Herrenhut)
Home|land ['ho:mlɛnd], das; -[s], -s ‹engl.› (*früher für* bestimmten Teilen der schwarzen Bevölkerung zugewiesenes Siedlungsgebiet in der Republik Südafrika)
Ho|mer (altgriech. Dichter); **Ho|me|ri|de,** der; -n, -n (↑R 126) ‹griech.› (Nachfolger Homers); **ho|me|risch;** homerisches Gelächter; homerische Gedichte (↑R 94); **Ho|me|ros** *vgl.* Homer
Home|rule ['ho:mru:l], die; - ‹engl.› („Selbstregierung“ als Schlagwort der irischen Unabhängigkeitsbewegung); **Home|spun** ['ho:mspan], das *od.* der; -s, -s (grobes Wollgewebe); **Home|trai|ner** ['ho:mtrɛ:nə(r)] (Sportgerät für häusliches Training)
Ho|mi|let, der; -en, -en (↑R 126) ‹griech.› (Kenner der Homiletik); **Ho|mi|le|tik,** die; - (Geschichte u. Theorie der Predigt); **ho|mi|le|tisch; Ho|mi|lie,** die; -, ...ien (erbaul. Bibelauslegung; Predigt über einen Bibeltext)

Ho|mi|ni|den *Plur.* ‹lat.› (*Biol.* Familie der Menschenartigen)
Hom|mage [ɔ'ma:ʒ], die; -, -n [...ʒ(ə)n] ‹franz.› (Veranstaltung, Werk als Huldigung für einen Menschen); - à (für) Miró
Ho|mo, der; -s, -s (*ugs. für* Homosexueller); **ho|mo...** ‹griech.› (gleich...); **Ho|mo...** (Gleich...)
Ho|mo|ero|tik (↑R 132), die; - (gleichgeschlechtl. Erotik); **ho|mo|ero|tisch**
ho|mo|fon usw. *eindeutschende Schreibung für* homophon usw.
ho|mo|gen (gleichartig, gleichmäßig zusammengesetzt); -es Feld; **ho|mo|ge|ni|sie|ren** (homogen machen, vermischen); **Ho|mo|ge|ni|sie|rung; Ho|mo|ge|ni|tät,** die; - (Gleichartigkeit)
ho|mo|log (übereinstimmend, entsprechend); **ho|mo|lo|gie|ren** ([einen Serienwagen] in die internationale Zulassungsliste zur Klasseneinteilung für Rennwettbewerbe aufnehmen); **Ho|mo|lo|gie|rung**
ho|mo|nym (↑R 132; gleich lautend [aber in der Bedeutung verschieden]); **Ho|mo|nym,** das; -s, -e (*Sprachw.* Wort, das mit einem anderen gleich lautet, z. B. „Heide“ = Nichtchrist *u.* „Heide“ = unbebautes Land); **ho|mo|ny|misch** *(älter für* homonym)
ho|mö|o... ‹griech.› (ähnlich...); **Ho|mö|o...** (Ähnlich...); **Ho|mö|o|path,** der; -en, -en; ↑R 126 (homöopath. Arzt, Anhänger der Homöopathie); **Ho|mö|o|pa|thie,** die; - (ein Heilverfahren); **Ho|mö|o|pa|thin; ho|mö|o|pa|thisch**
ho|mo|phil ‹griech.› (*svw.* homosexuell); **Ho|mo|phi|lie,** die; - (*svw.* Homosexualität)
ho|mo|phon (↑R 33); **Ho|mo|pho|nie,** die; - (Kompositionsstil mit nur einer führenden Melodiestimme)
Ho|mo sa|pi|ens [- 'za:pi̯ɛns], der; - - ‹lat.› (wissenschaftl. Bez. für den Menschen)
Ho|mo|se|xu|a|li|tät, die; - ‹griech.; lat.› (gleichgeschlechtliche Liebe [bes. des Mannes]); **ho|mo|se|xu|ell; Ho|mo|se|xu|el|le,** der *u.* die; -n, -n (↑R 5ff.)
ho|mo|zy|got (*Biol.* reinerbig)
Ho|mun|ku|lus, der; -, *Plur.* ...lusse *od.* ...li ‹lat.› (künstlich erzeugter Mensch)
Ho|nan (chines. Prov.); **Ho|nan|sei|de**
Hon|du|ra|ner (Bewohner von Honduras); **hon|du|ra|nisch; Hon|du|ras** (mittelamerik. Staat)

Ho|ne|cker (drittletzter Vorsitzender des Staatsrates der DDR)
Ho|neg|ger [*franz.* ɔnɛ'gɛ:r] (franz.-schweiz. Komponist)
ho|nen ‹engl.› ([Metallflächen] sehr fein schleifen)
ho|nett ‹franz.› (*veraltend für* ehrenhaft; anständig)
Hong|kong (chines. Hafenstadt)
Ho|ni|a|ra (Hptst. der Salomonen)
Ho|nig, der; -s, *Plur. (Sorten:)* -e; **Ho|nig|bie|ne; ho|nig|gelb; Ho|nig‿glas, ...ku|chen; Ho|nig|ku|chen|pferd;** *nur in* strahlen wie ein - (*ugs. für* über das ganze Gesicht strahlen); **Ho|nig|le|cken,** das; etwas ist kein Honiglecken *(ugs.);* **Ho|nig|mond** (*veraltend für* Flitterwochen); **Ho|nig|schle|cken,** das; *vgl.* Honiglecken; **Ho|nig|seim** *(veraltet);* **ho|nig|süß; Ho|nig‿tau** (der), **...wa|be, ...wein**
Hon|neurs [(h)ɔ'nø:rs] *Plur.* ‹franz.› (*veraltend für* [milit.] Ehrenerweisungen); die - machen (*geh. für* die Gäste begrüßen)
Ho|no|lu|lu (Hptst. von Hawaii)
ho|no|ra|bel ‹lat.› (*veraltet für* ehrbar; ehrenvoll); ...ab|le (↑R 130) Bedingungen; **Ho|no|rar,** das; -s, -e (Vergütung [für Arbeitsleistung in freien Berufen]); **Ho|no|rar|pro|fes|sor; Ho|no|ra|ti|o|ren** *Plur.* (Standespersonen, bes. in kleineren Orten); **ho|no|rie|ren** (belohnen; bezahlen; vergüten); **Ho|no|rie|rung; ho|no|rig** (*veraltend für* ehrenhaft; freigebig); **ho|no|ris cau|sa** (ehrenhalber; *Abk.* h. c.)
Ho|no|ri|us (röm. Kaiser)
Hoo|li|gan ['hu:ligən], der; -s, -s ‹engl.› (Randalierer, bes. bei Massenveranstaltungen)
Hoorn; Kap - (Südspitze Amerikas [auf der Insel Hoorn])
hop|fen (Bier mit Hopfen versehen); **Hop|fen,** der; -s, - (eine Kletterpflanze; Bierzusatz); **Hop|fen|stan|ge**
Ho|pi, der; -[s], -[s] (Angehöriger eines nordamerik. Indianerstammes)
Hop|lit (↑R 130), der; -en, -en (↑R 126) ‹griech.› (Schwerbewaffneter im alten Griechenland)
hopp!; hopp, hopp!; **hop|peln;** ich ...[e]le (↑R 16); **Hop|pel|pop|pel,** das; -s, - (*landsch. für* Bauernfrühstück; heißer Punsch); **hopp|hopp!; hop|la!; hopp|neh|men** (*ugs. für* festnehmen); **hops;** - (*ugs. für* verloren) sein; **Hops,** der; -es, -e; **hops!, hop|sa!, hop|sa|la!, hop|sa|sa!; hop|sen;** du hopst; **Hop|ser; Hop|se|rei;**

hops₋ge|hen (*ugs. für* umkommen; verloren gehen), **...neh|men** (*vgl.* hoppnehmen)
ho|ra ‹lat., „Stunde"›; *nur als Zeichen* (h) *in Abkürzungen von Maßeinheiten,* z. B. kWh [= Kilowattstunde], *u. als Zeitangabe,* z. B. 6 h *od.* 6ʰ (= 6 Uhr); **Ho|ra, Ho|re,** die; -, Horen *meist Plur.* (Stundengebet der kath. Geistlichen); die Horen beten
Hör|ap|pa|rat
Ho|ra|ti|us, Ho|raz (röm. Dichter); **ho|ra|zisch;** die horazischen Satiren (↑R 94)
hör|bar; Hör₋be|reich (der), **...bild, ...bril|le; horch!; hor|chen; Hor|cher; Hor|che|rin; Horch₋ge|rät, ...pos|ten**
[1]**Hor|de,** die; -, -n (Flechtwerk; Lattengestell; Rost, Sieb zum Dörren u. Lagern von Obst, Gemüse usw.); *vgl.* Hurde, Hürde
[2]**Hor|de,** die; -, -n ‹tatar.› (wilde Menge, ungeordnete Schar); **hor|den|wei|se**
Ho|re *vgl.* Hora; [1]**Ho|ren** (*eingedeutschter Plur. von* Hora)
[2]**Ho|ren** *Plur.* (*griech. Mythol.* Töchter des Zeus u. der Themis [Dike, Eunomia, Eirene; *vgl. d.*], Göttinnen der Jahreszeiten)
hö|ren; er hat von dem Unglück heute gehört; sie hat die Glocken läuten hören *od.* gehört; von sich - lassen; **Hö|ren|sa|gen,** das; *meist in* er weiß es vom -; **hö|rens|wert; Hö|rer; Hö|re|rin; Hö|rer|kreis; Hö|rer|schaft; Hör₋feh|ler, ...fol|ge, ...funk** (*für* Rundfunk im Ggs. zum Fernsehen); **Hör|ge|rät; Hör|ge|rä|te|akus|ti|ker** (↑R 132); **hör|ge|schä|digt; hö|rig; Hö|ri|ge,** der *u.* die; -n, -n; ↑R 5 ff. *(früher);* **Hö|rig|keit**
Ho|ri|zont, der; -[e]s, -e ‹griech.› (scheinbare Begrenzungslinie zwischen Himmel u. Erde; Gesichtskreis); **ho|ri|zon|tal** (waagerecht); **Ho|ri|zon|ta|le,** die; -, -n; drei -[n]; **Ho|ri|zon|tal|pen|del**
Hor|mon, das; -s, -e ‹griech.› (Drüsenstoff; ein körpereigener Wirkstoff); **hor|mo|nal,** hor|mo|nell; **Hor|mon|be|hand|lung; hor|mo|nell** *vgl.* hormonal; **Hor|mon₋for|schung, ...haus|halt, ...prä|pa|rat, ...spie|gel, ...sprit|ze**
Hör|mu|schel (am Telefon)
Horn, das; -[e]s, *Plur.* Hörner *u.* (*für* Hornarten:) -e; **Horn|ber|ger Schie|ßen;** *nur in* ausgehen wie das - - (ergebnislos enden); **Horn₋blen|de** (ein Mineral), **...bril|le; Hörn|chen; Hörndl|bau|er** (*österr. für* Bauer, der vorwiegend Viehzucht betreibt); **hor|nen** (*veraltet für* hörnern); **hör|nen** (das Gehörn abwerfen; *ugs. scherzh. für* [den Ehemann] betrügen); **hör|nern** (aus Horn); **Hör|ner₋schall, ...schlit|ten; Horn|haut; hor|nig**
Hor|nis|grin|de [*auch* 'hɔr...] (höchster Berg des nördl. Schwarzwaldes)
Hor|nis|se [*auch* 'hɔr...], die; -, -n (eine Wespenart); **Hor|nis|sen|nest**
Hor|nist, der; -en, -en; ↑R 126 (Hornbläser); **Hor|nis|tin; Horn|klee,** der; -s; **Horn₋ochs** *od.* **...och|se** (*derb für* dummer Mensch), **...si|gnal, ...tier**
Hor|nung, der; -s, -e (*alte dt. Bez. für* Februar)
Hor|nuß ['hɔrnu:s], der; -es, -e (*schweiz. für* Schlagscheibe); **hor|nu|ßen** (*schweiz. für* eine Art Schlagball spielen)
Horn|vieh (*auch svw.* Hornochse)
Hör|or|gan
Ho|ros (Sohn der Isis)
Ho|ro|skop (↑R 132), das; -s, -e ‹griech.› (astrolog. Voraussage nach der Stellung der Gestirne)
hor|rend ‹lat.› (schauderhaft; übermäßig); -e Preise; **hor|ri|bel** (furchtbar); ...ib|le (↑R 130) Zustände; **hor|ri|bi|le dic|tu** (schrecklich zu sagen)
hor|ri|do! (ein Jagdruf); **Hor|ri|do,** das; -s, -s
Hör|rohr
Hor|ror, der; -s ‹lat.› (Schauder, Abscheu); **Hor|ror|film; Hor|ror|trip** (*ugs. für* Drogenrausch mit Angst- u. Panikgefühlen; höchst unangenehmes Erlebnis); **Hor|ror va|cui** [- 'va:kui], der; - - (Scheu vor der Leere)
Hör|saal
hors con|cours [ɔr kɔ̃'ku:r] ‹franz.› (außer Wettbewerb); **Hors|d'œuv|re** [ɔr'dœ:vr(ə), *auch* o:r...] (↑R 130), das; -[s], -s [...vr(ə)] (appetitanregende Vorspeise)
Hör|sel, die; - (r. Nebenfluss der Werra); **Hör|sel|ber|ge** *Plur.* (Höhen im nördl. Vorland des Thüringer Waldes)
Hör|spiel
[1]**Horst** (m. Vorn.)
[2]**Horst,** der; -[e]s, -e (Greifvogelnest; Strauchwerk)
hors|ten (nisten [von Greifvögeln])
Horst|mar (m. Vorn.)
Hör|sturz (*Med.* plötzlich auftretende Schwerhörigkeit od. Taubheit)
Hort, der; -[e]s, -e (Schatz; Ort, Stätte; *kurz für* Kinderhort)
hört!; hört, hört!
hor|ten ([Geld usw.] aufhäufen)
Hor|ten|sia (w. Vorn.); **Hor|ten|sie** [...iə], die; -, -n (ein Zierstrauch); **Hor|ten|si|us** (m. Vorn.)
hört, hört!; Hört|hört|ruf
Hort|ne|rin (Erzieherin in einem Kinderhort); **Hor|tung** ‹*zu* horten›
ho ruck!, hau ruck!
Ho|rus *vgl.* Horos
Hor|váth ['hɔrva:t], Ödön von (österr. Schriftsteller)
Hör|wei|te; in -
ho|san|na! usw. *vgl.* hosianna!
Hös|chen; Ho|se, die; -, -n
Ho|sea (bibl. Prophet)
Ho|sen₋an|zug, ...band (das; *Plur.* ...bänder); **Ho|sen|band|or|den; Ho|sen₋bein, ...bo|den, ...bund** (der; -[e]s, ...bünde), **...knopf, ...la|den** (*ugs. auch für* Hosenschlitz), **...lupf** (*schweiz. für* Ringkampf [Schwingen]; Kräftemessen), **...matz, ...naht, ...rock, ...rol|le** (von einer Frau gespielte Männerrolle), **...schei|ßer** (*derb für* sehr ängstlicher Mensch), **...schlitz, ...stall** *(ugs. scherzh.),* **...ta|sche, ...trä|ger** *(meist Plur.)*
ho|si|an|na!, *ökum.* ho|san|na! ‹hebr.› (Gebets- u. Freudenruf); **Ho|si|an|na,** *ökum.* Ho|san|na, das; -s, -s
Hos|pi|tal, das; -s, *Plur.* -e *u.* ...täler ‹lat.› (Krankenhaus; *früher für* Armenhaus, Altersheim); **hos|pi|ta|li|sie|ren** (*Amtsspr.* in ein Hospital einweisen); **Hos|pi|ta|lis|mus,** der; - (*Med.* seel. u. körperl. Schäden, bes. bei Kindern, durch längere Krankenhaus- od. Heimunterbringung); **Hos|pi|tant,** der; -en, -en; ↑R 126 (Gast[hörer an Hochschulen]; Parlamentarier, der sich als Gast einer Fraktion anschließt); **Hos|pi|tan|tin; hos|pi|tie|ren** (als Gast [in Schulen] zuhören); **Hos|piz,** das; -es, -e ([in christl. Geist geführter] Beherbergungsbetrieb)
Hos|po|dar, Gos|po|dar, der; *Gen.* -s *u.* -en (↑R 126), *Plur.* -e[n] (ehem. slaw. Fürstentitel in der Moldau u. Walachei)
Hos|tess [*auch* 'hɔ...], die; -, -en ‹engl.› ([sprachkundige] Begleiterin, Betreuerin, Führerin [auf einer Ausstellung, in Hotels o. Ä.]; *verhüll. auch für* Prostituierte)
Hos|tie [...iə], die; -, -n ‹lat.› (Abendmahlsbrot)
Hot, der; -s ‹amerik.› (*kurz für* Hotjazz)

Hot|dog, *auch* **Hot Dog,** das, *auch* der; -s, -s ‹amerik.› (heißes Würstchen in einem Brötchen)
Ho|tel, das; -s, -s ‹franz.›; **Ho|tel-bar, ...be|sit|zer, ...be|sit|ze|rin, ...be|trieb, ...bett, ...de|tek|tiv, ...dieb, ...die|bin, ...di|rek|tor, ...di|rek|to|rin, ...fach, ...fach-schu|le, ...füh|rer** (*svw.* Hotelverzeichnis); **Ho|tel gar|ni** [hɔ'tɛl gar'ni:], das; - -, -s -s [hɔ'tɛl gar'ni:] (Hotel, das neben der Übernachtung nur Frühstück anbietet); **Ho|tel-ge|wer|be, ...hal|le; Ho|te|li|er** [...'li̯e:], der; -s, -s (Hotelbesitzer); **Ho|tel-kauf|frau, ...kauf|mann, ...ket|te; Ho|tel|le|rie,** die; - (Gast-, Hotelgewerbe); **Ho|tel-nach|weis, ...rech|nung, ...ver|zeich|nis, ...zim|mer**
Hot|jazz, *auch* **Hot Jazz** ['hɔt-'dʒɛs], der; - ‹amerik.› (scharf akzentuierter, oft synkopischer Jazzstil)
Hot|line ['hɔt'lain], die; -, -s ‹engl.› (Telefonanschluss für rasche Serviceleistungen, z. B. von Computerfirmen)
Hot|pants, *auch* **Hot Pants** ['hɔt-'pɛnts] *Plur.* ‹engl., „heiße Hosen"› (modische, kurze u. enge Damenhose)
hott! (*Zuruf an Zugtiere* rechts!); - und har!; - und hüst!; - und hü!
Hot|te, die; -, -n (*bes. südwestd. für* Bütte, Tragkorb); *vgl.* Hutte
hot|te|hü!; Hot|te|hü, das; -s, -s (*Kinderspr.* Pferd)
hot|ten ‹amerik.› (Hotjazz spielen, danach tanzen)
Hot|ten|tot|te, der; -n, -n; ↑R 126 (Angehöriger eines Mischvolkes in Südwestafrika); **hot|ten|tot-tisch**
Hot|ter, der; -s, - (*ostösterr. für* Gemeindegrenze)
hot|to!; Hot|to, das; -s, -s (*Kinderspr.* Pferd)
Ho|va|wart ['ho:fa...], der; -s, -s (eine Hunderasse)
Höx|ter (Stadt im Weserbergland)
h. p., *früher* **HP** = horsepower ['hɔ:(r)spau̯ə(r)] ‹engl., „Pferdestärke"› (mechan. Leistungseinheit = 745,7 Watt, nicht gleichzusetzen mit PS = 736 Watt); *vgl.* PS
hPa = Hektopascal
Hptst. = Hauptstadt
Hr. = Herr
HR = Hessischer Rundfunk
Hra|ban [r...] (dt. Gelehrter des MA.); **Hra|ba|nus Mau|rus** (*lat. Name für* Hraban)
Hrad|schin ['(h)ratʃi:n] (↑R 132) der; -s (Stadtteil von Prag mit Burg)
Hrd|lic|ka ['hirdlitʃka] (österr. Bildhauer u. Grafiker)
Hrn. = Herrn *Dat. u. Akk.; vgl.* Herr
Hros|wi|tha [r...] (↑R 132); *vgl.* Roswith
hrsg., hg. = herausgegeben;
Hrsg., Hg. = Herausgeber
Hs. = Handschrift; **Hss.** = Handschriften
HTL = höhere technische Lehranstalt (Technikum, Ingenieurschule in der Schweiz u. in Österreich)
hu!; hu|hu!
hü! (*Zuruf an Zugtiere, meist* vorwärts!); *vgl.* hott
Hub, der; -[e]s, Hübe (Weglänge eines Kolbens usw.)
Hub|bel, der; -s, - (*landsch. für* Unebenheit; kleiner Hügel); **hub-bel|ig**
Hub|brü|cke (Brücke, deren Verkehrsbahn angehoben werden kann)
Hu|be, die; -, -n (*südd., österr. für* Hufe)
Hu|bel, Hü|bel, der; -s, - (*veraltet, noch landsch.; vgl.* Hubbel)
hü|ben; - und drüben
Hu|ber, Hüb|ner, der; -s, - (*südd., österr. für* Hufner, Hüfner)
Hu|bert, Hu|ber|tus (m. Vorn.)
Hu|ber|tus|burg, die; - (Schloss in Sachsen); der Friede von -; **Hu-ber|tus-jagd** (festl. Treibjagd, ursprüngl. am Hubertustag), **...man|tel** (*österr. für* grüner Lodenmantel), **...tag** (3. November)
Hub|hö|he
Hüb|ner *vgl.* Huber
Hub|raum; Hub|raum|steu|er, die
hübsch; Hübsch|heit, die; -
Hub|schrau|ber; Hub|stap|ler; Hub|vo|lu|men (Hubraum)
huch!
Huch, Ricarda (dt. Schriftstellerin)
Hu|chen, der; -s, - (ein Raubfisch)
Hu|cke, die; -, -n (*landsch. für* Rückentrage, auf dem Rücken getragene Last); jmdm. die - voll lügen (*ugs.*); **Hu|cke|bein** (*landsch. für* Hinkebein); Hans - (Gestalt bei W. Busch); **hu|cken** (*landsch. für* auf den Rücken laden); **hu|cke|pack;** - (*ugs. für* auf dem Rücken) tragen; **Hu|cke-pack|ver|kehr** (*Eisenb.* Transport von Straßenfahrzeugen auf Waggons)
Hu|de, die; -, -n (*landsch. für* Weideplatz)
Hu|del, der; -s, -[n] (*veraltet, noch landsch. für* Lappen, Lumpen; liederlicher Mensch); **Hu|de|lei; Hu|de|ler** *vgl.* Hudler; **hu|de|lig** *vgl.* hudlig; **hu|deln** (*landsch. für* nachlässig sein od. handeln); ich ...[e]le (↑R 16)
hu|dern (die Jungen unter die Flügel nehmen); sich - (im Sand baden [von Vögeln])
Hud|ler, Hu|de|ler ‹*zu* hudeln›; **hud|lig,** hu|de|lig (*landsch.*)
Hud|son|bai ['hads(ə)n...] (↑R 95), die; - (nordamerik. Binnenmeer)
huf!, *auch* **hüf!** (*Zuruf an Zugtiere* zurück!)
Huf, der; -[e]s, -e; **Huf|be|schlag**
Hu|fe, die; -, -n (ehem. Durchschnittsmaß bäuerlichen Grundbesitzes; *veraltet für* Acker, Landbesitz); *vgl.* Hube
Huf|ei|sen; huf|ei|sen|för|mig
Hu|fe|land (dt. Arzt)
hu|fen ‹*zu* huf!› (*veraltet, noch landsch. für* zurückweichen)
Huf-lat|tich (ein Wildkraut u. eine Heilpflanze), **...na|gel**
Huf|ner, Hüf|ner (*früher für* Besitzer einer Hufe); *vgl.* Huber, Hübner
Huf-schlag, ...schmied
Hüf|te, die; -, -n; **Hüft-ge|lenk, ...gür|tel, ...hal|ter; hüft|hoch; Hüft|horn** *Plur.* ...hörner; *vgl.* Hifthorn
Huf|tier
Hüft-kno|chen, ...lei|den, ...weh, ...wei|te
Hü|gel, der; -s, -; **hü|gel-ab, ...an, ...auf; hü|ge|lig,** hüg|lig; **Hü|gel-ket|te, ...land** (*Plur.* ...länder)
Hu|ge|not|te, der; -n, -n (↑R 126) ‹franz.› (franz. Reformierter); **Hu|ge|not|tin; hu|ge|not|tisch**
Hughes|te|le|graf ['hju:s...] (↑R 95) ‹nach dem engl. Physiker Hughes› (erster Drucktelegrafenapparat)
Hu|gin ‹„der Denker"› (*nord. Mythol.* einer der beiden Raben Odins); *vgl.* Munin
hüg|lig, hü|ge|lig
[1]**Hu|go** (m. Vorn.)
[2]**Hu|go** [y'go:], Victor (franz. Schriftsteller)
Huhn, das; -[e]s, Hühner; **Hühn-chen; Hüh|ner-au|ge, ...brü|he, ...brust, ...dreck, ...ei, ...fri|kas-see, ...ha|bicht, ...hof, ...hund, ...lei|ter** (die), **...stall; Hüh|ner-stei|ge** *od.* **...stie|ge; Hüh|ner-volk, ...zucht**
hu|hu!
hui! [hui̯], *aber* (↑R 49): im Hui, in einem Hui
Hu|ka, die; -, -s ‹arab.› (ind. Wasserpfeife)
Huk|boot ‹niederl.› *u.* **Hu|ker,** der; -s, - (größeres Fischerfahrzeug)
Hu|la, die; -, -s *od.* der; -s, -s ‹hawaiisch› (Eingeborenentanz auf Hawaii); **Hu|la-Hoop** [...'hu:p] *u.*

Hula-Hopp, der *od.* das; -s ‹hawaiisch; engl.› (ein Reifenspiel); **Hula-Hoop-Reifen; Hulamädchen** (↑R 24)
Hülbe, die; -, -n (*schwäb. für* flacher Dorfteich, Wasserstelle)
Huld, die; - (*veraltend für* Wohlwollen, Freundlichkeit)
Hulda (w. Vorn.)
huldigen; Huldigung; huld‿reich, ...voll
Hulk, Holk, die; -, -e[n] *od.* der; -[e]s, -e[n] ‹engl.› (ausgedientes, für Kasernen- u. Magazinzwecke verwendetes Schiff)
Hüllblatt; Hülle, die; -, -n; **hüllen;** sich in etwas -; **hüllenlos; Hüllwort** *Plur.* ...wörter (*für* Euphemismus)
Hülschen; Hülse, die; -, -n (Kapsel[frucht]); **hülsen;** du hülst; **Hülsenfrucht; Hülsenfrüchtler** *(Bot.);* **hülsig**
Hultschin [*auch* 'hul...] (↑R 132; Ort in Mähren); **Hultschiner** [*auch* 'hul...] (↑R 103); Hultschiner Ländchen
human ‹lat.› (menschlich; menschenfreundlich; mild, gesittet, zugänglich); **Humangenetik** (Teilgebiet der Genetik); **humanisieren** (gesittet, menschlich machen; zivilisieren); **Humanisierung,** die; -; **Humanismus,** der; - (auf das Bildungsideal der griech.-röm. Antike gegründetes Denken u. Handeln; Humanität; geistige Strömung zur Zeit der Renaissance, als Neuhumanismus im 18. Jh.); **Humanist,** der; -en, -en; ↑R 126 (Vertreter des Humanismus; Kenner der alten Sprachen); **Humanistin; humanistisch;** -es Gymnasium; **humanitär** (menschenfreundlich; wohltätig); **Humanität,** die; - (Menschlichkeit; humane Gesinnung); **Humanitäts‿denken, ...duselei** *(abwertend),* **...ideal** (↑R 132); **Human‿medizin** (die; -), **...wissenschaft**
Humbert (m. Vorn.)
Humboldt (Familienn.); **humboldtisch, humboldtsch;** die humboldt[i]schen Schriften (↑R 94); **Humboldt-Universität** (↑R 132), die; - (in Berlin)
Humbug, der; -s ‹engl.› (*ugs. für* Schwindel; Unsinn)
Hume [hju:m] (engl. Philosoph)
Humerale, das; -s, *Plur.* ...lien [...iən] *u.* ...lia ‹lat.› (liturg. Schultertuch des kath. Priesters)
humid *u.* **humide** ‹lat.› (*Geogr.* feucht, nass); **Humidität,** die; -
Humifikation, die; - ‹lat.› (Vermoderung; Humusbildung); **humifizieren; Humifizierung,** die; - (*svw.* Humifikation)
Hummel, die; -, -n
Hummer, der; -s, -; **Hummer‿mayonnaise, ...suppe**
[1]**Humor,** der; -s, -e *Plur. selten* ‹engl.› (heitere Gelassenheit, fröhliche Wesensart; [gute] Laune); [2]**Humor,** der; -s, ...ores [...re:s] ‹lat.› (*Med.* Feuchtigkeit, Körperflüssigkeit); **humoral** (*Med.* die Körperflüssigkeiten betreffend); **Humoralpathologie,** die; - (antike Lehre von den Körpersäften als Ausgangspunkt der Krankheiten); **Humoreske,** die; -, -n ‹*zu* [1]Humor› (kleine humoristische Erzählung; Musikstück von heiterem Charakter); **humorig** (launig, mit Humor); **Humorist,** der; -en, -en; ↑R 126 (jmd., der mit Humor schreibt, spricht, vorträgt usw.); **humoristisch; humorlos; Humorlosigkeit,** die; -; **humorvoll**
humos ‹lat.› (reich an Humus)
Hümpel, der; -s, - (*nordd. für* Haufen)
Humpelei; humpelig, humplig (*landsch. für* uneben, holperig); **humpeln;** ich ...[e]le (↑R 16)
Humpen, der; -s, -
Humperdinck (dt. Komponist)
humplig *vgl.* humpelig
Humus, der; - ‹lat.› (fruchtbarer Bodenbestandteil, organ. Substanz im Boden); **Humus‿boden, ...erde; humusreich**
Hund, der; -[e]s, -e (*Bergmannsspr. auch* Förderwagen); (↑R 108:) der Große -, der Kleine - (Sternbilder); **Hündchen; Hundeart; hundeelend** (↑R 132; *ugs. für* sehr elend); **Hunde‿halter** *(Amtsspr.),* **...hütte; hundekalt** (*ugs. für* sehr kalt); **Hunde‿kälte** *(ugs.),* **...kot, ...kuchen, ...leine, ...marke** (*scherzh. auch für* Erkennungsmarke); **hundemüde,** hundsmüde (*ugs. für* sehr müde); **Hunde‿rasse, ...rennen**
hundert (*als römisches Zahlzeichen* C); [vier] von hundert; bis hundert zählen; Tempo hundert (*für* hundert Stundenkilometer); *Klein- oder Großschreibung bei unbestimmten (nicht in Ziffern schreibbaren) Mengen:* ein paar hundert *od.* Hundert; einige, viele hunderte *od.* Hunderte; einige hundert *od.* Hundert Büroklammern (Packungen von je hundert Stück); [viele] hunderte *od.* Hunderte von Menschen; ein paar hundert *od.* Hundert Bäume, Menschen; sie strömten zu hunderten *od.* Hunderten herein; *Zusammenschreibung mit bestimmten Zahlwörtern:* einhundert, zweihundert [Mann, Menschen]; hundert[und]eins, hundert[und]siebzig; hundert[und]ein Salutschuss, mit hundertundeinem Salutschuss *od.* mit hundert[und]ein Salutschüssen; hundert[und]eine Deutsche Mark; hundertunderster Tag; *vgl.* aber; [1]**Hundert,** das; -s, -e; [vier] vom Hundert (*Abk.* v. H., p. c.; *Zeichen* %); *vgl.* hundert; [2]**Hundert,** die; -, -en (Zahl); *vgl.* [1]Acht; **hundertein[s],** hundertundein[s]; *vgl.* hundert; **Hunderter,** der; -s, -; *vgl.* Achter; **hunderterlei;** auf - Weise; **Hunderterpackung; hundertfach; Hundertfache,** das; -n; *vgl.* Achtfache; **hundertfältig; hundertfünfzigprozentig** (*ugs. für* übertrieben, fanatisch); **Hundertjahrfeier** (*mit Ziffern* 100-Jahr-Feier; ↑R 28); **hundertjährig;** der hundertjährige Kalender (↑R 56); *vgl.* achtjährig; **Hundertkilometertempo,** das; -s *(ugs.);* im -; **hundertmal;** einhundertmal; vielhundertmal, (↑R 48:) viele hundert *od.* Hundert Mal[e]; viel hundert *od.* Hundert Male; ein halbes Hundert Mal; *vgl.* achtmal; **hundertmalig; Hundert‿markschein** (*mit Ziffern* 100-Mark-Schein; ↑R 28), **...meterlauf** (↑R 28); **hundertprozentig** (*mit Ziffer:* 100-prozentig, 100%ig); **Hundertsatz,** Vomhundertsatz (*für* Prozentsatz); **Hundertschaft; hundertste;** die hundertste Folge; der Hundertste; vom Hundertsten ins Tausendste kommen; *vgl.* achte; **hundertstel;** *vgl.* achtel; **Hundertstel,** das, *schweiz. meist* der; -s, -; *vgl.* Achtel; **Hundertstelsekunde** (*mit Ziffer:* 100stel-Sekunde); *auch* hundertstel Sekunde (100stel Sekunde); **hundertstens; hunderttausend;** mehrere hunderttausend DM; *vgl.* tausend; **Hunderttausendmannheer,** das; -[e]s (Reichsheer in der Weimarer Republik); **hundert[und]ein[s];** *vgl.* hundert
Hunde‿salon, ...scheiße *(derb),* **...schlitten, ...schnauze, ...sperre, ...steuer** (die), **...wache** (*Seemannsspr.* Nachtwache), **...wetter** (das; -s; *ugs.*), **...zucht; Hündin; hündisch**
Hundredweight ['handrədwe:t] (↑R 130), das; -, -s (engl. Handelsgewicht; *Abk.* cwt, cwt. [*eigtl. für* centweight])

Hunds|fott, der; -[e]s, *Plur.* -e *u.* ...fötter (*derb für* gemeiner Kerl, Schurke); **Hunds|föt|te|rei; hunds|föt|tisch; hunds|ge|mein** *(ugs.),* **Hunds|ka|mil|le; hunds‿mi|se|ra|bel** *(ugs.),* **...mü|de** (*vgl.* hundemüde); **Hunds‿ro|se** (wilde Rose), **...stern, ...ta|ge** (*Plur.;* vom 23. Juli bis zum 23. August), **...vei|gerl** (das; -s, -n; *österr. ugs.*) *u.* **...veil|chen** (duftloses Veilchen)

Hü|ne, der; -n, -n (↑R 126); **Hü|nen‿ge|stalt, ...grab; hü|nen|haft**

Hun|ger, der; -s; vor Hunger sterben; *aber* hungers sterben; **Hun|ger‿blüm|chen** *od.* **...blu|me** (eine Pflanze); **Hun|ger‿ge|fühl, ...künst|ler, ...kur, ...lei|der** (*ugs. für* armer Schlucker), **...lohn; hun|gern;** ich ...ere (↑R 16); mich hungert; **Hun|ger|ödem** (↑R 132); **Hun|gers|not; Hun|ger‿streik, ...tod, ...tuch** (*Plur.* ...tücher; Fastentuch), **...turm** *(früher);* **hung|rig**

Hun|ne, der; -n, -n; ↑R 126 (*früher* Angehöriger eines eurasischen Nomadenvolkes); **Hun|nen‿kö|nig, ...zug; hun|nisch**

Hu|nold (m. Vorn.)

Huns|rück, der; -s (Teil des westl. Rhein. Schiefergebirges); **Huns|rü|cker** (↑R 103)

Hunt, der; -[e]s, -e (*Nebenform von* Hund [Förderwagen])

Hun|ter ['han...], der; -s, - ⟨engl.⟩ (*Reiten* Jagdpferd; ein Jagdhund)

hun|zen (*veraltet, noch landsch. für* wie einen Hund behandeln; beschimpfen); du hunzt

Hu|pe, die; -, -n; **hu|pen; Hu|pe|rei**

Hupf, der; -[e]s, -e (*veraltet, noch landsch. für* Sprung); **Hupf|doh|le** (*ugs. scherzh. für* [Revue]tänzerin); **hup|fen** (*südd., österr., sonst veraltet für* hüpfen); das ist gehupft wie gesprungen (*ugs. für* das ist völlig gleich); **hüp|fen; Hup|fer** *(südd., österr.),* **Hüp|fer** (kleiner Sprung); **Hüp|fer|ling** (eine Krebsart)

Hup|kon|zert (*ugs. für* gleichzeitiges Hupen mehrerer Autofahrer)

Hür|chen ⟨*zu* Hure⟩

Hur|de, die; -, -n (Flechtwerk; *südwestd. u. schweiz. für* [1]Horde); **Hür|de**, die; -, -n (Flechtwerk; tragbare Einzäunung [für Schafe]; Hindernis beim Hürdenlauf); *vgl.* [1]Horde; **Hür|den‿lauf, ...läu|fer, ...läu|fe|rin**

Hu|re, die; -, -n; **hu|ren; Hu|ren‿bock** (Schimpfwort), **...kind** (*Druckerspr.* [einen Absatz beschließende] Einzelzeile am Anfang einer neuen Seite od. Spalte); **Hu|ren‿sohn** (Schimpfwort), **...wei|bel** (*früher* Aufseher über den Tross im Landsknechtsheer); **Hu|re|rei**

Hu|ri, die; -, -s ⟨arab.⟩ (schönes Mädchen im Paradies des Islams)

hür|nen (*veraltet für* aus Horn)

Hu|ro|ne, der; -n, -n; ↑R 126 (Angehöriger eines nordamerik. Indianerstammes); **hu|ro|nisch**

hur|ra! [*auch* 'hu...]; **Hur|ra**, das; -s, -s; viele -s; Hurra, *auch* hurra schreien; **Hur|ra‿pat|ri|o|tis|mus, ...ruf** [*auch* 'hu...]

Hur|ri|kan [*engl.* 'harikən], der; -s, *Plur.* -e, *bei engl. Ausspr.* -s ⟨indian.⟩ (Wirbelsturm in Amerika)

hur|tig; Hur|tig|keit, die; -

Hus, Jan (tschech. Reformator)

Hu|sar, der; -en, -en (↑R 126) ⟨ung.⟩ (*früher* Angehöriger einer leichten Reitertruppe in ungarischer Nationaltracht); **Hu|sa|ren‿ritt, ...streich** (waghalsiges Unternehmen, tollkühner Handstreich), **...stück|chen**

husch!; husch, husch!; **Husch**, der; -[e]s, -e *Plur. selten* (ugs.); auf einen - (für kurze Zeit) besuchen; im - (rasch); **Hu|sche**, die; -, -n (*landsch. für* Regenschauer); **hu|sche|lig,** hu|schig, husch|lig (*landsch. für* oberflächlich, eilfertig); **Hu|sche|lig|keit,** Husch|lig|keit; **hu|scheln** (*landsch. für* ungenau arbeiten); ich ...[e]le (↑R 16); sich - (*landsch. für* sich in einen Mantel usw. wickeln); **hu|schen;** du huschst; **hu|schig, husch|lig** *vgl.* huschelig; **Husch|lig|keit** *vgl.* Huscheligkeit

Hus|ky ['haski], der; -s, -s ⟨engl.⟩ (Eskimohund)

hus|sa!; hus|sa|sa!; hus|sen (*österr. ugs. für* aufwiegeln, hetzen); du husst

Hus|serl (dt. Philosoph)

Hus|sit, der; -en, -en; ↑R 126 (Anhänger von J. Hus); **Hus|si|ten|krieg**

hüst! (*Zuruf an Zugtiere* links!)

hüs|teln; ich ...[e]le (↑R 16); **hus|ten; Hus|ten**, der; -s, - *Plur. selten;* **Hus|ten‿an|fall, ...bon|bon, ...mit|tel** (das), **...reiz** (der; -es), **...saft**

Hu|sum (Stadt an der Nordsee); **Hu|su|mer** (↑R 103)

[1]**Hut**, der; -[e]s, Hüte (Kopfbedeckung); [2]**Hut**, die; - (*geh. für* Schutz, Aufsicht); auf der - sein; **Hut‿ab|tei|lung, ...band** (das; *Plur.* ...bänder); **Hüt|chen; Hüt|chen|spiel; Hüt|chen|spie|ler; Hü|te‿hund, ...jun|ge** (der); **hü|ten;** sich -; **Hü|ter; Hü|te|rin; Hut‿kof|fer, ...krem|pe, hut|los; Hut‿ma|cher, ...ma|che|rin, ...na|del, ...schach|tel**

[1]**Hut|sche, Hüt|sche** *vgl.* Hitsche; [2]**Hut|sche,** die; -, -n (*bayr., österr. für* Schaukel); **hut|schen** (*bayr., österr. für* schaukeln); du hutschst

Hut|schnur; *meist in* das geht über die - (*ugs. für* das geht zu weit)

Hutsch|pferd (*österr. für* Schaukelpferd)

Hütt|chen

Hut|te, die; -, -n (*schweiz. mdal. für* Rückentragkorb); *vgl.* Hotte

Hüt|te, die; -, -n (*auch kurz für* Eisenhütte, Glashütte u. a.)

Hut|ten (dt. Humanist)

Hüt|ten‿ar|bei|ter, ...be|trieb, ...dorf, ...in|dust|rie, ...kä|se, ...kun|de (die; -), **...schuh, ...werk, ...we|sen** (das; -s); **Hütt|ner** (*veraltet für* Häusler; Kleinbauer); **Hütt|rach**, das; -s (*österr. ugs. für* Arsen)

Hu|tung (*Landw.* dürftige Weide); **Hü|tung** (Bewachung); **Hut|wei|de** (Gemeindeweide, auf die das Vieh täglich getrieben wird)

Hut|zel, die; -, -n (*landsch. für* Tannenzapfen; Dörrobstschnitzel; *auch für* alte Frau); **Hut|zel|brot** (mit Hutzeln [Dörrobstschnitzeln] gebackenes Brot; südd. Festgebäck); **hut|ze|lig,** hutz|lig (*landsch. für* dürr, welk; alt); **Hut|zel|männ|chen** (*auch für* Heinzelmännchen); **hut|zeln** (*landsch. für* dörren; schrumpfen); ich ...[e]le (↑R 16); **hutz|lig** *vgl.* hutzelig

Hut|zu|cker

Hux|ley ['haksli], Aldous ['ɔ:ldəs] (engl. Schriftsteller)

Huy [hy:], der; -s (Höhenzug nördl. des Harzes)

Huy|gens ['hɔyg(ə)ns, *niederl.* 'hœyxəns] (niederl. Physiker u. Mathematiker); das huygenssche Prinzip (↑R 94)

Huy|wald [hy:...], der; -[e]s; *vgl.* Huy

Hu|zu|le, der; -n, -n; ↑R 126 (Angehöriger eines ukrain. Volksstammes)

Hwang|ho, der; -[s] ⟨chin., „gelber Fluss"⟩ (Strom in China)

Hy|a|den *Plur.* ⟨griech., „Regensterne"⟩ (Töchter des Atlas)

hy|a|lin ⟨griech.⟩ (*Med.* durchsichtig wie Glas, glasartig); **Hy|a|lit** [*auch* ...'lit], der; -s, -e (*Geol.* ein heller, glasartiger Opal)

Hy|ä|ne, die; -, -n ⟨griech.⟩ (ein Raubtier)

[1]**Hy|a|zinth** (Liebling Apollos);

²Hy|a|zinth, der; -[e]s, -e ‹griech.› (rötlich brauner Zirkon); **³Hy|a-zinth,** der; -s, -e (schöner Jüngling); **Hy|a|zin|the,** die; -, -n (eine Zwiebelpflanze)

¹hyb|rid (↑R 130) ‹griech.› (Hybris zeigend)

²hyb|rid (↑R 130) ‹lat.› (von zweierlei Herkunft; zwitterhaft); -e Bildung (*Sprachw.* Zwitterbildung; zusammengesetztes Wort, dessen Teile versch. Sprachen angehören); **Hyb|ri|de,** die; -, -n, *auch* der; -n, -n; ↑R 126 (*Biol.* Bastard [Pflanze od. Tier] als Ergebnis von Kreuzungen); **Hyb-ri|di|sa|ti|on;** **hyb|ri|di|sie|ren;** **Hyb|rid|rech|ner** (*EDV* Rechenanlage, die sowohl analog als auch digital arbeiten kann); **Hyb|rid-schwein, ...züch|tung**

Hyb|ris (↑R 130), die; - ‹griech.› (frevelhafter Übermut)

Hyde|park ['haid...], der; -[e]s (Park in London)

hyd|r... (↑R 130); *vgl.* hydro...; **Hyd|r...** *vgl.* Hydro; **¹Hyd|ra,** die; - ‹griech.› (sagenhafte Seeschlange; ein Sternbild); **²Hyd|ra,** die; -, ...dren (ein Süßwasserpolyp); **Hyd|rä|mie,** die; -, ...ien ‹griech.› (*Med.* erhöhter Wassergehalt des Blutes); **Hyd|rant,** der; -en, -en; ↑R 126 (Anschluss an die Wasserleitung); **Hyd|rar|gy|rum,** das; -s (Quecksilber, chem. Element; *Zeichen* Hg); **Hyd|rat,** das; -[e]s, -e (Verbindung chem. Stoffe mit Wasser); **Hyd|ra|[ta]|ti|on,** die; -, -en (Bildung von Hydraten); **hyd|ra|ti|sie|ren;** **Hyd|rau-lik,** die; - (Lehre von der Bewegung der Flüssigkeiten; deren techn. Anwendung); **hyd|rau-lisch** (mit Flüssigkeitsdruck arbeitend); -e Bremse; -e Presse; -er Mörtel (Wassermörtel)

Hyd|ra|zin (↑R 130), das; -s (chem. Verbindung von Stickstoff mit Wasserstoff; Bestandteil im Raketentreibstoff)

Hyd|rier|ben|zin (↑R 130); **hyd-rie|ren** (*Chemie* Wasserstoff anlagern); **Hyd|rie|rung;** **Hyd|rier-ver|fah|ren, ...werk**

hyd|ro... (↑R 130) ‹griech.›, *vor Vokalen* hyd|r... (wasser...); **Hyd-ro...** *vor Vokalen* Hyd|r... (Wasser...)

Hyd|ro|bi|o|lo|gie (↑R 130) ‹griech.› (Lehre von den im Wasser lebenden Organismen)

Hyd|ro|chi|non (↑R 130), das; -s ‹griech.; indian.› (*Chemie* besonders als fotogr. Entwickler verwendete organische Verbindung)

Hyd|ro|dy|na|mik (↑R 130) ‹griech.› (Strömungslehre); **hyd-ro|dy|na|misch**

Hyd|ro|gen, **Hyd|ro|ge|ni|um** (↑R 130), das; -s ‹griech.› (Wasserstoff; chem. Element; *Zeichen* H); **Hyd|ro|gra|phie,** die; - (Gewässerkunde); **hyd|ro|gra-phisch**

Hyd|ro|kul|tur (↑R 130), die; - ‹griech.› (Wasserkultur; Pflanzenzucht in Nährlösungen ohne Erde)

Hyd|ro|lo|gie (↑R 130), die; - ‹griech.› (Lehre vom Wasser); **hyd|ro|lo|gisch;** **Hyd|ro|ly|se,** die; -, -n (Spaltung chem. Verbindungen durch Wasser); **hyd|ro-ly|tisch**

Hyd|ro|me|cha|nik (↑R 130), die; - ‹griech.› (Mechanik der Flüssigkeiten); **Hyd|ro|me|ter,** das; -s, - (Gerät zur Messung der Fließgeschwindigkeit von Wasser); **Hyd-ro|met|rie,** die; -; **hyd|ro|met-risch**

Hyd|ro|path (↑R 130), der; -en, -en (↑R 126) ‹griech.› (hydropathisch Behandelnder); **Hyd|ro-pa|thie,** die; - (*svw.* Hydrotherapie); **hyd|ro|pa|thisch;** **hyd|ro-phil** (*Biol.* im od. am Wasser lebend); **hyd|ro|phob** (*Biol.* das Wasser meidend); **Hyd|roph-thal|mus,** der; -, ...mi (*Med.* Augenwassersucht); **Hyd|ro|phyt,** der; -en, -en; ↑R 126 (Wasserpflanze); **hyd|ro|pisch** (*Med.* wassersüchtig); **hyd|ro|pneu|ma-tisch** (*Technik* durch Wasser u. Luft [betrieben]); **Hyd|rops,** der; - *u.* **Hyd|rop|sie,** die; - (*Med.* Wassersucht)

Hyd|ro|sphä|re (↑R 130), die; - (Wasserhülle der Erde); **Hyd-ro|sta|tik** (*Physik* Lehre von den Gleichgewichtszuständen bei Flüssigkeiten); **hyd|ro|sta|tisch;** -e Waage (zum Bestimmen des Auftriebs)

Hyd|ro|tech|nik (↑R 130), die; - ‹griech.› (Wasserbau[kunst]); **hyd|ro|the|ra|peu|tisch;** **Hyd-ro|the|ra|pie,** die; -, -n (*Med.* Heilbehandlung durch Anwendung von Wasser; *nur Sing.:* Wasserheilkunde)

Hyd|ro|xid (↑R 130), das; -[e]s, -e ‹griech.› (chem. Verbindung); *vgl.* Oxid; **Hyd|ro|xyl|grup|pe** ‹griech.; dt.› (Wasserstoff-Sauerstoff-Gruppe)

Hyd|ro|ze|phal|lus (↑R 130), der; -, ...alen ‹griech.› (*Med.* Wasserkopf); **Hyd|ro|zo|on,** das; -s, ...zoen *meist Plur.* (*Zool.* Nesseltier)

Hy|e|to|gra|phie, die; - ‹griech.› (*Meteor.* Beschreibung der Verteilung von Niederschlägen); **Hy|e-to|me|ter,** das; -s, -; (Regenmesser)

Hy|gi|eia (griech. Göttin der Gesundheit); **Hy|gi|e|ne,** die; - ‹griech.› (Gesundheitslehre, -fürsorge, -pflege); **Hy|gi|e|ni|ker;** **hy|gi|e|nisch**

Hyg|ro|me|ter (↑R 130), das; -s, - ‹griech.› (Luftfeuchtigkeitsmesser); **Hyg|ro|phyt,** der; -en, -en; ↑R 126 (*Bot.* Landpflanze mit hohem Wasserverbrauch); **Hyg|ro-skop** (↑R 132), das; -s, -e (*Meteor.* Luftfeuchtigkeitsmesser); **hyg|ro|sko|pisch** (Feuchtigkeit an sich ziehend)

Hyk|sos *Plur.* (ein asiat. Erobervolk im alten Ägypten)

¹Hy|men, Hy|me|nai|os *u.* Hy|me|nä|us (griech. Hochzeitsgott); **²Hy|men,** der; -s, - ‹griech.› (antiker Hochzeitsgesang); **³Hy|men,** das, *auch* der; -s, - (*Med.* Jungfernhäutchen); **Hy|me|nai|os** [*auch* hy'mɛnaiɔs], **Hy|me|nä|us** *vgl.* ¹Hymen; **Hy|me|nop|te|ren** (↑R 132) *Plur.* (*Zool.* Hautflügler)

Hym|ne, die; -, -n *u.* Hym|nus, der; -, ...nen ‹griech.› (Festgesang; christl. Lobgesang; Weihelied); **Hym|nik** (Kunstform der Hymne); **hym|nisch;** **Hym|no-lo|gie,** die; - (Hymnenkunde); **hym|no|lo|gisch;** **Hym|nus** *vgl.* Hymne

Hy|os|cy|a|min, **Hy|os|zy|a|min** [*beide* ...tsya...], das; -s; ‹griech.› (Alkaloid, Heilmittel)

hyp... (↑R 132); *vgl.* hypo...; **Hyp...** *vgl.* Hypo...

Hy|pal|la|ge [*auch* hy'palage] (↑R 132), die; - ‹griech.› (*Sprachw.* Vertauschung eines attributiven Genitivs mit einem attributivischen Adjektiv u. umgekehrt, z. B. jagdliche Ausdrücke *statt* Ausdrücke der Jagd)

hy|per... ‹griech.› (über...); **Hy-per...** (Über...); **Hy|per|aci|di|tät** (↑R 132), die; - (*Med.* übermäßig hoher Säuregehalt im Magen); **Hy|per|al|ge|sie,** die; -, ...ien (*Med.* gesteigertes Schmerzempfinden); **hy|per|al|ge|tisch** (schmerzüberempfindlich); **Hy-per|äs|the|sie,** die; -, ...ien (*Med.* Überempfindlichkeit); **hy|per-äs|the|tisch**

Hy|per|bel, die; -, -n ‹griech.› (*Stilk.* Übertreibung des Ausdrucks; *Math.* Kegelschnitt); **hy|per|bo|lisch** (hyperbelartig; im Ausdruck übertreibend); -e Funktion *(Math.)*; **Hy|per|bo|lo-id,** das; -[e]s, -e (*Math.* Körper, der durch Drehung einer Hyperbel um ihre Achse entsteht)

Hy|per|bo|re|er (Angehöriger eines sagenhaften Volkes des hohen Nordens); **hy|per|bo|re|isch** (*veraltet für* im hohen Norden ansässig, gelegen)

Hy|per|dak|ty|lie, die; -, ...ien ‹griech.› (*Med.* Bildung von mehr als je fünf Fingern od. Zehen)

Hy|per|eme|sis (↑R 132), die; - ‹griech.› (*Med.* übermäßiges Erbrechen)

Hy|per|funk|ti|on, die; -, -en ‹griech.› (*Med.* Überfunktion eines Organs)

hy|per|go|lisch ‹griech.; lat.›; *(Chemie);* -er Treibstoff (Raketentreibstoff, der bei Berührung mit einem Sauerstoffträger sofort zündet)

Hy|pe|ri|on [*auch* ...'rio:n] (Titan, Vater des Helios)

hy|per|ka|ta|lek|tisch ‹griech.› (*Verslehre* mit überzähliger Silbe versehen); **hy|per|kor|rekt** (überkorrekt); **hy|per|kri|tisch** (überstreng, tadelsüchtig)

Hy|per|me|ter, der; -s, - ‹griech.› (Vers, der um eine Silbe zu lang ist u. mit der Anfangssilbe des folgenden Verses durch Elision verbunden wird); **hy|per|me|trisch**

Hy|per|met|ro|pie (↑R 130), die; - (*Med.* Weit-, Übersichtigkeit); **hy|per|met|ro|pisch**

hy|per|mo|dern (übermodern, übertrieben neuzeitlich)

Hy|pe|ron, das; -s, ...onen ‹griech.› (*Kernphysik* überschweres Elementarteilchen)

Hy|per|pla|sie, die; -, ...ien ‹griech.› (*Med., Biol.* abnorme Vermehrung von Zellen)

hy|per|sen|si|bel (überaus sensibel, empfindsam); **hy|per|so|nisch** ‹griech.; lat.› (*Physik* Überschall...)

Hy|per|to|nie, die; -, ...ien ‹griech.› (*Med.* gesteigerter Blutdruck; gesteigerte Muskelspannung; vermehrte Spannung im Augapfel); **hy|per|troph** (überspannt, überzogen; *Med., Biol.* durch Zellenwachstum vergrößert); **Hy|per|tro|phie,** die; -, ...ien ‹griech.› (übermäßige Vergrößerung von Geweben u. Organen; Überernährung)

Hy|phe, die; -, -n ‹griech.› (*Bot.* Pilzfaden)

Hy|phen (↑R 132), das; -[s], - ‹griech.› (Bindestrich bei zusammengesetzten Wörtern)

Hyp|no|pä|die, die; - ‹griech.› (Schlaflernmethode); **hyp|no|pä|disch; Hyp|nos** (griech. Gott des Schlafes); **Hyp|no|se,** die; -, -n ([durch Suggestion herbeigeführter] schlafähnlicher Bewusstseinszustand); **Hyp|no|tik,** die; - (Lehre von der Hypnose); **Hyp|no|ti|kum,** das; -s, ...ka (Schlafmittel); **hyp|no|tisch; Hyp|no|ti|seur** [...'zø:r], der; -s, -e ‹franz.› (die Hypnose Bewirkender); **hyp|no|ti|sie|ren** (in Hypnose versetzen; beeinflussen, widerstandslos machen); **Hyp|no|tis|mus,** der; - ‹griech.› (Lehre von der Hypnose; Beeinflussung)

hy|po... ‹griech.›, *vor Vokalen* hyp... (unter...); **Hy|po...,** *vor Vokalen* Hyp... (Unter...)

Hy|po|chon|der [...x...], der; -s, - ‹griech.› (Schwermütiger; eingebildeter Kranker); **Hy|po|chond|rie** (↑R 130), die; -, ...ien (Einbildung, krank zu sein; Trübsinn, Schwermut); **hy|po|chond|risch**

Hy|po|gast|ri|um (↑R 130), das; -s, ...ien [...iən] ‹griech.› (*Med.* Unterleib)

Hy|po|gä|um, das; -s, ...gäen ‹griech.-lat.› (unterirdisches Gewölbe; unterirdischer Grabraum, Kultraum)

hy|po|kaus|tisch ‹griech.›; **Hy|po|kaus|tum,** das; -s, ...sten (Fußbodenheizung der Antike); **Hy|po|ko|tyl,** das; -s, -e (*Bot.* Keimstängel der Samenpflanzen); **Hy|po|kri|sie,** die; -, ...ien (Heuchelei); **Hy|po|krit,** der; -en, -en; ↑R 126 (Heuchler); **hy|po|kri|tisch**

Hy|po|phy|se, die; -, -n ‹griech.› (*Med.* Hirnanhang)

Hy|pos|ta|se (↑R 132), die; -, -n ‹griech.› (Verdinglichung von Begriffen; Personifizierung göttlicher Eigenschaften od. religiöser Vorstellungen); **hy|pos|ta|sie|ren** (personifizieren; gegenständlich machen, verdinglichen); **hy|pos|ta|tisch** (vergegenständlichend, gegenständlich); **Hy|pos|ty|lon,** das; -s, ...la *u.* **Hy|pos|ty|los,** der; -, ...loi [...lɔy] (*Archit.* gedeckter Säulengang; Säulenhalle; Tempel mit Säulengang)

hy|po|tak|tisch ‹griech.› (*Sprachw.* unterordnend); **Hy|po|ta|xe,** die; -, -n, *älter* **Hy|po|ta|xis,** die; -, ...taxen (*Sprachw.* Unterordnung)

Hy|po|te|nu|se, die; -, -n (*Math.* im rechtwinkligen Dreieck die Seite gegenüber dem rechten Winkel)

Hy|po|tha|la|mus, der; -, ...mi (*Med.* Teil des Zwischenhirns)

Hy|po|thek, die; -, -en ‹griech.› (im Grundbuch eingetragenes Pfandrecht an einem Grundstück; *übertr. für* ständige Belastung); **Hy|po|the|kar,** der; -s, -e (Hypothekengläubiger); **hy|po|the|ka|risch; Hy|po|the|ken-bank** (*Plur.* ...banken), **...[pfand]brief, ...zins**

Hy|po|ther|mie, die; -, ...ien ‹griech.› (*Med.* unternormale Körperwärme); **Hy|po|the|se,** die; -, -n ([unbewiesene] Annahme, Vermutung; Vorentwurf für eine Theorie); **hy|po|the|tisch** (angenommen; zweifelhaft); **Hy|po|to|nie,** die; -, ...ien (*Med.* Verminderung des Blutdrucks; herabgesetzte Muskelspannung); **Hy|po|tra|che|li|on,** das; -s, ...ien [...iən] (*Archit.* Säulenhals unter dem Kapitell); **Hy|po|tro|phie,** die; -, ...ien (*Med.* Unterernährung, Unterentwicklung)

Hy|po|zent|rum (unter der Erdoberfläche liegender Erdbebenherd); **Hy|po|zyk|lo|i|de,** die; -, -n ‹griech.› (*Math.* eine geometr. Kurve)

Hyp|si|pho|bie, die; -, ...ien ‹griech.› (*Med.* Höhenangst); **Hyp|so|me|ter,** das; -s, - (Höhenmesser); **Hyp|so|met|rie,** die; -; **hyp|so|me|trisch**

Hyr|ka|ni|en [...iən] ‹griech.› (*im Altertum Bez. für* die südöstl. Küste des Kaspischen Meeres); **hyr|ka|nisch,** *aber* (↑R 102): das Hyrkanische Meer (alter Name für das Kaspische Meer)

Hys|te|ral|gie (↑R 132), die; -, ...ien ‹griech.› (*Med.* Gebärmutterschmerz); **Hys|te|rek|to|mie,** die; -, ...ien (operative Entfernung der Gebärmutter)

Hys|te|re|se, Hys|te|re|sis, die; - ‹griech.› (*Physik* Fortdauer einer Wirkung nach Aufhören der Ursache); **Hys|te|rie,** die; -, ...ien (abnorme seel. Verhaltensweise; nervöse Aufgeregtheit, Überspanntheit); **Hys|te|ri|ker; Hys|te|ri|ke|rin; hys|te|risch** (an Hysterie leidend; überspannt)

Hys|te|ron-Pro|te|ron, das; -s, Hystera-Protera ‹griech.› (*Philos.* Scheinbeweis; *Rhet.* Redefigur, bei der das [nach der Logik] Spätere zuerst steht)

Hys|te|rop|to|se (↑R 132), die; -, -n ‹griech.› (*Med.* Senkung der Gebärmutter)

Hys|te|ro|sko|pie, die; -, -n ‹griech.› (*Med.* Untersuchung der Gebärmutterhöhle); **Hys|te|ro|to|mie,** die; - (*Med.* Gebärmutterschnitt)

Hz = Hertz

I

I (Buchstabe); das I, des I, die I, *aber* das i in Bild; der Buchstabe I, i; der Punkt auf dem i (↑R 60); i-Punkt (↑R 25)
i (*Math.: Zeichen für* imaginäre Zahl)
i!; i bewahre!; i wo!
I = *chem. Zeichen für* Iod; *vgl.* Jod
I (röm. Zahlzeichen) = 1
I, ι = Iota
i. = in, im (*bei Ortsnamen,* z. B. Immenstadt i. Allgäu); *vgl.* i. d.
I a = *(ugs.);* das ist I a *od.* eins a
Ia. = Iowa
i. A.[1] = im Auftrag[e]
i|ah!; i|a|hen; der Esel [hat] iaht
i. Allg. = im Allgemeinen
Iam|be usw. *vgl.* Jambe usw.
...i|a|na *vgl.* ...ana
Ia|son *vgl.* Jason
I|at|rik (↑R 130), die; - ‹griech.› (*Med.* Heilkunst); **i|at|ro|gen** (*Med.* durch ärztliche Einwirkung verursacht)
ib., ibd. = ibidem
I|be|rer (Angehöriger der vorindogermanischen Bevölkerung der Iberischen Halbinsel); **i|be|risch,** *aber* (↑R 102): die Iberische Halbinsel; **I|be|ro|ame|ri|ka** (↑R 132; Lateinamerika); **i|be|ro|ame|ri|ka|nisch** (↑R 106 *u.* 132)
i|bi|dem [*auch* 'i(:)bi...] ‹lat.› (ebenda; *Abk.* ib., ibd.)
I|bis, der; Ibisses, Ibisse ‹ägypt.› (ein Schreitvogel)
I|bi|za (eine Baleareninsel; *vgl.* Eivissa); **I|bi|zen|ker,** der; -s, - (Einwohner von Ibiza); **i|bi|zen|kisch**
Ibn ‹arab., „Sohn"› (Teil von arab. Personennamen)
Ib|ra|him [*auch* ...'hi:m] (↑R 130; m. Vorn.)
Ib|sen (norw. Schriftsteller)
I|by|kos, I|by|kus (altgriech. Dichter)
IC = Intercityzug; **ICE** = Intercityexpresszug

[1] *Diese Abkürzung wird so geschrieben, wenn sie unmittelbar der Grußformel oder der Bezeichnung einer Behörde, Firma u. dgl. folgt. Sie wird im ersten Bestandteil großgeschrieben* (I. A.), *wenn sie nach einem abgeschlossenen Text allein vor einer Unterschrift steht.*

ich; Ich, das; -[s], -[s]; das liebe Ich; mein anderes Ich; **ich|be|zogen; Ich|er|zäh|ler** (↑R 24); **Ich-form** (↑R 24), die; -; Erzählung in der -; **Ich|ge|fühl** (↑R 24), das; -[e]s; **Ich|laut** (↑R 24), der; -[e]s, -e
Ich|neu|mon, der *od.* das; -s, *Plur.* -e *u.* -s ‹griech.› (eine Schleichkatze); **Ich|no|gramm** (*Med.* Gipsabdruck des Fußes)
Ich|ro|man (↑R 24), der; -s, -e (Roman in der Ichform); **Ich-sucht** (↑R 24), die; -; **ich|süch|tig**
Ich|thy|o|dont, der; -en, -en (↑R 126) ‹griech.› (versteinerter Fischzahn); **Ich|thy|o|lith** [*auch* ...'lit], der; *Gen.* -s *u.* -en, *Plur.* -e[n] (↑R 126; versteinerter Fisch[rest]); **Ich|thy|o|lo|ge,** der; -n, -n; ↑R 126; **Ich|thy|o|lo|gie,** die; - (Wissenschaft von den Fischen); **Ich|thy|o|sau|ri|er,** der; -s, - *u.* **Ich|thy|o|sau|rus,** der; -, ...rier [...i̯ər] (ausgestorbenes fischförmiges Kriechtier); **Ich-thy|o|se, Ich|thy|o|sis,** die; -, ...osen (*Med.* eine Hautkrankheit)
I|cing ['ai̯siŋ], das; -s, -s ‹engl.-amerik.› (*Eishockey* Befreiungsschlag)
id. = [1]idem, [2]idem
Id. = Idaho
i. d. = in der (*bei Ortsnamen,* z. B. Neumarkt i. d. Opf. [in der Oberpfalz])
[1]**I|da,** der; - (Berg auf Kreta; [im Altertum] Gebirge in Kleinasien)
[2]**I|da** (w. Vorn.); **I|da|feld,** das; -[e]s (*nord. Mythol.* Wohnort der Asen)
I|da|ho ['ai̯dəho:] (Staat in den USA; *Abk.* Id.)
i|dä|isch ‹*zu* [1]Ida›
ide. = indoeuropäisch
i|de|al ‹griech.› (nur in der Vorstellung existierend; der Idee entsprechend; musterhaft, vollkommen); **I|de|al,** das; -s, -e (dem Geiste vorschwebendes Muster der Vollkommenheit, Wunschbild; als ein höchster Wert erkanntes Ziel); **I|de|al‿bild, ...fall** (der), **...fi|gur, ...ge|stalt, ...ge|wicht; i|de|a|li|sie|ren** (der Idee od. dem Ideal annähern; verklären); **I|de|a|li|sie|rung; I|de|a|lis|mus,** der; - (Überordnung der Gedanken-, Vorstellungswelt über die wirkliche; Streben nach Verwirklichung von Idealen); **I|de|a|list,** der; -en, -en (↑R 126); **I|de|a|lis|tin; i|de-a|lis|tisch; I|de|a|li|tät,** die; - (ideale Beschaffenheit; *Philos.* das Sein als Idee oder Vorstellung); **I|de|al‿kon|kur|renz** (die; -; *Rechtsw.*), **...li|nie** *(bes. Sport),* **...lö|sung, ...maß, ...staat; i|de|al|ty|pisch; I|de|al‿ty|pus, ...vor|stel|lung, ...wert** (Kunstwert), **...zu|stand; I|dee,** die; -, Ideen ([Ur]begriff, Urbild; [Leit-, Grund]gedanke; Einfall, Plan); eine - (*ugs. auch für* eine Kleinigkeit); **I|dée fixe** [ide: 'fiks], die; - -, -s -s [ide: 'fiks] ‹franz.› (Zwangsvorstellung; leitmotivisches Kernthema eines musikalischen Werkes); **i|de|ell** (nur gedacht, geistig); **i|de|en|arm; I|de|en‿ar-mut, ...as|so|zi|a|ti|on** (Gedankenverbindung); **I|de|en‿dra-ma, ...flucht** (die; -; krankhaftes sprunghaftes Denken; *vgl.* [2]Flucht); **I|de|en‿fül|le, ...ge|halt** (der), **...gut; i|de|en|los; I|de|en-lo|sig|keit,** die; -; **i|de|en|reich; I|de|en‿reich|tum** (der; -s), **...welt**
[1]**i|dem** ‹lat.› (derselbe; *Abk.* id.); [2]**i|dem** (dasselbe; *Abk.* id.)
I|den, I|dus ['i:du:s] *Plur.* ‹lat.› (13. od. 15. Monatstag des altröm. Kalenders); die Iden des März (15. März)
I|den|ti|fi|ka|ti|on, die; -, -en ‹lat.›, I|den|ti|fi|zie|rung (Gleichsetzung, Feststellung der Identität); **i|den|ti|fi|zie|ren** (einander gleichsetzen; [die Persönlichkeit] feststellen; genau wieder erkennen); sich -; **I|den|ti|fi|zie|rung** *vgl.* Identifikation; **i|den|tisch** ([ein und] derselbe; übereinstimmend; völlig gleich); **I|den|ti|tät,** die; - (völlige Gleichheit); **I|den-ti|täts‿kar|te** (*österr. u. schweiz. für* Personalausweis), **...kri|se, ...nach|weis** *(Zollw.),* **...ver|lust**
I|de|o|gramm ‹griech.› (Schriftzeichen, das für einen Begriff, nicht für eine bestimmte Lautung steht); **I|de|o|gra|phie,** die; -, ...i̯en *Plur. selten* (aus Ideogrammen gebildete Schrift); **i|de|o-gra|phisch;** -e Schrift; **I|de|o|lo-ge,** der; -n, -n; ↑R 126 (Lehrer od. Anhänger einer Ideologie); **I|de|o|lo|gie,** die; -, ...i̯en (System von Weltanschauungen, [polit.] Grundeinstellungen u. Wertungen); **i|de|o|lo|gie‿frei, ...ge-bun|den; I|de|o|lo|gie|kri|tik,** die; -; **I|de|o|lo|gin; i|de|o|lo-gisch** (eine Ideologie betreffend); **i|de|o|lo|gi|sie|ren** (ideologisch durchdringen, interpretieren); **I|de|o|lo|gi|sie|rung; i|de|o|mo-to|risch** ‹griech.; lat.› (*Psych.* unbewusst ausgeführt)
id est ‹lat.› (*veraltend für* das ist, das heißt; *Abk.* i. e.)
idg. = indogermanisch

i|di|o... ‹griech.› (eigen..., sonder...); **I|di|o...** (Eigen..., Sonder...); **I|di|o|blast,** der; -en, -en; ↑R 126 (*Biol.* Pflanzenzelle mit bes. Funktion, die in andersartiges Gewebe eingelagert ist); **I|di|o|lat|rie** (↑R 130), die; - (Selbstvergötterung); **I|di|o|lekt,** der; -[e]s, -e (*Sprachw.* individueller Sprachgebrauch); **i|di|o|lek|tal**

I|di|om, das; -s, -e ‹griech.› (feste Redewendung; eigentümliche Sprache od. Sprechweise; Mundart); **I|di|o|ma|tik,** die; - (Lehre von den Idiomen; Gesamtbestand der Idiome einer Sprache; Sammlung von Idiomen); **i|di|o|ma|tisch; i|di|o|ma|ti|siert; I|di|o|ma|ti|sie|rung**

i|di|o|morph ‹griech.› (*Mineralogie* von eigenen echten Kristallflächen begrenzt); **I|di|o|plas|ma,** das; -s (*Biol.* Gesamtheit der im Zellplasma vorhandenen Erbanlagen); **I|di|o|syn|kra|sie,** die; -, ...ien (*Med.* Überempfindlichkeit gegen bestimmte Stoffe u. Reize); **i|di|o|syn|kra|tisch**

I|di|ot, der; -en, -en (↑R 126) ‹griech.› (Dummkopf; schwachsinniger Mensch); **i|di|o|ten|haft; I|di|o|ten|hü|gel** (*ugs. scherzh. für* Hügel, an dem Anfänger sich im Skifahren üben); **i|di|o|ten|si|cher** (*ugs. für* so beschaffen, dass niemand etwas falsch machen kann); **I|di|o|ten|test** (*ugs. für* MPU); **I|di|o|tie,** die; -, ...ien (Schwachsinn; Dummheit)

I|di|o|ti|kon, das; -s, *Plur.* ...ken, *auch* ...ka ‹griech.› (Mundartwörterbuch)

I|di|o|tin ‹griech.›; **i|di|o|tisch; I|di|o|tis|mus,** der; -, ...men (Äußerung der Idiotie; *Sprachw. veraltet* Eigenheit eines Idioms)

I|di|o|va|ri|a|ti|on [...v...], die; -, -en ‹griech.; lat.› (*Biol.* erbliche Veränderung eines Gens)

I|do, das; -s (eine künstl. Weltsprache)

I|dok|ras (↑R 130), der; -, -e ‹griech.› (ein Mineral)

I|dol, das; -s, -e ‹griech.› (Gegenstand der Verehrung; Publikumsliebling, Schwarm; Götzenbild, Abgott); **I|do|lat|rie,** I|do|lo|lat|rie (↑R 130), die; -, ...ien (Bilderanbetung; Götzendienst); **i|do|li|sie|ren; I|do|lo|lat|rie** *vgl.* Idolatrie

i-Dötz|chen (*rhein. für* Abc-Schütze)

I|du|mäa *vgl.* Edom

I|dun, *latinisiert* **I|du|na** (nord. Göttin der ewigen Jugend)

I|dus *vgl.* Iden

I|dyll, das; -s, -e ‹griech.› (Bereich, Zustand eines friedl. und einfachen, meist ländl. Lebens); **I|dyl|le,** die; -, -n (Schilderung eines Idylls in Literatur u. bildender Kunst; *auch svw.* Idyll); **I|dyl|lik,** die; - (idyllischer Zustand); **i|dyl|lisch** (das Idyll, die Idylle betreffend; ländlich; friedlich; einfach; beschaulich)

i. e. = id est

i.-e. = indoeuropäisch

I. E., IE = internationale Einheit

i. f. = ipse fecit

I|for, die; - ‹engl.; *Kurzwort für* Implementation Force [impləmenˈteːʃ(ə)n fɔː(r)s]› (internationale Truppe unter NATO-Führung in Bosnien u. Herzegowina); **I|for-Frie|dens|trup|pe**

I-för|mig (in Form eines lat. I); ↑R 25

IG = Industriegewerkschaft

I|gel, der; -s, -; **I|gel‿fisch, ...kak|tus, ...stel|lung** (ringförmige Verteidigungsstellung)

i|gitt!, i|git|ti|gitt!

Ig|lu, der *od.* das; -s, -s ‹eskim.› (runde Schneehütte der Eskimos)

Ig|na|ti|us (↑R 130; Name von Heiligen); Ignatius von Loyola (Gründer der Gesellschaft Jesu); **Ig|naz** [*auch* igˈnaːts] (m. Vorn.)

ig|no|rant ‹lat.› (↑R 130; von Unwissenheit zeugend); **Ig|no|rant,** der; -en, -en; ↑R 126 ‹„Nichtwisser“› (Dummkopf); **Ig|no|ran|ten|tum,** das; -s; **Ig|no|ran|tin; Ig|no|ranz,** die; - (Unwissenheit, Dummheit; Kenntnislosigkeit); **ig|no|rie|ren** (nicht wissen [wollen], absichtlich nicht beachten)

I|gor (m. Vorn.); **I|gor|lied,** das; -[e]s; ↑R 95 (ein altruss. Heldenepos)

I|gu|a|no|don (↑R 132), das; -s, *Plur.* -s *od.* ...odonten ‹indian.; griech.› (Pflanzen fressender Dinosaurier)

i. H. = im Haus[e]

IHK = Industrie- u. Handelskammer *(vgl. d.);* Internationale Handelskammer

Ih|le, der; -n, -n; ↑R 126 (Hering, der abgelaicht hat)

ihm; ihn; ih|nen; er folgte ihnen; *Großschreibung als Anrede (entsprechend Sie):* ich wäre Ihnen dankbar, wenn Sie ...

[1]**ihr, ih|re, ihr;** ihres, ihrem, ihren, ihrer; Ihre Majestät (*Abk.* I. M.); *Großschreibung als Anrede (entsprechend Sie):* geben Sie mir Ihr Ehrenwort, Ihren Schlüssel, Ihre Adresse (↑R 53); *vgl.* dein; [2]**ihr;** *(auch in Briefen kleingeschrieben;* ↑R 5:) ihr lieben Kinder; (↑R 6:) ihr Hilflosen; **ih|re**[1], ih|ri|ge[1]; *vgl.* deine, deinige; **ih|rer|seits**[1]; **ih|res|glei|chen**[1]; **ih|res|teils**[1]; **ih|ret|hal|ben**[1] *(veraltend);* **ih|ret|we|gen**[1]; **ih|ret|wil|len**[1]; um ihretwillen; **ih|ri|ge**[1], ihre[1]; *vgl.* deine, deinige; **Ih|ro** (*veraltet für* Ihre); Ihro Gnaden; **ihr|zen** (mit „Ihr“ anreden); du ihrzt

IHS = *IH(ΣOY)Σ* = Jesus

I. H. S. = in hoc salus; in hoc signo

i. J. = im Jahre

I|job *vgl.* Hiob

Ijs|sel, *niederl.* IJs|sel [ˈaisəl, *niederl.* ˈɛisəl], die; - (Flussarm im Rheindelta); **Ijs|sel|meer,** das; -[e]s (durch Abschlussdeich gebildeter See in Holland)

i|ka|risch ‹*zu* Ikarus›, *aber* das Ikarische Meer; **I|ka|ros, I|ka|rus** (Gestalt der griech. Sage)

I|ke|ba|na, das; -[s] ‹jap.› (Kunst des Blumensteckens)

I|kon, das; -s, -e ‹griech.› (*seltener für* Ikone); **I|ko|ne,** die; -, -n (Kultbild der Ostkirche); **I|ko|nen|ma|le|rei; I|ko|no|du|lie,** die; - (Bilderverehrung); **I|ko|no|graph,** der; -en, -en; ↑R 126; **I|ko|no|gra|phie,** die; -, ...ien (wiss. Bestimmung, Beschreibung, Erklärung von Ikonen); **I|ko|no|klas|mus,** der; -, ...men (Bildersturm); **I|ko|no|klast,** der; -en, -en; ↑R 126 (Bilderstürmer); **i|ko|no|klas|tisch; I|ko|no|lat|rie** (↑R 130), die; - (*svw.* Ikonodulie); **I|ko|no|lo|gie,** die; - (*svw.* Ikonographie); **I|ko|no|skop,** das; -s, -e (*Fernsehen* Bildspeicherröhre); **I|ko|nos|tas,** der; -, -e *u.* **I|ko|nos|ta|se** (↑R 132), die; -, -n (dreitürige Bilderwand in orthodoxen Kirchen)

I|ko|sa|e|der, das; -s, - ‹griech.› (*Math.* Zwanzigflächner); **I|ko|si|tet|ra|e|der,** das; -s, - (Vierundzwanzigflächner)

ikr = isländische Krone

IKRK = Internationales Komitee vom Roten Kreuz (in Genf)

IKS = Interkantonale Kontrollstelle für Heilmittel (in der Schweiz)

Ik|tus, der; -, *Plur.* - [ˈiktuːs] *u.* Ikten ‹lat.› (*Verslehre* Betonung der Hebung im Vers; *Med.* unerwartet u. plötzlich auftretendes Krankheitszeichen)

I|lang-I|lang-Öl *vgl.* Ylang-Ylang-Öl

Il|de|fons, Hil|de|fons (m. Vorn.)

I|ler, der; -s, - (Schabeisen der Kammmacher)

---

[1] *Als Anrede (entsprechend „Sie“) stets großgeschrieben* (↑R 52 f.).

I|le|us ['i:le|us], der; -, Ileen [...eən] ⟨griech.⟩ (*Med.* Darmverschluss)
I|lex, die, *auch* der; -, - ⟨lat.⟩ (Stechpalme)
I|li|as, *auch* I|li|a|de, die; - ([Homers] Heldengedicht über den Krieg gegen Ilion); **I|li|on** (*griech. Name von* Troja); **I|li|um** (*latinisierte Form von* Ilion)
Il|ja (m. Vorn.)
Il|ka (w. Vorn.)
Ill, die; - (r. Nebenfluss des Rheins; l. Nebenfluss des Rheins)
ill. = illustriert
Ill. = Illinois; Illustration, Illustrierte[n]
il|le|gal [*auch* ...'ga:l] ⟨lat.⟩ (gesetzwidrig); **Il|le|ga|li|tät** [*auch* 'il...], die; -, -en; in der - leben; **il|le|gi|tim** [*auch* ...'ti:m] (unrechtmäßig; unehelich); **Il|le|gi|ti|mi|tät** [*auch* 'il...], die; -
Il|ler, die; - (r. Nebenfluss der Donau)
il|lern (*landsch. für* [verstohlen] gucken); ich ...ere (↑R 16)
il|li|be|ral [*auch* ...'ra:l] ⟨lat.⟩ (*selten für* engherzig); **Il|li|be|ra|li|tät** [*auch* 'il...], die; -
Il|li|nois [...'nɔy(z)] (Staat in den USA; *Abk.* Ill.)
il|li|quid [*auch* ...'kvi:t] ⟨lat.⟩ ([vorübergehend] zahlungsunfähig); **Il|li|qui|di|tät** [*auch* 'il...], die; -
Il|li|te|rat [*auch* ...'ra:t], der; -en, -en (↑R 126) ⟨lat.⟩ (*selten für* Ungelehrter, Ungebildeter)
Il|lo|ku|ti|on, die; -, -en ⟨lat.⟩ (*Sprachw.* Sprechakt im Hinblick auf die kommunikative Funktion); **il|lo|ku|ti|o|när; il|lo|ku|tiv;** -er Akt (Illokution)
il|lo|yal ['iloaja:l, *auch* ...'ja:l] ⟨franz.⟩ (den Staat, eine Instanz o. Ä. nicht respektierend; unredlich, untreu; Vereinbarungen nicht einhaltend); **Il|lo|ya|li|tät** [*auch* 'il...], die; -
Il|lu|mi|nat, der; -en, -en (↑R 126) ⟨lat.⟩ (Angehöriger verschiedener früherer Geheimverbindungen, bes. des Illuminatenordens); **Il|lu|mi|na|ten|or|den,** der; -s (aufklärerisch-freimaurerische geheime Gesellschaft des 18. Jh.s); **Il|lu|mi|na|ti|on,** die; -, -en (Festbeleuchtung; Ausmalung); **Il|lu|mi|na|tor,** der; -s, ...oren (mittelalterl. Ausmaler von Büchern); **il|lu|mi|nie|ren** (festlich erleuchten; bunt ausmalen); **Il|lu|mi|nie|rung**
Il|lu|si|on, die; -, -en ⟨lat.⟩ (Wunschvorstellung; Wahn, Sinnestäuschung); **il|lu|si|o|när** (auf Illusion beruhend); **Il|lu|si|o|nis|mus,** der; - (*Philos.* Lehre, dass die Außenwelt nur Illusion sei); **Il|lu|si|o|nist,** der; -en, -en; ↑R 126 (Träumer; Zauberkünstler); **il|lu|si|o|nis|tisch; il|lu|si|ons|los; il|lu|so|risch** (nur in der Illusion bestehend; trügerisch)
il|lus|ter ⟨lat.⟩ (glänzend, vornehm); ...ust|re (↑R 130) Gesellschaft; **Il|lust|ra|ti|on** (↑R 130), die; -, -en (Erläuterung, Bildbeigabe, Bebilderung); *Abk.* Ill.; **il|lust|ra|tiv** (erläuternd, anschaulich); **Il|lust|ra|tor,** der; -s, ...oren (Künstler, der ein Buch mit Bildern schmückt); **Il|lust|ra|to|rin; il|lust|rie|ren** ([durch Bilder] erläutern; [ein Buch] mit Bildern schmücken; bebildern); **il|lust|riert** (*Abk.* ill.); **Il|lust|rier|te,** die; -n, -n; zwei Illustrierte, *auch* Illustrierten; *Abk.* Ill.; **Il|lust|rie|rung** (Vorgang des Illustrierens)
Il|ly|rer, Il|ly|ri|er [...i̯ər] (Angehöriger idg. Stämme in Illyrien); **Il|ly|ri|en** [...i̯ən] (das heutige Dalmatien u. Albanien); **il|ly|risch**
Ilm, die; - (l. Nebenfluss der Saale; r. Nebenfluss der Donau); **¹Il|me|nau;** ↑R 132 (Stadt im Thüringer Wald); **²Il|me|nau,** die; - (l. Nebenfluss der unteren Elbe)
Il|me|nit [*auch* ...'nit], der; -s, -e ⟨nach dem russ. Ilmengebirge⟩ (ein Mineral)
Il|o|na ['i(:)..., *auch* i'lo:na] (w. Vorn.)
Il|se (w. Vorn.)
Il|tis, der; Iltisses, Iltisse (kleines Raubtier; Pelz aus dessen Fell)
im (in dem; *Abk.* i. [*bei Ortsnamen,* z. B. Königshofen i. Grabfeld]); im Auftrag[e] (*Abk.* i. A.[1] *od.* I. A.[1]); im Grunde [genommen]; im Haus[e] (*Abk.* i. H.); im Argen liegen; im Allgemeinen (*Abk.* i. Allg.); im Besonderen; *vgl. auch* einzeln, ganz, gering, klar usw.
IM = inoffizieller Mitarbeiter (des Staatssicherheitsdienstes der ehem. DDR)
I. M. = Ihre Majestät; Innere Mission
I|mage ['imitʃ, *engl.* 'imidʒ], das; -[s], -s ['imitʃ(s), *engl.* 'imidʒiz] ⟨engl.⟩ (Vorstellung, Bild von jmdm. od. etw. [in der öffentlichen Meinung]); **I|mage|pfle|ge; i|ma|gi|na|bel** [imagi...] ⟨lat.⟩ (vorstellbar, erdenklich); ...ab|le (↑R 130) Vorgänge; **i|ma|gi|när** (nur in der Vorstellung bestehend; scheinbar); -e Zahl (*Math.; Zeichen* i); **I|ma|gi|na|ti|on,** die; -, -en ([dichter.] Einbildung[skraft]); **i|ma|gi|nie|ren** ([sich] vorstellen, einbilden); **I|ma|go,** die; -, ...gines [...gine:s] (*Biol.* fertig ausgebildetes, geschlechtsreifes Insekt)
im All|ge|mei|nen (*Abk.* i. Allg.; ↑R 47)
I|mam, der; -s, *Plur.* -s *u.* -e ⟨arab.⟩ (Vorbeter in der Moschee; Titel für Gelehrte des Islams; Prophet u. religiöses Oberhaupt der Schiiten)
I|man, das; -s ⟨arab.⟩ (Glaube [im Islam])
im Auf|trag, im Auf|tra|ge (*Abk.* i. A.[1] *od.* I. A.[1])
im Be|griff, im Be|grif|fe; - - sein
im Be|son|de|ren *vgl.* besondere
im|be|zil, im|be|zill ⟨lat.⟩ (*Med.* mittelgradig schwachsinnig); **Im|be|zil|li|tät,** die; -
Im|bi|bi|ti|on, die; -, -en ⟨lat.⟩ (*Bot.* Quellung von Pflanzenteilen; *Geol.* Durchtränken von Gestein mit magmatischen Gasen od. wässrigen Lösungen)
Im|biss, der; -es, -e; **Im|biss‿hal|le, ...stand** (↑R 136), **...stu|be** (↑R 136)
im Ein|zel|nen *vgl.* einzeln
im Fall *od.* **Fal|le[,] dass** (↑R 88)
im Grun|de; im Grunde genommen
I|mi|tat, das; -[e]s, -e, **I|mi|ta|ti|on,** die; -, -en ⟨lat.⟩ ([minderwertige] Nachahmung); **I|mi|ta|tor,** der; -s, ...oren (Nachahmer); **i|mi|ta|to|risch; i|mi|tie|ren; i|mi|tiert** (nachgeahmt, unecht)
im Jah|re (*Abk.* i. J.)
Im|ke (w. Vorn.)
Im|ker, der; -s, - (Bienenzüchter); **Im|ke|rei; Im|ke|rin; im|kern;** ich ...ere (↑R 16)
Im|ma (w. Vorn.)
im|ma|nent ⟨lat.⟩ (innewohnend, in etwas enthalten); **Im|ma|nenz,** die; - (das Innewohnen)
Im|ma|nu|el (m. Vorn.)
Im|ma|te|ri|a|li|tät [*auch* 'im...], die; - ⟨franz.⟩ (unkörperliche Beschaffenheit); **im|ma|te|ri|ell** [*auch* 'im...] (unstofflich; geistig)
Im|mat|ri|ku|la|ti|on (↑R 130), die; -, -en ⟨lat.⟩ (Einschreibung an einer Hochschule; *schweiz. auch für* amtliche Zulassung eines Kraftfahrzeugs); **im|mat|ri|ku|lie|ren; Im|mat|ri|ku|lie|rung**
Im|me, die; -, -n (*landsch. für* Biene)
im|me|di|at ⟨lat.⟩ (*veraltend für* unmittelbar [dem Staatsoberhaupt unterstehend, vortragend usw.]); **Im|me|di|at|ge|such** (unmittelbar an die höchste Behörde gerichtetes Gesuch)

[1] *Vgl.* S. 363, Anm. 1.

im|mens ‹lat.› (unermesslich [groß]); -er Reichtum; **Im|men|si|tät,** die; - (*veraltet für* Unermesslichkeit)
Im|men|stock *Plur.* ...stöcke ‹*zu* Imme›
im|men|su|ra|bel ‹lat.› (unmessbar); **Im|men|su|ra|bi|li|tät,** die; -
im|mer; immer wieder; immer mehr; noch immer; für immer; ein immer währender Frühling; der immer währende Kalender; **im|mer|dar** *(veraltend);* **im|mer|fort; im|mer|grün;** -e Blätter, *aber* immer grün bleiben; **Im|mer|grün,** das; -s, -e (eine Pflanze); **im|mer|hin**
Im|mer|si|on, die; -, -en ‹lat.› (Ein-, Untertauchen, z. B. eines Himmelskörpers in den Schatten eines anderen)
im|mer wäh|rend *vgl.* immer; **im|mer|zu** (fortwährend)
Im|mig|rant (↑R 130), der; -en, -en (↑R 126) ‹lat.› (Einwanderer); **Im|mig|ran|tin; Im|mig|ra|ti|on,** die; -, -en; **im|mig|rie|ren**
im|mi|nent ‹lat.› (*Med.* bevorstehend, drohend [z. B. von Fehlgeburten])
Im|mis|si|on, die; -, -en ‹lat.› (Einwirkung von Verunreinigungen, Lärm o. Ä. auf Lebewesen); **Im|mis|si|ons|schutz,** der; -es
Im|mo (m. Vorn.)
im|mo|bil [*auch* ...'bi:l] ‹lat.› (unbeweglich; *Milit.* nicht für den Krieg bestimmt od. ausgerüstet); **Im|mo|bi|li|ar‿kre|dit** (lat.; ital.; durch Grundbesitz gesicherter Kredit), **...ver|si|che|rung** (Versicherung von Gebäuden gegen Feuerschäden); **Im|mo|bi|lie** [...i̯ə], die; -, -n ‹lat.› (Grundstück, Grundbesitz); **Im|mo|bi|li|en‿händ|ler, ...händ|le|rin; im|mo|bi|li|sie|ren; Im|mo|bi|lis|mus,** der; - *u.* **Im|mo|bi|li|tät,** die; - (Unbeweglichkeit)
im|mo|ra|lisch; Im|mo|ra|lis|mus, der; - ‹lat.› (Ablehnung moralischer Grundsätze); **Im|mo|ra|li|tät** [*auch* 'im...], die; - (Gleichgültigkeit gegenüber moral. Grundsätzen)
Im|mor|ta|li|tät [*auch* 'im...], die; - (Unsterblichkeit); **Im|mor|tel|le,** die; -, -n ‹franz.› (eine Sommerblume mit strohtrockenen Blüten)
im|mun ‹lat.› (unempfänglich [für Krankheit]; unter Rechtsschutz stehend; unempfindlich); **Im|mun|bi|o|lo|gie; im|mu|ni|sie|ren** (unempfänglich machen [für Krankheiten]); **Im|mu|ni|sie|rung; Im|mu|ni|tät,** die; - (Unempfindlichkeit gegenüber Krankheitserregern; Persönlichkeitsschutz der Abgeordneten in der Öffentlichkeit); **Im|mu|ni|täts|for|schung; Im|mun|kör|per** (*Med.* Antikörper); **Im|mu|no|lo|ge,** der; -n, -n (↑R 126); **Im|mu|no|lo|gie,** die; - (*Med.* Lehre von der Immunität); **im|mu|no|lo|gisch; Im|mun|schwä|che; Im|mun|sys|tem**
im Nach|hi|nein *vgl.* Nachhinein
Imp, der; -s, - (*bayr., österr. mdal. für* Biene); *vgl.* Imme
imp. = imprimatur
Imp. = Imperator
Im|pal|la, die; -, -s ‹afrik.› (eine Antilopenart)
im|pas|tie|ren ‹ital.› (Farbe [mit dem Spachtel] dick auftragen); **Im|pas|to,** das; -s, *Plur.* -s *u.* ...sti (dickes Auftragen von Farben)
Im|pe|danz, die; -, -en ‹lat.› (elektr. Scheinwiderstand)
im|pe|ra|tiv ‹lat.› (befehlend, zwingend); imperatives Mandat (Mandat, das den Abgeordneten an den Auftrag seiner Wähler bindet); **Im|pe|ra|tiv** [*auch* ...'ti:f], der; -s, -e [...və] (*Sprachw.* Befehlsform, z. B. „lauf!, lauft!"; *Philos.* unbedingt gültiges sittliches Gebot); **im|pe|ra|ti|visch** [...v..., *auch* 'im...] (befehlend; Befehls...); **Im|pe|ra|tiv|satz; Im|pe|ra|tor,** der; -s, ...oren (*im alten Rom* Oberfeldherr; *später für* Kaiser; *Abk.* Imp.); **im|pe|ra|to|risch; Im|pe|ra|tor Rex** (Kaiser [und] König; *Abk.* I. R.)
Im|per|fekt [*auch* ...'fɛkt], das; -s, -e ‹lat.› (*Sprachw.* Präteritum); **im|per|fek|tisch** [*auch* ...'fɛk...]
im|pe|ri|al ‹lat.› (das Imperium betreffend; kaiserlich); **Im|pe|ri|a|lis|mus,** der; - (das Streben von Großmächten nach wirtschaftl., polit. u. militär. Vorherrschaft); **Im|pe|ri|a|list,** der; -en, -en; **im|pe|ri|a|lis|tisch; Im|pe|ri|um,** das; -s, ...ien [...i̯ən] (*im alten Rom* Oberbefehl; [röm.] Kaiserreich; Weltreich)
im|per|me|a|bel [*auch* 'im...] ‹lat.› (*fachspr. für* undurchlässig); ...able (↑R 130) Schicht; **Im|per|me|a|bi|li|tät,** die; -
Im|per|so|na|le, das; -s, *Plur.* ...lien [...i̯ən] *u.* ...lia ‹lat.› (*Sprachw.* unpersönliches Verb, Verb, das mit unpersönlichem „es" konstruiert wird, z. B. „es schneit")
im|per|ti|nent ‹lat.› (ungehörig, frech, unausstehlich); **Im|per|ti|nenz,** die; -, -en
Im|pe|ti|go, die; -, ...gines [...gine:s] ‹lat.› (eine Hautkrankheit)
im|pe|tu|o|so ‹ital.› (*Musik* stürmisch); **Im|pe|tus,** der; - ‹lat.› (Ungestüm, Antrieb, Drang)
Impf‿ak|ti|on, ...arzt; imp|fen; Impf|ka|len|der; Impf|ling; Impf‿pass, ...pflicht (die; -), **...pis|to|le, ...schein, ...stoff; Imp|fung; Impf|zwang,** der; -[e]s
Im|plan|tat, das; -[e]s, -e ‹lat.› (*Med.* dem Körper eingepflanztes Gewebestück o. Ä.); **Im|plan|ta|ti|on,** die; -, -en (Einpflanzung von Gewebe o. Ä. in den Körper); **im|plan|tie|ren**
im|ple|men|tie|ren ‹engl.› (einführen, einsetzen; einbauen); Anwendungsprogramme - *(EDV);* **Im|ple|men|tie|rung** (das Implementieren)
Im|pli|ka|ti|on, die; -, -en ‹lat.› (das Einbeziehen); **im|pli|zie|ren** (einschließen, mit einbegreifen); **im|pli|zit** (inbegriffen, eingeschlossen, mitgemeint; *Ggs.* explizit); **im|pli|zi|te** [...te] (mit einbegriffen, eingeschlossen); etwas - (zugleich mit) sagen
im|plo|die|ren ‹lat.› (durch äußeren Überdruck eingedrückt und zertrümmert werden); **Im|plo|si|on,** die; -, -en
im|pon|de|ra|bel ‹lat.› (*veraltet für* unwägbar, unberechenbar); ...able (↑R 130) Faktoren; **Im|pon|de|ra|bi|li|en** [...i̯ən] *Plur.* (Unwägbarkeiten, Gefühls- u. Stimmungswerte); **Im|pon|de|ra|bi|li|tät,** die; - (Unwägbarkeit)
im|po|nie|ren ‹lat.› (Achtung einflößen, Eindruck machen); **Im|po|nier|ge|ha|be** (*Zool.* bei männl. Tieren vor der Paarung)
Im|port, der; -[e]s, -e ‹engl.› (Einfuhr); Im- u. Export (↑R 23); **im|port|ab|hän|gig; Im|port‿ab|hän|gig|keit, ...be|schrän|kung; Im|por|te,** die; -, -n *meist Plur.* (*veraltend für* eingeführte Ware, bes. Zigarre); **Im|por|teur** [...'tø:r], der; -s, -e ‹franz.› ([Groß]händler, der Waren einführt); **Im|port‿ge|schäft, ...han|del** (*vgl.* [1]Handel); **im|por|tie|ren**
im|por|tun ‹lat.› (ungeeignet, ungelegen; *Ggs.* opportun)
im|po|sant ‹franz.› (eindrucksvoll; großartig)
im|po|tent [*auch* ...'tɛnt] ‹lat.› (zum Koitus, zur Zeugung nicht fähig); **Im|po|tenz,** die; -, -en
impr. = imprimatur
Im|präg|na|ti|on (↑R 130), die; -, -en ‹lat.› (*Geol.* feine Verteilung von Erdöl od. Erz in Spalten od. Poren eines Gesteins; *Med.* Eindringen des Spermiums in das rei-

fe Ei, Befruchtung); **im|präg|nie|ren** (mit einem Schutzmittel [gegen Feuchtigkeit, Zerfall] durchtränken); **Im|präg|nie|rung**
im|prak|ti|ka|bel [*auch* 'im...] ‹lat.; griech.› (unausführbar, unanwendbar); ...ab|le (↑R 130) Anordnung
Im|pre|sa|rio, der; -s, *Plur.* -s *od.* ...ri, *auch* ...rien [...i̯ən] ‹ital.› ([Theater-, Konzert]agent)
Im|pres|sen (*Plur. von* Impressum); **Im|pres|si|on,** die; -, -en ‹lat.› (Eindruck; Empfindung; Sinneswahrnehmung); **im|pres|si|o|na|bel** (für Eindrücke empfänglich; erregbar); ...ab|le (↑R 130) Naturen; **Im|pres|si|o|nis|mus,** der; - (Kunstrichtung der 2. Hälfte des 19. Jh.s); **Im|pres|si|o|nist,** der; -en, -en (↑R 126); **Im|pres|si|o|nis|tin; im|pres|si|o|nis|tisch; Im|pres|sum,** das; -s, ...ssen (*Buchw.* Erscheinungsvermerk; Angabe über Verleger, Drucker usw. in Druckerzeugnissen); **Im|pri|ma|tur** ‹„es werde gedruckt"› (Vermerk auf dem letzten Korrekturabzug); *Abk.* impr. *u.* imp.); **Im|pri|ma|tur,** das; -s (Druckerlaubnis); **im|pri|mie|ren** (das Imprimatur erteilen)
Im|promp|tu [ɛ̃prɔ̃'ty:], das; -s, -s ‹franz.› (*Musik* Phantasiekomposition)
Im|pro|vi|sa|ti|on [...v...], die; -, -en ‹ital.› (unvorbereitetes Handeln; Stegreifdichtung, -rede, -musizieren); **Im|pro|vi|sa|ti|ons|ta|lent; Im|pro|vi|sa|tor,** der; -s, ...oren (jmd., der improvisiert; Stegreifdichter usw.); **im|pro|vi|sie|ren**
Im|puls, der; -es, -e ‹lat.› (Antrieb; Anregung; [An]stoß; Anreiz); **im|pul|siv** (von plötzl. Einfällen abhängig; lebhaft, rasch); **Im|pul|si|vi|tät** [...v...], die; -
Imst (österr. Stadt)
im|stand *(bes. südd.),* **im|stan|de,** *auch* **im Stand, im Stan|de;** imstand[e], *auch* im Stand[e] sein; *vgl.* Stand
im Üb|ri|gen *vgl.* übrig
im Vo|raus [*auch* - ...'raus] (↑R 49)
im Vor|hi|nein (im Voraus; ↑R 49)
[1]**in** (*Abk.* i. [*bei Ortsnamen,* z. B. Weißenburg i. Bay.]); *Präp. mit Dat. u. Akk.:* ich gehe in dem (im) Garten auf und ab, *aber* ich gehe in den Garten; im (in dem); ins (in das); *vgl.* ins
[2]**in** ‹engl.›; in sein (*ugs. für* dazugehören; zeitgemäß, modern sein)
in, in. = Inch
In = *chem. Zeichen für* Indium
...in (z. B. Lehrerin, die; -, -nen)
I|na (w. Vorn.)
in ab|sen|tia ‹lat.› (in Abwesenheit [des Angeklagten])
in abs|trac|to ‹lat.› (im Allgemeinen betrachtet; rein begrifflich); *vgl.* abstrakt
in|adä|quat [*auch* ...'kva:t] (↑R 132) ‹lat.› (nicht passend; nicht entsprechend); **In|adä|quat|heit,** die; -, -en
in ae|ter|num [- ɛ...] ‹lat.› (auf ewig)
in|ak|ku|rat [*auch* ...'ra:t] ‹lat.› (ungenau)
in|ak|tiv [*auch* ...'ti:f] ‹lat.› (untätig, passiv; unwirksam; ruhend; außer Dienst); **in|ak|ti|vie|ren** [...v...] (*Chemie, Med.* unwirksam machen); **In|ak|ti|vi|tät** [*auch* 'in...], die; - (Untätigkeit, Unwirksamkeit)
in|ak|tu|ell [*auch* ...'ɛl] (nicht aktuell)
in|ak|zep|ta|bel [*auch* ...'ta:b(ə)l] ‹lat.› (unannehmbar); ...ab|le (↑R 130) Bedingungen
i|nan (↑R 132) ‹lat.› (*Philos.* nichtig, leer)
In|an|griff|nah|me, die; -, -n
In|an|spruch|nah|me, die; -, -n
in|ar|ti|ku|liert [*auch* ...'li:rt] ‹lat.› (ungegliedert; undeutlich [ausgesprochen])
In|au|gen|schein|nah|me, die; -, -n
In|au|gu|ral|dis|ser|ta|ti|on, die; -, -en ‹lat.› (wissenschaftliche Arbeit zur Erlangung der Doktorwürde); **In|au|gu|ra|ti|on,** die; -, -en ([feierl.] Einsetzung in ein hohes [polit. od. akadem.] Amt); **in|au|gu|rie|ren** (einsetzen; beginnen, einleiten)
in bar; etwas in bar bezahlen
In|be|griff, der; -[e]s, -e (absolute Verkörperung; Musterbeispiel); **in|be|grif|fen** *vgl.* einbegriffen
In|be|sitz|nah|me, die; -, -n
in Be|treff *vgl.* Betreff
In|be|trieb|nah|me, die; -, -n; **In|be|trieb|set|zung**
in Be|zug *vgl.* Bezug
In|bild (*geh. für* Ideal)
In|brunst, die; -; **in|brüns|tig**
In|bus|schlüs|sel ® (ein Werkzeug)
Inc. = incorporated [in'kɔ:(r)pəre:tid] ‹engl.-amerik.› (*amerik. Bez. für* eingetragen [von Vereinen o. Ä.])
In|cen|tive [in'sɛntiv], das; -s, -s ‹engl.› ([wirtschaftlicher] Anreiz; Ansporn; Gratifikation)
Inch [intʃ], der; -, -es [intʃis] ‹engl.› (angelsächs. Längenmaß; *Abk.* in, in.; *Zeichen* "); 4 -[es] (↑R 90)
in|cho|a|tiv ‹lat.›; -e Aktionsart; **In|cho|a|tiv** ['inkoa..., *auch* ...'ti:f], das; -s, -e [...və] (*Sprachw.* Verb, das den Beginn eines Geschehens ausdrückt, z. B. „erwachen")
in|ci|pit [...ts...] ‹lat., „es beginnt"› (Vermerk am Anfang von Handschriften u. Frühdrucken)
incl. *vgl.* inkl.
in con|cert [- 'kɔnsə(r)t] ‹engl.› (in einem öffentlichen Konzert; bei einem öffentlichen Konzert aufgenommen)
in con|cre|to ‹lat.› (in Wirklichkeit; tatsächlich); *vgl.* konkret
in con|tu|ma|ci|am [- ...ts...] ‹lat.› *(Rechtsspr.);* - - urteilen (in Abwesenheit des Beklagten ein Urteil fällen)
in cor|po|re [- ...re] ‹lat.› (insgesamt; alle gemeinsam)
Ind. = Indiana; Indikativ
I. N. D. = in nomine Dei; in nomine Domini
In|danth|ren ® (↑R 130 *u.* 132), das; -s, -e (ein licht- u. waschechter Farbstoff); **in|danth|ren|far|ben; In|danth|ren|farb|stoff**
In|de|fi|nit|pro|no|men [*auch* 'in...] ‹lat.› (*Sprachw.* unbestimmtes Fürwort, z. B. „jemand")
in|de|kli|na|bel [*auch* 'in...] ‹lat.› (*Sprachw.* nicht beugbar); ein ...ab|les (↑R 130) Wort
in|de|li|kat [*auch* ...ka:t] ‹franz.› (unzart; unfein)
in|dem; er diktierte den Brief, indem (während) er im Zimmer umherging (↑R 78); *aber* er diktierte den Brief, in dem (in welchem) ...
in|dem|ni|sie|ren ‹lat.› (*veraltet für* entschädigen, vergüten; Indemnität erteilen); **In|dem|ni|tät,** die; - (nachträgliche Billigung eines zuvor vom Parlament [als verfassungswidrig] abgelehnten Regierungsaktes; Straflosigkeit [der Abgeordneten])
In-den-Ap|ril-Schi|cken, das; -s (↑R 28)
In-den-Tag-hi|nein-Le|ben, das; -s (↑R 28)
In|dent|ge|schäft ‹engl.; dt.› (eine Art des Exportgeschäftes)
In|de|pen|dence Day [indi'pɛndəns 'de:], der; - - ‹engl.-amerik.› (Unabhängigkeitstag der USA [4. Juli]); **In|de|pen|den|ten** *Plur.* ‹engl.› (Anhänger einer engl. puritan. Richtung des 17. Jh.s); **In|de|pen|denz,** die; - ‹lat.› (*veraltet für* Unabhängigkeit)
In|der, der; -s, - (Bewohner Indiens); **In|de|rin**
in|des, in|des|sen

in|de|ter|mi|na|bel [*auch* 'in...] ‹lat.› (unbestimmbar); ...ab|ler (↑R 130) Begriff; **In|de|ter|mi|na|ti|on** [*auch* 'in...], die; - (Unbestimmtheit); **in|de|ter|mi|niert** [*auch* 'in...] (unbestimmt, nicht festgelegt, nicht abgegrenzt, frei); **In|de|ter|mi|nis|mus** [*auch* 'in...], der; - (*Philos.* Lehre von der Willensfreiheit)

In|dex, der; -[es], *Plur.* -e *u.* ...dizes, *auch* ...dices [...tse:s] ‹lat.› (alphabet. Namen-, Sachverzeichnis; Liste verbotener Bücher; statistische Messziffer); das Buch steht auf dem -; **In|dex₋wäh|rung** *(Wirtsch.),* **...zif|fer**

in|de|zent ‹lat.› (nicht taktvoll, nicht feinfühlig); **In|de|zenz,** die; -, -en (Mangel an Takt)

In|di|a|ca ® [...ka], das; -s (eine Art Volleyballspiel, Handtennis)

In|di|an, der; -s, -e (*bes. österr. für* Truthahn)

In|di|a|na (Staat in den USA; *Abk.* Ind.); **In|di|a|na|po|lis|start** (fliegender Start beim Autorennen; ↑R 105); **In|di|a|ner,** der; -s, - (Angehöriger der Urbevölkerung Amerikas [außer den Eskimos]); *vgl. auch* Indio; **In|di|a|ner₋buch, ...ge|schich|te, ...häupt|ling, ...krap|fen** (*österr. für* Mohrenkopf), **...re|ser|vat** *od.* **...re|ser|va|ti|on, ...schmuck, ...spra|che, ...stamm; in|di|a|nisch; In|di|a|nist,** der; -en, -en; ↑R 126 (Erforscher der indian. Sprachen und Kulturen); **In|di|a|nis|tik,** die; -

In|di|en [...iən] (Staat in Südasien); *vgl. auch* Bharat

In|dienst|nah|me, die; -, -n *(Amtsspr.);* **In|dienst|stel|lung**

in|dif|fe|rent [*auch* ...'rɛnt] ‹lat.› (unbestimmt, gleichgültig, teilnahmslos; wirkungslos); **In|dif|fe|ren|tis|mus,** der; - (Gleichgültigkeit [gegenüber bestimmten Dingen, Meinungen, Lehren]); **In|dif|fe|renz** [*auch* ...'rɛnts], die; -, -en (Unbestimmtheit, Gleichgültigkeit; Wirkungslosigkeit)

In|di|ges|ti|on [*auch* 'in...], die; -, -en ‹lat.› (*Med.* Verdauungsstörung)

In|dig|na|ti|on (↑R 130), die; - ‹lat.› (Unwille, Entrüstung); **in|dig|niert** (peinlich berührt, unwillig, entrüstet); **In|dig|ni|tät,** die; - (*Rechtsspr.* Erbunwürdigkeit; *veraltet für* Unwürdigkeit)

In|di|go, der *od.* das; -s, *Plur.* (*für* Indigoarten:) -s ‹span.› (ein blauer Farbstoff); **in|di|go|blau; In|di|go|blau; In|di|go|lith** [*auch* ...'lit], der; *Gen.* -s *u.* -en, *Plur.* -e[n]; ↑R 126 (ein Mineral); **In|di|go|tin,** das; -s ‹nlat.› (Indigo)

In|dik, der; -s (Indischer Ozean)

In|di|ka|ti|on, die; -, -en ‹lat.› (Merkmal; *Med.* Heilanzeige); **In|di|ka|ti|ons|mo|dell** (Modell zur Freigabe des Schwangerschaftsabbruchs unter bestimmten Voraussetzungen); **In|di|ka|tiv,** der; -s, -e [...və] (*Sprachw.* Wirklichkeitsform; *Abk.* Ind.); **in|di|ka|ti|visch** [...v..., *auch* ...'ti:...] (die Wirklichkeitsform betreffend); **In|di|ka|tor,** der; -s, ...oren (Merkmal, das etwas anzeigt; Gerät zum Messen physikal. Vorgänge; Stoff, der durch Farbwechsel das Ende einer chem. Reaktion anzeigt); **In|di|ka|tor|di|a|gramm** (Leistungsbild [einer Maschine]); **In|di|kat|rix** (↑R 130), die; - (math. Hilfsmittel zur Feststellung einer Flächenkrümmung)

In|dio, der; -s, -s ‹span.› (süd- u. mittelamerik. Indianer)

in|di|rekt [*auch* ...'rɛkt] ‹lat.› (mittelbar; auf Umwegen; abhängig; nicht geradezu); -e Wahl; -e Rede (*Sprachw.* abhängige Rede); -er Fragesatz (abhängiger Fragesatz); **In|di|rekt|heit**

in|disch; indische Musik, *aber* (↑R 102): der Indische Ozean; **In|disch|rot** (eine Anstrichfarbe)

in|dis|kret [*auch* ...'kre:t] ‹franz.› (nicht verschwiegen; taktlos; zudringlich); **In|dis|kre|ti|on** [*auch* 'in...], die; -, -en (Vertrauensbruch; Taktlosigkeit)

in|dis|ku|ta|bel [*auch* ...'ta:b(ə)l] ‹franz.› (nicht der Erörterung wert); ...ab|le (↑R 130) Forderung

in|dis|po|ni|bel [*auch* ...'ni:b(ə)l] ‹lat.› (nicht verfügbar; festgelegt); eine ...ib|le (↑R 130) Menge; **in|dis|po|niert** (in schlechter körperlich-seelischer Verfassung; nicht zu etwas aufgelegt); **In|dis|po|si|ti|on,** die; -, -en (schlechte körperlich-seel. Verfassung)

in|dis|pu|ta|bel [*auch* ...'ta:b(ə)l] ‹lat.› (*veraltet für* unbestreitbar)

in|dis|zip|li|niert [*auch* ...'ni:rt] ‹lat.›

In|di|um, das; -s (chem. Element, Metall; *Zeichen* In)

in|di|vi|du|a|li|sie|ren [...v...] ‹franz.› (die Individualität bestimmen; das Besondere, Eigentümliche hervorheben); **In|di|vi|du|a|li|sie|rung; In|di|vi|du|a|lis|mus,** der; - ‹lat.› (Anschauung, die dem Individuum den Vorrang vor der Gemeinschaft gibt); **In|di|vi|du|a|list,** der; -en, -en (Vertreter des Individualismus; Einzelgänger); **In|di|vi|du|a|lis|tin; in|di|vi|du|a|lis|tisch** (nur das Individuum berücksichtigend; das Besondere, Eigentümliche betonend); **In|di|vi|du|a|li|tät,** die; -, -en ‹franz.› (*nur Sing.:* Einzigartigkeit der Persönlichkeit; Eigenart; Persönlichkeit); **In|di|vi|du|al₋psy|cho|lo|gie** (die; -), **...recht** (Persönlichkeitsrecht), **...sphä|re; In|di|vi|du|a|ti|on,** die; -, -en (Entwicklung der Einzelpersönlichkeit, Vereinzelung); **in|di|vi|du|ell** ‹franz.› (dem Individuum eigentümlich; vereinzelt; besonders geartet; *regional für* privat, nicht staatlich); **In|di|vi|du|um** [...duum], das; -s, ...duen [...duən] ‹lat.› (Einzelwesen, einzelne Person; *abwertend für* Kerl, Lump)

In|diz, das; -es, -ien [...iən] ‹lat.› (Anzeichen; Verdacht erregender Umstand); **In|di|zes** (*Plur. von* Index); **In|di|zi|en** (*Plur. von* Indiz); **In|di|zi|en|be|weis** (auf zwingenden Verdachtsmomenten beruhender Beweis); **In|di|zi|en₋ket|te, ...pro|zess; in|di|zie|ren** (auf den Index setzen; mit einem Index versehen; anzeigen; *Med.* als angezeigt erscheinen lassen); **in|di|ziert** (*Med.* angezeigt, ratsam); **In|di|zie|rung**

In|do|chi|na (ehem. franz. Gebiet in Hinterindien); **In|do|eu|ro|pä|er** *vgl.* Indogermane; **in|do|eu|ro|pä|isch** (*Abk.* ide., i.-e.); *vgl.* indogermanisch; **In|do|ger|ma|ne** (Angehöriger einer westasiatisch-europäischen Sprachfamilie); **in|do|ger|ma|nisch** (*Abk.* idg.); **In|do|ger|ma|nisch,** das; -[s]; *vgl.* Deutsch; **In|do|ger|ma|ni|sche,** das; -n; *vgl.* Deutsche, das; **In|do|ger|ma|nist,** der; -en, -en (↑R 126); **In|do|ger|ma|nis|tik** (Wissenschaft, die die indogermanischen Sprachen erforscht); **In|do|ger|ma|nis|tin**

In|dokt|ri|na|ti|on (↑R 130), die; -, -en (massive [ideologische] Beeinflussung); **in|dokt|ri|na|tiv; in|dokt|ri|nie|ren; In|dokt|ri|nie|rung**

In|dol, das; -s (chem. Verbindung)

in|do|lent [*auch* ...'lɛnt] ‹lat.› (unempfindlich; gleichgültig; träge); **In|do|lenz** [*auch* ...'lɛnts], die; -

In|do|lo|ge, der; -n, -n (↑R 126) ‹griech.› (Erforscher der Sprachen u. Kulturen Indiens); **In|do|lo|gie,** die; -; **In|do|lo|gin**

In|do|ne|si|en (Inselstaat in Südostasien); **In|do|ne|si|er; In|do|ne|si|e|rin; in|do|ne|sisch**

in|do|pa|zi|fisch (um den Indischen u. Pazifischen Ozean gelegen); der -e Raum

In|dos|sa|ment, das; -s, -e ‹ital.› (*Bankw.* Wechselübertragungsvermerk); **In|dos|sant,** der; -en, -en; ↑R 126 (Wechselüberschreiber); **In|dos|sat,** der; -en, -en (↑R 126) *u.* **In|dos|sa|tar,** der; -s, -e (durch Indossament ausgewiesener Wechselgläubiger); **in|dos|sie|ren** ([einen Wechsel] durch Indossament übertragen); **In|dos|sie|rung; In|dos|so,** das; -s, *Plur.* -s *u.* ...dossi (Übertragungsvermerk auf einem Wechsel)

In|dra (↑R 130; ind. Hauptgott der wedischen Zeit)

in du|bio ‹lat.› (im Zweifelsfalle); **in du|bio pro reo** ‹„im Zweifel für den Angeklagten"› (ein alter Rechtsgrundsatz); In-dubio-pro-reo-Grundsatz (↑R 28)

In|duk|tanz, die; - ‹lat.› (*Elektrotechnik* rein induktiver Widerstand); **In|duk|ti|on,** die; -, -en (*Logik* Herleitung von allgemeinen Regeln aus Einzelfällen; *Elektrotechnik* Erregung elektr. Ströme u. Spannungen durch bewegte Magnetfelder); **In|duk|ti|ons‿ap|pa|rat** (*svw.* Induktor), **...be|weis** *(Logik),* **...krank|heit** *(Med.),* **...ofen** (↑R 132; *Technik*), **...strom** (durch Induktion erzeugter Strom); **in|duk|tiv** [*auch* 'in...] (auf Induktion beruhend); **In|duk|ti|vi|tät** [...v...], die; -, -en (Größe, die für die Stärke des Induktionsstromes mit maßgebend ist); **In|duk|tor,** der; -s, ...oren (Transformator zur Erzeugung hoher Spannung)

in dul|ci ju|bi|lo [- 'dultsi -] ‹lat., „in süßem Jubel"› (*übertr. für* herrlich u. in Freuden)

in|dul|gent ‹lat.› (nachsichtig); **In|dul|genz,** die; -, -en (Nachsicht; Straferlass; Ablass der zeitl. Sündenstrafen); **In|dult,** der *od.* das; -[e]s, -e (Frist; vorübergehende Befreiung von einer kirchengesetzlichen Verpflichtung)

In|du|ra|ti|on, die; -, -en ‹lat.› (*Med.* Gewebe- od. Organverhärtung)

In|dus, der; - (Strom in Vorderindien)

In|du|si, die; - ‹*Kurzw. aus* induktive Zugsicherung› (*Eisenb.* Zugsicherungseinrichtung)

In|du|si|um, das; -s, ...ien [...iən] ‹lat.› (*Bot.* häutiger Auswuchs der Blattunterseite von Farnen)

In|dust|ri|al|de|sign [in'dastri(ə)ldi'zain], *auch* **In|dust|ri|al De|sign** (↑R 130), das; -s ‹engl.› (Formgebung der Gebrauchsgegenstände); **In|dust|ri|al|de|sig|ner** [...di'zainə(r)], *auch* **In|dust|ri|al De|sig|ner,** der; -s, - (Formgestalter für Gebrauchsgegenstände); **in|dust|ri|a|li|sie|ren** ‹franz.› (Industrie ansiedeln, einführen); **In|dust|ri|a|li|sie|rung; In|dust|ri|a|lis|mus,** der; - (Prägung einer Volkswirtschaft durch die Industrie)

In|dust|rie (↑R 130), die; -, ...ien; **In|dust|rie‿an|la|ge, ...ar|bei|ter, ...ar|chä|o|lo|gie** (die; -; Erhaltung u. Erforschung von industriellen Bauwerken, Maschinen o. Ä.); **In|dust|rie‿aus|stel|lung, ...bau** (*Plur.* ...bauten), **...be|trieb, ...de|sign** (Gestaltung von Gebrauchsgegenständen), **...er|zeug|nis, ...ge|biet, ...ge|werk|schaft** (*Abk.* IG), **...ka|pi|tän** *(ugs.),* **...kauf|frau, ...kauf|mann** (*Plur.* ...leute), **...kom|bi|nat** *(ehem. in der DDR),* **...la|den** *(ehem. in der DDR),* **...land, ...land|schaft**

in|dust|ri|ell (↑R 130; die Industrie betreffend); die erste, zweite industrielle Revolution; **In|dust|ri|el|le,** der; -n, -n; ↑R 5 ff. (Inhaber eines Industriebetriebes)

In|dust|rie‿ma|gnat (↑R 130), **...müll, ...pro|dukt, ...ro|bo|ter, ...staat, ...stadt; In|dust|rie- und Han|dels|kam|mer** (*so die von den Richtlinien der Rechtschreibung* [↑R 28] *abweichende übliche Schreibung; Abk.* IHK); **In|dust|rie‿un|ter|neh|men, ...zeit|al|ter, ...zweig**

in|du|zie|ren ‹lat.› (*Verb zu* Induktion)

in|ef|fek|tiv [*auch* ...'ti:f] ‹lat.› (unwirksam, frucht-, nutzlos)

in ef|fi|gie [- ...gie, *auch* - ...giə] ‹lat., „im Bilde"› (bildlich)

in|ef|fi|zi|ent [*auch* ...'tsient] ‹lat.› (unwirksam; unwirtschaftlich); **In|ef|fi|zi|enz,** die; -, -en

in|egal [*auch* ...'ga:l] (↑R 132) ‹franz.› (ungleich[mäßig])

in|ei|nan|der (↑R 132): ineinander fließen, fügen, greifen usw.; ineinander verschlungen sein; *aber* das Ineinandergreifen der Zahnräder

in eins; in eins setzen (gleichsetzen); **In|eins|set|zung** *(geh.)*

i|nert (↑R 132) ‹lat.› (*veraltet für* untätig, träge; unbeteiligt); **I|nert|gas** (*Chemie* reaktionsträges Gas)

I|nes (w. Vorn.)

in|es|sen|ti|ell *auch* in|es|sen|zi|ell [*auch* ...'tsiɛl] ‹lat.› (unwesentlich)

in|exakt [*auch* ...'ksakt] (↑R 132) ‹lat.› (ungenau)

in|exis|tent [*auch* ...'stɛnt] (↑R 132) ‹lat.› (nicht vorhanden); **In|exis|tenz,** die; - (das Nichtvorhandensein; *Philos.* das Dasein, Enthaltensein in etwas)

in ex|ten|so ‹lat.› (ausführlich, vollständig)

in ext|re|mis (↑R 130) ‹lat.› (*Med.* im Sterben [liegend])

in|fal|li|bel ‹lat.› (unfehlbar [vom Papst]); eine ...ib|le (↑R 130) Entscheidung; **In|fal|li|bi|li|tät,** die; - ([päpstliche] Unfehlbarkeit)

in|fam ‹lat.› (ehrlos; niederträchtig, schändlich); **In|fa|mie,** die; -, ...ien

In|fant, der; -en, -en (↑R 126) ‹span., „Kind"› (*früher* Titel span. u. port. Prinzen); **In|fan|te|rie** [*auch* ...'ri:], die; -, ...ien ‹franz.› (*Milit.* Fußtruppe); **In|fan|te|rie|re|gi|ment** (*Abk.* IR.); **In|fan|te|rist** [*auch* ...'rist], der; -en, -en; ↑R 126 (Fußsoldat); **in|fan|te|ris|tisch; in|fan|til** ‹lat.› (kindlich; unentwickelt, unreif); **In|fan|ti|lis|mus,** der; -, ...men (Stehenbleiben auf kindlicher Entwicklungsstufe); **In|fan|ti|li|tät,** die; -; **In|fan|tin** ‹span.› (*früher* Titel span. u. port. Prinzessinnen)

In|farkt, der; -[e]s, -e ‹lat.› (*Med.* Absterben eines Gewebeteils infolge Gefäßverschlusses)

In|fekt, der; -[e]s, -e ‹lat.› (*Med.* Infektionskrankheit; *kurz für* Infektion); grippaler -; **In|fek|ti|on,** die; -, -en (Ansteckung durch Krankheitserreger); **In|fek|ti|ons‿ge|fahr, ...herd, ...krank|heit; in|fek|ti|ös** (ansteckend)

In|fel *vgl.* Inful

In|fe|ri|o|ri|tät, die; - ‹lat.› (untergeordnete Stellung; Minderwertigkeit)

in|fer|nal (*seltener für* infernalisch); **in|fer|na|lisch** ‹lat.› (höllisch; teuflisch); **In|fer|no,** das; -s ‹ital., „Hölle"› (entsetzliches Geschehen)

in|fer|til [*auch* 'in...] ‹lat.› (*Med.* unfruchtbar); **In|fer|ti|li|tät,** die; -

In|fight ['infait], der; -[s], -s *u.* **In|figh|ting** ['infaitiŋ], das; -[s], -s ‹engl.› (*Boxen* Nahkampf)

In|filt|ra|ti|on (↑R 130), die; -, -en ‹lat.› (Eindringen, z. B. von fremdartigen [krankheitserregenden] Substanzen in Zellen u. Gewebe; [ideologische] Unterwanderung); **In|filt|ra|ti|ons‿an|äs|the|sie** (*Med.* Betäubung durch Einspritzungen), **...ver|such; in|filt|rie|ren** (eindringen; durchtränken); **In|filt|rie|rung,** die; -, -en

in|fi|nit [*auch* ...'ni:t] ‹lat.› (*Sprachw.* unbestimmt); -e Form

(Form des Verbs, die im Ggs. zur finiten Form [*vgl.* finit] nicht nach Person u. Zahl bestimmt ist, z. B. „schwimmen" [*vgl.* Infinitiv], „schwimmend" u. „geschwommen" [*vgl.* Partizip]); **in|fi|ni|te|si|mal** (*Math.* zum Grenzwert hin unendlich klein werdend); **In|fi|ni|te|si|mal|rech|nung** *(Math.);* **In|fi|ni|tiv** [*auch* ...'ti:f], der; -s, -e [...və] (*Sprachw.* Grundform [des Verbs], z. B. „schwimmen"); **In|fi|ni|tiv|kon|junk|ti|on** (z. B. „zu", „ohne zu", „anstatt zu"); **In|fi|ni|tiv|satz** (satzwertiger Infinitiv)

In|fix [*auch* 'in...], das; -es, -e ⟨lat.⟩ (in den Wortstamm eingefügtes Sprachelement)

in|fi|zie|ren ⟨lat.⟩ (anstecken; mit Krankheitserregern verunreinigen); **In|fi|zie|rung**

in fla|gran|ti (↑R 130) ⟨lat.⟩ (auf frischer Tat); - - ertappen

in|flam|ma|bel ⟨lat.⟩ (entzündbar); ...ab|le (↑R 130) Stoffe

In|fla|ti|on, die; -, -en (übermäßige Ausgabe von Zahlungsmitteln; Geldentwertung); **in|fla|ti|o|när, in|fla|ti|o|nis|tisch, in|fla|to|risch** (Inflation bewirkend)

in|fle|xi|bel [*auch* ...'ksi:b(ə)l] ⟨lat.⟩ (*selten für* unbiegsam; unveränderlich; *Sprachw.* nicht beugbar); ...ib|les (↑R 130) Wort; **In|fle|xi|bi|li|tät** [*auch* 'in...], die; - (Unbiegsamkeit; Unbeugbarkeit)

In|flu|enz, die; -, -en ⟨lat.⟩ (Beeinflussung eines elektr. ungeladenen Körpers durch die Annäherung eines geladenen); **In|flu|en|za,** die; - ⟨ital.⟩ (*veraltet für* Grippe); **In|flu|enz|ma|schi|ne** (Maschine zur Erzeugung hoher elektr. Spannung)

In|fo, das; -s, -s (*ugs. kurz für* Informationsblatt)

in|fol|ge (↑R 41); *mit Gen. od. mit* „von": infolge des schlechten Wetters; infolge übermäßigen Alkoholgenusses; infolge von Krieg; das Hochwasser, infolge dessen die Straßen unpassierbar waren; *aber* **in|fol|ge|des|sen;** die Straßen waren überflutet und infolgedessen unpassierbar

In|fo|mo|bil, das; -s, -e (Fahrzeug als fahrbarer Informationsstand)

In|for|mand, der; -en, -en (↑R 126) ⟨lat.⟩ (eine Person, die informiert wird); **In|for|mant,** der; -en, -en; ↑R 126 (jmd., der [geheime] Informationen liefert); **In|for|ma|tik,** die; - (Wissenschaft von der Informationsverarbeitung, insbes. mithilfe von Computern); **In|for|ma|ti|ker;** **In|for|ma|ti|ke|rin; In|for|ma|ti|on,** die; -, -en (Auskunft; Nachricht; Belehrung); **in|for|ma|ti|o|nell; In|for|ma|ti|ons‿aus|tausch, ...be|dürf|nis, ...blatt, ...bü|ro, ...fluss** (der; -es), **...ge|halt** (der), **...ma|te|ri|al, ...quel|le, ...the|o|rie** (die; -), **...ver|ar|bei|tung; in|for|ma|tiv** (belehrend; Auskunft gebend; aufschlussreich); **In|for|ma|tor,** der; -s, ...oren (jmd., von dem man Informationen bezieht); **in|for|ma|to|risch** (der [vorläufigen] Unterrichtung dienend)

In|for|mel [ɛ̃fɔr'mɛl], das; - ⟨franz.⟩ (informelle Kunst; *vgl.* ²informell)

¹**in|for|mell** ⟨lat.⟩ (informierend, mitteilend)

²**in|for|mell** [*auch* ...'mɛl] ⟨franz.⟩ (nicht förmlich; auf Formen verzichtend); -e Kunst (eine Richtung der modernen Malerei)

in|for|mie|ren ⟨lat.⟩ (belehren; Auskunft geben; benachrichtigen); sich - (sich unterrichten, Auskünfte, Erkundigungen einziehen); **In|for|miert|heit,** die; -; **In|for|mie|rung; In|fo|tain|ment** [...'te:nmənt], das; -s ⟨engl.-dt.; *Kurzw. aus* Information *u.* Entertainment⟩ (unterhaltende Darbietung von Information)

in|fra|ge, *auch* **in Fra|ge;** infrage, *auch* in Frage kommen, stehen, stellen; das kommt nicht infrage, *auch* in Frage; die infrage, *auch* in Frage kommenden Personen; die infrage, *auch* in Frage gestellte Regelung

inf|ra|rot ⟨lat.; dt.⟩, *auch* **ult|ra|rot** (↑R 130; zum Infrarot gehörend); **Inf|ra|rot,** *auch* **Ult|ra|rot** (unsichtbare Wärmestrahlen, die im Spektrum zwischen dem roten Licht u. den kürzesten Radiowellen liegen); **Inf|ra|rot‿film, ...hei|zung, ...strah|ler** (ein Elektrogerät), **...strah|lung** (die; -); **Inf|ra|schall,** der; -[e]s (Schallwellenbereich unterhalb von 16 Hertz); **Inf|ra|struk|tur** (wirtschaftlich-organisatorischer Unterbau einer hoch entwickelten Wirtschaft; Gesamtheit milit. Anlagen); **inf|ra|struk|tu|rell**

In|ful, die; -, -n ⟨lat.⟩ (altröm. weiße Stirnbinde; *Bez. der* Mitra mit herabhängenden Bändern); **in|fu|liert** (zum Tragen der Inful berechtigt)

in|fun|die|ren ⟨lat.⟩ (*Med.* durch Infusion in den Körper einführen); **In|fus,** das; -es, -e (Aufguss; Tee); **In|fu|si|on,** die; -, -en (Zufuhr von Flüssigkeit in den Körper mittels einer Hohlnadel); **In|fu|si|ons|tier|chen** *u.* **In|fu|so|ri|um,** das; -s, ...ien [...iən] *meist Plur.* (Aufgusstierchen [einzelliges Wimpertierchen]); **In|fu|sum,** das; -s, ...sa (*svw.* Infus)

Ing. = Ingenieur

In|ga (w. Vorn.)

In|gang‿hal|tung (die; -), **...set|zung** (die; -)

In|gä|wo|nen usw. *vgl.* Ingwäonen usw.

Ing|bert (m. Vorn.); **In|ge, In|ge|borg** (w. Vorn.)

In|ge|brauch|nah|me, die; -, -n

In|ge|lo|re (w. Vorn.); ↑R 92

in ge|ne|re [*auch* - 'ge:...] ⟨lat.⟩ (im Allgemeinen)

In|ge|ni|eur [inʒe'niø:r], der; -s, -e ⟨franz.⟩ (*Abk.* Ing.); **In|ge|ni|eur‿aka|de|mie** (↑R 132), **...bau** (*Plur.* ...bauten), **...bü|ro; In|ge|ni|eu|rin; In|ge|ni|eur|öko|nom** (↑R 132; *ehem. in der DDR* auch auf techn. Gebiet ausgebildeter Wirtschaftswissenschaftler); **In|ge|ni|eur|schu|le; in|ge|ni|ös** [inge...] ⟨lat.⟩ (sinnreich; erfinderisch; scharfsinnig); **In|ge|ni|o|si|tät,** die; - (Erfindungsgabe, Scharfsinn); **In|ge|ni|um,** das; -s, ...ien [...iən] (natürl. Begabung, Erfindungskraft; Genie)

In|ges|ti|on, die; - ⟨lat.⟩ (*Med.* Nahrungsaufnahme)

in|ge|züch|tet ⟨*zu* Inzucht⟩

In|go, In|go|mar (m. Vorn.)

In|got ['iŋgɔt], der; -s, -s ⟨engl.⟩ (Metallblock, -barren)

In|grain|pa|pier [in'gre:n...] ⟨engl.; dt.⟩ (raues Zeichenpapier mit farbigen od. schwarzen Wollfasern)

In|gre|di|ens [...diɛns], das; -, ...ienzien [...iən] *meist Plur. u.* **In|gre|di|enz,** die; -, -en *meist Plur.* ⟨lat.⟩ (Zutat; Bestandteil)

Ing|res ['ɛ̃:gr(ə)] (↑R 130; franz. Maler)

In|gress, der; -es, -e ⟨lat.⟩ (*veraltet für* Eingang, Zutritt); **In|gres|si|on,** die; -, -en (*Geol.* das Eindringen von Meerwasser in Landsenken)

Ing|rid (w. Vorn.)

In|grimm, der; -[e]s (*veraltend für* Grimm); **in|grim|mig**

in gros|so ⟨ital.⟩ (*veraltend für* en gros)

Ing|wä|o|nen *Plur.* (Kultgemeinschaft westgerm. Stämme); **ing|wä|o|nisch**

Ing|wer, der; -s, - ⟨sanskr.⟩ (eine Gewürzpflanze; ein Likör; *nur Sing.:* ein Gewürz); **Ing|wer‿bier, ...öl**

In|ha|ber; In|ha|be|rin; In|ha|ber|pa|pier *(Bankw.)*

in|haf|tie|ren (in Haft nehmen);

In|haf|tier|te, der *u.* die; -n, -n (↑R 5 ff.); **In|haf|tie|rung; In|haft|nah|me,** die; -, -n *(Amtsspr.)*
In|ha|la|ti|on, die; -, -en ‹lat.› (*Med.* Einatmung meist dampfförmiger od. zerstäubter Heilmittel); **In|ha|la|ti|ons|ap|pa|rat; In|ha|la|to|ri|um,** das; -s, ...ien [...iən] (Raum zum Inhalieren); **in|ha|lie|ren** (*auch für* [beim Zigarettenrauchen] den Rauch [in die Lunge] einziehen)
In|halt, der; -[e]s, -e; **in|halt|lich; In|halts|an|ga|be; in|halts|arm; in|halts|los; in|halts‿reich, ...schwer; In|halts‿über|sicht** (↑R 132), **...ver|zeich|nis; in|halt[s]|voll**
in|hä|rent ‹lat.› (anhaftend; innewohnend); **In|hä|renz,** die; - (*Philos.* die Zugehörigkeit der Eigenschaften zu ihren Trägern); **in|hä|rie|ren** (anhaften)
in hoc sa|lus ‹lat., „in diesem [ist] Heil"› (*Abk.* I. H. S.)
in hoc sig|no (↑R 130) ‹lat., „in diesem Zeichen"› (*Abk.* I. H. S.)
in|ho|mo|gen [*auch* ...'ge:n] ‹lat.; griech.› (ungleichartig); **In|ho|mo|ge|ni|tät** [*auch* 'in...], die; -
in ho|no|rem ‹lat.› (zu Ehren)
in|hu|man [*auch* ...'ma:n] ‹lat.› (unmenschlich; rücksichtslos); **In|hu|ma|ni|tät** [*auch* 'in...], die; -, -en
in in|fi|ni|tum *vgl.* ad infinitum
I|ni|ti|al (↑R 132) *vgl.* Initiale; **I|ni|ti|al|buch|sta|be; I|ni|ti|a|le,** die; -, -n ‹lat.›, *seltener* I|ni|ti|al, das; -s, -e (großer [meist verzierter] Anfangsbuchstabe); **I|ni|ti|al‿spreng|stoff** (Zündstoff für Initialzündungen), **...wort** (*Plur.* ...wörter; *Sprachw.*), **...zel|len** *(Plur.; Bot.)*, **...zün|dung** (Zündung eines schwer entzündlichen Sprengstoffs durch einen leicht entzündlichen)
I|ni|ti|and (↑R 132), der; -en, -en; ↑R 126 (Einzuweihender; Anwärter auf eine Initiation); **I|ni|ti|ant,** der; -en, -en; ↑R 126 (jemand, der die Initiative ergreift); **I|ni|ti|a|ti|on,** die; -, -en (*Soziol.* Aufnahme in eine Gemeinschaft; *Völkerk.* Reifefeier bei den Naturvölkern); **I|ni|ti|a|ti|ons|ri|tus** *meist Plur.*
i|ni|ti|a|tiv (↑R 132; Initiative ergreifend, besitzend); initiativ werden; **I|ni|ti|a|tiv|an|trag** (die parlamentarische Diskussion eines Problems einleitender Antrag); **I|ni|ti|a|ti|ve** [...və], die; -, -n ‹franz.› (erste tätige Anregung zu einer Handlung; Entschlusskraft, Unternehmungsgeist; *schweiz. auch für* Begehren nach Erlass, Änderung od. Aufhebung eines Gesetzes od. Verfassungsartikels); die Initiative ergreifen; **I|ni|ti|a|tiv|recht,** das; -[e]s (das Recht, Gesetzentwürfe einzubringen)
I|ni|ti|a|tor (↑R 132), der; -s, ...oren ‹lat.› (Urheber; Anstifter); **I|ni|ti|a|to|rin; I|ni|ti|en** *Plur.* (Anfänge; Anfangsgründe); **i|ni|ti|ie|ren** (den Anstoß geben; einleiten; [in ein Amt] einführen; einweihen)
In|jek|ti|on, die; -, -en ‹lat.› (*Med.* Einspritzung; *Geol.* Eindringen von Magma in Gesteinsspalten; *Bauw.* Bodenverfestigung durch das Einspritzen von Zement); **In|jek|ti|ons‿lö|sung** *(Med.)*, **...sprit|ze; In|jek|tor,** der; -s, ...oren (*Technik* Pressluftzubringer in Saugpumpen; Pumpe, die Wasser in einen Dampfkessel einspritzt); **in|ji|zie|ren** (einspritzen)
In|ju|rie [...iə], die; -, -n ‹lat.› (Unrecht, Beleidigung); **in|ju|ri|ie|ren** (*veraltet für* beleidigen)
In|ka, der; -[s], -[s] (Angehöriger der ehem. indian. Herrscher- u. Adelsschicht in Peru); **In|ka|bein** *od.* In|ka|kno|chen (*Med.* ein Schädelknochen); **in|ka|isch; In|ka|kno|chen** *vgl.* Inkabein
In|kar|di|na|ti|on, die; -, -en ‹lat.› (Zuteilung eines kath. Geistlichen an eine Diözese)
in|kar|nat ‹lat.› (*Kunstw., sonst veraltet für* fleischfarben); **In|kar|nat,** das; -[e]s (Fleischton [auf Gemälden]); **In|kar|na|ti|on,** die; -, -en ‹„Fleischwerdung"› (Verkörperung; *Rel.* Menschwerdung [Christi]); **In|kar|nat|rot,** das; -s; **in|kar|nie|ren,** sich (verkörpern); **in|kar|niert** (*Rel.* Fleisch geworden)
In|kas|sant, der; -en, -en (↑R 126) ‹ital.› (*österr. für* jmd., der Geld kassiert); **In|kas|san|tin; In|kas|so,** das; -s, *Plur.* -s *od., österr. auch,* ...kassi (*Bankw.* Einziehung von Geldforderungen); **In|kas|so‿bü|ro, ...voll|macht**
In|kauf|nah|me, die; -
inkl. = inklusive
In|kli|na|ti|on, die; -, -en ‹lat.› (Vorliebe, Zuneigung; *Physik* Neigung einer frei aufgehängten Magnetnadel zur Waagerechten; *Math.* Neigung zweier Ebenen od. einer Linie u. einer Ebene gegeneinander)
in|klu|si|ve [...və] ‹lat.› (einschließlich, inbegriffen; *Abk.* inkl.); *Präp. mit Gen.:* inklusive des Verpackungsmaterials; *ein allein stehendes, stark gebeugtes Substantiv steht im Sing. ungebeugt:* inklusive Porto; *mit Dat., wenn der Gen. nicht erkennbar ist:* inklusive Getränken
in|ko|gni|to (↑R 130) ‹ital., „unerkannt"› (unter fremdem Namen); - reisen; **In|ko|gni|to,** das; -s, -s
in|ko|hä|rent [*auch* ...'rɛnt] ‹lat.› (unzusammenhängend); **In|ko|hä|renz** [*auch* ...'rɛnts], die; -, -en
In|koh|lung (*Geol.* Umwandlung von Pflanzen in Kohle unter Luftabschluss)
in|kom|men|su|ra|bel ‹lat.› (nicht messbar; nicht vergleichbar); ...rab|le (↑R 130) Größen *(Math.)*
in|kom|mo|die|ren ‹lat.› (*veraltend für* belästigen; bemühen); sich - (sich Mühe machen); **In|kom|mo|di|tät,** die; -, -en (Unbequemlichkeit, Lästigkeit)
in|kom|pa|ra|bel [*auch* ...'ra:...] ‹lat.› (*veraltend für* unvergleichbar; *Sprachw.* nicht steigerungsfähig); ...ab|le (↑R 130) Verhältnisse
in|kom|pa|ti|bel [*auch* ...'ti:...] ‹lat.› (unverträglich; unvereinbar); ...ib|le (↑R 130) Blutgruppen; **In|kom|pa|ti|bi|li|tät,** die; -, -en
in|kom|pe|tent [*auch* ...'tɛnt] ‹lat.› (nicht zuständig, nicht befugt); **In|kom|pe|tenz** [*auch* ...'tɛnts], die; -, -en
in|kom|plett [*auch* ...'plɛt] ‹franz.› (unvollständig)
in|kom|pres|si|bel [*auch* ...'si:...] ‹lat.› (*Physik* nicht zusammenpressbar); ...ib|le (↑R 130) Materialien; **In|kom|pres|si|bi|li|tät,** die; -
in|kon|gru|ent [*auch* ...'ɛnt] ‹lat.› (nicht übereinstimmend; *Math.* nicht deckungsgleich); **In|kon|gru|enz** [*auch* ...'ɛnts], die; -, -en
in|kon|se|quent [*auch* ...'kvɛnt] ‹lat.› (nicht folgerichtig; widersprüchlich; wankelmütig); **In|kon|se|quenz** [*auch* ...'kvɛnts], die; -, -en
in|kon|sis|tent [*auch* ...'stɛnt] ‹lat.› (unbeständig; unhaltbar; widersprüchlich); **In|kon|sis|tenz** [*auch* ...'stɛnts], die; -
in|kon|stant [*auch* ...'stant] ‹lat.› (veränderlich, unbeständig); **In|kon|stanz** [*auch* ...'stants], die; - (inkonstante Beschaffenheit)
In|kon|ti|nenz [*auch* ...'nɛnts], die; -, -en ‹lat.› (*Med.* Unvermögen, Harn, Stuhl zurückzuhalten)
in|kon|ver|ti|bel [*auch* ...'ti:...] ‹lat.› (*Wirtsch.* nicht austauschbar [von Währungen]); ...ib|le (↑R 130) Währungen
in|kon|zi|li|ant [*auch* ...'liant] ‹lat.› (nicht umgänglich)

in|kor|po|ral ‹lat.› (*Med.* im Körper [befindlich]); **In|kor|po|ra|ti|on,** die; -, -en (Einverleibung; Aufnahme); **in|kor|po|rie|ren; In|kor|po|rie|rung**

in|kor|rekt [*auch* ...ˈrɛkt] ‹lat.› ([sprachlich] ungenau, fehlerhaft; unangemessen); **In|kor|rekt|heit** [*auch* ...ˈrɛkt...]

in Kraft *vgl.* Kraft; **In|kraft|set|zung** *(Amtsspr.);* **In-Kraft-Tre|ten,** das; -s (eines Gesetzes; ↑R 28 *u.* 50); *vgl. auch* Kraft

In|kreis, der; -es, -e (*Math.* einer Figur einbeschriebener Kreis)

In|kre|ment, das; -[e]s, -e ‹lat.› (*Math.* Betrag, um den eine Größe zunimmt)

In|kret, das; -[e]s, -e ‹lat.› (*Med.* von Drüsen ins Blut abgegebener Stoff, Hormon); **In|kre|ti|on,** die; - (innere Sekretion); **in|kre|to|risch** (die innere Sekretion betreffend, auf ihr beruhend)

in|kri|mi|nie|ren ‹lat.› (beschuldigen; unter Anklage stellen); **in|kri|mi|niert** (beschuldigt)

In|krus|ta|ti|on, die; -, -en ‹lat.› (farbige Verzierung von Flächen durch Einlagen; *Geol.* Krustenbildung); **in|krus|tie|ren**

In|ku|ba|ti|on, die; -, -en ‹lat.› (Tempelschlaf in der Antike; *Zool.* Bebrütung von Vogeleiern; *Med.* das Sichfestsetzen von Krankheitserregern im Körper; *auch kurz für* Inkubationszeit); **In|ku|ba|ti|ons|zeit** (Zeit von der Infektion bis zum Ausbruch einer Krankheit); **In|ku|ba|tor,** der; -s, ...oren (Brutkasten [für Frühgeburten]; Brutschrank); **In|ku|bus,** der; -, Inkuben (Buhlteufel des mittelalterl. Hexenglaubens); *vgl.* Sukkubus

in|ku|lant [*auch* ...ˈlant] ‹franz.› ([geschäftlich] ungefällig); **In|ku|lanz** [*auch* ...ˈlants], die; -, -en

In|kul|pant, der; -en, -en (↑R 126) ‹lat.› (*Rechtsspr. veraltet* Ankläger); **In|kul|pat,** der; -en, -en; ↑R 126 (*Rechtsspr. veraltet* Angeschuldigter)

In|ku|na|bel, die; -, -n *meist Plur.* ‹lat.› (Wiegen-, Frühdruck, Druck aus der Zeit vor 1500)

in|ku|ra|bel [*auch* ...ˈra:...] ‹lat.› (*Med.* unheilbar); ...ab|le (↑R 130) Krankheit

In|laid, der; -s, -e ‹engl.› (durchgemustertes Linoleum)

In|land, das; -[e]s; **In|land|eis; In|län|der,** der; **In|län|de|rin; In|land|flug; in|län|disch; In|lands‿brief, ...ge|spräch, ...markt, ...por|to, ...preis, ...rei|se**

In|laut; in|lau|tend

In|lay [ˈinle:], das; -s, -s ‹engl., „Einlegestück“› (aus Metall od. Porzellan gegossene Zahnfüllung)

In|lett, das; -[e]s, *Plur.* -e *od.* -s (Baumwollstoff [für Federbetten u. -kissen])

in|lie|gend *vgl.* einliegend; **In|lie|gen|de,** das; -n (↑R 5 ff.)

In|li|ner [ˈinlaɪnə(r)], der; -s, - ‹engl.› (Rollschuh mit schmalen, in einer Linie hintereinander angeordneten Rädchen)

in ma|io|rem Dei glo|ri|am *vgl.* ad maiorem Dei gloriam

in me|di|as res ‹lat., „mitten in die Dinge hinein“› ([unmittelbar] zur Sache)

in me|mo|ri|am ‹lat., „zum Gedächtnis“› (zum Andenken); - - Maria Theresia

in|mit|ten *(geh.);* ↑R 41; *als Präp. mit Gen.:* inmitten des Sees

Inn, der; -[s] (r. Nebenfluss der Donau)

in na|tu|ra ‹lat.› (in Wirklichkeit; *ugs. für* in Form von Naturalien)

in|ne (↑R 39); inne sein *(geh.);* er ist dieses Erlebnisses inne gewesen; ehe er dessen inne ist, inne war; *vgl. aber* innehaben, innewerden usw.; mitteninne; **in|ne|ha|ben;** seit er dieses Amt innehat; er hat dieses Amt innegehabt; **in|ne|hal|ten;** er hat mitten im Satz innegehalten

in|nen; von, nach innen; innen und außen; **In|nen‿an|ten|ne, ...ar|bei|ten** *(Plur.),* **...ar|chi|tekt, ...ar|chi|tek|tin, ...ar|chi|tek|tur** (die; -), **...auf|nah|me, ...aus|stat|tung, ...bahn** *(Sport),* **...dienst, ...ein|rich|tung, ...flä|che, ...hand** *(Boxen),* **...hof, ...kan|te, ...kur|ve, ...le|ben** (das; -s), **...mi|nis|ter, ...mi|nis|te|rin, ...mi|nis|te|ri|um, ...po|li|tik** (die; -); **in|nen|po|li|tisch,** in|ner|po|li|tisch; **In|nen‿raum, ...rist** (*bes. Fußball* innere Seite des Fußrückens), **...sei|te, ...spie|gel, ...stadt, ...stür|mer, ...ta|sche, ...tem|pe|ra|tur, ...ver|tei|di|ger, ...welt** (die; -)

In|ner|asi|en (↑R 132); **in|ner‿be|trieb|lich, ...deutsch, ...dienst|lich; in|ne|re;** innerste; zuinnerst; die innere Medizin; innere Angelegenheiten eines Staates; innere Führung (*Bez. für* geistige Rüstung u. zeitgemäße Menschenführung in der dt. Bundeswehr); die äußere und die innere Mission, *aber* (↑R 108): die Innere Mission (Organisation der ev. Kirche; *Abk.* I. M.); (↑R 102:) die Innere Mongolei; **In|ne|re,** das; ...r[e]n; das Ministerium des Innern; im Inner[e]n (↑R 5 ff.); **In|ne|rei|en** *Plur.* (z. B. Leber, Herz, Gedärme von Schlachttieren); **in|ner|halb;** *als Präp. mit Gen.:* innerhalb eines Jahres, zweier Jahre; *im Plur. mit Dat., wenn der Gen. nicht erkennbar ist:* innerhalb vier Jahren, vier Tagen; **in|ner|lich; In|ner|lich|keit,** die; -; **in|ner|orts** (*bes. schweiz. für* innerhalb des Ortes); **In|ner|ös|ter|reich** (*hist. Bez. für* Steiermark, Kärnten, Krain, Görz; *heute westösterr. für* Ostösterreich); **in|ner|par|tei|lich; in|ner|po|li|tisch,** in|nen|po|li|tisch; **In|ner|rho|den** (*kurz für* Appenzell Innerrhoden); **in|ner‿sek|re|to|risch** (↑R 130; *Med.* die innere Sekretion betreffend, auf ihr beruhend), **...staat|lich; In|ner|stadt** (*schweiz. veraltend für* Innenstadt); **in|ner|städ|tisch;** der -e Verkehr; **In|ners|te,** das; -n (↑R 5 ff.); im Innersten; bis ins Innerste; **in|nert** (*schweiz. u. westösterr. für* innerhalb, binnen); innert eines Jahres *od.* innert einem Jahre; innert drei Tagen

In|ner|va|ti|on [...v...], die; -, -en ‹lat.› (*Med.* Versorgung der Körperteile mit Nerven; Reizübertragung durch Nerven); **in|ner|vie|ren** (mit Nerven od. Nervenreizen versehen; *übertr. auch für* anregen, Auftrieb geben)

in|ne sein *vgl.* inne; **in|ne|wer|den** *(geh.);* er ist sich seines schlechten Verhaltens innegeworden; ehe er dessen innewurde; **in|ne|woh|nen** *(geh.);* auch diesen alten Methoden hat Gutes innegewohnt

in|nig; In|nig|keit, die; -; **in|nig|lich; in|nigst**

in no|mi|ne ‹lat., „im Namen“› (im Auftrage); - - Dei (in Gottes Namen; *Abk.* I. N. D.); - - Domini (im Namen des Herrn; *Abk.* I. N. D.)

In|no|va|ti|on [...v...], die; -, -en ‹lat.› (Erneuerung; Neuerung [durch Anwendung neuer Verfahren u. Techniken]); **In|no|va|ti|ons|spross** ‹lat.; dt.› (*Bot.* Erneuerungsspross einer mehrjährigen Pflanze); **in|no|va|tiv** (Innovationen betreffend, schaffend); **in|no|va|to|risch** (Innovationen anstrebend)

In|no|zenz (m. Vorn.)

Inns|bruck (Hptst. von Tirol)

in nu|ce [- ˈnu:tsə] ‹lat.› (im Kern; in Kürze, kurz und bündig)

In|nung; In|nungs|meis|ter

Inn|vier|tel, das; -s; ↑R 105 (Landschaft in Österreich)

in|of|fen|siv [*auch* ...'zi:f] ‹lat.› (nicht offensiv)
in|of|fi|zi|ell [*auch* ...'tsi̯ɛl] ‹franz.› (nicht amtlich; außerdienstlich; vertraulich; nicht förmlich); **in|of|fi|zi|ös** [*auch* ...'tsi̯ø:s] (nicht offiziös)
in|ope|ra|bel [*auch* ...'ra:b(ə)l] (↑R 132) ‹franz.› (*Med.* nicht operierbar); ...ab|le (↑R 130) Verletzungen
in|op|por|tun [*auch* ...'tu:n] ‹lat.› (ungelegen, unangebracht); **In|op|por|tu|ni|tät** [*auch* 'in...], die; -, -en
I|no|sit [*auch* ...'zit], der; -s, -e ‹griech.› (in pflanzl. u. tierischen Geweben vorkommender Zucker); **I|nos|u|rie**, die; -, ...i̯en (*Med.* Auftreten von Inosit im Harn)
in per|pe|tu|um [- ...tu|um] ‹lat.› (auf immer)
in per|so|na ‹lat.› (persönlich)
in pet|to ‹ital.›; etwas in petto (*ugs. für* im Sinne, bereit) haben
in ple|no ‹lat.› (in, vor der Vollversammlung, vollzählig)
in pra|xi ‹lat.; griech.› (im wirklichen Leben; tatsächlich)
in punc|to ‹lat.› (hinsichtlich); in puncto puncti („im Punkte des Punktes"; *scherzh. für* hinsichtlich der Keuschheit)
In|put, der, *auch* das; -s, -s ‹engl.› (*Wirtsch.* von außen bezogene u. im Betrieb eingesetzte Produktionsmittel; *EDV* Eingabe); **In|put-Out|put-A|na|ly|se** ['input-'autput...]
in|qui|rie|ren ‹lat.› (*veraltend für* untersuchen, verhören); **In|qui|si|ten|spi|tal** (*österr. für* Gefangenenkrankenhaus); **In|qui|si|ti|on**, die; -, -en (*nur Sing.*: mittelalterl. kath. Ketzergericht; Untersuchung [dieses Gerichts]); **In|qui|si|ti|ons|ge|richt; In|qui|si|tor**, der; -s, ...oren (Richter der Inquisition); **in|qui|si|to|risch**
I. N. R. I. = Jesus Nazarenus Rex Judaeorum
ins; ↑R 13 (in das); eins ins andre gerechnet
in sal|do ‹ital.› (*veraltet für* im Rückstand)
In|sas|se, der; -n, -n (↑R 126); **In|sas|sen|ver|si|che|rung; In|sas|sin**
ins|be|son|de|re, ins|be|sond|re (↑R 67); insbesond[e]re[,] wenn (↑R 88)
in|schal|lah ‹arab.› (wenn Allah will [muslim. Redensart])
In|schrift; In|schrif|ten‿kun|de (die; -), **...samm|lung; in|schrift|lich**

In|sekt, das; -[e]s, -en ‹lat.› (Kerbtier); Insekten fressende Pflanzen, Tiere; **In|sek|ta|ri|um**, das; -s, ...ien [...i̯ən] (Anlage für Insektenaufzucht); **In|sek|ten‿be|kämp|fung, ...fraß; In|sek|ten fres|send** *vgl.* Insekt; **In|sek|ten‿fres|ser, ...gift, ...haus** (Anlage zur Aufzucht u. zum Studium der Insekten; Insektarium), **...kun|de** (die; -), **...pla|ge, ...pul|ver, ...stich, ...ver|til|gungs|mit|tel** (das); **[1]In|sek|ti|vo|re** [...v...], der; -n, -n *meist Plur.* (*Zool.* Insektenfresser); **[2]In|sek|ti|vo|re**, die; -n, -n *meist Plur.* (*Bot.* Insekten fressende Pflanze); **In|sek|ti|zid**, das; -s, -e (Insekten tötendes Mittel)
In|sel, die; -, -n ‹lat.›; **In|sel‿berg, ...be|woh|ner, ...grup|pe; In|sel|land** *Plur.* ...länder
In|sels|berg, der; -[e]s (im Thüringer Wald)
In|sel|staat *Plur.* ...staaten
In|se|mi|na|ti|on, die; -, -en ‹lat.› ([künstl.] Befruchtung)
in|sen|si|bel [*auch* ...zi:b(ə)l] ‹lat.› (unempfindlich; gefühllos); **In|sen|si|bi|li|tät** [*auch* 'in...], die; -
In|se|rat, das; -[e]s, -e ‹lat.› (Anzeige [in Zeitungen usw.]); **In|se|ra|ten|teil**, der; **In|se|rent**, der; -en, -en; ↑R 126 (jmd., der ein Inserat aufgibt); **In|se|ren|tin; in|se|rie|ren** (ein Inserat aufgeben); **In|sert**, das; -s, -s ‹engl.› (Inserat mit beigehefteter Bestellkarte; im Fernsehen eingeblendete Schautafel); **In|ser|ti|on**, die; -, -en ‹lat.› (Aufgeben einer Anzeige; *Med.* Muskelansatz); **In|ser|ti|ons|preis**
ins|ge|heim [*österr.* 'ins...]; **ins|ge|mein** [*österr.* 'ins...] (*veraltet*); **ins|ge|samt** [*österr.* 'ins...]
In|side ['insai̯d], der; -[s], -s ‹engl.› (*schweiz. für* Innenstürmer); **In|si|der** ['insai̯də(r)], der; -s, - (jmd., der interne Kenntnisse von etwas besitzt; Eingeweihter); **In|side|sto|ry** ['insai̯d...] (Geschichte, die aufgrund interner Kenntnis von etwas geschrieben wurde)
In|sie|gel (*veraltet für* Siegelbild; *Jägerspr.* Fährtenzeichen des Rotwildes)
In|si|gni|en [...i̯ən] (↑R 130) *Plur.* ‹lat.› (Abzeichen, Symbole der Macht u. Würde); **in|si|gni|fi|kant** [*auch* ...'kant] (unwichtig)
in|sis|tent ‹lat.› (beharrlich); **In|sis|tenz**, die; - (Beharrlichkeit, Hartnäckigkeit); **in|sis|tie|ren** (auf etwas bestehen, dringen)
in si|tu ‹lat., „in [natürlicher] Lage"› (*bes. Med., Archäol.*)

in|skri|bie|ren ‹lat.› (in eine Liste aufnehmen; *bes. österr. für* sich für das laufende Semester als Hörer an einer Universität anmelden); **In|skrip|ti|on**, die; -, -en
ins|künf|tig (*schweiz., sonst veraltet für* zukünftig, fortan)
in|so|fern [*auch* ...'fɛrn *od., österr. nur,* 'in...]; insofern hast du Recht; insofern du nichts dagegen hast, werden wir ...; insofern[,] als (↑R 88)
In|so|la|ti|on, die; -, -en ‹lat.› (*Meteor.* Sonnenbestrahlung; *Med.* Sonnenstich)
in|so|lent [*auch* ...'lɛnt] ‹lat.› (anmaßend, unverschämt); **In|so|lenz** [*auch* ...'lɛnts], die; -, -en
in|sol|vent [*auch* ...'vɛnt] ‹lat.› (*Wirtsch.* zahlungsunfähig); **In|sol|venz** [*auch* ...'vɛnts], die; -, -en
in Son|der|heit *vgl.* Sonderheit
in|so|weit [*auch* ...'vai̯t *od., österr. nur,* 'in...]; insoweit hast du Recht; insoweit es möglich ist, ...; insoweit[,] als (↑R 88)
in spe [- 'spe:] ‹lat., „in der Hoffnung"› (zukünftig)
In|spek|teur [...'tø:r] (↑R 132), der; -s, -e ‹franz.› (Leiter einer Inspektion; Dienststellung der ranghöchsten Offiziere der Bundeswehr); **In|spek|ti|on**, die; -, -en ‹lat.› (Besichtigung; [regelmäßige] Wartung [eines Kraftfahrzeugs]; Dienststelle); **In|spek|ti|ons‿fahrt, ...gang** (der), **...rei|se; In|spek|tor**, der; -s, ...oren (jmd., der etwas inspiziert; Verwaltungsbeamter); **In|spek|to|rin**
In|spi|ra|ti|on (↑R 132), die; -, -en ‹lat.› (Eingebung; Erleuchtung); **In|spi|ra|tor**, der; -s, ...oren (jmd., der andere zu etwas anregt); **in|spi|rie|ren**
In|spi|zi|ent (↑R 132), der; -en, -en (↑R 126) ‹lat.› (*Theater, Fernsehen usw.* jmd., der für den reibungslosen Ablauf einer Aufführung verantwortlich ist); **In|spi|zi|en|tin; in|spi|zie|ren** (prüfen); **In|spi|zie|rung**
in|sta|bil [*auch* ...'bi:l] ‹lat.› (nicht konstant bleibend; unbeständig); **In|sta|bi|li|tät** [*auch* 'in...], die; -, -en *Plur. selten* (Unbeständigkeit)
In|stal|la|teur [...'tø:r] (↑R 132), der; -s, -e ‹franz.› (Handwerker für Installationen); **In|stal|la|teu|rin** [...'tø:rin]; **In|stal|la|ti|on**, die; -, -en (Einrichtung, Einbau, Anlage, Anschluss von techn. Anlagen); **in|stal|lie|ren**
in|stand, *auch* **in Stand;** etwas instand, *auch* in Stand halten, setzen, (*schweiz.:* stellen); ein Haus

instand, *auch* in Stand besetzen (*ugs. für* widerrechtlich besetzen und wieder bewohnbar machen); **In|stand|be|set|zer** *(ugs.);* **in-stand hal|ten** *vgl.* instand; **In-stand|hal|tung; In|stand|hal-tungs|kos|ten** *Plur.*
in|stän|dig (eindringlich; flehentlich); **In|stän|dig|keit,** die; -
in|stand set|zen *vgl.* instand; **In-stand|set|zung; in|stand stel-len** *vgl.* instand; **In|stand|stel-lung** (*schweiz. neben* Instandsetzung)
in|stant [*auch* 'instənt] ‹engl.› (sofort löslich, in kürzester Zeit zum Genuss bereit); *nur als nachgestellte Beifügung,* z. B. Haferflocken instant; **In|stant...** (*in Zusammensetzungen,* z. B. Instantgetränk, Instantkaffee)
In|stanz, die; -, -en ‹lat.› (zuständige Stelle bei Behörden od. Gerichten); **In|stan|zen|weg** (Dienstweg)
in sta|tu nas|cen|di [- ˌsta:tu: nas'tsɛndi] ‹lat.› (im Zustand des Entstehens); **in sta|tu quo** (im gegenwärtigen Zustand); **in sta|tu quo an|te** (im früheren Zustand)
Ins|te, der; -n, -n; ↑R 126 (*nordd. früher für* Gutstagelöhner)
In|stil|la|ti|on, die; -, -en ‹lat.› (*Med.* Einträufelung); **in|stil|lie-ren**
Ins|tinkt (↑R 132), der; -[e]s, -e ‹lat.› (angeborene Verhaltensweise [bes. bei Tieren]; *auch für* sicheres Gefühl); **ins|tinkt|haft; Ins|tinkt|hand|lung; ins|tink|tiv** (trieb-, gefühlsmäßig, unwillkürlich); **ins|tinkt|los; Ins|tinkt|lo-sig|keit; ins|tinkt|mä|ßig; ins-tinkt|si|cher**
in|sti|tu|ie|ren ‹lat.› (einrichten); **In|sti|tut,** das; -[e]s, -e (Unternehmen; Bildungs-, Forschungsanstalt); **In|sti|tu|ti|on,** die; -,-en (öffentliche [staatliche, kirchliche o. Ä.] Einrichtung); **in|sti|tu|ti|o-na|li|sie|ren** (in eine feste, auch starre Institution verwandeln); **In|sti|tu|ti|o|na|li|sie|rung; in-sti|tu|ti|o|nell** (die Institution betreffend); **In|sti|tuts‿bib|li|o-thek, ...di|rek|tor, ...di|rek|to|rin, ...lei|ter** (der), **...lei|te|rin**
Inst|mann, der; -[e]s, ...leute ‹*zu* Inste› (*nordd. früher für* Gutstagelöhner)
in|stru|ie|ren ‹lat.› (unterweisen; anleiten); **In|struk|teur** [...'tø:r], der; -s, -e ‹franz.› (jmd., der andere instruiert); **In|struk|ti-on,** die; -, -en ‹lat.› (Anleitung; [Dienst]anweisung); **in|struk|tiv** (lehrreich); **In|struk|tor,** der; -s, ...oren (*österr. u. schweiz. für* Instrukteur)
In|stru|ment, das; -[e]s, -e ‹lat.›; **in|stru|men|tal** (Musikinstrumente verwendend); **In|stru-men|tal,** der; -s, -e (*Sprachw.* Fall, der das Mittel bezeichnet); **In|stru|men|tal|be|glei|tung; In-stru|men|ta|lis,** der; -, ...les [...le:s]; *vgl.* Instrumental; **In-stru|men|ta|list,** der; -en, -en (↑R 126); **In|stru|men|ta|lis|tin; In|stru|men|tal‿mu|sik** (die; -), **...satz** (*Sprachw.* Umstandssatz des Mittels); **In|stru|men|ta|ri-um,** das; -s, ...ien [...iən] (Gesamtheit der zur Verfügung stehenden Instrumente); **In|stru|men|ta|ti-on,** die; -, -en (Instrumentierung); **in|stru|men|tell** (mit Instrumenten); **In|stru|men|ten-‿bau** (der; -[e]s), **...brett, ...flug** *(Flugw.),* **...ma|cher, ...ma|che-rin; in|stru|men|tie|ren** ([ein Musikstück] für Orchesterinstrumente einrichten; mit [techn.] Instrumenten ausstatten); **In|stru-men|tie|rung**
In|sub|or|di|na|ti|on [*auch* 'in...], die; -, -en ‹lat.› (mangelnde Unterordnung; Ungehorsam im Dienst)
in|suf|fi|zi|ent [*auch* ...'tsiɛnt] ‹lat.› (unzulänglich); **In|suf|fi|zi|enz** [*auch* ...'tsiɛnts], die; -, -en (Unzulänglichkeit; *Med.* mangelhafte Funktion eines Organs; *Rechtsspr.* Überschuldung)
In|su|la|ner ‹lat.› (Inselbewohner); **in|su|lar** (eine Insel od. Inseln betreffend, inselartig); **In|su|lin,** das; -s (ein Hormon; ® ein Arzneimittel); **In|su|lin‿man|gel** (der; -s; *Med.*), **...prä|pa|rat, ...schock**
In|sult, der; -[e]s, -e ‹lat.› ([schwere] Beleidigung; *Med.* [Schlag]anfall); **In|sul|ta|ti|on,** die; -, -en; **in|sul|tie|ren** ([schwer] beleidigen)
in sum|ma ‹lat.› (*veraltend für* insgesamt)
In|sur|gent, der; -en, -en (↑R 126) ‹lat.› (Aufständischer); **in|sur-gie|ren** (zum Aufstand anstacheln; einen Aufstand machen); **In|sur|rek|ti|on,** die; -, -en (Aufstand)
in|sze|na|to|risch ‹lat.; griech.› (die Inszenierung betreffend); **in-sze|nie|ren** (eine Bühnenaufführung vorbereiten; geschickt ins Werk setzen); **In|sze|nie|rung**
In|tag|lio [in'taljo] (↑R 130), das; -s, ...ien [in'taljən] ‹ital.› (Gemme mit eingeschnittenen Figuren)
in|takt ‹lat.› (unversehrt, unberührt; funktionsfähig); **In|takt-heit,** die; -; **In|takt|sein,** das; -s
In|tar|sia, *häufiger* **In|tar|sie** [...iə], die; -, ...ien [...iən] *meist Plur.* ‹ital.› (Einlegearbeit); **In|tar-si|en|ma|le|rei**
in|te|ger ‹lat.› (unbescholten; unversehrt); ein in|teg|rer (↑R 130) Charakter
in|teg|ral (↑R 130; ein Ganzes ausmachend; vollständig; für sich bestehend); **In|teg|ral,** das; -s, -e (*Math.; Zeichen* ∫); **In|teg|ral-‿glei|chung, ...helm** (Kopf u. Hals bedeckender Schutzhelm bes. für Motorradfahrer), **...rech-nung; In|teg|ra|ti|on,** die; -, -en (Vervollständigung; Eingliederung, Vereinigung); **in|teg|ra|tiv** (eingliedernd); **in|teg|rier|bar; in|teg|rie|ren** (ergänzen; eingliedern; *Math.* das Integral berechnen); **in|teg|rie|rend** (notwendig [zu einem Ganzen gehörend]); ein integrierender Bestandteil; **in-teg|riert;** integrierte Gesamtschule; integrierte Schaltung *(Elektronik);* **In|teg|rie|rung; In-teg|ri|tät,** die; - (Unbescholtenheit; Unverletzlichkeit)
In|te|gu|ment, das; -s, -e ‹lat.› (*Biol.* Hautschichten von Tier u. Mensch; *Bot.* Hülle um die Samenanlage)
In|tel|lekt, der; -[e]s ‹lat.› (Verstand; Erkenntnis-, Denkvermögen); **In|tel|lek|tu|a|lis|mus,** der; - (philos. Lehre, die dem Intellekt den Vorrang gibt; einseitig verstandesmäßiges Denken); **in|tel-lek|tu|ell** ‹franz.› (den Intellekt betreffend; [einseitig] verstandesmäßig; geistig); **In|tel|lek|tu|el-le,** der *u.* die; -n, -n; ↑R 5 ff. ([einseitiger] Verstandesmensch; geistig Geschulte[r]); **in|tel|li|gent** ‹lat.› (verständig; klug, begabt); -e Maschinen (computergesteuerte Automaten); **In|tel|li|genz,** die; -, -en (besondere geistige Fähigkeit, Klugheit; *meist Plur.:* Vernunftwesen; *nur Sing.:* Schicht der Intellektuellen); **In|tel|li|genz|bes-tie** (*salopp für* Person, die ihre Intelligenz in auffallender Weise nach außen hin zeigt); **In|tel|li-genz‿grad, ...leis|tung; In|tel|li-genz|ler,** der; -s, - ‹lat.› (*oft abwertend für* Angehöriger der Intelligenz); **In|tel|li|genz‿quo|ti-ent** (Maß für die intellektuelle Leistungsfähigkeit; *Abk.* IQ), **...test; in|tel|li|gi|bel** (*Philos.* nur durch den Intellekt, nicht sinnlich wahrnehmbar); die ...ib|le (↑R 130) Welt (Ideenwelt)
In|ten|dant, der; -en, -en (↑R 126)

‹franz.› (Leiter eines Theaters, eines Rundfunk- od. Fernsehsenders); **In|ten|dan|tin; In|ten|dan|tur,** die; -, -en (*veraltet für* Amt eines Intendanten; Verwaltungsbehörde eines Heeres); **In|ten|danz,** die; -, -en (Amt, Büro eines Intendanten); **in|ten|die|ren** ‹lat.› (beabsichtigen, anstreben)

In|ten|si|me|ter, das; -s, - ‹lat.; griech.› (Messgerät für Röntgenstrahlen); **In|ten|si|on,** die; -, -en ‹lat.› (Anspannung; Eifer); **In|ten|si|tät,** die; -, -en *Plur. selten* (Stärke, Kraft; Wirksamkeit); **in|ten|siv** (eindringlich; kräftig; gründlich; durchdringend); -e Bewirtschaftung (*Landw.* Form der Bodennutzung mit großem Einsatz von Arbeitskraft u. Kapital); **In|ten|siv‿an|bau** (der; -s), **...hal|tung** (die; -); **in|ten|si|vie|ren** [...v...] (verstärken, steigern); **In|ten|si|vie|rung; In|ten|siv‿kurs, ...pfle|ge, ...sta|ti|on; In|ten|si|vum** [...vum], das; -s, ...va [...va] (*Sprachw.* Verb, das die Intensität eines Geschehens kennzeichnet, z. B. „schnitzen" = kräftig schneiden)

In|ten|ti|on, die; -, -en ‹lat.› (Absicht; Plan; Vorhaben); **in|ten|ti|o|nal** (zweckbestimmt; zielgerichtet)

in|ter|agie|ren (↑R 132) ‹lat.› (*Psych., Soziol.* Interaktion betreiben); **In|ter|ak|ti|on,** die; -, -en (Wechselbeziehung zwischen Personen u. Gruppen); **in|ter|ak|tiv; In|ter|ak|ti|vi|tät,** die; - (*bes. EDV* Dialog zwischen Computer und Benutzer)

in|ter|al|li|iert [*auch* 'in...] ‹lat.› (mehrere Alliierte betreffend; aus Verbündeten bestehend)

In|ter|ci|ty [...'siti], der; -s, -s ‹engl.-amerik.›; *kurz für* Intercityzug; **In|ter|ci|ty|ex|press|zug** (besonders schneller Intercityzug; *Abk.* ICE); **In|ter|ci|ty|zug** (schneller, zwischen bestimmten Großstädten [im Stundentakt] eingesetzter Eisenbahnzug; *Abk.* IC)

in|ter|de|pen|dent ‹lat.› (voneinander abhängend); **In|ter|de|pen|denz,** die; -, -en (gegenseitige Abhängigkeit)

In|ter|dikt, das; -[e]s, -e ‹lat.› (Verbot kirchlicher Amtshandlungen als Strafmaßnahme der kath. Kirchenbehörde)

in|ter|dis|zip|li|när [*auch* 'in...] ‹lat.› (zwischen Disziplinen bestehend, mehrere Disziplinen betreffend)

in|te|res|sant (↑R 132) ‹franz.›; **in|te|res|san|ter|wei|se; In|te|res|sant|heit,** die; -

In|te|res|se (↑R 132), das; -s, -n ‹lat.›; - an, für etwas haben; *vgl.* Interessen; **in|te|res|se|hal|ber; in|te|res|se|los; In|te|res|se|lo|sig|keit,** die; -; **In|te|res|sen** *Plur.* (*veraltet für* Zinsen); **In|te|res|sen‿aus|gleich, ...ge|biet, ...ge|mein|schaft** (Zweckverband), **...grup|pe, ...kon|flikt, ...la|ge, ...sphä|re** (Einflussgebiet)

In|te|res|sent (↑R 132), der; -en, -en (↑R 126); **In|te|res|sen|ten|kreis; In|te|res|sen|tin**

In|te|res|sen‿ver|band (↑R 132), **...ver|tre|tung**

in|te|res|sie|ren (↑R 132; Teilnahme erwecken); jmdn. an, für etwas -; sich - (Anteil nehmen, Sinn haben) für ...; **in|te|res|siert** (Anteil nehmend; beteiligt); **In|te|res|siert|heit,** die; -

In|ter|face [...fe:s], das; -, ...ces [..səs, *engl.* ...siz] ‹engl.› (*EDV svw.* Schnittstelle)

In|ter|fe|renz, die; -, -en ‹lat.› (*Physik* Überlagerung von Wellen; *Sprachw.* Abweichung von der Norm durch den Einfluss anderer sprachlicher Elemente; Verwechslung, falscher Gebrauch); **in|ter|fe|rie|ren** (überlagern; einwirken); **In|ter|fe|ro|me|ter,** das; -s, - ‹lat.; griech.› (ein physikal. Messgerät); **In|ter|fe|ron,** das; -s, -e (*Biol., Med.* bei Infektionen wirksame, körpereigene Abwehrsubstanz)

In|ter|flug, die; - ‹lat.; dt.› (ehem. Luftfahrtgesellschaft der DDR)

in|ter|frak|ti|o|nell ‹lat.› (zwischen Fraktionen bestehend, ihnen gemeinsam)

in|ter|ga|lak|tisch ‹lat.; griech.› (*Astron.* zwischen mehreren Galaxien gelegen)

in|ter|gla|zi|al ‹lat.› (*Geol.* zwischeneiszeitlich); **In|ter|gla|zi|al|zeit,** die; -

In|ter|ho|tel ‹lat.; franz.› (*ehem. in der DDR* besonders gut ausgestattetes Hotel [für internationale Gäste])

In|te|ri|eur [ɛ̃te'ri̯ø:r], das; -s, *Plur.* -s *u.* -e ‹franz.› (Inneres; Ausstattung eines Innenraumes; einen Innenraum darstellendes Bild)

In|te|rim, das; -s, -s ‹lat.› (Zwischenzeit, -zustand; vorläufige Regelung); **in|te|ri|mis|tisch** (vorläufig, einstweilig); **In|te|rims‿kon|to, ...lö|sung, In|te|rims|re|ge|lung** *od.* ...reg|lung; **...re|gie|rung, ...schein** (vorläufiger Anteilschein statt der eigentlichen Aktie)

In|ter|jek|ti|on, die; -, -en ‹lat.› (*Sprachw.* Ausrufe-, Empfindungswort, z. B. „au", „bäh")

in|ter|ka|lar ‹lat.› (eingeschaltet [von Schaltjahren])

in|ter|kan|to|nal ‹lat.; franz.› (*schweiz. für* mehrere [od. alle] Kantone betreffend)

In|ter|ko|lum|nie [...i̯ə], die; -, -n *u.* **In|ter|ko|lum|ni|um,** das; -s, ...ien [...i̯ən] ‹lat.› (*Archit.* Säulenabstand bei einem antiken Tempel)

in|ter|kom|mu|nal ‹lat.› (zwischen Gemeinden bestehend)

in|ter|kon|fes|si|o|nell ‹lat.› (das Verhältnis verschiedener Konfessionen zueinander betreffend)

in|ter|kon|ti|nen|tal ‹lat.› (Erdteile verbindend); **In|ter|kon|ti|nen|tal|ra|ke|te** (*Milit.* Rakete mit sehr großer Reichweite)

in|ter|kos|tal ‹lat.› (*Med.* zwischen den Rippen)

in|ter|kur|rent ‹lat.› (*Med.* hinzukommend); -e Krankheit

In|ter|la|ken (schweiz. Kurort)

in|ter|li|ne|ar ‹lat.› (zwischen die Zeilen des Urtextes geschrieben); **In|ter|li|ne|ar‿glos|se** (zwischen die Zeilen geschriebene Glosse; *vgl.* Glosse), **...über|set|zung** (↑R 132), **...ver|si|on**

In|ter|lock|wa|re ‹engl.; dt.› (feine Wirkware für Trikotagen)

In|ter|lu|di|um, das; -s, ...ien [...i̯ən] ‹lat.› (*Musik* Zwischenspiel)

In|ter|lu|ni|um, das; -s, ...ien [...i̯ən] ‹lat.› (Zeit des Neumondes)

In|ter|ma|xil|lar|kno|chen ‹lat.; dt.› (*Med.* Zwischenkiefer)

in|ter|me|di|är ‹lat.› (*fachspr. für* dazwischen befindlich; ein Zwischenglied bildend)

In|ter|mez|zo, das; -s, *Plur.* -s *u.* ...zzi ‹ital.› (Zwischenspiel, -fall)

in|ter|mi|nis|te|ri|ell (zwischen Ministerien bestehend, mehrere Ministerien betreffend)

in|ter|mit|tie|rend ‹lat.› (zeitweilig aussetzend); -es Fieber

in|tern ‹lat.› (nur die inneren, eigenen Verhältnisse angehend; vertraulich; *Med.* innerlich; *veraltend für* im Internat wohnend [von Schülern]); **In|ter|na** (*Plur. von* Internum); **in|ter|na|li|sie|ren** (*Psych.* sich [unbewusst] zu eigen machen); **In|ter|nat,** das; -[e]s, -e (einer [höheren] Schule angeschlossenes Wohnheim; Internatsschule)

in|ter|na|ti|o|nal ‹lat.› (zwischenstaatlich, nicht national begrenzt); internationales Recht; eine internationale Vereinbarung; internationales Einheitensystem (*Abk.* SI *(vgl. d.)*); internationale Einheit (*Abk.* I. E. *od.* IE *(vgl. d.)*); *aber* (↑R 108): Internationale Handelskammer (*Abk.* IHK); Internationales Olympisches Komitee (*Abk.* IOK); Internationales Rotes Kreuz (*Abk.* IRK); der Internationale Frauentag; [1]**In|ter|na|ti|o|na|le,** die; -, -n (internationale Vereinigung von Arbeiterbewegungen; *nur Sing.:* Kampflied der Arbeiterbewegung); [2]**In|ter|na|ti|o|na|le,** der *u.* die; -n, -n; ↑R 5 ff. (*Sport* Sportler[in] in der Nationalmannschaft); **in|ter|na|ti|o|na|li|sie|ren** (international gestalten); **In|ter|na|ti|o|na|li|sie|rung,** die; -; **In|ter|na|ti|o|na|lis|mus,** der; -, *Plur.* (*für Wörter:*) ...men (Streben nach überstaatl. Gemeinschaft; *Sprachw.* ein international gebräuchliches Wort)

In|ter|nats|schu|le ([höhere] Schule mit Wohnheim)

In|ter|ne, der *u.* die; -n, -n (↑R 5 ff.) ‹lat.› (Schüler[in] eines Internats)

In|ter|net, das; -s, -s ‹engl.› ([internationales] Computernetzwerk)

in|ter|nie|ren ‹lat.› (in staatl. Gewahrsam, in Haft nehmen; [Kranke] isolieren); **In|ter|nier|te,** der *u.* die; -n, -n (↑R 5 ff.); **In|ter|nie|rung; In|ter|nie|rungs|la|ger; In|ter|nist,** der; -en, -en; ↑R 126 (Facharzt für innere Krankheiten); **In|ter|nis|tin**

In|ter|no|di|um, das; -s, ...ien [...i̯ən] ‹lat.› (*Bot.* Sprossabschnitt zwischen zwei Blattknoten)

In|ter|num, das; -s, ...na *meist Plur.* ‹lat.› (nicht für Außenstehende bestimmte Angelegenheit)

In|ter|nun|ti|us, der; -, ...ien [...i̯ən] ‹lat.› (päpstl. Gesandter in kleineren Staaten)

in|ter|oze|a|nisch (↑R 132) ‹lat.; griech.› (Weltmeere verbindend)

in|ter|par|la|men|ta|risch ‹lat.; engl.› (die Parlamente der einzelnen Staaten umfassend)

In|ter|pel|lant, der; -en, -en (↑R 126) ‹lat.› (Fragesteller [in einem Parlament]); **In|ter|pel|la|ti|on,** die; -, -en ([parlamentar.] Anfrage; *früher für* Einspruch); **in|ter|pel|lie|ren**

in|ter|pla|ne|tar, in|ter|pla|ne|ta|risch (zwischen den Planeten befindlich); -e Materie; -er Raum

In|ter|pol, die; - (*Kurzw. für* Internationale Kriminalpolizeiliche Organisation; Zentralstelle zur internationalen Koordination der Ermittlungsarbeit in der Verbrechensbekämpfung)

In|ter|po|la|ti|on, die; -, -en ‹lat.› (nachträgl. Einfügung od. Änderung [in Texten]; *Math.* Bestimmung von Zwischenwerten); **in|ter|po|lie|ren**

In|ter|pret, der; -en, -en (↑R 126) ‹lat.› (Ausleger, Deuter; reproduzierender Künstler); **In|ter|pre|ta|ti|on,** die; -, -en; **in|ter|pre|tie|ren; In|ter|pre|tin**

in|ter|pun|gie|ren ‹lat.› (*seltener für* interpunktieren); **in|ter|punk|tie|ren** (Satzzeichen setzen); **In|ter|punk|ti|on,** die; - (Zeichensetzung); **In|ter|punk|ti|ons‿re|gel, ...zei|chen**

In|ter|rail|kar|te [...'re:l...] ‹engl.; dt.› (*Eisenb.* verbilligte Jugendfahrkarte für Fahrten in Europa)

In|ter|re|gio, der; -s, -s *u.* **In|ter|re|gi|o|zug** ‹lat. [dt.]› (schneller Eisenbahnzug; *Abk.* IR)

In|ter|re|gnum (↑R 130), das; -s, *Plur.* ...gnen *u.* ...gna ‹lat.› (Zwischenregierung; kaiserlose Zeit [1254–1273])

in|ter|ro|ga|tiv ‹lat.› (fragend); **In|ter|ro|ga|tiv,** das; -s, -e [...və] (*Sprachw.* Frage[für]wort, z. B. „wer?“, „welcher?“); **In|ter|ro|ga|tiv‿ad|verb** (Frageumstandswort), **...pro|no|men** (Fragefürwort), **...satz** (Fragesatz)

In|ter|rup|ti|on, die; -, -en ‹lat.› (Unterbrechung)

In|ter|sex [*auch* 'in...], das; -es, -e ‹lat.› (*Biol.* Organismus mit Intersexualität); **In|ter|se|xu|a|li|tät,** die; - (das Auftreten männl. Geschlechtsmerkmale bei einem weibl. Organismus u. umgekehrt); **in|ter|se|xu|ell** (zwischengeschlechtlich)

In|ter|shop [...ʃɔp], der; -[s], -s ‹lat.; engl.› (*ehem. in der DDR* Spezialgeschäft mit konvertierbarer Währung als Zahlungsmittel)

in|ter|stel|lar (zwischen den Sternen befindlich); -e Materie

in|ter|sti|ti|ell ‹lat.› (*Med., Biol.* dazwischenliegend); **In|ter|sti|ti|um,** das; -s, ...ien [...i̯ən] (*Biol.* Zwischenraum [zwischen Organen]; *nur Plur.: kath. Kirche* vorgeschriebene Zwischenzeit zwischen dem Empfang zweier geistl. Weihen)

in|ter|sub|jek|tiv ‹lat.› (*Psych.* dem Bewusstsein mehrerer Personen gemeinsam)

in|ter|ter|ri|to|ri|al ‹lat.› (zwischenstaatlich)

In|ter|tri|go, die; -, ...trigines [...ne:s] ‹lat.› (*Med.* Hautwolf)

in|ter|ur|ban [*auch* 'in...] ‹lat.› *(veraltend);* -es Telefongespräch (Ferngespräch)

In|ter|u|su|ri|um, das; -s, ...ien [...i̯ən] ‹lat.› (*BGB* Zwischenzinsen)

In|ter|vall [...v...], das; -s, -e ‹lat.› (Zeitabstand, Zeitspanne, Zwischenraum; Frist; Abstand [zwischen zwei Tönen]); **In|ter|vall|trai|ning** *(Sport)*

In|ter|ve|ni|ent [...v...], der; -en, -en (↑R 126) ‹lat.› (jmd., der sich in [Rechts]streitigkeiten [als Mittelsmann] einmischt); **in|ter|ve|nie|ren** (vermitteln; *Politik* Protest anmelden; sich einmischen); **In|ter|vent,** der; -en, -en (↑R 126) ‹lat.-russ.› (*nach ehem. DDR-Sprachgebrauch* Staat, der sich gewaltsam in die Belange eines anderen einmischt); **In|ter|ven|ti|on,** die; -, -en ‹lat.› (Vermittlung; staatl. Einmischung in die Angelegenheiten eines fremden Staates; Eintritt in eine Wechselverbindlichkeit); **In|ter|ven|ti|ons|krieg**

In|ter|view [...vju:, *auch* ...'vju:], das; -s, -s ‹engl.› (Unterredung [von Reportern] mit [führenden] Persönlichkeiten über Tagesfragen usw.; Befragung); **in|ter|vie|wen** [...'vju:..., *auch* 'in...]; interviewt; **In|ter|vie|wer; In|ter|vie|we|rin**

In|ter|vi|si|on [...v...], die; - ‹*Kurzw. aus* international und Television› osteurop. Organisation zur Gemeinschaftsübertragung von Fernsehsendungen)

in|ter|ze|die|ren ‹lat.› (*veraltend für* vermitteln; sich verbürgen)

in|ter‿zel|lu|lar, ...zel|lu|lär (lat.; *Biol., Med.* zwischen den Zellen gelegen); **In|ter|zel|lu|lar|raum**

In|ter|zes|si|on, die; -, -en ‹lat.› (*Rechtsw.* Schuldübernahme)

in|ter|zo|nal ‹lat.; griech.› (zwischen den Zonen); **In|ter|zo|nen‿han|del** *(früher),* **...ver|kehr** *(früher),* **...zug** *(früher)*

in|tes|ta|bel ‹lat.› (*Rechtsspr. veraltet* unfähig, ein Testament zu machen od. als Zeuge aufzutreten); ...ab|le (↑R 130) Personen; **In|tes|tat|er|be,** der (natürlicher, gesetzl. Erbe)

in|tes|ti|nal ‹lat.› (*Med.* zum Darmkanal gehörend)

In|thro|ni|sa|ti|on, die; -, -en ‹lat.; griech.› (Thronerhebung, feierliche Einsetzung); **in|thro|ni|sie|ren; In|thro|ni|sie|rung**

In|ti, der; -[s], -s ‹südamerik. India-

nerspr.⟩ (Währungseinheit in Peru); 5 - (↑R 90)
in|tim ⟨lat.⟩ (vertraut; innig, eng verbunden; vertraulich; das Geschlechtsleben betreffend); **In|ti|ma,** die; -, ...mä (*veraltend für* vertraute Freundin; *nur Sing.: Med.* innerste Haut der Gefäße); **In|ti|ma|ti|on,** die; -, -en (*veraltet für* gerichtl. Ankündigung, Aufforderung); **In|tim‿be|reich** (der), **...hy|gi|e|ne; In|ti|mi** (*Plur. von* Intimus); **In|ti|mi|tät,** die; -, -en ⟨*zu* intim⟩; **In|tim‿sphä|re** (vertraut-persönlicher Bereich), **...spray; In|ti|mus,** der; -, ...mi (vertrauter Freund)
in|to|le|ra|bel [*auch* ...'ra:b(ə)l]; ...ab|le (↑R 130) Verhältnisse; **in|to|le|rant** [*auch* ...'rant] (unduldsam); **In|to|le|ranz** [*auch* ...'rants], die; -, -en
In|to|na|ti|on, die; -, -en ⟨lat.⟩ (*Musik* das An-, Abstimmen; *Sprachw.* die Veränderung des Tones nach Höhe u. Stärke beim Sprechen von Silben oder ganzen Sätzen, Tongebung); **in|to|nie|ren** (anstimmen)
in to|to ⟨lat.⟩ (im Ganzen)
In|to|xi|ka|ti|on, die; -, -en ⟨lat.; griech.⟩ (*Med.* Vergiftung)
In|tra|da, In|tra|de, die; -, ...den ⟨ital.⟩ (*Musik* instrumentales Einleitungsstück [der Barockzeit])
int|ra|kar|di|al (↑R 130) ⟨lat.; griech.⟩ (*Med.* innerhalb des Herzens)
int|ra|ku|tan (↑R 130) ⟨lat.⟩ (*Med.* im Innern, ins Innere der Haut)
int|ra|mo|le|ku|lar (↑R 130) ⟨lat.⟩ (*Chemie* sich innerhalb der Moleküle vollziehend); intramolekulare Prozesse
int|ra mu|ros (↑R 130) ⟨lat., „innerhalb der Mauern"⟩ (nicht öffentlich)
int|ra|mus|ku|lär (↑R 130) ⟨lat.⟩ (*Med.* im Innern, ins Innere des Muskels)
in|tran|si|gent ⟨lat.⟩ (starr, unnachgiebig); **In|tran|si|gent,** der; -en, -en; (starrer Parteimann; *nur Plur.:* extreme polit. Parteien); **In|tran|si|genz,** die; -
in|tran|si|tiv ⟨lat.⟩ (*Sprachw.* nicht zum persönlichen Passiv fähig; nichtzielend); -es Verb; **In|tran|si|tiv,** das; -s, -e [...və] *u.* **In|tran|si|ti|vum,** das; -s, ...va [...va] (nichtzielendes Verb, z. B. „blühen")
int|ra|oku|lar (↑R 130 *u.* 132) ⟨lat.⟩ (*Med.* im Augeninnern liegend)
int|ra|ute|rin (↑R 130 *u.* 132) ⟨lat.⟩ (*Med.* innerhalb der Gebärmutter liegend); **Int|ra|ute|rin|pes|sar**
int|ra|ve|nös [...v...] (↑R 130) ⟨lat.⟩ (*Med.* im Innern, ins Innere der Vene); intravenöse Einspritzung, Injektion
int|ra‿zel|lu|lar, ...zel|lu|lär (↑R 130; *Biol., Med.* innerhalb der Zelle liegend)
int|ri|gant (↑R 130) ⟨franz.⟩ (auf Intrigen sinnend; hinterhältig); **Int|ri|gant,** der; -en, -en (↑R 126); **Int|ri|gan|tin; Int|ri|ge,** die; -, -n (hinterhältige Machenschaften, Ränke[spiel]); **Int|ri|gen‿spiel, ...wirt|schaft; int|ri|gie|ren**
Int|ro|duk|ti|on (↑R 130), die; -, -en ⟨lat.⟩ (Einführung, Einleitung; *Musik* Vorspiel, Einleitungssatz); **int|ro|du|zie|ren**
Int|ro|i|tus (↑R 130), der; -, - [...tu:s] ⟨lat.⟩ (Eingangsgesang der katholischen Messe; Eingangsworte od. Eingangslied im evangelischen Gottesdienst)
Int|ro|spek|ti|on, (↑R 130), die; -, -en ⟨lat.⟩ (*Psych.* Selbstbeobachtung); **int|ro|spek|tiv**
Int|ro|ver|si|on [...v...] (↑R 130), die; -, -en ⟨lat.⟩ (*Psych.* Konzentration auf die eigene Innenwelt); **int|ro|ver|tiert**
In|tru|si|on, die; -, -en ⟨lat.⟩ (*Geol.* Eindringen von Magma in die Erdkruste); **In|tru|siv|ge|stein** (Tiefengestein)
In|tu|ba|ti|on, die; -, -en ⟨lat.⟩ (*Med.* Einführen eines Röhrchens in den Kehlkopf [bei Erstickungsgefahr]); **in|tu|bie|ren**
In|tu|i|ti|on, die; -, -en ⟨lat.⟩ (Eingebung, ahnendes Erfassen; unmittelbare Erkenntnis [ohne Reflexion]); **in|tu|i|tiv**
In|tu|mes|zenz, In|tur|ges|zenz, die; -, -en ⟨lat.⟩ (*Med.* Anschwellung)
in|tus ⟨lat.⟩ (inwendig, innen); etwas intus haben (*ugs. für* etwas im Magen haben; etwas begriffen haben); **In|tus|sus|zep|ti|on,** die; -, -en (*Bot.* Einlagerung neuer Teilchen zwischen bereits vorhandene; *Med.* Darmeinstülpung)
I|nu|it *Plur.* ⟨eskim., „Menschen"⟩ (Selbstbez. der Eskimos)
I|nu|lin, das; -s ⟨griech.⟩ (ein Fruchtzucker)
In|un|da|ti|on, die; -, -en ⟨lat.⟩ (*Geogr.* völlige Überflutung durch das Meer od. einen Fluss); **In|un|da|ti|ons|ge|biet**
In|unk|ti|on, die; -, -en ⟨lat.⟩ (*Med.* Einreibung)
in u|sum Del|phi|ni *vgl.* ad ...
inv. = invenit
In|va|gi|na|ti|on [...v...], die; -, -en ⟨lat.⟩ (*Med.* Darmeinstülpung)
in|va|lid, in|va|li|de [...v...] ⟨franz.⟩ ([durch Verwundung od. Unfall] dienst-, arbeitsunfähig); **In|va|li|de,** der *u.* die; -n, -n; ↑R 126 (Dienst-, Arbeitsunfähige[r]); **In|va|li|den‿ren|te, ...ver|si|che|rung** (die; -); **in|va|li|die|ren** (*veraltet für* ungültig machen; entkräften); **in|va|li|di|sie|ren** (zum Invaliden erklären); **In|va|li|di|sie|rung; In|va|li|di|tät,** die; - (Erwerbs-, Dienst-, Arbeitsunfähigkeit)
in|va|ri|a|bel [*auch* ...'ria:...] ⟨lat.⟩ (unveränderlich); ...ab|le (↑R 130) Größen; **In|va|ri|an|te,** die; -, -n (*Math.* unveränderliche Größe); **In|va|ri|an|ten|the|o|rie** *(Math.);* **In|va|ri|anz** [*auch* ...'riants], die; -, -en (Unveränderlichkeit)
In|va|si|on [...v...], die; -, -en ⟨franz.⟩ ([feindlicher] Einfall; *Med.* das Eindringen [von Krankheitserregern]); **in|va|siv** (*Med.* eindringend); **In|va|sor,** der; -s, ...oren *meist Plur.* ⟨lat.⟩ (Eroberer; eindringender Feind)
In|vek|ti|ve [invɛk'ti:və], die; -, -n ⟨lat.⟩ (Beleidigung, Schmähung)
in|ve|nit [...v...] ⟨lat., „hat [es] erfunden"⟩ (Vermerk auf grafischen Blättern vor dem Namen des Künstlers, der die Originalzeichnung schuf; *Abk.* inv.)
In|ven|tar [...v...], das; -s, -e ⟨lat.⟩ (Einrichtungsgegenstände [eines Unternehmens]; Vermögensverzeichnis; Nachlassverzeichnis); **In|ven|tar|er|be,** der; **In|ven|ta|ri|sa|ti|on,** die; -, -en (Bestandsaufnahme); **in|ven|ta|ri|sie|ren; In|ven|ta|ri|sie|rung; In|ven|tar‿recht** (das; -[e]s), **...ver|zeich|nis; In|ven|ti|on,** die; -, -en ([musikal.] Erfindung); **In|ven|tur,** die; -, -en (*Wirtsch.* Bestandsaufnahme des Vermögens eines Unternehmens); **In|ven|tur‿prü|fung, ...ver|kauf** (verbilligter Verkauf nach einer Inventur)
in|vers [...v...] ⟨lat.⟩ (umgekehrt); **In|ver|si|on,** die; -, -en (*fachspr. für* Umkehrung, Umstellung)
In|ver|teb|rat (↑R 130); *vgl.* Evertebrat
In|ver|ter [...v...], der; -s, - ⟨engl.⟩ (*EDV* Gerät zur Verschlüsselung des Sprechfunkverkehrs); **in|ver|tie|ren** ⟨lat.⟩ (umkehren); **in|ver|tiert** (umgekehrt; *Psych. svw.* homosexuell)
In|ver|tin [...v...], das; -s ⟨lat.⟩ (ein Enzym)
in Ver|tre|tung (*Abk.* i. V. *od.* I. V.; *Klein- od. Großschreibung vgl.* „i. V."[1])
In|vert|zu|cker [...v...] ⟨lat.; dt.⟩

(Gemisch von Trauben- u. Fruchtzucker)
In|ver|wahr|nah|me, die; -, -n *(Amtsspr.)*
in|ves|tie|ren [...v...] ‹lat.› ([Kapital] anlegen; in ein [geistl.] Amt einweisen); **In|ves|tie|rung; In|ves|ti|ti|on,** die; -, -en ‹lat.› (langfristige [Kapital]anlage); **In|ves|ti|ti|ons|gut** *meist Plur.* (Gut, das der Produktion dient); **In|ves|ti|ti|ons‿hil|fe, ...len|kung, ...pro|gramm; In|ves|ti|tur,** die; -, -en (Einweisung in ein [niederes geistl.] Amt; im MA. feierl. Belehnung mit dem Bischofsamt durch den König; in Frankreich Bestätigung des Ministerpräsidenten durch die Nationalversammlung); **In|ves|ti|tur|streit,** der; -s (im 11./12. Jh.); **in|ves|tiv** (für Investitionen bestimmt); **In|ves|tiv|lohn** (als Spareinlage gebundener Teil des Arbeitnehmerlohnes); **In|vest|ment,** das; -s, -s ‹engl.› *(engl. Bez. für* Investition); **In|vest|ment‿fonds** (Effektenbestand einer Kapitalanlagegesellschaft), **...ge|sell|schaft** (Kapitalverwaltungsgesellschaft), **...pa|pier; In|vest|ment|trust** [...trast], der; -s, -s *(svw.* Investmentgesellschaft); **In|vest|ment|zer|ti|fi|kat; In|ves|tor,** der; -s, ...oren ‹lat.› (Kapitalanleger)
in vi|no ve|ri|tas [- 'vi:no v...] ‹lat., „im Wein [ist, liegt] Wahrheit"›
In-vit|ro-Fer|ti|li|sa|ti|on [...'vi:...] (↑R 130), die; -, -en ‹lat.› *(Med.* Befruchtung außerhalb des Körpers; *Abk.* IVF)
in vi|vo [- 'vi:vo] ‹lat., „im Leben"› (am lebenden Objekt)
In|vo|ka|ti|on [...v...], die; -, -en ‹lat.› (Anrufung [Gottes]); **In|vo|ka|vit** [invo'ka:vit] (Bez. des ersten Fastensonntags)
in Voll|macht *(Abk.* i. V. *od.* I. V.; *Klein- od. Großschreibung vgl.* „i. V."[1])
In|vo|lu|ti|on [...v...], die; -, -en ‹lat.› *(bes. Med.* Rückbildung [eines Organs]); **in|vol|vie|ren** [invɔl'vi:...] (in sich schließen)
in|wärts
in|wen|dig; in- u. auswendig
in|wie|fern
in|wie|weit
In|woh|ner *(veraltet für* Bewohner; *österr. auch für* Mieter)
In|zah|lung|nah|me, die; -, -n
In|zest, der; -[e]s, -e ‹lat.› (Geschlechtsverkehr zwischen engsten Blutsverwandten); **In|zest|ta|bu; in|zes|tu|ös**
In|zi|si|on, die; -, -en ‹lat.› *(Med.* Einschnitt); **In|zi|siv,** der; -s, -en [...vən] *od.* **In|zi|siv|zahn** (Schneidezahn); **In|zi|sur,** die; -, -en (Einschnitt, Einkerbung)
In|zucht, die; -, -en *Plur. selten;* **In|zucht|scha|den**
in|zwi|schen
Io. = Iowa
IOC [i:o:'tse:, *engl.* aio:'si:] = International Olympic Committee [intə(r)'nɛʃ(ə)nəl o'limpik kə'miti] *(svw.* IOK)
Iod, Io|dat, Io|did *vgl.* Jod, Jodat, Jodid
IOK = Internationales Olympisches Komitee
Io|kas|te (Mutter u. Gattin des Ödipus)
Io|lan|the (w. Vorn.)
Ion, das; -s, -en ‹griech.› (elektr. geladenes atomares od. molekulares Teilchen); **Io|nen‿an|trieb, ...aus|tausch, ...strah|len** *(Plur.),* **...wan|de|rung**
Io|nes|co [jɔ'nɛsko] (franz. Dramatiker rumänischer Abstammung)
Io|ni|en (Küstenlandschaft Kleinasiens); **Io|ni|er**
Io|ni|sa|ti|on, die; -, -en ‹griech.› *(Physik, Chemie* Versetzung neutraler materieller Teilchen in elektr. geladenen Zustand)
[1]**io|nisch** ‹*zu* Ion›; -e Bindung *(Chemie)*
[2]**io|nisch** ‹*zu* Ionien›; -er Stil, *aber* (↑R 102): die Ionischen Inseln
io|ni|sie|ren ‹griech.› (Ionisation bewirken); **Io|ni|sie|rung**
Io|no|sphä|re, die; - ‹griech.› (oberste Schicht der Atmosphäre)
Io|ta usw. *vgl.* Jota usw.
I|o|wa ['aiɔwə] (Staat in den USA; *Abk.* Ia. *od.* Io.)
I|pe|ka|ku|an|ha [...'kuanja], die; - ‹indian.-port.› (Brechwurzel, eine Heilpflanze)
I|phi|ge|nie [...iə] (Tochter Agamemnons)
ip|se fe|cit ‹lat., „er hat [es] selbst gemacht"› (auf Kunstwerken; *Abk.* i. f.); **ip|so fac|to** ‹„durch die Tat selbst"› (eigenmächtig); **ip|so ju|re** ‹„durch das Recht selbst"› (ohne Weiteres)
i-Punkt, der; -[e]s, -e (↑R 25)
IQ = Intelligenzquotient
Ir = *chem. Zeichen für* Iridium
IR = Interregiozug
IR. = Infanterieregiment
i. R. = im Ruhestand
I. R. = Imperator Rex
I|ra (w. Vorn.)
IRA = Irisch-Republikanische Armee
I|ra|de, der *od.* das; -s, -n ‹arab.› *(früher* ein Erlass des Sultans)
I|rak [*auch* 'i:...] *meist mit Artikel* der; -[s] (vorderasiat. Staat); die Städte des Irak[s], *aber* die Städte Iraks; **I|ra|ker; I|ra|ke|rin; I|ra|ki** der; -[s], -[s] *u.* die; -, -[s]; **i|ra|kisch**
I|ran *meist mit Artikel* der; -[s] (asiat. Staat); *vgl.* Irak, Persien; **I|ra|ner; I|ra|ne|rin; i|ra|nisch; I|ra|nist,** der; -en, -en; ↑R 126 (Wissenschaftler auf dem Gebiet der Iranistik); **I|ra|nis|tik,** die; - (Wissenschaft von den Sprachen u. Kulturen des Irans); **I|ra|nis|tin**
Ir|bis, der; -ses, -se ‹mong.› (Schneeleopard)
ir|den (aus gebranntem Ton); **Ir|den‿ge|schirr, ...wa|re; ir|disch**
I|re, der; -n, -n; ↑R 126 (Irländer)
I|re|nä|us (griech. Kirchenvater)
I|re|ne (w. Vorn.); **I|re|nik,** die; - ‹griech.› (Friedenslehre; Friedensstreben, Aussöhnung [bei kirchl. Streitigkeiten]); **i|re|nisch**
ir|gend; wenn du irgend kannst, so ...; wenn irgend möglich; irgend so ein Bettler; **ir|gend|ein,** irgendeine, irgendeiner; **ir|gend|et|was** *(ugs. auch* irgendwas); **ir|gend|je|mand; ir|gend|wann; ir|gend|welch;** irgendwelche Fragen; irgendwelches dumme[s] Zeug (↑R 5 ff.); **ir|gend|wer; ir|gend|wie; ir|gend|wo;** irgendwo anders, irgendwo sonst; sonst irgendwo; **ir|gend|wo|hin**
I|ri|dek|to|mie (↑R 132), die; -, ...ien ‹griech.› *(Med.* Ausschneiden der Regenbogenhaut); **I|ri|di|um,** das; -s (chem. Element, Metall; *Zeichen* Ir); **I|ri|do|lo|ge,** der; -n, -n; ↑R 126 *(Med.* Augendiagnostiker); **I|ri|do|lo|gie,** die; -
I|rin (Irländerin)
I|ri|na (w. Vorn.)
[1]**I|ris** (griech. Götterbotin; w. Vorn.); [2]**I|ris,** die; -, *Plur.* -, *auch* Iriden *Plur. selten* ‹griech.› (Regenbogenhaut im Auge); [3]**I|ris,** die; -, - (Schwertlilie; Regenbogen); **I|ris|blen|de** *(Optik* verstellbare Blende an der Kamera)
i|risch; (↑R 104:) das irische Bad, *aber* (↑R 102): die Irische See; **I|risch-Re|pub|li|ka|ni|sche Ar|mee** (↑R 130; irische Untergrundorganisation; *Abk.* IRA); **I|rish|cof|fee** ['airiʃ'kɔfi], der; -, -s ‹engl.› (Kaffee mit einem Schuss Whisky u. Schlagsahne); **I|rish|stew** ['airiʃ'stju:], das; -[s], -s (Weißkraut mit Hammelfleisch u. a.)
i|ri|sie|ren ‹griech.› (in Regenbogenfarben schillern); **I|ri|tis,** die; -, ...itiden *(Med.* Entzündung der Regenbogenhaut)

IRK = Internationales Rotes Kreuz
Ir|kutsk [*österr.* 'ir...] (Stadt in Sibirien)
Ir|land (nordwesteurop. Insel; Staat auf dieser Insel); **Ir|län|der; Ir|län|de|rin; ir|län|disch,** *aber* (↑R 102): Irländisches Moos (*svw.* Karrag[h]een)
Ir|ma, Irm|gard (w. Vorn.)
Ir|min|säu|le, Ir|min|sul, die; - (ein germ. Heiligtum)
Irm|traud (w. Vorn.)
I|ro|ke|se, der; -n, -n; ↑R 126 (Angehöriger eines nordamerik. Indianerstammes)
I|ro|nie, die; -, ...ien ‹griech.› ([versteckter, feiner] Spott); **I|ro|ni|ker; i|ro|nisch; i|ro|ni|sie|ren**
irr *vgl.* irre
Ir|ra|di|a|ti|on, die; -, -en ‹lat.› (*Med., Psych.* Ausstrahlung [von Schmerzen, Gefühlen, Affekten]; *Fotogr.* Überbelichtung fotografischer Platten)
ir|ra|ti|o|nal [*auch* ...'na:l] ‹lat.› (verstandesmäßig nicht fassbar; vernunftwidrig); -e Zahl; **Ir|ra|ti|o|na|lis|mus,** der; - ([philosoph. Lehre vom] Vorrang des Gefühlsmäßigen vor dem logisch-rationalen Denken); **Ir|ra|ti|o|na|li|tät,** die; - (das Irrationale); **Ir|ra|ti|o|nal|zahl** *(Math.)*
ir|re, irr; irr[e] sein; *vgl. aber* irreführen, irregehen, irreleiten, irremachen, irrereden, irrewerden; **[1]Ir|re,** die; -; in die - gehen; **[2]Ir|re,** der *u.* die; -n, -n (↑R 5 ff.)
ir|re|al [*auch* ...'a:l] ‹lat.› (unwirklich); **Ir|re|al** [*auch* ...'a:l], der; -s, -e (*Sprachw.* Verbform, mit der man einen unerfüllbaren Wunsch o. Ä. ausdrückt); **Ir|re|a|li|tät** [*auch* 'ir...], die; - (Unwirklichkeit)
Ir|re|den|ta, die; -, ...ten ‹ital.› (polit. Bewegung, die den staatl. Anschluss abgetrennter Gebiete an das Mutterland erstrebt); **Ir|re|den|tis|mus,** der; - (Geisteshaltung der Irredenta; polit. Bewegung); **Ir|re|den|tist,** der; -en, -en (↑R 126); **ir|re|den|tis|tisch**
ir|re|du|zi|bel [*auch* ...'tsi:...] ‹lat.› (*Philos., Math.* nicht ableitbar); ...ib|le (↑R 130) Sätze
ir|re|füh|ren; seine Darstellungsweise hat mich irregeführt; eine irreführende Auskunft; **Ir|re|füh|rung; ir|re|ge|hen;** er ist irregegangen
ir|re|gu|lär [*auch* ...'lɛ:r] ‹lat.› (unregelmäßig, ungesetzmäßig); -e Truppen (die nicht zum eigentl. Heer gehören); **Ir|re|gu|lä|re,** der; -n, -n; ↑R 5 ff. (nicht zum eigentl. Heer Gehörender); **Ir|re|gu|la|ri|tät** [*auch* 'ir...], die; -, -en (Regellosigkeit; Abweichung)
ir|re|lei|ten; er hat die Polizei irregeleitet; ein irregeleitetes Kind
ir|re|le|vant [*auch* ...'vant] ‹lat.› (unerheblich); **Ir|re|le|vanz** [*auch* ...'vants], die; -, -en
ir|re|li|gi|ös [*auch* ...'giø:s] ‹lat.› (nicht religiös); ein -er Mann; **Ir|re|li|gi|o|si|tät** [*auch* 'ir...], die; -
ir|re|ma|chen; er hat mich irregemacht; **ir|ren;** sich -; (↑R 50:) Irren, *auch* irren ist menschlich; **Ir|ren‿an|stalt, ...arzt** *(veraltet),* **...haus; ir|ren|haus|reif** *(ugs.)*
ir|re|pa|ra|bel [*auch* ...'ra:...] ‹lat.› (unersetzlich, nicht wieder herstellbar); ...ab|ler (↑R 130) Schaden
ir|re|po|ni|bel [*auch* ...'ni:...] ‹lat.› (*Med.* nicht einrenkbar); ...ib|le (↑R 130) Gelenkköpfe
ir|re|re|den; er hat irregeredet; **ir|re sein** *vgl.* irre; **Ir|re|sein,** Irrsein, das; -s (↑R 50)
ir|re|spi|ra|bel [*auch* ...'ra:...] ‹lat.› (*Med.* zum Einatmen untauglich); ...ab|le (↑R 130) Luft
ir|re|ver|si|bel [...v..., *auch* ...'zi:...] ‹lat.› (nicht umkehrbar); ...ib|le (↑R 130) Prozesse
ir|re|**wer|den,** irr|wer|den; wenn man irrewird, irrwird; du bist an dir irregeworden, irrgeworden (↑R 38 f.); **Ir|re|wer|den,** Irr|werden, das; -s (↑R 50); **Irr‿fahrt, ...gang** (der), **...gar|ten, ...gast** *(Zool.),* **...glau|be[n]; irr|gläu|big; ir|rig**
Ir|ri|ga|ti|on, die; -, -en ‹lat.› (*Med.* Ab- od. Ausspülung); **Ir|ri|ga|tor,** der; -s, ...oren (Spülapparat)
ir|ri|ger|wei|se
ir|ri|ta|bel ‹lat.› (reizbar); ein ...abler (↑R 130) Mensch; **Ir|ri|ta|bi|li|tät,** die; -; **Ir|ri|ta|ti|on,** die; -, -en (Reiz, Erregung); **ir|ri|tie|ren** ([auf]reizen, verwirren, stören)
Irr‿läu|fer (falsch beförderter Gegenstand), **...leh|re, ...licht** (*Plur.* ...lichter); **irr|lich|te|lie|ren** (*in Goethes Faust svw.* irrlichtern); **irr|lich|tern** (wie ein Irrlicht funkeln, sich hin und her bewegen); es irrlichtert; geirrlichtert; **Irr|sal,** das; -[e]s, -e (*geh. für* Zustand des menschlichen Irrens); **irr sein** *vgl.* irre; **Irr|sein,** das; -s; *vgl.* Irresein; **Irr|sinn,** der; -[e]s; **irr|sin|nig; Irr|sin|nig|keit,** die; -; **Irr|tum,** der; -s, ...tümer; **irr|tüm|lich; irr|tüm|li|cher|wei|se; Ir|rung** (*veraltet für* Irrtum); **Irr|weg; irr|wer|den** *vgl.* irrewerden; **Irr|wer|den** *vgl.* Irrewerden; **Irr|wisch,** der; -[e]s, -e (Irrlicht; sehr lebhafter Mensch); **irr|wit|zig**
Ir|tysch [*auch* ir'tiʃ], der; -[s] (linker Nebenfluss des Ob)
Ir|vin|gi|a|ner (Anhänger E. Irvings); **Ir|vin|gi|a|nis|mus,** der; -
I|sa (*moslem. Name für* Jesus)
I|sa|ak ['i:zaak, *auch* 'i:za(:)k, *österr.* 'i:zak] (bibl. m. Vorn.)
I|sa|bel, I|sa|bel|la, [1]I|sa|bel|le (w. Vorn.); **[2]I|sa|bel|le,** die; -, -n (falbes Pferd); **i|sa|bell|far|ben, i|sa|bell|far|big** (falb, graugelb)
I|sa|i|as (*Schreibung der Vulgata für* Jesaja)
I|sar, die; - (r. Nebenfluss der Donau); **I|sar-A|then;** ↑R 106 (*scherzh. für* München)
I|sa|tin, das; -s ‹griech.› (*Chemie* eine Indigoverbindung)
I|sau|ri|en [...iən] (antike Landschaft in Kleinasien)
ISBN = internationale Standardbuchnummer
Is|chä|mie [isçɛ..., *auch* iʃɛ...] (↑R 132), die; -, ...ien ‹griech.› (*Med.* örtl. Blutleere)
I|scha|ri|ot [i'ʃa:...] (↑R 132) ‹hebr.›; *vgl.* Judas
I|sche ['i(:)ʃə], die; -, -n ‹hebr.-jidd.› (*ugs. für* Mädchen, Freundin)
Is|chia ['iskia] (ital. Insel)
Is|chi|a|di|kus[1] [is'çia:...], der; -, ...dizi ‹griech.› (Hüftnerv); **is|chi|a|disch** (den Ischias betreffend); **Is|chi|al|gie**[1] [isçial...], die; -, ...ien (Hüftschmerz); **Is|chi|as**[1] ['isçias], der, *auch* das, *fachspr. auch* die; - (*svw.* Ischialgie); **Is|chi|as|nerv**[1]
Ischl, Bad (österr. Badeort)
Isch|tar (babylon. Göttin)
Isch|u|rie [isçu...], die; -, ...ien ‹griech.› (*Med.* Harnverhaltung)
ISDN = Integrated services digital network ‹engl., Dienste integrierendes digitales [Nachrichten]netz› (der schnellen Übermittlung von Sprache, Text, Bild, Daten dienendes Kommunikationsnetz)
I|se|grim, der; -s, -e (der Wolf in der Tierfabel; *übertr. für* mürrischer Mensch)
I|sel, der; -[s] (Berg in Tirol)
I|ser, die; - (r. Nebenfluss der Elbe); **I|ser|ge|bir|ge,** das; -s
I|ser|lohn (Stadt im Sauerland)
I|si|dor (m. Vorn.)
I|sis (altägypt. Göttin)
Is|ka|ri|ot *vgl.* Judas
Is|lam [*auch* 'is...], der; -[s] ‹arab.› (Lehre Mohammeds); **Is|la|ma|bad** (Hptst. von Pakistan); **Is|la-**

[1] [*oft auch* iʃia...]

mi|sa|ti|on, die; -, -en (die Bekehrung zum Islam); is|la|misch; is|la|mi|sie|ren (zum Islam bekehren; unter die Herrschaft des Islams bringen); Is|la|mis|mus, der; - (*früher für* Islam); Is|la|mit, der; -en, -en (↑R 126); Is|la|mitin; is|la|mi|tisch

Is|land; Is|län|der; Is|län|de|rin; is|län|disch; die isländische Sprache, *aber* (↑R 108): Isländisch[es] Moos (eine Heilpflanze); **Is|län|disch,** das; -[s] (Sprache); *vgl.* Deutsch; **Is|län|di|sche,** das; -n; *vgl.* Deutsche, das

Is|ma|el [...e:l, *auch* ...ɛl] (bibl. m. Eigenn.); **Is|ma|i|lit** [isma|i...], der; -en, -en; (↑R 126; Angehöriger einer schiit. Sekte)

Is|me|ne (Tochter des Ödipus)

Is|mus, der; -, ...men ‹griech.› (*abwertend für* bloße Theorie)

ISO = International Organization for Standardization [intə(r)ˈnɛʃ(ə)nəl ɔ:(r)gənaiˈze:ʃ(ə)n fɔ:(r) stɛndə(r)daiˈze:ʃ(ə)n], die; - (internationale Normierungsorganisation)

i|so... ‹griech.› (gleich...); **I|so...** (Gleich...); **I|so|ba|re,** die; -, -n (*Meteor.* Verbindungslinie zwischen Orten gleichen Luftdrucks); **I|so|bu|tan,** das; -s (ein brennbares Gas, das zur Herstellung von Flugbenzin verwendet wird)

i|so|chrom [...ˈkro:m] ‹griech.› (*svw.* isochromatisch); **I|so|chro|ma|sie** [...kro...], die; - (gleiche Farbempfindlichkeit von fotogr. Material); **i|so|chro|ma|tisch** (gleichfarbig, farbtonrichtig); **i|so|chron** [...ˈkro:n] (*Physik* gleich lange dauernd); **I|so|chro|ne,** die; -, -n (Linie gleichzeitigen Auftretens [von Erdbeben u. a.])

I|so|dy|na|me, die; -, -n ‹griech.› (Verbindungslinie zwischen Orten mit gleicher magnet. Stärke); **I|so|dy|ne,** die; -, -n (*Physik* Linie, die Punkte gleicher Kraft verbindet)

I|so|ga|mie, die; -, ...ien ‹griech.› (*Biol.* Fortpflanzung durch gleich gestaltete Geschlechtszellen); **I|so|glos|se,** die; -, -n (*Sprachw.* Linie auf Sprachkarten, die Gebiete gleichen Wortgebrauchs begrenzt); **I|so|gon,** das; -s, -e (regelmäßiges Vieleck); **i|so|go|nal** (winkelgetreu; gleichwinklig); **I|so|go|ne,** die; -, -n (*Meteor.* Verbindungslinie zwischen Orten gleicher magnet. Abweichung od. gleicher Windrichtung)

I|so|hy|e|te, die; -, -n ‹griech.› (*Meteor.* Verbindungslinie zwischen Orten mit gleicher Niederschlagsmenge); **I|so|hyp|se,** die; -, -n (*Geogr.* Verbindungslinie zwischen Orten mit gleicher Höhe ü. d. M.)

I|so|kli|ne, die; -, -n ‹griech.› (*Geogr.* Verbindungslinie zwischen Orten mit gleicher Neigung der Magnetnadel)

I|so|la|ti|on, die; -, -en ‹franz.›, I|so|lie|rung ([politische u. a.] Absonderung; Abkapselung; Getrennthaltung; [Ab]dämmung, Sperrung); **I|so|la|ti|o|nis|mus,** der; - ‹engl.› (polit. Tendenz, sich vom Ausland abzuschließen); **I|so|la|ti|o|nist,** der; -en, -en (↑R 126); **i|so|la|ti|o|nis|tisch; I|so|la|ti|ons‿fol|ter, ...haft; I|so|la|tor,** der; -s, ...oren (Stoff, der Elektrizität schlecht od. gar nicht leitet)

I|sol|de (mittelalterl. Sagengestalt; w. Vorn.)

I|so|lier|band, das; *Plur.* ...bänder; **i|so|lie|ren** ‹franz.› (absondern; getrennt halten; abschließen, [ab]dichten, [ab]dämmen; durch entsprechendes Material schützen); **I|so|lie|rer; I|so|lier‿ma|te|ri|al, ...schicht, ...sta|ti|on; i|so|liert** (*auch für* vereinsamt); **I|so|liert|heit,** die; -; **I|so|lie|rung** *vgl.* Isolation

I|so|li|nie, die; -, -n ‹griech.; lat.› (Verbindungslinie zwischen Punkten gleicher Wertung od. Erscheinung auf geographischen u. a. Karten)

i|so|mer ‹griech.› (Isomerie aufweisend); **I|so|mer,** das; -s, -e *u.* **I|so|me|re,** das; -n, -n *meist Plur.* (eine Isomerie aufweisende chem. Verbindung); ein -; **I|so|me|rie,** die; - (*Bot.* Gleichzähligkeit in Bezug auf die Zahl der Glieder in den verschiedenen Blütenkreisen; *Chemie* unterschiedliches Verhalten chem. Verbindungen trotz der gleichen Anzahl gleichartiger Atome); **I|so|met|rie** (↑R 130), die; - (Längengleichheit, Längentreue, bes. bei Landkarten); **i|so|met|risch** (↑R 130); **i|so|morph** (gleichförmig, von gleicher Gestalt, bes. bei Kristallen); **I|so|mor|phie,** die; -; **I|so|mor|phis|mus,** der; - (Eigenschaft gewisser chem. Stoffe, gemeinsam die gleichen Kristalle zu bilden)

I|son|zo, der; -[s] (Zufluss des Golfs von Triest)

i|so|pe|ri|met|risch (↑R 130) ‹griech.› (*Math.* von gleichem Ausmaß [von Längen, Flächen u. Körpern]); **I|so|po|de,** der; -n, -n *meist Plur.;* ↑R 126 (*Zool.* Assel)

I|so|pren, das; -s ‹Kunstwort› (ein chem. Stoff, der zur Herstellung von synthet. Kautschuk verwendet wird)

I|so|seis|te, die; -, -n ‹griech.› (Verbindungslinie zwischen Orten mit gleicher Erdbebenstärke); **I|sos|ta|sie** (↑R 132), die; - (Gleichgewichtszustand der Krustenschollen der Erde)

I|so|ther|me, die; -, -n ‹griech.› (*Meteor.* Verbindungslinie zwischen Orten mit gleicher Temperatur); **I|so|ton,** das; -s, -e *meist Plur.* (Atomkern, der die gleiche Anzahl Neutronen wie ein anderer enthält); **i|so|to|nisch** (*Chemie* von gleichem osmot. Druck); **I|so|top,** das; -s, -e (Atom, das sich von einem andern des gleichen chem. Elements nur in seiner Masse unterscheidet); **I|so|to|pen‿di|ag|nos|tik** (*Med.*), **...the|ra|pie, ...tren|nung; I|sot|ron** (↑R 130 *u.* 132), das; -s, *Plur.* ...trone, *auch* -s (Gerät zur Isotopentrennung); **i|so|trop** (*Physik, Chemie* nach allen Richtungen hin gleiche Eigenschaften aufweisend); **I|so|tro|pie,** die; -

Is|ra|el [...e:l, *auch* ...ɛl] (Volk der Juden im A. T.; Staat in Vorderasien); das Volk Israel; die Kinder Israel[s]; **Is|ra|e|li,** der; -[s], -s *u.* die; -, -[s] (Angehörige[r] des Staates Israel); **is|ra|e|lisch** (zum Staat Israel gehörend); **Is|ra|e|lit,** der; -en, -en; (↑R 126; Angehöriger eines der semit. Stämme im alten Palästina); **is|ra|e|li|tisch**

Is|tan|bul [ˈistambu:l] (türk. Stadt)

Ist|auf|kom|men (↑R 24; der tatsächliche [Steuer]ertrag); **Ist|bestand** (↑R 24)

isth|misch ‹griech.›, *aber* Isthmische Spiele (↑R 108); **Isth|mus,** der; -, ...men (Landenge, bes. die von Korinth)

Ist|ri|en (↑R 130; Halbinsel im Adriatischen Meer)

Ist|stär|ke (↑R 24), die; -, -n

Ist|wä|o|nen *Plur.* (Kultgemeinschaft westgerm. Stämme); **istwä|o|nisch**

Is|wes|ti|ja, die; - ‹russ., „Nachrichten"› (eine russ. Tageszeitung)

it. = item

I|ta|ker, der; -s, - (*ugs. abwertend für* Italiener)

I|ta|la, die; - ‹lat.› (älteste lat. Bibelübersetzung); **I|ta|ler** (Einwohner des antiken Italien); **I|ta|lia** (*lat. u. ital. Form von* Italien); **i|ta|li|a|ni|sie|ren,** i|ta|li|e|ni|sie|ren [...lie...] (italienisch machen); **I|ta|li|en** [...iən]; **I|ta|li|e|ner; I|ta|li|e|ne-**

rin; i|ta|li|e|nisch; die italienische Schweiz; eine italienische Nacht (↑R 104); italienischer Salat (↑R 108), *aber* (↑R 102): die Italienische Republik; *vgl.* deutsch; *vgl. aber* italisch; **I|ta|li|e|nisch,** das; -[s] (Sprache); *vgl.* Deutsch; **I|ta|li|e|ni|sche,** das; -n; *vgl.* Deutsche, das; **i|ta|li|e|ni|sie|ren** *vgl.* italianisieren; **I|ta|li|enne** [...ˈli̯ɛn], die; - ‹franz.› (*Druckw.* eine Schriftart); **I|ta|li|ker** ‹lat.› (Italer); **I|ta|lique** [...ˈlik], die; - ‹franz.› (*Druckw.* eine Schriftart); **i|ta|lisch** ‹lat.› (das antike Italien betreffend); *vgl. aber* italienisch; **I|ta|lo|wes|tern** (Western in einem von italienischen Regisseuren geprägten Stil)

I|ta|zis|mus, der; - (Aussprache der altgriech. E-Laute wie langes i)

i|tem ‹lat.› (*veraltet für* ebenso, desgleichen; ferner; *Abk.* it.); **I|tem,** das; -s, -s (*veraltet für* das Fernere, Weitere, ein [Frage]punkt; Einzelangabe)

I|te|ra|ti|on, die; -, -en ‹lat.› (Wiederholung; *Math.* schrittweises Rechenverfahren zur Annäherung an die exakte Lösung); **i|te|ra|tiv** [*auch* ˈi...] (wiederholend); **I|te|ra|tiv,** das; -s, -e [...və] (*Sprachw.* Verb, das eine stete Wiederholung von Vorgängen ausdrückt, z. B. „sticheln“ = immer wieder stechen)

I|tha|ka (eine griech. Insel)

I|ti|ne|rar, das; -s, -e *u.* **I|ti|ne|ra|ri|um,** das; -s, ...ien [...i̯ən] ‹lat.› (Straßenverzeichnis der röm. Zeit; Aufzeichnung noch nicht vermessener Wege bei Forschungsreisen)

i. Tr. = in der Trockenmasse

i-Tüp|fel|chen (↑R 25); **i-Tüp|ferl,** das; -s, -n (*österr. für* i-Tüpfelchen); **i-Tüp|ferl-Rei|ter** (*österr. ugs. für* Pedant)

It|ze|hoe [...ˈho:] (Stadt in Schleswig-Holstein); **It|ze|ho|er** (↑R 103)

it|zo, itzt, it|zund (↑R 132; *veraltet für* jetzt)

i. v. = intravenös

IV = Invalidenversicherung (in der Schweiz)

i. V.[1] = in Vertretung; in Vollmacht

[1] *Diese Abkürzung wird so geschrieben, wenn sie unmittelbar der Grußformel oder der Bezeichnung einer Behörde, Firma u. dgl. folgt. Sie wird im ersten Bestandteil großgeschrieben* (I. V.), *wenn sie nach einem abgeschlossenen Text allein vor einer Unterschrift steht.*

IVF = In-vitro-Fertilisation

I|vo (m. Vorn.)

I|vo|rer, der; -s, - ‹eingedeutschte Form von franz. Ivoirien› (Einwohner der Republik Elfenbeinküste)

I|wan, der; -[s], -s (m. Vorn.; scherzh. Bez. für den Russen *od. [nur Sing.:]* die Russen)

I|wein (Ritter der Artussage)

i wo! (*ugs. für* keineswegs)

Iw|rit[h] (↑R 130), das; -[s] (Neuhebräisch; Amtssprache in Israel)

Iz|mir [is..., *auch* ˈis..., *österr.* ˈiz...] (heutiger Name von Smyrna)

J

J [jɔt, *österr.* je:] (Buchstabe); das J; des J, die J, *aber* das j in Boje (↑R 60); der Buchstabe J, j; *vgl. auch* Jot

J = chem. Zeichen für Jod; Joule

ja; jaja, *auch* ja, ja!; jawohl; ja freilich; ja doch; aber ja; na ja; nun ja; ach ja; *Großschreibung* (↑R 49): das Ja und [das] Nein; Ja, *auch* ja sagen; mit [einem] Ja antworten; mit Ja oder [mit] Nein stimmen; die Folgen seines Ja[s]; zu allem Ja und Amen, *auch* ja und amen sagen *(ugs.)*

Jab [dʒɛb], der; -s, -s ‹engl.› (*Boxen* kurzer, gerader Schlag)

Ja|bo, der; -s, -s (*kurz für* Jagdbomber)

Ja|bot [ʒaˈbo:], das; -s, -s ‹franz.› (Spitzenrüsche [an Hemden usw.])

Jacht, *Seemannsspr. auch* Yacht, die; -, -en ‹niederl.› ([luxuriös eingerichtetes] Schiff für Sport- u. Vergnügungsfahrten, *auch* Segelboot); **Jacht|klub**

Jack [dʒɛk] (m. Vorn.)

Jäck|chen; Ja|cke, die; -, -n ‹arab.-franz.›

Jä|ckel, der; -s, - ‹Koseform von Jakob› (*abwertend für* einfältiger Mensch)

Ja|cken‿kleid, ...ta|sche

Ja|cket|kro|ne [ˈdʒɛkit...] ‹engl.› (Porzellanmantelkrone, Zahnkronenersatz)

Ja|ckett [ʒa...], das; -s, *Plur.* -s, *selten* -e ‹franz.› (gefütterte Stoffjacke von Herrenanzügen); **Ja|ckett|ta|sche** (↑R 136); **Jäck|lein**

Jack|pot [ˈdʒɛk...], der; -s, -s ‹engl.› (Variante des Pokerspiels; bes. hoher [angesammelter] Gewinn bei einem Glücksspiel)

Jack|stag [ˈdʒɛk...], das; -[e]s, -e[n] ‹engl.; dt.› (*Seemannsspr.* Eisen zum Festmachen von Segeln; Gleitschiene)

Jac|quard [ʒaˈka:r], der; -[s], -s ‹nach dem franz. Seidenweber› (Gewebe mit großem Muster); **Jac|quard‿ge|we|be** (↑R 95), **...ma|schi|ne**

Jacque|line [ʒaˈklin] (w. Vorn.); **Jacques** [ʒak] (m. Vorn.)

[1]Ja|de, die; - (Zufluss der Nordsee)

[2]Ja|de, der; -[s] *u.* die; - ‹franz.› (ein Mineral; ein blassgrüner Schmuckstein)

Ja|de|bu|sen (Nordseebucht bei Wilhelmshaven); *vgl.* [1]Jade

ja|de|grün *vgl.* [2]Jade

Ja|fet *vgl.* Japhet

Jaf|fa (Teil der Stadt Tel Aviv-Jaffa in Israel); **Jaf|fa|ap|fel|si|ne** (↑R 105)

Jagd, die; -, -en; **Jagd|auf|se|her; jagd|bar; Jagd|bar|keit,** die; -; **Jagd‿beu|te, ...bom|ber** (*vgl.* Jabo), **...fie|ber, ...flie|ger, ...flin|te, ...flug|zeug, ...fre|vel, ...ge|schwa|der, ...ge|wehr, ...glück, ...grün|de** (*Plur.;* die ewigen -), **...horn** (*Plur.* ...hörner), **...hund, ...hüt|te; jagd|lich; Jagd‿mes|ser** (das), **...pan|zer, ...ren|nen** *(Pferdesport),* **...re|vier, ...schein, ...schloss, ...sprin|gen** *(Pferdesport),* **...staf|fel** (Verband von Kampfflugzeugen), **...tro|phäe, ...wurst, ...zeit**

Ja|gel|lo|ne, der; -n, -n; ↑R 126 (Angehöriger eines lit.-poln. Königsgeschlechtes)

ja|gen; er jagt; gejagt; **Ja|gen,** das; -s, - (forstl. Wirtschaftsfläche); **Jä|ger; Ja|ge|rei,** die; - (fortwährendes Hetzen); **Jä|ge|rei,** die; - (Jagdwesen; Jägerschaft); **Jä|ger|hut; Jä|ge|rin; Jä|ger‿la|tein, ...meis|ter, ...prü|fung; Jä|ger|schaft,** die; -; **Jä|ger|schnit|zel** (*Gastron.* Schnitzel mit würziger Soße und Pilzen); **Jä|gers|mann** *Plur.* ...leute *(veraltet, geh.);* **Jä|ger|spra|che,** die; -; **Ja|ger|tee** (*österr. für* Tee mit Schnaps)

Ja|gi|el|lo|ne *vgl.* Jagellone

Ja|go (m. Vorn.)

Jagst, die; - (r. Nebenfluss des Neckars)

Ja|gu|ar, der; -s, -e ‹indian.› (ein Raubtier)
jäh; Jä|he, die; - *(veraltet);* **Jäh|heit,** die; -; **jäh|lings**
Jahn; Turnvater -
Jahnn, Hans Henny (dt. Schriftsteller)
Jahr, das; -[e]s, -e; im -[e] (*Abk.* i. J.); laufenden Jahres (*Abk.* lfd. *od.* l. J.); künftigen -es (*Abk.* k. J.); nächsten -es (*Abk.* n. J.); ohne Jahr (*Abk.* o. J.); vorigen Jahres (*Abk.* v. J.); dieses -es (*Abk.* d. J.); das Jahr eins unserer Zeitrechnung; über Jahr und Tag; Jahr für Jahr; von Jahr zu Jahr; zwei, viele Jahre lang; er ist über (mehr als) 14 Jahre alt; Schüler ab 14 Jahre[n], bis zu 18 Jahren; freiwillige Helfer nicht unter 14 Jahren; das neue Jahr; zum neuen Jahr[e] Glück wünschen; *vgl.* achtziger; **jahr|aus;** *nur in* -, jahrein (jedes Jahr, immerzu); **Jahr|buch** (*Abk.* Jb.); **Jähr|chen; jahr|ein** *vgl.* jahraus; **jah|re|lang; jäh|ren,** sich; **Jah|res‿abon|ne|ment** (↑R 132), **...ab|schluss, ...an|fang, ...aus|gleich** *(Steuerwesen),* **...aus|klang, ...aus|stoß, ...be|ginn, ...bei|trag, ...be|richt, ...best|zeit** *(Sport),* **...ein|kom|men, ...en|de, ...frist** (innerhalb -), **...kar|te, ...ra|te, ...ring** *(meist Plur.),* **...tag, ...um|satz, ...ur|laub, ...wa|gen** (von einem Mitarbeiter eines Automobilwerks mit Preisnachlass erworbener neuer Pkw, den dieser erst nach einem Jahr veräußern darf); **Jah|res‿wech|sel, ...wen|de, ...zahl, ...zeit; jah|res|zeit|lich; Jahr|fünft,** das; -[e]s, -e; **Jahr‿gang** (der; *Abk.* Jg.; *Plur.* ...gänge [*Abk.* Jgg.]), **...gän|ger** (*südwestd., westösterr. u. schweiz. für* Person desselben Geburtsjahres); **Jahr|hun|dert,** das; -s, -e (*Abk.* Jh.); **jahr|hun|der|te|alt,** *aber* zwei, viele Jahrhunderte alt; **jahr|hun|der|te|lang; Jahr|hun|dert‿fei|er, ...mit|te, ...som|mer, ...wein, ...wen|de; jäh|rig** (*veraltet für* ein Jahr her; ein Jahr dauernd; ein Jahr alt); **...jäh|rig** (z. B. vierjährig, *mit Ziffer* 4-jährig [vier Jahre dauernd, vier Jahre alt]); ein Fünfjähriger (*mit Ziffer* 5-Jähriger); zwei dreijährige (*mit Ziffer* 3-jährige) Pferde; **jähr|lich** (jedes Jahr wiederkehrend); die -e Wiederkehr der Zugvögel; **...jähr|lich** (z. B. alljährlich [alle Jahre wiederkehrend], vierteljährlich); **Jähr|ling** (einjähriges Tier); **Jahr|markt; Jahr|markts|bu|de; Jahr|mil|li|o|nen** *Plur.;* in -;
Jahr|tau|send, das; -s, -e (*vgl.* Jahrhundert); **Jahr|wei|ser** (*geh. für* Kalender); **Jahr|zehnt,** das; -[e]s, -e; **jahr|zehn|te‿alt, ...lang**
Jah|ve, *ökum.* **Jah|we** [*beide* 'ja:ve] (Name Gottes im A. T.); *vgl. auch* Jehova
Jäh|zorn; jäh|zor|nig
Ja|i|rus (bibl. m. Eigenn.)
ja|ja *vgl.* ja
Jak, der; -s, -s ‹tibet.› (asiat. Hochgebirgsrind); *vgl. auch* Yak
Ja|ka|ran|da|holz ‹indian.; dt.› (*svw.* Palisander)
Ja|kar|ta [dʒa...] (Hptst. u. wichtigster Hafen Indonesiens)
Ja|ko, der; -s, -s ‹franz.› (eine Papageienart)
Ja|kob (m. Vorn.); (↑R 108:) der wahre - (*ugs. für* der rechte Mann, das Rechte); der billige - (*ugs. für* Verkäufer auf Jahrmärkten); **Ja|ko|bi,** das; - (Jakobitag); **Ja|ko|bi|ne** (w. Vorn.); **Ja|ko|bi|ner** (Angehöriger der radikalsten Partei in der Franz. Revolution); **Ja|ko|bi|ner|müt|ze; Ja|ko|bi|ner|tum,** das; -s; **ja|ko|bi|nisch; Ja|ko|bi|tag** *vgl.* Jakobstag; **Ja|kobs|lei|ter,** die; -, -n (Himmelsleiter; *Seemannsspr.* Strickleiter); **Ja|kobs|tag,** Ja|ko|bi|tag; **Ja|ko|bus** (Apostel); ↑R 93: - der Ältere, - der Jüngere
Ja|ku|te, der; -n, -n; ↑R 126 (Angehöriger eines Turkvolkes); **ja|ku|tisch**
Ja|la|pe, die; -, -n ‹span.› (trop. Windengewächs)
Ja|lon [ʒa'lõ:], der; -s, -s ‹franz.› (Absteckpfahl; Fluchtstab [für Vermessungen])
Ja|lou|set|te [ʒalu...], die; -, -n ‹franz.› (Jalousie aus Leichtmetall- od. Kunststofflamellen); **Ja|lou|sie,** die; -, ...ien ([hölzerner] Fensterschutz, Rollladen); **Ja|lou|sie‿schrank** (Rollschrank), **...schwel|ler** (bei der Orgel)
Jal|ta (Hafenstadt auf der Krim); **Jal|ta|ab|kom|men** (↑R 105)
Jam [dʒɛm], das; -s, -s *u.* die; -, -s ‹engl.› (*engl. Bez. für* Konfitüre)
Ja|mai|ka (Insel der Großen Antillen; Staat auf dieser Insel); **Ja|mai|ka|ner,** *auch* Ja|mai|ker; **Ja|mai|ka|ne|rin,** *auch* Ja|mai|ke|rin; **ja|mai|ka|nisch,** *auch* ja|mai|kisch; **Ja|mai|ka|rum,** der; -s (↑R 105); **Ja|mai|ker** usw. *vgl.* Jamaikaner usw.
Jam|be, die; -, -n ‹griech.› *u.* Jambus, der; -, ...ben (ein Versfuß); **jam|bisch**
Jam|bo|ree [dʒɛmbə'ri:], das; -[s], -s ‹engl.› ([Pfadfinder]treffen; Zusammenkunft)
Jam|bus *vgl.* Jambe
James [dʒe:ms, *auch* dʒe:mz] (m. Vorn.); **James Grieve** [- 'gri:v], der; --, - - ‹nach dem engl. Apfelzüchter› (eine Apfelsorte)
Jam|mer, der; -s; **Jam|mer‿bild, ...ge|stalt, ...lap|pen** (*ugs. für* ängstlicher Mensch, Schwächling); **jäm|mer|lich; Jäm|mer|lich|keit; Jäm|mer|ling; Jam|mer|mie|ne; jam|mern;** ich ...ere (↑R 16); er jammert mich; es jammert mich; **jam|mer|scha|de;** es ist -; **Jam|mer|tal,** das; -[e]s; **jam|mer|voll**
Jam|ses|sion ['dʒɛm'sɛʃ(ə)n], die; -, -s ‹engl.› (zwanglose Zusammenkunft von Jazzmusikern zu gemeinsamem Spiel)
Jams|wur|zel ‹engl.; dt.› (eine trop. Staude)
Jan (m. Vorn.)
Jan. = Januar
Ja|ná|ček ['jana:tʃɛk] (tschech. Komponist)
Jane [dʒe:n] (w. Vorn.); *vgl.* Mary Jane
Jan|ga|da [ʒaŋ'ga:da], die; -, -s ‹port.› (indian. Floßboot)
Jangt|se, der; -[s] *u.* **Jangt|se|ki|ang** [*auch* ...'ki̯aŋ] (↑R 132), der; -[s] (chin. Strom)
Jan|ha|gel [*auch* 'jan...], der; -s (*veraltet für* Pöbel)
Ja|ni|ku|lus [*auch* ja'nik...], der; - (Hügel in Rom)
Ja|nit|schar (↑R 132), der; -en, -en (↑R 126) ‹türk.› (Angehöriger der ehem. türk. [Kern]truppe); **Ja|nit|scha|ren|mu|sik**
Jan|ker, der; -s, - (*südd., österr. für* wollene Trachtenjacke)
Jan Maat, der; - -[e]s, *Plur.* - -e *u.* - -en, **Jan|maat** [*auch* 'jan...], der; -[e]s, *Plur.* -e *u.* -en ‹niederl.› (*scherzh. für* Matrose)
Jän|ner, der; -[s] ‹lat.› (*österr., seltener auch südd., schweiz. für* Januar)
Jan|se|nis|mus, der; - (eine kath.-theolog. Richtung); **Jan|se|nist,** der; -en, -en (↑R 126)
Ja|nu|ar, der; -[s], -e ‹lat.› (erster Monat im Jahr, Eismond, Hartung, Schneemond, Wintermonat; *Abk.* Jan.); *vgl.* Jänner; **Ja|nu|a|ri|us** (ital. Heiliger); **Ja|nus** (röm. Gott der Türen u. des Anfangs); **Ja|nus|ge|sicht, Ja|nus|kopf** (doppelgesichtiger Männerkopf); ↑R 95; **ja|nus|köp|fig; Ja|nus|köp|fig|keit,** die; -
Ja|pan *vgl.* Nippon; **Ja|pa|ner; Ja|pa|ne|rin; ja|pa|nisch,** *aber* (↑R 102): das Japanische Meer; *vgl.* deutsch; **Ja|pa|nisch,** das; -[s] (Sprache); *vgl.* Deutsch; **Ja-**

pa|ni|sche, das; -n; *vgl.* Deutsche, das; **Ja|pa|no|lo|ge,** der; -n, -n (↑R 126) ‹jap.; griech.› (Erforscher der jap. Sprache u. Kultur); **Ja|pa|no|lo|gie,** die; - (Japankunde); **Ja|pa|no|lo|gin; Ja|pan|pa|pier**
Ja|phet, *ökum.* Ja|fet (bibl. m. Eigenn.)
jap|pen (*nordd. für* japsen); **jap|sen** (*ugs. für* nach Luft schnappen); du japst; **Jap|ser**
Jar|di|ni|e|re [ʒar...], die; -, -n ‹franz.› (Schale für Blumenpflanzen)
Jar|gon [ʒarˈgõ:], der; -s, -s ‹franz.› ([saloppe] Sondersprache einer Berufsgruppe od. Gesellschaftsschicht)
Ja|ro|wi|sa|ti|on, die; -, -en ‹russ.› (Verfahren, mit dem das Wachstum von Saatgut beschleunigt wird); **ja|ro|wi|sie|ren**
Ja|sa|ger
Jas|min, der; -s, -e ‹pers.-span.› (ein Zierstrauch [mit stark duftenden Blüten])
Jas|mund (Halbinsel von Rügen); -er Bodden (↑R 103)
Ja|son (*griech. Sage* Führer der Argonauten)
Jas|pers (dt. Philosoph)
Jas|per|wa|re [ˈdʒɛs...] ‹engl.› (farbiges, weiß verziertes Steingut)
Jas|pis, der; *Gen.* - *u.* -ses, *Plur.* -se ‹semit.› (ein Edelstein)
Jass, der; -es (*schweiz., auch südd. u. westösterr.* ein Kartenspiel); **jas|sen** (Jass spielen); du jasst; er jasst; du jasstest; gejasst; jass! *u.* jasse!; **Jas|ser**
Ja|stim|me
Ja|ta|gan, der; -s, -e ‹türk.› (gekrümmter Türkensäbel)
jä|ten
Jau|che, die; -, -n; **jau|chen; Jau|che[n]‿fass, ...gru|be, ...wa|gen**
Jau|chert *vgl.* Juchart
jau|chig
jauch|zen; du jauchzt; **Jauch|zer**
Jauk, der; -s ‹slowen.› (*südösterr. für* Föhn)
Jau|kerl, das; -s, -n (*österr. ugs. für* Injektion)
jau|len (klagend winseln, heulen)
Ja|un|de (Hptst. von Kamerun)
Jau|se, die; -, -n ‹slowen.› (*österr. für* Zwischenmahlzeit, Vesper); **jau|sen** (du jaust) *u.* jaus|nen; **Jau|sen‿brot, ...sta|ti|on** (Gaststätte, in der man einen Imbiss einnehmen kann), **...zeit; jaus|nen** *vgl.* jausen
Ja|va [...v...] (eine der Großen Sundainseln); **Ja|va|ner; Ja|va|ne|rin; ja|va|nisch**

ja|wohl
Ja|wort *Plur.* ...worte
Jazz [dʒɛs, *auch* jats], der; - ‹amerik.› ([zeitgenöss.] Musikstil, der sich aus der Volksmusik der schwarzen Bevölkerung Amerikas entwickelt hat); **Jazz|band** [ˈdʒɛsbɛnt, *auch* ˈjats...], die; -, -s (Jazzkapelle); **jaz|zen** [ˈdʒɛs(ə)n, *auch* ˈjats(ə)n]; du jazzt; er jazzt; gejazzt; **Jaz|zer** [ˈdʒɛsər, *auch* ˈjatsər], der; -s, - (Jazzmusiker); **Jazz|fan** [ˈdʒɛsfɛn, *auch* ˈjats...]; **Jazz‿fes|ti|val, ...gym|nas|tik, ...ka|pel|le, ...kel|ler, ...mu|sik, ...mu|si|ker, ...trom|pe|ter**
Jb. = Jahrbuch
je; seit je; je Person; je drei; je zwei und zwei; je beschäftigten Arbeiter; je länger, je lieber (*vgl. aber* Jelängerjelieber); je mehr, desto lieber; je kürzer, umso schneller; je nachdem *(vgl. d.);* je nach ...; je nun
Jean [ʒã:] (m. Vorn.); **Jeanne** [ʒan] (w. Vorn.); **Jeanne d'Arc** [ʒanˈdark] (Jungfrau von Orleans); **Jean|nette** [ʒaˈnɛt] (w. Vorn.); **Jean Paul** [ʒã: -] ‹*eigtl.* Johann (Jean) Paul Friedrich Richter› (dt. Schriftsteller)
Jeans [dʒi:nz] *Plur. od.* die; -, - ‹amerik.› ([saloppe] Hose im Stil der Bluejeans); **Jeans‿an|zug, ...kleid**
jeck (*rhein. für* närrisch, verrückt); **Jeck,** der; -en, -en (*rhein. für* [Fastnachts]narr)
je|den|falls *vgl.* [1]Fall
je|der, jede, jedes; jedes Mal; zu jeder Stunde, Zeit; auf jeden Fall; zu Anfang jedes Jahres, *auch* jeden Jahres; (↑R 48:) das weiß ein jeder; jeder Beliebige kann daran teilnehmen; jeder Einzelne wurde gefragt; alles und jedes (alles ohne Ausnahme); **je|der|art; je|der|lei;** auf - Weise; **je|der|mann** (↑R 48); es ist nicht -s Sache; **je|der|zeit** (immer), *aber* zu jeder Zeit; **je|der|zei|tig; je|des Mal; je|des|ma|lig**
je|doch
jed|we|der (*veraltend für* jeder), jedwede, jedwedes; jedweden Inhalts; jedweder neue Versuch; jedweder Angestellte
Jeep ® [dʒi:p], der; -s, -s ‹amerik.› (kleiner [amerik.] Kriegs-, Geländekraftwagen)
jeg|li|cher; ↑R 48 (*veraltend für* jeder); ein jeglicher; jegliches; jeglichen Geschlechts; jeglicher Angestellte; frei von jeglichem neidischen Gefühl
je|her [*auch* ˈje:ˈhe:r]; von -
Je|ho|va [...va] (*durch Vokalveränderung entstandene Form von* Jahve)

jein (*ugs. für* ja *u.* nein)
Je|län|ger|je|lie|ber, das; -s, - (Geißblatt)
Jel|zin (russ. Politiker)
je|mals
je|mand; *Gen.* -[e]s, *Dat.* -em, *auch* -, *Akk.* -en, *auch* -; sonst jemand; *aber* irgendjemand; jemand anders; mit, von jemand anders, *auch* anderem; jemand Fremdes; *aber* ein gewisser Jemand; *vgl.* irgend
je mehr
Je|men *auch mit Artikel* der; -[s] (Staat auf der Arabischen Halbinsel); *vgl.* Irak; **Je|me|nit,** der; -en, -en (↑R 126); **je|me|ni|tisch**
je|mi|ne! ‹*entstellt aus lat.* Jesu domine! = „o Herr Jesus!"› *(ugs.);* ojemine!, herrjemine!
Jen *vgl.* Yen
Je|na (Stadt an der Saale)
je nach|dem; je nachdem[,] ob/wie (↑R 88)
Je|na|er, *auch* Je|nen|ser (↑R 103); Jenaer Glas; **je|na|isch; Je|nen|ser** *vgl.* Jenaer
je|ner, jene, jenes; in jener Zeit, Stunde; ich erinnere mich jenes Tages; (↑R 48:) da kam jener; jener war es, der ...
je|nisch (die Landfahrer betreffend; *rotwelsch für* klug, gewitzt); -e Sprache (Gaunersprache, Rotwelsch)
Je|nis|sei, Jo|nis|sej [*beide* ...se:j, *auch* ...ˈse:j], der; -[s] (sibir. Strom)
Jen|ni, *auch* **Jen|ny** (w. Vorn.); **Jens** (m. Vorn.)
jen|sei|tig[1]; **Jen|sei|tig|keit**[1], die; -; **jen|seits**[1]; *als Präp. mit Gen.:* - des Flusses; **Jen|seits**[1], das; -; **Jen|seits|glau|be**[1]
Je|re|mia, Je|re|mi|as (bibl. Prophet); die Klagelieder Jeremiä (des Jeremia); **Je|re|mi|a|de,** die; -, -n (Klagelied)
Je|re|wan [*auch* ...ˈvan] (Hptst. von Armenien)
Je|rez [ˈçe:rɛs], der; - (ein span. Wein); *vgl.* Sherry; **Je|rez de la Fron|te|ra** [xeˈrɛs de la -] (span. Stadt); **Je|rez|wein** (↑R 105)
Je|ri|cho (Stadt im Westjordanland); **Je|ri|cho|ro|se** (↑R 105)
Je|ri|chow [...ço] (Stadt südöstl. von Tangermünde)
Jé|rôme [ʒeˈro:m] (m. Vorn.)
[1]**Jer|sey** [ˈdʒœ:(r)zi], der; -[s], -s ‹engl.› (eine Stoffart); [2]**Jer|sey,** das; -s, -s (Trikot des Sportlers)
je|rum!; ojerum!

---
[1] [*auch* ˈjɛn...]

Je|ru|sa|lem (die Heilige Stadt der Juden, Christen u. Moslems)
Je|sa|ja (bibl. Prophet); *vgl.* Isaias
Je|su|it, der; -en, -en; ↑R 126 (Mitglied des Jesuitenordens); **Je|su|i|ten|or|den,** der; -s; (Gesellschaft Jesu; *Abk.* SJ); **Je|su|i|ten|tum,** das; -s; **je|su|i|tisch;**
Je|sus ‹„Gott hilft" [*vgl.* Josua]› (bibl. m. Eigenn.); **Je|sus Chris|tus;** *Gen.* Jesu Christi, *Dat.* - - *u.* Jesu Christo, *Akk.* - - *u.* Jesum Christum, *Anredefall* - - *u.* Jesu Christe; **Je|sus|kind,** das; -[e]s; **Je|sus Na|za|re|nus Rex Ju|dae|o|rum** [- - - judɛ...] ‹lat., „Jesus von Nazareth, König der Juden"›; *Abk.* I. N. R. I.; **Je|sus Peo|ple** [ˈdʒi:zəs ˈpi:p(ə)l] *Plur.* ‹engl.› (Anhänger der Jesus-People-Bewegung); **Je|sus-Peo|ple-Be|we|gung,** die; - (weltweit verbreitete religiöse Bewegung der Jugend); **Je|sus Si|rach** (Verfasser einer bibl. Spruchsammlung)
[1]Jet [dʒɛt], der; -[s], -s ‹engl.› (*ugs. für* Düsenflugzeug)
[2]Jet *vgl.* Jett
Jet|lag [dʒɛtlɛg], der; -s, -s ‹*zu* [1]Jet› (Beschwerden nach schnellem Überfliegen mehrerer Zeitzonen); **Jet|li|ner** [ˈdʒɛtlainə(r)], der; -s, - (Düsenverkehrsflugzeug)
Je|ton [ʒəˈtõ:], der; -s, -s ‹franz.› (Spielmarke)
Jet|set [ˈdʒɛtsɛt], der; -s ‹engl.› (Gruppe reicher, den Tagesmoden folgender Menschen, die, um immer „dabei zu sein", ständig [mit dem [1]Jet] reisen); **Jet|stream** [ˈdʒɛtstri:m], der; -[s], -s (starker Luftstrom in der Tropo- od. Stratosphäre)
Jett, *fachspr.* Jet [dʒɛt], der *od.* das; -[e]s ‹franz.-engl.› (Pechkohle, Gagat); **jett|ar|tig**
Jett|chen (w. Vorn.)
jet|ten [ˈdʒɛt(ə)n] ‹engl.› (mit dem [1]Jet fliegen); gejettet
jet|zig; jet|zo (*veraltet für* jetzt); **jetzt;** bis -; von - an; **Jetzt,** das; - (Gegenwart, Neuzeit); **Jetzt‿mensch, ...zeit** (die; -)
Jeu [ʒø:], das; -s, -s ‹franz.› ([Karten]spiel)
Jeu|nesse do|rée [ʒøˌnɛs dɔˈre:], die; - - ‹franz.› (*früher für* reiche, leichtlebige Jugend der Großstädte)
Je|ver [...f..., *auch* ...v...] (Stadt in Niedersachsen); **Je|ve|ra|ner; Je|ve|ra|ne|rin** [...v...]; **Je|ver|land,** das; -[e]s (Gebiet im nördl. Oldenburg); **Je|ver|län|der; je|ver|län|disch; je|versch**
je|wei|len (*veraltet für* dann und wann; *schweiz. neben* jeweils); **je|wei|lig; je|weils**
Jg. = Jahrgang; **Jgg.** = Jahrgänge
Jh. = Jahrhundert
jid|disch (jüd.-dt.); **Jid|disch,** das; -[s] (jüd.-dt. Schrift- u. Umgangssprache [in Osteuropa]); *vgl.* Deutsch; **Jid|di|sche,** das; -n; *vgl.* Deutsche, das; **Jid|dis|tik,** die; - (jiddische Literatur- und Sprachwissenschaft)
Jim [dʒim], **Jim|my** [ˈdʒimi] (m. Vorn.)
Jin|gle [ˈdʒiŋg(ə)l], der; -[s], -[s] ‹engl.› (kurze, einprägsame Melodie eines Werbespots)
Jit|ter|bug [ˈdʒitə(r)bag], der; -, -[s] ‹amerik.› (in Amerika entstandener Jazztanz)
Jiu-Jit|su [ˌdʒi:uˈdʒitsu(:)], das; -[s] ‹jap.› (*älter für* Jujutsu *[vgl. d.]*)
Jive [dʒaiv], der; -, -[s] ‹amerik.› (dem Jitterbug ähnlicher Tanz)
j. L. = jüngere[r] Linie (*Genealogie)*
J.-Nr. = Journalnummer
Jo|ab (bibl. m. Eigenn.)
Jo|a|chim [*auch* ˈjo:...]; (m. Vorn.); **Jo|a|chims|ta|ler,** der; -s, - ‹nach dem Ort St. Joachimsthal in Böhmen› (eine Münze); *vgl.* Taler
Jo|as, *ökum.* **Jo|asch** (bibl. m. Eigenn.)
[1]Job (*Schreibung der Vulgata für* Hiob, Ijob)
[2]Job [dʒɔp], der; -s, -s ‹engl.-amerik.› ([Gelegenheits]arbeit, Stelle); **job|ben** [ˈdʒɔ...] (*ugs. für* einen [2]Job ausüben); gejobbt; **Jobber** [ˈdʒɔbər], der; -s, - (Händler an der Londoner Börse, der nur in eigenem Namen Geschäfte abschließen darf; *auch allg. für* Börsenspekulant; *ugs. für* jmd., der jobbt); **Job|ber|tum,** das; -s; **Job|hop|ping** [...hɔpiŋ], das; -s, -s ‹engl.› (*ugs. für* häufiger Stellenwechsel); **Job|kil|ler** (*ugs. abwertend für* etwas, das Arbeitsplätze einspart, überflüssig macht); **Job|sha|ring** [...ʃɛ:riŋ], das; -[s] (Aufteilung eines Arbeitsplatzes unter mehrere Personen)
Job|si|a|de, die; - (komisches Heldengedicht von K. A. Kortum)
Jobst (m. Vorn.)
Joch, das; -[e]s, -e (*auch* ein älteres Feldmaß); ↑R 90: 9 Joch Acker, 3 Joch Ochsen; **Joch‿bein, ...bogen** *(Med.)*
Jo|chem, Jo|chen (m. Vorn.)
jo|chen (*landsch. für* ins Joch spannen)
Jo|ckei [ˈdʒɔke:, *engl.* ˈdʒɔki, *auch* ˈdʒɔkai *od.* ˈjɔkai], der; -s, -s ‹engl.› (berufsmäßiger Rennreiter); **Jo|ckey** *vgl.* Jockei
Jod, *chem. fachspr. auch* Iod, das; -[e]s ‹griech.› (chem. Element, Nichtmetall; *Zeichen* J, *auch* I); **Jo|dat,** *chem. fachspr. auch* Io|dat, das; -[e]s, -e (Salz der Jodsauerstoffsäure)
Jo|del, der; -s, *Plur.* - *u.* Jödel (*landsch. für* Jodelgesang); **jo|deln;** ich ...[e]le (↑R 16)
jod|hal|tig; Jo|did, *chem. fachspr. auch* Io|did, das; -[e]s, -e ‹griech.› (Salz der Jodwasserstoffsäure); **jo|die|ren** (mit Jod versehen); **Jo|dit** [*auch* ...ˈdit], das; -s, -e (ein Mineral)
Jod|ler; Jod|le|rin
Jo|do|form, das; -s (ein Mittel zur Wunddesinfektion)
Jo|dok, Jo|do|kus (m. Vorn.)
Jod|salz; Jod|tink|tur, die; - ([Wund]desinfektionsmittel)
Jo|el [...e:l, *auch* ...ɛl] (bibl. Prophet)
Jo|ga *vgl.* Yoga
jog|gen [ˈdʒɔ...] (Jogging betreiben); sie joggt, hat gejoggt; **Jog|ger; Jog|ging,** das; -s ‹amerik.› (Laufen in mäßigem Tempo [als Fitnesstraining]); **Jog|ging‿an|zug, ...be|klei|dung**
Jo|ghurt, *eindeutschend* Jo|gurt (↑R 33), der *u.*, *bes. österr. u. schweiz.*, das; -[s], *Plur. (Sorten:)* -[s], *bes. österr. auch* die; -, -[s] ‹türk.› (durch Zusatz von Bakterienkulturen gewonnene säuerliche Dickmilch)
Jo|gi, Jo|gin *vgl.* Yogi, Yogin
Jo|gurt *vgl.* Joghurt
Jo|hann [*auch* ˈjo:..., *österr. nur so*] (m. Vorn.); *vgl.* Johannes; **Jo|han|na, Jo|han|ne** (w. Vorn.); **jo|han|ne|isch;** johanneischer Geist, die johanneischen (von Johannes herrührenden) Briefe; **[1]Jo|han|nes** (m. Vorn.); - der Täufer; **[2]Jo|han|nes** (Apostel u. Evangelist)
Jo|han|nes|burg (größte Stadt der Republik Südafrika)
Jo|han|nes‿evan|ge|li|um (↑R 132; das; -s), **...pas|si|on**
Jo|hann|ge|or|gen|stadt (Stadt im westl. Erzgebirge)
Jo|han|ni[s], das; - (Johannistag); **Jo|han|nis‿bee|re, ...ber|ger** (ein Wein), **...brot** (Hülsenfrucht des Johannisbrotbaumes), **...feu|er, ...kä|fer, ...nacht, ...tag** (am 24. Juni), **...trieb, ...würm|chen; Jo|han|ni|ter,** der; -s, - (Angehöriger des Johanniterordens); **Jo|han|ni|ter|or|den,** der; -s; **Jo-**

han|ni|ter|un|fall|hil|fe, die; - (*eigene Schreibung der Organisation:* Johanniter-Unfall-Hilfe)
joh|len
John [dʒɔn] (m. Vorn.); - Bull („Hans Stier"; scherzh. Bez. des Engländers)
John|son (dt. Schriftsteller)
Joint [dʒɔynt], der; -s, -s ‹engl.› (Zigarette, deren Tabak mit Haschisch od. Marihuana vermischt ist)
Joint|ven|ture, *auch* **Joint Venture** [dʒɔynt'vɛntʃə(r)], das; -[s], -s (*Wirtsch.* Zusammenschluss von Unternehmen, Gemeinschaftsunternehmen)
Jo-Jo, das; -s, -s ‹amerik.› (Geschicklichkeitsspiel aus zwei miteinander verbundenen Scheiben und einer Schnur)
Jo|jo|ba, die; -, -s ‹mexik.› (ein Buchsbaumgewächs); **Jo|jo|ba|öl**
Jo|ker [*auch* dʒo:...], der; -s, - ‹engl.› (eine Spielkarte)
Jo|ko|ha|ma *vgl.* Yo|ko|ha|ma
jo|kos ‹lat.› (*veraltet für* scherzhaft); **Jo|kus,** der; -, -se (*ugs. für* Scherz, Spaß)
Jo|li|ot-Cu|rie [ʒɔ'ljo:ky'ri], Frédéric [frede'rik] *u.* Irène [i'rɛn] (franz. Physikerehepaar)
Jol|le, die; -, -n (kleines [einmastiges] Boot); **Jol|len|kreu|zer**
Jom Kip|pur, der; - - (hoher jüd. Feiertag)
Jo|na, *ökum.* [1]**Jo|nas** (bibl. Prophet); [2]**Jo|nas** (m. Vorn.)
[1]**Jo|na|than,** der; -s, - (ein Winterapfel); [2]**Jo|na|than,** *ökum.* Jo|natan (bibl. m. Eigenn.)
Jong|leur [ʒɔŋ'lø:r] (↑R 130), der; -s, -e ‹franz.› (Geschicklichkeitskünstler); **jong|lie|ren**
Jons|dorf, Kur|ort (im Zittauer Gebirge)
Jöpp|chen; Jop|pe, die; -, -n (Jacke); **Jöpp|lein**
Jor|dan, der; -[s] (größter Fluss Israels u. Jordaniens); **Jor|da|ni|en** (Staat in Vorderasien); *vgl. auch* Transjordanien; **Jor|da|ni|er; Jor|da|ni|e|rin; jor|da|nisch**
Jörg (m. Vorn.)
Jörn (m. Vorn.)
Jo|sa|phat, *ökum.* Jo|scha|fat (bibl. m. Eigenn.); das Tal - (östl. von Jerusalem)
Jo|schi|ja *vgl.* Josia
Jo|sef usw. *vgl.* Joseph usw.; [1]**Joseph,** [1]Jo|sef (m. Vorn.); [2]**Joseph,** *ökum.* [2]Jo|sef (bibl. m. Eigenn.); **Jo|se|pha** [*auch* jo'ze:fa], *auch u. österr. nur* Jo|se|fa [*auch* jo'ze:fa] (w. Vorn.); **Jo|se|phi|ne,** *auch u. österr. nur* Jo|se|fi|ne (w. Vorn.); **jo|se|phi|nisch;** Josephinisches Zeitalter (Zeitalter Josephs II.); **Jo|se|phi|nis|mus,** der; - (aufgeklärte kath. Staatskirchenpolitik im Österreich des 18. u. 19. Jh.s); **Jo|se|phus** (jüd. Geschichtsschreiber)
Jo|sia, Jo|si|as, *ökum.* Jo|schi|ja (bibl. m. Eigenn.)
Jost (m. Vorn.)
Jo|sua („Gott hilft" [*vgl.* Jesus]) (bibl. m. Eigenn.)
Jot, das; -, - ‹semit.› (Buchstabe); **Jo|ta,** das; -[s], -s (griech. Buchstabe: *I, ι*); kein - (nicht das Geringste); **Jo|ta|zis|mus** (*svw.* Itazismus)
Joule [dʒu:l], das; -[s], - ‹nach dem Engländer J. P. Joule› (*Physik* Maßeinheit für die Energie; *Zeichen* J)
Jour [ʒu:r], der; -s, -s ‹franz.› (*früher für* [Dienst-, Amts-, Empfangs]tag); - fixe (fester Tag in der Woche [für Gäste, die nicht besonders eingeladen werden]); *vgl.* du jour *u.* à jour; **Jour|nail|le** [ʒur'naljə, *auch* ...'naj, *österr.* ...'najjə], die; - (gewissenlos u. hetzerisch arbeitende Tagespresse); **Jour|nal** [ʒur...], das; -s, -e (Tagebuch in der Buchhaltung; [Mode]zeitschrift; *veraltet für* Zeitung); **Jour|nal‿be|am|te** (*österr. für* Dienst habender Beamter), **...dienst** (*österr. für* Bereitschafts-, Tagesdienst); **Jour|na|lis|mus,** der; - ([bes. Wesen, Eigenart der] Zeitungsschriftstellerei; Pressewesen); **Jour|na|list,** der; -en, -en; ↑R 126 (jmd., der beruflich für die Presse, den Rundfunk, das Fernsehen schreibt, publizistisch tätig ist); **Jour|na|lis|tik,** die; - (Zeitungswesen); **Jour|na|lis|tin; jour|na|lis|tisch; Jour|nal|num|mer** (Nummer eines kaufmänn. od. behördl. Tagebuchs; *Abk.* J.-Nr.)
jo|vi|al [...v..., *österr. u. schweiz.* ʒo...] ‹lat.› (leutselig, gönnerhaft); **Jo|vi|a|li|tät,** die; -
Joyce [dʒɔys], James (ir. Schriftsteller)
Joy|stick ['dʒɔystik], der; -s, -s ‹engl.› (Steuerhebel für Computer[spiele])
jr., jun. = junior
[1]**Ju|an** [xuan] (m. Vorn.); Don - (*vgl. d.*)
[2]**Ju|an** *vgl.* Yuan
Ju|bel, der; -s; **Ju|bel‿fei|er, ...ge|schrei, ...greis** (*ugs. für* lebenslustiger alter Mann); **Ju|bel|jahr** (*bei den Juden* jedes 50., *in der kath. Kirche* jedes 25. Jahr); alle -e (*ugs. für* ganz selten); **ju|beln;** ich ...[e]le (↑R 16); **Ju|bel‿paar, ...ruf; Ju|bi|lar,** der; -s, -e ‹lat.›; **Ju|bi|la|rin; Ju|bi|la|te** („jubelt!") (dritter Sonntag nach Ostern); **Ju|bi|lä|um,** das; -s, ...äen; **Ju|bi|lä|ums‿aus|ga|be, ...aus|stel|lung, ...fei|er; ju|bi|lie|ren** (jubeln; *auch* ein Jubiläum feiern)
[1]**Ju|chart, Ju|chert,** der; -s, -e (altes südwestd. Feldmaß); 10 - Ackerland (↑R 90); *vgl.* Jauchert; [2]**Ju|chart, Ju|char|te,** die; -, ...ten (*schweiz. für* [1]Juchart)
ju|chen (*landsch. für* jauchzen); **juch|he!; Juch|he,** das; -s, -s (*ugs. für* oberste Galerie im Theater); **juch|hei!; juch|hei|ras|sa!; juch|hei|ras|sas|sa!; juch|heisa!; juch|hei|ßa!**
juch|ten (aus Juchten); **Juch|ten,** der *od.* das; -s ‹russ.› (feines, wasserdichtes Leder); **Juch|ten‿leder, ...stie|fel**
juch|zen (*Nebenform von* jauchzen); du juchzt; **Juch|zer**
ju|cken; es juckt mich [am Arm]; die Hand juckt mir, *auch* mich; mir, *auch* mich juckt die Hand; es juckt mir, *auch* mich in den Fingern (*ugs. für* es drängt mich)[,] dir eine Ohrfeige zu geben; ihm, *auch* ihn juckt das Fell (*ugs. für* er scheint Prügel haben zu wollen); *aber (ohne nähere Angabe)* es juckt (reizt) mich[,] ihm einen Streich zu spielen
Ju|cker, der; -s, - (leichtes [ung.] Wagenpferd); **Ju|cker|ge|schirr**
Juck‿pul|ver, ...reiz
[1]**Ju|da** (bibl. m. Eigenn.); [2]**Ju|da** (Sitz des Stammes Juda in u. um Jerusalem); *vgl.* Judäa; **Ju|däa** (Bez. des alten Südpalästinas, später ganz Palästinas); **Ju|da|ika** *Plur.* (Bücher, Sammelobjekte der jüd. Kultur u. Religion); **Ju|da|is|mus,** der; - (jüdische Religion); **Ju|da|is|tik,** die; - (Wissenschaft von der jüdischen Religion, Kultur, Geschichte); [1]**Ju|das** (bibl. m. Eigenn.); - I|scha|ri|ot, *ökum.* - Is|ka|ri|ot (Apostel, Verräter Jesu); - Thaddäus (ein Apostel); [2]**Ju|das,** der; -, -se ‹nach Judas Ischariot› (Verräter); **Ju|das‿kuss, ...lohn** (der; -[e]s; ↑R 95); **Ju|de,** der; -n, -n (↑R 126); **Ju|den|chris|ten|tum; Ju|den|geg|ner** (*für* Antisemit); **Ju|den|heit,** die; -; **Ju|den‿kir|sche** (eine Zierpflanze), **...stern; Ju|den|tum,** das; -s; **Ju|den|ver|fol|gung**
Ju|di|ka ‹lat., „richte!"› (Passionssonntag, zweiter Sonntag vor Ostern); **Ju|di|ka|ti|ve** [...və], die; - (*Rechtsspr.* richterliche Gewalt

[im Staat]); **ju|di|ka|to|risch** (*veraltend für* richterlich); **Ju|di|ka|tur,** die; -, -en (Rechtsprechung) **Jü|din; jü|disch;** die jüdische Zeitrechnung; [1]**Ju|dith** (w. Vorn.); [2]**Ju|dith,** *ökum.* Ju|dit (bibl. w. Eigenn.)
ju|di|zie|ren ‹lat.› (*Rechtsspr.* urteilen, richten); **Ju|di|zi|um,** das; -s, ...ien [...i̯ən] (aus langjähriger Gerichtspraxis sich entwickelndes Rechtsfindungsvermögen)
[1]**Ju|do,** der; -s, -s (*Kurzw. für* Jungdemokrat)
[2]**Ju|do** [*österr. meist* ˈdʒu:...], das; -[s] ‹jap.› (sportl. Ausübung des Jujutsu); **Ju|do|griff; Ju|do|ka,** der; -[s], -[s] (Judosportler)
Ju|gend, die; -; **Ju|gend‿amt, ...ar|beits|lo|sig|keit, ...ar|beits|schutz|ge|setz, ...be|geg|nung, ...be|we|gung, ...bild, ...bild|nis, ...er|in|ne|rung, ...er|zie|her, ...ese|lei** (↑R 132; *ugs.*); **ju|gend|frei** (Prädikat für Filme); **Ju|gend‿freund** (*ehem. in der DDR auch* Anrede für ein Mitglied der FDJ), **...freun|din, ...für|sor|ge; ju|gend|ge|fähr|dend;** ein -er Film; **Ju|gend‿grup|pe, ...her|ber|ge** (*vgl.* DJH), **...klub, ...kri|mi|na|li|tät** (die; -); **ju|gend|lich; Ju|gend|li|che,** der *u.* die; -n, -n (↑R 5 ff.); **Ju|gend|lich|keit,** die; -; **Ju|gend‿lie|be, ...li|te|ra|tur, ...or|ga|ni|sa|ti|on, ...pfar|rer, ...pfle|ge, ...psy|cho|lo|gie, ...recht** (das; -[e]s), **...rich|ter, ...schutz, ...sek|te; Ju|gend|stil,** der; -[e]s (eine Kunstrichtung); **Ju|gend|stil|lam|pe; Ju|gend‿streich, ...sün|de, ...tor|heit, ...wei|he** (eine feierliche Veranstaltung beim Übergang der Jugendlichen in das Leben der Erwachsenen), **...werk, ...zeit, ...zent|rum**
Ju|gos|la|we (↑R 132), der; -n, -n (↑R 126); **Ju|gos|la|wi|en; Ju|gos|la|win; ju|gos|la|wisch**
Ju|gur|tha (König von Numidien); **Ju|gur|thi|ni|sche Krieg,** der; -n -[e]s
ju|he! (*schweiz. für* juchhe!); **ju|hu!** [*auch* ˈju...]
Juice [dʒu:s], der *od.* das; -, -s [...sis] ‹engl.› (Obst- od. Gemüsesaft); 3 [Glas] - (↑R 90)
Juist [jy:st] (eine der Ostfriesischen Inseln)
Ju|ju|be, die; -, -n ‹franz.› (ein Strauch; Beere)
Ju|jut|su, das; -[s] ‹jap.› (Technik der Selbstverteidigung ohne Waffen)
Juke|box [ˈdʒu:k...], die; -, -es [...sis] ‹engl.› (*svw.* Musikbox)
Jul|bock, der ‹schwed.› (eine skandinavische Weihnachtsfigur)
Jul|chen (w. Vorn.)
Ju|lei (*verdeutlichende Sprechform von* Juli)
Jul|fest (Fest der Wintersonnenwende); *vgl.* Julklapp
Ju|li, der; -[s], -s ‹lat.› (der siebte Monat im Jahr, Heue[r]t, Heumond, Sommermonat); *vgl.* Julei; **Ju|lia,** Ju|lie [...i̯ə] (w. Vorn.); **Ju|li|an,** Ju|li|a|nus (röm. Jurist); **Ju|li|a|na, Ju|li|a|ne** (w. Vorn.); **ju|li|a|nisch;** der julianische Kalender (↑R 94); **Ju|li|a|nus** *vgl.* Julian; **Ju|lie** *vgl.* Julia; [1]**Ju|li|enne** [ʒyˈli̯ɛn] ‹franz.› (w. Vorn.); [2]**Ju|li|enne,** die; - (*Gastron.* feine Gemüsestreifen als Suppeneinlage und für Soßen); **Ju|li|enne|sup|pe;** [1]**Ju|li|er** [...i̯ər], der; -s, - ‹lat.› (Angehöriger eines röm. [Kaiser]geschlechtes); [2]**Ju|li|er,** der; -s (schweiz. Alpenpass), *auch* **Ju|li|er|pass** der; -es; **ju|lisch,** *aber* (↑R 102): die Julischen Alpen; **Ju|li|us** (röm. Geschlechtername; m. Vorn.); **Ju|li|us|turm,** der; -[e]s (↑R 95) ‹nach einem Turm der früheren Zitadelle in Spandau, in dem der Kriegsschatz des Dt. Reiches lag› (*übertr. für* vom Staat angesparte Gelder)
Jul|klapp, der; -s ‹schwed.› ([scherzhaft mehrfach verpacktes] kleines Weihnachtsgeschenk, das am Julfest von unbekanntem Geber in die Stube geworfen wird); **Jul‿mond** (*alte Bez. für* Dezember), **...nacht**
Jum|bo, der; -s, -s ‹amerik.› (*Kurzform für* Jumbojet); **Jum|bo|jet** [...dʒɛt] (Großraumflugzeug)
Ju|me|lage [ʒyməˈla:ʒ], die; -, -n [...ˈla:ʒ(ə)n] ‹franz.› (Städtepartnerschaft)
jum|pen [ˈdʒam...] ‹engl.› (springen); gejumpt
Jum|per [*engl.* ˈdʒam..., *bes. südd., österr.* ˈdʒɛm...], der; -s, - ‹engl.› (blusen- od. pulloverähnliches Kleidungsstück); **Jum|per|kleid**
jun., jr. = junior
jung; jünger, jüngste (*vgl. d.*); von jung auf; er ist der jüngere, jüngste meiner Söhne; *aber* (↑R 47): Jung und Alt (jedermann); Junge und Alte; mein Jüngster; er ist nicht mehr der Jüngste; er gehört nicht mehr zu den Jüngsten; (↑R 93 *u.* 108:) Jung Siegfried; der Jüngere (*Abk. [bei Eigennamen]* d. J.); das Junge Deutschland (eine Dichtergruppe des 19. Jh.s); die Junge Union (gemeinsame Jugendorganisation von CDU u. CSU); *vgl. auch* jüngste; **Jung‿brun|nen, ...bür|ger** (*österr. für* jmd., der das Wahlalter erreicht hat); **Jung|chen** (*landsch.*); **Jung|de|mo|krat** (Mitglied der [ehemaligen] Jugendorganisation der F.D.P.; *Kurzw.* Judo); **Jung|de|mo|kra|tin;** [1]**Jun|ge,** der; -n (↑R 126), *Plur.* -n, *ugs. auch* Jungs *u.* -ns; [2]**Jun|ge,** das; -n, -n (↑R 5 ff.); **Jün|gel|chen** (*oft abwertend*); **jun|gen** (Junge werfen); die Katze jungt; **Jun|gen|ge|sicht; jun|gen|haft; Jun|gen|haf|tig|keit,** die; -; **Jun|gen‿schu|le, ...streich; Jün|ger,** der; -s, -; **Jün|ge|rin; Jün|ger|schaft; Jung|fer,** die; -, -n (*veraltet*); **jüng|fer|lich; Jung|fern|fahrt** (erste Fahrt, bes. die eines neu erbauten Schiffes); **Jung|fern|flug; jung|fern|haft; Jung|fern‿häut|chen** (*für* Hymen), **...kranz** (*veraltet für* Brautkranz), **...re|de; Jung|fern|schaft,** die; - (*veraltet*); **Jung|fern|zeu|gung** (*für* Parthenogenese); **Jung|frau; jung|fräu|lich; Jung|fräu|lich|keit,** die; -; **Jung|ge|sel|le; Jung|ge|sel|len‿bu|de** (*ugs.*), **...da|sein, ...wirt|schaft, ...woh|nung; Jung|ge|sel|lin; Jung|gram|ma|ti|ker** (Angehöriger der Leipziger Schule der indogermanischen u. allgemeinen Sprachwissenschaft um 1900); **Jung|he|ge|li|a|ner** (Angehöriger der radikalen Gruppe der Hegelianer); **Jung‿holz, ...leh|rer; Jüng|ling; Jüng|lings|al|ter,** das; -s; **jüng|ling[s]|haft; Jung|pflan|ze; jungsch** (*berlin. für* jung); **Jung|so|zi|a|list,** der; -en, -en (Angehöriger einer Nachwuchsorganisation der SPD; *Kurzw.* Juso); **Jung|so|zi|a|lis|tin; jüngst** (*veraltend*); **jüngs|te,** *aber* (↑R 108): das Jüngste Gericht, der Jüngste Tag; *vgl.* jung; **Jung|stein|zeit,** die; - (*für* Neolithikum); **Jüngs|ten|recht** (*für* Minorat); **jüngs|tens** (*veraltet für* jüngst); **jüngst|hin** (*veraltend*)
Jung-Stil|ling (dt. Gelehrter u. Schriftsteller)
jüngst|ver|gan|gen; in -er Zeit; **Jung‿tier, ...un|ter|neh|mer, ...ver|hei|ra|te|te, ...ver|mähl|te, ...vieh, ...vo|gel, ...wäh|ler, ...wäh|le|rin**
Ju|ni, der; -[s], -s ‹lat.› (der sechste Monat des Jahres, Brachet, Brachmonat); **Ju|ni|kä|fer**
ju|ni|or ‹lat., „jünger"› (*hinter Namen* der Jüngere; *Abk.* jr. *u.* jun.); Karl Meyer junior; **Ju|ni|or,** der; -s, ...oren (Sohn [im Verhältnis

zum Vater]; *Mode* Jugendlicher; *Sport* Sportler zwischen 18 u. 23 Jahren); **Ju|ni|o|rat,** das; -[e]s (*svw.* Minorat); **Ju|ni|or|chef** (Sohn des Geschäftsinhabers); **Ju|ni|o|ren‿meis|ter** *(Sport)*, **...meis|ter|schaft** *(Sport)*, **...ren|nen** *(Sport)*; **Ju|ni|o|rin; Ju|ni|or|part|ner**

Ju|ni|us (röm. m. Eigenn.)

Jun|ker, der; -s, -; **jun|ker|haft; jun|ker|lich; Jun|ker|schaft,** die; -; **Jun|ker|tum,** das; -s

Jun|kie ['dʒaŋki], der; -s, -s ‹engl.-amerik.› (*Jargon* Drogenabhängiger)

Junk|tim, das; -s, -s ‹lat.› (Verbindung mehrerer [parlamentar.] Anträge zur gleichzeitigen Erledigung); **Junk|tims|vor|la|ge**

[1]**Ju|no** (*verdeutlichende Sprechform von* Juni)

[2]**Ju|no** (höchste röm. Himmelsgöttin); [3]**Ju|no,** die; - (ein Planetoid); **ju|no|nisch** ([2]Juno betreffend; stolz, erhaben); junonische Gestalt, Schönheit

Jun|ta ['xunta, *auch* 'junta], die; -, ...ten ‹span.› (Regierungsausschuss, bes. in Südamerika; *kurz für* Militärjunta)

Jüp|chen (*landsch. für* Jäckchen für Säuglinge); **Jupe** [ʒy:p], der, *seltener* das; -s, -s ‹franz.› (*schweiz. für* Frauenrock)

[1]**Ju|pi|ter** *Gen.* -s, *auch* Jovis [...v...] (höchster röm. Gott); [2]**Ju|pi|ter,** der; -s (ein Planet); **Ju|pi|ter|lam|pe** ® ‹nach der Berliner Firma „Jupiterlicht"› (sehr starke elektr. Bogenlampe für Film- u. Fernsehaufnahmen)

Ju|pon [ʒypɔ̃], der; -s, -s ‹franz.› (*schweiz. für* Unterrock)

Jupp (m. Vorn.)

[1]**Ju|ra** (*Plur. von* [1]Jus)

[2]**Ju|ra,** der; -s (*Geol.* mittlere Formation des Mesozoikums); ↑R 108: der Weiße -, der Braune -, der Schwarze -; [3]**Ju|ra,** der; -[s] (Bez. von Gebirgen); ↑R 102: der Fränkische -, der Schwäbische -; (↑R 103:) der Schweizer -; [4]**Ju|ra,** der; -[s] (schweiz. Kanton); **Ju|ra|for|ma|ti|on,** die; -; **Ju|ras|si|er** (Bewohner des [3,4]Jura); **ju|ras|sisch** (zum Jura gehörend)

Ju|ra|stu|dent

Jür|gen (m. Vorn.)

ju|ri|disch ‹lat.› (*österr., sonst veraltend für* juristisch); **ju|rie|ren** (in einer Jury mitwirken); **Ju|ris|dik|ti|on,** die; -, -en (Rechtsprechung; Gerichtsbarkeit); **Ju|ris|pru|denz,** die; - (Rechtswissenschaft); **Ju|rist,** der; -en, -en; ↑R 126 (Rechtskundiger); **Ju|ris|ten|deutsch,** das; -[s]; **Ju|ris|te|rei,** die; - (*scherzh. für* Rechtswissenschaft, Rechtsprechung); **Ju|ris|tin; ju|ris|tisch;** -e Fakultät; -e Person (rechtsfähige Körperschaft; *Ggs.* natürliche Person); **Ju|ror,** der; -s, ...oren ‹engl.› (Mitglied einer Jury); **Ju|ro|rin**

Jur|te, die; -, -n ‹türk.› (rundes Filzzelt mittelasiatischer Nomaden)

Ju|ry [ʒy'ri:, *auch* 'ʒy:ri], die; -, -s (Preisrichter- bzw. Kampfrichterkollegium); **ju|ry|frei** (nicht von Fachleuten, ohne Jury zusammengestellt); eine juryfreie Ausstellung; [1]**Jus** [*österr.* jus], das; -, Jura ‹lat.› (Recht, Rechtswissenschaft); Jura, *österr. u. schweiz.* Jus studieren

[2]**Jus** [ʒy:], die; -, *südd. auch* das; -, *schweiz. meist* der; - ‹franz.› (konzentrierter, eingedickter Fleischsaft; Bratensaft; *schweiz. auch für* Fruchtsaft)

Ju|so, der; -s, -s (*Kurzw. für* Jungsozialist)

Jus|stu|dent (*österr. u. schweiz. für* Jurastudent)

just ‹lat.› (*veraltend für* eben, gerade; recht); das ist - das Richtige; **jus|ta|ment** ‹franz.› (*veraltet, noch landsch. für* richtig, genau; nun erst recht, nun gerade); **jus|tie|ren** (genau einstellen, einpassen, ausrichten); **Jus|tie|rer; Jus|tie|rung; Jus|tier|waa|ge** (Münzkontrollwaage); **Jus|ti|fi|ka|ti|on,** die; -, -en (*fachspr. für* Rechtfertigung; *auch* svw. Justifikatur); **Jus|ti|fi|ka|tur,** die; -, -en (*fachspr. für* Genehmigung von Rechnungen nach Prüfung); **jus|ti|fi|zie|ren** (rechtfertigen; [eine Rechnung] nach Prüfung genehmigen); **Jus|ti|ne** (w. Vorn.); **Jus|ti|ni|an, Jus|ti|ni|a|nus** (Name byzant. Kaiser); **Jus|ti|nus** (m. Vorn.); **Jus|ti|tia** (altröm. Göttin der Gerechtigkeit); **jus|ti|ti|a|bel, Jus|ti|ti|ar** usw. *vgl.* justiziabel, Justiziar usw.; **Jus|tiz,** die; - (Gerechtigkeit; Rechtspflege); **Jus|tiz‿be|am|te, ...be|am|tin, ...be|hör|de; jus|ti|zi|a|bel,** *auch* jus|ti|ti|a|bel (richterlicher Entscheidung unterworfen); ...ab|le (↑R 130) Vergehen; **Jus|ti|zi|ar,** *auch* Jus|ti|ti|ar, der; -s, -e (Rechtsbeistand, Syndikus); **Jus|ti|zi|a|ri|at,** *auch* Jus|ti|ti|a|ri|at, das; -[e]s, -e (Amt des Justiziars); **Jus|tiz|irr|tum; Jus|ti|zi|um,** *auch* Jus|ti|ti|um, das; -s, ...ien [...iən] (Stillstand der Rechtspflege); **Jus|tiz‿mi|nis|ter, ...mi|nis|te|rin, ...mi|nis|te|ri|um; Jus|tiz|mord** (Hinrichtung eines unschuldig Verurteilten); **Jus|tiz‿pa|last, ...voll|zugs|an|stalt** (*Abk.* JVA), **...wa|che|be|am|te** (*österr.*); **Jus|tus** (m. Vorn.)

Ju|te, die; - ‹bengal.-engl.› (Faserpflanze; Bastfaser dieser Pflanze)

Jü|te, der; -n, -n; ↑R 126 (Bewohner Jütlands)

Ju|te|garn

Jü|ter|bog (Stadt im Fläming)

Ju|te‿sack, ...spin|ne|rei, ...ta|sche

jü|tisch, *aber* (↑R 102): die Jütische Halbinsel; **Jüt|land** (festländ. Teil Dänemarks); **jüt|län|disch**

Jut|ta, Jut|te (w. Vorn.)

Ju|ve|nal [...v...] (röm. Satiriker); **ju|ve|na|lisch** (satirisch, spöttisch); die juvenalischen Satiren (↑R 94)

ju|ve|na|li|sie|ren [...v...] ‹lat.› (am Stil, Geschmack der Jugend orientieren); **Ju|ve|na|li|sie|rung; ju|ve|nil** [...v...] (*geh. für* jugendlich, für junge Menschen charakteristisch; *Geol.* dem Erdinnern entstammend)

ju|vi|val|le|ra! [ju(:)vi(:)'va..., *auch* ...'fa...] (Ausruf der Freude bes. in Volksliedern)

[1]**Ju|wel,** das, *auch* der; -s, -en *meist Plur.* ‹niederl.› (Edelstein; Schmuckstück); [2]**Ju|wel,** das; -s, -e (Person od. Sache, die von jmdm. besonders geschätzt wird); **Ju|we|len|dieb|stahl; Ju|we|lier,** der; -s, -e (Schmuckhändler; Goldschmied); **Ju|we|lier|ge|schäft; Ju|we|lie|rin; Ju|we|lier|la|den**

Jux, der; -es, -e *Plur. selten* ‹lat.› (*ugs. für* Scherz, Spaß); aus lauter Jux und Tollerei (aus Übermut); **ju|xen** (*ugs. für* scherzen, Spaß machen); du juxt

Jux|ta, die; -, ...ten ‹lat.› (Kontrollstreifen [an Lotterielosen usw.]); **Jux|ta|po|si|ti|on,** die; -, -en (*Sprachw.* Nebeneinanderstellung [im Ggs. zur Komposition]; *Mineralogie* Ausbildung von zwei miteinander verwachsenen Kristallen, die eine Fläche gemeinsam haben); **Jux|ta|po|si|tum,** das; -s, ...ta (*Sprachw.* durch Nebeneinanderstellung entstandene Zusammensetzung, z. B. „Dreikäsehoch"); **Jux|te** (*österr. für* Juxta)

JVA = Justizvollzugsanstalt

jwd [jɔtve:'de:] ‹*aus berlinisch* janz weit draußen› (*ugs. scherzh. für* abgelegen, nicht ohne großen Zeitaufwand zu erreichen); die Baustelle ist jwd

Vgl. auch **C** *und* **Z**

K (Buchstabe); das K; des K, die K, *aber* das k in Haken (↑R 60); der Buchstabe K, k
k = Kilo...
K = *chem. Zeichen für* Kalium; Kelvin
K, κ = Kappa
k. = kaiserlich *vgl. d.;* königlich (im ehem. Österreich-Ungarn)
Ka|a|ba, die; - ‹arab.› (Hauptheiligtum des Islams in Mekka)
Ka|ba|le, die; -, -n ‹hebr.› (*veraltet für* Intrige, Ränke)
Ka|ba|nos|si, die; -, - (Wurstsorte)
Ka|ba|rett [*auch* 'ka...], das; -s, *Plur.* -s *u.* -e, *auch [österr. nur so]* das; -s, -s, Cabaret [...'re:, *auch* 'kabare], das; -s, -s ‹franz.› (Kleinkunst[bühne]; Speiseplatte mit Fächern); **Ka|ba|ret|ti|er** [...rɛ'ti̯e:], der; -s, -s (Besitzer einer Kleinkunstbühne); **Ka|ba|ret|tist,** der; -en, -en; (↑R 126; Künstler an einer Kleinkunstbühne); **Ka|ba|ret|tis|tin; ka|ba|ret|tis|tisch**
Ka|bäus|chen (*westmitteld. für* kleines Haus od. Zimmer)
Kab|ba|la, die; - ‹hebr.› (mittelalterl. jüd. Geheimlehre); **kab|ba|lis|tisch**
Kab|be|lei (*bes. nordd. für* Zankerei, Streit); **kab|be|lig** (*Seemannsspr.* unruhig; ungleichmäßig); **kab|beln;** sich - (*bes. nordd. für* zanken, streiten); ich ...[e]le mich (↑R 16); die See kabbelt (ist ungleichmäßig bewegt); **Kab|be|lung** *(Seemannsspr.)*
Ka|bel, das; -s, - ‹franz.› (isolierte elektr. Leitung; starkes Tau od. Drahtseil; *veraltet für* Kabelnachricht); **Ka|bel‿an|schluss, ...fern|se|hen, ...gat[t]** (Schiffsraum für Tauwerk)
Ka|bel|jau, der; -s, *Plur.* -e *u.* -s ‹niederl.› (ein Fisch)
Ka|bel‿län|ge (seem. Maß), **...le|ger** (Kabel verlegendes Schiff), **...lei|tung; ka|beln** (*veraltend für* [nach Übersee] telegrafieren); ich ...[e]le (↑R 16); **Ka|bel‿nach|richt** *(veraltet),* **...netz, ...schuh** *(Elektrotechnik),* **...tau** (das; -[e]s, -e), **...trom|mel, ...tu|ner** *(Fernsehtechnik);* **Ka|bel-TV,** das; -[s]
Ka|bi|ne, die; -, -n ‹franz.› (Schlaf-, Wohnraum auf Schiffen; Zelle [in Badeanstalten usw.]; Abteil); **Ka|bi|nen|rol|ler** (ein Fahrzeug); **Ka|bi|nett,** das; -s, -e ‹franz.› (Gesamtheit der Minister; Raum für Sammlungen; Qualitätsstufe für Wein; *österr. für* kleines, einfenstriges Zimmer; *regional für* Fachunterrichtsraum; *früher für* Beraterkreis eines Fürsten, Geheimkanzlei); **Ka|bi|netts‿be|schluss, ...bil|dung, ...fra|ge** (*seltener für* Vertrauensfrage); **Ka|bi|netts|jus|tiz** ([unzulässige] Einwirkung der Regierung auf die Rechtsprechung); **Ka|bi|netts‿kri|se, ...or|der** (Befehl des Herrschers), **...sit|zung; Ka|bi|nett|stück** (Prachtstück; besonders geschicktes Handeln); **Ka|bi|netts|vor|la|ge; Ka|bi|nett|wein**
Ka|bis, der; - ‹lat.› (*südd., schweiz. für* Kohl); *vgl.* Kappes
Ka|bo|ta|ge [...'ta:ʒə], die; ‹franz.› (*Rechtsw.* Personen- u. Güterbeförderung innerhalb eines Landes); **ka|bo|tie|ren**
Kab|rio (↑R 130), das; -[s], -s (*Kurzform von* Kabriolett); **Kab|ri|o|lett** [*auch* ...'le:, *österr. nur so*], das; -s, -s ‹franz.› (Pkw mit zurückklappbarem Verdeck; *früher* leichter, zweirädriger Wagen); **Kab|ri|o|li|mou|si|ne**
Ka|buff, das; -s, *Plur.* -e *u.* -s (*landsch. für* kleiner, dunkler Nebenraum)
Ka|bul [*auch* 'ka:...] (Hptst. von Afghanistan)
Ka|bu|se, Ka|bü|se, die; -, -n (*nordd. für* kleiner, dunkler Raum; *auch für* Kombüse)
Ka|by|le, der; -n, -n (Angehöriger eines Berberstammes)
Ka|chel, die; -, -n; **ka|cheln;** ich ...[e]le (↑R 16); **Ka|chel|ofen** (↑R 132)
Ka|che|xie [kax...] (↑R 132), die; -, ...i̯en ‹griech.› (*Med.* Kräfteverfall)
Ka|cke, die; - (*derb für* Kot); **ka|cken** *(derb);* **Ka|cker** (derbes Schimpfwort); **kack|fi|del** (*derb für* sehr fidel)
Ka|da|ver [...vər], der; -s, - ‹lat.› (toter [Tier]körper, Aas); **Ka|da|ver‿ge|hor|sam** (blinder Gehorsam), **...mehl, ...ver|wer|tung**
Kad|disch, das; -s ‹hebr.› (jüdisches Gebet für Verstorbene)
Ka|denz, die; -, -en ‹ital.› (Schluss eines Verses, eines Musikstückes; unbegleitetes Improvisieren des Solisten im Konzert; *Sprachw.* Schlussfall der Stimme); **ka|den|zie|ren** (*Musik* eine Kadenz spielen)
Ka|der, der, *schweiz.* das; -s, - ‹franz.› (*ehem. in der DDR* Stamm von besonders ausgebildeten u. geschulten Nachwuchs- bzw. Führungskräften [in Wirtschaft, Staat u. Ä.]; *auch für* Angehöriger dieses Personenkreises; *Milit.* Stamm, Kerntruppe einer Armee; *Sport* Stamm von Sportlern, die für einen Wettkampf infrage kommen); **Ka|der|lei|ter,** der *(ehem. in der DDR);* **Ka|der|par|tie** (bestimmte Partie im Billard); **Ka|der|schmie|de** (*ugs. für* Ausbildungsstelle für Kader)
Ka|dett, der; -en, -en (↑R 126); ‹franz.› (*früher* Zögling einer militär. Erziehungsanstalt; *schweiz. für* Mitglied einer [Schul]organisation für militär. Vorunterricht; *ugs. scherzh. für* Bursche, Kerl); **Ka|det|ten‿an|stalt, ...korps, ...schu|le**
Ka|di, der; -s, -s ‹arab.› (Richter in islamischen Ländern; *ugs. für* Richter)
kad|mie|ren *od.* **ver|kad|men** ‹griech.› (Metalle mit einer Kadmiumschicht überziehen); **Kad|mi|um,** *chem. fachspr.* Cad|mium, das; -s (chem. Element, Metall; *Zeichen* Cd); **Kad|mi|um|le|gie|rung**
Kad|mos, Kad|mus (König u. Held der griech. Sage)
ka|du|zie|ren (*Rechtsw.* für verfallen erklären)
Ka|far|na|um *vgl.* Kapernaum
Kä|fer, der; -s, - (*ugs. auch für* Volkswagen); **Kä|fer|samm|lung**
[1]**Kaff,** das; -[e]s (*nordd. für* Spreu; Wertloses; Geschwätz)
[2]**Kaff,** das; -s, *Plur.* -s *u.* -e ‹zigeuner.› (*ugs. für* Dorf, armselige Ortschaft)
Kaf|fee [*auch, österr. nur,* ka'fe:], der; -s, *Plur. (Sorten:)* -s ‹arab.-franz.› (Kaffeestrauch, Kaffeebohnen; Getränk); 3 [Tassen] -; **Kaf|fee‿baum, ...boh|ne; kaf|fee|braun**
Kaf|fee|ern|te (↑R 136); **Kaf|fee|er|satz** (↑R 136); **Kaf|fee|ex|port** (↑R 136); **Kaf|fee|ex|trakt** (↑R 136)
Kaf|fee‿fahrt, ...fil|ter; Kaf|fee|haus (*österr. für* Café); **Kaf|fee‿kan|ne, ...klatsch** *(ugs. scherzh.),* **...kränz|chen, ...löf|fel, ...ma|schi|ne, ...müh|le, ...pau|se, ...satz, ...ser|vice; Kaf|fee|sie|der** (*österr. amtl., sonst meist abwertend für* Kaffeehausbesitzer); **Kaf|fee‿sor|te, ...strauch, ...tan|te** *(ugs. scherzh.),* **...tas|se,**

...trin|ker, ...was|ser (das; -s), **...zu|satz**

[1]**Kaf|fer,** der; -n, -n; ↑R 126 (*früher* Angehöriger eines Bantustammes in Südafrika)

[2]**Kaf|fer,** der; -s, - ‹hebr.-jidd.› (*ugs. für* dummer, blöder Kerl)

Kaf|fern|büf|fel

Kä|fig, der; -s, -e; **kä|fi|gen** (*fachspr. für* in einem Käfig halten); **Kä|fig|hal|tung**

Ka|fil|ler, der; -s, - (*Gaunerspr.* Schinder, Abdecker); **Ka|fil|le|rei** (*Gaunerspr.* Abdeckerei)

Ka|fir, der; -s, -n ‹arab.› (*abwertend für* jmd., der nicht dem islamischen Glauben angehört)

Kaf|ka (österr. Schriftsteller); **kaf|ka|esk** (nach Art der Schilderungen Kafkas)

Kaf|tan, der; -s, -e ‹pers.› (langes Obergewand der orthodoxen Juden; *ugs. für* langes, weites Kleidungsstück)

Käf|ter|chen (*mitteld. für* Kämmerchen; Verschlag)

kahl; kahl sein, werden, bleiben; die Raupen haben den Baum [völlig] kahl gefressen; sie ließen sich die Köpfe [ganz] kahl scheren; einen Wald kahl schlagen

Kah|len|berg, der; -[e]s (Berg bei Wien)

Kahl|fraß, der; -es; **kahl fres|sen** *vgl.* kahl; **Kahl|frost** (Frost ohne Schnee); **Kahl|heit,** die; -; **Kahl-˯hieb** (abgeholztes Waldstück), **...kopf; kahl|köp|fig; Kahl|köp|fig|keit,** die; -; **kahl sche|ren** *vgl.* kahl; **Kahl|schlag** (abgeholztes Waldstück); **kahl schla|gen** *vgl.* kahl; **Kahl|wild** (*Jägerspr.* weibl. Hirsche)

Kahm, der; -[e]s (*fachspr. für* hefeähnl. Pilz-, Bakterienart); **kah|men** (Kahm ansetzen); **Kahm|haut** (aus Kahm gebildete Haut auf Flüssigkeiten); **kah|mig**

Kahn, der; -[e]s, Kähne; Kahn fahren (↑R 39), *aber* das Kahnfahren; **Kähn|chen; Kahn|fahrt**

[1]**Kai** [*österr.* ke:], *auch* Quai [kɛ], der; -s, -s ‹niederl.› (befestigtes Hafenufer)

[2]**Kai,** Kay (m. od. w. Vorn.)

Kai|man, der; -s, -e ‹indian.› (Krokodil im trop. Südamerika)

Kai|mau|er

Kain (bibl. m. Eigenn.)

Kai|nit [*auch* ...'nit], der; -s, -e ‹griech.› (ein Mineral)

Kains˯mal (*Plur.* ...male), **...zei|chen**

Kai|phas, *ökum.* Ka|ja|fas (bibl. m. Eigenn.)

Kai|ro (Hptst. Ägyptens); **Kai|ro|er** (↑R 103)

Kai|ser, der; -s, -; des -s Hadrian; - Hadrians Bauten; **Kai|ser˯ad|ler** (ein Greifvogel), **...fleisch** (*österr. für* geräuchertes Bauchfleisch, Schweinebauch), **...ge|bir|ge** (das; -s; in Tirol); **Kai|se|rin; Kai|se|rin|mut|ter** *Plur.* ...mütter; **Kai|ser|kro|ne** (*auch* eine Zierpflanze); **kai|ser|lich;** kaiserlich deutsch; kaiserlich österreichische Staatskanzlei; *im Titel* (↑R 56): Kaiserlich; **kai|ser|lich-kö|nig|lich** (Abk.: k. k.), *im Titel* Kaiserlich-Königlich (Abk.: K. K.)

Kai|ser|ling (ein Pilz)

Kai|ser˯man|tel (ein Schmetterling), **...pfalz** (*vgl.* [1]Pfalz), **...reich, ...sa|ge, ...schmar|ren** (*österr., auch südd.* in kleine Stücke gerissener Eierkuchen)

Kai|ser|schnitt (Entbindung, bei der die Gebärmutter durch einen Bauchschnitt geöffnet wird)

Kai|ser|sem|mel *(österr.)*

Kai|sers|lau|te|rer (↑R 103); **Kai|sers|lau|tern** (Stadt in Rheinland-Pfalz)

Kai|ser|stuhl, der; -[e]s (Bergland in Baden-Württemberg); **Kai|ser|stüh|ler** (↑R 28)

Kai|ser|tum, das; -s, ...tümer

Ka|ja|fas *vgl.* Kaiphas

Ka|jak, der, *seltener* das; -s, -s ‹eskim.› (einsitziges Boot der Eskimos; Sportpaddelboot); **Ka|jak-˯ei|ner, ...zwei|er**

Ka|jal, das; -[s] ‹sanskr.› (Kosmetikfarbe zum Umranden der Augen); **Ka|jal|stift**

Ka|je, die; -, -n ‹niederl.› (*nordd. für* Uferbefestigung; Kai); **Ka|je|deich** ([niedriger] Hilfsdeich)

Ka|je|put|baum ‹malai.; dt.› (ein Myrtengewächs); **Ka|je|put|öl,** das; -[e]s

Ka|jüt˯boot, ...deck; Ka|jü|te, die; -, -n (Wohn-, Aufenthaltsraum auf Schiffen)

Kak, der; -[e]s, -e (*nordd. veraltet für* Pranger)

Ka|ka|du [*österr.* ...'du:], der; -s, -s ‹malai.-niederl.› (ein Papagei)

Ka|kao [ka'kau̯, *auch* ka'ka:o], der; -s, *Plur. (Sorten:)* -s ‹mexik.-span.› (eine tropische Frucht; ein Getränk); **Ka|kao˯baum, ...boh|ne, ...but|ter, ...pul|ver**

ka|keln (*nordd. ugs. für* über Dummes, Belangloses reden); ich ...[e]le (↑R 16)

Ka|ke|mo|no, das; -s, -s ‹jap.› (japan. Gemälde im Hochformat auf einer Rolle aus Seide od. Papier)

Ka|ker|lak (↑R 126), der; *Gen.* -s *u.* -en, *Plur.* -en (Küchenschabe; Tier, auch Mensch mit vollständigem Albinismus)

Ka|ki, ka|ki|far|ben, Ka|ki|ja|cke usw. *vgl.* Khaki, khakifarben, Khakijacke usw.

ka|ko... ‹griech.› (schlecht..., übel..., miss...); **Ka|ko...** (Schlecht..., Übel..., Miss...); **Ka|ko|dyl|ver|bin|dung,** die; -, -en *meist Plur.* (*Chemie* Arsenverbindung); **Ka|ko|pho|nie,** die; -, ...ien ‹griech.› (Missklang; *Ggs.* Euphonie); **ka|ko|pho|nisch**

Kak|tee, die; -, -n ‹griech.› *u.* **Kak|tus,** der; *Gen.* -, *ugs. auch* -ses, *Plur.* ...teen [*auch* ...'te:n], *ugs. auch* -se (eine [sub]trop. Pflanze); **Kak|tus|fei|ge** ([Frucht des] Feigenkaktus)

Ka|la-A|zar, die; - ‹Hindi› (eine trop. Infektionskrankheit)

Ka|la|bas|se *vgl.* Kalebasse

Ka|lab|re|se (↑R 130), der; -n, -n (↑R 126); *vgl.* Kalabrier; **Ka|lab|re|ser** (breitrandiger Filzhut); **Ka|lab|ri|en** (Landschaft in Italien); **Ka|lab|ri|er** (Bewohner Kalabriens); **ka|lab|risch**

Ka|la|fa|ti, der; - ‹ital.› (Figur im Wiener Prater)

Ka|la|ha|ri[|step|pe], die; - (in Südafrika)

Ka|la|mai|ka, die; -, ...ken ‹russ.› (slaw.-ung. Nationaltanz)

Ka|la|mit, der; -en, -en *meist Plur.* (↑R 126) ‹griech.› (ausgestorbener baumhoher Schachtelhalm des Karbons)

Ka|la|mi|tät, die; -, -en ‹lat.› (schlimme, missliche Lage)

Ka|lan|choe [...çoe], die; -, ...choen ‹griech.› (eine Zimmerpflanze)

Ka|lan|der, der; -s, - ‹franz.› (*Technik* Glätt-, Prägemaschine; Walzenanlage zur Herstellung von Kunststofffolien)

Ka|lan|der|ler|che ‹griech.; dt.› (Lerchenart im Mittelmeerraum)

ka|lan|dern (*fachspr. für* mit dem Kalander bearbeiten); ich ...ere (↑R 16); **ka|land|rie|ren** (↑R 130; Kunststoff zu Folie auswalzen)

Ka|la|sche, die; -, -n ‹russ.› (*landsch. für* Tracht Prügel); **ka|la|schen** (*landsch. für* prügeln)

Ka|lasch|ni|kow [...kɔf], die; -, -s ‹nach dem russ. Konstrukteur› (eine Schusswaffe)

Ka|lau|er, der; -s, - ‹*aus franz.* calembour *unter Anlehnung an die Stadt* Calau *umgebildet*› (*ugs. für* nicht sehr geistreicher [Wort]witz); **ka|lau|ern** (Kalauer machen); ich ...ere (↑R 16)

Kalb, das; -[e]s, Kälber; (↑R 108:) das Goldene - *(bibl.)*; **Kälb|chen; Kal|be,** die; -, -n (*svw.* Färse)

Kal|be (Mil|de) (Stadt in der Altmark); *vgl. aber* Calbe (Saale)
kal|ben (ein Kalb werfen); **Käl|ber|ma|gen; kal|bern, [1]käl|bern** (*ugs. für* umhertollen); ich ...ere (↑R 16); **[2]käl|bern** (*südd., österr. für* aus Kalbfleisch); **Käl|ber|ne,** das; -n; ↑R 5 ff. (*südd., österr. für* Kalbfleisch); **Käl|ber|zäh|ne** *Plur.* (*ugs. für* große Graupen); **Kalb|fell** *vgl.* Kalbsfell; **Kalb-fleisch; Kal|bin** (*südd., österr. svw.* Färse); **Kalb|le|der,** Kalbsle|der, das; -s; **Kälb|lein; Kalbs-˯bra|ten, ...bries, ...bries|chen** *od.* **...brös|chen, ...brust; Kalb[s]|fell** (*früher auch für* Trommel); **Kalbs˯fri|kas|see, ...hach|se** (*vgl.* Hachse), **...keu-le, ...le|ber, ...le|ber|wurst; Kalb[s]|le|der,** das; -s; **Kalbs-˯me|dail|lon, ...milch** (Bries-chen), **...nie|ren|bra|ten, ...nuss** (kugelförmiges Stück der Kalbskeule), **...schle|gel** (*landsch. für* Kalbskeule), **...schnit|zel** (*vgl.* [1]Schnitzel), **...steak, ...stel|ze** (*österr. für* Kalbshachse)
Kal|chas (griech. Sagengestalt)
Kalck|reuth (dt. Maler)
Kal|da|ri|um, das; -s, ...ien [...iən] ‹lat.› (altröm. Warmwasserbad; *veraltet für* warmes Gewächshaus)
Kal|dau|ne, die; -, -n *meist Plur.* ‹lat.› (*nordd., mitteld. für* essbares Eingeweidestück, Kuttelfleck)
Ka|le|bas|se, die; -, -n ‹arab.-franz.› (aus einem Flaschenkürbis hergestelltes Gefäß)
Ka|le|do|ni|en (*veraltet für* das nördl. Schottland); **Ka|le|do|ni-er; ka|le|do|nisch,** *aber* (↑R 108): der Kaledonische Kanal (in Schottland)
Ka|lei|do|skop (↑R 132), das; -s, -e ‹griech.› (optisches Spielzeug; lebendig-bunte [Bilder]folge); **ka-lei|do|sko|pisch**
Ka|lei|ka, das; -s ‹poln.› (*landsch. für* Aufheben, Umstände); [k]ein - machen
ka|len|da|risch ‹lat.› (nach dem Kalender); **Ka|len|da|ri|um,** das; -s, ...ien [...iən] (Kalender; Verzeichnis kirchl. Fest- u. Gedenktage); **Ka|len|den** *Plur.* (erster Tag des altröm. Monats); **Ka|len-der,** der; -s, -; der gregorianische, julianische Kalender; der hundertjährige Kalender; **Ka|len-der˯blatt, ...jahr, ...ma|cher, ...re|form, ...spruch, ...tag; ka-len|der|täg|lich; Ka|len|der|wo-che**
Ka|le|sche, die; -, -n ‹poln.› (leichte vierrädrige Kutsche)
Ka|le|va|la, *eingedeutscht* **Ka|le-wa|la,** die *od.* das; - (Titel des finn. Volksepos)
Kal|fak|ter, der; -s, - ‹lat.› *u.* **Kal-fak|tor,** der; -s, ...oren (*veraltend, oft abwertend für* jmd., der allerlei Arbeiten und Dienste verrichtet, z. B. im Gefängnis; *landsch. für* Aushorcher, Schmeichler)
kal|fa|tern ‹arab.-niederl.› (*Seemannsspr.* [hölzerne Schiffswände] in den Fugen abdichten); ich ...ere (↑R 16); **Kal|fa|te|rung; Kal|fat|ham|mer**
[1]Ka|li, das; -s ‹arab.› (*Sammelbez. für* Kalisalze [wichtige Ätz- u. Düngemittel])
[2]Ka|li (ind. Göttin, Gemahlin Schiwas)
Ka|li|an, Ka|li|un, der *od.* das; -s, -e ‹pers.› (pers. Wasserpfeife)
Ka|li|ban, der; -s, -e ‹*nach* Caliban, einer Gestalt in Shakespeares „Sturm“› (*selten für* Unhold, hässliches Ungeheuer)
Ka|li|ber, das; -s, - ‹griech.› (lichte Weite von Rohren; innerer Durchmesser; *auch für* Messgerät zur Bestimmung des Durchmessers; *ugs. übertr. für* Art, Schlag); **Ka|li|ber|maß,** das; **ka|lib|rie-ren** (↑R 130; *Technik* das Kaliber messen, [Werkstücke] auf genaues Maß bringen; [Messinstrumente] eichen); **...ka|lib|rig** (z. B. kleinkalibrig)
Ka|li|da|sa (altind. Dichter)
Ka|li|dün|ger
Ka|lif, der; -en, -en (↑R 126) ‹arab.› (ehem. Titel morgenländ. Herrscher); **Ka|li|fat,** das; -[e]s, -e (Reich, Herrschaft eines Kalifen); **Ka|li|fen|tum,** das; -s
Ka|li|for|ni|en [...iən] (mexikan. Halbinsel; Staat in den USA; *Abk.* Calif.); **Ka|li|for|ni|er; ka|li|for|nisch,** *aber* (↑R 108): der Kalifornische Meerbusen (*älterer Name für* Golf von Kalifornien)
Ka|li|in|dust|rie
Ka|li|ko, der; -s, -s ‹nach der ostind. Stadt Kalikut› (dichter Baumwollstoff)
Ka|li|lau|ge
Ka|li|man|tan (*indones. Name von* Borneo)
Ka|li|nin|grad [*auch* ...'gra:t] (russ. Stadt am Pregel; *vgl.* Königsberg)
Ka|li˯sal|pe|ter, ...salz; Ka|li|um, das; -s ‹arab.-nlat.› (chem. Element, Metall; *Zeichen* K); **Ka|li-um˯bro|mid, ...chlo|rat, ...hyd-ro|xid** (*vgl.* Oxid), **...per|man|ga-nat, ...ver|bin|dung**
Ka|li|un *vgl.* Kalian
Ka|lixt, Ka|lix|tus (Papstname)
Ka|lix|ti|ner, der; -s, - ‹lat.› (Anhänger der gemäßigten Hussiten)
Kalk, der; -[e]s, *Plur.* (*Sorten:*) -e; Kalk brennen; **Kalk|al|pen** *Plur.*; Nördliche, Südliche Kalkalpen
Kal|kant, der; -en, -en (↑R 126) ‹lat.› (Blasebalgtreter an der Orgel)
Kal|kar (Stadt in Nordrhein-Westfalen)
Kalk|bo|den; kal|ken; käl|ken (*Jägerspr.* Exkremente ausscheiden [von Greifvögeln]; *landsch. auch für* kalken); **Kalk|gru|be; kalk|hal|tig; kal|kig; Kalk˯man-gel, ...ofen** (↑R 132), **...sin-ter** (aus Wasser abgesetzter Kalk[spat]), **...spat** (ein Mineral), **...stein, ...tuff**
[1]Kal|kül, das, *auch* der; -s, -e ‹franz.› (Berechnung, Schätzung); **[2]Kal|kül,** der; -s, -e (*Math.* Methode zur systematischen Lösung bestimmter Probleme); **Kal-ku|la|ti|on,** die; -, -en ‹lat.› (Ermittlung der Kosten, [Kosten]-voranschlag); **Kal|ku|la|tor,** der; -s, ...oren (Angestellter des betriebl. Rechnungswesens); **kal-ku|la|to|risch** (rechnungsmäßig); -e Abschreibungen, Zinsen (*Wirtsch.*); **kal|ku|lier|bar; kal-ku|lie|ren** ([be]rechnen; veranschlagen; überlegen)
Kal|kut|ta (größte Stadt Indiens); **kal|kut|tisch**
Kalk|was|ser, das; -s; **kalk|weiß**
Kal|la *vgl.* Calla
Kal|le, die; -, -n ‹hebr.-jidd.› (*Gaunerspr.* Braut, Geliebte; Dirne)
Kal|li|graf, Kal|li|gra|fie usw. *eindeutschende Schreibung für* Kalligraph, Kalligraphie usw.; **Kal|li-graph** (↑R 33), der; -en, -en (↑R 126) ‹griech.› (Schönschreiber); **Kal|li|gra|phie** (↑R 33), die; - (Schönschreibkunst); **kal|li|gra-phisch** (↑R 33)
Kal|li|o|pe [ka'li:ope] (Muse der erzählenden Dichtkunst)
Kal|li|py|gos [*auch* ...'li(:)...] ‹griech., „mit schönem Gesäß“› (Beiname der Aphrodite)
kal|lös ‹lat.› (*Med.* schwielig); **Kal-lus,** der; -, -se (*Bot.* an Wundrändern von Pflanzen entstehendes Gewebe; *Med.* Schwiele; nach Knochenbrüchen neu gebildetes Gewebe)
Kál|mán (ung. Komponist)
[1]Kal|mar, der; -s, ...are ‹franz.› (eine Tintenfischart)
[2]Kal|mar (schwed. Hafenstadt); **Kal|ma|rer U|ni|on,** die; - *od.* **Kal|ma|ri|sche U|ni|on,** die; -n -
Kal|mäu|ser [*auch* ...mɔy...], der; -s, - (*veraltend, noch landsch. für*

jmd., der sehr zurückgezogen lebt und seinen Gedanken nachhängt)
Kal|me, die; -, -n ‹franz.› (*Meteor.* Windstille); **Kal|men‿gür|tel, ...zo|ne**
Kal|muck, der; -[e]s, -e (ein Gewebe); **Kal|mück, Kal|mü|cke,** der; ...cken, ...cken; ↑R 126 (Angehöriger eines westmongol. Volkes)
Kal|mus, der; -, -se ‹griech.› (eine Heilpflanze); **Kal|mus|öl**
Kal|my|ke, der; -n, -n *vgl.* Kalmück
Ka|lo|bi|o|tik, die; - ‹griech.› (bei den alten Griechen die Kunst, ein harmon. Leben zu führen); **Ka|lo|ka|ga|thie,** die; - (körperl. u. geistige Vollkommenheit als Bildungsideal im alten Griechenland)
Ka|lo|rie, die; -, ...ien ‹lat.› (*früher* physikal. Maßeinheit für die Wärmemenge; *auch* Maßeinheit für den Energiewert von Lebensmitteln; *Zeichen* cal); **ka|lo|ri|en‿arm, ...be|wusst; Ka|lo|ri|en‿ge|halt; Ka|lo|rik,** die; - (Wärmelehre); **Ka|lo|ri|me|ter,** das; -s, - ‹lat.; griech.› (*Physik* Wärmemessgerät); **Ka|lo|ri|met|rie** (↑R 130), die; - (*Physik* Lehre von der Messung von Wärmemengen); **ka|lo|ri|met|risch; ka|lo|risch** ‹lat.› (*Physik* die Wärme, die Kalorien betreffend); **ka|lo|ri|sie|ren** (*Chemie* auf Metallen eine Schutzschicht durch Glühen in Aluminiumpulver herstellen)
Ka|lot|te, die; -, -n ‹franz.› (Käppchen [der kath. Geistlichen]; *Archit.* flache Kuppel; *Med.* Schädeldach)
Kal|pak [*auch* 'kal...], **Kol|pak** [*auch* 'kɔl...], der; -s, -s ‹türk.› (asiat. Lammfell-, Filzmütze; Husarenmütze)
kalt; kälter, kälteste; kalte Ente (ein Getränk); kalte Fährte; kalte Küche; kalte Miete (Miete ohne Heizung); auf kalt und warm reagieren; kalter Schlag (nicht zündender Blitz); ein kalter (nicht mit Waffen geführter) Krieg, *aber* (↑R 56:) der Kalte Krieg (als historische Epoche). *Schreibung in Verbindung mit Verben und Partizipien* (↑R 38 f.): kalt bleiben; das Wetter war kalt geblieben; die Ereignisse haben sie [völlig] kalt gelassen *(ugs.)*; den Pudding über Nacht [sehr] kalt stellen; den Kühlschrank kälter stellen; er hat uns kalt lächelnd (*ugs. für* ohne Mitgefühl, skrupellos) die Tür gewiesen; *vgl. aber* kaltmachen, kaltstellen *sowie die fachsprachlichen Wörter* kaltschweißen, kaltwalzen; kaltgepresst, kaltgeschlagen; **Kalt|blut,** das; -[e]s (eine Pferderasse); **Kalt|blü|ter** *(Zool.)*; **kalt|blü|tig; Kalt|blü|tig|keit,** die; -; **Käl|te,** die; -; **Käl|te‿ein|bruch, ...grad, ...ma|schi|ne, ...pe|ri|o|de, ...pol** (kältester Ort der Erde)
Kal|ter (*bayr., österr. für* [Fisch]behälter)
Käl|te‿sturz, ...tech|nik, ...wel|le; Kalt|front *(Meteor.)*; **kalt|ge|presst** *(fachspr.)*; kaltgepresstes Öl; **kalt|ge|schla|gen** *(fachspr.)*; kaltgeschlagenes Öl; **Kalt|haus** (Gewächshaus mit Innentemperaturen um 12 °C); **kalt|her|zig; Kalt|her|zig|keit,** die; -; **kalt lä|chelnd** *vgl.* kalt; **kalt las|sen** *vgl.* kalt; **Kalt‿leim, ...luft** *(Meteor.)*; **kalt|ma|chen** (↑R 38 f.; *ugs. für* ermorden); er hat ihn kaltgemacht; **Kalt‿mam|sell** (kalte Mamsell; *vgl.* Mamsell), **...mie|te** (Miete ohne Heizung); **Kalt|na|del|ra|die|rung** (ein Kupferdruckverfahren); **Kalt|scha|le** (kalte süße Suppe); **kalt|schnäu|zig** *(ugs.)*; **Kalt|schnäu|zig|keit,** die; - *(ugs.)*; **kalt|schwei|ßen;** ↑R 37 *(Technik); nur im Infinitiv u. Partizip II gebr.*; kaltgeschweißt; **Kalt|start; kalt|stel|len** (*ugs. für* [politisch] einflusslos machen); *vgl. aber* kalt; **Kalt‿stel|lung** *(ugs.)*, **...ver|pfle|gung; kalt|wal|zen;** ↑R 37 *(Technik); nur im Infinitiv u. Partizip II gebr.*; kaltgewalzt; **Kalt|walz|werk; Kalt|was|ser,** das; -s; **Kalt|was|ser‿heil|an|stalt, ...kur; Kalt|wel|le** (mithilfe chem. Mittel hergestellte Dauerwelle)
Ka|lum|bin, das; -s ‹Bantuspr.-nlat.› (Bitterstoff der Kolombowurzel)
Ka|lu|met [*auch* kaly'mɛ], das; -s, -s ‹lat.-franz.› (Friedenspfeife der nordamerik. Indianer)
Ka|lup|pe, die; -, -n ‹tschech.› (*landsch. für* schlechtes, baufälliges Haus)
Kal|va|ri|en|berg [...'va:ri̯ən...], der; -[e]s, -e ‹lat. calvaria „Schädel"; dt.› (Kreuzigungsgruppe; *nur Sing.:* Kreuzigungsort Christi)
kal|vi|nisch, cal|vi|nisch [...v...] ‹nach dem Genfer Reformator J. Calvin›; das kalvinische, calvinische Bekenntnis; **Kal|vi|nis|mus,** Cal|vi|nis|mus, der; - (evangelisch-reformierter Glaube); **Kal|vi|nist,** Cal|vi|nist, der; -en, -en; ↑R 126 (Anhänger des Kalvinismus); **kal|vi|nis|tisch,** cal|vi|nis|tisch
Ka|ly|do|ni|sche E|ber, der; -n -s ‹nach der ätol. Stadt Kalydon› (Riesentier der griech. Sage)
Ka|lyp|so (griech. Nymphe); *vgl. aber* Calypso
Ka|lypt|ra (↑R 130), die; -, ...ren ‹griech.› (*Bot.* Wurzelhaube der Farn- u. Samenpflanzen); **Ka|lypt|ro|gen,** das; -s (Gewebeschicht, aus der sich die Kalyptra bildet)
Kal|ze|o|la|rie [...i̯ə], die; -, -n ‹lat.› (*Bot.* Pantoffelblume)
Kal|zi|na|ti|on, *chem. fachspr.* Cal|ci|na|ti|on, die; - ‹lat.› (Zersetzung einer chem. Verbindung durch Erhitzen; Umwandlung in kalkähnliche Substanz); **kal|zi|nie|ren,** *chem. fachspr.* cal|ci|nie|ren; kalzinierte Soda; **Kal|zi|nier|ofen,** *chem. fachspr.* Cal|ci|nier|ofen (↑R 132); **Kal|zi|nie|rung,** *chem. fachspr.* Cal|ci|nie|rung (*svw.* Kalzination); **Kal|zit,** *chem. fachspr.* Cal|cit [*auch* ...'tsit], der; -s, -e (Kalkspat); **Kal|zi|um,** *chem. fachspr.* Cal|ci|um, das; -s (chem. Element, Metall; *Zeichen* Ca); **Kal|zi|um‿chlo|rid, ...kar|bid, ...kar|bo|nat** (*chem. fachspr.* Cal|ci|um...)
Ka|mal|du|len|ser, der; -s, - ‹nach dem Kloster Camaldoli bei Arezzo› (Angehöriger eines kath. Ordens)
Ka|ma|ril|la [...'ril(j)a], die; -, ...llen [...'ril(j)ən] ‹span.› (*geh. für* einflussreiche, intrigierende Gruppe in der Umgebung einer Regierung; *veraltet für* Berater eines Fürsten)
Ka|ma|sut|ra (↑R 130), das; -[s] ‹sanskr.› (indisches Lehrbuch der Erotik)
Kam|bi|um, das; -s, ...ien ‹nlat.› (*Bot.* ein zeitlebens teilungsfähig bleibendes Pflanzengewebe)
Kam|bod|scha (↑R 130; Staat in Hinterindien); **Kam|bod|scha|ner; kam|bod|scha|nisch**
Kam|brik [*auch* 'ke:m...] (↑R 130), der; -s ‹*zu* Cambrai› (ein Gewebe); **Kamb|rik|ba|tist**
kamb|risch (↑R 130; zum Kambrium gehörend); **Kamb|ri|um,** das; -s ‹*zu* Cambria = *alter Name von* Wales› (*Geol.* älteste Stufe des Paläozoikums); ↑R 108: das Obere Kambrium usw.
Ka|mee, die; -, -n [...'me:ən, *auch* ...'me:n] ‹franz.› (Schmuckstein mit erhaben geschnittenem Bild); **Ka|me|en|schnei|der**
Ka|mel, das; -[e]s, -e ‹semit.› (ein Huftier); **Ka|mel|dorn** *Plur.* ...dorne (ein Steppenbaum); **Kä|mel|garn** *od.* Käm|mel|garn

(Garn aus den Haaren der Angoraziege [*früher* = Kamelziege]); **Ka|mel|haar**

Ka|me|lie [...i̯ə], die; -, -n ‹nach dem mährischen Jesuiten Kamel [*latinisiert* Camellus]› (eine Zierpflanze)

Ka|mel|le, die; -, -n (*rhein. für* Karamellbonbon)

Ka|mel|len *Plur.* ‹griech.›; olle - (*ugs. für* Altbekanntes)

Ka|mel|lie [...i̯ə] *vgl.* Kamelie

Ka|me|lo|pard, der; *Gen.* -[e]s *u.* -en (↑R 126) ‹griech.› (Sternbild der Giraffe)

Ka|me|lott, der; -s, -e (ein Gewebe)

Ka|menz (Stadt in Sachsen)

Ka|me|ra, die; -, -s ‹lat.›; *vgl.* Camera obscura

Ka|me|rad, der; -en, -en (↑R 126) ‹franz.›; **Ka|me|ra|den|dieb|stahl; Ka|me|ra|de|rie,** die; - (*meist abwertend für* Kameradschaft; Cliquengeist); **Ka|me|ra|din; Ka|me|rad|schaft; ka|me|rad|schaft|lich; Ka|me|rad|schaft|lich|keit,** die; -; **Ka|me|rad|schafts‿ehe** (↑R 132), **...geist** (der; -[e]s)

Ka|me|ra‿ein|stel|lung, ...frau, ...füh|rung

Ka|me|ra|list, der; -en, -en (↑R 126) ‹griech.› (Fachmann auf dem Gebiet der Kameralistik; *früher* Beamter einer fürstl. Kammer); **Ka|me|ra|lis|tik,** die; - (bei staatswirtschaftl. Abrechnungen gebr. System des Rechnungswesens; *veraltet für* Finanzwissenschaft); **ka|me|ra|lis|tisch; Ka|me|ral|wis|sen|schaft**

Ka|me|ra‿mann (*Plur.* ...männer *u.* ...leute), **...re|cor|der** (Kamera, mit der man Videofilme aufnehmen [und abspielen] kann), **...team, ...über|wa|chung** (↑R 132), **...ver|schluss**

Ka|me|run [*auch* ...'ru:n] (Staat im Westen Zentralafrikas); **Ka|me|ru|ner** (↑R 103); **ka|me|ru|nisch; Ka|me|run|nuss** (Erdnuss)

ka|mie|ren, ka|mi|nie|ren ‹ital.› (*Fechtsport* die gegnerische Klinge mit der eigenen umgehen)

Ka|mi|ka|ze, der; -, - ‹jap.› (jap. Kampfflieger im 2. Weltkrieg, der sich mit seinem Flugzeug auf das feindliche Ziel stürzte)

Ka|mil|la *vgl.* Camilla

Ka|mil|le, die; -, -n ‹griech.› (eine Heilpflanze); **Ka|mil|len‿öl** (das; -[e]s), **...tee**

Ka|mil|li|a|ner, der; -s, - ‹nach dem Ordensgründer Camillo de Lellis› (Angehöriger eines Krankenpflegerordens)

Ka|mil|lo *vgl.* Camillo

Ka|min, der (*schweiz. für* „Schornstein" *u.* „Felsenspalte" *meist* das); -s, -e ‹griech.› (offene Feuerstelle mit Rauchabzug; *landsch. für* Schornstein; *Alpinistik* steile und enge Felsenspalte); **Ka|min‿fe|ger** *(landsch., schweiz.),* **...feu|er; [1]ka|mi|nie|ren** (*Alpinistik* im Kamin klettern)

[2]ka|mi|nie|ren *vgl.* kamieren

Ka|min‿keh|rer *(landsch.),* **...kleid** (langes Hauskleid)

Ka|mi|sol, das; -s, -e ‹franz.› (*früher* Unterjacke, kurzes Wams)

Kamm, der; -[e]s, Kämme; **Kämm|chen**

Käm|mel|garn *vgl.* Kämelgarn

käm|meln ([Wolle] fein kämmen); ich ...[e]le (↑R 16); **käm|men;** sich -

Kam|mer, die; -, -n; **Kam|mer|bul|le** (*Soldatenspr.* Unteroffizier, der die Kleiderkammer unter sich hat); **Käm|mer|chen; Kam|mer|die|ner; Käm|me|rei** (Finanzverwaltung einer Gemeinde); **Käm|me|rer; Kam|mer‿frau** *(veraltet),* **...herr** *(veraltet);* **...kam|me|rig** (z. B. vielkammerig); **Kam|mer‿jä|ger, ...jung|fer** *(veraltet),* **...jun|ker** *(veraltet);* **Käm|mer|lein; Kam|mer|ling** (ein Wurzelfüßer); **Käm|mer|ling** (*früher für* Kammerdiener); **Kam|mer‿mu|sik** (die; -), **...or|ches|ter, ...rat** (*Plur.* ...räte; früherer Titel), **...sän|ger; Kam|mer|spiel** (in einem kleinen Theater aufgeführtes Stück mit wenigen Rollen); **Kam|mer‿spie|le** (*Plur.;* kleines Theater), **...ton** (der; -[e]s; Normalton zum Einstimmen der Instrumente), **...zo|fe**

Kamm‿fett (vom Kamm des Pferdes), **...garn; Kamm|garn|spin|ne|rei; Kamm‿gras** (das; -es), **...griff** (der; -[e]s; *Geräteturnen*), **...grind** (der; -[e]s; eine Geflügelkrankheit); **Kamm|la|ge; Kämm|ling** (Abfall von Kammgarn)

Kamm|ma|cher (↑R 136); **Kämm|ma|schi|ne** (↑R 136); **Kamm|molch** (↑R 136); **Kamm|mu|schel** (↑R 136)

Kamm|weg

Ka|mor|ra, die; - ‹ital.› (Geheimbund im ehem. Königreich Neapel)

Kamp, der; -s, Kämpe ‹lat.› (*nordd. für* abgegrenztes Stück Land, Feldstück)

Kam|pa|gne [...'panjə] (↑R 130), die; -, -n ‹franz.› (Presse-, Wahlfeldzug; polit. Aktion; *Wirtsch.* Hauptbetriebszeit; Arbeitsabschnitt bei Ausgrabungen; *veraltet für* milit. Feldzug)

Kam|pa|la (Hptst. von Uganda)

Kam|pa|ni|en [...i̯ən] (hist. ital. Landschaft)

Kam|pa|ni|le, der; -, - ‹ital.› (frei stehender Glockenturm [in Italien])

Käm|pe, der; -n, -n; ↑R 126 (*veraltet, noch scherzh. für* Kämpfer, Krieger)

Kam|pe|lei *(landsch.);* **kam|peln,** sich (*landsch. für* sich balgen; sich streiten, zanken); ich ...[e]le mich mit ihm (↑R 16)

Kam|pe|sche|holz, das; -es ‹nach dem Staat Campeche in Mexiko› (Färbeholz)

Käm|pe|vi|se ['kɛmpəvi:zə], die; -, -r *meist Plur.* ‹dän.› (skand., bes. dän. Ballade des Mittelalters mit Stoffen aus der Heldensage)

Kampf, der; -[e]s, Kämpfe; - ums Dasein; **Kampf‿ab|stim|mung, ...an|sa|ge, ...bahn** (*für* Stadion), **...be|gier[|de]** (die; -); **kampf‿be|reit, ...be|tont; kämp|fen**

Kamp|fer, der; -s ‹sanskr.› (eine in Medizin u. chem. Industrie verwendete harzartige Masse)

[1]Kämp|fer (Kämpfender)

[2]Kämp|fer, der; -s, - (*Archit.* Gewölbeauflage; Teil eines Fensters)

Kämp|fe|rin; kämp|fe|risch; Kämp|fer|na|tur

Kamp|fer‿öl, ...spi|ri|tus

Kamp|fes|lärm, Kampf|lärm; **Kamp|fes|lust,** Kampf|lust; **kampf|fä|hig; Kampf‿fä|hig|keit** (die; -), **...fisch, ...flie|ger, ...flug|zeug, ...ge|fähr|te, ...geist** (der; -[e]s), **...grup|pe, ...hahn, ...hand|lung** *(meist Plur.),* **...hund, ...kraft, ...lärm** (*od.* Kamp|fes|lärm), **...läu|fer** (ein Vogel); **kampf|los; Kampf‿lust** (*od.* Kamp|fes|lust), **...maß|nah|me** *(meist Plur.),* **...mo|ral, ...pan|zer, ...pau|se, ...platz, ...preis** *(Wirtsch.),* **...rich|ter, ...sport; kampf|stark; Kampf|stoff; kampf|un|fä|hig; Kampf|un|fä|hig|keit,** die; -

kam|pie|ren ‹franz.› ([im Freien] lagern; *ugs. für* wohnen, hausen)

Kam|pu|chea [...pu'tʃe:a], **Kam|put|schea** (↑R 130; zeitweiliger Name von Kambodscha)

Kam|sin, der; -s, -e ‹arab.› (heißtrockener Sandwind in der ägypt. Wüste)

Kamt|scha|da|le (↑R 130), der; -n, -n; ↑R 126 (Bewohner von Kamtschatka); **Kamt|schat|ka** (eine nordostasiat. Halbinsel)

Ka|muf|fel, das; -s, - (*Schimpfwort, svw.* Dummkopf)

Kan. = Kansas
Ka|na (bibl. Ort); Hochzeit zu -
Ka|na|an [...na|an] (das vorisraelitische Palästina); **ka|na|a|nä|isch; Ka|na|a|ni|ter; ka|na|a|ni|tisch**
Ka|na|da (Bundesstaat in Nordamerika); **Ka|na|da|bal|sam,** der; -s (↑R 105); **Ka|na|di|er** [...iər] (Bewohner von Kanada; *auch* offenes Sportboot; *österr. auch* ein Polstersessel); **ka|na|disch,** *aber* (↑R 102): der Kanadische Schild (Festlandskern Nordamerikas)
Ka|nail|le [ka'naljə, *österr.* ka'naij(ə)], die; -, -n ‹franz.› (Schurke; *nur Sing.: veraltet für* Gesindel)
Ka|na|ke, der; -n, -n (↑R 126) ‹polynes.› (Eingeborener der Südseeinseln; *Ausspr. meist* [ka'nakə]: *ugs. abwertend für* ausländischer Arbeitnehmer)
Ka|nal, der; -s, ...näle ‹ital.› (*Sing. auch für* Ärmelkanal); **Ka|nal|bau** *Plur.* ...bauten; **Ka|näl|chen** (kleiner Kanal); **Ka|nal‿de|ckel, ...ge|bühr; Ka|na|li|sa|ti|on,** die; -, -en (Anlage zur Ableitung der Abwässer); **ka|na|li|sie|ren** (eine Kanalisation bauen; schiffbar machen; *übertr. für* in eine bestimmte Richtung lenken); **Ka|na|li|sie|rung** (System von Kanälen; Ausbau zu Kanälen); **Ka|nal‿schacht, ...schleu|se, ...tun|nel** (unter dem Ärmelkanal)
ka|na|nä|isch, Ka|na|ni|ter, ka|na|ni|tisch *vgl.* kanaanäisch usw.
Ka|na|pee [*österr.* ...'pe:], das; -s, -s ‹franz.› (*veraltend für* Sofa; *meist Plur.:* pikant belegte [geröstete] Weißbrotscheibe)
Ka|na|ren *Plur.* (Kanarische Inseln); **Ka|na|ri,** der; -s, - (*südd., österr. ugs. für* Kanarienvogel); **Ka|na|rie** [...iə], die; -, -n (*fachspr. für* Kanarienvogel); **Ka|na|ri|en|vo|gel; Ka|na|ri|er** (Bewohner der Kanarischen Inseln); **ka|na|risch; Ka|na|ri|sche In|seln** *Plur.* (Inselgruppe vor der Nordwestküste Afrikas)
Kan|da|har-Ren|nen ‹nach dem Earl of Kandahar› (jährl. stattfindendes Skirennen); ↑R 95
Kan|da|re, die; -, -n ‹ung.› (Gebissstange des Pferdes); jmdn. an die - nehmen (streng behandeln)
Kan|del, der; -s, -n *od.* die; -, -n (*landsch. für* [Dach]rinne)
Kan|de|la|ber, der; -s, - ‹franz.› (Ständer für Kerzen od. Lampen)
kan|deln (*landsch. für* auskehlen, rinnenförmig aushöhlen); ich ...[e]le (↑R 16)
Kan|del|zu|cker (*landsch. für* Kandis[zucker])
Kan|di|dat, der; -en, -en (↑R 126) ‹lat.› (in der Prüfung Stehender; [Amts]bewerber, Anwärter; *Abk.* cand.); - der Medizin (*Abk.* cand. med.); - des [lutherischen] Predigtamtes (*Abk.* cand. [rev.] min. *od.* c. r. m.; *vgl.* Doktor); **Kan|di|da|ten|lis|te; Kan|di|da|tin; Kan|di|da|tur,** die; -, -en (Bewerbung [um ein Amt o. Ä.]); **kan|di|del** (*nordd. veraltet für* heiter, lustig); **kan|di|die|ren** (sich [um ein Amt o. Ä.] bewerben)
Kan|di|dus *vgl.* Candidus
kan|die|ren ‹arab.› ([Früchte] durch Zucker haltbar machen)
Kan|dins|ky (russ. Maler)
Kan|dis, der; - ‹arab.› *u.* **Kan|dis|zu|cker** (an Fäden auskristallisierter Zucker); **Kan|di|ten** *Plur.* (*bes. österr. für* überzuckerte Früchte; Süßigkeiten)
Ka|neel, der; -s, -e ‹sumer.› (beste Zimtsorte); **Ka|neel|blu|me**
Ka|ne|pho|re, die; -, -n ‹griech.› (*Archit.* weibliche Figur als Gebälkträger)
Ka|ne|vas ['kanəvas], der; *Gen.* - *u.* -ses, *Plur.* - *u.* -se ‹franz.› (Gittergewebe; Akt- u. Szeneneinteilung in der ital. Stegreifkomödie); **ka|ne|vas|sen** (aus Kanevas)
Kän|gu|ru ['kɛŋg...], das; -s, -s ‹austral.› (ein Beuteltier)
Ka|ni|den *Plur.* ‹lat.› (*Zool.; Sammelbez. für* Hunde u. hundeartige Tiere)
Ka|nin, das; -s, -e ‹iber.› (Kaninchenfell); **Ka|nin|chen**
Ka|nis|ter, der; -s, - ‹sumer.-ital.› (tragbarer Behälter für Flüssigkeiten)
Kan|ker, der; -s, - ‹griech.› (*svw.* Weberknecht)
Kan|na *vgl.* Canna
Kan|nä, das; -, - ‹nach dem Schlachtort des Altertums in Italien: Cannae› (*geh. für* vernichtende Niederlage); *vgl.* kannensisch
Kan|na|da, das; -[s] (eine Sprache in Indien)
Kann|be|stim|mung (↑R 24)
Känn|chen; Kan|ne, die; -, -n; **Kan|ne|gie|ßer** (*veraltend iron. für* polit. Schwätzer); **kan|ne|gie|ßern** *(veraltend iron.);* ich ...ere (↑R 16); gekannegießert
Kän|nel, der; -s, - (*bes. schweiz. für* Dachrinne); **kan|ne|lie|ren** (*Archit.* mit Kannelüren versehen; auskehlen; riefeln); **Kan|ne|lie|rung**
Kän|nel|koh|le, die; - ‹engl.; dt.› (eine Steinkohlenart)
Kan|ne|lur, die; -, -en ‹sumer.-franz.› *u.* **Kan|ne|lü|re,** die; -, -n (*Archit.* senkrechte Rille am Säulenschaft; Hohlkehle)
Kan|ne[n]|bä|cker|land, das; -[e]s (Landschaft im Westerwald)
Kan|nen|pflan|ze (eine Insekten fressende Pflanze)
kan|nen|sisch; kannensische Niederlage (*geh. für* vollständige Niederlage, wie die bei Cannae); *vgl.* Kannä
kan|nen|wei|se; das Öl wurde kannenweise abgegeben
Kan|ni|ba|le, der; -n, -n (↑R 126) ‹span.› (Menschenfresser; *übertr. für* roher, ungesitteter Mensch); **kan|ni|ba|lisch; Kan|ni|ba|lis|mus,** der; - (Menschenfresserei; *übertr. für* unmenschliche Rohheit; *Zool.* das Auffressen von Artgenossen)
Kan|nit|ver|stan, der; -s, -e ‹niederl., „kann nicht verstehen"› (Figur bei J. P. Hebel)
Känn|lein
Kann|vor|schrift (↑R 24)
Ka|noldt (dt. Maler)
[1]**Ka|non,** der; -s, -s ‹sumer.-lat.› (Maßstab, Richtschnur; Regel; Lied, bei dem mehrere Stimmen nacheinander mit der Melodie einsetzen; Liste der kirchl. anerkannten bibl. Schriften; in der kath. Liturgie das Hochgebet der Eucharistie; kirchenamtl. Verzeichnis der Heiligen; kirchenrechtliche Norm [*fachspr. Plur.* Kanones ('ka:none:s)]; Verzeichnis mustergültiger Schriftsteller); [2]**Ka|non,** die; - (ein alter Schriftgrad)
Ka|no|na|de, die; -, -n ‹sumer.-franz.› ([anhaltendes] Geschützfeuer); **Ka|no|ne,** die; -, -n ‹sumer.-ital.› (Geschütz; *ugs. für* Pistole, Revolver; Könner); **Ka|no|nen|boot; Ka|no|nen|boot|po|li|tik,** die; - (Demonstration militärischer Macht [durch Entsendung von Kriegsschiffen] zur Durchsetzung politischer Ziele); **Ka|no|nen‿don|ner, ...fut|ter** (*ugs. abwertend; vgl.* [1]Futter), **...ku|gel, ...öf|chen, ...rohr, ...schlag** (ein Feuerwerkskörper), **...schuss; Ka|no|nier,** der; -s, -e ‹sumer.-franz.› (Soldat, der ein Geschütz bedient); **ka|no|nie|ren** (*ugs. für* kraftvoll schießen, werfen [beim Fuß-, Handball usw.])
Ka|no|nik, die; - ‹sumer.-lat.› (Name der Logik bei Epikur); **Ka|no|ni|kat,** das; -[e]s, -e (Amt, Würde eines Kanonikers); **Ka|no|ni|ker,** der; -s, - *od.* **Ka|no|ni|kus,** der; -, ...ker (Mitglied eines geistl. Kapi-

tels, Chorherr); **Ka|no|ni|sa|ti|on,** die; -, -en (Heiligsprechung); **ka|no|nisch** (den [1]Kanon betreffend, ihm gemäß; mustergültig); kanonisches Recht; kanonische Schriften; **ka|no|ni|sie|ren** (heilig sprechen, in den [1]Kanon aufnehmen); **Ka|no|nis|se,** die; -, -n ‹sumer.-franz.› *u.* **Ka|no|nis|sin** (Stiftsdame); **Ka|no|nist,** der; -en, -en (↑R 126) ‹sumer.-lat.› (Lehrer des kanon. Rechtes)

Ka|no|pe, die; -, -n ‹griech.› (altägypt. u. etrusk. Urne); **Ka|no|pen|de|ckel; Ka|no|pos** *vgl.* [1]Kanopus; **[1]Ka|no|pus** (antiker Name eines Ortes an der Nilmündung); **[2]Ka|no|pus,** der; - (ein Stern)

Ka|nos|sa, das; -s, -s ‹nach der Felsenburg Canossa in Norditalien›; ein Gang nach - (*übertr. für* Demütigung); **Ka|nos|sa|gang,** der (↑R 105)

Kä|no|zo|i|kum, das; -s; ‹griech.› (*Geol.* Erdneuzeit [Tertiär u. Quartär]); **kä|no|zo|isch**

Kans. = Kansas

Kan|sas (Staat in den USA; *Abk.* Kan. u. Kans.)

Kant (dt. Philosoph); Kant-Gesellschaft, *aber* Kantstudium (↑R 95)

kan|ta|bel ‹ital.› (*Musik* sangbar; gesanglich vorgetragen); ...ab|les (↑R 130) Spiel; **Kan|ta|bi|li|tät,** die; - ‹lat.› (*Musik* die Sangbarkeit, gesanglicher Ausdruck, melod. Schönheit)

Kan|ta|brer [*auch* 'kan...] (↑R 130), der; -s, - (Angehöriger eines alten iber. Volkes); **kan|ta|brisch;** *aber* (↑R 102): das Kantabrische Gebirge

Kan|tar, der *od.* das; -s, -e ‹lat.-arab.› (altes Gewichtsmaß im Mittelmeerraum); 5 - (↑R 90)

[1]Kan|ta|te, die; -, -n ‹lat.› (mehrteiliges, von Instrumenten begleitetes Gesangsstück für eine Solostimme oder Solo- und Chorstimmen); **[2]Kan|ta|te** ‹„singet!"› (vierter Sonntag nach Ostern)

Kan|te, die; -, -n; **Kan|tel,** die; -, -n (Holzstück mit quadrat. od. rechteckigem Querschnitt für Stuhlbeine usw.); **kan|ten** (mit Kanten versehen, rechtwinklig behauen; auf die Kante stellen); **Kan|ten,** der; -s, - (*bes. nordd. für* Brotrinde; Anschnitt od. Endstück eines Brotes); **Kan|ten‿ball** *(Tischtennis),* **...ge|schie|be** *(Geol.),* **...win|kel** *(Kristallographie)*

[1]Kan|ter, der; -s, - (Gestell [für Fässer]; Verschlag)

[2]Kan|ter [*auch* 'kɛn...], der; -s, - ‹engl.› (*Reitsport* leichter, kurzer Galopp); **kan|tern** (kurz galoppieren); ich ...ere (↑R 16); **Kan|ter|sieg** (*Sport* müheloser [hoher] Sieg)

Kant|ha|ken (ein kurzer Eisenhaken); jmdn. beim - kriegen (*ugs. für* jmdn. gehörig zurechtweisen)

Kan|tha|ri|de, der; -n, -n *meist Plur.* ‹griech.› (*Zool.* Weichkäfer); **Kan|tha|ri|den|pflas|ter** *(Med.);* **Kan|tha|ri|din,** *fachspr.* Can|tha|ri|din, das; -s (früher als Heilmittel verwendete Drüsenabsonderung bestimmter Insekten)

Kant|holz

Kan|ti|a|ner (Schüler, Anhänger Kants)

kan|tig

Kan|ti|le|ne, die; -, -n ‹ital.› (gesangartige, getragene Melodie)

Kan|til|le [*auch* ...'tiljə], die; -, -n ‹lat.-franz.› (gedrehter, vergoldeter od. versilberter Draht [für Tressen u. Borten])

Kan|ti|ne, die; -, -n ‹franz.› (Speisesaal in Betrieben, Kasernen o. Ä.); **Kan|ti|nen‿es|sen, ...wirt**

kan|tisch ‹*zu* Kant›; die kantischen Werke

[1]Kan|ton [...tɔn] (chin. Stadt)

[2]Kan|ton, der; -s, -e ‹franz.› (Bundesland der Schweiz [*Abk.* Kt.]; Bezirk, Kreis in Frankreich u. Belgien); **kan|to|nal** (den Kanton betreffend); **Kan|to|nal|bank** *Plur.* ...banken; **kan|to|na|li|sie|ren** (der Verantwortung des Kantons unterstellen); **Kan|to|ni|e|re,** die; -, -n ‹ital.› (Straßenwärterhaus in den ital. Alpen); **kan|to|nie|ren** ‹franz.› (*veraltet für* Truppen unterbringen; in Standorte legen); **Kan|to|nist,** der; -en, -en; ↑R 126 (*veraltet für* ausgehobener Rekrut); unsicherer - (*ugs. für* unzuverlässiger Mensch); **Kan|tön|li|geist,** der; -[e]s (*schweiz. abwertend für* Kirchturmpolitik, Lokalpatriotismus); **Kan|ton|ne|ment** [...'mã:], das; -s, -s *u.* schweiz. [...'mɛnt], das; -[e]s, -e (*schweiz., sonst veraltet für* Truppenunterkunft); **Kan|tons‿ge|richt, ...rat** (*Plur.* ...räte), **...rä|tin, ...schu|le** (kantonale höhere Schule), **...spi|tal**

Kan|tor, der; -s, ...oren ‹lat.› (Vorsänger im gregorian. Choral; Leiter des Kirchenchores, Organist); **Kan|to|rat,** das; -[e]s, -e (Amt eines Kantors); **Kan|to|rei** (ev. Kirchenchor; kleine Singgemeinschaft); **Kan|to|ren|amt**

Kant|schu, der; -s, -s ‹türk.› (Riemenpeitsche)

Kant|stein (*nordd. für* Bordstein)

Kan|tus, der; -, -se ‹lat.› (*Studentenspr.* Gesang)

Ka|nu [*österr.* ka'nu:], das; -s, -s ‹karib.› (leichtes Boot der Indianer; Einbaum; *zusammenfassende Bez. für* Kajak *u.* Kanadier)

Ka|nü|le, die; -, -n ‹sumer.-franz.› (Röhrchen; Hohlnadel)

Ka|nu|sla|lom; Ka|nu|te, der; -n, -n (↑R 126) ‹karib.› (*Sport* Kanufahrer)

Kan|zel, die; -, -n ‹lat.›; **Kan|zel‿red|ner, ...ton** (der; -[e]s)

kan|ze|ro|gen (*svw.* karzinogen); **kan|ze|rös** (*Med.* krebsartig)

Kanz|lei (Büro eines Anwalts od. einer Behörde); **Kanz|lei‿aus|druck, ...be|am|te; kanz|lei|mä|ßig; Kanz|lei‿spra|che, ...stil** (der; -[e]s); **Kanz|ler; Kanz|ler|amts|mi|nis|ter; Kanz|ler|kan|di|dat; Kanz|ler|schaft,** die; -; **Kanz|list,** der; -en, -en; ↑R 126 (*veraltet für* Schreiber, Angestellter in einer Kanzlei); **Kanz|lis|tin**

Kan|zo|ne, die; -, -n ‹ital.› (Gedichtform; Gesangstück; Instrumentalkomposition)

Ka|o|lin, das *od.* der *(fachspr. nur so);* -s, *Plur. (Sorten:)* -e ‹chin.-franz.› (Porzellanerde); **Ka|o|li|ner|de** (*svw.* Kaolin)

Kap, das; -s, -s ‹niederl.› (Vorgebirge); Kap der Guten Hoffnung (an der Südspitze Afrikas); Kap Hoorn (Südspitze Südamerikas)

Kap. = Kapitel (Abschnitt)

Ka|paun, der; -s, -e (kastrierter Masthahn); **ka|pau|nen** (*svw.* kapaunisieren); kapaunt; **ka|pau|ni|sie|ren** (Hähne kastrieren)

Ka|pa|zi|tät, die; -, -en ‹lat.› (Aufnahmefähigkeit, Fassungsvermögen; hervorragender Fachmann, Experte); **Ka|pa|zi|täts‿aus|las|tung, ...er|wei|te|rung; ka|pa|zi|tiv** (*Physik* auf die [elektr.] Kapazität bezüglich)

Kap Ca|na|ve|ral [- kə'nɛvərəl] (amerik. Raketenstartplatz)

Ka|pee ‹franz.›; *nur in der Wendung* schwer von - sein (*ugs. für* begriffsstutzig sein)

Ka|pe|lan, der; -s, -e ‹franz.› (ein Lachsfisch, Lodde)

Ka|pel|la, die; - ‹lat.› (ein Stern)

[1]Ka|pel|le, die; -, -n ‹lat.› (kleiner kirchl. Raum; Orchester)

[2]Ka|pel|le, *älter* Ku|pel|le, die; -, -n ‹lat.› (*fachspr. für* Tiegel)

Ka|pell|meis|ter

[1]Ka|per, die; -, -n *meist Plur.* ‹griech.› ([eingelegte] Blütenknospe des Kapernstrauches)

[2]Ka|per, der; -s, - ‹niederl.› (*früher* Kaperschiff; Freibeuter, Seeräuber); **Ka|per|brief; Ka|pe|rei**

(*früher* Aufbringung feindlicher und Konterbande führender neutraler Handelsschiffe); **Ka̱|per₋fahrt, ...gut; ka̱|pern;** ich ...ere (↑R 16)
Ka|pe̱r|na|um, *ökum.* Ka|far|na|um (bibl. Ort)
Ka̱|pern₋so|ße, ...strauch
Ka̱|per|schiff *(früher);* **Ka̱|pe|rung**
Ka̱|pe|tin|ger [*auch* 'kap...], der; -s, - (Angehöriger eines franz. Königsgeschlechtes)
ka|pie̱|ren ‹lat.› (*ugs. für* fassen, begreifen, verstehen)
ka|pil|la̱r ‹lat.› (haarfein, z. B. von Blutgefäßen); **Ka|pil|la̱r|ana|ly|se** (↑R 132; *Chemie*); **Ka|pil|la̱|re,** die; -, -n (Haargefäß, kleinstes Blutgefäß; Haarröhrchen); **Ka|pil|la̱r|ge|fäß** (feinstes Blutgefäß); **Ka|pil|la|ri|tä̱t,** die; - (*Physik* Verhalten von Flüssigkeiten in engen Röhren); **Ka|pil|la̱r|mi|kro|sko|pie,** die; - (*Med.* mikroskop. Untersuchung der Kapillaren)
ka|pi|ta̱l ‹lat.› (hauptsächlich; groß, gewaltig); ein -er Hirsch; **Ka|pi|ta̱l,** das; -s, *Plur.* -e *u., österr. nur,* -ien [...i̯ən] (Vermögen; Geldsumme); **Ka|pi|tä̱l,** das; -s, -e (*seltener für* Kapitell); **Ka|pi|ta̱l₋an|la|ge, ...auf|sto|ckung, ...aus|fuhr; Ka|pi|ta̱l|band,** Kap|ta̱l|band, das; -[e]s, ...bänder (Schutz- u. Zierband am Buchrücken); **Ka|pi|ta̱l₋be|darf, ...bil|dung, ...buch|sta|be** (Großbuchstabe); **Ka|pi|tä̱l|chen** (lat. Großbuchstabe in der Größe eines kleinen Buchstabens); **Ka|pi|ta̱|le,** die; -, -n ‹franz.› (*veraltet für* Hauptstadt); **Ka|pi|ta̱l₋eig|ner, ...er|hö|hung, ...er|trag[s]|steu|er, ...ex|port, ...feh|ler** (besonders schwerer Fehler), **...flucht** (die; -), **...ge|ber, ...ge|sell|schaft, ...ge|winn, ...hirsch; ka|pi|ta̱l|in|ten|siv** (viel Kapital erfordernd); **Ka|pi|ta̱l|in|ves|ti|ti|on; Ka|pi|ta|li|sa|ti|o̱n,** die; -, -en (Umwandlung eines laufenden Ertrags od. einer Rente in einen einmaligen Betrag); **ka|pi|ta|li|sie̱|ren; Ka|pi|ta|li|sie̱|rung** *vgl.* Kapitalisation; **Ka|pi|ta|lis|mus,** der; - (Wirtschafts- u. Gesellschaftsordnung, deren treibende Kraft das Gewinnstreben Einzelner ist); **Ka|pi|ta|li̱st,** der; -en, -en; ↑R 126 (*oft abwertend für* Vertreter des Kapitalismus); **ka|pi|ta|li̱s|tisch; Ka|pi|ta̱l|kraft,** die; -; **ka|pi|ta̱l|kräf|tig; Ka|pi|ta̱l₋markt, ...ver|bre|chen** (schweres Verbrechen), **...zins** (*Plur.* ...zinsen)
Ka|pi|tä̱n, der; -s, -e ‹ital.-(-franz.)›; **Ka|pi|tä̱n|leut|nant; Ka|pi|tä̱ns₋ka|jü|te, ...pa|tent**
Ka|pi̱|tel, das; -s, - ‹lat.› ([Haupt]stück, Abschnitt [*Abk.* Kap.]; geistl. Körperschaft [von Domherren, Mönchen]); Kapitel XII; **ka|pi̱|tel|fest** (*ugs. für* fest im Wissen; bibelfest)
Ka|pi|te̱ll, das; -s, -e ‹lat.› (*Archit.* oberer Säulen-, Pfeilerabschluss)
ka|pi̱|teln ‹lat.› (*landsch. für* ausschelten); ich ...[e]le (↑R 16); **Ka|pi̱|tel₋saal** (Sitzungssaal im Kloster), **...über|schrift** (↑R 132)
Ka|pi|to̱l, das; -s (Burg Alt-Roms; Kongresspalast in Washington); **ka|pi|to|li̱|nisch;** die kapitolinischen Gänse, *aber* (↑R 108): der Kapitolinische Hügel, die Kapitolinische Wölfin
Ka|pi|tu|la̱nt, der; -en, -en (↑R 126) ‹lat.› (jmd., der vor Schwierigkeiten o. Ä. kapituliert); **Ka|pi|tu|la̱r,** der; -s, -e (Mitglied eines Kapitels, z. B. Domherr); **Ka|pi|tu|la̱|ri|en** *Plur.* (Gesetze u. Verordnungen der karoling. Könige); **Ka|pi|tu|la|ti|o̱n,** die; -, -en ‹franz.› (Übergabe [einer Truppe od. einer Festung], Aufgabe; Übergabevertrag); **ka|pi|tu|lie̱|ren** (sich ergeben, aufgeben)
Ka̱p|la|ken, das; -s, - ‹niederl.› (*Seemannsspr. veraltet* dem Kapitän zustehende Sondervergütung)
Kap|la̱n (↑R 130), der; -s, ...pläne ‹lat.› (kath. Hilfsgeistlicher)
Ka̱p|land, das; -[e]s (*svw.* Kapprovinz)
Ka̱|po, der; -s, -s ‹Kurzform von franz. capora̱l› (Unteroffizier; Häftling eines Konzentrationslagers, der ein Arbeitskommando leitete)
Ka|po|da̱s|ter, der; -s, - ‹ital.› (bei Lauten u. Gitarren über alle Saiten reichender, auf dem Griffbrett verschiebbarer Bund)
Ka̱|pok, der; -s ‹malai.› (Samenfaser des Kapokbaumes, ein Füllmaterial)
ka|po̱|res ‹hebr.-jidd.› (*ugs. für* entzwei); kapores gehen; kapores sein
Ka|po̱|si|sar|kom (↑R 95) ‹nach dem österr.-ungar. Hautarzt Moritz Kaposi› (*Med.* ein [bei Aidspatienten häufiger auftretender] Hautkrebs)
Ka|po̱t|te, die; -, -n ‹franz.› (um die Jahrhundertwende getragener Damenhut); **Ka|po̱tt|hut,** der
Ka̱p|pa, das; -[s], -s (griech. Buchstabe: *K, κ*)
Kap|pa|do̱|ki|en usw. *vgl.* Kappadozien usw.; **Kap|pa|do̱|zi|en** (antike Bez. einer Landschaft im östl. Kleinasien); **Kap|pa|do̱|zi|er; kap|pa|do̱|zisch**
Ka̱pp|beil *(Seemannsspr.)*
Kä̱pp|chen; Ka̱p|pe, die; -, -n ‹lat.›
ka̱p|pen (ab-, beschneiden; abhauen)
Ka̱p|pen|abend (↑R 132; eine Faschingsveranstaltung)
Ka̱p|pes, Ka̱p|pus, der; - ‹lat.› (*westd. für* Weißkohl)
Ka̱pp|hahn (Kapaun)
Kä̱p|pi, das; -s, -s (kleine, längliche [Uniform]mütze); **Kä̱pp|lein**
Ka̱pp|naht (eine doppelt genähte Naht)
Ka̱p|pro|vinz, die; - (größte Provinz der Republik Südafrika)
Ka̱p|pung
Ka̱p|pus *vgl.* Kappes
Ka̱pp|zaum ‹ital.› (*Reitsport* Halfterzaum ohne Mundstück)
Ka̱pp|zie|gel (luftdurchlässiger Dachziegel)
Kap|ri|ce [...pri:sə] (↑R 130), die; -, -n ‹franz.› (Laune)
Kap|ri|o̱|le (↑R 130), die; -, -n ‹ital.› (närrischer Einfall, Streich; Luftsprung; *Reitsport* besonderer Sprung der hohen Schule); **kap|ri|o̱|len** (*selten für* Kapriolen machen)
Kap|ri̱|ze (↑R 130; *österr. svw.* Kaprice); **kap|ri|zie̱|ren,** sich ‹franz.› (*veraltend für* eigensinnig auf etwas bestehen); **kap|ri|zi|ö̱s** (launenhaft, eigenwillig); **Kap|ri̱z|pols|ter,** der; -s, - (*österr. ugs. veraltet für* ein kleines Polster)
Kap|ru̱n (↑R 130; österr. Kraftwerk)
Ka̱p|sel, die; -, -n; **Kä̱p|sel|chen; ka̱p|sel|för|mig; ka̱p|se|lig,** kaps|lig; **Ka̱p|sel|riss** *(Med.);* **Ka̱p|se|lung** *(Technik)*
Ka̱p|si|kum, das; -s ‹lat.› (span. Pfeffer)
ka̱ps|lig *vgl.* kapselig
Ka̱p|stadt (Hptst. der Kapprovinz)
Kap|ta̱l, das; -s, -e ‹lat.› (Kapitalband); **Kap|ta̱l|band** *vgl.* Kapitalband
Kap|ta|ti|o̱n, die; -, -en ‹lat.› (*veraltet für* Erschleichung)
Kap|te̱in, Kä̱p|ten, der; -s, -s (*nordd. für* Kapitän)
Kap|ti|o̱n, die; -, -en ‹lat.› (*veraltet für* Fangfrage; verfänglicher Trugschluss); **kap|ti|ö̱s** (*veraltet für* verfänglich); eine kaptiöse Frage
Ka|pu̱t, der; -s, -e ‹roman.› (*schweiz. für* Soldatenmantel)
ka|pu̱tt ‹franz.› (*ugs. für* entzwei, zerbrochen; matt; zerrüttet; psy-

chisch angeschlagen); kaputt sein; **ka|putt|drü|cken;** kaputtgedrückt; **ka|putt|ge|hen; kaputtgegangen; Ka|putt|heit,** die; - *(ugs.);* **ka|putt|la|chen,** sich; kaputtgelacht; **ka|putt|machen;** sich -; kaputtgemacht; **kaputt|schla|gen;** kaputtgeschlagen; **ka|putt|tre|ten;** kaputtgetreten

Ka|pu|ze, die; -, -n ‹ital.› (an einen Mantel od. eine Jacke angearbeitete Kopfbedeckung); **Ka|pu|zi|na|de,** die; -, -n ‹franz.› *(veraltet für* Kapuzinerpredigt, [derbe] Strafrede); **Ka|pu|zi|ner,** der; -s, - ‹ital.› (Angehöriger eines kath. Ordens; *österr. auch für* Kaffee mit wenig Milch); **Ka|pu|zi|ner‿af|fe, ...kres|se, ...mönch, ...orden** (der; -s; *Abk.* O. [F.] M. Cap. *[vgl. d.]*)

Kap Ver|de [- v...] (Staat, der die Kapverdischen Inseln umfasst); **Kap|ver|den** *Plur.* (Kapverdische Inseln); **Kap|ver|di|er; kap|verdisch; Kap|ver|di|sche In|seln** *Plur.* (Inselgruppe vor der Westküste Afrikas)

Kap|wein (Wein aus der Kapprovinz)

Kar, das; -[e]s, -e (Mulde [an vergletscherten Hängen])

Ka|ra|bi|ner, der; -s, - ‹franz.› (kurzes Gewehr; *österr. auch für* Karabinerhaken); **Ka|ra|bi|ner‑ha|ken** (federnder Verschlusshaken); **Ka|ra|bi|ni|er** [...'nie:], der; -s, -s ([urspr. mit Karabiner ausgerüsteter] Reiter; Jäger zu Fuß); **Ka|ra|bi|ni|e|re,** der; -[s], ...ri ‹ital.› (Angehöriger einer ital. Polizeitruppe)

Ka|ra|cho [...xo], das; - ‹span.› *(ugs. für* große Geschwindigkeit, Tempo); mit -

Ka|rä|er, der; -s, - ‹hebr.› (Angehöriger einer jüd. Sekte)

Ka|raf|fe, die; -, -n ‹arab.-franz.› ([geschliffene] bauchige Glasflasche [mit Glasstöpsel]); **Ka|raf|fi|ne,** die; -, -n *(veraltet, noch landsch. für* kleine Karaffe)

Ka|ra|gös, der; - ‹türk.› (Hanswurst im türk.-arab. Schattenspiel)

Ka|ra|i|be *vgl.* Karibe; **ka|ra|ibisch** *vgl.* karibisch

Ka|ra|jan ['ka(:)...], Herbert von (österr. Dirigent)

Ka|ra|kal, der; -s, -s ‹turkotat.› (Wüstenluchs)

Ka|ra|kal|pa|ke, der; -n, -n; ↑R 126 (Angehöriger eines Turkvolkes)

Ka|ra|ko|rum [*auch* ...'rum], der; -[s] (Hochgebirge in Mittelasien)

Ka|ra|kul|schaf ‹nach dem See im Hochland von Pamir› (Schaf, dessen Lämmer den Persianerpelz liefern); ↑R 105

Ka|ra|kum, die; - (Wüstengebiet in Turkmenistan)

Ka|ram|bo|la|ge [...'la:ʒə], die; -, -n ‹franz.› *(ugs. für* Zusammenstoß; *Billard* Treffer [durch Karambolieren]; *veraltend für* Streit); **Ka|ram|bo|le,** die; -, -n *(Billard* roter Ball); **ka|ram|bo|lie|ren** *(ugs. für* zusammenstoßen; *Billard* mit dem Spielball die beiden anderen Bälle treffen)

Ka|ra|mell, der, *schweiz. auch* das; -s ‹franz.› (gebrannter Zucker); **Ka|ra|mell‿bier, ...bon|bon; Ka|ra|mel|le,** die; -, -n *meist Plur.* (Bonbon mit Zusatz aus Milch[produkten]); **ka|ra|mel|li|sie|ren** (Zucker[lösungen] trocken erhitzen; Karamell zusetzen); **Ka|ra|mell‿pud|ding, ...zucker**

Ka|ra|o|ke, das; -[s] ‹jap.› (Veranstaltung, bei der Laien zur Instrumentalmusik eines Schlagers den Text singen)

Ka|ra|see, die; - ‹nach dem Fluss Kara› (Teil des Nordpolarmeeres)

Ka|rat, das; -[e]s, -e ‹griech.› (Gewichtseinheit von Edelsteinen; Maß der Feinheit einer Goldlegierung); 24 Karat (↑R 90)

Ka|ra|te, das; -[s] ‹jap.› (eine sportliche Methode der waffenlosen Selbstverteidigung); **Ka|ra|te|ka,** der; -[s], -[s] (jmd., der Karate betreibt); **Ka|ra|te|kämp|fer**

...ka|rä|ter (z. B. Zehnkaräter, *mit Ziffern* 10-Karäter; ↑R 44); **...ka|rä|tig,** *österr. auch* ...ka|ra|tig (z. B. zehnkarätig; *mit Ziffern* 10-karätig; ↑R 44)

Ka|rat|schi (↑R 132; pakistan. Hafenstadt)

Ka|rau|sche, die; -, -n ‹lit.› (ein karpfenartiger Fisch)

Ka|ra|vel|le [...v...], die; -, -n ‹niederl.› (mittelalterl. Segelschiff)

Ka|ra|wa|ne, die; -, -n ‹pers.› (durch Wüsten u. Ä. ziehende Gruppe von Reisenden); **Ka|ra|wa|nen‿han|del, ...stra|ße**

Ka|ra|wan|ken *Plur.* (Berggruppe im südöstl. Teil der Alpen)

Ka|ra|wan|se|rei ‹pers.› (Unterkunft für Karawanen)

Kar|bat|sche, die; -, -n ‹türk.› (Riemenpeitsche)

[1]**Kar|bid,** das; -[e]s ‹lat.› (Kalziumkarbid); [2]**Kar|bid,** *chem. fachspr.* Car|bid, das; -[e]s, -e (Verbindung aus Kohlenstoff u. einem Metall od. Bor od. Silicium); **Kar|bid|lam|pe; kar|bo...** (kohlen...); **Kar|bo...** (Kohlen...); **Kar|bol,** das; -s *(ugs. für* Karbolsäure); **Kar|bo|li|ne|um,** das; -s (Imprägnierungs- und Schädlingsbekämpfungsmittel); **Kar|bol|mäus|chen** *(veraltend scherzh. für* Krankenschwester); **Kar|bol|säu|re,** die; - *(veraltet für* Phenol, ein Desinfektionsmittel); **Kar|bon,** das; -s *(Geol.* Steinkohlenformation); **Kar|bo|na|de,** die; -, -n ‹franz.› *(landsch. für* gebratenes Rippenstück); **Kar|bo|na|do,** der; -s, -s ‹span.› *(svw.* [1]Karbonat); **Kar|bo|na|ri** *Plur.* ‹ital.› (Angehörige eines im 19. Jh. für die Freiheit u. Einheit Italiens eintretenden Geheimbundes); [1]**Kar|bo|nat,** der; -[e]s, -e ‹lat.› (eine Diamantenart); [2]**Kar|bo|nat,** *chem. fachspr.* Car|bo|nat, das; -[e]s, -e (Salz der Kohlensäure); **Kar|bo|ni|sa|ti|on,** die; - (Verkohlung, Umwandlung in [2]Karbonat); **kar|bo|nisch** *(Geol.* das Karbon betreffend); **kar|bo|ni|sie|ren** (verkohlen lassen, in [2]Karbonat umwandeln; Zellulosereste in Wolle durch Schwefelsäure od. andere Chemikalien zerstören); **Kar|bon|pa|pier** *(österr. neben* Kohlepapier); **Kar|bon|säu|ren** *Plur.* (eine Gruppe organ. Säuren); **Kar|bo|rund,** das; -[e]s (Carborundum ®; ein Schleifmittel); **Kar|bun|kel,** der; -s, - (Häufung dicht beieinander liegender Furunkel); **kar|bu|rie|ren** *(Technik* die Leuchtkraft von Gasgemischen durch Zusatz von Kohlenstaub o. Ä. steigern)

Kar|da|mom, der *od.* das; -s, -e[n] *Plur. selten* ‹griech.› (ein scharfes Gewürz)

Kar|dan‿an|trieb ‹nach dem Erfinder G. Cardano› *(Technik),* **...ge|lenk** (Verbindungsstück zweier Wellen, das Kraftübertragung unter wechselnden Winkeln ermöglicht); **kar|da|nisch;** kardanische Aufhängung (Vorrichtung, die Schwankungen der aufgehängten Körper ausschließt); **Kar|dan‿tun|nel** (im Kraftfahrzeug), **...wel|le** (Antriebswelle [für Kraftfahrzeuge] mit Kardangelenk)

Kar|dät|sche, die; -, -n ‹ital.› (grobe [Pferde]bürste); *vgl. aber* Kartätsche; **kar|dät|schen** (striegeln); du kardätschst; *vgl. aber* kartätschen; **Kar|de,** die; -, -n ‹lat.› (eine distelähnliche, krautige Pflanze; *Textiltechnik* eine Maschine zum Aufteilen von Faserbüscheln)

Kar|deel, das; -s, -e ‹niederl.› (*Seemannsspr.* Strang einer Trosse)
kar|den, kar|die|ren ‹lat.› (rauen, kämmen [von Wolle]); **Kar|den-distel, ...ge|wächs**
kar|di... usw. *vgl.* kardio... usw.; **Kar|di|a|kum,** das; -s, ...ka ‹griech.-lat.› (*Med.* herzstärkendes Mittel); **kar|di|al** ‹griech.› (*Med.* das Herz betreffend); **Kar|di|al|gie,** die; -, ...ien (*Med.* Magenkrampf; Herzschmerzen)
kar|die|ren *vgl.* karden
kar|di|nal ‹lat.› (*veraltet für* grundlegend; hauptsächlich); **Kar|di|nal,** der; -s, ...äle (Titel der höchsten katholischer Würdenträger nach dem Papst); **Kar|di|nal...** (Haupt...; Grund...); **Kar|di|na|le,** das; -[s], ...lia *meist Plur.* (*veraltet für* Grundzahl); **Kar|di|nal-feh|ler, ...fra|ge, ...prob|lem, ...punkt; Kar|di|nals-hut, ...kol|le|gi|um, ...kon|gre|ga|ti|on** (eine Hauptbehörde der päpstlichen Kurie); **Kar|di|nal|staats|sek|re|tär; Kar|di|nal-tu|gend, ...vi|kar** (päpstlicher Generalvikar von Rom), **...zahl** (Grundzahl, z. B. null, eins, zwei)
kar|di[|o]... ‹griech.› (herz...; magen...); **Kar|di[|o]...** (Herz...; Magen...); **Kar|di|o|gramm,** das; -s, -e (*Med.* mittels des Kardiographen aufgezeichnete Kurve); **Kar|di|o|graph,** der; -en, -en; ↑R 126 (*Med.* Gerät zur Aufzeichnung des Herzrhythmus); **Kar|di|o|i|de,** die; -, -n (*Math.* [herzförmige] Kurve); **Kar|di|o|lo|gie,** die; - (*Med.* Lehre vom Herzen u. den Herzkrankheiten); **kar|di|o|lo|gisch** *(Med.)*; **Kar|di|o|spas|mus,** der; -, ...men (*Med.* Krampf des Mageneinganges); **Kar|di|tis,** die; -, ...tiden (*Med.* entzündliche Erkrankung des Herzens)
Ka|re|li|en (nordosteurop. Landschaft); **Ka|re|li|er,** der; -s, - (Angehöriger eines finn. Volksstammes); **ka|re|lisch**
Ka|ren (w. Vorn.)
Ka|renz, die; -, -en ‹lat.› (Wartezeit, Sperrfrist; Enthaltsamkeit, Verzicht); **Ka|renz|zeit**
Ka|rer (Bewohner Kariens)
ka|res|sie|ren ‹franz.› (*veraltet, aber noch landsch. für* liebkosen; schmeicheln)
Ka|ret|te, die; -, -n ‹franz.› (Meeresschildkröte); **Ka|rett|schild|krö|te**
Ka|rez|za, die; - ‹ital.› (Koitus, bei dem der Samenerguss vermieden wird)
Kar|fi|ol, der; -s ‹ital.› (*südd., österr. für* Blumenkohl)
Kar|frei|tag (Freitag vor Ostern)
Kar|fun|kel, der; -s, - ‹lat.› (*volkstüml. für* roter Granat; *ugs. auch für* Karbunkel); **kar|fun|kel|rot; Kar|fun|kel|stein**
karg; karger (*auch* kärger), kargste (*auch* kärgste)
Kar|ga|deur [...'dø:r] ‹span.-franz.›, **Kar|ga|dor,** der; -s, -e ‹span.› (*Seew.* Begleiter einer Schiffsladung, der den Transport bis zur Übergabe an den Empfänger überwacht)
kar|gen *(geh.)*; **Karg|heit,** die; -; **kärg|lich; Kärg|lich|keit,** die; -
Kar|go, *auch* Car|go, der; -s, -s ‹span.› (*Seew.* Schiffsladung)
Ka|ri|be, der; -n, -n; ↑R 126 (Angehöriger einer indian. Sprachfamilie u. Völkergruppe in Mittel- u. Südamerika); **Ka|ri|bik,** die; - (Karibisches Meer mit den Antillen); **ka|ri|bisch,** *aber* (↑R 102): das Karibische Meer
Ka|ri|bu, das; -s, -s ‹indian.› (kanadisches Ren)
Ka|ri|en (hist. Landschaft in Kleinasien)
ka|rie|ren ‹franz.› (*selten für* mit Würfelzeichnung mustern, kästeln); **ka|riert** (gewürfelt, gekästelt)
Ka|ri|es [...iɛs], die; - ‹lat.› (*Med.* Zerstörung der harten Zahnsubstanz bzw. von Knochengewebe)
Ka|ri|ka|tur, die; -, -en ‹ital.› (Zerr-, Spottbild, kritische od. satirische Darstellung); **Ka|ri|ka|tu|ren|zeich|ner; Ka|ri|ka|tu|rist,** der; -en, -en (↑R 126); **Ka|ri|ka|tu|ris|tin; ka|ri|ka|tu|ris|tisch; ka|ri|kie|ren**
Ka|rin (w. Vorn.)
Ka|ri|na (w. Vorn.)
ka|ri|o|gen ‹lat.; griech.› (*Med.* Karies hervorrufend); **ka|ri|ös** ‹lat.› (*Med.* von Karies befallen); -e Zähne
ka|risch (aus Karien)
Ka|ri|sche Meer, das; -n -[e]s (ältere Bez. der Karasee)
Ka|ri|tas, die; - ‹lat.› (Nächstenliebe; Wohltätigkeit); *vgl.* Caritas; **ka|ri|ta|tiv** (wohltätig)
kar|ju|ckeln (*landsch. für* gemächlich umherfahren); ich ...[e]le (↑R 16)
Kar|kas|se, die; -, -n ‹franz.› (*Technik* fester Unterbau [eines Fahrzeugreifens]; *Gastron.* Gerippe von zerlegtem Geflügel, Wild od. Fisch)
Karl (m. Vorn.); **Kar|la** (w. Vorn.); **Karl-Heinz,** *auch* Karl Heinz, Karl|heinz (m. Vorn.); **Kar|li|ne,** die; -, -n (*veraltendes Schimpfwort für* dumme weibl. Person)
kar|lin|gisch (*für* karolingisch)
Kar|list, der; -en, -en (↑R 126; Anhänger der spanischen Thronanwärter mit Namen Don Carlos aus einer bourbon. Seitenlinie)
Karl|mann (dt. m. Eigenn.)
Karl-Marx-Stadt (Name für Chemnitz [1953–1990])
Kar|lo|vy Va|ry [...vi 'va:ri] (Kurort in Böhmen); *vgl.* Karlsbad
Karls|bad (*tschech.* Karlovy Vary); **Karls|ba|der** (↑R 103); - Salz, - Oblaten
Karls|kro|na [...'kru:na] (schwed. Hafenstadt)
Karls|preis (internationaler Preis der Stadt Aachen für Verdienste um die Einigung Europas)
Karls|ru|he (Stadt in Baden-Württemberg); **Karls|ru|he-Rüp|purr**
Karls|sa|ge; Karls|sa|gen|kreis, der; -es
[1]**Karl|stadt** (Stadt am Main)
[2]**Karl|stadt** (dt. Reformator)
Kar|ma[n], das; -s ‹sanskr.› (in östl. Religionen [z. B. im Hinduismus] das den Menschen bestimmende Schicksal)
Kar|mel, der; -[s] (Gebirgszug in Palästina); **Kar|me|lit,** der; -en, -en (↑R 126) *u.* **Kar|me|li|ter,** der; -s, - (Angehöriger eines kath. Ordens); **Kar|me|li|ter|geist,** der; -[e]s (ein Heilkräuterdestillat); **Kar|me|li|te|rin,** Kar|me|li|tin; **Kar|me|li|ter|or|den; Kar|me|li|tin** *vgl.* Karmeliterin
Kar|men, das; -s, ...mina ‹lat.› (*veraltet für* Fest-, Gelegenheitsgedicht)
Kar|me|sin ‹pers.› (*svw.* Karmin); **kar|me|sin|rot** (*svw.* karminrot); **Kar|min,** das; -s ‹franz.› (ein roter Farbstoff); **kar|min|rot; Kar|min|säu|re,** die; -
kar|mo|sie|ren ‹arab.› ([einen Edelstein] mit weiteren kleinen Steinen umranden)
[1]**Karn,** die; -, -en (*nordd. für* Butterfass)
[2]**Karn,** das; -s ‹nach den Karnischen Alpen› (*Geol.* eine Stufe der alpinen Trias)
Kar|nal|lit [*auch* ...'lit], der; -s ‹nach dem Geologen R. v. Carnall› (ein Mineral)
Kar|na|ti|on, die; - ‹lat.› (*svw.* Inkarnat)
Kar|nau|ba|wachs, das; -es ‹indian.; dt.› (ein Pflanzenwachs)
Kar|ne|ol, der; -s, -e ‹ital.› (ein rot bis gelblich gefärbter Schmuckstein)
[1]**Kar|ner,** Ker|ner, der; -s, - (*Archit.* [Friedhofskapelle mit] Beinhaus; *landsch. veraltet für* Räucherkammer)

[2]**Kar|ner,** der; -s, - (Angehöriger eines ehem. kelt. Volkes in den Karnischen Alpen)

Kar|ne|val [...v...], der; -s, *Plur.* -e *u.* -s ‹ital.› (Fastnacht[szeit], Fasching); **Kar|ne|va|list,** der; -en, -en (↑R 126); **Kar|ne|va|lis|tin; kar|ne|va|lis|tisch; Kar|ne|vals-ge|sell|schaft, ...prinz, ...tru-bel, ...ver|ein, ...zeit** (die; -), **...zug**

Kar|ni|ckel, das; -s, - (*landsch. für* Kaninchen; *ugs. auch für* Sündenbock)

Kar|nies, das; -es, -e ‹roman.› (*Bauw.* Leiste od. Gesims mit s-förmigem Querschnitt); **Kar-nie|se,** die; -, -n (*österr. für* Gardinenleiste)

kar|nisch ‹*zu* [2]Karn› (*Geol.;* ↑R 102:) die Karnischen Alpen

Kar|ni|sche *vgl.* Karniese

kar|ni|vor [...v...] ‹lat.› (Fleisch fressend); [1]**Kar|ni|vo|re,** der; -n, -n; ↑R 126 (Fleisch fressendes Tier); [2]**Kar|ni|vo|re,** die; -, -n (Fleisch fressende Pflanze)

Kar|nöf|fel, Kar|nüf|fel, der; -s (ein altes Kartenspiel)

Kärn|ten (österr. Bundesland); **Kärn|te|ner,** Kärnt|ner; **kärn-tisch** *(selten),* **kärnt|ne|risch**

Kar|nüf|fel *vgl.* Karnöffel

[1]**Ka|ro** (Hundename)

[2]**Ka|ro,** das; -s, -s ‹franz.› (Raute, [auf der Spitze stehendes] Viereck; *nur Sing.:* eine Spielkartenfarbe); **Ka|ro|ass** [*auch* ...'as], das; -es, -e (↑R 24)

Ka|ro|be *vgl.* Karube

Ka|ro|la [*auch* 'ka:...] (w. Vorn.); **Ka|ro|li|ne** (w. Vorn.)

Ka|ro|li|nen *Plur.* (Inselgruppe im Pazifischen Ozean)

Ka|ro|lin|ger, der; -s, - (Angehöriger eines fränk. Herrschergeschlechtes); **Ka|ro|lin|ger|zeit,** die; -; **ka|ro|lin|gisch;** -e Minuskel; **ka|ro|li|nisch** (auf einen der fränk. Herrscher mit dem Namen Karl bezüglich)

Ka|ros|se, die; -, -n ‹franz.› (Prunkwagen; *kurz für* Staatskarosse; *ugs. für* Karosserie); **Ka-ros|se|rie,** die; -, ...ien (Wagenoberbau, -aufbau [von Kraftfahrzeugen]); **Ka|ros|se|rie|bau|er,** der; -s, -; **Ka|ros|si|er** [...'sie:], der; -s, -s (Karosserieentwerfer; *veraltet für* Kutschpferd); **ka|ros-sie|ren** (mit einer Karosserie versehen)

Ka|ro|tin, *fachspr.* Ca|ro|tin, das; -s ‹lat.› (ein gelbroter Farbstoff in Pflanzenzellen)

Ka|ro|tis, die; -, ...iden ‹griech.› (*Med.* Kopf-, Halsschlagader)

Ka|rot|te, die; -, -n ‹niederl.› (eine Mohrrübenart); **Ka|rot|ten-beet, ...ho|se** (lange Hose mit stark betonter Hüftweite u. enger Fußweite)

Kar|pa|ten *Plur.* (Gebirge in Mitteleuropa); **kar|pa|tisch**

Kar|pell, das; -s, *Plur.* ...pelle *u.* ...pella ‹nlat.› (*Bot.* die Samenanlage tragender Teil der Blüte; Fruchtblatt)

Karp|fen, der; -s, - (ein Fisch); **Karp|fen-teich, ...zucht**

Kar|po|lith [*auch* ...'lit], der; *Gen.* -s *od.* -en, *Plur.* -e[n] (↑R 126) ‹griech.› (*veraltet für* fossile Frucht); **Kar|po|lo|gie,** die; - (Lehre von den Pflanzenfrüchten)

Kar|ra|g[h]een [...'ge:n], das; -[s] ‹nach dem irischen Ort Carrageen ['kɛrəgi:n]› (ein Heilmittel aus getrockneten Algen)

kar|ra|risch *svw.* carrarisch

Kärr|chen; [1]**Kar|re,** die; -, -n *u.,* *österr. nur,* Kar|ren, der; -s, -

[2]**Kar|re,** die; -, -n *meist Plur.* (*Geol.* Rinne od. Furche in Kalkgestein)

Kar|ree, das; -s, -s ‹franz.› (Viereck; *bes. österr. für* Rippenstück)

kar|ren (mit einer Karre befördern); **Kar|ren** *vgl.* [1]Karre

Kar|ren|feld *(Geol.)*

Kar|re|te, die; -, -n ‹ital.› (*bes. ostmitteld. für* schlechter Wagen); **Kar|ret|te,** die; -, -n (*schweiz. für* Schubkarren; schmalspuriger Transportwagen der Gebirgstruppen)

Kar|ri|e|re, die; -, -n ‹franz.› ([bedeutende, erfolgreiche] Laufbahn; schnellste Gangart des Pferdes); **Kar|ri|e|re-frau** *(auch abwertend),* **...ma|cher; Kar|ri|e-ris|mus** [karie...], der; - (*abwertend für* rücksichtsloses Streben nach Erfolg); **Kar|ri|e|rist,** der; -en, -en; ↑R 126 (*abwertend für* rücksichtsloser Karrieremacher); **kar|ri|e|ris|tisch**

Kar|ri|ol, das; -s, -s *u.* **Kar|ri|o|le,** die; -, -n ‹franz.› (*veraltet für* leichtes, zweirädriges Fuhrwerk mit Kasten; Briefpostwagen); **kar|ri|o|len** (*veraltet für* mit Karriol[post] fahren; *übertr. für* umherfahren, drauflosfahren)

Kärr|lein; Kärr|ner (*veraltet für* Arbeiter, der harte körperliche Arbeit verrichten muss); **Kärr-ner|ar|beit**

Kar|sams|tag (Samstag vor Ostern)

[1]**Karst,** der; -[e]s, -e (*landsch. für* zweizinkige Erdhacke)

[2]**Karst,** der; -[e]s, -e (*nur Sing.:* Teil der Dinarischen Alpen; *Geol.* durch Wasser ausgelaugte, meist unbewachsene Gebirgslandschaft aus Kalkstein od. Gips)

Kars|ten (m. Vorn.)

Karst|höh|le; kars|tig; Karst-land|schaft

kart. = kartoniert

Kar|tät|sche, die; -, -n ‹ital. (-franz.-engl.)› (*früher* mit Bleikugeln gefülltes Artilleriegeschoss; *Bauw.* Brett zum Verreiben des Putzes); *vgl. aber* Kardätsche; **kar|tät|schen** (*früher für* mit Kartätschen schießen); du kartätschst; *vgl. aber* kardätschen

Kar|tau|ne, die; -, -n ‹ital.› (*früher* großes Geschütz)

Kar|tau|se, die; -, -n (Kartäuserkloster); **Kar|täu|ser** (Angehöriger eines kath. Einsiedlerordens; ein Kräuterlikör); **Kar|täu|ser-mönch, ...nel|ke**

Kärt|chen; Kar|te, die; -, -n; alles auf eine - setzen; die gelbe -, die rote - *(Sport);* Karten spielen (↑R 39); **Kar|tei** (Zettelkasten); **Kar|tei-kar|te, ...kas|ten, ...lei-che** *(scherzh.),* **...zet|tel**

Kar|tell, das; -s, -e ‹franz.› (Interessenvereinigung in der Industrie; Zusammenschluss von student. Verbindungen mit gleicher Zielsetzung); **Kar|tell-amt, ...ge-setz; kar|tel|lie|ren** (in Kartellen zusammenfassen); **Kar|tel|lie-rung; Kar|tell|ver|band**

kar|ten (*ugs. für* Karten spielen); **Kar|ten-blatt, ...block** (*vgl.* Block), **...brief, ...haus, ...le|gen** (das; -s), **...le|ge|rin, ...schlä|ge-rin** (*ugs. für* Kartenlegerin), **...spiel, ...te|le|fon, ...[vor|]ver-kauf, ...zeich|ner**

kar|te|si|a|nisch, kar|te|sisch ‹nach R. Cartesius (= Descartes) benannt›; kartesianisches *od.* kartesisches Blatt *(Math.);* kartesianischer *od.* kartesischer Teufel *od.* Taucher (↑R 94)

Kar|tha|ger, *veraltet* **Kar|tha|gi-ni|en|ser; kar|tha|gisch; Kar-tha|go** (antike Stadt in Nordafrika)

Kar|tha|min, *fachspr.* Car|tha|min, das; -s ‹arab.› (ein roter Farbstoff)

kar|tie|ren ‹franz.› (*Geogr.* vermessen u. auf einer Karte darstellen; *auch für* in eine Kartei einordnen); **Kar|tie|rung**

Kar|ting, das; -s ‹engl.› (Ausübung des Gokartsports)

Kar|tof|fel, die; -, -n; **Kar|tof|fel-acker** (↑R 132); **Kar|tof|fel|bo-vist** *od.* ...bo|fist, **...brei; Kar|töf-fel|chen; Kar|tof|fel-chip** *(meist Plur.),* **...ern|te, ...feu|er, ...hor-de, ...kä|fer, ...kloß, ...knö|del**

(*südd.*), **...mehl, ...mus, ...puf|fer, ...pü|ree, ...sack, ...sa|lat, ...scha|le, ...schnaps, ...stock** (der; -[e]s; *schweiz. für* Kartoffelbrei), **...sup|pe**

Kar|to|graf, Kar|to|gra|fie usw. *eindeutschende Schreibung für* Kartograph, Kartographie usw.

Kar|to|gramm, das; -s, -e ‹franz.; griech.› (Darstellung statistischer Daten auf Landkarten)

Kar|to|graph (↑R 33), der; -en, -en; ↑R 126 (Landkartenzeichner; wissenschaftl. Bearbeiter einer Karte); **Kar|to|gra|phie** (↑R 33), die; - (Technik, Lehre, Geschichte der Herstellung von Karten[bildern]); **kar|to|gra|phie|ren** (↑R 33; auf Karten aufnehmen); **Kar|to|gra|phin** (↑R 33); **kar|to|gra|phisch** (↑R 33)

Kar|to|man|tie, die; - (Kartenlegekunst); **Kar|to|me|ter,** das (Kurvenmesser); **Kar|to|met|rie** (↑R 130), die; - (Kartenmessung)

Kar|ton [...'tɔŋ, *auch, österr. nur,* ...'to:n], der; -s, *Plur.* -s, *seltener* -e [...'to:nə] ‹franz.› ([leichte] Pappe, Steifpapier; Kasten, Hülle od. Schachtel aus [leichter] Pappe; Vorzeichnung zu einem [Wand]gemälde); 5 Karton[s] Seife (↑R 90); **Kar|to|na|ge** [...'na:ʒə], die; -, -n (Pappverpackung; Einbandart); **Kar|to|na|ge|ar|beit; Kar|to|na|gen‿fab|rik, ...ma|cher; kar|to|nie|ren** (in Pappe [leicht] einbinden, steif heften); **kar|to|niert** (*Abk.* kart.)

Kar|to|thek, die; -, -en ‹franz.; griech.› (Kartei)

Kar|tu|sche, die; -, -n ‹franz.› (*Milit.* Metallhülse [mit der Pulverladung] für Artilleriegeschosse; *Kunstw.* schildförmiges Ornament des Barocks mit Laubwerk usw.)

Ka|ru|be, Ka|ro|be, die; -, -n ‹arab.› (Johannisbrot)

Ka|run|kel, die; -, -n ‹lat.› (*Med.* kleine Warze aus gefäßreichem Bindegewebe)

Ka|rus|sell, das; -s, *Plur.* -s *u.* -e ‹franz.› (Drehgestell mit kleinen Pferden, Fahrzeugen, an Ketten aufgehängten Sitzen o. Ä.); **Ka|rus|sell|pferd**

kar|weel|ge|baut usw. *vgl.* kraweelgebaut usw.

Kar|wen|del|ge|bir|ge, *auch* Kar|wen|del, das; -s (Gebirgsgruppe der Tirolisch-Bayer. Kalkalpen)

Kar|wo|che (Woche vor Ostern)

Ka|ry|a|ti|de, die; -, -n ‹griech.› (*Archit.* weibl. Säulenfigur als Gebälkträgerin)

Ka|ry|op|se, die; -, -n ‹griech.› (*Bot.* Frucht der Gräser)

Kar|zer, der; -s, - ‹lat.› (*früher für* Schul-, Hochschulgefängnis; *nur Sing.:* verschärfter Arrest)

kar|zi|no|gen ‹griech.› (*Med.* Krebs[geschwülste] erzeugend); **Kar|zi|no|gen,** das; -s, -e (Krebs erregende Substanz); **Kar|zi|no|lo|gie,** die; - (wissenschaftl. Erforschung der Krebserkrankungen); **Kar|zi|nom,** das; -s, -e (Krebs[geschwulst]; *Abk.* Ca. [*für* Carcinoma]); **kar|zi|no|ma|tös** (krebsartig); -e Geschwulst; **Kar|zi|no|se,** die; -, -n (über den Körper verbreitete Krebsbildung)

Ka|sach, Ka|sak, der; -[s], -s (handgeknüpfter kaukasischer Teppich); **Ka|sa|che,** der; -n, -n; ↑R 126 (Angehöriger eines Turkvolkes in Mittelasien); **ka|sa|chisch,** *aber* (↑R 102): die Kasachische Schwelle (mittelasiat. Berg- u. Hügellandschaft); **Ka|sachs|tan** (Staat in Mittelasien)

[1]**Ka|sack** (dt. Schriftsteller)

[2]**Ka|sack,** der; -s, -s ‹türk.› (dreiviertellange Damenbluse)

Ka|sak *vgl.* Kasach

Ka|san (Stadt an der Wolga)

Ka|sat|schok (↑R 130), der; -s, -s ‹russ.› (ein russ. Volkstanz)

Kas|ba[h], die; -, -s *od.* Ksa|bi ‹arab.› (arab. Altstadtviertel in nordafrik. Städten)

Kasch, der; -s *u.* **Ka|scha,** die; - ‹russ.› (Brei, Grütze)

ka|scheln (*landsch. für* [auf der Eisbahn] schlittern); ich ...[e]le (↑R 16)

Ka|schem|me, die; -, -n ‹zigeuner.› (Lokal mit schlechtem Ruf)

ka|schen (*ugs. für* ergreifen, verhaften); du kaschst

Käs|chen

Kä|scher, Ke|scher, der; -s, - (Fangnetz)

ka|schie|ren ‹franz.› (verdecken, verbergen; *Druckw.* überkleben; *Theater* nachbilden); **Ka|schie|rung**

[1]**Kasch|mir** (Landschaft in Vorderindien); [2]**Kasch|mir,** der; -s, -e (ein Gewebe); **Kasch|mir‿schal, ...wol|le**

Kasch|nitz, Marie Luise (dt. Schriftstellerin)

Ka|scho|long, der; -s, -s ‹mong.› (ein Halbedelstein)

Ka|schu|be, der; -n, -n; ↑R 126 (Angehöriger eines westslaw. Stammes); **Ka|schu|bin; ka|schu|bisch,** *aber* (↑R 102): die Kaschubische Schweiz (östl. Teil des Pommerschen Höhenrückens [in Polen])

Kä|se, der; -s, -; **Kä|se‿auf|schnitt, ...be|rei|tung, ...blatt** (*ugs. für* niveaulose Zeitung), **...ecke** (↑R 132), **...ge|bäck, ...glo|cke; Ka|se|in,** das; -s (Eiweißbestandteil der Milch); **Kä|se|ku|chen** (Quarkkuchen)

Ka|sel, die; -, -n ‹lat.› (liturg. Messgewand)

Kä|se|laib

Ka|se|mat|te, die; -, -n ‹franz.› (*Milit.* beschusssicherer Raum in Festungen; Geschützraum eines Kriegsschiffes)

Kä|se‿mes|ser (das), **...mil|be; kä|sen;** du käst; er käs|te; die Milch käst (gerinnt, wird zu Käse); [1]**Ka|ser** (*landsch., bes. österr. für* Käser); [2]**Ka|ser,** die; -, -n (*westösterr. mdal. für* Sennhütte); **Kä|ser** (Facharbeiter in der Käseherstellung; *landsch. auch für* Käsehändler, Senn o. Ä.); **Kä|se|rei** ([Betrieb für] Käseherstellung); **Kä|se|rin|de**

Ka|ser|ne, die; -, -n ‹franz.›; **Ka|ser|nen‿block** (*vgl.* Block), **...hof; Ka|ser|nen|hof|ton** (lauter, herrischer Ton); **ka|ser|nie|ren; Ka|ser|nie|rung**

Kä|se‿sah|ne|tor|te, ...stan|ge, ...stoff (*für* Kasein), **...tor|te** (Quarktorte); **kä|se|weiß** (*ugs. für* sehr bleich); **kä|sig**

Ka|si|mir (m. Vorn.)

Ka|si|no, das; -s, -s ‹ital., „Gesellschaftshaus"› (Speiseraum [für Offiziere]; *kurz für* Spielkasino)

Kas|ka|de, die; -, -n ‹franz.› ([künstlicher] stufenförmiger Wasserfall; *Artistik* wagemutiger Sprung, Sturzsprung); **kas|ka|den|för|mig; Kas|ka|den|schal|tung** (*Technik* Reihenschaltung gleichartiger Teile); **Kas|ka|deur** [...'dø:r], der; -s, -e (Artist, der eine Kaskade ausführt)

Kas|ka|rill|rin|de ‹span.; dt.› (ein westind. Gewürz)

Kas|ko, der; -s, -s ‹span.› (*Seemannsspr.* Schiffsrumpf od. Fahrzeug [im Ggs. zur Ladung]; Spielart des Lombers); **kas|ko|ver|si|chert; Kas|ko|ver|si|che|rung** (Versicherung gegen Schäden an Fahrzeugen)

Kas|par (m. Vorn.); **Kas|per,** der; -s, - (*ugs. für* alberner Kerl); **Kas|perl,** der; -s, -n *(österr. nur so),* **Kas|per|le,** das *od.* der; -s, -; **Kas|per|le|the|a|ter; Kas|per|li,** der; -s, - *(schweiz.);* **Kas|per|li|the|a|ter** *(schweiz.);* **Kas|perl|the|a|ter** *(österr.);* **kas|pern** (*ugs. für* sich wie ein Kasper benehmen); ich ...ere (↑R 16); **Kas|per|the|a|ter**

Kas|pisch (*in geogr. Namen* ↑R 102), z. B. das Kaspische Meer; **Kas|pi|sche Meer,** das; -n -[e]s *od.* **Kas|pi|see,** der; -s (östl. des Kaukasus)

Kas|sa, die; -, Kassen ⟨ital.⟩ (*österr. für* Kasse); *vgl.* per cassa; **Kas|sa‿buch** (*österr. für* Kassenbuch), **...ge|schäft** (*Börse, Wirtsch.* Geschäft, das sofort od. kurzfristig erfüllt werden soll)

Kas|sand|ra (↑R 130; *griech. Mythol.* eine Seherin, Tochter des Priamos); **Kas|sand|ra|ruf** (*übertr. für* Unheil verheißende Warnung)

[1]**Kas|sa|ti|on,** die; -, -en ⟨ital.⟩ (mehrsätziges instrumentales Musikstück im 18. Jh.)

[2]**Kas|sa|ti|on,** die; -, -en ⟨lat.⟩, Kas|sie|rung (*Rechtsw.* Ungültigmachung einer Urkunde; Aufhebung eines gerichtlichen Urteils; *früher für* unehrenvolle Dienstentlassung); **Kas|sa|ti|ons|hof** (*Rechtsw.* oberster Gerichtshof mancher romanischer Länder); **kas|sa|to|risch** (*Rechtsw.* die Kassation betreffend)

Kas|sa|zah|lung ⟨ital.; dt.⟩ (Barzahlung); **Kas|se,** die; -, -n ⟨ital.⟩ (Geldkasten, -vorrat; Zahlraum, -schalter; Bargeld); *vgl.* Kassa

Kas|sel (Stadt an der Fulda); **Kas|se|ler,** Kass|ler, *auch* Kas|se|la|ner (↑R 103); Kasseler Leberwurst; **Kas|se|ler Braun,** das; - -s; **Kas|se|ler Rip|pen|speer,** das *od.* der; - -[e]s (gepökeltes Schweinebruststück mit Rippen)

Kas|sen‿ab|rech|nung, ...arzt, ...be|stand, ...block (*vgl.* Block), **...bon, ...bril|le** (*ugs. für* von der Krankenkasse bezahlte Brille), **...buch, ...mag|net** (*ugs. für* Person od. Sache, die ein großes zahlendes Publikum anzieht), **...pa|ti|ent, ...schal|ter, ...schla|ger, ...sturz** (Feststellung des Kassenbestandes), **...zet|tel**

Kas|se|rol|le, die; -, -n, *landsch. auch* Kas|se|rol, das; -s, -e ⟨franz.⟩ (Schmortopf, -pfanne)

Kas|set|te, die; -, -n ⟨franz.⟩ (verschließbares Kästchen für Wertsachen; *Bauw.* vertieftes Feld [in der Zimmerdecke]; Schutzhülle für Bücher u. a.; Behältnis für Bild- od. Tonaufzeichnungen [auf Magnetband], Fotoplatten od. Filme); **Kas|set|ten‿deck,** (das; -s, -s; Kassettenrekorder ohne Verstärker u. Lautsprecher), **...de|cke** (*Bauw.*), **...film, ...re|kor|der; kas|set|tie|ren** (*Bauw.* mit Kassetten versehen, täfeln)

Kas|sia usw. *vgl.* Kassie usw.

Kas|si|ber, der; -s, - ⟨hebr.-jidd.⟩ (*Gaunerspr.* heiml. Schreiben von Gefangenen u. an Gefangene)

Kas|si|de, die; -, -n ⟨arab.⟩ (eine arab. Gedichtgattung)

Kas|sie [...i̯ə], Kas|sia, die; -, ...ien [...i̯ən] ⟨semit.⟩ (eine Heil- u. Gewürzpflanze); **Kas|si|en|baum,** Kas|si|a|baum; **Kas|si|en|öl,** Kas|si|a|öl, das; -[e]s

Kas|sier, der; -s, -e ⟨ital.⟩ (*österr., schweiz., südd. häufig für* Kassierer); **kas|sie|ren** (Geld einnehmen; [Münzen] für ungültig erklären; *ugs. für* wegnehmen; verhaften); **Kas|sie|rer; Kas|sie|re|rin; Kas|sie|rin** (*österr., schweiz., südd. häufig für* Kassiererin); **Kas|sie|rung;** *vgl. auch* [2]Kassation

[1]**Kas|si|o|peia** (Mutter der Andromeda); [2]**Kas|si|o|peia,** die; - ⟨griech.⟩ (ein Sternbild)

Kas|si|te, der; -n, -n; ↑R 126 (Angehöriger eines alten Gebirgsvolkes im Iran)

Kas|si|te|rit [*auch* ...'rit], der; -s, -e ⟨griech.⟩ (Zinnerz)

Kass|ler *vgl.* Kasseler

Kas|tag|net|te [...ta'njɛtə] (↑R 130), die; -, -n *meist Plur.* ⟨span.(-franz.)⟩ (kleines Rhythmusinstrument aus zwei Holzschälchen, die mit einer Hand aneinander geschlagen werden)

Kas|ta|lia (griech. Nymphe); **Kas|ta|li|sche Quel|le,** die; -n - (am Parnass)

Kas|ta|nie [...i̯ə], die; -, -n ⟨griech.⟩ (ein Baum u. dessen Frucht); **Kas|ta|ni|en|baum; kas|ta|ni|en|braun; Kas|ta|ni|en‿holz, ...wald**

Käst|chen

Kas|te, die; -, -n ⟨franz.⟩ (Gruppe in der hinduist. Gesellschaftsordnung; sich streng abschließende Gesellschaftsschicht)

kas|tei|en, sich (sich [zur Buße] Entbehrungen auferlegen; sich züchtigen); kasteit; **Kas|tei|ung**

Kas|tell, das; -s, -e ⟨lat.⟩ (fester Platz, Burg, Schloss [bes. in Südeuropa]; *früher* römische Grenzbefestigungsanlage); **Kas|tel|lan,** der; -s, -e (Aufsichtsbeamter in Schlössern u. öffentl. Gebäuden; *früher* Schloss-, Burgvogt); **Kas|tel|la|nei** (Schlossverwaltung)

käs|teln (karieren); ich ...[e]le (↑R 16); **Kas|ten,** der; -s, *Plur.* Kästen, *selten* - (*südd., österr., schweiz. auch für* Schrank); **Kas|ten|brot**

Kas|ten|geist, der; -[e]s (*abwertend für* Standesdünkel)

Kas|ten|wa|gen

Kas|ten|we|sen, das; -s

Kas|ti|li|en [...i̯ən] (ehem. Königreich im Innern der Iberischen Halbinsel); **kas|ti|lisch**

Käst|lein

Käst|ner (dt. Schriftsteller)

[1]**Kas|tor** (Held der griech. Sage); - und Pollux (Zwillingsbrüder der griech. Sage; *übertr. für* zwei eng befreundete Männer); [2]**Kas|tor,** der; -s (ein Stern); **Kas|tor|öl,** das; -[e]s (*Handelsbez. für* Rizinusöl)

Kast|rat (↑R 130), der; -en, -en (↑R 126) ⟨ital.⟩ (kastrierter Mann); **Kast|ra|ti|on,** die; -, -en ⟨lat.⟩ (Entfernung od. Ausschaltung der Keimdrüsen); **Kast|ra|ti|ons|angst; kast|rie|ren; Kast|rie|rung**

Ka|su|a|li|en [...i̯ən] *Plur.* ⟨lat.⟩ ([geistliche] Amtshandlungen aus besonderem Anlass)

Ka|su|ar [*auch* 'ka:...], der; -s, -e ⟨malai.-niederl.⟩ (straußenähnlicher Laufvogel); **Ka|su|a|ri|ne,** die; -, -n (austral.-ostind. Baum)

Ka|su|ist, der; -en, -en (↑R 126) ⟨lat.⟩ (Vertreter der Kasuistik; *übertr. für* Wortverdreher, Haarspalter); **Ka|su|is|tik,** die; - (Lehre von der Anwendung sittl. u. religiöser Normen auf den Einzelfall, bes. in Moraltheologie u. -philosophie; *Rechtsw.* Rechtsfindung aufgrund von Einzelfällen gleicher od. ähnl. Art; *Med.* Beschreibung von Krankheitsfällen; *übertr. für* Haarspalterei); **ka|su|is|tisch; Ka|sus,** der; -, - [...zu:s] (Fall; Vorkommnis); *vgl.* Casus Belli, Casus obliquus *u.* Casus rectus; **Ka|sus|en|dung** (*Sprachw.*)

Kat, der; -s, -s (*kurz für* Katalysator [an Kraftfahrzeugen])

Ka|ta|bo|lis|mus, der; - ⟨griech.⟩ (Abbau von Substanzen im Körper durch den Stoffwechsel)

Ka|ta|chre|se, Ka|ta|chre|sis [...ç...], die; -, ...chresen ⟨griech.⟩ (*Rhet., Stilk.* Bildbruch, Vermengung von nicht zusammengehörenden Bildern im Satz, z. B. „das schlägt dem Fass die Krone ins Gesicht"); **ka|ta|chres|tisch**

Ka|ta|falk, der; -s, -e ⟨franz.⟩ (schwarz verhängtes Gerüst für den Sarg bei Trauerfeiern)

Ka|ta|ka|na, das; -[s] *od.* die; - ⟨jap.⟩ (eine jap. Silbenschrift)

ka|ta|kaus|tisch ⟨griech.⟩ (*Optik* einbrennend); katakaustische Fläche (Brennfläche)

Ka|ta|kla|se, die; -, -n ⟨griech.⟩ (*Geol.* Zerbrechen u. Zerreiben eines Gesteins durch tekton. Kräfte); **Ka|ta|klas|struk|tur,**

die; - ‹griech.; lat.› (Trümmergefüge eines Gesteins); **ka|ta|klas|tisch**
Ka|ta|klys|mus, der; -, ...men ‹griech.› (erdgeschichtl. Katastrophe)
Ka|ta|kom|be, die; -, -n *meist Plur.* ‹ital.› (unterird. Begräbnisstätte)
Ka|ta|la|ne, der; -n, -n; ↑R 126 (Bewohner Kataloniens); **ka|ta|la|nisch; Ka|ta|la|nisch,** das; -[s] (Sprache); *vgl.* Deutsch; **Ka|ta|la|ni|sche,** das; -n; *vgl.* Deutsche, das
Ka|ta|la|se, die; -, -n ‹griech.› (*Biochemie* ein Enzym)
Ka|ta|lau|ni|sche Fel|der *Plur.* (Gegend in der Champagne, Kampfstätte der Hunnenschlacht i. J. 451)
ka|ta|lek|tisch ‹griech.› (*Verslehre* verkürzt, unvollständig); -er Vers
Ka|ta|lep|sie, die; -, ...ien ‹griech.› (*Med.* Muskelverkrampfung); **ka|ta|lep|tisch**
Ka|ta|le|xe, Ka|ta|le|xis [*auch* ...'lɛ...], die; -, ...lexen ‹griech.› (*Verslehre* Unvollständigkeit des letzten Versfußes)
Ka|ta|log, der; -[e]s, -e ‹griech.› (Verzeichnis [von Bildern, Büchern, Waren usw.]); **ka|ta|lo|gi|sie|ren** ([nach bestimmten Regeln] in einen Katalog aufnehmen); **Ka|ta|lo|gi|sie|rung**
Ka|ta|lo|ni|en (autonome Region im Nordosten der Iberischen Halbinsel; hist. span. Provinz)
Ka|tal|pa, Ka|tal|pe, die; -, ...pen ‹indian.› (Trompetenbaum)
Ka|ta|ly|sa|tor, der; -s, ...oren ‹griech.› (*Chemie* Stoff, der eine Reaktion auslöst od. beeinflusst; *Kfz-Technik* Gerät zur Abgasreinigung); geregelter - *(Kfz-Technik);* **Ka|ta|ly|sa|tor|au|to; Ka|ta|ly|se,** die; -, -n (*Chemie* die Herbeiführung, Beschleunigung od. Verlangsamung einer chem. Reaktion); **ka|ta|ly|sie|ren; ka|ta|ly|tisch**
Ka|ta|ma|ran [*auch* ka'ta:...], der; -s, -e ‹tamil.-engl.› (schnelles, offenes Segelboot mit Doppelrumpf)
Ka|tam|ne|se (↑R 132), die; -, -n ‹griech.› (*Med.* abschließender Krankenbericht)
Ka|ta|pho|re|se, die; -, -n ‹griech.› (*Physik* Wanderung positiv elektr. geladener Teilchen in einer Flüssigkeit)
Ka|ta|pla|sie, die; -, ...ien ‹griech.› (*Med.* Rückbildung)
Ka|ta|plas|ma, das; -s, ...men ‹griech.› (*Med.* heißer Breiumschlag)
ka|tap|lek|tisch (↑R 130 *u.* 132) ‹griech.› (*Med.* zur Kataplexie neigend); **Ka|tap|le|xie,** die; -, ...ien (durch Erschrecken o. Ä. ausgelöste Muskelerschlaffung)
Ka|ta|pult, das, *auch* der; -[e]s, -e ‹griech.› (Wurf-, Schleudermaschine); **Ka|ta|pult⌣flug** (Schleuderflug), **...flug|zeug; ka|ta|pul|tie|ren; Ka|ta|pult⌣schuh,** *(Leichtathletik),* **...sitz**
Ka|tar [*auch* 'ka:...] (Scheichtum am Persischen Golf)
[1]Ka|ta|rakt, der; -[e]s, -e ‹griech.› (Wasserfall; Stromschnelle); **[2]Ka|ta|rakt,** die; -, -e *u.* **Ka|ta|rak|ta,** die; -, ...ten (*Med.* grauer Star)
Ka|ta|rer (Einwohner von Katar); **ka|ta|risch**
Ka|tarrh, *auch* Ka|tarr (↑R 33), der; -s, -e ‹griech.› (*Med.* Schleimhautentzündung); **ka|tar|rha|lisch,** *auch* ka|tar|ra|lisch; **ka|tarrh|ar|tig,** *auch* ka|tarr|ar|tig
Ka|tas|ter, der *(österr. nur so) od.* das; -s, - ‹ital.› (amtl. Grundstücksverzeichnis); **Ka|tas|ter⌣amt, ...aus|zug, ...steu|ern** *(Plur.)*
Ka|tast|ral|ge|mein|de (↑R 130; *österr. für* Verwaltungseinheit [innerhalb einer Gemeinde], Steuergemeinde); **Ka|tast|ral|joch** (*österr. Amtsspr.* ein Feldmaß); *vgl.* Joch; **ka|tast|rie|ren** (in ein Kataster eintragen)
ka|ta|stro|phal ‹griech.› (verhängnisvoll; niederschmetternd; entsetzlich); **Ka|ta|stro|phe** (↑R 132), die; -, -n (Unglück[sfall] großen Ausmaßes; Zusammenbruch); **Ka|ta|stro|phen|alarm** (↑R 132); **ka|ta|stro|phen|ar|tig; Ka|ta|stro|phen⌣dienst, ...ein|satz, ...fall** (der), **...ge|biet, ...schutz**
Ka|ta|to|nie, die; -, ...ien ‹griech.› (*Med.* eine Geisteskrankheit)
Kät|chen, [1]Ka|te, Kä|te *vgl.* Käthchen, Kathe, Käthe
[2]Ka|te, die; -, -n (*nordd., oft abwertend für* kleines, ärmliches Bauernhaus)
Ka|te|che|se [...ç...], die; -, -n ‹griech.› (Religionsunterricht); **Ka|te|chet,** der; -en, -en; ↑R 126 (Religionslehrer, insbes. für die kirchl. Christenlehre außerhalb der Schule); **Ka|te|che|tik,** die; - (Lehre von der Katechese); **Ka|te|che|tin; ka|te|che|tisch; Ka|te|chi|sa|ti|on,** die; -, -en (*seltener für* Katechese); **ka|te|chi|sie|ren** (Religionsunterricht erteilen); **Ka|te|chis|mus,** der; -, ...men (in Frage u. Antwort abgefasstes Lehrbuch des christl. Glaubens); **Ka|te|chist,** der; -en, -en; ↑R 126 (einheimischer Laienhelfer in der kath. Mission); **Ka|te|chis|tin**
Ka|te|chu [...çu], das; -s, -s ‹malai.-port.› (*Biol., Pharm.* ein Gerbstoff)
Ka|te|chu|me|ne [*auch* ...'çu:...], der; -n, -n (↑R 126) ‹griech.› ([erwachsener] Taufbewerber im Vorbereitungsunterricht; Teilnehmer am Konfirmandenunterricht, bes. im 1. Jahr); **Ka|te|chu|me|nen|un|ter|richt**
ka|te|go|ri|al ‹griech.›; **Ka|te|go|rie,** die; -, ...ien (Klasse; Gattung; Begriffs-, Anschauungsform); **ka|te|go|risch** (nachdrücklich, entschieden; unbedingt gültig); kategorischer Imperativ (unbedingtes ethisches Gesetz); **ka|te|go|ri|sie|ren** (nach Kategorien ordnen); **Ka|te|go|ri|sie|rung**
Ka|ten, der; -s, - (*Nebenform von* [2]Kate)
Ka|te|ne, die; -, -n *meist Plur.* ‹lat.› (Sammlung von Bibelauslegungen alter Schriftsteller)
Ka|ter, der; -s, - (männl. Katze; *ugs.* Folge übermäßigen Alkoholgenusses); **Ka|ter⌣bum|mel** *(ugs.),* **...früh|stück** *(ugs.),* **...idee** (↑R 132; *ugs.*), **...stim|mung** *(ugs.)*
kat|e|xo|chen [...x...] ‹griech.› (schlechthin; beispielhaft)
Kat|gut [*auch* 'kɛtgat], das; -s ‹engl.› (*Med.* chirurg. Nähmaterial aus Darmsaiten)
kath. = katholisch
Ka|tha|rer [*auch* 'ka...], der; -s, - ‹griech.› (Angehöriger einer Sekte im MA.)
Ka|tha|ri|na, Ka|tha|ri|ne (w. Vorn.)
Ka|thar|sis ['ka(:)..., *auch* ...'tar...], die; - („Reinigung") (*Literaturw.* innere Läuterung als Wirkung des Trauerspiels; *Psych.* das Sichbefreien); **ka|thar|tisch**
Käth|chen, Ka|the, Kä|the, *auch* Kät|chen, Ka|te, Kä|te (w. Vorn.)
Ka|the|der, das *od.* der *(österr. nur so);* -s, - ‹griech.› ([Lehrer]pult, Podium); *vgl. aber* Katheter; **Ka|the|der|blü|te** (ungewollt komischer Ausdruck eines Lehrers); **Ka|thed|ra|le** (↑R 130), die; -, -n (bischöfl. Hauptkirche); **Ka|thed|ral⌣ent|schei|dung** (unfehlbare päpstl. Entscheidung), **...glas**
Ka|the|te, die; -, -n ‹griech.› (*Math.* eine der beiden Seiten im rechtwinkligen Dreieck, die die Schenkel des rechten Winkels bilden)

Ka|the|ter, der; -s, - ‹griech.› (*Med.* röhrenförmiges Instrument zur Entleerung od. Spülung von Körperhohlorganen); *vgl. aber* Katheder; **ka|the|te|ri|sie|ren** *u.* **ka|the|tern** (den Katheter einführen); ich ...ere (↑R 16)

Kä|thi, Ka|thin|ka, Ka|tin|ka (w. Vorn.)

Ka|tho|de, *fachspr. auch* Ka|to|de, die; -, -n ‹griech.› (*Physik* negative Elektrode, Minuspol); **Ka|tho|den|strahl,** *fachspr. auch* Ka|to|den|strahl *meist Plur.*

Ka|tho|lik, der; -en, -en (↑R 126) ‹griech.› (Anhänger der kath. Kirche u. Glaubenslehre); **Ka|tho|li|ken|tag** (Generalversammlung der Katholiken eines Landes); **Ka|tho|li|kin; ka|tho|lisch** (die kath. Kirche betreffend od. ihr angehörend; *Abk.* kath.); die katholische Kirche, *aber* (↑R 108): Katholisches Bibelwerk (ein Verlag); **ka|tho|li|sie|ren** (katholisch machen); **Ka|tho|li|zis|mus,** der; - (Geist u. Lehre des kath. Glaubens); **Ka|tho|li|zi|tät,** die; - (Rechtgläubigkeit im Sinne der kath. Kirche)

Kath|rein, Kath|rin [*auch* 'ka...], **Kath|ri|ne,** *auch* Kat|rein, Katrin, Kat|ri|ne (↑R 130; w. Vorn.)

ka|ti|li|na|risch ‹nach dem röm. Verschwörer Catilina›; eine katilinarische (heruntergekommene, zu verzweifelten Schritten neigende) Existenz; (↑R 56:) die Erste Katilinarische Verschwörung (66 v. Chr.)

Ka|tin|ka, Ka|thin|ka (w. Vorn.)

Kat|ion ‹griech.› (*Physik* positiv geladenes Ion)

Kat|ja (w. Vorn.)

Kat|man|du [*auch* ...'du:] (Hptst. von Nepal)

Kät|ner (*nordd. für* Häusler, Besitzer einer [2]Kate)

Ka|to|de usw. *vgl.* Kathode usw.

ka|to|nisch ‹nach dem röm. Zensor Cato›; katonische Reden; katonische Strenge

Kat|rein, Kat|rin [*auch* 'ka...], **Kat|ri|ne** *vgl.* Kathrein usw.

kat|schen, du katschst *od.* **kät|schen;** du kätschst (*landsch. für* schmatzend kauen)

Katt|an|ker (*Seemannsspr.* zweiter Anker)

Kat|te|gat, das; -s ‹*dän.,* „Katzenloch"› (Meerenge zwischen Schweden u. Jütland)

kat|ten (*Seemannsspr.* [Anker] hochziehen)

Kat|tun, der; -s, -e ‹arab.-niederl.› (feinfädiges, leinwandbindiges Gewebe aus Baumwolle od. Chemiefasern); **kat|tu|nen;** -er Stoff; **Kat|tun|kleid**

Ka|tyn (Ort bei Smolensk)

katz|bal|gen, sich *(ugs.);* ich katzbalge mich; gekatzbalgt; zu katzbalgen; **Katz|bal|ge|rei; katz|bu|ckeln** (*ugs. für* sich unterwürfig zeigen); er hat gekatzbuckelt; **Kätz|chen; Kat|ze,** die; -, -n; (↑R 13:) für die Katz (*ugs. für* umsonst); Katz und Maus mit jmdm. spielen *(ugs.)*

Kat|zel|ma|cher ‹ital.› (*bes. südd., österr. abwertend für* Italiener)

Kat|zen_au|ge (*auch* ein Mineral; *ugs. für* Rückstrahler am Fahrrad), **...bu|ckel** (höchster Berg des Odenwaldes), **...dreck, ...fell; kat|zen|freund|lich** (*ugs. für* heuchlerisch freundlich); **Kat|zen|fut|ter; kat|zen|gleich; kat|zen|haft; Kat|zen_jam|mer** *(ugs.),* **...klo** *(ugs.),* **...kopf; Kat|zen|kopf|pflas|ter; Kat|zen_mu|sik** *(ugs.),* **...sprung** *(ugs.),* **...tisch** *(ugs.),* **...wä|sche** *(ugs.),* **...zun|gen** (*Plur.;* Schokoladetäfelchen); **Kät|zin; Katz-und-Maus-Spiel** (↑R 28)

Kaub (Stadt am Mittelrhein)

Kau|be|we|gung

kau|dal ‹lat.› (*Zool.* den Schwanz betreffend; *Med.* fußwärts liegend)

kau|dern (*veraltet, aber noch landsch. für* unverständlich sprechen); ich ...ere (↑R 16); **Kau|der|welsch,** das; -[s]; ein Kauderwelsch sprechen; **kau|der|wel|schen** (*svw.* kaudern); du kauderwelschst; gekauderwelscht

kau|di|nisch; ein kaudinisches Joch (*übertr. für* schimpfliche Demütigung), *aber* (↑R 108): das Kaudinische Joch (Joch, durch das die bei Caudium geschlagenen Römer schreiten mussten); ↑R 102: die Kaudinischen Pässe

Kaue, die; -, -n (*Bergmannsspr.* Gebäude über dem Schacht; Wasch- u. Umkleideraum)

kau|en

kau|ern (hocken); ich ...ere (↑R 16); **Kau|er|start** *(Sportspr.)*

Kauf, der; -[e]s, Käufe; in - nehmen; **kau|fen;** du kaufst usw., *landsch.* käufst usw.; **kau|fens|wert; Käu|fer; Käu|fe|rin; Kauf|fah|rer** (*veraltet für* Handelsschiff); **Kauf|fahr|tei|schiff** (*veraltet für* Handelsschiff); **Kauf|frau** (weibl. Kaufmann; Bez. im Handelsregister, *Abk.* Kffr.); **Kauf_haus, ...in|te|res|sent, ...kraft; kauf|kräf|tig; Kauf|la|den** *(veraltend);* **käuf|lich; Käuf|lich|keit,** die; -; **kauf|lus|tig; Kauf|mann** *Plur.* ...leute; *Abk.* Kfm.; **kauf|män|nisch;** kaufmännischer Angestellter; kaufmännisches Rechnen; *Abk.* kfm.; **Kauf|mann|schaft,** die; - (*veraltend);* **Kauf|manns_ge|hil|fe** (*älter für* Handlungsgehilfe), **...gil|de** (*früher),* **...la|den, ...spra|che, ...stand** *(veraltend);* **Kauf_preis** (*vgl.* [2]Preis), **...rausch, ...sum|me**

Kau|fun|ger Wald, der; - -[e]s (Teil des Hessischen Berglandes)

Kauf_ver|trag, ...wert, ...zwang

Kau|gum|mi, der, *auch* das; -s, -[s]

Kau|kamm (*Bergmannsspr.* Grubenbeil)

Kau|ka|si|en [...iən] (Gebiet zwischen Schwarzem Meer u. Kaspischem Meer); **Kau|ka|si|er; kau|ka|sisch; Kau|ka|sus,** der; - (Hochgebirge in Kaukasien)

Kaul|barsch (ein Fisch); **Käul|chen** *vgl.* Quarkkäulchen; **Kau|le,** die; -, -n (*mitteld. für* Grube, Loch; Kugel)

kau|li|flor ‹lat.› (*Bot.* am Stamm ansetzend [von Blüten])

Kaul|quap|pe (Froschlarve)

kaum; das ist kaum glaublich; er war kaum hinausgegangen, da kam ...; kaum[,] dass (↑R 88)

Kau|ma|zit [*auch* ...'tsit], der; -s, *Plur. (Sorten:)* -e ‹griech.› (Braunkohlenkoks)

Kau|mus|kel

Kau|pe|lei (*ostmitteld. für* heimlicher Handel); **kau|peln** (*ostmitteld.);* ich ...[e]le (↑R 16)

Kau|ri, der; -s, -s *od.* die; -, -s ‹Hindi› (Porzellanschnecke; so genanntes Muschelgeld [in Asien u. Afrika])

Kau|ri|fich|te ‹maorisch; dt.› (*svw.* Kopalfichte)

Kau|ri_mu|schel, ...schne|cke

kau|sal ‹lat.› (ursächlich zusammenhängend; begründend); -e Konjunktion (*Sprachw.;* z. B. „denn"); **Kau|sal_be|zie|hung, ...ge|setz** (*bes. Philos.);* **Kau|sa|li|tät,** die; -, -en (Ursächlichkeit); **Kau|sal_ket|te, ...kon|junk|ti|on** *(Sprachw.),* **...ne|xus** (*fachspr. für* ursächl. Zusammenhang), **...satz** (*Sprachw.* Umstandssatz des Grundes), **...zu|sam|men|hang; kau|sa|tiv** [*auch* ...'ti:f] (*Sprachw.* bewirkend; als Kausativ gebraucht); **Kau|sa|tiv,** das; -s, -e [...və] (veranlassendes Verb, z. B. „tränken" = „trinken machen"); **Kau|sa|ti|vum** [...v...], das; -s, ...va (*älter für* Kausativ)

Kausch, Kau|sche, die; -, ...schen (*Seemannsspr.* Ring mit Hohlrand, zur Verstärkung von Tau- u. Seilschlingen)

Kaus|tik, die; - ‹griech.› (*Optik* Brennfläche; *svw.* Kauterisation); **Kaus|ti|kum,** das; -s, ...ka (*Med.* ein Ätzmittel); **kaus|tisch** (*Chemie* ätzend, brennend, scharf; *übertr. für* beißend, spöttisch); kaustischer Witz; **Kaus|to|bi|o|lith** [*auch* ...'lit], der; *Gen.* -s *od.* -en, *Plur.* -e[n]; *meist Plur.* ↑R 126 (brennbares Produkt fossiler Lebewesen; z. B. Torf)

Kau|ta|bak

Kau|tel, die; -, -en ‹lat.› (*Rechtsspr.* Vorsichtsmaßregel; Vorbehalt; Absicherung)

Kau|ter, der; -s, - ‹griech.› (*Med.* chirurgisches Instrument zum Ausbrennen von Gewebsteilen); **Kau|te|ri|sa|ti|on,** die; -, -en (Ätzung zu Heilzwecken); **kau|te|ri|sie|ren; Kau|te|ri|um,** das; -s, ...ien [...i̯ən] (*Chemie* ein Ätzmittel; *Med.* Brenneisen)

Kau|ti|on, die; -, -en ‹lat.› (Geldsumme als Bürgschaft, Sicherheit[sleistung]); **kau|ti|ons|fä|hig** (bürgfähig); **Kau|ti|ons|sum|me**

Kaut|schuk (↑R 130), der; -s, -e ‹indian.› (Milchsaft des Kautschukbaumes; Rohstoff zur Gummiherstellung); **Kaut|schuk-milch** (die; -), **...pa|ra|graph** (dehnbare Rechtsvorschrift), **...plan|ta|ge; kaut|schu|tie|ren** (mit Kautschuk überziehen; aus Kautschuk herstellen)

Kau|werk|zeu|ge *Plur.*

Kauz, der; -es, Käuze; **Käuz|chen; kau|zig**

Ka|val [...v...], der; -s, -s ‹ital.› (Spielkarte im Tarockspiel: Ritter); **Ka|va|lier,** der; -s, -e ‹franz.›; **Ka|va|liers|de|likt; ka|va|lier[s]|mä|ßig; Ka|va|lier[s]-start** (schnelles, geräuschvolles Anfahren mit dem Auto); **Ka|val|ka|de,** die; -, -n (Reiter[auf]zug); **Ka|val|le|rie** [*auch* 'ka...], die; -, ...i̯en (*Milit. früher* Reiterei; Reitertruppe); **Ka|val|le|rist,** der; -en, -en (↑R 126)

Ka|va|ti|ne [...v...], die; -, -n ‹ital.› (*Musik* [kurze] Opernarie; liedartiger Instrumentalsatz)

Ka|vel|ling [...v...], die; -, -en ‹niederl.› (*Wirtsch.* Mindestmenge[neinheit], die ein Käufer auf einer Auktion erwerben muss)

Ka|vents|mann [...v...] *Plur.* ...männer (*landsch. für* beleibter Mann; Prachtexemplar; *Seemannsspr.* bes. hoher Wellenberg)

Ka|ver|ne [...v...], die; -, -n ‹lat.› (Höhle, Hohlraum); **Ka|ver|nom,** das; -s, -e (*Med.* Blutgefäßgeschwulst); **ka|ver|nös** (Kavernen bildend; voll Höhlungen)

Ka|vi|ar [...v...], der; -s, -e ‹türk.› (Rogen des Störs); **Ka|vi|ar|bröt|chen**

Ka|vi|tät [...v...], die; -, -en ‹lat.› (*Med.* Hohlraum); **Ka|vi|ta|ti|on,** die; -, -en (*Technik* Hohlraumbildung)

Ka|wa, die; - ‹polynes.› (berauschendes Getränk der Polynesier)

Ka|wass, Ka|was|se, der; ...wassen, ...wassen (↑R 126) ‹arab.› (*früher* oriental. Polizeisoldat; Ehrenwache)

Ka|wi, das; -[s] *od.* **Ka|wi|spra|che,** die; - ‹sanskr.› (alte Schriftsprache Javas)

Kay, Kai [*beide* kai] (m. *od.* w. Vorn.)

Ka|zi|ke, der; -n, -n (↑R 126) ‹indian.› (Häuptling bei den süd- u. mittelamerik. Indianern; *auch* indian. Ortsvorsteher)

KB = Kilobyte

Kč = tschech. Krone

kcal = Kilokalorie

Keats [ki:ts] (engl. Dichter)

Ke|bab, der; -[s], -s ‹türk.› (am Spieß gebratene [Hammel]fleischstückchen)

keb|beln *vgl.* kibbeln

Keb|se, die; -, -n (*früher für* Nebenfrau); **Kebs-ehe** (↑R 132), **...weib**

keck

ke|ckern (zornige Laute ausstoßen [von Fuchs, Marder, Iltis])

Keck|heit; keck|lich (*veraltet*)

Ke|der, der; -s, - (Randverstärkung aus Leder od. Kunststoff)

Keep, die; -, -en (*Seemannsspr.* Kerbe, Rille)

Kee|per ['ki:pə(r)], der; -s, - ‹engl.› (*bes. österr. für* Torhüter); **Keep|smi|ling** [ki:p'smailiŋ], das; - („lächle weiter“) ([zur Schau getragene] optimistische Lebensanschauung)

Kees, das; -es, -e (*bayr. u. österr. für* Gletscher); **Kees|was|ser,** das; -s, ...wasser (*bayr. u. westösterr. für* Gletscherbach)

Ke|fe, die; -, -n (*schweiz. für* Zuckererbse)

Ke|fir, der; -s ‹tatar.› (aus Milch gewonnenes gegorenes Getränk)

Ke|gel, der; -s, - (*Druckw. auch* Stärke des Typenkörpers); mit Kind und Kegel; Kegel schieben, (*bayr., österr.:*) scheiben; ich schiebe Kegel; weil ich Kegel schob; ich habe Kegel geschoben; um Kegel zu schieben; **Ke|gel-bahn, ...bre|cher** (eine Zerkleinerungsmaschine); **ke|gel|för|mig; ke|ge|lig,** keglig; **Ke|gel-klub, ...ku|gel, ...man|tel** (*Math.*); **ke|geln;** ich ...[e]le (↑R 16); **Ke|gel|schei|ben,** das; -s (*bayr., österr.*); **Ke|gel schei|ben** *vgl.* Kegel; **Ke|gel|schie|ben** (das; -s); **Ke|gel schie|ben** *vgl.* Kegel; **Ke|gel-schnitt** (*Math.*), **...sport, ...statt** (*Plur.* ...stätten; *österr. neben* Kegelbahn), **...stumpf** (*Math.*); **Keg|ler; keg|lig** *vgl.* kegelig

Keh|din|gen *vgl.* Land Kehdingen

Kehl (Stadt am Oberrhein)

Kehl|chen; Keh|le, die; -, -n; **keh|len** (rinnenartig aushöhlen; [Fisch] aufschneiden u. ausnehmen); **Kehl|ho|bel; keh|lig; Kehl|kopf; Kehl|kopf-ka|tarrh** (↑R 33), **...krebs, ...mik|ro|fon, ...schnitt, ...spie|gel; Kehl-laut, ...leis|te; Keh|lung** (*svw.* Hohlkehle)

Kehr|aus, der; -; **Kehr|be|sen**

Keh|re, die; -, -n (Wendekurve; eine turnerische Übung); [1]**keh|ren** (umwenden); sich nicht an etwas - (*ugs. für* sich nicht um etwas kümmern)

[2]**keh|ren** (fegen); **Keh|richt,** der, *auch* das; -s; **Keh|richt-ei|mer, ...hau|fen, ...schau|fel; Kehr|ma|schi|ne**

Kehr|ord|nung (*schweiz. für* festgelegte Wechselfolge, Turnus); **Kehr-reim, ...schlei|fe** (*für* Serpentine), **...sei|te; kehrt!** (*auch Milit.*); rechtsum kehrt!; **kehrt|ma|chen** (umkehren); ich mache kehrt; kehrtgemacht; kehrtzumachen; **Kehrt|wen|dung; Kehr|wert** (*für* reziproker Wert); **Kehr|wie|der** der *od.* das; -s (Name von Sackgassen, Gasthäusern u. Ä.)

Kehr|wisch (*südd. für* Handbesen)

Keib, der; -en, -en; ↑R 126 (*schwäb. u. schweiz. mdal. für* Aas; Lump, Kerl [grobes Schimpfwort])

kei|fen; Kei|fe|rei; kei|fisch (*veraltet*)

Keil, der; -[e]s, -e; **Keil|bein** (Schädelknochen); **Kei|le,** die; - (*ugs. für* Prügel); - kriegen; **kei|len** (*ugs. für* stoßen; [für eine Studentenverbindung] anwerben); sich - (*ugs. für* sich prügeln); **Kei|ler** (*Jägerspr.* männl. Wildschwein); **Kei|le|rei** (*ugs. für* Prügelei); **keil|för|mig; Keil-haue** (*Bergmannsspr.*), **...ho|se, ...kis|sen, ...pols|ter** (*österr.*), **...rie|men, ...schrift**

Keim, der; -[e]s, -e; **Keim-blatt, ...drü|se; kei|men; keim-fä|hig, ...frei; keim|haft; Keim|ling; Keim|plas|ma** (*Biol.*); **Kei|mung; Keim|zel|le**

kein, -e, -, *Plur.* -e; kein and[e]rer; in keinem Falle, auf keinen Fall; zu keiner Zeit; keine unreifen Früchte; es bedarf keiner großen Erörterungen mehr. *Allein stehend* (↑R 48): keiner, keine, kein[e]s; keiner, keine, kein[e]s von beiden; keiner, der (*nicht:* welcher); **kei|ner|lei; kei|ner|seits; kei|nes|falls** *vgl.* [1]Fall; **kei|nes|wegs; kein|mal,** *aber* kein einziges Mal

...keit (z. B. Ähnlichkeit, die; -, -en)

Keks, der *od.* das; *Gen.* - *u.* -es, *Plur.* - *u.* -e, *österr.* das; -, -[e] ‹engl.›; **Keks|do|se**

Kelch, der; -[e]s, -e; **Kelch|blatt; kelch|för|mig; Kelch˷glas** (*Plur.* ...gläser), **...kom|mu|ni|on** *(kath. Rel.)*

Kel|heim (Stadt in Bayern)

Ke|lim, der; -s, -s ‹türk.› (ein oriental. Teppich); **Ke|lim|sti|cke|rei** (eine Wollgarnstickerei)

Kel|le, die; -, -n

[1]**Kel|ler** (schweiz. Schriftsteller)

[2]**Kel|ler,** der; -s, -; **Kel|ler|as|sel; Kel|le|rei; Kel|ler˷fal|te, ...fens|ter, ...ge|schoss;** [1]**Kel|ler|hals** (*svw.* Seidelbast); [2]**Kel|ler|hals** (Überbau od. ansteigendes Gewölbe über einer Kellertreppe); **Kel|ler˷kind, ...meis|ter, ...trep|pe, ...tür, ...woh|nung; Kell|ner,** der; -s, -; **Kell|ne|rin; kell|nern** *(ugs.);* ich ...ere (↑R 16)

Kel|logg|pakt *vgl.* Briand-Kellogg-Pakt (↑R 95)

Kelt, der; -[e]s, -e ‹kelt.-lat.› (*veraltet für* bronzezeitliches Beil)

Kel|te, der; -n, -n; ↑R 126 (Angehöriger eines indogerm. Volkes)

Kel|ter, die; -, -n (Weinpresse); **Kel|te|rei; Kel|te|rer; kel|tern;** ich ...ere (↑R 16)

Kelt|ibe|rer (↑R 132; Angehöriger eines Mischvolkes im alten Spanien); **kelt|ibe|risch; kel|tisch; Kel|tisch,** das; -[s] (Sprache); *vgl.* Deutsch; **Kel|ti|sche,** das; -n; *vgl.* Deutsche, das; **kel|to|ro|ma|nisch**

Kel|vin [...vin], das; -s, - ‹nach dem engl. Physiker W. T. Kelvin› (Maßeinheit der absoluten Temperaturskala; *Zeichen* K); 0 K = –273,15 °C

Ke|ma|lis|mus, der; - (von dem türk. Präsidenten Kemal Atatürk begründete polit. Richtung); **Ke|ma|list,** der; -en, -en; ↑R 126

Ke|me|na|te, die; -, -n ([Frauen]gemach einer Burg)

Ken, das; -, - ‹jap.› (jap. Verwaltungsbezirk, Präfektur)

Ken. = Kentucky

Ken|do, das; -[s] ‹jap.› (jap. Form des Fechtens mit Bambusstäben)

Ke|nia (Staat in Ostafrika); **Ke|ni|a|ner; Ke|ni|a|ne|rin; ke|ni|a|nisch**

Ken|ne|dy [ˈkɛnidi], John F. (Präsident der USA)

Ken|nel, der; -s, - ‹engl.› (Hundezwinger)

Ken|nel|ly [ˈkɛn(ə)li] (amerik. Ingenieur u. Physiker); **Ken|nel|ly-Hea|vi|side-Schicht** [ˈkɛn(ə)li-ˈhɛvisaid...], die; - (*Meteor.* elektr. leitende Schicht in der Atmosphäre); *vgl.* Heaviside

ken|nen; du kanntest; *selten* kenntest; gekannt; kenn[e]!; jmdn. kennen lernen; ich lerne kennen; ich habe ihn kennen gelernt; kennen zu lernen; **Ken|ner; Ken|ner|blick; Ken|ne|rin; ken|ne|risch; Ken|ner|mie|ne; Ken|ner|schaft,** die; -; **Kenn|far|be**

Ken|ning, die; -, *Plur.* -ar, *auch* -e ‹altnord.› (*altnord. Dichtung* bildl. Umschreibung eines Begriffes durch eine mehrgliedrige Benennung)

Kenn˷kar|te, ...mar|ke; Kenn|num|mer (↑R 136); **Kenn|sig|nal; kennt|lich;** - machen; **Kennt|lich|ma|chung; Kennt|nis,** die; -, -se; von etwas - nehmen; in - setzen; zur - nehmen; **Kennt|nis|nah|me,** die; -; **kennt|nis|reich; Kennt|nis|stand,** der; -[e]s; **Ken|nung** (charakteristisches Merkmal; typ. Kennzeichen von Leuchtfeuern usw.); **Kenn˷wort** (*Plur.* ...wörter), **...zahl, ...zei|chen; kenn|zeich|nen;** gekennzeichnet; zu kennzeichnen; **kenn|zeich|nen|der|wei|se; Kenn˷zeich|nung, ...zif|fer**

Ke|no|taph, *auch* Ze|no|taph, das; -s, -e ‹griech.› (Grabmal für einen andernorts bestatteten Toten)

Kent (engl. Grafschaft)

Ken|taur *vgl.* Zentaur

ken|tern (umkippen [von Schiffen]); **Ken|te|rung**

Ken|tu|cky [...ˈtaki] (Staat in den USA; *Abk.* Ken. *u.* Ky.)

Ken|tum|spra|che *meist Plur.* ‹lat.; dt.› (Sprache aus einer bestimmten Gruppe der indogerm. Sprachen)

[1]**Ke|pheus** (griech. Sagengestalt); [2]**Ke|pheus,** der; - (ein Sternbild)

Ke|phi|sos, der; - (griech. Fluss)

Kep|ler (dt. Astronom); das keplersche Gesetz (↑R 94)

kep|peln (*österr. ugs. für* fortwährend schimpfen; keifen); ich kepp[e]le (↑R 16); **Kep|pel|weib; Kepp|le|rin**

Ke|ra|bau, der; -s, -s ‹malai.› (ind. Wasserbüffel)

Ke|ra|mik, die; -, *Plur.* (*für* Erzeugnisse:) -en ‹griech.› ([Erzeugnis der] [Kunst]töpferei); **Ke|ra|mi|ker; Ke|ra|mi|ke|rin; ke|ra|misch**

Ke|ra|tin, das; -s, -e ‹griech.› (*Biochemie* Hornsubstanz); **Ke|ra|ti|tis,** die; -, ...itiden (*Med.* Hornhautentzündung des Auges); **Ke|ra|tom,** das; -s, -e (Horngeschwulst der Haut); **Ke|ra|to|skop,** das; -s, -e (Instrument zur Untersuchung der Hornhautkrümmung)

[1]**Kerb,** die; -, -en (*hess.-pfälz. für* Kirchweih); *vgl.* Kerwe

[2]**Kerb,** der; -[e]s, -e (*Technik neben* Kerbe); **Ker|be,** die; -, -n (Einschnitt)

Ker|bel, der; -s (eine Gewürzpflanze); **Ker|bel|kraut,** das; -[e]s

ker|ben (Einschnitte machen)

Ker|be|ros *vgl.* Zerberus

Kerb|holz; *fast nur noch in* etwas auf dem - haben (*ugs. für* etwas auf dem Gewissen haben); **Kerb˷schnitt** (der; -[e]s; Holzverzierung), **...tier; Ker|bung**

Ke|ren *Plur.* (griech. Schicksalsgöttinnen)

Kerf, der; -[e]s, -e (Kerbtier)

Ker|gue|len [...ˈge:...] *Plur.* (Inseln im Indischen Ozean)

Ker|ker, der; -s, - (*früher* sehr festes Gefängnis; *österr. für* schwere Freiheitsstrafe); **Ker|ker˷meis|ter, ...stra|fe**

Ker|kops, der; -, ...open ‹griech.› (Kobold der griech. Sage)

Ker|ky|ra (*griech. Name für* Korfu)

Kerl, der; -[e]s, *Plur.* -e, *landsch., bes. nordd.* -s; **Kerl|chen**

Ker|mes|bee|re ‹arab.; dt.› (Pflanze, deren Beeren zum Färben von Getränken verwendet werden); **Ker|mes˷ei|che** (Eichenart des Mittelmeergebietes), **...schild|laus** (auf der Kermeseiche lebende Schildlaus, aus der ein roter Farbstoff gewonnen wird)

Kern, der; -[e]s, -e; **Kern|bei|ßer** (ein Singvogel); **ker|nen** (*seltener für* auskernen); **Kern|ener|gie** (↑R 132; *svw.* Atomenergie)

[1]**Ker|ner,** der; -s, - ‹nach dem Dichter J. Kerner› (eine Rebsorte, Weinsorte)

[2]**Ker|ner** *vgl.* [1]Karner

Kern|ex|plo|si|on (Zertrümmerung eines Atomkerns); **Kern|fäu|le** (Fäule des Kernholzes von lebenden Bäumen); **Kern˷for|de|rung, ...for|schung** (Atomforschung), **...fra|ge, ...frucht, ...fu|si|on, ...ge|dan|ke, ...ge|häu|se; kern|ge|sund; Kern|holz; ker|nig; Kern|kraft‿geg|ner, ...werk; Kern|ling** (aus einem Kern gezogener Baum od. Strauch); **kern|los; Kern‿obst, ...phy|sik** (Lehre von den Atomkernen u. -kernreaktionen); **kern|phy|si|ka|lisch; Kern‿phy|si|ker, ...prob|lem, ...punkt, ...re|ak|ti|on, ...re|ak|tor, ...schat|ten** *(Optik, Astron.),* **...sei|fe, ...spal|tung, ...spruch, ...stadt, ...stück, ...tech|nik, ...tei|lung, ...trup|pe, ...um|wand|lung, ...ver|schmel|zung, ...waf|fen** *(Plur.)*

Ke|ro|plas|tik *vgl.* Zeroplastik; **Ke|ro|sin,** das; -s ‹griech.› (ein Treibstoff)

Ke|rou|ac ['kɛruɛk] (amerik. Schriftsteller)

Kers|tin (w. Vorn.)

Ke|rub *vgl.* Cherub

Ker|we, die; -, -n *(hess.-pfälz. für* Kirchweih)

Ke|ryg|ma, das; -s ‹griech.› *(Theol.* Verkündigung [des Evangeliums]); **ke|ryg|ma|tisch** (verkündigend, predigend); -e Theologie

Ker|ze, die; -, -n; **Ker|zen|be|leuch|tung; ker|zen|ge|ra|de,** *auch* **ker|zen|gra|de; Ker|zen‿hal|ter, ...licht** *(Plur.* ...lichter), **...schein** (der; -[e]s), **...stän|der**

Ke|scher *vgl.* Käscher

kess *(ugs. für* frech; schneidig; flott); ein kesses Mädchen

Kes|sel, der; -s, -; **Kes|sel‿bo|den, ...fleisch** *(landsch. für* Wellfleisch), **...fli|cker, ...haus, ...pau|ke, ...schmied, ...stein, ...trei|ben, ...wa|gen** *(Eisenb.)*

Kess|heit

Ket|chup *vgl.* Ketschup

Ke|ton, das; -s, -e *meist Plur.* (eine chem. Verbindung); **Ke|ton|harz**

Ketsch, die; -, -en ‹engl.› (eine zweimastige [Sport]segeljacht)

ket|schen *(Nebenform von* kätschen)

Ket|schua *vgl.* Quechua

Ket|schup (↑R 33), *auch* Ketchup ['kɛtʃap, *auch* 'kɛtʃup, *engl.* 'kɛtʃəp], der *od.* das; -[s], -s ‹malai.-engl.› (pikante [Tomaten]soße zum Würzen)

Kett|baum, Ket|ten|baum (Teil des Webstuhls); **Kett|car ®,** der *od.* das; -s, -s ‹dt.; engl.› (ein Kinderfahrzeug); **Kett|chen; Ket|te,** die; -, -n; **Ket|tel,** der; -s, - *od.* die; -, -n *(landsch. für* Krampe); **Ket|tel|ma|schi|ne; ket|teln** ([kettenähnlich] verbinden); ich ...[e]le (↑R 16); **ket|ten; Ket|ten|baum** *vgl.* Kettbaum; **Ket|ten‿blu|me** (Löwenzahn), **...brief, ...bruch** (der; *Math.*), **...brü|cke; Ket|ten|fa|den** *vgl.* Kettfaden; **Ket|ten|garn** *vgl.* Kettgarn; **Ket|ten‿glied, ...haus** *(Bauw.),* **...hemd, ...hund, ...pan|zer, ...rad, ...rau|chen** (das; -s), **...rau|cher, ...re|ak|ti|on, ...sä|ge, ...schutz, ...stich; Kett‿fa|den** *(Weberei),* **...garn** *(Weberei);* **Ket|tung**

Ket|zer; Ket|ze|rei; Ket|zer|ge|richt; Ket|ze|rin; ket|ze|risch; Ket|zer‿tau|fe, ...ver|fol|gung

keu|chen; Keuch|hus|ten

Keu|le, die; -, -n; **keu|len** *(Tiermed.* seuchenkranke Tiere töten); **Keu|len|är|mel; keu|len|för|mig; Keu|len‿gym|nas|tik, ...schlag, ...schwin|gen** (das; -s)

Keu|per, der; -s *(landsch. für* roter, sandiger Ton; *Geol.* oberste Stufe der Trias)

keusch

Keu|sche, die; -, -n *(österr. für* Bauernhäuschen, Kate)

Keusch|heit, die; -; **Keusch|heits‿ge|lüb|de, ...gür|tel** *(früher);* **Keusch|lamm|strauch**

Keusch|ler *(österr. für* Bewohner einer Keusche, Häusler)

Ke|ve|laer ['ke:vəla:r] (Stadt in Nordrhein-Westfalen)

Ke|vin ['kɛvin] (m. Vorn.)

Key|board ['ki:bɔ:(r)d], das; -s, -s ‹engl.› (elektronisches Tasteninstrument); **Key|boar|der**

Key|ser|ling ['kai...] (balt. Adelsgeschlecht)

Kffr. = Kauffrau

kfm. = kaufmännisch

Kfm. = Kaufmann

Kfz = Kraftfahrzeug; **Kfz-Schlos|ser; Kfz-Werk|statt**

kg = Kilogramm; 2-kg-Dose (↑R 28)

KG = Kommanditgesellschaft;

KGaA = Kommanditgesellschaft auf Aktien

KGB, der; -[s] ‹*Abk. aus* russ. Komitet gossudarstwennoi besopasnosti = Komitee für Staatssicherheit› (Geheimdienst der ehem. Sowjetunion)

kgl. = königlich, *im Titel* Kgl.

K-Grup|pe *meist Plur.* *(Bez. für* unabhängige kommunistische Organisationen in der Bundesrepublik Deutschland)

k. g. V., kgV = kleinstes gemeinsames Vielfaches

Khai|ber|pass ['kai...], der; -es (Gebirgspass zwischen Afghanistan und Pakistan)

[1]**Kha|ki** ['ka:...] (↑R 33), das; -[s] ‹pers.-engl.› (Erdfarbe, Erdbraun); [2]**Kha|ki,** der; -[s] (gelbbrauner Stoff [für die Tropenuniform]); **kha|ki‿far|ben** *od.* **...far|big; Kha|ki‿ja|cke, ...uni|form** (↑R 132)

Khan [ka:n], der; -s, -e ‹mong.› (mong.-türk. Herrschertitel); **Kha|nat,** das; -[e]s, -e (Amt, Land eines Khans)

Khar|toum ['kar..., *auch* ...'tu:m] (Hptst. von Sudan)

Khe|di|ve [ke'di:və], der; *Gen.* -s *u.* -n, *Plur.* -n; ↑R 126 (Titel des früheren Vizekönigs von Ägypten)

Khmer [kme:r], der; -, - (Angehöriger eines Volkes in Kambodscha); **Khmer-Re|pub|lik**

Kho|mei|ni [xɔ'me:ni] (iran. Schiitenführer)

kHz = Kilohertz

kib|beln, keb|beln *(landsch. Nebenform von* kabbeln)

Kib|buz, der; -, *Plur.* ...uzim *od.* -e ‹hebr.› (Gemeinschaftssiedlung in Israel); **Kib|buz|nik,** der; -s, -s (Angehöriger eines Kibbuz)

Ki|be|rer ‹Gaunerspr.› *(österr. ugs. für* Kriminalpolizist)

Ki|bit|ka, die; -, -s ‹russ.› *u.* **Ki|bit|ke,** die; -, -n (Filzzelt asiat. Nomadenstämme; russ. Bretterwagen, russ. Schlitten mit Mattendach)

Ki|che|rei

Ki|cher|erb|se

ki|chern; ich ...ere (↑R 16)

Kick, der; -[s], -s ‹engl.› *(ugs. für* Tritt, Stoß [beim Fußball]; Nervenkitzel); **Kick|bo|xen** (asiat. Sportart); **Kick-down,** *auch* **Kick|down** [...'daun], der *od.* das; -s, -s *(Kfz-Technik* plötzliches Durchtreten des Gaspedals)

Ki|ckel|hahn, der; -[e]s (ein Berg im Thüringer Wald)

ki|cken ‹engl.› *(ugs. für* Fußball spielen); **Ki|cker,** der; -s, -[s] *(ugs. für* Fußballspieler); **Ki|ckers** *Plur.* (Name von Fußballvereinen); **Kick-off,** *auch* **Kick|off,** der; -s, -s *(schweiz. für* Anstoß beim Fußballspiel); **kick|sen** *vgl.* gicksen; **Kick|star|ter** (Fußhebel zum Anlassen bei Motorrädern)

Kick|xia ['kiksia], die; -, ...ien [...iən] ‹nach dem belg. Botaniker Kickx› (ein Kautschukbaum)

Kid, das; -s, -s ‹engl.› ([Handschuh aus] Kalb-, Ziegen-, Schafleder; *meist Plur.: ugs. für* Jugendliche, Kinder); **kid|nap|pen** [...nɛpən] (entführen); gekidnappt; **Kid|nap|per,** der; -s, - (Entführer); **Kid|nap|ping,** das; -s, -s

Kid|ron (↑R 130; Bachtal östl. von Jerusalem)

Kids *vgl.* Kid

kie|big *(landsch. für* zänkisch,

schlecht gelaunt; frech, prahlerisch, aufbegehrend)
Kie|bitz, der; -es, -e (ein Vogel); **Kie|bitz|ei**
kie|bit|zen ‹Gaunerspr.› (*ugs. für* beim [Karten-, Schach]spiel zuschauen); du kiebitzt
kie|feln (*österr. ugs. für* nagen)
[1]**Kie|fer,** die; -, -n (ein Nadelbaum)
[2]**Kie|fer,** der; -s, - (ein Schädelknochen); **Kie|fer‿ano|ma|lie** (↑R 132; *Med.*), **...bruch, ...chi|rur|gie, ...höh|le; Kie|fer|höh|len|ent|zün|dung; Kie|fer|kno|chen**
kie|fern (aus Kiefernholz); **Kie|fern‿eu|le** (ein Schmetterling), **...holz, ...na|del** *(meist Plur.)*, **...schwär|mer** (ein Schmetterling), **...span|ner** (ein Schmetterling), **...spin|ner** (ein Schmetterling), **...wald, ...zap|fen**
Kie|fer|or|tho|pä|de
Kie|ke, die; -, -n (*nordd. für* Kohlenbecken zum Fußwärmen)
kie|ken (*nordd. für* sehen); **Kie|ker** (*Seemannsspr. u. landsch. für* Fernglas); jmdn. auf dem - haben (*ugs. für* jmdn. misstrauisch beobachten; jmdn. nicht leiden können); **Kiek|in|die|welt,** der; -s, -s (*ugs. scherzh. für* kleines Kind; unerfahrener Mensch)
[1]**Kiel,** der; -[e]s, -e (Blütenteil; Federschaft)
[2]**Kiel** (Hptst. von Schleswig-Holstein)
[3]**Kiel,** der; -[e]s, -e (Grundbalken der Wasserfahrzeuge); **Kiel|boot**
kie|len (*veraltet für* Kielfedern bekommen)
Kie|ler (von [2]Kiel); ↑R 103; Kieler Bucht; Kieler Förde; Kieler Sprotten; Kieler Woche
Kiel|fe|der
kiel|ho|len ([ein Schiff] umlegen [zum Ausbessern]; frühere seemänn. Strafe: jmdn. unter dem Schiff durchs Wasser ziehen); er wurde gekielholt
Kiel|kropf (*veraltet für* Missgeburt, Wechselbalg)
Kiel|li|nie (Formation von [Kriegs]schiffen); in - fahren; **kiel|oben** (↑R 132; *Seemannsspr.*); kieloben liegen; **Kiel|raum; Kiel|schwein** (*Seemannsspr.* auf dem Hauptkiel von Schiffen liegender Verstärkungsbalken oder -träger); **Kiel‿schwert** *(Seemannsspr.)*, **...was|ser** (das; -s; Wasserspur hinter einem fahrenden Schiff)
Kie|me, die; -, -n *meist Plur.* (Atmungsorgan im Wasser lebender Tiere); **Kie|men‿at|mer** *(Zool.)*, **...at|mung, ...spal|te**

[1]**Kien** ‹Herkunft unsicher›; *nur in* auf dem Kien sein (*landsch. für* wachsam sein, gut aufpassen)
[2]**Kien,** der; -[e]s (harzreiches [Kiefern]holz); **Kien‿ap|fel, ...fa|ckel, ...holz; kie|nig; Kien‿span, ...zap|fen**
Kie|pe, die; -, -n (*nordd., mitteld. für* auf dem Rücken getragener, hoher Tragekorb); **Kie|pen|hut,** der (ein Frauenhut, Schute)
Kier|ke|gaard [ˈkirkəgart, *dän.* ˈkɛrgəgɔ:r] (dän. Philosoph u. Theologe)
Kies, der; -es, *Plur.* (*für* Kiesarten:) -e (*ugs. auch für* Geld); **Kie|sel,** der; -s, -; **Kie|sel‿al|ge, ...er|de, ...gur** (die; -; Erdart aus den Panzern von Kieselalgen); **kie|seln** (mit Kies beschütten); ich ...[e]le (↑R 16); **Kie|sel‿säu|re** (die; -), **...stein;** [1]**kie|sen** (*svw.* kieseln); du kiest; er kies|te; gekiest; kies[e]!
[2]**kie|sen** (*veraltet für* wählen); du kiest; kies[e]!; du kor[e]st, körest; gekoren; *vgl.* küren
Kie|se|rit [*auch* ...ˈrit], der; -s, *Plur. (Sorten:)* -e (ein Mineral)
Kies‿gru|be, ...hau|fen; kie|sig; Kies|weg
Ki|ew [ˈki:ɛf] (Hptst. der Ukraine); **Ki|e|wer** (↑R 103)
Kiez, der; -es, -e ‹slaw.› (*nordostd. für* Ort[steil]; *ugs. für* Prostituiertenviertel)
kif|fen ‹arab.-amerik.› (*Jargon* Haschisch od. Marihuana rauchen); **Kif|fer**
Ki|ga|li (Hptst. von Ruanda)
ki|ke|ri|ki!; [1]**Ki|ke|ri|ki,** der; -s, -s (*Kinderspr.* Hahn); [2]**Ki|ke|ri|ki,** das; -s, -s (Hahnenschrei)
Ki|ki, der; -s (*ugs. für* überflüssiges Zeug; Unsinn)
Kil|bi, die; -, ...benen *vgl.* Chilbi; **Kil|bi|tanz**
Ki|li|an (m. Vorn.)
Ki|li|ki|en, Zi|li|zi|en [...i̯ən] (im Altertum Landschaft in Kleinasien); **ki|li|kisch,** zi|li|zisch
Ki|li|mand|scha|ro (↑R 132), der; -[s] (höchster Berg Afrikas)
kil|le|kil|le; - machen (*ugs. für* kitzeln; unterm Kinn streicheln)
[1]**kil|len** ‹engl.› (*ugs. für* töten); er hat ihn gekillt
[2]**kil|len** ‹niederd.› (*Seemannsspr.* leicht flattern [von Segeln])
Kil|ler (*ugs. für* Totschläger, [berufsmäßiger] Mörder); **Kil|ler‿al|ge** *(ugs.)*, **...sa|tel|lit** (*ugs. für* Satellit, der Flugkörper im All zerstören soll); **Kil|ler|vi|rus** *(ugs.)*
Kiln, der; -[e]s, -e ‹engl.› (Schachtofen zur Holzverkohlung od. Metallgewinnung)

ki|lo... ‹griech.› (tausend...); **Ki|lo,** das; -s, -[s] (*Kurzform für* Kilogramm); **Ki|lo...** (Tausend...; das Tausendfache einer Einheit, z. B. Kilometer = 1 000 Meter; *Zeichen* k)
Ki|lo|byte [...ˈbait, *auch* ˈki:...] (*EDV* Einheit von 1 024 Byte; *Abk.* KB)
Ki|lo|gramm [*auch* ˈki:...] (1 000 Gramm; Maßeinheit für Masse; *Zeichen* kg); 3 - (↑R 90)
Ki|lo|hertz [*auch* ˈki:...] (1 000 Hertz; Maßeinheit für die Frequenz; *Zeichen* kHz)
Ki|lo|joule [...ˈdʒu:l, *auch* ˈki:...] (1 000 Joule; *Zeichen* kJ); *vgl.* Joule
Ki|lo|ka|lo|rie [*auch* ˈki:...] (1 000 Kalorien; *Zeichen* kcal)
Ki|lo|li|ter [*auch* ˈki:...] (1 000 Liter; *Zeichen* kl)
Ki|lo|me|ter [*auch* ˈki:...], der; -s, - (1 000 m; *Zeichen* km); 80 Kilometer je Stunde (*Abk.* km/h); **Ki|lo|me|ter‿fres|ser** *(ugs.)*, **...geld; Ki|lo|me|ter|geld|pau|scha|le; ki|lo|me|ter|lang,** *aber* 3 Kilometer lang; **Ki|lo|me|ter‿mar|ke, ...stand, ...stein, ...ta|rif; ki|lo|me|ter|weit** *vgl.* kilometerlang; **Ki|lo|me|ter|zäh|ler**
ki|lo|met|rie|ren (↑R 130; [Straßen, Flüsse usw.] mit Kilometereinteilung versehen); **Ki|lo|met|rie|rung; ki|lo|met|risch**
Ki|lo|new|ton [...ˈnju:t(ə)n, *auch* ˈki:...] (1 000 Newton; *Zeichen* kN)
Ki|lo|ohm [*auch* ˈki:...] (1 000 Ohm; *Zeichen* kΩ)
Ki|lo|pas|cal [*auch* ˈki:...] (1 000 Pascal; *Zeichen* kPa)
Ki|lo|pond [*auch* ˈki:...] (1 000 Pond; ältere Maßeinheit für Kraft u. Gewicht; *Zeichen* kp); **Ki|lo|pond|me|ter** (ältere Einheit der Energie; *Zeichen* kpm)
Ki|lo‿volt [*auch* ˈki:...] (1 000 Volt; *Zeichen* kV), **...volt|am|pere** [...amˈpɛ:r] (1 000 Voltampere; *Zeichen* kVA)
Ki|lo|watt [*auch* ˈki:...] (1 000 Watt; *Zeichen* kW); **Ki|lo|watt|stun|de** (1 000 Wattstunden; *Zeichen* kWh)
[1]**Kilt,** der; -[e]s (*früher südwestd. u. schweiz. für* das Fensterln)
[2]**Kilt,** der; -[e]s, -s ‹engl.› (knielanger Rock der Bergschotten)
Kilt|gang ‹*zu* [1]Kilt›
Kim|ber usw. *vgl.* Zimber usw.
Kimm, die; - (*Seew.* Horizontlinie zwischen Meer u. Himmel; *Schiffbau* Krümmung des Schiffsrumpfes zwischen Bordwand u. Boden); **Kim|me,** die; -, -n (Ein-

schnitt; Kerbe; Teil der Visiereinrichtung); **Kimm|ho|bel; Kimmung** (*Seew.* Luftspiegelung; Horizont)
Ki|mon (athen. Feldherr)
Ki|mo|no [*auch* 'ki... *od.* ki'mo:no], der; -s, -s ‹jap.› (weitärmeliges Gewand); **Ki|mo|no˯är|mel** (weiter, angeschnittener Ärmel), **...blu|se**
Ki|nä|de, der; -n, -n (↑R 126) ‹griech.› (männl. Hetäre im alten Griechenland; Päderast)
Kin|äs|the|sie, die; - ‹griech.› (*Med.* Fähigkeit der unbewussten Steuerung von Körperbewegungen)
Kind, das; -[e]s, -er; an Kindes statt; von Kind auf; sich bei jmdm. lieb Kind machen (einschmeicheln); **Kind|bett,** das; -[e]s; *(veraltend);* **Kind|bet|te|rin** *(veraltet);* **Kind|bett|fie|ber,** das; -s *(veraltend);* **Kind|chen; Kindchen|sche|ma** *(Verhaltensforschung);* **Kin|del|bier** (*nordd. für* Bewirtung bei der Kindtaufe); **Kin|der˯ar|beit, ...arzt, ...bett, ...buch; Kin|der|chen** *Plur.;* **Kinder˯dorf, ...ehe** (↑R 132); **Kinde|rei; Kin|der|er|zie|hung; kinder|feind|lich; Kin|der|fräu|lein; kin|der|freund|lich; Kin|der˯gar|ten, ...gärt|ne|rin, ...geld; kin|der|ge|recht** (*svw.* kindgerecht); **Kin|der˯got|tes|dienst, ...heim, ...hort, ...klei|dung, ...krank|heit, ...krie|gen** (das; -s; *ugs.*), **...krip|pe, ...la|den** (*auch für* nicht autoritär geleiteter Kindergarten), **...läh|mung; kin|derleicht; Kin|der|lein** *Plur.;* **kinder˯lieb, ...los; Kin|der|lo|sigkeit,** die; -; **Kin|der˯mäd|chen, ...mund, ...nah|rung, ...pflege|rin, ...post; kin|der|reich; Kin|der˯reich|tum** (der; -s), **...schreck** (der; -s), **...schuh, ...schutz, ...sei|te** (einer Zeitung), **...sen|dung; kin|der|sicher;** ein -er Verschluss; **Kin|der˯spiel, ...spra|che, ...stu|be, ...ta|ges|stät|te, ...tel|ler; kinder|tüm|lich; Kin|der˯uhr, ...wa|gen, ...zeit, ...zim|mer; Kin|des˯al|ter, ...aus|set|zung, ...bei|ne** (*Plur.; in* von -n an), **...ent|zie|hung** *(Rechtsw.),* **...kind** (*veraltet für* Enkelkind), **...liebe, ...miss|hand|lung, ...mord, ...mör|de|rin, ...un|ter|schiebung; kind|ge|mäß; kind|gerecht; kind|haft; Kind|heit,** die; -; **Kind|heits|er|in|ne|rung; kindisch; Kind|lein; kind|lich; Kind|lich|keit,** die; -; **Kinds˯bewe|gung, ...kopf** *(ugs. abwertend);* **kinds|köp|fig** *(ugs. abwertend);* **Kinds˯pech** (Stuhlgang des neugeborenen Kindes), **...tod; Kind|tau|fe**
Ki|ne|ma|thek, die; -, -en ‹griech.› (Sammlung von Filmen; Filmarchiv); **Ki|ne|ma|tik,** die; - (*Physik* Lehre von den Bewegungen); **ki|ne|ma|tisch** (die Kinematik betreffend); **Ki|ne|ma|to|graph,** der; -en, -en; ↑R 126 (der erste Apparat zur Aufnahme u. Wiedergabe bewegter Bilder; *Kurzform* Kino); **Ki|ne|ma|to|graphie,** die; - (Filmwissenschaft u. -technik, Aufnahme u. Wiedergabe von Filmen); **ki|ne|ma|to|graphisch; Ki|ne|tik,** die; - (*Physik* Lehre von den Kräften, die nicht im Gleichgewicht sind); **ki|netisch** (die Kinetik betreffend); kinetische Energie (Bewegungsenergie); **Ki|ne|to|se,** die; -, -n (Bewegungs- od. Reisekrankheit)
King, der; -[s], -s ‹engl.› (*engl. für* König; *ugs. für* Anführer; jmd., der größtes Ansehen genießt); **King|size** [...saiz], die, *auch* das; - (Großformat, Überlänge [von Zigaretten])
Kings|ton [...tən] (Hptst. von Jamaika)
Kings|town [...taun] (Hptst. des Staates St. Vincent und die Grenadinen)
Kink, der, *auch* die; -en, -en (*Seemannsspr. u. nordd. für* Knoten, Fehler im Tau)
Kin|ker|litz|chen *Plur.* ‹franz.› (*ugs. für* Nichtigkeiten, Albernheiten)
Kinn, das; -[e]s, -e; **Kinn˯backe[n], ...ha|ken, ...la|de, ...riemen, ...spit|ze**
Ki|no, das; -s, -s (Lichtspieltheater); *vgl.* Kinematograph; **Ki|no˯be|sit|zer, ...be|su|cher, ...karte, ...pro|gramm, ...re|kla|me**
Kin|sha|sa [...'ʃa...] (Hptst. von Zaire)
Kin|topp, der; -s, *Plur.* -s *u.* ...töppe (*ugs. für* Kino, Film)
Kin|zig, die; - (r. Nebenfluss des unteren Mains; r. Nebenfluss des Oberrheins); **Kin|zi|git** [*auch* ...'git], der; -s (eine Gneisart)
Ki|osk [*auch* ...'ɔsk], der; -[e]s, -e ‹pers.› (Verkaufshäuschen; oriental. Gartenhaus)
Ki|o|to ['kjo:to] (jap. Stadt)
Kipf, der; -[e]s, -e (*südd. für* länglich geformtes [Weiß]brot); **Kipfel,** das; -s, - *u.* **Kip|ferl,** das; -s, -n (*österr. für* Hörnchen [Gebäck]); **Kipf|ler** *Plur.* (*österr. für* eine Kartoffelsorte)
Kip|ling (engl. Schriftsteller)
Kip|pe, die; -, -n (Spitze, Kante; eine Turnübung; *ugs. für* Zigarettenstummel); **kip|pe|lig,** kipp|lig; **kip|peln** *(ugs.);* ich ...[e]le (↑R 16); **kip|pen;** [1]**Kip|per** (*früher* jmd., der Münzen mit zu geringem Edelmetallgehalt in Umlauf brachte); Kipper und Wipper; [2]**Kip|per** (Wagen mit kippbarem Wagenkasten); **Kipp|fenster; kipp|lig** *vgl.* kippelig; **Kipp˯lo|re, ...pflug** (↑R 136), **...re|gel** (ein Vermessungsgerät), **...schalter, ...schwin|gun|gen** *(Plur.; Physik),* **...wa|gen**
Kips, das; -es, -e *meist Plur.* ‹engl.› (getrocknete Haut des Zebus)
Kir, der; -s, -s ‹nach dem Dijoner Bürgermeister Félix Kir› (Getränk aus Johannisbeerlikör und Weißwein)
Kir|be, die; -, -n (*bayr. für* Kirchweih)
Kir|che, die; -, -n; **Kir|chen˯ältes|te** (der *u.* die), **...amt, ...austritt, ...bann, ...bau** (*Plur.* ...bauten), **...be|su|cher, ...bu|ße, ...chor, ...die|ner, ...fab|rik** (Stiftungsvermögen einer kath. Kirche), **...fest, ...gän|ger** (*svw.* Kirchgänger), **...ge|schich|te** (die; -), **...glo|cke, ...jahr, ...lehrer; Kir|chen|licht** *Plur.* -er; er ist kein [großes] Kirchenlicht (*ugs. für* er ist nicht sehr klug); **Kirchen˯lied, ...maus, ...mu|sik, ...rat** (*Plur.* ...räte), **...recht, ...schiff, ...spren|gel** (*od.* Kirchspren|gel), **...staat** (der; -[e]s), **...steu|er** (die), **...tag** (z. B. Deutscher Evangelischer Kirchentag), **...tür, ...uhr; Kir|chen|va|ter** *meist Plur.* (besonders anerkannter Kirchenschriftsteller aus der Frühzeit der christlichen Kirche); **Kir|chen|vor|stand; Kirch˯gänger, ...geld, ...hof; Kirch|hofs˯mau|er, ...stil|le; kirch|lich; Kirch|lich|keit,** die; -; **Kirch|ner** (*veraltet für* Küster)
Kirch˯spiel (Kirchensprengel), **...spren|gel** (*od.* Kir|chen|sprengel), **...tag** (*südd., österr. für* Kirchweih), **...turm; Kirch|turmpo|li|tik,** die; - (auf engen Gesichtskreis beschränkte Politik); **Kirch|va|ter** (*landsch. für* Kirchenältester); **Kirch|weih,** die; -, -en
Kir|gi|se, der; -n, -n; ↑R 126; **Kirgi|si|en, Kir|gi|sis|tan** (Staat in Mittelasien); **kir|gi|sisch**
Ki|ri|ba|ti (Inselstaat im Pazifik)
Kir|ke *vgl.* Circe
Kir|mes, die; -, ...messen (*bes. mittel- u. nordd. für* Kirchweih); **Kirmes|ku|chen**

kir|nen (*landsch. für* buttern; [Erbsen] ausschoten)
kir|re (*ugs. für* zutraulich, zahm); jmdn. kirre machen; **kir|ren** (*noch ugs. für* kirre machen)
Kir ro|yal [kir roa'jal], der; - -[s], -s -s ‹*vgl.* Kir *u.* royal› (Getränk aus Johannisbeerlikör und Champagner)
Kir|rung (*Jägerspr.* Lockfutter)
Kirsch, der; -[e]s, - (ein Branntwein); **Kirsch‿baum, ...blü|te; Kir|sche,** die; -, -n; **Kir|schen|baum** usw. (*seltener für* Kirschbaum usw.); **Kirsch‿geist** (der; -[e]s; ein Branntwein), **...holz, ...kern, ...ku|chen, ...li|kör; kirsch|rot; Kirsch‿saft, ...was|ser** (das; -s, -; ein Branntwein)
Kirs|ten (m. od. w. Vorn.)
Kir|tag (*bayr., österr. für* Kirchweih)
Kis|met, das; -s ‹arab., „Zugeteiltes"› (Los; gottergeben hinzunehmendes Schicksal im Islam)
Kiss|chen; Kis|sen, das; -s, -; **Kis|sen‿be|zug, ...fül|lung, ...hül|le, ...schlacht, ...über|zug** (↑R 132)
Kis|te, die; -, -n; **Kis|ten‿de|ckel, ...grab; kis|ten|wei|se**
Ki|su|a|he|li, Ki|swa|hi|li, Swa|hili, das; -[s] (Suahelisprache)
Kit|fuchs *vgl.* Kittfuchs
Ki|tha|ra, die; -, *Plur.* -s *u.* ...tharen ‹griech.› (altgriech. Saiteninstrument); **Ki|tha|rö|de** (↑R 132), der; -n, -n; ↑R 126 (altgriech. Zitherspieler u. Sänger)
Ki|thä|ron, der; -s (griech. Gebirge)
Kitsch, der; -[e]s (süßlich-sentimentale, geschmacklose Kunst; geschmacklos gestalteter Gebrauchsgegenstand); **kit|schen** (*landsch. für* zusammenscharren); du kitschst; **kit|schig**
Kitt, der; -[e]s, -e
Kitt|chen, das; -s, - (*ugs. für* Gefängnis)
Kit|tel, der; -s, -; **Kit|tel|schür|ze**
kit|ten
Kitt|fuchs (Fuchs einer nordamerik. Art; Fell dieses Fuchses)
Kitz, das; -es, -e *u.* Kit|ze, die; -, -n (Junges von Reh, Gämse, Ziege)
Kitz|bü|hel (österr. Stadt)
Kitz|chen; Kit|ze *vgl.* Kitz
Kit|zel, der; -s, -; **kit|ze|lig,** kitzlig; **kit|zeln;** ich ...[e]le (↑R 16)
Kitz|lein
Kitz|ler (*für* Klitoris)
kitz|lig *vgl.* kitzelig
[1]**Ki|wi,** der; -s, -s ‹maorisch› (ein flugunfähiger Laufvogel in Neuseeland)
[2]**Ki|wi,** die; -, -s (eine exotische Frucht)
kJ = Kilojoule
k. J. = künftigen Jahres
Kjök|ken|möd|din|ger *vgl.* Kökkenmöddinger
k. k. = kaiserlich-königlich (im ehem. österr. Reichsteil von Österreich-Ungarn für alle Behörden); *vgl.* kaiserlich; *vgl.* k. u. k.; **K. K.** = Kaiserlich-Königlich; *vgl.* kaiserlich
KKW = Kernkraftwerk
kl = Kiloliter
Kl. = Klasse, *österr. auch* = Klappe (*für* Telefonnebenstelle, Apparat)
Kl.-8° = Kleinoktav
kla|bas|tern (*landsch. für* schwerfällig gehen); ich ...ere (↑R 16)
Kla|bau|ter|mann, der; -[e]s, ...männer (ein Schiffskobold)
klack!; klack, klack!; **kla|cken** (klack machen); **kla|ckern** (*landsch. für* gluckern *u.* klecksen); ich ...ere (↑R 16); **klacks!; Klacks,** der; -es, -e (*ugs. für* kleine Menge; klatschendes Geräusch)
Klad|de, die; -, -n (*landsch. für* Schmierheft; Geschäftsbuch)
Klad|de|ra|datsch [*auch* ...'datʃ], der; -[e]s, -e (*ugs. für* Durcheinander nach einem Zusammenbruch; Skandal, Aufregung)
Kla|do|ze|re, die; -, -n *meist Plur.* (*Zool.* Wasserfloh)
klaf|fen; kläf|fen; Kläf|fer (*ugs. abwertend);* **Klaff|mu|schel**
Klaf|ter, der *od.* das; -s, -, *selten* die; -, -n (altes Längen-, Raummaß); 5 - Holz (↑R 90); **Klaf|ter|holz,** das; -es; **klaf|ter|lang;** ein klafterlanger Riss, *aber* 3 Klafter lang; **klaf|tern;** ich ...ere (↑R 16) Holz (schichte es auf); **klaf|ter|tief**
klag|bar *(Rechtsspr.);* klagbar werden; **Klag|bar|keit,** die; - *(Rechtsspr.);* **Kla|ge,** die; -, -n; **Kla|ge|ge|schrei,** Klag|ge|schrei; **Kla|ge‿laut, ...lied, ...mau|er** (Überreste des Tempels in Jerusalem); **kla|gen**
Kla|gen|furt (Hptst. von Kärnten)
Kla|ge|punkt; Klä|ger; Kla|ger|he|bung *(BGB);* **Klä|ge|rin; klä|ge|risch; klä|ge|ri|scher|seits** *(Rechtsspr.);* **Klä|ger|schaft** *(bes. schweiz.);* **Kla|ge‿schrift, ...weg; Klag|ge|schrei** *vgl.* Klagegeschrei; **kläg|lich; Kläg|lich|keit,** die; -; **klag|los**
Klai|pe|da (Hafenstadt in Litauen; *vgl.* [2]Memel)
Kla|mauk, der; -s (*ugs. für* Lärm; Ulk)
klamm (feucht; steif [vor Kälte]); -e Finger; **Klamm,** die; -, -en (Felsenschlucht [mit Wasserlauf]); **Klam|mer,** die; -, -n; **Klam|mer‿af|fe, ...beu|tel; Kläm|mer|chen; klam|mern;** ich ...ere (↑R 16); sich an etw. *od.* jmdn. -; **klamm|heim|lich** (*ugs. für* ganz heimlich)
Kla|mot|te, die; -, -n (*ugs. für* [Gesteins]brocken; minderwertiges [Theater]stück; *meist Plur.:* [alte] Kleidungsstücke)
Klam|pe, die; -, -n (*Seemannsspr.* Holz- od. Metallstück zum Festmachen der Taue); **Klamp|fe,** die; -, -n (*volkstüml. für* Gitarre; *österr. für* Bauklammer)
kla|mü|sern (*nordd. ugs. für* nachsinnen); ich ...ere (↑R 16)
Klan (*eindeutschend für* Clan)
klan|des|tin ‹lat.› (*veraltet für* heimlich); klandestine Ehe (nicht nach kanon. Vorschrift geschlossene Ehe)
klang!; kling, klang!; **Klang,** der; -[e]s, Klänge; **Klang‿ef|fekt, ...far|be, ...fül|le, ...kör|per; klang|lich; klang|los; Klang|schön|heit,** die; -; **klang|voll; Klang|wir|kung**
Klapf, der; -s, Kläpfe (*südd., schweiz. mdal. für* Knall, Schlag, Ohrfeige); **kläp|fen** (*südd., schweiz. mdal. für* knallen, schlagen)
Kla|po|tetz, der; -[es], -e (*südösterr.,* ein Windrad)
klapp!; klipp, klapp!; **klapp|bar; Klapp|bett; Klap|pe,** die; -, -n (*österr. auch für* Nebenstelle eines Telefonanschlusses, *svw.* Apparat); **klap|pen; Klap|pen‿feh|ler** (*kurz für* Herzklappenfehler), **...horn** (*Plur.* ...hörner; ein älteres Musikinstrument), **...text** *(Buchw.);* **Klap|per,** die; -, -n; **klap|per|dürr; klap|pe|rig,** klapp|rig; **Klap|per‿kas|ten, ...kis|te** (*ugs. für* altes Auto, alte Schreibmaschine u. a.); **klap|pern;** ich ...ere (↑R 16); **Klap|per‿schlan|ge, ...storch** *(Kindersp r.);* **Klapp‿fahr|rad, ...fens|ter; Klapp|horn|vers** (Scherzvers in Form eines Vierzeilers, beginnend mit: Zwei Knaben ...); **Klapp‿hut** (der), **...lei|ter** (die), **...lie|ge, ...mes|ser** (das), **...rad; klapp|rig** *vgl.* klapperig; **Klapp‿ses|sel, ...sitz, ...stuhl, ...stul|le** *(landsch.),* **...tisch, ...ver|deck**
Klaps, der; -es, -e; **Kläps|chen; klap|sen; klap|sig** (*ugs. für* leicht verrückt); **Klaps‿mann** (*Plur.* ...männer; *ugs. für* leicht Verrückter), **...müh|le** (*ugs. für* Nervenheilanstalt)
klar; ich bin mir längst darüber

im Klaren; klar Schiff! (seemänn. Kommando); klar sein, klar werden; mir ist jetzt Verschiedenes klar geworden, klarer geworden; nicht mehr klar denken können; ein klar denkender Mensch; klar sehen (deutlich sehen; *auch ugs. für* völlig verstehen, Bescheid wissen); solange wir in dieser Sache nicht klarer sehen, ...; *aber* klargehen, klarkommen, klarlegen, klarmachen, klarstellen (↑R 38 f.); **Klar** *vgl.* Eiklar

Kla|ra (w. Vorn.)

Klär|an|la|ge; Klar|ap|fel; Klär|be|cken; Klar|blick

Klär|chen (w. Vorn.)

klar den|kend *vgl.* klar; **Kla|re,** der; -n, -n; ↑R 5 ff. (Schnaps); **klä|ren**

Kla|rett, der; -s, -s ‹franz.› (gewürzter Rotwein)

klar|ge|hen (*ugs. für* reibungslos ablaufen); es ist alles klargegangen (↑R 38 f.); **Klar|heit** *Plur. selten*

kla|rie|ren ‹lat.› (beim Ein- u. Auslaufen eines Schiffes die Zollformalitäten erledigen); ein Schiff -

Kla|ri|net|te, die; -, -n ‹ital.-(-franz.)› (ein Holzblasinstrument); **Kla|ri|net|tist,** der; -en, -en; ↑R 126 (Klarinettenbläser); **Kla|ri|net|tis|tin**

Kla|ris|sa (w. Vorn.); **Kla|ris|sen|or|den,** der; -s (*kath. Kirche);* **Kla|ris|sin** (Angehörige des Klarissenordens)

klar|kom|men (*ugs. für* zurechtkommen); ich bin damit, mit ihm klargekommen (↑R 38 f.); **klar|legen** (erklären); er hat ihm den Vorgang klargelegt (↑R 38 f.); **klär|lich** (*veraltet für* klar, deutlich); **klar|ma|chen** (deutlich machen; [Schiff] fahr-, gefechtsbereit machen); sie hat ihm die Sache klargemacht; das Schiff hat klargemacht (↑R 38 f.); **Klär|mit|tel,** das; **Klar|schiff,** das; -[e]s (*Seemannsspr.* Gefechtsbereitschaft); **Klär|schlamm; Klar|schrift|le|ser** (EDV-Eingabegerät, das Daten in lesbarer Form verarbeitet); **klar se|hen** *vgl.* klar; **Klar|sicht|do|se, ...fo|lie; klar|sich|tig; Klar|sicht|pa|ckung; klar|stel|len** (Irrtümer beseitigen); er hat das Missverständnis klargestellt (↑R 38 f.); **Klar|stel|lung; Klar|text,** der (entzifferter [dechiffrierter] Text); **Klä|rung; klar wer|den** *vgl.* klar

Klas (m. Vorn.)

Klass... (*südd. in Zusammensetzungen für* Klassen... [= Schulklasse], z. B. Klasslehrer); **klas|se** (*ugs. für* hervorragend, großartig); ein klasse Auto; er hat klasse gespielt; das finde ich klasse (*auch* Klasse; *vgl. d.*); **Klas|se,** die; -, -n ‹lat.(-franz.)› (*Abk.* Kl.); jmd. *od.* etwas ist, hat Klasse; ist ganz große Klasse (*ugs. für* ist großartig, hervorragend); **Klas|se|leis|tung** *(ugs.);* **Klas|se|ment** [...'mã:, *schweiz.* ...'mɛnt], das; -s, -s ‹franz.› (Einreihung; Reihenfolge); **Klas|sen‿äl|tes|te** (der *u.* die), **...ar|beit, ...auf|satz, ...bes|te** (der *u.* die), **...be|wusst|sein; klas|sen|bil|dend** *(Sprachw.);* **Klas|sen‿buch, ...ge|sell|schaft, ...hass, ...in|te|res|se, ...jus|tiz, ...ka|me|rad, ...kampf, ...leh|rer, ...lei|ter** (der); **klas|sen|los;** die klassenlose Gesellschaft; **Klas|sen‿lot|te|rie, ...sie|ger** *(Sport),* **...spre|cher, ...staat, ...tref|fen, ...vor|stand** (*österr. für* Klassenlehrer), **...wahl|recht; klas|sen|wei|se; Klas|sen‿ziel, ...zim|mer; klas|sie|ren** (in ein gegebenes System einordnen; *Bergmannsspr.* nach der Größe trennen); **Klas|sie|rung; Klas|si|fi|ka|ti|on,** die; -, -en (*vgl.* Klassifizierung); **klas|si|fi|zie|ren; Klas|si|fi|zie|rung** (Einteilung, Einordnung [in Klassen]); **...klas|sig** (z. B. erst-, zweitklassig); **Klas|sik,** die; - (Epoche kultureller Höchstleistungen u. ihre mustergültigen Werke); **Klas|si|ker** (maßgebender Künstler od. Schriftsteller [bes. der antiken u. der dt. Klassik]); **Klas|si|ke|rin; klas|sisch** (mustergültig; vorbildlich; die Klassik betreffend; typisch, bezeichnend; herkömmlich, traditionell); klassische Philologie; die klassischen Sprachen; klassischer Jazz; **Klas|si|zis|mus,** der; - (die Klassik nachahmende Stilrichtung, bes. der Stil um 1800); **klas|si|zis|tisch; Klas|si|zi|tät,** die; - (Mustergültigkeit); **...kläss|ler** (z. B. Erst-, Zweitklässler)

klas|tisch ‹griech.› *(Geol.);* klastisches Gestein (Trümmergestein)

Kla|ter, der; -s, -n (*nordd. für* Lumpen, zerrissenes Kleid; *nur Sing.:* Schmutz); **kla|te|rig, klat|rig** (*nordd. für* schmutzig; schlimm, bedenklich; elend)

klatsch!; klitsch, klatsch!; **Klatsch,** der; -[e]s, -e (*ugs. auch für* Rederei, Geschwätz); **Klatsch|ba|se** *(ugs. abwertend);* **Klat|sche,** die; -, -n (*kurz für* Fliegenklatsche; Klatschbase); **klat|schen;** du klatschst; Beifall -; **klat|sche|nass** *vgl.* klatschnass; **Klat|scher; Klat|sche|rei** *(ugs.);* **Klat|sche|rin; klatsch|haft** *(ugs.);* **Klatsch|haf|tig|keit,** die; -; **Klatsch‿ko|lum|nist, ...maul** (*ugs. abwertend für* geschwätzige Person), **...mohn** (der; -[e]s); **klatsch|nass** (*ugs. für* völlig durchnässt); **Klatsch|nest** (*ugs. für* kleiner Ort, in dem viel geklatscht wird); **Klatsch‿spal|te, ...sucht** (die; -); **klatsch|süch|tig; Klatsch‿tan|te** *(ugs. abwertend),* **...weib** *(ugs. abwertend)*

Klau, die; -, -en (*nordd. für* gabelförmiges Ende der Gaffel)

Klaub|ar|beit (*Bergmannsspr.* das Sondern des haltigen u. tauben Gesteins, der Steine aus der Kohle); **klau|ben** (sondern; mit Mühe heraussuchen; *österr. für* pflücken, sammeln); **Klau|ber; Klau|be|rei**

Klau|dia *vgl.* Claudia; **Klau|di|ne** *vgl.* Claudine

Klaue, die; -, -n; **klau|en** (*ugs. für* stehlen); **Klau|en|seu|che,** die; -; Maul- u. Klauenseuche (↑R 23); **...klau|ig** (z. B. scharfklauig)

Klaus (m. Vorn.)

Klau|se, die; -, -n ‹lat.› (Klosterzelle, Einsiedelei; Talenge); **Klau|sel,** die; -, -n (Nebenbestimmung; Einschränkung, Vorbehalt)

Klau|sen|pass, der; -es (ein Alpenpass)

Klaus|ner ‹lat.› (Bewohner einer Klause, Einsiedler); **Klaust|ro|pho|bie** (↑R 130), die; -, ...ien ‹lat.; griech.› (*Psych.* krankhafte Angst vor dem Aufenthalt in geschlossenen Räumen); **Klau|sur,** die; -, -en ‹lat.› (abgeschlossener Gebäudeteil [im Kloster]; *svw.* Klausurarbeit); **Klau|sur‿ar|beit** (Prüfungsarbeit in einem abgeschlossenen Raum), **...ta|gung** (geschlossene Tagung)

Kla|vi|a|tur [...v...], die; -, -en ‹lat.› (Tasten [eines Klaviers], Tastbrett); **Kla|vi|chord** [...vi'kɔrt], das; -[e]s, -e ‹lat.; griech.› (altes Tasteninstrument); **Kla|vier** [...v...], das; -s, -e ‹franz.›; Klavier spielen (↑R 39); *vgl.* Wohltemperiertes Klavier; **Kla|vier‿abend** (↑R 132), **...aus|zug, ...be|glei|tung; kla|vie|ren** (*ugs. für* an etwas herumfingern); **kla|vie|ris|tisch** (der Technik des Klavierspiels entsprechend); **Kla|vier‿kon|zert, ...leh|rer, ...so|na|te, ...spiel, ...spie|ler, ...stim|mer, ...stuhl, ...stun|de, ...un|ter|richt; Kla|vi|kel** [...v...], das; -s, - ‹lat.› (*veraltet für* Schlüsselbein); **Kla|vi|ku|la**, die; -, ...lä *u. med. fachspr.* Cla|vi|cu|la, die; -, ...lae [...lɛ] (Schlüsselbein); **kla|vi|ku|lar** (das Schlüsselbein betreffend); **Kla|vi|zim|bel** *svw.* Clavicembalo

Kle|be, die; - (*ugs. für* Klebstoff); **Kle|be|bin|dung** *(Buchw.)*; **Kle|be|mit|tel**, Kleb|mit|tel, das; **kle|ben**; kleben bleiben (*ugs. auch für* nicht versetzt werden); er ist in der dritten Klasse kleben geblieben; ohne kleben zu bleiben; *vgl.* festkleben; **Kle|ber** (*auch* Bestandteil des Getreideeiweißes); **Kle|be|strei|fen** *vgl.* Klebstreifen; **Kleb|mit|tel** *vgl.* Klebemittel; **kleb|rig**; **Kleb|rig|keit**, die; -; **Kleb|stoff**; **Kleb|strei|fen**, Kle|be|strei|fen; **Kle|bung**

[1]**kle|cken** (*landsch. für* ausreichen; vonstatten gehen); es kleckt

[2]**kle|cken** (*landsch. für* geräuschvoll fallen [von Flüssigkeiten]); **Kle|cker⌣be|trag** *(ugs.)*, **...frit|ze** *(ugs.)*; **kle|ckern** (*ugs. für* beim Essen od. Trinken Flecke machen, sich beschmutzen); ich ...ere (↑R 16); *vgl.* [2]klotzen; **kle|cker|wei|se** (*ugs. für* mehrmals in kleinen Mengen); **Klecks**, der; -es, -e; **kleck|sen** (Kleckse machen); **Kleck|ser**; **Kleck|se|rei**; **kleck|sig**; **Kleck|so|gra|phie** (↑R 33), die; -, ...ien (Tintenklecksbild für psycholog. Tests)

Kle|da|ge [...ˈdaːʒə], **Kle|da|sche**, die; -, -n *Plur. selten* (*nordd. für* Kleidung)

[1]**Klee** (dt. Maler)

[2]**Klee**, der; -s; **Klee|blatt**; **Klee|ein|saat** (↑R 136), die; -, -en; **Klee|ern|te** (↑R 136), die; -, -n; **Klee⌣gras** (mit Klee vermischtes Gras), **...salz** (das; -es; ein Fleckenbeseitigungsmittel)

Klei, der; -[e]s (*landsch. für* fetter, zäher Boden); **klei|ben** (*landsch. für* kleben [bleiben]); **Klei|ber** (ein Vogel; *landsch. für* Klebstoff); **Klei|bo|den** *(landsch.)*

Kleid, das; -[e]s, -er; **Kleid|chen**; **klei|den**; sich -; es kleidet mich gut usw.; **Klei|der⌣bad**, **...bü|gel**, **...bürs|te**; **Klei|der|chen** *Plur.*; **Klei|der⌣ha|ken**, **...kam|mer** *(bes. Milit.)*, **...kas|ten** (*südd., österr., schweiz. für* Kleiderschrank), **...ma|cher** (*österr., sonst veraltet für* Schneider), **...mot|te**, **...re|chen** (*österr. für* Kleiderhaken), **...schrank**, **...stän|der**, **...stoff**; **kleid|sam**; **Kleid|sam|keit**, die; -; **Klei|dung** *Plur. selten*; **Klei|dungs|stück**

Kleie, die; -, -n (Abfallprodukt beim Mahlen von Getreide); **Klei|en|brot**; **klei|ig** (von Klei od. Kleie)

klein; kleiner als (*Math.; Zeichen* <); kleiner[e]nteils. **I.** *Kleinschreibung:* **a)** (↑R 47:) am kleinsten; von klein auf; ein klein wenig; **b)** (↑R 108:) die kleine Anfrage (im Parlament); das Schiff macht kleine Fahrt *(Seemannsspr.)*; das sind kleine Fische (*ugs. für* Kleinigkeiten); der kleine Grenzverkehr; das kleine Latinum; er ist kleiner Leute Kind; das Auto für den kleinen Mann. **II.** *Großschreibung:* **a)** (↑R 47:) Groß und Klein; Kleine und Große; die Kleinen und die Großen; die Kleinen (*für* Kinder); die Kleine (*für* junges Mädchen); meine Kleine *(ugs.)*; die Gemeinde ist ein Staat im Kleinen; einen Kleinen sitzen haben (*ugs. für* leicht betrunken sein); vom Kleinen auf das Große schließen; es ist mir ein Kleines (eine kleine Mühe), dies zu tun; um ein Kleines (wenig); über ein Kleines (*veraltet für* bald); bis ins Kleinste (sehr eingehend); **b)** (↑R 47:) etwas, nichts, viel, wenig Kleines; **c)** (↑R 93 *u.* 108:) Pippin der Kleine; Klein Dora, Klein Udo; der Kleine Bär, der Kleine Wagen *(Astron.)*; die Kleine Strafkammer; **d)** (↑R 102:) Kleiner Belt; Kleines Walsertal; Kleine Sundainseln. **III.** *Schreibung in Verbindung mit dem Partizip II:* klein gemusterte, karierte Stoffe; ein klein gedruckter Text; (↑R 47:) das klein Gedruckte, *auch* Kleingedruckte lesen; *vgl. aber* kleindenkend, kleingewachsen, kleinkariert (↑R 40). **IV.** *Schreibung in Verbindung mit Verben* (↑R 37 f.): klein sein, werden; die Kosten klein (niedrig) halten; klein beigeben (nachgeben); kurz u. klein schlagen; die Kräuter klein hacken; klein, kleiner machen; die Zwiebeln werden klein geschnitten; versuche sehr klein (in geringer Schriftgröße) zu schreiben; Rücksichtnahme wird bei diesen Leuten klein geschrieben (*ugs. für* nicht wichtig genommen); *vgl. aber* kleinbekommen, kleinkriegen, kleinschreiben; (↑R 38 f.). **V.** *Über die Schreibung in Straßennamen* (↑R 122 *u.* 123); **Klein**, das; -s (*kurz für* Gänseklein o. Ä.); **Klein⌣ak|ti|o|när**, **...an|zei|ge**, **...ar|beit**; **klein|asi|a|tisch** (↑R 132); **Klein|asi|en** [...i̯ən] (↑R 105 *u.* 132); **Klein|bahn**; **klein|be|kom|men** (↑R 38; *svw.* kleinkriegen); *vgl.* klein, IV; **Klein|be|trieb**; **Klein|bild|ka|me|ra**; **Klein⌣buch|sta|be**, **...bür|ger**; **klein|bür|ger|lich**; **Klein⌣bür|ger|tum**, **...bus**; **Klein|chen** (kleines Kind); **klein|den|kend** (kleinlich); **Klei|ne**, der, die, das; -n, -n; ↑R 5 ff.; **Klei|ne|leu|te|mi|li|eu**; **Klein|emp|fän|ger** (ein Rundfunkgerät); **klei|ne|ren|teils**, **klei|nern|teils**; **Klein⌣fa|mi|lie**, **...feld** *(Sport)*, **...for|mat**, **...gar|ten**, **...gärt|ner**; **klein ge|druckt** *vgl.* klein, III; **Klein|ge|druck|te**, das; -n; *vgl.* klein III; **Klein⌣geist** *(abwertend)*, **...geld** (das; -[e]s); **klein ge|mus|tert** *vgl.* klein, III; **klein|ge|wach|sen** (kleinwüchsig); **klein|gläu|big**; **Klein|gläu|big|keit**, die; -; **klein ha|cken** *vgl.* klein, IV; **Klein⌣han|del** (*vgl.* [1]Handel), **...häus|ler** (*österr. für* Kleinbauer); **Klein|heit**, die; -; **klein|her|zig**; **Klein⌣hirn**, **...holz**; **Klei|nig|keit**; **Klei|nig|keits|krä|mer** *(abwertend)*; **Klein|ka|li|ber|schie|ßen**, das; -s; **klein|ka|lib|rig** (↑R 130); **klein|ka|riert** (engherzig, engstirnig); ein kleinkarierter Mensch, er ist der kleinkarierteste Mensch, den ich kenne; *aber* klein kariertes, noch kleiner kariertes Papier (↑R 40); *vgl.* klein, III; **Klein|kat|ze** (z. B. Luchs, Wildkatze); **Klein|kind**; **Klein|kle|ckers|dorf** (*ugs. für* unbedeutender Ort); **Klein⌣kli|ma** *(Meteor.)*, **...kraft|rad**, **...kraft|wa|gen**, **...kram** (der; -[e]s), **...krieg**; **klein|krie|gen** (↑R 38; *ugs. für* gefügig machen; aufbrauchen; zerstören); ich kriege den Kerl schon klein; sie hatten den Kuchen schnell kleingekriegt; der Teppich ist nicht kleinzukriegen; *vgl.* klein, IV; **Klein|kunst**, die; -; **Klein|kunst|büh|ne**; **klein|laut**; **klein|lich**; **Klein|lich|keit**; **klein ma|chen** *vgl.* klein, IV; **klein|maß|stä|big**, **klein|maß|stäb|lich**; **Klein⌣mö|bel**, **...mut** (der; -[e]s); **klein|mü|tig**; **Klein|mü|tig|keit**, die; -; **Klein|od**, das; -[e]s, *Plur.* (*für* Kostbarkeit:) -e, (*für* Schmuckstück:) ...odien [...i̯ən]; **Klein|ok|tav**, das; -s (*Abk.* Kl.-8°); **Klein-Pa|ris** (↑R 106; *Bez. für* Leipzig); **Klein⌣rech|ner**, **...rent|ner**; **klein schnei|den** *vgl.* klein, IV; **klein|schrei|ben** (↑R 38; mit kleinem Anfangsbuchstaben schreiben); das Wort wird kleingeschrieben; *vgl.* klein, IV; **Klein⌣schrei|bung**, **...sied|lung**, **...staat** (*Plur.* ...staaten); **Klein|staa|te|rei**, die; -; **Klein⌣stadt**, **...städ|ter**; **klein-**

städ|tisch; Kleinst‿be|trag, ...kind, ...le|be|we|sen; kleinstmög|lich, *dafür besser:* möglichst klein; *falsch:* kleinstmöglichst; **Klein|tier|zucht; Klein‿transpor|ter, ...vieh, ...wa|gen; klein‿weis** (*österr. ugs. für* im Kleinen, nach und nach), **...win|zig; Klein|woh|nung; Klein|wüchsi|ge,** der *u.* die (↑R 5)
Kleio *vgl.* Klio
Kleist (dt. Dichter)
Kleis|ter, der; -s, -; **kleis|te|rig,** kleistlrig; **kleis|tern;** ich ...ere (↑R 16); **Kleis|ter|topf**
kleis|to|gam ‹griech.› (*Bot.* selbst bestäubend, selbst befruchtend); **Kleis|to|ga|mie,** die; -
kleist|rig *vgl.* kleisterig
Kle|ma|tis [*auch* ...'ma:tis], die; -, - ‹griech.› (Waldrebe, eine Kletterpflanze)
Kle|mens, Kle|men|tia, [1]Klemen|ti|ne *vgl.* Clemens, Clementia, [1]Clementine
[2]Kle|men|ti|ne, die; -, -n ‹vermutl. nach dem franz. Trappistenmönch Père Clément› (kernlose Sorte der Mandarine)
Klem|me, die; -, -n (*ugs. auch für* Notlage, Verlegenheit); **klemmen; Klem|mer** (*landsch. für* Kneifer, Zwicker); **klem|mig** (*Bergmannsspr.* fest); es Gestein; **Klemm|map|pe** (↑R 136); **Klemm|schrau|be**
klem|pern (*veraltet für* Blech hämmern; lärmen); ich ...ere (↑R 16); **Klemp|ner** (Blechschmied); **Klemp|ne|rei; Klemp|ner|la|den** (*ugs. für* viele Orden u. Ehrenzeichen auf der Brust); **Klemp|nermeis|ter; klemp|nern** (Klempnerarbeiten ausführen); ich ...ere (↑R 16); **Klemp|ner|werk|statt**
Kleng|an|stalt (Darre zur Gewinnung von Nadelholzsamen); **klen|gen** (Nadelholzsamen gewinnen)
Kle|o|pat|ra (↑R 130; ägypt. Königin)
[1]Klep|per, der; -s, - (*ugs. für* ausgemergeltes Pferd)
[2]Klep|per ®; **Klep|per|boot;** ↑R 95 (Faltboot); **Klep|per|mantel;** ↑R 95 (wasser-, winddichter Mantel)
Klep|to|ma|ne, der; -n, -n (↑R 126) ‹griech.› (an Kleptomanie Leidender); **Klep|to|ma|nie,** die; - (krankhafter Trieb zum Stehlen); **Klep|to|ma|nin; klepto|ma|nisch**
kle|ri|kal ‹griech.› (die Geistlichkeit betreffend; [streng] kirchlich [gesinnt]); **Kle|ri|ka|lis|mus,** der; - (überstarker Einfluss des Klerus auf Staat u. Gesellschaft); **Kle|riker** (kath. Geistlicher); **Kle|ri|sei,** die; - (*veraltet für* Klerus); **Klerus,** der; - (kath. Geistlichkeit, Priesterschaft)
Kles|til (österr. Bundespräsident)
Klet|te, die; -, -n; **Klet|ten[|haft]ver|schluss** ‹zum ® „Kletten"› (*svw.* Klettverschluss); **Klet|tenwur|zel|öl,** das; -[e]s
Klet|te|rei; Klet|te|rer; Klet|ter‿farn, ...ge|rüst; Klet|te|rin; Klet|ter‿max (der; -es, -e) *od.* **...ma|xe** (der; -n, -n; *ugs. für* Einsteigdieb, Fassadenkletterer); **klet|tern;** ich ...ere (↑R 16); **Kletter‿par|tie, ...pflan|ze, ...ro|se, ...schuh, ...seil, ...stan|ge, ...tour**
Klett|ver|schluss ‹*zu* Klette› (Haftverschluss, z. B. an Schuhen)
Klet|ze, die; -, -n (*österr. für* getrocknete Birne); **Klet|zen|brot**
Kle|ve [...v...] (Stadt im westl. Niederrheinischen Tiefland); **Kle|ver** (↑R 103); **kle|visch**
Kle|wi|an, der; -[e]s, -e, *auch* die; -, -en (*Kurzw. für* kleine Windenergieanlage [zur Erzeugung von Elektrizität])
klick!; Klick, der; -s, -s *meist Plur.* ‹engl.› (*Sprachw.* Schnalzlaut); **kli|cken** (einen dünnen, kurzen Ton von sich geben)
Kli|cker, der; -s, - (*landsch. für* Ton-, Steinkügelchen zum Spielen); **kli|ckern;** ich ...ere (↑R 16)
klie|ben (*veraltet, aber noch landsch. für* [sich] spalten); du klobst *u.* kliebtest; du klöbest *u.* kliebtest; gekloben *u.* gekliebt; klieb[e]!
Kli|ent, der; -en, -en (↑R 126) ‹lat.› (Auftraggeber [eines Rechtsanwaltes]); **Kli|en|tel** [kliɛn...], die; -, -en (Auftraggeberkreis [eines Rechtsanwaltes]); **Kli|en|te|le,** die; -, -n (*schweiz. svw.* Klientel); **Kli|en|tin**
klie|ren (*landsch. für* unsauber, schlecht schreiben)
Klie|sche, die; -, -n (*Zool.* eine Schollenart)
Kliff, das; -[e]s, -e (*bes. nordd. für* steiler Abfall einer [felsigen] Küste)
Kli|ma, das; -s, *Plur.* -s *u. fachspr.* ...mate ‹griech.› (Gesamtheit der meteorol. Erscheinungen in einem best. Gebiet); **Kli|ma‿ände|rung, ...an|la|ge** (↑R 24), **...fak|tor** *(meist Plur.),* **...kammer** (Raum, in dem zu Versuchs- u. Heilzwecken ein Klima künstlich erzeugt wird); **...ka|ta|strophe; kli|mak|te|risch** (das Klimakterium betreffend); -e Jahre (Wechseljahre); **Kli|mak|te|rium,** das; -s (*Med.* Wechseljahre der Frau); **Kli|ma|schwan|kung; kli|ma|tisch; kli|ma|ti|sie|ren** (eine Klimaanlage einbauen; die Frischluftzufuhr, Temperatur u. Luftfeuchtigkeit in geschlossenen Räumen automatisch regeln); **Klima|ti|sie|rung; Kli|ma|to|lo|gie,** die; - (Lehre vom Klima); **Kli|mawech|sel; Kli|max,** die; -, -e *Plur. selten* (Steigerung; Höhepunkt; *auch für* Klimakterium)
Klim|bim, der; -s (*ugs. für* überflüssige Aufregung; lautes Treiben; unnützes Beiwerk)
Klim|me, die; -, -n (eine Kletterpflanze); **klim|men** (klettern); du klommst (*auch* klimmtest); du klömmest (*auch* klimmtest); geklommen (*auch* geklimmt); klimm[e]!; **Klimm|zug** (eine Turnübung)
Klim|pe|rei *(ugs.);* **Klim|per|kasten** (*ugs. scherzh. für* Klavier)
klim|per|klein (*landsch. für* sehr klein)
klim|pern (klingen lassen, z. B. mit Geld -; *ugs. für* [schlecht] auf dem Klavier, der Gitarre o. Ä. spielen); ich ...ere (↑R 16)
Klimt (österr. Maler)
kling!; kling, klang!
Klin|ge, die; -, -n
Klin|gel, die; -, -n; **Klin|gel‿beutel, ...draht; Klin|ge|lei** *(ugs.);* **Klin|gel|gangs|ter** [...gɛŋstər] (*ugs. für* Verbrecher, der an der Wohnungstür klingelt, den Öffnenden überfällt und in die Wohnung eindringt); **Klin|gel|knopf; klin|geln;** ich ...[e]le (↑R 16); **Klin|gel‿zei|chen, ...zug**
klin|gen; du klangst; es klang; es klänge; geklungen; kling[e]!; **kling, klang!; Kling|klang,** der; -[e]s; **kling|ling!**
Kling|sor, *bei Novalis* **Kling|sohr** (Name eines sagenhaften Zauberers)
Kli|nik, die; -, -en ‹griech.› ([Spezial]krankenhaus; *nur Sing.:* prakt. medizin. Unterricht am Krankenbett); **Kli|ni|ker** (in einer Klinik tätiger Arzt od. Medizinstudent); **Kli|ni|kum,** das; -s, *Plur.* ...ka *u.* ...ken (Komplex von Kliniken; *nur Sing.:* Hauptteil der ärztlichen Ausbildung); **kli|nisch**
Klin|ke, die; -, -n; **klin|ken; Klinken|put|zer** (*ugs. für* Vertreter; Bettler)
Klin|ker, der; -s, - (bes. hart gebrannter Ziegel); **Klin|ker‿bau** (*Plur.* ...bauten), **...boot** (mit ziegelartig übereinander greifenden Planken), **...stein**

Kli|no|chlor, das; -s, *Plur. (Sorten:)* -e ‹griech.› (ein Mineral); **Kli|no|me|ter,** das; -s, - (Neigungsmesser); **Kli|no|mo|bil,** das; -s, -e ‹griech.; lat.› (Notarztwagen mit klinischer Ausrüstung); **Kli|nos|tat** (↑R 132), der; *Gen.* -[e]s *u.* -en, *Plur.* -e[n]; ↑R 126 (Apparatur für Pflanzenversuche)

Klin|se, Klin|ze, Klun|se, die; -, -n (*landsch. für* Ritze, Spalte)

Klio (Muse der Geschichte)

klipp!; klipp, klapp!; klipp u. klar (*ugs. für* ganz deutlich, unmissverständlich)

Klipp, der; -s, -s ‹engl.› (Klemme; Schmuckstück [am Ohr])

Klip|pe, die; -, -n

klip|pen (*landsch. für* hell tönen)

Klip|pen|rand; klip|pen|reich

Klip|per, der; -s, - ‹engl.› (*früher* schnelles Segelschiff); *vgl. aber* Clipper

Klipp|fisch (luftgetrockneter Kabeljau od. Schellfisch)

klipp, klapp!

Klipp|kram (*veraltet für* Trödel-, Kleinkram)

Klipp|schlie|fer (mit den Huftieren verwandtes, einem Murmeltier ähnliches afrikan. Säugetier)

Klipp|schu|le (*landsch. u. abwertend für* Elementarschule)

Klips, der; -es, -e ‹engl.› (*svw.* Klipp [Schmuckstück])

klirr!; klir|ren; Klirr|fak|tor

Kli|schee, das; -s, -s ‹franz.› (Druckstock; Abklatsch; eingefahrene Vorstellung); **kli|schee|haft; Kli|schee‿vor|stel|lung, ...wort** (*Plur.* ...wörter); **kli|schie|ren** (ein Klischee anfertigen); **Kli|scho|graph,** der; -en, -en (↑R 126) ‹franz.; griech.› (eine elektr. Graviermaschine)

Klis|tier, das; -s, -e ‹griech.› (Einlauf); **klis|tie|ren** (einen Einlauf geben); **Klis|tier|sprit|ze**

Kli|to|ris, die; -, *Plur.* - *u.* ...orides [...de:s] ‹griech.› (*Med.* Teil der weibl. Geschlechtsorgane)

klitsch!; klitsch, klatsch!; **Klitsch,** der; -[e]s, -e (*mitteld. für* Schlag; breiige Masse); **Klit|sche,** die; -, -n (*ugs. für* [ärmliches] Landgut); **klit|schen** *(landsch.);* **klit|sche|nass** *vgl.* klitschnass; **klit|schig** (*landsch. für* feucht und klebrig; unausgebacken); **klitsch, klatsch!; klitsch|nass,** klit|sche|nass *(ugs.)*

klit|tern (*abwertend für* zerstückeln; *landsch. für* zerkleinern, schmieren); ich ...ere (↑R 16); **Klit|te|rung**

klit|ze|klein (*ugs. für* sehr klein)

Klit|zing|ef|fekt (↑R 95), der; -[e]s ‹nach dem dt. Physiker Klaus von Klitzing› (ein physikal. Effekt)

Kli|vie [...viə], die; -, -n (*eindeutschend für* Clivia)

KLM = Koninklijke Luchtvaart Maatschappij [ˈko:nəŋkləkə ˈlyxtfa:rt ˈma:tsxapɛi:] (Königliche Niederländische Luftfahrtgesellschaft)

Klo, das; -s, -s (*ugs. für* Klosett)

Klo|a|ke, die; -, -n ‹lat.› ([unterirdischer] Abwasserkanal; Senkgrube; *Zool.* gemeinsamer Ausgang für Darm-, Harn- u. Geschlechtswege); **Klo|a|ken|tier**

Klo|bas|se, Klo|bas|si, die; -, ...sen ‹slaw.› (*österr.* eine Wurstsorte)

Klo|ben, der; -s, - (Eisenhaken; gespaltenes Holzstück; *auch für* unhöflicher, ungehobelter Mensch); **Klö|ben,** der; -s, - (*nordd.* ein Hefegebäck); **klo|big**

Klo|frau ‹*zu* Klo› *(ugs.)*

Klon, der; -s, -e ‹engl.› (durch Klonen entstandenes Lebewesen)

Klon|dike [...daik], der; -[s] (Fluss in Kanada)

klo|nen ‹engl.› (durch künstl. herbeigeführte ungeschlechtl. Vermehrung genet. identische Kopien von Lebewesen herstellen)

klö|nen (*nordd. für* gemütlich plaudern; schwatzen)

klo|nie|ren *vgl.* klonen

klo|nisch ‹griech.› (*Med.* krampfartig); **Klo|nus,** der; -, ...ni (*Med.* krampfartige Zuckungen)

Kloot, der; -[e]s, -en (*nordd. für* Kloß, Kugel); **Kloot|schie|ßen,** das; -s (fries. Eis- od. Rasenspiel [Boßeln])

Klo|pein (Ort in Kärnten); **Klo|pei|ner See,** der; - -s

Klöp|fel, der; -s, - (*veraltet für* Klöppel); **klop|fen; Klop|fer; klopf|fest;** klopffestes Benzin; **Klopf‿fes|tig|keit** (die; -), **...peit|sche, ...zei|chen**

Klop|pe, die; - (*nordd., mitteld. für* ²Prügel); - kriegen; **Klöp|pel,** der; -s, -; **Klöp|pe|lei; Klöp|pel‿kis|sen, ...ma|schi|ne; klöp|peln;** ich ...[e]le (↑R 16); **Klöp|pel|spit|ze; klop|pen** (*nordd., mitteld. für* klopfen, schlagen); sich -; **Klop|pe|rei** (*nordd., mitteld. für* längeres Klopfen; Schlägerei); **Klöpp|le|rin; Klops,** der; -es, -e (Fleischkloß)

Klop|stock (dt. Dichter); **klop|sto|ckisch, klop|stocksch;** klopstock[i]sche Verse (nach der Art Klopstocks); eine klopstock[i]sche Ode (von Klopstock)

Klo|sett, das; -s, *Plur.* -s, *auch* -e ‹engl.›; **Klo|sett‿bril|le, ...bürs|te, ...de|ckel, ...pa|pier, ...schüs|sel**

Kloß, der; -es, Klöße; **Kloß|brü|he; Klöß|chen, Klöß|lein**

Klos|ter, das; -s, Klöster; **Klos|ter‿bib|li|o|thek, ...bru|der, ...frau, ...gar|ten, ...gut, ...kir|che; klös|ter|lich; Klos|ter‿pfor|te, ...re|gel**

Klos|ters (Kurort in Graubünden)

Klos|ter|schu|le

Klö|ten *Plur.* (*nordd. für* Hoden)

Kloth, der; -[e]s, -e (*österr. svw.* Cloth)

Klot|hil|de (w. Vorn.); *vgl.* Chlothilde

Klo|tho ‹griech.› (eine der drei Parzen)

Klotz, der; -es, *Plur.* Klötze, *ugs.* Klötzer; **Klotz|beu|te** (eine Art Bienenstock); **Klötz|chen**

[1]**klot|zen** (*Textiltechnik* färben [auf der Klotzmaschine])

[2]**klot|zen;** -, nicht kleckern (*ugs. für* ordentlich zupacken, statt sich mit Kleinigkeiten abzugeben); **klot|zig** (*ugs. auch für* sehr viel)

Klub, der; -s, -s ‹engl.› ([geschlossene] Vereinigung, auch deren Räume; *österr. auch für* Fraktion); **Klub‿gar|ni|tur** (Gruppe von [gepolsterten] Sitzmöbeln), **...haus, ...ja|cke, ...ka|me|rad, ...mit|glied, ...raum, ...ses|sel, ...zwang** (*österr. für* Fraktionszwang)

[1]**Kluft,** die; -, -en ‹hebr.-jidd.› (*ugs. für* [alte] Kleidung; Uniform)

[2]**Kluft,** die; -, Klüfte (Spalte); **kluf|tig** *(selten);* **klüf|tig** (*Bergbau, sonst veraltet für* zerklüftet)

klug; klüger, klügste; (↑R 47:) der Klügere, Klügste gibt nach; es ist das Klügste (*aber* am klügsten) nachzugeben; *Getrenntschreibung in Verbindung mit Verben* (↑R 38 f.): klug sein, werden; klug reden (verständig reden; *auch für* alles besser wissen wollen); **Klü|ge|lei; klü|geln;** ich ...[e]le (↑R 16); **klu|ger|wei|se,** *aber* in kluger Weise; **Klug|heit; Klüg|ler; klüg|lich** *(veraltet);* **klug reden** *vgl.* klug; **Klug|red|ner; klug|schei|ßen** (*derb für* klug reden); **Klug‿schei|ßer** *(derb),* **...schna|cker** (*nordd. für* Besserwisser), **...schwät|zer**

Klump, der; -s, *Plur.* -e *u.* Klümpe (*nordd. für* Klumpen); **Klum|patsch,** der; -es (*ugs. für* [ungeordneter, wertloser] Haufen); **Klümp|chen; klum|pen;** der Pudding klumpt; **Klum|pen,** der; -s, -; **klüm|pe|rig,** klümp|rig *(landsch.);* -er Pudding

Klum|pert *vgl.* Glumpert

Klụmp|fuß; klụmp|fü|ßig; klụm-pig; Klụ̈mp|lein; klụ̈mp|rig *vgl.* klümperig
Klụ̈n|gel, der; -s, - (*abwertend für* Gruppe, die Vettern-, Parteiwirtschaft betreibt; Sippschaft, Clique); **Klün|ge|lei** (Vettern-, Parteiwirtschaft); **klụ̈n|geln;** ich ...[e]le (↑R 16)
Klu|ni|a|zẹn|ser, der; -s, - ‹nach dem ostfranz. Kloster Cluny› (Anhänger einer mittelalterl. kirchl. Reformbewegung); **klu-ni|a|zẹn|sisch**
Klụn|ker, die; -, -n *od.* der; -s, - (*landsch. für* Quaste, Troddel; Klümpchen; *ugs. für* Schmuckstein, Juwel); **klụn|ke|rig, klụnk-rig** (*landsch. für* mit Klunkern)
Klụn|se *vgl.* Klinse
Klụnt|je, das; -s, -s (*nordd. für* weißes Kandiszuckerstück)
Klụp|pe, die; -, -n (zangenartiges Messgerät; *österr. ugs. für* Wäscheklammer); **klụp|pen** (*veraltet für* einzwängen); **Klụp|perl,** das; -s, - (*bayr. für* Wäscheklammer; *scherzh. für* Finger)
Klus, die; -, -en ‹lat.› (*schweiz. für* schluchtartiges Quertal, Gebirgseinschnitt); **Klü|se,** die; -, -n ‹niederl.› (*Seemannsspr.* Öffnung im Schiffsbug für die Ankerkette);
Klu|sil, der; -s, -e ‹lat.› (*Sprachw.* Verschlusslaut, z. B. p, t, k, b, d, g)
Klü|ten *Plur.* (*nordd. für* Klumpen)
Klü|ver [...v...], der; -s, - ‹niederl.› (*Seemannsspr.* dreieckiges Vorsegel); **Klü|ver|baum**
Kly̧s|ma, das; -s, ...men ‹griech.› (*Med.* Klistier)
Kly̧st|ron (↑R 130), das; -s, *Plur.* ...one, *auch* -s ‹griech.› (Elektronenröhre zur Erzeugung und Verstärkung von Mikrowellen)
Kly|täm|nẹst|ra (↑R 130; Gemahlin Agamemnons)
km = Kilometer
k. M. = künftigen Monats
km² = Quadratkilometer
km³ = Kubikkilometer
km/h = Kilometer je Stunde
km-Zahl (↑R 26 *u.* R 60)
kn = Knoten *(Seew.)*
kN = Kilonewton
knab|bern; ich ...ere (↑R 16); *vgl. auch* knappern, knuppern
Kna|be, der; -n, -n (↑R 126); **Kna-ben|al|ter,** das; -s; **kna|ben|haft; Kna|ben|haf|tig|keit,** die; -; **Kna|ben|kraut** (eine zu den Orchideen gehörende Pflanze); **Knäb|lein**
knạck!; Knạck, der; -[e]s, -e (kurzer, harter, heller Ton); **Knä|cke-brot; knạ|cken; Knạ|cker** (*ugs. abwertend für* Mann; *landsch. für* Knackwurst); alter -; **knạck-frisch; Knạ|cki,** der; -s, -s (*ugs. für* Vorbestrafter; Gefängnisinsasse); **knạ|ckig;** etwas ist knackig frisch; **Knạck‿laut, ...man-del, ...punkt** (*ugs. für* entscheidender, problematischer Punkt); **knạcks!;** knịcks, knạcks!; **Knạcks,** der; -es, -e (*svw.* Knack; *ugs. auch für* Riss, Schaden); **knạck|sen** (knacken); du knackst; **Knạck|wurst**
Knag|ge, die; -, -n *u.* **Knag|gen,** der; -s, - (*nordd. für* dreieckige Stütze, Leiste; Winkelstück)
Knäk|en|te (eine Wildente)
Knạll, der; -[e]s, -e; - und Fall (*ugs. für* unerwartet, sofort); **Knạll-bon|bon; knạll|bụnt; Knạll|ef-fekt** (*ugs. für* große Überraschung); **knạl|len; Knạll|erb|se; Knal|le|rei; Knạll‿frosch, ...gas; knạll|hạrt** (*ugs. für* sehr hart); **knạl|lig** (*ugs. für* grell; sehr, überaus; eng anliegend); **Knạll|kopp,** der; -s, ...köppe (*ugs. Schimpfwort* verrückter Kerl); **Knạll|kör|per; knạll|rot**
knạpp (↑R 39:) knapp sein, werden, schneiden usw.; ein knapp sitzender Anzug; eine [sehr] knapp gehaltene Beschreibung; du darfst den Jungen nicht zu knapp halten *(ugs.)*
Knạp|pe, der; -n, -n; ↑R 126 (Bergmann; *früher* noch nicht zum Ritter geschlagener jüngerer Adliger)
knạp|pern (*landsch. für* knabbern); ich ...ere (↑R 16)
knạpp hal|ten *vgl.* knapp; **Knạpp-heit,** die; -
Knạpp|sack (*veraltet für* Reisetasche, Brotsack)
Knạpp|schaft (Gesamtheit der Bergarbeiter eines Bergwerks od. Bergreviers); **knạpp|schaft|lich; Knạpp|schafts‿kas|se, ...ren-te, ...ver|ein, ...ver|si|che|rung**
knạps!; knịps, knạps!; **knạp|sen** (*ugs. für* geizen; eingeschränkt leben); du knapst
Knar|re, die; -, -n (Kinderspielzeug; *ugs. für* Gewehr); **knar|ren**
[1]Knạst, der; -[e]s, Knäste (*landsch. für* Knorren; Brotkanten)
[2]Knạst, der; -[e]s, *Plur.* Knäste, *auch* -e ‹jidd.› (*ugs. für* Gefängnis; *nur Sing.:* Freiheitsstrafe)
[1]Knạs|ter, der; -s, - ‹niederl.› (*ugs. für* [schlechter] Tabak)
[2]Knạs|ter, Knạs|te|rer, Knạst|rer (*landsch. für* verdrießlicher, mürrischer [alter] Mann); **Knạs|ter-bart** (*svw.* [2]Knaster); **Knạs|te|rer** *vgl.* [2]Knaster; **knạs|tern** (*landsch. für* verdrießlich brummen); ich ...ere (↑R 16); **Knạst|rer** *vgl.* [2]Knaster
Knatsch, der; -[e]s (*landsch. für* Ärger, Streit); **knat|schen** (*landsch. für* nörgeln, mit weinerl. Stimme reden); **knat|schig**
knạt|tern; ich ...ere (↑R 16)
Knäu|el, der *od.* das; -s, -; **Knäu-el|gras,** Knaul|gras; **knäu|eln** *(selten); vgl.* knäulen
Knauf, der; -[e]s, Knäufe; **Knäuf-chen, Knäuf|lein**
Knaul, der *od.* das; -s, *Plur.* -e *u.* Knäule (*landsch. für* Knäuel); **Knäul|chen; knäu|len** (*ugs. für* zusammendrücken); **Knaul|gras** *vgl.* Knäuelgras
Knau|pe|lei *(landsch.);* **knau|pe-lig,** knaup|lig (*landsch. für* kniff-lig, viel Geschicklichkeit erfordernd); **Knau|pel|kno|chen** *(landsch.);* **knau|peln** (*landsch. für* benagen; abknabbern; sich abmühen; schwer an etwas tragen); ich ...[e]le (↑R 16); **knaup-lig** *vgl.* knaupelig
Knau|ser *(ugs.);* **Knau|se|rei** *(ugs.);* **knau|se|rig,** knaus|rig *(ugs.);* **Knau|se|rig|keit,** Knaus-rig|keit; **knau|sern** (*ugs. für* übertrieben sparsam sein); ich ...ere (↑R 16)
Knaus-O|gi|no-Me|tho|de, die; - ‹nach den Gynäkologen H. Knaus (Österreich) u. K. Ogino (Japan)› (Methode zur Bestimmung der fruchtbaren u. unfruchtbaren Tage des weibl. Zyklus)
knaus|rig usw. *vgl.* knauserig usw.
Knau|tie [...i̯ə], die; -, -n ‹nach dem dt. Botaniker Chr. Knaut› (eine Feld- u. Wiesenblume)
knaut|schen (knittern; *landsch. für* schmatzend essen; verhalten weinen); du knautschst; **knaut-schig; Knautsch‿lack, ...zo|ne** *(Kfz-Technik)*
Kne|bel, der; -s, -; **Kne|bel|bart; kne|beln;** ich ...[e]le (↑R 16); **Kne|bel|lung, Kneb|lung**
Knẹcht, der; -[e]s, -e; **knẹch|ten; knẹch|tisch; Knẹcht Ru̲p|recht,** der; - -[e]s, - -e; **Knẹcht|schaft,** die; -; **Knẹchts|ge|stalt** *(veraltet);* **Knẹch|tung**
Kneif, der; -[e]s, -e ([Schuster]messer); *vgl.* Kneip; **knei|fen;** du kniffst; du kniffest; gekniffen; kneif[e]!; er kneift ihn (*auch* ihm) in den Arm; *vgl. auch* [1]kneipen; **Knei|fer** (*nordd. für* Klemmer, Zwicker); **Kneif|zan|ge; Kneip,** der; -[e]s, -e (*Nebenform von* Kneif)
Knei|pe, die; -, -n (*ugs. für* [einfaches] Lokal mit Alkoholaus-

schank; *auch für* student. Trinkabend)
[1]**kneilpen** (*landsch. für* kneifen, zwicken); ich kneipte (*auch* knipp); gekneipt (*auch* geknippen)
[2]**kneilpen** (*ugs. für* sich in Kneipen aufhalten; trinken); ich kneipte; gekneipt; **Kneilpen|wirt; Kneipe|rei** *(ugs.)*; **Kneilpi|er** [...'pi̯e:], der; -s, -s (Kneipenwirt)
Kneipp (dt. kath. Geistlicher u. Heilkundiger; ® ein von ihm entwickeltes Wasserheilverfahren); **kneip|pen** (eine Wasserkur nach Kneipp machen); **Kneipp|kur** (↑R 95)
Kneip|zan|ge (*landsch. für* Kneifzange)
Knes|set[h], die; - ‹hebr., „Versammlung"› (israel. Parlament)
knet|bar; Kne|te, die; - (*ugs. für* Knetmasse; *auch für* Geld); **kneten; Knet‿ma|schi|ne, ...mas|sa|ge, ...mas|se, ...mes|ser** (das)
knib|beln (*mitteld. für* sich mit den Fingern an etwas zu schaffen machen); ich ...[e]le (↑R 16)
Knick, der; -[e]s, *Plur.* (*für* Hecke:) -e *u.* -s (scharfer Falz, scharfe Krümmung, Bruch; *nordd. auch für* Hecke als Einfriedung); **Kni|cke|bein,** der; -s (Eierlikör [als Füllung in Pralinen u. Ä.]); **Knick|ei** (angeschlagenes Ei); **kni|cken;** [1]**Kni|cker** (Jagdmesser; *ugs. für* Geizhals)
[2]**Kni|cker,** der; -s, - (*nordd. für* Spielkugel, Murmel)
Kni|cker|bo|cker, *engl.* **Kni|cker|bo|ckers** ['ni...] *Plur.* (halblange Pumphose)
Kni|cke|rei *(ugs.)*; **kni|cke|rig,** knick|rig *(ugs.)*; **Kni|cke|rig|keit,** Knick|rig|keit, die; - *(ugs.)*; **kni|ckern** (*ugs. für* geizig sein); ich ...ere (↑R 16); **knick|rig** usw. *vgl.* knickerig usw.
knicks!; knicks, knacks!; **Knicks,** der; -es, -e; **knick|sen;** du knickst
Kni|ckung
Knie, das; -s, - ['kni:ə, *auch* kni:]; auf den Knien liegen; auf die Knie!; **Knie|beu|ge**
Knie|bis, der; - (Erhebung im nördl. Schwarzwald)
Knie|bre|che, die; - (mitteld. Name steiler Höhenwege); **Knie|bund[|ho|se]; Knie|fall,** der; **knie‿fäl|lig, ...frei; Knie‿gei|ge** (*für* Gambe), **...ge|lenk; Knie|ge|lenk|ent|zün|dung; knie|hoch;** der Schnee liegt kniehoch; **Knie‿holz** (das; -es; niedrige Bergkiefern), **...ho|se, ...keh|le; knie|lang; knie|lings** (*selten für* kniend); **knien** [kni:n, *auch* 'kni:ən]; ich knie ['kni:ə, *auch* kni:]; du kniest; kniend ['kni:ənt]; gekniet; knie!
Knie|pau|gen (*landsch. für* kleine, lebhafte Augen)
Knie|riem (*veraltet für* Knieriemen); *nur noch in* Meister Knieriem (*scherzh. für* Schuster); **Knie|rie|men**
Knies, der; -es (*landsch. für* Dreck; Streit)
Knie‿schei|be, ...scho|ner, ...schüt|zer, ...strumpf; knie|tief
kniet|schen, knit|schen (*landsch. für* zerdrücken, ausquetschen; weinerlich sein); du kni[e]tschst
Kniff, der; -[e]s, -e; **Knif|fe|lei** (kniffige Arbeit); **knif|fe|lig,** kniff|lig; **Knif|fe|lig|keit,** Kniff|lig|keit; **knif|fen;** geknifft; **kniff|lig** usw. *vgl.* kniffelig usw.
Kni|ge, der; -[s], - ‹nach Adolph Freiherr von Knigge› (Buch über Umgangsformen)
Knilch, Knülch, der; -s, -e (*ugs. für* unangenehmer Mensch)
knil|le *vgl.* knülle
knips!; knips, knaps!; **Knips,** der; -es, -e; **knip|sen** *(ugs.)*; du knipst; **Knip|ser** *(ugs.)*; **knips, knaps!**
Knirps, der; -es, -e (kleiner Junge od. Mann; ® ein zusammenschiebbarer Regenschirm)
knir|schen; du knirschst
knis|tern; ich ...ere (↑R 16)
knit|schen *vgl.* knietschen
Knit|tel, der; -s, -; *vgl.* Knüttel; **Knit|tel|vers** (vierhebiger, unregelmäßiger Reimvers)
Knit|ter, der; -s, -; **knit|ter|arm; Knit|ter|fal|te; knit|ter‿fest, ...frei; knit|te|rig,** knitt|rig; **knittern;** ich ...ere (↑R 16); **knitt|rig** *vgl.* knitterig
Kno|bel, der; -s, - (*landsch. für* [Finger]knöchel; Würfel); **Knobel|be|cher** (*scherzh. auch für* Militärstiefel); **kno|beln** ([aus]losen; würfeln; lange nachdenken); ich ...[e]le (↑R 16)
Knob|lauch ['kno:p..., *auch* 'knɔp...], der; -[e]s; **Knob|lauch‿but|ter, ...pil|le, ...salz, ...wurst, ...ze|he, ...zwie|bel**
Knö|chel, der; -s, -; **Knö|chelchen; knö|chel‿lang, ...tief; Kno|chen,** der; -s, -; **Kno|chen‿bau** (der; -[e]s), **...bruch** (der), **...er|wei|chung, ...fraß** (der; -es), **...ge|rüst** (*ugs. auch für* magerer Mensch); **kno|chen|hart** (sehr hart); **Kno|chen‿hau|er** (*nordd. veraltet für* Fleischer), **...haut; Kno|chen|haut|ent|zün|dung; Kno|chen‿mann** (der; -[e]s; *volkstüml. für* Tod als Gerippe), **...mark** (das), **...mehl, ...müh|le** (altes, ungefedertes Fahrzeug; Unternehmen, in dem strapaziöse Arbeit geleistet werden muss), **...na|ge|lung** *(Med.)*, **...schwund, ...split|ter; kno|chen|tro|cken** (*ugs. für* sehr trocken); **knö|che|rig,** knöch|rig (aus Knochen; knochenartig); **knö|chern** (aus Knochen); **kno|chig** (mit starken Knochen); **Kno|chig|keit,** die; -; **Knöch|lein; knöch|rig** *vgl.* knöcherig
knock-out, *auch* **knock|out** [nɔk-'aut] ‹engl.› (beim Boxkampf niedergeschlagen, kampfunfähig; *Abk.* k. o. [ka:'o:]; jmdn. k. o. schlagen; **Knock-out,** *auch* **Knock|out,** der; -[s], -s (Niederschlag; *übertr. für* völlige Vernichtung; *Abk.* K. o.); **Knock-out-Schlag,** *auch* **Knock|out|schlag** (*Abk.* K.-o.-Schlag, *auch* Ko.-Schlag; ↑R 28)
Knö|del, der; -s, - (*südd., österr. für* Kloß)
Knöll|chen; Knol|le, die; -, -n, *landsch.* **Knol|len,** der; -s, -; **Knol|len|blät|ter|pilz** (ein Giftpilz); **Knol|len|fäu|le** (Krankheit der Kartoffel); **knol|len|för|mig; Knol|len‿frucht, ...na|se; knol|lig**
Knopf, der; -[e]s, Knöpfe (*österr. ugs. auch für* Knoten); **Knopf|au|ge** *meist Plur.*; **Knöpf|chen; Knopf|druck;** ein - genügt; **knöpfen; Knöpf|lein; Knöpf|li** *Plur.* (*schweiz.* [eine Art] Spätzle); **Knopf|loch; Knopf|loch|sei|de**
Kno|per, die; -, -n (Gallapfel, z. B. an grünen Eichelkelchen)
knö|ren (*Jägerspr.* leise röhren [vom Hirsch])
knor|ke (*berlin. veraltet für* fein, tadellos)
Knor|pel, der; -s, -; **knor|pe|lig, knorp|lig**
Knorr-Brem|se ® ‹nach dem dt. Ingenieur G. Knorr› (↑R 95)
Knor|ren, der; -s, - (*landsch. für* Knoten, harter Auswuchs); **knorrig; Knorz,** der; -es, -e (*südd., landsch. für* Knorren); **knor|zen** (*schweiz. mdal. für* sich abmühen, knausern); du knorzt; **Knor|zer** ‹*zu* knorzen› (*landsch. auch für* kleiner Kerl); **knor|zig**
Knösp|chen; Knos|pe, die; -, -n; **knos|pen;** geknospt; **knos|pig; Knösp|lein; Knos|pung**
Knos|sos (altkret. Stadt)
Knöt|chen
Kno|te, der; -n, -n; ↑R 126 (*veraltet für* plumper, ungebildeter Mensch)
knö|teln (kleine Knoten sticken); ich ...[e]le (↑R 16); **kno|ten;** ge-

knotet; **Kno|ten,** der; -s, - (*auch* Marke an der Logleine, Seemeile je Stunde [*Zeichen* kn]); **Kno|tenamt** *(Postw.);* **kno|ten|för|mig; Kno|ten‿punkt, ...stock; Knöte|rich,** der; -s, -e (eine Pflanze); **kno|tig**
Knot|ten|erz (Buntsandstein mit eingesprengtem Bleiglanz)
Know-how [noːˈhau̯, *auch* ˈnoːhau̯], das; -[s] ‹engl.› (Wissen um die praktische Verwirklichung od. Anwendung einer Sache); **Know-how-Trans|fer** (↑R 28)
Knub|be, die; -, -n *u.* **Knub|ben,** der; -s, - (*nordd. für* Knorren; Knospe; Geschwulst); **knubbeln,** sich (*landsch. für* sich drängen); ich ...[e]le mich (↑R 16)
knud|deln (*landsch. für* umarmen [u. küssen]; zerknüllen); ich ...[e]le (↑R 16)
Knuff, der; -[e]s, Knüffe (*ugs. für* Puff, Stoß); **knuf|fen** *(ugs.)*
Knülch *vgl.* Knilch
knüll, knül|le (*Studentenspr. u. ugs. für* betrunken; *landsch. für* erschöpft); **knül|len** (zerknittern)
Knül|ler (*ugs. für* Sensation; tolle Sache)
Knüpf|ar|beit; knüp|fen; Knüpftep|pich; Knüp|fung; Knüpfwerk
Knüp|pel, der; -s, -; **Knüp|pelaus|dem|sack** [*auch* ...ˈsak], der; -; - spielen (*scherzh. für* prügeln); **Knüp|pel|damm; knüp|pel|dick** (*ugs. für* sehr schlimm); **knüppeln** (mit einem Knüppel schlagen; *ugs. auch für* gehäuft auftreten); ich ...[e]le (↑R 16); **Knüppel|schal|tung**
knup|pern (*landsch. für* knabbern); ich ...ere (↑R 16)
knur|ren; Knurr|hahn (ein Fisch; *ugs. für* mürrischer Mensch); **knur|rig;** ein -er Mensch; **Knurrig|keit,** die; -; **Knurr|laut**
knü|se|lig (*landsch. für* unsauber)
Knus|per|chen (Gebäck); **Knusper‿flo|cken** *(Plur.),* **...häuschen; knus|pe|rig** *vgl.* knusprig; **knus|pern;** ich ...ere (↑R 16); **knusp|rig,** knus|pe|rig
Knust, der; -[e]s, *Plur.* -e *u.* Knüste (*nordd. für* Endstück des Brotes)
Knut (m. Vorn.)
Knu|te, die; -, -n ‹germ.-russ.› (Lederpeitsche); unter jmds. - (von jmdm. unterdrückt); **knu|ten** (knechten, unterdrücken)
knut|schen (*ugs. für* heftig liebkosen); du knutschst; **Knut|scherei** *(ugs.);* **Knutsch|fleck** *(ugs.)*
Knüt|tel, der; -s, -; **Knüt|tel|vers** *vgl.* Knittelvers
k. o. = knock-out (*vgl. d.);* k. o. schlagen; **K. o.** = Knock-out *(vgl. d.);* K.-o.-Schlag, K.-o.-Niederlage
kΩ = Kiloohm
Ko|ad|ju|tor, der; -s, ...oren ‹lat.› (Amtsgehilfe eines kath. Geistlichen, bes. eines Bischofs)
Ko|a|gu|lat, das; -[e]s, -e ‹lat.› (*Chemie* aus kolloidaler Lösung ausgeflockter Stoff); **Ko|a|gu|lati|on,** die; -, -en (Ausflockung); **ko|a|gu|lie|ren; Ko|a|gu|lum,** das; -s, ...la (*Med.* Blutgerinnsel)
Ko|a|la, der; -s, -s ‹austr.› (kleiner austral. Beutelbär); **Ko|a|la|bär**
ko|a|lie|ren, ko|a|li|sie|ren ‹franz.› (verbinden; sich verbünden); **Ko|a|li|ti|on,** die; -, -en (Vereinigung, Bündnis; Zusammenschluss [von Staaten]); kleine, große Koalition; **Ko|a|li|ti|o|när,** der; -s, -e *meist Plur.* (Koalitionspartner); **Ko|a|li|ti|ons‿frei|heit, ...krieg, ...par|tei, ...part|ner, ...recht, ...re|gie|rung**
Ko|au|tor, *auch* Kon|au|tor ‹lat.› (Mitverfasser)
ko|axi|al (↑R 132) ‹lat.› (mit gleicher Achse); **Ko|axi|al|ka|bel** *(Technik)*
Kob, der; -s, -s (*kurz für* Kontaktbereichsbeamte)
Ko|balt, *chem. fachspr.* Co|balt, das; -s ‹*nach* Kobold *gebildet*› (chem. Element, Metall; *Zeichen* Co); **ko|balt|blau; Ko|balt‿bombe, ...ka|no|ne** (*Med.* ein Bestrahlungsgerät), **...ver|bin|dung**
Ko|bel, der; -s, - (Nest des Eichhörnchens; *südd., österr. für* Verschlag, Koben); **Ko|ben,** der; -s, - (Verschlag; Käfig; Stall)
Kø|ben|havn [købənˈhau̯n] (*dän. Form von* Kopenhagen)
Ko|ber, der; -s, - (*landsch. für* Korb [für Esswaren])
Ko|b|lenz (↑R 130; Stadt an der Mündung der Mosel); **Ko|b|lenzer** (↑R 103); **ko|b|len|zisch**
Ko|bold, der; -[e]s, -e (neckischer Geist); **ko|bold|haft; Ko|boldma|ki** *vgl.* Maki
Ko|bolz, der; *nur noch in* Kobolz schießen (Purzelbaum schlagen); **ko|bol|zen;** kobolzt
Ko|b|ra (↑R 130), die; -, -s ‹port.› (Brillenschlange)
[1]**Koch,** der; -[e]s, Köche; [2]**Koch,** das; -s (*bayr., österr. für* Brei); **Koch‿beu|tel, ...buch; kochecht; kö|cheln** (leicht kochen); die Soße köchelt
Kö|chel|ver|zeich|nis, das; -ses ‹nach dem Musikgelehrten Ludwig von Köchel› (Verzeichnis der Werke Mozarts; *Abk.* KV); ↑R 95
ko|chen; kochend heißes Wasser; das Wasser ist kochend heiß; [1]**Ko|cher** (Kochgerät)
[2]**Ko|cher,** der; -s (r. Nebenfluss des Neckars)
Kö|cher, der; -s, - (Behälter für Pfeile)
Ko|che|rei, die; -; **koch‿fer|tig, ...fest; Koch‿ge|le|gen|heit, ...ge|schirr; Kö|chin; Koch‿käse, ...kunst, ...kurs, ...löf|fel, ...müt|ze, ...ni|sche, ...plat|te, ...re|zept, ...salz** (das; -es); **kochsalz|arm; Koch‿topf, ...wä|sche** (die; -), **...zeit**
Ko|da, *auch* Co|da, die; -, -s ‹ital.› (*Musik* Schlussteil eines Satzes)
Ko|dak ® (fotograf. Erzeugnisse)
Ko|dály [ˈkɔdaːj], Zoltán [ˈzoltaːn] (ung. Komponist)
kod|de|rig, kodd|rig (*landsch. für* schlecht; unverschämt, frech; übel); **Kod|der|schnau|ze; kodd|rig** *vgl.* kodderig
Kode, *fachspr. meist* Code [*beide* koːt], der; -s, -s ‹franz.-engl.› (System verabredeter Zeichen; Schlüssel zum Dechiffrieren)
Ko|de|in, das; -s ‹griech.› (ein Beruhigungsmittel)
Kö|der, der; -s, - (Lockmittel); **Köder|fisch; kö|dern;** ich ...ere (↑R 16)
Ko|dex, der; *Gen.* -es *u.* -, *Plur.* -e *u.* ...dizes [ˈkoːditseːs] ‹lat.› (Handschriftensammlung; Gesetzbuch); **ko|die|ren,** *in der Technik meist* co|die|ren (durch einen Kode verschlüsseln); **Kodie|rung,** Co|die|rung; **Ko|di|fika|ti|on,** die; -, -en (zusammenfassende Regelung eines größeren Rechtsgebietes; Gesetzessammlung); **ko|di|fi|zie|ren; Ko|di|fizie|rung** (Kodifikation); **Ko|dizill,** das; -s, -e (*Rechtsw.* letztwillige Verfügung; Zusatz zum Testament)
Ko|edu|ka|ti|on [*auch* ...ˈtsi̯oːn] (↑R 132), die; - ‹engl.› (Gemeinschaftserziehung beider Geschlechter)
Ko|ef|fi|zi|ent, der; -en, -en (↑R 126) ‹lat.› (*Math.* Multiplikator der veränderl. Größe[n] einer Funktion; *Physik* kennzeichnende Größe, z. B. für die Ausdehnung eines Stoffes)
Ko|er|zi|tiv|feld|stär|ke, die; - ‹lat.; dt.› *(Physik)*
ko|exis|tent [*auch* ...ˈtɛnt] (↑R 132); **Ko|exis|tenz** [*auch* ...ˈtɛnts], die; - ‹lat.› (gleichzeitiges Vorhandensein unterschiedlicher Dinge; friedl. Nebeneinanderbestehen von Staaten mit unterschiedlichen Gesellschaftsordnungen); **koexis|tie|ren** [*auch* ...ˈtiː...]

Ko|fel, der; -s, - (*bayr. u. westösterr. für* Bergkuppe)
Ko|fen, der; -s, - (*nordd. für* Koben)
Kof|fe|in, das; -s ‹arab.› (Wirkstoff von Kaffee u. Tee); **kof|fe|in-frei, ...hal|tig**
Kof|fer, der; -s, - ‹franz.›; **Kof|fer|an|hän|ger; Köf|fer|chen; Kof|fer-de|ckel, ...ge|rät, ...kleid, ...ku|li** (Transportwagen auf Bahnhöfen, Flughäfen usw.); **Köf|fer|lein; Kof|fer-ra|dio, ...raum, ...schloss, ...schlüs|sel, ...schreib|ma|schi|ne**
Kog, der; -[e]s, Köge (*svw.* Koog)
[1]**Ko|gel**, der; -s, - (*südd., österr. für* Bergkuppe; kegelförmiger Berg); [2]**Ko|gel**, die; -, -n (*veraltet für* Kapuze)
Kog|ge, die; -, -n (dickbauchiges Hanseschiff)
Kog|nak ['kɔnjak] (↑R 130), der; -s, -s (*ugs. für* Weinbrand); drei Kognak (↑R 90); *vgl. aber* [2]Cognac; **Kog|nak-boh|ne, ...glas, ...kir|sche, ...schwen|ker**
Kog|nat (↑R 130 *u.* 132), der; -en, -en (↑R 126) ‹lat.› (Blutsverwandter, der nicht Agnat ist)
Kog|ni|ti|on (↑R 130 *u.* 132), die; -, -en ‹lat.› (das Erkennen, Wahrnehmen); **kog|ni|tiv** (die Erkenntnis betreffend)
Kog|no|men (↑R 130 *u.* 132), das; -s, *Plur.* - *u.* ...mina ‹lat.› (Beiname der Römer)
Ko|ha|bi|ta|ti|on, die; -, -en ‹lat.› (*Med.* Geschlechtsverkehr; *Politik* [in Frankreich] Zusammenarbeit des Staatspräsidenten mit einer Regierung einer anderen polit. Richtung); **ko|ha|bi|tie|ren**
ko|hä|rent ‹lat.› (zusammenhängend); -es Licht *(Physik)*; **Ko|hä|renz**, die; -; **ko|hä|rie|ren** (zusammenhängen; Kohäsion zeigen); **Ko|hä|si|on**, die; - (*Physik* Zusammenhalt der Moleküle eines Körpers); **ko|hä|siv**
Ko|hi|noor [...'nu:r], *auch* **Ko|hi|nur**, der; -s ‹pers.-engl.› (Name eines großen Diamanten)
[1]**Kohl**, der; -[e]s, *Plur. (Sorten:)* -e (ein Gemüse)
[2]**Kohl**, der; -[e]s ‹hebr.› (*ugs. für* Unsinn; Geschwätz); - reden
Kohl|dampf, der; -[e]s (*ugs. für* Hunger); - schieben
Koh|le, die; -, -n; Kohle führende Flöze; **Koh|le|ben|zin** (aus Kohle gewonnenes Benzin); **Koh|le|fa|den** usw. *vgl.* Kohlenfaden usw.; **Koh|le füh|rend** *vgl.* Kohle; **koh|le|hal|tig; Koh|le|herd**, Koh|len|herd; **Koh|le|hyd|rat** *vgl.* Kohlenhydrat; **Koh|le|hyd|rie|rung**, die; - *(Chemie)*; **Koh|le|im|port**, Koh|len|im|port; **Koh|le|kraft|werk**; [1]**koh|len** (nicht mit voller Flamme brennen, schwelen; *Seemannsspr.* Kohlen übernehmen)
[2]**koh|len** ‹*zu* [2]Kohl› (*ugs. für* aufschneiden, schwindeln)
Koh|len-be|cken, ...berg|bau, ...berg|werk, ...bun|ker; Koh|len-di|oxid (*vgl.* Oxid); **Koh|len|di|oxid|ver|gif|tung; Koh|len|ei|mer; Koh|le[n]|fa|den; Koh|le[n]|fa|den|lam|pe; Koh|len-feu|er, ...flöz, ...grus, ...hal|de, ...hand|lung, ...hei|zung; Koh|le[n]-herd, ...hyd|rat** (zucker- od. stärkeartige chem. Verbindung), **...im|port; Koh|len|mei|ler; Koh|len|mo|no|xid** *vgl.* Oxid; **Koh|len|mo|no|xid|ver|gif|tung; Koh|len|pott**, der; -s (*ugs. für* Ruhrgebiet); **koh|len|sau|er;** koh|len|sau|res Natron; **Koh|len-säu|re, ...schau|fel, ...staub, ...stift** (der; *Technik*), **...stoff** (der; -[e]s; chem. Element; *Zeichen* C), **...trim|mer; Koh|len|was|ser|stoff; Koh|le-pa|pier, ...pfen|nig** (der; -s; *ugs. für* dem Strompreis zugeschlagene Abgabe zugunsten des Kohlebergbaus); **Köh|ler; Köh|le|rei; Köh|ler|glau|be**, der; -ns (blinder Glaube); **Koh|le|stift**, der (ein Zeichenstift); **Koh|le-ver|flüs|si|gung, ...ver|ga|sung, ...zeich|nung**
Kohl-her|nie (eine Pflanzenkrankheit), **...kopf**
Kohl|mei|se (ein Vogel)
Kohl|ra|be (*für* Kolkrabe); **kohl|ra|ben|schwarz**
Kohl|ra|bi, der; -[s], -[s] ‹ital.› (ein Gemüse); **Kohl-rau|pe, ...rou|la|de, ...rü|be**
kohl|schwarz
Kohl-spros|se (*österr. für* Röschen des Rosenkohls), **...strunk, ...sup|pe, ...weiß|ling** (ein Schmetterling)
Ko|hor|te, die; -, -n ‹lat.› (der 10. Teil einer röm. Legion)
Koi|ne [kɔy'ne:], die; -, Koinai ‹griech.› (griech. Gemeinsprache der hellenist. Welt; *Sprachw.* übermundartl. Gemeinsprache)
ko|in|zi|dent ‹lat.› (*fachspr. für* zusammenfallend); **Ko|in|zi|denz**, die; -, -en (Zusammentreffen von Ereignissen); **ko|in|zi|die|ren**
ko|i|tie|ren ‹lat.› (*Med.* den Koitus vollziehen); **Ko|i|tus**, der; -, *Plur.* - [...tu:s] *u.* -se (*Med.* Geschlechtsakt)
Ko|je, die; -, -n ‹niederl.› (Schlafstelle [auf Schiffen]; Ausstellungsstand)
Ko|jo|te, der; -n, -n (↑R 126) ‹mexik.› (nordamerik. Präriewolf; Schimpfwort)
Ko|ka, die; -, - ‹indian.› (*kurz für* Kokastrauch); **Ko|ka|in**, das; -s (ein Betäubungsmittel; Rauschgift); **Ko|ka|i|nis|mus**, der; - (Kokainsucht)
Ko|kar|de, die; -, -n ‹franz.› (Abzeichen, Hoheitszeichen an Uniformmützen)
Ko|ka|strauch (ein Strauch mit Kokain enthaltenden Blättern)
ko|keln (*landsch. für* mit Feuer spielen); ich ...[e]le (↑R 16); *vgl.* gokeln
ko|ken ‹engl.› ([1]Koks herstellen)
[1]**Ko|ker**, der; -s, - (*Seemannsspr.* Öffnung im Schiffsheck für den Ruderschaft)
[2]**Ko|ker** (Koksarbeiter); **Ko|ke|rei** (Kokswerk; *nur Sing.:* Koksgewinnung)
ko|kett ‹franz.› (eitel, gefallsüchtig); **Ko|ket|te|rie**, die; -, ...ien; **ko|ket|tie|ren**
Ko|kil|le, die; -, -n ‹franz.› (mehrfach verwendbare Gussform); **Ko|kil|len|guss**
Kok|ke, die; -, -n *u.* Kok|kus, der; -n, Kokken *meist Plur.* ‹griech.› (kugelförmige Bakterie)
Kok|kels|kör|ner *Plur.* ‹griech.; dt.› (Giftsamen zum Fischfang)
Kök|ken|möd|din|ger *Plur.* ‹dän., „Küchenabfälle"› (steinzeitl. Abfallhaufen)
Kok|ko|lith [*auch* ...'lit], der; *Gen.* -s *u.* -en, *Plur.* -e[n] (↑R 126) ‹griech.› (*Geol.* aus Kalkalgen entstandenes Gestein der Tiefsee);
Kok|kus *vgl.* Kokke
Ko|ko|lo|res, der; - (*ugs. für* Umstände; Unsinn)
Ko|kon [ko'kõ:, *österr.* ko'ko:n], der; -s, -s ‹franz.› (Hülle der Insektenpuppen); **Ko|kon|fa|ser**
Ko|kos|bus|serl (*österr.* ein Gebäck)
Ko|kosch|ka [*auch* 'kɔ...] (österr. Maler u. Dichter)
Ko|ko|sette [...'zɛt], das; -s ‹span.› (*österr. für* Kokosflocken); **Ko|kos-fa|ser, ...fett, ...flo|cken** *(Plur.)*, **...läu|fer, ...mat|te, ...milch, ...nuss, ...öl** (das; -[e]s), **...pal|me, ...ras|pel** *(Plur.)*, **...tep|pich**
Ko|kot|te, die; -, -n ‹franz.› (*veraltet für* Dirne, Halbweltdame)
[1]**Koks**, der; -es, -e ‹engl.› (ein Brennstoff aus Kohle; *nur Sing.:* *ugs. scherzh. für* Geld)
[2]**Koks**, der; -es ‹indian.› (*ugs. für* Kokain)
[3]**Koks**, der; -[es], -e ‹jidd.› (*ugs. für* steifer Hut)

ko̱k|sen (*ugs. für* Kokain nehmen; schlafen, schnarchen); du kokst; **Ko̱k|ser** (*ugs. für* Kokainsüchtiger)

Ko̱ks‿ofen (↑R 132), **...staub**

Ko|ky|tos [*auch* ...'tɔs], der; - (ein Fluss der Unterwelt in der griech. Sage)

Kok|zi̱|die [...i̯ə], die; -, -n *meist Plur.* ‹griech.› (parasit., krankheitserregende Sporentierchen); **Kok|zi|di|o̱|se,** die; -, -n (durch Kokzidien verursachte Tierkrankheit)

[1]**Ko̱|la** (*Plur. von* Kolon)

[2]**Ko̱|la** (Halbinsel im NW Russlands)

Ko|la̱|ni, Co|la̱|ni, der; -s, -s (warmes, hüftlanges [Marine]jackett)

Ko̱|la‿nuss, ...strauch

Ko|la̱t|sche, die; -, -n ‹tschech.› (*österr. für* kleiner, gefüllter Hefekuchen)

Ko̱l|ben, der; -s, -; **Ko̱l|ben‿dampf|ma|schi|ne, ...fres|ser** (*ugs. für* Motorschaden durch festsitzenden Kolben), **...hieb, ...hirsch** *(Jägerspr.)*, **...hir|se, ...hub, ...ring, ...stan|ge; ko̱l|big**

Ko̱l|chis [...çis], die; - (antike Landschaft am Schwarzen Meer)

Kol|chos ['kɔlçɔs], der; -, ...ose [...'ço:zə] *u. (österr. nur)* Kol|cho̱|se [...ç...], die; -, -n ‹russ.› (landwirtschaftl. Produktionsgenossenschaft in der ehem. Sowjetunion); **Ko̱l|ohos|bau|er; Kol|cho̱|se** *vgl.* Kolchos

ko̱l|dern (*südd., schweiz. mdal. für* schelten, poltern, zanken); ich ...ere (↑R 16)

Ko|le|op|te̱|ren (↑R 132) *Plur.* ‹griech.› (*Zool.* Käfer)

Ko̱|li|bak|te|ri|en [...i̯ən] *Plur.* ‹griech.› ([Dick]darmbakterien)

Ko̱|lib|ri (↑R 130), der; -s, -s ‹karib.› (kleiner Vogel)

ko|li̱e|ren ‹lat.› (*Pharm.* [durch ein Tuch] seihen); **Ko|li̱er|tuch** *Plur.* ...tücher

Ko̱|lik [*auch* ko'li:k], die; -, -en ‹griech.› (Anfall von krampfartigen Leibschmerzen); **Ko|li̱|tis,** die; -, ...itiden (*Med.* Dickdarmentzündung)

Ko̱lk, der; -[e]s, -e (*nordd. für* Wasserloch)

Kol|ko|tha̱r, der; -s, -e ‹arab.› (rotes Eisenoxid)

Ko̱lk|ra|be

Koll. = Kolleg[e], Kollegin

Ko̱l|la, die; - ‹griech.› (*Chemie, Med.* Leim)

kol|la|bi̱e|ren ‹lat.› (*Med.* einen Kollaps erleiden)

Kol|la|bo|ra|teur [...'tø:r], der; -s, -e ‹franz.› (jmd., der mit dem Feind zusammenarbeitet); **Kol|la|bo|ra|ti|o̱n,** die; -, -en; **kol|la|bo|ri̱e|ren** ‹„mitarbeiten"› (mit dem Feind zusammenarbeiten)

kol|la|ge̱n ‹griech.› (*Med., Biol.* aus Kollagenen bestehend); **Kol|la|ge̱n,** das; -s, -e (leimartiges Eiweiß des Bindegewebes)

Ko̱l|laps [*auch* kɔ'laps], der; -es, -e ‹lat.› (plötzlicher Schwächeanfall durch Kreislaufversagen)

Kol|la̱r, das; -s, -e ‹lat.› (steifer Halskragen, bes. des kath. Geistlichen)

kol|la|te|ra̱l ‹lat.› (seitlich gelagert; *fachspr. für* nebenständig)

Kol|la|ti|o̱n, die; -, -en ‹lat.› ([Text]vergleich; Übertragung eines kirchl. Amtes); **kol|la|ti|o|ni̱e|ren** ([Abschrift mit der Urschrift] vergleichen); **Kol|la|tu̱r,** die; -, -en (Recht zur Verleihung eines Kirchenamtes)

Kol|lau|da|ti|o̱n, die; -, -en ‹lat.› (*schweiz. neben* Kollaudierung); **kol|lau|di̱e|ren; Kol|lau|di̱e|rung** (*österr. u. schweiz. für* amtl. Prüfung eines Bauwerkes, Schlussgenehmigung)

[1]**Kol|le̱g,** das; -s, *Plur.* -s *u.* -ien [...i̯ən] ‹lat.› (akadem. Vorlesung; Bildungseinrichtung); [2]**Ko̱l|leg,** das; -s, -s (*österr. für* Lehrgang, Kurzstudium nach dem Abitur); **Kol|le̱|ge,** der; -n, -n; ↑R 126 (*Abk.* Koll.); **Kol|le̱|gen|kreis; Kol|le̱|gen|schaft,** die; -; **Kol|le̱g|heft** (Vorlesungsheft); **kol|le|gi|a̱l** (einem [guten] Verhältnis zwischen Kollegen entsprechend); **Kol|le|gi|a|li|tä̱t,** die; -; **Kol|le|gi|a̱t,** der; -en, -en; ↑R 126 (Stiftsgenosse; Teilnehmer an einem [Funk]kolleg); **Kol|le̱|gin** (*Abk.* Kolln.); **Kol|le̱|gi|um,** das; -s, ...ien [...i̯ən] (Gruppe von Personen mit gleichem Amt od. Beruf; Lehrkörper [einer Schule]); **Kol|le̱|gi|ums|mit|glied; Kol|le̱g|map|pe**

Kol|lek|ta|ne̱|en [*auch* ...'ta:neən] *Plur.* ‹lat.› (*veraltet für* gesammelte literar. u. wissenschaftl. Auszüge); **Kol|le̱k|te,** die; -, -n (Sammlung von Geldspenden in der Kirche; liturg. Gebet); **Kol|lek|ti|o̱n,** die; -, -en ([Muster]sammlung [von Waren], Auswahl); **kol|lek|ti̱v** (gemeinschaftlich, gruppenweise, umfassend); **Kol|lek|ti̱v,** das; -s, *Plur.* -e [...və], *auch* -s (Team, Gruppe; Arbeits- u. Produktionsgemeinschaft, bes. in der sozialist. Wirtschaft); **Kol|lek|ti̱v‿ar|beit, ...be|wusst|sein, ...ei|gen|tum; kol|lek|ti|vi̱e|ren** [...v...] (Kollektivwirtschaften bilden, Privateigentum in Gemeineigentum überführen); **Kol|lek|ti|vi̱e|rung; Kol|lek|ti|vi̱s|mus,** der; - (starke Betonung des gesellschaftl. Ganzen im Gegensatz zum Individualismus); **Kol|lek|ti|vi̱st,** der; -en, -en; ↑R 126 (Anhänger des Kollektivismus); **kol|lek|ti|vi̱s|tisch; Kol|lek|ti|vi|tä̱t,** die; - (Gemeinschaft[lichkeit]); **Kol|lek|ti̱v‿no|te** (gemeinsame diplomatische Note), **...schuld, ...stra|fe; ...suf|fix** *(Sprachw.)*, **Kol|lek|ti̱|vum** [...vum], das; -s, ...va (*Sprachw.* Sammelbezeichnung, z. B. „Wald", „Gebirge"); **Kol|lek|ti̱v‿ver|trag, ...wirt|schaft; Kol|le̱k|tor,** der; -s, ...o̱ren (Stromabnehmer, -wender; Sammler für Strahlungsenergie); **Kol|lek|tu̱r,** die; -, -en (*österr. für* Lottogeschäftsstelle)

Kol|len|chy̱m [...ç...] (↑R 132), das; -s, -e ‹griech.› (*Bot.* pflanzl. Festigungsgewebe)

[1]**Ko̱l|ler,** das; -s, - (Schulterpasse; *veraltet, aber noch landsch. für* [breiter] Kragen; Wams)

[2]**Ko̱l|ler,** der; -s, - (eine Pferdekrankheit; *ugs. für* Wutausbruch)

Ko̱l|ler|gang, der (Mahlwerk)

ko̱l|le|rig, ko̱ll|rig (*ugs. für* leicht aufbrausend, erregbar); [1]**ko̱l|lern** (*veraltet für* den [2]Koller haben; knurrig sein); ich ...ere (↑R 16)

[2]**ko̱l|lern** (*landsch. für* kullern); ich ...ere (↑R 16)

Kol|le̱tt, das; -s, -e ‹franz.› (*veraltet für* Reitjacke)

[1]**Ko̱l|li** (*Plur. von* Kollo); [2]**Ko̱l|li,** das; -s, -[s] (*österr. für* Kollo)

kol|li|di̱e|ren ‹lat.› (zusammenstoßen; sich überschneiden)

Kol|li|er [kɔ'li̯e:], das; -s, -s ‹franz.› (ein Halsschmuck)

Kol|li|ma|ti|o̱n, die; -, -en ‹nlat.› (*fachspr.* Zusammenfallen zweier Linien, z. B. bei Einstellung des Fernrohrs); **Kol|li|ma|ti|o̱ns|feh|ler; Kol|li|ma̱|tor,** der; -s, ...o̱ren (astron. Hilfsfernrohr; Spaltrohr beim Spektralapparat)

Kol|li|si|o̱n, die; -, -en ‹lat.› (Zusammenstoß); **Kol|li|si|o̱ns|kurs,** der; -es; auf - gehen

Kolln. = Kollegin, Kollegen *(Plur.)*

Ko̱l|lo, das; -s, *Plur.* -s *u.* Kolli ‹ital.› (Frachtstück, Warenballen); *vgl.* Kolli

Kol|lo̱|di|um, das; -s ‹griech.› (eine klebrige, zähflüssige Zelluloselösung); **kol|lo|i̱d,** kol|lo|i|da̱l (*Chemie* fein zerteilt); **Kol|lo|i̱d,** das; -[e]s, -e (*Chemie* fein zerteilter Stoff [in Wasser od. Gas]); **Kol|lo|i̱d‿che|mie, ...re|ak|ti|o̱n**

Kol|lo|qui|um [*auch* ...'lo:...], das; -s, ...ien [...i̯ən] ‹lat.› (wissenschaftl. Gespräch; Zusammenkunft von Wissenschaftlern; *bes. österr.* kleinere Prüfung an Universitäten)

kol|rig *vgl.* kollerig

kol|lu|die|ren ‹lat.› (*Rechtsspr.* im geheimen Einverständnis stehen); **Kol|lu|si|on,** die; -, -en (Verschleierung einer Straftat; unerlaubte Verabredung)

Koll|witz (dt. Malerin u. Grafikerin)

Kolm, der; -[e]s, -e (*svw.* [1]Kulm)

kol|ma|tie|ren ‹franz.› (*fachspr. für* [Sumpfboden u. Ä.] aufhöhen); **Kol|ma|ti|on,** die; -, -en

Köln (Stadt am Rhein); **Köl|ner** (↑R 103); Kölner Messe; **Köl|ner Braun,** das; - -s (Umbra); **köl|nisch;** -es Wesen, kölnisch[es] Wasser; **Köl|nisch|braun** (Umbra); **Köl|nisch|was|ser** [*auch* ...'vasər], das; -s

Ko|lo|fo|ni|um *eindeutschende Schreibung für* Kolophonium

Ko|lo|man [*auch* 'kɔ...] (m. Vorn.)

Ko|lom|bi|ne, Ko|lum|bi|ne, die; -, -n ‹ital., „Täubchen"› (w. Hauptrolle des ital. Stegreiftheaters)

Ko|lom|bo|wur|zel ‹Bantuspr.; dt.› (ein Heilmittel)

Ko|lon, das; -s, *Plur.* -s *u.* Kola ‹griech.› (*veraltet für* Doppelpunkt; *Med.* Grimmdarm)

Ko|lo|nat, das, *auch* der; -[e]s, -e ‹lat.› (Rechtsverhältnis der Kolonen im alten Rom; Erbzinsgut); **Ko|lo|ne,** der; -n, -n; ↑R 126 (persönl. freier, aber an seinen Landbesitz gebundener Pächter in der röm. Kaiserzeit; Erbzinsbauer)

Ko|lo|nel, die; - ‹franz.› (*Druckw.* ein Schriftgrad)

Ko|lo|ni|a|kü|bel *vgl.* Coloniakübel

ko|lo|ni|al ‹lat.› (die Kolonie[n] betreffend; zu Kolonien gehörend; aus Kolonien stammend); **Ko|lo|ni|al‿ge|biet, ...herr|schaft** (die; -); **Ko|lo|ni|a|lis|mus,** der; - (auf Erwerb u. Ausbau von Kolonien ausgerichtete Politik eines Staates); **Ko|lo|ni|a|list,** der; -en, -en; ↑R 126 (Anhänger des Kolonialismus); **Ko|lo|ni|al‿krieg, ...po|li|tik, ...stil** (der; -s), **...wa|ren** *(Plur.; veraltend);* **Ko|lo|nie,** die; -, ...i̯en (auswärtige, bes. überseeische Besitzung eines Staates; Siedlung); **Ko|lo|ni|sa|ti|on,** die; -, -en; **Ko|lo|ni|sa|tor,** der; -s, ...oren; **ko|lo|ni|sa|to|risch; ko|lo|ni|sie|ren; Ko|lo|ni|sie|rung; Ko|lo|nist,** der; -en, -en; ↑R 126 (Ansiedler in einer Kolonie)

Ko|lon|na|de, die; -, -n ‹franz.› (Säulengang, -halle); **Ko|lon|ne,** die; -, -n; die fünfte - (Sabotage- u. Spionagetrupp); **Ko|lon|nen‿ap|pa|rat** (Destillierapparat), **...fah|ren** (das; -s), **...schrift** (z. B. das Chinesische), **...sprin|ger** (*ugs. für* in einer Kolonne ständig überholender Autofahrer)

[1]Ko|lo|phon, der; -s, -e ‹griech.› (Schlussformel mittelalterlicher Handschriften u. Frühdrucke mit Angabe über Verfasser, Druckort u. Druckjahr); **[2]Ko|lo|phon** (altgriech. Stadt in Lydien); **Ko|lo|pho|ni|um** (↑R 33), das; -s ‹nach der altgriech. Stadt Kolophon› (ein Harzprodukt)

Ko|lo|quin|te, die; -, -n ‹lat.› (Frucht einer subtrop. Kürbispflanze)

Ko|lo|ra|do|kä|fer ‹nach dem Staat Colorado in den USA› (Kartoffelkäfer); ↑R 105

Ko|lo|ra|tur, die; -, -en ‹ital.› (virtuose gesangl. Verzierung); **ko|lo|ra|tu|ren|si|cher** *(Musik);* **Ko|lo|ra|tur‿sän|ge|rin, ...sop|ran; ko|lo|rie|ren** (färben; aus-, bemalen); **Ko|lo|rie|rung; Ko|lo|ri|me|ter,** das; -s, - ‹lat.; griech.› (Gerät zur Bestimmung von Farbtönen); **Ko|lo|ri|met|rie** (↑R 130), die; -; **ko|lo|ri|met|risch; Ko|lo|rist,** der; -en, -en (↑R 126) ‹lat.› (jmd., der koloriert; Maler, der den Schwerpunkt auf das Kolorit legt); **ko|lo|ris|tisch; Ko|lo|rit** [*auch* ...'rit], das; -[e]s, *Plur.* -e, *auch* -s ‹ital.› (Farbgebung, -wirkung; Klangfarbe)

Ko|lo|skop, das; -s, -e ‹griech.› (*Med.* Gerät zur direkten Untersuchung des Grimmdarms)

Ko|loss [*auch* 'kɔ...], der; -es, -e ‹griech.› (Riesenstandbild; Riese, Ungetüm)

Ko|los|sä (im Altertum Stadt in Phrygien)

ko|los|sal ‹franz.› (riesig, gewaltig, Riesen...; übergroß); **Ko|los|sal‿bau** (*Plur.* ...bauten), **...fi|gur, ...film, ...ge|mäl|de; ko|los|sa|lisch** (*geh. für* kolossal); **Ko|los|sal|sta|tue**

Ko|los|ser (Einwohner von Kolossä); **Ko|los|ser|brief,** der; -[e]s *(N.T.)*

Ko|los|se|um, das; -s (Amphitheater in Rom)

Ko|lost|ral|milch (↑R 130), die; - ‹lat.; dt.› *u.* **Ko|lost|rum,** das; -s ‹lat.› (*Med.* Sekret der Brustdrüsen)

Ko|lo|to|mie, die; -, ...i̯en ‹griech.› (*Med.* operative Öffnung des Dickdarms)

Kol|pak *vgl.* Kalpak

Kol|ping (kath. Priester); **Kol|ping‿haus, ...ju|gend; Kol|pings|fa|mi|lie; Kol|ping|werk,** das; -[e]s (internationaler kath. Sozialverband)

Kol|pi|tis, die; -, ...iti̯den ‹griech.› (*Med.* Scheidenentzündung)

Kol|por|ta|ge [...'ta:ʒə, *österr.* ...'ta:ʒ], die; -, -n [...'ta:ʒ(ə)n] ‹franz.› (Verbreitung von Gerüchten); **kol|por|ta|ge|haft; Kol|por|ta|ge‿li|te|ra|tur, ...roman; Kol|por|teur** [...'tø:r], der; -s, -e (Verbreiter von Gerüchten); **kol|por|tie|ren**

Kol|po|skop, das; -s, -e ‹griech.› (*Med.* Spiegelgerät zur gynäkolog. Untersuchung); **Kol|po|sko|pie,** die; -, ...i̯en

[1]Kölsch, das; -[s] ‹„aus Köln, kölnisch"› (ein obergäriges Bier; Kölner Mundart); **[2]Kölsch,** der; -[e]s (*schweiz. für* gewürfelter Baumwollstoff)

[1]Kol|ter, der; -s, - *u.* die; -, -n ‹franz.› (*südwestd. für* Wolldecke, Steppdecke)

[2]Kol|ter, das; -s, - ‹franz.› (*bes. nordwestd. für* Messer vor der Pflugschar)

Ko|lum|ba|ri|um, das; -s, ...ien [...i̯ən] ‹lat.› (altröm. Grabkammer; *heute für* Urnenhalle eines Friedhofs)

Ko|lum|bi|a|ner, *auch* Ko|lum|bi|er; **Ko|lum|bi|a|ne|rin,** *auch* Ko|lum|bi|e|rin; **ko|lum|bi|a|nisch,** *auch* ko|lum|bisch; **Ko|lum|bi|en** (Staat in Südamerika); **Ko|lum|bi|er** usw. *vgl.* Kolumbianer usw.

Ko|lum|bi|ne *vgl.* Kolombine

ko|lum|bisch *vgl.* kolumbianisch

Ko|lum|bus (Entdecker Amerikas)

Ko|lum|ne, die; -, -n ‹lat., „Säule"› (senkrechte Reihe; [Druck]spalte); **Ko|lum|nen‿maß** (das), **...ti|tel; ko|lum|nen|wei|se** ([druck]spaltenweise); **Ko|lum|nist,** der; -en, -en; ↑R 126 (Journalist, dem ständig eine bestimmte Spalte einer Zeitung zur Verfügung steht); **Ko|lum|nis|tin**

Köm, der; -s, -s (*nordd. für* Kümmelschnaps); 3 Köm (↑R 90)

Ko|ma, das; -s, *Plur.* -s *u.* -ta ‹griech.› (*Med.* tiefe Bewusstlosigkeit)

Ko|man|tsche, der; -n, -n; ↑R 126 (Angehöriger eines nordamerik. Indianerstammes)

ko|ma|tös (in tiefer Bewusstlosigkeit befindlich); -er Zustand

Kom|bat|tant, der; -en, -en (↑R 126) ‹franz.› (*Rechtsspr. u. veraltet für* [Mit]kämpfer; Kriegsteilnehmer)

Kom|bi, der; -[s], -s (*kurz für* kombinierter Liefer- u. Personenwagen); **Kom|bi...** (kombiniert); **Kom|bi|nat**, das; -[e]s, -e ‹russ.› (Zusammenschluss produktionsmäßig eng zusammengehörender Betriebe in [den ehem.] sozialist. Staaten); **¹Kom|bi|na|ti|on**, die; -, -en ‹lat.› (berechnende Verbindung; gedankliche Folgerung; Zusammenstellung von sportl. Disziplinen, Farben u. a.; *Sport* planmäßiges, flüssiges Zusammenspiel); **²Kom|bi|na|ti|on** [*auch* ...'ne:ʃ(ə)n], die; -, *Plur.* -en, *bei engl. Ausspr.* -s ‹engl.› (Hemdhose; einteiliger [Schutz]anzug, bes. der Flieger); **Kom|bi|na|ti|ons‿ga|be** (die; -), **...schloss, ...spiel, ...ver|mö|gen** (das; -s); **kom|bi|na|to|risch** ‹lat.›; -er Lautwandel *(Sprachw.)*; **Kombine** [...'bain], die; -, -s, *auch* [...'bi:nə], die; -, -n *u.* Com|bine [kɔm'bain], die; -, -s ‹engl.› (landwirtschaftl. Maschine, die verschiedene Arbeitsgänge gleichzeitig ausführt; Mähdrescher); **kom|bi|nier|bar; kom|bi|nie|ren** ‹lat.› (vereinigen, zusammenstellen; berechnen; vermuten; *Sport* planmäßig zusammenspielen); **Kom|bi|nier|te**, der; -n, -n; ↑R 5 ff. (*Skisport* Teilnehmer an der nordischen Kombination); **Kom|bi|nie|rung; Kom|bi‿schrank, ...wa|gen, ...zan|ge**

Kom|bü|se, die; -, -n (*Seemannsspr.* Schiffsküche)

Ko|me|do (↑R 132), der; -s, ...onen ‹lat.› (*veraltet für* Fresser, Schlemmer; *Med., meist Plur.* Mitesser)

Ko|met, der; -en, -en (↑R 126) ‹griech.› (Schweifstern); **Ko|me|ten|bahn; ko|me|ten|haft; Ko|me|ten|schweif**

Kö|me|te|ri|on *vgl.* Zömeterium

Kom|fort [...'fo:r], der; -s ‹engl.› (Bequemlichkeiten, Annehmlichkeiten; Ausstattung mit einem gewissen Luxus); **kom|for|ta|bel**; ...ab|le (↑R 130) Wohnung

Ko|mik, die; - ‹griech.› (erheiternde, Lachen erregende Wirkung); **Ko|mi|ker; Ko|mi|ke|rin**

Kom|in|form, das; -s (= Kommunistisches Informationsbüro, 1947 bis 1956)

Kom|in|tern, die; - (= Kommunistische Internationale, 1919 bis 1943)

ko|misch ‹griech.› (belustigend, zum Lachen reizend; sonderbar, wunderlich, seltsam); **ko|mi|scher|wei|se**

Ko|mi|tat, das, *auch* der; -[e]s, -e ‹lat.› (*früher* feierliches Geleit, Ehrengeleit; Grafschaft; ehem. Verwaltungsbezirk in Ungarn)

Ko|mi|tee, das; -s, -s ‹franz.› (leitender Ausschuss)

Ko|mi|ti|en [...iən] *Plur.* ‹lat.› (altröm. Bürgerversammlungen)

Kom|ma, das; -s, *Plur.* -s, *auch* -ta ‹griech.› (Beistrich); **Kom|ma|ba|zil|lus** *(Med.)*

Kom|man|dant, der; -en, -en (↑R 126) ‹franz.› (Befehlshaber einer Festung, eines Schiffes usw.; *schweiz. auch svw.* Kommandeur); **Kom|man|dan|tur**, die; -, -en ‹lat.› (Dienstgebäude eines Kommandanten; Amt des Befehlshabers); **Kom|man|deur** [...'dø:r], der; -s, -e ‹franz.› (Befehlshaber eines größeren Truppenteils); **kom|man|die|ren**; (↑R 108:) der Kommandierende General (eines Armeekorps); **Kom|man|die|rung**

Kom|man|di|tär, der; -s, -e ‹franz.› (*schweiz. für* Kommanditist); **Kom|man|di|te**, die; -, -n (Zweiggeschäft, Nebenstelle; *veraltet für* Kommanditgesellschaft); **Kom|man|dit|ge|sell|schaft** (bestimmte Form der Handelsgesellschaft; *Abk.* KG); - auf Aktien (*Abk.* KGaA); **Kom|man|di|tist**, der; -en, -en; ↑R 126 (Gesellschafter einer Kommanditgesellschaft, dessen Haftung auf seine Einlage beschränkt ist)

Kom|man|do, das; -s, *Plur.* -s, *österr. auch* ...den ‹ital.› (Befehl; *Milit.* Einheit, Dienststelle; *nur Sing.:* Befehlsgewalt); **Kom|man|do‿brü|cke, ...ge|walt** (die; -), **...kap|sel** *(Raumfahrt)*; **Kom|man|do|sa|che**; geheime -; **Kom|man|do‿stand, ...stim|me, ...strich** (*svw.* Spiegelstrich), **...zent|ra|le**

Kom|mas|sa|ti|on, die; -, -en ‹lat.› (*fachspr. für* Zusammenlegung [von Grundstücken]); **kom|mas|sie|ren; Kom|mas|sie|rung** (*bes. österr. für* Kommassation)

Kom|ma|ta (*Plur. von* Komma)

Kom|me|mo|ra|ti|on, die; -, -en ‹lat.› (Fürbitte in der kath. Messe; kirchl. Gedächtnisfeier)

kom|men; du kamst; du kämest; gekommen; komm[e]!; kommen lassen; **Kom|men**, das; -s; wir warten auf sein Kommen; das Kommen und Gehen; im Kommen sein

Kom|men|de, die; -, -n ‹lat.› (*früher* kirchl. Pfründe ohne Amtsverpflichtung; Komturei)

Kom|men|sa|lis|mus, der; - ‹lat.› (*Biol.* Ernährungsgemeinschaft von Tieren od. Pflanzen)

kom|men|su|ra|bel ‹lat.› (mit gleichem Maß messbar; vergleichbar); ...ab|le (↑R 130) Größen; **Kom|men|su|ra|bi|li|tät**, die; -

Kom|ment [...'mã:], der; -s, -s ‹franz., „wie"› (*Studentenspr.* Brauch, Sitte, Regel)

Kom|men|tar, der; -s, -e ‹lat.› (Erläuterung, Auslegung; kritische Stellungnahme; *ugs. für* Bemerkung); **kom|men|tar|los; Kom|men|ta|tor**, der; -s, ...oren (Verfasser eines Kommentars; Journalist o. Ä., der regelmäßig kommentiert); **Kom|men|ta|to|rin; kom|men|tie|ren; Kom|men|tie|rung**

Kom|mers, der; -es, -e ‹franz.› (*Studentenspr.* feierlicher Trinkabend); **Kom|mers|buch** (student. Liederbuch)

Kom|merz, der; -es ‹lat.› (Wirtschaft, Handel u. Geschäftsverkehr); **Kom|merz|fern|se|hen** (*meist abwertend für* Privatfernsehen); **kom|mer|zi|a|li|sie|ren** (kommerziellen Interessen unterordnen; *Finanzw.* öffentliche Schulden in privatwirtschaftliche umwandeln); **Kom|mer|zi|a|li|sie|rung; Kom|mer|zi|al|rat** *Plur.* ...räte (*österr. für* Kommerzienrat); **kom|mer|zi|ell** (auf den Kommerz bezüglich); **Kom|mer|zi|en|rat** *Plur.* ...räte (*früher* Titel für Großkaufleute u. Industrielle)

Kom|mi|li|to|ne, der; -n, -n (↑R 126) ‹lat.› (*Studentenspr.* Studienkollege); **Kom|mi|li|to|nin**

Kom|mis [kɔ'mi:], der; - [kɔ'mi:(s)], - [kɔ'mi:s] ‹franz.› (*veraltet für* Handlungsgehilfe); **Kom|miss**, der; -es ‹lat.› (*ugs. für* Militär[dienst]); beim -; **Kom|mis|sar**, der; -s, -e ([vom Staat] Beauftragter; Dienstbez., z. B. Polizeikommissar); **Kom|mis|sär**, der; -s, -e ‹franz.› (*südd., schweiz., österr. für* Kommissar); **Kom|mis|sa|ri|at**, das; -[e]s, -e ‹lat.› (Amt[szimmer] eines Kommissars; *österr. für* Polizeidienststelle); **kom|mis|sa|risch** (beauftragt; auftragsweise, vorübergehend); kommissarischer Leiter; kommissarische Vernehmung *(Rechtsspr.)*; **Kom|miss|brot; Kom|mis|si|on**, die; -, -en (Ausschuss [von Beauftragten]; *Wirtsch.* Handel für fremde Rechnung); **Kom|mis|si|o|när**, der; -s, -e ‹franz.› (Händler auf fremde Rechnung; Kommissionsbuchhändler); **kom|mis|si|o|nie|ren** ‹lat.› (*österr. für* [einen Neubau] prüfen und zur Benutzung freigeben); **Kom|mis|si|ons⌣buch|han|del** (Zwischenbuchhandel [zwischen Verlag u. Sortiment]), **...ge|schäft** (Geschäft im eigenen Namen für fremde Rechnung), **...gut** (Ware, für die der Besteller ein Rückgaberecht hat), **...sen|dung** (Sendung von Kommissionsgut); **Kom|miss⌣stie|fel** (↑R 136; *veraltend*), **...zeit** *(veraltend);* **Kom|mit|tent,** der; -en, -en; ↑R 126 (Auftraggeber des Kommissionärs); **kom|mit|tie|ren** (beauftragen, [einen Kommissionär] bevollmächtigen)

kom|mod ‹franz.› (*bes. österr. für* bequem); **Kom|mo|de,** die; -, -n; **Kom|mo|den|schub|la|de;** **Kom|mo|di|tät,** die; -, -en (*veraltet, noch landsch. für* Bequemlichkeit)

Kom|mo|do|re, der; -s, *Plur.* -n *u.* -s ‹engl.› (Geschwaderführer; erprobter, älterer Kapitän bei großen Schifffahrtslinien)

kom|mun ‹lat.› (*veraltend für* gemeinschaftlich; gemein); **kom|mu|nal** (die Gemeinde[n] betreffend, Gemeinde..., gemeindeeigen); kommunale Angelegenheiten; **Kom|mu|nal⌣be|am|te,** **...be|hör|de;** **kom|mu|na|li|sie|ren** (in Gemeindebesitz od. -verwaltung überführen); **Kom|mu|na|li|sie|rung;** **Kom|mu|nal⌣po|li|tik,** **...ver|wal|tung,** **...wahl;** **Kom|mu|nar|de,** der; -n, -n (↑R 126) ‹franz.› (Anhänger der Pariser Kommune; Mitglied einer der frühen [Berliner] Wohngemeinschaften); **Kom|mu|ne,** die; -, -n (politische Gemeinde; Wohn- und Wirtschaftsgemeinschaft; *veraltend, abwertend für* Kommunisten; [*auch* kɔ'my:n(ə)] *nur Sing.:* Herrschaft des Pariser Gemeinderates 1789–1795 und 1871); **Kom|mu|ni|kant,** der; -en, -en (↑R 126) ‹lat.› (Teilnehmer am Abendmahl); **Kom|mu|ni|kan|tin;** **Kom|mu|ni|ka|ti|on,** die; -, -en (Verständigung untereinander; Verbindung, Zusammenhang); **Kom|mu|ni|ka|ti|ons⌣mit|tel** (das), **...stö|rung,** **...sys|tem,** **...tech|nik;** **kom|mu|ni|ka|ti|ons|tech|nisch;** **Kom|mu|ni|ka|ti|ons⌣tech|no|lo|gie,** **...zent|rum;** **kom|mu|ni|ka|tiv** (mitteilsam; die Kommunikation betreffend); **Kom|mu|ni|kee** *vgl.* Kommuniqué; **Kom|mu|ni|on,** die; -, -en (*kath. Kirche* [Teilnahme am] Abendmahl); **Kom|mu|ni|on⌣bank** (*Plur.* ...bänke), **...kind** (Erstkommunikant[in]); **Kom|mu|ni|qué** [...myni'ke:, ...mu...], *auch* Kom|mu|ni|kee (↑R 33), das; -s, -s ‹franz.› (Denkschrift; [regierungs]amtliche Mitteilung); **Kom|mu|nis|mus,** der; - (nach Karl Marx die auf den Sozialismus folgende, von Klassengegensätzen freie Entwicklungsstufe der Gesellschaft; politische Richtung, die sich gegen den Kapitalismus wendet und für eine zentral gelenkte Wirtschafts- und Sozialordnung eintritt); **Kom|mu|nist,** der; -en, -en (↑R 126); **Kom|mu|nis|tin;** **kom|mu|nis|tisch;** (↑R 108:) das Kommunistische Manifest; **Kom|mu|ni|tät,** die; -, -en ‹lat.› (ev. Bruderschaft; *veraltet für* Gemeinschaft; Gemeingut); **kom|mu|ni|zie|ren** (zusammenhängen, in Verbindung stehen; miteinander sprechen, sich verständigen; *kath. Kirche* die Kommunion empfangen); **kom|mu|ni|zie|rend;** -e (verbundene) Röhren

kom|mu|ta|bel ‹lat.› (veränderlich, vertauschbar); ...ab|le (↑R 130) Objekte; **Kom|mu|ta|ti|on,** die; -, -en (*bes. Math.* Umstellbarkeit, Vertauschbarkeit; bestimmter astron. Winkel); **kom|mu|ta|tiv** (vertauschbar); -e Gruppe; **Kom|mu|ta|tor,** der; -s, ...oren (*Technik* Stromwender, Kollektor); **kom|mu|tie|ren** (vertauschen; die Richtung des Stroms ändern); **Kom|mu|tie|rung**

Ko|mö|di|ant, der; -en, -en (↑R 126) ‹ital.(-engl.)› (Schauspieler; *auch für* jmd., der sich verstellt); **ko|mö|di|an|ten|haft;** **Ko|mö|di|an|ten|tum,** das; -s; **Ko|mö|di|an|tin;** **ko|mö|di|an|tisch;** **Ko|mö|die** [...iə], die; -, -n (Lustspiel; *auch für* Vortäuschung, Verstellung); **Ko|mö|di|en⌣dich|ter,** **...schrei|ber**

Ko|mo|ren *Plur.* (Inselgruppe u. Staat im Indischen Ozean); **Ko|mo|rer;** **ko|mo|risch**

Komp., Co., Co = Kompanie

Kom|pag|non ['kɔmpanjõ, *auch* ...'njõ:] (↑R 130), der; -s, -s ‹franz.› (*Kaufmannsspr.* [Geschäfts]teilhaber; Mitinhaber)

kom|pakt ‹franz.› (gedrungen; dicht, konzentriert; fest); **Kom|pakt|bau|wei|se;** **Kom|pakt|heit,** die; -; **Kom|pakt|schall|plat|te** (Schallplatte, die mithilfe eines Laserstrahls abgespielt wird); **Kom|pakt|se|mi|nar** (auf wenige Tage od. Stunden konzentrierte Lehr- od. Informationsveranstaltung)

Kom|pa|nie, die; -, ...ien ‹ital. *u.* franz.› (militärische Einheit [*Abk.* Komp.]; *Kaufmannsspr. veraltet für* [Handels]gesellschaft; *Abk. in Firmen* Co. *od.* Co, *seltener* Cie.); **Kom|pa|nie⌣chef,** **...füh|rer,** **...ge|schäft**

kom|pa|ra|bel ‹lat.› (vergleichbar; *Sprachw.* steigerungsfähig); ...able (↑R 130) Größen; **Kom|pa|ra|ti|on,** die; -, -en (*Sprachw.* Steigerung); **Kom|pa|ra|tis|tik,** die; - (vergleichende Literatur- od. Sprachwissenschaft); **Kom|pa|ra|tiv,** der; -s, -e [...və] (*Sprachw.* erste Steigerungsstufe, z. B. „schöner"); **Kom|pa|ra|tiv|satz** (*Sprachw.* Vergleichssatz); **Kom|pa|ra|tor,** der; -s, ...oren (Gerät zum Vergleichen von Längenmaßen); **kom|pa|rie|ren** (vergleichen; *Sprachw.* steigern)

Kom|par|se, der; -n, -n (↑R 126) ‹franz.› (Statist, stumme Person [bei Bühne und Film]); **Kom|par|se|rie,** die; -, ...ien (Gesamtheit der Komparsen); **Kom|par|sin**

Kom|pass, der; -es, -e ‹ital.› (Gerät zur Bestimmung der Himmelsrichtung); **Kom|pass⌣na|del,** **...ro|se**

kom|pa|ti|bel ‹franz.(-engl.)› (vereinbar, zusammenpassend, kombinierbar); ...ib|le (↑R 130) Ämter; **Kom|pa|ti|bi|li|tät,** die; -, -en (Vereinbarkeit [zweier Ämter in einer Person]; Kombinierbarkeit [verschiedener Computersysteme])

Kom|pat|ri|ot, der; -en, -en (↑R 126) ‹franz.› (*veraltet für* Landsmann)

kom|pen|di|a|risch, **kom|pen|di|ös** ‹lat.› (*veraltet für* zusammengefasst; gedrängt); **Kom|pen|di|um,** das; -s, ...ien [...iən] (Abriss, kurzes Lehrbuch)

Kom|pen|sa|ti|on, die; -, -en ‹lat.› (Ausgleich, Entschädigung; *BGB* Aufrechnung); **Kom|pen|sa|ti|ons|ge|schäft;** **Kom|pen|sa|tor,** der; -s, ...oren (Ausgleicher; Gerät zur Messung einer Spannung); **kom|pen|sa|to|risch** (ausgleichend); **kom|pen|sie|ren** (gegeneinander ausgleichen; *BGB* aufrechnen)

kom|pe|tent ‹lat.› (sachverständig; befähigt; zuständig, maßgebend, befugt); **Kom|pe|tenz,** die; -, -en (Sachverstand, Fähigkeiten; Zuständigkeit; *Sprachw., nur Sing.* Beherrschung eines Sprachsystems); **Kom|pe|tenz⌣be|reich** (der), **...fra|ge,** **...kom|pe|tenz** (*Rechtsspr.* Befugnis zur Bestimmung der Zuständigkeit), **...kon|flikt,** **...strei|tig|keit** *(meist Plur.)*

Kom|pi|la|ti|on, die; -, -en ‹lat.› (das Zusammentragen mehrerer [wissenschaftl.] Quellen; durch Zusammentragen entstandene Schrift [ohne wissenschaftl. Wert]); **Kom|pi|la|tor,** der; -s, ...oren (Zusammenträger); **kom|pi|la|to|risch; kom|pi|lie|ren**

Kom|ple|ment, das; -[e]s, -e ‹lat.› (Ergänzung); **kom|ple|men|tär** ‹franz.› (ergänzend); **Kom|ple|men|tär,** der; -s, -e (persönlich haftender Gesellschafter einer Kommanditgesellschaft; *ehem. in der DDR* Eigentümer einer privaten Firma, an der der Staat beteiligt ist); **Kom|ple|men|tär|far|be** (*Optik* Ergänzungsfarbe); **kom|ple|men|tie|ren** (ergänzen, vervollständigen); **Kom|ple|men|tie|rung; Kom|ple|ment|win|kel** (*Math.* Ergänzungswinkel); **¹Kom|plet** [kɔmˈpleː, *auch* kɔ̃ˈpleː], das; -[s], -s (Mantel [od. Jacke] u. Kleid aus gleichem Stoff); **²Kom|plet,** die; -, -e ‹lat.› (Abendgebet als Schluss der kath. kirchl. Tageszeiten); **kom|plett** ‹franz.› (vollständig, abgeschlossen; *österr. auch für* voll besetzt); **kom|plet|tie|ren** (vervollständigen; auffüllen); **Kom|plet|tie|rung; Kom|plett|preis** *(bes. Werbespr.)*

kom|plex ‹lat.› (zusammengefasst, umfassend; vielfältig verflochten; *Math.* aus reellen u. imaginären Zahlen zusammengesetzt); **Kom|plex,** der; -es, -e (zusammengefasster Bereich; [Sach-, Gebäude]gruppe; *Psych.* seelisch bedrückende, negative Vorstellung [in Bezug auf sich selbst]); **Kom|plex|bri|ga|de** (*ehem. in der DDR* Arbeitsgruppe aus verschiedenen Berufen); **Kom|ple|xi|on,** die; -, -en (*veraltet für* Zusammenfassung); **Kom|ple|xi|tät,** die; -; **Kom|plex|ver|bin|dung** *(Chemie)*

Kom|pli|ce usw. *vgl.* Komplize usw.

Kom|pli|ka|ti|on, die; -, -en ‹lat.› (Verwicklung; Erschwerung); **kom|pli|ka|ti|ons|los**

Kom|pli|ment, das; -[e]s, -e ‹franz.› (lobende, schmeichelnde Äußerung; *veraltet für* Gruß); **kom|pli|men|tie|ren** (*geh. für* mit höflichen Gesten und Worten [ins Zimmer o. Ä.] geleiten)

Kom|pli|ze, *auch* Kom|pli|ce [...ˈpliː(t)sə], der; -n, -n (↑R 126) ‹franz.› (*abwertend für* Mitschuldiger; Mittäter); **Kom|pli|zen|schaft,** die; -

kom|pli|zie|ren ‹lat.› (verwickeln; erschweren); **kom|pli|ziert** (verwickelt, schwierig, umständlich); **Kom|pli|ziert|heit,** die; -; **Kom|pli|zie|rung**

Kom|pli|zin *(abwertend)*

Kom|plott, das, *ugs. auch* der; -[e]s, -e ‹franz.› (heimlicher Anschlag, Verschwörung); **kom|plot|tie|ren** *(veraltet)*

Kom|po|nen|te, die; -, -n ‹lat.› (Teilkraft; Bestandteil eines Ganzen); **kom|po|nie|ren** (*Musik* [eine Komposition] schaffen; *geh. für* [kunstvoll] gestalten); **Kom|po|nist,** der; -en, -en; ↑R 126 (jmd., der komponiert); **Kom|po|nis|tin; Kom|po|si|te,** die; -, -n *meist Plur.* (*Bot.* Korbblütler); **Kom|po|si|ti|on,** die; -, -en (Zusammensetzung; Aufbau u. Gestaltung eines Kunstwerkes; *Musik* das Komponieren; Tonschöpfung); **kom|po|si|to|risch; Kom|po|si|tum,** das; -s, *Plur.* ...ta, *selten* ...siten (*Sprachw.* [Wort]zusammensetzung, z. B. „Haustür"); **Kom|post** [*auch* ˈkɔm...], der; -[e]s, -e ‹franz.› (natürl. Mischdünger); **Kom|post‿er|de, ...hau|fen; kom|pos|tier|bar; kom|pos|tie|ren** (zu Kompost verarbeiten); **Kom|pos|tie|rung; Kom|pott,** das; -[e]s, -e (gekochtes Obst); **Kom|pott|tel|ler** (↑R 136)

kom|press ‹lat.› (*veraltet für* eng zusammengedrängt; *Druckw.* ohne Durchschuss); **Kom|pres|se,** die; -, -n ‹franz.› (*Med.* feuchter Umschlag; Mullstück); **kom|pres|si|bel** ‹lat.› (*Physik* zusammenpressbar; verdichtbar); ...ible (↑R 130) Flüssigkeiten; **Kom|pres|si|bi|li|tät,** die; - (*Physik* Zusammendrückbarkeit); **Kom|pres|si|on,** die; -, -en (*Technik* Zusammendrückung; Verdichtung; *Skisport* flacherer Teil einer Abfahrtsstrecke [nach einem Steilhang]); **Kom|pres|si|ons‿di|a|gramm** *(Kfz-Technik),* **...strumpf** *(Med.),* **...ver|band** *(Med.);* **Kom|pres|sor,** der; -s, ...oren (*Technik* Verdichter); **Kom|pri|mat,** das; -[e]s, -e (*fachspr. für* Zusammengefasstes, -gepresstes); **kom|pri|mier|bar; kom|pri|mie|ren** (zusammenpressen; verdichten); **kom|pri|miert; Kom|pri|mie|rung**

Kom|pro|miss, der, *selten* das; -es, -e ‹lat.› (Übereinkunft; Ausgleich, Zugeständnis); **kom|pro|miss|be|reit; Kom|pro|miss‿be|reit|schaft, ...kan|di|dat** *(Politik);* **Kom|pro|miss|ler** (*abwertend für* jmd., der dazu neigt, Kompromisse zu schließen); **kom|pro|miss|le|risch** *(abwertend);* **kom|pro|miss|los; Kom|pro|miss‿lö|sung, ...ver|such, ...vor|schlag; kom|pro|mit|tie|ren** (bloßstellen)

Komp|ta|bi|li|tät, die; - ‹franz.› (Verantwortlichkeit, Rechenschaftspflicht [von der Verwaltung öffentl. Stellen])

Kom|so|mol, der; - ‹russ.› (kommunist. Jugendorganisation in der ehem. UdSSR); **Kom|so|mol|ze,** der; -n, -n (Mitglied des Komsomol); **Kom|so|mol|zin**

Kom|tess *u.* **Kom|tes|se** [*auch* kɔ̃ˈtɛs], die; -, ...tessen ‹franz.› (unverheiratete Gräfin)

Kom|tur, der; -s, -e ‹franz.› (Ordensritter; Leiter einer Komturei); **Kom|tu|rei** (Verwaltungsbezirk eines Ritterordens); **Kom|tur|kreuz** (Halskreuz eines Verdienstordens)

Ko|nak, der; -s, -e ‹türk.› (Palast, Amtsgebäude in der Türkei)

Kon|au|tor *vgl.* Koautor

Kon|cha [...ça], die; -, *Plur.* -s *u.* ...chen ‹griech.› (*svw.* Konche; *Med.* muschelähnliches Organ); **Kon|che,** die; -, -n (*Archit.* Nischenwölbung); **Kon|chi|fe|re,** die; -, -n *meist Plur.* ‹griech.; lat.› (*Zool.* Weichtier mit einheitlicher Schale); **kon|chi|form** (muschelförmig); **Kon|cho|i|de,** die; -, -n ‹griech.› (*Math.* einer Muschel ähnliche Kurve vierten Grades); **Kon|chy|lie** [...i̯ə], die; -, -n *meist Plur.* (*Zool.* Schale der Weichtiere); **Kon|chy|li|o|lo|ge,** der; -n, -n (↑R 126); **Kon|chy|li|o|lo|gie,** die; - (Lehre von den Gehäusen der Konchylien)

Kon|dem|na|ti|on, die; -, -en ‹lat.› (*veraltet für* Verurteilung, Verdammung; *Seew.* Erklärung eines Experten, dass die Reparatur eines beschädigten Schiffes nicht mehr lohnt)

Kon|den|sat, das; -[e]s, -e ‹lat.› (Niederschlag[swasser]); **Kon|den|sa|ti|on,** die; -, -en (Verdichtung; Verflüssigung); **Kon|den|sa|ti|ons|punkt** *(Physik);* **Kon|den|sa|tor,** der; -s, ...oren (Gerät zum Speichern von Elektrizität od. zum Verflüssigen von Dämpfen); **kon|den|sie|ren** (verdichten, eindicken; verflüssigen); **Kon|den|sie|rung; Kon|dens|milch; Kon|den|sor,** der; -s, ...oren (*Optik* Lichtsammler, -verstärker); **Kon|dens‿strei|fen, ...was|ser** (das; -s)

Kon|dik|ti|on, die; -, -en ‹lat.› (*Rechtsw.* Klage auf Rückgabe)

kon|di|tern (Konditorwaren herstellen; *ugs. für* eine Konditorei besuchen); ich ...ere (↑R 16)
Kon|di|ti|on, die; -, -en ‹lat.› (Bedingung; *nur Sing.:* körperlicher Zustand); *vgl.* à condition; **kon|di|ti|o|nal** (*Sprachw.* bedingend); **Kon|di|ti|o|nal,** der; -s, -e (*Sprachw.* Bedingungsform); **Kon|di|ti|o|na|lis|mus,** der; - (eine philos. Lehre); **Kon|di|ti|o|nal|satz** (*Sprachw.* Bedingungssatz); **kon|di|ti|o|nie|ren** (Werkstoffe vor der Bearbeitung an die erforderlichen Bedingungen anpassen); **kon|di|ti|o|niert** (beschaffen [von Waren]); **Kon|di|ti|o|nie|rung; Kon|di|ti|ons‿schwä|che, ...trai|ner, ...trai|ning**
Kon|di|tor, der; -s, ...oren ‹lat.›; **Kon|di|to|rei; Kon|di|to|rin** [*auch* ...'dito...]; **Kon|di|tor|meis|ter**
Kon|do|lenz, die; -, -en ‹lat.› (Beileid[sbezeigung]); **Kon|do|lenz‿be|such, ...buch, ...kar|te, ...schrei|ben; kon|do|lie|ren;** jmdm. -
Kon|dom, das *od.* der; -s, *Plur.* -e, *selten* -s ‹engl.› (Präservativ)
Kon|do|mi|nat, das *od.* der; -[e]s, -e ‹lat.› *u.* **Kon|do|mi|ni|um,** das; -s, ...ien [...iən] (Herrschaft mehrerer Staaten über dasselbe Gebiet; *auch* dieses Gebiet selbst)
Kon|dor, der; -s, -e ‹indian.› (sehr großer südamerik. Geier)
Kon|dot|ti|e|re, der; -s, ...ri ‹ital.› (italien. Söldnerführer im 14. u. 15. Jh.)
Kon|du|ite [*auch* kɔ̃'dyi:t], die; - ‹franz.› (*veraltet für* Führung)
Kon|dukt, der; -[e]s, -e ‹lat.› (*veraltend für* [feierl.] Geleit, Leichenzug); **Kon|duk|teur** [...'tø:r, *schweiz.* 'kɔn...], der; -s, -e ‹franz.› (*schweiz., sonst veraltet für* Schaffner); **Kon|duk|tor,** der; -s, ...oren ‹lat.› ([elektr.] Leiter; *Med.* Überträger einer Erbkrankheit)
Kon|du|ran|go, die; -, -s ‹indian.› (südamerik. Kletterstrauch, dessen Rinde ein Magenmittel liefert); **Kon|du|ran|go|rin|de**
Kon|dy|lom, das; -s, -e ‹griech.› (*Med.* Feigwarze)
Ko|nen (*Plur. von* Konus)
Kon|fekt, das; -[e]s, -e ‹lat.› (Pralinen; *südd., schweiz., österr. auch für* Teegebäck); **Kon|fek|ti|on,** die; -, -en *Plur. selten* ‹franz.› (industrielle Anfertigung von Kleidung; [Handel mit] Fertigkleidung; Bekleidungsindustrie); **Kon|fek|ti|o|när,** der; -s, -e (Hersteller von Fertigkleidung; Unternehmer, Angestellter in der Konfektion); **Kon|fek|ti|o|neu|se** [...'nø:zə], die; -, -n ([leitende] Angestellte in der Konfektion); **kon|fek|ti|o|nie|ren** (fabrikmäßig herstellen); **Kon|fek|ti|o|nie|rung; Kon|fek|ti|ons‿an|zug, ...ge|schäft, ...grö|ße**
Kon|fe|renz, die; -, -en ‹lat.› (Besprechung; Zusammenkunft von Experten); **Kon|fe|renz‿be|schluss, ...pau|se, ...saal, ...schal|tung** *(Fernmeldetechnik),* **...sen|dung** *(Rundf.),* **...teil|neh|mer, ...tisch, ...zim|mer; kon|fe|rie|ren** ‹franz.› (eine Konferenz abhalten; als Conférencier sprechen); *vgl.* conferieren
Kon|fes|si|on, die; -, -en ‹lat.› ([Glaubens]bekenntnis; [christl.] Bekenntnisgruppe); **Kon|fes|si|o|na|lis|mus,** der; - ([übermäßige] Betonung der eigenen Konfession); **kon|fes|si|o|nell** (zu einer Konfession gehörend); **kon|fes|si|ons|los; Kon|fes|si|ons|lo|sig|keit,** die; -; **Kon|fes|si|ons|schu|le**
Kon|fet|ti *Plur., heute meist* das; -[s] ‹ital.› (bunte Papierblättchen); **Kon|fet|ti‿pa|ra|de, ...re|gen**
Kon|fi|dent, der; -en, -en (↑R 126) ‹franz.› (*veraltet für* Vertrauter, Busenfreund; *österr. für* [Polizei]spitzel); **kon|fi|den|ti|ell** (*veraltet für* vertraulich)
Kon|fi|gu|ra|ti|on, die; -, -en ‹lat.› (*Astron., Astrol.* bestimmte Stellung der Planeten; *Med.* Verformung [z. B. des Schädels]; *Chemie* räumliche Anordnung der Atome eines Moleküls; *Kunst* Gestalt, Gestaltung)
Kon|fir|mand, der; -en, -en (↑R 126) ‹lat.›; **Kon|fir|man|den‿stun|de, ...un|ter|richt; Kon|fir|man|din; Kon|fir|ma|ti|on,** die; -, -en (Aufnahme jugendl. evangel. Christen in die Gemeinde der Erwachsenen); goldene -; **Kon|fir|ma|ti|ons‿an|zug, ...ge|schenk, ...spruch; kon|fir|mie|ren**
Kon|fi|se|rie [*auch* kɔ̃...], die; -, ...ien ‹franz.› (*schweiz.* [Geschäft für] Süßwaren, Pralinen u. Ä. aus eigener Herstellung); **Kon|fi|seur** [...'zø:r], der; -s, -e (Berufsbez.)
Kon|fis|ka|ti|on, die; -, -en ‹lat.› ([entschädigungslose] Enteignung; Beschlagnahmung); **kon|fis|zie|ren**
Kon|fi|tent, der; -en, -en (↑R 126) ‹lat.› (*veraltet für* Beichtender)
Kon|fi|tü|re, die; -, -n ‹franz.› (Marmelade mit Früchten od. Fruchtstücken)
kon|fli|gie|ren ‹lat.› (in Konflikt geraten); **Kon|flikt,** der; -[e]s, -e ‹lat., „Zusammenstoß"› (Zwiespalt, [Wider]streit); **Kon|flikt‿feld** (Spannungsfeld), **...for|schung, ...herd, ...kom|mis|si|on** (*ehem. in der DDR* außergerichtl. Schiedskommission); **kon|flikt‿los, ...scheu; Kon|flikt‿si|tu|a|ti|on, ...stoff**
Kon|flu|enz, die; -, -en ‹lat.› (*Geol.* Zusammenfluss zweier Gletscher)
Kon|fö|de|ra|ti|on, die; -, -en ‹lat., „Bündnis"› ([Staaten]bund); **kon|fö|de|rie|ren,** sich (sich verbünden); **Kon|fö|de|rier|te,** der *u.* die; -n, -n (↑R 5 ff.)
kon|fo|kal ‹lat.› (*Optik* mit gleichen Brennpunkten); -e Kegelschnitte
kon|form ‹lat.› (einig, übereinstimmend); konform gehen (übereinstimmen); **Kon|for|mis|mus,** der; - ([Geistes]haltung, die [stets] um Anpassung bemüht ist); **Kon|for|mist,** der; -en, -en; ↑R 126 (Anhänger der anglikan. Kirche; Vertreter des Konformismus); **kon|for|mis|tisch; Kon|for|mi|tät,** die; - (Übereinstimmung)
Kon|fra|ter ‹lat., „Mitbruder"› ([kath.] Amtsbruder); **Kon|fra|ter|ni|tät,** die; -, -en (*veraltet für* Bruderschaft kath. Geistlicher)
Kon|fron|ta|ti|on, die; -, -en ‹lat.› (Gegenüberstellung [von Angeklagten u. Zeugen]; Auseinandersetzung); **Kon|fron|ta|ti|ons|kurs; kon|fron|tie|ren;** mit jmdm., mit etwas konfrontiert werden; **Kon|fron|tie|rung**
kon|fus ‹lat.› (verwirrt, verworren, durcheinander); **Kon|fu|si|on,** die; -, -en (Verwirrung, Durcheinander; *BGB* Vereinigung von Forderung u. Schuld in einer Person); **Kon|fu|si|ons|rat** *Plur.* ...räte (*veraltend scherzh. für* Wirrkopf)
Kon|fut|se, Kon|fu|zi|us (chin. Philosoph); **kon|fu|zi|a|nisch;** konfuzianische Aussprüche (von Konfuzius); konfuzianische Philosophie (nach Art des Konfuzius); **Kon|fu|zi|a|nis|mus,** der; - (sich auf die Lehre von Konfuzius berufende Geisteshaltung); **kon|fu|zi|a|nis|tisch** (den Konfuzianismus betreffend); **Kon|fu|zi|us** *vgl.* Konfutse
kon|ge|ni|al [*auch* 'kɔn...] ‹lat.› (geistesverwandt; geistig ebenbürtig); **Kon|ge|ni|a|li|tät,** die; -
kon|ge|ni|tal ‹lat.› (*Med.* angeboren)
Kon|ges|ti|on, die; -, -en ‹lat.› (*Med.* Blutandrang); **kon|ges|tiv** (Blutandrang erzeugend)

Kon|glo|me|rat, das; -[e]s, -e ‹lat.› (Zusammenballung, Gemisch; *Geol.* Sedimentgestein)

[1]**Kon|go,** der; -[s] (Strom in Mittelafrika); [2]**Kon|go** *meist mit Artikel* der; -[s] (Staat in Mittelafrika); *vgl.* Irak, Zaire; **Kon|go|be|cken,** das; -s; **Kon|go|le|se,** der; -n, -n (↑R 126); **Kon|go|le|sin; kon|go|le|sisch; kon|go|rot; Kon|go|rot;** ↑R 105 (ein Farbstoff)

Kon|gre|ga|ti|on, die; -, -en ‹lat.› ([kath.] Vereinigung); **Kon|gre|ga|ti|o|na|list,** der; -en, -en (↑R 126) ‹engl.› (Angehöriger einer engl.-nordamerik. Freikirche); **Kon|gre|ga|ti|o|nist,** der; -en, -en (↑R 126) ‹lat.› (Angehöriger einer Kongregation)

Kon|gress, der; -es, -e ‹lat.› ([größere] fachl. od. polit. Versammlung; *nur Sing.:* Parlament in den USA); **Kon|gress|hal|le; Kon|gress|saal** (↑R 136); **Kon|gress|stadt** (↑R 136); **Kon|gress|teil|neh|mer**

kon|gru|ent ‹lat.› (übereinstimmend; *Math.* deckungsgleich); **Kon|gru|enz,** die; -, -en *Plur. selten* (Übereinstimmung; *Math.* Deckungsgleichheit); **Kon|gru|enz|satz** *(Geom.);* **kon|gru|ie|ren**

Ko|ni|die [...diə], die; -, -n *meist Plur.* ‹griech.› (*Bot.* Pilzspore)

K.-o.-Nie|der|la|ge; ↑R 28 (*Boxen* Niederlage durch K. o.); *vgl. auch* Knock-out-Schlag

Ko|ni|fe|re, die; -, -n *meist Plur.* ‹lat.› (*Bot.* Zapfen tragendes Nadelholzgewächs)

Kö|nig, der; -s, -e; **Kö|ni|gin; Kö|ni|gin‿mut|ter** (*Plur.* ...mütter), **...pas|te|te, ...wit|we** (↑R 24); **kö|nig|lich** (*Abk.* kgl.); das königliche Spiel (Schach); *im Titel* (↑R 108): Königlich (*Abk.* Kgl.); Königliche Hoheit (Anrede eines Fürsten od. Prinzen); *vgl.* kaiserlich; **Kö|nig|reich; Kö|nigs|ad|ler** (*svw.* Steinadler)

Kö|nigs|berg (*russ.* Kaliningrad); Königsberger Klopse (ein Fleischgericht); *vgl.* Kaliningrad

kö|nigs|blau; Kö|nigs‿blau, ...burg, ...farn, ...haus, ...hof, ...ker|ze (eine Heil- u. Zierpflanze), **...kro|ne, ...ku|chen, ...pal|me, ...schloss**

Kö|nigs|see, der; -s (in Bayern)

Kö|nigs|sohn; Kö|nigs|stuhl, der; -s (Kreidefelsen auf Rügen); **Kö|nig|stein,** der; -s (Tafelberg im Elbsandsteingebirge); die Festung -; **Kö|nigs‿thron, ...ti|ger, ...toch|ter; kö|nigs|treu; Kö|nigs‿was|ser** (das; -s; *Chemie*), **...weg** (bester, idealer Weg)

Kö|nigs Wus|ter|hau|sen (↑R 101; Stadt südöstl. Berlins); **Kö|nigs-Wus|ter|hau|se|ner** (↑R 103 *u.* 105)

Kö|nig|tum

Ko|ni|in, das; -s ‹griech.› (*Biol., Chemie* ein giftiges Alkaloid)

ko|nisch ‹griech.› (kegelförmig); konische Spirale

Konj. = Konjunktiv

Kon|jek|tur, die; -, -en ‹lat.› (*Literaturw.* verbessernder Eingriff in einen nicht einwandfrei überlieferten Text); **kon|jek|tu|ral; Kon|jek|tu|ral|kri|tik; kon|ji|zie|ren** (Konjekturen machen)

Kon|ju|ga|ti|on, die; -, -en (*Sprachw.* Beugung des Verbs); **Kon|ju|ga|ti|ons|en|dung; kon|ju|gier|bar** (beugungsfähig); **kon|ju|gie|ren** ([Verb] beugen); **kon|jun|gie|ren** (*veraltet für* verbinden); **Kon|junk|ti|on,** die; -, -en (*Sprachw.* Bindewort, z. B. „und“, „weil“; *Astron.* Stellung zweier Gestirne im gleichen Längengrad); **Kon|junk|ti|o|nal‿ad|verb, ...satz** (*Sprachw.* von einer Konjunktion eingeleiteter Nebensatz); **Kon|junk|tiv,** der; -s, -e [...və] (*Sprachw.* Möglichkeitsform; *Abk.* Konj.); **Kon|junk|ti|va** [...v...], die; -, ...vä (*Med.* Bindehaut [des Auges]); **kon|junk|ti|visch** [...viʃ] (*Sprachw.* den Konjunktiv betreffend, auf ihn bezüglich); **Kon|junk|ti|vi|tis** [...v...], die; -, ...itiden (*Med.* Bindehautentzündung [des Auges]); **Kon|junk|tiv|satz; Kon|junk|tur,** die; -, -en (wirtschaftl. Gesamtlage von bestimmter Entwicklungstendenz; wirtschaftl. Aufschwung); **kon|junk|tur|be|dingt; Kon|junk|tur|be|richt; kon|junk|tu|rell** (der Konjunktur gemäß); **Kon|junk|tur‿la|ge, ...po|li|tik; kon|junk|tur|po|li|tisch; Kon|junk|tur‿pro|gramm, ...rit|ter** *(abwertend),* **...schwan|kung, ...sprit|ze** (*ugs. für* Maßnahme zur Konjunkturbelebung), **...zu|schlag**

kon|kav ‹lat.› (*Optik* hohl, vertieft, nach innen gewölbt); **Kon|kav|glas** *Plur.* ...gläser; **Kon|ka|vi|tät** [...v...], die; - (konkaver Zustand); **Kon|kav|spie|gel**

Kon|kla|ve [...və], das; -s, -n ‹lat.› (Versammlung[sort] der Kardinäle zur Papstwahl)

kon|klu|dent ‹lat.› (schlüssig); -es Verhalten *(Rechtsw.);* **kon|klu|die|ren** (*Philos.* folgern); **Kon|klu|si|on,** die; -, -en (Schluss[folgerung]); **kon|klu|siv** (schließend, folgernd)

kon|kor|dant ‹lat.› (übereinstimmend); **Kon|kor|danz,** die; -, -en (*Biol.* Übereinstimmung; *Buchw.* alphabet. Verzeichnis von Wörtern od. Sachen zum Vergleich ihres Vorkommens u. Sinngehaltes an verschiedenen Stellen eines Buches, z. B. Bibelkonkordanz; *Geol.* gleich laufende Lagerung mehrerer Gesteinsschichten; *Druckw.* ein Schriftgrad); 5 Konkordanz (*Druckw.;* ↑R 90); **Kon|kor|dat,** das; -[e]s, -e (Vertrag zwischen Staat u. kath. Kirche; *schweiz. für* Vertrag zwischen Kantonen); **Kon|kor|dats|po|li|tik,** die; -; **Kon|kor|dia,** die; - (Name von Vereinen usw.); **Kon|kor|di|en|for|mel,** die; - (letzte lutherische Bekenntnisschrift von 1577)

Kon|kre|ment, das; -[e]s, -e ‹lat.› (*Med.* krankhaftes festes Gebilde, das in Körperflüssigkeiten u. -hohlräumen entsteht [z. B. Nierenstein]); **kon|kret** ‹lat.› (körperlich, gegenständlich, sinnfällig, anschaubar, greifbar); *vgl.* in concreto; konkrete Malerei; konkrete Musik; **Kon|kre|ti|on,** die; -, -en (*Med.* Verwachsung; *Geol.* mineralischer Körper in Gesteinen); **kon|kre|ti|sie|ren** (verdeutlichen; [im Einzelnen] ausführen); **Kon|kre|ti|sie|rung; Kon|kre|tum,** das; -s, ...ta (*Sprachw.* Substantiv, das etwas Gegenständliches benennt, z. B. „Tisch“)

Kon|ku|bi|nat, das; -[e]s, -e ‹lat.› (*Rechtsspr.* eheähnliche Gemeinschaft ohne Eheschließung); **Kon|ku|bi|ne,** die; -, -n (*veraltet für* im Konkubinat lebende Frau; *abwertend für* Geliebte)

Kon|ku|pis|zenz, die; - ‹lat.› (*Philos., Theol.* Begehrlichkeit; sinnl. Begierde)

Kon|kur|rent, der; -en, -en (↑R 126) ‹lat.› (Mitbewerber, [geschäftl.] Rivale); **Kon|kur|ren|tin; Kon|kur|renz,** die; -, -en (Wettbewerb; Zusammentreffen zweier Tatbestände od. Möglichkeiten; *nur Sing.:* Konkurrent, Gesamtheit der Konkurrenten); **Kon|kur|renz|be|trieb; kon|kur|renz|fä|hig; kon|kur|ren|zie|ren** (*österr., schweiz. für* jmdm. Konkurrenz machen); jmdn. -; **Kon|kur|ren|zie|rung** *(österr., schweiz.);* **Kon|kur|renz|kampf; kon|kur|renz|los; Kon|kur|renz‿neid, ...un|ter|neh|men; kon|kur|rie|ren** (wetteifern; miteinander in Wettbewerb stehen; zusammentreffen [von mehreren strafrechtl. Tatbeständen]); **Kon|kurs**, der; -es, -e (Zahlungseinstellung, -unfähigkeit); **Kon|kurs|er|öff|nung, ...mas|se, ...ver|fah|ren, ...ver|wal|ter**

kön|nen; du kannst; du konntest; du könntest; gekonnt, *aber* ich habe das nicht glauben können; **Kön|nen**, das; -s; **Kön|ner**; **Kön|ne|rin**; **Kön|ner|schaft**, die; -

Kon|ne|ta|bel, der; -s, -s ‹franz.› (franz. Kronfeldherr [bis ins 17. Jh.])

Kon|nex, der; -es, -e ‹lat.› (Zusammenhang, Verbindung; persönlicher Kontakt); **Kon|ne|xi|on**, die; -, -en *meist Plur.* (*selten für* [vorteilhafte] Beziehung)

kon|ni|vent [...v...] ‹lat.› (*Rechtsw.* nachsichtig); **Kon|ni|venz**, die; -, -en (Nachsicht); **kon|ni|vie|ren** (*veraltet für* Nachsicht üben)

Kon|nos|se|ment, das; -[e]s, -e ‹ital.› (*Seew.* Frachtbrief)

Kon|no|ta|ti|on, die; -, -en ‹lat.› (*Sprachw.* semant.-stilist. Färbung; mit einem Wort verbundene zusätzliche Vorstellung, z. B. „Nacht", „kühl" bei „Mond"); **kon|no|ta|tiv**; **kon|no|tie|ren** (eine Konnotation hervorrufen)

Kon|nu|bi|um, das; -s, ...ien [...i̯ən] ‹lat.› (*Rechtsspr. veraltet für* Ehe[gemeinschaft])

Ko|no|id, das; -[e]s, -e ‹griech.› (*Geom.* kegelähnlicher Körper)

Kon|quis|ta|dor [...k(v)i...], der; -en, -en (↑R 126) ‹span.› (span. Eroberer von Mittel- u. Südamerika im 16. Jh.)

Kon|rad (m. Vorn.); **Kon|ra|din** [...di:n] (m. Vorn.); **Kon|ra|di|ne** (w. Vorn.)

Kon|rek|tor, der; -s, ...oren ‹lat.› (Vertreter des Rektors einer Schule)

Kon|sek|ra|ti|on (↑R 130), die; -, -en ‹lat.› (liturg. Weihe einer Person od. Sache; Verwandlung von Brot u. Wein beim Abendmahl); **kon|sek|rie|ren**

kon|se|ku|tiv ‹lat.› (die Folge bezeichnend); **Kon|se|ku|tiv|satz** (*Sprachw.* Umstandssatz der Folge)

Kon|sens, der; -es, -e ‹lat.› (Meinungsübereinstimmung; *veraltend für* Genehmigung); **kon|sens|fä|hig**; **Kon|sen|sus**, der; -, - [...zu:s] (*svw.* Konsens); **kon|sen|tie|ren** (*veraltet für* einwilligen, genehmigen)

kon|se|quent ‹lat.› (folgerichtig; bestimmt; beharrlich, zielbewusst); **Kon|se|quenz**, die; -, -en (Folgerichtigkeit; Beharrlichkeit; Zielstrebigkeit; Folge[rung])

Kon|ser|va|ti|s|mus [...v...] ‹lat.› *vgl.* Konservativismus; **kon|ser|va|tiv** [*auch* 'kɔn...] (am Hergebrachten festhaltend; polit. dem Konservativismus zugehörend); eine konservative Partei; *aber* (↑R 108): die Konservative Partei (in Großbritannien); **Kon|ser|va|ti|ve**, der *u.* die; -n, -n (↑R 5 ff.); **Kon|ser|va|ti|vis|mus**, der; - (am Überlieferten orientierte Einstellung; auf Erhalt der bestehenden Ordnung gerichtete Haltung); **Kon|ser|va|ti|vi|tät**, die; -; **Kon|ser|va|tor**, der; -s, ...oren (für die Instandhaltung von Kunstdenkmälern verantwortl. Fachmann bzw. Beamter); **kon|ser|va|to|risch** (pfleglich; das Konservatorium betreffend); - gebildet (auf einem Konservatorium ausgebildet); **Kon|ser|va|to|rist**, der; -en, -en; ↑R 126 (Schüler eines Konservatoriums); **Kon|ser|va|to|ris|tin**; **Kon|ser|va|to|ri|um**, das; -s, ...ien [...i̯ən] ‹ital.› (Musik[hoch]schule); **Kon|ser|ve**, die; -, -n ‹mlat.› (haltbar gemachtes Nahrungs- od. Genussmittel; Konservenbüchse, -glas mit Inhalt; *ugs. für* auf Tonband, Schallplatte Festgehaltenes; *kurz für* Blutkonserve); **Kon|ser|ven|büch|se, ...do|se, ...fab|rik, ...glas, ...öff|ner, ...ver|gif|tung** *(Med.)*; **kon|ser|vie|ren** ‹lat.› (einmachen; haltbar machen; beibehalten); **Kon|ser|vie|rung**; **Kon|ser|vie|rungs|mit|tel**, das

Kon|sig|nant (↑R 130), der; -en, -en (↑R 126) ‹lat.› (*Wirtsch.* Versender von Konsignationsgut); **Kon|sig|na|tar**, **Kon|sig|na|tär**, der; -s, -e (Empfänger von Konsignationsgut); **Kon|sig|na|ti|on**, die; -, -en (Kommissionsgeschäft [bes. im Überseehandel]); **Kon|sig|na|ti|ons|gut**; **kon|sig|nie|ren** (Waren zum Verkauf übersenden)

Kon|si|li|a|ri|us, der; -, ...rii ‹lat.› (zur Beratung hinzugezogener Arzt); **Kon|si|li|um**, das; -s, ...ien [...i̯ən] (Beratung [von Ärzten]; beratende Versammlung); *vgl.* Consilium abeundi

kon|sis|tent ‹lat.› (fest, zäh zusammenhaltend; dickflüssig); **Kon|sis|tenz**, die; -

Kon|sis|to|ri|al|rat *Plur.* ...räte (ev. Titel); **Kon|sis|to|ri|um**, das; -s, ...ien [...i̯ən] ‹lat.› (außerordentl. Versammlung der Kardinäle unter Vorsitz des Papstes; oberste Verwaltungsbehörde mancher ev. Landeskirchen)

kon|skri|bie|ren ‹lat.› (*früher für* zum Heeres-, Kriegsdienst ausheben); **Kon|skri|bier|te**, der; -n, -n (↑R 5 ff.); **Kon|skrip|ti|on**, die; -, -en

Kon|sol, der; -s, -s *meist Plur.* ‹engl.› (Staatsschuldschein); **Kon|so|le**, die; -, -n ‹franz.› (Wandbrett; *Bauw.* herausragender Mauerteil); **Kon|so|li|da|ti|on**, die; -, -en ‹lat.(-franz.)› (Vereinigung mehrerer Staatsanleihen zu einer einheitlichen Anleihe; Umwandlung kurzfristiger Staatsschulden in Anleihen); **kon|so|li|die|ren** ([in seinem Bestand] sichern, festigen); **Kon|so|li|die|rung** (Sicherung, Festigung [eines Unternehmens]); **Kon|so|li|die|rungs|pha|se**; **Kon|sol|tisch**; **Kon|sol|tisch|chen**

Kon|som|mee [kɔ̃sɔ'me:] *vgl.* Consommé

kon|so|nant ‹lat.› (*Musik* harmonisch, zusammenklingend; *veraltet für* einstimmig, übereinstimmend); **Kon|so|nant**, der; -en, -en; ↑R 126 (*Sprachw.* Mitlaut, z. B. p, t, k); **Kon|so|nan|ten|häu|fung, ...schwund**; **kon|so|nan|tisch** (Konsonanten betreffend); **Kon|so|nanz**, die; -, -en (*Musik* harmonischer Gleichklang; *Sprachw.* Anhäufung von Mitlauten, Mitlautfolge)

Kon|sor|te, der; -n, -n ‹lat., „Genosse"› (*Wirtsch.* Mitglied eines Konsortiums; *nur Plur.: abwertend für* Mitbeteiligte, Mittäter); **Kon|sor|ti|um**, das; -s, ...ien [...i̯ən] (Genossenschaft; vorübergehende Vereinigung von Unternehmen, bes. von Banken, für größere Finanzierungsaufgaben)

Kon|spekt, der; -[e]s, -e ‹lat.› (Zusammenfassung, Inhaltsübersicht); **kon|spek|tie|ren** (einen Konspekt anfertigen)

Kon|spi|ra|ti|on, die; -, -en ‹lat.› (Verschwörung); **kon|spi|ra|tiv** (verschwörerisch); **kon|spi|rie|ren** (sich verschwören; eine Verschwörung anzetteln)

[1]**Kons|tab|ler** (↑R 130 *u.* 132), der; -s, - ‹lat.› (*früher für* Geschützmeister usw. [auf Kriegsschiffen]); [2]**Kons|tab|ler**, der; -s, - ‹engl.› (*veraltet für* Polizist in England u. in den USA)

kon|stant; ‹lat.› (beharrlich, fest[stehend], ständig, unveränderlich, stet[ig]); **Kon|stan|te**, die; -[n], *Plur.* -n, *ohne Artikel fachspr. auch* - (eine mathemat. Größe, deren Wert sich nicht ändert; *Ggs.* Veränderliche, Variable); zwei -[n]; **Kon|stan|tin** [*österr. nur so, auch* ...'ti:n] (m.

Vorn.); Konstantin der Große (röm. Kaiser); **kon|stan|ti|nisch,** *aber* (↑R 56): die Konstantinische Schenkung; **Kon|stan|ti|no|pel** (*früherer Name für* Istanbul); **Kon|stan|ti|no|pe|ler, Kon|stan|ti|nop|ler** (↑R 130), **Kon|stan|ti|no|po|li|ta|ner** (↑R 103); **[1]Kon|stanz,** die; - ⟨lat.⟩ (Beharrlichkeit, Unveränderlichkeit; Stetigkeit); **[2]Kon|stanz** (Stadt am Bodensee); **Kon|stan|ze** (w. Vorn.); **kon|sta|tie|ren** ⟨franz.⟩ (feststellen); **Kon|sta|tie|rung**

Kons|tel|la|ti|on (↑R 132), die; -, -en ⟨lat.⟩ (Zusammentreffen von Umständen; Lage; *Astron.* Stellung der Gestirne zueinander)

Kons|ter|na|ti|on (↑R 132), die; -, -en ⟨lat.⟩ (*veraltet für* Bestürzung); **kons|ter|nie|ren** (verblüffen, verwirren); jmdn. -; **kons|ter|niert** (bestürzt, betroffen)

Kons|ti|pa|ti|on (↑R 132), die; -, -en ⟨lat.⟩ (*Med.* Verstopfung)

Kon|sti|tu|an|te *vgl.* Constituante; **Kon|sti|tu|en|te,** die; -, -n ⟨lat.⟩ (*Sprachw.* sprachl. Bestandteil eines größeren Ganzen); **kon|sti|tu|ie|ren** ⟨lat.(-franz.)⟩ (einsetzen, festsetzen, gründen); sich - (zusammentreten [zur Beschlussfassung]); -de Versammlung; **Kon|sti|tu|ie|rung; Kon|sti|tu|ti|on,** die; -, -en (allgemeine, bes. körperliche Verfassung; *Med.* Körperbau; *Politik* Verfassung, Satzung); **Kon|sti|tu|ti|o|na|lis|mus,** der; - (Staatsform auf dem Boden einer Verfassung); **kon|sti|tu|ti|o|nell** ⟨franz.⟩ (verfassungsmäßig; *Med.* auf die Körperbeschaffenheit bezüglich; anlagebedingt); konstitutionelle Monarchie; **Kon|sti|tu|ti|ons|typ; kon|sti|tu|tiv** ⟨lat.⟩ (das Wesen einer Sache bestimmend)

Kon|strik|ti|on, die; -, -en ⟨lat.⟩ (*Med.* Zusammenziehung [eines Muskels]; *Biol.* Einschnürung, Verengung); **Kon|strik|tor,** der; -s, ...oren (*Med.* Schließmuskel); **kon|strin|gie|ren** [...st...] (*Med.* zusammenziehen [von Muskeln])

kon|stru|ie|ren ⟨lat.⟩ (gestalten; zeichnen; bilden; [künstlich] herstellen); **Kon|strukt,** das; -[e]s, *Plur.* -e *u.* -s (Arbeitshypothese); **Kon|struk|teur** [...'tø:r], der; -s, -e ⟨franz.⟩ (Erbauer, Erfinder, Gestalter); **Kon|struk|teu|rin** [...'tø:...]; **Kon|struk|ti|on,** die; -, -en ⟨lat.⟩; **kon|struk|ti|ons|be|dingt; Kon|struk|ti|ons‿bü|ro, ...feh|ler, ...zeich|nung; kon|struk|tiv** [*auch* 'kɔn...] (die Konstruktion betreffend; folgerichtig; aufbauend); konstruktives Misstrauensvotum; **Kon|struk|ti|vis|mus** [...v...], der; - (Richtung der bildenden Kunst u. der Architektur um 1920); **Kon|struk|ti|vist,** der; -en, -en (↑R 126); **kon|struk|ti|vis|tisch**

Kon|sub|stan|ti|a|ti|on, die; -, -en ⟨lat.⟩ (*ev. Rel.* [nach Luther] Verbindung der realen Gegenwart Christi mit Brot u. Wein beim Abendmahl)

Kon|sul, der; -s, -n ⟨lat.⟩ (höchster Beamter der röm. Republik; *Diplomatie* Vertreter eines Staates zur Wahrnehmung seiner [wirtschaftl.] Interessen in einem anderen Staat); **Kon|su|lar|agent** (↑R 132; *Diplomatie* Bevollmächtigter eines Konsuls); **kon|su|la|risch;** *aber* das Konsularische Korps (*Abk.* CC); **Kon|su|lar‿recht** (das; -[e]s), **...ver|trag; Kon|su|lat,** das; -[e]s, -e (Amt[sgebäude] eines Konsuls); **Kon|su|lats|ge|bäu|de; Kon|su|lent,** der; -en, -en; ↑R 126 (*veraltet für* [Rechts]berater); **Kon|su|lin; Kon|sul|tant,** der; -en, -en (fachmänn. Berater); **Kon|sul|ta|ti|on,** die; -, -en (Befragung, bes. eines Arztes; Beratung von Regierungen); **Kon|sul|ta|ti|ons|mög|lich|keit; kon|sul|ta|tiv** (beratend); **kon|sul|tie|ren** ([einen Arzt] befragen; zurate ziehen)

[1]Kon|sum, der; -s ⟨ital.⟩ (Verbrauch, Verzehr); **[2]Kon|sum** ['kɔnzum, *auch* ...zu:m, *österr.* ...'zu:m], der; -s, -s (*kurz für* [Verkaufsstelle einer] Konsumgenossenschaft); **Kon|sum|ar|ti|kel; Kon|su|ma|ti|on,** die; -, -en ⟨franz.⟩ (*österr. u. schweiz. für* Verzehr, Zeche); **Kon|sum|den|ken** (auf [1]Konsum ausgerichtete Lebenshaltung); **Kon|su|ment,** der; -en, -en (↑R 126) ⟨lat.⟩ (Verbraucher; Käufer); **kon|su|men|ten|freund|lich; Kon|su|men|tin; Kon|sum‿for|schung, ...ge|nos|sen|schaft** (Verbrauchergenossenschaft; *Kurzw.* [2]Konsum), **...ge|sell|schaft, ...gut** *(meist Plur.);* **Kon|sum|gü|ter|in|dust|rie; kon|su|mie|ren** (verbrauchen; verzehren); **Kon|su|mie|rung; Kon|sump|ti|on,** die; - (*Med.* starke Abmagerung); **Kon|sum|ti|on,** die; -, -en (Verbrauch); **kon|sum|tiv** (zum Verbrauch bestimmt); **Kon|sum|ver|ein** (Verbrauchergenossenschaft); *vgl.* [2]Konsum

Kon|ta|gi|on, die; -, -en ⟨lat.⟩ (*Med.* Ansteckung); **kon|ta|gi|ös** (*Med.* ansteckend, übertragbar); -e Krankheiten; **Kon|ta|gi|o|si|tät,** die; - (*Med.* Ansteckungsfähigkeit); **Kon|ta|gi|um,** das; -s, ...ien [...iən] (*Med. veraltet* bei Ansteckung wirksamer Stoff; Ansteckung); **Kon|takt,** der; -[e]s, -e ⟨lat.⟩ (Berührung, Verbindung); **Kon|takt‿ad|res|se, ...an|zei|ge; kon|takt|arm; Kon|takt‿ar|mut, ...auf|nah|me, ...be|reichs|be|am|te** (Revierpolizist; *Kurzw.* Kob); **kon|tak|ten** (*bes. Wirtsch.* kontaktieren); **Kon|tak|ter** *(Wirtsch.);* **kon|takt|freu|dig; Kon|takt‿gift** (das), **...glas** (*Plur.* ...gläser); **kon|tak|tie|ren** (Kontakt[e] aufnehmen); jmdn. *od.* mit jmdm. -; **Kon|takt‿in|fek|ti|on, ...lin|se; kon|takt|los; Kon|takt|lo|sig|keit,** die; -; **Kon|takt‿man|gel** (der; -s), **...mann** (*Plur.* ...männer *u.* ...leute); **Kon|takt|nah|me,** die; -, -n; **Kon|takt‿per|son, ...schal|le, ...schwä|che, ...schwel|le, ...sper|re, ...stoff, ...stö|rung, ...stu|di|um, ...zaun**

Kon|ta|mi|na|ti|on, die; -, -en ⟨lat.⟩ (*Sprachw.* Verschmelzung, Wortkreuzung, z. B. „Gebäulichkeiten“ aus „Gebäude“ u. „Baulichkeiten“; *fachspr. für* [radioaktive] Verunreinigung, Verseuchung); **kon|ta|mi|nie|ren**

kon|tant ⟨ital.⟩ (bar); **Kon|tan|ten** *Plur.* (ausländ. Münzen, die nicht als Zahlungsmittel, sondern als Ware gehandelt werden)

Kon|temp|la|ti|on (↑R 130), die; -, -en ⟨lat.⟩ (religiöse Versenkung, Versunkenheit; Beschaulichkeit, Betrachtung); **kon|temp|la|tiv**

Kon|ten (*Plur. von* Konto); **Kon|ten‿plan, ...rah|men**

Kon|ten|ten *Plur.* ⟨lat.⟩ (*Seew.* Ladeverzeichnisse der Seeschiffe); **Kon|ten|tiv|ver|band** (med. Stützverband)

Kon|ter, der; -s, - ⟨franz. u. engl.⟩ (*Sport* schneller Gegenangriff); **kon|ter...** (gegen...); **Kon|ter...** (Gegen...); **Kon|ter|ad|mi|ral** (Offiziersdienstgrad bei der Marine); **Kon|ter|an|griff** *(Sport);* **Kon|ter|ban|de,** die; - (*veraltet für* Schmuggelware); **Kon|ter|fei** [*auch* ...'fai], das; -s, -s (*veraltet, aber noch scherzh. für* [Ab]bild, Bildnis); **kon|ter|fei|en** [*auch* ...'faiən] (*veraltet, aber noch scherzh. für* abbilden); konterfeit; **Kon|ter|fuß|ball** (defensive, auf Konterangriffe ausgerichtete Spielweise); **kon|ter|ka|rie|ren** (hintertreiben); **Kon|ter|mi|ne** (*Festungswesen* Gegenmine; *Börse* Gegen-, Baissespekulation);

kon|tern (schlagfertig erwidern; sich zur Wehr setzen; *Druckw.* ein Druckbild umkehren; *Sport* den Gegner im Angriff durch gezielte Gegenschläge abfangen; durch eine Gegenaktion abwehren); ich ...ere (↑R 16); **Kon|ter|re|vo|lu|ti|on** (Gegenrevolution); **kon|ter|re|vo|lu|ti|o|när; Kon|ter|schlag** *(bes. Boxen)*

Kon|text [*auch* ...'tɛkst], der; -[e]s, -e ⟨lat.⟩ (umgebender Text; Zusammenhang; Inhalt [eines Schriftstücks]); **Kon|text|glos|se** (*Literaturw.* Glosse, die in den Text [einer Handschrift] eingefügt ist); **kon|tex|tu|ell** (den Kontext betreffend)

Kon|ti *(Plur. von* Konto); **kon|tie|ren** ⟨ital.⟩ (ein Konto benennen; auf ein Konto verbuchen)

Kon|ti|gu|i|tät, die; - ⟨lat.⟩ (*Psych.* zeitl. Zusammenfließen verschiedener Erlebnisinhalte)

Kon|ti|nent [*auch* 'kɔn...], der; -[e]s, -e ⟨lat.⟩ (Festland; Erdteil); **kon|ti|nen|tal; Kon|ti|nen|tal|eu|ro|pa; kon|ti|nen|tal|eu|ro|pä|isch; Kon|ti|nen|tal‿kli|ma** (das; -s), **...macht, ...plat|te** *(Geol.),* **...sper|re** (die; -; *früher*), **...ver|schie|bung** *(Geol.)*

Kon|ti|nenz, die; - ⟨lat.⟩ (*Med.* Fähigkeit, Stuhl u. Urin zurückzuhalten)

Kon|tin|gent, das; -[e]s, -e ⟨lat.⟩ (anteilig zu erbringende Menge, Leistung, Anzahl; Zahl der [von Einzelstaaten] zu stellenden Truppen); **kon|tin|gen|tie|ren** (das Kontingent festsetzen; [vorsorglich] ein-, zuteilen); **Kon|tin|gen|tie|rung; Kon|tin|gent[s]|zu|wei|sung**

Kon|ti|nu|a|ti|on, die; -, -en ⟨lat.⟩ (*Buchw., sonst veraltet für* Fortsetzung); **kon|ti|nu|ier|lich** (stetig, fortdauernd, unaufhörlich, durchlaufend); -er Bruch (*Math.* Kettenbruch); **Kon|ti|nu|i|tät,** die; - (lückenloser Zusammenhang, Stetigkeit, Fortdauer); **Kon|ti|nu|um** [...nu|um], das; -s, ...nua (lückenlos Zusammenhängendes, Stetiges)

Kon|to, das; -s, *Plur.* ...ten, *auch* -s *u.* ...ti ⟨ital.⟩ (Rechnung, Aufstellung über Forderungen u. Schulden); *vgl.* a conto; **Kon|to‿aus|zug, ...buch, ...in|ha|ber; Kon|to|kor|rent,** das; -s, -e (*Wirtsch.* laufende Rechnung); **Kon|to|num|mer; Kon|tor,** das; -s, -e ⟨niederl.⟩ (Handelsniederlassung im Ausland; *ehem. in der DDR* Handelszentrale als Mittler zwischen Industrie u. Einzelhandel); **Kon|to|rist,** der; -en, -en (↑R 126); **Kon|to|ris|tin**

Kon|tor|si|on, die; -, -en ⟨lat.⟩ (*Med.* Verdrehung, Verrenkung eines Gliedes); **Kon|tor|si|o|nist,** der; -en, -en; ↑R 126 (*Artistik* Schlangenmensch)

Kon|to|stand

kont|ra (↑R 130) ⟨lat.⟩ (gegen, entgegengesetzt); *vgl. auch* contra; **Kont|ra,** das; -s, -s (*Kartenspiel* Gegenansage); jmdm. Kontra geben; **Kont|ra‿alt** (tiefer Alt), **...bass** (Bassgeige), **...bas|sist; Kont|ra|dik|ti|on,** die; -, -en (*Philos.* Widerspruch); **kont|ra|dik|to|risch** (*Philos.* widersprechend); **Kont|ra|fa|gott** (tiefes Fagott); **Kont|ra|fak|tur,** die; -, -en (*Literaturw.* geistl. Nachdichtung eines weltl. Liedes [u. umgekehrt] unter Beibehaltung der Melodie)

Kon|tra|ha|ge [...'ha:ʒə], die; -, -n ⟨franz.⟩ (*Studentenspr. früher* Verabredung eines Duells); **Kon|tra|hent,** der; -en, -en (↑R 126) ⟨lat.⟩ (*Rechtsspr.* Vertragspartner; Gegner [im Streit]); **Kon|tra|hen|tin; kon|tra|hie|ren** (*Biol., Med.* sich zusammenziehen [von Muskeln, Fasern usw.]; einen Kontrakt abschließen, vereinbaren; *Studentenspr. früher* ein Duell verabreden, jmdn. fordern); sich - (sich zusammenziehen)

Kont|ra|in|di|ka|ti|on (↑R 130), die; -, -en ⟨lat., „Gegenanzeige"⟩ (*Med.* Umstand, der die Anwendung eines Medikaments o. Ä. verbietet)

kon|trakt ⟨lat.⟩ (*veraltet für* zusammengezogen; verkrümmt; gelähmt); **Kon|trakt,** der; -[e]s, -e (Vertrag, Abmachung); **Kon|trakt‿ab|schluss, ...bruch** (der); **kon|trakt|brü|chig; kon|trak|til** (*Med.* zusammenziehbar); **Kon|trak|ti|li|tät,** die; - (*Med.* Fähigkeit, sich zusammenzuziehen); **Kon|trak|ti|on,** die; -, -en (*Med.* Zusammenziehung [von Muskeln]; *Physik* Verringerung des Volumens); **Kon|trak|ti|ons|vor|gang; kon|trakt|lich** (vertragsgemäß); **Kon|trak|tur,** die; -, -en (*Med.* Verkürzung [von Muskeln, Sehnen]; Versteifung)

Kont|ra|post (↑R 130), der; -[e]s, -e ⟨ital.⟩ (*bild. Kunst* Ausgleich [bes. von Stand- u. Spielbein]); **kont|ra|pro|duk|tiv** (negativ, entgegenwirkend; ein gewünschtes Ergebnis verhindernd); **Kont|ra|punkt,** der; -[e]s ⟨lat.⟩ (*Musik* Führung mehrerer selbstständiger Stimmen im Tonsatz); **Kont|ra|punk|tik,** die; - (Lehre des Kontrapunktes; Kunst der kontrapunktischen Stimmführung); **kont|ra|punk|tisch; kont|rär** ⟨franz.⟩ (gegensätzlich; widrig); **Kont|ra|sig|na|tur,** die; -, -en ⟨lat.⟩ (*selten für* Gegenzeichnung); **kont|ra|sig|nie|ren** (*selten für* gegenzeichnen)

Kon|trast, der; -[e]s, -e ⟨franz.⟩ ([starker] Gegensatz; auffallender [Farb]unterschied); **Kon|trast‿brei** *(Med.),* **...far|be; kon|tras|tie|ren** ⟨franz.⟩ (sich unterscheiden, einen [starken] Gegensatz bilden); **kon|tras|tiv** ⟨engl.⟩ (*Sprachw.* gegenüberstellend, vergleichend); -e Grammatik; **Kon|trast‿mit|tel** (das; *Med.*), **...pro|gramm; kon|trast|reich**

Kont|ra|zep|ti|on (↑R 130), die; - ⟨lat.⟩ (*Med.* Empfängnisverhütung); **kont|ra|zep|tiv** (empfängnisverhütend); **Kont|ra|zep|tiv,** das; -s, -e [...və] *u.* **Kont|ra|zep|ti|vum** [...v...], das; -s, ...va (empfängnisverhütendes Mittel)

Kon|trek|ta|ti|ons|trieb ⟨lat.; dt.⟩ (*Med.* Trieb zur körperl. Berührung)

Kont|re|tanz (↑R 130; alter Gesellschaftstanz)

Kon|tri|bu|ti|on, die; -, -en ⟨lat.⟩ (Kriegssteuer, -entschädigung)

Kon|tri|ti|on, die; -, -en ⟨lat.⟩ (*kath. Kirche* tiefe Reue)

Kon|troll|ab|schnitt; Kon|troll‿ap|pa|rat, ...be|fug|nis, ...be|hör|de, ...da|tum; Kon|trol|le, die; -, -n ⟨franz.⟩ (Überwachung; Überprüfung; Beherrschung); **Kon|trol|ler,** der; -s, - ⟨engl.⟩ (*Technik* Steuerschalter an Elektromotoren); **Kon|trol|leur** [...'lø:r], der; -s, -e ⟨franz.⟩ (Aufsichtsbeamter, Prüfer); **Kon|trol|leu|rin** [...'lø:rin]; **Kon|troll|grup|pe** *(bes. Med., Psych.);* **kon|trol|lier|bar; Kon|trol|lier|bar|keit,** die; -; **kon|trol|lie|ren; Kon|troll‿kas|se, ...kom|mis|si|on; Kon|troll|lam|pe** (↑R 136); **Kon|troll|lis|te** (↑R 136); **Kon|troll|me|cha|nis|mus; Kon|trol|lor,** der; -s, -e ⟨ital.⟩ (*österr. für* Kontrolleur); **Kon|troll‿or|gan, ...pflicht, ...punkt; Kon|troll|rat,** der; -[e]s (oberstes Besatzungsorgan in Deutschland nach dem 2. Weltkrieg); **Kon|troll‿sta|ti|on, ...stel|le, ...stem|pel, ...sys|tem, ...turm, ...uhr, ...zent|rum**

kont|ro|vers [...v...] (↑R 130) ⟨lat.⟩ (entgegengesetzt; strittig; umstritten); **Kont|ro|ver|se,** die; -, -n (Meinungsverschiedenheit; [wissenschaftl.] Streit[frage])

Kon|tu|maz, die; - ‹lat.› (*veraltet für* Nichterscheinen vor Gericht; *österr. veraltet für* Quarantäne); *vgl.* in contumaciam; **Kon|tu|ma|zi|al|ver|fah|ren** (*Rechtsspr.* Gerichtsverfahren in Abwesenheit einer Partei od. des Beschuldigten)

Kon|tur, die; -, -en *meist Plur.* ‹franz.› (Umriss[linie]; andeutende Linie[nführung]); **Kon|tur|buch|sta|be** (nur im Umriss gezeichneter [Druck]buchstabe); **kon|tu|ren|reich; Kon|tu|ren‿schär|fe** (*Fotogr.*), **...stift** (zum Nachziehen der Lippenkonturen); **kon|tu|rie|ren** (die äußeren Umrisse ziehen; andeuten); **Kon|tur|schrift** (*Druckw.* Zierschrift mit Konturbuchstaben)

Kon|tu|si|on, die; -, -en ‹lat.› (*Med.* Quetschung)

Ko|nus, der; -, *Plur.* Konusse, *Technik auch* Konen ‹griech.› (Kegel, Kegelstumpf; bei Drucktypen die Seitenflächen des schriftbildtragenden Oberteils)

Kon|va|les|zent [...v...], der; -en, -en (↑R 126) ‹lat.› (*svw.* Rekonvaleszent); **Kon|va|les|zenz,** die; -, -en *Plur. selten* (*Rechtsw.* nachträgliches Gültigwerden von ungültigen Rechtsgeschäften; *Med. svw.* Rekonvaleszenz)

Kon|vek|ti|on [...v...], die; -, -en ‹lat., „Mitführung"› (*Physik* Transport von Energie od. elektr. Ladung durch die kleinsten Teilchen einer Strömung); **kon|vek|tiv; Kon|vek|tor,** der; -s, ...oren (ein Heizkörper)

kon|ve|na|bel [...v...] ‹franz.› (*veraltet für* schicklich; passend, bequem; annehmbar); ...ab|le (↑R 130) Preise; **Kon|ve|ni|at,** das; -s, -s ‹lat.› (Zusammenkunft der kath. Geistlichen eines Dekanats); **Kon|ve|ni|enz,** die; -, -en (*veraltet für* Herkommen; Schicklichkeit; Zuträglichkeit; Bequemlichkeit); **kon|ve|nie|ren** (*veraltet für* passen, annehmbar sein); **Kon|vent,** der; -[e]s, -e (*kath. Kirche* Versammlung der Mönche; Gesamtheit der Konventualen; *ev. Kirche* Zusammenkunft der Geistlichen zur Beratung; Versammlung einer Studentenverbindung; *nur Sing.:* Nationalversammlung in Frankreich 1792 bis 1795); **Kon|ven|ti|kel,** das; -s, - ([heimliche] Zusammenkunft; private religiöse Versammlung); **Kon|ven|ti|on,** die; -, -en ‹franz.› (Abkommen, [völkerrechtl.] Vertrag; *meist Plur.:* Herkommen, Brauch, Förmlichkeit); **kon|ven|ti|o|nal** ‹lat.› (die Konvention betreffend); **Kon|ven|ti|o|nal|stra|fe** (*Rechtsspr.* Vertragsstrafe); **kon|ven|ti|o|nell** ‹franz.› (herkömmlich, üblich; förmlich); **Kon|ven|tu|a|le,** der; -n, -n (↑R 126) ‹lat.› (stimmberechtigtes Klostermitglied; Angehöriger eines kath. Ordens)

kon|ver|gent [...v...] ‹lat.› (sich zuneigend, zusammenlaufend; übereinstimmend); **Kon|ver|genz,** die; -, -en (Annäherung, Übereinstimmung); **Kon|ver|genz|the|o|rie,** die; - (*Politik*); **kon|ver|gie|ren**

Kon|ver|sa|ti|on [...v...], die; -, -en ‹franz.› (gesellige Unterhaltung, Plauderei); **Kon|ver|sa|ti|ons‿le|xi|kon, ...stück; kon|ver|sie|ren** (*veraltet für* sich unterhalten)

Kon|ver|si|on [...v...], die; -, -en ‹lat.› (*Rel.* Glaubenswechsel; *Sprachw.* Übergang in eine andere Wortart ohne eine formale Änderung, z. B. „Dank" – „dank"); **Kon|ver|ter,** der; -s, - ‹engl.› (*Hüttenw.* Gerät zur Stahlherstellung; *Physik* Gerät zum Umformen von Frequenzen); **kon|ver|ti|bel** ‹franz.› (*svw.* konvertierbar); ...b|le (↑R 130) Währungen; **Kon|ver|ti|bi|li|tät,** die; - (Konvertierbarkeit); **kon|ver|tier|bar** (austauschbar zum jeweiligen Wechselkurs [von Währungen]); frei -e Währung; **Kon|ver|tier|bar|keit,** die; - (*Wirtsch.*); **kon|ver|tie|ren** ‹lat.(-franz.)› (*Rel.* den Glauben wechseln; *Wirtsch.* Währung zum Wechselkurs tauschen); **Kon|ver|tie|rung; Kon|ver|tit,** der; -en, -en (↑R 126) ‹engl.› (*Rel.* zu einem anderen Glauben Übergetretener); **Kon|ver|ti|ten|tum,** das; -s (*Rel.*)

kon|vex [...v...] ‹lat.› (*Optik* erhaben, nach außen gewölbt); **Kon|ve|xi|tät,** die; - (konvexer Zustand); **Kon|vex‿lin|se, ...spie|gel**

Kon|vikt [...v...], das; -[e]s, -e ‹lat.› (kirchl. Internat; *österr. für* Internat einer Klosterschule); **Kon|vik|tu|a|le,** der; -n, -n; ↑R 126 (*veraltet für* Angehöriger eines Konvikts); **Kon|vi|vi|um** [...'vi:vi̯um], das; -s, ...ien [...i̯ən] (*veraltet für* Gelage)

Kon|voi [...'vɔy, *auch* 'kɔn...], der; -s, -s ‹engl.› (*bes. Milit.* Geleitzug [für Schiffe]; Fahrzeugkolonne)

Kon|vo|ka|ti|on [...v...], die; -, -en ‹lat., „Zusammenrufen"› (*veraltet für* Einberufung)

Kon|vo|lut [...v...], das; -[e]s, -e ‹lat.› (*Buchw.* Bündel [von Schriftstücken od. Drucksachen]; Sammelband)

Kon|vul|si|on [...v...], die; -, -en ‹lat.› (*Med.* Schüttelkrampf); **kon|vul|siv, kon|vul|si|visch** (krampfhaft [zuckend])

kon|ze|die|ren ‹lat.› (zugestehen, einräumen)

Kon|ze|leb|ra|ti|on (↑R 130), die; -, -en ‹lat.› (*kath. Kirche* gemeinsame Eucharistiefeier durch mehrere Geistliche); **kon|ze|leb|rie|ren**

Kon|zent|rat (↑R 130), das; -[e]s, -e ‹lat.; griech.› (angereicherter Stoff, hochprozentige Lösung; hochprozentiger [Frucht- od. Pflanzen]auszug); **Kon|zent|ra|ti|on,** die; -, -en (Zusammenziehung [von Truppen]; [geistige] Sammlung; *Chemie* Gehalt einer Lösung); **Kon|zent|ra|ti|ons‿fä|hig|keit** (die; -), **...la|ger** (das; -s, -; *Abk.* KZ), **...man|gel** (der), **...schwä|che; kon|zent|rie|ren** ([Truppen] zusammenziehen, vereinigen; *Chemie* anreichern, gehaltreich machen); sich - (sich [geistig] sammeln); **kon|zent|riert** (*Chemie* angereichert, gehaltreich; *übertr. für* gesammelt, aufmerksam); **Kon|zent|riert|heit,** die; -; **Kon|zent|rie|rung; kon|zent|risch** (mit gemeinsamem Mittelpunkt); konzentrische Kreise; **Kon|zent|ri|zi|tät,** die; - (Gemeinsamkeit des Mittelpunktes)

Kon|zept, das; -[e]s, -e ‹lat.› (Entwurf; erste Fassung; grober Plan); **Kon|zep|ti|on,** die; -, -en ([künstlerischer] Einfall; Entwurf eines Werkes; *Med.* Empfängnis); **kon|zep|ti|o|nell; kon|zep|ti|ons|los; Kon|zep|ti|ons|lo|sig|keit,** die; -; **Kon|zept|pa|pier; kon|zep|tu|a|li|sie|ren** (als Konzept gestalten; ein Konzept entwerfen); **kon|zep|tu|ell** (auf ein Konzept bezogen)

Kon|zern, der; -[e]s, -e ‹engl.› (Zusammenschluss wirtschaftl. Unternehmen); **kon|zer|nie|ren** (zu einem Konzern zusammenschließen); **Kon|zer|nie|rung; Kon|zern|mut|ter** (*Wirtsch.* Muttergesellschaft eines Konzerns); **Kon|zern|toch|ter** (Tochtergesellschaft eines Konzerns)

Kon|zert, das; -[e]s, -e ‹ital.›; **Kon|zert‿abend** (↑R 132), **...agen|tur** (↑R 132); **kon|zer|tant** (konzertmäßig, in Konzertform); **Kon|zert|flü|gel; kon|zer|tie|ren** (ein Konzert geben); **kon|zer|tiert;** eine konzertierte Aktion (*Wirtsch.* gemeinsam zwischen Partnern abgestimmtes Handeln); **Kon|zer|ti|na**, die; -, -s (eine Handharmonika); **Kon|zert-meis|ter, ...pro|gramm; kon|zert|reif; Kon|zert-rei|fe, ...rei|se, ...saal, ...stück, ...tour|nee, ...ver|an|stal|tung**

Kon|zes|si|on, die; -, -en ‹lat.› (behördl. Genehmigung; *meist Plur.*: Zugeständnis); **Kon|zes|si|o|när**, der; -s, -e (Inhaber einer Konzession); **Kon|zes|si|o|nä|rin; kon|zes|si|o|nie|ren** (behördl. genehmigen); **Kon|zes|si|ons-be|reit|schaft, ...in|ha|ber; kon|zes|siv** (*Sprachw.* einräumend); -e Konjunktion; **Kon|zes|siv|satz** (Umstandssatz der Einräumung)

Kon|zil, das; -s, *Plur.* -e *u.* -ien [...iən] ‹lat.› (Versammlung kath. Würdenträger; Gremium an Universitäten); **kon|zi|li|ant** (versöhnlich, umgänglich, verbindlich); **Kon|zi|li|anz**, die; - (Umgänglichkeit, Entgegenkommen); **Kon|zi|li|a|ris|mus**, der; - (kirchenrechtl. Theorie, die das Konzil über den Papst stellt); **Kon|zils|va|ter** *meist Plur.* (stimmberechtigter Teilnehmer an einem Konzil)

kon|zinn ‹lat.› (*Rhet.* ebenmäßig gebaut; *veraltet für* gefällig)

Kon|zi|pi|ent, der; -en, -en (↑R 126) ‹lat.› (*veraltet für* Verfasser eines Schriftstückes; *österr. für* Jurist [zur Ausbildung] in einem Anwaltsbüro); **Kon|zi|pi|en|tin** *(österr.)*; **kon|zi|pie|ren** (verfassen, entwerfen; *Med.* schwanger werden)

kon|zis ‹lat.› (*Rhet.* kurz, gedrängt)

Koof|mich, der; -s, *Plur.* -e *u.* -s (*berlin. abwertend für* Kaufmann)

Koog, der; -[e]s, Köge (*nordd. für* dem Meer abgewonnenes eingedeichtes Land; Polder); *vgl.* Kog

Ko|ope|ra|ti|on (↑R 132), die; -, -en ‹lat.› (Zusammenarbeit); **Ko|ope|ra|ti|ons|ab|kom|men; ko|ope|ra|ti|ons|be|reit; Ko|ope|ra|ti|ons-be|reit|schaft, ...mög|lich|keit; ko|ope|ra|tiv; Ko|ope|ra|tiv**, das; -s, *Plur.* -e [...və], *auch* -s *u.* **Ko|ope|ra|ti|ve** [...və], die; -, -n (Arbeitsgemeinschaft, Genossenschaft); **Ko|ope|ra|tor**, der; -s, ...oren (*veraltet für* Mitarbeiter; *landsch. u. österr. für* kath. Hilfsgeistlicher, Vikar); **ko|ope|rie|ren** (zusammenarbeiten)

Ko|op|ta|ti|on, die; -, -en ‹lat.› (*selten für* Ergänzungs-, Zuwahl); **ko|op|tie|ren** (*selten für* hinzuwählen)

Ko|or|di|na|te, die; -, -n *meist Plur.* ‹lat.› (*Math.* Abszisse u. Ordinate; Zahl, die die Lage eines Punktes in der Ebene od. im Raum bestimmt); **Ko|or|di|na|ten-ach|se** *(Math.)*, **...sys|tem** *(Math.)*; **Ko|or|di|na|ti|on**, die; -, -en; **Ko|or|di|na|tor**, der; -s, ...natoren (jmd., der koordiniert); **ko|or|di|nie|ren** (in ein Gefüge einbauen; aufeinander abstimmen; nebeneinander stellen; *Sprachw.* beiordnen); koordinierende (nebenordnende) Konjunktion (z. B. „und"); **Ko|or|di|nie|rung**

Kop. = Kopeke

Ko|pa|i|va|bal|sam [...v...], der; -s, ‹indian; hebr.› (ein Harz)

Ko|pal, der; -s, -e ‹indian.-span.› (ein Harz); **Ko|pal-fich|te, ...harz, ...lack**

Ko|pe|ke, die; -, -n (↑R 90) ‹russ.› (russ. Münze; *Abk.* Kop.; 100 Kopeken = 1 Rubel)

Ko|pen|ha|gen (Hptst. Dänemarks); *vgl.* København; **Ko|pen|ha|ge|ner** (↑R 103)

Kö|pe|nick (Stadtteil von Berlin); **Kö|pe|ni|cker** (↑R 103); **Kö|pe|ni|cki|a|de**, die; -, -n ‹nach dem Hauptmann von Köpenick› (toller Streich)

Ko|pe|po|de, der; -n, -n *meist Plur.*; ↑R 126 ‹griech.› (*Zool.* Ruderfußkrebs)

Kö|per, der; -s, - ‹niederl.› (ein Gewebe); **Kö|per|bin|dung**

ko|per|ni|ka|nisch; das kopernikanische Weltsystem; eine kopernikanische (tief greifende) Wende; die kopernikanischen „Sechs Bücher über die Umläufe der Himmelskörper" (Hauptwerk des Kopernikus); **Ko|per|ni|kus** (dt. Astronom)

Kopf, der; -[e]s, Köpfe; von Kopf bis Fuß; auf dem Kopf stehen, das Bild, der Turner steht auf dem Kopf; Kopf stehen (einen Kopfstand machen; *ugs. für* völlig verwirrt sein); ich stehe Kopf, habe Kopf gestanden, um Kopf zu stehen; **Kopf-an-Kopf-Ren|nen** (↑R 28); **Kopf-ar|beit, ...ar|bei|ter, ...bahn|hof, ...ball; Kopf|ball|tor**, das; **Kopf-be|de|ckung, ...be|we|gung; Köpf|chen; Kopf-dün|ger** (zur Düngung während der Wachstumszeit), **...dün|gung; köp|feln** (*österr., schweiz. für* einen Kopfsprung machen; den Ball mit dem Kopf stoßen); ich ...[e]le (↑R 16); **köp|fen; Kopf-en|de, ...form, ...fü|ßer** *(Zool.)*, **...geld, ...grip|pe, ...haar, ...hal|tung; kopf|hän|ge|risch; Kopf-haut, ...hö|rer; ...köp|fig** (z. B. vielköpfig); **...köp|fisch** (z. B. rappelköpfisch); **Kopf-jä|ger, ...keil, ...kis|sen; kopf|las|tig; Kopf|las|tig|keit**, die; -; **Köpf|lein; Köpf|ler** (*österr. für* Kopfsprung; Kopfstoß); **kopf|los; Kopf|lo|sig|keit; Kopf-ni|cken** (das; -s), **...nuss, ...putz, ...quo|te; kopf|rech|nen** *nur im Infinitiv gebr.*; **Kopf-rech|nen** (das; -s), **...sa|lat; kopf|scheu; Kopf-schmerz** *(meist Plur.)*, **...schmuck, ...schup|pe** *(meist Plur.)*, **...schuss, ...schüt|teln** (das; -s); **kopf|schüt|telnd; Kopf-schutz, ...schüt|zer, ...sprung, ...stand; Kopf|ste|hen**, das; -s; **Kopf ste|hen** *vgl.* Kopf; **Kopf|stein|pflas|ter; Kopf-steu|er** (die), **...stim|me, ...stoß** *(Fußball, Boxen)*, **...stüt|ze, ...teil** (das *od.* der), **...tuch** (*Plur.* ...tücher); **kopf|über** (↑R 132); **kopf|un|ter; Kopf-ver|let|zung, ...wä|sche, ...weh** (das; -s), **...wei|de** (*vgl.* [1]Weide), **...wun|de, ...zahl; Kopf|zer|bre|chen**, das; -s; viel -

Koph|ta, der; -s, -s (geheimnisvoller ägypt. Magier); **koph|tisch**

Ko|pi|al|buch ‹lat.; dt.› (Buch für Abschriften von Urkunden, Rechtsfällen usw.); **Ko|pi|a|li|en** [...iən] *Plur.* (*veraltet für* Abschreibegebühren); **Ko|pi|a|tur**, die; -, -en (*veraltet für* Abschreiben); **Ko|pie** [*österr. auch* 'ko:piə], die; -, ...ien [ko'pi:ən, *österr. auch* 'ko:piən] (Abschrift; Abdruck; Nachbildung; *Film* Abzug); **Ko|pier|an|stalt; ko|pie|ren** (eine Kopie machen); **Ko|pie|rer** (*ugs. für* Kopiergerät); **Ko|pier-ge|rät, ...pa|pier, ...schutz** *(EDV)*, **...stift** (der)

Ko|pi|lot (zweiter Flugzeugführer; zweiter Fahrer); **Ko|pi|lo|tin**

ko|pi|ös ‹franz.› (*Med.* reichlich, in Fülle)

Ko|pist, der; -en, -en; ↑R 126 ‹lat.› (jmd., der eine Kopie anfertigt)

Kop|pe, die; -, -n (ein Fisch; *landsch. für* Kuppe, z. B. Schneekoppe)

[1]**Kop|pel**, die; -, -n (eingezäunte Weide; Riemen; durch Riemen verbundene Tiere); [2]**Kop|pel**, das; -s, -, *österr.* die; -, -n (Gürtel); **kop|pel|gän|gig** *(Jägerspr.)*; -er Hund; **kop|peln** (verbinden); ich ...[e]le (↑R 16); *vgl.* kuppeln; **Kop|pel|schloss; Kop|pe|lung**, Kopp|lung; **Kop|pe|lungs|ma|nö|ver** *od.* Kopp|lungs|ma|nö|ver; **Kop|pel-wei|de** (*vgl.* [2]Weide), **...wirt|schaft, ...wort** (*Plur.* ...wörter; *Sprachw.*)

kop|pen (Luft schlucken [eine Pferdekrankheit]) **kopp|hei|s|ter** (*nordd. für* kopfüber); koppheister schießen (einen Purzelbaum schlagen) **Kop|lung** *vgl.* Koppelung; **Kopp|lungs|ma|nö|ver** *vgl.* Koppelungsmanöver **Ko|pra** (↑R 130), die; - ‹tamil.-port.› (zerkleinertes u. getrocknetes Mark der Kokosnuss) **Ko|pro|duk|ti|on,** die; -, -en (Gemeinschaftsherstellung, bes. beim Film); **Ko|pro|du|zent,** der; -en, -en (↑R 126); **Ko|pro|du|zen|tin; ko|pro|du|zie|ren** **Kop|ro|lith** [*auch* ...ˈlit] (↑R 130), der; *Gen.* -s *od.* -en, *Plur.* -e[n] (↑R 126) ‹griech.› (versteinerter Kot [urweltl. Tiere]); **Kop|rom,** das; -s, -e (*Med.* Kotgeschwulst); **kop|ro|phag** (*Biol.* Kot essend); **Kop|ro|pha|ge,** der *u.* die; -n, -n; ↑R 5 ff. (*Biol., Psych.* Kotesser[in]); **Kop|ro|pha|gie,** die; - (Kotessen) **Kops,** der; -es, -e ‹engl.› (Spule, Spindel mit Garn) **Kop|te,** der; -n, -n (↑R 126) ‹griech.› (Angehöriger der christl. Kirche in Ägypten); **kop|tisch;** -e Kirche; -e Schrift **Ko|pu|la,** die; -, *Plur.* -s *u.* ...lae [...lɛː] ‹lat., „Band"› (*Sprachw.* Satzband); **Ko|pu|la|ti|on,** die; -, -en (*Biol.* Begattung; *Gartenbau* bestimmte Veredelung von Pflanzen); **ko|pu|la|tiv** (*Sprachw.* verbindend, anreihend); -e Konjunktion (anreihendes Bindewort, z. B. „und"); **Ko|pu|la|ti|vum** [...vum], das; -s, ...va [...va] (*Sprachw.* Zusammensetzung aus zwei gleichgeordneten Bestandteilen, z. B. „taubstumm", „Hemdhose"); **ko|pu|lie|ren** (*Verb zu* Kopulation) **Ko|rah,** *ökum.* Ko|rach (bibl. m. Eigenn.); eine Rotte Korah (*veraltet für* randalierender Haufen) **Ko|ral|le,** die; -, -n ‹griech.› (ein Nesseltier; aus seinem Skelett gewonnener Schmuckstein); **ko|ral|len** (aus Korallen, korallenrot); **Ko|ral|len‿bank** (*Plur.* ...bänke), **...baum, ...in|sel, ...ket|te, ...riff; ko|ral|len|rot** **ko|ram** ‹lat., „vor aller Augen"›; jmdn. koram nehmen (*veraltet für* scharf tadeln); *vgl.* coram publico **Ko|ran** [*auch* ˈkoːraːn], der; -s, -e ‹arab.› (das heilige Buch des Islams); **Ko|ran|su|re** **Korb,** der; -[e]s, Körbe; drei Korb Kabeljau (↑R 90); **Korb|ball; Korb|ball|spiel; Korb|blüt|ler; Körb|chen; Kor|ber** (*schweiz. für* Korbmacher); **Korb‿fla|sche, ...flech|ter** **Kor|bi|ni|an** [*auch* ...ˈbi...] (ein Heiliger; *auch* m. Vorn.) **Körb|lein; Korb‿ma|cher, ...ses|sel, ...stuhl, ...wa|gen, ...wei|de** (*vgl.* [1]Weide), **...wurf** [1]**Kord** (m. Vorn.) [2]**Kord** usw. *vgl.* Cord usw.; **Kord|an|zug** *vgl.* Cordanzug **Kor|de,** die; -, -n ‹franz.› (*veraltet für* schnurartiger Besatz); **Kor|del,** die; -, -n (gedrehte oder geflochtene Schnur; *landsch. für* Bindfaden; *österr. svw.* Korde); **Kör|del|chen** **Kor|de|lia, Kor|de|lie** *vgl.* Cordelia, Cordelie **Kord|ho|se** *vgl.* Cordhose **kor|di|al** ‹lat.› (*veraltet für* herzlich; vertraulich); **Kor|di|a|li|tät,** die; - **kor|die|ren** ‹franz.› (vertiefte Muster in zu glatte Griffe von Werkzeugen einarbeiten); **Kor|dier|ma|schi|ne** **Kor|dil|le|ren** [...diˈljeː...] *Plur.* ‹span.› (amerik. Gebirgszug) **Kor|dit** [*auch* ...ˈdit], der; -s ‹franz.› (ein Schießpulver) **Kor|don** [...ˈdɔ̃ː, *österr.* ...ˈdoːn], der; -s, *Plur.* -s, *österr.* -e ‹franz.› (Postenkette, Absperrung; Ordensband); **Kor|do|nett‿sei|de** (Zwirn-, Schnurseide), **...stich** (ein Zierstich) **Kord|samt** *vgl.* Cordsamt **Kor|du|la** *vgl.* Cordula **Ko|re,** die; -, -n ‹griech.› ([Gebälk tragende] Frauengestalt) **Ko|rea** (eine Halbinsel Ostasiens); **Ko|rea|krieg** (1950 bis 1953); **Ko|re|a|ner; Ko|re|a|ne|rin; ko|re|a|nisch** **Ko|re|fe|rat, Ko|re|fe|rent, ko|re|fe|rie|ren** *vgl.* Korreferat usw. **Ko|re|gis|seur** **kö|ren** (*fachspr. für* [männl. Haustiere] zur Zucht auswählen) **Kor|fi|ot,** der; -en, -en; ↑R 126 (Bewohner der Insel Korfu); **kor|fi|o|tisch; Kor|fu** (ionische Insel u. Stadt); *vgl.* Kerkyra **Kör‿ge|setz** (*fachspr.*), **...hengst** **Ko|ri|an|der,** der; -s, - *Plur. selten* ‹griech.› (Gewürzpflanze u. deren Samen); **Ko|ri|an|der‿öl, ...schnaps; Ko|ri|an|do|li,** das; -[s], - ‹ital.› (*österr. für* Konfetti) **Ko|rin|na** (altgriech. Dichterin); *vgl.* Corinna **Ko|rinth** (griech. Stadt); **Ko|rin|the,** die; -, -n *meist Plur.* (kleine Rosinenart); **Ko|rin|then|brot; Ko|rin|then|ka|cker** (*derb für* kleinlicher Mensch); **Ko|rin|ther** (↑R 103); **Ko|rin|ther|brief** (↑R 105); **ko|rin|thisch;** korinthische Säulenordnung, *aber* (↑R 102): der Korinthische Krieg **Kork,** der; -[e]s, -e (Rinde der Korkeiche; Korken); **Kork‿brand, ...ei|che; kor|ken** (aus Kork); **Kor|ken,** der; -s, - (Stöpsel aus Kork); **Kor|ken|geld** (*veraltend für* Entschädigung für den Wirt, wenn der Gast im Wirtshaus seinen eigenen Wein o. Ä. trinkt); **Kor|ken|zie|her; Kork‿geld** (*svw.* Korkengeld), **...gür|tel; kor|kig;** der Wein schmeckt korkig; **Kork‿soh|le, ...wes|te, ...zie|her** (*svw.* Korkenzieher) **Kor|mo|phyt,** der; -en, -en *meist Plur.;* ↑R 126 ‹griech.› (*Bot.* Sammelbezeichnung für Farn- u. Samenpflanzen) **Kor|mo|ran** [*österr.* ˈkɔr...], der; -s, -e ‹lat.› (ein Schwimmvogel) **Kor|mus,** der; - ‹griech.› (*Bot.* aus Wurzel u. Sprossachse bestehender Pflanzenkörper) [1]**Korn,** das; -[e]s, *Plur.* Körner *u.* (*für* Getreidearten:) -e; [2]**Korn,** das; -[e]s, -e *Plur. selten* (Teil der Visiereinrichtung); [3]**Korn,** der; -[e]s (*ugs. für* Kornbranntwein); 3 -; **Korn|äh|re** **Kor|nak,** der; -s, -s ‹singhal.› ([ind.] Elefantenführer) **Korn|blu|me; korn|blu|men|blau; Korn|brannt|wein; Körn|chen; Körndl|bau|er** (*österr. für* Bauer, der hauptsächlich Getreide anbaut) **Kor|nea** *vgl.* Cornea **Kor|ne|lia, Kor|ne|lie, Kor|ne|li|us** *vgl.* Cornelia, Cornelie, Cornelius **Kor|nel|kir|sche,** die; -, -n ‹lat.; dt.› (ein Zierstrauch) **kör|nen** **Kor|ner** *vgl.* Corner [1]**Kör|ner,** Theodor (dt. Dichter) [2]**Kör|ner** (Markierstift zum Ankörnen) **Kör|ner‿fres|ser, ...fut|ter** (*vgl.* [1]Futter) [1]**Kor|nett,** der; -[e]s, *Plur.* -e *u.* -s ‹franz.› (*früher* Fähnrich [bei der Reiterei]); [2]**Kor|nett,** das; -[e]s, *Plur.* -e *u.* -s (ein Blechblasinstrument); **Kor|net|tist,** der; -en, -en; ↑R 126 (Kornettspieler) **Korn|feld; kör|nig** **kor|nisch; Kor|nisch,** das; -[s] (früher in Cornwall gesprochene kelt. Sprache); *vgl.* Deutsch; **Kor|ni|sche,** das; -n; *vgl.* Deutsche, das **Korn|kam|mer; Körn|lein; Korn|ra|de** (ein Ackerwildkraut); **Korn|spei|cher; Kör|nung** (bestimmte Größe kleiner Materialteilchen; das Körnen; *Jägerspr.* Futter zur Wildfütterung; *auch für* Futterplatz)

Ko|rol|la, Ko|rol|le, die; -, ...llen ‹griech.› (Blumenkrone); **Ko|rol|lar**, das; -s, -e *u.* **Ko|rol|la|ri|um**, das; -s, ...ien [...iən] (*Logik* Satz, der selbstverständlich aus einem bewiesenen Satz folgt); **Ko|rol|le** *vgl.* Korolla

Ko|ro|man|del (vorderind. Küstengebiet); **Ko|ro|man|del˽holz, ...küs|te** (die; -)

[1]**Ko|ro|na**, die; -, ...nen ‹griech.-lat., „Kranz, Krone"› (*Kunstw.* Heiligenschein; *Astron.* Strahlenkranz [um die Sonne]; *ugs. für* [fröhliche] Runde, [Zuhörer]kreis; *auch für* Horde); [2]**Ko|ro|na** *vgl.* Corona; **ko|ro|nar** (*Med.* die Herzkranzgefäße betreffend); **Ko|ro|nar˽in|suf|fi|zi|enz, ...skle|ro|se**

Kör|per, der; -s, -; **Kör|per˽bau** (der; -[e]s), **...be|herr|schung; kör|per|be|hin|dert; Kör|per|be|hin|der|te**, der *u.* die; -n, -n (↑R 5 ff.); **kör|per|ei|gen**; -e Abwehrstoffe; **Kör|per˽ein|satz** *(Sport)*, **...er|zie|hung, ...fül|le, ...ge|ruch, ...ge|wicht, ...grö|ße; kör|per|haft; Kör|per˽hal|tung, ...kraft, ...kul|tur** (die; -), **...län|ge; kör|per|lich; Kör|per|lich|keit**, die; -; **kör|per|los; Kör|per|pfle|ge**, die; -; **Kör|per|schaft; kör|per|schaft|lich; Kör|per|schafts|steu|er, Kör|per|schaft|steu|er**, die (↑R 34); **Kör|per˽teil** (der), **...tem|pe|ra|tur, ...ver|let|zung, ...wär|me**

Kor|po|ra (*Plur. von* [2]Korpus)

Kor|po|ral, der; -s, *Plur.* -e, *auch* ...äle ‹franz.› (*früher* Führer einer Korporalschaft; Unteroffizier; *schweiz.* niederster Unteroffiziersgrad); **Kor|po|ral|schaft** (*früher* Untergruppe der Kompanie für den inneren Dienst)

Kor|po|ra|ti|on, die; -, -en ‹lat.› (Körperschaft; Studentenverbindung); **kor|po|ra|tiv** (körperschaftlich; einheitlich; eine Studentenverbindung betreffend); **kor|po|riert** (einer stud. Korporation angehörend); **Korps** [ko:r], das; - [ko:r(s)], - [ko:rs] ‹franz.› (Heeresabteilung; [schlagende] stud. Verbindung); **Korps˽bru|der, ...geist** (der; -[e]s), **...stu|dent; kor|pu|lent** ‹lat.› (beleibt); **Kor|pu|lenz**, die; - (Beleibtheit); [1]**Kor|pus**, der; -, ...pusse (Christusfigur am Kreuz; *fachspr. für* massiver Teil von Möbeln; *ugs. scherzh. für* Körper); [2]**Kor|pus**, das; -, ...pora (einer wissenschaftl. Untersuchung zugrunde liegender Text; *Musik [heute meist* der; *nur Sing.]* Klangkörper eines Instruments); [3]**Kor|pus**, die; - (ein alter Schriftgrad); **Kor|pus|kel**, das; -s, -n, *fachspr. häufig* die; -, -n ‹lat., „Körperchen"› (kleines Teilchen der Materie); **Kor|pus|ku|lar|strah|len** *Plur.* (*Physik* Strahlen aus elektr. geladenen Teilchen); **Kor|pus|ku|lar|the|o|rie**, die; - (Theorie, nach der das Licht aus Korpuskeln besteht)

Kor|ral, der; -s, -e ‹span.› ([Fang]gehege für Wildtiere)

Kor|ra|si|on, die; -, -en ‹lat.› (*Geol.* Abschabung, Abschleifung)

Kor|re|fe|rat [*auch* ...'ra:t], *landsch. u. österr.* Ko|re|fe|rat, das; -[e]s, -e ‹lat.› (zweiter Bericht; Nebenbericht); **Kor|re|fe|rent** [*auch* ...'rɛnt], *landsch. u. österr.* Ko|re|fe|rent, der; -en, -en; ↑R 126 (zweiter Referent; Mitgutachter); **kor|re|fe|rie|ren** [*auch* ...'ri:...], *landsch. u. österr.* ko|re|fe|rie|ren

kor|rekt ‹lat.›; **kor|rek|ter|wei|se; Kor|rekt|heit**, die; -; **Kor|rek|ti|on**, die; -, -en (*veraltet für* [Ver]besserung; Regelung); **kor|rek|tiv** (*veraltet für* bessernd; zurechtweisend); **Kor|rek|tiv**, das; -s, -e [...və] (Besserungs-, Ausgleichsmittel); **Kor|rek|tor**, der; -s, ...oren (Berichtiger von Manuskripten od. Druckabzügen); **Kor|rek|to|rat**, das; -[e]s, -e (Abteilung der Korrektoren); **Kor|rek|to|rin; Kor|rek|tur**, die; -, -en (Berichtigung [des Schriftsatzes], Verbesserung); Korrektur lesen; **Kor|rek|tur˽ab|zug, ...bo|gen, ...fah|ne, ...le|sen** (das; -s), **...vor|schrif|ten** *(Plur.)*, **...zei|chen**

kor|re|lat, kor|re|la|tiv ‹lat.› (einander wechselseitig erfordernd und bedingend); **Kor|re|lat**, das; -[e]s, -e (Ergänzung, Entsprechung; *Sprachw.* Wort, das auf ein anderes bezogen ist); **Kor|re|la|ti|on**, die; -, -en (Wechselbeziehung); **Kor|re|la|ti|ons|rech|nung** *(Math.)*; **kor|re|la|tiv** *vgl.* korrelat; **kor|re|lie|ren**

kor|re|pe|tie|ren ‹lat.› (*Musik* mit jmdm. eine Gesangspartie vom Klavier aus einüben); **Kor|re|pe|ti|tor**

kor|res|pek|tiv (↑R 132) ‹lat.› (*Rechtsspr.* gemeinschaftlich); korrespektives Testament

Kor|res|pon|dent (↑R 132), der; -en, -en (↑R 126) ‹lat.› (auswärtiger, fest engagierter Berichterstatter; Bearbeiter des [kaufmänn.] Schriftwechsels); **Kor|res|pon|den|tin; Kor|res|pon|denz**, die; -, -en (Briefverkehr, -wechsel; *regional für* Berichterstattung; *veraltend für* Übereinstimmung); **Kor|res|pon|denz|bü|ro; Kor|res|pon|denz|kar|te** (*österr. für* Postkarte); **kor|res|pon|die|ren** (im Briefverkehr stehen; übereinstimmen); korrespondierendes Mitglied (auswärtiges Mitglied [einer Akademie])

Kor|ri|dor, der; -s, -e ‹ital.› ([Wohnungs]flur, Gang; schmaler Gebietsstreifen); **Kor|ri|dor|tür**

Kor|ri|gend, der; -en, -en (↑R 126) ‹lat., „der zu Bessernde"› (*veraltet für* Sträfling); **Kor|ri|gen|da** *Plur.* ([Druck]fehler, Fehlerverzeichnis); **Kor|ri|gens**, das; -, *Plur.* ...gentia *u.* ...genzien [...iən] *meist Plur.* (*Pharm.* geschmackverbessernder Zusatz zu Arzneien); **kor|ri|gie|ren** (berichtigen; verbessern)

kor|ro|die|ren ‹lat.› (*fachspr. für* zersetzen, zerstören; der Korrosion unterliegen); **Kor|ro|si|on**, die; -, -en (Zersetzung, Zerstörung); **kor|ro|si|ons˽be|stän|dig, ...fest; Kor|ro|si|ons|schutz; kor|ro|si|on[s]|ver|hü|tend; kor|ro|siv** (zerfressend, zerstörend; durch Korrosion hervorgerufen)

kor|rum|pie|ren ‹lat.› ([charakterlich] verderben; bestechen); **kor|rum|piert** (verderbt [von Stellen in alten Texten]); **Kor|rum|pie|rung; kor|rupt** ([moralisch] verdorben; bestechlich); **Kor|rup|ti|on**, die; -, -en (Bestechlichkeit; das Verderben, Bestechung; [Sitten]verfall, -verderbnis); **Kor|rup|ti|ons|skan|dal**

Kor|sa|ge [...'za:ʒə], die; -, -n ‹franz.› (trägerloses, versteiftes Oberteil eines Kleides)

Kor|sar, der; -en, -en (↑R 126) ‹ital.› (*früher für* Seeräuber[schiff]; kleine Zweimannjolle)

Kor|se, der; -n, -n; ↑R 126 (Bewohner Korsikas)

Kor|se|lett, das; -s, *Plur.* -s, *auch* -e ‹franz.› (bequemes, leichtes Korsett); **Kor|sett**, das; -s, *Plur.* -s, *auch* -e (Mieder; *Med.* Stützvorrichtung für die Wirbelsäule); **Kor|sett|stan|ge**

Kor|si|ka (Insel im Mittelmeer); *vgl.* Corsica; **Kor|sin; kor|sisch**

Kor|so, der; -s, -s ‹ital.› (Schaufahrt; Umzug; Straße [für das Schaufahren])

Kors|te, die; -, -n (*landsch. für* Endstück des Brotes)

Kor|tex, der; -[es], *Plur.* -e, *auch* ...tizes [...tse:s] ‹lat.› (*Med.* äußere

Zellschicht eines Organs, bes. Hirnrinde); **kor|ti|kal** (den Kortex betreffend); **Kor|ti|son,** *fachspr.* Cor|ti|son, das; -s ‹Kunstw.› (*Pharm.* ein Hormonpräparat)
Ko|rund, der; -[e]s, -e ‹tamil.› (ein Mineral)
Kö|rung ‹*zu* kören›
Kor|vet|te [...v...], die; -, -n ‹franz.› (leichtes [Segel]kriegsschiff); **Kor|vet|ten|ka|pi|tän**
Kor|vey *vgl.* Corvey
Ko|ry|bant, der; -en, -en (↑R 126) ‹griech.› (Priester der Kybele); **ko|ry|ban|tisch** (wild begeistert, ausgelassen)
Ko|ry|phäe, die; -, -n ‹griech.› (bedeutende Persönlichkeit, hervorragender Gelehrter usw.)
Kos (Insel des Dodekanes)
Ko|sak, der; -en, -en (↑R 126) ‹russ.› (Angehöriger der militär. organisierten Grenzbevölkerung im zarist. Russland; leichter Reiter); **Ko|sa|ken‿müt|ze, ...pferd**
Ko|sche|nil|le [...'niljə], die; -, -n ‹span.› (eine Schildlaus; *nur Sing.:* ein roter Farbstoff); **Ko|sche|nil|le|laus**
ko|scher ‹hebr.-jidd.› (den jüd. Speisegesetzen gemäß [erlaubt]; *ugs. für* einwandfrei)
K.-o.-Schlag; ↑R 28 (*Boxen* Niederschlag); *vgl. auch* Knock-out-Schlag
Koś|ci|usz|ko [kɔʃ'tʃjuʃkɔ] (poln. Nationalheld)
Ko|se|form
Ko|se|kans, der; -, *Plur.* -, *auch* ...anten ‹lat.› (*Math.* Kehrwert des Sinus im rechtwinkligen Dreieck; *Zeichen* cosec)
ko|sen; du kost; **Ko|se‿na|me, ...wort** (*Plur.* ...wörter, *auch* ...worte)
K.-o.-Sie|ger (↑R 28); *vgl. auch* Knock-out-Schlag
Ko|si|ma *vgl.* Cosima
Ko|si|nus, der; -, *Plur.* - [...nu:s] *u.* -se *Plur. selten* ‹lat.› (*Math.* eine Winkelfunktion im rechtwinkligen Dreieck; *Zeichen* cos)
Kos|me|tik, die; - ‹griech.› (Körper- u. Schönheitspflege); **Kos|me|ti|ke|rin; Kos|me|tik‿sa|lon, ...ta|sche; Kos|me|ti|kum,** das; -s, ...ka ‹griech.-lat.› (Schönheitsmittel); **kos|me|tisch**
kos|misch ‹griech.› (im Kosmos; das Weltall betreffend; All...); -e Strahlung; **Kos|mo|bi|o|lo|gie** [*auch* 'kɔs...] (Lehre von den außerird. Einflüssen auf die Gesamtheit der Lebenserscheinungen); **Kos|mo|drom,** das; -s, -e ‹griech.-russ.› (Startplatz für Raumschiffe); **Kos|mo|go|nie,** die; -, ...ien ‹griech.› (Weltentstehungslehre); **kos|mo|go|nisch; Kos|mo|gra|phie,** die; -, ...ien (*veraltet für* Weltbeschreibung); **Kos|mo|lo|gie,** die; -, ...ien (Lehre von der Entstehung u. Entwicklung des Weltalls); **kos|mo|lo|gisch; Kos|mo|naut,** der; -en, -en (↑R 126) ‹griech.-russ.› (Weltraumfahrer); **Kos|mo|nau|tik,** die; -; **Kos|mo|nau|tin; Kos|mo|po|lit,** der; -en, -en (↑R 126) ‹griech.› (Weltbürger); **kos|mo|po|li|tisch; Kos|mo|po|li|tis|mus,** der; - (Weltbürgertum); **Kos|mos,** der; - (Weltall, Weltraum); **Kos|mo|the|is|mus,** der; - (philos. Anschauung, die Gott und die Welt als Einheit begreift); **Kos|mot|ron** [*auch* ...'tro:n] (↑R 130), das; -s, *Plur.* ...trone, *auch* -s (*Kernphysik* Teilchenbeschleuniger)
Kos|suth ['kɔʃut] (ung. Nationalheld)
Kost, die; -
kos|tal ‹lat.› (*Med.* zu den Rippen gehörend)
Kos|ta|ri|ka usw. (*eindeutschend für* Costa Rica usw.)
kost|bar; Kost|bar|keit
[1]**kos|ten** (schmecken)
[2]**kos|ten** (wert sein); es kostet mich viel [Geld], nichts, hundert Mark, das kostet ihn *od.* ihm die Stellung; **Kos|ten** *Plur.;* auf Kosten des ... *od.* von ...; (↑R 40:) Kosten sparende Maßnahmen; **Kos|ten‿an|schlag, ...be|rech|nung, ...dämp|fung; kos|ten|de|ckend; Kos|ten‿ent|wick|lung, ...er|stat|tung, ...ex|plo|si|on, ...fak|tor, ...fest|set|zung, ...fra|ge; kos|ten|frei; Kos|ten|grün|de** *Plur.;* aus -n; **kos|ten‿güns|tig, ...in|ten|siv, ...los; Kos|ten|mie|te; kos|ten|neut|ral; Kos|ten-Nut|zen-A|na|ly|se; kos|ten|pflich|tig; Kos|ten‿punkt, ...rah|men** (der; -s), **...sen|kung; Kos|ten spa|rend** *vgl.* Kosten; **Kos|ten‿stei|ge|rung, ...vor|an|schlag**
Kost‿gän|ger, ...ge|ber, ...geld
köst|lich; Köst|lich|keit
Kost|pro|be
kost|spie|lig; Kost|spie|lig|keit, die; -
Kos|tüm, das; -s, -e ‹franz.› (aus Rock und Jacke bestehende Damenkleidung; Verkleidung); **Kos|tüm‿bild|ner, ...bild|ne|rin, ...fest, ...film, ...fun|dus, ...ge|schich|te; kos|tü|mie|ren;** sich - ([ver]kleiden); **Kos|tü|mie|rung; Kos|tüm|ver|leih**
Kost|ver|äch|ter (*scherzh.*)
K.-o.-Sys|tem (Austragungsmodus sportl. Wettkämpfe, bei dem der jeweils Unterliegende aus dem Wettbewerb ausscheidet)
Kot, der; -[e]s, -e *Plur. selten*
Ko|tan|gens, der; -, - *Plur. selten* ‹lat.› (*Math.* eine Winkelfunktion im Dreieck; *Zeichen* cot)
Ko|tau, der; -s, -s ‹chin.› (demütige Ehrerweisung); - machen
[1]**Ko|te,** die; -, -n ‹franz.› (*Geogr.* Geländepunkt [einer Karte], dessen Höhenlage genau vermessen ist)
[2]**Ko|te,** die; -, -n *od.* Kot|ten, der; -s, - (*nordd. für* kleines Haus)
[3]**Ko|te,** die; -, -n ‹finn.› (Lappenzelt)
Kö|te, die; -, -n (*fachspr. für* hintere Seite der Zehe bei Rindern u. Pferden)
Kö|tel, der; -s, - (*nordd. für* Kotklümpchen)
Ko|te|lett [*auch* kɔt'lɛt], das; -s, -s ‹franz., „Rippchen"› (Rippenstück); **Ko|te|let|ten** *Plur.* (Backenbart)
Kö|ten|ge|lenk (*Zool.* Fesselgelenk)
Ko|ten|ta|fel (*Geogr.* Höhentafel)
Kö|ter, der; -s, - (*abwertend für* Hund)
Ko|te|rie, die; -, ...ien ‹franz.› (*veraltet für* Kaste; Klüngel)
Kot|flü|gel
Kö|then (Stadt südwestl. von Dessau); **Kö|the|ner** (↑R 103)
Ko|thurn, der; -s, -e ‹griech.› (dicksohliger Bühnenschuh der Schauspieler im antiken Theater); auf hohem Kothurn einhergehen (*geh. für* hochtrabend reden)
ko|tie|ren ‹franz.› (*Kaufmannsspr.* ein Wertpapier an der Börse zulassen); **Ko|tie|rung**
ko|tig
Ko|til|lon ['kɔtiljɔ̃, *auch* kɔtil'jɔ̃:], der; -s, -s ‹franz.› (ein alter Gesellschaftstanz)
Köt|ner (*nordd.; svw.* Kätner)
Ko|to, das; -s, -s, *auch* die; -, -s ‹jap.› (ein zitherähnliches jap. Musikinstrument)
Ko|ton [...'tɔ̃:], der; -s, -s ‹arab.-franz.› (*selten für* Baumwolle); *vgl. auch* Cotton; **ko|to|ni|sie|ren** [...toni...] (*Textilw.* baumwollähnlich machen); **Ko|to|ni|sie|rung**
Ko|tor, *auch* Cat|ta|ro (jugoslaw. Stadt)
Ko|to|rin|de ‹indian.; dt.› (ein altes Heilmittel)
Ko|trai|ner (*svw.* Assistenztrainer)
Kot‿sass *od.* **...sas|se** (*nordd.; svw.* Kötner)
Kot|schin|chi|na ‹„Kleinchina"›

(alte Bez. des Südteils von Vietnam); **Kot|schin|chi|na|huhn**

Kot|ten *vgl.* ²Kote; **Kot|ter,** der; -s, - (*nordd. veraltend für* ²Kote; *österr. für* Arrest); **Köt|ter** (*nordd. für* Inhaber einer ²Kote)

Ko|ty|le|do|ne, die; -, -n *meist Plur.* ‹griech.› (*Zool.* Zotte der tierischen Embryohülle; *Bot.* pflanzl. Keimblatt); **Ko|ty|lo|sau|ri|er** (ein ausgestorbenes eidechsenähnliches Kriechtier)

Kotz|bro|cken (*derb für* widerwärtiger Mensch)

¹Kot|ze, die; -, -n (*landsch. für* wollene Decke, Wollzeug; wollener Umhang); *vgl.* Kotzen

²Kot|ze, die; - (*derb für* Erbrochenes)

Köt|ze, die; -, -n (*mitteld. für* Rückentragkorb)

Kot|ze|bue [...bu] (dt. Dichter)

kot|zen (*derb für* sich übergeben); du kotzt

Kot|zen, der; -s, - (*Nebenform von* ¹Kotze); **kot|zen|grob** (*landsch. für* sehr grob)

Köt|zer, der; -s, - (*svw.* Kops)

kot|ze|rig (*derb für* zum Erbrechen übel); **kotz‿jäm|mer|lich, ...lang|wei|lig, ...übel** (↑R 132; *derb*)

Ko|va|ri|an|ten|phä|no|men [kova..., *auch* 'ko:va...] ‹lat.; griech.› (*Psych.* Täuschung der Raum-, Tiefenwahrnehmung); **Ko|va|ri|anz,** die; -, -en ‹lat.› (*Physik, Math.*)

Ko|xal|gie (↑R 132), die; -, ...ien ‹lat.; griech.› (*Med.* Hüftgelenkschmerz); **Ko|xi|tis,** die; -, ...itiden ‹lat.› (Hüftgelenkentzündung)

Ko|zy|tus *vgl.* Kokytos

kp = Kilopond

kPa = Kilopascal

KPD = Kommunistische Partei Deutschlands

kpm = Kilopondmeter

kr = Krone (Währungseinheit)

Kr = *chem. Zeichen für* Krypton

Kr., Krs. = Kreis

Kraal *vgl.* Kral

Krab|be, die; -, -n (ein Krebs, eine Garnele; *Archit.* Steinblume an Giebeln usw.; *ugs. für* Kind, junges Mädchen); **Krab|bel|al|ter; Krab|be|lei** *(ugs.)*; **krab|be|lig** *vgl.* krabblig; **Krab|bel|kind; krab|beln** (*ugs. für* sich kriechend fortbewegen; kitzeln; jucken); ich ...[e]le (↑R 16); es kribbelt u. krabbelt; *vgl. aber* grabbeln

krab|ben (*fachspr. für* [Geweben] Glätte u. Glanz verleihen)

Krab|ben‿fi|scher, ...kut|ter

krabb|lig, krab|be|lig *(ugs.)*

krach!; Krach, der; -[e]s, Kräche (*nur Sing.:* Lärm; *ugs. für* Streit; Zusammenbruch); mit Ach und - (mit Müh und Not); - schlagen; **kra|chen;** sich mit jmdm. - (*ugs. für* streiten); **Kra|chen,** der; -s, Krächen (*schweiz. mdal. für* Schlucht, kleines Tal); **Kra|cher** (*ugs. für* Knallkörper); **Kra|cherl,** das; -s, -n (*österr., bayr. für* Brauselimonade); **kra|chig; Krach|le|der|ne,** die; -n, -n (*bayr. für* kurze Lederhose); **Krach|man|del** *(landsch.)*; **kräch|zen;** du krächzt; **Kräch|zer** (*ugs. für* gekrächzter Laut; *scherzh. für* Mensch, der heiser, rau spricht)

Kra|cke, die; -, -n (*landsch. für* altes Pferd)

kra|cken [*auch* 'krɛ...] ‹engl.› (*Chemie* Schweröle in Leichtöle umwandeln); **Krä|cker,** der; -s, -; *vgl.* Cracker; **Kra|ckung** [*auch* 'krɛ...] *(Chemie)*; **Krack|ver|fah|ren**

Krad, das; -[e]s, Kräder (*Kurzform für* Kraftrad [bes. bei Militär u. Polizei]); **Krad‿fah|rer, ...mel|der** *(Milit.)*, **...schüt|ze**

kraft (↑R 46); *Präp. mit Gen.:* kraft meines Amtes; **¹Kraft,** die; -, Kräfte; in Kraft treten, das in Kraft getretene Gesetz; (↑R 50): das In-Kraft-Treten; etwas außer Kraft setzen; **²Kraft** (m. Vorn.); **Kraft‿akt, ...an|stren|gung, ...auf|wand, ...aus|druck, ...brü|he, ...drosch|ke** *(veraltend)*; **Kräf|te‿paar** *(Physik)*, **...pa|ral|le|lo|gramm** *(Physik)*; **kraft|er|füllt; Kräf|te|ver|hält|nis; kräf|te|zeh|rend; Kraft‿fah|rer, ...fah|re|rin; Kraft|fahr|zeug** (*Abk.* Kfz); **Kraft|fahr|zeug|brief; Kraft|fahr|zeug-Haft|pflicht|ver|si|che|rung** (↑R 24); **Kraft|fahr|zeug‿hal|ter, ...in|dust|rie, ...kenn|zei|chen, ...re|pa|ra|tur|werk|statt, ...schein, ...steu|er** (die), **...ver|si|che|rung; Kraft‿feld** *(Physik)*, **...fut|ter; kräf|tig; kräf|ti|gen; Kräf|ti|gung; Kräf|ti|gungs|mit|tel,** das; **kraft|los;** saft- und kraftlos (↑R 23); **Kraft|los|er|klä|rung** *(Rechtsw.)*; **Kraft|lo|sig|keit,** die; -; **Kraft‿mei|er** (*ugs.* jmd., der mit seiner Kraft protzt), **...mei|e|rei, ...post** *(früher)*, **...pro|be, ...protz, ...rad** (*Kurzform* Krad), **...sport, ...stoff; Kraft|stoff‿pum|pe, ...ver|brauch; Kraft|strom; kraft|strot|zend; Kraft|ver|kehr; kraft|voll; Kraft‿wa|gen, ...werk; Kraft|werk[s]|be|trei|ber; Kraft|wort** *Plur.* ...worte u. ...wörter

Kra|ge, die; -, -n (*Archit.* Konsole); **Krä|gel|chen, Krä|ge|lein; Kra|gen,** der; -s, *Plur.* -, *südd., österr. u. schweiz. auch* Krägen; **Kra|gen‿bär, ...knopf, ...num|mer, ...wei|te; Krag‿stein** (*Archit.* vorspringender, als Träger verwendeter Stein), **...trä|ger** (*Archit.* Konsole)

Krä|he, die; -, -n; **krä|hen; Krä|hen|fü|ße** *Plur.* (*ugs. für* Fältchen in den Augenwinkeln; unleserlich gekritzelte Schrift; kleine, spitze Eisenstücke, die die Reifen verfolgender Autos beschädigen sollen); **Krä|hen|nest** (*auch für* Ausguck am Schiffsmast)

Krähl, der; -[e]s, -e (*Bergmannsspr.* besonderer Rechen); **kräh|len**

Kräh|win|kel, das; -s, *meist ohne Artikel* ‹nach dem Ortsnamen in Kotzebues „Kleinstädtern"› (spießbürgerliche Kleinstadt); **Kräh|win|ke|lei** (spießiges Verhalten); **Kräh|wink|ler** (↑R 103)

Kraich|gau, der; -[e]s (Hügelland zwischen Odenwald u. Schwarzwald); **Kraich|gau|er** (↑R 103)

Krain (Westteil von Slowenien)

Kra|ka|tau [*auch* ...'tau] (vulkanische Insel zwischen Sumatra u. Java)

Kra|kau (Stadt in Polen); **Kra|kau|er,** die; -, - (eine Art Knackwurst)

Kra|ke, der; -n, -n (↑R 126) ‹norw.› (Riesentintenfisch)

Kra|keel, der; -s (*ugs. für* Lärm u. Streit; Unruhe); **kra|kee|len** *(ugs.)*; er hat krakeelt; **Kra|kee|ler** *(ugs.)*; **Kra|kee|le|rei** *(ugs.)*

Kra|kel, der; -s, - (*ugs. für* schwer leserliches Schriftzeichen)

Kra|ke|lee (*eindeutschend für* Craquelé)

Kra|ke|lei *(ugs.)*; **Kra|kel|fuß** *meist Plur.* (*ugs. für* krakeliges Schriftzeichen); **kra|ke|lig** *(ugs.)*; **kra|keln** *(ugs.)*; ich ...[e]le (↑R 16); **krak|lig** *(ugs.)*

Kra|ko|wi|ak, der; -s, -s ‹poln.› (poln. Nationaltanz)

Kral, der; -s, *Plur.* -e, *auch* -s ‹port.-afrikaans› (Runddorf afrik. Stämme)

Kräll|chen; Kral|le, die; -, -n; **kral|len** (mit den Krallen zufassen; *ugs. für* unerlaubt wegnehmen); sich an etwas *od.* jmdn. -; **Kral|len‿af|fe, ...frosch; kral|lig**

Kram, der; -[e]s

Kram|bam|bu|li, der; -[s], -[s] (*Studentenspr.* ein alkoholisches Mixgetränk)

kra|men (*ugs. für* durchsuchen; aufräumen); **Krä|mer** (*veraltet, aber noch landsch. für* Kleinhändler); **Kra|me|rei; Krä|me|rei** (*veraltet, aber noch landsch. für* kleiner Laden); **Krä|mer|geist,** der; -[e]s *(abwertend);* **krä|mer|haft; Krä|me|rin** *(veraltet);* **Krä|mer-⌣la|tein** (*veraltet, aber noch landsch. für* Kauderwelsch, Händlersprache), **...seel|e** (kleinlicher Mensch); **Kram|la|den** *(abwertend);* **Kram|markt**

Kram|mets|vo|gel (*landsch. für* Wacholderdrossel)

Kram|pe, die; -, -n (u-förmig gebogener Metallhaken); **kram|pen** (anklammern); **Kram|pen,** der; -s, - (*Nebenform von* Krampe; *bayr., österr. für* Spitzhacke)

Krampf, der; -[e]s, Krämpfe; **Krampf|ader** (↑R 132); **Krampf-ader|bil|dung** (↑R 132); **krampf-ar|tig; kramp|fen;** sich -; **krampf|haft; Krampf|hus|ten; kramp|fig; krampf|stil|lend**

[1]**Kram|pus,** der; -, ...pi (*Med.* Muskelkrampf)

[2]**Kram|pus,** der; *Gen.* - *u.* -ses, *Plur.* -se (*österr. für* Begleiter des Sankt Nikolaus; Knecht Ruprecht)

Kra|mu|ri, die; - (*österr. ugs. für* Kram, Gerümpel)

Kran, der; -[e]s, *Plur.* Kräne *u. (fachspr.)* Krane (Hebevorrichtung; *landsch. für* Zapfen, Zapfröhre, Wasserhahn); **kran|bar** (*Technik* was gekrant werden kann); **Krän|chen** (*landsch. für* Zapfen; *auch* das Gezapfte); **kra|nen** (*Technik* mit dem Kran transportieren)

Kra|ne|wit|ter, der; -s, - (*bayr., österr. für* Wacholderschnaps)

Kran|füh|rer

Kran|gel, der; -, -n (*Bergsteigen* verdrehte Stelle im Seil); **krangeln;** das Seil krangelt; **krän|gen** (*Seemannsspr.* sich seitwärts neigen [vom Schiff]); **Krän|gung**

kra|ni|al ‹griech.› (*Med.* den Schädel betreffend, Schädel...)

Kra|nich, der; -s, -e (ein Stelzvogel)

Kra|ni|o|lo|gie, die; - ‹griech.› (*Med.* Schädellehre); **Kra|ni|o-met|rie** (↑R 130), die; -, ...ien (Schädelmessung); **Kra|ni|o|te,** der; -n, -n *meist Plur.* (*Zool.* Wirbeltier mit Schädel); **Kra|ni|o|to-mie,** die; -, ...ien (*Med.* Schädelöffnung)

krank; kränker, kränkste (↑R 39:) krank sein, werden, liegen; sich krank ärgern, fühlen, stellen; weil die Belastungen uns krank machen; *vgl. aber* krankfeiern, kranklachen, krankmachen, krankmelden, krankschießen, krankschreiben; **Kran|ke,** der *u.* die; -n, -n (↑R 5ff.); **krän|keln;** ich ...[e]le (↑R 16); **kran|ken;** an etwas - (durch etwas beeinträchtigt sein; *veraltet für* an etwas erkrankt sein); **krän|ken** (beleidigen, verletzen); **Kran|ken⌣an|stalt, ...be-richt, ...be|such, ...bett, ...blatt; krän|kend; Kran|ken⌣geld, ...ge|schich|te, ...gut** (das; -[e]s; bestimmte Anzahl untersuchter Patienten), **...gym|nas|tik, ...gym-nas|tin, ...haus, ...kas|se, ...la-ger, ...pfle|ge, ...pfle|ger, ...pfle-ge|rin, ...sal|bung** (kath. Sakrament), **...schein, ...schwes|ter, ...trans|port; kran|ken|ver|si-chert; Kran|ken|ver|si|che-rung; kran|ken|ver|si|che-rungs|pflich|tig; Kran|ken⌣wa-gen, ...zim|mer; krank|fei|ern** (↑R 38 f.; *ugs. für* der Arbeit fernbleiben, ohne ernstlich krank zu sein; *landsch. für* arbeitsunfähig sein); er hat gestern krankgefeiert; **krank|haft; Krank|haf|tig-keit,** die; -; **Krank|heit; Krank-heits|bild; krank|heits|er|re-gend; Krank|heits|er|re|ger; krank|heits|hal|ber; krank|la-chen,** sich (↑R 38 f.; *ugs. für* heftig lachen); wir haben uns krankgelacht; **kränk|lich; Kränk|lich-keit,** die; -; **krank|ma|chen** (↑R 38 f.; *svw.* krankfeiern); er hat krankgemacht; *vgl. aber* krank; **krank|mel|den,** sich (↑R 38 f.); **Krank|mel|dung; krank|schie|ßen** (↑R 38 f.; *Jägerspr.* anschießen); er hat das Reh krankgeschossen; **krank-schrei|ben** (↑R 38 f.); sie wurde [für] eine Woche krankgeschrieben; **Krän|kung**

Kran⌣wa|gen, ...win|de

Kranz, der; -es, Kränze; **Kränz-chen; krän|zen** (*dafür häufiger* bekränzen); du kränzt; **Kranz-⌣ge|fäß** *(meist Plur.; Med.),* **...geld** *(Rechtsspr.),* **...ge|sims** *(Archit.),* **...jung|fer** (*landsch. für* Brautjungfer), **...ku|chen; Kranzl|jung|fer** (*bayr., österr. für* Brautjungfer); **Kranz⌣nie|der|le-gung, ...schlei|fe, ...spen|de**

Kräpf|chen; Kräp|fel, der; -s, - (*südd. für* Krapfen); *vgl.* Kräppel; **Krap|fen,** der; -s, - (ein Gebäck);

Krapp, der; -[e]s ‹niederl.› (eine Färberpflanze)

Kräp|pel, der; -s, - (*mitteld. für* Krapfen)

krap|pen *vgl.* krabben

krapp|rot ‹*zu* Krapp›

krass (extrem; außerordentlich scharf; grell); **Krass|heit**

[1]**Kra|ter,** der; -s, -e ‹griech.› (altgriech. Krug); [2]**Kra|ter,** der; -s, - (Vulkanöffnung; Abgrund); **Kra-ter⌣land|schaft, ...see** (der)

kra|ti|ku|lie|ren ‹lat.› (*Math.* durch ein Gitternetz ausmessen od. übertragen)

Kratt, das; -s, -e (*nordd. für* Eichengestrüpp)

Krat|ten, der; -s, - (*südd. u. schweiz. für* [kleinerer, enger u. tiefer] Korb)

Kratz, der; -es, -e (*landsch. für* Schramme); **Kratz⌣band** (das; *Bergmannsspr.* ein Fördergerät), **...bee|re** (*landsch. meist für* Brombeere), **...bürs|te; kratz-bürs|tig** (widerspenstig); **Kratz-bürs|tig|keit; Krätz|chen** (*Soldatenspr.* Feldmütze); **Krat|ze,** die; -, -n (ein Werkzeug)

[1]**Krät|ze,** die; -, -n (*südd. für* Korb)

[2]**Krät|ze,** die; - (Hautkrankheit; metallhaltiger Abfall); **Kratz|ei-sen; krat|zen;** du kratzt; sich -; **Krät|zen|kraut,** das; -[e]s; **Krat-zer** (*ugs. für* Schramme; *Biol.* ein Eingeweidewurm); **Krät|zer** (saurer Wein, gärender Weinmost); **Kratz|fuß** (*früher für* tiefe Verbeugung); **krat|zig; krät|zig; Krätz|mil|be; Kratz⌣putz** (*für* Sgraffito), **...spur**

krau|chen (*landsch. für* kriechen)

Kräu|el, der; -s, - (*landsch. für* Haken, Kratze); **krau|eln** *(selten);* ich ...[e]le (↑R 16); *vgl.* [2]kraulen; **krau|en** (mit den Fingerkuppen sanft kratzen)

Kraul, das; -[s] ‹engl.› (ein Schwimmstil); [1]**krau|len** (im Kraulstil schwimmen)

[2]**krau|len** (zart krauen)

Krau|ler; Kraul⌣schwim|men (das; -s), **...schwim|mer, ...sprint, ...staf|fel**

kraus

Kraus, Karl (österr. Schriftsteller)

Krau|se, die; -, -n; **Kräu|sel-⌣band, ...garn, ...krank|heit** (eine Pflanzenkrankheit), **...krepp; kräu|seln;** ich ...[e]le (↑R 16); das Haar kräuselt sich; **Kräu|se|lung; Krau|se|min|ze** (eine Heil- u. Gewürzpflanze); **krau|sen;** du kraust; er kraus|te; sich -; **Kraus-haar; kraus|haa|rig; Kraus-kopf; kraus|köp|fig**

Krauss, Clemens (österr. Dirigent)

[1]**Kraut,** der; -s (*nordd. für* Garnelen, Krabben)

[2]**Kraut,** das; -[e]s, Kräuter (*südd., österr. Sing. auch für* Kohl); **kraut|ar|tig; Kräut|chen; krau-ten** (*landsch. für* Unkraut jäten); **Krau|ter** (*scherzh. für* Sonderling); **Kräu|ter** *Plur.* (Gewürz- und Heilpflanzen); **Kräu|ter-**

˽buch, ...but|ter, ...kä|se, ...li|kör, ...tee; Kraut˽fäu|le (eine Kartoffelkrankheit), ...gar|ten (*landsch. für* Gemüsegarten), ...gärt|ner (*landsch. für* Gemüsegärtner), ...häup|tel (*österr. für* Kraut-, Kohlkopf); Kräu|ticht, das; -s, -e (*veraltet für* Bohnen-, Kartoffelkraut usw. nach der Ernte); krau|tig (krautartig); Kraut|kopf (*südd., österr. für* Kohlkopf); Kräut|lein Rühr-mich|nicht|an, das; -s -, - -; Kräut|ler (*österr. veraltend für* Gemüsehändler); Kraut|stie|le *Plur.* (*schweiz. für* Mangoldrippen [als Gemüse]); Kraut|wi|ckel (*südd., österr. für* Kohlroulade)

Kra|wall, der; -s, -e (Aufruhr; *nur Sing.: ugs. für* Lärm); Kra|wall-ma|cher

Kra|wat|te, die; -, -n ‹frz. cravate, zu dt. (mundartl.) Krawat = Kroate› ([Hals]binde, Schlips; *Ringkampf* verbotener drosselnder Halsgriff); Kra|wat|ten˽muf|fel *(Werbespr.)*, ...na|del, ...zwang (der; -[e]s)

Kra|weel|be|plan|kung, Karweel|be|plan|kung ‹*von* Karavelle› *(Schiffbau)*; kra|weel|ge|baut, kar|weel|ge|baut; -es Boot (mit aneinander stoßenden Planken)

Kra|xe, die; -, -n (*bayr., österr. für* Rückentrage); Kra|xe|lei *(ugs.)*; kra|xeln (*ugs. für* mühsam steigen; klettern); ich ...[e]le (↑R 16); Krax|ler

Kra|yon [krɛˈjõː], der; -s, -s ‹franz.› (*veraltet für* Blei-, Kreidestift); Kra|yon|ma|nier, die; - (*bild. Kunst* ein Radierverfahren)

Krä|ze, die; -, -n (*schweiz. mdal. für* Rückentragkorb); *vgl.* ¹Krätze

Kre|as, das; - ‹span.› (ungebleichte Leinwand)

Kre|a|tin, das; -s ‹griech.› (*Biol., Med.* organ. Verbindung in der Muskulatur)

Kre|a|ti|on, die; -, -en ‹lat.-(franz.)› (Modeschöpfung; *veraltend für* Erschaffung); kre|a|tiv (schöpferisch); Kre|a|ti|vi|tät [...v...], die; - (schöpferische Kraft); Kre|a|ti|vi|täts˽test, ...trai|ning; Kre|a|tiv|ur|laub [...f...] (Urlaub, in dem man eine künstlerische Tätigkeit erlernt od. ausübt); Kre|a|tur, die; -, -en ‹lat.› (Lebewesen, Geschöpf; willenloses, gehorsames Werkzeug); kre|a|tür|lich; Kre|a|tür|lich-keit, die; -

Krebs, der; -es, -e (Krebstier; bösartige Geschwulst; *nur Sing.:* Sternbild); (↑R 40:) eine Krebs erregende, *auch* krebserregende (karzinogene) Chemikalie; kreb|sar|tig; kreb|sen (Krebse fangen; *ugs. für* sich mühsam bewegen; erfolglos bleiben); du krebst; Krebs er|re|gend, *vgl.* Krebs; Krebs˽for|schung, ...früh|er|ken|nung, ...gang (der; -[e]s), ...ge|schwulst, ...geschwür; kreb|sig; krebs˽krank, ...rot; Krebs˽scha|den, ...suppe, ...übel (↑R 132), ...vor|sor-ge, ...zel|le

Kre|denz, die; -, -en ‹ital.› (*veraltend für* Anrichte); kre|den|zen (*geh. für* [ein Getränk] feierlich anbieten, darreichen, einschenken); du kredenzt; ¹Kre|dit [*auch* ...ˈdit], der; -[e]s, -e ‹franz.› (befristet zur Verfügung gestellter Geldbetrag; *nur Sing.:* Zahlungsaufschub; Vertrauenswürdigkeit in Bezug auf Zahlungsfähigkeit u. Zahlungsbereitschaft; *übertr. für* Glaubwürdigkeit); auf Kredit (auf Borg); ²Kre|dit, das; -s, -s ‹lat.› (die rechte Seite, Habenseite eines Kontos); Kre|dit˽an|stalt [*auch* ...ˈdit...], ...auf|nah|me, ...bank (*Plur.* ...banken), ...brief, ...bü|ro; kre|dit|fä|hig; Kre|dit-˽ge|ber, ...ge|be|rin, ...ge|nos-sen|schaft, ...ge|schäft; Kre-dit|hai (*ugs. für* skrupelloser, überhöhte Zinsen fordernder Geldverleiher); Kre|dit|hil|fe; kre|di|tie|ren ‹franz.› (Kredit gewähren, vorschießen); einem Schuldner [einen Betrag] kreditieren; Kre|di|tie|rung; Kre|dit˽in-sti|tut [*auch* ...ˈdit...], ...kar|te, ...kauf, ...markt, ...neh|mer, ...neh|me|rin; Kre|di|tor [*österr.* ...ˈdiː...], der; -s, ...oren ‹lat.› (Kreditgeber, Gläubiger); Kre|di|to-ren|kon|to; Kre|dit˽po|li|tik [*auch* ...ˈdit...], ...we|sen (das; -s); kre|dit|wür|dig; Kre|dit|wür-dig|keit, die; -; Kre|do, das; -s, -s ‹„ich glaube“› (Glaubensbekenntnis)

Kre|feld (Stadt in Nordrhein-Westfalen); Kre|fel|der (↑R 103)

kre|gel (*bes. nordd. für* gesund, munter)

Krehl, der; -s, -e (Gerät zum Jäten); *vgl. aber* Krähl

Krei|de, die; -, -n; krei|de|bleich; Krei|de˽fel|sen, ...for|ma|ti|on (die; -; *Geol.*), ...küs|te; krei|den (*selten für* mit Kreide bestreichen); Krei|de|strich; krei|de-weiß; Krei|de˽zeich|nung, ...zeit (die; -; *Geol.*); krei|dig

kre|ie|ren ‹lat.(-franz.)› ([er]schaffen); Kre|ie|rung

Kreis, der; -es, -e (*auch für* Verwaltungsgebiet; *Abk.* Kr., *auch* Krs.); Kreis˽ab|schnitt, ...amt, ...arzt, ...bahn, ...be|we|gung, ...bo|gen

krei|schen; du kreischst; er kreischte; gekreischt

Kreis|durch|mes|ser; Krei|sel, der; -s, -; Krei|sel˽kom|pass, ...lüf|ter (*für* Turboventilator); krei|seln; ich ...[e]le (↑R 16); Krei|sel˽pum|pe, ...ver|dich|ter (*für* Turbokompressor); krei-sen; du kreist; *vgl. aber* kreißen; Krei|ser (*Jägerspr.* jmd., der bei Neuschnee Wild ausmacht); Kreis|flä|che; kreis|för|mig; kreis|frei; eine kreisfreie Stadt; Kreis|in|halt

Kreis|ky (österr. Politiker)

Kreis|lauf; Kreis|läu|fer *(Handball)*; Kreis|lauf˽kol|laps, ...mit-tel (das), ...schwä|che, ...stö-rung, ...ver|sa|gen (das; -s); kreis|rund; Kreis|sä|ge

krei|ßen (*veraltet für* in Geburtswehen liegen); du kreißt; *vgl. aber* kreisen; Krei|ßen|de, die; -n, -n (↑R 5 ff.); Kreiß|saal (Entbindungsraum im Krankenhaus)

Kreis˽stadt, ...tag, ...um|fang, ...ver|kehr; Kreis|wehr|er|satz-amt

Krem, die; -, -s, *ugs. auch* der; -s, *Plur.* -e *od.* -s, *landsch. auch* Kre|me, die; -, -s usw. *vgl.* Creme usw.

Kre|ma|ti|on, die; -, -en ‹lat.› (Einäscherung [von Leichen]); Kre-ma|to|ri|um, das; -s, ...ien [...i̯ən] (Anlage für Feuerbestattungen); kre|mie|ren (*schweiz., sonst veraltet für* einäschern)

kre|mig ‹*zu* Krem›; *vgl.* cremig

Kreml [*auch* kreːml], der; -[s], - ‹russ.› (burgartiger Stadtteil in russ. Städten, bes. in Moskau; *nur Sing.: übertr. für* Regierung Russlands); Kreml|füh|rung

Krem|pe, die; -, -n ‹*zu* Krampe› ([Hut]rand)

¹Krem|pel, der; -s (*ugs. für* [Trödel]kram)

²Krem|pel, die; -, -n (*Textilw.* Maschine zum Auflockern der Faserbüschel); ¹krem|peln (Faserbüschel auflockern); ich ...[e]le (↑R 16)

²krem|peln ([nach oben] umschlagen); ich ...[e]le (↑R 16); krem-pen (*veraltet für* ²krempeln); Kremp|ling (ein Pilz)

Krems an der Do|nau (österr. Stadt)

Krem|ser, der; -s, - ‹nach dem Berliner Fuhrunternehmer› (offener Wagen mit Verdeck)

Krem|ser Weiß, das; - -[es] (Bleiweiß)

Kren, der; -[e]s ‹slaw.› (*südd., österr. für* Meerrettich)
Kře|nek [ˈkrʃɛnɛk] (österr. Komponist)
Kren|fleisch (*österr. für* gekochtes Schweinefleisch mit Meerrettich)
Kren|gel, der; -s, - (*Nebenform von* Kringel; *landsch. für* Brezel); **kren|geln,** sich (*landsch. für* sich winden, sich herumdrücken; umherschlendern); ich ...[e]le mich (↑R 16)
kren|gen usw. (*Nebenform von* krängen usw.)
Kre|ol, das; -s (*Sprachw.* auf [ehemals] französischen Karibikinseln gesprochene Mischsprache auf der Grundlage des Französischen); **Kre|o|le,** der; -n, -n (↑R 126) ‹franz.› (in Mittel- u. Südamerika urspr. Abkömmling roman. Einwanderer; *auch für* Abkömmling von schwarzen Sklaven in Brasilien); **Kre|o|lin; kre|o|lisch; Kre|o|lisch,** das; -[s] (Sprache); *vgl.* Deutsch; **Kre|o|li|sche,** das; -n; *vgl.* Deutsche, das; **Kre|o|lis|tik,** die; - (Wissenschaft von den kreol. Sprachen u. Literaturen)
Kre|o|pha|ge, der; -n, -n (↑R 126) ‹griech.› (*svw.* Karnivore); **Kre|o|sot,** das; -[e]s (*Med., Pharm.* ein Desinfektions- u. Arzneimittel)
kre|pie|ren ‹ital.› (bersten, platzen, zerspringen [von Sprenggeschossen]; *derb für* verenden); **Kre|pi|ta|ti|on,** die; -, -en ‹lat.› (*Med.* Reiben u. Knirschen [bei Knochenbrüchen usw.])
Krepp, der; -s, *Plur.* -s *u.* -e ‹franz.› (krauses Gewebe; *auch: eindeutschende Schreibung für* [2]Crêpe); **krepp|ar|tig; krep|pen** (zu Krepp, Krepppapier verarbeiten); **Krepp‿flor, ...gummi; Krepp|pa|pier** (↑R 136); **Krepp|soh|le**
Kre|sol, das; -s (*Chemie* ein Desinfektionsmittel)
[1]**Kres|se,** die; -, -n (Name verschiedener Pflanzen)
[2]**Kres|se,** die; -, -n (*landsch. svw.* Kressling); **Kress|ling** (Gründling)
Kres|zen|tia (w. Vorn.); [1]**Kres|zenz,** die; -, -en ‹lat., „Wachstum"› (Herkunft [edler Weine]); [2]**Kres|zenz** (w. Vorn.)
Kre|ta (eine griech. Insel)
kre|ta|ze|isch, kre|ta|zisch ‹lat.› (*Geol.* zur Kreideformation gehörend)
Kre|te, die; -, -n ‹franz.› (*schweiz. für* Geländekamm, -grat)
Kre|ter (Bewohner Kretas); **Kre|te|rin**
Kre|thi und Ple|thi *Plur., auch Sing., ohne Artikel* ‹nach den „Kretern und Philistern" in Davids Leibwache› (*abwertend für* alle möglichen Leute; jedermann); Krethi und Plethi war[en] da; mit Krethi und Plethi verkehren
Kre|ti|kus, der; -, ...izi ‹griech.› (*Verslehre* ein antiker Versfuß)
Kre|tin [kreˈtɛ̃:], der; -s, -s ‹franz.› (Schwachsinniger); **Kre|ti|nis|mus** [...ti...], der; - (*Med.*); **kre|ti|no|id** (*Med.* kretinartig)
kre|tisch (von Kreta); **Kre|ti|zi** (*Plur. von* Kretikus)
Kre|ton, der; -s, -e (*österr. für* Cretonne); **Kre|tonne** [kreˈtɔn] (*eindeutschend für* Cretonne)
Kret|scham, Kret|schem, der; -s, -e ‹slaw.› (*ostmitteld. für* Schenke); **Kretsch|mer,** der; -s, - (*ostmitteld. für* Wirt)
kreuchst (*veraltet für* kriechst); **kreucht** (*veraltet für* kriecht); was da kreucht u. fleucht
Kreut|zer|so|na|te, die; - (von Beethoven dem franz. Geiger R. Kreutzer gewidmet); ↑R 95
Kreuz, das; -es, -e ‹lat.›; (↑R 108:) das Blaue, Rote, Weiße, Eiserne Kreuz; über Kreuz; in die Kreuz und [in die] Quere [laufen], *aber* (↑R 46): kreuz und quer; **Kreuz‿ab|nah|me, ...ass, ...auf|fin|dung** (die; -; kath. Fest), **...band** (das; *Plur.* ...bänder; *Med.*), **...bein** (*Med.*), **...blu|me** (*Archit.*), **...blüt|ler** (eine Pflanzenfamilie); **kreuz‿brav** (*ugs.*), **...ehr|lich** (*ugs.*); **kreu|zen** (über Kreuz legen; *Biol.* paaren; *Seemannsspr.* im Zickzackkurs fahren); du kreuzt; sich kreuzen (sich überschneiden); **Kreu|zer** (ehem. Münze; Kriegsschiff; größere Segeljacht); großer, kleiner Kreuzer; **Kreuz|er|hö|hung,** die; - (kath. Fest); **Kreu|zes‿tod, ...weg** (Christi Weg zum Kreuz; *vgl.* Kreuzweg); **Kreu|zes|zei|chen** *vgl.* Kreuzzeichen; **Kreuz‿fah|rer, ...fahrt, ...feu|er; kreuz|fi|del** (*ugs.*); **kreuz|för|mig; Kreuz‿gang** (der), **...ge|lenk, ...ge|wöl|be; kreu|zi|gen; Kreu|zi|gung; kreuz|lahm; Kreuz‿ot|ter** (die), **...rit|ter; kreuz|sai|tig** (beim Klavier); **Kreuz|schlitz|schrau|be; Kreuz‿schlüs|sel** (für die Radmuttern beim Auto), **...schmerz** (*meist Plur.*), **...schna|bel** (ein Vogel), **...spin|ne, ...stich** (ein Zierstich); **kreuz und quer;** *vgl.* Kreuz; **Kreu|zung; kreuz|un|glück|lich** (*ugs.*); **kreu|zungs|frei; Kreu|zungs|punkt; Kreuz‿ver|band, ...ver|hör, ...weg** (*auch für* Darstellung des Leidens Christi; *vgl.* Kreuzesweg); **kreuz|wei|se; Kreuz|wort|rät|sel; Kreuz|zei|chen,** Kreu|zes|zei|chen; **Kreuz|zug**
Kre|vet|te [...v...], die; -, -n ‹franz.› (eine Garnelenart)
Krib|be, die; -, -n (*nordd. für* Buhne)
krib|be|lig, kribb|lig (*ugs. für* ungeduldig, gereizt); **Krib|bel|krank|heit,** die; - (*Med.* Mutterkornvergiftung); **krib|beln** (*ugs. für* prickeln, jucken; wimmeln); es kribbelt mich; es kribbelt u. krabbelt; **kribb|lig** *vgl.* kribbelig
Kri|ckel, das; -s, -[n] *meist Plur.* (*Jägerspr.* Horn der Gämse); *vgl.* Krucke
kri|cke|lig, krick|lig (*ostmitteld. für* unzufrieden; tadelsüchtig, nörgelnd); **Kri|ckel|kra|kel,** das; -s, - (*ugs. für* unleserliche Schrift); **kri|ckeln** (*landsch. für* streiten, nörgeln; *ugs. auch für* kritzeln); ich ...[e]le (↑R 16)
Kri|ckel|wild (Gamswild)
Krick|en|te, *auch* Kriek|en|te (eine Wildente)
Kri|cket, das; -s ‹engl.› (ein Ballspiel); **Kri|cket‿ball, ...spie|ler**
krick|lig *vgl.* krickelig
Kri|da, die; - ‹mlat.› (*österr. für* Konkursvergehen); **Kri|dar, Kri|da|tar,** der; -s, -e (*österr. für* Gemeinschuldner)
Krie|bel|mü|cke
Krie|che, die; -, -n (*landsch.* eine Pflaumensorte)
krie|chen; du krochst; du kröchest; gekrochen; kriech[e]!; *vgl.* kreuchst usw.; **Krie|cher** (*abwertend*); **Krie|che|rei; Krie|che|rin; krie|che|risch**
Krie|cherl, das; -s, -n (*österr. für* Krieche); **Krie|cherl|baum**
Kriech‿spur, ...strom (*Elektrotechnik*), **...tier**
Krieg, der; -[e]s, -e; die Krieg führenden Parteien; [1]**krie|gen** (*veraltet für* Krieg führen); [2]**krie|gen** (*ugs. für* erhalten, bekommen); **Krie|ger; Krie|ger‿denk|mal** (*Plur.* ...mäler), **...grab; Krie|ge|rin; krie|ge|risch; Krie|ger|tum,** das; -s; **Krie|ger|wit|we;** Krieg füh|rend *vgl.* Krieg; **Krieg|füh|rung,** Kriegs|füh|rung; **Kriegs‿an|lei|he, ...aus|bruch** (der; -[e]s); **kriegs|be|dingt; Kriegs‿be|ginn, ...beil, ...be|ma|lung, ...be|richt, ...be|richt|er|stat|ter; kriegs|be|schä|digt; Kriegs|be|schä|dig|te,** der *u.* die; -n, -n (↑R 5ff.); **Kriegs|be|schä|dig-**

ten|für|sor|ge; **Kriegs₋blin|de,** **...dienst;** **Kriegs|dienst₋ver|wei|ge|rer,** **...ver|wei|ge|rung;** **Kriegs₋ein|wir|kung,** **...en|de,** **...er|klä|rung,** **...flot|te,** **...frei|wil|li|ge;** **Kriegs|füh|rung** *vgl.* Kriegführung; **Kriegs|fuß;** *nur in* auf [dem] Kriegsfuß mit jmdm. *od.* etwas stehen; **kriegs|ge|fan|gen;** **Kriegs₋ge|fan|ge|ne,** **...ge|fan|gen|schaft,** **...geg|ner,** **...ge|richt,** **...ge|schrei,** **...ge|winn|ler** *(abwertend);* **Kriegs|grä|ber|für|sor|ge;** **Kriegs₋ha|fen** (*vgl.* ²Hafen), **...het|ze** (die; -), **...hin|ter|blie|be|ne;** **Kriegs|hin|ter|blie|be|nen|für|sor|ge;** **Kriegs₋in|va|li|de,** **...ka|me|rad,** **...kunst,** **...list,** **...ma|ri|ne,** **...op|fer,** **...pfad,** **...rat** (der; -[e]s), **...recht** (das; -[e]s), **...ro|man,** **...scha|den,** **...schau|platz,** **...schiff,** **...schuld,** **...teil|neh|mer,** **...to|te,** **...trau|ung,** **...trei|ber,** **...ver|bre|cher,** **...ver|let|zung,** **...ver|sehr|te;** **kriegs|ver|wen|dungs|fä|hig** (*Abk.* kv.); **Kriegs₋wai|se,** **...wir|ren** *(Plur.),* **...zu|stand** *(Plur. selten)*

Kriek|en|te *vgl.* Krickente

Kriem|hild, **Kriem|hil|de** (w. Vorn.)

Kri|ko|to|mie, die; -, ...ien ‹griech.› (*Med.* operative Spaltung des Ringknorpels der Luftröhre)

Krill, der; -[e]s ‹norw.› (tierisches Plankton)

Krim, die; - (Halbinsel im Süden der Ukraine)

Kri|mi [*auch* 'kri:mi], der; -s, -s, *selten* -, - (*ugs. für* Kriminalroman, -film); **kri|mi|nal** ‹lat.› (Verbrechen, schwere Vergehen, das Strafrecht, das Strafverfahren betreffend); **Kri|mi|nal,** das; -s, -e (*österr. veraltend für* Strafanstalt, Zuchthaus); **Kri|mi|nal|be|am|te;** **Kri|mi|na|le,** der; -n, -n (↑R 5 ff.) *u.* **Kri|mi|na|ler,** der; -s, - (*ugs. für* Kriminalbeamte); **Kri|mi|nal₋film,** **...ge|schich|te;** **kri|mi|na|li|sie|ren** (etwas als kriminell hinstellen); **Kri|mi|na|list,** der; -en, -en; ↑R 126 (Kriminalpolizist; Strafrechtslehrer); **Kri|mi|na|lis|tik,** die; - (Lehre vom Verbrechen, von seiner Aufklärung usw.); **Kri|mi|na|lis|tin;** **kri|mi|na|lis|tisch;** **Kri|mi|na|li|tät,** die; -; **Kri|mi|nal₋kom|mis|sar,** **...mu|se|um,** **...po|li|zei** (*Kurzw.* Kripo), **...pro|zess** (*veraltet für* Strafprozess), **...psy|cho|lo|gie,** **...recht** (das; -[e]s; *veraltet für* Strafrecht), **...ro|man;** **kri|mi|nell** ‹franz.›; **Kri|mi|nel|le,** der *u.* die; -n, -n; ↑R 5 ff. (straffällig Gewordene[r]); ein Krimineller; **Kri|mi|no|lo|gie,** die; - ‹lat.; griech.› (Wissenschaft vom Verbrechen); **kri|mi|no|lo|gisch**

Krim|krieg, der; -[e]s; ↑R 105

krim|meln *(nordd.); nur in* es krimmelt u. wimmelt

Krim|mer, der; -s, - ‹nach der Halbinsel Krim› (*urspr.* ein Lammfell, *heute* ein Wollgewebe)

krim|pen (*nordd. für* einschrumpfen [lassen]; sich von West nach Ost drehen [vom Wind]); gekrimpt u. gekrumpen

Krim|sekt

Krims|krams, der; -[es] (*ugs. für* Plunder, durcheinander liegendes, wertloses Zeug)

Krin|gel, der; -s, - ([kleiner, gezeichneter] Kreis; *auch für* [Zucker]gebäck); **krin|ge|lig** (sich ringelnd); sich kringelig lachen *(ugs.);* **krin|geln** ([sich] zu Kringeln formen); ich ...[e]le (↑R 16); sich - (*ugs. für* sich [vor Vergnügen] wälzen)

Kri|no|i|de, der; -n, -n *meist Plur.* ‹griech.› (*Zool.* Haarstern od. Seelilie, ein Stachelhäuter)

Kri|no|li|ne, die; -, -n ‹franz.› (*früher* Reifrock)

Kri|po = Kriminalpolizei; **Kri|po|chef** *(ugs.)*

Krip|pe, die; -, -n; **krip|pen** (*veraltet für* [einen Deich] mit Flechtwerk sichern); **Krip|pen₋bei|ßer** (Pferd, das die Unart hat, die Zähne aufzusetzen u. Luft hinunterzuschlucken), **...platz,** **...set|zer** (*svw.* Krippenbeißer), **...spiel** (Weihnachtsspiel)

Kris, der; -es, -e ‹malai.› (Dolch der Malaien)

Kri|se, **Kri|sis,** die; -, Krisen ‹griech.›; **kri|seln;** es kriselt; **kri|sen₋an|fäl|lig,** **...fest;** **Kri|sen|ge|biet;** **kri|sen|haft;** **Kri|sen₋herd,** **...ma|nage|ment,** **...si|tu|a|ti|on,** **...stab,** **...zei|chen,** **...zeit;** **Kri|sis** *vgl.* Krise

kris|peln (*Gerberei* narben, die Narben herausarbeiten); ich ...[e]le (↑R 16)

¹Kris|tall, der; -s, -e ‹griech.› (fester, regelmäßig geformter, von ebenen Flächen begrenzter Körper); **²Kris|tall,** das; -s (geschliffenes Glas); **kris|tall|ar|tig;** **Kris|tall|che|mie;** **Kris|täll|chen;** **kris|tal|len** (aus, von Kristall[glas]; kristallklar, wie Kristall); **Kris|tall₋git|ter** *(Chemie),* **...glas** (*Plur.* ...gläser); **kris|tal|lin,** **kris|tal|li|nisch** (aus vielen kleinen Kristallen bestehend); kristalline Schiefer, Flüssigkeiten; **Kris|tal|li|sa|ti|on,** die; -, -en (Kristallbildung); **Kris|tal|li|sa|ti|ons₋punkt,** **...vor|gang;** **kris|tal|lisch** (*seltener für* kristallen); **kris|tal|li|sier|bar;** **kris|tal|li|sie|ren** (Kristalle bilden); **Kris|tal|li|sie|rung;** **Kris|tal|lit** [*auch* ...'lit], der; -s, -e (kristallähnliches Gebilde); **kris|tall|klar**

Kris|tall|leuch|ter (↑R 136); **Kris|tall|lin|se** (↑R 136); **Kris|tall|lüs|ter,** *österr.* **Kris|tall|lus|ter** (↑R 136)

Kris|tall|nacht, die; - (*nationalsoz.* Nacht vom 9. zum 10. November 1938, in der von den Nationalsozialisten ein Pogrom gegen die deutschen Juden veranstaltet wurde); **Kris|tal|lo|gra|phie,** die; - (Lehre von den Kristallen); **kris|tal|lo|gra|phisch;** **Kris|tal|lo|id,** das; -[e]s, -e (kristallähnlicher Körper); **Kris|tall|phy|sik;** **Kris|tall₋va|se,** **...zu|cker**

¹Kris|ti|a|nia (Name Oslos bis 1924); *vgl.* Christiania; **²Kris|ti|a|nia,** der; -s, -s ‹*nach* Kristiania = Oslo› (früher üblicher Querschwung beim Skilauf); **Kris|tin** (w. Vorn.)

Kri|te|ri|um, das; -s, ...ien [...iən] ‹griech.› (Prüfstein, unterscheidendes Merkmal; *bes. im Radsport* Zusammenfassung mehrerer Wertungsrennen zu einem Wettkampf); **Kri|tik** [*auch* ...'tik], die; -, -en (kritische Beurteilung; *nur Sing.:* Gesamtheit der Kritiker); **Kri|ti|kas|ter,** der; -s, - (kleinlicher Kritiker, Nörgler); **Kri|ti|ker** [*auch* 'kri...]; **Kri|ti|ke|rin;** **kri|tik|fä|hig** [*auch* ...'tik...]; **Kri|tik|fä|hig|keit,** die; -; **kri|tik|los;** **Kri|tik|lo|sig|keit,** die; -; **Kri|tik|punkt;** **kri|tisch** [*auch* 'kri...] (streng beurteilend, prüfend, wissenschaftl. verfahrend; *oft für* anspruchsvoll; die Wendung [zum Guten od. Schlimmen] bringend; gefährlich, bedenklich); kritische Ausgabe; kritische Geschwindigkeit; kritische Temperatur; **kri|ti|sie|ren;** **Kri|ti|sie|rung;** **Kri|ti|zis|mus,** der; - (philos. Verfahren)

Krit|te|lei; **Krit|te|ler,** Krittler; **krit|te|lig,** krittlig; **krit|teln** (mäkelnd urteilen); ich ...[e]le (↑R 16); **Krit|tel|sucht,** die; -

Krit|ze|lei *(ugs.);* **krit|ze|lig,** kritzlig *(ugs.);* **krit|zeln** *(ugs.);* ich ...[e]le (↑R 16); **kritz|lig** *vgl.* kritzelig

Kro|a|te, der; -n, -n; ↑R 126 (Einwohner Kroatiens); **Kro|a|ti|en** [...iən] (Staat im Südosten Europas); **Kro|a|tin;** **kro|a|tisch;** **Kro|a|tisch,** das; -[s] (Sprache);

vgl. Deutsch; **Kro|a|ti|sche,** das; -n; *vgl.* Deutsche, das
Kro|atz|bee|re *vgl.* Kratzbeere
Kro|cket [*auch* ...'kɛt], das; -s ‹engl.› (ein Ballspiel); **kro|ckie|ren** (beim Krocketspiel [die Kugel] wegschlagen)
Kro|kant, der; -s ‹franz.› (knusprige Masse aus zerkleinerten Mandeln od. Nüssen)
Kro|ket|te, die; -, -n *meist Plur.* ‹franz.› (gebackenes längliches Klößchen [aus Kartoffelbrei, Fisch, Fleisch o. Ä.])
Kro|ki, das; -s, -s ‹franz.› (*fachspr. für* Riss, Plan, einfache Geländezeichnung); **kro|kie|ren; Kro|ki|zeich|nung**
Kro|ko, das; -[s], -s (*kurz für* Krokodilleder); **Kro|ko|dil,** das; -s, -e ‹griech.›; **Kro|ko|dil|le|der; Kro|ko|dils|trä|ne** *meist Plur.* (heuchlerische Träne); -n weinen; **Kro|ko|dil|wäch|ter** (ein Vogel)
Kro|kus, der; -, *Plur.* - *u.* -se ‹griech.› (eine früh blühende Gartenpflanze)
Krol|le, die; -, -n (*rhein. u. nordd. für* Locke)
Krom|lech ['krɔmlɛk, *auch* ...lɛç *od.* 'kro:m...], der; -s, *Plur.* -e *u.* -s ‹kelt.› (jungsteinzeitliche Kultstätte)
Kro|nach (↑R 132; Stadt in Oberfranken)
Krön|chen; [1]**Kro|ne,** die; -, -n ‹griech.› (Kopfschmuck usw.); (↑R 108:) die Nördliche -, die Südliche - (Sternbilder); [2]**Kro|ne,** die; -, -n (dän., isländ., norw., schwed., slowak., tschech. Währungseinheit; *Abk.* [mit Ausnahme der slowak. u. tschech.]: kr); dän. - (*Abk.* dkr); isländ. - (*Abk.* ikr); norw. - (*Abk.* nkr); schwed. - (*Abk.* skr); slowak. - (*Abk.* Ks); tschech. - (*Abk.* Kč); **krö|nen; Kro|nen|kor|ken,** Kron|kor|ken; **Kro|nen‿mut|ter** (*Plur.* ...muttern), **...or|den** (ehem. Verdienstorden); **Kro|nen|ta|ler,** Kron|taler (ehem. Münze); **Kron‿er|be** (der), **...glas** (das; -es; ein optisches Glas)
Kro|ni|de, der; -n, *Plur.* (*für* Nachkommen des Kronos:) -n (↑R 126) ‹griech.› (Beiname des Zeus); **Kro|ni|on** (Zeus)
Kron‿ju|wel (*meist Plur.*), **...ko|lo|nie, ...kor|ken** (*vgl.* Kronenkorken); **Kron|land** *Plur.* ...länder; **Kron|leuch|ter**
Kro|nos (Vater des Zeus)
Kron‿prä|ten|dent (Thronbewerber), **...prinz, ...prin|zes|sin; kron|prin|zess|lich; kron|prinz|lich; Kron|rat,** der; -[e]s
Krons|bee|re (*nordd. für* Preiselbeere)
Kron|schatz; Kron|ta|ler *vgl.* Kronentaler; **Krö|nung; Krö|nungs‿man|tel, ...or|nat; Kron|zeu|ge** (Hauptzeuge)
Krö|pel, der; -s, - (*nordd. für* Krüppel)
Kropf, der; -[e]s, Kröpfe; **Kröpf|chen; kröp|fen** (*Technik u. Bauw.* krumm biegen, in gebrochenen Linien führen; fressen [von Greifvögeln]); **Kröp|fer** (männl. Kropftaube); **krop|fig; Kropf‿stein** (*Bauw.*), **...tau|be; Kröp|fung** (*fachspr.*)
Kropp|zeug, das; -[e]s (*ugs., oft scherzh. für* kleine Kinder; *ugs. abwertend für* Pack, Gesindel, nutzloses Zeug)
Krö|se, die; -, -n (steife Halskrause; *Böttcherei* Einschnitt in den Fassdauben); **Krö|se|ei|sen** (ein Böttcherwerkzeug); **krö|seln** ([Glas] wegbrechen); ich ...[e]le (↑R 16); **Krö|sel|zan|ge** (ein Glaserwerkzeug)
kross (*nordd. für* knusprig)
[1]**Krö|sus** ‹griech.› (König von Lydien); [2]**Krö|sus,** der; *Gen.* -, *auch* -ses, *Plur.* -se (sehr reicher Mann)
Krot, die; -, -en (*österr. mdal. für* Kröte); **Krö|te,** die; -, -n; **Krö|ten** *Plur.* (*ugs. für* Geld); **Krö|ten‿stein** (*volkstüml. für* tierische Versteinerung), **...wan|de|rung**
Kro|ton, der; -s, -e ‹griech.› (ein ostasiat. Wolfsmilchgewächs); **Kro|ton|öl,** das; -[e]s (ein Abführmittel)
Kröv (Ort an der Mosel); **Krö|ver** [...vər]; - Nacktarsch (ein Wein)
Kro|wot, der; -en, -en; ↑R 126 (*österr. mdal. für* Kroate)
Krs., Kr. = Kreis
Kru|ke, die; -, -n *meist Plur.* (*Jägerspr.* Horn der Gämse); *vgl.* Krickel; **Krü|cke,** die; -, -n; **Kru|cken|kreuz** *od.* **Krü|cken|kreuz; Krück|stock** *Plur.* ...stöcke
krud, kru|de ‹lat.› (*veraltet für* grob, roh); **Kru|di|tät,** die; -, -en
[1]**Krug,** der; -[e]s, Krüge (ein Gefäß)
[2]**Krug,** der; -[e]s, Krüge (*landsch., bes. nordd. für* Schenke)
Krü|gel, das; -s, - (*österr. für* Bierglas mit Henkel); zwei - Bier; **Krü|gel|chen**
Krü|ger (*nordd. für* Wirt; Pächter)
Kru|ke, die; -, -n (*nordd. für* großer Krug; Tonflasche; ulkiger, eigenartiger Mensch)
Krul|le, die; -, -n (*früher für* Halskrause); **Krüll‿schnitt** (ein Tabakschnitt), **...ta|bak**
Krüm|chen; Kru|me, die; -, -n;
Krü|mel, der; -s, -, *landsch. auch* das; -s, - (kleine Krume); **Krü|mel|chen; krü|me|lig,** krüm|lig; **krü|meln;** ich ...[e]le (↑R 16); **Krü|mel|zu|cker; Krüm|lein; krüm|lig** *vgl.* krümelig
krumm; krummer (*landsch.* krümmer), krummste (*landsch.* krümmste); krumm (gekrümmt) gehen; (↑R 39:) etwas krumm biegen; wir mussten uns [sehr] krumm legen (*ugs. für* sehr einschränken); diese Bemerkung hat er dir [äußerst] krumm genommen (*ugs. für* übel genommen); *vgl.* krummlachen; **krumm|bei|nig; Krum|me,** der; -n, -n; ↑R 5 ff. (*Jägerspr. scherzh. für* Feldhase); **krüm|men;** sich -; **Krüm|mer** (gebogenes Rohrstück; Gerät zur Bodenbearbeitung); **Krumm|holz** (von Natur gebogenes Holz); **Krumm|holz|kie|fer,** die; *vgl.* Latsche; **Krumm|horn** *Plur.* ...hörner (altes Holzblasinstrument); **krumm|la|chen,** sich (*ugs. für* sehr lachen); **krumm le|gen,** sich *vgl.* krumm; **Krümm|ling** (*fachspr. für* gebogener Teil von Treppenwangen u. -geländern); **krumm‿li|nig, ...na|sig; krumm neh|men** *vgl.* krumm; **Krumm‿schwert, ...stab; Krüm|mung; Krüm|mungs‿kreis, ...ra|di|us**
krum|pe|lig, krump|lig (*landsch. für* zerknittert); **krum|peln** (*landsch. für* knittern); ich ...[e]le (↑R 16)
Krüm|per (vor 1813 kurzfristig ausgebildeter preuß. Wehrpflichtiger); **Krüm|per|sys|tem,** das; -s
krumpf|echt (nicht einlaufend [von Geweben]); **krump|fen** (einlaufen lassen); **krumpf|frei**
krump|lig *vgl.* krumpelig
Krupp, der; -s ‹engl.› (*Med.* akute [diphtherische] Entzündung der Schleimhaut des Kehlkopfes)
Krup|pa|de, die; -, -n ‹franz.› (*Reitsport* Sprung der hohen Schule); **Krup|pe,** die; -, -n (Kreuz [des Pferdes])
Krüp|pel, der; -s, -; **krüp|pel|haft; Krüp|pel|holz; krüp|pe|lig,** krüpp|lig; **Krüp|pel|walm|dach** (eine Dachform); **krüpp|lig** *vgl.* krüppelig
krup|pös ‹engl.› (*Med.* krupparti g); -er Husten
kru|ral ‹lat.› (*Med.* zum Schenkel gehörend; Schenkel...)
krüsch (*nordd. für* wählerisch im Essen)
Krü|sel|wind (*nordd. für* kreiselnder, sich drehender Wind)
Krus|ta|zee, die; -, ...een *meist*

Plur. ‹lat.› (*Zool.* Krebstier); **Krüst|chen; Krus|te,** die; -, -n; **Krus|ten|tier; krus|tig**

Krux *vgl.* Crux; **Kru|zi|fe|re,** die; -, -n *meist Plur.* ‹lat.› (*Bot.* Kreuzblütler); **Kru|zi|fix** [*auch* ...'fiks, *österr. nur so*], das; -es, -e (plastische Darstellung des gekreuzigten Christus); **Kru|zi|fi|xus,** der; - (*Kunstw.* Christus am Kreuz); **Kru|zi|tür|ken!** (ein Fluch)

Kry|o|bi|o|lo|gie ‹griech.› (Teilgebiet der Biologie, das sich mit der Einwirkung sehr tiefer Temperaturen auf Organismen befasst); **Kry|o|chi|rur|gie** (*Med.* Kältechirurgie); **Kry|o|lith** [*auch* ...'lit], der; *Gen.* -s *od.* -en, *Plur.* -e[n]; ↑R 126 (ein Mineral); **Kry|o|the|ra|pie,** die; - (Anwendung von Kälte zur Zerstörung von krankem Gewebe); **Kry|ot|ron** (↑R 130), das; -s, *Plur.* ...one, *auch* -s (*EDV* ein Schaltelement)

Kryp|ta, die; -, ...ten ‹griech.› (Gruft, unterirdischer Kirchenraum); **Kryp|ten** *Plur.* (*Med.* verborgene Einbuchtungen in den Rachenmandeln; Drüsen im Darmkanal); **kryp|tisch** (unklar, schwer zu deuten); **kryp|to...** (geheim, verborgen); **Kryp|to...** (Geheim...); **Kryp|to|ga|me,** die; -, -n *meist Plur.* (*Bot.* Sporenpflanze); **kryp|to|gen, kryp|to|ge|ne|tisch** (*Biol.* von unbekannter Entstehung); **Kryp|to|gramm,** das; -s, -e (Verstext mit verborgener Nebenbedeutung; *veraltet für* Geheimtext); **Kryp|to|graph,** der; -en, -en; ↑R 126 (*veraltet für* Geheimschriftmaschine); **Kryp|to|gra|phie,** die; -, ...ien (*Psychol.* absichtslos entstandene Kritzelzeichnung bei Erwachsenen; Disziplin der Informatik; *veraltet für* Geheimschrift); **kryp|to|kris|tal|lin, kryp|to|kris|tal|li|nisch** (*Geol.* erst bei mikroskop. Untersuchung als kristallinisch erkennbar); **Kryp|ton** [*auch* ...'to:n], das; -s (chem. Element, Edelgas; *Zeichen* Kr); **Kryp|tor|chis|mus** [...ç...] (↑R 132), der; -, ...men (*Med.* Zurückbleiben des Hodens in Bauchhöhle od. Leistenkanal)

Ks = slowak. Krone

KSZE = Konferenz über Sicherheit und Zusammenarbeit in Europa (frühere Bez. für OSZE [*vgl. d.*]); **KSZE-Schluss|ak|te,** die; - (↑R 26)

Kt. = ²Kanton

Kte|no|id|schup|pe ‹griech.; dt.› (*Zool.* Kammschuppe vieler Fische)

Kto. = Konto

Ku = Kurtschatovium

k.u. = königlich ungarisch (im ehem. Reichsteil Ungarn von Österreich-Ungarn für alle Behörden); *vgl.* k.k.; *vgl.* k. u. k.

Ku|a|la Lum|pur (Hptst. von Malaysia)

Ku|ba (mittelamerik. Staat; Insel der Großen Antillen); **Ku|ba|ner; Ku|ba|ne|rin; ku|ba|nisch**

Ku|ba|tur, die; -, -en ‹griech.› (*Math.* Erhebung zur dritten Potenz; Berechnung des Rauminhalts von [Rotations]körpern)

Küb|bung, die; -, -en (*Archit.* Seitenschiff des niedersächs. Bauernhauses)

Ku|be|be, die; -, -n ‹arab.› (Frucht eines indones. Pfefferstrauchs)

Kü|bel, der; -s, -; **kü|beln** (*ugs. auch für* viel [Alkohol] trinken); ich ...[e]le (↑R 16); **Kü|bel‿pflan|ze, ...wa|gen**

Ku|ben (*Plur. von* Kubus); **ku|bie|ren** ‹griech.› (*Forstw.* den Rauminhalt eines Baumstammes ermitteln; *Math.* zur dritten Potenz erheben); **Ku|bie|rung; Ku|bik|de|zi|me|ter** [*auch* ku'bik...] (*Zeichen* dm^3); **Ku|bik|fuß,** der; -es; 3 - (↑R 90); **Ku|bik|ki|lo|me|ter** (*Zeichen* km^3); **Ku|bik|maß,** das; **Ku|bik|me|ter** (*Zeichen* m^3); **Ku|bik|mil|li|me|ter** (*Zeichen* mm^3); **Ku|bik‿wur|zel** (*Math.* dritte Wurzel), **...zahl; Ku|bik|zen|ti|me|ter** (*Zeichen* cm^3)

Ku|bin [*auch* ku'bi:n] (österr. Zeichner u. Schriftsteller)

ku|bisch (würfelförmig; *Math.* in der dritten Potenz vorliegend); kubische Gleichung; **Ku|bis|mus,** der; - (Kunststil, der in kubischen Formen gestaltet); **Ku|bist,** der; -en, -en (↑R 126); **ku|bis|tisch**

ku|bi|tal ‹lat.› (*Med.* zum Ellbogen gehörend)

Ku|bus, der; -, Kuben ‹griech.› (Würfel; *Math.* dritte Potenz)

Kü|che, die; -, -n; **¹Kü|chel|chen** (kleine Küche)

²Kü|chel|chen *vgl.* ³Küchlein; **kü|cheln** (*schweiz. für* Fettgebackenes bereiten); ich küchle; **Ku|chen,** der; -s, -

Kü|chen|ab|fall *meist Plur.*

Ku|chen‿bä|cker, ...blech, ...brett

Kü|chen‿bü|fett, ...buf|fet, ...bul|le (*ugs., Soldatenspr.* Koch einer Großküche, Kantine u. Ä.), **...chef, ...fee** (*scherzh. für* Köchin), **...fens|ter**

Ku|chen‿form, ...ga|bel

Kü|chen‿hand|tuch, ...herd, ...hil|fe, ...ka|bi|nett (*geh. scherzh. für* [inoffizieller] Beraterstab, bes. eines Politikers), **...kraut** (*meist Plur.*), **...la|tein** (*scherzh. für* schlechtes Latein), **...mes|ser** (das), **...per|so|nal, ...scha|be** (ein Insekt)

Kü|chen|schel|le, die; -, -n (eine Pflanze)

Kü|chen‿schrank, ...schür|ze

Ku|chen‿teig, ...tel|ler

Kü|chen‿tisch, ...tuch, ...uhr, ...waa|ge, ...wa|gen (Gerätewagen der Feldküche), **...zei|le, ...zet|tel**

¹Küch|lein (*vgl.* ¹Küken)

²Küch|lein (kleine Küche)

³Küch|lein (kleiner Kuchen)

ku|cken (*nordd. für* gucken)

Kü|cken *vgl.* ¹Küken

ku|ckuck!; Ku|ckuck, der; -s, -e; **Ku|ckucks‿blu|me** (Pflanzenname), **...ei, ...uhr**

Ku'|damm, der; -[e]s (↑R 15; *ugs. kurz für* Kurfürstendamm)

Kud|del|mud|del, der *od.* das; -s (*ugs. für* Durcheinander, Wirrwarr)

Ku|del|kraut *vgl.* Kuttelkraut

Ku|der, der; -s, - (*Jägerspr.* männl. Wildkatze)

Ku|du, der; -s, -s ‹afrikaans› (afrik. Antilope)

Kues [ku:s], Nikolaus von (dt. Philosoph u. Theologe)

¹Ku|fe, die; -, -n (Gleitschiene [eines Schlittens])

²Ku|fe, die; -, -n (*landsch. für* Bottich, Kübel); **Kü|fer** (*südwestd. u. schweiz. für* Böttcher; *auch svw.* Kellermeister); **Kü|fe|rei; Kuff,** die; -, -e (breit gebautes Küstenfahrzeug)

ku|fi|sche Schrift, die; -n - ‹nach Kufa, einer ehem. Stadt bei Bagdad› (eine alte arab. Schrift)

Kuf|stein [*auch* 'ku:f...] (Stadt im Unterinntal, Österreich)

Ku|gel, die; -, -n; Kugel scheiben (*österr. für* Murmeln spielen); **Ku|gel|blitz; Kü|gel|chen; Ku|gel|fang; ku|gel|fest; Ku|gel‿fisch, ...form** (die; -); **ku|gel|för|mig; Ku|gel|ge|lenk**

Kü|gel|gen (dt. Maler)

Ku|gel|ha|gel; ku|ge|lig, kuglig; **Ku|gel|kopf; Ku|gel|kopf|ma|schi|ne** (eine Schreibmaschine); **Ku|gel|la|ger; ku|geln;** ich ...[e]le (↑R 16); sich -; **Ku|gel|re|gen; ku|gel|rund; Ku|gel schei|ben** *vgl.* Kugel; **Ku|gel|schrei|ber; ku|gel|si|cher; ku|gel|sto|ßen** *nur im Infinitiv gebräuchlich;* **Ku|gel|sto|ßen,** das; -s; **kug|lig** *vgl.* kugelig

Ku|gu|ar, der; -s, -e ‹indian.› (Puma)

Kuh, die; -, Kühe; die Kuh vom

Eis kriegen (*ugs. für* ein schwieriges Problem lösen); **Kuh‿dorf** *(abwertend),* **...dung, ...eu|ter, ...fla|den, ...fuß** (*fachspr. für* Brechstange), **...glo|cke, ...han|del** (*vgl.* [1]Handel; *ugs. für* kleinliches Aushandeln von Vorteilen); **kuh|han|deln** *(ugs.);* ich ...[e]le (↑R 16); gekuhhandelt; **Kuh|haut;** das geht auf keine - (*ugs. für* das ist unerhört); **kuh|hes|sig** (wie bei den [2]Hessen der Kuh eng zusammenstehend [Fehler der Hinterbeine von Haustieren]); **Kuh|hirt**

kühl; (↑R 47:) im Kühlen; ins Kühle setzen; **Kühl‿ag|gre|gat, ...an|la|ge**

Kuh|le, die; -, -n (*ugs. für* Grube, Loch)

Küh|le, die; -; **küh|len; Küh|ler** (Kühlvorrichtung); **Küh|ler‿fi|gur, ...grill, ...hau|be; Kühl‿flüs|sig|keit, ...haus, ...ket|te** (die; -; Gefrierkette), **...mit|tel, ...raum, ...rip|pe, ...schiff, ...schlan|ge** (*Technik* Röhrenkühlanlage), **...schrank, ...ta|sche; Kühl|te,** die; -, -n (*Seemannsspr.* mäßiger Wind); **Kühl‿tru|he, ...turm; Küh|lung,** die; -

Küh|lungs|born, **Ost|see|bad** (westl. von Rostock)

Kühl‿wa|gen, ...was|ser (das; -s)

Kuh‿milch, ...mist

kühn; Kühn|heit; kühn|lich *(veraltet)*

Kuh‿po|cken *(Plur.),* **...rei|gen** *od.* **...rei|hen, ...schel|le** (*svw.* Küchenschelle), **...stall; kuh|warm;** -e Milch

Ku|jon, der; -s, -e ⟨franz.⟩ (*veraltend für* Schuft); **ku|jo|nie|ren** (*ugs. abwertend für* verächtlich behandeln; schikanieren)

k. u. k. = kaiserlich u. königlich (im ehem. Österreich-Ungarn beide Reichsteile betreffend); *vgl.* k. k.

[1]Kü|ken, *österr.* Kü|cken, das; -s, - (das Junge des Huhnes; *ugs. für* kleines, unerfahrenes Mädchen); **[2]Kü|ken,** das; -s, - (*Technik* drehbarer Teil, Kegel des [Fass]hahns)

Ku-Klux-Klan [*selten engl.* 'kju:klaks'klɛn], der; -[s] ⟨engl.-amerik.⟩ (terroristischer Geheimbund in den USA)

Ku|ku|mer, die; -, -n ⟨lat.⟩ (*südwestd. für* Gurke)

Ku|ku|ruz [*auch* 'ku:...], der; -[es] ⟨slaw.⟩ (*bes. österr. für* Mais)

Ku|lak, der; -en, -en (↑R 126) ⟨russ.⟩ (Großbauer im zaristischen Russland)

Ku|lan, der; -s, -e ⟨kirgis.⟩ (asiat. Wildesel)

ku|lant ⟨franz.⟩ (entgegenkommend, großzügig [im Geschäftsverkehr]); **Ku|lanz,** die; -

[1]Ku|li, der; -s, -s ⟨Hindi⟩ (Tagelöhner in Südostasien; *abwertend für* rücksichtslos Ausgenutzter)

[2]Ku|li, der; -s, -s (*ugs. kurz für* Kugelschreiber)

Ku|lier|wa|re ⟨franz.; dt.⟩ (Wirkware)

ku|li|na|risch ⟨lat.⟩ (auf die [feine] Küche, die Kochkunst bezüglich; ausschließlich dem Genuss dienend); kulinarische Genüsse

Ku|lis|se, die; -, -n ⟨franz.⟩ (*Theater* Teil der Bühnendekoration; *Technik* Hebel mit verschiebbarem Drehpunkt; *Börse* Personen, die sich auf eigene Rechnung am Börsenverkehr beteiligen; *übertr. für* Rahmen, Hintergrund); **Ku|lis|sen‿schie|ber, ...wech|sel**

Kul|ler, die; -, -n (*landsch. für* kleine Kugel); **Kul|ler|au|gen** *Plur.* (*ugs. für* erstaunte, große, runde Augen); **kul|lern** (*ugs. für* rollen)

[1]Kulm, der *od.* das; -[e]s, -e ⟨slaw. u. roman.⟩ (abgerundete [Berg]kuppe)

[2]Kulm, das; -s ⟨engl.⟩ (*Geol.* schieferige Ausbildung der Steinkohlenformation)

Kulm|bach (Stadt in Oberfranken); **Kulm|ba|cher** (↑R 103); **Kulm|ba|cher,** das; -s (ein Bier)

Kul|mi|na|ti|on, die; -, -en ⟨lat.⟩ (Erreichung des Höhe-, Scheitel-, Gipfelpunktes; *Astron.* höchster und tiefster Stand eines Gestirns); **Kul|mi|na|ti|ons|punkt** (Höhepunkt); **kul|mi|nie|ren** (den Höhepunkt erreichen, gipfeln)

Kult, der; -[e]s, -e *u.* Kul|tus, der; -, Kulte ⟨lat.⟩ (Verehrung; Form der Religionsausübung; *auch für* übertriebene Verehrung); **Kult|fi|gur; Kult|film** ([von einem bestimmten Publikum] als besonders eindrucksvoll beurteilter und immer wieder angesehener Film); **Kult|hand|lung; kul|tisch; Kul|ti|va|tor** [...v...], der; -s, ...oren (*Landw.* Bodenbearbeitungsgerät); **kul|ti|vie|ren** ⟨franz.⟩ ([Land] bearbeiten, urbar machen; [aus]bilden; pflegen); **kul|ti|viert** (gesittet; hochgebildet); **Kul|ti|vie|rung** *Plur. selten;* **Kult|stät|te; Kul|tur,** die; -, -en; **Kul|tur‿ab|kom|men, ...at|ta|ché, ...aus|tausch, ...ba|nau|se, ...be|trieb** (der; -s), **...beu|tel** (Behälter für Toilettensachen), **...denk|mal; kul|tu|rell; Kul|tur‿er|be** (das), **...film, ...flüch|ter** (*Biol.* Pflanzen- od. Tierart, die von der Kulturlandschaft verdrängt wird), **...fol|ger** (*Biol.* Pflanzen- od. Tierart, die den menschlichen Kulturbereich als Lebensraum bevorzugt), **...form, ...ge|schich|te** (die; -); **kul|tur|ge|schicht|lich; Kul|tur|gut; kul|tur|his|to|risch; Kul|tur|kampf,** der; -[e]s (zwischen dem protestant. preuß. Staat u. der kath. Kirche 1871 bis 1887); **Kul|tur‿kri|tik** (die; -), **...land|schaft, ...le|ben** (das; -s); **kul|tur|los; Kul|tur|lo|sig|keit,** die; -; **Kul|tur‿mi|nis|te|ri|um, ...pflan|ze, ...po|li|tik** (die; -), **...re|vo|lu|ti|on** (radikale kulturelle Umgestaltung, bes. 1965–69 in China), **...schaf|fen|de** (der *u.* die; -n, -n; ↑R 5ff.; *regional*), **...spon|so|ring, ...tou|ris|mus; Kul|tus** *vgl.* Kult; **Kul|tus‿frei|heit** (die; -; *Rechtsspr.*), **...ge|mein|de, ...mi|nis|ter, ...mi|nis|te|rin, ...mi|nis|te|ri|um**

Ku|ma|ne, der; -n, -n; ↑R 126 (Angehöriger eines in südosteurop. Völkern aufgegangenen Turkvolkes)

Ku|ma|rin, das; -s ⟨indian.⟩ (pflanzl. Duft- u. Wirkstoff); **Ku|ma|ron,** das; -s (*Chemie* Bestandteil des Steinkohlenteers); **Ku|ma|ron|harz**

Kumm, der; -[e]s, -e (*nordd. für* Kasten; tiefe, runde Schüssel, Futtertrog); **Kum|me,** die; -, -n (*Seemannsspr. u. nordd. für* Schüssel)

Küm|mel, der; -s, - (Gewürzpflanze; ein Branntwein); **Küm|mel|brannt|wein** (der; -[e]s), **...brot; küm|meln** (mit Kümmel zubereiten; *ugs. für* [Alkohol] trinken); ich ...[e]le (↑R 16); **Küm|mel|tür|ke** (*veraltet* Schimpfwort; *abwertend für* Türke, türkischer Gastarbeiter)

Kum|mer, der; -s

Kum|mer|bund, der; -[e]s, -e ⟨Hindi-engl.⟩ (breite Leibbinde aus Seide)

Küm|me|rer (verkümmernde Pflanze; in der Entwicklung zurückgebliebenes Tier); **Küm|mer|form** *(Biol.);* **küm|mer|lich; Küm|mer|ling** (schwaches, zurückgebliebenes Geschöpf; Kümmerer); **küm|mern** (in der Entwicklung zurückbleiben [von Pflanzen u. Tieren]); sich [um jmdn., etwas] - ([für jmdn., etwas] sorgen); ich kümmere mich um sie (↑R 16); es kümmert mich nicht; **[1]Küm|mer|nis,** die; -, -se *(geh.)*

[2]Küm|mer|nis, Kum|mer|nus (eine legendäre Heilige)

Kum|mer|speck (*ugs. für* aus

Kummer angegessenes Übergewicht); **kum|mer|voll**

Kum|met, das, *schweiz.* der; -s, -e (gepolsterter Bügel um den Hals von Zugtieren)

Kü|mo, das; -s, -s (*kurz für* Küstenmotorschiff)

Kump, das; -s, -e (*landsch. für* kleines, rundes Gefäß, [Milch]schale; *Technik* Form zum Wölben von Platten); *vgl.* Kumpf

Kum|pan, der; -s, -e (*ugs. für* Kamerad, Gefährte; *abwertend für* Helfershelfer; Mittäter); **Kum|pa|nei** *(ugs., meist abwertend);* **Kum|pa|nin; Kum|pel,** der; -s, *Plur.* -, *ugs.* -s (Bergmann; *ugs. auch für* Arbeitskollege u. Freund)

küm|peln (*Technik* [Platten] wölben u. formen); ich ...[e]le (↑R 16); **Kum|pen,** der; -s, - (*nordd. für* Gefäß, Schüssel); **Kumpf,** der; -[e]s, *Plur.* -e *u.* Kümpfe (*südd., österr. für* Gefäß, Behälter [für den Wetzstein])

Kum|ran, *auch* Qum|ran (Ruinenstätte am Nordwestufer des Toten Meeres)

Kumst, der; -[e]s (*landsch. für* [Sauer]kohl)

Kumt, das; -[e]s, -e (*svw.* Kummet)

Ku|mu|la|ti|on, die; -, -en ‹lat.› (*fachspr. für* Anhäufung, Speicherung); **ku|mu|la|tiv** (anhäufend); **ku|mu|lie|ren** (anhäufen); kumulierende (sich ständig vergrößernde) Bibliographie; sich -; **Ku|mu|lie|rung; Ku|mu|lo|nim|bus** (*Meteor.* Gewitterwolke); **Ku|mu|lus,** der; -, ...li (*Meteor.* Haufen[wolke])

Ku|mys, Ku|myss [*auch* ...'mys], der; - ‹russ.› (gegorene Stutenmilch)

kund; kund und zu wissen tun; *vgl.* kundgeben usw.; **künd|bar** (die Möglichkeit einer Kündigung enthaltend); ein -er Vertrag; [1]**Kun|de,** der; -n, -n; ↑R 126 (Käufer; *Gaunerspr.* Landstreicher; *abwertend für* Kerl); [2]**Kun|de,** die; -, -n *Plur. selten* (Kenntnis, Lehre, Botschaft); [3]**Kun|de,** die; -, -n (*österr. für* Kundschaft); **kün|den** (*geh. für* kundtun; *schweiz. veraltend für* kündigen); **Kun|den‿be|ra|tung, ...be|such, ...dienst, ...fang** (der; -[e]s); **kun|den|freund|lich; Kun|den‿ge|spräch, ...kreis, ...spra|che** (Gaunersprache), **...wer|bung; Kün|der** *(geh.);* **Kund‿fahrt** (*österr. für* [wissenschaftliche] Exkursion), **...ga|be** (die; -); **kund|ge|ben** *(geh.);* ich gebe kund; kundgegeben; kundzugeben; ich gebe etwas kund, *aber* ich gebe Kunde von etwas; **Kund|ge|bung; kun|dig; Kun|di|ge,** der *u.* die; -n, -n (↑R 5 ff.); **kün|di|gen;** er kündigt ihm; er kündigt ihm das Darlehen, die Wohnung; es wurde ihm *od.* ihm wurde gekündigt; **Kün|di|gung;** *vgl.* vierteljährig *u.* vierteljährlich; **Kün|di|gungs‿frist, ...grund, ...schrei|ben, ...schutz, ...ter|min; Kun|din** (Käuferin); **kund|ma|chen** (*österr. Amtsspr., sonst geh. für* bekannt geben); ich mache kund; kundgemacht; kundzumachen; **Kund|ma|chung** (*südd., österr. für* Bekanntmachung); **Kund|schaft; kund|schaf|ten;** gekundschaftet; **Kund|schaf|ter; Kund|schaf|te|rin; kund|tun;** ich tue kund; kundgetan; kundzutun; **kund|wer|den** *(geh.);* es wird kund; es ist kundgeworden; kundzuwerden

ku|ne|i|form ‹lat.› (*Med.* keilförmig)

Kü|net|te, die; -, -n ‹franz.› (Abflussgraben)

künf|tig; künftigen Jahres (*Abk.* k. J.); künftigen Monats (*Abk.* k. M.); **künf|tig|hin**

Kun|ge|lei; kun|geln (*ugs. abwertend für* heimliche, unlautere Geschäfte abschließen); ich ...[e]le (↑R 16)

Kung-Fu, das; -[s] ‹chin.-engl.› (eine sportliche Methode der Selbstverteidigung)

Ku|ni|bert (m. Vorn.); **Ku|ni|gund, Ku|ni|gun|de** (w. Vorn.)

Kun|kel, die; -, -n (*südd. u. westd. für* Spindel, Spinnrocken)

Kün|ne|ke (dt. Operettenkomponist)

Ku|no (m. Vorn.)

Kunst, die; -, Künste; **Kunst‿aka|de|mie** (↑R 132), **...aus|stel|lung, ...bau** (*Plur.* ...bauten; *Technik*), **...be|trach|tung, ...darm, ...denk|mal, ...druck** (*Plur.* ...drucke); **Kunst|druck|pa|pier; Kunst|dün|ger; Kunst|eis|bahn; Küns|te|lei; küns|teln;** ich ...[e]le (↑R 16); **Kunst‿er|zie|her, ...er|zie|he|rin, ...er|zie|hung, ...fäl|schung, ...fa|ser, ...feh|ler; kunst|fer|tig; Kunst‿fer|tig|keit** (die; -), **...flug, ...ge|gen|stand, ...ge|lehr|te** (der *u.* die); **kunst‿ge|mäß, ...ge|recht; Kunst‿ge|schich|te** (die; -), **...ge|wer|be** (das; -s); **Kunst|ge|wer|be|mu|se|um; Kunst‿ge|werb|ler, ...ge|werb|le|rin; kunst|ge|werb|lich; Kunst‿griff, ...han|del** (*vgl.* [1]Handel), **...händ|ler, ...händ|le|rin, ...hand|lung, ...hand|werk, ...harz, ...his|to|ri|ker, ...his|to|ri|ke|rin, ...ho|nig, ...horn** (*Plur.* ...horne; chem. gehärtetes Kasein), **...kopf** *(Rundfunk),* **...kri|tik, ...kri|ti|ker, ...kri|ti|ke|rin; Künst|ler; Künst|le|rin; künst|le|risch; Künst|ler‿knei|pe, ...ko|lo|nie, ...mäh|ne** *(ugs.),* **...na|me, ...pech** *(ugs.);* **Künst|ler|tum,** das; -s; **künst|lich;** künstliche Befruchtung; künstliche Niere; künstliche Intelligenz; **Künst|lich|keit; Kunst|licht,** das; -[e]s; **kunst|los; Kunst‿ma|ler, ...markt; kunst|mä|ßig; Kunst|pau|se; kunst|reich; Kunst‿samm|ler, ...samm|le|rin, ...samm|lung, ...schatz, ...schu|le, ...sei|de; kunst|sin|nig; Kunst‿spra|che, ...stein, ...stoff; Kunst|stoff|fla|sche** (↑R 136); **Kunst|stoff|fo|lie** (↑R 136); **Kunst|stoff|ra|sen; kunst|stop|fen** *nur im Infinitiv u. Partizip II gebräuchlich;* kunstgestopft; **Kunst‿stück, ...stu|dent, ...stu|den|tin, ...tisch|ler, ...tisch|le|rin, ...tur|nen, ...ver|ein, ...ver|lag, ...ver|stand; kunst‿ver|stän|dig, ...voll; Kunst‿werk, ...wis|sen|schaft, ...wis|sen|schaft|ler, ...wis|sen|schaft|le|rin, ...wort** (*Plur.* ...wörter), **...zeit|schrift**

kun|ter|bunt (durcheinander, gemischt); **Kun|ter|bunt,** das; -s

Kunz (m. Vorn.); *vgl.* Hinz

Kü|pe, die; -, -n ‹lat.› (Färbekessel; Färbebad, Lösung eines Küpenfarbstoffes)

Ku|pee, das; -s, -s (*eindeutschend für* Coupé)

Ku|pel|le *vgl.* [2]Kapelle; **ku|pel|lie|ren** ‹franz.› (unedle Metalle aus Edelmetallen herausschmelzen)

Kü|pen|farb|stoff (ein wasch- u. lichtechter Farbstoff für Textilien); **Kü|per** (*nordd. für* Küfer, Böttcher; *auch für* Warenkontrolleur in Häfen)

Kup|fer, das; -s, - (*kurz für* Kupferstich; *nur Sing.:* chem. Element, Metall; *Zeichen* Cu); **Kup|fer‿draht, ...druck** (*Plur.* ...drucke), **...erz; kup|fer|far|ben; Kup|fer|geld,** das; -[e]s; **kup|fe|rig,** kupfrig; **Kup|fer‿kan|ne, ...kes|sel, ...mün|ze; kup|fern** (aus Kupfer); kupferne Hochzeit, *aber* (↑R 108): Kupferner Sonntag (*früher* drittletzter Sonntag vor Weihnachten); **kup|fer|rot; Kup|fer‿schmied, ...ste|cher, ...stich; Kup|fer|stich|ka|bi|nett; Kup|fer|tief|druck; Kup|fer|vit|ri|ol,** das; -s; **kupf|rig** *vgl.* kupferig

ku|pie|ren ⟨franz.⟩ ([Ohren, Schwanz bei Hunden oder Pferden] stutzen; *Med.* [Krankheit] im Entstehen unterdrücken); **ku|piert;** -es ([von Gräben usw.] durchschnittenes) Gelände
Ku|pol|ofen, Kup|pel|ofen (↑R 132) ⟨ital.; dt.⟩ (Schmelz-, Schachtofen)
Ku|pon, *auch* Cou|pon [ku'pɔŋ, *auch* ku'pɔ̃:, *österr.* ku'po:n], der; -s, -s ⟨franz.⟩ (abtrennbarer Zettel; [Stoff]abschnitt; Zinsschein)
Kup|pe, die; -, -n
Kup|pel, die; -, -n ⟨lat.⟩; **Kup|pel|bau** *Plur.* ...bauten
Kup|pe|lei (*veraltend abwertend für* Vermittlung einer Heirat durch unlautere Mittel; *Rechtsspr.* strafbare Förderung zwischenmenschlicher sexueller Handlungen)
Kup|pel|grab
kup|peln (*svw.* koppeln; *veraltend auch für* Kuppelei betreiben); ich ...[e]le (↑R 16)
Kup|pel|ofen (↑R 132) *vgl.* Kupolofen
Kup|pel|pelz; *meist in der Wendung* sich einen (den) - verdienen (*abwertend für* eine Heirat vermitteln); **Kup|pe|lung** *vgl.* Kupplung
kup|pen (stutzen, die Kuppe abhauen); Bäume kuppen
Kupp|ler *(abwertend);* **Kupp|le|rin; kupp|le|risch; Kupp|lung,** *seltener* Kup|pe|lung; **Kupp|lungs‿au|to|mat, ...be|lag, ...he|bel, ...pe|dal, ...scha|den, ...schei|be**
Kup|ris|mus (↑R 130), der; - (*Med.* Kupfervergiftung)
¹Kur, die; -, -en ⟨lat.⟩ (Heilverfahren; [Heil]behandlung, Pflege)
²Kur, die; -, -en (*veraltet für* Wahl); *noch in* kurbrandenburgisch, Kurfürst usw.; **Kür,** die; -, -en (Wahl; Wahlübung im Sport); sie muss noch [ihre] Kür laufen, ist schon Kür gelaufen; *aber* sie ist beim Kürlaufen gestürzt
ku|ra|bel ⟨lat.⟩ (*Med.* heilbar); ...ab|le (↑R 130) Krankheit; **Kur|an|stalt** *(veraltet)*
ku|rant ⟨lat.⟩ (*veraltet für* in Umlauf befindlich; *Abk.* crt.); **Ku|rant,** das; -[e]s, -e (*veraltet für* Währungsmünze, deren Metallwert dem aufgeprägten Wert entspricht); zwei Mark Kurant
Ku|ra|re, das; -[s] ⟨indian.-span.⟩ (ein [Pfeil]gift, als Narkosehilfsmittel verwendet)
Kü|rass, der; -es, -e ⟨franz.⟩ (Brustharnisch); **Kü|ras|sier,** der; -s, -e (*früher für* Panzerreiter; schwerer Reiter)
Ku|rat, der; -en, -en (↑R 126) ⟨lat.⟩ (wie ein Pfarrer eingesetzter kath. Seelsorgegeistlicher mit eigenem Seelsorgebezirk); **Ku|ra|tel,** die; -, -en (*veraltet für* Vormundschaft; Pflegschaft); **Ku|ra|tie,** die; -, ...ien (Seelsorgebezirk eines Kuraten); **ku|ra|tiv** (*Med.* heilend, Heil-); eine kurative Behandlung; **Ku|ra|tor,** der; -s, ...oren (Verwalter einer Stiftung; Vertreter des Staates in der Universitätsverwaltung; *österr. auch für* Treuhänder; *früher für* Vormund; Pfleger); **Ku|ra|to|ri|um,** das; -s, ...ien [...iən] (Aufsichtsbehörde)
Kur|auf|ent|halt
Kur|bel, die; -, -n; **Kur|be|lei,** die; -; **kur|beln;** ich ...[e]le (↑R 16); **Kur|bel‿stan|ge, ...wel|le**
Kur|bet|te, die; -, -n ⟨franz.⟩ (Bogensprung [eines Pferdes]); **kur|bet|tie|ren**
Kür|bis, der; -ses, -se (eine Kletter- od. Kriechpflanze); **Kür|bis‿fla|sche, ...kern**
Kur|de, der; -n, -n; ↑R 126 (Angehöriger eines Volkes in Vorderasien); **Kur|din; kur|disch; Kur|dis|tan** (↑R 132; Gebirgs- u. Hochland in Vorderasien)
ku|ren (eine Kur machen)
kü|ren (*geh. für* wählen); du kürtest, *seltener* korst, korest; du kürtest, *seltener* körest; gekürt, *seltener* gekoren; kür[e]!; *vgl.* kiesen
Kü|ret|ta|ge [...'ta:ʒə], die; -, -en ⟨franz.⟩ (*Med.* Ausschabung der Gebärmutter mit der Kürette); **Kü|ret|te,** die; -, -n (ein med. Instrument); **kü|ret|tie|ren**
Kur|fürst; der Große - (↑R 93); **Kur|fürs|ten|damm,** der; -[e]s (eine Straße in Berlin; *ugs. Kurzform* Ku'damm [↑R 15]); **Kur|fürs|ten|tum; kur|fürst|lich;** kurfürstlich sächsische Staatskanzlei; *im Titel* (↑R 108): Kurfürstlich
Kur‿gast (*Plur.* ...gäste), **...haus**
Kur‿hes|se[1], **...hes|sen**[1] (früheres Kurfürstentum Hessen-Kassel); **kur|hes|sisch**[1]
ku|ri|al ⟨lat.⟩ (zur päpstl. Kurie gehörend); **Ku|ri|al|stim|me** (*früher für* Gesamtstimme eines Wahlkörpers); **Ku|rie** [...iə], die; - ([Sitz der] päpstl. Zentralbehörde); **Ku|ri|en|kar|di|nal**
Ku|rier, der; -s, -e ⟨franz.⟩ (Bote [im Militär- od. Staatsdienst])

[1] [*auch* kur'hɛs...]

ku|rie|ren ⟨lat.⟩ (ärztlich behandeln; heilen)
Ku|rier‿flug|zeug, ...ge|päck
Ku|ri|len *Plur.* (Inseln im Pazifischen Ozean)
ku|ri|os ⟨lat.(-franz.)⟩ (seltsam, sonderbar); **Ku|ri|o|si|tät,** die; -, -en; **Ku|ri|o|si|tä|ten‿händ|ler, ...ka|bi|nett; Ku|ri|o|sum,** das; -s, ...sa
ku|risch, *aber* (↑R 102): das Kurische Haff, die Kurische Nehrung
Kur‿ka|pel|le, (Orchester eines Kurortes), **...kar|te, ...kli|nik**
Kur|köln[1] (Erzbistum Köln vor 1803); **kur|köl|nisch**[1]
Kur|kon|zert
Kur|ku|ma, die; -, Kur|ku|men ⟨arab.⟩ (Gelbwurzel; ein Gewürz); **Kur|ku|ma‿gelb, ...pa|pier**
Kur|laub, der; -[e]s, -e (mit einer Kur verbundener Urlaub)
Kür|lauf *(Sport);* **Kür|lau|fen,** das; -s; **Kür lau|fen** *vgl.* Kür
Kur|mainz[1] (Erzbistum Mainz vor 1803)
Kur|mark, die; - (Hauptteil der ehem. Mark Brandenburg); **Kur|mär|ker; kur|mär|kisch**
Kur|mit|tel, das; **Kur|mit|tel|haus; Kur‿or|ches|ter, ...ort** (der; -[e]s, -e), **...park**
Kur|pfalz[1], die; - (ehem. Kurfürstentum Pfalz); **Kur|pfäl|zer**[1] (↑R 103); **kur|pfäl|zisch**[1]
kur|pfu|schen *(abwertend);* ich kurpfusche; gekurpfuscht; zu kurpfuschen; **Kur|pfu|scher; Kur|pfu|sche|rei; Kur|pfu|sche|rin; Kur|pfu|scher|tum,** das; -s
Kur|prinz (Erbprinz eines Kurfürstentums); **kur|prinz|lich**
Kur|pro|me|na|de
Kur|re, die; -, -n (*Seemannsspr.* Grundschleppnetz)
Kur|ren|da|ner ⟨lat.⟩ (Mitglied einer Kurrende); **Kur|ren|de,** die; -, -n (*früher* Knabenchor, der vor Häusern, bei Begräbnissen o. Ä. gegen Geld geistl. Lieder singt; *heute* ev. Kinderchor)
kur|rent ⟨lat.⟩ (*österr. für* in deutscher Schrift); **Kur|rent|schrift** (*veraltet für* „laufende", d. h. Schreibschrift; *österr. für* deutsche Schreibschrift)
kur|rig (*landsch. für* mürrisch, launisch)
Kur|ri|ku|lum, das; -s, ...la ⟨lat.⟩ (*veraltet für* Laufbahn); *vgl.* Curriculum *u.* Curriculum vitae
Kurs, der; -es, -e ⟨lat.⟩; **Kurs‿ab|schlag** (*für* Deport), **...ab|wei-**

[1] [*auch* 'ku:r...]

chung, ...än|de|rung, ...an|stieg; Kur|sant, der; -en, -en; ↑R 126 (*regional für* Kursteilnehmer); Kurs-auf|schlag (*für* Report [*Börse*]), ...buch

Kürsch, das; -[e]s (*Heraldik* Pelzwerk)

Kur|schat|ten (*ugs. scherzh. für* Person, die sich während eines Kuraufenthaltes einem Kurgast des anderen Geschlechts anschließt)

Kürsch|ner (Pelzverarbeiter); Kürsch|ne|rei; Kürsch|ne|rin

Kur|se (*Plur. von* Kurs *u.* Kursus); Kurs-ein|bu|ße, ...ge|winn; kur|sie|ren ‹lat.› (umlaufen, im Umlauf sein); kursierende Gerüchte; Kur|sist, der; -en, -en; ↑R 126 (*veraltet für* Teilnehmer an einem Kursus); kur|siv (laufend, schräg); Kur|siv|druck, der; -[e]s; Kur|si|ve [...və], die; -, -n (schräg liegende Druckschrift); Kur|siv|schrift; Kurs|kor|rek|tur; kur|so|risch (fortlaufend, rasch durchlaufend); Kurs-rück|gang, ...stei|ge|rung, ...sturz, ...sys|tem (*Schulw.*)

Kürs|te, die; -, -n (*landsch. für* [harte] Brotrinde)

Kurs|teil|neh|mer; Kur|sus, der; -, Kurse ‹lat.› (Lehrgang, zusammenhängende Vorträge; *auch für* Gesamtheit der Lehrgangsteilnehmer); Kurs-ver|lust, ...wa|gen, ...wech|sel, ...wert, ...zet|tel

Kurt (m. Vorn.)

Kur|ta|ge [...'taːʒə] *vgl.* Courtage

Kur|ta|xe

Kur|ti|sa|ne, die; -, -n ‹franz.› (*früher für* Geliebte am Fürstenhof)

Kur|trier[1] (Erzbistum Trier vor 1803); kur|trie|risch[1]

Kurt|scha|to|vi|um [...v...] (↑R 132), das; -s ‹nach dem russ. Atomphysiker Kurtschatow› (chem. Element, Transuran; *Zeichen* Ku)

Kur|tur|nen (Turnen mit freier Wahl der Übungen); Kur|übung (↑R 132)

ku|ru|lisch ‹lat.›; -er Stuhl (Amtssessel der höchsten Beamten im alten Rom)

Ku|rus [ku'ruʃ], der; -, - ‹türk.› (Untereinheit des türk. Pfundes)

Kur|va|tur [...v...], die; -, -en ‹lat.› (*Med.* Krümmung eines Organs, bes. des Magens); Kur|ve [...v..., *auch* ...f...], die; -, -n (krumme Linie, Krümmung; Bogen[linie]; [gekrümmte] Bahn; Flugbahn); ballistische Kurve (Flug-, Geschossbahn); kur|ven; gekurvt; Kur|ven|dis|kus|si|on (*Math.*); kur|ven|för|mig; Kur|ven-li|ne|al, ...mes|ser (der); kur|ven|reich; Kur|ven-schar (*Math.*; *vgl.* ²Schar), ...tech|nik, ...vor|ga|be (*Leichtathletik*)

Kur|ver|wal|tung

kur|vig [...v...]; Kur|vi|me|ter, das; -s, - (Kurvenmesser)

Kur|wür|de, die; - (Würde eines Kurfürsten)

kurz; kürzer, kürzeste; kurz und gut; kurz und bündig; kurz und klein schlagen; zu kurz kommen; kurz angebunden; kurz entschlossen; kurz gesagt; am kürzesten; über kurz oder lang; binnen, in, seit, vor kurzem; den Kürzer[e]n ziehen; etwas Kurzes spielen, vortragen; (↑R 108:) Pippin der Kurze. *Schreibung in Verbindung mit Verben:* kurz schneiden; sie hat das Kleid zu kurz geschnitten; sich kurz fassen; ihre Gesundheit zwang sie kurz zu treten, kürzer zu treten (sich zu schonen); finanziell kürzer treten (sich einschränken) müssen; jmdn. kurz halten (jmdm. wenig Geld od. Essen geben); *vgl. aber* kurzarbeiten, kurzschließen. *Schreibung in Verbindung mit Partizipien:* kurz gebratenes Fleisch; eine kurz gefasste Erklärung; kurz geschnittene Haare; Kurz|ar|beit, die; -; kurz|ar|bei|ten; ↑R 38 (aus Betriebsgründen eine kürzere Arbeitszeit einhalten); ich arbeite kurz; kurzgearbeitet; kurzzuarbeiten; Kurz|ar|bei|ter; kurz-är|me|lig *od.* ...ärm|lig; ...at|mig; Kurz|at|mig|keit, die; -; Kurz-be|richt, ...bi|o|gra|phie; Kur|ze, der; -n, -n; ↑R 5 ff. (*ugs. für* kleines Glas Branntwein; Kurzschluss); Kür|ze, die; -; in -; Kür|zel, das; -s, - (festgelegtes [stenograph.] Abkürzungszeichen; *vgl.* Sigel); kür|zen; du kürzt; kur|zer|hand; kür|zer tre|ten *vgl.* kurz; Kurz-er|zäh|lung, ...fas|sung, ...film, ...flüg|ler (*Zool.*); kurz|fris|tig; kurz ge|bra|ten *vgl.* kurz; kurz ge|fasst *vgl.* kurz; Kurz|ge|schich|te; kurz ge|schnit|ten *vgl.* kurz; kurz|haa|rig; kurz|hal|sig; kurz hal|ten *vgl.* kurz; kurz|hin (*veraltet für* kurz, beiläufig); kurz|le|big; Kurz|le|big|keit, die; -; kürz|lich; Kurz-mel|dung, ...nach|richt, ...par|ker, ...pass (*Ballspiele*), ...pro|gramm (*Eiskunstlauf*); kurz|schlie|ßen (↑R 38); einen Stromkreis kurzschließen; ich schließe kurz; kurzgeschlossen; kurzzuschließen; Kurz|schluss; Kurz|schluss-hand|lung, ...re|ak|ti|on; Kurz|schrift (*für* Stenographie); Kurz|schrift|ler (*für* Stenograph); kurz|schrift|lich (*für* stenographisch); kurz|sich|tig; Kurz|sich|tig|keit, die; -; kurz-sil|big (*übertr. auch für* wortkarg), ...stäm|mig; Kurz|stre|cke; Kurz|stre|cken-lauf, ...läu|fer, ...läu|fe|rin, ...ra|ke|te; Kurz-streck|ler (*Sportspr.* Kurzstreckenläufer), ...stun|de (*Schulw.*); Kurz|tag|pflan|ze (*Bot.*); kurz tre|ten *vgl.* kurz; kurz|um [*auch* 'kurts'um]; Kür|zung; Kurz|ur|laub; Kurz|wa|ren|hand|lung; kurz|weg [*auch* 'kurts'vɛk]; Kurz|weil, die; -; kurz|wei|lig; Kurz|wel|le (*Physik, Rundf.*); Kurz|wel|len-sen|der, ...the|ra|pie (*Med.*); kurz|wel|lig; Kurz|wort *Plur.* ...wörter; Kurz|zeit|ge|dächt|nis, das; -ses (*Psych.*); kurz|zei|tig; ein kurzzeitiger Engpass

kusch! (*Befehl an den Hund* leg dich still nieder!); *vgl.* kuschen

Ku|schel, Kus|sel, die; -, -n (*nordd. für* niedrige [verkrüppelte] Kiefer; Gebüsch)

ku|sche|lig, kusch|lig (gut zum Kuscheln); ku|scheln; sich - (sich anschmiegen); ich ...[e]le mich (↑R 16); Ku|schel|tier (weiches Stofftier); ku|schen (sich lautlos hinlegen [vom Hund]; *ugs. auch für* stillschweigen); du kuschst; kusch dich! (leg dich still nieder!); kusch|lig *vgl.* kuschelig

Ku|sel (Stadt im Saar-Nahe-Bergland); Kuseler Schichten (*Geol.*)

Ku|sin|chen; Ku|si|ne (*eindeutschende Schreibung für* Cousine)

¹Kus|kus, der; -, - ‹westindones.› (ein Beuteltier)

²Kus|kus, der *u.* das; -, - ‹arab.› (ein nordafrik. Gericht)

Küs|nacht (ZH) (Ort am Zürichsee); *vgl. aber* Küssnacht

Kuss, der; -es, Küsse; Küss|chen; kuss|echt

Kus|sel *vgl.* Kuschel

küs|sen; du küsst, er küsst; du küsstest; geküsst; küsse! *u.* küss mich!; küss die Hand! (*österr. veraltend*); sie küsst ihn auf die Stirn; Kuss-hand, ...händ|chen

Küss|nacht am Ri|gi (Ort am Vierwaldstätter See); *vgl. aber* Küsnacht

Küs|te, die; -, -n; Küs|ten-be|feu|e|rung (Kennzeichnung durch Leuchtfeuer u. a.), ...fah|rer (Schiff), ...fi|sche|rei, ...ge|bir|ge, ...mo|tor|schiff, ...nä|he, ...schiff|fahrt, ...strich

[1] [*auch* 'kuːr...]

Kụs|ter (Kirchendiener); **Küs|te|rei;** [1]**Kus|to|de,** die; -, -n ‹lat.› (*früher* Kennzeichen der einzelnen Lagen einer Handschrift; *Druckw. Nebenform von* Kustos); [2]**Kus|to|de,** der; -n, -n; ↑R 126 (*Nebenform von* Kustos [wissenschaftl. Sachbearbeiter]); **Kụs|tos,** der; -, Kustoden ‹lat., „Wächter"› (wissenschaftlicher Sachbearbeiter an Museen u. Ä.; *Druckw. früher für* Silbe od. Wort am Fuß einer Seite zur Verbindung mit der folgenden Seite; *veraltet für* Küster, Kirchendiener)

Ku|te, die; -, -n (*nordd., bes. berlin. für* Vertiefung; Grube)

Ku|ti|ku|la, die; -, *Plur.* -s *u.* ...lä ‹lat.› (*Biol.* Häutchen der äußeren Zellschicht bei Pflanzen u. Tieren); **Ku|tis,** die; - (*Biol.* Lederhaut der Wirbeltiere; nachträglich verkorktes Pflanzengewebe [z. B. an Wurzeln])

Kụtsch|bock; Kụt|sche, die; -, -n ‹nach dem ung. Ort Kocs [kɔtʃ], d. h. Wagen aus Kocs›; **kụt|schen** (*veraltet für* kutschieren); du kutschst; **Kụt|schen|schlag; Kụt|scher; Kụt|scher‿knei|pe, ...sitz; kut|schie|ren; Kụtsch|kas|ten**

Kụt|te, die; -, -n

Kụt|tel, die; -, -n *meist Plur.* (*südd., österr., schweiz. für* Kaldaune); **Kụt|tel|fleck,** der; -[e]s, -e *meist Plur.* (*südd., österr. für* Kaldaune); **Kut|tel‿hof** (*veraltet für* Schlachthof), **...kraut** (das; *österr. mdal. für* Thymian)

Kụt|ter, der; -s, - ‹engl.› (ein kleines Fischereifahrzeug)

Kü|ve|la|ge [kyvə'la:ʒə], die; -, -n ‹franz.› (*Bergbau* Ausbau eines wasserdichten Schachtes mit gusseisernen Ringen); **kü|ve|lie|ren** [...v...]; **Kü|ve|lie|rung** (*svw.* Küvelage)

Ku|vert [ku've:r, ku'vɛ:r, *auch* ku'vɛrt], das; -s, -s, *bei dt. Ausspr.* -[e]s, -e ‹franz.› ([Brief]umschlag; [Tafel]gedeck für eine Person); **ku|ver|tie|ren** [...v...] (mit einem Umschlag versehen); **Ku|ver|tü|re,** die; -, -n (Überzugsmasse [aus Schokolade] für Kuchen, Gebäck u. a.)

Kü|vẹt|te [...v...], die; -, -n ‹franz.› (*veraltet für* Innendeckel [der Taschenuhr]; kleines Gefäß, Trog)

Ku|wait, Ku|weit [*auch* 'ku:... *od.* ...'ve:t] (Scheichtum am Persischen Golf); **Ku|wai|ter,** Ku|weiter; **ku|wai|tisch,** ku|wei|tisch

Kụx, der; -es, -e ‹tschech.-mlat.› (börsenmäßig gehandelter Bergwerksanteil)

kv. = kriegsverwendungsfähig

kV = Kilovolt

KV = Köchelverzeichnis

kVA = Kilovoltampere

kW = Kilowatt

Kwạss, der; *Gen.* - *u.* -es ‹russ.› (gegorenes Getränk)

kWh = Kilowattstunde

Ky. = Kentucky

Ky|a|ni|sa|ti|on, die; - ‹nach dem engl. Erfinder J. H. Kyan› (ein Imprägnierungsverfahren für Holz); **ky|a|ni|sie|ren**

Ky|a|thos, der; -, - (antiker einhenkliger Becher)

Ky|be|le [...le:, *auch* ...'be(:)...] (phryg. Göttin)

Ky|ber|ne|tik, die; - ‹griech.› (wissenschaftliche Forschungsrichtung, die vergleichende Betrachtungen über Steuerungs- u. Regelungsvorgänge anstellt; *ev. Theol.* Lehre von der Kirchen- u. Gemeindeleitung); **Ky|ber|ne|ti|ker; Ky|ber|ne|ti|ke|rin; ky|ber|ne|tisch**

Kyff|häu|ser ['kif...], der; -[s] (Bergrücken südl. des Harzes)

Kyk|la|den (↑R 130) *Plur.* (Inselgruppe in der Ägäis)

Kyk|li|ker (↑R 130) *vgl.* Zykliker

Kyk|lop (↑R 130) *vgl.* Zyklop

Ky|ma, das; -s, -s *u.* **Ky|ma|ti|on,** das; -s, *Plur.* -s *u.* ...ien [...i̯ən] ‹griech.› (*Archit.* Zierleiste aus stilisierten Blattformen [bes. am Gesims griech. Tempel])

Ky|mo|gramm, das; -s, -e ‹griech.› (*Med.* Röntgenbild von sich bewegenden Organen); **Ky|mo|graph,** der; -en, -en; ↑R 126 (Gerät zur mechanischen Aufzeichnung von rhythm. Bewegungen, z. B. des Pulsschlages); **Ky|mo|gra|phie,** die; - (Röntgenverfahren zur Darstellung von Organbewegungen)

Kym|re, der; -n, -n; ↑R 126 (keltischer Bewohner von Wales); **kym|risch; Kym|risch,** das; -[s] (Sprache); *vgl.* Deutsch; **Kym|ri|sche,** das; -n; *vgl.* Deutsche, das

Ky|ni|ker ‹griech.› (Angehöriger der von Antisthenes gegründeten Philosophenschule); *vgl. aber* Zyniker; **Ky|no|lo|ge,** der; -n, -n (↑R 126); **Ky|no|lo|gie,** die; - (Lehre von Zucht, Dressur u. Krankheiten der Hunde)

Ky|pho|se, die; -, -n ‹griech.› (*Med.* Wirbelsäulenverkrümmung nach hinten)

Ky|re|na|i|ka *vgl.* Cyrenaika

Ky|rie ['ky:ri̯ə], das; -, -s ‹griech.› (*kurz für* Kyrieeleison); **Ky|rie e|lei|son!** [*auch* - e'leizɔn], **Ky|rie|e|lei|son** (↑R 132), das; -s, -s (Bittruf); **Ky|ri|e|leis!** ‹„Herr, erbarme dich!"› (Bittformel im gottesdienstlichen Gesang); *vgl.* Leis

ky|ril|lisch ‹nach dem Slawenapostel Kyrill›; kyrillische Schrift (↑R 94); **Ky|ril|lisch,** das; -s (die kyrillische Schrift); in Kyrillisch

Ky|ros (pers. König)

Ky|the|ra (alter Name der griech. Insel Kithira)

KZ = Konzentrationslager

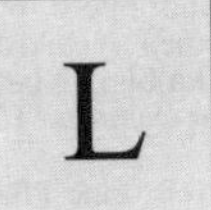

l = lävogyr; Leu; Liter

L (Buchstabe); das L; des L, die L, *aber*: das l in Schale (↑R 60); der Buchstabe L, l

L (röm. Zahlzeichen) = 50

Λ, λ = Lambda

£, £Stg = Pfund (Livre) Sterling

l. = lies!; links

L. = Linné; [1]Lira *Sing. u.* Lire *Plur.*; Lucius *od.* Luzius

La = *chem. Zeichen für* Lanthan

LA = Lastenausgleich

La. = Louisiana

l. a. = lege artis

Laa an der Tha|ya [- - - 'ta:ja] (österr. Stadt)

Laa|cher See, der; - -s (See in der Eifel)

Laa|ser Mar|mor, der; - -s

Lab, das; -[e]s, -e (*Biol.* Enzym im [Kälber]magen)

La Bam|ba, die; - -, - -s, *ugs. auch* der; - -[s], - -s ‹bras.› (ein Modetanz)

La|ban (bibl. m. Eigenn.); langer Laban (*ugs. für* hochgewachsene, hagere männliche Person)

lab|be|rig, labb|rig (*nordd. für* schwach; fade [vom Geschmack]; weichlich; breiig); **lab|bern** (*nordd. für* schlürfend essen od. trinken; *Seemannsspr.* schlaff werden); ich ...ere (↑R 16); **labb|rig** *vgl.* labberig

Lab|da|num *vgl.* Ladanum

La|be, die; - (*geh.*); **La|be|fla|sche** (*Radsport*)

La|bel ['le:b(ə)l], das; -s, -s ‹engl.› (Klebemarke; Schallplattenetikett; *auch für* Schallplattenfirma)

la|ben; sich -

La|ber|dan, der; -s, -e ‹niederl.› (eingesalzener Kabeljau)
la|bern (*ugs. für* schwatzen, unaufhörlich u. einfältig reden); ich ...ere (↑R 16)
La|be|trunk
la|bi|al ‹lat.› (die Lippen betreffend); **La|bi|al,** der; -s, -e *u.* **La|bi|al|laut** (*Sprachw.* Lippenlaut, mit den Lippen gebildeter Laut, z. B. p, m); **La|bi|al|pfei|fe** (eine Orgelpfeife); **La|bi|a|te,** die; -, -n *meist Plur.* (*Bot.* Lippenblütler)
la|bil ‹lat.› (schwankend; veränderlich, unsicher); -es Gleichgewicht; **La|bi|li|tät,** die; -, -en *Plur. selten*
La|bi|o|den|tal ‹lat.› *u.* **La|bi|o|den|tal|laut** (*Sprachw.* Lippenzahnlaut, mit Unterlippe u. oberen Schneidezähnen gebildeter Laut, z. B. f, w); **La|bi|o|ve|lar** *u.* **La|bi|o|ve|lar|laut** (*Sprachw.* Lippengaumenlaut)
Lab‿kraut (das; -[e]s; eine Pflanzengattung), **...ma|gen** (Teil des Magens der Wiederkäuer)
La|boe [la'bø:] (Ostseebad); **Laboer** [la'bø:ər]
La|bor [*österr. auch, schweiz. meist* 'la:...], das; -s, *Plur.* -s, *auch* -e ‹lat.› (*Kurzform von* Laboratorium); **La|bo|rant,** der; -en, -en; ↑R 126 (Laborgehilfe); **La|bo|ran|tin; La|bo|ra|to|ri|um,** das; -s, ...ien [...iən] (Arbeitsstätte; [bes. chem.] Versuchsraum; Forschungsstätte); **La|bor|be|fund; la|bo|rie|ren;** an einer Krankheit - (*ugs. für* an einer Krankheit leiden u. sie zu überwinden suchen); an einer Arbeit - (*ugs. für* sich abmühen); **La|bor‿tier, ...ver|such**
La Bos|tel|la, die; - -, - -s, *ugs. auch* der; - -[s], - -s ‹Herkunft unsicher› (ein Modetanz)
La|bour Par|ty ['le:bə(r) 'pa:(r)ti], die; - - ‹engl.› (engl. Arbeiterpartei)
[1]**Lab|ra|dor** (↑R 130; eine nordamerik. Halbinsel); [2]**Lab|ra|dor,** der; -s, -e *u.* **Lab|ra|do|rit** [*auch* ...'rit], der; -s, -e (ein Mineral, ein Schmuckstein); **Lab|ra|dor|hund**
Lab|sal, das; -[e]s, -e, *österr. u. südd. auch* die; -, -e
lab|sal|ben ‹niederl.› (*Seemannsspr.* [zum Schutz] teeren); ich labsalbe; gelabsalbt; zu -
Labs|kaus, das; - ‹engl.› (ein seemänn. Eintopfgericht)
La|bung
La|by|rinth, das; -[e]s, -e ‹griech.› (Irrgang, -garten; Durcheinander; *Med.* inneres Ohr); **La|by|rinth|fisch; la|by|rin|thisch**
La Chaux-de-Fonds [la ʃod'fɔ̃:] (Stadt im Schweizer Jura)

[1]**La|che,** die; -, -n (Gelächter)
[2]**La|che** [*auch* 'la:xə], die; -, -n (Pfütze)
[3]**La|che,** *fachspr. meist* **Lach|te,** die; -, -n (*Forstw.* Einschnitt [in Baumrinde])
lä|cheln; ich ...[e]le (↑R 16); **lachen;** Tränen lachen; er hat gut lachen; **La|chen,** das; -s; das ist zum Lachen; **La|cher; Lach|er|folg; lä|cher|lich;** ins Lächerliche ziehen; **lä|cher|li|cher|wei|se; Lä|cher|lich|keit; lä|chern** (*landsch. für* zum Lachen reizen)
La|che|sis (eine der drei Parzen)
Lach|fält|chen *meist Plur.*; **Lachgas; lach|haft; Lach|haf|tig|keit,** die; -; **Lach‿krampf, ...lust** (die; -), **...mö|we, ...num|mer** (*ugs. für* lächerliche, unsinnige Angelegenheit)
Lachs, der; -es, -e (ein Fisch)
Lach|sal|ve
Lachs‿bröt|chen, ...fang; lachs‿far|ben *od.* **...far|big, ...rosa, ...rot; Lachs‿schin|ken, ...schnit|zel** *(Plur.)*
Lach|tau|be
Lach|te *vgl.* [3]Lache
Lach|ter, die; -, -n *od.* das; -s, - (altes bergmänn. Längenmaß)
la|cie|ren [la'si:...] ‹franz.› (einschnüren; mit Band durchflechten)
Lack, der; -[e]s, -e ‹sanskr.›; **Lack|af|fe** *(ugs.)*; **Lack|ar|beit**
La|cke, die; -, -n (*österr. ugs. für* [2]Lache)
La|ckel, der; -s, - (*südd., österr. ugs. für* grober, auch unbeholfener, tölpelhafter Mensch)
la|cken (*seltener für* lackieren); gelackt; **lack|glän|zend; Lack|gür|tel; la|ckie|ren** (Lack auftragen; *ugs. für* anführen; übervorteilen); **La|ckie|rer; La|ckie|re|rei; La|ckie|rung; La|ckier‿werk|statt** *od.* **...werk|stät|te; Lack‿le|der, ...man|tel; lack|mei|ern;** *vgl.* gelackmeiert
Lack|mus, der *od.* das; - ‹niederl.› (chem. Reagens); **Lack|mus|papier**
Lack‿scha|den, ...schuh, ...stiefel
Lac|ri|mae Chris|ti [...mε: k...] (↑R 130), der; - -, - - ‹lat., „Christustränen“› (Wein von den Hängen des Vesuvs); **lac|ri|mo|so** ‹ital.› (↑R 130; *Musik* klagend); **Lac|ri|mo|so,** das; -[s], ...si
Lac|rosse [la'krɔs] (↑R 130), das; - ‹franz.› (ein amerik. Ballspiel)
Lac|tam, das; -s, -e ‹lat.; griech.› (eine chem. Verbindung)
La|dakh (Hochplateau in Nordindien)

La|da|num, das; -s ‹griech.› (ein Harz)
Läd|chen (kleine Lade; kleiner Laden); **La|de,** die; -, -n (*landsch. für* Truhe, Schublade); **La|de‿baum, ...flä|che, ...ge|rät, ...gewicht, ...gut, ...hem|mung, ...kon|trol|le, ...lu|ke, ...mast** (der); [1]**la|den** (aufladen); du lädst, er lädt; du ludst; du lüdest; geladen; lad[e]!
[2]**la|den** (einladen); du lädst, er lädt (*veraltet, aber noch landsch.* du ladest, er ladet); du ludst; du lüdest; geladen; lad[e]!
La|den, der; -s, *Plur.* Läden, *selten auch* -; **La|den‿dieb, ...diebstahl, ...hü|ter** (schlecht absetzbare Ware), **...kas|se, ...ket|te, ...pas|sa|ge, ...preis** (*vgl.* [2]Preis), **...schluss** (*der;* -es); **La|den|schluss‿ge|setz, ...zeit; La|den‿schwen|gel** (*abwertend für* junger Verkäufer), **...stra|ße, ...tisch, ...zent|rum**
La|de|platz; La|der (Auflader); **La|de‿ram|pe, ...raum, ...stock** (*Plur.* ...stöcke; Teil der früheren Gewehre; *Bergbau* runder Holzstock zum Einführen der Sprengstoffpatronen in die Bohrlöcher)
lä|die|ren ‹lat.› (verletzen; beschädigen); lädiert sein; **Lä|die|rung**
La|din, das; -s (ladinische Sprache); **La|di|ner** (Angehöriger eines rätoroman. Volksteils in Südtirol); **la|di|nisch; La|di|nisch,** das; -[s] (Sprache); *vgl.* Deutsch; **La|di|ni|sche,** das; -n; *vgl.* Deutsche, das
La|dis|laus (m. Vorn.)
Lad|ne|rin, die; -, -nen (*südd. u. österr. veraltend* Verkäuferin)
La|do|ga|see, der; -s (nordöstl. von Sankt Petersburg)
La|dung
La|dy ['le:di], die; -, -s (Titel der engl. adligen Frau; *selten für* Dame); **la|dy|like** ['le:dilaik] (nach Art einer Lady; vornehm)
La|er|tes (Vater des Odysseus)
La Fa|yette, La|fa|yette [lafa'jεt] (franz. Staatsmann)
La|fet|te, die; -, -n ‹franz.› (Untergestell der Geschütze)
[1]**Laf|fe,** der; -n, -n; ↑R 126 (*ugs. für* Geck); [2]**Laf|fe,** die; -, -n (*südwestd. für* Schöpfteil des Löffels; Ausguss; *schweiz. für* Bug, Schulterstück vom Rind, Schwein usw.)
La Fon|taine [la fɔ̃'tε:n] (franz. Dichter); die la-fontaineschen Fabeln (↑R 96)
LAG = Lastenausgleichsgesetz
La|ge, die; -, -n; in der - sein; **La|ge‿be|richt, ...be|spre|chung**
Lä|gel, das; -s, - (*landsch. für* Fäss-

chen [für Fische]; Traggefäß; ein altes Maß, Gewicht)

La|gen‿schwim|men (das; -s), **...staf|fel; la|gen|wei|se; La|ge|plan;** *vgl.* ²Plan; **La|ger,** das; -s, *Plur.* - u. (*Kaufmannsspr. für* Warenvorräte:) Läger; etwas auf - halten; **La|ger|bier; la|ger‿fä|hig, ...fest; La|ger‿feu|er, ...ge|bühr, ...haft, ...hal|le, ...hal|tung, ...haus, ...in|sas|se; La|ge|rist,** der; -en, -en; ↑R 126 (Lagerverwalter); **La|ge|ris|tin; La|ger|kol|ler**

La|ger|löf, Selma (schwed. Schriftstellerin)

la|gern; ich ...ere (↑R 16); sich -; **La|ger‿obst, ...platz, ...raum, ...schild** (der; -es, -e; *Technik*), **...statt** (*Plur.* ...stätten; *geh. für* Bett, Lager), **...stät|te** (*Plur.* ...stätten; *Geol.* Fundort; *seltener für* Lagerstatt); **La|ge|rung; La|ger|ver|wal|ter; La|ge|skiz|ze**

La|go Mag|gio|re [- ma'dʒo:rə], der; - - ⟨ital.⟩ (ital.-schweiz. See); *vgl.* Langensee

La|gos (Hptst. von Nigeria)

lag|ri|mo|so (↑R 130) *vgl.* lacrimoso

Lag|ting, das; -s ⟨norw.⟩ (das norw. Oberhaus)

La|gu|ne, die; -, -n ⟨ital.⟩ (durch einen Landstreifen vom offenen Meer getrennter flacher Meeresteil); **La|gu|nen|stadt**

lahm; ein lahmes Pferd; den Verkehr lahm legen; eine Demonstration hat den Verkehr lahm gelegt; **lahm|ar|schig** (*derb für* träge); **Läh|me,** die; - (eine Jungtierkrankheit); **lah|men** (lahm gehen); **läh|men** (lahm machen); **Lahm|heit,** die; -; **lahm le|gen** *vgl.* lahm; **Lahm|le|gung; Läh|mung; Läh|mungs|er|schei|nung** *meist Plur.*

¹**Lahn,** die; - (r. Nebenfluss des Rheins)

²**Lahn,** der; -[e]s, -e ⟨franz.⟩ (*fachspr.* ein Metalldraht)

³**Lahn,** die; -, -en (*bayr. u. österr. mdal. für* Lawine); **lah|nen** (*bayr. u. österr. mdal. für* tauen)

Lahn|spu|le (*zu* ²Lahn)

Lah|nung (*Wasserbau* ins Meer hineingebauter Damm)

Lahn|wind (*bayr. u. österr. mdal. für* Tauwind)

Lahr (Stadt am Westrand des Schwarzwaldes); -er Hinkender Bote (Name eines Kalenders)

Laib, der; -[e]s, -e; ein - Brot, Käse

Lai|bach (*slowen.* Ljubljana)

Laib|chen (*österr.* ein kleines, rundes Gebäck)

Lai|bung, *auch* Lei|bung (innere Mauerfläche bei Wandöffnungen; innere Wölbfläche bei Wölbungen)

Laich, der; -[e]s, -e (Eier von Wassertieren); **lai|chen** (Laich absetzen); **Laich‿kraut, ...platz, ...zeit**

Laie, der; -n, -n (↑R 126) ⟨griech.⟩ (Nichtfachmann; Nichtpriester); **Lai|en‿apos|to|lat** (↑R 132), **...bre|vier, ...bru|der, ...büh|ne, ...chor; lai|en|haft; Lai|en‿kunst, ...pries|ter, ...rich|ter, ...spiel, ...stand** (der; -[e]s); **lai|si|e|ren** (einen Kleriker regulär od. strafweise in den Laienstand versetzen); **Lai|i|sie|rung**

Lais|ser-al|ler [lɛsea'le:], das; - ⟨franz.⟩ (das [Sich]gehenlassen); **Lais|ser-faire** [...'fɛ:r], das; - (das Gewähren-, Treibenlassen; *veraltet für* Ungezwungenheit, Ungebundenheit); **Lais|sez-pas|ser** [...pa'se:], der; -, - (*veraltet für* Passierschein)

La|i|zis|mus [lai...], der; - ⟨griech.⟩ (weltanschauliche Richtung, die die radikale Trennung von Kirche u. Staat fordert); **la|i|zis|tisch**

La|kai, der; -en, -en (↑R 126) ⟨franz.⟩ (*abwertend für* Kriecher; *früher für* herrschaftl. Diener [in Livree]); **la|kai|en|haft**

La|ke, die; -, -n (Salzlösung zum Einlegen von Fisch, Fleisch)

La|ke|dä|mon (anderer Name für den altgriech. Stadtstaat Sparta); **La|ke|dä|mo|ni|er** (Bewohner von Lakedämon); **la|ke|dä|mo|nisch**

La|ken, das; -s, - (*nordd., mitteld. für* Betttuch; Tuch)

Lak|ko|lith [*auch* ...'lit], der; *Gen.* -s *u.* -en, *Plur.* -e[n] (↑R 126) ⟨griech.⟩ (*Geol.* ein Tiefengesteinskörper)

La|ko|da, der; -[s], -s ⟨nach einer Insellandschaft im Beringmeer⟩ (ein Robbenpelz)

La|ko|ni|en [...iən] (Verwaltungsbezirk im Peloponnes); **La|ko|nik,** die; - ⟨griech.⟩ (*geh. für* lakonische Art des Ausdrucks); **la|ko|nisch** (*auch für* kurz u. treffend); **La|ko|nis|mus,** der; -, ...men (Kürze des Ausdrucks)

Lak|rit|ze, die; -, -n, *landsch.* Lakritz, der, *auch* das; -es, -e (↑R 130) ⟨griech.⟩ (eingedickter Süßholzsaft); **Lak|rit|zen|saft,** der; -[e]s; **Lak|rit|zen|stan|ge** *od.* **Lak|ritz|stan|ge**

lakt... ⟨lat.⟩ (milch...); **Lakt...** (Milch...); **Lak|tam** *vgl.* Lactam; **Lak|ta|se,** die; -, -n (ein Enzym); **Lak|ta|ti|on,** die; -, -en (Milchabsonderung; Zeit des Stillens); **lak|tie|ren** (Milch absondern; säugen); **Lak|to|me|ter,** das; -s, - (Vorrichtung zur Milchprüfung); **Lak|to|se,** die; - (Milchzucker); **Lak|to|skop,** das; -s, -e ⟨lat.; griech.⟩ (Vorrichtung zur Milchprüfung); **Lak|tos|u|rie,** die; -, ...ien (*Med.* Ausscheidung von Milchzucker mit dem Harn)

la|ku|när ⟨lat.⟩ (*Med., Biol.* Gewebelücken bildend, höhlenartig, buchtig); **La|ku|ne,** die; -, -n (*Sprachw.* Lücke in einem Text; *Med., Biol.* Hohlraum in Geweben); **la|kust|risch** (↑R 130; *Geol., Biol.* in Seen sich bildend od. vorkommend [von Gesteinen u. Lebewesen])

la|la (*ugs.*); es ging ihm so - (einigermaßen)

lal|len; Lall‿pe|ri|o|de (*Päd.* [frühkindl.] Lebensphase), **...wort** (*Sprachw.*)

L. A. M. = Liberalium Artium Magister

¹**La|ma,** das; -s, -s ⟨peruan.⟩ (eine südamerik. Kamelart; ein flanellartiges Gewebe)

²**La|ma,** der; -[s], -s ⟨tibet.⟩ (buddhist. Priester od. Mönch in Tibet u. der Mongolei); **La|ma|is|mus,** der; - (Form des Buddhismus); **la|ma|is|tisch**

La|mäng ⟨nach franz. la main „die Hand"⟩; *in* aus der [kalten] Lamäng (*scherzh. für* aus dem Stegreif, sofort)

La|man|tin, der; -s, -e ⟨indian.⟩ (amerik. Seekuh)

La|marck (franz. Naturforscher); **La|mar|ckis|mus,** der; - (von Lamarck begründete Abstammungslehre)

Lam|ba|da, die; -, -s, *auch* der; -[s], -s ⟨port.⟩ (ein Modetanz)

Lam|ba|re|ne (Ort in Gabun; Wirkungsstätte Albert Schweitzers)

Lamb|da, das; -[s], -s ⟨griech. Buchstabe: Λ, λ⟩; **Lamb|da‿naht** (*Med.*), **...son|de** (beim Abgaskatalysator); **Lamb|da|zis|mus,** der; - ⟨griech.⟩ (fehlerhafte Aussprache des R als L)

Lam|bert, Lamb|recht, Lamp|recht (↑R 132; m. Vorn.); **Lam|ber|ta** (w. Vorn.)

Lam|berts|nuss ⟨*zu* lombardisch⟩ (Nuss einer Haselnussart)

Lamb|recht *vgl.* Lambert

Lamb|re|quin [lãbrə'kɛ̃:] (↑R 130), der; -s, -s ⟨franz.⟩ (*veraltet für* [gezackter] Querbehang [über Fenstern])

Lamb|rie (↑R 130), Lam|pe|rie die; -, ...ien ⟨franz.⟩ (*landsch. für* Lambris); **Lamb|ris** [lã'bri:], der; - [...'bri:(s)], - [...'bri:s], *österr.* die; -, *Plur.* - u. ...ien (untere Wandverkleidung aus Holz, Marmor od. Stuck)

Lamb|rus|co (↑R 130), der; - ⟨ital.⟩ (ein ital. Rotwein)

Lamb|skin ['lɛmskin], das; -[s], -s ⟨engl.⟩ (Lammfellimitation); **Lambs|wool** ['lɛmzwul], die; - (zarte Lamm-, Schafwolle)

la|mé [la'me:], *eindeutschend* lamee ⟨franz.⟩ (mit Lamé durchwirkt); **La|mé,** *eindeutschend* Lamee, der; -s, -s (Gewebe aus Metallfäden, die mit [Kunst]seide übersponnen sind); **la|mel|lar** ⟨lat.⟩ (streifig, schichtig, geblättert); **La|mel|le,** die; -, -n ⟨franz.⟩ (Streifen, dünnes Blättchen; Blatt unter dem Hut von Blätterpilzen); **la|mel|len|för|mig; La|mel|len|ver|schluss** *(Fotogr.)*

la|men|ta|bel ⟨lat.⟩ *(veraltet für* jämmerlich, kläglich; beweinenswert); ...ab|le (↑R 130) Lage; **La|men|ta|ti|on,** die; -, -en *(veraltet für* Jammern, Wehklagen); **la|men|tie|ren** *(ugs. für* laut klagen, jammern); **La|men|to,** das; -s, *Plur.* -s *od.* *(für* Klagelieder:) ...ti ⟨ital.⟩ *(ugs. für* [lautes] Gejammer; *Musik* Klagelied)

La|met|ta, das; -s ⟨ital.⟩ (Metallfäden [als Christbaumschmuck]); **La|met|ta|syn|drom** (eine durch Umweltvergiftung hervorgerufene Baumkrankheit)

la|mi|nar ⟨lat.⟩ *(Physik* ohne Wirbel nebeneinander herlaufend); -e Strömung; **La|mi|na|ria,** die; -, ...ien [...i̯ən] *(Bot.* eine Gattung der Braunalgen); **la|mi|nie|ren** ⟨franz.⟩ *(Weberei* [Material] strecken, um die Fasern längs zu richten; *fachspr. für* [Werkstoffe] mit einer [Deck]schicht überziehen; *Buchw.* [ein Buch] mit Glanzfolie überziehen)

Lamm, das; -[e]s, Lämmer; **Lamm|bra|ten; Lämm|chen; lam|men** (ein Lamm werfen); **Läm|mer|gei|er** (ein Greifvogel); **Läm|mer|ne,** das; -n; ↑R 5 ff. *(bes. österr. für* Lammfleisch); **Läm|mer|wol|ke** *meist Plur.;* **Lam|mes|ge|duld** *(svw.* Lammsgeduld); **Lamm‿fell, ...fleisch; lamm|fromm** *(ugs.);* **Lamm|ko|te|lett; Lämm|lein; Lamms|ge|duld** *(ugs. für* große Geduld); **Lam|mung,** die; -

Lam|pas, der; -, - ⟨franz.⟩ (ein Damastgewebe); **Lam|pas|sen** [*österr.* 'lam...] *Plur.* (breite Streifen an [Uniform]hosen)

Lämp|chen (kleine [2]Lampe)

[1]**Lam|pe** *(Kurzform von* Lampert; der Hase der Tierfabel); Meister -

[2]**Lam|pe,** die; -, -n; **Lam|pen‿docht, ...fie|ber, ...licht** (das; -[e]s), **...schein** (der; -[e]s), **...schirm, ...stu|be** *(Bergmannsspr.)*

Lam|pe|rie *vgl.* Lambrie

Lam|pi|on [...'pi̯ɔŋ, *auch* ...'pi̯õ:, *österr.* ...'pi̯o:n], der, *seltener* das; -s, -s ⟨franz.⟩ ([Papier]laterne); **Lam|pi|on|blu|me**

Lamp|recht *vgl.* Lambert

Lamp|re|te (↑R 130), die; -, -n ⟨mlat.⟩ (ein Fisch)

Lan|ça|de [lã'sa:də], die; -, -n ⟨franz.⟩ (ein Sprung eines Pferdes in der hohen Schule)

Lan|cas|ter ['lɛŋkəstə(r)] (engl. Herzogsfamilie; engl. Stadt)

Lan|ci|er [lã'si̯e:], der; -s, -s ⟨franz., „Lanzenreiter"⟩ (ein Tanz; *früher für* Ulan); **lan|cie|ren** [lã'si:...] (fördern; zu Anerkennung, Verbreitung verhelfen; gezielt in die Öffentlichkeit dringen lassen); **lan|ciert;** -e (in bestimmter Art gemusterte) Gewebe; **Lan|cie|rung**

Land, das; -[e]s, *Plur.* Länder *u.* (geh.) Lande; aus aller Herren Länder[n]; außer Landes; hier zu Lande, *auch* hierzulande; die Halligen melden „Land unter" (Überflutung); zu Lande u. zu Wasser; bei uns zu Lande; **land|ab** *vgl.* landauf; **Land‿adel** (↑R 132), **...am|bu|la|to|ri|um** *(ehem. in der DDR),* **...am|mann** *(schweiz.* Titel des Präsidenten einiger Kantonsregierungen), **...ar|beit, ...ar|bei|ter, ...arzt**

Lan|dau|er (↑R 132; viersitziger Wagen)

land|auf; -, landab (überall); **Land|auf|ent|halt**

Lan|dau in der Pfalz (↑R 132; Stadt im Vorland der Haardt)

land|aus; -, landein (überall); **Land‿bau** (der; -[e]s), **...be|sitz, ...be|völ|ke|rung, ...be|woh|ner, ...brot; Länd|chen; Lan|de,** die; -, -n *(landsch. für* Landungsplatz); **Lan|de‿bahn, ...er|laub|nis, ...fäh|re; Land‿ei|gen|tü|mer, ...ei|gen|tü|me|rin; land|ein** *vgl.* landaus; **land|ein|wärts; Lan|de‿kap|sel** *(Raumfahrt),* **...klap|pe** (am Flugzeug), **...ma|nö|ver; lan|den; län|den** *(landsch. u. schweiz. für* landen, ans Ufer bringen); **Land|en|ge; Lan|de‿pis|te, ...platz; Län|de|rei|en** *Plur.;* **Län|der‿kampf** *(Sport),* **...kun|de** (die; -; Wissenschaftsfach); **län|der|kun|dig** (die Länder kennend); **län|der|kund|lich** (die Länderkunde betreffend); **Län|der‿na|me, ...spiel** *(Sport)*

Landes [lã:d] *Plur.* (eine franz. Landschaft)

Lan|des‿amt, ...art (die; -), **...auf|nah|me** *(svw.* Landvermessung), **...bank** *(Plur.* ...banken), **...be|hör|de, ...bi|schof, ...brauch; Lan|de|schlei|fe** *(Flugw.);* **Lan|des‿ebe|ne** (↑R 132; auf - verhandeln), **...far|ben** *(Plur.),* **...feind; lan|des|flüch|tig,** landflüch|tig; **Lan|des‿fürst, ...fürs|tin, ...ge|richt** *(österr. svw.* Landgericht), **...ge|richts|rat** *(österr. svw.* Landgerichtsrat), **...ge|schich|te, ...gren|ze, ...haupt|mann** *(Plur.* ...leute *od.* ...männer; *österr. für* Regierungschef eines Bundeslandes), **...haupt|stadt, ...herr, ...her|rin; lan|des|herr|lich; Lan|des‿ho|heit, ...hym|ne** *(österr. für* offz. Hymne eines Bundeslandes), **...in|ne|re, ...kind, ...kir|che**

Lan|des|kro|ne (Berg bei Görlitz)

Lan|des|kun|de, die; - (Wissenschaftsfach); **lan|des|kun|dig** (das Land kennend); **lan|des|kund|lich** (die Landeskunde betreffend); **Lan|des‿lis|te, ...meis|ter|schaft, ...mut|ter** *(Plur.* ...mütter), **...par|la|ment, ...pla|nung, ...pro|dukt, ...rat** *(österr. für* Mitglied einer Landesregierung), **...recht** (das; -[e]s; Recht der Länder im Gegensatz zum Bundesrecht), **...re|gie|rung, ...schul|rat** *(österr. für* oberste Schulbehörde eines Bundeslandes), **...sit|te, ...so|zi|al|ge|richt** *(Abk.* LSG), **...spra|che, ...tracht, ...trau|er; lan|des|üb|lich; Lan|des‿va|ter, ...ver|rat, ...ver|rä|ter, ...ver|si|che|rungs|an|stalt** *(Abk.* LVA), **...ver|tei|di|gung, ...ver|wei|sung; lan|des|ver|wie|sen; Lan|des‿wäh|rung, ...wap|pen; lan|des|weit; Lan|des|zent|ral|bank** *(Abk.* LZB); **Lan|de|ver|bot; Land‿fah|rer, ...fah|re|rin; land|fein** *(Seemannsspr.);* sich - machen; **Land|flucht,** die; - (Abwanderung der ländl. Bevölkerung in die [Groß]städte); **land|flüch|tig** *vgl.* landesflüchtig; **Land|frau; Land|frau|en|schu|le; land|fremd; Land|frie|de[n]; Land|frie|dens|bruch,** der; **Land‿gang** *(Seemannsspr.),* **...ge|mein|de, ...ge|richt** *(Abk.* LG), **...ge|richts|rat** *(Plur.* ...räte); **land|ge|stützt** (von Raketen); **Land‿ge|win|nung, ...graf** *(früher),* **...gut, ...haus, ...heim, ...jä|ger** (eine Dauerwurst; *früher für* Landpolizist, Gendarm), **...kaf|fee** (kaffeeähnliches Getränk), **...kar|te**

Land Kẹh|din|gen, das; -es (Teil der Elbmarschen)

Lạnd‿kind, ...kli|ma, ...kom|mu|ne, ...kreis; lạnd|läu|fig; Lạnd|le|ben, das; -s; **Lạ̈nd|ler** (ein Volkstanz); **lạ̈nd|lich; Lạ̈nd|lich|keit,** die; -; **lạnd|lie|bend** *(Zool.)*; **Lạnd‿luft, ...macht, ...mann** (*Plur.* ...leute; *veraltet für* Bauer), **...ma|schi|ne, ...mes|ser** (der; *veraltend*), **...nah|me** (die; -; *früher für* Inbesitznahme von Land durch ein Volk), **...par|tie, ...pfar|rer, ...pfle|ger** *(bibl.)*, **...pla|ge, ...po|me|ran|ze** (*ugs. für* Mädchen vom Lande, Provinzlerin), **...pra|xis, ...rat** (*Plur.* ...räte), **...rä|tin, ...rat|te** (*Seemannsspr.* Nichtseemann), **...recht** (im MA.), **...re|gen, ...rich|ter** *(veraltet)*

Land|ro|ver ® ['lɛndro:wə(r)], der; -[s], - ‹engl.› (ein geländegängiges Kraftfahrzeug)

Lạnd|rü|cken; lạnd|säs|sig *(veraltet)*

Lạnds|berg a. Lẹch (Stadt in Oberbayern)

Lạnd|schaft; Lạnd|schaf|ter (*veraltet für* Landschaftsmaler); **lạnd|schaft|lich; Lạnd|schafts‿gärt|ner, ...gärt|ne|rin, ...ma|ler, ...ma|le|rin, ...pfle|ge, ...schutz|ge|biet** (*Abk.* LSG); **Lạnd|schrei|ber** (*schweiz. für* Kanzleivorsteher eines Landkantons, Bezirks); **Lạnd|schu|le; Lạnd|schul|heim; Lạnd|see,** der; **Lạnd|ser** (*ugs. für* Soldat); **Lạnds|ge|mein|de** (*schweiz. für* Versammlung der stimmfähigen Bürger eines Kantons, Bezirks)

Lạnds|hut (Stadt a. d. Isar)

Lạnd|sitz; Lạnds|knecht

Lands|mål ['lantsmo:l], das; -[s] ‹norw., „Landessprache"› (*ältere Bez. für* Nynorsk *[vgl. d.]*)

Lạnds‿mann (*Plur.* ...leute; Landes-, Heimatgenosse), **...män|nin; lạnds|män|nisch; Lạnds|mann|schaft; lạnds|mann|schaft|lich; Lạnd|stadt; Lạnd|stän|de** *Plur. (früher)*

Lands|ting ['lanstɛŋ], das; -s ‹dän.› (bis 1953 der Senat des dän. Reichstages)

Lạnd|stör|zer (*veraltet für* Fahrender); **Lạnd|stör|ze|rin; Lạnd‿stra|ße, ...strei|cher; Lạnd|strei|che|rei,** die; -; **Lạnd‿strei|che|rin, ...streit|kräf|te** *(Plur.)*, **...strich, ...sturm** (*vgl.* [1]Sturm); **Lạnd|sturm|mann** *Plur.* ...männer; **Lạnd|tag;** der Hessische - (↑R 108); der - von Baden-Württemberg; **Lạnd|tags‿ab|ge|ord|ne|te, ...wahl; Lạn|dung; Lạn|dungs‿boot, ...brü|cke, ...steg; Lạnd‿ur|laub, ...ver|mes|ser, ...ver|mes|se|rin, ...ver|mes|sung, ...vogt** *(früher)*, **...volk** (das; -[e]s); **lạnd|wärts; Lạnd-Wạs|ser-Tier** (↑R 28); **Lạnd|wehr,** die *(früher)*; **Lạnd|wehr|mann** *Plur.* ...männer; **Lạnd‿wein, ...wind, ...wirt, ...wir|tin, ...wirt|schaft; lạnd|wirt|schaft|lich;** landwirtschaftliche Produktionsgenossenschaft (*ehem. in der DDR; Abk.* LPG), *aber* (↑R 108): „Landwirtschaftliche Produktionsgenossenschaft Einheit"; **Lạnd|wirt|schafts‿aus|stel|lung, ...kam|mer, ...mi|nis|ter, ...mi|nis|te|rin; Lạnd|zun|ge**

lạng; länger, längste; (↑R 47): am längsten; über kurz oder lang; seit langem; seit längerem. **I.** *Großschreibung:* **a)** (↑R 47:) in Lang (*ugs. für* im langen Abendkleid) gehen; ein Langes und Breites (viel) reden; sich des Langen und Breiten, des Längeren und Breiteren über etwas äußern; **b)** (↑R 108:) der Lange Marsch (der Marsch der chin. Kommunisten quer durch China 1934/35). **II.** *Getrennt- und Zusammenschreibung:* **a)** allzu lang; ein Gummiband lang ziehen/länger ziehen; jmdm. die Hammelbeine lang ziehen (*ugs. für* jmdn. heftig tadeln); jmdm. die Ohren lang ziehen (jmdn. [an den Ohren ziehend] strafen); ein lang gehegter Wunsch; ein lang gestrecktes Gebäude; eine lang gezogene Kurve; **b)** langhin; meterlang, jahrelang, tagelang usw., *aber* einen Fuß lang, zehn Meter lang, zwei Jahre lang usw.; langgehen *(vgl. d.)*; langlegen, sich *(vgl. d.)*; *vgl.* lange; **lạng‿är|me|lig** *od.* **...ärm|lig; lạng‿ar|mig, ...at|mig, ...bär|tig; Lạng‿baum** (*svw.* Langwied[e]), **...bein** *(scherzh.)*; **lạng|bei|nig; lạn|ge,** lạng; länger, am längsten (↑R 47); lang ersehnte Hilfe, lang anhaltender Beifall usw.; es ist lange her; lang, lang ists her; **Lạ̈n|ge,** die; -, -n; **lạ̈n|ge|lang** (*ugs. für* der Länge nach); - hinfallen

lạn|gen (*ugs. für* ausreichen; [nach etwas] greifen)

lạ̈n|gen (länger machen; *veraltet für* länger werden); **Lạ̈n|gen‿grad, ...kreis, ...maß** (das)

Lạn|gen|see, der; -s (*dt. Name für* Lago Maggiore)

Lan|ge|oog [...'o:k] (eine der Ostfries. Inseln)

lạ̈n|ger|fris|tig

Lan|get|te, die; -, -n ‹franz.› (Randstickerei als Abschluss; Trennungswand zwischen zwei Schornsteinen); **lan|get|tie|ren** (mit Randstickereien versehen); **Lan|get|tie|rung**

Lan|ge|wei|le [*auch* 'laŋə...], Lang|wei|le, die; *Gen.* der Lang[e]weile *u.* Langenweile; aus - *u.* Langerweile; **Lan|ge|zeit,** die; *zur Beugung vgl.* Langeweile (*schweiz. für* Sehnsucht, Heimweh); **lạng|fä|dig** (*schweiz. für* weitschweifig, langatmig); **Lạng|fin|ger** (*ugs. für* Dieb); **lạng‿fin|ge|rig** *od.* **...fing|rig; lạng|fris|tig**

Lạng|gäs|ser (dt. Dichterin)

lạng ge|hegt *vgl.* lang; **lạng|ge|hen** (*ugs. für* entlanggehen); wissen, wo es langgeht; **lạng ge|streckt, ge|zo|gen,** *vgl.* lang; **lạng‿glie|de|rig** *od.* **...glied|rig; Lạng|haar|da|ckel; lạng‿haa|rig, ...hal|sig; Lạng|haus** *(Archit.)*; **lạng|hịn;** ein langhin rollendes Echo; **Lạng|holz; lạng‿jäh|rig, ...köp|fig; Lạng|lauf** *(Sport)*; **Lạng|lauf|ski; lạng|le|big; Lạng|le|big|keit,** die; -; **lạng|le|gen,** sich (*ugs. für* sich zum Ausruhen hinlegen); **lạ̈ng|lich;** länglich rund; **lạng|mäh|nig; Lạng|mut,** die; - *(geh.)*; **lạng|mü|tig; Lạng|mü|tig|keit,** die; -; **lạng|na|sig**

Lan|go|bar|de, der; -n, -n; ↑R 126 (Angehöriger eines westgerm. Volkes); **lan|go|bar|disch**

Lạng|ohr, das; -[e]s, -en (*scherzh. für* Hase; Esel); **Lạng‿pferd** *(Turnen)*, **...ril|le** (*scherzh. für* Langspielplatte); **lạng|rip|pig; lạ̈ngs** (der Länge nach); etwas längs trennen; *als Präp. mit Gen.:* längs des Weges, *gelegentl. mit Dat.:* längs dem Wege; ein längs gestreifter Stoff; **Lạ̈ngs|ach|se**

lạng|sam; -er Walzer; **Lạng|sam|keit,** die; -

lạng‿schä|de|lig *od.* **...schäd|lig; Lạng‿schäf|ter** (Stiefel mit langem Schaft), **...schlä|fer, ...schlä|fe|rin; lạng‿schnä|be|lig** *od.* **...schnäb|lig; lạ̈ngs|deck[s]** (*Seemannsspr.* auf dem Deck entlang); **Lạng|sei|te; Lạ̈ngs‿fa|den, ...fal|te;** längs **ge|streift** *vgl.* längs; **Lạ̈ngs|li|nie; Lạng|spiel|plat|te** (*Abk.* LP); **Lạ̈ngs|rich|tung; lạ̈ngs|schiffs** (*Seemannsspr.* in Kielrichtung); **Lạ̈ngs|schnitt; lạ̈ngs|seit** (*Seemannsspr.* an der langen Seite, an die lange Seite des Schiffes); **Lạ̈ngs|sei|te; lạ̈ngs|seits** (parallel zur Längsrichtung); *als Präp. mit Gen.:* - des Schiffes; **Lạ̈ngs|strei|fen; lạ̈ngst** (seit langem);

lang⌣stän|ge|lig *od.* **...stäng|lig; längs|tens** (*landsch. für* längst; spätestens); **lang|stie|lig** (*ugs. auch für* langweilig, einförmig); **Lang|stre|cke; Lang|stre|cken⌣bom|ber, ...flug, ...lauf, ...läu|fer, ...läu|fe|rin; Lang|streck|ler** (*Sportspr.* Langstreckenläufer); **Längs|wand**

Langue|doc [lãg'dɔk], das *od.* die; - (eine südfranz. Landschaft); **Langue|doc|wein** (↑ R 105)

Lan|gus|te, die; -, -n ‹franz.› (ein Krebs)

Lang|wei|le *vgl.* Langeweile; **lang|wei|len;** du langweilst; gelangweilt; zu -; sich -; **Lang|wei|ler** (*ugs. für* langweiliger Mensch); **lang|wei|lig; Lang|wei|lig|keit,** die; -; **Lang|wel|le** *(Physik, Rundf.)*; **lang|wel|lig; Lang|wied, Lang|wie|de,** die; -, ...den (*landsch. für* langes Rundholz, das Vorder- u. Hintergestell eines großen Leiterwagens verbindet); **lang|wie|rig; Lang|wie|rig|keit; Lang|zei|le; Lang|zeit⌣ar|beits|lo|se, ...ge|dächt|nis** *(Psych.)*, **...kran|ke, ...pro|gramm, ...scha|den** *(meist Plur.)*, **...stu|die, ...wir|kung; lang zie|hen** *vgl.* lang

La|no|lin, das; -s ‹lat.› (Wollfett, Salbengrundstoff)

Lan|ta|na, die; - ‹nlat.› (Wandelröschen, ein Zierstrauch)

Lan|than, das; -s ‹griech.› (chem. Element, Metall; *Zeichen* La); **Lan|tha|nit** [*auch* ...'nit], der; -s, -e (ein Mineral)

La|nu|go, die; -, ...gines [...ne:s] ‹lat.› (Wollhaarflaum des Embryos)

Lan|ze, die; -, -n; **Lan|zen⌣farn, ...rei|ter, ...spit|ze, ...stich, ...stoß; Lan|zet|te,** die; -, -n ‹franz.› (ein chirurg. Instrument); **Lan|zett⌣fens|ter** *(Archit.)*, **...fisch; lan|zett|för|mig**

lan|zi|nie|ren ‹lat.› (*Med.* blitzartig und heftig schmerzen [bes. bei Rückenmarksschwindsucht]); -de Schmerzen

La|o|ko|on [...koɔn] (griech. Sagengestalt)

La O|la, die; - -, - -s *meist ohne Artikel* ‹span., „die Welle"› (besondere Art der Begeisterungsbezeigung in Sportstadien); **La-O|la-Wel|le** (↑ R 28)

Laon [lã:] (franz. Stadt)

La|os (Staat in Hinterindien); **La|o|te,** der; -n, -n (↑ R 126); **la|o|tisch**

La|ot|se [*auch* 'lau...] (↑ R 132; chin. Weiser)

La|pa|ro|skop, das; -s, -e ‹griech.› (*Med.* ein Instrument zur Untersuchung der Bauchhöhle); **La|pa|ro|to|mie,** die; -, ...ien (*Med.* Bauchschnitt)

La Paz [- 'pa(:)s] (größte Stadt u. Regierungssitz von Bolivien)

la|pi|dar ‹lat.› (einfach, elementar; kurz u. bündig); **La|pi|där,** der; -s, -e (ein Schleif- u. Poliergerät der Uhrmacher); **La|pi|da|ri|um,** das; -s, ...ien [...i̯ən] (*fachspr. für* Sammlung von Steindenkmälern); **La|pi|dar⌣schrift** (Versalschrift, meist auf Stein), **...stil** (der; -[e]s); **La|pil|li** *Plur.* ‹ital.› (kleine Steinchen, die bei einem Vulkanausbruch ausgeworfen werden); **La|pis|la|zu|li,** der; -, - (*svw.* Lasurit)

La|pi|the, der; -n, -n; ↑ R 126 (Angehöriger eines myth. Volkes in Thessalien)

La|place [la'pla:s] (franz. Astronom und Mathematiker); die laplacesche Theorie (↑ R 94)

[1]La Pla|ta (Stadt in Argentinien); **[2]La Pla|ta,** der; - - (*svw.* Rio de la Plata; *vgl. d.*); **La-Pla|ta-Staa|ten** *Plur.*; ↑ R 28 (Argentinien, Paraguay, Uruguay)

Lapp, der; -en, -en; ↑ R 126 (*bayr., österr. mdal. für* einfältiger, tölpelhafter Mensch)

Lap|pa|lie [...i̯ə], die; -, -n (Kleinigkeit; Nichtigkeit); **Läpp|chen** (kleiner Lappen)

Lap|pe, der; -n, -n; ↑ R 126 (Angehöriger eines Volksstammes im nördl. Nordeuropa; *vgl.* [1]Same)

Lap|pen, der; -s, -

läp|pen (*fachspr. für* metallische Werkstoffe fein bearbeiten)

Lap|pen|zelt ‹*zu* Lappe›

Lap|pe|rei (*seltener für* Läpperei); **Läp|pe|rei** (*landsch. für* Kleinigkeit; Wertloses); **läp|pern** (*landsch. für* schlürfen; in kleinen Teilen sammeln; zusammenkommen); ich ...ere (↑ R 16); es läppert sich

lap|pig

lap|pisch ‹*zu* Lappe›

läp|pisch

Lapp|land (Landschaft in Nordeuropa); **Lapp|län|der** (Bewohner Lapplands); **lapp|län|disch**

Läpp|ma|schi|ne (Maschine zum Läppen)

Lap|sus, der; -, - [...su:s] ‹lat.› ([geringfügiger] Fehler, Versehen); **Lap|sus Ca|la|mi,** der; - -, - [...su:s] - (Schreibfehler); **Lap|sus Lin|gu|ae** [- 'liŋguɛ:], der; - -, [...su:s] - (das Sichversprechen); **Lap|sus Me|mo|ri|ae** [- ...riɛ:], der; - -, - [...su:s] - (Gedächtnisfehler)

Lap|top ['lɛptɔp], der; -s, -s ‹engl.› (kleiner, tragbarer Personalcomputer)

Lar, der; -s, -en ‹malai.› (ein Langarmaffe, Weißhandgibbon)

La|ra (w. Vorn.)

Lär|che, die; -, -n (ein Nadelbaum); *vgl. aber* Lerche

La|ren *Plur.* ‹lat.› (altröm. Schutzgeister)

large [la:rʒ] ‹franz.› (*bes. schweiz. für* großzügig, weitherzig); **Large|heit**

lar|ghet|to [...'gɛto] ‹ital.› (*Musik* etwas breit, etwas langsam); **Lar|ghet|to,** das; -s, *Plur.* -s *u.* ...tti; **lar|go** (*Musik* breit, langsam); **Lar|go,** das; -s, *Plur.* -s, *auch* ...ghi [...gi]

la|ri|fa|ri! (*ugs. für* Geschwätz!, Unsinn!); **La|ri|fa|ri,** das; -s

Lärm, der; *Gen.* -s, *seltener* -es; **lärm|arm; Lärm⌣be|kämp|fung, ...be|läs|ti|gung; lärm|emp|find|lich; lär|men; lär|mig** (*schweiz., sonst veraltet für* lärmend laut); **Lärm⌣ma|cher, ...min|de|rung**

lar|mo|yant [...moa'jant] ‹franz.› (*geh. für* weinerlich, rührselig); **Lar|mo|yanz,** die; - *(geh.)*

Lärm⌣pe|gel, ...quel|le, ...schutz, ...schutz|wall, ...schutz|zaun

Lars (m. Vorn.)

L'art pour l'art [la:r pur 'la:r], das; - ‹franz., „die Kunst für die Kunst"› (die Kunst als Selbstzweck)

lar|val [...'va:l] ‹lat.› (*Biol.* die Tierlarve betreffend); **Lar|ve** [...fə], die; -, -n (Gespenst, Maske; *oft abwertend für* Gesicht; *Zool.* Jugendstadium bestimmter Tiere); **lar|ven|ähn|lich**

La|ryn|gal, der; -s, -e ‹griech.› *u.* **La|ryn|gal|laut** (*Sprachw.* Laut, der in der Stimmritze [im Kehlkopf] gebildet wird, Stimmritzen-, Kehlkopflaut); **La|ryn|gen** (*Plur. von* Larynx); **La|ryn|gi|tis,** die; -, ...itiden (*Med.* Kehlkopfentzündung); **La|ryn|go|skop,** das; -s, -e (*Med.* Kehlkopfspiegel); **la|ryn|go|sko|pisch; La|rynx,** der; -, Laryngen (*Med.* Kehlkopf)

La|sag|ne [la'sanjə] (↑ R 130) *Plur.* ‹ital.› (ein ital. Nudelgericht)

Las|caux [las'ko:] (Steinzeithöhle in Südfrankreich)

lasch (*ugs. für* schlaff, lässig; *landsch. für* fade, nicht gewürzt)

La|sche, die; -, -n (ein Verbindungsstück); **la|schen** (durch Lasche[n] verbinden); du laschst; **La|schen|kupp|lung** *(Bergbau)*

Lasch|heit ‹*zu* lasch›

La|schung (Verbindung durch Lasche[n])

La|se, die; -, -n (*mitteld. für* [Bier]gefäß)
La|ser ['le:zə(r), *auch* 'la:...], der; -s, - ‹engl.› (*Physik* Gerät zur Verstärkung von Licht od. zur Erzeugung eines scharf gebündelten Lichtstrahles); **La|ser‿chi|rur|gie, ...dru|cker, ...im|puls, ...strahl, ...tech|nik, ...waf|fe**
la|sie|ren ‹pers.› (mit Lasur versehen); **La|sie|rung**
Lä|si|on, die; -, -en ‹lat.› (*Med.* Verletzung)
Las|kar, der; -s, ...karen ‹anglo-ind.› (*früher* ostind. Matrose, Soldat)
Las|ker-Schü|ler (dt. Dichterin)
Las Pal|mas (Hptst. der span. Insel Gran Canaria)
lass (*geh. für* matt, müde, schlaff)
Las|sa|fie|ber, das; -s (↑R 105) ‹nach dem Ort Lassa in Nigeria› (eine Infektionskrankheit)
Las|salle [la'sal] (Mitbegründer der dt. Arbeiterbewegung); **Las|sal|le|a|ner** (Anhänger Lassalles)
las|sen; du lässt, *veraltet* lässest, er lässt; du ließest, er ließ; gelassen; lasse! *u.* lass!; ich lass sie nicht; ich habe es gelassen (unterlassen), *aber* ich habe dich rufen lassen; ich habe ihn dies wissen lassen; *vgl.* bleiben, fahren, fallen usw.
Lass|heit, die; - ‹*zu* lass›; **läs|sig; Läs|sig|keit,** die; -; **läss|lich** (*bes. Rel.* verzeihlich); -e (kleinere) Sünde; **Läss|lich|keit**
Las|so, das, *österr. nur so, seltener* der; -s, -s ‹span.› (Wurfschlinge; Figur im Eis- u. Rollkunstlauf)
Last, die; -, -en (*Seemannsspr. auch* Vorratsraum unter Deck); zu meinen Lasten; zulasten, *auch* zu Lasten des *od.* von ...; **Last|au|to; las|ten; Las|ten‿auf|zug, ...aus|gleich** (*Abk.* LA); **Las|ten|aus|gleichs|ge|setz** (*Abk.* LAG); **las|ten|frei; Las|ten|seg|ler;** [1]**Las|ter,** der; -s, - (*ugs. für* Lastkraftwagen)
[2]**Las|ter,** das; -s, -; **Läs|te|rei; Läs|te|rer; las|ter|haft; Las|ter|haf|tig|keit,** die; -; **Las|ter|höh|le; Läs|te|rin; Las|ter|le|ben,** das; -s; **läs|ter|lich; Läs|ter|lich|keit; Läs|ter|maul** (*ugs. für* jmd., der viel lästert); **läs|tern;** ich ...ere (↑R 16); **Läs|te|rung; Läs|ter|zun|ge**
Last|esel
Las|tex, das; - ‹Kunstwort› ([Gewebe aus] Gummifäden, die mit Kunstseiden- od. Chemiefasern umsponnen sind); **Las|tex|ho|se**
Last|fuh|re; läs|tig; ...las|tig (z. B. zweilastig; *Flugw.* schwanzlastig); **Las|tig|keit,** die; - (Fluglage eines Flugzeugs; Schwimmlage eines Schiffs); **Läs|tig|keit**
Las|ting, der; -s, -s ‹engl.› (ein Gewebe)
Last‿kahn, ...kraft|wa|gen (*Abk.* Lkw, *auch* LKW)
last, not least ['la:st nɔt 'li:st] ‹engl., „als Letzter [Letztes], nicht Geringster [Geringstes]"› (zuletzt der Stelle, nicht dem Wert nach)
Last‿pferd, ...schiff, ...schrift (*Buchhaltung);* **Last|schrift|zet|tel; Last‿spit|ze** (größte Belastung eines Kraftwerks in einer bestimmten Zeit), **...tier, ...trä|ger, ...wa|gen** (Lastkraftwagen), **...zug**
La|sur, die; -, -en ‹pers.› (durchsichtige Farbschicht); **La|sur|far|be; La|su|rit** [*auch* ...'rit] *od.* La|sur|stein (ein blauer Schmuckstein); **La|sur|lack** (durchsichtige Farbe); **La|sur|stein** *vgl.* Lasurit
Las Ve|gas [- v...] (Stadt in Nevada)
las|ziv ‹lat.› (schlüpfrig, anstößig; übertrieben sinnlich); **Las|zi|vi|tät** [...v...], die; -
Lä|ta|re ‹lat., „freue dich!"› (dritter Sonntag vor Ostern)
La|tein, das; -s; **La|tein|ame|ri|ka** (↑R 132; Gesamtheit der spanisch- od. portugiesischsprachigen Staaten von Amerika); **la|tein|ame|ri|ka|nisch** (↑R 132); **La|tei|ner** (jmd., der Latein kennt, spricht); **la|tei|nisch;** -e Schrift; *vgl.* deutsch; **La|tei|nisch,** das; -[s] (Sprache); *vgl.* Deutsch; **La|tei|ni|sche,** das; -n; *vgl.* Deutsche, das; **La|tein‿schrift, ...schu|le, ...se|gel** (dreieckiges Segel), **...un|ter|richt**
La-Tène-Zeit [...'tɛ:n...], die; - ‹nach der Untiefe im Neuenburger See› (Abschnitt der Eisenzeit); ↑R 105; **La-Tène-zeit|lich**
la|tent ‹lat.› (vorhanden, aber [noch] nicht in Erscheinung tretend); ein -er Gegensatz; -es Bild (*Fotogr.);* eine -e Krankheit; -e (gebundene) Wärme; **La|tenz,** die; -; **La|tenz‿pe|ri|o|de, ...zeit**
la|te|ral ‹lat.› (*fachspr. für* seitlich)
La|te|ran, der; -s (ehem. Palast des Papstes in Rom); **La|te|ran‿kon|zil, ...pa|last, ...ver|trä|ge** (*Plur.)*
La|te|rit [*auch* ...'rit], der; -s, -e ‹lat.› (ein roter Verwitterungsboden); **La|te|rit|bo|den**
La|ter|na ma|gi|ca, die; - -, ...nae ...cae [...nɛ: ...tsɛ:] ‹lat.› (einfachster Projektionsapparat); **La|ter|ne,** die; -, -n ‹griech.› (*Archit. auch* turmartiger Aufsatz); **La|ter|nen‿ga|ra|ge** *(ugs.),* **...licht** (das; -[e]s), **...pfahl**
La|tex, der; -, Latizes [...tse:s] ‹griech.› ([Anstrichstoff aus] Kautschukmilch); **la|te|xie|ren**
La|tier|baum (Stange im Pferdestall zur Abgrenzung der Plätze)
La|ti|fun|di|en|wirt|schaft, die; -; **La|ti|fun|di|um,** das; -s, ...ien [...iən] ‹lat.› (Landgut im Röm. Reich; Großgrundbesitz)
La|ti|ner, der; -s, - (Angehöriger eines altitalischen Volkes in Latium); **la|ti|nisch; la|ti|ni|sie|ren** ‹lat.› (in lat. Sprachform bringen); **La|ti|ni|sie|rung; La|ti|nis|mus,** der; -, ...men (dem Lateinischen eigentümlicher Ausdruck in einer nichtlat. Sprache); **La|ti|nist,** der; -en, -en; ↑R 126 (Kenner u. Erforscher des Lateinischen); **La|ti|nis|tin; La|ti|ni|tät,** die; - ([klassische, mustergültige] lateinische Schreibweise, desgl. Schrifttum);
La|tin|lo|ver, der; -[s], -s, *auch* **La|tin Lo|ver** ['lɛtinlavə(r)], der; -[s], - - ‹engl.› (feuriger, südländischer Liebhaber); **La|ti|num,** das; -s ([Ergänzungs]prüfung im Lateinischen); das kleine, große -
Lä|ti|tia (w. Vorn.)
La|ti|um (hist. Landschaft in Mittelitalien)
Lat|ri|ne (↑R 130), die; -, -n ‹lat.› (Abort, Senkgrube); **Lat|ri|nen‿ge|rücht** *(ugs.),* **...pa|ro|le** *(ugs.)*
Latsch, der; -[e]s, -e (*ugs. für* nachlässig gehender Mensch; Hausschuh); [1]**Lat|sche,** die; -, -n *u.* Lat|schen, der; -s, - (*ugs. für* Hausschuh, abgetretener Schuh)
[2]**Lat|sche,** die; -, -n (Krummholzkiefer, Legföhre)
lat|schen (*ugs. für* nachlässig, schleppend gehen); du latschst
Lat|schen *vgl.* [1]Latsche
Lat|schen‿ge|büsch, ...kie|fer (die); **Lat|schen[|kie|fern]|öl,** das; -[e]s
lat|schig (*ugs. für* nachlässig in Gang u. Wesen)
Lat|te, die; -, -n; **Lat|ten‿holz, ...kis|te, ...kreuz** (*Sport* von Pfosten u. Querlatte gebildete Ecke des Tores), **...rost** (*vgl.* [1]Rost), **...schuss** (*Sport* Schuss an die Querlatte des Tores), **...zaun**
Lat|tich, der; -s, -e ‹lat.› (ein Korbblütler)
La|tüch|te, die; -, -n (*ugs. für* Laterne, Licht)
Lat|wer|ge, die; -, -n ‹griech.› (eine breiförmige Arznei; *veraltet, aber noch landsch. für* Fruchtmus)
Latz, der; -es, *Plur.* Lätze, *österr. auch* Latze (Kleidungsteil [z. B. Brustlatz]); **Lätz|chen; Latz|ho|se; Latz|schür|ze**
lau

Laub, das; -[e]s; (↑R 40:) Laub tragende Bäume; **Laub|baum**

[1]**Lau|be,** die; -, -n

[2]**Lau|be,** der; -n, -n; ↑R 126 (ein Fisch, Ukelei)

Lau|ben‿gang (der), **...haus, ...ko|lo|nie, ...pie|per** (*landsch. für* Kleingärtner)

Laub‿fall (der; -[e]s), **...fär|bung, ...frosch, ...ge|höl|ze** (*Plur.; Bot.*), **...holz; Laub|hüt|ten|fest** (jüd. Fest); **lau|big** (*veraltet für* [viel] Laub tragend); **Laub|sä|ge; Laub tra|gend** *vgl.* Laub; **Laub‿wald, ...werk**

Lauch, der; -[e]s, -e (eine Zwiebelpflanze); **lauch|grün**

Lau|da|num, das; -s ‹lat.› (in Alkohol gelöstes Opium)

Lau|da|tio, die; -, ...io̱nes [...ne:s] ‹lat., „Lob[rede]"› (feierl. Würdigung); **Lau|des** [...de:s] *Plur.* ‹„Lobgesänge"› (Morgengebet des kath. Breviers)

[1]**Lau|er,** die; -; auf der - sein, liegen (*ugs.*)

[2]**Lau|er,** der; -s, - ‹lat.› (Tresterwein)

lau|ern; ich ...ere (↑R 16)

Lauf, der; -[e]s, Läufe; im Lauf[e] der Zeit; 100-m-Lauf (↑R 28); **Lauf‿ar|beit** (die; -; *Sport*), **...bahn, ...brett, ...bur|sche** (*abwertend*); **Läuf|chen**

Läu|fel, die; -, - (*südwestd. für* äußere [grüne] Schale, bes. der Walnuss)

lau|fen; du läufst, er läuft; du liefst (liefest); du liefest; gelaufen; lauf[e]!; laufen lassen (*ugs. auch für* lossagen, freigeben); ich habe sie laufen lassen, *seltener* laufen gelassen; er beabsichtigt, sie laufen zu lassen; **lau|fend** (*Abk.* lfd.); laufendes Jahr *u.* laufenden Jahres (*Abk.* lfd. J.); laufender Meter *u.* laufenden Meters (*Abk.* lfd. M.); laufender Monat *u.* laufenden Monats (*Abk.* lfd. M.); laufende Nummer *u.* laufender Nummer (*Abk.* lfd. Nr.); am laufenden Band arbeiten; (↑R 47:) auf dem Laufenden sein, bleiben, halten; **lau|fen las|sen** *vgl.* laufen; **Läu|fer** (*auch für* längerer, schmaler Teppich); **Lau|fe|rei** (*ugs.*); **Läu|fe|rin; läu|fe|risch; Lauf‿feu|er, ...flä|che; lauf|freu|dig** (*Sportspr.*); **Lauf‿gang, ...ge|wicht, ...git|ter, ...gra|ben; läu|fig** (brünstig [von der Hündin]); **Läu|fig|keit,** die; - (Brunst der Hündin); **Lauf‿kä|fer, ...kat|ze** (*Technik*), **...kund|schaft** (die; -), **...ma|sche, ...pass** (*nur in ugs.* jmdm. den - geben), **...pen|sum** (*Sportspr.*), **...plan|ke, ...rad, ...schie|ne, ...schrift** (sich bewegende Leuchtschrift), **...schritt, ...ställ|chen, ...steg, ...stil** (*Sport*), **...stuhl, ...vo|gel, ...werk** (*Technik, EDV*), **...wett|be|werb, ...zeit, ...zet|tel**

Lau|ge, die; -, -n (alkal. [wässrige] Lösung; Auszug); **lau|gen** (*veraltend*); **lau|gen|ar|tig; Lau|gen‿bad, ...bre|zel** (*landsch.*), **...bröt|chen, ...was|ser** (das; -s)

Lau|heit, die; -

Lau|mann (*ugs. für* Mensch ohne eigene Meinung)

Lau|ne, die; -, -n ‹lat.›; **lau|nen|haft; Lau|nen|haf|tig|keit,** die; -; **lau|nig** (humorvoll); **lau|nisch** (launenhaft)

Lau|ra (w. Vorn.)

Lau|re|at, der; -en, -en; ↑R 126 ‹lat.› ([öffentl.] ausgezeichneter Wissenschaftler; *früher für* lorbeergekrönter Dichter); *vgl.* Poeta laureatus

Lau|re̱n|tia (w. Vorn.)

lau|re̱n|tisch ‹nach dem latinisierten Namen des Sankt-Lorenz-Stromes›; -e Gebirgsbildung (am Ende des Archaikums)

Lau|re̱n|ti|us (m. Vorn.)

lau|re|ta|nisch (aus Loreto), *aber* (↑R 108): Lauretanische Litanei (in Loreto entstandene Marienlitanei)

Lau|rin (Zwergenkönig, mittelalterl. Sagengestalt)

Lau|rus, der; *Gen.* - *u.* -ses, *Plur.* - [...ru:s] *u.* -se ‹lat.› (*Bot.* Lorbeerbaum)

Laus, die; -, Läuse

Lau|sanne [lo'zan] (Stadt am Genfer See); **Lau|sa̱n|ner** (↑R 103)

Laus|bub, *auch* **Laus|bu|be** (*ugs.*); **Laus|bu|ben|streich; Laus|bü|be|rei; laus|bü|bisch**

Lau|scha|er Gla̱s|wa|ren *Plur.* ‹nach dem Ort Lauscha im Thüringer Wald›

Lausch‿ak|ti|on, ...an|griff (heimliches Anbringen von Abhörgeräten [in einer Privatwohnung])

Lau|sche, die; - (höchster Berg im Zittauer Gebirge)

lau|schen; du lauschst

Läus|chen

Lau|scher (Lauschender; *Jägerspr.* Ohr des Haarwildes); **Lau|sche|rin; lau|schig** (gemütlich)

Läu|se|be|fall; Lau|se‿ben|gel *od.* **...jun|ge** *od.* **...kerl** (*ugs.*); **Läu|se|kraut,** das; -[e]s (eine Pflanzengattung); **lau|sen;** du laust; **Lau|se|pack** (*abwertend*); **Lau|ser** (*landsch. für* Lausbub); **Lau|se|rei** (*ugs.*); **lau|sig** (*ugs. auch für* äußerst; schäbig, erbärmlich, schlecht); - kalt; -e Zeiten

Lau|sitz, die; -, -en (Landschaft um Bautzen u. Görlitz [Oberlausitz] u. um Cottbus [Niederlausitz]); **Lau|sit|zer** (↑R 103); das Lausitzer Bergland; **lau|sit|zisch**

[1]**laut;** etwas laut werden lassen;

[2]**laut** (↑R 46; *Abk.* lt.); *Präp. mit Gen., auch mit Dativ:* laut [des] ärztlichen Gutachtens, *auch* laut ärztlichem Gutachten; laut amtlicher Nachweise, *auch* laut amtlichen Nachweisen; *ein allein stehendes, stark gebeugtes Substantiv steht im Sing. gewöhnlich ungebeugt:* laut Befehl, laut Übereinkommen, *im Plur. aber mit Dativ:* laut Berichten; **Laut,** der; -[e]s, -e; - geben (*Jägerspr. u. ugs.*); **Laut|ar|chiv** (Tonbandsammlung zur gesprochenen Sprache); **lautbar** (*veraltet*); - werden; **Laut|bil|dung** (*für* Artikulation)

Lau|te, die; -, -n (ein Saiteninstrument)

lau|ten; die Antwort lautet ...; das Urteil lautet auf drei Jahre Freiheitsstrafe; **läu|ten;** die Glocken läuten; er läutet die Glocken

Lau|te|ni̱st, der; -en, -en; ↑R 126 (Lautenspieler); **Lau|te|ni̱s|tin; Lau|ten|spiel,** das; -[e]s

[1]**lau|ter** (*geh. für* rein, ungemischt; ungetrübt); -er Wein; -e Gesinnung; [2]**lau|ter** (nur, nichts als); - (nur) Jungen; - (nichts als) Wasser; **Lau|ter|keit,** die; -; **läu|tern** (*geh. für* reinigen; von Fehlern befreien); ich ...ere (↑R 16); **Läu|te|rung** (*geh.*)

Läu|te|werk, Läut|werk; **Laut|ge|setz; laut|ge|treu,** laut|treu; **laut|hals** (aus voller Kehle); **lau|tie|ren** (Worte, Text nach Lauten zergliedern); **Lau|tier|me|tho|de; Laut|leh|re** (*für* Phonetik *u.* Phonologie); **laut|lich; laut|los; Laut|lo|sig|keit,** die; -; **laut|ma|lend; Laut|ma|le|rei; laut|nach|ah|mend; Laut‿schrift, ...spre|cher; Laut|spre|cher‿box, ...wa|gen; laut|stark; Laut|stär|ke; Laut|stär|ke|reg|ler; laut|treu** *vgl.* lautgetreu; **Lau|tung; Laut‿ver|än|de|rung, ...ver|schie|bung** (*Sprachw.*), **...wan|del, ...wech|sel; Läut|werk** *vgl.* Läutewerk; **Laut|zei|chen**

lau|warm

La|va [...va], die; -, Laven ‹ital.› (feurig-flüssiger Schmelzfluss aus Vulkanen u. das daraus entstandene Gestein)

La|va̱|bel [...v...], der; -s ‹franz.› (feinfädiges, waschbares Kreppgewebe in Leinwandbindung); **La|va|bo** [la'va:..., *schweiz.* 'la:...], das; -[s], -s ‹lat.› (Handwaschung

des Priesters in der Messe u. das dazu verwendete Waschbecken mit Kanne; *schweiz. für* Waschbecken)
La|va|bom|be *(Geol.)*
La|vant [...f...], die; - (l. Nebenfluss der Drau); **La|vant|tal**
La|va|strom
La|va|ter ['la:va:..., *schweiz.* 'la:fa...] (schweiz. Schriftsteller)
La|ven *(Plur. von* Lava)
la|ven|del [...v...] ‹ital.› (blauviolett); ein lavendel Kleid; *vgl. auch* beige; **La|ven|del,** der; -s, - (Heil- u. Gewürzpflanze); **La|ven|del-öl** (das; -[e]s), **...was|ser** (das; -s)
[1]**la|vie|ren** [...v...] ‹niederl.› (sich mit Geschick durch Schwierigkeiten hindurchwinden; *veraltet für* gegen den Wind kreuzen)
[2]**la|vie|ren** [...v...] ‹ital.› (aufgetragene Farben auf einem Bild verwischen; *auch für* mit verlaufenden Farbflächen arbeiten); lavierte Zeichnung
La|vi|nia [...v...] (röm. w. Eigenn.)
lä|vo|gyr [...v...] ‹griech.› *(Chemie* linksdrehend; *Zeichen* l)
La|voir [la'voa:r], das; -s, -s ‹franz.› *(veraltet für* Waschschüssel)
Lä|vu|lo|se [...v...], die; - ‹griech.› (Fruchtzucker)
La|wi|ne, die; -, -n ‹lat.›; **la|wi-nen|ar|tig; La|wi|nen-ge|fahr** (die; -), **...hund** *(svw.* Lawinensuchhund), **...ka|ta|stro|phe, ...schutz; la|wi|nen|si|cher; La-wi|nen|such|hund**
Lawn|ten|nis ['lɔ:n...] ‹engl.› (Rasentennis)
Law|ren|ci|um [lɔ'rentsium], das; -s ‹nach dem amerik. Physiker Lawrence› (künstliches radioaktives chem. Element, ein Transuran; *Zeichen* Lr)
lax ‹lat.› (schlaff, lässig; locker, lau [von Sitten]); **La|xans,** das; -, *Plur.* ...antia *u.* ...anzien [...iən] *u.* **La|xa|tiv,** das; -s, -e [...və] *u.* **La-xa|ti|vum** [...v...], das; -s, ...va *(Med.* Abführmittel); **Lax|heit** (Schlaffheit; Lässigkeit); **la|xie-ren** *(Med.* abführen)
Lax|ness, Halldór (isländ. Schriftsteller)
Lay-out, *auch* **Lay|out** [le:'aut, *auch* 'le:aut], das; -s, -s ‹engl.› *(Druckw.* [skizzenhafter Entwurf für] Text- und Bildgestaltung); **Lay|ou|ter** (Gestalter eines Layouts); **Lay|ou|te|rin**
La|za|rett, das; -[e]s, -e ‹franz.› (Militärkrankenhaus); **La|za-rett-schiff, ...zug; La|za|rist,** der; -en, -en; ↑R 126 (Angehöriger einer kath. Kongregation);
[1]**La|za|rus** (bibl. m. Eigenn.); der arme -; [2]**La|za|rus,** der; -[ses], -se (schwer leidender, bedauernswerter Mensch)
La|ze|dä|mo|ni|er usw. *vgl.* Lakedämonier usw.
La|ze|ra|ti|on, die; -, -en ‹lat.› *(Med.* Einriss); **la|ze|rie|ren**
La|zer|te, die; -, -n ‹lat.› *(Zool.* Eidechse)
La|zu|lith [*auch* ...'lit], der; *Gen.* -s *od.* -en, *Plur.* -e[n] (↑R 126) ‹lat.; griech.› (ein Mineral)
Laz|za|ro|ne, der; *Gen.* -[n] *u.* -s, *Plur.* -n *u.* ...ni ‹ital.› (Gelegenheitsarbeiter, Bettler in Neapel)
l. c. = loco citato
LCD-An|zei|ge ‹aus engl. liquid crystal display› (Flüssigkristallanzeige)
Ld. = limited
LDPD = Liberal-Demokratische Partei Deutschlands *(ehem. in der DDR)*
Lea (bibl. w. Eigenn.; w. Vorn.)
Lead [li:d], das; -[s] ‹engl.› (die Führungsstimme im Jazz [oft Trompete od. Kornett]); **Lea|der,** der; -s, - *(kurz für* Bandleader; *österr. u. schweiz. Sportspr.* Tabellenführer); **Lead|gi|tar|rist**
Le|an|der (griech. m. Eigenn.; m. Vorn.)
Lear [li:r] (sagenhafter kelt. König, Titelheld bei Shakespeare)
lea|sen ['li:...] ‹engl.› (mieten, pachten); leas|te, geleast; ein Auto leasen; **Lea|sing,** das; -s, -s (Vermietung von [Investitions]gütern [mit Anrechnung der Mietzahlungen bei späterem Kauf]); **Lea|sing|fir|ma**
Le|be|da|me; Le|be|hoch, das; -s, -s; er rief ein herzliches Lebehoch, *aber* er rief: „Er lebe hoch!“; **Le|be|mann** *Plur.* ...männer; **le|be|män|nisch; le-ben;** leben und leben lassen; lebend gebärende Tiere; *vgl.* hochleben, wohl; **Le|ben,** das; -s, -; mein Leben lang; am Leben bleiben; das süße Leben; die Leben spendende Kraft der Sonne; eine [alles] Leben zerstörende Strahlung (↑R 40); **le|ben|be|ja|hend** *vgl.* lebensbejahend (↑R 40); **le|bend ge|bä|rend** *vgl.* leben; **Le|bend|ge|wicht,** das; -[e]s; **le|ben|dig;** lebendig gebärende Tiere; **Le|ben|dig|keit,** die; -; **Le|bend|mas|se; Le|bend|vieh; Le|bens-abend** (↑R 132), **...ab-schnitt, ...ader** (↑R 132), **...al|ter, ...angst, ...ar|beit, ...ar|beits|zeit** (die; -), **...art, ...auf|fas|sung, ...auf|ga|be, ...bahn, ...baum** (ein symbolisches Ornament; *auch für* Thuja), **...be|din|gung** *(meist Plur.);* **le|bens-be|dro|hend, ...be|droh|lich, ...be|ja|hend; Le-bens-be|ja|hung, ...be|reich, ...be|schrei|bung, ...bild, ...bund** (der; *geh.*), **...dau|er, ...ele|ment** (↑R 132), **...eli|xier** (↑R 132), **...en|de** (das; -s), **...er|fah|rung, ...er|in|ne|run|gen** *(Plur.),* **...er-war|tung; le|bens|fä|hig; Le-bens|fä|hig|keit,** die; -; **le|bens-feind|lich, ...fern; Le|bens-form, ...fra|ge; le|bens|fremd; Le|bens|freu|de; le|bens|froh; Le|bens|ge|fahr,** die; -; **le|bens-ge|fähr|lich; Le|bens-ge|fähr-te, ...ge|fähr|tin, ...ge|fühl, ...geis|ter** *(Plur.),* **...ge|mein-schaft, ...ge|nuss, ...ge|wohn-heit** *(meist Plur.);* **le|bens|groß; Le|bens|grö|ße; Le|bens|hal-tung; Le|bens|hal|tungs-in-dex, ...kos|ten** *(Plur.);* **Le|bens-hil|fe, ...hun|ger, ...in|halt, ...in-te|res|se** *(meist Plur.),* **...jahr, ...kampf, ...kraft** (die), **...kreis, ...künst|ler, ...la|ge; le|bens-lang** (auf -), **...läng|lich** (zu „lebenslänglich“ verurteilt werden; „lebenslänglich“ erhalten); **Le-bens-lauf, ...licht** (das; -[e]s), **...lust** (die; -); **le|bens|lus|tig; Le|bens|mit|tel,** das *meist Plur.;* **Le|bens|mit|tel-che|mie, ...ver-gif|tung; le|bens|mü|de; Le-bens|mut; le|bens|nah; Le-bens-nerv, ...ni|veau; le|bens-not|wen|dig; Le|bens-part|ner, ...part|ne|rin; Le|ben spen|dend** *vgl.* Leben; **Le|bens-pfad** *(geh.),* **...phi|lo|so|phie; le|ben|sprü-hend** (↑R 40); **Le|bens-qua|li-tät** (die; -), **...raum, ...ret|ter, ...ret|te|rin; Le|bens|ret|tungs-me|dail|le; Le|bens-schick|sal, ...stan|dard** (der; -s), **...stel|lung, ...stil; le|bens-tüch|tig, ...über-drüs|sig** (↑R 132); **Le|bens-un-ter|halt, ...ver|si|che|rung; Le-bens|ver|si|che|rungs|ge|sell-schaft; le|bens|wahr; Le|bens-wan|del, ...weg, ...wei|se** (die), **...weis|heit, ...werk; le|bens-wert, ...wich|tig; Le|bens-wil-le, ...zei|chen, ...zeit** (auf -), **...ziel, ...zu|ver|sicht, ...zweck;** **Le|ben zer|stö|rend** *vgl.* Leben
Le|ber, die; -, -n; **Le|ber-abs-zess, ...bal|sam** (Name verschiedener Pflanzen), **...blüm|chen** (eine Anemonenart), **...di|ät** (die; -)
Le|be|recht, Leb|recht (m. Vorn.)
Le|ber-egel (↑R 132), **...fleck, ...ha|ken** *(Boxen),* **...kä|se** *(bes. südd. u. österr.* ein Fleischgericht), **...knö|del, ...krebs, ...lei|den,**

...pas|te|te, **...tran,** **...wert** *(Med.),* **...wurst, ...zir|rho|se**
Le|be|we|sen; Le|be|wohl, das; -[e]s, *Plur.* -e *u.* -s; jmdm. Lebewohl sagen; er rief ein herzliches Lebewohl, *aber* er rief: „Leb[e] wohl!"; **leb|haft; Leb|haf|tig|keit,** die; -; **...le|big** (z. B. kurzlebig)
Leb|ku|chen; Leb⌣küch|ler *od.* **...küch|ner** *(fränk. für* Lebkuchenbäcker); **Leb|küch⌣le|rei** *od.* **...küch|ne|rei; Leb|küch|ner** *vgl.* Lebküchler; **Leb|küch|ne|rei** *vgl.* Lebküchlerei
leb|los; Leb|lo|sig|keit, die; -
Leb|recht *vgl.* Leberecht
Leb|tag, der *(ugs.);* ich denke mein *(nicht:* meinen) Lebtag daran; meine Lebtag[e], *landsch.* meiner Lebtage
Le|bus [*auch* 'le:...] (Stadt an der Oder); **Le|bu|ser** (↑R 103)
Leb|zei|ten *Plur.;* bei - seines Vaters; zu seinen -
Leb|zel|ten, der; -s, - *(österr. veraltend für* Lebkuchen); **Leb|zel|ter** *(österr. veraltend für* Lebkuchenbäcker)
Lech, der; -s (r. Nebenfluss der Donau); **Lech|feld,** das; -[e]s (Ebene bei Augsburg)
lech|zen; du lechzt
Le|ci|thin *vgl.* Lezithin
leck *(Seemannsspr.* undicht); *vgl.* leckschlagen; **Leck,** das; -[e]s, -s *(Seemannsspr.* undichte Stelle [bei Schiffen, an Gefäßen, Kraftmaschinen u. a.]); **Le|cka|ge** [lɛ'ka:ʒə, *österr.* lɛ'ka:ʒ], die; -, -n [lɛ'ka:ʒ(ə)n] (Gewichtsverlust bei flüssigen Waren durch Verdunsten od. Aussickern; Leck)
Le|cke, die; -, -n (Stelle od. Trog, wo das Wild od. das Vieh Salz leckt, Salzstein)
[1]**le|cken** *(Seemannsspr.* leck sein); das Boot leckt
[2]**le|cken** (mit der Zunge); **le|cker** (wohlschmeckend); **Le|cker** *(Jägerspr.* Zunge beim Schalenwild); **Le|cker|bis|sen; Le|cke|rei** (Leckerbissen); **Le|cker|li,** das; -s, - *(schweiz.);* Basler - (in kleine Rechtecke geschnittenes, honigkuchenähnliches Gebäck); **Le|cker|maul** *(ugs. für* jmd., der/die gern Süßigkeiten isst)
leck|schla|gen (leck werden [vom Schiff]); leckgeschlagen
Le Cor|bu|si|er [lə kɔrby'zie:] (franz.-schweiz. Architekt)
led. = ledig
Le|da (sagenhafte Königin von Sparta)
Le|de, die; -, -n ‹niederl.› *(nordd. für* Brache, Heide)
Le|der, das; -s, -; die Leder verarbeitende Industrie; **le|der|ar|tig; Le|der⌣ball, ...band** (der); **le|der|braun; Le|der|ein|band; Le|de|rer** *(landsch. veraltend für* Gerber); **le|der⌣far|ben** *od.* **...far|big; Le|der⌣fett, ...gür|tel, ...hand|schuh, ...haut** (Schicht der menschl. u. tierischen Haut); **Le|der|her|stel|lung;** (↑R 23:) Lederherstellung u. -vertrieb; **Le|der|ho|se; le|de|rig, led|rig** (lederartig); **Le|der⌣ja|cke, ...man|tel, ...map|pe;** [1]**le|dern** (mit einem Lederlappen putzen, abreiben; *landsch. für* prügeln); ich ...ere (↑R 16); [2]**le|dern** (aus Leder; zäh, langweilig); **Le|der⌣pols|ter, ...rie|men, ...schuh, ...schurz, ...ses|sel, ...soh|le, ...ta|sche; Le|der ver|ar|bei|tend** *vgl.* Leder
le|dig *(Abk.* led.); - sein, bleiben; jmdn. seiner Sünden - sprechen; ledig gehend (aus beruflichen Gründen vorübergehend getrennt lebend); **Le|di|ge,** der *u.* die; -n, -n (↑R 5 ff.); **Le|di|gen|heim; le|dig ge|hend** *vgl.* ledig; **le|dig|lich**
Le|di|schiff *(schweiz. für* Lastschiff)
led|rig *vgl.* lederig
Lee, die; -, *auch (Geogr. nur:)* das; -s *(Seemannsspr.* die dem Wind abgekehrte Seite; *Ggs.* Luv); *meist ohne Artikel* in, nach -
leer; den Teller leer essen; das Glas leer trinken; ein Gefäß leer laufen (auslaufen) lassen; die Maschine ist leer (ohne Leistung) gelaufen; leer machen, räumen, stehen usw.; eine leer stehende Wohnung; ins Leere gehen; **Lee|re,** die; - (Leerheit); **lee|ren** (leer machen); sich -; **Leer⌣for|mel** *(Soziol.),* **...ge|wicht, ...gut** (das; -[e]s); **Leer|heit,** die; -; **Leer|lauf; leer lau|fen, leer ste|hend** *vgl.* leer; **Leer|stel|le** *(Sprachw.* nicht besetzte Stelle); **Leer|tas|te** (bei der Schreibmaschine); **Lee|rung; Leer⌣woh|nung, ...zim|mer**
Lee|sei|te *(Seemannsspr.* die dem Wind abgekehrte Seite); **lee|wärts**
Le Fort [lə 'fɔ:r], Gertrud von (dt. Schriftstellerin)
Lef|ze, die; -, -n (Lippe bei Tieren)
leg. = legato
le|gal ‹lat.› (gesetzlich, gesetzmäßig); **Le|ga|li|sa|ti|on,** die; -, -en (Beglaubigung von Urkunden); **le|ga|li|sie|ren** (gesetzlich machen); **Le|ga|li|sie|rung; Le|ga|lis|mus** *(geh. für* striktes Befolgen der Gesetze); **le|ga|lis|tisch** (übertrieben, in kleinlicher Weise legal); **Le|ga|li|tät,** die; - (Gesetzlichkeit, Rechtsgültigkeit); **Le|ga|li|täts|prin|zip,** das; -s *(Rechtsw.)*
le|gas|then (↑R 132) ‹lat.; griech.› *(Med.* legasthenisch); **Le|gas|the|nie,** die; -, ...ien (Lese- u. Rechtschreibschwäche); **Le|gas|the|ni|ker** (an Legasthenie Leidender); **Le|gas|the|ni|ke|rin; le|gas|the|nisch**
[1]**Le|gat,** der; -en, -en (↑R 126) ‹lat.› *(im alten Rom* Gesandter, Unterfeldherr; *heute* päpstl. Gesandter); [2]**Le|gat,** das; -[e]s, -e *(Rechtsspr.* Vermächtnis); **Le|ga|tar,** der; -s, -e (Vermächtnisnehmer); **Le|ga|ti|on,** die; -, -en ([päpstl.] Gesandtschaft); **Le|ga|ti|ons|rat** *Plur.* ...räte
le|ga|to ‹ital.› *(Musik* gebunden; *Ggs.* staccato; *Abk.* leg.); **Le|ga|to,** das; -s, *Plur.* -s *u.* ...ti
le|ge ar|tis ‹lat.› (nach den Regeln der Kunst; *Abk.* l. a.)
Le|ge|bat|te|rie (in mehreren Etagen angeordnete Drahtkäfige zur Haltung von Legehennen); **Le|ge|hen|ne,** Leg|hen|ne
Le|gel, der *od.* das; -s, - *(Seemannsspr.* Ring zum Befestigen eines Segels)
le|gen; gelegt; *vgl. aber* gelegen
Le|gen|dar, das; -s, -e (Legendenbuch: Sammlung von Heiligenleben); **le|gen|där** ‹lat.› (legendenhaft; unwahrscheinlich); **Le|gen|da|ri|um,** das; -s, ...ien [...iən] *(älter für* Legendar); **Le|gen|de,** die; -, -n ([Heiligen]erzählung; [fromme] Sage; Umschrift [von Münzen, Siegeln]; Zeichenerklärung [auf Karten usw.]); **Le|gen|den|er|zäh|ler; le|gen|den|haft**
le|ger [le'ʒɛ:r] ‹franz.› (ungezwungen, [nach]lässig)
Le|ger ‹*zu* legen›
Le|ges [...ge:s] *(Plur. von* Lex)
Le|ge|zeit
Leg|föh|re *(svw.* [2]Latsche)
Leg|gings, Leg|gins *Plur.* ‹engl.› (hosenähnliches ledernes Kleidungsstück der nordamerik. Indianer; Strumpfhose ohne Füßlinge)
Leg|hen|ne *vgl.* Legehenne
Leg|horn, das; -s, *Plur.* -[s], *landsch. auch* Leghörner ‹nach dem engl. Namen der ital. Stadt Livorno› (Huhn der Rasse Leghorn)
le|gie|ren ‹ital.› ([Metalle] verschmelzen; [Suppen, Soßen] mit Eigelb anrühren, binden); **Le|gie|rung**
Le|gi|on, die; -, -en ‹lat.› (röm. Heereseinheit; *in der Neuzeit für* Freiwilligentruppe, Söldnerschar;

große Menge); **Le|gi|o|nar,** der; -s, -e (Soldat einer röm. Legion); **Le|gi|o|när,** der; -s, -e ‹franz.› (Soldat einer Legion [z. B. der Fremdenlegion]); **Le|gi|o|närs-krank|heit,** die; - (*Med.* eine Infektionskrankheit); **Le|gi|o|nel-le,** die; -, -n *meist Plur.* (Erreger der Legionärskrankheit); **Le|gi-ons|sol|dat**
le|gis|la|tiv ‹lat.› (gesetzgebend); **Le|gis|la|ti|ve** [...və], die; -, -n (gesetzgebende Versammlung, gesetzgebende Gewalt); **le|gis|la-to|risch** (gesetzgeberisch); **Le-gis|la|tur,** die; -, -en (*selten für* Gesetzgebung; *früher auch für* gesetzgebende Körperschaft); **Le-gis|la|tur|pe|ri|o|de** (Amtsdauer einer Volksvertretung); **le|gi|tim** (gesetzlich; rechtmäßig; als ehelich anerkannt; begründet); **Le-gi|ti|ma|ti|on,** die; -, -en (Echtheitserklärung, Beglaubigung; [Rechts]ausweis; *im BGB für* Nachweis der Empfangsberechtigung, Befugnis; Ehelichkeitserklärung); **Le|gi|ti|ma|ti|ons|kar-te; le|gi|ti|mie|ren** (beglaubigen; [Kinder] als ehelich erklären); sich - (sich ausweisen); **Le|gi|ti-mie|rung; Le|gi|ti|mis|mus,** der; - (Lehre von der Unabsetzbarkeit des angestammten Herrscherhauses); **Le|gi|ti|mist,** der; -en, -en (↑R 126); **le|gi|ti|mis|tisch; Le-gi|ti|mi|tät,** die; - (Rechtmäßigkeit einer Staatsgewalt; Gesetzmäßigkeit [eines Besitzes o. Ä.])
Le|gu|an [*auch* 'le:...], der; -s, -e ‹karib.› (trop. Baumeidechse)
Le|gu|min, das; -s ‹lat.› (Eiweiß der Hülsenfrüchte); **Le|gu|mi|no-se,** die; -, -n *meist Plur.* (*Bot.* Hülsenfrüchtler)
Leg|war|mer ['lɛgwɔ:(r)mə(r)], der; -s, -[s] *meist Plur.* ‹engl.› (langer Wollstrumpf ohne Füßling)
Le|hár [le'ha:r, *ung. u. österr.* 'lɛha:r] (ung. Operettenkomponist)
Le Hav|re [lə '(h)a:vr(ə)] (↑R 130; franz. Hafenstadt)
Leh|de *vgl.* Lede
Le|hen, das; -s, -; **Le|hens|we-sen** *vgl.* Lehnswesen
Lehm, der; -[e]s, -e; **Lehm‿bat-zen, ...bo|den; lehm|gelb; leh-mig**
Leh|ne, die; -, -n; **leh|nen;** sich -
Lehn|gut *vgl.* Lehnsgut; **Lehns-eid** *(früher)*
Lehn|ses|sel
Lehns|gut *od.* Lehn|gut; **Lehns-‿herr, ...mann** (*Plur.* ...männer *u.* ...leute), **...trä|ger, ...treue**
Lehn|stuhl
Lehns|we|sen, Le|hens|we|sen, das; -s *(früher);* **Lehn‿über|set-zung** (↑R 132; *Sprachw.*), **...über-tra|gung** (↑R 132), **...wort** (*Plur.* ...wörter)
Lehr, das; -[e]s, -e (*Bauw., Technik svw.* [2]Lehre); **Lehr|amt; Lehr-amts|an|wär|ter; Lehr‿an|ge-bot, ...an|stalt, ...auf|trag, ...aus|bil|der; lehr|bar; Lehr|bar-keit,** die; -; **Lehr‿be|fä|hi|gung, ...be|helf** (*österr. für* Lehrmittel), **...be|ruf, ...bo|gen** (*Bauw.* Gerüst für Bogen-, Gewölbebau; *zu* [2]Lehre), **...brief, ...bub** (*regional für* Lehrjunge), **...buch, ...dorn** (Prüfgerät für Bohrungen; *zu* [2]Lehre); **[1]Leh|re,** die; -, -n (Unterricht, Unterweisung; Lehrmeinung); **[2]Leh|re,** die; -, -n (Messwerkzeug); **leh|ren** (unterweisen); jmdn., *auch* jmdm. etwas lehren; er lehrt ihn, *auch* ihm das Lesen; *jedoch nur:* er lehrt ihn lesen; er hat gelehrt; er hat ihn reiten gelehrt, *selten* lehren; er lehrt ihn ein, *seltener* einen Helfer der Armen sein; er lehrt ihn[,] ein Helfer der Armen zu sein (↑R 75); **Leh|rer; Leh|rer|aus|bil-dung; leh|rer|haft; Leh|re|rin; Leh|re|rin|nen|schaft,** die; -; **Leh|rer‿kol|le|gi|um, ...kon-fe|renz; Leh|rer|schaft,** die; -; **Leh|rers|frau; Leh|rer|zim|mer; Lehr‿fach, ...film, ...frei|heit** (die; -), **...gang** (der); **Lehr-gangs|teil|neh|mer; Lehr‿ge-dicht, ...geld, ...ge|rüst** (beim Stahlbetonbau; *zu* [2]Lehre); **lehr-haft; Lehr|haf|tig|keit,** die; -; **Lehr‿hau|er** (angehender Bergmann), **...herr** (Ausbildender), **...jahr, ...jun|ge** (der), **...kan|zel** (*österr. für* Lehrstuhl), **...kör|per, ...kraft; Lehr|ling** (Auszubildende[r]); **Lehr|lings[|wohn]|heim; Lehr‿mäd|chen, ...mei|nung, ...meis|ter, ...meis|te|rin, ...me-tho|de, ...mit|tel** (das; Hilfsmittel für den Lehrenden); **Lehr|mit-tel|frei|heit; Lehr‿pfad, ...plan** (*vgl.* [2]Plan), **...pro|be; lehr|reich; Lehr‿satz, ...stel|le, ...stoff, ...stück, ...stuhl, ...tä|tig|keit, ...toch|ter** (*schweiz. für* Lehrmädchen), **...ver|an|stal|tung, ...ver|trag** (Ausbildungsvertrag), **...werk|statt, ...zeit**
[1]Lei [lej] (*Plur. von* [2]Leu)
[2]Lei, die; -, -en (*rhein. für* Fels; Schiefer); Lorelei (*vgl.* Loreley)
Leib, der; -[e]s, -er (Körper; *veraltet auch für* Leben); (↑R 41:) gut bei Leibe (wohlgenährt) sein, *aber* beileibe nicht; jmdm. zu Leibe rücken; Leib und Leben wagen; **Leib‿arzt, ...bin|de; Leib|chen** (*auch* ein Kleidungsstück, *österr. u. schweiz. für* Unterhemd, Trikot; *vgl.* Leiberl); **leib|ei|gen** *(früher);* **Leib|ei|ge|ne,** der *u.* die; -n, -n (↑R 5 ff.); **Leib|ei|gen-schaft,** die; -; **lei|ben;** *nur in* wie er leibt u. lebt; **Lei|berl,** das; -s, -n (*österr. für* Leibchen); **Lei|bes-‿er|be** (der), **...er|zie|her, ...er-zie|hung, ...frucht, ...fül|le, ...kräf|te** (*Plur; nur in* aus *od.* nach Leibeskräften), **...stra|fe** (*veraltet;* bei -), **...übun|gen** (↑R 132; *Plur.*), **...um|fang, ...vi-si|ta|ti|on; leib|feind|lich; Leib-‿gar|de, ...gar|dist, ...ge|richt; leib|haft** (*selten für* leibhaftig); **leib|haf|tig**[1]; **Leib|haf|ti|ge**[1], der; -n (*verhüllend für* Teufel); **Leib|haf|tig|keit**[1], die; -; **...lei|big** (z. B. dickleibig); **Leib|koch; leib-lich; Leib|lich|keit,** die; -
Leib|nitz (österr. Stadt)
Leib|niz (dt. Philosoph); **leib|ni-zisch** (↑R 94); leibnizisches Denken; die leibnizische Philosophie
Leib‿pferd, ...ren|te (lebenslängliche Rente), **...rie|men** (*veraltet für* Gürtel), **...rock** *(veraltet),* **...schmerz** (*meist Plur.*), **...schnei|den** (das; -s; *landsch. für* Leibschmerzen); **Leib-See-le-Prob|lem,** das; -s; ↑R 28 *(Psych.);* **leib|see|lisch; Leib-spei|se** (*svw.* Leibgericht)
leibt *vgl.* leiben
Lei|bung *vgl.* Laibung
Leib‿wa|che, ...wäch|ter, ...wä-sche (die; -), **...weh, ...wi|ckel**
Lei|ca ®, die; -, -s (*Kurzw. für* Leitz-Camera [der Firma Ernst Leitz])
Leich, der; -[e]s, -e (eine mittelhochd. Liedform)
Leich|dorn, der; -[e]s, *Plur.* -e *u.* ...dörner (*mitteld. für* Hühnerauge); **Lei|che,** die; -, -n; **Lei|chen-‿acker** (↑R 132; *landsch.*), **...be-gäng|nis, ...be|schau|er, ...bit-ter** (*veraltend für* Person, die zur Beerdigung einlädt); **Lei|chen-bit|ter|mie|ne** (*ugs. für* düsterer, trauriger Gesichtsausdruck); **lei|chen‿blass, ...fahl; Lei-chen|fled|de|rei** ‹Gaunerspr.› (*Rechtsw.* Ausplünderung toter od. schlafender Menschen); **Lei-chen‿fled|de|rer, ...frau, ...gift, ...hal|le, ...hemd, ...öff|nung** (*für* Obduktion), **...pass, ...re|de, ...schän|dung, ...schau|haus, ...schmaus** *(ugs.),* **...trä|ger, ...tuch, ...ver|bren|nung, ...wa-gen, ...wär|ter, ...zug; Leich-nam,** der; -[e]s, -e

[1] [*auch* 'laip...]

leicht; am leichtesten; leichte Artillerie; leichtes Heizöl; leichte Musik; *Großschreibung* (↑R 47): er isst gern etwas Leichtes; es ist mir ein Leichtes (fällt mir sehr leicht); *Schreibung in Verbindung mit Verben, Partizipien u. Adjektiven* (↑R 39 *u.* 40): leicht atmen; sie hat leicht geatmet; leicht, leichter fallen, er ist nur leicht gefallen; es ist mir leicht gefallen (hat mich keine Anstrengung gekostet); er hat es sich leicht gemacht (hat sich wenig Mühe gemacht); etwas leicht nehmen (keine Mühe darauf verwenden); ich habe mir *od.* mich leicht getan dabei (es ohne Schwierigkeiten, Hemmungen bewältigt); leicht beschwingte Musik; ein leicht bewaffneter Soldat; ein leicht entzündlicher Stoff; das Mädchen ging leicht geschürzt *(meist scherzh.)*; eine leicht verdauliche Speise; leicht verderbliche Waren; eine leicht verständliche Sprache; eine leicht verletzte Sportlerin; ein leicht verwundeter Offizier; die leicht Verletzten, *auch* Leichtverletzten; die leicht Verwundeten, *auch* Leichtverwundeten (↑R 47)

Leicht|ath|let; Leicht|ath|le|tik; Leicht|ath|le|tin; leicht|ath|le|tisch

Leicht|bau, der; -s (*svw.* Leichtbauweise); **Leicht|bau|plat|te** (*Bauw.* Platte aus leichtem Material); **Leicht|ben|zin; leicht be|schwingt, be|waff|net** *vgl.* leicht; **Leicht|be|waff|ne|te**, der; -n, -n (↑R 5ff.); **leicht|blü|tig;** [1]**Leich|te**, die; - (*geh. für* Leichtheit); [2]**Leich|te**, die; -, -n (*nordd. für* Tragriemen beim Schubkarrenfahren); **leicht ent|zünd|lich** *vgl.* leicht; **Leich|ter**, Lich|ter (*Seemannsspr.* [kleineres] Wasserfahrzeug zum Leichtern); **leich|tern**, lich|tern (größere Schiffe entfrachten); ich ...ere (↑R 16); **leicht fal|len** *vgl.* leicht; **leicht|fer|tig; Leicht~fer|tig|keit, ...flug|zeug; leicht|flüs|sig** *(fachspr.)* leichtflüssige Legierungen; **Leicht|fuß** *(ugs. scherzh.)*; **leicht|fü|ßig; Leicht|fü|ßig|keit**, die; -; **leicht|gän|gig;** eine -e Lenkung; **leicht ge|schürzt** *vgl.* leicht; **Leicht|ge|wicht** (Körpergewichtsklasse in der Schwerathletik); **Leicht|ge|wicht|ler; leicht|gläu|big; Leicht|gläu|big|keit**, die; -; **Leicht|heit**, die; -; **leicht|her|zig; Leicht|her|zig|keit**, die; -; **leicht|hin; Leich|tig|keit**, die; -; **Leicht|in|dust|rie; leicht|le|big; Leicht|le|big|keit**, die; -; **leicht|lich** (*veraltend für* mühelos); **Leicht|lohn|grup|pe** (unterste Tarifgruppe, bes. für Frauen); **leicht ma|chen** *vgl.* leicht; **Leicht~mat|ro|se, ...me|tall; leicht neh|men** *vgl.* leicht; **Leicht~öl, ...schwer|ge|wicht** (Körpergewichtsklasse beim Gewichtheben), **...sinn** (der; -[e]s); **leicht|sin|nig; Leicht|sin|nig|keit**, die; -; **Leicht|sinns|feh|ler; leicht tun** *vgl.* leicht; **leicht ver|dau|lich, ver|derb|lich, ver|letzt** *vgl.* leicht; **Leicht|ver|letz|te**, der u. die; -n, -n (↑R 5ff.); *vgl.* leicht; **leicht ver|ständ|lich, ver|wun|det** *vgl.* leicht; **Leicht|ver|wun|de|te**, der *u.* die; -n, -n (↑R 5ff.); *vgl.* leicht

leid (*als Adjektiv schweiz. mdal. für* hässlich, ungut, unlieb; *vgl.* Leid); (↑R 46:) leid sein, werden; es sich nicht leid sein lassen; **Leid**, das; -[e]s; es tut mir Leid; weil es ihm Leid tut; (↑R 40:) jmdm. etwas zuleide, *auch* zu Leide tun; [sich] ein Leid, *veraltet* Leids [an]tun; (↑R 13:) [in] Freud und Leid; *aber* (↑R 46:) ich bin es leid, das immer wieder zu hören

Lei|de|form (*für* Passiv); **lei|den;** du littst; du littest; gelitten; leid[e]!; Not -; [1]**Lei|den**, das; -s, - (Krankheit); Freuden u. Leiden

[2]**Lei|den** [*niederl.* 'lɛidə] (niederl. Stadt)

lei|dend; Lei|den|de, der *u.* die; -n, -n (↑R 5ff.)

Lei|de|ner ‹*zu* [2]Leiden› (↑R 103); - Flasche *(Physik)*

Lei|den|schaft; lei|den|schaft|lich; Lei|den|schaft|lich|keit, die; -; **lei|den|schafts|los; lei|dens|fä|hig; Lei|dens|fä|hig|keit**, die; -; **Lei|dens~ge|fähr|te, ...ge|fähr|tin, ...ge|nos|se, ...ge|nos|sin, ...ge|schich|te, ...ge|sicht, ...mie|ne, ...weg, ...zeit; lei|der;** - Gottes ‹*entstanden aus* (bei dem) Leiden Gottes›; **leid|ge|prüft; lei|dig** (unangenehm); **Leid|kar|te** (*schweiz. für* Trauerkarte); **leid|lich** (gerade noch ausreichend); **leid|tra|gend;** (↑R 40); **Leid|tra|gen|de**, der *u.* die; -n, -n (↑R 5ff.); **Leid tun** *vgl.* Leid; **leid|voll** *(geh.)*; **Leid|we|sen**, das; *nur in* zu meinem, seinem usw. - (Bedauern)

Lei|er, die; -, -n ‹griech.› (ein Saiteninstrument; *auch* ein Sternbild); **Lei|e|rei** *(ugs.)*; **Lei|e|rer; Lei|er|kas|ten; Lei|er|kas|ten|mann** *Plur.* ...männer; **lei|ern;** ich ...ere (↑R 16); **Lei|er|schwanz** (ein austral. Vogel)

Leif (m. Vorn.)

Leih~amt, ...ar|bei|ter, ...bib|li|o|thek, ...bü|che|rei; Lei|he, die; -, -n (*BGB* unentgeltliches Verleihen; *ugs. für* Leihhaus); **lei|hen;** du leihst; du liehst; du liehest; geliehen; leih[e]!; ich leihe mir einen Frack; **Leih~ga|be, ...ge|ber, ...ge|bühr, ...haus, ...mut|ter** (Frau, die [nach künstlicher Befruchtung] ein Kind für eine andere Frau austrägt); **Leih~schein, ...stim|me** *(Politik)*, **...ver|kehr, ...ver|trag, ...wa|gen; leih|wei|se**

Leik (*selten für* Liek)

Lei|kauf, Leit|kauf, der; -[e]s, ...käufe ‹zu dem veralteten Wort „Leit" = Obstwein› (*landsch. für* Trunk zur Bestätigung eines Vertragsabschlusses)

Lei|lach, Lei|lak, das; -[e]s, -e[n] ‹*aus* Leinlachen = Leinenlaken› (*nordd. veraltet für* Leintuch)

Leim, der; -[e]s, -e; **lei|men; Leim|far|be; lei|mig; Leim~ring, ...ru|te, ...sie|der** (*landsch. für* langweiliger Mensch), **...topf**

...lein (z. B. Brüderlein, das; -s, -)

Lein, der; -[e]s, *Plur. (Sorten:)* -e (Flachs); **Lein|acker** (↑R 132)

[1]**Lei|ne**, die; - (l. Nebenfluss der Aller)

[2]**Lei|ne**, die; -, -n (Strick); [1]**lei|nen** (aus Leinen); [2]**lei|nen** (an die Leine nehmen); **Lei|nen**, das; -s, -; **Lei|nen~band** (der; *Abk.* Ln., Lnbd.), **...bin|dung** (*svw.* Leinwandbindung), **...ein|band, ...garn, ...kleid, ...tuch** (*Plur.* ...tücher; Tuch aus Leinen; *vgl. aber* Leintuch), **...we|ber** (*svw.* Leinweber), **...we|be|rei, ...zeug; Lei|ne|we|ber** (*svw.* Leinweber); **Lein~ku|chen, ...öl; Lein|öl|brot; Lein~pfad** (Treidelweg), **...saat, ...sa|men, ...tuch** (*Plur.* ...tücher; *landsch. für* Betttuch; *vgl. aber* Leinentuch); **Lein|wand** (*für* Maler-, Kinoleinwand u. Ä. *Plur.* ...wände); **lein|wand|bin|dig; Lein|wand~bin|dung** (die; -; einfachste u. festeste Webart), **...grö|ße** (*scherzh. für* bekannter Filmstar); **Lein|we|ber** (Weber, der Leinwand herstellt)

Leip|zig (Stadt in Sachsen); **Leip|zi|ger** (↑R 103); - Allerlei; - Messe

leis *vgl.* leise

Leis, der; *Gen.* - *u.* -es, *Plur.* -e[n] ‹*aus* Kyrieleis *(vgl. d.)*› (mittelalterl. geistl. Volkslied)

lei|se (↑R 47:) nicht im Leisesten (durchaus nicht) zweifeln; **Lei|se|tre|ter; Lei|se|tre|te|rei**, die; -; **lei|se|tre|te|risch**

Leist, der; -[e]s (eine Pferdekrankheit)
Leis|te, die; -, -n
leis|ten; ich leiste mir ein neues Auto; **Leis|ten,** der; -s, -
Leis|ten‿beu|ge, ...bruch (der), **...ge|gend** (die; -), **...zer|rung**
Leis|tung; Leis|tungs‿ab|fall, ...an|stieg, ...bi|lanz *(Wirtsch.),* **...druck** (der; -[e]s); **leis|tungsfä|hig; Leis|tungs|fä|hig|keit,** die; -; **leis|tungs|ge|recht; Leistungs‿ge|sell|schaft, ...gren|ze** (die; -), **...knick, ...kon|trol|le, ...kraft** (die), **...kurs** *(Schulw.),* **...kur|ve** (Arbeitskurve), **...lohn; leis|tungs|ori|en|tiert** (↑R 132); **Leis|tungs‿prä|mie, ...prin|zip, ...prü|fung, ...schau, ...sport** (der; -[e]s); **leis|tungs|stark; Leis|tungs‿stei|ge|rung, ...test, ...trä|ger, ...ver|gleich, ...vermö|gen** (das; -s), **...wett|bewerb, ...zent|rum** *(Sport),* **...zula|ge, ...zu|schlag**
Leit|an|trag (*bes. Politik;* von einem leitenden Gremium eingebrachter Antrag, dessen Inhalt für alle weiteren gestellten Anträge als Leitlinie gilt); **Leit|ar|ti|kel** (Stellungnahme der Zeitung zu aktuellen Fragen); **Leit|ar|tik|ler** (*ugs. für* Verfasser von Leitartikeln); **leit|bar; Leit|bar|keit,** die; -; **Leit‿bild, ...bün|del** *(Bot.)*
Lei|te, die; -, -n (*südd., österr. für* Berghang)
Leit|ein|rich|tung *(Verkehrsw.);* **lei|ten;** leitender Angestellter; **Lei|ten|de,** der *u.* die; -n, -n (↑R 5 ff.); **[1]Lei|ter,** der
[2]Lei|ter, die; -, -n (ein Steiggerät); **lei|ter|ar|tig; Lei|ter|baum**
Lei|te|rin
Lei|ter|plat|te *(Elektronik)*
Lei|ter‿spros|se, ...wa|gen
Leit|fa|den *Plur.* ...fäden; **leit|fähig; Leit‿fä|hig|keit** (die; -), **...figur, ...form, ...fos|sil** (*Geol.* für bestimmte Gesteinsschichten charakteristisches Fossil)
Leit|geb, der; -en, -en (↑R 126) *u.* **Leit|ge|ber** ‹zu dem veralteten Wort „Leit" = Obstwein› (*landsch. veraltet für* Wirt)
Leit‿ge|dan|ke, ...ge|we|be *(Biol.)*
Lei|tha, die; - (r. Nebenfluss der Donau); **Lei|tha|ge|bir|ge,** das; -s
Leit‿ham|mel, ...idee (↑R 132)
Leit|kauf *vgl.* Leikauf
Leit‿ke|gel (an Straßenbaustellen), **...li|nie, ...mo|tiv; leit|mo|tivisch; Leit‿plan|ke, ...satz, ...schnur** (die; -), **...spruch, ...stel|le, ...stern** (*vgl.* [2]Stern), **...strahl** *(Funkw., Math., Physik),* **...tier** (führendes Tier einer Herde), **...ton** (*Plur.* ...töne)
Lei|tung; Lei|tungs‿draht, ...mast (der), **...netz, ...rohr, ...strom, ...was|ser** (das; -s); **Leit‿ver|mö|gen, ...wäh|rung** *(Wirtsch.),* **...werk, ...wert** *(Physik),* **...wort** (*Plur.* ...wörter), **...zins** *(Wirtsch.)*
[1]Lek, der; - (Mündungsarm des Rheins)
[2]Lek, der; -, - ‹alban.› (alban. Währungseinheit)
Lek|ti|on, die; -, -en ‹lat.› (Unterricht[sstunde]; Lernabschnitt, Aufgabe; Zurechtweisung); **Lektor,** der; -s, ...oren (Lehrer für praktische Übungen [in neueren Sprachen usw.] an einer Hochschule; wissenschaftl. Mitarbeiter zur Begutachtung der bei einem Verlag eingehenden Manuskripte; *kath. Kirche* jemand, der liturg. Lesungen hält; *ev. Kirche* jemand, der Lesegottesdienste hält); **Lek|to|rat,** das; -[e]s, -e (Lehrauftrag eines Lektors; Verlagsabteilung, in der eingehende Manuskripte geprüft u. bearbeitet werden); **lek|to|rie|ren** (ein Manuskript prüfen u. bearbeiten); **Lek|to|rin; Lek|tü|re,** die; -, -n ‹franz.› (Lesestoff; *nur Sing.:* Lesen); **Lek|tü|re|stun|de**
Le|ky|thos, die; -, Lekythen ‹griech.› (altgriech. Salbengefäß)
Le Mans [lə 'mã:] (franz. Stadt)
Lem|ma, das; -s, -ta ‹griech.› (*Sprachw.* Stichwort; *Logik* Vordersatz eines Schlusses; *veraltet für* Überschrift); **lem|ma|ti|sieren** (mit einem Stichwort versehen)
Lem|ming, der; -s, -e ‹dän. *u.* norw.› (skand. Wühlmaus)
Lem|nis|ka|te, die; -, -n ‹griech.› (eine math. Kurve)
Le|mur, der; -en, -en, **Le|mu|re,** der; -n, -n *meist Plur.;* ↑R 126 ‹lat.› (Geist eines Verstorbenen, Gespenst; Halbaffe); **le|mu|renhaft; Le|mu|ria,** die; - (für die Triaszeit vermutete Landmasse zwischen Vorderindien u. Madagaskar); **le|mu|risch**
[1]Le|na, die; - (Strom in Sibirien)
[2]Le|na, Le|ne, Le|ni (w. Vorn.)
Le|nau (österr. Lyriker)
Len|de, die; -, -n; **Len|den|braten; len|den|lahm; Len|den‿schmerz, ...schurz** *(Völkerk.),* **...stück, ...wir|bel**
Le|ne *vgl.* [2]Lena
Leng, der; -[e]s, -e (ein Fisch)
Le|ni *vgl.* [2]Lena
Le|nin (sowjet. Politiker); **Le|ningrad** *vgl.* Sankt Petersburg; **Lenin|gra|der** (↑R 103); Leningrader Sinfonie (von Schostakowitsch); **Le|ni|nis|mus,** der; - (Lehre Lenins; Bolschewismus); **Le|ni|nist,** der; -en, -en (↑R 126); **le|ni|nis|tisch**
Le|nis, die; -, Lenes ['le:ne:s] ‹lat.› (*Sprachw.* mit geringer Intensität gesprochener Verschluss- od. Reibelaut, z. B. b, w; *Ggs.* Fortis *[vgl. d.]*)
Lenk|ach|se; lenk|bar; Lenk|barkeit, die; -; **len|ken; Len|ker; Len|ke|rin; Lenk|rad; Lenk|rad‿schal|tung, ...schloss; lenksam; Lenk|sam|keit,** die; -; **Lenk|stan|ge; Len|kung; Lenkwaf|fe**
Len|ne, die; - (l. Nebenfluss der Ruhr)
Le|no|re (w. Vorn.)
len|tan|do ‹ital.› (*Musik* nach u. nach langsamer [werdend]); **Lentan|do,** das; -s, *Plur.* -s *u.* ...di; **len|to** (langsam, gedehnt); **Lento,** das; -s, *Plur.* -s *u.* ...ti
lenz (*Seemannsspr.* leer [von Wasser])
Lenz, der; -es, -e (*geh. für* Frühjahr, Frühling; *Plur. auch für* Jahre); **[1]len|zen** (*geh. für* Frühling werden); es lenzt
[2]len|zen (*Seemannsspr.* vor schwerem Sturm mit stark gerefften Segeln laufen; leer pumpen); du lenzt
Len|zing, der; -s, -e; **Lenz‿mo|nat** *od.* **...mond** (*alte Bez. für* März)
Lenz|pum|pe *(Seemannsspr.)*
Lenz|tag *(geh.)*
Leo (m. Vorn.)
Le|o|ben (österr. Stadt)
Le|on (m. Vorn.)
Le|o|nar|do da Vin|ci *vgl.* Vinci
Le|on|ber|ger ‹nach der baden-württembergischen Stadt Leonberg› (eine Hunderasse)
Le|on|hard, Lien|hard (m. Vorn.)
Le|o|ni|das (spartan. König)
Le|o|ni|den *Plur.* ‹lat.› (Sternschnuppenschwarm im November)
[1]le|o|ni|nisch ‹lat.; nach einem mittelalterl. Dichter namens Leo *od.* nach einem Papst Leo›; *in der Fügung* leoninischer Vers (ein Vers, dessen Mitte u. Ende sich reimen); **[2]le|o|ni|nisch** ‹nach einer Fabel Äsops›; *in der Fügung* leoninischer Vertrag (Vertrag, bei dem der eine Teil allen Nutzen, den „Löwenanteil", hat)
le|o|nisch ‹nach der span. Stadt León›; leonische Gespinste, Fäden (Metallfäden)
Le|o|no|re (w. Vorn.)

Le|o|pard, der; -en, -en (↑R 126) ‹lat.› (asiat. u. afrik. Großkatze)
Le|o|pold (m. Vorn.)
Le|o|pol|di|na, die; - ‹nach dem dt. Kaiser Leopold I.› (*kurz für* Deutsche Akademie der Naturforscher „Leopoldina")
Le|o|pol|di|ne (w. Vorn.)
Lé|o|pold|ville [...'vil] (*früherer Name von* Kinshasa)
[1]**Le|po|rel|lo** (Diener in Mozarts „Don Giovanni"); [2]**Le|po|rel|lo,** das; -s, -s (*kurz für* Leporelloalbum); **Le|po|rel|lo|al|bum;** ↑R 95 (harmonikaartig zusammenzufaltende Bilderreihe)
Le|pra (↑R 130), die; - ‹griech.› (*Med.* Aussatz); **Lep|rom,** das; -s, -e (Lepraknoten); **lep|ros, lep|rös** (aussätzig); -e Kranke; **Lep|ro|so|ri|um,** das; -s, ...ien [...iən] (Krankenhaus für Leprakranke)
Lep|ta (*Plur. von* [1]Lepton); **lep|to...** ‹griech.› (schmal...); **Lep|to...** (Schmal...); **Lep|to|kar|di|er** [...iər] *Plur.* (*Zool.* Lanzettfischchen); [1]**Lep|ton,** das; -s, Lepta (altgriech. Gewicht; alt- u. neugriech. Münze [100 Lepta = 1 Drachme]); [2]**Lep|ton,** das; -s, ...onen („leichtes" Elementarteilchen); **lep|to|som** (*Anthrop., Med.* schmal-, schlankwüchsig); -er Typ; **Lep|to|so|me,** der *u.* die; -n, -n; ↑R 5 ff. (Schmalgebaute[r]); **lep|to|ze|phal** (*Biol., Med.* schmalköpfig); **Lep|to|ze|pha|le,** der *u.* die; -n, -n; ↑R 5 ff. (Schmalköpfige[r]); **Lep|to|ze|pha|lie,** die; -
Ler|che, die; -, -n (ein Vogel); *vgl. aber* Lärche; **Ler|chen|sporn** *Plur.* ...sporne (eine Zierstaude)
Ler|nä|i|sche Schlan|ge, die; -n - ‹nach dem Sumpfsee Lerna› (ein Ungeheuer der griech. Sage)
lern|bar; Lern|be|gier[|de], die; -; **lern‿be|gie|rig, ...be|hin|dert** (*Päd.*); **Lern|be|hin|der|te,** der *u.* die; -n, -n *meist Plur.* (↑R 5 ff.); **Lern|ei|fer; lern|eif|rig; ler|nen;** ein gelernter Tischler; Deutsch lernen; lesen (*auch* [das] Lesen) lernen, Klavier spielen (*auch* [das] Klavierspielen) lernen, Schlittschuh laufen (*auch* [das] Schlittschuhlaufen) lernen; ich habe gelernt; kennen lernen; lieben lernen; schätzen lernen; um sie kennen zu lernen; wir haben ihn schätzen und lieben gelernt; **Ler|ner** (*Sprachw.*); **lern|fä|hig; Lern|mit|tel,** das (Hilfsmittel für den Lernenden); **Lern|mit|tel|frei|heit,** die; -; **Lern‿pro|zess, ...schritt, ...schwes|ter, ...stoff, ...zeit, ...ziel**
Les|art; les|bar; Les|bar|keit, die; -
Les|be, die; -, -n (*ugs. für* Lesbierin); **Les|bi|er** [...iər] (Bewohner von Lesbos); **Les|bi|e|rin** (Bewohnerin von Lesbos; homosexuell veranlagte Frau); **les|bisch;** -e Liebe (Homosexualität bei Frauen); **Les|bos** (eine Insel im Ägäischen Meer)
Le|se, die; -, -n (Weinernte); **Le|se‿abend** (↑R 132), **...au|to|mat, ...bril|le, ...buch, ...dra|ma, ...ecke** (↑R 132), **...frucht, ...ge|rät, ...hun|ger, ...lam|pe, ...lu|pe; le|sen;** du liest, er liest; du lasest; du läsest; gelesen; lies! (*Abk.* l.); **le|sens|wert; Le|se‿pro|be, ...pult; Le|ser; Le|se|rat|te** (*ugs. für* leidenschaftlicher Leser); **Le|ser|brief; Le|se-Recht|schreib-Schwä|che;** ↑R 28 (*Med., Psych.* Lernstörung beim Lesen od. Rechtschreiben von Wörtern; *Abk.* LRS); *vgl. auch* Legasthenie; **Le|se|rei,** die; -; **Le|se|rin; Le|ser|kreis; le|ser|lich; Le|ser|lich|keit,** die; -; **Le|ser|schaft; Le|ser‿wunsch, ...zu|schrift; Le|se‿saal** (*Plur.* ...säle), **...stoff, ...wut** (*ugs.*), **...zei|chen, ...zim|mer, ...zir|kel**
Le|so|ther; le|so|thisch; Le|so|tho (Staat in Afrika)
Les|sing (dt. Dichter); **les|singsch;** lessingsches Denken; lessingsche Dramen (↑R 94)
Le|sung
le|tal ‹lat.› (*Med.* tödlich)
Le|thar|gie, die; - ‹griech.› (Schlafsucht; Trägheit, Teilnahms-, Interesselosigkeit); **le|thar|gisch;**
Le|the, die; - ‹nach dem Unterweltfluss der griech. Sage› (*geh. für* Vergessenheit[strank])
Let|kiss, der; - ‹finn.-engl.› (ein Modetanz)
let|schert (*österr. ugs. für* kraftlos; schlapp)
Let|scho, das, *auch* der; -[s] ‹ungar.› (ungar. Gemüsegericht)
Let|te, der; -n, -n; ↑R 126 (Angehöriger eines balt. Volkes)
Let|ten, der; -s, - (Ton, Lehm)
Let|ter, die; -, -n ‹lat.› (Druckbuchstabe); **Let|tern‿gieß|ma|schi|ne, ...gut** (das; -[e]s), **...me|tall**
Let|te-Ver|ein (↑R 95), der; -s (von W. A. Lette 1866 gegründeter Verein zur Förderung der Berufsausbildung von Mädchen)
let|tig ‹*zu* Letten› (ton-, lehmhaltig)
Let|tin; let|tisch; -e Sprache; *vgl.* deutsch; **Let|tisch,** das; -[s] (Sprache); *vgl.* Deutsch; **Let|ti|sche,** das; -n; *vgl.* Deutsche, das; **Lett|land**
Lett|ner, der; -s, - ‹lat.› (Schranke zwischen Chor u. Langhaus in mittelalterl. Kirchen)
letz; letzer, letzeste (*südd. u. schweiz. mdal. für* verkehrt, falsch; *österr. mdal. für* schlecht, mühsam)
let|zen (*veraltet für* laben, erquicken); du letzt; sich -
Letzt, die; - (*veraltet für* Abschiedsmahl); *noch in* zu guter Letzt; auf die Letzt (*österr. mdal. für* schließlich)
letz|te; der letzte Schrei; das letzte Stündlein; die letzte Ruhestätte; letzte Ehre; letzten Endes; eine Ausgabe letzter Hand (*Buchw.*); der letzte Wille (Testament); die letzten Dinge (nach kath. Lehre); das letzte Mal; zum letzten Mal (*vgl.* Mal); die zwei letzten Tage des Urlaubs waren besonders ereignisreich; die letzten zwei Tage habe ich fast nichts gegessen; *Großschreibung* (↑R 47): der Letzte, der gekommen ist; als Letzter fertig werden; er ist der Letzte, den ich wählen würde; dies ist das Letzte, was ich tun würde; den Letzten beißen die Hunde; die Letzten werden die Ersten sein; sein Letztes hergeben; ein Letztes habe ich zu sagen; am, zum Letzten (zuletzt); im Letzten (zutiefst); bis ins Letzte (genau); bis zum Letzten (sehr) angespannt sein; bis zum Letzten (Äußersten) gehen; fürs Letzte (zuletzt); der Letzte des Monats; das ist das Letzte (das Schlimmste); (↑R 108:) das Letzte Gericht; die Letzte Ölung (*vgl.* Ölung); **letzt|end|lich; letz|tens; letz|te|re;** der letztere (zuletzt genannte) Fall; (↑R 47:) Letzterer *od.* der Letztere kommt nicht in Betracht; Letzteres muss noch geprüft werden; **letzt|ge|nannt; Letzt|ge|nann|te,** der *u.* die; -n, -n (↑R 5 ff.); **letzt|hän|dig** (noch zu Lebzeiten eigenhändig vorgenommen); **letzt|hin; letzt|jäh|rig; letzt|lich; letzt|ma|lig; letzt|mals; letzt|mög|lich; letzt|wil|lig;** -e Verfügung
[1]**Leu,** der; -en, -en; ↑R 126 (*geh. für* Löwe)
[2]**Leu** [leu], der; -, Lei [lej] ‹rumän., „Löwe"› (rumän. Währungseinheit; *Abk.* l)
Leucht‿ba|ke, ...bo|je, ...bom|be; Leuch|te, die; -, -n; **leuch|ten; leuch|tend;** leuchtend blaue Augen; **Leuch|ter; Leucht‿far|be, ...feu|er, ...gas** (das; -es), **...kä-**

fer, ...kraft (die; -), **...ku|gel, ...pis|to|le, ...ra|ke|te, ...re|klame, ...röh|re, ...schirm, ...schrift, ...sig|nal, ...spur, ...stoff|lam|pe, ...turm, ...zif|fer, ...zif|fer|blatt**
leug|nen; Leug|ner; Leug|nung
leuk... ‹griech.› (weiß...); **Leuk...** (Weiß...); **Leu|kä|mie** (↑R 132), die; -, ...ien (*Med.* „Weißblütigkeit", Blutkrebs); **leu|kä|misch** (an Leukämie leidend); **leu|koderm** (*Med.* hellhäutig); **Leu|koder|ma,** das; -s, ...men (Auftreten weißer Flecken auf der Haut); **Leu|kom,** das; -s, -e (weißer Hornhautfleck); **Leu|ko|pa|thie,** die; -, -ien (*svw.* Leukoderma); [1]**Leu|ko|plast,** der; -en, -en; ↑R 126 (*Biol.* Bestandteil der Pflanzenzelle); [2]**Leu|ko|plast** ®, das; -[e]s, -e (Heftpflaster); **Leukor|rhö**[1], **Leu|kor|rhöe** [...'rø:], die; -, ...rrhöen (*Med.* weißer [Aus]fluss bei Gebärmutterkatarrh); **leu|kor|rhö|isch; Leu|koto|mie,** Lo|bo|to|mie, die; -, ...ien (*Med.* chirurg. Eingriff in die weiße Gehirnsubstanz); **Leu|ko|zyt,** der; -en, -en *meist Plur.;* ↑R 126 (*Med.* weißes Blutkörperchen); **Leu|ko|zy|to|se,** die; - (krankhafte Vermehrung der weißen Blutkörperchen)
Leu|mund, der; -[e]s (Ruf); **Leumunds|zeug|nis**
Leu|na (Stadt an der Saale; ®)
Leut|chen *Plur.* (*ugs.); **Leu|te** Plur.;* **leu|te|scheu; Leu|teschin|der** *(abwertend)*
Leut|nant, der; -s, *Plur.* -s, *seltener* -e ‹franz.› (unterster Offiziersgrad; *Abk.* Lt., Ltn.); **Leutnants‿rang** (der; -[e]s), **...uniform** (↑R 132)
Leut|pries|ter (*veraltet für* Weltgeistlicher, Laienpriester)
leut|se|lig; Leut|se|lig|keit, die; -
Leu|wa|gen, der; -s, - (*nordd. für* Schrubber)
Leu|zit [*auch* ...'tsit], der; -s, -e ‹griech.› (ein Mineral)
Le|va|de [...v...], die; -, -n ‹franz.› (*Reitsport* Aufrichten des Pferdes auf der Hinterhand)
Le|van|te [...v...], die; - ‹ital.› (Mittelmeerländer östl. von Italien); **Le|van|ti|ne,** die; - (ein Gewebe); **Le|van|ti|ner;** ↑R 103 (Bewohner der Levante); **le|van|ti|nisch**
Le|vee [lə've:], die; -, -s ‹franz.› (*früher für* Aushebung von Rekruten)
Le|vel [...v...], der; -s, -s ‹engl.› (Niveau; [Schwierigkeits]stufe)

[1] *Vgl. die Anmerkung zu* „Diarrhö, Diarrhöe".

Le|ver [lə've:], das; -s, -s ‹franz.› (*früher* Morgenempfang bei Fürsten)
Le|ver|ku|sen [...v..., *auch* ...'ku:...] (Stadt am Niederrhein)
Le|vi ['le:vi] (bibl. m. Eigenn.)
Le|vi|a|than, *ökum.* Le|vi|a|tan [le'via:tan, *auch* levia'ta:n], der; -s ‹hebr.› (Ungeheuer der altoriental. Mythol.)
Le|vin [...v...], Le|win (m. Vorn.)
Le|vi|rats|ehe [...v...] (↑R 132) ‹lat.; dt.› (Ehe eines Mannes mit der Frau seines kinderlos verstorbenen Bruders [im A.T. u. bei Naturvölkern])
Le|vit [le'vi(:)t], der; -en, -en; ↑R 126 (Angehöriger des jüd. Stammes Levi; Tempeldiener im A.T.; *Plur.: kath. Kirche früher* Helfer des Priesters beim feierlichen Hochamt)
Le|vi|ta|ti|on [...v...], die; -, -en ‹lat.› (*Parapsychologie* [vermeintliche] Aufhebung der Schwerkraft)
Le|vi|ten [....'vi(:)...] ‹*zu* Levit›; *nur in* jmdm. die - lesen ‹nach den Verhaltensvorschriften des Levitikus› (*ugs. für* [ernste] Vorhaltungen machen); **Le|vi|ti|kus,** der; - (3. Buch Mosis); **le|vi|tisch** (auf die Leviten bezüglich)
Lev|koie [lɛf'kɔyə] (*älter für* Levkoje); **Lev|ko|je,** die; -, -n ‹griech.› (eine Zierpflanze)
Lew [lɛf], der; -[s], Lewa ['lɛva] ‹bulgar., „Löwe"› (bulgar. Währungseinheit; *Abk.* Lw)
Le|win *vgl.* Levin
Lex, die; -, Leges [...ge:s] ‹lat.› (Gesetz; Gesetzesantrag); - Heinze
Lex.-8° = Lexikonoktav, Lexikonformat
Le|xem, das; -s, -e ‹russ.› (*Sprachw.* lexikal. Einheit, Wortschatzeinheit im Wörterbuch);
Le|xik, die; - (Wortschatz einer [Fach]sprache); **le|xi|kal** (*seltener für* lexikalisch); **le|xi|ka|lisch** (das Lexikon betreffend, in der Art eines Lexikons); **le|xi|ka|lisiert** (*Sprachw.* als Worteinheit festgelegt [z. B. Zaunkönig, hochnäsig]); **Le|xi|ko|graf, Le|xi|kogra|fie** usw. *eindeutschende Schreibung für* Lexikograph, Lexikographie usw.; **Le|xi|kograph,** der; -en, -en; ↑R 126 (Verfasser eines Wörterbuches od. Lexikons); **Le|xi|ko|gra|phie,** die; - ([Lehre von der] Abfassung eines Wörterbuches [auch eines Lexikons]); **Le|xi|ko|gra|phin; le|xiko|gra|phisch; Le|xi|ko|lo|ge,** der; -n, -n (Wissenschaftler auf dem Gebiet der Lexikologie); **Lexi|ko|lo|gie** (Lehre von Aufbau und Struktur des Wortschatzes); **Le|xi|ko|lo|gin; le|xi|ko|lo|gisch;**
Le|xi|kon, das; -s, *Plur.* ...ka, *auch* ...ken (alphabetisch geordnetes allgemeines Nachschlagewerk; *auch für* Wörterbuch); **Le|xi|kon‿for|mat** (das; -[e]s) *od.* **...ok|tav** (das; -s; *Abk.* Lex.-8°); **le|xisch** (die Lexik betreffend)
Le|zi|thin, *fachspr.* Le|ci|thin, das; -s ‹griech.› (*Chemie, Biol.* phosphorhaltiger Nährstoff)
lfd. = laufend *(vgl. d.)*
lfr *vgl.* Franc
LG = Landgericht
Lha|sa (Hptst. Tibets)
Li = *chem. Zeichen für* Lithium
Li|ai|son [liɛ'zɔ̃:], die; -, -s ‹franz.› (*veraltend für* Verbindung; Liebesverhältnis)
[1]**Li|a|ne,** die; -, -n *meist Plur.* ‹franz.› (eine Schlingpflanze)
[2]**Li|a|ne** (w. Vorn.)
Li|as, der *od.* die; - ‹franz.› (*Geol.* untere Abteilung der Juraformation); **Li|as|for|ma|ti|on; li|assisch** (zum Lias gehörend)
Li|ba|ne|se, der; -n, -n (↑R 126); **Li|ba|ne|sin; li|ba|ne|sisch;** [1]**Liba|non,** *meist mit Artikel* der; -[s] (Staat im Vorderen Orient); [2]**Liba|non,** der; -[s] (Gebirge im Vorderen Orient)
Li|ba|ti|on, die; -, -en ‹lat.› (altröm. Trankopfer)
Li|bell, das; -s, -e ‹lat., „Büchlein"› (Klageschrift im alten Rom; Schmähschrift)
Li|bel|le, die; -, -n ‹lat.› (ein Insekt; Teil der Wasserwaage); **Li|bellen|waa|ge**
Li|bel|list, der; -en, -en (↑R 126) ‹lat.› (*veraltet für* Verfasser einer Schmähschrift)
li|be|ral ‹lat.› (vorurteilslos; freiheitlich; den Liberalismus vertretend); eine liberale Partei; *aber* (↑R 108:) Liberal-Demokratische Partei Deutschlands (*ehem. in der DDR; Abk.* LDPD); das Liberale Forum *(österr.);* **Li|be|ra|le,** der *u.* die; -n, -n; ↑R 5 ff. (Anhänger[in] des Liberalismus); **li|be|ra|li|sieren** (von Einschränkungen befreien, freiheitlich gestalten); **Libe|ra|li|sie|rung** (das Liberalisieren; *Wirtsch.* Aufhebung der staatl. Außenhandelsbeschränkungen); **Li|be|ra|lis|mus,** der; - (Denkrichtung, die die freie Entfaltung des Individuums fordert und staatliche Eingriffe auf ein Minimum beschränkt sehen will); **Li|be|ra|list,** der; -en, -en (↑R 126); **li|be|ra|lis|tisch** (freiheitlich im Sinne des Liberalis-

mus; *auch für* extrem liberal); **Li|be|ra|li|tät**, die; - (Freiheitlichkeit; Vorurteilslosigkeit)
Li|be|ra|li|um Ar|ti|um Ma|gis|ter ⟨lat.⟩ (Magister der freien Künste; *Abk.* L. A. M.)
Li|be|ria (Staat in Westafrika); **Li|be|ri|a|ner,** *auch* Li|be|ri|er; **Li|be|ri|a|ne|rin,** *auch* Li|be|ri|e|rin; **li|be|ri|a|nisch,** *auch* li|be|risch; **Li|be|ri|er** usw. *vgl.* Liberianer usw.
Li|be|ro, der; -s, -s ⟨ital.⟩ (*Fußball* nicht mit Spezialaufgaben betrauter freier Verteidiger)
Li|ber|tas (röm. Göttin der Freiheit); **Li|ber|tät,** die; -, -en ⟨franz.⟩ (*früher für* ständische Freiheit); **Li|ber|té, É|ga|li|té, Fra|ter|ni|té** [...'te:, egali'te:, ...'te:] („Freiheit, Gleichheit, Brüderlichkeit", die drei Losungsworte der Franz. Revolution)
Li|ber|tin [...'tɛ̃:], der; -s, -s ⟨franz.⟩ (*veraltet für* Freigeist; Wüstling); **Li|ber|ti|na|ge** [...'na:ʒə], die; -, -n (*geh. für* Liederlichkeit, Zügellosigkeit)
Li|bi|di|nist, der; -en, -en (↑R 126) ⟨lat.⟩ (*Psych.* sexuell triebhafter Mensch); **li|bi|di|nös; Li|bi|do** [*auch* li'bi:do], die; - (Begierde, Trieb; Geschlechtstrieb)
Lib|ra|ti|on (↑R 130), die; -, -en ⟨lat.⟩ (*Astron.* scheinbare Mondschwankung)
Lib|ret|tist (↑R 130), der; -en, -en (↑R 126) ⟨ital.⟩ (Verfasser von Librettos); **Lib|ret|to,** das; -s, *Plur.* -s *u.* ...tti (Text[buch] von Opern, Operetten usw.)
Lib|re|ville [...'vil] (↑R 130; Hauptstadt von Gabun)
Li|bus|sa (sagenhafte tschech. Königin)
Li|by|en (Staat in Nordafrika); **Li|by|er; Li|by|e|rin; li|bysch,** *aber* (↑R 102): die Libysche Wüste
lic. (*schweiz. für* Lic.); **Lic.** = Licentiatus; *vgl.* [2]Lizentiat
li|cet ['li:tsɛt] ⟨lat.⟩ („es ist erlaubt")
...lich (z. B. weiblich)
Li|che|no|lo|ge [...ç...], der; -n, -n (↑R 126) ⟨lat.⟩ (*Bot.* Flechtenkundler); **Li|che|no|lo|gie,** die; - (Flechtenkunde)
licht; es wird licht; ein lichter Wald; im Lichten (↑R 47; im Hellen; im Inneren gemessen); -e Weite (Abstand von Wand zu Wand bei einer Röhre u. a.); -e Höhe (lotrechter Abstand von Kante zu Kante bei einem Tor u. a.); **Licht,** das; -[e]s, *Plur.* -er, *veraltet u. geh.* Lichte (*auch Jägerspr. für* Auge des Schalenwildes [*Plur. nur* Lichter]); **Licht|an|la|ge; licht|arm; Licht‿bad** *(Med.),* **...be|hand|lung** *(Med.);* **licht|be|stän|dig; Licht|bild** (*für* Passbild; Fotografie; Diapositiv); **Licht|bil|der|vor|trag; licht|blau; Licht|blick; licht|blond; Licht|bo|gen** *(Technik);* **licht|braun; licht|bre|chend** (*für* dioptrisch); **Licht|bre|chung** *(Physik);* **Licht|chen; Licht|druck** *Plur.* ...drucke; **licht‿durch|flu|tet, ...durch|läs|sig; Lich|te,** die; - (lichte Weite); **licht|echt; Licht‿echt|heit** (die; -), **...ef|fekt, ...ein|fall; licht|elekt|risch** (↑R 132; *Physik*); **lich|teln** (*landsch. für* Kerzen brennen lassen); **licht|emp|find|lich;** [1]**lich|ten** (licht machen); das Dunkel lichtet sich
[2]**lich|ten** (*Seemannsspr.* leicht machen, anheben); den Anker -
Lich|ten|berg (dt. Physiker u. Schriftsteller)
Lich|ten|stein (Schloss südlich von Reutlingen); *vgl. aber* Liechtenstein
Lich|ter *vgl.* Leichter
Lich|ter|baum (Weihnachtsbaum); **Lich|ter‿fest** (jüd. Fest der Tempeleinweihung), **...glanz, ...ket|te; lich|ter|loh; Lich|ter|meer**
lich|tern *vgl.* leichtern
Licht‿fil|ter, ...ge|schwin|dig|keit (die; -), **...ge|stalt; licht‿grau, ...grün; Licht‿hof, ...hu|pe, ...jahr** (astron. Längeneinheit; *Zeichen* ly), **...ke|gel, ...kreis, ...leh|re** (die; -; *für* Optik); **Licht|lein; Licht|lei|tung; licht|los; Licht‿man|gel** (der), **...ma|schi|ne; Licht|mess** (kath. Fest); **Licht‿mes|sung** (*für* Photometrie), **...nel|ke, ...or|gel, ...pau|se; Licht[|putz]|sche|re; Licht‿quel|le, ...re|flex, ...re|kla|me, ...satz** (*Druckw.* fotograf. Setzverfahren), **...schacht, ...schal|ter, ...schein; licht|scheu; Licht‿schim|mer, ...schran|ke** *(Elektrotechnik),* **...schutz|fak|tor** (bei Sonnenschutzmitteln und Kosmetika), **...sig|nal; Licht|spiel‿haus, ...the|a|ter** (*veraltend für* Kino); **Licht‿stär|ke, ...strahl, ...tech|nik; licht|tech|nisch; Licht|the|ra|pie; licht|trun|ken** *(geh.);* **Lich|tung; Licht|ver|hält|nis|se** *Plur.;* **licht|voll** *(geh.);* **licht|wen|dig** (*für* phototropisch); **Licht|wen|dig|keit,** die; - (*für* Phototropismus); **Licht|zei|chen** (*svw.* Lichtsignal)
Lic. theol. = Licentiatus theologiae; *vgl.* [2]Lizentiat
Lid, das; -[e]s, -er (Augendeckel); *vgl. aber* Lied
Li|di|ce ['lidjitsɛ] (tschech. Ort)
Lid|krampf (*Med.* krampfhaftes Schließen der Augenlider)
Li|do, der; -s, *Plur.* -s, *auch* Lidi ⟨ital.⟩ (Nehrung, bes. die bei Venedig)
Lid‿rand, ...sack, ...schat|ten, ...spal|te, ...strich
lieb; am liebsten; sich bei jmdm. lieb Kind machen; der liebe Gott; lieb haben; sie haben sich [sehr] lieb gehabt; sie hat ihn immer lieb behalten; er wird sie lieb gewinnen; eine lieb gewordene Gewohnheit; *vgl. aber* liebäugeln, liebkosen; *Großschreibung* (↑R 47:) viel, nichts Liebes; mein Lieber, meine Liebe, mein Liebes; es ist mir das Liebste (sehr lieb), wenn ...; (↑R 108:) [Kirche] Zu Unsrer Lieben Frau[en]; **Lieb,** das; -s (Geliebte[r]); mein Lieb; **lieb|äu|geln** (↑R 37); er hat mit diesem Plan geliebäugelt; zu liebäugeln; **lieb be|hal|ten** *vgl.* lieb; **Lieb|chen; Lieb|den,** die; - (*veraltet* ehrende Anrede an Adlige); Euer -; **Lie|be,** die; -, *Plur.* (*ugs. für* Liebschaften:) -n; Lieb und Lust (↑R 13); (↑R 41:) mir zuliebe; jmdm. etwas zuliebe tun; **lie|be|be|dürf|tig; Lie|be|die|ner** (*abwertend für* Schmeichler, unterwürfiger Mensch); **Lie|be|die|ne|rei; lie|be|die|ne|risch; lie|be|die|nern** (unterwürfig schmeicheln); er hat geliebedienert; zu liebedienern; **lie|be|leer; Lie|be|lei; lie|beln** (*veraltet für* flirten); ich ...[e]le (↑R 16); **lie|ben;** sie haben sich lieben gelernt (↑R 39); **Lie|ben|de,** der *u.* die; -n, -n (↑R 5 ff.); **lie|ben ler|nen** *vgl.* lieben; **lie|bens‿wert, ...wür|dig; lie|bens|wür|di|ger|wei|se; Lie|bens|wür|dig|keit; lie|ber** *vgl.* gern
Lie|ber|mann (dt. Maler)
Lie|bes‿aben|teu|er (↑R 132), **...af|fä|re, ...akt** *(geh.),* **...ap|fel, ...ban|de** *(Plur.; geh.),* **...be|zei|gung** *(veraltet),* **...be|zie|hung, ...bo|te, ...brief, ...die|ne|rin** (*ugs. für* Prostituierte), **...dienst, ...ent|zug** *(Psych.),* **...er|klä|rung, ...film, ...ga|be, ...ge|dicht, ...ge|schich|te, ...gott, ...göt|tin, ...hei|rat, ...kno|chen** (*landsch. für* Eclair), **...kum|mer, ...lau|be, ...le|ben** (das; -s), **...lied, ...müh** *od.* **...mü|he, ...nacht, ...nest, ...paar, ...per|len** (*Plur.;* zur Verzierung von Gebäck), **...ro|man, ...spiel; lie|bes|toll; Lie|bes|tö|ter** *Plur.* (*ugs. scherzh. für* lange,

warme Unterhose); **lie|bes|trunken; Lie|bes‿ver|hält|nis, ...zauber; lie|be|voll; Lieb|frau|en|kirche** (Kirche Zu Unsrer Lieben Frau[en]); **Lieb|frau|en|milch** (ein Wein); *als* ®: Liebfraumilch; **lieb ge|win|nen, ge|wor|den, ha|ben** *vgl.* lieb; **Lieb|ha|ber; Lieb|ha|ber|büh|ne; Lieb|ha|be|rei; Lieb|ha|be|rin; Lieb|ha|ber‿preis, ...wert**

Lieb|hard (m. Vorn.)

Lie|big (dt. Chemiker; ®)

Lieb|knecht, Wilhelm (Mitbegründer der Sozialist. Arbeiterpartei Deutschlands)

lieb|ko|sen [*auch* 'li:p...] (↑R 37); er hat liebkost (*auch* geliebkost); **Lieb|ko|sung; lieb|lich; Lieb|lich|keit,** die; -; **Lieb|ling; Lieb|lings‿buch, ...dich|ter, ...dich|te|rin, ...far|be, ...ge|richt, ...kind, ...lied, ...platz, ...schü|ler, ...schü|le|rin, ...wort** (*Plur.* ...wörter); **lieb|los; Lieb|lo|sig|keit; lieb|reich; Lieb|reiz,** der; -es; **lieb|rei|zend; Lieb|schaft; Liebs|te,** der *u.* die; -n, -n (↑R 5 ff.)

Lieb|stö|ckel, das *od.* der; -s, - (eine Heil- u. Gewürzpflanze)

lieb|wert *(veraltet)*

Liech|ten|stein ['liç...] (Fürstentum); *vgl. aber* Lichtenstein; **Liech|ten|stei|ner; liech|ten|stei|nisch**

Lied, das; -[e]s, -er (Gedicht; Gesang); *vgl. aber* Lid; **Lied|chen; Lie|der‿abend** (↑R 132), **...buch, ...hand|schrift**

Lie|der|jan, Lied|ri|an, der; -[e]s, -e (*ugs. für* liederlicher Mensch); **lie|der|lich; Lie|der|lich|keit**

Lie|der‿ma|cher, ...ma|che|rin; lie|der|reich; lied|haft; Lied|lein

Lied|ri|an *vgl.* Liederjan

Lie|fe|rant, der; -en, -en (↑R 126) ⟨*zu* liefern, mit lat. Endung⟩ (Lieferer); **Lie|fe|ran|tin; lie|fer|bar; Lie|fer‿be|din|gun|gen** *(Plur.)*, **...be|trieb; Lie|fe|rer; Lie|fer‿fir|ma, ...frist; Lie|fe|rin; lie|fern;** ich ...ere (↑R 16); **Lie|fer‿schein, ...stopp, ...ter|min; Lie|fe|rung; Lie|fe|rungs‿ort** (der; -[e]s, -e), **...sper|re; lie|fe|rungs|wei|se; Lie|fer‿ver|trag, ...wa|gen, ...zeit**

Lie|ge, die; -, -n (ein Möbelstück); **Lie|ge‿geld** *(Seew.)*, **...hal|le, ...kur; lie|gen;** du lagst; du lägest; gelegen; lieg[e]!; ich habe (*südd., österr., schweiz.* bin) gelegen; ich habe zwanzig Flaschen Wein im Keller liegen; *Getrenntschreibung in Verbindung mit Verben* (↑R 39): die Brille ist liegen geblieben; er hat den Schlüssel liegen lassen; sie hat ihn links liegen lassen, *seltener* liegen gelassen (vergessen, nicht beachtet); **liegend;** -es Gut, -e Güter; **Lie|gen|de,** das; -n; ↑R 5 ff. (*Bergmannsspr.; Ggs.* Hangende); **lie|gen las|sen** *vgl.* liegen; **Lie|gen|schaft** (Grundbesitz); **Lie|ge‿platz** *(Seew.)*, **...pols|ter; Lie|ger** (*Seemannsspr.* Wächter auf einem außer Dienst befindlichen Schiff; großes Trinkwasserfass [als Notvorrat]); **Lie|ge‿sitz, ...so|fa, ...statt** (die; -, ...stätten), **...stuhl, ...stütz** (der; -es, -e; *Sport*), **...wa|gen, ...wie|se, ...zeit**

Liek, das; -[e]s, -en (*Seemannsspr.* Tauwerk als Einfassung eines Segels); *vgl.* Leik

Li|en ['li:en, *auch* 'lie:n], der; -s, Lienes ⟨lat.⟩ (*Med.* Milz); **li|e|nal** (die Milz betreffend)

Lien|hard *vgl.* Leonhard

Li|e|ni|tis, die; -, ...itiden ⟨griech.⟩ (*Med.* Milzentzündung)

Li|enz (Stadt in Österreich)

lies! (*Abk.* l.)

Liesch, das; -[e]s (eine Grasgattung); [1]**Lie|schen** *Plur.* (Vorblätter am Maiskolben)

[2]**Lies|chen** (w. Vorn.); *vgl.* fleißig

[1]**Lie|se,** die; -, -n (*Bergmannsspr.* enge [2]Kluft)

[2]**Lie|se, Lie|sel,** Liesl, Lise (w. Vorn.); **Lie|se|lot|te** [*auch* ...'lɔtə]; ↑R 92 (w. Vorn.); *vgl.* Liselotte

Lie|sen *Plur.* (*nordd. für* Schweinefett)

Liesl *vgl.* Liesel

Lies|tal (Hptst. des Halbkantons Basel-Landschaft)

Life|style ['laifstail], der; -s ⟨engl.⟩ (Lebensstil); **Life|time|sport** ['laiftaim...], der; -s (Sportart, die man lebenslang ausüben kann)

Lift, der; -[e]s, *Plur.* -e *u.* -s ⟨engl.⟩ (Fahrstuhl, Aufzug); **Lift|boy** [...bɔy]; **lif|ten** (heben, stemmen)

Li|ga, die; -, ...gen ⟨span.⟩ (Bund, Bündnis; *Sport* Bez. einer Wettkampfklasse); **Li|ga|de,** die; -, -n (*Fechten* Zurseitedrücken der gegnerischen Klinge); **Li|ga|ment,** das; -[e]s, -e ⟨lat.⟩ *u.* **Li|ga|men|tum,** das; -s, ...ta (*Med.* Band); **Li|ga|tur,** die; -, -en (*Druckw.* [Buchstaben]verbindung; *Med.* Unterbindung [einer Ader usw.]; *Musik* Verbindung zweier gleicher Töne zu einem)

Li|ge|ti (ungar. Komponist)

Light|show ['laitʃo:], die; -, -s ⟨engl.⟩ (Show mit besonderen Lichteffekten)

li|gie|ren ⟨lat.⟩ (*Fechten* die gegnerische Klinge zur Seite drücken); **Li|gist,** der; -en, -en; ↑R 126 (Angehöriger einer Liga; Verbündeter); **li|gis|tisch**

Lig|nin (↑R 130), das; -s, -e ⟨lat.⟩ (Holzstoff); **Lig|nit** [*auch* ...'nit], der; -s, -e (Braunkohle mit Holzstruktur)

Lig|ro|in (↑R 130), das; -s ⟨Kunstwort⟩ (ein Leichtöl)

Li|gu|rer, der; -s, - (Angehöriger eines voridg. Volkes in Südfrankreich u. Oberitalien); **Li|gu|ri|en** [...iən] (ital. Region); **li|gu|risch,** *aber* (↑R 102): das Ligurische Meer

Li|gus|ter, der; -s, - ⟨lat.⟩ (ein Ölbaumgewächs mit weißen Blütenrispen); **Li|gus|ter‿he|cke, ...schwär|mer** (ein Schmetterling)

li|ie|ren ⟨franz.⟩ (eng verbinden); sich -; **Li|ier|te,** der *u.* die; -n, -n; ↑R 5 ff. (*veraltet für* Vertraute[r]); **Li|ie|rung** (enge Verbindung)

Li|kör, der; -s, -e ⟨franz.⟩ (süßer Branntwein); **Li|kör‿es|senz, ...fla|sche, ...glas** (*Plur.* ...gläser)

Lik|tor, der; -s, ...oren (Diener der Obrigkeit im alten Rom); **Lik|to|ren|bün|del**

li|la ⟨franz.⟩ (fliederblau; *ugs. für* mittelmäßig); ein lila Kleid; *vgl.* blau; *vgl. auch* beige; **Li|la,** das; -s, *Plur.* -, *ugs.* -s (ein fliederblauer Farbton); **li|la‿far|ben** *od.* **...far|big; Li|lak,** der; -s, -s (span. Flieder)

Li|li *vgl.* Lilli

Li|lie [...iə], die; -, -n ⟨lat.⟩ (eine [Garten]blume)

Li|li|en|cron (dt. Dichter)

Li|li|en|ge|wächs

Li|li|en|thal (dt. Luftfahrtpionier)

li|li|en|weiß

Li|li|put ⟨nach engl. Lilliput⟩ (Land der Däumlinge in J. Swifts Buch „Gullivers Reisen"); **Li|li|pu|ta|ner** (Bewohner von Liliput; kleiner Mensch; Zwerg); **Li|li|put‿bahn, ...for|mat**

Lille [lil] (franz. Stadt)

Lil|li, Lili, **Lil|ly,** Lilly (w. Vorn.)

Li|long|we [...ve] (Hptst. von Malawi)

Li|ly *vgl.* Lilly

lim = [2]Limes

lim., Lim. = limited

Li|ma (Hptst. von Peru)

Lim|ba, das; -s (ein Furnierholz)

Lim|bi (*Plur. von* [2]Limbus)

Lim|bo, der; -s, -s ⟨karib.⟩ (akrobatischer Tanz unter einer niedrigen Querstange hindurch)

Lim|burg (belg. u. niederl. Landschaft; Stadt in Belgien)

Lim|burg a. d. Lahn (Stadt in Hessen)
¹Lim|bur|ger (↑R 103); - Käse (urspr. aus der belg. Landschaft Limburg); **²Lim|bur|ger,** der; -s, - (ein Käse)
¹Lim|bus, der; - ‹lat.› (Teil der Unterwelt; *christl. Rel.* Vorhölle); **²Lim|bus,** der; -, ...bi (*Technik* Gradkreis, Teilkreis an Winkelmessinstrumenten)
Li|me|rick, der; -[s], -s ‹*engl.*; nach der irischen Stadt Limerick› (fünfzeiliges Gedicht grotesk-komischen Inhalts)
¹Li|mes, der; - ‹lat.› (von den Römern angelegter Grenzwall [vom Rhein bis zur Donau]); **²Li|mes,** der; -, - (*Math.* Grenzwert; *Zeichen* lim); **Li|mes|kas|tell**
Li|met|te, *auch* Li|met|ta, die; -, ...tten ‹pers.-ital.› (westind. Zitrone); **Li|met|ten|saft**
Li|mit, das; -s, *Plur.* -s *u.* -e ‹engl.› (Grenze, Begrenzung; *Kaufmannsspr.* Preisgrenze, äußerster Preis); **Li|mi|ta|ti|on,** die; -, -en ‹lat.› (Begrenzung, Beschränkung); **Li|mi|te,** die; -, -n ‹franz.› (*schweiz. svw.* Limit); **li|mi|ted** [...tid] ‹engl.› (*in engl. u. amerik. Firmennamen* „mit beschränkter Haftung"; *Abk.* Ltd., lim., Lim., Ld.); **li|mi|tie|ren** ‹lat.› ([den Preis] begrenzen; beschränken); limitierte Auflage (z. B. einer Grafik); **Li|mi|tie|rung**
Lim|mat, die; - (r. Nebenfluss der Aare)
Lim|ni|me|ter, das; -s, - ‹griech.› (Pegel zum Messen des Wasserstandes eines Sees); **lim|nisch** (*Biol., Geol.* im Süßwasser lebend, abgelagert); **Lim|no|graph,** der; -en, -en; ↑R 126 (*svw.* Limnimeter); **Lim|no|lo|ge,** der; -n, -n; ↑R 126 (Kenner u. Erforscher der stehenden Gewässer); **Lim|no|lo|gie,** die; - (Süßwasser-, Seenkunde); **lim|no|lo|gisch** (auf Binnengewässer bezüglich); **Lim|no|plank|ton** *(Biol.)*
Li|mo, die; -, -s (*ugs. Kurzform für* Limonade); **Li|mo|na|de,** die; -, -n ‹pers.›; **Li|mo|ne,** die; -, -n (*svw.* Limette; *auch für* Zitrone)
Li|mo|nit [*auch* ...'nit], der; -s, -e ‹griech.› (ein Mineral)
li|mos, li|mös ‹lat.› (*Biol.* schlammig, sumpfig)
Li|mou|si|ne [limu...], die; -, -n ‹franz.› (Pkw mit festem Verdeck)
Li|na, Li|ne (w. Vorn.); **Lin|chen** (w. Vorn.)
Lin|cke (dt. Komponist)
Lin|coln ['liŋkən] (Präsident der USA)
lind; ein -er Regen
Lin|da (w. Vorn.)
Lin|dau (Bo|den|see) (↑R 132; Stadt in Bayern)
Lin|de, die; -, -n; **lin|den** (aus Lindenholz); **Lin|den‿al|lee, ...baum, ...blatt, ...blü|te; Lin|den|blü|ten|tee; Lin|den‿holz, ...ho|nig**
lin|dern; ich ...ere (↑R 16); **Lin|de|rung; Lin|de|rungs|mit|tel,** das
lind|grün ‹*zu* Linde›
Lind|heit, die; -
Lind|wurm (Drache in der Sage)
Li|ne *vgl.* Lina
Li|ne|al, das; -s, -e ‹lat.›; **li|ne|ar** (geradlinig; auf gerader Linie verlaufend; linienförmig); lineare Gleichung *(Math.)*; lineare Programmierung *(Math.)*; **Li|ne|ar‿be|schleu|ni|ger** *(Kernphysik)*, **...mo|tor** *(Elektrotechnik)*, **...zeich|nung** (Umrisszeichnung, Riss); **Li|ne|a|tur,** die; -, -en (Linierung; Linienführung)
...ling (z. B. Frühling, der; -s, -e)
Lin|ga[m], das; -s ‹sanskr.› (Phallus als Sinnbild des ind. Gottes der Zeugungskraft)
Lin|ge|rie [lɛ̃ʒ(ə)ri:], die; -, ...ien (*schweiz. für* Wäscheraum, betriebsinterne Wäscherei; Wäschegeschäft)
...lings (z. B. jählings)
lin|gu|al [liŋ'gua:l] ‹lat.› (auf die Zunge bezüglich, Zungen...); **Lin|gu|al,** der; -s, -e *u.* **Lin|gu|al|laut** (*Sprachw.* Zungenlaut); **Lin|gu|ist** [...'guist], der; -en, -en; ↑R 126 (Sprachwissenschaftler); **Lin|gu|is|tik,** die; - (Sprachwissenschaft); **Lin|gu|is|tin; lin|gu|is|tisch**
Li|nie [...iə], die; -, -n ‹lat.›; - halten *(Druckw.)*; absteigende, aufsteigende Linie *(Genealogie)*; **Li|ni|en‿ball** *(Tennis)*, **...blatt, ...bus, ...dienst, ...flug, ...flug|zeug, ...füh|rung, ...netz, ...pa|pier, ...rich|ter, ...rich|te|rin** *(Sport)*, **...schiff, ...spie|gel** (*österr. für* Linienblatt), **...ste|cher** (*für* Guillocheur), **...tau|fe** (Äquatortaufe); **li|ni|en|treu** (einer politischen Ideologie genau u. engstirnig folgend); **Li|ni|en|ver|kehr; li|nie|ren,** *auch* li|ni|ie|ren (mit Linien versehen; Linien ziehen); liniertes, liniiertes Papier; **Li|nier‿ma|schi|ne, ...plat|te; Li|nie|rung** (*österr. nur so*), **Li|ni|ie|rung; ...li|nig** (z. B. geradlinig)
Li|ni|ment, das; -[e]s, -e ‹lat.› (*Med.* Mittel zum Einreiben)
link; linker Hand (links); **¹Lin|ke,** der *u.* die; -n, -n; ↑R 5 ff. (Angehörige[r] einer links stehenden Partei od. Gruppe); **²Lin|ke,** die; -n, -n; ↑R 5 ff. (linke Hand; linke Seite; *Politik* Bez. für links stehende Parteien, auch für die links stehende Gruppe einer Partei); zur Linken; in meiner Linken; er traf ihn mit einer blitzschnellen Linken *(Boxen)*; die radikale Linke (im Parlament); die neue Linke (*vgl.* neu); **Lin|ke|hand|re|gel,** die; - *(Physik)*; **lin|ken** (*ugs. für* täuschen); **lin|ker Hand; lin|ker|seits; lin|kisch**
links (*Abk.* l.); links von mir, vom Eingang; von, nach links; von links nach rechts; von links her, nach links hin; an der Kreuzung gilt rechts vor links; er weiß nicht, was rechts und was links ist; links außen spielen, stürmen *(Sport)*; links um! (milit. Kommando; *vgl. aber* linksum); *als Präp. mit Gen.:* links des Waldes; links sein (*ugs.* Linkshänder sein); [politisch] links stehende Abgeordnete; etwas mit links (*ugs.* mit Leichtigkeit) machen; **Links|ab|bie|ger** *(Verkehrsw.)*; **Links|aus|la|ge,** die; - *(Boxen)*; **Links|aus|le|ger; links au|ßen** *vgl.* links; **Links|au|ßen,** der; -, - *(Sport)*; er spielt -; **links|bün|dig; Links|drall; links|dre|hend,** *aber* nach links drehend; **Links|dre|hung; Lin|ker** (*ugs. für* Linkshänder); **links|ext|rem; Links‿ext|re|mis|mus** (der; -), **...ext|re|mist, ...ga|lopp; links|ge|rich|tet; Links‿ge|win|de, ...hän|der, ...hän|de|rin; links|hän|dig; Links|hän|dig|keit,** die; -; **links|her** (*veraltet für* von links her); **links|he|rum;** linksherum drehen, *aber* nach links herumdrehen; **links|hin** (*veraltet für* nach links hin); **Links|hörn|chen** (eine Schnecke); **Links‿in|tel|lek|tu|el|le, ...kurs, ...kur|ve; links‿las|tig, ...läu|fig, ...li|be|ral** (-e Koalition); **Links|par|tei; links|ra|di|kal; Links‿ra|di|ka|le, ...ra|di|ka|lis|mus; Links-rechts-Kom|bi|na|ti|on** *(Boxen)*; **links|rhei|nisch** (auf der linken Rheinseite); **Links|ruck** *(Politik)*; **links‿rum** *(ugs.)*, **...sei|tig; links ste|hend** *vgl.* links; **links|uf|rig; links|um** [*auch* 'liŋks...]; - machen; - kehrt! *vgl. aber* links; **Links‿un|ter|zeich|ne|te** (*vgl.* Unterzeichnete), **...ver|kehr, ...wen|dung**
Lin|né [li'ne:] (schwed. Naturforscher; *Abk. hinter biol. Namen* L.); linnésches System (↑R 94)
lin|nen (*geh. für* leinen); **Lin|nen,** das; -s, - (*geh. für* Leinen)
Li|no|le|um [...le|um, *österr. meist*

...'le:um] (↑R 132), das; -s ‹lat.› (ein Fußbodenbelag); **Li|no|le|um|be|lag; Li|nol|schnitt** (ein graph. Verfahren u. dessen Ergebnis)
Li|non [li'nɔ̃:, *auch* 'linɔn], der; -[s], -s ‹franz.› (Baumwollgewebe [mit Leinencharakter])
Li|no|type ® ['lainotaip], die; -, -s ‹engl.› (Setz- u. Zeilengießmaschine); **Li|no|type-Setz|ma|schi|ne** (↑R 24), die; -, -n
Lin|se, die; -, -n; **lin|sen** (*ugs. für* schauen, scharf äugen); **Lin|sen|feh|ler** *(Optik);* **lin|sen|för|mig; Lin|sen‿ge|richt, ...sup|pe, ...trü|bung** *(Med.);* **...lin|sig** (z. B. vierlinsig, *mit Ziffer* 4-linsig)
Linth, die; - (Oberlauf der Limmat)
Li|nus (m. Vorn.)
Linz (Hptst. von Oberösterreich)
Linz am Rhein (Stadt am Mittelrhein)
Lin|zer (↑R 103); - Torte
Li|o|ba (w. Vorn.)
Li|on ['laiən], der; -s, -s (Mitglied des Lions Clubs); **Li|ons Club** [*engl.* 'laiənz 'klab], der; - -s *u.* **Li|ons In|ter|na|tio|nal** [*engl.* - intə(r)'nɛʃ(ə)nəl], der; - - (karitativ tätige, um internationale Verständigung bemühte Vereinigung führender Persönlichkeiten des öffentlichen Lebens)
Li|pä|mie (↑R 132), die; -, ...ien ‹griech.› (*Med.* Vermehrung des Fettgehaltes im Blut); **li|pä|misch** (fettblütig)
Li|pa|ri|sche In|seln, *auch* Äo|li|sche In|seln *Plur.* (im Mittelmeer)
Lip|gloss, das; -, - ‹engl.› (Kosmetikmittel, das den Lippen Glanz verleiht)
Li|piz|za|ner, der; -s, - (Vollblutpferd einer bestimmten Rasse)
li|po|id ‹griech.› (fettähnlich); **Li|po|id,** das; -s, -e *meist Plur.* (*Biol.* fettähnlicher, lebenswichtiger Stoff im Körper); **Li|pom,** das; -s, -e *u.* **Li|po|ma,** das; -s, -ta (*Med.* Fettgeschwulst); **Li|po|ma|to|se,** die; -, -n (*Med.* Fettsucht)
[1]**Lip|pe,** die; -, -n (Rand der Mundöffnung)
[2]**Lip|pe** (Land des ehem. Deutschen Reiches); [3]**Lip|pe,** die; - (r. Nebenfluss des Niederrheins)
Lip|pen‿be|kennt|nis, ...blüt|ler (der; -s, -), **...laut** (*für* Labial), **...stift** (der), **...syn|chro|ni|sa|ti|on** *(Film)*
Lip|pe-Sei|ten|ka|nal (↑R 105)
Lipp|fisch; ...lip|pig (z. B. mehrlippig)
lip|pisch ‹*zu* [2]Lippe›, *aber* (↑R 102): Lippischer Wald

Lip|tau (deutscher Name einer slowak. Landschaft); **Lip|tau|er** (↑R 103); - Käse; **Lip|tau|er,** der; -s, - (ein Käse)
Lip|u|rie, die; -, ...ien ‹griech.› (*Med.* Ausscheidung von Fett durch den Harn)
liq., Liq. = Liquor; **Li|que|fak|ti|on,** die; -, -en ‹lat.› (Verflüssigung); **li|quid,** li|qui|de (flüssig; fällig; verfügbar); -e Gelder, -e Forderung; **Li|qui|da,** die; -, *Plur.* ...dä *u.* ...quiden *u.* Li|quid|laut (*Sprachw.* Fließlaut, z. B. l, r); **Li|qui|da|ti|on,** die; -, -en ([Kosten]abrechnung freier Berufe; Tötung [aus polit. Gründen]; Auflösung [eines Geschäftes]); **Li|qui|da|ti|ons|ver|hand|lung; Li|qui|da|tor,** der; -s, ...oren (jmd., der eine Liquidation durchführt); **li|qui|de** *vgl.* liquid; **li|qui|die|ren** ([eine Forderung] in Rechnung stellen; [einen Verein o. Ä.] auflösen; Sachwerte in Geld umwandeln; beseitigen, tilgen; [aus polit. Gründen] töten); **Li|qui|die|rung** (*bes. für* Beseitigung [einer Person]; Beilegung eines Konflikts); **Li|qui|di|tät,** die; - (Verhältnis der Verbindlichkeiten eines Unternehmens zu den liquiden Vermögensbestandteilen); **Li|quid|laut** *vgl.* Liquida; **Li|quor,** der; -s, ...ores (*Med.* Körperflüssigkeit; *Pharm.* flüssiges Arzneimittel; *Abk.* liq., Liq. [auf Rezepten])
[1]**Li|ra,** die; -, Lire (ital. Währungseinheit; *Abk.* L., Lit *[für Sing. u. Plur.]*); [2]**Li|ra,** die; -, - (türk. Währungseinheit [türk. Pfund]; *Abk.* TL)
Lis|beth [*auch* 'lis...] (w. Vorn.)
Lis|boa [*port.* liʒ'boa] (*port. Name für* Lissabon)
Li|se *vgl.* [2]Liese; **Li|se|lot|te** [*auch* ...'lɔtə]; Liselotte von der Pfalz; *vgl.* Lieselotte
Li|se|ne, die; -, -n ‹franz.› (*Archit.* pfeilerartiger Mauerstreifen)
Li|set|te (w. Vorn.)
Lis|mer, der; -s, - (*schweiz. mdal. für* Strickweste)
lis|peln; ich ...[e]le (↑R 16); **Lis|pel|ton** *Plur.* ...töne; **Lisp|ler**
Lis|sa|bon [*auch* ...'bɔn] (Hptst. Portugals); *vgl. auch* Lisboa; **Lis|sa|bon|ner** (↑R 103); **lis|sa|bon|nisch**
Lis|se, die; -, -n (*landsch. für* Stützleiste an Leiterwagen)
[1]**List,** die; -, -en
[2]**List** (dt. Volkswirt); *vgl.* Liszt
Lis|te, die; -, -n; die schwarze -; **lis|ten** (in Listenform bringen); gelistet; **Lis|ten‿platz, ...preis**
lis|ten|reich

Lis|ten‿ver|bin|dung *(Politik),* **...wahl**
lis|tig; lis|ti|ger|wei|se; Lis|tig|keit, die; -
Liszt [list] (ung. Komponist)
Lit = [1]Lira *Sing. u.* Lire *Plur.*
Lit. = Litera; Literatur
Li|ta|nei, die; -, -en ‹griech.› (Wechsel-, Bittgebet; eintöniges Gerede; endlose Aufzählung)
Li|tau|en[1]; **Li|tau|er**[1]; **li|tau|isch**[1]; -e Sprache; *vgl.* deutsch; **Li|tau|isch**[1], das; -[s] (Sprache); *vgl.* Deutsch; **Li|tau|i|sche**[1], das; -n; *vgl.* Deutsche, das
Li|ter[1], der, *schweiz. nur so, auch* das; -s, - ‹griech.› (1 Kubikdezimeter; *Zeichen* l); ein halber, *auch* halbes Liter, ein viertel Liter
Li|te|ra, die; -, *Plur.* -s *u.* ...rä ‹lat.› (Buchstabe; *Abk.* Lit.); **Li|te|rar|his|to|ri|ker; li|te|rar|his|to|risch; li|te|ra|risch** (schriftstellerisch, die Literatur betreffend); **Li|te|rar|kri|tik** (Verfahren zur Rekonstruktion bes. von bibl. Texten; *auch svw.* Literaturkritik); **Li|te|rat,** der; -en, -en; ↑R 126 (*oft abwertend für* Schriftsteller); **Li|te|ra|ten|tum,** das; -s; **Li|te|ra|tur,** die; -, -en; **Li|te|ra|tur‿an|ga|be** *(meist Plur.),* **...bei|la|ge, ...denk|mal** (*Plur.* ...mäler, *geh.* ...male), **...gat|tung, ...ge|schich|te; li|te|ra|tur|ge|schicht|lich; Li|te|ra|tur‿hin|weis, ...kri|tik, ...kri|ti|ker, ...kri|ti|ke|rin, ...preis, ...spra|che, ...ver|zeich|nis, ...wis|sen|schaft; li|te|ra|tur|wis|sen|schaft|lich; Li|te|ra|tur|zeit|schrift**
Li|ter‿fla|sche[1], **...leis|tung** (Leistung, die aus jeweils 1 000 cm³ Hubraum eines Kfz-Motors erzielt werden kann); **li|ter|wei|se**[1]
Li|tew|ka [li'tɛfka], die; -, ...ken ‹poln.› (*früher* ein Uniformrock)
Lit|faß|säu|le ‹nach dem Berliner Buchdrucker E. Litfaß› (Anschlagsäule)
lith... ‹griech.› (stein...); **Lith...** (Stein...); **Li|thi|a|sis,** die; -, ...iasen (*Med.* Steinbildung [in Galle, Niere usw.]); **Li|thi|um,** das; -s (chem. Element, Metall; *Zeichen* Li)
Li|tho, das; -s, -s ‹griech.› (*Kurzform für* Lithographie [als Kunstblatt]); **Li|tho|graf, Li|tho|gra|fie** usw. *eindeutschende Schreibung für* Lithograph, Lithographie usw.; **Li|tho|graph** (↑R 33), der; -en, -en (Steinzeichner); **Li|tho|gra|phie** (↑R 33), die; -, -ien

[1] [*auch* 'li...]

(Steinzeichnung; *nur Sing.:* Herstellung von Platten für den Steindruck; Kunstblatt in Steindruck); **li|tho|gra|phie|ren** (↑R 33); **li|tho|gra|phisch** (↑R 33)

Li|tho|klast, der; -en, -en; ↑R 126 ‹griech.› (*Med.* Instrument zum Zertrümmern von Blasensteinen); **Li|tho|lo|ge,** der; -n, -n; ↑R 126 (Kenner u. Erforscher der Gesteine); **Li|tho|lo|gie,** die; - (Gesteinskunde); **Li|tho|ly|se,** die; -, -n (*Med.* Auflösung von Nieren- und Harnsteinen durch Arzneien); **li|tho|phag** (*Zool.* sich in Gestein einbohrend); **Li|tho|po|ne,** die; - (lichtechte Weißfarbe); **Li|tho|sphä|re,** die; - (*Geol.* Gesteinsmantel der Erde); **Li|tho|tom,** der *od.* das; -s, -e (*Med.* chirurg. Messer zur Durchführung der Lithotomie); **Li|tho|to|mie,** die; -, ...ien ([Blasen]steinoperation); **Li|tho|trip|sie,** die; -, ...ien ([Blasen]steinzertrümmerung); **Li|tho|trip|ter,** der; -s, - (Lithoklast); **Li|thur|gik** (↑R 132), die; - (Lehre von der Verwendung u. Verarbeitung von Gesteinen u. Mineralien); *vgl. aber* Liturgik

li|to|ral ‹lat.› (*Geogr.* der Küste angehörend); **Li|to|ral,** das; -s, -e (Uferzone [Lebensraum im Wasser]); **Li|to|ra|le,** das; -s, -s ‹ital.› (Küstenland); **Li|to|ral|fau|na** ‹lat.›; **Li|to|ral|flo|ra; Li|to|ri|na,** die; -, ...nen (*Zool.* Uferschnecke); **Li|to|ri|na|meer,** das; -[e]s (Entwicklungsstufe der Ostsee mit der Litorina als Leitfossil)

Li|to|tes [...tɛs], die; -, - ‹griech.› (*Rhet.* Bejahung durch doppelte Verneinung, z. B. nicht unklug)

Lit|schi, die; -, -s ‹chin.› (pflaumengroße, erdbeerähnlich schmeckende Frucht)

Li|turg, der; -en, -en; ↑R 126 ‹griech.›; (den Gottesdienst haltender Geistlicher); **Li|tur|gie,** die; -, ...ien (die amtliche od. gewohnheitsrechtliche Form des kirchl. Gottesdienstes, bes. der am Altar gehaltene Teil); **Li|tur|gi|en|samm|lung; Li|tur|gik,** die; - (*Theol.* Theorie u. Geschichte der Liturgie); *vgl. aber* Lithurgik; **Li|tur|gin; li|tur|gisch;** -e Gefäße

Lit|ze, die; -, -n ‹lat.›

Li|u|dol|fin|ger (*svw.* Ludolfinger)

live [laif] ‹engl.› (*Rundf. u. Fernsehen* direkt, original); live senden

Li|ve [...və], der; -n, -n; ↑R 126 (Angehöriger eines finn. Volksstammes)

Live|auf|zeich|nung ['laif...] (↑R 24; *Rundfunk, Fernsehen*); **Live|mit|schnitt; Live|mu|sik**

Li|ver|pool ['livə(r)pu:l] (engl. Stadt)

Live|sen|dung ['laif...] (↑R 24) ‹engl.; dt.› (*Rundfunk, Fernsehen* Direktsendung, Originalübertragung); **Live|show** (↑R 33)

Li|via [...via] (Gemahlin des Kaisers Augustus)

li|visch [...v...] ‹*zu* Live›

Li|vi|us [...vius] (röm. Geschichtsschreiber)

Liv|land [...f...]; **Liv|län|der** (↑R 103); **liv|län|disch**

Liv|re ['li:vr(ə)] (↑R 130), der *od.* das; -[s], -[s] ‹franz.› (alte franz. Münze); 6 - (↑R 90)

Liv|ree [...v...] (↑R 130), die; -, ...een ‹franz.› (uniformartige Dienerkleidung); **liv|riert** (in Livree [gekleidet])

Li|zen|ti|at *vgl.* [1,2]Lizenziat; **Li|zenz,** die; -, -en ‹lat.› ([behördl.] Erlaubnis, Genehmigung, bes. zur Nutzung eines Patents od. zur Herausgabe einer Zeitung, Zeitschrift od. eines Buches); **Li|zenz‿aus|ga|be, ...ge|ber, ...ge|bühr;** [1]**Li|zen|zi|at,** *auch* Li|zen|ti|at, das; -[e]s, -e (akadem. Grad in der Schweiz und bei einigen kath.-theol. Fakultäten); - der Theologie; [2]**Li|zen|zi|at** *auch* Li|zen|ti|at, der; -en, -en; ↑R 126 (Inhaber des [1]Lizentiats; *Abk.* Lic. [theol.], *schweiz.* lic. phil. usw.); **li|zen|zie|ren** (Lizenz erteilen); **Li|zenz‿in|ha|ber, ...neh|mer, ...num|mer, ...spie|ler** (*Fußball*), **...trä|ger, ...ver|trag**

Ljubl|ja|na (↑R 130; Hptst. Sloweniens; *vgl.* Laibach)

Lkw, *auch* **LKW,** der; -[s], *Plur.* -s, *selten* - = Lastkraftwagen

Lla|ne|ro [lja...], der; -s, -s ‹span.› (Bewohner der Llanos); **Lla|no** ['lja:...], der; -s, -s *meist Plur.* (baumarme Hochgrassteppe in [Süd]amerika)

Lloyd [lɔyt], der; -[s] ‹nach dem Londoner Kaffeehausbesitzer E. Lloyd› (Name von Seeversicherungs-, auch von Schifffahrtsgesellschaften; Name von Zeitungen [mit Schiffsnachrichten]); Norddeutscher -, *jetzt* Hapag-Lloyd AG

lm = Lumen

Ln., Lnbd. = Leinen[ein]band

[1]**Lob,** das; -[e]s, -e *Plur. selten;* -spenden

[2]**Lob,** der; -[s], -s ‹engl.› (*Tennis* einen hohen Bogen beschreibender Ball); **lob|ben** (einen [2]Lob schlagen)

Lob|by ['lɔbi], die; -, -s ‹engl.› (Wandelhalle im [engl. od. amerik.] Parlament; *auch für* Gesamtheit der Lobbyisten); **Lob|by|is|mus,** der; - (Versuch, Gepflogenheit, Zustand der Beeinflussung von Abgeordneten durch Interessengruppen); **Lob|by|ist,** der; -en, -en; ↑R 126 (jmd., der Abgeordnete für seine Interessen zu gewinnen sucht)

Lo|be|lie [...iə], die; -, -n ‹nach dem flandrischen Botaniker M. de l'Obel› (eine Zierpflanze)

lo|ben; lo|bens‿wert, ...wür|dig; lo|be|sam (*veraltet*); **Lo|bes‿er|he|bung** (*meist Plur.; geh.*), **...hym|ne; Lob‿ge|sang, ...gier; lob|gie|rig; Lob|hu|de|lei** (*abwertend*); **lob|hu|deln** (*abwertend für* übertrieben loben); ich ...[e]le (↑R 16); gelobhudelt; zu -; **Lob|hud|ler** (*abwertend*); **löb|lich; Lob|lied**

Lo|bo|to|mie *vgl.* Leukotomie

Lob|preis; lob|prei|sen (*geh.*); du lobpreist; du lobpreistest *u.* lobpriesest; gelobpreist *u.* lobgepriesen; zu lobpreisen; lobpreise!; **Lob|prei|sung** (*geh.*); **Lob‿re|de, ...red|ner; lob|red|ne|risch; lob|sin|gen;** du lobsingst; du lobsangst (lobsangest); lobgesungen; zu lobsingen; lobsinge!; **Lob|spruch** *meist Plur.*

Lo|car|ner (↑R 103) *u.* **Lo|car|ne|se,** der; -n, -n (Bewohner von Locarno); **Lo|car|no** (Stadt am Lago Maggiore)

Loc|cum (Ort südl. von Nienburg [Weser])

Loch, das; -[e]s, Löcher; **Lö|chel|chen; lo|chen; Lo|cher** (Gerät zum Lochen; Person, die Lochkarten locht); **lö|che|rig** (*svw.* löchrig); **Lo|che|rin; lö|chern;** ich ...ere (↑R 16)

Lo|chi|en [...xiən] *Plur.* ‹griech.› (*Med.* Wochenfluss nach der Geburt)

Loch‿ka|me|ra, ...kar|te; Loch|kar|ten|ma|schi|ne; Loch|leh|re (Gerät zur Prüfung der Durchmesser von Bolzen)

Loch Ness, der; -[s] - (ein See in Schottland)

löch|rig; Loch‿sti|cke|rei, ...strei|fen; Lo|chung; Loch|zan|ge

Löck|chen; Lo|cke, die; -, -n; [1]**lo|cken** (lockig machen)

[2]**lo|cken** (anlocken)

lö|cken (mit den Füßen ausschlagen); *noch in* wider den Stachel - (*geh.*)

Lo|cken‿haar, ...kopf; lo|cken|köp|fig; Lo|cken‿pracht, ...stab, ...wi|ckel *od.* **...wick|ler**

lo|cker (*auch ugs. für* entspannt, zwanglos); locker sein, sitzen, werden; (einen Knoten, das Seil) locker lassen, machen; die Zügel locker/lockerer lassen; *vgl. aber* lockerlassen, lockermachen (↑R 38 f.); **Lo|cker|heit,** die; -; **lo|cker|las|sen** (↑R 38 f.; *ugs. für* nachgeben); er hat nicht lockergelassen; *aber* die Zügel locker/ lockerer lassen; *vgl.* locker; **lo|cker|ma|chen** (↑R 38 f.; *ugs. für* hergeben; von jmdm. erlangen); er hat viel Geld lockergemacht; *vgl.* locker; **lo|ckern;** ich ...ere (↑R 16); **Lo|cke|rung; Lo|cke|rungs‿mit|tel,** (das; zum Auflockern des Teiges), **...übung** (↑R 132)

lo|ckig

Lock‿mit|tel (das), **...ruf, ...spei|se** (*geh. für* Köder), **...spit|zel** *(abwertend);* **Lo|ckung; Lock|vo|gel; Lock|vo|gel|wer|bung**

Lock|wel|le (Lockenfrisur mit kleineren Wellen)

lo|co ['lo:ko, *auch* 'lɔko] ‹lat.› (*Kaufmannsspr.* am Ort; hier; greifbar; vorrätig); - Berlin (ab Berlin); *vgl. aber* Lokoverkehr; **lo|co ci|ta|to** (am angeführten Orte; *Abk.* l. c.)

Lod|de, die; -, -n; (*svw.* Kapelan)

Lod|del, der; -s, - (*ugs. für* Zuhälter)

lod|de|rig (*landsch. für* lotterig)

Lo|de, die; -, -n (Schössling)

Lo|den, der; -s, - (ein Wollgewebe); **Lo|den‿man|tel, ...stoff**

lo|dern; ich ...ere (↑R 16)

Lodz [lɔtʃ], *auch* Lodsch (*dt. Schreibung von* Łódź); **Łódź** [uutʃç] (Stadt in Polen)

Löf|fel, der; -s, -; **Löf|fel‿bag|ger, ...bis|kuit, ...en|te, ...kraut; löf|feln;** ich ...[e]le (↑R 16); **Löf|fel‿rei|her** (*vgl.* Löffler), **...stiel; löf|fel|wei|se; Löff|ler** (ein Stelzvogel)

Lo|fo|ten [*auch* lo'fo:...] *Plur.* (norw. Name der Lofotinseln); **Lo|fot|in|seln** *Plur.* (Gebiet u. Inselgruppe vor der Küste Nordnorwegens)

log = Logarithmus

Log, das; -s, -e ‹engl.› (Fahrgeschwindigkeitsmesser eines Schiffes)

Lo|ga|rith|men|ta|fel (↑R 132; *Math.);* **lo|ga|rith|mie|ren** ‹griech.› (mit Logarithmen rechnen; den Logarithmus berechnen); **lo|ga|rith|misch; Lo|ga|rith|mus,** der; -, ...men (math. Größe; *Zeichen* log)

Log|buch ‹engl.; dt.› (Schiffstagebuch)

Lo|ge ['lo:ʒə, *österr.* lo:ʒ], die; -, -n ['lo:ʒ(ə)n] ‹franz.› (Pförtnerraum; Theaterraum; [geheime] Gesellschaft); **Lo|ge|ment** [lɔʒə'mã:], das; -s, -s (*veraltet für* Wohnung, Bleibe); **Lo|gen‿bru|der** (Freimaurer), **...platz, ...schlie|ßer** (Beschließer [im Theater])

Log|gast, der; -[e]s, -en (Matrose zur Bedienung des Logs); **Log|ge,** die; -, -n (*seltener für* Log); **log|gen** (*Seemannsspr.* mit dem Log messen)

Log|ger, der; -s, - ‹niederl.› (*Seemannsspr.* ein Fischereifahrzeug)

Log|gia ['lɔdʒ(i)a], die; -, ...ien ['lɔdʒ(ə)n, *auch* 'lɔdʒiən] ‹ital., „Laube"› (*Archit.* halb offene Bogenhalle; nach einer Seite offener, überdeckter Raum am Haus)

Log|glas *Plur.* ...gläser (*Seemannsspr.* Sanduhr zum Loggen)

Lo|gi|cal ['lɔdʒik(ə)l], das; -s, -s ‹anglisierend› (nach den Gesetzen der Logik aufgebautes Rätsel)

Lo|gier|be|such [lo'ʒi:r...]; **lo|gie|ren** ‹franz.› ([vorübergehend] wohnen; *veraltend für* beherbergen); **Lo|gier|gast** *Plur.* ...gäste

Lo|gik, die; - ‹griech.› (Lehre von den Gesetzen, der Struktur, den Formen des Denkens; folgerichtiges Denken); **Lo|gi|ker** (Lehrer der Logik; scharfer, klarer Denker)

Lo|gis [lo'ʒi:], das; - [lo'ʒi:(s)], - [lo'ʒi:s] ‹franz.› (Wohnung, Bleibe; *Seemannsspr. veraltend* Mannschaftsraum auf Schiffen)

lo|gisch ‹griech.› (folgerichtig; denknotwendig; *ugs. für* natürlich, selbstverständlich, klar); **lo|gi|scher|wei|se; Lo|gis|mus,** der; -, ...men (*Philos.* Vernunftschluss); [1]**Lo|gis|tik,** die; - (Behandlung der logischen Gesetze mithilfe von math. Symbolen; math. Logik)

[2]**Lo|gis|tik,** die; - ‹nlat.› (militär. Nachschubwesen; *Wirtsch.* Gesamtheit aller Aktivitäten eines Unternehmens von der Beschaffung der Materialien bis zur Auslieferung von Fertigprodukten)

Lo|gis|ti|ker ‹griech.› (Vertreter der [1]Logistik); [1]**lo|gis|tisch** (die [1]Logistik betreffend)

[2]**lo|gis|tisch** ‹nlat.› (die [2]Logistik betreffend); -e Kette

Log|lei|ne *(Seemannsspr.)*

lo|go (*Schülerspr.* logisch); das ist doch -; **Lo|go,** der *od.* das; -s, -s ‹engl.› (Firmenzeichen, Signet); **Lo|go|griph,** der; *Gen.* -s *u.* -en, *Plur.* -e[n] (↑R 126) ‹griech.› (Buchstabenrätsel); **Lo|go|pä|de,** der; -n, -n; ↑R 126 (Sprachheilkundiger); **Lo|go|pä|die,** die; - (Sprachheilkunde); **Lo|go|pä|din; lo|go|pä|disch; Lo|gor|rhö**[1], **Lo|gor|rhöe** [...'rø:], die; -, ...rrhöen (*Med.* krankhafte Geschwätzigkeit); **Lo|gos,** der; -, ...goi [...gɔy] *Plur. selten* (sinnvolle Rede; Vernunft; Wort)

...loh (*in Ortsnamen* Gelände mit strauchartigem Baumbewuchs, z. B. Gütersloh)

Loh‿bei|ze *(Gerberei),* **...blü|te** (Schleimpilz); [1]**Lo|he,** die; -, -n (Gerbrinde)

[2]**Lo|he,** die; -, -n (*geh. für* Glut, Flamme); **lo|hen** *(geh.)*

Lo|hen|grin (altd. Sagen- u. Epengestalt)

loh|gar (mit [1]Lohe gegerbt); **Loh|ger|ber**

Lohn, der; -[e]s, Löhne; **lohn|ab|hän|gig; Lohn|ab|hän|gi|ge,** der *u.* die; -n, -n (↑R 5 ff.); **Lohn‿ab|zug, ...an|pas|sung, ...aus|fall, ...aus|gleich, ...aus|zah|lung, ...buch|hal|ter, ...buch|hal|tung, ...bü|ro, ...emp|fän|ger; loh|nen;** es lohnt den Einsatz; es lohnt die, der Mühe nicht; der Einsatz lohnt [sich]; **löh|nen** (Lohn auszahlen); **loh|nens|wert; Lohn‿er|hö|hung, ...for|de|rung, ...fort|zah|lung** (bei Krankheit), **...grup|pe; lohn|in|ten|siv; Lohn‿kür|zung, ...ne|ben|kos|ten, ...ni|veau, ...pfän|dung; Lohn-Preis-Spi|ra|le** (↑R 28); **Lohn‿ska|la, ...steu|er** (die); **Lohn|steu|er‿jah|res|aus|gleich, ...kar|te; Lohn|stopp; Lohn|sum|men|steu|er,** die; **Lohn|tü|te; Löh|nung; Lohn‿ver|hand|lung, ...ver|zicht, ...zet|tel**

Loh|rin|de (*zu* [1]Lohe)

Loi|pe ['lɔypə], die; -, -n ‹norw.› (*Skisport* Langlaufbahn, -spur); **Loi|pen|be|trei|ber**

Loire [lo̯a:r], die; - (franz. Fluss)

Lok, die; -, -s (*Kurzform von* Lokomotive)

lo|kal ‹lat.› (örtlich; örtlich beschränkt); **Lo|kal,** das; -[e]s, -e (Örtlichkeit; [Gast]wirtschaft); **Lo|kal‿an|äs|the|sie** (*Med.* örtl. Betäubung), **...au|gen|schein** (*österr. für* Lokaltermin), **...bahn, ...be|richt, ...der|by** *(Sport);* **Lo|ka|le,** das; -n (*in Zeitungen* Nachrichten aus dem Ort); **Lo|ka|li|sa|ti|on,** die; -, -en (örtl. Beschränkung, Ortsbestimmung, -zuordnung); **lo|ka|li|sie|ren; Lo|ka|li|sie|rung** (*svw.* Lokalisation); **Lo|ka|li|tät,** die; -, -en (Örtlichkeit; Raum; *scherzh. für* Lokal); **Lo|kal‿ko|lo|rit, ...ma|ta|dor** (ört-

[1] *Vgl. die Anmerkung zu* „Diarrhö, Diarrhöe".

liche Berühmtheit), **...pat|ri|o|tis|mus, ...pres|se, ...re|dak|ti|on, ...re|por|ter, ...re|por|te|rin, ...satz** (*Sprachw.* Umstandssatz des Ortes), **...sei|te, ...ter|min** (*Rechtsspr.*), **...zei|tung; Lo|ka|ti|on,** die; -, -en (Bohrstelle [bei der Erdölförderung]; moderne Wohnsiedlung); **Lo|ka|tiv** [*auch* ...'ti:f], der; -s, -e [...və] (*Sprachw.* Ortsfall); **Lo|ka|tor,** der; -s, ...oren (*im MA.* [Kolonial]land verteilender Ritter)

Lok|füh|rer (*Kurzform von* Lokomotivführer)

Lo|ki (germ. Gott)

lo|ko *vgl.* loco; **Lo|ko|ge|schäft** (*Kaufmannsspr.* zur sofortigen Erfüllung abgeschlossenes Geschäft); **Lo|ko|mo|ti|on,** die; -, -en (*Med.* Gang[art], Fortbewegung); **Lo|ko|mo|ti|ve** [...və, *auch* ...fə], die; -, -n ⟨engl.⟩ (*Kurzform* Lok); **Lo|ko|mo|tiv‿füh|rer** (*Kurzform* Lokführer), **...schup|pen; lo|ko|mo|to|risch** ⟨lat.⟩ (*Med.* die Fortbewegung, den Gang betreffend); **Lo|ko‿ver|kehr, ...wa|re** (*Kaufmannsspr.* sofort lieferbare Ware); **Lo|kus,** der; *Gen.* - *u.* -ses, *Plur.* - *u.* -se (*ugs. für* [1]Abort)

Lo|la (w. Vorn.)

Lolch, der; -[e]s, -e ⟨lat.⟩ (*Bot.* eine Grasart)

Lo|li|ta, die; -, -s ⟨nach einer Romanfigur⟩ (Kindfrau)

Lol|li, der; -s, -s (*bes. nordd. ugs. für* Lutscher)

Lom|bard [*auch* ...'bart], der *od.* das; -[e]s, -e (*Bankw.* Kredit gegen Verpfändung beweglicher Sachen); **Lom|bar|de,** der; -n, -n; ↑R 126 (Bewohner der Lombardei); **Lom|bar|dei,** die; - (ital. Region); **Lom|bard|ge|schäft** [*auch* ...'bart...] (*Bankw.*); **lom|bar|die|ren** (bewegliche Sachen beleihen); **lom|bar|disch** (aus der Lombardei), *aber* (↑R 102): die Lombardische Tiefebene; **Lom|bard‿lis|te** [*auch* ...'bart...] (*Bankw.*), **...satz, ...zins|fuß**

Lom|ber, das; -s ⟨franz.⟩ (ein Kartenspiel); **Lom|ber|spiel,** das; -[e]s

Lo|mé ['lo:me] (Hptst. von Togo)

Lom|matzsch [...matʃ] (Stadt in Sachsen); **Lom|matz|scher Pfle|ge,** die; - - (Ebene nordwestl. von Meißen)

Lo|mo|nos|sow [...ɔf] (russ. Gelehrter); **Lo|mo|nos|sow|uni|ver|si|tät** (↑R 95 *u.* 132), die; - (in Moskau)

Lon|don (Hptst. von Großbritannien); **Lon|do|ner** (↑R 103)

Long|drink ⟨engl.⟩ (mit Soda, Eiswasser o. Ä. verlängerter Drink); **Long|drink|glas** *Plur.* ...gläser

Lon|ge ['lɔ̃:ʒə], die; -, -n ⟨franz.⟩ (*Reiten* Laufleine für Pferde; *Akrobatik* Sicherheitsleine); **lon|gie|ren** [lɔ̃'ʒi:...] (*Reiten* ein Pferd an der Longe laufen lassen)

Lon|gi|met|rie (↑R 130), die; - ⟨lat.; griech.⟩ (*Physik* Längenmessung)

lon|gi|tu|di|nal ⟨lat.⟩ (in der Längsrichtung); **Lon|gi|tu|di|nal‿schwin|gung** (*Physik* Längsschwingung), **...wel|le**

long|line [...lain] ⟨engl.⟩ (*Tennis* an der Seitenlinie entlang); den Ball - spielen; **Long|line,** der; -[s], -s (entlang der Seitenlinie gespielter Ball)

Long|sel|ler, der; -s, - ⟨anglisierend⟩ (lange zu den Bestsellern gehörendes Buch)

Lo|ni (w. Vorn.)

Löns [*auch* lœns] (dt. Schriftsteller)

Look [luk], der; -s, -s ⟨engl.⟩ (bestimmtes Aussehen; Moderichtung)

Loo|ping ['lu:...], der, *auch* das; -s, -s ⟨engl.⟩ (*Flugw.* senkrechter Schleifenflug, Überschlagrolle)

Loos (österr. Architekt)

Lo|pe de Ve|ga [- - 've:ga] (span. Dichter)

Lor|bass, der; -es, -e ⟨lit.⟩ (*nordostd. für* Lümmel, Taugenichts)

Lor|beer, der; -s, -en ⟨lat.⟩ (ein Baum; ein Gewürz); **Lor|beer‿baum, ...blatt; lor|beer|grün; Lor|beer‿kranz, ...zweig**

Lor|chel, die; -, -n (ein Pilz)

Lor|chen (w. Vorn.)

Lord, der; -s, -s ⟨engl.⟩ (hoher engl. Adelstitel); **Lord|kanz|ler** (höchster engl. Staatsbeamter); **Lord May|or** [- 'me:ə(r)], der; - -s, - -s (Titel der Oberbürgermeister mehrerer engl. Großstädte)

Lor|do|se, die; -, -n ⟨griech.⟩ (*Med.* Rückgratverkrümmung nach vorn)

Lord|ship [...ʃip], die; - ⟨engl.⟩ (Lordschaft; Würde od. Herrschaft eines Lords)

[1]Lo|re, die; -, -n ⟨engl.⟩ (offener Eisenbahngüterwagen, Feldbahnwagen)

[2]Lo|re (w. Vorn.)

Lo|re|ley [...'lai, *auch* 'lo:...], *auch* Lo|re|lei [*auch* 'lo:...], die; - (Rheinnixe der dt. Sage; Felsen am rechten Rheinufer bei St. Goarshausen)

Lo|renz (m. Vorn.); **Lo|renz|strom** (↑R 105); *vgl.* Sankt-Lorenz-Strom

Lo|re|to (Wallfahrtsort in Italien)

Lo|ret|to|hö|he, die; - ⟨franz.⟩ (Anhöhe bei Arras)

Lorg|net|te [lɔr'njɛtə] (↑R 130), die; -, -n ⟨franz.⟩ (Stielbrille); **lorg|net|tie|ren** [lɔrnjɛ'ti:...] *früher für* durch die Lorgnette betrachten; scharf mustern); **Lorg|non** [lɔr'njɔ̃:], das; -s, -s (Stieleinglas, -brille)

[1]Lo|ri, der; -s, -s ⟨karib.-span.⟩ (ein Papagei)

[2]Lo|ri, der; -s, -s ⟨niederl.⟩ (ein schwanzloser Halbaffe)

Lork, der; -[e]s, Lörke (*nordd. für* Kröte)

Lor|ke, die; - (*landsch. für* dünner, schlechter Kaffee)

Lo|ro|kon|to ⟨ital.⟩ (das bei einer Bank geführte Kontokorrentkonto einer anderen Bank)

Lort|zing (dt. Komponist)

los; *Adj., nur prädikativ* (*vgl. aber* lose): der Knopf ist los (abgetrennt); der Hund ist [von der Kette] los; los und ledig sein; *ugs.* er wird die Sorgen bald los sein (*selten* haben); auf dem Fest ist nichts los gewesen; *Adverb:* los!; los (weg) von Rom; *vgl.* losbinden (er bindet los, losgebunden, loszubinden), losfahren usw.

...los (z. B. arbeitslos)

Los, das; -es, -e; das große Los (↑R 108)

Los An|ge|les [lɔs 'ɛndʒələs] (größte Stadt Kaliforniens, USA)

lös|bar; Lös|bar|keit, die; -

los|be|kom|men; ich habe den Deckel nicht -

los|bin|den; losgebunden

los|brau|sen (*ugs.*)

los|bre|chen; ein Sturm brach los

Lösch‿ap|pa|rat, ...ar|beit (*meist Plur.*); **lösch|bar; Lösch‿blatt, ...boot; [1]lö|schen** (einen Brand ersticken); du löschst, er löscht; du löschtest; gelöscht; lösch[e]!; **[2]lö|schen** (*nur noch geh. für* erlöschen); du lischst; er lischt; du loschst; du löschest; geloschen; lisch!

[3]lö|schen ⟨*zu* los⟩ (*Seemannsspr.* ausladen); du löschst; du löschtest; gelöscht; lösch[e]!

Lö|scher; Lösch‿fahr|zeug, ...ge|rät, ...kalk, ...pa|pier, ...tas|te; Lö|schung; Lösch‿was|ser (das; -s), **...zug**

lo|se; das lose Blatt; lose Ware (nicht in Originalpackung, sondern einzeln); eine lose Zunge haben (leichtfertig reden); die Zügel lose (locker) halten; der Knopf ist lose, *landsch. auch:* los (locker); *vgl. aber* los

Lo|se, die; -n, -n (*Seemannsspr.* schlaffes Tau[stück])

Lo|se|blatt|aus|ga|be (↑R 28); der Lose[n]blattausgabe; die Lose[n]blattausgaben

Lö|se|geld

los|ei|sen (*ugs. für* mit Mühe frei machen, abspenstig machen); er eis|te los; sich -; ich habe mich endlich von ihnen losgeeist

Lö|se|mit|tel, das

lo|sen (das Los ziehen); du lost; er los|te; gelost; los[e]!

lö|sen (*auch für* befreien; *Bergmannsspr.* entwässern, mit frischer Luft beschicken); du löst; er lös|te; gelöst; lös[e]!

Los|ent|scheid

los|fah|ren; er ist losgefahren

los|ge|hen (*ugs. auch für* anfangen); der Streit ist losgegangen

los|ha|ben (*ugs. für* etwas verstehen; mit Leichtigkeit können); sie hat in ihrem Beruf viel losgehabt

los|heu|len (*ugs. auch für* zu weinen beginnen); die Sirene heulte los

...lo|sig|keit (z. B. Regellosigkeit, die; -, -en)

Los|kauf; los|kau|fen; die Gefangenen wurden losgekauft

los|kom|men; er ist von diesem Gedanken nicht losgekommen

los|krie|gen (*ugs.*); den Deckel nicht -

los|las|sen; sie hat den Hund [von der Kette] losgelassen

los|lau|fen; er ist losgelaufen

los|le|gen (*ugs. für* ungestüm beginnen); sie hat ordentlich losgelegt (z. B. energisch geredet)

lös|lich; Lös|lich|keit, die; -

los|lö|sen; sich -; er hat die Briefmarke losgelöst; du hast dich von diesen Anschauungen losgelöst; **Los|lö|sung**

los|ma|chen; er hat das Brett losgemacht; mach los! (*ugs. für* beeile dich!)

los|mar|schie|ren; er ist sofort losmarschiert

Los|num|mer

los|rei|ßen; du hast dich losgerissen

Löss, *auch* **Löß**, der; -es, -e (*Geol.* kalkhaltige Ablagerung des Pleistozäns)

los|sa|gen; sich von etwas -; du hast dich von ihm losgesagt; **Los|sa|gung**

Löss|bo|den, *auch* **Löß|bo|den**

los|schi|cken; er hat den Trupp losgeschickt

los|schie|ßen (*ugs.*); sie ist auf mich losgeschossen

los|schla|gen; er hat das Brett losgeschlagen; die Feinde haben losgeschlagen (mit dem Kampf begonnen)

los|schrau|ben; sie hat den Griff losgeschraubt

los sein *vgl.* los

lös|sig, *auch* **lö|ßig** (*Geol.*); **Löss|kin|del**, *auch* **Löß|kin|del**, das; -s, - (Konkretion im Löss); **Löss|land|schaft**, *auch* **Löß|land|schaft**

Löß|nitz, die; - (Landschaft nordwestl. von Dresden)

los|spre|chen (von Schuld); er hat ihn losgesprochen; **Los|spre|chung** (*für* Absolution)

Löss|schicht (↑R 136), *auch* **Löß|schicht** (*Geol.*)

los|steu|ern; auf ein Ziel -

los|stür|zen (*ugs.*); er ist losgestürzt, als ...

Lost, der; -[e]s (Deckname für einen chem. Kampfstoff)

Los|tag (nach dem Volksglauben für die Wetterprophezeiung bedeutsamer Tag); **Los|trom|mel**;

[1]**Lo|sung** (Wahl-, Leitspruch; Erkennungswort)

[2]**Lo|sung** (*Jägerspr.* Kot des Wildes u. des Hundes; *Kaufmannsspr.* Tageseinnahme [in Kaufhäusern]); **Lö|sung; Lö|sungs‿mit|tel** (das), **...ver|such**

Lo|sungs|wort *Plur.* ...worte

Los-von-Rom-Be|we|gung, die; - (↑R 28)

los|wer|den; etwas loswerden (von etwas befreit werden; *ugs. für* etwas verkaufen); sie ist ihn glücklich losgeworden; ..., damit du alle Sorgen loswirst; sie muss sehen, wie sie die Ware loswird

los|zie|hen (*ugs. für* sich zu einer [vergnüglichen] Unternehmung aufmachen); er ist losgezogen; gegen jmdn. losziehen (*ugs. für* gehässig von ihm reden)

[1]**Lot**, das; -[e]s, -e (metall. Bindemittel; Vorrichtung zum Messen der Wassertiefe u. zur Bestimmung der Senkrechten; *früher* [Münz]gewicht, Hohlmaß); 3 - Kaffee (↑R 90)

[2]**Lot**, das; -[s], -s ‹engl.› (ein Posten Ware, bes. bei Briefmarken)

[3]**Lot** (bibl. m. Eigenn.)

lo|ten (senkrechte Richtung bestimmen; Wassertiefe messen)

lö|ten (durch Lötmetall verbinden); **Löt‿fu|ge, ...ge|rät**

Lo|thar; ↑R 92 (m. Vorn.)

Loth|rin|gen; Loth|rin|ger (↑R 103); **loth|rin|gisch**

...lö|tig (z. B. sechzehnlötig)

Lo|ti|on [*auch* engl. 'lo:ʃən], die; -, *Plur.* -en, *bei engl. Aussprache* -s ‹engl.› (flüssiges Reinigungs-, Pflegemittel für die Haut)

Löt‿kol|ben, ...lam|pe, ...me|tall

Lo|to|pha|ge, der; -n, -n (↑R 126) ‹griech., „Lotosesser"› (Angehöriger eines sagenhaften Volkes in Homers Odyssee); **Lo|tos**, der; -, - (eine Seerose); **Lo|tos‿blu|me, ...blü|te, ...sitz**

lot|recht; Lot|rech|te, die; -n, -n; vier -[n]

Löt|rohr; Löt|rohr|ana|ly|se (↑R 132; ein chemisches Prüfverfahren)

Lötsch|berg‿bahn (die; -), **...tun|nel** (der; -s); ↑R 105; **Löt|schen|pass**, der; -es

Lot|se, der; -n, -n (↑R 126) ‹engl.›; **lot|sen**; du lotst; gelotst; **Lot|sen‿boot, ...dienst, ...fisch, ...sta|ti|on**

Löt|stel|le

Lott|chen, Lot|te, Lot|ti (w. Vorn.)

Lot|ter, der; -s, - (*noch landsch. für* Herumtreiber, Faulenzer); **Lot|ter‿bett** (*veraltet, noch scherzh. für* Sofa), **...bu|be** (*abwertend*); **Lot|te|rei** (*abwertend*)

Lot|te|rie, die; -, ...ien ‹niederl.› (Glücksspiel, Verlosung); **Lot|te|rie‿ein|neh|mer, ...los, ...spiel**

lot|te|rig, lott|rig (*ugs. für* unordentlich); **Lot|te|rig|keit**, die; - (*ugs.*); **Lot|ter|le|ben**, das; -s (*abwertend*); **lot|tern** (*landsch. für* ein Lotterleben führen; *schweiz. für* lose sein, aus den Fugen gehen); ich ...ere (↑R 16); **Lot|ter|wirt|schaft**, die; - (*abwertend*)

Lot|ti *vgl.* Lotte

Lot|to, das; -s, -s ‹ital.› (Zahlenlotterie; Gesellschaftsspiel); **Lot|to‿an|nah|me|stel|le** (↑R 24), **...fee** (*scherzh. für* Fernsehansagerin bei der Ziehung der Lottozahlen), **...ge|winn, ...kol|lek|tur** (*österr. für* Geschäftsstelle für das Lottospiel), **...schein, ...spiel, ...zah|len** (*Plur.*), **...zet|tel**

lott|rig *vgl.* lotterig

Lo|tung

Lö|tung

Lo|tus, der; -, - ‹griech.› (Hornklee; *auch svw.* Lotos)

lot|wei|se

Löt|zinn

[1]**Lou|is** ['lu:i] (m. Vorn.); [2]**Lou|is**, der; - ['lu:i(s)], - ['lu:is] (*ugs. für* Zuhälter); **Lou|is|dor** [lu̯i'do:r], der; -s, -e (eine alte franz. Münze); 6 - (↑R 90)

Lou|i|si|a|na [lu̯i'zia:na, *auch* ...'zi̯ɛnə] (Staat der USA; *Abk.* La.)

Lou|is-qua|torze [lu̯ika'tɔrs], das; - ‹franz.› (Stil zur Zeit Ludwigs XIV.); **Lou|is-quinze** [lu̯i'kɛ̃(:)z], das; - (Stil zur Zeit Ludwigs XV.); **Lou|is-seize** [lu̯i'sɛ:s], das; - (Stil zur Zeit Ludwigs XVI.)

Lounge [laundʒ], die; -, -s [...dʒiz] ‹engl.› ([Hotel]halle)
Lourdes [lurd] (franz. Wallfahrtsort); **Lourdes|grot|te**
Louv|re ['lu:vr(ə)] (↑R 130), der; -[s] (ein Museum in Paris)
Love|sto|ry ['lav‚stɔ:ri] ‹engl.› (Liebesgeschichte)
Lö|we, der; -n, -n (↑R 126) ‹griech.›; **Lö|wen‿an|teil** (*ugs. für* Hauptanteil), **...bän|di|ger, ...bräu; Lö|wen|herz** (m. Eigenn.); **Lö|wen‿jagd, ...kä|fig, ...mäh|ne, ...maul** (das; -[e]s; eine Gartenblume), **...mäul|chen** (*svw.* Löwenmaul), **...mut; lö|wen|stark; Lö|wen|zahn,** der; -[e]s (eine Wiesenblume); **Lö|win**
lo|yal [loa'ja:l] ‹franz.› (redlich, [regierungs]treu); **Lo|ya|li|tät** [loajali...], die; -, -en; **Lo|ya|li|täts|er|klä|rung**
Lo|yo|la [lo'jo:la]; Ignatius von -
LP = Läuten u. Pfeifen (Eisenbahnzeichen); Langspielplatte
LPG = landwirtschaftliche Produktionsgenossenschaft *(ehem. in der DDR)*
Lr = Lawrencium
LRS = Lese-Rechtschreib-Schwäche
LSD = Lysergsäurediäthylamid (ein Rauschgift)
LSG = Landessozialgericht; Landschaftsschutzgebiet
lt. = ²laut
Lt. = Leutnant
Ltd. = limited
Ltn. = Leutnant
Lu = *chem. Zeichen für* Lutetium
Lu|an|da (Hptst. von Angola)
Lu|ba, *auch* Ballu|ba, der; -[s], -[s] (Angehöriger eines Bantustammes in Zaire)
Lü|beck (Hafenstadt an der Ostsee); **Lü|be|cker** (↑R 103); die - Bucht; **lü|be|ckisch, lü|bisch** (von Lübeck); -e Währung
Lüb|ke (zweiter dt. Bundespräsident)
Luch, die; -, Lüche ['ly:çə] *od.* das; -[e]s, -e (*landsch. für* Sumpf)
Luchs, der; -es, -e (ein Raubtier); **Luchs|au|ge** *(auch ugs. übertr.)*; **luchs|äu|gig; luch|sen** (*ugs. für* sehr genau aufpassen); du luchst
Lucht, die; -, -en ‹niederl.› (*nordd. für* Dachboden)
Lu|cia usw. *vgl.* Luzia usw.; *vgl. auch* Santa Lucia; **Lu|ci|an** *vgl.* Lukian; **Lu|ci|a|ner** (Einwohner von St. Lucia); **lu|ci|a|nisch; Lu|ci|us** [...tsius] (röm. m. Vorn.; *Abk.* L.)
Lü|cke, die; -, -n; **Lü|cken|bü|ßer** (*ugs. für* Ersatzmann); **lü|cken|haft; Lü|cken|haf|tig|keit,** die; -; **lü|cken|los; Lü|cken|lo|sig|keit,** die; -; **Lü|cken|test** *(Psych.)*; **lu|ckig** (*Bergmannsspr.* großporig); -es Gestein
Luc|re|tia (↑R 130) *vgl.* Lukretia; **Luc|re|ti|us,** *eindeutschend auch* Luk|rez (altröm. Dichter); **Luc|re|zia** *vgl.* Lukretia
Lu|cul|lus (röm. Feldherr); *vgl.* Lukullus
Lu|de, der; -n, -n; ↑R 126 (*Gaunerspr.* Zuhälter)
Lu|der, das; -s, - (*Jägerspr.* Köder, Aas; *auch* Schimpfwort); **Lu|derer** (*veraltet für* liederlicher Mensch); **lu|der|haft** *(veraltet)*; **Lu|der|jan** (*svw.* Liederjan); **Lu|der|le|ben,** das; -s; **lu|der|mä|ßig** (*landsch. für* sehr, überaus); **lu|dern** (*veraltet für* liederlich leben); ich ...ere (↑R 16)
Lud|ger (m. Vorn.)
Lud|mil|la (w. Vorn.)
Lu|dolf (m. Vorn.)
Lu|dol|fin|ger (Angehöriger eines mittelalterl. dt. Herrschergeschlechtes)
lu|dolf|sche Zahl, die; -n -, *auch* **Lu|dolf|zahl** (↑R 95), die; - ‹nach dem Mathematiker Ludolf van Ceulen ['kø:lən]› (*selten für* die Zahl π [Pi])
Lu|do|wi|ka (w. Vorn.)
Lu|do|win|ger (Angehöriger eines thüring. Landgrafengeschlechtes)
Lud|wig (m. Vorn.); **Lud|wi|ga** (w. Vorn.); **Lud|wigs|burg** (Stadt nördl. von Stuttgart); **Lud|wigs|ha|fen am Rhein** (Stadt in Rheinland-Pfalz)
Lu|es, die; - ‹lat.› (*Med.* Syphilis); **lu|e|tisch,** lu|isch (syphilitisch)
Luf|fa, die; -, -s ‹arab.› (eine kürbisartige Pflanze); **Luf|fa|schwamm** (schwammartige Frucht der Luffa)
Luft, die; -, Lüfte; **Luft‿ab|wehr, ...alarm** (↑R 132), **...an|griff, ...auf|klä|rung, ...auf|nah|me, ...auf|sicht, ...bad, ...bal|lon, ...be|we|gung** *(Meteor.)*, **...bild, ...bla|se; Luft-Bo|den-Ra|ke|te; Luft|brü|cke; Lüft|chen; luft|dicht;** - verschließen; **Luft‿dich|te, ...druck** (der; -[e]s); **luft|durch|läs|sig; Luft‿elek|tri|zi|tät** (↑R 132), **...em|bo|lie; lüf|ten; Lüf|ter; Luft|fahrt,** die; -, *Plur.* (*für* Fahrten durch die Luft:) -en; **Luft|fahrt‿for|schung, ...in|dust|rie, ...me|di|zin; Luft‿fahr|zeug, ...feuch|te** (die; -), **...feuch|tig|keit** (die; -), **...fil|ter, ...flot|te, ...fracht; luft|ge|kühlt;** -er Motor; **luft|ge|schützt;** ein -er Ort; **luft|ge|trock|net;** -e Wurst; **Luft‿ge|wehr, ...ha|fen** (*vgl.* ²Hafen), **...han|sa** (*für* Deutsche Lufthansa AG), **...hei|zung, ...ho|heit** (die; -), **...hül|le; luf|tig; Luf|tig|keit,** die; -; **Luf|ti|kus,** der; -[ses], -se (*scherzh. für* oberflächlicher Mensch); **Luft‿kampf, ...kis|sen; Luft|kis|sen|fahr|zeug; Luft‿klap|pe** (*für* Ventil), **...kor|ri|dor, ...krank|heit, ...krieg, ...küh|lung** (die; -), **...kur|ort** (der; -[e]s, ...orte); **Luft|lan|de|trup|pe** (für die Landung aus der Luft bes. ausgebildete u. ausgerüstete militär. Einheit); **luft|leer; Lüft|lein; Luft|li|nie; Lüftl|ma|le|rei** (Fassadenmalerei in Bayern); **Luft‿loch, ...man|gel** (der; -s), **...ma|sche, ...mat|rat|ze, ...mi|ne, ...pi|rat, ...po|li|zist, ...pols|ter, ...post** (die; -), **...pum|pe, ...qua|li|tät** (die; -), **...raum, ...röh|re, ...sack** *(Zool.)*, **...schacht, ...schau|kel** (*landsch. für* Schiffsschaukel), **...schicht, ...schiff, ...schif|fer; Luft|schiff|fahrt** (↑R 136), die; -, *Plur.* (*für* Fahrten mit dem Luftschiff:) -en; **Luft‿schlacht, ...schlan|ge** *(meist Plur.)*, **...schloss, ...schrau|be** (*für* Propeller), **...schutz; Luft|schutz‿bun|ker, ...kel|ler, ...raum; Luft|sper|re; Luft|sperr|ge|biet; Luft‿spie|ge|lung** *od.* **...spieg|lung, ...sprung, ...streit|kräf|te** *(Plur.)*, **...ta|xi, ...tem|pe|ra|tur; luft|tüch|tig;** ein -es Flugzeug; **Lüf|tung; Lüf|tungs|klap|pe; Luft‿ver|än|de|rung, ...ver|kehr; Luft|ver|kehrs|ge|sell|schaft; Luft‿ver|schmut|zung, ...waf|fe, ...wech|sel, ...weg** (auf dem -[e]), **...wi|der|stand, ...wir|bel, ...wur|zel, ...zu|fuhr** (die; -), **...zug**
¹Lug, der; -[e]s (Lüge); [mit] Lug und Trug
²Lug, der; -s, -e (*landsch. für* Ausguck)
Lu|ga|ner (↑R 103); **Lu|ga|ner See,** der; - -s; **Lu|ga|ne|se,** der; -n, -n; ↑R 126 (Luganer); **lu|ga|ne|sisch; Lu|ga|no** (Stadt in der Schweiz)
Lug|aus, der; -, - (*landsch., auch geh. für* Aussichtsturm)
Lü|ge, die; -, -n; jmdn. Lügen strafen (der Unwahrheit überführen)
lu|gen (*landsch. für* ausschauen, spähen)
lü|gen; du logst; du lögest; gelogen; lüg[e]!; **Lü|gen|bold,** der; -[e]s, -e *(abwertend)*; **Lü|gen|de|tek|tor** (Gerät, mit dem unwillkürliche körperliche Reaktionen eines Befragten gemessen werden

können); **Lü|gen‿dich|tung, ...ge|bäu|de, ...ge|schich|te, ...ge|spinst, ...ge|we|be; lü|gen|haft; Lü|gen|haf|tig|keit,** die; -; **Lü|gen|maul** (*ugs. für* Lügner); **Lü|ge|rei** (*ugs.*)
Lug|ins|land, der; -[e]s, -e (*veraltend für* Wachtturm, Aussichtsturm)
Lüg|ner; Lüg|ne|rin; lüg|ne|risch
lu|isch *vgl.* luetisch
Lu|is|chen, Lu|i|se (w. Vorn.)
Lu|it|gard (w. Vorn.); **Lu|it|ger** (m. Vorn.); **Lu|it|pold** (m. Vorn.)
Luk, das; -[e]s, -e; *vgl.* Luke
Lu|kar|ne, die; -, -n ‹franz.› (*landsch. für* Dachfenster, -luke)
Lu|kas (Evangelist); Evangelium Lucä [...tsɛ:] (des Lukas)
Lu|ke, die; -, -n (kleines Dach- od. Kellerfenster; Öffnung im Deck od. in der Wand des Schiffes)
Lu|ki|an (griech. Satiriker)
Luk|ma|ni|er [...i̯ər], der; -s, *auch* **Luk|ma|ni|er|pass,** der; -es (ein schweiz. Alpenpass)
luk|ra|tiv (↑R 130) ‹lat.› (Gewinn bringend)
Luk|re|tia, Luc|re|tia, Luc|re|zia (↑R 130; w. Vorn.); **Luk|rez** *vgl.* Lucretius; **Luk|re|zia** (w. Vorn.)
lu|kul|lisch (üppig); -es Mahl; **Lu|kul|lus,** der; -, -se (Schlemmer [nach Art des Lucullus])
Lu|latsch, der; -[e]s, -e (*ugs. für* langer, schlaksiger Mann)
Lul|le, die; -, -n (*ugs. für* Zigarette)
lul|len (*volkstüml. für* leise singen); das Kind in den Schlaf -
Lul|ler (*südd., österr. für* Schnuller)
Lu|lu [*auch* lu'lu:] (w. Vorn.)
Lum|ba|go, die; - ‹lat.› (*Med.* Schmerzen in der Lendengegend; Hexenschuss); **lum|bal** (die Lenden[gegend] betreffend); **Lum|bal‿an|äs|the|sie, ...punk|ti|on**
lum|be|cken ‹nach dem dt. Erfinder E. Lumbeck› (Bücher durch das Aneinanderkleben der einzelnen Blätter binden); gelumbeckt
Lum|ber|jack ['lambə(r)dʒɛk], der; -s, -s ‹engl.› (eine Art Jacke)
Lu|men, das; -s, *Plur.* - *u.* ...mina ‹lat., „Licht"› (*Physik* Einheit des Lichtstromes [*Zeichen* lm]; *Biol., Med.* innerer Durchmesser [lichte Weite] od. Hohlraum von Zellen od. Organen); **Lu|mi|nes|zenz,** die; -, -en (*Physik* jede Lichterscheinung, die nicht durch erhöhte Temperatur bewirkt ist); **lu|mi|nes|zie|ren**
Lum|me, die; -, -n ‹nord.› (ein arktischer Seevogel)
Lum|mel, der; -s, - (*südd. für* Lendenfleisch, -braten)
Lüm|mel, der; -s, -; **Lüm|me|lei; lüm|mel|haft; lüm|meln,** sich (*ugs.*); ich ...[e]le mich (↑R 16)
Lump, der; -en, -en; ↑R 126 (schlechter Mensch); **Lum|pa|zi|us,** der; -, -se (*scherzh. veraltend für* Lump); **Lum|pa|zi|va|ga|bun|dus** [...v...], der; -, *Plur.* -se *u.* ...di (Landstreicher); **lum|pen** (*ugs. für* liederlich leben); sich nicht - lassen (*ugs. für* freigebig sein; Geld ausgeben); **Lum|pen,** der; -s, - (Lappen); **Lum|pen‿ge|sin|del, ...händ|ler** (*ugs. für* Altwarenhändler), **...kerl, ...pack** (das), **...pro|le|ta|ri|at** (*marxist. Theorie*), **...sack, ...samm|ler** (*auch übertr. scherzh. für* letzte [Straßen]bahn, letzter Omnibus in der Nacht); **Lum|pe|rei; lum|pig**
Lu|na ‹lat.› (röm. Mondgöttin; *geh. für* Mond; Name sowjetischer unbemannter Mondsonden); **lu|nar** (den Mond betreffend, Mond...); **lu|na|risch** (*älter für* lunar); **Lu|na|ri|um,** das; -s, ...ien [...i̯ən] (Gerät zur Veranschaulichung der Mondbewegung); **Lu|na|tis|mus,** der; - (*Med.* Mondsüchtigkeit)
Lunch [lantʃ], der; *Gen.* -[e]s *od.* -, *Plur.* -[e]s *od.* -e ‹engl.› (leichte Mittagsmahlzeit [in angelsächsischen Ländern]); **lun|chen** ['lantʃ...]; du lunchst; **Lunch‿pa|ket, ...zeit**
[1]**Lund** (Stadt in Schweden)
[2]**Lund,** der; -[e]s, -e (Papageitaucher, ein Vogel)
Lü|ne|burg (Stadt am Nordrand der Lüneburger Heide); **Lü|ne|bur|ger Hei|de,** die; - -; ↑R 103 (Teil des Norddeutschen Tieflandes)
Lü|net|te, die; -, -n ‹franz.› (*Technik* Stütze für lange Werkstücke auf der Drehbank; *Archit.* Bogenfeld, Stichkappe; *früher* eine Grundrissform im Festungsbau)
Lun|ge, die; -, -n; die eiserne -; **Lun|gen‿bläs|chen, ...bra|ten** (*österr. für* Lendenbraten), **...ent|zün|dung, ...fisch** (*Zool.*), **...flü|gel, ...ha|schee; lun|gen|krank; Lun|gen|krebs; lun|gen|lei|dend; Lun|gen‿ödem** (↑R 132), **...schwind|sucht, ...spit|zen|ka|tarrh** (↑R 33); **Lun|gen-Tbc** (↑R 26); **Lun|gen‿tu|ber|ku|lo|se, ...tu|mor, ...zug**
lun|gern (*ugs.*); ich ...ere (↑R 16)
Lü|ning, der; -s, -e (*nordd. für* Sperling)
Lun|ker, der; -s, - (fehlerhafter Hohlraum in Gussstücken)
Lün|se, die; -, -n (Achsnagel)
Lünt, die; - (*landsch. für* Schweinenierenfett)
Lun|te, die; -, -n (ein Zündmittel; *Jägerspr.* Schwanz des Fuchses); - riechen (*ugs. für* Gefahr wittern); **Lun|ten|schnur** *Plur.* ...schnüre
Lu|pe, die; -, -n ‹franz.› (Vergrößerungsglas); **lu|pen|rein** (sehr rein, ganz ohne Mängel [von Edelsteinen]; *übertr. für* einwandfrei, hundertprozentig)
Lu|per|ka|li|en [...i̯ən] *Plur.* (ein altröm. Fest)
Lupf, der; -[e]s, -e (*südd. u. schweiz. für* das Hochheben; Last, die man eben noch heben kann; *auch für* Hosenlupf); **lup|fen** (*südd., schweiz., österr. für* lüpfen); **lüp|fen** (leicht anheben, kurz hochheben, lüften)
Lu|pi|ne, die; -, -n ‹lat.› (eine Futter- od. Zierpflanze); **Lu|pi|nen‿feld, ...krank|heit** (die; -); **Lu|pi|no|se,** die; - (Leberentzündung bei Wiederkäuern)
Lup|pe, die; -, -n (*Technik* Eisenklumpen); **lup|pen** (gerinnen lassen)
Lu|pu|lin, das; -s ‹lat.› (Bitterstoff der Hopfenpflanze)
Lu|pus, der; -, *Plur.* - *u.* -se ‹lat.› (*Med.* tuberkulöse Hautflechte); **Lu|pus in fa|bu|la,** der; - - - ‹„der Wolf in der Fabel"› (jemand, der kommt, wenn man gerade von ihm spricht)
[1]**Lurch,** der; -[e]s, -e (Amphibie)
[2]**Lurch,** der; -[e]s (*österr. ugs. für* zusammengeballter, mit Fasern durchsetzter Staub); den - wegkehren
Lu|re, die; -, -n ‹nord.› (ein altes nord. Blasinstrument)
Lu|rex ®, das; - ‹Kunstwort› (Garn mit metallisierten Fasern)
Lu|sa|ka (Hptst. von Sambia)
Lu|sche, die; -, -n (*ugs. für* Spielkarte [von geringem Wert]); **lu|schig** (*landsch. für* liederlich, flüchtig)
Lu|si|ta|ner, Lu|si|ta|ni|er [...i̯ər], der; -s, - (Angehöriger eines iber. Volksstammes); **Lu|si|ta|ni|en** [...i̯ən] (röm. Provinz, das heutige Portugal); **Lu|si|ta|ni|er** *vgl.* Lusitaner; **lu|si|ta|nisch**
Lust, die; -, Lüste; Lust haben; **Lust|bar|keit** (*veraltend*); **lust|be|tont**
Lus|ter, der; -s, - ‹franz.› (*österr. für* Kronleuchter); **Lüs|ter,** der; -s, - (Kronleuchter; Glanzüberzug auf Glas-, Ton-, Porzellanwaren; glänzendes Gewebe); **Lüs|ter‿far|be, ...glas** (*Plur.* ...gläser), **...klem|me**
lüs|tern; er hat -e Augen; der Mann ist -; **Lüs|tern|heit,** die; -
lust|feind|lich; Lust‿feind|lich-

keit (die; -), **...gar|ten** (*früher für* parkartiger Garten), **...ge|fühl,** **...ge|winn** (der; -[e]s), **...greis** *(ugs. abwertend);* **lus|tig;** *vgl.* Bruder Lustig; **Lus|tig|keit,** die; -; **Lüst|ling** *(abwertend);* **lust|los; Lust|lo|sig|keit,** die; -; **Lust‿molch** *(ugs., oft scherzh.),* **...mord, ...mör|der, ...ob|jekt, ...prin|zip** (das; -s; *Psych.*)

Lus|tra (↑R 130; *Plur. von* Lustrum); **Lust|ra|ti|on,** die; -, -en ⟨lat.⟩ (*Rel.* feierliche Reinigung [durch Sühneopfer]); **Lus|tren** (*Plur. von* Lustrum); **lust|rie|ren** (*Rel.* feierlich reinigen); **lüs|trie|ren** ⟨franz.⟩ (*Textilind.* [Baumwoll- u. Leinengarne] fest u. glänzend machen); **Lus|trum,** das; -s, *Plur.* ...ren *u.* ...ra ⟨lat.⟩ (altröm. Sühneopfer; Zeitraum von fünf Jahren)

Lust‿schloss, ...spiel; Lust|spiel|dich|ter; lust|voll; lust|wan|deln *(veraltend);* ich ...[e]le (↑R 16); er ist gelustwandelt; zu -

Lu|te|in, das; -s ⟨lat.⟩ (gelber Farbstoff in Pflanzenblättern u. im Eidotter)

Lu|te|tia (w. Eigenn.; *lat. Name von* Paris); **Lu|te|ti|um,** das; -s (chem. Element; *Zeichen* Lu)

Lu|ther (dt. Reformator); **Lu|the|ra|ner; lu|ther|feind|lich** (↑R 96); **lu|the|risch** [*auch* noch ...ˈteː...]; eine lutherische Kirche; die lutherische *od.* luthersche Bibelübersetzung (↑R 94); **Lu|ther|ro|se** (ein ev. Sinnbild); **Lu|ther|stadt Wit|ten|berg** *vgl.* Wittenberg; **Lu|ther|tum,** das; -s

Lutsch|beu|tel; lut|schen *(ugs.);* du lutschst; **Lut|scher**

lütt (*nordd. ugs. für* klein)

Lut|te, die; -, -n (*Bergmannsspr.* Röhre zur Lenkung des Wetterstromes)

Lut|ter, der; -s, - (noch unreines Spiritusdestillat)

Lut|ter am Ba|ren|ber|ge (Ort nordwestl. von Goslar)

Lüt|tich (Stadt in Belgien)

[1]**Lutz** (m. Vorn.)

[2]**Lutz,** der; -, - ⟨nach dem österr. Eiskunstläufer A. Lutz⟩ (Drehsprung beim Eiskunstlauf)

Lüt|zel|burg (*ehem. dt. Name von* Luxemburg)

Lüt|zow [...tso:] (Familienn.); die -schen Jäger (ein Freikorps)

Luv [lu:f], die; -, *auch (Geogr. nur:)* das; -s (*Seemannsspr., Geogr.* die dem Wind zugekehrte Seite [bes. eines Schiffes, eines Gebirges]; *Ggs.* Lee); *meist ohne Artikel* in, von -; **lu|ven** [...f...] (*Seemannsspr.* das Schiff mehr an den Wind bringen); **Luv|sei|te; luv|wärts** (dem Winde zugekehrt)

Lux, das; -, - ⟨lat.⟩ (Einheit der Beleuchtungsstärke; *Zeichen* lx)

Lu|xa|ti|on, die; -, -en ⟨lat.⟩ (*Med.* Verrenkung)

[1]**Lu|xem|burg** (belg. Provinz); [2]**Lu|xem|burg** (Großherzogtum); [3]**Lu|xem|burg** (Hptst. von [2]Luxemburg); **Lu|xem|bur|ger** (↑R 103); **lu|xem|bur|gisch**

lu|xie|ren ⟨lat.⟩ (*Med.* verrenken, ausrenken)

Lux|me|ter, das; -s, - ⟨lat.; griech.⟩ (Gerät zum Messen der Beleuchtungsstärke)

Lu|xor (ägypt. Stadt)

lu|xu|rie|ren ⟨lat.⟩ (*Bot.* üppig wachsen [bes. von Pflanzenbastarden]; *veraltet für* schwelgen); **lu|xu|ri|ös; Lu|xus,** der; - (Verschwendung, Prunksucht); **Lu|xus‿ar|ti|kel, ...aus|ga|be, ...damp|fer, ...ge|gen|stand, ...gü|ter** *(Plur.),* **...ho|tel, ...jacht, ...li|mou|si|ne, ...steu|er** (die), **...vil|la, ...wa|gen, ...woh|nung**

Lu|zern (Kanton u. Stadt in der Schweiz); **Lu|zern|biet,** das; -s (*schweiz. mdal. für* Kanton Luzern)

Lu|zer|ne, die; -, -n ⟨franz.⟩ (eine Futterpflanze); **Lu|zer|nen|heu**

Lu|zer|ner (↑R 103); **lu|zer|nisch**

Lu|zia, Lu|zie [...tsi, *auch* ...tsiə] (w. Vorn.)

Lu|zi|an *vgl.* Lukian

lu|zid ⟨lat.⟩ (klar, einleuchtend); **Lu|zi|di|tät,** die; - (luzide Beschaffenheit)

Lu|zie *vgl.* Luzia

[1]**Lu|zi|fer,** der; -s ⟨lat., „Lichtbringer"⟩ (*röm. Mythol.* Morgenstern); [2]**Lu|zi|fer** (Satan); **Lu|zi|fe|rin,** das; -s (*Biol., Chemie* Leuchtstoff vieler Tiere u. Pflanzen); **lu|zi|fe|risch** (teuflisch)

Lu|zi|us *vgl.* Lucius

LVA = Landesversicherungsanstalt

Lw = Lew

lx = Lux

ly = Lichtjahr

Ly|der, Ly|di|er [...iər] (Einwohner Lydiens); **Ly|dia** (w. Vorn.); **Ly|di|en** [...iən] (*früher* Landschaft in Kleinasien); **Ly|di|er** *vgl.* Lyder; **ly|disch**

Ly|ki|en [...iən] (*früher* Landschaft in Kleinasien); **Ly|ki|er** [...iər]; **ly|kisch**

Ly|ko|po|di|um, das; -s, ...ien [...iən] ⟨griech.⟩ (*Bot.* Bärlapp)

Ly|kurg (Gesetzgeber Spartas; ein athen. Redner); **ly|kur|gisch;** die lykurgischen Reden (↑R 94)

lym|pha|tisch ⟨griech.⟩ (*Med.* auf Lymphe, Lymphknötchen, -drüsen bezüglich, sie betreffend); **Lymph‿bahn, ...drai|na|ge, ...drü|se** (*veraltet für* Lymphknoten); **Lym|phe,** die; -, -n (weißliche Körperflüssigkeit, ein Impfstoff); **Lymph‿ge|fäß, ...kno|ten; lym|pho|gen** (lymphatischen Ursprungs); **lym|pho|id** (lymphartig); **Lym|pho|zyt,** der; -en, -en *meist Plur.;* ↑R 126 (bes. Form der weißen Blutkörperchen); **Lym|pho|zy|to|se,** die; -, -n (krankhafte Vermehrung der Lymphozyten)

lyn|chen [ˈlynç(ə)n, *auch* ˈlin...] ⟨wahrscheinlich nach dem amerik. Friedensrichter Charles Lynch⟩ (ungesetzliche Volksjustiz ausüben); du lynchst; er wurde gelyncht; **Lynch‿jus|tiz, ...mord**

Lyn|keus [*auch* lyŋˈkɔys] ⟨griech., „Luchs"⟩ (scharfsichtiger Steuermann der Argonauten in der griech. Sage)

Ly|on [liˈɔ̃:] (Stadt in Frankreich); [1]**Ly|o|ner** [liˈo:nər]; ↑R 103 (Bewohner von Lyon); [2]**Ly|o|ner,** die; - (*Kurzform von* Lyoner Wurst); **Ly|o|ner Wurst; Ly|o|ne|ser** *vgl.* Lyoner; **ly|o|ne|sisch**

ly|o|phil ⟨griech.⟩ (*Chemie* leicht löslich); **ly|o|phob** (*Chemie* schwer löslich)

Ly|ra, die; -, ...ren ⟨griech.⟩ (ein altgriech. Saiteninstrument; Leier; *nur Sing.:* ein Sternbild); **Ly|rik,** die; - ([liedmäßige] Dichtung); **Ly|ri|ker** (lyrischer Dichter); **Ly|ri|ke|rin; ly|risch** (der persönlichen Stimmung u. dem Erleben unmittelbaren Ausdruck gebend; gefühl-, stimmungsvoll; liedartig); -es Drama; -e Dichtung

Ly|san|der (spartan. Feldherr u. Staatsmann)

Ly|sin, das; -s, -e *meist Plur.* ⟨griech.⟩ (*Med.* ein Bakterien auflösender Antikörper); **Ly|sis,** die; -, Lysen (*Med.* langsamer Fieberabfall; *Psych.* Persönlichkeitszerfall)

Ly|sis|tra|ta (↑R 130; Titelheldin einer Komödie von Aristophanes)

Ly|sol ®, das; -s (ein Desinfektionsmittel)

Lys|sa, die; - ⟨griech.⟩ (*Med., Tiermed.* Tollwut, Raserei)

Ly|ze|um, das; -s, ...een ⟨griech.⟩ (*veraltet für* höhere Schule für Mädchen; *schweiz. auch für* Oberstufe des Gymnasiums)

Ly|zi|en usw. *vgl.* Lykien usw.

LZ = Ladezone

Lz. = Lizenz

LZB = Landeszentralbank

M (Buchstabe); das M; des M, die M, *aber* das m in Wimpel (↑R 60); der Buchstabe M, m
m = Meter; Milli...
µ = Mikro...; Mikron
M (römisches Zahlzeichen) = 1 000
M = Mark; Modell (bei Schusswaffen); Mega...; Mille
M, µ = [1]My
M. = Markus; Monsieur
M', Mc = Mac
m² (*früher auch* qm) = Quadratmeter
m³ (*früher auch* cbm) = Kubikmeter
ma. = mittelalterlich
Ma = Machzahl
mA = Milliampere
MA. = Mittelalter
M. A. = Magister Artium; Master of Arts
[1]**Mä|an|der,** der; -[s] (alter Name eines Flusses in Kleinasien); [2]**Mä|an|der,** der; -s, - (geschlängelter Flusslauf; ein bandförmiges Ornament); **Mä|an|der|li|nie; mä|an|dern, mä|and|rie|ren** (↑R 130; *Geogr.* in [2]Mäandern verlaufen; *Kunstw.* mit mäanderförmigen Ornamenten verzieren); **mä|and|risch**
Maar, das; -[e]s, -e (*Geogr.* [wassergefüllte] kraterförmige Senke)
Maas, die; - (ein Fluss); **Maastricht** [*auch* 'ma:s...] (↑R 132; niederl. Stadt an der Maas)
Maat, der; -[e]s, *Plur.* -e *u.* -en (*Seemannsspr.* Schiffsmann; Unteroffizier auf Schiffen)
Mac [mɛk, *vor dem Namen* mək] ‹kelt., „Sohn"› (Bestandteil von schottischen [auch irischen] Namen [z. B. MacLeod]; *Abk.* M', Mc)
Ma|cau, *älter* Ma|cao [*beide* ma'kau̯] (port. verwaltetes Territorium an der südchines. Küste)
Mac|beth [mək'bɛθ] (König von Schottland; Titelheld eines Dramas von Shakespeare)
Mac|chie ['maki̯ə], *auch* Mac|chia ['maki̯a], die; -, Macchien [...i̯ən] ‹ital.› (immergrüner Buschwald des Mittelmeergebietes)
Mach, das; -[s], - (*Kurzform für* Machzahl)
Ma|chan|del, der; -s, - (*nordd. für* Wacholder); **Ma|chan|del|baum**
Mach|art; mach|bar; Mach|bar|keit, die; -; **Ma|che,** die; - (*ugs. für* Schein, Vortäuschung)
Ma|che|ein|heit; ↑R 95 ‹nach dem österr. Physiker H. Mache› (*früher* Maßeinheit für radioaktive Strahlung; *Zeichen* ME)
ma|chen; er hat es gemacht; du hast mich lachen gemacht, *selten* machen; **Ma|chen|schaft,** die; -, -en *meist Plur.;* **Ma|cher** (Person, die etwas [bedenkenlos] zustande bringt; tatkräftiger, durchsetzungsfähiger Mensch [in einer Führungsposition]); **...ma|cher** (z. B. Schuhmacher); **Ma|cher|lohn**
Ma|che|te [ma'xe:tə, *auch* ma'tʃe:tə], die; -, -n ‹span.› (Buschmesser)
Ma|chi|a|vel|li [maki̯a'vɛli] (ital. Politiker, Schriftsteller u. Geschichtsschreiber); **Ma|chi|a|vel|lis|mus,** der; - (polit. Lehre Machiavellis; *auch für* durch keine Bedenken gehemmte Machtpolitik); **ma|chi|a|vel|lis|tisch**
Ma|chi|na|ti|on [...x...], die; -, -en ‹lat.› (*nur Plur.:* Machenschaften; *veraltet für* Kniff, Trick)
Ma|chis|mo [ma'tʃismo], der; -[s] ‹span.› (übersteigertes Männlichkeitsgefühl); **Ma|cho** ['matʃo], der; -s, -s (sich betont männlich gebender Mann)
Ma|chor|ka [...x...], der; -s, -s ‹russ.› (ein russ. Tabak)
Macht, die; -, Mächte; alles in unserer Macht Stehende; **Macht‿an|spruch, ...be|fug|nis, ...be|reich** (der), **...block** (*Plur.* ...blöcke, *selten* ...blocks); **Mäch|te‿grup|pe, ...grup|pie|rung; Macht‿ent|fal|tung, ...er|grei|fung, ...fra|ge, ...fül|le; Macht|ha|ber; Macht|hun|ger; mäch|tig; Mäch|tig|keit,** die; -; **Mäch|tig|keits|sprin|gen** (*Pferdesport*); **Macht|kampf; macht|los; Macht|lo|sig|keit,** die; -; **Macht‿mit|tel** (das), **...po|si|ti|on, ...pro|be, ...spruch, ...stel|lung, ...stre|ben, ...über|nah|me** (↑R 132); **macht|voll; Macht‿voll|kom|men|heit, ...wech|sel, ...wil|le, ...wort** (*Plur.* ...worte)
ma|chul|le [...x...] ‹hebr.-jidd.› (*ugs. für* bankrott; *landsch. für* ermüdet; verrückt)
Ma|chu Pic|chu ['matʃu 'piktʃu] (Ruinenstadt der Inka in Peru)
Mach|werk (*abwertend für* minderwertiges [geistiges] Produkt)
Mach|zahl (↑R 95) ‹nach dem österr. Physiker u. Philosophen E. Mach› (Verhältnis der Geschwindigkeit einer Strömung od. eines [Flug]körpers zur Schallgeschwindigkeit; *Kurzform* Mach; *Abk.* Ma; 1 Mach = Schallgeschwindigkeit, 2 Mach = doppelte Schallgeschwindigkeit)
[1]**Ma|cke,** die; -, -n ‹hebr.-jidd.› (*ugs. für* Tick; Fehler)
[2]**Ma|cke** (dt. Maler)
Ma|cker (*ugs. für* Freund [bes. eines Mädchens]; Kerl); **mack|lich** (*nordd. für* ruhig, behaglich; *Seemannsspr.* ruhig im Wasser liegend)
MAD = Militärischer Abschirmdienst
Ma|da|gas|kar (Insel u. Staat östl. von Afrika); **Ma|da|gas|se,** der; -n, -n; ↑R 126 (Bewohner von Madagaskar); **ma|da|gas|sisch**
Ma|dam, die; -, *Plur.* -s *u.* -en ‹franz.› (*veraltet, aber noch ugs. für* Hausherrin; gnädige Frau; *scherzh. für* [dickliche, behäbige] Frau); **Ma|dam|chen** (*ugs. scherzh.);* **Ma|dame** [...'dam] (franz. Anrede für eine Frau, *svw.* „gnädige Frau"; *als Anrede ohne Artikel; Abk. [nur in Verbindung mit dem Namen]* Mme. *[schweiz. ohne Punkt]*); *Plur.* Mesdames [mɛ'dam] (*Abk.* Mmes. *[schweiz. ohne Punkt]*)
Mäd|chen; - für alles; **Mäd|chen|au|ge** (*auch* eine Blume); **mäd|chen|haft; Mäd|chen|haf|tig|keit,** die; -; **Mäd|chen‿han|del** (*vgl.* [1]Handel), **...händ|ler, ...herz, ...klas|se, ...na|me, ...pen|si|o|nat, ...schu|le, ...zim|mer**
Ma|de, die; -, -n (Insektenlarve)
made in Ger|ma|ny ['me:d in 'dʒœ:(r)məni] ‹engl., „hergestellt in Deutschland"› (ein Warenstempel)
[1]**Ma|dei|ra** [...'de:ra], Ma|de|ra (Insel im Atlantischen Ozean); [2]**Ma|dei|ra** [...'de:ra], Ma|de|ra, der; -s, -s (Süßwein aus Madeira); **Ma|dei|ra|wein**
Mä|del, das; -s, *Plur.* - *od. (bes. nordd.)* -s *u. bayr., österr.* -n
Made|leine [ma'dlɛ(:)n] (w. Vorn.)
Ma|de|moi|selle [mad(ə)moa̯'zɛl] ‹franz.› (*franz. Bez. für* unverheiratete Frau; *als Anrede ohne Artikel; Abk. [nur in Verbindung mit dem Namen]* Mlle. *[schweiz. ohne Punkt]*); *Plur.* Mesdemoiselles [mɛd(ə)moa̯'zɛl] (*Abk.* Mlles. *[schweiz. ohne Punkt]*)
Ma|den|wurm
Ma|de|ra usw. *vgl.* Madeira usw.
Mä|de|süß, das; -, - (ein Rosengewächs)
ma|dig; jmdn. - machen (*ugs. für*

in schlechten Ruf bringen); jmdm. etwas - machen (*ugs. für* verleiden)

Mad|jar [*ung. Schreibung* Magyar usw.], der; -en, -en; ↑R 126 (Ungar); **Mad|ja|ren|reich,** das; -[e]s; **mad|ja|risch; mad|ja|ri|sie|ren** (ungarisch machen); **Mad|ja|ri|sie|rung,** die; -

Ma|don|na, die; -, ...nnen ‹ital., „meine Herrin"› (*nur Sing.:* Maria, Mutter Gottes; *bild. Kunst* Mariendarstellung [mit Jesuskind]); **Ma|don|nen‿bild, ...gesicht; ma|don|nen|haft; Ma|don|nen|li|lie**

Mad|ras (↑R 130; Stadt in Vorderindien); **Mad|ras|ge|we|be**

Mad|re|po|re (↑R 130), die; -, -n *meist Plur.* ‹franz.› (*Zool.* Steinkoralle); **Mad|re|po|ren|kalk** (*Geol.* Korallenkalk der Juraformation)

Mad|rid (↑R 130; Hptst. Spaniens); **Mad|ri|der** (↑R 103)

Mad|ri|gal (↑R 130), das; -s, -e ‹ital.› ([Hirten]lied; mehrstimmiges Gesangstück); **Mad|ri|gal|chor; Mad|ri|gal|stil**

ma|es|to|so [maɛ...] ‹ital.› (*Musik* feierlich, würdevoll); **Ma|es|to|so,** das; -s, *Plur.* -s *u.* ...si

Ma|est|ro [ma'ɛs...] (↑R 130), der; -s, *Plur.* -s, *auch* ...stri ‹ital., „Meister"› (großer Musiker, Komponist *[bes. als Anrede]*)

Mä|eu|tik, die; - ‹griech.› (Fragemethode des Sokrates); **mä|eu|tisch**

Ma|fia, *auch* Maf|fia, die; -, -s ‹ital.› (erpresserische Geheimorganisation [in Sizilien]); **Ma|fi|a|me|tho|den,** *auch* Maf|fi|a|me|tho|den (↑R 132) *Plur.*; **ma|fi|os** (nach Art der Mafia); **Ma|fi|o|so,** der; -[s], ...si (Mitglied der Mafia)

Mag. = Magister

Ma|gal|hães [...'ljœiʃ] (port. Seefahrer); **Ma|gal|hães|stra|ße,** die; -; ↑R 105 (Meeresstraße zwischen dem südamerik. Festland u. Feuerland); *vgl. auch* Magellanstraße

Ma|ga|zin, das; -s, -e ‹arab.-ital.›; **Ma|ga|zi|ner** (*schweiz. für* Magazinarbeiter); **Ma|ga|zi|neur** [...'nø:r], der; -s, -e ‹franz.› (*österr. für* Magazinverwalter); **ma|ga|zi|nie|ren** (einspeichern; lagern)

Magd, die; -, Mägde

Mag|da (w. Vorn.); **Mag|da|la** (Dorf am See Genezareth); **Mag|da|le|na, Mag|da|le|ne** (w. Vorn.); **Mag|da|le|nen‿stift** (das), **...strom** (der; -[e]s; in Kolumbien); **Mag|da|lé|ni|en** [...le'niɛ̃:], das; -[s] ‹franz.› (Kultur der Älteren Steinzeit)

Mag|de|burg (Stadt an der mittleren Elbe); **Mag|de|bur|ger** (↑R 103); **Mag|de|bur|ger Bör|de** (Gebiet westl. der Elbe); **mag|de|bur|gisch**

Mäg|de|lein *(veraltet);* **Mäg|de|stu|be** *(früher);* **Mägd|lein** *vgl.* Mägdelein; **Magd|tum,** das; -s (*veraltet für* Jungfräulichkeit)

Ma|gel|lan|stra|ße [*auch* magɛl'ja:n... *u.* 'magɛljan...] (↑R 105), die; - (*eindeutschende Schreibung für* Magalhãesstraße)

Ma|ge|lo|ne (neapolitan. Königstochter; Gestalt des franz. u. dt. Volksbuches)

Ma|gen, der; -s, *Plur.* Mägen, *auch* -; **Ma|gen‿aus|gang, ...aus|he|be|rung** (*vgl.* aushebern), **...be|schwer|den** *(Plur.),* **...bit|ter** (der; -s, -; bitterer Kräuterlikör); **Ma|gen-Darm-Ka|tarrh** (↑R 28 *u.* 33; *Med.*); **Ma|gen‿drü|cken, ...ein|gang, ...er|wei|te|rung** *(Med.),* **...fahr|plan** (*ugs.* feststehender Küchenzettel für eine bestimmte Zeit), **...fis|tel** *(Med.),* **...ge|gend** (die; -), **...ge|schwür, ...gru|be, ...ka|tarrh** (↑R 33), **...knur|ren** (das; -s), **...krampf; ma|gen|krank; Ma|gen‿krebs, ...lei|den; ma|gen|lei|dend; Ma|gen‿ope|ra|ti|on** (↑R 132), **...saft, ...säu|re, ...schleim|haut, ...schleim|haut|ent|zün|dung, ...schmerz** *(meist Plur.),* **...spie|ge|lung, ...spü|lung**

Ma|gen|ta [ma'dʒɛnta], das; -s ‹nach einem ital. Ort› (Anilinrot)

Ma|gen‿ver|stim|mung, ...wand

ma|ger; Ma|ger|keit, die; -; **Ma|ger‿koh|le, ...milch, ...quark, ...sucht** (die; -)

Mag|gi [*schweiz.* 'madʒi] (Familienn.; ®)

Mag|gie ['mɛgi] (w. Vorn.)

Magh|reb (↑R 130), der; - ‹arab., „Westen"› (der Westteil der arab.-moslem. Welt: Tunesien, Nordalgerien, Marokko); **magh|re|bi|nisch**

Ma|gie, die; - ‹pers.› (Zauber-, Geheimkunst); **Ma|gi|er** (Zauberer); **ma|gisch;** -es Quadrat

Ma|gis|ter, der; -s, - ‹lat., „Meister"› (akadem. Grad; *veraltet für* Lehrer; *Abk. [bei Titeln]* Mag.); Magister Artium (akadem. Grad; *Abk.* M. A., z. B.: Ernst Meier M. A.; *österr.* Mag. art.); - der Philosophie (*österr., Abk.* Mag. phil.); - der Naturwissenschaften (*österr., Abk.* Mag. rer. nat.); - der Theologie (*österr., Abk.* Mag. theol.); - der Philosophie der theolog. Fakultät (*österr., Abk.* Mag. phil. fac. theol.); - der Rechte (*österr., Abk.* Mag. jur.); - der Sozial- und Wirtschaftswissenschaften (*österr., Abk.* Mag. rer. soc. oec.); - der Tierheilkunde (*österr., Abk.* Mag. med. vet.); - der Pharmazie (*österr., Abk.* Mag. pharm.); - der Architektur (*österr., Abk.* Mag. arch.)

Ma|gist|ra|le (↑R 130), die; -, -n (*regional u. fachspr. für* Hauptverkehrsstraße, -linie); [1]**Ma|gist|rat,** der; -[e]s, -e (Stadtverwaltung, -behörde); [2]**Ma|gist|rat,** der; -en, -en; ↑R 126 (*schweiz. für* Inhaber eines hohen öffentlichen Amtes); **Ma|gist|rats|be|schluss**

Mag|ma, das; -s, ...men ‹griech.› (*Geol.* Gesteinsschmelzfluss des Erdinnern); **mag|ma|tisch**

Mag|na Char|ta [- k...] (↑R 130), die; - - ‹lat.› (englisches [Grund]gesetz von 1215; *geh. für* Grundgesetz, Verfassung); **mag|na cum lau|de** (↑R 130) ‹lat., „mit großem Lob"› (zweitbeste Note der Doktorprüfung)

Mag|nat (↑R 130), der; -en, -en; ↑R 126 ‹lat.› (Grundbesitzer, Großindustrieller)

[1]**Mag|ne|sia** [*auch* maŋ'ne:...] (↑R 130; Landschaft Thessaliens; *heute* Magnisia); [2]**Mag|ne|sia,** die; - (Magnesiumoxid); **Mag|ne|sit** [*auch* ...'zit], der; -s, -e (ein Mineral); **Mag|ne|si|um,** das; -s (chem. Element, Metall; *Zeichen* Mg); **Mag|ne|si|um|le|gie|rung**

Mag|net (↑R 130), der; *Gen.* -en *u.* -[e]s, *Plur.* -e, *seltener* -en; ↑R 126 ‹griech.›; **Mag|net‿band** (das; *Plur.* ...bänder), **...berg, ...ei|sen|stein, ...feld** *(Physik);* **mag|ne|tisch;** -e Feldstärke; -er Pol; -er Sturm; **Mag|ne|ti|seur** [...'zø:r] *vgl.* Magnetopath; **mag|ne|ti|sie|ren** (*Physik* magnetisch machen; *Med.* mit magnetischer Kraft behandeln); **Mag|ne|ti|sie|rung; Mag|ne|tis|mus,** der; - (Gesamtheit der magnetischen Erscheinungen; ein Heilverfahren); **Mag|ne|tit** [*auch* ...'tit], der; -s, -e (Magneteisenstein); **Mag|net‿kar|te, ...na|del; Mag|ne|to|me|ter,** das; -s, - *(Physik);* **Mag|ne|ton** [*auch* ...'to:n], das; -s, -[s] (*Physik* Einheit des magnetischen Moments); 2 - (↑R 90); **Mag|ne|to|path,** der; -en, -en (↑R 126) *u.* Mag|ne|ti|seur [...'zø:r], der; -s, -e (mit magnetischen Kräften behandelnder Heilkundiger); **Mag|ne|to|phon** ®, das; -s, -e (ein Tonbandgerät); **Mag|ne|to|sphä|re,** die; - (*Meteor.* höchster Teil der Atmosphäre); **Mag|net|ron** [*auch* ...'tro:n] (↑R 130), das;

-s, Plur. ...one, auch -s (*Physik* Elektronenröhre, die magnetische Energie verwendet [für hohe Impulsleistungen]); **Mag|net|ton-ge|rät, ...ver|fah|ren**

mag|ni|fik [manji...] (↑R 130) ‹franz.› (*veraltet für* herrlich, prächtig, großartig); **Mag|ni|fi-kat** [mag...], das; -[s], -s ‹lat.› (Lobgesang Marias); **Mag|ni|fi-kus,** der; -, ...fizi (*veraltet für* Rektor einer Hochschule); *vgl.* Rector magnificus; **Mag|ni|fi-zenz,** die; -, -en (Titel für Hochschulrektoren u. a.); *als Anrede* Euer, Eure (*Abk.* Ew.) -

Mag|ni|sia (↑R 130); *vgl.* [1]Magnesia

Mag|no|lie [...iə] (↑R 130), die; -, -n ‹nach dem franz. Mediziner u. Botaniker Magnol› (ein Zierbaum)

Mag|num (↑R 130), die; -, ...gna ‹lat.› (Wein- oder Sektflasche mit 1,5 l Fassungsvermögen; *Waffentechnik* spezielle Patrone mit verstärkter Ladung)

Mag|nus (↑R 130; m. Vorn.)

Ma|gog (Reich des Gog); *vgl.* Gog

Mag. pharm. = Magister pharmaciae (österr. akadem. Titel)

Mag. phil. = Magister philosophiae (österr. akadem. Titel)

Mag. rer. nat. = Magister rerum naturalium (österr. akadem. Titel)

Mag|ritte [ma'grit] (↑R 130; belg. Maler)

Mag. theol. = Magister theologiae (österr. akadem. Titel)

Mag|yar [ma'dja:r] usw. *vgl.* Madjar usw.

mäh!; mäh, mäh!; mäh schreien

Ma|ha|go|ni, das; -s ‹indian.› (ein Edelholz); **Ma|ha|go|ni-holz, ...mö|bel**

Ma|ha|rad|scha (↑R 130), der; -s, -s ‹sanskr.› (ind. Großfürst); **Ma-ha|ra|ni,** die; -, -s (Frau eines Maharadschas, ind. Fürstin); **Ma|ha-ri|schi,** der; -[s], -s ‹Hindi› (ein ind. religiöser Ehrentitel)

Ma|hat|ma, der; -s, -s ‹sanskr.› (ind. Ehrentitel für geistig hoch stehende Männer); Mahatma Gandhi

Mäh|bin|der; [1]**Mahd,** die; -, -en (*landsch. für* das Mähen; das Abgemähte [meist Gras]); [2]**Mahd,** das; -[e]s, Mähder (*schweiz. u. österr. für* Bergwiese); [1]**Mäh|der** (*Plur. von* [2]Mahd); [2]**Mäh|der** (*landsch. für* Mäher)

Mah|di ['maxdi, *auch* 'ma:di], der; -[s], -s (von den Moslems erwarteter Welt-, Glaubenserneuerer)

Mäh|dre|scher; Mäh|drusch; [1]**mä|hen** ([Gras] schneiden)

[2]**mä|hen** (*ugs. für* mäh schreien)

Mä|her

Mahl, das; -[e]s, *Plur.* Mähler *u.* -e (Gastmahl)

mah|len (Korn u. a.); gemahlen

Mah|ler (österr. Komponist u. Dirigent)

Mahl-gang (der; *Technik*), **...geld, ...gut**

mäh|lich (*geh. für* allmählich)

Mahl-knecht (*veraltet*), **...sand** (*Seemannsspr.*)

Mahl|schatz (*Rechtsspr. veraltet für* Brautgabe); **Mahl|statt** *od.* **...stät|te** (Gerichts- u. Versammlungsstätte der alten Germanen)

Mahl-stein, ...steu|er (die; eine frühere Steuer), **...strom** (Strudel), **...werk** (*Technik*), **...zahn** (*für* Molar)

Mahl|zeit; gesegnete Mahlzeit!

Mäh|ma|schi|ne

Mahn-be|scheid (*Rechtsw.* Zahlungsbefehl), **...brief**

Mäh|ne, die; -, -n

mah|nen

mäh|nen|ar|tig

Mah|ner; Mah|ne|rin; Mahn|ge-bühr

mäh|nig ‹*zu* Mähne›

Mahn-mal (*Plur.* ...male, *selten* ...mäler), **...ruf** (*geh.*), **...schrei-ben; Mah|nung; Mahn-ver-fah|ren** (*Rechtsspr.*), **...wa|che, ...wort** (*Plur.* ...worte, *meist Plur.*; *geh.*), **...zei|chen**

Ma|ho|nie [...iə], die; -, -n ‹nach dem amerik. Gärtner B. MacMahon› (ein Zierstrauch)

Mahr, der; -[e]s, -e (quälendes Nachtgespenst, [1]Alb)

[1]**Mäh|re,** die; -, -n ([altes, abgemagertes] Pferd)

[2]**Mäh|re,** der; -n, -n (↑R 126); **Mäh|ren** (Gebiet in der Tschechischen Republik); **Mäh|rer** (*svw.* [2]Mähre); **Mäh|re|rin, Mäh|rin; mäh|risch,** *aber* (↑R 102): die Mährische Pforte

Mai, der; *Gen.* -[e]s *u.* - (*geh. gelegentl. noch* -en), *Plur.* -e ‹lat.› (der fünfte Monat des Jahres, Wonnemond, Weidemonat); (↑R 108:) der Erste Mai (Feiertag); **Ma|ia** *vgl.* [2]Maja; **Mai|an|dacht** (*kath. Kirche*); **Mai|baum**[1]; **Mai|blu-me**[1]; **Mai|blu|men|strauß; Mai-bow|le**

Maid, die; -, -en (*veraltet, noch scherzh. für* Mädchen)

Mai|de|monst|ra|ti|on; Maie, die; -, -n (*veraltend für* Maibaum); **mai|en** (*geh.*); es grünt und mait; **Mai|en,** der; -s, - (*schweiz. mdal. für* Blumenstrauß); **mai|en|haft;**

[1] *Geh. auch* Maien...

Mai|en|nacht (*geh.*); **Mai|en-säß,** das; -es, -e (*schweiz. für* Frühlingsbergweide); **Mai-fei|er, ...glöck|chen, ...kä|fer, ...kätz-chen**

Mai|ke, Mei|ke (w. Vorn.)

Mai-kö|ni|gin[1], **...kund|ge|bung**

Mai|land (ital. Stadt); *vgl.* Milano; **Mai|län|der** (↑R 103); Mailänder Scala; **mai|län|disch**

Mail|box ['me:l...], die; -, -en ‹engl.› (*EDV* „Briefkasten" für den Austausch von Nachrichten in Computersystemen); **Mai|ling** ['me:liŋ], das; -[s] (Versenden von Werbematerial durch die Post)

Mail|lol [ma'jɔl] (franz. Bildhauer u. Grafiker)

Mai|luft[1]

Main, der; -[e]s (r. Nebenfluss des Rheins)

Mai|nacht[1]

Mai|nau (↑R 132), die; - (Insel im Bodensee)

Main-Do|nau-Ka|nal, der; -s (↑R 105)

Maine [me:n] (Staat in den USA; *Abk.* Me.)

Main|fran|ken; Main|li|nie, die; -

Mainz (Stadt am Rhein); **Main-zer** (↑R 103); **main|zisch**

Maire [mɛ:r], der; -s, -s ‹franz.› (Bürgermeister in Frankreich); **Mai|rie** [mɛ:'ri:], die; -, ...ien (*franz. Bez. für* Rathaus)

Mais, der; -es, *Plur.* (*Sorten:*) -e ‹indian.› (eine Getreidepflanze); **Mais-bir|ne** (Trainingsgerät für Boxer), **...brei, ...brot**

Maisch, der; -[e]s, -e (*selten für* Maische); **Maisch|bot|tich; Mai-sche,** die; -, -n (Gemisch zur Wein-, Bier- od. Spiritusherstellung); **mai|schen;** du maischst

mais|gelb; Mais-kol|ben, ...korn, ...mehl

Mai|so|nette, *auch* **Mai|son-nette** [mɛzɔ'nɛt], die; -, *Plur.* -s ‹franz.› (zweistöckige Wohnung)

Maiß, der; -es, -e *od.* die; -, -en (*bayr., österr. für* Holzschlag; Jungwald)

Mais-stär|ke, ...stroh

Maît|re de Plai|sir ['mɛ:trə də plɛ-'zi:r] (↑R 130), der; - - -, -s ['mɛ:trə] - - ‹franz.› (*veraltet, noch scherzh. für* jmd., der ein Unterhaltungsprogramm leitet)

[1]**Ma|ja,** die; - ‹sanskr.› (*ind. Philos.* [als verschleierte Schönheit dargestellte] Erscheinungswelt, Blendwerk)

[2]**Ma|ja** (röm. Göttin des Erdwachstums; *griech. Mythol.* Mutter des Hermes)

[1] *Geh. auch* Maien...

Ma|ja|ko̤ws|ki (↑R 132; russ. Dichter)
Maj|da|nek [maj'da(:)...] (im 2. Weltkrieg Konzentrationslager der Nationalsozialisten in Polen)
Ma|jes|tä̲t, die; -, *Plur.* (als Titel u. Anrede von Kaisern u. Königen:) -en ‹lat.› (Herrlichkeit, Erhabenheit); Seine - (*Abk.* S[e]. M.), Ihre - (*Abk.* I. M.), Euer - *od.* Eure - (*Abk.* Ew. M.); **ma|jes|tä̲|tisch** (herrlich, erhaben); **Ma|jes|tä̲tsbe|lei|di|gung**
Ma|jo̲|li|ka, die; -, *Plur.* ...ken *u.* -s ‹nach der Insel Mallorca› (Töpferware mit Zinnglasur)
Ma|jo|nä̲|se, *auch* Ma|yon|nai|se [majɔ'nɛ:zə, *österr.* ...'nɛ:z] (↑R 33), die; -, -n ‹franz.; nach der Stadt Mahón [ma'ɔn] auf Menorca› (kalte, dicke Soße aus Eigelb u. Öl)
Ma|jo̲r, der; -s, -e ‹lat.-span.› (unterster Stabsoffizier)
Ma̲|jo|ran [*auch* ...'ra:n], *seltener* Me̲i|ran, der; -s, -e *Plur. selten* ‹mlat.› (eine Gewürzpflanze; deren getrocknete Blätter)
Ma|jo|ra̲t, das; -[e]s, -e ‹lat.› (*Rechtsspr.* Vorrecht des Ältesten auf das Erbgut; nach dem Ältestenrecht zu vererbendes Gut; *Ggs.* Minorat); **Ma|jo|ra̲ts|gut**
Ma|jor|do̲|mus, der; -, - ‹lat.› (Hausmeier; Stellvertreter der fränk. Könige); **ma|jo|re̤nn** (*Rechtsspr. veraltet für* volljährig, mündig); **Ma|jo|ren|ni|tä̲t,** die; - (*veraltet für* Volljährigkeit, Mündigkeit); **Ma|jo|rette** [...'rɛt], die; -, *Plur.* -s *u.* -n [...'rɛt(ə)n] ‹franz.› (junges Mädchen in Uniform, das bei festlichen Umzügen paradiert); **Ma|jo|re̤t|ten|grup|pe; ma|jo|ri|sie̲|ren** ‹lat.› (überstimmen, durch Stimmenmehrheit zwingen); **Ma|jo|ri|tä̲t,** die; -, -en ([Stimmen]mehrheit); **Ma|jo|ritä̲ts‿be|schluss, ...prin|zip** (das; -s), **...wahl** (Mehrheitswahl)
Ma|jo̲rs|rang, der; -[e]s
Ma|jo̤rz, der; -es ‹lat.› (*schweiz. für* Mehrheitswahlsystem)
Ma|ju̲s|kel, die; -, -n ‹lat.› (Großbuchstabe)
ma|ka̲|ber; makab[e]rer, makaberste ‹franz.› (unheimlich; Schauder erregend; frivol); makab|res (↑R 130) Aussehen
Ma|ka|da̤m, der *od.* das; -s, -e ‹nach dem schott. Ingenieur McAdam› (Straßenbelag); **maka|da|mi|sie̲|ren** (mit Makadam versehen, belegen)
Ma̲|kak, der; *Gen.* -s *u.* ...ka̤ken, *Plur.* ...ka̤ken; ↑R 126 ‹afrik.-port.› (meerkatzenartiger Affe)
Ma|ka̲|me, die; -, -n ‹arab.› (*Literaturw.* kunstvolle alte arab. Stegreifdichtung)
[1]Ma|ka̲o [*auch* ma'kau], der; -s, -s ‹Hindi-port.› (ein Papagei)
[2]Ma|ka̲o [*auch* ma'kau], das; -s ‹*nach* Macau *(vgl. d.)*› (ein Glücksspiel)
Ma̤|kart (österr. Maler); **Ma̤|kartbu|kett** (↑R 95; Strauß aus getrockneten Blumen)
Ma|ke|do̲|ni|en, *auch* Ma|ze|do̲|ni|en (Balkanlandschaft; Staat im Süden des ehem. Jugoslawien); **Ma|ke|do̲|ni|er,** *auch* Ma|ze|do̲|ni|er; **ma|ke|do̲|nisch,** *auch* maze|do̲|nisch
Ma̲|kel, der; -s, - (*geh. für* Schande; Fleck; Fehler)
Mä|ke|le̲i (*svw.* Nörgelei); **mä̲|kelig, mä̲k|lig** (gern mäkelnd)
ma̲|kel|los; Ma̲|kel|lo|sig|keit, die; -
ma̲|keln (Vermittlergeschäfte machen); ich ...[e]le (↑R 16); **mä̲keln** (*svw.* nörgeln); ich ...[e]le (↑R 16); **Mä̲|kel|sucht,** die; -; **mä̲|kel|süch|tig**
Ma|ke̤t|te, die; -, -n (*eindeutschend für* Maquette)
Make-up [me:k'ap], das; -s, -s ‹engl.› (kosmet. Verschönerung; kosmet. Präparat)
Ma̲|ki, der; -s, -s ‹madagass.-franz.› (ein Halbaffe)
Ma|ki|mo̲|no, das; -s, -s ‹jap.› (ostasiat. Rollbild im Querformat auf Seide od. Papier)
Mak|ka|bä̲|er, der; -s, - (Angehöriger eines jüd. Geschlechtes); **Mak|ka|bä̲|er|mün|ze; mak|kabä̲|isch; Mak|ka̲|bi,** der; -[s], -s ‹hebr.› (Name jüd. Sportvereinigungen); **Mak|ka|bi|a̲|de,** die; -, -n (jüd. Sporttreffen nach Art der Olympiade)
Mak|ka|ro̲|ni *Plur.* ‹ital.› (röhrenförmige Nudeln); **mak|ka|ro̲nisch** (aus lateinischen [u. lateinisch deklinierten] Wörtern lebender Sprachen gemischt); -e Dichtung
Ma̲k|ler (Geschäftsvermittler); **[1]Mä̲k|ler** (*selten für* Makler); **[2]Mä̲k|ler** (*svw.* Nörgler); **Ma̲kler|ge|bühr; Ma̲k|le|rin; Ma̲kler|pro|vi|si|on; mä̲k|lig** *vgl.* mäkelig
Ma̲|ko, die; -, -s *od.* der *od.* das; -[s], -s ‹nach dem Ägypter Mako Bey› (ägypt. Baumwolle); **Ma̤|kobaum|wol|le**
Ma|ko|ré [...'re:], das; -[s] ‹franz.› (afrik. Hartholz)
Mak|ra|mee̲ (↑R 130), das; -[s], -s ‹arab.-ital.› (Knüpfarbeit [mit Fransen])
Mak|re̲|le (↑R 130), die; -, -n ‹niederl.› (ein Fisch)
mak|ro... (↑R 130) ‹griech.› (lang..., groß...); **Mak|ro...** (Lang..., Groß...); **Mak|ro|bi|o̲tik,** die; - (*Med.* Kunst, das Leben zu verlängern); **mak|ro|bi|o̲tisch; mak|ro|ke|pha̲l** usw. *vgl.* makrozephal usw.; **Mak|ro|klima** ['ma(:)kro...] (Großklima); **mak|ro|ko̤s|misch** [*auch* 'ma(:)kro...]; **Mak|ro|kos|mos, Makro|kos|mus,** der; - (die große Welt, Weltall; *Ggs.* Mikrokosmos); **Mak|ro|mo|le|kü̲l** [*auch* 'ma(:)kro...] (*Chemie* aus 1 000 u. mehr Atomen aufgebautes Molekül); **mak|ro|mo|le|ku|la̲r**
Mak|ro̲|ne (↑R 130), die; -, -n ‹ital.› (ein Gebäck)
mak|ro|se̲is|misch [*auch* 'ma(:)kro...] (↑R 130) ‹griech.› (*Geol.* ohne Instrumente wahrnehmbar [von starken Erdbeben]); **makro|sko̲|pisch** (mit freiem Auge sichtbar); **Mak|ro|spo̲|re** [*auch* 'ma(:)kro...] *meist Plur.* (*Bot.* große weibliche Spore einiger Farnpflanzen); **Mak|ro|struk|tur** ['ma(:)kro...] (*fachspr. für* ohne optische Hilfsmittel erkennbare Struktur); **mak|ro|ze|pha̲l** (*Med.* großköpfig); **Mak|ro|ze|pha̲|le,** der *u.* die; -n, -n (↑R 5 ff.); **Makro|ze|pha|li̲e,** die; -, ...i̲en; **Makru|li̲e,** die; -, ...i̲en (*Med.* Wucherung des Zahnfleisches)
Ma|ku|la|tu̲r, die; -, -en ‹lat.› (*Druckw.* beim Druck schadhaft gewordene u. fehlerhafte Bogen, Fehldruck; Altpapier); **ma|kuli̲e|ren** (zu Makulatur machen)
ma̲l; acht mal zwei (*mit Ziffern [u. Zeichen]:* 8 mal 2, 8 × 2 *od.* 8 · 2); acht mal zwei ist, macht, gibt (*nicht:* sind, machen, geben) sechzehn; eine Fläche von drei mal fünf Metern (*mit Ziffern [u. Zeichen]:* 3 m × 5 m); *vgl. aber* achtmal und [1]Mal; mal (*ugs. für* einmal [*vgl.* [1]Mal], z. B. komm mal her!; wenn das mal gut geht!; das ist nun mal so; öfter mal was Neues; sag das noch mal!); **[1]Ma̲l,** das; -[e]s, -e. **I.** *Groß- und Getrenntschreibung als Substantiv:* das erste, zweite usw. Mal; das and[e]re, einzige, letzte, nächste, vorige usw. Mal; das eine Mal; e̲in Ma̲l (beide Wörter sind betont, sonst: e̲inmal); ein erstes usw. Mal; ein and[e]res, einziges, letztes Mal; ein Mal über das and[e]re, ein ums and[e]re Mal; von Mal zu Mal; Mal für Mal; dieses, manches, nächstes, voriges Mal; manches liebe, manch liebes

Mal; mit einem Mal[e]; beim, zum ersten, zweiten, letzten, ander[e]n, soundsovielten, x-ten Mal[e]; die letzten, nächsten Male; alle, einige, etliche, mehrere, unendliche, unzählige, viele, viele tausend, wie viele Mal[e]; ein Dutzend Mal; Millionen Mal; ein paar, ein paar Dutzend, eine Million Mal[e], drei Millionen Mal[e]; ein oder mehrere Mal[e]; ein für alle Mal[e]; zu fünf Dutzend Malen; zu verschiedenen, wiederholten Malen. **II.** *Zusammenschreibung als Adverb:* einmal; zweimal (*mit Ziffer* 2-mal); drei- bis viermal (*mit Ziffern* 3- bis 4-mal *od.* 3–4-mal); fünfundsiebzigmal; [ein]hundertmal; noch einmal, noch einmal so viel; keinmal; manchmal; vielmal, sovielmal, wievielmal, vieltausendmal, x-mal; allemal, diesmal; ein andermal, ein paarmal; auf einmal; **²Mal**, das; -[e]s, *Plur.* -e *u.* Mäler (Fleck; Merkmal; *geh. für* Denkmal; *Sport* Ablaufstelle)

Ma|la|bar|küs|te, die; - (südl. Teil der Westküste Vorderindiens)

Ma|la|bo (Hptst. von Äquatorialguinea)

Ma|la|chi|as [...x...], *ökum.* Male|a|chi (bibl. Prophet)

Ma|la|chit [...'xi:t, *auch* ...'xit], der; -s, -e ⟨griech.⟩ (ein Mineral); **ma|la|chit|grün; Ma|la|chit|va|se**

ma|lad (*selten für* malade); **ma|la|de** ⟨franz.⟩ (*ugs. für* krank, sich unwohl fühlend)

ma|la fi|de ⟨lat.⟩ (in böser Absicht; wider besseres Wissen)

Ma|la|ga, der; -s, -s (ein Süßwein); **Má|la|ga** (span. Provinz u. Hafenstadt)

Ma|la|gas|si, das; - (Sprache der Madagassen)

Ma|la|ga|wein

Ma|la|gue|ña [...'gɛnja], die; -, -s ⟨span.⟩ (ein südspan., dem Fandango ähnl. Tanz)

Ma|laie, der; -n, -n; ↑R 126 (Angehöriger mongol. Völker Südostasiens); **Ma|lai|in; ma|lai|isch**, *aber* (↑R 102): der Malaiische Archipel; Malaiischer Bund

Ma|lai|se (↑R 33) ma'lɛ:zə, *schweiz.* malɛ:z], die; -, -n, *schweiz.* das; -s, -s ⟨franz.⟩ (Misere; Missstimmung)

Ma|la|ja|lam, das; -[s] (eine drawid. Sprache in Südindien)

Ma|lak|ka (südostasiat. Halbinsel)

Ma|la|ko|lo|gie, die; - ⟨griech.⟩ (Lehre von den Weichtieren)

Ma|la|ria, die; - ⟨ital.⟩ (eine trop. Infektionskrankheit); **Ma|la|ri|a|er|re|ger; ma|la|ri|a|krank; Ma|la|ri|a|lo|gie**, die; - (Erforschung der Malaria)

Ma|lä|se *eindeutschende Schreibung für* Malaise

Ma|la|wi (Staat in Afrika); **Ma|la|wi|er** [...iər]; **ma|la|wisch**

Mal|axt (Axt zum Bezeichnen der zu fällenden Bäume)

Ma|lay|sia [...'lai...] (Föderation in Südostasien); **Ma|lay|si|er; ma|lay|sisch**

Mal|buch

Mal|chen *vgl.* Melibocus

Mal|chus (bibl. m. Eigenn.)

Ma|le ['ma:le(:)] (Hptst. der Malediven)

Ma|le|a|chi [...xi] *vgl.* Malachias

Ma|le|di|ven [...v...] *Plur.* (Inselstaat im Ind. Ozean); **Ma|le|di|ver; ma|le|di|visch**

Ma|le|fiz|kerl ⟨lat.; dt.⟩ (*landsch. für* Draufgänger)

ma|len (Bilder usw.); gemalt

Ma|le|par|tus, der; - (Wohnung des Fuchses in der Tierfabel)

Ma|ler; Ma|ler|ar|beit; Ma|le|rei; Ma|ler‿email (↑R 132; Schmelzmalerei), **...far|be; Ma|le|rin; ma|le|risch; Ma|ler|meis|ter; ma|lern** (*ugs. für* Malerarbeiten ausführen); ich ...lere (↑R 16)

Ma|le|sche, die; -, -n ⟨franz., „Malaise"⟩ (*nordd. für* Ungelegenheit, Unannehmlichkeit)

Mal|feld *(Rugby)*

Mal|grund *(Kunstw.)*

Mal|heur [ma'lø:r], das; -s, *Plur.* -e *u.* -s ⟨franz.⟩ (*ugs. für* [kleines] Missgeschick; Unglück)

mal|ho|nett ⟨franz.⟩ (*veraltet für* unfein, unredlich)

Ma|li (Staat in Afrika)

Ma|li|ce [ma'li:sə], die; -, -n ⟨franz.⟩ (*veraltet für* Bosheit)

Ma|li|er [...iər] (Bewohner von Mali)

...ma|lig (z. B. dreimalig [*mit Ziffer* 3-malig])

ma|lig|ne (↑R 130) ⟨lat.⟩ (*Med.* bösartig); **Ma|lig|ni|tät**, die; - (Bösartigkeit [einer Krankheit, bes. einer Geschwulst])

ma|lisch ⟨*zu* Mali⟩

ma|li|zi|ös (boshaft, hämisch)

Mal|kas|ten

mal|kon|tent ⟨franz.⟩ (*veraltet, noch landsch. für* [mit polit. Zuständen] unzufrieden)

mall ⟨niederl.⟩ (*Seew.* umspringend, verkehrt, verdreht [vom Wind]; *nordd. übertr. für* von Sinnen, verrückt); **Mall**, das; -[e]s, -e (*Seemannsspr.* Modell für Schiffsteile, Spantenschablone)

Mal|lar|mé [...'me:] (franz. Dichter)

mal|len (*Seemannsspr.* nach dem Mall bearbeiten; umspringen [vom Wind])

Mal|lor|ca [ma'jɔrka, *auch* ma'lɔrka] (Hauptinsel der Balearen); **Mal|lor|qui|ner** [majɔr'ki:..., *auch* malɔr'ki:...] (Einwohner Mallorcas); **mal|lor|qui|nisch**

Mal|lung (*Seemannsspr.* Hinundherspringen des Windes)

Malm, der; -[e]s ⟨engl.⟩ (*Geol.* obere Abteilung der Juraformation; Weißer Jura); **mal|men** (*selten für* zermalmen, knirschen)

Mal|mö (schwed. Hafenstadt)

mal|neh|men (vervielfachen); ich nehme mal; malgenommen; malzunehmen

Ma|loc|chio [ma'lɔkio], der; -s, *Plur.* -s *u.* ...occhi [ma'lɔki] ⟨ital.⟩ (*ital. Bez. für* böser Blick)

Ma|lo|che [*auch* ...'lɔ...], die; - ⟨hebr.-jidd.⟩ (*ugs. für* schwere Arbeit); **ma|lo|chen** (*ugs. für* schwer arbeiten, schuften); **Ma|lo|cher** (*ugs. für* Arbeiter)

¹Ma|lo|ja (Ort in Graubünden); **²Ma|lo|ja**, der; -[s] (schweiz. Pass) *u.* **Ma|lo|ja|pass**, der; -es (↑R 105)

Ma|los|sol, der; -s ⟨russ.⟩ (schwach gesalzener Kaviar)

mal|pro|per ⟨franz.⟩ (*veraltet, noch landsch. für* unsauber); malpropre (↑R 130) Schürze

...mals (z. B. mehrmals)

Mal|säu|le (*veraltet für* Grenzstein; Gedenksäule)

Mal|ta (Insel u. Staat im Mittelmeer); **Mal|ta|fie|ber** (↑R 105)

Mal|te (m. Vorn.)

Mal|tech|nik

Mal|ter, der *od.* das; -s, - (altes Getreide-, Kartoffelmaß; *österr. ugs. auch für* Mörtel)

Mal|te|ser (Bewohner von Malta; Angehöriger des Malteserordens); (↑R 103:) Malteser Hündchen; **Mal|te|ser-Hilfs|dienst; Mal|te|ser‿kreuz, ...or|den** (der; -s), **...rit|ter; mal|te|sisch**, *aber* (↑R 102): Maltesische Inseln

Mal|thus [*engl.* 'mɛlθəs] (engl. Sozialphilosoph); **Mal|thu|si|a|ner** (Vertreter des Malthusianismus); **Mal|thu|si|a|nis|mus**, der; -; **mal|thu|sisch;** malthusisches Bevölkerungsgesetz

Mal|to|se, die; - (*Chemie* Malzzucker)

malt|rä|tie|ren (↑R 130) ⟨franz.⟩ (misshandeln, quälen); **Malt|rä|tie|rung**

Ma|lus, der; *Gen.* - *u.* -ses, *Plur.* - *u.* -se ⟨lat.⟩ (*Kfz-Versicherung* Prämienzuschlag bei Häufung von Schadensfällen)

Mal|uten|si|li|en (↑R 132) *Plur.*

Mal|va|sie̲r [...v...], der; -s (ein Süßwein); **Mal|va|sie̲r|wein**
Ma̤l|ve [...v...], die; -, -n ‹ital.› (eine Zier-, Heilpflanze); **ma̤l|ven|far|ben** *od.* **...far|big**
Mal|vi̲|nen [...v...] *Plur.* (*svw.* Falklandinseln)
Mal|wi̲|ne (w. Vorn.)
Ma̤lz, das; -es; **Ma̤lz˯bier, ...bon|bon**
Ma̲l|zei|chen (Multiplikationszeichen; *Zeichen* · *od.* ×)
Mä̲l|zel (dt. Instrumentenmacher); Mälzels Metronom, *auch* Metronom - (*Abk.* M. M.)
mä̤l|zen (Malz bereiten); du mälzt; **Mä̤l|zer; Mäl|ze|re̲i; Mäl|ze|rin; Ma̤lz˯ex|trakt, ...kaf|fee**
Ma̤|ma [*veraltend u. geh.* ma'ma:], die; -, -s; **Ma|ma̲|chen**
Ma̤m|ba, die; -, -s ‹Zulu› (eine afrik. Giftschlange)
Ma̤m|bo, der; -[s], -s, *auch* die; -, -s ‹kreol.› (ein südamerik. Tanz)
Ma|me|lṳck, der; -en, -en (↑R 126) ‹arab.-ital.› (Söldner islam. Herrscher)
Ma|me̤r|tus (ein Heiliger)
Ma̤|mi (*Kinderspr.*)
Mam|ma̤|lia *Plur.* ‹lat.› (*Zool.* Sammelbez. für alle Säugetiere); **Mam|mo|gra|phi̲e**, die; -, ...i̲en (*Med.* Röntgenuntersuchung der weibl. Brust)
Ma̤m|mon, der; -s ‹aram.› (*abwertend für* Reichtum; Geld); **Mam|mo|ni̤s|mus**, der; - (Geldgier, -herrschaft)
Ma̤m|mut, das; -s, *Plur.* -e *u.* -s ‹russ.-franz.› (Elefant einer ausgestorbenen Art); **Ma̤m|mut...** (*auch für* Riesen...); **Ma̤m|mut˯baum, ...kno|chen, ...pro|gramm, ...pro|zess, ...schau, ...ske|lett, ...un|ter|neh|men, ...ver|an|stal|tung, ...zahn**
ma̤mp|fen (*ugs. für* [mit vollen Backen] essen)
Mam|se̤ll, die; -, *Plur.* -en *u.* -s ‹franz.› (Angestellte im Gaststättengewerbe; *veraltet, noch scherzh. für* unverheiratete Frau, Hausgehilfin); (↑R 108:) kalte Mamsell, *auch* Kaltmamsell (Angestellte für die Zubereitung der kalten Speisen)
[1]**ma̤n** (↑R 48); *Dat.* einem, *Akk.* einen; man kann nicht wissen, was einem zustoßen wird; du siehst einen an, als ob man ...
[2]**ma̤n** (*nordd. ugs. für* nur, mal); das lass man bleiben
[1]**Man** [mɛn] (Insel in der Irischen See)
[2]**Ma̤n**, der *od.* das; -s, -s ‹pers.› (früheres pers. Gewicht); 3 - (↑R 90)

m. A. n. = meiner Ansicht nach
Mä|na̲|de, die; -, -n ‹griech.› (rasendes Weib [im Kult des griech. Weingottes Dionysos])
Ma|nage|ment ['mɛnɛdʒmənt], das; -s, -s ‹engl.-amerik.› (Leitung eines Unternehmens); **Ma|nage|ment-Buy-out** [...ba̯i'a̯ut], das; -[s] (Übernahme einer Firma durch die eigene Geschäftsleitung); **ma|na|gen** ['mɛnɛdʒ(ə)n] (*ugs. für* leiten, unternehmen; zustande bringen); gemanagt; **Ma|na|ger**, der; -s, - (Leiter [eines großen Unternehmens]; Betreuer [eines Berufssportlers]); **Ma|na|ge|rin; Ma|na|ger|krank|heit**
Ma|na|gua [ma'na(:)...] (Hptst. von Nicaragua)
Ma|na̲|ma (Hptst. von Bahrain)
Ma|na̤s|se (bibl. m. Eigenn.)
ma̤nch; -er, -e, -es; in manchem; manche sagen (↑R 48); so mancher, so manches; manch einer; mancher Tag; mancher Art; manche Stunde; manches *u.* manch Buch; mancher, der; manches, was. *Beugung:* manch guter Vorsatz; mancher gute Vorsatz; mit manch gutem Vorsatz, mit manchem guten Vorsatz; manch böses Wort, manches böse Wort; manchmal; manches Mal; manch liebes Mal, manches liebe Mal; manch Schönes *u.* manches Schöne; mit manch Schönem *u.* mit manchem Schönen; mancher stimmfähiger (*auch noch* stimmfähigen) Mitglieder, für manche ältere (*auch noch* älteren) Leute; manche Stimmberechtigte (*auch* Stimmberechtigten)
Ma̤n|cha [...tʃa], die; - (span. Landschaft)
ma̤n|chen|o̤rts; ma̤n|cher *vgl.* manch; **ma̤n|cher|le̲i**; mancherlei, was; **ma̤n|cher|o̤r|ten**, *häufiger* **ma̤n|cher|o̤rts; ma̤n|ches** *vgl.* manch
[1]**Man|ches|ter** ['mɛntʃɛstə(r), *engl.* 'mɛntʃistə] (engl. Stadt); [2]**Man|ches|ter** [man'ʃɛstər], der; -s (ein Gewebe); **Man|ches|ter|ho|se; Man|ches|ter|tum** ['mɛntʃɛstə(r)...], das; -s (liberalistische volkswirtschaftliche Anschauung)
ma̤nch|mal *vgl.* manch
Ma̤n|da|la, das; -[s], -s ‹sanskr.› (Bild als Meditationshilfe)
Man|da̤nt, der; -en, -en (↑R 126) ‹lat.› (*Rechtsspr.* Auftraggeber; Vollmachtgeber); **Man|da̤n|tin**
Man|da|ri̲n, der; -s, -e ‹sanskr.-port.› (*früher* europ. Bezeichnung hoher chin. Beamter); **Man|da|ri̲|ne**, die; -, -n (kleine apfelsinenähnliche Frucht); **Man|da|ri̲|nen|öl**, das; -[e]s; **Man|da|ri̲n|en|te** (eine asiat. Ente)

Man|da̲t, das; -[e]s, -e ‹lat.› (Auftrag, Vollmacht; Sitz im Parlament; in Treuhand von einem Staat verwaltetes Gebiet); **Man|da|ta̲r**, der; -s, -e (jmd., der im Auftrag eines anderen handelt; Rechtsanwalt; *österr. für* Abgeordneter); **Man|da|ta̲r|staat**; *vgl.* [1]Staat; **man|da|ti̲e|ren** (*veraltet für* zum Mandatar machen); **Man|da̲ts˯ge|biet, ...trä|ger, ...ver|lust**
[1]**Ma̤n|del**, die; -, -n ‹griech.› (Kern einer Steinfrucht; *meist Plur.:* Gaumenmandeln)
[2]**Ma̤n|del**, die; -, -[n] ‹mlat.› (altes Zählmaß; Gruppe von etwa 15 Garben; kleine Mandel = 15 Stück, große Mandel = 16 Stück); 3 Mandel[n] Eier (↑R 90)
Man|de̲|la, Nelson (südafrik. schwarzer Bürgerrechtler u. Politiker)
Ma̤n|del|au|ge; ma̤n|del|äu|gig; Ma̤n|del˯baum, ...blü|te, ...ent|zün|dung; ma̤n|del|för|mig; -e Augen; **Ma̤n|del˯ge|bäck, ...kern, ...kleie, ...öl** (das; -[e]s), **...ope|ra|ti|on** (↑R 132)
Ma̤n|derl *vgl.* Mandl
Man|di̲|beln *Plur.* ‹lat.› (*Biol.* Oberkiefer der Gliederfüßer); **man|di|bu|la̲r, man|di|bu|lä̲r** (zum Unterkiefer gehörend)
Ma̤ndl, Ma̤n|derl, das; -s, -n (*bayr. u. österr. ugs. für* Männlein; Wild-, Vogelscheuche; Wegzeichen aus Steinen)
Man|do̲|la, die; -, ...len ‹ital.› (eine Oktave tiefer als die Mandoline klingendes Zupfinstrument); **Man|do|li̲|ne**, die; -, -n ‹franz.› (ein Saiteninstrument)
Ma̤n|dor|la, die; -, ...do̤rlen ‹ital.› (mandelförmiger Heiligenschein)
Mand|ra̤|go|ra, Mand|ra|go̲|re (↑R 130), die; -, ...o̲ren ‹griech.› (ein Nachtschattengewächs)
Mand|ri̤ll (↑R 130), der; -s, -e ‹engl.› (ein in Westafrika heimischer Affe)
[1]**Ma̤nd|schu** (↑R 130), der; -[s], - (Angehöriger eines mongol. Volkes); [2]**Ma̤nd|schu**, das; -[s] (Sprache); **Mand|schṳ|kuo** (Name der Mandschurei als Kaiserreich 1934–45); **Mand|schu|re̲i**, die; - (nordostchin. Tiefland); **mand|schu̲|risch**; -es Fleckfieber
Ma|ne|ge [ma'ne:ʒə], die; -, -n ‹franz.› (runde Vorführfläche od. Reitbahn im Zirkus)

Ma|nen *Plur.* ‹lat.› (die guten Geister der Toten im altröm. Glauben)
ma|nes|sisch; *aber* (↑R 108): die Manessische Handschrift (eine Minnesängerhandschrift)
Ma|net [ma'ne:, *franz.* ma'nɛ], Edouard [e'dua:r] (franz. Maler)
Man|fred (m. Vorn.)
mang (*nordd. ugs. für* unter, dazwischen); mittenmang *(vgl. d.)*
Man|ga|be, die; -, -n ‹afrik.› (ein afrik. Affe)
Man|gan, das; -s ‹griech.› (chem. Element, Metall; *Zeichen* Mn); **Man|ga|nat,** das; -s, -e (Salz der Mangansäure); **Man|gan|ei|sen; Man|ga|nit** [*auch* ...'nit], der; -s, -e (ein Mineral)
Man|ge, die; -, -n (*südd., schweiz. für* [1]Mangel); [1]**Man|gel,** die; -, -n ([Wäsche]rolle)
[2]**Man|gel,** der; -s, Mängel (Fehler, Unvollkommenheit; *nur Sing.:* das Fehlen); **Man|gel‿be|ruf, ...er|schei|nung; man|gel|frei; man|gel|haft;** *vgl.* ausreichend; **Man|gel|haf|tig|keit,** die; -; **Män|gel|haf|tung** *(Rechtsw.)*
Man|gel|holz
Man|gel|krank|heit
[1]**man|geln** ([Wäsche] rollen); ich ...[e]le (↑R 16)
[2]**man|geln** (nicht [ausreichend] vorhanden sein); es hat an allem gemangelt
Män|gel|rü|ge (Klage über mangelhafte Ware od. Arbeit); **man|gels** (↑R 46); *Präp. mit Gen.:* mangels des nötigen Geldes, - eindeutiger Beweise; *im Plur. mit Dat., wenn der Gen. nicht erkennbar ist:* mangels Beweisen; **Man|gel|wa|re**
Man|gel|wä|sche, die; -; **man|gen** (*landsch. für* [1]mangeln)
Mang‿fut|ter (*landsch. für* Mischfutter; *vgl.* [1]Futter), **...ge|trei|de**
Mang|le|rin ‹*zu* [1]mangeln›
Man|go, die; -, *Plur.* ...gonen *od.* -s ‹tamil.-port.› (eine tropische Frucht); **Man|go|baum**
Man|gold, der; -[e]s, -e *Plur. selten* (ein Blatt- u. Stängelgemüse)
Mang|ro|ve [...v...] (↑R 130), die; -, -n ‹engl.› (immergrüner Laubwald in Meeresbuchten u. Flussmündungen tropischer Gebiete); **Mang|ro|ve[n]‿baum, ...küs|te**
Man|gus|te, die; -, -n ‹Marathi› (in Südeurasien u. Afrika heimische Schleichkatze)
Man|hat|tan [mɛn'hɛt(ə)n] (Stadtteil von New York)
Ma|ni (babylonischer Religionsstifter); **Ma|ni|chä|er** [...ç...] (Anhänger des Manichäismus); **Ma|ni|chä|is|mus,** der; - (von Mani gestiftete Religionsform)
Ma|nie, die; -, ...ien ‹griech.› (Sucht; Besessenheit)
Ma|nier, die; - ‹franz.› (Art u. Weise, Eigenart; Unnatur, Künstelei); **Ma|nie|ren** *Plur.* (Umgangsformen, [gutes] Benehmen); **ma|nie|riert** (gekünstelt; unnatürlich); **Ma|nie|riert|heit; Ma|nie|ris|mus,** der; - ‹lat.› (Stilbegriff für die Kunst der Zeit zwischen Renaissance u. Barock; gekünstelte Anwendung eines Stils); **Ma|nie|rist,** der; -en, -en (↑R 126; Vertreter des Manierismus); **ma|nie|ris|tisch; ma|nier|lich** (gesittet; fein; wohlerzogen)
ma|ni|fest ‹lat.› (handgreiflich, offenbar, deutlich); **Ma|ni|fest,** das; -es, -e (öffentl. Erklärung, Kundgebung; *Seew.* Verzeichnis der Güter auf einem Schiff); das Kommunistische Manifest; **Ma|ni|fes|tant,** der; -en, -en (↑R 126; *veraltet für* den Offenbarungseid Leistender; *schweiz., sonst veraltet für* Teilnehmer an einer politischen Kundgebung); **Ma|ni|fes|ta|ti|on,** die; -, -en (Offenbarwerden; *Rechtsw.* Offenlegung; Bekundung; *Med.* Erkennbarwerden [von Krankheiten]; *regional u. schweiz. für* politische Kundgebung); **ma|ni|fes|tie|ren** (offenbaren; bekunden; *veraltet für* den Offenbarungseid leisten; *regional u. schweiz. für* demonstrieren); sich manifestieren (deutlich werden, sich zu erkennen geben)
Ma|ni|kü|re, die; -, -n ‹franz.› (Handpflege, bes. Nagelpflege; Etui mit Geräten für die Nagelpflege; Hand-, Nagelpflegerin); **ma|ni|kü|ren;** manikürt
Ma|ni|la (Hptst. der Philippinen); **Ma|ni|la|hanf** (↑R 105; Spinnfaser der philippin. Faserbanane)
Ma|nil|le [ma'niljə], die; -, -n ‹franz.› (Trumpfkarte im Lomberspiel)
Ma|ni|ok, der; -s, -s ‹indian.-franz.› (eine tropische Nutzpflanze); **Ma|ni|ok‿mehl** (das; -[e]s), **...wur|zel**
[1]**Ma|ni|pel,** der; -s, - ‹lat.› (Teil der röm. Kohorte); [2]**Ma|ni|pel,** der; -s, -, *auch* die; -, -n (Teil der kath. Priestergewandung); **Ma|ni|pu|lant,** der; -en, -en (↑R 126); **Ma|ni|pu|la|ti|on,** die; -, -en (Hand-, Kunstgriff; Verfahren; *meist Plur.:* Machenschaft); **ma|ni|pu|la|tiv; Ma|ni|pu|la|tor,** der; -s, ...oren (*Technik* Vorrichtung zur Handhabung gefährlicher Substanzen hinter Schutzwänden; *veraltet für* fingerfertiger Zauberkünstler); **ma|ni|pu|lier|bar; Ma|ni|pu|lier|bar|keit,** die; -; **ma|ni|pu|lie|ren;** manipulierte (gesteuerte) Währung; der manipulierte Mensch; **Ma|ni|pu|lie|rung**
ma|nisch ‹griech.› (*Psych., Med.* an einer Manie erkrankt; abnorm heiter erregt); **ma|nisch-de|pres|siv** (↑R 27; *Psych.* abwechselnd manisch und depressiv)
Ma|nis|mus, der; - ‹lat.› (*Völkerk.* Ahnenkult, Totenverehrung)
Ma|ni|to|ba [*auch engl.* mɛni'to:bə] (kanad. Provinz)
Ma|ni|tu, der; -s ‹indian.› (zauberhafte Macht des indian. Glaubens, oft ohne Artikel personifiziert als „Großer Geist“)
Man|ko, das; -s, -s ‹ital.› (Fehlbetrag; Ausfall; Mangel); **Man|ko|geld** (pauschaler Ausgleich für Fehlbeträge)
[1]**Mann,** Heinrich u. Thomas (dt. Schriftsteller)
[2]**Mann,** der; -[e]s, *Plur.* Männer *u.* (*früher für* Lehnsleute, ritterl. Dienstmannen *od. scherzh.:*) Mannen; (↑R 90:) vier Mann hoch *(ugs.),* alle - an Bord, an Deck!, tausend -; er ist -s genug; seinen - stehen, stellen
Man|na, das; -[s], *österr. nur so, od.* die; - ‹hebr.› (legendäres [vom Himmel gefallenes] Brot der Israeliten; Pflanzensaft)
mann|bar; Mann|bar|keit, die; -; **Männ|chen; Mann|de|ckung** *(Sport);* **Män|ne** (*Koseform zu* Mann); **man|nen** (*Seemannsspr.* von Mann zu Mann reichen)
Man|ne|quin ['manəkɛ̃(:), *auch* ...'kɛ̃:], das, *selten* der; -s, -s ‹franz.› (Frau, die Modellkleider u. Ä. vorführt; *veraltet für* Gliederpuppe)
Män|ner‿be|kannt|schaft, ...be|ruf, ...bund; Män|ner|chen *Plur. (ugs.);* **Män|ner‿chor** (der), **...fang** (*meist nur in* auf Männerfang ausgehen); **män|ner|feind|lich; Män|ner‿freund|schaft, ...haus** *(Völkerk.),* **...heil|kun|de** (die; -); **män|ner|mor|dend** *(ugs. scherzh.);* **Män|ner‿sa|che, ...stim|me; Män|ner|treu,** die; -, -, *schweiz.* das; -s, - (Name verschiedener Pflanzen); **Man|nes‿al|ter** (das; -s), **...kraft, ...stamm** (männl. Linie einer Familie), **...stär|ke, ...treue, ...wort** (*Plur.* ...worte), **...zucht; mann|haft; Mann|haf|tig|keit,** die; -
Mann|heim (Stadt am Rhein); **Mann|hei|mer** (↑R 103); - Schule *(Musik)*
Mann|heit, die; - *(veraltet)*

man|nig|fach; man|nig|fal|tig; Man|nig|fal|tig|keit, die; - **män|nig|lich** (*veraltet für* jeder); **Män|nin,** die; - *(nur bibl.);* **...män|nisch** (z. B. bergmännisch)
Man|nit, der; -s, -e ‹hebr.› (sechswertiger Alkohol im Manna)
Männ|lein; Männlein und Weiblein *(Plur.);* **männ|lich;** -es Geschlecht; **Männ|lich|keit,** die; -; **Männ|lich|keits|wahn,** der; -[e]s (*svw.* Machismo); **Mann|loch** (Öffnung zum Einsteigen in große Behälter wie Kessel, Tanks o. Ä.); **Manns|bild** *(ugs.);* **Mann|schaft; mann|schaft|lich; Mann|schafts‿auf|stel|lung, ...geist** (der; -[e]s), **...ka|pi|tän, ...raum, ...sie|ger, ...stär|ke, ...stu|be, ...wa|gen, ...wer|tung; manns|dick; manns|hoch; Manns|hö|he;** in -; **Manns‿leu|te** *(Plur.; ugs.),* **...per|son; manns|toll; Manns|volk**
Man|nus (Gestalt der germ. Mythol.)
Mann|weib (*abwertend für* männlich wirkende Frau)
Ma|no|me|ter, das; -s, - ‹griech.› (*Physik* ein Druckmessgerät); **ma|no|me|trisch** (↑R 130)
Ma|nö|ver [...v...], das; -s, - ‹franz.› (größere Truppen-, Flottenübung; Bewegung, die mit einem Schiff, Flugzeug usw. ausgeführt wird; Winkelzug); **Ma|nö|ver‿kri|tik** (*auch* Besprechung mit kritischem Rückblick), **...scha|den**
ma|növ|rie|ren (↑R 130; Manöver vornehmen; geschickt zu Werke gehen); **ma|növ|rier|fä|hig; Ma|növ|rier‿fä|hig|keit** (die; -), **...mas|se**
Man|sard|dach ‹nach dem franz. Baumeister Mansart› (Dach mit gebrochenen Flächen); **Man|sar|de,** die; -, -n (Dachgeschoss, -zimmer); **Man|sar|den‿woh|nung, ...zim|mer**
Mansch, der; -[e]s (*ugs. für* Schneewasser; breiige Masse); **man|schen** (*ugs. für* mischen; im Wasser planschen); du manschst; **Man|sche|rei** *(ugs.)*
Man|schet|te, die; -, -n ‹franz.› (Ärmelaufschlag; Papierkrause für Blumentöpfe; unerlaubter Würgegriff beim Ringkampf); Manschetten haben (*ugs. für* Angst haben); **Man|schet|ten|knopf**
Mans, Le [lə 'mã:] (franz. Stadt); Le Mans' [lə 'mã:s] Umgebung (↑R 107)
Man|tel, der; -s, Mäntel; **Män|tel|chen; Man|tel‿fut|ter** (*vgl.* [2]Futter), **...ge|setz** (Rahmengesetz), **...kra|gen, ...rohr** *(Technik),* **...sack** (*veraltet für* Reisetasche); **Man|tel|ta|rif** *(Wirtsch.);* **Man|tel|ta|rif|ver|trag; Man|tel|ta|sche; Man|tel-und-De|gen-Film** (↑R 28; Abenteuerfilm, der in der Zeit der degentragenden Kavaliere spielt)
Man|tik, die; - ‹griech.› (Seher-, Wahrsagekunst)
Man|til|le [...'til(j)ə], die; -, -n ‹span.› (Schleiertuch)
Man|tis|se, die; -, -n ‹lat.› (*Math.* hinter dem Komma stehende Ziffern der Logarithmen)
Man|tua (ital. Stadt); **Man|tu|a|ner; man|tu|a|nisch**
Ma|nu|al, das; -s, -e ‹lat.› (Handklaviatur der Orgel; *veraltet für* Handbuch, Tagebuch)
Ma|nu|el [...ɛl] (m. Vorn.); **Ma|nu|e|la** (w. Vorn.)
ma|nu|ell ‹lat.› (mit der Hand; Hand...); manuelle Fertigkeit (Handfertigkeit); **Ma|nu|fakt,** das; -[e]s, -e (*veraltet für* handgearbeitetes Erzeugnis); **Ma|nu|fak|tur,** die; -, -en ([vorindustrieller] gewerblicher Großbetrieb mit Handarbeit; *veraltet für* in Handarbeit hergestelltes Erzeugnis); **Ma|nu|fak|tur|be|trieb; ma|nu|fak|tu|rie|ren** (*veraltet für* anfertigen; verarbeiten); **Ma|nu|fak|tu|rist,** der; -en, -en (↑R 126; *früher für* Leiter einer Manufaktur; Händler in Manufakturwaren); **Ma|nu|fak|tur|wa|ren** *Plur.* (Textilwaren)
Ma|nul|druck *Plur.* ...drucke (besonderes Druckverfahren; danach hergestelltes Druckwerk)
ma|nu pro|pria [*auch* - 'prɔ...] (↑R 130) ‹lat.› (mit eigener Hand; eigenhändig; *Abk.* m. p.); **Ma|nus,** das; -, - (*österr. u. schweiz. Kurzform von* Manuskript); **Ma|nu|skript,** das; -[e]s, -e ‹lat.› (hand- od. maschinenschriftl. Ausarbeitung; Urschrift; Satzvorlage; *Abk.* Ms. [*Plur.* Mss.] *od.* Mskr.); **Ma|nu|skript‿blatt, ...sei|te**
Ma|nu|ti|us (ital. Buchdrucker); *vgl.* Aldine usw.
Manx [maŋks, *engl.* mɛŋks], das; - (kelt. Sprache auf der Insel Man)
Man|za|nil|la [man(t)sa'nilja], der; -s ‹span.› (ein span. Weißwein)
Ma|o|is|mus, der; - (kommunist. Ideologie in der chin. Ausprägung von Mao Tse-tung); **Ma|o|ist,** der; -en, -en (↑R 126; Anhänger des Maoismus); **Ma|o|is|tin; ma|o|is|tisch**
[1]**Ma|o|ri** [*auch* 'mauri], der; -[s], -[s] (Polynesier auf Neuseeland); [2]**Ma|o|ri,** das; - (Sprache der Maoris); **ma|o|risch**
Mao Tse-tung [*auch* mao dzə'duŋ], *in neuerer Umschrift* **Mao Ze|dong** (chin. Staatsmann)
Ma|pai, die; - ‹hebr.› (gemäßigte sozialist. Partei Israels); **Ma|pam,** die; - (Arbeiterpartei Israels)
Mäpp|chen; Map|pe, die; -, -n
Ma|pu|to (Hptst. von Mosambik)
Ma|quet|te [ma'kɛt(ə)], die; -, -n ‹franz.› (Entwurf für ein Kunstwerk)
Ma|quis [ma'ki:], der; - [ma'ki:(s)] ‹franz., „Gestrüpp, Unterholz“› (franz. Widerstandsorganisation im 2. Weltkrieg); **Ma|qui|sard** [maki'za:r], der; -, *Plur.* -s *u.* -en [...'za:rdən] (Angehöriger des Maquis)
Mär, Mä|re, die; -, Mären (*veraltet, heute noch scherzh. für* Kunde, Nachricht; Sage)
Ma|ra|bu, der; -s, -s ‹arab.› (ein Storchvogel); **Ma|ra|but,** der; *Gen.* - *od.* -[e]s, *Plur.* - *od.* -s (moslem. Einsiedler, Heiliger)
Ma|ra|cu|ja, die; -, -s ‹indian.› (essbare Frucht der Passionsblume)
ma|ra|na|tha!, *ökum.* ma|ra|na|ta! ‹aram., „unser Herr, komm!“› (Gebetsruf der altchristlichen Abendmahlsfeier); **Ma|ra|na|tha,** *ökum.* Ma|ra|na|ta, das; -s, -s
Ma|rä|ne, die; -, -n ‹slaw.› (ein Fisch)
Ma|ran|te, *auch* Ma|ran|ta, die; -, ...ten ‹nach dem venezian. Arzt Maranta› (Pfeilwurz, eine Zimmerpflanze)
ma|ran|tisch (*svw.* marastisch)
Ma|ras|chi|no [maras'ki:no], der; -s, -s ‹ital.› (ein Kirschlikör)
Ma|ras|mus, der; - ‹griech.› (*Med.* Entkräftung, [Alters]schwäche); **ma|ras|tisch** (an Marasmus leidend, entkräftet, erschöpft)
Ma|rat [ma'ra] (franz. Revolutionär)
Ma|ra|thi, das; -[s] (Eingeborenensprache des mittleren Indien)
[1]**Ma|ra|thon** ['ma(:)...] (Ort nördl. von Athen); [2]**Ma|ra|thon,** der; -s, -s (*kurz für* Marathonlauf); [3]**Ma|ra|thon,** das; -s, -s (etwas durch übermäßig lange Dauer Anstrengendes); **Ma|ra|thon‿lauf** (↑R 105; leichtathletischer Wettlauf über 42,195 km), **...läu|fer, ...läu|fe|rin, ...re|de, ...sit|zung, ...ver|an|stal|tung**
Mar|bel, Mär|bel, Mar|mel, Mur|mel, die; -, -n (*landsch. für* kleine [marmorne] Kugel zum Spielen)

Mar|bod (markomann. König)
Mar|burg ['ma(:)r...] (Stadt in Hessen); **Mar|bur|ger** (↑R 103)
[1]**Marc** (dt. Maler u. Grafiker)
[2]**Marc** (m. Vorn.)
mar|ca|to ‹ital.› (*Musik* markiert, betont)
Mar|cel [mar'sɛl] (m. Vorn.)
[1]**March,** die; - (l. Nebenfluss der Donau)
[2]**March,** die; - (Gebiet am Ostende des Zürichsees)
[3]**March,** die; -, -en (*schweiz. für* Flurgrenze, Grenzzeichen)
Mär|chen; Mär|chen‿buch, ...dich|tung (die; -), **...er|zäh|ler, ...er|zäh|le|rin, ...film, ...for|schung; mär|chen|haft; Mär|chen‿land** (das; -[e]s), **...on|kel** (*ugs. auch für* jmd., der [häufig] Märchen erzählt), **...pracht, ...prinz, ...prin|zes|sin, ...stun|de, ...tan|te**
Mar|che|sa [...'ke:za], die; -, *Plur.* -s *u.* ...sen ‹ital.› (*w. Form von* Marchese); **Mar|che|se** [...'ke:zə], der; -, -n (hoher ital. Adelstitel)
March|feld, das; -[e]s (Ebene in Niederösterreich)
March|zins *Plur.* ...zinsen (*schweiz. Bankw.* Stückzins [beim Verkauf eines festverzinslichen Wertpapiers] seit dem letzten Zinstag)
Mar|co|ni (ital. Physiker)
Mar|co Po|lo (ital. Reisender)
Mar|der, der; -s, -; **Mar|der|fell**
Mä|re *vgl.* Mär
Ma|rees [ma're:] (dt. Maler)
Ma|rel|le (*Nebenform von* Morelle *u.* Marille)
Ma|rem|men *Plur.* ‹ital.› (sumpfige Küstengegend in Mittelitalien); **Ma|rem|men|land|schaft**
mä|ren (*landsch. für* in etwas herumwühlen; langsam sein; umständlich reden)
Ma|ren (w. Vorn.)
Ma|ren|de, die; -, -n ‹ital.› (*tirol. für* Zwischenmahlzeit, Vesper)
Ma|ren|go, der; -s ‹nach dem oberital. Ort› (grau melierter Kammgarnstoff)
Mä|re|rei ‹*zu* mären›
Mar|ga|re|ta, Mar|ga|re|te (w. Vorn.); **Mar|ga|re|ten|blu|me**
Mar|ga|ri|ne, die; - ‹franz.›; **Mar|ga|ri|ne‿fab|rik, ...wür|fel**
Mar|ge ['marʒə], die; -, -n ‹franz.› (Abstand, Spielraum; *Wirtsch.* Spanne zwischen zwei Preisen, Handelsspanne)
Mar|ge|ri|te [*auch* ...'ritə], die; -, -n ‹franz.› (eine Wiesenblume, Wucherblume); **Mar|ge|ri|ten‿strauß, ...wie|se**
Mar|ghe|ri|ta [...ge...] (w. Vorn.)
mar|gi|nal ‹lat.› (auf dem Rand stehend; am Rand liegend; *Bot.* randständig); **Mar|gi|nal‿be|mer|kung, ...glos|se** (an den Rand der Seite geschriebene od. gedruckte Glosse *[vgl. d.]*); **Mar|gi|na|lie** [...iə], die; -, -n *meist Plur.* (Randbemerkung auf der Seite einer Handschrift od. eines Buches); **mar|gi|na|li|sie|ren** (*auch für* [politisch] ins Abseits schieben)
Mar|git, Mar|git|ta, Mar|got, Mar|grit, Mar|gue|rite [margə'rit] (w. Vorn.)
Ma|ria (w. Vorn.; gelegentl. zusätzlicher m. Vorn.); Mariä (der Maria) Himmelfahrt (kath. Fest); die Himmelfahrt Mariens; *vgl.* Marie
Ma|ri|a|ge [...'aʒə], die; -, -n (König-Dame-Paar in Kartenspielen)
Ma|riä-Him|mel|fahrts-Fest, das; -[e]s (↑R 95)
Ma|ria Laach (Benediktinerabtei in der Eifel)
Ma|ri|a|nen *Plur.* (Inselgruppe im Pazifischen Ozean)
ma|ri|a|nisch ‹*zu* Maria›; marianische Frömmigkeit, *aber* (↑R 108): Marianische Kongregation; **Ma|ri|an|ne** (w. Vorn.; symbol. Verkörperung der Französischen Republik)
ma|ria-the|re|si|a|nisch; Ma|ri|a-the|re|si|en|ta|ler (frühere Münze)
Ma|ri|a|zell (Wallfahrtsort in der Steiermark)
Ma|rie, Ma|rie|chen, Ma|rie-Lu|i|se, *auch* Ma|rie|lu|i|se (w. Vorn.); **Ma|ri|en‿bild, ...dich|tung, ...fest, ...kä|fer; Ma|ri|en|kir|che** (↑R 95), *aber* St.-Marien-Kirche; **Ma|ri|en‿kult, ...le|ben** *(Kunstw.),* **...le|gen|de, ...tag, ...ver|eh|rung**
Ma|ri|en|wer|der (Stadt am Ostrand des Weichseltales); **Ma|ri|en|wer|der|stra|ße** (↑R 123)
Ma|ri|et|ta (w. Vorn.)
Ma|rig|na|no [mari'nja:no] (↑R 130; berühmter Schlachtort in Italien)
Ma|ri|hu|a|na [*mexik.* ...xu'a:na], das; -s ‹mexik.; aus den Vornamen Maria u. Juana [xu'a:na = Johanna]› (ein Rauschgift)
Ma|ri|ka (w. Vorn.)
Ma|ril|le, die; -, -n ‹ital.› (*bes. österr. für* Aprikose); **Ma|ril|len‿knö|del, ...mar|me|la|de, ...schnaps**
Ma|rim|ba, die; -, -s ‹afrik.-span.› (dem Xylophon ähnliches Musikinstrument); **Ma|rim|ba|phon,** das; -s, -e (Marimba mit Resonanzkörpern aus Metall)
ma|rin ‹lat.› (zum Meer gehörend, Meer[es]...)
[1]**Ma|ri|na** (w. Vorn.)
[2]**Ma|ri|na,** die; -, -s ‹lat.-engl.› (Jacht-, Motorboothafen)
Ma|ri|na|de, die; -, -n ‹franz.› (Flüssigkeit mit Essig, Kräutern, Gewürzen zum Einlegen von Fleisch, Gurken usw.; Salatsoße; eingelegter Fisch)
Ma|ri|ne, die; -, -n ‹franz.› (Seewesen eines Staates; Flottenwesen; Kriegsflotte, Flotte); **Ma|ri|ne‿ar|til|le|rie, ...at|ta|ché; ma|ri|ne|blau** (dunkelblau); **Ma|ri|ne‿flie|ger, ...in|fan|te|rie, ...ma|ler, ...of|fi|zier;** [1]**Ma|ri|ner,** der; -s, - (*Jargon* Matrose, Marinesoldat); [2]**Ma|ri|ner** ['mɛrinə(r)], der; -s, - ‹amerik.› (unbemannte amerik. Raumsonde zur Planetenerkundung); **Ma|ri|ne‿sol|dat, ...stück** (*svw.* Seestück), **...stütz|punkt, ...uni|form** (↑R 132)
ma|ri|nie|ren ‹franz.› (in Marinade einlegen)
Ma|rio (m. Vorn.)
Ma|ri|o|lat|rie (↑R 130), die; - ‹griech.› (relig. Marienverehrung); **Ma|ri|o|lo|ge,** der; -n, -n; ↑R 126 (Vertreter der Mariologie); **Ma|ri|o|lo|gie,** die; - (kath.-theol. Lehre von der Gottesmutter); **ma|ri|o|lo|gisch**
Ma|ri|on (w. Vorn.); **Ma|ri|o|net|te,** die; -, -n ‹franz.› (Gliederpuppe; willenloser Mensch als Werkzeug anderer); **Ma|ri|o|net|ten|büh|ne; ma|ri|o|net|ten|haft; Ma|ri|o|net|ten‿re|gie|rung, ...spiel, ...the|a|ter**
Ma|ri|otte [ma'riɔt] (franz. Physiker); mariottesches Gesetz (↑R 94)
Ma|rist, der; -en, -en; ↑R 126 ‹*zu* Maria› (Angehöriger einer kath. Missionskongregation)
Ma|ri|ta (w. Vorn.)
ma|ri|tim ‹lat.› (das Meer, das Seewesen betreffend; Meer[es]..., See...); -es Klima
Ma|ri|us (röm. Feldherr u. Staatsmann)
Mar|jell, die; -, -en, **Mar|jell|chen** ‹lit.› (*ostpreuß. für* Mädchen)
[1]**Mark,** die; -, *Plur.* -, *ugs. scherzh.* Märker (Währungseinheit; *Abk. [ehem. in der DDR]* M); Deutsche Mark (*Abk.* DM). *Zur Schreibung der Dezimalstellen* ↑R 135
[2]**Mark,** die; -, -en (*früher für* Grenzland); die Mark Brandenburg
[3]**Mark,** das; -[e]s (*Med., Bot.; auch übertr. für* das Innerste, Beste)

[4]Mark (m. Vorn.)
mar|kant ‹franz.› (stark ausgeprägt)
Mar|ka|sit [*auch* ...'zit], der; -s, -e ‹arab.› (ein Mineral)
Mark Au|rel (röm. Kaiser)
mark|durch|drin|gend; -er Schrei
Mar|ke, die; -, -n (Zeichen; Handels-, Waren-, Wertzeichen); **Mär|ke,** die; -, -n (*österr. für* [Namens]zeichen); **mär|ken** (*österr. für* mit einer Märke versehen); **Mar|ken‿ar|ti|kel, ...but|ter, ...er|zeug|nis, ...fab|ri|kat, ...samm|ler, ...schutz, ...wa|re, ...zei|chen**
Mar|ker, der; -s, -[s] ‹engl.› (Stift zum Markieren; *fachspr. für* Merkmal)
Mär|ker (Bewohner der [2]Mark)
mark|er|schüt|ternd; -e Schreie
Mar|ke|ten|der, der; -s, - ‹ital.› (*früher* Händler bei der Feldtruppe); **Mar|ke|ten|de|rei; Mar|ke|ten|de|rin; Mar|ke|ten|der‿wa|gen, ...wa|re**
Mar|ke|te|rie, die; -, ...ien ‹franz.› (*Kunstw.* Einlegearbeit [von farbigem Holz usw.])
Mar|ke|ting, das; -[s] ‹engl.› (*Wirtsch.* Ausrichtung eines Unternehmens auf die Förderung des Absatzes)
Mark‿graf (*früher für* Verwalter einer [2]Mark), **...grä|fin; Mark|gräf|ler,** der; -s, - (ein südbad. Wein); **Mark|gräf|ler Land,** das; - -[e]s (Landschaft am Oberrhein); **mark|gräf|lich; Mark|graf|schaft** *(früher)*
mar|kie|ren ‹franz.› (be-, kennzeichnen; eine Rolle o. Ä. [bei der Probe] nur andeuten; *österr. für* [eine Fahrkarte] entwerten, stempeln; *ugs. für* vortäuschen; *Sport* [einen Treffer] erzielen, [einen Gegenspieler] decken); **Mar|kier|ham|mer** *(Forstw.)*; **Mar|kie|rung; Mar|kie|rungs‿fähn|chen, ...li|nie, ...punkt**
mar|kig; Mar|kig|keit, die; -
mär|kisch (aus der [2]Mark stammend, sie betreffend); märkische Heimat, *aber* (↑R 108): das Märkische Museum
Mar|ki|se, die; -, -n ‹franz.› ([leinenes] Sonnendach, Schutzdach, -vorhang); *vgl. aber* Marquise; **Mar|ki|sen|stoff; Mar|ki|set|te** (*eindeutschend für* Marquisette)
Mark|ka ['marka], die; -, -; *aber* 10 Markkaa [...ka] ‹germ.-finn.› (*svw.* Finnmark; *Abk.* mk)
Mark‿klöß|chen (eine Suppeneinlage), **...kno|chen; mark|los**
Mar|ko (m. Vorn.)
Mar|ko|brun|ner (ein Rheinwein)
[1]Mar|kolf (m. Vorn.)
[2]Mar|kolf, der; -[e]s, -e (*landsch. für* Häher)
Mar|ko|man|ne, der; -n, -n; ↑R 126 (Angehöriger eines germ. Volksstammes)
Mar|kör, der; -s, -e ‹franz.› (Aufseher, Punktezähler beim Billardspiel; *Landw.* Gerät zum Anzeichnen von Pflanzreihen)
Mark|ran|städt (Stadt südwestl. von Leipzig)
Mark|schei|de (Grenze [eines Grubenfeldes]); **Mark|schei|de‿kun|de** (die; -), **...kunst** (die; -; *Bergmannsspr.* Vermessung, Darstellung der Lagerungs- u. Abbauverhältnisse); **Mark|schei|der** (Vermesser im Bergbau); **mark|schei|de|risch**
Mark|stamm|kohl (als Grün- od. Gärfutter verwendete Form des Kohls)
Mark|stein
Mark|stück; mark|stück|groß; *vgl.* fünfmarkstückgroß
Markt, der; -[e]s, Märkte; zu Markte tragen; **Markt‿ab|spra|che, ...ana|ly|se** (↑R 132), **...an|teil; markt|be|herr|schend; Markt‿be|richt, ...brun|nen, ...bu|de, ...chan|ce; mark|ten** (abhandeln, feilschen); **Markt‿fah|rer** (*österr. u. schweiz. für* Wanderhändler), **...fle|cken, ...for|schung, ...frau; markt|füh|rend; Markt|füh|rer; markt|gän|gig; Markt‿hal|le, ...la|ge, ...lü|cke**
Markt|ober|dorf (↑R 132; Stadt im Allgäu)
Markt|ord|nung; markt|ori|en|tiert (↑R 132); **Markt‿ort** (der; -[e]s, -e), **...platz, ...preis** (*vgl.* [2]Preis), **...recht, ...schrei|er; markt|schrei|e|risch; Markt‿seg|ment, ...tag; markt|üb|lich**
Mark Twain [- 'twe:n] (amerik. Schriftsteller)
Markt‿weib, ...wert, ...wirt|schaft (Wirtschaftssystem mit freiem Wettbewerb); freie -; soziale -; **markt|wirt|schaft|lich**
Mar|kung (*veraltet für* Grenze)
Mar|kus (Evangelist; röm. m. Vorn. [*Abk.* M.]); Evangelium Marci [...tsi] (des Markus); **Mar|kus|kir|che** (↑R 95)
Mark|ward (m. Vorn.)
Marl|bo|rough ['mɔ:lbərо, *engl.* 'mɔ:lbərə] (engl. Feldherr u. Staatsmann)
Mär|lein (*veraltet für* Märchen)
Mar|le|ne (w. Vorn.)
Mar|lies, Mar|lis (w. Vorn.)
Mar|lowe ['ma(:)rlo:] (engl. Dramatiker)
Mar|ma|ra|meer, das; -[e]s (zwischen Bosporus und Dardanellen)
[1]Mar|mel *vgl.* Marbel; **[2]Mar|mel,** der; -s, - ‹lat.› (*veraltet für* Marmor)
Mar|me|la|de, die; -, -n; **Mar|me|la|de[n]‿brot, ...ei|mer, ...glas** (*Plur.* ...gläser), **...re|zept**
mar|meln ‹lat.› (*landsch. für* mit [1]Marmeln spielen); ich ...[e]le (↑R 16); **Mar|mel|stein** (*veraltet für* Marmor); **Mar|mor,** der; -s, -e (Gesteinsart); **mar|mor|ar|tig; Mar|mor‿block** (*Plur.* ...blöcke), **...büs|te; mar|mo|rie|ren** (marmorartig bemalen, ädern); **Mar|mor|ku|chen; mar|morn** (aus Marmor); **Mar|mor‿plat|te, ...säu|le, ...sta|tue, ...trep|pe**
Mar|ne [*franz.* marn], die; - (franz. Fluss)
Ma|ro|cain [...'kɛ̃:], der *od.* das; -s, -s ‹franz.› (fein gerippter Kleiderstoff)
ma|rod (*österr. ugs. für* leicht krank); **ma|ro|de** ‹franz.› (*Soldatenspr. für* marschunfähig; *veraltend für* ermattet, erschöpft, verkommen); **Ma|ro|deur** [...'dø:r], der; -s, -e (*Soldatenspr.* plündernder Nachzügler); **ma|ro|die|ren**
Ma|rok|ka|ner; ma|rok|ka|nisch; Ma|rok|ko (Staat in Nordwestafrika)
[1]Ma|ro|ne, die; -, *Plur.* -n, *landsch. auch* ...ni ‹franz.› ([geröstete] essbare Kastanie); **[2]Ma|ro|ne,** die; -, -n (ein Pilz); **Ma|ro|nen|pilz; Ma|ro|ni,** die; -, - (*südd., österr. svw.* [1]Marone); **Ma|ro|ni|bra|ter**
Ma|ro|nit, der; -en, -en (↑R 126) ‹nach dem hl. Maro› (Angehöriger der mit Rom unierten syrischen Kirche im Libanon); **ma|ro|ni|tisch;** -e Liturgie
Ma|ro|quin [...'kɛ̃:], der, *auch* das; -s ‹franz., „aus Marokko"› (Ziegenleder)
Ma|rot|te, die; -, -n ‹franz.› (Schrulle, wunderliche Neigung, Grille)
Mar|quis [...'ki:], der; - [...'ki:(s)], - [...'ki:s] ‹franz., „Markgraf"› (franz. Titel); **Mar|qui|sat** [...ki...], das; -[e]s, -e (Würde, Gebiet eines Marquis); **Mar|qui|se,** die; -, -n ‹„Markgräfin"› (franz. Titel); *vgl. aber* Markise; **Mar|qui|set|te,** die; -, *auch* der; -s (ein Gardinengewebe)
Mar|ra|kesch (Stadt u. Provinz in Marokko)
Mar|ro|ni (*schweiz. für* Maroni)
[1]Mars (röm. Kriegsgott); **[2]Mars,** der; - (ein Planet)
[3]Mars, der; -, -e, *auch* die; -, -en ‹niederd.› (*Seemannsspr.* Platt-

form zur Führung u. Befestigung der Marsstenge)
[1]**Mar|sa̲|la** (ital. Stadt); [2]**Mar|sa̲|la,** der; -s, -s (ein Süßwein); **Mar|sa̲|la|wein** (↑R 105)
marsch!; marsch, marsch!; vorwärts marsch!; [1]**Marsch,** der; -[e]s, Märsche
[2]**Marsch,** die; -, -en (vor Küsten angeschwemmter fruchtbarer Boden)
Mar|schall, der; -s, ...schälle ‹„Pferdeknecht"› (hoher milit. Dienstgrad; Haushofmeister); **Mar|schall[s]‿stab, ...wür|de**
Marsch|be|fehl; marsch|be|reit; Marsch‿be|reit|schaft (die; -), **...block** (*Plur.* ...blocks)
Marsch|bo|den; Mar|schen|dorf
marsch|fer|tig; Marsch|flug|kör|per *(Milit.)*; **Marsch|ge|päck; mar|schie̲|ren; Mar|schie̲|rer; Marsch‿ko|lon|ne, ...kom|pass**
Marsch|land *Plur.* ...länder (*svw.* [2]Marsch)
Marsch|lied; marsch|mä|ßig; Marsch‿mu|sik, ...ord|nung, ...rich|tung, ...rou|te, ...tem|po, ...tritt, ...ver|pfle|gung, ...ziel
Mar|seil|lai|se [marsɛˈjɛ:z(ə)], die; - (franz. Revolutionslied, dann Nationalhymne); **Mar|seille** [...ˈsɛ:j] (franz. Stadt); **Mar|seil|ler** [...ˈsɛ:jər] (↑R 103)
Mars|feld, das; -[e]s (Versammlungs- u. Übungsplatz im alten Rom; großer Platz in Paris)
Mar|shall|in|seln [ˈmarʃal..., *engl.* ˈma:(r)ʃ(ə)l...] *Plur.* (↑R 105; Inseln im Pazifischen Ozean)
Mar|shall|plan [ˈmarʃal..., *engl.* ˈma:(r)ʃ(ə)l...] (↑R 95), der; -[e]s ‹nach dem amerik. Außenminister G. C. Marshall› (amerik. Hilfsprogramm für Westeuropa nach dem 2. Weltkrieg)
Mars‿mensch, ...son|de
Mars|sten|ge (*Seemannsspr.* erste Verlängerung des Mastes)
Mar|stall, der; -[e]s, ...ställe ‹„Pferdestall"› (Pferdehaltung eines Fürsten u. a.)
Mar|sy|as (altgriech. Meister des Flötenspiels)
Mar|ta *vgl.* [2]Martha
Mär|te, die; -, -n (*mitteld. für* Mischmasch; Kaltschale)
Mar|ten|si̲t [*auch* ...ˈzit], der; -s, -e ‹nach dem dt. Ingenieur Martens› (beim Härten von Stahl entstehendes Gefüge von Eisen und Kohlenstoff)
Mar|ter, die; -, -n; **Mar|ter|in|stru|ment; Mar|terl,** das; -s, -n (*bayr. u. österr. für* Tafel mit Bild und Inschrift zur Erinnerung an Verunglückte; Pfeiler mit Nische für Kruzifix od. Heiligenbild); **mar|tern;** ich ...ere (↑R 16); **Mar|ter‿pfahl, ...qual, ...tod; Mar|te|rung; mar|ter|voll; Mar|ter|werk|zeug**
[1]**Mar|tha;** ↑R 92 (w. Vorn.); [2]**Mar|tha,** *ökum.* Mar|ta (bibl. w. Eigenn.)
mar|ti|a̲|lisch ‹lat.› (kriegerisch; grimmig; verwegen)
[1]**Mar|tin** (m. Vorn.)
[2]**Mar|tin** [marˈtɛ̃:] (schweiz. Komponist)
Mar|ti̲|na (w. Vorn.)
Mar|tin|gal, das; -s, *Plur.* -e *u.* -s ‹franz.› (*Reiten* zwischen den Vorderbeinen des Pferdes durchlaufender Sprungzügel)
Mar|tin-Horn ® *vgl.* Martinshorn
Mar|ti̲|ni, das; - (Martinstag)
Mar|ti|nique [...ˈnik] (Insel der Kleinen Antillen)
Mar|tins‿gans, ...horn (als ®: Martin-Horn; *Plur.* ...hörner), **...tag** (11. Nov.)
Mär|ty|rer[1], der; -s, - ‹griech.› (jmd., der wegen seines Glaubens od. seiner Überzeugung Verfolgung od. den Tod erleidet); **Mär|ty|[re]|rin**[1]; **Mär|ty|rer‿kro|ne, ...tod; Mär|ty|rer|tum,** das; -s; **Mar|ty̲|ri|um,** das; -s, ...ien [...i̯ən] (schweres Leiden [um des Glaubens od. der Überzeugung willen]); **Mar|ty|ro|lo̲|gi|um,** das; -s, ...ien [...i̯ən] (Verzeichnis der Märtyrer u. Heiligen u. ihrer Feste)
Ma|run|ke, die; -, -n (*ostmitteld.* eine Pflaume)
Marx, Karl (dt. Philosoph, Begründer der nach ihm benannten Lehre vom Kommunismus); die marxsche Philosophie (↑R 94); **Mar|xis|mus,** der; - (die von Marx u. Engels begründete Theorie des Kommunismus); **Mar|xis|mus-Le|ni|nis|mus,** der; - (in den [ehem.] sozialistischen Ländern gebräuchl. Bez. für die kommunist. Ideologie nach Marx, Engels u. Lenin); **Mar|xist,** der; -en, -en (↑R 126); **Mar|xis|tin; mar|xis|tisch; Mar|xist-Le|ni|nist,** der; Marxisten-Leninisten, *Plur.* Marxisten-Leninisten (↑R 126)
Ma|ry [ˈmɛri] (w. Vorn.); **Ma|ry Jane** [- ˈdʒe:n], die; - - ‹engl.› (Marihuana *[vgl. d.]*); **Ma|ry|land** [ˈmɛrilɛnd] (Staat der USA; *Abk.* Md.)
März, der; *Gen.* -[es], *geh. auch noch* -en, *Plur.* -e ‹lat.; nach dem röm. Kriegsgott Mars› (dritter Monat im Jahr, Lenzing, Lenzmond, Frühlingsmonat); **März|be|cher,** Mär|zen|be|cher (eine Frühlingsblume); **März|bier, Mär|zen|bier; März‿feld** (das; -[e]s; merowing. Wehrmännerversammlung), **...ge|fal|le|ne** (der; -n, -n; ↑R 5 ff.; der Revolution von 1848), **...glöck|chen** (eine Frühlingsblume)
Mar|zi|pa̲n [*auch,* österr. nur, ˈmar...], das, *österr., sonst selten,* der; -s, -e ‹arab.› (süße Masse aus Mandeln u. Zucker); **Mar|zi|pan‿kar|tof|fel, ...schwein|chen**
märz|lich; März‿nacht, ...re|vo|lu|ti|on (1848), **...son|ne** (die; -), **...veil|chen**
Ma|sa|ryk [...rik] (tschechoslowak. Soziologe u. Staatsmann)
Mas|cag|ni [...ˈkanji] (↑R 130; ital. Komponist)
[1]**Mas|ca̲|ra,** die; -, -s ‹span.-engl.› (Wimperntusche); [2]**Mas|ca̲|ra,** der; -, -s (Stift od. Bürste zum Auftragen von Wimperntusche)
Mas|car|po̲|ne, der; -s ‹ital.› (ein ital. Weichkäse)
Ma|schans|ker, der; -s, - ‹tschech.› (*österr.* eine Apfelsorte)
Ma|sche, die; -, -n (Schlinge; *österr. u. schweiz. auch für* Schleife; *ugs. für* Lösung; Trick); das ist die neu[e]ste Masche
Ma|schek|sei|te *vgl.* Maschikseite
Ma|schen‿draht (Drahtgeflecht), **...mo|de, ...netz, ...pan|zer, ...wa|re; Ma|scherl,** das; -s, -n (*österr. für* Schleife); **ma|schig**
Ma|schik|sei|te, Ma|schek|sei|te ‹ung.› (*ostösterr. für* entgegengesetzte Seite, Rückseite)
Ma|schi̲|ne, die; -, -n ‹franz.›; ich schreibe Maschine; weil er Maschine schreibt; ich habe Maschine geschrieben; Maschine zu schreiben; *aber* ein maschinegeschriebener Brief; *vgl.* maschinengeschrieben; **ma|schi|nell** (maschinenmäßig [hergestellt]); **Ma|schi̲|nen‿bau** (der; -[e]s), **...fab|rik; ma|schi̲|nen‿ge|schrie|ben** (*od.* maschine..., *österr.* maschingeschrieben; *vgl.* Maschine u. maschinschreiben), **...ge|stickt, ...ge|strickt; Ma|schi̲|nen‿ge|wehr** (*Abk.* MG), **...haus; ma|schi̲|nen|les|bar** *(EDV)*; **ma|schi̲|nen|mä|ßig; Ma|schi̲|nen‿meis|ter, ...nä|he|rin, ...öl, ...pis|to|le** (*Abk.* MP, MPi), **...re|vi|si|on** (*Druckw.* Überprüfung der Druckbogen vor Druckbeginn); **Ma|schi̲|nen|satz** (zwei miteinander starr gekoppelte Maschinen; *Druckw., nur Sing.:* mit der Setzmaschine hergestellter

[1] *Kath. Kirche auch* Martyrer usw.

Schriftsatz); **Ma|schi|nen‿scha|den, ...schlos|ser, ...schlos|se|rin; Ma|schi|ne[n]‿schrei|ben** (das; -s; *Abk.* Masch.-Schr.), **...schrei|ber, ...schrei|be|rin; Ma|schi|nen|schrift; ma|schi|nen|schrift|lich; Ma|schi|nen‿set|zer** *(Druckw.),* **...spra|che** *(EDV),* **...te|le|graf, ...wär|ter, ...zeit|al|ter; Ma|schi|ne|rie,** die; -, ...ien (maschinelle Einrichtung; Getriebe); **Ma|schi|ne|schrei|ben** usw. *vgl.* Maschine[n]schreiben usw.; **Ma|schi|ne schrei|ben** *vgl.* Maschine; **Ma|schi|nist,** der; -en, -en; ↑R 126 (Maschinenmeister); **ma|schin|schrei|ben** (*österr. für* Maschine schreiben); **Ma|schin|schrei|ben,** das; -s *(österr.);* **Ma|schin|schrei|ber** *(österr.);* **ma|schin|schrift|lich** *(österr.);* **Masch.-Schr.** = Maschine[n]schreiben (↑R 26)

[1]**Ma|ser** ['me:zə(r), *auch* 'ma:...], der; -s, - ‹engl.› (*Physik* Gerät zur Verstärkung oder Erzeugung von Mikrowellen)

[2]**Ma|ser,** die; -, -n (Zeichnung [im Holz]; Narbe)

Ma|se|reel ['masəre:l], Frans (belg. Grafiker u. Maler)

Ma|ser|holz; ma|se|rig; ma|sern; ich ...ere (↑R 16); gemasertes Holz; **Ma|sern** *Plur.* (eine Kinderkrankheit)

Ma|se|ru (Hptst. von Lesotho)

Ma|se|rung (Zeichnung des Holzes)

Mas|ka|rill, der; -[s], -e ‹span.› (span. Lustspielgestalt)

Mas|ka|ron, der; -s, -e ‹franz.› (*Archit.* Menschen- od. Fratzengesicht)

Mas|kat (Hptst. von Oman); **Mas|kat und Oman** (*frühere Bez. für* Oman)

Mas|ke, die; -, -n ‹franz.› (künstl. Hohlgesichtsform; Verkleidung; kostümierte Person); **Mas|ken‿ball, ...bild|ner, ...bild|ne|rin; mas|ken|haft; Mas|ken‿kos|tüm, ...spiel, ...ver|leih; Mas|ke|ra|de,** die; -, -n ‹span.› (Verkleidung; Maskenfest; Mummenschanz); **mas|kie|ren** ‹franz.› ([mit einer Maske] unkenntlich machen; verkleiden; verbergen, verdecken); sich -; **Mas|kie|rung**

Mas|kott|chen ‹franz.› (Glück bringender Talisman, Anhänger; Puppe u. a. [als Amulett]); **Mas|kot|te,** die; -, -n (*svw.* Maskottchen)

mas|ku|lin [*auch* ...'li:n] ‹lat.› (männlich); **mas|ku|li|nisch** (*älter für* maskulin); **Mas|ku|li|num,** das; -s, ...na (*Sprachw.* männl. Substantiv, z. B. „der Wagen"; *nur Sing.:* männl. Geschlecht)

Ma|so|chis|mus [...x...], der; - ‹nach dem österr. Schriftsteller L. v. Sacher-Masoch› (geschlechtl. Erregung durch Erdulden von Misshandlungen); **Ma|so|chist,** der; -en, -en (↑R 126); **Ma|so|chis|tin; ma|so|chis|tisch**

Ma|so|wi|en [...iən] (hist. Gebiet beiderseits der Weichsel um Warschau)

[1]**Maß,** das; -es, -e ‹*zu* messen›; Maß halten; er hält Maß; dass er Maß hält; Maß gehalten; Maß zu halten; eine Maß haltende Forderung; Maß nehmen, *aber* (↑R 50): das Maßnehmen; [2]**Maß,** die; -, -[e] (*bayr. u. österr.* ein Flüssigkeitsmaß); 2 Maß Bier (↑R 90)

Mass. = Massachusetts

Mas|sa|chu|setts [mɛsə'tʃu:sɛts] (Staat in den USA; *Abk.* Mass.)

Mas|sa|ge [ma'sa:ʒə, *österr.* ma'sa:ʒ], die; -, -n [ma'sa:ʒ(ə)n] ‹franz.› (Heilbehandlung durch Streichen, Kneten usw. des Körpergewebes); **Mas|sa|ge‿in|sti|tut, ...sa|lon, ...stab**

Mas|sai [*auch* 'mas...], der; -, - (Angehöriger eines Nomadenvolkes in Ostafrika)

Mas|sa|ker, das; -s, - ‹franz.› (Gemetzel); **mas|sak|rie|ren** (↑R 130; niedermetzeln); **Mas|sak|rie|rung**

Maß|ana|ly|se (↑R 132; *Chemie*); **maß|ana|ly|tisch; Maß‿an|ga|be, ...an|zug, ...ar|beit, ...band** (*Plur.* ...bänder), **...be|zeich|nung; Mäß|chen** (altes Hohlmaß); **Ma|ße,** die; -, -n (*veraltet für* Mäßigkeit; Art u. Weise); *noch in* in, mit, ohne Maßen; über die -n; über alle -n

Mas|se, die; -, -n; **Mas|se|gläu|bi|ger** *Plur. (Wirtsch.)*

Maß‿ein|heit, ...ein|tei|lung

[1]**Mas|sel,** der; -s ‹hebr.-jidd.› (*Gaunerspr.* Glück)

[2]**Mas|sel,** die; -, -n (Form für Roheisen; Roheisenbarren)

mas|se|los; -e Elementarteilchen

ma|ßen (*veraltet für* weil); **Ma|ßen** (*Plur. von* Maße); **...ma|ßen** (z. B. einigermaßen)

Mas|sen‿ab|fer|ti|gung, ...ab|satz, ...an|drang, ...ar|beits|lo|sig|keit, ...ar|ti|kel, ...auf|ge|bot, ...be|darf, ...be|darfs|ar|ti|kel, ...ent|las|sung, ...fab|ri|ka|ti|on, ...ge|sell|schaft *(Soziol.),* **...grab; mas|sen|haft; Mas|sen‿hin|rich|tung, ...ka|ram|bo|la|ge, ...kund|ge|bung, ...me|di|um** *(meist Plur.),* **...mord, ...mör|der, ...or|ga|ni|sa|ti|on, ...pro|duk|ti|on** (die; -), **...psy|cho|se, ...quar|tier, ...sport, ...ster|ben, ...tou|ris|mus, ...ver|an|stal|tung, ...ver|kehrs|mit|tel; mas|sen|wei|se; Mas|se|schul|den** *Plur.* (Wirtsch.)

Mas|set|te, die; -, -n (*österr. für* Eintrittskartenblock)

Mas|seur [ma'sø:r], der; -s, -e ‹franz.› (die Massage Ausübender); **Mas|seu|rin** [ma'sø:rin], die; -, -nen *(offz. Berufsbez.);* **Mas|seu|se** [ma'sø:zə], die; -, -n

Maß|ga|be, die; - (*Amtsspr. für* Bestimmung); mit der -; nach - (entsprechend); **maß|ge|bend; maß|geb|lich; maß|ge|recht; maß|ge|schnei|dert; Maß hal|ten[d]** *vgl.* [1]Maß; **maß|hal|tig** (*Technik* das Maß einhaltend); **Maß|hal|tig|keit,** die; -

Maß|hol|der, der; -s, - (Feldahorn)

[1]**mas|sie|ren** ‹franz.› (durch Massage behandeln, kneten)

[2]**mas|sie|ren** ‹franz.› (Truppen zusammenziehen; verstärken, intensivieren); **Mas|sie|rung**

mas|sig

mä|ßig; ...mä|ßig (z. B. behelfsmäßig); **mä|ßi|gen;** sich -

Mas|sig|keit, die; -

Mä|ßig|keit, die; -; **Mä|ßi|gung,** die; -

mas|siv ‹franz.› (schwer; voll [nicht hohl]; fest, dauerhaft; roh, grob); **Mas|siv,** das; -s, -e [...və] (Gebirgsstock); **Mas|siv|bau** *Plur.* ...bauten; **Mas|siv|bau|wei|se; Mas|si|vi|tät** [...v...], die; -

Maß‿kon|fek|ti|on, ...krug; maß|lei|dig (*südd. für* verdrossen)

Maß|lieb, das; -[e]s, -e ‹niederl.› (eine Blume); **Maß|lieb|chen**

maß|los; Maß|lo|sig|keit; Maß|nah|me, die; -, -n; **Maß|nah|men|ka|ta|log; Maß|neh|men,** das; -s; *vgl.* Maß

Mas|sör usw. *vgl.* Masseur usw.

Mas|so|ra, die; - ‹hebr.› ([jüd.] Textkritik des A. T.); **Mas|so|ret,** der; -en, -en; ↑R 126 (mit der Massora beschäftigter jüd. Schriftgelehrter u. Textkritiker); **mas|so|re|tisch**

Mas|sö|se *vgl.* Masseuse

Maß|re|gel; maß|re|geln; ich maßreg[e]le (↑R 16); gemaßregelt; zu maßregeln; **Maß|re|ge|lung, Maß|reg|lung; Maß‿sa|chen** *(Plur.; ugs.),* **...schnei|der, ...stab; maß|stäb|lich; ...maß|stäb|lich,** *gelegentlich auch* ...maß|stä|big (z. B. großmaßstäblich, *gelegentl. auch* großmaßstäbig); **maß|stab[s]‿ge|recht, ...ge|treu; maß|voll; Maß|werk,**

das; -[e]s (Ornament an gotischen Bauwerken)
[1]**Mast**, der; -[e]s, *Plur.* -en, *auch* -e (Mastbaum)
[2]**Mast**, die; -, -en (Mästung)
Mas|ta|ba, die; -, *Plur.* -s *u.* ...taben ‹arab.› (altägypt. Grabkammer)
Mast|baum
Mast|darm; Mast|darm|fis|tel; mäs|ten; Mast|en|te
Mas|ten|wald
Mas|ter, der; -s, - ‹engl., „Meister"› (engl. Anrede an junge Leute; akadem. Grad in England u. in den USA; Leiter bei Parforcejagden); Master of Arts (akadem. Grad; *Abk.* M. A.; *vgl.* Magister)
...mas|ter (z. B. Dreimaster)
Mäs|ter; Mäs|te|rei; Mast‿fut|ter (*vgl.* [1]Futter), **...gans, ...huhn**
Mas|tiff, der; -s, -s ‹engl.› (Hund einer doggenartigen Rasse)
mas|tig (*landsch. für* fett, feist; *auch für* feucht [von Wiesen])
Mas|ti|ka|tor, der; -s, ...oren ‹lat.› (Knetmaschine); **Mas|tix**, der; -[es] (ein Harz)
Mast|korb
Mast‿kur, ...och|se
Mas|to|don (↑R 132), das; -s, ...donten ‹griech.› (ausgestorbene Elefantenart)
Mast|schwein
Mast|spit|ze
Mäs|tung
Mas|tur|ba|ti|on, die; -, -en ‹lat.› (geschlechtliche Selbstbefriedigung); **mas|tur|ba|to|risch; mas|tur|bie|ren**
Mast|vieh
Ma|su|re, der; -n, -n; ↑R 126 (Bewohner Masurens); **Ma|su|ren** (Landschaft im ehem. Ostpreußen); **ma|su|risch**, *aber* (↑R 102): die Masurischen Seen; **Ma|sur|ka** (↑R 33), die; -, *Plur.* ...ken *u.* -s ‹poln.› (poln. Nationaltanz)
Ma|sut, das; -[e]s ‹russ.› (Erdölrückstand, der zum Heizen von Kesseln verwendet wird)
Ma|ta|dor, der; *Gen.* -s, *auch* -en, *Plur.* -e, *auch* -en ‹span.› (Hauptkämpfer im Stierkampf; Hauptperson)
Match [mɛtʃ, *schweiz. auch* matʃ], das, *schweiz.* der; -[e]s, *Plur.* -s, *auch* -e, *österr. u. schweiz. auch* -es [...is] ‹engl.› (Wettkampf, -spiel); **Match‿ball** (['mɛtʃ...] spielentscheidender Ball [Aufschlag] beim Tennis), **...beu|tel, ...sack, ...stra|fe** (Feldverweis für die gesamte Spieldauer beim Eishockey); **Match|win|ner**, der; -s, - (Gewinner eines Matchs)
[1]**Ma|te**, der; - ‹indian.› (ein Tee);
[2]**Ma|te**, die; -, -n (südamerik. Stechpalmengewächs, Teepflanze); **Ma|te‿baum, ...blatt**
Ma|ter, die; -, -n ‹lat.› (*Druckw.* Papptafel mit negativer Prägung eines Schriftsatzes; Matrize; *Med.* die das Hirn einhüllende Haut); **Ma|ter do|lo|ro|sa**, die; - - ‹„schmerzensreiche Mutter"› (*christl. Rel.* Beiname Marias, der Mutter Jesu)
ma|te|ri|al ‹lat.› (stofflich, inhaltlich, sachlich); materiale Ethik; **Ma|te|ri|al**, das; -s, ...ien [...iən]; **Ma|te|ri|al‿aus|ga|be, ...be|darf, ...be|schaf|fung, ...ein|spa|rung, ...er|mü|dung** *(Technik)*, **...feh|ler; Ma|te|ri|a|li|sa|ti|on**, die; -, -en (Verkörperung, Verstofflichung; *Physik* Umwandlung von Energie in materielle Teilchen; *Parapsychologie* Entwicklung körperhafter Gebilde in Abhängigkeit von einem Medium); **ma|te|ri|a|li|sie|ren; Ma|te|ri|a|lis|mus**, der; - (philos. Anschauung, die alles Wirkliche auf Kräfte od. Bedingungen der Materie zurückführt; auf Besitz und Gewinn ausgerichtete Haltung); **Ma|te|ri|a|list**, der; -en, -en (↑R 126); **Ma|te|ri|a|lis|tin; ma|te|ri|a|lis|tisch; Ma|te|ri|al‿kos|ten** *(Plur.)*, **...man|gel, ...prü|fung, ...samm|lung, ...schlacht; Ma|te|rie** [...iə], die; -, -n (Stoff; Inhalt; Gegenstand [einer Untersuchung]; *Philos.*, *nur Sing.*: Urstoff; die außerhalb unseres Bewusstseins vorhandene Wirklichkeit); **ma|te|ri|ell** ‹franz.› (stofflich; wirtschaftlich, finanziell; auf den eigenen Nutzen bedacht)
[1]**ma|tern** ‹lat.› (*Druckw.* von einem Satz Matern herstellen); ich ...ere (↑R 16); [2]**ma|tern** (*Med.* mütterlich); **Ma|ter|ni|tät**, die; - (*Med.* Mutterschaft)
Ma|te|tee
Math. = Mathematik
Ma|the, die; - (*Schülerspr.* Mathematik); **Ma|the|ma|tik** [...'ti(:)k, *österr.* ...'matik], die; - ‹griech.› (Wissenschaft von den Raum- u. Zahlengrößen; *Abk.* Math.); **Ma|the|ma|ti|ker; Ma|the|ma|ti|ke|rin; ma|the|ma|tisch** [*österr.* ...'matiʃ]; -er Zweig; **ma|the|ma|ti|sie|ren**
Mat|hil|de; ↑R 92 (w. Vorn.)
Ma|ti|nee [*auch* 'ma...], die; -, ...een ‹franz.› (am Vormittag stattfindende künstlerische Veranstaltung)
Ma|tisse [ma'tis] (franz. Maler)
Mat|jes|he|ring ‹niederl.; dt.› (junger Hering)
Mat|rat|ze (↑R 130), die; -, -n (Bettpolster); **Mat|rat|zen|la|ger**
Mät|res|se (↑R 130), die; -, -n ‹franz.› (*früher* Geliebte [eines Fürsten]); **Mät|res|sen|wirt|schaft**, die; -
mat|ri|ar|cha|lisch (↑R 130) ‹lat.; griech.› (das Matriarchat betreffend); **Mat|ri|ar|chat**, das; -[e]s, -e *Plur. selten* (Mutterherrschaft, Mutterrecht); **Mat|ri|kel** [*auch, österr. nur,* ma'trikəl], die; -, -n ‹lat.› (Verzeichnis; *österr. für* Personenstandsregister); **Mat|rix**, die; -, *Plur.* Matrizes, *auch* Matrices [...tse:s] *u.* Matrizen (*Math.* geordnetes Schema von Werten, für das bestimmte Rechenregeln gelten; *Med.* Keimschicht); **Mat|ri|ze**, die; -, -n ‹franz.› (*Druckw.* bei der Setzmaschine Hohlform [zur Aufnahme der Patrize]; die von einem Druckstock zur Anfertigung eines Galvanos hergestellte [Wachs]form); **Mat|ri|zen|rand**
Matr|josch|ka *vgl.* Matroschka
Mat|ro|ne (↑R 130), die; -, -n ‹lat.› (ältere, ehrwürdige Frau, Greisin; *abwertend für* [ältere] korpulente Frau); **mat|ro|nen|haft**
Mat|rosch|ka (↑R 130), *seltener auch* Matr|josch|ka, die; -, -s ‹russ.› (Holzpuppe mit ineinander gesetzten kleineren Puppen)
Mat|ro|se (↑R 130), der; -n, -n; ↑R 126 ‹niederl.›; **Mat|ro|sen‿an|zug, ...blu|se, ...kra|gen, ...müt|ze, ...uni|form** (↑R 132)
matsch ‹ital.› (*ugs. für* völlig verloren; schlapp, erschöpft); - sein; [1]**Matsch**, der; -[e]s, -e (gänzlicher Verlust beim Kartenspiel)
[2]**Matsch**, der; -[e]s (*ugs. für* weiche Masse; nasser Straßenschmutz); **mat|schen** *(ugs.);* du matschst; **mat|schig** *(ugs.)*
matsch|kern (*ostösterr. ugs. für* schimpfen, maulen)
Matsch-und-Schnee-Rei|fen; ↑R 28 (*Abk.* M-und-S-Reifen);
Matsch|wet|ter
matt ‹arab.› (schwach; kraftlos; glanzlos); jmdn. matt setzen (handlungsunfähig machen); Schach und matt!; mattblau u. a.; **Matt**, das; -s, -s
Mat|tä|us *vgl.* Matthäus
[1]**Mat|te**, die; -, -n (Decke, Unterlage; Bodenbelag)
[2]**Mat|te**, die; -, -n (*geh. für* Weide [in den Hochalpen]; *schweiz. für* Wiese)
[3]**Mat|te**, die; - (*mitteld. für* Quark)
Mat|ter|horn, das; -[e]s (Berg in den Walliser Alpen)
Matt‿glas, ...gold; matt|gol|den
Mat|thä|us, *ökum.* Mat|tä|us

(Apostel u. Evangelist); Evangelium Matthäi (des Matthäus); bei jmdm. ist Matthäi am Letzten ‹mit Bezug auf das letzte Kapitel des Matthäusevangeliums› (*ugs. für* jmd. ist finanziell am Ende); **Mat|thä|us|pas|si|on** (Vertonung der Leidensgeschichte Christi nach Matthäus)
Matt|heit, die; -; **matt|her|zig**
¹Mat|thi|as (m. Vorn.); **²Mat|thi|as**, *ökum.* **Mat|ti|as** (bibl. m. Eigenn.)
mat|tie|ren ‹franz.› (matt, glanzlos machen); **Mat|tie|rung; Mat|tig|keit**, die; -; **Matt|schei|be;** [eine] - haben (*übertr. ugs. für* begriffsstutzig, benommen sein)
Ma|tur, das; -s, *schweiz.* die; - *u.* Ma|tu|rum, das; -s ‹lat.› (Reife-, Schlussprüfung); **Ma|tu|ra**, die; - (*österr. u. schweiz. für* Reifeprüfung); **Ma|tu|rand**, der; -en, -en; ↑R 126 (*schweiz., sonst veraltet für* Abiturient); **Ma|tu|rant**, der; -en, -en; ↑R 126 (*österr. für* Abiturient); **ma|tu|rie|ren** (*österr., sonst veraltet für* die Reifeprüfung ablegen); **Ma|tu|ri|tas prae|cox** [- ˈprɛːkɔks], die; - - (*Med., Psych.* [sexuelle] Frühreife); **Ma|tu|ri|tät**, die; - (*veraltet für* Reife; *schweiz. für* Hochschulreife); **Ma|tu|ri|täts‿prü|fung, ...zeug|nis; Ma|tu|rum** *vgl.* Matur
Ma|tu|tin, die; -, -e[n] ‹lat.› (nächtliches Stundengebet)
Matz, der; -es, *Plur.* -e *u.* Mätze *(scherzh.); meist in Zusammensetzungen,* z. B. Hosenmatz; **Mätzchen;** - machen (*ugs. für* Ausflüchte machen, sich sträuben)
Mat|ze, die; -, -n *u.* **Mat|zen**, der; -s, - ‹hebr.› (ungesäuertes Passahbrot der Juden)
mau (*ugs. für* schlecht; dürftig); *nur in* das ist -; mir ist -
Maud [mɔːd] (w. Vorn.)
Mau|er, die; -, -n; **Mau|er|ar|beit**, Mau|rer|ar|beit; **Mau|er‿as|sel, ...blüm|chen** (*veraltend für* Mädchen, das selten zum Tanzen aufgefordert wird; jmd., der wenig beachtet wird); **Mäu|er|chen; Mau|e|rei**, Mau|re|rei, die; - (das Mauern); **Mau|er|ha|ken; Mau|er|kel|le**, Mau|rer|kel|le; **Mau|er|kro|ne; Mau|er|loch; Mau|er|meis|ter**, Mau|rer|meis|ter; **mau|ern;** ich ...ere (↑R 16); **Mau|er|po|lier**, Mau|rer|po|lier (Vorarbeiter); **Mau|er‿rit|ze, ...seg|ler** (ein Vogel); **Mau|er|specht** (*ugs. für* jmd., der Stücke aus der Berliner Mauer [als Souvenirs] herausbrach); **Mau|e|rung; Mau|er‿vor|sprung, ...werk**
Maugham [mɔːm] (engl. Schriftsteller)
Mau|ke, die; - (eine Hauterkrankung bei Tieren)
Maul, das; -[e]s, Mäuler; **Maul|af|fen** *Plur.; meist in* - feilhalten (*ugs. für* mit offenem Mund dastehen u. nichts tun)
Maul|beer|baum; Maul|bee|re; Maul|beer|sei|den|spin|ner
Maul|bronn (Stadt in Baden-Württemberg)
Mäul|chen (kleiner Mund); **mau|len** (*ugs. für* murren, widersprechen)
Maul|esel (↑R 132; Kreuzung aus Pferdehengst u. Eselstute)
maul|faul *(ugs.);* **Maul|held** *(ugs.);* **Maul|korb; Maul|korb|er|lass** *(ugs.);* **Maul‿schel|le** *(ugs.),* **...sper|re** *(ugs.),* **...ta|sche** (*meist Plur.;* schwäb. Pastetchen aus Nudelteig)
Maul|tier (Kreuzung aus Eselhengst u. Pferdestute)
Maul|trom|mel (ein Musikinstrument); **Maul- und Klau|en|seu|che**, die; -; ↑R 23 (*Abk.* MKS); **Maul|werk** *(ugs.)*
Maul|wurf, der; -[e]s, ...würfe (*auch für* Spion); **Maul|wurfs‿gril|le, ...hau|fen**
¹Mau-Mau *Plur.* ‹afrik.› (Geheimbund in Kenia)
²Mau-Mau, das; -[s] (ein Kartenspiel)
maun|zen (*landsch. für* winseln, weinerlich sein, klagen [von Kindern und Wehleidigen, auch von Katzen]); du maunzt
Mau|pas|sant [mopaˈsãː] (franz. Schriftsteller)
Mau|re, der; -n, -n; ↑R 126 (Angehöriger eines nordafrik. Mischvolkes)
Mau|rer; Mau|[r]er|ar|beit; Mau|re|rei, Mau|e|rei, die; -; **Mau|rer‿ge|sel|le, ...hand|werk** (das; -[e]s); **mau|re|risch** (freimaurerisch), *aber* (↑R 108): Maurerische Trauermusik (Orchesterstück von W. A. Mozart); **Mau|[r]er|kel|le; Mau|[r]er|meis|ter; Mau|[r]er|po|lier; Mau|rer|zunft**
Mau|res|ke *vgl.* Moreske
Mau|re|ta|ni|en (im Altertum Name Marokkos; *heute* selbstständiger Staat in Afrika); **Mau|re|ta|ni|er; mau|re|ta|nisch**
Mau|rice [moˈriːs] (m. Vorn.)
Mau|rin ‹*zu* Maure›
Mau|ri|ner, der; -s, - ‹nach dem hl. Patron Maurus› (Angehöriger einer Kongregation der Benediktiner)
mau|risch (die Mauren betreffend); -er Bau, -er Stil
Mau|ri|ti|er [...t͡si̯ər] (Bewohner von ¹Mauritius); **mau|ri|tisch; ¹Mau|ri|ti|us** (Insel u. Staat im Ind. Ozean); die blaue Mauritius (bestimmte Briefmarke der Insel Mauritius aus dem Jahre 1847)
²Mau|ri|ti|us ‹lat.› (ein Heiliger)
Maus, die; -, Mäuse
Mau|schel, der; -s, - ‹hebr.-jidd., „Moses"› (armer Jude); **Mau|schel|be|te**, die; -, -n ‹jidd.; franz.› (*Kartenspiel* doppelter Strafsatz beim Mauscheln); **Mau|schel|lei** ‹hebr.-jidd.› ([heimliches] Aushandeln von Vorteilen, Geschäften); **mau|scheln** (jiddisch sprechen; [heimlich] Vorteile aushandeln, Geschäfte machen; *übertr. für* unverständlich sprechen; Mauscheln spielen); ich ...[e]le (↑R 16); **Mau|scheln**, das; -s (ein Kartenglücksspiel)
Mäus|chen; mäus|chen|still; Mäu|se|bus|sard; Mau|se|fal|le, *seltener* **Mäu|se|fal|le; Mäu|se‿fraß, ...gift; mäu|seln** (*Jägerspr.* das Pfeifen der Mäuse nachahmen); ich ...[e]le (↑R 16); **Mau|se|loch**, *seltener* **Mäu|se|loch; mau|sen** (*ugs. scherzh. für* stehlen; *landsch. für* Mäuse fangen); du maust; er maus|te; **Mäu|se‿nest, ...pla|ge**
¹Mau|ser, die; - ‹lat.› (jährlicher Ausfall und Ersatz der Federn bei Vögeln)
²Mau|ser (Familienn.; ®); *vgl.* Mauserpistole
Mau|se|rei (*ugs. scherzh. für* Stehlerei); **Mäu|se|rich**, der; -s, -e (männliche Maus)
mau|sern, sich
Mau|ser|pis|to|le (↑R 95); *vgl.* ²Mauser)
Mau|se|rung
mau|se|tot, *österr. auch* maus|tot *(ugs.);* - schlagen; **Mäu|se|turm**, der; -[e]s (Turm auf einer Rheininsel bei Bingen); **maus‿far|ben** *od.* **...far|big, ...grau**
mau|sig; sich - machen (*ugs. für* frech, vorlaut sein)
Mau|so|le|um, das; -s, ...een ‹griech.; nach dem König Mausolos› (monumentales Grabmal)
maus|tot (*österr. neben* mausetot)
Maut, die; -, -en (*veraltet für* Zoll; *bayr., österr. für* Gebühr für Straßen- u. Brückenbenutzung); **maut|bar** (*veraltet für* zollpflichtig); **Maut|ge|bühr** *(österr.)*
Maut|hau|sen (Ort in Oberösterreich; im 2. Weltkrieg Konzentrationslager der Nationalsozialisten)
Maut|in|kas|so *(österr.)*
Maut|ner (*veraltet für* Zöllner);

Maut⌣stel|le *(österr.),* **...stra|ße** *(österr. für* Straße, die nur gegen Gebühr befahren werden darf)
mauve [mo:v] ‹franz.› (malvenfarbig); ein mauve Kleid; *vgl. auch* beige; in Mauve (↑R 47); **mauve|far|ben; Mau|ve|in** [move'i:n], das; -s (ein Anilinfarbstoff)
mau|zen (*svw.* maunzen); du mauzt
m. a. W. = mit ander[e]n Worten
Max, Mäx|chen (m. Vorn.)
ma|xi (*Mode* knöchellang); der Rock ist maxi; **¹Ma|xi,** das; -s, -s (*ugs. für* Maxikleid; *meist ohne Artikel, nur Sing.:* knöchellange Kleidung); Maxi tragen; **²Ma|xi,** der; -s, -s (*ugs. für* Maxirock, -mantel usw.); **Ma|xi...** (bis zu den Knöcheln reichend, z. B. Maxirock)
Ma|xil|la, die; -, ...llae [...lɛ:] ‹lat.› (*Med.* Oberkiefer); **ma|xil|lar**
Ma|xi|ma (*Plur. von* Maximum); **ma|xi|mal** ‹lat.› (sehr groß, größt..., höchst...); **Ma|xi|mal⌣be|las|tung, ...for|de|rung, ...hö|he, ...leis|tung, ...pro|fit, ...stra|fe, ...wert; Ma|xi|me,** die; -, -n (allgemeiner Grundsatz, Hauptgrundsatz); **ma|xi|mie|ren** (maximal machen); **Ma|xi|mie|rung; Ma|xi|mi|li|an** (m. Vorn.); **Ma|xi|mum,** das; -s, ...ma (Höchstwert, -maß); barometrisches Maximum (*Meteor.* Hoch); **Ma|xi|sin|gle,** die (²Single von der Größe einer LP für längere Stücke der Popmusik)
Max-Planck-Ge|sell|schaft, die; -; ↑R 95 (*kurz für* Max-Planck-Gesellschaft zur Förderung der Wissenschaften; *früher* Kaiser-Wilhelm-Gesellschaft); **Max-Planck-In|sti|tut,** das; -[e]s, -e; **Max-Planck-Me|dail|le,** die; -, -n (seit 1929 für besondere Verdienste um die theoretische Physik verliehen)
Max|well ['mɛkswəl] (engl. Physiker)
May (dt. Schriftsteller)
Ma|ya ['ma:ja], der; -[s], -[s] (Angehöriger eines indian. Kulturvolkes in Mittelamerika); **Ma|ya|kul|tur,** die; -
May|day ['me:de:] ‹engl.› (internationaler Notruf im Funksprechverkehr)
Ma|yon|nai|se *vgl.* Majonäse
May|or ['mɛ(:)ə(r)], der; -s, -s ‹engl.› (Bürgermeister in England u. in den USA); *vgl.* Lord Mayor
MAZ, die; - (*Fernsehen, Kurzwort für* magnetische Bildaufzeichnung)
Maz|daz|nan [masdas...], das, *auch* der; -s (von O. Hanish begründete, auf der Lehre Zarathustras fußende religiöse Heilsbewegung)
Ma|ze|do|ni|en usw. *vgl.* Makedonien usw.
Mä|zen, der; -s, -e ‹lat.; nach dem Römer Maecenas› (Kunstfreund; freigebiger Gönner); **Mä|ze|na|ten|tum,** das; -s; **mä|ze|na|tisch; Mä|ze|nin**
Ma|ze|ra|ti|on, die; -, -en ‹lat.› (*Med.* Aufweichung von Gewebe durch Flüssigkeit; Auslaugung); **ma|ze|rie|ren**
Ma|zis, der; - ‹franz.› *u.* **Ma|zis|blü|te,** die; -, -n (getrocknete Samenhülle des Muskatnussbaumes [als Gewürz und Heilmittel verwendet])
Ma|zur|ka [ma'zurka] *vgl.* Masurka
Maz|zi|ni (ital. Politiker u. Freiheitskämpfer)
mb = Millibar
MB = Megabyte
Mba|ba|ne (Hptst. von Swasiland)
mbH = mit beschränkter Haftung
Mbyte, MByte = Megabyte
Mc, M' = Mac
MC, die; -, -[s] (*kurz für* Musikkassette)
m. c. = mensis currentis, *dafür besser* laufenden Monats (lfd. M.)
Mc|Car|thy|is|mus [məka:(r)θi'ismus], der; - ‹nach dem amerik. Politiker McCarthy› (zu Beginn der 50er-Jahre in den USA betriebene Verfolgung von Kommunisten u. Linksintellektuellen)
Mc|Kin|ley *vgl.* Mount McKinley
Md = *chem. Zeichen für* Mendelevium
MD = Musikdirektor
Md. = Maryland
Md., Mia., Mrd. = Milliarde[n]
mdal. = mundartlich
MdB, M. d. B. = Mitglied des Bundestages
MdL, M. d. L. = Mitglied des Landtages
MDR = Mitteldeutscher Rundfunk
Me. = Maine
ME = Macheeinheit
m. E. = meines Erachtens
Me|cha|nik, die; -, -en ‹griech.› (*nur Sing.:* Lehre von den Kräften u. Bewegungen; *auch für* Getriebe, Trieb-, Räderwerk); **Me|cha|ni|ker; Me|cha|ni|ke|rin; me|cha|nisch** (den Gesetzen der Mechanik entsprechend; maschinenmäßig; unwillkürlich, gewohnheitsmäßig, gedankenlos); -es Lernen; **me|cha|ni|sie|ren** ‹franz.› (auf mechanischen Ablauf umstellen); **Me|cha|ni|sie|rung; Me|cha|ni|sie|rungs|pro|zess; Me|cha|nis|mus,** der; -, ...men (sich bewegende techn. Einrichtung; [selbsttätiger] Ablauf, Zusammenhang; *früher* eine Richtung der Naturphilosophie); **me|cha|nis|tisch** (nur mechan. Ursachen anerkennend)
Me|cheln, *amtl.* Me|che|len (Stadt in Belgien)
Mecht|hild, Mecht|hil|de (w. Vorn.)
meck!; meck, meck!
Me|cke|rei; Me|cke|rer *(ugs. abwertend);* **Me|cker|frit|ze** *(ugs. abwertend);* **me|ckern;** ich ...ere (↑R 16; *ugs. abwertend*); **Me|cker⌣stim|me, ...zie|ge**
Meck|len|burg ['me:k..., *auch* 'mɛk...]; **Meck|len|bur|ger** (↑R 103); **meck|len|bur|gisch,** *aber* (↑R 102): die Mecklenburgische Seenplatte; die Mecklenburgische Schweiz; **Meck|len|burg-Schwe|rin; Meck|len|burg-Stre|litz; Meck|len|burg-Vor|pom|mer** (↑R 103); **meck|len|burg-vor|pom|me|risch** *vgl.* pommerisch; **Meck|len|burg-Vor|pom|mern** (↑R 106)
Me|dail|le [me'daljə, *österr.* me'dailjə], die; -, -n (Gedenk-, Schaumünze; Auszeichnung); **Me|dail|len⌣ge|win|ner, ...spie|gel** ([inoffz.] Tabelle über die Verteilung der Medaillen auf die teilnehmenden Länder bei Sportveranstaltungen); **Me|dail|leur** [medal'jø:r], der; -s, -e (Stempelschneider); **Me|dail|lon** [medal'jõ:], das; -s, -s (Bildkapsel; Rundbild[chen]; *Kunstw.* rundes od. ovales Relief; kleine, runde Fleischschnitte)
Me|dard, Me|dar|dus (Heiliger)
Me|dea (griech. Sagengestalt, kolchische Königstochter)
Me|den|spie|le (*Plur.;* ↑R 95) ‹nach dem ersten Präsidenten des Deutschen Tennis-Bundes, C. A. von der Meden› (Mannschaftswettkampf im Tennis)
Me|der, der; -s, - (Bewohner von ³Medien)
Me|dia, die; -, *Plur.* ...diä *u.* ...dien [...iən] ‹lat.› (*Sprachw.* stimmhafter Laut, der durch die Aufhebung eines Verschlusses entsteht, z. B. b; *Med.* mittlere Schicht der Gefäßwand); **me|di|al** (*Sprachw.* von passiv. Form in aktiv. Bedeutung; *Med.* nach der Körpermitte hin gelegen; *Parapsychologie* das spiritistische Medium betreffend); **me|di|an** (*Med.* in der Mittellinie des Körpers gelegen);

Me|di|an|ebe|ne (↑R 132; *Med.* Symmetrieebene des menschl. Körpers); **Me|di|an|te,** die; -, -n ‹ital.› (*Musik* Mittelton der Tonleiter; *auch für* Dreiklang über der 3. Stufe)
Me|di|a|ti|on, die; -, -en ‹lat.› (Vermittlung eines Staates in einem Konflikt zwischen anderen Staaten; Vermittlung zwischen Streitenden [z. B. Scheidungswilligen]); **me|di|a|ti|sie|ren** ‹franz.› (*früher* [reichsunmittelbare Besitzungen] der Landeshoheit unterwerfen); **Me|di|a|ti|sie|rung**
me|di|ä|val [...v...] ‹lat.› (mittelalterlich); **Me|di|ä|val** [*Druckw. meist* meˈdi̯ɛvəl], die; - (eine Schriftgattung); **Me|di|ä|vist,** der; -en, -en; ↑R 126 (Erforscher u. Kenner des MA.); **Me|di|ä|vis|tik,** die; - (Erforschung des MA.); **Me|di|ä|vis|tin**
Me|di|ce|er [...ˈt͡se:ər, *auch, österr. nur* ...ˈt͡ʃe:ər], der; -s, - *u.* **Me|di|ci** [ˈme:dit͡ʃi], der; -, - (Angehöriger eines florentin. Geschlechts); **me|di|ce|isch** [...ˈt͡se:iʃ, *auch, österr. nur,* ...ˈt͡ʃe:iʃ]; die Mediceische Venus (↑R 108)
[1]**Me|di|en** [...i̯ən] *Plur.* (*zusammenfassende Bez. für* Film, Funk, Fernsehen, Presse)
[2]**Me|di|en** [...i̯ən] (*Plur. von* [1]Media *u.* Medium)
[3]**Me|di|en** [...i̯ən] (*früher* Land im Iran)
me|di|en|ge|recht [...i̯ən...]; **Me|di|en‿land|schaft** (die; -), **...spek|ta|kel** (das; *ugs.*), **...verbund** (Kombination, Verbindung verschiedener [1]Medien)
Me|di|ka|ment, das; -[e]s, -e ‹lat.› (Arzneimittel); **me|di|ka|men|tös;** -e Behandlung; **Me|di|ka|ti|on,** die; -, -en (Arzneimittelverabreichung, -verordnung); **Me|di|kus,** der; -, *Plur.* Medizi, *ugs.* -se (*scherzh. für* Arzt)
[1]**Me|di|na** (saudiarab. Stadt)
[2]**Me|di|na,** die; -, -s ‹arab.› (islam. Stadt od. alte islam. Stadtteile im Ggs. zu den Europäervierteln)
me|dio ‹ital., „in der Mitte"› (*Kaufmannsspr.*); medio (Mitte) Mai; **Me|dio,** der; -[s], -s (*Kaufmannsspr.* Monatsmitte); zum - abschließen
me|di|o|ker ‹franz.› (*selten für* mittelmäßig); ...ok|re (↑R 130) Leistung; **Me|di|o|kri|tät** (↑R 130), die; -, -en
Me|di|o|wech|sel (*Kaufmannsspr.* in der Mitte eines Monats fälliger Wechsel)
Me|di|ta|ti|on, die; -, -en ‹lat.› (Nachdenken; sinnende Betrachtung; religiöse Versenkung); **me|di|ta|tiv**
me|di|ter|ran ‹lat., „mittelländisch"› (mit dem Mittelmeer zusammenhängend); **Me|di|ter|ran|flo|ra,** die; - (Pflanzenwelt der Mittelmeerländer)
me|di|tie|ren ‹lat.› (nachdenken; Meditation üben)
me|di|um [ˈmi:djəm] ‹engl.› (*Gastron.* halb durchgebraten); **Me|di|um,** das; -s, ...ien [...i̯ən] ‹lat.› (Mittel[glied]; Mittler[in], Mittelsperson [bes. beim Spiritismus]; Kommunikationsmittel; *Sprachw.* Mittelform zwischen Aktiv u. Passiv)
Me|di|zi (*Plur. von* Medikus); **Me|di|zin,** die; -, -en ‹lat.› (Arznei; *nur Sing.:* Heilkunde); **Me|di|zi|nal‿rat** (*Plur.* ...räte), **...sta|tis|tik, ...we|sen** (das; -s); **Me|di|zin|ball** (großer, schwerer, nicht elastischer Lederball); **Me|di|zi|ner** (Arzt; *auch für* Medizinstudent); **Me|di|zi|ne|rin; me|di|zi|nisch; me|di|zi|nisch-tech|nisch** (↑R 27); -e Assistentin (*Abk.* MTA); **Me|di|zin‿mann** (*Plur.* ...männer), **...schränk|chen, ...stu|dent, ...stu|den|tin, ...stu|di|um, ...tech|nik**
Med|ley [ˈmɛdli], das; -s, -s ‹engl.› (Melodienstrauß, Potpourri)
Me|doc [meˈdɔk], der; -s, -s ‹nach der franz. Landschaft Médoc› (franz. Rotwein)
Med|re|se, Med|res|se (↑R 130), die; -, -n ‹arab.› (islam. jurist. u. theolog. Hochschule; Koranschule einer Moschee)
Me|du|sa,[1]**Me|du|se,** die; - (eine der Gorgonen); [2]**Me|du|se,** die; -, -n (*Zool.* Qualle); **Me|du|sen‿blick, ...haupt** (das; -[e]s); **me|du|sisch** (*geh. für* medusenähnlich, schrecklich)
Meer, das; -[e]s, -e
Mee|ra|ne (Stadt bei Zwickau)
Meer‿bu|sen, ...en|ge; Mee|res‿al|ge, ...arm, ...bi|o|lo|gie, ...bo|den, ...bucht, ...for|schung, ...frei|heit (die; -; *Völkerrecht*), **...früch|te** (*Plur.*), **...grund** (der; -[e]s), **...kun|de** (die; -; *für* Ozeanographie), **...leuch|ten** (das; -s), **...ober|flä|che** (↑R 132; die; -), **...spie|gel** (der; -s; über dem - [*Abk.* ü. d. M.]; unter dem - [*Abk.* u. d. M.]), **...strand, ...stra|ße, ...strö|mung, ...tie|fe; Meer‿frau, ...gott; meer|grün; Meer‿jung|frau, ...kat|ze** (ein Affe)
Meer|ret|tich (Heil- u. Gewürzpflanze); **Meer|ret|tich|so|ße**
Meer|salz, das; -es
Meers|burg (Stadt am Bodensee); [1]**Meers|bur|ger** (↑R 103); [2]**Meers|bur|ger,** der; -s (ein [Rot]wein)
Meer|schaum, der; -[e]s; **Meer|schaum‿pfei|fe, ...spit|ze; Meer|schwein|chen; meer|um|schlun|gen** (*geh.*); **meer|wärts; Meer|was|ser,** das; -s; **Meer|was|ser|wel|len|bad; Meer‿weib** (Meerjungfrau), **...zwie|bel** (ein Liliengewächs)
Mee|ting [ˈmi:...], das; -s, -s ‹engl., „[Zusammen]treffen"› (Versammlung; Sportveranstaltung; *regional für* Kundgebung)
me|ga... ‹griech.› (groß...); **Me|ga...** (Groß...; das Millionenfache einer Einheit; z. B. Megawatt = 10^6 Watt; *Zeichen* M); **Me|ga|byte** [*auch* ˈmɛ... *u.* ...ˈbait], das; -[s], -[s] (2^{20} Byte; *Zeichen* MB, MByte, Mbyte); **Me|ga|elekt|ro|nen|volt** [*auch* ˈmɛ... *u.* ...ˈtro:...] (↑R 130 *u.* 132; 1 Million Elektron[en]volt; *Zeichen* MeV); **Me|ga|fon** *vgl.* Megaphon; **Me|ga|hertz** [*auch* ˈmɛ... *u.* ...ˈhɛrt͡s] (1 Million Hertz; *Zeichen* MHz); **Me|ga|joule** [*auch* ˈmɛ... *u.* ...ˈd͡ʒu:l] (1 Million Joule; *Zeichen* MJ)
Me|ga|lith [...ˈli:t, *auch* ...ˈlit], der; *Gen.* -s *u.* -en, *Plur.* -e[n] (↑R 126) ‹griech.› (großer Steinblock bei vorgeschichtlichen Grabanlagen); **Me|ga|lith|grab** (vorgeschichtl., aus großen Steinen angelegtes Grab); **Me|ga|li|thi|ker,** der; -s, - (Träger der Megalithkultur [Großsteingräberleute]); **me|ga|li|thisch; Me|ga|lith|kul|tur,** die; -
Me|ga|lo|ma|nie, die; -, ...ien ‹griech.› (*Psych.* Größenwahn)
Me|ga|lo|po|lis, die; -, ...polen ‹griech.› (Zusammenballung von benachbarten Millionenstädten, Riesenstadt)
Me|ga|ohm [*auch* ˈmɛ...], *auch* Me|ohm [*auch* ˈmɛk..., *beide auch* ...ˈo:m] (1 Million Ohm; *Zeichen* MΩ); **Me|ga|pas|cal** [*auch* ˈmɛ... *u.* ...ˈkal] (1 Million Pascal; *Zeichen* MPa)
Me|ga|phon, *eindeutschend* Me|ga|fon (↑R 33), das; -s, -e ‹griech.› (Sprachrohr)
[1]**Me|gä|re** (*griech. Mythol.* eine der drei Erinnyen); [2]**Me|gä|re,** die; -, -n (*geh. für* böses Weib)
Me|ga|the|ri|um, das; -s, ...ien [...i̯ən] ‹griech.› (ein ausgestorbenes Riesenfaultier)
Me|ga|ton|ne [*auch* ˈmɛ... *u.* ...ˈtɔnə] (das Millionenfache einer Tonne; *Abk.* Mt; 1 Mt = 1 000 000 t); **Me|ga|ton|nen|bom|be; Me|ga|volt** [*auch* ˈmɛ...

u. ...'vɔlt] (1 Million Volt; *Zeichen* MV); **Me|ga|watt** [*auch* 'mɛ... *u.* ...'vat] (1 Million Watt; *Zeichen* MW); **Meg|ohm** *vgl.* Megaohm

Mehl, das; -[e]s, *Plur.* *(Sorten:)* -e; **mehl|ar|tig; Mehl⌣bee|re, ...brei; meh|lig; Mehl⌣kleis|ter, ...papp** *(landsch.),* **...sack, ...schwit|ze** (Einbrenne, in Fett gebräuntes Mehl), **...sor|te, ...spei|se** (mit Mehl zubereitetes Gericht; *österr. für* Süßspeise, Kuchen); **Mehl|tau,** der (durch bestimmte Pilze hervorgerufene Pflanzenkrankheit); *vgl. aber* Meltau; **Mehl|wurm**

mehr; mehr Freunde als Feinde; mehr Geld; mit mehr Hoffnung; mehr oder weniger (minder); umso mehr; mehr denn je; wir können nicht mehr als arbeiten; **Mehr,** das; -[s] *(auch für* Mehrheit); ein Mehr an Kosten; das Mehr oder Weniger; **Mehr⌣ar|beit, ...auf|wand, ...aus|ga|be, ...be|darf, ...be|las|tung; mehr|deu|tig; Mehr|deu|tig|keit; mehr|di|men|si|o|nal; Mehr|di|men|si|o|na|li|tät,** die; -; **Mehr|ein|nah|me; meh|ren** *(geh.);* **Meh|rer** *(geh.);* **meh|re|re;** ↑R 48 (einige, eine Anzahl); mehrere sagten, dass ...; mehrere Bücher, Mark; mehrere tüchtige Menschen; mehrerer tüchtiger, *seltener* tüchtigen Menschen; mehrere Abgeordnete, mehrerer Abgeordneter, *seltener* Abgeordneten; **meh|re|res** (↑R 48); ich habe noch mehreres zu tun; **Meh|re|rin** *(geh.);* **meh|rer|lei** *(ugs.);* **Mehr⌣er|lös, ...er|trag; mehr|fach;** *vgl. auch* Mehrfache; **mehr|fach|be|hin|dert** *(Amtsspr.);* **Mehr|fach|be|hin|der|te,** der *u.* die; -n, -n; ↑R 5 ff. *(Amtsspr.);* **Mehr|fa|che,** das; -n; um ein Mehrfaches vergrößern; um das Mehrfache vergrößern; *vgl.* Achtfache; **Mehr|fach⌣impf|stoff, ...nut|zung, ...spreng|kopf; Mehr|fa|mi|li|en|haus; Mehr|far|ben|druck** *Plur.* ...drucke; **mehr|far|big,** *österr.* **mehr|fär|big; mehr⌣glied|rig** *od.* ...glie|de|rig; **Mehr|heit;** einfache, qualifizierte, absolute -; die schweigende -; **mehr|heit|lich; Mehr|heits⌣be|schaf|fer** (Gruppe, Partei o. Ä., mit deren Hilfe eine Mehrheit zustande kommt), **...be|schluss; mehr|heits|fä|hig;** eine -e Partei, Gesetzesvorlage; **Mehr|heits|wahl|recht; mehr|jäh|rig; Mehr⌣kampf** *(Sport),* **...kämp|fer** *(Sport),* **...kämp|fe|rin** *(Sport),* **...kos|ten** *(Plur.),* **...la|der** (eine Feuerwaffe), **...leis|tung; Mehr|ling** (Zwilling, Drilling usw.); **Mehr|lings|ge|burt; mehr|ma|lig; mehr|mals; Mehr|par|tei|en|sys|tem; Mehr|pha|sen|strom** (mehrfach verketteter Wechselstrom); **mehr⌣sil|big, ...spra|chig; Mehr|spra|chig|keit,** die; -; **mehr⌣stim|mig, ...stö|ckig; Mehr|stu|fe** *(für* Komparativ); **Mehr|stu|fen|ra|ke|te; mehr⌣stu|fig, ...stün|dig, ...tä|gig; Mehr|tei|ler** (mehrteiliges Fernsehspiel u. Ä.); **mehr|tei|lig; Meh|rung,** die; - *(geh.);* **Mehr|völ|ker|staat** *(für* Nationalitätenstaat; *Plur.* ...staaten); **Mehr|weg|fla|sche** *(svw.* Pfandflasche); **Mehr|wert,** der; -[e]s *(Wirtsch.);* **Mehr|wert|steu|er,** die *(Abk.* MwSt. *od.* Mw.-St.); **mehr|wö|chig; Mehr|zahl,** die; - *(auch für* Plural); **mehr⌣zei|lig, ...zel|lig; Mehr|zweck⌣ge|rät, ...hal|le, ...ma|schi|ne, ...mö|bel, ...raum, ...tisch**

mei|den; du miedst; du miedest; gemieden; meid[e]!

Mei|er *(veraltet für* Gutspächter, -verwalter); **Mei|e|rei** *(veraltet für* Pachtgut; *landsch. für* Molkerei); **Mei|er|hof; Mei|e|rin**

Mei|ke (w. Vorn.)

Mei|le, die; -, -n (ein Längenmaß); **mei|len|lang** [*auch* 'mailən'laŋ], *aber* drei Meilen lang; **Mei|len⌣stein, ...stie|fel** *(seltener für* Siebenmeilenstiefel); **mei|len|weit** [*auch* 'mailən'vait], *aber* zwei Meilen weit

Mei|ler, der; -s, - (zum Verkohlen bestimmter Holzstoß); **Mei|ler|ofen** (↑R 132)

mein, meine, mein; mein Ein u. [mein] Alles; *vgl.* dein *u.* deine; **mei|ne,** mei|ni|ge; *vgl.* deine, deinige

Mein|eid (Falscheid); **mein|ei|dig; Mein|ei|dig|keit,** die; -

mei|nen; ich meine es gut mit ihm

mei|ner *(Gen. von* „ich"); gedenke meiner; **mei|ner An|sicht nach** *(Abk.* m. A. n.); **mei|ner|seits; mei|nes Er|ach|tens** *(Abk.* m. E.); *falsch* meines Erachtens nach; **mei|nes|glei|chen; mei|nes|teils; mei|nes Wis|sens** *(Abk.* m. W.); **mei|net|hal|ben** *(veraltend);* **mei|net|we|gen; mei|net|wil|len;** um meinetwillen

Mein|hard (m. Vorn.); **Mein|hild, Mein|hil|de** (w. Vorn.)

mei|ni|ge *vgl.* meine

Mei|nin|gen (Stadt an der oberen Werra); **Mei|nin|ger** (↑R 103); **mei|nin|gisch**

Mei|nolf, Mei|nulf (m. Vorn.); **Mein|rad** (m. Vorn.); **Mei|nulf** (m. Vorn.)

Mei|nung; Mei|nungs⌣äu|ße|rung, ...aus|tausch; mei|nungs|bil|dend; Mei|nungs⌣bil|dung, ...for|scher, ...for|sche|rin, ...for|schung, ...for|schungs|in|sti|tut, ...frei|heit (die; -), **...streit, ...test, ...um|fra|ge, ...ver|schie|den|heit, ...viel|falt**

Mei|o|se, die; -, -n ‹griech.› *(Biol.* Reifeteilung der Keimzellen)

Mei|ran *vgl.* Majoran

Mei|se, die; -, -n (ein Singvogel); **Mei|sen|nest**

Meis|je, das; -s, -s ‹niederl.› (holländ. Mädchen)

Mei|ßel, der; -s, -; **mei|ßeln;** ich ...[e]le (↑R 16); **Mei|ße|lung**

Mei|ßen (Stadt an der Elbe); **Mei|ße|ner,** Meiß|ner (↑R 103); Meiß[e]ner Porzellan; **mei|ße|nisch,** meiß|nisch

[1]**Meiß|ner,** der; -s (Teil des Hessischen Berglandes); der Hohe -

[2]**Meiß|ner** *vgl.* Meißener; **meiß|nisch** *vgl.* meißenisch

meist; meist kommt er viel zu spät; *vgl.* meiste; **meist|be|güns|tigt; Meist|be|güns|ti|gung** (eine Bestimmung in internationalen Handelsverträgen); **Meist|be|güns|ti|gungs|klau|sel; meist|be|tei|ligt; meist|bie|tend;** meistbietend verkaufen, versteigern, *aber* Meistbietender bleiben; **Meist|bie|ten|de,** der *u.* die; -n, -n (↑R 5 ff.); **meis|te;** der meiste Kummer, die meiste Zeit, das meiste Geld; die meisten Menschen; (↑R 47:) am meisten; (↑R 48:) die meisten glauben, ...; das meiste ist bekannt; **meis|ten|orts; meis|tens; meis|ten|teils**

Meis|ter; Meis|ter⌣be|trieb, ...brief, ...de|tek|tiv, ...dieb, ...ge|sang (der; -[e]s; *vgl.* Meistersang); **meis|ter|haft; Meis|ter|haf|tig|keit,** die; -; **Meis|ter|hand;** von - [gefertigt]; **Meis|te|rin; Meis|ter⌣klas|se, ...leis|tung; meis|ter|lich** *(veraltend);* **Meis|ter|ma|cher** *(ugs. für* sehr erfolgreicher Trainer); **meis|tern;** ich ...ere (↑R 16); **Meis|ter|prü|fung; Meis|ter⌣sang** (der; -[e]s; Kunstdichtung des 15. u. 16. Jh.s), **...sän|ger** *(vgl.* Meistersinger); **Meis|ter|schaft; Meis|ter|schafts⌣kampf, ...spiel, ...ti|tel; Meis|ter⌣schü|ler, ...schü|le|rin, ...schuss, ...sin|ger** (Dichter des Meistersangs), **...stück, ...ti|tel** *(Handw.; Sport);* **Meis|te|rung,** die; -; **Meis|ter⌣werk, ...wür|de** (die; -), **...wurz** (ein Doldengewächs)

Meist|ge|bot; meist₋ge|bräuch|lich, ...ge|fragt, ...ge|kauft, ...ge|le|sen, ...ge|nannt; Meist|stu|fe (*für* Superlativ)

[1]**Mek|ka** (saudiarab. Stadt); [2]**Mek|ka,** das; -s, -s (Zentrum, das viele Besucher anlockt); ein - der Touristen

Me|kong [*auch* meˈkɔŋ], der; -[s] (Fluss in Südostasien); **Me|kong|del|ta,** das; -s

Me|la|min|harz ⟨Kunstwort⟩ (ein Kunstharz)

Me|lan|cho|lie [melaŋko...], die; -, ...ien ⟨griech.⟩ (Trübsinn, Schwermut); **Me|lan|cho|li|ker; me|lan|cho|lisch**

Me|lanch|thon (↑R 132) ⟨griech.⟩ (eigtl. Name Schwarzert; dt. Humanist u. Reformator)

Me|la|ne|si|en [...i̯ən] ⟨griech.⟩ (westpazif. Inseln nordöstlich von Australien); **Me|la|ne|si|er** [...i̯ər]; **me|la|ne|sisch**

Me|lan|ge [meˈlã:ʒə, *österr.* meˈlã:ʒ], die; -, -n [...ʒ(ə)n] (Mischung, Gemisch; *österr. für* Milchkaffee)

Me|la|nie [ˈme:lani:, *auch* melaˈni: *od.* meˈla:ni̯ə] (w. Vorn.)

Me|la|nin, das; -s, -e ⟨griech.⟩ (*Biol.* brauner od. schwarzer Farbstoff); **Me|la|nis|mus,** der; -, ...men *u.* Me|la|no|se, die; -, -n (*Med.* krankhafte Dunkelfärbung der Haut); **Me|la|nit** [*auch* ...ˈnit], der; -s, -e (ein Mineral); **Me|la|nom,** das; -s, -e (*Med.* bösartige Geschwulst an der Haut od. den Schleimhäuten); **Me|la|no|se** *vgl.* Melanismus; **Me|la|phyr,** der; -s, -e (ein Gestein); **Me|las|ma,** das; -s, *Plur.* ...men *u.* ...lasmata (*Med.* schwärzliche Hautflecken)

Me|las|se, die; -, -n ⟨franz.⟩ (Rückstand bei der Zuckergewinnung)

Me|la|to|nin, das; -s ⟨griech.⟩ (ein den Stoffwechsel senkendes Hormon)

Mel|ber, der; -s, - (*bayr. für* Mehlhändler)

Mel|bourne [ˈmɛlbərn] (austr. Stadt)

Mel|chi|or (m. Vorn.)

Mel|chi|se|dek [*auch, österr. nur,* ...çi:...] (bibl. m. Eigenn.)

Melch|ter, die; -, -n (*schweiz. für* Melkeimer)

Mel|de, die; -, -n (eine Pflanzengattung)

Mel|de₋amt, ...bü|ro, ...fah|rer, ...frist, ...hund; mel|den; Mel|de|pflicht; polizeiliche -; **mel|de|pflich|tig;** meldepflichtige Krankheit; **Mel|der; Mel|de₋rei|ter, ...schluss, ...stel|le, ...ter|min, ...zet|tel** (*österr. für* Formular, Bestätigung für polizeiliche Anmeldung); **Mel|dung**

Me|li|bo|cus *auch* **Me|li|bo|kus,** der; - *od.* Mal|chen, der; -s (Berg im Odenwald)

me|lie|ren ⟨franz.⟩ (mischen; sprenkeln); **me|liert** (aus verschiedenen Farben gemischt; leicht ergraut [vom Haar]); grau meliert

Me|li|nit [*auch* ...ˈnit], der; -s ⟨griech.⟩ (Gelberde)

Me|li|o|ra|ti|on, die; -, -en ⟨lat.⟩ (*Landw.* [Boden]verbesserung); **me|li|o|rie|ren** ([Ackerboden] verbessern)

Me|lis, der; - ⟨griech.⟩ (Verbrauchszucker aus verschiedenen Zuckersorten)

me|lisch ⟨*zu* Melos; griech.⟩ (*Musik, Literaturw.* liedhaft); **Me|lis|ma,** das; -s, ...men (*Musik* melod. Verzierung, Koloratur); **Me|lis|ma|tik,** die; - (Kunst der melod. Verzierung); **me|lis|ma|tisch**

Me|lis|sa (w. Vorn.); **Me|lis|se,** die; -, -n ⟨griech.⟩ (eine Heil- u. Gewürzpflanze); **Me|lis|sen|geist ®**, der; -[e]s (ein Heilkräuterdestillat); **Me|lit|ta** (w. Vorn.)

melk (*veraltet für* Milch gebend, melkbar); eine melke Kuh

Melk (österr. Stadt)

Melk|ei|mer; mel|ken; du melkst, *veraltet* milkst; du melktest, *veraltend* molkst; du melktest, *veraltet* mölkest; gemolken, *auch* gemelkt; melk[e]!, *veraltet* milk!; frisch gemolkene Milch; eine melkende Kuh (*ugs. für* gute Einnahmequelle); **Mel|ker; Mel|ke|rei** (das Melken; Milchwirtschaft); **Mel|ke|rin; Melk₋kü|bel, ...ma|schi|ne, ...sche|mel**

Me|lo|die, die; -, ...ien ⟨griech.⟩ (sangbare, in sich geschlossene Folge von Tönen); **Me|lo|di|en₋fol|ge, ...rei|gen; Me|lo|dik,** die; - (Lehre von der Melodie); **me|lo|di|ös; me|lo|disch;** (wohlklingend); **Me|lo|dram, Me|lo|dra|ma,** das; -s, ...men (Schauspiel mit Musikbegleitung; pathetisch inszeniertes Schauspiel); **Me|lo|dra|ma|tik; me|lo|dra|ma|tisch**

Me|lo|ne, die; -, -n ⟨griech.⟩ (großes Kürbisgewächs; *ugs. scherzh. für* runder, steifer Hut)

Me|los [*auch* ˈmɛ...], das; - ⟨griech.⟩ (*Musik* Melodie, melodische Eigenschaft)

Mel|po|me|ne [...ne:] (Muse des Trauerspiels)

Mel|tau, der; -[e]s (Blattlaushonig, Honigtau); *vgl. aber* Mehltau

Me|lu|si|ne (altfranz. Sagengestalt, Meerfee)

Mel|ville [...vil], Herman (amerik. Schriftsteller)

Mem|bran, die; -, -en ⟨lat.⟩, *seltener* **Mem|bra|ne** (↑R 130), die; -, -n (gespanntes Häutchen; Schwingblatt)

[1]**Me|mel,** die; - (ein Fluss); [2]**Me|mel** (*lit.* Klaipeda); **Me|me|ler** (↑R 103)

Me|men|to, das; -s, -s ⟨lat.⟩ (Erinnerung, Mahnruf); **me|men|to mo|ri** ⟨lat., „gedenke des Todes!"⟩ (häufige Grabsteininschrift); **Me|men|to mo|ri,** das; - -, - - (etwas, was an den Tod gemahnt)

Mem|me, die; -, -n (*ugs. abwertend für* Feigling)

mem|meln (*bayr. für* mummeln); ich ...[e]le (↑R 16)

mem|men|haft (*ugs. abwertend);* **Mem|men|haf|tig|keit,** die; -

Mem|non (sagenhafter äthiop. König); **Mem|nons|säu|len** *Plur.* (bei Luxor in Ägypten); ↑R 95

Me|mo, das; -s, -s (*kurz für* Memorandum); **Me|moire** [meˈmo̯a:r], das; -s, -s ⟨franz.⟩ (Memorandum); **Me|moi|ren** [meˈmo̯a:rən] *Plur.* (Lebenserinnerungen); **Me|mo|ra|bi|li|en** [...i̯ən] *Plur.* ⟨lat.⟩ (Denkwürdigkeiten); **Me|mo|ran|dum,** das; -s, *Plur.* ...den *u.* ...da (Denkschrift); [1]**Me|mo|ri|al,** das; -s, *Plur.* -e *u.* -ien [...i̯ən] ⟨lat.⟩ (*veraltet für* Tagebuch; [Vor]merkbuch); [2]**Me|mo|ri|al** [miˈmɔ:ri̯əl], das; -s, -s ⟨engl.⟩ (sportl. Veranstaltung zum Gedenken an einen Verstorbenen; Denkmal); **me|mo|rie|ren** (*veraltend für* auswendig lernen)

Mem|phis (altägypt. Stadt westl. des Nils)

Me|na|ge [meˈna:ʒə, *österr.* meˈna:ʒ], die; -, -n [meˈna:ʒ(ə)n] ⟨franz.⟩ (Gewürzständer; *veraltet für* Haushalt; *österr. für* [Truppen]verpflegung); **Me|na|ge|rie** [menaʒə...], die; -, ...ien (Tierschau, Tiergehege); **me|na|gie|ren** [menaˈʒi:...] (*veraltet, aber noch landsch. für* sich selbst verköstigen; *österr. für* Essen fassen [beim Militär]); sich - (*veraltet für* sich mäßigen)

Me|nar|che (↑R 132), die; -, -n ⟨griech.⟩ (*Med.* erster Eintritt der Regelblutung)

Men|del (österr. Biologe)

Men|de|le|vi|um [...v...], das; -s ⟨nach dem russ. Chemiker Mendelejew⟩ (chem. Element, ein Transuran; *Zeichen* Md)

Men|de|lis|mus, der; - (mendelsche Vererbungslehre); **men|deln** (*Biol.* nach den Vererbungsregeln Mendels in Erscheinung treten); **men|delsch** (↑R 94); mendelsche Regeln

Men|dels|sohn Bar|thol|dy[1] (dt. Komponist)

Men|di|kant, der; -en, -en (↑R 126) ‹lat.› (Bettelmönch); **Men|di|kan|ten|or|den**

Me|ne|la|os (griech. Sagengestalt, König von Sparta); **Me|ne|la|us** *vgl.* Menelaos

Me|ne|te|kel, das; -s, - ‹aram.› (unheildrohendes Zeichen)

Men|ge, die; -, -n

men|gen (mischen)

Men|gen‿an|ga|be, ...be|zeich|nung, ...kon|junk|tur *(Wirtsch.),* **...leh|re** (die; -; *Math., Logik*); **men|gen|mä|ßig** (*für* quantitativ); **Men|gen‿preis** (*vgl.* ²Preis), **...ra|batt**

Meng|sel, das; -s, - (*landsch. für* Gemisch)

Men|hir, der; -s, -e ‹breton.-franz.› (unbehauene vorgeschichtliche Steinsäule)

Me|nin|gi|tis, die; -, ...itiden ‹griech.› (*Med.* Hirnhautentzündung)

me|nip|pisch (↑R 94); menippische Satire, die menippische Philosophie; **Me|nip|pos** (altgriech. Philosoph)

Me|nis|kus, der; -, ...ken ‹griech.› (*Med.* Zwischenknorpel im Kniegelenk; *Physik* gewölbte Flüssigkeitsoberfläche); **Me|nis|kus‿ope|ra|ti|on** (↑R 132; *Med.*), **...riss** (eine Sportverletzung)

Men|jou|bärt|chen ['mɛnʒu...] ‹nach dem amerik. Filmschauspieler A. Menjou› (schmaler, gestutzter Schnurrbart); ↑R 95

Men|ken|ke, die; - (*landsch. ugs. für* Durcheinander; Umstände)

Men|ni|ge, die; - ‹iber.› (Bleiverbindung; rote Malerfarbe); **Men|nig|rot**

Men|no|nit, der; -en, -en (↑R 126) ‹nach dem Gründer Menno Simons› (Angehöriger einer evangelischen Freikirche)

Me|no|pau|se, die; -, -n ‹griech.› (*Med.* Aufhören der Regelblutungen im Klimakterium)

Me|no|ra, die; -, - ‹hebr.› (siebenarmiger Leuchter der jüd. Liturgie)

Me|nor|ca (eine Baleareninsel); **Me|nor|qui|ner** [...'ki:...] (Einwohner Menorcas); **me|nor|qui|nisch**

Me|nor|rhö[1], **Me|nor|rhöe** [...'rø:], die; -, ...rrhöen ‹griech.› (*Med.* Menstruation); **me|nor|rhö|isch;** **Me|no|sta|se** (↑R 132), die; -, -n (Ausbleiben der Monatsblutung)

Me|not|ti (amerik. Komponist ital. Herkunft)

Men|sa, die; -, *Plur.* -s *u.* ...sen ‹lat.› (restaurantähnliche Einrichtung an Universitäten [für die Studenten]; *Kunstw.* Altarplatte); **Men|sa|es|sen**

[1]**Mensch,** der; -en, -en (↑R 126); [2]**Mensch,** das; -[e]s, -er (*abwertend für* weibliche Person); **menscheln** (*ugs. für* menschl. Schwächen deutlich werden lassen); es menschelt; **Men|schen|af|fe; men|schen|ähn|lich; Men|schen|al|ter; men|schen|arm; Men|schen‿auf|lauf, ...feind, ...fleisch, ...fres|ser, ...freund; men|schen|freund|lich; Men|schen‿füh|rung** (die; -), **...ge|den|ken** (seit -), **...geist** (der; -[e]s), **...ge|schlecht** (das; -[e]s), **...ge|stalt** (in -), **...ge|wühl, ...hand** (von -), **...han|del** (*vgl.* [1]Handel), **...händ|ler, ...herz** *(geh.),* **...ken|ner, ...kennt|nis** (die; -), **...ket|te, ...kind, ...kun|de** (die; -; *für* Anthropologie), **...le|ben; men|schen|leer; Men|schen‿lie|be, ...mas|se** *(meist Plur.),* **...men|ge; men|schen|mög|lich;** was menschenmöglich war, wurde getan; *aber* er hat das Menschenmögliche getan; **Men|schen‿op|fer, ...pflicht, ...ras|se, ...raub; Men|schen|recht** *meist Plur.;* **Men|schen|rechts‿er|klä|rung, ...ver|let|zung; men|schen|scheu; Men|schen‿scheu, ...schlag** (der; -[e]s), **...see|le** (keine -); **Men|schens|kind!** (ugs. Ausruf); **Men|schen|sohn,** der; -[e]s (Selbstbezeichnung Jesu Christi); **Men|schen|tum,** das; -s; **men|schen|un|wür|dig; Men|schen‿ver|ach|tung, ...werk** *(geh.),* **...wür|de** (die; -); **men|schen|wür|dig**

Men|sche|wik, der; -en (↑R 126), *Plur.* -en *u.* -i ‹russ.› (Anhänger des Menschewismus); **Men|sche|wis|mus,** der; - (ehem. gemäßigter russ. Sozialismus); **Men|sche|wist,** der; -en, -en; ↑R 126 (*svw.* Menschewik); **men|sche|wis|tisch**

Mensch|heit, die; -; **mensch|heit|lich; Mensch|heits‿ent|wick|lung** (die; -), **...ge|schich|te** (die; -), **...traum; mensch|lich;** Menschliches, Allzumenschliches (↑R 47); **Mensch|lich|keit,** die; -; **Mensch|wer|dung,** die; -

men|sen|die|cken (nach der Methode von B. Mensendieck Gymnastik treiben); ich ...diecke

men|sis cur|ren|tis ‹lat.› (*veraltet für* laufenden Monats; *Abk.* m. c.)

menst|ru|al (↑R 130; *Med.* zur Menstruation gehörend); **Menst|ru|al|blu|tung; Menst|ru|a|ti|on,** die; -, -en; (Monatsblutung, Regel); **menst|ru|ie|ren**

Men|sur, die; -, -en ‹lat.› (Abstand der beiden Fechter; stud. Zweikampf; Zeitmaß der Noten; Maßverhältnis bei Musikinstrumenten; *Chemie* Messglas); **men|su|ra|bel** (*geh. für* messbar); ...ab|le (↑R 130) Größe; **Men|su|ra|bi|li|tät,** die; - *(geh.);* **Men|su|ral|mu|sik,** die; - (die in Mensuralnotenschrift aufgezeichnete Musik des 13. bis 16. Jh.s); **Men|su|ral|no|ta|ti|on,** die; - (im 13. Jh. ausgebildete, die Tondauer angebende Notenschrift)

men|tal ‹lat.› (geistig; gedanklich); **Men|ta|li|tät,** die; -, -en (Denk-, Anschauungsweise; Sinnes-, Geistesart); **Men|tal|re|ser|va|ti|on** (*Rechtsspr.* stiller Vorbehalt)

Men|thol, das; -s ‹lat.› (Bestandteil des Pfefferminzöls)

[1]**Men|tor** ‹griech.› (Erzieher des Telemach); [2]**Men|tor,** der; -s, ...oren (Erzieher; Ratgeber)

Me|nü, das; -s, -s ‹franz.› (Speisenfolge; *EDV* auf dem Bildschirm angebotene Programmauswahl); **Me|nu|ett,** das; -[e]s, *Plur.* -e, *auch* -s (ein Tanz)

Me|nu|hin [*auch* ...'hi:n], Yehudi (amerik. Geigenvirtuose u. Dirigent)

Men|zel (dt. Maler u. Grafiker)

Me|phis|to, Me|phis|to|phe|les (Teufel in Goethes „Faust"); **me|phis|to|phe|lisch**

Me|ran (Stadt in Südtirol)

Mer|ca|tor (flandrischer Geograph); **Mer|ca|tor|pro|jek|ti|on** (↑R 95; *Geogr.* Netzentwurf von Landkarten)

Mer|ce|des-Benz ® (Kraftfahrzeuge)

Mer|ce|rie [mɛrsə...], die; -, ...ien ‹franz.› (*schweiz. für* Kurzwaren[handlung])

Mer|ce|ri|sa|ti|on usw. *vgl.* Merzerisation usw.

Mer|chan|di|sing ['mœ(r)tʃəndaiziŋ], das; -s ‹engl.› (*Wirtsch.* verkaufsfördernde Maßnahmen)

[1] *Eigene Schreibung des Komponisten; sonst als Familienname mit Bindestrich.*

[1] *Vgl. die Anmerkungen zu* „Diarrhö, Diarrhöe".

mer|ci! [mɛrˈsiː] ‹franz.› (danke!)
Mer|cu|ry|kap|sel [ˈmœː(r)kjuri...] ‹amerik.; dt.› (↑R 95; erste bemannte amerik. Raumkapsel)
Me|re|dith [ˈmɛrədiθ] (engl. Schriftsteller); ↑R 17
Mer|gel, der; -s, - (aus Ton u. Kalk bestehendes Sedimentgestein); **Mer|gel|bo|den; mer|ge|lig, merg|lig**
Me|ri|an, Maria Sibylla (dt. Malerin, Kupferstecherin u. Naturforscherin)
Me|ri|an d. Ä., Matthäus (schweiz. Kupferstecher u. Buchhändler)
Me|ri|di|an, der; -s, -e ‹lat.› (*Geogr., Astron.* Mittags-, Längenkreis); **Me|ri|di|an|kreis** (astron. Messinstrument); **me|ri|di|o|nal** (*Geogr.* den Längenkreis betreffend)
Mé|ri|mée [meriˈmeː], Prosper [prɔsˈpɛːr] (franz. Schriftsteller)
Me|rin|ge, die; -, -n ‹franz.›, **Me|rin|gel,** das; -s, -, *schweiz.* **Meringue** [ˈmɛrɛŋ, *franz.* məˈrɛ̃ːg], die; -, -s (ein Schaumgebäck)
Me|ri|no, der; -s, -s ‹span.› (Schaf einer span. Rasse); **Me|ri|no‿schaf, ...wol|le**
Me|ris|tem, das; -s, -e ‹griech.› (*Bot.* pflanzl. Bildungsgewebe); **me|ris|te|ma|tisch** (*Bot.* teilungsfähig [von pflanzl. Geweben])
Me|ri|ten (*Plur. von* Meritum); **me|ri|to|risch** ‹lat.› (*veraltet für* verdienstvoll); **Me|ri|tum,** das; -s, ...iten *meist Plur.* (das Verdienst)
[1]**Merk,** der; -s, -e (ein Doldengewächs)
[2]**Merk,** das; -s, -e (*veraltet für* Merkzeichen, Marke)
mer|kan|til, *veraltet* **mer|kan|ti|lisch** ‹lat.› (kaufmännisch; Handels...); **Mer|kan|ti|lis|mus,** der; - (Wirtschaftspolitik in der Zeit des Absolutismus); **Mer|kan|ti|list,** der; -en, -en (↑R 126); **mer|kan|ti|lis|tisch; Mer|kan|til|sys|tem,** das; -s
merk|bar; Merk‿blatt, ...buch; mer|ken; ich merke mir etwas; **Mer|ker** (*ugs. iron. für* jmd., der alles bemerkt); **Merk‿heft, ...hil|fe; merk|lich;** merkliche Besserung; *aber* um ein Merkliches; **Merk‿mal** (*Plur.* ...male), **...satz, ...spruch**
[1]**Mer|kur** (röm. Gott des Handels; Götterbote); [2]**Mer|kur,** der; -s (ein Planet); [3]**Mer|kur,** der *od.* das; -s (*[alchimist.] Bez. für* Quecksilber); **Mer|ku|ri|a|lis|mus,** der; - (Quecksilbervergiftung); **Mer|kur|stab**
Merk‿vers, ...wort (*Plur.* ...wörter); **merk|wür|dig; merk|wür|di|ger|wei|se; Merk‿wür|dig|keit** (die; -, -en), **...zei|chen, ...zet|tel**
Mer|lan, der; -s, -e ‹franz.› (*svw.* Wittling)
Mer|le, die; -, -n ‹lat.› (*landsch. für* Amsel)
[1]**Mer|lin** [*auch* ˈmɛr...] (kelt. Sagengestalt, Zauberer)
[2]**Mer|lin** [*auch* ˈmɛr...], der; -s, -e ‹engl.› (ein Greifvogel)
Me|ro|win|ger, der; -s, - (Angehöriger eines fränk. Königsgeschlechtes); **Me|ro|win|ger|reich,** das; -[e]s; **me|ro|win|gisch**
Mer|se|burg (Stadt an der Saale); **Mer|se|bur|ger** (↑R 103); Merseburger Zaubersprüche; **mer|se|bur|gisch**
Mer|ten (m. Vorn.)
Mer|ze|ri|sa|ti|on, die; -, -en ‹nach dem engl. Erfinder Mercer› (Veredlungsverfahren [bes. bei Baumwolle]); **mer|ze|ri|sie|ren; Mer|ze|ri|sie|rung**
Merz‿schaf, ...vieh (zur Zucht nicht geeignetes Vieh)
Me|sal|li|ance [mezaˈli̯ãːs] (↑R 132), die; -, -n ‹franz.› (*bes. früher* nicht standesgemäße Ehe; *übertr. für* unglückliche Verbindung)
me|schant ‹franz.› (*landsch. für* boshaft, ungezogen)
me|schug|ge ‹hebr.-jidd.› (*ugs. für* verrückt)
Mes|dames [mɛˈdam] (*Plur. von* Madame); **Mes|de|moi|selles** [mɛd(ə)moaˈzɛl, *österr. nur* mɛdmoa...] (*Plur. von* Mademoiselle)
Me|sen|chym [...ˈçyːm] (↑R 132), das; -s, -e ‹griech.› (*Biol., Med.* embryonales Bindegewebe)
Me|se|ta, die; -, *Plur.* ...ten, *auch* ...tas (*span. Bez. für* Hochebene)
Mes|ka|lin, das; -s ‹indian.-span.› (Alkaloid einer mexikan. Kaktee, ein Rauschmittel)
Mes|mer, der; -s, - (*schweiz. für* Mesner)
Mes|me|ris|mus, der; - ‹nach dem dt. Arzt Mesmer› (Lehre von der heilenden Wirkung magnetischer Kräfte)
Mes|ner, Mess|ner ‹mlat.› (*landsch. für* Kirchendiener); **Mes|ne|rei,** Mess|ne|rei (*landsch. für* Amt und Wohnung des Mesners)
me|so... ‹griech.› (mittel..., mitten...); **Me|so...** (Mittel..., Mitten...); **Me|so|derm,** das; -s, -e (*Biol., Med.* mittleres Keimblatt in der menschl. u. tier. Embryonalentwicklung); **Me|so|karp,** das; -s, -e (*Bot.* Mittelschicht von Pflanzenfrüchten); **Me|so|ke|pha|lie** *vgl.* Mesozephalie; **Me|so|li|thi|kum** [*auch* ...ˈlit...], das; -s (*Geol.* Mittelsteinzeit); **me|so|li|thisch**
Me|son, *älter* **Me|sot|ron** (↑R 130), das; -s, ...onen *meist Plur.* ‹griech.› (*Physik* instabiles Elementarteilchen mittlerer Masse)
Me|so|phyt, der; -en, -en (↑R 126) ‹griech.› (*Bot.* Pflanze, die Böden mittleren Feuchtigkeitsgrades bevorzugt)
Me|so|po|ta|mi|en [...i̯ən] (hist. Landschaft im Irak [zw. Euphrat u. Tigris]); **Me|so|po|ta|mi|er** [...i̯ər]; **me|so|po|ta|misch**
Me|so|sphä|re, die; - ‹griech.› (*Meteor.* in etwa 50 bis 80 km Höhe liegende Schicht der Erdatmosphäre)
Me|sot|ron (↑R 130); *vgl.* Meson; **Me|so|ze|pha|lie,** die; - ‹griech.› (*Med.* mittelhohe Kopfform); **Me|so|zo|i|kum,** das; -s (*Geol.* Mittelalter der Erde); **me|so|zo|isch**
Mes|sage [ˈmɛsidʒ], die; -, -s [...dʒiz] ‹engl.› (Nachricht; Information; *auch für* Gehalt, Aussage eines Kunstwerks u. Ä.)
[1]**Mes|sa|li|na** (Gemahlin des Kaisers Claudius); [2]**Mes|sa|li|na,** die; -, ...nen (*veraltet für* ausschweifend lebende, sittenlose Frau)
Mess|band, das; *Plur.* ...bänder; **mess|bar; Mess|bar|keit,** die; -; **Mess‿be|cher, ...brief** (*Seew.* amtl. Bescheinigung über die Vermessung eines Schiffes)
Mess|buch (*für* Missale)
Mess|da|ten *Plur.*
Mess|die|ner; Mess|die|ne|rin; [1]**Mes|se,** die; -, -n ‹lat.› (kath. Gottesdienst mit Eucharistiefeier; Chorwerk); die, eine - lesen, *aber* (↑R 50): das Messelesen; [2]**Mes|se,** die; -, -n (Großmarkt, Ausstellung)
[3]**Mes|se,** die; -, -n ‹engl.› (Speise- u. Aufenthaltsraum der Schiffsbesatzung; Tischgesellschaft der Schiffsbesatzung)
Mes|se‿aus|weis, ...be|su|cher, ...ge|län|de, ...hal|le, ...ka|ta|log
Mes|se|le|sen, das; -s
mes|sen; du misst, er misst; ich maß, du maßest; du mäßest; gemessen; miss!; sich [mit jmdm.] -
Mes|se|ni|en (altgriech. Landschaft des Peloponnes); **mes|se|nisch** (↑R 104); die messenischen Kriege
[1]**Mes|ser,** der ‹*zu* messen› (Messender, Messgerät; *fast nur als*

2. Bestandteil in Zusammensetzungen, z. B. Zeitmesser)
²**Mes|ser,** das; -s, - (ein Schneidwerkzeug); **Mes|ser-bänk|chen, ...[form|]schnitt** (ein [kurzer] Haarschnitt), **...held** *(abwertend);* **mes|ser|scharf; Mes|ser-schmied, ...spit|ze, ...ste|cher, ...ste|che|rei, ...stich, ...wer|fer**
Mes|se-schla|ger, ...stadt, ...stand
Mess-feh|ler, ...füh|ler *(Technik),* **...ge|rät**
Mess|ge|wand
Mess|glas
Mes|si|a|de, die; -, -n; (Dichtung vom Messias)
Mes|siaen [mɛ'sjã:] (franz. Komponist)
mes|si|a|nisch (auf den Messias bezüglich); **Mes|si|a|nis|mus,** der; - (geistige Bewegung, die die [rel. od. polit.] Erlösung von einem Messias erwartet); **Mes|si|as,** der; -, -se ‹hebr., „Gesalbter"› *(nur Sing.:* Beiname Jesu Christi; *A. T.* der verheißene Erlöser; *auch für* Befreier)
Mes|si|dor, der; -[s], -s ‹„Erntemonat"› (10. Monat des Kalenders der Franz. Revolution: 19. Juni bis 18. Juli)
Mes|sieurs [mɛ'siø:] *(Plur. von* Monsieur; *Abk.* MM)
Mes|si|na (Stadt auf Sizilien); **Mes|si|na|ap|fel|si|ne** (↑ R 105)
Mes|sing, das; -s, *Plur. (Sorten:)* -e (Kupfer-Zink-Legierung); **Messing-bett, ...draht; mes|singen;** eine messing[e]ne Platte; **Mes|sing-griff, ...leuch|ter, ...schild** (das), **...stan|ge**
Mess-in|stru|ment, ...lat|te
Mess|ner *vgl.* Mesner
Mess|op|fer (kath. Feier der Eucharistie)
Mess-satz (↑ R 136; mehrere zusammengefasste Messgeräte), **...schie|ber** (↑ R 136; Schieblehre), **...schnur** (↑ R 136; *Plur.* ...schnüre), **...schrau|be** (↑ R 136; ein Feinmessgerät), **...stab** (↑ R 136); **...tech|nik, ...tisch; Mess|tisch|blatt; Mes|sung; Mess-ver|fah|ren, ...wert, ...zy|lin|der**
Mes|te, die; -, -n (altes mitteld. Maß; ein [Holz]gefäß)
Mes|ti|ze, der; -n, -n (↑ R 126) ‹lat.-span.› (Nachkomme eines weißen u. eines indianischen Elternteils); **Mes|ti|zin**
MESZ = mitteleuropäische Sommerzeit
Met, der; -[e]s (gegorener Honigsaft)
Me|ta (w. Vorn.)

me|ta... ‹griech.› (zwischen..., mit..., um..., nach...); **Me|ta...** (Zwischen..., Mit..., Um..., Nach...); **me|ta|bol, me|ta|bolisch** *(Biol.* veränderlich; *Biol., Med.* den Stoffwechsel betreffend); **Me|ta|bo|lis|mus,** der; - *(Biol., Med.* Stoffwechsel)
Me|ta|ge|ne|se, die; -, -n ‹griech.› *(Biol.* eine besondere Form des Generationswechsels bei vielzelligen Tieren); **me|ta|ge|ne|tisch**
Me|ta|ge|schäft ‹ital.; dt.› *(Kaufmannsspr.* gemeinschaftlich durchgeführtes Waren- od. Bankgeschäft zweier Firmen mit gleichmäßiger Verteilung von Gewinn u. Verlust)
Me|ta|kri|tik *[auch* ...'tik, *auch* 'mɛta...], die; - ‹griech.› (auf die Kritik folgende Kritik; Kritik der Kritik); **Me|ta|lep|se, Me|talep|sis,** die; -, ...epsen *(Rhet.* Verwechslung)
Me|tall, das; -s, -e ‹griech.›; die Metall verarbeitende Industrie; **Me|tall-ar|bei|ter, ...ar|bei|te|rin, ...be|ar|bei|tung** (die; -), **...block** *(Plur.* ...blöcke); **me|tallen** (aus Metall); **Me|tal|ler** *(ugs. für* Metallarbeiter; Angehöriger der IG Metall); **Me|tal|le|rin; Me|tall|guss; me|tall|hal|tig; Me|tall|hal|tig|keit,** die; -; **metal|lic** [...lik] (metallisch schimmernd [lackiert]); ein Auto in Blau metallic *od.* in Blaumetallic, in metallic Blau *od.* in Metallicblau; **Me|tal|lic|la|ckie|rung; Me|tall|in|dust|rie** (↑ R 130); **Me|tal|li|sa|ti|on,** die; -, -en *(Technik* Vererzung beim Versteinerungsvorgang); **me|tal|lisch** (metallartig); **mé|tal|li|sé** [metali'ze:] (metallic); **me|tal|li|sie|ren** *(Technik* mit Metall überziehen); **Me|tal|li|sie|rung; Me|tall|kun|de,** die; -; **Me|tall|kund|ler; Metall|le|gie|rung** (↑ R 136); **Metal|lo|chro|mie,** die; - *(Technik* galvanische Metallfärbung); **Metal|lo|gie,** die; - (Metallkunde); **Me|tal|lo|gra|phie,** die; - (Zweig der Metallkunde); **Me|tal|lo|id,** das; -[e]s, -e *(veraltete Bez. für* nichtmetall. Grundstoff); **Metall-ski, ...über|zug** (↑ R 132); **Me|tal|lurg, Me|tal|lur|ge** (↑ R 132), der; ...gen, ...gen; ↑ R 126; **Me|tal|lur|gie,** die; - (Hüttenkunde); **me|tal|lur|gisch** (hüttenkundlich, Hütten...); **Metall ver|ar|bei|tend** *vgl.* Metall
me|ta|morph, me|ta|mor|phisch ‹griech.› (die Gestalt, den Zustand wandelnd); **Me|ta|mor|phis|mus,** der; -, ...men *(svw.* Metamorphose); **Me|ta|mor|pho|se,** die; -, -n (Umgestaltung, Verwandlung); **me|ta|mor|pho|sie|ren; Me|ta|pha|se,** die; -, -n *(Biol.* zweite Phase der indirekten Zellkernteilung); **Me|ta|pher,** die; -, -n *(Sprachw.* Wort mit übertragener Bedeutung, bildliche Wendung, z. B. „Haupt der Familie"); **Me|ta|pho|rik,** die; - (Verbildlichung, Übertragung in eine Metapher); **me|ta|pho|risch** (bildlich, im übertragenen Sinne); **Me|ta|phra|se,** die; -, -n (Umschreibung); **me|ta|phras|tisch** (umschreibend); **Me|ta|phy|sik,** die; -, -en *Plur. selten* (philos. Lehre von den letzten, nicht erfahr- u. erkennbaren Gründen u. Zusammenhängen des Seins); **Me|ta|phy|si|ker; me|ta|physisch; Me|ta|plas|mus,** der; -, ...men *(Sprachw.* Umbildung von Wortformen); **Me|ta|psy|chik,** die; - *(svw.* Parapsychologie); **me|ta|psy|chisch; Me|ta|psycho|lo|gie,** die; - *(svw.* Parapsychologie); **Me|ta|se|quo|ia** [...ia], die; -, ...oien [...iən] (Vertreter einer Gattung der Sumpfzypressengewächse); **Me|ta|spra|che** *(EDV, Sprachw., Math.* Sprache, die zur Beschreibung einer anderen Sprache benutzt wird); **me|ta|sprach|lich**
Me|tas|ta|se (↑ R 132), die; -, -n *(Med.* Tochtergeschwulst); **metas|ta|sie|ren** (Tochtergeschwülste bilden); **me|tas|ta|tisch**
Me|ta|the|se, Me|ta|the|sis, die; -, ...esen *(Sprachw.* Lautumstellung, z. B. „Born"–„Bronn"); **Me|ta|tro|pis|mus,** der; - *(Psych.* Umkehrung des geschlechtl. Empfindens; Vertauschung der Rollen von Frau u. Mann); **meta|zent|risch** (das Metazentrum betreffend); **Me|ta|zent|rum** *(Schiffbau* Schwankpunkt); **Meta|zo|on,** das; -s ...zoen *meist Plur.* (mehrzelliges [höheres] Tier)
Me|tem|psy|cho|se (↑ R 132), die; -, -n ‹griech.› (Seelenwanderung)
Me|te|or, der, *selten* das; -s, -e ‹griech.› (Leuchterscheinung beim Eintritt eines Meteoriten in die Erdatmosphäre); **Me|te|oreisen; me|te|o|risch** (auf Lufterscheinungen, -verhältnisse bezüglich); **Me|te|o|rit** *[auch* ...'rit], der; *Gen.* -en *u.* -s, *Plur.* -en *u.* -e (in die Erdatmosphäre eindringender kosmischer Körper); **mete|o|ri|tisch** (von einem Meteor stammend, meteorartig); **Mete|o|ro|lo|ge,** der; -n, -n (↑ R 126); **Me|te|o|ro|lo|gie,** die; -

(Lehre von Wetter u. Klima); **Me|te|o|ro|lo|gin; me|te|o|ro|lo|gisch; me|te|o|ro|trop** (wetter-, klimabedingt); **Me|te|o|ro|tro|pis|mus,** der; -, ...men (wetterbedingter Krankheitszustand); **Me|te|or|stein**

Me|ter, der, *schweiz. nur so, auch* das; -s, - ‹griech.› (Längenmaß; *Zeichen* m); eine Länge von zehn Metern, *auch* Meter (↑R 90); eine Mauer von drei Meter Höhe; von 10 Meter, *auch* Metern an (↑R 90); ein[en] Meter lang, acht Meter lang; laufender Meter (*Abk.* lfd. M.); **...me|ter** (z. B. Zentimeter); **me|ter|dick;** -e Mauern; *aber* die Mauern sind zwei Meter dick; **me|ter|hoch;** der Schnee liegt -; *aber* drei Meter hoch; **me|ter|lang,** *aber* ein[en] Meter lang; **Me|ter_lat|te** (Geh- und Messstock des Grubensteigers), **...maß** (das), **...wa|re** (die; -); **me|ter|wei|se; me|ter|weit,** *aber* drei Meter weit; **Me|ter|zent|ner** (*österr. veraltet für* Doppelzentner [100 kg]; *Zeichen* q [*vgl.* Quintal]); *vgl.* Zentner

Me|than, das; -s ‹griech.› (Gruben-, Sumpfgas); **Me|than|gas; Me|tha|nol,** das; -s (Methylalkohol)

Me|tho|de, die; -, -n ‹griech.› (wissenschaftlich planmäßiges u. folgerichtiges Verfahren; Art des Vorgehens); **Me|tho|den|leh|re; Me|tho|dik,** die; -, -en (Verfahrenslehre, -weise; Vortrags-, Unterrichtslehre; *nur Sing.*: methodisches Vorgehen); **Me|tho|di|ker** (planmäßig Verfahrender; Begründer einer Methode); **me|tho|disch** (planmäßig; überlegt, durchdacht); **me|tho|di|sie|ren; Me|tho|dist,** der; -en, -en; ↑R 126 (Angehöriger der Methodistenkirche); **Me|tho|dis|ten|kir|che** (eine ev. Freikirche); **me|tho|dis|tisch; Me|tho|do|lo|gie,** die; -, ...ien (Lehre von den wissenschaftl. Methoden); **me|tho|do|lo|gisch**

Me|tho|ma|nie, die; - ‹griech.› (*Med.* Säuferwahnsinn)

[1]**Me|thu|sa|lem,** *ökum.* Me|tu|sche|lach (bibl. Eigenname); [2]**Me|thu|sa|lem,** der; -[s], -s (*übertr. für* sehr alter Mann)

Me|thyl, das; -s ‹griech.› (einwertiger Methanrest in zahlreichen organ.-chem. Verbindungen); **Me|thyl|al|ko|hol,** der; -s (Holzgeist, Methanol); **Me|thy|la|min** (↑R 132), das; -s, -e (einfachste organ. Base); **Me|thy|len|blau** (ein synthet. Farbstoff)

Me|ti|er [me'ti̯e:], das; -s, -s ‹franz.› (Handwerk; Beruf; Geschäft)

Me|tist, der; -en, -en (↑R 126) ‹ital.› (Teilnehmer an einem Metageschäft)

Me|tö|ke (↑R 132), der; -n, -n (↑R 126) ‹griech.› (eingesessener Fremdling ohne polit. Rechte [in altgriech. Städten])

Me|ton (altgriech. Mathematiker); **me|to|ni|scher Zyk|lus** (↑R 94), der; -n - (alter Kalenderzyklus [Zeitraum von 19 Jahren], der der Berechnung des christl. Osterdatums zugrunde liegt)

Me|to|no|ma|sie (↑R 132), die; -, ...ien ‹griech.› (Namensveränderung durch Übersetzung in eine fremde Sprache); **Me|to|ny|mie,** die; -, ...ien (*Stilk.* Ersetzung eines Wortes durch einen verwandten Begriff, z. B. „Dolch" durch „Stahl"); **me|to|ny|misch**

Me|to|pe (↑R 132), die; -, -n ‹griech.› (*Archit.* Zwischenfeld in einem antiken Tempelfries)

Me|tra, Me|tren (↑R 130; *Plur. von* Metrum); **Me|trik,** die; -, -en ‹griech.› (Verslehre, -kunst; *Musik* Lehre vom Takt); **Me|tri|ker; me|trisch** (die Verslehre, das Versmaß, den Takt betreffend; in Versen abgefasst; nach dem Meter messbar); -er Raum; -es System

Me|tro [*auch* 'mɛ...] (↑R 130), die; -, -s ‹griech.-franz.› (Untergrundbahn, bes. in Paris u. Moskau)

Met|ro|lo|gie (↑R 130), die; - ‹griech.› (Maß- u. Gewichtskunde); **met|ro|lo|gisch**

Met|ro|nom (↑R 130), das; -s, -e ‹griech.› (*Musik* Taktmesser); *vgl.* Mälzel

Met|ro|po|le (↑R 130), die; -, -n ‹griech.› (Hauptstadt, Weltstadt); **Met|ro|po|lis,** die; -, ...polen (*veraltet für* Metropole); **Met|ro|po|lit,** der; -en, -en (↑R 126; Erzbischof); **Met|ro|po|li|tan|kir|che**

Me|trum (↑R 130), das; -s, *Plur.* ...tren, *älter* ...tra ‹griech.› (Versmaß; *Musik* Takt)

Mett, das; -[e]s (*nordd. für* gehacktes Schweinefleisch)

Met|ta|ge [mɛ'ta:ʒə], die; -, -n [...'ta:ʒ(ə)n] ‹franz.› (*Druckw.* Umbruch [in einer Zeitungsdruckerei])

Met|te, die; -, -n ‹lat.› (nächtl. Gottesdienst; nächtl. Gebet)

Met|ter|nich (österr. Staatskanzler)

Met|teur [mɛ'tø:r], der; -s, -e ‹franz.› (*Druckw.* Umbrecher, Hersteller der Seiten)

Mett|wurst

Me|tu|sche|lach *vgl.* [1]Methusalem

Metz [*franz.* mɛs] (franz. Stadt)

[1]**Met|ze,** die; -, -n, *südd. u. österr.* Met|zen, der; -s, - (altes Getreidemaß)

[2]**Met|ze,** die; -, -n (*veraltet für* Prostituierte)

Met|ze|lei (*ugs.*); **met|zeln** (*landsch. für* schlachten; *selten für* niedermachen, morden); ich ...[e]le (↑R 16); **Met|zel|sup|pe** (*südd. für* Wurstsuppe)

Met|zen *vgl.* [1]Metze

Metzg, die; -, -en (*schweiz. für* Metzge); **Metz|ge,** die; -, -n (*südd. für* Metzgerei, Schlachtbank); **metz|gen** (*landsch. u. schweiz. für* schlachten); **Metz|ger** (*westmitteld., südd., schweiz. für* Fleischer); **Metz|ge|rei** (*westmitteld., südd., schweiz.*); **Metz|ger|meis|ter; Metz|ger[s]|gang,** der (*landsch. für* erfolglose Bemühung); **Metz|ge|te,** die; -, -n (*schweiz. für* Schlachtfest; Schlachtplatte); **Met|zig,** die; -, -en (*svw.* Metzge); **Metz|ler** (*rhein. für* Fleischer)

Meub|le|ment [møblə'mã:] (↑R 130), das; -s, -s ‹franz.› (*veraltet für* Zimmer-, Wohnungseinrichtung)

Meu|chel_mord, ...mör|der; meu|cheln (*veraltend für* heimtückisch ermorden); ich ...[e]le (↑R 16); **Meuch|ler; meuch|le|risch; meuch|lings** (*veraltend für* heimtückisch)

Meu|ni|er [mø'ni̯e:] (belg. Bildhauer u. Maler)

Meu|te, die; -, -n (*Jägerspr.* Gruppe von Hunden; *übertr. abwertend für* größere Zahl von Menschen); **Meu|te|rei; Meu|te|rer; meu|tern;** ich ...ere (↑R 16)

MeV = Megaelektronenvolt

Me|xi|ka|ner; Me|xi|ka|ne|rin; me|xi|ka|nisch; Me|xi|ko (Staat in Nord- u. Mittelamerika u. dessen Hptst.)

Mey|er, Conrad Ferdinand (schweiz. Schriftsteller)

Mey|er|beer (dt. Komponist)

MEZ = mitteleuropäische Zeit

Mez|za|nin, das; -s, -e ‹ital.› (Halb-, Zwischengeschoss, bes. in der Baukunst der Renaissance u. des Barocks, *in Österr.* auch noch in älteren Wohnhäusern); **Mez|za|nin|woh|nung**

mez|za vo|ce [- vo:tʃə] ‹ital.› (*Musik* mit halber Stimme; *Abk.* m. v.); **mez|zo|for|te** (*Musik* halbstark; *Abk.* mf); **Mez|zo|gior|no** [...'dʒɔrno], der; - (der

Teil Italiens südl. von Rom, einschließlich Siziliens); **mez|zo|pi|a|no** (*Musik* halbleise; *Abk.* mp); **Mez|zo|sop|ran** [*auch* ...'pra:n]; mittlere Frauenstimme zwischen Sopran u. Alt; Sängerin der mittleren Stimmlage); **Mez|zo|tịn|to,** das; -[s], *Plur.* -s *od.* ...ti (*nur Sing.:* Schabkunst, bes. Technik des Kupferstichs; *auch für* Erzeugnis dieser Technik)
mf = mezzoforte
µF = Mikrofarad
mg = Milligramm
µg = Mikrogramm
Mg = *chem. Zeichen für* Magnesium
MG = Maschinengewehr; MG-Schütze (↑R 26)
¹Mgr. = Monseigneur
²Mgr., Msgr. = Monsignore
mhd. = mittelhochdeutsch
MHz = Megahertz
Mi. = Mittwoch
Mia (w. Vorn.)
Mia., Md., Mrd. = Milliarde[n]
Mi|a|mi [mai'ɛmi] (Badeort u. Hafenstadt an der Küste Floridas)
Mi|as|ma, das; -s, ...men ‹griech.› (früher angenommene giftige Ausdünstung des Bodens); **mi|as|ma|tisch** (giftig)
mi|au!; mi|au|en; die Katze hat miaut
mich (*Akk. von* „ich")
Mich. = Michigan
Mi|cha (bibl. Prophet)
Mi|cha|el [...ça|e:l, *auch* ...ça|ɛl] (einer der Erzengel; m. Vorn.); **Mi|cha|e|la** (w. Vorn.); **Mi|cha|e|li[s],** das; - (Michaelstag); **Mi|cha|els|tag** (29. Sept.); **¹Mi|chel** (m. Vorn.); **²Mi|chel,** der; -s, - (*Spottname für* den Deutschen); deutscher -
Mi|chel|an|ge|lo Bu|o|nar|ro|ti [mike'landʒelo -] (ital. Künstler)
Mi|chelle [mi'ʃɛl] (w. Vorn.)
Mi|chels|tag (*landsch. für* Michaelstag)
Mi|chi|gan ['miʃigən] (Staat in den USA; *Abk.* Mich.); **Mi|chi|gan|see,** der; -s
mi|cke|rig, mick|rig (*ugs. für* schwach, zurückgeblieben); **Mi|cke|rig|keit,** Mick|rig|keit, die; -; **mi|ckern** (*landsch. für* sich schlecht entwickeln); ich ...ere (↑R 16); die Pflanze mickert
Mic|ki|e|wicz [mitsˈkiɛvitʃ] (poln. Dichter)
mick|rig *vgl.* mickerig; **Mick|rig|keit** *vgl.* Mickerigkeit
Mi|cky|maus, die; -, ...mäuse (eine Trickfilm- u. Comicfigur)
Mi|das (phryg. König); **Mi|das|oh|ren** *Plur.;* ↑R 95 (Eselsohren)
Mid|der, das; -s (*landsch. für* Kalbsmilch)
Mid|gard, der; - (*nord. Mythol.* die Welt der Menschen, die Erde); **Mid|gard|schlan|ge,** die; - (Sinnbild des die Erde umschlingenden Meeres)
Mi|di... (*Mode* bis zu den Waden reichend, halblang, z. B. Midikleid)
Mi|di|a|ni|ter, der; -s, -; (Angehöriger eines nordarab. Volkes im A. T.)
Mi|di|nette [...'nɛt], die; -, -n [...'nɛt(ə)n] ‹franz.› (Pariser Modistin; *veraltet für* leichtlebiges Mädchen)
Mid|life|cri|sis, *auch* **Mid|life-Cri|sis** ['midlaif'kraisis], die; - ‹engl.-amerik.› (Krise in der Mitte des Lebens)
Mid|ship|man [...ʃipmən], der; -s, ...men (unterster brit. Marineoffiziersrang; nordamerik. Seeoffiziersanwärter)
Mie|der, das; -s, -; **Mie|der‿ho|se, ...wa|ren** *(Plur.)*
Mief, der; -[e]s (*ugs. für* schlechte Luft); **mie|fen** *(ugs.);* es mieft; **mie|fig**
Mie|ke (w. Vorn.)
Mie|ne, die; -, -n (Gesichtsausdruck); **Mie|nen|spiel**
Mie|re, die; -, -n (Name einiger Pflanzen)
mies ‹hebr.-jidd.› (*ugs. für* hässlich, übel, schlecht); miese Laune; mies machen (*ugs. für* schlecht machen, herumnörgeln); er hat das Buch mies gemacht
¹Mies, die; -, -en (*Nebenform von* Miez, Mieze)
²Mies, das; -es, -e (*südd. für* Sumpf, Moor)
Mies|chen *vgl.* Miezchen
Mie|se *Plur.;* ↑R 5 (*ugs. für* Minuspunkte, Minusbetrag); in den -n sein
Mie|se|kat|ze *vgl.* Miezekatze
Mie|se|pe|ter, der; -s, - (*ugs. für* stets unzufriedener Mensch); **mie|se‿pe|te|rig** *od.* **...pet|rig** *(ugs.);* **Mie|sig|keit,** die; - *(ugs.);* **mies ma|chen** *vgl.* mies; **Mies|ma|cher** (*ugs. abwertend für* Schwarzseher); **Mies|ma|che|rei** *(ugs. abwertend)*
Mies|mu|schel (Pfahlmuschel)
Mies van der Ro|he (dt.-amerik. Architekt)
Miet‿aus|fall, ...au|to, ...be|trag;
¹Mie|te, die; -, -n (Preis, der für das Benutzen von Wohnungen u. a. zu zahlen ist)
²Mie|te, die; -, -n ‹lat.› (gegen Frost gesicherte Grube u. a. zur Aufbewahrung von Feldfrüchten)
¹mie|ten; eine Wohnung -
²mie|ten ‹lat.› (*landsch. für* einmieten, Feldfrüchte in Mieten setzen)
Mie|ten|re|ge|lung, Miet|re|ge|lung; **Mie|ter; Miet|er|hö|hung; Mie|te|rin; Mie|ter|schutz; Mie|ter|schutz|ge|setz; Miet‿er|trag, ...fi|nan|zie|rung** (besondere Form des Leasings); **miet|frei; Miet‿ge|setz, ...kauf; Miet|ling** (*veraltet für* gedungener Knecht); **Miet‿par|tei, ...preis; Miet|preis|po|li|tik; Miet|recht; Miet|re|ge|lung,** Mie|ten|re|ge|lung; **Miets‿haus, ...ka|ser|ne** (*abwertend für* großes Mietshaus); **Miet|spie|gel** (Tabelle ortsüblicher Mieten); **Miet[s]‿stei|ge|rung, ...strei|tig|kei|ten** *(Plur.);* **Mie|tung; Miet‿ver|lust, ...ver|trag, ...wa|gen, ...woh|nung, ...wu|cher, ...zah|lung, ...zins** (*Plur.* ...zinse; *südd., österr., schweiz. für* ¹Miete)
Miez *vgl.* Mieze; **Miez|chen** (Kätzchen); **Mie|ze,** die; -, -n (*fam. für* Katze; *ugs. für* Freundin, Mädchen); **Mie|ze|kätz|chen** *(Kinderspr.);* **Mie|ze|kat|ze**
MiG, die; -, -[s] ‹nach den Konstrukteuren Mikojan und Gurewitsch› (*Bez. für* Flugzeugtypen der ehem. Sowjetunion)
Mig|non ['minjɔ̃, *auch* min'jɔ̃:] (↑R 130; w. Vorn.; Gestalt aus Goethes „Wilhelm Meister"); **Mig|no|nette** [minjɔ'nɛt], die; -, -s (schmale Zwirnspitze); **Mig|non|fas|sung** (für kleine Glühlampen)
Mig|rä|ne (↑R 130), die; -, -n ‹griech.› ([halb-, einseitiger] heftiger Kopfschmerz)
Mig|ra|ti|on (↑R 130), die; -, -en ‹lat.› (*Biol., Soziol.* Wanderung)
Mig|ros ['migro] (↑R 130), die; - ‹franz.› (eine schweiz. Verkaufsgenossenschaft)
Mi|guel [mi'gɛl] (m. Vorn.)
Mijn|heer [mə'ne:r], der; -s, -s ‹niederl., „mein Herr"› (*ohne Artikel:* niederl. Anrede; *auch scherzh. Bez. für* den Holländer)
¹Mi|ka|do, der; -s, -s ‹jap.› (*frühere Bez. für* den jap. Kaiser); *vgl.* Tenno; **²Mi|ka|do,** das; -s, -s (ein Geschicklichkeitsspiel mit Holzstäbchen); **³Mi|ka|do,** der; -s, -s (Hauptstäbchen im ²Mikado)
Mike [maik] (m. Vorn.)
Mi|ko, der; -, -s (*ugs. Kurzw. für* Minderwertigkeitskomplex)
mik|ro... (↑R 130) ‹griech.› (klein...); **Mik|ro...** (Klein...; ein Millionstel einer Einheit, z. B. Mikrometer = 10^{-6} Meter; *Zei-*

chen µ); **Mik|ro|be,** die; -, -n (*svw.* Mikroorganismus); **mik|ro|bi|ell** (*Biol.* die Mikroben betreffend, durch Mikroben); **Mik|ro-bi|o|lo|gie**[1] (Wissenschaft von den Mikroorganismen), **...che|mie**[1] (Zweig der Chemie, der die Analyse kleinster Mengen von Substanzen zum Gegenstand hat); **Mik|ro-chip, ...com|pu|ter; Mik|ro|elekt|ro|nik**[1] (↑R 130 *u.* 132); **mik|ro|elekt|ro|nisch**[1]; **Mik|ro-fa|rad**[1] (ein millionstel Farad; *Zeichen* µF), **...fau|na**[1] (*Biol.* Kleintierwelt); **Mik|ro|fiche** (*svw.* [3]Fiche); **Mik|ro|film; Mik|ro|fon**[1], *auch* Mik|ro|phon (↑R 33), das; -s, -e (Gerät, durch das Töne, Geräusche u. Ä. auf Tonband, über Lautsprecher u. Ä. übertragen werden können); **mik|ro|fo|nisch,** *auch* mik|ro|pho|nisch; **Mik|ro|gramm**[1] (ein millionstel Gramm; *Zeichen* µg); **mik|ro|ke|phal** usw. *vgl.* mikrozephal usw.; **Mik|ro|kli|ma** (*Meteor.* Kleinklima, Klima der bodennahen Luftschicht); **Mik|ro-kok|kus**[1] (der; -, ...kokken; *Biol.* Kugelbakterie), **...ko|pie**[1] (fotogr. Kleinaufnahme, meist von Buchseiten); **mik|ro|kos|misch**[1]; **Mik|ro|kos|mos**[1], **Mik|ro|kos|mus**[1], der; - (Welt des Menschen als verkleinertes Abbild des Universums; *Ggs.* Makrokosmos; *Biol.* Welt der Kleinlebewesen); [1]**Mik|ro|me|ter,** das; -s, - (ein Feinmessgerät); [2]**Mik|ro|me|ter**[1], das; -s, - (ein millionstel Meter; *Zeichen* µm); **Mik|ro|me|ter|schrau|be** (ein Feinmessgerät); **Mik|ron,** das; -s, - (*veraltet für* [2]Mikrometer; *Kurzform* My; *Zeichen* µ)

Mik|ro|ne|si|en (↑R 130) ‹„Kleininselland"› (Inselgruppe im Pazifischen Ozean); **Mik|ro|ne|si|er; mik|ro|ne|sisch**

Mik|ro|or|ga|nis|mus[1] (↑R 130) *meist Plur.* ‹griech.› (*Biol.* kleinstes, meist einzelliges Lebewesen); **Mik|ro|phon**[1] *vgl.* Mikrofon; **mik|ro|pho|nisch** *vgl.* mikrofonisch; **Mik|ro|phy|sik**[1] (Physik der Moleküle u. Atome); **Mik|ro|phyt,** der; -en, -en (*Biol.* pflanzl. Mikroorganismus); **Mik|ro|pro|zes|sor**[1], der; -s, ...oren *(EDV);* **Mik|ro|ra|di|o|me|ter**[1], das; -s, - (Messgerät für kleinste Strahlungsmengen); **mik|ro|seis|misch**[1] (nur mit Instrumenten wahrnehmbar [von Erdbeben])

Mik|ro|skop (↑R 130 *u.* 132), das; -s, -e (opt. Vergrößerungsgerät);

[1] [*auch* 'mi:kro...]

mik|ro|sko|pie|ren (mit dem Mikroskop arbeiten, untersuchen); **mik|ro|sko|pisch** (verschwindend klein; mithilfe des Mikroskops durchgeführt)

Mik|ro|spo|re[1] (↑R 130; kleine männl. Spore einiger Farnpflanzen); **Mik|ro|tom,** der *od.* das; -s,-e (Gerät zur Herstellung feinster Schnitte für mikroskop. Untersuchungen); **Mik|ro|wel|le** (elektromagnet. Welle mit einer Wellenlänge zwischen 10 cm und 1 m); **Mik|ro|wel|len-ge|rät, ...herd; Mik|ro|zen|sus** ‹griech.; lat.› (vierteljährlich durchgeführte statistische Repräsentativerhebung der Bevölkerung u. des Erwerbslebens); **mik|ro|ze|phal** (*Med.* kleinköpfig); **Mik|ro|ze|pha|le,** der *u.* die; -n, -n (↑R 5 ff.); **Mik|ro|ze|pha|lie,** die; - (*Med.* Kleinköpfigkeit)

[1]**Mi|lan** [*auch* mi'la:n], der; -s, -e ‹franz.› (ein Greifvogel)

[2]**Mi|lan** (m. Vorn.)

Mi|la|no (*ital. Form von* Mailand)

Mil|be, die; -, -n (ein Spinnentier); **mil|big**

Milch, die; -, *Plur. (fachspr.)* -e[n]; **Milch-bar** (die), **...bart** (*svw.* Milchgesicht), **...brei, ...bröt|chen, ...drü|se, ...eis, ...ei|weiß;** [1]**mil|chen** (aus Milch); [2]**mil|chen** (*landsch. für* Milch geben); [1]**Mil|cher** *vgl.* Milchner; [2]**Mil|cher** (*landsch. für* Melker); **Mil|che|rin** *(landsch.);* **Milch-er|trag, ...fla|sche, ...frau** *(ugs.),* **...ge|biss, ...ge|sicht** (unreifer junger Bursche), **...glas** (*Plur.* ...gläser); **mil|chig; Milch-kaf|fee, ...känn|chen, ...kan|ne, ...kuh, ...kur; Milch|ling** (ein Pilz); **Milch|mäd|chen; Milch|mäd|chen|rech|nung** (*ugs. für* auf Trugschlüssen beruhende Rechnung); **Milch|mann** *Plur.* ...männer; **Milch|mix|ge|tränk; Milch|napf; Milch|ner,** Mil|cher (männl. Fisch); **Milch-pro|dukt, ...pul|ver, ...pum|pe, ...reis, ...saft** *(Bot.),* **...säu|re; Milch|säu|re|bak|te|ri|en** *Plur.;* **Milch-scho|ko|la|de, ...stra|ße** (die; -; *Astron.*), **...tü|te; milch|weiß; Milch-wirt|schaft, ...zahn, ...zu|cker**

mild, mil|de; Mil|de, die; -; **mil|dern;** ich ...ere (↑R 16); mildernde Umstände *(Rechtsspr.);* **Mil|de|rung; Mil|de|rungs|grund; mild|her|zig; Mild|her|zig|keit,** die; -; **mild|tä|tig; Mild|tä|tig|keit,** die; -

[1] [*auch* 'mi:kro...]

Mi|le|na [*auch* 'mi:...] (w. Vorn.)

Mi|le|si|er [...iər] (Bewohner von Milet); **Mi|let** (altgriech. Stadt)

Mil|haud [mi'jo], Darius [da'riys] (franz. Komponist)

Mi|li|ar|tu|ber|ku|lo|se ‹lat.› (*Med.* meist rasch tödlich verlaufende Allgemeininfektion des Körpers mit Tuberkelbazillen)

Mi|li|eu [mi'liø:], das; -s, -s ‹franz.› (Umwelt; *bes. schweiz. auch für* Dirnenwelt); **mi|li|eu|be|dingt; Mi|li|eu|for|schung; mi|li|eu|ge|schä|digt; Mi|li|eu|ge|schä|dig|te,** der *u.* die; -n, -n (↑R 5 ff.); **Mi|li|eu-scha|den** *(Psych.),* **...the|o|rie**

mi|li|tant ‹lat.› (kämpferisch); **Mi|li|tanz,** die; -; [1]**Mi|li|tär,** der; -s, -s ‹franz.› (höherer Offizier); [2]**Mi|li|tär,** das; -s (Soldatenstand; Streitkräfte); **Mi|li|tär-ad|mi|nist|ra|ti|on, ...aka|de|mie** (↑R 132), **...arzt, ...at|ta|ché, ...block** (*Plur.* ...blöcke, *selten* ...blocks), **...bud|get, ...bünd|nis, ...dienst, ...dik|ta|tur, ...etat** (↑R 132), **...flug|ha|fen** (*vgl.* [2]Hafen), **...ge|richts|bar|keit; Mi|li|ta|ria** *Plur.* ‹lat.› (Bücher über das Militärwesen; milit. Sammlerstücke; *veraltet für* Heeresangelegenheiten); **mi|li|tä|risch** ‹franz.›; **mi|li|ta|ri|sie|ren** (milit. Anlagen errichten, Truppen aufstellen); **Mi|li|ta|ri|sie|rung; Mi|li|ta|ris|mus,** der; - ‹lat.› (Vorherrschen milit. Gesinnung); **Mi|li|ta|rist,** der; -en, -en (↑R 126); **mi|li|ta|ris|tisch; Mi|li|tär-jun|ta** (von Offizieren [nach einem Putsch] gebildete Regierung), **...marsch, ...mis|si|on, ...mu|sik, ...pflicht** (die; -); **mi|li|tär|pflich|tig; Mi|li|tär|pflich|ti|ge,** der; -n, -n (↑R 5 ff.); **Mi|li|tär-po|li|zei, ...re|gie|rung, ...schu|le, ...seel|sor|ge; Mi|li|ta|ry** ['militəri], die; -, -s ‹engl.› (Vielseitigkeitsprüfung [im sportl. Reiten]); **Mi|li|tär|zeit,** die; -; **Mi|liz,** die; -, -en ‹lat.› (kurz ausgebildete Truppen, Bürgerwehr; *in einigen [ehemals] sozialistischen Staaten auch für* Polizei); **Mi|liz|heer; Mi|li|zi|o|när,** der; -s, -e; (Angehöriger der Miliz); **Mi|liz|sol|dat**

Mil|ke, die; -, *auch* **Mil|ken,** der; -s (*schweiz. für* Kalbsmilch)

Mill., Mio. = Million[en]

Mil|le, das; -, - ‹lat.› (Tausend; *Zeichen* M; *ugs. für* tausend Mark); 5 -; *vgl.* per, pro mille

Mil|le|fi|o|ri|glas *Plur.* ...gläser ‹ital.; dt.› (vielfarbiges Mosaikglas)

[1]**Mille|fleurs** [mil'flœ:r], das; - ‹franz.› (Streublumenmuster);

²Mille|fleurs, der; - (Stoff mit Streublumenmuster)
Mil|le Mig|lia [- 'milja] (↑R 130) *Plur.* ‹ital.› (Langstreckenrennen für Sportwagen in Italien)
Mil|len|ni|um (↑R 132), das; -s, ...ien [...i̯ən] ‹lat.› (*selten für* Jahrtausend); **Mil|len|ni|um[s]|fei|er** (Tausendjahrfeier)
Mil|li (w. Vorn.)
Mil|li... ‹lat.› (ein Tausendstel einer Einheit, z. B. Millimeter = 10^{-3} Meter; *Zeichen* m); **Mil|li|am|pere** [...am'pɛ:r, *auch* 'mili...] (Maßeinheit kleiner elektr. Stromstärken; *Zeichen* mA); **Mil|li|am|pere|me|ter** [...pɛ:r'me:tər, *auch* 'mili...], das; -s, - (Gerät zur Messung geringer Stromstärken)
Mil|li|ar|där, der; -s, -e ‹franz.› (Besitzer eines Vermögens von mindestens einer Milliarde); **Mil|li|ar|dä|rin; Mil|li|ar|de,** die; -, -n (1 000 Millionen; *Abk.* Md., Mrd. *u.* Mia.); **Mil|li|ar|den₋an|lei|he, ...be|trag, ...hö|he** (in -); **mil|li|ards|te;** *vgl.* achte; **mil|li|ards|tel;** *vgl.* achtel; **Mil|li|ards|tel;** *vgl.* Achtel
Mil|li|bar, das (¹/₁₀₀₀ Bar; alte Maßeinheit für den Luftdruck; *Abk.* mbar, *in der Meteor. nur* mb); **Mil|li|gramm** [*auch* 'mili...] (¹/₁₀₀₀ g; *Zeichen* mg); 10 -; **Mil|li|li|ter** [*auch* 'mili...] (¹/₁₀₀₀ l; *Zeichen* ml); **Mil|li|me|ter** (¹/₁₀₀₀ m; *Zeichen* mm); **Mil|li|me|ter₋ar|beit** (die; -; *ugs.*), **...pa|pier; Mil|li|mol** [*auch* 'mili...] (¹/₁₀₀₀ mol; *Zeichen* mmol)
Mil|li|on, die; -, -en ‹ital.› (1 000 mal 1 000; *Abk.* Mill. *u.* Mio.); eine Million; ein[und]dreiviertel Millionen; zwei Millionen fünfhunderttausend; mit 0,8 Millionen; **Mil|li|o|när,** der; -s, -e ‹franz.› (Besitzer eines Vermögens von mindestens einer Million; sehr reicher Mann); **Mil|li|o|nä|rin; Mil|li|o|nen₋auf|la|ge, ...auf|trag, ...be|trag; mil|li|o|nen|fach; Mil|li|o|nen₋ge|schäft, ...ge|winn, ...heer, ...hö|he** (in -); **Mil|li|o|nen Mal;** *vgl.* ¹Mal; **Mil|li|o|nen|scha|den; mil|li|o|nen|schwer; Mil|li|o|nen|stadt; mil|li|ons|te;** *vgl.* achte; **mil|li|on[s]|tel;** *vgl.* achtel; **Mil|li|on[s]|tel,** das, *schweiz. meist* der; -s, -; *vgl.* Achtel
Mil|lö|cker (österr. Komponist)
Mill|statt (österr. Ort); **Mill|stät|ter** (↑R 103); - See
Mil|ly (w. Vorn.)
Mil|reis, das; -, - ‹port.› (1 000 Reis; ehem. Währungseinheit in Portugal u. Brasilien)
Mil|ti|a|des (athen. Feldherr)
Mil|ton ['milt(ə)n] (engl. Dichter)
Milz, die; -, -en (Organ); **Milz₋brand** (der; -[e]s; eine gefährliche Infektionskrankheit), **...quet|schung, ...riss**
¹Mi|me (*eingedeutschte Form von* Mimir)
²Mi|me, der; -n, -n (↑R 126) ‹griech.› (*veraltend für* Schauspieler); **mi|men** (*veraltend für* als Mime wirken; *ugs. für* so tun, als ob); **Mi|men** (*Plur. von* ²Mime *u.* Mimus); **Mi|me|se,** die; -, -n (*Zool.* Nachahmung des Aussehens von Gegenständen od. Lebewesen bei Tieren [zum Schutz]); **Mi|me|sis,** die; -, ...esen (Nachahmung); **mi|me|tisch** (die Mimese betreffend; nachahmend); **Mi|mik,** die; - (Gebärden- u. Mienenspiel [des Schauspielers]); **Mi|mi|ker** *vgl.* Mimus; **Mi|mik|ry** [...kri] (↑R 130), die; - ‹engl.› (*Zool.* Nachahmung wehrhafter Tiere durch nichtwehrhafte in Körpergestalt u. Färbung; *übertr. für* Anpassung)
Mi|mir (Gestalt der nord. Mythol.; Gestalt der germ. Heldensage)
mi|misch ‹griech.› (schauspielerisch; mit Gebärden)
Mi|mo|se, die; -, -n ‹griech.› (Pflanzengattung; Blüte der Silberakazie; *übertr. für* überempfindlicher Mensch); **mi|mo|sen|haft** (zart, fein; [über]empfindlich)
Mi|mus, der; -, ...men ‹griech.› (Possenreißer der Antike; *auch* die Posse selbst)
min, Min. = Minute
Mi|na, Mi|ne (w. Vorn.)
Mi|na|rett, das; -s, *Plur.* -e *u.* -s ‹arab.-franz.› (Moscheeturm)
Min|chen (w. Vorn.)
Min|da|nao (eine Philippineninsel)
Min|den (Stadt a. d. Weser); **Min|de|ner** (↑R 103)
min|der; minder gut, minder wichtig; **min|der₋be|deu|tend, ...be|gabt; Min|der|be|gab|te,** der *u.* die; -n, -n (↑R 5 ff.); **min|der|be|mit|telt; Min|der|be|mit|tel|te,** der *u.* die; -n, -n (↑R 5 ff.); **Min|der₋bru|der** (Angehöriger des I. Ordens des hl. Franz von Assisi), **...ein|nah|me; Min|der|heit; Min|der|hei|ten₋fra|ge, ...schutz; Min|der|heits|re|gie|rung; min|der|jäh|rig; Min|der|jäh|ri|ge,** der *u.* die; -n, -n (↑R 5 ff.); **Min|der|jäh|rig|keit,** die; -; **Min|der|leis|tung; min|dern;** ich ...ere (↑R 16); **Min|de|rung; Min|der|wert; min|der|wer|tig;** -es Fleisch; **Min|der|wer|tig|keit; Min|der|wer|tig|keits₋ge|fühl, ...kom|plex** (*ugs. Kurzw.* Miko); **Min|der|zahl,** die; -; **Min|dest₋ab|stand, ...al|ter, ...an|for|de|rung, ...bei|trag, ...be|steu|e|rung, ...be|trag; Min|dest|bie|ten|de,** der *u.* die; -n, -n (↑R 5 ff.); **min|des|te;** das Mindeste, *auch* mindeste; zum Mindesten, *auch* mindesten; nicht im Mindesten, *auch* mindesten; **min|des|tens; Min|dest|for|dern|de,** der *u.* die; -n, -n (↑R 5 ff.); **Min|dest₋for|de|rung, ...ge|bot, ...ge|schwin|dig|keit, ...grö|ße, ...lohn, ...maß** (das), **...preis** (*vgl.* ²Preis), **...re|ser|ve** (*meist Plur.; Bankw.*), **...satz, ...stra|fe, ...zahl, ...zeit**
min|disch (aus Minden)
¹Mi|ne, die; -, -n ‹franz.› (unterird. Gang [mit Sprengladung]; Bergwerk; Sprengkörper; Kugelschreiber-, Bleistifteinlage)
²Mi|ne, die; -, -n ‹griech.› (altgriech. Münze, Gewicht)
³Mi|ne *vgl.* Mina
Mi|nen₋ar|bei|ter, ...feld, ...le|ger, ...räum|boot, ...stol|len, ...such|boot, ...such|ge|rät, ...wer|fer
Mi|ne|ral, das; -s, *Plur.* -e *u.* -ien [...i̯ən] ‹franz.› (anorganischer, chem. einheitlicher u. natürlich gebildeter Bestandteil der Erdkruste); **Mi|ne|ral₋bad, ...dün|ger; Mi|ne|ra|li|en|samm|lung** [...i̯ən...]; **mi|ne|ra|lisch; Mi|ne|ra|lo|ge,** der; -n, -n (↑R 126) ‹franz.; griech.›; **Mi|ne|ra|lo|gie,** die; - (Wissenschaft von den Mineralen); **Mi|ne|ra|lo|gin; mi|ne|ra|lo|gisch; Mi|ne|ral|öl; Mi|ne|ral|öl₋ge|sell|schaft, ...in|dust|rie, ...steu|er** (die); **Mi|ne|ral₋quel|le, ...stoff, ...was|ser** (*Plur.* ...wässer)
Mi|ner|va [...va] (röm. Göttin des Handwerks, der Weisheit u. der Künste)
Mi|nest|ra (↑R 130), die; -, ...ren ‹ital.› (*svw.* Minestrone; *österr. auch für* Kohlsuppe); **Mi|nest|ro|ne,** die; -, -n (ital. Gemüsesuppe)
Mi|net|te, die; -, -n ‹franz.› (Eisenerz); **Mi|neur** [mi'nø:r], der; -s, -e (*früher für* im Minenbau ausgebildeter Pionier)
mi|ni (*Mode* sehr kurz); der Rock ist mini; **¹Mi|ni,** das; -s, -s (*ugs. für* Minikleid; *meist ohne Artikel, nur Sing.:* sehr kurze Kleidung); Mini tragen; **²Mi|ni,** der; -s, -s (*ugs. für* Minirock); **Mi|ni...** (sehr klein; *Mode* äußerst kurz, z. B. Minirock); **Mi|ni|a|tur,** die; -, -en

(kleines Bild; [kleine] Illustration); **Mi|ni|a|tur‿aus|ga|be** (kleine[re] Ausgabe), **...bild; mi|ni|a|tu|ri|sie|ren** (*Elektrotechnik* verkleinern); **Mi|ni|a|tu|ri|sie|rung; Mi|ni|a|tur|ma|le|rei**

Mi|ni|bar, die (kleiner Kühlschrank im Hotelzimmer; Wagen mit Esswaren und Getränken in Fernzügen); **Mi|ni|bi|ki|ni,** der; -s, -s (sehr knapper Bikini); **Mi|ni|break** [...bre:k], das; -s, -s *(Tennis);* **Mi|ni|car,** der; -s, -s ‹engl.› (Kleintaxi); **Mi|ni|com|pu|ter**

mi|nie|ren ‹franz.› (unterirdische Gänge, Stollen anlegen); *vgl.* [1]Mine

Mi|ni|golf (Miniaturgolfanlage; Kleingolfspiel)

Mi|ni|ki|ni, der; -s, -s (Damenbadebekleidung ohne Oberteil); **Mi|ni|kleid**

mi|nim ‹lat.› (*schweiz., sonst veraltet für* geringfügig, minimal); **Mi|ni|ma** [*auch* 'mini...] (*Plur. von* Minimum); **mi|ni|mal** (sehr klein, niedrigst, winzig); **Mi|ni|mal|art,** *auch* **Mi|ni|mal Art** ['miniməl a:(r)t], die; - (Kunstrichtung, die mit einfachsten Grundformen arbeitet); **Mi|ni|mal‿be|trag, ...for|de|rung, ...kon|sens; Mi|ni|mal|mu|sic,** *auch* **Mi|ni|mal Mu|sic** ['miniməl 'mju:zik], die; - (Musikrichtung, die mit einfachsten Grundformen arbeitet); **Mi|ni|mal‿pro|gramm, ...wert; mi|ni|mie|ren** (minimal machen); **Mi|ni|mie|rung; Mi|ni|mum** [*auch* 'mini...], das; -s, ...ma ‹„das Geringste, Kleinste"› (Mindestpreis, -maß, -wert); **Mi|ni|mum|ther|mo|me|ter; Mi|ni‿rock, ...slip, ...spi|on** (Kleinstabhörgerät)

Mi|nis|ter, der; -s, - ‹lat.› (einen bestimmten Geschäftsbereich leitendes Regierungsmitglied); **Mi|nis|ter‿amt, ...ebe|ne** (↑R 132; auf -); **Mi|nis|te|ri|al‿be|am|te, ...di|rek|tor, ...di|ri|gent; Mi|nis|te|ri|a|le,** der; -n, -n (↑R 126; Angehöriger des mittelalterl. Dienstadels); **Mi|nis|te|ri|al|rat** *Plur.* ...räte; **mi|nis|te|ri|ell** ‹franz.› (von einem Minister od. Ministerium ausgehend usw.); **Mi|nis|te|rin; Mi|nis|te|ri|um,** das; -s, ...ien [...iən] ‹lat.› (höchste [Verwaltungs]behörde des Staates mit bestimmtem Aufgabenbereich); **Mi|nis|ter‿prä|si|dent, ...prä|si|den|tin, ...rat** (*Plur.* ...räte)

mi|nist|ra|bel (↑R 130; fähig, Minister zu werden); **Mi|nist|rant,** der; -en, -en; ↑R 126 (kath. Messdiener); **Mi|nist|ran|tin; mi|nist|rie|ren** (als Messdiener tätig sein)

Mi|ni|um, das; -s ‹lat.› (Mennige)

Mink, der; -s, -e ‹engl.› (amerik. Nerz)

Min|ka (w. Vorn.)

Mink|fell

Minn. = Minnesota

Min|na (w. Vorn.); *vgl.* grün, I, b

Min|ne, die; - (*mhd. Bez. für* Liebe; *heute noch scherzh.*); **Min|ne‿dienst, ...lied; min|nen** *(noch scherzh.);* **Min|ne|sang,** der; -[e]s; **Min|ne|sän|ger, Min|ne|sin|ger**

Min|ne|so|ta (Staat in den USA; *Abk.* Minn.)

min|nig|lich (*veraltet für* wonnig, liebevoll)

mi|no|isch ‹nach dem sagenhaften altgriech. König Minos auf Kreta›; -e Kultur

Mi|no|rat, das; -[e]s, -e ‹lat.› (Vorrecht des Jüngsten auf das Erbgut; nach dem Jüngstenrecht zu vererbendes Gut; *Ggs.* Majorat); **mi|no|renn** (*veraltet für* minderjährig); **Mi|no|ren|ni|tät,** die; - *(veraltet);* **Mi|no|rist,** der; -en, -en; ↑R 126 (kath. Kleriker, der eine niedere Weihe erhalten hat); **Mi|no|rit,** der; -en, -en; ↑R 126 (Minderbruder); **Mi|no|ri|tät,** die; -, -en (Minderzahl, Minderheit)

Mi|no|taur, der; -s *u.* **Mi|no|tau|rus,** der; - ‹griech.› (Ungeheuer der griech. Sage, halb Mensch, halb Stier)

Minsk (Hptst. von Weißrussland)

Minst|rel (↑R 130), der; -s, -s ‹engl.› (Spielmann, Minnesänger in England)

Mi|nu|end, der; -en, -en (↑R 126) ‹lat.› (Zahl, von der etwas abgezogen werden soll); **mi|nus** (weniger; *Zeichen* – [negativ]; *Ggs.* plus); fünf minus drei ist, macht, gibt (*nicht* sind, machen, geben) zwei; minus 15 Grad *od.* 15 Grad minus; **Mi|nus,** das; -, - (Minder-, Fehlbetrag, Verlust); **Mi|nus|be|trag; Mi|nus|kel,** die; -, -n (Kleinbuchstabe); **Mi|nus‿pol, ...punkt, ...re|kord, ...zei|chen** (Subtraktionszeichen); **Mi|nu|te,** die; -, -n (1/60 Stunde; *Zeichen* min, *Abk.* Min.; *Geom.* 1/60 Grad; *Zeichen* '); **mi|nu|ten|lang;** -er Beifall; *aber* mehrere Minuten lang; **Mi|nu|ten|zei|ger; ...mi|nü|tig,** *auch* **...mi|nu|tig** (z. B. fünfminütig, *mit Ziffer* 5-minütig [fünf Minuten dauernd]); **mi|nu|ti|ös** ‹franz.› *auch* mi|nu|zi|ös (peinlich genau); **mi|nüt|lich** (jede Minute); **...mi|nüt|lich,** *auch* **...mi|nut|lich** (z. B. fünfminütlich, *mit Ziffer* 5-minütlich [alle fünf Minuten wiederkehrend]); **Mi|nu|zi|en** *Plur.* ‹lat.› (*veraltet für* Kleinigkeiten); **Mi|nu|zi|en|stift,** der (Aufstecknadel für Insektensammlungen); **mi|nu|zi|ös** *vgl.* minutiös

Min|ze, die; -, -n (Name verschiedener Pflanzenarten)

Mio., Mill. = Million[en]

mi|o|zän ‹griech.› (*Geol.* zum Miozän gehörend); **Mi|o|zän,** das; -s (*Geol.* zweitjüngste Abteilung des Tertiärs)

mir (*Dat. des Pronomens* „ich"); mir nichts, dir nichts; (↑R 5:) mir alten, *selten* alter Frau; mir jungem, *auch* jungen Menschen; mir Geliebten (weibl.; *selten* Geliebter); mir Geliebtem (männl.; *auch* Geliebten)

[1]**Mir,** der; -s ‹russ.› (Dorfgemeinschaft mit Gemeinschaftsbesitz im zarist. Russland)

[2]**Mir** ‹*russ. für* Frieden› Name der 1986 gestarteten sowjet.-russ. Raumstation

Mi|ra, die; - ‹lat.› (ein Stern)

Mi|ra|beau [...'bo:] (franz. Publizist u. Politiker)

Mi|ra|bel|le, die; -, -n ‹franz.› (eine kleine, gelbe Pflaume); **Mi|ra|bel|len‿kom|pott, ...schnaps**

Mi|rage [mi'ra:ʒ], die; -, -s ‹franz.› (ein franz. Jagdbomber)

Mi|ra|kel, das; -s, - ‹lat.› (*veraltend für* Wunder[werk]); **Mi|ra|kel|spiel** (mittelalterl. Drama); **mi|ra|ku|lös** (*veraltet für* wunderbar)

Mi|ra|ma|re ‹ital.› (Schloss unweit von Triest)

Mi|ró [mi'ro], Joan ['xoan] (span. Maler)

Mir|za, der; -s, -s ‹pers., „Fürstensohn"› (*vor dem Namen* Herr; *hinter dem Namen* Prinz)

Mi|sand|rie (↑R 130 *u.* 132), die; - ‹griech.› (Männerhass, -scheu)

Mi|santh|rop (↑R 130 *u.* 132), der; -en, -en (↑R 126) ‹griech.› (Menschenhasser, -feind); **Mi|santh|ro|pie,** die; -, ...ien; **mi|santh|ro|pisch**

Misch‿bat|te|rie, ...be|cher, ...blut, ...brot, ...ehe (↑R 132; Ehe zwischen Angehörigen verschiedener Konfessionen od. Kulturkreise); **mi|schen;** du mischst; sich -; **Mi|scher; Mi|sche|rei; Misch|far|be; misch|far|ben** *od.* **...far|big; Misch‿form, ...fut|ter** (*vgl.* [1]Futter), **...gas** (Leuchtgas), **...ge|mü|se, ...ge|tränk, ...ge|we|be, ...kal|ku|la|ti|on, ...krug, ...kul|tur; Misch|ling** (Bastard); **Misch|masch,** der; -[e]s, -e (*ugs. für* Durcheinander verschiedener Dinge)

Misch|na, die; - ⟨hebr.⟩ (grundlegender Teil des Talmuds)

Misch|po|che [...x...], **Misch|po|ke,** die; - ⟨hebr.-jidd.⟩ (*ugs. für* Verwandtschaft; üble Gesellschaft)

Misch‿pult *(Rundfunk, Film),* **...ras|se, ...spra|che, ...trom|mel** (zum Mischen des Baustoffs); **Mi|schung; Mi|schungs|ver|hält|nis; Misch|wald**

Mi|se ['mi:zə], die; -, -n ⟨franz.⟩ (Einmalprämie bei der Lebensversicherung; Spieleinsatz)

Mi|sel, das; -s, -s ⟨elsäss., „Mäuschen"⟩ ([bei Goethe:] junges Mädchen, Liebchen)

mi|se|ra|bel ⟨franz.⟩ (*ugs. für* erbärmlich [schlecht]; nichtswürdig); ...ab|ler (↑R 130) Kerl; **Mi|se|re,** die; -, -n (Jammer, Not[lage], Elend, Armseligkeit); **Mi|se|re|or,** das; -[s] ⟨lat., „ich erbarme mich"⟩ (kath. Fastenopferspende für die Entwicklungsländer); **Mi|se|re|re,** das; -[s] ⟨„erbarme dich!"⟩ (Anfang u. Bez. des 51. Psalms [Bußpsalm] in der Vulgata; *Med.* Kotbrechen); **Mi|se|ri|cor|di|as Do|mi|ni** [...'kɔrdias -] ⟨„die Barmherzigkeit des Herrn" [Psalm 89,2]⟩ (zweiter Sonntag nach Ostern); **Mi|se|ri|kor|die** [...iə], die; -, -n (Vorsprung an den Klappsitzen des Chorgestühls als Stütze während des Stehens)

Mi|so|gam, der; *Gen.* -s *u.* -en, *Plur.* -e[n]; ↑R 126 ⟨griech.⟩ (*Psych.* jmd., der eine krankhafte Abscheu vor der Ehe hat); **Mi|so|ga|mie,** die; - (*Med., Psych.* Ehescheu); **mi|so|gyn** (*Psych.* frauenfeindlich); **Mi|so|gyn,** der; *Gen.* -s *u.* -en, *Plur.* -e[n]; ↑R 126 (*Psych.* Frauenfeind); **Mi|so|gy|nie,** die; - (*Med., Psych.* Frauenhass, -scheu)

Mi|sox, das; - (Tal im Südwesten von Graubünden; *ital.* Val Mesolcina)

Mis|pel, die; -, -n ⟨griech.⟩ (Obstgehölz, Frucht)

Mis|ra|chi [...xi], die; - ⟨hebr.⟩ (eine Weltorganisation orthodoxer Zionisten)

Miss, die, -, -es ['misis] ⟨engl.⟩ (*[engl. u. nordamerik.] für* unverheiratete Frau; *ohne Artikel als Anrede vor dem Eigenn.* Fräulein; *in Verbindung mit einem Länder- od. Ortsnamen für* Schönheitskönigin, z. B. Miss Australien)

miss... (*Vorsilbe von Verben; zum Verhältnis von Betonung und Partizip II vgl.* missachten)

Miss. = [2]Mississippi

Mis|sa, die; -, Missae ['misɛ] ⟨lat.⟩ (*kirchenlat. Bez. der* Messe); - solem|nis (feierliches Hochamt; *auch* Titel eines Werkes von Beethoven)

miss|ach|ten; ich missachte; ich habe missachtet; zu missachten; *seltener* missachten, gemissachtet, zu missachten; **Miss|ach|tung,** die; -

[1]**Mis|sal,** das; -s, -e *u.* Mis|sa|le, das; -s, *Plur.* -n *u.* ...alien [...iən] ⟨lat.⟩ (kath. Messbuch); [2]**Mis|sal,** die; - (*Druckw.* ein Schriftgrad); **Mis|sa|le** *vgl.* [1]Missal

miss|be|ha|gen; es missbehagt mir; es hat mir missbehagt; misszubehagen; **Miss|be|ha|gen; miss|be|hag|lich**

miss|be|schaf|fen; Miss|be|schaf|fen|heit, die; -

Miss|bil|dung

miss|bil|li|gen; ich missbillige; ich habe missbilligt; zu missbilligen; **Miss|bil|li|gung; Miss|bil|li|gungs|an|trag** *(Politik)*

Miss|brauch; miss|brau|chen; ich missbrauche; ich habe missbraucht; zu missbrauchen; **miss|bräuch|lich; miss|bräuch|li|cher|wei|se**

miss|deu|ten; ich missdeute; ich habe missdeutet; zu missdeuten; **Miss|deu|tung**

mis|sen; du misst; gemisst; misse! *od.* miss!

Miss|er|folg

Miss|ern|te

Mis|ses (*Plur. von* Miss)

Mis|se‿tat *(veraltend),* **...tä|ter, ...tä|te|rin**

miss|fal|len; ich missfalle, missfiel; ich habe missfallen; zu missfallen; es missfällt mir; **Miss|fal|len,** das; -s; **Miss|fal|lens‿äu|ße|rung, ...kund|ge|bung; miss|fäl|lig** (mit Missfallen)

Miss|far|be; miss‿far|ben *od.* **...far|big**

miss|ge|bil|det

Miss|ge|burt

miss|ge|launt; Miss|ge|launt|heit, die; -

Miss|ge|schick

miss|ge|stalt (*selten für* missgestaltet); **Miss|ge|stalt; miss|ge|stal|ten;** er missgestaltet; er hat missgestaltet; misszugestalten; **miss|ge|stal|tet** (hässlich)

miss|ge|stimmt

miss|ge|wach|sen, miss|wach|sen ein -er Mensch

miss|glü|cken; es missglückt; es ist missglückt; zu missglücken

miss|gön|nen; ich missgönne; ich habe missgönnt; zu missgönnen

Miss|griff

Miss|gunst; miss|güns|tig

miss|han|deln; ich misshand[e]le (↑R 16); ich habe misshandelt; zu misshandeln; **Miss|hand|lung**

Miss|hei|rat

miss|hel|lig (*veraltet für* nicht übereinstimmend, unharmonisch); **Miss|hel|lig|keit,** die; -, -en *meist Plur.*

Mis|sile ['misail], das; -s, -s (*kurz für* Cruisemissile)

Mis|sing|link, *auch* **Mis|sing Link,** das; - ⟨engl.⟩ (*Biol.* fehlende Übergangsform in tier. u. pflanzl. Stammbäumen)

mis|singsch; Mis|singsch, das; -[s] (der Schriftsprache angenäherte [niederdeutsche] Sprachform)

Mis|sio ca|no|ni|ca, die; - - ⟨lat.⟩ (Ermächtigung zur Ausübung der kirchl. Lehrgewalt); **Mis|si|on,** die; -, -en (Sendung; Auftrag, Botschaft; diplomatische Vertretung im Ausland; *nur Sing.:* Glaubensverkündung [unter Andersgläubigen]); die Innere Mission (Organisation der ev. Kirche; *Abk.* I. M.); **Mis|si|o|nar,** *auch, bes. österr.* **Mis|si|o|när,** der; -s, -e (Sendbote; in der Mission tätiger Geistlicher); **Mis|si|o|na|rin; mis|si|o|na|risch; mis|si|o|nie|ren** (eine Glaubenslehre verbreiten); **Mis|si|o|nie|rung; Mis|si|ons‿chef, ...sta|ti|on, ...wis|sen|schaft** (die; -), **...zelt**

[1]**Mis|sis|sip|pi,** der; -[s] (nordamerik. Strom); [2]**Mis|sis|sip|pi** (Staat in den USA; *Abk.* Miss.)

Miss|klang

Miss|kre|dit, der; -[e]s (schlechter Ruf); jmdn. in - bringen

miss|lau|nig

Miss|laut (*svw.* Misston)

miss|lei|ten; ich missleite; ich habe missleitet, *auch* missgeleitet (*vgl.* miss...); zu missleiten; **Miss|lei|tung**

miss|lich (unangenehm); die Verhältnisse sind -; **Miss|lich|keit**

miss|lie|big (unbeliebt); **Miss|lie|big|keit**

miss|lin|gen; es misslingt; es misslang; es misslänge; es ist misslungen; zu misslingen; **Miss|lin|gen,** das; -s

Miss|ma|nage|ment (schlechtes Management)

Miss|mut; miss|mu|tig

[1]**Mis|sou|ri** [mi'su:ri], der; -[s] (r. Nebenstrom des Mississippi); [2]**Mis|sou|ri** (Staat in den USA; *Abk.* Mo.)

Miss|pi|ckel, der; -s (Arsenkies, ein Mineral)

miss|ra|ten (schlecht geraten); es missrät; der Kuchen ist missraten; zu missraten

Miss|stand (↑R 136)
Miss|stim|mung (↑R 136)
Miss|ton *Plur.* ...töne; **miss|tö|nend; miss|tö|nig**
miss|trau|en; ich misstraue; ich habe misstraut; zu misstrauen; **Miss|trau|en**, das; -s; - gegen jmdn. hegen; **Miss|trau|ens‿an|trag, ...vo|tum; miss|trau|isch**
Miss|ver|gnü|gen, das; -s; **miss|ver|gnügt**
Miss|ver|hält|nis
miss|ver|ständ|lich; Miss|ver|ständ|nis; miss|ver|ste|hen; ich missverstehe; ich habe missverstanden; misszuverstehen; sich -
Miss|wachs, der; -es (*Landw.* dürftiges Wachstum); **miss|wach|sen** *vgl.* missgewachsen
Miss|wahl ‹*zu* Miss›
Miss|wei|sung (*für* Deklination [Abweichung der Magnetnadel])
Miss|wirt|schaft
Miss|wuchs, der; -es (fehlerhafter Wuchs)
miss|zu|frie|den *(veraltet)*
Mist, der; -[e]s (*österr. auch für* Kehricht, Müll); **Mist|beet**
Mis|tel, die; -, -n (eine immergrüne Schmarotzerpflanze); **Mis|tel‿ge|wächs, ...zweig**
mis|ten
Mis|ter *vgl.* Mr
Mist‿fink (der; *Gen.* -en, *auch* -s, *Plur.* -en; *svw.* Mistkerl), **...for|ke** *(nordd.)*, **...ga|bel, ...hau|fen, ...hund** (Schimpfwort); **mis|tig** (*landsch. für* schmutzig); **Mis|tig|keit**, die; - *(landsch.)*; **Mist‿jau|che, ...kä|fer, ...kerl** (gemeiner Kerl [Schimpfwort]), **...kü|bel** (*österr. für* Abfalleimer)
Mist|ral (↑R 130), der; -s, -e ‹franz.› (kalter, stürmischer Nord[west]wind im Rhonetal)
Mist|ress (↑R 130) *vgl.* Mrs
Mist‿schau|fel (*österr. für* Kehrichtschaufel), **...stock** (*Plur.* ...stöcke; *schweiz. für* Misthaufen), **...stück** (gemeiner Mensch, Luder [Schimpfwort]), **...vieh** (Schimpfwort), **...wet|ter** (*ugs. für* sehr schlechtes Wetter)
Mis|zel|la|ne|en [*auch* ...'la:neən], **Mis|zel|len** *Plur.* ‹lat.› (Vermischtes; kleine Aufsätze verschiedenen Inhalts)
mit; **I.** *Präp. mit Dat.:* mit anderen Worten (*Abk.* m. a. W.). **II.** *(getrennt geschriebenes) Adverb; drückt die vorübergehende Beteiligung oder den Gedanken des Anschlusses aus (svw. auch), z. B.:* mit nach oben gehen; das kann ich nicht mit ansehen; das muss mit eingeschlossen werden; das ist mit zu berücksichtigen. **III.** *mit Verben zusammengeschrieben; vgl.* mitarbeiten, mitbringen, mitfahren, mitreißen, mitteilen usw.
Mit|an|ge|klag|te; Mit|ar|beit, die; -; **mit|ar|bei|ten**; er hat an diesem Werk mitgearbeitet; **Mit‿ar|bei|ter, ...ar|bei|te|rin; Mit|ar|bei|ter|stab; Mit‿au|tor, ...au|to|rin, ...be|grün|der, ...be|grün|de|rin; mit|be|kom|men; mit|be|nut|zen**, *bes. südd.* **mit|be|nüt|zen; Mit|be|nut|zung; mit be|rück|sich|ti|gen** *vgl.* mit; **Mit‿be|sit|zer, ...be|sit|ze|rin; mit|be|stim|men; Mit|be|stim|mung**, die; -; **Mit|be|stim|mungs‿ge|setz, ...recht; Mit‿be|wer|ber, ...be|wer|be|rin, ...be|woh|ner, ...be|woh|ne|rin**
mit|brin|gen; er hat mir die Vase von der Reise mitgebracht; **Mit|bring|sel**, das; -s, -
Mit|bür|ger; Mit|bür|ge|rin; Mit|bür|ger|schaft, die; -
mit|den|ken
mit|dür|fen; die Kinder haben nicht mitgedurft
Mit‿ei|gen|tum, ...ei|gen|tü|mer, ...ei|gen|tü|me|rin
mit|ei|nan|der (↑R 132); *in Verbindung mit Verben immer getrennt geschrieben:* miteinander (einer mit dem andern) auskommen, gehen, leben usw.; *vgl.* aneinander; **Mit|ei|nan|der** [*auch* 'mit...], das; -[s]
Mit‿emp|fin|den, ...er|be (der)
mit|er|le|ben
mit|es|sen; Mit|es|ser
mit|fah|ren; Mit‿fah|rer, ...fah|re|rin, ...fahr|ge|le|gen|heit, ...fahrt
mit|füh|len; mit|füh|lend
mit|füh|ren
mit|ge|ben
mit|ge|fan|gen; mitgefangen, mitgehangen; **Mit|ge|fan|ge|ne**
Mit|ge|fühl, das; -[e]s
mit|ge|hen
mit|ge|nom|men; er sah sehr - (ermattet) aus
Mit|gift, die; -, -en (*veraltend für* Mitgabe; Aussteuer); **Mit|gift|jä|ger** *(abwertend)*
Mit|glied; - des Bundestages (*Abk.* M. d. B. *od.* MdB); - des Landtages (*Abk.* M. d. L. *od.* MdL); **Mit|glie|der‿kar|tei, ...lis|te, ...schwund, ...ver|samm|lung, ...ver|zeich|nis, ...zahl; Mit|glieds‿aus|weis, ...bei|trag; Mit|glied|schaft**, die; -, -en; **Mit|glieds‿kar|te, ...land** (*Plur.* ...länder); **Mit|glieds|staat, Mit|glied|staat** *Plur.* ...staaten
mit|ha|ben; alle Sachen -
mit|hal|ten; mit jmdm. -
mit|hel|fen; Mit‿hel|fer, ...hel|fe|rin
Mit‿he|raus|ge|ber, ...he|raus|ge|be|rin
mit|hil|fe, *auch* mit Hil|fe; mithilfe, *auch* mit Hilfe einiger Zeugen; *vgl. auch* Hilfe
Mit|hil|fe, die; -
mit|hin (somit)
mit|hö|ren; am Telefon -
Mith|ra[s] (↑R 130; altiran. Lichtgott)
Mith|ri|da|tes (↑R 130; König von Pontus)
Mi|ti|li|ni *vgl.* Mytilene
Mit‿in|ha|ber, ...in|ha|be|rin
Mit‿kämp|fer, ...kämp|fe|rin
Mit‿klä|ger, ...klä|ge|rin
mit|klin|gen
mit|kom|men
mit|kön|nen; mit jmdm. nicht - (*ugs. für* nicht konkurrieren können)
mit|krie|gen (*ugs. für* mitbekommen)
mit|lau|fen; Mit‿läu|fer, ...läu|fe|rin
Mit|laut (*für* Konsonant)
Mit|leid, das; -[e]s; (↑R 40:) sie waren in einem Mitleid erregenden, *auch* mitleiderregenden Zustand; **Mit|lei|den**, das; -s *(geh.)*; **Mit|lei|den|schaft**; *nur in* etwas *od.* jmdn. in - ziehen; **Mit|leid er|re|gend** *vgl.* Mitleid; **mit|lei|dig; mit|leid[s]‿los, ...voll**
mit|le|sen
mit|lie|fern
mit|ma|chen *(ugs.)*
Mit|mensch, der; **mit|mensch|lich; Mit|mensch|lich|keit**, die; -
mit|mi|schen (*ugs. für* sich aktiv an etwas beteiligen)
mit|mö|gen (*ugs. für* mitgehen, mitkommen mögen)
mit|müs|sen; auf die Wache -
Mit|nah|me, die; - (das Mitnehmen); **Mit|nah|me|preis; mit|neh|men** *vgl.* mitgenommen; **Mit|neh|me|preis** (Mitnahmepreis); **Mit|neh|mer** *(Technik)*
mit|nich|ten *(veraltend) vgl.* nicht
Mi|to|se, die; -, -n ‹griech.› (*Biol.* eine Art der Zellkernteilung)
Mit‿pas|sa|gier, ...pas|sa|gie|rin
Mit‿pa|ti|ent, ...pa|ti|en|tin
Mit|ra (↑R 130), die; -, ...tren ‹griech.› (Bischofsmütze; *Med.* haubenartiger Kopfverband)
Mit|rail|leur [mitra'jø:r] (↑R 130), der; -s, -e ‹franz.› (*schweiz. für* Maschinengewehrschütze); **Mit|rail|leu|se** [mitra(l)'jø:zə], die; -, -n (ein Vorläufer des Maschinengewehrs)
mit|rau|chen; (↑R 50:) passives Mitrauchen

mit|rech|nen
mit|re|den; bei etwas - können
mit|rei|sen; sie ist mit ihnen mitgereist; **Mit|rei|sen|de**
mit|rei|ßen; von der Menge mitgerissen werden; der Redner riss alle Zuhörer mit; **mit|rei|ßend;** eine mitreißende Musik
Mit|ro|pa (↑R 130), die; - (Mitteleuropäische Schlaf- u. Speisewagen-Aktiengesellschaft)
mit|sam|men (*landsch. für* zusammen, gemeinsam); **mit|samt;** *Präp. mit Dat.* (gemeinsam mit): mitsamt seinem Eigentum
mit|schlei|fen
mit|schlep|pen
mit|schnei|den (vom Rundf. od. Fernsehen Gesendetes auf Tonband aufnehmen); **Mit|schnitt**
mit|schrei|ben
Mit|schuld, die; -; **mit|schul|dig; Mit|schul|di|ge**
Mit‿schü|ler, ...schü|le|rin
mit|schwin|gen
mit|sin|gen
mit|sol|len; weil der Hund mitsoll
mit|spie|len; lasst die Kleine -; **Mit‿spie|ler, ...spie|le|rin**
Mit|spra|che, die; -; **Mit|spra|che|recht; mit|spre|chen**
mit|ste|no|gra|phie|ren
Mit‿strei|ter, ...strei|te|rin
Mitt|acht|zi|ger *vgl.* Mittdreißiger
[1]**Mit|tag,** der; -s, -e; über Mittag wegbleiben; [zu] Mittag essen; Mittag (*ugs. für* Mittagspause) machen; des Mittags, eines Mittags; (↑R 45): [bis, von] gestern, heute, morgen Mittag; *(Zusammenschreibung:)* Dienstagmittag; *vgl.* Dienstagabend; mittags; [2]**Mit|tag,** das; -s (*ugs. für* Mittagessen); ein karges -; **Mit|tag‿brot** *(landsch.),* **...es|sen; mit|tä|gig** *vgl.* ...tägig; **mit|täg|lich** *vgl.* ...täglich; **mit|tags** (↑R 46); 12 Uhr mittags; *aber* des Mittags; *(Zusammenschreibung:)* dienstagmittags; *vgl.* Abend, Dienstagabend; **Mit|tags|brot** *(landsch.);* **Mit|tags‿hit|ze, ...kreis** (*für* Meridian), **...li|nie** (*für* Meridianlinie); **Mit|tag[s]|mahl** *(geh.);* **Mit|tags|pau|se; Mit|tag[s]‿schicht, ...schlaf** (*vgl.* [2]Schlaf), **...son|ne, ...stun|de; Mit|tags‿tisch, ...zeit**
Mit‿tä|ter, ...tä|te|rin, ...tä|ter|schaft
Mitt|drei|ßi|ger (Mann in der Mitte der Dreißigerjahre); **Mitt|drei|ßi|ge|rin**
Mit|te, die; -, -n; in der Mitte; Mitte Januar; Mitte dreißig, Mitte der Dreißiger; Seite 3 [in der] Mitte, Obergeschoss Mitte

mit|tei|len (melden); er hat ihm das Geheimnis mitgeteilt; **mit|tei|lens|wert; mit|teil|sam; Mit|teil|sam|keit,** die; -; **Mit|tei|lung; Mit|tei|lungs‿be|dürf|nis** (das; -ses), **...drang**
mit|tel (*nur adverbial; ugs. für* mittelmäßig); [1]**Mit|tel,** das; -s, -; sich ins Mittel legen; [2]**Mit|tel,** die; - (*Druckw.* ein Schriftgrad)
mit|tel|alt; mittelalter Gouda; **Mit|tel|al|ter,** das; -s (*Abk.* MA.); **mit|tel|al|te|rig,** mit|tel|alt|rig (in mittlerem Alter stehend); **mit|tel|al|ter|lich** (dem Mittelalter angehörend; *Abk.* ma.); **mit|tel|alt|rig** *vgl.* mittelalterig
Mit|tel|ame|ri|ka (↑R 132)
mit|tel|bar
Mit|tel|bau, der; -[e]s, -ten (*Bauw.* mittlerer Flügel eines Gebäudes; *nur Sing.: Hochschulw.* Gruppe der Assistenten u. akademischen Räte)
Mit|tel|be|trieb
Mit|tel|chen
mit|tel|deutsch *vgl.* deutsch; **Mit|tel|deutsch,** das; -[s] (Sprache); *vgl.* Deutsch; **Mit|tel|deut|sche,** das; -n; *vgl.* Deutsche, das; **Mit|tel|deutsch|land**
Mit|tel|ding
Mit|tel|eu|ro|pa; Mit|tel|eu|ro|pä|er; mit|tel|eu|ro|pä|isch; -e Zeit (*Abk.* MEZ)
mit|tel|fein *(Kaufmannsspr.)*
Mit|tel|feld *(bes. Sport);* **Mit|tel|feld‿spie|ler, ...spie|le|rin**
Mit|tel|fin|ger
Mit|tel|fran|ken
mit|tel|fris|tig (auf eine mittlere Zeitspanne begrenzt)
Mit|tel|fuß; Mit|tel|fuß|kno|chen
Mit|tel|ge|bir|ge; Mit|tel‿ge|wicht (Körpergewichtsklasse in der Schwerathletik), **...ge|wicht|ler, ...glied; mit|tel‿groß, ...gut**
Mit|tel|hand, die; -; in der - sitzen *(Kartenspiel)*
mit|tel|hoch|deutsch (*Abk.* mhd.); *vgl.* deutsch; **Mit|tel|hoch|deutsch,** das; -[s] (Sprache); *vgl.* Deutsch; **Mit|tel|hoch|deut|sche,** das; -n; *vgl.* Deutsche, das
Mit|te-links-Bünd|nis ([Regierungs]bündnis von Parteien der polit. Mitte u. der polit. Linken)
Mit|tel|in|stanz
Mit|tel|klas|se; Mit|tel|klas|se|wa|gen
Mit|tel|kreis *(bes. Fußball, Eishockey)*
mit|tel|län|disch; -es Klima, *aber* (↑R 102): das Mittelländische Meer
Mit|tel|land|ka|nal, der; -s

Mit|tel|la|tein; mit|tel|la|tei|nisch (*Abk.* mlat.)
Mit|tel|läu|fer *(Sport)*
Mit|tel|li|nie
mit|tel|los; Mit|tel|lo|sig|keit, die; -
Mit|tel|maß, das; -es; **mit|tel|mä|ßig; Mit|tel|mä|ßig|keit**
Mit|tel|meer, das; -[e]s; **mit|tel|mee|risch; Mit|tel|meer‿kli|ma, ...raum**
mit|tel|nie|der|deutsch (*Abk.* mnd.)
Mit|tel|ohr, das; -[e]s; **Mit|tel|ohr‿ent|zün|dung, ...ver|ei|te|rung**
mit|tel|präch|tig *(ugs.)*
mit|tel|prei|sig; -e Produkte
Mit|tel|punkt; Mit|tel|punkt|schu|le; Mit|tel|punkts|glei|chung *(Astron.)*
mit|tels ⟨*erstarrter Gen. zu* Mittel⟩, *auch noch* mit|telst (↑R 46); *Präp. mit Gen.:* mittels eines Löffels; *besser:* mit einem Löffel; mittels Wasserkraft; mittels Drahtes; *ein allein stehendes, stark gebeugtes Substantiv steht im Sing. meist ungebeugt:* mittels Draht, *im Plur. mit Dat., da der Gen. nicht erkennbar ist:* mittels Drähten
Mit|tel‿schel|tel, ...schicht *(Soziol.),* **...schiff, ...schu|le** (Realschule; *schweiz. für* höhere Schule); **Mit|tel|schul‿leh|rer, ...leh|re|rin**
mit|tel|schwer; -e Verletzungen
Mit|tels‿mann (*Plur.* ...leute *od.* ...männer; Vermittler), **...per|son**
mit|telst *vgl.* mittels
Mit|tel|stand, der; -[e]s; **mit|tel|stän|dig** (*Bot., Genetik für* intermediär); -e Blüte; **mit|tel|stän|disch** (den Mittelstand betreffend); **Mit|tel|ständ|ler**
mit|tels|te; die mittelste Säule; *vgl.* mittlere
Mit|tel‿stein|zeit (*svw.* Mesolithikum), **...stel|lung, ...stim|me** *(Musik),* **...stre|cke, Mit|tel|stre|cken‿flug|zeug, ...lauf, ...läu|fer, ...läu|fe|rin, ...ra|ke|te; Mit|tel‿streck|ler** (*Sportspr.* Mittelstreckenläufer), **...strei|fen, ...stück, ...stu|fe, ...stür|mer, ...stür|me|rin** *(Fußball),* **...teil** (der); **Mit|te|lung** (Bestimmung des Mittelwertes); **Mit|tel|was|ser** *Plur.* ...wasser (Wasserstand zwischen Hoch- u. Niedrigwasser; durchschnittlicher Wasserstand); **Mit|tel‿weg, ...wel|le** *(Rundf.),* **...wert, ...wort** (*Plur.* ...wörter; *für* Partizip)
mit|ten; ↑R 46; inmitten *(vgl. d.). Getrennt- oder Zusammenschreibung* (↑R 37 f.): mitten darein,

mitten darin, mitten darunter; *vgl. aber* mittendrein, mittendrin, mittendrunter; mitten entzweibrechen; mitten hindurchgehen; er will mitten durch den dunklen Wald gehen; *vgl. aber* mittendurch; mitten in dem Becken liegen; *vgl. aber* mitteninne; **mit|ten|dre̲i̲n** (mitten hinein); er hat den Stein mittendre̲i̲n geworfen; *vgl. aber* mitten; **mit|ten|drịn** (mitten darin); sie befand sich mittendrịn; *vgl. aber* mitten; **mit|ten|drụn|ter** (mitten darunter); er geriet mittendrunter; *vgl. aber* mitten; **mit|ten|dụrch** (mitten hindurch); sie lief mittendụrch; der Stab brach mittendụrch; *vgl. aber* mitten; **mit|ten|ịn|ne** *(veraltend);* mitteninne sitzen; *vgl. aber* mitten; **mit|ten|mạng** (*nordd. für* mitten dazwischen); er befand sich mittenmạng

Mịt|ten|wald (Ort an der Isar)

Mịt|te-rẹchts-Bünd|nis *vgl.* Mitte-links-Bündnis

Mịt|ter|nacht, die; -; um Mitternacht; *vgl.* Abend; **mịt|ter|näch|tig** (*seltener für* mitternächtlich); **mịt|ter|nächt|lich; mịt|ter|nachts** (↑R 46), *aber* des Mitternachts; **mịt|ter|nachts|blau; Mịt|ter|nachts‿got|tes|dienst, ...mes|se, ...son|ne** (die; -), **...stun|de**

Mịt|ter|rand [...ˈrã:] (franz. Staatsmann)

Mịt|te|strich (Binde-, Gedankenstrich der Schreibmaschine)

Mịtt|fas|ten *Plur.* (Mittwoch vor Lätare od. Lätare selbst)

Mịtt|fünf|zi|ger *vgl.* Mittdreißiger

mịt|tig (*Technik für* zentrisch)

Mịtt|ler (*geh. für* Vermittler; *Sing. auch für* Christus); **mịtt|le|re;** die mittlere Reife (Abschluss der Realschule od. der Mittelstufe der höheren Schule), *aber* (↑R 108): der Mittlere Osten; *vgl.* mittelste; **Mịtt|le|rin; Mịtt|ler|rol|le; Mịtt|ler|tum,** das; -s

mịtt|ler|we̲i̲|le

mịtt|schiffs (*Seemannsspr.* in der Mitte des Schiffes)

Mịtt|sech|zi|ger, Mịtt|sieb|zi|ger *vgl.* Mittdreißiger

Mịtt|som|mer; Mịtt|som|mer|nacht; Mịtt|som|mer|nachts|traum *vgl.* Sommernachtstraum; **mịtt|som|mers** (↑R 46)

mịt|tun *(ugs.);* er hat mịtgetan

Mịtt|vier|zi|ger *vgl.* Mittdreißiger

Mịtt|win|ter; Mịtt|win|ter|käl|te; mịtt|win|ters (↑R 46)

Mịtt|woch, der; -[e]s, -e; *Abk.* Mi.; *vgl.* Dienstag; **mịtt|wochs** (↑R 46); *vgl.* Dienstag; **Mịtt|wochs|lot|to,** das; -s (Lotto, bei dem mittwochs die Gewinnzahlen gezogen werden)

Mịtt|zwan|zi|ger *vgl.* Mittdreißiger

mit|ụn|ter (zuweilen)

mịt|ver|ant|wort|lich; Mịt|ver|ant|wort|lich|keit; Mịt|ver|ant|wor|tung

mịt|ver|die|nen; - müssen

Mịt‿ver|fas|ser, ...ver|fas|se|rin

Mịt|ver|gan|gen|heit (*österr. für* Imperfekt)

Mịt|ver|schul|den

Mịt‿ver|schwo|re|ne *od.* **...verschwor|ne; Mịt|ver|schwö|rer**

mịt|ver|si|chert; Mịt|ver|si|che|rung

Mịt|welt, die; -

mịt|wir|ken; Mịt|wir|ken|de, der *u.* die; -n, -n (↑R 5 ff.); **Mịt|wir|kung,** die; -; **Mịt|wir|kungs|recht**

Mịt|wis|ser; Mịt|wis|se|rin; Mịt|wis|ser|schaft, die; -

mịt|wol|len; er hat mitgewollt

mịt|zäh|len

Mịt|zi (w. Vorn.)

mịt|zie|hen

Mịx, der; -, -e (*fachspr.* Gemisch, spezielle Mischung); **Mịx|becher; Mixed** [mikst], das; -[s], -[s] ‹engl.› (*Sport* gemischtes Doppel); **Mixed|grịll,** *auch* **Mixed Grịll** [ˈmikst...], der; -[s], -s (*Gastron.* Gericht aus verschiedenen gegrillten Fleischstücken [u. Würstchen]); **Mixed|pi|ckles,** *auch* **Mixed Pi|ckles** [ˈmikstˈpik(ə)ls] u. Mix|pi|ckles [ˈmikspik(ə)ls] *Plur.* (in Essig eingemachtes Mischgemüse); **mị|xen** ([Getränke] mischen; *Film, Funk, Fernsehen* verschiedene Tonaufnahmen zu einem Klangbild vereinigen); du mixt; **Mị|xer,** der; -s, - (Barmixer; Gerät zum Mixen; *Film, Funk, Fernsehen* Tonmischer); **Mịx|ge|tränk; Mịx|pi|ckles** *vgl.* Mixedpickles; **Mịx|tum com|po̲|si|tum,** das; - -, ...ta ...ta ‹lat.› (Durcheinander, buntes Gemisch); **Mix|tu̲r,** die; -, -en (flüssige Arzneimischung; gemischte Stimme der Orgel)

MJ = Megajoule

Mjọ̈ll|nir, der; -s ‹„Zermalmer"› (Thors Hammer [Waffe])

mk = Markka

MKS = Maul- und Klauenseuche

MKS-Sys|te̲m, das; -s (älteres physikal. Maßsystem, das auf den Grundeinheiten Meter [M], Kilogramm [K] u. Sekunde [S] aufgebaut ist; *vgl.* CGS-System)

ml = Milliliter

mlat. = mittellateinisch

Mlle.[1] = Mademoiselle

Mlles.[1] = Mesdemoiselles

mm = Millimeter

µm = ²Mikrometer

mm² = Quadratmillimeter

mm³ = Kubikmillimeter

MM. = Messieurs (*vgl.* Monsieur)

m. m. = mutatis mutandis

M. M. = Mälzels Metronom, Metronom Mälzel

Mme.[1] = Madame

Mmes.[1] = Mesdames

MMM = Messe der Meister von morgen (*ehem. in der DDR* techn. Leistungsschau der Jugend)

mmol = Millimol

Mn = *chem. Zeichen für* Mangan

mnd. = mittelniederdeutsch

Mne̲|me, die; - ‹griech.› (Erinnerung, Gedächtnis); **Mne|mịs|mus,** der; - (Lehre von der Mneme); **Mne|mo̲|nik,** Mne|mo|tẹch|nik, die; - (die Kunst, das Gedächtnis durch Hilfsmittel zu unterstützen); **Mne|mo̲|ni|ker,** Mne|mo|tẹch|ni|ker; **mne|mo̲|nisch,** mne|mo|tẹch|nisch; **Mne|mo|sy̲|ne** (griech. Göttin des Gedächtnisses, Mutter der Musen); **Mne|mo|tẹch|nik** usw. *vgl.* Mnemonik usw.

Mo = *chem. Zeichen für* Molybdän

Mo. = ²Missouri; Montag

MΩ = Megaohm

Mo̲a, der; -[s], -s ‹Maori› (ausgestorbener straußenähnlicher Vogel)

Mo̲|ab (Landschaft östl. des Jordans); **Mo|a|bi̲t** (Stadtteil von Berlin); **Mo|a|bi̲|ter** (Bewohner von Moab; Bewohner von Berlin-Moabit); ↑R 103

Mo̲|ar, der; -s, -e ‹bayr., „Meier"› (Kapitän einer Moarschaft); **Mo̲|ar|schaft,** die; -, -en (Vierermannschaft beim Eisschießen)

Mọb, der; -s ‹engl.› (Pöbel, randalierender Haufen); **mọb|ben** (Arbeitskolleg[inn]en ständig schikanieren [mit der Absicht, sie von ihrem Arbeitsplatz zu vertreiben]); **Mọb|bing,** das; -s

Mö̲|bel, das; -s, - *meist Plur.* ‹franz.›; **Mö̲|bel‿fab|rik, ...firma, ...ge|schäft, ...händ|ler, ...la|ger, ...pa|cker, ...po|li|tur, ...spe|di|teur, ...stoff, ...stück, ...tisch|ler, ...wa|gen; mo|bi̲l** ‹lat.› (beweglich, munter; *ugs. für* wohlauf; *Milit.* auf Kriegsstand gebracht); mobil machen (auf Kriegsstand bringen); **Mo̲|bi|le,** das; -s, -s ‹engl.› (von der Decke

[1] *Schweiz. meist (nach franz. Regel) ohne Punkt.*

hängendes, durch Luftzug in Schwingung geratendes Gebilde aus Fäden, Stäben u. Figuren); **Mo|bi|li|ar,** das; -s, -e ‹lat.› (bewegliche Habe; Hausrat, Möbel); **Mo|bi|li|ar‿kre|dit, ...ver|si|che|rung; Mo|bi|li|en** [...i̯ən] *Plur.* (*veraltet für* Hausrat, Möbel); **Mo|bi|li|sa|ti|on,** die; -, -en; **mo|bi|li|sie|ren** (*Milit.* auf Kriegsstand bringen; [Kapital] flüssig machen; aktivieren, in Gang bringen; wieder beweglich machen); **Mo|bi|li|sie|rung; Mo|bi|li|tät,** die; - ([geistige] Beweglichkeit; Häufigkeit des Wohnsitzwechsels); **Mo|bil|ma|chung** *(Milit.)*; **Mo|bil|te|le|fon** (drahtloses Telefon für unterwegs)

möb|lie|ren (↑R 130) ‹franz.› ([mit Hausrat] einrichten, ausstatten); **möb|liert;** möbliertes Zimmer; **Möb|lie|rung**

Mobs|ter, der; -s, - ‹amerik.› (Gangster)

Mo|çam|bique [mosamˈbik] *vgl.* Mosambik

Moc|ca (*österr. auch für* ²Mokka)

Mo|cha [*auch* ˈmɔka], der; -s ‹nach der jemenit. Hafenstadt, heute Mokka› (ein Mineral)

Möch|te|gern, der; -[s], *Plur.* -e *od.* -s *(ugs.)*; **Möch|te|gern‿ca|sa|no|va, ...künst|ler, ...renn|fah|rer**

Mo|cke, die; -, -n (*fränk. für* Zuchtschwein)

Mo|cken, der; -s, - (*südd. u. schweiz. mdal. für* Brocken, dickes Stück)

Mock|tur|tle|sup|pe [ˈmɔktœrt(ə)l...] ‹engl.› (unechte Schildkrötensuppe)

mod. = moderato

mo|dal ‹lat.› (die Art u. Weise bezeichnend); **Mo|dal|be|stim|mung** *(Sprachw.)*; **Mo|da|li|tät** *meist Plur.* (Art u. Weise, Ausführungsart); **Mo|da|li|tä|ten|lo|gik** (Zweig der math. Logik); **Mo|dal|satz** (*Sprachw.* Umstandssatz der Art u. Weise); **Mo|dal|verb** (Verb, das vorwiegend ein anderes Sein od. Geschehen modifiziert, z. B. „wollen" in: „wir wollen weitermachen")

Mod|der, der; -s (*nordd. für* Morast, Schlamm); **mod|de|rig, modd|rig**

Mo|de, die; -, -n ‹franz.› (als zeitgemäß geltende Art, sich zu kleiden; etwas, was dem gerade herrschenden Geschmack entspricht); in Mode sein, kommen; **Mo|de‿ar|ti|kel, ...aus|druck; mo|de|be|wusst; Mo|de‿cen|ter, ...de|sig|ner, ...de|sig|ne|rin, ...far|be, ...fim|mel** *(ugs.)*, **...ge|schäft, ...haus, ...heft, ...jour|nal, ...krank|heit**

¹Mo|del, der; -s, - ‹lat.› (Backform; Hohlform für Gusserzeugnisse; erhabene Druckform für Zeugdruck; *auch* svw. ¹Modul); **²Mo|del,** das; -s, -s ‹engl.› (Fotomodell); **Mo|dell,** das; -s, -e ‹ital.› (Muster, Vorbild, Typ; Entwurf, Nachbildung; Gießform; nur einmal in dieser Art hergestelltes Kleidungsstück; Person od. Sache als Vorbild für ein Kunstwerk; Mannequin); Modell stehen; **Mo|dell‿bau** (der; -s), **...bau|er** (*vgl.* ¹Bauer), **...ei|sen|bahn; Mo|del|leur** [...ˈløːr], der; -s, -e ‹franz.› (*svw.* Modellierer); **Mo|dell‿fall** (der), **...flug|zeug; mo|dell|haft; Mo|del|lier|bo|gen; mo|del|lie|ren** (künstlerisch formen, bilden; ein Modell herstellen); **Mo|del|lie|rer** ([Muster]former); **Mo|del|lier‿holz, ...mas|se; Mo|del|lie|rung; mo|dell|ig** (in der Art eines Modells [von Kleidungsstücken]); **Mo|dell‿kleid, ...pup|pe, ...schutz, ...the|a|ter, ...tisch|ler, ...tisch|le|rin, ...ver|such, ...zeich|nung; mo|deln** ‹lat.› (*selten für* gestalten, in eine Form bringen); ich ...[e]le (↑R 16); **Mo|del|tuch** *Plur.* ...tücher (*älter für* Stickmustertuch); **Mo|del|lung**

Mo|dem, der, *auch* das; -s, -s ‹engl.› (Gerät zur Datenübertragung über Fernsprechleitungen)

Mo|de|ma|cher

Mo|de|na (ital. Stadt); **Mo|de|na|er** (↑R 103); **mo|de|na|isch**

Mo|den‿haus (*svw.* Modehaus), **...heft** (*svw.* Modeheft), **...schau, ...zeit|schrift** (*svw.* Modezeitschrift); **Mo|de‿püpp|chen, ...pup|pe**

Mo|der, der; -s (Faulendes, Fäulnisstoff)

Mo|de|ra|men, das; -s, *Plur.* - *u.* ...mina ‹lat.› (Vorstandskollegium einer ev. reformierten Synode); **mo|de|rat** (gemäßigt); **Mo|de|ra|ti|on,** die; -, -en (*Rundf., Fernsehen* Tätigkeit des Moderators; *veraltet für* Mäßigung); **mo|de|ra|to** ‹ital.› (*Musik* mäßig [bewegt]; *Abk.* mod.); **Mo|de|ra|to,** das; -s, *Plur.* -s *u.* ...ti; **Mo|de|ra|tor,** der; -s, ...oren ‹lat.› (*Rundf., Fernsehen* jmd., der eine Sendung moderiert; *Kernphysik* bremsende Substanz in Kernreaktoren); **Mo|de|ra|to|rin**

Mo|der|ge|ruch

mo|de|rie|ren ‹lat.› (*Rundf., Fernsehen* durch eine Sendung führen, [eine Sendung] mit einleitenden u. verbindenden Worten versehen; *veraltet, aber noch landsch. für* mäßigen)

mo|de|rig, mod|rig; ¹mo|dern (faulen); es modert

²mo|dern ‹franz.› (modisch, der Mode entsprechend; neu[zeitlich]; zeitgemäß); moderner Fünfkampf *(Sport)*; **Mo|der|ne,** die; - (moderne Richtung [in der Kunst]; moderner Zeitgeist); **mo|der|ni|sie|ren** (modisch machen; auf einen neueren [technischen] Stand bringen); **Mo|der|ni|sie|rung; Mo|der|nis|mus,** der; - ‹lat.› (moderner Geschmack, Bejahung des Modernen; Bewegung innerhalb der kath. Kirche); **Mo|der|nist,** der; -en, -en (↑R 126); **Mo|der|ni|tät** (neuzeitl. Gepräge; Neues; Neuheit); **Mo|dern|jazz,** *auch* **Mo|dern Jazz** [...ˈdʒɛs], der; - ‹engl.› (nach 1945 entstandener Jazzstil)

Mo|der|sohn (dt. Maler u. Grafiker); **Mo|der|sohn-Be|cker** (dt. Malerin)

Mo|de‿sa|che, ...sa|lon, ...schaf|fen, ...schau (*vgl.* Modenschau), **...schmuck, ...schöp|fer, ...schöp|fe|rin**

mo|dest ‹lat.› (*veraltet für* bescheiden, sittsam)

Mo|de‿tanz, ...tor|heit, ...trend, ...wa|re, ...welt (die; -; Welt, die nach der Mode lebt), **...wort** (*Plur.* ...wörter), **...zeich|ner, ...zeich|ne|rin, ...zeit|schrift**

Mo|di (*Plur. von* Modus); **Mo|di|fi|ka|ti|on,** die; -, -en, **Mo|di|fi|zie|rung** ‹lat.›; **mo|di|fi|zie|ren** (abwandeln, auf das richtige Maß bringen; [ab]ändern)

Mo|dig|li|a|ni [modiˈljaːni] (↑R 130; ital. Maler)

mo|disch ‹*zu* Mode› (in od. nach der Mode); **Mo|dist,** der; -en, -en (↑R 126); **Mo|dis|tin** (Hutmacherin)

mod|rig *vgl.* moderig

¹Mo|dul, der; -s, -n ‹lat.› (Model; Verhältniszahl math. od. techn. Größen; Materialkonstante); **²Mo|dul,** das; -s, -e ‹lat.-engl.› (*bes. Elektrotechnik* Bau- od. Schaltungseinheit); **mo|du|lar** (in der Art eines ²Moduls); **Mo|du|la|ti|on,** die; -, -en (*Musik* das Steigen u. Fallen der Stimme, des Tones; Übergang in eine andere Tonart; *Technik* Änderung einer Schwingung); **Mo|du|la|ti|ons|fä|hig|keit,** die; - (Anpassungsvermögen, Biegsamkeit [der Stimme]); **mo|du|lie|ren** (abwandeln; in eine andere Tonart übergehen)

Mo|dus [*auch* 'mɔ...], der; -, Modi ‹lat.› (Art u. Weise; *Sprachw.* Aussageweise; *mittelalterl. Musik* Melodie, Kirchentonart); **Modus Pro|ce|den|di** [- ...tse...], der; - -, Modi - (Art und Weise des Verfahrens); **Mo|dus Vi|ven|di** [- vi'vɛndi], der; - -, Modi - (erträgliche Übereinkunft; Verständigung)

Moers [mø:rs] (Stadt westl. von Duisburg)

Mo|fa, das; -s, -s (*Kurzw. für* Motorfahrrad); **mo|feln** (*ugs. für* mit dem Mofa fahren); ich ...[e]le (↑R 16)

Mo|fet|te, die; -, -n ‹franz.› (*Geol.* Kohlensäureausströmung in vulkan. Gebiet)

Mo|ga|di|schu (Hptst. von Somalia)

Mo|ge|lei; mo|geln (*ugs. für* betrügen [beim Spiel], nicht ehrlich sein, nicht korrekt handeln); ich ...[e]le (↑R 16); **Mo|gel|pa|ckung** (*ugs.*)

mö|gen; ich mag, du magst, er mag; du mochtest; du möchtest; du hast es nicht gemocht, *aber* das hätte ich hören mögen

Mog|ler ‹*zu* mogeln› (*ugs.*)

mög|lich; so viel wie, *älter* als möglich; so gut wie, *älter* als möglich; wo möglich (*Auslassungssatz* wenn es möglich ist), *vgl. aber* womöglich; im Rahmen des Möglichen; Mögliches und Unmögliches verlangen; Mögliches und Unmögliches zu unterscheiden wissen; das Mögliche (im Gegensatz zum Unmöglichen) tun; etwas, nichts Mögliches; wir haben das Mögliche (alles), alles Mögliche (viel, allerlei) getan, versucht; man sollte alles Mögliche (alle Möglichkeiten) bedenken; er wird sein Möglichstes tun; **mög|lichen|falls** *vgl.* Fall, der; **mög|licher|wei|se; Mög|lich|keit;** nach -; **Mög|lich|keits|form** (*für* Konjunktiv); **mög|lichst;** möglichst schnell; möglichst viel Geld verdienen

Mo|gul [*auch, bes. österr.* ...'gu:l], der; -s, -n ‹pers.› (*früher* Beherrscher eines oriental. Reiches)

Mo|hair *vgl.* Mohär

Mo|ham|med (Stifter des Islams); **Mo|ham|me|da|ner** (Anhänger [der Lehre] Mohammeds); **mo|ham|me|da|nisch;** mohammedanische Zeitrechnung; **Mo|ham|me|da|nis|mus,** der; - (*svw.* Islam)

Mo|här, *auch* Mo|hair [mo'hɛ:r] (↑R 33), der; -s, -e ‹arab.-ital.-engl.› (Wolle der Angoraziege)

Mo|hi|ka|ner, der; -s, - (Angehöriger eines ausgestorbenen nordamerik. Indianerstammes); der Letzte der Mohikaner *od.* der letzte Mohikaner (*auch scherzh. für* das letzte Stück [Geld])

Mohn, der; -[e]s, *Plur. (Sorten:)* -e; **Mohn‿beu|gel** *(österr.),* **...blu|me, ...bröt|chen, ...kip|ferl** *(österr.),* **...ku|chen, ...öl, ...saft, ...sa|men, ...stru|del** *(österr.),* **...zopf**

Mohr, der; -en, -en (*veraltet für* dunkelhäutiger Afrikaner)

Möh|re, die; -, -n (eine Gemüsepflanze)

Moh|ren‿hir|se, ...kopf (ein Gebäck); **moh|ren|schwarz** *(veraltet);* **Moh|ren|wä|sche** (Versuch, einen offensichtlich Schuldigen durch Scheinbeweise rein zu waschen); **Moh|rin** *(veraltet)*

Mohr|rü|be (*svw.* Möhre)

Mohs|här|te (↑R 95), die; - ‹nach dem dt. Mineralogen F. Mohs› (Skala zur Bestimmung der Härtegrade von Mineralien)

Moi|ra ['mɔyra], die; -, ...ren *meist Plur.* ‹griech.› (griech. Schicksalsgöttin [Atropos, Klotho, Lachesis])

Moi|ré [moa're:], der *od.* das; -s, -s ‹franz.› (Gewebe mit geflammtem Muster; *Druckw.* fehlerhaftes Fleckenmuster in der Bildreproduktion); **moi|rie|ren** [moa...] (flammen); **moi|riert** (geflammt)

mo|kant ‹franz.› (spöttisch)

Mo|kas|sin [*auch* 'mɔ...], der; -s, *Plur.* -s *u.* -e ‹indian.› (lederner Halbschuh der nordamerikan. Indianer)

Mo|kett, der; -s ‹franz.› (Möbel-, Deckenplüsch)

Mo|kick, das; -s, -s ‹*Kurzw. aus* Motor *u.* Kickstarter› (kleines Motorrad)

mo|kie|ren, sich ‹franz.› (sich abfällig od. spöttisch äußern); ich mokiere mich über sein Verhalten

[1]**Mok|ka** (Stadt im Jemen); [2]**Mokka,** der; -s, -s (eine Kaffeesorte; sehr starker Kaffee); *vgl.* Mocca; **Mok|ka|tas|se**

Mol, das; -s, -e (*früher svw.* Grammmolekül; Einheit der Stoffmenge; *Zeichen* mol); ↑R 90; **mo|lar** ‹lat.› (auf das Mol bezüglich; je 1 Mol)

Mo|lar, der; -s, -en ‹lat.› (*Med.* [hinterer] Backenzahn, Mahlzahn); **Mo|lar|zahn**

Mo|las|se, die; - ‹franz.› (*Geol.* Tertiärschicht)

Molch, der; -[e]s, -e (im Wasser lebender Lurch)

[1]**Mol|dau,** die; - (l. Nebenfluss der Elbe); [2]**Mol|dau** (Republik Moldau; Staat in Osteuropa); **mol|dau|isch; Mol|da|wi|en** (*für* Republik Moldau)

[1]**Mo|le,** die; -, -n ‹ital.› (Hafendamm); *vgl.* Molo

[2]**Mo|le,** die; -, -n ‹griech.› (*Med.* abgestorbene, fehlentwickelte Leibesfrucht)

Mo|le|kel, die; -, -n, *österr. auch* das; -s, - ‹lat.› (*älter für* Molekül); **Mo|le|kül,** das; -s, -e ‹franz.› (kleinste Einheit einer chem. Verbindung); **mo|le|ku|lar; Mo|le|ku|lar‿bi|o|lo|ge, ...bi|o|lo|gie, ...bi|o|lo|gin, ...ge|ne|tik, ...ge|wicht**

Mo|len|kopf (Ende der [1]Mole)

Mole|skin ['mo:lskin], der *od.* das; -s, -s ‹engl.› (Englischleder, aufgerautes Baumwollgewebe)

Mo|les|ten *Plur.* ‹lat.› (*veraltet für* Beschwerden; Belästigungen); **mo|les|tie|ren** (*veraltet für* belästigen)

Mo|let|te, die; -, -n ‹franz.› (Prägwalze; Mörserstößel)

Mo|li *vgl.* Molo

Mo|lière [mɔ'ljɛ:r] (franz. Lustspieldichter); **mo|li|e|risch;** die molierischen Charaktere, Komödien (↑R 94)

Mol|ke, die; - (bei der Käseherstellung übrig bleibende Milchflüssigkeit); **Mol|ken,** der; -s (*landsch. für* Molke); **Mol|ken|kur; Mol|ke|rei; Mol|ke|rei‿but|ter, ...ge|nos|sen|schaft, ...pro|dukt** (*meist Plur.*); **mol|kig**

[1]**Moll,** das; - ‹lat.› (*Musik* Tongeschlecht mit kleiner Terz); a-Moll; a-Moll-Tonleiter (↑R 28); *vgl.* Dur

[2]**Moll,** der; -[e]s, *Plur.* -e *u.* -s (*svw.* Molton)

Moll‿ak|kord *(Musik),* **...drei|klang**

Mol|le, die; -, -n (*nordd. für* Mulde, Backtrog; *berlin. für* Bierglas, ein Glas Bier); **Mol|len|fried|hof** (*berlin. scherzh. für* Bierbauch)

Möl|ler, der; -s, - (*Hüttenw.* Gemenge von Erz u. Zuschlag); **möl|lern** (mengen); ich ...ere (↑R 16)

mol|lert (*bayr., österr. für* mollig)

Möl|le|rung *(Hüttenw.)*

mol|lig (*ugs. für* behaglich; angenehm warm; rundlich, vollschlank)

Moll‿ton|art, ...ton|lei|ter

Mol|lus|ke, die; -, -n *meist Plur.* ‹lat.› (*Biol.* Weichtier); **mol|lus|ken|ar|tig**

Mol|ly (w. Vorn.)

Mo|lo, der; -s, Moli (*österr. für* [1]Mole)

[1]**Mo|loch** [*auch* 'mɔ...] (ein semit. Gott); [2]**Mo|loch,** der; -s, -e (Macht, die alles verschlingt)
Mo|lo|tow|cock|tail [...tɔf...] (↑R 95) ‹nach dem ehemaligen sowjet. Außenminister W. M. Molotow› (mit Benzin [u. Phosphor] gefüllte Flasche, die wie eine Handgranate verwendet wird)
Molt|ke (Familienn.); **molt|kesch** (↑R 94); die moltkeschen Briefe
mol|to ‹ital.› (*Musik* sehr); - allegro (sehr schnell); - vivace [- vi'va:tʃə] (sehr lebhaft)
Mol|ton, der; -s, -s ‹franz.› (ein Gewebe)
Mol|to|pren ®, das; -s, -e (ein leichter, druckfester, schaumartiger Kunststoff)
Mo|luk|ken *Plur.* (eine indones. Inselgruppe)
Mo|lyb|dän, das; -s ‹griech.› (chem. Element, Metall; *Zeichen* Mo)
Mom|ba|sa (Hafenstadt in Kenia)
[1]**Mo|ment,** der; -[e]s, -e ‹lat.› (Augenblick; Zeit[punkt]; kurze Zeitspanne); [2]**Mo|ment,** das; -[e]s, -e ([ausschlaggebender] Umstand; Merkmal; Gesichtspunkt; Produkt aus zwei physikal. Größen); **mo|men|tan** (augenblicklich; vorübergehend); **Mo|ment˯auf|nah|me, ...bild**
Momm|sen (dt. Historiker)
Mo|na (w. Vorn.)
[1]**Mo|na|co** [*auch* 'mo:...] (Staat in Südeuropa); [2]**Mo|na|co** (Stadtbezirk von [1]Monaco); *vgl.* Monegasse
Mo|na|de, die; -, -n ‹griech.› (*Philos.* das Einfache, Unteilbare; [bei Leibniz:] die letzte, in sich geschlossene, vollendete Ureinheit); **Mo|na|den|leh|re,** die; -; **Mo|na|do|lo|gie,** die; - (Lehre von den Monaden)
Mo|na|ko *vgl.* Monaco
Mo|na Li|sa, die; - - (Gemälde von Leonardo da Vinci)
Mo|narch (↑R 132), der; -en, -en (↑R 126) ‹griech.› (gekröntes Staatsoberhaupt); **Mo|nar|chie,** die; -, ...ien; **Mo|nar|chin; mo|nar|chisch; Mo|nar|chis|mus,** der; -; **Mo|nar|chist,** der; -en, -en; ↑R 126 (Anhänger der monarchischen Regierungsform); **mo|nar|chis|tisch**
Mo|nas|te|ri|um, das; -s, ...ien [...iən] ‹griech.› (Kloster[kirche], Münster)
Mo|nat, der; -[e]s, -e; alle zwei Monate; dieses Monats (*Abk.* d. M.); laufenden -s (*Abk.* lfd. M.); künftigen -s (*Abk.* k. M.); nächsten -s (*Abk.* n. M.); vorigen -s (*Abk.* v. M.); **mo|na|te|lang,** *aber* viele Monate lang; **...mo|na|tig** (z. B. dreimonatig, *mit Ziffer* 3-monatig [drei Monate dauernd]); **mo|nat|lich; ...mo|nat|lich** (z. B. dreimonatlich, *mit Ziffer* 3-monatlich [alle drei Monate wiederkehrend]); **Mo|nats˯an|fang, ..bei|trag, ...bin|de, ...blu|tung, ...ein|kom|men, ...en|de, ...ers|te, ...frist** (innerhalb -), **...ge|halt** (das), **...hälf|te, ...heft, ...kar|te, ...letz|te, ...lohn, ...na|me, ...ra|te, ...schrift, ...wech|sel; mo|nat[s]|wei|se**
mo|nau|ral (↑R 132) ‹griech.; lat.› (ein Ohr betreffend; *Tontechnik* einkanalig)
Mo|na|zit [*auch* ...'tsit], der; -s, -e ‹griech.› (ein Mineral)
Mönch, der; -[e]s, -e ‹griech.› (Angehöriger eines geistl. Ordens)
Mön|chen|glad|bach (Stadt in Nordrhein-Westfalen)
mön|chisch; Mönchs˯klos|ter, ...kut|te, ...la|tein (mittelalterl. [schlechtes] Latein), **...or|den, ...rob|be; Mönch[s]|tum,** das; -s; **Mönchs˯we|sen, ...zel|le**
[1]**Mond,** der; -[e]s, -e (ein Himmelskörper); [2]**Mond,** der; -[e]s, -e (*veraltet für* Monat)
mon|dän ‹franz.› (betont [u. übertrieben] elegant); **Mon|dä|ni|tät,** die; -
Mond˯auf|gang, ...bahn; mond|be|schie|nen (↑R 40); **Mond|blind|heit** (Augenentzündung, bes. bei Pferden); **Mon|den|schein,** der; -[e]s *(geh.)*; **Mon|des|fins|ter|nis** (*österr. meist für* Mondfinsternis); **Mon|des|glanz** *(geh.)*; **Mond˯fäh|re, ...fins|ter|nis, ...flug; mond˯för|mig, ...hell; Mond˯jahr, ...kalb** (tierische Missgeburt; *ugs. für* Dummkopf), **...kra|ter, ...lan|de|fäh|re, ...land|schaft, ...lan|dung, ...licht** (das; -[e]s); **mond|los; Mond˯mo|bil** (das; -[e]s, -e), **...nacht, ...ober|flä|che** (↑R 132) **...or|bit, ...pha|se, ...preis** (*ugs. für* willkürlich festgesetzter [überhöhter] [2]Preis), **...ra|ke|te**
Mon|dri|an (↑R 130; niederl. Maler)
Mond|schein, der; -[e]s; **Mond|schein|ta|rif** (verbilligter Telefontarif in den Abend- u. Nachtstunden [bis 1980])
Mond|see (österr. Ort und See); **Mond|se|er** [...ze:ər] (↑R 103 *u.* 105); - Rauchhaus; *vgl.* Monseer
Mond˯si|chel, ...son|de (zur Erkundung des Mondes gestarteter, unbemannter Raumflugkörper); **Mond˯stein** (*svw.* Adular), **...sucht** (die; -); **mond|süch|tig; Mond˯süch|tig|keit, ...um|lauf|bahn, ...un|ter|gang, ...wech|sel**
Mo|ne|gas|se, der; -n, -n; ↑R 126 (Bewohner Monacos); **Mo|ne|gas|sin; mo|ne|gas|sisch**
Mo|net [mɔ'ne:, *franz.* mɔ'nɛ], Claude [klo:d] (franz. Maler)
mo|ne|tär ‹lat.› (das Geld betreffend, geldlich); **Mo|ne|ten** *Plur.* (*ugs. für* [Bar]geld)
Mon|go|le, der; -n, -n; ↑R 126 (Angehöriger einer Völkergruppe in Asien); **Mon|go|lei,** die; - (Hochland u. Staat in Zentralasien); ↑R 102: die Innere, Äußere -; **Mon|go|len˯fal|te, ...fleck; mon|go|lid** (*Anthropol.* zu dem vorwiegend in Asien, Grönland u. im arkt. Nordamerika verbreiteten Rassenkreis gehörend); -er Rassenkreis; **Mon|go|li|de,** der *u.* die; -n, -n (↑R 5 ff.); **mon|go|lisch,** *aber* (↑R 102): die Mongolische Volksrepublik; **Mon|go|lis|mus,** der; - (*svw.* Downsyndrom); **mon|go|lo|id** (den Mongolen ähnlich; die Merkmale des Mongolismus aufweisend, an Mongolismus leidend); **Mon|go|lo|i|de,** der *u.* die; -n, -n (↑R 5 ff.)
Mo|nier|bau|wei|se [*auch* mɔ'nje:...], die; - (↑R 95) ‹nach dem franz. Gärtner J. Monier› (Stahlbetonbauweise); **Mo|nier|ei|sen** (*veraltet für* in [Stahl]beton eingebettetes [Rund]eisen)
mo|nie|ren ‹lat.› (mahnen; rügen; beanstanden)
Mo|nier|zan|ge [*auch* mɔ'nje:...] (↑R 95) ‹nach dem franz. Gärtner J. Monier› (Zange für Eisendrahtarbeiten mit kleinem Zangenkopf u. langen Griffen)
Mo|ni|ka (w. Vorn.)
Mo|ni|lia, die; - ‹lat.› (Pilz, der eine Erkrankung an Obstbäumen hervorruft)
Mo|nis|mus, der; - ‹griech.› (philos. Lehre, die jede Erscheinung auf ein einheitliches Prinzip zurückführt); **Mo|nist,** der; -en, -en; ↑R 126 (Anhänger des Monismus); **mo|nis|tisch**
Mo|ni|ta (*Plur. von* Monitum)
Mo|ni|teur [...'tø:r], der; -s, -e ‹franz.› (Anzeiger [Name franz. Zeitungen]); **Mo|ni|tor,** der; -s, *Plur.* ...oren, *auch* -e ‹engl.› (Kontrollgerät, bes. beim Fernsehen; Strahlennachweis- u. -messgerät; *Bergbau* Wasserwerfer zum Losspülen von Gestein); **Mo|ni|to|ri|um,** das; -s, ...ien [...iən] ‹lat.› (*veraltet für* Erinnerungs-, Mahnschreiben); **Mo|ni|tum,** das; -s, ...ta (Rüge, Beanstandung)

mo|no [*auch* 'mo:no] ‹griech.› (*kurz für* monophon); die Schallplatte wurde mono aufgenommen; **Mo|no,** das; -s (*kurz für* Monophonie); **mo|no...** (allein...); **Mo|no...** (Allein...)

Mo|no|chord [...'kɔrt], das; -[e]s, -e ‹griech.› (ein Instrument zur Ton- und Intervallmessung)

mo|no|chrom [...'kro:m] ‹griech.› (einfarbig)

mo|no|co|lor ‹griech.; lat.› (*österr. ugs.*); eine monocolore Regierung (Einparteienregierung)

Mo|no|die (↑R 132), die; - ‹griech.› (*Musik* einstimmiger Gesang; einstimmige Melodieführung); **mo|no|disch**

mo|no|fil ‹griech.; lat.› (aus einer einzigen Faser bestehend)

mo|no|gam; Mo|no|ga|mie, die; - ‹griech.› (Zusammenleben mit nur einem Geschlechtspartner; Einehe; *Ggs.* Polygamie); **mo|no|ga|misch**

mo|no|gen ‹griech.› (*Genetik* durch nur ein Gen bedingt); **Mo|no|ge|ne|se, Mo|no|go|nie,** die; - (*Biol.* ungeschlechtl. Fortpflanzung)

Mo|no|gra|fie usw. *eindeutschende Schreibung für* Monographie usw.; **Mo|no|gramm,** das; -s, -e ‹griech.› (Namenszug; [ineinander verschlungene] Anfangsbuchstaben eines Namens); **Mo|no|gra|phie** (↑R 33), die; -, ...ien (wissenschaftliche Untersuchung über einen einzelnen Gegenstand); **mo|no|gra|phisch**

mo|no|kau|sal ‹griech.; lat.› (auf nur einer Ursache beruhend)

Mo|no|kel (↑R 132), das; -s, - ‹franz.› (Augenglas für nur ein Auge)

mo|no|klin ‹griech.› (*Geol.* mit einer geneigten Achse; *Bot.* gemischtgeschlechtig [Staub- u. Fruchtblätter in einer Blüte tragend])

mo|no|klo|nal ‹griech.› (*Med.* aus einem Zellklon gebildet)

Mo|no|ko|ty|le|do|ne, die; -, -n ‹griech.› (*Bot.* einkeimblättrige Pflanze)

mo|no|ku|lar [*auch* 'mɔn...] (↑R 132) ‹griech.; lat.› (mit einem Auge, für ein Auge)

Mo|no|kul|tur [*auch* 'mo:...] ‹griech.; lat.› (einseitiger Anbau einer bestimmten Wirtschafts- od. Kulturpflanze)

Mo|no|lat|rie (↑R 130), die; - ‹griech.› (Verehrung nur eines Gottes)

Mo|no|lith [...'li:t, *auch* ...'lit], der; *Gen.* -s *od.* -en, *Plur.* -e[n] (↑R 126) ‹griech.› (Säule, Denkmal aus einem einzigen Steinblock); **mo|no|li|thisch**

Mo|no|log, der; -s, -e ‹griech.› (Selbstgespräch [bes. im Drama]); **mo|no|lo|gisch; mo|no|lo|gi|sie|ren**

Mo|nom, Mo|no|nom, das; -s, -e ‹griech.› (*Math.* eingliedrige Zahlengröße)

mo|no|man, mo|no|ma|nisch ‹griech.› (*Psych.* an Monomanie leidend); **Mo|no|ma|ne,** der; -n, -n; ↑R 126; **Mo|no|ma|nie,** die; - (krankhaftes Besessensein von einer Wahnvorstellung, fixe Idee); **Mo|no|ma|nin; mo|no|ma|nisch** *vgl.* monoman

mo|no|mer ‹griech.› (*Chemie* aus einzelnen, voneinander getrennten, selbstständigen Molekülen bestehend); **Mo|no|mer,** das; -s, -e *u.* **Mo|no|me|re,** das; -n, -n *meist Plur.* (Stoff, dessen Moleküle monomer sind)

mo|no|misch, mo|no|no|misch ‹griech.› (*Math.* eingliedrig); **Mo|no|nom** *vgl.* Monom; **mo|no|no|misch** *vgl.* monomisch

mo|no|phon ‹griech.› (*Tontechnik* einkanalig); **Mo|no|pho|nie,** die; -

Mo|noph|thong (↑R 132), der; -s, -e ‹griech.› (*Sprachw.* einfacher Vokal, z. B. a, i; *Ggs.* Diphthong); **mo|noph|thon|gie|ren** ([einen Diphthong] zum Monophthong umbilden); **Mo|noph|thon|gie|rung**

mo|no|phy|le|tisch ‹griech.› (*Biol.* auf eine Urform zurückgehend)

Mo|no|ple|gie, die; -, ...ien ‹griech.› (*Med.* Lähmung eines einzelnen Gliedes)

Mo|no|pol, das; -s, -e ‹griech.› (das Recht auf Alleinhandel u. -verkauf; Vorrecht, alleiniger Anspruch); **Mo|no|pol‿bren|ne|rei, ...in|ha|ber; mo|no|po|li|sie|ren** (ein Monopol aufbauen, die Entwicklung von Monopolen vorantreiben); **Mo|no|po|li|sie|rung; Mo|no|po|list,** der; -en, -en; ↑R 126 (Besitzer eines Monopols); **mo|no|po|lis|tisch; Mo|no|pol‿ka|pi|tal, ...ka|pi|ta|lis|mus, ...ka|pi|ta|list; mo|no|pol|ka|pi|ta|lis|tisch; Mo|no|pol|stel|lung; Mo|no|po|ly** ®, das; - ‹engl.› (ein Gesellschaftsspiel)

Mo|no|pos|to, der; -s, -s ‹ital.› (*Automobilrennsport* Einsitzer mit unverkleideten Rädern)

Mo|nop|te|ros (↑R 132), der; -, ...eren ‹griech.› (von einer Säulenreihe umgebener antiker Tempel)

mo|no|sem ‹griech.› (*Sprachw.* nur eine Bedeutung habend); **Mo|no|se|mie,** die; - (Eindeutigkeit sprachl. Einheiten)

mo|nos|ti|chisch (↑R 132); ‹griech.› (*Verslehre* in Einzelversen [abgefasst usw.]); **Mo|nos|ti|chon,** das; -s, ...cha (Einzelvers)

mo|no|syl|la|bisch ‹griech.› (*Sprachw.* einsilbig)

mo|no|syn|de|tisch ‹griech.› (*Sprachw.* nur im letzten Glied einer Reihung durch eine Konjunktion verbunden, z. B. „Ehre, Macht und Ansehen")

Mo|no|the|is|mus, der; - ‹griech.› (Glaube an einen einzigen Gott); **Mo|no|the|ist,** der; -en, -en (↑R 126); **mo|no|the|is|tisch**

mo|no|ton ‹griech.› (eintönig; gleichförmig; ermüdend); **Mo|no|to|nie,** die; -, ...ien

Mo|no|tre|men *Plur.* ‹griech.› (*Zool.* Kloakentiere)

mo|no|trop ‹griech.› (*Biol.* beschränkt anpassungsfähig)

Mo|no|type ® [...taip], die; -, -s ‹griech.-engl.› (*Druckw.* Gieß- u. Setzmaschine für Einzelbuchstaben); **Mo|no|ty|pie** [...ty...], die; -, ...ien (ein graph. Verfahren)

mo|no|va|lent [...v..., *auch* 'mo:-no...] (*fachspr. für* einwertig)

Mo|no|xid, *nichtfachsprachlich auch* **Mo|no|xyd** [*auch* ...'ksy:t] (↑R 132) ‹griech.› (Oxid, das ein Sauerstoffatom enthält)

Mo|no|zel|le [*auch* 'mo:...] ‹griech.; dt.› (kleines elektrochemisches Element als Stromquelle)

Mo|nö|zie (↑R 132), die; - ‹griech.› (*Bot.* Einhäusigkeit, Vorkommen männl. u. weibl. Blüten auf einer Pflanze); **mo|nö|zisch** (einhäusig)

Mo|no|zyt, der; -en, -en *meist Plur.* ‹griech.› (*Med.* größtes [weißes] Blutkörperchen); **Mo|no|zy|to|se,** die; -, -n (krankhafte Vermehrung der Monozyten)

Mon|roe|dok|trin ['mɔnro:...] (↑R 95), die; - (von dem nordamerik. Präsidenten Monroe 1823 verkündeter Grundsatz der gegenseitigen Nichteinmischung)

Mon|ro|via [...via] (Hptst. von Liberia)

Mon|se|er [...ze:ər]; **Mon|see-Wie|ner Frag|men|te** (altd. Schriftdenkmal); *vgl.* Mondsee

Mon|seig|neur [mɔ̃sɛ'njø:r] (↑R 130), der; -s, *Plur.* -e *u.* -s ‹franz.› (Titel u. Anrede hoher franz. Geistlicher, Adliger u. hoch gestellter Personen; *Abk.* Mgr.)

Mon|ser|rat *vgl.* Montserrat

Mon|si|eur [mə'sjø:], der; -[s], Messieurs [mɛ'sjø:] ‹franz., „mein

Herr") (*franz. Bez. für* Herr; *als Anrede ohne Artikel; Abk.* M., *Plur.* MM.); **Mon|si|gno|re** [mɔnsi'njo:rə] (↑R 130), der; -[s], ...ri ‹ital.› (Titel hoher Würdenträger der kath. Kirche; *Abk.* Mgr., Msgr.)

Mons|ter, das; -s, - ‹engl.› (Ungeheuer); **Mons|ter...** (riesig, Riesen...)

Mons|te|ra, die; -, ...rae [...rɛ] ‹nlat.› (eine Zimmerpflanze)

Mons|ter‿bau (*Plur.* ...bauten), **...film, ...kon|zert, ...pro|gramm, ...pro|zess, ...schau; Mons|tra** (↑R 130; *Plur. von* Monstrum)

Monst|ranz (↑R 130), die; -, -en ‹lat.› (Gefäß zum Tragen u. Zeigen der geweihten Hostie)

monst|rös (↑R 130); ‹lat.(-franz.)› (Furcht erregend scheußlich; ungeheuer aufwändig; *Med.* missgebildet); **Monst|ro|si|tät,** die; -, -en (monströse Beschaffenheit; *Med.* Missbildung); **Monst|rum,** das; -s, *Plur.* ...ren *u.* ...ra (Ungeheuer; *Med.* Missbildung, Missgeburt)

Mon|sun, der; -s, -e ‹arab.› (jahreszeitlich wechselnder Wind, bes. im Indischen Ozean); **mon|su|nisch; Mon|sun|re|gen**

Mont. = Montana

Mon|ta|baur [*auch* ...'bauər] (Stadt im Westerwald)

Mon|ta|fon, das; -s (Alpental in Vorarlberg); **mon|ta|fo|ne|risch**

Mon|tag, der; -[e]s, -e; *Abk.* Mo.; *vgl.* Dienstag

Mon|ta|ge [mɔn'ta:ʒə, *auch* mɔ̃..., *österr.* mɔn'ta:ʒ], die; -, -n [...'ta:ʒ(ə)n] ‹franz.› (Aufstellung [einer Maschine], Auf-, Zusammenbau); **Mon|ta|ge‿band** (das), **...bau|wei|se, ...hal|le, ...zeit**

mon|tä|gig; *vgl.* ...tägig; **mon|täg|lich;** *vgl.* ...täglich

Mon|tag|nard [mɔ̃ta'nja:r] (↑R 130), der; -s, -s (Mitglied der „Bergpartei" der Franz. Revolution)

mon|tags (↑R 46); *vgl.* Dienstag; **Mon|tags‿aus|ga|be, ...au|to** (*scherzh. für* Auto mit Produktionsfehlern), **...de|monst|ra|ti|on** (bes. in Leipzig [1989]), **...wa|gen** (*svw.* Montagsauto)

Mon|taig|ne [mɔ̃'tɛnj(ə)] (↑R 130; franz. Schriftsteller u. Philosoph)

mon|tan, mon|ta|nis|tisch ‹lat.› (Bergbau u. Hüttenwesen betreffend)

Mon|ta|na (Staat in den USA; *Abk.* Mont.)

Mon|tan‿ge|sell|schaft (Berggesellschaft), **...in|dust|rie** (Gesamtheit der bergbaulichen Industrieunternehmen); **Mon|ta|nis|mus,** der; - ‹nach dem Begründer Montanus› (schwärmer. altkirchl. Bewegung in Kleinasien); **Mon|ta|nist,** der; -en, -en; ↑R 126 (Sachverständiger im Bergbau- u. Hüttenwesen; Anhänger des Montanus); **mon|ta|nis|tisch** *vgl.* montan; **Mon|tan‿mit|be|stim|mung, ...uni|on** (↑R 132; die; -; Europäische Gemeinschaft für Kohle u. Stahl)

Mon|ta|nus (Gründer einer altchristl. Sekte)

Mont|blanc [mɔ̃'blã:], der; -[s] ‹franz.› (höchster Gipfel der Alpen u. Europas)

Mont|bre|tie [mɔ̃'bre:tsiə], die; -, -n ‹nach dem franz. Naturforscher de Montbret› (ein Irisgewächs)

Mont Ce|nis [mɔ̃ se'ni:], der; - - (ein Alpenpass); **Mont-Ce|nis-Stra|ße,** die; - (↑R 105)

Mon|te Car|lo (Stadtbezirk von [1]Monaco)

Mon|te Cas|si|no, *ital. Schreibung* **Mon|te|cas|si|no,** der; - (Berg u. Kloster bei Cassino)

Mon|te|cris|to, *franz.* **Mon|te-Cris|to** [mɔ̃təkris'to:], *bei Dumas in dt. Übersetzung* Mon|te Chris|to (Insel im Ligurischen Meer)

Mon|te|neg|ri|ner (↑R 130); **mon|te|neg|ri|nisch; Mon|te|neg|ro** (Gliedstaat Jugoslawiens)

Mon|te Ro|sa, der; - - (Gebirgsmassiv in den Westalpen)

Mon|tes|qui|eu [mɔ̃tɛs'kiø:] (franz. Staatsphilosoph und Schriftsteller)

Mon|teur [mɔn'tø:r, *auch* mɔ̃...], der; -s, -e (Montagefacharbeiter); **Mon|teur|an|zug**

Mon|te|ver|di [...v...] (ital. Komponist)

Mon|te|vi|deo [...v...] (Hptst. von Uruguay)

Mon|te|zu|ma (aztek. Herrscher); -s Rache (*ugs. scherzh. für* Erkrankung an Durchfall [beim Aufenthalt in Lateinamerika])

Mont|gol|fi|e|re [mɔ̃gɔl...], die; -, -n ‹nach den Brüdern Montgolfier› (ein Heißluftballon)

mon|tie|ren [mɔn..., *auch* mɔ̃...] ‹franz.› ([eine Maschine, ein Gerüst u. a.] [auf]bauen, aufstellen, zusammenbauen); **Mon|tie|rer; Mon|tie|rung**

Mont|mart|re [mɔ̃'martr(ə)] (↑R 130; Stadtteil von Paris)

Mont|re|al [*engl.* mɔntrɪ'ɔ:l] (Stadt in Kanada)

Mont|reux [mɔ̃'trø:] (↑R 130; Stadt am Genfer See)

Mont-Saint-Mi|chel [mɔ̃sɛ̃mi'ʃɛl] (Felsen u. Ort an der franz. Kanalküste)

Mont|sal|wätsch, der; -[es] ‹altfranz.› (Name der Gralsburg in der Gralsdichtung)

Mont|ser|rat [mɔntse'rat], *auch* Mon|ser|rat [mɔnse'rat] (Berg u. Kloster bei Barcelona)

Mon|tur, die; -, -en ‹franz.› (*ugs. für* [Arbeits]kleidung; *österr., sonst veraltet für* Dienstkleidung, Uniform)

Mo|nu|ment, das; -[e]s, -e ‹lat.› (Denkmal); **mo|nu|men|tal** (gewaltig; großartig); **Mo|nu|men|tal‿aus|ga|be, ...bau** (*Plur.* ...bauten), **...film, ...ge|mäl|de; Mo|nu|men|ta|li|tät,** die; - (Großartigkeit)

Moon|boot ['mu:nbu:t], der; -s, -s *meist Plur.* ‹engl.› (dick gefütterter Winterstiefel [aus Kunststoff])

Moor, das; -[e]s, -e; **Moor|bad; moor|ba|den** *(nur im Infinitiv gebräuchlich);* **Moor|bo|den**

Moore [mu:(r)], Henry (engl. Bildhauer)

moo|rig; Moor‿ko|lo|nie, ...kul|tur, ...lei|che, ...pa|ckung, ...sied|lung

[1]**Moos,** das; -es, *Plur.* -e *u.* (*für* Sumpf usw.:) Möser (eine Pflanze; *bayr., österr., schweiz. auch für* Sumpf, [2]Bruch)

[2]**Moos,** das; -es ‹hebr.-jidd.› (*ugs. für* Geld)

Moos|art; moos|ar|tig; moos|be|deckt (↑R 40); **Moos‿bee|re, ...farn, ...flech|te; moos|grün; moo|sig; Moos‿krepp, ...pols|ter, ...ro|se**

Mop *frühere Schreibung für* Mopp

Mo|ped [*auch* ...pe:t], das; -s, -s (leichtes Motorrad); **Mo|ped|fah|rer**

Mopp, der; -s, -s ‹engl.› (Staubbesen mit langen Fransen)

Mop|pel, der; -s, - (*ugs. für* kleiner, dicklicher Mensch)

mop|pen (mit dem Mopp reinigen)

Mops, der; -es, Möpse (ein Hund); **Möps|chen; möp|seln** (*landsch. für* muffig riechen); ich ...[e]le (↑R 16); **mop|sen** (*ugs. für* stehlen); du mopst; sich - (*ugs. für* sich langweilen; sich ärgern); **mops|fi|del** (*ugs. für* sehr fidel); **Mops|ge|sicht; mop|sig** (*ugs. für* langweilig; dick)

Mo|quette [mo'kɛt] *vgl.* Mokett

[1]**Mo|ra,** die; - ‹ital.› (ein Fingerspiel)

[2]**Mo|ra,** die; -, ...ren ‹lat.› (kleinste Zeiteinheit im Verstakt)

Mo|ral, die; -, -en *Plur. selten* ‹lat.›

(Sittlichkeit; Sittenlehre; sittl. Nutzanwendung); **Mo|ral|be|griff; Mo|ra|lin,** das; -s (spießige Entrüstung in moral. Dingen); **mo|ra|lin|sau|er;** ...sau|res Gehabe; **mo|ra|lisch** ‹lat.› (der Moral gemäß; sittlich); moralische Maßstäbe; **mo|ra|li|sie|ren** ‹franz.› (moral. Betrachtungen anstellen; den Sittenprediger spielen); **Mo|ra|lis|mus,** der; - ‹lat.› (Anerkennung der Sittlichkeit als Zweck u. Sinn des menschl. Lebens; [übertrieben strenge] Beurteilung aller Dinge unter moral. Gesichtspunkten); **Mo|ra|list,** der; -en, -en; ↑R 126 (jmd., der den Moralismus vertritt; Sittenprediger); **mo|ra|lis|tisch; Mo|ra|li|tät,** die; -, -en ‹franz.› (*nur Sing.*: Sittenlehre, Sittlichkeit; *meist Plur.*: mittelalterl. geistl. Schauspiel); **Mo|ral_ko|dex, ...pau|ke** *(ugs.),* **...phi|lo|so|phie, ...pre|di|ger, ...pre|digt, ...the|o|lo|gie**

Mo|rä|ne, die; -, -n ‹franz.› (*Geol.* Gletschergeröll); **Mo|rä|nen|land|schaft**

Mo|rast, der; -[e]s, *Plur.* -e *u.* Moräste (sumpfige schwarze Erde, Sumpf[land]); **mo|ras|tig**

Mo|ra|to|ri|um, das; -s, ...ien [...i̯ən] ‹lat.› (befristete Stundung [von Schulden]; Aufschub)

mor|bid ‹lat.› (krank[haft]; kränklich; brüchig, im [moral.] Verfall begriffen); **Mor|bi|dez|za,** die; - ‹ital.› (*bes. Malerei* Zartheit [der Farben]); **Mor|bi|di|tät,** die; - ‹lat.› (*Med.* Krankheitsstand; Erkrankungsziffer); **mor|bi|phor** (ansteckend); **Mor|bo|si|tät,** die; - ‹lat.› (Kränklichkeit, Siechtum); **Mor|bus,** der; -, ...bi (Krankheit)

Mor|chel, die; -, -n (ein Pilz)

Mord, der; -[e]s, -e; **Mord_an|kla|ge, ...an|schlag; mord|[be|]gie|rig; Mord_bren|ner** (*veraltet für* jmd., der einen Brand legt und dadurch Menschen tötet), **...bu|be** (*veraltet für* Mörder), **...dro|hung; mor|den**

Mor|dent, der; -s, -e ‹ital.› (*Musik* Wechsel zwischen Hauptnote u. nächsttieferer Note, Triller)

Mör|der; Mör|der|gru|be; aus seinem Herzen keine Mördergrube machen (*ugs. für* mit seiner Meinung nicht zurückhalten); **Mör|der|hand;** *nur in* durch, von Mörderhand (durch einen Mörder); **Mör|de|rin; mör|de|risch** (*veraltend für* mordend; *ugs. für* schrecklich, furchtbar, sehr stark, gewaltig); -e Kälte; er schimpfte mörderisch; **mör|der|lich** (*ugs. für* mörderisch); er hat ihn mörderlich verprügelt; **Mord_fall** (der), **...gier; mord|gie|rig** *vgl.* mordbegierig; **Mord|in|stru|ment; mor|dio!** (*veraltet für* Mord!; zu Hilfe!); *vgl.* zetermordio; **Mord_kom|mis|si|on, ...lust, ...nacht, ...pro|zess; mords..., Mords...** (*ugs. für* sehr groß, gewaltig); **Mords_ar|beit, ...ding, ...durst, ...du|sel, ...gau|di, ...ge|schrei, ...hit|ze, ...hun|ger, ...kerl, ...krach; mords|mä|ßig** (*ugs. für* sehr, ganz gewaltig); das war ein mordsmäßiger Lärm; **Mords_schreck** *od.* **...schre|cken, ...spaß** (*ugs. für* großer Spaß), **...spek|ta|kel; mords|we|nig** (*ugs. für* sehr wenig); er hatte mordswenig zu sagen; **Mords|wut; Mord_tat, ...ver|dacht, ...ver|such, ...waf|fe**

Mo|rel|le, die; -, -n ‹ital.› (eine Sauerkirschenart)

Mo|ren (*Plur. von* [2]Mora)

mo|ren|do ‹ital.› (*Musik* immer leiser werdend); **Mo|ren|do,** das; -s, *Plur.* -s *u.* ...di

Mo|res [...re:s] *Plur.* ‹lat., „[gute] Sitten"›; *nur in* jmdn. - lehren (*ugs. für* jmdn. zurechtweisen)

Mo|res|ke, Mau|res|ke, die; -, -n ‹franz.› (*svw.* Arabeske)

mor|ga|na|tisch ‹mlat.› (zur linken Hand [getraut]); -e Ehe (standesungleiche Ehe)

Mor|gar|ten, der; -s (schweiz. Berg)

mor|gen (am folgenden Tag); (↑R 45:) morgen Abend, morgen Mittag, morgen Nachmittag; *aber* morgen früh; bis, für, zu morgen; die Technik von morgen (der nächsten Zukunft), Entscheidung für morgen (die Zukunft); *vgl.* Abend *u.* Dienstag; **[1]Mor|gen,** der; -s, - (Tageszeit); guten Morgen! (Gruß); (↑R 45:) heute, gestern Morgen; (↑R 46:) morgens; morgens früh; *vgl.* Abend *u.* früh; **[2]Mor|gen,** der; -s, - ‹*urspr.* Land, das ein Gespann an einem Morgen pflügen kann› (ein altes Feldmaß); fünf Morgen Land; **[3]Mor|gen,** das; - (die Zukunft); das Heute und das Morgen; **Mor|gen_an|dacht, ...aus|ga|be; mor|gend** (*veraltet für* morgig); der morgende Tag; **Mor|gen|däm|me|rung; mor|gend|lich** (am Morgen geschehend); **Mor|gen_duft** (der; -[e]s; eine Apfelsorte), **...es|sen** (*schweiz. für* Frühstück); **mor|gen|frisch; Mor|gen_frü|he, ...ga|be** *(früher),* **...grau|en, ...gym|nas|tik, ...land** (das; -[e]s; *veraltet für* Orient; Land, in dem die Sonne aufgeht); **Mor|gen|län|der** *(veraltet);* **mor|gen|län|disch** *(veraltet);* **Mor|gen_licht** (das; -[e]s), **...luft, ...man|tel, ...muf|fel** (*ugs. für* jmd., der morgens nach dem Aufstehen mürrisch ist), **...ne|bel, ...rock** (*vgl.* [1]Rock), **...rot** *od.* **...rö|te; mor|gens** (↑R 46), *aber* des Morgens; *vgl.* [1]Morgen, Abend, Dienstag; **Mor|gen_son|ne, ...spa|zier|gang, ...stern** (ein Stern; mittelalterl. Schlagwaffe; *vgl.* [2]Stern), **...stun|de**

Mor|gen|thau|plan (↑R 95), der; -[e]s ‹nach dem US-Finanzminister Henry Morgenthau› (Vorschlag, Deutschland nach dem 2. Weltkrieg in einen Agrarstaat umzuwandeln)

Mor|gen|zei|tung

mor|gig; der morgige Tag

Mo|ria, die; - ‹griech.› (*Med.* krankhafte Geschwätzigkeit und Albernheit)

mo|ri|bund ‹lat.› (*Med.* im Sterben liegend)

Mö|ri|ke (dt. Dichter)

Mo|rio-Mus|kat, der; -s ‹nach dem dt. Züchter P. Morio› (eine Reb- u. Weinsorte)

Mo|ris|ke, der; -n, -n (↑R 126) ‹span.› (in Spanien sesshaft gewordener Maure)

Mo|ri|tat, die; -, -en [*auch* ...'ta:t(ə)n] ([zu einer Bildertafel] vorgetragenes Lied über ein schreckliches od. rührendes Ereignis); **Mo|ri|ta|ten|sän|ger** [*auch* ...'ta:...]

Mo|ritz, *österr. auch* **Mo|riz** (m. Vorn.); der kleine - (*ugs. für* einfältiges, schlichtes Gemüt)

Mor|mo|ne, der; -n, -n; ↑R 126 (Angehöriger einer nordamerik. Sekte); **Mor|mo|nen|tum,** das; -s

Mo|ro|ni (Hptst. der Komoren)

mo|ros ‹lat.› (*veraltet für* verdrießlich); **Mo|ro|si|tät,** die; -

Mor|phe, die; - ‹griech.› (Gestalt, Form); **Mor|phem,** das; -s, -e (*Sprachw.* kleinste bedeutungstragende Einheit in der Sprache)

Mor|pheus [...fɔys] (griech. Gott des Traumes); in Morpheus' Armen; **Mor|phin,** das; -s ‹*nach* Morpheus› (Hauptalkaloid des Opiums; Schmerzlinderungsmittel); **Mor|phi|nis|mus,** der; - ‹griech.› (Morphiumsucht); **Mor|phi|nist,** der; -en, -en (↑R 126); **Mor|phi|nis|tin; Mor|phi|um,** das; -s (*allgemeinsprachlich für* Morphin); **Mor|phi|um_sprit|ze, ...sucht** (die; -); **mor|phi|um|süch|tig; Mor|pho|ge|ne|se, Mor|pho|ge|ne|sis** [*auch* ...'ge:...], die; -, ...nesen (*Biol.* Ursprung und Entwicklung von Organen od. Geweben eines pflanzl. od. tierischen Organismus); **mor|pho|ge|ne|tisch** (gestaltbildend); **Mor|pho|ge|nie,** die; -, ...ien (*svw.* Morphogenese); **Mor|pho|lo|ge,** der; -n, -n (↑R 126); **Mor|pho|lo|gie,** die; - (*Biol.* Gestaltlehre; *Sprachw.* Formenlehre); **mor|pho|lo|gisch** (die äußere Gestalt betreffend)

morsch; Morsch|heit, die; -

Mor|se|al|pha|bet (↑R 95) ‹nach dem nordamerik. Erfinder Morse› (Alphabet für die Telegrafie); **Mor|se|ap|pa|rat** (Telegrafengerät); **mor|sen** (den Morseapparat bedienen); du morst

Mör|ser, der; -s, - (schweres Geschütz; schalenförmiges Gefäß zum Zerkleinern); **mör|sern;** ich ...ere (↑R 16); **Mör|ser|stö|ßel**

Mor|se|zei|chen

Mor|ta|del|la, die; -, -s ‹ital.› (eine Wurstsorte)

Mor|ta|li|tät, die; - ‹lat.› (*Med.* Sterblichkeit[sziffer])

Mör|tel, der; -s, *Plur. (Sorten:)* -; **Mör|tel‿kas|ten, ...kel|le; mör|teln;** ich ...[e]le (↑R 16); **Mör|tel|pfan|ne**

Mo|ru|la, die; - ‹lat.› (*Biol.* Entwicklungsstufe des Embryos)

Mo|sa|ik, das; -s, *Plur.* -en, *auch* -e ‹griech.-franz.› (Bildwerk aus bunten Steinchen; Einlegearbeit); **Mo|sa|ik|ar|beit; mo|sa|ik|ar|tig; Mo|sa|ik‿bild, ...fuß|bo|den, ...stein**

mo|sa|isch (nach Moses benannt; jüdisch); mosaisches Bekenntnis; die mosaischen Bücher (↑R 94); **Mo|sa|is|mus,** der; - (*veraltet für* Judentum)

Mo|sam|bik (Staat in Ostafrika); **Mo|sam|bi|ka|ner,** Mo|sam|bi|ker; **Mo|sam|bi|ka|ne|rin,** Mo|sam|bi|ke|rin; **mo|sam|bi|ka|nisch,** mo|sam|bi|kisch; **Mo|sam|bi|ker** usw. *vgl.* Mosambikaner usw.

Mosch, der; -[e]s (*landsch. für* allerhand Abfälle, Überbleibsel)

Mo|schaw, der; -s, ...wim ‹hebr.› (Genossenschaftssiedlung von Kleinbauern mit Privatbesitz in Israel)

Mo|schee, die; -, ...scheen ‹arab.-franz.› (islam. Bethaus)

Mo|schus, der; - ‹sanskr.› (ein Riechstoff); **mo|schus|ar|tig; Mo|schus‿ge|ruch, ...och|se**

Mo|se *vgl.* Moses

Mö|se, die; -, -n (*derb für* weibl. Scham)

[1]**Mo|sel,** die; - (l. Nebenfluss des Rheins); [2]**Mo|sel,** der; -s, - (*kurz für* Moselwein); **Mo|sel|la|ner,** *auch* **Mo|sel|la|ner** (Bewohner des Mosellandes); **Mo|sel|wein**

Mö|ser (*Plur. von* [1]Moos)

mo|sern ‹hebr.-jidd.› (*ugs. für* nörgeln); ich ...ere (↑R 16)

[1]**Mo|ses,** *ökum.* Mo|se (jüd. Gesetzgeber im A. T.); fünf Bücher Mosis (des Moses) *od.* Mose; [2]**Mo|ses,** der; -, - (*Seemannsspr.* Beiboot einer Jacht; *auch für* jüngstes Besatzungsmitglied an Bord, Schiffsjunge)

Mos|kau (Hptst. Russlands); **Mos|kau|er** (↑R 103); Moskauer Zeit; **mos|kau|isch**

Mos|ki|to, der; -s, -s *meist Plur.* ‹span.› (eine trop. Stechmücke); **Mos|ki|to|netz**

Mos|ko|wi|ter (*veraltend für* Bewohner von Moskau); **Mos|ko|wi|ter|tum,** das; -s; **mos|ko|wi|tisch;** [1]**Mosk|wa,** die; - (russ. Fluss); [2]**Mosk|wa** (*russ. Form von* Moskau)

Mos|lem, der; -s, -s ‹arab.› (Anhänger des Islams); *vgl. auch* Muslim; **Mos|lem|bru|der|schaft,** die; -, -en (ägypt. polit. Vereinigung); **mos|le|mi|nisch** (*veraltet*), **mos|le|misch** *vgl. auch* muslimisch; **Mos|li|me,** die; -, -n (Anhängerin des Islams); *vgl. auch* Muslime

mos|so ‹ital.› (*Musik* bewegt, lebhaft)

Mos|sul *vgl.* Mosul

Most, der; -[e]s, -e (unvergorener Frucht-, bes. Traubensaft; *südd., österr. u. schweiz. für* Obstwein, -saft); **Most|bir|ne; mos|ten; Mos|tert,** der; -s (*nordwestd. für* Senf); **Most|rich,** der; -[e]s (*nordostd. für* Senf)

Mo|sul, Mos|sul (Stadt im Irak)

Mo|tel [*auch* mo'tɛl], das; -s, -s ‹amerik.; *aus* motorists' hotel› (an Autobahnen o. Ä. gelegenes Hotel [für Autoreisende])

Mo|tet|te, die; -, -n ‹ital.› (geistl. Chorwerk); **Mo|tet|ten|stil**

Mo|ti|li|tät, die; - ‹lat.› (*Med.* unwillkürlich gesteuerte Muskelbewegungen); **Mo|ti|on,** die; -, -en ‹franz.› (*Sprachw.* Abwandlung des Adjektivs nach dem jeweiligen Geschlecht; *schweiz. für* gewichtigste Form des Antrags in einem Parlament); **Mo|ti|o|när,** der; -s, -e (*schweiz. für* jmd., der eine Motion einreicht)

Mo|tiv, das; -s, -e [...və] ‹lat.-(-franz.)› ([Beweg]grund, Antrieb, Ursache; Leitgedanke; Gegenstand, Thema einer [künstler.] Darstellung; kleinstes musikal. Gebilde); **Mo|ti|va|ti|on** [...v...], die; -, -en ‹lat.› (die Beweggründe, die das Handeln eines Menschen bestimmen); **Mo|tiv|for|schung,** die; - (Zweig der Marktforschung); **mo|ti|vie|ren** [...v...] ‹franz.› (begründen; anregen, anspornen); **Mo|ti|vie|rung; Mo|ti|vik,** die; - ‹lat.› (Kunst der Motivverarbeitung [in einem Tonwerk]); **mo|ti|visch; Mo|tiv|samm|ler** (*Philatelie*)

Mo|to, das; -s, -s ‹franz.› (*schweiz. Kurzform von* Motorrad)

Mo|to|cross, *auch* **Mo|to-Cross,** das; -, -e ‹engl.› (Geschwindigkeitsprüfung im Gelände für Motorradsportler); **Mo|to|drom,** das; -s, -e ‹franz.› (Rennstrecke [Rundkurs]); **Mo|tor,** der; -s, ...toren, *auch* [mo'to:r], der; -s, -e ‹lat.› (Antriebskraft erzeugende Maschine; *übertr. für* vorwärts treibende Kraft); **Mo|tor‿block**[1] (*Plur.* ...blöcke), **...boot; Mo|to|ren‿bau** (der; -[e]s), **...ge|räusch, ...lärm, ...öl; Mo|tor‿fahr|zeug**[1], **...hau|be; ...mo|to|rig** (z. B. zweimotorig, *mit Ziffer* 2-motorig); **Mo|to|rik,** die; - (Gesamtheit der Bewegungsabläufe des menschl. Körpers; Bewegungslehre); **Mo|to|ri|ker** (*Psych.* jmd., dessen Erinnerungen, Assoziationen o. Ä. vorwiegend von Bewegungsvorstellungen geleitet werden); **mo|to|risch;** -es Gehirnzentrum (Sitz der Bewegungsantriebe); **mo|to|ri|sie|ren** (mit Kraftmaschinen, -fahrzeugen ausstatten); **Mo|to|ri|sie|rung; Mo|tor‿jacht**[1], **...leis|tung, ...öl** (*vgl.* Motorenöl), **...rad; Mo|tor|rad‿bril|le**[1], **...fah|rer, ...fah|re|rin, ...ren|nen; Mo|tor‿rol|ler**[1], **...sä|ge, ...scha|den, ...schiff, ...schlep|per, ...schlit|ten, ...seg|ler, ...sport, ...sprit|ze**

Mot|sche|kieb|chen, das; -s, - (*landsch. für* Marienkäfer)

Mot|te, die; -, -n

mot|ten (*südd. u. schweiz. für* schwelen, glimmen)

mot|ten‿echt, ...fest; Mot|ten‿fif|fi (der; -s, -s; *ugs. scherzh. für* Pelzmantel), **...fraß, ...kis|te, ...ku|gel, ...pul|ver**

Mot|to, das; -s, -s ‹ital.› (Denk-, Wahl-, Leitspruch; Devise)

Mo|tu|pro|p|rio (↑R 130), das; -s, -s ‹lat.› (ein nicht auf Eingaben beruhender päpstl. Erlass)

mot|zen (*ugs. für* nörgelnd schimpfen; *landsch. auch für* schmollen); du motzt; **mot|zig** (*ugs.*)

---

[1] [*auch* ...'to:r...]

Mouche [muʃ], die; -, -s [muʃ] ‹franz.› (Schönheitspflästerchen)
mouil|lie|ren [muˈji:...] ‹franz.› (*Sprachw.* erweichen; ein „j" nachklingen lassen, z. B. nach l in „brillant" = [briˈljant]); **Mouil|lie|rung** [muˈji:...]
Mou|la|ge [muˈla:ʒə], der; -, -s, *auch* die; -, -n ‹franz.› (*Med.* Abdruck, Abguss, bes. farbiges anatom. Wachsmodell)
Mou|li|né [muliˈne:], der; -s, -s (Garn, Gewebe); **mou|li|nie|ren** [muli...] (Seide zwirnen)
Moun|tain|bike [ˈmauntinbaik], das; -s, -s ‹engl.› (Fahrrad für Gelände- bzw. Gebirgsfahrten)
Mount E|ve|rest [maunt ˈɛvərist], der; - -[s] ‹engl.› (höchster Berg der Erde); **Mount Mc|Kin|ley** [- məˈkinli], der; - -[s] (höchster Berg Nordamerikas)
Mousse [mus], die; -, -s [mus] ‹franz.› (schaumige [Schokoladen]süßspeise; Vorspeise aus püriertem Fleisch)
Mous|se|line [mus(ə)lin], die; - ‹franz.› (*schweiz. für* Musselin)
mous|sie|ren ‹franz.› (schäumen)
Mous|té|ri|en [musteˈriɛ̃:], das; -[s] ‹franz.› (Kulturstufe der älteren Altsteinzeit)
mo|vie|ren [...v...] (*Sprachw.* die weibliche Form zu einer männlichen Personenbezeichnung bilden; z. B. Lehrerin); **Mo|vie|rung**
Mö|we, die; -, -n (ein Vogel); **Mö|wen‿ei, ...ko|lo|nie, ...schrei**
Moz|ara|ber [*auch* motsˈara...] *meist Plur.* (↑R 132; Angehöriger der „arabisierten" span. Christen der Maurenzeit); **moz|ara|bisch**
Mo|zart (österr. Komponist); **Mo|zar|te|um**, das; -s (Musikinstitut in Salzburg); **mo|zar|tisch** (↑R 94): mozartische Kompositionen; **Mo|zart|kon|zert|abend** (↑R 95 *u.* 132); **Mo|zart|ku|gel** (↑R 95); **Mo|zart|zopf** (↑R 95; am Hinterkopf mit einer Schleife zusammengebundener Zopf)
Moz|za|rel|la, der; -s, -s ‹ital.› (ein ital. Käse aus Büffel- od. Kuhmilch)
mp = mezzopiano
m. p. = manu propria
MP, MPi = Maschinenpistole
MPU = medizinisch-psychologische Untersuchung (z. B. nach einem Führerscheinentzug)
Mr = Mister ‹engl.› (engl. Anrede *[nur mit Eigenn.]*)
Mrd., Md., Mia. = Milliarde[n]
Mrs = Mistress [ˈmisis] ‹engl.› (engl. Anrede für verheiratete Frauen *[nur mit Eigenn.]*)
m. S. = multiple Sklerose; *vgl.* MS
Ms (schriftl. engl. Anrede für verheiratete od. unverheiratete Frauen *[nur mit Eigenn.]*)
Ms., Mskr. = Manuskript
MS = Motorschiff; multiple Sklerose; *vgl.* m. S.
m/s = Meter je Sekunde
Msgr., Mgr. = Monsignore
Mskr., Ms. = Manuskript
Mss. = Manuskripte
Mt = Megatonne
MTA = medizinisch-technische[r] Assistent[in]
Mu|ba = Schweizerische Mustermesse Basel
Much|tar, der; -s, -s ‹arab.› (Dorfschulze)
Mu|ci|us [ˈmu:tsius] (altröm. m. Eigenn.); - Scävola [- ˈstsɛ:vɔla] (röm. Sagengestalt)
Muck *vgl.* Mucks
Mu|cke, die; -, -n (*ugs. für* Grille, Laune; Kleinigkeit, Nebengeschäft [*vgl. auch* Mugge]; *südd. für* Mücke); **Mü|cke**, die; -, -n
Mu|cke|fuck, der; -s (*ugs. für* Ersatzkaffee; sehr dünner Kaffee)
mu|cken (*ugs. für* leise murren)
Mü|cken‿dreck (*ugs. für* Kleinigkeit, lächerliche Angelegenheit), **...pla|ge, ...schiss** (*derb für* Mückendreck), **...stich**
Mu|cker (heuchlerischer Frömmler; Duckmäuser); **mu|cke|risch; Mu|cker|tum**, das; -s; **muckisch** (*veraltet, aber noch landsch. für* launisch, unfreundlich); **Mucks**, der; -es, -e, *auch* Muck, der; -s, -e *u.* Muck|ser, der; -s, - (*ugs. für* leiser, halb unterdrückter Laut); keinen - tun; **mucksch** (*svw.* muckisch); **muck|schen** (*landsch. für* muckisch sein); **muck|sen** (*ugs. für* einen Laut geben; eine Bewegung machen); er hat sich nicht gemuckst (*ugs. für* er hat sich kleinlaut verhalten, sich nicht gerührt); **Muck|ser** *vgl.* Mucks; **mucks|mäus|chen|still** (*ugs. für* ganz still)
Mud, der; -s (*nordd. für* Schlamm [an Flussmündungen]; Morast); **mud|dig** (*nordd. für* schlammig)
mü|de; sich müde arbeiten; einer Sache müde (überdrüssig) sein; ich bin es (*vgl.* „es" *[alter Gen.]*) müde; **Mü|dig|keit**, die; -
Mu|dir, der; -s, -e ‹arab.(-türk.)› (Leiter eines Verwaltungsbezirkes [in Ägypten])
M. U. Dr. *(österr.)* = medicinae universae doctor (Doktor der gesamten Medizin)
Mud|scha|hed (↑R 132), der; -, ...din ‹arab., „Kämpfer"› (Freischärler [im islam. Raum])
Mü|es|li (*schweiz. Form von* Müsli)
Mu|ez|zin [*auch, österr. nur,* ˈmu...], der; -s, -s ‹arab.› (Gebetsrufer im Islam)
[1]**Muff**, der; -[e]s (*nordd. für* [1]Schimmel, Kellerfeuchtigkeit)
[2]**Muff**, der; -[e]s, -e ‹niederl.› (Handwärmer); **Muf|fe**, die; -, -n (Rohr-, Ansatzstück); Muffe haben (*ugs. für* Angst haben)
[1]**Muf|fel**, der; -s, - (*Jägerspr.* kurze Schnauze; *Zool.* unbehaarter Teil der Nase bei manchen Säugetieren; *ugs. für* mürrischer Mensch)
[2]**Muf|fel**, die; -, -n (Schmelztiegel)
[3]**Muf|fel**, das; -s, - (*dt. Form für* Mufflon)
muf|fe|lig, muff|lig (*nordd. für* den Mund verziehend; mürrisch); [1]**muf|feln** (*ugs. für* ständig [mit sehr vollem Mund] kauen; mürrisch sein); ich ...[e]le (↑R 16)
[2]**muf|feln** (*österr. für* müffeln); **müf|feln** (*landsch. für* dumpf riechen); ich ...[e]le (↑R 16)
Muf|fel|ofen (↑R 132) ‹*zu* [2]Muffel›
Muf|fel|wild (Mufflon)
muf|fen (*landsch. für* dumpf riechen)
Muf|fen|sau|sen, das; -s *(derb)*; - haben (Angst haben)
[1]**muf|fig** (*landsch. für* mürrisch)
[2]**muf|fig** (dumpf, nach Muff [[1]Schimmel] riechend)
Muf|fig|keit, die; - ‹*zu* [1,2]muffig›
muff|lig *vgl.* muffelig
Muff|lon, der; -s, -s ‹franz.› (ein Wildschaf)
Muf|ti, der; -s, -s ‹arab.› (islam. Gesetzeskundiger)
Mu|gel, der; -s, -[n] (*österr. ugs. für* Hügel); **mu|ge|lig**, mug|lig (*österr. ugs. für* hügelig; *fachspr. für* mit gewölbter Fläche)
Mug|ge, die; -, -n (*landsch. für* Gelegenheit, Nebengeschäft [bes. für Musiker]; *vgl. auch* Mucke)
Müg|gel|see, der; -s (südöstl. von Berlin)
mug|lig *vgl.* mugelig
muh!; muh machen, muh schreien
Mü|he, die; -, -n; mit Müh und Not (↑R 13); es kostet mich keine Mühe; ich gebe mir redlich Mühe; **mü|he|los; Mü|he|lo|sig|keit**, die; -
mu|hen (muh schreien)
mü|hen, sich; ich mühe mich; **mü|he|voll; Mü|he|wal|tung**
Muh|kuh (*Kinderspr. für* Kuh)
Mühl|bach; Müh|le, die; -, -n; **Müh|len|rad** usw. *vgl.* Mühlrad usw.; **Müh|le|spiel; Mühl|graben**
Mühl|hau|sen, Tho|mas-Münt|zer-Stadt (Stadt in Thüringen); **Mühl|häu|ser**

Mühl|heim a. Main (Stadt bei Offenbach)
Mühl|heim an der Do|nau (Stadt in Baden-Württemberg)
Mühl‿rad, ...stein, ...wehr (das), **...werk**
Muh|me, die; -, -n (*veraltet für* Tante)
Müh|sal, die; -, -e; **müh|sam; Müh|sam|keit,** die; -; **müh|se-lig; Müh|se|lig|keit**
Muk|den (*früher für* Schenjang)
mu|kös ‹lat.› (*Med.* schleimig); **Mu|ko|sa,** die; -, ...sen (Schleimhaut)
Mu|lat|te, der; -n, -n (↑R 126) ‹span.› (Nachkomme eines weißen u. eines schwarzen Elternteils); **Mu|lat|tin**
Mulch, der; -[e]s, -e (Schicht aus zerkleinerten Pflanzen, Torf o. Ä. auf dem Acker- od. Gartenboden); **Mulch|blech** (Laubzerkleinerer an Rasenmähern); **mul-chen** (mit Mulch bedecken)
Mul|de, die; -, -n; **mul|den|för-mig**
Mu|le|ta, die; -, -s ‹span.› (rotes Tuch der Stierkämpfer)
Mül|hau|sen (Stadt im Elsass)
Mül|heim (Ort bei Koblenz)
Mül|heim a. d. Ruhr (Stadt im Ruhrgebiet)
[1]**Mu|li,** das; -s, -[s] ‹lat.› (*südd., österr. für* Mulus [Maulesel]); [2]**Mu|li** (*Plur. von* Mulus)
[1]**Mull,** der; -[e]s, -e ‹Hindi-engl.› (ein Baumwollgewebe)
[2]**Mull,** der; -[e]s, -e (*nordd. für* weicher, lockerer Humusboden)
[3]**Mull,** *auch* Gold|mull, der; -s, -e (ein maulwurfähnlicher Insektenfresser)
Müll, der; -[e]s (Abfälle [der Haushalte, der Industrie]); **Müll‿ab-fuhr, ...ab|la|de|platz**
Mul|lah, der; -s, -s ‹arab.› (Titel von islam. Geistlichen u. Gelehrten)
Mul|lat|schag, der; -s, -s ‹ung.› (*ostösterr. für* ausgelassenes Fest)
Müll‿au|to, ...berg, ...beu|tel
Mull|bin|de
Müll‿con|tai|ner, ...de|po|nie, ...ei|mer
Mül|ler; Mül|ler‿bursch *od.* **...bur|sche; Mül|le|rei; Mül|le-rin; Mül|le|rin|art;** *in den Wendungen* auf *od.* nach - (in Mehl gewendet, gebraten u. mit Butter übergossen)
Mül|ler-Thur|gau [*auch* ...'tu:r...], der; - ‹nach dem schweiz. Pflanzenphysiologen H. Müller-Thurgau› (eine Reb- u. Weinsorte)
Mull|gar|di|ne
Müll‿gru|be, ...hau|fen
Müll|heim (Stadt in Baden-Württemberg)
Müll|kip|pe
Mull|läpp|chen (↑R 136)
Müll‿mann (*ugs.; Plur.* ...männer), **...schlu|cker, ...ton|ne, ...ver-bren|nung; Müll|ver|bren-nungs|an|la|ge; Müll‿wa|gen, ...wer|ker** (Berufsbezeichnung)
Mull|win|del
Mulm, der; -[e]s (lockere Erde; faules Holz); **mul|men** (zu Mulm machen; in Mulm zerfallen); **mul|mig** (*ugs. auch für* bedenklich; unwohl); mir ist - (*ugs.*)
Mul|ti, der; -s, -s ‹lat.› (*ugs. Kurzwort für* multinationaler Konzern); **mul|ti|funk|ti|o|nal** (vielen Funktionen gerecht werdend); **mul|ti|kul|tu|rell** (viele Kulturen, Angehörige mehrerer Kulturen umfassend, aufweisend); **mul|ti-la|te|ral** (mehrseitig); -e Verträge; **Mul|ti|me|dia,** das; -[s] (*Informatik* Zusammenwirken verschiedener Medientypen [Texte, Bilder, Grafiken, Tonsequenzen, Animationen, Videoclips] in einem System, in dem diese Informationen gespeichert, präsentiert u. manipuliert werden können); **mul|ti|me|di|al** (viele Medien betreffend, berücksichtigend; für viele Medien bestimmt); **Mul|ti-me|di|a|sys|tem** (System, das mehrere Medien [z. B. Fernsehen u. Bücher] verwendet); **Mul|ti-mil|li|o|när; mul|ti|na|ti|o|nal** (aus vielen Nationen bestehend; in vielen Staaten vertreten); -e Unternehmen; **mul|ti|pel** (vielfältig); ...ip|le (↑R 130) Sklerose (Gehirn- u. Rückenmarkskrankheit; *Abk.* MS, m. S.); **Mul|ti|ple-choice|ver|fah|ren,** *auch* **Mul|ti-ple-Choice-Ver|fah|ren** ['maltip(ə)l'tʃɔys...] ‹engl.; dt.› ([Prüfungs]verfahren, bei dem von mehreren vorgegebenen Antworten eine od. mehrere als richtig zu kennzeichnen sind); **mul|ti|plex;** (*veraltet für* vielfältig); *vgl.* Dr. [h.c.] mult.; **Mul|ti|plex,** das; -[es], -e (großes Kinozentrum); **Mul|ti|pli|kand,** der; -en, -en; ↑R 126 (*Math.* Zahl, die mit einer anderen multipliziert werden soll); **Mul|ti|pli|ka|ti|on,** die; -, -en (Vervielfachung); **Mul|ti|pli-ka|ti|vum** [...v...], das; -s, ...va (*Sprachw.* Vervielfältigungszahlwort); **Mul|ti|pli|ka|tor,** der; -s, ...oren (Zahl, mit der eine vorgegebene Zahl multipliziert werden soll; jmd., der Wissen, Informationen weitergibt und verbreitet); **mul|ti|pli|zie|ren** (malnehmen, vervielfachen); zwei multipliziert mit zwei ist, macht, gibt (*nicht:* sind, machen, geben) vier; **mul|ti-va|lent** [...v...] (*Psych.* mehr-, vielwertig [von Tests, die mehrere Lösungen zulassen]); **Mul|ti|va-lenz,** die; -, -en (*bes. Psych.* Mehrwertigkeit [von psychischen Eigenschaften, Schriftmerkmalen, Tests]); **Mul|ti|vib|ra|tor,** der; -s, ...oren (ein Bauelement in elektron. Rechenanlagen u. Fernsehgeräten); **Mul|ti|vi|si|ons|wand** (Projektionswand, auf die mehrere Dias gleichzeitig projiziert werden)
mul|tum, non mul|ta ‹lat., „viel [= ein Gesamtes], nicht vielerlei [= viele Einzelheiten]“› (Gründlichkeit, nicht Oberflächlichkeit)
Mu|lus, der; -, Muli ‹lat.› (Maulesel)
Mu|mie [...iə], die; -, -n ‹pers.-ital.› ([durch Einbalsamieren usw.] vor Verwesung geschützter Leichnam); **mu|mi|en|haft** [...iən...]; **Mu|mi|en|sarg; Mu|mi|fi|ka|ti-on,** die; -, -en ‹pers.-ital.; lat.› (*seltener für* Mumifizierung; *Med.* Gewebeeintrocknung); **mu|mi|fi-zie|ren; Mu|mi|fi|zie|rung** (Einbalsamierung)
Mumm, der; -s (*ugs. für* Mut, Schneid); keinen Mumm haben
[1]**Mum|me,** die; - (*landsch. für* Malzbier); Braunschweiger -
[2]**Mum|me,** die; -, -n (*veraltet für* Larve; Vermummter)
Mum|mel, die; -, -n (Teichrose)
Mum|mel|greis (*ugs. für* alter [zahnloser] Mann); **Müm|mel-mann,** der; -[e]s, ...männer (*scherzh. für* Hase); **mum|meln** (*landsch. für* murmeln; behaglich kauen, wie ein Zahnloser kauen; *auch für* mummen); ich ...[e]le (↑R 16); **müm|meln** (fressen [vom Hasen, Kaninchen])
Mum|mel|see, der; -s
mum|men (*veraltet für* einhüllen); **Mum|men|schanz,** der; -es (*veraltend für* Maskenfest)
Mum|pitz, der; -es (*ugs. für* Unsinn; Schwindel)
Mumps, der, *landsch. auch* die; - ‹engl.› (eine Infektionskrankheit)
Munch [muŋk], Edvard (norweg. Maler)
Mün|chen (Stadt a.d. Isar); München-Schwabing (↑R 106); **Mün-che|ner,** Münch|ner (↑R 103); Münch[e]ner Kindl; Münch[e]ner Straße (↑R 123)
[1]**Münch|hau|sen,** Karl Friedrich Hieronymus von, *genannt* „Lügenbaron“ (Verfasser unglaubhafter Abenteuergeschichten);

[2]**Münch|hau|sen,** der; -, - (Aufschneider); **Münch|hau|se|ni|a|de, Münch|hau|si|a|de** (Erzählung in Münchhausens Art); **münch|hau|sisch;** die münchhausischen Schriften (↑R 94)
Münch|ner *vgl.* Münchener
[1]**Mund,** der; -[e]s, *Plur.* Münder, *selten auch* Munde *u.* Münde; einen, zwei, ein paar Mund voll [Brot] nehmen; den Mund [zu] voll nehmen (großsprecherisch sein)
[2]**Mund,** Munt, die; - (Schutzverhältnis im germ. Recht); *vgl.* Mundium
Mund|art (Dialekt); **Mund|art‿dich|ter, ...dich|te|rin, ...dich|tung; Mund|ar|ten|for|schung, Mund|art|for|schung; mund|art|lich** (*Abk.* mdal.); **Mund|art‿spre|cher, ...spre|che|rin, ...wör|ter|buch; Münd|chen; Mund|du|sche**
Mün|del, das, BGB *(für beide Geschlechter)* der; -s, -, *für ein Mädchen selten auch* die; -, -n ‹*zu* [2]Mund, Munt› (*Rechtsspr.* unter Vormundschaft stehende Person); **Mün|del|geld; mün|del|si|cher** *(Bankw.);* **Mün|del|si|cher|heit,** die; -
mun|den (*geh.* *für* schmecken); **mün|den**
Mün|den (Stadt am Zusammenfluss der Fulda u. der Werra zur Weser; *vgl.* Hann. Münden); **Mün|de|ner** (↑R 103)
mund|faul (*ugs.* *für* wortkarg); **Mund|fäu|le** (eitrige Entzündung der Mundschleimhaut u. des Zahnfleisches); **mund|fer|tig; Mund|flo|ra** (*Med.* die Bakterien und Pilze in der Mundhöhle); **mund|ge|recht; Mund‿ge|ruch, ...har|mo|ni|ka, ...höh|le**
mün|dig; mündig sein, werden; er wurde mündig gesprochen; **Mün|dig|keit,** die; -; **Mün|dig|keits|er|klä|rung; mün|dig spre|chen** *vgl.* mündig; **Mün|dig|spre|chung**
Mun|di|um, das; -s, *Plur.* ...ien [...i̯ən] *u.* ...ia ‹germ.-mlat.› (Schutzverpflichtung, -gewalt im frühen dt. Recht); *vgl.* [2]Mund
Mund|kom|mu|ni|on *(kath. Kirche);* **münd|lich; Münd|lich|keit,** die; -; **Mund‿öff|nung** *(Zool.),* **...par|tie, ...pfle|ge, ...pro|pa|gan|da, ...raub** (der; -[e]s), **...rohr** (*veraltet für* Mundstück)
Mund|schaft (*früher* Verhältnis zwischen Schützer u. Beschütztem; Schutzverhältnis)
Mund‿schenk (*früher* an Fürstenhöfen für die Getränke verantwortlicher Hofbeamter), **...schleim|haut, ...schutz** (der; -s, -e *Plur. selten; Med., Boxen*)
M-und-S-Rei|fen = Matsch-und-Schnee-Reifen
Mund|stück; mund|tot; jmdn. mundtot machen (zum Schweigen bringen); **Mund|tuch** *Plur.* ...tücher (*veraltet für* Serviette)
Mün|dung; Mün|dungs‿feu|er, ...scho|ner; Mund voll *vgl.* Mund; **Mund‿vor|rat, ...was|ser** (*Plur.* ...wässer); **Mund|werk,** das; -s, -e; ein großes Mundwerk haben (*ugs. für* großsprecherisch sein); **Mund‿werk|zeug** *(meist Plur.),* **...win|kel; Mund-zu-Mund-Be|at|mung** (↑R 28); **Mund-zu-Na|se-Be|at|mung** (↑R 28)
Mung|ge|nast [ˈmuŋənast] (↑R 132; österr. Barockbaumeisterfamilie)
[1]**Mun|go,** der; -s, -s ‹angloind.› (eine Schleichkatze)
[2]**Mun|go,** der; -[s], -s ‹engl.› (Garn, Gewebe aus Reißwolle)
Mu|ni, der; -s, - (*schweiz. für* Zuchtstier)
Mu|nin ‹„der Erinnerer"› (*nord. Mythol.* einer der beiden Raben Odins); *vgl.* Hugin
Mu|ni|ti|on, die; -, -en ‹franz.›; **mu|ni|ti|o|nie|ren** (mit Munition versehen); **Mu|ni|ti|o|nie|rung; Mu|ni|ti|ons‿de|pot, ...fab|rik, ...la|ger, ...zug**
mu|ni|zi|pal ‹lat.› (*veraltet für* städtisch; Verwaltungs...); **Mu|ni|zi|pi|um,** das; -s, ...ien [...i̯ən] (altröm. Landstadt mit Selbstverwaltung)
Mun|kel|lei *(ugs.);* **mun|keln** (*ugs. für* im Geheimen reden); ich ...[e]le (↑R 16)
Müns|ter, das, *selten* der; -s, - (Stiftskirche, Dom)
Müns|te|ra|ner (Einwohner von Münster [Westf.])
Müns|ter|bau *Plur.* ...bauten
Müns|ter|kä|se, der; -s, - ‹nach der franz. Stadt Munster im Elsass› (ein Weichkäse)
Müns|ter|land, das; -[e]s (Teil der Westfälischen Bucht)
Müns|ter|turm
Müns|ter (Westf.) (Stadt im Münsterland)
Munt *vgl.* [2]Mund
mun|ter; Mun|ter|keit, die; -; **Mun|ter|ma|cher** (*ugs. für* Anregungsmittel)
Münt|zer, Thomas (dt. ev. Theologe)
Münz‿amt, ...an|stalt, ...ap|pa|rat, ...au|to|mat; Mün|ze, die; -, -n (Zahlungsmittel, Geld; Geldprägestätte); **mün|zen;** du münzt; das ist auf mich gemünzt (*ugs. für* das zielt auf mich ab); **Mün|zen|samm|lung; Mün|zer** (*veraltet für* Münzenpräger); **Münz‿fern|spre|cher, ...fuß** (Verhältnis zwischen Gewicht u. Feingehalt bei Münzen), **...ge|wicht, ...ho|heit, ...ka|bi|nett, ...kun|de** (die; -; *für* Numismatik); **münz|mä|ßig; Münz‿recht, ...samm|lung** (*vgl.* Münzensammlung), **...sor|tier|ma|schi|ne, ...stät|te, ...tank, ...tech|nik, ...ver|bre|chen, ...wechs|ler, ...we|sen** (das; -s)
Mur, die; - (l. Nebenfluss der Drau)
Mu|rä|ne, die; -, -n ‹griech.› (ein Fisch)
mürb, *häufiger* **mür|be;** mürbes Gebäck; er hat ihn mürbe gemacht (*ugs. für* seinen Widerstand gebrochen); **Mür|be,** die; -; **Mür|be‿bra|ten** (*nordd. für* Lendenbraten), **...teig; Mürb|heit,** die; -; **Mür|big|keit,** die; - *(veraltet)*
Mur|bruch, der; -[e]s, ...brüche
Mu|re, die; -, -n (*Geol.* Schutt- od. Schlammstrom im Hochgebirge)
mu|ren ‹engl.› (*Seew.* mit einer Muring verankern)
mu|ri|a|tisch ‹lat.› (kochsalzhaltig)
mu|rig ‹*zu* Mure›; -es Gelände
Mu|ril|lo [muˈriljo] (span. Maler)
Mu|ring, die; -, -e ‹engl.› (*Seew.* Vorrichtung zum Verankern mit zwei Ankern); **Mu|rings‿bo|je, ...schä|kel**
Mü|ritz, die; - (See in Mecklenburg)
Mur|kel, der; -s, - (*landsch. für* kleines Kind; unansehnlicher [kleiner] Mensch); **mur|ke|lig, murk|lig** (*landsch. für* klein u. unansehnlich)
Murks, der; -es (*ugs. für* unordentliche Arbeit; fehlerhaftes Produkt); **murk|sen** *(ugs.);* du murkst; **Murk|ser**
Mur|mansk (russ. Hafenstadt)
Mur|mel, die; -, -n (*landsch. für* Spielkügelchen)
[1]**mur|meln;** ich ...[e]le (↑R 16) (leise u. undeutlich sprechen); vor sich hin murmeln
[2]**mur|meln;** ich ...[e]le (↑R 16) (*landsch. für* mit Murmeln spielen)
Mur|mel|tier (ein Nagetier); schlafen wie ein -
Mur|ner, der; -s (Kater in der Tierfabel)
Murr, die; - (r. Nebenfluss des Neckars)
mur|ren; mür|risch; Mür|risch-

keit, die; -; **Murr|kopf** (*veraltet für* mürrischer Mensch); **murr|köp|fig, murr|köp|fisch**

Mur|ten (Stadt im Kanton Freiburg); **Mur|ten|see**, der; -s

Mürz, die; - (l. Nebenfluss der Mur)

Mus, das, *landsch. auch* der; -es, -e

Mu|sa, die; - ‹arab.› (Bananenart); **Mu|sa|fa|ser** (Manilahanf)

[1]**Mu|sa|get** (↑R 132), der; -en (↑R 126) ‹griech., „Musen[an]führer"› (Beiname Apollos); [2]**Mu|sa|get** (↑R 132), der; -en, -en; ↑R 126 (*veraltet für* Freund u. Förderer der Künste u. Wissenschaften)

mus|ar|tig

Mus|ca|det [myska'dɛ], der; -[s], -s (ein trockener franz. Weißwein)

[1]**Mu|sche**, die; -, -n ‹franz.› (*vgl.* Mouche)

[2]**Mu|sche**, die; -, -n (*landsch. für* leichtlebige Frau; Prostituierte)

Mu|schel, die; -, -n; **Mu|schel|bank** *Plur.* ...bänke; **Mü|schel|chen; mu|schel|för|mig; mu|sche|lig, musch|lig; Mu|schel‿kalk** (der; -[e]s; *Geol.* mittlere Abteilung der Triasformation), **...samm|lung, ...scha|le, ...werk** (das; -[e]s; *Kunstw.*)

Mu|schi, die; -, -s (*Kinderspr.* Katze; *ugs. für* Vulva)

Mu|schik [*auch* mu'ʃik], der; -s, -s ‹russ.› (Bauer im zarist. Russland)

Mu|schir, der; -s, -e ‹arab.› (*früher* türk. Feldmarschall)

Musch|ko|te, der; -n, -n (↑R 126) ‹*zu* Musketier› (*veraltend für* Soldat [ohne Rang]; einfacher Mensch)

musch|lig *vgl.* muschelig

Mu|se, die; -, -n ‹griech.› (eine der [neun] griech. Göttinnen der Künste); die zehnte Muse (*scherzh. für* Kleinkunst, Kabarett); **mu|se|al** (zum, ins Museum gehörend; Museums...); **Mu|se|en** (*Plur. von* Museum)

Mu|sel|man ['mu:z(ə)lma:n], der; -en, Muselmanen ‹arab.; *verderbt aus* Moslem› (*veraltet für* Anhänger des Islams); *vgl.* Moslem *u.* Muslim; **Mu|sel|ma|nin** *vgl.* Moslime *u.* Muslime; **mu|sel|ma|nisch; Mu|sel|mann** *Plur.* ...männer (*veraltet; eindeutschend für* Muselman); **Mu|sel|män|nin; mu|sel|män|nisch**

Mu|sen|al|ma|nach; Mu|sen‿sohn (*scherzh. für* Dichter), **...tem|pel** (*scherzh. für* Theater); **Mu|se|o|lo|gie**, die; - (Museumskunde); **mu|se|o|lo|gisch**

Mu|sette [my'zɛt], die; -, *Plur.* -s *od.* -n [...t(ə)n] ‹franz.› (franz. Tanz im $^3/_4$- od. $^6/_8$-Takt)

Mu|se|um, das; -s, ...een ‹griech.› ([der Öffentlichkeit zugängliche] Sammlung von Altertümern, Kunstwerken o. Ä.); **Mu|se|ums‿auf|se|her, ...bau** (*Plur.* ...bauten), **...die|ner** (*veraltend*), **...füh|rer, ...ka|ta|log; mu|se|ums|reif; Mu|se|ums|stück**

Mu|si|cal ['mju:zik(ə)l], das; -s, -s ‹amerik.› (populäres Musiktheater[stück], das von operetten- u. revuehaften Elementen bestimmt ist); **Mu|sic|box** ['mju:zik...], die; -, -es [...bɔksiz] ‹amerik.› (*svw.* Musikbox)

mu|siert ‹griech.› (*svw.* musivisch)

Mu|sik, die; -, -en ‹griech.› (*nur Sing.:* Tonkunst; Komposition, Musikstück); ein Musik liebender Mensch (↑R 40); **Mu|sik|aka|de|mie** (↑R 132); **Mu|si|ka|li|en** *Plur.* (gedruckte Musikwerke); **Mu|si|ka|li|en|hand|lung; mu|si|ka|lisch** (tonkünstlerisch; musikbegabt, Musik liebend); **Mu|si|ka|li|tät**, die; - (musikal. Wirkung; musikal. Empfinden od. Nacherleben); **Mu|si|kant**, der; -en, -en; ↑R 126 (Musiker, der zum Tanz u. dgl. aufspielt); **Mu|si|kan|ten|kno|chen** (*ugs. für* schmerzempfindlicher Ellenbogenknochen); **Mu|si|kan|tin; mu|si|kan|tisch** (musizierfreudig); **Mu|sik‿au|to|mat, ...bib|li|o|thek; Mu|sik|box** (Schallplattenapparat in Gaststätten); **Mu|sik‿di|rek|tor** (*Abk.* MD), **...dra|ma; Mu|si|ker; Mu|si|ke|rin; Mu|sik‿er|zie|hung, ...ge|schich|te** (die; -), **...hoch|schu|le, ...in|stru|ment; Mu|sik|in|stru|men|ten|in|dust|rie; Mu|sik‿ka|pel|le, ...kas|set|te, ...kon|ser|ve, ...kri|ti|ker, ...kri|ti|ke|rin, ...leh|rer, ...leh|re|rin, ...le|xi|kon; Mu|sik lie|bend** *vgl.* Musik; **Mu|sik|lieb|ha|ber; Mu|si|ko|lo|ge**, der; -n, -n; ↑R 126 (Musikwissenschaftler); **Mu|si|ko|lo|gie**, die; - (Musikwissenschaft); **Mu|si|ko|lo|gin; Mu|sik‿preis** (*vgl.* [2]Preis), **...stück, ...the|a|ter** (das; -s), **...tru|he, ...über|tra|gung** (↑R 132), **...un|ter|richt; Mu|si|kus**, der; -, *Plur.* ...sizi *u.* ...kusse (*scherzh. für* Musiker); **Mu|sik|ver|lag; mu|sik|ver|stän|dig; Mu|sik‿werk, ...wis|sen|schaft** (die; -), **...wis|sen|schaft|ler, ...wis|sen|schaft|le|rin, ...zeit|schrift**

Mu|sil (österr. Schriftsteller)

mu|sisch ‹griech.› (künstlerisch [durchgebildet, hoch begabt usw.]; die schönen Künste betreffend); -es Gymnasium

Mu|siv‿ar|beit (eingelegte Arbeit, Mosaik), **...gold** (unechtes Gold); **mu|si|visch** [...viʃ] ‹griech.› (eingelegt); -e Arbeit; **Mu|siv|sil|ber** (Legierung aus Zinn, Wismut u. Quecksilber zum Bronzieren)

mu|si|zie|ren; Mu|si|zier|stil

Mus|kat [*österr. u. schweiz.* 'mus...], der; -[e]s, -e ‹sanskr.-franz.› (ein Gewürz); **Mus|kat|blü|te** [*österr. u. schweiz.* 'mus...]; **Mus|ka|te**, die; -, -n (*veraltet für* Muskatnuss); **Mus|ka|tel|ler**, der; -s, - ‹ital.› (eine Reb- u. Weinsorte); **Mus|ka|tel|ler|wein; Mus|kat|nuss** [*österr. u. schweiz.* 'mus...]; **Mus|kat|nuss|baum**

Mus|kel, der; -s, -n ‹lat.›; **Mus|kel‿at|ro|phie** (*Med.* Muskelschwund), **...fa|ser, ...ka|ter** (*ugs. für* Muskelschmerzen), **...kraft, ...krampf, ...mann** (*Plur.* ...männer; *ugs. für* muskulöser [starker] Mensch), **...pa|ket** (*ugs. svw.* Muskelmann), **...protz** (*ugs. für* jmd., der mit seinen Muskeln prahlt), **...riss, ...schwund, ...zer|rung**

Mus|ke|te, die; -, -n ‹franz.› (*früher* schwere Handfeuerwaffe); **Mus|ke|tier**, der; -s, -e (*früher* Fußsoldat)

Mus|ko|vit [...v...], *auch* **Mus|ko|wit** [*beide auch* ...'vit], der; -s, -e (heller Glimmer)

mus|ku|lär ‹lat.› (auf die Muskeln bezüglich, sie betreffend); **Mus|ku|la|tur**, die; -, -en (Muskelgefüge, starke Muskeln); **mus|ku|lös** ‹franz.› (mit starken Muskeln versehen; äußerst kräftig)

Müs|li, das; -s, - ‹schweiz.› (ein Rohkostgericht, bes. aus Getreideflocken); *vgl.* Müesli

Mus|lim, der; -[s], *Plur.* -e *u.* -s (*fachspr. für* Moslem); **Mus|li|me, mus|li|misch** (*fachspr. für* Moslime, moslemisch *[vgl. d.]*)

Mus|pel|heim (*nord. Mythol.* Welt des Feuers, Reich der Feuerriesen); **Mus|pil|li**, das; -s ‹„Weltbrand"› (altd. Gedicht vom Weltuntergang)

Muss, das; - (Zwang); es ist ein Muss (notwendig); wenn nicht das harte Muss dahinter stünde; **Muss|be|stim|mung** (↑R 24)

Mu|ße, die; - (freie Zeit, [innere] Ruhe)

Muss|ehe (↑R 132; *ugs.*)

Mus|se|lin, der; -s, -e ‹nach der Stadt Mosul› (ein Gewebe); **mus|se|li|nen** (aus Musselin)

müs|sen; ich muss; du musst; du

muss|test; du müsstest; gemusst; müsse!; ich habe gemusst, *aber* was habe ich hören müssen!
Mus|se|ron [...'rɔ̃:], der; -s, -s ‹franz.› (ein Pilz)
Mu|ße|stun|de
Muss|hei|rat *(ugs.)*
mü|ßig; müßig sein; müßig gehen (*auch für* faulenzen); er ist zu lange müßig gegangen; **mü|ßi|gen;** *nur noch in* sich gemüßigt (veranlasst, genötigt) sehen; **Mü|ßig-gang** (der; -[e]s), **...gän|ger, ...gän|ge|rin; mü|ßig|gän|ge|risch; mü|ßig ge|hen** *vgl.* müßig; **Mü|ßig|keit,** die; - *(geh.)*
Mus|sorgs|ki (russ. Komponist)
Mus|sprit|ze (*ugs. für* Regenschirm)
Muss|vor|schrift (↑R 24)
Mus|ta|fa (m. Vorn.)
Mus|tang, der; -s, -s ‹engl.› (wild lebendes Präriepferd)
Mus|ter, das; -s, -; nach -; **Mus|ter-bei|spiel, ...be|trieb, ...bild, ...brief, ...buch, ...ehe** (↑R 132), **...exemp|lar** (↑R 132; *meist iron.*), **...gat|te** *(meist iron.);* **mus|ter|gül|tig; Mus|ter|gül|tig|keit,** die; -; **mus|ter|haft; Mus|ter|haf|tig|keit,** die; -; **Mus|ter-kar|te, ...kna|be** *(iron.),* **...kof|fer, ...land, ...mes|se** (*vgl.* ²Messe); **mus|tern;** ich ...ere (↑R 16); **Mus|ter-pro|zess, ...schü|ler, ...schü|le|rin, ...schutz, ...stück; Mus|te|rung; Mus|te|rungs|be|scheid; Mus|ter-zeich|ner, ...zeich|nung**
Mus|topf; aus dem Mustopf kommen (*ugs. für* ahnungslos sein)
Mut, der; -[e]s; jmdm. Mut machen; guten Mut[e]s sein; mir ist traurig zumute, *auch* zu Mute
Mu|ta, die; -, ...tä ‹lat.› (*Sprachw.* Explosivlaut); - cum liquida (Verbindung von Verschluss- u. Fließlaut, z. B. pl, pr)
mu|ta|bel ‹lat.› (veränderlich); ...ab|le (↑R 130) Merkmale; **Mu|ta|bi|li|tät,** die; - (Veränderlichkeit); **Mu|tant,** der; -en, -en (*svw.* Mutante; *bes. österr. auch für* Jugendlicher im Stimmwechsel); **Mu|tan|te,** die; -, -n (*Biol.* durch Mutation entstandenes Lebewesen); **Mu|ta|ti|on,** die; -, -en (*Biol.* spontan entstandene od. künstlich erzeugte Veränderung im Erbgefüge; *Med.* Stimmwechsel; *schweiz. für* Änderung im Personal- od. Mitgliederbestand); **mu|ta|tis mu|tan|dis** (mit den nötigen Abänderungen; *Abk.* m. m.)
Müt|chen, das; -s; an jmdm. sein Mütchen kühlen (an jmdm. seinen Zorn auslassen)
mu|ten (*Bergmannsspr.* die Genehmigung zum Abbau beantragen; *Handw.* um die Erlaubnis nachsuchen, das Meisterstück zu machen); [wohl] gemutet (*veraltet für* gestimmt, gesinnt) sein, *aber* wohlgemut sein; **Mu|ter** (*Bergmannsspr.* jmd., der Mutung einlegt)
mut|er|füllt
Mut|geld (*veraltet für* Abgabe für das Meisterstück); *vgl.* muten
mu|tie|ren ‹lat.› (*Biol.* sich spontan im Erbgefüge ändern; *Med.* die Stimme wechseln)
mu|tig; ...mü|tig (z. B. wehmütig)
Müt|lein *vgl.* Mütchen
mut|los; Mut|lo|sig|keit, die; -
mut|ma|ßen (vermuten); du mutmaßt; gemutmaßt; zu -; **mut|maß|lich;** der mutmaßliche Täter; **Mut|ma|ßung**
Mut|pro|be
Mut|schein (*Bergmannsspr.* Urkunde über die Genehmigung zum Abbau)
Mutt|chen (*landsch. Koseform von* ²Mutter)
¹Mut|ter, die; -, -n (Schraubenteil)
²Mut|ter, die; -, Mütter; Mutter Erde, Mutter Natur; **Müt|ter|be|ra|tungs|stel|le; Mut|ter|bo|den,** der; -s (humusreiche oberste Bodenschicht); **Müt|ter|chen; Mut|ter|er|de,** die; - (*svw.* Mutterboden); **Mut|ter|freu|den** *Plur.; in* - entgegensehen (*geh. für* schwanger sein); **Müt|ter|ge|ne|sungs|heim; Müt|ter-Ge|ne|sungs|werk;** Deutsches -; **Mut|ter-ge|sell|schaft** *(Wirtsch.),* **...ge|stein; Mut|ter Got|tes,** die; - -, *auch* **Mut|ter|got|tes,** die; -; **Mut|ter|got|tes|bild; Mut|ter-herz, ...kir|che, ...korn** (*Plur.* ...korne), **...ku|chen** (*für* Plazenta), **...land** (*Plur.* ...länder), **...leib** (der; -[e]s); **Müt|ter|lein; müt|ter|lich; müt|ter|li|cher|seits; Müt|ter|lich|keit,** die; -; **Mut|ter|lie|be; mut|ter|los; Mut|ter-mal** (*Plur.* ...male), **...milch, ...mund** (der; -[e]s; *Med.*)
Mut|tern-fab|rik, ...schlüs|sel
Mut|ter-pass, ...pflan|ze, ...recht (das; -[e]s), **...schaf; Mut|ter|schaft,** die; -; **Mut|ter|schafts|ur|laub; Mut|ter-schiff, ...schutz; Mut|ter|schutz|ge|setz; Mut|ter|schwein; mut|ter|see|len|al|lein** (ganz allein); **Mut|ter-söhn|chen** *(abwertend),* **...spra|che, ...stel|le** (an jmdm. - vertreten), **...tag, ...tier, ...witz** (der; -es); **Mut|ti,** die; -, -s (*Koseform von* ²Mutter)
mu|tu|al, mu|tu|ell ‹lat.› (wechselseitig); **Mu|tu|a|lis|mus,** der; - (*Biol.* Beziehung zwischen Lebewesen verschiedener Art zu beiderseitigem Nutzen); **mu|tu|ell** *vgl.* mutual
Mu|tung (*Bergmannsspr.* Antrag auf Erteilung des Abbaurechts); - einlegen (Antrag stellen)
Mut|wil|le, der; -ns; **mut|wil|lig; Mut|wil|lig|keit**
Mutz, der; -es, -e (*landsch. für* Tier mit gestutztem Schwanz)
Mütz|chen; Müt|ze, die; -, -n; **Müt|zen|schirm**
m. v. = mezza voce
MV = Megavolt
m. W. = meines Wissens
MW = Megawatt
MwSt., Mw.-St. = Mehrwertsteuer
¹My, das; -[s], -s (griech. Buchstabe: *M, μ*); **²My** (*kurz für* Mikron *[vgl. d.]*)
My|al|gie, die; -, ...ien ‹griech.› (*Med.* Muskelschmerz)
My|an|mar (Staat in Hinterindien)
My|as|the|nie, die; -, ...ien (*Med.* krankhafte Muskelschwäche); **My|ato|nie,** die; -, ...ien (*Med.* [angeborene] Muskelerschlaffung)
My|e|li|tis, die; -, ...litiden ‹griech.› (*Med.* Entzündung des Rückenod. Knochenmarks)
My|ke|nä, My|ke|ne (griech. Ort u. antike Ruinenstätte); **my|ke|nisch**
My|ko|lo|ge, der; -n, -n (↑R 126) ‹griech.› (Kenner u. Erforscher der Pilze); **My|ko|lo|gie,** die; - (Pilzkunde); **my|ko|lo|gisch; My|kor|rhi|za,** die; -, ...zen (*Bot.* Lebensgemeinschaft zwischen den Wurzeln von höheren Pflanzen u. Pilzen); **My|ko|se,** die; -, -n (*Med.* Pilzerkrankung)
My|la|dy [mi'le:di] ‹engl.› (frühere engl. Anrede an eine Dame = gnädige Frau)
My|lo|nit [*auch* ...'nit], der; -s, -e ‹griech.› (*Geol.* Gestein)
My|lord [mi...] ‹engl.› (frühere engl. Anrede an einen Herrn = gnädiger Herr)
Myn|heer [mə'ne:r] ‹niederl.› *vgl.* Mijnheer
My|o|kard, das; -[e]s, -e *u.* My|o|kar|di|um, das; -s, ...dia ‹griech.› (*Med.* Herzmuskel); **My|o|kar|die,** die; -, ...ien *u.* My|o|kar|do|se, die; -, -n (nichtentzündliche Herzmuskelerkrankung); **My|o|kard|in|farkt** (Herzinfarkt); **My|o|kar|di|tis,** die; -, ...itiden (Herzmuskelentzündung); **My|o|kar|do|se** *vgl.* Myokardie; **My|o|kard|scha|den; My|o|lo|gie,** die;

- (*Med.* Muskellehre); **My|om,** das; -s, -e (gutartige Muskelgewebsgeschwulst); **my|o|morph** (muskelfaserig)

My|on, das; -s, ...onen *meist Plur.* ‹griech.› (*Kernphysik* instabiles Elementarteilchen)

my|op, my|o|pisch ‹griech.› (*Med.* kurzsichtig); **My|o|pe,** der *od.* die; -n, -n; ↑R 5 ff. (Kurzsichtige[r]); **My|o|pie,** die; - (Kurzsichtigkeit); **my|o|pisch** *vgl.* myop

My|o|sin, das; -s (Muskeleiweiß); **My|o|si|tis,** die; -, ...itiden ‹griech.› (*Med.* Muskelentzündung); **My|o|to|mie,** die; -, ...ien (operative Muskeldurchtrennung); **My|o|to|nie,** die; -, ...ien (Muskelkrampf)

My|ri|a... ‹griech.› (10 000 Einheiten enthaltend); **My|ri|a|de,** die; -, -n (Anzahl von 10 000; *meist Plur.: übertr. für* unzählig große Menge); **My|ri|a|po|de, My|ri|o|po|de,** der; -n, -n *meist Plur.;* ↑R 126 (*Zool.* Tausendfüßer)

Myr|me|ko|lo|gie, die; - ‹griech.› (*Zool.* Ameisenkunde)

Myr|mi|do|ne, der; -n, -n; ↑R 126 (Angehöriger eines antiken Volksstammes)

My|ro|ba|la|ne, die; -, -n ‹griech.› (Gerbstoff enthaltende Frucht vorderind. Holzgewächse)

Myr|rhe, *auch* Myr|re (↑R 33), die; -, -n ‹semit.› (ein aromat. Harz); **Myr|rhen‿öl** (das; -[e]s), **...tinktur** (die; -)

Myr|te, die; -, -n (immergrüner Baum od. Strauch des Mittelmeergebietes u. Südamerikas); **Myr|ten‿kranz, ...zweig**

Mys|te|ri|en|spiel ‹griech.; dt.› (mittelalterliches geistliches Drama); **mys|te|ri|ös** ‹franz.› (geheimnisvoll; rätselhaft); **Mys|te|ri|um,** das; -s, ...ien [...iən] ‹griech.› (unergründliches Geheimnis [religiöser Art]); **Mys|ti|fi|ka|ti|on,** die; -, -en ‹griech.; lat.› (Täuschung; Vorspiegelung); **mys|ti|fi|zie|ren** (mystisch betrachten; täuschen, vorspiegeln); **Mys|ti|fi|zie|rung; Mys|tik,** die; - ‹griech.› (*urspr.* Geheimlehre; relig. Richtung, die den Menschen durch Hingabe u. Versenkung zu persönl. Vereinigung mit Gott zu bringen sucht); **Mys|ti|ker** (Anhänger der Mystik); **Mys|ti|ke|rin; mys|tisch** (geheimnisvoll; dunkel); **Mys|ti|zis|mus,** der; - (Wunderglaube, [Glaubens]schwärmerei); **mys|ti|zis|tisch**

My|the, die; -, -n (*älter für* Mythos)

My|then [ˈmiː...], der; -s, - (Gebirgsstock bei Schwyz); der Große, der Kleine -

My|then‿bil|dung, ...for|schung (die; -); **my|then|haft; my|thisch** ‹griech.› (sagenhaft, erdichtet); **My|tho|lo|gie,** die; -, ...ien (wissenschaftl. Behandlung der Götter-, Helden-, Dämonensage; Götterlehre); **my|tho|lo|gisch** (sagen-, götterkundlich); **my|tho|lo|gi|sie|ren** (in mythischer Form darstellen, mythologisch erklären); **My|thos,** *auch* **My|thus,** der; -, ...then (Sage u. Dichtung von Göttern, Helden u. Geistern; legendäre, glorifizierte Person od. Sache)

My|ti|le|ne, *neugriech.* Mi|ti|li|ni (Hptst. von Lesbos)

Myx|ödem (↑R 132) ‹griech.› (*Med.* körperl. u. geistige Erkrankung mit heftigen Hautanschwellungen); **My|xo|ma|to|se,** die; -, -n (tödlich verlaufende Viruskrankheit bei Hasen- u. [Wild]kaninchen); **My|xo|my|zet,** der; -en, -en; ↑R 126 (*Bot.* ein Schleimpilz)

My|zel, das; -s, -ien [...iən] ‹griech.› *u.* **My|ze|li|um,** das; -s, ...lien [...iən] (*Bot.* [unter der Erde wachsendes] Fadengeflecht der Pilze); **My|zet,** der; -en, -en; ↑R 126 (*selten für* Pilz); **My|ze|tis|mus,** der; -, ...men (*Med.* Pilzvergiftung)

N

N (Buchstabe); das N; des N, die N, *aber* das n in Wand (↑R 60); der Buchstabe N, n

N = Nahschnellverkehrszug; Nationalstraße; Newton; Nitrogenium (*chem. Zeichen für* Stickstoff); Nord[en]

n = Nano...; Neutron

N, *ν* = Ny

'n; ↑R 13 (*ugs. für* ein, einen)

Na = *chem. Zeichen für* Natrium

na!; na, na!; na ja!; na und?; na gut!; na, so was!

na! (*bayr., österr. ugs. für* nein!); *vgl.* ne!

Naab, die; - (l. Nebenfluss der Donau); **Naab|eck** (Ortsn.); *aber* **Nab|burg** (Stadt an der Naab)

Na|be, die; -, -n (Mittelhülse des Rades); **Na|bel,** der; -s, -; **Nabel‿bin|de, ...bruch** (der), **...schau** (*ugs.*); **Na|bel|schnur** *Plur.* ...schnüre; **Na|ben|boh|rer**

Na|bob, der; -s, -s ‹Hindi-engl.› (Provinzgouverneur in Indien; reicher Mann)

Na|bo|kov (amerik. Schriftsteller)

Na|buc|co (*ital. Kurzform von* Nabucodonosor = Nebukadnezar; Oper von Verdi)

nach; nach und nach; nach wie vor; *Präp. mit Dat.:* nach ihm; nach Hause *od.* Haus, *österr., schweiz. auch* nachhause; nach langem, schwerem Leiden (↑R 7); nacheinander; nachher

nach... (*in Zus. mit Verben,* z. B. nachmachen, du machst nach, nachgemacht, nachzumachen)

nach|äf|fen (*ugs. für* nachahmen); **Nach|äf|fe|rei; Nach|äf|fung**

nach|ah|men; er hat ihn nachgeahmt; **nach|ah|mens|wert; Nach|ah|mer; Nach|ah|me|rin; Nach|ah|mung; Nach|ah|mungs|trieb; nach|ah|mungs|wür|dig**

nach|ar|bei|ten

Nach|bar, der; *Gen.* -n (↑R 126), *seltener* -s, *Plur.* -n; **Nach|bar‿dorf, ...gar|ten, ...haus; Nach|ba|rin; Nach|bar|land** *Plur.* ...länder; **nach|bar|lich; Nach|bar‿ort** (*vgl.* ¹Ort), **...recht** (das; -[e]s); **Nach|bar|schaft,** die; -; **nach|bar|schaft|lich; Nach|bar|schafts‿heim, ...hil|fe; Nach|bars‿fa|mi|lie, ...frau, ...kind, ...leu|te** (*Plur.*); **Nach|bar‿staat** (*Plur.* ...staaten), **...stadt, ...wis|sen|schaft**

Nach|be|ben (nach einem Erdbeben)

nach|be|han|deln; Nach|be|hand|lung

nach|be|kom|men (*ugs.*)

nach|be|rei|ten (*Päd.* [den bereits behandelten Unterrichtsstoff] vertiefen, ergänzen o. Ä.); **Nach|be|rei|tung**

nach|bes|sern; ich bessere *od.* bessre nach; **Nach|bes|se|rung, Nach|bess|rung**

nach|be|stel|len; Nach|be|stel|lung

nach|be|ten; Nach|be|ter

nach|be|zeich|net (*bes. Kaufmannsspr.*); nachbezeichnete Waren

nach|bil|den; Nach|bil|dung

nach|blei|ben (*landsch. für* zurückbleiben; nachsitzen)

nach|bli|cken
nach|blu|ten; Nach|blu|tung
nach|boh|ren (*auch für* hartnäckig nachfragen)
nach|börs|lich (nach der Börsenzeit)
nach Chris|ti Ge|burt (*Abk.* n. Chr. G.); **nach|christ|lich; nach Chris|to, nach Chris|tus** (*Abk.* n. Chr.)
nach|da|tie|ren (mit einem früheren, *auch* späteren Datum versehen); sie hat das Schreiben nachdatiert; *vgl.* zurückdatieren *u.* vorausdatieren; **Nach|da|tie|rung**
nach|dem; je nachdem; je nachdem[,] ob ... *od.* wie ... (↑R 88)
nach|den|ken; nach|denk|lich; Nach|denk|lich|keit, die; -
nach|dich|ten; Nach|dich|tung
nach|die|seln; *vgl.* dieseln
nach|dop|peln (*schweiz. für* nachbessern; zum zweiten Mal in Angriff nehmen); ich dopp[e]le nach
nach|drän|gen
nach|dre|hen; eine Szene -
Nach|druck, der; -[e]s, *Plur.* *(Druckw.:)* ...drucke; **nach|drucken; Nach|druck|er|laub|nis; nach|drück|lich; Nach|drück|lich|keit,** die; -; **nach|drucks|voll; Nach|druck|ver|fah|ren**
nach|dun|keln; der Anstrich ist *od.* hat nachgedunkelt
Nach|durst (nach Alkoholgenuss)
nach|ei|fern; nach|ei|ferns|wert; Nach|ei|fe|rung
nach|ei|len
nach|ei|nan|der (↑R 132); *in Verbindung mit Verben immer getrennt* (↑R 39): nacheinander starten; die Schüler wurden nacheinander aufgerufen usw.
nach|eis|zeit|lich
nach|emp|fin|den; Nach|emp|fin|dung
Na|chen, der; -s, - (*landsch. u. geh. für* Kahn)
nach|ent|rich|ten; Versicherungsbeiträge -; **Nach|ent|rich|tung**
Nach|er|be, der; **Nach|erb|schaft**
nach|er|le|ben
Nach|ern|te
nach|er|zäh|len; Nach|er|zäh|lung
N[a]chf. = Nachfolger, Nachfolgerin
Nach|fahr, der; *Gen.* -en, *selten* -s, *Plur.* -en *u.* **Nach|fah|re,** der; -n, -n; ↑R 126 (*selten für* Nachkomme); **nach|fah|ren; Nach|fah|ren|ta|fel**
Nach|fall, der (*Bergmannsspr.* Gestein, das bei der Kohlegewinnung nachfällt und die Kohle verunreinigt)
nach|fär|ben
nach|fas|sen (*auch für* hartnäckig weitere Fragen stellen)
Nach|fei|er; nach|fei|ern
nach|fi|nan|zie|ren; Nach|fi|nan|zie|rung
Nach|fol|ge, die; -; **nach|fol|gen; nach|fol|gend;** die nachfolgenden Bestimmungen; (↑R 47:) das Nachfolgende, Nachfolgendes gilt nur mit Einschränkungen; im Nachfolgenden (weiter unten) ist zu lesen ...; **Nach|fol|gen|de,** der *u.* die; -n, -n (↑R 5 ff.); **Nach|fol|ge|or|ga|ni|sa|ti|on; Nach|fol|ger** (*Abk.* N[a]chf.); **Nach|fol|ge|rin** (*Abk.* N[a]chf.); **Nach|fol|ger|schaft; Nach|fol|ge|staat** *Plur.* ...staaten
nach|for|dern; Nach|for|de|rung
nach|for|men; eine Plastik -
nach|for|schen; Nach|for|schung
Nach|fra|ge; nach|fra|gen
nach|füh|len; nach|füh|lend
nach|fül|len; Nach|fül|lung
Nach|gang; im Nachgang (*Amtsspr.* als Nachtrag)
nach|gä|ren; Nach|gä|rung
nach|ge|ben
nach|ge|bo|ren; nachgebor[e]ner Sohn; **Nach|ge|bo|re|ne,** der *u.* die; -n, -n (↑R 5 ff.)
Nach|ge|bühr (z. B. Strafporto)
Nach|ge|burt
Nach|ge|fühl
nach|ge|hen; einer Sache -
nach|ge|las|sen (*veraltend für* hinterlassen); ein -es Werk
nach|ge|ord|net (*Amtsspr.* dem Rang nach folgend); die nachgeordneten Behörden
nach|ge|ra|de
nach|ge|ra|ten; jmdm. -
Nach|ge|schmack, der; -[e]s
nach|ge|wie|se|ner|ma|ßen
nach|gie|big; Nach|gie|big|keit, die; -
nach|gie|ßen
nach|grü|beln
nach|gu|cken *(ugs.)*
nach|ha|ken (*ugs. auch für* eine [weitere] Frage stellen)
Nach|hall; nach|hal|len
nach|hal|tig; Nach|hal|tig|keit, die; -
nach|hän|gen; ich hing nach, du hingst nach; nachgehangen; einer Sache nachhängen; *vgl.* [1]hängen
nach Haus *od.* **nach Hau|se,** *österr., schweiz. auch* **nach|hau|se; Nach|hau|se|weg**
nach|hel|fen
nach|her [*auch, österr. nur,* 'na:xhe:r]; **nach|he|rig**
Nach|hil|fe; Nach|hil|fe‿schü|ler, ...schü|le|rin, ...stun|de, ...un|ter|richt
Nach|hi|nein (↑R 49 *u.* 132); *nur in:* im Nachhinein (hinterher, nachträglich)
nach|hin|ken
Nach|hol|be|darf; nach|ho|len; Nach|hol|spiel *(Sport)*
Nach|hut, die; -, -en *(Milit.)*
nach|ja|gen; dem Glück -
nach|kar|ten (*ugs. für* eine nachträgliche Bemerkung machen)
Nach|kauf; nach|kau|fen; man kann alle Teile des Geschirrs -
Nach|klang
Nach|klapp, der; -s, -s (*ugs. für* Nachtrag)
nach|klin|gen
Nach|kom|me, der; -n, -n (↑R 126); **nach|kom|men; Nach|kom|men|schaft; Nach|kömm|ling**
Nach|kon|trol|le; nach|kon|trol|lie|ren
Nach|kriegs‿er|schei|nung, ...ge|ne|ra|ti|on, ...zeit
Nach|kur
nach|la|den
Nach|lass, der; -es, *Plur.* ...lasse *u.* ...lässe; **nach|las|sen; Nach|las|ser** (*selten für* Erblasser); **Nach|lass|ge|richt; nach|läs|sig; nach|läs|si|ger|wei|se; Nach|läs|sig|keit; Nach|lass‿pfle|ger, ...pfle|ge|rin; Nach|las|sung; Nach|lass‿ver|wal|ter, ...ver|wal|te|rin**
nach|lau|fen; Nach|läu|fer
nach|le|ben; einem Vorbild -; **Nach|le|ben,** das; -s (Leben eines Verstorbenen in der Erinnerung der Hinterbliebenen)
nach|le|gen
Nach|le|se; nach|le|sen
nach|lie|fern; Nach|lie|fe|rung
nach|lö|sen
nachm., nm. = nachmittags
nach|ma|chen (*ugs. für* nachahmen)
Nach|mahd (*landsch. für* Grummet)
nach|ma|len
nach|ma|lig (*veraltend für* später);
nach|mals (*veraltet für* später)
nach|mes|sen; Nach|mes|sung
Nach‿mie|ter, ...mie|te|rin
Nach|mit|tag; (↑R 46:) nachmittags; (*Abk.* nachm., *bei Raummangel* nm.); *aber* des Nachmittags; (↑R 45:) gestern, heute, morgen Nachmittag; *vgl.* [1]Mittag;
nach|mit|tä|gig *vgl.* ...tägig;
nach|mit|täg|lich *vgl.* ...täglich;
nach|mit|tags *vgl.* Nachmittag;
Nach|mit|tags‿kaf|fee, ...schlaf, ...stun|de, ...vor|stel|lung
Nach|nah|me, die; -, -n; **Nach|nah|me‿ge|bühr, ...sen|dung**

Nach|na|me (Familienname)
nach|plap|pern *(ugs.)*
nach|po|lie|ren
Nach|por|to
nach|prä|gen; Nach|prä|gung
nach|prüf|bar; Nach|prüf|bar|keit, die; -; **nach|prü|fen; Nach|prü|fung**
Nach|raum, der; -[e]s (*Forstw.* Ausschuss)
nach|rech|nen; Nach|rech|nung
Nach|re|de; üble -; **nach|re|den**
nach|rei|chen; Unterlagen -
Nach|rei|fe; nach|rei|fen
nach|rei|sen
nach|ren|nen
Nach|richt, die; -, -en; **Nach|rich|ten‿agen|tur** (↑R 132), **...bü|ro; Nach|rich|ten|dienst;** Allgemeiner Deutscher - (*ehem. in der DDR; Abk.* ADN); **nach|rich|ten|dienst|lich; Nach|rich|ten‿ma|ga|zin, ...sa|tel|lit, ...sen|dung, ...sper|re, ...spre|cher, ...spre|che|rin, ...tech|nik, ...über|mitt|lung** (↑R 132), **...we|sen** (das; -s); **nach|richt|lich**
nach|rü|cken; Nach|rü|cker; Nach|rü|cke|rin
Nach|ruf, der; -[e]s, -e; **nach|ru|fen**
Nach|ruhm; nach|rüh|men
nach|rüs|ten (nachträglich mit einem Zusatzgerät versehen; die militärische Bewaffnung ergänzen, ausbauen); **Nach|rüs|tung**
nach|sa|gen; jmdm. etwas -
Nach|sai|son
nach|sal|zen
Nach|satz
[1]**nach|schaf|fen** (ein Vorbild nachgestalten); *vgl.* [2]schaffen; [2]**nach|schaf|fen** (nacharbeiten); *vgl.* [1]schaffen
nach|schau|en
nach|schen|ken; Wein -
nach|schi|cken
nach|schie|ben
Nach|schlag, der; -[e]s, Nachschläge (*Musik; ugs. für* zusätzliche Essensportion); **nach|schla|gen;** er ist seinem Vater nachgeschlagen (nachgeartet); er hat in einem Buch nachgeschlagen; **Nach|schla|ge|werk**
nach|schlei|chen
Nach|schlüs|sel; Nach|schlüs|sel|dieb|stahl (Diebstahl mithilfe von Nachschlüsseln)
nach|schmei|ßen *(ugs.)*
Nach|schöp|fung
nach|schrei|ben; Nach|schrift (*Abk.* NS)
Nach|schub, der; -[e]s, Nachschübe *Plur. selten;* **Nach|schub‿ko|lon|ne, ...trup|pe, ...weg**
Nach|schuss (*Wirtsch.* zusätzliche Einzahlung über die Stammeinlage hinaus; *Sportspr.* erneuter Schuss auf das Tor); **Nach|schuss|pflicht** *(Wirtsch.)*
nach|schwat|zen
nach|schwin|gen
nach|se|hen; jmdm. etwas -; **Nach|se|hen,** das; -s
Nach|sen|de|auf|trag; nach|sen|den; Nach|sen|dung
nach|set|zen; jmdm. - (jmdn. verfolgen)
Nach|sicht, die; -; **nach|sich|tig; Nach|sich|tig|keit,** die; -; **nach|sichts|voll**
Nach|sicht|wech|sel *(Bankw.)*
Nach|sil|be
nach|sin|gen
nach|sin|nen (*geh. für* nachdenken)
nach|sit|zen (zur Strafe nach dem Unterricht noch dableiben müssen); er hat nachgesessen
Nach|som|mer
Nach|sor|ge, die; - *(Med.)*
Nach|spann (*Film, Fernsehen* einem Film o. Ä. folgende Angaben über die Mitwirkenden, den Autor o. Ä.); *vgl.* Vorspann
Nach|spei|se
Nach|spiel; nach|spie|len
nach|spi|o|nie|ren *(ugs.)*
nach|spre|chen; Nach|spre|cher
nach|spü|len
nach|spü|ren
[1]**nächst;** nächsten Jahres (*Abk.* n. J.), nächsten Monats (*Abk.* n. M.), nächstes Mal, das nächste Mal (*vgl.* Mal, I); nächstdem; die nächsthöhere Nummer; bei nächstbester Gelegenheit; der nächste Beste; das kommt der Wahrheit am nächsten; (↑R 48:) der Nächste, die Nächste, bitte!; das Nächste [zu tun] wäre ...; das Nächstbeste [zu tun] wäre ...; als Nächstes; *vgl.* Nächste; [2]**nächst** (hinter, gleich nach); *Präp. mit Dat.:* nächst dem Hause, nächst ihm; **nächst|bes|ser;** die nächstbessere Platzierung; **nächst|bes|te** *vgl.* nächst; **Nächst|bes|te,** der *u.* die *u.* das; -n, -n (↑R 5 ff.); **nächst|dem; Nächs|te,** der; -n, -n; ↑R 5 ff. (Mitmensch); liebe deinen Nächsten
nach|ste|hen; nach|ste|hend; die nachstehende Erläuterung; *aber* (↑R 48:) ich möchte Ihnen Nachstehendes (Folgendes) zur Kenntnis bringen; Einzelheiten werden im Nachstehenden (weiter unten) behandelt; das Nachstehende muss geprüft werden
nach|stei|gen (*ugs. für* folgen)
nach|stel|len; er hat ihm nachgestellt; **Nach|stel|lung**
Nächs|ten|lie|be; nächs|tens; nächs|tes Mal, das nächste Mal; *vgl.* Mal, I; **nächst|fol|gend; Nächst|fol|gen|de,** der *u.* die *u.* das; -n, -n (↑R 5 ff.); **nächst‿ge|le|gen, ...hö|her; Nächst|hö|he|re,** der *u.* die *u.* das; -n, -n (↑R 5 ff.); **nächst|jäh|rig; nächst|lie|gend** *vgl.* nahe liegend; **Nächst|lie|gen|de,** das; -n (↑R 5 ff.); **nächst|mög|lich;** zum nächstmöglichen Termin; *falsch:* nächstmöglichst
nach|sto|ßen
nach|stür|zen
nach|su|chen; Nach|su|chung
Nacht, die; -, Nächte; bei, über Nacht; die Nacht über; Tag und Nacht; es wird Nacht; des Nachts, eines Nachts; (↑R 45:) [bis, von] gestern, heute, morgen Nacht; Dienstagnacht; *vgl.* nachts; **Nacht|ab|sen|kung** (bei der Zentralheizung); **nacht|ak|tiv;** nachtaktive Säugetiere; **Nacht‿an|griff, ...ar|beit** (die; -), **...asyl** (↑R 132), **...aus|ga|be, ...bar** (die); **nacht‿blau, ...blind; Nacht‿blind|heit, ...dienst; nacht|dun|kel**
Nach|teil, der; **nach|tei|lig**
näch|te|lang; *aber* drei Nächte lang; **nach|ten** (*schweiz. u. geh. für* Nacht werden); **näch|tens** (*geh. für* nachts); **Nacht|es|sen** (*bes. südd., schweiz. für* Abendessen); **Nacht|eu|le** (*ugs. auch für* jmd., der bis spät in die Nacht hinein aufbleibt); **Nacht‿fahrt, ...fal|ter; nacht|far|ben;** -er Stoff; **Nacht‿frost, ...ge|bet, ...ge|schirr, ...ge|spenst, ...ge|wand** *(geh.);* **Nacht|glei|che,** die; -, -n (*svw.* Tagundnachtgleiche); **Nacht‿hemd, ...him|mel**
Nach|ti|gall, die; -, -en (ein Singvogel); **Nach|ti|gal|len|schlag,** der; -[e]s
näch|ti|gen (übernachten); er hat bei uns genächtigt
Nach|tisch, der; -[e]s
Nacht‿ka|ba|rett, ...käst|chen (*bes. österr. für* Nachttisch), **...ker|ze** (eine Heil- und Zierpflanze), **...kli|nik** (Klinik, in der berufstätige Patienten übernachten und behandelt werden); **Nacht‿klub, ...küh|le, ...la|ger** (*Plur.* ...lager), **...le|ben** (das; -s); **nächt|lich; nächt|li|cher|wei|le; Nacht‿licht** (*Plur.* ...lichter), **...lo|kal, ...luft, ...mahl** *(bes. österr.);* **nacht|mah|len** (*österr. für* zu Abend essen); ich nachtmahle; genachtmahlt; zu nachtmahlen; **Nacht‿mahr** (Spukgestalt im Traum), **...marsch,**

...mensch, ...mu|sik, ...müt|ze, ...por|ti|er, ...quar|tier
Nach|trag, der; -[e]s, ...träge; **nach|tra|gen; nach|trä|ge|risch** (*geh. für* nachtragend, nicht vergebend); **nach|träg|lich** (hinterdrein, später, danach); **Nach|trags|haus|halt**
nach|trau|ern
Nacht|ru|he
Nach|trupp
nachts (↑R 46), *aber* des Nachts, eines Nachts; nachtsüber (↑R 46), *aber* die Nacht über; *vgl.* Abend; **Nacht|schat|ten** (eine Pflanze); **Nacht|schat|ten|ge|wächs** *meist Plur.* (eine Pflanzengattung); **Nacht˯schicht, ...schlaf; nacht|schla|fend;** zu, bei nachtschlafender Zeit; **Nacht˯schränk|chen, ...schwär|mer** (*scherzh. für* jmd., der sich die Nacht über vergnügt); **Nacht˯schwes|ter, ...spei|cher|ofen** (↑R 132), **...strom** (der; -[e]s); **nachts|über** (↑R 132); *vgl.* nachts; **Nacht˯ta|rif, ...tier, ...tisch, ...topf, ...tre|sor**
nach|tun; es jmdm. nachtun
Nacht-und-Ne|bel-Ak|ti|on
Nacht˯vi|o|le (eine Zierpflanze), **...vo|gel, ...vor|stel|lung, ...wa|che, ...wäch|ter; Nacht|wäch|ter|lied; nacht|wan|deln;** ich ...[e]le (↑R 16); ich bin, *auch* habe genachtwandelt; zu nachtwandeln; **Nacht˯wan|de|rung, ...wand|ler, ...wand|le|rin; nacht|wand|le|risch;** mit -er Sicherheit; **Nacht˯wä|sche, ...zeit** (zur Nachtzeit), **...zug, ...zu|schlag**
nach|un|ter|su|chen; Nach|un|ter|su|chung
Nach|ver|an|la|gung *(Finanzw.)*
nach|ver|si|chern; Nach|ver|si|che|rung
nach|voll|zieh|bar; nach|voll|zie|hen
nach|wach|sen
Nach|wahl
Nach|we|hen *Plur.*
nach|wei|nen
Nach|weis, der; -es, -e; **nach|weis|bar; nach|wei|sen** (beweisen); er hat den Tatbestand nachgewiesen; **nach|weis|lich**
nach|wei|ßen (nochmals weißen)
Nach|welt, die; -
nach|wer|fen
nach|wie|gen
nach|win|ken
Nach|win|ter; nach|win|ter|lich
nach|wir|ken; Nach|wir|kung
nach|wol|len (*ugs. für* folgen wollen); er hat ihm nachgewollt
Nach|wort *Plur.* ...worte
Nach|wuchs, der; -es; **Nach|wuchs˯au|tor, ...fah|rer, ...ka|der** *(ehem. in der DDR)*, **...kraft** (die), **...man|gel** (der; -s), **...spie|ler, ...spie|le|rin**
nach|wür|zen
nach|zah|len; nach|zäh|len; Nach|zah|lung; Nach|zäh|lung
nach|zeich|nen; Nach|zeich|nung
Nach|zei|tig|keit, die; - *(Sprachw.)*
nach|zie|hen
Nach|zoll
nach|zot|teln *(ugs.)*
Nach|zucht, die; -
Nach|zug; Nach|züg|ler; nach|züg|le|risch; Nach|zugs|ver|bot
Na|cke|dei, der; -s, -s (*scherzh. für* nacktes Kind; Nackte[r])
Na|cken, der; -s, -
na|ckend (*landsch. für* nackt)
Na|cken˯haar *(meist Plur.)*, **...schlag, ...schutz, ...stüt|ze, ...wir|bel**
na|ckert (*landsch. für* nackt); **Nack|frosch** *vgl.* Nacktfrosch; **na|ckig** (*ugs. für* nackt)
...na|ckig (z. B. kurznackig)
nackt; nackt|ar|mig; Nackt|ba|den, das; -s; *aber* sie gehen gern nackt baden; **Nackt|ba|de|strand; Nackt|frosch,** *seltener* Nack|frosch (*scherzh. für* nacktes Kind); **Nackt|heit,** die; -; **Nackt˯kul|tur** (die; -), **...mo|dell; Nackt|sa|mer,** der; -s, - *meist Plur.* (*Bot.* Pflanze, deren Samenanlage offen an den Fruchtblättern sitzt); **nackt|sa|mig** *(Bot.)*; **Nackt˯schne|cke, ...tän|ze|rin**
Na|del, die; -, -n; **Na|del˯ar|beit, ...baum, ...büch|se; Nä|del|chen; na|del˯fein, ...fer|tig** (zum Nähen vorbereitet [von Stoffen]), **...för|mig; Na|del˯ge|höl|ze** *(Plur.; Bot.)*, **...geld** (*früher* eine Art Taschengeld für Frau od. Tochter), **...holz** (*Plur.* ...hölzer); **na|de|lig,** nad|lig *(fachspr.)*; -e Baumarten; **Na|del˯kis|sen, ...ma|le|rei** (gesticktes buntes Bild); **na|deln** (Nadeln verlieren [von Tannen u. a.]); **Na|del˯öhr, ...spit|ze, ...stich, ...strei|fen** (sehr feiner Streifen in Stoffen), **...wald**
Na|de|rer (*österr. ugs. für* Spitzel, Verräter)
Na|di|ne (w. Vorn.)
Na|dir, der; -s ⟨arab.⟩ (*Astron.* Fußpunkt, Gegenpunkt des Zenits an der Himmelskugel)
Nad|ja (w. Vorn.)
Nad|ler (*früher für* Nadelmacher); **nad|lig** *vgl.* nadelig
NAFTA, die, - ⟨engl.; *Kurzwort für* North American Free Trade Agreement [nɔ:(r)θ əˈmɛrikən fri: tre:d əˈgri:mənt]⟩ (Freihandelsabkommen zwischen den USA, Kanada und Mexiko)
Naf|ta|li *vgl.* Naphthali
Na|gai|ka, die; -, -s ⟨russ.⟩ (Lederpeitsche [der Kosaken u. Tataren])
Na|ga|na, die; - ⟨Zuluspr.⟩ (eine afrik. Viehseuche)
Na|ga|sa|ki (jap. Stadt; am 9. 8. 1945 durch eine Atombombe fast völlig zerstört)
Na|gel, der; -s, Nägel; **Na|gel˯bett** (*Plur.* ...betten, *seltener* ...bette), **...boh|rer, ...bürs|te; Nä|gel|chen** (kleiner Nagel); **Na|gel˯falz, ...fei|le; na|gel|fest;** *nur in* niet- u. nagelfest (↑R 23); **Na|gel|fluh** (*Geol.* ein Gestein); **Na|gel|haut; Na|gel|haut|ent|fer|ner; Nä|gel|kau|en,** das; -s; **Na|gel˯kopf, ...lack; Na|gel|lack|ent|fer|ner; na|geln;** ich ...[e]le (↑R 16); **na|gel|neu** *(ugs.)*; **Na|gel˯pfle|ge, ...pro|be** (Prüfstein für etwas), **...rei|ni|ger, ...ring** (der; -[e]s; Schwert der german. Heldensage), **...sche|re, ...schuh, ...stie|fel, ...wur|zel**
na|gen; Na|ger; Na|ge|tier
Näg|lein (*veraltet für* Nelke; *vgl. auch* Nägelchen)
NAGRA, der; -s (*Kurzwort für* Fachnormenausschuss für das graphische Gewerbe)
nah *vgl.* nahe
Näh|ar|beit
Näh˯auf|nah|me, ...be|reich (der), **...bril|le** (z. B. für Weitsichtige); [1]**na|he,** *seltener* nah; näher *(vgl. d.)*; nächst *(vgl. d.)*; nächstens; nahebei, nahehin, nahezu; nah[e] daran sein; von nah und fern; nahe bekannt, nah verwandte Personen usw.; von nahem; *aber* (↑R 108): der Nahe Osten. *Getrenntschreibung in Verbindung mit Verben und Partizipien* (↑R 38 f.): z. B. nahe bringen (erläutern, vertraut machen; Verständnis erwecken); der Dichter wurde uns in der Schule nahe gebracht; nahe gehen (in die Nähe gehen); der Tod seines Freundes ist ihm nahe gegangen (hat ihn seelisch ergriffen); sie sind sich menschlich nahe gekommen; sie hat ihm die Erfüllung eurer Bitte nahe gelegt (empfohlen); die Lösung hat nahe gelegen (war leicht zu finden); ein nahe liegendes Gehöft, ein nahe liegender Gedanke; jmdm. bedrohlich näher rücken; weil der Termin jetzt nahe rückt; er weiß, dass ich ihm nahe stehe; ein mir nahe stehender Mensch;

eine nahe stehendes (in der Nähe stehendes) Haus; jmdm. nahe treten (befreundet, vertraut werden); jmdm. zu nahe treten (jmdn. verletzen, beleidigen); ²**na|he,** *selten* nah; *Präp. mit Dat.:* nahe dem Ufer

Na|he, die; - (l. Nebenfluss des Rheins)

Nä|he, die; -; in der -; **na|he|bei;** er wohnt nahebei, *aber* er wohnt nahe bei der Post; **na|he bringen** *vgl.* ¹nahe; **na|he ge|hen** *vgl.* ¹nahe; **Nah|ein|stel|lung** *(Fotogr.);* **na|he kom|men** *vgl.* ¹nahe; **na|he le|gen** *vgl.* ¹nahe; **nahe lie|gen** *vgl.* ¹nahe; **na|he liegend;** näher liegend, am nächsten liegend; *aber* nächstliegend; *vgl. auch* ¹nahe; **na|hen** *(geh.);* sich [jmdm.] -

nä|hen

nä|her; nähere Erläuterungen; *aber* (↑R 47): Näheres folgt; das Nähere findet sich bei ...; ich kann mich des Näher[e]n (der besonderen Umstände) nicht entsinnen; jmdm. etw. des Näher[e]n (genauer) auseinander setzen; alles Nähere können Sie der Gebrauchsanweisung entnehmen. *Getrenntschreibung in Verbindung mit Verben* (↑R 38 f.): z. B. näher kommen (in größere Nähe kommen); dem Abgrund immer näher kommen; weil der Termin schon wieder näher gekommen ist; sie werden sich schon näher kommen (verstehen lernen); jmdm. die moderne Kunst näher bringen (erklären, leichter verständlich machen); ... weil es näher liegt zu gehen als zu bleiben; sie hat mir näher gestanden als ihm (war mir vertrauter); er wird diesem Vorschlag näher treten (sich damit befassen, darauf eingehen)

Nä|he|rei

Nah|er|ho|lungs|ge|biet

Nä|he|rin

nä|her kom|men, lie|gen *vgl.* näher; **nä|her lie|gend** *vgl.* nahe liegend; **nä|hern;** sich -; ich ...ere mich (↑R 16); **nä|her ste|hen, treten** *vgl.* näher; **Nä|he|rung** *(Math.* Annäherung); **Nä|he|rungs|wert** *(Math.);* **na|he stehen** *vgl.* ¹nahe; **na|he ste|hend;** näher stehend, am nächsten stehend; *aber* nächststehend; *vgl. auch* ¹nahe; **na|he tre|ten** *vgl.* ¹nahe

Na|he|wein

na|he|zu

Näh‿fa|den, ...garn

Nah|kampf; Nah|kampf|mit|tel

Näh|käst|chen; aus dem - plaudern (*ugs. für* Geheimnisse ausplaudern); **Näh‿kas|ten, ...kissen, ...korb, ...ma|schi|ne; Nähma|schi|nen|öl; Näh|na|del**

Nah|ost (der Nahe Osten); für, in, nach, über Nahost; **nah|öst|lich**

Nähr‿bo|den, ...creme; näh|ren; sich -; **nahr|haft; Nähr‿he|fe, ...lö|sung, ...mit|tel** (das; *meist Plur.*), **...prä|pa|rat, ...salz, ...stoff** *(meist Plur.);* **nähr|stoff‿arm, ...reich; Nah|rung,** die; -, *Plur. (fachspr.:)* -en; **Nah|rungs‿auf|nah|me** (die; -), **...ket|te** *(Biol.),* **...man|gel** (der), **...mit|tel** (das; *meist Plur.*); **Nah|rungs‿mit|tel‿che|mie, ...in|dust|rie, ...ver|gif|tung; Nah|rungs‿quel|le, ...su|che; Nähr|wert**

Nah|schnell|ver|kehrs|zug (*Eisenb. früher; Zeichen* N)

Näh|sei|de; Naht, die; -, Nähte; **Näh|te|rin** (*veraltet für* Näherin); **Näh|tisch; naht|los; Naht|stel|le**

Na|hum (bibl. Prophet)

Nah|ver|kehr, der; -[e]s; **nah verwandt** *vgl.* ¹nahe

Näh|zeug

Nah‿ziel, ...zo|ne

Na|lm, *ökum.* **Na|in** (bibl. Ort in Galiläa)

Nai|ro|bi (Hptst. von Kenia)

na|iv ‹lat.-franz.› (natürlich; unbefangen; kindlich; einfältig); naive Malerei; naive u. sentimentalische Dichtung (bei Schiller); **Na|ive** [...və], die; -n, -n; ↑R 5 ff. (Darstellerin, die das Rollenfach der jugendlichen Liebhaberin vertritt); **Na|i|vi|tät,** die; -; **Na|iv|ling** (gutgläubiger, törichter Mensch)

na ja!

Na|ja|de, die; -, -n *meist Plur.* ‹griech.› (*griech. Mythol.* Quellnymphe; *Zool.* Flussmuschel)

Na|ma, der; -[s], -[s] (Angehöriger eines Hottentottenstammes); **Na|ma|land,** das; -[e]s

Na|me, der; -ns, -n; im Namen; mit Namen; **Na|men,** der; -s, - (*seltener für* Name); **Na|men‿buch, ...for|schung** (*auch* Na|mens|for|schung), **...ge|bung** (*auch* Na|mens|ge|bung), **...gedächt|nis; Na|men-Je|su-Fest** (↑R 95); **Na|men|kun|de,** die; -; **na|men|kund|lich; Na|men|lis|te; na|men|los; Na|men|lo|se,** der *u.* die; -n, -n (↑R 5 ff.); **Na|men|lo|sig|keit,** die; -; **Na|men‿nen|nung** (*seltener für* Namensnennung), **...re|gis|ter; na|mens;** ↑R 46 (im Namen, im Auftrag [von]; mit Namen); *Präp. mit Gen. (Amtsspr.):* namens der Regierung; **Na|mens‿ak|tie** (Aktie, die auf den Namen des Aktionärs ausgestellt ist), **...än|de|rung, ...fest** (*svw.* Namenstag), **...form, ...for|schung** (*vgl.* Namenforschung), **...ge|bung** (*vgl.* Namengebung), **...nen|nung** (die; -), **...pa|pier** (*für* Rektapapier), **...pat|ron, ...schild** (*Plur.* ...schilder), **...tag, ...vet|ter, ...zei|chen, ...zug; na|ment|lich;** namentlich[,] wenn (↑R 67 *u.* 88); **Na|men‿ver|wechs|lung, ...verzeich|nis, ...wort** (*Plur.* ...wörter; *svw.* Nomen); **nam|haft;** jmdn. namhaft machen; **Nam|haft|machung** *(Amtsspr.)*

Na|mi|bia (Republik in Südwestafrika); **Na|mi|bi|er; na|mi|bisch**

...na|mig (z.B. vielnamig); **nämlich;** nämlich[,] dass/wenn (↑R 67 *u.* 88); (↑R 47:) er ist noch der Nämliche (*veraltend* derselbe); er sagt immer das Nämliche (*veraltend* dasselbe); **Näm|lich|keit,** die; - (*Amtsspr. selten für* Identität); **Näm|lich|keits|be|schei|nigung** (*Zollw. svw.* Identitätsnachweis)

Na|mur [na'my:r] (belg. Stadt)

na, na!

¹**Nan|cy** ['nã:si, *auch* nã'si] (Stadt in Frankreich)

²**Nan|cy** ['nɛnsi] (w. Vorn.)

Nan|du, der; -s, -s ‹indian.-span.› (ein südamerik. straußenähnl. Laufvogel)

Nan|ga Par|bat, der; - - (Berg im Himalaja)

Nä|nie [...i̯ə], die; -, -n ‹lat.› ([altröm.] Totenklage, Klagegesang)

Na|nis|mus, der; - ‹griech.› (*Med., Biol.* Zwergwuchs)

¹**Nan|king** (chines. Stadt); ²**Nanking,** der; -s, *Plur.* -e *u.* -s (ein Baumwollgewebe)

Nan|net|te (w. Vorn.); **Nan|ni, Nan|ny** (w. Vorn.)

Na|no... ‹griech.› (ein Milliardstel einer Einheit, z. B. Nanometer = 10^{-9} Meter; *Zeichen* n); **Na|no‿fa|rad** (*Zeichen* nF), **...me|ter** (*Zeichen* nm), **...se|kun|de** (*Zeichen* ns)

Nan|sen (norw. Polarforscher); **Nan|sen|pass** (↑R 95; Ausweis für Staatenlose)

Nantes [nã:t] (franz. Stadt); das Edikt von -

na|nu!

Na|palm ®, das; -s ‹*Kurzwort aus* Naphthensäure u. Palmitinsäure› (hochwirksamer Füllstoff für Benzinbrandbomben); **Na|palm|bom|be**

Napf, der; -[e]s, Näpfe; **Näpfchen; Napf|ku|chen**

Naph|tha, das; -s *od.* die; - ‹pers.› (Roherdöl)
Naph|tha|li, *ökum.* Naf|ta|li (bibl. m. Eigenn.)
Naph|tha|lin, das; -s ‹pers.› (*Chemie* aus Steinkohlenteer gewonnener Kohlenwasserstoff); **Naph|the|ne** *Plur.* (gesättigte Kohlenwasserstoffe); **Naph|tho|le** *Plur.* (aromat. Alkohole zur Herstellung künstlicher Farbstoffe)
Na|po|le|on (Kaiser der Franzosen); **Na|po|le|on|dor**, der; -s, -e ‹franz.› (unter Napoleon I. u. III. geprägte Goldmünze); fünf - (↑R 90); **Na|po|le|o|ni|de**, der; -n, -n; (↑R 126; Abkömmling der Familie Napoleons); **na|po|le|o|nisch;** napoleonischer Eroberungsdrang, die napoleonischen Feldzüge; **Na|po|le|on|kra|gen** (↑R 95)
Na|po|li (*ital. Form von* Neapel); **Na|po|li|tain** [...'tɛ̃:], das; -s, -s ‹franz.› (Schokoladentäfelchen); **Na|po|li|taine** [...'tɛ:n], die; - (ein Gewebe)
Nap|pa, das; -[s], -s ‹nach der kaliforn. Stadt Napa› (*kurz für* Nappaleder); **Nap|pa|le|der**
Nar|be, die; -, -n; **nar|ben** (*Gerberei* [Leder] mit Narben versehen); **Nar|ben**, der; -s, - (*Gerberei für* Narbe); **Nar|ben‿bil|dung, ...ge|we|be, ...le|der; nar|big**
Nar|bonne [...'bɔn] (franz. Stadt)
Nar|cis|sus (*lat. Form von* Narziss)
Nar|de, die; -, -n ‹semit.› (*Bez. für* verschiedene wohlriechende Pflanzen, die schon im Altertum für Salböle verwendet wurden); **Nar|den|öl**
Nar|gi|leh [*auch* ...'gi:le], die; -, -[s] *od.* das; -s, -s ‹pers.› (oriental. Wasserpfeife)
Nar|ko|ma|nie, die; - ‹griech.› (*Med.* Sucht nach Narkotika); **Nar|ko|se**, die; -, -n (*Med.* Betäubung); **Nar|ko|se‿ap|pa|rat, ...arzt** (*für* Anästhesist), **...ärz|tin, ...ge|wehr** *(Tiermed.)*, **...mas|ke, ...mit|tel** (das), **...schwes|ter; Nar|ko|ti|kum**, das; -s, ...ka (Rausch-, Betäubungsmittel); **nar|ko|tisch** (berauschend, betäubend); **nar|ko|ti|sie|ren** (betäuben)
Narr, der; -en, -en (↑R 126)
nar|ra|tiv ‹lat.› (erzählend)
nar|ren (*geh. für* anführen, täuschen); **Nar|ren|frei|heit; nar|ren|haft; Nar|ren‿haus, ...kap|pe; nar|ren|si|cher** *(ugs.)*; **Nar|ren[s]|pos|se;** -n treiben; **Nar|ren|streich; Nar|ren|tum**, das; -s; **Nar|ren|zep|ter; Nar|re|tei** (*veraltend für* Scherz; Unsinn); **Narr|hal|la|marsch**, der; -[e]s (auf Karnevalssitzungen gespielter Marsch); **Narr|heit; När|rin; när|risch**
Nar|vik ['narvik] (norw. Hafenstadt)
Nar|wal ‹nord.› (Wal einer bestimmten Art)
[1]**Nar|ziss** ‹griech.› (in sein Bild verliebter schöner Jüngling der griech. Sage); [2]**Nar|ziss**, der; *Gen.* - *u.* -es, *Plur.* -e (jmd., der sich selbst bewundert u. liebt); **Nar|zis|se**, die; -, -n (eine Frühjahrsblume); **Nar|zis|sen|blü|te; Nar|ziss|mus**, der; - (krankhafte Verliebtheit in die eigene Person); **Nar|zisst**, der; -en, -en (↑R 126); **nar|ziss|tisch**
NASA, die; - (= National Aeronautics and Space Administration [ˌnɛʃ(ə)nəl ɛ:rəˈnɔ:tiks ənd ˈspe:s adminisˈtre:ʃ(ə)n]; Nationale Luft- und Raumfahrtbehörde der USA)
na|sal ‹lat.› (durch die Nase gesprochen, genäselt; zur Nase gehörend); **Na|sal**, der; -s, -e *u.* Na|sal|laut (*Sprachw.* mit Beteiligung des Nasenraumes od. durch die Nase gesprochener Laut, z. B. m, ng); **na|sa|lie|ren** ([einen Laut] durch die Nase aussprechen, näseln); **Na|sa|lie|rung; Na|sal‿laut** (*vgl.* Nasal), **...vo|kal** (Vokal mit nasaler Färbung, z. B. o in Bon [*franz.* bɔ̃:])
na|schen; du naschst
Näs|chen
Na|scher, *älter* **Nä|scher; Na|sche|rei** (wiederholtes Naschen *[nur Sing.]; auch für* Näscherei); **Nä|sche|rei** *meist Plur.* (*veraltend für* Süßigkeit); **Na|sche|rin**, *älter* **Nä|sche|rin; nasch|haft; Nasch|haf|tig|keit**, die; -; **Nasch‿kat|ze** (jmd., der gerne nascht), **...maul** (*derb svw.* Naschkatze), **...sucht** (die; -); **nasch|süch|tig; Nasch|werk**, das; -[e]s (*veraltet für* Süßigkeiten)
Na|se, die; -, -n; **na|se|lang** *vgl.* nasenlang; **nä|seln;** ich ...[e]le (↑R 16); **Na|sen‿bär, ...bein, ...blu|ten** (das; -s), **...du|sche, ...flü|gel, ...höh|le; na|sen|lang**, nas[e]lang *(ugs.)*; *nur in* alle nasenlang, alle naselang, alle naslang (sich in kurzen Abständen wiederholend); *vgl.* all; **Na|sen‿län|ge, ...laut** (*für* Nasal), **...loch; Na|sen-Ra|chen-Raum** (↑R 28); **Na|sen‿ring, ...rü|cken, ...schei|de|wand, ...schleim|haut, ...schmuck** *(Völkerk.)*, **...spie|gel** *(Med.)*, **...spit|ze, ...stü|ber, ...trop|fen, ...wur|zel; Na|se|rümp|fen**, das; -s; **na|se|rümp|fend**, *aber* (↑R 40): die Nase rümpfend; **na|se|weis; Na|se|weis**, der; -es, -e (*ugs. für* neugieriger Mensch); Herr, Jungfer Naseweis *(scherzh.)*; **nas|füh|ren;** ich nasführe; genasführt; zu nasführen; **Nas|horn** *Plur.* ...hörner; **Nas|horn‿kä|fer, ...vo|gel; ...na|sig** (z. B. langnasig); **...nä|sig** (z. B. hochnäsig)
Na|si-go|reng, *auch* **Na|si|go|reng**, das; -[s], -s ‹malai.› (indonesisches Reisgericht)
Na|si|rä|er, der; -s, - ‹hebr.› (*im alten Israel* Träger eines besonderen Gelübdes der Enthaltsamkeit)
nas|lang *vgl.* nasenlang
nass; nasser, *auch* nässer, nasseste, *auch* nässeste; sich nass machen; nass geschwitzt sein; **Nass**, das; -es (Wasser); gut Nass! (Gruß der Schwimmer)
[1]**Nas|sau** (Stadt a. d. Lahn; ehem. Herzogtum); [2]**Nas|sau** [*engl.* 'nɛsɔ:] (Hptst. der Bahamas); [1]**Nas|sau|er** (↑R 103); [2]**Nas|sau|er** (*ugs. für* jmd., der nassauert; *scherzh. für* Regenschauer); **nas|sau|ern** (*ugs. für* auf Kosten anderer leben); ich ...ere (↑R 16); **nas|sau|isch**
Näs|se, die; -; **näs|seln** (*veraltet, noch landsch. für* ein wenig nass sein, werden); es nässelt; **näs|sen;** du nässt (nässest), er nässt; du nässtest; genässt; nässe! *u.* näss!; **nass|fest;** nassfestes Papier; **nass|forsch** (*ugs. für* übertrieben forsch); **nass geschwitzt** *vgl.* nass; **Nass-in-Nass-Druck** *Plur.* ...drucke *(Druckw.)*; ↑R 28; **nass|kalt; näss|lich** (ein wenig feucht); **Nass‿ra|sie|rer, ...ra|sur**
Nass|schnee (↑R 136); **Nass|spinn|ver|fah|ren** (↑R 136; *Textiltechnik*)
Nass‿wä|sche, ...zel|le (*Bauw.* Raum, in dem Wasserleitungen liegen)
Nas|tie, die; - ‹griech.› (*Bot.* durch Reiz ausgelöste Bewegung von Teilen einer Pflanze)
Nas|tuch *Plur.* ...tücher (*südd. neben, schweiz. für* Taschentuch)
nas|zie|rend ‹lat.› (entstehend, im Werden begriffen)
Na|tal (Provinz der Republik Südafrika)
Na|ta|lie ['natali:, *auch* na'ta:li̯ə *u.* ...'li:] (w. Vorn.)
Na|ta|li|tät, die; - ‹lat.› (*Statistik* Geburtenhäufigkeit)
Na|tan *vgl.* Nathan
Na|ta|na|el *vgl.* Nathanael

Na|ta|scha (w. Vorn.)
Na|than, *ökum.* Na|tan (bibl. Prophet)
[1]**Na|tha|na|el** [...e:l, *auch* ...ɛl], *ökum.* Na|ta|na|el (Jünger Jesu); [2]**Na|tha|na|el** (m. Vorn.)
Na|ti|on, die; -, -en ‹lat.› (Staatsvolk); **na|ti|o|nal;** nationales Interesse; nationale Unabhängigkeit, Einigung, Kultur; (↑R 108): Nationale Front (*ehem. in der DDR* Zusammenschluss aller polit. Parteien u. Organisationen); Nationales Olympisches Komitee (*Abk.* NOK); **na|ti|o|nal|bewusst; Na|ti|o|nal‿be|wusst|sein, ...cha|rak|ter; na|ti|o|nal|de|mo|kra|tisch; Na|ti|o|nal‿denk|mal, ...dress** (*svw.* Nationaltrikot); **Na|ti|o|na|le,** das; -s, - (*österr. für* Personalangaben, Personenbeschreibung); **Na|ti|o|nal‿ein|kom|men, ...elf** (*vgl.* [3]Elf), **...epos** (↑R 132), **...far|ben** (*Plur.*), **...fei|er|tag, ...flag|ge, ...gar|de, ...ge|fühl** (das; -[e]s), **...ge|richt, ...ge|tränk, ...hei|ligtum, ...held, ...hym|ne; na|ti|o|na|li|sie|ren** (einbürgern; verstaatlichen); **Na|ti|o|na|li|sie|rung; Na|ti|o|na|lis|mus,** der; - (übertriebenes Nationalbewusstsein); **Na|ti|o|na|list,** der; -en, -en (↑R 126); **na|ti|o|na|lis|tisch; Na|ti|o|na|li|tät,** die; -, -en (Staatsangehörigkeit; nationale Minderheit); **Na|ti|o|na|li|tä|ten‿fra|ge** (*ohne Plur.*), **...po|li|tik, ...staat** (*Plur.* ...staaten; Mehr-, Vielvölkerstaat); **Na|ti|o|na|li|täts|prin|zip,** das; -s; **Na|ti|o|nal‿kir|che, ...kon|vent; na|ti|o|nal|li|be|ral; Na|ti|o|nal‿li|ga** (in der Schweiz die höchste Spielklasse im Fußball), **...li|te|ratur, ...mann|schaft, ...öko|nom** (↑R 132; Volkswirtschaftler), **...öko|no|mie** (↑R 132; Volkswirtschaftslehre), **...park, ...preis** (*früher* höchste Auszeichnung der DDR); **Na|ti|o|nal|preis|trä|ger** (*Abk.* NPT); **Na|ti|o|nal|rat** (Bez. von Volksvertretungen in der Schweiz u. in Österreich; *auch für* deren Mitglied); **Na|ti|o|nal‿so|zi|a|lis|mus** (*Abk.* NS), **...so|zi|a|list; na|ti|o|nal|so|zi|a|lis|tisch; Na|ti|o|nal‿spie|ler** (*Sport*), **...spie|le|rin, ...sport, ...sprache, ...staat** (*Plur.* ...staaten); **na|ti|o|nal|staat|lich; Na|ti|o|nal‿stolz, ...stra|ße** (*schweiz. für* Autobahn, Autostraße; *Zeichen* N 1, N 2 usw.), **...tanz, ...the|a|ter, ...tracht, ...tri|kot, ...ver|samm|lung**
Na|ti|vis|mus [...v...], der; - ‹lat.› (*Psych.* Lehre, nach der es angeborene Vorstellungen, Begriffe, Grundeinsichten usw. gibt); **Na|ti|vist,** der; -en, -en (↑R 126); **na|ti|vis|tisch; Na|ti|vi|tät,** die; -, -en (*Astrologie* Stand der Gestirne bei der Geburt eines Menschen)
NATO, *auch* **Na|to,** die; - ‹engl.; *Kurzwort für* North Atlantic Treaty Organization [nɔ:(r)θ ət'lɛntik 'tri:ti ɔ:(r)gənai'ze:ʃ(ə)n]› (Organisation der Signatarmächte des Nordatlantikpakts, Verteidigungsbündnis); **na|to|grün** (graugrün)
Nat|ri|um (↑R 130), das; -s ‹ägypt.› (chem. Element, Metall; *Zeichen* Na); **Nat|ri|um|chlo|rid,** das; -[e]s, -e (Kochsalz); **Nat|ron,** das; -s (*ugs. für* doppeltkohlensaures Natrium); **Nat|ron|lau|ge**
Nat|schal|nik (↑R 132), der; -s, -s ‹russ.› (*russ. Bez. für* Chef, Vorgesetzter)
Nat|té [na'te:], der; -[s], -s ‹franz.› (*Textilw.* feines, glänzendes Gewebe [mit Würfelmusterung])
Nat|ter, die; -, -n; **Nat|tern‿brut, ...ge|zücht** (*abwertend*)
Na|tur, die; -, -en ‹lat.›; *vgl. auch* in natura; **Na|tu|ral‿ab|ga|ben** (*Plur.*), **...be|zü|ge** (*Plur.*; Sachbezüge), **...ein|kom|men; Na|tu|ra|li|en** *Plur.* (Natur-, Landwirtschaftserzeugnisse); **Na|tu|ra|li|en‿ka|bi|nett** (naturwissenschaftliche Sammlung), **...samm|lung; Na|tu|ra|li|sa|ti|on,** die; -, -en (*svw.* Naturalisierung); **na|tu|ra|li|sie|ren; Na|tu|ra|li|sie|rung** (Einbürgerung, Aufnahme in den Staatsverband; allmähl. Anpassung von Pflanzen u. Tieren); **Na|tu|ra|lis|mus,** der; -, ...men (Naturglaube; *nur Sing.:* Wirklichkeitstreue; nach naturgetreuer Darstellung strebende Kunstrichtung); **Na|tu|ra|list,** der; -en, -en (↑R 126); **Na|tu|ra|lis|tin; na|tu|ra|lis|tisch; Na|tu|ral‿lohn, ...wirt|schaft; Na|tur‿apos|tel** (↑R 132), **...arzt; Na|tur|be|gabung; na|tur|be|las|sen; Na|tur‿be|o|bach|tung, ...be|schreibung; na|tur|blond; Na|tur‿bursche, ...darm, ...denk|mal, ...dün|ger; na|ture** [na'ty:r] ‹franz.›; Schnitzel nature (ohne Panade); **Na|tu|rell** [natu...], das; -s, -e (Veranlagung; Wesensart); **Na|tur‿er|eig|nis, ...er|schei|nung; na|tur|far|ben;** -es Holz; **Na|tur‿far|ben|druck** (Farbendruck nach fotografischen Farbaufnahmen), **...fa|ser, ...film, ...for|scher, ...for|sche|rin, ...freund, ...freun|din, ...gas** (*svw.* Erdgas), **...ge|fühl** (das; -[e]s); **na|tur‿ge|ge|ben, ...gemäß; Na|tur|ge|schich|te,** die; -; **na|tur|ge|schicht|lich; Na|tur|ge|setz; na|tur|ge|treu; na|tur|haft; Na|tur‿haus|halt, ...heil|kun|de** (die; -), **...heil|ver|fah|ren; na|tur|iden|tisch** (↑R 132), natürliche und naturidentische Aromastoffe; **Na|tu|ris|mus,** der; - (Freikörperkultur); **Na|tu|rist,** der; -en, -en (↑R 126); **Na|tur‿ka|ta|stro|phe, ...kind, ...kraft** (die), **...kun|de** (die; -); **na|tur|kund|lich; Na|tur|leh|re** (*veraltet für* physikalisch-chemischer Teil des naturwissenschaftlichen Unterrichts an Schulen); **Na|tur|lehr|pfad; na|tür|lich;** natürliche Geometrie, Gleichung (*Math.*); natürliche Person (*Ggs.* juristische Person); **na|tür|li|cher|wei|se; Na|tür|lich|keit,** die; -; **Na|tur|mensch,** der; **na|tur|nah; Na|tur‿nä|he, ...not|wen|dig|keit, ...park, ...phi|lo|so|phie, ...pro|dukt, ...recht** (das; -[e]s); **na|tur|rein; Na|tur‿re|li|gi|on, ...schau|spiel, ...schön|heit, ...schutz, ...schüt|zer; Na|tur|schutz‿ge|biet** (*Abk.* NSG), **...ge|setz, ...park; Na|tur‿sei|de, ...ta|lent, ...the|a|ter** (Freilichtbühne), **...treue, ...trieb; na|tur‿trüb, ...ver|bun|den, ...voll, ...wid|rig; Na|tur‿wis|sen|schaft** (*meist Plur.*), **...wis|sen|schaft|ler, ...wis|sen|schaft|le|rin; na|tur|wis|sen|schaft|lich;** der naturwissenschaftliche Zweig; **na|tur|wüch|sig; Na|tur|wüch|sig|keit,** die; -; **Na|tur‿wun|der, ...zer|stö|rung** (die; -), **...zu|stand** (der; -[e]s)
Nau|arch, der; -en, -en (↑R 126) ‹griech.› (Schiffsbefehlshaber im alten Griechenland)
Naue, die; -, -n *u., schweiz. nur,* **Nau|en,** der; -s, - (*südd. neben* Nachen, Kahn; *schweiz. für* großer [Last]kahn auf Seen)
'**nauf;** ↑R 13 (*landsch. für* hinauf)
Naum|burg (Stadt an der Saale); **Naum|bur|ger** (↑R 103); - Dom
Naup|li|us (↑R 130), der; -, ...ien [...iən] ‹griech.› (*Zool.* Krebstierlarve)
Na|u|ru (Inselrepublik im Stillen Ozean); **Na|u|ru|er; na|u|ru|isch**
'**naus;** ↑R 13 (*landsch. für* hinaus)
Nau|sea, die; - ‹griech.› (*Med.* Übelkeit; Seekrankheit)
Nau|si|kaa [...kaa] (phäakische Königstochter in der griech. Sage)
Nau|tik, die; - ‹griech.› (Schiff-

fahrtskunde); **Nau|ti|ker; Nau|ti|lus,** der; -, *Plur.* - *u.* -se (Tintenfisch); **nau|tisch;** nautisches Dreieck (*svw.* sphärisches Dreieck)

Na|va|ho, Na|va|jo [*beide* ˈnɛvəho:, *auch* naˈvaxo], der; -[s], -[s] (Angehöriger eines nordamerik. Indianerstammes)

Na|var|ra [...v...] (nordspan. Provinz; *auch für* hist. Provinz in den Westpyrenäen); **Na|var|re|se,** der; -n, -n (↑R 126); **Na|var|re|sin; na|var|re|sisch**

Na|vel [ˈna:vəl, *engl.* ˈne:vəl], die; -, -s ‹engl.› (*Kurzform von* Navelorange); **Na|vel|oran|ge** (↑R 132; kernlose Orange, die eine zweite kleine Frucht einschließt)

Na|vi|ga|ti|on [...v...], die; - ‹lat.› (Orts- u. Kursbestimmung von Schiffen u. Flugzeugen); **Na|vi|ga|ti|ons‿feh|ler, ...in|stru|men|te** *(Plur.)*, **...of|fi|zier** (für die Navigation verantwortlicher Offizier), **...schu|le** (Seefahrtsschule); **Na|vi|ga|tor,** der; -s, ...oren (*Flugw., Seew.* für die Navigation verantwortliches Besatzungsmitglied); **na|vi|ga|to|risch; na|vi|gie|ren** (ein Schiff od. Flugzeug führen)

na|xisch (von Naxos); **Na|xos** (griech. Insel)

[1]**Na|za|rä|er,** *ökum.* Na|zo|rä|er, der; -s ‹hebr.› (Beiname Jesu); [2]**Na|za|rä|er,** *ökum.* Na|zo|rä|er, der; -s, - (Mitglied der frühen Christengemeinden); [1]**Na|za|re|ner,** der; -s (Beiname Jesu); [2]**Na|za|re|ner,** der; -s, - (Angehöriger einer Künstlergruppe der Romantik); **Na|za|reth,** *ökum.* **Na|za|ret** (Stadt in Israel)

Na|zi, der; -s, -s (*kurz für* Nationalsozialist); **Na|zi‿bar|ba|rei, ...dik|ta|tur, ...herr|schaft** (die; -), **...par|tei, ...re|gime; Na|zis|mus,** der; - (*abwertend für* Nationalsozialismus); **na|zis|tisch** (*abwertend für* nationalsozialistisch); **Na|zi‿ver|bre|cher, ...zeit**

Na|zo|rä|er *vgl.* [1]Nazaräer *u.* [2]Nazaräer

Nb = *chem. Zeichen für* Niob

NB = notabene!

n. Br., nördl. Br. = nördlicher Breite; 50° n. Br.

N. C. = North Carolina; *vgl.* Nordkarolina

Nchf., Nachf. = Nachfolger

n. Chr. = nach Christus, nach Christo; *vgl.* Christus; **n. Chr. G.** = nach Christi Geburt; *vgl.* Christus

Nd = *chem. Zeichen für* Neodym

nd. = niederdeutsch

N. D. = North Dakota; *vgl.* Norddakota

N'Dja|me|na [ndʒaˈme:na, *auch* ...ˈna] (Hptst. von Tschad)

NDR = Norddeutscher Rundfunk

Ne = *chem. Zeichen für* Neon

ne!, nee! (*ugs. für* nein!)

'ne; ↑R 13 (*ugs. für* eine)

Ne|an|der|ta|ler ‹nach dem Fundort Neandertal bei Düsseldorf› (vorgeschichtlicher Mensch)

Ne|a|pel (ital. Stadt); *vgl.* Napoli; **Ne|a|pe|ler, Ne|ap|ler,** [1]**Ne|a|po|li|ta|ner** (↑R 103); [2]**Ne|a|po|li|ta|ner, Ne|a|po|li|ta|ner|schnit|te** (*österr. für* gefüllte Waffel); **ne|a|po|li|ta|nisch**

Ne|ark|tis, die; - ‹griech.› (tiergeographisches Gebiet, das Nordamerika u. Mexiko umfasst); **ne|ark|tisch;** -e Region

neb|bich ‹jidd.› (*ugs. für* nun, wenn schon!; was macht das!); **Neb|bich,** der; -s, -s (*ugs. für* Nichtsnutz; unbedeutender Mensch)

Ne|bel, der; -s, -; **Ne|bel‿bank** (*Plur.* ...bänke), **...bil|dung, ...bo|je** *(Seew.)*, **...de|cke, ...feld, ...fet|zen; ne|bel|grau; ne|bel|haft; Ne|bel|horn** *Plur.* ...hörner *(Seew.)*; **ne|be|lig** *vgl.* neblig; **Ne|bel‿kam|mer** *(Atomphysik)*, **...kap|pe** (Tarnkappe), **...ker|ze** *(Milit.)*, **...krä|he, ...lam|pe, ...mo|nat** *od.* **...mond** (*alte Bez. für* November); **ne|beln;** es nebelt; **Ne|bel|näs|sen,** das; -s (nieselndes Regnen bei dichtem Nebel); **Ne|bel‿schein|wer|fer, ...schlei|er, ...schluss|leuch|te, ...schwa|den, ...strei|fen; Ne|bel|lung,** Neb|lung, der; -s, -e (*alte Bez. für* November; *vgl.* Nebelmond); **ne|bel|ver|han|gen; Ne|bel|wand**

Ne|bel|wer|fer ‹nach dem Erfinder R. Nebel› (*Milit.* ein Raketenwerfer)

ne|ben; *Präp. mit Dat. u. Akk.:* neben dem Hause stehen, *aber* neben das Haus stellen; *als Adverb in Zusammensetzungen wie* nebenan, nebenbei u. a.; **Ne|ben‿ab|re|de** *(Rechtsspr.)*, **...ab|sicht, ...amt; ne|ben|amt|lich; ne|ben|an; Ne|ben‿an|schluss, ...ar|beit, ...aus|ga|be, ...aus|gang, ...bahn, ...be|deu|tung; ne|ben|bei;** nebenbei bemerkt; **Ne|ben|be|ruf; ne|ben|be|ruf|lich; Ne|ben‿be|schäf|ti|gung, ...buh|ler, ...buh|le|rin, ...buh|ler|schaft, ...ef|fekt; ne|ben|ei|nan|der;** *in Verbindung mit Verben immer getrennt geschrieben* (↑R 39): nebeneinander herunterrutschen, die Sachen nebeneinander legen; nebeneinander schalten; nebeneinander liegen, stehen, stellen, hergehen; *vgl.* nebeneinanderher; **Ne|ben|ei|nan|der** [*auch* ˈne:...], das; -s; **ne|ben|ei|nan|der|her;** sie haben nebeneinanderher gelebt; sie sind nebeneinanderher über die Wiese gegangen; **ne|ben|ei|nan|der schal|ten** *vgl.* nebeneinander; **Ne|ben|ei|nan|der|schal|tung; ne|ben|ei|nan|der sit|zen, ste|hen, stel|len** *vgl.* nebeneinander; **Ne|ben‿ein|künf|te** *(Plur.)*, **...er|schei|nung, ...er|werb; Ne|ben|er|werbs|land|wirt|schaft; Ne|ben‿er|zeug|nis, ...fach, ...fi|gur, ...fluss, ...form, ...frau, ...ge|dan|ke, ...ge|lass, ...ge|räusch, ...ge|stein** (*Bergmannsspr.* Gestein unmittelbar über u. unter dem Flöz), **...gleis, ...hand|lung, ...haus; ne|ben|her; ne|ben|her‿fah|ren, ...ge|hen, ...lau|fen; ne|ben|hin;** etwas nebenhin sagen; **Ne|ben‿höh|le** (an die Nasenhöhle angrenzender Hohlraum), **...job, ...kla|ge, ...klä|ger, ...klä|ge|rin, ...kos|ten** *(Plur.)*, **...kra|ter, ...kriegs|schau|platz, ...li|nie, ...mann** (*Plur.* ...männer *u.* ...leute), **...mensch** (der), **...me|tall, ...nie|re, ...nut|zung; ne|ben|ord|nen** *(Sprachw.)*; nebenordnende Konjunktionen; **Ne|ben‿ord|nung** *(Sprachw.)*, **...pro|dukt, ...raum, ...rol|le, ...sa|che; ne|ben|säch|lich; Ne|ben|säch|lich|keit; Ne|ben‿sai|son, ...satz** *(Sprachw.)*; **ne|ben|schal|ten** (*für* parallel schalten); **Ne|ben|schal|tung** (*für* Parallelschaltung); **Ne|ben‿spie|ler, ...spie|le|rin; ne|ben|ste|hend;** (↑R 48:) Nebenstehendes, das Nebenstehende bitte vergleichen; im Nebenstehenden (*Amtsspr.* hierneben); **Ne|ben‿stel|le, ...stra|ße, ...stre|cke, ...tä|tig|keit, ...tisch, ...ton** (*Plur.* ...töne); **ne|ben|to|nig; Ne|ben‿ver|dienst** (der), **...weg, ...wir|kung, ...woh|nung, ...zim|mer, ...zweck**

neb|lig, ne|be|lig; **Neb|lung** *vgl.* Nebelung

Nebr. = Nebraska

Neb|ras|ka (↑R 130; Staat in den USA; *Abk.* Nebr.)

nebst; *Präp. mit Dat. (veraltend):* nebst seinem Hunde; **nebst|bei** (*österr. neben* nebenbei)

Ne|bu|kad|ne|zar, *ökum.* **Ne|bu|kad|nez|zar** [...ˈnɛtsar] (Name babylon. Könige); *vgl.* Nabucco

ne|bu|los, ne|bu|lös ‹lat.› (unklar, verschwommen)
Ne|ces|saire [nesɛ'sɛ:r], *auch* Nes|ses|sär (↑R 33), das; -s, -s ‹franz.› ([Reise]behältnis für Toiletten-, Nähutensilien u. a.)
Ne|cho ['ne:ço, *auch* 'nɛço] (ägypt. Pharao)
n-Eck (↑R 25; *Math.*)
Neck, der; -en, -en; ↑R 126 (ein Wassergeist)
Ne|ckar, der; -s (rechter Nebenfluss des Rheins); **Ne|ckar|sulm** (Stadt an der Mündung der Sulm in den Neckar)
ne|cken; Ne|cke|rei
Ne|cking, das; -[s], -s ‹amerik.› (Austausch von Zärtlichkeiten)
ne|ckisch
Ned|bal (tschech. Komponist)
nee! *vgl.* ne!
Neer, die; -, -en (*nordd. für* Wasserstrudel mit starker Gegenströmung); **Neer|strom**
Nef|fe, der; -n, -n (↑R 126)
Ne|ga|ti|on, die; -, -en ‹lat.› (Verneinung, Verwerfung einer Aussage; Verneinungswort, z. B. „nicht"); **ne|ga|tiv** [*auch* 'nɛ... *od.* ...'ti:f] (verneinend; ergebnislos; *Math.* kleiner als Null; *Elektrotechnik: Ggs. zu* positiv); **Ne|ga|tiv,** das; -s, -e [...və] (*Fotogr.* Gegen-, Kehrbild); **Ne|ga|tiv|bild; Ne|ga|ti|ve** [...və], die; -, -n (*veraltet für* Verneinung); **Ne|ga|tiv|image** [*auch* 'nɛ...] (↑R 132); **Ne|ga|ti|vi|tät** [...v...], die; -
Ne|geb [*auch* 'nɛgɛp], der; -, *auch* die; - (Wüstenlandschaft im Süden Israels)
Ne|ger, der; -s, - ‹lat.› *(auch abwertend);* **Ne|ger|haar; Ne|ge|rin; ne|ge|risch; Ne|ger‿kuss** (schokoladeüberzogenes Schaumgebäck), **...skla|ve**
Ne|gev [*auch* 'nɛgɛf] *vgl.* Negeb
ne|gie|ren ‹lat.› (verneinen; bestreiten); **Ne|gie|rung**
Neg|li|gé *vgl.* Negligee; **neg|li|geant** [negli'ʒant] (*veraltend für* nachlässig); **Neg|li|gee,** *auch* Neg|li|gé [negli'ʒe:] (↑R 33 *u.* 130), das; -s, -s ‹franz.› (Hauskleid; leichter Morgenmantel); **neg|li|gen|te** [...'dʒɛntə] ‹ital.› (*Musik* flüchtig, darüber hinhuschend); **neg|li|gie|ren** [...'ʒi:...] (*veraltend für* vernachlässigen)
neg|rid ‹lat.› (↑R 130); negrider Rassenkreis *(Anthropol.; veraltend);* **Neg|ri|de,** der *u.* die; -n, -n (↑R 5 ff.); **Neg|ri|to,** der; -[s], -[s] (zwergwüchsiger u. dunkelhäutiger Mensch [auf den Philippinen]); **Né|gri|tude** [negri'ty:d], die; - ‹franz.› (aus der Rückbesinnung auf afrikanische Traditionen entstandene Forderung nach kultureller Eigenständigkeit der Französisch sprechenden Länder Afrikas); **neg|ro|id** (den Negriden ähnlich); **Neg|ro|i|de,** der *u.* die; -n, -n (↑R 5 ff.); **Neg|ro|spi|ri|tu|al** ['ni:gro:'spiritjuəl], das, *auch* der; -s, -s ‹lat.-engl.-amerik.› (geistl. Lied der Schwarzen im Süden der USA)
Ne|gus, der; -, *Plur.* - *u.* -se (*früher* Kaiser von Äthiopien)
Ne|he|mia, *auch* **Ne|he|mi|as** (Gestalt des A. T.)
neh|men; du nimmst, er nimmt; ich nahm, du nahmst; du nähmest; genommen; nimm!; ich nehme es an mich; (↑R 50:) Geben (*auch* geben) ist seliger denn Nehmen (*auch* nehmen); **Neh|mer** (*auch für* Käufer); **Neh|mer|qua|li|tä|ten** *Plur. (Boxen)*
Neh|ru (indischer Staatsmann)
Neh|rung, die; -, -en (schmale Landzunge)
Neid, der; -[e]s; **nei|den; Nei|der; neid|er|füllt** (↑R 40); **Neid|ham|mel** (*ugs. für* neidischer Mensch); **Neid|hard,** [1]**Neid|hart** (m. Vorn.); [2]**Neid|hart,** der; -[e]s, -e (*veraltet für* Neider); **nei|dig** (*veraltet für* beneidend); jmdm. neidig sein; **nei|disch; neid|los; Neid|lo|sig|keit,** die; -
Neid|na|gel (*Nebenform von* Niednagel)
neid|voll
Nei|ge, die; -, -n; zur Neige gehen; **nei|gen;** sich -; **Nei|gung; Nei|gungs‿ehe** (↑R 132), **...win|kel**
nein; nein, nein; (↑R 49:) das Ja und das Nein; Nein sagen, *auch* nein sagen; mit [einem] Nein antworten; mit Nein stimmen; das ist die Folge seines Neins
'nein; ↑R 13 (*landsch. für* hinein)
Nein|sa|gen, das; -s; **Nein|sa|ger; Nein|stim|me**
Nei|ße, die; - (ein Flussname); die Oder-Neiße-Grenze (↑R 105)
Nek|ro|bi|o|se (↑R 130), die; - ‹griech.› (*Biol.* langsames Absterben einzelner Zellen); **Nek|ro|log,** der; -[e]s, -e (Nachruf); **Nek|ro|lo|gi|um,** das; -s, ...ien [...iən] (Totenverzeichnis in Klöstern und Stiften); **Nek|ro|mant,** der; -en, -en; ↑R 126 (Toten-, Geisterbeschwörer, bes. des Altertums); **Nek|ro|man|tie,** die; - (Toten-, Geisterbeschwörung); **Nek|ro|phi|lie,** die; - (*Psych.* auf Leichen gerichteter Sexualtrieb); **Nek|ro|po|le,** die; -, ...polen (Totenstadt, Gräberfeld alter Zeit); **Nek|rop|sie,** die; -, ...ien (Leichenbesichtigung, -öffnung); **Nek|ro|se,** die; -, -n (*Med.* das Absterben von Geweben, Organen od. Organteilen); **Nek|ro|sper|mie,** die; - (*Med.* das Abgestorbensein od. die Funktionsunfähigkeit der männl. Samenzellen; Zeugungsunfähigkeit); **nek|ro|tisch** (*Med.* abgestorben)
Nek|tar, der; -s, -e ‹griech.› (zuckerhaltige Blütenabsonderung; *nur Sing.: griech. Mythol.* ewige Jugend spendender Göttertrank); **Nek|ta|ri|ne,** die; -, -n (eine Pfirsichart mit glatthäutigen Früchten); **Nek|ta|ri|um,** das; -s, ...ien [...iən] (Nektardrüse bei Blütenpflanzen)
Nek|ton, das; -s ‹griech.› (*Biol.* die Gesamtheit der im Wasser sich aktiv bewegenden Tiere); **nek|to|nisch**
Nel|ke, die; -, -n (eine Blume; ein Gewürz); **Nel|ken‿öl, ...strauß** (*Plur.* ...sträuße), **...wurz** (eine Pflanze)
Nell, das; -s, - (*schweiz. für* Trumpfneun beim Jass)
Nel|li, Nel|ly (w. Vorn.)
[1]**Nel|son** ['nɛlzən, *engl.* 'nɛls(ə)n] (engl. Admiral)
[2]**Nel|son,** der; -[s], -[s] ‹engl.› (Ringergriff)
Ne|ma|to|de, der; -n, -n (↑R 126) *meist Plur.* ‹griech.› (*Zool.* Fadenwurm)
ne|me|isch (aus Nemea [Tal in Argolis]); *aber* (↑R 108): der Nemeische Löwe *(griech. Mythologie)*
[1]**Ne|me|sis** (griech. Rachegöttin); [2]**Ne|me|sis,** die; - ‹griech.› (ausgleichende Gerechtigkeit)
NE-Me|tall [ɛn'e:...] (↑R 26; *kurz für* Nichteisenmetall)
'nen; ↑R 13 (*ugs. für* einen)
Ne|na (w. Vorn.)
Nenn|be|trag; nen|nen; du nanntest; *selten* du nenntest; genannt; nenn[e]!; er nannte ihn einen Dummkopf; **nen|nens|wert; Nen|ner** *(Math.);* **Nenn|form** (*für* Infinitiv); **Nenn|form|satz** (*für* Infinitivsatz); **Nenn‿leis|tung** *(Technik),* **...on|kel, ...tan|te; Nen|nung; Nenn‿wert, ...wort** (*Plur.* ...wörter; *für* Nomen)
Nen|ze, der; -n, -n; ↑R 126 (Angehöriger eines Volkes im Nordwesten Sibiriens); *vgl.* Samojede
ne|o... ‹griech.› (neu...); **Ne|o...** (Neu...); **Ne|o|dym,** das; -s (chem. Element, Metall; *Zeichen* Nd); **Ne|o‿fa|schis|mus** (*Bez. für* die faschist. Bestrebungen nach dem 2. Weltkrieg), **...fa|schist** (↑R 126); **ne|o|fa|schis-**

tisch; Ne|o|gen, das; -s (*Geol.* Jungtertiär); **Ne|o‿klas|si|zis|mus, ...ko|lo|ni|a|lis|mus, ...li|be|ra|lis|mus** *(Wirtsch.)*; **Ne|o|li|thi|kum,** das; -s (*Urgesch.* Jungsteinzeit); **ne|o|li|thisch** (jungsteinzeitlich); **Ne|o|lo|gis|mus,** der; -, ...men (sprachl. Neubildung); **Ne|o|mar|xis|mus,** der; -

Ne|on, das; -s (chem. Element, Edelgas; *Zeichen* Ne)

Ne|o‿na|zi, ...na|zis|mus, ...na|zist; ne|o|na|zis|tisch

Ne|on‿fisch, ...lam|pe, ...licht (*Plur.* ...lichter), **...re|kla|me, ...röh|re**

Ne|o|phyt, der; -en, -en; ↑R 126 (erwachsener Neugetaufter im Urchristentum); **Ne|o|plas|ma** (*Med.* [bösartige] Geschwulst); **Ne|o|po|si|ti|vis|mus; Ne|o|te|nie,** die; - (*Med.* unvollkommener Entwicklungszustand eines Organs; *Biol.* Eintritt der Geschlechtsreife im Larvenstadium); **ne|o|tro|pisch** (den Tropen der Neuen Welt angehörend); neotropische Region (tiergeographisches Gebiet, das Mittel- u. Südamerika umfasst); **Ne|o|vi|ta|lis|mus** (Lehre von den Eigengesetzlichkeiten des Lebendigen); **Ne|o|zo|i|kum,** das; -s (*svw.* Känozoikum); **ne|o|zo|isch** (*svw.* känozoisch)

Ne|pal [*auch* ne'pa:l] (Himalajastaat); **Ne|pa|ler** *vgl.* Nepalese; **Ne|pa|le|se,** der; -n, -n (↑R 126), *auch* Ne|pa|ler; **ne|pa|le|sisch,** *auch* **ne|pa|lisch**

Ne|per, das; -s, - ‹nach dem schott. Mathematiker J. Napier› (eine physikalische Maßeinheit; *Abk.* Np)

Ne|phe|lin, der; -s, -e ‹griech.› (ein Mineral); **Ne|phe|lo|met|rie** (↑R 130), die; - (*Chemie* Messung der Trübung von Flüssigkeiten od. Gasen); **Ne|pho|graph,** der; -en, -en; ↑R 126 (*Meteor.* Gerät, das die verschiedenen Arten u. die Dichte der Bewölkung fotogr. aufzeichnet); **Ne|pho|skop,** das; -s, -e (Gerät zur Bestimmung der Zugrichtung u. -geschwindigkeit von Wolken)

Neph|ral|gie (↑R 132), die; -, ...ien ‹griech.› (*Med.* Nierenschmerzen); **Neph|rit,** der; -s, -e (ein Mineral); **Neph|ri|tis,** die; -, ...iti|den (*Med.* Nierenentzündung); **Neph|ro|se,** die; -, -n (Nierenerkrankung mit Gewebeschädigung)

Ne|po|muk (m. Vorn.)

Ne|po|tis|mus, der; - ‹lat.› (Vetternwirtschaft)

Nepp, der; -s; **nep|pen** (durch weit überhöhte Preisforderungen übervorteilen); **Nep|per; Nep|pe|rei; Nepp|lo|kal**

[1]**Nep|tun** (röm. Gott des Meeres); [2]**Nep|tun,** der; -s (ein Planet); **nep|tu|nisch** (durch Einwirkung des Wassers entstanden); -e Gesteine (*veraltet für* Sedimentgesteine); **Nep|tu|ni|um,** das; -s (chem. Element, ein Transuran; *Zeichen* Np)

Ne|re|i|de, die; -, -n *meist Plur.*; (meerbewohnende Tochter des Nereus); **Ne|reus** [*auch* ne:'rɔys] (griech. Meergott)

Nerf|ling (ein Fisch)

Nernst|lam|pe; ↑R 95 ‹nach dem dt. Physiker u. Chemiker›

Ne|ro (röm. Kaiser)

Ne|ro|li|öl, das; -[e]s ‹ital.; dt.› (Pomeranzenblütenöl)

ne|ro|nisch ‹*zu* Nero›; neronische Christenverfolgung (↑R 94)

Ner|thus (germ. Göttin)

Ne|ru|da, Pablo (chilen. Lyriker)

Nerv [nɛrf], der; -s, -en ‹lat.›

Ner|va [...va] (röm. Kaiser)

Ner|va|tur [...v...], die; -, -en ‹lat.› (Aderung des Blattes, der Insektenflügel); **ner|ven** [...f...] (*ugs. für* nervlich strapazieren; belästigen); **Ner|ven‿an|span|nung, ...arzt, ...ärz|tin; ner|ven‿auf|peit|schend, ...auf|rei|bend; Ner|ven‿bahn, ...be|las|tung; ner|ven|be|ru|hi|gend** (↑R 40); **Ner|ven‿be|ru|hi|gungs|mit|tel, ...bün|del, ...chi|rur|gie** (die; -), **...ent|zün|dung, ...gas, ...gift** (das), **...heil|an|stalt, ...kit|zel, ...kli|nik, ...kos|tüm** (das; -s; *ugs. scherzh.*), **...kraft** (die); **ner|ven|krank; Ner|ven‿krank|heit, ...krieg, ...kri|se, ...lei|den; ner|ven|lei|dend; Ner|ven‿nah|rung, ...pro|be, ...sa|che** (*ugs.; meist in* das ist -), **...sä|ge** *(ugs.)*, **...schmerz** *(meist Plur.)*, **...schock** (der); **ner|ven|schwach; Ner|ven|schwä|che,** die; -; **ner|ven|stark; Ner|ven‿stär|ke** (die; -), **...sys|tem** (vegetatives -), **...zu|sam|men|bruch; ner|vig** [...f..., *auch* ...v...] (sehnig, kräftig); **nerv|lich** [...f...] (das Nervensystem betreffend); **ner|vös** [...v...] (nervenschwach; unruhig, gereizt; *Med. svw.* nervlich); **Ner|vo|si|tät,** die; -; **nerv|tö|tend; Ner|vus Re|rum** [...v...], der; - - (Hauptsache; *scherzh. für* Geld)

Nerz, der; -es, -e ‹slaw.› (Pelz[tier]); **Nerz‿farm, ...fell, ...kra|gen, ...man|tel, ...sto|la**

Nes|ca|fé ®, der; -s, -s ‹nach der schweiz. Firma Nestlé› (löslicher Kaffeeextrakt)

Nes|chi ['nɛski, *auch* 'nɛsçi], das *od.* die; - ‹arab.› (arab. Schreibschrift)

[1]**Nes|sel,** die; -, -n; [2]**Nes|sel,** der; -s, - (ein Gewebe); **Nes|sel‿aus|schlag, ...fa|den** *(Zool.)*, **...fie|ber, ...pflan|ze, ...qual|le, ...stoff, ...sucht** (die; -), **...tier**

Nes|ses|sär *eindeutschende Schreibung für* Necessaire

Nes|sus|ge|wand; ↑R 95 ‹nach dem vergifteten Gewand des Herakles in der griech. Sage› (Verderben bringende Gabe)

Nest, das; -[e]s, -er; **Nest|bau** *Plur.* ...bauten; **Nest|be|schmut|zer** (*abwertend für* jmd., der schlecht über das eigene Land u. Ä. spricht); **Nest|chen**

Nes|tel, die; -, -n (*landsch. für* Schnur); **nes|teln;** ich ...[e]le (↑R 16)

Nes|ter|chen *Plur.*; **Nest‿flüch|ter, ...häk|chen** (das jüngste Kind in der Familie), **...ho|cker, ...jun|ge** (*vgl.* [2]Junge); **Nest|ling** (noch nicht flügger Vogel)

[1]**Nes|tor** (greiser König der griech. Sage); [2]**Nes|tor,** der; -s, ...oren (ältester [anerkannter] Vertreter einer bestimmten Wissenschaft, eines künstlerischen Fachs)

Nes|to|ri|a|ner, der; -s, - (Anhänger des Nestorius); **Nes|to|ri|a|nis|mus,** der; - (Lehre des Nestorius); **Nes|to|ri|us** (Patriarch von Konstantinopel)

Nest|roy ['nɛstrɔy] (↑R 130; österr. Bühnendichter)

Nest|treue; nest|warm; -e Eier; **Nest|wär|me,** die; -

nett

Nett|chen, Net|te (w. Vorn.)

net|ter|wei|se *(ugs.)*; **Net|tig|keit** ‹*zu* nett›; **net|to** ‹ital.› (rein, nach Abzug der Verpackung, der Unkosten, der Steuern u. Ä.); **Net|to‿ein|kom|men, ...er|trag, ...ge|wicht, ...ge|winn, ...lohn, ...mas|se** (die; -), **...preis** (*vgl.* [2]Preis), **...raum|zahl** (*Abk.* NRZ), **...re|gis|ter|ton|ne** (*früher für* Nettoraumzahl; *Abk.* NRT), **...ver|dienst** (der)

Netz, das; -es, -e; **Netz|an|schluss; Netz|an|schluss|ge|rät** *(Rundfunk)*; **netz|ar|tig; Netz|ball** *(Sport)*

net|zen (*geh. für* nass machen, befeuchten); du netzt

Netz|flüg|ler, der; -s, - (*für* Neuropteren); **netz|för|mig; Netz‿ge|rät** (*kurz für* Netzanschlussgerät), **...gleich|rich|ter** *(Rundfunk)*, **...haut; Netz|haut‿ab|lö-**

sung, ...ent|zün|dung; Netz‿hemd, ...kar|te *(Verkehrsw.)*
Netz|mit|tel, das (Stoff, der die Oberflächenspannung von Flüssigkeiten verringert)
Netz|plan *(Wirtsch.);* **Netz|plan|tech|nik,** die; - *(Wirtsch.);* **Netz‿rol|ler** *(bes. Tennis),* **...span|nung, ...spie|ler** *(Sport),* **...spie|le|rin, ...ste|cker, ...werk**
neu; neuer, neu[e]ste; neu[e]stens; (↑R 47:) etwas auf neu herrichten; neu für alt *(Kaufmannsspr.);* seit neuestem; von neuem; sie hat es aufs Neue (wieder) versucht; er ist aufs Neue (auf Neuerungen) erpicht; das Alte und das Neue; etwas, nichts, allerlei Neues; auf ein Neues. *Kleinschreibung in mehrteiligen Fügungen* (↑R 108:) das neue Jahr fängt gut an; ein gutes neues Jahr! (Glückwunsch); die neue Armut; die neue Linke (neomarxistische, im Ggs. zu den traditionellen sozialistischen u. kommunistischen Parteien stehende philosophische u. politische Richtung); die neue Mathematik (auf der formalen Logik u. der Mengenlehre basierende Mathematik); die neuen Medien (z. B. Kabelfernsehen, Bildschirmtext); die neuen Bundesländer; neue Sprachen. *Großschreibung in Namen* (↑R 108:) der Neue Bund *(christl. Rel.);* das Neue Forum (1989 in der damaligen DDR gegründete Bürgerbewegung; *Abk.* NF); die Neue Welt (Amerika); das Neue Testament (*Abk.* N. T.). *In Verbindung mit Verben und Partizipien gilt in der Regel Getrenntschreibung* (↑R 39 *u.* 40): z. B. neu bauen, neu bearbeiten, neu hinzukommen; neu entstehende Siedlungen; das Geschäft ist neu eröffnet; das neu eröffnete Zweiggeschäft; das [völlig] neu bearbeitete Werk; die neu geschaffenen Anlagen; die neu vermählten Ehepaare; *vgl. aber* neugeboren
Neu‿an|fang, ...an|fer|ti|gung, ...an|kömm|ling, ...an|la|ge, ...an|schaf|fung; neu|apos|to|lisch (↑R 132); *aber* (↑R 56:) die Neuapostolische Gemeinde (eine christl. Religionsgemeinschaft); **neu|ar|tig; Neu|ar|tig|keit,** die; -; **Neu‿auf|la|ge, ...auf|nah|me, ...aus|ga|be; Neu|bau** *Plur.* ...bauten; **Neu|bau‿vier|tel, ...woh|nung; neu be|ar|bei|tet** *vgl.* neu; **Neu‿be|ar|bei|tung, ...be|ginn; Neu|be|kehr|te,** der *u.* die; -n, -n (↑R 5 ff.); **Neu‿be|set|zung, ...bil|dung**
Neu|bran|den|burg (Stadt in Mecklenburg-Vorpommern)
Neu|braun|schweig (kanad. Provinz)
Neu|bür|ger
Neu|châ|tel [nøʃaˈtɛl] (*franz. Name von* Neuenburg)
Neu-De|lhi (südl. Stadtteil von Delhi, Regierungssitz der Republik Indien)
neu|deutsch; Neu|druck (*Plur.* ...drucke)
Neue, die; - (*Jägerspr.* frisch gefallener Schnee)
Neu‿ein|stel|lung, ...ein|stu|die|rung
Neue Ker|ze (bis 1948 dt. Lichtstärkeeinheit [*heute* Candela])
Neu|en|ahr, Bad (Stadt an der Ahr)
Neu|en|burg (Kanton u. Stadt in der Schweiz; *franz.* Neuchâtel); **Neu|en|bur|ger** (↑R 103); **Neu|en|bur|ger See,** der; - -s
Neu|eng|land (die nordöstl. Staaten der USA)
neu|eng|lisch; *vgl.* deutsch
Neu‿ent|de|ckung, ...ent|wick|lung
neu|er|dings (kürzlich; *südd., österr., schweiz. für* von neuem);
Neu|e|rer; Neu|e|rer|be|we|gung, die; - *(ehem. in der DDR);* **neu|er|lich** (von neuem); **neu|ern** (*veraltend für* erneuern); ich ...ere (↑R 16); **neu er|öff|net** *vgl.* neu; **Neu‿er|öff|nung, ...er|schei|nung; Neu|e|rung; Neu|e|rungs|sucht,** die; -; **Neu‿er|werb, ...er|wer|bung; neu[|e]s|tens** *(selten)*
Neu‿fas|sung, ...fest|set|zung; neu|fran|zö|sisch; *vgl.* deutsch
Neu|fund|land (kanad. Provinz); **Neu|fund|län|der** (Bewohner Neufundlands; *auch* eine Hunderasse); **neu|fund|län|disch**
neu|ge|bo|ren (↑R 40); die neugeborenen Kinder; sich wie neugeboren fühlen; **Neu|ge|bo|re|ne,** das; -n, -n; ↑R 5 ff. (Säugling); **Neu|ge|burt; neu ge|schaf|fen** *vgl.* neu; **Neu‿ge|stal|tung, ...ge|würz** (das; -es; *österr. für* Piment); **Neu|gier, Neu|gier|de,** die; -; **neu|gie|rig; Neu‿glie|de|rung, ...go|tik; Neu|grad** *vgl.* Gon
neu|grie|chisch; *vgl.* deutsch; **Neu|grie|chisch,** das; -[s] (Sprache); *vgl.* Deutsch; **Neu|grie|chi|sche,** das; -n; *vgl.* Deutsche, das
Neu|grün|dung
Neu|gui|nea [...gi...]; ↑R 105 (Insel nördl. von Australien); **Neu|gui|ne|er; Neu|gui|ne|e|rin; neu|gui|ne|isch**
neu|heb|rä|isch; *vgl.* deutsch; **Neu|heb|rä|isch,** das; -[s] (Sprache); *vgl.* Deutsch; **Neu|heb|rä|i|sche,** das; -n; *vgl.* Deutsche, das; *vgl.* Iwrith
Neu|he|ge|li|a|ner; neu|he|ge|li|a|nisch; Neu|he|ge|li|a|nis|mus, der; -
Neu|heit; neu|hoch|deutsch (*Abk.* nhd.); *vgl.* deutsch; **Neu|hoch|deutsch,** das; -[s] (Sprache); *vgl.* Deutsch; **Neu|hoch|deut|sche,** das; -n; *vgl.* Deutsche, das; **Neu|hu|ma|nis|mus; Neu|ig|keit; Neu|in|sze|nie|rung; Neu|jahr; Neu|jahrs‿an|spra|che, ...bot|schaft, ...fest, ...glück|wunsch, ...gruß, ...kar|te, ...tag, ...wunsch**
Neu|ka|le|do|ni|en [...i̯ən] (Inselgruppe östlich von Australien)
Neu‿kan|ti|a|ner, ...kan|ti|a|nis|mus (der; -; philos. Schule), **...kauf** *(Kaufmannsspr.),* **...klas|si|zis|mus**
Neu|kölln (Stadtteil von Berlin)
Neu|kon|struk|ti|on; Neu|land, das; -[e]s
Neu|la|tein; neu|la|tei|nisch (*Abk.* nlat.); *vgl.* deutsch
neu|lich; Neu|ling
Neu|mark, die; - (hist. Landschaft in der Mark Brandenburg)
Neu|me, die; -, -n *meist Plur.* ⟨griech.⟩ (mittelalterl. Notenzeichen)
neu|mo|disch
Neu|mond, der; -[e]s
neun, *ugs.* neu|ne; alle neun[e]!; wir sind zu neunen *od.* zu neunt; *vgl.* acht; **Neun,** die; -, -en (Ziffer, Zahl); *vgl.* [1]Acht; **Neun|au|ge** (ein Fisch); **neun‿bän|dig, ...eckig** (↑R 132); **neun|ein|halb,** neun|und|ein|halb; **Neu|ner** *(ugs.);* einen Neuner schieben (beim Kegeln); *vgl.* Achter; **neu|ner|lei; neun|fach; Neun|fa|che,** das; -n; *vgl.* Achtfache; **neun|hun|dert; neun|mal;** *vgl.* achtmal; **neun|ma|lig; neun|mal|klug** (*ugs. für* überklug); **neun|schwän|zig;** *in* die -e Katze (*Seemannsspr.* Peitsche mit neun Riemen); **neun‿stel|lig, ...stö|ckig, ...stün|dig; neunt;** *vgl.* neun; **neun|tä|gig; neun|tau|send; neun|te;** *vgl.* achte; **neun|tel;** *vgl.* achtel; **Neun|tel,** das, *schweiz. meist* der; -s, -; *vgl.* Achtel; **neun|tens; Neun|tö|ter** (ein Vogel); **neun|[und|]ein|halb; neun|und|zwan|zig;** *vgl.* acht; **neun|zehn;** *vgl.* acht; **neun|zig** usw. *vgl.* achtzig usw.
Neu‿ord|nung, ...or|ga|ni|sa|ti|on, ...ori|en|tie|rung (↑R 132)

Neu-phi|lo|lo|ge, ...phi|lo|lo|gie; neu|phi|lo|lo|gisch; Neu-pla|to|ni|ker, ...pla|to|nis|mus (der; -), **...prä|gung, ...preis**

neu|r... (↑R 132) *vgl.* neuro...; **Neu|r...** *vgl.* Neuro...; **Neu|ral|gie,** die; -, ...ien ‹griech.› (*Med.* in Anfällen auftretender Nervenschmerz); **Neu|ral|gi|ker** (an Neuralgie Leidender); **neu|ral|gisch; Neu|ras|the|nie,** die; -, ...ien (*Med.* krankhafte Übererregbarkeit, Nervenschwäche); **Neu|ras|the|ni|ker** (an Nervenschwäche Leidender); **neu|ras|the|nisch**

Neu|re|ge|lung, Neu|reg|lung; neu|reich; Neu|rei|che, der *u.* die; -n, -n (↑R 5ff.)

Neu|ries (Papiermaß; 1 000 Bogen)

Neu|rin, das; -s ‹griech.› (starkes Fäulnisgift); **Neu|ri|tis,** die; -, ...itiden (*Med.* Nervenentzündung); **neu|ro...,** *vor Vokalen* neu|r... (↑R 132; nerven...); **Neu|ro...,** *vor Vokalen* Neu|r... (Nerven...); **Neu|ro|bi|o|lo|gie,** die; -; **Neu|ro|chi|rur|gie,** die; - (Chirurgie des Nervensystems); **Neu|ro|der|mi|tis,** die; -, ...itiden (entzündliche Hauterkrankung); **neu|ro|gen** (*Med.* von den Nerven ausgehend); **Neu|ro|lo|ge,** der; -n, -n; ↑R 126 (Nervenarzt); **Neu|ro|lo|gie,** die; - (Lehre von den Nerven und ihren Erkrankungen); **Neu|ro|lo|gin; neu|ro|lo|gisch; Neu|rom,** das; -s, -e (*Med.* Nervenfasergeschwulst)

Neu-ro|man|tik, ...ro|man|ti|ker; neu|ro|man|tisch

Neu|ron, das; -s, *Plur.* ...one, *auch* ...onen ‹griech.› (*Med.* Nervenzelle); **neu|ro|nal; Neu|ro|pa|thie,** die; -, ...ien (*Med.* Nervenleiden, nervöse Veranlagung); **neu|ro|pa|thisch; Neu|ro|pa|tho|lo|gie,** die; - (Lehre von den Nervenkrankheiten); **Neu|rop|te|ren** (↑R 132) *Plur.* (*Zool.* Netzflügler); **Neu|ro|se,** die; -, -n (*Med., Psych.* psychische Störung); **Neu|ro|ti|ker** (an Neurose Leidender); **Neu|ro|ti|ke|rin; neu|ro|tisch; Neu|ro|to|mie,** die; -, ...ien (*Med.* Nervendurchtrennung)

Neu|rup|pin (Stadt in Brandenburg); **Neu|rup|pi|ner** (↑R 103); - Bilderbogen; **neu|rup|pi|nisch**

Neu-satz *(Druckw.),* **...schnee**

Neu|scho|las|tik (Erneuerung der Scholastik; *vgl. d.*)

Neu|schöp|fung

Neu|schott|land (kanad. Prov.)

Neu|schwan|stein (Schloss König Ludwigs II. von Bayern)

Neu|see|land; ↑R 105 (Inselgruppe u. Staat im Pazifischen Ozean); **Neu|see|län|der** (↑R 103); **Neu|see|län|de|rin; neu|see|län|disch**

Neu|siedl am See (österr. Stadt); **Neu|sied|ler See,** der; - -s (in Österreich u. Ungarn)

Neu|sil|ber (eine Legierung); **neu|sil|bern;** -e Uhr; **Neu|sprach|ler** (Lehrer, Kenner der neueren Sprachen); **neu|sprach|lich;** -er Unterricht, Zweig

Neuss, *bis 1970* **Neuß** (Stadt am Niederrhein); **Neus|ser**

neu|s|tens *vgl.* neuestens

Neu|stre|litz (Stadt in Mecklenburg)

Neust|ri|en (↑R 130; alter Name für das westliche Frankenreich)

Neu|struk|tu|rie|rung

Neu|süd|wales [...we:ls]; ↑R 105 (Gliedstaat des Australischen Bundes)

Neu|tes|ta|ment|ler; neu|tes|ta|ment|lich; Neu|tö|ner (Vertreter neuer Musik); **neu|tö|ne|risch** (*auch für* ganz modern)

Neut|ra [*österr.* 'ne|u...] (↑R 130; *Plur. von* Neutrum); **neut|ral** ‹lat.› (keiner der Krieg führenden Parteien angehörend; unparteiisch; keine besonderen Merkmale aufweisend); ein neutrales Land; die neutrale Ecke *(Boxen);* **Neut|ra|li|sa|ti|on,** die; -, -en; **neut|ra|li|sie|ren; Neut|ra|li|sie|rung; Neut|ra|lis|mus,** der; - (Grundsatz der Nichteinmischung in fremde Angelegenheiten [vor allem in der Politik]); **Neut|ra|list,** der; -en, -en; ↑R 126 (Verfechter u. Vertreter des Neutralismus); **neut|ra|lis|tisch**

Neut|ra|li|tät (↑R 130), die; -; **Neut|ra|li|täts-ab|kom|men, ...bruch** (der), **...er|klä|rung, ...po|li|tik, ...ver|let|zung; Neut|ren** (*Plur. von* Neutrum); **Neut|ri|no,** das; -s, -s ‹ital.› (*Kernphysik* masseloses Elementarteilchen ohne elektrische Ladung); **Neut|ron,** das; -s, ...onen ‹lat.› (*Kernphysik* Elementarteilchen ohne elektrische Ladung als Baustein des Atomkerns; *Zeichen* n); **Neut|ro|nen|bom|be; Neut|ro|nen|strah|len** (*Plur.* Neutronen hoher Geschwindigkeit); **Neut|ro|nen|waf|fe**

Neut|rum [*österr.* 'ne|u...] (↑R 130), das; -s, *Plur.* ...tra, *auch* ...tren (*Sprachw.* sächliches Substantiv, z. B. „das Buch"; *nur Sing.:* sächl. Geschlecht)

neu ver|mählt *vgl.* neu; **Neu|ver|mähl|te,** der *u.* die; -n, -n (↑R 5ff.); **Neu-ver|schul|dung, ...wa|gen, ...wahl; neu|wa|schen** (*landsch. für* frisch gewaschen); **Neu|wert; neu|wer|tig; Neu|wert|ver|si|che|rung**

Neu-Wien (↑R 105); **Neu-Wie|ner; neu-wie|ne|risch**

Neu|wort *Plur.* ...wörter

Neu|zeit, die; -; **neu|zeit|feind|lich; neu|zeit|lich; Neu-züch|tung, ...zu|gang, ...zu|las|sung, ...zu|stand** (der; -[e]s)

Nev. = Nevada

Ne|va|da [...v...] (Staat in den USA; *Abk.* Nev.)

Ne|wa [*auch* nɪɛ'va], die; - (Abfluss des Ladogasees)

New|age, *auch* **New Age** ['nju:'e:dʒ] (↑R 33), das; - ‹engl.› (neues Zeitalter als Inbegriff eines neuen integralen Weltbildes); **New|co|mer** ['nju:kamə(r)], der; -s, - (Neuling); **New Deal** [nju: 'di:l], der; - - ‹amerik.› (Reformprogramm des amerik. Präsidenten F. D. Roosevelt); **New Hamp|shire** [nju: 'hɛmpʃə(r)] (Staat in den USA; *Abk.* N. H.); **New Jer|sey** [nju: 'dʒœ:(r)zi] (Staat in den USA; *Abk.* N. J.); **New|look,** *auch* **New Look** [nju:'luk] (↑R 33), der *od.* das; -[s] ‹amerik.› (neue Moderichtung nach dem 2. Weltkrieg); **New Me|xi|co** [nju: -] (Staat in den USA; *Abk.* N. Mex.); **New Or|leans** [nju: ɔ:(r)'li:ns, *auch* ...'li:nz bzw. 'ɔ:(r)...] (Stadt in Louisiana); **New-Or|leans-Jazz** [...dʒɛs], der; - (frühester, improvisierender Jazzstil der nordamerik. Schwarzen); **News** [nju:z] *Plur.* ‹engl.› (Nachrichten)

[1]**New|ton** ['nju:t(ə)n] (engl. Physiker); [2]**New|ton,** das; -s, - (Einheit der Kraft; *Zeichen* N); **New|ton|me|ter** (Einheit der Energie; *Zeichen* Nm)

New York [nju: 'jɔ:(r)k] (Staat [*Abk.* N. Y.] u. Stadt in den USA); **New-Yor|ker,** New Yorker (↑R 105)

Ne|xus, der; -, - ['nɛksu:s] ‹lat.› (Zusammenhang, Verbindung)

nF = Nanofarad

NF = Neues Forum (*vgl.* neu)

N. F. = Neue Folge

n-fach (↑R 25)

Ngo|ro|ngo|ro|kra|ter (Kraterhochland in Tansania, Zentrum eines Wildreservats)

N. H. = New Hampshire; Normalhöhenpunkt

nhd. = neuhochdeutsch

Ni = *chem. Zeichen für* Nickel

Ni|a|ga|ra|fäl|le [*österr. auch* ni'aga...] *Plur.*

Nia|mey [nja'mɛ:] (Hptst. von Niger)
Ni|am-Ni|am *Plur.* (Volksstamm im Sudan)
nib|beln ‹engl.› ([Bleche o. Ä.] schneiden od. abtrennen); ich ...[e]le (↑R 16); **Nibb|ler** (Gerät zum Schneiden von Blechen)
ni|beln (*südd. für* nebeln, fein regnen); es nibelt
Ni|be|lun|gen (germ. Sagengeschlecht; die Burgunden); **Ni|belun|gen‿hort** (der; -[e]s), **...lied** (das; -[e]s), **...sa|ge** (die; -), **...treue**
Nib|lick (↑R 130), der; -s, -s ‹engl.› (Golfschläger mit Eisenkopf)
Ni|cäa [ni'tsɛ:a] usw. *vgl.* Nizäa usw.
Ni|ca|ra|gua (Staat in Mittelamerika); **Ni|ca|ra|gu|a|ner** (↑R 103); **Ni|ca|ra|gu|a|ne|rin; ni|ca|ra|gu|a|nisch**
nicht; nicht wahr?; gar nicht; mitnichten, zunichte machen, werden. *Die Verbindungen von „nicht" mit einem Adjektiv können getrennt oder zusammengeschrieben werden,* z. B. die Darstellung war nicht amtlich (*auch* nichtamtlich); dieses Kind ist nicht ehelich (*auch* nichtehelich); nicht berufstätige (*auch* nichtberufstätige) Frauen; nicht flektierbare (*auch* nichtflektierbare) Wörter; nicht kommunistische (*auch* nichtkommunistische) Staaten; die Sitzung war nicht öffentlich (*auch* nichtöffentlich) usw. *Die Verbindungen von „nicht" mit einem Partizip werden in der Regel getrennt geschrieben* (↑R 40): nicht leitende Stoffe; die nicht organisierten Arbeiter; nicht rostende Stähle; die nicht Krieg führenden (neutralen) Parteien; sein nicht veröffentlichter Aufsatz; eine nicht zutreffende Behauptung; nicht Zutreffendes, *auch* Nichtzutreffendes streichen; *vgl. aber* nichtzielend
Nicht|ach|tung
nicht|amt|lich, nicht amt|lich; *vgl. auch* nicht
Nicht|an|er|ken|nung, die; -
Nicht|an|griffs|pakt [*auch* ...'an...]
Nicht|be|ach|tung, die; -; **Nicht|be|fol|gung,** die; -; **nicht|be|rufs|tä|tig, nicht be|rufs|tä|tig;** *vgl. auch* nicht; **Nicht|be|rufs|tä|ti|ge,** der *u.* die; -n, -n (↑R 5 ff.)
Nicht|christ, der; **nicht|christ|lich, nicht christ|lich;** *vgl. auch* nicht
Nich|te, die; -, -n
nicht|ehe|lich (↑R 132; *Rechtsspr. für* unehelich); *vgl. auch* nicht
Nicht|ein|brin|gungs|fall (*österr. Amtsspr.* Zahlungsunfähigkeit); im -
Nicht|ein|hal|tung
Nicht|ein|mi|schung
Nicht|ei|sen|me|tall
Nicht|er|fül|lung
Nicht|er|schei|nen, das; -s
nicht|euk|li|disch, nicht euk|li|disch *(Math.);* die nichteuklidische *od.* nicht euklidische Geometrie; *vgl. auch* nicht
Nicht|fach|mann
nicht|flek|tier|bar, nicht flek|tier|bar (*Sprachw.* unbeugbar); *vgl. auch* nicht
Nicht|ge|fal|len, das; -s *(Kaufmannsspr.);* bei -
Nicht|ge|schäfts|fä|hi|ge, der *u.* die; -n, -n (↑R 5 ff.)
Nicht|ge|wünsch|te, das; -n (↑R 5 ff.)
Nicht-Ich, das; -[s], -[s] (↑R 24; *Philos.*)
nich|tig; null u. -; **Nich|tig|keit; Nich|tig|keits|kla|ge**
Nicht|in|an|spruch|nah|me *(bes. Amtsspr.)*
Nicht|ka|tho|lik
nicht|kom|mu|nis|tisch, nicht kom|mu|nis|tisch; *vgl. auch* nicht
nicht lei|tend *vgl.* nicht; **Nicht|lei|ter,** der (*für* Isolator)
Nicht|me|tall; Nicht|mit|glied
nicht|öf|fent|lich, nicht öf|fent|lich; *vgl. auch* nicht
nicht or|ga|ni|siert *vgl.* nicht
Nicht|rau|cher; Nicht|rau|cher‿ab|teil, ...gast|stät|te; Nicht|rau|che|rin; Nicht|rau|cher|zo|ne
nicht ros|tend *vgl.* nicht
nichts; für nichts; zu nichts; gar nichts; um nichts und [um] wieder nichts; sich in nichts auflösen, unterscheiden; nichts tun; mir nichts, dir nichts (ohne weiteres); viel Lärm um nichts; nach nichts aussehen; (↑R 47): nichts Genaues, nichts Näheres, nichts Neues u. a., *aber* (↑R 48): nichts and[e]res; nichts weniger als; (↑R 40): ein nichts sagendes Gesicht; ein nichts ahnender Besucher; **Nichts,** das; -, -e; wir stehen vor dem Nichts; **nichts ahnend** *vgl.* nichts
Nicht|schwim|mer; Nicht|schwim|mer|be|cken; Nicht|schwim|me|rin
nichts|des|to|min|der *(selten);* **nichts|des|to|trotz** *(ugs.);* **nichts|des|to|we|ni|ger**
nicht|selbst|stän|dig, nicht selbst|stän|dig *vgl. auch* nicht *u.* selbstständig
Nicht|sess|haf|te, der *u.* die; -n, -n (↑R 5 ff.)
Nichts|kön|ner; Nichts|nutz, der; -es, -e; **nichts|nut|zig** *(veraltend);* **Nichts|nut|zig|keit; nichts sagend** *vgl.* nichts; **Nichts|tu|er** *(ugs.);* **nichts|tu|e|risch; Nichts|tun,** das; -s; **nichts|wür|dig; Nichts|wür|dig|keit**
Nicht|tän|zer
Nicht|ver|fol|ger|land *Plur.* ...länder (Land, in dem keine [polit.] Verfolgung stattfindet)
Nicht|wei|ter|ga|be, die; -
nicht|zie|lend; ↑R 40 (*für* intransitiv); nichtzielendes Verb
Nicht|zu|las|sung
Nicht|zu|stan|de|kom|men
Nicht|zu|tref|fen|de, das; -n (↑R 5 ff. *u.* 47); Nichtzutreffendes streichen; *vgl.* nicht
[1]**Ni|ckel,** der; -s, - (*landsch. für* boshaftes Kind); [2]**Ni|ckel,** das; -s (chem. Element, Metall; *Zeichen* Ni); [3]**Ni|ckel,** der; -s, - (früheres Zehnpfennigstück); **Ni|ckel‿bril|le, ...hoch|zeit** (nach zwölfeinhalbjähriger Ehe); **ni|cke|lig, nick|lig** ‹*zu* [1]Nickel› (*landsch.* frech, mutwillig); **Ni|cke|lig|keit,** Nick|lig|keit; **Ni|ckel|mün|ze**
ni|cken; Ni|cker (*ugs. für* Kopfnicken); **Ni|cker|chen** (*ugs. für* kurzer Schlaf); **Nick|fän|ger** (*Jägerspr.* Genickfänger); **Nick|haut** (drittes Augenlid vieler Wirbeltiere)
Ni|cki, der; -s, -s (Pullover aus samtartigem Baumwollstoff)
nick|lig usw. *vgl.* nickelig usw.
Ni|col ['ni:kɔl], das; -s, -s ‹nach dem engl. Erfinder› (*Optik* Prisma zur Polarisation des Lichts)
Ni|cole [ni'kɔl] (w. Vorn.)
Ni|co|sia *vgl.* Nikosia
Ni|co|tin *vgl.* Nikotin
nid (*südd. u. schweiz. veraltet für* unter[halb]); nid dem Berg
Ni|da|ti|on, die; -, -en ‹lat.› (*Med.* Einnistung der befruchteten Eizelle in die Gebärmutterschleimhaut)
[1]**Nid|da,** die; - (r. Nebenfluss des Mains); [2]**Nid|da** (Stadt an der [1]Nidda)
Ni|del, der; -s *od.* die; -, *auch* **Nid|le,** die; - (*schweiz. mdal. für* Sahne)
Nid|wal|den *vgl.* Unterwalden nid dem Wald; **Nid|wald|ner** (↑R 103); **nid|wald|ne|risch**
nie; nie mehr; nie u. nimmer
nie|der; nieder mit ihm!; auf und nieder
nie|der... (*in Zus. mit Verben,* z. B. niederlegen, du legst nieder, niedergelegt, niederzulegen)

Nie|der|bay|ern (↑R 105)
nie|der|beu|gen; sich -
nie|der|bren|nen
nie|der|brin|gen; einen Schacht - (*Bergmannsspr.* herstellen)
nie|der|deutsch (*Abk.* nd.); *vgl.* deutsch; **Nie|der|deutsch,** das; -[s] (Sprache); *vgl.* Deutsch; **Nie|der|deut|sche,** das; -n; *vgl.* Deutsche, das; **Nie|der|deutsch|land** (↑R 105)
Nie|der|druck, der; -[e]s; **nie|der|drü|cken; nie|der|drü|ckend; Nie|der|druck|hei|zung**
nie|de|re; niederer, niederste; (↑R 108:) die niedere Jagd; aus niederem Stande; der niedere Adel; (↑R 47:) Hoch und Nieder (jedermann); Hohe und Niedere trafen sich zum Fest; (↑R 102:) die Niedere Tatra (Teil der Westkarpaten); die Niederen Tauern *Plur.* (Teil der Zentralalpen)
nie|der|fal|len
Nie|der|flur|wa|gen *(Technik)*
Nie|der|fran|ken
nie|der|fre|quent *(Physik);* **Nie|der|fre|quenz**
Nie|der|gang, der
nie|der|ge|drückt
nie|der|ge|hen; eine Lawine ist niedergegangen
Nie|der|ge|las|se|ne, der *u.* die; -n, -n; ↑R 5 ff. (*schweiz. für* Einwohner mit dauerndem Wohnsitz)
nie|der|ge|schla|gen (bedrückt, traurig); sie ist sehr -; **Nie|der|ge|schla|gen|heit,** die; -
nie|der|hal|ten; die Empörung wurde niedergehalten; **Nie|der|hal|tung,** die; -
nie|der|hau|en; er hieb den Flüchtenden nieder
nie|der|ho|len; die Flagge wurde niedergeholt
Nie|der⌣holz (das; -es; Unterholz), **...jagd** (die; -; *Jägerspr.* Jagd auf Kleinwild)
nie|der|kämp|fen
nie|der|kau|ern, sich
nie|der|knal|len
nie|der|kni|en; er ist niedergekniet
nie|der|knüp|peln
nie|der|kom|men; sie ist [mit Zwillingen] niedergekommen *(veraltend);* **Nie|der|kunft,** die; -, ...künfte (*veraltend für* Geburt)
Nie|der|la|ge
Nie|der|lan|de *Plur.;* **Nie|der|län|der** (↑R 103); **Nie|der|län|de|rin; nie|der|län|disch,** *aber* (↑R 108): Niederländisches Dankgebet (ein Lied aus dem niederländischen Freiheitskampf gegen Spanien); **Nie|der|län|disch,** das; -[s] (Sprache); *vgl.* Deutsch; **Nie|der|län|di|sche,** das; -n; *vgl.* Deutsche, das
nie|der|las|sen; sich auf dem *od.* auf den Stuhl niederlassen; der Vorhang wurde niedergelassen; **Nie|der|las|sung; Nie|der|las|sungs|frei|heit,** die; -
nie|der|läu|fig; eine -e Hunderasse
Nie|der|lau|sitz [*auch* ...'lau...] (↑R 105; Landschaft um Cottbus; *Abk.* N. L.)
nie|der|le|gen; etwas auf der *od.* auf die Platte -; er hat den Kranz niedergelegt; sich -; **Nie|der|le|gung**
nie|der|ma|chen *(ugs.)*
nie|der|mä|hen
nie|der|met|zeln
Nie|der|ös|ter|reich (↑R 105; österr. Bundesland)
nie|der|pras|seln
nie|der|reg|nen
nie|der|rei|ßen; das Haus wurde niedergerissen
Nie|der|rhein; nie|der|rhei|nisch, *aber* (↑R 102): die Niederrheinische Bucht (Tiefland in Nordrhein-Westfalen)
nie|der|rin|gen; der Feind wurde niedergerungen
Nie|der|sach|se; Nie|der|sach|sen (↑R 105); **Nie|der|säch|sin; nie|der|säch|sisch**
nie|der|schie|ßen; der Adler ist auf die Beute niedergeschossen; er hat ihn niedergeschossen
Nie|der|schlag, der; -[e]s, ...schläge; **nie|der|schla|gen;** sich -; der Prozess wurde dann niedergeschlagen; **nie|der|schlags⌣arm, ...frei; Nie|der|schlags|men|ge; nie|der|schlags|reich; Nie|der|schla|gung**
Nie|der|schle|si|en (↑R 105)
nie|der|schmet|tern; jmdn., etwas niederschmettern; diese Nachricht hat ihn niedergeschmettert
nie|der|schrei|ben
nie|der|schrei|en; die Menge hat ihn niedergeschrien
Nie|der|schrift
nie|der|set|zen; ich habe mich niedergesetzt
nie|der|sin|ken
nie|der|sit|zen (*landsch. für* sich [nieder]setzen)
Nie|der|span|nung *(Elektrotechnik)*
nie|ders|te; *vgl.* niedere
nie|der|stei|gen; sie ist niedergestiegen
nie|der|stim|men; einen Antrag -
nie|der|sto|ßen; er hat ihn niedergestoßen
nie|der|stre|cken; er hat ihn niedergestreckt
Nie|der|sturz; nie|der|stür|zen; die Lawine ist niedergestürzt
nie|der|tou|rig *(Technik)*
Nie|der|tracht, die; -; **nie|der|träch|tig; Nie|der|träch|tig|keit**
nie|der|tram|peln
nie|der|tre|ten
Nie|de|rung; Nie|de|rungs|moor
Nie|der|wald, der; -[e]s (Teil des Rheingaugebirges); **Nie|der|wald|denk|mal,** das; -[e]s
nie|der|wal|zen
nie|der|wärts
nie|der|wer|fen; der Aufstand wurde niedergeworfen; **Nie|der|wer|fung**
Nie|der|wild
nie|der|zie|hen
nie|der|zwin|gen
nied|lich; Nied|lich|keit, die; -
Nied|na|gel (am Fingernagel losgelöstes Hautstückchen)
nied|rig; das Brett niedrig[er] halten; (↑R 108:) niedrige Absätze; niedrige Beweggründe; von niedrigem Niveau; niedriger Wasserstand; (↑R 47:) Hoch und Niedrig (jedermann); Hohe und Niedrige. *In Verbindung mit dem Partizip II Getrenntschreibung:* niedrig gesinnt sein, die niedrig gesinnten Gegner; niedrig stehendes Wasser (↑R 40); **Nied|rig|hal|tung,** die; -; **Nied|rig|keit; Nied|rig|lohn|land** *Plur.* ...länder; **nied|rig|prei|sig;** -e Produkte; **nied|rig|pro|zen|tig; nied|rig ste|hend** *vgl.* niedrig; **Nied|rig|was|ser** *Plur.* ...wasser
Ni|el|lo, das; -[s], *Plur.* -s *u.* ...llen, *auch* ...lli ‹ital.› (eine Verzierungstechnik der Goldschmiedekunst *[nur Sing.];* mit dieser Technik verziertes Kunstwerk); **Ni|el|lo|ar|beit**
Niels (m. Vorn.)
nie|mals
nie|mand (↑R 48); *Gen.* -[e]s; *Dat.* -em, *auch* -; *Akk.* -en, *auch* -; (↑R 47:) niemand Fremdes usw., *aber* (↑R 48): niemand anders; niemand kann es besser wissen als er; **Nie|mand,** der; -[e]s; er ist ein Niemand; der böse Niemand (*auch für* Teufel); **Nie|mands|land,** das; -[e]s (Kampfgebiet zwischen feindlichen Linien; unerforschtes, herrenloses Land)
Nie|re, die; -, -n; eine künstliche Niere (med. Gerät); **Nie|ren|be|cken; Nie|ren⌣be|cken|ent|zün|dung, ...bra|ten, ...ent|zün|dung, ...fett; nie|ren|för|mig; Nie|ren|ko|lik; nie|ren|krank; Nie|ren⌣sen|kung, ...stein, ...tisch, ...trans|plan|ta|ti|on, ...tu|ber|ku|lo|se; nie|rig** (nieren-

förmig [von Mineralien]); **Nierndl,** das; -s, -n (*österr. für* Niere [als Gericht])
Nier|stei|ner (ein Rheinwein)
nie|seln (*ugs. für* leise regnen); es nieselt; **Nie|sel|re|gen**
nie|sen; du niest; er nies|te; geniest; **Nies‿pul|ver, ...reiz**
Nieß|brauch, der; -[e]s ‹*zu* nießen = genießen› (*Rechtsspr.* Nutzungsrecht); **Nieß|nutz,** der; -es; **Nieß|nut|zer**
Nies|wurz, die; -, -en ‹*zu* niesen› (eine Pflanzengattung)
Niet, der, *auch* das; -[e]s, -e (*fachspr. für* [1]Niete); **[1]Nie|te,** die; -, -n (Metallbolzen zum Verbinden von Werkstücken)
[2]Nie|te, die; -, -n ‹niederl.› (Los, das nichts gewonnen hat; Reinfall, Versager)
nie|ten; Nie|ten|ho|se; Nie|ter (Berufsbez.); **Niet‿ham|mer, ...ho|se** (*selten für* Nietenhose), **...na|gel, ...pres|se; niet- und na|gel|fest** (↑R 23); **Nie|tung**
Nietz|sche (dt. Philosoph); **Nietzsche-Ar|chiv** (↑R 95)
Ni|fe ['ni:fe(:)], das; - ‹*Kurzw. aus* Ni[ckel] *u.* Fe [Eisen]› (*Bez. für* den nach älterer Theorie aus Nickel u. Eisen bestehenden Erdkern); **Ni|fe|kern**
Nifl|heim [*auch* 'ni...], das; -[e]s („Nebelheim") (*nord. Mythol.* Reich der Kälte; *auch für* Totenreich)
ni|gel|na|gel|neu (*schweiz. für* funkelnagelneu)
[1]Ni|ger, der; -[s] (afrik. Strom); **[2]Ni|ger** (*auch mit Artikel:* der, -s; Staat in Westafrika); *vgl.* Nigrer; **Ni|ge|ria** (Staat in Westafrika); **Ni|ge|ri|a|ner; Ni|ge|ri|a|ne|rin; ni|ge|ri|a|nisch**
Ni|ger, der; -s, - ‹amerik.› (*abwertend für* Schwarzer)
Night|club ['naitklab], der; -s, -s ‹engl.› (Nachtlokal)
Ni|grer (↑R 130) ‹*zu* [2]Niger›; **nigrisch**
Nig|ro|sin (↑R 130), das; -s, -e ‹lat.› (ein Farbstoff)
Ni|hi|lis|mus, der; - ‹lat.› (Philosophie, die alles Bestehende für nichtig, sinnlos hält; völlige Verneinung aller Normen u. Werte); **Ni|hi|list,** der; -en, -en (↑R 126); **ni|hi|lis|tisch**
Nij|me|gen ['nɛime:xə] (niederl. Stadt); *vgl.* Nimwegen
Ni|käa usw. *vgl.* Nizäa usw.
Ni|ka|ra|gua usw. *vgl.* Nicaragua usw.
Ni|ke (griech. Siegesgöttin)
Ni|ki|ta (m. Vorn.)
Nik|las (↑R 130; m. Vorn.); **Nik|laus** (*schweiz. für* hl. Nikolaus; *auch* m. Vorn.)
Ni|ko|ba|ren *Plur.* (Inselgruppe im Ind. Ozean)
Ni|ko|de|mus (Jesus anhängender jüd. Schriftgelehrter)
Ni|kol *vgl.* Nicol
[1]Ni|ko|laus, der; -, *Plur.* -e, *ugs. scherzh. auch* ...läuse ‹griech.› (als hl. Nikolaus verkleidete Person; den hl. Nikolaus darstellende Figur aus Schokolade, Marzipan u. a.); **[2]Ni|ko|laus** (m. Vorn.); **Ni|ko|laus|tag** (6. Dez.); **Ni|ko|lo** [*auch* ...'lo:], der; -s, -s ‹ital.› (*österr. für* hl. Nikolaus); **Ni|ko|lo‿abend** (↑R 132), **...tag**
Ni|ko|sia [*auch* ...'ko:zia] (Hptst. von Zypern)
Ni|ko|tin, *chem. fachspr.* Ni|co|tin, das; -s ‹nach dem franz. Gelehrten Nicot› (Alkaloid im Tabak); **ni|ko|tin‿arm, ...frei; Ni|ko|tin|ge|halt,** der; **ni|ko|tin|hal|tig; Ni|ko|tin|hal|tig|keit,** die; -; **Ni|ko|tin|ver|gif|tung**
Nil, der; -[s] (afrik. Fluss); **Nil‿del|ta** (das; -s; ↑R 105), **...gans**
Nil|gau, der; -[e]s, -e ‹Hindi› (antilopenartiger ind. Waldbock)
nil|grün; Ni|lo|te, der; -n, -n; ↑R 126 (Angehöriger negrider Völker am oberen Nil); **ni|lo|tisch; Nil|pferd**
Nils (m. Vorn.)
Nim|bus, der; -, -se ‹lat.› (besonderes Ansehen, Ruf; *bild. Kunst* Heiligenschein, Strahlenkranz)
nim|mer (*landsch. für* niemals; nicht mehr); nie und nimmer; **Nim|mer|leins|tag** (*ugs.*); am, bis zum Nimmerleinstag; **nim|mermehr** (*landsch. für* niemals); nie und nimmermehr, nun und nimmermehr; **Nim|mer|mehrs|tag** *vgl.* Nimmerleinstag; **nim|mer|mü|de; Nim|mer|satt,** der; *Gen.* - *u.* -[e]s, *Plur.* -e (jmd., der nicht genug bekommen kann); **Nimmer|wie|der|se|hen,** das; -s; auf Nimmerwiedersehen (*ugs.*)
[1]Nim|rod ‹hebr.› (*A. T.* Herrscher von Babylon, Gründer Ninives); **[2]Nim|rod,** der; -s, -e ([leidenschaftlicher] Jäger)
Nim|we|gen (*dt. Form von* Nijmegen)
Ni|na (w. Vorn.)
nin|geln (*mitteld. für* wimmern); ich ...[e]le (↑R 16)
Ni|ni|ve [...ve:] (Hptst. des antiken Assyrerreiches); **Ni|ni|vit** [...v...], der; -en, -en; ↑R 126 (Bewohner von Ninive); **ni|ni|vi|tisch**
Nin|ja, der; -[s], -[s] ‹jap.› (*früher in Japan* in Geheimbünden organisierter Krieger)
Ni|ob, *chem. fachspr.* Ni|o|bi|um, das; -s ‹*nach* Niobe› (chem. Element, Metall; *Zeichen* Nb)
Ni|o|be [...be:, *auch* ni'o(:)be:] (griech. w. Sagengestalt); **Ni|o|bide,** der *u.* die; -n, -n; ↑R 126 (Kind der Niobe)
Ni|o|bi|um *vgl.* Niob
Nipf (*österr. ugs. für* Mut); jmdm. den - nehmen
Nip|pel, der; -s, - (kurzes Rohrstück mit Gewinde; ab- od. vorstehendes [Anschluss]stück)
nip|pen
Nip|pes ['nip(ə)s] *Plur.* ‹franz.› (kleine Ziergegenstände [aus Porzellan])
Nipp|flut (*nordd. für* geringe Flut)
Nip|pon (*jap. Name von* Japan)
Nipp|sa|chen *Plur.* (*svw.* Nippes)
Nipp|ti|de (*svw.* Nippflut)
nir|gend (*veraltend für* nirgends); **nir|gend|her; nir|gend|hin; nirgends; nir|gends|her** usw. *vgl.* nirgendher usw.; **nir|gend|wo; nir|gend|wo|her; nir|gend|wohin**
Ni|ros|ta ®, der; -s (*Kurzw. aus* nicht rostender Stahl)
Nir|wa|na, das; -[s] ‹sanskr.› (völlige, selige Ruhe als Endzustand des gläubigen Buddhisten)
Ni|sche, die; -, -n ‹franz.›
Ni|schel, der; -s, - (*bes. mitteld. für* Kopf)
Ni|schen|al|tar
Nisch|ni Now|go|rod (Stadt a. d. Wolga [*früherer Name* Gorki])
Nis|se, die; -, -n, *älter* Niss, die; -, -e (Ei der Laus)
Nis|sen|hüt|te (↑R 95) ‹nach dem engl. Offizier P. N. Nissen› (halbrunde Wellblechbaracke)
nis|sig (voller Nisse[n], filzig)
nis|ten; Nist‿höh|le, ...kas|ten, ...platz, ...stät|te, ...zeit
Nit|hard (fränk. Geschichtsschreiber)
Nit|rat (↑R 130), das; -[e]s, -e ‹ägypt.› (*Chemie* Salz der Salpetersäure); **Nit|rid,** das; -[e]s, -e (Verbindung von Stickstoff mit einem Metall); **nit|rie|ren** (mit Salpetersäure behandeln); **Nit|rifi|ka|ti|on,** die; -, -en (Salpeterbildung durch Bodenbakterien); **nitri|fi|zie|ren** ([durch Bodenbakterien] Salpeter bilden); nitrifizierende Bakterien; **Nit|ri|fi|zierung; Nit|ril,** das; -s, -e (Zyanverbindung); **Nit|rit** [*auch* ni'trit], das; -s, -e (Salz der salpetrigen Säure); **Nit|ro|ge|la|ti|ne** ['ni:troʒə..., *auch* ...'ti:nə] (ein Sprengstoff); **Nit|ro|ge|ni|um** [...'ge:...], das; -s (Stickstoff; *Zeichen* N); **Nit|ro|gly|ze|rin** [*auch* ...'ri:n] (ein

Heilmittel; ein Sprengstoff); **Nitrollack** (gelöste Nitrozellulose enthaltender Lack); **Nit|ro|phos|phat** [*auch* 'ni:...] (Düngemittel)

Nit|ro|sa|mi|ne (↑R 130 *u.* 132) *Plur.* (eine Gruppe chem. Verbindungen)

Nit|ro|zel|lu|lo|se (↑R 130; ein sehr schnell verbrennender Stoff, Schießbaumwolle); **Nit|rum,** das; -s (*veraltet für* Salpeter)

nit|scheln *(Textiltechnik);* ich ...[e]le (↑R 16); **Nit|schel|werk** (Maschine, mit der man Fasern zum Spinnen vorbereitet)

nit|sche|wo! (↑R 132) ‹russ.› (*scherzh. für* macht nichts!, hat nichts zu bedeuten!)

Ni|veau [ni'vo:], das; -s, -s ‹franz.› (waagerechte Fläche auf einer gewissen Höhenstufe; Höhenlage; [Bildungs]stand, Rang, Stufe); **Niveau|dif|fe|renz; ni|veau|frei** (*Verkehrsw.* sich nicht in gleicher Höhe kreuzend); **Ni|veau|ge|fälle; ni|veau|gleich; Ni|veau|li|nie** (Höhenlinie); **ni|veau|los; Niveau|un|ter|schied; ni|veau|voll; Ni|vel|le|ment** [nivɛl(ə)'mã:], das; -s, -s (Ebnung, Gleichmachung; Höhenmessung); **ni|vel|lie|ren** (gleichmachen; ebnen; Höhenunterschiede [im Gelände] bestimmen); **Ni|vellier|in|stru|ment; Ni|vel|lie|rung**

Ni|vose [ni'vo:z], der; -, -s [ni'vo:z] ‹franz., „Schneemonat"› (4. Monat des Kalenders der Franz. Revolution: 21. Dez. bis 19. Jan.)

nix (*ugs. für* nichts)

Nix, der; -es, -e (germ. Wassergeist); **Nix|chen; Ni|xe,** die; -, -n (Meerjungfrau; [badendes] Mädchen); **ni|xen|haft**

Ni|zäa (Stadt [*jetziger Name* Isnik] im alten Bithynien); **ni|zä|isch,** *aber* (↑R 108): Nizäisches Glaubensbekenntnis; **ni|zä|nisch** *vgl.* nizäisch; **Ni|zä|num, Ni|zä|um,** das; -s (Nizäisches Glaubensbekenntnis)

Niz|za (franz. Stadt); **Niz|za|er** (↑R 103); **niz|za|isch**

n. J. = nächsten Jahres

N. J. = New Jersey

Njas|sa, der; -[s] (afrik. See); **Njas|sa|land,** das; -[e]s (*früherer Name von* Malawi)

Nje|men, der; -[s] (russ. Name der Memel)

NK = Neue Kerze

nkr = norwegische Krone

NKWD, der; - ‹*Abk. aus* russ. Narodny Komissariat Wnutrennich [...x] Del [diel] = Volkskommissariat des Innern› (sowjet. polit. Geheimpolizei [1934–46])

N. L. = Niederlausitz

nlat. = neulateinisch

nm = Nanometer

nm., nachm. = nachmittags

n. M. = nächsten Monats

Nm = Newtonmeter

N. Mex. = New Mexico

N. N. = nomen nescio [- 'nɛstsio] ‹lat., „den Namen weiß ich nicht"› *od.* nomen nominandum ‹„der zu nennende Name"› (z. B. Herr N. N.)

N. N., NN = Normalnull

NNO = Nordnordost[en]

NNW = Nordnordwest[en]

No = Nobelium

No., N° = Numero

NO = Nordost[en]

NÖ = Niederösterreich

No|ah, *ökum.* No|ach (bibl. m. Eigenn.); *Gen.:* des -, *aber (ohne Artikel)* Noah[s] *u.* Noä; die Arche Noah

no|bel ‹franz.› (edel, vornehm; *ugs. für* freigebig); ein nob|ler (↑R 130) Mensch

[1]**No|bel,** der; -s (Löwe in der Tierfabel)

[2]**No|bel** (schwed. Chemiker)

No|bel‿her|ber|ge (*ugs. für* luxuriöses Hotel), **...ho|tel**

No|be|li|um, das; -s ‹*zu* [2]Nobel› (chem. Element, Transuran; *Zeichen* No); **No|bel|preis; No|bel|preis|trä|ger; No|bel|stif|tung,** die; -

No|bi|li|tät, die; -, -en ‹lat.› (Adel); **no|bi|li|tie|ren** (*früher für* adeln)

Nob|les|se (↑R 130), die; -, -n ‹franz.› (*veraltet für* Adel; *nur Sing.: veraltend für* vornehmes Benehmen); **nob|lesse ob|lige** [nɔblɛsɔ'bli:ʒ] (Adel verpflichtet)

No|bo|dy, der; -s, -s ‹engl.› (jmd., der unbedeutend, ein Niemand ist)

noch; noch nicht; noch immer; noch mehr; noch und noch; noch einmal; noch einmal so viel; noch mal (*ugs. für* noch einmal); **Noch|ge|schäft** *(Börse);* **noch|ma|lig; noch|mals**

[1]**Nock,** das; -[e]s, -e, *auch* die; -, -en ‹niederl.› (*Seemannsspr.* Ende eines Rundholzes)

[2]**Nock,** der; -s, -e (*bayr. u. österr. für* Felskopf, Hügel)

Nöck *vgl.* Neck

No|cke, die; -, -n, [1]**No|cken,** die; -, - (*österr. ugs. für* dumme, eingebildete Frau); [2]**No|cken,** der; -s, - (*Technik* Vorsprung an einer Welle oder Scheibe); **No|cken|wel|le**

No|ckerl, das; -s, -n (*österr. für* Klößchen; naives Mädchen); **No|ckerl|sup|pe** *(österr.)*

Noc|turne [nɔk'tyrn], das; -s, -s *od.* die; -, -s ‹franz., „Nachtstück"› (*Musik* lyrisches, stimmungsvolles Klavierstück)

No|e|sis, die; - ‹griech.› (*Philos.* geistiges Wahrnehmen, Denken, Erkennen); **No|e|tik,** die; - (Lehre vom Denken, vom Erkennen geistiger Gegenstände); **no|e|tisch**

Nof|re|te|te (↑R 130; altägypt. Königin)

no fu|ture ['no: 'fju:tʃə(r)] ‹engl., „keine Zukunft"› (Schlagwort meist arbeitsloser Jugendlicher); **No|fu|ture|ge|ne|ra|ti|on,** *auch* **No-Fu|ture-Ge|ne|ra|ti|on,** die; -

no i|ron ['no: airən] ‹engl.› (nicht bügeln, bügelfrei [Hinweis an Kleidungsstücken])

Noi|sette [noa'zɛt], die; -, *Plur. (Sorten:)* -s ‹franz.›, **Noi|sette|scho|ko|la|de** (Milchschokolade mit fein gemahlenen Haselnüssen)

NOK = Nationales Olympisches Komitee

Nol|de (dt. Maler u. Grafiker)

nö|len (*nordd. ugs. abwertend für* [im Reden u. a.] langsam sein)

no|lens vo|lens [- v...] ‹lat., „nicht wollend wollend"› (wohl oder übel); **No|li|me|tan|ge|re** [...'taŋgərə], das; -, - ‹„rühr mich nicht an"› (Springkraut)

Nö|lie|se, die; -, -n; **Nöl|pe|ter,** der; -s, - (*nordd. ugs. abwertend für* langsamer, schwerfälliger, langweiliger Mensch)

Nom. = Nominativ

No|ma|de, der; -n, -n (↑R 126) ‹griech.› (Angehöriger eines Hirten-, Wandervolkes); **No|ma|den|da|sein; no|ma|den|haft; No|ma|den‿le|ben** (das; -s), **...volk; No|ma|din; no|ma|disch** (umherziehend, unstet); **no|ma|di|sie|ren** (umherziehen)

No|men, das; -s, *Plur.* ...mina *od.* - ‹lat., „Name"› (*Sprachw.* Nennwort, Substantiv, z. B. „Haus"; *häufig auch für* Adjektiv u. andere deklinierbare Wortarten); **No|men ac|ti** [- 'akti], das; - -, ...mina - (*Sprachw.* Substantiv, das den Abschluss od. das Ergebnis eines Geschehens bezeichnet, z. B. „Lähmung, Guss"); **No|men ac|ti|o|nis** [- ak...], das; - -, ...mina - (*Sprachw.* Substantiv, das ein Geschehen bezeichnet, z. B. „Schlaf"); **No|men a|gen|tis,** das; - -, ...mina - (*Sprachw.* Substantiv, das den Träger eines Geschehens bezeichnet, z. B. „Schläfer"); **no|men est o|men** (der Name deutet schon darauf hin); **No|men in|stru|men|ti,** das; - -,

...mina - (*Sprachw.* Substantiv, das ein Werkzeug od. Gerät bezeichnet, z. B. „Bohrer"); **No|men|kla|tor,** der; -s, ...oren (Verzeichnis für die in einem Wissenschaftszweig vorkommenden gültigen Namen); **no|men|kla|to|risch; No|men|kla|tur,** die; -, -en (Zusammenstellung, System von [wissenschaftl.] Fachausdrücken); **No|men|kla|tu|ra,** die; - ⟨russ.⟩ (*ehem. in der Sowjetunion* Verzeichnis der wichtigsten Führungspositionen; *übertr. für* Oberschicht); **No|men|kla|tur|ka|der** (*ehem. in der DDR);* **No|men pro|pri|um** [*auch* - 'prɔ...] (↑R 130), das; - -, ...mina ...pria ⟨lat.⟩ (Eigenname); **No|mi|na** (*Plur. von* Nomen); **no|mi|nal** (zum Namen gehörend; *Wirtsch.* zum Nennwert); **No|mi|nal|be|trag** (Nennbetrag); **No|mi|na|lis|mus,** der; - (eine philos. Lehre); **No|mi|na|list,** der; -en, -en (↑R 126); **No|mi|nal‿lohn, ...stil** (der; -[e]s; Stil, der das Substantiv, das Nomen, bevorzugt; *Ggs.* Verbalstil), **...wert; No|mi|na|ti|on,** die; -, -en (*früher* [das Recht der] Benennung von Anwärtern auf höhere Kirchenämter durch die Landesregierung; *seltener für* Nominierung); **No|mi|na|tiv,** der; -s, -e [...və] (*Sprachw.* Werfall, 1. Fall; *Abk.* Nom.); **no|mi|nell** ([nur] dem Namen nach [bestehend], vorgeblich; zum Nennwert); *vgl.* nominal; **no|mi|nie|ren** (benennen, bezeichnen; ernennen); **No|mi|nie|rung**

No|mo|gramm, das; -s, -e ⟨griech.⟩ (*Math.* Schaubild od. Zeichnung zum graph. Rechnen)

Non, No|ne, die; -, Nonen ⟨lat.⟩ (Teil des kath. Stundengebets)

No|na|gon, das; -s, -e ⟨lat.; griech.⟩ (Neuneck)

No-Name-Pro|dukt ['no:'ne:m...] ⟨engl.; lat.⟩ (neutral verpackte Ware ohne Marken- od. Firmenzeichen)

Non-Book-Ab|tei|lung ['nɔn-'buk...] ⟨engl.; dt.⟩ (Abteilung in Buchläden, in der Schallplatten, Poster o. Ä. verkauft werden)

Non|cha|lance [nɔ̃ʃa'lɑ̃:s], die; - ⟨franz.⟩ (Lässigkeit, formlose Ungezwungenheit); **non|cha|lant** [...'lɑ̃:, *attributiv* ...'lant]; nonchalanteste [...'lantəstə] (formlos, ungezwungen, [nach]lässig)

No|ne, die; -, -n ⟨lat.⟩ (*Musik* neunter Ton [vom Grundton an]; ein Intervall); *vgl.* Non; **No|nen** *Plur.* (*im altröm. Kalender* neunter Tag vor den Iden); **No|nen|ak|kord** (*Musik);* **No|nett,** das; -[e]s, -e (Musikstück für neun Instrumente; *auch* die neun Ausführenden)

Non-Food-Ab|tei|lung ['nɔn-'fu:d...] ⟨engl.; dt.⟩ (Abteilung in Einkaufszentren, in der keine Lebensmittel, sondern andere Gebrauchsgüter verkauft werden)

No|ni|us, der; -, *Plur.* ...ien [...iən] *u.* -se ⟨nach dem Portugiesen Nunes⟩ (verschiebbarer Messstabzusatz)

Non|kon|for|mis|mus [*auch* 'no:n...] ⟨lat.-engl.⟩ (von der herrschenden Meinung unabhängige Einstellung); **Non|kon|for|mist,** der; -en, -en (↑R 126); **non|kon|for|mis|tisch**

Non|ne, die; -, -n; **non|nen|haft; Non|nen‿klos|ter, ...zie|gel** (ein Dachziegel)

Non|pa|reille [nɔ̃pa'rɛ:j], die; - ⟨franz.⟩ (*Druckw.* ein Schriftgrad)

Non|plus|ult|ra (↑R 130), das; - ⟨lat.⟩ (Unübertreffbares, Unvergleichliches)

Non|pro|li|fe|ra|tion [nɔnpro:lifə-'re:ʃ(ə)n], die; - ⟨engl.-amerik.⟩ (Nichtweitergabe [von Atomwaffen])

non schol|ae, sed vi|tae dis|ci|mus [- 'sço:lɛ:, *auch* 'sko:lɛ: - 'vi:tɛ: 'distsi...] ⟨lat., „nicht für die Schule, sondern für das Leben lernen wir"⟩

Non|sens, der; *Gen.* - *u.* -es ⟨lat.-engl.⟩ (Unsinn; törichtes Gerede)

non|stop ⟨engl.⟩ (ohne Halt, ohne Pause); nonstop fliegen, spielen; **Non|stop|flug,** *auch* **Non-Stop-Flug** (Flug ohne Zwischenlandung); **Non|stop|ki|no,** *auch* **Non-Stop-Ki|no** (Kino mit fortlaufenden Vorführungen und durchgehendem Einlass)

non trop|po ⟨ital.⟩ (*Musik* nicht zu viel)

Non|va|leur [nɔ̃va'lø:r], der; -s, -s ⟨franz.⟩ (entwertetes Wertpapier; Investition, die keinen Ertrag abwirft)

non|ver|bal [*auch* 'nɔn...] (nicht mithilfe der Sprache)

Noor, das; -[e]s, -e ⟨dän.⟩ (*nordd. für* Haff)

Nop|pe, die; -, -n (Knoten in Geweben); **Nopp|ei|sen; nop|pen** (Knoten aus dem Gewebe entfernen); **Nop|pen‿garn, ...ge|we|be, ...glas** (*Plur.* ...gläser), **...stoff; nop|pig; Nopp|zan|ge**

No|ra (w. Vorn.)

Nor|bert (m. Vorn.)

Nör|chen ⟨*zu* nören⟩ (*nordwestd. für* Schläfchen)

¹Nord (Himmelsrichtung; *Abk.* N); Nord und Süd; der kalte Wind kommt aus Nord (*fachspr.);* Autobahnausfahrt Frankfurt Nord, *auch* Frankfurt-Nord; *vgl.* Norden; **²Nord,** der; -[e]s, -e *Plur. selten* (*geh. für* Nordwind); **Nord‿af|ri|ka, ...ame|ri|ka** (↑R 132); **nord|ame|ri|ka|nisch,** *aber* (↑R 108): der Nordamerikanische Bürgerkrieg (Sezessionskrieg); **Nord|at|lan|tik|pakt,** der; -[e]s (*vgl.* NATO); **Nord|aust|ra|li|en** [...iən]; **Nord|ba|den;** *vgl.* Baden; **Nord|bra|bant** (niederl. Prov.); **Nord|da|ko|ta** (Staat in den USA; *Abk.* N. D.); **nord|deutsch,** *aber* (↑R 102): das Norddeutsche Tiefland, *auch* die Norddeutsche Tiefebene; (↑R 108:) der Norddeutsche Bund; *vgl.* deutsch; **Nord|deutsch|land; Nor|den,** der; -s (*Abk.* N); das Gewitter kommt aus Norden; sie zogen gen -; *vgl.* Nord; **Nor|den|skiöld** ['nu:rdən-ʃœld] (schwed. Polarforscher); **Nor|der|dith|mar|schen** (Teil von Dithmarschen); **Nor|der|ney** [...'nai]; ↑R 129 (eine der Ostfriesischen Inseln); **Nord‿eu|ro|pa, ...frank|reich; nord|frie|sisch,** *aber* (↑R 102): die Nordfriesischen Inseln; **Nord|fries|land; Nord|ger|ma|ne; nord|ger|ma|nisch; Nord|hang; Nord|häu|ser** ⟨nach der Stadt Nordhausen⟩ ([Korn]branntwein); **Nord|ir|land; nor|disch** (den Norden betreffend); nordische Kälte; die nordischen Sprachen; nordische Kombination (*Skisport* Sprunglauf u. 15-km-Langlauf), *aber* (↑R 108): der Nordische Krieg (1700–21); **Nor|dist,** der; -en, -en; ↑R 126 (Kenner u. Erforscher der nord. Sprachen und Kulturen sowie der nord. Altertumskunde); **Nor|dis|tik,** die; -; **Nor|dis|tin; Nord|ita|li|en** (↑R 132); **Nord|kap,** das; -s (auf einer norweg. Insel); **Nord|ka|ro|li|na** (Staat in den USA; *Abk.* N. C.); **Nord|ko|rea** (↑R 105; *nichtamtl. Bez. für* Demokratische Volksrepublik Korea); **Nord|ko|re|a|ner; Nord|ko|re|a|ne|rin; nord|ko|re|a|nisch; Nord|küs|te; Nord|län|der,** der; **Nord|län|de|rin; Nord|land|fahrt; nord|län|disch; Nord|land|rei|se; n[ördl]. Br.** = nördlicher Breite; **nörd|lich;** nördlich des Meeres, nördlich vom Meer; nördlich von München, *selten* nördlich Münchens; nördlicher Breite (*Abk.* n[ördl]. Br.); nördlicher Stern[en]himmel, *aber* (↑R 102): das Nördliche Eismeer (*älter für* Nordpolarmeer); **Nörd|li|che Dwi|na,** die; -n - (russischer Strom; *vgl.* Dwina); **Nord|licht** *Plur.* ...lichter (*auch scherzh. für* Norddeutscher); **Nörd|lin|gen** (Stadt im Ries in Bayern); **Nörd|lin|ger** (↑R 103); **[1]Nord|nord|ost** (Himmelsrichtung; *Abk.* NNO); *vgl.* Nordnordosten; **[2]Nord|nord|ost,** der; -[e]s, -e *Plur. selten* (Nordnordostwind; *Abk.* NNO); **Nord|nord|os|ten,** der; -s (*Abk.* NNO); *vgl.* Nordnordost; **[1]Nord|nord|west** (Himmelsrichtung; *Abk.* NNW); *vgl.* Nordnordwesten; **[2]Nord|nord|west,** der; -[e]s, -e *Plur. selten* (Nordnordwestwind; *Abk.* NNW); **Nord|nord|wes|ten,** der; -s (*Abk.* NNW); *vgl.* Nordnordwest; **[1]Nord|ost** (Himmelsrichtung; *Abk.* NO); *vgl.* Nordosten; **[2]Nord|ost,** der; -[e]s, -e *Plur. selten* (Nordostwind); **Nord|os|ten,** der; -s (*Abk.* NO); *vgl.* Nordost; **nord|öst|lich,** *aber* (↑R 102): die Nordöstliche Durchfahrt; **Nord-Ost|see-Ka|nal,** der; -s; **Nord|ost|wind; Nord|pol,** der; -s; **Nord|po|lar‿ge|biet** (das; -[e]s), **...meer; Nord|pol‿ex|pe|di|ti|on, ...fah|rer; Nord|punkt,** der; -[e]s; **Nord|rhein-West|fa|len** (↑R 106); **nord|rhein-west|fä|lisch; Nord|rho|de|si|en** [...iən] (*früherer Name von* Sambia); **Nord|see,** die; - (Meer); **Nord|see|ka|nal,** der; -s; **Nord|sei|te; Nord-Süd-Ge|fäl|le** (wirtschaftl. Gefälle zwischen Industrie- u. Entwicklungsländern); **nord|süd|lich;** in nordsüdlicher Richtung; **Nord|ter|ri|to|ri|um** (in Australien); **Nord|wand; nord|wärts; [1]Nord|west** (Himmelsrichtung; *Abk.* NW); *vgl.* Nordwesten; **[2]Nord|west,** der; -[e]s, -e *Plur. selten* (Nordwestwind); **Nord|wes|ten,** der; -s (*Abk.* NW); *vgl.* Nordwest; **nord|west|lich,** *aber* (↑R 102): die Nordwestliche Durchfahrt; **Nord|west|ter|ri|to|ri|en** [...iən] *Plur.* (in Kanada); **Nord|west|wind; Nord|wind**

nö|ren (*nordwestd. für* schlummern); *vgl.* Nörchen

Nör|ge|lei; Nör|gel|frit|ze, der; -n, -n *(ugs.);* **nör|ge|lig,** nörglig; **nör|geln;** ich ...[e]le (↑R 16); **Nörg|ler; Nörg|le|rin; nörg|le|risch; Nörg|ler|tum,** das; -s; **nörg|lig** *vgl.* nörgelig

no|risch (ostalpin); *aber* (↑R 102:) die Norischen Alpen

Norm, die; -, -en ‹griech.-lat.› (Richtschnur, Regel; sittliches Gebot oder Verbot als Grundlage der Rechtsordnung; Größenanweisung in der Technik; *Druckerspr.* Bogensignatur); **nor|mal** (der Norm entsprechend, vorschriftsmäßig; gewöhnlich, üblich, durchschnittlich; geistig gesund); **Nor|mal,** das; -s, -e (besonders genauer Maßstab; *meist ohne Artikel, nur Sing.: kurz für* Normalbenzin); **Nor|mal‿aus|füh|rung, ...ben|zin, ...bür|ger, ...druck** (*Plur.* ...drücke); **Nor|ma|le,** die; -[n], -n; zwei Normale[n] (*Math.* Senkrechte); **nor|ma|ler|wei|se; Nor|mal‿fall** (der), **...film, ...form** *(Sport),* **...ge|wicht, ...grö|ße, ...hö|he; Nor|mal|hö|hen|punkt,** der; -[e]s (*Zeichen* N. H.); **Nor|mal|ho|ri|zont** (Ausgangsfläche für Höhenmessungen); **Nor|ma|lie** [...iə], die; -, -n (*Technik* nach einem bestimmten System vereinheitlichtes Bauelement; *meist Plur.:* Grundform, Vorschrift); **nor|ma|li|sie|ren** (wieder normal gestalten); sich normalisieren (wieder normal werden); **Nor|ma|li|sie|rung; Nor|ma|li|tät,** die; - (normaler Zustand); **Nor|mal‿maß** (das), **...null** (das; -s; *Abk.* N. N., NN), **...pro|fil** (Walzeisenquerschnitt), **...spur** (die; -; *Eisenb.* Vollspur); **nor|mal|spu|rig** (vollspurig); **Nor|mal‿tem|pe|ra|tur, ...ton** (*Plur.* ...töne), **...uhr, ...ver|brau|cher, ...zeit** (Einheitszeit), **...zu|stand**

Nor|man (m. Vorn.)

Nor|man|die [*auch* ...mã'di:], die; - (Landschaft in Nordwestfrankreich); **Nor|man|ne,** der; -n, -n; ↑R 126 (Angehöriger eines nordgerman. Volkes); **nor|man|nisch;** normannischer Eroberungszug, *aber* (↑R 102): die Normannischen Inseln

nor|ma|tiv ‹griech.› (maßgebend, als Richtschnur dienend); **Nor|ma|tiv,** das; -s, -e (*regional für* Richtschnur, Anweisung); **Norm|blatt; nor|men** (einheitlich festsetzen, gestalten; [Größen] regeln); **Nor|men‿aus|schuss, ...kon|trol|le** *(Rechtsspr.);* **Nor|men|kon|troll|kla|ge; nor|mie|ren** (normgerecht gestalten); **Nor|mie|rung; Nor|mung** (das Normen)

Nor|ne, die; -, -n *meist Plur.* ‹altnord.› (nord. Schicksalsgöttin [Urd, Werdandi, Skuld])

Nor|thum|ber|land [nɔ:(r)'θambə(r)lənd] (↑R 132; engl. Grafschaft)

Nor|we|gen; Nor|we|ger (↑R 103); **Nor|we|ge|rin; Nor|we|ger|mus|ter** (ein Strickmuster); **Nor|we|ger|tuch,** das; -[e]s; ↑R 105 (Stoff für Skianzüge); **nor|we|gisch; Nor|we|gisch,** das; -[s] (Sprache); *vgl.* Deutsch; **Nor|we|gi|sche,** das; -n; *vgl.* Deutsche, das

No|se|ma|seu|che ‹griech.; dt.› (eine Bienenkrankheit)

No|so|gra|phie, die; - ‹griech.› (Krankheitsbeschreibung); **No|so|lo|gie,** die; - (Lehre von den Krankheiten, systematische Beschreibung der Krankheiten); **no|so|lo|gisch**

No-Spiel (↑R 24) ‹jap.-dt.› (eine Form des klassischen jap. Theaters)

Nos|sack (dt. Schriftsteller)

Nö|ßel, der *od.* das; -s, - (altes Flüssigkeitsmaß)

Nos|tal|gie, die; -, ...ien ‹griech.› ([sehnsuchtsvolle] Rückwendung zu früheren Zeiten u. Erscheinungen, z. B. in Kunst, Musik, Mode); **Nos|tal|gie|wel|le; Nos|tal|gi|ker; nos|tal|gisch**

Nost|ra|da|mus (↑R 130; franz. Astrologe des 16. Jh.s)

Nost|ri|fi|ka|ti|on (↑R 130), die; -, -en ‹lat.› (Einbürgerung; Anerkennung eines ausländischen Diploms); **nost|ri|fi|zie|ren; Nost|ri|fi|zie|rung** (*svw.* Nostrifikation)

Nost|ro‿gut|ha|ben *od.* **...kon|to** (↑R 130) ‹ital.› (Eigenguthaben im Verkehr zwischen Banken)

Not, die; -, Nöte; in Not, in Nöten sein; zur Not; wenn Not am Mann ist; seine [liebe] Not haben; Not leiden, die Not leidende Bevölkerung; alle Notleidenden, *auch* Not Leidenden; (↑R 46:) Not sein, Not tun, Not werden (*veraltend für* nötig sein, werden); *aber* das ist vonnöten

No|ta, die; -, -s ‹lat.› (*Wirtsch.* [kleine] Rechnung, Vormerkung); *vgl.* ad notam; **No|ta|beln** *Plur.* ‹franz.› (durch Bildung, Rang u. Vermögen ausgezeichnete Mitglieder des [franz.] Bürgertums); **no|ta|be|ne** ‹lat., „merke wohl!"› (übrigens; *Abk.* NB); **No|ta|be|ne,** das; -[s], -[s] (Merkzeichen, Vermerk, Denkzettel); **No|ta|bi|li|tät,** die; -, -en (*nur Sing.:* Vornehmheit; *meist Plur.:* hervorragende Persönlichkeit)

Not|an|ker

No|tar, der; -s, -e ‹lat.› (Amtsperson zur Beurkundung von Rechtsgeschäften); **No|ta|ri|at,** das; -[e]s, -e (Amt eines Notars); **No|ta|ri|ats‿ge|hil|fe, ...ge|hil-**

fin; no|ta|ri|ell (von einem Notar [ausgefertigt]); notariell beglaubigt; **No|ta|rin; no|ta|risch** (*seltener für* notariell)

Not₋arzt, ...ärz|tin; Not|arzt|wagen

No|ta|ti|on, die; -, -en (Aufzeichnung [in Notenschrift]; System von Zeichen od. Symbolen)

Not|auf|nah|me; Not|auf|nah|me|la|ger *Plur.* ...lager; **Not₋aus|gang, ...aus|rüs|tung, ...be|helf, ...be|leuch|tung, ...bett, ...brem|se, ...brem|sung, ...brü|cke**

Not|burg, Not|bur|ga (w. Vorn.)

Not|dienst; ärztlicher -; **Notdurft,** die; - (*veraltend für* Drang, den Darm, die Blase zu entleeren; Stuhlgang); **not|dürf|tig**

No|te, die; -, -n ‹lat.›; *vgl.* ausreichend *u.* drei

Note|book ['no:tbuk], das; -s, -s ‹engl.› (Personalcomputer im Buchformat)

No|ten *Plur.* ‹lat.› (*ugs. für* Musikalien); **No|ten₋aus|tausch, ...bank** (*Plur.* ...banken), **...blatt, ...durch|schnitt, ...heft, ...li|nie** (*meist Plur.*), **...pult, ...satz** (der; -es), **...schlüs|sel, ...schrift, ...stän|der, ...ste|cher** (Berufsbez.), **...sys|tem, ...um|lauf, ...wech|sel**

Not₋er|be (der; Erbe, der nicht übergangen werden darf), **...fall** (der); **Not|fall|me|di|zin,** die; -; **not|falls** (*vgl.* Fall, der *u.* R 46); **Not₋feu|er, ...ge|biet; not|ge|drun|gen; Not₋geld, ...ge|mein|schaft, ...gro|schen, ...ha|fen** (*vgl.* [2]Hafen); **Not|hel|fer;** die vierzehn Nothelfer (Heilige); **Not₋hel|fe|rin, ...hil|fe** (die; -)

no|tie|ren ‹lat.› (aufzeichnen; vormerken; *Kaufmannsspr.* den Kurs eines Papiers, den Preis einer Ware festsetzen; einen bestimmten Kurswert, Preis haben); **No|tie|rung; No|ti|fi|ka|ti|on,** die; -, -en (*veraltet für* Anzeige; Benachrichtigung); **no|ti|fi|zie|ren** (*veraltet*)

no|tig (*südd., österr. ugs. für* arm, in Not); **nö|tig;** für nötig halten; etwas nötig haben, machen; das Nötigste (↑R 47); **nö|ti|gen; nö|ti|gen|falls; Nö|ti|gung**

No|tiz, die; -, -en ‹lat.›; von etwas - nehmen; **No|tiz₋block** (*vgl.* Block), **...buch; No|tiz|samm|lung,** No|ti|zen|samm|lung; **No|tiz|zet|tel**

Not|ker (m. Vorn.)

Not|la|ge; not|lan|den; ich notlande; notgelandet; notzulanden; **Not|lan|dung; Not lei|dend** *vgl.* Not; **Not₋lei|den|de** (↑R 47), **...lei|ter** (die), **...licht** (*Plur.* ...lichter), **...lö|sung, ...lü|ge, ...maß|nah|me, ...na|gel** (*ugs. für* jmd., mit dem man in einer Notlage vorlieb nimmt), **...ope|ra|ti|on** (↑R 132), **...op|fer**

no|to|risch ‹lat.› (offenkundig, allbekannt; berüchtigt)

Not₋pfen|nig, ...pro|gramm

Not|re-Dame [nɔtr(ə)'dam] (↑R 130), die; - (*franz. Bez.* der Jungfrau Maria; Name vieler franz. Kirchen)

not|reif; Not₋rei|fe, ...ruf; Not|ruf₋an|la|ge, ...num|mer, ...säu|le; not|schlach|ten; ich notschlachte; notgeschlachtet; notzuschlachten; **Not₋schlach|tung, ...schrei, ...sig|nal, ...si|tu|a|ti|on, ...sitz, ...stand; Not|stands₋ge|biet, ...ge|setz|ge|bung, ...hil|fe** (*österr.*); **Not|strom|ag|gre|gat; Not|tau|fe; not|tau|fen;** ich nottaufe; notgetauft; notzutaufen; **Not|tür**

Not|tur|no, das; -s, *Plur.* -s *u.* ...ni ‹ital.› (*svw.* Nocturne)

Not₋un|ter|kunft, ...ver|band, ...ver|ord|nung; not|voll; not|was|sern; ich notwassere; notgewassert; notzuwassern; **Not|was|se|rung; Not|wehr,** die; -; **not|wen|dig** [*auch* ...'vɛn...]; (↑R 47:) [sich] auf das, aufs Notwendigste beschränken; es fehlt am Notwendigsten; alles Notwendige tun; **not|wen|di|gen|falls; not|wen|di|ger|wei|se; Not|wen|dig|keit** [*auch* ...'vɛn...]; **Not₋zei|chen, ...zucht** (die; -); **not|züch|ti|gen;** genotzüchtigt; zu -

Nou|ak|chott [nuak'ʃɔt] (Hptst. von Mauretanien)

Nou|gat *vgl.* Nugat

Nou|veau|té [nuvo'te:], die; -, -s ‹franz.› (Neuheit, Neuigkeit)

Nou|velle Cu|i|sine [nu'vɛl kÿi'zi:n], die; - - ‹franz.› (moderne Richtung der Kochkunst)

Nov. = November

[1]**No|va** ['no:va], die; -, ...vä ‹lat.› (neuer Stern); [2]**No|va** [*auch* 'nɔ...] (*Plur. von* Novum; Neuerscheinungen im Buchhandel)

No|va|lis [...v...] (dt. Dichter)

No|va|ti|on [...v...], die; -, -en ‹lat.› (*Rechtsw.* Schuldumwandlung, Aufhebung eines bestehenden Schuldverhältnisses durch Schaffung eines neuen)

No|ve|cen|to [nove'tʃɛnto], das; -[s] ‹ital.› ([Kunst]zeitalter des 20. Jh.s in Italien)

No|vel|le [...v...], die; -, -n ‹lat.› (Prosaerzählung; Nachtragsgesetz); **no|vel|len|ar|tig; No|vel|len₋band** (der), **...dich|ter, ...form, ...samm|lung, ...schrei|ber; No|vel|let|te,** die; -, -n (kleine Novelle); **no|vel|lie|ren** (durch ein Nachtragsgesetz ändern, ergänzen); **No|vel|lie|rung; No|vel|list,** der; -en, -en; ↑R 126 (Novellenschreiber); **no|vel|lis|tisch** (novellenartig; unterhaltend)

No|vem|ber [...v...], der; -[s], - ‹lat.› (elfter Monat im Jahr; Nebelmond, Neb[e]lung, Windmonat, Wintermonat; *Abk.* Nov.); **no|vem|ber|haft; no|vem|ber|lich; No|vem|ber₋ne|bel, ...re|vo|lu|ti|on**

No|ve|ne [...v...], die; -, -n ‹lat.› (neuntägige kath. Andacht)

No|vi|lu|ni|um [...v...], das; -s, ...ien [...i̯ən] ‹lat.› (*Astron.* erstes Sichtbarwerden der Mondsichel nach Neumond)

No|vi|tät [...v...], die; -, -en ‹lat.› (Neuerscheinung; Neuheit [der Mode u. a.]; *veraltet für* Neuigkeit); **No|vi|ze,** der; -n, -n (↑R 126) *u.* die; -, -n (Mönch od. Nonne während der Probezeit; Neuling); **No|vi|zen|meis|ter; No|vi|zi|at,** das; -[e]s, -e (dem Ordensgelübde vorausgehende Probezeit [im Kloster]); **No|vi|zi|at|jahr; No|vi|zin; No|vum** [*auch* 'nɔ...], das; -s, ...va (absolute Neuheit, noch nie Dagewesenes); *vgl.* [2]Nova

No|wa|ja Semlja (↑R 132) ‹russ.› (russ. Inselgruppe im Nordpolarmeer)

No|wo|si|birsk (Stadt in Sibirien)

No|xe, die; -, -n ‹lat.› (*Med.* krankheitserregende Ursache); **No|xin,** das; -s, -e (*Med.* aus abgestorbenem Körpereiweiß stammender Giftstoff)

Np = *chem. Zeichen für* Neptunium; Neper

NPD = Nationaldemokratische Partei Deutschlands

Nr. = Nummer; **Nrn.** = Nummern

NRT = Nettoregistertonne

NRZ = Nettoraumzahl

ns = Nanosekunde

NS = Nachschrift; *auf Wechseln* nach Sicht; Nationalsozialismus

NSG = Naturschutzgebiet

n. St. = neuen Stils (*Zeitrechnung* nach dem gregorianischen Kalender)

NS-Ver|bre|cher (↑R 26; Naziverbrecher)

N. T. = Neues Testament

n-te (↑R 25); *vgl.* x-te

nu (*ugs. für* nun); **Nu,** der (sehr kurze Zeitspanne); *nur in* im Nu, in einem Nu

Nu|an|ce [ny'ã:sə, *österr.* ny'ã:s], die; -, -n [...s(ə)n] ‹franz.› (feiner Unterschied; Feinheit; Kleinigkeit); **nu|an|cen|reich; nu|an|cie|ren; Nu|an|cie|rung**
Nu|ba, der; -[s], -[s] (Angehöriger eines Mischvolkes im Sudan)
'nü|ber; ↑R 13 (*landsch. für* hinüber)
Nu|bi|en (Landschaft in Nordafrika); **Nu|bi|er; Nu|bi|e|rin; nu|bisch,** *aber* (↑R 102): die Nubische Wüste
Nu|buk, das; -[s] ‹engl.› (wildlederartiges Kalbsleder); **Nu|buk|le|der**
nüch|tern; Nüch|tern|heit, die; -
Nu|cke, Nü|cke, die; -, -n (*landsch. für* Laune, Schrulle)
Nu|ckel, der; -s, - (*ugs. für* Schnuller); **nu|ckeln** (*ugs. für* saugen); ich ...[e]le (↑R 16)
Nu|ckel|pin|ne, die; -, -n (*ugs. für* altes, klappriges Auto)
nü|ckisch ‹*zu* Nucke›
Nud|del, der; -s, - (*landsch. für* Schnuller); **nud|deln** (*landsch. für* nuckeln); ich ...[e]le (↑R 16)
Nu|del, die; -, -n; **Nu|del|brett; nu|del|dick** (*ugs. für* sehr dick); **Nu|del|holz; nu|deln;** ich ...[e]le (↑R 16); **Nu|del‿sa|lat, ...sup|pe, ...teig, ...wal|ker** (*österr. für* Nudelholz)
Nu|dis|mus, der; - ‹lat.› (Freikörperkultur); **Nu|dist,** der; -en, -en (↑R 126); **Nu|dis|tin; Nu|di|tät** (*selten für* [anzügliche] Nacktheit)
Nu|gat, *auch* Nougat ['nu:gat] (↑R 33), der *od.* das; -s, -s ‹franz.› (süße Masse aus Zucker und Nüssen oder Mandeln); **Nu|gat‿fül|lung, ...scho|ko|la|de**
Nug|get ['nagit], das; -[s], -s ‹engl.› (natürlicher Goldklumpen)
Nug|gi ['nuki], der; -s, - (*schweiz. mdal. für* Schnuller)
nuk|le|ar (↑R 130) ‹lat.› (den Atomkern, Kernwaffen betreffend); nukleare Waffen; **Nuk|le|ar‿macht, ...me|di|zin** (die; -; Teilgebiet der Strahlenmedizin), **...spreng|kopf, ...waf|fe** (*meist Plur.*); **Nuk|le|a|se,** die; -, -n (*Chemie* Nukleinsäuren spaltendes Enzym); **Nuk|le|in,** das; -s, -e (*svw.* Nukleoproteid); **Nuk|le|in|säu|re; Nuk|le|on,** das; -s, ...onen (Atomkernbaustein); **Nuk|le|o|nik,** die; - (Atomlehre); **Nuk|le|o|pro|te|id,** das; -[e]s, -e (*Biochemie* Eiweißverbindung des Zellkerns); **Nuk|le|us,** der; -, ...ei [...e|i] (*Biol.* [Zell]kern)
Nu|ku'a|lo|fa (Hptst. von Tonga)
null ‹lat.›; null und nichtig; null Fehler haben; null Grad, null Uhr, null Sekunden; der Wert der Gleichung geht gegen null; die erste Ableitung gleich null setzen; null Komma eins (0,1); sie verloren drei zu null (3:0); die Stunde null; das Thermometer steht auf null; die Temperaturen sinken unter null; in null Komma nichts (*ugs. für* sehr schnell); *in der Jugendsprache auch für* „kein“: null Ahnung haben, null Bock (keine Lust) auf etwas haben; [1]**Null,** die; -, -en (Ziffer; Wertloses); die Zahl Null; er ist eine Null (*ugs. für* Versager); eine Zahl mit fünf Nullen; [2]**Null,** der, *auch* das; -[s], -s (*Skat* Nullspiel); **null|acht|fünf|zehn,** *in Ziffern* 08/15 (*ugs. für* wie üblich, Allerwelts...); **Null|acht|fünf|zehn-So|ße** *(ugs.)*
nul|la poe|na si|ne le|ge [- 'pø:na - -] ‹lat., „keine Strafe ohne Gesetz“›
Null-Bock-Ge|ne|ra|ti|on, die; - (*ugs. für* junge Generation, die durch Unlust u. Desinteresse gekennzeichnet ist); **Null|di|ät,** die; - (*Med.* [fast] völlig kalorienfreie Diät); **nul|len** (mit dem Nullleiter verbinden; *ugs. für* ein neues Jahrzehnt beginnen); **Nul|lerl,** das; -s, -n (*österr. ugs. für* Mensch, der nichts zu sagen hat, nichts bedeutet); **Null|feh|ler|ritt** *(Reitsport);* **Nul|li|fi|ka|ti|on,** die; -, -en; **nul|li|fi|zie|ren** (zunichte machen, für nichtig erklären); **Nul|li|tät,** die; -, -en (*selten für* Nichtigkeit; Ungültigkeit)
Null|la|ge (↑R 136), die; - (Nullstellung bei Messgeräten); **Null|lei|ter** (↑R 136), der *(Elektrotechnik);* **Null|li|nie** (↑R 136), die; -, -n; **Null|lö|sung** (↑R 136)
Null|men|ge *(Mengenlehre);* **Null|me|ri|di|an,** der; -s; **Null ou|vert** [- u'vɛ:r], der, *auch* das; - -[s], - -s ‹lat.; franz.› (offenes Nullspiel [beim Skat]); **Null|punkt;** die Stimmung sank auf den - *(ugs.);* **Null‿run|de** (*ugs. für* Lohnrunde ohne [reale] Lohnerhöhung), **...se|rie** (erste Versuchsserie einer Fertigung), **...spiel** *(Skat),* **...ta|rif** (kostenlose Gewährung bes. der Benutzung öffentlicher Verkehrsmittel); **null|te** (*Math.* Ordnungszahl zu null); **Null|wachs|tum,** das; -s *(Wirtsch.)*
Nul|pe, die; -, -n (*ugs. für* dummer, langweiliger Mensch)
Nu|me|ra|le, das; -s, *Plur.* ...lien [...i̯ən] *u.* ...lia ‹lat.› (*Sprachw.* Zahlwort, z. B. „eins“); **Nu|me|ri** [*auch* 'nu:...] (*Plur. von* Numerus; Name des 4. Buches Mosis); **nu|me|rie|ren, Nu|me|rie|rung** *frühere Schreibung für* nummerieren, Nummerierung; **Nu|me|rik,** die; - (*EDV* numerische Steuerung); **nu|me|risch** (zahlenmäßig, der Zahl nach; mit Ziffern [verschlüsselt]); **Nu|me|ro** [*auch* 'nu:...], das; -s, -s ‹ital.› (*veraltet für* Zahl; *Abk.* No., N°); *vgl.* Nummer; **Nu|me|rus** [*auch* 'nu:...], der; -, ...ri ‹lat., „Zahl“› (*Sprachw.* Zahlform des Substantivs [Singular, Plural]; *Math.* die zu logarithmierende Zahl); **Nu|me|rus clau|sus,** der; - - (zahlenmäßig beschränkte Zulassung [bes. zum Studium])
Nu|mi|der [*auch* 'nu(:)...], **Nu|mi|di|er; Nu|mi|di|en** (antikes nordafrik. Reich); **nu|mi|disch**
nu|mi|nos ‹lat.› (*Theol.* [auf das Göttliche bezogen] schauervoll und anziehend zugleich)
Nu|mis|ma|tik, die; - ‹griech.› (Münzkunde); **Nu|mis|ma|ti|ker; nu|mis|ma|tisch**
Num|mer, die; -, -n ‹lat.› (Zahl; *Abk.* Nr., *Plur.* Nrn.); Nummer fünf; etwas ist Gesprächsthema Nummer eins *(ugs.);* Nummer null; auf Nummer Sicher, *auch* auf Nummer sicher gehen (*ugs. für* nichts tun, ohne sich abzusichern); laufende Nummer (*Abk.* lfd. Nr.); *vgl.* Numero; **num|me|rie|ren** (beziffern, [be]nummern); nummerierte Ausgabe *(Druckw.);* **Num|me|rie|rung; num|me|risch** (*für* numerisch); **num|mern** (*für* nummerieren); ich ...ere (↑R 16); **Num|mern‿girl** (im Varieté), **...kon|to, ...schei|be, ...schild** (das), **...stem|pel, ...ta|fel; Num|me|rung** (*für* Nummerierung)
Num|mu|lit [*auch* ...'lit], der; *Gen.* -s *u.* -en, *Plur.* -e[n] ‹lat.› (versteinerter Wurzelfüßer im Eozän)
nun; nun [ein]mal; nun wohlan!; nun und nimmer[mehr]; von nun an
Nun|cha|ku [...'tʃa(:)ku], das; -s, -s ‹jap.›, **Nun|cha|ku|holz** (asiat. Verteidigungswaffe aus zwei mit einer Schnur od. Kette verbundenen Holzstäben)
nun|mehr *(geh.);* **nun|meh|rig** *(geh.)*
'nun|ter; ↑R 13 (*landsch. für* hinunter)
Nun|ti|a|tur, die; -, -en ‹lat.› (Amt und Sitz eines Nuntius); **Nun|ti|us,** der; -, ...ien [...i̯ən] (ständiger Botschafter des Papstes bei weltlichen Regierungen)
nup|ti|al ‹lat.› (*veraltet für* ehelich, hochzeitlich)

nur; nur Gutes empfangen; nur mehr (*landsch. für* nur noch); warum nur? nur zu!
Nür|burg|ring, der; -[e]s (↑R 105; Autorenn- u. -teststrecke in der Eifel)
Nur|haus|frau
Nürn|berg (Stadt in Mittelfranken); **Nürn|ber|ger** (↑R 103); Nürnberger Lebkuchen; Nürnberger Trichter
Nurse [nœ:(r)s], die; -, *Plur.* -s [ˈnœ:(r)siz] *u.* -n [...s(ə)n] ‹engl.› (*engl. Bez. für* Kinderpflegerin)
nu|scheln (*ugs. für* undeutlich sprechen); ich ...[e]le (↑R 16)
Nuss, die; -, Nüsse; **Nuss‿baum,** **...beu|gel** *(österr.)*; **nuss|braun;** **Nüss|chen;** **Nuss‿fül|lung,** **...gip|fel** *(schweiz.)*; **nus|sig;** ein nussiger Geschmack; **Nuss‿kip|ferl** *(österr.)*, **...kna|cker,** **...koh|le,** **...ku|chen;** **Nüss|li|sa|lat** (*schweiz. für* Feldsalat)
Nuss|scha|le (↑R 136; *auch für* kleines Boot); **Nuss|schin|ken;** **Nuss|scho|ko|la|de;** **Nuss|stru|del** *(österr.)*
Nuss|tor|te
Nüs|ter [*auch* ˈny:...], die; -, -n *meist Plur.*
Nut, die; -, -en *(in der Technik nur so) u.* Nu|te, die; -, -n (Furche, Fuge)
Nu|ta|ti|on, die; -, -en ‹lat.› (*Astron.* Schwankung der Erdachse gegen den Himmelspol; *Bot.* Wachstumsbewegung der Pflanze)
Nu|te *vgl.* Nut; **Nut|ei|sen;** **nu|ten;** **Nu|ten|frä|ser**
Nu|the, die; - (l. Nebenfluss der Havel)
Nut|ho|bel
[1]**Nut|ria** (↑R 130), die; -, -s ‹span.› (Biberratte); [2]**Nut|ria,** der; -s, -s (Pelz aus dem Fell der [1]Nutria)
Nut|ri|ment (↑R 130), das; -[e]s, -e ‹lat.› (*Med.* Nahrungsmittel); **Nut|ri|ti|on,** die; -, -en (Ernährung); **nut|ri|tiv** (nährend, nahrungsmäßig)
Nut|sche, die; -, -n (*Chemie* Filtriereinrichtung, Trichter); **nut|schen** (*ugs. u. landsch. für* lutschen; *Chemie* durch einen Filter absaugen); du nutschst
Nut|te, die; -, -n (*derb für* Prostituierte); **nut|ten|haft,** **nut|tig** (*derb für* wie eine Nutte)
nutz; zu nichts nutz sein (*südd., österr. für* zu nichts nütze sein); *vgl.* Nichtsnutz; **Nutz,** der (*veraltet für* Nutzen); zu Nutz und Frommen; (↑R 41:) sich etwas zunutze, *auch* zu Nutze machen; **Nutz|an|wen|dung;** **nutz|bar;** nutzbar machen; **Nutz|bar|keit,** die; -; **Nutz|bar|ma|chung;** **Nutz|bau** *Plur.* ...bauten; **nutz|brin|gend;** **nüt|ze;** [zu] nichts nütze; **Nutz|ef|fekt** (Nutzleistung, Wirkungsgrad); **nut|zen** (du nutzt), *häufiger* **nüt|zen** (du nützt; es nützt mir nichts); **Nut|zen,** der; -s; es ist von [großem, geringem] -; **Nut|zen-Kos|ten-A|na|ly|se** *(Wirtsch.)*; **Nut|zer;** **Nut|ze|rin;** **Nutz‿fahr|zeug,** **...flä|che,** **...gar|ten,** **...holz,** **...kos|ten** *(Wirtsch.)*, **...last,** **...leis|tung** *(Technik)*; **nütz|lich;** sich nützlich machen; **Nütz|lich|keit,** die; -; **Nütz|lich|keits‿den|ken,** **...prin|zip** (das; -s); **Nütz|ling** (*Ggs.* Schädling); **nutz|los;** **Nutz|lo|sig|keit,** die; -; **nutz|nie|ßen** (*geh. für* von etwas Nutzen haben); du nutznießt; genutznießt; **Nutz|nie|ßer;** **Nutz|nie|ße|rin;** **nutz|nie|ße|risch;** **Nutz|nie|ßung** (*auch Rechtsspr.* Nießbrauch); **Nutz‿pflan|ze,** **...tier;** **Nut|zung;** **Nut|zungs‿aus|fall,** **...dau|er,** **...recht** *(Rechtsspr.)*; **Nutz|wert**
n. V. = nach Verlängerung *(Sport)*
NVA = Nationale Volksarmee (*ehem.* Streitkräfte der DDR)
NW = Nordwest[en]
Ny, das; -[s], -s (griech. Buchstabe; *N, ν*)
N. Y. = New York (Staat)
Nyk|ta|lo|pie (↑R 132), die; - ‹griech.› (*Med.* Nachtblindheit); **Nyk|to|pho|bie,** die; - (*Med., Psych.* [krankhafte] Furcht vor Dunkelheit)
Ny|lon ® [ˈnailɔn], das; -[s] ‹engl.› (haltbare synthet. Textilfaser); **Ny|lons** *Plur.* (*ugs. veraltend für* Nylonstrümpfe); **Ny|lon|strumpf**
Nym|phäa, **Nym|phäe,** die; -, ...äen ‹griech.› (*Bot.* Seerose); **Nym|phä|um,** das; -s, ...äen (Brunnentempel [in der Antike]); **Nym|phe,** die; -, -n (griech. Naturgottheit; *Zool.* Entwicklungsstufe [der Libelle]); **Nym|phen|burg** (Schlossanlage in München); **nym|phen|haft;** **Nym|phen|sit|tich** (austral. Papagei); **nym|pho|man** (an Nymphomanie leidend); **Nym|pho|ma|nie,** die; - (krankhaft gesteigerter Geschlechtstrieb bei der Frau); **Nym|pho|ma|nin** (nymphomane Frau); **nym|pho|ma|nisch**
Ny|norsk, das; - ‹norw.› (norw. Schriftsprache, die auf den Dialekten beruht; *vgl.* Landsmål)
Nys|tag|mus, der; - ‹griech.› (*Med.* Zittern des Augapfels)
Nyx (griech. Göttin der Nacht)

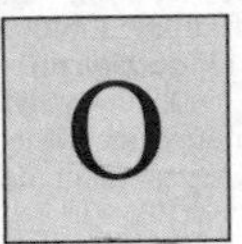

O (Buchstabe); das O; des O, die O, *aber* das o in Tor (↑R 60); der Buchstabe O, o
Ö (Buchstabe; Umlaut); das Ö; des Ö, die Ö, *aber* das ö in König (↑R 60); der Buchstabe Ö, ö
o *vgl.* oh
O = Ost[en]
O = Oxygenium (*chem. Zeichen für* Sauerstoff)
O, o = Omikron
Ω, ω = Omega
Ω = Ohm (elektr. Einheit)
O' ‹„Nachkomme"› (Bestandteil irischer Eigennamen, z. B. O'Neill [o:ˈni:l])
o. a. = oben angeführt
o. Ä. = oder Ähnliche[s] (*vgl.* ähnlich)
ÖAMTC = Österr. Automobil-, Motorrad- und Touring-Club
OAPEC = Organization of the Arab Petroleum Exporting Countries [ɔ:(r)gənaiˈze:ʃ(ə)n əv ði ˈɛrəb piˈtro:liəm ɛksˈpɔ:(r)tiŋ ˈkantri:z], die; - (Organisation der arabischen Erdöl exportierenden Länder)
O|a|se, die; -, -n ‹ägypt.› (Wasserstelle in der Wüste)
OAU = Organization of African Unity [ɔ:(r)gənaiˈze:ʃ(ə)n əv ˈɛfrikən ˈju:niti] (Organisation für Afrikanische Einheit); **OAU-Staa|ten** (↑R 26)
[1]**ob;** (↑R 49:) das Ob und Wann
[2]**ob;** *Präp. mit Dat.* (*veraltet, noch landsch. für* oberhalb, über), z. B. ob dem Walde, Rothenburg ob der Tauber; *Präp. mit Gen., seltener mit Dat.* (*veraltend für* über, wegen), z. B. ob des Glückes, ob gutem Fang erfreut sein
Ob, der; -[s] (Strom in Sibirien)
OB = Oberbürgermeister(in)
o. B. = ohne Befund
O|bacht (↑R 132), die; -; Obacht geben
O|bad|ja (bibl. Prophet)
ÖBB = Österr. Bundesbahnen
obd. = oberdeutsch
Ob|dach, das; -[e]s (*veraltend für* Unterkunft, Wohnung); **ob|dach|los;** **Ob|dach|lo|se,** der *u.* die; -n, -n (↑R 5 ff.); **Ob|dach|lo|sen‿asyl** (↑R 132), **...für|sor|ge,** **...heim;** **Ob|dach|lo|sig|keit,** die; -

Ob|duk|ti|on, die; -, -en ‹lat.› (*Med.* Leichenöffnung); **Ob|duk|ti|ons|be|fund; ob|du|zie|ren**

O|be|di|enz (↑R 132), die; - ‹lat.› (*kath. Kirche* kanonischer Gehorsam der Kleriker gegenüber den geistl. Oberen)

O-Bei|ne *Plur.* (↑R 25); **o-bei|nig,** *auch* **O-bei|nig**

O|be|lisk, der; -en, -en (↑R 126) ‹griech.› (vierkantige, nach oben spitz zulaufende Säule)

o|ben; nach, von, bis oben; nach oben hin, zu; von oben her, herab; alles Gute kommt von oben; man wusste kaum noch, was oben und was unten war; oben ohne (*ugs. für* busenfrei); oben sein, bleiben, liegen, stehen usw.; die oben angeführte, oben erwähnte, gegebene, oben genannte, stehende, zitierte Erklärung; das [weiter] oben Erwähnte, die oben Genannten, im oben Stehenden, oben Stehendes gilt weiterhin, *auch* das Obenerwähnte, die Obengenannten, im Obenstehenden, Obenstehendes

o|ben|an; obenan stehen, sitzen; **o|ben|auf;** obenauf liegen; obenauf (*ugs. für* gesund, guter Laune) sein; obenauf, *auch* obenaus schwingen (*schweiz. für* die Oberhand gewinnen, an der Spitze liegen); **o|ben|aus** *vgl.* obenauf; **o|ben|drauf;** obendrauf liegen, stellen; **o|ben|drein; o|ben|drü|ber;** obendrüber legen; **o|ben|durch; o|ben er|wähnt** *vgl.* oben; **o|ben ge|nannt** (*Abk.* o. g.); *vgl.* oben; **o|ben|her;** du musst obenher gehen, *aber* von oben her; **o|ben|he|rum** (↑R 132; *ugs. für* im oberen Teil; oben am Körper); **o|ben|hin** (flüchtig), *aber* nach oben hin; **O|ben-oh|ne-Ba|de|an|zug** (↑R 28); **O|ben-oh|ne-Lo|kal; o|ben|rum** (*svw.* obenherum); **o|ben ste|hend, zitiert** *vgl.* oben

[1]**o|ber** (*österr. für* über); *Präp. mit Dat.,* z. B. das Schild hängt ober der Tür

[2]**o|ber** *vgl.* obere

O|ber, der; -s, - ([Ober]kellner; eine Spielkarte)

O|ber|am|mer|gau; ↑R 105 (Ort am Oberlauf der Ammer)

O|ber‿arm, ...arzt, ...ärz|tin, ...auf|sicht, ...bau (*Plur.* ...bauten), **...bauch**

O|ber|bay|ern (↑R 105)

O|ber‿be|fehl (der; -[e]s), **...befehls|ha|ber, ...be|griff, ...beklei|dung; O|ber|berg|amt; O|ber‿bett, ...bür|ger|meis|ter** ([*auch* ...'byr...] *Abk.* OB, OBM)

O|ber|deck

o|ber|deutsch (*Abk.* obd.); *vgl.* deutsch; **O|ber|deutsch,** das; -[s] (Sprache); *vgl.* Deutsch; **O|ber|deut|sche,** das; -n; *vgl.* Deutsche, das

O|ber|dorf

o|be|re; der obere Stock; die ober[e]n Klassen; *aber* (↑R 102): das Obere Eichsfeld; [1]**O|be|re,** das; -n (Höheres); [2]**O|be|re,** der; -n, -n; ↑R 5 ff. (Vorgesetzter)

o|ber|faul (*ugs. für* sehr verdächtig)

O|ber|flä|che; o|ber|flä|chen|ak|tiv *(Chemie, Physik);* **O|ber|flä|chen‿be|hand|lung, ...span|nung, ...struk|tur, ...ver|bren|nung, ...was|ser** (das; -s; *Ggs.* Grundwasser); **o|ber|fläch|lich; O|ber|fläch|lich|keit**

O|ber|förs|ter

O|ber|fran|ken (↑R 105)

o|ber|gä|rig; -es Bier; **O|ber‿ge|frei|te, ...ge|richt** (*schweiz. svw.* Kantonsgericht), **...ge|schoss, ...ge|wand, ...gren|ze**

o|ber|halb; *als Präp. mit Gen.:* der Neckar oberhalb Heidelbergs (von Heidelberg aus flussaufwärts)

O|ber|hand, die; -

O|ber‿haupt, ...haus (im Zweikammerparlament), **...hemd, ...herr|schaft** (die; -)

O|ber|hes|sen (↑R 105)

O|ber|hit|ze; bei - backen

O|ber|hof|meis|ter [*auch* ...'ho:f...]; **O|ber|ho|heit,** die; -

O|be|rin (Oberschwester; Leiterin eines Nonnenklosters)

O|ber‿in|ge|ni|eur (*Abk.* Ob.-Ing.), **...in|spek|tor** (*Abk.* Ob.-Insp.)

o|ber|ir|disch

O|ber|ita|li|en (↑R 105 *u.* 132)

o|ber|kant *(schweiz.); Präp. mit Gen.:* oberkant des Fensters, *auch* oberkant Fenster; **O|ber‿kan|te, ...kell|ner, ...kie|fer** (der), **...kir|chen|rat** [*auch* ...'kir...], **...kom|man|die|ren|de** (der; -n, -n; ↑R 5 ff.), **...kom|man|do, ...kör|per, ...kreis|di|rek|tor** [*auch* ...'krais...]

O|ber|land, das; -[e]s; **O|ber|län|der,** der; -s, - (Bewohner des Oberlandes)

O|ber|lan|des|ge|richt [*auch* ...'lan...] (*Abk.* OLG)

O|ber|län|ge

o|ber|las|tig (*Seemannsspr.* zu hoch beladen); -es Schiff

O|ber|lauf, der; -[e]s, ...läufe

O|ber|lau|sitz [*auch* ...'lau...]; ↑R 105 (Landschaft zwischen Bautzen u. Görlitz; *Abk.* O. L.)

O|ber‿le|der, ...leh|rer; o|ber|leh|rer|haft; O|ber|lei|tung; O|ber|lei|tungs|om|ni|bus (*Kurzform* Obus); **O|ber‿leut|nant** (*Abk.* Oblt.; - z. [zur] See), **...licht, ...li|ga, ...li|gist, ...lip|pe, ...maat, ...ma|te|ri|al**

O|be|ron (König der Elfen)

O|ber|ös|ter|reich; ↑R 105 (österr. Bundesland)

O|ber|pfalz, die; -; ↑R 105 (Regierungsbezirk des Landes Bayern)

O|ber‿post|di|rek|ti|on [*auch* ...'pɔst...], **...pries|ter, ...pri|ma** [*auch* ...'pri:ma], **...rat** (Akademischer -), **...rä|tin** (Wissenschaftliche -), **...re|al|schu|le** [*auch* ...re'a:l...], **...re|gie|rungs|rat** [*auch* ...'gi:...]

O|ber|rhein; o|ber|rhei|nisch, *aber* (↑R 102): das Oberrheinische Tiefland

O|bers, das; - (*bayr. u. österr. für* Sahne)

O|ber|schen|kel; O|ber|schen|kel|hals; O|ber|schen|kel|hals|bruch; O|ber|schicht; o|ber|schläch|tig (durch Wasser von oben angetrieben); -es Mühlrad; **o|ber|schlau** (*ugs. für* sich für besonders schlau haltend)

O|ber|schle|si|en (↑R 105)

O|ber‿schul|amt [*auch* ...'ʃu:l...], **...schu|le, ...schü|ler, ...schü|le|rin, ...schwes|ter, ...sei|te; o|ber|seits** (an der Oberseite); **O|ber|se|kun|da** [*auch* ...'kunda]

o|berst *vgl.* oberste; **O|berst,** der; *Gen.* -en (↑R 126) *u.* -s, *Plur.* -en, *seltener* -e

O|ber‿staats|an|walt [*auch* ...'ʃta:ts...], **...stabs|arzt** [*auch* ...'ʃta:bs...], **...stadt|di|rek|tor** [*auch* ...'ʃtat...], **o|ber|stän|dig** *(Bot.)*

O|berst|dorf (Ort in den Allgäuer Alpen)

o|bers|te; oberstes Stockwerk; dort das Buch, das oberste, hätte ich gern; die obersten Gerichtshöfe; *aber* (↑R 108): der Oberste Gerichtshof; (↑R 47:) das Oberste zuunterst, das Unterste zuoberst kehren; **O|bers|te,** der *u.* die; -n, -n; ↑R 5 ff. (Vorgesetzter, Vorgesetzte)

O|ber‿stei|ger *(Bergbau),* **...stim|me**

O|berst|leut|nant [*auch* ...'lɔyt...]

O|ber|stock, der; -[e]s (Stockwerk); **O|ber|stüb|chen;** *meist in* im - nicht ganz richtig sein (*ugs. für* nicht ganz normal sein)

O|ber|stu|di|en‿di|rek|tor[1], **...di|rek|to|rin, ...rat, ...rä|tin**

---

[1] [*auch* ...'ʃtu:...]

O|ber‿stu|fe, ...teil (das, *auch* der), **...ter|tia** [*auch* ...'tɛr...], **...ton** (*Plur.* ...töne), **...ver|wal|tungs|ge|richt** [*auch* ...'val...]

O|ber|vol|ta [...v...] (*früher für* Burkina Faso); **O|ber|vol|ta|er; o|ber|vol|ta|isch**

o|ber|wärts (*veraltet für* oberhalb)

O|ber|was|ser, das; -s; - haben, bekommen (*ugs. für* im Vorteil sein, in Vorteil kommen); **O|ber|wei|te**

O|ber|wie|sen|thal, Kur|ort (im Erzgebirge)

Ob|frau (*svw.* Obmännin)

ob|ge|nannt (*österr. Amtsspr., sonst veraltet für* oben genannt)

ob|gleich

Ob|hut, die; - *(geh.)*

O|bi, der *od.* das; -[s], -s ‹jap.› (Kimonogürtel; *Judo* Gürtel der Kampfbekleidung)

o|big; die obigen Paragraphen; der Obige (der oben Genannte; *Abk.* d. O.); Obiges gilt auch weiterhin; im Obigen (*Amtsspr.* weiter oben); *vgl.* folgend

Ob.-Ing. = Oberingenieur

Ob.-Insp. = Oberinspektor

Ob|jekt, das; -[e]s, -e ‹lat.› (Ziel, Gegenstand; *ehem. in der DDR auch für* für die Allgemeinheit geschaffene Einrichtung [z. B. Verkaufsstelle, Ferienheim]; *österr. Amtsspr. auch für* Gebäude; *Sprachw.* Ergänzung); **Ob|jek|te|ma|cher** *(Kunstw.)*; **ob|jek|tiv** [*auch* 'ɔp...] (gegenständlich; tatsächlich; sachlich); **Ob|jek|tiv,** das; -s, -e [...və] (bei opt. Instrumenten die dem Gegenstand zugewandte Linse); **Ob|jek|ti|va|ti|on** [...v...], die; -, -en (Vergegenständlichung); **ob|jek|ti|vie|ren** (vergegenständlichen; von subjektiven Einflüssen befreien); **Ob|jek|ti|vie|rung; Ob|jek|ti|vis|mus,** der; - (philosoph. Denkrichtung, die vom Subjekt unabhängige objektive Wahrheiten u. Werte annimmt); **ob|jek|ti|vis|tisch** (in der Art des Objektivismus); **Ob|jek|ti|vi|tät,** die; - (strenge Sachlichkeit; Vorurteilslosigkeit); **Ob|jekt|kunst,** die; - (moderne Kunstrichtung, die statt der Darstellung eines Gegenstandes diesen selbst präsentiert); **Ob|jekt|satz** (*Sprachw.* Nebensatz in der Funktion eines Objektes); **Ob|jekt|schutz** ([polizeil.] Schutz für Gebäude, Sachwerte o. Ä.); **Ob|jekts|ge|ni|tiv; Ob|jekt‿spra|che** *(Sprachw.)*, **...tisch** (am Mikroskop), **...trä|ger** (Glasplättchen [mit zu mikroskopierendem Objekt])

[1]**Ob|la|te** [*österr.* 'ɔ...], die; -, -n ‹lat.› (ungeweihte Hostie; dünnes, rundes Gebäck; Unterlage für Konfekt, Lebkuchen); [2]**Ob|la|te,** der; -n, -n; ↑R 126 (Laienbruder; Angehöriger einer kath. Genossenschaft); **Ob|la|ti|on,** die; -, -en (Darbringungsgebet, Teil der kath. Messe)

Ob|leu|te (*Plur. von* Obmann)

ob|lie|gen [*auch, österr. nur,* ɔp'li:...]; es liegt, lag mir ob, es hat mir obgelegen; obzuliegen (*od., österr. nur,* es obliegt, oblag mir, es hat mir oblegen; zu obliegen); **Ob|lie|gen|heit**

ob|li|gat ‹lat.› (unerlässlich, unvermeidlich, unentbehrlich); mit -er Flöte *(Musik)*; **Ob|li|ga|ti|on,** die; -, -en (*Rechtsspr.* persönl. Haftung für eine Verbindlichkeit; *Wirtsch.* Wertpapier mit fester Verzinsung); **Ob|li|ga|ti|o|nen|recht,** das; -[e]s (*schweiz. für* Schuldrecht; *Abk.* OR); **ob|li|ga|to|risch** (verbindlich; *auch svw.* obligat); -e Stunden (Pflichtstunden); **Ob|li|ga|to|ri|um,** das; -s, ...ien [...iən] (*schweiz. für* Verpflichtung; Pflichtfach, -leistung); **Ob|li|go** [*auch* 'ɔb...], das; -s, -s ‹ital.› (*Wirtsch.* Haftung; Verpflichtung); ohne Obligo (unverbindlich; ohne Gewähr; *Abk.* o. O.), *österr.* außer Obligo

ob|lique [o'bli:k] ‹lat.›; -r [o'bli:kvər] Kasus (*Sprachw.* abhängiger Fall); *vgl.* Casus obliquus; **Ob|li|qui|tät** [...kvi...], die; -

Ob|li|te|ra|ti|on, die; -, -en ‹lat.› (*Wirtsch.* Tilgung; *Med.* Verstopfung von Hohlräumen, Kanälen, Gefäßen des Körpers)

ob|long ‹lat.› (*veraltet für* länglich, rechteckig)

Oblt. = Oberleutnant

OBM = Oberbürgermeister(in)

Ob‿mann (*Plur.* ...männer *u.* ...leute), **...män|nin**

O|boe [*österr.* 'o:...], die; -, -n ‹ital.› (ein Holzblasinstrument); **O|bo|ist,** der; -en, -en; ↑R 126 (Oboebläser); **O|bo|is|tin**

O|bo|lus, der; -, *Plur.* - *u.* -se ‹griech.› (kleine Münze im alten Griechenland; *übertr. für* kleine Geldspende)

O|bot|rit (↑R 130), der; -en, -en; ↑R 126 (Angehöriger eines westslaw. Volksstammes)

Ob|rig|keit (Träger der Macht, der Regierungsgewalt); **ob|rig|keit|lich; Ob|rig|keits‿den|ken, ...staat**

Ob|rist (↑R 130), der; -en, -en; ↑R 126 (*veraltet für* Oberst; *auch für* Mitglied einer Militärjunta)

ob|schon

Ob|ser|vant [...v...], der; -en, -en (↑R 126) ‹lat.› (Mönch der strengeren Ordensregel); **Ob|ser|vanz,** die; -, -en (*Rechtsspr.* örtl. begrenztes Gewohnheitsrecht; Befolgung der strengeren Regel eines Mönchsordens); **Ob|ser|va|ti|on,** die; -, -en ([wissenschaftl.] Beobachtung); **Ob|ser|va|tor,** der; -s, ...oren (wissenschaftl. Beobachter an einem Observatorium); **Ob|ser|va|to|ri|um,** das; -s, ...ien [...iən] ([astron., meteorolog., geophysikal.] Beobachtungsstation); **ob|ser|vie|ren** (*auch für* polizeilich überwachen)

Ob|ses|si|on, die; -, -en ‹lat.› (*Psych.* Zwangsvorstellung)

Ob|si|di|an, der; -s, -e ‹lat.› (ein Gestein)

ob|sie|gen [*auch* 'ɔp...] (*veraltend für* siegen, siegreich sein); ich obsieg[t]e, habe obsiegt, zu obsiegen *(österr. nur so)*; *auch* ich sieg[t]e ob, habe obgesiegt, obzusiegen

obs|kur (↑R 132) ‹lat.› (dunkel; verdächtig; fragwürdig); *vgl.* Clair-obscur; **Obs|ku|ran|tis|mus,** der; - (Aufklärungs- u. Wissenschaftsfeindlichkeit); **Obs|ku|ri|tät,** die; -, -en (Dunkelheit, Unklarheit)

ob|so|let ‹lat.› (nicht mehr üblich; veraltet)

Ob|sor|ge, die; - (*österr. Amtsspr., sonst veraltet für* sorgende Aufsicht)

Obst, das; -[e]s; **Obst‿an|bau, ...bau** (der; -[e]s); **obst|bau|lich; Obst‿baum, ...blü|te, ...ern|te, ...es|sig**

Obs|te|trik (↑R 130 *u.* 132), die; - ‹lat.› (*Med.* Lehre von der Geburtshilfe)

Obst‿gar|ten, ...händ|ler

obs|ti|nat (↑R 132) ‹lat.› (starrsinnig, widerspenstig)

Obs|ti|pa|ti|on (↑R 132), die; -, -en ‹lat.› (*Med.* Stuhlverstopfung); **obs|ti|piert** (verstopft)

Obst|ku|chen; Obst|ler, Öbst|ler (*landsch. für* Obsthändler; aus Obst gebrannter Schnaps); **Obst|le|rin, Öbst|le|rin** (*landsch. für* Obstverkäuferin); **Obst‿mes|ser** (das), **...plan|ta|ge; obst|reich**

ob|stru|ie|ren ‹lat.› ([Parlamentsbeschlüsse] zu verhindern suchen; hemmen); **Ob|struk|ti|on,** die; -, -en (Verschleppung [der Arbeiten], Verhinderung [der Beschlussfassung]; *Med.* Verstopfung); **Ob|struk|ti|ons‿po|li|tik** (die; -), **...tak|tik; ob|struk|tiv** (hemmend; *Med.* verstopfend)

Obst‿saft, ...sa|lat, ...schaum|wein, ...tag, ...tor|te, ...wein
obs|zön (↑R 132) ‹lat.› (unanständig, schamlos, schlüpfrig); **Obs|zö|ni|tät,** die; -, -en
O|bus, der; -ses, -se (*Kurzform von* Oberleitungsomnibus)
Ob|wal|den *vgl.* Unterwalden ob dem Wald; **Ob|wald|ner** (↑R 103); **ob|wald|ne|risch**
ob|wal|ten [*auch* ...'val...] *(veraltend);* es waltet[e] ob, *auch* es obwaltet[e]; obgewaltet; obzuwalten; **ob|wal|tend;** unter den -en Umständen
ob|wohl; ob|zwar *(veraltend)*
Oc|ca|si|on, die; -, -en ‹franz.› (*schweiz. für* Okkasion [Gelegenheitskauf, Gebrauchtware])
och!
Och|lo|kra|tie [...x...], die; -, ...ien ‹griech.› (Pöbelherrschaft [im alten Griechenland]); **och|lo|kra|tisch**
o|chots|kisch [...x...] (die russ. Hafenstadt Ochotsk betreffend); *aber* das Ochotskische Meer
Ochs, der; -en, -en; ↑R 126 (*landsch. u. österr. für* Ochse); **Öchs|chen; Och|se,** der; -n, -n (↑R 126); **och|sen** (*ugs. für* angestrengt arbeiten); du ochst; **Och|sen|au|ge** (*Archit.* ovales od. rundes Dachfenster; *landsch. für* Spiegelei); **Och|sen‿brust, ...fie|sel** (der; -s, -; *landsch. für* Ochsenziemer), **...fleisch, ...frosch, ...kar|ren, ...maul; Och|sen|maul|sa|lat; Och|sen|schlepp,** der; -[e]s, -e (*österr. für* Ochsenschwanz); **Och|sen|schlepp|sup|pe** *(österr.);* **Och|sen|schwanz; Och|sen|schwanz|sup|pe; Och|sen|tour** (*ugs. für* langsame, mühselige Arbeit, [Beamten]laufbahn); **Och|sen|zie|mer; Och|se|rei** *(ugs.);* **och|sig** (*ugs. für* dumm; plump)
Öchs|le, das; -s, - ‹nach dem Mechaniker› (Maßeinheit für das spezif. Gewicht des Mostes); 90° Öchsle; **Öchs|le|grad** (↑R 95)
o|cker ‹griech.› (gelbbraun); eine ocker Wand; *vgl. auch* beige; **O|cker,** der *od. österr. nur,* das; -s, - (zur Farbenherstellung verwendete Tonerde; gelbbraune Malerfarbe); in Ocker (↑R 47); **o|cker|braun; O|cker|far|be; o|cker‿far|ben** *od.* **...far|big; o|cker|gelb; o|cker|hal|tig**
Ock|ham ['ɔkɛm] (engl. mittelalterl. Theologe); **Ock|ha|mis|mus,** der; - (Lehre des Ockham)
Oc|ta|via usw. *vgl.* Oktavia usw.
Od, das; -[e]s (angebliche Ausstrahlung des menschl. Körpers)
od. = oder
öd *vgl.* öde
O|da (w. Vorn.)
O|dal, das; -s, -e (*germ. Recht* Sippeneigentum an Grund und Boden)
O|da|lis|ke, die; -, -n ‹türk.› (*früher für* weiße türk. Haremssklavin)
Odd Fel|low [- ...lo:], der; - -s, - -s *u.* **Odd|fel|low,** der; -s, -s ‹engl.› (Angehöriger einer urspr. engl. humanitären Bruderschaft)
Odds *Plur.* ‹engl.› (*Sport* Vorgaben [bes. bei Pferderennen])
O|de, die; -, -n ‹griech.› (feierliches Gedicht)
ö|de, *auch* öd; **Ö|de,** die; -, -n
O|del *vgl.* ²Adel
O|dem, der; -s (*geh. für* Atem)
Ö|dem, das; s, -e ‹griech.› (*Med.* Gewebewassersucht); **ö|de|ma|tös** (ödemartig)
ö|den (*ugs. für* langweilen; *landsch. für* roden)
Ö|den|burg (*ung.* Sopron)
O|den|wald, der; -[e]s (Bergland östl. des Oberrheinischen Tieflandes); **O|den|wäl|der,** der
O|de|on, das; -s, -s ‹franz.› (*svw.* Odeum; *auch* Name von Gebäuden für Tanzveranstaltungen u. Ä.)
o|der (*Abk.* od.); *vgl.* ähnlich *u.* entweder
O|der, die; - (ein Strom); **O|der|bruch,** das, *auch* der; -[e]s; **O|der|haff;** *vgl.* Stettiner Haff
O|der|men|nig, A|cker|men|nig, der; -[e]s, -e (eine Heilpflanze)
O|der-Nei|ße-Gren|ze, die; - (↑R 105); **O|der-Spree-Ka|nal,** der; -s (↑R 105)
O|des|sa (ukrain. Hafenstadt am Schwarzen Meer)
O|de|um, das; -s, Odeen ‹griech.-lat.› (im Altertum rundes, theaterähnliches Gebäude für Musik- u. Theateraufführungen)
O|deur [o'dø:r], das; -s, *Plur.* -s *u.* -e ‹franz.› (wohlriechender Duft)
OdF = Opfer des Faschismus
Öd|heit, die; -; **Ö|dig|keit,** die; -
O|di|lia, O|di|lie [...iə] (w. Vorn.);
O|di|lo (m. Vorn.)
O|din (*nord. Form für* Wodan)
o|di|os, o|di|ös ‹lat.› (widerwärtig, verhasst)
ö|di|pal *(Psychoanalyse);* die -e Phase (Entwicklungsphase des Kindes); **Ö|di|pus** (in der griech. Sage König von Theben); **Ö|di|pus|kom|plex** (zu starke Bindung eines Kindes an den gegengeschlechtlichen Elternteil)
O|di|um, das; -s ‹lat.› (übler Beigeschmack, Makel)
Öd|land, das; -[e]s; **Öd|nis,** die; - *(geh.)*
O|do (m. Vorn.)
O|do|a|ker (germ. Heerführer)
O|do|ar|do (m. Vorn.)
O|don|to|lo|ge, der; -n, -n; ↑R 126 ‹griech.›; **O|don|to|lo|gie,** die; - (Zahnheilkunde)
O|dys|see, die; -, ...sseen (*nur Sing.:* griech. Heldengedicht; *übertr. für* Irrfahrt); **o|dys|se|isch** (die Odyssee betreffend); **O|dys|seus** [...sɔys] (in der griech. Sage König von Ithaka); *vgl.* Ulixes, Ulysses
Oe|bis|fel|de [ø:...] (Stadt in der Altmark)
OECD = Organization for Economic Cooperation and Development [ɔ:(r)gənai'ze:ʃ(ə)n fɔr ikə'nɔmik ko:ɔpə're:ʃ(ə)n ənd di'vɛləpmənt] ‹engl.› (Organisation für wirtschaftliche Zusammenarbeit und Entwicklung)
Oels|nitz ['œls...] (Stadt im Vogtland); **Oels|nitz (Erz|ge|bir|ge)** (Stadt am Rande des Erzgebirges)
Oe|so|pha|gus [ø...] *vgl.* Ösophagus
Œuv|re ['œ:vr(ə)] (↑R 130), das; -, -s ‹franz.› ([Gesamt]werk eines Künstlers); **Œuv|re‿ka|ta|log, ...ver|zeich|nis**
Oeyn|hau|sen ['ø:n...], **Bad** (Badeort im Ravensberger Land)
OEZ = osteuropäische Zeit
Öf|chen; O|fen, der; -s, Öfen; **O|fen|bank** *Plur.* ...bänke; **o|fen|frisch** (frisch aus dem Backofen); **O|fen‿hei|zung, ...ka|chel, ...rohr, ...röh|re, ...set|zer, ...tür**
off ‹engl.› (*bes. Film, Fernsehen* nicht sichtbar [von einem Sprecher]; *Ggs.* on); **Off,** das; - (das Unsichtbarbleiben des Sprechers; *Ggs.* On); im, aus dem Off sprechen; **Off|beat** ['ɔfbi:t], der; - (rhythm. Eigentümlichkeit der Jazzmusik)
of|fen; ein offener Brief; das offene Meer; ein offener Wein (im Ausschank); offene Rücklage *(Wirtsch.);* auf offener Straße, Strecke; Beifall auf offener Bühne, Szene; Tag der offenen Tür; offene Handelsgesellschaft (*Abk.* OHG); mit offenen Karten spielen (*übertr. für* ohne Hintergedanken handeln); *Schreibung in Verbindung mit Verben* (↑R 39): das Fenster muss [weit] offen bleiben; die wichtigste Frage ist [völlig] offen geblieben; sie mussten ihre Vermögensverhältnisse [völlig] offen legen; offen halten, lassen, sein, stehen; offen gestanden, gesagt

Of|fen|bach, Jacques (dt.-franz. Komponist)
Of|fen|bach am Main; Of|fen|ba|cher (↑R 103)
of|fen|bar [*auch* ...'ba:r]; **öf|fen|bar; of|fen|ba|ren** [*österr. u. schweiz.* 'ɔf...]; du offenbarst; offenbart, *auch noch* geoffenbart; zu -; sich -; **Of|fen|ba|rung; Of|fen|ba|rungs|eid; of|fen blei|ben, hal|ten** *vgl.* offen; **Of|fen|heit,** die; -; **of|fen|her|zig; Of|fen|her|zig|keit,** die; -; **of|fen|kun|dig** [*auch* ...'kun...]; **Of|fen|kun|dig|keit,** die; -; **of|fen las|sen, le|gen** *vgl.* offen; **Of|fen|le|gung; Of|fen|markt|po|li|tik** *(Bankw.)*; **of|fen|sicht|lich** [*auch* ...'ziçt...]; **Of|fen|sicht|lich|keit,** die; -
of|fen|siv ‹lat.› (angreifend); **Of|fen|siv|bünd|nis; Of|fen|si|ve** [...və], die; -, -n ([militär.] Angriff); **Of|fen|siv⌣krieg** [...f...], **...spiel** *(Sport)*, **...ver|tei|di|ger** *(Fußball)*, **...waf|fe**
Of|fen|stall; of|fen ste|hen *vgl.* offen; **öf|fent|lich;** die öffentliche Meinung; die öffentliche Hand; im öffentlichen Dienst; (↑R 23:) öffentliche und Privatmittel, *aber* Privat- und öffentliche Mittel; **Öf|fent|lich|keit,** die; -; **Öf|fent|lich|keits|ar|beit,** die; - (*für* Publicrelations); **öf|fent|lich-recht|lich** (↑R 27); die öffentlich-rechtlichen Rundfunkanstalten
Of|fe|rent, der; -en, -en (*Kaufmannsspr.* jmd., der eine Offerte macht); **of|fe|rie|ren** ‹lat.› (anbieten, darbieten); **Of|fert,** das; -[e]s, -e *(österr.)* u. **Of|fer|te,** die; -, -n ‹franz.› (Angebot, Anerbieten); **Of|fer|ten|ab|ga|be; Of|fer|to|ri|um,** das; -s, ...ien [...i̯ən] ‹lat.› (Teil der kath. Messe)
[1]**Of|fice** ['ɔfis], das; -, -s [...sis] ‹engl.› (*engl. Bez. für* Büro); [2]**Of|fice** ['ɔfis], das; -, -s ['ɔfis] ‹franz.› (*schweiz. für* Anrichteraum im Gasthaus); **Of|fi|zi|al,** der; -s, -e ‹lat.› (Beamter, bes. Vertreter des Bischofs bei Ausübung der Gerichtsbarkeit; österr. Beamtentitel, z. B. Postoffizial); **Of|fi|zi|al|ver|tei|di|ger** (amtlich bestellter Verteidiger); **Of|fi|zi|ant,** der; -en, -en; ↑R 126 (einen Gottesdienst haltender kath. Priester; *veraltet für* Unterbeamter, Bediensteter); **of|fi|zi|ell** ‹franz.› (amtlich; verbürgt; förmlich)
Of|fi|zier [*österr. auch* ...'si:r], der; -s, -e ‹franz.›; **Of|fi|zie|rin; Of|fi|ziers⌣an|wär|ter**[1], **...ka|si|no, ...korps, ...lauf|bahn, ...mes|se** (*vgl.* [3]Messe), **...rang**
Of|fi|zin, die; -, -en ‹lat.› (*veraltet für* [größere] Buchdruckerei; Apotheke); **of|fi|zi|nal, of|fi|zi|nell** (arzneilich; als Heilmittel anerkannt)
of|fi|zi|ös ‹lat.› (halbamtlich; nicht verbürgt); **Of|fi|zi|um,** das; -s, ...ien [...i̯ən] (*kath. Kirche* [1]Messe [an hohen Feiertagen]; Stunden-, Chorgebet; *veraltet für* [Dienst]-pflicht); *vgl.* ex officio
off li|mits! ‹engl.› (Eintritt verboten!, Sperrzone!); **off|line** [...la̯in] (*EDV* getrennt von der Datenverarbeitungsanlage arbeitend); **Off|line|be|trieb**
öff|nen; sich -; **Öff|ner; Öff|nung; Öff|nungs⌣win|kel, ...zeit**
Off|road|fahr|zeug [ɔf'ro:d-] ‹engl.› (Geländefahrzeug); **Off|set|druck** ['ɔfsɛt...] *Plur.* ...drucke ‹engl.; dt.› (Flachdruck[verfahren]); **Off|set|druck|ma|schi|ne; Off|shore|boh|rung** ['ɔfʃɔ:(r)...] (Bohrung [nach Erdöl] von einer Bohrinsel aus); **off|side** ['ɔfsa̯id] ‹engl.› (*schweiz. Sportspr.* abseits); **Off|side,** das; -s, -s (*schweiz. Sportspr.* Abseits); **Off|spre|cher** (↑R 24) ‹engl.; dt.› *(Fernsehen, Film)*; **Off|stim|me**
O|fir *vgl.* Ophir
O. F. M. = Ordinis Fratrum Minorum ‹lat., „vom Orden der Minderbrüder"› (Franziskanerorden)
O. [F.] M. Cap. = Ordinis [Fratrum] Minorum Capucinorum ‹lat., „vom Orden der Minderen Kapuziner[brüder]"› (Kapuzinerorden)
o-för|mig, *auch* **O-för|mig;** ↑R 25
oft; öfter *(vgl. d.)*, öftest *(vgl. d.)*; wie oft; so oft (*vgl.* sooft); **öf|ter;** öfter als ...; (↑R 47:) öfter mal was Neues; des Öfter[e]n; **öf|ters** (*landsch. für* öfter); **öf|test;** am öftesten (*selten für* am häufigsten); **oft|ma|lig; oft|mals**
o. g. = oben genannt
ÖGB = Österr. Gewerkschaftsbund
O|ger, der; -s, - ‹franz.› (Menschenfresser in franz. Märchen)
o|gi|val [...'va:l, *auch* ɔʒi'val] ‹franz.› (*Kunstw.* spitzbogig); **O|gi|val|stil** (Baustil der [franz.] Gotik)
oh!; oh, das ist schade; ein überraschtes Oh; *(in Verbindung mit anderen Wörtern oft auch ohne h geschrieben:)* oh ja!, oh nein!, oh weh!; *auch* o ja!, o nein!, o weh!
Oh. = Ohio
o|ha!
O|heim, der; -s, -e (*veraltet für* Onkel); *vgl. auch* [4]Ohm
OHG = offene Handelsgesellschaft
[1]**O|hio** [o'ha̯io], der; -[s] (Nebenfluss des Mississippis); [2]**O|hio** (Staat in den USA; *Abk.* Oh.)
o[h], là, là! [ola'la] ‹franz.› (Ausruf der Verwunderung)
[1]**Ohm,** das; -[e]s, -e ‹griech.› (früheres Flüssigkeitsmaß); 3 - (↑R 90)
[2]**Ohm** (dt. Physiker); [3]**Ohm,** das; -[s], - (Einheit für den elektr. Widerstand; *Zeichen* Ω); *vgl.* ohmsch
[4]**Ohm,** der; -[e]s, -e (*veraltet für* Onkel; *vgl.* Oheim); **Öhm,** der; -[e]s, -e (*westd. für* Oheim)
Öhmd, das; -[e]s (*südwestd. für* das zweite Mähen); **öhm|den** (*südwestd. für* nachmähen)
Ohm|me|ter, das; -s, - *zu* [3]Ohm› (Gerät zur Messung des elektr. Widerstandes)
O. H. M. S. = On His (Her) Majesty's Service [- - (hœ:[r]) 'mɛdʒistiz 'sœ:(r)vis] ‹engl., „Im Dienste Seiner [Ihrer] Majestät"› (amtlich)
ohmsch ‹*zu* [2]Ohm›; der ohmsche Widerstand; das ohmsche Gesetz (↑R 94)
oh|ne; *Präp. mit Akk.:* ohne ihren Willen; ohne dass (↑R 88); ohne weiteres; oben ohne (*ugs. für* busenfrei); zweifelsohne; **oh|ne Befund** (*Abk.* o. B.); **oh|ne|dem** (*veraltet für* ohnedies); **oh|ne|dies; oh|ne|ei|nan|der** (↑R 132); ohneeinander auskommen; **oh|ne|glei|chen; Oh|ne|halt|flug; oh|ne|hin; oh|ne Jahr** (bei Buchtitelangaben; *Abk.* o. J.); **Oh|ne-mich-Stand|punkt** (↑R 28); **oh|ne Ob|li|go** [*auch* - 'ɔb...] (ohne Verbindlichkeit; *Abk.* o. O.); **oh|ne Ort** (bei Buchtitelangaben; *Abk.* o. O.); **oh|ne Ort und Jahr** (bei Buchtitelangaben; *Abk.* o. O. u. J.); **oh|ne wei|te|res; oh|ne|wei|ters** (*österr. für* ohne weiteres)
Ohn|macht, die; -, -en; **ohn|mäch|tig; Ohn|machts|an|fall**
o|ho!
Ohr, das; -[e]s, -en; **Öhr,** das; -[e]s, -e (Nadelloch); **Öhr|chen** (kleines Ohr od. kleines Öhr)
Ohr|druf (Stadt in Thüringen)
Oh|ren⌣arzt, ...beich|te; oh|ren|be|täu|bend; Oh|ren|blä|ser (*veraltend für* heimlicher Aufhetzer, Zuträger); **Oh|ren|ent|zün|dung; oh|ren|fäl|lig; Oh|ren⌣heil|kun|de** (die; -), **...klap|pe; Oh|ren|klipp** *vgl.* Ohrklipp; **oh|ren|krank; Oh|ren⌣krie|cher**

[1] Beim Militär meist ohne Fugen-s.

(Ohrwurm), ...**sau|sen** (das; -s), ...**schmalz** (das; -es), ...**schmaus** (der; -es; *ugs. für* Genuss für die Ohren), ...**schmerz** *(meist Plur.)*, ...**schüt|zer**, ...**ses|sel**, ...**zeu|ge**; **Ohr|fei|ge**; **ohr|fei|gen**; er hat mich geohrfeigt; **Ohr|fei|gen|ge|sicht** *Plur.* ...gesichter (*ugs. für* dümmlich-freches Gesicht); **Ohr|ge|hän|ge**; ...**oh|rig** (z. B. langohrig); **Ohr|klipp**, Oh|ren|klipp (Ohrschmuck); **Ohr|läpp|chen**; **Ohr‿luft|du|sche**, ...**mar|ke** (bei Zuchttieren), ...**mu|schel**, ...**ring**, ...**schmuck**, ...**spei|chel|drü|se**, ...**spü|lung**, ...**ste|cker**, ...**trom|pe|te**, ...**wa|schel** (das; -s, -n; *österr. ugs. für* Ohrläppchen, Ohrmuschel), ...**wurm** (*ugs. auch für* leicht eingängige Melodie)

O|ie [ˈɔyə], die; -, -n (Insel); Greifswalder Oie

Oist|rach [ˈɔy...] (↑R 130; russ. Geiger)

o. J. = ohne Jahr

o|je!; **o|je|mi|ne!** *vgl.* jemine; **o|je|rum**

o. k., O. K. = okay

O|ka [*auch* ˈɔka], die; - (r. Nebenfluss der Wolga)

O|ka|pi, das; -s, -s ‹afrik.› (kurzhalsige Giraffenart)

O|ka|ri|na, die; -, *Plur.* -s *u.* ...nen ‹ital.› (tönernes Blasinstrument)

o|kay [oˈke:] ‹amerik.› (richtig, in Ordnung; *Abk.* o. k. *od.* O. K.); **O|kay**, das; -[s], -s; sein - geben

O|ke|a|ni|de, *auch* O|ze|a|ni|de, die; -, -n ‹griech.› (*griech. Mythol.* Meernymphe); **O|ke|a|nos** (Weltstrom; Gott des Weltstromes)

O|ker, die; - (l. Nebenfluss der Aller); **O|ker|tal|sper|re**, die; -; ↑R 105

Ok|ka|si|on, die; -, -en ‹lat.› (*veraltet für* Gelegenheit, Anlass; *Kaufmannsspr.* Gelegenheitskauf); **Ok|ka|si|o|na|lis|mus**, der; - (eine philos. Lehre); **Ok|ka|si|o|na|list**, der; -en, -en (↑R 126); **ok|ka|si|o|nell** ‹franz.› (gelegentlich, Gelegenheits...)

Ok|ki|ar|beit ‹ital.; dt.› (Handarbeit, bei der aus Knoten gefertigte Bogen und Ringe eine Spitze bilden)

ok|klu|die|ren ‹lat.› (*veraltet für* einschließen, verschließen); **Ok|klu|si|on**, die; -, -en (*Med.* normale Schlussbissstellung der Zähne; *Meteor.* Zusammentreffen von Kalt- u. Warmfront); **ok|klu|siv**; **Ok|klu|siv**, der; -s, -e [...və] (*Sprachw.* Verschlusslaut, z. B. p, t, k)

ok|kult ‹lat.› (verborgen; heimlich, geheim); **Ok|kul|tis|mus**, der; - (Lehre vom Übersinnlichen); **Ok|kul|tist**, der; -en, -en (↑R 126); **Ok|kul|tis|tin**; **ok|kul|tis|tisch**

Ok|ku|pant, der; -en, -en ‹lat.› (*abwertend für* jmd., der fremdes Gebiet okkupiert); **Ok|ku|pa|ti|on**, die; -, -en (Besetzung [fremden Gebietes] mit od. ohne Gewalt; *Rechtsw.* Aneignung herrenlosen Gutes); **Ok|ku|pa|ti|ons‿heer**, ...**macht**; **ok|ku|pie|ren**

Okla. = Oklahoma

Ok|la|ho|ma (↑R 130; Staat in den USA; *Abk.* Okla.)

Ö|ko|la|den (Laden, in dem nur umweltfreundliche Waren verkauft werden); **Ö|ko|lo|ge**, der; -n, -n ‹griech.› (Wissenschaftler auf dem Gebiet der Ökologie); **Ö|ko|lo|gie**, die; - (Lehre von den Beziehungen der Lebewesen zur Umwelt); **Ö|ko|lo|gin**; **ö|ko|lo|gisch**

Ö|ko|nom, der; -en, -en (↑R 126) ‹griech.› (Wirtschaftswissenschaftler; *veraltend für* [Land]wirt); **Ö|ko|no|mie**, die; -, ...ien (Wirtschaftlichkeit, sparsame Lebensführung *[nur Sing.]*; Lehre von der Wirtschaft; *veraltet für* Landwirtschaft[sbetrieb]); **Ö|ko|no|mie|rat** (österr. Titel); **Ö|ko|no|mik**, die; - (Wirtschaftswissenschaft, -theorie; wirtschaftliche Verhältnisse [eines Landes, Gebietes]; *nach marxist. Lehre* Produktionsweise einer Gesellschaftsordnung); **Ö|ko|no|min**; **ö|ko|no|misch**; **Ö|ko|pax|be|we|gung** (Bewegung, die für die Erhaltung der natürlichen Umwelt und die Bewahrung des Friedens eintritt); **Ö|ko|sys|tem** (zwischen Lebewesen und ihrem Lebensraum bestehende Wechselbeziehung)

Okt. = Oktober

Ok|ta|e|der, das; -s, - ‹griech.› (Achtflächner); **ok|ta|ed|risch** (↑R 130); **Ok|ta|gon** *vgl.* Oktogon; **Ok|tant**, der; -en, -en (↑R 126) ‹lat.› (achter Teil des Kreises od. der Kugel; nautisches Winkelmessgerät); **Ok|tan|zahl** (Maßzahl für die Klopffestigkeit von Treibstoffen); [1]**Ok|tav**, das; -s (*Buchw.* Achtelbogengröße [Buchformat]; *Zeichen* 8°, z. B. Lex.-8°); in -; Großoktav *(vgl. d.)*; [2]**Ok|tav**, die; -, -en (kath. Feier; *österr. auch svw.* Oktave); **Ok|ta|va** [...va], die; -, ...ven (*österr. für* 8. Klasse des Gymnasiums); **Ok|tav‿band** (der; *Buchw.*), ...**bo|gen**; **Ok|ta|ve** [...və], *österr.* Ok|tav, die; -, -en (*Musik* achter Ton [vom Grundton an]; ein Intervall; *svw.* Ottaverime); **Ok|tav|for|mat** [...f...] (*Buchw.* Achtelgröße)

Ok|ta|via [...v...], Ok|ta|vie [...iə] (röm. w. Eigenn.); **Ok|ta|vi|an**, **Ok|ta|vi|a|nus** (röm. Kaiser)

ok|ta|vie|ren [...v...] ‹lat.› (in die Oktave überschlagen [von Blasinstrumenten]); **Ok|tett**, das; -[e]s, -e ‹ital.› (Komposition für acht Soloinstrumente od. -stimmen; Gruppe von acht Instrumentalsolisten; Achtergruppe von Elektronen in der Außenschale der Atomhülle); **Ok|to|ber**, der; -[s], - ‹lat.› (zehnter Monat im Jahr; Gilbhard, Weinmonat, Weinmond; *Abk.* Okt.); **Ok|to|ber‿fest** (in München), ...**re|vo|lu|ti|on** (1917 in Russland); **Ok|to|de**, die; -, -n ‹griech.› (Elektronenröhre mit acht Elektroden); **Ok|to|gon**, das; -s, -e (Achteck; Bau mit achteckigem Grundriss); **ok|to|go|nal** (achteckig); **Ok|to|po|de**, der; -n, -n (↑R 126) (*Zool.* Achtfüßer)

okt|ro|yie|ren [...troaˈji:...] (↑R 130) ‹franz.› (aufdrängen, aufzwingen)

o|ku|lar ‹lat.› (mit dem Auge, fürs Auge); **O|ku|lar**, das; -s, -e (die dem Auge zugewandte Linse eines optischen Gerätes); **O|ku|la|ti|on**, die; -, -en (Pflanzenveredelungsart); **O|ku|li** ‹„Augen"› (vierter Sonntag vor Ostern); **o|ku|lie|ren** (durch Okulation veredeln, äugeln); **O|ku|lier|mes|ser**, das; **O|ku|lie|rung**

Ö|ku|me|ne, die; - ‹griech.› (die bewohnte Erde; Gesamtheit der Christen; ökumenische Bewegung); **ö|ku|me|nisch** (allgemein; die ganze bewohnte Erde betreffend, Welt...); ökumenische Bewegung (zwischen- u. überkirchl. Bestrebungen christlicher Kirchen u. Konfessionen zur Einigung in Fragen des Glaubens u. der religiösen Arbeit); ökumenisches Konzil (allgemeine kath. Kirchenversammlung), *aber* (↑R 108): der Ökumenische Rat der Kirchen; **Ö|ku|me|nis|mus**, der; - (*kath. Kirche* Gesamtheit der Bemühungen um die Einheit der Christen)

Ok|zi|dent [*auch* ...ˈdɛnt], der; -s ‹lat.› (Abendland; Westen; *vgl.* Orient); **ok|zi|den|tal**, **ok|zi|den|ta|lisch**

ö. L. = östlicher Länge

O. L. = Oberlausitz

Öl, das; -[e]s, -e

O|laf (m. Vorn.)

Öl‿alarm (↑R 132), ...**baum**, ...**be-**

häl|ter; Öl|berg, der; -[e]s (bei Jerusalem); **Öl‿bild, ...boh|rung**

Ol|den|burg (Landkreis in Niedersachsen); **[1]Ol|den|bur|ger** (↑R 103); **[2]Ol|den|bur|ger,** der; -s, - (eine Pferderasse); **Ol|den|bur|ger Geest,** die; - - (Gebiet in Niedersachsen); **Ol|den|burg (Hol|stein)** (Stadt in Schleswig-Holstein); **ol|den|bur|gisch,** *aber* (↑R 102): Oldenburgisches Münsterland; **Ol|den|burg (Ol|den|burg)** (Stadt in Niedersachsen)

Ol|des|loe [...lo:], **Bad** (Stadt in Schleswig-Holstein); **Ol|des|lo|er** [...lo:ər] (↑R 103)

Ol|die ['o:ldi], der; -s, -s ‹engl.-amerik.› (noch immer od. wieder beliebter alter Schlager)

Öl|druck; Öl|druck|brem|se *(Kfz-Technik)*

Old|ti|mer ['o:ldtaimə(r)], der; -s, - ‹engl.› (altes Modell eines Fahrzeugs [bes. Auto]; *auch scherzh. für* langjähriges Mitglied, älterer Mann)

o|lé! ‹span.› (los!, auf!, hurra!)

O|lea *(Plur. von* Oleum)

O|le|an|der, der; -s, - ‹ital.› (ein immergrüner Strauch od. Baum, Rosenlorbeer); **O|le|an|der|schwär|mer** (ein Schmetterling)

O|le|at, das; -[e]s, -e ‹griech.› *(Chemie* Salz der Ölsäure); **O|le|fin,** das; -s, -e (ein ungesättigter Kohlenwasserstoff); **o|le|fin|reich; O|le|in,** das; -s, -e (ungereinigte Ölsäure); **ö|len; O|le|um** ['o:leum], das; -s, Olea (Öl; rauchende Schwefelsäure)

ol|fak|to|risch ‹lat.› *(Med.* den Geruchssinn betreffend)

Öl|far|be; Öl|far|ben|druck *Plur.* ...drucke; **Öl‿feu|e|rung, ...film** (dünne Ölschicht), **...fleck, ...för|de|rung, ...frucht**

OLG = Oberlandesgericht

Ol|ga (w. Vorn.)

Öl|ge|mäl|de; Öl|göt|ze; *nur in* dastehen, dasitzen wie ein - *(ugs. für* stumm, unbeteiligt, verständnislos dastehen, dasitzen); **Öl‿haut, ...hei|zung; öl|höf|fig** (erdölhöffig)

O|li|fant [*auch* ...'fant], der; -[e]s, -e ([Rolands] elfenbeinernes Hifthorn)

ö|lig

O|li|gä|mie (↑R 132), die; -, ...ien ‹griech.› *(Med.* Blutarmut); **O|li|garch,** der; -en, -en; ↑R 126 (Anhänger der Oligarchie); **O|li|gar|chie,** die; -, ...ien (Herrschaft einer kleinen Gruppe); **o|li|gar|chisch; O|li|go|phre|nie,** die; -, ...ien *(Med.* Schwachsinn); **O|li|go|pol,** das; -s, -e *(Wirtsch.* Beherrschung des Marktes durch wenige Großunternehmen); **o|li|go|troph** (nährstoffarm [von Ackerböden]); **o|li|go|zän** (das Oligozän betreffend); **O|li|go|zän,** das; -s *(Geol.* mittlerer Teil des Tertiärs)

O|lim ‹lat., „ehemals"›; *nur in* seit, zu Olims Zeiten *(scherzh. für* vor langer Zeit)

Öl|in|dust|rie

o|liv ‹griech.› (olivenfarben); ein oliv Kleid; *vgl. auch* beige; **O|liv,** das; -s, *Plur. -, ugs.* -s; ein Kleid in Oliv (↑R 47)

O|li|ve [...v..., *österr.* ...f...], die; -, -n ‹griech.› (Frucht des Ölbaumes); **O|li|ven‿baum, ...ern|te; o|li|ven|far|ben** *od.* **...far|big; O|li|ven|öl**

O|li|ver [...vər, *auch* 'ɔ...] (m. Vorn.)

o|liv‿grau, ...grün

O|li|vin [...'vi:n], der; -s, -e ‹griech.› (ein Mineral)

Öl‿kan|ne, ...kri|se, ...ku|chen

oll *(landsch. für* alt); olle Kamellen *(vgl.* Kamellen)

Öl|lam|pe

Ol|le, der *u.* die; -n, -n; ↑R 5ff. *(landsch. für* Alte)

Öl‿lei|tung, ...luft|pum|pe

Olm, der; -[e]s, -e (ein Lurch)

Ol|ma = Ostschweizerische land- und milchwirtschaftliche Ausstellung *(heute* Schweizerische Messe für Land- und Milchwirtschaft, St. Gallen)

Öl‿ma|le|rei, ...mess|stab, ...müh|le, ...mul|ti *(ugs.; vgl.* Multi), **...ofen** (↑R 132), **...pal|me, ...pa|pier, ...pest** (die; -; Verschmutzung von Meeresküsten durch [auf dem Wasser treibendes] Rohöl); **Öl‿pflan|ze, ...platt|form, ...preis, ...quel|le, ...raf|fi|ne|rie, ...sar|di|ne, ...säu|re** (die; -), **...scheich** *(ugs.),* **...schicht, ...stand, ...tank, ...tan|ker**

Ol|ten (schweiz. Stadt); **Ol|te|ner,** Olt|ner (↑R 103)

Öl|tep|pich

Olt|ner *vgl.* Oltener

Ö|lung; die Letzte Ölung *(kath. Kirche früher für* Krankensalbung); **Öl‿vor|kom|men, ...wan|ne** *(Technik),* **...wech|sel**

O|lymp, der; -s (Gebirgsstock in Griechenland; Wohnsitz der Götter; *scherzh. für* Galerieplätze im Theater); **[1]O|lym|pia** (altgriech. Nationalheiligtum); **[2]O|lym|pia,** das; -[s] *(geh. für* Olympische Spiele); **O|lym|pi|a|de,** die; -, -n (Olympische Spiele; *selten für* Zeitraum von vier Jahren zwischen zwei Olympischen Spielen; *auch regional für* Wettbewerb [für Schüler]); **O|lym|pi|a‿dorf, ...jahr, ...mann|schaft, ...me|dail|le, ...norm; o|lym|pi|a|reif; O|lym|pi|a‿sieg, ...sie|ger, ...sie|ge|rin, ...sta|di|on, ...stadt, ...teil|neh|mer, ...teil|neh|me|rin; o|lym|pi|a|ver|däch|tig** *(ugs. für* sportlich hervorragend); **O|lym|pi|a|zwei|te,** der *u.* die; -n, -n (↑R 5ff.); **O|lym|pi|er** [...iər] (Beiname der griech. Götter, bes. des Zeus; gelegentlicher Beiname Goethes); **O|lym|pi|o|ni|ke,** der; -n, -n; ↑R 126 (Sieger in od. Teilnehmer an den Olympischen Spielen); **O|lym|pi|o|ni|kin; o|lym|pisch** (göttlich, himmlisch; die Olympischen Spiele betreffend); olympische Ruhe, olympischer Eid, olympisches Dorf, *aber* (↑R 108): die Olympischen Spiele, Internationales Olympisches Komitee *(Abk.* IOK); Nationales Olympisches Komitee *(Abk.* NOK)

O|lynth (altgriech. Stadt); **o|lyn|thisch;** die olynthischen Reden des Demosthenes

Öl‿zeug, ...zweig

O|ma, die; -, -s *(fam. für* Großmutter)

O|mai|ja|de, der; -n, -n; ↑R 126 (Angehöriger eines arab. Herrschergeschlechtes)

O|ma|ma, die; -, -s *(svw.* Oma)

O|man (Staat auf der Arabischen Halbinsel); **O|ma|ner; o|ma|nisch**

O|mar [*auch* 'ɔ...] (arab. Eigenn.)

Omb|ro|graph (↑R 130), der; -en, -en (↑R 126) ‹griech.› *(Meteor.* Gerät zur Aufzeichnung des Niederschlags)

Om|buds|frau (w. Form von Ombudsmann); **Om|buds|mann,** der; -[e]s, *Plur.* ...männer, *selten* ...leute ‹schwed.› (jmd., der die Rechte des Bürgers gegenüber den Behörden wahrnimmt)

O. M. Cap. *vgl.* O. [F.] M. Cap.

O|me|ga, das; -[s], -s (griech. Buchstabe [langes O]; *Ω, ω*); *vgl.* Alpha

O|me|lett [ɔm(ə)...], das; -[e]s, *Plur.* -e *u.* -s *u., österr., schweiz. nur,* **Ome|lette** [ɔm'lɛt], die; -, -n ‹franz.› (Eierkuchen); Omelette aux fines herbes [- ofin'zɛrb] (Eierkuchen mit Kräutern)

O|men, das; -s, *Plur.* - *u.* Omina ‹lat.› (Vorzeichen; Vorbedeutung)

O|mi, die; -, -s *(Koseform von* Oma)

O|mik|ron [*auch* 'ɔ...] (↑R 130),

das; -[s], -s (griech. Buchstabe [kurzes O]: *O, o*)
O|mi|na (*Plur. von* Omen); **o|mi|nös** ‹lat.› (von schlimmer Vorbedeutung; unheilvoll; anrüchig)
O|mis|siv|de|likt ‹lat.› (*Rechtsw.* Unterlassungsdelikt)
Om ma|ni pad|me hum (mystische Formel des lamaistischen Buddhismus)
om|nia ad ma|io|rem Dei glo|ri|am *vgl.* ad maiorem ...
Om|ni|bus, der; -ses, -se ‹lat.› (*Kurzw.* Bus); **Om|ni|bus‿bahn|hof, ...fahrt, ...li|nie; om|ni|po|tent** (allmächtig); **Om|ni|po|tenz,** die; - (Allmacht); **om|ni|prä|sent** (allgegenwärtig); **Om|ni|prä|senz,** die; - (Allgegenwart); **Om|ni|um,** das; -s, ...ien [...iən] (*Radsport* aus mehreren Bahnwettbewerben bestehender Wettkampf); **Om|ni|vo|re** [...v...], der; -n, -n *meist Plur.;* ↑R 126 (*Zool.* Allesfresser)
Om|pha|le [...le] (lydische Königin)
Om|pha|li|tis, die; -, ...itiden ‹griech.› (*Med.* Nabelentzündung)
Omsk (Stadt in Sibirien)
on ‹engl.› (*bes. Fernsehen* sichtbar [von einem Sprecher]; *Ggs.* off); **On,** das; - (das Sichtbarsein des Sprechers; *Ggs.* Off); im On
O|na|ger, der; -s, - ‹lat.› (Halbesel in Südwestasien)
O|nan (bibl. m. Eigenn.); **O|na|nie,** die; - ‹nach der bibl. Gestalt Onan› (geschlechtl. Selbstbefriedigung); **o|na|nie|ren; O|na|nist,** der; -en, -en (↑R 126); **o|na|nis|tisch**
ÖNB = Österr. Nationalbank, Österr. Nationalbibliothek
On|dit [õ'di:], das; -, -s ‹franz.› (Gerücht); einem - zufolge
On|du|la|ti|on, die; -, -en ‹franz.› (das Wellen der Haare mit der Brennschere); **on|du|lie|ren; On|du|lie|rung**
O|ne|ga|see [*russ.* ɔ'nʲega...], der; -s (See in Russland)
O|nei|da|see, der; -s (See im Staat New York)
O'Neill [o:'ni:l] (amerik. Dramatiker)
One|step ['wanstɛp], der; -s, -s ‹engl.› (ein Tanz)
On|kel, der; -s, *Plur.* -, *ugs. auch* -s; **On|kel|ehe** (↑R 132; *volkstüml. für* Zusammenleben einer Witwe mit einem Mann, den sie aus Versorgungsgründen nicht heiraten will); **on|kel|haft**
On|ko|lo|ge, der; -n, -n ‹griech.›; **On|ko|lo|gie,** die; - (*Med.* Lehre von den Geschwülsten); **on|ko|lo|gisch**
on|line [...lain] ‹engl.› (*EDV* in direkter Verbindung mit der Datenverarbeitungsanlage arbeitend); **On|line|be|trieb**
ONO = Ostnordost[en]
Ö|no|lo|gie, die; - ‹griech.› (Wein[bau]kunde); **ö|no|lo|gisch; Ö|no|ma|nie,** die; - (*Med.* Säuferwahnsinn)
O|no|ma|si|o|lo|gie, die; - ‹griech.› (*Sprachw.* Bezeichnungslehre); **o|no|ma|si|o|lo|gisch; O|no|mas|tik,** die; - (Namenkunde); **O|no|mas|ti|kon,** das; -s, *Plur.* ...ken *u.* ...ka (Wörterverzeichnis der Antike u. des Mittelalters); **o|no|ma|to|po|e|tisch** (laut-, klang-, schallnachahmend); **O|no|ma|to|pö|ie,** die; -, ...ien (Bildung eines Wortes durch Lautnachahmung, Lautmalerei, z. B. „Kuckuck")
Ö|no|me|ter, das; -s, - ‹griech.› (Weinmesser [zur Bestimmung des Alkoholgehaltes])
Ö|norm (österr. Norm)
On|spre|cher (↑R 24) ‹engl.; dt.› (*Fernsehen, Film*)
On|ta|rio [*engl.* ɔn'tɛ:rio:] (kanad. Provinz); **On|ta|ri|o|see,** der; -s
on the rocks [- ðə -] ‹engl.› (mit Eiswürfeln [bei Getränken])
On|to|ge|ne|se, On|to|ge|nie, die; - ‹griech.› (*Biol.* Entwicklung des Einzelwesens); **on|to|ge|ne|tisch; On|to|lo|gie,** die; - (*Philos.* Wissenschaft vom Seienden); **on|to|lo|gisch**
O|nyx, der; -[es], -e ‹griech.› (ein Halbedelstein)
o. O. = ohne Obligo; ohne Ort
o. ö. = ordentlicher öffentlicher (z. B. Professor [*Abk.* o. ö. Prof.])
OÖ = Oberösterreich
O|o|ge|ne|se, die; - ‹griech.› (*Med.* Entwicklung der Eizelle); **o|o|ge|ne|tisch; O|o|lith** [*auch* ...'lit], der; *Gen.* -s *u.* -en, *Plur.* -e[n]; ↑R 126 (ein Gestein); **O|o|lo|gie,** die; - (Wissenschaft vom Vogelei)
o. ö. Prof. = ordentlicher öffentlicher Professor
o. O. u. J. = ohne Ort und Jahr
op. = opus; *vgl.* Opus
o. P. = ordentlicher Professor; *vgl.* Professor
OP = Operationssaal
O. P., O. Pr. = Ordinis Praedicatorum ‹lat., „vom Orden der Prediger"› (Dominikanerorden)
O|pa, der; -s, -s (*fam. für* Großvater)
o|pak ‹lat.› (*fachspr. für* undurchsichtig, lichtundurchlässig)
O|pal, der; -s, -e ‹sanskr.› (ein Schmuckstein; ein Gewebe); **o|pa|len** (aus Opal, durchscheinend wie Opal); **O|pa|les|zenz,** die; - (opalartiges Schillern); **o|pa|les|zie|ren,** o|pa|li|sie|ren; **O|pal|glas** *Plur.* ...gläser
O|pan|ke, die; -, -n ‹serb.› (sandalenartiger Schuh [mit am Unterschenkel kreuzweise gebundenen Lederriemen])
O|pa|pa, der; -s, -s (*svw.* Opa)
Op-Art ['ɔp|a:(r)t] (↑R 24), die; - ‹amerik.› (eine moderne Kunstrichtung)
O|pa|zi|tät, die; - ‹*zu* opak› (*fachspr. für* Undurchsichtigkeit)
OPEC = Organization of the Petroleum Exporting Countries [ɔ:(r)gənai'ze:ʃ(ə)n əv ðə pi't-ro:liəm ɛks'pɔ:(r)tiŋ 'kantri:z], die; - ‹engl.› (Organisation der Erdöl exportierenden Länder)
O|pel ® (Kraftfahrzeuge)
O|pen|air, *auch* **O|pen Air** ['o:p(ə)n 'ɛ:(r)] (↑R 24 *u.* 33), das; -s, -s (*kurz für* Openairfestival od. -konzert); **O|pen|air|fes|ti|val,** *auch* **O|pen-Air-Fes|ti|val** [...'fɛstiv(ə)l] ‹engl.› (Folklore-, Popmusik- od. Jazzveranstaltung im Freien); **O|pen|air|kon|zert,** *auch* **O|pen-Air-Kon|zert; o|pen end** ['o:p(ə)n 'ɛnd] (ohne festgelegten Schluss der Veranstaltung); **O|pen|end|dis|kus|si|on,** *auch* **O|pen-End-Dis|kus|si|on**
O|per, die; -, -n ‹ital.›; **O|pe|ra** (*Plur. von* Opus)
o|pe|ra|bel ‹lat.› (so, dass man damit arbeiten kann; *Med.* operierbar)
O|pe|ra buf|fa, die; - -, ...re ...ffe [...re ...fe] ‹ital.› (komische Oper)
O|pe|rand, der; -en, -en ‹lat.› (*Math., EDV* Gegenstand einer Operation)
O|pe|ra se|ria, die; - -, ...re ...rie [...re ...rie] (ernste Oper)
O|pe|ra|teur [...'tø:r], der; -s, -e ‹franz.› (eine Operation vornehmender Arzt; Kameramann; Filmvorführer; *auch für* Operator); **O|pe|ra|ti|on,** die; -, -en ‹lat.› (chirurg. Eingriff; [militärische] Unternehmung; Rechenvorgang; Verfahren); **o|pe|ra|ti|o|nal** (sich durch bestimmte Verfahren vollziehend); **o|pe|ra|ti|o|na|li|sie|ren** (durch Angabe der Verfahren präzisieren); **O|pe|ra|ti|ons‿ba|sis, ...saal** (*Abk.* OP), **...schwes|ter, ...tisch; o|pe|ra|tiv** (auf chirurgischem Wege, durch Operation; planvoll tätig; strategisch); -er Eingriff; **O|pe|ra|tor** [*engl.* 'ɔpəre:tə(r)], der; -s, *Plur.* ...oren, *bei engl.*

Ausspr. -s (jmd., der eine EDV-Anlage überwacht u. bedient); **O|pe|ra|to|rin**

O|pe|ret|te, die; -, -n ‹ital.› (heiteres musikal. Bühnenwerk); **o|pe|ret|ten|haft; O|pe|ret|ten‿kom|po|nist, ...me|lo|die, ...mu|sik, ...staat** (*Plur.* ...staaten; *scherzh.*)

o|pe|rie|ren ‹lat.› (eine Operation durchführen; in bestimmter Weise vorgehen; mit etwas arbeiten)

O|pern‿arie (↑R 132), **...ball, ...füh|rer, ...glas** (*Plur.* ...gläser), **...gu|cker** (*ugs. für* Opernglas); **o|pern|haft; O|pern‿haus, ...me|lo|die, ...mu|sik, ...sän|ger, ...sän|ge|rin**

Op|fer, das; -s, -; - des Faschismus (*Abk.* OdF); **op|fer|be|reit; Op|fer‿be|reit|schaft** (die; -), **...freu|dig|keit, ...gang** (der), **...geist** (der; -[e]s), **...geld** (das; -[e]s), **...lamm, ...mut; op|fern;** ich ...ere (↑R 16); sich -; **Op|fer‿pfen|nig, ...schal|le, ...sinn** (der; -[e]s), **...stock** (*Plur.* ...stöcke; in Kirchen aufgestellter Sammelkasten), **...tier, ...tod; Op|fe|rung; Op|fer|wil|le; op|fer|wil|lig; Op|fer|wil|lig|keit,** die; -

O|phe|lia (Frauengestalt bei Shakespeare)

O|phi|o|lat|rie (↑R 130), die; - ‹griech.› (religiöse Schlangenverehrung)

O|phir, *ökum.* O|fir ‹hebr.› (Goldland im A. T.)

O|phit, der; -en, -en (↑R 126) ‹griech.› (Schlangenanbeter, Angehöriger einer Sekte); **O|phi|u|chus,** der; - („Schlangenträger") (ein Sternbild)

Oph|thal|mi|at|rie, Oph|thal|mi|at|rik (↑R 130), die; - ‹griech.› (*Med.* Augenheilkunde); **Oph|thal|mie,** die; -, ...ien (Augenentzündung); **Oph|thal|mo|lo|ge,** der; -n, -n; ↑R 126 (Augenarzt); **Oph|thal|mo|lo|gie,** die; - (Lehre von den Augenkrankheiten); **oph|thal|mo|lo|gisch**

O|pi|at, das; -[e]s, -e ‹griech.› (opiumhaltiges Arzneimittel); **O|pi|um,** das; -s (ein Betäubungsmittel u. Rauschgift); **O|pi|um|ge|setz; o|pi|um|hal|tig; O|pi|um‿han|del** (*vgl.* [1]Handel), **...krieg** (der; -[e]s; 1840–42), **...pfei|fe, ...rau|cher, ...schmug|gel, ...sucht** (die; -)

Op|la|den (Stadt in Nordrhein-Westfalen)

ÖPNV = öffentlicher Personennahverkehr

O|po|le (poln. Stadt an der Oder; *vgl.* Oppeln)

O|pos|sum, das; -s, -s ‹indian.› (amerik. Beutelratte; *auch für* Pelz dieses Tieres)

Op|peln (*poln.* Opole); **Op|pel|ner** (↑R 103)

Op|po|nent, der; -en, -en (↑R 126) ‹lat.› (Gegner [im Redestreit]); **Op|po|nen|tin; op|po|nie|ren** (widersprechen; sich widersetzen)

op|por|tun ‹lat.› (passend, nützlich, angebracht; zweckmäßig; *Ggs.* importun); **Op|por|tu|nis|mus,** der; - (prinzipienloses Anpassen an die jeweilige Lage, Handeln nach Zweckmäßigkeit); **Op|por|tu|nist,** der; -en, -en (↑R 126); **Op|por|tu|nis|tin; op|por|tu|nis|tisch; Op|por|tu|ni|tät,** die; -, -en (günstige Gelegenheit, Vorteil, Zweckmäßigkeit); **Op|por|tu|ni|täts|prin|zip** (strafrechtlicher Grundsatz, nach dem die Erhebung einer Anklage in das Ermessen der Anklagebehörde gestellt ist)

Op|po|si|ti|on, die; -, -en ‹lat.›; **op|po|si|ti|o|nell** ‹franz.› (gegensätzlich; gegnerisch; zum Widerspruch neigend); **Op|po|si|ti|ons‿füh|rer, ...füh|re|rin, ...geist** (der; -[e]s), **...par|tei, ...wort** (*Plur.* ...wörter; *für* Antonym)

Op|pres|si|on, die; -, -en ‹lat.› (*veraltet für* Unterdrückung; *Med.* Beklemmung)

O. Pr. *vgl.* O. P.

OP-Schwes|ter (*Med.*)

Op|tant, der; -en, -en (↑R 126) ‹lat.› (jmd., der optiert); **Op|ta|tiv,** der; -s, -e [...və] (*Sprachw.* Wunsch-, *auch* Möglichkeitsform des Verbs); **op|tie|ren** (sich für etwas [bes. für eine Staatsangehörigkeit] entscheiden; die Voranwartschaft auf etwas geltend machen)

Op|tik, die; -, -en *Plur. selten* ‹griech.› (Lehre vom Licht; Linsensystem eines opt. Gerätes; optischer Eindruck, optische Wirkung); **Op|ti|ker** (Hersteller od. Verkäufer von Brillen u. optischen Geräten); **Op|ti|ke|rin**

Op|ti|ma (*Plur. von* Optimum); **op|ti|ma fi|de** ‹lat., „in bestem Glauben"›; **op|ti|mal** (bestmöglich); **Op|ti|mat,** der; -en, -en; ↑R 126 (Angehöriger der herrschenden Geschlechter im alten Rom); **op|ti|mie|ren** (optimal gestalten); **Op|ti|mie|rung; Op|ti|mis|mus,** der; - (*Ggs.* Pessimismus); **Op|ti|mist,** der; -en, -en (↑R 126); **Op|ti|mis|tin; op|ti|mis|tisch; Op|ti|mum,** das; -s, ...tima (höchster erreichbarer Wert; *Biol.* beste Lebensbedingungen)

Op|ti|on, die; -, -en ‹lat.› (Wahl einer bestimmten Staatsangehörigkeit; *Rechtsw.* Voranwartschaft auf Erwerb od. zukünftige Lieferung einer Sache); **op|ti|o|nal** (nicht zwingend, nicht verbindlich; nach eigener Wahl)

op|tisch ‹griech.› (die Optik, das Sehen betreffend); -e Täuschung; -e Erscheinung; **Op|to|me|ter,** das; -s, - (*Med.* Sehweitenmesser); **Op|to|met|rie** (↑R 130), die; - (Sehkraftbestimmung)

o|pu|lent ‹lat.› (reich[lich], üppig); **O|pu|lenz,** die; -

O|pun|tie [...i̯ə], die; -, -n ‹griech.› (Feigenkaktus)

O|pus [*auch* 'ɔ...], das; -, Opera ‹lat.› ([musikal.] Werk; *Abk. in der Musik* op.)

O|ra|dour-sur-Glane [...dursyr'glan] (franz. Ort)

o|ra et la|bo|ra! ‹lat., „bete und arbeite!"› (Mönchsregel des Benediktinerordens)

O|ra|kel, das; -s, - ‹lat.› (rätselhafte Weissagung; *auch* Ort, an dem Seherinnen od. Priester Weissagungen verkünden); **o|ra|kel|haft; o|ra|keln** (in dunklen Andeutungen sprechen); ich ...[e]le (↑R 16); **O|ra|kel|spruch**

o|ral ‹lat.› (*Med.* den Mund betreffend, durch den Mund)

o|ran|ge [o'rãːʒ(ə), *österr.* o'rãːʒ] ‹pers.-franz.› (goldgelb; orangenfarbig); ein orange Band; *vgl. auch* beige; **[1]O|ran|ge** [o'raŋʒə], die; -, -n (*bes. südd., österr. u. schweiz. für* Apfelsine); **[2]O|ran|ge** [o'rãːʒ(ə), *österr.* o'rãːʒ], das; -, *Plur.* -, *ugs.* -s (orange Farbe); in Orange (↑R 26); **O|ran|gea|de** [oraŋ..., *auch* orã'ʒaːdə], die; -, -n (unter Verwendung von Orangensaft bereitetes Getränk); **O|ran|geat** [oraŋ..., *auch* orã'ʒaːt], das; -s, *Plur. (Sorten:)* -e (eingezuckerte Apfelsinenschalen); **o|ran|gen** [o'raŋ..., *auch* o'rãːʒ(ə)n]; der Himmel färbt sich -; **O|ran|gen‿baum, ...blü|te; o|ran|ge[n]|far|ben** *od.* **...far|big; O|ran|gen‿mar|me|la|de, ...saft, ...scha|le; O|ran|ge|rie** [oraŋ..., *auch* orãʒə'riː], die; -, ...ien (Gewächshaus zum Überwintern von Orangenbäumen u. empfindlichen Pflanzen); **o|ran|ge|rot** [o'raŋʒ..., *auch* o'rãːʒ...]

O|rang-U|tan, der; -s, -s ‹malai.› (ein Menschenaffe)

O|ra|ni|en [...i̯ən] (niederl. Fürstengeschlecht); **O|ra|ni|er** [...i̯ər], der; -s, - (zu Oranien Gehörender); **O|ran|je,** der; -[s] (Fluss in Südafrika); **O|ran|je|frei|staat,**

der; -[e]s; ↑R 105 (Provinz der Republik Südafrika)
o|ra pro no|bis! ‹lat., „bitte für uns!"›
O|ra|tio ob|li|qua [- ...kva], die; - - ‹lat.› (*Sprachw.* indirekte Rede); **O|ra|tio rec|ta,** die; - - (*Sprachw.* direkte Rede); **O|ra|to|ri|a|ner,** der; -s, - (Angehöriger einer kath. Weltpriestervereinigung); **o|ra|to|risch** (rednerisch; *Musik* in der Art eines Oratoriums); **O|ra|to|ri|um,** das; -s, ...ien [...iən] (episch-dramat. Komposition für Solostimmen, Chor u. Orchester; *kath. Kirche* Andachtsraum)
ORB = Ostdeutscher Rundfunk Brandenburg
Or|bis pic|tus, der; - - ‹lat., „gemalte Welt"› (Unterrichtsbuch des Comenius); **Or|bit,** der; -s, -s ‹engl.› (*Raumfahrt* Umlaufbahn); **Or|bi|ta,** die; -, ...tae [...tɛ:] ‹lat.› (*Med.* Augenhöhle); **or|bi|tal** (*Raumfahrt* den Orbit betreffend, für ihn bestimmt; *Med.* zur Augenhöhle gehörend); **Or|bi|tal-bahn, ...bom|be, ...ra|ke|te**
Or|ches|ter [ɔr'kɛs..., *österr. auch* ...'çɛs...], das; -s, - ‹griech.› (Vereinigung einer größeren Zahl von Instrumentalmusikern; vertiefter Raum für die Musiker vor der Bühne); **Or|ches|ter-be|glei|tung, ...gra|ben, ...lei|ter** (der)
Or|chest|ra [ɔr'çɛs...] (↑R 130), die; -, ...stren (Tanzraum des Chors im altgriech. Theater); **or|chest|ral** [ɔrkɛs..., *österr. auch* ...çɛs...] (zum Orchester gehörend); **or|chest|rie|ren** (für Orchester bearbeiten, instrumentieren); **Or|chest|rie|rung; Or|chest|ri|on** [...'çɛs...], das; -s, ...ien [...iən] (ein mechan. Musikinstrument)
Or|chi|dee [*auch* ...'de:], die; -, -n ‹griech.› (eine exotische Zierpflanze); **Or|chi|de|en|art; Or|chis,** die; -, - (Knabenkraut); **Or|chi|tis,** die; -, ...itiden (*Med.* Hodenentzündung)
Or|dal, das; -s, ...ien [...iən] ‹angels.› (mittelalterl. Gottesurteil)
Or|den, der; -s, - ‹lat.› ([klösterliche] Gemeinschaft mit bestimmten Regeln; Ehrenzeichen); **or|den|ge|schmückt** (↑R 40); **Or|dens-band** (das; ...bänder), **...bru|der, ...frau, ...mann** (*Plur.* ...männer *od.* ...leute), **...re|gel, ...rit|ter, ...schwes|ter, ...span|ge, ...stern** (*vgl.* ²Stern), **...tracht, ...ver|lei|hung**
or|dent|lich; ordentliches (zuständiges) Gericht; ordentlicher Professor (*Abk.* o. P.); ordentlicher öffentlicher Professor (*Abk.* o. ö. Prof.); **or|dent|li|cher|wei|se; Or|dent|lich|keit,** die; -
Or|der, die; -, *Plur.* -n *od. (Kaufmannsspr. nur:)* -s ‹franz.› (Befehl; *Kaufmannsspr.* Bestellung, Auftrag); - parieren (*veraltet für* einen Befehl ausführen); **Or|der-buch, ...ein|gang; or|dern** (*Kaufmannsspr.* bestellen); ich ...ere (↑R 16); **Or|der|pa|pier** (Wertpapier, das die im Papier bezeichnete Person durch Indossament übertragen kann)
Or|di|na|le, das; -[s], ...lia *meist Plur.* ‹lat.› (*selten für* Ordinalzahl); **Or|di|nal|zahl** (Ordnungszahl, z. B. „zweite"); **or|di|när** ‹franz.› (gewöhnlich, alltäglich; unfein, unanständig); **Or|di|na|ri|at,** das; -[e]s, -e ‹lat.› (Amt eines ordentlichen Hochschulprofessors; eine kirchl. Behörde); **Or|di|na|ri|um,** das; -s, ...ien [...iən] (ordentlicher Staatshaushalt); **Or|di|na|ri|us,** der; -, ...ien [...iən] (ordentlicher Professor an einer Hochschule); **Or|di|när|preis** (vom Verleger festgesetzter Buchverkaufspreis; Marktpreis im Warenhandel); **Or|di|na|te,** die; -, -n (*Math.* auf der Ordinatenachse abgetragene zweite Koordinate eines Punktes); **Or|di|na|ten|ach|se** (senkrechte Achse des rechtwinkligen Koordinatensystems); **Or|di|na|ti|on,** die; -, -en (Weihe, Einsetzung [eines Geistlichen] ins Amt; ärztliche Verordnung, Sprechstunde; *österr. auch für* ärztl. Behandlungsräume, einschließlich Wartezimmer usw.); **Or|di|na|ti|ons-hil|fe** *(österr.)*, **...zim|mer** *(österr.)*; **or|di|nie|ren** (*Verb zu* Ordination)
ord|nen; Ord|ner; Ord|nung; - halten; **Ord|nungs|amt; ord|nungs|ge|mäß; ord|nungs|hal|ber,** *aber* der Ordnung halber; **Ord|nungs-hü|ter** (*scherzh. für* Polizist), **...lie|be; ord|nungs|lie|bend; Ord|nungs-po|li|zei, ...prin|zip, ...ruf, ...sinn** (der; -[e]s), **...stra|fe; ord|nungs|wid|rig; Ord|nungs-wid|rig|keit, ...zahl** (*für* Ordinalzahl)
Or|don|nanz, *auch* **Or|do|nanz,** die; -, -en ‹franz.› (*Milit.* zu dienstlichen Zwecken, bes. zur Befehlsübermittlung abkommandierter Soldat; *schweiz., sonst veraltet für* Anordnung, Befehl); **Or|don|nanz|of|fi|zier,** *auch* **Or|do|nanz|of|fi|zier; Ord|re** (↑R 130), die; -, -s; *vgl.* Order
Ö|re, das; -s, -, *auch* die; -, - (dän., norw., schwed. Münze; 100 Öre = 1 Krone); 5 -
O|re|a|de, die; -, -n *meist Plur.* ‹griech.› (*griech. Mythol.* Bergnymphe)
Oreg. = Oregon
O|re|ga|no, der; - ‹ital.› (eine Gewürzpflanze)
O|re|gon ['ɔrigən] (Staat in den USA; *Abk.* Oreg.)
O|rest, O|res|tes (Sohn Agamemnons); **O|res|tie,** die; - (eine Trilogie des Äschylus)
ORF = Österr. Rundfunk
Or|fe, die; -, -n ‹griech.› (ein Fisch)
Orff, Carl (dt. Komponist)
Or|gan, das; -s, -e ‹griech.› (Körperteil; Sinn, Empfänglichkeit; Stimme; Beauftragter; Fachblatt, Vereinsblatt); **Or|gan|bank** *Plur.* ...banken *(Med.)*
Or|gan|din, der; -s (*österr. svw.* Organdy); **Or|gan|dy,** der; -s ‹engl.› (ein Baumwollgewebe)
Or|ga|nell, das; -s, -en ‹griech.› *u.* **Or|ga|nel|le,** die; -, -n (*Biol.* organartige Bildung des Zellplasmas von Einzellern); **Or|gan-emp|fän|ger, ...ent|nah|me; Or|ga|ni|gramm,** das; -s, -e (schematische Darstellung des Aufbaus einer wirtschaftlichen Organisation); **Or|ga|nik,** die; - (Wissenschaft von den Organismen); **Or|ga|ni|sa|ti|on,** die; -, -en ‹franz.› (Anlage, Aufbau, planmäßige Gestaltung, Einrichtung, Gliederung *[nur Sing.]*; Gruppe, Verband mit bestimmten Zielen); **Or|ga|ni|sa|ti|ons-bü|ro, ...feh|ler, ...form, ...ga|be** (die; -), **...plan** (*vgl.* ²Plan), **...ta|lent; Or|ga|ni|sa|tor,** der; -s, ...oren; **Or|ga|ni|sa|to|rin; or|ga|ni|sa|to|risch; or|ga|nisch** ‹griech.› (belebt, lebendig; auf ein Organ od. auf den Organismus bezüglich); -e Verbindung *(Chemie)*; **or|ga|ni|sie|ren** ‹franz.› (*auch ugs. für* auf nicht ganz redliche Weise beschaffen); sich -; **or|ga|ni|siert** (einer polit. od. gewerkschaftl. Organisation angehörend); **Or|ga|ni|sie|rung; or|ga|nis|misch** (zu einem Organismus gehörend); **Or|ga|nis|mus,** der; -, ...men (Gefüge; einheitliches, gegliedertes [lebendiges] Ganzes; Lebewesen)
Or|ga|nist, der; -en, -en (↑R 126) ‹griech.› (Orgelspieler); **Or|ga|nis|tin**
Or|gan-kon|ser|ve *(Med.)*, **...kon|ser|vie|rung, ...man|dat** (*österr. Amtsspr.* vom Polizisten direkt verfügtes Strafmandat); **or|ga|no|gen** (Organe bildend; organi-

schen Ursprungs); **Or|ga|no|gra|phie**, die; -, ...ien (*Med.* Beschreibung der Organe und ihrer Entstehung; *auch svw.* Organigramm); **or|ga|no|gra|phisch; Or|ga|no|lo|gie**, die; - (*Med., Biol.* Organlehre; *Musik* Orgel[bau]kunde); **or|ga|no|lo|gisch**

Or|gan|sin, der *od.* das; -s ‹franz.› (Kettenseide)

Or|gan‿spen|der, ...straf|ver|fü|gung (*vgl.* Organmandat)

Or|gan|tin (*österr. svw.* Organdy)

Or|gan‿trans|plan|ta|ti|on, ...ver|pflan|zung

Or|gan|za, der; -s ‹ital.› (ein Seidengewebe)

Or|gas|mus, der; -, ...men ‹griech.› (Höhepunkt der geschlechtl. Erregung); **or|gas|tisch**

Or|gel, die; -, -n ‹griech.›; **Or|gel‿bau|er** (der; -s, -), **...bau|e|rin, ...kon|zert, ...mu|sik; or|geln** (*veraltet für* auf der Orgel spielen; *Jägerspr.* Brunstlaute ausstoßen [vom Rothirsch]; *derb für* koitieren); ich ...[e]le (↑R 16); **Or|gel|pfei|fe**; wie die -n (*scherzh. für* [in einer Reihe] der Größe nach); **Or|gel‿punkt** (*Musik*), **...re|gis|ter, ...spiel**

Or|gi|as|mus, der; -, ...men ‹griech.› (ausschweifende kult. Feier in antiken Mysterien); **or|gi|as|tisch** (schwärmerisch; wild, zügellos); **Or|gie** [...iə], die; -, -n (ausschweifendes Gelage; Ausschweifung)

O|ri|ent [ˈoːriɛnt, *auch* oˈriɛnt], der; -s ‹lat.› (die vorder- u. mittelasiat. Länder; östl. Welt; *veraltet für* Osten; *vgl.* Okzident); (↑R 102:) der Vordere Orient; **O|ri|en|ta|le** [oriɛn...], der; -n, -n; ↑R 126 (Bewohner der Länder des Orients); **O|ri|en|ta|lin; o|ri|en|ta|lisch** (den Orient betreffend, östlich); orientalische Sprachen, *aber* (↑R 108): das Orientalische Institut (in Rom); **O|ri|en|ta|list**, der; -en, -en; ↑R 126 (Kenner der oriental. Sprachen u. Kulturen); **O|ri|en|ta|lis|tik**, die; - (Wissenschaft von den oriental. Sprachen und Kulturen); **O|ri|en|ta|lis|tin; o|ri|en|ta|lis|tisch; O|ri|ent|ex|press** [*auch* oˈriɛnt...] (↑R 105); **o|ri|en|tie|ren**; sich -; auf etw. - (*regional*); **O|ri|en|tie|rung; O|ri|en|tie|rungs‿hil|fe, ...lauf** (*Sport*); **o|ri|en|tie|rungs|los; O|ri|en|tie|rungs|lo|sig|keit**, die; -; **O|ri|en|tie|rungs‿marsch, ...sinn** (der; -[e]s), **...stu|fe** (*Schulw.*), **...ver|mö|gen** (das; -s);

O|ri|ent|kun|de [*auch* oˈriɛnt...], die; -; **O|ri|ent|tep|pich**

O|ri|ga|no *vgl.* Oregano

o|ri|gi|nal ‹lat.› (ursprünglich, echt; urschriftlich); original Lübecker Marzipan; original französischer Sekt; **O|ri|gi|nal**, das; -s, -e (Urschrift; Urbild, Vorlage; Urtext; eigentümlicher Mensch); **O|ri|gi|nal‿auf|nah|me, ...aus|ga|be, ...do|ku|ment, ...druck** (*Plur.* ...drucke), **...fas|sung; o|ri|gi|nal|ge|treu; O|ri|gi|na|li|tät**, die; -, -en *Plur. selten* ‹franz.› (Selbständigkeit; Ursprünglichkeit; Besonderheit, wesenhafte Eigentümlichkeit); **O|ri|gi|nal‿pro|gramm** (*Eiskunstlauf*), **...spra|che, ...text** (der), **...ton** (der; -[e]s), **...treue, ...zeich|nung; o|ri|gi|när** ‹lat.› (grundlegend neu; eigenständig); **o|ri|gi|nell** ‹franz.› (eigenartig, einzigartig; urwüchsig; komisch)

O|ri|no|ko, der; -[s] (Strom in Venezuela)

[1]**O|ri|on** (Held der griech. Sage); [2]**O|ri|on**, der; -[s] (ein Sternbild); **O|ri|on|ne|bel**, der; -s

Or|kan, der; -[e]s, -e ‹karib.› (stärkster Sturm); **or|kan|ar|tig; Or|kan|stär|ke**

Ork|ney|in|seln [...ni...] *Plur.* (Inselgruppe nördl. von Schottland)

[1]**Or|kus** (in der röm. Sage Beherrscher der Unterwelt); [2]**Or|kus**, der; - (Unterwelt)

Or|le|a|ner; ↑R 103 (Einwohner von Orleans); **Or|le|a|nist**, der; -en, -en; ↑R 126 (Anhänger des Hauses Orleans); [1]**Or|le|ans** [ˈɔrleã, *franz.* ɔrleˈã], *franz.* [1]**Or|lé|ans** (franz. Stadt); [2]**Or|le|ans**, der; - (ein Gewebe); [3]**Or|le|ans**, *franz.* [2]**Or|lé|ans**, der; -, - (Angehöriger eines Zweiges des ehem. franz. Königshauses)

Or|log, der; -s, *Plur.* -e *u.* -s ‹niederl.› (*veraltet für* Krieg); **Or|log|schiff** (*früher für* Kriegsschiff)

Or|muzd (spätpers. Name für den altiran. Gott Ahura Masdah)

Or|na|ment, das; -[e]s, -e ‹lat.› (Verzierung; Verzierungsmotiv); **or|na|men|tal** (schmückend, zierend); **or|na|ment|ar|tig; Or|na|men|ten|stil**, der; -[e]s; **Or|na|ment|form; or|na|men|tie|ren** (mit Verzierungen versehen); **Or|na|men|tik**, die; - (Verzierungskunst); **Or|na|ment|stich**

Or|nat, der, *auch* das; -[e]s, -e ‹lat.› (feierl. [kirchl.] Amtstracht)

Or|nis, die; - ‹griech.› (*Zool.* Vogelwelt [einer Landschaft]); **Or|ni|tho|lo|ge**, der; -n, -n (↑R 126); **Or|ni|tho|lo|gie**, die; - (Vogelkunde); **Or|ni|tho|lo|gin; or|ni|tho|lo|gisch** (vogelkundlich); **Or|ni|tho|phi|lie**, die; - (*Biol.* Blütenbefruchtung durch Vögel)

o|ro... ‹griech.› (berg..., gebirgs...); **O|ro...** (Berg..., Gebirgs...); **O|ro|ge|ne|se**, die; -, -n (*Geol.* Gebirgsbildung); **O|ro|gra|phie**, die; -, ...ien (*Geogr.* Beschreibung der Reliefformen eines Landes); **o|ro|gra|phisch; O|ro|hyd|ro|gra|phie** (↑R 130), die; -, ...ien (*Geogr.* Gebirgs- und Wasserlaufbeschreibung); **o|ro|hyd|ro|gra|phisch**

Or|pheus [ˈɔrfɔys] (sagenhafter griech. Sänger); **Or|phi|ker**, der; -s, - (Anhänger einer altgriech. Geheimsekte); **or|phisch** (geheimnisvoll)

Or|ping|ton [...t(ə)n], das; -s, -s ‹engl.› (Huhn einer bestimmten Rasse)

Orp|lid [*auch* ˈɔr...] (↑R 130; von Mörike u. seinen Freunden erfundener Name einer Wunsch- u. Märcheninsel)

[1]**Ort**, der; -[e]s, *Plur.* -e, *bes. Seemannsspr. u. Math.* Örter (Ortschaft; Stelle); geometrische Örter; am angeführten, *auch* angegebenen Ort (*Abk.* a. a. O.); an Ort und Stelle; höher[e]n Ort[e]s; allerorten, allerorts

[2]**Ort**, das; -[e]s, Örter (*Bergmannsspr.* Ende einer Strecke, Arbeitsort); vor -

[3]**Ort**, der *od.* das; -[e]s, -e (*schweiz. früher für* Bundesglied, Kanton); die 13 Alten Orte

[4]**Ort**, der *od.* das; -[e]s, -e ([Schuster]ahle, Pfriem; *in erdkundlichen Namen für* Spitze, z. B. Darßer Ort [Nordspitze der Halbinsel Darß])

Ort‿band (das; -[e]s, ...bänder; Beschlag an der Spitze der Säbelscheide), **...brett** (*landsch. für* Eckbrett)

Ört|chen

Or|te|ga y Gas|set [- i -] (span. Philosoph u. Soziologe)

or|ten (die Position, Lage ermitteln, bestimmen); **Or|ter** (mit dem Orten Beauftragter)

Ör|ter|bau, der; -[e]s (*Bergmannsspr.* Abbauverfahren, bei dem ein Teil der Lagerstätte stehen bleibt); **ör|tern** (Strecken anlegen); ich ...ere (↑R 16)

or|tho... ‹griech.› (gerade..., aufrecht...; richtig..., recht...); **Or|tho...** (Gerade..., Aufrecht...; Richtig..., Recht...); **Or|tho|chro|ma|sie** [...k...], die; - (Fähigkeit einer fotogr. Schicht, für alle Farben außer Rot empfindlich zu sein); **or|tho|chro|ma|tisch; or|tho|dox** (recht-, strenggläubig); die orthodoxe Kirche; **Or|tho|do|xie,** die; -; **Or|tho|e|pie,** die; - (*Sprachw.* Lehre von der richtigen Aussprache der Wörter); **Or|tho|e|pik,** die; - (*seltener für* Orthoepie); **or|tho|e|pisch; Or|tho|ge|ne|se,** die; -, -n (*Biol.* Hypothese, nach der die stammesgeschichtl. Entwicklung der Lebewesen durch zielgerichtete innere Faktoren bestimmt ist); **Or|tho|gna|thie,** die; - (*Med.* gerade Kieferstellung); **Or|tho|gon,** das; -s, -e (*Geom.* Rechteck); **or|tho|go|nal** (rechtwinklig)

Or|tho|gra|phie, *auch* Or|tho|gra|fie (↑R 33), die; -, ...ien (Rechtschreibung); **or|tho|gra|phisch,** *auch* or|tho|gra|fisch (rechtschreiblich)

Or|tho|klas, der; -es, -e (*Mineral.* ein Feldspat); **Or|tho|pä|de,** der; -n, -n; ↑R 126 (Facharzt für Orthopädie); **Or|tho|pä|die,** die; - (Lehre u. Behandlung von Fehlbildungen u. Erkrankungen der Bewegungsorgane); **Or|tho|pä|die‿me|cha|ni|ker, ...schuh|ma|cher; Or|tho|pä|din; or|tho|pä|disch; Or|tho|pä|dist,** der; -en, -en; ↑R 126 (Hersteller orthopädischer Geräte); **Or|thop|te|re,** die; -, -n *u.* **Or|thop|te|ron** (↑R 132), das; -s, ...pteren *beide meist Plur.* (*Zool.* Geradflügler)

Or|thop|tist (↑R 132), der; -en, -en; ↑R 126 (Mitarbeiter des Arztes bei der Heilbehandlung von Sehstörungen); **Or|thop|tis|tin**

Or|tho|sko|pie, die; - (*Optik* unverzerrte Abbildung durch Linsen); **or|tho|sko|pisch**

Ort|ler, der; -s (höchster Gipfel der Ortlergruppe); **Ort|ler|grup|pe,** die; - (Gebirgsgruppe der Zentralalpen)

ört|lich; Ört|lich|keit

Ort|lieb (m. Vorn.)

Or|to|lan, der; -s, -e ⟨ital.⟩ (ein Vogel)

Or|trud (w. Vorn.); **Ort|run** (w. Vorn.)

Orts|an|ga|be; orts|an|säs|sig; Orts‿aus|gang, ...bei|rat, ...be|stim|mung; orts|be|weg|lich; Ort|schaft

Ort|scheit *Plur.* ...scheite (Querholz zur Befestigung der Geschirrstränge am Fuhrwerk)

Orts‿durch|fahrt, ...ein|gang, ...et|ter (*vgl.* Etter); **orts‿fest, ...fremd; Orts‿ge|spräch, ...grup|pe, ...kennt|nis, ...kern, ...klas|se; Orts|kran|ken|kas|se;** Allgemeine - (↑R 108; *Abk.* AOK); **Orts|kun|de,** die; -; **orts|kun|dig; Orts|na|me; Orts|na|men|for|schung,** die; -; **Orts|netz** *(Telefonwesen);* **Orts|netz|kenn|zahl** *(Telefonwesen);* **Orts‿sinn** (der; -[e]s), **...ta|fel, ...teil** (der)

Ort|stein (durch Witterungseinflüsse verfestigte Bodenschicht)

orts|üb|lich; Orts‿um|ge|hung, ...ver|ein, ...ver|kehr, ...vor|ste|her, ...wech|sel, ...zeit, ...zu|schlag

Or|tung ⟨*zu* orten⟩; **Or|tungs|kar|te**

Ort|win (m. Vorn.)

Ort|zie|gel (ein Dachziegel)

Or|well [ˈɔ:(r)wəl] (engl. Schriftsteller)

Os = *chem. Zeichen für* Osmium

Os, der, *auch* das; -[es], -er *meist Plur.* ⟨schwed.⟩ (*Geol.* durch Schmelzwasser der Eiszeit entstandener Höhenrücken)

öS = österr. Schilling

O-Saft *(ugs.)* = Orangensaft

Ō|sa|ka (jap. Stadt)

OSB, *auch* **O.S.B.** = Ordinis Sancti Benedicti ⟨lat., „vom Orden des hl. Benedikt"⟩ (Benediktinerorden)

Os|car, der; -[s], -s ⟨amerik.⟩ (amerik. Filmpreis)

Ö|se, die; -, -n

Ö|sel (estnische Insel)

Ö|ser (*Plur. von* Os)

O|si|ris (ägypt. Gott des Nils und des Totenreiches)

Os|kar (m. Vorn.)

Os|ker, der; -s, - (Angehöriger eines idg. Volksstammes in Mittelitalien); **os|kisch**

Os|ku|la|ti|on, die; -, -en ⟨lat.⟩ (*Math.* Berührung zweier Kurven); **os|ku|lie|ren**

Os|lo (Hptst. Norwegens); **Os|lo|er**

OSM, *auch* **O. S. M.** = Ordinis Servorum *od.* Servarum Mariae ⟨lat., „vom Orden der Diener[innen] Marias"⟩ *vgl.* Servit, Servitin

Os|man (Gründer des Türk. Reiches); **Os|ma|ne,** der; -n, -n; ↑R 126 (Stammesgenosse Osmans, Türke); **Os|ma|nen|tum,** das; -s; **os|ma|nisch,** *aber* (↑R 108): das Osmanische Reich

Os|mi|um, das; -s ⟨griech.⟩ (chem. Element, Metall; *Zeichen* Os); **Os|mo|lo|gie,** die; - (Lehre von den Riechstoffen u. vom Geruchssinn); **Os|mo|se,** die; - (*Chemie, Biol.* Übergang des Lösungsmittels einer Lösung in eine stärker konzentrierte Lösung durch eine feinporige Scheidewand); **os|mo|tisch**

Os|na|brück (Stadt in Niedersachsen)

Os|ning, der; -s (mittlerer Teil des Teutoburger Waldes)

OSO = Ostsüdost[en]

Ö|so|pha|gus, *fachspr.* Oe|so|phagus [ø...], der; -, ...gi ⟨griech.⟩ (*Med.* Speiseröhre)

Os|sa|ri|um, Os|su|a|ri|um, das; -s, ...ien [...i̯ən] ⟨lat.⟩ (Beinhaus auf Friedhöfen, antike Gebeinurne)

Os|ser|va|to|re Ro|ma|no [...v... -], der; - - ⟨„Röm. Beobachter"⟩ (päpstl. Zeitung)

Os|se|te, der; -n, -n (Angehöriger eines Bergvolkes im Kaukasus); **os|se|tisch**

Os|si, der; -s, -s (*ugs. für* Bewohner der ehem. DDR; Ostdeutscher)

Os|si|an [*auch* ɔˈsi̯a:n] (sagenhafter kelt. Barde)

Os|si|etz|ky, Carl von (dt. Publizist)

Os|si|fi|ka|ti|on, die; -, -en ⟨lat.⟩ (*Med.* Knochenbildung, Verknöcherung); **os|si|fi|zie|ren**

Os|su|a|ri|um *vgl.* Ossarium

[1]**Ost** (Himmelsrichtung; *Abk.* O); Ost und West; *fachspr.:* der Wind kommt aus Ost; Autobahnausfahrt Saarbrücken Ost (↑R 106); *vgl.* Osten; [2]**Ost,** der; -[e]s, -e *Plur. selten* (*geh. für* Ostwind); **Ost|af|ri|ka; ost|asi|a|tisch** (↑R 132); **Ost|asi|en** (↑R 132); **ost|bal|tisch;** -e Rasse; **Ost|ber|lin** (↑R 105); **Ost|ber|li|ner; Ost|block,** der; -[e]s (*früher* Gesamtheit der Staaten des Warschauer Pakts); **Ost|block‿land** (*Plur.* ...länder), **...staat** (*Plur.* ...staaten); **Ost|chi|na; ost|deutsch; Ost|deutsch|land**

Os|te|al|gie, die; -, ...ien ⟨griech.⟩ (*Med.* Knochenschmerzen)

Ost|el|bi|en; Ost|el|bi|er (*früher für* Großgrundbesitzer und Junker); **ost|el|bisch; os|ten** (*Bauw.* nach Osten [aus]richten); **Os|ten,** der; -s (Himmelsrichtung; *Abk.* O); ↑R 108: der Ferne Osten; der Nahe Osten; der Mittlere Osten; *vgl.* Ost

Ost|en|de (Seebad in Belgien)

os|ten|si|bel ⟨lat.⟩ (zur Schau gestellt, auffällig); ...ib|le (↑R 130) Gegenstände; **os|ten|siv** (*veraltend für* augenscheinlich, offensichtlich); **Os|ten|ta|ti|on,** die; -, -en (*veraltend für* Schaustellung; Prahlerei); **os|ten|ta|tiv** (betont; herausfordernd)

Os|te|o|lo|gie, die; - ⟨griech.⟩ (*Med.* Knochenlehre); **Os|te|o|ma|la|zie,** die; -, ...ien (Knochenerweichung)

Os|te|o|my|e|li|tis (↑R 132), die; -, ...itiden (Knochenmarkentzündung); **Os|te|o|plas|tik** (operatives Schließen von Knochenlücken); **os|te|o|plas|tisch; Os|te|o|po|ro|se,** die; -, -n (Knochenschwund)

Os|ter‿brauch, ...ei, ...fest, ...feu|er, ...glo|cke, ...ha|se

Os|te|ria, die; -, *Plur.* -s *u.* ...ien (Gasthaus [in Italien])

Os|ter‿in|sel (die; -; im Pazif. Ozean), **...ker|ze** *(kath. Kirche),* **...lamm; ös|ter|lich; Os|ter|lu|zei** [*auch* ...ˈtsai], die; -, -en (ein Schlinggewächs); **Os|ter‿marsch** (der), **...mar|schie|rer, ...mes|se; Os|ter|mo|nat** *od.* **...mond** *(alte Bez. für* April), **...mon|tag; Os|tern,** das; -, - (Osterfest); Ostern ist bald vorbei; *landsch., bes. österr. u. schweiz. als Plur.:* nach den Ostern; *in Wunschformeln auch allg. als Plur.:* fröhliche Ostern!; zu Ostern *(bes. nordd.),* an Ostern *(bes. südd.)*

Ös|ter|reich; Ös|ter|rei|cher; Ös|ter|rei|che|rin; ös|ter|rei|chisch, *aber* (↑R 108): die Österreichischen Bundesbahnen (*Abk.* ÖBB); **ös|ter|rei|chisch-un|ga|risch;** die -e Monarchie; **Ös|ter|reich-Un|garn** (ehem. Doppelmonarchie)

Os|ter‿sonn|tag, ...spiel, ...ver|kehr, ...was|ser (das; -s), **...wo|che** (Woche nach Ostern; *auch für* Karwoche)

Ost|eu|ro|pa; ost|eu|ro|pä|isch; osteuropäische Zeit (*Abk.* OEZ); **Ost|fa|le,** der; -n, -n; ↑R 126 (Angehöriger eines altsächsischen Volksstammes); **Ost|fa|len; ost|fä|lisch; Ost|flan|dern** (belg. Prov.); **Ost|fran|ken** (hist. Landschaft); **ost|frän|kisch; Ost|frie|se; Ost|frie|sen|witz; Ost|frie|sin; ost|frie|sisch,** *aber* (↑R 102): die Ostfriesischen Inseln; **Ost|fries|land; Ost|geld,** das; -[e]s; *vgl.* [2]Ostmark; **Ost|ger|ma|ne; ost|ger|ma|nisch**

Os|tia (Hafen des alten Roms)

os|ti|nat, os|ti|na|to ‹ital.› (*Musik* stetig wiederkehrend, ständig wiederholt [vom Bassthema])

Ost|in|di|en; ost|in|disch; ostindische Waren, *aber* (↑R 108): die Ostindische Kompanie *(früher)*

Os|ti|tis, die; -, ...itiden ‹griech.› (*Med.* Knochenentzündung)

Ost|ja|ke, der; -n, -n; ↑R 126 (Angehöriger eines finn.-ugr. Volkes in Westsibirien)

Ost‿kir|che, ...küs|te; öst|lich; östlich des Waldes, östlich vom Wald; östlicher Länge (*Abk.* ö. L.); **[1]Ost|mark** (hist. Landschaft); **[2]Ost|mark,** die; -, - *(früher ugs. für* Währung der DDR); **[1]Ost|nord|ost** (Himmelsrichtung; *Abk.* ONO); *vgl.* Ostnordosten; **[2]Ost|nord|ost,** der; -[e]s, -e *Plur. selten* (Ostnordostwind; *Abk.* ONO); **Ost|nord|os|ten,** der; -s (*Abk.* ONO); *vgl.* [1]Ostnordost; **Ost|po|li|tik; Ost|preu|ßen; ost|preu|ßisch**

Ost|ra|zis|mus (↑R 130), der; - ‹griech.› (Scherbengericht, altathen. Volksgericht)

Öst|ro|gen (↑R 130), das; -s, -e ‹griech.› (*Med.* w. Geschlechtshormon)

Ost|rom; ost|rö|misch, *aber* (↑R 108): das Oströmische Reich

Ost|rows|ki (↑R 130; russ. Dramatiker)

Ost|see, die; -; **Ost|see|bad;** Ostseebad Prerow [...ro:] (↑R 105); **Ost|see|in|sel; Ost|sei|te; [1]Ost|süd|ost** (Himmelsrichtung; *Abk.* OSO); *vgl.* Ostsüdosten; **[2]Ost|süd|ost,** der; -[e]s, -e *Plur. selten* (Ostsüdostwind; *Abk.* OSO); **Ost|süd|os|ten,** der; -s (*Abk.* OSO); *vgl.* [1]Ostsüdost; **Ost|ti|rol; Os|tung,** die; - ‹*zu* osten›

Ost|wald (dt. Chemiker); ostwaldsche Farbenlehre

ost|wärts; Ost-West-Ge|spräch, das; -[e]s, -e; ↑R 28; **ost|west|lich;** in -er Richtung; **Ost‿wind, ...zo|ne** *(veraltet für* sowjetische Besatzungszone)

Os|wald (m. Vorn.); **Os|win** (m. Vorn.)

OSZE = Organisation für Sicherheit und Zusammenarbeit in Europa

Os|zil|la|ti|on, die; -, -en ‹lat.› (*Physik* Schwingung); **Os|zil|la|tor,** der; -s, ...toren (Gerät zur Erzeugung elektrischer Schwingungen); **os|zil|lie|ren** (schwingen, pendeln, schwanken); **Os|zil|lo|gramm,** das; -s, -e ‹lat.; griech.› (Schwingungsbild); **Os|zil|lo|graph,** der; -en, -en; ↑R 126 (Schwingungsschreiber)

Ö|ta, der; -[s] (mittelgriech. Gebirge)

O|tal|gie (↑R 132), die; -, ...ien ‹griech.› (*Med.* Ohrenschmerz)

Ot|fried (m. Vorn.)

O|thel|lo (Titelheld bei Shakespeare)

Oth|mar *vgl.* Otmar

O|tho (röm. Kaiser)

O|ti|at|rie (↑R 130 *u.* 132), die; - ‹griech.› (*Med.* Ohrenheilkunde); **O|ti|tis,** die; -, ...itiden (Ohrenentzündung)

Ot|mar, Oth|mar (↑R 92), Ot|tomar (m. Vorn.)

O|to|lith [*auch* ...ˈlit], der; *Gen.* -s *od.* -en, *Plur.* -e[n] (↑R 126) ‹griech., „Gehörsteinchen"› (Teil des Gleichgewichtsorgans); **O|to|lo|gie,** die; - (*svw.* Otiatrie)

O-Ton = Originalton

O|to|skop, das; -s, -e ‹griech.› (*Med.* Ohrenspiegel)

Öt|scher, der; -s (Berg in Niederösterreich)

Ot|ta|ve|ri|me [...v...] *Plur.* ‹ital.› (*Verslehre* Stanze)

[1]Ot|ta|wa, der; -[s] (Fluss in Kanada); **[2]Ot|ta|wa** (Hptst. Kanadas); **[3]Ot|ta|wa,** der; -[s], -[s] (Angehöriger eines nordamerik. Indianerstammes)

[1]Ot|ter, der; -s, - (eine Marderart)

[2]Ot|ter, die; -, -n (eine Schlange); **Ot|tern‿brut, ...ge|zücht** *(bibl.)*

Ot|ter|zun|ge (versteinerter Fischzahn)

Ott|heln|rich (m. Vorn.)

Ot|ti|lia, Ot|ti|lie [...iə] (w. Vorn.); **Ot|to** (m. Vorn.); - Normalverbraucher *(ugs. für* Durchschnittsmensch); **Ot|to|kar** (m. Vorn.)

Ot|to|man, der; -s, -e ‹türk.› (ein Ripsgewebe); **[1]Ot|to|ma|ne,** die; -, -n *(veraltet für* niedriges Sofa); **[2]Ot|to|ma|ne,** der; -n, -n; ↑R 126 (*svw.* Osmane)

Ot|to|mar *vgl.* Otmar

Ot|to|mo|tor ® (↑R 95) ‹nach dem Erfinder› (Vergasermotor)

Ot|to|ne, der; -n, -n; ↑R 126 (Bez. für einen der sächsischen Kaiser Otto I., II. und III.); **ot|to|nisch**

Ötz|tal; Ötz|ta|ler; - Alpen

Oua|ga|dou|gou [wagaˈdu:gu] (Hptst. von Burkina Faso)

out [aut] ‹engl.› (*österr., sonst veraltet für* aus, außerhalb des Spielfeldes [bei Ballspielen]; *ugs. für* unzeitgemäß, unmodern); **Out,** das; -[s], -[s]; **Out|back** [autbɛk], das; -s (das Landesinnere Australiens); **Out|cast** [ˈautka:st], der; -s, -s (von der Gesellschaft Ausgestoßener); **Out|ein|wurf** *(österr. Sportspr.);* **ou|ten** [ˈautən]; jmdn. - (jmds. Homosexualität o. Ä. ohne dessen Zustimmung öffentlich bekannt machen); **Out|fit,** das; -[s], -s (Kleidung; Ausrüstung); **Ou|ting,** das; -s (das [Sich]outen); **Out|law** [ˈautlɔ:], der; -[s], -s (Geächteter, Verbrecher); **Out|li|nie** *(österr. Sportspr.);* **Out|put,** der, *auch* das; -s, -s (*Wirtsch.* Produktion[smenge]; *EDV* Arbeitsergebnisse einer Datenverarbeitungsanlage, Ausgabe)

out|rie|ren [u...] (↑R 130) ‹franz.› *(veraltet für* übertreiben)

Out|si|der ['au̯tsaɪ̯də(r)], der; -s, - ⟨engl.⟩ (Außenseiter); **Out|wach|ler** (*österr. ugs. für* Linienrichter)
Ou|ver|tü|re [uvɛr...], die; -, -n ⟨franz., „Öffnung"⟩ (instrumentales Eröffnungsstück)
Ou|zo ['u:zo], der; -[s], -s ⟨griech.⟩ (griech. Anisbranntwein)
o|val [...v...] ⟨lat.⟩ (eirund, länglich rund); **O|val**, das; -s, -e; **O|var**, das; -s, -e; *vgl.* Ovarium; **O|va|ri|um**, das; -s, ...ien [...i̯ən] (*Biol., Med.* Eierstock)
O|va|ti|on [...v...], die; -, -en ⟨lat.⟩ (begeisterter Beifall)
O|ver|all ['o:vərɔ:l, *auch* ...al], der; -s, -s ⟨engl.⟩ (einteiliger [Schutz]anzug); **o|ver|dressed** ['o:və(r)drɛst] (zu gut, fein angezogen); **O|ver|drive** ['o:və(r)draɪ̯v], der; -[s], -s (*Kfz-Technik* Schnellgang); **O|ver|head|pro|jek|tor** ['o:və(r)hɛd...] (Projektor, der transparente Vorlagen auf eine hinter dem Vortragenden liegende Fläche projiziert); **O|ver|kill** ['o:və(r)kil], der; -[s] (*Milit.* das Vorhandensein von mehr Waffen, als nötig sind, um den Gegner zu vernichten)
O|vid [o'vi:t] (röm. Dichter); **o|vi|disch**; die ovidischen Liebeselegien
o|vi|par [...v...] ⟨lat.⟩ (*Biol.* Eier legend, sich durch Eier fortpflanzend); **o|vo|id, o|vo|i|disch** ⟨lat.; griech.⟩ (eiförmig); **o|vo|vi|vi|par** ⟨lat.⟩ (Eier mit schon weit entwickelten Embryonen legend)
ÖVP = Österreichische Volkspartei
O|vu|la|ti|on [...v...], die; -, -en ⟨lat.⟩ (*Biol.* Ausstoßung des reifen Eies aus dem Eierstock); **O|vu|la|ti|ons‿hem|mer** *(Med.)*, **...zyk|lus**
...ow [...o:, *österr.* ...of] (*in geograph. Namen,* z. B. Teltow; ↑R 131)
Ow|en ['au̯ən] (Stadt in Baden-Württemberg)
O|xa|lit [*auch* ...'lit], der; -s, -e ⟨griech.⟩ (ein Mineral); **O|xal|säu|re**, die; - ⟨griech.; dt.⟩ (Kleesäure)
O|xer, der; -s, - ⟨engl.⟩ (Zaun zwischen Viehweiden; *Pferdesport* Hindernis bei Springprüfungen)
Ox|ford (engl. Stadt)
Ox|hoft, das; -[e]s, -e (altes Flüssigkeitsmaß); 10 - (↑R 90)
O|xid *nichtfachspr. auch* O|xyd, das; -[e]s, -e ⟨griech.⟩ (Sauerstoffverbindung); **O|xi|da|ti|on**, *nichtfachspr. auch* O|xy|da|ti|on, die; -, -en (*svw.* Oxidierung); **o|xi|die|ren**, *nichtfachspr. auch* o|xy|dieren (sich mit Sauerstoff verbinden, Sauerstoff aufnehmen; bewirken, dass sich eine Substanz mit Sauerstoff verbindet); **O|xi|die|rung**, *nichtfachspr. auch* O|xy|die|rung (Vorgang, Ergebnis des Oxidierens); **o|xi|disch**, *nichtfachspr. auch* o|xy|disch; **o|xy...** (scharf...; sauerstof...), **O|xy...** (Scharf...; Sauerstoff...); **O|xy|gen**, **O|xy|ge|ni|um**, das; -s (*griech.-lat. Bez. für* Sauerstoff; chem. Element; *Zeichen* O); **O|xy|hä|mo|glo|bin** ⟨griech.; lat.⟩ (sauerstoffhaltiger Blutfarbstoff); **O|xy|mo|ron**, das; -s, ...ra ⟨griech.⟩ (*Rhet.* Zusammenstellung zweier sich widersprechender Begriffe als rhet. Figur, z. B. „bittersüß"); **O|xy|to|non**, das; -s, ...na (*Sprachw.* auf der letzten, kurzen Silbe betontes Wort)
Oy|bin [ɔy'bi:n], **Kurort** (am gleichnamigen Berg im Zittauer Gebirge)
O|za|lid ® (*Markenbez. für* Papiere, Gewebe, Filme mit lichtempfindlichen Emulsionen); **O|za|lid‿pa|pier, ...ver|fah|ren**
O|ze|an, der; -s, -e ⟨griech.⟩ (Weltmeer); der große (endlos scheinende) Ozean, *aber* (↑R 102): der Große (Pazifische) Ozean; **O|ze|a|na|ri|um**, das; -s, ...ien [...i̯ən] (Anlage mit Meerwasseraquarien); **O|ze|a|naut**, der; -en, -en (*svw.* Aquanaut); **O|ze|an‿damp|fer; O|ze|a|ni|de** *vgl.* Okeanide; **O|ze|a|ni|en** [...i̯ən] (die Pazifikinseln zwischen Amerika, den Philippinen u. Australien); **o|ze|a|nisch** (Meeres...; zu Ozeanen gehörend); **O|ze|a|no|gra|phie**, die; - (Meereskunde); **o|ze|a|no|gra|phisch**
O|zel|le, die; -, -n ⟨lat.⟩ (*Zool.* Lichtsinnesorgan bei Insekten u. Spinnentieren)
O|ze|lot [*auch* 'ɔ...], der; -s, *Plur.* -e *u.* -s ⟨aztek.⟩ (ein katzenartiges Raubtier Nord- u. Südamerikas; *auch für* Pelz dieses Tieres)
O|zo|ke|rit [*auch* ...'rit], der; -s ⟨griech.⟩ (Erdwachs; natürlich vorkommendes mineral. Wachs)
O|zon, der *od.* (*fachspr. nur:*) das; -s ⟨griech.⟩ (besondere Form des Sauerstoffs); **O|zon‿alarm** (↑R 132), **...ge|halt**, der; -[e]s; **o|zon|hal|tig**, *österr.* **o|zon|häl|tig; o|zo|ni|sie|ren** (mit Ozon behandeln); **O|zon|loch** (bes. durch Treibgase verursachte Zerstörung der oberen Schichten der Erdatmosphäre); **o|zon|reich; O|zon‿schicht**, die; - *(Meteor.)*, **...the|ra|pie** *(Med.)*

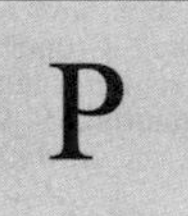

P (Buchstabe); das P; des P, die P, *aber* das p in hupen (↑R 60); der Buchstabe P, p
p = [1]Para; Penni; Penny *(nur für den neuen Penny im engl. Dezimalsystem);* piano; Pico..., Piko...; Pond; typographischer Punkt
P *(auf dt. Kurszetteln)* = Papier (*vgl.* B); Peta...; *chem. Zeichen für* Phosphor; Poise
p. = pinxit
p., pag. = Pagina
Π, π = [1]Pi; *π* = [2]Pi
P. = Pastor; Pater; [2]Papa
Pa = *chem. Zeichen für* Protactinium; Pascal
Pa. = Pennsylvanien
p. a. = pro anno
p. A. = per Adresse, *besser:* bei
Pä|an, der; -s, -e ⟨griech.⟩ (altgriech. Hymne)
[1]**paar** ⟨lat.⟩ (einige; ↑R 46); ein paar Leute, für ein paar Mark, mit ein paar Worten; ein paar Dutzend Mal[e]; ein paar Mal[e] (*vgl.* [1]Mal); die paar Groschen;
[2]**paar** (*Biol. selten für* paarig); paare Blätter; **Paar**, das; -[e]s, -e (zwei zusammengehörende Personen od. Dinge); ein Paar Schuhe; ein Paar neue, *selten* neuer Schuhe; für zwei Paar neue, *selten* neuer Schuhe; mit einem Paar Schuhe[n]; mit einem Paar wollenen Strümpfen *od.* wollener Strümpfe; mit zwei Paar neuen Schuhen *od.* neuer Schuhe; zu Paaren treiben (*veraltend für* bändigen, bewältigen); **Paar|bil|dung; paa|ren;** sich -; **Paar|hu|fer** *(Zool.);* **paa|rig** (paarweise vorhanden); **Paa|rig|keit**, die; -; **Paar|lauf** *(Sport);* **paar|lau|fen** *nur im Infinitiv u. im Partizip II gebr.;* **Paar|läu|fer** *(Sport);* **Paar|läu|fe|rin; paar Mal** *vgl.* [1]paar u. [1]Mal; **Paa|rung; paa|rungs|be|reit; paar|wei|se; Paar|ze|her** (*svw.* Paarhufer)
Pace [pe:s], die; - ⟨engl.⟩ (Gangart des Pferdes; Renntempo); **Pace|ma|cher** (Pferd, das das Renntempo bestimmt); **Pace|ma|ker** [...me:kə(r)], der; -s, - (Pacemacher; *Med.* Herzschrittmacher)
Pacht, die; -, -en; **pach|ten; Päch|ter; Päch|te|rin; Pacht-**

‿geld, ...gut, ...land (das; -[e]s), **...sum|me; Pach|tung; Pacht|ver|trag; pacht|wei|se; Pacht|zins** *Plur.* ...zinsen

Pa|chul|ke, der; -n, -n (↑R 126) ⟨slaw.⟩ (*landsch. für* ungehobelter Bursche, Tölpel)

¹Pack, der; -[e]s, *Plur.* -e *u.* Päcke (Gepacktes; Bündel); **²Pack,** das; -[e]s (*abwertend für* Gesindel, Pöbel); **Pa|ckage|tour** ['pɛkidʒtu:r], die; -, -s ⟨engl.⟩ (durch ein Reisebüro vorbereitete Reise im eigenen Auto mit vorher bezahlten Unterkünften u. sonstigen Leistungen); **Päck|chen; Pack|eis** ([übereinander geschobenes] Scholleneis)

Pa|cke|lei (*österr. ugs. für* heimliches Paktieren); **pa|ckeln** ([heimlich] paktieren)

Pa|ckeln *Plur.* (*österr. ugs.* Fußballschuhe); **pa|cken;** sich - (*ugs. für* sich fortscheren); **Pa|cken,** der; -s, -; **Pa|cker; Pa|cke|rei; Pa|cke|rin; Pack|esel** (↑R 132; *ugs. für* jmd., dem alles aufgepackt wird)

Pack|fong, das; -s ⟨chin.⟩ (im 18. Jh. aus China eingeführte Kupfer-Nickel-Zink-Legierung)

Pack|kis|te; Pack‿lein|wand, ...pa|pier, ...raum, ...set (das; -s, -s; von der Post angebotener Karton mit Kordel u. Aufkleber für Pakete u. Päckchen); **Pack|tisch; Pa|ckung** (*ugs. auch für* hohe Niederlage im Sport); **Pack‿wagen, ...werk** (*Wasserbau*), **...zettel** (*Wirtsch.*)

Pä|da|go|ge (↑R 132), der; -n, -n (↑R 126) ⟨griech.⟩ (Erzieher; Lehrer; Erziehungswissenschaftler); **Pä|da|go|gik,** die; - (Erziehungslehre, -wissenschaft); **Pä|da|go|gi|kum,** das; -s, ...ka (Prüfung in Erziehungswissenschaften für Lehramtskandidat[inn]en); **Pä|da|go|gin; pä|da|go|gisch** (erzieherisch); pädagogische Fähigkeit; pädagogische Maßnahmen; [eine] pädagogische Hochschule, *aber* (↑R 108): die Pädagogische Hochschule (*Abk.* PH) in Münster; **pä|da|go|gi|sie|ren; Pä|da|go|gi|um,** das; -s, ...ien [...i̯ən] (*früher* Vorbereitungsschule für das Studium an einer pädagogischen Hochschule)

Pad|del, das; -s, - ⟨engl.⟩; **Pad|del|boot; Pad|del|boot|fahrt; pad|deln;** ich ...[e]le (↑R 16); **Padd|ler**

Pad|dock ['pɛdɔk], der; -s, -s ⟨engl.⟩ (umzäunter Auslauf [für Pferde])

¹Pad|dy ['pɛdi], der; -s ⟨malai.-engl.⟩ (ungeschälter Reis)

²Pad|dy ['pɛdi], der; -s, -s ⟨engl.; Koseform des m. Vornamens Patrick⟩ (Spitzname des Iren)

Pä|de|rast (↑R 132), der; -en, -en (↑R 126) ⟨griech.⟩ (Homosexueller mit bes. auf männl. Jugendliche gerichtetem Sexualempfinden); **Pä|de|ras|tie,** die; -

Pa|der|born (Stadt in Nordrhein-Westfalen)

Pä|di|a|ter (↑R 132), der; -s, - ⟨griech.⟩ (Kinderarzt); **Pä|di|a|trie** (↑R 130 *u.* 132), die; - (Kinderheilkunde); **pä|di|a|trisch**

Pa|di|schah, der; -s, -s ⟨pers.⟩ (*früher* Titel islam. Fürsten)

Pä|do|ge|ne|se, *auch* **Pä|do|ge|ne|sis** [*auch* ...ge:...], die; - ⟨griech.⟩ (*Biol.* Fortpflanzung im Larvenstadium)

pä|do|phil; Pä|do|phi|le, der; -n, -n (↑R 5 ff.); **Pä|do|phi|lie,** die; - ⟨griech.⟩ (auf Kinder gerichteter Sexualtrieb Erwachsener)

Pa|douk [pa'dauk], das; -s ⟨birman.⟩ (ein Edelholz)

Pa|dua (ital. Stadt); **Pa|du|a|ner** (↑R 103); **pa|du|a|nisch**

Pa|el|la [pa'ɛlja], die; -, -s ⟨span.⟩ (span. Reisgericht mit verschiedenen Sorten Fleisch, Fisch, Gemüse u. a.)

Pa|fe|se, Po|fe|se, die; -, -n *meist Plur.* ⟨ital.⟩ (*bayr. u. österr. für* gebackene Weißbrotschnitte)

paff *vgl.* baff

paff!; piff, paff!

paf|fen (*ugs. für* [schnell u. stoßweise] rauchen)

pag., p. = Pagina

Pa|ga|ni|ni (ital. Geigenvirtuose u. Komponist)

Pa|ga|nis|mus, der; -, ...men ⟨lat.⟩ (*nur Sing.:* Heidentum; *auch für* heidnische Elemente im christl. Glauben u. Brauchtum)

Pa|gat, der; -[e]s, -e ⟨ital.⟩ (Karte im Tarockspiel)

pa|ga|to|risch ⟨lat.-ital.⟩ (*Wirtsch.* auf Zahlungsvorgänge bezogen); pagatorische Buchhaltung

Pa|ge ['pa:ʒə], der; -n, -n (↑R 126) ⟨franz.⟩ (livrierter junger [Hotel]diener; *früher* Edelknabe); **Pa|gen‿dienst, ...fri|sur, ...kopf**

Pa|gi|na, die; -, -s ⟨lat.⟩ (*veraltet für* [Buch-, Blatt]seite; *Abk.* p. *od.* pag.); **pa|gi|nie|ren** (mit Seitenzahl[en] versehen); **Pa|gi|nier|ma|schi|ne; Pa|gi|nie|rung**

¹Pa|go|de, die; -, -n ⟨drawid.-port.⟩ ([buddhist.] Tempel in Indien, China u. Japan); **²Pa|go|de,** die; -, -n, *auch* der; -n, -n; ↑R 126 (*veraltet, aber noch österr. für* ostasiat. Götterbild; kleine sitzende Porzellanfigur mit beweglichem Kopf); **Pa|go|den‿dach, ...kragen** (aus mehreren in Stufen übereinander gelegten Teilen bestehender Kragen)

pah!, bah!

Pail|let|te [pa'jɛtə], die; -, -n *meist Plur.* ⟨franz.⟩ (glitzerndes Metallblättchen zum Aufnähen); **pail|let|ten|be|setzt; Pail|let|ten|kleid**

Pair [pɛ:r], der; -s, -s ⟨franz.⟩ (*früher* Mitglied des höchsten franz. Adels); *vgl.* Peer; **Pai|rie,** die; -, ...i̯en (Würde eines Pairs); **Pairs|wür|de,** die; -

Pak, die; -, -[s] (*Kurzw. für* Panzerabwehrkanone)

Pa|ket, das; -[e]s, -e; **Pa|ket‿ad|res|se, ...an|nah|me, ...boot; pa|ke|tie|ren** (zu einem Paket machen, verpacken); **Pa|ke|tier|ma|schi|ne; Pa|ket‿kar|te, ...post, ...zu|stel|lung**

Pa|kis|tan (↑R 132; Staat in Asien); **Pa|kis|ta|ner; Pa|kis|ta|ne|rin; Pa|kis|ta|ni,** der; -[s], -[s] *u.* die; -, -[s] (Pakistaner[in]); **pa|kis|ta|nisch**

Pa|ko, der; -s, -s ⟨indian.-span.⟩ (*svw.* ¹Alpaka)

Pakt, der; -[e]s, -e ⟨lat.⟩ (Vertrag; Bündnis); **pak|tie|ren** (einen Vertrag schließen; gemeinsame Sache machen); **Pak|tie|rer**

pa|lä|ark|tisch ⟨griech.⟩; -e Region (*Tiergeogr.* Europa, Nordafrika, Asien außer Indien)

Pa|la|din [*auch* 'pa...], der; -s, -e ⟨lat.⟩ (Angehöriger des Heldenkreises am Hofe Karls d. Gr.; treuer, ergebener Anhänger); **Pa|lais** [pa'lɛ:], das; - [pa'lɛ:(s)], - [pa'lɛ:s] ⟨franz.⟩ (Palast, Schloss)

Pa|lan|kin, der; -s, *Plur.* -e *u.* -s ⟨Hindi⟩ (ind. Tragsessel; Sänfte)

pa|lä|o... ⟨griech.⟩ (alt..., ur...); **Pa|lä|o...** (Alt..., Ur...); **Pa|lä|o‿bi|o|lo|gie** (Biologie ausgestorbener Lebewesen), **...bo|ta|nik** (Botanik ausgestorbener Pflanzen), **...ge|o|gra|phie** (Geographie der Erdgeschichte); **Pa|lä|o|graph,** der; -en, -en; ↑R 126 (Wissenschaftler auf dem Gebiet der Paläographie); **Pa|lä|o|gra|phie,** die; - (Lehre von den Schriftarten des Altertums u. des MA.); **pa|lä|o|gra|phisch** (↑R 33); **Pa|lä|o‿his|to|lo|gie** (die; -; Lehre von den Geweben der fossilen Lebewesen), **...kli|ma|to|lo|gie** (die; -; Lehre von den Klimaten der Erdgeschichte); **Pa|lä|o|lith** [*auch* ...'lit], der; *Gen.* -s *od.* -en, *Plur.* -e[n] (Steinwerkzeug des Paläolithikums); **Pa|lä|o|li|thi|kum** [*auch* ...'liti...], das; -s (Altsteinzeit); **pa|lä|o|li|thisch; Pa|lä|on|to|lo|ge,** der; -n, -n (↑R 126); **Pa|lä|on|to|lo|gie,** die; - (Lehre von den Lebewesen vergangener Erdperioden); **Pa|lä|on|to|lo|gin; pa|lä|on|to|lo|gisch; Pa|lä|o|phy|ti|kum,** das; -s (Frühzeit der Pflanzenentwicklung im Verlauf der Erdgeschichte); **Pa|lä|o|zän,** Pa|le|o|zän, das; -s (*Geol.* älteste Abteilung des Tertiärs); **Pa|lä|o|zo|i|kum,** das; -s (erdgeschichtl. Altertum); **pa|lä|o|zo|isch; Pa|lä|o|zo|o|lo|gie,** die; - (Zoologie der fossilen Tiere)

Pa|las, der; -, -se ‹lat.› (Hauptgebäude der mittelalterl. Burg); **Pa|last,** der; -[e]s, Paläste (Schloss; Prachtbau)

Pa|läs|ti|na (Gebiet zwischen Mittelmeer u. Jordan); **Pa|läs|ti|na|pil|ger; Pa|läs|ti|nen|ser; Pa|läs|ti|nen|ser|füh|rer; Pa|läs|ti|nen|se|rin; pa|läs|ti|nen|sisch; pa|läs|ti|nisch**

Pa|läst|ra (↑R 130), die; -, ...ren ‹griech.› (altgriech. Ring-, Fechtschule)

Pa|last‿re|vol|te, ...re|vo|lu|ti|on, ...wa|che

pa|la|tal ‹lat.› (den Gaumen betreffend, Gaumen...); **Pa|la|tal,** der; -s, -e *u.* **Pa|la|tal|laut,** der; -[e]s, -e (*Sprachw.* am vorderen Gaumen gebildeter Laut, z. B. j)

[1]**Pa|la|tin,** der; -s ‹lat.› (ein Hügel in Rom); [2]**Pa|la|tin,** der; -s, -e (*früher* Pfalzgraf); **Pa|la|ti|na,** die; - (Heidelberger [kurpfälzische] Bücherei); **Pa|la|ti|nat,** das; -[e]s, -e (*früher* Würde eines Pfalzgrafen); **pa|la|ti|nisch** (pfälzisch), *aber* (↑R 102): der Palatinische Hügel (in Rom)

Pa|lat|schin|ke (↑R 130 *u.* 132), die; -, -n *meist Plur.* ‹ung.› (*österr. für* gefüllter Eierkuchen)

Pa|la|ver [...vər], das; -s, - ‹lat.-port.-engl.› (Ratsversammlung afrikan. Stämme; *ugs. für* endloses Gerede u. Verhandeln); **pa|la|vern** *(ugs.);* sie haben palavert

Pa|laz|zo, der; -[s], ...zzi ‹ital.› (*ital. Bez. für* Palast)

Pa|le, die; -, -n (*nordd. für* Schote, Hülse)

Pale Ale ['pe:l 'e:l], das; - - ‹engl.› (helles engl. Bier)

pa|len (*nordd. für* [Erbsen] aus den Hülsen [Palen] lösen)

Pa|le|o|zän *vgl.* Paläozän

Pa|ler|mer (↑R 103); **pa|ler|misch; Pa|ler|mo** (Stadt auf Sizilien)

Pa|lest|ri|na (↑R 130; ital. Komponist)

Pa|le|tot ['paləto:, *auch, österr. nur,* pal(ə)'to:], der; -s, -s (taillierter doppelreihiger Herrenmantel [mit Samtkragen]; dreiviertellanger Damen- od. Herrenmantel)

Pa|let|te, die; -, -n ‹franz.› (Farbenmischbrett; genormtes Lademittel für Stückgüter; *übertr. für* bunte Mischung)

pa|let|ti; *in* alles paletti (*ugs. für* in Ordnung)

pa|let|tie|ren ‹franz.› (Versandgut auf einer Palette stapeln)

Pa|li, das; -[s] (Schriftsprache der Buddhisten in Sri Lanka u. Hinterindien)

pa|lim..., pa|lin... ‹griech.› (wieder...); **Pa|lim...,** Pa|lin... (Wieder...); **Pa|limp|sest** (↑R 132), der *od.* das; -es, -e (von Neuem beschriebenes Pergament); **Pa|lind|rom** (↑R 130 *u.* 132), das; -s, -e (Wort[folge] od. Satz, die vorwärts wie rückwärts gelesen [den gleichen] Sinn ergeben, z. B. Reittier; Leben – Nebel; Rentner; Reliefpfeiler); **Pa|lin|ge|ne|se,** die; -, -n (*Rel.* Wiedergeburt; *Biol.* Auftreten von Merkmalen stammesgeschichtl. Vorfahren während der Keimesentwicklung; *Geol.* Aufschmelzung eines Gesteins u. Bildung einer neuen Gesteinsschmelze); **Pa|li|no|die** (↑R 132), die; -, ...ien (*Literaturw.* [dichterischer] Widerruf)

Pa|li|sa|de, die; -, -n ‹franz.› (aus Pfählen bestehendes Hindernis); **Pa|li|sa|den‿pfahl, ...wand**

Pa|li|san|der, der; -s, - ‹indian.-franz.› (brasil. Edelholz); **Pa|li|san|der|holz; pa|li|san|dern** (aus Palisander)

[1]**Pal|la|di|um,** das; -s, ...ien [...iən] ‹griech.› (Bild der Pallas; Schutzbild; schützendes Heiligtum); [2]**Pal|la|di|um,** das; -s (chem. Element, Metall; *Zeichen* Pd)

Pal|las ‹griech.› (Beiname der Athene)

Pal|lasch, der; -[e]s, -e ‹ung.› (schwerer Säbel)

Pal|la|watsch, Bal|la|watsch, der; -s (*österr. ugs. für* Durcheinander, Blödsinn)

Pal|li|a|tiv, das; -s, -e [...və], **Pal|li|a|ti|vum** [...v...], das; -s, ...va ‹lat.› (*Med.* Linderungsmittel); **Pal|li|um,** das; -s, ...ien [...iən] (Schulterbinde des erzbischöfl. Ornats)

Pal|lot|ti|ner, der; -s, - ‹nach dem ital. Priester Pallotti› (Angehöriger einer kath. Vereinigung); **Pal|lot|ti|ne|rin; Pal|lot|ti|ner|or|den,** der; -s

Palm, der; -s, -e ‹lat., „flache Hand"› (altes Maß zum Messen von Rundhölzern); 10 - (↑R 90);

Palm|art *vgl.* Palmenart; **Pal|ma|rum** (Palmsonntag); **Palm|baum** (*veraltet für* Palme); **Palm|blatt; Pal|me,** die; -, -n; **Pal|men|art; pal|men|ar|tig; Pal|men|blatt** *vgl.* Palmblatt; **Pal|men‿hain, ...her|zen** (*Plur.; svw.* Palmherzen), **...rol|ler** (eine südasiatische Schleichkatze); **Pal|men|we|del** *vgl.* Palmwedel; **Pal|men|zweig** *vgl.* Palmzweig; **Pal|met|te,** die; -, -n ‹franz.› (*Kunstw.* [palmblattartige] Verzierung; *Gartenbau* fächerförmig gezogener Spalierbaum); **Palm|her|zen** *Plur.* (als Gemüse od. Salat zubereitetes Mark bestimmter Palmen); **pal|mie|ren** ‹lat.› ([bei einem Zaubertrick] in der Handfläche verbergen); **Pal|mi|tin,** das; -s (Hauptbestandteil der meisten Fette); **Palm‿kätz|chen, ...öl** (das; -[e]s); **Palm|sonn|tag** [*auch* 'palm...]; **Palm|we|del,** *auch* Pal|men|we|del; **Palm‿wei|de, ...wein**

Pal|my|ra ([Ruinen]stadt in der Syrischen Wüste); **Pal|my|ra|pal|me; Pal|my|rer; pal|my|risch**

Palm|zweig, *auch* Pal|men|zweig

Pa|lo|lo|wurm ‹polynes.; dt.› (ein trop. Borstenwurm)

pal|pa|bel ‹lat.› (*Med.* tast-, fühl-, greifbar); **...ab|le** (↑R 130) Organe; **Pal|pa|ti|on,** die; -, -en (*Med.* Untersuchung durch Abtasten); **Pal|pe,** die; -, -n (*Zool.* Taster [bei Gliederfüßern]); **pal|pie|ren** (*Med.* betastend untersuchen); **Pal|pi|ta|ti|on,** die; -, -en (Pulsschlag, Herzklopfen); **pal|pi|tie|ren** (schlagen, pulsieren)

Pa|mel|la, Pa|mel|le [*beide auch* pa'mɛ...] (w. Vorn.)

Pa|mir [*auch* 'pa:...], der, *auch* das; -[s] (Hochland in Innerasien)

Pamp, der; -[e]s (*nordd. für* Pamps)

Pam|pa, die; -, -s *meist Plur.* ‹indian.› (baumlose Grassteppe in Südamerika); **Pam|pa[s]|gras**

Pam|pe, die; - (*nordd., mitteld. für* Schlamm, Sand- u. Schmutzbrei)

Pam|pel|mu|se [*auch* 'pam...], die; -, -n ‹niederl.› (eine Zitrusfrucht)

Pam|per|letsch *vgl.* Bamperletsch

Pampf, der; -[e]s (*südd. für* Pamps)

Pamph|let (↑R 130), das; -[e]s, -e ‹franz.› (Streit-, Schmähschrift); **Pamph|le|tist,** der; -en, -en; ↑R 126 (Verfasser von Pamphleten)

pam|pig (*nordd., mitteld. für* breiig; *ugs. für* frech, patzig)

Pamps, der; -[e]s (*landsch. für* dicker Brei [zum Essen])

Pam|pu|sche *vgl.* Babusche
[1]**Pan** (griech. Hirten-, Waldgott)
[2]**Pan,** der; -s, -s ‹poln.› (*früher in Polen* Besitzer eines kleineren Landgutes; *poln. [in Verbindung mit dem Namen]:* Herr); *vgl.* Panje
pan... ‹griech.› (gesamt..., all...); **Pan...** (Gesamt..., All...)
Pa|na|ché [...'ʃe:] *vgl.* Panaschee
Pa|na|de, die; -, -n ‹franz.› (Weißbrotbrei zur Bereitung von Füllungen; Mischung aus Ei u. Semmelmehl zum Panieren); **Pa|na|del|sup|pe** (*südd. u. österr. für* Suppe mit Weißbroteinlage)
pan|af|ri|ka|nisch; (↑R 108:) Panafrikanische Spiele; **Pan|af|ri|ka|nis|mus,** der; -; *vgl.* Panamerikanismus
Pa|na|ma (Staat u. dessen Hptst. in Mittelamerika); **Pa|na|ma|er** (↑R 103); **Pa|na|ma|hut,** der (↑R 105); **pa|na|ma|isch; Pa|na|ma|ka|nal,** der; -s (↑R 105)
pan|ame|ri|ka|nisch (↑R 132); -e Bewegung; **Pan|ame|ri|ka|nis|mus,** der; - (Bestreben, die wirtschaftl. u. polit. Zusammenarbeit aller amerik. Staaten zu verstärken)
pan|ara|bisch (↑R 132); -e Bewegung; **Pan|ara|bis|mus,** der; -; *vgl.* Panislamismus
Pa|na|ri|ti|um, das; -s, ...ien [...i̯ən] ‹griech.› (*Med.* eitrige Entzündung am Finger)
Pa|nasch, der; -[e]s, -e ‹franz.› (Feder-, Helmbusch); **Pa|na|schee,** das; -s, -s (*veraltet für* gemischtes, mehrfarbiges Eis; Kompott, Gelee aus verschiedenen Obstsorten); **pa|na|schie|ren** (bei einer Wahl seine Stimme für Kandidaten verschiedener Parteien abgeben); **Pa|na|schier|sys|tem,** das; -s (ein Wahlsystem); **Pa|na|schie|rung,** die; -, -en, **Pa|na|schü|re,** die; -, -n (*Bot.* weiße Musterung auf Pflanzenblättern durch Mangel an Blattgrün)
Pan|athe|nä|en (↑R 132), *Plur.* ‹griech.› (Fest zu Ehren der Athene im alten Athen)
Pa|na|zee [*auch* ...'t͜se:] (↑R 132), die; -, -n [...'t͜se:ən] ‹griech.› (Allheil-, Wundermittel)
pan|chro|ma|tisch ‹griech.› (*Fotogr.* empfindlich für alle Farben u. Spektralbereiche)
Panc|ra|ti|us *vgl.* Pankratius
Pan|da, der; -s, -s (asiat. Bärenart)
Pan|dai|mo|ni|on, Pan|dä|mo|ni|um, das; -s, ...ien [...i̯ən] ‹griech.› (Aufenthalt od. Gesamtheit der [bösen] Geister)
Pan|da|ne, die; -, -n ‹malai.› (eine Zierpflanze)
Pan|dek|ten *Plur.* ‹griech.› (Sammlung altröm. Rechtssprüche)
Pan|de|mie, die; -, ...ien ‹griech.› (*Med.* Epidemie größeren Ausmaßes); **pan|de|misch** (sehr weit verbreitet); eine -e Seuche
Pan|dit, der; -s, -e *u.* -s ‹sanskr.-Hindi› ([Titel] brahman. Gelehrter)
Pan|do|ra (*griech. Mythol.* die Frau, die alles Unheil auf die Erde brachte); die Büchse der -
Pand|schab [pan'd͜ʒa:p, *auch* 'pan...] (↑R 130), das; -s ‹sanskr., „Fünfstromland"› (Landschaft in Vorderindien); **Pand|scha|bi,** das; -[s] (eine neuind. Sprache)
Pan|dur, der; -en, -en (↑R 126) ‹ung.› (*früher* ung. Leibdiener; leichter ung. Fußsoldat)
Pa|neel, das; -s, -e ‹niederl.› (Täfelung der Innenwände); **pa|nee|lie|ren**
Pa|ne|gy|ri|ker (↑R 132) ‹griech.› (Verfasser eines Panegyrikus); **Pa|ne|gy|ri|kon,** das; -[s], ...ka (liturg. Buch der orthodoxen Kirche mit predigtartigen Lobreden auf die Heiligen); **Pa|ne|gy|ri|kos** *vgl.* Panegyrikus; **Pa|ne|gy|ri|kus,** der; -, *Plur.* ...ken *u.* ...zi (Fest-, Lobrede; Fest-, Lobgedicht); **pa|ne|gy|risch**
Pa|nel ['pɛn(ə)l], das; -s, -s ‹engl.› (repräsentative Personengruppe für die Meinungsforschung); **Pa|nel|tech|nik,** die; - (Methode der Meinungsforscher, die gleiche Gruppe von Personen innerhalb eines bestimmten Zeitraums mehrfach zu befragen)
pa|nem et cir|cen|ses [- - ...ze:s] ‹lat., „Brot u. Zirkusspiele"› (Lebensunterhalt u. Vergnügungen als Mittel zur Zufriedenstellung des Volkes)
Pan|en|the|is|mus, der; - ‹griech.› (Lehre, nach der das All in Gott eingeschlossen ist); **pan|en|the|is|tisch**
Pa|net|to|ne, der; -[s], ...ni ‹ital.› (ein ital. Kuchen)
Pan|eu|ro|pa (erstrebte Gemeinschaft der europäischen Staaten)
Pan|flö|te ([antike] Hirtenflöte aus aneinander gereihten Pfeifen)
Pan|has, der; - (niederrhein.-westfäl. Gericht aus Wurstbrühe u. Buchweizenmehl)
Pan|hel|le|nis|mus, der; - (Bewegung zur polit. Einigung der griech. Staaten [in der Antike]); **pan|hel|le|nis|tisch**
[1]**Pa|nier,** das; -s, -e ‹germ.-franz.› (*veraltet für* Banner; *geh. für* Wahlspruch)
[2]**Pa|nier,** die; - ‹franz.› (*österr. für* Hülle aus Ei u. Semmelbröseln); **pa|nie|ren** (in Ei u. Semmelbröseln wenden); **Pa|nier|mehl; Pa|nie|rung**
Pa|nik, die; -, -en ‹*nach* [1]Pan› (durch plötzl. Schrecken entstandene, unkontrollierte [Massen]angst); **pa|nik|ar|tig; Pa|nik‿ma|che, ...re|ak|ti|on, ...stim|mung; pa|nisch** (lähmend); panischer Schrecken
Pan|is|la|mis|mus, der; - (Streben, alle islam. Völker zu vereinigen)
Pan|je, der; -s, -s ‹slaw.› (*veraltet für* poln. od. russ. Bauer; *poln. Anrede [ohne Namen]:* Herr); *vgl.* [2]Pan; **Pan|je|pferd** (poln. od. russ. Landpferd); **Pan|je|wa|gen**
Pan|kar|di|tis, die; -, ...iti̯den ‹griech.› (*Med.* Entzündung aller Schichten der Herzwand)
Pan|kow [...ko:] (Stadtteil von Berlin)
Pank|ra|ti|on (↑R 130), das; -s, -s ‹griech.› (altgriech. Ring- u. Faustkampf)
Pank|ra|ti|us, Pank|raz [*österr.* 'pan...] (↑R 130 *u.* 132; m. Vorn.)
Pank|re|as (↑R 130 *u.* 132), das; - ‹griech.› (*Med.* Bauchspeicheldrüse); **Pank|re|a|ti|tis,** die; -, ...iti̯den (Entzündung der Bauchspeicheldrüse)
Pan|lo|gis|mus, der; - ‹griech.› (philos. Lehre, nach der das ganze Weltall als Verwirklichung der Vernunft aufzufassen ist)
Pan|mi|xie, die; -, ...i̯en ‹griech.› (*Biol.* Kreuzung mit jedem beliebigen Partner der gleichen Tierart)
Pan|ne, die; -, -n ‹franz.› (Unfall, Schaden, Störung [bes. bei Fahrzeugen]; Missgeschick); **Pan|nen|dienst; pan|nen|frei; Pan|nen‿kof|fer, ...kurs** (Lehrgang über das Beheben von Autopannen)
Pan|no|ni|en [...i̯ən] (*früher* röm. Donauprovinz); **pan|no|nisch**
Pa|nop|ti|kum (↑R 132), das; -s, ...ken ‹griech.› (Sammlung von Sehenswürdigkeiten; Wachsfigurenschau); **Pa|no|ra|ma,** das; -s, ...men (Rundblick; Rundgemälde; [fotogr.] Rundbild); **Pa|no|ra|ma‿bus, ...fens|ter, ...spie|gel**
Pan|ple|gie, die; - ‹griech.› (*Med.* allgemeine, vollständige Muskellähmung)
Pan|psy|chis|mus, der; - ‹griech.› (*Philos.* Lehre, nach der auch die unbelebte Natur beseelt ist)

pan|schen, *auch* pant|schen (*ugs. für* mischend verfälschen, verdünnen; mit den Händen od. Füßen im Wasser patschen, planschen); du pan[t]schst; **Pan|scher,** *auch* Pant|scher *(ugs.);* **Pan|sche|rei,** *auch* Pant|sche|rei *(ugs.)*

Pan|sen, der; -s, - (Magenteil der Wiederkäuer); *vgl.* Panzen

Pan|se|xu|a|lis|mus, der; - ⟨griech.; lat.⟩ (psychoanalyt. Richtung, die in der Sexualität den Auslöser für alle psychischen Vorgänge sieht)

Pans|flö|te *vgl.* Panflöte

Pan|sla|wis|mus, der; - (Streben im 19. Jh., alle slaw. Völker zu vereinigen); **pan|sla|wis|tisch**

Pan|so|phie, die; - ⟨griech., „Gesamtwissenschaft"⟩ (vom 16. bis zum 18. Jh. Bewegung mit dem Ziel einer Gesamtdarstellung aller Wissenschaften)

Pan|sper|mie, die; - ⟨griech.⟩ (Theorie von der Entstehung des Lebens auf der Erde durch Keime von anderen Planeten)

Pan|ta|le|on (ein Heiliger)

Pan|ta|lo|ne, der; -[s], *Plur.* -s *u.* ...ni ⟨ital.⟩ (Figur des ital. Volkslustspieles); **Pan|ta|lons** [pãta'lõ:s *od.* 'pantalõ:s] *Plur.* ⟨franz.⟩ (in der Franz. Revolution aufgekommene lange Männerhose)

pan|ta rhei ⟨griech., „alles fließt"⟩ (Heraklit [fälschlich?] zugeschriebener Grundsatz, nach dem das Sein als ewiges Werden, ewige Bewegung gedacht wird)

Pan|ter usw. *vgl.* Panther usw.

Pan|the|is|mus, der; - ⟨griech.⟩ (Weltanschauung, nach der Gott u. Welt eins sind); **Pan|the|ist,** der; -en, -en (↑R 126); **pan|the|is|tisch; Pan|the|on,** das; -s, -s (*früher* Tempel für alle Götter; Ehrentempel)

Pan|ther, *auch* Pan|ter, der; -s, - ⟨griech.⟩ (*svw.* Leopard); **Pan|ther|fell,** *auch* Pan|ter|fell

Pan|ti|ne, die; -, -n *meist Plur.* ⟨niederl.⟩ (*nordd. für* Holzschuh, -pantoffel)

pan|to... ⟨griech.⟩ (all...); **Pan|to...** (All...)

Pan|tof|fel, der; -s, *Plur.* -n, *ugs.* - ⟨franz.⟩ (Hausschuh); **Pan|tof|fel|blu|me; Pan|töf|fel|chen; Pan|tof|fel‿held** (*ugs. für* Mann, der von der Ehefrau beherrscht wird), **...ki|no** (*ugs. scherzh. für* Fernsehen), **...tier|chen** *(Biol.)*

Pan|to|graph (↑R 33), der; -en, -en (↑R 126) ⟨griech.⟩ (Storchschnabel, Instrument zum Übertragen von Zeichnungen im gleichen, größeren od. kleineren Maßstab); **Pan|to|gra|phie,** die; -, ...ien (mit dem Pantographen hergestelltes Bild)

Pan|to|let|te, die; -, -n *meist Plur.* ⟨Kunstwort⟩ (leichter Sommerschuh ohne Fersenteil)

[1]**Pan|to|mi|me,** die; -, -n ⟨griech. (-franz.)⟩ (Darstellung einer Szene nur mit Gebärden u. Mienenspiel); [2]**Pan|to|mi|me,** der; -n, -n; ↑R 126 (Darsteller einer Pantomime); **Pan|to|mi|mik,** die; - (Gebärdenspiel; Kunst der Pantomime); **pan|to|mi|misch**

Pant|ry ['pɛntri] (↑R 130), die; -, -s ⟨engl.⟩ (Speise-, Anrichtekammer [auf Schiffen])

pant|schen usw. *vgl.* panschen usw.

Pant|schen-La|ma, der; -[s], -s ⟨tibet.⟩ (zweites, kirchl. Oberhaupt des tibet. Priesterstaates)

Pan|ty ['pɛnti], die; -, -s ['pɛnti:s] ⟨engl.⟩ (Miederhose)

Pän|ul|ti|ma, die; -, *Plur.* ...mä *u.* ...men ⟨lat.⟩ (*Sprachw.* vorletzte Silbe eines Wortes)

Pan|zen, der; -s, - (*landsch. für* dicker Bauch); **Pan|zer** (Kampffahrzeug; feste Hülle, Schutzumkleidung; *früher* Rüstung, Harnisch); **Pan|zer|ab|wehr; Pan|zer|ab|wehr‿ka|no|ne** (*Kurzw.* Pak), **...ra|ke|te; pan|zer|bre|chend;** -e Munition; **Pan|zer‿di|vi|si|on, ...ech|se, ...faust** *(Milit.),* **...glas** (das; -es), **...gra|ben, ...gra|na|te, ...gre|na|dier, ...hemd** *(früher),* **...jä|ger, ...kampf|wa|gen, ...kreu|zer; pan|zern;** ich ...ere (↑R 16); **Pan|zer‿plat|te, ...schiff, ...schrank, ...späh|wa|gen, ...sper|re; Pan|ze|rung; Pan|zer|wa|gen**

Pä|o|nie [...iə], die; -, -n ⟨griech.⟩ (Pfingstrose)

[1]**Pa|pa** [*veraltend u. geh.* pa'pa:], der; -s, -s ⟨franz.⟩ (Vater); [2]**Pa|pa,** der; -s ⟨griech., „Vater"⟩ (kirchl. Bez. des Papstes; *Abk.* P.); **Pa|pa|bi|li** *Plur.* ⟨lat.⟩ (ital. Bez. der als Papstkandidaten infrage kommenden Kardinäle); **Pa|pa|chen**

Pa|pa|gal|lo, der; -[s], *Plur.* -s *u.* ...lli ⟨ital.⟩ (ital. [junger] Mann, der erotische Abenteuer mit Touristinnen sucht); **Pa|pa|gei** [*österr. u. schweiz. auch* 'pa...], der; *Gen.* -en *u.* -s, *Plur.* -en, *seltener* -e ⟨franz.⟩; **Pa|pa|gei|en|grün,** das; -s; **pa|pa|gei|en|haft; Pa|pa|gei|en|krank|heit,** die; - (von Papageien übertragene Viruskrankheit); **Pa|pa|gei‿fisch, ...tau|cher** (ein Vogel)

Pa|pa|ge|no (Vogelhändler in Mozarts „Zauberflöte")

pa|pal ⟨lat.⟩ (päpstlich); **Pa|pal|sys|tem,** das; -s; **Pa|pat,** der, *auch* das; -[e]s (Amt u. Würde des Papstes)

Pa|pa|ve|ra|ze|en [...v...] *Plur.* ⟨lat.⟩ (*Bot.* Familie der Mohngewächse); **Pa|pa|ve|rin,** das; -s (Opiumalkaloid)

Pa|pa|ya, die; -, -s ⟨span.⟩ (der Melone ähnliche Frucht)

Pap|chen (*Koseform für* [1]Papa)

Pa|per ['pe:pə(r)], das; -s, -s ⟨engl.⟩ (Schriftstück; schriftl. Unterlage); **Pa|per|back** ['pe:pə(r)bɛk], das; -s, -s (kartoniertes Buch, insbes. Taschenbuch)

Pa|pe|te|rie, die; -, ...ien ⟨franz.⟩ (*schweiz. für* Papier-, Schreibwaren[geschäft])

pa|phisch (aus Paphos)

Paph|la|go|ni|en [...iən] (↑R 130; antike Landschaft in Kleinasien)

Pa|phos (im Altertum Stadt auf Zypern)

Pa|pi, der; -s, -s (*Koseform von* [1]Papa)

Pa|pier, das; -s, -e (*Abk. auf dt. Kurszetteln* P); die Papier verarbeitende Industrie; **Pa|pier‿bahn, ...block** (*vgl.* Block), **...blu|me, ...bo|gen, ...deutsch** (umständliches, geschraubtes Deutsch); **pa|pie|ren** (aus Papier); papier[e]ner Stil; papier[e]nes Gesetz; **Pa|pier‿fab|rik, ...fet|zen, ...for|mat, ...geld** (das; -[e]s), **...in|dust|rie, ...korb, ...krieg** (*ugs. für* lange dauernder Schriftverkehr); **Pa|pier|ma|ché** [papie:ma'ʃe:, *auch* pa'pi:r...], das; -s, -s ⟨franz.⟩ (verformbare Papiermasse); **Pa|pier‿mes|ser** (das), **...müh|le, ...sack, ...sche|re, ...schlan|ge, ...schnip|sel** *(ugs.),* **...schnit|zel** (*vgl.* [2]Schnitzel), **...ser|vi|et|te, ...ta|schen|tuch, ...ti|ger** (*übertr. für* nur dem Schein nach starke Person, Macht); **Pa|pier ver|ar|bei|tend** *vgl.* Papier; **Pa|pier|ver|ar|bei|tung; Pa|pier|wa|ren** *Plur.;* **Pa|pier|wa|ren|hand|lung; Pa|pier‿win|del, ...wol|le** (Verpackungsmaterial)

pa|pil|lar ⟨lat.⟩ (*Med.* warzenartig, -förmig); **Pa|pil|lar‿ge|schwulst, ...kör|per, ...li|ni|en** (*Plur.;* feine Hautlinien auf Hand- u. Fußflächen); **Pa|pil|le,** die; -, -n (Warze); **Pa|pil|lom,** das; -s, -e (warzenartige Geschwulst der Schleimhaut)

Pa|pil|lon [papi'jõ:], der; -s, -s ⟨franz., „Schmetterling"⟩ (weicher Kleiderstoff; Zwergspaniel); **Pa|pil|lo|te** [papi'jo:tə], die; -, -n (Haarwickel; *Gastron.* Hülle aus

Pergamentpapier für das Braten od. Grillen)
Pa|pin|topf [pa'pɛ̃:...] (↑R 95) ‹nach dem franz. Physiker Papin› (fest schließendes Gefäß zum Erhitzen von Flüssigkeiten über deren Siedepunkt hinaus)
Pa|pi|ro|sa, die; -, ...ossy [...si] (russ. Zigarette mit langem Pappmundstück)
Pa|pis|mus, der; - ‹griech.› (*abwertend für* Papsttum); **Pa|pist,** der; -en, -en; ↑R 126 (Anhänger des Papsttums); **pa|pis|tisch**
papp; nicht mehr papp sagen können (*ugs. für* sehr satt sein)
Papp, der; -[e]s, -e *Plur. selten* (*landsch. für* Brei; Kleister); **Papp|band,** der (in Pappe gebundenes Buch; *Abk.* Pp[bd].); **Papp|be|cher; Papp|de|ckel,** Pap|pen|de|ckel; **Pap|pe,** die; -, -n (steifes, papierähnliches Material)
Pap|pel, die; -, -n ‹lat.› (ein Laubbaum); **Pap|pel‿al|lee, ...holz; pap|peln** (aus Pappelholz)
päp|peln (*landsch. für* [ein Kind] füttern); ich ...[e]le (↑R 16); **pap|pen** (*ugs. für* kleistern, kleben); der Schnee pappt; **Pap|pen|de|ckel** *vgl.* Pappdeckel
Pap|pen|hei|mer, der; -s, - (Angehöriger des Reiterregiments des dt. Reitergenerals Graf zu Pappenheim); ich kenne meine - (*ugs. für* ich kenne diese Leute; ich weiß Bescheid)
Pap|pen|stiel (*ugs. für* Wertloses); kein - sein
pap|per|la|papp!
pap|pig *(ugs.);* **Papp‿ka|me|rad** (*ugs. für* Figur aus Pappe für Schießübungen), **...kar|ton; Papp|ma|ché** [...maʃe:], *eindeutschend* **Papp|ma|schee** (↑R 33); *vgl.* Papiermaché; **Papp|na|se; Papp|pla|kat** (↑R 136); **Papp‿schach|tel, ...schnee** (der; -s), **...tel|ler**
Pap|pus, der; -, *Plur.* - *u.* -se ‹griech.› (*Bot.* Haarkrone der Frucht von Korbblütlern)
[1]**Pap|ri|ka** (↑R 130), der; -s, -[s] ‹serb.-ung.› (ein Gewürz; ein Gemüse); [2]**Pap|ri|ka,** die; -, -[s] (*kurz für* Paprikaschote); **Pap|ri|ka‿schnit|zel, ...scho|te** (*vgl.* [3]Schote); **pap|ri|zie|ren** (*bes. österr. für* mit Paprika würzen)
Paps, der; -, -e (*Kinderspr. für* [1]Papa; *meist als Anrede*)
Papst, der; -[e]s, Päpste ‹griech.› (Oberhaupt der kath. Kirche; *auch übertr. für* anerkannte Autorität); **Papst|fa|mi|lie** (Umgebung des Papstes); **Päps|tin; Papst|ka|ta|log** (Verzeichnis der Päpste); **päpst|lich,** *aber* (↑R 108): das Päpstliche Bibelinstitut; **Papst|na|me; Papst|tum,** das; -s; **Papst|wahl**
Pa|pua [*auch* pa'pu:a], der; -[s], -[s] (Eingeborener Neuguineas); **Papua-Neu|gui|nea** [...gi...] (Staat auf Neuguinea); **pa|pu|a|nisch; Pa|pu|a|spra|che**
Pa|py|rin, das; -s ‹griech.› (Pergamentpapier); **Pa|py|ro|lo|gie,** die; - (Wissenschaft vom Papyrus); **Pa|py|rus,** der; -, ...ri (Papierstaude; Papyrusrolle); **Pa|py|rus‿rol|le, ...stau|de**
Par, das; -[s], -s ‹engl.› (*Golf* festgesetzte Anzahl von Schlägen für ein Loch)
par..., pa|ra... ‹griech.› (bei..., neben..., falsch...); **Par..., Pa|ra...** (Bei..., Neben..., Falsch...)
Pa|ra, der; -s, -s ‹franz.› (*Kurzform für* parachutiste [paraʃy'tist] = franz. Fallschirmjäger)
Pa|ra|ba|se, die; -, -n ‹griech.› (Teil der attischen Komödie)
Pa|ra|bel, die; -, -n ‹griech.› (Gleichnis[rede]; *Math.* Kegelschnittkurve)
Pa|ra|bel|lum ®, die; -, -s ‹lat.› (Pistole mit Selbstladevorrichtung); **Pa|ra|bel|lum|pis|to|le**
Pa|ra|bol|an|ten|ne, die; -, -n (Antenne in der Form eines Parabolspiegels); **pa|ra|bo|lisch** ‹griech.› (gleichnisweise; *Math.* parabelförmig gekrümmt); **Pa|ra|bo|lo|id,** das; -[e]s, -e (*Math.* gekrümmte Fläche); **Pa|ra|bol|spie|gel** (Hohlspiegel)
pa|ra|cel|sisch [...'tsɛl...]; paracelsische Schriften (↑R 94); **Pa|ra|cel|sus** (dt. Naturforscher, Arzt u. Philosoph); **Pa|ra|cel|sus|aus|ga|be** (↑R 95); **Pa|ra|cel|sus-Me|dail|le** (↑R 95)
Pa|ra|de, die; -, -n ‹franz.› (Truppenschau, prunkvoller Aufmarsch; *Reitsport* kürzere Gangart des Pferdes, Anhalten; *Sport* Abwehrbewegung); **Pa|ra|de‿bei|spiel, ...dis|zi|plin** *(Sport)*
Pa|ra|dei|ser, der; -s, - (*österr. für* Tomate); **Pa|ra|deis‿sa|lat, ...sup|pe** *(österr.)*
Pa|ra|de‿kis|sen, ...marsch (der)
Pa|ra|den|to|se *vgl.* Parodontose
Pa|ra|de‿pferd (*ugs. für* Person, Sache, mit der man renommieren kann), **...stück, ...uni|form** (↑R 132); **pa|ra|die|ren** ‹franz.› (*Milit.* in einer Parade vorüberziehen; *geh. für* aufgereiht sein)
Pa|ra|dies, das; -es, -e ‹pers.› (*nur Sing.:* der Garten Eden, Himmel; *übertr. für* Ort der Seligkeit; *Archit.* Portalvorbau an mittelalterl. Kirchen); **Pa|ra|dies|ap|fel** (*landsch. für* Tomate; *auch* Zierapfel); **pa|ra|die|sisch** (wonnig, himmlisch); **Pa|ra|dies|vo|gel** (*ugs. auch für* Person, die durch ihr Äußeres od. Gebaren auffällt, fremdartig wirkt)
Pa|ra|dig|ma, das; -s, *Plur.* ...men, *auch* -ta ‹griech.› (Beispiel, Muster; *Sprachw.* Beugungsmuster); **pa|ra|dig|ma|tisch** (beispielhaft; als Muster dienend)
pa|ra|dox ‹griech.› ([scheinbar] widersinnig; *ugs. für* sonderbar); **Pa|ra|dox,** das; -es, -e (etwas, was einen Widerspruch in sich enthält; *auch svw.* Paradoxon); **pa|ra|do|xer|wei|se; Pa|ra|do|xie,** die; -, ...ien (Widersinnigkeit); **Pa|ra|do|xon,** das; -s, ...xa (scheinbar falsche Aussage, die aber auf eine höhere Wahrheit hinweist; *auch svw.* Paradox)
Pa|raf|fin (↑R 132), das; -s, -e ‹lat.› (wachsähnlicher Stoff; *meist Plur.: Chemie* gesättigter, aliphatischer Kohlenwasserstoff, z. B. Methan, Propan, Butan); **pa|raf|fi|nie|ren** (mit Paraffin behandeln); **pa|raf|fi|nisch; Pa|raf|fin‿ker|ze, ...öl** (das; -[e]s)
Pa|ra|gli|ding [...glaidiŋ], das; -s ‹engl.› (Fliegen vom Berg mit fallschirmähnlichen Gleitsegeln)
Pa|ra|graf usw. *eindeutschende Schreibung für* Paragraph usw.
Pa|ra|gramm, das; -s, -e ‹griech.› (Buchstabenänderung in einem Wort od. Namen, wodurch ein scherzhaft-komischer Sinn entstehen kann)
Pa|ra|graph (↑R 33), der; -en, -en; ↑R 126 ([in Gesetzestexten u. wissenschaftl. Werken] fortlaufend nummerierter Absatz, Abschnitt; *Zeichen* §, *Plur.* §§); **Pa|ra|gra|phen‿di|ckicht, ...dschun|gel, ...rei|ter** (*abwertend für* sich übergenau an Vorschriften haltender Mensch); **pa|ra|gra|phen|wei|se; Pa|ra|gra|phen|zei|chen** *vgl.* Paragraphzeichen; **Pa|ra|gra|phie,** die; - (*Med.* Störung des Schreibvermögens); **pa|ra|gra|phie|ren** (in Paragraphen einteilen); **Pa|ra|gra|phie|rung; Pa|ra|graph|zei|chen,** Pa|ra|gra|phen|zei|chen (das Zeichen §)
[1]**Pa|ra|gu|ay** [...'guai, *auch* 'pa(:)...], der; -[s] (r. Nebenfluss des Paraná); [2]**Pa|ra|gu|ay** (südamerik. Staat); **Pa|ra|gu|ay|er** (↑R 103); **Pa|ra|gu|ay|e|rin; pa|ra|gu|ay|isch**
Pa|ra|ki|ne|se, die; -, -n ‹griech.› (*Med.* Koordinationsstörungen im Bewegungsablauf)

Pa|ra|kla|se, die; -, -n ‹griech.› (*Geol.* Verwerfung)

Pa|rak|let (↑R 130), der; *Gen.* -[e]s *u.* -en, *Plur.* -e[n] (↑R 126) ‹griech.› (*nur Sing.:* Heiliger Geist; Helfer, Fürsprecher vor Gott)

Pa|ra|la|lie, die; - ‹griech.› (*Med., Psych.* Wort- u. Lautverwechslung)

Pa|ra|le|xie, die; - ‹griech.› (*Med., Psych.* Lesestörung mit Verwechslung der gelesenen Wörter)

Pa|ra|li|po|me|non, das; -s, ...mena *meist Plur.* ‹griech.› (*Literaturw.* Ergänzung, Nachtrag; Randbemerkung)

pa|ral|lak|tisch (↑R 132) ‹griech.› (die Parallaxe betreffend); **Pa|ral|la|xe,** die; -, -n (*Physik* Winkel, den zwei Gerade bilden, die von verschiedenen Standorten zu einem Punkt gerichtet sind; *Astron.* Entfernungsbestimmung u. -angabe von Sternen; *Fotogr.* Unterschied zwischen dem Bildausschnitt im Sucher u. auf dem Film)

pa|ral|lel (↑R 132) ‹griech.› (gleich laufend, gleichgerichtet; genau entsprechend); [mit etwas] parallel laufen; parallel laufende Geraden; zwei völlig parallel geschaltete Systeme; **Pa|ral|le|le,** die; -, -n (Gerade, die zu einer anderen Geraden in gleichem Abstand u. ohne Schnittpunkt verläuft; Vergleich, vergleichbarer Fall); vier Parallele[n]

Pa|ral|lel|epi|ped [...pe:t] (↑R 132), das; -[e]s, -e *u.* **Pa|ral|lel|epi|pe|don** (↑R 132), das; -s, *Plur.* ...da *u.* ...peden (*Math.* Parallelflach); **Pa|ral|lel‿er|schei|nung, ...fall** (der), **...flach** (das; -[e]s, -e; *Math.* von drei Paaren paralleler Ebenen begrenzter Raumteil); **pa|ral|le|li|sie|ren** ([vergleichend] nebeneinander stellen, zusammenstellen); **Pa|ral|le|li|sie|rung; Pa|ral|le|lis|mus,** der; -, ...men ([formale] Übereinstimmung verschiedener Dinge od. Vorgänge; *Sprachw.* inhaltlich u. grammatisch gleichmäßiger Bau von Satzgliedern od. Sätzen); **Pa|ral|le|li|tät,** die; - (Eigenschaft zweier paralleler Geraden; Gleichlauf); **Pa|ral|lel‿klas|se, ...kreis** (*Geogr.* Breitenkreis); **pa|ral|lel lau|fend** *vgl.* parallel; **Pa|ral|lel|li|nie; Pa|ral|le|lo,** der; -[s], -s ‹ital.› (*veraltet für* längs gestrickter Pullover); **Pa|ral|le|lo|gramm,** das; -s, -e ‹griech.› (*Math.* Viereck mit paarweise parallelen Seiten); **Pa|ral|lel|pro|jek|ti|on** (*Math.*); **pa|ral|lel schal|ten** *vgl.* parallel; **Pa|ral|lel‿schal|tung** (*Elektrotechnik* Nebenschaltung), **...schwung** (*Skisport*); **...sla|lom** (*Skisport*); **...stel|le, ...stra|ße, ...ton|art** (*Musik*)

Pa|ra|lo|gie, die; -, ...ien ‹griech.› (Vernunftwidrigkeit); **Pa|ra|lo|gis|mus,** der; -, ...men (*Logik* auf Denkfehlern beruhender Fehlschluss); **Pa|ra|ly|se,** die; -, -n (*Med.* Lähmung; Endstadium der Syphilis, Gehirnerweichung); **pa|ra|ly|sie|ren; Pa|ra|ly|ti|ker** (an Paralyse Erkrankter); **pa|ra|ly|tisch**

pa|ra|mag|ne|tisch ‹griech.› (*Physik*); **Pa|ra|mag|ne|tis|mus,** der; - (Verstärkung des Magnetismus)

Pa|ra|ma|ri|bo (Hptst. von ²Surinam)

Pa|ra|ment, das; -[e]s, -e *meist Plur.* ‹lat.› (Altar- u. Kanzeldecke; liturg. Kleidung); **Pa|ra|men|ten|ma|cher**

Pa|ra|me|ter, der; -s, - ‹griech.› (*Math.* konstante od. unbestimmt gelassene Hilfsvariable; *Technik* die Leistungsfähigkeit einer Maschine charakterisierende Kennziffer)

pa|ra|mi|li|tä|risch (halbmilitärisch, militärähnlich)

Pa|ra|ná [...'na], der; -[s] (südamerik. Strom)

Pa|ra|noia [...'nɔya], die; - ‹griech.› (*Med.* Geistesgestörtheit); **pa|ra|no|id** (der Paranoia ähnlich); **Pa|ra|no|i|ker; pa|ra|no|isch** (geistesgestört)

pa|ra|nor|mal ‹griech.› (*Parapsychologie* übersinnlich)

Pa|ra|nuss ‹nach dem bras. Ausfuhrhafen Pará›; ↑R 105 (dreikantige Nuss des Paranussbaumes); **Pa|ra|nuss|baum**

Pa|ra|phe, die; -, -n ‹griech.› (Namenszeichen; [Stempel mit] Namenszug); **pa|ra|phie|ren** (mit der Paraphe versehen, zeichnen); **Pa|ra|phie|rung**

Pa|ra|phra|se, die; -, -n ‹griech.› (*Sprachw.* verdeutlichende Umschreibung; *Musik* ausschmückende Bearbeitung); **pa|ra|phra|sie|ren**

Pa|ra|ple|gie, die; -, ...ien ‹griech.› (*Med.* doppelseitige Lähmung)

Pa|rap|luie [...'ply:] (↑R 130 *u.* 132), der *od.* das; -s, -s ‹franz.› (*veraltet für* Regenschirm)

Pa|ra|psy|cho|lo|gie, die; - ‹griech.› (Psychologie der okkulten seelischen Erscheinungen); **pa|ra|psy|cho|lo|gisch**

Pa|ra|sit, der; -en, -en (↑R 126) ‹griech.› (Schmarotzer[pflanze, -tier]); **pa|ra|si|tär** ‹franz.› (schmarotzerhaft; durch Schmarotzer hervorgebracht); **Pa|ra|si|ten|tum,** das; -s ‹griech.›; **pa|ra|si|tisch** (schmarotzerartig); **Pa|ra|si|tis|mus,** der; - (Schmarotzertum); **Pa|ra|si|to|lo|gie,** die; - (Lehre von den [krankheitserregenden] Schmarotzern)

Pa|ra|ski, der; - (*Sport* Kombination aus Fallschirmspringen und Riesenslalom)

¹Pa|ra|sol, der *od.* das; -s, -s ‹franz.› (*veraltet für* Sonnenschirm); **²Pa|ra|sol,** der; -s, *Plur.* -e *u.* -s (Schirmpilz); **Pa|ra|sol|pilz**

Pa|räs|the|sie (↑R 132), die; -, ...ien ‹griech.› (*Med.* anormale Körperempfindung, z. B. Einschlafen der Glieder)

Pa|ra|sym|pa|thi|kus, der; - ‹griech.› (*Med.* Teil des Nervensystems)

pa|rat ‹lat.› (bereit; fertig); etwas parat haben

pa|ra|tak|tisch ‹griech.› (*Sprachw.* nebenordnend, -geordnet); **Pa|ra|ta|xe,** *älter* **Pa|ra|ta|xis,** die; -, ...taxen (Nebenordnung)

Pa|ra|ty|phus, der; - ‹griech.› (*Med.* dem Typhus ähnliche Erkrankung)

Pa|ra|vent [...'vã:], der *od.* das; -s, -s ‹franz.› (*veraltet für* Wind-, Ofenschirm, spanische Wand)

par a|vi|on [- a'viõ:] ‹franz., „durch Luftpost“›

pa|ra|zent|risch ‹griech.› (*Math.* um den Mittelpunkt liegend od. beweglich)

par|bleu! [...'blø:] ‹franz.› (*veraltend für* Donnerwetter!)

par|boiled ['pa:(r)bɔyld] ‹engl.› (vitaminschonend vorbehandelt [vom Reis])

Pär|chen ‹*zu* Paar›

Par|cours [...'ku:r], der; - [...'ku:r(s)], - [...'ku:rs] ‹franz.› (*Reitsport* Hindernisbahn für Springturniere; *schweiz. Sportspr.* Renn-, Laufstrecke)

par|dauz!

Par|del, Par|der, der; -s, - (*veraltend für* Leopard)

par dis|tance [- dis'tã:s] ‹franz.› (aus der Ferne)

Par|don [...'dõ:, *auch* ...'dɔŋ, *österr. auch* ...'do:n], der, *auch* das; -s ‹franz.› (*veraltend für* Verzeihung; Gnade; Nachsicht); Pardon geben; um Pardon bitten; Pardon! (*landsch. für* Verzeihung!); **par|do|nie|ren** [...'ni:...] (*veraltet für* verzeihen, begnadigen)

Par|dun, das; -[e]s, -s ⟨niederl.⟩ *u.* **Par|du|ne,** die; -, -n (*Seemannsspr.* Tau, das die Masten od. Stengen nach hinten hält)
Pa|ren|chym [...ç...] (↑R 132), das; -s, -e ⟨griech.⟩ (*Biol.* pflanzl. u. tier. Grundgewebe; *Bot.* Schwammschicht des Blattes)
Pa|ren|tel, die; -, -en ⟨lat.⟩ (*Rechtsw.* Gesamtheit der Abkömmlinge eines Stammvaters); **Pa|ren|tel|sys|tem,** das; -s (*Rechtsw.* für die 1. bis 3. Ordnung gültige Erbfolge)
Pa|ren|the|se (↑R 132), die; -, -n ⟨griech.⟩ (*Sprachw.* Redeteil, der außerhalb des eigtl. Satzverbandes steht; Einschaltung; Klammer[zeichen]); in - setzen; **pa|ren|the|tisch** (eingeschaltet; nebenbei [gesagt])
Pa|reo, der; -s, -s ⟨polynes.-span.⟩ (Wickeltuch)
Pa|re|re, das; -[s], -[s] ⟨ital.⟩ (*österr. für* medizin. Gutachten)
Par|er|ga, *Plur.* ⟨griech.⟩ (*veraltet für* Beiwerk, Anhang; gesammelte kleine Schriften)
par ex|cel|lence [- ɛksɛ'lã:s] ⟨franz.⟩ (vorzugsweise, vor allem andern, schlechthin)
Par|fait [par'fɛ], das; -s, -s ⟨franz.⟩ (gefrorene Speiseeismasse; gebundene u. erstarrte Masse aus fein gehacktem Fleisch od. Fisch)
par force [- 'fɔrs] ⟨franz.⟩ (*geh. für* mit Gewalt; unbedingt); **Par|force‿horn, ...jagd** (Hetzjagd), **...rei|ter, ...ritt**
Par|fum [...'fœ̃:], das; -s, -s, **Par|füm,** das; -s, *Plur.* -e *u.* -s ⟨franz.⟩ (wohlriechender Duft[stoff]); **Par|fü|me|rie,** die; -, ...ien (Geschäft für Parfüms u. Kosmetikartikel; Betrieb zur Herstellung von Parfümen; *nur Plur.: fachspr. für* das Parfümieren, Parfümerieprodukte); **Par|fü|meur** [...'mø:r], der; -s, -e (Fachkraft der Parfümherstellung); **Par|fum|fla|sche** [...'fœ̃:...], **Par|füm|fla|sche; par|fü|mie|ren;** sich -; **Par|füm|zer|stäu|ber**
pa|ri ⟨ital.⟩ (*Bankw.* zum Nennwert; gleich); über, unter pari; die Chancen stehen pari; *vgl.* al pari
Pa|ria, der; -s, -s ⟨tamil.-angloind.⟩ (kastenloser Inder; *übertr. für* von der menschlichen Gesellschaft Ausgestoßener); **Pa|ri|a|tum,** das; -s
¹pa|rie|ren ⟨franz.⟩ ([einen Hieb] abwehren; *Reiten* [ein Pferd] zum Stehen bringen)
²pa|rie|ren ⟨lat.⟩ (unbedingt gehorchen)
Pa|ri|e|tal|au|ge [...i|e...] (*Biol.* lichtempfindl. Sinnesorgan niederer Wirbeltiere)
Pa|ri|kurs (*Wirtsch.* Nennwert eines Wertpapiers)
¹Pa|ris (griech. Sagengestalt)
²Pa|ris (Hptst. Frankreichs)
pa|risch (von der Insel Paros)
¹Pa|ri|ser (↑R 103); - Verträge (von 1954); **²Pa|ri|ser,** der; -s, - (*ugs. für* Präservativ); **Pa|ri|ser Blau,** das; - -s; **pa|ri|se|risch** (nach Art des ¹Parisers); **Pa|ri|si|enne** [...'ziɛn], die; - (Seidengewebe; franz. Freiheitslied); **pa|ri|sisch** (von [der Stadt] Paris)
pa|ri|syl|la|bisch ⟨lat.; griech.⟩ (*Sprachw.* gleichsilbig in allen Beugungsfällen); **Pa|ri|syl|la|bum,** das; -s, ...ba (in Sing. u. Plur. parisyllabisches Wort)
Pa|ri|tät, die; -, -en ⟨lat.⟩ (Gleichstellung, -berechtigung; *Wirtsch.* Austauschverhältnis zwischen zwei od. mehreren Währungen); **pa|ri|tä|tisch** (gleichgestellt, -berechtigt); - getragene Kosten; *aber* (↑R 108): Deutscher Paritätischer Wohlfahrtsverband
Pa|ri|wert (*Bankw.*)
Park, der; -s, *Plur.* -s, *seltener* -e, *schweiz.* Pärke ⟨franz.(-engl.)⟩ (großer Landschaftsgarten; Depot [*meist in Zusammensetzungen,* z. B. Wagenpark])
Par|ka, der; -s, -s *od.* die; -, -s ⟨eskim.⟩ (knielanger, warmer Anorak mit Kapuze)
Park-and-ride-Sys|tem ['pa:(r)kənd'raid...] ⟨engl.-amerik.⟩ (Verkehrssystem, bei dem die Autofahrer am Stadtrand parken u. mit öffentl. Verkehrsmitteln in die Innenstadt weiterfahren); **Park|an|la|ge; park|ar|tig; Park‿bahn** (*Raumfahrt* Umlaufbahn, von der aus eine Raumsonde gestartet wird), **...bank** (*Plur.* ...bänke), **...bucht, ...deck; par|ken** (ein Kraftfahrzeug abstellen); **Par|ker**
Par|kett, das; -[e]s, *Plur.* -e *u.* -s ⟨franz.⟩ (im Theater meist vorderer Raum zu ebener Erde; getäfelter Fußboden); **Par|kett|bo|den; Par|ket|te,** die; -, -n (*österr. für* Einzelbrett des Parkettfußbodens); **par|ket|tie|ren** (mit Parkettfußboden versehen); **Par|kett‿le|ger, ...le|ge|rin; Par|kett|sitz**
Park|haus; par|kie|ren (*schweiz. für* parken); **Par|king|me|ter,** der; -s, - ⟨engl.⟩ (*schweiz. für* Parkuhr)
Par|kin|son ['pa:(r)kins(ə)n] (engl. Chirurg); **Par|kin|son|krank|heit** (↑R 96), die; - *od.* **par|kin|son|sche Krank|heit,** die; -n -
Park‿kral|le (Vorrichtung zum Blockieren der Räder eines [falsch parkenden] Autos), **...leit|sys|tem, ...leuch|te, ...licht** (*Plur.* ...lichter), **...lü|cke; Par|ko|me|ter,** das, *auch* der; -s, - (Parkuhr); **Park‿platz, ...raum, ...schei|be, ...stu|di|um** (*ugs. für* Studium in einem nicht gewünschten Fach, bis man den eigentlich erstrebten Studienplatz bekommt); **Park‿sün|der, ...uhr, ...ver|bot, ...wäch|ter, ...weg, ...zeit**
Par|la|ment, das; -[e]s, -e ⟨engl.⟩ (gewählte Volksvertretung); **Par|la|men|tär,** der; -s, -e ⟨franz.⟩ (Unterhändler); **Par|la|men|tär|flag|ge; Par|la|men|ta|ri|er,** der; -s, - ⟨engl.⟩ (Abgeordneter, Mitglied des Parlamentes); **Par|la|men|ta|ri|e|rin; par|la|men|ta|risch** (das Parlament betreffend); eine parlamentarische Anfrage; parlamentarischer Staatssekretär (aber ↑R 56); der Parlamentarische Rat (Versammlung von Ländervertretern, die das Grundgesetz ausarbeiteten; ↑R 108); **par|la|men|ta|risch-de|mo|kra|tisch** (↑R 27); **Par|la|men|ta|ris|mus,** der; - (Regierungsform, in der die Regierung dem Parlament verantwortlich ist); **par|la|men|tie|ren** ⟨franz.⟩ (*veraltet für* unter-, verhandeln; *landsch. für* hin u. her reden); **Par|la|ments‿aus|schuss, ...be|schluss, ...de|bat|te, ...fe|ri|en** (*Plur.*), **...mit|glied, ...sit|zung, ...wahl** (*meist Plur.*)
par|lan|do ⟨ital.⟩ (*Musik* mehr gesprochen als gesungen); **Par|lan|do,** das; -s, *Plur.* -s *u.* ...di
Pär|lein ⟨zu Paar⟩
par|lie|ren ⟨franz.⟩ (*veraltend für* Konversation machen; in einer fremden Sprache reden)
Par|ma (ital. Stadt); **Par|ma|er** (↑R 103); **par|ma|isch**
Par|mä|ne, die; -, -n (eine Apfelsorte)
Par|me|san, der; -[s] (*kurz für* Parmesankäse); **Par|me|sa|ner** *vgl.* Parmaer; **par|me|sa|nisch** *vgl.* parmaisch; **Par|me|san|kä|se** (ein Reibkäse)
Par|nass, der; *Gen.* - *u.* -es (mittelgriech. Gebirgszug; Musenberg, Dichtersitz); **par|nas|sisch; Par|nas|sos, Par|nas|sus,** der; -; *vgl.* Parnass
pa|ro|chi|al [...x...] (↑R 132) ⟨griech.⟩ (zur Pfarrei gehörend); **Pa|ro|chi|al|kir|che** (Pfarrkirche); **Pa|ro|chie,** die; -, ...ien (Pfarrei; Amtsbezirk eines Geistlichen)

Pa|ro|die (↑R 132), die; -, ...ien ‹griech.› (komische Umbildung ernster Dichtung; scherzh. Nachahmung; *Musik* Vertauschung geistl. u. weltl. Texte u. Kompositionen [zur Zeit Bachs]); **Pa|ro|die|mes|se** (Messenkomposition unter Verwendung eines schon vorhandenen Musikstücks); *vgl.* [1]Messe; **pa|ro|die|ren** (auf scherzhafte Weise nachahmen); **Pa|ro|dist,** der; -en, -en; ↑R 126 (jmd., der parodiert); **Pa|ro|dis|tik,** die; -; **pa|ro|dis|tisch**

Pa|ro|don|ti|tis (↑R 132), die; -, ...itiden ‹griech.› (*Med.* Zahnbettentzündung); **Pa|ro|don|to|se,** *älter* Pa|ra|den|to|se, die; -, -n (Zahnbetterkrankung mit Lockerung der Zähne)

Pa|ro|le, die; -, -n ‹franz.› (milit. Kennwort; Losung; *auch für* Leit-, Wahlspruch); **Pa|ro|le|aus|ga|be;** **Pa|role d'hon|neur** [paˈrɔldɔˈnøːr], das; - - ‹franz.› (*veraltend für* Ehrenwort)

Pa|ro|li, das; -s, -s ‹franz.›; *nur in* Paroli bieten (Widerstand entgegensetzen)

Pa|rö|mie (↑R 132), die; -, ...ien ‹griech.› ([altgriech.] Sprichwort, Denkspruch); **Pa|rö|mi|o|lo|gie,** die; - (Sprichwortkunde); **Pa|ro|no|ma|sie,** die; -, ...ien (*Rhet.* Zusammenstellung lautlich gleicher od. ähnlich klingender Wörter von gleicher Herkunft); **Pa|ro|ny|ma, Pa|ro|ny|me** (*Plur. von* Paronymon); **Pa|ro|ny|mik,** die; - (Lehre von der Ableitung der Wörter); **pa|ro|ny|misch** (stammverwandt); **Pa|ro|ny|mon,** das; -s, *Plur.* ...ma *u.* ...onyme (*veraltet für* mit anderen Wörtern vom gleichen Stamm abgeleitetes Wort)

Pa|ros (griech. Insel)

Pa|ro|tis (↑R 132), die; -, ...iden ‹griech.› (*Med.* Ohrspeicheldrüse); **Pa|ro|ti|tis,** die; -, ...itiden (*Med.* Entzündung der Ohrspeicheldrüse; Mumps); **Pa|ro|xys|mus,** der; -, ...men (*Med.* anfallartige Steigerung von Krankheitserscheinungen; *Geol.* aufs Höchste gesteigerte Tätigkeit eines Vulkans); **Pa|ro|xy|to|non,** das; -s, ...tona (*Sprachw.* auf der vorletzten Silbe betontes Wort)

Par|se, der; -n, -n (↑R 126) ‹pers.› (Anhänger des Zarathustra)

Par|sec, das; -, - ‹*Kurzw. aus* Parallaxe *u.* Sekunde› (astron. Längenmaß; *Abk.* pc)

Par|si|fal (*von Richard Wagner gebrauchte Schreibung für* Parzival)

par|sisch (die Parsen betreffend); **Par|sis|mus,** der; - (Religion der Parsen)

Pars pro to|to, das; - - - ‹lat.› (*Sprachw.* Redefigur, die einen Teil für das Ganze setzt)

Part, der; -s, *Plur.* -s, *auch* -e ‹franz.› (Anteil; Stimme eines Instrumental- od. Gesangstücks)

part. = parterre

Part. = Parterre

[1]Par|te, die; -, -n ‹ital.› (*österr. für* Todesanzeige); **[2]Par|te,** die; -, -n (*landsch. für* Mietpartei)

Par|tei, die; -, -en ‹franz.›; **Par|tei‿ab|zei|chen, ...amt; par|tei|amt|lich; Par|tei‿an|hän|ger, ...ap|pa|rat, ...aus|weis, ...buch, ...bü|ro, ...chef, ...che|fin, ...chi|ne|sisch** (das; -[s]; *iron. für* dem Außenstehenden unverständliche Parteisprache); **Par|tei|dis|zi|plin,** die; -; **Par|tei|en‿fi|nan|zie|rung, ...kampf, ...land|schaft, ...staat** (*Plur.* ...staaten), **...ver|kehr** (der; -s; *österr. für* Amtsstunden); **Par|tei‿freund, ...freun|din, ...füh|rer, ...füh|re|rin, ...füh|rung** (die; -), **...funk|ti|o|när, ...funk|ti|o|nä|rin, ...gän|ger, ...gän|ge|rin, ...ge|nos|se, ...ge|nos|sin, ...ide|o|lo|ge** (↑R 132), **...in|stanz; par|tei|in|tern; par|tei|isch** (nicht neutral, nicht objektiv; voreingenommen; der einen od. der anderen Seite zugeneigt); **Par|tei‿ka|der, ...kon|gress, ...lehr|jahr** (*ehemals in der DDR* obligator. Schulung der SED-Mitglieder), **...lei|tung; par|tei|lich** (im Sinne einer polit. Partei, eine Partei betreffend); **Par|tei|lich|keit,** die; -; **Par|tei|li|nie; par|tei|los; Par|tei|lo|se,** der *u.* die; -n, -n (↑R 5 ff.); **Par|tei|lo|sig|keit,** die; -; **par|tei|mä|ßig; Par|tei|mit|glied; Par|tei|nah|me,** die; -, -n; **Par|tei‿or|gan, ...or|ga|ni|sa|ti|on** (die; -), **...po|li|tik; par|tei|po|li|tisch;** - neutral sein; **Par|tei‿prä|si|di|um, ...pro|gramm, ...pro|pa|gan|da, ...sek|re|tär, ...sek|re|tä|rin, ...spit|ze, ...tag; Par|tei|tags|be|schluss; Par|tei|ung** (*selten für* Zerfall in Parteien; [politische] Gruppierung); **Par|tei‿ver|samm|lung, ...vor|sit|zen|de, ...vor|stand, ...zent|ra|le**

par|terre [...ˈtɛr] ‹franz.› (zu ebener Erde; *Abk.* part.); parterre wohnen; **Par|ter|re** [...ˈtɛr(ə)], das; -s, -s (Erdgeschoss [*Abk.* Part.]; Saalplatz im Theater; Plätze hinter dem Parkett); **Par|terre|ak|ro|ba|tik** [...ˈtɛr...] (artistisches Bodenturnen); **Par|ter|re|woh|nung** [...tɛr(ə)...]

Par|te|zet|tel (*österr. svw.* [1]Parte)

Par|the|no|ge|ne|se, *auch noch* **Par|the|no|ge|ne|sis** [*auch* ...ˈgeː...], die; - ‹griech.› (*Biol.* Jungfernzeugung, Entwicklung aus unbefruchteten Eizellen); **par|the|no|ge|ne|tisch; Par|the|non,** der; -s (Tempel der Athene); **Par|the|no|pe** [...pe] (*veraltet für* Neapel); **par|the|no|pe|isch,** *aber* (↑R 108): die Parthenopeische Republik (1799)

Par|ther, der; -s, - (Angehöriger eines nordiran. Volksstammes im Altertum); **Par|thi|en** (Land der Parther); **par|thisch**

par|ti|al ‹lat.› (*veraltet für* partiell); **Par|ti|al...** (Teil...); **Par|ti|al‿bruch** (der; -[e]s, ...brüche; *Math.* Teilbruch eines Bruches mit zusammengesetztem Nenner), **...ob|li|ga|ti|on** (*Bankw.* Teilschuldverschreibung), **...tö|ne** (*Plur.; Musik* Obertöne, Teiltöne eines Klanges); **Par|tie,** die; -, ...ien ‹franz.› (Teil, Abschnitt; bestimmte Bühnenrolle; *Kaufmannsspr.* Posten, größere Menge einer Ware; *österr. auch für* für eine bestimmte Aufgabe zusammengestellte Gruppe von Arbeitern; *Sport* Durchgang, Spiel; *veraltend für* Ausflug); eine gute Partie machen (reich heiraten); **Par|tie‿be|zug** (der; -[e]s; *Kaufmannsspr.*), **...füh|rer** (*österr. auch für* Vorarbeiter); **par|ti|ell** (teilweise [vorhanden]); partielle Sonnenfinsternis; **par|ti|en|wei|se; Par|tie|preis; Par|tie|wa|re** (*Kaufmannsspr.* fehlerhafte Ware); **par|tie|wei|se; [1]Par|ti|kel** [*auch* ...ˈtikəl], die; -, -n ‹lat.› (*kath. Kirche* Teilchen der Hostie, Kreuzreliquie; *Sprachw.* unflektierbare Wortart, z. B. Präposition); **[2]Par|ti|kel,** das; -s, -, *auch* die; -, -n (*Physik* Elementarteilchen); **par|ti|ku|lar, par|ti|ku|lär** (einen Teil betreffend, einzeln); **Par|ti|ku|la|ris|mus,** der; - (Sonderbestrebungen staatl. Teilgebiete, Kleinstaaterei); **Par|ti|ku|la|rist,** der; -en, -en (↑R 126); **par|ti|ku|la|ris|tisch; Par|ti|ku|lar|recht** (*veraltet für* Einzel-, Sonderrecht); **Par|ti|ku|lier,** der; -s, -e ‹franz.› (selbstständiger Schiffseigentümer; Selbstfahrer in der Binnenschifffahrt); **Par|ti|men|to,** das *u.* der; -[s], ...ti ‹ital.› (*Musik* Generalbassstimme); **Par|ti|san,** der; *Gen.* -s *u.* -en, *Plur.* -en (↑R 126) ‹franz.› (bewaffneter Widerstandskämpfer im feindlich besetzten Hinterland); **Par|ti|sa|ne,** die; -, -n (spießartige Stoßwaffe des 15. bis 18. Jh.s); **Par|ti|sa|nen₋ge|biet, ...kampf, ...krieg; Par|ti|sa|nin; Par|ti|ta,** die; -, ...iten ‹ital.› (*Musik svw.* Suite); **Par|ti|te,** die; -, -n (*Kaufmannsspr.* einzelner Posten einer Rechnung); **Par|ti|ti|on,** die; -, -en ‹lat.› (*geh. für* Teilung, Einteilung; *Logik* Zerlegung des Begriffsinhaltes in seine Teile od. Merkmale); **par|ti|tiv** (*Sprachw.* die Teilung bezeichnend); **Par|ti|tur,** die; -, -en ‹ital.› (Zusammenstellung aller zu einem Musikstück gehörenden Stimmen); **Par|ti|zip,** das; -s, -ien [...iən] ‹lat.› (*Sprachw.* Mittelwort); Partizip I (Partizip Präsens, Mittelwort der Gegenwart, z. B. „sehend"); Partizip II (Partizip Perfekt, Mittelwort der Vergangenheit, z. B. „gesehen"); **Par|ti|zi|pa|ti|on,** die; -, -en (das Teilhaben); **Par|ti|zi|pa|ti|ons₋ge|schäft** *(Wirtsch.),* **...kon|to** *(Wirtsch.);* **par|ti|zi|pi|al** (*Sprachw.* mittelwörtlich, Mittelwort...); **Par|ti|zi|pi|al₋bil|dung, ...grup|pe** (*vgl.* [1]Gruppe), **...kon|struk|ti|on, ...satz; par|ti|zi|pie|ren** (Anteil haben, teilnehmen); **Par|ti|zi|pi|um,** das; -s, ...pia (*älter für* Partizip); **Part|ner,** der; -s, - ‹engl.› (Gefährte; Teilhaber; Teilnehmer; Mitspieler); **Part|ne|rin; Part|ner₋land, ...look** (der; -s; *Mode*); **Part|ner|schaft; part|ner|schaft|lich; Part|ner₋staat** (*Plur.* ...staaten), **...stadt, ...tausch, ...wahl, ...wech|sel**

par|tout [...'tu:] ‹franz.› (*ugs. für* durchaus; um jeden Preis)

Par|ty ['pa:(r)ti], die; -, -s ‹engl.-amerik.› (zwangloses [privates] Fest); **Par|ty₋girl, ...lö|we** (jmd., der auf Partys umschwärmt wird), **...ser|vice** (Unternehmen, das Speisen u. Getränke für Festlichkeiten ins Haus liefert)

Pa|ru|sie (↑R 132), die; - ‹griech.› (*christl. Rel.* Wiederkunft Christi beim Jüngsten Gericht)

Par|ve|nü [...v...] *u., österr. nur,* **Par|ve|nu** [...'ny:], der; -s, -s ‹franz.› (Emporkömmling; Neureicher)

Par|ze, die; -, -n *meist Plur.* ‹lat.› (röm. Schicksalsgöttin [Atropos, Klotho, Lachesis]); *vgl.* Moira

Par|zel|lar|ver|mes|sung; Par|zel|le, die; -, -n ‹lat.› (vermessenes Grundstück, Baustelle); **Par|zel|len|wirt|schaft; par|zel|lie|ren** (in Parzellen zerlegen)

Par|zi|val [...fal] (Held der Artussage); *vgl.* Parsifal

Pas [pa], der; - [pa(s)], - [pas] ‹franz.› ([Tanz]schritt)

[1]**Pas|cal** [...'kal] (franz. Mathematiker u. Philosoph); [2]**Pas|cal,** das; -s, - (Einheit des Drucks; *Zeichen* Pa)

PASCAL, das; -s ‹Kunstw., an [1]Pascal angelehnt› (eine Programmiersprache)

Pasch, der; -[e]s, *Plur.* -e *u.* Päsche ‹franz.› (Wurf mit gleicher Augenzahl auf mehreren Würfeln; *Domino* Stein mit Doppelzahl)

[1]**Pas|cha** usw. *vgl.* Passah usw.

[2]**Pa|scha,** der; -s, -s ‹türk.› (früherer oriental. Titel; *ugs. für* rücksichtsloser, herrischer Mann, der sich [von Frauen] bedienen lässt); **Pa|scha|al|lü|ren** *Plur.*

Pa|scha|lis [*auch* pas'ça:...] ‹hebr.› (Papstname)

[1]**pa|schen** ‹franz.› (würfeln; *bayr. u. österr. mdal. für* klatschen); du paschst

[2]**pa|schen** ‹hebr.› (*ugs. für* schmuggeln); du paschst; **Pa|scher; Pa|sche|rei**

pa|scholl! ‹russ.› (*ugs. veraltend für* pack dich!; vorwärts!)

Pasch|tu, das; -s (Amtssprache in Afghanistan)

Pas de Ca|lais [pa də ka'lɛ:], der; - - - ‹franz.› (franz. Name der Straße von Dover)

Pas de deux [pa də 'dø:], der; - - -, - - - ‹franz.› (Tanz od. Ballett für zwei)

Pas|lack, der; -s, -s ‹slaw.› (*nordostd. für* jmd., der für andere schwer arbeiten muss)

Pa|so do|ble (↑R 130), der; - -, - - ‹span.› (ein Tanz)

Pas|pel, die; -, -n, *selten* der; -s, - ‹franz.› *u., bes. österr.,* Passe|poil [pas'poal], der; -s, -s (schmaler Nahtbesatz bei Kleidungsstücken); **pas|pe|lie|ren,** *bes. österr. u. schweiz.* passe|poil|lie|ren (mit Paspeln versehen); **Pas|pe|lie|rung,** Passe|poil|lie|rung; **pas|peln;** ich pasp[e]le (↑R 16)

Pas|quill, das; -s, -e ‹ital.› (*veraltend für* Schmäh-, Spottschrift); **Pas|quil|lant,** der; -en, -en; ↑R 126 (Verfasser od. Verbreiter eines Pasquills)

Pass, der; -es, Pässe ‹lat.› (Bergübergang; Ausweis [für Reisende]; gezielte Ballabgabe beim Fußball); *vgl. aber* zupass, zupasse kommen

Pas|sa usw. *vgl.* Passah usw.

pas|sa|bel ‹lat.› (annehmbar; leidlich); ...a|ble (↑R 130) Gesundheit

Pas|sa|cag|lia [...'kalja] (↑R 130), die; -, ...ien [...jən] ‹ital.› (*Musik* Instrumentalstück aus Variationen über einem ostinaten Bass)

Pas|sa|ge [pa'sa:ʒə], die; -, -n ‹franz.› (Durchfahrt, -gang; Überfahrt mit Schiff od. Flugzeug; schnelle Tonfolge in einem Musikstück; fortlaufender Teil einer Rede od. eines Textes; *Reitsport* Gangart in der hohen Schule); **pas|sa|ger** [pasa'ʒe:r] (*Med.* nur vorübergehend auftretend); **Pas|sa|gier** [...'ʒi:r], der; -s, -e ‹ital.(-franz.)› (Schiffsreisender, Fahrgast, Fluggast); **Pas|sa|gier₋damp|fer, ...flug|zeug, ...gut; Pas|sa|gie|rin; Pas|sa|gier|lis|te**

Pas|sah, *ökum.* Pas|cha ['pasça], das; -s ‹hebr.› (jüd. Fest zum Gedenken an den Auszug aus Ägypten; das beim Passahmahl gegessene Lamm); **Pas|sah₋fest** (*od.* Pas|cha|fest), **...lamm** (*od.* Pas|cha|lamm), **...mahl** (*od.* Pas|cha|mahl; *Plur.* ...mahle)

Pass|amt

Pas|sant, der; -en, -en (↑R 126) ‹franz.› (Fußgänger; Vorübergehender); **Pas|san|tin**

Pas|sat, der; -[e]s, -e ‹niederl.› (gleichmäßig wehender Tropenwind); **Pas|sat|wind**

Pas|sau (Stadt am Zusammenfluss von Donau, Inn u. Ilz); **Pas|sau|er** (↑R 103)

Pass|bild

pas|sé [pa'se:] *vgl.* pas|see

Pas|se, die; -, -n ‹franz.› (glattes Hals- u. Schulterteil an Kleidungsstücken)

pas|see, *auch* pas|sé (↑R 33) ‹franz.› (*ugs. für* vorbei, abgetan); das ist -

Pas|sei|er, das; -s *u.* **Pas|sei|er|tal,** das; -[e]s (Alpental in Südtirol)

pas|sen ‹franz.› (*auch Kartenspiel* auf ein Spiel verzichten; *bes. Fußball* den Ball genau zuspielen); du passt; gepasst; passe! *u.* passt!; das passt sich nicht *(ugs.);* **passend;** etwas Passendes; **Passe|par|tout** [paspar'tu:], das, *schweiz.* der; -s, -s (Umrahmung aus leichter Pappe für Grafiken, Zeichnungen u. a.; *schweiz. auch für* Dauerkarte; Hauptschlüssel)

Passe|poil usw. *vgl.* Paspel usw.

Pas|ser, der; -s, - (*Druckw.* das genaue Übereinanderliegen der einzelnen Formteile u. Druckelemente, bes. beim Mehrfarbendruck); **Pass₋form, ...fo|to; Pass|gang,** der (Gangart, bei der beide Beine einer Seite gleichzeitig vorgesetzt werden [bes. bei Reittieren]); **Pass|gän|ger; pass|ge|recht; Pass|hö|he; Pas|sier|ball** *(Tennis);* **pas|sier|bar** (überschreitbar); **pas|sie|ren** ‹franz.› (vorübergehen, -fahren;

durchqueren, überqueren; geschehen; *Gastron.* durch ein Sieb drücken; *Tennis* den Ball am Gegner vorbeischlagen); **Pas|sier₋ge|wicht** (*Münzwesen* Mindestgewicht), **...ma|schi|ne, ...schein; Pas|sier|schein₋ab|kom|men, ...stel|le; Pas|sier₋schlag** *(Tennis),* **...sieb**

pas|sim ‹lat.› ([im angegebenen Werk] da u. dort zerstreut)

Pas|si|on, die; -, -en ‹lat.› (*nur Sing.:* Leidensgeschichte Christi; Leidenschaft, leidenschaftliche Hingabe); **pas|si|o|na|to** ‹ital.› (*Musik* mit Leidenschaft); **Pas|si|o|na|to,** das; -s, *Plur.* -s *u.* ...ti; **pas|si|o|niert** ‹franz.› (leidenschaftlich, begeistert); **Pas|si|ons₋blu|me, ...frucht, ...sonn|tag** (*auch für* zweiter Sonntag vor Ostern, *vgl.* Judika), **...spiel** (Darstellung der Leidensgeschichte Christi), **...weg, ...wo|che, ...zeit**

pas|siv [*auch* ...'si:f] ‹lat.› (untätig; teilnahmslos; duldend; *seltener für* passivisch); passive [...və] Bestechung; -e [Handels]bilanz; passives Wahlrecht (Recht, gewählt zu werden); **Pas|siv,** das; -s, -e [...və] *Plur. selten* (*Sprachw.* Leideform); **Pas|si|va** [...va], Pas|si|ven [...vən] *Plur.* (*Kaufmannsspr.* Schulden, Verbindlichkeiten); **Pas|siv₋bil|dung** *(Sprachw.),* **...ge|schäft** *(Bankw.),* **...han|del** (*Kaufmannsspr.; vgl.* ¹Handel); **pas|si|vie|ren** [...v...] ([Verbindlichkeiten] in der Bilanz erfassen u. ausweisen; *Chemie* Metalle auf [elektro]chem. Wege korrosionsbeständig machen); **pas|si|visch** [*auch* ...'si:viʃ] (*Sprachw.* das Passiv betreffend); **Pas|si|vi|tät,** die; - (passives Verhalten); **Pas|siv₋le|gi|ti|ma|ti|on** *(Rechtsw.),* **...mas|se, ...pos|ten** *(Kaufmannsspr.),* **...rau|chen** (das; -s), **...sal|do** (Verlustvortrag), **...zin|sen** *(Plur.)*

Pass|kon|trol|le; pass|lich (*veraltet für* angemessen; bequem); **Pass|stel|le** (↑R 136), **Pass|stra|ße** (↑R 136); **Pas|sung** (*Technik* Beziehung zwischen zusammengefügten Maschinenteilen); **Pas|sus,** der; -, - ['pasu:s] ‹lat.› (Schriftstelle, Absatz); **pass|wärts; Pass₋wort** (*Plur.* ...wörter; *EDV, Bildschirmtext* Kennwort), **...zwang** (der; -[e]s)

¹Pas|ta *vgl.* Paste; **²Pas|ta,** die; - ‹ital.› (ital. Bez. für Teigwaren); **Pas|ta a|sciut|ta** [- a'ʃuta], die; - -, ...te ...tte [...tə a'ʃutə], **Pas|ta|sciut|ta** [pasta'ʃuta] (↑R 132), die; -, ...tte (ital. Spaghettigericht); **Pas|te,** *selten* Pas|ta, die; -, ...sten (streichbare Masse; Teigmasse als Grundlage für Arzneien und kosmetische Mittel); **Pas|tell,** das; -[e]s, -e ‹ital.(-franz.)› (mit Pastellfarben gemaltes Bild); **pas|tel|len; Pas|tell|far|be; pas|tell|far|ben; pas|tel|lig; Pas|tell₋ma|le|rei, ...stift** (*vgl.* ¹Stift), **...ton** (*Plur.* ...töne)

Pas|ter|nak (russ. Schriftsteller)

Pas|ter|ze, die; - (größter österr. Gletscher am Großglockner)

Pas|tet|chen; Pas|te|te, die; -, -n ‹roman.› (Fleisch-, Fischspeise u. a. [in Teighülle])

Pas|teur [...'tø:r] (franz. Bakteriologe); **Pas|teu|ri|sa|ti|on,** die; -, -en; **pas|teu|ri|sie|ren;** pasteurisierte Milch; **Pas|teu|ri|sie|rung** (Entkeimung)

Pas|til|le, die; -, -n ‹lat.› (Kügelchen, Plätzchen, Pille)

Pas|ti|nak, der; -s, -e *häufiger* **Pas|ti|na|ke,** die; -, -n ‹lat.› (krautige Pflanze, deren Wurzeln als Gemüse u. Viehfutter dienen)

Past|milch (*schweiz. Kurzform von* pasteurisierte Milch)

Pas|tor [*auch* ...'to:r], der; -s, *Plur.* ...oren, *auch* ...ore, *landsch. auch* ...öre ‹lat.› (ev. od. kath. Geistlicher; *Abk.* P.); **pas|to|ral** (seelsorgerisch; [übertrieben] feierlich); **Pas|to|ral|brief** *(christl. Rel.);* **¹Pas|to|ra|le,** das; -s, -s *od.* die; -, -n ‹ital.› (ländlich-friedvolles Tonstück; Schäferspiel); **²Pas|to|ra|le,** das; -s, -s (Hirtenstab des kath. Bischofs); **Pas|to|ral|the|o|lo|gie,** die; - (praktische Theologie); **Pas|to|rat,** das; -[e]s, -e (*bes. nordd. für* Pfarramt, -wohnung); **Pas|to|rel|le,** die; -, -n ‹ital.› (mittelalterl. Hirtenliedchen); **Pas|to|rin; Pas|tor pri|ma|ri|us,** der; - -, ...ores ...rii [...re:s ...ri̯i] (Hauptpastor; Oberpfarrer; *Abk.* P. prim.)

pas|tos ‹ital.› (*bild. Kunst* dick aufgetragen); **pas|tös** ‹franz.› (breiig, dickflüssig; *Med.* gedunsen)

Pa|ta|go|ni|en [...i̯ən] (südlichster Teil Amerikas); **Pa|ta|go|ni|er** [...i̯ər]; **pa|ta|go|nisch**

Pat|chen (Patenkind)

Patch|work ['pɛtʃwœ:(r)k], das; -s, -s ‹amerik.› (aus bunten Flicken zusammengesetzter Stoff, auch Leder in entsprechender Verarbeitung)

¹Pa|te, der; -n, -n; ↑R 126 (Taufzeuge, *auch für* Patenkind); **²Pa|te,** die; -, -n (*svw.* Patin)

Pa|tel|la, die; -, ...llen ‹lat.› (*Med.* Kniescheibe); **Pa|tel|lar|re|flex**

Pa|ten₋be|trieb (*ehem. in der DDR),* **...bri|ga|de** *(ehem. in der DDR)*

Pa|te|ne, die; -, -n ‹griech.› (*christl. Kirche* Hostienteller)

Pa|ten₋ge|schenk, ...kind, ...on|kel; Pa|ten|schaft; Pa|ten|schafts|ver|trag (*ehem. in der DDR* Vertrag zwischen einem Betrieb u. einer Bildungseinrichtung zum Zwecke gegenseitiger Hilfe sowie kultureller u. polit. Zusammenarbeit); **Pa|ten|sohn**

pa|tent ‹lat.› (*ugs. für* praktisch, tüchtig, brauchbar; *landsch. für* fein, elegant); **Pa|tent,** das; -[e]s, -e (Urkunde über die Berechtigung, eine Erfindung allein zu verwerten; Bestallungsurkunde eines [Schiffs]offiziers); **Pa|tent|amt**

Pa|ten|tan|te

Pa|tent|an|walt; pa|tent|fä|hig; pa|ten|tie|ren (durch ein Patent schützen); **Pa|tent₋in|ha|ber, ...in|ha|be|rin, ...knopf, ...lö|sung** *(ugs.)*

Pa|ten|toch|ter

Pa|tent₋recht, ...re|zept *(ugs.),* **...rol|le, ...schrift, ...schutz** (der; -es), **...ver|schluss**

Pa|ter, der; -s, *Plur.* - *u.* Pat|res ['pa:tre:s] (↑R 130) ‹lat.› (kath. Ordensgeistlicher; *Abk.* P., *Plur.* PP.); **Pa|ter|fa|mi|li|as,** der; -, - (*veraltet scherzh. für* Familienoberhaupt, Hausherr); **Pa|ter|ni|tät,** die; - (*veraltet für* Vaterschaft); **¹Pa|ter|nos|ter,** das; -s, - (Vaterunser); **²Pa|ter|nos|ter,** der; -s, - (ständig umlaufender Aufzug); **Pa|ter|nos|ter|auf|zug; pa|ter, pec|ca|vi** [- pɛ'ka:vi] („Vater, ich habe gesündigt"); pater, peccavi sagen (flehentlich um Verzeihung bitten); **Pa|ter|pec|ca|vi,** das; -, - (reuiges Geständnis)

Pa|the|tik, die; - ‹griech.› (übertriebene, gespreizte Feierlichkeit); **Pa|thé|tique** [pate'ti:k], die; - ‹franz.› (Titel einer Klaviersonate Beethovens u. einer Sinfonie Tschaikowskys); **pa|the|tisch** ‹griech.› (voller Pathos; [übertrieben] feierlich); **pa|tho|gen** (*Med.* krankheitserregend); pathogene Bakterien; **Pa|tho|ge|ne|se,** die; -, -n (Entstehung u. Entwicklung einer Krankheit); **Pa|tho|ge|ni|tät,** die; - (Fähigkeit, Krankheiten hervorzurufen); **pa|tho|gno|mo|nisch, pa|tho|gnos|tisch** (für eine Krankheit kennzeichnend); **Pa|tho|lo|ge,** der; -n, -n (↑R 126); **Pa|tho|lo|gie,** die; -, ...ien (*nur Sing.:* allgemeine Lehre von den Krankheiten; pathologisches Institut); **Pa|tho|lo|gin; pa|tho|lo|gisch** (die Pathologie betreffend; krankhaft); pathologische Anatomie; **Pa|tho|pho|bie,** die; -, ...ien (*Psych.* Furcht vor Krankheiten); **Pa|tho|phy|si|o|lo|gie** (Lehre von den Krankheitsvorgängen u. Funktionsstörungen [in einem Organ]); **Pa|tho|psy|cho|lo|gie** (*svw.* Psychopathologie); **Pa|thos,** das; - ([übertriebene] Gefühlserregung; feierliche Ergriffenheit)

Pa|ti|ence [pa'siã:s], die; -, -n [...s(ə)n] ‹franz.› (Geduldsspiel mit Karten); **Pa|ti|ence|spiel; Pa|ti|ent** [pa'tsiɛnt], der; -en, -en (↑R 126) ‹lat.› (vom Arzt behandelte od. betreute Person); **Pa|ti|en|tin**

Pa|tin

Pa|ti|na, die; - ‹ital.› (ein grünlicher Überzug auf Kupfer, Edelrost); **pa|ti|nie|ren** (mit einer künstlichen Patina versehen)

Pa|tio, der; -s, -s ‹span.› (Innenhof eines [span.] Hauses)

Pa|tis|se|rie, die; -, ...ien ‹franz.› ([in Hotels] Raum zur Herstellung von Backwaren; *schweiz. für* feines Gebäck; Konditorei); **Pa|tis|si|er** [...'sie:], der; -s, -s ([Hotel]konditor)

Pat|mos (griech. Insel)

Pat|na|reis ‹nach der ind. Stadt› ([langkörniger] Reis); ↑R 105

Pa|tois [pa'toa], das; -, - ‹franz.› (*franz. Bez. für* Sprechweise der Landbevölkerung)

Pat|ras (↑R 130; griech. Stadt)

Pa|tres (↑R 130; *Plur. von* Pater); **Pat|ri|arch,** der; -en, -en (↑R 126) ‹griech.› (Stammvater im A. T.; Ehren-, Amtstitel einiger Bischöfe; Titel hoher orthodoxer Geistlicher); **pat|ri|ar|cha|lisch** (altväterlich; ehrwürdig; väterlich-bestimmend; männlich-autoritativ); **Pat|ri|ar|cha|kir|che** (Hauptkirche); **Pat|ri|ar|chat,** das, *in der Theol. auch* der; -[e]s, -e (Würde, Sitz u. Amtsbereich eines Patriarchen; Vaterherrschaft, -recht); **pat|ri|ar|chisch** (einem Patriarchen entsprechend)

Pat|ri|cia (↑R 130) ‹lat.› (w. Vorn.); **Pat|rick** (m. Vorn.)

pat|ri|mo|ni|al (↑R 130) ‹lat.› (erbherrlich); **Pat|ri|mo|ni|al|ge|richts|bar|keit** (*früher* Rechtsprechung durch den Grundherrn); **Pat|ri|mo|ni|um,** das; -s, ...ien [...iən] (*röm. Recht* väterl. Erbgut); **[1]Pat|ri|ot,** der; -en, -en (↑R 126) ‹griech.› (jmd., der für sein Vaterland eintritt); **[2]Pat|ri|ot** ['pɛtriət], die; -, -s ‹engl.› (eine amerik. Flugabwehrrakete); **pat|ri|o|tisch** [pa...] ‹griech.›; **Pat|ri|o|tis|mus,** der; -

Pat|ris|tik (↑R 130), die; - (Wissenschaft von den Schriften u. Lehren der Kirchenväter); **Pat|ris|ti|ker** (Kenner, Erforscher der Patristik); **pat|ris|tisch**

Pat|ri|ze (↑R 130), die; -, -n ‹lat.› (*Druckw.* Stempel, Prägestock; Gegenform zur Matrize)

Pat|ri|zia (↑R 130) ‹lat.› (w. Vorn.)

Pat|ri|zi|at (↑R 130), das; -[e]s, -e ‹lat.› (Gesamtheit der altröm. Adelsgeschlechter; ratsfähige Bürgerfamilien der dt. Städte im MA.); **Pat|ri|zi|er** (Angehöriger des Patriziats); **Pat|ri|zi|er‿ge|schlecht, ...haus; Pat|ri|zi|e|rin; pat|ri|zisch**

Pat|rok|los [*auch* 'pa...] (↑R 130; Freund Achills); **Pat|ro|klus** [*auch* 'pa...] *vgl.* Patroklos

Pat|ro|lo|gie (↑R 130), die; - ‹griech.› (*svw.* Patristik); **[1]Pat|ron,** der; -s, -e ‹lat.› (Schutzherr, -heiliger; Stifter einer Kirche; *veraltet für* Gönner; *ugs. für* übler Kerl, Bursche); **[2]Pat|ron** [patrõ], der; -s, -s ‹franz.› (*schweiz. für* Betriebsinhaber, Dienstherr); **Pat|ro|na,** die; -, ...nä ‹lat.› ([heilige] Beschützerin); **Pat|ro|na|ge,** [...'na:ʒə], die; -, -n ‹franz.› (Günstlingswirtschaft, Protektion); **Pat|ro|nanz,** die; - ‹lat.› (*österr. meist für* Schirmherrschaft); **Pat|ro|nat,** das; -[e]s, -e (Würde, Amt, Recht eines Schutzherrn [im alten Rom]; Rechtsstellung des Stifters einer christlichen Kirche od. seines Nachfolgers; Schirmherrschaft); **Pat|ro|nats‿fest, ...herr**

Pat|ro|ne (↑R 130), die; -, -n ‹franz.› (Geschoss u. Treibladung enthaltende [Metall]hülse; Musterzeichnung auf kariertem Papier bei der Jacquardweberei; Behälter [z. B. für Tinte, Kleinbildfilm]); **Pat|ro|nen‿gurt, ...hül|se, ...kam|mer, ...ta|sche, ...trom|mel; pat|ro|nie|ren** (*österr. für* [Wände] mithilfe von Schablonen bemalen); **Pat|ro|nin** ‹lat.› (Schutzherrin, Schutzheilige); **pat|ro|ni|sie|ren** (*veraltet für* beschützen; begünstigen); **Pat|ro|ny|mi|kon, Pat|ro|ny|mi|kum,** das; -s, ...ka ‹griech.› (nach dem Namen des Vaters gebildeter Name, z. B. Petersen = Peters Sohn); **pat|ro|ny|misch**

Pat|rouil|le [pa'truljə, *österr.* pa'tru:jə] (↑R 130), die; -, -n ‹franz.› (Spähtrupp; Kontrollgang); **Pat|rouil|len‿boot, ...fahrt, ...flug, ...füh|rer, ...gang** (der); **pat|rouil|lie|ren** [patru'(l)ji:..., *österr.* patru'ji:...] (auf Patrouille gehen; [als Posten] auf u. ab gehen)

Pat|ro|zi|ni|um (↑R 130), das; -s, ...ien [...iən] ‹lat.› (im alten Rom die Vertretung durch einen Patron vor Gericht; Schutzherrschaft eines Heiligen über eine kath. Kirche; Patronatsfest); **Pat|ro|zi|ni|ums|fest**

patsch!; pitsch, patsch!; **[1]Patsch,** der; -[e]s, -e (klatschendes Geräusch); **[2]Patsch,** der; -en, -en (*österr. ugs. für* Tolpatsch); **Pat|sche,** die; -, -n (*ugs. für* Hand; Gegenstand zum Schlagen [z. B. Feuerpatsche]; *nur Sing.:* Schlamm, Matsch); in der - sitzen (*ugs. für* in einer unangenehmen Lage sein); **pät|scheln** (*landsch. für* [spielerisch] rudern); ich ...[e]le (↑R 16); **pat|schen** *(ugs.);* du patschst; **Pat|schen,** der; -s, - (*österr. für* Hausschuh; Reifendefekt); **pat|sche|nass** *vgl.* patschnass; **Pat|scherl,** das; -s, -n (*österr. ugs. für* ungeschicktes Kind); **pat|schert** (*österr. ugs. für* unbeholfen); **Patsch|hand, Patsch|händ|chen** *(Kinderspr.);* **patsch|nass,** pat|sche|nass (*ugs. für* klatschnass)

Pat|schu|li, das; -s, -s ‹tamil.› (Duftstoff aus der Patschulipflanze); **Pat|schu|li‿öl, ...pflan|ze** (eine asiat. Pflanze)

patt ‹franz.› (*Schach* nicht mehr in der Lage, einen Zug zu machen, ohne seinen König ins Schach zu bringen); patt sein; **Patt,** das; -s, -s (*auch für* Situation, in der keine Partei einen Vorteil erringen kann)

Pat|te, die; -, -n ‹franz.› (Taschenklappe, Taschenbesatz)

Pat|tern ['pɛtərn], das; -s, -s ‹engl.› (*Psych.* [Verhaltens]muster, [Denk]schema; *Sprachw.* Sprachmuster)

Patt|si|tu|a|ti|on *vgl.* Patt

pat|zen (*ugs. für* kleinere Fehler machen); du patzt; **Pat|zen,** der; -s, - (*bayr. u. österr. für* Klecks, Klumpen); **Pat|zer** (*ugs. für* jmd., der patzt; Fehler); **Pat|ze|rei** *(ugs.);* **pat|zig** (*ugs. für* frech, grob; *südd. auch für* klebrig, breiig); **Pat|zig|keit** *(ugs.)*

Pau|kant, der; -en, -en; ↑R 126 (*Studentenspr.* Fechter bei einer Mensur); **Pauk‿arzt** *(Studentenspr.),* **...bo|den, ...bril|le; Pau|ke,** die; -, -n; auf die - hauen (*ugs. für* ausgelassen sein); **pau|ken** (die Pauke schlagen; *Studentenspr.* eine Mensur fechten; *ugs.*

für angestrengt lernen); **Pau|ken⌣fell, ...höh|le** (*Med.* Teil des Mittelohrs), **...schall, ...schlag, ...schlä|gel, ...schlä|ger, ...wir|bel; Pau|ker** (*Schülerspr. auch für* Lehrer); **Pau|ke|rei; Pau|kist,** der; -en, -en; ↑R 126 (Paukenspieler); **Pauk|tag** *(Studentenspr.)*

Paul (m. Vorn.); **Pau|la, Pau|li|ne** (w. Vorn.); **pau|li|nisch** ‹*zu* Paulus›; paulinische Briefe, Schriften (↑R 94); **Pau|li|nis|mus,** der; - (*christl. Theol.* Lehre des Apostels Paulus)

Pau|low|nia, die; -, ...ien [...iən] ‹nach der russ. Großfürstin Anna Pawlowna› (ein Zierbaum)

Pauls|kir|che, die; -; **Pau|lus** (Apostel); Pauli (des Paulus) Bekehrung (kath. Fest)

Pau|pe|ris|mus, der; - ‹lat.› (*veraltend für* Massenarmut)

Pau|sa|ni|as (spartan. Feldherr u. Staatsmann; griech. Reiseschriftsteller)

Paus|back, der; -[e]s, -e (*landsch. für* pausbäckiger Mensch); **Paus|ba|cken** *Plur.* (*landsch. für* dicke Wangen); **paus|ba|ckig,** *häufiger* **paus|bä|ckig**

pau|schal (alles zusammen; rund); **Pau|schal⌣ab|schrei|bung, ...be|steu|e|rung, ...be|wer|tung; Pau|scha|le,** die; -, -n ‹*latinisierende Bildung zu dt.* Pauschsumme› (geschätzte Summe; Gesamtbetrag); **pau|scha|lie|ren** (abrunden); **pau|scha|li|sie|ren** (stark verallgemeinern); **Pau|scha|li|tät,** die; - (Undifferenziertheit); **Pau|schal⌣preis, ...rei|se, ...sum|me, ...tou|ris|mus, ...ur|teil, ...ver|si|che|rung; Pausch|be|trag; Pau|sche,** die; -, -n (Wulst am Sattel; Handgriff am Seitpferd); **Päu|schel** *vgl.* Bäuschel; **Pau|schen|pferd** (*bes. schweiz. für* Seitpferd); **Pausch⌣quan|tum, ...sum|me**

[1]**Pau|se,** die; -, -n ‹griech.› (Ruhezeit; Unterbrechung); die große - (in der Schule, im Theater)

[2]**Pau|se,** die; -, -n ‹franz.› (Kopie mittels Durchzeichnung); **pau|sen** (durchzeichnen); du paust; er paus|te

Pau|sen⌣brot (bes. für Schüler), **...fül|ler** *(ugs.)*, **...gym|nas|tik, ...hal|le; pau|sen|los; Pau|sen⌣pfiff** *(Sport)*, **...raum, ...stand** *(Sport)*, **...tee** *(Sport)*, **...zei|chen; pau|sie|ren** ‹griech.› (innehalten, ruhen, zeitweilig aufhören)

Paus⌣pa|pier, ...zeich|nung

Pa|va|ne, die; -, -n ‹franz.› (langsamer Schreittanz; *später* Einleitungssatz der Suite)

Pa|via [pa'vi:a] (ital. Stadt)

Pa|vi|an [...v...], der; -s, -e ‹niederl.› (ein Affe)

Pa|vil|lon ['paviljɔ̃:, *österr.* 'pavijɔ̃:], der; -s, -s ‹franz.› (kleiner, frei stehender, meist runder Bau; Ausstellungsgebäude; Festzelt; *Archit.* vorspringender Gebäudeteil); **Pa|vil|lon|sys|tem** *(Archit.)*

Paw|lat|sche, die; -, -n ‹tschech.› (*österr. für* Bretterbühne; baufälliges Haus); **Paw|lat|schen|the|a|ter** *(österr.)*

Paw|low (russ. Physiologe); **paw|lowsch;** die pawlowschen Hunde (↑R 94)

Pax, die; - ‹lat., „Frieden"› (*kath. Kirche* Friedensgruß, -kuss); **Pax vo|bis|cum!** [- v...] ‹„Friede [sei] mit euch!"›

Pay|ing|guest ['pe:iŋ'gɛst], (↑R 33), der; -, -s ‹engl.› (jmd., der bei einer Familie als Gast wohnt, aber für Unterkunft u. Verpflegung bezahlt); **Pay-TV** ['pe:tivi:] (nur gegen Gebühr zu empfangendes Privatfernsehen)

Pa|zi|fik [*auch* 'pa:...], der; -s ‹lat.-engl.› (Großer od. Pazifischer Ozean); **Pa|zi|fik|bahn,** die; -; **pa|zi|fisch;** pazifische Inseln, *aber* (↑R 102): der Pazifische Ozean; **Pa|zi|fis|mus,** der; - ‹lat.› (Ablehnung des Krieges aus religiösen od. ethischen Gründen); **Pa|zi|fist,** der; -en, -en (↑R 126); **Pa|zi|fis|tin; pa|zi|fis|tisch; pa|zi|fi|zie|ren** (*veraltend für* beruhigen; befrieden); **Pa|zi|fi|zie|rung**

Pb = Plumbum (*chem. Zeichen für* Blei)

P. b. b. = Postgebühr bar bezahlt (Österreich)

pc = Parsec

PC [pe:'tse:], der; -[s], -[s] (Personalcomputer)

p. c., %, v. H. = pro centum; *vgl.* Prozent

PCB = polychlorierte Biphenyle (bestimmte giftige, Krebs erregende chemische Verbindungen)

p. Chr. [n.] = post Christum [natum]

Pd = *chem. Zeichen für* [2]Palladium

PdA = Partei der Arbeit (kommunistische Partei in der Schweiz)

PDS = Partei des Demokratischen Sozialismus

Pea|nuts ['pi:nats] *Plur.* ‹engl., „Erdnüsse"› (*ugs. für* Kleinigkeiten; unbedeutende Geldsumme)

Pearl Har|bor ['pœ:(r)l 'ha:(r)bə(r)] (amerik. Flottenstützpunkt im Pazifik)

Pech, das; *Gen.* -s, *seltener* -es, *Plur. (Arten:)* -e; **Pech⌣blen|de** (ein Mineral), **...draht, ...fa|ckel; pech|fins|ter** *(ugs.)*; **pe|chig; Pech⌣koh|le, ...nel|ke; pech|ra|ben|schwarz** *(ugs.)*; **pech|schwarz** *(ugs.)*; **Pech⌣sträh|ne** *(ugs.)*, **...vo|gel** (*ugs. für* Mensch, der [häufig] Unglück hat)

Pe|dal, das; -s, -e ‹lat.› (Fußhebel; Teil an der Fahrradtretkurbel); **Pe|dal|weg** *(Kfz-Technik)*

pe|dant (*österr. für* pedantisch); **Pe|dant,** der; -en, -en (↑R 126) ‹griech.› (ein in übertriebener Weise genauer, kleinlicher Mensch); **Pe|dan|te|rie,** die; -, ...ien; **Pe|dan|tin; pe|dan|tisch**

Ped|dig|rohr, das; -[e]s (Markrohr der Rotangpalme zum Flechten von Korbwaren)

Pe|dell, der; -s, -e, *österr. meist* der; -en, -en (*veraltend für* Hausmeister einer [Hoch]schule)

Pe|dig|ree ['pɛdigri] (↑R 130), der; -s, -s ‹engl.› (Stammbaum bei Tieren u. Pflanzen)

Pe|di|kü|re, die; -, -n ‹franz.› (*nur Sing.:* Fußpflege; Fußpflegerin); **pe|di|kü|ren;** er hat pedikürt; **Pe|di|ment,** das; -s, -e ‹lat.› (*Geogr.* terrassenartige Fläche am Fuß eines Gebirges); **Pe|do|graph,** der; -en, -en (↑R 126) ‹lat.› (Wegmesser); **Pe|do|me|ter,** das; -s, - (Schrittzähler)

Ped|ro (↑R 130; m. Vorn.)

Pee|ling ['pi:...], das; -s, -s ‹engl.› (kosmetische Schälung der [Gesichts]haut)

Pee|ne, die; - (Fluss in Mecklenburg-Vorpommern)

Peep|show ['pi:pʃo:], die; -, -s ‹engl.› (Möglichkeit, gegen Geldeinwurf durch ein Guckloch eine unbekleidete Frau zu betrachten)

[1]**Peer,** Per (m. Vorn.); *vgl.* Peer Gynt

[2]**Peer** [pi:(r)], der; -s, -s ‹engl.› (Mitglied des höchsten engl. Adels; Mitglied des engl. Oberhauses); *vgl.* Pair; **Pee|rage** ['pi:ridʒ], die; - (Würde eines Peers; Gesamtheit der Peers); **Pee|ress** ['pi:rɛs], die; -, -es [...rɛsis] (Gattin eines Peers)

Peer Gynt (norweg. Sagengestalt)

Peers|wür|de ['pi:(r)s...], die; -

Pe|ga|sos ‹griech.›; *vgl.* Pegasus; [1]**Pe|ga|sus,** der; - (geflügeltes Ross der griech. Sage; Dichterross); [2]**Pe|ga|sus,** der; - (ein Sternbild)

Pe|gel, der; -s, - (Wasserstandsmesser); **Pe|gel⌣hö|he, ...stand**

Peg|ma|tit [*auch* ...'tit], der; -s, -e ‹griech.› (ein grobkörniges Gestein)

[1]**Peg|nitz,** die; - (r. Nebenfluss der

Rednitz [Regnitz]); ²**Peg|nitz** (Stadt an der Pegnitz); **Peg|nitzor|den,** der; -s (↑R 105)
Peh|le|wi ['pɛç...], das; -s (Mittelpersisch)
Pei|es *Plur.* ‹hebr.› (Schläfenlocken [der orthodoxen Ostjuden])
pei|len (Richtung, Entfernung, Wassertiefe bestimmen); **Pei|ler** (Einrichtung zum Peilen; jmd., der peilt); **Peil˯fre|quenz, ...linie, ...rah|men** *(Funkwesen);* **Peilung**
Pein, die; - (Schmerz, Qual); **peini|gen; Pei|ni|ger; Pei|ni|ge|rin; Pei|ni|gung; pein|lich;** *Rechtsspr. veraltet:* peinliches Recht (Strafrecht), peinliche Gerichtsordnung (Strafprozessordnung); **Peinlich|keit; pein|sam; pein|voll**
Pei|sis|tra|tos (↑R 130; athen. Tyrann)
Peit|sche, die; -, -n; **peit|schen;** du peitschst; **Peit|schen˯hieb, ...knall, ...leuch|te** (Straßenlaterne mit gebogenem Mast), **...schlag, ...stiel, ...wurm** (ein Fadenwurm)
pe|jo|ra|tiv (*Sprachw.* verschlechternd, abwertend); **Pe|jo|ra|tivum** [...vum], das; -s, ...va (Wort mit abwertendem Sinn)
Pe|ka|ri, das; -s, -s ‹karib.-franz.› (amerik. Wildschwein)
Pe|ke|sche, die; -, -n ‹poln.› (Schnürrock; student. Festjacke)
Pe|ki|ne|se, der; -n, -n (↑R 126) ‹nach der chin. Hptst. Peking› (Hunderasse); **Pe|king** (Hptst. Chinas); **Pe|king˯mensch** *(Anthropol.),* **...oper** (↑R 132)
Pek|ten|mu|schel ‹lat.; dt.› (*Zool.* Kammmuschel)
Pek|tin, das; -s, -e *meist Plur.* ‹griech.› (gelierender Pflanzenstoff in Früchten, Wurzeln u. a.)
pek|to|ral ‹lat.› (*Med.* die Brust betreffend; Brust...); **Pek|to|ra|le,** das; -[s], *Plur.* -s *u.* ...lien [...i̯ən] (Brustkreuz kath. geistl. Würdenträger; ein mittelalterl. Brustschmuck)
pe|ku|ni|är ‹lat.-franz.› (geldlich; in Geld bestehend; Geld...)
pek|zie|ren ‹lat.› (*landsch. für* etwas anstellen); *vgl.* pexieren
Pe|la|gi|al, das; -s ‹griech.› (*Ökologie* das freie Wasser der Meere u. Binnengewässer)
Pe|la|gi|a|ner (Anhänger der Lehre des Pelagius); **Pe|la|gi|a|nismus,** der; -
pe|la|gisch ‹griech.› (*Biol.* im freien Wasser lebend), *aber* (↑R 102): Pelagische Inseln (Inselgruppe südl. von Sizilien)
Pe|la|gi|us (engl. Mönch)
Pe|lar|go|nie [...i̯ə], die; -, -n ‹griech.› (eine Zierpflanze)
Pe|las|ger *meist Plur.* (Angehöriger einer Urbevölkerung Griechenlands); **pe|las|gisch**
pêle-mêle [pɛ(:)l'mɛ(:)l] ‹franz.› (*selten für* durcheinander); **Pelemele** [pɛl'mɛl], das; - (Mischmasch; eine Süßspeise)
Pe|le|ri|ne, die; -, -n ‹franz.› ([ärmelloser] Umhang; *veraltend für* Regenmantel)
Pe|leus ['pe:lɔys] (Vater des Achill); **Pe|li|de,** der; -n; ↑R 126 (Beiname des Achill)
Pe|li|kan [*auch* ...'ka:n], der; -s, -e ‹griech.› (ein Vogel)
Pe|li|on, der; -s (Gebirge in Thessalien)
Pel|lag|ra (↑R 130), das; -[s] ‹griech.› (*Med.* Krankheit durch Mangel an Vitamin B_2); **Pel|le,** die; -, -n ‹lat.› (*landsch. für* Haut, Schale); jmdm. auf die Pelle rücken (*ugs. für* energisch zusetzen); jmdm. auf der Pelle sitzen (*ugs. für* lästig sein); **pel|len** (*landsch. für* schälen)
Pel|let, das; -s, -s *meist Plur.* ‹engl.› (Kügelchen, kleiner Zylinder o. Ä., bes. aus gepresstem Tierfutter); **pel|le|tie|ren**
Pell|kar|tof|fel
Pe|lo|pon|nes, der; -[es], *fachspr. auch* die; - (südgriech. Halbinsel); **pe|lo|pon|ne|sisch,** *aber* (↑R 108): der Peloponnesische Krieg;
Pe|lops (Sohn des Tantalus)
Pe|lo|ta, die; - ‹span.› (ein baskisches Ballspiel)
Pe|lo|ton [...'tõ:], das; -s, -s ‹franz.› (*früher für* kleine milit. Einheit; *Radsport* geschlossenes Fahrerfeld bei Straßenrennen); **Pe|lotte,** die; -, -n (*Med.* ballenförmiges Druckpolster)
Pel|sei|de, die; - ‹ital.; dt.› (geringwertiges Rohseidengarn)
Pel|tast, der; -en, -en (↑R 126) ‹griech.› (altgriech. Leichtbewaffneter)
Pe|lusch|ke, die; -, -n ‹slaw.› (*landsch. für* Ackererbse)
Pelz, der; -es, -e; jmdm. auf den - rücken (*ugs. für* jmdn. drängen); **Pelz|be|satz; pelz|be|setzt;** ¹**pel|zen** (*fachspr. für* den Pelz abziehen; *ugs. für* faulenzen); du pelzt
²**pel|zen** (*landsch. für* pfropfen); du pelzt
pelz|ge|füt|tert; pel|zig; Pelz˯kap|pe, ...kra|gen, ...man|tel; Pelz|mär|te, der; -s, -n *u.* **Pelzmär|tel,** der; -s, - ‹nach dem hl. Martin› (*südd. für* Knecht Ruprecht); **Pelz˯müt|ze, ...ni|ckel** (*vgl.* Belznickel), **...sto|la, ...tier; Pelz|tier|farm; pelz|ver|brämt; Pelz˯ver|brä|mung, ...wa|re, ...werk** (das; -[e]s)
Pem|mi|kan, der; -s ‹indian.› (haltbarer Dauerproviant nordamerik. Indianer aus getrocknetem Fleisch u. Fett)
Pem|phi|gus, der; - ‹griech.› (*Med.* eine Hautkrankheit)
PEN, P.E.N. [pɛn], der; -[s] ‹engl.; *Kurzw. aus* poets, essayists, novelists› (internationale Schriftstellervereinigung)
Pe|nal|ty ['pɛnəlti, *schweiz. meist* pɛ'nalti], der; -[s], -s ‹engl.› (*Sport, bes. Eishockey* Strafstoß)
Pe|na|ten *Plur.* ‹lat.› (röm. Hausgötter; *übertr. für* häuslicher Herd, Wohnung, Heim)
Pence [pɛns] (*Plur. von* Penny)
PEN-Club, P.E.N.-Club
Pen|dant [pã'dã:], das; -s, -s ‹franz.› ([ergänzendes] Gegenstück; *veraltet für* Ohrgehänge)
Pen|del, das; -s, - ‹lat.› (um eine Achse od. einen Punkt frei schwingender Körper); **Pen|del˯ach|se** *(Kfz-Technik),* **...lam|pe; pen|deln** (schwingen; zwischen Wohnort und Arbeitsplatz hin- und herfahren); ich ...[e]le (↑R 16); **Pen|del˯sä|ge, ...schwin|gung, ...tür, ...uhr, ...ver|kehr** (der; -s); **pen|dent** ‹ital.› (*schweiz. für* schwebend, unerledigt); **Pen|den|tif** [pãdã'ti:f], das; -s, -s (*Archit.* Zwickel); **Pen|denz** [pɛn...], die; -, -en ‹ital.› (*schweiz. für* schwebendes Geschäft, unerledigte Aufgabe)
Pen|de|rec|ki [...'rɛtski], Krzysztof ['kʃiʃtɔf] (poln. Komponist)
Pend|ler; Pend|le|rin; Pend|lerver|kehr, der; -s; **Pen|du|le** [pã'dylə], **Pen|dü|le** [pɛn...], die; -, -n ‹franz.› (Pendel-, Stutzuhr)
Pe|ne|lo|pe [...pe:] (Frau des Odysseus)
Pe|ne|plain ['piniple:n], die; -, -s ‹engl.› (*svw.* Fastebene)
Pe|nes (*Plur. von* Penis)
pe|net|rant (↑R 130) ‹franz.› (durchdringend; aufdringlich); **Pe|net|ranz,** die; -, -en (Aufdringlichkeit; *Genetik* Häufigkeit, mit der ein Erbfaktor wirksam wird); **Pe|net|ra|ti|on,** die; -, -en ‹lat.› (Durchdringung; das Eindringen); **pe|net|rie|ren**
peng!; peng, peng!
Pen|hol|der|griff [...ho:l...] ‹engl.; dt.› (*Tischtennis* Schlägerhaltung, bei der der Griff zwischen Daumen u. Zeigefinger nach oben zeigt)
pe|ni|bel ‹franz.› (sehr genau, fast

kleinlich; *landsch. für* peinlich); ...ib|le (↑R 130) Lage; **Pe|ni|bi|li|tät,** die; - (Genauigkeit)
Pe|ni|cil|lin *vgl.* Penizillin
Pen|in|su|la, die; -, ...suln ‹lat.› (*veraltet für* Halbinsel)
Pe|nis, der; -, *Plur.* -se *u.* Penes [ˈpeːneːs] ‹lat.› (männl. Glied); **Pe|nis|neid** *(Psych.)*
Pe|ni|zil|lin, *fachspr. u. österr.* Pe|ni|cil|lin, das; -s, -e ‹lat.› (ein Antibiotikum); **Pe|ni|zil|lin‿am|pul|le, ...sprit|ze**
Pen|nal, das; -s, -e ‹lat.› (*österr., sonst veraltet für* Federbüchse; *Schülerspr. früher für* höhere Lehranstalt); **Pen|nä|ler,** der; -s, - (*ugs. für* Schüler einer höheren Lehranstalt); **pen|nä|ler|haft**
Penn|bru|der (*svw.* Penner); [1]**Pen|ne,** die; -, -n ‹jidd.› (*ugs. für* behelfsmäßiges Nachtquartier)
[2]**Pen|ne,** die; -, -n ‹lat.› (*Schülerspr.* Schule)
pen|nen (*ugs. für* schlafen); **Pen|ner** (*ugs. für* Stadt-, Landstreicher; *auch* Schimpfwort)
Pen|ni, der; -[s], -[s] (finn. Münze; *Abk.* p; 100 Penni = 1 Markka)
Penn|syl|va|nia [...silˈveːni̯ə], *eingedeutscht* **Penn|syl|va|ni|en** [...zilˈvaːni̯ən] (Staat in den USA; *Abk.* Pa.); **penn|syl|va|nisch**
Pen|ny [ˈpɛni], der; -s, *Plur.* (*für einige Stücke:*) Pennys *u.* (*bei* Wertangabe:) Pence [pɛns] ‹engl.› (engl. Münze; *Abk.* p, *früher* d [= denarius])
Pen|sa (*Plur. von* Pensum)
pen|see [pãˈseː] ‹franz.› (dunkellila); ein pensee Kleid; *vgl.* blau *u.* beige; **Pen|see,** das; -s, -s (*franz. Bez. für* Gartenstiefmütterchen); **pen|see|far|big; Pen|see|kleid**
Pen|sen (*Plur. von* Pensum); **Pen|si|on** [paŋˈzi̯oːn, *auch* pã..., *südd., österr. nur, schweiz. auch* pɛn...], die; -, -en ‹franz.› (Ruhestand *[nur Sing.];* Ruhe-, Witwengehalt; kleineres Hotel, Fremdenheim); **Pen|si|o|när,** der; -s, -e (Ruheständler; *bes. schweiz. für* Kostgänger, [Dauer]gast einer Pension); **Pen|si|o|nä|rin; Pen|si|o|nat,** das; -[e]s, -e (Internat, bes. für Mädchen); **pen|si|o|nie|ren** (in den Ruhestand versetzen); **Pen|si|o|nie|rung; Pen|si|o|nist** [pɛn...], der; -en, -en; ↑R 126 (*österr., schweiz. für* Ruheständler); **Pen|si|ons‿al|ter** [paŋˈzi̯oːns..., *auch* pã...; *südd., österr. nur, schweiz. auch* pɛn...], **...an|spruch; pen|si|ons|be|rech|tigt; Pen|si|ons|gast; Pen|si|ons|ge|schäft** (*Bankw.* Verkauf von Wechseln od. Effekten mit einer Rückkaufverpflichtung); **Pen|si|ons|kas|se** (betrieblicher Fonds für die Altersversorgung der Beschäftigten); **Pen|si|ons|preis; pen|si|ons|reif** *(ugs.);* **Pen|si|ons|rück|stel|lun|gen** *Plur. (Wirtsch.);* **Pen|sum,** das; -s, *Plur.* ...sen *u.* ...sa ‹lat.› (zugeteilte Arbeit; Lehrstoff)
pent..., pen|ta... ‹griech.› (fünf...); **Pent..., Pen|ta...** (Fünf...); **Pen|ta|de,** die; -, -n (Zeitraum von fünf Tagen); **Pen|ta|e|der,** das; -s, - (Fünfflach); [1]**Pen|ta|gon,** das; -s, -e (Fünfeck); [2]**Pen|ta|gon,** das; -s (das auf einem fünfeckigen Grundriss errichtete amerik. Verteidigungsministerium); **Pen|ta|gon|do|de|ka|e|der** [...goːn...] (von zwölf Fünfecken begrenzter Körper); **Pen|ta|gramm,** das; -s, -e, **Pent|al|pha,** das; -, -s (fünfeckiger Stern; Drudenfuß); **Pen|ta|me|ron** (↑R 132), das; -s (neapolitan. Volksmärchensammlung); **Pen|ta|me|ter,** der; -s, - (ein fünffüßiger Vers); **Pen|tan,** das; -s, -e (ein Kohlenwasserstoff); **Pen|tar|chie** (↑R 132), die; -, ...ien (Herrschaft von fünf Mächten); **Pen|ta|teuch,** der; -s (die fünf Bücher Mose im A.T.); **Pen|tath|lon** [*auch* ...ˈaːtlɔn] (↑R 132), das; -s (antiker Fünfkampf); **Pen|ta|to|nik,** die; - (Fünftonmusik); **Pen|te|kos|te,** die; - ‹griech.› (50. Tag nach Ostern; Pfingsten)
Pen|te|li|kon, der; -s (Gebirge in Attika); **pen|te|lisch;** -er Marmor
Pen|te|re, die; -, -n ‹griech., „Fünfruderer"› (antikes Kriegsschiff)
Pent|haus, das; -es, ...häuser (*eingedeutscht für* Penthouse)
Pen|the|si|lea, Pen|the|si|leia ‹griech.› (eine Amazonenkönigin in der griech. Sage)
Pent|house [ˈpɛnthaus], das; -, -s [...ziz] ‹amerik.› (exklusive Dachterrassenwohnung über einem Etagenhaus)
Pen|to|de (↑R 132), die; -, -n ‹griech.› (Elektronenröhre mit 5 Elektroden)
Pe|nun|ze, die; -, -n *meist Plur.* ‹poln.› (*ugs. für* Geld)
pen|zen (*österr. ugs. für* betteln, bitten; ständig ermahnen)
Pep, der; -[s] ‹amerik.; *von* pepper = Pfeffer› (Schwung, Elan); **Pe|pe|ro|ne,** der; -, ...oni, *häufiger* **Pe|pe|ro|ni,** die; -, - *meist Plur.* ‹ital.› (scharfe, kleine [in Essig eingemachte] Paprikaschote)
Pe|pi|ta, der *od.* das; -s, -s ‹span.› (kariertes Gewebe); **Pe|pi|ta‿kleid, ...kos|tüm**
Pep|lon (↑R 130), das; -s, *Plur.* ...len *u.* -s ‹griech.› *u.* **Pep|los,** der; -, *Plur.* ...len *u.* - (altgriech. Umschlagtuch der Frauen)
Pep|mit|tel (*ugs. für* Aufputschmittel); **pep|pig** (mit Pep); **Pep|pil|le** *(ugs.)*
Pep|ping (dt. Komponist u. Musikschriftsteller)
Pep|po (m. Vorn.)
Pep|sin, das; -s, -e ‹griech.› (Enzym des Magensaftes; ein Arzneimittel); **Pep|sin|wein; Pep|ti|sa|ti|on,** die; - *(Chemie);* **pep|tisch** (verdauungsfördernd); **pep|ti|sie|ren** (in kolloide Lösung überführen); **Pep|ton,** das; -s, -e (Abbaustoff des Eiweißes); **Pep|ton|u|rie,** die; - (*Med.* Ausscheidung von Peptonen im Harn)
per ‹lat.› *Präp. mit Akk.* (durch, mit, gegen, für); *häufig in der Amts- u. Kaufmannsspr.,* z. B. per Adresse ([*Abk.* p. A.], *besser:* bei); per Monat (*besser:* jeden Monat, im Monat, monatlich); per Stück (*besser:* das, je *od.* pro Stück); per ersten Januar (*besser:* für ersten Januar, zum ersten Januar); per eingeschriebenen (*besser:* als eingeschriebenen) Brief
[1]**Per,** Peer (m. Vorn.)
[2]**Per,** das; -s (*kurz für* bes. bei der chem. Reinigung verwendetes Perchloräthylen)
per as|pe|ra ad as|tra (↑R 130) ‹lat., „auf rauen Wegen zu den Sternen"›
Per|bo|rat, das; -[e]s, -e *meist Plur.* ‹lat.; pers.› (chem. Verbindung aus Wasserstoffperoxid u. Boraten); **Per|bor|säu|re,** die; -
per cas|sa ‹ital.› ([gegen] bar, bei Barzahlung); *vgl.* Kassa
Perche|akt [ˈpɛrʃ...] (↑R 24), der; -[e]s, -e ‹franz.› (artistische Darbietung an einer langen, elastischen [Bambus]stange)
Per|chlor|äthy|len (↑R 132; *Chemie* ein Lösungsmittel bes. für Fette u. Öle); *vgl.* Äthylen *u.* [2]Per
Percht, die; -, -en (myth. Gestalt); **Perch|ten‿lauf** (Umzug u. Tänze in Perchtenmasken [zur Fastnachtszeit]), **...mas|ke**
per con|to ‹ital.› (*Kaufmannsspr.* auf Rechnung)
Per|cus|sion [pœː(r)ˈkaʃ(ə)n], die; -, -s *meist Plur.* ‹engl.› (*Musik* Gruppe von Schlaginstrumenten); *vgl. auch* Perkussion
per de|fi|ni|ti|o|nem ‹lat.› (erklärtermaßen)
per|du [pɛrˈdyː] ‹franz.› (*ugs. für* verloren, weg, auf und davon)

Pe|rem[p]|ti|on (↑R 132), die; -, -en ‹lat.› (*veraltet für* Verjährung); **pe|rem[p]|to|risch** (aufhebend; endgültig)

pe|ren|nie|rend (↑R 132) ‹lat.› (*Bot.* ausdauernd; mehrjährig [von Stauden- u. Holzgewächsen])

Pe|rest|roi|ka [...ˈstrɔyka] (↑R 130 *u.* 132), die; - ‹russ., „Umbau"› (Umbildung, Neugestaltung [ursprünglich des sowjetischen politischen u. wirtschaftlichen Systems])

per|fekt ‹lat.› (vollendet, vollkommen [ausgebildet]; abgemacht; gültig); **Per|fekt** [*auch* ...ˈfɛkt], das; -[e]s, -e *Plur. selten* (*Sprachw.* Vollendung in der Gegenwart, Vorgegenwart); **per|fek|ti|bel** (vervollkommnungsfähig); ...tible (↑R 130) Dinge; **Per|fek|ti|bi|lis|mus,** der; - (*Philos.* Lehre von der Vervollkommnung [des Menschengeschlechtes]); **Per|fek|ti|bi|list,** der; -en, -en (↑R 126); **Per|fek|ti|bi|li|tät,** die; - (Vervollkommnungsfähigkeit); **Per|fek|ti|on,** die; - (Vollendung, Vollkommenheit); **per|fek|ti|o|nie|ren;** **Per|fek|ti|o|nis|mus,** der; - (übertriebenes Streben nach Vervollkommnung); **Per|fek|ti|o|nist,** der; -en, -en (↑R 126); **Per|fek|ti|o|nis|tin;** **per|fek|ti|o|nis|tisch** (in übertriebener Weise Perfektion anstrebend; bis in alle Einzelheiten vollständig, umfassend); **per|fek|tisch** (das Perfekt betreffend); **per|fek|tiv;** *in der Fügung* perfektive Aktionsart (*Sprachw.* Aktionsart eines Verbs, die eine zeitl. Begrenzung des Geschehens ausdrückt, z. B. „verblühen"); **per|fek|ti|visch** [...viʃ] (perfektisch; *veraltet für* perfektiv)

per|fid, *österr. nur so, od.* **per|fi|de** ‹lat.-franz.› (niederträchtig, gemein); **Per|fi|die,** die; -, ...ien (Niedertracht, Gemeinheit); **Per|fi|di|tät,** die; -, -en (*selten für* Perfidie)

Per|fo|ra|ti|on, die; -, -en ‹lat.› (Durchbohrung; Lochung; Reiß-, Trennlinie; Zähnung [bei Briefmarken]); **Per|fo|ra|tor,** der; -s, ...oren (Gerät zum Perforieren); **per|fo|rie|ren;** **Per|fo|rier|ma|schi|ne**

Per|for|mance [pœ(r)ˈfɔ:(r)məns], die; -, -s [...siz] ‹engl., „Vorführung"› (einem Happening ähnliche künstlerische Aktion); **Per|for|manz,** die; - ‹lat.› (*Sprachw.* Sprachverwendung in einer bestimmten Situation); **per|for|ma|tiv, per|for|ma|to|risch** (eine mit einer Äußerung beschriebene Handlung zugleich vollziehend, z. B. „ich gratuliere dir")

per|ga|me|nisch (aus Pergamon); **Per|ga|ment,** das; -[e]s, -e ‹griech.› (bearbeitete Tierhaut; alte Handschrift [auf Tierhaut]); **Per|ga|ment|band** *Plur.* ...bände; **per|ga|men|ten** (aus Pergament); **Per|ga|ment|pa|pier;** **Per|ga|min,** das; -s (durchscheinendes, pergamentartiges Papier); **Per|ga|mon** (antike Stadt in Nordwestkleinasien); **Per|ga|mon‿al|tar, ...mu|se|um,** (das; -s; ↑R 105)

Per|gel, das; -s, - ‹ital.› (*südd. für* Weinlaube); **Per|go|la,** die; -, ...len (Weinlaube; berankter Laubengang)

per|hor|res|zie|ren ‹lat.› (verabscheuen, zurückschrecken)

Pe|ri, der; -s, -s *od.* die; -, -s *meist Plur.* ‹pers.› (feenhaftes Wesen der altpers. Sage)

pe|ri... ‹griech.› (um..., herum...); **Pe|ri...** (Um..., Herum...)

Pe|ri|arth|ri|tis (↑R 130), die; -, ...itiden ‹griech.› (*Med.* Entzündung in der Umgebung von Gelenken)

Pe|ri|car|di|um *vgl.* Perikard

Pe|ri|chond|ri|tis [...çɔn...], (↑R 130), die; -, ...itiden ‹griech.› (*Med.* Knorpelhautentzündung); **Pe|ri|chond|ri|um,** das; -s, ...ien [...iən] (*Med.* Knorpelhaut)

pe|ri|cu|lum in mo|ra ‹lat.› (Gefahr besteht, wenn man zögert)

Pe|ri|derm, das; -s, -e ‹griech.› (*Bot.* ein Pflanzengewebe)

Pe|ri|dot, der; -s ‹franz.› (ein Mineral); **Pe|ri|do|tit** [*auch* ...ˈtit], der; -s, -e (ein Tiefengestein)

Pe|ri|gast|ri|tis (↑R 130), die; -, ...itiden ‹griech.› (*Med.* Entzündung des Bauchfellüberzuges des Magens)

Pe|ri|gä|um, das; -s, ...äen ‹griech.› (*Astron.* der Punkt der größten Erdnähe des Mondes od. eines Satelliten; *Ggs.* Apogäum); **Pe|ri|gon,** das; -s, -e *u.* **Pe|ri|go|ni|um,** das; -s, ...ien [...iən] (*Bot.* Blütenhülle aus gleichartigen Blättern); **Pe|ri|hel,** das; -s, -e (*Astron.* der Punkt einer Planeten- od. Kometenbahn, der der Sonne am nächsten liegt; *Ggs.* Aphel); **Pe|ri|he|pa|ti|tis,** die; -, ...itiden (*Med.* Entzündung des Bauchfellüberzuges der Leber); **Pe|ri|kard,** das; -s, -e *u.* Pe|ri|kar|di|um, *med. fachspr.* Pe|ri|car|di|um, das; -s, ...ien [...iən] (*Med.* Herzbeutel); **Pe|ri|kar|di|tis,** die; -, ...itiden (*Med.* Herzbeutelentzündung); **Pe|ri|kar|di|um** *vgl.* Perikard; **Pe|ri|karp,** das; -s, -e (*Bot.* [äußere] Hülle der Früchte von Samenpflanzen); **Pe|ri|klas,** der; *Gen.* - *u.* -es, *Plur.* -e (ein Mineral)

pe|rik|le|isch (↑R 130); perikleischer Geist, perikleische Verwaltung (↑R 94); **Pe|rik|les** (athen. Staatsmann)

Pe|ri|ko|pe, die; -, -n ‹griech.› (zu gottesdienstl. Verlesung vorgeschriebener Bibelabschnitt; *Verslehre* Strophengruppe)

Pe|ri|me|ter [*schweiz.* ˈpɛri...], das, *schweiz.* der; -s, - (*Med.* Vorrichtung zur Messung des Gesichtsfeldes; *schweiz. für* Umfang eines [Planungs]gebietes); **pe|ri|met|rie|ren** (↑R 130); **pe|ri|met|risch**

pe|ri|na|tal (*Med.* die Zeit während, kurz vor u. nach der Geburt betreffend); perinatale Medizin

Pe|ri|o|de, die; -, -n ‹griech.› (Umlauf[szeit] eines Gestirns, Kreislauf; Zeit[abschnitt, -raum]; Menstruation; [kunstvolles] Satzgefüge; Schwingungsdauer; unendlicher Dezimalbruch); **Pe|ri|o|den‿er|folg** *(Wirtsch.),* **...rech|nung** *(Wirtsch.),* **...sys|tem** *(Chemie),* **...zahl** *(Elektrotechnik);* **...pe|ri|o|dig** (z. B. zweiperiodig); **Pe|ri|o|dik,** die; - (*svw.* Periodizität); **Pe|ri|o|di|kum,** das; -s, ...ka *meist Plur.* (periodisch erscheinende [Zeit]schrift); **pe|ri|o|disch** (regelmäßig auftretend, wiederkehrend); periodischer Dezimalbruch; periodisches System *(Chemie);* **pe|ri|o|di|sie|ren** (in Zeitabschnitte einteilen); **Pe|ri|o|di|sie|rung;** **Pe|ri|o|di|zi|tät,** die; - (regelmäßige Wiederkehr)

Pe|ri|o|don|ti|tis, die; -, ...itiden ‹griech.› (*Med.* Entzündung der Zahnwurzelhaut); **Pe|ri|ö|ke,** der; -n, -n; ↑R 126 ‹„Umwohner"› (freier, aber polit. rechtloser Bewohner im alten Sparta); **pe|ri|o|ral** (↑R 132; *Med.* um den Mund herum); **Pe|ri|ost,** das; -[e]s, -e (*Med.* Knochenhaut); **Pe|ri|os|ti|tis,** die; -, ...itiden (*Med.* Knochenhautentzündung)

Pe|ri|pa|te|ti|ker ‹griech.› (Philosoph aus der Schule des Aristoteles); **pe|ri|pa|te|tisch;** **Pe|ri|pa|tos,** der; - (Wandelgang; Teil der Schule in Athen, wo Aristoteles lehrte); **Pe|ri|pe|tie,** die; -, ...ien (entscheidender Wendepunkt, Umschwung [in einem Drama]); **pe|ri|pher** (am Rande befindlich, Rand...); **Pe|ri|phe|rie,** die; -, ...ien ([Kreis]umfang; Umkreis;

Randgebiet [der Großstädte], Stadtrand); **pe|ri|phe|risch** (*veraltet für* peripher); **Pe|ri|phra|se,** die; -, -n (*Rhet.* Umschreibung); **pe|ri|phra|sie|ren; pe|ri|phras|tisch** (umschreibend); **Pe|rip|te|ros** (↑R 132), der; -, *Plur.* - *od.* ...teren (griechischer Tempel mit einem umlaufenden Säulengang)

Pe|ri|skop (↑R 132), das; -s, -e ‹griech.› (Fernrohr [für Unterseeboote] mit geknicktem Strahlengang); **pe|ri|sko|pisch**

Pe|ris|po|me|non (↑R 132), das; -s, ...na (*Sprachw.* auf der letzten, langen Silbe betontes Wort)

Pe|ris|tal|tik (↑R 132), die; - (*Med.* wellenförmig fortschreitendes Zusammenziehen, z. B. der Speiseröhre, des Darms); **pe|ris|tal|tisch**

Pe|ris|ta|se (↑R 132), die; -, -n (*Biol., Med.* die auf die Entwicklung des Organismus einwirkende Umwelt); **pe|ris|ta|tisch** (umweltbedingt); **Pe|ris|te|ri|um,** das; -s, ...ien [...iən] (mittelalterl. Hostiengefäß in Gestalt einer Taube); **Pe|ris|tyl,** das; -s, -e, **Pe|ris|ty|li|um,** das; -s, ...ien [...iən] (von Säulen umgebener Innenhof des antiken Hauses)

Pe|ri|to|ne|um, das; -s, ...neen (*Med.* Bauchfell); **Pe|ri|to|ni|tis,** die; -, ...itiden (*Med.* Bauchfellentzündung)

Per|kal, der; -s, -e ‹pers.› (ein Baumwollgewebe); **Per|ka|lin,** das; -s, -e (stark appretiertes Gewebe [für Bucheinbände])

Per|ko|lat, das; -[e]s, -e ‹lat.› (*Pharm.* durch Perkolation gewonnener Pflanzenextrakt); **Per|ko|la|ti|on,** die; -, -en (Herstellung konzentrierter Pflanzenextrakte); **Per|ko|la|tor,** der; -s, ...oren (Gerät zur Perkolation); **per|ko|lie|ren**

Per|kus|si|on, die; -, -en ‹lat.› (Zündung durch Stoß od. Schlag [beim Perkussionsgewehr des 19. Jh.s]; ärztl. Organuntersuchung durch Beklopfen der Körperoberfläche; Anschlagvorrichtung beim Harmonium); *vgl. auch* Percussion; **Per|kus|si|ons‿ge|wehr, ...ham|mer** (*Med.*), **...in|stru|ment** (Schlaginstrument), **...schloss, ...zün|dung; per|kus|so|risch** (*Med.* durch Perkussion nachweisbar)

per|ku|tan ‹lat.› (*Med.* durch die Haut hindurch)

per|ku|tie|ren ‹lat.› (*Med.* abklopfen); **per|ku|to|risch** (*svw.* perkussorisch)

Perl, die; - (*Druckw.* ein Schriftgrad); **Per|le,** die; -, -n; **¹per|len** (tropfen; Bläschen bilden); **²per|len** (aus Perlen [hergestellt]); **per|len‿be|setzt, ...be|stickt; Per|len‿fi|scher, ...fi|sche|rin, ...ket|te, ...kol|li|er, ...schnur** (*Plur.* ...schnüre); **Per|len‿sti|cke|rei, ...tau|cher, ...tau|che|rin; Perl|garn; perl|grau; Perl|huhn; per|lig; Per|lit** [*auch* ...'lit], der; -s, -e ‹lat.› (ein Gestein; Gefügebestandteil des Eisens); **Per|lit|guss** (Spezialgusseisen für hohe Beanspruchungen); **Perl|mu|schel; Perl|mutt** [*auch* ...'mut], das; -s ‹*verkürzt aus* „Perlmutter"›; **Perl|mut|ter** [*auch* ...'mutər], die; - *od.* das; -s (glänzende Innenschicht von Perlmuschel- u. Seeschneckenschalen); **Perl|mut|ter|fal|ter** (ein Schmetterling); **perl|mut|ter|far|ben; Perl|mut|ter|knopf** (*svw.* Perlmuttknopf); **perl|mut|tern** (aus Perlmutter); **Perl|mutt|knopf**

Per|lon ®, das; -s (eine synthet. Textilfaser); **Per|lon|strumpf; per|lon|ver|stärkt**

Perl‿schrift (die; -), **...stich**

Per|lus|tra|ti|on, die; -, -en ‹lat.›, Per|lust|rie|rung (↑R 130; *österr., sonst veraltet für* Durchmusterung, genaue Untersuchung [eines Verdächtigen]); **per|lust|rie|ren**

Perl|wein; perl|weiß; Perl|zwie|bel

¹Perm (Stadt in Russland); **²Perm,** das; -s (*Geol.* jüngster Teil des Paläozoikums)

per|ma|nent ‹lat.› (dauernd, ununterbrochen, ständig); **Per|ma|nent‿gelb** (das; -s; lichtechtes Gelb), **...weiß** (das; -[es]); **Per|ma|nenz,** die; - (Dauer[haftigkeit]); in - (dauernd, ständig); **Per|ma|nenz|the|o|rie,** die; - (*Geol.*)

Per|man|ga|nat, das; -s, -e ‹lat.; griech.› (chem. Verbindung, die als Oxidations- u. Desinfektionsmittel verwendet wird)

per|me|a|bel ‹lat.› (durchdringbar, durchlässig); ...ab|le (↑R 130) Körper; **Per|me|a|bi|li|tät,** die; -

per mil|le (*svw.* pro mille)

perm|isch ‹*zu*² Perm›

Per|mis|si|on, die; -, -en ‹lat.› (*veraltend für* Erlaubnis); **per|mis|siv** (*Soziol., Psych.* nachgiebig, frei gewähren lassend); **Per|mis|si|vi|tät,** die; -; **per|mit|tie|ren** (*veraltend für* erlauben, zulassen)

per|mu|ta|bel ‹lat.› (umstellbar, aus-, vertauschbar); ...tab|le (↑R 130) Größen; **Per|mu|ta|ti|on,** die; -, -en (Umstellung, Vertauschung; *Math.* Umstellung von Elementen einer geordneten Menge); **per|mu|tie|ren**

Per|nam|bu|co (*früherer Name von* Recife); **Per|nam|buk|holz,** Fer|nam|buk|holz

Per|nio, der; -, *Plur.* ...iones *u.* ...ionen ‹lat.› (*Med.* Frostbeule); **Per|ni|o|sis,** die; -, ...sen (Frostschaden der Haut)

per|ni|zi|ös ‹franz.› (bösartig, schlimm); perniziöse Anämie (*Med.*)

Per|nod ® [...'no:], der; -[s], -[s] ‹franz.› (ein alkohol. Getränk)

Pe|ro|nis|mus, der; - ‹nach dem ehem. argentinischen Staatspräsidenten Perón› (eine polit.-soziale Bewegung in Argentinien); **Pe|ro|nist,** der; -en, -en; ↑R 126 (Anhänger des Peronismus); **pe|ro|nis|tisch**

Pe|ro|nos|po|ra (↑R 132), die; - ‹griech.› (Gattung Pflanzen schädigender Algenpilze)

per|oral (↑R 132) ‹lat.› (*Med.* durch den Mund)

Per|oxid, *nichtfachspr. auch* Per|oxyd (↑R 132), das; -[e]s, -e ‹lat.; griech.› (sauerstoffreiche chem. Verbindung)

per pe|des [a|pos|to|lo|rum] ‹lat., „zu Fuß [wie die Apostel]"›

Per|pen|di|kel, der *od.* das; -s, - ‹lat.› (Uhrpendel; Senk-, Lotrechte); **per|pen|di|ku|lar, per|pen|di|ku|lär** (senk-, lotrecht)

Per|pe|tua (eine Heilige)

per|pe|tu|ie|ren ‹lat.› (ständig weitermachen; fortdauern); **Per|pe|tu|um mo|bi|le** [...tu|um ...le:], das; - -[s], *Plur.* - -[s] *u.* ...tua ...bilia (utopische Maschine, die ohne Energieverbrauch dauernd Arbeit leistet; *Musik* in kurzwertigen Noten verlaufendes virtuoses Instrumentalstück)

per|plex ‹lat.› (*ugs. für* verwirrt, verblüfft; bestürzt); **Per|ple|xi|tät,** die; - (Bestürzung, Verwirrung)

per pro|cu|ra ‹lat.› (*Kaufmannsspr.* in Vollmacht; *Abk.* pp., ppa.); *vgl.* Prokura

Per|ron [pɛ'rɔ̃:, *österr.* pɛ'ro:n, *schweiz.* 'pɛrɔ̃], der; -s, -s ‹franz.› (*veraltet, noch schweiz. für* Bahnsteig; *veraltet für* Plattform der Straßenbahn)

per sal|do ‹ital.› (*Kaufmannsspr.* als Rest zum Ausgleich [auf einem Konto])

per se ‹lat.› (von selbst); das versteht sich per se

Per|sen|ning, die; -, *Plur.* -e[n] *od.* -s ‹niederl.› (*nur Sing.:* Gewebe für Segel, Zelte u. a.; *See-*

mannsspr. Schutzbezug aus Persenning)
Per|se|pho|ne [...ne] (griech. Göttin der Unterwelt)
Per|se|po|lis (Hptst. Altpersiens); **Per|ser** (Bewohner von Persien; Perserteppich); **Per|se|rin; Per|ser-kat|ze, ...krieg, ...tep|pich**
[1]**Per|seus** [...zɔys] (Held der griech. Sage); [2]**Per|seus,** der; - (Sternbild)
Per|se|ve|ranz [...v...], die; - ‹lat.› (*veraltend für* Beharrlichkeit, Ausdauer); **Per|se|ve|ra|ti|on,** die; -, -en (*Psych.* [krankhaftes] Verweilen bei einem bestimmten Gedanken); **per|se|ve|rie|ren**
Per|shing [ˈpœ:(r)ʃiŋ], die; -, -s ‹nach dem amerik. General› (eine militär. Mittelstreckenrakete)
Per|si|a|ner (Karakulschafpelz [früher über Persien gehandelt]); **Per|si|a|ner|man|tel; Per|si|en** [...iən] (*ältere Bez. für* Iran)
Per|sif|la|ge [...ˈfla:ʒə] (↑R 130), die; -, -n ‹franz.› (Verspottung); **per|sif|lie|ren**
Per|si|ko, der; -s, -s ‹franz.› (aus Pfirsich- od. Bittermandelkernen bereiteter Likör)
Per|sil|schein ‹nach dem Waschmittel Persil ®› (*ugs. für* entlastende Bescheinigung)
Per|si|mo|ne, die; -, -n ‹indian.› (essbare Frucht einer nordamerik. Dattelpflaumenart)
Per|si|pan [*auch* ˈpɛr...], das; -s, -e ‹nach lat. persicus (Pfirsich) *u.* Marzipan gebildet› (Ersatz für Marzipan aus Pfirsich- od. Aprikosenkernen)
per|sisch; persischer Teppich, *aber* (↑R 102): der Persische Golf; **Per|sisch,** das; -[s] (Sprache); *vgl.* Deutsch; **Per|si|sche,** das; -n; *vgl.* Deutsche, das
per|sis|tent ‹lat.› (anhaltend, dauernd, beharrlich); **Per|sis|tenz,** die; -, -en
Per|son, die; -, -en ‹etrusk.-lat.› (Mensch; Wesen); *vgl.* in persona; **Per|so|na gra|ta,** die; - - (gern gesehener Mensch; Diplomat, gegen den vonseiten des Gastlandes kein Einwand erhoben wird); **Per|so|na in|gra|ta,** Per|so|na non gra|ta, die; - - (unerwünschte Person; Diplomat, dessen Aufenthalt vom Gastland nicht mehr gewünscht wird); **per|so|nal** (persönlich; Persönlichkeits...); im personalen Bereich; **Per|so|nal,** das; -s (Belegschaft, alle Angestellten [eines Betriebes]); **Per|so|nal-ab|bau** (der; -[e]s), **...ab|tei|lung, ...ak|te** (*meist Plur.*), **...aus|weis, ...bü|ro, ...com|pu|ter** (*Abk.* PC), **...de|cke** (Gesamtheit der zur Verfügung stehenden Personen in einem Betrieb o. Ä.), **...di|rek|tor, ...ein|spa|rung, ...form** (*vgl.* finite Form); **Per|so|na|li|en** *Plur.* (Angaben über Lebenslauf u. Verhältnisse eines Menschen); **per|so|nal|in|ten|siv;** -e Betriebe; **per|so|na|li|sie|ren** (auf eine Person beziehen od. ausrichten); **Per|so|na|li|tät,** die; -, -en (Persönlichkeit); **Per|so|na|li|täts|prin|zip,** das; -s (*Rechtsw.*); **per|so|na|li|ter** (*veraltet für* persönlich); **Per|so|na|li|ty|show** [pœ:(r)səˈnɛlitiʃo:], die; -, -s ‹amerik.› (Show, die von der Persönlichkeit eines Künstlers getragen wird [und bes. dessen Vielseitigkeit zeigen soll]); **Per|so|nal-kos|ten** (*Plur.*), **...lei|ter** (der), **...pla|nung, ...po|li|tik, ...pro|no|men** (*Sprachw.* persönliches Fürwort, z. B. „er, wir"), **...rat** (*Plur.* ...räte), **...re|fe|rent, ...uni|on** (↑R 132; Vereinigung mehrerer Ämter in einer Person; *früher* [durch Erbfolge bedingte] Vereinigung selbstständiger Staaten unter einem Monarchen); **Per|so|nal|ver|wal|tung; Per|so|na non gra|ta** *vgl.* Persona ingrata; **Per|sön|chen; per|so|nell** ‹franz.› (das Personal betreffend); **Per|so|nen-auf|zug, ...be|för|de|rung; Per|so|nen|be|för|de|rungs|ge|setz; Per|so|nen-be|schrei|bung, ...fir|ma** (Firma, deren Name aus einem od. mehreren Personennamen besteht; *Ggs.* Sachfirma); **per|so|nen|ge|bun|den; Per|so|nen-kraft|wa|gen** (*Abk.* Pkw, *auch* PKW), **...kreis, ...kult, ...na|me, ...scha|den** (*Ggs.* Sachschaden), **...schiff|fahrt, ...schutz, ...stand** (der; -[e]s; Familienstand); **Per|so|nen|stands|re|gis|ter; Per|so|nen-ver|kehr, ...ver|si|che|rung** (*Versicherungsw.*), **...waa|ge, ...wa|gen, ...zahl, ...zug; Per|so|ni|fi|ka|ti|on,** die; -, -en; **per|so|ni|fi|zie|ren; Per|so|ni|fi|zie|rung** (Verkörperung); **per|sön|lich** (in [eigener] Person; eigen[artig]; selbst); persönliches Fürwort (*für* Personalpronomen); **Per|sön|lich|keit; per|sön|lich|keits|be|wusst; Per|sön|lich|keits|ent|fal|tung; per|sön|lich|keits|fremd** (einer Person wesensfremd); **Per|sön|lich|keits-kult** (*selten für* Personenkult), **...recht, ...wahl, ...wert; Per|sons|be|schrei|bung** (*österr. für* Personenbeschreibung)
Per|spek|tiv, das; -s, -e [...və] ‹lat.› (kleines Fernrohr); **Per|spek|ti|ve** [...və], die; -, -n (Darstellung von Raumverhältnissen in der ebenen Fläche; Sicht, Blickwinkel; Aussicht [für die Zukunft]); **per|spek|ti|visch** (die Perspektive betreffend); perspektivische Verkürzung; **Per|spek|tiv|lo|sig|keit; Per|spek|tiv|pla|nung** (*Wirtsch.* langfristige Globalplanung)
Per|spi|ra|ti|on, die; - ‹lat.› (*Med.* Hautatmung); **per|spi|ra|to|risch**
Per|sua|si|on, die; -, -en ‹lat.› (Überredung[skunst]); **per|sua|siv** (der Überredung dienend)
[1]**Perth** [pœ:(r)θ] (schott. Grafschaft u. deren Hptst.)
[2]**Perth** [pœ:(r)θ] (Hptst. Westaustraliens)
Pe|ru (südamerik. Staat); **Pe|ru|a|ner; Pe|ru|a|ne|rin; pe|ru|a|nisch; Pe|ru|bal|sam,** der; -s (↑R 105)
Pe|rü|cke, die; -, -n ‹franz.› (Haarersatz, künstl. Haartracht); **Pe|rü|cken|ma|cher**
Pe|ru|gia [...dʒa] (ital. Stadt)
Pe|ru|rin|de, die; - (↑R 105; *svw.* Chinarinde)
per|vers [...v...] ‹lat.(-franz.)› ([geschlechtlich] abartig, widernatürlich; verderbt); **Per|ver|si|on,** die; -, -en; **Per|ver|si|tät,** die; -, -en; **per|ver|tie|ren** (vom Normalen abweichen); **Per|ver|tiert|heit; Per|ver|tie|rung**
Per|zent, das; -[e]s, -e ‹lat.› usw. (*österr. neben* Prozent usw.)
per|zep|ti|bel ‹lat.› (wahrnehmbar; fassbar); ...ib|le (↑R 130) Geräusche; **Per|zep|ti|bi|li|tät,** die; - (Wahrnehmbarkeit; Fasslichkeit); **Per|zep|ti|on,** die; -, -en (sinnliche Wahrnehmung); **per|zep|tiv, per|zep|to|risch** (wahrnehmend); **Per|zi|pi|ent,** der; -en, -en; ↑R 126 (*veraltet für* Empfänger); **per|zi|pie|ren** (erfassen; wahrnehmen)
Pe|sa|de, die; -, -n ‹franz.› (*Reiten* Figur der hohen Schule)
pe|san|te ‹ital.› (*Musik* schleppend, wuchtig); **Pe|san|te,** das; -s, -s
Pe|sel, der; -s, - (*nordd. für* bäuerl. Wohnraum)
pe|sen (*ugs. für* eilen, rennen); du pest; er pes|te
Pe|se|ta, *auch* **Pe|se|te,** die; -, ...ten ‹span.› (span. Währungseinheit; *Abk.* Pta); **Pe|so,** der; -[s], -[s] (südamerik. Währungseinheit)
Pes|sar, das; -s, -e ‹griech.› (*Med.*

[Kunststoff]ring o. Ä., der den Gebärmuttermund zur Empfängnisverhütung verschließt)
Pes|si|mis|mus, der; - ‹lat.› (seelische Gedrücktheit; Schwarzseherei; *Ggs.* Optimismus); **Pes|si|mist,** der; -en, -en (↑R 126); **Pes|si|mis|tin; pes|si|mis|tisch; Pes|si|mum,** das; -s, ...ma (*Biol.* schlechteste Umweltbedingungen)
[1]**Pest,** die; - ‹lat.› (eine Seuche)
[2]**Pest** (Stadtteil von Budapest)
Pes|ta|loz|zi (schweiz. Pädagoge u. Sozialreformer)
pest|ar|tig; -er Gestank; **Pest‿beu|le, ...hauch; Pes|ti|lenz,** die; -, -en ‹lat.› (*veraltet für* [1]Pest); **pes|ti|len|zi|a|lisch; Pes|ti|zid,** das; -s, -e (Schädlingsbekämpfungsmittel); **pest|krank; Pest|kran|ke**
Pe|ta... ‹griech.› (das Billiardenfache einer Einheit, z. B. Petajoule = 10^{15} Joule)
Pe|tar|de, die; -, -n ‹franz.› (*früher* Sprengmörser, -ladung)
Pe|tent, der; -en, -en (↑R 126) ‹lat.› (*Amtsspr.* Antrag-, Bittsteller)
Pe|ter (m. Vorn.)
Pe|ter|le, das; -[s] (*landsch. für* Petersilie)
Pe|ter|männ|chen (ein Fisch)
Pe|ter-Paul-Kir|che (↑R 95)
Pe|ters|burg (*kurz für* Sankt Petersburg)
Pe|ters|fisch (ein Speisefisch)
Pe|ter|sil, der; -s ‹griech.› (*österr. neben* Petersilie); **Pe|ter|si|lie** [...i̯ə], die; -, -n (ein Küchenkraut); **Pe|ter|si|li|en‿kar|tof|feln** *(Plur.),* **...wur|zel**
Pe|ters‿kir|che, ...pfen|nig; Pe|ter-und-Paul-Kir|che (↑R 95); **Pe|ter-und-Pauls-Tag;** ↑R 95 (kath. Fest)
Pe|ter|wa|gen (*ugs. für* Funkstreifenwagen)
Pe|tit [pəˈtiː], die; - ‹franz.› (*Druckw.* ein Schriftgrad); **Pe|ti|tes|se,** die; -, -n (Geringfügigkeit)
Pe|ti|ti|on, die; -, -en ‹lat.› (Gesuch); **pe|ti|ti|o|nie|ren; Pe|ti|ti|ons‿aus|schuss, ...recht** (Bittrecht, Beschwerderecht)
Pe|tit|satz [pəˈtiː...], der; -es; **Pe|tit|schrift** *(Druckw.)*
Pe|tits Fours [pəti ˈfuːr] *Plur.* ‹franz.› (feines Kleingebäck)
Pe|tő|fi [ˈpetøːfi] (ungar. Lyriker)
Pe|t|ra (↑R 130; w. Vorn.)
Pet|rar|ca (↑R 130; ital. Dichter u. Gelehrter)
Pet|ras|si (↑R 130; ital. Komponist)
Pet|re|fakt (↑R 130), das; -[e]s, -e[n] ‹griech.; lat.› (*veraltet für* Versteinerung von Pflanzen od. Tieren)
Pe|t|ri (↑R 130) *vgl.* Petrus
Pet|ri|fi|ka|ti|on (↑R 130), die; -, -en ‹griech.; lat.› (Versteinerungsprozess); **pet|ri|fi|zie|ren** (versteinern)
Pe|t|ri Heil! (↑R 130) *vgl.* Petrus; **Pe|t|ri|jün|ger** (*scherzh. für* Angler); **Pe|t|ri|kir|che, pet|ri|nisch;** petrinischer Lehrbegriff, petrinische Briefe (↑R 94)
Pet|ro|che|mie (↑R 130) ‹griech.› (Wissenschaft von der chem. Zusammensetzung der Gesteine; *auch für* Petrolchemie); **pet|ro|che|misch; Pe|t|ro|dol|lar** [*auch* ˈpɛ...] (von Erdöl fördernden Staaten eingenommenes Geld in amerik. Währung); **Pet|ro|ge|ne|se,** die; -, -n (Gesteinsbildung); **pet|ro|ge|ne|tisch**
Pet|ro|graph (↑R 130), der; -en, -en; ↑R 126 (Kenner u. Forscher auf dem Gebiet der Petrographie); **Pet|ro|gra|phie,** die; - (Gesteinskunde, -beschreibung); **pet|ro|gra|phisch**
Pet|rol (↑R 130), das; -s (*schweiz. neben* Petroleum); **Pet|rol|che|mie** (auf Erdöl u. Erdgas beruhende techn. Rohstoffgewinnung in der chem. Industrie); **pet|rol|che|misch; Pet|ro|le|um** [...leum], das; -s (*auch veraltet für* Erdöl); **Pet|ro|le|um‿ko|cher, ...lam|pe, ...ofen** (↑R 132)
Pet|ro|lo|ge (↑R 130), der; -n, -n (↑R 126); **Pet|ro|lo|gie,** die; - (Wissenschaft von der Bildung u. Umwandlung der Gesteine)
Pe|t|rus (↑R 130; Apostel); Petri Heil! (Anglergruß); Petri (des Petrus) Stuhlfeier (kath. Fest), Petri Kettenfeier (kath. Fest), *aber* Petrikirche usw.
Pet|schaft, das; -s, -e ‹tschech.› (Stempel zum Siegeln); **pet|schie|ren** (mit einem Petschaft schließen); **pet|schiert** (*österr. ugs. für* in einer peinlichen Situation, ruiniert); petschiert sein
Pet|ti|coat [ˈpɛtikoːt], der; -s, -s ‹engl.› (steifer Taillenunterrock)
Pet|ting, das; -[s], -s ‹amerik.› (sexuelles Liebesspiel ohne eigentlichen Geschlechtsverkehr)
pet|to *vgl.* in petto
Pe|tu|nie [...i̯ə], die; -, -n ‹indian.› (eine Zierpflanze)
Petz, der; -es, -e (*scherzh. für* Bär); Meister Petz; [1]**Pet|ze,** die; -, -n (*landsch. für* Hündin)
[2]**Pet|ze,** die; -, -n *(Schülerspr.);* [1]**pet|zen** (*Schülerspr.* mitteilen, dass jmd. etwas Unerlaubtes getan hat); du petzt
[2]**pet|zen** (*landsch. für* zwicken, kneifen); du petzt
Pet|zer ‹*zu* [1]petzen›
peu à peu [pø: a ˈpøː] ‹franz.› (*ugs. für* nach und nach, allmählich)
pe|xie|ren (*svw.* pekzieren)
pF = Pikofarad
Pf = Pfennig
Pfad, der; -[e]s, -e; **Pfäd|chen; pfa|den** (*schweiz. für* [einen Weg] begeh-, befahrbar machen); **Pfa|der** (*schweiz. Kurzform für* Pfadfinder); **Pfad|fin|der; Pfad|fin|de|rin; pfad|los**
Pfaf|fe, der; -n, -n; ↑R 126 (*abwertend für* Geistlicher); **Pfaf|fen‿hüt|chen** (ein giftiger Zierstrauch), **...knecht** *(abwertend);* **Pfaf|fen|tum,** das; -s *(abwertend);* **pfäf|fisch** *(abwertend)*
Pfahl, der; -[e]s, Pfähle; **Pfahl‿bau** (*Plur.* ...bauten), **...bau|er** (der; -s, -), **...bür|ger** (*veraltend für* Kleinbürger); **pfäh|len; Pfahl‿gra|ben, ...grün|dung** *(Bauw.),* **...mu|schel; Pfäh|lung; Pfahl‿werk, ...wur|zel**
[1]**Pfalz,** die; -, -en ‹lat.› ([kaiserl.] Palast; Hofburg für kaiserl. Hofgericht; Gebiet, auch Burg des Pfalzgrafen); [2]**Pfalz,** die; - (südl. Teil des Bundeslandes Rheinland-Pfalz); **Pfäl|zer** (↑R 103); - Wein; **Pfäl|zer Wald,** *auch* **Pfäl|zer|wald; Pfalz|graf** (im MA.); **pfalz|gräf|lich; pfäl|zisch**
Pfand, das; -[e]s, Pfänder; **pfänd|bar; Pfänd|bar|keit,** die; -; **Pfand‿brief** *(Bankw.),* **...bruch** (der; -[e]s, ...brüche; Beseitigung gepfändeter Sachen), **...ef|fek|ten** *(Plur.; Bankw.);* **pfän|den;**
[1]**Pfän|der** (*südd. für* Gerichtsvollzieher)
[2]**Pfän|der,** der; -s (Berg bei Bregenz)
Pfän|der|spiel; Pfand‿fla|sche, ...geld, ...haus; Pfand|kehr, die; - *(Rechtsspr.);* **Pfand‿leih|an|stalt** *(österr.),* **...lei|he, ...lei|her, ...recht, ...schein; Pfän|dung; Pfän|dungs‿auf|trag, ...schutz** (Schutz vor zu weit gehenden Pfändungen), **...ver|fü|gung; pfand|wei|se; Pfand|zet|tel**
Pfänn|chen; Pfan|ne, die; -, -n; jmdn. in die Pfanne hauen (*ugs. für* jmdn. zurechtweisen, erledigen, ausschalten); **Pfan|nen‿ge|richt, ...stiel; Pfän|ner** (*früher* Besitzer einer Saline); **Pfän|ner|schaft** (*früher* Genossenschaft zur Nutzung der Solquellen); **Pfann|ku|chen**
Pfarr‿ad|mi|nist|ra|tor, ...amt;

Pfar|re, die; -, -n *(landsch.)*; **Pfar|rei**; **pfar|rei|lich**; **Pfar|rer**; **Pfar|re|rin**; **Pfar|rers-frau** *(svw.* Pfarrfrau), **...kö|chin, ...toch|ter**; **Pfarr-frau, ...haus, ...hel|fer, ...hel|fe|rin, ...herr** *(veraltet)*, **...hof, ...kir|che**; **pfarr|lich**; **Pfarr|vi|kar**
Pfau, der; -[e]s, -en, *österr.* der; *Gen.* -[e]s *od.* -en, *Plur.* -e *od.* -en (ein Vogel)
pfau|chen *(österr. für* fauchen)
Pfau|en-au|ge, ...fe|der, ...rad, ...thron (der; -[e]s; Thron früherer Herrscher des Iran); **Pfau-hahn, ...hen|ne**
Pfd., ℔ = Pfund
Pfef|fer, der; -s, *Plur. (Sorten:)* - (eine Pflanze; Gewürz); Pfeffer u. Salz; schwarzer, weißer - (↑R 108); **Pfef|fer|fres|ser** *(für* Tukan); **pfef|fe|rig** *vgl.* pfeffrig; **Pfef|fer|ku|chen**; **Pfef|fer|ku|chen|häus|chen**; **Pfef|fer|ling** *(selten für* Pfifferling [Pilz]); **[1]Pfef|fer|minz[1]**, der; -es, -e (ein Likör); 3 - (↑R 90); **[2]Pfef|fer|minz[1]**, das; -es, -e (Bonbon, Plätzchen mit Pfefferminzgeschmack); **Pfef|fer|minz|bon|bon[1]**; **Pfef|fer|min|ze[1]**, die; - (eine Heil- u. Gewürzpflanze); **Pfef|fer|minz-li|kör[1], ...pas|til|le, ...tee**; **Pfef|fer-müh|le, ...mu|schel**; **pfef|fern**; ich ...ere (↑R 16); **Pfef|fer|nuss**; **Pfef|fe|ro|ne,** der; -, *Plur.* ...oni, *selten* -n *(svw.* Pfefferoni); **Pfef|fe|ro|ni,** der; -, - ‹sanskr.; ital.› *(österr. für* Peperoni); **Pfef|fer-sack** *(veraltend für* Großkaufmann), **...steak, ...strauch**; **Pfef|fer-und-Salz-Mus|ter** (↑R 28); **pfeff|rig,** pfef|fe|rig
Pfei|fe, die; -, -n *(ugs. auch für* ängstlicher Mensch; Versager); **pfei|fen**; du pfiffst; du pfiffest; gepfiffen; pfeif[e]!; auf etwas - *(ugs. für* an etwas nicht interessiert sein); **Pfei|fen-be|steck, ...de|ckel, ...kopf, ...kraut, ...mann** *(Plur.* ...männer; *ugs. für* Schiedsrichter), **...rau|cher, ...rei|ni|ger, ...stän|der, ...stop|fer, ...ta|bak**; **Pfei|fer**; **Pfei|fe|rei**; **Pfeif-kes|sel, ...kon|zert, ...ton** *(Plur.* ...töne)
Pfeil, der; -[e]s, -e
Pfei|ler, der; -s, -; **Pfei|ler-ba|si|li|ka, ...bau** (der; -[e]s; *Bergmannsspr.* ein Abbauverfahren)
pfeil-ge|ra|de, ...ge|schwind; **Pfeil-gift** (das), **...hecht, ...kraut, ...rich|tung**; **pfeil|schnell**; **Pfeil|wurz** (eine trop. Staude)

[1] [*auch* ...'min...]

pfel|zen *(österr. landsch. für* pfropfen)
Pfen|nig, der; -s, -e (Münze; *Abk.* Pf; 100 Pf = 1 [Deutsche] Mark); 6 Pfennig (↑R 90); **Pfen|nig-ab|satz** *(ugs. für* hoher, dünner Absatz bei Damenschuhen), **...be|trag, ...fuch|ser** *(ugs. für* Geizhals); **Pfen|nig|fuch|se|rei**; **pfen|nig|groß**; **Pfen|nig|stück**; **pfen|nig|stück|groß**; **Pfen|nig|wa|re** (Kleinigkeit); **pfen|nig|wei|se**
Pferch, der; -[e]s, -e (Einhegung, eingezäunte Fläche); **pfer|chen** (hineinzwängen)
Pferd, das; -[e]s, -e; zu -e; **Pfer|de-ap|fel, ...bahn** *(früher* von Pferden gezogene Straßenbahn), **...drosch|ke, ...fleisch, ...fuß, ...ge|biss** *(ugs.)*, **...ge|sicht** *(ugs.)*, **...kop|pel, ...kur** *(svw.* Rosskur; *vgl.* [1]Kur), **...län|ge** *(Reitsport)*, **...na|tur** *(ugs.)*, **...ren|nen, ...schwanz** *(auch für* eine Frisur), **...sport, ...stall, ...stär|ke** (frühere techn. Maßeinheit; *Abk.* PS; *vgl.* HP), **...strie|gel, ...wirt, ...zucht**; **...pfer|dig** (z. B. sechspferdig); **Pferd|sprung** *(Turnen)*
Pfet|te, die; -, -n (waagerechter, tragender Balken im Dachstuhl); **Pfet|ten|dach**
pfet|zen *(landsch. für* kneifen)
Pfiff, der; -[e]s, -e
Pfif|fer|ling (ein Pilz); keinen Pfifferling wert sein *(ugs. für* wertlos sein)
pfif|fig; **Pfif|fig|keit,** die; -; **Pfif|fi|kus,** der; -[ses], -se *(ugs. für* schlauer Mensch)
Pfings|ten, das; -, - ‹griech.› (christl. Feiertag am 50. Tag nach Ostern); Pfingsten fällt früh; Pfingsten ist bald vorüber; *landsch., bes. österr. u. schweiz. als Plur.:* die[se] Pfingsten fallen früh; nach den Pfingsten; *in Wunschformeln auch allg. als Plur.:* fröhliche Pfingsten!; zu Pfingsten *(bes. nordd.)*, an Pfingsten *(bes. südd.)*; **Pfingst|fest**; **Pfingst|ler** (Anhänger einer religiösen Bewegung); **pfingst|lich**; **Pfingst|mon|tag**; **Pfingst-och|se, ...ro|se** (Päonie); **Pfingst|sonn|tag**; **Pfingst-ver|kehr, ...wo|che**
Pfir|sich, der; -s, -e; - Melba (Pfirsich mit Vanilleeis und Himbeermark); **Pfir|sich-baum, ...blü|te, ...bow|le**; **pfir|sich|far|ben**; **Pfir|sich|haut** *(übertr. auch für* samtige, rosige Gesichtshaut)
Pfit|scher Joch, das; - -s (Alpenpass in Südtirol)
Pfitz|ner (dt. Komponist)

Pflanz, der; - *(österr. ugs. für* Hohn, Schwindel)
Pflänz|chen; **Pflan|ze,** die; -, -n; **pflan|zen** *(österr. ugs. auch für* zum Narren halten); du pflanzt; **pflan|zen|ar|tig**; **Pflan|zen-bau** (der; -[e]s), **...de|cke, ...ex|trakt, ...fa|ser, ...fett, ...fres|ser, ...gift** (das), **...grün, ...kost, ...krank|heit, ...kun|de** (die; -; *für* Botanik), **...milch, ...öl, ...reich** (das; -[e]s), **...schutz**; **Pflan|zen|schutz|mit|tel,** das; **Pflan|zer**; **Pflan|ze|rin**; **Pflanz-gar|ten, ...kar|tof|feln** *(Plur.)*; **pflanz|lich**; -e Kost; **Pflänz|ling**; **Pflanz-stadt** *(veraltet für* [antike] Kolonie), **...stock** *(Plur.* ...stöcke); **Pflan|zung** *(auch für* Plantage)
Pflas|ter, das; -s, - (Heil- od. Schutzverband; Straßenbelag); ein teures Pflaster *(ugs. für* Stadt mit teuren Lebensverhältnissen); **Pfläs|ter|chen**; **Pflas|te|rer,** *landsch. u. schweiz.* **Pfläs|te|rer**; **Pflas|ter|ma|ler** (jmd., der auf Bürgersteige o. Ä. [Kreide]bilder malt); **pflas|ter|mü|de**; **pflas|tern,** *landsch. u. schweiz.* **pfläs|tern**; ich ...ere (↑R 16); **Pflas|ter-stein, ...tre|ter** *(veraltend für* müßig Herumschlendernder); **Pflas|te|rung,** *landsch. und schweiz.* **Pfläs|te|rung**
Pflatsch, der; -[e]s, -e *u.* **Pflat|schen,** der; -s, - *(landsch. für* Fleck durch verschüttete Flüssigkeit; jäher Regenguss); **pflat|schen** *(landsch. für* klatschend aufschlagen); du pflatschst
Pfläum|chen; **Pflau|me,** die; -, -n; **pflau|men** *(ugs. für* scherzhafte Bemerkungen machen); **Pflau|men|au|gust** *(abwertend für* nichts sagender, charakterloser Mann); *vgl.* [2]August; **Pflau|men-baum, ...brannt|wein** (Slibowitz), **...ku|chen, ...mus, ...schnaps**; **pflau|men|weich**
Pfle|ge, die; -; **Pfle|ge|amt**; **pfle|ge-arm, ...be|dürf|tig**; **Pfle|ge|be|foh|le|ne,** der *u.* die; -n, -n (↑R 5 ff.); **Pfle|ge-el|tern** *(Plur.)*, **...fall** (der), **...geld, ...heim, ...kind**; **pfle|ge|leicht**; **Pfle|ge|mut|ter**; **pfle|gen**; du pflegtest; gepflegt; pfleg[e]!; *in der Wendung* „der Ruhe pflegen" *auch* du pflogst; du pflögest; gepflogen; **Pfle|ge|per|so|nal**; **Pfle|ger** *(auch* Vormund); **Pfle|ge|rin**; **pfle|ge|risch**; **Pfle|ge-satz, ...sohn, ...sta|ti|on, ...stät|te, ...toch|ter, ...va|ter, ...ver|si|che|rung**; **pfleg|lich**; **Pfleg|ling**; **pfleg|sam** *(selten für* sorgsam); **Pfleg|schaft** *(Rechtsspr.)*

Pflicht, die; -, -en ⟨*zu* pflegen⟩; **Pflicht‿ar|beit, ...be|such; pflicht|be|wusst; Pflicht‿bewusst|sein, ...ei|fer; pflicht|eif|rig; Pflicht|ein|stel|lung; Pflich|ten‿heft, ...kreis; Pflicht‿er|fül|lung** (die; -), **...exemp|lar** (↑R 132), **...fach, ...ge|fühl** (das; -[e]s); **pflicht|ge|mäß; ...pflich|tig** (z. B. schulpflichtig); **Pflicht‿jahr** (das; -[e]s), **...kür** *(Sport),* **...lauf** *(Sport),* **...lau|fen** (das; -s; *Sport*), **...leis|tung, ...lek|tü|re, ...platz** (Arbeitsplatz, der mit einem Schwerbeschädigten besetzt werden muss); **Pflicht|re|ser|ve** *meist Plur. (Wirtsch.)*; **pflicht|schul|dig, pflicht|schul|digst; Pflicht|teil,** der, *österr. nur so, od.* das; **pflicht|treu; Pflicht‿treue, ...übung** (↑R 132), **...um|tausch** (vorgeschriebener Geldumtausch bei Reisen in bestimmte Länder); **pflicht|ver|ges|sen;** der -e Mensch; **Pflicht‿ver|ges|sen|heit, ...ver|let|zung; pflicht|ver|si|chert; Pflicht‿ver|si|che|rung, ...ver|tei|di|ger; pflicht|wid|rig;** -es Verhalten

Pflock, der; -[e]s, Pflöcke; **Pflöck|chen; pflo|cken, pflö|cken**

Pflotsch, der; -[e]s *(schweiz. mdal. für* Schneematsch)

Pflü|cke, die; -, -n (Pflücken [des Hopfens]); **pflü|cken; Pflü|cker; Pflü|cke|rin; Pflück‿rei|fe, ...salat**

Pflug, der; -[e]s, Pflüge; **pflü|gen; Pflü|ger; Pflug‿mes|ser** (das), **...schar** (die; -, -en, *landw. auch* das; -[e]s, -e), **...sterz** (der; -es, -e; *vgl.* ²Sterz)

Pfort|ader (↑R 132; *Med.*); **Pfört|chen; Pfor|te,** die; -, -n; (↑R 108:) die Burgundische -; **Pfor|ten|ring** *(früher* Klopfring an einer Pforte); **Pfört|ner; Pfört|ne|rin; Pfört|ner|lo|ge**

Pforz|heim (Stadt am Nordrand des Schwarzwaldes)

Pföst|chen; Pfos|ten, der; -s, -; **Pfos|ten|schuss** *(Sport)*

Pföt|chen; Pfo|te, die; -, -n

Pfriem, der; -[e]s, -e (ein [Schuster]werkzeug); *vgl.* Ahle; **pfrie|meln** (*landsch. für* mit den Fingerspitzen hin und her drehen; zwirbeln); **Pfrie|men|gras**

Pfril|le, die; -, -n (*svw.* Elritze)

Pfropf, der; -[e]s, -e (zusammengepresste Masse, die etwas verstopft, verschließt); **Pfröpf|chen**

¹**pfrop|fen** (durch Einsetzen eines wertvolleren Sprosses veredeln)

²**pfrop|fen** ([eine Flasche] verschließen); **Pfrop|fen,** der; -s, - (Kork, Stöpsel)

Pfröpf|ling; Pfropf‿mes|ser (das), **...reis** (das)

Pfrün|de, die; -, -n (Einkommen durch ein Kirchenamt; *auch scherzh. für* [fast] müheloses Einkommen); **Pfrün|der** (*schweiz. für* Pfründner); **Pfründ|haus** (*landsch. für* Altersheim, Armenhaus); **Pfründ|ner** (*landsch. für* Insasse eines Pfründhauses); **Pfründ|ne|rin**

Pfuhl, der; -[e]s, -e (große Pfütze; Sumpf; *landsch. für* Jauche)

Pfühl, der, *auch* das; -[e]s, -e (*veraltet für* Kissen)

pfui!; pfui, pfui!; pfui Teufel!; pfui, schäm dich!; **Pfui,** das; -s, -s; Pfui, *auch* pfui rufen; ein verächtliches Pfui ertönte; **Pfui|ruf**

Pful|men, der; -s, - (*schweiz. für* breites Kopfkissen)

Pfund[1], das; -[e]s, -e ⟨lat.⟩ (Gewichtseinheit; *Abk.* Pfd.; *Zeichen:* ℔; Münzeinheit [*vgl.* Pfund Sterling]); 4 Pfund Butter (↑R 90); **Pfünd|chen; ...pfün|der** (z. B. Zehnpfünder, *mit Ziffern* 10-Pfünder; ↑R 44); **pfun|dig** (*ugs. für* großartig, toll); **...pfün|dig** (z. B. zehnpfündig, *mit Ziffern* 10-pfündig; ↑R 44); **Pfund|no|te; Pfunds‿kerl** *(ugs.),* **...spaß** *(ugs.);* **Pfund Ster|ling** [- ˈster... *bzw.* ˈʃtɛr..., *engl.* -ˈstœ:(r)...], das; - -, - - (brit. Währungseinheit; *Zeichen u. Abk.* £); **pfund|wei|se**

Pfusch, der; -[e]s (Pfuscherei); **Pfusch|ar|beit; pfu|schen** (*ugs. für* liederlich arbeiten; *österr. u. landsch. für* schwarzarbeiten); du pfuschst; **Pfu|scher; Pfu|sche|rei; pfu|scher|haft; Pfu|sche|rin**

pfutsch (*österr. für* futsch)

Pfütz|chen; Pfüt|ze, die; -, -n; **Pfütz|ei|mer** (*Bergmannsspr.* Schöpfeimer); **Pfüt|zen|was|ser,** das; -s; **pfüt|zig** *(veraltet)*

PGH = Produktionsgenossenschaft des Handwerks *(regional)*

PGiroA = Postgiroamt

ph = Phot

PH = pädagogische Hochschule; *vgl.* pädagogisch

Phä|a|ke, der; -n, -n; ↑R 126 (Angehöriger eines [glücklichen, genussliebenden] Seefahrervolkes der griech. Sage; *übertr. für* sorgloser Genießer); **Phä|a|ken|le|ben,** das; -s

Phä|don (altgriech. Philosoph)

Phäd|ra (↑R 130; Gattin des Theseus)

[1] *In Deutschland und in der Schweiz als amtliche Gewichtsbezeichnung abgeschafft.*

Phäd|rus (↑R 130; röm. Fabeldichter)

Pha|e|thon (griech. Sagengestalt; Sohn des Helios)

Pha|ge, der; -n, -n (*svw.* Bakteriophage)

Pha|go|zyt, der; -en, -en *meist Plur.* ⟨griech.⟩ ↑R 126 (*Med.* weißes Blutkörperchen, das bes. Bakterien unschädlich macht)

Pha|lanx, die; -, ...langen ⟨griech.⟩ (geschlossene Schlachtreihe *[bes. übertr.]; Med.* Finger-, Zehenglied)

Pha|le|ron (Vorstadt vom antiken Athen)

phal|lisch ⟨griech.⟩ (den Phallus betreffend); **Phal|lo|kra|tie,** die; - (*abwertend für* gesellschaftliche Vorherrschaft des Mannes); **Phal|los,** der; -, *Plur.* ...lloi [ˈfalɔy] *u.* ...llen; *vgl.* Phallus; **Phal|lus,** der; -, *Plur.* ...lli *u.* ...llen, *auch* -se ([erigiertes] männl. Glied); **Phal|lus‿kult** (*Völkerk.* relig. Verehrung des Phallus als Sinnbild der Naturkraft), **...sym|bol** *(bes. Psych.)*

Pha|ne|ro|ga|me, die; -, -n ⟨griech.⟩ (*Bot.* Samenpflanze)

Phä|no|lo|gie, die; - ⟨griech.⟩ (Lehre von den Erscheinungen des jahreszeitl. Ablaufs in der Pflanzen- u. Tierwelt, z. B. der Laubverfärbung der Bäume); **Phä|no|men,** das; -s, -e ([Natur]erscheinung; seltenes Ereignis; Wunder[ding]; *übertr. für* Genie); **phä|no|me|nal** (außerordentlich, außergewöhnlich, erstaunlich); **Phä|no|me|na|lis|mus,** der; - (philos. Lehre, nach der nur die Erscheinungen der Dinge, nicht diese selbst erkannt werden können); **Phä|no|me|no|lo|gie,** die; - (Lehre von den Wesenserscheinungen der Dinge); **phä|no|me|no|lo|gisch; Phä|no|me|non,** das; -s, ...na (*svw.* Phänomen); **Phä|no|typ** *vgl.* Phänotypus; **phä|no|ty|pisch; Phä|no|ty|pus,** der; -, ...pen (*Biol.* Erscheinungsbild, -form eines Organismus)

Phan|ta|sie, *auch* Fan|ta|sie *(vgl. d.),* die; -, ...ien ⟨griech.⟩ (Vorstellung[skraft], Einbildung[skraft]; Trugbild); **phan|ta|sie|be|gabt,** *auch* fan|ta|sie|begabt; **Phan|ta|sie|ge|bil|de,** *auch* Fan|ta|sie|ge|bil|de; **phan|ta|sie|los,** *auch* fan|ta|sie|los; **Phan|ta|sie|lo|sig|keit,** *auch* Fan|ta|sie|lo|sig|keit; die; -; **phan|ta|sie|ren,** *auch* fan|ta|sie|ren (sich [dem Spiel] der Einbildungskraft hingeben; irrereden; *Musik* frei über eine Melodie od. über ein Thema musizieren); **phan|ta|sie|voll,** *auch* fan|ta|sie|voll; **Phan|ta|sie|vor|stel|lung,** *auch* Fan|ta|sie|vor|stel|lung; **Phan|tas|ma,** das; -s, ...men (Trugbild); **Phan|tas|ma|go|rie,** die; -, ...ien (Zauber, Truggebilde; künstl. Darstellung von Trugbildern, Gespenstern u. a.); **phan|tas|ma|go|risch;** **Phan|ta|sos** *vgl.* Phantasus; **Phan|tast,** *auch* Fan|tast; der; -en, -en; ↑R 126 (Träumer, Schwärmer); **Phan|tas|te|rei,** *auch* Fan|tas|te|rei; **Phan|tas|tik,** *auch* Fan|tas|tik; die; -; **phan|tas|tisch,** *auch* fan|tas|tisch (schwärmerisch; überspannt; unwirklich; *ugs. für* großartig); **Phan|ta|sus** (griech. Traumgott); **Phan|tom,** das; -s, -e (Trugbild; *Med.* Nachbildung eines Körperteils od. Organs für Versuche od. für den Unterricht); **Phan|tom‿bild** (*Kriminalistik* nach Zeugenaussagen gezeichnetes Porträt eines gesuchten Täters), **...schmerz** (*Med.* Schmerzgefühl an einem amputierten Glied)

¹**Pha|rao,** der; -s, ...onen ‹ägypt.› (altägypt. König); ²**Pha|rao,** das; -s ‹franz.› (altes franz. Kartenglücksspiel); **Pha|ra|o|amei|se** (↑R 132); **Pha|ra|o|nen‿grab, ...rat|te** (*für* Ichneumon), **...reich; pha|ra|o|nisch**

Pha|ri|sä|er ‹hebr.› (Angehöriger einer altjüd., streng gesetzesfrommen Partei; *übertr. für* hochmütiger, selbstgerechter Heuchler; heißer Kaffee mit Rum u. Schlagsahne); **pha|ri|sä|er|haft; Pha|ri|sä|er|tum,** das; -s *(geh.)*; **pha|ri|sä|isch; Pha|ri|sä|is|mus,** der; - (Lehre der Pharisäer; *übertr. für* Selbstgerechtigkeit, Heuchelei)

Phar|ma|in|dust|rie ‹griech.; lat.› (Arzneimittelindustrie); **Phar|ma|kant,** der; -en, -en (↑R 126) ‹griech.› (Facharbeiter in der Pharmaindustrie); **Phar|ma|kan|tin; Phar|ma|ko|lo|ge,** der; -n, -n; ↑R 126 (Wissenschaftler auf dem Gebiet der Pharmakologie); **Phar|ma|ko|lo|gie,** die; - (Arzneimittelkunde); **Phar|ma|ko|lo|gin; phar|ma|ko|lo|gisch; Phar|ma|kon,** das; -s, ...ka (Arzneimittel; Gift); **Phar|ma|ko|pöe** [...'pø:, *selten* ...'pø:ə], die; -, -n [...'pø:ən] (amtl. Arzneibuch); **Phar|ma|re|fe|rent** (Arzneimittelvertreter); **Phar|ma|re|fe|ren|tin; Phar|ma|zeut,** der; -en, -en; ↑R 126 (Arzneikundiger); **Phar|ma|zeu|tik,** die; - (Arzneimittelkunde); **Phar|ma|zeu|ti|kum,** das; -s, ...ka (Arzneimittel); **Phar|ma|zeu|tin; phar|ma|zeu|tisch; phar|ma|zeu|tisch-tech|nisch** (↑R 27); -er Assistent (*Abk.* PTA); **Phar|ma|zie,** die; - (Lehre von der Arzneimittelzubereitung, Arzneimittelkunde)

Pha|ro, das; -s (*verkürzte Bildung zu* ²Pharao)

Pha|rus, der; -, *Plur.* - *u.* -se ‹nach der Insel Pharus› (*veraltet für* Leuchtturm)

Pha|ryn|gis|mus [...ŋg...], der; -, ...men ‹griech.› (*Med.* Schlundkrampf); **Pha|ryn|gi|tis,** die; -, ...itiden (Rachenentzündung); **Pha|ryn|go|skop,** das; -s, -e (Endoskop zur Untersuchung des Rachens); **Pha|ryn|go|sko|pie,** die; -, ...ien (Ausspiegelung des Rachens); **Pha|rynx,** der; -, ...ryngen [fa'ryŋən] (Rachen)

Pha|se, die; -, -n ‹griech.› (Abschnitt einer [stetigen] Entwicklung, [Zu]stand; *Physik* Schwingungszustand beim Wechselstrom); **Pha|sen‿bild** *(Film)*, **...mes|ser** (der), **...ver|schie|bung; ...pha|sig** (z. B. einphasig)

Phei|di|as *vgl.* Phidias

Phe|na|ce|tin [...ts...] (↑R 132), das; -s ‹griech.-nlat.› (Schmerzen stillender Wirkstoff); **Phe|nol,** das; -s ‹griech.› (Karbolsäure); **Phe|nolph|tha|le|in** (↑R 132), das; -s (chem. Indikator); **Phe|no|plast,** der; -[e]s, -e *meist Plur.* (ein Kunstharz); **Phe|nyl|grup|pe** (*Chemie* einwertige Atomgruppe in vielen aromat. Kohlenwasserstoffen)

Phe|ro|mon, das; -s, -e ‹griech.-nlat.› (*Biol.* Wirkstoff, der auf andere Individuen der gleichen Art Einfluss hat, sie z. B. anlockt)

Phi [fi:], das; -[s], -s (griech. Buchstabe: Φ, ϕ)

Phi|a|le, die; -, -n ‹griech.› (altgriech. flache [Opfer]schale)

Phi|di|as (altgriech. Bildhauer); **phi|di|as|sisch;** die phidiassische Athenastatue (↑R 94)

phil..., phi|lo... ‹griech.› (...liebend); **Phil...,** Phi|lo... (...freund)

Phi|la|del|phia (↑R 132; Stadt in Pennsylvanien); **Phi|la|del|phi|er; phi|la|del|phisch**

Phi|lanth|rop (↑R 130 *u.* 132), der; -en, -en (↑R 126) ‹griech.› (Menschenfreund); **Phi|lanth|ro|pie,** die; - (Menschenliebe); **Phi|lanth|ro|pi|nis|mus** (*svw.* Philanthropismus); **phi|lanth|ro|pisch** (menschenfreundlich); **Phi|lanth|ro|pis|mus,** der; - ([von Basedow u. a. geforderte] Erziehung zu Natürlichkeit, Vernunft u. Menschenfreundlichkeit)

Phi|la|te|lie (↑R 132), die; - ‹griech.› (Briefmarkenkunde); **Phi|la|te|list,** der; -en, -en; ↑R 126 (Briefmarkensammler); **phi|la|te|lis|tisch**

Phi|le|mon (phryg. Sagengestalt; Gatte der Baucis); **Phi|le|mon und Bau|cis** (antikes Vorbild ehelicher Liebe u. Treue sowie selbstloser Gastfreundschaft)

Phil|har|mo|nie, die; -, ...ien ‹griech.› (Name von musikalischen Gesellschaften, von Orchestern u. ihren Konzertsälen); **Phil|har|mo|ni|ker** [*österr. auch* 'fil...] (Künstler, der in einem philharmonischen Orchester spielt); **phil|har|mo|nisch**

Phil|hel|le|ne, der; -n, -n (↑R 126) ‹griech.› (Freund der Griechen [der den Befreiungskampf gegen die Türken unterstützte]); **Phil|hel|le|nis|mus,** der; -

Phi|lipp [*auch* 'fi...] (↑R 132; m. Vorn.); **Phi|lip|per|brief,** der; -[e]s; ↑R 105 (Brief des Paulus an die Gemeinde von Philippi); **Phi|lip|pi** (im Altertum Stadt in Makedonien); **Phi|lip|pi|ka,** die; -, ...ken (Kampfrede [des Demosthenes gegen König Philipp von Makedonien]; Strafrede); **Phi|lip|pi|ne** (w. Vorn.); **Phi|lip|pi|nen** *Plur.* (Inselgruppe u. Staat in Südostasien); **Phi|lip|pi|ner** *vgl.* Filipino; **phi|lip|pi|nisch; phi|lip|pisch;** philippische Reden (↑R 94; Philippiken des Demosthenes); **Phi|lip|pus** (Apostel)

Phi|lis|ter, der; -s, - (Angehöriger des Nachbarvolkes der Israeliten im A. T.; *übertr. für* Spießbürger; *Studentenspr.* im [engen] Berufsleben stehender Alter Herr); **Phi|lis|te|rei; phi|lis|ter|haft; Phi|lis|te|ri|um,** das; -s (*Studentenspr.* das spätere [enge] Berufsleben eines Studenten); **Phi|lis|ter|tum,** das; -s; **phi|lis|trös** (↑R 130; beschränkt; spießig)

Phil|lu|me|nie, die; - ‹griech.; lat.› (das Sammeln von Streichholzschachteln od. deren Etiketten); **Phil|lu|me|nist,** der; -en, -en (↑R 126)

phi|lo... usw. *vgl.* phil... usw.

Phi|lo|den|dron (↑R 130), der, *auch* das; -s, ...ren ‹griech.› (eine Blattpflanze)

Phi|lo|lo|ge, der; -n, -n (↑R 126) ‹griech.› (Sprach- u. Literaturforscher); **Phi|lo|lo|gie,** die; -, ...ien (Sprach- und Literaturwissenschaft); **Phi|lo|lo|gin; phi|lo|lo|gisch**

[1]**Phi|lo|me|la,** [1]**Phi|lo|me|le,** die; -, ...len ⟨griech.⟩ (*veraltet für* Nachtigall); [2]**Phi|lo|me|la,** [2]**Phi|lo|me|le** (w. Vorn.)
Phi|lo|me|na (w. Vorn.)
Phi|lo|se|mit, der; -en, -en (↑R 126) ⟨griech.⟩; **phi|lo|se|mi|tisch; Phi|lo|se|mi|tis|mus,** der; - (judenfreundl. Bewegung im 18. Jh.; unkrit. Haltung gegenüber der Politik Israels)
Phi|lo|soph, der; -en, -en (↑R 126) ⟨griech.⟩ (jmd., der nach Erkenntnis strebt, nach dem letzten Sinn fragt, forscht); **Phi|lo|so|phas|ter,** der; -s, - (Scheinphilosoph); **Phi|lo|so|phem,** das; -s, -e (Ergebnis philos. Lehre, Ausspruch des Philosophen); **Phi|lo|so|phie,** die; -, ...ien (Streben nach Erkenntnis des Zusammenhanges der Dinge in der Welt; Denk-, Grundwissenschaft); **phi|lo|so|phie|ren; Phi|lo|so|phi|kum,** das; -s, ...ka (philosophisch-pädagogische Zwischenprüfung); **Phi|lo|so|phin; phi|lo|so|phisch**
Phi|mo|se, die; -, -n ⟨griech.⟩ (*Med.* Verengung der Vorhaut)
Phi|o|le, die; -, -n ⟨griech.⟩ (bauchiges Glasgefäß mit langem Hals)
Phle|bi|tis, die; -, ...itiden ⟨griech.⟩ (*Med.* Venenentzündung)
Phleg|ma, das; -s ⟨griech.⟩ (Ruhe, [Geistes]trägheit, Gleichgültigkeit, Schwerfälligkeit); **Phleg|ma|ti|ker** (körperlich träger, geistig wenig regsamer Mensch); **Phleg|ma|ti|kus,** der; -, -se (*ugs. scherzh. für* träger, schwerfälliger Mensch); **phleg|ma|tisch**
Phlox, der; -es, -e, *auch* die; -, -e ⟨griech.⟩ (eine Zierpflanze); **Phlo|xin,** das; -s (ein roter Farbstoff)
Phnom Penh [pnɔm 'pɛn] (Hauptstadt von Kambodscha)
Phö|be (griech. Mondgöttin; Beiname der Artemis)
Pho|bie, die; -, ...ien ⟨griech.⟩ (*Med.* krankhafte Angst)
Phö|bos *vgl.* Phöbus; **Phö|bus** (Beiname Apollos)
phon..., pho|no... (↑R 33) ⟨griech.⟩ (laut...); **Phon,** *eindeutschend* Fon, das; -s, -s (Maßeinheit für die Lautstärke); 50 Phon (↑R 90); **Phon...,** Pho|no... (Laut...); **Pho|nem,** das; -s, -e (*Sprachw.* Laut, kleinste bedeutungsdifferenzierende sprachl. Einheit); **Pho|ne|ma|tik,** die; - (*svw.* Phonologie); **pho|ne|ma|tisch** (das Phonem betreffend); **pho|ne|misch; Pho|ne|tik,** die; - (Lehre von der Lautbildung); **Pho|ne|ti|ker; pho|ne|tisch**
Pho|ni|a|ter ⟨griech.⟩; **Pho|ni|at|rie** (↑R 130), die; - (*Med.* Lehre von den Erkrankungen des Stimmapparates)
Phö|ni|ker *vgl.* Phönizier
pho|nisch ⟨griech.⟩ (die Stimme, den Laut betreffend)
Phö|nix, der; -[es], -e ⟨griech.⟩ (Vogel der altägypt. Sage, der sich im Feuer verjüngt)
Phö|ni|zi|en [...iən] (im Altertum Küstenland an der Ostküste des Mittelmeeres); **Phö|ni|zi|er; phö|ni|zisch**
pho|no... (↑R 33) usw. *vgl.* phon... usw.; **Pho|no|dik|tat,** *eindeutschend* Fo|no|dik|tat ⟨griech.; lat.⟩ (auf Tonband o. Ä. gesprochenes Diktat); **Pho|no|gramm,** das; -s, -e ⟨griech.⟩ (Aufzeichnung von Schallwellen auf Schallplatte, Tonband usw.); **Pho|no|graph,** der; -en, -en; ↑R 126 (von Edison 1877 erfundenes Tonaufnahmegerät); **Pho|no|gra|phie,** die; -, ...ien (*veraltet für* Lautschrift, lautgetreue Schreibung); **pho|no|gra|phisch,** *eindeutschend* fo|no|gra|fisch (lautgetreu; die Phonographie betreffend); **Pho|no|lith** [*auch* ...'lit], der; *Gen.* -s *u.* -en, *Plur.* -e[n]; ↑R 126 (ein Ergussgestein); **Pho|no|lo|gie,** die; - (Wissenschaft, die das System u. die bedeutungsmäßige Funktion der Laute untersucht); **pho|no|lo|gisch; Pho|no|me|ter,** das; -s, - (Lautstärkemesser); **Pho|no|met|rie** (↑R 130), die; - (Messung akust. Reize u. Empfindungen); **Pho|no|tech|nik,** *eindeutschend* Fo|no|tech|nik; **Pho|no|thek,** die; -, -en (*svw.* Diskothek); **Pho|no|ty|pis|tin,** *eindeutschend* Fo|no|ty|pis|tin (weibl. Schreibkraft, die vorwiegend nach einem Diktiergerät schreibt); **phon|stark** (*vgl.* Phon); **Phon|zahl** (*vgl.* Phon)
Phos|gen, das; -s ⟨griech.⟩ (ein giftiges Gas); **Phos|phat,** das; -[e]s, -e (Salz der Phosphorsäure); **phos|phat|hal|tig; Phos|phin,** das; -s (Phosphorwasserstoff); **Phos|phit** [*auch* ...'fit], das; -s, -e (Salz der phosphorigen Säure); **Phos|phor,** der; -s (chem. Grundstoff; *Zeichen* P); **Phos|pho|res|zenz,** die; - (Nachleuchten vorher bestrahlter Stoffe); **phos|pho|res|zie|ren; phos|phor|hal|tig; phos|pho|rig; Phos|pho|ris|mus,** der; -, ...men (Phosphorvergiftung); **Phos|pho|rit** [*auch* ...'rit], der; -s, -e (ein Sedimentgestein); **Phos|phor|säu|re** (die; -), **...ver|gif|tung**
Phot, das; -s, - ⟨griech.⟩ (alte Leuchtstärkeeinheit; *Zeichen* ph)
pho|to... (↑R 33; licht...); **Pho|to...** (Licht...); **Pho|to** *vgl.* Foto; **Pho|to|al|bum** usw. *vgl.* Fotoalbum usw.; **Pho|to|che|mie** [*auch* 'fo:...] (Lehre von der chem. Wirkung des Lichtes); **Pho|to|che|mi|gra|phie** [*auch* 'fo:...] (Herstellung von Ätzungen aller Art auf fotograf. Wege); **pho|to|che|mi|gra|phisch** [*auch* 'fo:...]; **pho|to|che|misch** [*auch* 'fo:...] (durch Licht bewirkte chem. Reaktionen betreffend); **Pho|to|ef|fekt** (Austritt von Elektronen aus bestimmten Stoffen durch Lichteinwirkung); **Pho|to|elek|tri|zi|tät** [*auch* 'fo:...] (↑R 132); **Pho|to-elekt|ron** (↑R 132; bei Lichteinwirkung frei werdendes Elektron), **...ele|ment** (↑R 132; elektr. Element [Halbleiter], das Lichtenergie in elektr. Energie umwandelt); **pho|to|gen** (durch Licht entstanden); *vgl. auch* fotogen usw.; **Pho|to|gramm,** das; -s, -e (Messbild); **Pho|to|gramm|met|rie** (↑R 130 *u.* 136), die; - (Herstellung von Grund- u. Aufrissen, Karten aus Lichtbildern); **pho|to|gramm|met|risch** (↑R 136); **Pho|to|graph** usw. *vgl.* Fotograf usw.; **Pho|to|gra|vü|re** (*svw.* Heliogravüre); **Pho|to|in|dust|rie** *vgl.* Fotoindustrie; **Pho|to|ko|pie** usw. *vgl.* Fotokopie usw.; **Pho|to|li|tho|gra|phie** (Verfahren zur Herstellung von Druckformen für den Flachdruck); **pho|to|me|cha|nisch** [*auch* 'fo:...]; -es Verfahren (Anwendung der Fotografie zur Herstellung von Druckformen); **Pho|to|me|ter,** das; -s, - (Gerät zur Lichtmessung); **Pho|to|met|rie,** *eindeutschend* Fo|to|met|rie (↑R 130), die; -; **pho|to|met|risch; Pho|to|mo|dell** *vgl.* Fotomodell; **Pho|to|mon|ta|ge** *vgl.* Fotomontage; **Pho|ton** [*auch* fɔ'to:n], das; -s, ...onen (kleinstes Energieteilchen einer elektromagnet. Strahlung); **Pho|to|phy|si|o|lo|gie** [*auch* 'fo:...] (modernes Teilgebiet der Physiologie); **Pho|to|re|por|ter** *vgl.* Fotoreporter; **Pho|to|satz,** der; -es (*Druckw.* Lichtsatz); **Pho|to|sphä|re** [*auch* 'fo:...], die; - (strahlende Gashülle der Sonne); **Pho|to|syn|the|se,** *eindeutschend* Fo|to|syn|the|se [*auch* 'fo:...] (Aufbau chem. Verbindungen durch Lichteinwirkung); **pho|to|tak|tisch;** -e Bewegungen (Bewegungen von Pflanzenteilen zum Licht hin); **Pho|to|thek** *vgl.* Fotothek;

Pho|to|the|ra|pie [*auch* 'fo:...], die; - (*Med.* Lichtheilverfahren); **pho|to|trop, pho|to|tro|pisch** (Phototropismus zeigend, lichtwendig); *vgl.* fototrop; **Pho|to|tro|pis|mus,** der; -, ...men (*Biol.* Krümmungsreaktion von Pflanzenteilen bei einseitigem Lichteinfall); **Pho|to|vol|ta|ik,** *eindeutschend* Fo|to|vol|ta|ik, die; - (Teilgebiet der Elektronik); **Pho|to|zeit|schrift** *vgl.* Fotozeitschrift; **Pho|to|zel|le,** *eindeutschend* Fo|to|zel|le

Phra|se, die; -, -n ‹griech.› (leere Redensart, nichts sagende Äußerung; Redewendung; *Musik* selbstständige Tonfolge); **Phra|sen|dre|sche|rei** (nichts sagendes Gerede); **phra|sen|haft; phra|sen|reich; Phra|se|o|lo|gie,** die; -, ...ien (Lehre od. Sammlung von den eigentümlichen Redewendungen einer Sprache); **phra|se|o|lo|gisch; phra|sie|ren** (*Musik* der Gliederung der Motive [u. a.] entsprechend interpretieren); **Phra|sie|rung** (melodisch-rhythmische Einteilung eines Tonstücks)

Phre|ne|sie, die; - ‹griech.› (*Med.* Wahnsinn); **phre|ne|tisch** (wahnsinnig); *vgl. aber* frenetisch; **Phre|ni|tis,** die; -, ...itiden (Zwerchfellentzündung)

Phry|gi|en (antikes Reich in Nordwestkleinasien); **Phry|gi|er; phry|gisch;** -e Mütze (Sinnbild der Freiheit bei den Jakobinern)

Phry|ne (griech. Hetäre)

Phthi|sis, die; -, ...sen ‹griech.› (*Med.* Schwindsucht)

pH-Wert [pe:'ha:...]; ↑R 25 (Maßzahl für die Konzentration der Wasserstoffionen in einer Lösung)

Phy|ko|lo|gie, die; - ‹griech.› (Algenkunde)

Phy|le, die; -, -n ‹griech.› (Geschlechterverband im antiken Griechenland); **phy|le|tisch** (*Biol.* die Abstammung betreffend)

Phyl|lis (w. Eigenn.)

Phyl|lit [*auch* ...'lit], der; -s, -e ‹griech.› (ein Gestein); **Phyl|lo|kak|tus** (ein Blattkaktus); **Phyl|lo|kla|di|um,** das; -s, ...ien [...iən] (*Bot.* blattähnlicher Pflanzenspross); **Phyl|lo|pha|ge,** der; -n, -n; ↑R 126 (*Zool.* Pflanzen-, Blattfresser); **Phyl|lo|po|de,** der; -n, -n *meist Plur.;* ↑R 126 (*Zool.* Blattfüßer [Krebs]); **Phyl|lo|ta|xis,** die; -, ...xen (*Bot.* Blattstellung); **Phyl|lo|xe|ra,** die; -, ...ren (*Zool.* Reblaus)

Phy|lo|ge|ne|se, die; -, -n ‹griech.› (*svw.* Phylogenie); **phy|lo|ge|ne|tisch; Phy|lo|ge|nie,** die; -, ...ien (Stammesgeschichte der Lebewesen); **Phy|lum,** das; -s, ...la (*Biol.* Tier- oder Pflanzenstamm)

Phy|sa|lis, die; -, *Plur.* - u. ...alen ‹griech.› (*Bot.* Blasen-, Judenkirsche; Kapstachelbeere)

Phy|si|a|ter, der; -s, - ‹griech.› (Naturarzt); **Phy|si|at|rie** (↑R 130), die; - (Naturheilkunde); **Phy|sik,** die; - (Wissenschaft von der Struktur u. der Bewegung der unbelebten Materie); **phy|si|ka|lisch;** physikalische Chemie, physikalische Maßeinheit, *aber* (↑R 108): das Physikalische Institut der Universität Frankfurt; **Phy|si|ker; Phy|si|ke|rin; Phy|si|ko|che|mie** (physikalische Chemie); **phy|si|ko|che|misch; Phy|si|kum,** das; -s, ...ka (Vorprüfung der Medizinstudenten); **Phy|si|kus,** der; -, -se (*veraltet für* Kreis-, Bezirksarzt)

Phy|si|og|nom (↑R 130), der; -en, -en (↑R 126) ‹griech.› (Deuter der äußeren Erscheinung eines Menschen); **Phy|si|og|no|mie,** die; -, ...ien (äußere Erscheinung eines Lebewesens, bes. Gesichtsausdruck); **Phy|si|og|no|mik,** die; - (Ausdrucksdeutung [Kunst, von der Physiognomie her auf seelische Eigenschaften zu schließen]); **Phy|si|og|no|mi|ker** (*svw.* Physiognom); **phy|si|og|no|misch**

Phy|si|o|krat, der; -en, -en (↑R 126) ‹griech.› (Vertreter des Physiokratismus); **phy|si|o|kra|tisch; Phy|si|o|kra|tis|mus,** der; - (volkswirtschaftl. Theorie des 18. Jh.s, die die Landwirtschaft als die Quelle des Nationalreichtums ansah)

Phy|si|o|lo|ge, der; -n, -n (↑R 126) ‹griech.› (Erforscher der Lebensvorgänge); **Phy|si|o|lo|gie,** die; - (Lehre von den Lebensvorgängen); **Phy|si|o|lo|gin; phy|si|o|lo|gisch** (die Physiologie betreffend); **Phy|si|o|the|ra|peut** (jmd., der die Physiotherapie anwendet); **Phy|si|o|the|ra|peu|tin; phy|si|o|the|ra|peu|tisch; Phy|si|o|the|ra|pie** (Heilbehandlung mit Licht, Luft, Wasser, Bestrahlungen, Massage usw.); **Phy|sis,** die; - (Körper; körperliche Beschaffenheit, Natur); **phy|sisch** (natürlich; körperlich)

phy|to|gen ‹griech.› (aus Pflanzen entstanden); **Phy|to‿ge|o|gra|phie** (Pflanzengeographie), **...me|di|zin, ...pa|tho|lo|gie** (Wissenschaft von den Pflanzenkrankheiten); **phy|to|pa|tho|lo|gisch; phy|to|phag** (*Zool.* Pflanzen fressend); **Phy|to|pha|ge,** der; -n, -n *meist Plur.;* ↑R 126 (*Zool.* Pflanzenfresser); **Phy|to‿phar|ma|zie, ...plank|ton** (Gesamtheit der im Wasser lebenden pflanzl. Organismen), **...the|ra|pie** (die; -; Pflanzenheilkunde)

[1]Pi, das; -[s], -s (griech. Buchstabe: Π, π); **[2]Pi,** das; -[s] (*Math.* Zahl, die das Verhältnis von Kreisumfang zu Kreisdurchmesser angibt; $\pi = 3{,}1415...$)

Pia (w. Vorn.)

Pi|af|fe, die; -, -n ‹franz.› (*Reiten* Trab auf der Stelle); **pi|af|fie|ren** (die Piaffe ausführen)

Pi|a|ni|no, das; -s, -s ‹ital.› (kleines [2]Piano); **pi|a|nis|si|mo** (*Musik* sehr leise; *Abk.* pp); **Pi|a|nis|si|mo,** das; -s, *Plur.* -s *u.* ...mi; **Pi|a|nist,** der; -en, -en; ↑R 126 (Klavierspieler, -künstler); **Pi|a|nis|tin; pi|a|nis|tisch** (die Technik, Kunst des Klavierspielens betreffend); **pi|a|no** (*Musik* leise; *Abk.* p); **[1]Pi|a|no,** das; -s, *Plur.* -s *u.* ...ni (leises Spielen, Singen); **[2]Pi|a|no,** das; -s, -s (*Kurzform von* Pianoforte); **Pi|a|no|for|te,** das; -s, -s (*veraltet für* Klavier); *vgl.* Fortepiano; **Pi|a|no|la,** das; -s, -s (selbsttätig spielendes Klavier)

Pi|a|rist, der; -en, -en (↑R 126) ‹lat.› (Angehöriger eines kath. Lehrordens)

Pi|as|sa|va [...va], die; -, ...ven ‹indian.-port.› (Palmenblattfaser); **Pi|as|sa|va|be|sen**

Pi|ast, der; -en, -en; ↑R 126 (Angehöriger eines poln. Geschlechtes)

Pi|as|ter, der; -s, - ‹griech.› (Währungseinheit im Libanon, Sudan, in Syrien u. Ägypten)

Pi|a|ve [...və], die, *auch* der; - (ital. Fluss)

Pi|az|za, die; -, ...zze ‹ital.› ([Markt]platz); **Pi|az|zet|ta,** die; -, ...tte[n] (kleine Piazza)

Pi|ca ['pi:ka], die; - ‹lat.› (eine genormte Schriftgröße bei der Schreibmaschine)

Pi|car|de, der; -n, -n (↑R 126); **Pi|car|die,** die; - (hist. Provinz in Nordfrankreich); **pi|car|disch**

Pi|cas|so, Pablo (span. Maler u. Grafiker)

Pic|ca|dil|ly [pikə'dili] (eine Hauptstraße in London)

Pic|card [pi'ka:r] (schweiz. Physiker)

Pic|co|lo *vgl.* [1,2]Pikkolo

Pic|co|lo|mi|ni, der; -[s], - (Angehöriger eines ital. Geschlechtes)

Pi|che|lei *(ugs.);* **Pi|che|ler** *vgl.* Pichler; **pi|cheln** (*ugs. für* trinken); ich ...[e]le (↑R 16)
Pi|chel|stei|ner Fleisch, das; - -[e]s, **Pi|chel|stei|ner Topf,** der; - -[e]s (ein Eintopfgericht)
[1]**pi|chen** (*landsch. für* mit Pech überziehen); [2]**pi|chen** (kleben, heften)
Pich|ler, Pi|che|ler (*ugs. für* Trinker)
[1]**Pick** *vgl.* [2]Pik
[2]**Pick,** der; -s (*österr. ugs. für* Klebstoff)
Pi|cke, die; -, -n (Spitzhacke); [1]**Pi|ckel,** der; -s, - (Spitzhacke)
[2]**Pi|ckel,** der; -s, - (Hautpustel, Mitesser)
Pi|ckel|hau|be (früherer [preuß.] Infanteriehelm)
Pi|ckel|he|ring (gepökelter Hering; *übertr. für* Spaßmacher im älteren Lustspiel)
pi|cke|lig, pick|lig ‹*zu* [2]Pickel›
pi|ckeln (*landsch. für* mit der Spitzhacke arbeiten); ich ...[e]le (↑R 16)
pi|cken (*österr. ugs. auch für* kleben, haften); **Pi|ckerl,** das; -s, -n (*österr. für* Klebeetikett)
pi|ckern (*landsch. für* essen); ich ...ere (↑R 16)
Pick|ham|mer (*Bergmannsspr.* Abbauhammer)
Pick|les *vgl.* Mixedpickles
pick|lig *vgl.* pickelig
Pick|nick, das; -s, *Plur.* -e *u.* -s ‹franz.› (Essen im Freien); **pick|ni|cken;** gepicknickt; **Pick|nick|korb**
pick|süß ‹ital.; dt.› (*österr. für* sehr süß); das picksüße Hölzel (die Piccoloklarinette)
Pick-up [pik'ap], der; -s, -s ‹engl.› (elektr. Tonabnehmer für Schallplatten; kleinerer Lieferwagen mit Pritsche)
Pi|co... *vgl.* Piko...
pi|co|bel|lo ‹niederd.; ital.› (*ugs. für* tadellos)
Pi|cot [pi'ko:], der; -s, -s ‹franz.› (Spitzenmasche)
Pic|pus|mis|si|o|nar ['pikpys...] (↑R 95) ‹nach dem ersten Haus in der Picpusstraße in Paris› (Angehöriger der kath. Genossenschaft der hl. Herzen Jesu u. Mariä)
Pid|gin|eng|lisch ['pidʒin...], das; -[s] (vereinfachte Mischsprache aus Englisch u. einer anderen Sprache)
Pi|e|ce ['pi̯ɛ:s(ə)], die; -, -n ‹franz.› ([musikal.] Zwischenspiel; Theaterstück)
Pi|e|des|tal [pi̯e...], das; -s, -e ‹franz.› (Sockel; Untersatz)
Pief|ke, der; -s, -s (*landsch. für* Dummkopf, Angeber; *österr. abwertend für* [Nord]deutscher)
Piek, die; -, -en (*Seemannsspr.* unterster Teil des Schiffsraumes)
Pie|ke, die; -, -n (*svw.* [2]Pik)
piek‿fein (*ugs. für* besonders fein), **...sau|ber** (*ugs. für* besonders sauber)
Pi|e|mont [pi̯e...] (Landschaft in Nordwestitalien); **Pi|e|mon|te|se,** der; -n, -n (↑R 126); **pi|e|mon|te|sisch,** *auch* **pi|e|mon|tisch**
piep!; piep, piep!; **Piep,** der; *nur in ugs. Wendungen wie* einen Piep haben (*ugs. für* nicht recht bei Verstand sein); er tut, sagt, macht keinen Piep mehr (*ugs. für* er ist tot); **pie|pe, piep|egal** (↑R 132; *ugs. für* gleichgültig); das ist mir piepegal
Pie|pel, der; -s, -[s] (*landsch. für* kleiner Junge; Penis)
pie|pen; es ist zum Piepen (*ugs. für* es ist zum Lachen); **Pie|pen** *Plur.* (*ugs. für* Geld); **Piep‿hahn** (*landsch. für* Penis), **...matz** (*ugs. für* Vogel); **pieps** *(ugs.);* er kann nicht mehr pieps sagen; **Pieps,** der; -es, -e *(ugs.);* keinen Pieps von sich geben; **piep|sen;** du piepst; **Piep|ser; piep|sig** (*ugs. für* hoch u. dünn [von der Stimme]; winzig); **Piep|sig|keit,** die; - *(ugs.);* **Piep|vo|gel** *(Kinderspr.)*
[1]**Pier,** der; -s, *Plur.* -e *od.* -s, *in der Seemannsspr.* die; -, -s ‹engl.› (Hafendamm; Landungsbrücke)
[2]**Pier,** der; -[e]s, -e (*nordd. für* Sandwurm als Fischköder)
Pi|erre [pi̯ɛ:r] (m. Vorn.)
Pi|er|ret|te [pi̯ɛ...], die; -, -n ‹franz.› (weibl. Lustspielfigur); **Pi|er|rot** [pi̯ɛ'ro:], der; -s, -s (männl. Lustspielfigur)
pie|sa|cken (*ugs. für* quälen); gepiesackt; **Pie|sa|cke|rei**
pie|seln (*ugs. für* regnen; urinieren); ich ...[e]le (↑R 16)
Pie|se|pam|pel, der; -s, - (*landsch. abwertend für* dummer, engstirniger Mensch)
Pies|por|ter (ein Moselwein)
Pi|e|ta, *ital.* **Pi|e|tà** [*beide* pi̯e'ta], die; -, -s ‹ital.› (Darstellung der Maria mit dem Leichnam Christi auf dem Schoß; Vesperbild); **Pi|e|tät,** die; - ‹lat.› (Respekt, taktvolle Rücksichtnahme); **pi|e|tät|los; Pi|e|tät|lo|sig|keit,** die; -; **pi|e|tät|voll; Pi|e|tis|mus,** der; - (ev. Erweckungsbewegung; *auch für* schwärmerische Frömmigkeit); **Pi|e|tist,** der; -en, -en (↑R 126); **pi|e|tis|tisch**
Pietsch, der; -[e]s, -e (*landsch. für* Trinker); **piet|schen** (*landsch. für* ausgiebig Alkohol trinken); du pietschst
pi|e|zo|e|lekt|risch (↑R 132) ‹griech.›; **Pi|e|zo‿elekt|ri|zi|tät** (↑R 132; die; -; *Physik* durch Druck entstehende Elektrizität an der Oberfläche bestimmter Kristalle), **...me|ter** (das; -s, -; Druckmesser), **...quarz**
piff, paff!
Pig|ment, das; -[e]s, -e ‹lat.› (Farbstoff, -körper); **Pig|men|ta|ti|on,** die; -, -en (Färbung); **Pig|ment‿druck** (*Plur.* ...drucke; Kohledruck, fotogr. Kopierverfahren u. dessen Erzeugnis), **...far|be, ...fleck; pig|men|tie|ren** (Pigment bilden; sich durch Pigmente einfärben); **Pig|men|tie|rung; pig|ment|los; Pig|ment|mal** *Plur.* ...male (Muttermal)
Pig|no|le [pi'njo:lə] (↑R 130), die; -, -n ‹ital.› (Piniennuss); **Pig|no|lie** [pi'njo:li̯ə], die; -, -n (*österr. für* Pignole)
Pi|ja|cke, die; -, -n ‹engl.› (*nordd. für* blaue Seemannsüberjacke)
[1]**Pik,** der; -s, *Plur.* -e *u.* -s ‹franz.› (Bergspitze); *vgl.* Piz; [2]**Pik,** der; -s, -e (*ugs. für* heimlicher Groll); einen Pik auf jmdn. haben; [3]**Pik,** das; -[s], *österr. auch* die; - (Spielkartenfarbe); **pi|kant** (scharf [gewürzt]; prickelnd; reizvoll; anzüglich; schlüpfrig); pikantes Abenteuer; **Pi|kan|te|rie,** die; -, ...i̯en; **pi|kan|ter|wei|se**
Pi|kar|de usw. (*eindeutschend für* Picarde usw.)
pi|ka|resk, pi|ka|risch ‹span.›; -er Roman (*Literaturw.* Schelmenroman)
Pik|ass [*auch* 'pi:k'as], das; -es, -e (↑R 24); [1]**Pi|ke,** die; -, -n ‹franz.› (Spieß [des Landsknechts]); von der Pike auf dienen (*ugs. für* im Beruf bei der untersten Stellung anfangen); [2]**Pi|ke,** die; -, -n (*Nebenform von* [2]Pik); [1]**Pi|kee,** der, *österr. auch* das; -s, -s ([Baumwoll]gewebe); [2]**Pi|kee** *vgl.* Piqué; **pi|kee|ar|tig; Pi|kee‿kra|gen, ...wes|te; pi|ken,** pik|sen (*ugs. für* stechen); du pikst; **Pi|ke|nier,** der; -s, -e (mit der [1]Pike bewaffneter Landsknecht); **Pi|kett,** das; -[e]s, -e (ein Kartenspiel; *schweiz. für* einsatzbereite Mannschaft [bei Militär u. Feuerwehr]); **Pi|kett|stel|lung** (*schweiz. für* Bereitschaftsstellung); **pi|kie|ren** (*Gartenbau* [zu dicht stehende junge Pflanzen] in größeren Abständen neu einpflanzen); **pi|kiert** (ein wenig beleidigt, gekränkt, verstimmt)
[1]**Pik|ko|lo,** der; -s, -s ‹ital.› (Kell-

nerlehrling); ²Pịk|ko|lo, das; -s, -s (*kurz für* Pikkoloflöte); **Pịk|ko|lo-˘fla|sche** (kleine Sektflasche für eine Person), **...flö|te** (kleine Querflöte)

Pik|ko|lo|mi|ni (*dt. Schreibung für* Piccolomini)

Pi|ko..., Pi|co... ⟨ital.⟩ (ein Billionstel einer Einheit; *Zeichen* p; *vgl.* Pikofarad); **Pi|ko|fa|rad,** Pi|co-fa|rad (ein billionstel Farad; *Abk.* pF)

Pi|kör, der; -s, -e ⟨franz.⟩ (Vorreiter bei der Parforcejagd)

Pik|rat (↑R 130), das; -[e]s, -e ⟨griech.⟩ (*Chemie* Pikrinsäuresalz); **Pik|rin|säu|re,** die; - (organ. Verbindung, die früher als Färbemittel u. Sprengstoff verwendet wurde)

pịk|sen *vgl.* piken

Pik|sie|ben; dastehen wie Piksieben (*ugs. für* verwirrt, hilflos sein)

Pịk|te, der; -n, -n; ↑R 126 (Angehöriger der ältesten Bevölkerung Schottlands)

Pik|to|gramm, das; -s, -e ⟨lat.; griech.⟩ (graph. Symbol [mit international festgelegter Bed.], z. B. Totenkopf für „Gift")

Pi|kul, der *od.* das; -s, - ⟨malai.⟩ (Gewicht in Ostasien)

Pi|lar, der; -en, -en (↑R 126) ⟨span.⟩ (*Reiten* Pflock zum Anbinden der Halteleine bei der Abrichtung der Pferde); **Pi|las|ter,** der; -s, - ⟨lat.⟩ ([flacher] Wandpfeiler)

¹**Pi|la|tus** (röm. Landpfleger in Palästina); *vgl. auch* Pontius Pilatus

²**Pi|la|tus,** der; - (Berg bei Luzern)

Pi|lau, Pi|law, der; -s ⟨pers. *u.* türk.⟩ (oriental. Reiseintopf)

Pịl|ger (Wallfahrer; *auch* Wanderer); **Pịl|ger|fahrt; Pịl|ge|rin; pil|gern;** ich ...ere (↑R 16); **Pịl|ger-schaft,** die; -; **Pịl|gers|mann** *Plur.* ...männer *u.* ...leute (*älter für* Pilger); **Pịl|ger|stab; Pịlg|rim** (↑R 130), der; -s, -e (*veraltet für* Pilger)

pil|lie|ren ⟨franz.⟩ (zerstoßen, schnitzeln [bes. Rohseife])

Pịl|ke, die; -, -n (fischförmiger, mit vier Haken versehener Köder beim Hochseeangeln); **pịl|ken** (mit der Pilke angeln)

Pịl|le, die; -, -n ⟨lat.⟩ ([kugelförmiges] Arzneimittel; *nur Sing., meist mit bestimmtem Artikel: kurz für* Antibabypille); **Pịl|len˘dre|her** (ein Käfer; *ugs. scherzh. für* Apotheker), **...knick** (*ugs. für* Geburtenrückgang durch Verbreitung der Antibabypille), **...schach|tel; pil|lie|ren** (*Landw.* Saatgut zu Kügelchen rollen); **Pil|lie|rung;**

Pịl|ling, das; -s ⟨engl.⟩ (Knötchenbildung in Textilien); **pịl|ling|frei**

Pi|lot, der; -en, -en (↑R 126) ⟨franz.⟩ (Flugzeugführer; Rennfahrer; Lotsenfisch; *veraltet für* Lotse, Steuermann); **Pi|lot˘an|la|ge** (*Technik* Versuchsanlage), **...bal|lon** (unbemannter Ballon zur Feststellung des Höhenwindes)

Pi|lo|te, die; -, -n ⟨franz.⟩ (*Bauw.* Rammpfahl)

Pi|lo|ten|schein; Pi|lot|film (Testfilm für eine geplante Fernsehserie); ¹**pi|lo|tie|ren** ([ein Auto, Flugzeug] steuern)

²**pi|lo|tie|ren** ⟨*zu* Pilote⟩ ([Piloten] einrammen); **Pi|lo|tie|rung**

Pi|lo|tin; Pi|lot˘sen|dung, ...stu|die (vorläufige, wegweisende Untersuchung), **...ton** (zur synchronen Steuerung von Bild u. Ton bei Film u. Fernsehen; *vgl.* ¹Ton), **...ver|such**

Pịls, das; -, - (*Kurzform von* Pils[e]ner Bier); 3 Pils; **Pịl|sen** (*tschech.* Plzeň); ¹**Pịl|se|ner,** Pilsner (↑R 103); ²**Pịl|se|ner, Pịls-ner,** das; -s, - (Bier)

Pịlz, der; -es, -e; **Pịlz˘fa|den, ...ge-richt; pil|zig; Pịlz˘kopf** (*ugs. veraltend für* Beatle), **...krank|heit, ...kun|de** (die; -), **...samm|ler, ...ver|gif|tung**

Pi|mẹnt, der *od.* das; -[e]s, -e ⟨lat.⟩ (Nelkenpfeffer, Küchengewürz)

Pịm|mel, der; -s, - (*ugs. für* Penis)

pịm|pe (*nordd. für* gleichgültig)

Pim|pe|lei (*ugs.*); **pịm|pe|lig,** pịmp|lig (*ugs.*); **pịm|peln** (*ugs. für* zimperlich, wehleidig sein); ich ...[e]le (↑R 16)

Pịm|per|lin|ge *Plur.* (*ugs. für* Geld)

¹**pịm|pern** (*bayr. für* klimpern; klingeln); ich ...ere (↑R 16)

²**pịm|pern** (*derb für* koitieren)

Pim|per|nẹll, der; -s, -e *u.* Pim|pinẹl|le, die; -, -n ⟨sanskr.⟩ (eine Küchen- u. Heilpflanze)

Pịm|per|nuss ⟨*zu* ¹pimpern⟩ (ein Zierstrauch)

Pịmpf, der; -[e]s, -e (kleiner Junge; jüngster Angehöriger einer Jugendbewegung)

Pim|pi|nẹl|le *vgl.* Pimpernell

pịmp|lig *vgl.* pimpelig

Pịn, der; -s, -s ⟨engl.⟩ (*fachspr. für* [Verbindungs]stift; [getroffener] Kegel beim Bowling)

PIN = personal identification number (persönliche Geheimzahl für Geldautomaten o. Ä.)

Pi|na|ko|id, das; -[e]s, -e ⟨griech.⟩ (eine Kristallform); **Pi|na|ko-thek,** die; -, -en (Bilder-, Gemäldesammlung)

Pi|nạs|se, die; -, -n ⟨niederl.⟩ (Beiboot [von Kriegsschiffen])

Pin|ce|nez [pɛ̃s(ə)'ne:], das; - [...'ne:(s)], - [...'ne:s] ⟨franz.⟩ (*veraltet für* Klemmer, Kneifer)

Pịn|dar (altgriech. Lyriker); **pin-da|risch;** pindarische Verse (↑R 94); **Pịn|da|ros** *vgl.* Pindar

Pịn|ge *vgl.* Binge

pịn|ge|lig (*ugs. für* kleinlich, pedantisch; empfindlich); **Pịn|ge-lig|keit,** die; -

Pịng|pong [*österr.* ...'pɔŋ], das; -s ⟨engl.⟩ (*veraltet für* Tischtennis); **Ping|pong˘plat|te, ...schlä|ger**

Pịn|gu|in, der; -s, -e (ein Vogel der Antarktis)

Pi|nie [...i̯ə], die; -, -n ⟨lat.⟩ (Kiefer einer bestimmten Art); **Pi|ni|en-˘wald, ...zap|fen**

pịnk ⟨engl.⟩ (rosa); ein pink Kleid; *vgl. auch* beige; ¹**Pịnk,** das; -s, -s (kräftiges Rosa); in Pink (↑R 47)

²**Pịnk,** die; -, -en *u.* ¹**Pịn|ke,** die; -, -n (*nordd. für* Segelschiff; Fischerboot)

²**Pịn|ke,** Pịn|ke|pịn|ke, die; - (*ugs. für* Geld)

¹**Pịn|kel,** der; -s, - (*ugs.*); *meist in* feiner Pinkel (vornehm tuender Mensch)

²**Pịn|kel,** die; -, -n (*nordd.* eine fette, gewürzte Wurst)

pịn|keln (*ugs. für* urinieren); ich ...[e]le (↑R 16); **Pịn|kel|pau|se** (*ugs.*)

pịn|ken (*landsch. für* hämmern)

Pịn|ke|pịn|ke *vgl.* ²Pinke

Pịn|ne, die; -, -n ([Kompass]stift; Teil des Hammers; *bes. nordd. für* Reißzwecke; *Seemannsspr.* Hebelarm am Steuerruder); **pịn|nen** (*bes. nordd. für* mit Pinnen versehen, befestigen); **Pịnn|wand** (Tafel [aus Kork], an der man Merkzettel u. a. anheftet)

Pi|noc|chio [pi'nɔki̯o], der, -[s] ⟨ital.⟩ (eine Märchengestalt)

Pi|no|le, die; -, -n ⟨ital.⟩ (*Technik* Teil der Spitzendrehmaschine)

Pịn|scher, der; -s, - (eine Hunderasse)

¹**Pịn|sel,** der; -s, - (*ugs. für* törichter Mensch, Dummkopf)

²**Pịn|sel,** der; -s, - ⟨lat.⟩; **pịn|sel|ar-tig;** ¹**Pin|se|lei** (*abwertend für* das Pinseln, Malerei)

²**Pin|se|lei** (*veraltet für* große Dummheit)

Pịn|se|ler, Pịns|ler; **pịn|seln;** ich ...[e]le (↑R 16); **Pịn|sel˘stiel, ...strich; Pịns|ler** *vgl.* Pinseler

¹**Pint,** der; -s, -e (*ugs. für* Penis)

²**Pint** [pai̯nt], das; -s, -s ⟨engl.⟩ (engl. u. amerik. Hohlmaß; *Abk.* pt); **Pin|te** ['pintə], die; -, -n (*landsch. für* Wirtshaus, Schenke)

Pin-up-Girl [pin'apgœ:(r)l], das; -s, -s ⟨engl.-amerik.⟩ (leicht bekleidetes Mädchen auf [Illustrierten]bildern, die man an die Wand heften kann)

pinx. = pinxit; **pin|xit** ⟨lat., „hat es gemalt"⟩ (neben dem Namen des Künstlers auf Gemälden; *Abk.* p. *od.* pinx.)

Pin|zet|te, die; -, -n ⟨franz.⟩ (kleine Greif-, Federzange)

Pinz|gau, der; -[e]s (österr. Landschaft)

Pi|om|bi *Plur.* ⟨ital.⟩ (*hist. Bez. für* die Staatsgefängnisse im Dogenpalast von Venedig)

Pi|o|nier, der; -s, -e ⟨franz.⟩ (Soldat der techn. Truppe; *übertr. für* Wegbereiter, Vorkämpfer, Bahnbrecher; *ehem. in der DDR* Angehöriger einer Kinderorganisation); **Pi|o|nier‿ab|tei|lung, ...arbeit, ...geist** (der; -[e]s), **...la|ger** (*Plur.* ...lager; *ehem. in der DDR*), **...lei|ter** (der; *ehem. in der DDR*), **...pflan|ze** *(Bot.),* **...trup|pe** *(Milit.),* **...zeit**

Pi|pa|po, das; -s (*ugs. für* was dazugehört); mit allem Pipapo

[1]**Pi|pe,** die; -, -n (*österr. für* Fass-, Wasserhahn)

[2]**Pipe** [paip], das *od.* die; -, -s ⟨engl.⟩ (engl. u. amerik. Hohlmaß für Wein u. Branntwein); **Pipeline** ['paiplain], die; -, -s (Rohrleitung [für Gas, Erdöl]); **Pi|pet|te** [pi...], die; -, -n ⟨franz.⟩ (Saugröhrchen, Stechheber)

Pi|pi, das; -s *(Kinderspr.);* - machen

Pi|pi|fax, der; - (*ugs. für* überflüssiges Zeug; Unsinn)

Pip|pau, der; -[e]s (eine Pflanzengattung)

Pip|pin [*auch, österr. nur,* 'pi...] (Name fränk. Fürsten)

Pips, der; -es (eine Geflügelkrankheit); **pip|sig**

Pi|qué [pi'ke:], das; -s, -s ⟨franz.⟩ (Reinheitsgrad für Diamanten)

Pi|ran|del|lo (ital. Schriftsteller)

Pi|ran|ha [pi'ranja] ⟨indian.-port.⟩, Pi|ra|lya [...ja], der; -[s], -s ⟨indian.⟩ (ein Raubfisch)

Pi|rat, der; -en, -en (↑R 126) ⟨griech.⟩ (Seeräuber); **Pi|ra|ten‿schiff, ...sen|der; Pi|ra|tentum,** das; -s; **Pi|ra|te|rie,** die; -, ...ien ⟨franz.⟩

Pi|rä|us, der; - (Hafen von Athen)

Pi|ra|ya *vgl.* Piranha

Pir|ma|sens (Stadt in Rheinland-Pfalz)

Pi|ro|ge, die; -, -n ⟨karib.-franz.⟩ (indian. Einbaum)

Pi|rog|ge, die; -, -n ⟨russ.⟩ (eine Pastetenart; ein russ. Gericht)

Pi|rol, der; -s, -e (ein Singvogel)

Pi|rou|et|te [piru...], die; -, -n ⟨franz.⟩ (*Tanz, Eiskunstlauf* schnelle Drehung um die eigene Achse; *Reiten* Drehung in der hohen Schule); **pi|rou|et|tie|ren**

Pirsch, die; -, -en (Schleichjagd); auf der - sein; **pir|schen;** du pirschst; **Pirsch|gang,** der

Pi|sa (ital. Stadt); der Schiefe Turm von - (↑R 108); **Pi|sa|ner** (↑R 103)

Pi|sang, der; -s, -e ⟨malai.-niederl.⟩ (eine Bananenart)

pi|sa|nisch ⟨*zu* Pisa⟩

Pi|see|bau, der; -[e]s ⟨franz.; dt.⟩ (Bauweise, bei der die Mauern aus festgestampftem Lehm o. Ä. bestehen)

pis|pern (*landsch. für* wispern); ich ...ere (↑R 16)

Piss, der; -es (*svw.* Pisse)

Pis|sar|ro (franz. Maler)

Pis|se, die; - (*derb für* Harn); **pissen** *(derb);* du pisst; **Pis|soir** [pi'soa:r], das; -s, *Plur.* -e *u.* -s ⟨franz.⟩ (öffentl. Toilette für Männer)

Pis|ta|zie [...iə], die; -, -n ⟨pers.⟩ (ein Baum mit essbaren Samen; der Samenkern dieses Baumes); **Pis|ta|zi|en|nuss**

Pis|te, die; -, -n ⟨franz.⟩ (Ski-, Rad- od. Autorennstrecke; Rollbahn auf Flugplätzen; unbefestigter Verkehrsweg [z. B. durch die Wüste]; Rand der Manege); **Pis|ten‿sau** (*Plur.* ...säue), **...schwein** (*derb für* rücksichtsloser Skifahrer)

Pis|till, das; -s, -e ⟨lat.⟩ (*Pharm.* Stampfer, Keule; *Bot.* Blütenstempel)

Pis|to|ia (ital. Stadt); **Pis|to|ia|er** [...jaər] (↑R 103); **pis|to|ia|isch** [...jaiʃ]

[1]**Pis|to|le,** die; -, -n ⟨tschech.-roman.⟩ (alte Goldmünze); [2]**Pis|tole,** die; -, -n ⟨tschech.⟩ (kurze Handfeuerwaffe); jmdm. die Pistole auf die Brust setzen (*ugs. für* jmdn. zu einer Entscheidung zwingen); wie aus der Pistole geschossen (*ugs. für* spontan, sehr schnell, sofort); **Pis|to|len‿griff, ...knauf, ...lauf, ...schuss, ...tasche**

Pis|ton [...'tõ:], das; -s, -s ⟨franz.⟩ (Pumpenkolben; Zündstift bei Perkussionsgewehren; Pumpenventil der Blechinstrumente; *franz. Bez. für* [2]Kornett); **Pis|tonblä|ser**

Pi|ta|val [...'val], der; -[s], -s ⟨nach dem franz. Rechtsgelehrten⟩ (Sammlung berühmter Rechtsfälle); Neuer -

Pitch|pine ['pitʃpain], die; -, -s ⟨engl.⟩ (nordamerik. Pechkiefer); **Pitch|pine|holz**

Pi|the|kan|thro|pus (↑R 132), der; -, ...pi ⟨griech.⟩ (javan. u. chin. Frühmensch des Diluviums); **pi|the|ko|id** (affenähnlich)

pit|sche|nass, pit|sche|pat|sche|nass, pitsch|nass *(ugs.);* **pitsch, patsch** *(Kinderspr.);* **pitsch|patsch|nass** *(ugs.)*

pit|to|resk ⟨franz.⟩ (malerisch)

Pi|us (m. Vorn.)

Pi|vot [pi'vo:], der *od.* das; -s, -s ⟨franz.⟩ (*Technik* Schwenkzapfen an Drehkränen u. a.)

Piz, der; -es, -e ⟨ladin.⟩ (Bergspitze); **Piz Bu|in** (Gipfel in der Silvrettagruppe); **Piz Pa|lü** (Gipfel in der Berninagruppe); *vgl.* [1]Pik

Piz|za, die; -, *Plur.* -s, *auch* Pizzen ⟨ital.⟩ (gebackener Hefeteig mit Tomaten, Käse, Sardellen o. Ä.); **Piz|za|bä|cker; Piz|ze|ria,** die; -, *Plur.* -s, *auch* ...rien (Lokal, in dem Pizzas angeboten werden)

piz|zi|ca|to ⟨ital.⟩ (*Musik* mit den Fingern gezupft); **Piz|zi|ka|to,** das; -s, *Plur.* -s *u.* ...ti

Pjöng|jang (Hptst. von Nordkorea)

Pkt. = Punkt

Pkw, *auch* **PKW,** der; -[s], *Plur.* -s, *selten* - = Personenkraftwagen

pl., Pl., Plur. = Plural

Pla|ce|bo, das; -s, -s ⟨lat.⟩ (*Med.* Scheinmedikament ohne Wirkstoffe)

Pla|ce|ment [plas(ə)'mã:], das; -s, -s ⟨franz.⟩ (*Wirtsch.* Anlage von Kapitalien; Absatz von Waren)

Pla|cet *vgl.* Plazet

pla|chan|dern (*ostd. für* plaudern; [einfältig] reden)

Pla|che *vgl.* Blahe

Pla|ci|dia [...ts...] (altröm. w. Eigenn.); **Pla|ci|dus** (altröm. m. Vorn.)

pla|cie|ren [pla'tsi:..., *selten* ...'si:...] usw. *frühere Schreibung für* platzieren usw.

pla|cken, sich (*ugs. für* sich sehr abmühen)

Pla|cken, der; -s, - ; (*landsch. für* großer [schmutziger od. bunter] Fleck)

Pla|cke|rei *(ugs.)*

pla|dauz! (*nordwestd. für* pardauz!)

plad|dern (*nordd. für* heftig, in großen Tropfen regnen); es pladdert)

plä|die|ren; auf schuldig plädieren; **Plä|do|yer** [...doa'je:], das; -s, -s (zusammenfassende Rede des Strafverteidigers od. Staatsanwaltes vor Gericht)

Pla|fond [...'fõ:, *österr. meist*

...'fo:n], der; -s, -s ⟨franz.⟩ (oberer Grenzbetrag bei der Kreditgewährung; *landsch. für* [Zimmer]decke); **pla|fo|nie|ren** [...fo'ni:...] (nach oben hin begrenzen); **Pla|fo|nie|rung**

Pla|ge, die; -, -n; **Pla|ge|geist** *Plur.* ...geister; **pla|gen;** sich -; **Pla|ge|rei**

Plag|ge, die; -, -n (*nordd. für* ausgestochenes Rasenstück)

Pla|gi|at, das; -[e]s, -e ⟨lat.⟩ (Diebstahl geistigen Eigentums); **Pla|gi|a|tor,** der; -s, ...oren; **pla|gi|a|to|risch; pla|gi|ie|ren** (ein Plagiat begehen)

Pla|gi|o|klas, der; -es, -e ⟨griech.⟩ (ein Mineral)

Plaid [ple:t], das, *älter* der; -s, -s ⟨engl.⟩ ([Reise]decke; *auch* großes Umhangtuch aus Wolle)

Pla|kat, das; -[e]s, -e ⟨niederl.⟩ (großformatiger öffentlicher Aushang od. Anschlag zu Informations-, Werbe-, Propagandazwecken o. Ä.); **pla|ka|tie|ren** (Plakate ankleben; durch Plakat bekannt machen; öffentl. anschlagen); **Pla|ka|tie|rung; pla|ka|tiv** (bewusst herausgestellt, sehr auffällig); **Pla|kat₋kunst** (die; -), **...ma|le|rei, ...säu|le, ...schrift, ...wand, ...wer|bung; Pla|ket|te,** die; -, -n ⟨franz.⟩ (kleine [meist geprägte] Platte mit einer Reliefdarstellung; Abzeichen; *auch für* Aufkleber [als Prüfzeichen])

Pla|ko|der|men *Plur.* ⟨griech.⟩ (ausgestorbene Panzerfische); **Pla|ko|dont** (↑R 132), der; -en, -en; ↑R 126 ⟨„Breitzahner"⟩ (ausgestorbene Echsenart); **Pla|ko|idschup|pe** (Schuppe der Haie)

plan ⟨lat.⟩ (flach, eben); plan geschliffene Fläche; **[1]Plan,** der; -[e]s, Pläne (*veraltet für* Ebene; Kampfplatz); *noch in Wendungen wie* auf den Plan rufen (zum Erscheinen veranlassen)

[2]Plan, der; -[e]s, Pläne (Grundriss, Entwurf, Karte; Absicht, Vorhaben)

Pla|na|rie [...i̯ə], die; -, -n (ein Strudelwurm)

Planche [plã:ʃ], die; -, -n [...ʃ(ə)n] ⟨franz.⟩ (Fechtbahn)

Plan|chet|te [plã'ʃɛtə], die; -, -n ⟨franz.⟩ (Miederstäbchen)

Planck (dt. Physiker); plancksches Strahlungsgesetz (↑R 94)

Pla|ne, die; -, -n ([Wagen]decke)

Plä|ne, die; -, -n ⟨franz.⟩ (*veraltet für* Ebene)

pla|nen; Pla|ner

Plä|ner, der; -s (heller Mergel)

Plan|er|fül|lung (*ehem. in der DDR*); **pla|ne|risch; Plä|neschmied, ...schmie|den** (das; -s)

Pla|net, der; -en, -en (↑R 126) ⟨griech.⟩ (sich um eine Sonne bewegender Himmelskörper; Wandelstern); **pla|ne|tar** *vgl.* planetarisch; **pla|ne|ta|risch;** -er Nebel; **Pla|ne|ta|ri|um,** das; -s, ...ien [...i̯ən] (Instrument zur Darstellung der Bewegung der Gestirne; Gebäude dafür); **Pla|ne|ten₋bahn, ...ge|trie|be** (*Technik*), **...jahr, ...kon|stel|la|ti|on, ...sys|tem; Pla|ne|to|id,** der; -en, -en; ↑R 126 (kleiner Planet)

Plan|fest|stel|lung; Plan|fest|stel|lungs|ver|fah|ren

Plan|film (flach gelagerter Film im Gegensatz zum Rollfilm); **plan|ge|mäß; Plan|heit,** die; - (Flächigkeit); **Pla|nier|bank** *Plur.* ...bänke (*Technik*); **pla|nie|ren** ⟨lat.⟩ ([ein]ebnen); **Pla|nier₋rau|pe, ...schild** (der); **Pla|nie|rung; Pla|ni|fi|ka|teur** [...'tø:r], der; -s, -e ⟨franz.⟩ (Fachmann für volkswirtschaftliche Gesamtplanung); **Pla|ni|fi|ka|ti|on,** die; -, -en ⟨lat.⟩ (wirtschaftl. Rahmenplanung des Staates als Orientierungshilfe für die privaten Unternehmen)

Pla|ni|glob, das; -s, -en ⟨lat.⟩ *u.* **Pla|ni|glo|bi|um,** das; -s, ...ien [...i̯ən] (kreisförmige Karte einer Erdhalbkugel)

Pla|ni|me|ter, das; -s, - ⟨lat.; griech.⟩ (Gerät zum Messen des Flächeninhaltes, Flächenmesser); **Pla|ni|met|rie** (↑R 130), die; - (Geometrie der Ebene); **pla|ni|me|trisch**

Plan|kal|ku|la|ti|on (Kalkulation mithilfe der Plankostenrechnung)

Plan|ke, die; -, -n (starkes Brett, Bohle; Bretterzaun)

Plän|ke|lei; plän|keln (sich streiten; ein Gefecht austragen); ich ...[e]le (↑R 16)

Plan|ken|zaun

Plänk|ler (*veraltet*)

Plan|kos|ten *Plur.*; **Plan|kos|ten|rech|nung**

Plank|ton, das; -s ⟨griech.⟩ (*Biol.* Gesamtheit der im Wasser schwebenden niederen Lebewesen); **plank|to|nisch; Plank|ton|netz; Plank|tont,** der; -en, -en; ↑R 126 (im Wasser schwebendes Lebewesen)

plan|los; Plan|lo|sig|keit; plan|mä|ßig; Plan|mä|ßig|keit; Plan|num|mer

pla|no ⟨lat.⟩ (*fachspr. für* glatt, ungefalzt [bes. von Druckbogen u. Karten])

Plan₋quad|rat, ...rück|stand (*ehem. in der DDR*)

Plansch|be|cken, *auch* Plantschbe|cken; **plan|schen,** *auch* plantschen; du planschst, *auch* plantschst

Plan₋schul|den (*Plur.; ehem. in der DDR*), **...soll** (*ehem. in der DDR; vgl.* [2]Soll), **...spiel, ...stel|le**

Plan|ta|ge [...'ta:ʒə, *österr.* ...'ta:ʒ], die; -, -n [...'ta:ʒ(ə)n] ⟨franz.⟩ ([An]pflanzung, landwirtschaftl. Großbetrieb [in trop. Gegenden]); **Plan|ta|gen₋be|sit|zer, ...wirt|schaft**

plan|tar ⟨lat.⟩ (*Med.* die Fußsohle betreffend)

Plantsch|be|cken usw. *vgl.* Planschbecken usw.

Pla|num, das; -s ⟨lat.⟩ (eingeebnete Untergrundfläche beim Straßen- u. Gleisbau)

Pla|nung; Pla|nungs₋bü|ro, ...kom|mis|si|on, ...rech|nung (*Math.*), **...sta|di|um; plan|voll**

Plan|wa|gen

Plan|wirt|schaft (zentral geleitete Wirtschaft, z. B. ehem. in der DDR); **plan|zeich|nen** (Grundrisse, Karten o. Ä. zeichnen *[nur im Infinitiv gebräuchlich]*); **Plan₋zeich|ner, ...zeich|nung, ...ziel**

Plap|pe|rei (*ugs.*); **Plap|pe|rer, Plapp|rer** (*ugs.*); **plap|per|haft;** (*ugs.*); **Plap|per|haf|tig|keit,** die; - (*ugs.*); **Plap|pe|rin** (*ugs.*); **Plap|per₋maul** (*ugs. für* jmd., der plappert), **...mäul|chen** (*ugs.*); **plap|pern** (*ugs. für* viel u. gerne reden); ich ...ere (↑R 16); **Plap|per|ta|sche** (*ugs. svw.* Plappermaul); **Plapp|rer** *vgl.* Plapperer

Plaque [plak], die; -, -s [plak] ⟨franz.⟩ (*Med.* Zahnbelag; Hautfleck)

plär|ren (*ugs.*); **Plär|rer**

Plä|san|te|rie, die; -, ...ien ⟨franz.⟩ (*veraltet für* Scherz); **Plä|sier,** das; -s, *Plur.* -e, *österr.* -s (*veraltend, noch scherzh. für* Vergnügen; Spaß, Unterhaltung); **plä|sier|lich** (*veraltet für* vergnüglich, heiter)

Plas|ma, das; -s, ...men ⟨griech.⟩ (Protoplasma; flüssiger Bestandteil des Blutes; leuchtendes, elektrisch leitendes Gasgemisch); **Plas|ma₋che|mie, ...phy|sik; Plas|mo|di|um,** das; -s, ...ien [...i̯ən] (vielkernige Protoplasmamasse)

Plast, der; -[e]s, -e *meist Plur.* ⟨griech.⟩ (*regional für* Kunststoff); **Plas|te,** die; -, -n (*regional für* [2]Plastik); **Plas|te|tü|te** (*regional*); **Plas|tics** ['plɛstiks] *Plur.* ⟨engl.⟩ (*engl. Bez. für* Kunststoffe); **Plas|ti|de** [pla...], die; -, -n *meist Plur.* ⟨griech.⟩ (*Bot.* Bestandteil der

Pflanzenzelle); [1]**Plas|tik,** die; -, -en (*nur Sing.*: Bildhauerkunst; Bildwerk; *übertr. für* Körperlichkeit; *Med.* operativer Ersatz von zerstörten Gewebs- u. Organteilen); [2]**Plas|tik,** das; -s (Kunststoff); **Plas|tik‿beu|tel, ...bom|be, ...ein|band; Plas|ti|ker** (Bildhauer); **Plas|tik‿fo|lie, ...geld** (das; -[e]s), **...helm, ...sack, ...tra|ge|ta|sche, ...tü|te; Plas|ti|lin,** das; -s, *österr. nur so, u.* **Plas|ti|li|na,** die; - (Knetmasse zum Modellieren); **plas|tisch** (knetbar; körperlich, deutlich hervortretend; anschaulich; einprägsam); plastische Masse; eine plastische Sprache; **Plas|ti|zi|tät,** die; - (Formbarkeit, Körperlichkeit; Bildhaftigkeit, Anschaulichkeit)

Plast|ron [...'strɔ̃:, *österr.* ...'stro:n] (↑R 130), der *od.* das; -s, -s ‹franz.› (breite [weiße] Krawatte; gestickter Brustlatz an Frauentrachten; eiserner Brust- od. Armschutz im MA.; Stoßkissen zu Übungszwecken beim Fechten)

Pla|täa (im Altertum Stadt in Böotien); **Pla|tä|er**

Pla|ta|ne, die; -, -n ‹griech.› (ein Laubbaum); **Pla|ta|nen|blatt**

Pla|teau [...'to:], das; -s, -s ‹franz.› (Hochebene, Hochfläche; Tafelland); **pla|teau|för|mig**

Pla|te|resk, das; -[e]s ‹span.› (Baustil der span. Spätgotik u. der ital. Frührenaissance)

Pla|tin [*österr.* ...'ti:n], das; -s ‹span.› (chem. Element, Edelmetall; *Zeichen* Pt); **pla|tin|blond** (weißblond); **Pla|tin|draht**

Pla|ti|ne, die; -, -n ‹griech.› (Montageplatte für elektrische Bauteile; Teil der Web- od. Wirkmaschine; *Hüttenw.* Formteil)

pla|ti|nie|ren (mit Platin überziehen); **Pla|ti|no|id,** das; -[e]s, -e ‹span.; griech.› (eine Legierung)

Pla|ti|tu|de *vgl.* Plattitüde; **Pla|ti|tü|de** *frühere Schreibung für* Plattitüde

Pla|to *vgl.* Platon; **Pla|ton** (altgriech. Philosoph); **Pla|to|ni|ker** (Anhänger der Lehre Platos); **pla|to|nisch;** platonische (geistige) Liebe; platonisches Jahr; platonische Schriften (↑R 94); **Pla|to|nis|mus,** der; - (Weiterentwicklung u. Abwandlung der Philosophie Platos)

platsch!; plat|schen *(ugs.);* du platschst; **plät|schern;** ich ...ere (↑R 16); **platsch|nass** *(ugs.)*

platt (flach); die Nase platt drücken; da bist du platt! (*ugs. für* da bist du sprachlos, sehr erstaunt!); er hat einen Platten (*ugs. für* eine Reifenpanne); das platte (flache) Land; **Platt,** das; -[s] (das Niederdeutsche; Dialekt); **Plätt|brett; Plätt|chen; platt|deutsch;** *vgl.* deutsch; **Platt|deutsch,** das; -[s] (Sprache); *vgl.* Deutsch; **Platt|deut|sche,** das; -n; *vgl.* Deutsche, das; **Plat|te,** die; -, -n (*österr. ugs. auch für* [Gangster]-bande); **Plät|te,** die; -, -n (*landsch. für* Bügeleisen; *bayr. u. österr. für* flaches Schiff); **Plat|tei** ([Adrema]plattensammlung); **Plätt|ei|sen** *(landsch.);* **plät|teln** (mit Platten, Fliesen auslegen od. verkleiden); ich ...[e]le (↑R 16); **plat|ten** (*landsch. für* platt machen; Platten legen); **plät|ten** (*landsch. für* bügeln); **Plat|ten‿al|bum, ...ar|chiv, ...bau** (*Plur.* ...bauten), **...bau|wei|se** (die; -), **...be|lag, ...hül|le, ...le|ger, ...samm|lung, ...schrank**

Plat|ten|see, der; -s (ung. See); *vgl.* Balaton; [1]**Plat|ten|se|er** (↑R 103, 105 *u.* 131); [2]**Plat|ten|se|er,** der; -s (ein Wein)

Plat|ten‿spie|ler, ...ste|cher (ein Lehrberuf), **...tel|ler, ...wechs|ler, ...weg**

Platt|erb|se; plat|ter|dings (*veraltet für* glatterdings); **Plät|te|rei** *(landsch.);* **Plät|te|rin** *(landsch.);* **Platt‿fisch, ...form, ...frost** (Frost ohne Schnee), **...fuß; platt|fü|ßig; Platt|fuß|in|di|a|ner** *(ugs.);* **Platt|heit; Platt|hirsch** (*Jägerspr.* geweihloser Rothirsch); **plat|tie|ren** ‹franz.› ([mit Metall] überziehen; umspinnen); **Plat|tie|rung; Plat|tier|ver|fah|ren; plat|tig** (glatt [von Felsen]); **Plat|ti|tü|de,** *nach franz. Schreibung auch* Pla|ti|tu|de [...'ty:də], die; -, -n ‹franz.› (*geh. für* Plattheit, Seichtheit); **Platt|ler** (ein Älplertanz); **Plätt|ma|schi|ne** *(landsch.);* **platt|na|sig; Platt|stich;** Platt- und Stielstich; **Platt|[stich|]sti|cke|rei; Platt‿wan|ze, ...wurm**

Platz, der; -es, Plätze (*landsch. auch für* Kuchen, Plätzchen); *Schreibung in Straßennamen:* ↑R 123; Platz finden, greifen, haben; Platz machen, nehmen; am Platz[e] sein; eine Platz sparende Lösung (↑R 40); **Platz‿angst** (die; -), **...an|wei|ser, ...an|wei|se|rin, ...be|darf; Plätz|chen; Platz|deck|chen**

Plat|ze; *in Wendungen wie* die - kriegen (*landsch. für* wütend werden); **plat|zen;** du platzt; **plät|zen** (*landsch. für* mit lautem Knall schießen; Bäume durch Abschlagen eines Rindenstückes zeichnen; den Boden mit den Vorderläufen aufscharren [vom Schalenwild]); du plätzt

...plät|zer (*schweiz. für* ...sitzer); **Platz‿hal|ter** *(bes. Sprachw.),* **...hirsch** (stärkster Hirsch eines Brunftplatzes); **plat|zie|ren** ‹franz.› (aufstellen, an einen bestimmten Platz stellen, bringen; *Kaufmannsspr.* [Kapitalien] unterbringen, anlegen); sich platzieren (*Sport* einen vorderen Platz erreichen); **plat|ziert** (*Sport* genau gezielt); ein platzierter Schuss, Schlag; **Plat|zie|rung; Plat|zie|rungs|vor|schrift** (für Werbeanzeigen o. Ä.); **...plät|zig** *schweiz. für*...sitzig); **Platz‿kar|te, ...kon|zert, ...kos|ten|rech|nung** (*Wirtsch.* Berechnung der Kosten für einzelne Abteilungen eines Betriebes); **Plätz|li,** das; -s, - (*schweiz. mdal. für* flaches Stück, *bes. für* Plätzchen, Schnitzel); **Platz‿man|gel** (der; -s), **...mie|te** (*vgl.* [1]Miete), **...ord|ner**

Platz‿pat|ro|ne, ...re|gen

Platz|run|de *(bes. Sport);* **Platz spa|rend** *vgl.* Platz; **Platz‿ver|hält|nis|se** *(Plur.),* **...ver|tre|tung** *(Kaufmannsspr.),* **...ver|weis** *(Sport),* **...vor|schrift** (*svw.* Platzierungsvorschrift), **...wart** (der; -[e]s, -e), **...wech|sel, ...wet|te**

Platz|wun|de

Platz|zif|fer *(Sport)*

Plau|de|rei; Plau|de|rer, Plaudrer; **Plau|de|rin,** Plaud|re|rin; **plau|dern;** ich ...ere (↑R 16); **Plau|der‿stünd|chen, ...ta|sche** (*ugs. scherzh. für* jmd., der gerne plaudert, geschwätzig ist), **...ton** (der; -[e]s); **Plaud|rer** *vgl.* Plauderer; **Plaud|re|rin** *vgl.* Plauderin

Plau|en (Stadt im Vogtland); **Plau|e|ner** (↑R 103); - Spitzen; **plau|ensch,** *auch* plau|isch; -e Ware

Plau|en|sche Grund, der; -n -[e]s (bei Dresden)

Plau|er Ka|nal, der; - -s ‹*nach* Plaue (Ortsteil von Brandenburg)›

Plau|er See, der; - -s ‹*nach* Plau (Stadt in Mecklenburg)›

Plau|e|sche Grund, der; -n -[e]s; (bei Erfurt)

plau|isch *vgl.* plauensch

Plausch, der; -[e]s, -e *Plur. selten* (*bes. südd., österr. für* gemütl. Plauderei; *schweiz. mdal. für* Vergnügen, Spaß); **plau|schen** (*bes. südd., österr. für* gemütl. plaudern); du plauschst

plau|si|bel ‹lat.› (annehmbar, einleuchtend, begreiflich); ...ib|le

(↑R 130) Gründe; **Plau|si|bi|li|tät,** die; -

plaus|tern (*landsch. für* plustern)

Plau|tus (röm. Komödiendichter)

plauz!; Plauz, der; -es, -e (*ugs. für* Fall; Schall); einen - tun

Plau|ze, die; -, -n ‹slaw.› (*landsch. für* Lunge; Bauch); *bes. in Wendungen wie* es auf der Plauze haben (stark erkältet sein)

plau|zen ‹*zu* Plauz›; du plauzt

Play-back, *auch* **Play|back** ['ple:-bɛk], das; -, -s ‹engl.› (*nur Sing.: Film u. Fernsehen* Verfahren der synchronen Bild- u. Tonaufnahme zu einer bereits vorliegenden Tonaufzeichnung; Bandaufzeichnung); **Play-back-Ver|fah|ren,** *auch* **Play|back|ver|fah|ren;**

Play|boy ['ple:bɔy], der; -s, -s ‹engl.-amerik.› ([reicher jüngerer] Mann, der vor allem seinem Vergnügen lebt u. sich entsprechend darstellt); **Play|girl** ['ple:gœ:(r)l], das; -s, -s (leichtlebiges, attraktives Mädchen [das sich meist in Begleitung reicher Männer befindet]); **Play-off** [ple:'ɔf], das; -, - (System von Ausscheidungsspielen in bestimmten Sportarten); **Play-off-Run|de**

Pla|zen|ta, die; -, *Plur.* -s *u.* ...ten ‹griech.› (*Med., Biol.* Mutterkuchen, Nachgeburt); **pla|zen|tal, pla|zen|tar**

Pla|zet, das; -s, -s ‹lat.› (Bestätigung, Erlaubnis)

pla|zie|ren usw. *frühere Schreibung für* platzieren usw.

Ple|be|jer, der; -s, - ‹lat.› (Angehöriger der niederen Schichten [im alten Rom]; ungehobelter Mensch); **ple|be|jisch** (ungebildet, ungehobelt, pöbelhaft); **Ple|bis|zit,** das; -[e]s, -e (Entscheidung durch Volksabstimmung); **ple|bis|zi|tär; [1]Plebs** [*auch* ple:ps], der; -es, *österr.* die; - (Volk; Pöbel); **[2]Plebs,** die; - (das [arme] Volk im alten Rom)

Plei|nair [plɛ'nɛ:r] (↑R 132), das; -s, -s ‹franz.› (Freilichtmalerei); **Plei|nair|ma|le|rei**

Plei|ße, die; - (r. Nebenfluss der Weißen Elster)

pleis|to|zän ‹griech.›; **Pleis|to|zän,** das; -s (*Geol.* Eiszeitalter)

plei|te ‹hebr.-jidd.› (*ugs. für* zahlungsunfähig); pleite sein, werden; er ist pleite; **Plei|te,** die; -, -n (*ugs.*); Pleite gehen, Pleite machen; er geht Pleite, macht Pleite; das ist ja eine Pleite (ein Reinfall); **Plei|te|gei|er** (*ugs.*)

Ple|ja|de, die; - (griech. Regengöttin); **Ple|ja|den** *Plur.* (Siebengestirn [eine Sterngruppe])

Plek|tron (↑R 130), das; -s, *Plur.* ...tren *u.* ...tra ‹griech.› (Stäbchen od. Plättchen, mit dem die Saiten mancher Zupfinstrumente angerissen werden); **Plek|trum** *vgl.* Plektron

Plem|pe, die; -, -n (*ugs. für* dünnes, fades Getränk); **plem|pern** (*landsch. für* spritzen, [ver]schütten; seine Zeit mit nichtigen Dingen vertun; herumlungern); ich ...ere (↑R 16)

plem|plem (*ugs. für* verrückt)

Ple|nar_saal ‹lat.; dt.›, **...sit|zung** (Vollsitzung), **...ver|samm|lung** (Vollversammlung); **ple|ni|po|tent** (*veraltet für* ohne Einschränkung bevollmächtigt, allmächtig); **Ple|ni|po|tenz,** die; -

ple|no or|ga|no ‹lat.› (mit vollen Registern [bei der Orgel])

ple|no ti|tu|lo ‹lat.› (*österr., sonst veraltet für* mit vollem Titel; *Abk.* P. T.)

Plen|te, die; -, -n ‹ital.› (*südd. für* Brei aus Mais- od. Buchweizenmehl)

Plen|ter|be|trieb (*svw.* Femelbetrieb); **plen|tern** (*Forstw.* einzelne Bäume schlagen); ich ...ere (↑R 16)

Ple|num, das; -s, ...nen ‹lat.› (Gesamtheit [des Parlaments, Gerichts u. a.], Vollversammlung); *vgl.* in pleno

Ple|o|chro|is|mus [...k...], der; - ‹griech.› (Eigenschaft gewisser Kristalle, Licht nach mehreren Richtungen in verschiedene Farben zu zerlegen); **ple|o|morph** usw. *vgl.* polymorph usw.; **Ple|o|nas|mus,** der; -, ...men (*Rhet.* überflüssige Häufung sinngleicher od. sinnähnlicher Ausdrücke; z. B. weißer Schimmel, Einzelindividuum); **ple|o|nas|tisch** (überflüssig gesetzt; überladen); **Ple|o|ne|xie** (↑R 132), die; - (Habsucht; Geltungssucht)

Ple|si|o|sau|ri|er, Ple|si|o|sau|rus, der; -, ...rier [...iər] ‹griech.› (ein ausgestorbenes Reptil)

Ple|thi *vgl.* Krethi

Ple|tho|ra, die; -, *Plur.* ...ren, *fachspr.* ...rae [...rɛ:] ‹griech.› (*Med.* vermehrter Blutandrang)

Ple|thys|mo|graph, der; -en, -en; ↑R 126 ‹griech.› (*Med.* Apparat zur Messung von Umfangsveränderungen eines Gliedes od. Organs)

Pleu|el, der; -s, - (*Technik* Schubstange); **Pleu|el|stan|ge**

Pleu|ra, die; -, ...ren ‹griech.› (*Med.* Brust-, Rippenfell)

Pleu|reu|se [plø'rø:zə], die; -, -n ‹franz.› (*früher* Trauerbesatz an Kleidern; lange [herabhängende] Straußenfeder auf Frauenhüten)

Pleu|ri|tis, die; -, ...itiden ‹griech.› (*Med.* Brust-, Rippenfellentzündung); **Pleu|ro|dy|nie** (↑R 132), die; -, ...ien (Seitenschmerz, Seitenstechen); **Pleu|ro|pneu|mo|nie,** die; -, ...ien (Rippenfell- u. Lungenentzündung)

ple|xi|form ‹lat.› (*Med.* geflechtartig)

Ple|xi|glas ® ‹lat.; dt.› (ein glasartiger Kunststoff)

Ple|xus, der; -, - ['plɛksu:s] ‹lat.› (*Med.* Gefäß- od. Nervengeflecht)

Pli, der; -s ‹franz.› (*landsch. für* Gewandtheit [im Benehmen])

Plicht, die; -, -en (offener Sitzraum hinten in Motor- u. Segelbooten)

plie|ren (*nordd. für* mit den Augen kneifen, blinzeln; weinen); **plie|rig** (*nordd. für* blinzelnd; verweint, triefäugig); plierige Augen

plietsch (*nordd. für* pfiffig)

Plie|vi|er [...'vie:] (dt. Schriftsteller)

Pli|ni|us (röm. Schriftsteller)

plin|kern (*nordd. für* blinzeln)

Plin|se, die; -, -n ‹slaw.› (*landsch. für* Eier- od. Kartoffelspeise)

plin|sen (*nordd. für* weinen); du plinst

Plin|sen|teig (*landsch.*)

Plin|the, die; -, -n ‹griech.› ([Säulen]platte; Sockel[mauer])

Plin|ze, die; -, -n (*Nebenform von* Plinse)

pli|o|zän ‹griech.›; **Pli|o|zän,** das; -s (*Geol.* jüngste Stufe des Tertiärs)

Plis|see, das; -s, -s ‹franz.› (in Fältchen gelegtes Gewebe); **Plis|see|rock; plis|sie|ren**

PLO = Palestine Liberation Organization ['pɛləstain libə're:ʃ(ə)n ɔ:(r)gənai'ze:ʃ(ə)n] (palästinensische Befreiungsbewegung)

Plock|wurst (eine Dauerwurst)

Plom|be, die; -, -n ‹franz.› (Bleisiegel, -verschluss; *veraltend für* [Zahn]füllung); **plom|bie|ren; Plom|bie|rung**

Plo|ni (w. Vorn.)

Plör|re, die; -, -n (*nordd. für* wässriges, fades Getränk)

Plot, der, *auch* das; -s, -s ‹engl.› (*Literaturw.* Handlung[sablauf]; *EDV* graph. Darstellung); **Plot|ter** (*EDV*)

Plöt|ze, die; -, -n ‹slaw.› (ein Fisch)

plötz|lich; Plötz|lich|keit, die; -

Plu|der|ho|se; plu|de|rig, plud|rig; **plu|dern** (sich bauschen)

Plum|bum, das; -s ‹lat.› (*lat. Bez. für* Blei; *Zeichen* Pb)

Plu|meau [ply'mo:], das; -s, -s ‹franz.› (Federdeckbett)

plump; eine plumpe Falle
Plum|pe, die; -, -n (*ostmitteld. für* Pumpe); **plum|pen** (*ostmitteld. für* pumpen)
Plump|heit; plumps!; Plumps, der; -es, -e *(ugs.);* **Plump|sack** (im Kinderspiel); **plump|sen** (*ugs. für* dumpf fallen); du plumpst; **Plumps|klo** (*ugs. für* Toilette ohne Spülung)
Plum|pud|ding ['plam...] ‹engl.› (engl. Süßspeise)
plump|ver|trau|lich (↑R 27)
Plun|der, der; -s, -n (*nur Sing.: ugs. für* altes Zeug; Backwerk aus Blätterteig mit Hefe); **Plun|der|bre|zel; Plün|de|rei; Plün|de|rer,** Plünd|rer; **Plun|der|ge|bäck; Plün|de|rin,** Plünd|re|rin; **Plun|der_kam|mer** *(veraltet),* **...markt** *(veraltet);* **plün|dern;** ich ...ere (↑R 16); **Plun|der|teig; Plün|de|rung; Plünd|rer** *vgl.* Plünderer; **Plünd|re|rin** *vgl.* Plünderin
Plün|nen *Plur.* (*nordd. für* [alte] Kleider)
Plun|ze, die; -, -n (*ostmitteld. für* Blutwurst); **Plun|zen,** die; -, - (*bayr. für* Blutwurst; *scherzh. für* dicke, schwerfällige Person)
Plur. = Plural; **plu|ral** *vgl.* pluralistisch; **Plu|ral,** der; -s, -e ‹lat.› (*Sprachw.* Mehrzahl; *Abk.* pl., Pl., Plur.); **Plu|ral|en|dung; Plu|ra|le|tan|tum,** das; -s, *Plur.* -s *u.* Pluraliatantum (*Sprachw.* nur in der Mehrzahl vorkommendes Wort, z. B. „die Leute"); **plu|ra|lisch** (in der Mehrzahl [gebraucht, vorkommend]); **Plu|ra|li|sie|rung; Plu|ra|lis Ma|jes|ta|tis,** der; - -, ...les - [...le:s -] (auf die eigene Person angewandte Mehrzahlform); **Plu|ra|lis|mus,** der; - (philos. Meinung, dass die Wirklichkeit aus vielen selbstständigen Weltprinzipien besteht; Vielgestaltigkeit gesellschaftlicher, politischer u. anderer Phänomene); **plu|ra|lis|tisch;** pluralistische Gesellschaft; **Plu|ra|li|tät,** die; -, -en (Mehrheit; Vielfältigkeit); **Plu|ral|wahl|recht** (Wahlrecht, bei dem bestimmte Wählergruppen zusätzliche Stimmen haben); **plu|ri|form** (vielgestaltig); **Plu|ri|pa|ra,** die; -, ...paren ‹lat.› (*Med.* Frau, die mehrmals geboren hat); **plus** (und; *Zeichen* + [positiv]; *Ggs.* minus); drei plus drei ist, macht, gibt (*nicht:* sind, machen, geben) sechs; plus 15 Grad *od.* 15 Grad plus; **Plus,** das; -, - (Mehr, Überschuss, Gewinn; Vorteil); **Plus|be|trag**
Plüsch [ply(:)ʃ], der; -[e]s, -e ‹franz.› (Florgewebe); **Plüsch_au|gen** *Plur.* (*ugs. für* sanft blickende [große] Augen); **plüschen** (aus Plüsch); **plü|schig** (wie Plüsch); **Plüsch_ses|sel, ...so|fa, ...tep|pich, ...tier**
Plus_pol, ...punkt
Plus|quam|per|fekt, das; -s, -e ‹lat.› (*Sprachw.* Vollendung in der Vergangenheit, Vorvergangenheit)
plus|tern; die Federn plustern (sträuben, aufrichten); sich -; *vgl.* plaustern
Plus|zei|chen (Zusammenzähl-, Additionszeichen; *Zeichen* +)
Plu|tarch (↑R 132; griech. philosophischer Schriftsteller); **Plu|tar|chos** *vgl.* Plutarch
¹Plu|to (Beiname des Gottes Hades; griech. Gott des Reichtums und des Überflusses); **²Plu|to,** der; - (ein Planet); **Plu|to|krat,** der; -en, -en (↑R 126) ‹griech.› (jmd., der durch seinen Reichtum politische Macht ausübt); **Plu|to|kra|tie,** die; -, ...ien (Geldherrschaft; Geldmacht); **Plu|ton** *vgl.* ¹Pluto; **plu|to|nisch** (der Unterwelt zugehörig); plutonische Gesteine (Tiefengesteine); **Plu|to|nis|mus,** der; - (Tiefenvulkanismus; veraltete geol. Lehre, nach der die Gesteine ursprünglich in glutflüssigem Zustand waren); **Plu|to|ni|um,** das; -s (chem. Element, Transuran; *Zeichen* Pu)
Plut|zer (*österr. mdal. für* Kürbis; Steingutflasche; grober Fehler)
plu|vi|al [...v...] ‹lat.› (*Geol.* als Regen fallend); **Plu|vi|a|le,** das; -s, -[s]; (Vespermantel des kath. Priesters; Krönungsmantel); **Plu|vi|al|zeit** (*Geol.* in den subtrop. Gebieten eine den Eiszeiten der höheren Breiten entsprechende Periode mit kühlerem Klima u. stärkeren Niederschlägen); **Plu|vi|o|graph,** der; -en, -en (↑R 126) ‹lat.; griech.› (*Meteor.* Regenmesser); **Plu|vi|o|me|ter,** das; -s, - (*Meteor.* Regenmesser); **Plu|vi|o|ni|vo|me|ter** [...nivo...], das; -s, - (*Meteor.* Gerät zur Aufzeichnung des als Regen od. Schnee fallenden Niederschlags); **Plu|vi|ose** [ply'vi̯o:s, *auch* ...'vi̯o:z], der; -, -s [...'vi̯o:zəs, *auch* ...'vi̯o:z] ‹franz., „Regenmonat"› (5. Monat des Kalenders der Franz. Revolution: 20. Jan. bis 18. Febr.); **Plu|vi|us** ‹lat.› (Beiname Jupiters)
Ply|mouth ['pliməθ] (engl. Stadt); **Ply|mouth Rocks** *Plur.* (eine Hühnerrasse)
PLZ = Postleitzahl
Plzeň ['p(ə)lzɛn] (Hptst. des Westböhm. Kreises; *vgl.* Pilsen)
p. m. = post meridiem; post mortem; pro memoria
p. m., v. T., ‰ = per *od.* pro mille
Pm = *chem. Zeichen für* Promethium
Pneu, der; -s, -s ‹griech.› (*kurz für* ²Pneumatik *od.* Pneumothorax); **Pneu|ma,** das; -s ‹Hauch› (*Theol.* Heiliger Geist); **¹Pneu|ma|tik,** die; - (Lehre von den Luftbewegungen u. vom Verhalten der Gase; deren Anwendung in der Technik, z. B. als Luftdruckmechanik bei der Orgel); **²Pneu|ma|tik** [*österr.* ...'ma...], der; -s, -s, *österr.* die; -, -en (Luftreifen; *Kurzform* Pneu); **pneu|ma|tisch** (die Luft, das Atmen betreffend; durch Luft[druck] bewegt, bewirkt); pneumatische Bremse (Luftdruckbremse); pneumatische Kammer (luftdicht abschließbare Kammer mit regulierbarem Luftdruck); **Pneu|mo|graph,** der; -en, -en; ↑R 126 (*Med.* Vorrichtung zur Aufzeichnung der Atembewegungen); **Pneu|mo|kok|kus,** der; -, ...kken (Erreger der Lungenentzündung); **Pneu|mo|ko|ni|o|se,** die; - (Staublunge); **Pneu|mo|nie,** die; -, ...ien (Lungenentzündung); **Pneu|mo|pe|ri|kard,** das; -[e]s (Luftansammlung im Herzbeutel); **Pneu|mo|pleu|ri|tis,** die; -, ...itiden (Rippenfellentzündung bei leichter Lungenentzündung); **Pneu|mo|tho|rax,** der; -[es], -e (krankhafte od. künstl. Luft-, Gasansammlung im Brustfellraum; *Kurzform* Pneu)
¹Po, der; -[s] (ital. Fluss)
²Po, der; -s, -s (*kurz für* Popo)
Po = *chem. Zeichen für* Polonium
P. O. = Professor ordinarius (ordentlicher Professor; *vgl. d.*)
Pö|bel, der; -s ‹franz.› (Pack, Gesindel); **Pö|be|lei; pö|bel|haft; Pö|bel|haf|tig|keit,** die; -; **Pö|bel|herr|schaft,** die; -; **pö|beln** (*ugs. für* durch beleidigende Äußerungen provozieren); ich ...[e]le (↑R 16)
Poch, das, *auch* der; -[e]s (ein Kartenglücksspiel); **Poch|brett; Po|che,** die; -, -n (*landsch. für* Schläge); **po|chen**
po|chie|ren [pɔ'ʃi:...] ‹franz.› (*Gastron.* Speisen, bes. aufgeschlagene Eier, in kochendem Wasser gar werden lassen)
Poch_stem|pel (Balken zum Zerkleinern von Erzen), **...werk** *(Bergbau)*
Po|cke, die; -, -n (Eiterbläschen; Impfpustel); **Po|cken** *Plur.* (eine Infektionskrankheit); **Po|cken-**

..imp|fung, ...nar|be; po|cken-nar|big; Po|cken..schutz|imp-fung, ...vi|rus

Po|cket|ka|me|ra ⟨engl.; lat.⟩ (Taschenkamera)

Pock|holz (Guajakholz, ein trop. Holz); **po|ckig**

po|co ⟨ital.⟩ (*Musik* [ein] wenig); poco a poco (nach und nach); poco largo (ein wenig langsam)

Po|dag|ra (↑R 130 *u.* 132), das; -s ⟨griech.⟩ (*Med.* Fußgicht); **po-dag|risch; Po|dal|gie** (↑R 132), die; -, ...ien (Fußschmerzen)

Po|dest, das, *österr. nur so, auch* der; -[e]s, -e ⟨griech.⟩ ([Treppen]absatz; größere Stufe)

Po|des|ta, *ital.* **Po|des|tà** [...'ta], der; -[s], -s ⟨ital.⟩ (*ital. Bez. für* Bürgermeister)

Po|dex, der; -[es], -e ⟨lat.⟩ (*scherzh. für* Gesäß)

Po|di|um, das; -s, ...ien [...iən] ⟨griech.⟩ (trittartige Erhöhung [für Musiker, Redner usw.]); **Po|di|ums..dis|kus|si|on, ...ge-spräch; Po|do|me|ter,** das; -s, - ⟨griech.⟩ (Schrittzähler)

Pod|sol, der; -s ⟨russ.⟩ (graue bis weiße Bleicherde)

Poe [po:], Edgar Allan ['ɛdgər 'ɛlən] (amerik. Schriftsteller)

Po|ebe|ne (↑R 132), die; -; ↑R 105 (Ebene des Flusses Po)

Po|em, das; -s, -e ⟨griech.⟩ (*veraltend, noch scherzh. für* größere lyrisch-epische Dichtung); **Po|e-sie,** die; -, ...ien (Dichtung; Dichtkunst; dicht. Stimmungsgehalt, Zauber); **Po|e|sie|al|bum; po|e|sie|los; Po|e|sie|lo|sig|keit,** die; -; **Po|et,** der; -en, -en; ↑R 126 (*oft scherzh. für* [lyrischer] Dichter); **Po|e|ta lau|re|a|tus,** der; - -, ...tae [...tɛ] ...ti ⟨lat.⟩ ([lorbeer]gekrönter, mit einem Ehrentitel ausgezeichneter Dichter); **Po|e|tas-ter,** der; -s, - ⟨griech.⟩ (*abwertend für* schlechter Dichter); **Po|e|tik,** die; -, -en ([Lehre von der] Dichtkunst); **Po|e|tin** *vgl.* Poet; **po|e-tisch** (dichterisch); er hat eine poetische Ader (*ugs. für* dichterische Veranlagung); **po|e|ti|sie-ren** (dichterisch ausschmücken; dichtend erfassen)

Po|fel, der; -s (*südd. u. österr. svw.* Bafel; Wertloses)

po|fen (*ugs. für* schlafen)

Po|fe|se *vgl.* Pafese

Po|gat|sche, die; -, -n ⟨ung.⟩ (*österr. für* eine Süßspeise)

Pog|rom (↑R 130), der *od.* das; -s, -e ⟨russ.⟩ (Ausschreitungen gegen nationale, religiöse, rassische Gruppen); **Pog|rom..het-ze, ...nacht, ...op|fer**

poi|ki|lo|therm [pɔy...] ⟨griech.⟩ (wechselwarm [von Tieren])

Poi|lu [poa'ly:], der; -[s], -s ⟨franz.⟩ (Spitzname des franz. Soldaten)

Point [poɛ̃:], der; -s, -s ⟨franz.⟩ (*Würfelspiel* Auge; *Kartenspiel* Stich; *Kaufmannsspr.* Notierungseinheit von Warenpreisen an Produktenbörsen); **Point d'Hon|neur** [poɛ̃ dɔ'nø:r], der; - - (*veraltet für* Punkt, an dem sich jmd. in seiner Ehre getroffen fühlt); **Poin|te** ['poɛ̃:tə], die; -, -n (springender Punkt; überraschendes Ende eines Witzes, einer Erzählung); **Poin|ter** ['pɔyntə(r)], der; -s, - ⟨engl.⟩ (Vorstehhund); **poin|tie|ren** [poɛ̃'ti:...] ⟨franz.⟩ (unterstreichen, betonen); **poin-tiert** (betont; zugespitzt); **Poin-til|lis|mus** [poɛ̃ti'jis..., *auch* ...'lis...], der; - (Richtung der impressionist. Malerei); **Poin|til-list,** der; -en, -en; ↑R 126 (Vertreter des Pointillismus); **poin|til|lis-tisch**

Poi|se ['poa:z(ə)], das; -, - ⟨nach dem franz. Arzt Poiseuille⟩ (alte Maßeinheit der Viskosität; *Zeichen* P)

Po|jatz, der; -, -e (*landsch. für* Bajazzo, Hanswurst)

Po|kal, der; -s, -e ⟨ital.⟩ (Trinkgefäß mit Fuß; Sportpreis); **Po|kal-..end|spiel, ...sie|ger, ...spiel, ...sys|tem, ...ver|tei|di|ger, ...wett|be|werb**

Pö|kel, der; -s, - ([Salz]lake); **Pö-kel..fleisch, ...he|ring, ...la|ke; pö|keln;** ich ...[e]le (↑R 16)

Po|ker, das; -s ⟨amerik.⟩ (ein Kartenglücksspiel)

Pö|ker, der; -s, - (*nordd. Kinderspr. für* Podex, Gesäß)

Po|ker..face [...fe:s], **...ge|sicht, ...mie|ne; po|kern** ⟨amerik.⟩; ich ...ere (↑R 16); **Po|ker|spiel**

po|ku|lie|ren ⟨lat.⟩ (*veraltet für* bechern, zechen)

[1]**Pol,** der; -s, -e ⟨griech.⟩ (Drehpunkt; Endpunkt der Erdachse; *Math.* Bezugspunkt; *Elektrotechnik* Aus- u. Eintrittspunkt des Stromes)

[2]**Pol,** der; -s, -e ⟨franz.⟩ (Oberseite von Samt u. Plüsch, die den Flor trägt)

Po|lack, der; -en, -en ⟨poln.⟩ (*abwertende Bez. für* Pole)

po|lar ⟨griech.⟩ (am Pol befindlich, die Pole betreffend; entgegengesetzt wirkend); polare Strömungen; polare Luftmassen; **Po|la|re,** die; -, -n (*Math.* Verbindungslinie der Berührungspunkte zweier Tangenten an einem Kegelschnitt); zwei Polare[n]; **Po-lar..eis, ...ex|pe|di|ti|on, ...fau-na, ...for|scher, ...for|sche|rin, ...front** (*Meteor.* Front zwischen polarer Kaltluft u. trop. Warmluft), **...fuchs, ...ge|biet, ...ge-gend, ...hund; Po|la|ri|sa|ti|on,** die; -, -en (deutliches Hervortreten von Gegensätzen; *Physik* das Herstellen einer festen Schwingungsrichtung aus sonst unregelmäßigen Schwingungen des natürlichen Lichtes); **Po|la|ri|sa|ti-ons..ebe|ne** (↑R 132), **...fil|ter, ...mik|ro|skop, ...strom; Po|la|ri-sa|tor,** der; -s, ...oren (Vorrichtung, die polarisierte Strahlung aus natürlicher erzeugt); **po|la|ri-sie|ren** (der Polarisation unterwerfen); sich - (in seiner Gegensätzlichkeit immer stärker hervortreten); **Po|la|ri|sie|rung; Po|la-ri|tät,** die; -, -en (Vorhandensein zweier [1]Pole, Gegensätzlichkeit); **Po|lar..kreis, ...land** (*Plur.* ...länder), **...licht** (*Plur.* ...lichter), **...luft** (die; -), **...meer, ...nacht**

Po|la|ro|id|ka|me|ra ® [*auch* ...'rɔyt...] (Fotoapparat, der kurz nach der Aufnahme das fertige Bild liefert)

Po|lar..stern (der; -[e]s; *vgl.* [2]Stern), **...zo|ne**

Pol|del (m. Vorn.)

Pol|der, der; -s, - ⟨niederl.⟩ (eingedeichtes Land); **Pol|der|deich**

Po|le, der; -n, -n (↑R 126)

Po|lei, der; -[e]s, -e ⟨lat.⟩ (Bez. verschiedener Heil- u. Gewürzpflanzen); **Po|lei|min|ze**

Po|le|mik, die; -, -en ⟨griech.⟩ (wissenschaftl., literar. Fehde, Auseinandersetzung; [unsachlicher] Angriff); **Po|le|mi|ker; Po|le|mi-ke|rin; po|le|misch; po|le|mi-sie|ren**

po|len ⟨griech.⟩ (an einen elektr. Pol anschließen)

Po|len

Po|len|ta, die; -, *Plur.* -s *u.* ...ten ⟨ital.⟩ (ein Maisgericht)

Po|len|te, die; - ⟨jidd.⟩ (*ugs. für* Polizei)

Pole|po|si|tion ['po:lpə'ziʃ(ə)n], die; - ⟨engl.⟩ (beste Startposition beim Autorennen)

Po|les|je, Po|less|je, die; - (osteurop. Wald- u. Sumpflandschaft)

Pol|gar (österr. Schriftsteller)

Pol|hö|he (*Geogr.*)

Po|li|ce [...sə], die; -, -n ⟨franz.⟩ (Versicherungsschein)

Po|li|ci|nel|lo [...tʃi...], der; -s, ...lli ⟨ital.⟩ (*veraltete Nebenform von* Pulcinella)

Po|lier, der; -s, -e ⟨franz.⟩ (Vorarbeiter der Maurer u. Zimmerleute; Bauführer)

Po|lie̲r|bürs|te; po|lie̲|ren ‹franz.› (reiben, putzen; glänzend, blank machen); **Po|lie̲|rer; Po|lie̲|re|rin; Po|lie̲r‿mit|tel** (das), **...stahl** *(Druckw.)*, **...wachs**

Po̲|li|kli|nik [*auch* 'pɔ...] (medizin. Einrichtung zur ambulanten Behandlung); **po|li|kli|nisch**

Po̲|lin

Po̲|lio, die; - (*Kurzform von* Poliomyelitis); **Po̲|li|o|in|fek|ti|on; Po|li|o|my|e|li̲|tis,** die; -, ...iti̲den ‹griech.› (*Med.* Kinderlähmung)

Po̩|lis, die; -, Poleis ‹griech.› (altgriech. Stadtstaat)

Po|li̩t|bü|ro ‹*Kurzw. für* Politisches Büro› (Führungsorgan von kommunist. Parteien)

[1]**Po|li|te̩s|se,** die; - ‹franz.› (*veraltet für* Höflichkeit, Artigkeit)

[2]**Po|li|te̩s|se,** die; -, -n ‹aus Polizei u. Hostess› (Angestellte einer Gemeinde, die bes. die Einhaltung des Parkverbots kontrolliert)

Po|li̲|ti|cal Cor|re̩ct|ness (↑R 33) [...kəl -], die; - - ‹engl.› (von einer bestimmten Öffentlichkeit als richtig angesehene Gesinnung)

po|li|tie̲|ren ‹lat.-franz.› (*ostösterr. für* mit Politur einreiben u. glänzend machen)

Po|li|ti̲k [*auch* ...'tik], die; -, -en *Plur. selten* ‹griech.› ([Lehre von der] Staatsführung; zielgerichtetes Verhalten); **Po|li|ti|ka̩s|ter,** der; -s, - (*abwertend für* jmd., der viel von Politik spricht, ohne etwas davon zu verstehen); **Po|li̲|ti|ker** [*auch* pɔ'li...]; **Po|li|ti|ke|rin; po|li|ti̲k|fä|hig; Po|li|ti̲k|fä|hig|keit,** die; -; **Po|li̲|ti|kum,** das; -s, ...ka (Tatsache, Vorgang von polit. Bedeutung); **Po|li̲|ti|kus,** der; -, -se (*ugs. scherzh. für* jmd., der sich gern mit Politik beschäftigt); **Po|li|ti̲k|ver|ständ|nis,** das; -ses; **po|li̲|tisch** (die Politik betreffend; staatsmännisch; staatsklug); politische Karte (Staatenkarte); politische Wissenschaft; politische Geographie; politische Geschichte; politische Ökonomie; politisch korrekt (*auch iron.* niemanden durch eine [möglicherweise] als abwertend empfundene Benennung diskriminierend); poli̲tisch-gese̩llschaftlich (↑R 27); **po|li|ti|sie̲|ren** (von Politik reden; politisch behandeln); **Po|li|ti|sie̲|rung,** die; -; **Po|li̩t|of|fi|zier** *(ehem. in der DDR);* **Po|li|to|lo̲|ge,** der; -n, -n; ↑R 126 (Wissenschaftler auf dem Gebiet der Politologie); **Po|li|to|lo|gie̲,** die; - (Wissenschaft von der Politik); **Po|li|to|lo̲|gin; Po|li̩t‿por|no|gra|phie, ...re|vue; Po|lit|ru̩k,** der; -s, -s ‹russ.› (*früher* polit. Führer in einer sowjet. Truppe)

Po|li|tu̲r, die; -, -en ‹lat.› (Glätte, Glanz; Poliermittel; *nur Sing.:* äußerer Anstrich, Lebensart)

Po|li|ze̲i, die; -, -en *Plur. selten* ‹griech.›; **Po|li|ze̲i‿ak|ti|on, ...ap|pa|rat, ...auf|ge|bot, ...au|to, ...be|am|te, ...be|am|tin, ...be|hör|de, ...chef, ...di|rek|ti|on, ...ein|satz, ...es|kor|te, ...funk, ...ge|wahr|sam, ...griff, ...hund, ...kom|mis|sar, ...kom|mis|sa|rin, ...kon|tin|gent, ...kon|trol|le, ...kräf|te** *(Plur.);* **po|li|ze̲i|lich;** polizeiliches Führungszeugnis; polizeiliche Meldepflicht; **Po|li|ze̲i‿meis|ter, ...ober|meis|ter** (↑R 132), **...or|gan, ...prä|si|dent, ...prä|si|di|um, ...re|vier, ...schutz** (der; -es), **...si|re|ne, ...spit|zel, ...staat** (*Plur.* ...staaten), **...strei|fe, ...stun|de** (die; -), **...ver|ord|nung, ...wa|che, ...we|sen** (das; -s); **po|li|ze̲i|wid|rig; Po|li|zi̩st,** der; -en, -en (↑R 126); **Po|li|zi̩s|tin**

Po|li̩z|ze, die; -, -n (*österr. für* Police)

Pölk, das *od.* der; -[e]s, -e (*nordd. für* halberwachsenes, männliches kastriertes Schwein)

Po̩l|ka, die; -, -s ‹poln.-tschech.› (ein Tanz)

po̩l|ken (*nordd. für* bohren, mit den Fingern entfernen)

Po̩l|lack, der; -s, -s (eine Schellfischart)

Po̩l|len, der; -s, - ‹lat.› (Blütenstaub); **Po̩l|len‿al|ler|gie, ...ana|ly|se** (↑R 132), **...korn** (das; *Plur.* ...körner), **...schlauch**

Po̩l|ler, der; -s, - (*Seemannsspr.* Holz- od. Metallpfosten zum Befestigen der Taue; Markierungsklotz für den Straßenverkehr)

Pol|lu|ti|o̲n, die; -, -en ‹lat.› (*Med.* unwillkürlicher [nächtl.] Samenerguss)

[1]**Po̩l|lux** (Held der griech. Sage); Kastor und Pollux (Zwillingsbrüder; *übertr. für* eng befreundete Männer); [2]**Po̩l|lux,** der; - (Zwillingsstern im Sternbild Gemini)

po̩l|nisch; polnische Wurst, *aber* (↑R 108): der Polnische Erbfolgekrieg; **Po̩l|nisch,** das; -[s] (Sprache); *vgl.* Deutsch; **Po̩l|ni|sche,** das; -n; *vgl.* Deutsche, das

Po̲|lo, das; -s ‹engl.› (Ballspiel vom Pferd aus); **Po̲|lo|hemd** (kurzärmeliges Trikothemd)

Po|lo|nai|se [...'nɛ:zə], *eindeutschend* **Po|lo|nä̲|se,** die; -, -n ‹franz.› (ein Reihentanz); **Po|lo̲|nia** (lat. Name von Polen); **po|lo|ni|sie̲|ren** (polnisch machen); **Po|lo|ni̩st,** der; -en, -en; ↑R 126 (Wissenschaftler auf dem Gebiet der Polonistik); **Po|lo|ni̩s|tik,** die; - (Wissenschaft von der poln. Sprache u. Kultur); **Po|lo|ni̩s|tin; po|lo|ni̩s|tisch; Po|lo̲|ni|um,** das (chem. Element, Halbmetall; *Zeichen* Po)

Po̲|lo|spiel, das; -[e]s (*svw.* Polo)

Po̩ls|ter, das, *österr.* der; -s, *Plur.* -, *österr. auch* Pölster (*österr. auch für* Kissen); **Pö̩ls|ter|chen; Po̩ls|te|rer; Po̩ls|ter|gar|ni|tur; Po̩ls|te|rin; Po̩ls|ter|mö|bel; po̩ls|tern;** ich ...ere (↑R 16); **Po̩ls|ter‿ses|sel, ...stoff, ...stuhl; Po̩ls|te|rung**

Po̩l|ter, der *od.* das; -s, - (*südwestd. für* Holzstoß)

Po̩l|ter|abend (↑R 132); **Po̩l|te|rer; Po̩l|ter|geist** *Plur.* ...geister; **po̩l|te|rig,** po̩lt|rig; **po̩l|tern;** ich ...ere (↑R 16); **po̩lt|rig** *vgl.* polterig

Po̲l‿wechs|ler *od.* **...wen|der** *(Elektrotechnik)*

po|ly... ‹griech.› (viel...); **Po|ly...** (Viel...)

Po|ly|ac|ryl, das; -s ‹griech.› (ein Kunststoff)

Po|ly|ami̲d ® (↑R 132), das; -[e]s, -e ‹griech.› (ein elastischer, fadenbildender Kunststoff)

Po|ly|and|rie̲ (↑R 130), die; - ‹griech.› (*Völkerk.* Vielmännerei)

Po|ly|arth|ri̲|tis, die; -, ...iti̲den ‹griech.› (*Med.* Entzündung mehrerer Gelenke)

Po|ly|äs|the|sie̲, die; -, ...ien ‹griech.› (*Med.* das Mehrfachempfinden eines Berührungsreizes)

Po|ly|äthy|le̲n, *chem. fachspr.* Po|ly|ethy|le̲n (↑R 132), das; -s, -e ‹griech.› (thermoplastischer, säure- und laugenbeständiger Kunststoff)

Po|ly̲|bi|os, Po|ly̲|bi|us (griech. Geschichtsschreiber)

po|ly|chro̲m [...k...] ‹griech.› (vielfarbig, bunt); **Po|ly|chro|mie̲,** die; -, ...ien (Vielfarbigkeit; bunte Bemalung von Bau- u. Bildwerken); **po|ly|chro|mie̲|ren** (vielfarbig, bunt ausstatten)

Po|ly|dak|ty|lie̲, die; - ‹griech.› (*Med.* Bildung von überzähligen Fingern od. Zehen)

Po|ly|deu̲|kes (griech. Name von [1]Po̩llux)

Po|ly|e̲|der, das; -s, - ‹griech.› (*Math.* Vielflächner); **Po|ly|e̲|der|krank|heit,** die; - (*Biol.* eine Raupenkrankheit); **po|ly|e̲d|risch** (↑R 130; *Math.* vielflächig)

Po|ly|e̩s|ter, der; -s, - ‹griech.› (aus Säuren u. Alkoholen gebildete

Verbindung mit hohem Molekulargewicht, ein Kunststoff)

Po|ly|ethy|len (↑R 132) *vgl.* Polyäthylen

po|ly|fon *eindeutschende Schreibung für* polyphon

po|ly|gam ‹griech.› (mehr-, vielehig); **Po|ly|ga|mie,** die; - (Mehr-, Vielehe); **Po|ly|ga|mist,** der; -en, -en (↑R 126)

po|ly|gen ‹griech.› (vielfachen Ursprungs; *Biol.* durch mehrere Erbfaktoren bedingt)

po|ly|glott ‹griech.› (vielsprachig; viele Sprachen sprechend); [1]**Po|ly|glot|te,** der *u.* die; -n, -n; ↑R 126 (jmd., der viele Sprachen spricht); [2]**Po|ly|glot|te,** die; -, -n (*Buchw.* mehrsprachige Ausgabe von Texten); **Po|ly|glot|ten|bi|bel**

Po|ly|gon, das; -s, -e ‹griech.› (*Math.* Vieleck); **po|ly|go|nal** (vieleckig); **Po|ly|gon‿aus|bau** (der; -[e]s; *Bergmannsspr.*), **...bo|den** *(Geol.)*

Po|ly|graph, der; -en, -en (↑R 126) ‹griech.› (Gerät zur gleichzeitigen Registrierung mehrerer [medizin. od. psych.] Vorgänge); **Po|ly|gra|phie,** die; -, ...ien (*Med.* Röntgenuntersuchung mit mehrmaliger Belichtung zur Darstellung von Organbewegungen; *nur Sing.: regional für* Gesamtheit des graph. Gewerbes)

Po|ly|gy|nie, die; - ‹griech.› (*Völkerk.* Vielweiberei)

Po|ly|his|tor, der; -s, ...oren ‹griech.› (*veraltet für* in vielen Fächern bewanderter Gelehrter)

Po|ly|hym|nia, Po|lym|nia (Muse des ernsten Gesanges)

po|ly|karp, *auch* po|ly|kar|pisch ‹griech.› (*Bot.* in einem bestimmten Zeitraum mehrmals Blüten und Früchte ausbildend)

Po|ly|karp (ein Heiliger)

Po|ly|kla|die, die; - ‹griech.› (*Bot.* Bildung von Seitensprossen nach Verletzung einer Pflanze)

Po|ly|kon|den|sa|ti|on, die; -, -en ‹griech.; lat.› (*Chemie* Zusammenfügen einfachster Moleküle zu größeren zur Gewinnung von Kunststoffen)

Po|ly|kra|tes (ein Tyrann von Samos)

po|ly|mer ‹griech.› (*Chemie* aus größeren Molekülen bestehend); **Po|ly|mer,** das; -s, -e *u.* **Po|ly|me|re,** das; -n, -n *meist Plur.;* ↑R 5 ff. (*Chemie* eine Verbindung aus Riesenmolekülen); **Po|ly|me|rie,** die; -, ...jen (*Biol.* das Zusammenwirken mehrerer gleichartiger Erbfaktoren bei der Ausbildung eines Merkmals; *Chemie* Bez. für die besonderen Eigenschaften polymerer Verbindungen); **Po|ly|me|ri|sat,** das; -[e]s, -e (*Chemie* durch Polymerisation entstandener neuer Stoff); **Po|ly|me|ri|sa|ti|on,** die; -, -en (auf Polymerie beruhendes chem. Verfahren zur Herstellung von Kunststoffen); **po|ly|me|ri|sier|bar; po|ly|me|ri|sie|ren; Po|ly|me|ri|sie|rung**

Po|ly|me|ter, das; -s, - ‹griech.› (meteor. Messgerät); **Po|ly|met|rie** (↑R 130), die; -, ...ien (*Verslehre, Musik* Vielfalt in Metrik u. Takt)

Po|lym|nia *vgl.* Polyhymnia

po|ly|morph ‹griech.› (viel-, verschiedengestaltig); **Po|ly|mor|phie,** die; - *u.* **Po|ly|mor|phis|mus,** der; - (Vielgestaltigkeit, Verschiedengestaltigkeit)

Po|ly|ne|si|en ‹griech.› (Inselwelt im mittleren Pazifik); **Po|ly|ne|si|er; Po|ly|ne|si|e|rin; po|ly|ne|sisch**

Po|ly|nom, das; -s, -e ‹griech.› (*Math.* vielgliedrige Größe); **po|ly|no|misch**

po|ly|nuk|le|är (↑R 130) ‹griech.; lat.› (*Med.* vielkernig)

Po|lyp, der; -en, -en (↑R 126) ‹griech.› (ein Nesseltier mit Fangarmen; *veraltet für* Tintenfisch; *Med.* gestielte Geschwulst, [Nasen]wucherung; *ugs. für* Polizeibeamter); **po|ly|pen|ar|tig**

Po|ly|pha|ge, der; -n, -n *meist Plur.* (↑R 126) ‹griech.› (*Zool.* sich von verschiedenartigen Pflanzen od. Beutetieren ernährendes Tier); **Po|ly|pha|gie,** die; -

Po|ly|phem, Po|ly|phe|mos (griechische Sagengestalt; Zyklop)

po|ly|phon (↑R 33) ‹griech.› (*Musik* mehrstimmig, vielstimmig); polyphoner Satz; **Po|ly|pho|nie,** die; - (Mehrstimmigkeit, Vielstimmigkeit; ein Kompositionsstil); **po|ly|pho|nisch** (*veraltend für* polyphon)

Po|ly|pi|o|nie, die; - ‹griech.› (*Med.* Fettsucht)

po|ly|plo|id ‹griech.› (*Biol.* mit mehrfachem Chromosomensatz [von Zellen])

Po|ly|re|ak|ti|on ‹griech.; lat.› (*Chemie* Bildung hochmolekularer Verbindungen)

Po|ly|rhyth|mik ‹griech.› (*Musik* verschiedenartige, aber gleichzeitig ablaufende Rhythmen in einer Komposition); **po|ly|rhyth|misch**

Po|ly|sac|cha|rid, Po|ly|sa|cha|rid [*beide* ...zaxa...], das; -[e]s, -e ‹griech.› (Vielfachzucker, z. B. Stärke, Zellulose)

po|ly|sem, po|ly|se|man|tisch ‹griech.› (*Sprachw.* Polysemie besitzend; mehr-, vieldeutig); **Po|ly|se|mie,** die; - (Mehrdeutigkeit [von Wörtern])

Po|ly|sty|rol, das; -s, -e ‹griech.; lat.› (*Chemie* ein Kunststoff)

po|ly|syn|de|tisch ‹griech.› (*Sprachw.* durch Konjunktionen verbunden); **Po|ly|syn|de|ton,** das; -s, ...ta (durch Konjunktionen verbundene Wort- od. Satzreihe)

po|ly|syn|the|tisch ‹griech.› (*Sprachw.* vielfach zusammengesetzt); polysynthetische Sprachen; **Po|ly|syn|the|tis|mus,** der; - (Verschmelzung von Bestandteilen des Satzes in ein großes Satzwort)

Po|ly|tech|ni|ker ‹griech.› (Besucher des Polytechnikums); **Po|ly|tech|ni|kum** (technische Fachhochschule); **po|ly|tech|nisch** (viele Zweige der Technik umfassend); polytechnische Oberschule (*ehem. in der DDR* zehnklassige Schule; *Abk.* POS); polytechnischer Lehrgang (9. Jahr der allgemeinen Schulpflicht in Österr.)

Po|ly|the|is|mus ‹griech.› (Glaube an viele Götter); **Po|ly|the|ist; po|ly|the|is|tisch**

Po|ly|to|na|li|tät, die; - ‹griech.› (*Musik* gleichzeitiges Auftreten mehrerer Tonarten in den verschiedenen Stimmen eines Tonstücks)

po|ly|trop ‹griech.› (*Biol.* vielfach anpassungsfähig)

Po|ly|vi|nyl|chlo|rid [...v...], das; -[e]s ‹griech.› (*Chemie* ein säurefester Kunststoff; *Abk.* PVC)

pöl|zen (*österr. für* [durch Stützen, Verschalung] abstützen); du pölzt; einen Stollen -

Po|ma|de, die; -, -n ‹franz.› ([Haar]fett); **Po|ma|den|hengst** (*ugs. für* geschniegelter Mann); **po|ma|dig** (mit Pomade eingerieben; *ugs. für* träge; blasiert); **po|ma|di|sie|ren** (mit Pomade einreiben)

Po|me|ran|ze, die; -, -n ‹ital.› (apfelsinenähnl. Zitrusfrucht); **Po|me|ran|zen|öl**

Pom|mer, der; -n, -n (↑R 126); **Pom|me|rin; pom|me|risch,** pom|mersch, *aber* (↑R 102): die Pommersche Bucht; **Pom|mer|land,** das; -[e]s; **Pom|mern; pom|mersch** *vgl.* pommerisch

Pom|mes *Plur.* (*ugs. für* Pommes frites); **Pommes Cro|quettes** [pɔm krɔ'kɛt] *Plur.* ‹franz.›

(Kroketten aus Kartoffelbrei); **Pommes Dau|phine** [pɔm doˈfi(:)n] *Plur.* (eine Art Kartoffelkroketten); **Pommes frites** [pɔm ˈfrit] *Plur.* (in Fett gebackene Kartoffelstäbchen)

Po|mo|lo|gie, die; - ⟨lat.; griech.⟩ (Obst[bau]kunde); **Po|mo|na** (röm. Göttin der Baumfrüchte)

Pomp, der; -[e]s ⟨franz.⟩ (prachtvolle Ausstattung; [übertriebener] Prunk)

[1]**Pom|pa|dour** [pɔ̃paˈdu:r] (Mätresse Ludwigs XV.); [2]**Pom|pa|dour** [ˈpɔmpadu:r], der; -s, *Plur.* -e *u.* -s (*früher* beutelartige Handtasche)

Pom|pei *vgl.* Pompeji; **Pom|pe|ja|ner** (*seltener für* Pompejer); **pom|pe|ja|nisch** (*seltener für* pompejisch); **Pom|pe|jer** (↑R 103); **Pom|pe|ji,** Pom|pei (Stadt u. Ruinenstätte am Vesuv); **pom|pe|jisch**

Pom|pe|jus (röm. Feldherr u. Staatsmann)

pomp|haft; Pomp|haf|tig|keit, die; -

Pom|pon [pɔ̃ˈpɔ̃:, *auch* pɔmˈpɔ̃:], der; -s, -s ⟨franz.⟩ (knäuelartige Quaste aus Wolle od. Seide)

pom|pös ⟨franz.⟩ ([übertrieben] prächtig; prunkhaft)

Po|mu|chel, der; -s, - ⟨slaw.⟩ (*nordostd. für* Dorsch); **Po|mu|chels|kopp,** der; -s, ...köppe (*nordostd. für* dummer, plumper Mensch)

pö|nal ⟨griech.⟩ (*veraltet für* die Strafe, das Strafrecht betreffend); **Pö|na|le,** das; -s, *Plur.* ...lien [...iən], *österr.* - (*österr., sonst veraltet für* Strafe, Buße); **Pö|nal|ge|setz** *(kath. Moraltheol.)*

Po|na|pe (eine Karolineninsel)

pon|ceau [pɔ̃ˈso:] ⟨franz.⟩ (leuchtend orangerot); ein ponceau Kleid; *vgl. auch* beige; **Pon|ceau,** das; -s, -s (leuchtendes Orangerot); in Ponceau (↑R 47)

Pon|cho [ˈpɔntʃo], der; -s, -s ⟨indian.⟩ (capeartiger [Indio]mantel)

pon|cie|ren [pɔ̃ˈsi:...] ⟨franz.⟩ (mit Bimsstein abreiben; mit Kohlenstaubbeutel durchpausen)

Pond, das; -s, - ⟨lat.⟩ (alte physikal. Krafteinheit; *Zeichen* p); **pon|de|ra|bel** (*veraltet für* wägbar); ...able (↑R 130) Angelegenheiten; **Pon|de|ra|bi|li|en** [...iən] *Plur.* (*veraltet* kalkulierbare, wägbare Dinge)

Pon|gau, der; -[e]s (salzburgische Alpenlandschaft)

Pö|ni|tent, der; -en, -en (↑R 126) ⟨lat.⟩ (*kath. Kirche veraltend für* Büßender, Beichtender); **Pö|ni|ten|ti|ar,** der; -s, -e (*veraltend für* Beichtvater); **Pö|ni|tenz,** die; -, -en (*veraltend für* Buße, Bußübung)

Pon|te, die; -, -n ⟨lat.⟩ (*landsch. für* breite Fähre); **Pon|ti|cel|lo** [...ˈtʃɛlo], der; -s, *Plur.* -s *u.* ...lli ⟨ital.⟩ (*Musik* Steg der Streichinstrumente); **Pon|ti|fex,** der; -, ...tifizes, *auch* ...tifices (Oberpriester im alten Rom); **Pon|ti|fex ma|xi|mus,** der; - -, ...tifices [...tse:s] ...mi (oberster Priester im alten Rom; *nur Sing.:* Titel des röm. Kaisers u. danach des Papstes); **Pon|ti|fi|ces** (*Plur. von* Pontifex); **pon|ti|fi|kal** (*kath. Kirche* bischöflich); *vgl.* in pontificalibus; **Pon|ti|fi|kal|amt,** das; -[e]s (eine von einem Bischof od. Prälaten gehaltene feierl. Messe); **Pon|ti|fi|ka|le,** das; -[s], ...lien [...iən] (liturg. Buch für die bischöflichen Amtshandlungen); **Pon|ti|fi|ka|li|en** *Plur.* (die den kath. Bischof auszeichnenden liturg. Gewänder u. Abzeichen); **Pon|ti|fi|kat,** das *od.* der; -[e]s, -e (Amtsdauer u. Würde des Papstes od. eines Bischofs); **Pon|ti|fi|zes** (*Plur. von* Pontifex)

Pon|ti|ni|sche Sümp|fe *Plur.* (ehem. Sumpfgebiet bei Rom)

pon|tisch ⟨griech.⟩ (steppenhaft, aus der Steppe stammend)

Pon|ti|us Pi|la|tus (röm. Landpfleger in Palästina); von Pontius zu Pilatus laufen (*ugs. für* mit einem Anliegen [vergeblich] von einer Stelle zur anderen gehen)

Pon|ton [pɔnˈtɔŋ, *auch* pɔ̃ˈtɔ̃:, *österr.* pɔnˈto:n], der; -s, -s ⟨franz.⟩ (Brückenschiff); **Pon|ton‿brü|cke, ...form; Pon|to|nier,** der; -s, -e (*schweiz. Milit.* Soldat einer Spezialtruppe für das Übersetzen über Flüsse und Seen und den Bau von Kriegsbrücken)

Pont|re|si|na (↑R 130; schweiz. Kurort)

Pon|tus (im Altertum Reich in Kleinasien); **Pon|tus Eu|xi|nus,** der; - - ⟨lat.⟩ (im Altertum das Schwarze Meer)

[1]**Po|ny** [*selten* ˈpo:ni], das; -s, -s ⟨engl.⟩ (Kleinpferd); [2]**Po|ny,** der; -s, -s (fransenartig in die Stirn gekämmtes Haar); **Po|ny‿fran|sen** *(Plur.)*, **...fri|sur**

[1]**Pool** [pu:l], der; -s, -s ⟨engl.⟩ (*kurz für* Swimmingpool); [2]**Pool,** der; -s, -s (*Wirtsch.* Gewinnverteilungskartell); **Pool|bil|lard** (Billard, bei dem die Kugeln in Löcher am Rand des Spieltisches gespielt werden müssen)

Pop, der; -[s] ⟨engl.⟩ (*kurz für* Popmusik, Pop-Art u. a.)

Po|panz, der; -es, -e ⟨slaw.⟩ ([vermummte] Schreckgestalt; *ugs. für* willenloser Mensch)

Pop-Art [ˈpɔpa:(r)t], die; - ⟨amerik.⟩ (eine moderne Kunstrichtung)

Pop|corn, das; -s ⟨engl.⟩ (Puffmais)

Po|pe, der; -n, -n (↑R 126) ⟨griech.-russ.⟩ (niederer Geistlicher der russisch-orthodoxen Kirche; *auch abwertend für* Geistlicher)

Po|pel, der; -s, - (*ugs. für* verhärteter Nasenschleim; *landsch. für* schmutziger kleiner Junge); **po|pe|lig,** pop|lig (*ugs. für* armselig, schäbig; gewöhnlich; knauserig); ein popeliges Geschenk

Po|pe|lin, der; -s, -e ⟨franz.⟩ *u.* **Po|pe|li|ne** [...ˈli:n(ə), *österr. beide* poˈpli:n], der; -s, - [...nə] *u.* die; -, - [...nə] (*Sammelbez. für* feinere ripsartige Stoffe in Leinenbindung)

po|peln (*ugs. für* in der Nase bohren); ich ...[e]le (↑R 16)

Pop|far|be; pop|far|ben; Pop‿fes|ti|val, ...grup|pe, ...kon|zert, ...kunst (die; -)

pop|lig *vgl.* popelig

Pop‿mo|de, ...mu|sik (die; -)

Po|po, der; -s, -s (*fam. für* Gesäß)

Po|po|ca|te|petl, der; -[s] (Vulkan in Mexiko)

Pop|per, der; -s, - ⟨*zu* Pop⟩ (Jugendlicher, der sich durch modische Kleidung und gepflegtes Äußeres bewusst von den Punkern abheben will *[bes. 80er Jahre]*); **pop|pig** (mit Stilelementen der Pop-Art; auffallend); ein poppiges Plakat; poppige Farben; **Pop‿sän|ger, ...sän|ge|rin, ...star** (*vgl.* [2]Star), **...sze|ne**

po|pu|lär ⟨lat.⟩ (volkstümlich; beliebt; gemeinverständlich); eine populäre Darstellung; ein populärer Politiker; **po|pu|la|ri|sie|ren** (gemeinverständlich darstellen; in die Öffentlichkeit bringen); **Po|pu|la|ri|sie|rung; Po|pu|la|ri|tät,** die; - (Volkstümlichkeit, Beliebtheit); **po|pu|lär|wis|sen|schaft|lich;** eine -e Buchreihe; **Po|pu|la|ti|on,** die; -, -en (*Biol.* Gesamtheit der Individuen einer Art in einem eng begrenzten Bereich; *veraltet für* Bevölkerung); **Po|pu|la|ti|ons|dich|te** *(Biol.);* **Po|pu|lis|mus,** der; - (opportunistische Politik, die die Gunst der Massen zu gewinnen sucht); **Po|pu|list,** der; -en, -en; ↑R 126; **po|pu|lis|tisch**

Por|cia [...tsia] (altröm. w. Eigenn.)

Po|re, die; -, -n ‹griech.› (feine [Haut]öffnung); **po|ren|tief** *(Werbesprache);* - sauber; **po|rig** (Poren aufweisend, löchrig)

Pör|kel[t], Pör|költ, das; -s ‹ung.› (dem Gulasch ähnliches Fleischgericht mit Paprika)

Por|ling (ein Baumpilz)

Por|no, der; -s, -s (*Kurzform für* pornographischer Film, Roman u. Ä.); **Por|no...** (*kurz für* Pornographie..., z. B. Pornofilm, Pornoheft, Pornostück); **Por|no|graf, Por|no|gra|fie** usw. *eindeutschend für* Pornograph, Pornographie usw.; **Por|no|graph** (↑R 33), der; -en, -en ‹griech.› (Verfasser pornographischer Werke); **Por|no|gra|phie** (↑R 33), die; - (einseitig das Sexuelle darstellende Schriften od. Bilder); **por|no|gra|phisch** (↑R 33); **por|no|phil** (Pornographie liebend)

po|rös ‹griech.› (durchlässig, löchrig); **Po|ro|si|tät,** die; -

Por|phyr [*auch, österr. nur,* ...'fy:r], der; -s, -e ‹griech.› (ein Ergussgestein); **Por|phy|rit** [*auch* ...'rit], der; -s, -e (ein Ergussgestein)

Por|ree, der; -s, -s ‹franz.› (eine Gemüsepflanze)

Por|ridge ['pɔritʃ, *engl.* 'pɔridʒ], der, *auch* das; -s ‹engl.› (Haferbrei)

Por|sche (dt. Autokonstrukteur)

Porst, der; -[e]s, -e (ein Heidekrautgewächs)

Port, der; -[e]s, -e ‹lat.› (*veraltet für* Hafen, Zufluchtsort); **Por|ta,** die; - (*Kurzform von* Porta Westfalica)

Por|ta|ble ['pɔ(r)təb(ə)l], der, *auch* das; -s, -s ‹engl.› (tragbares Rundfunk- od. Fernsehgerät)

Por|ta Hun|ga|ri|ca, die; - - ‹lat., „Ungarische Pforte"› (Donautal zwischen Wiener Becken u. Oberungarischem Tiefland); **Por|tal,** das; -s, -e ([Haupt]eingang, [prunkvolles] Tor)

Por|ta|men|to, das; -s, *Plur.* -s *od.* ...ti ‹ital.› (*Musik* Hinüberschleifen von einem Ton zum anderen)

Por|ta Ni|gra (↑R 130), die; - - ‹lat., „schwarzes Tor"› (monumentales röm. Stadttor in Trier)

Por|ta|tiv, das; -s, -e [...və] ‹lat.› (kleine tragbare Zimmerorgel); **por|ta|to** ‹ital.› (*Musik* getragen, abgehoben, ohne Bindung)

Port-au-Prince [pɔrto'prɛ̃:s] (Hptst. von Haiti)

[1]**Por|ta West|fa|li|ca,** die; - - ‹lat.›, *auch* West|fä|li|sche Pfor|te, die; -n - (Weserdurchbruch zwischen Weser- u. Wiehengebirge); [2]**Por|ta West|fa|li|ca** (Stadt an der [1]Porta Westfalica)

Porte|chai|se [pɔrt'ʃɛ:zə], die; -, -n ‹franz.› (*veraltet für* Tragsessel, Sänfte); **Porte|feuille** [pɔrt'fø:j], das; -s, -s (*veraltet für* Brieftasche; Mappe; *auch für* Geschäftsbereich eines Ministers); **Porte|mon|naie,** *eindeutschend* Port|mo|nee [pɔrtmɔ'ne:, *auch* 'pɔrt...] (↑R 33), das; -s, -s (Geldtäschchen, Börse); **Por|te|pee** (↑R 132), das; -s, -s (*früher* Degen-, Säbelquaste); **Por|te|pee|trä|ger** (*früher* Offizier od. höherer Unteroffizier)

Por|ter, der, *auch* das; -s, - ‹engl.› (starkes [engl.] Bier); **Por|ter|house|steak** ['pɔ:tə(r)haus|ste:k] ([auf dem Rost gebratene] dicke Scheibe aus dem Rippenstück des Rinds mit [Knochen u.] Filet)

Por|ti (*Plur. von* Porto)

Por|ti|ci ['pɔrtitʃi] (ital. Stadt); Die Stumme von - (Oper von Auber)

Por|ti|er [...'ti̯e:, *österr.* ...'ti:r], der; -s, *Plur.* -s, *österr.* -e ‹franz.› (Pförtner; Hauswart); **Por|ti|e|re,** die; -, -n (Türvorhang)

por|tie|ren ‹franz.› (*schweiz. für* zur Wahl vorschlagen)

Por|ti|ers|frau [...'ti̯e:s..., *österr.* ...'ti:rs...]

Por|ti|kus, der, *fachspr. auch* die; -, *Plur.* - [...ku:s] *od.* ...ken ‹lat.› (Säulenhalle)

Por|ti|on, die; -, -en ‹lat.› ([An]teil, abgemessene Menge); er ist nur eine halbe Portion (*ugs. für* er ist sehr klein, er zählt nicht); **Por|ti|ön|chen; por|ti|o|nen|wei|se** *vgl.* portionsweise; **por|ti|o|nie|ren** (in Portionen einteilen); **por|ti|ons|wei|se**

Por|ti|un|ku|la [...tsi̯...], die; - (Marienkapelle bei Assisi); **Por|ti|un|ku|la|ab|lass,** der; -es (vollkommener Ablass)

Port|juch|he, das; -s, -s (*ugs. scherzh. für* Portemonnaie)

Port|land|ze|ment, der; -[e]s

Port Lou|is [- 'lu:is] (Hptst. von Mauritius)

Port|mo|nee *vgl.* Portemonnaie

Port Mores|by [- 'mɔ:(r)zbi] (Hptst. von Papua-Neuguinea)

Por|to, das; -s, *Plur.* -s *u.* ...ti ‹ital.› (Beförderungsentgelt für Postsendungen, Postgebühr, -geld); **Por|to|buch; por|to|frei**

Port of Spain [- əv 'spe:n] (Hptst. von Trinidad u. Tobago)

Por|to|kas|se

Por|to No|vo [- 'no:vo] (Hptst. von Benin)

por|to|pflich|tig

Por|to Ri|co [- 'ri:ko] (*alter Name für* Puerto Rico)

Port|rät [...'trɛ:] (↑R 130), das; -s, -s ‹franz.› (Bildnis eines Menschen); **Port|rät|auf|nah|me; port|rä|tie|ren** [...'ti:...]; **Port|rä|tist,** der; -en, -en; ↑R 126 (Porträtmaler); **Port|rät‿ma|ler, ...sta|tue, ...stu|die, ...zeich|nung**

Port Said (ägypt. Stadt)

Ports|mouth ['pɔ:(r)tsməθ] (engl. u. amerikan. Ortsn.)

Port Su|dan (Stadt am Roten Meer)

Por|tu|gal; Por|tu|ga|le|ser, der; -s, - (alte Goldmünze); **Por|tu|gie|se,** der; -n, -n; ↑R 126 (Bewohner von Portugal); **Por|tu|gie|ser** (eine Reb- und Weinsorte); **Por|tu|gie|sin; por|tu|gie|sisch; Por|tu|gie|sisch,** das; -[s] (Sprache); *vgl.* Deutsch; **Por|tu|gie|si|sche,** das; -n; *vgl.* Deutsche, das; **Por|tu|gie|sisch-Gui|nea** [...gi...]; ↑R 105 (*früherer Name von* Guinea-Bissau)

Por|tu|lak, der; -s, *Plur.* -e *u.* -s ‹lat.› (eine Gemüse- u. Zierpflanze)

Port|wein ‹nach der portugies. Stadt Porto›

Por|zel|lan, das; -s, -e ‹ital.›; echt Meißner Porzellan; chinesisches -; **por|zel|la|nen** (aus Porzellan); **Por|zel|lan‿er|de, ...fi|gur, ...la|den, ...ma|le|rei, ...ma|nu|fak|tur, ...schne|cke, ...tel|ler**

Por|zia (w. Vorn.)

POS = polytechnische Oberschule; *vgl.* polytechnisch

Pos. = Position

Po|sa|da, die; -, ...den ‹span.› (Wirtshaus)

Po|sa|ment, das; -[e]s, -en *meist Plur.* ‹lat.› (Besatz zum Verzieren von Kleidung, Polstermöbeln u. Ä., z. B. Borte, Schnur); **Po|sa|men|ter,** der; -s, - *u.* Po|sa|men|tier, der; -s, -e, *österr. nur* Po|sa|men|tie|rer (Posamentenhersteller und -händler); **Po|sa|men|te|rie,** die; -, ...ien ([Geschäft für] Posamenten); **Po|sa|men|tier** *vgl.* Posamenter; **Po|sa|men|tier|ar|beit; po|sa|men|tie|ren; Po|sa|men|tie|rer** *vgl.* Posamenter

Po|sau|ne, die; -, -n ‹lat.› (ein Blechblasinstrument); die Posaunen des [Jüngsten] Gerichtes; **po|sau|nen;** ich habe posaunt; **Po|sau|nen‿blä|ser, ...chor** (der), **...en|gel** (*meist übertr. scherzh. für* pausbäckiges Kind), **...schall; Po|sau|nist,** der; -en, -en (↑R 126); **Po|sau|nis|tin**

[1]**Po|se,** die; -, -n (*nordd. für* Feder[kiel], Bett; *Angeln* an der Schnur befestigter Schwimmer)

[2]**Po|se,** die; -, -n ‹franz.› ([gekünstelte] Stellung, Körperhaltung)

Po|sei|don (griech. Gott des Meeres)

Po|se|mu|ckel [*auch* ˈpo:...], **Po|se|mu|kel** [*auch* ˈpo:...] (*ugs. für* kleiner, unbedeutender Ort)

po|sen (*svw.* posieren); er pos|te;

Po|seur [poˈzø:r], der; -s, -e ‹franz.› (*veraltend für* Wichtigtuer); **po|sie|ren** (eine [2]Pose einnehmen, schauspielern)

Po|si|lip (*eindeutschend für* Posillipo); **Po|sil|li|po,** *auch* Po|si|li|po, der; -[s] (Bergrücken am Golf von Neapel)

Po|si|ti|on, die; -, -en ‹franz.› ([An]stellung, Stelle, Lage; Einzelposten [*Abk.* Pos.]; Stück, Teil; Standort eines Schiffes od. Flugzeuges; [philosoph.] Standpunkt, grundsätzl. Auffassung); eine führende Position; er hat eine starke -; **po|si|ti|o|nell** (die Position betreffend); **po|si|ti|o|nie|ren** (in eine bestimmte Position bringen; ein Produkt auf dem Markt einordnen); **Po|si|ti|o|nie|rung; Po|si|ti|ons₋be|stim|mung, ...lam|pe, ...la|ter|ne, ...licht** (*Plur.* ...lichter), **...win|kel** *(Astron.);* **po|si|tiv** [*auch* ...ˈti:f] ‹lat.› (zustimmend; günstig; bestimmt, gewiss; *auch für* HIV-positiv); positives Ergebnis; positive Theologie; *(Math.:)* positive Zahlen; *(Physik:)* positiver Pol; (↑R 47:) im Positiven wie im Negativen; [1]**Po|si|tiv**[1], das; -s, -e [...və] (kleine Standorgel ohne Pedal im Gegensatz zum Portativ; *Fotogr.* vom Negativ gewonnenes, seitenrichtiges Bild); [2]**Po|si|tiv**[1], der; -s, -e [...və] (*Sprachw.* Grundstufe, nicht gesteigerte Form, z. B. „schön"); **Po|si|ti|vis|mus** [...v...], der; - (philosoph. Position, die allein das Tatsächliche als Gegenstand der Erkenntnis zulässt); **Po|si|ti|vist,** der; -en, -en (↑R 126); **po|si|ti|vis|tisch; Po|si|ti|vum,** das; -s, ...va [...va] ‹lat.› (das Positive); **Po|sit|ron** (↑R 130), das; -s, ...onen ‹lat.; griech.› (*Kernphysik* positiv geladenes Elementarteilchen); **Po|si|tur,** die; -, -en ‹lat.› ([herausfordernde] Haltung; *landsch. für* Gestalt, Figur, Statur; *vgl.* Postur); sich in Positur setzen, stellen

Pos|se, die; -, -n (derb-komisches Bühnenstück)

Pos|se|kel, der; -s, - (*nordostd. für* großer Schmiedehammer)

Pos|sen, der; -s, - (derber, lustiger Streich); jmdm. einen Possen spielen; - reißen; **pos|sen|haft; Pos|sen|haf|tig|keit; Pos|sen|rei|ßer**

Pos|ses|si|on, die; -, -en ‹lat.› (*Rechtsspr.* Besitz); **pos|ses|siv** [*auch* ...ˈsi:f] (*Sprachw.* besitzanzeigend); **Pos|ses|siv,** das; -s, -e [...və] (*bes. fachspr. svw.* Possessivpronomen); **Pos|ses|siv|pro|no|men** (*Sprachw.* besitzanzeigendes Fürwort, z. B. „mein"); **Pos|ses|si|vum** [...v...], das; -s, ...va [...va] (*älter für* Possessivpronomen); **pos|ses|so|risch** (*Rechtsspr.* den Besitz betreffend)

pos|sier|lich (spaßhaft, drollig); **Pos|sier|lich|keit,** die; -

Pöß|neck (Stadt in Thüringen)

Post, die; - ‹ital.›; (↑R 108:) er wohnt im Gasthaus „Zur Alten Post"; **Post|ab|hol|ler; pos|ta|lisch** (die Post betreffend, von der Post ausgehend, Post...)

Pos|ta|ment, das; -[e]s, -e ‹ital.› (Unterbau)

Post|amt; post|amt|lich; Post₋an|stalt, ...an|wei|sung, ...ar|beit (*österr. für* dringende Arbeit), **...auf|trag, ...au|to, ...bank** (*Plur.* ...banken), **...bar|scheck, ...be|am|te, ...be|am|tin, ...be|zirk, ...be|zug, ...bo|te, ...bo|tin, ...brief|kas|ten, ...bus**

Pöst|chen (kleiner Posten)

post Chris|tum [na|tum] ‹lat.› (*veraltet für* nach Christi Geburt; *Abk.* p. Chr. [n.]); **post|da|tie|ren** (*veraltet für* nachdatieren)

Post₋dienst, ...di|rek|ti|on

post|emb|ry|o|nal ‹lat.; griech.› (*Med.* nach dem embryonalen Stadium)

pos|ten ‹ital.› (*schweiz. mdal. für* einkaufen); **Pos|ten,** der; -s, - (bestimmte Menge einer Ware; Rechnungsbetrag; Amt, Stellung; Wache; Schrotsorte); ein Posten Kleider; [auf] Posten stehen (↑R 39); **Pos|ten₋dienst, ...ket|te**

Pos|ter [*engl.* ˈpo:stə(r)], das *od.* der; -s, *Plur.* -, *bei engl. Ausspr.* -s ‹engl.› (plakatartiges, großformatig gedrucktes Bild)

poste res|tante [pɔst rɛsˈtã:t] ‹franz.› (*franz. Bez. für* postlagernd)

Pos|te|ri|o|ra *Plur.* ‹lat.› (*veraltet, noch scherzh. für* Gesäß); **Pos|te|ri|o|ri|tät,** die; -; (*veraltet für* niedrigerer Rang); **Pos|te|ri|tät,** die; -, -en (*veraltet für* Nachkommenschaft, Nachwelt)

Post|fach

post fes|tum ‹lat., „nach dem Fest"› (hinterher, zu spät)

Post₋flug|zeug, ...form|blatt; **post|frisch** *(Philatelie);* **Post₋ge|bühr, ...ge|heim|nis** (das; -ses); **Post|gi|ro₋amt** (*Abk.* PGiroA), **...dienst, ...kon|to, ...ver|kehr**

post|gla|zi|al ‹lat.› (*Geol.* nacheiszeitlich)

Post₋gut, ...hal|ter *(früher);* **Post|hal|te|rei** *(früher);* **Post|horn** *Plur.* ...hörner

post|hum *vgl.* postum

pos|tie|ren ‹franz.› (aufstellen); sich postieren; **Pos|tie|rung**

Pos|til|le, die; -, -n ‹lat.› (Erbauungs-, Predigtbuch)

Pos|til|li|on [*österr. nur so, auch* ...ˈjo:n], der; -s, -e ‹ital. (-franz.)› (*früher für* Postkutscher); **Pos|til|lon d'A|mour** [pɔstiˌjɔ̃: daˈmu:r], der; - -, -s [...jɔ̃:] - ‹franz.› (Liebesbote, Überbringer eines Liebesbriefes)

post|kar|bo|nisch ‹lat.› (*Geol.* nach dem Karbon [liegend])

Post|kar|te; Post|kar|ten₋grö|ße (die; -), **...gruß; Post|kas|ten** *(landsch.)*

Post|kom|mu|ni|on ‹lat.› (ein Schlussgebet der kath. Messe)

Post|kon|fe|renz (Zusammenkunft in größeren Betrieben zur Postbearbeitung u. -verteilung)

post|kul|misch ‹lat.; engl.› (*Geol.* nach dem Kulm [liegend])

Post₋kun|de (der), **...kut|sche; post|la|gernd;** postlagernde Sendungen

Post|leit|zahl (*Abk.* PLZ); **Post|ler** (*bes. südd. u. österr. ugs. für* bei der Post Beschäftigter); **Pöst|ler** (*schweiz. svw.* Postler); **Post|meil|len|säu|le; Post|meis|ter** *(früher)*

post me|ri|di|em [- ...diɛm] ‹lat.› (nachmittags; *Abk.* p. m.)

Post|mi|nis|ter; Post|mi|nis|te|ri|um

post|mo|dern ‹engl.›; postmoderne Architektur; **Post|mo|der|ne,** die; - ([umstrittene] Bez. für verschiedene Strömungen der gegenwärtigen Architektur, Kunst und Kultur)

post|mor|tal ‹lat.› (*Med.* nach dem Tode eintretend); **post mor|tem** (nach dem Tode; *Abk.* p. m.); **post|na|tal** (*Med.* nach der Geburt auftretend)

Post|ne|ben|stel|le

post|nu|me|ran|do ‹lat.› (*Wirtsch.* nachträglich [zahlbar]); **Post|nu|me|ra|ti|on,** die; -, -en (Nachzahlung)

Pos|to ‹ital.›; *in der Wendung* Posto fassen (*veraltet für* sich aufstellen)

---

[1] [*auch* ...ˈti:f]

post|ope|ra|tiv (↑R 132) ‹lat.› (*Med.* nach der Operation)

Post⌣pa|ket, ...rat (*Plur.* ...räte), **...re|gal** (das; -s; Recht des Staates, das gesamte Postwesen in eigener Regie zu führen); **Post⌣sack, ...schaff|ner** *(Postw.),* **...scheck; Post|scheck⌣amt** (*früher für* Postgiroamt; *Abk.* PSchA), **...kon|to** (*früher für* Postgirokonto), **...ver|kehr** (*früher für* Postgiroverkehr); **Post⌣schiff, ...schließ|fach** (*Abk.* PSF)

Post|skript, das; -[e]s, -e *u., österr. nur,* **Post|skrip|tum,** das; -s, *Plur.* ...ta, *österr. auch* ...te ‹lat.› (Nachschrift; *Abk.* PS)

Post⌣spar|buch, ...spa|ren (das; -s), **...spar|kas|se; Post|spar|kas|sen⌣amt, ...dienst; Post|stem|pel**

Post|sze|ni|um, das; -s, ...ien [...iən] ‹lat.; griech.› (Raum hinter der Bühne; *Ggs.* Proszenium)

post|ter|ti|är ‹lat.› (*Geol.* nach dem Tertiär [liegend]); **post|trau|ma|tisch** ‹lat.; griech.› (*Med.* nach einer Verletzung auftretend)

Pos|tu|lant, der; -en, -en (↑R 126) ‹lat.› (*veraltet für* Bewerber); **Pos|tu|lat,** das; -[e]s, -e (Forderung); **pos|tu|lie|ren; Pos|tu|lie|rung**

pos|tum ‹lat.› (nach jmds. Tod erfolgend; nachgelassen)

Pos|tur, die; -, -en (*schweiz. mdal. für* Statur; *vgl.* Positur)

post ur|bem con|di|tam ‹lat.› (nach Gründung der Stadt [Rom]; *Abk.* p. u. c.)

Post⌣ver|bin|dung, ...ver|ein, ...ver|kehr; Post|ver|wal|tungs⌣ge|setz (das; -es), **...rat** (der; -[e]s); **Post|voll|macht; post|wen|dend; Post⌣wert|zei|chen, ...we|sen** (das; -s), **...wurf|sen|dung, ...zug, ...zu|stel|lung**

[1]Pot, das; -s ‹engl.› (*ugs. für* Marihuana)

[2]Pot, der; -s ‹engl.› (*ugs. für* Summe aller Gewinneinsätze)

po|tem|kin|sche Dör|fer [*auch* pa'tjɔm... -] *Plur.* (↑R 94) ‹nach dem russ. Fürsten› (Trugbilder, Vorspiegelungen)

po|tent ‹lat.› (mächtig, einflussreich; zahlungskräftig, vermögend; *Med.* zum Geschlechtsverkehr fähig, zeugungsfähig); **Po|ten|tat,** der; -en, -en; ↑R 126 (Machthaber; Herrscher); **po|ten|ti|al** usw. *vgl.* potenzial usw.; **Po|ten|ti|al|dif|fe|renz** (*Physik* Unterschied elektrischer Kräfte bei aufgeladenen Körpern); **Po|ten|ti|a|lis,** der; -, ...les [...le:s]; (*Sprachw.* Modus der Möglichkeit; Möglichkeitsform); **Po|ten|ti|a|li|tät,** die; -, -en (*bes. Philos.* Möglichkeit); **po|ten|ti|ell** *vgl.* potenziell

Po|ten|til|la, die; -, ...llen ‹lat.› (Fingerkraut)

Po|ten|ti|o|me|ter, das; -s, - ‹lat.; griech.› (*Elektrotechnik* regelbarer Widerstand als Spannungsteiler); **po|ten|ti|o|me|t|risch** (↑R 130); **Po|tenz,** die; -, -en ‹lat., „Macht"› (*nur Sing.:* Fähigkeit des Mannes, den Geschlechtsverkehr auszuüben, Zeugungsfähigkeit; innewohnende Kraft, Leistungsfähigkeit; *Med.* Bez. des Verdünnungsgrades eines homöopath. Mittels; *Math.* Produkt aus gleichen Faktoren); **Po|tenz|ex|po|nent** (*Math.* Hochzahl einer Potenz); **po|ten|zi|al,** *auch* po|ten|ti|al (↑R 33; möglich; die [bloße] Möglichkeit bezeichnend); **Po|ten|zi|al,** *auch* Po|ten|ti|al (↑R 33), das; -s, -e (Leistungsfähigkeit; *Physik* Maß für die Stärke eines Kraftfeldes); **po|ten|zi|ell,** *auch* po|ten|ti|ell (↑R 33) ‹franz.› (möglich [im Gegensatz zu wirklich]; der Anlage nach); potentielle Energie (*Physik* Energie, die ein Körper wegen seiner Lage in einem Kraftfeld besitzt); **po|ten|zie|ren** (verstärken, erhöhen, steigern; *Math.* zur Potenz erheben, mit sich selbst vervielfältigen); **Po|ten|zie|rung; Po|tenz⌣schwä|che, ...schwie|rig|kei|ten** *(Plur.);* **po|tenz|stei|gernd**

Po|te|rie, die; -, -s ‹franz.› (*veraltet für* Töpferware; Töpferwerkstatt)

Po|ti|phar, *ökum.* Po|ti|far (bibl. m. Eigenn.)

Pot|pour|ri ['pɔtpuri, *österr.* ...'ri:], das; -s, -s ‹franz.› (Allerlei; aus populären Melodien zusammengesetztes Musikstück)

Pots|dam (Hptst. von Brandenburg); **Pots|da|mer** (↑R 103); das Potsdamer Abkommen

Pott, der; -[e]s, Pötte (*bes. nordd. ugs. für* Topf; [altes] Schiff); **Pott|asche** (↑R 132), die; - (Kaliumkarbonat); **Pott|bä|cker** (*landsch. für* Töpfer); **Pott|harst** *vgl.* Potthast; **pott|häss|lich** (*ugs. für* sehr hässlich); **Pott|hast,** Pott|harst, der; -[e]s, -e (westfäl. Schmorgericht aus Gemüse und Rindfleisch); **Pott|sau** *Plur.* ...säue (derbes Schimpfwort); **Pott|wal** (ein Zahnwal)

potz Blitz!; potz|tau|send!

Po|ufer (↑R 105 *u.* 132) ‹*zu* [1]Po›

Pou|lard [pu'la:r], das; -s, -s ‹franz.›, *häufiger* **Pou|lar|de** [pu'lardə], die; -, -n (noch nicht geschlechtsreifes Masthuhn); **Poule** [pu:l], die; -, -n ([Spiel]einsatz [beim Billard o. Ä.]); **Pou|let** [pu'le:], das; -s, -s (junges Masthuhn)

Pour le Mé|rite [pu:r lə me'rit], der; - - - (hoher preuß. Verdienstorden)

Pous|sa|de [pu'sa:də], die; -, -n, **Pous|sa|ge** [pu'sa:ʒə], die; -, -n ‹franz.› (*veraltet für* Geliebte; Liebelei); **pous|sie|ren** [pu'si:...] (*ugs. veraltend für* flirten); **Pous|sier|stän|gel** (*ugs. veraltend für* jmd., der eifrig poussiert)

Pou|voir [pu'vo̯a:r], das; -s, -s ‹franz.› (*österr. für* Handlungsvollmacht)

po|wer ‹franz.› (*landsch. für* armselig); pow[e]re Leute

Pow|er ['paụə(r)], die; - ‹engl.› (*ugs. für* Stärke, Leistung, Wucht); **pow|ern** ['paụə(r)n] (große Leistung entfalten; mit großem Einsatz unterstützen); **Pow|er|play** ['paụə(r)ple:], das; -[s] (*bes. Eishockey* anhaltender gemeinsamer Ansturm auf das gegnerische Tor); **Pow|er|slide** ['paụə(r)slaịd], das; -[s] (eine Kurvenfahrtechnik bei Autorennen)

Po|widl, der; -s, - ‹tschech.› (*ostösterr. für* Pflaumenmus); **Po|widl|knö|del**

Poz|z[u|]o|la|ner|de *vgl.* Puzzolanerde

pp = pianissimo

pp. = per|ge, per|ge ‹lat., „fahre fort"› (und so weiter)

pp., ppa. = per procura

Pp., Ppbd. = Pappband

PP. = Patres

P. P. = praemissis praemittendis

ppa., pp. = per procura

Ppbd., Pp. = Pappband

P. prim. = Pastor primarius

Pr = *chem. Zeichen für* Praseodym

PR = Publicrelations

Prä, das; -s ‹lat., „vor"›; *meist in* das Prä haben (*ugs. für* den Vorrang haben); **prä...** (vor...); **Prä...** (Vor...); **Prä|am|bel,** die; -, -n (feierl. Einleitung; Vorrede)

PR-Ab|tei|lung ‹*zu* PR = Publicrelations›

Pra|cher, der; -s, - ‹slaw.› (*bes. nordd. für* zudringlicher Bettler); **pra|chern** (*bes. nordd. für* betteln); ich ...ere (↑R 16)

Pracht, die; -; eine kalte Pracht; eine wahre - *(ugs.);* **Pracht⌣aus|ga|be, ...band** (der), **...bau** (*Plur.* ...bauten), **...exem|plar** (↑R 132); **präch|tig; Präch|tig|keit,** die; -; **Pracht⌣jun|ge** (der), **...kerl** *(ugs.);* **Pracht|lie|be,** die; -;

Pracht.mensch *(ugs.)*, **...straße, ...stück; prachtlvoll; Pracht.weib** *(ugs.)*, **...werk**
pralcken (*österr. ugs. für* schlagen); **Pralcker** (*österr. ugs. für* Teppichklopfer)
Präldesltilnaltilon, die; - ‹lat.› (Vorherbestimmung); **Präldesltinaltilonsllehlre,** die; - *(Theol.)*; **präldesltilnielren; präldesltiniert** (vorherbestimmt; wie geschaffen [für etwas]); **Präldesltinielrung,** die; - (*svw.* Prädestination)
Präldilkant, der; -en, -en (↑R 126) ‹lat.› ([Hilfs]prediger); **Präldikanltenlorlden,** der; -s (*selten für* Dominikanerorden); **Präldilkat,** das; -[e]s, -e ([gute] Zensur, Beurteilung; *kurz für* Adelsprädikat; *Sprachw.* Satzaussage); **präldikaltilsielren** ([einen Film o.Ä.] mit einem Prädikat versehen); **präldilkaltiv** (aussagend; das Prädikat betreffend); **Präldilkativ,** das; -s, -e [...və] (*Sprachw.* auf das Subjekt od. Objekt bezogener Teil des Prädikats); **Präldilkaltivsatz** *(Sprachw.)*; **Präldilkaltilvum** [...vum], das; -s, ...va [...va] (*älter für* Prädikativ); **Präldilkats.examen** (↑R 132; mit einer sehr guten Note bestandenes Examen), **...nolmen** (*älter für* Prädikativ), **...wein**
präldislpolnielren ‹lat.› (im Vorhinein festlegen; empfänglich machen, bes. für Krankheiten); **Prädislpolsiltilon,** die; -, -en (*Med.* Anlage, Empfänglichkeit [für eine Krankheit])
Praldo, der; -[s] (span. Nationalmuseum in Madrid)
präldolmilnielren ‹lat.› (vorherrschen, überwiegen)
praelmislsis praelmitltenldis [prɛ... prɛ...] ‹lat.› (*veraltet für* der gebührende Titel sei vorausgeschickt; *Abk.* P.P.)
Prälexisltenz (↑R 132), die; - ‹lat.› (*Philos., Theol.* das Existieren in einem früheren Leben)
prälfablrilzielren (im Voraus festlegen)
Prälfaltilon, die; -, -en ‹lat.› (Dankgebet als Teil der kath. Eucharistiefeier u. des ev. Abendmahlsgottesdienstes)
Prälfekt, der; -en, -en (↑R 126) ‹lat.› (hoher Beamter im alten Rom; oberster Verwaltungsbeamter eines Departements in Frankreich, einer Provinz in Italien; Leiter des Chors als Vertreter des Kantors); **Prälfekltur,** die; -, -en (Amt, Bezirk, Amtsräume eines Präfekten)
prälfelrenltilell *vgl.* präferenziell; **Prälfelrenz,** die; -, -en (Vorzug, Vorrang; *Wirtsch.* Bevorzugung im Handelsverkehr); **prälfelrenzilell,** *auch* prälfelrenltilell (↑R 33) ‹lat.› (vorrangig); **Prälfelrenz.lislte, ...spanlne** *(Wirtsch.)*, **...stellllung, ...zoll** (Zoll, der einen Handelspartner bes. begünstigt); **prälfelrielren** (den Vorzug geben)
Prälfix [*auch* ...'fiks], das; -es, -e ‹lat.› (*Sprachw.* Vorsilbe, z.B. „be-" in „beladen")
Prälforlmaltilon, die; -, -en ‹lat.› (*Biol.* angenommene Vorherbildung des fertigen Organismus im Keim); **prälforlmielren** (im Keim vorbilden); **Prälforlmierung**
Prag (Hptst. der Tschechischen Republik); *vgl.* Praha
prägbar; Prägbarlkeit, die; -; **Präge.bild** *(Münzw.)*, **...druck** *(Druckw.)*, **...eilsen** (Prägestempel), **...form** *(Münzw.)*, **...maschilne** (Prägestock); **prälgen; Prälgelpreslse** *(Druckw.)*
Pralger ‹*zu* Prag› (↑R 103); der Prager Fenstersturz
Prälger; Präge.stätlte, ...stempel, ...stock (der; -[e]s, ...stöcke)
prälglalzilal ‹lat.› (*Geol.* voreiszeitlich)
Praglmaltik, die; -, -en ‹griech.› (*nur Sing.*: Orientierung auf das Nützliche, Sachbezogenheit; *Sprachw.* Lehre vom sprachlichen Handeln; *österr. auch für* Dienstpragmatik); **Praglmaltiker; Praglmaltilkelrin; praglmaltisch** (auf praktisches Handeln gerichtet; sachbezogen); pragmatische (den ursächlichen Zusammenhang darlegende) Geschichtsschreibung; *aber* (↑R 108): Pragmatische Sanktion (Grundgesetz des Hauses Habsburg von 1713); **praglmaltilsielren** (*österr. für* [auf Lebenszeit] fest anstellen); **Praglmaltilsielrung** *(österr.)*; **Praglmaltislmus,** der; - (philos. Richtung, die alles Denken u. Handeln vom Standpunkt des prakt. Nutzens aus beurteilt); **Praglmaltist,** der; -en, -en (↑R 126)
präglnant (↑R 130) ‹lat.› (knapp und treffend); **Präglnanz,** die; -
Prälgung
Pralha (*tschech. Form von* Prag)
Prälhisltolrie [...i̯ə, *auch, österr. nur,* 'prɛ:...], die; - ‹lat.› (Vorgeschichte); **Prälhisltolrilker; Prälhisltolrilkelrin; prälhisltolrisch** (vorgeschichtlich)
prahllen; Prahller; Prahllelrei; Prahllelrin; prahllelrisch; Prahl.hans (der; -es, ...hänse; *ugs. für* jmd., der gern prahlt), **...sucht** (die; -); **prahllsüchltig**
Prahm, der; -[e]s, *Plur.* -e *od.* Prähme ‹tschech.› (flaches Wasserfahrzeug für Arbeitszwecke)
Pralia ['prai̯ə] (Hptst. von Kap Verde)
Prailrilal [prɛ'ri̯al], der; -[s], -s ‹franz., „Wiesenmonat"› (9. Monat des Kalenders der Franz. Revolution: 20. Mai bis 18. Juni)
Präljuldiz, das; -es, *Plur.* -e *od.* -ien [...i̯ən] ‹lat.› (Vorentscheidung; hochrichterl. Entscheidung, die bei Beurteilung künftiger ähnl. Rechtsfälle herangezogen wird); **präljuldilzilell** ‹franz.› (bedeutsam für die Beurteilung eines späteren Sachverhalts); **präljuldilzieren** ‹lat.› (der [richterl.] Entscheidung vorgreifen); präjudizierter Wechsel (*Bankw.* nicht eingelöster Wechsel, dessen Protest versäumt wurde)
prälkamblrisch (*Geol.* vor dem Kambrium [liegend]); **Prälkambrilum,** das; -s (vor dem Kambrium liegender erdgeschichtlicher Zeitraum)
prälkarlbolnisch ‹lat.› (*Geol.* vor dem Karbon [liegend])
prälkarldilal, prälkorldilal (*Med.* vor dem Herzen [liegend]); **Prälkarldilallgie,** die; -, ...ien ‹lat.; griech.› (Schmerzen in der Herzgegend)
prälklueldielren ‹lat.› (*Rechtsspr.* jmdm. die Geltendmachung eines Rechtes gerichtlich verweigern); **Prälklulsilon,** die; -, -en (Ausschließung; Rechtsverwirkung); **prälklulsiv,** prälklulsilvisch [...viʃ]; **Prälklulsivlfrist**
prälkollumlbisch (die Zeit vor der Entdeckung Amerikas durch Kolumbus betreffend)
prälkorldilal *vgl.* präkardial; **Prälkorldilallangst** *(Med.)*
Praklrit (↑R 130), das; -s (*Sammelbez. für* die mittelind. Volkssprachen)
prakt. Arzt *vgl.* praktisch; **prakltilfilzielren** ‹griech.; lat.› (in die Praxis umsetzen, verwirklichen); **Prakltilfilzielrung; Prakltik,** die; -, -en ‹griech.› (Art der Ausübung von etwas; Handhabung; Verfahrensweise; *meist Plur.*: nicht einwandfreies [unerlaubtes] Vorgehen); **Prakltilka** (*Plur. von* Praktikum); **prakltilkalbel** (brauchbar; benutzbar; zweckmäßig); ...ablle (↑R 130) Einrichtung; **Prakltilkabel,** das; -s, - (*Theater* fest gebauter, begehbarer Teil der Bühnen-

dekoration); **Prak|ti|ka|bi|li|tät,** die; -; **Prak|ti|kant,** der; -en, -en; ↑R 126 (jmd., der ein Praktikum absolviert); **Prak|ti|kan|tin; Prak|ti|ker** (Mann der praktischen Arbeitsweise und Erfahrung; *Ggs.* Theoretiker); **Prak|ti|kum,** das; -s, ...ka (praktische Übung an der Hochschule; im Rahmen einer Ausbildung außerhalb der [Hoch]schule abzuleistende praktische Tätigkeit); **Prak|ti|kus,** der; -, -se (*scherzh. für* jmd., der immer u. überall Rat weiß); **prak|tisch** (auf die Praxis bezüglich; zweckmäßig, gut zu handhaben; geschickt; tatsächlich, in Wirklichkeit); praktischer Arzt (nicht spezialisierter Arzt, Arzt für Allgemeinmedizin; *Abk.* prakt. Arzt); praktisches Jahr (einjähriges Praktikum); praktisches (tätiges) Christentum; (↑R 47:) etwas Praktisches schenken; sie hat praktisch (*ugs. für* so gut wie) kein Geld; **prak|ti|zie|ren** (in der Praxis anwenden, in die Praxis umsetzen; als Arzt usw. tätig sein; ein Praktikum durchmachen); ein praktizierender Arzt

prä|kul|misch ‹lat.; engl.› (*Geol.* vor dem ²Kulm [liegend])

Prä|lat, der; -en, -en (↑R 126) ‹lat.› (geistl. Würdenträger); **Prä|la|tur,** die; -, -en (Amt, Sitz eines Prälaten)

Prä|li|mi|nar|frie|den ‹lat.; dt.› (vorläufiger Frieden); **Prä|li|mi|na|ri|en** *Plur.* ‹lat.› ([diplomatische] Vorverhandlungen; Einleitung)

Pra|li|ne, die; -, -n ‹nach dem franz. Marschall du Plessis-Praslin› (mit Schokolade überzogene Süßigkeit); **Pra|li|nee,** das; -s, -s (*österr. u. schweiz., sonst veraltend für* Praline)

prall (voll; stramm); **Prall,** der; -[e]s, -e (heftiges Auftreffen); **pral|len; Pral|ler, Prall|tril|ler** (*Musik* Wechsel zwischen Hauptnote u. nächsthöherer Note); **prall|voll** *(ugs.)*

prä|lu|die|ren ‹lat.› (*Musik* einleitend spielen); **Prä|lu|di|um,** das; -s, ...ien [...iən] (Vorspiel)

Prä|ma|tu|ri|tät, die; - ‹lat.› (*Med.* Frühreife)

Prä|mie [...iə], die; -, -n ‹lat.› (Belohnung, Preis; [Zusatz]gewinn; zusätzliche Vergütung; Versicherungsbeitrag); **Prä|mi|en‿an|lei|he** *(Wirtsch.),* **...aus|lo|sung; prä|mi|en|be|güns|tigt;** -es Sparen; **Prä|mi|en|de|pot** *(Versicherungsw.);* **prä|mi|en|frei;** -e Versicherung; **Prä|mi|en‿ge|schäft** *(Kaufmannsspr.),* **...kurs** *(Börse),* **...lohn** *(Wirtsch.);* **Prä|mi|en|lohn|sys|tem; Prä|mi|en‿los, ...rück|ge|währ** (Gewähr für Beitragsrückzahlung), **...schein; prä|mi|en|spa|ren** *meist nur im Infinitiv gebr.;* **Prä|mi|en‿spa|ren** (das; -s), **...spa|rer, ...spar|ver|trag, ...zah|lung, ...zu|schlag; prä|mie|ren,** prä|mi|ie|ren; **Prä|mie|rung,** Prä|mi|ie|rung; **prä|mi|ie|ren** *vgl.* prämieren; **Prä|mi|ie|rung** *vgl.* Prämierung

Prä|mis|se, die; -, -n ‹lat.› (Voraussetzung; Vordersatz eines logischen Schlusses)

Prä|monst|ra|ten|ser (↑R 130), der; -s, - ‹nach dem franz. Kloster Prémontré› (Angehöriger eines kath. Ordens)

prä|na|tal ‹lat.› (*Med.* der Geburt vorausgehend)

Prand|tau|er (österr. Barockbaumeister)

Prandtl|rohr (↑R 95) ‹nach dem dt. Physiker› (*Physik* Gerät zum Messen des Drucks in einer Strömung)

pran|gen

Pran|ger, der; -s, - (*MA.* Schandpfahl); *noch in Wendungen wie* an den Pranger stellen

Pran|ke, die; -, -n (Klaue, Tatze; *ugs. für* große, derbe Hand); **Pran|ken|hieb**

Prä|no|men, das; -s, ...mina ‹lat.› (Vorname [der alten Römer])

prä|nu|me|ran|do ‹lat.› (*Wirtsch.* im Voraus [zu zahlen]); **Prä|nu|me|ra|ti|on,** die; -, -en (Vorauszahlung); **prä|nu|me|rie|ren**

Pranz, der; -es (*landsch. für* Prahlerei); **pran|zen; Pran|zer**

Prä|pa|rand, der; -en, -en (↑R 126) ‹lat.› (*früher* jmd., der sich auf das Lehrerseminar vorbereitet); **Prä|pa|rat,** das; -[e]s, -e (zubereitete Substanz, z. B. Arzneimittel; *Biol.* zu Lehrzwecken konservierter Pflanzen- od. Tierkörper; *Med.* zum Mikroskopieren vorbereiteter Gewebeteil); **Prä|pa|ra|ten|samm|lung; Prä|pa|ra|ti|on,** die; -, -en (*bes. Biol., Med.* Herstellung eines Präparates); **Prä|pa|ra|tor,** der; -s, ...oren (Hersteller von Präparaten); **Prä|pa|ra|to|rin; prä|pa|rie|ren;** einen Stoff, ein Kapitel präparieren (vorbereiten); sich - (vorbereiten); Körper- od. Pflanzenteile - (dauerhaft, haltbar machen)

prä|peln (*landsch. für* [etwas Gutes] essen)

Prä|pon|de|ranz, die; - ‹lat.› (*veraltet für* Übergewicht)

Prä|po|si|ti|on, die; -, -en ‹lat.› (*Sprachw.* Verhältniswort, z. B. „auf, bei, in, vor, zwischen"); **prä|po|si|ti|o|nal; Prä|po|si|ti|o|nal‿at|tri|but, ...fall** (der), **...ge|fü|ge, ...ka|sus, ...ob|jekt; Prä|po|si|tur,** die; -, -en (Stelle eines Präpositus); **Prä|po|si|tus,** der; -, ...ti (Vorgesetzter; Propst)

prä|po|tent ‹lat.› (*veraltet für* übermächtig, *österr. für* überheblich, aufdringlich); **Prä|po|tenz,** die; -

Prä|pu|ti|um, das; -s, ...ien [...iən] ‹lat.› (*Med.* Vorhaut)

Prä|raf|fa|e|lit [...fa|e...], der; -en, -en (↑R 126) ‹lat.; ital.› (*Kunstw.* Nachahmer des vorraffaelischen Malstils)

PR-Ar|beit ‹*zu* PR = Publicrelations›

Prä|rie, die; -, ...ien ‹franz.› (Grasebene in Nordamerika); **Prä|rie‿aus|ter** (ein Mixgetränk), **...gras, ...hund** (ein Nagetier), **...in|di|a|ner, ...wolf** (der)

Prä|ro|ga|tiv, das; -s, -e [...və] ‹lat.› *u.* **Prä|ro|ga|ti|ve** [...və], die; -, -n (Vorrecht; *früher* nur dem Herrscher vorbehaltenes Recht)

Prä|sens, das; -, *Plur.* ...sentia *od.* ...senzien [...iən] ‹lat.› (*Sprachw.* Gegenwart); **Prä|sens|par|ti|zip** *vgl.* Partizip Präsens; **prä|sent** (anwesend; gegenwärtig); präsent sein; etwas - haben; **Prä|sent,** das; -[e]s, -e ‹franz.› (Geschenk; kleine Aufmerksamkeit); **prä|sen|ta|bel** (*veraltend für* ansehnlich; vorzeigbar); ...ab|le (↑R 130) Ergebnisse; **Prä|sen|tant,** der; -en, -en (↑R 126) ‹lat.› (*Wirtsch.* jmd., der einen fälligen Wechsel vorlegt); **Prä|sen|ta|ti|on,** die; -, -en (das Vorstellen, das Präsentieren; *Wirtsch.* Vorlegung eines fälligen Wechsels); **Prä|sen|ta|ti|ons|recht,** das; -[e]s (*kath. Kirche* Vorschlagsrecht); **Prä|sen|tia** (*Plur. von* Präsens); **prä|sen|tie|ren** ‹franz.› (vorstellen; überreichen, anbieten; vorlegen [bes. einen Wechsel]; milit. Ehrenbezeigung [mit dem Gewehr] machen); sich präsentieren (sich zeigen); **Prä|sen|tier|tel|ler;** *nur noch in der Wendung* auf dem - sitzen (*ugs. für* allen Blicken ausgesetzt sein); **Prä|sen|tie|rung; prä|sen|tisch** ‹lat.› (*Sprachw.* das Präsens betreffend); **Prä|sent|korb; Prä|senz,** die; - (Gegenwart, Anwesenheit); **Prä|senz|bib|li|o|thek** (Bibliothek, deren Bücher nicht nach Hause mitgenommen werden dürfen); **Prä|senz‿die|ner** (*österr. für* Soldat im Grundwehrdienst des österr. Bundesheeres), ...**dienst** (*österr. für* Grundwehrdienst); **Prä|sen|zi|en** (*Plur. von* Präsens); **Prä|senz_lis|te** (Anwesenheitsliste), ...**pflicht** (die; -), ...**stär|ke** (augenblickliche Personalstärke [bei der Truppe])

Pra|se|o|dym, das; -s ‹griech.› (chem. Element, Seltenerdmetall; *Zeichen* Pr)

Prä|ser (*ugs. kurz für* Präservativ); **prä|ser|va|tiv** [...v...] ‹lat.› (vorbeugend, verhütend); **Prä|ser|va|tiv,** das; -s, -e [...və] (Gummischutz für das männl. Glied zur Empfängnisverhütung); **Prä|ser|ve,** die; -, -n *meist Plur.* (Halbkonserve); **prä|ser|vie|ren** (*veraltet für* haltbar machen, erhalten; schützen)

Prä|ses, der; -, *Plur.* ...sides [...de:s] *u.* ...siden ‹lat.› (*kath. u. ev. Kirche* Vorsitzender, Vorstand); **Prä|si|de,** der; -n, -n; ↑R 126 (*Studentenspr.* Leiter einer Kneipe, eines Kommerses); **Prä|si|dent,** der; -en, -en; ↑R 126 (Vorsitzender; Staatsoberhaupt in einer Republik); **Prä|si|den|ten|wahl; Prä|si|den|tin; Prä|si|dent|schaft; Prä|si|dent|schafts|kan|di|dat; Prä|si|des** (*Plur. von* Präses); **prä|si|di|al** (den Präsidenten, das Präsidium betreffend); **Prä|si|di|al_de|mo|kra|tie, ...ge|walt, ...re|gie|rung, ...sys|tem** (Regierungsform, bei der das Staatsoberhaupt gleichzeitig Regierungschef ist); **prä|si|die|ren** (den Vorsitz führen, leiten); einem (*schweiz.* einen) Ausschuss präsidieren; **Prä|si|di|um,** das; -s, ...ien [...iən] (leitendes Gremium; Vorsitz; Amtsgebäude eines [Polizei]präsidenten)

prä|si|lu|risch ‹nlat.› (*Geol.* vor dem Silur [liegend])

prä|skri|bie|ren ‹lat.› (vorschreiben; verordnen); **Prä|skrip|ti|on,** die; -, -en; **prä|skrip|tiv** (vorschreibend; regelnd)

Prass, der; -es (*veraltet für* wertloses Zeug, Plunder)

pras|seln; es prasselt

pras|sen (schlemmen); du prasst, er prasst; du prasstest; geprasst; prasse! *u.* prass!; **Pras|ser; Pras|se|rei**

prä|sta|bi|lie|ren ‹lat.› (*veraltet für* vorher festsetzen); prästabilierte Harmonie (Leibniz)

Prä|stant, der; -en, -en; ↑R 126 (große, zinnerne Orgelpfeife)

prä|su|mie|ren ‹lat.› (*Philos., Rechtsw.* annehmen; voraussetzen); **Prä|sum|ti|on,** die; -, -en (Annahme; Vermutung; Voraussetzung); **prä|sum|tiv** (mutmaßlich)

Prä|ten|dent, der; -en, -en (↑R 126) ‹lat.› (jmd., der Anspruch auf eine Stellung, ein Amt, bes. auf einen Thron, erhebt); **prä|ten|die|ren; Prä|ten|ti|on,** die; -, -en (Anspruch; Anmaßung); **prä|ten|ti|ös** (anspruchsvoll, anmaßend, selbstgefällig)

Pra|ter, der; -s (Park mit Vergnügungsplatz in Wien)

Prä|te|ri|tio, die; -, ...onen ‹lat.›, **Prä|te|ri|ti|on** (↑R 132), die; -, ...onen (*Rhet.* scheinbare Übergehung); **Prä|te|ri|to|prä|sens,** das; -, *Plur.* ...sentia *od.* ...senzien [...iən] (*Sprachw.* Verb, dessen Präsens [Gegenwart] ein früheres starkes Präteritum [Vergangenheit] ist u. dessen neue Vergangenheitsformen schwach gebeugt werden, z. B. „können, wissen"); **Prä|te|ri|tum,** das; -s, ...ta (*Sprachw.* Vergangenheit)

prä|ter|prop|ter ‹lat.› (etwa, ungefähr)

Prä|tor, der; -s, ...oren ‹lat.› (höchster [Justiz]beamter im alten Rom); **Prä|to|ri|a|ner** (Angehöriger der Leibwache der röm. Feldherren od. Kaiser)

Prät|ti|gau, das; -s (Talschaft in Graubünden)

Prä|tur, die; -, -en ‹lat.› (Amt eines Prätors)

Prat|ze, die; -, -n (*svw.* Pranke)

Prau, die; -, -e ‹malai.› (Boot der Malaien)

Prä|ven|ti|on [...v...], die; -, -en ‹lat.› (Vorbeugung, Verhütung); **prä|ven|tiv; Prä|ven|tiv_an|griff, ...be|hand|lung** (*Med.*), ...**krieg, ...maß|nah|me, ...me|di|zin** (die; -), ...**mit|tel** (das), ...**schlag** (*svw.* Präventivangriff), ...**ver|kehr** (der; -s; Geschlechtsverkehr mit Anwendung eines Verhütungsmittels); **prä|ver|bal;** präverbale Periode (erste Lebenszeit eines Kindes, bevor es sprechen lernt)

Praw|da (↑R 130), die; - ‹russ., „Wahrheit"› (Moskauer Tageszeitung)

Pra|xe|dis [*auch* 'pra...] (eine Heilige)

Pra|xis, die; -, ...xen ‹griech.› (*nur Sing.:* Tätigkeit, Ausübung, Erfahrung, *Ggs.* Theorie; Tätigkeitsbereich des Arztes od. Anwalts; Räumlichkeiten für die Berufsausübung dieser Personen); *vgl.* in praxi; **pra|xis|be|zo|gen; Pra|xis|be|zug; pra|xis_fern, ...fremd, ...ge|recht, ...nah, ...ver|bun|den**

Pra|xi|te|les (altgriech. Bildhauer)

Prä|ze|dens, das; -, ...denzien [...iən] ‹lat.› (früherer Fall, früheres Beispiel; Beispielsfall); **Prä|ze|denz_fall** (der; Präzedens), ...**strei|tig|keit** (Rangstreitigkeit); **Prä|zep|tor,** der; -s, ...oren (*veraltet für* Lehrer; Erzieher); **Prä|zes|si|on,** die; -, -en (*Astron.* das Fortschreiten des Frühlingspunktes); **Prä|zi|pi|tat,** das; -[e]s, -e (*Chemie* Bodensatz, Niederschlag); **Prä|zi|pi|ta|ti|on,** die; - (Ausfällung); **prä|zi|pi|tie|ren** (ausfällen, ausflocken); **Prä|zi|pi|tin,** das; -s, -e (*Med.* immunisierender Stoff im Blut)

prä|zis, *österr. nur so, auch* **prä|zi|se** ‹lat.› (genau; pünktlich; eindeutig); **prä|zi|sie|ren** (genau[er] angeben; knapp zusammenfassen); **Prä|zi|sie|rung; Prä|zi|si|on,** die; - (Genauigkeit); **Prä|zi|si|ons_ar|beit, ...in|stru|ment, ...ka|me|ra, ...mes|sung, ...mo|tor, ...uhr, ...waa|ge**

Pré|cis [pre'si:], der; - [...'si:(s)], - [...'si:(s)] ‹franz.› (kurze Inhaltsangabe)

Pre|del|la, die; -, *Plur.* -s *u.* ...llen ‹ital.› (Sockel eines Altaraufsatzes)

pre|di|gen; Pre|di|ger; Pre|di|ge|rin; Pre|di|ger_or|den (der; -s), ...**se|mi|nar; Pre|digt,** die; -, -en; **Pre|digt_amt, ...stuhl** (*veraltet für* Kanzel), ...**text**

Pre|fe|rence [...'rã:s], die; -, -n [...s(ə)n] ‹franz.› (ein franz. Kartenspiel)

Pre|gel, der; -s (ein Fluss)

prei|en ‹niederl.› (*Seemannsspr.);* ein Schiff preien (anrufen)

Preis, der; -es, -e (Geldbetrag; Belohnung; *geh. für* Lob); um jeden, keinen Preis; Preis freibleibend (*Kaufmannsspr.);* er gewann den ersten Preis; **Preis_ab|bau** (der; -[e]s), ...**ab|schlag, ...ab|spra|che, ...an|ga|be, ...an|ord|nung** (*ehem. in der DDR; Abk.* PAO), ...**an|stieg, ...auf|ga|be, ...auf|trieb** (*Wirtsch.);* **Preis|aus|schrei|ben,** das; -s, -; **preis|be|güns|tigt; Preis_be|hör|de, ...be|we|gung; preis|be|wusst; Preis_bil|dung** (*Wirtsch.*), ...**bin|dung, ...bo|xer** (*früher*), ...**bre|cher**

Prei|sel|bee|re

Preis|emp|feh|lung; unverbindliche -

prei|sen; du preist, er preist; du priesest, er pries; gepriesen; preis[e]!

Preis_ent|wick|lung, ...er|hö|hung, ...er|mä|ßi|gung, ...ex-

plo|si|on, ...fah|ren (das; -s, -; eine sportl. Veranstaltung), **...frage**

Preis|ga|be, die; -; **preis|ge|ben;** du gibst preis; preisgegeben; preiszugeben

preis|ge|bun|den; Preis‿ge|fälle, ...ge|fü|ge; preis|ge|krönt; Preis‿geld, ...ge|richt, ...ge|staltung, ...gren|ze; preis|güns|tig; ...prei|sig (*in* hochpreisig, mittelpreisig, niedrigpreisig); **Preis‿index** (*Plur.* ...indizes, *auch* ...indices; *Wirtsch.*), **...kal|ku|la|ti|on, ...kar|tell** *(Wirtsch.)*; **preis|kegeln** *nur im Infinitiv und Partizip II gebräuchlich;* wir wollen preiskegeln; **Preis|ke|geln,** das; -s; **Preis‿klas|se, ...kon|junk|tur** *(Wirtsch.)*, **...kon|trol|le, ...kon|ven|ti|on** *(Wirtsch.)*, **...kor|rek|tur; preis|kri|tisch; Preis|la|ge;** Waren in jeder Preislage; **Preis-Leis|tungs-Ver|hält|nis; preis|lich** (den Preis betreffend, im Preis); preisliche Unterschiede; **Preis‿lied, ...lis|te; Preis-Lohn-Spi|ra|le,** die; -; ↑R 28 *(Wirtsch.)*; **Preis‿nachlass** (*für* Rabatt), **...ni|veau, ...po|li|tik, ...rät|sel, ...rich|ter, ...rich|te|rin, ...rück|gang, ...schie|ßen, ...schild** (das), **...schla|ger** (*ugs. für* besonders preiswertes Angebot), **...schrift, ...sen|kung, ...skat; preis|stabil; Preis‿sta|bi|li|tät, ...stei|ge|rung, ...stei|ge|rungs|ra|te** *(Wirtsch.)*, **...stopp** (Verbot der Preiserhöhung); **Preis|stopp|ver|ord|nung; Preis‿sturz, ...tafel, ...trä|ger, ...trä|ge|rin; preis|trei|bend; Preis|trei|ber; Preis|trei|be|rei; Preis‿über|wachung** (↑R 132), **...un|ter|grenze, ...ver|gleich, ...ver|lei|hung, ...ver|tei|lung, ...ver|zeich|nis, ...vor|schrift; preis|wert; Preis|wu|cher; preis|wür|dig; Preis|wür|dig|keit,** die; -

pre|kär ‹franz.› (misslich, schwierig, bedenklich)

Prell‿ball (der; -[e]s; dem Faustball ähnliches Mannschaftsspiel), **...bock** *(Eisenb.)*; **prel|len; Prel|ler; Prel|le|rei; Prell‿schuss, ...stein; Prel|lung**

Pré|lude [pre'lyd], das; -s, -s ‹franz.› (der Fantasie ähnliches Klavier- od. Instrumentalstück; *auch* svw. Präludium)

Pre|mi|er [prə'mi̯e:, pre...], der; -s, -s ‹franz.› (Premierminister); **Pre|mi|e|re** [*österr.* ...'mi̯ɛ:r], die; -, -n (Erst-, Uraufführung); **Pre|mi|e|ren‿abend** (↑R 132), **...be|su|cher, ...pub|li|kum; Pre|mi|er|mi|nis|ter** [prə'mi̯e:..., pre...]; **Pre|mi|er|mi|nis|te|rin; pre|mium** ‹lat.-engl.› (von besonderer, bester Qualität)

Pres|by|ter, der; -s, - ‹griech.› ([urchristl.] Gemeindeältester; Priester; Mitglied des Presbyteriums); **Pres|by|te|ri|al|ver|fassung** *(ev.-reformierte Kirche);* **Pres|by|te|ri|a|ner,** der; -s, - (Angehöriger protestant. Kirchen mit Presbyterialverfassung in England u. Amerika); **Pres|by|te|ri|a|ne|rin; pres|by|te|ri|a|nisch; Pres|by|te|rin; Pres|by|te|ri|um,** das; -s, ...ien [...i̯ən] (Versammlung[sraum] der Presbyter; Kirchenvorstand; Chorraum)

pre|schen (*ugs. für* rennen, eilen); du preschst

Pre|shave ['pri:ʃe:v], das; -[s], -s ‹engl.› (*kurz für* Preshavelotion); **Pre|shave|lo|tion** [...lo:ʃən], die; -, -s (Gesichtswasser zum Gebrauch vor der Rasur)

press (*Sportspr.* eng, nah); jmdn. press decken

pres|sant ‹franz.› (*veraltet, aber noch landsch. für* dringlich, eilig)

Press|ball (*Fußball* von zwei Spielern gleichzeitig getretener Ball)

Preß|burg (*slowak.* Bratislava)

Pres|se, die; -, -n (*kurz für* Druck-, Obst-, Ölpresse usw.; *ugs. für* Privatschule, die [schwächere Schüler] auf Prüfungen vorbereitet; *nur Sing.:* Gesamtheit der period. Druckschriften; *nur Sing.:* Zeitungs-, Zeitschriftenwesen); die freie Presse; **Pres|se‿agen|tur** (↑R 132), **...amt, ...aus|weis, ...be|richt, ...be|richt|er|stat|ter, ...bü|ro** (Agentur), **...chef, ...dienst, ...empfang, ...er|klä|rung, ...fo|to|graf, ...fo|to|gra|fin, ...frei|heit** (die; -), **...ge|setz, ...in|for|ma|ti|on, ...kam|pag|ne, ...kom|men|tar, ...kon|fe|renz, ...land|schaft, ...mel|dung; pres|sen;** du presst, er presst; du presstest; gepresst; presse! *u.* press!; **Pres|se‿no|tiz, ...or|gan, ...recht** (das; -[e]s), **...re|fe|rent, ...re|fe|ren|tin, ...schau, ...spre|cher, ...spre|che|rin, ...stel|le** (Abteilung für Presseinformation), **...stim|me, ...tri|bü|ne, ...ver|tre|ter, ...we|sen** (das; -s), **...zen|sur** (die; -), **...zent|rum; Press‿form, ...glas** (*Plur.* ...gläser), **...he|fe, ...holz; pres|sie|ren** (*bes. südd., österr. u. schweiz. für* drängen, treiben, eilig sein); es pressiert; **Pres|si|on,** die; -, -en ‹lat.› (Druck; Nötigung, Zwang); **Press‿koh|le, ...kopf** (der; -[e]s; eine Wurstart); **Press|ling** (*für* Brikett); **Press|luft,** die; -; **Press|luft‿boh|rer, ...fla|sche, ...ham|mer; Press‿sack** (↑R 136; der; -[e]s; *svw.* Presskopf), **...schlag** (↑R 136; *Fußball*), **...span** (↑R 136), **...span|plat|te** (↑R 136), **...stoff** (↑R 136), **...stroh** (↑R 136); **Pres|sung; Pres|sure|group** ['prɛʃə(r)gru:p] (↑R 33), die; -, -s ‹engl.-amerik.› (Interessenverband, der [oft mit Druckmitteln] auf Parteien, Parlamente u. a. Einfluss zu gewinnen sucht); **Press‿we|he** *(meist Plur.; Med.)*, **...wurst** (*svw.* Presskopf)

Pres|ti (*Plur. von* Presto)

Pres|ti|ge [prɛs'ti:ʒ(ə)], das; -s ‹franz.› (Ansehen, Geltung); **Pres|ti|ge‿den|ken, ...ge|winn, ...grund** *(meist Plur.)*, **...sa|che, ...ver|lust**

pres|tis|si|mo ‹ital.› (*Musik* sehr schnell); **Pres|tis|si|mo,** das; -s, *Plur.* -s *u.* ...mi; **pres|to** (*Musik* schnell); **Pres|to,** das; -s, *Plur.* -s *u.* ...ti

Prêt-à-por|ter [prɛtapɔr'te:], das; -s, -s ‹franz.› (von einem Modeschöpfer entworfenes Konfektionskleid)

pre|ti|ös *vgl.* preziös; **Pre|ti|o|sen** *vgl.* Preziosen

Pre|to|ria (Hptst. von Transvaal u. Regierungssitz der Republik Südafrika)

Preu|ße, der; -n, -n (↑R 126); **Preu|ßen; Preu|ßin; preu|ßisch;** preußische Reformen, *aber* (↑R 102): der Preußische Höhenrücken; **Preu|ßisch|blau**

pre|zi|ös, *auch* pre|ti|ös ‹franz.› (kostbar; gekünstelt); **Pre|zi|o|sen,** *auch* Pre|ti|o|sen *Plur.* ‹lat.› (Kostbarkeiten; Geschmeide)

Pri|a|mel, die; -, -n, *auch* das; -s, - ‹lat.› (Spruchgedicht, bes. des dt. Spätmittelalters)

Pri|a|mos, Pri|a|mus (griech. Sagengestalt)

pri|a|pe|isch ‹griech.› (den Priapus betreffend; *veraltet für* unzüchtig); priapeische Gedichte; **Pri|a|pos, Pri|a|pus** (griech.-röm. Gott der Fruchtbarkeit)

Pri|cke, die; -, -n (Markierung in flachen Küstengewässern)

Pri|ckel, der; -s, - (Reiz, Erregung); **pri|cke|lig,** prick|lig (prickelnd); **pri|ckeln;** (↑R 50:) ein Prickeln auf der Haut empfinden; **pri|ckelnd;** (↑R 47:) etwas Prickelndes für den Gaumen; **[1]pri|cken** (*landsch., bes. nordd. für* [aus]stechen; abstecken)

[2]pri|cken (ein Fahrwasser mit Pricken versehen)

prick|lig *vgl.* prickelig
[1]**Priel,** der; -s (Bergname); (↑R 102:) der Große Priel, der Kleine Priel
[2]**Priel,** der; -[e]s, -e (schmaler Wasserlauf im Wattenmeer)
Priem, der; -[e]s, -e ‹niederl.› (Stück Kautabak); **prie|men** (Tabak kauen); **Priem|ta|bak**
Prieß|nitz (Begründer einer Naturheilmethode); **Prieß|nitz‿kur** (↑R 95; eine Kaltwasserkur), **...um|schlag**
Pries|ter, der; -s, -; **Pries|ter|amt,** das; -[e]s; **pries|ter|haft; Pries|te|rin; Pries|ter‿kon|gre|ga|ti|on, ...kö|nig; pries|ter|lich; Pries|ter|schaft,** die; -; **Pries|ter|se|mi|nar; Pries|ter|tum,** das; -s; **Pries|ter|wei|he**
Priest|ley ['pri:stli] (engl. Schriftsteller)
Prig|nitz, die; - (Landschaft in Nordostdeutschland)
Prim, die; -, -en ‹lat.› (Fechthieb; Morgengebet im kath. Brevier; *svw.* Prime *[Musik]*)
Prim. = Primar, Primararzt, Primarius; Primaria
pri|ma ‹ital.› (*Kaufmannsspr. veraltend für* vom Besten, erstklassig; *Abk.* Ia; *ugs. für* ausgezeichnet, großartig); ein prima Kerl; prima Essen; **Pri|ma,** die; -, ...men ‹lat.› (*veraltende Bez. für* die beiden oberen Klassen [*in Österr. für* die erste Klasse] eines Gymnasiums); **Pri|ma|bal|le|ri|na,** die; -, ...nen ‹ital.› (erste Tänzerin); **Pri|ma|don|na,** die; -, ...nnen (erste Sängerin)
Pri|ma|ge [...'ma:ʒə], die; -, -n ‹franz.› (Primgeld)
Pri|ma|ner ‹lat.› (Schüler der Prima); **pri|ma|ner|haft** (unerfahren, unreif); **Pri|ma|ne|rin; Pri|mar,** der; -s, -e (*österr. für* Chefarzt einer Abteilung eines Krankenhauses; *Abk.* Prim.); **pri|mär** ‹franz.› (die Grundlage bildend, wesentlich; ursprünglich, erst...); **Pri|mar|arzt** *(österr.); vgl.* Primar; **Pri|mar|ärz|tin** *(österr.); vgl.* Primaria; **Pri|mär|ener|gie** (↑R 132; Energiegehalt der natürlichen Energieträger, z.B. Wasserkraft); **Pri|ma|ria,** die; -, ...iae [...riɛ:] ‹lat.› (*österr. für* weibl. Primar; *Abk.* Prim.); **Pri|ma|ri|us,** der; -, ...ien [...iən] ‹lat.› (erster Geiger im Streichquartett; *österr. svw.* Primar); **Pri|mar|leh|rer** *(schweiz.);* **Pri|mär|li|te|ra|tur** (der eigtl. dichterische Text; *Ggs.* Sekundärliteratur); **Pri|mar|schu|le** (*schweiz. für* allgemeine Volksschule); **Pri|mär|strom** *(Elektrotechnik);* **Pri|mar|stu|fe** (1. bis 4. Schuljahr); **Pri|mär|wick|lung** *(Elektrotechnik);* [1]**Pri|mas,** der; -, *Plur.* -se, *auch* ...aten ‹der Erste, Vornehmste› (Ehrentitel bestimmter Erzbischöfe); [2]**Pri|mas,** der; -, -se (Solist u. Vorgeiger einer Zigeunerkapelle); [1]**Pri|mat,** der *od.* das; -[e]s, -e (Vorrang, bevorzugte Stellung; [Vor]herrschaft; oberste Kirchengewalt des Papstes); [2]**Pri|mat,** der; -en, -en *meist Plur.;* ↑R 126 (*Biol.* Herrentier, höchstentwickeltes Säugetier); **Pri|ma‿wa|re** *(Kaufmannsspr.),* **...wech|sel** *(Bankw.);* **Pri|me,** die; -, -n (*Musik* erster Ton der diaton. Tonleiter; Intervall im Einklang; *Druckerspr.* am Fuß der ersten Seite eines Bogens stehende Kurzfassung des Buchtitels; *vgl. auch* Norm); **Pri|mel,** die; -, -n (eine Frühjahrsblume); **Pri|men** (*Plur. von* Prim, Prima *u.* Prime); **Prim|gei|ger** (erster Geiger im Streichquartett)
Prim|geld ‹lat.› (Sondervergütung für den Schiffskapitän)
Pri|mi (*Plur. von* Primus); **pri|mis|si|ma** ‹ital.› (*ugs. für* ganz prima, ausgezeichnet); **pri|mi|tiv** ‹lat.› (einfach, dürftig; *abwertend für* von geringem geistig-kulturellem Niveau); ein -er Mensch; ein -es Bedürfnis; ein -es Volk; **Pri|mi|ti|ve** [...və], der *u.* die; -n, -n *meist Plur.;* ↑R 5 ff. (Angehörige[r] eines naturverbundenen, auf einer niedrigen Zivilisationsstufe stehenden Volkes); **pri|mi|ti|vi|sie|ren** [...v...]; **Pri|mi|ti|vi|sie|rung; Pri|mi|ti|vis|mus,** der; - (moderne Kunstrichtung, die sich von der Kunst der Primitiven anregen lässt); **Pri|mi|ti|vi|tät,** die; -; **Pri|mi|tiv|kul|tur; Pri|mi|tiv|ling** *(ugs.);* **Pri|mi|ti|vum** [...vum], das; -s, ...va (*Sprachw.* Stamm-, Wurzelwort); **Pri|miz,** die; -, -en (*kath. Kirche* erste [feierl.] Messe des Primizianten); **Pri|miz|fei|er; Pri|mi|zi|ant,** der; -en, -en; ↑R 126 (neu geweihter kath. Priester); **Pri|mi|zi|en** *Plur.* (den römischen Göttern dargebrachte „Erstlinge" von Früchten u. Ä.); **Pri|mo|ge|ni|tur,** die; -, -en (*früher* Erbfolgerecht des Erstgeborenen u. seiner Nachkommen); **Pri|mus,** der; -, *Plur.* ...mi *u.* -se (Klassenbester); **Pri|mus in|ter Pa|res,** der; - - -, ...mi - - (der Erste unter Gleichen, ohne Vorrang); **Prim|zahl** (nur durch 1 u. durch sich selbst teilbare Zahl)
Prince of Wales ['prins əv 'wɛ:lz], der; - - - (Titel des engl. Thronfolgers)
Prin|te, die; -, -n *meist Plur.* ‹niederl.› (ein Gebäck); Aachener -n; **Prin|ted in Ger|ma|ny** ['printid in 'dʒœ:(r)məni] ‹engl.› (in Deutschland gedruckt [Vermerk in Büchern]); **Prin|ter,** der; -s, - (automat. Kopiergerät; Drucker); **Print|me|di|um** *meist Plur.* (Zeitungen, Zeitschriften und Bücher)
Prinz, der; -en, -en (↑R 126) ‹lat.›; **Prin|zen|gar|de** (Garde eines Karnevalsprinzen); **Prin|zen|in|seln** *Plur.* (im Marmarameer); **Prin|zen|paar,** das; -[e]s, -e (Prinz u. Prinzessin [im Karneval]); **Prin|zess,** die; -, -en (*veraltet für* Prinzessin); **Prin|zess|boh|ne** *meist Plur.;* **Prin|zes|sin; Prin|zess|kleid; Prinz|ge|mahl** (Ehemann einer regierenden Herrscherin); **Prinz-Hein|rich-Müt|ze** ‹nach dem preuß. Prinzen› (Schiffermütze); **Prin|zip,** das; -s, *Plur.* -ien [...iən], *seltener* -e (Grundlage; Grundsatz); [1]**Prin|zi|pal,** der; -s, -e (*veraltet für* Lehrherr; Geschäftsinhaber, -leiter); [2]**Prin|zi|pal,** das; -s, -e (Hauptregister der Orgel); **Prin|zi|pal|gläu|bi|ger** (Hauptgläubiger); **Prin|zi|pa|lin** (*veraltet für* Geschäftsführerin; Theaterleiterin); **prin|zi|pa|li|ter** (*veraltet für* vor allem, in erster Linie); **Prin|zi|pat,** das, *auch* der; -[e]s, -e (*veraltet für* Vorrang; röm. Verfassungsform der ersten Kaiserzeit); **prin|zi|pi|ell** (grundsätzlich); **prin|zi|pi|en|fest; Prin|zi|pi|en|fra|ge; prin|zi|pi|en|los; Prin|zi|pi|en|lo|sig|keit,** die; -; **Prin|zi|pi|en‿rei|ter** (jmd., der kleinlich auf seinen Prinzipien beharrt), **...rei|te|rei, ...streit; prin|zi|pi|en|treu; Prin|zi|pi|en|treue; prinz|lich; Prinz|re|gent**
Pri|or, der; -s, Prioren ‹lat.› ([Kloster]oberer, -vorsteher; *auch für* Stellvertreter eines Abtes); **Pri|o|rat,** das; -[e]s, -e (Amt, Würde eines Priors; meist von einer Abtei abhängiges [kleineres] Kloster); **Pri|o|rin** [*auch* 'pri:...]; **Pri|o|ri|tät,** die; -, -en ‹franz.› (Vor[zugs]recht, Erstrecht, Vorrang; *nur Sing.:* zeitl. Vorhergehen); Prioritäten setzen (festlegen, was vorrangig ist); **Pri|o|ri|tä|ten** *Plur.* (Wertpapiere mit Vorzugsrechten); **Pri|o|ri|tä|ten|lis|te; Pri|o|ri|täts‿ak|ti|en** *(Plur.),* **...ob|li|ga|ti|o|nen** *(Plur.),* **...recht**

Pris|chen (kleine Prise [Tabak u. a.]); **Pri|se,** die; -, -n ‹franz.› (*Seew.* [im Krieg] erbeutetes [Handels]schiff od. -gut; so viel [Tabak, Salz u. a.], wie zwischen Daumen u. Zeigefinger zu greifen ist); **Pri|sen‿ge|richt** *(Seew.),* **...kom|man|do, ...recht** (das; -[e]s)

Pris|ma, das; -s, ...men ‹griech.› (*Math.* Polyeder; *Optik* Licht brechender Körper); **pris|ma|tisch** (prismenförmig); **Pris|ma|to|id,** das; -[e]s, -e (prismenähnlicher Körper); **Pris|men‿fern|rohr, ...form, ...glas** (*Plur.* ...gläser), **...su|cher** (bei Spiegelreflexkameras)

Prit|sche, die; -, -n (flaches Schlagholz [beim Karneval]; hölzerne Liegestatt; Ladefläche eines Lkw); **prit|schen** (*landsch. für* mit der Pritsche schlagen; *Sport* den Volleyball mit den Fingern weiterspielen); du pritschst; **Prit|schen|wa|gen; Prit|sch|meis|ter** (*landsch. für* Hanswurst)

pri|vat [...v...] ‹lat.› (persönlich; nicht öffentlich, außeramtlich; vertraulich; vertraut); eine private Meinung, Angelegenheit; die private Wirtschaft; sich privat versichern; ein privat versicherter Patient; (↑R 47:) Verkauf an, Kauf von privat; **Pri|vat‿ad|res|se, ...an|ge|le|gen|heit, ...au|di|enz, ...bahn, ...bank** (*Plur.* ...banken), **...be|sitz, ...brief, ...de|tek|tiv, ...do|zent** (Hochschullehrer ohne Beamtenstelle), **...do|zen|tin, ...druck** (*Plur.* ...drucke); **Pri|va|te,** der *u.* die; -n, -n; ↑R 5 ff. (Privatperson); **Pri|vat‿ei|gen|tum, ...fern|se|hen, ...flug|zeug, ...ge|brauch** (der; -[e]s), **...ge|lehr|te, ...ge|spräch, ...gläu|bi|ger, ...hand** (*nur in* aus, von, in -), **...haus; Pri|va|ti|er** [...ˈtie:], der; -s, -s (*veraltet für* Privatmann, Rentner); **pri|va|tim** (*veraltend für* [ganz] persönlich, unter vier Augen, vertraulich); **Pri|vat‿ini|ti|a|ti|ve** (↑R 132), **...in|te|res|se; Pri|va|ti|on,** die; -, -en (*veraltet für* Beraubung; Entziehung); **pri|va|ti|sie|ren** (staatl. Vermögen in Privatvermögen umwandeln; als Rentner[in] od. als Privatperson vom eigenen Vermögen leben); **Pri|va|ti|sie|rung; pri|va|tis|si|me** [...me] (im engsten Kreise; streng vertraulich; ganz allein); **Pri|va|tis|si|mum,** das; -s, ...ma (Vorlesung für einen ausgewählten Kreis; *übertr. für* Ermahnung); **Pri|va|tist,** der; -en, -en; ↑R 126 (*österr. für* Schüler, der sich ohne Schulbesuch auf die Prüfung an einer Schule vorbereitet); **Pri|vat‿kla|ge, ...kli|nik, ...kon|tor, ...kund|schaft, ...le|ben** (das; -s), **...leh|rer, ...leh|re|rin, ...leu|te** *(Plur.),* **...mann** (*Plur.* ...leute, *selten* ...männer); **Pri|vat|mit|tel** *Plur.;* (↑R 23:) Privat- u. öffentliche Mittel, *aber* öffentliche und Privatmittel; **Pri|vat‿pa|ti|ent, ...pa|ti|en|tin, ...per|son, ...quar|tier, ...recht** (das; -[e]s); **pri|vat|recht|lich; Pri|vat‿sa|che, ...schu|le, ...sek|re|tär, ...sek|re|tä|rin, ...sphä|re** (die; -), **...sta|ti|on, ...stun|de, ...un|ter|richt, ...ver|gnü|gen, ...ver|mö|gen; pri|vat ver|si|chert** *vgl.* privat; **Pri|vat‿ver|si|che|rung, ...weg, ...wirt|schaft; pri|vat|wirt|schaft|lich; Pri|vat‿woh|nung, ...zim|mer**

Pri|vi|leg [...v...], das; -[e]s, *Plur.* -ien [...i̯ən], *auch* -e ‹lat.› (Vor-, Sonderrecht); **pri|vi|le|gie|ren; pri|vi|le|giert; Pri|vi|le|gi|um,** das; -s, ...ien [...i̯ən] (*älter für* Privileg)

Prix [pri:], der; -, - ‹franz.› (*franz. Bez. für* Preis); Prix Goncourt [- gõˈku:r] (franz. Literaturpreis); *vgl.* Grand Prix

PR-Mann, *Plur.* PR-Leute ‹*zu* PR = Publicrelations› (*ugs. für* für die Öffentlichkeitsarbeit zuständiger Mitarbeiter)

pro *Präp. mit Akk.* ‹lat.› (für, je); pro Stück; pro männlichen Angestellten; **Pro,** das; - (Für); das Pro und Kontra (das Für und Wider); **pro...** (z. B. proamerikanisch, prowestlich); **pro an|no** (*veraltet für* jährlich; *Abk.* p. a.)

pro|ba|bel ‹lat.› (*veraltet für* wahrscheinlich); ...ab|le (↑R 130) Gründe; **Pro|ba|bi|lis|mus,** der; - (*Philos.* Wahrscheinlichkeitslehre; *kath. Moraltheologie* Lehre, nach der in Zweifelsfällen eine Handlung erlaubt ist, wenn gute Gründe dafür sprechen); **Pro|ba|bi|li|tät,** die; -, -en (Wahrscheinlichkeit); **Pro|band,** der; -en, -en; ↑R 126 (Testperson, an der etwas ausprobiert od. gezeigt wird; *Genealogie* jmd., für den eine Ahnentafel aufgestellt werden soll); **Pro|ban|din; pro|bat** (erprobt; bewährt); **Pröb|chen; Pro|be,** die; -, -n; zur, auf Probe; [einen Wagen] Probe fahren; wir sind Probe gefahren; ohne Probe zu fahren; lass die Maschine Probe laufen; die Maschine ist Probe gelaufen; wir mussten [eine Seite] Probe schreiben; sie haben vormittags Probe geturnt; wann wollen Sie Probe singen?; hat sie schon Probe gesungen?; **Pro|be‿ab|zug, ...alarm** (↑R 132), **...ar|beit, ...auf|nah|me, ...boh|rung, ...druck** (*Plur.* ...drucke), **...exemp|lar** (↑R 132); **Pro|be fah|ren** *vgl.* Probe; **Pro|be|fahrt; pro|be|hal|ber; pro|be|hal|tig** (*veraltet für* die Probe bestehend, aushaltend); **Pro|be‿jahr, ...lauf; Pro|be lau|fen** *vgl.* Probe; **Pro|be|leh|rer** (*österr. für* Lehrer an einer höheren Schule im Probejahr); **Pro|be|lek|ti|on; prö|beln** (*schweiz. für* allerlei Versuche anstellen); ich ...[e]le (↑R 16); **pro|ben; Pro|ben‿ar|beit, ...ent|nah|me; Pro|be|num|mer; Pro|be schrei|ben** *vgl.* Probe; **Pro|be‿sei|te** *(Druckw.),* **...sen|dung; Pro|be sin|gen** *vgl.* Probe; **Pro|be|stück; Pro|be tur|nen** *vgl.* Probe; **pro|be|wei|se; Pro|be|zeit; pro|bie|ren** (versuchen, kosten, prüfen); (↑R 50:) Probieren *(auch* probieren) geht über Studieren *(auch* studieren); **Pro|bie|rer** (Prüfer); **Pro|bier‿glas** (*Plur.* ...gläser), **...stu|be**

Prob|lem (↑R 130), das; -s, -e ‹griech.› (zu lösende Aufgabe; Frage[stellung]; unentschiedene Frage; Schwierigkeit); **Prob|le|ma|tik,** die; -, -en (Gesamtheit von Problemen; Schwierigkeit [etwas zu klären]); **prob|le|ma|tisch; prob|le|ma|ti|sie|ren** (die Problematik von etwas aufzeigen); **Prob|lem‿be|reich, ...be|wusst|sein, ...den|ken, ...film, ...grup|pe, ...haar, ...haut** (die; -), **...kind, ...kreis; prob|lem|los; Prob|lem‿lö|sung, ...müll; prob|lem|ori|en|tiert** (↑R 132); **Prob|lem‿schach, ...stel|lung, ...stück, ...zo|ne**

Probst|zel|la (Ort im nordwestl. Frankenwald)

Pro|ce|de|re [...ˈtse:...], *eindeutschend* Pro|ze|de|re, das; -, - ‹lat.› (Verfahrensordnung, -weise; Prozedur)

pro cen|tum [- ˈtsɛ...] ‹lat.› (für hundert, für das Hundert; *Abk.* p. c., v. H.; *Zeichen* %); *vgl.* Prozent

Pro|de|kan, der; -s, -e ‹lat.› (Vertreter des Dekans an einer Hochschule)

pro do|mo ‹lat.› (in eigener Sache; zum eigenen Nutzen, für sich selbst); - - reden

Pro|drom, das; -s, -e ‹griech.›, **Pro|dro|mal|symp|tom** (*Med.* Vorbote, Vorläufer einer Krankheit)

Pro|du|cer [proˈdju:sə(r)], der; -s, -

⟨engl.⟩ (*engl. Bez. für* Hersteller, [Film]produzent, Fabrikant); **Pro|duct|place|ment,** *auch* **Product-Place|ment** ['prɔdakt 'ple:smənt] (↑R 24), das; -s, -s ⟨engl.⟩ (Werbemaßnahme im Film u. im Fernsehen, bei der ein Produkt als Requisit in die Spielhandlung einbezogen wird); **Produkt,** das; -[e]s, -e ⟨lat.⟩ (Erzeugnis; Ertrag; Folge, Ergebnis [*Math.* der Multiplikation]); **Produk|ten‿bör|se** (*Wirtsch.* Warenbörse), **...han|del** (*vgl.* [1]Handel), **...markt; Pro|duk|ti|on,** die; -, -en (Herstellung, Erzeugung); **Pro|duk|ti|ons‿an|la|gen** *(Plur.),* **...ap|pa|rat, ...aus|fall, ...ba|sis, ...bri|ga|de** *(ehem. in der DDR),* **...er|fah|rung, ...fak|tor, ...form, ...gang, ...ge|nos|sen|schaft, ...gü|ter** *(Plur.),* **...ka|pa|zi|tät, ...kol|lek|tiv** *(ehem. in der DDR),* **...kos|ten** *(Plur.),* **...leis|tung, ...men|ge, ...me|tho|de, ...mittel** (das), **...plan** (*vgl.* [2]Plan), **...pro|zess, ...stät|te, ...stei|gerung, ...ver|fah|ren, ...ver|hältnis|se** *(Plur.),* **...vo|lu|men, ...wei|se, ...wert, ...zif|fer, ...zweig; pro|duk|tiv** (ergiebig; fruchtbar, schöpferisch); **Produk|ti|vi|tät** [...v...], die; -; **Produk|ti|vi|täts‿ef|fekt, ...ren|te** (Rente, die der wirtschaftl. Produktivität angepasst wird), **...steige|rung, ...stu|fe; Pro|duk|tiv‿kraft** (die; -, ...kräfte), **...kre|dit** (Kredit, der Unternehmen der gewerbl. Wirtschaft zur Errichtung von Anlagen od. zur Bestreitung der laufenden Betriebsausgaben gewährt wird); **Pro|du|zent,** der; -en, -en; ↑R 126 (Hersteller, Erzeuger); **Pro|du|zen|tin; pro|duzie|ren** ([Güter] hervorbringen, [er]zeugen, schaffen); sich produzieren (die Aufmerksamkeit auf sich lenken)

Pro|en|zym, das; -s, -e ⟨lat.; griech.⟩ (Vorstufe eines Enzyms)

Prof. = Professor

pro|fan ⟨lat.⟩ (unheilig, weltlich; nicht außergewöhnlich, alltäglich); **Pro|fa|na|ti|on,** Pro|fa|nierung, die; -, -en (Entweihung); **Pro|fan|bau** *Plur.* ...bauten (*Kunstw.* nichtkirchl. Bauwerk; *Ggs.* Sakralbau); **Pro|fa|ne,** der *u.* die; -n, -n; ↑R 5 ff. (Unheilige[r], Ungeweihte[r]); **pro|fa|nie|ren** (entweihen; säkularisieren); **Profa|nie|rung** *vgl.* Profanation; **Pro|fa|ni|tät,** die; - (Unheiligkeit, Weltlichkeit; Alltäglichkeit)

pro|fa|schis|tisch (dem Faschismus zuneigend)

Pro|fer|ment, das; -s, -e ⟨lat.⟩ (*veraltend für* Proenzym)

[1]**Pro|fess,** der; -en, -en (↑R 126) ⟨lat.⟩ (Mitglied eines geistl. Ordens nach Ablegung der Gelübde); [2]**Pro|fess,** die; -, -e (Ablegung der [Ordens]gelübde); **Profes|si|on,** die; -, -en ⟨franz.⟩ (*veraltet für* Beruf; Gewerbe); **Profes|si|o|nal** [*engl.* prəˈfɛʃ(ə)nəl], der; -s, *Plur.* -e, *bei engl.Ausspr.* -s ⟨engl.⟩ (Berufssportler; *Kurzw.* Profi); **pro|fes|si|o|na|li|sie|ren** (zum Beruf machen, als Erwerbsquelle ansehen); **Pro|fes|si|o|nali|sie|rung; Pro|fes|si|o|na|lismus,** der; - ⟨lat.⟩ (Berufssportlertum); **Pro|fes|si|o|na|li|tät,** die; - (das Professionellsein); **pro|fessi|o|nell** ⟨franz.⟩ (berufsmäßig; fachmännisch); **pro|fes|si|oniert** (*selten für* gewerbsmäßig); **Pro|fes|si|o|nist,** der; -en, -en; ↑R 126 (*österr., sonst nur landsch. für* Handwerker, Facharbeiter); **pro|fes|si|ons|mä|ßig; Pro|fessor,** der; -s, ...oren ⟨lat.⟩ (Hochschullehrer; Titel für verdiente Lehrkräfte, Forscher u. Künstler; *österr. auch für* definitiv angestellter Lehrer an höheren Schulen; *Abk.* Prof.); ordentlicher öffentlicher Professor (*Abk.* o. ö. Prof.); ordentlicher Professor (*Abk.* o. P.); außerordentlicher Professor (*Abk.* ao., a. o. Prof.); ein emeritierter Professor; **pro|fesso|ral** (professorenhaft, würdevoll); **Pro|fes|so|ren|kol|le|gium; pro|fes|so|ren|mä|ßig; Profes|so|ren|schaft** (Gesamtheit der Professoren einer Hochschule); **Pro|fes|so|ren|ti|tel,** Pro|fessor|ti|tel; **Pro|fes|so|rin** [*auch* ...ˈfɛ...] (*im Titel u. in der Anrede auch* Frau Professor); **Pro|fessors|frau; Pro|fes|sor|ti|tel** *vgl.* Professorentitel; **Pro|fes|sur,** die; -, -en (Lehrstuhl, -amt); **Profi,** der; -s, -s ⟨*Kurzw. für* Professional⟩ (Berufssportler; jmd., der etwas fachmännisch betreibt); **Pro|fi‿bo|xer, ...fuß|ball, ...geschäft; pro|fi|haft**

Pro|fil, das; -s, -e ⟨ital.(-franz.)⟩ (Seitenansicht; Längs- od. Querschnitt; Riffelung bei Gummireifen; charakteristisches Erscheinungsbild); geologisches Profil (senkrechter Geländeschnitt)

Pro|fi|la|ger, das; -s *(Sport);* ins - wechseln

Pro|fil‿bild, ...ei|sen; pro|fi|lieren ⟨franz.⟩ (im Querschnitt darstellen); sich profilieren (sich ausprägen, hervortreten); **pro|fi|liert** (*auch für* gerillt, geformt; scharf umrissen; von ausgeprägter Art); **Pro|fi|lie|rung; pro|fil|los; Profil|neu|ro|se** (*Psych.* übertriebene Sorge um die Profilierung der eigenen Persönlichkeit); **Pro|fil‿soh|le, ...stahl** *(Technik),* **...tiefe** *(Kfz-Technik)*

Pro|fi|sport, der; -[e]s

Pro|fit [*auch* ...ˈfit], der; -[e]s, -e ⟨franz.⟩ (Nutzen; Gewinn; Vorteil); ein Profit bringendes Geschäft, *aber* ein äußerst profitbringendes Geschäft (↑R 40); **pro|fi|ta|bel** (*veraltet für* Gewinn bringend); ...ab|les (↑R 130) Geschäft; **Pro|fit brin|gend** *vgl.* Profit; **Pro|fit|chen** (*meist für* nicht ganz ehrlicher Gewinn); **Pro|fiteur** [...ˈtøːr], der; -s, -e ⟨franz.⟩; **Pro|fit|gier; pro|fi|tie|ren** (Nutzen ziehen); **Pro|fit|jä|ger** (jmd., der profitgierig ist); **pro|fit|lich** (*landsch. für* sparsam; nur auf den eigenen Vorteil bedacht); **Pro|fit‿ma|cher** *(ugs.),* **...ra|te, ...streben** (das; -s)

pro for|ma ⟨lat.⟩ (der Form wegen, zum Schein); **Pro-for|ma-Ankla|ge** (↑R 28)

Pro|fos, der; *Gen.* -es *u.* -en, *Plur.* -e[n] (↑R 126) ⟨niederl.⟩ (*früher* Verwalter der Militärgerichtsbarkeit)

pro|fund ⟨lat.⟩ (tief, gründlich; *Med.* tief liegend); **pro|fus** (*Med.* reichlich, übermäßig; stark)

Pro|ge|ni|tur, die; -, -en ⟨lat.⟩ (*Med.* Nachkommen[schaft])

Pro|ges|te|ron, das; -s (Gelbkörperhormon, das die Schwangerschaftsvorgänge reguliert)

Prog|no|se (↑R 130), die; -, -n ⟨griech.⟩ ([wissenschaftl.] Vorhersage); **Prog|nos|tik,** die; - (Lehre von der Prognose); **Prog|nos|tikon, Prog|nos|ti|kum,** das; -s, *Plur.* ...ken *u.* ...ka (Vorzeichen); **prog|nos|tisch; prog|nos|ti|zieren; Prog|nos|ti|zie|rung**

Pro|gramm, das; -s, -e ⟨griech.⟩ (Plan; Darlegung von Grundsätzen; Ankündigung; Spiel-, Sende-, Fest-, Arbeits-, Vortragsfolge; Tagesordnung; *EDV* Folge von Anweisungen für einen Computer); **Pro|gramm‿ab|lauf, ...än|de|rung, ...an|zei|ger; Program|ma|tik,** die; -, -en (Zielsetzung, -vorstellung); **Pro|gramma|ti|ker; pro|gram|ma|tisch** (dem Programm gemäß; einführend; richtungweisend); **Programm‿di|rek|tor** *(bes. Fernsehen),* **...fol|ge; pro|gramm|füllend; Pro|gramm|fül|ler** (*Fernsehen* Kurzfilm, der eingesetzt werden kann, um Lücken im Programm zu füllen); **pro|gramm|ge|mäß; Pro|gramm|ge|stal|tung; pro|gramm|ge|steu|ert** *(EDV);* **Pro|gramm‿heft, ...hin|weis; pro|gram|mier|bar; Pro|gram|mier|be|reich** *(EDV);* **pro|gram|mie|ren** ([im Ablauf] festlegen; [einen Computer] mit Informationen, mit einem Programm versorgen); **Pro|gram|mie|rer** (Fachmann, der Schaltungen u. Ablaufpläne für Computer erarbeitet); **Pro|gram|mie|re|rin; Pro|gram|mier|spra|che; Pro|gram|mie|rung; pro|gramm|mä|ßig** (↑R 136); **Pro|gramm|mu|sik** (↑R 136), die; **Pro|gramm‿punkt, ...steu|e|rung** (automatische Steuerung); **...vor|schau, ...zeit|schrift, ...zet|tel**

Pro|gress, der; -es, -e ‹lat.› (Fortschritt; Fortgang); **Pro|gres|si|on,** die; -, -en (das Fortschreiten; [Stufen]folge, Steigerung; *Math. veraltet* Aufeinanderfolge von Zahlen usw.); arithmetische -; geometrische -; **Pro|gres|sis|mus,** der; - ([übertriebene] Fortschrittlichkeit); **Pro|gres|sist,** der; -en, -en; ↑R 126; **pro|gres|sis|tisch; pro|gres|siv** ‹franz.› (stufenweise fortschreitend, sich entwickelnd; fortschrittlich); **Pro|gres|si|vist** [...'vist], der; -en, -en (↑R 126); **Pro|gres|siv|steu|er** [...f...], die *(Wirtsch.)*

Pro|gym|na|si|um, das; -s, ...ien [...i̯ən] (Gymnasium ohne Oberstufe)

pro|hi|bie|ren ‹lat.› (*veraltet für* verhindern; verbieten); **Pro|hi|bi|ti|on,** die; -, -en (Verbot, bes. von Alkoholherstellung u. -abgabe); **Pro|hi|bi|ti|o|nist,** der; -en, -en (↑R 126); **pro|hi|bi|tiv** (verhindernd, abhaltend, vorbeugend); **Pro|hi|bi|tiv‿maß|re|gel, ...zoll** (Sperr-, Schutzzoll)

Pro|jekt, das; -[e]s, -e ‹lat.› (Plan[ung], Entwurf, Vorhaben); **Pro|jek|tant,** der; -en, -en; ↑R 126 (Planer); **Pro|jek|te[n]|ma|cher; Pro|jekt|grup|pe** (Arbeitsgruppe, die sich für ein bestimmtes Projekt einsetzt); **pro|jek|tie|ren; Pro|jek|tie|rung; Pro|jek|til,** das; -s, -e ‹franz.› (Geschoss); **Pro|jek|ti|on,** die; -, -en ‹lat.› (Darstellung auf einer Fläche; Vorführung mit dem Bildwerfer); **Pro|jek|ti|ons‿ap|pa|rat** (Bildwerfer), **...ebe|ne** (↑R 132; *Math.*), **...lam|pe, ...schirm, ...ver|fah|ren, ...wand; Pro|jek|tor,** der; -s, ...oren (Bildwerfer); **pro|ji|zie|ren** (auf einer Fläche darstellen; mit dem Projektor vorführen); **Pro|ji|zie|rung**

Pro|kla|ma|ti|on, die; -, -en ‹lat.› (amtl. Bekanntmachung, Verkündigung; Aufruf); **pro|kla|mie|ren; Pro|kla|mie|rung**

Pro|kli|se, Pro|kli|sis, die; -, ...klisen ‹griech.› (*Sprachw.* Anlehnung eines unbetonten Wortes an das folgende betonte; *Ggs.* Enklise); **Pro|kli|ti|kon,** das; -s, ...ka (unbetontes Wort, das sich an das folgende betonte anlehnt, z. B. „und 's Mädchen [= und das Mädchen] sprach"); **pro|kli|tisch**

Pro|kof|jew [...jɛf] (↑R 132), Sergej [sjɛr'gjei̯] (russ. Komponist)

pro|kom|mu|nis|tisch (dem Kommunismus zuneigend)

Pro|kon|sul, der; -s, -n ‹lat.› (gewesener Konsul; Statthalter einer röm. Provinz); **Pro|kon|su|lat,** das; -[e]s, -e (Amt des Prokonsuls; Statthalterschaft)

Pro|kop, Pro|ko|pi|us (byzant. Geschichtsschreiber)

pro Kopf; Pro-Kopf-Ver|brauch (↑R 28)

Pro|krus|tes (Gestalt der griech. Sage); **Pro|krus|tes|bett,** das; -[e]s; ↑R 95 (Schema, in das jmd. od. etwas hineingezwängt wird)

Prok|tal|gie (↑R 132), die; -, ...ien ‹griech.› (*Med.* neuralg. Schmerzen in After u. Mastdarm); **Prok|ti|tis,** die; -, ...itiden (Mastdarmentzündung); **Prok|to|lo|ge,** der; -n, -n; ↑R 126 (Facharzt für Erkrankungen im Bereich des Mastdarms); **Prok|to|lo|gie,** die; -; **prok|to|lo|gisch; Prok|to|spas|mus,** der; -, ...men (Krampf des Afterschließmuskels); **Prok|tos|ta|se** (↑R 132), die; - (Kotzurückhaltung im Mastdarm)

Pro|ku|ra, die; -, ...ren ‹lat.-ital.› (Handlungsvollmacht; Recht, den Geschäftsinhaber zu vertreten); in Prokura; *vgl.* per procura; **Pro|ku|ra|ti|on,** die; -, -en (Stellvertretung durch einen Bevollmächtigten; Vollmacht); **Pro|ku|ra|tor,** der; -s, ...oren (Statthalter einer röm. Provinz; hoher Staatsbeamter der Republik Venedig; Vermögensverwalter eines Klosters); **Pro|ku|rist,** der; -en, -en; ↑R 126 (Inhaber einer Prokura); **Pro|ku|ris|ten|stel|le; Pro|ku|ris|tin**

Pro|ky|on, der; -[s] ‹griech.› (ein Stern)

Pro|laps, der; -es, -e ‹lat.› *u.* **Pro|lap|sus,** der; -, - [...su:s] (*Med.* Vorfall, Heraustreten von inneren Organen)

Pro|le|go|me|na [*auch* ...'gɔ...] *Plur.* ‹griech.› (einleitende Vorbemerkungen usw.)

Pro|lep|se, Pro|lep|sis [*auch* 'pro:...], die; -, ...lepsen ‹griech.› (*Rhet.* Vorwegnahme eines Satzgliedes); **pro|lep|tisch** (vorgreifend; vorwegnehmend)

Pro|let, der; -en, -en (↑R 126) ‹lat.› (*veraltet für* Proletarier; *abwertend für* ungebildeter, ungehobelter Mensch); **Pro|le|ta|ri|at,** das; -[e]s, -e (Gesamtheit der Proletarier); **Pro|le|ta|ri|er,** der; -s, - (Angehöriger der wirtschaftlich unselbstständigen, besitzlosen Klasse); **Pro|le|ta|ri|er‿kind, ...vier|tel; pro|le|ta|risch; pro|le|ta|ri|sie|ren** (zu Proletariern machen); **Pro|le|ta|ri|sie|rung,** die; -; **Pro|let|kult,** der; -[e]s (von der russ. Oktoberrevolution ausgehende kulturrevolutionäre Bewegung der 20er Jahre)

[1]**Pro|li|fe|ra|ti|on,** die; -, -en ‹lat.› (*Med.* Sprossung, Wucherung); [2]**Pro|li|fe|ra|tion** [pro:lifə're:ʃ(ə)n], die; - ‹engl.-amerik.› (Weitergabe von Atomwaffen od. Mitteln zu ihrer Herstellung); **pro|li|fe|rie|ren** ‹lat.› (*Med.* sprossen, wuchern)

Pro|log, der; -[e]s, -e ‹griech.› (Einleitung; Vorwort, -spiel, -rede; *Radsport* Rennen zum Auftakt einer Etappenfahrt)

Pro|lon|ga|ti|on, die; -, -en ‹lat.› (*Wirtsch.* Verlängerung [einer Frist, bes. einer Kreditfrist], Aufschub, Stundung); **Pro|lon|ga|ti|ons‿ge|schäft, ...wech|sel; pro|lon|gie|ren** (verlängern; stunden); **Pro|lon|gie|rung**

pro me|mo|ria ‹lat.› (zum Gedächtnis; *Abk.* p. m.); **Pro|me|mo|ria,** das; -s, *Plur.* ...ien [...i̯ən] *u.* -s (*veraltet für* Denkschrift; Merkzettel)

Pro|me|na|de, die; -, -n ‹franz.› (Spazierweg; Spaziergang); *Schreibung in Straßennamen:* ↑R 123; **Pro|me|na|den‿deck** (auf Schiffen), **...kon|zert, ...mi|schung** (*ugs. scherzh. für* nicht reinrassiger Hund), **...weg; pro|me|nie|ren** (spazieren gehen)

Pro|mes|se, die; -, -n ‹franz.› (*Rechtsspr.* Schuldverschreibung; Urkunde, in der eine Leistung versprochen wird); **Pro|mes|sen|ge|schäft**

pro|me|the|isch ‹griech.›; ↑R 94 (*auch für* himmelstürmend); prometheisches Ringen; **Pro|me|theus** [...tɔys] (griech. Sagengestalt); **Pro|me|thi|um,** das; -s (chem. Element, Metall; *Zeichen* Pm)

pro mil|le ‹lat.› (für tausend, für das Tausend, vom Tausend; *Abk.* p. m., v. T.; *Zeichen* ‰); **Pro|mil|le,** das; -[s], - (Tausendstel); 2 - (↑R 90); **Pro|mil|le‿gren|ze, ...satz** (Vomtausendsatz)
pro|mi|nent ‹lat.› (hervorragend, bedeutend, maßgebend); **Pro|mi|nen|te,** der *u.* die; -n, -n; ↑R 5 ff. (hervorragende, bedeutende, bekannte Persönlichkeit); **Pro|mi|nenz,** die; - (Gesamtheit der Prominenten; *veraltet für* [hervorragende] Bedeutung); **Pro|mi|nen|zen** *Plur.* (hervorragende Persönlichkeiten)
Pro|mis|ku|i|tät, die; - ‹lat., „Vermischung"› (Geschlechtsverkehr mit häufig wechselnden Partnern); **pro|mis|ku|i|tiv**
pro|mis|so|risch ‹lat.› (*Rechtsspr. veraltet für* versprechend); promissorischer Eid (vor der Aussage geleisteter Eid)
Pro|mo|ter [prə'mo:tə(r)], der; -s, - ‹engl.› (Veranstalter von Berufssportwettkämpfen); **¹Pro|mo|ti|on** [pro...], die; -, -en ‹lat.› (Erlangung, Verleihung der Doktorwürde); Promotion sub auspiciis [praesidentis] (*österr. für* Ehrenpromotion in Anwesenheit des Bundespräsidenten); **²Pro|mo|tion** [prə'mo:ʃən], die; - ‹amerik.› (*Wirtsch.* Absatzförderung durch gezielte Werbemaßnahmen); **Pro|mo|tor** [pro...], der; -s, ...oren ‹lat.› (Förderer, Manager); **Pro|mo|vend** [...v...], der; -en, -en (jmd., der die Doktorwürde anstrebt); **pro|mo|vie|ren** (die Doktorwürde erlangen, verleihen); ich habe promoviert; ich bin [von der ... Fakultät zum Doktor ...] promoviert worden
prompt ‹lat.› (unverzüglich; schlagfertig; pünktlich; sofort; rasch); prompte (schnelle) Bedienung; **Prompt|heit,** die; -
Pro|mul|ga|ti|on, die; -, -en ‹lat.› (*veraltend für* Verbreitung, Veröffentlichung [eines Gesetzes]); **pro|mul|gie|ren**
Pro|no|men, das; -s, *Plur.* -, *älter* ...mina ‹lat.› (*Sprachw.* Fürwort, z. B. „ich, mein"); **pro|no|mi|nal** (fürwörtlich); **Pro|no|mi|nal|ad|jek|tiv** (unbestimmtes Für- od. Zahlwort, nach dem das folgende [substantivisch gebrauchte] Adjektiv wie nach einem Pronomen oder wie nach einem Adjektiv gebeugt wird, z. B. „manche": „manche geeignete, *auch noch:* geeigneten Einrichtungen"); **Pro|no|mi|nal|ad|verb** (Adverb, das für eine Fügung aus Präposition u. Pronomen steht, z. B. „darüber" = „über das" od. „über es")
pro|non|cie|ren [...nõ'si:...] ‹franz.› (*veraltet für* deutlich aussprechen; scharf betonen); **pro|non|ciert**
Pro|ö|mi|um, das; -s, ...ien [...iən] ‹griech.› (Vorrede; Einleitung)
Pro|pä|deu|tik, die; -, -en ‹griech.› (Einführung in die Vorkenntnisse, die zu einem Studium gehören); **Pro|pä|deu|ti|kum,** das; -s, ...ka (*schweiz. für* medizin. Vorprüfung); **pro|pä|deu|tisch**
Pro|pa|gan|da, die; - ‹lat.› (Werbung für polit. Grundsätze, kulturelle Belange od. wirtschaftl. Zwecke); **Pro|pa|gan|da‿ap|pa|rat, ...chef, ...feld|zug, ...film, ...lü|ge, ...ma|te|ri|al, ...schrift, ...sen|dung; pro|pa|gan|da|wirk|sam; Pro|pa|gan|dist,** der; -en, -en; ↑R 126 (jmd., der Propaganda treibt, Werber); **Pro|pa|gan|dis|tin; pro|pa|gan|dis|tisch; Pro|pa|ga|tor,** der; -s, ...oren (jmd., der etwas propagiert); **pro|pa|gie|ren** (verbreiten, werben für etwas); **Pro|pa|gie|rung**
Pro|pan, das; -s ‹griech.› (ein Brenn-, Treibgas); **Pro|pan|gas,** das; -es
Pro|pa|ro|xy|to|non (↑R 132), das; -s, ...tona ‹griech.› (*Sprachw.* auf der drittletzten, kurzen Silbe betontes Wort)
Pro|pel|ler, der; -s, - ‹engl.› (Antriebsschraube bei [Luft]fahrzeugen; Schiffsschraube); **Pro|pel|ler‿an|trieb, ...flug|zeug, ...tur|bi|ne**
Pro|pen *vgl.* Propylen
pro|per, prop|re (↑R 130) ‹franz.› (sauber, ordentlich); **Pro|per|ge|schäft** (*Wirtsch.* Geschäft für eigene Rechnung)
Pro|pe|ris|po|me|non (↑R 132), das; -s, ...mena ‹griech.› (*Sprachw.* auf der vorletzten, langen Silbe betontes Wort)
Pro|pha|se, die; -, -n ‹griech.› (*Biol.* erste Phase der indirekten Zellkernteilung)
Pro|phet, der; -en, -en (↑R 126) ‹griech.› (Weissager, Seher; Mahner); ein falscher Prophet; ein guter Prophet, *aber* (↑R 108): die Großen Propheten (z. B. Jesaja), die Kleinen Propheten (z. B. Hosea); **Pro|phe|ten|ga|be,** die; -; **Pro|phe|tie,** die; -, ...ien (Weissagung); **Pro|phe|tin; pro|phe|tisch** (seherisch, weissagend, vorausschauend); **pro|phe|zei|en** (weis-, voraussagen); er hat prophezeit; **Pro|phe|zei|ung**
Pro|phy|lak|ti|kum, das; -s, ...ka ‹griech.› (*Med.* vorbeugendes Mittel); **pro|phy|lak|tisch** (vorbeugend, verhütend); **Pro|phy|la|xe,** die; -, -n (Maßnahme[n] zur Vorbeugung, [Krankheits]verhütung)
Pro|pi|on|säu|re (ein Konservierungsmittel)
Pro|po|nent, der; -en, -en (↑R 126) ‹lat.› (*veraltet für* Antragsteller); **pro|po|nie|ren**
Pro|pon|tis, die; - ‹griech.› (Marmarameer)
Pro|por|ti|on, die; -, -en ‹lat.› ([Größen]verhältnis; *Math.* Verhältnisgleichung); **pro|por|ti|o|nal** (verhältnismäßig; in gleichem Verhältnis stehend; entsprechend); **Pro|por|ti|o|na|le,** die; -, -n (*Math.* Glied einer Verhältnisgleichung); drei Proportionale[n]; mittlere -; **Pro|por|ti|o|na|li|tät,** die; -, -en (Verhältnismäßigkeit, proportionales Verhältnis); **Pro|por|ti|o|nal|wahl** (Verhältniswahl); **pro|por|ti|o|nell** (*österr. für* dem Proporz entsprechend); **pro|por|ti|o|niert** (bestimmte Proportionen aufweisend); gut, schlecht proportioniert; **Pro|por|ti|o|niert|heit,** die; -; **Pro|por|ti|ons|glei|chung** *(Math.);* **Pro|porz,** der; -es, -e (Verteilung von Sitzen u. Ämtern nach dem Stimmenverhältnis bzw. dem Verhältnis der Partei- oder Konfessionszugehörigkeit; *bes. österr. u. schweiz. für* Verhältniswahlsystem); **Pro|porz‿den|ken, ...wahl** (Verhältniswahl)
Pro|po|si|ti|on, die; -, -en ‹lat.› (Ausschreibung bei Pferderennen; *veraltet für* Vorschlag, Antrag; *Sprachw.* Satzinhalt); **Pro|po|si|tum,** das; -s, ...ta (*veraltet für* Äußerung, Rede)
Prop|pen, der; -s, - (*nordd. für* Pfropfen); **prop|pen|voll** (*ugs. für* ganz voll; übervoll)
Pro|prä|tor, der; -s, ...oren (röm. Provinzstatthalter, der vorher Prätor war)
prop|re (↑R 130) *vgl.* proper; **Prop|re|ge|schäft** *vgl.* Propergeschäft; **Prop|re|tät,** die; - ‹franz.› (*veraltet, aber noch landsch. für* Reinlichkeit, Sauberkeit); **Prop|ri|e|tär,** der; -s, -e (*veraltet für* Eigentümer); **Prop|ri|e|tät,** die; -, -en (*veraltet für* Eigentum, Eigentumsrecht); **Prop|ri|e|täts|recht; Prop|ri|um** [*auch* 'prɔ...], das; -s ‹lat.› (*Psych.* Identität, Selbstgefühl; *kath. Kirche* die wechselnden Texte u. Gesänge der Messe)
Propst, der; -[e]s, Pröpste ‹lat.›

(Kloster-, Stiftsvorsteher; Superintendent); **Props|tei,** die; -, -en (Amt[ssitz], Sprengel, Wohnung eines Propstes); **Pröps|tin**

Pro|pusk [*auch* ...'pusk], der; -s, -e ‹russ.› (*russ. Bez. für* Passierschein, Ausweis)

Pro|py|lä|en *Plur.* ‹griech.› (Vorhalle griech. Tempel)

Pro|py|len, Pro|pen, das; -s ‹griech.› (ein gasförmiger ungesättigter Kohlenwasserstoff)

Pro|rek|tor, der; -s, ...oren ‹lat.› (Stellvertreter des Rektors); **Pro|rek|to|rat,** das; -[e]s, -e (Amt u. Würde eines Prorektors)

Pro|ro|ga|ti|on, die; -, -en ‹lat.› (*veraltet für* Aufschub, Verlängerung); **pro|ro|ga|tiv** (aufschiebend); **pro|ro|gie|ren**

Pro|sa, die; - ‹lat.› (Rede [Schrift] in ungebundener Form; *übertr. für* Nüchternheit); **Pro|sa|dich|tung; Pro|sa|i|ker** (nüchterner Mensch; *älter für* Prosaist); **pro|sa|isch** (in Prosa; *übertr. für* nüchtern); **Pro|sa|ist,** der; -en, -en; ↑R 126 (Prosa schreibender Schriftsteller); **Pro|sa|is|tin; Pro|sa‿schrift|stel|ler, ...werk**

Pro|sec|co, der; -[s], -s ‹ital.› (ein ital. Schaum-, Perl- *od.* Weißwein)

Pro|sek|tor [*auch* ...'zɛk...], der; -s, ...oren ‹lat.› (Arzt, der Sektionen durchführt; Leiter der Prosektur); **Pro|sek|tur,** die; -, -en (Abteilung eines Krankenhauses, in der Sektionen durchgeführt werden)

Pro|se|ku|ti|on, die; -, -en ‹lat.› (*Rechtsw. selten für* Strafverfolgung); **Pro|se|ku|tor,** der; -s, ...oren (*Rechtsw. selten für* Staatsanwalt [als Ankläger])

Pro|se|lyt, der; -en, -en (↑R 126) ‹griech.› (*im Altertum* ein zum Judentum übergetretener Heide; Neubekehrter); **Pro|se|ly|ten‿ma|cher, ...ma|che|rei** (*abwertend*)

Pro|se|mi|nar, das; -s, -e ‹lat.› (Seminar, Übung für Studienanfänger)

Pro|ser|pi|na (*lat. Form von* Persephone)

pro|sit!, prost! ‹lat.› (wohl bekomm's!); pros[i]t Neujahr!; pros[i]t allerseits!; prost Mahlzeit! (*ugs.*); **Pro|sit,** das; -s, -s *u.* Prost, das; -[e]s, -e (Zutrunk); ein - der Gemütlichkeit!

pro|skri|bie|ren ‹lat.› (ächten); **Pro|skrip|ti|on,** die; -, -en (Ächtung)

Pro|so|die (↑R 132), die; -, ...ien ‹griech.› (Silbenmessung[slehre]; Lehre von der metrisch-rhythmischen Behandlung der Sprache); **Pro|so|dik,** die; -, -en (*seltener für* Prosodie); **pro|so|disch**

Pros|pekt (↑R 132), der, *österr. auch* das; -[e]s, -e ‹lat.› (Werbeschrift; Ansicht [von Gebäuden, Straßen u. a.]; *russ. Bez. für* lange, breite [Haupt]straße; Bühnenhintergrund; Pfeifengehäuse der Orgel; *Wirtsch.* allgemeine Darlegung der Lage eines Unternehmens); **pros|pek|tie|ren; Pros|pek|tie|rung, Pros|pek|ti|on,** die; -, -en (Erkundung nutzbarer Bodenschätze; *Wirtsch.* Drucksachenwerbung); **pros|pek|tiv** (der Aussicht, Möglichkeit nach); **Pros|pek|tor,** der; -s, ...oren (jmd., der Bodenschätze erkundet)

pros|pe|rie|ren (↑R 132) ‹lat.› (gedeihen, vorankommen); **Pros|pe|ri|tät,** die; - (Wohlstand, wirtschaftl. Aufschwung, [Wirtschafts]blüte)

Pro|sper|mie, die; -, ...ien ‹griech.› (*Med.* vorzeitiger Samenerguss)

prost! *vgl.* prosit!; **Prost** *vgl.* Prosit

Pros|ta|ta (↑R 132), die; -, ...tae [...tɛ:] ‹griech.-lat.› (Vorsteherdrüse); **Pros|ta|ti|ker** (*Med.* jmd., der an einer übermäßigen Vergrößerung der Prostata leidet); **Pros|ta|ti|tis,** die; -, ...itiden (Entzündung der Prostata)

pros|ten; prös|ter|chen! (*ugs.*); **Prös|ter|chen**

pros|ti|tu|ie|ren (↑R 132) ‹lat.› (herabwürdigen); sich - (sich preisgeben); **Pros|ti|tu|ier|te,** die; -n, -n; ↑R 5 ff. (Frau, die Prostitution betreibt); **Pros|ti|tu|ti|on,** die; - ‹franz.› (gewerbsmäßige Ausübung sexueller Handlungen; Herabwürdigung)

Prost|ra|ti|on (↑R 130), die; -, -en ‹lat.› (*kath. Kirche* Niederwerfung, Fußfall; *Med.* hochgradige Erschöpfung)

Pro|sze|ni|um, das; -s, ...ien [...iən] ‹griech.› (vorderster Teil der Bühne, Vorbühne); **Pro|sze|ni|ums|lo|ge** (Bühnenloge)

prot. = protestantisch

Pro|tac|ti|ni|um (↑R 132), das; -s ‹griech.› (radioaktives chem. Element, Metall; *Zeichen* Pa)

Pro|ta|go|nist (↑R 132), der; -en, -en (↑R 126) ‹griech.› (*altgriech. Theater* erster Schauspieler; zentrale Gestalt; Vorkämpfer); **Pro|ta|go|nis|tin** (zentrale Gestalt; Vorkämpferin)

Pro|tak|ti|ni|um (↑R 132) *vgl.* Protactinium

Pro|te|gé [...'ʒe:], der; -s, -s ‹franz.› (Günstling; Schützling); **pro|te|gie|ren** [...'ʒi:...]

Pro|te|id, das; -[e]s, -e ‹griech.› (mit anderen chem. Verbindungen zusammengesetzter Eiweißkörper); **Pro|te|in,** das; -s, -e (vorwiegend aus Aminosäuren aufgebauter Eiweißkörper)

pro|te|isch (in der Art des [1]Proteus, wandelbar, unzuverlässig)

Pro|tek|ti|on, die; -, -en ‹lat.› (Gönnerschaft; Förderung; Schutz); **Pro|tek|ti|o|nis|mus,** der; - (Politik, die z. B. durch Schutzzölle die inländische Wirtschaft begünstigt); **Pro|tek|ti|o|nist,** der; -en, -en (↑R 126); **pro|tek|ti|o|nis|tisch; Pro|tek|tor,** der; -s, ...oren (Beschützer; Förderer; Schutz-, Schirmherr; Ehrenvorsitzender); **Pro|tek|to|rat,** das; -[e]s, -e (Schirmherrschaft; Schutzherrschaft; das unter Schutzherrschaft stehende Gebiet)

Pro|te|ro|zo|i|kum, das; -s ‹griech.› (*Geol.* Abschnitt der erdgeschichtl. Frühzeit)

Pro|test, der; -[e]s, -e ‹lat.-ital.› (Einspruch; Missfallensbekundung; *Wirtsch.* [beurkundete] Verweigerung der Annahme od. der Zahlung eines Wechsels od. Schecks); zu Protest gehen (von Wechseln); **Pro|test|ak|ti|on; Pro|tes|tant,** der; -en, -en (↑R 126) ‹lat.› (Angehöriger des Protestantismus); **Pro|tes|tan|tin; pro|tes|tan|tisch** (*Abk.* prot.); **Pro|tes|tan|tis|mus,** der; - (Gesamtheit der auf die Reformation zurückgehenden ev. Kirchengemeinschaften); **Pro|tes|ta|ti|on,** die; -, -en (*veraltet für* Protest); **Pro|test‿be|we|gung, ...de|monst|ra|ti|on, ...hal|tung; pro|tes|tie|ren** (Einspruch erheben, Verwahrung einlegen); einen Wechsel protestieren (*Wirtsch.* Nichtzahlung od. Nichtannahme eines rechtzeitig vorgelegten Wechsels beurkunden [lassen]); **Pro|test|kund|ge|bung; Pro|test|ler** (*ugs.*); **Pro|test‿marsch** (der), **...no|te, ...re|so|lu|ti|on, ...ruf, ...sän|ger, ...sän|ge|rin, ...schrei|ben, ...song, ...streik, ...sturm, ...ver|samm|lung, ...wäh|ler, ...wel|le**

[1]**Pro|teus** [...tɔys] (verwandlungsfähiger griech. Meergott); [2]**Pro|teus,** der; -, - (Mensch, der leicht seine Gesinnung ändert); **pro|teus|haft**

Prot|evan|ge|li|um (↑R 132) *vgl.* Protoevangelium

Pro|the|se, die; -, -n ‹griech.› (künstlicher Ersatz eines fehlenden Körperteils; Zahnersatz; *Sprachw.* Bildung eines neuen Lautes am Wortanfang); **Pro|the|sen|trä|ger; Pro|the|tik,** die; - (Wissenschaftsbereich, der sich mit der Entwicklung u. Herstellung von Prothesen befasst); **pro|the|tisch**

Pro|tist, der; -en, -en (↑R 126) ‹griech.› (*Biol.* Einzeller)

Pro|to|evan|ge|li|um (↑R 132), das; -s ‹griech.› (*kath. Kirche* erste Verkündigung des Erlösers [1. Mose, 3, 15])

pro|to|gen ‹griech.› (*Geol.* am Fundort entstanden [von Erzlagern])

Pro|to|koll, das; -s, -e ‹griech.› (förml. Niederschrift, Tagungsbericht; Beurkundung einer Aussage, Verhandlung u. a.; *nur Sing.:* Gesamtheit der im diplomat. Verkehr gebräuchl. Formen); zu Protokoll geben; **Pro|to|koll|ab|tei|lung; Pro|to|kol|lant,** der; -en, -en; ↑R 126 ([Sitzungs]schriftführer); **Pro|to|kol|lan|tin; pro|to|kol|la|risch** (durch Protokoll festgestellt, festgelegt); **Pro|to|koll‿be|am|te, ...chef, ...füh|rer** (Schriftführer); **pro|to|kol|lie|ren** (ein Protokoll aufnehmen; beurkunden); **Pro|to|kol|lie|rung**

Pro|ton, das; -s, ...onen ‹griech.› (*Kernphysik* stabiles, positiv geladenes Elementarteilchen als Baustein des Atomkerns); **Pro|to|nen|be|schleu|ni|ger; Pro|to|no|tar,** der; -s, -e ‹griech.; lat.› (Notar der päpstl. Kanzlei; *auch* Ehrentitel); **Pro|to|phy|te,** die; -, -n ‹griech.› *u.* **Pro|to|phy|ton,** das; -s, ...yten *meist Plur.* (*Bot.* einzellige Pflanze); **Pro|to|plas|ma,** das; -s (*Biol.* Lebenssubstanz aller pflanzl., tier. u. menschl. Zellen); **Pro|to|typ** [*selten* ...'ty:p], der; -s, -en (Muster; Urbild; Inbegriff); **pro|to|ty|pisch; Pro|to|zo|on,** das; -s, ...zoen *meist Plur.* (*Biol.* Urtierchen)

pro|tra|hie|ren ‹lat.› (*Med.* verzögern)

Pro|tu|be|ranz, die; -, -en *meist Plur.* ‹lat.› (aus dem Sonneninnern ausströmende glühende Gasmasse; *Med.* stumpfer Vorsprung an Organen, bes. an Knochen)

Protz, der; *Gen.* -es, *älter* -en, *Plur.* -e, *älter* -en; ↑R 126 (*ugs. für* Angeber; *landsch. für* Kröte)

Prot|ze, die; -, -n ‹ital.› (*früher* Vorderwagen von Geschützen u. a.)

prot|zen (*ugs.);* du protzt; **protzen|haft; Prot|zen|haf|tig|keit,** die; -; **Prot|zen|tum,** das; -s; **Prot|ze|rei; Prot|zer|tum** (*svw.* Protzentum); **prot|zig; Prot|zigkeit**

Protz‿kas|ten, ...wa|gen (*Milit. früher)*

Proust [pru:st] (franz. Schriftsteller)

Prov. = Provinz

Pro|vence [...'vã:s], die; - (franz. Landschaft)

Pro|ve|ni|enz [...v...], die; -, -en ‹lat.› (Herkunft, Ursprung)

Pro|ven|za|le [...v...], der; -n, -n; ↑R 126 (Bewohner der Provence); **Pro|ven|za|lin; pro|ven|za|lisch**

Pro|verb [...v...], das; -s, -en ‹lat.› *u.* Pro|ver|bi|um, das; -s, ...ien [...iən] (*veraltet für* Sprichwort); **pro|ver|bi|al, pro|ver|bi|a|lisch, pro|ver|bi|ell** (*veraltet für* sprichwörtlich); **Pro|ver|bi|um** *vgl.* Proverb

Pro|vi|ant [...v...], der; -s, -e *Plur. selten* ‹ital. *u.* franz.› ([Mund]vorrat; Wegzehrung; Verpflegung); **pro|vi|an|tie|ren** (*veraltet für* verproviantieren); **Pro|vi|ant|wa|gen**

Pro|vinz [...v...], die; -, -en ‹lat.› (Land[esteil]; größeres staatliches od. kirchliches Verwaltungsgebiet; das Land im Gegensatz zur Hauptstadt; *abwertend für* [kulturell] rückständige Gegend; *Abk.* Prov.); **Pro|vinz‿be|woh|ner, ...büh|ne; Pro|vin|zi|al,** der; -s, -e (*kath. Kirche* Vorsteher einer Ordensprovinz); **Pro|vin|zi|a|le,** der; -n, -n; ↑R 126; (*veraltet für* Provinzbewohner); **pro|vin|zi|a|li|sie|ren; Pro|vin|zi|a|lis|mus,** der; -, ...men (*Sprachw.* [auf eine Landschaft beschränkter] vom hochsprachl. Wortschatz abweichender Ausdruck; *nur Sing.: abwertend für* provinzielles Denken, Verhalten); **pro|vin|zi|ell** ‹franz.› (die Provinz betreffend; landschaftlich; mundartlich; *abwertend für* hinterwäldlerisch); **Pro|vinz|ler** (*abwertend für* Provinzbewohner; [kulturell] rückständiger Mensch); **pro|vinz|le|risch; Pro|vinz‿nest** *(abwertend),* **...stadt, ...the|a|ter**

Pro|vi|si|on [...v...], die; -, -en ‹ital.› (Vergütung [für Geschäftsbesorgung], [Vermittlungs]gebühr); **Pro|vi|si|ons|ba|sis;** *meist in* auf - [arbeiten]; **pro|vi|si|ons|frei; Pro|vi|si|ons|rei|sen|de; Pro|vi|sor,** der; -s, ...oren ‹lat.› (*früher* erster Gehilfe des Apothekers; *österr. für* als Vertreter amtierender Geistlicher); **pro|vi|so|risch** (vorläufig); **Pro|vi|so|ri|um,** das; -s, ...ien [...iən] (vorläufige Einrichtung; Übergangslösung)

Pro|vi|ta|min [...v...], das; -s, -e (Vorstufe eines Vitamins)

Pro|vo [...v...], der; -s, -s ‹lat.-niederl.› (Vertreter einer [1965 in Amsterdam entstandenen] antibürgerlichen Protestbewegung); **pro|vo|kant** ‹lat.› (provozierend); **Pro|vo|ka|teur** [...'tø:r], der; -s, -e ‹franz.› (jmd., der provoziert); **Pro|vo|ka|ti|on,** die; -, -en (Herausforderung; Aufreizung); **pro|vo|ka|tiv, pro|vo|ka|to|risch** (herausfordernd); **pro|vo|zie|ren** (herausfordern, reizen; auslösen); **Pro|vo|zie|rung**

pro|xi|mal ‹lat.› (*Med.* der [Körper]mitte zu gelegen)

Pro|ze|de|re *vgl.* Procedere; **pro|ze|die|ren** ‹lat.› (*veraltet für* zu Werke gehen, verfahren); **Pro|ze|dur,** die; -, -en (Verfahren, [schwierige, unangenehme] Behandlungsweise)

Pro|zent, das; -[e]s, -e ‹ital.› ([Zinsen, Gewinn] vom Hundert, Hundertstel; *Abk.* p. c., v. H.; *Zeichen* %); 5 Prozent (↑R 90) *od.* 5 %; *vgl.* Fünfprozentklausel; **...pro|zen|tig** (z. B. fünfprozentig [*mit Ziffer* 5-prozentig]; eine 5 %ige *od.* 5 %-Anleihe usw.); **pro|zen|tisch** *vgl.* prozentual; **Pro|zent‿kurs** *(Börse),* **...punkt** (Prozent [als Differenz zweier Prozentzahlen]), **...rech|nung** (die; -), **...satz** (Hundertsatz, Vomhundertsatz), **...span|ne** *(Wirtsch.);* **pro|zen|tu|al,** *österr.* pro|zen|tu|ell (im Verhältnis zum Hundert, in Prozenten ausgedrückt); an einem Unternehmen prozentual beteiligt sein (einen in Prozenten festgelegten Anteil vom Reinertrag erhalten); **pro|zen|tu|a|li|ter** (*veraltet für* prozentual); **pro|zen|tu|ell** *vgl.* prozentual; **pro|zen|tu|ie|ren** (in Prozenten ausdrücken); **Pro|zent|wert**

Pro|zess, der; -es, -e ‹lat.› (Vorgang, Ablauf; Verfahren; Entwicklung; gerichtl. Durchführung von Rechtsstreitigkeiten); **Pro|zess‿ak|te, ...be|richt; Pro|zess|be|tei|lig|te,** der *u.* die; -n, -n (↑R 5 ff.); **pro|zess|be|voll|mäch|tigt; Pro|zess|be|voll|mäch|tig|te,** der *u.* die; -n, -n (↑R 5 ff.); **pro|zess|fä|hig; Pro|zess|fä|hig|keit,** die; -; **pro|zess|füh|rend;** die -en Parteien; **Pro|zess|füh|rungs|klau|sel**

(*Versicherungswesen*); **Pro|zess‿geg|ner, ...han|sel** (der; -s, -[n]; *ugs. für* jmd., der bei jeder Gelegenheit prozessiert); **pro|zes|sie|ren** (einen Prozess führen); **Pro|zes|si|on,** die; -, -en ([feierl. kirchl.] Umzug, Bitt- od. Dankgang); **Pro|zes|si|ons‿kreuz** (*kath. Kirche*), **...spin|ner** (ein Schmetterling); **Pro|zess|kos|ten** *Plur.*; **Pro|zes|sor,** der; -s, ...oren (zentraler Teil einer Datenverarbeitungsanlage); **Pro|zess‿ord|nung, ...par|tei, ...rech|ner** (besonderer Computer für industrielle Fertigungsabläufe), **...recht** (das; -[e]s); **pro|zes|su|al** (auf einen Rechtsstreit bezüglich); **Pro|zess‿ver|fah|ren, ...ver|gleich, ...ver|schlep|pung, ...voll|macht**

pro|zyk|lisch [*auch* ...'tsyk...] (*Wirtsch.* einem bestehenden Konjunkturzustand gemäß)

prü|de ‹franz.› (zimperlich, spröde [in sittl.-erot. Beziehung])

Pru|de|lei (*landsch. für* Pfuscherei); **pru|de|lig,** prudlig (*landsch. für* unordentlich); **pru|deln** (*für* pfuschen); ich ...[e]le (↑R 16)

Pru|den|tia (w. Vorn.); **Pru|den|ti|us** (christl.-lat. Dichter)

Prü|de|rie, die; - ‹franz.› (Zimperlichkeit, Ziererei)

prud|lig *vgl.* prudelig

Prüf|au|to|mat; prüf|bar; Prüf|be|richt; prü|fen; Prü|fer; Prü|fer|bi|lanz, Prü|fungs|bi|lanz; **Prü|fe|rin; Prüf‿feld, ...ge|rät; Prüf|ling; Prüf‿me|tho|de, ...norm, ...stand, ...stein; Prü|fung;** mündliche, schriftliche -; **Prü|fungs‿angst, ...ar|beit, ...auf|ga|be, ...be|din|gun|gen** (*Plur.*), **...bi|lanz** (*vgl.* Prüferbilanz), **...fach, ...fahrt, ...fra|ge, ...ge|bühr, ...kom|mis|si|on, ...ord|nung, ...ter|min, ...un|ter|la|gen** (*Plur.*), **...ver|fah|ren, ...ver|merk, ...zeug|nis; Prüf‿ver|fah|ren, ...vor|schrift**

[1]**Prü|gel,** der; -s, - (Stock); [2]**Prü|gel** *Plur.* (*ugs. für* Schläge); **Prü|ge|lei; Prü|gel|kna|be** (jmd., der an Stelle des Schuldigen bestraft wird); **prü|geln;** ich ...[e]le (↑R 16); sich -; **Prü|gel‿stra|fe, ...sze|ne**

Prü|nel|le, die; -, -n ‹franz.› (entsteinte, getrocknete Pflaume)

Prunk, der; -[e]s; **Prunk‿bau** (*Plur.* ...bauten), **...bett; prun|ken; Prunk‿ge|mach, ...ge|wand; prunk|haft; prunk|los; Prunk|lo|sig|keit,** die; -; **Prunk‿saal, ...ses|sel, ...sit|zung** (im Karneval), **...stück, ...sucht** (die; -; *abwertend*); **prunk‿süch|tig, ...voll; Prunk|wa|gen**

Prunt|rut (↑R 130) (Stadt im Kanton Jura; *franz.* Porrentruy)

Pru|ri|go, die; -, Prurigines [...ne:s] *od.* der; -s -s ‹lat.› (*Med.* Juckflechte); **Pru|ri|tus,** der; - (Hautjucken)

prus|ten (stark schnauben)

Pruth, der; -[s] (l. Nebenfluss der Donau)

Pru|ze, der; -n, -n *meist Plur.* (*alte Bez. für* Preuße [Angehöriger eines zu den baltischen Völkern gehörenden Stammes])

Pry|ta|ne, der; -n, -n (↑R 126) ‹griech.› (Mitglied der in altgriech. Staaten regierenden Behörde); **Pry|ta|nei|on,** das; -s, ...eien *u.* **Pry|ta|ne|um,** das; -s, ...een (Versammlungshaus der Prytanen)

PS = Pferdestärke; Postskript[um]

Psa|li|gra|phie, die; - ‹griech.› (Kunst des Scherenschnittes); **psa|li|gra|phisch**

Psalm, der; -s, -en ‹griech.› (geistl. Lied); **Psal|men‿dich|ter, ...sän|ger; Psal|mist,** der; -en, -en; ↑R 126 (Psalmendichter, -sänger)

Psal|mo|die (↑R 132), die; -, ...ien (Psalmengesang); **psal|mo|die|ren** (Psalmen vortragen; eintönig singen); **psal|mo|disch**

Psal|ter, der; -s, - (Buch der Psalmen im A.T.; ein Saiteninstrument; *Zool.* Blättermagen der Wiederkäuer)

PSchA = Postscheckamt

pscht!, pst!

pseud..., pseu|do... ‹griech.› (falsch...); **Pseud...,** Pseu|do... (Falsch...); **Pseu|de|pi|gra|phen** (↑R 132), *Plur.* (Schriften aus der Antike, die einem Autor fälschlich zugeschrieben wurden); **pseu|do...** usw. *vgl.* pseud... usw.; **Pseu|do|krupp** (*Med.* Anfall von Atemnot u. Husten bei Kehlkopfentzündung); **Pseu|do|lo|gie,** die; -, ...ien (*Med.* krankhaftes Lügen); **pseu|do|morph** (*Mineralogie* Pseudomorphose zeigend); **Pseu|do|mor|pho|se,** die; -, -n (*Mineralogie* [Auftreten eines] Mineral[s] in der Kristallform eines anderen Minerals)

pseu|do|nym (↑R 132; unter einem Decknamen [verfasst]); **Pseu|do|nym,** das; -s, -e (Deckname, Künstlername)

Pseu|do|po|di|um, das; -s, ...ien [...iən] (*Biol.* Scheinfüßchen mancher Einzeller); **pseu|do|wis|sen|schaft|lich**

PSF = Postschließfach

[1]**Psi,** das; -[s], -s (griech. Buchstabe: Ψ, ψ); [2]**Psi,** das; -[s] *meist ohne Artikel* (bestimmendes Element parapsychologischer Vorgänge)

Psi|lo|me|lan, der; -s, -e ‹griech.› (ein Manganerz)

Psi|phä|no|men ‹griech.› (parapsychol. Erscheinung)

Psit|ta|ko|se, die; -, -n ‹griech.› (*Med.* Papageienkrankheit)

Pso|ri|a|sis, die; -, ...iasen ‹griech.› (*Med.* Schuppenflechte); **Pso|ri|a|ti|ker; Pso|ri|a|ti|ke|rin**

PS-stark (↑R 26 *u.* 60)

pst!, pscht!

Psy|cha|go|ge (↑R 132), der; -n, -n ‹griech.› (↑R 126); **Psy|cha|go|gik,** die; - (pädagogisch-therapeutische Betreuung zum Abbau von Verhaltensstörungen o. Ä.); **Psy|cha|go|gin**

[1]**Psy|che** ['psy:çe:] (*griech. Mythol.* Gattin des Eros); [2]**Psy|che,** die; -, -n (Seele; *österr. für* mit Spiegel versehene Frisiertoilette); **psy|che|de|lisch** (in einem [durch Rauschmittel hervorgerufenen] euphorischen, tranceartigen Gemütszustand befindlich; Glücksgefühle hervorrufend); psychedelische Mittel

Psy|chi|a|ter (↑R 132), der; -s, -; (Facharzt für Psychiatrie); **Psy|chi|a|te|rin**

Psy|chi|a|trie (↑R 130 *u.* 132), die; -, ...ien; (*nur Sing.*: Lehre von den seelischen Störungen, von den Geisteskrankheiten; *ugs. für* psychiatrische Klinik); **psy|chi|a|trie|ren;** jmdn. - (*österr.* von einem Psychiater in Bezug auf den Geisteszustand untersuchen lassen); **psy|chi|a|trisch**

psy|chisch (seelisch); psychische Krankheiten, Störungen; die psychische Gesundheit

Psy|cho|ana|ly|se (↑R 132), die; - (Verfahren zur Untersuchung u. Behandlung seelischer Störungen); **psy|cho|ana|ly|sie|ren; Psy|cho|ana|ly|ti|ker** (die Psychoanalyse vertretender od. anwendender Psychologe, Arzt); **Psy|cho|ana|ly|ti|ke|rin; psy|cho|ana|ly|tisch**

Psy|cho|di|ag|nos|tik die; - (Lehre von den Methoden zur Erkenntnis u. Erforschung psychischer Besonderheiten); **Psy|cho|dra|ma,** das; -s, ...men; **psy|cho|gen** (seelisch bedingt); **Psy|cho|ge|ne|se, Psy|cho|ge|ne|sis** [*auch* ...'ge:...], die; -, ...nesen (Entstehung u. Entwicklung der Seele, des Seelenlebens [Forschungsgebiet der Entwicklungspsychologie]); **Psy|cho|gramm,** das; -s, -e (graph. Darstellung von Fähigkeiten u. Eigenschaften einer Persönlichkeit [z. B. in einem Koordinatensystem]; psychologische Persönlichkeitsstudie [im Fernsehen od. Film]); **Psy|cho|graph,** der; -en, -en; ↑R 126 (Gerät zum automat. Buchstabieren u. Niederschreiben angeblich aus dem Unbewussten stammender Aussagen); **psy|cho|id** (seelenartig, seelenähnlich); **Psy|cho|ki|ne|se,** die; - (parapsycholog. seel. Einflussnahme auf Bewegungsvorgänge ohne physikal. Ursache); **Psy|cho|kri|mi** (*ugs. kurz für* psychologischer Kriminalfilm, -roman); **Psy|cho|lin|gu|is|tik,** die; - (Wissenschaft von den psychischen Vorgängen bei Gebrauch und Erlernen der Sprache); **Psy|cho|lo|ge,** der; -n, -n (↑R 126); **Psy|cho|lo|gie,** die; - (Wissenschaft von den psych. Vorgängen); **Psy|cho|lo|gin; psy|cho|lo|gisch;** ein -er Roman; **psy|cho|lo|gi|sie|ren** (nach psychologischen Gesichtspunkten untersuchen od. darstellen); **Psy|cho|lo|gi|sie|rung; Psy|cho|lo|gis|mus,** der; - (Überbewertung der Psychologie als Grundwissenschaft einer Wissenschaft); **Psy|cho|man|tie,** die; - (*svw.* Nekromantie); **Psy|cho|met|rie** (↑R 130), die; - (Messung seel. Vorgänge; Hellsehen durch Betasten von Gegenständen); **Psy|cho|neu|ro|se,** die; -, -n (seel. bedingte Neurose); **Psy|cho|path,** der; -en, -en (↑R 126); **Psy|cho|pa|thie,** die; - (Abweichen des geistig-seel. Verhaltens von der Norm); **Psy|cho|pa|thin; psy|cho|pa|thisch; Psy|cho|pa|tho|lo|gie,** die; - (Lehre von krankhaften Erscheinungen u. deren Ursachen im Seelenleben; Lehre von den durch körperliche Krankheiten bedingten seelischen Störungen); **Psy|cho|phar|ma|kon,** das; -s, ...ka (auf die Psyche einwirkendes Arzneimittel); **Psy|cho|phy|sik,** die; - (Lehre von den Wechselbeziehungen des Physischen u. des Psychischen); **psy|cho|phy|sisch; Psy|cho|se,** die; -, -n (Seelenstörung; Geistes- od. Nervenkrankheit); **Psy|cho|so|ma|tik,** die; - (Wissenschaft von der Bedeutung seel. Vorgänge für Entstehung u. Verlauf körperl. Krankheiten); **psy|cho|so|ma|tisch; Psy|cho|ter|ror,** der; -s (Einschüchterung mit psychischen Mitteln); **Psy|cho|the|ra|peut,** der; -en, -en; ↑R 126 (Facharzt für Psychotherapie); **Psy|cho|the|ra|peu|tik,** die; - (Seelenheilkunde); **Psy|cho|the|ra|peu|tin; psy|cho|the|ra|peu|tisch; Psy|cho|the|ra|pie,** die; -, ...ien (seel. Heilbehandlung); **Psy|cho|thril|ler** (mit psychologischen Effekten spannend gemachter Kriminalfilm od. -roman); **psy|cho|tisch** (zur Psychose gehörend; geistes-, gemütskrank)

Psych|ro|me|ter [...çro...] (↑R 132), das; -s, - ⟨griech.⟩ (*Meteor.* Luftfeuchtigkeitsmesser)

pt = Pint

Pt = *chem. Zeichen für* Platin

P. T. = pleno titulo

Pta = Peseta

PTA = pharmazeutisch-technische[r] Assistent[in]

Ptah (ägypt. Gott)

Pte|ra|no|don (↑R 132), das; -s, ...donten ⟨griech.⟩ (Flugsaurier der Kreidezeit); **Pte|ro|dak|ty|lus,** der; -, ...ylen (Flugsaurier des Juras); **Pte|ro|po|de,** die; -, -n *meist Plur.* (*Zool.* Ruderschnecke); **Pte|ro|sau|ri|er** *meist Plur.* (urzeitliche Flugechse); **Pte|ry|gi|um,** das; -s, ...ia (*Zool.* Flug-, Schwimmhaut)

Pto|le|mä|er, der; -s, - (Angehöriger eines makedon. Herrschergeschlechtes im alten Ägypten); **pto|le|mä|isch;** das ptolemäische Weltsystem; **Pto|le|mä|us** (altägypt. Geograph, Astronom u. Mathematiker in Alexandria)

Pto|ma|in, das; -s, -e ⟨griech.⟩ (*Med.* Leichengift)

PTT (*schweiz. Abk. für* Post, Telefon, Telegraf)

Pty|a|lin, das; -s ⟨griech.⟩ (Speichelenzym)

Pu = *chem. Zeichen für* Plutonium

Pub [pab], das, *auch* der; -s, -s ⟨engl.⟩ (Wirtshaus im engl. Stil, Bar)

pu|ber|tär ⟨lat.⟩ (mit der Geschlechtsreife zusammenhängend); **Pu|ber|tät,** die; - ([Zeit der eintretenden] Geschlechtsreife; Reifezeit); **Pu|ber|täts|zeit; pu|ber|tie|ren** (in die Pubertät eintreten, sich in ihr befinden); **Pu|bes|zenz,** die; - (*Med.* Geschlechtsreifung)

pu|bli|ce [...tse] (↑R 130) ⟨lat.⟩ (öffentlich [von bestimmten Universitätsvorlesungen]); **Pub|li|ci|ty** [pa'blisiti], die; - ⟨engl.⟩ (Öffentlichkeit; Reklame, [Bemühung um] öffentl. Aufsehen; öffentl. Verbreitung); **pub|li|ci|ty|scheu; Pub|lic|re|la|tions,** *auch* **Pub|lic Re|la|tions** ['pablikri'le:ʃ(ə)ns] (↑R 24) *Plur.* ⟨amerik.⟩ (Öffentlichkeitsarbeit; Kontaktpflege; *Abk.* PR); **pub|lik** [pu...] ⟨franz.⟩ (öffentlich; offenkundig; allgemein bekannt); publik machen, werden; **Pub|li|ka|ti|on,** die; -, -en (Veröffentlichung; Schrift); **Pub|li|ka|ti|ons‿mit|tel** (das), **...or|gan; pub|li|ka|ti|ons|reif; Pub|li|ka|ti|ons|ver|bot**

Pub|li|kum (↑R 130), das; -s ⟨lat.⟩ (teilnehmende Menschenmenge; Zuhörer-, Leser-, Besucher[schaft], Zuschauer[menge]; *auch für* die Umstehenden); das breite -; **Pub|li|kums‿er|folg, ...ge|schmack, ...in|te|res|se, ...lieb|ling, ...ver|kehr** (der; -s); **pub|li|kums|wirk|sam; pub|li|zie|ren** (veröffentlichen, herausgeben; *seltener für* publik machen, bekannt machen); **pub|li|zier|freu|dig; Pub|li|zist,** der; -en, -en; ↑R 126 (polit. Schriftsteller; Tagesschriftsteller; Journalist); **Pub|li|zis|tik,** die; -; **Pub|li|zis|tin; pub|li|zis|tisch; Pub|li|zi|tät,** die; - (Öffentlichkeit, Bekanntheit)

p. u. c. = post urbem conditam

Puc|ci|ni [pu'tʃi:ni], Giacomo ['dʒa:komo] (ital. Komponist)

Puck, der; -s, -s ⟨engl.⟩ (Kobold; Hartgummischeibe beim Eishockey)

pu|ckern (*ugs. für* klopfen, stoßweise schlagen); eine -de Wunde

Pud, das; -, - ⟨russ.⟩ (altes russ. Gewicht); 5 - (↑R 90)

Pud|del|ei|sen ⟨engl.; dt.⟩ (*Hüttenw.*)

[1]**pud|deln** (*bes. westmitteld. für* jauchen; im Wasser planschen)

[2]**pud|deln** ⟨engl.⟩ (*Hüttenw.* aus Roheisen Schweißstahl gewinnen); ich ...[e]le (↑R 16); **Pud|del|ofen** (↑R 132)

Pud|ding, der; -s, *Plur.* -e *u.* -s ⟨engl.⟩ (eine Süß-, Mehlspeise); **Pud|ding‿form, ...pul|ver**

Pu|del, der; -s, - (eine Hunderasse; *ugs. für* Fehlwurf [beim Kegeln]); **Pu|del|müt|ze; pu|deln** (*ugs. für* vorbeiwerfen [beim Kegeln]); ich ...[e]le (↑R 16); **pu|del‿nackt** (*ugs.*), **...nass** (*ugs.*), **...wohl** (*ugs.*; sich pudelwohl fühlen)

Pu|der, der, *ugs. auch* das; -s, - ⟨franz.⟩ (feines Pulver); **Pu|der|do|se; pu|de|rig,** pud|rig; **pu|dern;** ich ...ere (↑R 16); sich -; **Pu|der|quas|te; Pu|de|rung; Pu|der|zu|cker,** der; -s; **pud|rig** *vgl.* puderig

Pu|eb|lo [pu'e:blo] (↑R 130), der;

-s, -s ‹span.› (Dorf der Puebloindianer); **Pu|eb|lo|in|di|a|ner** (Angehöriger eines Indianerstammes im Südwesten Nordamerikas)

pu|e|ril [pu|e...] ‹lat.› (knabenhaft; kindlich); **Pu|e|ri|li|tät**, die; - (kindliches, kindisches Wesen); **Pu|er|pe|ral|fie|ber**, das; -s (*Med.* Kindbettfieber); **Pu|er|pe|ri|um**, das; -s, ...ien [...i̯ən] (*Med.* Wochenbett)

Pu|er|to|ri|ca|ner (Bewohner von Puerto Rico); **Pu|er|to|ri|ca|ne|rin; pu|er|to|ri|ca|nisch; Pu|er|to Ri|co** (Insel der Großen Antillen)

puff!; ¹Puff, der; -[e]s, -e (*veraltet, aber noch landsch. für* Bausch; *landsch. für* gepolsterter Wäschebehälter); **²Puff**, das; -[e]s (ein Brett- u. Würfelspiel); **³Puff**, der, *auch* das; -s, -s (*ugs. für* Bordell); **⁴Puff**, der; -[e]s, *Plur.* Püffe, *seltener* Puffe (*ugs. für* Stoß); **Puff‿är|mel, ...boh|ne; Püff|chen** (kleiner ¹,⁴Puff); **Puf|fe**, die; -, -n (Bausch); **puf|fen** (bauschen; *ugs. für* stoßen); er pufft (stößt) ihn, *auch* ihm in die Seite; **Puf|fer** (federnde, Druck u. Aufprall abfangende Vorrichtung [an Eisenbahnwagen u. a.]; *kurz für* Kartoffelpuffer); **Püf|fer|chen; Puf|fer‿staat** (*Plur.* ...staaten), **...zo|ne; puf|fig** (bauschig); **Puff‿mais, ...mut|ter** (*Plur.* ...mütter; *ugs.; zu* ³Puff), **...ot|ter** (die; eine Schlange), **...reis** (der; -es), **...spiel** (*zu* ²Puff)

puh!

Pul, der; -, -s ‹pers.› (afghan. Münze; 1 Pul = 0,01 Afghani); 5 - (↑R 90)

Pül|cher, der; -s, - (*österr. ugs. für* Strolch)

Pul|ci|nell [pultʃi...], der; -s, -e (*eindeutschend für* Pulcinella); **Pul|ci|nel|la**, der; -[s], ...lle ‹ital.› (komischer Diener, Hanswurst in der ital. Komödie); *vgl.* Policinello

pu|len (*nordd. für* bohren, herausklauben)

Pu|lit|zer (amerik. Journalist u. Verleger); **Pu|lit|zer|preis**

Pulk, der; -[e]s, *Plur.* -s, *selten auch* -e ‹slaw.› (Verband von Kampfflugzeugen od. milit. Kraftfahrzeugen; Anhäufung; Schar)

Pul|le, die; -, -n ‹lat.› (*ugs. für* Flasche)

¹pul|len (*nordd. für* rudern; *Reiten* in unregelmäßiger Gangart vorwärts drängen [vom Pferd])

²pul|len, pul|lern (*landsch. für* urinieren)

Pul|li, der; -s, -s (*ugs. für* leichter Pullover)

Pull|man|kap|pe (*österr. für* Baskenmütze); **Pull|man|wa|gen** ‹nach dem amerik. Konstrukteur›; ↑R 95 (sehr komfortabler [Schnellzug]wagen)

Pul|lo|ver [...v...] (↑R 132), der; -s, - ‹engl.›; **Pul|lo|ver|hemd** (leichter modischer Pullover mit hemdartigem Einsatz); **Pul|lun|der** (↑R 132), der; -s, - (meist kurzer, ärmelloser Pullover)

pul|mo|nal ‹lat.› (*Med.* die Lunge betreffend, Lungen...)

Pulp, der; -s, -en ‹engl.› *u.* Pul|pe ‹lat.›, Pül|pe, die; -, -n ‹franz.› (breiige Masse mit Fruchtstücken zur Herstellung von Obstsaft od. Konfitüre); **Pul|pa**, die; -, ...pae [...pɛ] ‹lat.› (*Med.* weiche, gefäßreiche Gewebemasse im Zahn u. in der Milz); **Pul|pe, Pül|pe** *vgl.* Pulp; **Pul|pi|tis**, die; -, ...itiden (*Med.* Zahnmarkentzündung); **pul|pös** (*Med.* fleischig; markig; aus weicher Masse bestehend)

Pul|que [...kə], der; -[s] ‹indian.-span.› (gegorener Agavensaft)

Puls, der; -es, -e ‹lat., „Stoß, Schlag"› (Aderschlag; Pulsader am Handgelenk); **Puls|ader** (↑R 132; Schlagader); **Pul|sar**, der; -s, -e (*Astron.* kosmische Radioquelle mit periodischen Strahlungspulsen); **Pul|sa|ti|on**, die; -, -en (*Med.* Pulsschlag; *Astron.* Veränderung eines Sterndurchmessers); **Pul|sa|tor**, der; -s, ...oren (Gerät zur Erzeugung pulsierender Bewegungen, z. B. bei der Melkmaschine); **pul|sen, pul|sie|ren** (rhythmisch schlagen, klopfen; an- und abschwellen); du pulst; **Pul|si|on**, die; -, -en (*fachspr. für* Stoß, Schlag); **Pul|so|me|ter**, das; -s, - ‹lat.; griech.› (eine kolbenlose Dampfpumpe); **Puls‿schlag, ...wär|mer, ...zahl**

Pult, das; -[e]s, -e ‹lat.›; **Pult|dach**

Pul|ver [...f..., *auch* ...v...], das; -s, - ‹lat.›; **Pül|ver|chen; Pul|ver‿dampf** (der; -[e]s), **...fass; pul|ver|fein**; -er Kaffee; **pul|ve|rig**, pulv|rig; **Pul|ve|ri|sa|tor** [...v...], der; -s, ...oren (Maschine zur Herstellung von Pulver durch Stampfen od. Mahlen); **pul|ve|ri|sie|ren** (zu Pulver zerreiben, [zer]pulvern); **Pul|ve|ri|sie|rung; Pul|ver‿kaf|fee, ...ma|ga|zin, ...müh|le** (*früher* Fabrik für die Herstellung von Schießpulver); **pul|vern**; ich ...ere (↑R 16); **Pul|ver|schnee; pul|ver|tro|cken; Pul|ver|turm** (*früher*); **pulv|rig** *vgl.* pulverig

Pu|ma, der; -s, -s ‹peruan.› (ein Raubtier)

Pum|mel, der; -s, - (*ugs. für* rundliches Kind); **Pum|mel|chen; pum|me|lig, pumm|lig** (*ugs. für* dicklich)

Pump, der; -s, -e; auf Pump leben (*ugs. für* von Geborgtem leben); **Pum|pe**, die; -, -n; **pum|pen** (*ugs. auch für* borgen); **Pum|pen‿haus, ...schwen|gel**

pum|perl|ge|sund (*bayr. u. österr. ugs. für* kerngesund)

pum|pern (*landsch., bes. südd., österr. ugs. für* laut u. heftig klopfen, rumoren); ich ...ere (↑R 16); **Pum|per|ni|ckel**, der; -s, - (ein Schwarzbrot)

Pump|ho|se (weite Hose [mit Kniebund])

Pumps [pœmps], der; -, - ‹engl.› (ausgeschnittener Damenschuh mit höherem Absatz)

Pump‿spei|cher|werk, ...werk

Pu|muckl (Kobold aus einem bekannten Kinderbuch)

Pu|na, die; - ‹indian.› (Hochfläche der südamerik. Anden mit Steppennatur)

Punch [pantʃ], der; -s, -s ‹engl.› (Boxhieb; große Schlagkraft); **Pun|cher**, der; -s, - (Boxer, der besonders kraftvoll schlagen kann); **Pun|ching|ball** (Übungsgerät für Boxer)

Punc|tum sa|li|ens [- ...i̯ens], das; - - ‹lat., „springender Punkt"› (Kernpunkt; Entscheidendes)

Pu|ni|er [...i̯ər] (Karthager); **pu|nisch**; -e Treue (*iron. für* Untreue, Wortbrüchigkeit), *aber* (↑R 108): die Punischen Kriege; der Erste, Zweite, Dritte Punische Krieg

Punk [paŋk], der; -[s], -s ‹engl.› (*nur Sing.*: bewusst primitiv-exaltierte Rockmusik; Punker); **Punker** (Jugendlicher, der durch Verhalten und Aufmachung [z. B. grell gefärbte Haare] seine antibürgerliche Einstellung ausdrückt); **Pun|ke|rin; pun|kig; Punk|rock**, der; -[s]; *vgl.* ²Rock

Punkt, der; -[e]s, -e ‹lat.› (*Abk.* Pkt.); Punkt 8 Uhr; typographischer Punkt (*Druckw.* frühere Maßeinheit für Schriftgröße u. Zeilenabstand; *Abk.* p); (↑R 90:) 2 Punkt Durchschuss; (↑R 60:) der Punkt auf dem i; **Punk|tal|glas** ® *Plur.* ...gläser (*Optik*); **Punk|ta|ti|on**, die; -, -en (*Rechtsw.* Vorvertrag, Vertragsentwurf); **Punkt|ball** (Übungsgerät für Boxer); **Pünkt|chen; Pun|kte|kampf** (*Sport*); **punk|ten; Pun|kte|spiel** (*Sport*);

punkt|gleich *(Sport);* **Punkt|gleich|heit,** die; -; **punk|tie|ren** (mit Punkten versehen, tüpfeln; *Med.* eine Punktion ausführen); punktierte Note *(Musik);* **Punk|tier|na|del** *(Med.);* **Punk|tie|rung; Punk|ti|on,** Punk|tur, die; -, -en (*Med.* Einstich in eine Körperhöhle zur Entnahme von Flüssigkeiten); **Punkt|lan|dung** (*bes. Raumfahrt* Landung genau am vorausberechneten Punkt); **pünkt|lich; Pünkt|lich|keit,** die; -; **Punkt|nie|der|la|ge** *(Sport);* **punk|to** (*schweiz., sonst veraltet; svw.* betreffs); *Präp. mit Gen.:* punkto gottloser Reden; *ungebeugt bei allein stehenden, stark gebeugten Substantiven im Singular:* punkto Geld; *vgl.* in puncto; **Punkt‿rich|ter** *(Sport),* **...rol|ler** (ein Massagegerät), **...schrift** (Blindenschrift); **punkt|schwei|ßen** *nur im Infinitiv u. im Partizip II gebr.;* punktgeschweißt; **Punkt‿schwei|ßung, ...sieg** *(Sport),* **...spiel** *(Sport),* **...sys|tem; Punk|tu|a|li|tät,** die; - (*veraltet für* Genauigkeit, Strenge); **punk|tu|ell** (punktweise; einzelne Punkte betreffend); **Punk|tum;** *nur in* [und damit] Punktum! (und damit Schluss!); **Punk|tur** *vgl.* Punktion; **Punkt‿ver|lust, ...wer|tung, ...zahl**

Punsch, der; -[e]s, *Plur.* -e, *auch* Pünsche ‹engl.› (ein alkohol. Getränk); **Punsch‿es|senz, ...glas, ...schüs|sel**

Punz|ar|beit; Pun|ze, die; -, -n (Stahlstäbchen für Treibarbeit; eingestanztes Zeichen zur Angabe des Edelmetallgehalts); **pun|zen,** pun|zie|ren (Metall treiben; ziselieren; den Feingehalt von Gold- u. Silberwaren kennzeichnen); du punzt; **Punz|ham|mer; pun|zie|ren** *vgl.* punzen

Pup, der; -[e]s, -e *u.* Pups, der; -es, *Plur.* -e *u.* Pup|ser (*ugs. für* abgehende Blähung)

Pu|pe, der *od.* die; -n, -n (*derb für* Homosexueller; *berlin. auch für* verdorbenes Weißbier)

pu|pen, pup|sen (*ugs. für* eine Blähung abgehen lassen); du pupst

pu|pil|lar ‹lat.› (zur Pupille gehörend); **Pu|pil|le,** die; -, -n (Sehöffnung im Auge); **Pu|pil|len‿er|wei|te|rung, ...ver|en|gung**

pu|pi|ni|sie|ren ‹nach dem amerik. Elektrotechniker Pupin› (Pupinspulen einbauen); **Pu|pin|spu|le;** ↑R 95 (eine Induktionsspule)

pu|pi|par ‹lat.› *(Zool.);* -e Insekten (Insekten, deren Larven sich gleich nach der Geburt verpuppen); **Püpp|chen; Pup|pe,** die; -, -n; **pup|pen** (*landsch. für* mit Puppen spielen); du puppst; **Pup|pen‿dok|tor, ...film, ...ge|sicht; pup|pen|haft; Pup|pen‿haus, ...kli|nik, ...kü|che, ...mut|ter** (*Plur.* ...mütter), **...spiel, ...spie|ler, ...spie|le|rin, ...stu|be, ...the|a|ter, ...wa|gen, ...woh|nung**

pup|pern (*ugs. für* zittern, sich zitternd bewegen); ich ...ere (↑R 16)

pup|pig (*ugs. für* klein u. niedlich)

Pups *vgl.* Pup; **pup|sen** *vgl.* pupen; **Pup|ser** *vgl.* Pup

pur ‹lat.› (rein, unverfälscht, lauter); die pure (reine) Wahrheit; -es Gold; Whisky pur; **Pü|ree,** das; -s, -s ‹franz.› (Brei, breiförmige Speise); **Pur|gans,** das; -, *Plur.* ...anzien [...iən] *u.* ...antia *u.* **Pur|ga|tiv,** das; -s, -e [...və] ‹lat.› (*Med.* Abführmittel); **Pur|ga|to|ri|um,** das; -s (Fegefeuer); **pur|gie|ren** (*Med.* abführen; *veraltet für* reinigen); **Pur|gier|mit|tel,** das; **pü|rie|ren** (zu Püree machen); **Pu|ri|fi|ka|ti|on,** die; -, -en (liturg. Reinigung); **pu|ri|fi|zie|ren** (*veraltet für* reinigen, läutern)

Pu|rim [*auch* 'pu:...], das; -s ‹hebr.› (ein jüd. Fest)

Pu|rin, das; -s, -e *meist Plur.* ‹lat.› (*Chemie* eine organ. Verbindung)

Pu|ris|mus, der; - ‹lat.› (Reinigungseifer; [übertriebenes] Streben nach Sprachreinheit); **Pu|rist,** der; -en, -en (↑R 126); **Pu|ris|tin; pu|ris|tisch; Pu|ri|ta|ner** (Anhänger des Puritanismus); **Pu|ri|ta|ne|rin; pu|ri|ta|nisch** (sittenstreng); **Pu|ri|ta|nis|mus,** der; - (streng kalvinistische Richtung im England des 16./17. Jh.s); **Pu|ri|tät,** die; - (*veraltet für* Reinheit; Sittenreinheit)

Pur|pur, der; -s ‹griech.› (hochroter Farbstoff; prächtiges, purpurfarbiges Gewand); **pur|pur|far|ben, pur|pur|far|big; Pur|pur|man|tel; pur|purn; pur|pur|rot; Pur|pur‿rö|te, ...schne|cke**

pur|ren (*landsch. für* stochern; necken, stören; *Seemannsspr.* [zur Wache] wecken)

Pur|ser ['pœ:(r)sə(r)], der; -s, - ‹engl.› (Zahlmeister auf einem Schiff; Chefsteward im Flugzeug)

pu|ru|lent ‹lat.› (*Med.* eitrig)

Pur|zel, der; -s, - (*fam. für* kleiner Kerl)

Pür|zel, der; -s, - (*Jägerspr.* Schwanz des Wildschweins)

Pur|zel|baum; pur|zeln; ich ...[e]le (↑R 16)

Pu|schel, Pü|schel, der; -s, - *u.* die; -, -n (*landsch. für* Quaste; fixe Idee, Steckenpferd)

pu|schen; du puschst; *vgl.* pushen

Pusch|kin (russ. Dichter)

Pusch|lav, das; -s (Tal im Süden von Graubünden; *ital.* Val [di] Poschiavo)

pu|shen [...ʃ...], *auch* puschen ‹engl.-amerik.› (mit Rauschgift handeln; *auch für* in Schwung bringen, propagieren); du pushst; **Pu|sher,** der; -s, - (Rauschgifthändler)

Pus|sel|ar|beit (*ugs. für* mühsame Arbeit); **Pus|sel|chen** (*fam. für* kleines Kind od. Tier); **pus|se|lig,** puss|lig (*ugs. für* Geschicklichkeit erfordernd, umständlich); **Pus|sel|kram** *(ugs.);* **pus|seln** (*ugs. für* sich mit Kleinigkeiten beschäftigen; herumbasteln); ich pussele *u.* pussle (↑R 16); **puss|lig** *vgl.* pusselig

Pus|te, die; - (*ugs. für* Atem; *übertr. für* Kraft, Vermögen, Geld); aus der - (außer Atem) sein; [ja,] Puste, Pustekuchen! (*ugs. für* aber nein, gerade das Gegenteil); **Pus|te|blu|me** (*Kinderspr.* Löwenzahn); **Pus|te|ku|chen** *(ugs.); nur in* [ja,] Pustekuchen! (*vgl.* Puste)

Pus|tel, die; -, -n ‹lat.› (Hitze-, Eiterbläschen, [2]Pickel)

pus|ten (*landsch. für* blasen; schnaufen, heftig atmen)

Pus|ter|tal, das; -[e]s (ein Alpental)

pus|tu|lös ‹lat.› (voll Hitze-, Eiterbläschen); -e Haut

Pusz|ta ['pusta], die; -, ...ten ‹ung.› (Grassteppe, Weideland in Ungarn)

pu|ta|tiv ‹lat.› (*Rechtsspr.* vermeintlich, irrigerweise für gültig gehalten); **Pu|ta|tiv‿ehe** (↑R 132), **...not|wehr**

Put|bus (Ort auf Rügen); **Put|bus|ser,** *auch* Put|bu|ser (↑R 103)

Pu|te, die; -, -n (Truthenne); **Pu|ter** (Truthahn); **pu|ter|rot;** - werden

put, put (Lockruf für Hühner); **Put|put,** das; -s, -[s] (Lockruf; *Kinderspr.* Huhn)

Put|re|fak|ti|on, die; -, -en, **Put|res|zenz** (↑R 130), die; -, -en ‹lat.› (*Med.* Verwesung, Fäulnis); **put|res|zie|ren**

Putsch, der; -[e]s, -e (polit. Handstreich); **put|schen;** du putschst

püt|sche|rig (*nordd. für* kleinlich, umständlich); **püt|schern** (*nordd. für* umständlich arbeiten, ohne etwas zustande zu bringen)

Put|schist, der; -en, -en (↑R 126); **Putsch|ver|such**

Putt [*auch* pat], der; -[s], -s ‹engl.› (*Golf* Schlag mit dem Putter)

Pụtt, der; -s, *Plur.* -e, *auch* -s (*rhein. u. westfäl. für* Bergwerk)
Pụt|te, die; -, -n ‹ital.› *u.* Pụt|to, der; -s, *Plur.* ...tti *u.* ...tten (*bild. Kunst* nackte Kinder-, kleine Engelsfigur)
pụt|ten [*auch* 'patən] ‹engl.› (*Golf* den Ball mit dem Putter schlagen); **Pụt|ter** [*auch* 'patə(r)] der; -s, - (Spezialgolfschläger [für das Einlochen])
Pụt|to *vgl.* Putte
Pụtz, der; -es
Pụ̈tz, Pụ̈t|ze, die; -, ...tzen (*Seemannsspr.* Eimer)
pụt|zen; du putzt; sich putzen; **Pụt|zer; Put|ze|rei** (*österr. auch für* chem. Reinigung); **Pụtz_fim|mel** (*ugs.*), **...frau**
pụt|zig (*ugs. für* drollig)
Pụtz_kas|ten, ...lap|pen, ...ma|cher (*veraltet für* Modist), **...ma|che|rin** (*veraltet für* Modistin), **...mit|tel** (das); **pụtz|mụn|ter** (*ugs. für* sehr munter); **Pụtz|sucht,** die; -; **pụtz|süch|tig; Pụtz_tag, ...teu|fel** (*ugs. für* jmd., der übertrieben oft u. gründlich sauber macht), **...tuch** (*Plur.* ...tücher), **...wol|le, ...zeug**
puz|zeln ['pas(ə)ln, *auch* 'pu...] ‹engl.› (ein Puzzle zusammensetzen); ich puzz[e]le (↑R 16); **Puz|zle** ['pas(ə)l, *auch* 'pu...], das; -s, -s (ein Geduldsspiel); **Puzz|ler; Puz|zle|spiel**
Puz|zo|la|ner|de, die; - ‹nach Pozzuoli bei Neapel› (ein Sedimentgestein, Aschentuff)
PVC = Polyvinylchlorid
Py|ä|mie, die; -, ...ien ‹griech.› (*Med.* herdbildende Form einer Allgemeininfektion durch Eitererreger in der Blutbahn)
Py|e|li|tis, die; -, ...itiden ‹griech.› (*Med.* Entzündung des Nierenbeckens); **Py|e|lo|grạmm,** das; -s, -e (Röntgenbild von Nierenbecken und Harnwegen); **Py|e|lo|gra|phie,** die; - (Röntgenaufnahme des Nierenbeckens); **Py|e|lo|neph|ri|tis,** die; -, ...itiden (Entzündung von Nierenbecken u. Nieren); **Py|e|lo|zys|ti|tis,** die; -, ...itiden (Entzündung von Nierenbecken u. Blase)
Pyg|mäe, der; -n, -n (↑R 126) ‹griech.› (Angehöriger einer kleinwüchsigen Bevölkerungsgruppe in Afrika); **pyg|mä|en|haft; pyg|mä|isch** (zwerghaft, zwergwüchsig)
Pyg|ma|li|on (griech. Sagengestalt)
Pyhrn|pass, der; -es (österr. Alpenpass)
Py|ja|ma [py(d)ʒ..., *auch* py'ja:ma], der, *österr. u. schweiz. auch* das; -s, -s ‹Hindi-engl.› (Schlafanzug); **Py|ja|ma_ho|se, ...ja|cke**
Pỵk|ni|ker (↑R 130) ‹griech.› (*Anthropol.* kräftiger, gedrungen gebauter Mensch); **pỵk|nisch; Pyk|no|me|ter,** das; -s, - (*Physik* Dichtemesser); **pyk|no|tisch** (*Med.* dicht zusammengedrängt)
Py|la|des (Freund des Orest in der griech. Sage)
Py|lon, der; -en, -en (↑R 126) ‹griech.› *u.* **Py|lo|ne,** die; -, -n (großes, von Ecktürmen flankiertes Eingangstor altägypt. Tempel u. Paläste; torähnlicher, tragender Pfeiler einer Hängebrücke; kegelförmige Absperrmarkierung auf Straßen)
Py|lo|rus, der; -, ...ren ‹griech.› (*Med.* Pförtner; Schließmuskel am Magenausgang)
py|o|gen ‹griech.› (*Med.* Eiterungen verursachend); **Py|or|rhö**[1], **Py|or|rhöe** [...'rø:], die; -, ...rrhöen (eitriger Ausfluss); **py|or|rho|isch**
py|ra|mi|dal ‹ägypt.› (pyramidenförmig; *ugs. für* gewaltig, riesenhaft); **Py|ra|mi|de,** die; -, -n (ägypt. Grabbau; geometr. Körper); **py|ra|mi|den|för|mig; Py|ra|mi|den|stumpf** (*Math.*)
Py|ra|no|me|ter (↑R 132), das; -s, - ‹griech.› (*Meteor.* Gerät zur Messung der Sonnen- u. Himmelsstrahlung)
Py|re|nä|en *Plur.* (Gebirge zwischen Spanien u. Frankreich); **Py|re|nä|en|halb|in|sel,** die; -; **py|re|nä|isch**
Py|reth|rum (↑R130), das; -s, ...ra ‹griech.› (aus einer Chrysantheme gewonnenes Insektizid)
Py|re|ti|kum, das; -s, ...ka ‹griech.› (*Med.* Fieber erzeugendes Arzneimittel); **py|re|tisch** (Fieber erzeugend); **Py|re|xie** (↑R 132), die; -, ...ien (Fieber[anfall])
Py|rit [*auch* ...'rit], der; -s, -e ‹griech.› (Eisen-, Schwefelkies)
Pyr|mont, Bad (Stadt im Weserbergland)
py|ro|gen ‹griech.› (*Geol.* magmatisch entstanden; *Med. auch svw.* pyretisch); **Py|ro|ly|se,** die; -, -n (*Chemie* Zersetzung von Stoffen durch Hitze); **Py|ro|ma|ne,** der; -n, -n; ↑R 126 (an Pyromanie Leidender); **Py|ro_ma|nie** (die; -; krankhafter Brandstiftungstrieb), **...me|ter** (das; -s, -; Messgerät für hohe Temperaturen); **py|ro|phor** (selbstentzündlich, in feinster Verteilung an der Luft aufglühend); **Py|ro|phor,** der; -s, -e (Stoff mit pyrophoren Eigenschaften); **Py|ro|tech|nik** [*auch* 'py:...], die; - (Herstellung u. Gebrauch von Feuerwerkskörpern); **Py|ro|tech|ni|ker; py|ro|tech|nisch; Py|ro|xen,** der; -s, -e *meist Plur.* (gesteinsbildendes Mineral)
Pỵr|rhus (König von Epirus); **Pỵr|rhus|sieg** (↑R 95; Scheinsieg, zu teuer erkaufter Sieg)
Pyr|rol, das; -s ‹griech.› (eine chem. Verbindung)
Py|tha|go|rä|er usw. *vgl.* Pythagoreer usw.; [1]**Py|tha|go|ras** (altgriech. Philosoph); [2]**Py|tha|go|ras,** der; - (*kurz für* pythagoreischer Lehrsatz); **Py|tha|go|re|er,** *österr.* Py|tha|go|rä|er (Anhänger der Lehre des Pythagoras); **py|tha|go|re|isch,** *österr.* py|tha|go|rä|isch; (↑R 94:) die pythagoreische Philosophie; pythagoreischer Lehrsatz (grundlegender Satz der Geometrie)
[1]**Py|thia** (Priesterin in Delphi); [2]**Py|thia,** die; -, ...ien [...iən] (Frau, die orakelhafte Anspielungen macht); **py|thisch** (dunkel, orakelhaft); pythische Worte, *aber* (↑R 108): Pythische (zu Pytho [Delphi] gefeierte) Spiele; **Py|thon,** der; -s, -s (eine Riesenschlange)
Pỵ|xis, die; -, *Plur.* ...iden, *auch* ...ides [...de:s] ‹griech.› (Hostienbehälter)

Q [ku:, *österr. [außer Math.]* kve:] (Buchstabe); das Q; des Q, die Q, *aber* das q in verquer (↑R 60); der Buchstabe Q, q
Q, Ø = [2]Quetzal
q = Quintal
q (*österr.*) = Meterzentner
Q. = Quintus
qcm *vgl.* cm^2; **qdm** *vgl.* dm^2
q. e. d. = quod erat demonstrandum
Qin|dar ['kin...], der; -s, -ka [...'darka] (Münzeinheit in Albanien; 100 Qindarka = 1 Lek)

[1] *Vgl. die Anmerkung zu* „Diarrhö, Diarrhöe".

qkm *vgl.* km²; **qm** *vgl.* m²; **qmm** *vgl.* mm²
qua ‹lat.› ([in der Eigenschaft] als; gemäß); qua Beamter; qua amtliche, *auch* amtlicher Befugnis
Quab|be, die; -, -n (*nordd. für* Fettwulst); **quab|be|lig,** quabblig (*für* schwabbelig, fett); **quab|beln;** ich ...[e]le (↑R 16); **quab|big; quabb|lig** *vgl.* quabbelig
Qua|cke|lei (*landsch. für* ständiges, törichtes Reden); **Qua|cke|ler,** Quack|ler (*landsch. für* Schwätzer); **qua|ckeln** (*landsch. für* viel u. töricht reden); ich ...[e]le (↑R 16); **Quack|sal|ber** (*svw.* Kurpfuscher); **Quack|sal|be|rei; Quack|sal|be|rin; quack|sal|be|risch; quack|sal|bern;** ich ...ere (↑R 16); gequacksalbert; zu quacksalbern
Quad|del, die; -, -n (juckende Anschwellung der Haut)
Qua|de, der; -n, -n; ↑R 126 (Angehöriger eines westgermanischen Volkes)
Qua|der, der; -s, *Plur.* -, *österr.* -n *od.* die; -, -n ‹lat.› (*Math.* ein von sechs Rechtecken begrenzter Körper; behauener [viereckiger] Bruchsteinblock); **Qua|der|bau** *Plur.* ...bauten; **Qua|der|stein**
Quad|ra|ge|si|ma (↑R 130), die; - ‹lat.› (vierzigtägige christl. Fastenzeit vor Ostern)
Quad|ran|gel (↑R 130), das; -s, - ‹lat.› (*svw.* Viereck)
Quad|rant (↑R 130), der; -en, -en (↑R 126) ‹lat.› (*Math.* Viertelkreis); **Quad|rant|sys|tem,** das; -s (Maßsystem)
[1]**Quad|rat** (↑R 130), das; -[e]s, -e ‹lat.› (Viereck mit vier rechten Winkeln u. vier gleichen Seiten; zweite Potenz einer Zahl); [2]**Quad|rat,** das; -[e]s, -e[n] (*Druckw.* Geviert, Bleistück zum Ausfüllen nicht druckender Stellen); **Quad|rat|de|zi|me|ter** (*Zeichen* dm²); **quad|rä|teln** (mit Geviertstücken würfeln [Würfelspiel der Buchdrucker u. Setzer]); ich ...[e]le (↑R 16); **Quad|ra|ten|kas|ten** (*Druckw.*); **Quad|rat|fuß,** der; -es; 10 - (↑R 90); *vgl.* Fuß; **quad|ra|tisch;** quadratische Gleichung (Gleichung zweiten Grades); **Quad|rat‿ki|lo|me|ter** (*Zeichen* km²), **...lat|schen** (*Plur.; ugs. scherzh. für* große, unförmige Schuhe), **...mei|le, ...me|ter** (*Zeichen* m²), **...mil|li|me|ter** (*Zeichen* mm²), **...schä|del** (*ugs. für* breiter, eckiger Kopf; *übertr. für* starrsinniger, begriffsstutziger Mensch); **Quad|ra|tur,** die; -, -en (Verfahren zur Flächenberechnung); **Quad|ra|tur|ma|le|rei** (*Kunstwiss.*); **Quad|rat‿wur|zel, ...zahl, ...zen|ti|me|ter** (*Zeichen* cm²)
Quad|ri|en|na|le (↑R 130), die; -, -n ‹ital.› (alle vier Jahre stattfindende Veranstaltung od. Ausstellung); **Quad|ri|en|ni|um,** das; -s, ...ien [...iən] ‹lat.› (*veraltet für* Zeit von vier Jahren)
quad|rie|ren (↑R 130) ‹lat.› (*Math.* [eine Zahl] in die zweite Potenz erheben)
Quad|ri|ga (↑R 130), die; -, ...gen ‹lat.› (von einem Streit-, Renn- od. Triumphwagen [der Antike] aus gelenktes Viergespann)
Quad|ril|le [k(v)a'driljə, *österr.* ka'dril] (↑R 130), die; -, -n ‹span.-franz.› (ein Tanz)
Quad|ril|li|on (↑R 130), die; -, -en ‹franz.› (vierte Potenz einer Million); **Quad|ri|nom,** das; -s, -e ‹lat.; griech.› (*Math.* die Summe aus vier Gliedern); **Quad|ri|re|me,** die; -, -n ‹lat.› (antikes Kriegsschiff mit vier übereinander liegenden Ruderbänken); **Quad|ri|vi|um** [...vium], das; -s (im mittelalterl. Universitätsunterricht die vier höheren Fächer Arithmetik, Geometrie, Astronomie, Musik)
Quad|ro ['kva(:)...] (↑R 130), das; -s ‹lat.› (*Kurzw. für* Quadrophonie); **quad|ro|fon** usw. *eindeutschende Schreibung für* quadrophon usw.; **quad|ro|phon** (↑R 33) ‹lat.; griech.› (*svw.* quadrophonisch); **Quad|ro|pho|nie,** die; - (Vierkanalstereophonie); **quad|ro|pho|nisch; Quad|ro|sound** ['kva(:)drosaunt], der; -s ‹engl.-amerik.› (quadrophonische Klangwirkung)
Quad|ru|pe|de (↑R 130), der; -n, -n *meist Plur.;* ↑R 126 ‹lat.› (*Zool. veraltet für* Vierfüß[l]er); [1]**Quad|ru|pel,** das; -s, - ‹franz.› (vier zusammengehörende math. Größen); [2]**Quad|ru|pel,** der; -s, - (frühere span. Goldmünze); **Quad|ru|pel|al|li|anz** (Allianz zwischen vier Staaten)
Quag|ga, das; -s, -s ‹hottentott.› (ein ausgerottetes Zebra)
Quai [kɛ], der *od.* das; -s, -s ‹franz.› (*schweiz. für* Uferstraße); *vgl.* Kai; **Quai d'Or|say** [ke dɔr'sɛ:], der; - - ‹franz.› (Straße in Paris; *übertr. für* das franz. Außenministerium)
quak!; Quä|ke, die; -, -n (Instrument zum Nachahmen des Angstschreis der Hasen); **Quä|kel|chen** (*fam. für* kleines Kind); **quä|keln** (*landsch. für* undeutlich reden); ich ...[e]le (↑R 16); **qua|ken;** der Frosch quakt; **quä|ken;** quäkende Stimme
Quä|ker, der; -s, - ‹engl.› (Angehöriger einer christl. Glaubensgemeinschaft); **quä|ke|risch**
Quak|frosch (*Kinderspr. für* Frosch)
Qual, die; -, -en; **quä|len;** sich -; **Quä|ler; Quä|le|rei; Quä|le|rin; quä|le|risch; Quäl|geist** *Plur.* ...geister (*ugs.*)
Qua|li|fi|ka|ti|on, die; -, -en ‹lat.› (Befähigung[snachweis]; Teilnahmeberechtigung für sportl. Wettbewerbe); **Qua|li|fi|ka|ti|ons‿ren|nen, ...run|de, ...spiel; qua|li|fi|zie|ren** (als etw. bezeichnen, klassifizieren; befähigen); sich - (sich eignen; sich als geeignet erweisen; eine Qualifikation erwerben); **qua|li|fi|ziert;** ein qualifizierter Arbeiter; eine qualifizierte Mehrheit; qualifiziertes Vergehen (*Rechtsspr.* Vergehen unter erschwerenden Umständen); **Qua|li|fi|zie|rung** (*auch für* fachl. Aus- u. Weiterbildung); **Qua|li|tät,** die; -, -en (Beschaffenheit, Güte, Wert); erste, zweite, mittlere -; **qua|li|ta|tiv** [*auch* 'kva...] (dem Wert, der Beschaffenheit nach); **Qua|li|täts|ar|beit** (Wertarbeit); **qua|li|täts|be|wusst; Qua|li|täts‿be|wusst|sein, ...be|zeich|nung, ...ein|bu|ße, ...er|zeug|nis, ...kon|trol|le, ...min|de|rung, ...norm, ...stei|ge|rung, ...stu|fe, ...wa|re, ...wein** (- mit Prädikat)
Quall, der; -[e]s, -e (*veraltet, noch landsch. für* emporquellendes Wasser); **Qual|le,** die; -, -n (ein Nesseltier); **qual|lig**
Qualm, der; -[e]s; **qual|men; qual|mig**
Quals|ter, der; -s, - (*nordd. für* Schleim, Auswurf); **quals|te|rig,** qualst|rig; **quals|tern;** ich ...ere (↑R 16)
qual|voll
Quant, das; -s, -en ‹lat.› (*Physik* kleinste Energiemenge); **Quänt|chen** (eine kleine Menge); ein Quäntchen Glück; **quan|teln** (eine Energiemenge in Quanten aufteilen); **Quan|ten** (*Plur. von* Quant *u.* Quantum); **Quan|ten‿bi|o|lo|gie, ...me|cha|nik** (die; -), **...the|o|rie** (die; -; Theorie der mikrophysikal. Erscheinungen u. Objekte); **quan|ti|fi|zie|ren** ([Eigenschaften] in Zahlen u. messbare Größen umsetzen); **Quan|ti|fi|zie|rung; Quan|ti|tät,** die; -, -en (*nur Sing.:* Menge, Größe; *Sprachw.* Dauer, Länge eines Lautes od. einer Silbe); **quan|ti-**

ta|ti̱v [*auch* 'kvan...] (der Quantität nach, mengenmäßig); **Quan|ti|täts˷glei|chung** *(Wirtsch.)*, **...the|o|rie** (die; -; *Wirtsch.* Theorie, nach der ein Kausalzusammenhang zwischen Geldmenge u. Preisniveau besteht); **Quan|ti|té nég|li|gea|ble** [kãti'te: negli'ʒa:b(ə)l] (↑R 130), die; - - ‹franz.› (wegen ihrer Kleinheit außer Acht zu lassende Größe, Belanglosigkeit); **quan|ti|ti̱e|ren** [kvanti...] ‹lat.› (*Sprachw.* die Silben [nach der Länge od. Kürze] messen); **Quan|tum,** das; -s, ...ten (Menge, Anzahl, Maß, Summe, Betrag)

Quap|pe, die; -, -n (ein Fisch; eine Lurchlarve, Kaulquappe)

Qua|ran|tä̱|ne [ka...], die; -, -n (vorübergehende Isolierung von Personen od. Tieren, die eine ansteckende Krankheit haben [könnten]); **Qua|ran|tä̱|ne|sta|ti|on**

Quar|gel, der; -s, - (*österr. für* kleiner, runder Käse)

[1]**Quark** [kwɔ:(r)k], das; -s, -s ‹engl.› (*Physik* hypothetisches Elementarteilchen)

[2]**Quark,** der; -s (aus saurer Milch hergestelltes Nahrungsmittel; *ugs. auch für* Wertloses); red nicht solchen - (Unsinn); **Quark|brot; quar|kig; Quark˷kä|se, ...käul|chen** (*landsch. für* gebackenes [3]Küchlein aus Kartoffeln u. Quark), **...kü|chen** *(landsch.)*, **...schnit|te, ...spei|se**

Quar|re, die; -, -n (*nordd. für* weinerliches Kind; zänkische Frau); **quar|ren; quar|rig;** das Kind ist -

[1]**Quart,** die; -, -en ‹lat.› (Fechthieb); *vgl. auch* Quarte; [2]**Quart,** das; -s, -e (altes Flüssigkeitsmaß; *nur Sing.:* Viertelbogengröße [Buchformat]; *Abk.* 4°); 3 - (↑R 90); in -; Großquart (*Abk.* Gr.-4°); **Quar|ta,** die; -, ...ten (*veraltende Bez. für* die dritte [*in Österr.* vierte] Klasse eines Gymnasiums); **Quar|ta̱l,** das; -s, -e (Vierteljahr); **Quar|ta̱l[s]˷ab|schluss, ...säu|fer** *(ugs.)*; **quar|ta̱l[s]|wei|se** (vierteljahrsweise); **Quar|ta̱|na,** die; - (*Med.* Viertagefieber, Art der Malaria); **Quar|ta̱|ner** (Schüler der Quarta); **Quar|ta̱|ne|rin; Quar|ta̱n|fie|ber,** das; -s (*svw.* Quartana); **quar|tä̱r** (zum Quartär gehörend); **Quar|tä̱r,** das; -s (*Geol.* obere Formation des Neozoikums); **Quar|tä̱r|for|ma|ti|on,** die; -; **Quart˷band** (der; *Buchw.*), **...blatt; Quar|te,** die; -, -n *u.* Quart, die; -, -en (*Musik* vierter Ton der diaton. Tonleiter; Intervall im Abstand von 4 Stufen); **Quar|tel,** das; -s, - (*bayr. für* kleines Biermaß); **Quar|ten** (*Plur. von* Quart, Quarte *u.* Quarta); **Quar|ter** ['kwɔ:(r)tə(r)], der; -s, - (altes engl. u. amerik. Hohlmaß u. Gewicht); **Quar|ter|deck** ['kvar...] (Hinterdeck); **Quar|tett,** das; -[e]s, -e ‹ital.› (Musikstück für vier Stimmen od. vier Instrumente; *auch für* die vier Ausführenden; ein Kartenspiel); **Quart|for|mat** *(Buchw.)*; **Quar|ti̱er,** das; -s, -e ‹franz.› (Unterkunft, bes. von Truppen; *schweiz., österr. auch für* Stadtviertel); **quar|ti̱e|ren** (*selten für* einquartieren); **Quar|ti̱er|ma|cher; Quar|ti̱ers˷frau, ...wirt; Quart|sext|ak|kord** *(Musik)*

Quarz, der; -es, -e (ein Mineral); **Quarz˷fels** (der; -), **...fil|ter, ...gang** (der); **quarz|ge|steu|ert; Quarz|glas** *Plur.* ...gläser; **quarz|hal|tig; quarz|häl|tig** *(österr.)*; **quar|zig; Quar|zi̱t** [*auch* ...'tsit], der; -s, -e (ein Gestein); **Quarz˷kris|tall, ...lam|pe, ...steu|e|rung** *(Elektrotechnik)*, **...uhr**[1]

Quas, der; -es, -e ‹slaw.› (*landsch. für* Gelage, Schmaus; bes. Pfingstbier mit festl. Tanz); *vgl. aber* Kwass

Qua|sar, der; -s, -e ‹lat.› (sternenähnliches Objekt im Kosmos mit extrem starker Radiofrequenzstrahlung)

qua|sen (*landsch. für* prassen; vergeuden); du quast

qua|si ‹lat.› (gewissermaßen, gleichsam, sozusagen); **Qua|si|mo|do|ge|ni|ti** („wie die neugeborenen [Kinder]") (erster Sonntag nach Ostern); **qua|si|of|fi|zi|ell** (gewissermaßen offiziell); **qua|si|op|tisch** (*Physik* ähnlich den Lichtwellen sich ausbreitend); **Qua|si|sou|ve|rä|ni|tät,** die; -, -en (scheinbare Souveränität)

Quas|se|lei (*ugs. für* [dauerndes] Quasseln); **quas|seln** (*ugs. für* unaufhörlich u. schnell reden, schwatzen); ich quassele *u.* quassle (↑R 16); **Quas|sel|strip|pe,** die; -, -n (*ugs. für* Telefon; *auch für* jmd., der viel redet)

Quas|sie [...iə], die; -, -n ‹nach dem angebl. Entdecker› (südamerik. Baum, dessen Holz Bitterstoff enthält)

Quast, der; -[e]s, -e (*nordd. für* [Borsten]büschel, breiter Pinsel); **Quäst|chen; Quas|te,** die; -, -n (Troddel, Schleife); **Quas|ten˷be|hang, ...flos|ser** *(Zool.)*; **quas|ten|för|mig**

Quäs|ti|o̱n, die; -, -en ‹lat.› (wissenschaftl. Streitfrage)

Quäs|tor, der; -s, ...oren ‹lat.› (altröm. Beamter; Schatzmeister an Hochschulen; *schweiz. geh. für* Kassenwart eines Vereins); **Quäs|tu̱r,** die; -, -en (Amt eines Quästors; Kasse an einer Hochschule)

Qua|tem|ber, der; -s, - ‹lat.› (vierteljährlicher kath. Fasttag); **Qua|tem|ber|fas|ten,** das; -s

qua|ter|nä̱r ‹lat.› (*Chemie* aus vier Teilen bestehend); **Qua|ter|ne,** die; -, -n (Reihe von vier gesetzten od. gewonnenen Nummern in der alten Zahlenlotterie); **Qua|ter|nio,** der; -s, ...onen (Zahl, Ganzes aus vier Einheiten)

quatsch! (Schallwort)

[1]**Quatsch,** der; -[e]s (*landsch. für* Matsch)

[2]**Quatsch,** der; -[e]s (*ugs. für* dummes Gerede, Unsinn; *auch für* Albere i); - reden; das ist ja -!; ach -!

[1]**quat|schen** *(landsch.)*; der Boden quatscht unter den Füßen

[2]**quat|schen** *(ugs.)*; du quatschst; **Quat|sche|rei** *(ugs.)*; **Quatsch|kopf** *(ugs.)*

quatsch|nass (*ugs. für* sehr nass)

Quat|tro|cen|tist [...tʃɛn...], der; -en, -en; ↑R 126 (Dichter, Künstler des Quattrocentos); **Quat|tro|cen|to** [...'tʃɛnto], das; -[s] (*Kunstw.* das 15. Jh. in Italien [als Stilbegriff], Frührenaissance)

Que|bec [kvi'bɛk] (Provinz u. Stadt in Kanada); **Que|be|cer**

Queb|ra|cho [ke'bratʃo] (↑R 130), das; -s ‹span.› (gerbstoffreiches Holz eines südamerik. Baumes); **Queb|ra|cho|rin|de** (ein Arzneimittel)

[1]**Que|chua** ['kɛtʃua], der; -[s], -[s] (Angehöriger eines indian. Volkes in Peru); [2]**Que|chua,** das; -[s] (eine indian. Sprache)

queck (*für* quick); **Que|cke,** die; -, -n (eine Graspflanze); **que|ckig** (voller Quecken); **Queck|sil|ber** (ein chem. Element, Metall; *Zeichen* Hg); **Queck|sil|ber|dampf; Queck|sil|ber|dampf|lam|pe; queck|sil|ber|hal|tig; queck|sil|be|rig** *vgl.* quecksilbrig; **queck|sil|bern** (aus Quecksilber); **Queck|sil|ber˷prä|pa|rat, ...sal|be, ...säu|le, ...ver|gif|tung; queck|silb|rig** ([unruhig] wie Quecksilber)

Qued|lin|burg (Stadt im nördl. Harzvorland)

[1] *In Werbetexten oft mit der englischen tz-Schreibung.*

Queen [kwi:n], die; -, -s (engl. Königin)
Quee|ne, die; -, -n (*nordd. für* Färse)
Queens|land ['kwi:nslənt] (Staat des Australischen Bundes)
Queich, die; - (l. Nebenfluss des Oberrheins)
Queis, der; - (l. Nebenfluss des ²Bobers)
Quell, der; -[e]s, -e *Plur. selten* (*geh. für* Quelle); **Quell|be|wöl|kung; Quell|chen; Quel|le**, die; -, -n; Nachrichten aus amtlicher, erster -; **¹quel|len** (schwellen, größer werden; hervordringen, sprudeln); du quillst, du quollst; du quöllest; gequollen; quill!; Wasser quillt; **²quel|len** (im Wasser weichen lassen); du quellst; du quelltest; gequellt; quell[e]!; ich quelle Bohnen; **Quel|len‿an|ga|be, ...for|schung, ...kri|tik** (die; -), **...kun|de** (die; -); **quel|len|mä|ßig; Quel|len|ma|te|ri|al; quel|len|reich; Quel|len‿samm|lung, ...steu|er** (die; Steuer, die in dem Staat erhoben wird, wo der Gewinn, die Einnahme erwirtschaftet wurde); **Quel|len|stu|di|um; Quel|ler** (eine Strandpflanze); **Quell‿fas|sung, ...fluss; quell|frisch; Quell‿ge|biet, ...nym|phe; Quel|lung; Quell‿was|ser** (*Plur.* ...wasser), **...wol|ke**
Quem|pas, der; - ⟨lat.⟩ (ein weihnachtl. Wechselgesang); **Quem|pas|lied**
Quen|del, der; -s, - (Name verschiedener Pflanzen)
Quen|ge|lei; quen|ge|lig, quenglig; **quen|geln** (*ugs. für* weinerlich nörgelnd immer wieder um etwas bitten, keine Ruhe geben [meist von Kindern]); ich ...[e]le (↑R 16); **Queng|ler; queng|lig** *vgl.* quengelig
Quent, das; -[e]s, -e ⟨lat.⟩ (altes dt. Gewicht); 5 - (↑R 90); **Quent|chen** *frühere Schreibung für* Quäntchen
quer; kreuz und quer; quer [über die Straße] gehen; ihm ist alles quer gegangen (*ugs. für* missglückt); ein Ast hatte sich quer gelegt; ich will mich nicht länger quer legen (*ugs. für* mich nicht länger widersetzen); einer muss doch immer quer schießen! (*ugs. für* Schwierigkeiten machen); einen Wechsel quer schreiben (*bes. Bankw.* akzeptieren); ein quer gestreifter (↑R 40) Pullover; **quer|ab** (*Seemannsspr.* rechtwinklig zur Längsrichtung [des Schiffs]); **Quer‿bahn|steig, ...bal|ken, ...bau** (*Plur.* ...bauten), **...baum** (älteres Turngerät); **quer|beet** (*ugs. für* ohne festgelegte Richtung; nicht vorgegeben); **Quer|den|ker** (jmd., der eigenständig u. originell denkt); **Quer|den|ke|rin; quer|durch;** er ist einfach querdurch gelaufen, *aber* er läuft quer durch die Felder; **Que|re**, die; - (*ugs.*); *meist in* in die Quere kommen; in die Kreuz und [in die] Quer[e]
Que|re|le, die; -, -n *meist Plur.* ⟨lat.⟩ (Klage; Streit; *nur Plur.:* Streitigkeiten)
que|ren (*veraltend für* überschreiten, überschneiden); **quer|feld|ein; Quer|feld|ein‿lauf, ...ren|nen, ...ritt; Quer‿flö|te, ...for|mat, ...gang** (der; *auch für* Klettertour auf einer waagerecht verlaufenden Route); **quer ge|hen** *vgl.* quer; **quer ge|streift** *vgl.* quer; **Quer‿haus, ...holz, ...kopf** (*ugs. für* jmd., der ärgerlicherweise immer anders handelt, der sich nicht einordnet); **quer|köp|fig; Quer|köp|fig|keit**, die; - (*ugs.*); **Quer‿la|ge** (*Med.*), **...lat|te; quer le|gen** *vgl.* quer; **Quer‿li|nie, ...pass** (*Sportspr.*), **...pfei|fe, ...rin|ne; quer schie|ßen** *vgl.* quer; **Quer|schiff** (Teil einer Kirche); **quer|schiffs** (*Seemannsspr.*); **Quer‿schlag** (*Bergmannsspr.* Gesteinsstrecke, die [annähernd] senkrecht zu den Schichten verläuft), **...schlä|ger** (abprallendes od. quer aufschlagendes Geschoss), **...schnitt; quer|schnitt[s]|ge|lähmt; Quer|schnitt[s]‿ge|lähm|te, ...läh|mung; quer schrei|ben** *vgl.* quer; **Quer‿schuss, ...stra|ße, ...strich, ...sum|me, ...trei|ber** (jmd., der gegen etwas handelt, etwas zu durchkreuzen trachtet); **Quer|trei|be|rei; quer|über** (↑R 132; *veraltend*); querüber liegt ein Haus, *aber* er geht quer über den Hof
Que|ru|lant, der; -en, -en (↑R 126) ⟨lat.⟩ (Nörgler, Quengler); **Que|ru|lan|tin; Que|ru|la|ti|on**, die; -, -en (*veraltet für* Beschwerde, Klage); **que|ru|lie|ren** (nörgeln)
Quer‿ver|bin|dung, ...ver|weis, ...wand
Que|se, die; -, -n (*nordd. für* durch Quetschung entstandene Blase; Schwiele; Finne des Quesenbandwurms, die bei Schafen die Drehkrankheit verursacht); **que|sen** (*nordd. für* quengeln); du quest; **Que|sen|band|wurm; que|sig** (*nordd. auch für* quengelig)
Quetsch, der; -[e]s, -e (*westmitteld., südd. für* Zwetschenschnaps); **¹Quet|sche**, die; -, -n (*landsch. für* Zwetsche)
²Quet|sche, die; -, -n (*landsch. für* Presse; *ugs. für* kleines Geschäft, kleiner Betrieb); **quet|schen;** du quetschst; **Quetsch‿fal|te, ...kar|tof|feln** (*Plur.; landsch. für* Kartoffelpüree), **...kom|mo|de** (*ugs. scherzh. für* Ziehharmonika); **Quet|schung; Quetsch|wun|de**
¹Quet|zal [kɛ...], der; -s, -s ⟨indian.-span.⟩ (bunter Urwaldvogel; Wappenvogel von Guatemala); **²Quet|zal** [kɛ...], der; -[s], -[s] (Münzeinheit in Guatemala; *Abk.* Q, Q); 5 - (↑R 90)
¹Queue [kø:], das, *auch* der; -s, -s ⟨franz.⟩ (Billardstock); **²Queue**, die; -, -s (*veraltend für* Menschenschlange, Ende einer [Marsch]kolonne)
Quiche [kiʃ], die; -, -s [kiʃ] ⟨franz.⟩ (Speckkuchen aus Mürbe- od. Blätterteig)
Qui|chotte *vgl.* Don Quichotte
quick (*landsch. für* lebendig, rege, schnell); **Quick|born**, der; -[e]s, -e (*veraltet für* Jungbrunnen); **quick|le|ben|dig; Quick|stepp** [...stɛp], der; -s, -s ⟨engl.⟩ (ein Tanz)
Quick|test ⟨nach dem amerik. Arzt A. J. Quick⟩ (*Med.* Verfahren zur Bestimmung der Gerinnungszeit des Blutes); **Quick|wert**
Qui|dam, der; - ⟨lat.⟩; ein gewisser - (*veraltet für* ein gewisser Jemand)
Quid|pro|quo, das; -s, -s ⟨lat.⟩ (Verwechslung, Ersatz)
Quie, die; -, Quien (*svw.* Queene)
quiek!; quiek, quiek!; **quie|ken, quiek|sen;** du quiekst; **Quiek|ser** (*ugs.*)
Qui|e|tis|mus [kvi|e...], der; - ⟨lat.⟩ (inaktive Haltung; religiöse Bewegung); **Qui|e|tist**, der; -en, -en (↑R 126; Anhänger des Quietismus); **qui|e|tis|tisch; Qui|e|tiv**, das; -s, -e [...və] (*Med.* Beruhigungsmittel)
quiet|schen; du quietschst; **Quiet|scher** (*ugs.*); **quietsch‿fi|del, ...ver|gnügt** (*ugs. für* sehr vergnügt)
Qui|jo|te *vgl.* Don Quijote
Quil|la|ja, die; -, -s ⟨indian.⟩ (ein chilen. Seifenbaum); **Quil|la|ja|rin|de**
quil|len (*veraltet, noch landsch. für* ¹quellen)
Quilt, der; -s, -s ⟨engl.⟩ (eine Art Steppdecke); **Quilt|de|cke; quil|ten** (Quilts herstellen)

Quilnar, der; -s, -e ‹lat.› (eine altröm. Münze)
quinlkellielren, quinlquillielren ‹lat.› *(bes. nordd. für* hell u. leise singen)
Quinlqualgelsilma, die; *Gen.* -, *bei Gebrauch ohne Artikel auch* ...mä ‹lat., „fünfzigster" [Tag]› (siebter Sonntag vor Ostern); **Quinlquenlnilum,** das; -s, ...ien [...iən] *(veraltet für* Jahrfünft)
quinlquillielren *vgl.* quinkelieren
Quinlquilllilon, die; -, -en ‹lat.› (5. Potenz der Million); **Quint,** die; -, -en (Fechthieb); *vgl. auch* Quinte; **Quinlta,** die; -, ...ten *(veraltend für* zweite *[in Österr.* fünfte] Klasse eines Gymnasiums); **Quinltal** *[franz.* kẽ..., *span. u. port.* kin'tal], der; -s, -[e] ‹roman.› (Gewichtsmaß [Zentner] in Frankreich, Spanien u. in mittel- u. südamerik. Staaten; *Zeichen* q); 2 - (↑R 90); **Quinltalna,** die; - ‹lat.› *(Med.* Fünftage[wechsel]fieber); **Quinltalner** (Schüler der Quinta); **Quinltalnelrin; Quintanlfielber,** das; -s *(svw.* Quintana); **Quinlte,** die; -, -n *u.* Quint, die; -, -en *(Musik* fünfter Ton der diaton. Tonleiter; Intervall im Abstand von 5 Stufen); **Quinlten** *(Plur. von* Quinta *u.* Quint); **Quintenlzirlkel,** der; -s *(Musik);* **Quinterlne,** die; -, -n (Reihe von fünf gesetzten od. gewonnenen Nummern in der alten Zahlenlotterie); **Quintleslsenz,** die; -, -en ‹lat.› ([als Ergebnis] das Wesentliche einer Sache); **Quinltett,** das; -[e]s, -e ‹ital.› (Musikstück für fünf Stimmen od. fünf Instrumente; *auch für* die fünf Ausführenden)
Quinltililan, **Quinltililalnus** (röm. Redner, Verfasser eines lat. Lehrbuches der Rhetorik); **Quintililus** (altröm. m. Eigenn.)
Quinltilllilon, die; -, -en *(svw.* Quinquillion); **Quinltolle,** die; -, -n ‹lat.› (Gruppe von fünf Tönen, die einen Zeitraum von drei, vier od. sechs Tönen gleichen Taktwertes in Anspruch nehmen); **Quintlsextlaklkord** *(Musik)*
Quinltus (altröm. m. Vorn.; *Abk.* Q.)
Quilprolquo, das; -s, -s ‹lat.› (Verwechslung einer Person mit einer anderen)
Quilpu ['kipu], das; -[s], -[s] ‹indian.› (Knotenschrift der Inkas)
Quilrin, Quilrilnus (röm. Gott; röm. Tribun; ein Heiliger); **Quirilnal,** der; -s (Hügel in Rom; Sitz des ital. Staatspräsidenten)
Quilrilte, der; -n, -n; ↑R 126 (altröm. Vollbürger)
Quirl, der; -[e]s, -e; **quirllen; quirlig** *(ugs. für* lebhaft, unruhig)
Quilsilsalna, das; - ‹ital.› (Name von Kur- und Gasthäusern)
Quislling, der; -s, -e ‹nach dem norw. Faschistenführer› *(abwertend für* Kollaborateur)
Quislquililen [...iən] *Plur.* ‹lat.› (Kleinigkeiten)
Quilto ['ki:to] (Hptst. Ecuadors)
quitt ‹franz.› (ausgeglichen, fertig, befreit); wir sind quitt *(ugs.);* mit jmdm. quitt sein
Quitlte *[österr. auch* 'kitə], die; -, -n (ein Obstbaum; dessen Frucht); **quitltelgelb** *od.* quitltenlgelb; **Quitltenˍbrot** (das; -[e]s; in Stücke geschnittene, feste Quittenmarmelade), **...gellee, ...kälse** (der; -es; *österr. für* Quittenbrot), **...marlmellalde, ...mus**
quitltielren ‹franz.› ([den Empfang] bescheinigen; *veraltend für* [ein Amt] niederlegen); etwas mit einem Achselzucken - (hinnehmen); **Quitltung** (Empfangsbescheinigung); **Quitltungsˍblock** *(vgl.* Block), **...forlmullar**
Quilvive [ki'vi:f] ‹franz.› (Werdaruf); *nur in* auf dem - sein *(ugs. für* auf der Hut sein)
Quiz [kvis], das; -, - ‹engl.› (Frage-und-Antwort-Spiel); **Quizlfralge; Quizlmaslter** ['kvisma:stə(r)], der; -s, - (Fragesteller u. Conférencier] bei einer Quizveranstaltung); **Quizlsenldung; quizlzen** ['kvis(ə)n] *(ugs.)*
Qumlran *vgl.* Kumran
quod elrat delmonstlranldum (↑R 130) ‹lat., „was zu beweisen war"› *(Abk.* q. e. d.)
Quodllilbet, das; -s, -s ‹lat.› (Durcheinander, Mischmasch; ein Kartenspiel; *Musik* scherzh. Zusammenstellung verschiedener Melodien u. Texte)
quorlren *(Jägerspr.* balzen [von der Schnepfe])
Quolrum, das; -s ‹lat.› *(bes. schweiz. für* die zur Beschlussfassung in einer Körperschaft erforderl. Anzahl anwesender Mitglieder)
Quoltaltilon, die; -, -en ‹lat.› (Kursnotierung an der Börse); **Quolte,** die; -, -n (Anteil [von Personen], der bei Aufteilung eines Ganzen auf den Einzelnen od. eine Einheit entfällt); **Quotenˍkarltell** *(Wirtsch.),* **...relgellung** (Festlegung eines angemessenen Anteils von Frauen in [polit.] Gremien); **Quoltilent,** der; -en, -en; ↑R 126 (Zahlenausdruck, bestehend aus Zähler u. Nenner); **quoltielren** (den Preis angeben od. mitteilen); **Quoltielrung** *(svw.* Quotation); **quoltilsielren** (in Quoten aufteilen); **Quoltisielrung**
quo valdis? [- v...] ‹lat., „wohin gehst du?"› (wohin wird das führen, was wird daraus?)

R (Buchstabe); das R; des R, die R, *aber* das r in fahren (↑R 60); der Buchstabe R, r
R = ²Rand; Reaumur
® = registered [trademark] ‹engl., „eingetragenes Warenzeichen"›
P, ϱ = Rho
r, R = Radius
r. = rechts
R., Reg[t]., Rgt. = Regiment
Ra *vgl.* ¹Re
Ra = *chem. Zeichen für* Radium
¹Raab (Stadt in Ungarn); **²Raab,** die; - (r. Nebenfluss der Donau)
Raalbe (dt. Schriftsteller)
Rab (eine dalmatin. Insel)
Ralbalnus Maulrus *vgl.* Hrabanus Maurus
Ralbat [ra'ba(:)t] (Hptst. von Marokko)
Ralbatt, der; -[e]s, -e ‹ital.› (Preisnachlass); **Ralbatlte,** die; -, -n ‹niederl.› ([Rand]beet); **ralbattielren** ‹ital.› (Rabatt gewähren); **Ralbatltielrung; Ralbattlmarlke**
Ralbatz, der; -es *(ugs. für* lärmendes Treiben, Unruhe, Krach); - machen; **Ralbau,** der; *Gen.* -s *u.* -en, *Plur.* -e[n]; ↑R 126 *(niederrhein. für* kleine graue Renette; Rabauke); **Ralbaulke,** der; -n, -n; ↑R 126 *(ugs. für* Rüpel, gewalttätiger Mensch)
Rablbi, der; -[s], *Plur.* -s *u.* ...inen ‹hebr.› *(nur Sing.:* Ehrentitel jüd. Gesetzeslehrer u. a.; Träger dieses Titels); **Rablbilnat,** das; -[e]s, -e (Amt, Würde eines Rabbi[ners]); **Rablbilner,** der; -s, - (jüd. Gesetzes-, Religionslehrer, Geistlicher, Prediger); **rablbinisch**
Räblchen *(landsch. auch für* frecher Bengel); **Ralbe,** der; -n, -n (↑R 126)

Rä|be, die; -, -n (*schweiz. für* Weiße Rübe)
Ra|bea (w. Vorn.)
Ra|be|lais [rab(ə)'lɛ] (franz. Satiriker)
Ra|ben‿aas (Schimpfwort), **...el|tern** (*Plur.;* lieblose Eltern), **...krä|he, ...mut|ter** (*Plur.* ...mütter; lieblose Mutter)
Ra|ben|schlacht, die; - (Schlacht bei Raben [Ravenna])
ra|ben|schwarz *(ugs.);* **Ra|ben‿stein** ([Richtstätte unter dem] Galgen), **...va|ter** (liebloser Vater), **...vo|gel**
ra|bi|at ‹lat.› (wütend; grob, gewalttätig)
Ra|bitz|wand; ↑R 95 ‹nach dem Erfinder› (Gipswand mit Drahtnetzeinlage)
Ra|bu|list, der; -en, -en (↑R 126) ‹lat.› (Wortverdreher, Haarspalter); **Ra|bu|lis|te|rei; Ra|bu|lis|tik,** die; -; **ra|bu|lis|tisch** (spitzfindig, wortklauberisch)
Ra|che, die; -; [an jmdm.] - nehmen; **Ra|che‿akt, ...durst; ra|che|dürs|tend** (↑R 40); **ra|che|durs|tig; Ra|che‿en|gel, ...ge|dan|ke, ...ge|lüs|te** *(Plur.),* **...göt|tin**
Ra|chel (w. Vorn.)
Ra|chen, der; -s, -
rä|chen; gerächt (*veraltet, aber noch scherzh.* gerochen); sich -
Ra|chen‿blüt|ler *(Bot.),* **...ka|tarrh** (↑R 33), **...man|del** (*vgl.* [1]Mandel), **...put|zer** (*ugs. scherzh. für* scharfes alkohol. Getränk)
Ra|che|plan; *vgl.* [2]Plan; **Rä|cher; Rä|che|rin; Ra|che|schwur; Rach|gier; rach|gie|rig**
Ra|chi|tis [...x...], die; -, ...itiden ‹griech.› (*Med.* durch Mangel an Vitamin D hervorgerufene Krankheit); **ra|chi|tisch**
Rach|ma|ni|now [...nɔf] (russ.-amerik. Komponist)
Rach|sucht, die; -; **rach|süch|tig**
Ra|cine [ra'si:n] (franz. Dramendichter)
Rack [rɛk], das; -s, -s ‹engl.› (Regal für eine Stereoanlage)
Ra|cke, die; -, -n (ein Vogel)
Ra|ckel‿huhn, ...wild
Ra|cker, der; -s, - (*fam. od. scherzh. für* Schlingel); **Ra|cke|rei,** die; - (*ugs. für* schwere, mühevolle Arbeit, Schinderei); **ra|ckern** (*ugs. für* sich abarbeiten); ich ...ere (↑R 16)
Ra|cket ['rɛkət], das; -s, -s ‹engl.› ([Tennis]schläger)
Rac|lette ['raklɛt, *auch* ...'klɛt] (↑R 130), die; -, -s, *auch* das; -s, -s ‹franz.› (ein Walliser Käsegericht); **Rac|lette|kä|se**
rad = Radiant
Rad, das; -[e]s, Räder; Rad fahren, ich fahre Rad, sie ist Rad gefahren, um Rad zu fahren, *aber* sie ist beim Radfahren verunglückt; Rad schlagen, ich schlage [ein] Rad, er hat [ein] Rad geschlagen, um Rad zu schlagen, *aber* er hat sich beim Radschlagen verletzt; wir kamen zu Rad [und nicht zu Fuß]; unter die Räder kommen (*ugs. für* völlig herunterkommen; eine empfindliche Niederlage hinnehmen müssen)
Ra|dar [*auch, österr. nur,* 'ra:...], der *od.* das; -s, -e ‹*aus engl.* radio detection and ranging›; **Ra|dar‿ast|ro|no|mie, ...fal|le** *(ugs.),* **...ge|rät, ...kon|trol|le, ...me|te|o|ro|lo|gie, ...pei|lung, ...schirm, ...sta|ti|on, ...tech|ni|ker, ...wa|gen**
Ra|dau, der; -s (*ugs. für* Lärm; Krach); - machen; **Ra|dau‿bru|der** (jmd., der Krach macht, randaliert), **...ma|cher**
Rad‿ball, ...bal|ler, ...ball|spiel; Rad‿brem|se, ...bruch (der); **Räd|chen; Rad|damp|fer**
Ra|de, die; -, -n (*kurz für* Kornrade)
ra|de|bre|chen; du radebrechst; du radebrechtest; geradebrecht; zu radebrechen
Ra|de|gund, Ra|de|gun|de (w. Vorn.)
Ra|de|ha|cke (*ostmitteld. für* Rodehacke)
ra|deln (Rad fahren); ich ...[e]le (↑R 16); **rä|deln** (ausradeln); ich ...[e]le (↑R 16)
Rä|dels|füh|rer
Ra|den|thein (österr. Ort)
Rä|der|chen *Plur.;* **Rä|der|ge|trie|be; ...rä|de|rig, ...räd|rig** (z. B. dreiräderig); **rä|dern** (*früher* durch das Rad hinrichten); ich ...ere (↑R 16); **Rä|der‿tier** (*meist Plur.;* Rundwurm), **...werk**
Ra|detz|ky (österr. Feldherr); **Ra|detz|ky|marsch,** der; -es (↑R 95)
Rad fah|ren *vgl.* Rad; **Rad|fah|ren** das; -s; **Rad|fah|rer; Rad|fah|rer|ho|se; Rad|fah|re|rin; Rad|fahr|weg; Rad|fel|ge**
Ra|di, der; -s, - (*bayr. u. österr. für* Rettich); einen - kriegen (*bayr. u. österr. ugs. für* gerügt werden)
ra|di|al ‹lat.› (auf den Radius bezogen, strahlenförmig; von einem Mittelpunkt ausgehend); **Ra|di|al‿ge|schwin|dig|keit, ...li|nie** (*österr. für* Straße, Straßenbahnlinie u. dgl., die von der Stadtmitte zum Stadtrand führt); **Ra|di|al‿rei|fen, ...sym|met|rie** (die; -);
Ra|di|ant, der; -en, -en; ↑R 126 (*Astron.* scheinbarer Ausgangspunkt der Sternschnuppen; *Math.* Einheit des ebenen Winkels; *Zeichen* rad); **ra|di|är** ‹franz.› (strahlig); **Ra|di|a|ti|on,** die; -, -en (Strahlung); **Ra|di|a|tor,** der; -s, ...oren (ein Heizkörper)
Ra|dic|chio [ra'dikio], der; -s ‹ital.› (eine ital. Zichorienart)
Ra|di|en (*Plur. von* Radius)
ra|die|ren ‹lat.›; **Ra|die|rer** (Künstler, der Radierungen anfertigt); **Ra|dier‿gum|mi** (der), **...kunst** (die; -; Ätzkunst), **...mes|ser** (das), **...na|del; Ra|die|rung** (mit einer geätzten Platte gedruckte Grafik)
Ra|dies|chen ‹lat.› (eine Pflanze);
ra|di|kal (politisch, weltanschaulich extrem; gründlich; rücksichtslos); **Ra|di|kal,** das; -s, -e (Atomgruppe chemischer Verbindungen); **Ra|di|ka|le,** der *u.* die; -n, -n (↑R 5 ff.); **Ra|di|ka|len|er|lass,** der; -es (Erlass, nach dem Mitglieder extremistischer Organisationen nicht im öffentlichen Dienst beschäftigt werden dürfen); **Ra|di|ka|lins|ki,** der; -s, -s (*ugs. für* Radikaler); **ra|di|ka|li|sie|ren** (radikal machen); **Ra|di|ka|li|sie|rung** (Entwicklung zum Radikalen); **Ra|di|ka|lis|mus,** der; -, ...men (rücksichtslos bis zum Äußersten gehende [politische, religiöse usw.] Richtung); **Ra|di|ka|list,** der; -en, -en (↑R 126); **Ra|di|ka|li|tät,** die; -; **Ra|di|kal‿kur, ...ope|ra|ti|on** (↑R 132); **Ra|di|kand,** der; -en, -en; ↑R 126 (*Math.* Zahl, deren Wurzel gezogen werden soll)
ra|di|o... ‹lat.›, **Ra|di|o...** (Strahlen..., [Rund]funk...); **Ra|dio,** das (*südd., österr. ugs., schweiz. für das Gerät auch* der); -s, -s (Rundfunk[gerät]); **ra|di|o|ak|tiv;** radioaktiver Niederschlag; radioaktive Stoffe; **Ra|di|o|ak|ti|vi|tät,** die; - (Eigenschaft der Atomkerne instabiler Isotope, sich ohne äußere Einflüsse umzuwandeln und dabei bestimmte Strahlen auszusenden); **Ra|di|o‿ama|teur** (↑R 132), **...ap|pa|rat, ...ast|ro|no|mie, ...che|mie, ...ele|ment** (↑R 132; radioaktives chem. Element), **...ge|rät; Ra|di|o|gramm,** das; -s, -e ‹lat.; griech.› (Röntgenbild); **Ra|di|o|gra|phie,** die; - (Untersuchung mit Röntgenstrahlen); **ra|di|o|gra|phisch; Ra|di|o|la|rie** [...iə], die; -, -n *meist Plur.* ‹lat.› (*Zool.* Strahlentierchen); **Ra|di|o|lo|ge,** der; -n, -n (↑R 126) ‹lat.; griech.› (*Med.*

Facharzt für Röntgenologie u. Strahlenheilkunde); **Ra|di|o|lo|gie**, die; - (Strahlenkunde); **Ra|di|o|lo|gin; ra|di|o|lo|gisch; Ra|di|o|me|te|o|ro|lo|gie; Ra|di|o|me|ter**, das; -s, - (*Physik* Strahlungsmessgerät); **Ra|di|o|met|rie** (↑R 130), die; -; **Ra|di|o|pho|nie**, die; - (*veraltet für* drahtlose Telefonie); **Ra|di|o‿pro|gramm, ...re|kor|der, ...röh|re, ...sen|der, ...son|de** *(Meteor., Physik)*, **...sta|ti|on, ...stern, ...tech|nik; Ra|di|o‿te|le|fo|nie** (*svw.* Radiophonie), **...te|le|gra|fie, ...te|le|skop** *(Astron.)*, **...the|ra|pie** (die; -, ...ien; Heilbehandlung durch Bestrahlung); **Ra|di|um**, das; -s ‹lat.› (radioaktives chem. Element, Metall; *Zeichen* Ra); **Ra|di|um‿be|strah|lung, ...ema|na|ti|on** (↑R 132; die; -; *ältere Bez. für* Radon); **ra|di|um|hal|tig; Ra|di|us**, der; -, ...ien [...iən] (Halbmesser des Kreises; *Abk. r, R*)

Ra|dix, die; -, ...izes [...tse:s] ‹lat.› (*fachspr. für* Wurzel); **ra|di|zie|ren** (*Math.* die Wurzel aus einer Zahl ziehen)

Rad‿kap|pe, ...kas|ten, ...kranz; [1]Rad|ler (Radfahrer); **[2]Rad|ler** (*landsch., bes. südd. für* Erfrischungsgetränk aus Bier u. Limonade); **Rad|ler|ho|se; Rad|le|rin; Rad|ler|maß**, die (*svw.* [2]Radler); **Rad‿ma|cher** (*landsch. für* Stellmacher), **...man|tel**

Ra|dolf, Ra|dulf (m. Vorn.)

Ra|dom, das; -s, -s ‹engl.› (Radarschutzkuppel, Traglufthalle)

Ra|don [*auch* ...'do:n], das; -s ‹lat.› (radioaktives chem. Element, Edelgas; *Zeichen* Rn)

Rad|renn|bahn; Rad|ren|nen; ...räd|rig *vgl.* ...räderig

Rad|scha [*auch* 'ra:...] (↑R 132), der; -s, -s ‹sanskr.› (ind. Fürstentitel)

Rad schla|gen *vgl.* Rad; **Rad|schla|gen**, das; -s; **Rad‿schuh** (Bremsklotz aus Holz od. Eisen), **...sport** (der; -[e]s), **...sport|ler**

Rad|stadt (Stadt im österr. Bundesland Salzburg); **Rad|städ|ter Tau|ern** *Plur.*

Rad‿stand, ...sturz, ...tour

Ra|dulf, Ra|dolf (m. Vorn.)

Rad‿wan|de|rung, ...wech|sel, ...weg

Raes|feld ['ra:s...] (Ort in Nordrhein-Westfalen)

RAF = Rote-Armee-Fraktion

R. A. F. = Royal Air Force

Räf, das; -s, -e (*schweiz. für* [1]Reff *u.* [2]Reff)

Ra|fa|el (*ökumen. u. österr. für* Raphael); *vgl. aber* Raffael

Raf|fa|el [...e:l, *auch* ...ɛl] (ital. Maler); *vgl. aber* Raphael; **raf|fa|e|lisch**; die raffaelische Madonna (↑R 94)

Raf|fel, die; -, -n (*landsch. für* großer, hässlicher Mund; loses Mundwerk; geschwätzige [alte] Frau; Gerät zum Abstreifen von Heidelbeeren; Reibeisen; Klapper); **raf|feln** (*landsch. für* raspeln; rasseln; schwatzen); ich ...[e]le (↑R 16)

raf|fen; Raff|gier; raff|gie|rig; raf|fig (*landsch. für* raff-, habgierig)

Raf|fi|na|de, die; -, -n ‹franz.› (gereinigter Zucker); **Raf|fi|nat**, das; -[e]s, -e (Produkt der Raffination); **Raf|fi|na|ti|on**, die; -, -en (Verfeinerung, Veredelung); **Raf|fi|ne|ment** [...'mã:], das; -s, -s (Überfeinerung; durchtriebene Schlauheit); **Raf|fi|ne|rie**, die; -, ...ien (Anlage zum Reinigen von Zucker od. zur Verarbeitung von Rohöl); **Raf|fi|nes|se**, die; -, -n (Durchtriebenheit, Schlauheit); **Raf|fi|neur** [...'nø:r], der; -s, -e (Maschine zum Feinmahlen von Holzsplittern [zur Papierherstellung]); **raf|fi|nie|ren** (Zucker reinigen; Rohöl zu Brenn- od. Treibstoff verarbeiten); **Raf|fi|nier‿ofen** (↑R 132), **...stahl** (der; -[e]s); **raf|fi|niert** (gereinigt; durchtrieben, schlau); -er Zucker; ein -er Betrüger; **Raf|fi|niert|heit; Raf|fi|no|se**, die; - (zuckerartige chem. Verbindung)

Raff|ke, der; -s, -s (*ugs. für* raffgieriger Mensch); **Raff|sucht**, die; -; **Raf|fung; Raff|zahn** (*landsch. für* stark überstehender Zahn; *ugs. für* raffgieriger Mensch)

Raft, das; -s, -s ‹engl.› (schwimmende Insel aus Treibholz); **Raf|ting**, das; -s (das Wildwasserfahren einer Gruppe im Schlauchboot)

Rag [rɛg], der; -s (*Kurzform von* Ragtime)

Ra|gaz, Bad (schweiz. Badeort)

Ra|ge ['ra:ʒə, *österr.* ra:ʒ], die; - ‹franz.› (*ugs. für* Wut, Raserei); in der -; in - bringen

ra|gen

Ra|gio|ne [ra'dʒo:nə], die; -, -n ‹ital.› (*schweiz. für* Firma, die im Handelsregister eingetragen ist); **Ra|gio|nen|buch** (*schweiz. für* Verzeichnis der Ragionen)

Rag|lan [*engl.* 'rɛglən] (↑R 130), der; -s, -s ‹engl.› ([Sport]mantel mit angeschnittenem Ärmel); **Rag|lan‿är|mel, ...schnitt**

Rag|na|rök, die; - ‹altnord.› (*nord. Mythol.* Weltuntergang)

Ra|gout [ra'gu:], das; -s, -s ‹franz.› (Gericht aus Fleisch-, Wild-, Geflügel- od. Fischstückchen in pikanter Soße); **Ra|gout fin**, *fachspr.* **Ra|goût fin** [ra.gu 'fɛ̃:], das; - -, -s -s [- 'fɛ̃:] (feines Ragout [aus Kalbfleisch])

Rag|time ['rɛgtaim], der; - ‹amerik.› (afroamerikanischer Stil populärer Klaviermusik)

Ra|gu|sa (*ital. Name von* Dubrovnik)

Rag|wurz (eine Orchideengattung)

Rah, Ra|he, die; -, Rahen (*Seemannsspr.* Querstange am Mast für das Rahsegel)

Ra|hel (w. Vorn.)

Rahm, der; -[e]s (*landsch. für* Sahne)

Rähm, der; -[e]s, -e (*Bauw.* waagerechter Teil des Dachstuhls); **Rähm|chen; rah|men; Rah|men**, der; -s, -; **Rah|men‿ab|kom|men, ...an|ten|ne, ...be|din|gung** *(meist Plur.)*, **...bruch** (der; -[e]s, ...brüche), **...er|zäh|lung; rah|men|ge|näht**; -e Schuhe; **Rah|men‿ge|setz, ...naht, ...plan** (*vgl.* [2]Plan), **...pro|gramm, ...richt|li|nie** *(meist Plur.)*, **...ta|rif, ...ver|ein|ba|rung**

rah|mig (*landsch. für* sahnig); **Rahm‿kä|se, ...so|ße, ...spei|se** *(landsch.)*

Rah|mung

Rah|ne, die; -, -n (*südd., österr. für* rote Rübe); *vgl.* Rande

Rah|se|gel *(Seemannsspr.)*

Raid [re:d], der; -s, -s ‹engl.› (Überraschungsangriff)

Raiff|ei|sen (Familienn.); **Raiff|ei|sen|bank** *Plur.* ...banken

Rai|gras, das; -es ‹engl.; dt.› (Name verschiedener Grasarten)

[1]Rai|mund, Rei|mund (m. Vorn.)

[2]Rai|mund (österr. Dramatiker)

Rain, der; -[e]s, -e (Ackergrenze; *schweiz. u. südd. für* Abhang)

Rai|nald, Rei|nald (m. Vorn.); Rainald von Dassel (Kanzler Friedrichs I. Barbarossa)

rai|nen (*veraltet für* ab-, umgrenzen)

Rai|ner, Rei|ner (m. Vorn.)

Rain|farn (eine Pflanze); **Rai|nung** (*veraltet für* Festsetzung der Ackergrenze); - und Steinung *(veraltet)*; **Rain|wei|de** (Liguster)

Rai|son [rɛ'zõ:] usw. *vgl.* Räson usw.

ra|jo|len (*svw.* rigolen)

Ra|ke *vgl.* Racke

Ra|kel, die; -, -n (*Druckw.* Vorrichtung zum Abstreichen überschüssiger Farbe von der eingefärbten Druckform)

rä|keln *vgl.* rekeln
Ra|ke|te, die; -, -n ‹ital.› (ein Feuerwerkskörper; ein Flugkörper); **Ra|ke|ten‿ab|schuss|ram|pe, ...ab|wehr, ...an|griff, ...an|trieb, ...ap|pa|rat** *(Rettungswesen),* **...au|to, ...ba|sis; ra|ke|ten|be|stückt** (↑R 40); **Ra|ke|ten‿flug|zeug, ...schlit|ten, ...start, ...stu|fe, ...stütz|punkt, ...treib|stoff, ...trieb|werk, ...waf|fe, ...wer|fer, ...zeit|al|ter** (das; -s)
Ra|kett, das; -[e]s, *Plur.* -e *u.* -s *(eindeutschend für* Racket)
Ra|ki, der; -[s], -s ‹türk.› (ein Branntwein aus Rosinen u. Anis)
Ralf (m. Vorn.)
Ral|le, die; -, -n (ein Vogel)
ral|li|ie|ren ‹franz.› *(veraltet für* zerstreute Truppen sammeln); **Ral|lye** ['rali, *auch* 'rɛli], die; -, -s, *schweiz.* das; -s, -s ‹engl.-franz.› (Autosternfahrt); **Ral|lye|cross,** das; -, -e (Autorennen auf Rennstrecken mit wechselndem Streckenbelag); **Ral|lye‿fah|rer, ...fah|re|rin**
Ralph (m. Vorn.)
RAM, das; -[s], -[s] ‹*aus engl.* random access memory› *(EDV* Informationsspeicher mit wahlfreiem Zugriff)
Ra|ma|dan, der; -[s] ‹arab.› (Fastenmonat der Moslems)
Ra|ma|ja|na, das; - ‹sanskr.› (ind. religiöses Nationalepos)
Ra|ma|su|ri, die; - ‹ital.› *(bayr. u. österr. ugs. für* großes Durcheinander; Trubel)
Ram|bo, der; -s, -s ‹nach dem amerik. Filmhelden› *(ugs. für* jmd., der sich rücksichtslos [u. mit Gewalt] durchsetzt)
Ram|bouil|let [rãbu'je:] (franz. Stadt); **Ram|bouil|let|schaf** (ein feinwolliges Schaf); ↑R 105
Ram|bur, der; -s, -e ‹franz.› (Apfel einer bestimmten säuerlichen Sorte)
Ra|mes|si|de, der; -n, -n; ↑R 126 (Herrscher aus dem Geschlecht des Ramses)
Ra|mie, die; -, ...ien ‹malai.-engl.› (Bastfaser, Chinagras)
Ramm, der; -[e]s, -e (Rammsporn [früher an Kriegsschiffen]); **Ramm‿bär** (der; -s, *Plur.* -en, *fachspr. auch* -e), **...bock, ...bug; ramm|dö|sig** *(ugs. für* benommen; überreizt); **Ram|me,** die; -, -n (Fallklotz); **[1]Ram|mel,** die; -, -n *(veraltet für* Ramme); **[2]Ram|mel,** der; -s, - *(landsch. für* ungehobelter Kerl, Tölpel); **Ram|me|lei** *(ugs.);* **ram|meln** *(auch Jägerspr.* belegen, decken [bes. von Hasen und Kaninchen]; *derb für* koitieren); **ram|men** (mit der Ramme eintreiben; [mit Wucht] gegen ein Hindernis stoßen); **Ramm‿ham|mer, ...klotz; Ramm|ler** (Männchen von Hasen u. Kaninchen); **Ramm|ma|schi|ne** (↑R 136); **Ramms|kopf** (Pferdekopf mit stark gekrümmtem Nasenrücken); **Ramm|sporn,** der; -[e]s, -e
Ram|pe, die; -, -n ‹franz.› (schiefe Ebene zur Überwindung von Höhenunterschieden; Auffahrt; Verladebühne; *Theater* Vorbühne); **Ram|pen|licht,** das; -[e]s
ram|po|nie|ren ‹ital.› *(ugs. für* stark beschädigen)
Ram|sau [*auch* 'ramsau] (↑R 132; Name verschiedener Orte in Südbayern u. Österreich)
[1]Ramsch, der; -[e]s, -e *Plur. selten (ugs. für* wertloses Zeug; minderwertige Ware)
[2]Ramsch, der; -[e]s, -e ‹franz.› (Spielart beim Skat, mit dem Ziel, möglichst wenig Punkte zu bekommen)
[1]ram|schen ‹*zu* [1]Ramsch› *(ugs. für* Ramschware billig aufkaufen); du ramschst
[2]ram|schen (einen [2]Ramsch spielen); du ramschst
Ram|scher ‹*zu* [1]Ramsch› *(ugs. für* Aufkäufer zu Schleuderpreisen); **Ramsch|la|den; Ramsch|wa|re; ramsch|wei|se**
Ram|ses (Name ägypt. Könige)
ran; ↑R 13 *(ugs. für* heran)
Ran *(nord. Mythol.* Gattin des Meerriesen Ägir)
Ranch [rɛntʃ], die; -, -[e]s ‹amerik.› (nordamerik. Viehwirtschaft, Farm); **Ran|cher,** der; -s, -[s] (nordamerik. Viehzüchter, Farmer)
[1]Rand, der; -[e]s, Ränder; außer Rand und Band sein *(ugs.);* zurande, *auch* zu Rande kommen
[2]Rand [rɛnd], der; -s, -[s] ‹engl.› (Währungseinheit der Republik Südafrika; *Abk.* R); 5 - (↑R 90)
Ran|dal, der; -s, -e *(veraltet für* Lärm, Gejohle); **Ran|da|le,** die; -; *meist in der Wendung* - machen *(ugs. für* randalieren); **ran|da|lie|ren; Ran|da|lie|rer**
Rand‿al|ko|ho|li|ker, ...aus|gleich, ...be|din|gung *(meist Plur.),* **...beet, ...be|mer|kung, ...be|zirk; Ränd|chen**
Ran|de, die; -, -n *(schweiz. für* Rote Rübe); *vgl.* Rahne
Rän|del|mut|ter *Plur.* ...muttern; **rän|deln** (mit einer Randverzierung versehen; riffeln); ich ...[e]le (↑R 16); **Rän|del‿rad, ...schrau|be; Rän|de|lung**
Rän|der *(Plur. von* [1]Rand); **...rän|de|rig** *vgl.* ...randig; **rän|dern;** ich ...ere (↑R 16); **Rand‿er|schei|nung, ...fi|gur, ...ge|biet, ...ge|bir|ge, ...glos|se, ...grup|pe** *(bes. Soziologie);* **...ran|dig,** *auch* ...rän|de|rig, ...rdnd|rig (z. B. breitrandig, *auch* -ränd[e]rig); **Rand|la|ge; Rand|leis|te; rand|los;** -e Brille; **Rand‿lö|ser** (an der Schreibmaschine), **...no|tiz**
Ran|dolf, Ran|dulf (m. Vorn.)
...ränd|rig *vgl.* ...randig; **Rand‿sied|lung, ...staat** *(Plur.* ...staaten), **...stein, ...stel|ler** (an der Schreibmaschine), **...strei|fen**
Ran|dulf, Ran|dolf (m. Vorn.)
Rand|ver|zie|rung; rand|voll; ein randvolles Glas; **Rand‿wäh|ler, ...zeich|nung, ...zo|ne**
Ranft, der; -[e]s, Ränfte *(landsch. für* Brotkanten, -kruste); **Ränft|chen, Ränft|lein**
Rang, der; -[e]s, Ränge ‹franz.›; jmdm. den - ablaufen (jmdn. überflügeln, übertreffen); der erste, zweite -; ein Sänger von -; **Rang‿ab|zei|chen, ...äl|tes|te**
Ran|ge, die; -, -n, *selten* der; -n, -n; ↑R 126 *(landsch. für* unartiges Kind)
ran|ge|hen; ↑R 13 *(ugs. für* herangehen; etwas energisch anpacken)
Ran|ge|lei; ran|geln *(für* sich balgen, raufen); ich ...[e]le (↑R 16)
Ran|ger ['re:ndʒə(r)], der; -s, -s ‹amerik.› (Soldat mit Spezialausbildung; Aufseher in Nationalparks; *früher* Angehöriger einer Polizeitruppe in Nordamerika [z. B. Texas Ranger])
Rang‿er|hö|hung, ...fol|ge; rang|gleich; Rang|höchs|te, der *u.* die; -n, -n (↑R 5 ff.); **rang|hö|her**
Ran|gier|bahn|hof [raŋ'ʒi:..., *österr.* ran'ʒi:..., *selten* rã'ʒi:...]; **ran|gie|ren** ‹franz.› (einen Rang innehaben [vor, hinter jmdm.]; *Eisenb.* verschieben; *landsch. für* ordnen); **Ran|gie|rer; Ran|gier‿gleis, ...lok, ...lo|ko|mo|ti|ve, ...meis|ter; Ran|gie|rung**
...ran|gig (z. B. zweitrangig); **Rang‿lis|te, ...lo|ge; rang|mä|ßig; Rang‿ord|nung, ...stu|fe**
Ran|gun [raŋ'gu:n] (Hptst. von Birma); **Ran|gun|reis,** der
Rang|un|ter|schied
ran|hal|ten, sich; ↑R 13 *(ugs. für* sich beeilen)
rank *(geh. für* schlank; geschmeidig); rank und schlank
Rank, der; -[e]s, Ränke *(schweiz. für* Wegkrümmung; Kniff, Trick); den Rank (eine geschickte Lösung) finden; *vgl.* Ränke
Ran|ke, die; -, -n (Pflanzenteil)

Rän|ke *Plur.* (*veraltend für* Intrigen, Machenschaften); Ränke schmieden; *vgl.* Rank
ran|ken; sich -
Ran|ken, der; -s, - (*landsch. für* dickes Stück Brot)
ran|ken|ar|tig; Ran|ken₋ge|wächs, ...werk (das; -[e]s; ein Ornament)
Rän|ke₋schmied *(veraltend),* **...spiel, ...sucht** (die; -); **rän|ke₋süch|tig, ...voll**
ran|kig
ran|klot|zen; ↑R 13 (*ugs. für* viel arbeiten); **ran|krie|gen;** ↑R 13 (*ugs. für* zur Verantwortung ziehen; hart arbeiten lassen)
Ran|kü|ne, die; -, -n ‹franz.› (*veraltend für* Groll, heimliche Feindschaft; Rachsucht)
ran|las|sen; ↑R 13 (*ugs. für* jmdm. die Gelegenheit geben, seine Fähigkeiten zu beweisen; sich zum Geschlechtsverkehr bereit finden); **ran|müs|sen;** ↑R 13 (*ugs. für* [mit]arbeiten müssen); **ran|schmei|ßen,** sich; ↑R 13 (*ugs. für* sich anbiedern)
Ra|nun|kel, die; -, -n ‹lat.› (ein Hahnenfußgewächs)
Ränz|chen; Rän|zel, das, *nordd. auch* der; -s, - (kleiner Ranzen)
ran|zen (*Jägerspr.* begatten [von Fuchs, Marder u. anderen Raubtieren])
Ran|zen, der; -s, - (Schultasche; *ugs. für* dicker Bauch)
Ran|zer (*landsch. für* grober Tadel)
ran|zig ‹niederl.›; -es Öl, -e Butter
Ran|zi|on, die; -, -en ‹franz.› (*früher für* Lösegeld); **ran|zi|o|nie|ren** (*früher für* freikaufen)
Ränz|lein
Ranz|zeit ‹*zu* ranzen›
Ra|oul [ra'u:l] (m. Vorn.)
Rap [rɛp], der; -[s], -s ‹engl.-amerik.› (rhythmischer Sprechgesang in der Popmusik)
Ra|pal|lo (Seebad bei Genua); **Ra|pal|lo|ver|trag,** der; -[e]s
Rap|fen, der; -s, - (ein Karpfenfisch)
Ra|pha|el, *ökum. u. österr.* Ra|fa|el [...e:l, *auch* ...ɛl] (einer der Erzengel); *vgl. aber* Raffael
Ra|phia, die; -, ...ien [...i̯ən] ‹madagass.› (afrik. Bastpalme, Nadelpalme); **Ra|phi|a|bast**
Ra|phi|den *Plur.* ‹griech.› (*Bot.* nadelförmige Kristalle in Pflanzenzellen)
ra|pid, *österr. nur so, od.* **ra|pi|de** ‹lat.› (überaus schnell); **Ra|pi|di|tät,** die; -
Ra|pier, das; -s, -e ‹franz.› (Fechtwaffe, Degen)
Rapp, der; -s, -e (*landsch. für* Traubenkamm, entbeerte Traube)
Rap|pe, der; -n, -n; ↑R 126 (schwarzes Pferd)
Rap|pel, der; -s, - (*ugs. für* plötzlicher Zorn; Verrücktheit); **rap|pe|lig,** rapp|lig *(ugs.);* **Rap|pel|kopf** (*ugs. für* aufbrausender Mensch); **rap|pel|köp|fisch** *(ugs.);* **rap|peln** (klappern; *österr. für* verrückt sein); ich ...[e]le (↑R 16); **rap|pel|tro|cken** (völlig trocken)
Rap|pen, der; -s, - (schweiz. Münze; *Abk.* Rp.; 100 Rappen = 1 Schweizer Franken); **Rap|pen|spal|ter** (*schweiz. für* Pfennigfuchser)
Rap|per ['rɛpə], der; -s, - ‹*zu* Rap› (Rapsänger); **Rap|ping** ['rɛpɪŋ], das; -s (*svw.* Rap)
rapp|lig *vgl.* rappelig
Rap|port, der; -[e]s, -e ‹franz.› (Bericht, dienstl. Meldung; *Textiltechnik* Musterwiederholung bei Geweben); **rap|por|tie|ren**
Rapp|schim|mel (Pferd)
raps!; rips, raps!
Raps, der; -es, *Plur. (Sorten:)* -e (eine Ölpflanze); **Raps₋acker** (↑R 132), **...blü|te**
rap|schen (*landsch. für* hastig wegnehmen; du rapschst) *u.* **rapsen** (du rapst)
Raps₋erd|floh, ...feld, ...glanz|käfer, ...ku|chen *(Landw.),* **...öl** (das; -[e]s)
Rap|tus, der; -, *Plur.* - [...tu:s] *u.* (*für* Rappel:) -se ‹lat.› (*Med.* Anfall von Raserei; *scherzh. für* Rappel)
Ra|pünz|chen (Feldsalat); **Ra|pünz|chen|sa|lat; Ra|pun|ze,** die; -, -n; *vgl.* Rapunzel; **Ra|pun|zel,** die; -, -n (*landsch. für* Rapünzchen)
Ra|pu|se, die; - ‹tschech.›; *in den Wendungen* in die - kommen *od.* gehen (*landsch. für* verloren gehen); in die - geben (*landsch. für* preisgeben)
rar ‹lat.› (selten); sich rar machen (*ugs. für* selten kommen); **Ra|ri|tät,** die; -, -en (seltenes Stück, seltene Erscheinung); **Ra|ri|tä|ten₋ka|bi|nett, ...samm|lung**
Ras, der; -, - ‹arab.› (Vorgebirge; Berggipfel; *früher* äthiop. Fürstentitel)
ra|sant ‹lat.› (*ugs. für* sehr schnell; schnittig; schwungvoll, begeisternd; sehr flach, gestreckt verlaufend [von Geschossbahnen]); **Ra|sanz,** die; -
ra|sau|nen (*landsch. für* lärmen, poltern); er hat rasaunt
rasch
ra|scheln; ich ...[e]le (↑R 16)
ra|sches|tens; Rasch|heit, die; -; **rasch₋le|big, ...wüch|sig**
ra|sen (wüten; toben; sehr schnell fahren, rennen); du rast; er ras|te
Ra|sen, der; -s, -; **Ra|sen|bank** *Plur.* ...bänke; **ra|sen₋be|deckt, ...be|wach|sen; Ra|sen|blei|che**
ra|send (wütend; schnell); rasend werden, *aber* (↑R 50): es ist zum Rasendwerden
Ra|sen₋de|cke, ...flä|che, ...mäher, ...spiel, ...sport (der; -[e]s), **...spren|ger, ...strei|fen, ...tennis, ...tep|pich**
Ra|ser (*ugs. für* unverantwortlich schnell Fahrender); **Ra|se|rei**
Ra|sier₋ap|pa|rat, ...creme; ra|sie|ren ‹franz.›; sich -; **Ra|sie|rer** (*kurz für* Rasierapparat); **Ra|sier₋klin|ge, ...mes|ser** (das), **...pin|sel, ...schaum** (der; -[e]s), **...sei|fe, ...sitz** (*ugs. scherzh. für* Sitz in der ersten Reihe im Kino), **...spie|gel, ...was|ser** (*Plur.* ...wasser *od.* ...wässer), **...zeug**
ra|sig (mit Rasen bewachsen)
Rä|son [rɛ'zɔŋ, *auch* rɛ'zõ:], die; - ‹franz.› (*veraltend für* Vernunft, Einsicht); jmdn. zur Räson bringen; **Rä|so|neur** [...'nø:r], der; -s, -e (*veraltet für* jmd., der ständig räsoniert); **rä|so|nie|ren** (sich wortreich äußern; *ugs. für* ständig schimpfen); **Rä|son|ne|ment** [...'mã:], das; -s, -s (*veraltend für* vernünftige Überlegung, Erwägung)
Ras|pa, die; -, -s, *ugs. auch* der; -s, -s ‹span.› (ein lateinamerik. Gesellschaftstanz)
[1]Ras|pel, die; -, -n (ein Werkzeug); **[2]Ras|pel,** der; -s, - *meist Plur.* (geraspeltes Stückchen [von Schokolade, Kokosnuss u. a.]); **ras|peln;** ich ...[e]le (↑R 16)
Ras|pu|tin [*russ.* ...'pu...] (russ. Eigenn.)
raß *(südd.),* **räß** (*südd., schweiz. mdal. für* scharf gewürzt, beißend [von Speisen])
Ras|se, die; -, -n ‹franz.›; die weiße, gelbe, schwarze, rote -; **Ras|se|hund**
Ras|sel, die; -, -n (Knarre, Klapper); **Ras|sel|ban|de,** die; -, -n (*scherzh. für* übermütige, zu Lärm u. Streichen aufgelegte Kinderschar); **Ras|se|lei; Ras|se|ler,** Rass|ler; **ras|seln;** ich rass[e]le (↑R 16)
Ras|sen₋dis|kri|mi|nie|rung (die; -), **...for|scher, ...for|schung, ...fra|ge, ...ge|setz, ...hass, ...het|ze, ...kra|wall, ...kreuzung, ...kun|de** (die; -), **...merkmal, ...mi|schung, ...prob|lem,**

...tren|nung, ...un|ru|hen (Plur.); **Ras|se|pferd; ras|se|rein; Ras|se|rein|heit**, die; -; **ras|se|ver|e|delnd; ras|sig** (von ausgeprägter Art); vgl. reinrassig; **ras|sisch** (der Rasse entsprechend, auf die Rasse bezogen); **Ras|sis|mus**, der; - (übersteigertes Rassenbewusstsein, Rassenhetze); **Ras|sist**, der; -en, -en; ↑R 126 (Vertreter des Rassismus); **Ras|sis|tin; ras|sis|tisch**

Rass|ler vgl. Rasseler

Rast, die; -, -en; ohne Rast und Ruh

Ra|statt (Stadt im Oberrhein. Tiefland); **Ra|stat|ter** (↑R 103)

Ras|te, die; -, -n (Stützkerbe)

Ras|tel, das; -s, - ‹ital.› (*österr. für* Schutzgitter, Drahtgeflecht); **Ras|tel|bin|der** (*österr. veraltet für* Siebmacher, Kesselflicker)

ras|ten

[1]**Ras|ter**, der; -s, - ‹lat.› (Glasplatte od. Folie mit engem Liniennetz zur Zerlegung eines Bildes in Rasterpunkte); [2]**Ras|ter**, das; -s, - (Fläche des Fernsehbildschirmes, die sich aus Lichtpunkten zusammensetzt); **Ras|ter‿ät|zung** (Autotypie), **...fahn|dung** (mithilfe von Computern durchgeführte Überprüfung eines großen Personenkreises); **Ras|ter|mik|ro|skop; ras|tern** (ein Bild durch Raster in Rasterpunkte zerlegen); ich ...ere (↑R 16); **Ras|ter‿plat|te, ...punkt; Ras|te|rung**

Rast‿haus, ...hof; rast|los; Rast|lo|sig|keit, die; -; **Rast|platz**

Rast|ral (↑R 130), das; -s, -e ‹lat.› (Gerät zum Ziehen von Notenlinien); **rast|rie|ren**

Rast‿stät|te, ...tag

Ra|sur, die; -, -en ‹lat.› (Tilgung durch Schaben od. Radieren mit einer Klinge; das Rasieren)

Rat, der; -[e]s, *Plur.* (*für* Personen u. Institutionen:) Räte; sich Rat holen (↑R 39); sich Rat suchend an jmd. wenden; einen Rat Suchenden, *auch* Ratsuchenden nicht abweisen; zurate, *auch* zu Rate gehen, ziehen; jmdn. um Rat fragen; (↑R 108:) der Große Rat (*schweiz. Bez. für* Kantonsparlament); der Hohe Rat (in Jerusalem zur Zeit Jesu)

Rät, Rhät, das; -s ‹nach den Rätischen Alpen› (jüngste Stufe des Keupers)

Ra|tan|hi|a|wur|zel [ra'tani̯a...] ‹indian.; dt.› ([als Heilmittel verwendete] Wurzel einer südamerik. Pflanze)

Ra|ta|touille [rata'tuj], die; -, -s *u.* das; -s, -s ‹franz.› (*Gastron.* Gemüse aus Tomaten, Auberginen, Paprika usw.)

Ra|te, die; -, -n ‹ital.› (Teilzahlung; Teilbetrag)

Rä|te|de|mo|kra|tie

ra|ten; du rätst, er rät; du rietst; du rietest, er riet; geraten; rat[e]!

Ra|ten‿be|trag, ...ge|schäft, ...kauf, ...wech|sel; ra|ten|wei|se; Ra|ten|zah|lung; Ra|ten|zah|lungs|kre|dit

Ra|ter

Rä|ter (Bewohner des alten Rätien)

Rä|te‿re|gie|rung, ...re|pub|lik; Ra|te|rin; Rä|te|russ|land; Ra|te|spiel; Rä|te‿staat (*Plur.* ...staaten), **...sys|tem; Ra|te|team; Rat‿ge|ber, ...ge|be|rin; Rat|haus; Rat|haus|saal**

Ra|the|nau (dt. Staatsmann)

Ra|the|now [...no:] (Stadt an der Havel)

Rä|ti|en [...i̯ən] (altröm. Prov., *auch für* Graubünden); vgl. Räter u. rätisch

Ra|ti|fi|ka|ti|on, die; -, -en ‹lat.› (Genehmigung; Bestätigung, Anerkennung, bes. von völkerrechtl. Verträgen); **Ra|ti|fi|ka|ti|ons|ur|kun|de; ra|ti|fi|zie|ren; Ra|ti|fi|zie|rung**

Rä|ti|kon, das; -s, *auch* der; -[s] (Teil der Ostalpen an der österr.-schweiz. Grenze)

Rä|tin (Titel)

Ra|ti|né [...'ne:], der; -s, -s ‹franz.› (ratiniertes Gewebe); **ra|ti|nie|ren** (*Textiltechnik* Knötchen od. Wellen [auf Gewebe] erzeugen)

Ra|tio, die; - ‹lat.› (Vernunft; logischer Verstand); vgl. Ultima Ratio; **Ra|ti|on**, die; -, -en ‹franz.› (zugeteiltes Maß, [An]teil; täglicher Verpflegungssatz); die eiserne -; **ra|ti|o|nal** ‹lat.› (vernünftig, aus der Vernunft stammend; begrifflich fassbar); rationale Zahlen (*Math.*); **Ra|ti|o|na|li|sa|tor**, der; -s, ...oren (jmd., der rationalisiert); **ra|ti|o|na|li|sie|ren** ‹franz.› (zweckmäßiger u. wirtschaftlicher gestalten); **Ra|ti|o|na|li|sie|rung; Ra|ti|o|na|li|sie|rungs|maß|nah|me; Ra|ti|o|na|lis|mus**, der; - ‹lat.› (Geisteshaltung, die das rationale Denken als einzige Erkenntnisquelle ansieht); **Ra|ti|o|na|list**, der; -en, -en (↑R 126); **Ra|ti|o|na|lis|tin; ra|ti|o|na|lis|tisch; Ra|ti|o|na|li|tät**, die; - (rationales, vernünftiges Wesen; Vernünftigkeit); **ra|ti|o|nell** ‹franz.› (zweckmäßig, wirtschaftlich); **ra|ti|o|nen|wei|se** *od.* ra|ti|ons|wei|se; **ra|ti|o|nie|ren** (einteilen; in relativ kleinen Mengen zuteilen); **Ra|ti|o|nie|rung**

rä|tisch ‹*zu* Räter, Rätien›, *aber* (↑R 102): die Rätischen Alpen

rät|lich (*veraltend für* ratsam); **rat|los; Rat|lo|sig|keit**, die; -

Rä|to|ro|ma|ne[1], der; -n, -n; ↑R 106 *u.* 126 (Angehöriger eines Alpenvolkes mit eigener roman. Sprache); **rä|to|ro|ma|nisch**[1]; **Rä|to|ro|ma|nisch**[1], das; -[s] (Sprache); vgl. Deutsch; **Rä|to|ro|ma|ni|sche**[1], das; -n; vgl. Deutsche, das

rat|sam; Rats|be|schluss

ratsch!; ritsch, ratsch!; **Rat|sche** (*südd., österr.*), **Rät|sche** [*schweiz.* 'rɛt͡ʃə], die; -, -n (*südd., schweiz. für* Rassel, Klapper; *ugs. auch für* schwatzhafte Person); **rat|schen** (*südd., österr.*), **rät|schen** [*schweiz.* 'rɛt͡ʃən] (*südd., schweiz. ugs. auch für* schwatzen, über jmdn. reden); du ratschst

Rat|schlag, der; -[e]s, ...schläge; **rat|schla|gen** (*veraltend*); du ratschlagst; du ratschlagtest; geratschlagt; zu ratschlagen; **Rat|schluss; Rats|die|ner**

Rät|sel, das; -s, -; Rätsel raten, *aber* (↑R 50): das Rätselraten; **Rät|sel‿ecke** (↑R 132), **...fra|ge, ...freund; rät|sel|haft; Rät|sel|haf|tig|keit; Rät|sel|lö|ser; Rät|sel|lö|sung; rät|seln**; ich ...[e]le (↑R 16); **Rät|sel|ra|ten**, das; -s; **rät|sel|voll; Rät|sel‿zeit|schrift, ...zei|tung**

Rats‿herr (*veraltend*), **...kel|ler, ...schrei|ber** (*veraltet, noch landsch.*), **...sit|zung; Rat su|chend** vgl. Rat; **Rat|su|chen|de**, der *u.* die; -n, -n (↑R 5 ff.); vgl. Rat; **Rats|ver|samm|lung**

Rat|tan, das; -s, -e ‹malai.› (*svw.* Peddigrohr)

Rat|te, die; -, -n; **Rat|ten‿be|kämp|fung, ...fal|le, ...fän|ger, ...gift** (das), **...kö|nig** (*auch ugs. übertr. für* unentwirrbare Schwierigkeit), **...schwanz** (*ugs. übertr. für* endlose Folge), **...schwänz|chen** (*scherzh. für* kurzer, dünner Haarzopf)

Rät|ter, der; -s, -, *auch* die; -, -n (*Technik* Sieb)

rat|tern; ich ...ere (↑R 16)

rät|tern (mit dem Rätter sieben); ich ...ere (↑R 16); **Rät|ter|wä|sche** (ein Siebverfahren)

Ratt|ler, der; -s, - (*veraltet* für den Rattenfang geeigneter Hund)

Ratz, der; -es, -e (*landsch. für* Ratte, Hamster; *Jägerspr.* Iltis); **Rat|ze**, die; -, -n (*ugs. für* Ratte)

---

[1] [*auch* 'rɛ:...]

Rat|ze|fum|mel, der; -s, - (*Schülerspr.* Radiergummi)
rat|ze|kahl ⟨*umgebildet aus* radikal⟩ (*ugs. für* gänzlich leer, kahl);
Rät|zel, das; -s, - (*landsch. für* zusammengewachsene Augenbrauen; Mensch mit solchen Brauen);
[1]**rat|zen** (*ugs. für* schlafen); du ratzt
[2]**rat|zen** (*landsch. für* ritzen); du ratzt
rau; ein raues Wesen; ein rauer Ton; eine raue Luft; ein noch raueres Klima; die rau[e]sten Sitten
Raub, der; -[e]s, -e
Rau|bank *Plur.* ...bänke (langer Hobel); **Rau|bauz,** der; -es, -e (*ugs. für* grober Mensch); **rau|bau|zig** (*ugs. für* grob, derb)
Raub|bau, der; -[e]s; - treiben; **Raub|druck,** der; -[e]s, -e
Rau|bein, das; -[e]s, -e (äußerlich grober, aber im Grunde gutmütiger Mensch); **rau|bei|nig**
rau|ben; Räu|ber; Räu|ber|ban|de; Räu|be|rei; Räu|ber‿ge|schich|te, ...haupt|mann, ...höh|le; Räu|be|rin; räu|be|risch; räu|bern; ich ...ere (↑R 16); **Räu|ber‿pis|to|le** (Räubergeschichte), **...zi|vil** (*ugs. scherzh. für* sehr legere Kleidung); **Raub‿fisch, ...gier; raub|gie|rig; Raub‿kat|ze, ...ko|pie, ...mord, ...mör|der**
rau|bors|tig
Raub‿pres|sung (von Schallplatten), **...rit|ter; Raub|rit|ter|tum,** das; -s; **raub|süch|tig; Raub‿tier, ...über|fall** (↑R 132), **...vo|gel** (*ältere Bez. für* Greifvogel), **...wild** (*Jägerspr.* alle jagdbaren Raubtiere), **...zeug** (das; -[e]s; *Jägerspr.* alle nicht jagdbaren Raubtiere), **...zug**
Rauch, der; -[e]s; **Rauch‿ab|zug, ...bier, ...bom|be; rau|chen;** rauchende Schwefelsäure; **Rau|cher; Räu|cher|aal; Rau|cher‿ab|teil, ...bein; Rau|che|rei; Räu|che|rei; Räu|cher|fisch; Rau|cher|hus|ten,** der; -s; **räu|che|rig; Rau|che|rin; Räu|cher‿kam|mer, ...ker|ze, ...lachs, ...männ|chen** (Holzfigur, in der eine Räucherkerze abgebrannt wird); **räu|chern;** ich ...ere (↑R 16); **Räu|cher‿pfan|ne, ...schal|le, ...schin|ken, ...speck** (der; -[e]s), **...stäb|chen; Räu|che|rung; Räu|cher|wa|re; Rauch‿fah|ne, ...fang** (*österr. für* Schornstein); **Rauch|fang|keh|rer** (*österr. für* Schornsteinfeger); **rauch|far|ben, rauch|far|big; Rauch‿fass** (ein kult. Gerät), **...fleisch; rauch|frei; Rauch|gas** (*meist Plur.*); **rauch|ge|schwärzt; Rauch|glas; rauch|grau; rau|chig; rauch|los; Rauch‿mas|ke, ...mel|der**
Rauch|näch|te *vgl.* Raunächte
Rauch‿op|fer, ...quarz (dunkler Bergkristall), **...sa|lon, ...säu|le, ...schwa|den, ...schwal|be, ...sig|nal, ...ta|bak, ...tisch, ...to|pas** (*vgl.* Rauchquarz), **...ver|bot, ...ver|gif|tung, ...ver|zeh|rer**
Rauch|wa|re *meist Plur.* (Pelzware)
Rauch|wa|ren *Plur.* (*ugs. für* Tabakwaren)
Rauch|wa|ren‿han|del (*vgl.* [1]Handel), **...mes|se; Rauch|werk,** das; -[e]s (Pelzwerk)
Rauch‿wol|ke, ...zei|chen, ...zim|mer
Räu|de, die; -, -n (Krätze, Grind); **räu|dig; Räu|dig|keit,** die; -
Raue, die; -, -n (*landsch. für* Leichenschmaus)
rau|en (rau machen); **Rau|e|rei**
rauf; ↑R 13 (*ugs. für* herauf, hinauf)
Rau|fa|ser; Rau|fa|ser|ta|pe|te
Rauf|bold, der; -[e]s, -e (jmd., der gern mit anderen rauft); **Rau|fe,** die; -, -n (Futterkrippe); **räu|feln** *vgl.* aufräufeln; **rau|fen** (*auch für* mit jmdm. [prügelnd u. ringend] kämpfen); **Rau|fer; Rau|fe|rei; Rauf‿han|del** (*veraltet für* Rauferei; *vgl.* [2]Handel), **...lust** (die; -); **rauf|lus|tig**
Rau‿frost, ...fut|ter (das; -s)
Rau|graf (früherer oberrhein. Grafentitel)
rauh usw. *frühere Schreibung für* rau usw.; **Rau|haar|da|ckel; rau|haa|rig; Rau|heit; Rauh|putz, Rauh|reif** usw. *frühere Schreibungen für* Rauputz, Raureif usw.; **Rau|ig|keit**
Rau|ke, die; -, -n (eine Pflanze)
raum; raumer Wind (*Seemannsspr.* Wind, der schräg von hinten weht); raumer Wald (*Forstw.* offener, lichter Wald);
Raum, der; -[e]s, Räume; eine Raum sparende Lösung, *aber* eine noch raumsparendere Lösung (↑R 40); *vgl. auch* raumgreifend; **Raum‿akus|tik** (↑R 132), **...an|ga|be** (*Sprachw.* adverbiale Bestimmung des Raumes, des Ortes), **...an|zug, ...auf|tei|lung, ...aus|stat|ter** (Berufsbez.), **...aus|stat|te|rin, ...bild; Raum|bild|ver|fah|ren** (Herstellung von Bildern, die einen räumlichen Eindruck hervorrufen); **Räum|boot** (zum Beseitigen von Minen); **Räum|chen; Raum|de|ckung** (*Sport*); **räu|men; Räu|mer; Raum‿er|spar|nis, ...fäh|re, ...fah|rer, ...fahrt; Raum|fahrt‿be|hör|de, ...me|di|zin** (die; -), **...pro|gramm, ...tech|ni|ker; Raum|fahr|zeug; Räum|fahr|zeug** (zum Schneeräumen u. a.); **Raum‿flug, ...for|schung** (die; -), **...ge|fühl** (das; -[e]s), **...ge|stal|tung, ...glei|ter; raum|grei|fend;** -e Schritte; **Raum‿in|halt, ...kap|sel; Räum|kom|man|do; Raum‿kunst** (die; -), **...leh|re** (die; -; *für* Geometrie); **räum|lich; Räum|lich|keit; Raum|man|gel;** *vgl.* [2]Mangel; **Räum|ma|schi|ne; Raum‿maß** (das), **...me|ter** (*alte Maßeinheit für* 1 m³ geschichtetes Holz mit Zwischenräumen, im Gegensatz zu Festmeter; *Zeichen* Rm, *früher* rm); **Raum‿ord|nung, ...ord|nungs|plan** (*vgl.* [2]Plan), **...pend|ler, ...pfle|ge|rin, ...pla|nung, ...pro|gramm, ...schiff; Raum|schiff|fahrt** (die; -), **...sinn** (der; -[e]s), **...son|de** (unbemanntes Raumfahrzeug); **Raum spa|rend** *vgl.* Raum; **Raum|sta|ti|on; Räum|te,** die; -, -n (*Seemannsspr.* verfügbarer [Schiffs]laderaum); **Raum‿tei|ler** (frei stehendes Regal), **...tem|pe|ra|tur, ...trans|por|ter; Räu|mung; Räu|mungs‿ar|bei|ten** (*Plur.*), **...frist, ...kla|ge, ...ver|kauf; Raum‿wahr|neh|mung, ...wirt|schafts|the|o|rie** (die; -), **...zahl** (Maßzahl für den Rauminhalt von Schiffen)
Rau|näch|te, Rauch|näch|te *Plur.* (im Volksglauben die „Zwölf Nächte“ zwischen dem 25. Dez. und dem 6. Jan.)
rau|nen (dumpf, leise sprechen; flüstern); **Rau|nen,** das; -s
raun|zen (*landsch. für* widersprechen, nörgeln; *ugs. für* sich grob u. laut äußern); du raunzt; **Raun|zer; Raun|ze|rei; raun|zig**
Räup|chen; Rau|pe, die; -, -n; **rau|pen** (*landsch. für* von Raupen befreien); **rau|pen|ar|tig; Rau|pen‿bag|ger, ...fahr|zeug, ...fraß** (der; -es), **...ket|te, ...schlep|per**
Rau|putz
Rau|ra|ker, Rau|ri|ker, der; -s, - (Angehöriger eines kelt. Volksstammes)
Rau|reif, der; -[e]s
raus; ↑R 13 (*ugs. für* heraus, hinaus)
Rausch, der; -[e]s, Räusche (Betrunkensein; Zustand der Erregung, Begeisterung)
rausch|arm (*Technik*)

Rausch‿bee|re (Moorbeere), **...brand** (der; -[e]s; eine Tierkrankheit)
Rau|sche|bart (*veraltend scherzh. für* [Mann mit] Vollbart)
rau|schen (*auch Jägerspr.* brünstig sein [vom Schwarzwild]); du rauschst; **rau|schend;** ein -es Fest *(ugs.);* **Rau|scher,** der; -s (*rhein. für* schäumender Most)
Rausch|gelb, das; -s (ein Mineral [Auripigment])
Rausch|gift, das; **Rausch|gift‿be|kämp|fung** (die; -), **...han|del, ...händ|ler; rausch|gift|süch|tig; Rausch|gift|süch|ti|ge,** der *u.* die; -n, -n (↑R 5 ff.); **Rausch|gold** (dünnes Messingblech); **Rausch|gold|en|gel; rausch|haft; Rausch‿nar|ko|se** (*Med.* kurze Narkose für kleine chirurg. Eingriffe), **...sil|ber** (dünnes Neusilberblech), **...tat** *(Rechtsspr.),* **...zeit** (Brunstzeit des Schwarzwildes), **...zu|stand**
raus‿ekeln (↑R 13 *u.* 132; *ugs.*), **...feu|ern** *(ugs.),* **...flie|gen** *(ugs.),* **...hal|ten** *(ugs.),* **...kom|men** *(ugs.),* **...krie|gen** *(ugs.)*
Räus|pe|rer; räus|pern, sich; ich ...ere mich (↑R 16)
raus‿rü|cken (↑R 13; *ugs.*), **...schmei|ßen** *(ugs.);* **Raus|schmei|ßer** (*ugs. für* jmd., der randalierende Gäste aus dem Lokal entfernt; letzter Tanz); **Raus|schmiss** *(ugs.);* **raus|wer|fen;** ↑R 13 (*ugs. für* hinauswerfen)
[1]**Rau|te,** die; -, -n ‹lat.› (eine Pflanze)
[2]**Rau|te,** die; -, -n (schiefwinkliges gleichseitiges Viereck, Rhombus)
Rau|ten|de|lein (elfisches Wesen; Gestalt bei Gerhart Hauptmann)
rau|ten|för|mig
Rau|ten‿kranz, ...kro|ne *(Heraldik)*
Rau|wa|cke (eine Kalksteinart); **Rau|wa|re** (*landsch. für* Rauchware)
Rave [re:v], der *od.* das; -[s], -s ‹engl.› (größere Tanzveranstaltung zu Technomusik)
Ra|vel [ra'vɛl] (franz. Komponist)
Ra|ven|na [ra'vɛ...] (ital. Stadt)
Ra|vens|berg [...v...] (ehem. westfäl. Grafschaft); **Ra|vens|ber|ger** (↑R 103); - Land; **ra|vens|ber|gisch; Ra|vens|brück** (Frauenkonzentrationslager der Nationalsozialisten); **Ra|vens|burg** (Stadt in Oberschwaben)
Ra|vi|o|li [...v...] *Plur.* ‹ital.› (gefüllte kleine Nudelteigtaschen)
rav|vi|van|do [ravi'vando] ‹ital.› (*Musik* wieder belebend, schneller werdend)
Ra|wal|pin|di (Stadt in Pakistan)
Rax, die; - (österr. Berg)
Ra|yé [rɛ'je:], der; -[s], -s ‹franz.› (ein gestreiftes Gewebe)
Ray|gras *vgl.* Raigras
Ra|yon [rɛ'jɔ̃:, *österr. meist* ra'jo:n], der; -s, -s ‹franz.› (*österr. u. schweiz., sonst veraltet für* Bezirk, [Dienst]bereich; *selten für* Warenhausabteilung); **Ra|yon|chef** (*selten für* Abteilungsleiter [im Warenhaus]); **ra|yo|nie|ren** [rɛjɔ'ni:...] (*österr., sonst veraltet für* einteilen; zuweisen)
Ra|yonne [rɛjɔn], die; - ‹franz.› (*schweiz. für* Reyon)
Ra|yons|in|spek|tor [ra'jo:ns..., *auch* rɛ'jɔ̃:...] *(österr.)*
ra|ze|mös ‹lat.› (*Bot.* traubenförmig); -e Blüte
Raž|nji|ći ['raʒnitʃi], das; -[s], -[s] ‹serbokroat.› (ein jugoslaw. Fleischgericht)
Raz|zia, die; -, *Plur.* ...ien [...i̯ən], *seltener* -s ‹arab.-franz.› (überraschende Fahndung der Polizei in einem Gebäude od. Gebiet)
Rb = *chem. Zeichen für* Rubidium
RB = Radio Bremen
Rbl = Rubel
rd. = rund
[1]**Re** (ägyptischer Sonnengott)
[2]**Re,** das; -s, -s ‹lat.› (*Kartenspiel* Erwiderung auf ein Kontra)
Re = *chem. Zeichen für* Rhenium
Rea|der ['ri:də(r)], der; -s, - ‹engl.› (Buch mit Auszügen aus der [wissenschaftlichen] Literatur u. verbindendem Text); **Rea|der's Di|gest** ['ri:də(r)s 'daid͡ʒɛst], der *od.* das; - - (amerik. Monatsschrift mit Aufsätzen u. mit Auszügen aus neu erschienenen Büchern)
Re|a|gens, das; -, ...genzien [...i̯ən] *u.* **Re|a|genz,** das; -es, -ien [...i̯ən] ‹lat.› (*Chemie* Stoff, der mit einem anderen eine bestimmte chem. Reaktion herbeiführt u. diesen so identifiziert); **Re|a|genz|glas** *Plur.* ...gläser (Prüfglas, Probierglas für [chem.] Versuche); **Re|a|genz|pa|pier; re|a|gie|ren** (aufeinander einwirken); auf etwas - (für etwas empfindlich sein, auf etwas ansprechen; auf etwas eingehen); **Re|ak|tanz,** die; -, -en (*Elektrotechnik* Blindwiderstand); **Re|ak|ti|on,** die; -, -en (Rück-, Gegenwirkung, Gegenströmung, -druck, Rückschlag; chem. Umsetzung; Rückschritt; *nur Sing.:* Gesamtheit aller nicht fortschrittl. polit. Kräfte); eine chemische Reaktion; **re|ak|ti|o|när** ‹franz.› (Gegenwirkung erstrebend od. ausführend; *abwertend für* nicht fortschrittlich); **Re|ak|ti|o|när,** der; -s, -e (*abwertend für* jmd., der sich jeder fortschrittl. Entwicklung entgegenstellt); **re|ak|ti|ons|fä|hig; Re|ak|ti|ons‿ge|schwin|dig|keit, ...psy|cho|se; re|ak|ti|ons‿schnell, ...trä|ge; Re|ak|ti|ons‿ver|mö|gen** (das; -), **...zeit; re|ak|tiv** ‹lat.› (rückwirkend; auf Reize reagierend); **re|ak|ti|vie|ren** [...v...] (wieder in Tätigkeit setzen; wieder anstellen; chem. wieder umsetzungsfähig machen); **Re|ak|ti|vie|rung; Re|ak|ti|vi|tät,** die; -, -en ‹*zu* reaktiv›; **Re|ak|tor,** der; -s, ...oren (Vorrichtung, in der eine chemische od. eine Kernreaktion abläuft); **Re|ak|tor‿block** (*Plur.* ...blöcke), **...geg|ner, ...phy|sik, ...tech|nik** (die; -), **...un|fall**
re|al ‹lat.› (wirklich, tatsächlich; dinglich, sachlich)
[1]**Re|al,** der; -s, -es ‹span.› (alte span. Münze); [2]**Re|al,** der; -s, Reis ‹port.› (alte port. Münze)
[3]**Re|al,** das; -[e]s, -e (*landsch. für* Regal [Gestell mit Fächern])
Re|al‿akt *(Rechtsspr.),* **...ein|kom|men, ...en|zyk|lo|pä|die** (Sachwörterbuch)
Re|al|gar, der; -s, -e ‹arab.› (ein Mineral)
Re|al|ge|mein|de (land- od. forstwirtschaftliche Genossenschaft)
Re|al|gym|na|si|um (Form der höheren Schule); **Re|a|li|en** *Plur.* ‹lat.› (wirkliche Dinge; naturwissenschaftliche Unterrichtsfächer; Sachkenntnisse); **Re|a|li|en|buch; Re|al‿in|dex** (*veraltet für* Sachverzeichnis), **...in|ju|rie** (*Rechtsspr.* tätliche Beleidigung); **Re|a|li|sa|ti|on,** die; -, -en (Verwirklichung; *Wirtsch.* Umwandlung in Geld); **Re|a|li|sa|tor,** der; -s, ...oren (jmd., der etwas, bes. einen Film, eine Fernsehsendung verwirklicht); **re|a|li|sier|bar; Re|a|li|sier|bar|keit,** die; -; **re|a|li|sie|ren** (verwirklichen; erkennen, begreifen; *Wirtsch.* in Geld umwandeln); **Re|a|li|sie|rung** *Plur. selten;* **Re|a|lis|mus,** der; - ([nackte] Wirklichkeit; Kunstdarstellung des Wirklichen; Wirklichkeitssinn; Bedachtsein auf die Wirklichkeit, den Nutzen); **Re|a|list,** der; -en, -en (↑R 126); **Re|a|lis|tik,** die; - ([ungeschminkte] Wirklichkeitsdarstellung); **Re|a|lis|tin; re|a|lis|tisch; Re|a|li|tät,** die; -, -en (Wirklichkeit, Gegebenheit); **Re|a|li|tä|ten** *Plur.* (Gegebenheiten; *bes. österr. auch für* Grundstücke, Häuser); **Re|a|li|tä|ten|händ|ler** (*österr. für* Grundstücksmakler); **re|a|li|täts-**

˷be|zo|gen, ...fern, ...fremd; Re|a|li|täts˷sinn (der; -[e]s), **...ver|lust; re|a|li|ter** (in Wirklichkeit)
Re|a|li|ty-TV [riˈɛliti-], das; -[s] ‹engl.› (Fernsehprogramm, das tatsächlich Geschehendes [bes. nach Unglücksfällen] live zeigt oder später nachstellt)
Re|al˷ka|pi|tal, ...ka|ta|log *(Bibliothekswesen),* **...kon|kor|danz** *(Theol.),* **...kon|kur|renz** (die; -; *Rechtsspr.*), **...kont|rakt** *(Rechtsspr.),* **...kre|dit, ...last** *(meist Plur.),* **...le|xi|kon** (Sachwörterbuch), **...lohn; Re|a|lo,** der; -s, -s (*ugs. für* Realpolitiker, pragmatischer Politiker [bes. bei den Grünen]); **Re|al˷po|li|tik** (die; -; Politik auf realen Grundlagen), **...pro|dukt** *(Wirtsch.),* **...schu|le** (Schule, die mit der 10. Klasse u. der mittleren Reife abschließt), **...schü|ler, ...schü|le|rin; Re|al|schul˷leh|rer, ...leh|re|rin; Re|al˷steu|er** (die; *meist Plur.*), **...wert, ...wör|ter|buch** (Sachwörterbuch)
re|ama|teu|ri|sie|ren [...tø...]; ↑R 132 *(Sport)*
Re|ani|ma|ti|on (↑R 132), die; -, -en ‹lat.› (*Med.* Wiederbelebung); **Re|ani|ma|ti|ons|zent|rum; re|ani|mie|ren** (wieder beleben); **Re|ani|mie|rung**
Re|au|mur [ˈreːomyːr] ‹nach dem franz. Physiker› (Einheit der Grade beim heute veralteten 80-teiligen Thermometer; *Zeichen* R; *fachspr.* °R); 3° R, *fachspr.* 3 °R
Reb|bach *vgl.* Reibach
Reb|bau, der; -[e]s; **Reb|berg; Re|be,** die; -, -n
Re|bek|ka (w. Vorn.)
Re|bell, der; -en, -en (↑R 126) ‹franz.› (Aufrührer, Aufständischer); **re|bel|lie|ren; Re|bel|lin; Re|bel|li|on,** die; -, -en; **re|bel|lisch**
re|beln ([Trauben u. a.] abbeeren); ich ...[e]le (↑R 16); *vgl.* Gerebelte; **Re|ben˷blü|te, ...hü|gel, ...saft** (der; -[e]s)
Reb|hen|del, das; -s, -n (*österr. neben* Rebhuhn); **Reb|huhn** [*österr. nur so, sonst auch* ˈrɛp...]
Reb|laus (ein Insekt); **Reb|ling** (Rebenschössling)
Re|bound [riˈbaunt], der; -s, -s ‹engl.› (*Basketball* vom Brett od. Korbring abprallender Ball)
Reb˷pfahl, ...schnitt
Reb|schnur, die; -, ...schnüre (*österr. für* starke Schnur)
Reb˷schu|le, ...sor|te, ...stock (*Plur.* ...stöcke)
Re|bus, der *od.* das; -, -se ‹lat.› (Bilderrätsel)
Rec., Rp. = recipe
Re|cei|ver [riˈsiːvə(r)], der; -s, - ‹engl.› (Hochfrequenzteil für den Satellitenempfang; Empfänger u. Verstärker für Hi-Fi-Wiedergabe)
Re|chaud [reˈʃoː], der *od.* das; -s, -s ‹franz.› (Wärmeplatte; *südd., österr. u. schweiz für* [Gas]kocher)
re|chen (*landsch. für* harken); gerecht; **Re|chen,** der; -s, - (*landsch. für* Harke)
Re|chen˷an|la|ge, ...auf|ga|be, ...au|to|mat, ...brett, ...buch, ...exem|pel (↑R 132), **...feh|ler, ...heft, ...künst|ler, ...ma|schi|ne, ...ope|ra|ti|on** (↑R 132); **Re|chen|schaft,** die; -; **Re|chen|schafts˷be|richt, ...le|gung, ...pflicht; re|chen|schafts|pflich|tig; Re|chen˷schei|be, ...schie|ber, ...stab**
Re|chen|stiel (Stiel des Rechens)
Re|chen˷stun|de, ...ta|fel, ...un|ter|richt, ...zei|chen, ...zent|rum
Re|cher|che [reˈʃɛrʃə], die; -, -n *meist Plur.* ‹franz.› (Nachforschung); **Re|cher|cheur** [...ˈʃøːr], der; -s, -e; **re|cher|chie|ren**
rech|nen; gerechnet; **Rech|nen,** das; -s; **Rech|ner; Rech|ne|rei; rech|ner˷ge|steu|ert, ...ge|stützt; rech|ne|risch; Rech|nung;** einer Sache - tragen; **Rech|nungs|ab|gren|zung** (in der Buchführung); **Rech|nungs|ab|gren|zungs|pos|ten; Rech|nungs˷ab|la|ge, ...amt, ...art, ...be|trag, ...block** (*vgl.* Block), **...buch, ...ein|heit** *(Finanzw.),* **...füh|rer** (Buchhalter), **...füh|rung, ...hof, ...jahr, ...le|gung, ...num|mer, ...pos|ten, ...prü|fer, ...prü|fe|rin, ...prü|fung, ...we|sen** (das; -s)
recht; erst recht; das ist [mir] durchaus, ganz, völlig recht; das geschieht ihm recht; es ist [nur] recht und billig; ich kann ihm nichts recht machen; du hast recht daran getan; gehe ich recht in der Annahme, dass ...; ein rechter Winkel; jmds. rechte Hand sein *(übertr.);* zur rechten Hand, rechter Hand (rechts); **Recht,** das; -[e]s, -e; im Recht sein; mit, ohne Recht; nach Recht und Gewissen; Recht finden, sprechen, suchen; Recht haben, behalten, bekommen; jmdm. Recht geben; von Rechts wegen; zu Recht bestehen, erkennen; sie ist zu Recht auf den zweiten Platz gekommen, *aber* sie ist allein gut zurechtgekommen; *vgl. auch* rechtens *u.* zurechtbiegen, zurechtfinden usw.; **recht|dre|hend** *(Meteor.);* -er Wind (sich in Uhrzeigerrichtung drehender Wind, z. B. von Nord auf Nordost; *Ggs.* rückdrehend);
[1]Rech|te, der, die, das; -n; du bist mir der Rechte; an den Rechten kommen; das Rechte treffen, tun; etwas, nichts Rechtes können, wissen; nach dem Rechten sehen;
[2]Rech|te, die; -n, -n; ↑R 5 ff. (rechte Hand; rechte Seite; *Politik* die rechts stehenden Parteien, eine rechts stehende Gruppe in einer Partei); zur Rechten; in meiner Rechten; er traf ihn mit einer blitzschnellen Rechten *(Boxen);* die gemäßigte, äußerste Rechte; er gehört der Rechten an *(Politik);*
Recht|eck; recht|eckig (↑R 132); **Rech|te|hand|re|gel,** die; - *(Physik);* **rech|ten; rech|tens** (rechtmäßig, zu Recht); er wurde rechtens verurteilt; die Gebührenerhöhung war rechtens, wurde für nicht rechtens gehalten; **rech|ter Hand** *vgl.* recht; **rech|ter|seits**
recht|fer|ti|gen; er hat sich vor uns allen gerechtfertigt; **Recht|fer|ti|gung; Recht|fer|ti|gungs˷schrift, ...ver|such**
recht|gläu|big; Recht|gläu|big|keit, die; -
Recht|ha|ber; Recht|ha|be|rei, die; -; **recht|ha|be|risch**
Recht|kant, das *od.* der; -[e]s, -e
recht|läu|fig (*Astron.* entgegen dem Uhrzeigersinn laufend)
recht|lich; rechtliches Gehör (*Rechtsspr.* verfassungsrechtl. garantierter Anspruch des Staatsbürgers, seinen Standpunkt vor Gericht vorzubringen); **Recht|lich|keit,** die; -; **recht|los; Recht|lo|sig|keit,** die; -; **recht|mä|ßig; Recht|mä|ßig|keit,** die; -
rechts (*Abk.* r.); rechts von mir, vom Eingang; *auch mit Gen.:* rechts des Waldes, der Isar, des Mains; von, gegen, nach rechts; von rechts nach links; an der Kreuzung gilt rechts vor links; er weiß nicht, was rechts und was links ist; politisch rechts stehende Parteien; rechts außen spielen, stürmen *(Sport); vgl. auch* Rechtsaußen, rechtsum; **Rechts|ab|bie|ger** *(Verkehrsw.)*
Rechts˷ab|tei|lung, ...akt, ...an|ge|le|gen|heit, ...an|glei|chung, ...an|schau|ung, ...an|spruch, ...an|walt, ...an|wäl|tin; Rechts|an|walt[s]˷bü|ro, ...kam|mer, ...kanz|lei, ...pra|xis; Rechts˷an|wen|dung, ...auf|fas|sung, ...aus|kunft
Rechts˷aus|la|ge *(Boxen),* **...aus-**

le|ger *(Boxen);* **rechts au|ßen** *vgl.* rechts; **Rechts|au|ßen,** der; -, - *(Sport);* er spielt den klassischen Rechtsaußen
rechts|be|flis|sen *(veraltet, noch scherzh.);* **Rechts-bei|stand, ...be|leh|rung, ...be|ra|ter, ...be|ra|te|rin, ...be|ra|tung, ...be|schwer|de, ...beu|gung, ...be|wusst|sein, ...bre|cher, ...bre|che|rin, ...bruch** (der)
rechts|bün|dig
recht|schaf|fen *(veraltend);* ein rechtschaffener Beruf; **Recht|schaf|fen|heit,** die; -
Recht|schreib|buch, Recht|schrei|be|buch; recht|schrei|ben *nur im Infinitiv gebr.;* er kann nicht rechtschreiben, *aber* er kann nicht recht schreiben (er schreibt unbeholfen); **Recht|schrei|ben,** das; -s; **Recht|schreib-feh|ler, ...fra|ge; recht|schreib|lich; Recht|schreib|re|form; Recht|schrei|bung**
Rechts|drall, der; -[e]s, -e; **rechts|dre|hend,** *aber* nach rechts drehend; *vgl.* rechtdrehend; **Rechts|dre|hung; rechts|el|bisch** (auf der rechten Elbseite)
Rechts|emp|fin|den
Recht|ser *(ugs. für* Rechtshänder)
rechts|er|fah|ren
Recht|set|zung, Rechts|set|zung
rechts|ext|rem; Rechts-ext|re|mis|mus (der; -), **...ext|re|mist; rechts|ext|re|mis|tisch**
rechts|fä|hig; Rechts|fä|hig|keit, die; -; **Rechts|fall** (der)
Rechts|ga|lopp
Rechts-gang (der; *für* gerichtliches Verfahren), **...ge|lehr|sam|keit** *(veraltet);* **rechts|ge|lehrt; Rechts-ge|lehr|te, ...ge|schäft; rechts|ge|schäft|lich; Rechts|ge|schich|te,** die; -
Rechts|ge|win|de
Rechts-grund, ...grund|satz; rechts|gül|tig; Rechts|gül|tig|keit, die; -; **Rechts-gut, ...han|del** *(vgl.* ²Handel)
Rechts-hän|der, ...hän|de|rin; rechts|hän|dig; Rechts|hän|dig|keit, die; -
rechts|hän|gig (gerichtlich noch nicht abgeschlossen)
rechts|her *(veraltet für* von rechts her); **rechts|he|rum;** rechtsherum drehen, *aber* nach rechts herumdrehen
Rechts|hil|fe; Rechts|hil|fe-ab|kom|men, ...ord|nung
rechts|hin *(veraltet für* nach rechts hin)
Rechts-his|to|ri|ker, ...kon|su|lent (der; -en, -en; ↑R 126; *svw.* Rechtsbeistand); **Rechts|kraft,** die; -; formelle (äußere) -; materielle (sachliche) -; **rechts|kräf|tig; rechts|kun|dig**
Rechts-kurs, ...kur|ve
Rechts|la|ge *(Rechtsw.)*
rechts-las|tig, ...läu|fig
Rechts-leh|re (die; -), **...mit|tel** (das); **Rechts|mit|tel|be|leh|rung; Rechts-nach|fol|ge, ...nach|fol|ger, ...nach|fol|ge|rin, ...norm, ...ord|nung**
Rechts|par|tei
Rechts-pfle|ge (die; -), **...pfle|ger, ...pfle|ge|rin, ...phi|lo|so|phie** (die; -); **Recht|spre|chung**
rechts|ra|di|kal; Rechts-ra|di|ka|le, ...ra|di|ka|lis|mus; rechts|rhei|nisch (auf der rechten Rheinseite); **Rechts|ruck** *(Politik);* **rechts|rum** *(ugs.)*
Rechts-sa|che, ...satz, ...schrift, ...schutz (der; -es); **Rechts|schutz|ver|si|che|rung**
rechts|sei|tig; - gelähmt
Rechts-set|zung *(auch* Rechtsetzung), **...si|cher|heit** (die; -), **...spra|che** (die; -), **...spruch, ...staat** *(Plur.* ...staaten); **rechts|staat|lich; Rechts|staat|lich|keit,** die; -; **Rechts|stand|punkt**
rechts ste|hend *vgl.* rechts
Rechts-stel|lung, ...streit, ...ti|tel, ...trä|ger *(Rechtsw.);* **recht|su|chend;** der -e Bürger, *aber* der sein Recht suchende Bürger
rechts|uf|rig; rechts|um [*auch* rɛçts...]; rechtsum machen; rechtsum! (milit. Kommando); rechtsum kehrtmachen *(schweiz. auch übertr. für* den entgegengesetzten Weg einschlagen)
Rechts|un|si|cher|heit, die; -
Rechts|un|ter|zeich|ne|te; *vgl.* Unterzeichnete
rechts|ver|bind|lich; Rechts-ver|bind|lich|keit (die; -), **...ver|dre|her** *(abwertend),* **...ver|fah|ren**
Rechts|ver|kehr
Rechts-ver|let|zung, ...ver|ord|nung, ...ver|wei|ge|rung, ...vor|schlag *(schweiz. für* Einspruch gegen Zwangsvollstreckung); **Rechts-vor|schrift, ...vor|stel|lung, ...weg**
Rechts|wen|dung
Rechts|we|sen, das; -s; **rechts|wid|rig; rechts|wirk|sam; Rechts|wis|sen|schaft,** die; -
recht|wink|lig
recht|zei|tig
Re|ci|fe [re'sifi] (Hptst. von Pernambuco)
re|ci|pe! ['re:tsipe:] ‹lat., „nimm!"› (auf ärztl. Rezepten; *Abk.* Rec. *u.* Rp.)
Re|ci|tal [ri'sait(ə)l], das; -s, -s, *eindeutschend* Re|zi|tal, das; -s, *Plur.* -e *od.* -s ‹engl.› (Solistenkonzert)
re|ci|tan|do [retʃi...] ‹ital.› *(Musik* vortragend, sprechend, rezitierend)
Reck, das; -[e]s, *Plur.* -e, *auch* -s (ein Turngerät)
Re|cke, der; -n, -n; ↑R 126 (Held [bes. in der Sage])
re|cken; Wäsche - *(landsch. für* gerade legen); sich -
re|cken|haft ‹*zu* Recke›
Reck|ling|hau|sen (Stadt im Ruhrgebiet); **Reck|ling|häu|ser** (↑R 103)
Reck-stan|ge, ...tur|nen, ...tur|ner, ...übung (↑R 132)
Re|cor|der *vgl.* Rekorder
rec|te ‹lat.› *(veraltet für* richtig); **Rec|to** *vgl.* Rekto
Rec|tor mag|ni|fi|cus (↑R 130), der; - -, ...ores ...fici [...re:s ...tsi] ‹lat.› (Titel des Hochschulrektors)
re|cy|cel|bar [ri'saik...] ‹engl.›; **re|cy|celn** (einem Recycling zuführen); **Re|cyc|ling** (↑R 130), das; -s (Wiederverwendung bereits benutzter Rohstoffe); **Re|cyc|ling-an|la|ge, ...pa|pier, ...ver|fah|ren**
Re|dak|teur [...'tø:r], der; -s, -e ‹franz.› (jmd., der in Presse, Buchverlagen, im Rundfunk od. Fernsehen Manuskripte be- u. ausarbeitet); **Re|dak|teu|rin** [...'tø:rin]; **Re|dak|ti|on,** die; -, -en (Tätigkeit des Redakteurs; Gesamtheit der Redakteure u. deren Arbeitsraum); **re|dak|ti|o|nell; Re|dak|ti|ons-as|sis|tent, ...as|sis|ten|tin, ...ge|heim|nis, ...schluss** (der; -es), **...sta|tut; Re|dak|tor,** der; -s, ...oren ‹lat.› (Herausgeber; *schweiz. auch svw.* Redakteur)
Red|der, der; -s, - *(nordd., nur noch in Straßennamen* enger Weg [zwischen Hecken])
Red|di|ti|on, die; -, -en ‹lat.› *(veraltet für* Rückgabe)
Re|de, die; -, -n; - und Antwort stehen; zur - stellen; **Re|de-blü|te, ...du|ell, ...fi|gur, ...fluss** (der; -es), **...frei|heit** (die; -), **...ga|be** (die; -); **re|de-ge|wal|tig, ...ge|wandt; Re|de-ge|wandt|heit, ...kunst**
Re|demp|to|rist (↑R 132), der; -en, -en (↑R 126) ‹lat.› (Angehöriger einer kath. Kongregation)
re|den; gut reden haben; von sich reden machen; (↑R 50:) jmdn. zum Reden bringen; nicht viel Redens von einer Sache machen; **Re|dens|art; re|dens|art|lich; Re|de|rei; Re|de-schwall** (der;

-[e]s), **...strom** (der; -[e]s), **...verbot, ...wei|se** (die), **...wen|dung, ...zeit**
re|di|gie|ren ‹franz.› (druckfertig machen; abfassen; bearbeiten; als Redakteur tätig sein)
Re|din|gote [redɛ̃'gɔt, *auch* rə...], die; -, -n [...tən], *auch* der; -[s], -s ‹franz.› (taillierter Damenmantel mit Reverskragen)
Re|dis|fe|der (*österr.* eine Schreibfeder für Tusche u. Ä.)
re|dis|kon|tie|ren ‹ital.› ([einen diskontierten Wechsel] an- od. weiterverkaufen); **Re|dis|kon-tie|rung**
re|di|vi|vus [...'vi:vus] ‹lat.› (wieder erstanden)
red|lich; Red|lich|keit, die; -
Red|ner; Red|ner‿büh|ne, ...gabe (die; -); **Red|ne|rin; red|nerisch; Red|ner‿lis|te, ...pult, ...tri|bü|ne**
Re|dou|te [re'du:tə], die; -, -n ‹franz.› (*früher für* geschlossene Schanze; *veraltet für* Saal für Feste u. Tanzveranstaltungen; *österr., sonst veraltet für* Maskenball)
re|dres|sie|ren ‹franz.› (*Med.* wieder einrenken)
red|se|lig; Red|se|lig|keit, die; -
Re|du|it [re'dyi:], das; -s, -s ‹franz.› (*früher* Verteidigungsanlage im Kern einer Festung)
Re|duk|ti|on, die; -, -en ‹lat.› (*zu* reduzieren); **Re|duk|ti|o|nis-mus; re|duk|ti|o|nis|tisch; Re-duk|ti|ons‿di|ät, ...mit|tel** (das; *Chemie*), **...ofen** (↑R 132; *Technik*), **...tei|lung** *(Biol.)*
re|dun|dant (↑R 132) ‹lat.› (überreichlich, üppig; weitschweifig); **Re|dun|danz,** die; -, -en (Überladung, Überfluss; *EDV* nicht notwendiger Teil einer Information); **re|dun|danz|frei**
Re|dup|li|ka|ti|on (↑R 130), die; -, -en ‹lat.› (*Sprachw.* Verdoppelung eines Wortes oder einer Anlautsilbe, z. B. „Bonbon"); **re|dup|li-zie|ren**
re|du|zi|bel ‹lat.› *(Math.);* **re|du-zie|ren** (zurückführen; herabsetzen, einschränken; vermindern; *Chemie* Sauerstoff entziehen); **Re|du|zie|rung; Re|du|zier|ven-til** *(Technik)*
ree!, rhe! (Segelkommando)
Ree|de, die; -, -n (Ankerplatz vor dem Hafen); **Ree|der** (Schiffseigner); **Ree|de|rei** (Schifffahrtsunternehmen); **Ree|de|rei|flag|ge**
re|ell ‹franz.› (anständig, ehrlich; ordentlich; wirklich [vorhanden], echt); -e Zahlen *(Math.);* **Re|el|li-tät** [reɛ...], die; -
Reep, das; -[e]s, -e (*nordd. für* Seil, Tau); **Ree|per|bahn** (*nordd. für* Seilerbahn; Straße in Hamburg); **Reep|schlä|ger** (*nordd. für* Seiler); *vgl.* Rebschnur
Reet, das; -s (*nordd. für* Ried); **Reet|dach** *(nordd.)*
ref., reform. = reformiert
REFA, die [*Abk. für* Reichsausschuss für Arbeitszeitermittlung, *später* Reichsausschuss für Arbeitsstudien] (Verband für Arbeitsstudien u. Betriebsorganisation e. V.); **REFA-Fach|mann** (↑R 26)
Re|fak|tie [...i̯ə], die; -, -n ‹niederl.› (*Kaufmannsspr.* Gewichts- od. Preisabzug wegen beschädigter oder fehlerhafter Ware; Frachtnachlass, Rückvergütung); **re-fak|tie|ren** (einen Frachtnachlass gewähren)
REFA-Leh|re; *vgl.* REFA
Re|fek|to|ri|um, das; -s, ...ien [...i̯ən] ‹lat.› (Speisesaal [in Klöstern])
Re|fe|rat, das; -[e]s, -e ‹lat.› (Bericht, Vortrag, [Buch]besprechung; Sachgebiet eines Referenten); **Re|fe|ree** [refə'ri:, *auch* 'rɛfəri], der; -s, -s ‹engl.› (*Sport* Schieds-, Ringrichter); **Re|fe-ren|dar,** der; -s, -e ‹lat.› (Anwärter auf die höhere Beamtenlaufbahn nach der ersten Staatsprüfung); **Re|fe|ren|da|ri|at,** das; -[e]s, -e (Vorbereitungsdienst für Referendare); **Re|fe|ren|da|rin; Re|fe|ren|dum,** das; -s, *Plur.* ...den *u.* ...da (Volksabstimmung, Volksentscheid [insbes. in der Schweiz]); **Re|fe|rent,** der; -en, -en; ↑R 126 (Berichterstatter; Sachbearbeiter); *vgl. aber* Reverend; **Re|fe|ren|tin; Re|fe|renz,** die; -, -en (Beziehung, Empfehlung; *auch für* jmd., der eine Referenz erteilt); *vgl. aber* Reverenz; **Re|fe|ren|zen|lis|te; re|fe|rie-ren** ‹franz.› (berichten; vortragen; [ein Buch] besprechen)
¹Reff, das; -[e]s, -e (*ugs. für* hagere [alte] Frau)
²Reff, das; -[e]s, -e (*landsch. für* Rückentrage)
³Reff, das; -[e]s, -s (*Seemannsspr.* Vorrichtung zum Verkürzen eines Segels); **ref|fen**
re|fi|nan|zie|ren (*Finanzw.* fremde Mittel aufnehmen, um damit selbst Kredit zu geben); **Re|fi-nan|zie|rung**
Re|fla|ti|on, die; -, -en ‹lat.› (*Finanzw.* Erhöhung der im Umlauf befindlichen Geldmenge); **re|fla-ti|o|när**
Re|flek|tant, der; -en, -en (↑R 126) ‹lat.› (*veraltend für* Bewerber, Kauflustiger); **re|flek-tie|ren** ([zu]rückstrahlen, wiedergeben, spiegeln; nachdenken, erwägen; in Betracht ziehen; Absichten haben auf etwas); **Re|flek|tor,** der; -s, ...oren ([Hohl]spiegel; Teil einer Richtantenne; Fernrohr mit Parabolspiegel); **re|flek|to|risch** (durch einen Reflex bedingt, Reflex...); **Re|flex,** der; -es, -e ‹franz.› (Widerschein, Rückstrahlung zerstreuten Lichts; unwillkürliches Ansprechen auf einen Reiz); **re|flex|ar|tig; Re|flex‿be|we-gung, ...hand|lung; Re|fle|xi|on,** die; -, -en ‹lat.› (Rückstrahlung von Licht, Schall, Wärme u. a.; Vertiefung in einen Gedankengang, Betrachtung); **Re|fle|xi-ons|win|kel** *(Physik);* **re|fle|xiv** (*Psych.* durch Reflexion gewonnen, durch [Nach]denken u. Erwägen; *Sprachw.* rückbezüglich); -es Verb (rückbezügliches Verb, z. B. „sich schämen"); **Re|fle|xiv,** das; -s, -e [...və] (*svw.* Reflexivpronomen); **Re|fle|xiv|pro|no-men** (*Sprachw.* rückbezügliches Fürwort, z. B. „sich" *in* „er wäscht sich"); **Re|fle|xi|vum** [...v...], das; -s, ...va [...va] (*älter für* Reflexivpronomen); **Re|flex-schal|tung** (*Elektrotechnik* Wendeschaltung)
Re|form, die; -, -en ‹lat.› (Umgestaltung; Verbesserung des Bestehenden; Neuordnung); **re|form.,** ref. = reformiert; **Re|for|ma|ti-on,** die; -, -en (Umgestaltung; *nur Sing.:* christl. Glaubensbewegung des 16. Jh.s, die zur Bildung der ev. Kirchen führt); **Re|for|ma|ti-ons‿fest, ...tag** (31. Okt.), **...zeit** (die; -), **...zeit|al|ter** (das; -s); **Re|for|ma|tor,** der; -s, ...oren; **re|for|ma|to|risch; re|form|be-dürf|tig; Re|form‿be|dürf|tig-keit, ...be|stre|bung** (*meist Plur.*), **...be|we|gung; Re|for-mer** ‹engl.› (Verbesserer, Erneuerer); **Re|for|me|rin; re|for|me-risch; re|form|freu|dig; Re-form|haus; re|for|mie|ren** ‹lat.›; **re|for|miert** (*Abk.* ref., reform.); -e Kirche (↑R 108); **Re|for|mier-te,** der *u.* die; -n, -n; ↑R 5 ff. (Anhänger[in] der reformierten Kirche); **Re|for|mie|rung; Re|for-mis|mus,** der; - (Bewegung zur Verbesserung eines Zustandes od. Programms, bes. die Bestrebungen innerhalb der Arbeiterbewegung, soziale Verbesserungen durch Reformen, nicht durch Revolutionen zu erreichen); **Re|for-mist,** der; -en, -en (↑R 126);

re|for|mis|tisch; Re|form_klei|dung, ...kom|mu|nis|mus, ...kon|zil, ...kost, ...pä|da|go|gik, ...po|li|tik (die; -), **...wa|re** *(meist Plur.)*
Ref|rain [rə'frɛ̃:] (↑R 130 *u.* 132), der; -s, -s ‹franz.› (Kehrreim)
re|frak|tär ‹lat.› (*Med.* unempfindlich; unempfänglich für neue Reize); **Re|frak|ti|on,** die; -, -en (*Physik* [Strahlen]brechung an Grenzflächen zweier Medien); **Re|frak|to|me|ter,** das; -s, - (*Optik* Gerät zur Messung des Brechungsvermögens); **Re|frak|tor,** der; -s, ...oren (aus Linsen bestehendes Fernrohr); **Re|frak|tu|rie|rung** (*Med.* erneutes Brechen eines schlecht geheilten Knochens)
Ref|ri|ge|ra|tor (↑R 130 *u.* 132), der; -s, ...oren ‹lat.› (Kühler; Gefrieranlage)
Re|fu|gié [refy'ʒie:], der; -s, -s ‹franz.› (Flüchtling, bes. aus Frankreich geflüchteter Protestant [17. Jh.]); **Re|fu|gi|um** [re'fu:gium], das; -s, ...ien [...iən] ‹lat.› (Zufluchtsort)
re|fun|die|ren ‹lat.› (*österr. für* [Spesen, Auslagen] ersetzen, zurückerstatten)
Re|fus, Re|füs [rə'fy:, re...], der; - [...'fy:(s)], - [...'fy:s] ‹franz.› (*veraltet für* abschlägige Antwort, Ablehnung; Weigerung); **re|fü|sie|ren** *(veraltet)*
reg. = registered
Reg., Regt., Rgt. = Regiment
Reg, die; -, - ‹hamit.› (Geröllwüste)
[1]**Re|gal,** das; -s, -e ([Bücher-, Waren]gestell mit Fächern)
[2]**Re|gal,** das; -s, -e ‹franz.› (kleine, nur aus Zungenstimmen bestehende Orgel; Zungenregister der Orgel)
[3]**Re|gal,** das; -s, ...lien [...iən] *meist Plur.* ‹lat.› (*früher* [wirtschaftlich nutzbares] Hoheitsrecht, z. B. Zoll-, Münz-, Postrecht)
Re|gal|brett
re|ga|lie|ren ‹franz.› (*landsch. für* reichlich bewirten); sich - (sich an etwas satt essen, gütlich tun)
Re|ga|li|tät, die; -, -en ‹lat.› (*veraltet für* Anspruch auf Hoheitsrechte)
Re|gal_teil (das), **...wand**
Re|gat|ta, die; -, ...tten ‹ital.› (Bootswettfahrt); **Re|gat|ta|strecke**
Reg.-Bez. = Regierungsbezirk (↑R 26)
re|ge; reger, regste; - sein, werden; er ist körperl. und geistig -
Re|gel, die; -, -n ‹lat.›; **Re|gel|anfra|ge** *(Amtsspr.)*; **re|gel|bar; Re|gel|bar|keit,** die; -; **Re|gel|blu|tung; Re|gel|fall,** der; -[e]s; **re|gel|los; Re|gel|lo|sig|keit; re|gel|mä|ßig;** regelmäßige Verben *(Sprachw.)*; **Re|gel|mä|ßig|keit; re|geln;** ich ...[e]le (↑R 16); sich -; **re|gel|recht; Re|gel_satz** (Richtsatz für die Bemessung von Sozialhilfeleistungen), **...schu|le, ...stu|di|en|zeit** (die; -), **...tech|nik** (die; -), **...tech|ni|ker, ...über|wa|chung** (↑R 132); **Re|ge|lung,** Reglung; **Re|ge|lungs|tech|nik,** die; - (*svw.* Regeltechnik); **re|gel|wid|rig; Re|gel|wid|rig|keit**
re|gen; sich -; sich - bringt Segen
[1]**Re|gen** (l. Nebenfluss der Donau)
[2]**Re|gen,** der; -s, -; saurer - (Niederschlag, der schweflige Säure enthält); **re|gen|arm;** ...ärmer, ...ärmste; **Re|gen|bo|gen; re|gen|bo|gen_far|ben** *od.* ...farbig; **Re|gen|bo|gen|far|ben** *Plur.*; in allen - schillern; **Re|gen|bo|gen|haut** (*für* [2]Iris); **Re|gen|bo|gen|haut|ent|zün|dung; Re|gen|bo|gen|pres|se,** die; - (vorwiegend triviale Unterhaltung, Gesellschaftsklatsch, Sensationsmeldungen u. a. druckende Wochenzeitschriften); **Re|gen|bo|gen|tri|kot,** das (Trikot des Radweltmeisters); **Re|gen_cape, ...dach; re|gen|dicht**
Re|ge|ne|rat, das; -[e]s, -e ‹lat.› (durch chem. Aufbereitung gewonnenes Material); **Re|ge|ne|ra|ti|on,** die; -, -en (Neubildung [tier. od. pflanzl. Körperteile und zerstörter menschl. Körpergewebe]; Neubelebung; Wiederherstellung); **re|ge|ne|ra|ti|ons|fä|hig; Re|ge|ne|ra|ti|ons_fä|hig|keit** (die; -), **...zeit; Re|ge|ne|ra|tiv|ver|fah|ren** (*Technik* Verfahren zur Rückgewinnung von Wärme); **Re|ge|ne|ra|tor,** der; -s, ...oren (Wärmespeicher; Luftvorwärmer); **re|ge|ne|rie|ren** (erneuern, neu beleben); sich -
Re|gen_fall (der; *meist Plur.*), **...fass, ...front, ...guss, ...haut** ® (wasserdichter Regenmantel), **...kar|te, ...man|tel, ...men|ge; re|gen|nass; Re|gen|pfei|fer** (ein Vogel); **re|gen|reich; Re|gen|rin|ne**
Re|gens, der; -, *Plur.* Regentes [...te:s] *u.* ...enten ‹lat.› (Vorsteher, Leiter [bes. kath. Priesterseminare])
Re|gens|burg (Stadt an der Donau); [1]**Re|gens|bur|ger** (↑R 103); - Domspatzen; [2]**Re|gens|bur|ger,** die; -, - (eine Wurstsorte)
Re|gen_schat|ten (die regenarme Seite eines Gebirges), **...schau|er** (der), **...schirm**
Re|gens Cho|ri [- 'ko:ri], der; - -, Regentes - ‹lat.› (Chorleiter in der kath. Kirche); **Re|gens|cho|ri,** der; -, - (*österr. für* Regens Chori)
Re|gen|schutz, der; -es; **re|gen|schwer;** -e Wolken
Re|gent, der; -en, -en (↑R 126) ‹lat.› (Staatsoberhaupt; Herrscher)
Re|gen|tag
Re|gen|tes (*Plur. von* Regens); **Re|gen|tin**
Re|gen_ton|ne, ...trop|fen
Re|gent|schaft, die; -, -en; **Re|gent|schafts|rat** *Plur.* ...räte
Re|gen_wald, ...was|ser (das; -s), **...wet|ter** (das; -s), **...wol|ke, ...wurm, ...zeit**
Re|ger (dt. Komponist)
Re|gest, das; -[e]s, -en *meist Plur.* ‹lat.› (zusammenfassende Inhaltsangabe einer Urkunde)
Reg|gae ['rɛge:], der; -[s] ‹engl.› (auf Jamaika entstandene Stilrichtung der Popmusik)
Re|gie [re'ʒi:], die; - ‹franz.› (Spielleitung [bei Theater, Film, Fernsehen usw.]; verantwortliche Führung, Verwaltung); **Re|gie_an|wei|sung, ...as|sis|tent, ...as|sis|ten|tin, ...be|trieb** (Betrieb der öffentlichen Hand), **...ein|fall, ...feh|ler, ...kos|ten** (*Plur.*; Verwaltungskosten); **re|gie|lich; Re|gi|en** [re'ʒi:ən] *Plur.* (*österr. für* Regie-, Verwaltungskosten)
re|gier|bar; re|gie|ren ‹lat.› (lenken; [be]herrschen; *Sprachw.* einen bestimmten Fall fordern); (↑R 56:) Regierender Bürgermeister (*im Titel, sonst:* regierender Bürgermeister); **Re|gie|rung; Re|gie|rungs_an|tritt, ...bank** (*Plur.* ...bänke), **...be|am|te, ...be|zirk** (*Abk.* Reg.-Bez.), **...bil|dung, ...bünd|nis, ...chef, ...che|fin, ...de|le|ga|ti|on, ...di|rek|tor, ...er|klä|rung; re|gie|rungs|fä|hig; Re|gie|rungs|form; re|gie|rungs|freund|lich; Re|gie|rungs_ge|bäu|de, ...ge|walt, ...ko|a|li|ti|on, ...kri|se, ...par|tei, ...prä|si|dent, ...prä|si|di|um, ...pro|gramm, ...rat** (*Plur.* ...räte; [höherer] Verwaltungsbeamter [*Abk.* Reg.-Rat]; *schweiz. für* Kantonsregierung und deren Mitglied); **re|gie|rungs|sei|tig** (*Amtsspr.* von [vonseiten] der Regierung); **Re|gie|rungs_sitz, ...spit|ze, ...spre|cher, ...spre|che|rin, ...sys|tem; re|gie|rungs|treu; Re|gie|rungs_um|bil|dung, ...vier|tel, ...vor|la|ge,**

...wech|sel, ...zeit; Re|gier|werk (Gesamtheit von Pfeifen, Manualen u. Pedalen, Traktur u. Registratur einer Orgel)

Re|gime [re'ʒi:m], das; -s, *Plur.* - [re'ʒi:mə], *selten noch* -s ⟨franz.⟩ (*abwertend für* [diktatorische] Regierungsform; Herrschaft); **Regime‿kri|ti|ker, ...kri|ti|ke|rin**

Re|gi|ment, das; -[e]s, *Plur.* -e *u.* (*für* Truppeneinheiten:) -er ⟨lat.⟩ (Regierung; Herrschaft; größere Truppeneinheit; *Abk.* R., Reg[t]., Rgt.); **re|gi|men|ter|wei|se; Re|gi|ments‿arzt** *(Milit.),* **...kom|man|deur, ...stab**

Re|gi|na (w. Vorn.)

Re|gi|nald (m. Vorn.)

Re|gi|ne (w. Vorn.)

Re|gi|o|lekt, der; -[e]s, -e ⟨lat.; griech.⟩ (Dialekt in rein geographischer Hinsicht); **Re|gi|on,** die; -, -en ⟨lat.⟩ (Gegend; Bereich); **re|gi|o|nal** (gebietsmäßig, -weise); **Re|gi|o|na|lis|mus,** der; - (Ausprägung landschaftlicher Sonderbestrebungen; Heimatkunst der Zeit nach 1900); **Re|gi|o|na|list,** der; -en, -en (↑R 126); **Re|gi|o|nal‿li|ga** *(Sport),* **...pla|nung** (Planung der räumlichen Ordnung und Entwicklung einer Region), **...pro|gramm** *(Rundf., Fernsehen)*

Re|gis|seur [reʒi'sø:r], der; -s, -e ⟨franz.⟩ (Spielleiter [bei Theater, Film, Fernsehen usw.]); **Re|gis|seu|rin**

Re|gis|ter, das; -s, - ⟨lat.⟩ ([alphabet. Inhalts]verzeichnis, Sach- od. Wortweiser, Liste; Stimmenzug bei Orgel und Harmonium); **re|gis|tered** ['rɛdʒistəd] ⟨engl.⟩ (in ein Register eingetragen; patentiert; gesetzlich geschützt; *Abk.* reg.); **Re|gis|ter|hal|ten,** das; -s (*Druckw.* genaues Aufeinanderpassen von Farben beim Mehrfarbendruck od. von Vorder- und Rückseite); **Re|gis|ter|ton|ne** (*Seew.* Einheit des Volumens für die Schiffsvermessung)

Re|gist|ra|tor (↑R 130), der; -s, ...oren (*früher* Register führender Beamter; *auch für* Ordner[mappe]); **Re|gist|ra|tur,** die; -, -en (Aufbewahrungsstelle für Akten; Aktengestell, -schrank; die die Register und Koppeln auslösende Schaltvorrichtung bei Orgel und Harmonium); **Re|gist|rier|bal|lon** (*Meteor.* [unbemannter] mit Messinstrumenten bestückter Treibballon zur Erforschung der höheren Luftschichten); **re|gist|rie|ren** ([in ein Register] eintragen; selbsttätig aufzeichnen; einordnen; *übertr. für* bewusst wahrnehmen; *bei Orgel u. Harmonium* Stimmkombinationen einschalten, Register ziehen); **Re|gist|rier|kas|se; Re|gist|rie|rung**

Reg|le|ment [reglə'mã:, *schweiz.* ...'mɛnt] (↑R 130), das; -s, *Plur.* -s, *schweiz.* -e ⟨franz.⟩ ([Dienst]vorschrift; Geschäftsordnung); **reg|le|men|ta|risch** (den Vorschriften, Bestimmungen genau entsprechend); **reg|le|men|tie|ren** (durch Vorschriften regeln); **Reg|le|men|tie|rung; reg|le|ment‿mä|ßig** [reglə'mã:...], **...wid|rig**

Reg|ler

Reg|let|te (↑R 130), die; -, -n ⟨franz.⟩ (*Druckw.* Bleistreifen für den Zeilendurchschuss)

reg|los

Reg|lung *vgl.* Regelung

reg|nen; Reg|ner (ein Bewässerungsgerät); **reg|ne|risch**

Reg.-Rat = Regierungsrat (↑R 26)

Re|gress, der; -es, -e ⟨lat.⟩ (Ersatzanspruch, Rückgriff); **Re|gress|an|spruch** (Ersatzanspruch); **Re|gres|si|on,** die; -, -en (Rückbildung, -bewegung); **re|gres|siv** (zurückgehend, rückläufig; rückwirkend; rückschrittlich); **Re|gress|pflicht; re|gress|pflich|tig**

reg|sam; Reg|sam|keit, die; -

Regt., Rgt., R. = Regiment

Re|gu|la (w. Vorn.)

Re|gu|lar, der; -s, -e ⟨lat.⟩ (Mitglied eines katholischen Ordens); **re|gu|lär** (der Regel gemäß; vorschriftsmäßig, üblich); -es System (*Mineral.* Kristallsystem mit drei gleichen, aufeinander senkrecht stehenden Achsen); -e Truppen (gemäß dem Wehrgesetz eines Staates aufgestellte Truppen); **Re|gu|lar|geist|li|che; Re|gu|la|ri|en** [...jən] *Plur.* (auf der Tagesordnung stehende, regelmäßig abzuwickelnde Vereinsangelegenheiten); **Re|gu|la|ri|tät,** die; -, -en (Regelmäßigkeit; Richtigkeit); **Re|gu|la|ti|on,** die; -, -en (*Biol., Med.* die Regelung der Organsysteme eines lebendigen Körpers durch verschiedene Steuerungseinrichtungen; Anpassung eines Lebewesens an Störungen); **Re|gu|la|ti|ons‿stö|rung, ...sys|tem; re|gu|la|tiv** (ein Regulativ darstellend, regulierend); **Re|gu|la|tiv,** das; -s, -e [...və] (regelnde Vorschrift; steuerndes Element); **Re|gu|la|tor,** der; -s, ...oren (regulierende Kraft, Vorrichtung; eine besondere Art Pendeluhr); **re|gu|lier|bar; re|gu|lie|ren** (regeln, ordnen; [ein]stellen); **Re|gu|lie|rung**

[1]**Re|gu|lus** (altröm. Feldherr); [2]**Re|gu|lus,** der; -, -se (*nur Sing.:* ein Stern; *veraltet für* gediegenes Metall)

Re|gung; re|gungs|los; Re|gungs|lo|sig|keit, die; -

Reh, das; -[e]s, -e

Re|ha, die; -, -s (*kurz für* Rehabilitation, Rehabilitationsklinik); **Re|ha|bi|li|tand,** der; -en, -en (↑R 126) ⟨lat.⟩ (jmd., dem die Wiedereingliederung in das berufl. u. gesellschaftl. Leben ermöglicht werden soll); **Re|ha|bi|li|tan|din; Re|ha|bi|li|ta|ti|on,** die; -, -en (Gesamtheit der Maßnahmen, die mit der Wiedereingliederung in die Gesellschaft zusammenhängen; *auch für* Rehabilitierung); **Re|ha|bi|li|ta|ti|ons‿kli|nik, ...zent|rum; re|ha|bi|li|tie|ren;** sich - (sein Ansehen wieder herstellen); **Re|ha|bi|li|tie|rung** (Wiedereinsetzung [in die ehemaligen Rechte, in den früheren Stand]; Ehrenrettung); **Re|ha|kli|nik** (*kurz für* Rehabilitationsklinik)

Reh‿bein (*Tiermed.* Überbein beim Pferd), **...bock, ...bra|ten; reh|braun; Reh|brunft**

Re|he, die; - (*Tiermed.* eine Hufkrankheit)

reh|far|ben, reh|far|big; Reh‿geiß, ...jun|ge (das; -n; *österr. für* Rehklein), **...kalb, ...keu|le, ...kitz, ...klein** (das; -s; ein Gericht); **reh|le|dern; Reh|ling** (*landsch. für* Pfifferling); **Reh‿pos|ten** (grober Schrot), **...rü|cken, ...zie|mer** (Rehrücken)

Rei|bach, der; -s ⟨hebr.-jidd.⟩ (*ugs. für* Verdienst, Gewinn)

Reib|ah|le; Rei|be, die; -, -n; **Rei|be|brett** (zum Glätten des Putzes); **Reib|ei|sen; Rei|be‿ku|chen** (*landsch., bes. rhein. für* Kartoffelpuffer), **...laut** (*für* Frikativ); **rei|ben;** du riebst; du riebest; gerieben; reib[e]!; (↑R 50:) durch kräftiges Reiben säubern; **Rei|ber** (*auch landsch. für* Reibe); **Rei|be|rei** *meist Plur.* (kleine Streitigkeit); **Reib‿flä|che, ...gers|tel** (das; -s; *österr.* eine Suppeneinlage), **...kä|se; Rei|bung; Rei|bungs‿elekt|ri|zi|tät** (↑R 132), **...flä|che; rei|bungs|los; Rei|bungs|lo|sig|keit,** die; -; **Rei|bungs‿ver|lust, ...wär|me, ...wi|der|stand; Reib|zun|ge** (*Zool.* Zunge von Weichtieren)

reich; Arm und Reich (*veraltet für* jedermann), Arme und Reiche; ein [mit Blumen] reich geschmückter Altar; reich verzierte Fassaden

Reich, das; -[e]s, -e; von -s wegen; (↑R 108:) das Deutsche -; das Römische -; das Heilige Römische - Deutscher Nation

Rei|che, der *u.* die; -n, -n (↑R 5 ff.)

rei|chen (geben; sich erstrecken; auskommen; genügen)

Rei|che|nau (↑R 132), die; - (eine Insel im Bodensee)

reich ge|schmückt *vgl.* reich; **reich|hal|tig; Reich|hal|tig|keit,** die; -; **reich|lich**

Reichs‿abt *(früher),* **...äb|tis|sin** *(früher),* **...acht** (*früher; vgl.* [3]Acht), **...ad|ler, ...ap|fel** (der; -s; Teil der Reichsinsignien), **...archiv** (das; -[e]s; Sammelstelle der Reichsakten [1871 bis 1945]), **...bahn** *(früher),* **...bann** *(früher),* **...frei|herr** *(früher),* **...ge|richt** (das; -[e]s; höchstes dt. Gericht [1879 bis 1945]), **...grenze, ...grün|dung, ...in|sig|ni|en** (*Plur.; früher*); **Reichs|kam|merge|richt,** das; -[e]s (höchstes dt. Gericht [1495 bis 1806]); **Reichs‿kanz|ler** (leitender dt. Reichsminister [1871 bis 1945]), **...klein|odi|en** (*Plur.; früher*); **Reichs|kris|tall|nacht** (*vgl.* Kristallnacht); **Reichs|mark** (dt. Währungseinheit [1924 bis 1948]; *Abk.* RM); **reichs|mit|tel|bar** *(früher);* **Reichs‿pfen|nig** (dt. Münzeinheit [1924 bis 1948]), **...prä|si|dent** (dt. Staatsoberhaupt [1919 bis 1934]), **...rat** (der; -[e]s; Vertretung der dt. Länder beim Reich [1919 bis 1934]), **...stadt** (*Bez. für* die früheren reichsunmittelbaren Städte), **...stän|de** (*Plur.; früher* die reichsunmittelbaren Fürsten, Städte u. a. des Deutschen Reiches), **...tag** (*früher* Versammlung der Reichsstände [bis 1806]; *nur Sing.:* dt. Volksvertretung [1871 bis 1945]; Parlament bestimmter Staaten); **Reichs|tags|brand,** der; -[e]s (Brand des Berliner Reichstagsgebäudes am 27. 2. 1933); **reichs|un|mit|tel|bar** (*früher* Kaiser und Reich unmittelbar unterstehend); **Reichs|ver|si|che|rungs|ord|nung,** die; - (Gesetz zur Regelung der öffentl.-rechtl. Invaliden-, Kranken- und Unfallversicherung; *Abk.* RVO); **Reichs|wehr,** die; - (Bez. des dt. 100 000-Mann-Heeres [1921 bis 1935])

Reich|tum, der; -s, ...tümer; **reich ver|ziert** *vgl.* reich

Reich|wei|te

Rei|der|land, *auch* Rhei|der|land, das; -[e]s (Teil Ostfrieslands)

reif (voll entwickelt; geeignet)

[1]**Reif,** der; -[e]s (gefrorener Tau)

[2]**Reif,** der; -[e]s, -e (*geh. für* Reifen, Diadem, Fingerring)

Rei|fe, die; - (z. B. von Früchten); mittlere Reife (Abschluss der Realschule od. der 10. Klasse der höheren Schule); **Rei|fe|grad;** [1]**rei|fen** (reif werden); die Frucht ist gereift; ein gereifter Mann

[2]**rei|fen** ([1]Reif ansetzen); es hat gereift

Rei|fen, der; -s, -; **Rei|fen‿druck, ...pan|ne, ...pro|fil, ...scha|den, ...spiel, ...wech|sel**

Rei|fe|prü|fung; Rei|fe|rei (*fachspr.* Raum, in dem bereits geerntete Früchte [bes. Bananen] nachreifen); **Rei|fe‿zeit, ...zeug|nis**

Reif|glät|te

reif|lich

Reif|rock *(veraltet)*

Rei|fung, die; - (das Reifwerden); **Rei|fungs|pro|zess**

Rei|gen, *veraltet* Rei|hen, der; -s, - (ein Tanz); **Rei|gen‿füh|rer, ...tanz**

Rei|he, die; -, -n; in, außer der -; der - nach; an der - sein; an die - kommen; in Reih und Glied (↑R 13); arithmetische -, geometrische -, unendliche - *(Math.);* [1]**rei|hen** (in Reihen ordnen; lose, vorläufig nähen); er reihte, hat gereiht, *landsch. u. fachspr. auch* rieh, hat geriehen

[2]**rei|hen** (*Jägerspr.* während der Paarungszeit zu mehreren einer Ente folgen [von Erpeln])

[1]**Rei|hen,** der; -s, - (*südd. für* Fußrücken)

[2]**Rei|hen** *vgl.* Reigen

Rei|hen‿bil|dung, ...dorf, ...folge, ...grab, ...haus, ...mo|tor, ...schal|tung (*für* Serienschaltung), **...sied|lung, ...un|ter|suchung; rei|hen|wei|se**

Rei|her, der; -s, - (ein Vogel); **Reiher‿bei|ze** (*Jägerspr.* Reiherjagd), **...fe|der, ...horst** (*vgl.* [2]Horst); **rei|hern** (*ugs. für* erbrechen); **Rei|her|schna|bel** (eine Pflanze)

Reih‿fa|den, ...garn

...rei|hig (z. B. einreihig); **reih|um;** es geht -; **Rei|hung**

Reih|zeit (*Jägerspr.* Paarungszeit der Enten)

Reim, der; -[e]s, -e; ein stumpfer (männlicher) Reim, ein klingender (weiblicher) Reim *(Verslehre);* **Reim‿art, ...chro|nik** (im MA.); **rei|men;** sich -; **Rei|mer** (*veraltet für* jmd., der Verse schreibt); **Rei|me|rei; Reim|le|xi|kon; reim|los**

Re|im|plan|ta|ti|on [re(:)im...], die; -, -en ‹lat.› (*Med.* Wiedereinpflanzung [z. B. von Zähnen]); **re|im|plan|tie|ren**

Re|im|port [re(:)im...], der; -[e]s, -e ‹lat.› (Wiedereinfuhr bereits ausgeführter Güter); **re|im|por|tie|ren**

Reims [*franz.* rɛ̃:s] (franz. Stadt)

Reim|schmied (*scherzh. für* Versemacher)

Reim|ser ‹*zu* Reims› (↑R 103)

Rei|mund *vgl.* [1]Raimund

Reim|wort *Plur.* ...wörter

[1]**rein;** ↑R 13 (*ugs. für* herein, hinein)

[2]**rein;** rein halten; rein machen, *aber* das große Rein[e]machen; sich rein waschen (seine Unschuld beweisen; ↑R 39); ins Reine bringen, kommen, schreiben; mit etwas, mit jmdm. im Reinen sein; rein Schiff! (seemänn. Kommando); (↑R 5:) reinen Sinnes; (↑R 40:) ein rein goldener, rein silberner (*auch* reingoldener, reinsilberner) Ring; rein leinen, rein seiden, rein wollen (*auch* reinleinen, reinseiden, reinwollen) u. a.; [3]**rein** (*ugs. für* durchaus, ganz, gänzlich); er ist rein toll; er war rein weg (ganz hingerissen); *vgl.* rein[e]weg

Rein, die; -, -en (*südd. u. österr. ugs. für* flacher Kochtopf)

Rei|nald, Rai|nald (m. Vorn.)

rein|but|tern; ↑R 13 (*ugs. für* [Geld] hineinstecken)

Rein|del, Reindl, das; -s, -n (*südd. u. österr. Verkleinerungsform von* Rein); **Reind|ling** (*südostösterr.* ein Hefekuchen)

Rei|ne, die; - (*geh. für* Reinheit)

Rei|nec|lau|de [rɛnə'klo:də] (↑R 130 *u.* 132) *vgl.* Reneklode

Rein|ein|nah|me *(Wirtsch.)*

Rei|ne|ke Fuchs (Name des Fuchses in der Tierfabel)

Rei|ne|ma|che|frau, Rein|ma|che|frau; **Rei|ne|ma|chen,** Rein|ma|chen, das; -s *(landsch.); vgl.* [2]rein

Rei|ner, Rai|ner (m. Vorn.)

rein|er|big (*für* homozygot); **Rein‿er|hal|tung** (die; -), **...er|lös, ...er|trag**

Rei|net|te [rɛ'nɛtə] *vgl.* Renette

rei|ne|weg, rein|weg (*ugs. für* ganz und gar); das ist rein[e]weg zum Tollwerden; *vgl.* [3]rein

Rein|fall, der; ↑R 13 *(ugs.);* **rein|fal|len** *(ugs.)*

Re|in|farkt [re(:)in...], der; -[e]s, -e ‹lat.› (*Med.* wiederholter Infarkt)

Re|in|fek|ti|on [re(:)in...], die; -, -en ‹lat.› (*Med.* erneute Infektion); **re|in|fi|zie|ren;** sich -

Rein|ge|schmeck|te *vgl.* Hereingeschmeckte

Rein‿ge|wicht, ...ge|winn; rein|gol|den; *vgl.* [2]rein; **Rein|hal|tung,** die; -
rein|hän|gen, sich; ↑R 13 (*ugs. für* sich einer Sache annehmen, sich engagieren)
Rein|hard (m. Vorn.)
Rein|hardt (österr. Schauspieler u. Theaterleiter)
Rein|heit, die; -; **Rein|heits|ge|bot,** das; -[e]s (Gesetz für das Brauen von Bier in Deutschland)
Rein|hild, Rein|hil|de (w. Vorn.); **Rein|hold** (m. Vorn.)
rei|ni|gen; Rei|ni|ger; Rei|ni|gung; die rituelle - *(Rel.)*; **Rei|ni|gungs‿creme, ...in|sti|tut, ...milch, ...mit|tel** (das)
Re|in|kar|na|ti|on [re(:)in...], die; -, -en ‹lat.› (Wiederverkörperung von Gestorbenen)
rein|knien, sich; ↑R 13 *(ugs.)*; **rein|kom|men** *(ugs.)*; **rein|kön|nen** *(ugs.)*; **rein|krie|gen** *(ugs.)*
Rein|kul|tur
rein|las|sen; ↑R 13 *(ugs.)*; **rein|le|gen** *(ugs.)*
rein|lei|nen; *vgl.* [2]rein; **rein|lich; Rein|lich|keit,** die; -; **rein|lich|keits|lie|bend; Rein|ma|che|frau** *vgl.* Reinemachefrau; **Rein|ma|chen** *vgl.* Reinemachen
Rein|mar (m. Eigenn.)
Rein|ni|ckel, das
Rei|nold (m. Vorn.)
rein|ras|sig; Rein|ras|sig|keit, die; -
rein|rei|ßen; ↑R 13 *(ugs.)*; **rein|rei|ten** (*ugs. für* in eine unangenehme Lage bringen)
Rein|schiff, das (gründliche Schiffsreinigung); **Rein|schrift; rein|schrift|lich; rein|sei|den;** *vgl.* [2]rein; **rein|sil|bern;** *vgl.* [2]rein; **Rein|ver|mö|gen** *(Wirtsch.)*; **rein wa|schen** *vgl.* [2]rein; **rein|weg** *vgl.* reineweg; **rein|wol|len;** *vgl.* [2]rein; **Rein|zucht**
[1]**Reis** (*Plur. von* [2]Real)
[2]**Reis,** Johann Philipp (Erfinder des Telefons)
[3]**Reis,** das; -es, -er (kleiner, dünner Zweig; Pfropfreis)
[4]**Reis,** der; -es, *Plur.* (*für* Reisarten:) -e ‹griech.› (ein Getreide); **Reis|bau,** der; -[e]s
Reis|be|sen (*svw.* Reisigbesen)
Reis‿brannt|wein, ...brei
Rei|se, die; -, -n; **Rei|se‿an|den|ken, ...apo|the|ke** (↑R 132), **...be|glei|ter, ...be|glei|te|rin, ...be|kannt|schaft, ...be|richt, ...be|schrei|bung, ...be|steck, ...buch, ...buch|han|del, ...bü|ro, ...bus, ...de|cke, ...dip|lo|ma|tie, ...er|leb|nis; rei|se|fer|tig; Rei|se‿fie|ber, ...füh|rer, ...füh|re|rin, ...geld, ...ge|päck; Rei|se|ge|päck|ver|si|che|rung; Rei|se‿ge|schwin|dig|keit, ...ge|sell|schaft, ...ka|der** (*ehem. in der DDR* jmd., der zu Reisen ins [westl.] Ausland zugelassen war), **...kos|ten** *(Plur.)*, **...krank|heit** (die; -), **...kre|dit|brief, ...land** (*Plur.* ...länder), **...lei|ter** (der), **...lei|te|rin, ...lek|tü|re, ...lust** (die; -); **rei|se|lus|tig; rei|sen;** du reist; du reis|test; gereist; reis[e]!; **Rei|sen|de,** der *u.* die; -n, -n (↑R 5 ff.); **Rei|se‿ne|ces|saire, ...on|kel** (*scherzh. für* Mann, der oft und gern reist), **...pass, ...plan** (*vgl.* [2]Plan), **...pros|pekt, ...pro|vi|ant**
Rei|ser|be|sen (*svw.* Reisigbesen)
Rei|ser|chen *Plur.*
Rei|se|rei (dauerndes Reisen)
rei|sern (*Jägerspr.* Witterung [von Zweigen u. Ästen] nehmen)
Rei|se‿rou|te, ...ruf, ...sai|son, ...scheck, ...schreib|ma|schi|ne, ...spe|sen *(Plur.)*, **...ta|sche, ...ver|an|stal|ter, ...ver|kehr** (der; -s); **Rei|se|ver|kehrs‿kauf|frau, ...kauf|mann; Rei|se‿vor|be|rei|tun|gen** *(Plur.)*, **...we|cker, ...wet|ter** (das; -s), **...wet|ter|be|richt, ...wet|ter|ver|si|che|rung, ...zeit, ...ziel**
Reis|feld
Reis|holz, das; -es (*veraltet für* Reisig)
rei|sig (*veraltet für* beritten)
Rei|sig, das; -s; **Rei|sig‿be|sen, ...bün|del**
Rei|si|ge, der; -n, -n; ↑R 5 ff. (*im Mittelalter* berittener Söldner)
Rei|sig|holz, das; -es
Reis|korn *Plur.* ...körner
Reis|lauf, der; -[e]s (*früher bes. in der Schweiz* Eintritt in fremden Dienst als Söldner); **Reis|läu|fer**
Reis|lein ‹*zu* [3]Reis›
Reis‿mehl, ...pa|pier, ...rand *(Gastron.)*
Reiß|ah|le; Reiß|aus; *nur in* - nehmen (*ugs. für* davonlaufen); **Reiß‿bahn** (*Flugw.* abreißbarer Teil der Ballonhülle), **...blei** (das; Graphit), **...brett** (Zeichenbrett)
Reis‿schleim, ...schnaps
rei|ßen; du reißt, er reißt; du rissest, er riss; gerissen; reiß[e]!; reißende (wilde) Tiere; *vgl. auch* hinreißen; **Rei|ßen,** das; -s (*ugs. auch für* Rheumatismus); **rei|ßend;** -er Strom; -e Schmerzen; -er Absatz; **Rei|ßer** (*ugs. für* besonders spannender, effektvoller Film, Roman u. a.); **rei|ße|risch;** -e Schlagzeilen; **Reiß|fe|der; reiß|fest; Reiß|fes|tig|keit,** die; -; **Reiß‿lei|ne** (am Fallschirm u. an der Reißbahn), **...li|nie** (*für* Perforation), **...na|gel** (*svw.* Reißzwecke), **...schie|ne, ...teu|fel** (*ugs. für* jmd., der seine Kleidung rasch verschleißt)
Reis‿stroh|tep|pich, ...sup|pe
Reiß|ver|schluss; Reiß|ver|schluss|sys|tem (↑R 136), das; -s *(Straßenverkehr)*; sich nach dem - einfädeln; **Reiß‿wolf** (der), **...wol|le, ...zahn, ...zeug, ...zir|kel, ...zwe|cke**
Reis|te, die; -, -n (*schweiz. für* Holzrutsche, [3]Riese); **reis|ten** (*schweiz. für* Holz von den Bergen niederrutschen lassen)
Reis|wein (Sake)
Reit|bahn
Rei|tel, der; -s, - (*mitteld. für* Drehstange, Knebel); **Rei|tel|holz** *(mitteld.)*
rei|ten; du reitest; du rittst (rittest), er ritt; du rittest; geritten; reit[e]!; **rei|tend;** -e Artillerie, -e Post; [1]**Rei|ter**
[2]**Rei|ter,** die; -, -n (*landsch., bes. österr. für* [Getreide]sieb)
Rei|ter|an|griff; Rei|te|rei; Rei|te|rin; rei|ter|lich; rei|ter|los; Rei|ter|re|gi|ment; Rei|ters|mann *Plur.* ...männer *u.* ...leute; **Rei|ter|stand|bild; Reit‿ger|te, ...ho|se**
Reit im Winkl (Ort in Bayern)
Reit‿leh|rer, ...leh|re|rin, ...peit|sche, ...pferd, ...schu|le (*südwestd. u. schweiz. auch für* Karussell), **...sport** (der; -[e]s), **...stall, ...stie|fel, ...stun|de, ...tier, ...tur|nier; Reit- und Fahr|tur|nier** (↑R 23); **Reit- und Spring|tur|nier** (↑R 23); **Reit‿un|ter|richt, ...weg**
Reiz, der; -es, -e; (↑R 47:) der Reiz des Neuen; **reiz|bar; Reiz|bar|keit,** die; -; **rei|zen;** du reizt; **rei|zend; Reiz‿gas, ...hus|ten**
Reiz|ker, der; -s, - ‹slaw.› (ein Pilz)
Reiz|kli|ma; reiz|los; Reiz|lo|sig|keit, die; -; **Reiz|mit|tel,** das; **Reiz‿schwel|le** *(Psych., Physiol.)*, **...stoff, ...the|ma** (*vgl.* Reizwort), **...the|ra|pie, ...über|flu|tung** (↑R 132); **Rei|zung; reiz|voll; Reiz‿wä|sche, ...wort** (Emotionen auslösendes Wort)
Re|ka|pi|tu|la|ti|on, die; -, -en ‹lat.› (Wiederholung, Zusammenfassung); **re|ka|pi|tu|lie|ren**
Re|kel, der; -s, - (*nordd. für* grober, ungeschliffener Mensch); **Re|ke|lei; re|keln,** sich (sich behaglich recken und dehnen); ich ...[e]le mich (↑R 16)
Re|kla|mant, der; -en, -en (↑R 126) ‹lat.› (*Rechtsw.* Beschwerdeführer); **Re|kla|ma|ti|on,** die; -, -en (Beanstandung);

Re|kla|me, die; -, -n (Werbung; Anpreisung von Waren); **Re|kla|me‿feld|zug, ...flä|che; re|kla|me|haft; Re|kla|me‿pla|kat, ...rum|mel** *(ugs.),* **...trick; Re|kla|me|trom|mel;** die - rühren (Reklame machen); **re|kla|mie|ren** ([zurück]fordern; beanstanden)

re|kog|nos|zie|ren (↑R 130 *u.* 132) ‹lat.› (*veraltet für* [die Echtheit] anerkennen; *scherzh. für* auskundschaften; *früher, heute noch schweiz. für* erkunden, aufklären [beim Militär]); **Re|kog|nos|zie|rung**

Re|kom|man|da|ti|on, die; -, -en ‹franz.› (*veraltet für* Empfehlung); **Re|kom|man|da|ti|ons|schrei|ben** *(veraltet);* **re|kom|man|die|ren** (*veraltet, aber noch landsch. für* empfehlen; *österr. für* [einen Brief] einschreiben lassen)

Re|kom|pens, die; -, -en ‹lat.› (*Wirtsch.* Entschädigung); **Re|kom|pen|sa|ti|on; re|kom|pen|sie|ren**

re|kon|stru|ier|bar; re|kon|stru|ie|ren ‹lat.› ([den ursprüngl. Zustand] wieder herstellen od. nachbilden; den Ablauf eines früheren Ereignisses wiedergeben; *regional auch für* renovieren, sanieren); **Re|kon|stru|ie|rung; Re|kon|struk|ti|on,** die; -, -en

re|kon|va|les|zent [...v...] ‹lat.› (*Med.* genesend); **Re|kon|va|les|zent,** der; -en, -en (↑R 126); **Re|kon|va|les|zen|tin; Re|kon|va|les|zenz,** die; -; **re|kon|va|les|zie|ren**

Re|kord, der; -[e]s, -e ‹engl.›; **Re|kord|be|such; Re|kor|der** (Gerät zur elektromagnet. Speicherung u. Wiedergabe von Bild- u. Tonsignalen); **Re|kord‿er|geb|nis, ...ern|te, ...flug, ...hal|ter, ...hö|he, ...in|ter|na|ti|o|na|le** (der *u.* die; -n, -n; *Sport*), **...leis|tung, ...mar|ke, ...ver|such, ...wei|te, ...zahl, ...zeit**

Re|kre|a|ti|on, die; -, -en ‹lat.› (*veraltet für* Erholung; Erfrischung); **re|kre|ie|ren** *(veraltet)*

Rek|rut (↑R 130 *u.* 132), der; -en, -en (↑R 126) ‹franz.› (Soldat in der ersten Zeit der Ausbildung); **Rek|ru|ten‿aus|bil|der, ...aus|bil|dung, ...zeit; rek|ru|tie|ren** (*Milit. veraltet für* Rekruten ausheben, mustern); sich - (sich zusammensetzen, sich bilden); **Rek|ru|tie|rung**

Rek|ta (*Plur. von* Rektum); **rek|tal** ‹lat.› (*Med.* auf den Mastdarm bezüglich); **Rek|tal‿er|näh|rung, ...nar|ko|se, ...tem|pe|ra|tur; rek|tan|gu|lär** (↑R 132; *veraltet für* rechtwinklig); **Rek|ta|pa|pier** (*Bankw.* Wertpapier, auf dem der Besitzer namentlich genannt ist); **Rek|tas|zen|si|on** (↑R 132), die; -, -en (*Astron.* gerades Aufsteigen eines Sternes); **Rek|ta|wech|sel** (*Bankw.* auf den Namen des Inhabers ausgestellter Wechsel); **Rek|ti|fi|ka|ti|on,** die; -, -en (*veraltet für* Berichtigung; *Chemie* Reinigung durch wiederholte Destillation; *Math.* Bestimmung der Länge einer Kurve); **Rek|ti|fi|zier|an|la|ge** (Reinigungsanlage); **rek|ti|fi|zie|ren** (*zu* Rektifikation); **Rek|ti|on,** die; -, -en ‹lat.› (*Sprachw.* Fähigkeit eines Wortes [z. B. eines Verbs, einer Präposition], den Kasus des von ihm abhängenden Wortes zu bestimmen); **Rek|to,** das; -s, -s (*fachspr. für* [Blatt]vorderseite); **Rek|tor,** der; -s, ...oren (Leiter einer [Hoch]schule; kath. Geistlicher an einer Nebenkirche u. Ä.); **Rek|to|rat,** das; -[e]s, -e (Amt[szimmer], Amtszeit eines Rektors); **Rek|to|rats|re|de** (Rede eines Hochschulrektors bei der Übernahme seines Amtes); **Rek|to|ren|kon|fe|renz; Rek|to|rin; Rek|tor|re|de; Rek|to|skop** (↑R 132), das; -s, -e ‹lat.; griech.› (*Med.* Spiegel zur Mastdarmuntersuchung); **Rek|to|sko|pie,** die; -, ...ien; **Rek|tum,** das; -s, ...ta ‹lat.› (Mastdarm)

re|kul|ti|vie|ren [...v...] ‹franz.› (unfruchtbar gewordenen Boden wieder nutzbar machen); **Re|kul|ti|vie|rung**

Re|ku|pe|ra|tor, der; -s, ...oren ‹lat.› (Wärmeaustauscher zur Rückgewinnung der Wärme heißer Abgase)

re|kur|rie|ren ‹lat.› (auf etwas zurückkommen; zu etwas seine Zuflucht nehmen); **Re|kurs,** der; -es, -e (das Zurückgehen, Zuflucht; *Rechtsw.* Beschwerde, Einspruch); **Re|kurs|an|trag; re|kur|siv** (*Math.* zurückgehend bis zu bekannten Werten)

Re|lais [rəˈlɛː], das; - [rəˈlɛː(s)], - [rəˈlɛːs] ‹franz.› (*Elektrotechnik* Schalteinrichtung; *Postw. früher* Auswechslung[sstelle] der Pferde); **Re|lais|sta|ti|on**

Re|la|ti|on, die; -, -en ‹lat.› (Beziehung, Verhältnis); **Re|la|ti|ons|be|griff** (*Philos.* Begriff der Vergleichung und Entgegensetzung); **re|la|tiv** [*auch* ˈreː...] (bezüglich; verhältnismäßig; vergleichsweise; bedingt); -e (einfache) Mehrheit; **Re|la|tiv,** das; -s, -e [...və] (*Sprachw.* Relativpronomen; Relativadverb); **Re|la|tiv|ad|verb** (*Sprachw.* bezügliches Umstandswort, z. B. „wo" in „dort, wo der Fluss tief ist"); **re|la|ti|vie|ren** [...v...] (in eine Beziehung bringen; einschränken); **Re|la|ti|vis|mus,** der; - (philosophische Lehre, für die alle Erkenntnis nur relativ, nicht allgemein gültig ist); **re|la|ti|vis|tisch; Re|la|ti|vi|tät,** die; -, -en (Bezüglichkeit, Bedingtheit; *nur Sing.:* das Relativsein); **Re|la|ti|vi|täts|the|o|rie,** die; - (von Einstein begründete physikalische Theorie); **Re|la|tiv|pro|no|men** (*Sprachw.* bezügliches Fürwort, z. B. „das" in: „Ein Buch, das ich kenne."); **Re|la|tiv|satz**

re|laxed [riˈlɛkst] ‹engl.› (*ugs. für* entspannt); **re|la|xen** [riˈlɛksən] (sich entspannen); **Re|la|xing,** das; -s (das Relaxen)

Re|lease [riˈliːs], das; -, -s [...sis] ‹engl.› (Einrichtung zur Heilung Rauschgiftsüchtiger); **Re|lease|cen|ter; Re|lea|ser** (Psychotherapeut od. Sozialarbeiter, der bei der Behandlung Rauschgiftsüchtiger mitwirkt); **Re|lease|zent|rum** (*svw.* Releasecenter)

Re|le|ga|ti|on, die; -, -en ‹lat.› (Verweisung von der [Hoch]schule; *Sport* Relegationsspiele); **Re|le|ga|ti|ons|spiel** (*Sport* über Ab- od. Aufstieg entscheidendes Qualifikationsspiel); **re|le|gie|ren** (von der [Hoch]schule verweisen)

re|le|vant [...v...] ‹lat.› (erheblich, wichtig); **Re|le|vanz,** die; -

Re|li|ef, das; -s, *Plur.* -s *u.* -e ‹franz.› (über eine Fläche erhaben hervortretendes Bildwerk; *Geogr.* Form der Erdoberfläche, plastische Nachbildung der Oberfläche eines Geländes); **re|li|ef|ar|tig; Re|li|ef‿druck** (*Plur.* ...drucke; Hoch-, Prägedruck), **...glo|bus, ...kar|te** *(Kartographie),* **...kli|schee** *(Druckw.),* **...pfei|ler, ...sti|cke|rei**

Re|li|gi|on, die; -, -en ‹lat.›; natürliche, [ge]offenbarte, positive, monotheistische -; **Re|li|gi|ons‿be|kennt|nis, ...buch, ...frei|heit** (die; -), **...frie|de, ...ge|mein|schaft, ...ge|schich|te** (die; -), **...krieg, ...leh|re, ...leh|rer, ...leh|re|rin; re|li|gi|ons|los; Re|li|gi|ons|lo|sig|keit,** die; -; **Re|li|gi|ons‿phi|lo|so|phie, ...psy|cho|lo|gie, ...so|zi|o|lo|gie, ...stif|ter, ...strei|tig|kei|ten** *(Plur.),* **...stun|de, ...un|ter|richt, ...wis|sen|schaft** (die; -); **re|li|gi|ons|wis|sen|schaft|lich; Re|li|gi|ons|zu|ge|hö|rig|keit; re|li|gi-**

ös ‹franz.›; eine -e Bewegung; **Re|li|gi|o|se,** der *u.* die; -n, -n *meist Plur.;* ‹lat.› (Mitglied einer Ordensgemeinschaft); **Re|li|gi|o|si|tät,** die; -

re|likt ‹lat.› (*Biol.* in Resten vorkommend [von Tieren, Pflanzen]); **Re|likt,** das; -[e]s, -e (Rest; Überbleibsel); **Re|lik|ten** *Plur.* (*veraltet für* Hinterbliebene; Hinterlassenschaft); **Re|lik|ten‿fau|na** (die; -; *Zool.* Überbleibsel einer früheren Tierwelt), **...flo|ra** (die; -; *Bot.*)

Re|ling, die; -, *Plur.* -s, *seltener* -e ([Schiffs]geländer, Brüstung)

Re|li|qui|ar, das; -s, -e ‹lat.› (Reliquienbehälter); **Re|li|quie** [...iə], die; -, -n (Überrest, Gegenstand eines Heiligen); **Re|li|qui|en‿be|häl|ter, ...schrein**

Re|lish ['rɛlɪʃ], das; -s, -es [...ʃɪs] ‹engl.› (würzige Soße aus Gemüsestückchen)

Re|ma|gen (Stadt am Mittelrhein)

Re|make [ri'me:k], das; -s, -s ‹engl.› (Neuverfilmung; Neufassung einer künstlerischen Produktion)

Re|ma|nenz, die; - ‹lat.› (*Physik* Restmagnetismus)

Re|marque [rə'mark] (dt. Schriftsteller)

Re|ma|su|ri *vgl.* Ramasuri

Rem|bours [rã'bu:r], der; - [rã'bu:r(s)], - [rã'bu:rs] (*Überseehandel* Finanzierung u. Geschäftsabwicklung über eine Bank); **Rem|bours‿ge|schäft, ...kre|dit**

Rem|brandt (niederl. Maler); - van Rijn [fan *od.* van 'rɛin]

Re|me|di|um, das; -s, *Plur.* ...ien [...iən] *u.* ...ia ‹lat.› (*Med.* Arzneimittel; *Münzw.* zulässiger Mindergehalt [der Münzen an edlem Metall]); **Re|me|dur,** die; -, -en (*veraltend für* Abhilfe); - schaffen

Re|mi|gi|us (ein Heiliger)

Re|mig|rant (↑R 130), der; -en, -en (↑R 126) ‹lat.› (Rückwanderer, zurückgekehrter Emigrant); **Re|mig|ran|tin**

re|mi|li|ta|ri|sie|ren ‹franz.› (wieder bewaffnen; das aufgelöste Heerwesen eines Landes von neuem organisieren); **Re|mi|li|ta|ri|sie|rung,** die; -

Re|mi|nis|zenz, die; -, -en ‹lat.› (Erinnerung; Anklang); **Re|mi|nis|ze|re** („gedenke!") (fünfter Sonntag vor Ostern)

re|mis [rə'mi:] ‹franz.› (unentschieden); **Re|mis,** das; - [rə'mi:(s)], *Plur.* - [rə'mi:s] *u.* -en [...zən] (unentschiedenes Spiel); **Re|mi|se,** die; -, -n (*veraltend für* Geräte-, Wagenschuppen; *Jägerspr.* Schutzgehölz für Wild); **Re|mis|si|on,** die; -, -en ‹lat.› (*Buchw.* Rücksendung von Remittenden; *Med.* vorübergehendes Nachlassen von Krankheitserscheinungen; *Physik* das Zurückwerfen von Licht an undurchsichtigen Flächen); **Re|mit|ten|de,** die; -, -n (*Buchw.* beschädigtes od. fehlerhaftes Druckerzeugnis, das an den Verlag zurückgeschickt wird); **Re|mit|tent,** der; -en, -en; ↑R 126 (*Wirtsch.* Wechselnehmer); **re|mit|tie|ren** (*Buchw.* zurücksenden; *Med.* nachlassen [vom Fieber])

Rem|mi|dem|mi, das; -s (*ugs. für* lärmendes Treiben, Trubel)

re|mon|tant [*auch* remõ'tant] ‹franz.› (*Bot.* zum zweiten Mal blühend); **Re|mon|tant|ro|se;** **Re|mon|te** [*auch* re'mõ:tə], die; -, -n (*früher* junges Militärpferd); **re|mon|tie|ren** [*auch* remõ...] (*Bot.* zum zweiten Mal blühen od. fruchten; *früher* den militär. Pferdebestand durch Jungpferde ergänzen); **Re|mon|tie|rung; Re|mon|toir|uhr** [remõ'toa:r...] (*veraltet für* ohne Schlüssel aufziehund stellbare Taschenuhr)

Re|mor|queur [...'kø:r], der; -s, -e ‹franz.› (*österr. für* kleiner Schleppdampfer)

Re|mou|la|de [...mu...], die; -, -n ‹franz.› (eine Kräutermajonäse); **Re|mou|la|den|so|ße**

Rem|pe|lei (*ugs.*); **rem|peln** (*ugs. für* absichtlich stoßen); ich ...[e]le (↑R 16); **Remp|ler** (*ugs. für* Stoß)

Remp|ter *vgl.* Remter

Rems, die; - (r. Nebenfluss des Neckars)

Rem|scheid (Stadt in Nordrhein-Westfalen)

Rem|ter, der; -s, - ‹lat.› (Speise-, Versammlungssaal [in Burgen und Klöstern])

Re|mu|ne|ra|ti|on, die; -, -en ‹lat.› (*veraltet, noch österr. für* Entschädigung, Vergütung); *vgl. aber* Renumeration; **re|mu|ne|rie|ren** (*veraltet, noch österr.*)

Re|mus (Zwillingsbruder des Romulus)

[1]**Ren** [re:n, rɛn], das; -s, *Plur.* Rene *u.* -s [rɛns] ‹nord.› (ein nordländ. Hirsch)

[2]**Ren,** der; -s, -es [...ne:s] ‹lat.› (*Med.* Niere)

Re|nais|sance [rənɛ'sã:s], die; -, -n [...sən] ‹franz.› (*nur Sing.:* auf der Antike aufbauende kulturelle Bewegung vom 14. bis 16. Jh.; erneutes Aufleben); **Re|nais|sance‿dich|ter, ...ma|ler, ...stil** (der; -[e]s), **...zeit** (die; -)

Re|na|ta, Re|na|te (w. Vorn.)

re|na|tu|rie|ren ‹lat.› (in einen naturnahen Zustand zurückführen); **Re|na|tu|rie|rung**

Re|na|tus (m. Vorn.)

Re|nault ® [rə'no:] (Kraftfahrzeugmarke)

Ren|cont|re (↑R 130) *vgl.* Renkontre

Ren|dant, der; -en, -en (↑R 126) ‹franz.› (Rechnungsführer); **Ren|dan|tur,** die; -, -en ‹lat.› (*veraltet für* Gelder einnehmende u. auszahlende Behörde); **Ren|de|ment** [rãdə'mã:], das; -s, -s ‹franz.› (Gehalt an reinen Bestandteilen, bes. Gehalt an reiner Wolle); **Ren|dez|vous,** *schweiz. auch* **Ren|dez-vous** [rãde'vu:], das; - [...'vu:(s)], - [...'vu:s] (Verabredung [von Verliebten]; Begegnung von Raumfahrzeugen im Weltall); **Ren|dez|vous‿ma|nö|ver, ...tech|nik; Ren|di|te** [rɛn...], die; -, -n ‹ital.› (*Wirtsch.* Verzinsung, Ertrag); **Ren|di|ten|haus** (*schweiz. für* Mietshaus); **Ren|di|te|ob|jekt**

Re|né [rə'ne:] (m. Vorn.)

Re|ne|gat, der; -en, -en (↑R 126) ‹lat.› (jmd., der seine bisherige politische od. religiöse Überzeugung wechselt; Abtrünniger); **Re|ne|ga|ten|tum,** das; -s

Re|nek|lo|de, *auch* Rei|nec|lau|de [rɛnə'klo:də] (↑R 130 *u.* 132), die; -, -n ‹franz.› (eine Edelpflaume); *vgl.* Ringlotte

Re|net|te, die; -, -n ‹franz.› (ein Apfel); *vgl.* Reinette

Ren|for|cé [rãfɔr'se:], der *od.* das; -s, -s ‹franz.› (ein Baumwollgewebe)

re|ni|tent ‹lat.› (widerspenstig, widersetzlich); **Re|ni|ten|te,** der *u.* die; -n, -n (↑R 5 ff.); **Re|ni|tenz,** die; - (renitentes Verhalten)

Ren|ke, die; -, -n *u.* Ren|ken, der; -s, - (ein Fisch in den Voralpenseen)

ren|ken (*veraltet für* drehend hin und her bewegen)

Ren|kont|re [rã'kõ:tər, *auch* ...trə] (↑R 130), das; -s, -s ‹franz.› (*veraltend für* feindliche Begegnung; Zusammenstoß)

Renk|ver|schluss (*für* Bajonettverschluss)

Renn‿au|to, ...bahn, ...boot; ren|nen; du ranntest; *selten:* du renntest; gerannt; renn[e]!; **Ren|nen,** das; -s, -; **Ren|ner** (*ugs. auch für* etwas, was erfolgreich, beliebt ist; Verkaufsschlager); **Ren|ne|rei; Renn‿fah|rer, ...fah|re|rin, ...fie|ber** (das; -s), **...jacht, ...lei|ter** (der), **...ma|schi|ne** (Motorrad für Rennen), **...pferd, ...pis|te, ...platz, ...rad, ...rei|ter, ...ro|deln** (das; -s), **...sport** (der; -[e]s), **...stall**

Renn|steig, *auch* **Renn|stieg** *od.* Renn|weg, der; -[e]s (Kammweg auf der Höhe des Thüringer Waldes u. Frankenwaldes)

Renn‿stre|cke, ...wa|gen

Renn|weg *vgl.* Rennsteig

Re|noir [rə'noa:r] (franz. Maler u. Grafiker)

Re|nom|ma|ge [...'ma:ʒə], die; -, -n ‹franz.› (*veraltet für* Prahlerei); **Re|nom|mee,** das; -s, -s ([guter] Ruf, Leumund); **re|nom|mie|ren** (prahlen); **Re|nom|mier|stück; re|nom|miert** (berühmt, angesehen, namhaft); **Re|nom|mist,** der; -en, -en; ↑R 126 (Prahlhans); **Re|nom|mis|te|rei**

Re|non|ce [re'nɔ̃:s(ə)], die; -, -n ‹franz.› (*Kartenspiel* Fehlfarbe)

Re|no|va|ti|on [...v...], die; -, -en ‹lat.› (*schweiz., sonst veraltet für* Renovierung); **re|no|vie|ren** (erneuern, instand setzen); **Re|no|vie|rung**

Ren|seig|ne|ment [rɑ̃sɛnjə'mɑ̃:] (↑R 130), das; -s, -s ‹franz.› (*veraltet für* Auskunft, Nachweis)

ren|ta|bel (zinstragend; einträglich); ein ...ab|les (↑R 130) Geschäft; **Ren|ta|bi|li|tät,** die; - (*Wirtsch.* Einträglichkeit, [Höhe der] Verzinsung); **Ren|ta|bi|li|täts‿ge|sichts|punkt, ...prü|fung, ...rech|nung; Rent|amt** (*früher* Rechnungsamt); **Ren|te,** die; -, -n ‹franz.› (regelmäßiges Einkommen [aus Vermögen od. rechtl. Ansprüchen]); eine lebenslängliche -; **Ren|tei** (*svw.* Rentamt); **Ren|ten‿al|ter** (im - sein), **...an|lei|he** (Anleihe des Staates, für die kein Tilgungszwang besteht), **...an|pas|sung, ...an|spruch, ...bank** (*Plur.* ...banken), **...ba|sis, ...be|mes|sungs|grund|la|ge, ...be|ra|ter, ...be|ra|tung, ...emp|fän|ger, ...emp|fän|ge|rin, ...mark** (die; -, -; dt. Währungseinheit [1923]), **...markt** (Handel mit festverzinsl. Wertpapieren), **...pa|pier** (*svw.* Rentenwert); **ren|ten|pflich|tig; Ren|ten‿rech|nung** *(Math.)*, **...re|form, ...schein, ...ver|schrei|bung** (ein Wertpapier, das die Zahlung einer Rente verbrieft), **...ver|si|che|rung, ...wert** (ein Wertpapier mit fester Verzinsung), **...zah|lung**

[1]**Ren|tier** [*auch* 'rɛn...] (*svw.* [1]Ren)

[2]**Ren|ti|er** [...'tie:], der; -s, -s ‹franz.› (*veraltend für* Rentner; jmd., der von den Erträgen seines Vermögens lebt); **ren|tie|ren** [...'ti:...] (Gewinn bringen); sich - (sich lohnen)

Ren|tier|flech|te [*auch* 'rɛn...] ([Futter für das [1]Ren liefernde] Flechte nördlicher Länder)

ren|tier|lich (*svw.* rentabel); **Rent|ner; Rent|ne|rin**

Re|nu|me|ra|ti|on, die; -, -en ‹lat.› (*Wirtsch.* Rückzahlung); *vgl. aber* Remuneration; **re|nu|me|rie|ren** (zurückzahlen)

Re|nun|ti|a|ti|on, Re|nun|zi|a|ti|on, die; -, -en ‹lat.› (Abdankung [eines Monarchen]); **re|nun|zie|ren**

Re|ok|ku|pa|ti|on, die; -, -en ‹lat.› (Wiederbesetzung); **re|ok|ku|pie|ren**

Re|or|ga|ni|sa|ti|on, die; -, -en *Plur. selten* ‹lat.; franz.› (Neugestaltung, Neuordnung); **Re|or|ga|ni|sa|tor,** der; -s, ...oren; **re|or|ga|ni|sie|ren**

Rep, der; -s, *Plur.* -s, u. *(ugs.)* Repse (*kurz für* Republikaner [Mitglied einer rechtsgerichteten Partei])

re|pa|ra|bel ‹lat.› (sich reparieren lassend, ersetzbar); ...ab|le (↑R 130) Schäden; **Re|pa|ra|teur** [...'tø:r], der; -s, -e (jmd., der etwas berufsmäßig repariert); **Re|pa|ra|ti|on,** die; -, -en (Wiederherstellung; *nur Plur.:* Kriegsentschädigung); **Re|pa|ra|ti|ons‿leis|tung, ...zah|lung; Re|pa|ra|tur,** die; -, -en; **re|pa|ra|tur|an|fäl|lig; Re|pa|ra|tur|an|nah|me; re|pa|ra|tur|be|dürf|tig; Re|pa|ra|tur‿kos|ten** *(Plur.)*, **...werk|statt; re|pa|rie|ren**

re|par|tie|ren ‹franz.› (*Börse* Wertpapiere aufteilen, zuteilen); **Re|par|ti|ti|on,** die; -, -en

re|pas|sie|ren ‹franz.› (Laufmaschen aufnehmen); **Re|pas|sie|re|rin** (Arbeiterin, die Laufmaschen aufnimmt)

re|pat|ri|ie|ren (↑R 130) ‹lat.› (die frühere Staatsangehörigkeit wieder verleihen; Kriegs-, Zivilgefangene in die Heimat entlassen); **Re|pat|ri|ie|rung**

Re|per|kus|si|on, die; -, -en ‹lat.› (*Musik* Sprechton beim Psalmenvortrag; Durchführung des Themas durch alle Stimmen der Fuge)

Re|per|toire [...'toa:r], das; -s, -s ‹franz.› (Vorrat einstudierter Stücke usw., Spielplan); **Re|per|toire|stück** (populäres, immer wieder gespieltes Stück); **Re|per|to|ri|um,** das; -s, ...ien [...iən] ‹lat.› (wissenschaftl. Nachschlagewerk)

Re|pe|tent, der; -en, -en (↑R 126) ‹lat.› (Schüler, der eine Klasse wiederholt; *veraltet für* Repetitor); **re|pe|tie|ren** (wiederholen); **Re|pe|tier‿ge|wehr, ...uhr** (Taschenuhr mit Schlagwerk); **Re|pe|ti|ti|on,** die; -, -en (Wiederholung); **Re|pe|ti|tor,** der; -s, ...oren (jmd., der mit Studenten den Lehrstoff [zur Vorbereitung auf das Examen] wiederholt; *auch für* Korrepetitor); **Re|pe|ti|to|ri|um,** das; -s, ...ien [...iən] (*veraltend für* Wiederholungsunterricht, -buch)

Rep|lik (↑R 130), die; -, -en ‹franz.› (Gegenrede, Erwiderung; vom Künstler selbst angefertigte Nachbildung eines Originals); **rep|li|zie|ren** ‹lat.›

re|po|ni|bel ‹lat.› (*Med.* sich reponieren lassend); ...ib|ler (↑R 130) Bruch; **re|po|nie|ren** ([Knochen, Organe] wieder in die normale Lage zurückbringen)

Re|port, der; -[e]s, -e ‹franz.› (Bericht, Mitteilung; *Börse* Kursaufschlag bei der Verlängerung von Termingeschäften); **Re|por|ta|ge** [...'ta:ʒə, *österr.* ...'ta:ʒ], die; -, -n [...'ta:ʒ(ə)n] (Bericht[erstattung] über ein aktuelles Ereignis); **Re|por|ter,** der; -s, - ‹engl.› (Zeitungs-, Fernseh-, Rundfunkberichterstatter); **Re|por|te|rin**

Re|po|si|ti|on, die; -, -en ‹lat.› (*Med.* das Reponieren)

re|prä|sen|ta|bel ‹franz.› (würdig; stattlich; wirkungsvoll); ...ab|le (↑R 130) Erscheinung; **Re|prä|sen|tant,** der; -en, -en; ↑R 126 (Vertreter, Abgeordneter); **Re|prä|sen|tan|ten|haus; Re|prä|sen|tan|tin; Re|prä|sen|tanz,** die; -, -en ([geschäftl.] Vertretung); **Re|prä|sen|ta|ti|on,** die; -, -en ([Stell]vertretung; *nur Sing.:* standesgemäßes Auftreten, gesellschaftl. Aufwand); **Re|prä|sen|ta|ti|ons‿auf|wen|dung, ...gel|der** *(Plur.)*, **...schluss** (*Statistik* bei Stichproben u. Schätzungen angewandtes Schlussverfahren); **re|prä|sen|ta|tiv** (vertretend; typisch; wirkungsvoll); -e Demokratie; **Re|prä|sen|ta|tiv‿bau** (*Plur.* ...bauten), **...be|fra|gung** *(Statistik)*, **...er|he|bung, ...ge|walt** (die; -; *Politik*); **Re|prä|sen|ta|ti|vi|tät** [...v...], die; -; **Re|prä|sen|ta|tiv‿sys|tem** *(Politik)*, **...um|fra|ge; re|prä|sen|tie|ren** (vertreten; etwas darstellen; standesgemäß auftreten)

Re|pres|sa|lie [...iə], die; -, -n *meist Plur.* ‹lat.› (Vergeltungsmaßnahme, Druckmittel); **Re|pres|si|on,** die; -, -en (Unterdrückung [von Kritik, polit. Bewegungen u. Ä.]); **re|pres|si|ons|frei; Re|pres|si|ons|in|stru|ment; re|pres|siv** (unterdrückend, Druck ausübend); repressive Maßnahmen; **Re|pres|siv|zoll** (Schutzzoll)

Re|print, der; -s, -s ‹engl.› (*Buchw.* unveränderter Nachdruck, Neudruck)

Re|pri|se, die; -, -n ‹franz.› (*Börse* Kurserholung; *Musik* Wiederholung; *Theater, Film* Wiederaufnahme [eines Stückes] in den Spielplan; Neuauflage einer Schallplatte)

re|pri|va|ti|sie|ren [...v...] ‹franz.› (staatliches od. gesellschaftliches Eigentum in Privatbesitz zurückführen); **Re|pri|va|ti|sie|rung**

Re|pro, die; -, -s *u.* das; -s, -s ‹*Kurzform von* Reproduktion› (*Druckw.* fotografische Reproduktion einer Bildvorlage)

Re|pro|ba|ti|on, die; -, -en ‹lat.› (*Rechtsspr. veraltet für* Missbilligung); **re|pro|bie|ren**

Re|pro|duk|ti|on, die; -, -en ‹lat.› (Nachbildung; Wiedergabe eines Originals [bes. durch Druck]; Vervielfältigung); **Re|pro|duk|ti|ons‿fak|tor** *(Kernphysik),* **...for|schung, ...me|di|zin, ...tech|nik, ...ver|fah|ren; re|pro|duk|tiv; re|pro|du|zie|ren** (*zu* Reproduktion); **Re|pro|gra|phie** (↑R 33), die; -, ...ien (Sammelbezeichnung für verschiedene Kopierverfahren)

Reps, der; -es, *Plur. (Sorten:)* -e (*südd. für* Raps)

Rep|til, das; -s, *Plur.* -ien [...i̯ən], *selten* -e ‹franz.› (Kriechtier); **Rep|ti|li|en|fonds** (*iron. für* Geldfonds, über dessen Verwendung hohe Regierungsstellen keine Rechenschaft abzulegen brauchen)

Re|pu|blik (↑R 130), die; -, -en ‹franz.›; **Re|pu|bli|ka|ner; Re|pu|bli|ka|ne|rin; re|pu|bli|ka|nisch; Re|pu|bli|ka|nis|mus,** der; - (*veraltend für* Streben nach einer republikanischen Verfassung); **Re|pu|blik|flucht** (*ehemals* Flucht aus der DDR); *vgl.* [2]Flucht; **re|pu|blik|flüch|tig; Re|pu|blik|flücht|ling**

Re|pu|di|a|ti|on, die; -, -en ‹lat.› (*Wirtsch.* Verweigerung der Annahme von Geld wegen geringer Kaufkraft)

Re|pul|si|on, die; -, -en ‹franz.› (*Technik* Ab-, Zurückstoßung); **Re|pul|si|ons|mo|tor; re|pul|siv** (zurück-, abstoßend)

Re|pun|ze, die; -, -n ‹lat.; ital.› (Stempel [für Feingehalt bei Waren aus Edelmetall]); **re|pun|zie|ren** (mit einem Feingehaltsstempel versehen)

Re|pu|ta|ti|on, die; - ‹lat.-franz.› ([guter] Ruf, Ansehen); **re|pu|tier|lich** (*veraltet für* ansehnlich; achtbar; ordentlich)

Re|qui|em [...i̯em], das; -s, *Plur.* -s, *österr.* ...quien [...i̯ən] ‹lat.› (*kath. Kirche* Totenmesse; *Musik* [1]Messe); **re|qui|es|cat in pa|ce** [...kat -ˈpaːt͡sə] ‹„er [sie] ruhe in Frieden!“› (*Abk.* R. I. P.)

re|qui|rie|ren ‹lat.› (beschlagnahmen [für milit. Zwecke]; *veraltet für* um Rechtshilfe ersuchen); **Re|qui|sit,** das; -[e]s, -en (Zubehör; Gegenstand, der für eine Theateraufführung od. eine Filmszene verwendet wird); **Re|qui|si|te,** die; -, -n (Requisitenkammer; für die Requisiten zuständige Stelle beim Theater); **Re|qui|si|ten|kam|mer; Re|qui|si|teur** [...ˈtøːr], der; -s, -e ‹franz.› (*Theater, Film* Verwalter der Requisiten); **Re|qui|si|ti|on,** die; -, -en (*zu* requirieren)

resch (*bayr. u. österr. für* knusprig, lebhaft, munter)

Re|schen|pass, der; -es *u.* **Re|schen|schei|deck,** das; -s (österr.-ital. Alpenpass)

Re|se|da, die; -, *Plur.* ...den, *selten* -s ‹lat.› (eine Pflanze); **re|se|da|far|ben; Re|se|de,** die; -, -n (Reseda)

Re|sek|ti|on, die; -, -en ‹lat.› (*Med.* operative Entfernung kranker Organteile)

Re|ser|va|ge [...vaːʒə], die; - ‹franz.› (*Textilwirtsch.* Schutzbeize, die das Aufnehmen von Farbe verhindert); **Re|ser|vat** [...v...], das; -[e]s, -e ‹lat.› (Vorbehalt; Sonderrecht; großes Freigehege für gefährdete Tierarten; *auch für* Reservation); **Re|ser|va|tio men|ta|lis,** die; - -, ...tiones [...neːs] ...tales [...leːs] (*svw.* Mentalreservation); **Re|ser|va|ti|on,** die; -, -en (Vorbehalt; den Indianern vorbehaltenes Gebiet in Nordamerika); **Re|ser|vat|recht** (Sonderrecht); **Re|ser|ve,** die; -, -n ‹franz.› (Ersatz; Vorrat; *Milit.* nicht aktive Wehrpflichtige; *Wirtsch.* Rücklage; *nur Sing.:* Zurückhaltung, Verschlossenheit); in - (vorrätig); [Leutnant usw.] der - (*Abk.* d. R.); **Re|ser|ve‿bank** *(Sport),* **...fonds** (*Wirtsch.* Rücklage), **...ka|nis|ter, ...of|fi|zier, ...rad, ...rei|fen, ...spie|ler, ...spie|le|rin, ...tank, ...übung** (↑R 132); **re|ser|vie|ren** ‹lat.› (aufbewahren; vormerken, vorbestellen, [Platz] freihalten); **re|ser|viert** (*auch für* zurückhaltend, kühl); **Re|ser|viert|heit,** die; -; **Re|ser|vie|rung; Re|ser|vist,** der; -en, -en; ↑R 126 (Soldat der Reserve); **Re|ser|vo|ir** [...ˈvoaːr], das; -s, -e ‹franz.› (Sammelbecken, Behälter)

re|se|zie|ren ‹lat.› (*Verb zu* Resektion)

Re|si (w. Vorn.)

Re|si|dent, der; -en, -en (↑R 126) ‹franz.› (*veraltet für* Geschäftsträger; *veraltend für* Regierungsvertreter, Statthalter); **Re|si|denz,** die; -, -en ‹lat.› (Wohnsitz des Staatsoberhauptes, eines Fürsten, eines hohen Geistlichen; Hauptstadt); **Re|si|denz‿pflicht** (die; -), **...stadt, ...the|a|ter; re|si|die|ren** (seinen Wohnsitz haben [bes. von regierenden Fürsten]); **re|si|du|al** (*Med.* zurückbleibend, restlich); **Re|si|du|um** [...du̯um], das; -s, ...duen [...du̯ən] (Rest [als Folge einer Krankheit])

Re|sig|na|ti|on (↑R 130), die; -, -en *Plur. selten* ‹lat.› (Ergebung in das Schicksal; Verzicht); **re|sig|na|tiv** (durch Resignation gekennzeichnet); **re|sig|nie|ren; re|sig|niert** (mutlos, niedergeschlagen)

Re|si|nat, das; -[e]s, -e ‹lat.› (*Chemie* Salz der Harzsäure)

Ré|sis|tance [rezisˈtãːs], die; - ‹franz.› (franz. Widerstandsbewegung gegen die deutsche Besatzung im 2. Weltkrieg); **re|sis|tent** ‹lat.› (widerstandsfähig); **Re|sis|tenz,** die; -, -en (Widerstand[sfähigkeit]); passive -; **re|sis|tie|ren** (widerstehen; ausdauern); **re|sis|tiv** (widerstehend, hartnäckig)

Re|skript, das; -[e]s, -e ‹lat.› (feierl. Rechtsentscheidung des Papstes od. eines Bischofs)

re|so|lut ‹lat.› (entschlossen, beherzt, tatkräftig); **Re|so|lut|heit,** die; -; **Re|so|lu|ti|on,** die; -, -en (Beschluss, Entschließung); **re|sol|vie|ren** [...v...] (*veraltet für* beschließen)

Re|so|nanz, die; -, -en ‹lat.› (*Musik, Physik* Mittönen, -schwingen; Widerhall, Zustimmung); **Re|so|nanz‿bo|den** (*Musik* Schallboden), **...fre|quenz** *(Physik),* **...kas|ten** *(Musik),* **...kör|per, ...raum; Re|so|na|tor,** der; -s, ...oren (mitschwingender Körper)

Re|so|pal ®, das; -s (ein Kunststoff)

re|sor|bie|ren ‹lat.› (ein-, aufsaugen); **Re|sorp|ti|on,** die; -, -en (Aufnahme [gelöster Stoffe in die

Blut- bzw. Lymphbahn]); **Re|sorp|ti|ons|fä|hig|keit**

re|so|zi|a|li|sie|r|bar; re|so|zi|a|li|sie|ren; Re|so|zi|a|li|sie|rung ‹lat.› (schrittweise Wiedereingliederung von Straffälligen in die Gesellschaft)

resp. = respektive

Res|pekt (↑R 132), der; -[e]s ‹franz.› (Achtung; Ehrerbietung; *Buchw., Kunstw.* leerer Rand [bei Drucksachen, Kupferstichen]); (↑R 40:) eine Respekt einflößende Persönlichkeit; **res|pek|ta|bel** (ansehnlich; angesehen); ...ab|le (↑R 130) Größe; **Res|pek|ta|bi|li|tät,** die; - (Ansehen); **Res|pekt|blatt** (*Buchw.* leeres Blatt am Anfang eines Buches); **Res|pekt ein|flö|ßend** *vgl.* Respekt; **res|pek|tie|ren** (achten, in Ehren halten; *Wirtsch.* einen Wechsel bezahlen); **res|pek|tier|lich** (*veraltend für* ansehnlich, achtbar); **Res|pek|tie|rung,** die; -; **res|pek|tiv** ‹lat.› (*veraltet für* jeweilig); **res|pek|ti|ve** [...və] (beziehungsweise; oder; und; *Abk.* resp.); **res|pekt|los; Res|pekt|lo|sig|keit; Res|pekts|per|son; res|pekt|voll**

Res|pi|ghi [...gi] (ital. Komponist)

Re|spi|ra|ti|on, die; - ‹lat.› (*Med.* Atmung); **Re|spi|ra|ti|ons|ap|pa|rat; Re|spi|ra|tor,** der; -s, ...oren (Beatmungsgerät); **re|spi|ra|to|risch** (die Atmung betreffend, auf ihr beruhend); **re|spi|rie|ren** (atmen)

res|pon|die|ren (↑R 132) ‹lat.› (*veraltet für* antworten); **Res|pons,** der; -es, -e (auf eine Initiative o. Ä. hin erfolgende Reaktion); **res|pon|sa|bel** (*veraltet für* verantwortlich); **Res|pon|so|ri|um,** das; -s, ...ien [...i̯ən] (liturg. Wechselgesang)

Res|sen|ti|ment [rɛsãtiˈmã:], das; -s, -s ‹franz.› (gefühlsmäßige Abneigung)

Res|sort [rɛˈso:r], das; -s, -s ‹franz.› (Geschäfts-, Amtsbereich); **res|sor|tie|ren** [rɛsɔrˈti:...] (*veraltend für* zugehören, unterstehen); **Res|sort|lei|ter** [rɛˈso:r...], der; **res|sort|mä|ßig** ([amts]zuständig); **Res|sort|mi|nis|ter**

Res|sour|ce [rɛˈsursə], die; -, -n *meist Plur.* ‹franz.› (Rohstoff-, Erwerbsquelle; Geldmittel)

Rest, der; -[e]s, *Plur.* -e *u.* (*Kaufmannsspr., bes. von Schnittwaren:*) -er, *schweiz.* -en ‹lat.›; **Rest‿ab|schnitt, ...al|ko|hol** (der; -s); **Res|tant** (↑R 132), der; -en, -en; ↑R 126 (*Bankw.* rückständiger Schuldner; nicht abgeholtes Wertpapier; *Wirtsch.* Ladenhüter); **Res|tan|ten|lis|te**

Res|tau|rant [rɛstoˈrã:], das; -s, -s ‹franz.› (Gaststätte); **Res|tau|rant|füh|rer**

Res|tau|ra|teur [...toraˈtø:r], der; -s, -e (*schweiz., sonst veraltet für* Gastwirt); **Res|tau|ra|ti|on** [...tau̯...], die; -, -en ‹lat.› (Wiederherstellung eines Kunstwerkes; Wiederherstellung der alten Ordnung nach einem Umsturz; *österr., sonst veraltet für* Gastwirtschaft); **Res|tau|ra|ti|ons|ar|beit** *meist Plur.*; **Res|tau|ra|ti|ons|be|trieb; Res|tau|ra|ti|ons‿po|li|tik** (die; -), **...zeit; Res|tau|ra|tor,** der; -s, ...oren (Wiederhersteller [von Kunstwerken]); **Res|tau|ra|to|rin; res|tau|rie|ren** (wieder in den ursprünglichen Zustand bringen, ausbessern [bes. von Kunstwerken]); **Res|tau|rie|rung**

Rest‿be|stand, ...be|trag; Res|ten, Res|ter (*Plur. von* Rest); **Res|te‿ver|kauf, ...ver|wer|tung; Rest‿for|de|rung, ...grup|pe, ...harn**

re|sti|tu|ie|ren ‹lat.› (wieder einsetzen; zurückerstatten, ersetzen); **Re|sti|tu|ti|on,** die; -, -en; **Re|sti|tu|ti|ons‿edikt** (↑R 132; das; -[e]s; von 1629), **...kla|ge** (*Rechtsw.* Klage auf Wiederaufnahme eines Verfahrens)

Rest|kos|ten|rech|nung (ein betriebswirtschaftliches Kalkulationsverfahren); **rest|lich; Rest|loch** *(Bergbau);* **rest|los; Rest|müll; Rest|nut|zungs|dau|er** *(Wirtsch.)*

Rest|pos|ten

Rest|rik|ti|on (↑R 130 *u.* 132), die; -, -en ‹lat.› (Einschränkung, Vorbehalt); **Rest|rik|ti|ons|maß|nah|me** *(Politik);* **rest|rik|tiv** (ein-, beschränkend, einengend); -e Konjunktion (*Sprachw.* einschränkende Konjunktion, z. B. „insofern“); **rest|rin|gie|ren** (*selten für* einschränken)

Rest|ri|si|ko

re|struk|tu|rie|ren ‹lat.› (neu gestalten, neu ordnen, neu strukturieren); **Re|struk|tu|rie|rung** (Umgestaltung, Neuordnung)

Rest‿stra|fe, ...sum|me, ...sü|ße (die; -; *Weinbau*), **...ur|laub, ...wär|me**

Re|sul|tan|te, die; -, -n ‹franz.› (*Physik* Ergebnisvektor von verschieden gerichteten Bewegungs- od. Kraftvektoren); **Re|sul|tat,** das; -[e]s, -e (Ergebnis); **re|sul|ta|tiv** (ein Resultat bewirkend); -e Verben (*Sprachw.* Verben, die das Ergebnis eines Vorgangs mit einschließen, z. B. „aufessen“); **re|sul|tat|los; re|sul|tie|ren** (sich [als Schlussfolgerung] ergeben; folgen); **Re|sul|tie|ren|de,** die; -n, -n; ↑R 5 ff. (*svw.* Resultante)

Re|sü|mee, das; -s, -s ‹franz.› (Zusammenfassung); **re|sü|mie|ren**

Ret *vgl.* Reet

Re|ta|bel, das; -s, - ‹franz.› (*Kunstw.* Altaraufsatz)

Re|tard [rəˈta:r], der; -s ‹franz.› (Verzögerung [bei Uhren]); den Hebel auf - stellen; **Re|tar|da|ti|on,** die; -, -en ([Entwicklungs]verzögerung, Verlangsamung); **re|tar|die|ren** (verzögern, zurückbleiben); retardierendes Moment (bes. im Drama)

Re|ten|ti|on, die; -, -en ‹lat.› (*Med.* Zurückhaltung von auszuscheidenden Stoffen im Körper)

Re|thel (dt. Maler)

Re|ti|kül, der *od.* das; -s, *Plur.* -e *u.* -s ‹franz.› (*svw.* Ridikül); **re|ti|ku|lar, re|ti|ku|lär** ‹lat.› (*Med.* netzartig, netzförmig); **re|ti|ku|liert** (mit netzartigem Muster); -e Gläser; **Re|ti|na,** die; -, ...nae [...nɛ] (*Med.* Netzhaut des Auges); **Re|ti|ni|tis,** die; -, ...itiden (Netzhautentzündung)

Re|ti|ra|de, die; -, -n ‹franz.› (*veraltet für* Toilette); **re|ti|rie|ren** (*veraltet, noch scherzh. für* sich zurückziehen)

Re|tor|si|on, die; -, -en ‹lat.› (*Rechtsspr.* Gegenmaßnahme; Vergeltung); **Re|tor|te,** die; -, -n ‹franz.› (Destillationsgefäß); **Re|tor|ten‿ba|by** (durch künstl. Befruchtung außerhalb des Mutterleibes entstandenes Kind), **...gra|phit** (der; -s; *Chemie* graphitähnlich aussehender Stoff aus fast reinem Kohlenstoff), **...koh|le** (die; -; *svw.* Retortengraphit)

re|tour [reˈtu:r] ‹franz.› (*landsch., österr., schweiz., sonst veraltet für* zurück); **Re|tour|bil|lett** (*schweiz., sonst veraltet für* Rückfahrkarte); **Re|tou|re** [reˈtu:rə], die; -, -n *meist Plur.* (*Wirtsch.* Rücksendung an den Verkäufer); **Re|tour‿[fahr|]kar|te** (*österr., sonst veraltet für* Rückfahrkarte), **...gang** (*österr. für* Rückwärtsgang), **...kut|sche** (*ugs. für* Zurückgeben eines Vorwurfs, einer Beleidigung); **re|tour|nie|ren** [retur...] (*Wirtsch.* zurücksenden [an den Verkäufer]; *Tennis* den vom Gegner geschlagenen Ball zurückschlagen); **Re|tour‿sen|dung** [reˈtu:r...], **...spiel** (*österr. u. schweiz. für* Rückspiel)

Re|trai|te [rəˈtrɛ:tə], die; -, -n

⟨franz.⟩ (*Milit. veraltet für* Rückzug; Zapfenstreich der Kavallerie)

Re|trak|ti|on, die; -, -en ⟨lat.⟩ (*Med.* Schrumpfung)

Re|tri|bu|ti|on, die; -, -en ⟨lat.⟩ (*veraltet für* Wiedererstattung)

Ret|rie|val [ri'tri:v(ə)l] (↑R 130), das; -s ⟨engl.⟩ (*EDV* das Suchen u. Auffinden gespeicherter Daten); **Ret|rie|ver** [rit...], der; -s, - (brit. Jagdhund)

ret|ro|da|tie|ren (↑R 130) ⟨lat.⟩ (*veraltet für* zurückdatieren); **Ret|ro|fle|xi|on**, die; -, -en (*Med.* Rückwärtsknickung von Organen); **ret|ro|grad** (rückläufig; rückgebildet); **Ret|ro|spek|ti|on**, die; -, -en (Rückschau, Rückblick); **ret|ro|spek|tiv** (rückschauend, rückblickend); **Ret|ro|spek|ti|ve** [...və], die; -, -n (*svw.* Retrospektion; *auch für* Präsentation des [Früh]werks eines Künstlers o. Ä.); **Ret|ro|ver|si|on**, [...v...] die; -, -en (*Med.* Rückwärtsneigung, bes. der Gebärmutter); **ret|ro|ver|tie|ren** (zurückwenden, zurückneigen); **ret|ro|ze|die|ren** (*veraltet für* zurückweichen; [etwas] wieder abtreten; *Wirtsch.* rückversichern); **Ret|ro|zes|si|on**, die; -, -en (*veraltet für* Wiederabtretung; *Wirtsch.* bes. Form der Rückversicherung)

Ret|si|na, der; -[s], *Plur. (Sorten:)* -s ⟨neugriech.⟩ (geharzter griech. Weißwein)

ret|ten; Ret|ter; Ret|te|rin

Ret|tich, der; -s, -e ⟨lat.⟩

rett|los (*Seemannsspr.* unrettbar); -es Schiff; **Ret|tung** (*nur Sing.*: *österr. auch kurz für* Rettungsdienst); **Ret|tungs‿ak|ti|on, ...an|ker, ...arzt, ...ba|ke, ...bom|be** (*Bergbau*), **...boot, ...dienst, ...flug|zeug, ...gür|tel, ...hub|schrau|ber, ...in|sel; ret|tungs|los; Ret|tungs‿mann|schaft, ...ring, ...sa|ni|tä|ter, ...schlauch** (der Feuerwehr), **...schlit|ten** (der Bergwacht); **Ret|tungs|schuss;** *in der Fügung* finaler - (*Amtsspr.* Todesschuss, der in einer Notsituation zur Rettung einer Person auf den Täter abgegeben werden kann); **Ret|tungs‿schwim|men** (das; -s), **...schwim|mer, ...sta|ti|on, ...wa|che**

Re|turn [ri'tœ:(r)n], der; -s, -s ⟨engl.⟩ (*[Tisch]tennis* nach dem Aufschlag des Gegners zurückgeschlagener Ball)

Re|tu|sche, die; -, -n ⟨franz.⟩ (Nachbesserung [bes. von Fotografien]); **Re|tu|scheur** [...'ʃø:r], der; -s, -e; **re|tu|schie|ren** (nachbessern [bes. Fotografien])

Reuch|lin (dt. Humanist)

Reue, die; -; **reu|en;** es reut mich; **reu|e|voll; Reu|geld** (*Rechtsw.* Abstandssumme); **reu|ig; Reu|kauf** (*Wirtsch.* Kauf mit Rücktrittsrecht gegen Zahlung eines Reugeldes)

reu|mü|tig

re|unie|ren [re|y'ni:...] (↑R 132) ⟨franz.⟩ (*veraltet für* [wieder]vereinigen, versöhnen; sich versammeln); [1]**Re|uni|on** [re|u'ni̯o:n], die; -, -en (*veraltet für* [Wieder]vereinigung); [2]**Re|uni|on** [re|y'ni̯ɔ̃:], die; -, -s (*veraltet für* gesellige Veranstaltung)

Ré|uni|on [re|y'ni̯ɔ̃] (↑R 132; Insel im Ind. Ozean)

Re|uni|ons|kam|mern (↑R 132), *Plur.* (durch Ludwig XIV. eingesetzte franz. Gerichte zur Durchsetzung von Annexionen)

Reu|se, die; -, -n (Korb zum Fischfang)

[1]**Reuß**, die; - (r. Nebenfluss der Aare)

[2]**Reuß** (Name zweier früherer Thüringer Fürstentümer)

Reu|ße, der; -n, -n (*früher für* Russe)

re|üs|sie|ren ⟨franz.⟩ (gelingen; Erfolg, Glück haben)

reu|ßisch ⟨*zu* [2]Reuß⟩

reu|ten (*südd., österr., schweiz. für* roden)

Reu|ter (niederd. Mundartdichter)

Reu|ter|bü|ro; ↑R 95 (engl. Nachrichtenbüro)

Reut|lin|gen (Stadt in Baden-Württemberg)

Reut|te (Ort in Tirol)

Reut|ter (dt. Komponist)

Rev. = Reverend

Re|vak|zi|na|ti|on [...v...], die; -, -en ⟨lat.⟩ (*Med.* Wiederimpfung); **re|vak|zi|nie|ren**

Re|val ['re:val] (*dt. Name von* Tallinn)

re|va|lie|ren [...v...] ⟨lat.⟩ (*veraltend für* sich für eine Auslage schadlos halten; *Kaufmannsspr.* [eine Schuld] decken); **Re|va|lie|rung** (*Kaufmannsspr.* Deckung [einer Schuld]); **Re|val|va|ti|on**, die; -, -en (*Wirtsch.* Aufwertung); **re|val|vie|ren**

Re|van|che [re'vã:ʃ(ə)], die; -, -n ⟨franz.⟩ (Vergeltung; Rache); **Re|van|che‿foul** (*Sport*), **...krieg; re|van|che|lus|tig; Re|van|che‿po|li|tik** (die; -), **...spiel; re|van|chie|ren,** sich (sich rächen; einen Gegendienst erweisen); **Re|van|chis|mus**, der; - (nationalist. Vergeltungspolitik); **Re|van|chist**, der; -en, -en (↑R 126); **re|van|chis|tisch**

Re|ve|nue [rəvə'ny:], die; -, -n [...'ny:ən] ⟨franz.⟩ (Einkommen, Einkünfte)

Re|ve|rend [...v...], der; -s, -s ⟨lat.⟩ (*nur Sing.*: Titel der Geistlichen in England und Amerika; *Abk.* Rev.; Träger dieses Titels); **Re|ve|renz**, die; -, -en (Ehrerbietung; Verbeugung); *vgl. aber* Referenz

Re|ve|rie [...v...], die; -, ...ien ⟨franz., „Träumerei"⟩ (*Musik* Fantasiestück)

[1]**Re|vers** [rə'vɛ:r], das, *österr.* der; - [rə'vɛ:r(s)], - [rə'vɛ:rs] ⟨franz.⟩ (Umschlag od. Aufschlag an Kleidungsstücken); [2]**Re|vers** [re'vɛrs, *franz.* rə'vɛ:r], der; *Gen.* -es, *bei franz. Ausspr.* - [rə'vɛ:r(s)], *Plur.* -e, *bei franz. Ausspr.* - [rə'vɛ:rs] (Rückseite [einer Münze]); [3]**Re|vers** [re'vɛrs], der; -es, -e (schriftl. Erklärung rechtlichen Inhalts); **re|ver|si|bel** ⟨lat.⟩ (umkehrbar; *Med.* heilbar); ...ib|le (↑R 130) Prozesse; **Re|ver|si|bi|li|tät**, die; -; [1]**Re|ver|si|ble** [...'zi:b(ə)l], der; -s, -s (beidseitig verwendbares Gewebe mit einer glänzenden u. einer matten Seite); [2]**Re|ver|si|ble**, das; -s, -s (Kleidungsstück, das beidseitig getragen werden kann); **Re|ver|si|on**, die; -, -en (*fachspr. für* Umkehrung); **Re|vers|sys|tem** (*Wirtsch.*)

Re|vi|dent [...v...], der; -en, -en (↑R 126) ⟨lat.⟩ (*Rechtsw.* jmd., der Revision beantragt; *österr.* ein Beamtentitel); **re|vi|die|ren** (durchsehen, überprüfen); sein Urteil - (korrigieren)

Re|vier [re'vi:r], das; -s, -e ⟨niederl.⟩ (Bezirk, Gebiet, Bereich; *kurz für* Forst-, Jagd-, Polizeirevier; *Bergbau* großes Gebiet, in dem Bergbau betrieben wird; *Milit.* Krankenstube); **re|vie|ren** (in einem Revier nach Beute suchen [von Jagdhunden]); **Re|vier|förs|ter; re|vier|krank** (*Soldatenspr.*); **Re|vier|kran|ke**, der

Re|view [ri'vju:], die; -, -s ⟨engl.⟩ (Titel[bestandteil] engl. u. amerik. Zeitschriften)

Re|vi|re|ment [revirə'mã:, *österr.* revir'mã:], das; -s, -s (Umbesetzung von [staatlichen] Ämtern)

Re|vi|si|on [...v...], die; -, -en ⟨lat.⟩ ([nochmalige] Durchsicht; Prüfung; Änderung [einer Ansicht]; *Rechtsw.* Überprüfung eines Urteils); **Re|vi|si|o|nis|mus**, der; - (Streben nach Änderung eines bestehenden Zustandes oder eines Programms; eine Strömung in der Arbeiterbewegung); **Re|vi|si|o|nist**, der; -en, -en; ↑R 126 (Verfechter des Revisionismus); **re|vi|si|o|nis|tisch; Re|vi|si|ons‿frist** *(Rechtsw.)*, **...ge|richt, ...ver|fah|ren, ...ver|hand|lung; Re|vi|sor**, der; -s, ...oren (Wirtschaftsprüfer; *Druckw.* Korrektor der Umbruchfahnen)

re|vi|ta|li|sie|ren [...v...] ‹lat.› (*Med.* wieder kräftigen, funktionsfähig machen); **Re|vi|ta|li|sie|rung**, die; -

Re|vi|val [ri'vaivəl], das; -s, -s ‹engl.› (Erneuerung, Wiederbelebung)

Re|vo|ka|ti|on [...v...], die; -, -en ‹lat.› (Widerruf)

Re|vol|te [...v...], die; -, -n ‹franz.› (Empörung, Auflehnung, Aufruhr); **re|vol|tie|ren; Re|vo|lu|ti|on**, die; -, -en ‹lat.›; **re|vo|lu|ti|o|när** ‹franz.› ([staats]umwälzend); **Re|vo|lu|ti|o|när**, der; -s, -e; **Re|vo|lu|ti|o|nä|rin; re|vo|lu|ti|o|nie|ren; Re|vo|lu|ti|o|nie|rung; Re|vo|lu|ti|ons‿füh|rer, ...ge|richt, ...rat, ...re|gie|rung, ...tri|bu|nal, ...wir|ren** *(Plur.)*; **Re|vo|luz|zer**, der; -s, - ‹ital.› (*abwertend für* jmd., der sich als Revolutionär gebärdet)

Re|vol|ver [re'vɔlvər], der; -s, - ‹engl.› (kurze Handfeuerwaffe; drehbarer Ansatz an Werkzeugmaschinen); **Re|vol|ver‿blatt** (*abwertend für* reißerisch aufgemachte Zeitung), **...dreh|bank, ...held, ...knauf, ...lauf, ...pres|se** (*vgl.* Revolverblatt), **...schal|tung, ...schnau|ze** (*derb für* freches, vorlautes Mundwerk; unverschämter, vorlauter Mensch); **re|vol|vie|ren** (*Technik* zurückdrehen); **Re|vol|ving|ge|schäft** [ri'vɔlviŋ...] (*Wirtsch.* mithilfe von Revolvingkrediten finanziertes Geschäft); **Re|vol|ving|kre|dit** (Kredit in Form von immer wieder prolongierten kurzfristigen Krediten)

re|vo|zie|ren [revo...] ‹lat.› (zurücknehmen, widerrufen)

Re|vue [rə'vy:], die; -, -n [rə'vy:ən] ‹franz.› (Zeitschrift mit allgemeinen Überblicken; musikal. Ausstattungsstück); - passieren lassen (vor seinem geistigen Auge vorbeiziehen lassen); **Re|vue‿büh|ne, ...film, ...girl, ...the|a|ter**

Rex|ap|pa|rat ® (*österr. für* Einkochapparat); **Rex|glas** ® *Plur.* ...gläser (*österr. für* Einkochglas)

Reyk|ja|vík ['raikjavi:k, *auch* 'rɛikjavi:k] (Hptst. Islands)

Re|yon [rɛ'jɔ̃:], der *od.* das; - ‹franz.› (Kunstseide aus Viskose)

Re|zen|sent, der; -en, -en (↑R 126) ‹lat.› (Verfasser einer Rezension); **Re|zen|sen|tin; re|zen|sie|ren; Re|zen|si|on**, die; -, -en (kritische Besprechung von Büchern, Theateraufführungen u. a.; Durchsicht eines alten Textes); **Re|zen|si|ons‿exem|plar** (↑R 132), **...stück** (Besprechungsstück)

re|zent ‹lat.› (*Biol.* gegenwärtig lebend, auftretend; *landsch. für* säuerlich, pikant); rezente Kulturen (*Völkerk.* noch bestehende altertüml. Kulturen)

Re|zept, das; -[e]s, -e ‹lat.› ([Arznei-, Koch]vorschrift, Verordnung); **Re|zept‿block** (*vgl.* Block), **...buch; re|zept|frei; re|zep|tie|ren** (Rezepte ausschreiben); **Re|zep|ti|on**, die; -, -en (Auf-, An-, Übernahme; verstehende Aufnahme eines Textes, eines Kunstwerks; Empfangsbüro im Hotel); **re|zep|tiv** (aufnehmend, empfangend; empfänglich); **Re|zep|ti|vi|tät** [...vi...], die; - (Aufnahmefähigkeit, Empfänglichkeit); **Re|zep|tor**, der; -s, ...oren (*Biol., Physiol.* reizaufnehmende Zelle als Bestandteil eines Gewebes, z. B. der Haut od. eines Sinnesorgans); **Re|zept|pflicht**, die; -; **re|zept|pflich|tig; Re|zep|tur**, die; -, -en (Anfertigung von Rezepten; Arbeitsraum in der Apotheke)

Re|zess, der; -es, -e ‹lat.› (*Rechtsw.* Auseinandersetzung, Vergleich, Vertrag); **Re|zes|si|on**, die; -, -en (*Wirtsch.* Rückgang der Konjunktur); **Re|zes|si|ons|pha|se; re|zes|siv** (*Biol.* zurücktretend; nicht in Erscheinung tretend [von Erbfaktoren])

re|zi|div ‹lat.› (*Med.* wiederkehrend [von Krankheiten]); **Re|zi|div**, das; -s, -e [...və] (Rückfall); **re|zi|di|vie|ren** [...v...] (in Abständen wiederkehren)

Re|zi|pi|ent, der; -en, -en (↑R 126) ‹lat.› (jmd., der einen Text, ein Musikstück o. Ä. rezipiert; *Physik* Glasglocke, die zu Versuchszwecken luftleer gepumpt werden kann); **re|zi|pie|ren** (etwas als Hörer, Leser, Betrachter aufnehmen, übernehmen)

re|zip|rok (↑R 130) ‹lat.› (wechselseitig, gegenseitig, aufeinander bezüglich); -er Wert (*Math.* Kehrwert [durch Vertauschung von Zähler u. Nenner]); -es Pronomen (*Sprachw.* wechselbezügl. Fürwort, z. B. „einander"); **Re|zip|ro|zi|tät**, die; - (Wechselseitigkeit)

Re|zi|tal *vgl.* Recital; **re|zi|tan|do** *vgl.* recitando; **Re|zi|ta|ti|on**, die; -, -en ‹lat.› (künstler. Vortrag einer Dichtung); **Re|zi|ta|ti|ons|abend; Re|zi|ta|tiv**, das; -s, -e [...və] ‹ital.› ([dramat.] Sprechgesang); **re|zi|ta|ti|visch** [...v...] (in der Art des Rezitativs); **Re|zi|ta|tor**, der; -s, ...oren ‹lat.› (jmd., der rezitiert); **re|zi|tie|ren**

Re|zyk|lat (↑R 130), das; -[e]s, -e ‹lat.; griech.› (Produkt eines Recyclingverfahrens); **re|zyk|lie|ren** *vgl.* recyceln

rf., rfz. = rinforzando

R-Ge|spräch; ↑R 105 (Ferngespräch, das der Angerufene bezahlt)

Rgt., Reg[t]., R. = Regiment

RGW = Rat für gegenseitige Wirtschaftshilfe (bis 1991)

rh, Rh *vgl.* Rhesusfaktor

Rh = *chem. Zeichen für* Rhodium

Rha|ba|nus Mau|rus *vgl.* Hrabanus Maurus

Rha|bar|ber, der; -s ‹griech.›; **Rha|bar|ber‿kom|pott, ...ku|chen**

Rhab|dom, das; -s, -e ‹griech.› (*Med.* Sehstäbchen in der Netzhaut des Auges)

Rha|da|man|thys (Totenrichter in der griech. Sage)

Rha|ga|de, die; -, -n ‹griech.› (*Med.* Einriss in der Haut)

Rhap|so|de, der; -n, -n (↑R 126) ‹griech.› (fahrender Sänger im alten Griechenland); **Rhap|so|die**, die; -, ...ien (erzählendes Gedicht, Heldenlied; [aus Volksweisen zusammengesetztes] Musikstück); (↑R 108:) die Ungarische Rhapsodie (Musikstück von Liszt); **rhap|so|disch** (zum Rhapsoden, zur Rhapsodie gehörend; in Rhapsodieform; unzusammenhängend, bruchstückartig); -e Dichtung

Rhät usw. *vgl.* Rät, Räter, Rätien, Rätikon *u.* rätisch

rhe! *vgl.* ree!

Rhe|da-Wie|den|brück (Stadt im Münsterland)

Rhe|de (Ort östl. von Bocholt)

Rhei|der|land *vgl.* Reiderland

Rheidt (Ort nördl. von Bonn)

Rhein, der; -[e]s (ein Strom); **rhein|ab[|wärts]; Rhein|an|ke**, die; -, -n (ein Fisch); **rhein|auf[|wärts]; Rhein‿bund** (der; -[e]s; ↑R 105; dt. Fürstenbund unter franz. Führung), **...fall** (der), **...gau** (der, *landsch.* das; -[e]s; eine Landschaft in Hessen); **Rhein-Her|ne-Ka|nal**, der; -s (↑R 105); **Rhein|hes|sen; rhei|nisch**, *aber* (↑R 102): das Rheinische Schiefergebirge; (↑R 108:) Rheinischer Merkur; Rheinische Stahlwerke; **Rhei|nisch-Ber|gi|sche Kreis,** der; -n -es (Landkreis im Reg.-Bez. Köln); **rhei|nisch-west|fä|lisch** (↑R 106), *aber* (↑R 108): das Rheinisch-Westfälische Elektrizitätswerk (*Abk.* RWE); Rheinisch-Westfälisches Industriegebiet; **Rhein|land,** das; -[e]s (*Abk.* Rhld.); **Rhein|lan|de** *Plur.* (Siedlungsgebiete der Franken beiderseits des Rheins); **Rhein|län|der** (*auch* ein Tanz); **Rhein|län|de|rin; rhein|län|disch; Rhein|land-Pfalz; rhein|land-pfäl|zisch** (↑R 106); **Rhein-Main-Do|nau-Groß|schiff|fahrts|weg,** der; -[e]s (↑R 105); **Rhein-Main-Flug|ha|fen,** der; -s (↑R 105); **Rhein-Mar|ne-Ka|nal,** der; -s (↑R 105); **Rhein‿pfalz, ...pro|vinz** (die; -; ehem. preußische Provinz beiderseits des Mittel- und Niederrheins); **Rhein-Rho|ne-Ka|nal,** der; -s (↑R 105); **Rhein-Schie-Ka|nal** [...'sxi:...], der; -s (↑R 105); **Rhein|sei|ten|ka|nal,** der; -s (↑R 105); **Rhein|wald,** das; -s (oberste Talstufe des Hinterrheins); **Rhein|wein**

rhe|na|nisch ⟨lat.⟩ (*veraltet für* rheinisch); **Rhe|ni|um,** das; -s (chem. Element, Metall; *Zeichen* Re)

Rhe|o|lo|gie, die; - ⟨griech.⟩ (Teilgebiet der Physik, das Fließerscheinungen von Stoffen unter Einwirkung äußerer Kräfte untersucht); **Rhe|os|tat** (↑R 132), der; *Gen.* -[e]s *u.* -en, *Plur.* -e[n] (stufenweise veränderlicher elektr. Widerstand)

Rhe|sus, der; -, - ⟨nlat.⟩ (*svw.* Rhesusaffe); **Rhe|sus|af|fe** (in Süd- u. Ostasien vorkommender, meerkatzenartiger Affe); **Rhe|sus|fak|tor,** der; -s (*Med.* erbliches Merkmal der roten Blutkörperchen; *kurz* Rh-Faktor; *Zeichen* Rh = Rhesusfaktor positiv, rh = Rhesusfaktor negativ)

Rhe|tor, der; -s, ...oren ⟨griech.⟩ (Redner der Antike); **Rhe|to|rik,** die; - (Redekunst; Lehre von der wirkungsvollen Gestaltung der Rede); **Rhe|to|ri|ker; rhe|to|risch;** -e Frage (Frage, auf die keine Antwort erwartet wird)

Rheu|ma, das; -s ⟨griech.⟩ (*Kurzw. für* Rheumatismus); **Rheu|ma|de|cke; Rheu|ma|ti|ker** (an Rheumatismus Leidender); **Rheu|ma|ti|ke|rin; rheu|ma|tisch; Rheu|ma|tis|mus,** der; -, ...men; ↑R 126 (schmerzhafte Erkrankung der Gelenke, Muskeln, Nerven, Sehnen); **Rheu|ma|to|lo|ge,** der; -n, -n; ↑R 126 (Arzt mit speziellen Kenntnissen auf dem Gebiet der Rheumatologie); **Rheu|ma|to|lo|gie,** die; - (Lehre vom Rheumatismus); **Rheu|ma|to|lo|gin; rheu|ma|to|lo|gisch; Rheu|ma|wä|sche,** die; -

Rheydt [rait] (Stadt bei Mönchengladbach)

Rh-Fak|tor (*Med. svw.* Rhesusfaktor; ↑R 26)

Rhi|ni|tis, die; -, ...itiden ⟨griech.⟩ (*Med.* Nasenschleimhautentzündung, Schnupfen); **Rhi|no|lo|gie,** die; - (Nasenheilkunde); **Rhi|no|plas|tik,** die; -, -en (chirurgische Korrektur od. Neubildung der Nase); **Rhi|no|skop,** das; -s, -e (Nasenspiegel); **Rhi|no|sko|pie,** die; -, ...ien (Untersuchung mit dem Rhinoskop); **Rhi|no|ze|ros,** das; *Gen.* - *u.* -ses, *Plur.* -se (Nashorn)

Rhi|zom, das; -s, -e ⟨griech.⟩ (*Bot.* bewurzelter unterird. Spross); **Rhi|zo|po|de,** der; -n, -n *meist Plur.*; ↑R 126 (*Zool.* Wurzelfüßer [Einzeller])

Rhld. = Rheinland

Rh-ne|ga|tiv (den Rhesusfaktor nicht aufweisend)

Rho, das; -[s], -s (griech. Buchstabe: *P, ρ*)

Rho|da|mi|ne (↑R 132) *Plur.* ⟨griech.; lat.⟩ (*Chemie* Gruppe lichtechter Farbstoffe); **Rho|dan,** das; -s ⟨griech.⟩ (eine einwertige Gruppe in chem. Verbindungen)

Rhode Is|land [ro:d 'ailənd] (Staat in den USA; *Abk.* R. I.); **Rho|de|län|der** ['ro:də...], das; -s, - (rotbraunes, schweres Haushuhn)

Rho|de|si|en [...iən] ⟨nach Cecil Rhodes⟩ (früherer Name von Simbabwe); **rho|de|sisch**

rho|di|nie|ren ⟨griech.⟩ (mit Rhodium überziehen)

rho|disch ⟨*zu* Rhodos⟩

Rho|di|um, das; -s ⟨griech.⟩ (chem. Element, Metall; *Zeichen* Rh)

Rho|do|den|dron (↑R 130), der, *auch* das; -s, ...ren ⟨griech.⟩ (eine Zierpflanze)

Rho|do|pen *Plur.* (Gebirge in Bulgarien u. Griechenland)

Rho|dos (eine Mittelmeerinsel)

rhom|bisch ⟨griech.⟩ (rautenförmig); **Rhom|bo|e|der,** das; -s, - (von sechs Rhomben begrenzte Kristallform); **Rhom|bo|id,** das; -[e]s, -e (*Math.* schiefwinkliges Parallelogramm mit paarweise ungleichen Seiten); **Rhom|bus,** der; -, ...ben ([2]Raute; *Math.* gleichseitiges Parallelogramm)

Rhön, die; - (Teil des Hessischen Berglandes)

Rho|ne, *franz.* Rhône [ro:n], die; - (schweiz.-franz. Fluss); *vgl.* Rotten

Rhön|rad (ein Turngerät)

Rho|ta|zis|mus, der; -, ...men ⟨griech.⟩ (*Sprachw.* Übergang eines zwischen Vokalen stehenden stimmhaften s zu r, z. B. griech. „genēseos" gegenüber lat. „generis")

Rh-po|si|tiv (den Rhesusfaktor aufweisend)

Rhus, der; - ⟨griech.⟩ (Essigbaum; ein immergrüner [Zier]strauch)

Rhyth|men (*Plur. von* Rhythmus); **Rhyth|mik,** die; - ⟨griech.⟩ (Art des Rhythmus; *auch* Lehre vom Rhythmus); **Rhyth|mi|ker; rhyth|misch** (den Rhythmus betreffend, gleich-, taktmäßig); rhythmische Gymnastik; **rhyth|mi|sie|ren** (in einen bestimmten Rhythmus bringen); **Rhyth|mus,** der; -, ...men (regelmäßige Wiederkehr; geregelter Wechsel; Zeit-, Gleich-, Ebenmaß; taktmäßige Gliederung); **Rhyth|mus‿gi|tar|re, ...grup|pe, ...in|stru|ment**

R. I. = Rhode Island

Ria (w. Vorn.)

Ri|ad (Hptst. von Saudi-Arabien)

Ri|al, der; -[s], -s ⟨pers. *u.* arab.⟩ (iran. Münzeinheit; 1 Rial = 100 Dinar; *Abk.* Rl); 100 - (↑R 90); *vgl.* Riyal

RIAS, der; - ⟨Rundfunksender im amerik. Sektor⟩ (in Berlin [bis 1992])

Ri|bat|tu|ta, die; -, ...ten ⟨ital.⟩ (*Musik* langsam beginnender, allmählich schneller werdender Triller)

rib|bel|fest; rib|beln (*landsch. für* zwischen Daumen und Zeigefinger rasch [zer]reiben); ich ...[e]le (↑R 16)

Ri|bi|sel, die; -, -n ⟨arab.-ital.⟩ (*österr. für* Johannisbeere); **Ri|bi|sel|saft** (*österr.*)

Ri|bo|fla|vin [...v...], das; -s ⟨Kunstwort⟩ (Vitamin B_2); **Ri|bo|nuk|le|in|säu|re** (↑R 130), die; -, -n (wichtiger Bestandteil des Kerneiweißes der Zelle; *Abk.* RNS)

Ri|car|da (w. Vorn.); **Ri|chard** (m. Vorn.)

Ri|chard-Wag|ner-Fest|spie|le *Plur.* (↑R 95)

Ri|che|li|eu [riʃə'liø:] (franz. Staatsmann); **Ri|che|li|eu|sti|cke|rei** ['riʃəliø...]; ↑R 95 (Weißstickerei mit ausgeschnittenen Mustern)

Richt_an|ten|ne, ...ba|ke, ...baum, ...beil (ein Stellmacherwerkzeug; Henkerbeil), **...blei** (das; *Bauw.*), **...block** (*Plur.* ...blöcke); **Rich|te,** die; - (*landsch. für* gerade Richtung); in die - bringen usw.; **rich|ten;** sich -; richt[1] euch! (milit. Kommando); **Rich|ter; Rich|ter|amt,** das; -[e]s; **Rich|te|rin; rich|ter|lich; Rich|ter|schaft,** die; -

Rich|ter|ska|la (↑R 95) ⟨nach dem amerik. Seismologen⟩ (Skala zur Messung der Erdbebenstärke)

Rich|ter_spruch, ...stuhl (der; -[e]s); **Richt_fest, ...feu|er, ...funk, ...ge|schwin|dig|keit; rich|tig;** das Richtige (richtig) sein; das Richtige tun; es wäre das Richtigste, wenn ...; *aber* es wäre am richtigsten, wenn ...; eine Uhr, die richtig geht; eine richtig gehende Uhr; *vgl. aber* richtiggehend; wir haben mit der Schätzung richtig gelegen *(ugs.)*; eine Behauptung richtig stellen; **rich|tig|ge|hend;** das war eine richtiggehende (durchaus so zu nennende) Blamage; **Rich|tig|keit,** die; -; **rich|tig lie|gen, ma|chen, stel|len** *vgl.* richtig; **Rich|tig|stel|lung** (Berichtigung); **Richt_ka|no|nier, ...kranz, ...lat|te, ...li|nie** *(meist Plur.)*; **Richt|li|ni|en|kom|pe|tenz; Richt_mik|ro|fon, ...platz, ...preis** (*vgl.* [2]Preis), **...satz, ...scheit** (*Bauw.*; *svw.* Richtlatte), **...schmaus, ...schnur** (*Plur.* ...schnuren), **...schüt|ze** (*svw.* Richtkanonier), **...schwert, ...stät|te, ...strah|ler** (eine Antenne für Kurzwellensender), **...stre|cke** (*Bergmannsspr.* waagerechte Strecke, die möglichst geradlinig angelegt wird); **Rich|tung;** sie flohen [in] Richtung Heimat; **rich|tung|ge|bend** (↑R 40); **Rich|tungs_än|de|rung, ...an|zei|ger** (Blinkleuchte), **...fahr|bahn** *(Verkehrsw.)*; **rich|tungs|los; Rich|tungs|lo|sig|keit,** die; -; **Rich|tungs|pfeil; rich|tungs|sta|bil** *(Kfz-Technik)*; **Rich|tungs_sta|bi|li|tät, ...ver|kehr** (der; -s), **...wahl** (Wahl, von der eine Wende in der polit. Richtung erwartet wird), **...wech|sel; rich|tung|wei|send** (↑R 40); **Richt_waa|ge, ...wert, ...zahl**

Rick, das; -[e]s, *Plur.* -e, *auch* -s (*landsch. für* Stange; Gestell)

Ri|cke, die; -, -n (weibl. Reh)

ri|di|kül ⟨franz.⟩ (*veraltet für* lächerlich); **Ri|di|kül,** der *od.* das; -s, *Plur.* -e *u.* -s (*früher für* Arbeitsbeutel; Strickbeutel)

riech|bar; rie|chen; du rochst; du röchest; gerochen; riech[e]!; **Rie|cher** (*ugs. für* Nase *[bes. im übertr. Sinne]*); einen guten - für etwas haben (etwas gleich merken); **Riech_fläsch|chen, ...kol|ben** (*ugs. scherzh. für* Nase), **...or|gan, ...salz, ...stoff, ...was|ser** (*Plur.* ...wasser)

[1]**Ried,** das; -[e]s, -e (Schilf, Röhricht); [2]**Ried,** die; -, -en *u.* **Rie|de,** die; -, -n (*österr. für* Nutzfläche in den Weinbergen); **Ried|gras**

Rie|fe, die; -, -n (Längsrinne; Streifen, Rippe); **rie|feln;** ich ...[e]le (↑R 16) *u.* **rie|fen** (mit Rillen versehen); **Rie|fe|lung; rie|fen** *vgl.* riefeln; **Rie|fen|samt** (*landsch. für* Kordsamt); **rie|fig**

Rie|ge, die; -, -n (Turnerabteilung)

Rie|gel, der; -s, -; **Rie|gel|chen**

Rie|gel|hau|be (*früher* bayr. Frauenhaube)

Rie|gel|haus (*schweiz. für* Fachwerkhaus); **rie|geln** (*veraltet, noch landsch., bes. schweiz. für* verriegeln); ich ...[e]le (↑R 16); **Rie|gel_stel|lung** *(Milit.)*, **...werk** (*landsch. für* Fachwerk)

Rie|gen|füh|rer; rie|gen|wei|se

Riem|chen (*Bauw. auch* schmales Bauelement, z. B. Fliese); [1]**Rie|men,** der; -s, - (Lederstreifen)

[2]**Rie|men,** der; -s, - ⟨lat.⟩ (längeres, mit beiden Händen bewegtes Ruder); sich in die Riemen legen

Rie|men_an|trieb, ...schei|be (Radscheibe am Riemenwerk)

Rie|men|schnei|der, Tilman (dt. Bildhauer u. Holzschnitzer)

Rie|mer (*landsch. für* Riemenmacher)

ri|en ne va plus [riẽnəva'ply(:)] ⟨franz., „nichts geht mehr"⟩ (beim Roulettspiel die Ansage des Croupiers, dass nicht mehr gesetzt werden kann)

Ri|en|zi (röm. Volkstribun)

[1]**Ries,** das; -es (Becken zwischen Schwäb. u. Fränk. Alb); Nördlinger Ries

[2]**Ries,** das; -es, -e ⟨arab.⟩ (Papiermaß); 4 - Papier (↑R 90)

[1]**Rie|se** ⟨*eigtl.* Ries⟩, Adam (dt. Rechenmeister); 2 mal 2 ist nach Adam Riese (richtig gerechnet) 4

[2]**Rie|se,** der; -n, -n; ↑R 126 (außergewöhnl. großer Mensch; *auch für* sagenhaftes, myth. Wesen, Märchengestalt)

[3]**Rie|se,** die; -, -n (*südd., österr. für* [Holz]rutsche im Gebirge)

Rie|sel|feld; rie|seln

rie|sen (*südd. für* mit Holzrutschen herablassen)

Rie|sen_an|stren|gung *(ugs.)*, **...ar|beit** (die; -; *ugs.*), **...dumm|heit** *(ugs.)*, **...fel|ge** *(Turnen)*, **...ge|bir|ge** (das; -s); **rie|sen|groß; rie|sen|haft; Rie|sen|hun|ger** *(ugs.)*; **Rie|sen_rad, ...ross** (Schimpfwort), **...schild|krö|te, ...schlan|ge, ...schritt, ...sla|lom** *(Skisport)*, **...spaß** *(ugs.)*; **rie|sen|stark; rie|sig** (gewaltig groß; hervorragend, toll); **Rie|sin; rie|sisch** (*selten für* zu den Riesen gehörend)

Ries|ling, der; -s, -e (eine Reb- u. Weinsorte)

Ries|ter, der; -s, - (*veraltend für* Lederflicken auf dem Schuh)

ries|wei|se ⟨*zu* [2]Ries⟩

Riet, das; -[e]s, -e (Weberkamm); **Riet|blatt**

Rif, das; -s ⟨arab.⟩ *u.* **Rif|at|las,** der; - (Gebirge in Marokko)

[1]**Riff,** das; -[e]s, -e (Felsenklippe; Sandbank)

[2]**Riff,** der; -[e]s, -s ⟨engl.⟩ (*bes. Jazz, Popmusik* ständig wiederholte, rhythmische Tonfolge)

Rif|fel, die; -, -n (Flachs-, Reffkamm; rippenähnlicher Streifen; *bayr. u. österr. für* gezackter Berggrat [bes. in Bergnamen, z. B. die Hohe Riffel]); **Rif|fel_glas** (*Plur.* ...gläser), **...kamm, ...ma|schi|ne; rif|feln** ([Flachs] kämmen; aufrauen; mit Riefen versehen); ich ...[e]le (↑R 16); **Rif|fe|lung**

Ri|fi|fi, das; -s ⟨franz.⟩ (raffiniertes Verbrechen)

Rif|ka|by|le (Bewohner des Rifatlas)

Ri|ga (Hptst. von Lettland); **Ri|ga|er** (↑R 103); - Bucht; **ri|ga|isch,** *aber* (↑R 102): der Rigaische Meerbusen (*svw.* Rigaer Bucht)

Ri|gel, der; - ⟨arab.⟩ (ein Stern)

Rigg, das; -s, -s, **Rig|gung** ⟨engl.⟩ (*Seemannsspr.* Takelung; Segel[werk]); **rig|gen** ([auf]takeln)

Ri|gi, der; -[s], *auch* die; - (Gebirgsmassiv in der Schweiz)

ri|gid, ri|gi|de ⟨lat.⟩ (streng; steif, starr); **Ri|gi|di|tät,** die; - (starres Festhalten, Strenge; *Med.* Versteifung, [Muskel]starre)

Ri|gips|plat|te ® (Gipskartonplatte zur Verkleidung von Innenwänden)

Ri|go|le, die; -, -n ⟨franz.⟩ (*Landw.* tiefe Rinne, Abzugsgraben); **ri|go|len** (tief pflügen oder umgraben); ich habe rigolt

Ri|go|let|to (Titelheld in der gleichnamigen Oper von Verdi)

Ri|gol|pflug

Ri|go|ris|mus, der; - ⟨lat.⟩ (übertriebene Strenge; strenges Festhalten an Grundsätzen); **Ri|go-**

[1] *So die Schreibung der Bundeswehr.*

rist, der; -en, -en; **ri|go|ris|tisch** (überaus streng); **ri|go|ros** ([sehr] streng); **Ri|go|ro|si|tät,** die; -; **Ri|go|ro|sum,** das; -s, *Plur.* ...sa, *österr.* ...sen (mündl. Examen bei der Promotion)

Rig|we|da, der; -[s] ‹sanskr.› (Sammlung der ältesten ind. Opferhymnen)

Ri|je|ka (Hafenstadt in Kroatien); *vgl.* Fiume

Rijs|wijk [ˈrais̯vaik, *niederl.* ˈrɛiswɛik] (niederl. Stadt)

Ri|kam|bio, der; -s, ...ien [...i̯ən] ‹ital.› (*Bankw.* Rückwechsel)

Ri|ke (w. Vorn.)

Rik|scha, die; -, -s ‹jap.› (zweirädriger Wagen, der von einem Menschen gezogen wird u. zur Beförderung von Personen dient)

Riks|mål [ˈri:ksmo:l], das; -[s] ‹norw.› (*ältere Bez. für* Bokmål)

Ril|ke, Rainer Maria (österr. Dichter)

Ril|le, die; -, -n; **ril|len; ril|len|för|mig; Ril|len|pro|fil; ril|lig** (*selten für* gerillt)

Rim|baud [rɛ̃ˈbo:] (franz. Dichter)

Ri|mes|se, die; -, -n ‹ital.› (*Wirtsch.* in Zahlung gegebener Wechsel); **Ri|mes|sen|wech|sel**

Ri|mi|ni (ital. Hafenstadt)

Rims|ki-Kor|sa|kow [...kɔf] (russ. Komponist)

Ri|nal|do Ri|nal|di|ni (Held eines Räuberromans von Chr. A. Vulpius)

Rind, das; -[e]s, -er

Rin|de, die; -, -n; **Rin|den‿boot, ...hüt|te; rin|den|los**

Rin|der|bra|ten, *südd., österr. u. schweiz.* Rinds|bra|ten; **Rin|der‿brust, ...gu|lasch, ...hack|fleisch, ...her|de; rin|de|rig** (brünstig [von der Kuh]); **Rin|der|le|ber; rin|dern** (brünstig sein [von der Kuh]); **Rin|der‿pest** (die), **...ras|se, ...talg, ...wahn** (*kurz für* Rinderwahnsinn), **...wahn|sinn** (eine Rinderkrankheit); **Rind|fleisch**

rin|dig (mit Rinde versehen)

Rind|le|der *vgl.* Rindsleder; **rind|le|dern** *vgl.* rindsledern; **Rinds|bra|ten** usw. (*südd., österr. u. schweiz. für* Rinderbraten usw.); **Rinds|le|der; rinds|le|dern** (aus Rindsleder); **Rind|stück** (Beefsteak); **Rind|sup|pe** (*österr. für* Fleischbrühe); **Rind|viech** (Schimpfwort); **Rind|vieh** (*auch* Schimpfwort)

rin|for|zan|do ‹ital.› (*Musik* stärker werdend; *Abk.* rf., rfz.); **Rin|for|zan|do,** das; -s, *Plur.* -s *u.* ...di

ring (*südd., schweiz. mdal. für* leicht, mühelos)

Ring, der; -[e]s, -e; **ring|ar|tig; Ring‿arzt** (*Boxen*), **...bahn, ...buch; Rin|gel,** der; -s, - (kleineres ringförmiges od. spiraliges Gebilde); **Rin|gel|blu|me; Rin|gel|chen** *vgl.* Ringlein; **rin|ge|lig,** ring|lig; **Rin|gel|lo|cke; rin|geln;** ich ...[e]le (↑R 16); sich -; **Rin|gel|nat|ter**

Rin|gel|natz (dt. Dichter); Ringelnatz’ Gedichte (↑R 98)

Rin|gel|piez, der; -[es], -e (*ugs. scherzh. für* anspruchsloses Tanzvergnügen); - mit Anfassen; **Rin|gel‿pul|li, ...rei|gen** *od.* **...rei|hen** (*österr. nur so*), **...schwanz, ...söck|chen** (*meist Plur.*), **...spiel** (*österr. für* Karussell), **...ste|chen** (das; -s, -; früheres ritterliches Spiel), **...tau|be, ...wurm**

rin|gen; du rangst; du rängest; gerungen; ring[e]!; **Rin|gen,** das; -s; **Rin|ger; Rin|ger|griff; rin|ge|risch;** seine -en Qualitäten

Ring|fahn|dung (Großfahndung der Polizei in einem größeren Gebiet); **Ring|fin|ger; Ring|flü|gel|flug|zeug** (*für* Coleopter); **ring|för|mig; Ring‿ge|schäft, ...gra|ben**

ring|hö|rig (*schweiz. mdal. für* schalldurchlässig, hellhörig)

Ring‿kampf, ...kämp|fer

Ring|knor|pel (Kehlkopfknorpel); **Ring|lein** (kleiner Ring); **ring|lig** *vgl.* ringelig

Rin|glot|te [riŋˈglɔtə], die; -, -n (*landsch. u. österr. für* Reneklode)

Ring‿mau|er, ...rich|ter (*Boxen*); **rings;** *vgl.* ringsum; **Ring|sen|dung** (*Rundf., Fernsehen*); **rings|he|rum** (↑R 132); **Ring|stra|ße; rings|um;** ringsum (rundherum) läuft ein Geländer; ringsum (überall) stehen blühende Sträucher, *aber* die Kinder standen rings um ihren Lehrer; rings um den See standen Bäume; **rings|um|her**

Ring‿tausch, ...ten|nis, ...vor|le|sung, ...wall

Rink, der; -en, -en (↑R 126) *u.* **Rin|ke,** die; -, -n (*landsch. für* Schnalle, Spange); **rin|keln** (*veraltet für* schnallen); ich ...[e]le (↑R 16); **Rin|ken,** der; -s, - (*svw.* Rink)

Rin|ne, die; -, -n; **rin|nen;** es rann; es ränne, *selten* rönne; geronnen; rinn[e]!; **Rinn|sal,** das; -[e]s, -e (*geh. für* kleines fließendes Gewässer); **Rinn|stein**

Rio de Ja|nei|ro [- - ʒaˈne:ro] (Stadt in Brasilien); **Rio de la Pla|ta,** der; - - - - (gemeinsame Mündung der Flüsse Paraná u. Uruguay); **Rio-de-la-Pla|ta-Bucht,** die; - (↑R 105); **Rio Gran|de do Sul** (Bundesstaat in Brasilien)

R. I. P. = requiescat in pace!

Ri|pos|te, die; -, -n ‹ital.› (*Fechten* unmittelbarer Gegenangriff); **ri|pos|tie|ren**

Ripp|chen; Rip|pe, die; -, -n

rip|peln, sich (*landsch. für* sich regen, sich beeilen); ich ...[e]le mich (↑R 16)

rip|pen (mit Rippen versehen); gerippt; **Rip|pen‿bo|gen, ...bruch** (der), **...fell; Rip|pen|fell|ent|zün|dung; Rip|pen|heiz|kör|per; Rip|pen|speer,** der *od.* das; -[e]s (gepökeltes Schweinebruststück mit Rippen); *vgl.* Kasseler Rippe[n]speer; **Rip|pen‿stoß, ...stück; Ripp|li,** das; -s, - (*schweiz. für* Schweinerippchen)

rips!; rips, raps!

Rips, der; -es, -e ‹engl.› (geripptes Gewebe)

ri|pu|a|risch ‹lat.› (am [Rhein]ufer wohnend); -e Franken (um Köln)

ri|ra|rutsch!

Ri|sa|lit, der; -s, -e ‹ital.› (*Bauw.* Vorbau, Vorsprung)

ri|scheln (*landsch. für* rascheln, knistern); es rischelt

Ri|si|ko, das; -s, *Plur.* -s *od.* ...ken, *österr.* Risken, *auch* -s ‹ital.›; **Ri|si|ko‿ana|ly|se** (↑R 132), **...be|reit|schaft** (die; -), **...fak|tor; ri|si|ko|frei; Ri|si|ko‿ge|burt, ...grup|pe** (*Med., Soziol.*), **...leh|re** (Lehre von den Ursachen u. der Eindämmung der möglichen Folgen eines Risikos); **ri|si|ko|los; Ri|si|ko‿pa|ti|ent** (besonders gefährdeter Patient), **...prä|mie** (*Wirtsch.*)

Ri|si-Pi|si *od., bes. österr.,* **Ri|si|pi|si,** das; -[s], - ‹ital.› (ein Gericht aus Reis u. Erbsen)

ris|kant ‹franz.› (gefährlich, gewagt); **ris|kie|ren** (wagen, aufs Spiel setzen)

Ri|skont|ro (↑R 130) *vgl.* Skontro

Ri|sor|gi|men|to [risɔrdʒi...], das; -[s] ‹ital.› (italienische Einigungsbewegung im 19. Jh.)

Ri|sot|to, der; -[s], -s, *österr. auch* das; -s, -[s] ‹ital.› (Reisspeise)

Ris|pe, die; -, -n (Blütenstand); **ris|pen|för|mig; Ris|pen|gras; ris|pig**

Riss, der; -es, -e; **riss|fest; ris|sig**

Ris|so|le, die; -, -n (*Gastron.* kleine, halbmondförmige Pastete)

Rist, der; -es, -e (*bes. Sport* Fuß-, Handrücken; *kurz für* Widerrist)

Ris|te, die; -, -n (*landsch. für* Flachsbündel)

Rist|griff (*Turnen*)

ri|stor|nie|ren ‹ital.› (*Wirtsch.* einen irrig eingetragenen Posten

zurückschreiben); **Ri|stor|no,** der *od.* das; -s, -s (*Wirtsch.* Gegen-, Rückbuchung, Rücknahme)
ris|veg|li|an|do [risvɛl'jando] (↑R 130 *u.* 132) ‹ital.› (*Musik* aufgeweckt, munter, lebhaft werdend); **ris|veg|li|a|to** [...'ja:to] (*Musik* [wieder] munter, lebhaft)
rit. = ritardando, ritenuto
Ri|ta (w. Vorn.)
ri|tar|dan|do ‹ital.› (*Musik* langsamer werdend; *Abk.* rit.); **Ri|tar|dan|do,** das; -s, *Plur.* -s *u.* ...di
ri|te ‹lat.› (in üblicher, ordnungsgemäßer Weise; genügend [geringstes Prädikat beim Rigorosum]); **Ri|ten** (*Plur. von* Ritus)
ri|ten., rit. = ritenuto
Ri|ten|kon|gre|ga|ti|on, die; - (eine päpstl. Behörde)
ri|te|nu|to ‹ital.› (*Musik* zurückgehalten, plötzlich langsamer; *Abk.* rit., riten.); **Ri|te|nu|to,** das; -s, *Plur.* -s *u.* ...ti
Ri|tor|nell, das; -s, -e ‹ital.› (*Verslehre* dreizeilige Strophe; *Musik* sich [mehrfach] wiederholender Teil eines Musikstücks)
Ri|trat|te, die; -, -n ‹ital.› (*svw.* Rikambio)
ritsch!; ritsch, ratsch!
Rit|scher, der; -s *u.* **Rit|schert,** das; -s (*österr. für* Speise aus Graupen und Hülsenfrüchten)
Ritt, der; -[e]s, -e
Ritt|ber|ger, der; -s, - ‹nach dem dt. Eiskunstläufer› (Drehsprung im Eiskunstlauf)
Rit|ter; die Ritter des Pour le Mérite; der Ritter von der traurigen Gestalt (Don Quichotte); arme Ritter (eine Süßspeise); **Rit|ter‿burg, ...dich|tung, ...gut; Rit|ter|guts|be|sit|zer; rit|ter|lich; Rit|ter|lich|keit; Rit|ter|ling** (ein Pilz); **Rit|ter‿or|den, ...roman, ...rüs|tung; Rit|ter|schaft,** die; -; **rit|ter|schaft|lich; Rit|ter|schlag; Rit|ters|mann** *Plur.* ...leute; **Rit|ter|sporn** *Plur.* ...sporne (eine Blume); **Rit|ter|tum,** das; -s; **Rit|ter-und-Räu|ber-Ro|man** (↑R 28); **Rit|ter‿we|sen** (das; -s), **...zeit** (die; -); **rit|tig** (zum Reiten geschult, reitgerecht [von Pferden]); **Rit|tig|keit,** die; -; **Rit|tig|keits|ar|beit,** die; - *(Pferdesport);* **ritt|lings; Ritt|meis|ter** *(Milit. früher)*
Ri|tu|al, das; -s, *Plur.* -e *u.* -ien [...iən] ‹lat.› (religiöser Brauch; Zeremoniell); **Ri|tu|al‿buch, ...hand|lung; Ri|tu|a|lis|mus,** der; - (Richtung der anglikan. Kirche); **Ri|tu|a|list,** der; -en, -en (↑R 126); **Ri|tu|al|mord; ri|tu|ell** ‹franz.› (zum Ritus gehörend; durch den Ritus geboten); **Ri|tus,** der; -, ...ten ‹lat.› (gottesdienstlicher [Fest]brauch; Zeremoniell)
Ritz, der; -es, -e (Kerbe, Schramme, Kratzer; *auch für* Ritze); **Rit|ze,** die; -, -n (sehr schmale Spalte od. Vertiefung); **Rit|zel,** das; -s, - (*Technik* kleines Zahnrad); **rit|zen;** du ritzt; **Rit|zer** (*ugs. für* kleine Schramme); **Rit|zung**
Ri|u|ki|u|in|seln *Plur.* (Inselkette im Pazifik)
Ri|va|le [...v...], der; -n, -n (↑R 126) ‹franz.› (Nebenbuhler, Mitbewerber); **Ri|va|lin; ri|va|li|sie|ren** (um den Vorrang kämpfen); **Ri|va|li|tät,** die; -, -en
Ri|ver|boat|shuf|fle ['rivə(r)bo:t-ʃaf(ə)l], die; -, -s ‹amerik.› (Vergnügungsfahrt auf einem [Fluss]schiff, bei der eine Jazzband spielt)
ri|ver|so [...v...] ‹ital.› (*Musik* umgekehrt, vor- und rückwärts zu spielen)
Ri|vi|e|ra [...v...], die; -, ...ren *Plur. selten* (ein Küstengebiet am Mittelmeer)
Ri|yal, der; -[s], -s ‹arab.› (Münzeinheit in Saudi-Arabien; *Abk.* SRl, Rl); 100 - (↑R 90); *vgl.* Rial
Ri|zi|nus [*österr.* ri'tsi:...], der; -, *Plur.* - *u.* -se ‹lat.› (ein Wolfsmilchgewächs, Heilpflanze); **Ri|zi|nus|öl,** das; -[e]s
r.-k., röm.-kath. = römisch-katholisch
RKW = Rationalisierungs-Kuratorium der Deutschen Wirtschaft
Rl = Rial; Riyal
Rm, *früher* rm = Raummeter
RM = Reichsmark
Rn = *chem. Zeichen für* Radon
RNS = Ribonukleinsäure
Roa|die ['ro:di], der; -s, -s ‹amerik.› (*kurz für* Roadmanager); **Road|ma|na|ger** ['ro:d...] (für die Bühnentechnik u. deren Transport verantwortlicher Begleiter einer Rockgruppe); **Roads|ter** ['ro:dstə(r)], der; -s, - ‹engl.› (offener, zweisitziger Sportwagen)
Roa|ring Twen|ties ['rɔ:riŋ 'twenti:z] *Plur.* ‹engl., „die stürmischen zwanziger (Jahre)"› (die 20er Jahre des 20. Jh. in den USA u. in Westeuropa)
Roast|beef ['ro:stbi:f, 'rɔst...], das; -s, -s ‹engl.› (Rostbraten)
Rob|be, die; -, -n (Seesäugetier)
Robbe-Gril|let [rɔbgri'jɛ] (franz. Schriftsteller)
rob|ben (robbenartig kriechen); er robbt; **Rob|ben‿fang, ...fän|ger, ...fell, ...jagd, ...jä|ger, ...schlag** (Erlegung der Robbe mit einem Knüppel), **...ster|ben**
Rob|ber, der; -s, - ‹engl.› (*svw.* [1]Rubber)
Ro|be, die; -, -n ‹franz.› (kostbares, langes [Abend]kleid; Amtstracht, bes. für Richter, Anwälte, Geistliche)
Ro|bert (m. Vorn.); **Ro|ber|ta, Ro|ber|ti|ne** (w. Vorn.)
Ro|bes|pi|erre [rɔbɛs'pjɛ:r] (Führer in der Franz. Revolution)
Ro|bi|nie [...iə], die; -, -n ‹nach dem franz. Botaniker Robin› (ein Zierbaum od. -strauch)
Ro|bin|so|na|de, die; -, -n ‹neulat.› (Robinsongeschichte); **Ro|bin|son Cru|soe** [- 'kru:zo] (Held in einem Roman von Daniel Defoe); **Ro|bin|son|lis|te** (Liste von Personen, die keine Werbesendungen erhalten möchten)
Ro|bot, die; -, -en ‹tschech.› (*veraltet für* Frondienst); **ro|bo|ten** (*ugs. für* schwer arbeiten); er hat gerobotet, *auch* robotet; **Ro|bo|ter** (elektron. gesteuerter Automat); **ro|bo|ter|haft**
Ro|bu|rit [*auch* ...'rit], der; -s ‹lat.› (ein Sprengstoff); **ro|bust** (stark, widerstandsfähig); **Ro|bust|heit**
Ro|caille [rɔ'ka:j], das *od.* die; -, -s ‹franz.› (*Kunst* Muschelwerk; Rokokoornament)
Ro|cha|de [...x..., *auch* ...ʃ...], die; -, -n ‹arab.-span.-franz.› (*Schach* Doppelzug von König und Turm)
Roche|fort [rɔʃ'fɔ:r] (franz. Stadt)
rö|cheln; ich ...[e]le (↑R 16)
Ro|chen, der; -s, - (ein Seefisch)
Ro|chett [...ʃ...], das; -s, -s ‹franz.› (Chorhemd des kath. Geistlichen)
ro|chie|ren [...x..., *auch* ...ʃ...] ‹arab.-span.-franz.› (die Rochade ausführen; die Positionen wechseln [z. B. beim Fußball])
Ro|chus (Heiliger); einen - auf jmdn. haben (*ugs. für* zornig auf jmdn. sein)
[1]Rock, der; -[e]s, Röcke
[2]Rock, der; -[s] ‹amerik.› (Stilrichtung der Popmusik); **Rock and Roll,** Rock 'n' Roll ['rɔk (ɛ)n(d) 'ro:l], der; - - -[s], - - -[s] (stark synkopierter amerik. Tanz)
Röck|chen
ro|cken ([2]Rock spielen)
Ro|cken, der; -s, - (Spinngerät)
Ro|cken|bol|le, die; -, -n (*nordd. für* Perlzwiebel)
Ro|cken|stu|be (Spinnstube)
Ro|cker, der; -s, - ‹engl.› (Angehöriger einer Gruppe von Jugendlichen [mit Lederkleidung u. Motorrad als Statussymbolen]; Rockmusiker); **Ro|cker‿ban|de** (*vgl.* [2]Bande), **...braut** (*ugs. für* Freundin eines Rockers); **Rock‿grup|pe, ...kon|zert**

Röck|lein
Rock|mu|sik; Rock|mu|si|ker;
Rock 'n' Roll *vgl.* Rock and Roll; **Rock-'n'-Roll-Meis|ter|schaft;**
Rock|oper (↑R 132)
Rocks *Plur.* ‹engl.› (Fruchtbonbons)
Rock‿sän|ger, ...sän|ge|rin
Rock‿saum, ...schoß, ...ta|sche
Ro|cky Moun|tains [ˌrɔki ˈmauntins] *Plur.* (nordamerik. Gebirge)
Rock|zip|fel
Ro|de|ha|cke
[1]**Ro|del,** der; -s, Rödel (*südwestd. u. schweiz. für* Liste, Verzeichnis)
[2]**Ro|del,** der; -s, - (*bayr. für* Schlitten); [3]**Ro|del,** die; -, -n (*österr. für* kleiner Schlitten; *landsch. für* Kinderrassel); **Ro|del|bahn; ro|deln;** ich ...[e]le (↑R 16); **Ro|del|schlit|ten**
ro|den
Ro|deo, der *od.* das; -s, -s ‹engl.› (Reiterschau der Cowboys in den USA)
Ro|der (Gerät zum Roden [von Kartoffeln, Rüben])
Ro|de|rich (m. Vorn.)
Ro|din [rɔˈdɛ̃ː] (franz. Bildhauer)
Rod|ler; Rod|le|rin
Ro|do|mon|ta|de, die; -, -n ‹franz.› (*veraltet für* Aufschneiderei, Großsprecherei); **ro|do|mon|tie|ren** (*veraltet für* aufschneiden)
Ro|don|ku|chen [roˈdɔŋ...], der; -s, - ‹franz.; dt.› (*landsch.* ein Napfkuchen)
Rod|ri|go (↑R 130; m. Vorn.)
Ro|dung
Ro|ga|te ‹lat., „bittet!"› (fünfter Sonntag nach Ostern); **Ro|ga|ti|on,** die; -, -en (*veraltet für* Fürbitte; kath. Bittumgang)
Ro|gen, der; -s, - (Fischeier); **Ro|ge|ner,** Rog|ner (weibl. Fisch); **Ro|gen|stein** (rogenartige Versteinerung)
Ro|ger [*franz.* rɔˈʒeː, *engl.* ˈrɔdʒə(r)] (m. Vorn.)
Rög|gel|chen (*rhein. für* Roggenbrötchen); **Rog|gen,** der; -s, *Plur. (Sorten:)* - (ein Getreide); **Rog|gen‿brot, ...bröt|chen, ...ern|te, ...feld, ...mehl**
Rog|ner *vgl.* Rogener
roh; roh behauener, bearbeiteter Stein; aus dem Rohen arbeiten; im Rohen fertig; **Roh‿ar|beit, ...bau** (*Plur.* ...bauten), **...bi|lanz** *(Wirtsch.),* **...di|a|mant, ...ei|sen** (das; -s); **Roh|ei|sen|ge|win|nung; Ro|heit** *frühere Schreibung für* Rohheit; **Roh‿ent|wurf, ...er|trag; ro|her|wei|se; Roh|ge|wicht; Roh|heit; Roh|kost; Roh|köst|ler; Roh|köst|le|rin; Roh|ling; Roh‿ma|te|ri|al, ...öl, ...pro|dukt; Roh|pro|duk|ten|händ|ler**
Rohr, das; -[e]s, -e (Schilf; Pflanzenschaft; langer Hohlzylinder; *landsch., bes. österr. für* Backröhre); **Rohr‿am|mer** (ein Vogel), **...bruch** (der); **Röhr|chen** (kleines Rohr; kleine Röhre); **Rohr|dom|mel,** die; -, -n (ein Vogel); **Röh|re,** die; -, -n; [1]**röh|ren** (*veraltet für* mit Röhren versehen)
[2]**röh|ren** (brüllen [vom Hirsch zur Brunftzeit])
Röh|ren|be|wäs|se|rung; Röh|ren|blüt|ler, der; -s, - *(Bot.);* **Röh|ren‿brun|nen** (Brunnen, aus dem das Wasser ständig rinnt), **...ho|se, ...kno|chen, ...pilz; rohr|far|ben** (*für* beige); **Rohr‿flech|ter, ...flö|te, ...ge|flecht; Röh|richt,** das; -s, -e (Rohrdickicht); **...röh|rig** (z. B. vielröhrig); **Rohr‿kol|ben, ...kre|pie|rer** (*Soldatenspr.* Geschoss, das im Geschützrohr u. Ä. explodiert), **...le|ger, ...lei|tung; Röhr|li,** das; -s, -[s] (knöchelhoher mod. Damenstiefel); **Röhr|ling** (ein Pilz); **Rohr‿post** (die; -), **...rück|lauf** (der; -[e]s; beim Geschütz), **...sän|ger** (ein Singvogel); **Rohr|spatz;** *in* schimpfen wie ein - (*ugs. für* aufgebracht, laut schimpfen); **Rohr‿stock** (*Plur.* ...stöcke), **...stuhl, ...wei|he** (ein Greifvogel), **...zan|ge, ...zu|cker**
Roh‿schrift (*für* Konzept), **...sei|de; roh|sei|den;** ein -es Kleid; **Roh‿stahl** (*vgl.* [1]Stahl), **...stoff; roh|stoff|arm;** ...ärmer, ...ärmste; **Roh|stoff‿fra|ge** (↑R 136), **...man|gel** (der), **...markt; roh|stoff|reich; Roh|stoff|ver|ar|bei|tung; Roh‿ta|bak, ...zu|cker, ...zu|stand** (der; -[e]s)
ro|jen (*Seemannsspr.* rudern)
Ro|kam|bo|le, die; -, -n ‹franz.› (Perlzwiebel)
Ro|kit|no|sümp|fe *Plur.* (in der Polesje)
Ro|ko|ko [*auch* roˈkɔko, *österr.* ...ˈkoː], das; *Gen.* -s, *fachspr. auch* - ‹franz.› ([Kunst]stil des 18. Jh.s); **Ro|ko|ko‿kom|mo|de, ...stil, ...zeit** (die; -)
Ro|land (m. Vorn.); **Ro|lands|lied,** das; -[e]s; **Ro|land[s]|säu|le**
Rolf (m. Vorn.)
Rol|la|den *frühere Schreibung für* Rollladen
Roll|back [ˈroːlbɛk], das; -[s], -s ‹engl.› (Rückzug, erzwungenes Zurückweichen; Rückgang)
Roll‿bahn, ...bal|ken (*österr. für* Rollladen), **...ball** (der; -s; Mannschaftsballspiel), **...bra|ten; Roll|brett** (*svw.* Rollerbrett); **Röll|chen; Rol|le,** die; -, -n; **rol|len;** (↑R 50:) der Wagen kommt ins Rollen; **Rol|len‿be|set|zung** *(Theater),* **...fach** *(Theater);* **rol|len‿för|mig, ...spe|zi|fisch; Rol|len‿spiel** *(Soziol.),* **...tausch, ...ver|tei|lung; Rol|ler** (Motorroller; Kinderfahrzeug; männl. [Kanarien]vogel mit rollendem Schlag; *österr. für* Rollo; *österr. auch svw.* Rollfähre); [mit dem] Roller fahren, *aber* (↑R 50): das Rollerfahren; **Rol|ler|brett** (*für* Skateboard); **rol|lern;** ich ...ere (↑R 16); **Rol|ler|skate** [roːlə(r)skeːt], das; -s, -s ‹engl.› (*svw.* Diskoroller); **Roll‿fäh|re** (*österr. für* Seilfähre), **...feld, ...film; Roll|fuhr‿dienst** *(veraltend),* **...mann** (*Plur.* ...männer *u.* ...leute; *veraltend*); **Roll‿geld, ...gut, ...ho|ckey**
rol|lie|ren ‹lat.› (umlaufen; *Schneiderei* den Rand einrollen)
Roll‿kom|man|do, ...kra|gen; Roll|kra|gen|pull|over; Roll‿kunst|lauf (der; -[e]s), **...kur** *(Med.)*
Roll|la|den (↑R 136), der; -s, *Plur.* ...läden, *seltener* ...laden; **Roll|la|den|kas|ten; Roll|la|den|schrank**
Roll|loch (↑R 136; *Bergmannsspr.* steil abfallender Grubenbau)
Roll|mops (gerollter eingelegter Hering)
Rol|lo [*auch, österr. nur,* rɔˈloː], das; -s, -s (aufrollbarer Vorhang [z. B. an Fenstern])
Roll‿schie|ne, ...schin|ken, ...schnell|lauf, ...schrank; Roll|schuh; - laufen, *aber* (↑R 50): das Rollschuhlaufen; **Roll|schuh‿bahn, ...sport** (der; -[e]s); **Roll‿sitz, ...ski, ...splitt** (der; -[e]s), **...sport** (der; -[e]s; *svw.* Rollschuhsport)
Rolls-Royce ® [rɔlsˈrɔys, *engl.* ˈroːls...], der; -, - (engl. Kraftfahrzeugmarke)
Roll‿stuhl, ...trep|pe
[1]**Rom** (Hptst. Italiens)
[2]**Rom,** der; -, -a ‹Zigeunerspr.› (Zigeuner [mit nichtdeutscher Staatsangehörigkeit])
ROM, das; -[s], -[s] ‹aus engl. read-only memory› (*EDV* Informationsspeicher, dessen Inhalt nur abgelesen, aber nicht verändert werden kann)
Ro|ma (*Plur. von* [2]Rom)
Ro|ma|dur [*österr.* ...ˈduːr], der; -[s], -s ‹franz.› (ein Weichkäse)
Ro|mag|na [roˈmanja] (↑R 130), die; - (eine ital. Landschaft)
Ro|man, der; -s, -e ‹franz.›; ein historischer -; **ro|man|ar|tig; Ro-**

man˽au|tor, ...au|to|rin; Ro|män|chen; Ro|man|ci|er [romã'sie:], der; -s, -s (Romanschriftsteller); **Ro|mand** [rɔmã], der; -, -s (Schweizer mit franz. Muttersprache); **Ro|ma|ne,** der; -n, -n (↑R 126) ‹lat.› (Angehöriger eines Volkes mit roman. Sprache); **Ro|ma|nen|tum,** das; -s; **Ro|man˽fi|gur, ...ge|stalt; ro|man|haft; Ro|man˽held, ...hel|din**

Ro|ma|ni [*auch* 'rɔ...], das; -[s] ‹Zigeunerspr.› (Zigeunersprache)

Ro|ma|nik, die; - ‹lat.› (Kunststil vom 11. bis 13. Jh.; Zeit des roman. Stils); **Ro|ma|nin; ro|ma|nisch** (zu den Romanen gehörend; im Stil der Romanik, die Romanik betreffend; *schweiz. auch für* rätoromanisch [*vgl.* romantsch]); -e Sprachen; **ro|ma|ni|sie|ren** (römisch, romanisch machen); **Ro|ma|nist,** der; -en, -en; ↑R 126 (Kenner und Erforscher der roman. Sprachen u. Literaturen; Kenner und Erforscher des römischen Rechts); **Ro|ma|nis|tik,** die; - (Wissenschaft von den romanischen Sprachen u. Literaturen; Wissenschaft vom röm. Recht); **Ro|ma|nis|tin; ro|ma|nis|tisch; Ro|man˽le|ser, ...li|te|ra|tur** (die; -)

Ro|ma|now [...nɔf, *auch, österr. nur,* 'rɔ...] (ehem. russ. Herrschergeschlecht)

Ro|man˽schrei|ber, ...schrei|be|rin, ...schrift|stel|ler, ...schrift|stel|le|rin; Ro|man|tik, die; - ‹lat.› (Kunst- und Literaturrichtung von etwa 1800 bis 1830; gefühlsbetonte Stimmung); keinen Sinn für - haben; **Ro|man|ti|ker** (Anhänger, Dichter usw. der Romantik; *abwertend für* Phantast, Gefühlsschwärmer); **Ro|man|ti|ke|rin; ro|man|tisch** (zur Romantik gehörend; gefühlsbetont, schwärmerisch; abenteuerlich); **ro|man|ti|sie|ren** (romantisch darstellen, gestalten); **ro|mantsch** (rätoromanisch); **Ro|mantsch,** das; -[s] (rätoroman. Sprache [in Graubünden]); **Ro|ma|nus** (m. Vorn.); **Ro|man|ze,** die; -, -n ‹franz.› (erzählendes volkstüml. Gedicht; liedartiges Musikstück mit besonderem Stimmungsgehalt; romantisches Liebeserlebnis); **Ro|man|zen˽dich|ter, ...samm|lung; Ro|man|ze|ro,** der; -s, -s ‹span.› (span. Romanzensammlung)

Ro|meo (Gestalt bei Shakespeare)

¹Rö|mer (Einwohner Roms; Angehöriger des Römischen Reiches; *auch für* eine Dachziegelart); **²Rö|mer,** der; -s (das alte Rathaus in Frankfurt am Main); **³Rö|mer** (bauchiges Kelchglas für Wein); **Rö|mer|brief,** der; -[e]s (↑R 105; *N. T.*); **Rö|me|rin; Rö|mer|stra|ße** (↑R 123); **Rö|mer|topf** ® (↑R 105); **Rö|mer|tum,** das; -s; **Rom˽fah|rer, ...fahrt** (↑R 105); **rö|misch** (auf Rom, auf die alten Römer bezogen); römische Zeitrechnung, römische Zahlen, römisches Bad, römisches Recht, die römischen Kaiser, *aber* (↑R 108): das Römische Reich, das Heilige Römische Reich Deutscher Nation; **rö|misch-iri|sch** (↑R 27); römisch-irisches Bad (ein Heißluftbad); **rö|misch-ka|tho|lisch** (↑R 27; *Abk.* r.-k., röm.-kath.); die römisch-katholische Kirche; **röm.-kath.** = römisch-katholisch

Rom|mé, *eindeutschend* **Rommee** ['rɔme:, *auch* rɔ'me:] (↑R 33), das; -s, -s ‹franz.› (ein Kartenspiel)

Ro|mu|ald, Ru|mold (m. Vorn.)

Ro|mu|lus (in der röm. Sage Gründer Roms); Romulus und Remus; Romulus Augustulus (letzter weströmischer Kaiser)

Ro|nald (m. Vorn.)

Ron|ces|valles ['rɔ̃səval, *span.* rɔnθez'valjɛs] (span. Ort)

Ron|de ['rɔndə, *auch* 'rɔ̃:də], die; -, -n ‹franz.› (*früher für* Runde, Rundgang; Wachen u. Posten kontrollierender Offizier); **Ron|deau** [rɔn'do:], das; -s, -s (*österr. für* rundes Beet, runder Platz); **Ron|dell, Run|dell,** das; -s, -e (Rundteil [an der Bastei]; Rundbeet); **Ron|den|gang,** der (*svw.* Ronde); **Ron|do,** das; -s, -s ‹ital.› (mittelalterl. Tanzlied; Instrumentalsatz mit mehrfach wiederkehrendem Thema)

Ron|ka|li|sche Fel|der *Plur.* (Ebene in Oberitalien)

rönt|gen (mit Röntgenstrahlen durchleuchten); du röntgst; **Rönt|gen** (dt. Physiker); **Rönt|gen˽ap|pa|rat** (↑R 95), **...arzt, ...ärz|tin, ...auf|nah|me, ...be|hand|lung, ...be|strah|lung, ...bild, ...di|ag|nos|tik; rönt|ge|ni|sie|ren** (*österr. für* röntgen); **Rönt|gen|ki|ne|ma|to|gra|phie,** die; - (Filmen des durch Röntgenstrahlen entstehenden Bildes); **Rönt|ge|no|gramm,** das; -s, -e (Röntgenbild); **Rönt|ge|no|gra|phie,** die; - (fotogr. Aufnahme mit Röntgenstrahlen); **rönt|ge|no|gra|phisch; Rönt|ge|no|lo|ge,** der; -n, -n (↑R 126); **Rönt|ge|no|lo|gie,** die; - (Lehre von den Röntgenstrahlen); **Rönt|ge|no|lo|gin; rönt|ge|no|lo|gisch; Rönt|ge|no|sko|pie,** die; -, ...ien (Durchleuchtung mit Röntgenstrahlen); **Rönt|gen˽pass** (*Plur.* ...pässe), **...rei|hen|un|ter|su|chung, ...schirm, ...schwes|ter, ...spekt|rum, ...strah|len** (*Plur.*), **...struk|tur|ana|ly|se** (↑R 132; röntgenolog. Untersuchung der Struktur von Kristallen), **...tie|fen|the|ra|pie** (die; -), **...un|ter|su|chung**

Roo|ming-in [.ru(:)miŋ'in], das; -[s], -s ‹engl.› (gemeinsame Unterbringung von Mutter und Kind im Krankenhaus)

Roo|se|velt ['ro:z(ə)vɛlt] (Name zweier Präsidenten der USA)

Roque|fort ['rɔkfo:r, *auch* rɔk'fo:r], der; -s, -s ‹nach dem franz. Ort› (ein Käse); **Roque|fort|kä|se** (↑R 105)

Ror|schach (schweiz. Stadt)

Ror|schach|test ‹nach dem Schweizer Psychiater› (ein psycholog. Testverfahren)

ro|sa ‹lat.› (rosenfarbig, blassrot); ein rosa Kleid; die rosa Kleider; *vgl. auch* beige; in Rosa (↑R 47); **¹Ro|sa,** das; -s, *Plur.* -, *ugs.* -s (rosa Farbe); *vgl.* Blau; **²Ro|sa** (w. Vorn.); **ro|sa|far|ben, ro|sa|far|big; Ro|sa|lia, Ro|sa|lie** [...i̯ə] (w. Vorn.); **Ro|sa|li|en|ge|bir|ge,** das; -s (nördl. Ausläufer der Zentralalpen); **Ro|sa|lin|de** (w. Vorn.); **Ro|sa|mund, Ro|sa|mun|de** (w. Vorn.); **Ro|sa|ni|lin** (↑R 132), das; -s (ein Farbstoff); **Ro|sa|ri|um,** das; -s, ...ien [...i̯ən] (Rosenpflanzung; kath. Rosenkranzgebet); **ro|sa|rot** (↑R 27); **Ro|sa|zee,** die; -, -n (*Bot.* Rosengewächs)

rösch [*auch* rø:ʃ] (*Bergmannsspr.* grob [zerkleinert]; *bes. südd., auch schweiz. mdal. für* knusprig)

Rö|sche, die; -, -n (*Bergmannsspr.* Graben od. stollenartiger Gang, der Wasser zu- od. abführt)

Rös|chen (kleine Rose; *kurz für* Blumenkohlröschen); **¹Ro|se,** die; -, -n; **²Ro|se** (w. Vorn.); **ro|sé** [ro'ze:] ‹franz.› (rosig, zartrosa); rosé Spitze; *vgl. auch* beige; in Rosé (↑R 47); **¹Ro|sé,** das; -[s], -[s] (rosé Farbe); **²Ro|sé,** der; -s, -s (Roséwein)

Ro|seau [ro:'zo:] (Hptst. von Dominica)

Ro|see|wein *vgl.* Roséwein

Ro|seg|ger [*auch* ro'zɛ..., 'rɔ...] (österr. Schriftsteller)

Ro|sel (w. Vorn.); **Ro|se|ma|rie** (w. Vorn.); **Ro|sen˽blatt, ...busch, ...duft; ro|sen|far|ben,**

ro|sen|far|big; Ro|sen‿gar|ten, ...hoch|zeit (*ugs. für* 10. Jahrestag der Eheschließung), **...holz, ...kohl** (der; -[e]s), **...kranz**

Ro|sen|mon|tag ⟨*zu* rasen = tollen⟩ (Fastnachtsmontag); **Rosen|mon|tags|zug**

Ro|se|no|bel [*auch* ...'no:...], der; -s, - ⟨engl.⟩ (alte engl. Goldmünze)

Ro|sen‿öl, ...pap|ri|ka (der; -s), **...quarz** (ein Schmuckstein); **rosen|rot; Ro|sen‿schau, ...stock** (*Plur.* ...stöcke), **...strauch, ...strauß** (*Plur.* ...sträuße), **...was|ser** (*Plur.* ...wässer), **...züch|ter**

Ro|se|o|le, die; -, -n ⟨lat.⟩ (*Med.* ein Hautausschlag)

[1]**Ro|sette** [ro'zɛt] (Stadt in Unterägypten)

[2]**Ro|set|te,** die; -, -n ⟨franz.⟩ (Verzierung in Rosenform; Bandschleife; Edelsteinschliff); **Ro|séwein** [ro'ze:...], *amtl.* Ro|see|wein (blassroter Wein); **Ro|si** (w. Vorn.); **ro|sig;** eine rosig weiße Blüte

Ro|si|nan|te, die; -, -n ⟨span.⟩ (Don Quichottes Pferd; *selten für* Klepper)

Ro|si|ne, die; -, -n ⟨franz.⟩ (getrocknete Weinbeere); **Ro|sinen‿brot, ...bröt|chen, ...kuchen; ro|sin|far|ben**

Rös|lein *vgl.* Röschen

Ros|ma|rin [*auch* ...'ri:n], der; -s ⟨lat.⟩ (eine Gewürzpflanze); **Rosma|rin|öl**

Ro|so|lio, der; -s, -s ⟨ital.⟩ (ein Likör)

Roß, das; -es, -e *u.* Ro|ße, die; -, -n (*mitteld. für* Wabe)

Ross, das; -es, *Plur.* Rosse, *landsch.* Rösser (*südd., österr. u. schweiz., sonst geh. für* Pferd)

Ross‿ap|fel (*landsch. scherzh. für* Pferdekot), **...arzt** (*veraltet für* Tierarzt im Heer), **...brei|ten** (*Plur.;* windschwache Zone im subtropischen Hochdruckgürtel); **Röss|chen,** Röss|lein, Rös|sel, Rössl (kleines Ross)

Ro|ße *vgl.* Roß

Rös|sel *vgl.* Rösschen; **Ros|selen|ker** *(geh.);* **Rös|sel|sprung** (Rätselart); **ros|sen** (brünstig sein [von der Stute]); die Stute rosst; **Ross|haar; Ross|haarmat|rat|ze; ros|sig** ⟨*zu* rossen⟩

Ros|si|ni (ital. Komponist)

Ross‿kamm (Pferdestriegel; *spött. für* Pferdehändler), **...kasta|nie, ...kur** (*ugs. für* mit drastischen Mitteln durchgeführte Kur; *vgl.* [1]Kur); **Rössl, Röss|lein** *vgl.* Rösschen; **Ross‿schlach|ter** *od.* **...schläch|ter** (↑R 136; *landsch. für* Pferdeschlächter); **Ross|täuscher** (*veraltet für* Pferdehändler); **Ross|täu|sche|rei; Rosstäu|scher|trick; Ross|trap|pe,** die; - (ein Felsen im Harz)

[1]**Rost** [*schweiz.* ro:st], der; -[e]s, -e ([Heiz]gitter; *landsch. für* Stahlmatratze)

[2]**Rost,** der; -[e]s (Zersetzungsschicht auf Eisen; Pflanzenkrankheit); **Rost|an|satz; rost|bestän|dig; Rost|bil|dung**

Rost‿bra|ten, ...brat|wurst

rost|braun

Röst|brot [*auch* 'rœst...]; **Rös|te** [*auch* 'rœ...], die; -, -n (Röstvorrichtung; Erhitzung von Erzen; Rotten [von Flachs])

ros|ten (Rost ansetzen)

rös|ten [*auch* 'rœ...] (braten; bräunen [Kaffee, Brot u. a.]; [Erze u. Hüttenprodukte] erhitzen; [Flachs] rotten); **Rös|ter,** der; -s, - (*österr. für* Kompott od. Mus aus Holunderbeeren od. Zwetschen); **Rös|te|rei**

rost|far|ben, rost|far|big; Rost‿fleck, ...fraß; rost|frei; -er Stahl

röst|frisch [*auch* 'rœst...]; -er Kaffee; **Rös|ti,** die; - (*schweiz.* [grob geraspelte] Bratkartoffeln)

ros|tig

Röst|kar|tof|fel [*auch* 'rœst...] *meist Plur.* (*landsch. für* Bratkartoffel)

Rost|lau|be (*ugs. für* Auto mit vielen Roststellen)

Ros|tock (Hafenstadt an der Ostsee)

Ros|tow [*auch* ...'tɔf] (Name zweier Städte in Russland); - am Don

Rost|pilz (Erreger von Pflanzenkrankheiten)

Ros|tra (↑R 130), die; -, ...ren ⟨lat.⟩ (Rednerbühne im alten Rom)

Rost|ro|po|witsch, Mstislaw (↑R 130; russ. Cellist u. Dirigent)

rost|rot; - färben

Röst|schnit|te [*auch* 'rœst...]

Rost‿schutz (der; -es), **...schutzmit|tel** (das), **...stel|le**

Rös|tung [*auch* 'rœ...]

Ros|with, Ros|wi|tha (↑R 132; w. Vorn.)

rot; röter, röteste, *seltener* roter, roteste.; rote Farbe; rote Grütze; *vgl. aber* ↑R 56); die rote Karte *(bes. Fußball);* der rote Faden; der rote Hahn (Feuer); das rote Ass *(Kartenspiel);* er wirkt auf sie wie ein rotes Tuch; er hat keinen roten Heller (Pfennig) mehr; sie hat sich die Augen rot geweint; (↑R 40:) rot geweinte Augen; die rot glühende Sonne; ein rot gestreifter Pullover; *vgl.* rotbraun, rotgrün u. rotsehen; *Großschreibung* (↑R 47, 102 *u.* 108): die Roten (*ugs. für* die Sozialisten, Kommunisten u. a.); das Rote Meer; die Rote Erde (Bezeichnung für Westfalen); der Rote Fluss (in Vietnam); die Rote Wand (in Österreich); der Rote Planet (Mars); das Rote Kreuz; der Rote Halbmond; die Rote Armee (Sowjetarmee); Rote Be[e]te; *vgl.* blau; **Rot,** das; -s, *Plur.* -, *ugs.* -s (rote Farbe); bei Rot ist das Überqueren der Straße verboten; die Ampel steht auf, zeigt Rot; er spielte Rot aus *(Kartenspiel); vgl.* Blau; **Röt,** das; -[e]s (*Geol.* Stufe der unteren Triasformation)

Ro|ta, die; - ⟨ital.⟩ *u.* Ro|ta Ro|mana, die; - - ⟨lat.⟩ (höchster Gerichtshof der kath. Kirche)

Rot|al|ge (rötlich gefärbte Alge)

Ro|tang, der; -s, -e ⟨malai.⟩ (eine Palmenart); **Ro|tang|pal|me**

Ro|ta|print ® ⟨lat.; engl.⟩ (Offsetdruck- und Vervielfältigungsmaschinen)

Ro|ta|ri|er [...i̯ər] (Mitglied des Rotary Clubs); **ro|ta|risch**

Rot|ar|mist, der; -en, -en; ↑R 126 *(früher)*

Ro|ta Ro|ma|na *vgl.* Rota

Ro|ta|ry Club [*engl.* 'ro:təri 'klab], der; - -[s], - -s ⟨engl.⟩ (Vereinigung führender Persönlichkeiten unter dem Gedanken des Dienstes am Nächsten); **Ro|ta|ry In|ter|natio|nal** ['ro:təry intə(r)'nɛʃ(ə)nəl] (internationale Dachorganisation der Rotary Clubs)

Ro|ta|ti|on, die; -, -en ⟨lat.⟩ (Drehung, Umlauf); **Ro|ta|ti|ons‿ach|se, ...be|we|gung, ...druck** (*Plur.* ...drucke), **...el|lip|so|id** *(Math.);* **Ro|ta|ti|ons|kol|benmo|tor** *(Technik);* **Ro|ta|ti|ons‿kör|per, ...ma|schi|ne, ...pa|rabo|lo|id** *(Math.),* **...pres|se, ...prin|zip** *(Politik);* **Ro|ta|to|ri|en** *Plur.* (*Zool.* Rädertierchen)

Rot|au|ge (ein Fisch); **rot‿backig** *od.* **...bä|ckig; Rot‿barsch, ...bart; rot‿bär|tig, ...blau, ...blond, ...braun** (↑R 27); **Rotbu|che**

Rot|chi|na [...'çi:...], das; -s (*für* Volksrepublik China)

Rot|dorn *Plur.* ...dorne; **Rö|te,** die; -

Ro|te-Ar|mee-Frak|ti|on[1], die; - (eine terrorist. Vereinigung); er gehört zur Rote[n]-Armee-Fraktion

Ro|te-Be[e]|te-Sa|lat[1], der; Rote[n]-Be[e]te-Salat[e]s, Rote[n]-Be[e]te-Salate

[1] ↑R 28

Ro|te-Kreuz-Los[1], das; Rote[n] Kreuz-Loses, Rote[n]-Kreuz-Lose; **Ro|te-Kreuz-Lot|te|rie**[1], die; Rote[n]-Kreuz-Lotterie, Rote[n]-Kreuz-Lotterien; **Ro|te-Kreuz-Schwes|ter**[1], die; Rote[n]-Kreuz-Schwester, Rote[n]-Kreuz-Schwestern; *vgl.* Rotkreuzschwester

Rö|tel, der; -s, - (roter Mineralfarbstoff, Zeichenstift); **Rö|teln** *Plur.* (eine Infektionskrankheit); **Rö|tel‿stift** (*vgl.* [1]Stift), **...zeich|nung; rö|ten;** sich -

Ro|ten|burg a. d. Ful|da (Stadt in Hessen); **Ro|ten|burg (Wüm|me)** (Stadt in Niedersachsen); *vgl. aber* Rothenburg

Ro|te|turm|pass, der (in den Karpaten)

Rot‿fe|der (ein Fisch), **...fil|ter** *(Fotogr.),* **...fo|rel|le, ...fuchs** (*ugs. auch für* rothaariger Mensch), **...gar|dist** *(früher);* **rot|ge|sich|tig; rot ge|weint, glü|hend** *vgl.* rot; **Rot|glut**, die; -

rot|grün (↑R 27); ein rotgrünes Bündnis (zwischen Sozialdemokraten u. Grünen); **Rot|grün|blind|heit**, die; -; ↑R 27 (Farbenfehlsichtigkeit, bei der Rot u. Grün verwechselt werden)

Rot|gül|dig|erz, *fachspr. auch* **Rot|gül|tig|erz** (ein Silbererz); **Rot|guss** (Gussbronze)

[1]**Roth**, Eugen (dt. Schriftsteller)

[2]**Roth**, Joseph (österr. Schriftsteller)

Rot|haar|ge|bir|ge, das; -s (Teil des Rhein. Schiefergebirges)

rot|haa|rig; Rot|haut (*scherzh. für* Indianer)

Ro|then|burg ob der Tau|ber (Stadt in Bayern); **Ro|then|burg (Ober|lau|sitz)** [*auch* ...'lau...] (Stadt an der Lausitzer Neiße); *vgl. aber* Rotenburg

Rot|hirsch

Roth|schild (Bankiersfamilie)

ro|tie|ren ‹lat.› (umlaufen, sich um die eigene Achse drehen)

Ro|tis|se|rie, die; -, ...ien ‹franz.› (Grillrestaurant)

Rot‿ka|bis (*schweiz. für* Rotkohl), **...käpp|chen** (eine Märchengestalt), **...kehl|chen** (ein Singvogel), **...kohl** (der; -[e]s), **...kopf** (Mensch mit roten Haaren), **...kraut** (das; -[e]s); **Rot|kreuz|schwes|ter**, Ro|te-Kreuz-Schwes|ter *(vgl. d.);* **Rot|lauf**, der; -[e]s ([Tier]krankheit); **röt|lich;** rötlich braun usw. **Rot|licht**, das; -[e]s; **Rot|lie|gen|de**, das; -n; ↑R 5 ff. (*Geol.* untere Abteilung der Permformation); **Röt|ling** (ein Pilz); **rot|na|sig**

Ro|tor, der; -s, ...oren ‹lat.› (sich drehender Teil von [elektr.] Maschinen); **Ro|tor‿an|ten|ne, ...blatt, ...schiff**

Ro|traud (w. Vorn.)

Rot‿rü|be (*landsch. für* Rote Rübe), **Rot‿schwanz** *od.* **...schwänz|chen** (ein Singvogel); **rot|se|hen** (↑R 38; *ugs. für* wütend werden); er sieht rot; rotgesehen; rotzusehen; **Rot|spon**, der; -[e]s, -e (*ugs. für* Rotwein); **Rot‿stift** (*vgl.* [1]Stift), **...sün|der** (*bes. für* Fußballspieler, der die rote Karte bekommen hat), **...tan|ne**

Rot|te, die; -, -n (ungeordnete Schar, Gruppe von Menschen); [1]**rot|ten** (*veraltet für* eine Rotte bilden)

[2]**rot|ten, röt|ten** (*Landw.* [Flachs] der Zersetzung aussetzen, um die Fasern herauszulösen)

Rot|ten, der; -s (dt. Name des Oberlaufes der Rhone)

Rot|ten|burg a. d. Laa|ber (Ort in Niederbayern); **Rot|ten|burg am Ne|ckar** (Stadt in Baden-Württemberg)

Rot|ten|füh|rer *(Eisenb.);* **rot|ten|wei|se**

Rot|ter|dam [*auch* 'rɔ...] (niederl. Stadt); **Rot|ter|da|mer** (↑R 103); der - Hafen

Rot|tier (*Jägerspr.* Hirschkuh)

Rott|wei|ler, der; -s, - (eine Hunderasse)

Ro|tun|de, die; -, -n ‹lat.› (*Archit.* Rundbau; runder Saal)

Rö|tung; rot|wan|gig; Rot|wein

rot|welsch; Rot|welsch, das; -[es] (Gaunersprache); *vgl.* Deutsch; **Rot|wel|sche**, das; -n; *vgl.* Deutsche, das

Rot‿wild, ...wurst (*landsch. für* Blutwurst)

Rotz, der; -es ([Tier]krankheit; *derb für* Nasenschleim); **Rotz|ben|gel** (*derb für* ungepflegter, unerzogener Junge); **rot|zen** (*derb für* sich die Nase putzen; [Schleim] ausspucken); du rotzt; **Rotz|fah|ne** (*derb für* Taschentuch); **rotz|frech** (*derb für* sehr frech); **rot|zig** *(derb);* **Rotz‿jun|ge** (der; *svw.* Rotzbengel), **...krank|heit** *(Tiermed.),* **...löf|fel** (*svw.* Rotzbengel), **...na|se** (*derb; auch übertr. für* naseweises, freches Kind); **rotz|nä|sig** *(derb)*

Rot|zun|ge (ein Fisch)

Roué [rue:], der; -s, -s ‹franz.› (*veraltet für* Lebemann)

Rou|en [ru'ã:] (franz. Stadt an der unteren Seine)

Rouge [ru:ʒ], das; -s, -s ‹franz.› (rote Schminke)

Rouge et noir [ru:ʒ e 'noa:r], das; - - - ‹franz., „Rot und Schwarz"› (ein Glücksspiel)

Rou|la|de [ru...], die; -, -n ‹franz.› (gerollte u. gebratene Fleischscheibe; *Musik* virtuose Gesangspassage); **Rou|leau** [ru'lo:], das; -s, -s (*ältere Bez. für* Rollo); **Rou|lett**, das; -[e]s, *Plur.* -e *u.* -s *od.* **Rou|lette** [ru'lɛ:t], das; -s, -s (ein Glücksspiel); **rou|lie|ren** (*svw.* rollieren)

Round|ta|ble|ge|spräch, *auch* **Round-Ta|ble-Ge|spräch** (↑R 28) [raund'te:b(ə)l...] ‹engl.› (Gespräch am runden Tisch zwischen Gleichberechtigten); **Round|ta|ble|kon|fe|renz,** *auch* **Round-Ta|ble-Kon|fe|renz**

[1]**Rous|seau** [ru'so:], Jean-Jacques (schweiz.-franz. Schriftsteller)

[2]**Rous|seau** [ru'so:], Henri (franz. Maler)

Rou|te ['ru:tə], die; -, -n ‹franz.› (festgelegte Wegstrecke); **Rou|ten|ver|zeich|nis; Rou|ti|ne**, die; - (durch längere Erfahrung erworbene Gewandtheit, Fertigkeit; gewohnheitsmäßige Ausführung einer Tätigkeit); **Rou|ti|ne‿an|ge|le|gen|heit, ...kon|trol|le; rou|ti|ne|mä|ßig; Rou|ti|ne‿sa|che, ...über|prü|fung** (↑R 132), **...un|ter|su|chung; Rou|ti|ni|er** [...'nie:], der; -s, -s (jmd., der Routine hat); **rou|ti|niert** (gerissen, gewandt)

Row|dy ['raudi], der; -s, -s ‹engl.› ([jüngerer] gewalttätiger Mensch); **row|dy|haft; Row|dy|tum**, das; -s

ro|yal [roa'ja:l] ‹franz.› (königlich; königstreu); **Ro|yal Air Force** [ˌrɔy(ə)l 'ɛ:(r) fɔ:(r)s], die; - - ‹engl., „Königl. Luftwaffe"› (Bez. der brit. Luftwaffe; *Abk.* R. A. F.); **Ro|ya|lis|mus** [roa-ja...], der; - ‹franz.› (Königstreue); **Ro|ya|list**, der; -en, -en (↑R 126); **ro|ya|lis|tisch** (königstreu)

Rp = Rupiah

Rp. = Rappen

Rp., Rec. = recipe!

RP *(bei Telegrammen)* = Réponse payée [re'pɔ̃:s pɛ'je:] ‹franz., „Antwort bezahlt"›

RSFSR = Russische Sozialistische Föderative Sowjetrepublik (1918 bis 1991)

RT = Registertonne

Ru = *chem. Zeichen für* Ruthenium

Ru|an|da (Staat in Zentralafrika); **Ru|an|der; ru|an|disch**

---

[1] ↑R 28

ru|ba|to ‹ital.› (*Musik* nicht im strengen Zeitmaß); **Ru|ba|to,** das; -s, *Plur.* -s *u.* ...ti
rub|be|lig (*landsch. für* rau; uneben); **Rub|bel|los** (Lotterielos, bei dem die Gewinnzahl o. Ä. von einer abreibbaren Schutzschicht verdeckt ist); **rub|beln** (*landsch. für* kräftig reiben); ich ...[e]le (↑R 16)
[1]**Rub|ber** ['rabə(r)], der; -s, - ‹engl.› (Doppelpartie im Whist od. Bridge); [2]**Rub|ber,** der; -s (*engl. Bez. für* Gummi)
Rüb|chen; Rü|be, die; -, -n
Ru|bel, der; -s, - ‹russ.› (russ. Währungseinheit; *Abk.* Rbl; 1 Rubel = 100 Kopeken)
Ru|ben (bibl. m. Eigenn.)
Rü|ben|acker (↑R 132); **rü|ben|ar|tig; Rü|ben˯feld, ...kraut** (das; -[e]s; *landsch. für* Sirup)
Ru|bens (fläm. Maler)
Rü|ben|si|rup
ru|bensch; rubenssche Farbgebung; rubenssche Gemälde (↑R 94)
Rü|ben|zu|cker, der; -s
rü|ber; ↑R 13 (*ugs. für* herüber, hinüber); **rü|ber˯brin|gen, ...kom|men** *(ugs.)*
Rü|be|zahl (Berggeist des Riesengebirges)
Ru|bi|di|um, das; -s ‹lat.› (chem. Element, Metall; *Zeichen* Rb)
Ru|bi|kon, der; -[s] (ital. Fluss); den - überschreiten (*übertr. für* eine wichtige Entscheidung treffen)
Ru|bin, der; -s, -e ‹lat.› (ein Edelstein); **Ru|bin|glas** *Plur.* ...gläser; **ru|bin|rot**
Rüb|kohl, der; -[e]s (*schweiz. für* Kohlrabi)
Ru|bra, Ru|bren (↑R 130; *Plur. von* Rubrum); **Rub|rik,** die; -, -en ‹lat.› (Spalte, Kategorie [in die etwas eingeordnet wird]); **rub|ri|zie|ren** (einordnen, einstufen; *früher für* Überschriften u. Initialen malen); **Rub|ri|zie|rung; Ru|brum,** das; -s, *Plur.* ...ra *u.* ...ren (*veraltet für* [Akten]aufschrift; kurze Inhaltsangabe)
Rüb|sa|me[n], der; ...mens *od.* **Rüb|sen,** der; -s (eine Ölpflanze)
Ruch [*auch* rux], der; -[e]s, Rüche (*selten für* Geruch; zweifelhafter Ruf)
ruch|bar [*auch* 'rux...] (bekannt, offenkundig); ruchbar werden
Ruch|gras (eine Grasgattung)
ruch|los [*auch* 'rux...] (*geh. für* niedrig, gemein, böse, verrucht); **Ruch|lo|sig|keit**
Rück (*svw.* Rick)
ruck!; hau ruck!, ho ruck!; **Ruck,** der; -[e]s, -e; mit einem -
Rück˯an|sicht, ...ant|wort
ruck|ar|tig
Rück|äu|ße|rung; Rück|bau, der; -[e]s; **rück|bau|en** (durch Baumaßnahmen in einen früheren [naturnäheren] Zustand bringen); **Rück˯be|för|de|rung, ...be|sin|nung; rück|be|züg|lich;** -es Fürwort (*für* Reflexivpronomen); **Rück|bil|dung; Rück|bleib|sel,** das; -s, - (*veraltet für* Rückstand); **Rück|blen|de** *(Film);* **rück|blen|den; Rück|blick; rück|bli|ckend; rück|bu|chen; Rück|bu|chung; rück|da|tie|ren;** er hat den Brief rückdatiert; **Rück|de|ckungs|ver|si|che|rung** (*Wirtsch.* eine Risikoversicherung); **rück|dre|hend** *(Meteor.);* -er Wind (sich gegen den Uhrzeigersinn drehender Wind, z. B. von Nord auf Nordwest; *Ggs.* rechtdrehend)
ru|ckeln (*landsch. für* leicht, ein wenig [2]rucken)
[1]**ru|cken,** rucksen (gurren [von Tauben])
[2]**ru|cken** ([sich] ruckartig bewegen)
rü|cken; jmdm. zu Leibe -
Rü|cken, der; -s, -; **Rü|cken˯aus|schnitt, ...de|ckung, ...flos|se; rü|cken|frei;** ein -es Kleid; **Rü|cken˯la|ge, ...leh|ne, ...mark,** (das); **Rü|cken|mark|ent|zün|dung,** Rü|cken|marks|ent|zün|dung; **Rü|cken|mark|schwind|sucht,** Rü|cken|marks|schwind|sucht; **Rü|cken|mark|sub|stanz; Rü|cken˯mus|kel, ...mus|ku|la|tur, ...schmerz** *(meist Plur.);* **rü|cken|schwim|men;** *im Allg. nur im Infinitiv gebr.;* er kann nicht -; **Rü|cken|schwim|men,** das; -s; **Rü|cken|stär|kung**
Rück|ent|wick|lung
Rü|cken|wind, der; -[e]s; **Rü|cken|wir|bel**
Rück|er|bit|tung *(Amtsspr.);* unter - (*Abk.* u. R.); **Rück˯er|in|ne|rung, ...er|o|be|rung, ...er|stat|tung, ...fahr|kar|te; Rück|fahr|schein|wer|fer; Rück˯fahrt, ...fall** (der); **rück|fäl|lig; Rück|fäl|lig|keit; Rück|fall˯kri|mi|na|li|tät, ...tä|ter; Rück˯flug, ...fluss, ...fra|ge; rück|fra|gen;** er hat noch einmal rückgefragt
Rück|front
Rück˯füh|rung, ...ga|be; Rück|ga|be|recht, das; -[e]s; **Rück|gang,** der; **rück|gän|gig;** -e Geschäfte; etw. - machen; **Rück|gän|gig|ma|chung; rück|ge|bil|det; Rück|ge|win|nung**
Rück|grat, das; -[e]s, -e; **rück|grat|los; Rück|grat|ver|krüm|mung**
Rück˯griff (*auch für* Regress), **...halt; Rück|hal|te|be|cken** (*Wasserwirtsch.*); **rück|halt|los; Rück˯hand** (die; -; *bes.* [*Tisch*]*tennis*), **...kampf, ...kauf; Rück|kaufs˯recht, ...wert; Rück|kehr,** die; -; **rück|keh|ren** (*seltener für* zurückkehren); **Rück|keh|rer; Rück|keh|re|rin; Rück|kehr|hil|fe** (finanzielle Zuwendung für ausländ. Arbeitnehmer, die freiwillig in ihre Heimat zurückkehren); **Rück|kehr|prä|mie** (*svw.* Rückkehrhilfe); **rück|kop|peln;** ich ...[e]le (↑R 16); **Rück˯kop|pe|lung** *od.* **...kopp|lung** *(fachspr.);* **rück|kreu|zen; Rück|kreu|zung; Rück|kunft,** die; - (*geh. für* Rückkehr); **Rück˯la|ge** (zurückgelegter Betrag), **...lauf; rück|läu|fig;** -e Bewegung; -e Entwicklung; **Rück|läu|fig|keit; Rück˯leuch|te, ...licht** (*Plur.* ...lichter)
rück|lings
Rück˯marsch (der), **...mel|dung; Rück|nah|me,** die; -, -n; **Rück˯pass** *(Sport),* **...por|to, ...rei|se, ...ruf, ...run|de** (*Sport; Ggs.* Hinrunde)
Ruck|sack; Ruck|sack˯tou|rist, ...ur|lau|ber
Rück˯schau, ...schein (*Postw.* Empfangsbestätigung für den Absender), **...schlag; Rück|schlag|ven|til** (Ventil, das ein Gas od. eine Flüssigkeit nur in einer Richtung durchströmen lässt); **Rück˯schluss, ...schritt; rück|schritt|lich; Rück|schritt|lich|keit,** die; -
Rück|sei|te; rück|sei|tig
ruck|sen *vgl.* [1]rucken
Rück|sen|dung
Rück|sicht, die; -, -en; ohne, in, mit - auf; - nehmen; **rück|sicht|lich** (*Amtsspr.* mit Rücksicht auf); *Präp. mit Gen.:* - seiner Fähigkeiten; **Rück|sicht|nah|me,** die; -; **rück|sichts|los; Rück|sichts|lo|sig|keit; rück|sichts|voll;** er ist ihr gegenüber *od.* gegen sie immer sehr rücksichtsvoll
Rück|sied|lung
Rück˯sitz, ...spie|gel
Rück˯spiel (*Sport; Ggs.* Hinspiel), **...spra|che** (mit jmdm. - nehmen)
Rück|stand; im Rückstand bleiben, in Rückstand kommen; die Rückstände aufarbeiten; **rück|stand|frei; rück|stän|dig; rück|stands|frei** (*svw.* rückstandfrei)
Rück|stau; Rück|stell|tas|te; Rück|stel|lung (*Wirtsch.* Passivposten in der Bilanz zur Berücksichtigung ungewisser Verbindlichkeiten); **Rück|stoß; Rück-**

stoß|an|trieb (*für* Raketenantrieb); **Rück-strah|ler** (Schlusslicht), **...tas|te, ...trans|port, ...tritt; Rück|tritt|brem|se; Rück|tritts-dro|hung, ...gesuch, ...recht** (das; -[e]s); **rück|über|set|zen** (↑R 132); ich werde den Text -; der Text ist rückübersetzt; **Rück|über|set|zung** (↑R 132); **rück|ver|gü|ten** *(Wirtsch.);* ich werde ihm den Betrag rückvergüten; der Betrag wurde ihm rückvergütet; **Rück|ver|gü|tung; rück|ver|si|chern,** sich; ich rückversichere mich; rückversichert; rückzuversichern; **Rück|ver|si|che|rung**

Rück|wand

Rück-wan|de|rung, ...wa|re (*Wirtsch.* in das Zollgebiet zurückkehrende Ware)

rück|wär|tig; -e Verbindungen; **rück|wärts;** rückwärts fahren, gehen usw.; sie ist rückwärts gegangen; mit dem Umsatz ist es immer mehr rückwärts gegangen (er hat sich verschlechtert); eine rückwärts gewandte Politik; **Rück|wärts|gang,** der; **rück|wärts ge|hen, rück|wärts gewandt** *vgl.* rückwärts

Rück-wech|sel (*für* Rikambio), **...weg**

ruck|wei|se

Rück|wen|dung; rück|wir|kend; Rück|wir|kung; rück|zahl|bar; Rück|zah|lung; Rück|zie|her; einen - machen (*ugs. für* zurückweichen; *Fußball* den Ball über den Kopf nach hinten spielen)

ruck, zuck!

Rück|zug; Rück|zugs-ge|biet *(Völkerk., Biol.),* **...ge|fecht**

rü|de, *österr. auch* rüd ‹franz.› (roh, grob, ungesittet)

Rü|de, der; -n, -n; ↑R 126 (männl. Hund, Hetzhund)

Ru|del, das; -s, -; **ru|del|wei|se**

Ru|der, das; -s, -; ans - (*ugs. für* in eine leitende Stellung) kommen

Ru|de|ral|pflan|ze ‹lat.; dt.› (Pflanze, die auf stickstoffreichen Schuttplätzen gedeiht)

Ru|der-bank (*Plur.* ...bänke), **...blatt, ...boot; Ru|de|rer,** Rudrer; **Ru|der-fü|ßer** *(Zool.),* **...gän|ger** (*Segeln* jmd., der das Ruder bedient), **...haus; ...ru|derig,** ...rud|rig (z. B. achtrud[e]rig); **Ru|de|rin,** Rud|re|rin; **Ru|der-klub, ...ma|schi|ne; ru|dern;** ich ...ere (↑R 16); **Ru|der-re|gat|ta, ...sport** (der; -[e]s), **...verband** (Deutscher -), **...ver|ein**

Rü|des|heim am Rhein (Stadt in Hessen); [1]**Rü|des|hei|mer** (↑R 103); [2]**Rü|des|hei|mer** (Wein)

Rüd|heit

Ru|di (m. Vorn.)

Rü|di|ger (m. Vorn.)

Ru|di|ment, das; -[e]s, -e ‹lat.› (Überbleibsel, Rest; verkümmertes Organ); **ru|di|men|tär** (nicht ausgebildet, verkümmert)

Ru|dolf (m. Vorn.); **Ru|dol|fi|nische Ta|feln** *Plur.* (von Kepler für Kaiser Rudolf II. zusammengestellte Tafeln über Sternenbahnen)

Ru|dol|stadt (Stadt a. d. Saale); **Ru|dol|städ|ter** (↑R 103)

Rud|rer *vgl.* Ruderer; **Rud|re|rin** *vgl.* Ruderin; **...rud|rig** *vgl.* ...ruderig

Rüeb|li, das; -s, - (*schweiz. für* Karotte)

Ruf, der; -[e]s, -e; **Ruf|be|reitschaft**

Rü|fe, die; -, -n (*schweiz. für* Mure)

ru|fen; du rufst; du riefst; du riefest; gerufen; ruf[e]!; er ruft mich, den Arzt rufen; **Ru|fer; Ru|fe|rin**

Rüf|fel, der; -s, - (*ugs. für* Verweis, Tadel); **rüf|feln;** ich ...[e]le (↑R 16); **Rüff|ler**

Ruf-mord (schwere Verleumdung), **...nä|he, ...na|me, ...nummer, ...säu|le; ruf|schä|di|gend; Ruf-schä|di|gung, ...wei|te** (die; -), **...zei|chen**

Rug|by [ˈrakbi, *auch* ˈragbi], das; -[s] ‹engl.› (ein Ballspiel)

Rü|ge, die; -, -n

Ru|gel, der; -s, - (*schweiz. für* Rundholz)

rü|gen

Rü|gen (Insel vor der vorpommerschen Ostseeküste); **Rü|ge|ner** (↑R 103); **rü|gensch,** *auch* rügisch

rü|gens|wert; Rü|ger

Ru|gi|er (Angehöriger eines ostgerm. Volksstammes)

rü|gisch *vgl.* rügensch

Ru|he, die; -; jmdn. zur [letzten] Ruhe betten (*geh. für* beerdigen); sich zur Ruhe setzen; **Ru|he-bank** (*Plur.* ...bänke), **...be|dürfnis** (das; -ses); **ru|he|be|dürf|tig; Ru|he-bett** (*veraltet für* Liegesofa), **...ge|halt** (das; *svw.* Pension); **ru|he|ge|halt[s]|fä|hig** *(Amtsspr.);* **Ru|he-geld** (Altersrente), **...ge|nuss** (*österr. Amtsspr.* Pension), **...kis|sen, ...la|ge; ru|he|los; Ru|he|lo|sigkeit,** die; -; **Ru|he|mas|se** *(Physik);* **ru|hen;** ruht! (*österr. für* rührt euch!); sie hat den Fall ruhen lassen (*seltener* ruhen gelassen); die Angelegenheit wird ihn nicht ruhen lassen; wir wollen Großvater ein wenig ruhen lassen; **ru|hend;** er ist der -e Pol; der -e Verkehr; **ru|hen las|sen** *vgl.* ruhen; **Ru|he-pau|se, ...platz, ...raum; Ru|he|sitz; Ru|hestand,** der; -[e]s; des -[e]s (*Abk.* d. R.); im - (*Abk.* i. R.); **Ru|heständ|ler; Ru|he|statt** *od.* **Ru|he|stät|te** *(geh.);* **Ru|he|stellung** *(Milit.);* **ru|he|stö|rend;** -er Lärm (↑R 40); **Ru|he|stö|rer; Ru|he-stö|rung, ...tag, ...zeit; ru|hig;** ruhig sein, werden, bleiben usw.; einen Patienten ruhig stellen (*Med.* durch Medikamente beruhigen); **Ru|hig|stel|lung,** die; - *(Med.)*

Ruh|la (Stadt in Thüringen)

Ruhm, der; -[e]s

Ruh|mas|se (*svw.* Ruhemasse)

ruhm|be|deckt (↑R 40); **Ruhmbe|gier[|de],** die; -; **ruhm|be|gie|rig** (↑R 40); **rüh|men;** sich seines Wissens rühmen; (↑R 50:) nicht viel Rühmens von einer Sache machen; **rüh|mens|wert; Ruh|mes-blatt** (*meist in* kein - sein), **...hal|le, ...tat; rühm|lich; ruhm|los; Ruhm|lo|sig|keit,** die; -; **ruhm|re|dig** (*geh. für* prahlerisch); **Ruhm|re|dig|keit,** die; - *(geh.);* **ruhm|reich; Ruhm|sucht,** die; -; **ruhm|süch|tig; ruhm|voll**

[1]**Ruhr,** die; -, -en *Plur. selten* (Infektionskrankheit des Darmes)

[2]**Ruhr,** die; - (r. Nebenfluss des Rheins); *vgl. aber* Rur

Rühr|ei; rüh|ren; sich -; etwas schaumig rühren; den Teig glatt rühren; **rüh|rend**

Ruhr|ge|biet, das; -[e]s

rüh|rig; Rüh|rig|keit, die; -

Ruhr|koh|le

ruhr|krank

Rühr-löf|fel, ...ma|schi|ne

Rühr|mich|nicht|an, das; -, - (Springkraut); das Kräutlein -

Ruhr|ort (Stadtteil von Duisburg)

rühr|sam (*veraltet für* rührselig); **rühr|se|lig; Rühr-se|lig|keit** (die; -), **...stück, ...teig; Rührung,** die; -; **Rühr|werk**

Ru|in, der; -s ‹lat.-franz.› (Zusammenbruch, Verfall; Verderb, Verlust [des Vermögens]); **Ru|i|ne,** die; -, -n (zerfallen[d]es Bauwerk, Trümmer); **ru|i|nen|ar|tig; Ru|i|nen|grund|stück; ru|i|nen|haft; ru|i|nie|ren** ‹lat.› (zerstören, verwüsten); sich -; **ru|i|nös** (zum Ruin führend)

Ruis|dael [ˈrœizda:l] (niederl. Maler)

Ru|län|der, der; -s (eine Reb- u. Weinsorte)

Rülps, der; -es, -e (*ugs. für* hörbares Aufstoßen; *landsch. derb für* Flegel); **rülp|sen** *(ugs.);* du rülpst; **Rülp|ser** *(ugs.)*

rum; ↑R 13 (*ugs. für* herum)
Rum [*südd. u. österr. auch, schweiz. nur,* ru:m], der; -s, *Plur.* -s, *österr.* -e ‹engl.› (Branntwein [aus Zuckerrohr])
Ru|mä|ne, der; -n, -n (↑R 126); **Ru|mä|ni|en** [...iən]; **Ru|mä|nin; ru|mä|nisch; Ru|mä|nisch,** das; -[s] (Sprache); *vgl.* Deutsch; **Ru|mä|ni|sche,** das; -n; *vgl.* Deutsche, das
Rum|ba, die; -, -s, *ugs. auch, österr. nur,* der; -s, -s ‹kuban.› (ein Tanz)
Rum|fla|sche
rum|hän|gen; ↑R 13 (*ugs. für* sich irgendwo ohne ersichtlichen Grund, zum Zeitvertreib aufhalten)
rum|krie|gen; ↑R 13 (*ugs. für* zu etwas bewegen; hinter sich bringen)
Rum|ku|gel (eine Süßigkeit mit Rum[aroma])
rum|ma|chen; ↑R 13 (*ugs. für* sich auf diese od. jene Weise beschäftigen; herumbasteln)
Rum|mel, der; -s (*ugs. für* lärmender Betrieb; Durcheinander); **rum|meln** (*landsch. für* lärmen); ich ...[e]le (↑R 16); **Rum|mel|platz** *(ugs.)*
Rum|my ['rœmi, *auch* 'rami], das; -s, -s ‹engl.› (*österr. für* Rommee)
Ru|mold *vgl.* Romuald
Ru|mor, der; -s ‹lat.› (*veraltet, aber noch landsch. für* Lärm, Unruhe); **ru|mo|ren;** er hat rumort
[1]**Rum|pel,** der; -s (*südd. u. mitteld. für* Gerumpel; Gerümpel); [2]**Rum|pel,** die; -, -n (*mitteld. für* Waschbrett); **rum|pe|lig,** rumplig (*landsch. für* holprig); **Rum|pel|kam|mer** *(ugs.)*; **rum|peln** *(ugs.)*; ich ...[e]le (↑R 16); **Rum|pel|stilz|chen,** das; -s (eine Märchengestalt)
Rumpf, der; -[e]s, Rümpfe
rümp|fen; die Nase -
Rumpf|krei|sen, das; -s (eine gymnast. Übung)
rump|lig *vgl.* rumpelig
Rump|steak [...ste:k], das; -s, -s ‹engl.› ([gebratene] Rindfleischscheibe)
rums!; rum|sen (*landsch. für* krachen); es rumst
Rum‿topf, ...ver|schnitt
Run [ran], der; -s, -s ‹engl.› (Ansturm [auf etwas Begehrtes])
rund ([*im Sinne von* etwa] *Abk.* rd.); Gespräch am runden Tisch; rund um die Uhr (*ugs. für* im 24-Stunden-Betrieb); rund um die Welt, *aber* rundum; *vgl.* rundgehen; **Rund,** das; -[e]s, -e; **Run|da,** das; -s, -s (Rundgesang; Volkslied im Vogtland); **Rund‿bank** (*Plur.* ...bänke), **...bau** (*Plur.* ...bauten), **...beet** (*für* Rondell), **...blick, ...bo|gen; Rund|bo|gen|fens|ter; Run|de,** die; -, -n; die - machen; die erste -; **Rün|de,** die; - (*veraltet für* Rundsein); **Run|dell** *vgl.* Rondell; **run|den** (rund machen); sich -; **Run|den‿re|kord** *(Sport)*, **...zeit** *(Sport)*; **Rund|er|lass; rund|er|neu|ert;** -e Reifen; **Rund‿er|neu|e|rung, ...fahrt, ...flug, ...fra|ge**
Rund|funk, der; -s; **Rund|funk‿an|stalt, ...ap|pa|rat, ...emp|fän|ger, ...ge|bühr, ...ge|rät, ...hö|rer, ...hö|re|rin, ...kom|men|ta|tor, ...kom|men|ta|to|rin, ...or|ches|ter, ...pro|gramm, ...sen|der, ...spre|cher, ...spre|che|rin, ...sta|ti|on, ...tech|nik** (die; -), **...teil|neh|mer, ...teil|neh|me|rin, ...über|tra|gung** (↑R 132), **...wer|bung, ...zeit|schrift**
Rund|gang, der; **rund|ge|hen** (↑R 38 f.); es geht rund (*ugs. für* es ist viel Betrieb); es ist rundgegangen; **Rund|ge|sang; Rund|heit,** die; -; **rund|he|raus;** etwas rundheraus sagen; **rund|he|rum; Rund‿holz, ...ho|ri|zont** *(Theater)*, **...kurs, ...lauf** (ein Turngerät); **rund|lich; Rund|lich|keit,** die; -; **Rund|ling** (Dorfanlage); **Rund‿rei|se, ...rü|cken** *(Med.)*; **...ruf, ...schä|del, ...schau ...schild, ...schlag, ...schrei|ben, ...schrift, ...sicht, ...spruch** (der; -[e]s; *schweiz. für* Rundfunk), **...stre|cke; rund|stri|cken; Rund‿strick|na|del, ...stück** (*nordd. für* Brötchen), **...tanz; rund|um; rund|um|her; Rund|um|schlag; Run|dung; Rund|wan|der|weg; rund|weg; Rund|weg**
Ru|ne, die; -, -n ‹altnord.› (germ. Schriftzeichen); **Ru|nen‿al|pha|bet, ...for|schung, ...schrift, ...stein**
Run|ge, die; -, -n ([senkrechte] Stütze an der Wagenseite); **Run|gen|wa|gen**
ru|nisch ‹*zu* Rune›
Run|kel, die; -, -n (*österr. u. schweiz. für* Runkelrübe); **Run|kel|rü|be**
Run|ken, der; -s, - (*mitteld. für* unförmiges Stück Brot); **Runks,** der; -es, -e (*ugs. für* ungeschliffener Mensch); **runk|sen** (*ugs. für* sich wie ein Runks benehmen); du runkst
Run|ning|gag ['raniŋgɛk], der; -s, -s (Gag, der sich immer wiederholt)
Ru|no|lo|ge, der; -n, -n (↑R 126) ‹altnord.; griech.› (Runenforscher); **Ru|no|lo|gie,** die; - (Runenkunde od. -forschung)
Runs, der; -es, -e, *häufiger* **Run|se,** die; -, -n (*südd., österr., schweiz. für* Rinne an Berghängen mit Wildbach)
run|ter; ↑R 13 (*ugs. für* herunter, hinunter); **run|ter|fal|len** *(ugs.)*; **run|ter|flie|gen** *(ugs.)*; **run|ter|hau|en** *(ugs.)*; jmdm. eine -; **run|ter|ho|len** *(ugs.)*; **run|ter|kom|men** *(ugs.)*; **run|ter|las|sen** *(ugs.)*; **run|ter|put|zen** *(ugs.)*; **run|ter|rut|schen** *(ugs.)*; **run|ter|schlu|cken** *(ugs.)*
Run|zel, die; -, -n; **run|ze|lig; run|zeln;** ich ...[e]le (↑R 16); **runz|lig** (*svw.* runzelig)
Ru|od|lieb (Gestalt des ältesten [lateinisch geschriebenen] Romans der dt. Literatur)
Rü|pel, der; -s, -; **Rü|pe|lei; rü|pel|haft; Rü|pel|haf|tig|keit,** die; -
Ru|pert, Ru|precht (↑R 130; m. Vorn.); Knecht Ruprecht
[1]**rup|fen;** Gras -; [2]**rup|fen** (aus Rupfen); **Rup|fen,** der; -s, - (Jutegewebe); **Rup|fen|lein|wand**
Ru|pi|ah, die; -, - ‹Hindi› (indones. Währungseinheit; 1 Rupiah = 100 Sen; *Abk.* Rp); **Ru|pie** [...iə], die; -, -n (Währungseinheit in Indien, Sri Lanka u. a.)
rup|pig; Rup|pig|keit; Rupp|sack (*ugs. für* ruppiger Mensch)
Rup|recht *vgl.* Rupert *u.* Knecht Ruprecht
Rup|tur, die; -, -en ‹lat.› (*Med.* Zerreißung)
Rur, die; - (r. Nebenfluss der Maas); *vgl. aber* [2]Ruhr
ru|ral ‹lat.› (*veraltet für* ländlich)
Rus, die; - ‹russ.› (alte Bez. der ostslaw. Stämme im 9./10. Jh.); Kiewer Rus
Rusch, der; -[e]s, -e ‹lat.› (*nordd. für* Binse); in - und Busch
Rü|sche, die; -, -n (gefältelter [Stoff]besatz)
Ru|schel, die; -, -n, *auch* der; -s, - (*landsch. für* ruschelige Person); **ru|sche|lig,** rusch|lig (*landsch. für* unordentlich, schlampig); **ru|scheln** *(landsch.)*; ich ...[e]le (↑R 16)
Rü|schen‿blu|se, ...hemd
rusch|lig *vgl.* ruschelig
Rush|hour ['raʃauə(r)], die; -, -s ‹engl.› (Hauptverkehrszeit)
Ruß, der; -es, *Plur. (fachspr.)* -e; **ruß|be|schmutzt** (↑R 40); **ruß|braun**
[1]**Rus|se,** der; -n, -n; ↑R 126 (Einwohner Russlands; Angehöriger

eines ostslaw. Volkes); [2]**Rus|se,** der; -n, -n; ↑R 126 (*landsch. für* [1]Schabe)

Rüs|sel, der; -s, -; **rüs|sel|för|mig; Rüs|sel|kä|fer**

ru|ßen (*schweiz. auch für* entrußen); du rußt; es rußt

Rus|sen‿blu|se, ...kit|tel

ruß|far|ben, ruß|far|big; Ruß|fil|ter; ruß|ge|schwärzt; ru|ßig; Ru|ßig|keit, die; -

Rus|sin; rus|sisch; russische Eier; russischer Salat; russisches Roulett, *aber* (↑R 108): der Russisch-Türkische Krieg (1877/78); *vgl.* deutsch; **Rus|sisch,** das; -[s] (Sprache); *vgl.* Deutsch; **Rus|sisch|brot,** das; -[e]s (ein Gebäck); **Rus|si|sche,** das; -n; *vgl.* Deutsche, das; **Rus|sisch|grün; rus|sisch-or|tho|dox;** -e Kirche; **rus|sisch-rö|misch** (↑R 27); *in* -es Bad; **Russ|ki** (*ugs. für* Russe, russischer Soldat); **Russ|land**

ruß|schwarz

Rüst|an|ker (*Seemannsspr.* Ersatzanker)

[1]**Rüs|te,** die; - (*landsch. für* Rast, Ruhe); *noch in* zur - gehen (*veraltet für* untergehen [von der Sonne], zu Ende gehen)

[2]**Rüs|te,** die; -, -n (*Seemannsspr.* starke Planke an der Schiffsaußenseite zum Befestigen von Ketten od. Stangen)

rüs|ten; sich rüsten *(geh.);* Gemüse rüsten (*schweiz. für* putzen, vorbereiten)

Rüs|ter [*auch* 'ry:...], die; -, -n (Ulme); **rüs|tern** (aus Rüsterholz); **Rüs|ter[n]|holz**

rüs|tig; Rüs|tig|keit, die; -

Rus|ti|ka, die; - ‹lat.› (*Archit.* Mauerwerk aus Quadern mit roh bearbeiteten Außenflächen); **rus|ti|kal** (ländlich, bäuerlich)

Rüst‿kam|mer, ...tag *(jüd. Rel.);* **Rüs|tung; Rüs|tungs‿ab|bau, ...auf|trag, ...aus|ga|be** *(meist Plur.),* **...be|gren|zung, ...fab|rik, ...geg|ner, ...in|dust|rie, ...kon|trol|le, ...spi|ra|le, ...wett|lauf; Rüst‿zeit, ...zeug**

Rut *vgl.* [2]Ruth

Ru|te, die; -, -n (Gerte; altes Längenmaß; männl. Glied bei Tieren; *Jägerspr.* Schwanz); **Ru|ten‿bün|del, ...gän|ger** ([Quellen-, Gestein-, Erz]sucher mit der Wünschelrute)

[1]**Ruth** (w. Vorn.); [2]**Ruth,** *ökum.* Rut (biblischer w. Eigenn.); das Buch -

Rut|hard (m. Vorn.)

Ru|the|ne, der; -n, -n; ↑R 126 (*früher Bez. für* im ehem. Österreich-Ungarn lebender Ukrainer); **ru|the|nisch; Ru|the|ni|um,** das; -s (chem. Element, Metall; *Zeichen* Ru)

Ru|ther|ford ['raðə(r)fə(r)d] (engl. Physiker); **Ru|ther|for|di|um,** das; -s ‹nach dem engl. Physiker› (*svw.* Kurtschatovium)

Ru|til, der; -s, -e ‹lat.› (ein Mineral); **Ru|ti|lis|mus,** der; - (*Med.* Rothaarigkeit)

Ru|tin, das; -s ‹lat.› (*Pharmazie* ein pflanzlicher Wirkstoff)

Rüt|li, das; -s (Bergmatte am Vierwaldstätter See); **Rüt|li|schwur,** der; -[e]s; ↑R 105 (sagenumwobener Treueschwur bei der Gründung der Schweiz. Eidgenossenschaft)

rutsch!; Rutsch, der; -[e]s, -e; guten Rutsch [ins neue Jahr]!; **Rutsch|bahn; Rut|sche,** die; -, -n (Gleitbahn); **rut|schen;** du rutschst; **Rut|scher** (*früher* ein alter Tanz; *österr. ugs. für* kurze Fahrt, Abstecher); **Rut|sche|rei; rutsch|fest; Rutsch|ge|fahr,** die; -; **rut|schig; Rutsch|par|tie** *(ugs.);* **rutsch|si|cher**

Rut|te, die; -, -n (ein Fisch)

Rüt|tel|be|ton; Rüt|te|lei; Rüt|tel|fal|ke; rüt|teln; ich ...[e]le (↑R 16); **Rüt|tel|sieb; Rütt|ler** (ein Baugerät)

[1]**Ru|wer,** die; - (r. Nebenfluss der Mosel); [2]**Ru|wer,** der; -s, - (eine Weinsorte)

Ruys|dael *vgl.* Ruisdael

RVO = Reichsversicherungsordnung

RWE = Rheinisch-Westfälisches Elektrizitätswerk

S

S (Buchstabe); das S; des S, die S, *aber* das s in Hase (↑R 60); der Buchstabe S, s

s = Sekunde

s, sh = Shilling

S = Schilling; Sen; [2]Siemens; Süd[en]; Sulfur (*chem. Zeichen für* Schwefel)

$ = Dollar

Σ, σ, ς = Sigma

s. = sieh[e]!

S. = San, Sant', Santa, Santo, São; Seite

S., Se. = Seine (Exzellenz usw.)

Sa. = Summa; Sachsen; Samstag, Sonnabend

s. a. = sine anno

Saal, der; -[e]s, Säle; *aber* Sälchen *(vgl. d.);* **Saal|bau** *Plur.* ...bauten

Saal|burg, die; - (röm. Grenzbefestigung im Taunus)

Saa|le, die; - (l. Nebenfluss der Elbe); **Saal|feld (Saa|le)** (Stadt in Thüringen)

Saal‿ord|ner, ...schlacht, ...toch|ter (*schweiz. für* Kellnerin im Speisesaal), **...tür**

Saa|ne, die; - (l. Nebenfluss der Aare); **Saa|nen** (schweiz. Ort); **Saa|nen|kä|se**

Saar, die; - (r. Nebenfluss der Mosel); **Saar|brü|cken** (Hptst. des Bundeslandes Saarland); **Saar|brü|cker** (↑R 103); **Saar|ge|biet,** das; -[e]s; **Saar|land,** das; -[e]s; **Saar|län|der; Saar|län|de|rin; saar|län|disch,** *aber* (↑R 108): Saarländischer Rundfunk; **Saar|louis** [...'lui] (Stadt im Saarland); **Saar|louis|er** [...'luiər]; **Saar-Na|he-Berg|land** (↑R 105)

Saat, die; -, -en; **Saa|ten‿pfle|ge** (die; -), **...stand** (der; -[e]s); **Saat‿ge|trei|de, ...gut** (das; -[e]s), **...kar|tof|fel, ...korn** (*Plur.* ...körner), **...krä|he**

Sa|ba (hist. Land in Südarabien); **Sa|bä|er,** der; -s, - (Angehöriger eines alten Volkes in Südarabien)

Sab|bat, der; -s, -e ‹hebr., „Ruhetag"› (Samstag, jüd. Feiertag); **Sab|ba|ta|ri|er** [...iər] *u.* **Sab|ba|tist,** der; -en, -en; ↑R 126 (Angehöriger einer christl. Sekte); **Sab|bat‿jahr** *(jüd. Rel.),* **...stil|le**

Sab|bel, der; -s, - (*nordd. für* Mund; *nur Sing.: svw.* Sabber); **Sab|bel|lätz|chen** (*nordd. für* Sabberlätzchen); **sab|beln** (*nordd. für* [unaufhörlich] schwatzen; Speichel ausfließen lassen); ich ...[e]le (↑R 16); **Sab|ber,** der; -s (*ugs. für* ausfließender Speichel); **Sab|ber|lätz|chen** *(fam.);* **sab|bern** (*ugs. für* Speichel ausfließen lassen; [unaufhörlich] schwatzen); ich ...[e]re (↑R 16)

Sä|bel, der; -s, - ‹ung.-poln.›; **Sä|bel|bei|ne** *Plur.* (O-Beine); **sä|bel|bei|nig; Sä|bel|fech|ten,** das; -s; **sä|bel|för|mig; Sä|bel‿ge|ras|sel** *(abwertend),* **...hieb; sä|beln** (*ugs. für* unsachgemäß, ungeschickt schneiden); ich ...[e]le (↑R 16); **Sä|bel|ras|seln,** das; -s *(abwertend);* **sä|bel|ras|selnd; Sä|bel|rass|ler**

Sa|be|na, die; - ‹franz.; *Kurzwort*

für Société Anonyme Belge d'Exploitation de la Navigation Aérienne [sɔsje'te: anɔ'nim 'bɛlʒ dɛksploata'sjɔ̃: də la naviga'sjɔ̃: aer'jɛn]⟩ (belg. Luftfahrtgesellschaft)

Sa|bi|na, Sa|bi|ne (w. Vorn.); **Sa|bi|ner** (Angehöriger eines ehem. Volksstammes in Mittelitalien); **Sa|bi|ner Ber|ge** *Plur.; Sa|bi|ne|rin; sa|bi|nisch*

Sa|bot [...'bo:], der; -[s], -s ⟨franz.⟩ (hinten offener, hochhackiger Damenschuh)

Sa|bo|ta|ge [...'ta:ʒə, *österr.* ...'ta:ʒ], die; -, -n [...ʒ(ə)n] ⟨franz.⟩ (vorsätzl. Schädigung od. Zerstörung von wirtschaftl. u. militär. Einrichtungen); **Sa|bo|ta|ge|akt; Sa|bo|teur** [...'tø:r], der; -s, -e; **sa|bo|tie|ren**

Sa|bre (↑R 130), der; -s, -s ⟨hebr.⟩ (in Israel geborener Nachkomme jüd. Einwanderer)

Sab|ri|na (↑R 130; w. Vorn.)

SAC = Schweizer Alpen-Club

Sac|cha|ra|se, Sa|cha|ra|se [*beide* zaxa...], die; - ⟨sanskr.⟩ (ein Enzym); **Sac|cha|ri|me|ter,** Sa|cha|ri|me|ter, das; -s, - ⟨sanskr.; griech.⟩ (ein Gerät zur Bestimmung des Zuckergehaltes); **Sac|cha|ri|met|rie,** Sa|cha|ri|met|rie (↑R 130), die; - (Bestimmung des Zuckergehaltes einer Lösung); **Sac|cha|rin,** Sa|cha|rin, das; -s (ein Süßstoff)

Sa|cha|lin [...x..., *auch* 'sa...] (ostasiat. Insel)

Sach|an|la|ge *meist Plur.*, **Sach|an|la|ge|ver|mö|gen** *(Wirtsch.)*

Sa|cha|ra|se usw. *vgl.* Saccharase usw.

Sa|char|ja (jüd. Prophet)

Sach₋be|ar|bei|ter, ...be|ar|bei|te|rin, ...be|reich (der), **...be|schä|di|gung; sach|be|zo|gen; Sach₋be|zü|ge** *(Plur.)*, **...buch; sach|dien|lich; Sach|dis|kus|si|on; Sa|che,** die; -, -n; in Sachen Meyer [gegen Müller]; zur - kommen; **Sach|ein|la|ge** (*Wirtsch.* Sachwerte, die bei der Gründung einer AG eingebracht werden); **Sä|chel|chen; Sa|chen|recht,** das; -[e]s *(Rechtsw.)*; **Sach|er|klä|rung**

Sa|cher|tor|te ⟨nach dem Wiener Hotelier Sacher⟩ (eine Schokoladentorte); ↑R 95

Sach|fir|ma (Firma, deren Name den Gegenstand des Unternehmens angibt; *Ggs.* Personenfirma); **Sach|fra|ge; sach|fremd; Sach|ge|biet; sach₋ge|mäß, ...ge|recht; Sach₋grün|dung** (*Wirtsch.* Gründungsform einer AG), **...ka|ta|log, ...kennt|nis, ...kun|de** (die; -); **Sach|kun|de|un|ter|richt; sach|kun|dig; Sach₋la|ge** (die; -), **...le|gi|ti|ma|ti|on** *(Rechtsw.)*, **...leis|tung; sach|lich** (zur Sache gehörend; *auch für* objektiv); -e Kritik; -er Ton; -er Unterschied; -e Angaben; **säch|lich;** -es Geschlecht *(Sprachw.)*; **Sach|lich|keit,** die; -; die Neue - *(Kunstw.)*; **Sach|män|gel|haf|tung,** die; -; **Sach₋mit|tel** *(Plur.)*, **...re|gis|ter**

[1]**Sachs** (dt. Meistersinger); Hans Sachs' Gedichte (↑R 98)

[2]**Sachs,** der; -es, -e (german. Eisenmesser, kurzes Schwert)

Sach|scha|den (*Ggs.* Personenschaden)

Sach|se, der; -n, -n (↑R 126); **säch|seln** (sächsisch sprechen); ich ...[e]le (↑R 16); **Sach|sen** (*Abk.* Sa.); **Sach|sen-An|halt;** ↑R 106; **Sach|sen-An|hal|ter** *od.* Sach|sen-An|hal|ti|ner; **Sach|sen-An|hal|te|rin** *od.* Sach|sen-An|hal|ti|ne|rin; **sach|sen-an|hal|tisch** *od.* sach|sen-an|hal|ti|nisch; **Sach|sen|hau|sen** (Konzentrationslager der Nationalsozialisten); **Sach|sen|spie|gel,** der; -s (eine Rechtssammlung des dt. MA.); **Sach|sen|wald,** der; -[e]s (Waldgebiet östl. von Hamburg); **Säch|sin; säch|sisch,** *aber* (↑R 102): die Sächsische Schweiz (Teil des Elbsandsteingebirges)

Sach|spen|de

sacht (leise, unmerklich); **sacht|chen** (*obersächs. für* ganz sachte); **sach|te** *(ugs.)*; sachte voran!

Sach₋ver|halt (der; -[e]s, -e), **...ver|si|che|rung, ...ver|stand; sach|ver|stän|dig; Sach|ver|stän|di|ge,** der *u.* die; -n, -n (↑R 5 ff.); **Sach|ver|stän|di|gen|gut|ach|ten; Sach₋ver|zeich|nis, ...wal|ter, ...wal|te|rin; sach|wal|te|risch; Sach₋wei|ser** (*selten für* Sachregister), **...wert, ...wör|ter|buch, ...zu|sam|men|hang, ...zwang** *(meist Plur.; Soziol.)*

Sack, der; -[e]s, Säcke; 5 Sack Mehl (↑R 90); mit Sack und Pack; **Sack|bahn|hof; Säck|chen; Sä|ckel,** der; -s, - (*landsch., bes. südd., österr. für* Hosentasche; Geldbeutel); **Sä|ckel|meis|ter** (*südd., österr. u. schweiz. für* Kassenwart, Schatzmeister); **sä|ckeln** (*landsch. für* in Säcke füllen); ich ...[e]le (↑R 16); **Sä|ckel|wart,** der; -[e]s, -e (*landsch. für* Kassenwart); [1]**sa|cken** (*landsch. für* in Säcke füllen)

[2]**sa|cken** (sich senken; sinken)

sä|cken (*veraltet für* in einem Sack ertränken)

sa|cker|lot! *vgl.* sapperlot!; **sa|cker|ment!** *vgl.* sapperment!

sä|cke|wei|se (in Säcken); **sack|för|mig; Sack|gas|se; sack|grob** (*ugs. für* sehr grob); **sack|hüp|fen** *nur im Infinitiv u. Part. I gebr.*; **Sack|hüp|fen,** das; -s

Sä|ckin|gen (bad. Stadt am Hochrhein); **Sä|ckin|ger**

Sack₋kar|re, ...kar|ren, ...kleid, ...lau|fen (das; -s); **sack|lei|nen; Sack|lei|nen; Sack|lein|wand; Säck|ler** (*landsch. für* Lederarbeiter); **Sack₋pfei|fe** (*für* Dudelsack), **...tuch** (*Plur.* ...tücher; grobes Tuch; *südd., österr. ugs. neben* Taschentuch); **sack|wei|se**

Sad|du|zä|er, der; -s, - ⟨hebr.⟩ (Angehöriger einer altjüd. Partei)

Sa|de|baum ⟨lat.; dt.⟩ (ein wacholderartiger Nadelbaum)

Sad|hu, der; -[s], -s ⟨sanskr.⟩ (als Eremit u. bettelnder Asket lebender Hindu)

Sa|dis|mus, der; -, *Plur.* (*für* Handlungen:) ...men ⟨nach dem franz. Schriftsteller de Sade⟩ (Lust am Quälen, an Grausamkeiten [als abnorme sexuelle Befriedigung]); **Sa|dist,** der; -en, -en (↑R 126); **Sa|dis|tin; sa|dis|tisch; Sa|do|ma|so|chis|mus** [...x...], der; -, ...men (Verbindung von Sadismus u. Masochismus); **sa|do|ma|so|chis|tisch**

Sa|do|wa (Dorf bei Königgrätz)

sä|en; du säst, er sät; du sätest; gesät; säe!; **Sä|er; Sä|e|rin**

Sa|fa|ri, die; -, -s ⟨arab.⟩ (Gesellschaftsreise zum Jagen, Fotografieren [in Afrika]); **Sa|fa|ri|park** (Tierpark, den der Besucher mit dem Auto durchquert)

Safe [se:f], der, *auch* das; -s, -s ⟨engl.⟩ (Geldschrank, Stahlkammer, Sicherheitsfach); **Sa|fer|sex,** *auch* **Sa|fer Sex** ['se:fə(r) 'seks], der; -es (die Gefahr einer Aidsinfektion minderndes Sexualverhalten)

Saf|fi|an, der; -s ⟨pers.⟩ (feines Ziegenleder); **Saf|fi|an|le|der**

Saf|lor (↑R 130), der; -s, -e ⟨arab.-ital.⟩ (Färberdistel); **saf|lor|gelb**

Saf|ran (↑R 130), der; -s, -e ⟨pers.⟩ (Krokus; Farbstoff; *nur Sing.*: ein Gewürz); **saf|ran|gelb**

Saft, der; -[e]s, Säfte (*österr. auch für* Bratensoße); **Saft|bra|ten; saf|ten; Saft|fut|ter** *vgl.* [1]Futter; **saft|grün; saf|tig** (*ugs. auch für* derb); **Saf|tig|keit; Saft₋kur** (mit Obst- oder Gemüsesäften durchgeführte [2]Kur), **...la|den**

(*ugs. abwertend für* schlecht funktionierender Betrieb); **saft|los;** saft- u. kraftlos (↑R 23); **Saft‿pres|se, ...tag**

Sa|ga ['za(:)ga], die; -, -s ⟨altnord.⟩ (altisländ. Prosaerzählung)

sag|bar; Sa|ge, die; -, -n

Sä|ge, die; -, -n; **Sä|ge‿blatt, ...bock, ...fisch, ...mehl** (das; -[e]s), **...müh|le**

sa|gen; es kostet sage und schreibe (tatsächlich) zwanzig Mark

sä|gen

Sa|gen‿buch, ...dich|tung (die; -), **...for|scher, ...ge|stalt; sa|gen|haft** (*ugs. auch für* unvorstellbar); ein -er Reichtum; **Sa|gen|kreis; sa|gen|um|wo|ben** (↑R 40)

Sä|ger; Sä|ge|rei; Sä|ge‿spä|ne (*Plur.*), **...werk, ...wer|ker, ...zahn**

sa|git|tal ⟨lat.⟩ (*Biol., Med.* parallel zur Mittelachse liegend); **Sa|git|tal|ebe|ne** (↑R 132; der Mittelebene des Körpers parallele Ebene)

Sa|go, der, *österr. meist* das; -s ⟨indones.⟩ (gekörntes Stärkemehl aus Palmenmark od. aus Kartoffelstärke); **Sa|go‿pal|me, ...sup|pe**

Sa|ha|ra [*auch* 'za:...], die; - ⟨arab.⟩ (Wüste in Nordafrika)

Sa|hel [*auch* 'za:hɛl], der; -[s] ⟨arab.⟩ (Gebiet südl. der Sahara); **Sa|hel|zo|ne,** die; -

Sa|hib, der; -[s], -s ⟨arab.-Hindi⟩ (*in Indien u. Pakistan titelähnliche Bez. für* Europäer; *ohne Artikel auch* Anrede)

Sah|ne, die; -; **Sah|ne‿bon|bon, ...eis, ...häub|chen, ...känn|chen, ...kä|se, ...meer|ret|tich** (der; -s); **sah|nen; Sah|ne‿so|ße, ...tor|te; sah|nig**

Saib|ling (ein Fisch); *vgl.* Salbling

Sai|gon [*od.* 'zai...] (*früherer Name von* Ho-Chi-Minh-Stadt)

[1]**Saint** [s(ə)nt] ⟨engl., „heilig"⟩ (*männl. u. weibl. Form; in engl. u. amerik. Heiligennamen u. auf solche zurückgehenden Ortsnamen,* z. B. Saint Louis[1] [s(ə)nt 'lu:is] = Stadt in Missouri, Saint Anne[1] [- 'ɛn]; *Abk.* St.); *vgl.* San, Sankt, São; [2]**Saint** [sɛ̃:] ⟨franz., „heilig"⟩ (*männl. Form*) *u.* **Sainte** [sɛ̃:t] (*weibl. Form; in franz. Heiligennamen u. auf solche zurückgehenden Ortsnamen,* z. B. Saint-Cyr[1] [sɛ̃:'si:r] = Kriegsschule in Frankreich, Sainte-Marie[1]; *Abk.* St *bzw.* Ste); *vgl.* San, Sankt, São

Saint-E|xu|pé|ry [sɛ̃:tɛgzype'ri] (franz. Schriftsteller)

Saint Geor|ge's [s(ə)nt 'dʒɔ:(r)dʒiz] (Hptst. von Grenada)

Saint John's [s(ə)nt 'dʒɔnz] (Hptst. von Antigua und Barbuda)

Saint Lou|is [s(ə)nt 'lu:is] (Stadt in Missouri)

Saint-Saëns [sɛ̃'sã:s] (franz. Komponist)

Saint-Si|mo|nis|mus [sɛ̃si...], der; - ⟨nach dem franz. Sozialreformer Saint-Simon⟩ (sozialist. Lehre); **Saint-Si|mo|nist,** der; -en, -en (↑R 126)

Sa|is (altägypt. Stadt im Nildelta)

Sai|son [zɛ'zɔŋ, *auch* sɛ'zɔ̃:, *österr. auch* zɛ'zo:n], die; -, *Plur.* -s, *österr. auch* ...onen ⟨franz.⟩ (Hauptbetriebs-, Hauptreise-, Hauptgeschäftszeit, Theaterspielzeit); **sai|son|ab|hän|gig; sai|so|nal** [...zo'na:l]; **Sai|son‿ar|beit, ...ar|bei|ter, ...auf|takt, ...aus|ver|kauf** (Winter-, Sommerschlussverkauf); **sai|son|be|dingt; Sai|son|be|ginn,** der; -s; **sai|son|be|rei|nigt** (*Amtsspr.*); **Sai|son‿be|trieb, ...en|de** (das; -s), **...er|öff|nung; Sai|so|ni|er** *vgl.* Saisonnier; **Sai|son‿in|dex** (*Wirtsch.*), **...kre|dit** (*Bankw.*); **Sai|son|ni|er** [...'nie:] (*schweiz. für* Saisonarbeiter); **Sai|son‿schluss, ...wan|de|rung** (saisonbedingte Wanderung von Arbeitskräften); **sai|son|wei|se**

Sai|te, die; -, -n (gedrehter Tierdarm, Metall od. Kunststoff [zur Bespannung von Musikinstrumenten]); *vgl. aber* Seite; **Sai|ten‿hal|ter** (Teil eines Saiteninstrumentes), **...in|stru|ment, ...spiel** (das; -[e]s); **...sai|tig** (z. B. fünfsaitig); **Sait|ling** (Schafdarm)

Sa|ke, der; - ⟨jap.⟩ (aus Reis hergestellter japanischer Wein)

Sak|ko [*österr.* za'ko:], der, *auch, österr. nur,* das; -s, -s (Herrenjackett); **Sak|ko|an|zug**

sak|ra! ⟨lat.⟩ (↑R 130; *südd. ugs. für* verdammt!); **sak|ral** (den Gottesdienst betreffend; *Med.* zum Kreuzbein gehörend); **Sak|ral|bau** *Plur.* ...bauten (*Kunstw.* kirchl. Bauwerk; *Ggs.* Profanbau); **Sak|ra|ment,** das; -[e]s, -e (eine gottesdienstl. Handlung); **sak|ra|men|tal; Sak|ra|men|ta|li|en** *Plur.* (*kath. Kirche* sakramentähnliche Zeichen u. Handlungen, z. B. Wasserweihe; *auch Bez. für* geweihte Dinge, z. B. Weihwasser); **Sak|ra|men|ter,** der; -s, - (*landsch. für* jmd., über den man sich ärgert; Schimpfwort); **sak|ra|ment|lich; Sak|ra|ments|häus|chen; sak|rie|ren** (*veraltet für* weihen, heiligen); **Sak|ri|fi|zi|um,** das; -s, ...ien [...iən] (*svw.* [Mess]opfer); **Sak|ri|leg,** das; -s, -e *u.* Sak|ri|le|gi|um, das; -s, ...ien [...iən] (Vergehen gegen Heiliges; Kirchenraub; Gotteslästerung); **sak|ri|le|gisch; sak|risch** (*südd. für* verdammt); **Sak|ris|tan,** der; -s, -e (kath. Küster, Mesner); **Sak|ris|ta|nin; Sak|ris|tei** (Kirchenraum für den Geistlichen u. die gottesdienstl. Geräte); **sak|ro|sankt** (unverletzlich)

sä|ku|lar ⟨lat.⟩ (alle hundert Jahre wiederkehrend; weltlich); **Sä|ku|lar|fei|er** (Hundertjahrfeier); **Sä|ku|la|ri|sa|ti|on,** die; -, -en (Einziehung geistl. Besitzungen; Verweltlichung); **sä|ku|la|ri|sie|ren** (kirchl. Besitz in weltl. umwandeln); **Sä|ku|la|ri|sie|rung** (Verweltlichung; Loslösung aus den Bindungen an die Kirche; Erlaubnis für Angehörige eines Ordens, das Kloster zu verlassen u. ohne Bindung an die Gelübde zu leben); **Sä|ku|lum,** das; -s, ...la (Jahrhundert)

Sa|la|din ⟨arab.⟩ (ein Sultan)

Sa|lam ⟨arab.⟩ (arab. Grußwort); - alaikum! (Heil, Friede mit euch!)

Sa|la|man|ca (span. Stadt u. Provinz)

Sa|la|man|der, der; -s, - ⟨griech.⟩ (ein Schwanzlurch)

Sa|la|mi, die; -, -[s], *schweiz. auch* der; -s, - ⟨ital.⟩ (eine Dauerwurst)

Sa|la|mi|ni|er [...iər]; **Sa|la|mis** (griech. Insel; Stadt auf der Insel Salamis)

Sa|la|mi|tak|tik, die; - (*ugs. für* Taktik, bei der man durch mehrere kleinere Übergriffe od. Forderungen ein größeres [polit.] Ziel zu verwirklichen sucht); **Sa|la|mi|wurst**

Sa|lär, das; -s, -e ⟨franz.⟩ (*schweiz. für* Gehalt, Lohn); **sa|la|rie|ren** (*schweiz. für* besolden)

Sa|lat, der; -[e]s, -e; gemischter -; **Sa|lat‿be|steck, ...blatt, ...gur|ke; Sa|la|tie|re,** die; -, -n (*veraltet für* Salatschüssel); **Sa|lat‿kar|tof|fel** (*meist Plur.*), **...kopf, ...öl, ...pflan|ze, ...plat|te, ...schüs|sel, ...so|ße, ...tel|ler**

Sal|ba|der (*abwertend für* langweiliger [frömmelnder] Schwätzer); **Sal|ba|de|rei; sal|ba|dern;** ich ...ere (↑R 16); er hat salbadert

Sal|band, das; *Plur.* ...bänder (Gewebekante, -leiste; *Geol.* Berüh-

[1] *Hinter* „Saint" *steht in franz. Namen ein Bindestrich, in engl. u. amerik. nicht. Hinter* „Sainte" *steht immer ein Bindestrich.*

rungsfläche eines Ganges mit dem Nebengestein)
Sal|be, die; -, -n
Sal|bei [*österr. nur so, sonst auch* ...'bai], der; -s, *österr. nur so, sonst auch* die; - ‹lat.› (eine Heil- u. Gewürzpflanze); **Sal|bei|tee**
sal|ben; Sal|ben|do|se
Salb|ling (*svw.* Saibling)
Salb|öl *(kath. Kirche);* **Sal|bung; sal|bungs|voll** (übertrieben würdevoll)
Säl|chen (kleiner Saal)
Sal|chow [...ço], der; -[s], -s ‹nach dem schwed. Eiskunstläufer U. Salchow› (ein Drehsprung beim Eiskunstlauf); einfacher, doppelter, dreifacher -
Sal|den‿bi|lanz *(Wirtsch.),* **...lis|te** *(Wirtsch.);* **sal|die|ren** ‹ital.› ([eine Rechnung] ausgleichen, abschließen; *österr. für* die Bezahlung einer Rechnung bestätigen); **Sal|die|rung; Sal|do,** der; -s, *Plur.* ...den, -s *u.* ...di (Unterschied der beiden Seiten eines Kontos); **Sal|do‿an|er|kennt|nis** (das; *Wirtsch.* Schuldanerkenntnis dem Gläubiger gegenüber), **...kon|to** (Kontokorrentbuch), **...über|trag** (↑R 132), **...vor|trag**
Sä|le (*Plur. von* Saal)
Sa|lem *vgl.* Salam
Sa|lep, der; -s, -s ‹arab.› (getrocknete Orchideenknolle, die für Heilzwecke verwendet wird)
Sa|le|si|a|ner (Mitglied der Gesellschaft des hl. Franz von Sales; Angehöriger einer kath. Priestergenossenschaft)
Sales|ma|na|ger ['se:lz...], der; -s, - ‹engl.› (*Wirtsch.* Verkaufsleiter, [Groß]verkäufer); **Sales|man|ship** ['se:lzmənʃip], das; -s (eine in den USA entwickelte Verkaufslehre); **Sales|pro|mo|ter** ['se:lzprə.mo:tə(r)], der; -s, - (Vertriebskaufmann mit bes. Kenntnissen auf dem Gebiet der Marktbeeinflussung); **Sales|pro|mo|tion** [...prə.mo:ʃ(ə)n], die; - (Verkaufsförderung)
Sa|let|tel, Sa|lettl, das; -s, -n ‹ital.› (*bayr. u. österr. für* Pavillon, Laube, Gartenhäuschen)
Sä|li, das; -s, - (*schweiz. für* besonderer Raum in Gastwirtschaften)
Sa|li|cyl|säu|re *vgl.* Salizylsäure
[1]**Sa|li|er** *Plur.* ‹lat.› (altröm. Priester)
[2]**Sa|li|er,** der; -s, - (Angehöriger der salischen Franken; Angehöriger eines dt. Kaisergeschlechtes)
Sa|li|ne, die; -, -n ‹lat.› (Anlage zur Salzgewinnung); **Sa|li|nen|salz**
Sa|ling, die; -, -s (*Seemannsspr.* Stange am Mast zur Abstützung der Wanten)
sa|li|nisch (*selten für* salzartig, -haltig)
sa|lisch; -e Franken; -e Gesetze, *aber* (↑R 108): das Salische Gesetz (über die Tronfolge)
Sa|li|zyl|säu|re, *chem. fachspr.* Sa|li|cyl|säu|re [...'tsy:l...], die; - ‹lat.; griech.; dt.› (eine organ. Säure)
Sal|kan|te (Gewebeleiste)
Salk|vak|zi|ne [*engl.* 'sɔ:(l)k...] (↑R 95; Impfstoff des amerik. Bakteriologen J. Salk gegen Kinderlähmung)
Sal|leis|te (Gewebeleiste)
Sal|lust (röm. Geschichtsschreiber); **Sal|lus|ti|us** *vgl.* Sallust
Sal|ly (m. *od.* w. Vorn.)
[1]**Salm,** der; -[e]s, -e ‹lat.› (ein Fisch)
[2]**Salm,** der; -s, -e *Plur. selten* ‹*zu* Psalm› (*ugs. für* umständliches Gerede)
Sal|ma|nas|sar (Name assyr. Könige)
Sal|mi|ak [*auch, österr. nur,* 'zal...], der, *auch* das; -s ‹lat.› (eine Ammoniakverbindung); **Sal|mi|ak‿geist** (der; -[e]s; Ammoniaklösung), **...lö|sung, ...pas|til|le**
Salm|ler (ein Fisch)
Sal|mo|nel|len *Plur.* ‹nach dem amerik. Pathologen u. Bakteriologen Salmon› (Darmkrankheiten hervorrufende Bakterien); **Sal|mo|nel|lo|se,** die; -, -n (*Med.* durch Salmonellen verursachte Erkrankung)
Sal|mo|ni|den *Plur.* ‹lat.; griech.› (*Zool.* Familie der Lachsfische)
Sa|lo|me [...me] (Stieftochter des Herodes); **Sa|lo|mon,** *ökum.* Sa|lo|mo (bibl. König, Sohn Davids); *Gen.* Salomo[n]s *u.* Salomonis; **Sa|lo|mo|nen** *Plur.* (Inselstaat östl. von Neuguinea); **Sa|lo|mon|in|seln** *Plur.;* **sa|lo|mo|nisch;** salomonische Schriften; salomonisches (weises) Urteil; salomonische Weisheit; **Sa|lo|mon[s]|sie|gel** (Weißwurz, ein Liliengewächs)
Sa|lon [za'lɔŋ, *auch* sa'lɔ̃:, *südd., österr.* za'lo:n], der; -s, -s ‹franz.› (Gesellschafts-, Empfangszimmer; Friseur-, Mode-, Kosmetikgeschäft; [Kunst]ausstellung); **Sa|lon|da|me** *(Theater);* **sa|lon|fä|hig**
Sa|lo|ni|ker, Sa|lo|ni|ki|er [...iər] (↑R 103); **Sa|lo|ni|ki** (nordgriech. Stadt); *vgl.* Thessaloniki
Sa|lon‿kom|mu|nist *(iron.),* **...lö|we** *(abwertend),* **...mu|sik** (die; -), **...or|ches|ter, ...wa|gen** *(Eisenb.)*
Sa|loon [sə'lu:n], der; -s, -s ‹amerik.› (Lokal im Wildweststil)
sa|lopp ‹franz.› (ungezwungen; nachlässig; bequem); -es Benehmen; -e Kleidung; **Sa|lopp|heit**
Sal|pe, die; -, -n ‹griech.› (ein walzenförmiges Meerestier)
Sal|pe|ter, der; -s ‹lat.› (*Bez. für* einige Salze der Salpetersäure); **Sal|pe|ter‿dün|ger, ...er|de; sal|pe|ter|hal|tig; sal|pe|te|rig** *vgl.* salpetrig; **Sal|pe|ter|säu|re,** die; -; **sal|pet|rig;** -e Säure
Sal|pinx, die; -, ...ingen ‹griech.› (*Med.* [Ohr]trompete; Eileiter)
Sal|sa, der; - ‹span.› (Art der lateinamerik. Rockmusik; ein Tanz)
Sal|se, die; -, -n ‹ital.› (*Geol.* Schlammsprudel, -vulkan)
Sal|siz, das; -es, -e (Graubündener Wurstsorte)
Salt, SALT [*engl.* sɔ:lt] = Strategic Arms Limitation Talks [strə'ti:dʒik 'a:(r)mz limi'te:ʃ(ə)n 'tɔ:ks] (Gespräche über die Begrenzung der strategischen Rüstung)
Sal|ta, das; -s ‹lat., „spring!"› (ein Brettspiel); **Sal|ta|rel|lo,** der; -s, ...lli ‹ital.› (ital. u. span. Springtanz); **Sal|ta|to,** das; -s, *Plur.* -s *u.* ...ti (*Musik* Spiel mit hüpfendem Bogen)
Salt-Kon|fe|renz [*engl.* 'sɔ:lt...], **SALT-Kon|fe|renz**
Sal|to, der; -s, *Plur.* -s *u.* ...ti ‹ital.› (freier Überschlag; Luftrolle); **Sal|to mor|ta|le,** der; - -, *Plur.* - - *u.* ...ti ...li (meist dreifacher Salto in großer Höhe)
sa|lü! ['saly, *auch* sa'ly] (*bes. schweiz.* Grußformel)
Sa|lut, der; -[e]s, -e ‹franz.› ([milit.] Ehrengruß); **Sa|lu|ta|ti|on,** die; -, -en ‹lat.› (*veraltet für* feierl. Begrüßung); **sa|lu|tie|ren** (militärisch grüßen); **Sa|lut|schuss**
Sal|va|dor, El usw. *vgl.* El Salvador usw.; **Sal|va|do|ri|a|ner; sal|va|do|ri|a|nisch**
Sal|va|ti|on [...v...], die; -, -en ‹lat.› (*veraltet für* Rettung; Verteidigung); [1]**Sal|va|tor,** der; -s (Jesus als Retter, Erlöser); [2]**Sal|va|tor** ®, das *od.* der; -s (ein bayr. Starkbier); **Sal|va|tor‿bier** (*als* ®: Salvator-Bier), **...bräu** (*als* ®: Salvator-Bräu); **Sal|va|to|ri|a|ner** (Angehöriger einer kath. Priesterkongregation für Seelsorge u. Mission; *Abk.* SDS *[vgl. d.]*); **sal|va|to|risch** (*Rechtsspr.* nur ergänzend geltend); -e Klausel
sal|va ve|nia [...va 've:...] ‹lat.› (*veraltet für* mit Erlaubnis, mit Verlaub [zu sagen]; *Abk.* s. v.)

sal|ve! [...ve] ⟨lat., „sei gegrüßt!"⟩ (lat. Gruß); **Sal|ve** [...və], die; -, -n ⟨franz.⟩ (gleichzeitiges Schießen von mehreren Feuerwaffen [auch als Ehrengruß]); **sal|vie|ren** ⟨lat.⟩ (*veraltet für* retten); *noch in* sich - (sich von einem Verdacht reinigen), salviert sein; **sal|vo ti|tu|lo** (*veraltet für* mit Vorbehalt des richtigen Titels; *Abk.* S. T.)
Sal|wei|de (eine Weidenart)
Salz, das; -es, -e
Sal|zach (↑R 132), die; - (r. Nebenfluss des Inns)
Salz|ader (↑R 132); **salz‿arm, ...ar|tig; Salz‿bad, ...berg|bau, ...berg|werk, ...bo|den, ...bre|zel**
Salz|burg (österr. Bundesland u. dessen Hptst.); **Salz|bur|ger** (↑R 103); - Festspiele
Salz|det|furth, Bad (Stadt südl. von Hildesheim)
sal|zen; du salzt; gesalzen (*in übertr. Bedeutung nur so,* z. B. die Preise sind gesalzen, ein gesalzener Witz), *auch* gesalzt; **Säl|zer** (*veraltet für* Salzsieder, -händler; jmd., der [Fleisch, Fische] einsalzt); **Salz‿fass, ...fleisch, ...gar|ten** (Anlage zur Salzgewinnung), **...ge|halt** (der), **...ge|win|nung, ...gru|be** (Salzbergwerk), **...gur|ke; salz|hal|tig; Salz|he|ring; sal|zig**
Salz|kam|mer|gut, das; -s (österr. Alpenlandschaft)
Salz‿kar|tof|fel (*meist Plur.*), **...korn** (*Plur.* ...körner), **...ko|te** (*früher* Salzsiedehaus; *vgl.* [2]Kote), **...la|ke, ...le|cke** (*vgl.* Lecke); **salz|los; Salz‿lö|sung, ...man|del, ...pfan|ne, ...pflan|ze; salz|sau|er** (Salzsäure enthaltend); **Salz‿säu|le, ...säu|re** (die; -), **...see, ...sie|der, ...so|le, ...stan|ge, ...steu|er** (die), **...streu|er, ...teig**
Salz|uf|len, Bad (Stadt am Teutoburger Wald)
Salz‿was|ser (*Plur.* ...wässer), **...wüs|te, ...zoll**
...sam (z. B. langsam)
Sam [sɛm] (m. Vorn.); Onkel - (*scherzh. Bez. für* USA; *vgl.* Uncle Sam)
Sa|ma|el [...e:l, *auch* ...ɛl] *vgl.* Samiel
Sä|mann *Plur.* ...männer
Sa|ma|ria [*auch* ...'ri:a] (antike Stadt u. hist. Landschaft in Palästina); **Sa|ma|ri|ta|ner** (Angehöriger eines Volkes in Palästina); *vgl.* Samariter; **sa|ma|ri|ta|nisch;** der -e Pentateuch (*Rel.*); **Sa|ma|ri|ter** (Bewohner von Samaria; [freiwilliger] Krankenpfleger, -wärter); barmherziger Samariter; **Sa|ma|ri|ter|dienst; Sa|ma|ri|ter|tum,** das; -s
Sa|ma|ri|um, das; -s (chem. Element, Metall; *Zeichen* Sm)
[1]**Sa|mar|kand** (Stadt in Usbekistan); [2]**Sa|mar|kand,** der; -[s], -s (ein Teppich)
Sä|ma|schi|ne
Sam|ba, die; -, -s, *auch u. österr. nur* der; -s, -s ⟨afrik.-port.⟩ (ein Tanz)
Sam|be|si, der; -[s] (Strom in Afrika)
Sam|bia (Staat in Afrika); **Sam|bi|er; sam|bisch**
[1]**Sa|me,** der; -n, -n (Lappe)
[2]**Sa|me,** der; -ns, -n (*geh. für* Samen); **Sa|men,** der; -s, -; **Sa|men‿an|la|ge, ...bank** (*Plur.* ...banken; *Med.*), **...er|guss, ...fa|den, ...flüs|sig|keit, ...hand|lung, ...kap|sel** (*Bot.*), **...kern, ...korn** (*Plur.* ...körner), **...lei|ter** (der; *Med.*), **...pflan|ze, ...strang** (*Med.*), **...zel|le, ...zucht** (die; -); **Sä|me|rei,** die; -, -en
Sa|mi|el, Sa|ma|el [*beide* ...e:l, *auch* ...ɛl], der; -s ⟨hebr.⟩ (böser Geist, Teufel)
...sa|mig (z. B. vielsamig)
sä|mig (seimig; dickflüssig); **Sä|mig|keit,** die; -
sa|misch (von Samos)
sä|misch ⟨slaw.⟩ (fettgegerbt); **Sä|misch‿ger|ber, ...le|der**
Sa|mis|dat, der; - ⟨russ.⟩ (im Selbstverlag erschienene [verbotene] Literatur in der ehem. Sowjetunion)
Sam|land, das; -[e]s (Halbinsel zwischen dem Frischen u. dem Kurischen Haff); **Sam|län|der,** der; **sam|län|disch**
Säm|ling (aus Samen gezogene Pflanze)
Sam|mel‿al|bum, ...an|schluss (*Postw.*), **...auf|trag** (*Postw.*), **...band** (der), **...be|cken, ...be|griff, ...be|stel|lung, ...be|zeich|nung, ...büch|se, ...de|pot** (*Bankw.* eine Form der Wertpapierverwahrung); **Sam|me|lei; Sam|mel‿ei|fer, ...frucht** (*Bot.*), **...grab, ...gut; Sam|mel|gut|ver|kehr,** der; -s; **Sam|mel‿kon|to, ...la|ger, ...lei|den|schaft** (die; -), **...lin|se** (*Optik*), **...map|pe; sam|meln;** ich ...[e]le (↑R 16); **Sam|mel‿na|me** (*Sprachw.*), **...num|mer** (*Postw.*), **...platz, ...schie|ne** (*Elektrotechnik*), **...stel|le; Sam|mel|su|ri|um,** das; -s, ...ien [...iən] (*ugs. für* Unordnung, Durcheinander); **Sam|mel‿tas|se, ...trans|port, ...trieb** (der; -[e]s), **...über|wei|sung** (↑R 132; *Postw.*), **...werk, ...wert|be|rich|ti|gung** (*Bankw.*), **...wut**
Sam|met, der; -s, -e (*veraltet für* Samt)
Samm|ler; Samm|ler‿fleiß, ...freu|de; Samm|le|rin; Samm|lung
Sam|my ['sɛmi] (m. Vorn.)
Sam|ni|te, der; -n, -n (↑R 126) *od.* **Sam|ni|ter,** der; -s, - (Angehöriger eines italischen Volkes)
Sa|moa (Inselgruppe im Pazifischen Ozean); **Sa|mo|a|in|seln** *Plur.* (↑R 105); **Sa|mo|a|ner; sa|mo|a|nisch**
Sa|mo|je|de, der; -n, -n; ↑R 126 (*früher für* Nenze)
[1]**Sa|mos** (griech. Insel); [2]**Sa|mos,** der; -, - (Wein von [1]Samos); **Sa|mo|thra|ke** (griech. Insel)
Sa|mo|war [*auch* 'sa...], der; -s, -e ⟨russ.⟩ (russ. Teemaschine)
Sam|pan, der; -s, -s ⟨chin.⟩ (chin. Wohnboot)
Sam|ple ['zamp(ə)l, *engl.* 'sa:m...], das; -[s], -s ⟨engl.⟩ (Stichprobe; repräsentative Gruppe; Warenprobe, Muster)
Sam|son *vgl.* Simson
Sams|tag, der; -[e]s, -e ⟨hebr., „Sabbattag"⟩ (*Abk.* Sa.); langer, kurzer -; *vgl.* Dienstag; **sams|tags** (↑R 46); *vgl.* Dienstag
samt; - und sonders; *Präp. mit Dat.:* - dem Geld
Samt, der; -[e]s, -e (ein Gewebe); **samt|ar|tig; Samt|band; sam|ten** (aus Samt); ein -es Band
Samt|ge|mein|de (Gemeindeverband [in Niedersachsen])
Samt|hand|schuh; jmdn. mit -en anfassen (jmdn. vorsichtig behandeln); **Samt|ho|se; sam|tig** (samtartig); eine -e Haut; **Samt‿ja|cke, ...kleid**
sämt|lich; -er aufgehäufte Sand, der Verlust -er vorhandenen Energie, mit -em gesammelten Material, -es vorhandene Eigentum; -e vortrefflichen, *seltener* vortreffliche Einrichtungen, -er vortrefflicher, *auch* vortrefflichen Einrichtungen; -e Stimmberechtigten, *auch* Stimmberechtigte; sie waren - erschienen
Samt‿pföt|chen, ...tep|pich; samt|weich
Sa|mu|el [...e:l, *auch* ...ɛl] (bibl. Eigenn.)
Sa|mum [*auch* za'mu:m], der; -s, *Plur.* -s *u.* -e ⟨arab.⟩ (*Geogr.* ein heißer Wüstenwind)
Sa|mu|rai, der; -[s], -[s] ⟨jap.⟩ (Angehöriger des jap. Adels)
San ⟨lat., „heilig"⟩; *in Heiligennamen u. auf solche zurückgehenden Ortsnamen:* **I.** *Im Italienischen:* **a)**

San (*vor Konsonanten [außer* Sp... *u.* St...] *in männl. Namen; Abk.* S.), z. B. San Giuseppe [- dʒu...], S. Giuseppe; **b)** Sant' (*vor Vokalen in männl. u. weibl. Namen; Abk.* S.), z. B. Sant' Angelo [- 'andʒelo], S. Angelo; Sant' Agata, S. Agata; **c)** Santa (*vor Konsonanten in weibl. Namen; Abk.* S.), z. B. Santa Lucia [- lu'tʃi:a], S. Lucia; **d)** Sante *Plur.* (*vor weibl. Namen; Abk.* SS.), z. B. Sante Maria e Maddalena, SS. Maria e Maddalena; **e)** Santi *Plur.* (*vor männl. Namen; Abk.* SS.), z. B. Santi Pietro e Paolo, SS. Pietro e Paolo; **f)** Santo (*vor* Sp... *u.* St... *in männl. Namen; Abk.* S.), z. B. Santo Spirito, S. Spirito; Santo Stefano, S. Stefano. **II.** *Im Spanischen:* **a)** San (*vor männl. Namen [außer vor* Do... *u.* To...]; *Abk.* S.), z. B. San Bernardo, S. Bernardo; **b)** Santa (*vor weibl. Namen; Abk.* Sta.), z. B. Santa Maria, Sta. Maria; **c)** Santo (*vor* Do... *u.* To... *in männl. Namen; Abk.* Sto.), z. B. Santo Domingo, Sto. Domingo; Santo Tomás, Sto. Tomás. **III.** *Im Portugiesischen:* **a)** Santa (*vor weibl. Namen; Abk.* Sta.), z. B. Santa Clara, Sta. Clara; **b)** Santo [...tu] (*vor männl. Namen, bes. vor Vokal; Abk.* S.), z. B. Santo André, S. André; *vgl.* Saint, Sankt *u.* São

Sa|na (Hptst. von Jemen)

Sa|na|to|ri|um, das; -s, ...ien [...iən] ⟨lat.⟩ (Heilanstalt; Genesungsheim)

San Ber|nar|di|no, der; - - (ital. Name des Sankt-Bernhardin-Passes)

San|cho Pan|sa ['santʃo -] (Knappe Don Quichottes)

Sanc|ta Se|des, die; - - ⟨lat.⟩ (*lat. Bez. für* Heiliger [Apostolischer] Stuhl); **sanc|ta simp|li|ci|tas!** (↑R 130) ⟨„heilige Einfalt!"⟩; **Sanc|ti|tas,** die; - ⟨„Heiligkeit"⟩ (Titel des Papstes); **Sanc|tus,** das; -, - (Lobgesang der kath. Messe)

Sand, der; -[e]s, -e; **Sand|aal** (ein Fisch)

San|da|le, die; -, -n *meist Plur.* ⟨griech.⟩ (leichte Fußbekleidung [mit Lederriemen]); **San|da|let|te,** die; -, -n *meist Plur.* (sandalenartiger Sommerschuh)

San|da|rak, der; -s ⟨griech.⟩ (ein trop. Harz)

Sand‿bad, ...bahn; Sand|bahn|ren|nen *(Sport);* **Sand‿bank** (*Plur.* ...bänke), **...blatt** (beim Tabak), **...bo|den, ...burg, ...dorn** (der; -[e]s, ...dorne; eine Pflanzengattung)

San|del|holz, das; -es ⟨sanskr.; dt.⟩ (duftendes Holz verschiedener Sandelbaumgewächse); **San|del|holz|öl,** das; -[e]s

[1]**san|deln** (*österr. ugs. für* langsam arbeiten, faulenzen)

[2]**san|deln** *(südd.),* **sän|deln** (*schweiz. für* im Sand spielen); ich ...[e]le (↑R 16)

San|del|öl (*svw.* Sandelholzöl)

san|den (*mdal. u. schweiz. für* mit Sand bestreuen; *auch für* Sand streuen); **sand|far|ben** *od.* ...farbig (*für* beige); **Sand‿förm|chen** (ein Kinderspielzeug), **...gru|be, ...ha|se** (Fehlwurf beim Kegeln; *Soldatenspr. veraltend für* Infanterist), **...hau|fen, ...ho|se** (Sand führender Wirbelsturm); **san|dig**

San|di|nist, der; -en, -en ⟨nach C. A. Sandino, der 1927 einen Kleinkrieg gegen die amerik. Truppen in Nicaragua führte⟩ (Anhänger einer polit. Bewegung in Nicaragua)

Sand|kas|ten; Sand|kas|ten|spiel; Sand‿korn (*Plur.* ...körner), **...ku|chen**

Sand|ler (*österr. für* Obdachloser)

Sand‿mann (der; -[e]s), **...männ|chen** (das; -s; eine Märchengestalt), **...pa|pier, ...platz**

Sand|ra (↑R 130; w. Vorn.)

Sand‿sack, ...schie|fer, ...stein; Sand|stein‿fels *od.* **...fel|sen, ...ge|bir|ge; sand|strah|len;** *nur im Infinitiv u. im Partizip II gebr.;* gesandstrahlt, *fachspr. auch* sandgestrahlt; **Sand|strahl|ge|blä|se; Sand‿strand, ...tor|te, ...uhr**

Sand|wich ['zɛntvitʃ], das *od.* der; *Gen.* -[e]s *od.* -, *Plur.* -[e]s, *auch* -e ⟨engl.⟩ (belegte Weißbrotschnitte); **Sand|wich‿bau|wei|se** (die; -; *Technik*), **...we|cken** (*österr. für* langes, dünnes Weißbrot)

Sand|wüs|te

san|fo|ri|sie|ren ⟨nach dem amerik. Erfinder Sanford Cluett⟩ ([Gewebe] krumpfecht machen)

San Fran|cis|co (Stadt in den USA; *Kurzform* Frisco); **San Fran|zis|ko** (*eindeutschend für* San Francisco; *Kurzform* Frisko)

sanft; Sänf|te, die; -, -n (Tragstuhl); **Sänf|ten|trä|ger; Sanft|heit,** die; -; **sänf|ti|gen** *(veraltet);* **Sanft|mut,** die; -; **sanft|mü|tig; Sanft|mü|tig|keit,** die; -

Sang, der; -[e]s, Sänge *(veraltet);* mit - und Klang; **sang|bar; Sän|ger;** fahrender -; **Sän|ger‿bund** (der), **...chor** (der), **...fest; Sän|ge|rin; Sän|ger|schaft; San|ges|bru|der; san|ges|freu|dig; San|ges|freund; san|ges‿froh, ...kun|dig; San|ges|lust,** die; -; **san|ges|lus|tig; sang|los;** *nur in* sang- u. klanglos (↑R 23; *ugs. für* plötzlich, unbemerkt) abtreten

Sang|ria (↑R 130), die; -, -s ⟨span.⟩ (Rotweinbowle); **Sang|ri|ta** ®, die; -, -s (gewürzter [Tomaten]saft mit Fruchtfleisch)

San|gu|i|ni|ker [zaŋ'gui:...] ⟨lat.⟩ (heiterer, lebhafter Mensch); **san|gu|i|nisch**

San|hed|rin (↑R 130), der; -s (*hebr. Form von* Synedrion)

San|he|rib (ein assyr. König)

Sa|ni, der; -s, -s (*bes. Soldatenspr. kurz für* Sanitäter); **sa|nie|ren** ⟨lat.⟩ (gesund machen; gesunde Lebensverhältnisse schaffen; durch Renovierung u. Modernisierung den neuen Lebensverhältnissen anpassen; wieder leistungsfähig, rentabel machen); sich - (*ugs. für* großen Gewinn machen; wirtschaftlich gesunden); **Sa|nie|rung; sa|nie|rungs|be|dürf|tig; Sa|nie|rungs‿bi|lanz, ...ge|biet, ...maß|nah|me, ...ob|jekt, ...plan; sa|nie|rungs|reif; sa|ni|tär** ⟨franz.⟩ (gesundheitlich); -e Anlagen; **Sa|ni|tär|ein|rich|tun|gen** *Plur.;* **sa|ni|ta|risch** ⟨lat.⟩ (*schweiz. für* den amtl. Gesundheitsdienst betreffend); **Sa|ni|tät,** die; - (*schweiz. u. österr. für* [milit.] Sanitätswesen); **Sa|ni|tä|ter** (in der ersten Hilfe Ausgebildeter, Krankenpfleger); **Sa|ni|täts‿au|to, ...be|hör|de** (Gesundheitsbehörde), **...dienst, ...ein|heit, ...ge|frei|te, ...ko|lon|ne, ...kom|pa|nie, ...korps, ...kraft|wa|gen** (*Kurzw.* Sank[r]a), **...of|fi|zier, ...rat** (*Plur.* ...räte; *Abk.* San.-Rat), **...sol|dat, ...trup|pe, ...wa|che, ...wa|gen, ...zelt**

San Jo|sé [- xo'se:] (Hptst. von Costa Rica); **San-Jo|sé-Schild|laus,** die; -, ...läuse (↑R 105)

San|ka, San|kra, der; -s, -s (*Soldatenspr.* Sanitätskraftwagen)

Sankt ⟨lat., „heilig"⟩; *In Heiligennamen u. auf solche zurückgehenden Ortsnamen Schreibung ohne Bindestrich; in Ableitungen wird ein Bindestrich gesetzt, der bei Formen auf -er auch entfallen kann.* Sankt Peter, Sankt Elisabeth, Sankt Gallen; die Sankt-Gallener, *auch* Sankt Gallener *od.* Sankt-Galler, *auch* Sankt Galler Handschrift; (↑R 105:) die Sankt-Gotthard-Gruppe; *Abk.* St., z. B. St. Paulus, St. Elisabeth, St. Pölten, *aber* (↑R 95): das St.-Elms-Feuer, die St.-Marien-Kirche; (↑R 105:) die St.-Andreasberger, *auch* St. Andreasberger Bergwerke; *vgl.* Saint, San *u.* São

Sankt And|re|as|berg (Stadt im Harz)
Sankt Bern|hard, der; - -[s] (Name zweier Pässe in der Schweiz); der Große, der Kleine - -; **Sankt-Bern|har|din-Pass**, der; -es
Sankt Bla|si|en (Stadt im südl. Schwarzwald); **Sankt-Bla|si|en Stra|ße** (↑R 123)
Sankt Flo|ri|an (österr. Stift); **Sankt-Flo|ri|ans-Prin|zip**, das; -s; ↑R 123 (der Grundsatz, Unangenehmes von sich wegzuschieben, auch wenn andere dadurch geschädigt werden)
Sankt Gal|len (Kanton u. Stadt in der Schweiz); **Sankt-Gal|le|ner**, *in der Schweiz nur* Sankt-Gal|ler (↑R 103 *u.* 105); Sankt-Gallener *od.* Sankt-Galler Handschrift; *vgl. auch* Sankt; **sankt-gal|lisch** (↑R 105)
Sankt Gott|hard, der; - -[s] (schweiz. Alpenpass)
Sankt He|le|na (Insel im südl. Atlant. Ozean)
Sank|ti|on, die; -, -en (Bestätigung; Erteilung der Gesetzeskraft; *meist Plur.:* Zwangsmaßnahme); **sank|ti|o|nie|ren** (bestätigen; Sanktionen verhängen); **Sank|ti|o|nie|rung; Sank|tis|si|mum**, das; -s (*kath. Rel.* Allerheiligstes, geweihte Hostie)
Sankt-Lo|renz-Strom, der; -[e]s; ↑R 105 (in Nordamerika)
Sankt Mär|gen (Ort im südl. Schwarzwald)
Sankt-Mi|cha|e|lis-Tag, der; -[e]s, -e; ↑R 95 (29. Sept.)
Sankt Mo|ritz [*schweiz.* - mo'rits] (Ort im Oberengadin); *vgl.* Sankt
Sankt-Nim|mer|leins-Tag, der; -[e]s; ↑R 95 *(ugs. scherzh.)*; am -; bis zum -
Sankt Pau|li (Stadtteil von Hamburg)
Sankt Pe|ters|burg (russ. Stadt an der Newa)
Sankt Pöl|ten (Hptst. von Niederösterreich)
Sank|tu|a|ri|um, das; -s, ...ien [...iən] ‹lat.› (Altarraum in der kath. Kirche; [Aufbewahrungsort eines] Reliquienschrein[s])
Sankt-Wolf|gang-See, *auch* Wolf|gang|see *od.* Al|ber|see, der; -s; ↑R 105 (im Salzkammergut)
San-Ma|ri|ne|se, der; -n, -n (↑R 105 *u.* 126; Einwohner von San Marino); **san-ma|ri|ne|sisch** (↑R 105); **San Ma|ri|no** (Staat u. seine Hptst. auf der Apenninenhalbinsel)
San.-Rat = Sanitätsrat
San Sal|va|dor [- ...v...] (Hptst. von El Salvador)
Sans|cu|lot|te [sãsky...], der; -n, -n (↑R 126) ‹franz., „Ohne[knie]hose"› (*Bez. für* einen Revolutionär der Franz. Revolution)
San|se|vi|e|ria [...'vie:...], **San|se|vi|e|rie** [...iə], die; -, ...rien [...iən] ‹nach dem ital. Gelehrten Raimondo di Sangro, Fürst von San Severo› (ein trop. Liliengewächs, Zimmerpflanze)
sans gêne [sã 'ʒɛn] ‹franz.› (*veraltet für* zwanglos; nach Belieben)
San|si|bar (Insel an der Ostküste Afrikas); **San|si|ba|rer** (↑R 103); **san|si|ba|risch**
Sansk|rit [*österr.* ...'krit] (↑R 130), das; -s (Literatur- u. Gelehrtensprache des Altindischen); **Sansk|rit|for|scher; sansk|ri|tisch; Sansk|ri|tist**, der; -en, -en; ↑R 126 (Kenner u. Erforscher des Sanskrits); **Sansk|ri|tis|tik**, die; - (Wissenschaft vom Sanskrit); **Sansk|ri|tis|tin**
Sans|sou|ci ['sã:susi] ‹franz., „sorgenfrei"› (Schloss in Potsdam)
Sant' *vgl.* San, I, b; **San|ta** *vgl.* San, I, c; II, b; III, a
San|ta Claus [ˌsɛntə 'klɔ:z], der; - -, - - ‹amerik.› (*amerik. Bez. für* Weihnachtsmann)
San|ta Lu|cia [- lu'tʃi:a], die; - - (neapolitan. Schifferlied)
San|tan|der (↑R 132; span. Stadt u. Provinz)
San|te *vgl.* San, I, d; **San|ti** *vgl.* San, I, e
San|ti|a|go, *auch* **San|ti|a|go de Chi|le** [- - 'tʃi:le(:)] (↑R 132; Hptst. von Chile)
San|ti|a|go de Com|pos|te|la (↑R 132, span. Stadt)
Sän|tis, der; - (schweiz. Alpengipfel)
San|to *vgl.* San, I, f; II, c
San|to Do|min|go (Hptst. der Dominikanischen Republik)
San|to|rin (griech. Insel)
San|tos (brasil. Stadt)
São ['sa:u, *port.* sɐ̃u] ‹port., „heilig"› (*vor Konsonanten in port. männl. Heiligennamen u. auf solche zurückgehenden Ortsnamen; Abk.* S.), São Paulo, S. Paulo
Saône [so:n], die; - (franz. Fluss)
São To|mé [ˌsa:u to'me:] (Hptst. von São Tomé und Príncipe); **São To|mé und Prín|ci|pe** [- - - 'prinsipə] (westafrik. Inselstaat)
Sa|phir [*auch, österr. nur,* za'fi:r], der; -s, -e ‹semit.-griech.› (ein Edelstein); **Sa|phir|na|del**
sa|pi|en|ti sat! ‹lat., „genug für den Verständigen!"› (es bedarf keiner weiteren Erklärung für den Eingeweihten)
Sa|pin, der; -s, -e, **Sa|pi|ne**, die; -, -n *od.* Sap|pel, der; -s, - ‹ital.› (*österr. für* Werkzeug zum Wegziehen gefällter Bäume)
Sa|po|nin, das; -s, -e ‹lat.› (ein pflanzl. Wirkstoff)
Sap|pe, die; -, -n ‹franz.› (*Milit. früher* Lauf-, Annäherungsgraben)
Sap|pel *vgl.* Sapin
sap|per|lot!, sa|cker|lot! ‹franz.› (*veraltet, aber noch landsch.* ein Ausruf des Unwillens od. des Erstaunens); **sap|per|ment!**, sa|cker|ment! (*svw.* sapperlot)
Sap|peur [za'pø:r], der; -s, -e ‹franz.› (*früher* Soldat für den Sappenbau; *schweiz.* Soldat der techn. Truppe, Pionier)
sap|phisch ['zafiʃ, *auch* 'zapfiʃ] (↑R 94); -e Strophe, -es Versmaß; **Sap|pho** [...f..., *auch* ...pf...] (griech. Dichterin)
Sap|po|ro (jap. Stadt)
sap|ris|ti! (↑R 130) ‹franz.› (*veraltet* Ausruf des Erstaunens, Unwillens)
Sap|ro|bie [...iə] (↑R 130), die; -, -n *meist Plur.* ‹griech.› (*Biol.* von faulenden Stoffen lebender tier. od. pflanzl. Organismus); **Sap|ro|bi|ont**, der; -en, -en; ↑R 126 (*svw.* Saprobie); **sap|ro|gen** (Fäulnis erregend); **Sap|ro|pel**, das; -s, -e (Faulschlamm, der unter Sauerstoffabschluss in Seen u. Meeren entsteht); **Sap|ro|pha|gen** *Plur.* (Pflanzen od. Tiere, die sich von faulenden Stoffen ernähren); **sap|ro|phil** (auf, in od. von faulenden Stoffen lebend); **Sap|ro|phyt**, der; -en, -en; ↑R 126 (pflanzl. Organismus, der von faulenden Stoffen lebt)
Sa|ra (w. Vorn.)
Sa|ra|ban|de, die; -, -n ‹pers.-arab.-span.-franz.› (ein alter Tanz)
Sa|ra|gos|sa (*eindeutschend für* Zaragoza)
Sa|ra|je|vo [...vo] (Hptst. von Bosnien und Herzegowina)
Sa|ra|sa|te (span. Geiger u. Komponist)
Sa|ra|ze|ne, der; -n, -n (↑R 126) ‹arab.› (*veraltet für* Araber, Muslim); **sa|ra|ze|nisch**
Sar|da|na|pal (assyr. König)
Sar|de, der; -n, -n (↑R 126) *u.* Sar|di|ni|er [...iər] (Bewohner Sardiniens)
Sar|del|le, die; -, -n ‹ital.› (ein Fisch); **Sar|del|len‿but|ter, ...fi|let, ...pas|te**
Sar|des (Hptst. des alten Lydiens)
Sar|din *u.* Sar|di|ni|e|rin
Sar|di|ne, die; -, -n ‹ital.› (ein Fisch); **Sar|di|nen|büch|se**

Sar|di|ni|en [...iən] (ital. Insel im Mittelmeer); **Sar|di|ni|er** *vgl.* Sarde; **Sar|di|ni|e|rin** *vgl.* Sardin; **sar|di|nisch, sar|disch**

sar|do|nisch ⟨lat.⟩ (boshaft, hämisch); -es (*Med.* krampfhaftes) Lachen

Sar|do|nyx (↑R 132), der; -[es], -e ⟨griech.⟩ (ein Schmuckstein)

Sarg, der; -[e]s, Särge; **Sarg‿de|ckel, ...na|gel** (*ugs. scherzh. auch für* Zigarette), **...trä|ger, ...tuch**

Sa|ri, der; -[s], -s ⟨sanskr.-Hindi⟩ (gewickeltes, auch den Kopf umhüllendes Gewand der Inderin)

Sar|kas|mus, der; -, ...men ⟨griech.⟩ (*nur Sing.:* [beißender] Spott; sarkastische Äußerung); **sar|kas|tisch** (spöttisch)

Sar|kom, das; -s, -e *u.* **Sar|ko|ma,** das; -s, -ta ⟨griech.⟩ (*Med.* bösartige Geschwulst); **sar|ko|ma|tös; Sar|ko|ma|to|se,** die; - (*Med.* ausgebreitete Sarkombildung); **Sar|ko|phag,** der; -s, -e (Steinsarg, [Prunk]sarg)

Sar|ma|te, der; -n, -n; ↑R 126 (Angehöriger eines ehem. asiat. Nomadenvolkes); **Sar|ma|ti|en** [...iən] (alter Name des Landes zwischen Weichsel u. Wolga); **sar|ma|tisch**

Sar|nen (Hauptort des Halbkantons Obwalden)

Sa|rong, der; -[s], -s ⟨malai.⟩ (um die Hüfte geschlungenes, buntes, oft gebatiktes Tuch der Malaien)

Sar|rass, der; -es, -e ⟨poln.⟩ (Säbel mit schwerer Klinge)

Sar|raute [sa'ro:t], Nathalie [...'li:] (franz. Schriftstellerin)

Sart|re ['sartr(ə)] (↑R 130), Jean-Paul ['ʒã'pɔl] (franz. Philosoph u. Schriftsteller)

SAS = Scandinavian Airlines System [skendi'ne:viən 'ɛ:(r)lainz 'sistəm] (Skandinavische Luftlinien)

Sa|scha (m. Vorn.)

Sas|kat|che|wan [səs'kɛtʃiwən] ⟨engl.⟩ (kanad. Provinz)

Sa-Sprin|gen [ɛs'a:...] ⟨*Kurzw. für* schweres Springen der Kategorie a⟩ (*Reiten* schwere Springprüfung)

Sass, Sas|se, der; -en, -en; ↑R 126 (*früher* Besitzer von Grund und Boden, Grundbesitzer; Ansässiger)

Sas|saf|ras (↑R 130), der; -, - ⟨franz.⟩ (nordamerik. Laubbaum); **Sas|saf|ras|öl,** das; -[e]s (ätherisches Öl aus dem Holz des Sassafras)

Sas|sa|ni|de, der; -n, -n; ↑R 126 (Angehöriger eines alten pers. Herrschergeschlechtes); **sas|sa|ni|disch**

[1]**Sas|se** *vgl.* Sass; [2]**Sas|se,** die; -, -n (*Jägerspr.* Hasenlager)

Saß|nitz (Hafenstadt a. d. Ostküste von Rügen)

Sa|tan, der; -s, -e ⟨hebr.⟩ *u.* **Sa|ta|nas,** der; -, -se (*nur Sing.:* Teufel; boshafter Mensch)

Sa|tang, der; -[s], -[s] ⟨siam.⟩ (Münze in Thailand; *Abk.* St. *od.* Stg.; 100 Satangs = 1 Baht); 100 - (↑R 90)

sa|ta|nisch (teuflisch); **Sa|tans‿bra|ten** (*ugs. scherzh. für* pfiffiger, durchtriebener Kerl; Schlingel), **...kerl, ...pilz, ...weib**

Sa|tel|lit [*auch* ...'lit], der; -en, -en (↑R 126) ⟨lat.⟩ (*Astron.* [1]Mond der Planeten; *Raumfahrt* künstlicher Mond, Raumsonde; *kurz für* Satellitenstaat); **Sa|tel|li|ten‿bahn, ...bild, ...fern|se|hen, ...flug, ...fo|to, ...funk, ...pro|gramm, ...schüs|sel** *(ugs.)*, **...staat** (*Plur.* ...staaten; von einer Großmacht abhängiger, formal selbstständiger Staat), **...stadt** (Trabantenstadt), **...über|tra|gung** (↑R 132; Übertragung über einen Fernsehsatelliten)

Sa|tem|spra|che (Sprache aus einer bestimmten Gruppe der idg. Sprachen)

Sa|ter|land, das; -[e]s (oldenburg. Landschaft)

Sa|ter|tag, der; -[e]s, -e ⟨lat.⟩ (*westf., ostfries. für* Sonnabend)

Sa|tin [sa'tɛ̃:, *auch* za'tɛŋ], der; -s, -s ⟨arab.-franz.⟩ (*Sammelbez. für* Gewebe in Atlasbindung mit glänzender Oberfläche); **Sa|ti|na|ge** [za..., *auch* sati'na:ʒə], die; -, -n (Glättung [von Papier u. a.]); **Sa|tin‿blu|se** [sa'tɛ̃:..., *auch* za'tɛŋ...], **...holz** (eine glänzende Holzart); **sa|ti|nie|ren** [...ti...] ([Papier] glätten); **Sa|ti|nier|ma|schi|ne**

Sa|ti|re, die; -, -n ⟨lat.⟩ (iron.-witzige literar. od. künstler. Darstellung menschlicher Schwächen u. Laster; *nur Sing.:* literar. Kritik an Personen u. Zuständen durch Übertreibung, Ironie u. Spott); **Sa|ti|ri|ker** (Verfasser von Satiren); **sa|ti|risch**

Sa|tis|fak|ti|on, die; -, -en ⟨lat.⟩ (Genugtuung); **sa|tis|fak|ti|ons|fä|hig**

Sat|rap (↑R 130), der; -en, -en (↑R 126) ⟨pers.⟩ (altpers. Statthalter); **Sat|ra|pen|wirt|schaft,** die; - (*abwertend für* Behördenwillkür); **Sat|ra|pie,** die; -, ...ien (altpers. Statthalterschaft)

Sat|su|ma, die; -, -s ⟨nach der früheren jap. Provinz Satsuma⟩ (Mandarine[nart])

satt; ein sattes Blau; sich satt essen; satt sein (*ugs. auch für* völlig betrunken sein); ich bin *od.* habe es satt (*ugs. für* habe keine Lust mehr); sich an einer Sache satt sehen *(ugs.);* etwas satt bekommen, haben *(ugs.);* sattblau usw.

Sat|te, die; -, -n (*nordd. für* größere, flache Schüssel)

Sat|tel, der; -s, Sättel; **Sät|tel|chen; Sat|tel‿dach, ...de|cke; sat|tel|fest** (*auch für* kenntnissicher, -reich); **Sat|tel‿gurt, ...kis|sen, ...knopf; sat|teln;** ich ...[e]le (↑R 16); **Sat|tel‿pferd** (das im Gespann links gehende Pferd), **...schlep|per, ...ta|sche; Sat|tel|lung,** Satt|lung; **Sat|tel|zeug**

satt|grün; Satt|heit, die; -; **sät|ti|gen;** eine gesättigte Lösung *(Chemie);* **Sät|ti|gung; Sät|ti|gungs‿ge|fühl** (das; -[e]s), **...grad**

Satt|ler; Satt|ler|ar|beit; Satt|le|rei; Satt|ler|hand|werk, das; -[e]s; **Satt|le|rin; Satt|ler|meis|ter; Satt|lung** *vgl.* Sattelung

satt|rot; satt|sam (hinlänglich)

Sa|tu|ra|ti|on, die; -, -en ⟨lat., „Sättigung"⟩ (ein besonderes Verfahren bei der Zuckergewinnung); **sa|tu|rie|ren** (sättigen; [Ansprüche] befriedigen); **sa|tu|riert** (zufrieden gestellt)

[1]**Sa|turn,** der; -s ⟨lat.⟩ (ein Planet); [2]**Sa|turn** *vgl.* Saturnus; [3]**Sa|turn,** die; -, -s (*kurz für* Saturnrakete); **Sa|tur|na|li|en** [...iən] *Plur.* (altröm. Fest zu Ehren des Gottes Saturn); **sa|tur|nisch;** saturnischer Vers; saturnisches Zeitalter (das goldene Zeitalter in der antiken Sage); **Sa|turn|ra|ke|te** (amerik. Trägerrakete); **Sa|tur|nus** (röm. Gott der Aussaat)

Sa|tyr, der; *Gen.* -s *u.* -n, *Plur.* -n (↑R 126) ⟨griech.⟩ (derb-lüsterner, bocksgestaltiger Waldgeist u. Begleiter des Dionysos in der griech. Sage); **sa|tyr|ar|tig; Sa|ty|ri|a|sis,** die; - (*Med.* krankhafte Steigerung des männl. Geschlechtstriebes); **Sa|tyr|spiel**

Satz, der; -es, Sätze; ein verkürzter, elliptischer -; **Satz‿aus|sa|ge** (*svw.* Prädikat), **...ball** *(Sport)*, **...band** (das; *Plur.* ...bänder; *für* Kopula), **...bau** (der; -[e]s), **...bau|plan, ...bruch** (der; *für* Anakoluth); **Sätz|chen; Satz|er|gän|zung; satz|fer|tig;** ein -es Manuskript; **Satz‿ge|fü|ge, ...ge|gen|stand, ...glied; ...sät|zig** (*Musik,* z. B. viersätzig); **Satz‿kon|struk|ti|on, ...leh|re** (die; -; *für* Syntax); **Satz‿rei|he, ...spie|gel** *(Druckw.)*, **...tech|nik, ...teil**

(der); **Satz|zung; satz|zungs|ge|mäß; Satz|ver|bin|dung; satz|wei|se; satz|wer|tig;** -er Infinitiv; -es Partizip; **Satz‿zei|chen, ...zu|sam|men|hang**
[1]**Sau**, die; -, *Plur.* Säue *u.* (*bes. von* Wildschweinen:) -en
[2]**Sau** (*frühere dt. Bez. für* [2]Save)
sau|ber; saub[e]rer, sauberste; saubere (nicht verschmutzte) Umwelt; *Getrenntschreibung in Verbindung mit Verben:* sauber halten; ich halte sauber; sauber gehalten; sauber zu halten; sauber machen; **Sau|ber|keit,** die; -; **säu|ber|lich; sau|ber ma|chen** *vgl.* sauber; **Sau|ber|mann** *Plur.* ...männer (*scherzh.; auch für* jmd., der auf die Wahrung der Moral achtet); **säu|bern;** ich ...ere (↑R 16); **Säu|be|rung; Säu|be|rungs‿ak|ti|on, ...wel|le**
sau|blöd, sau|blö|de (*derb für* sehr blöd[e]); **Sau|boh|ne**
Sau|ce [ˈzo:sə, *österr.* zo:s], die; -, -n [ˈzo:s(ə)n] (*franz. Schreibung von* Soße); **Sauce bé|ar|naise** [zo:s bearˈnɛ:z], die; - - ‹franz.› (eine weiße Kräutersoße); **Sauce hol|lan|daise** [- ɔlãˈdɛ:z], die; - - (eine weiße Soße)
Säu|chen
Sau|ci|e|re [zoˈsi̯ɛ:rə, *österr.* zoˈsi̯ɛ:r], die; -, -n [...r(ə)n] ‹franz.› (Soßenschüssel, -napf); **sau|cie|ren** [zoˈsi:...] ([Tabak] mit einer Soße behandeln); **Sau|cis|chen** [zo..., *auch* soˈsi:s...] (kleine Bratwurst, Würstchen)
Sau|di, der; -s, -s *u.* **Sau|di-A|ra|ber** [*auch* ...ˈara...] (Bewohner von Saudi-Arabien); **Sau|di-A|ra|bi|en** [...i̯ən] (↑R 105; arab. Staat); **sau|di-a|ra|bisch**
sau|dumm (*derb für* sehr dumm);
sau|en (*vom Schwein* Junge bekommen)
sau|er; saure Gurken, Heringe; saurer Regen; (↑R 47:) gib ihm Saures! (*ugs. für* prügle ihn!); **Sau|er,** das; -s (*Druckerspr.* bezahlte, aber noch nicht geleistete Arbeit; *fachspr. kurz für* Sauerteig); **Sau|er‿amp|fer, ...bra|ten, ...brun|nen, ...dorn** (*Plur.* ...dorne)
Sau|e|rei (*derb*)
Sau|er‿kir|sche, ...klee (der; -s), **...kohl** (der; -[e]s; *landsch.*), **...kraut** (das; -[e]s)
Sau|er|land, das; -[e]s (westfäl. Landschaft); **Sau|er|län|der,** der; **sau|er|län|disch**
säu|er|lich; Säu|er|lich|keit, die; -; **Säu|er|ling** (kohlensaures Mineralwasser; Sauerampfer); **Sau|er|milch,** die; -; **säu|ern** (sauer machen; *auch für* sauer werden); ich ...ere (↑R 16); das Brot wird gesäuert; **Säu|er|nis,** die; -; **Sau|er|rahm; Sau|er|stoff,** der; -[e]s (chem. Element, Gas; *Zeichen* O); **Sau|er|stoff‿ap|pa|rat, ...bad, ...du|sche; Sau|er|stoff|fla|sche** (↑R 136); **Sau|er|stoff‿ge|halt** (der), **...ge|rät; sau|er|stoff|hal|tig; Sau|er|stoff‿man|gel** (der; -s), **...mas|ke, ...tank, ...ver|sor|gung, ...zelt, ...zu|fuhr; sau|er|süß** [*auch* ˈzauərˈzy:s] (↑R 27); **Sau|er|teig; sau|er|töp|fisch** (griesgrämig); **Säu|e|rung; Sau|er|was|ser** *Plur.* ...wässer
Sauf|aus, der; -, - (*veraltend für* Trinker); **Sauf|bold,** der; -[e]s, -e (*svw.* Saufaus)
Sau|fe|der (*Jägerspr.* Spieß zum Abfangen des Wildschweines)
sau|fen (*derb in Bezug auf Menschen, bes. für* Alkohol trinken); du säufst; du soffst; du söffest; gesoffen; sauf[e]!; **Säu|fer** (*derb*); **Säu|fer|bal|ken** (*ugs.* im Führerschein); **Sau|fe|rei** (*derb*); **Säu|fe|rin** (*derb*); **Säu|fer‿le|ber** (*ugs.*), **...wahn, ...wahn|sinn; Sauf‿ge|la|ge** (*derb*), **...kum|pan** (*derb*)
Sau|fraß (*derb* schlechtes Essen)
Saug|am|me; Saug|bag|ger; sau|gen; du saugst; du sogst, *auch* saugtest; du sögest; gesogen, *auch* gesaugt (*Technik nur* saugte, gesaugt); saug[e]!; **säu|gen; Sau|ger** (saugendes Junges; Schnuller); **Säu|ger** (Säugetier); **Säu|ge|tier; saug|fä|hig; Saug‿fä|hig|keit** (die; -), **...fla|sche, ...glo|cke** (*Med.*), **...he|ber** (*Chemie*), **...kap|pe, ...kraft, ...lei|tung; Säug|ling** (Kind im 1. Lebensjahr); **Säug|lings‿gym|nas|tik, ...heim, ...pfle|ge, ...schwes|ter, ...sterb|lich|keit, ...waa|ge; Saug‿mas|sa|ge, ...napf** (Haftorgan bei bestimmten Tieren), **...pum|pe**
sau|grob (*derb für* sehr grob)
Saug‿rohr, ...wir|kung
Sau|hatz (*Jägerspr.*); **Sau‿hau|fen** (*derb*), **...hund** (*derb*); **säu|isch** (*derb für* sehr unanständig); **Sau|jagd** (*Jägerspr.*); **sau|kalt** (*ugs. für* sehr kalt); **Sau|kerl** (*derb*)
Saul (bibl. König)
Säul|chen; Säu|le, die; -, -n (Stütze; stützendes Mauerwerk u. Ä.)
Säu|len|ab|schluss (*für* Kapitell); **säu|len|för|mig; Säu|len‿fuß, ...gang** (der), **...hal|le, ...hei|li|ge** (*svw.* Stylit), **...kak|tus, ...schaft** (der; *vgl.* [1]Schaft), **...tem|pel; ...säu|lig** (z. B. mehrsäulig)
Sau|lus (bibl. m. Eigenn.)
[1]**Saum,** der; -[e]s, Säume (Rand; Besatz)
[2]**Saum,** der; -[e]s, Säume (*veraltet für* Last)
Sau|ma|gen (*Gastron.* gefüllter Schweinemagen); **sau|mä|ßig** (*derb*)
Säum|chen (kleiner [2]Saum)
[1]**säu|men** (mit einem Rand, Besatz versehen)
[2]**säu|men** (*veraltet für* mit Saumtieren Lasten befördern)
[3]**säu|men** (*geh. für* zögern)
[1]**Säu|mer** (Zusatzteil der Nähmaschine)
[2]**Säu|mer** (*veraltet für* Saumtier, Lasttier; Saumtiertreiber)
[3]**Säu|mer** (*geh. für* Säumender, Zögernder); **säu|mig; Säu|mig|keit,** die; -
Saum|naht
Säum|nis, die; -, -se *od.* das; -ses, -se (*Rechtsw., sonst veraltend*); **Säum|nis|zu|schlag**
Saum|pfad ‹*zu* [2]Saum› (Gebirgsweg für Saumtiere)
Saum|sal, die; -, -e *od.* das; -[e]s, -e (*veraltet für* Säumigkeit, Nachlässigkeit); **saum|se|lig; Saum|se|lig|keit**
Saum|tier ‹*zu* [2]Saum› (Tragtier)
Sau|na, die; -, *Plur.* -s *od.* ...nen ‹finn.› (Heißluftbad); **Sau|na|bad; sau|nen, sau|nie|ren** (in die Sauna gehen, sich in der Sauna aufhalten); **Sau|nist; Sau|nis|tin**
Sau|rach, der; -[e]s, -e (ein Strauch)
Säu|re, die; -, -n; **säu|re‿arm, ...be|stän|dig, ...fest, ...frei; Säu|re|ge|halt,** der; **Sau|re-Gur|ken-Zeit** (↑R 28), die; -, -en (*scherzh. für* polit. od. geschäftl. ruhige Zeit); **säu|re|hal|tig; Säu|re‿man|gel** (der), **...man|tel** (*Med.*), **...mes|ser** (der), **...schutz|an|zug, ...über|schuss** (↑R 132), **...ver|gif|tung**
Sau|ri|er [...i̯ər], der; -s, - (urweltl. [Riesen]echse)
Saus; *nur in der Wendung* in - und Braus (sorglos prassend) leben
Sau|se, die; -, -n (*ugs. für* ausgelassene Feier); eine - machen
säu|seln; ich ...[e]le (↑R 16); **sau|sen;** du saust; er saus|te; sausen lassen (*ugs. für* aufgeben); **Sau|ser** (*landsch. für* neuer Wein u. dadurch hervorgerufener Rausch); **Sau|se|schritt;** *nur in* im - (sehr schnell); **Sau|se|wind** (*auch für* unsteter, lebhafter junger Mensch)
Saus|sure [soˈsy:r], Ferdinand de (schweiz. Sprachwissenschaftler)

Sau|stall (*meist übertr. derb für* schmutzige Verhältnisse, Unordnung)
Sau|ternes [soˈtɛrn], der; -, - ‹nach der gleichnamigen Ortschaft› (ein franz. Wein)
Sau|wet|ter, das; -s (*derb für* sehr schlechtes Wetter); **sau|wohl** (*ugs. für* sehr wohl); **Sau|wut** (*derb für* heftige Wut)
Sa|van|ne [...v...], die; -, -n ‹indian.› (Steppe mit einzeln od. gruppenweise stehenden Bäumen)
[1]**Save** [sa:v] (l. Nebenfluss der Garonne)
[2]**Sa|ve** [ˈza:və] (r. Nebenfluss der Donau)
Sa|vig|ny [ˈzavinji] (↑R 130), Friedrich Carl von (dt. Jurist)
Sa|voir-viv|re [savoarˈvi:vr(ə)] (↑R 130), das; - ‹franz.› (feine Lebensart, Lebensklugheit)
Sa|vo|na|ro|la [...v...] (ital. Bußprediger u. Reformator)
Sa|vo|yar|de [zavoˈjardə], der; -n, -n (↑R 126) ‹franz.› (Savoyer); **Sa|voy|en** [zaˈvɔyən] (hist. Provinz in Ostfrankreich); **Sa|voy|er** (↑R 103); **Sa|voy|er|kohl**, der; -[e]s (Wirsingkohl); **sa|voy|isch**
Sa|xi|fra|ga (↑R 130), die; -, ...fragen ‹lat.› (*Bot.* Steinbrech)
Sa|xo|fon *eindeutschende Schreibung für* Saxophon
Sa|xo|ne, der; -n, -n; ↑R 126 (Angehöriger einer altgerm. Stammesgruppe; [Alt]sachse)
Sa|xo|phon (↑R 33), das; -s, -e ‹nach dem belg. Erfinder A. Sax› (ein Blasinstrument); **Sa|xo|pho|nist**, der; -en, -en; ↑R 126 (Saxophonbläser); **Sa|xo|pho|nis|tin**
Sa|zer|do|ti|um, das; -s ‹lat.› (Priestertum, -amt; im MA. die geistl. Gewalt des Papstes)
sb = Stilb
Sb = Stibium (*chem. Zeichen für* Antimon)
SB = Selbstbedienung (z. B. SB-Markt, SB-Tankstelle [↑R 26])
S-Bahn, die; -, -en (Schnellbahn); **S-Bahn|hof**; **S-Bahn-Wa|gen**, der; -s, - (↑R 28)
SBB = Schweizerische Bundesbahnen
Sbir|re, der; -n, -n (↑R 126) ‹ital.› (*früher für* ital. Polizeidiener)
s. Br., südl. Br. = südlicher Breite; 50° s. Br.
Sbrinz, der; -[es] (ein [Schweizer] Hartkäse)
Sc = *chem. Zeichen für* Scandium
sc., scil. = scilicet
sc., sculps. = sculpsit
S. C. = South Carolina; *vgl.* Südkarolina
Sca|la, die; - ‹ital., „Treppe"›; Mailänder Scala (Mailänder Opernhaus); *vgl. auch* Skala
Scam|pi *Plur.* ‹ital.› (*ital. Bez. für* eine Art kleiner Krebse)
Scan|di|um, das; -s (chem. Element, Metall; *Zeichen* Sc)
scan|nen [ˈskɛn...] ‹engl.› (mit einem Scanner abtasten); **Scan|ner** [ˈskɛnər], der; -s, - (ein elektron. Gerät); **Scan|ning**, das; -[s], -s (das Scannen)
Sca|pa Flow [ˈska:pa ˈflo:] (Bucht zwischen den Orkneyinseln)
Scar|lat|ti (Name verschiedener ital. Komponisten)
Scene [si:n], die; -, -s *Plur. selten* ‹engl.› (*ugs. für* durch bestimmte Moden, Lebensformen u. a. geprägtes Milieu)
[1]**Scha|be**, Schwa|be, die; -, -n (ein Insekt); [2]**Scha|be**, die; -, -n (ein Werkzeug)
Schä|be, die; -, -n (Holzteilchen vom Flachs)
Scha|be|fleisch; **Schab|ei|sen**; **Scha|be|mes|ser** (*svw.* Schabmesser); **scha|ben**; **Scha|ber**; **Scha|be|rei**
Scha|ber|nack, der; -[e]s, -e (übermütiger Streich, Possen)
schä|big (*abwertend*); **Schä|big|keit**
Schab|kunst, die; - (eine graph. Technik); **Schab|kunst|blatt**
Scha|b|lo|ne (↑R 130), die; -, -n (ausgeschnittene Vorlage; Muster; Schema, Klischee); **Schab|lo|nen_ar|beit**, **...druck** (*Plur.* ...drucke); **schab|lo|nen|haft**; **schab|lo|nen|mä|ßig**; **schab|lo|nie|ren**, **schab|lo|ni|sie|ren** (nach der Schablone [be]arbeiten, behandeln)
Schab|mes|ser, das
Scha|bot|te, die; -, -n ‹franz.› (schweres Fundament für Maschinenhämmer)
Schab|ra|cke (↑R 130), die; -, -n ‹türk.› (verzierte Satteldecke; *ugs. für* abgenutzte, alte Sache, alte Frau); **Schab|ra|cken|ta|pir**
Schab|sel, das; -s, -; **Schab|zie|ger**, *schweiz.* **Schab|zi|ger** (harter [Schweizer] Kräuterkäse)
Schach, das; -s, -s ‹pers.› (Brettspiel; Bedrohung des Königs im Schachspiel); - spielen, bieten; im *od.* in - halten (nicht gefährlich werden lassen); Schach und matt!; **Schach_auf|ga|be**, **...brett**; **schach|brett|ar|tig**; **Schach|brett|mus|ter**; **Schach|com|pu|ter**
Scha|chen, der; -s, - (*südd., österr. mdal. u. schweiz. für* Waldstück, -rest; *schweiz. auch für* Niederung, Uferland)
Scha|cher, der; -s ‹hebr.› (übles, feilschendes Geschäftemachen)
Schä|cher (*bibl. für* Räuber, Mörder)
Scha|che|rei ‹hebr.›; **Scha|che|rer**; **scha|chern** (*abwertend für* feilschend handeln); ich ...ere (↑R 16)
Schach|fi|gur; **schach|matt** (*ugs. auch für* sehr matt); **Schach_meis|ter**, **...meis|te|rin**, **...meis|ter|schaft**, **...par|tie**, **...prob|lem**, **...spiel**, **...spie|ler**, **...spie|le|rin**
Schacht, der; -[e]s, Schächte; - kriegen (*nordd. für* Prügel bekommen)
Schach|tel, die; -, -n; alte - (*ugs. abwertend für* alte, ältere Frau); **Schäch|tel|chen**; **Schach|tel|di|vi|den|de** (*Wirtsch.*); **Schäch|tel|lein**; **Schach|tel|ge|sell|schaft** (*Wirtsch.*)
Schach|tel|halm
schach|teln; ich ...[e]le (↑R 16); **Schach|tel|satz** (*Sprachw.*)
schach|ten (eine Grube, einen Schacht graben)
schäch|ten ‹hebr.› (nach jüd. Vorschrift schlachten); **Schäch|ter**
Schach|tisch
Schacht_meis|ter, **...meis|te|rin**, **...ofen** (↑R 132)
Schäch|tung ‹*zu* schächten›
Schach_tur|nier, **...uhr**, **...welt|meis|ter**, **...welt|meis|ter|schaft**, **...zug**
Schad|bild; -er an Nadelbäumen
scha|de (↑R 46); es ist schade um jmdn. *od.* um etwas; schade, dass ...; ich bin mir dafür zu schade; o wie schade!; es ist jammerschade!; **Scha|de**, der (*veraltet für* Schaden); *nur noch in* es soll, wird dein - nicht sein
Schä|del, der; -s, -; **Schä|del|ba|sis** (*Med.*); **Schä|del|ba|sis|bruch**, der; *vgl.* [1]Bruch; **Schä|del_bruch** (der; *vgl.* [1]Bruch), **...dach**, **...de|cke**, **...form**; **...schä|de|lig**, ...schäd|lig (z. B. langschäd[e]lig); **Schä|del|stät|te** (*eindeutschend für* Golgatha)
scha|den; jmdm. -; **Scha|den**, der; -s, Schäden; zu Schaden kommen (*Amtsspr.*); **Scha|den|be|gren|zung**, Scha|dens|be|gren|zung; **Scha|den|be|rech|nung**, Scha|dens|be|rech|nung; **Scha|den|be|richt**, Scha|dens|be|richt; **Scha|den|er|satz** (*BGB* Schadensersatz); **Scha|den|er|satz_an|spruch**, **...leis|tung**, **...pflicht** (die; -); **scha|den|er|satz|pflich|tig**; **Scha|den|fest|stel|lung**, Scha|dens|fest|stel|lung; **Scha|den|feu|er**; **Scha|den|frei|heits|ra|batt**; **Scha-**

den|freu|de, die; -; **scha|den|froh; Scha|den|nach|weis,** Scha|dens|nach|weis; **Scha|dens|be|gren|zung,** Scha|den|be|gren|zung; **Scha|dens|be|rech|nung,** Scha|den|be|rech|nung; **Scha|dens|be|richt,** Scha|den|be|richt; **Scha|dens|er|satz** (*BGB für* Schadenersatz); **Scha|dens|fall; Scha|dens|fest|stel|lung,** Scha|den|fest|stel|lung; **Scha|dens|nach|weis,** Scha|den|nach|weis; **Scha|den⌣ver|hü|tung, ...ver|si|che|rung; Schad|fraß,** der; -es; **schad|haft; Schad|haf|tig|keit,** die; -; **schä|di|gen; Schä|di|ger; Schä|di|gung; Schad|in|sekt; schäd|lich; Schäd|lich|keit,** die; -
...schäd|lig *vgl.* ...schädelig
Schäd|ling; Schäd|lings|be|kämp|fung, die; -; **Schäd|lings|be|kämp|fungs|mit|tel,** das; **schad|los;** sich - halten; **Schad|los⌣bür|ge** (*Wirtsch.* Bürge bei der Ausfallbürgschaft), **...hal|tung** (die; -)
Scha|dor *vgl.* Tschador
Scha|dow [...do] (dt. Bildhauer)
Schad|stoff; schad|stoff|arm; Schad|stoff⌣aus|stoß (der; -[e]s), **...be|las|tung, ...emis|si|on** (↑R 132); **schad|stoff|frei** (↑R 136); **Schad|stoff|ge|halt,** der; -[e]s; **schad|stoff⌣hal|tig, ...re|du|ziert; Schad|stoff|re|du|zie|rung**
Schaf, das; -[e]s, -e; **Schaf|bock; Schäf|chen;** seine Schäfchen ins Trockene bringen (*ugs. auch für* sich großen Gewinn verschaffen), im Trockenen haben (*ugs. auch für* sich seinen Vorteil gesichert haben); **Schäf|chen|wol|ke** *meist Plur.*; **Schä|fer; Schä|fer|dich|tung; Schä|fe|rei; Schä|fer|hund; Schä|fe|rin; Schä|fer⌣kar|ren, ...ro|man, ...spiel, ...stünd|chen** (heimliches Beisammensein von Verliebten)
Schaff, das; -[e]s, -e (*südd., österr. für* [offenes] Gefäß; *landsch. für* Schrank); *vgl.* ²Schaft *u.* Schapp; **Schäff|chen** ⟨*zu* Schaff⟩; **Schaf|fel,** das; -s, -n (*österr. mdal. für* [kleines] Schaff)
Schaf|fell
¹schaf|fen (vollbringen; *landsch. für* arbeiten; in [reger] Tätigkeit sein; *Seemannsspr.* essen); du schafftest; geschafft; schaff[e]!; er hat den ganzen Tag geschafft *(landsch.)*; sie haben es geschafft; er hat die Kiste auf den Boden geschafft; diese Sorgen sind aus der Welt geschafft (sind beseitigt); ich möchte mit dieser Sache nichts mehr zu schaffen haben; ich habe mir daran zu schaffen gemacht;
²schaf|fen (schöpferisch, gestaltend hervorbringen); du schufst; du schüfest; geschaffen; schaff[e]!; Schiller hat „Wilhelm Tell" geschaffen; er ist zum Lehrer wie geschaffen; er stand da, wie ihn Gott geschaffen hat; sie schuf, *auch* schaffte [endlich] Abhilfe, Ordnung, Platz, Raum; es muss [endlich] Abhilfe, Ordnung, Platz, Raum geschaffen, *selten* geschafft werden; **Schaf|fen,** das; -s; **Schaf|fens⌣drang** (der; -[e]s), **...freu|de** (die; -); **schaf|fens|freu|dig; Schaf|fens|kraft,** die; -; **schaf|fens|kräf|tig; Schaf|fens|lust,** die; -; **schaf|fens|lus|tig; Schaf|fer** (*landsch. für* tüchtiger Arbeiter; *Seemannsspr.* Mann, der die Schiffsmahlzeit besorgt und anrichtet; *österr. veraltet für* Aufseher auf einem Gutshof); **Schaf|fe|rei** (*Seemannsspr.* Schiffsvorratskammer; *landsch. für* [mühseliges] Arbeiten); **Schaf|fe|rin** *(landsch.)*
Schaff|hau|sen (Kanton u. Stadt in der Schweiz); **Schaff|hau|ser; schaff|hau|se|risch**
schaf|fig (*landsch. u. schweiz. mdal. für* arbeitsam)
Schäff|ler (*bayr. für* Böttcher); **Schäff|ler|tanz** (Zunfttanz der Münchener Schäffler)
Schaff|ner (Kassier- u. Kontrollbeamter bei öffentl. Verkehrsbetrieben; *veraltet für* Verwalter; Aufseher); **Schaff|ne|rei** (*veraltet für* Schaffneramt, -wohnung); **Schaff|ne|rin; schaff|ner|los;** ein -er Zug; **Schaf|fung,** die; -
Schaf|gar|be, die; -, -n (eine Heilpflanze); **Schaf⌣her|de, ...hirt**
Scha|fi|it, der; -en, -en; ↑R 126 (Angehöriger einer islam. Rechtsschule)
Schaf|käl|te, Schafs|käl|te (Mitte Juni auftretender Kaltlufteinbruch); **Schaf|kä|se** *vgl.* Schafskäse; **Schaf|kopf,** Schafs|kopf, der; -[e]s (ein Kartenspiel); **Schaf|le|der; Schäf|lein; Schaf|milch,** Schafs|milch, die; -
Scha|fott, das; -[e]s, -e ⟨niederl.⟩ (Gerüst für Hinrichtungen)
Schaf⌣pelz, ...que|se (Drehwurm), **...schur; Schafs|käl|te** *vgl.* Schafkälte; **Schafs|kä|se,** Schaf|kä|se; **Schafs⌣kleid** (*nur in* der Wolf im -), **...kopf** (Schimpfwort; *vgl.* Schafkopf); **Schafs|milch** *vgl.* Schafmilch; **Schafs⌣na|se** (*auch* eine Apfel-, Birnensorte; *auch für* dummer Mensch), **...pelz; Schaf|stall**
¹Schaft, der; -[e]s, Schäfte (z. B. Lanzenschaft)
²Schaft, der; -[e]s, Schäfte (*südd. u. schweiz. für* Gestell[brett], Schrank); *vgl. auch* Schaff *u.* Schapp
...schaft (z. B. Landschaft)
Schäft|chen; schäf|ten (mit einem Schaft versehen; [Pflanzen] veredeln; *landsch. für* prügeln); **Schaft|le|der; Schaft|stie|fel**
Schaf⌣wei|de, ...wol|le (die; -), **...zucht**
Schah, der; -s, -s ⟨pers., „König"⟩ (pers. Herrschertitel; *meist kurz für* Schah-in-schah); **Schah-in-schah,** der; -s, -s ⟨„König der Könige"⟩ (*früher* Titel des Herrschers des Iran)
Scha|kal, der; -s, -e ⟨sanskr.⟩ (ein hundeartiges Raubtier)
Scha|ke, die; -, -n (*Technik* Ring, Kettenglied); **Schä|kel,** der; -s, - (*Seemannsspr.* U-förmiges Verbindungsglied aus Metall); **schä|keln** (mit einem Schäkel verbinden); ich ...[e]le (↑R 16)
Schä|ker ⟨hebr.-jidd.⟩; **Schä|ke|rei; Schä|ke|rin; schä|kern** (scherzen); ich ...ere (↑R 16)
schal; ein -es (abgestandenes) Bier; ein -er (fader) Witz
Schal, der; -s, *Plur.* -s, *auch* -e ⟨pers.-engl.⟩ (langes, schmales Halstuch)
Scha|lan|der, der; -s, - (*landsch. für* Pausenraum in Brauereien)
Schal|brett (für Verschalungen verwendetes rohes Brett)
¹Schäl|chen (kleiner Schal)
²Schäl|chen (kleine Schale)
¹Scha|le, die; -, -n (flaches Gefäß; *südd. u. österr. auch für* Tasse)
²Scha|le, die; -, -n (Hülle; *Jägerspr.* Huf beim Schalenwild); **Schäl|ei|sen** (ein Werkzeug); **schä|len; Scha|len⌣bau|wei|se** (die; -), **...guss** (ein Hartguss)
Scha|len|kreuz (Teil des Windgeschwindigkeitsmessers)
scha|len|los (ohne ²Schale); **Scha|len|obst** (Obst mit harter, holziger ²Schale, z. B. Nüsse)
Scha|len⌣ses|sel ⟨*zu* ¹Schale⟩, **...sitz**
Scha|len|wild (*Jägerspr.* Rot-, Schwarz-, Steinwild)
Schal|heit, die; - ⟨*zu* schal⟩
Schäl|hengst (Zuchthengst)
Schal|holz; ...scha|lig (z. B. dünnschalig)
Schalk, der; -[e]s, *Plur.* -e *u.* Schälke (Spaßvogel, Schelm)
Schal|ke, die; -, -n (*Seemannsspr.* wasserdichter Abschluss einer Luke); **schal|ken** (wasserdicht schließen)

schalk|haft; Schalk|haf|tig|keit, die; -; **Schalk|heit,** die; -
Schal‿kra|gen, ...kra|wat|te
Schalks|narr *(veraltet)*
Schäl|kur *(Kosmetik)*
Schall, der; -[e]s, *Plur.* -e *od.* Schälle; **Schall‿be|cher** (bei Blasinstrumenten), **...bo|den; schall|däm|mend** (↑R 40); **Schall‿däm|mung, ...dämp|fer, ...de|ckel; schall|dicht; Schall|do|se; schal|len;** es schallt; es schallte, *seltener* scholl; es schallte, *seltener* schölle; geschallt; schall[e]!; schallendes Gelächter; **schal|lern** *(ugs. für* laut knallen); jmdm. eine - (jmdm. eine Ohrfeige geben); **schall|ge|dämpft;** -er Motor; **Schall|ge|schwin|dig|keit; Schall|leh|re** (↑R 136), die; -; **Schall|lei|ter** (↑R 136), der; **Schall|loch** (↑R 136), das; -[e]s, Schalllöcher; **Schall|mau|er,** die; - (extrem hoher Luftwiderstand bei einem die Schallgeschwindigkeit erreichenden Flugobjekt); die - durchbrechen
schal|los *vgl.* schalenlos
Schall|plat|te; Schall|plat|ten‿al|bum, ...ar|chiv, ...auf|nah|me, ...in|dust|rie, ...mu|sik; schall|schlu|ckend (↑R 40); **schall|si|cher; schall|tot;** -er Raum; **Schall‿trich|ter** (trichterförmiges Gerät zur Schallverstärkung), **...wel|le** *(meist Plur.),* **...wort** *(Plur.* ...wörter; durch Lautnachahmung entstandenes Wort), **...zei|chen** *(Amtsspr. svw.* Hupzeichen)
Schalm, der; -[e]s, -e *(Forstw.* in die Rinde eines Baumes geschlagenes Zeichen)
Schal|mei, die; -, -en (ein Holzblasinstrument; *auch für* Register der Klarinette u. der Orgel); **Schal|mei|blä|ser; Schal|mei|en|klang**
schal|men *(Forstw.* einen Baum mit einem Schalm versehen)
Schal|obst *vgl.* Schalenobst
scha|lom! ⟨hebr., „Friede"⟩ (hebr. Begrüßungsformel)
Schal|lot|te, die; -, -n ⟨franz.⟩ (eine kleine Zwiebel)
Schalt‿an|la|ge, ...bild, ...brett, ...ele|ment (↑R 132); **schal|ten;** er hat geschaltet (beim Autofahren den Gang gewechselt; *ugs. für* begriffen, verstanden, reagiert); sie hat damit nach Belieben geschaltet [u. gewaltet]; **Schal|ter; Schal|ter‿be|am|te, ...dienst, ...hal|le, ...raum, ...schluss** (der; -es), **...stun|den** *(Plur.);* **Schalt‿ge|trie|be, ...he|bel**
Schal|tier (Muschel; Schnecke)
Schalt‿jahr, ...knüp|pel, ...kreis, ...plan *(vgl.* [2]Plan), **...pult, ...satz** *(Sprachw.),* **...sche|ma** (Schaltplan), **...skiz|ze, ...stel|le, ...ta|fel, ...tag, ...tisch, ...uhr; Schal|tung; Schal|tungs|über|sicht** (↑R 132); **Schalt‿werk, ...zei|chen** *(Elektrotechnik),* **...zent|ra|le**
Scha|lung (Bretterverkleidung); **Schä|lung** (Entfernung der Schale, der Haut u. a.)
Scha|lup|pe, die; -, -n ⟨franz.⟩ (Küstenfahrzeug; *auch für* größeres [Bei]boot)
Schal|wild *vgl.* Schalenwild
Scham, die; -
Scha|ma|de, die; -, -n ⟨franz.⟩ *(früher für* [mit der Trommel oder Trompete gegebenes] Zeichen der Kapitulation); - schlagen, blasen *(übertr. für* klein beigeben, aufgeben)
Scha|ma|ne, der; -n, -n (↑R 126) ⟨sanskr.-tungus.⟩ (Zauberpriester bei [asiat.] Naturvölkern); **Scha|ma|nis|mus,** der; - (eine Religionsform)
Scham‿bein *(Med.),* **...berg, ...drei|eck; schä|men,** sich; er schämte sich seines Verhaltens, *heute meist* wegen seines Verhaltens
scham|fi|len *(Seemannsspr.* scheuern); er hat schamfilt
Scham‿ge|fühl (das; -s), **...ge|gend** (die; -), **...haar** *(meist Plur.);* **scham|haft; Scham|haf|tig|keit,** die; -; **schä|mig** *(landsch. für* verschämt); **Schä|mig|keit,** die; -; **Scham|lip|pe** *meist Plur.* (äußeres weibl. Geschlechtsorgan); **scham|los; Scham|lo|sig|keit**
Scham|mes, der; -, - ⟨hebr.-jidd.⟩ (Diener in einer Synagoge u. Assistent des jüd. Gemeindevorstehers)
Scha|mott, der; -s ⟨jidd.⟩ *(ugs. für* Kram, Zeug, wertlose Sachen)
Scha|mot|te, die; - ⟨ital.⟩ (feuerfester Ton); **Scha|mot|te‿stein, ...zie|gel; scha|mot|tie|ren** *(österr. für* mit Schamottesteinen auskleiden)
Scham|pon, das; -s, -s *(eindeutschend für* Shampoo); **scham|po|nie|ren** ⟨hindi-engl.⟩ (mit Shampoo einschäumen, waschen); **Scham|pun** *(eindeutschend für* Shampoo); **scham|pu|nie|ren** *vgl.* schamponieren
Scham|pus, der; - *(ugs. für* Champagner)
scham|rot; Scham‿rö|te, ...tei|le *(Plur.);* **scham|ver|let|zend; scham|voll**
schand|bar; Schand|bu|be *(veraltet);* **Schan|de,** die; -; zuschanden, *auch* zu Schanden gehen, machen, werden
Schan|deck, Schan|de|ckel *(Seemannsspr.* oberste Schiffsplanke)
schän|den; Schän|der; Schand|fleck; schänd|lich; Schänd|lich|keit; Schand‿mal *(Plur.* ...male *u.* ...mäler), **...maul** *(ugs. abwertend),* **...pfahl** *(früher),* **...tat; Schän|dung; Schand|ur|teil**
Schan|figg, das; -s (Tal zwischen Arosa und Chur)
Schang|hai, *postamtlich* Shanghai [ʃaŋˈhai] (Stadt in China); **schang|hai|en** *(Seemannsspr.* Matrosen gewaltsam heuern); sie wurden schanghait
Scha|ni, der; -s, - *(ostösterr. ugs. für* Diener; Kellner); **Scha|ni|gar|ten** *(ostösterr. für* kleiner Garten vor dem Lokal für die Bewirtung im Freien)
[1]**Schank,** der; -[e]s, Schänke *(veraltet für* Ausschank); *vgl.* Schenke; [2]**Schank,** die; -, -en *(österr. für* Raum für den Ausschank, Theke); **Schank|be|trieb; Schän|ke** *vgl.* Schenke
Schan|ker, der; -s, - ⟨lat.-franz.⟩ *(Med.* Geschwür bei Geschlechtskrankheiten); harter, weicher -
Schank‿er|laub|nis|steu|er (die), **...ge|rech|tig|keit** *(veraltet für* Schankkonzession), **...kon|zes|si|on** (behördl. Genehmigung, alkoholische Getränke auszuschenken); **Schank|stu|be,** Schänk|stu|be, Schenk|stu|be; **Schank|tisch,** Schänk|tisch, Schenk|tisch; **Schank|wirt,** Schänk|wirt, Schenk|wirt; **Schank|wirt|schaft,** Schänk|wirt|schaft, Schenk|wirt|schaft
Schan|si (chin. Provinz)
Schan|tung, Shan|tung [ʃ...], der; -s, -s ⟨nach der chin. Provinz⟩ (ein Seidengewebe); **Schan|tung|sei|de**
Schanz|ar|beit *meist Plur. (Milit.);* **Schanz|bau** *Plur.* ...bauten
[1]**Schan|ze,** die ⟨altfranz.⟩ *(veraltet für* Glückswurf, -umstand); *nur noch in* in die - schlagen (aufs Spiel setzen)
[2]**Schan|ze,** die; -, -n *(Milit. früher* geschlossene Verteidigungsanlage; *Seemannsspr.* Oberdeck des Achterschiffes; *kurz für* Sprungschanze); **schan|zen** *(früher* an einer [2]Schanze arbeiten); du schanzt; **Schan|zen‿bau** *(vgl.* Schanzbau), **...re|kord** *(Sport),* **...tisch** (Absprungfläche einer Sprungschanze); **Schan|zer** *(Milit. früher);* **Schanz‿kleid** *(See-*

mannsspr. Schiffsschutzwand), **...werk** (*früher für* Festungsanlage), **...zeug** *(Milit. früher)*
Schapf, der; -[e]s, -e *u.* **Schap|fe,** die; -, -n (*landsch. für* Schöpfgefäß mit langem Stiel)
Schap|ka, die; -, -s ‹slaw.› (Kappe, Mütze [aus Pelz]); *vgl. aber* Tschapka
Schapp, der *od.* das; -s, -s (*Seemannsspr.* Schrank, Fach); *vgl. auch* Schaff *u.* [2]Schaft
[1]**Schap|pe,** die; -, -n ‹franz.› (ein Gewebe aus Seidenabfall)
[2]**Schap|pe,** die; -, -n (*Bergmannsspr.* Tiefenbohrer)
Schap|pel, das; -s, - ‹franz.› (*landsch. für* Kopfschmuck)
Schap|pe|sei|de (*svw.* [1]Schappe)
[1]**Schar,** die; -, -en (größere Anzahl, Menge, Gruppe); [2]**Schar,** die; -, -en, *fachspr.* das; -[e]s, -e (Pflugschar)
Scha|ra|de, die; -, -n ‹franz.› (Worträtsel, bei dem das zu erratende Wort in Silben od. Teile zerlegt wird)
Schär|baum (*Weberei* Garn- od. Kettbaum)
Schar|be, die; -, -n (Kormoran)
Schar|bock, der; -[e]s ‹niederl.› (*veraltet für* Skorbut); **Scharbocks|kraut,** das; -[e]s
Schä|re, die; -, -n *meist Plur.* ‹schwed.› (kleine, der Küste vorgelagerte Felsinsel)
scha|ren, sich
schä|ren (*Weberei* Kettfäden aufziehen)
Schä|ren‿kreu|zer (ein Segelboot), **...küs|te**
scha|ren|wei|se
scharf; schärfer, schärfste; ein scharfes Getränk; scharfes S (*für* Eszett); (↑R 47): er ist ein Scharfer (*ugs. für* ein strenger Polizist, Beamter u. Ä.); etwas aufs, auf das Schärfste, *auch* schärfste verurteilen; (↑R 39): scharf durchgreifen, sehen, schießen usw.; *vgl. aber* scharfmachen; **scharf|äugig** *(selten);* **Scharf|blick,** der; -[e]s; **Schär|fe,** die; -, -n; **Scharfein|stel|lung,** die; -; **schär|fen; Schär|fen|tie|fe,** die; - *(Fotogr.);* **scharf|kan|tig**
scharf|ma|chen; ↑R 38 f. (*ugs. für* aufhetzen, scharfe Maßregeln befürworten); ich mache scharf; scharfgemacht, scharfzumachen; *vgl. aber* das Messer scharf machen (schärfen); **Scharfma|cher; Scharf|ma|che|rei; Scharf‿rich|ter** (*für Henker),* **...schie|ßen** (das; -s), **...schüt|ze; scharf|sich|tig; Scharf|sich|tigkeit,** die; -; **Scharf|sinn,** der; -[e]s; **scharf|sin|nig; Schärfung; scharf‿za|ckig, ...zah|nig, ...zün|gig; Scharf|zün|gig|keit,** die; -
Schär|has|pel ‹*zu* schären›
Scha|ria, Sche|ria, die; - ‹arab.› (religiöses Gesetz des Islam)
[1]**Schar|lach,** der, *österr.* das; -s ‹mlat.› (lebhaftes Rot); [2]**Scharlach,** der; -s (eine Infektionskrankheit); **Schar|lach|ausschlag; schar|la|chen** (hochrot); **Schar|lach|far|be,** die; -; **scharlach‿far|ben** *od.* **...far|big; Schar|lach|fie|ber,** das; -s; **schar|lach|rot**
Schar|la|tan, der; -s, -e ‹franz.› (Schwindler, der bestimmte Fähigkeiten vortäuscht); **Schar|la|ta|ne|rie,** die; -, ...ien
Scharm *vgl.* Charme; **schar|mant** *vgl.* charmant
Schär|ma|schi|ne *(Weberei); vgl.* schären
schar|mie|ren (*veraltet für* bezaubern; entzücken)
Schar|müt|zel, das; -s, - (kurzes, kleines Gefecht, Plänkelei); **schar|müt|zeln** *(veraltet);* ich ...[e]le (↑R 16); **schar|mut|zieren** (*veraltet, aber noch landsch. für* flirten)
Scharn, der; -[e]s, -e *u.* Schar|ren, der; -s, - (*landsch. für* Verkaufsstand für Fleisch od. Brot)
Scharn|horst (preuß. General)
Schar|nier, das; -s, -e ‹franz.› (Drehgelenk [für Türen]); **Scharnier‿band** (das; *Plur.* ...bänder), **...ge|lenk**
Schär|pe, die; -, -n (um Schulter od. Hüften getragenes breites Band)
Schar|pie, die; - ‹franz.› (*früher für* zerzupfte Leinwand als Verbandmaterial)
Schär|rah|men ‹*zu* schären›
Schar|re, die; -, -n (ein Werkzeug zum Scharren); **Scharr|ei|sen; schar|ren**
Schar|ren *vgl.* Scharn
Schar|rer; Scharr|fuß (*veraltet für* Kratzfuß); **scharr|fü|ßeln** *(veraltet);* ich ...[e]le (↑R 16); gescharrfüßelt
Schar|rier|ei|sen (ein Steinmetzwerkzeug); **schar|rie|ren** ‹franz.› (mit dem Scharriereisen bearbeiten)
Schar|schmied (Schmied, der Pflugscharen herstellt)
Schar|te, die; -, -n (Einschnitt; [Mauer]lücke; schadhafte Stelle [an einer Schneide]); eine - auswetzen (*ugs. für* einen Fehler wieder gutmachen; eine Niederlage o. Ä. wettmachen)
Schar|te|ke, die; -, -n (wertloses Buch, Schmöker; *abwertend für* ältliche, unsympathische Frau)
schar|tig
Schär|trom|mel ‹*zu* schären›
Scha|rung (*Geogr.* spitzwinkliges Zusammenlaufen zweier Gebirgszüge)
Schar|wen|zel, Scher|wen|zel, der; -s, - ‹tschech.› (*landsch. für* Unter, Bube [in Kartenspielen]; *veraltend für* übertrieben dienstbeflissener Mensch); **schar|wenzeln,** scher|wen|zeln (*ugs. für* sich dienernd hin u. her bewegen; herumscharwenzeln); ich ...[e]le (↑R 16); er hat scharwenzelt, scherwenzelt
Schar|werk (*veraltet für* Fronarbeit; harte Arbeit); **schar|werken** (*landsch. für* Gelegenheitsarbeiten ausführen); gescharwerkt; **Schar|wer|ker** *(landsch.)*
Schasch|lik, der *od.* das; -s, -s ‹russ.› (am Spieß gebratene oder gegrillte Fleischstückchen mit Zwiebelringen, Paprika u. Speckscheiben)
schas|sen ‹franz.› (*ugs. für* [von der Schule, der Lehrstätte, aus dem Amt] jagen); du schasst, er schasst; du schasstest; geschasst; schasse! *u.* schass!; **schas|sieren** (mit kurzen, gleitenden Schritten geradlinig tanzen)
schat|ten (*geh. für* Schatten geben); geschattet; **Schat|ten,** der; -s, -; Schatten spenden; der Baum spendet Schatten, hat Schatten gespendet; Schatten zu spenden; ein Schatten spendender Baum; **Schat|ten‿bild, ...bo|xen** (das; -s), **...da|sein; schat|ten|haft; schat|ten|halb** (*schweiz. für* auf der Schattenseite eines Bergtals); **Schat|ten‿ka|bi|nett, ...kö|nig; schat|ten|los; Schat|ten‿mo|rel|le** (eine Sauerkirschsorte), **...pflan|ze** *(Bot.),* **...re|gie|rung; schat|ten|reich; Schat|tenreich** *(Mythol.);* **Schat|ten‿riss, ...sei|te; schat|ten|sei|tig; Schat|ten spen|dend** *vgl.* Schatten; **Schat|ten‿spiel, ...the|a|ter, ...wirt|schaft** (die; -; Gesamtheit der wirtschaftlichen Betätigungen, die nicht amtl. erfasst werden können [z. B. Schwarzarbeit]); **schat|tie|ren** ([ab]schatten); **Schat|tie|rung; schat|tig; Schatt|sei|te** (*österr. u. schweiz. neben* Schattenseite); **schatt|seitig** (*österr. u. schweiz. neben* schattenseitig)
Scha|tul|le, die; -, -n ‹mlat.› (Geld-, Schmuckkästchen; *früher für* Privatkasse eines Fürsten)

Schatz, der; -es, Schätze; **Schatz-amt, ...an|wei|sung; schätz-bar; Schätz|bar|keit**, die; -; **Schätz|chen; schat|zen** (*veraltet für* mit Abgaben belegen); du schatzt; **schät|zen;** du schätzt; schätzen lernen; sie haben sich schätzen gelernt; **schät|zens-wert; Schät|zer; Schatz-grä-ber, ...in|sel, ...kam|mer, ...kanz-ler** (*in Großbritannien*); **Schatz-käst|chen** *od.* **...käst|lein; Schatz-meis|ter, ...meis|te|rin; Schätz|preis; Schatz-su|che, ...su|cher; Schat|zung** (*veraltet für* Belegung mit Abgaben; *schweiz. für* [amtliche] Schätzung des Geldwerts); **Schät|zung; schät|zungs|wei|se; Schatz-wech|sel** (*Bankw.* Schatzanweisung in Wechselform mit kurzer Laufzeit); **Schätz|wert**

schau (*ugs. veraltend für* ausgezeichnet, wunderbar); **Schau**, die; -, -en (Ausstellung, Überblick; Vorführung); zur Schau stehen, stellen, tragen; jmdm. die Schau stehlen (*ugs. für* ihn um die Beachtung u. Anerkennung der anderen bringen)

Schaub, der; -[e]s, Schäube (*südd., österr., schweiz. mdal. für* Garbe, Strohbund); 3 - (↑R 90)

schau|bar (*veraltet für* sichtbar)

Schau|be, die; -, -n ‹arab.› (weiter, vorn offener Mantelrock des MA.)

Schau|be|gier; schau|be|gie|rig (*geh. für* schaulustig)

Schau|ben|dach (*veraltet für* Strohdach)

Schau-bild, ...brot (*meist Plur.; jüd. Rel.*), **...bu|de, ...büh|ne**

Schau|der, der; -s, -; Schauder erregen; der Film erregt Schauder, hat Schauder erregt; Schauder zu erregen; ein Schauder erregendes Ereignis; **schau|der|bar** (*ugs. scherzh. für* schauderhaft); **Schau|der er|re|gend** *vgl.* Schauder; **Schau|der|ge|schich-te; schau|der|haft; schau|dern;** ich ...ere (↑R 16); mir *od.* mich schaudert; **schau|der|voll** (*geh.*)

schau|en

¹**Schau|er**, der; -s, - (*Seemannsspr.* Hafen-, Schiffsarbeiter)

²**Schau|er** (*selten für* Schauender)

³**Schau|er**, der; -s, - (Schreck; Regenschauer)

⁴**Schau|er**, der *od.* das; -s, - (*landsch. für* Schutzdach; *auch für* offener Schuppen)

schau|er|ar|tig; -e Regenfälle; **Schau|er-bild, ...ge|schich|te; schau|er|lich; Schau|er|lich-keit**

Schau|er|mann, der; -[e]s, ...leute (*Seemannsspr.* Hafen-, Schiffsarbeiter)

Schau|er|mär|chen; schau|ern; ich ...ere (↑R 16); mir *od.* mich schauert; **Schau|er|ro|man; schau|er|voll**

Schau|fel, die; -, -n; **Schau|fel-bag|ger, ...blatt; Schäu|fe|le**, das; -s, - (*Gastron.* geräuchertes od. gepökeltes Schulterstück vom Schwein); **schau|fel|för|mig; schau|fe|lig**, schauf|lig; **Schau-fel|la|der; schau|feln;** ich ...[e]le (↑R 16); **Schau|fel|rad; Schau-fel|rad|damp|fer**

Schau|fens|ter; Schau|fens|ter-aus|la|ge, ...bum|mel, ...de|ko-ra|ti|on, ...pup|pe, ...wett|be-werb

Schauf|ler (Damhirsch)

schauf|lig *vgl.* schaufelig

Schau|ge|schäft, das; -[e]s

Schau|ins|land (Berg im südl. Schwarzwald)

Schau-kampf, ...kas|ten

Schau|kel, die; -, -n; **Schau-kel|be|we|gung; Schau|ke|lei; schau|ke|lig**, schauk|lig; **schau-keln;** ich ...[e]le (↑R 16); **Schau-kel-pferd, ...po|li|tik** (die; -), **...reck, ...stuhl; Schauk|ler; schauk|lig** *vgl.* schaukelig

schau|lau|fen *nur im Infinitiv u. Partizip gebr.*; **Schau-lau|fen** (das; -s; *Eiskunstlauf*), **...lust** (die; -); **schau|lus|tig;** eine -e Menge; **Schau|lus|ti|ge**, der *u.* die; -n, -n (↑R 5 ff.)

Schaum, der; -[e]s, Schäume; **Schaum|bad; schäum|bar;** -e Stoffe; **schaum|be|deckt** (↑R 40); **Schaum-bla|se, ...blu-me** (beim Bier)

Schaum|burg-Lip|pe (Landkreis in Niedersachsen); **schaum-burg-lip|pisch**

schäu|men; Schaum-ge|bäck, ...ge|bo|re|ne (die; -n; Beiname der aus dem Meer aufgetauchten Aphrodite [*vgl.* Anadyomene]); **schaum|ge|bremst;** -e Waschmittel; **Schaum-gold, ...gum|mi** (der; -s, -[s]); **schau|mig; Schaum-kel|le, ...kraut, ...kro-ne, ...löf|fel, ...lösch|ge|rät, ...rol|le** (*österr. für* mit Schlagsahne gefülltes Gebäck), **...schlä|ger** (ein Küchengerät; *auch für* Angeber, Blender); **Schaum|schlä-ge|rei** (*abwertend*); **Schaum-spei|se, ...stoff, ...stoff|kis-sen, ...tep|pich** (*Flugw.*)

Schau|mün|ze

Schaum|wein; Schaum|wein-steu|er, die

Schau-ob|jekt, ...or|ches|ter, ...pa|ckung, ...platz, ...pro-gramm, ...pro|zess

schau|rig; schaurig-schön (↑R 27); **Schau|rig|keit**, die; -

Schau-sei|te, ...spiel; Schau-spie|ler; Schau|spie|ler|be|ruf; Schau|spie|le|rei, die; -; **Schau-spie|le|rin; schau|spie|le|risch; schau|spie|lern;** ich ...ere (↑R 16); geschauspielert; zu -; **Schau|spiel-haus, ...kunst, ...schu|le, ...schü|ler, ...schü|le-rin, ...un|ter|richt; Schau-stel-ler, ...stel|le|rin, ...stel|lung, ...stück, ...ta|fel, ...tanz**

Schau|te *vgl.* ¹Schote

Schau-tur|nen (das; -s), **...tur-nier**

¹**Scheck**, *schweiz.* Cheque, *auch* Check [ʃɛk], der; -s, -s ‹engl.› (Zahlungsanweisung [an eine Bank]); ein ungedeckter -

²**Scheck**, der; -en, -en; *vgl.* ¹Schecke

Scheck-ab|tei|lung, ...be|trug, ...be|trü|ger, ...be|trü|ge|rin, ...buch, ...dis|kon|tie|rung

¹**Sche|cke**, der; -n, -n ‹franz.› (scheckiges Pferd od. Rind);

²**Sche|cke**, die; -, -n (scheckige Stute od. Kuh)

Scheck-fä|hig|keit (die; -), **...fäl-schung, ...heft; scheck|heft|ge-pflegt;** ein -es Auto

sche|ckig; das Pferd ist scheckig braun (↑R 40)

Scheck-in|kas|so, ...kar|te, ...recht (das; -[e]s), **...ver|kehr**

Scheck|vieh (scheckiges Vieh)

Sched|bau, Shed|bau [ʃ...] *Plur.* ...bauten ‹engl.; dt.› (eingeschossiger Bau mit Scheddach); **Sched|dach**, Shed|dach (sägezahnförmiges Dach)

scheel (*ugs. für* missgünstig, geringschätzig); scheel blicken; ich blicke scheel; scheel geblickt; scheel zu blicken; ein scheel blickender Mensch

Scheel (vierter dt. Bundespräsident)

scheel|äu|gig (*svw.* scheel blickend); **scheel bli|ckend** *vgl.* scheel; **Scheel|sucht**, die; - (*veraltend für* Neid, Missgunst); **scheel|süch|tig** (*veraltend*)

Sche|fe, die; -, -n (*südd. für* ³Schote)

Schef|fel, der; -s, - (ein altes Hohlmaß); **schef|feln** (*ugs. für* [geizig] zusammenraffen); ich ...[e]le (↑R 16); es scheffelt (es kommt viel ein); **schef|fel|wei|se**

Sche|he|ra|za|de, Sche|he|re|za-de [*beide* ...'za:də] ‹pers.› (Märchenerzählerin aus Tausendundeiner Nacht)

Scheib|band, das; -[e]s, ...bänder (*österr. für* Brustriemen zum Karrenziehen); **Scheib|chen; scheib|chen|wei|se; Schei|be**, die; -, -n; **schei|ben** (*bayr., österr. für* rollen, [Kegel] schieben); **Schei|ben‿brem|se, ...brot** (Schnittbrot); **schei|ben|för|mig; Schei|ben‿gar|di|ne, ...han|tel, ...ho|nig, ...kleis|ter** (der; -s; *verhüllend für* Scheiße), **...kupp|lung, ...schie|ßen** (das; -s); **Schei|ben|wasch|an|la|ge; Schei|ben‿wa|scher, ...wi|scher; schei|big; Scheib|tru|he** (*österr. für* Schubkarren)

Scheich, der; -s, *Plur.* -e *u.* -s ‹arab.› ([Stammes]oberhaupt in arab. Ländern; *ugs. für* Freund, Liebhaber); **Scheich|tum**

Schei|de, die; -, -n; **Schei|de|brief** (*veraltet für* Scheidungsurkunde)

Schei|degg, die; - (Name zweier Pässe in der Schweiz); die Große -, die Kleine -

Schei|de‿kunst (die; -; alter Name der Chemie), **...mün|ze** (*veraltet*); **schei|den**; du schiedst; du schiedest; geschieden (*vgl. d.*); scheid[e]!; **Schei|den|ent|zün|dung** (*Med.*); **Schei|de‿wand, ...was|ser** (*Plur.* ...wässer; *Chemie*), **...weg; Schei|ding**, der; -s, -e (*alte Bez. für* September); **Schei|dung; Schei|dungs‿an|walt, ...grund, ...kla|ge, ...pro|zess, ...rich|ter, ...ur|teil**

Scheik *vgl.* Scheich

Schein, der; -[e]s, -e; **Schein‿an|griff, ...ar|chi|tek|tur** (die nur gemalten Architekturteile auf Wand od. Decke), **...ar|gu|ment, ...asy|lant** (↑R 132); **schein|bar** (nur dem [der Wirklichkeit nicht entsprechenden] Scheine nach); er hörte scheinbar aufmerksam zu (in Wirklichkeit gar nicht), *aber* er hörte anscheinend (= augenscheinlich, offenbar) aufmerksam zu; **Schein‿be|schäf|ti|gung, ...blü|te, ...da|sein; schei|nen**; du schienst; du schienest; geschienen; schein[e]!; die Sonne schien, hat geschienen; sie kommt scheint's (*ugs. für* anscheinend) erst morgen; **Schein‿fir|ma, ...frie|de, ...frucht** (*Biol.*), **...füß|chen** (bei Amöben), **...ge|fecht, ...ge|schäft, ...ge|sell|schaft, ...ge|sell|schaf|ter, ...ge|winn, ...grund, ...grün|dung; schein|hei|lig; Schein|hei|li|ge**, der *u.* die; -n, -n (↑R 5 ff.); **Schein|hei|lig|keit**, die; -; **Schein‿kauf, ...kauf|mann** (*Rechtsspr.*), **...prob|lem, ...tod** (der; -[e]s); **schein|tot; Schein|to|te**, der *u.* die; -en, -en (↑R 5 ff.); **Schein‿ver|trag, ...welt, ...wer|fer; Schein|wer|fer‿ke|gel, ...licht** (das; -[e]s); **Schein|wi|der|stand** (*Elektrotechnik*)

Scheiß, der; - (*derb für* unangenehme Sache; Unsinn); **Scheiß|dreck** (*derb*); **Schei|ße**, die; - (*derb*); **scheiß|egal** (↑R 132; *derb*); **schei|ßen** (*derb*); ich schiss; du schissest; geschissen; scheiß[e]!; **Schei|ßer** (*derb*); **Schei|ße|rei**, die; - (*derb*); **scheiß|freund|lich** (*derb für* übertrieben freundlich); **Scheiß‿haus** (*derb*), **...kerl** (*derb*), **...la|den** (*derb*); **scheiß‿li|be|ral** (*derb*), **...vor|nehm; Scheiß|wet|ter** (*derb*)

Scheit, das; -[e]s, *Plur.* -e, *bes. österr. u. schweiz.* -er (Holzscheit; *landsch. für* Spaten)

Schei|tel, der; -s, -; **Schei|tel‿bein** (ein Schädelknochen), **...li|nie; schei|teln**; ich ...[e]le (↑R 16); **Schei|tel|punkt; schei|tel|recht** (*veraltet für* senkrecht); **Schei|tel‿wert, ...win|kel**

schei|ten (*schweiz. für* Holz spalten); **Schei|ter|hau|fen; schei|tern**; ich ...ere (↑R 16); **Scheit|holz; scheit|recht** (*veraltet für* waagerecht u. geradlinig); **Scheit|stock**, der; -[e]s, ...stöcke (*schweiz. für* Holzklotz zum Holzspalten)

Sche|kel, der; -s, - ‹hebr.› (israel. Währungseinheit); *vgl.* Sekel

Schelch, der *od.* das; -[e]s, -e (*rhein., ostfränk. für* größerer Kahn)

Schel|de, die; - (Zufluss der Nordsee)

Schelf, der *od.* das; -s, -e ‹engl.› (*Geogr.* Festlandsockel; Flachmeer entlang der Küste)

Schel|fe, Schil|fe, die; -, -n (*landsch. für* [Frucht]hülse, [2]Schale); **schel|fen**, schil|fen (*seltener für* schelfern, schilfern); **schel|fe|rig**, schelf|rig, schil|fe|rig, schilf|rig (*landsch.*); **schel|fern**, schil|fern (*landsch. für* in kleinen Teilen od. Schuppen abschälen); ich ...ere (↑R 16); **schelf|rig** *vgl.* schelferig

Schel|lack, der; -[e]s, -e ‹niederl.› (ein Harz)

[1]**Schel|le**, die; -, -n (ringförmige Klammer [an Rohren u. a.])

[2]**Schel|le**, die; -, -n (Glöckchen; *landsch. für* Ohrfeige); **schel|len; Schel|len** *Plur., als Sing. gebraucht* (eine Spielkartenfarbe); -sticht; **Schel|len‿ass, ...baum** (Instrument der Militärkapelle); **Schel|len|ge|läut** *od.* **...ge|läu|te; Schel|len‿kap|pe, ...kö|nig**

Schell|fisch

Schell|ham|mer (ein Werkzeug)

Schell|hengst *vgl.* Schälhengst

Schel|ling (dt. Philosoph)

Schell|kraut, das; -[e]s (*älter für* Schöllkraut); **Schell|wurz**

Schelm, der; -[e]s, -e (Spaßvogel, Schalk); **Schel|men‿ro|man, ...streich, ...stück; Schel|me|rei; schel|misch**

Schels|ky (dt. Soziologe)

Schel|te, die; -, -n (scharfer Tadel; ernster Vorwurf); **schel|ten** (schimpfen, tadeln); du schiltst, er schilt; du schaltst, er schalt; du schöltest; gescholten; schilt!

Schel|to|pu|sik, der; -s, -e ‹russ.› (eine Schleiche)

Schelt‿re|de (*geh.*), **...wort** (*Plur.* ...wörter *u.* ...worte; *geh.*)

Sche|ma, das; -s, *Plur.* -s *u.* -ta, *auch* Schemen ‹griech.› (Muster, Aufriss; Konzept); nach - F (gedankenlos u. routinemäßig); **Sche|ma|brief; sche|ma|tisch**; eine -e Zeichnung; **sche|ma|ti|sie|ren** (nach einem Schema behandeln; [zu sehr] vereinfachen); **Sche|ma|ti|sie|rung; Sche|ma|tis|mus**, der; -, ...men (gedankenlose Nachahmung eines Schemas; statist. Handbuch einer kath. Diözese od. eines geistl. Ordens, *österr. auch* der öffentlichen Bediensteten)

Schem|bart (Maske mit Bart); **Schem|bart‿lau|fen** (das; -s), **...spiel**

Sche|mel, der; -s, -

[1]**Sche|men**, der; -s, - (Schatten[bild]; *landsch. für* Maske)

[2]**Sche|men** (*Plur. von* Schema)

sche|men|haft ‹*zu* [1]Schemen›

Schen|jang (Stadt in Nordostchina)

Schenk, der; -en, -en; ↑R 126 (*veraltet für* Diener [zum Einschenken]; Wirt); **Schen|ke**, *auch* Schän|ke, die; -, -n

Schen|kel, der; -s, -; **Schen|kel‿bruch** (der), **...druck** (der; -[e]s; beim Reiten), **...hals; Schen|kel|hals|bruch**, der; **Schen|kel‿kno|chen, ...stück**

schen|ken (als Geschenk geben; *älter für* einschenken)

Schen|ken|dorf (dt. Dichter)

Schen|ker (*veraltet für* Bierwirt, Biereinschenker; *Rechtsspr.* jmd., der eine Schenkung macht); **Schen|kin** (*veraltet*); **Schenk|stu|be** usw. *vgl.* Schankstube usw.; **Schen|kung; Schen|kungs|brief; Schen|kungs|steu|er**, (die); **Schen|kung-**

steu|er (*Amtsspr.;* die); **Schen|kungs|ur|kun|de**
schepp (*landsch. für* schief)
schep|pern (*ugs. für* klappern, klirren); ich ...ere (↑R 16)
Scher, der; -[e]s, -e (*südd., österr. für* Maulwurf); *vgl.* Schermaus
Scher|baum (Stange der Gabeldeichsel)
Scher|be, die; -, -n (Bruchstück aus Glas, Ton o. Ä.); **Scher|bel**, der; -s, - (*landsch. für* Scherbe); **scher|beln** (*landsch. für* tanzen; *schweiz. für* spröde klingen; klirren, rascheln); ich ...[e]le (↑R 16); **Scher|ben**, der; -s, - (*südd., österr. für* Scherbe; *Keramik* gebrannter, noch nicht glasierter Ton); **Scher|ben|ge|richt**, das; -[e]s (*für* Ostrazismus); ein - veranstalten (streng mit jmdm. ins Gericht gehen); **Scher|ben|hau|fen**
Scher|bett *vgl.* Sorbett
Sche|re, die; -, -n; **¹sche|ren** (abschneiden); du scherst, er schert; du schorst, *selten* schertest; du schörest, *selten* schertest; geschoren, *selten* geschert; scher[e]!
²sche|ren, sich (*ugs. für* sich fortmachen; sich um etwas kümmern); scher dich zum Teufel!; er hat sich nicht im Geringsten darum geschert
Sche|ren‿arm *(Technik)*, **...fern|rohr**, **...git|ter**, **...schlag** *(Fußball)*, **...schlei|fer**, **...schnitt**, **...zaun**; **Sche|rer**
Sche|re|rei *meist Plur.* (*ugs. für* Unannehmlichkeit)
Scher|fes|tig|keit *(Technik)*
Scherf|lein (*veraltend für* kleiner Geldbetrag, Spende); sein - beitragen
Scher|ge, der; -n, -n; ↑R 126 (Handlanger, Vollstrecker der Befehle eines Machthabers); **Scher|gen|dienst** *(abwertend)*
Sche|ria *vgl.* Scharia
Sche|rif, der; *Gen.* -s *u.* -en, *Plur.* -s *u.* -e[n] (↑R 126) ‹arab.› (ein arab. Titel)
Scher‿kopf (am elektr. Rasierapparat), **...kraft** (die), **...ma|schi|ne**, **...maus** (Wühlmaus, Wasserratte; *vgl.* Scher), **...mes|ser** (das)
Sche|rung *(Math., Physik)*
Scher|wen|zel usw. *vgl.* Scharwenzel usw.
Scher|wol|le
¹Scherz, der; -es, -e (*bayr., österr. ugs. für* Brotanschnitt, Kanten)
²Scherz, der; -es, -e; aus, im -; **scher|zan|do** [skɛr...] ‹ital.› (*Musik* heiter [vorzutragen]); **Scherz|ar|ti|kel**; **Scherz|bold**, der; -[e]s, -e *(ugs.)*
Scher|zel, das; -s, - (*bayr., österr. für* Brotanschnitt, Kanten; *österr. auch für* Schwanzstück vom Rind)
scher|zen; du scherzt, du scherztest; **Scherz‿fra|ge**, **...ge|dicht**; **scherz|haft**; **scherz|haf|ter|wei|se**; **Scherz|haf|tig|keit**, die; -; **Scher|zo** [ˈskɛrtso], das; -s, *Plur.* -s *u.* ...zi ‹ital.› (heiteres Tonstück); **Scherz‿rät|sel**, **...re|de**; **scherz|wei|se**; **Scherz|wort** *Plur.* ...worte
sche|sen (*landsch. für* eilen); du schest
scheu; - sein, werden; - machen; **Scheu**, die; - (Angst, banges Gefühl); ohne -; **Scheu|che**, die; -, -n (Schreckbild, -gestalt [auf Feldern usw.]); **scheu|chen**; **scheu|en**; sich -; das Pferd hat gescheut; ich habe mich vor dieser Arbeit gescheut
Scheu|er, die; -, -n (*landsch. für* Scheune)
Scheu|er‿be|sen, **...frau**, **...lap|pen**, **...leis|te**
Scheu|er|mann|krank|heit (↑R 95), die; - *u.* **scheu|er|mann|sche Krank|heit**, die; -n - ‹nach dem dän. Orthopäden› (die Wirbelsäule betreffende Entwicklungsstörung bei Jugendlichen)
scheu|ern; ich ...ere (↑R 16); **Scheu|er‿sand**, **...tuch** (*Plur.* ...tücher)
Scheu‿klap|pe *(meist Plur.)*, **...le|der** (*svw.* Scheuklappe)
Scheu|ne, die; -, -n; **Scheu|nen|dre|scher**; *nur in* [fr]essen wie ein - (*ugs. für* sehr viel essen); **Scheu|nen|tor**, das
Scheu|re|be (eine Reb- u. Weinsorte)
Scheu|sal, das; -s, *Plur.* -e, *ugs.* ...säler; **scheuß|lich**; **Scheuß|lich|keit**
Schi usw. *vgl.* Ski usw.
Schib|bo|leth, das; -s, *Plur.* -e *u.* -s ‹hebr.› (*selten für* Erkennungszeichen, Losungswort)
Schicht, die; -, -en (Gesteinsschicht; Überzug; Arbeitszeit, bes. des Bergmanns; Belegschaft); die führende Schicht; Schicht arbeiten; zur Schicht gehen; **Schicht‿ar|beit** (die; -), **...ar|bei|ter**, **...ar|bei|te|rin**, **...be|trieb**, **...dienst**; **Schich|te**, die; -, -n (*österr. für* [Gesteins]schicht); **schich|ten**; **Schich|ten‿fol|ge** *(Geol.)*, **...kopf** *(Bergmannsspr.)*; **schich|ten|spe|zi|fisch** *(Soziol., Sprachw.)*; **schich|ten|wei|se** *vgl.* schichtweise; **Schicht‿ge|stein** *(Geol.)*, **...holz** *(Forstw.)*; **schich|tig** (*für* lamellar); **...schich|tig** (z. B. zweischichtig); **Schicht‿kä|se**, **...lohn**; **Schich|tung**; **Schicht‿un|ter|richt**, **...wech|sel**; **schicht|wei|se**, schich|ten|wei|se; **Schicht‿wol|ke** (*für* Stratuswolke), **...zeit**
schick (fein; modisch, elegant); ein -er Mantel; **Schick**, der; -[e]s ([modische] Feinheit); diese Dame hat -; **schi|cken**; es schickt sich nicht; er hat sich schnell in diese Verhältnisse geschickt; **schi|cker** (*ugs. für* leicht betrunken); **Schi|cke|ria**, die; - ‹ital.› (bes. modebewusste obere Gesellschaftsschicht); **Schi|cki|mi|cki**, der; -s, -s (*ugs. für* jmd., der viel Wert auf modische, schicke Dinge legt; modischer Kleinkram); **schick|lich** *(geh.)*; ein -es Betragen; **Schick|lich|keit**, die; - *(geh.)*; **Schick|sal**, das; -s, -e; **schick|sal|haft**; **schick|sal[s]|er|ge|ben**; **Schick|sals‿fra|ge**, **...fü|gung**, **...ge|fähr|te**, **...ge|fähr|tin**, **...ge|mein|schaft**, **...glau|be**, **...göt|tin**, **...schlag**; **schick|sals|schwan|ger** *(geh.)*; **Schick|sals|tra|gö|die**; **schick|sals|ver|bun|den**; **Schick|sals|ver|bun|den|heit**, die; -; **schick|sals|voll**; **Schick|sals|wahl** (*Politik* Wahl, von der man eine Entscheidung über das polit. Schicksal einer Regierung o. Ä. erwartet); **Schick|sals|wen|de**; **Schick|schuld**, die; - (*Rechtsspr.* Bringschuld, bei der das Geld an den Gläubiger zu senden ist)
Schick|se, die; -, -n ‹jidd.› (*ugs. abwertend für* leichtlebige Frau)
Schi|ckung (*geh. für* Fügung, Schicksal)
Schie|be‿bock (*landsch. für* Schubkarre), **...büh|ne**, **...dach**, **...de|ckel**, **...fens|ter**; **schie|ben**; du schobst; du schöbest; geschoben; schieb[e]!; **Schie|ber** (Riegel, Maschinenteil; ein Tanz; *ugs. auch für* gewinnsüchtiger Geschäftemacher, Betrüger); **Schie|be|rei**; **Schie|ber|müt|ze** *(ugs.)*; **Schie|be‿tür**, **...wi|der|stand** *(Physik)*; **Schieb|leh|re** (ein Messgerät; Messschieber); **Schie|bung** (*ugs. für* betrügerischer Handel, Betrug)
schiech (*bayr. u. österr. für* hässlich, zornig, Furcht erregend)
Schie|dam [ˈsxiː...] (niederl. Stadt); **¹Schie|da|mer** (↑R 103); **²Schie|da|mer** (ein Branntwein)
schied|lich (*veraltet für* friedfertig); - und friedlich; **schied|lich-fried|lich** (↑R 27); **Schieds‿frau**, **...ge|richt**, **...klau|sel**, **...mann** (*Plur.* ...leute *u.* ...män-

ner), **...rich|ter; Schieds|rich|ter-ball, ...be|lei|di|gung, ...ent|schei|dung; Schieds|rich|te|rin; schieds|rich|ter|lich; schieds|rich|tern;** ich ...ere (↑R 16); er hat gestern das Spiel geschiedsrichtert; **Schieds|rich|ter-stuhl, ...ur|teil; Schieds-spruch, ...stel|le, ...ur|teil, ...ver|fah|ren**

schief; die schiefe Ebene; ein schiefer Winkel; er macht ein schiefes (missvergnügtes) Gesicht; ein schiefer (scheeler) Blick; schiefe (nicht zutreffende) Vergleiche; in ein schiefes Licht geraten (falsch beurteilt werden), *aber* (↑R 108): der Schiefe Turm von Pisa. *Getrenntschreibung in Verbindung mit Verben und Partizipien* (↑R 39): schief sein, werden, stehen, halten, ansehen, urteilen, denken; die Sache ist [total] schief gegangen (misslungen); das Unternehmen ist [ziemlich] schief gelaufen (*ugs. für* missglückt); da hast du wohl [ganz] schief gelegen (*ugs. für* einen falschen Standpunkt vertreten); schief geladen haben (*ugs. für* betrunken sein); er hat die Absätze [schon sehr] schief getreten, er hat den Draht schief gewickelt; da bist du aber [ganz] schief gewickelt (*ugs. für* sehr im Irrtum); die Decke hat schief gelegen; *vgl. aber* schieflachen; **Schie|fe,** die; -

Schie|fer, der; -s, - (ein Gestein; *landsch. auch für* Holzsplitter); **Schie|fer-bruch** (der), **...dach, ...ge|bir|ge; schie|fer|grau; schie|fe|rig,** schief|rig; **schie|fern** (schieferig sein; *Weinbau* Erde mit [zerkleinertem] Schiefer bestreuen); ich ...ere (↑R 16); **Schie|fer-öl, ...plat|te, ...ta|fel; Schie|fe|rung**

schief ge|hen, schief ge|wi|ckelt *vgl.* schief; **Schief|hals** *(Med.)*; **Schief|heit; schief|la|chen,** sich (*ugs. für* heftig lachen); **schief lau|fen, lie|gen** *vgl.* schief; **schief|mäu|lig** (*veraltend für* missgünstig)

schief|rig *vgl.* schieferig

schief tre|ten *vgl.* schief; **schief|wink|lig**

schie|gen (*landsch. für* mit einwärts gekehrten Beinen gehen, [Schuhe] schief treten)

schiel|äu|gig

Schie|le (österr. Maler)

schie|len; sie schielt

Schie|mann, der; -[e]s, ...männer (*nordd. veraltend für* Bootsmannsmaat)

Schien|bein; Schien|bein-bruch (der), **...scho|ner, ...schüt|zer; Schie|ne,** die; -, -n; **schie|nen; Schie|nen-bahn, ...brem|se, ...bus, ...er|satz|ver|kehr, ...fahr|zeug; schie|nen|ge|bun|den;** -e Fahrzeuge; **schie|nen|gleich;** -er Bahnübergang; **Schie|nen-netz, ...räu|mer, ...stoß** (Stelle, an der zwei Schienen aneinander gefügt sind), **...strang, ...ver|kehr, ...weg**

[1]schier (bald, beinahe, gar); das ist schier unmöglich; **[2]schier** (*landsch. für* unvermischt, rein); schieres Fleisch

Schi|er (*Plur. von* Schi)

Schier|ling (eine Giftpflanze); **Schier|lings-be|cher, ...tan|ne** (*vgl.* Tsuga)

Schier|mon|ni|koog [sxi:rmɔnik'o:x] (↑R 132; eine der Westfriesischen Inseln)

Schieß-aus|bil|dung, ...baum|wol|le (die; -), **...be|fehl, ...bu|de; Schieß|bu|den-be|sit|zer, ...fi|gur** (*ugs. für* komische Figur); **Schieß|ei|sen** (*ugs. für* Schusswaffe); **schie|ßen** (*auch Bergmannsspr.* sprengen; *südd., österr. auch für* verbleichen); du schießt, er schießt; du schossest, er schoss; du schössest; geschossen; schieß[e]!; schießen lassen (↑R 39; *auch ugs. für* aufgeben); sie hat ihren Plan schießen lassen; **Schie|ßen,** das; -s, -; (↑R 50:) es ist zum - (*ugs. für* es ist zum Lachen); **schie|ßen las|sen** *vgl.* schießen; **Schie|ßer** (*Jargon* Fixer); **Schie|ße|rei; Schieß-ge|wehr, ...hund** (*veraltet für* Hund, der angeschossenes Wild aufspürt); *noch in* aufpassen wie ein - *(ugs.)*; **Schieß-meis|ter** (*Bergmannsspr.* Sprengmeister), **...platz, ...prü|gel** (der; *scherzh. für* Gewehr), **...pul|ver, ...schar|te, ...schei|be, ...sport** (der; -[e]s), **...stand, ...übung** (↑R 132); **schieß|wü|tig**

Schiet, der; -s ‹„Scheiße"› (*nordd. für* Kot, Dreck; Unangenehmes); **Schiet|kram**

Schi|fah|rer usw. *vgl.* Skifahrer usw.

Schiff, das; -[e]s, -e; **schiff|bar;** -machen; **Schiff|bar|keit,** die; -; **Schiff|bar|ma|chung,** die; -; **Schiff|bau** *(bes. fachspr.)*, Schiffs|bau, der; -[e]s; **Schiff-bau|er, ...bau|e|rin; Schiff|bau-in|ge|ni|eur, ...we|sen** (das; -s); **Schiff|bruch,** der; **schiff|brü|chig; Schiff|brü|chi|ge,** der *u.* die; -n, -n (↑R 5 ff.); **Schiff|brü|cke; Schiff|chen** (*auch für* eine milit. Kopfbedeckung); **Schiff|chen|ar|beit** (*svw.* Okkiarbeit); **schif|feln** (*landsch. für* Kahn fahren); ich ...[e]le (↑R 16); **schif|fen** (*veraltet für* zu Wasser fahren; *derb für* urinieren); **Schif|fer; Schif|fe|rin; Schif|fer-kla|vier** (*ugs. für* Ziehharmonika), **...kno|ten, ...müt|ze, ...schei|ße** (*derb; nur in der Wendung* dumm wie - [sehr dumm] sein); **Schiff|fahrt** (↑R 136; Verkehr zu Schiff); **Schiff|fahrts-ge|richt, ...ge|sell|schaft, ...kun|de** (die; -; *für* Navigation), **...li|nie, ...recht** (das; -[e]s), **...stra|ße, ...weg, ...zei|chen; Schiff|lein; Schiffs-agent** (↑R 132; Vertreter einer Reederei), **...arzt, ...aus|rüs|ter, ...bau** (*Plur.* ...bauten; *vgl.* Schiffbau), **...be|sat|zung, ...brief; Schiff|schau|kel,** Schiffs|schaukel (eine große Jahrmarktsschaukel); **Schiffs-eig|ner, ...fahrt** (Fahrt mit einem Schiff), **...fracht, ...glo|cke, ...hal|ter, ...he|be|werk, ...jour|nal** (Logbuch), **...jun|ge** (der), **...ka|pi|tän, ...ka|ta|stro|phe, ...koch** (der), **...la|dung, ...last, ...lis|te, ...mak|ler, ...ma|ni|fest** (für die Verzollung im Seeverkehr benötigte Aufstellung der geladenen Waren), **...mann|schaft, ...ma|schi|ne, ...mo|dell, ...na|me, ...of|fi|zier, ...pa|pie|re** *(Plur.)*, **...plan|ke, ...raum, ...re|gis|ter, ...rei|se, ...rumpf, ...schau|kel** (*vgl.* Schiffschaukel), **...schrau|be, ...ta|ge|buch, ...tau** (das), **...tau|fe, ...ver|kehr, ...werft, ...zer|ti|fi|kat, ...zim|mer|mann, ...zwie|back**

Schi|flie|gen *vgl.* Skifliegen

schif|ten (*Bauw.* [Balken] nur durch Nägel verbinden; [zu]spitzen, dünner machen; *Seemannsspr.* die Stellung des Segels verändern; verrutschen [von der Ladung]); **Schif|ter** (*Bauw.* Dachsparren); **Schif|tung**

Schi|ha|serl *vgl.* Skihaserl

Schi|is|mus, der; - ‹arab.› (eine Glaubensrichtung des Islam); **Schi|it** der; -en, -en; ↑R 126 (Anhänger des Schiismus); **Schi|i|tin; schi|i|tisch**

Schi|ka|ne, die; -, -n ‹franz.› (böswillig bereitete Schwierigkeit; *Sport* [eingebaute] Schwierigkeit in einer Autorennstrecke); **Schi|ka|neur** [...'nø:r], der; -s, -e (jmd., der andere schikaniert); **schi|ka|nie|ren; schi|ka|nös**

Schi|kjö|ring, Schi|jö|ring *vgl.* Skikjöring

Schi|ko|ree *vgl.* Chicorée

Schi|kurs *vgl.* Skikurs; **Schi|lauf** usw. *vgl.* Skilauf usw.

Schilcher (*österr. für* ²Schiller [hellroter Wein])

¹Schild, das; -[e]s, -er (Erkennungszeichen, Aushängeschild u. a.); **²Schild,** der; -[e]s, -e (Schutzwaffe)

Schild|bür|ger ‹„mit Schild bewaffneter Städter"; *später* auf die Stadt Schilda[u] bezogen› (engstirniger Mensch, Spießer); **Schild|bür|ger|streich**

Schild|drü|se; Schild|drü|sen‿hor|mon, ...über|funk|ti|on (↑R 132); **Schil|der|brü|cke** (die Fahrbahn überspannende Beschilderung); **Schil|de|rei** (*veraltet für* bildl. Darstellung); **Schil|de|rer; Schil|der|haus** *od.* **...häus|chen** (*für* Holzhäuschen für die Schildwache); **Schil|der|ma|ler; schil|dern;** ich ...ere (↑R 16); **Schil|de|rung; Schil|der|wald** (*ugs. für* Häufung von Verkehrszeichen); **Schild‿farn, ...knap|pe** *(früher);* **Schild|krot,** das; -[e]s (*landsch. für* Schildpatt); **Schild|krö|te; Schild|krö|ten|sup|pe; Schild‿laus, ...patt** (das; -[e]s; Hornplatte einer Seeschildkröte); **Schild|wa|che** *od.* **...wacht** (*veraltet für* milit. Wachposten [bes. vor einem Eingang])

Schi|leh|rer usw. *vgl.* Skilehrer usw.

Schilf, das; -[e]s, -e *Plur. selten* ‹lat.› (eine Grasart); **schilf|bedeckt** (↑R 40); **Schilf|dach**

Schil|fe *vgl.* Schelfe

¹schil|fen *vgl.* schelfen

²schil|fen (aus Schilf)

schil|fe|rig, schilf|rig *vgl.* schelferig usw.; **schil|fern,** schelfern (*landsch. für* in kleinen Teilen od. Schuppen abschälen; abschilfern); ich ...ere (↑R 16)

Schilf‿gras, ...halm; schil|fig

schilf|rig *vgl.* schelferig usw.

Schilf|rohr; Schilf|rohr|sän|ger (ein Vogel)

Schi|lift *vgl.* Skilift

Schill, der; -[e]s, -e (ein Flussfisch, Zander)

Schil|le|bold, der; -[e]s, -e (*nordd. für* Libelle)

¹Schil|ler (dt. Dichter)

²Schil|ler, der; -s, - (Farbenglanz; *landsch. für* zwischen Rot u. Weiß spielender Wein); **schil|le|rig,** schill|rig (*selten für* schillernd)

schil|le|risch, schil|lersch; schiller[i]sche Balladen (Balladen von Schiller); ihm gelangen Verse von schiller[i]schem Pathos (nach Schillers Art)

Schil|ler‿kra|gen (↑R 95), **...locke** (Gebäck; geräuchertes Fischstück); **Schil|ler|mu|se|um**

schil|lern; das Kleid schillert in vielen Farben

schil|lersch *vgl.* schillerisch

Schil|ler|wein

Schil|ling, der; -s, -e (österr. Währungseinheit; *Abk.* S, öS); 6 - (↑R 90); *vgl. aber* Shilling

schill|rig *vgl.* schillerig

Schil|lum, das; -s, -s ‹pers.› (Rohr zum Rauchen von Haschisch)

schil|pen (*svw.* tschilpen)

Schil|ten *Plur., als Sing. gebraucht* (*schweiz. für* eine Farbe der dt. Spielkarten; Schellen)

Schi|mä|re, die; -, -n ‹griech.› (Trugbild, Hirngespinst); *vgl.* Chimära usw.; **schi|mä|risch** (trügerisch)

¹Schim|mel, der; -s (weißl. Pilzüberzug auf organ. Stoffen); **²Schim|mel,** der; -s, - (weißes Pferd); **Schim|mel‿be|lag, ...bo|gen** (*Druckw.* nicht od. nur einseitig bedruckter Bogen), **...gespann; schim|me|lig,** schimmlig; **schim|meln;** das Brot schimmelt; **Schim|mel‿pilz, ...rei|ter** (der; -s; geisterhaftes Wesen der dt. Sage; Beiname Wodans)

Schim|mer; schim|mern; ein Licht schimmert

schimm|lig *vgl.* schimmelig

Schim|pan|se, der; -n, -n (↑R 126) ‹afrik.› (ein Menschenaffe)

Schimpf, der; -[e]s; *meist in* mit - und Schande; **schimp|fen; Schimp|fer; Schimp|fe|rei; schimp|fie|ren** (*veraltet für* verunglimpfen); **Schimpf|ka|no|nade; schimpf|lich** (schändlich, entehrend); **Schimpf‿na|me, ...wort** (*Plur.* ...worte *u.* ...wörter)

Schi|na|kel, das; -s, -[n] ‹ung.› (*österr. ugs. für* kleines Boot)

Schind|an|ger (*veraltet für* Platz, wo Tiere abgehäutet werden)

Schin|del, die; -, -n; **Schin|del|dach; schin|deln;** ich ...[e]le (↑R 16)

schin|den; du schindetest, *seltener* schund[e]st; geschunden; schind[e]!; **Schin|der** (jmd., der andere quält; *veraltet für* Abdecker); **Schin|de|rei**

Schin|der|han|nes; ↑R 97 (Führer einer Räuberbande am Rhein um 1800)

Schin|der|kar|re[n] *(früher)*

schin|dern (*obersächs. für* auf dem Eise gleiten); ich ...ere (↑R 16)

Schind|lu|der; *nur in Wendungen wie* mit jmdm. - treiben (*ugs. für* jmdn. schmählich behandeln); **Schind|mäh|re** (altes, verbrauchtes Pferd)

Schin|kel (dt. Baumeister u. Maler)

Schin|ken, der; -s, -; **Schin|ken‿brot, ...bröt|chen, ...klop|fen** (das; -s; ein Spiel), **...kno|chen, ...röll|chen, ...speck** (der; -[e]s), **...wurst**

Schinn, der; -s (*bes. nordd. für* Kopfschuppen); **Schin|ne,** die; -, -n *meist Plur.* (*bes. nordd. für* Kopfschuppe)

Schin|to|is|mus, der; - ‹jap.› (jap. Religion); **Schin|to|ist;** -en, -en (↑R 126); **schin|to|is|tisch**

Schi|pis|te *vgl.* Skipiste

Schipp|chen; ein - machen *od.* ziehen (das Gesicht mit aufgeworfener Unterlippe zum Weinen verziehen [von Kindern]); **Schip|pe,** die; -, -n (Schaufel; *ugs. scherzh. für* unmutig aufgeworfene Unterlippe); **schip|pen; Schip|pen** *Plur., als Sing. gebraucht* (eine Spielkartenfarbe; ³Pik); - sticht; **Schip|pen|ass** [*auch* 'ʃipən'as]

schip|pern (*ugs. für* mit dem Schiff fahren); ich ...ere (↑R 16)

Schi|ras, der; -, - ‹nach der Stadt in Iran› (ein Teppich; Fettschwanzschaf, dessen Fell als Halbpersianer gehandelt wird)

Schi|ri, der; -s, -s (*ugs. Kurzw. für* Schiedsrichter)

schir|ken (*landsch. für* einen flachen Stein über das Wasser hüpfen lassen)

Schirm, der; -[e]s, -e; **Schirm|bild; Schirm|bild‿fo|to|gra|fie, ...ge|rät** (Röntgengerät), **...rei|hen|un|ter|su|chung; Schirm|dach; schir|men** (*veraltend für* schützen); **Schir|mer; Schir|me|rin; Schirm‿fab|rik, ...fut|te|ral; Schirm|git|ter|röh|re** (*Elektrotechnik);* **Schirm‿herr, ...her|rin, ...herr|schaft, ...hül|le; Schirm|ling** (Schirmpilz); **Schirm‿macher, ...ma|che|rin, ...müt|ze, ...pilz, ...stän|der; Schir|mung**

Schi|rok|ko, der; -s, -s ‹arab.-ital.› (ein warmer Mittelmeerwind)

schir|ren (*selten für* anschirren, [an]spannen); **Schirr|meis|ter** (*früher* für Fahrzeuge u. Geräte verantwortlicher Unteroffizier); **Schir|rung**

Schir|ting, der; -s, *Plur.* -e *u.* -s ‹engl.› (ein Baumwollgewebe)

Schir|wan, der; -[s], -s ‹nach der aserbaidschanischen Steppe› (ein Teppich)

Schis|ma[1], das; -s, *Plur.* ...men *u.* ...ta ‹griech.› ([Kirchen]spaltung); **Schis|ma|ti|ker**[1] (Abtrünniger); **schis|ma|tisch**[1]

Schi|sport usw. *vgl.* Skisport usw.

Schiss, der; -es, -e *Plur. selten*

---

[1] [*auch* sçi...]

(*derb für* Kot; *nur Sing.: ugs. für* Angst); **Schis|ser,** der; -s, - (*derb für* Angsthase)

Schiss|la|weng *vgl.* Zislaweng

Schi|stock *vgl.* Skistock

Schi|wa ‹sanskr.› (eine der Hauptgottheiten des Hinduismus)

Schi|wachs *vgl.* Skiwachs

schi|zo|gen[1] ‹griech.› (*Biol.* durch Spaltung entstanden); **Schi|zo|go|nie**[1], die; - (eine Form der ungeschlechtl. Fortpflanzung); **schi|zo|id**[1] (nicht einheitlich, seelisch zerrissen); **Schi|zo|pha|sie**[1], die; - (*Med.* Sprachverwirrtheit); **schi|zo|phren**[1] (an Schizophrenie erkrankt); **Schi|zo|phre|nie**[1], die; -, ...ien (*Med.* Bewusstseinsspaltung)

Schlab|ber, die; -, -n (*landsch. für* Mundwerk); **Schlab|be|rei; schlab|be|rig,** schlabb|rig; **schlab|bern** (*ugs. für* schlürfend trinken u. essen; *landsch. für* [fortwährend] reden, schwatzen); ich ...ere (↑R 16); **schlabb|rig** *vgl.* schlabberig

Schlacht, die; -, -en

Schlach|ta, die; - ‹poln.› (der ehem. niedere Adel in Polen)

Schlacht|bank *Plur.* ...bänke; **schlacht|bar; schlach|ten; Schlach|ten‿bumm|ler** *(ugs.),* **...ma|ler; Schlach|ter, Schläch|ter** (*nordd. für* Fleischer); **Schlach|te|rei, Schläch|te|rei** (*nordd. für* Fleischerei; Gemetzel, Metzelei); **Schlacht‿feld, ...fest, ...ge|sang, ...ge|schrei, ...ge|wicht, ...haus, ...hof, ...kreu|zer, ...mes|ser** (das), **...op|fer, ...plan** (*vgl.* [2]Plan), **...plat|te; schlacht|reif; Schlacht‿ross** (das; -es, -e), **...ruf, ...schiff**

Schlacht|schitz, der; -en, -en; ↑R 126 ‹poln.› (Angehöriger der Schlachta)

Schlacht‿tag, ...tier; Schlach|tung; Schlacht|vieh; Schlacht|vieh|be|schau

schlack (*bayr. u. schwäb. für* träge; schlaff); **Schlack,** der; -[e]s (*nordd. für* breiige Masse; Schneeregen); **Schlack|darm** (*nordd. für* Mastdarm)

Schla|cke, die; -, -n (Rückstand beim Verbrennen, bes. von Koks); **schla|cken;** geschlackt; **Schla|cken‿bahn** *(Sport),* **...erz; schla|cken|frei; Schla|cken‿gru|be, ...hal|de; schla|cken|reich; Schla|cken|rost**

[1]**schla|ckern** (*landsch. für* schlenkern); ich ...ere (↑R 16); mit den Ohren -

[2]**schla|ckern** (*nordd. für* nass schneien); es schlackert; **Schla|cker‿schnee, ...wet|ter** (das)

schla|ckig; Schlack|wurst

Schlad|ming (Stadt im Ennstal); **Schlad|min|ger** (↑R 103)

Schlaf, der; -[e]s; **Schlaf|an|zug; Schlaf|an|zug‿ho|se, ...ja|cke; Schlaf|au|ge** *meist Plur.* (bei Puppen; *ugs. auch für* versenkbarer Autoscheinwerfer); **Schlaf|baum** (Baum, auf dem bestimmte Vögel regelmäßig schlafen); **Schläf|chen; Schlaf|couch**

Schlä|fe, die; -, -n (Schädelteil)

schla|fen; du schläfst; du schliefst; du schliefest; geschlafen; schlaf[e]!; schlafen gehen; [sich] schlafen legen

Schlä|fen‿ader (↑R 132), **...bein, ...ge|gend** (die; -)

Schla|fen|ge|hen, das; -s; vor dem -; **Schla|fens|zeit; Schlä|fer; Schlä|fe|rin; schlä|fern** *(selten);* mich schläfert

schlaff; Schlaff|heit, die; -

Schlaf‿gän|ger (*veraltet für* Mieter einer Schlafstelle), **...gast** (*Plur.* ...gäste), **...ge|le|gen|heit, ...ge|mach** *(geh.)*

Schla|fittchen ‹*aus* „Schlagfittich" = Schwungfedern›; *in Wendungen wie* jmdn. am *od.* beim - nehmen, kriegen, packen (*ugs. für* jmdn. packen)

Schlaf|krank|heit, die; -; **Schläf|lein; Schlaf|lied; schlaf|los; Schlaf|lo|sig|keit,** die; -; **Schlaf‿mit|tel** (das), **...müt|ze** (*auch scherzh. für* Viel-, Langschläfer; träger, schwerfälliger Mensch); **schlaf|müt|zig; Schlaf|müt|zig|keit,** die; -; **Schlaf‿pup|pe, ...rat|te** (*ugs. für* Langschläfer), **...ratz** (*svw.* Schlafratte); **schläf|rig; Schläf|rig|keit,** die; -; **Schlaf‿rock** (*vgl.* [1]Rock), **...saal, ...sack, ...stadt** (Trabantenstadt mit geringen Möglichkeiten zur Freizeitgestaltung); **Schlaf‿stel|le, ...stel|lung, ...stö|rung** *(meist Plur.),* **...sucht** (die; -); **schlaf|süch|tig; Schlaf‿tab|let|te, ...tier, ...trunk; schlaf|trun|ken; Schlaf|trun|ken|heit,** die; -; **Schlaf-wach-Rhyth|mus** *(Physiol.);* **Schlaf|wa|gen; schlaf|wan|deln;** ich ...[e]le (↑R 16); er schlafwandelte; er hat (*auch* ist) geschlafwandelt; zu -; **Schlaf|wand|ler; Schlaf|wand|le|rin; schlaf|wand|le|risch; Schlaf‿zent|rum, ...zim|mer; Schlaf|zim|mer|blick,** der; -[e]s (*ugs. für* betont sinnlicher Blick mit nicht ganz geöffneten Lidern); **Schlaf|zim|mer|ein|rich|tung**

[1]**Schlag,** der; -[e]s, Schläge; Schlag 2 Uhr; Schlag auf Schlag; [2]**Schlag,** der; -[e]s (*österr.; kurz für* Schlagobers); Kaffee mit -; **Schlag‿ab|tausch** *(Sportspr., auch übertr.),* **...ader** (↑R 132), **...an|fall; schlag|ar|tig; Schlag|ball; schlag|bar; Schlag‿baum, ...boh|rer, ...bohr|ma|schi|ne, ...bol|zen; Schla|ge,** die; -, -n (*landsch. für* Hammer); **Schlag|ei|sen** *(Jägerspr.);* **Schlä|gel,** der; -s, - ([Bergmanns]hammer; *auch für* Trommelschlägel); *vgl.* Schlegel; **Schlä|gel|chen** (kleiner Schlag); **schla|gen;** du schlägst; du schlugst; du schlügest; er hat geschlagen; schlag[e]!; er schlägt ihn (*auch* ihm) ins Gesicht; schlagende Wetter (*Bergmannsspr.* explosives Gemisch aus Grubengas und Luft); **Schla|ger** ([Tanz]lied, das in Mode ist; etwas, das sich gut verkauft, großen Erfolg hat); **Schlä|ger** (Raufbold; Fechtwaffe; Sportgerät); **Schlä|ge|rei; Schla|ger‿fes|ti|val, ...mu|sik** (die; -); **schlä|gern** (*österr. für* Bäume fällen, schlagen); ich ...ere (↑R 16); **Schla|ger‿sän|ger, ...sän|ge|rin, ...spiel** *(Sport),* **...star** (*vgl.* [2]Star), **...text, ...tex|ter** (Verfasser von Schlagertexten); **Schlä|ger‿trupp, ...trup|pe, ...typ; Schlä|ge|rung** *(österr.);* **Schla|ge|tot,** der; -s, -s (*veraltet für* brutaler Schläger, Raufbold); **schlag|fer|tig; Schlag|fer|tig|keit,** die; -; **schlag|fest; Schlag‿fluss** (*veraltet für* Schlaganfall), **...ham|mer, ...hand** *(Boxen),* **...holz, ...in|stru|ment, ...kraft** (die; -); **schlag|kräf|tig; Schlag|licht** *Plur.* ...lichter; **schlag|licht|ar|tig; Schlag‿loch, ...mann** (*Plur.* ...männer; *Rudersport*); **Schlag|obers** (↑R 132; *österr. für* Schlagsahne); **Schlag‿rahm, ...ring, ...sah|ne, ...schat|ten, ...sei|te, ...stock, ...werk** (Uhr), **...wet|ter** (*Plur.;* schlagende Wetter); **Schlag|wort** *Plur.* ...worte *u.* (*für* Stichwörter eines Schlagwortkatalogs:) ...wörter; **Schlag|wort|ka|ta|log; Schlag‿zahl** *(Rudern),* **...zei|le, ...zeug** (Gruppe von Schlaginstrumenten), **...zeu|ger, ...zeu|ge|rin**

Schlaks, der; -es, -e (*ugs. für* lang aufgeschossener, ungeschickter Mensch); **schlak|sig**

Schla|mas|sel, der, *auch, österr. nur,* das; -s ‹jidd.› (*ugs. für* Unglück, verfahrene Situation); **Schla|mas|tik,** die; -, -en (*landsch. für* Schlamassel)

[1] [*auch* sçi...]

Schlamm, der; -[e]s, *Plur.* -e *u.* Schlämme; **Schlamm_bad, ...bei|ßer** (ein Fisch); **schlam|men** (mit Wasser aufbereiten; Schlamm absetzen); **schläm|men** (von Schlamm reinigen); **schlam|mig; Schlämm|krei|de,** die; -; **Schlamm|mas|se** (↑R 136); **Schlamm|pa|ckung; Schlämm|putz** (dünner, aufgestrichener Putzüberzug); **Schlamm|schlacht** ([Fußball]spiel auf aufgeweichtem Spielfeld; mit herabsetzenden und unsachlichen Äußerungen geführter Streit); **Schlamm|ver|fu|gung** *(Bauw.)*

Schlamp, der; -[e]s, -e (*landsch. für* unordentlicher Mensch); **schlam|pam|pen** (*landsch. für* schlemmen); er hat schlampampt; **Schlam|pe,** die; -, -n (*ugs. für* unordentliche Frau); **schlam|pen** (*ugs. für* unordentlich sein); **Schlam|per** (*landsch. für* unordentlich Arbeitender; Mensch mit unordentlicher Kleidung); **Schlam|pe|rei** (*ugs. für* Nachlässigkeit; Unordentlichkeit); **schlam|pert** (*österr. ugs. für* schlampig); **schlam|pig** (*ugs. für* unordentlich; schluderig); **Schlam|pig|keit** *(ugs.)*

Schlan|ge, die; -, -n; Schlange stehen (↑R 39); **Schlän|gel|chen; schlän|ge|lig,** schläng|lig; **schlän|geln,** sich; ich ...[e]le (↑R 16) mich durch die Menge; **schlan|gen|ar|tig; Schlan|gen_be|schwö|rer, ...biss, ...brut, ...farm, ...fraß** (der; -es; *ugs. für* schlechtes Essen), **...gift, ...gru|be** (Ort, wo Gefahren drohen; gefährliche Situation), **...gur|ke** (*svw.* Salatgurke); **schlan|gen|haft; Schlan|gen_le|der, ...li|nie, ...mensch, ...tanz; schläng|lig** *vgl.* schlängelig

schlank; auf die schlanke Linie achten; - machen; **Schlan|kel,** der; -s, -[n] (*österr. ugs. für* Schelm, Schlingel); **schlan|ker|hand** (*veraltend für* ohne Weiteres); **Schlank|heit,** die; -; **Schlank|heits|kur; Schlank|ma|cher** (*ugs. für* Mittel, das das Abnehmen erleichtern soll); **schlank|weg** (*ugs. für* ohne Weiteres)

Schlap|fen, der; -s, - (*bayr., österr. ugs. für* Schlappen)

schlapp (*ugs. für* schlaff, müde, abgespannt); *vgl.* schlappmachen; **Schläpp|chen** (*landsch. für* kleiner Schlappen); **Schlap|pe,** die; -, -n ([geringfügige] Niederlage); **schlap|pen** (*ugs. für* lose sitzen [vom Schuh]; *landsch. für* schlurfend gehen); **Schlap|pen,** der; -s, - (*ugs. für* bequemer Hausschuh); **Schlap|per|milch,** die; - (*landsch. für* saure Milch); **schlap|pern** (*landsch. für* schlürfend trinken u. essen; lecken; *ugs. für* schwätzen); ich ...ere (↑R 16); **Schlapp|heit; Schlapp|hut,** der; **schlap|pig** (*landsch. für* nachlässig); **schlapp|ma|chen** (↑R 39; *ugs. für* nicht durchhalten, am Ende seiner Kräfte sein; sie haben bald schlappgemacht; **Schlapp_ohr** (*scherzh. für* Hase), **...schuh** (Schlappen), **...schwanz** (*ugs. für* willensschwacher, energieloser Mensch)

Schla|raf|fe, der; -n, -n; ↑R 126 (*veraltet für* [auf Genuss bedachter] Müßiggänger; Mitglied der Schlaraffia); **Schla|raf|fen_land** (das; -[e]s), **...le|ben** (das; -s); **Schla|raf|fia,** die; - (Schlaraffenland; Vereinigung zur Pflege der Geselligkeit unter Künstlern u. Kunstfreunden)

Schlar|fe, Schlar|pe, die; -, -n (*landsch. für* Pantoffel)

schlau

Schlau|be, die; -, -n (*landsch. für* Fruchthülle, [2]Schale); **schlau|ben** (*landsch. für* enthülsen)

Schlau|ber|ger (*ugs. für* schlauer, pfiffiger Mensch); **Schlau|ber|ge|rei,** die; - *(ugs.)*

Schlauch, der; -[e]s, Schläuche; ein - sein (*ugs. für* sehr anstrengend sein); **schlauch|ar|tig; Schlauch|boot; Schläu|chel|chen; schlau|chen** (*ugs. für* sehr anstrengend sein; *landsch. für* auf jmds. Kosten leben); **schlauch|för|mig; Schlauch|lei|tung; schlauch|los;** schlauchlose Reifen; **Schlauch_pilz, ...rol|le** (Aufrollgerät für den Wasserschlauch), **...wa|gen, ...wurm**

Schlau|der, die; -, -n (*Bauw.* eiserne Verbindung an Bauwerken); **schlau|dern** (durch Schlaudern befestigen); ich ...ere (↑R 16)

Schläue, die; - (Schlauheit); **schlau|er|wei|se**

Schlau|fe, die; -, -n (Schleife)

Schlau|fuchs (*svw.* Schlauberger); **Schlau|heit; Schlau|ig|keit** (*veraltet);* **Schlau_kopf** (*svw.* Schlauberger), **...mei|er** (*svw.* Schlauberger)

Schla|wi|ner (*ugs. für* Nichtsnutz, pfiffiger, durchtriebener Mensch)

schlecht; eine schlechte Ware; der schlechte Ruf; schlechte Zeiten; schlecht (schlicht) und recht. *Großschreibung* (↑R 47): im Schlechten und im Guten; etwas, nichts, viel, wenig Schlechtes. *Getrenntschreibung in Verbindung mit Verben und dem Partizip II* (↑R 39 f.): er wird schlecht sein, werden, singen usw.; du wirst mit ihnen schlecht auskommen; er kann in diesen Schuhen schlecht gehen; es wird ihr sicher [sehr] schlecht gehen (sie befindet sich in einer üblen Lage); du hast die Aufgabe schlecht gemacht (schlecht ausgeführt); sie hat ihn überall [ziemlich] schlecht gemacht (herabgesetzt); mit der Lösung waren wir schlecht beraten; ein schlecht bezahlter Job; der [ausgesprochen] schlecht gelaunte Besucher; **schlech|ter|dings** (durchaus); **schlecht ge|hen, schlecht ge|launt** *vgl.* schlecht; **Schlecht|heit,** die; -; **schlecht|hin** (in typischer Ausprägung; an sich; geradezu); **schlecht|hin|nig** (*Amtsspr.* absolut, völlig); **Schlech|tig|keit; schlecht ma|chen** *vgl.* schlecht; **schlecht|weg** (geradezu, einfach); **Schlecht|wet|ter,** das; -s; bei -; **Schlecht|wet|ter_front, ...geld** *(Bauw.),* **...pe|ri|o|de**

Schleck, der; -s, -e (*südd. u. schweiz. für* Leckerbissen); **schle|cken; Schle|cker** (*ugs. für* Schleckermaul); **Schle|cke|rei; schle|cker|haft** (*landsch. für* naschhaft); **Schle|cker|maul** (*ugs. für* jmd., der gern nascht); **schle|ckern;** ich ...ere (↑R 16); **schle|ckig** (*landsch. für* naschhaft); **Schleck|werk,** das; -[e]s *(landsch.)*

Schle|gel, der; -s, - (*landsch. u. österr., schweiz. für* [Kalbs-, Reh]keule); *vgl.* Schlägel

Schleh|dorn *Plur.* ...dorne (ein Strauch); **Schle|he,** die; -, -n (Schlehdorn; dessen Frucht); **Schle|hen_blü|te, ...li|kör**

[1]**Schlei,** die; - (Förde an der Ostküste Schleswigs)

[2]**Schlei** *vgl.* Schleie

Schlei|che, die; -, -n (schlangenähnliche Echse); **schlei|chen;** du schlichst; du schlichest; geschlichen; schleich[e]!; eine schleichende Krankheit; **Schlei|cher** (*svw.* Leisetreter); **Schlei|che|rei** *(ugs.);* **Schleich_han|del** (der; -s), **...kat|ze, ...pfad, ...tem|po, ...weg** (auf -en), **...wer|bung** (die; -)

Schleie, die; -, -n, *auch* Schlei, der; -[e]s, -e (ein Fisch)

Schlei|er, der; -s, -; **Schlei|er|eu|le; schlei|er|haft** (*ugs. für* rätselhaft, unbegreiflich); **Schlei|er|kraut** (eine Pflanze)

Schlei|er|ma|cher (dt. Theologe, Philosoph u. Pädagoge)
Schlei|er-schwanz (ein Fisch), **...stoff, ...tanz**
Schleif-ap|pa|rat, ...au|to|mat, ...band (das; *Plur.* ...bänder), **...bank** (*Plur.* ...bänke)
¹Schlei|fe, die; -, -n (Schlinge)
²Schlei|fe, die; -, -n (*landsch. für* Schlitterbahn); **¹schlei|fen** (schärfen; *Soldatenspr.* scharf drillen; *landsch. für* schlittern); du schliffst; du schliffest; geschliffen; schleif[e]!; **²schlei|fen** (über den Boden ziehen; sich am Boden [hin] bewegen; [eine Festung] dem Erdboden gleichmachen); du schleiftest; geschleift; schleif[e]!
Schlei|fen-fahrt, ...flug
Schlei|fer (jmd., der etw. schleift; alter Bauerntanz; *Musik* kleine Verzierung; *Soldatenspr.* rücksichtsloser Ausbilder); **Schlei|fe|rei; Schleif-kon|takt** *(Elektrotechnik)*, **...lack; Schleif|lack|mö|bel; Schleif-ma|schi|ne, ...mit|tel** (das), **...pa|pier, ...ring, ...spur, ...stein; Schlei|fung**
Schleim, der; -[e]s, -e; **Schleim|beu|tel; Schleim|beu|tel|ent|zün|dung; Schleim|drü|se; schlei|men; Schlei|mer** (*ugs. für* Schmeichler); **Schlei|me|rin; Schleim-fisch, ...haut; schlei|mig; schleim|lö|send;** -e Mittel; **Schleim-pilz, ...schei|ßer** (*derb für* Schmeichler), **...sup|pe**
Schlei|ße, die; -, -n (dünner Span; *früher* Schaft der Feder nach Abziehen der Fahne); **schlei|ßen** (*veraltet für* abnutzen, zerreißen; *landsch. für* auseinander reißen; spalten); du schleißt; er schleißt; du schlissest *u.* schleißtest, er schliss *u.* schleißte; geschlissen *u.* geschleißt; schleiß[e]!; Federn -; **Schlei|ße|rin** *(veraltet)*; **Schleiß|fe|der; schlei|ßig** (*landsch. für* verschlissen, abgenutzt)
Schleiz (Stadt im Vogtland); **Schlei|zer** (↑R 103)
Schle|mihl [*auch* 'ʃle:...], der; -s, -e ⟨hebr.-jidd.⟩ (Pechvogel; *landsch. für* gerissener Kerl)
schlemm ⟨engl.⟩; *nur in* - machen, werden; **Schlemm,** der; -s, -e *(Bridge, Whist)*; großer - (alle Stiche); kleiner - (alle Stiche bis auf einen)
schlem|men (gut u. reichlich essen); **Schlem|mer; Schlem|me|rei; Schlem|me|rin; schlem|me|risch; Schlem|mer-lo|kal, ...mahl[|zeit]**
Schlem|pe, die; -, -n (Rückstand bei der Spirituserzeugung; Viehfutter)
schlen|dern; ich ...ere (↑R 16); **Schlen|der|schritt; Schlend|ri|an,** der; -[e]s (*ugs. für* Schlamperei)
Schlen|ge, die; -, -n (*nordd. für* Reisigbündel; Buhne)
Schlen|ke, die; -, -n (*Geol.* Wasserrinne im Moor)
Schlen|ker (schlenkernde Bewegung; kurzer Umweg); **Schlen|ke|rich,** Schlenk|rich, der; -s, -e (*obersächs. für* Stoß, Schwung); **schlen|kern;** ich ...ere (↑R 16); die Arme, mit den Armen -; **Schlenk|rich** *vgl.* Schlenkerich
schlen|zen (*Eishockey u. Fußball* den Ball od. Puck [ohne auszuholen] mit einer schiebenden od. schlenkernden Bewegung spielen); du schlenzt; **Schlen|zer,** der; -s, -
Schlepp, der; *nur in den Wendungen* in - nehmen, im - haben, im - fahren; **Schlepp-an|ten|ne** *(Flugw.)*, **...damp|fer; Schlep|pe,** die; -, -n; **schlep|pen; Schlep|pen|kleid; Schlep|per** (*auch für* jmd., der einem unseriösen Unternehmen Kunden od. Besucher zuführt); **Schlep|pe|rei** *(ugs.)*; **Schlepp-kahn, ...kleid** (*svw.* Schleppenkleid), **...lift** *(Skisport)*, **...netz; Schlepp|pin|sel** (↑R 136), der; -s, - (Pinsel für den Steindruck); **Schlepp-schiff, ...schiff|fahrt** (↑R 136; die; -), **...seil, ...start** (Segelflugstart durch Hochschleppen mit einem Motorflugzeug), **...tau** (das; -[e]s, -e), **...zug**
Schle|si|en; Schle|si|er; Schle|si|e|rin; schle|sisch; (↑R 104:) schlesisches Himmelreich (ein Gericht), *aber* (↑R 108): der Erste Schlesische Krieg
Schles|wig; Schles|wi|ger (↑R 103); **Schles|wig-Hol|stein; Schles|wig-Hol|stei|ner** (↑R 103); **Schles|wig-Hol|stei|ne|rin; schles|wig-hol|stei|nisch** (↑R 106), *aber* (↑R 108): der Schleswig-Holsteinische Landtag; **schles|wi|gisch, schles|wigsch**
schlet|zen (*schweiz. mdal. für* [die Tür] zuschlagen); du schletzt
Schleu|der, die; -, -n; **Schleu|der-ball, ...be|ton, ...brett** *(Sport)*; **Schleu|de|rei; Schleu|de|rer,** Schleud|rer; **Schleu|der-gang** (der; bei der Waschmaschine), **...ge|fahr, ...ho|nig, ...kurs** (für Autofahrer), **...ma|schi|ne** (*für* Zentrifuge); **schleu|dern;** ich ...ere (↑R 16); **Schleu|der-preis** (*vgl.* ²Preis), **...pum|pe** (*für* Zentrifugalpumpe), **...sitz, ...start** *(Flugw.)*, **...wa|re** *(ugs.)*; **Schleud|rer** *vgl.* Schleuderer
schleu|nig (schnell); **schleu|nigst** (auf dem schnellsten Wege)
Schleu|se, die; -, -n; **schleu|sen;** du schleust; **Schleu|sen-kam|mer, ...tor** (das), **...wär|ter**
schleuß! (*veraltet für* schließ[e]!); **schleußt** (*veraltet für* schließt)
Schlich, der; -[e]s, -e (feinkörniges Erz; *nur Plur.: ugs. für* List, Trick); **Schli|che** *vgl.* Schlich
schlicht; ein -es Kleid; -e Leute; -e Eleganz; **Schlich|te,** die; -, -n (Klebflüssigkeit zum Glätten u. Verfestigen der Gewebe); **schlich|ten** (vermittelnd beilegen; *auch für* mit Schlichte behandeln); einen Streit -; **Schlich|ter; Schlich|te|rin; Schlicht|heit,** die; -; **Schlicht|ho|bel; Schlich|tung; Schlich|tungs-aus|schuss, ...ver|fah|ren, ...ver|such; schlicht|weg**
Schlick, der; -[e]s, -e (an organ. Stoffen reicher Schlamm am Boden von Gewässern; Schwemmland); **schli|cken** ([sich] mit Schlick füllen); **schli|cke|rig,** schlick|rig *(nordd.)*; **Schli|cker|milch,** die; - (*landsch. für* Sauermilch); **schli|ckern** (*landsch. für* schwanken; schlittern); ich ...ere (↑R 16); **schli|ckig** (*nordd. für* voller Schlick); **schlick|rig** *vgl.* schlickerig; **Schlick|watt**
Schlief, der; -[e]s, -e (*landsch. für* klitschige Stelle [im Brot]); *vgl.* Schliff; **schlie|fen** (*Jägerspr. u. südd., österr. ugs. für* in den Bau schlüpfen, kriechen); du schloffst; du schlöffest; geschloffen; schlief[e]!; **Schlie|fen,** das; -s (*Jägerspr.* Einfahren des Hundes in den [Dachs]bau); **Schlie|fer** (*Jägerspr.* Hund, der in den [Dachs]bau schlieft)
Schlief|fen (ehem. Chef des dt. Generalstabes)
schlie|fig (*landsch. für* klitschig [vom Brot])
Schlie|mann (dt. Altertumsforscher)
Schlier, der; -s (*bayr. u. österr. für* Mergel); **Schlie|re,** die; -, -n (*nur Sing.: landsch. für* schleimige Masse; streifige Stelle [im Glas]); **schlie|ren** (*Seemannsspr.* gleiten, rutschen); **schlie|rig** (*landsch. für* schleimig, schlüpfrig); **Schlier|sand,** der; -[e]s (*österr. für* feiner [Schwemm]sand)
¹Schlier|see (Ort am ²Schliersee); **²Schlier|see,** der; -s; **Schlier|se|er** [...ze:ər] (↑R 103 *u.* 105)
Schließ|an|la|ge; schließ|bar; Schlie|ße, die; -, -n; **schlie|ßen;**

du schließt, er schließt (*veraltet* er schleußt); du schlossest, er schloss; du schlössest; geschlossen; schließ[e]! (*veraltet* schleuß!); **Schlie|ßer; Schlie|ße|rin; Schließ₋fach, ...frucht** (*Bot.* Frucht, die sich bei der Reife nicht öffnet), **...ket|te, ...korb; schließ|lich; Schließ₋mus|kel, ...rah|men** (*Druckw.*); **Schlie|ßung; Schließ₋zeit, ...zy|lin|der** (im Sicherheitsschloss)

Schliff, der; -[e]s, -e (geschliffene Fläche [im Glas]; Schleifen; *nur Sing.:* Geschliffensein; *landsch. für* klitschige Stelle [im Brot], Schlief; *nur Sing.: ugs. für* gute Umgangsformen); **Schliff|flä|che** (↑R 136); **schlif|fig** (*svw.* schliefig)

schlimm; - sein, stehen; im schlimmsten Fall[e]; schlimme Zeiten; eine schlimme Lage; er ist am schlimmsten d[a]ran; *aber* es ist das Schlimmste (sehr schlimm), dass ...; das ist noch lange nicht das Schlimmste; ich bin auf das, aufs Schlimmste gefasst; sie wurde auf das, aufs Schlimmste, *auch* schlimmste getäuscht; das Schlimmste fürchten; zum Schlimmsten kommen; sich zum Schlimmen wenden; etwas, wenig, nichts Schlimmes; **schlimms|ten|falls** *vgl.* Fall, der

Schling|be|schwer|den *Plur.*

Schlin|ge, die; -, -n; [1]**Schlin|gel,** das; -s, - (*landsch. für* Öse)

[2]**Schlin|gel,** der; -s, - (*scherzh. für* übermütiger Junge; freches Kerlchen); **Schlin|gel|chen, Schlin|gel|lein**

schlin|gen; du schlangst; du schlängest; sie hat geschlungen; schling[e]!

Schlin|gen|stel|ler

Schlin|ger₋be|we|gung, ...kiel (Seitenkiel zur Verminderung des Schlingerns); **schlin|gern** (um die Längsachse schwanken [von Schiffen]); das Schiff schlingert; **Schlin|ger|tank** (Tank zur Verminderung des Schlingerns)

Schling|pflan|ze

Schlipf, der; -[e]s, -e (*schweiz. für* [Berg-, Fels-, Erd]rutsch)

Schlipp, der; -[e]s, -e ⟨engl.⟩ (*Seemannsspr.* schiefe Ebene für den Stapellauf eines Schiffes)

Schlip|pe, die; -, -n (*nordd. für* Rockzipfel; *landsch. für* enger Durchgang)

schlip|pen (*Seemannsspr.* lösen, loslassen)

Schlip|per, der; -s (*landsch. für* abgerahmte, dicke Milch); **schlip|pe|rig,** schlipp|rig (*landsch. für* gerinnend); **Schlip|per|milch,** die; - (*landsch.*); **schlipp|rig** *vgl.* schlipperig

Schlips, der; -es, -e (Krawatte); **Schlips|na|del**

Schlit|tel, das; -s, - (*landsch. für* kleiner Schlitten); **schlit|teln** (*schweiz. für* rodeln); ich ...[e]le (↑R 16); - lassen (laufen lassen, sich um etwas nicht kümmern); **schlit|ten** (*landsch.*); **Schlit|ten,** der; -s, - (↑R 39:) - fahren; ich bin Schlitten gefahren; **Schlit|ten₋bahn, ...fah|ren** (das; -s), **...fahrt, ...hund; Schlit|ter|bahn; schlit|tern** ([auf dem Eis] gleiten); ich ...ere (↑R 16); **Schlitt|schuh;** - laufen (↑R 39); ich bin Schlittschuh gelaufen; **Schlitt|schuh₋lau|fen** (das; -s), **...läu|fer, ...läu|fe|rin**

Schlitz, der; -es, -e; **Schlitz|au|ge; schlitz|äu|gig; schlit|zen;** du schlitzt; **Schlitz|ohr** (*ugs. für* gerissener Kerl); **schlitz|oh|rig** (*ugs.*); ein schlitzohriger Geschäftsmann; **Schlitz|oh|rig|keit,** die; - (*ugs.*); **Schlitz|ver|schluss** (*Fotogr.*)

schloh|weiß (ganz weiß)

Schlor|re, die; -, -n (*landsch. für* Hausschuh); **schlor|ren** (*landsch. für* schlurfen)

Schloss, das; -es, Schlösser; **Schlöss|chen**

Schlo|ße, die; -, -n *meist Plur.* (*landsch. für* Hagelkorn); **schlo|ßen** (*landsch.*); es schloßt; es hat geschloßt

Schlos|ser; Schlos|ser|ar|beit; Schlos|se|rei; Schlos|ser|hand|werk, das; -[e]s; **Schlos|se|rin; schlos|sern;** ich schlossere *u.* schlossre (↑R 16); **Schlos|ser|werk|statt; Schloss₋gar|ten, ...herr, ...her|rin, ...hof, ...hund** (*nur in der Wendung* heulen wie ein -), **...ka|pel|le, ...kir|che, ...park, ...ru|i|ne**

Schlot, der; -[e]s, *Plur.* -e, *seltener* Schlöte (*ugs. auch für* Nichtsnutz; unangenehmer Mensch); **Schlot|ba|ron** (*abwertend veraltend für* Großindustrieller [im Ruhrgebiet]); **Schlot|fe|ger** (*landsch. für* Schornsteinfeger)

Schlot|te, die; -, -n (Zwiebelblatt; *Bergmannsspr.* Hohlraum im Gestein); **Schlot|ten|zwie|bel**

schlot|te|rig, schlott|rig; **schlot|tern;** ich ...ere (↑R 16)

schlot|zen (*bes. schwäb. für* genüsslich trinken); du schlotzt

Schlucht, die; -, -en

schluch|zen; du schluchzt; **Schluch|zer; Schluck,** der; -[e]s, *Plur.* -e, *selten* Schlücke; **Schluck|auf,** der; -s; **Schluck|be|schwer|den** *Plur.*; **Schlück|chen; schlu|cken; Schlu|cken,** der; -s (Schluckauf); **Schlu|cker** (*ugs.*); *meist in* armer - (mittelloser, bedauernswerter Mensch); **Schluck|imp|fung; schluck|sen** (*ugs. für* Schluckauf haben); du schluckst; **Schluck|ser,** der; -s (*ugs. für* Schluckauf); **Schluck|specht** (*ugs. scherzh. für* Trinker); **schluck|wei|se**

Schlu|der|ar|beit; Schlu|de|rei; schlu|de|rig, schlud|rig (*ugs. für* nachlässig); **schlu|dern** (*ugs. für* nachlässig arbeiten); ich ...ere (↑R 16)

Schluff, der; -[e]s, *Plur.* -e *u.* Schlüffe (Ton; [Schwimm]sand; *landsch. für* enger Durchlass; *südd. veraltend für* Muff)

Schluft, die; -, Schlüfte (*veraltet für* Schlucht, Höhle)

Schlum|mer, der; -s; **Schlum|mer₋kis|sen, ...lied; schlum|mern;** ich ...ere (↑R 16); **Schlum|mer₋rol|le, ...stünd|chen, ...trunk**

Schlumpf, der; -[e]s, Schlümpfe (zwergenhafte Comicfigur)

Schlumps (*landsch. für* unordentlicher, wenig sympathischer Mensch)

Schlund, der; -[e]s, Schlünde

Schlun|ze, die; -, -n (*landsch. für* unordentliche Frau); **schlun|zig** (*landsch. für* unordentlich)

Schlup *vgl.* Slup

Schlupf, der; -[e]s, *Plur.* Schlüpfe *u.* -e *Plur. selten* (*veraltend für* Unterschlupf); **schlup|fen** (*südd., österr.*), *häufiger* **schlüp|fen; Schlüp|fer** ([Damen]unterhose); **Schlupf₋ja|cke, ...loch; schlüpf|rig** (*auch für* zweideutig, anstößig); **Schlüpf|rig|keit; Schlupf₋stie|fel, ...wes|pe, ...win|kel, ...zeit**

Schlup|pe, die; -, -n (*landsch. für* [Band]schleife)

schlur|fen (schleppend gehen); er hat geschlurft; er ist dorthin geschlurft; **schlür|fen** ([Flüssigkeit] geräuschvoll in den Mund einsaugen; *landsch. für* schlurfen); **Schlur|fer** (Schlurfender); **Schlür|fer** (Schlürfender; *auch landsch. für* Schlurfer); **schlur|ren** (*landsch., bes. nordd. für* schlurfen); **Schlur|ren,** der; -s, - (*nordd. für* Pantoffel)

Schlu|se, die; -, -n (*landsch. für* Schale, Hülle; *auch für* Falschgeld)

Schluss, der; -es, Schlüsse; **Schluss₋ab|stim|mung, ...ak|kord, ...akt, ...ball, ...be|ar|bei-**

tung, ...be|mer|kung, ...be|spre|chung, ...bi|lanz *(Kaufmannsspr.),* **...bild, ...brief** *(Kaufmannsspr.),* **...drit|tel** *(Eishockey);* **Schlüs|sel,** der; -s, -; **Schlüs|sel‿bart, ...bein; Schlüs|sel|bein|bruch; Schlüs|sel‿blu|me, ...brett, ...bund** (der, *österr. nur so, od.* das; -[e]s, -e); **Schlüs|sel|chen; Schlüs|sel|dienst; Schlüs|sel|er|leb|nis** *(Psych.);* **schlüs|sel|fer|tig** (bezugsfertig [von Neubauten]); **Schlüs|sel‿fi|gur, ...fra|ge, ...ge|walt** (die; -), **...in|dust|rie, ...kind** (Kind mit eigenem Wohnungsschlüssel, das nach der Schule unbeaufsichtigt ist, weil beide Eltern berufstätig sind); **Schlüs|sel|loch; schlüs|seln** (*fachspr. für* nach einem bestimmten Verhältnis [Schlüssel] aufteilen); ich schlüssele *u.* schlüssle (↑R 16); **Schlüs|sel‿po|si|ti|on, ...reiz** (*Psych.* Reiz, der eine bestimmte Reaktion bewirkt), **...ring, ...ro|man, ...stel|lung; Schlüs|se|lung; Schlüs|sel|wort** (*vgl.* Wort); **schluss|end|lich** (*landsch. für* schließlich); **Schluss‿fei|er, ...fol|ge** (*svw.* Schlussfolgerung); **schluss|fol|gern;** ich schlussfolgere (↑R 16); du schlussfolgerst; geschlussfolgert; um zu schlussfolgern; **Schluss‿fol|ge|rung, ...for|mel; schlüs|sig;** - sein; [sich] - werden; ich wurde mir darüber -; ein -er Beweis; **Schluss‿ka|pi|tel, ...kurs** *(Börse),* **...läu|fer** *(Sport),* **...läu|fe|rin** *(Sport),* **...leuch|te, ...licht** (*Plur.* ...lichter), **...mann** (*Plur.* ...männer *od.* ...leute), **...no|te** *(Rechtsw.),* **...no|tie|rung** *(Börse),* **...pfiff** *(Sport),* **...pha|se, ...punkt, ...rech|nung, ...re|dak|teur, ...re|dak|teu|rin, ...re|dak|ti|on; Schluss-s,** das; -, - (↑R 25)

Schluss|satz (↑R 136); **Schluss|sig|nal** (↑R 136; *fachspr., bes. Funkw.*); **Schluss|si|re|ne** (↑R 136); **Schluss|spurt** (↑R 136; *Sport*); **Schluss|stein** (↑R 204; *Archit.*); **Schluss|strich** (↑R 136); **Schluss|sze|ne** (↑R 136)

Schluss‿ver|kauf, ...ver|tei|lung *(Rechtsw.),* **...wort** (*Plur.* ...worte), **...zei|chen**

Schlütt|li, das; -s, - (*schweiz. für* Säuglingsjäckchen)

Schmach, die; -; **schmach|be|deckt;** ↑R 40 *(geh.);* **schmach|be|la|den;** ↑R 40 *(geh.)*

schmach|ten *(geh.);* **Schmacht|fet|zen** (*ugs. für* rührseliges Lied); **schmäch|tig; Schmacht‿korn** (*Plur.* ...körner; *Landw.* verkümmertes Korn), **...lap|pen** (*ugs. für* Hungerleider; verliebter Jüngling), **...lo|cke** (*ugs. für* in die Stirn gekämmte Locke), **...rie|men** (*ugs. für* Gürtel, Koppel)

schmach|voll *(geh.)*

[1]**Schmack,** der; -[e]s, -e (Mittel zum Schwarzfärben); *vgl.* Sumach

[2]**Schmack, Schma|cke,** die; -, -n (*früher* kleines Küsten- od. Fischerfahrzeug); **Schma|ckes** *Plur.* (*landsch. für* Schwung, Wucht; *auch für* Hiebe, Prügel)

schmack|haft; Schmack|haf|tig|keit, die; -

Schmad|der, der; -s (*bes. nordd. für* [nasser] Schmutz); **schmad|dern** (*bes. nordd. für* kleckern, sudeln); ich ...ere (↑R 16)

Schmäh, der; -s, -[s] (*österr. ugs. für* Trick); einen - führen (Witze machen); **schmä|hen; schmäh|lich; Schmäh|lich|keit; Schmäh‿re|de, ...schrift, ...sucht** (die; -); **schmäh|süch|tig; Schmäh|tand|ler** (*österr. ugs. für* jmd., der billige Tricks oder Witze macht); **Schmä|hung; Schmäh|wort** (*Plur.* ...worte)

schmal; schmaler *u.* schmäler, schmalste, *auch* schmälste; **schmal|brüs|tig; schmä|len** (*veraltend für* zanken; herabsetzen; *Jägerspr.* schrecken [vom Rehwild]); **schmä|lern** (verringern, verkleinern); ich ...ere (↑R 16); **Schmä|le|rung; Schmal|film; Schmal|fil|mer; Schmal|film|ka|me|ra; Schmal|hans;** *nur in* da ist - Küchenmeister (*ugs. für* jmd. muss sparsam leben); **Schmal|heit,** die; -

Schmal|kal|den (Stadt am Südwestrand des Thüringer Waldes); **Schmal|kal|de|ner, Schmal|kal|der** (↑R 103); **schmal|kal|disch,** *aber* (↑R 108): die Schmalkaldischen Artikel (von Luther); der Schmalkaldische Bund (1531)

schmal|lip|pig; schmal|ran|dig; Schmal‿reh (*Jägerspr.; vgl.* Schmaltier), **...sei|te, ...spur** (die; -; *Eisenb.*); **Schmal|spur‿aka|de|mi|ker** (↑R 132; *abwertend),* **...bahn; schmal|spu|rig**

Schmal|te, die; -, -n ‹ital.› (Kobaltschmelze, ein Blaufärbemittel [für Porzellan u. Keramik]); **schmal|ten** (*veraltend für* emaillieren)

Schmal‿tier (*Jägerspr.* weibl. Rot-, Dam- od. Elchwild vor dem ersten Setzen), **...vieh** (*veraltend für* Kleinvieh)

Schmalz, das; -es, -e; **Schmalz|brot; Schmäl|ze,** die; -, -n (zum Schmälzen der Wolle benutzte Flüssigkeit); *vgl. aber* Schmelze; **schmal|zen** (Speisen mit [heißem] Schmalz zubereiten, übergießen); du schmalzt; geschmalzt *u.* geschmalzen (*in übertr. Bedeutung nur so,* z. B. es ist mir zu geschmalzen [*ugs. für* zu teuer]); gesalzen und geschmalzen; **schmäl|zen** (*auch für* Wolle vor dem Spinnen einfetten); du schmälzt; geschmälzt; **Schmalz|fleisch; Schmalz|ge|ba|cke|ne,** das; -n (↑R 5 ff.); **schmal|zig** (*abwertend für* übertrieben gefühlvoll, sentimental); **Schmalz|ler,** der; -s (*bes. bayr. für* fettdurchsetzter Schnupftabak)

Schmand usw. *vgl.* Schmant usw.

Schman|kerl, das; -s, -n (*bayr. u. österr. für* eine süße Mehlspeise; Leckerbissen)

Schmant, *auch* Schmand, der; -[e]s (*landsch. für* Sahne; *ostmitteld. für* Matsch, Schlamm); **Schmant|kar|tof|feln** *Plur.*

schma|rot|zen (auf Kosten anderer leben); du schmarotzt; du schmarotztest; er hat schmarotzt; **Schma|rot|zer; schma|rot|zer|haft; Schma|rot|ze|rin; schma|rot|ze|risch; Schma|rot|zer‿pflan|ze, ...tier; Schma|rot|zer|tum,** das; -s; **Schma|rot|zer|wes|pe**

Schmar|re, die; -, -n (*landsch. für* lange Hiebwunde, Narbe); **Schmar|ren,** der; -s, - (*bayr. u. österr. für* eine Mehlspeise; *ugs. für* wertloses Zeug; Unsinn)

Schma|sche, die; -, -n ‹poln.› (*fachspr. für* Fell eines tot geborenen Lammes)

Schmatz, der; -es, *Plur.* -e, *auch* Schmätze (*ugs. für* [lauter] Kuss); **Schmätz|chen; schmat|zen;** du schmatzt; **Schmät|zer** (ein Vogel)

Schmauch, der; -[e]s (*landsch. für* qualmender Rauch); **schmau|chen; Schmauch|spu|ren** *Plur.* (*Kriminalistik* Reste unverbrannten Pulvers nach einem Schuss)

Schmaus, der; -es, Schmäuse (*veraltend, noch scherzh. für* reichhaltiges u. gutes Mahl); **schmau|sen** (*veraltend, noch scherzh. für* vergnügt u. mit Genuss essen); du schmaust; **Schmau|se|rei** *(veraltend)*

schme|cken

Schmei|che|lei; schmei|chel|haft; Schmei|chel‿kätz|chen *od.* **...kat|ze** *(fam.);* **schmei|cheln;** ich ...[e]le (↑R 16); **Schmei|chel|wort** *Plur.* ...worte;

Schmeich|ler; Schmeich|le|rin; schmeich|le|risch
schmei|dig (*veraltet für* geschmeidig); **schmei|di|gen** (*veraltend für* geschmeidig machen)
[1]**schmei|ßen** (*ugs. für* werfen; *auch für* aufgeben; misslingen lassen); du schmeißt; du schmissest, er schmiss; geschmissen; schmeiß[e]!; [2]**schmei|ßen** (*Jägerspr.* Kot auswerfen); der Habicht schmeißt, schmeißte, hat geschmeißt; **Schmeiß|flie|ge**
Schmelz, der; -es, -e; **Schmelzbad** *(Technik);* **schmelz|bar; Schmelz|bar|keit,** die; -; **Schmelz|but|ter; Schmel|ze,** die; -, -n; *vgl. aber* Schmälze; [1]**schmel|zen** (flüssig werden); du schmilzt, er schmilzt; du schmolzest; du schmölzest; geschmolzen; schmilz!; [2]**schmel|zen** (flüssig machen); du schmilzt, *auch* schmelzt; er schmilzt, *auch* schmelzt; du schmolzest, *auch* schmelztest; du schmölzest, *auch* schmelzest; geschmolzen, *auch* geschmelzt; schmilz!, *auch* schmelze!; **Schmel|zer; Schmel|ze|rei; Schmelz‿far|be, ...glas** (*Plur.* ...gläser; Email), **...hüt|te, ...kä|se, ...ofen** (↑R 132), **...punkt, ...schwei|ßung, ...tie|gel; Schmel|zung; Schmelz‿wär|me, ...was|ser** (*Plur.* ...wasser), **...zo|ne**
Schmer, der *od.* das; -s (*landsch. für* Bauchfett des Schweines); **Schmer‿bauch** (*ugs. svw.* Fettbauch), **...fluss** (der; -es; *für* Seborrhö)
Schmer|le, die; -, -n (ein Fisch)
Schmer|ling (ein Speisepilz)
Schmerz, der; -es, -en; schmerzlindernd, *aber* den Schmerz lindernd; schmerzstillend, *aber* den Schmerz stillend (↑R 40); **schmerz‿arm** (-e Geburt), **...emp|find|lich; Schmerz|emp|find|lich|keit,** die; -; **Schmerzemp|fin|dung; schmer|zen;** du schmerzt; die Füße schmerzten ihm *od.* ihn vom langen Stehen; die Wunde schmerzte ihn; **schmer|zen|reich** *vgl.* schmerzensreich; **Schmer|zens‿geld** (das; -[e]s), **...kind** *(veraltend),* **...laut, ...mann** (der; -[e]s; *Kunst* Darstellung des leidenden Christus), **...mut|ter** (die; -; *Kunst* Darstellung der trauernden Maria); **schmer|zens|reich** *(geh.);* **Schmer|zens|schrei; schmerz‿er|füllt, ...frei** (der Patient ist heute -); **Schmerz‿ge|fühl, ...gren|ze; schmerz|haft;** -e Operation; **Schmerz|haf|tig|keit,** die; -; **Schmerz|kli|nik** (Klinik für Patienten mit bestimmten sehr schmerzhaften Krankheiten); **schmerz|lich;** -er Verlust; **Schmerz|lich|keit,** die; -; **schmerz|lin|dernd** (↑R 40); *vgl.* Schmerz; **schmerzlos; Schmerz|lo|sig|keit,** die; -; **Schmerz‿mit|tel** (das); **...schwel|le; schmerz|stil|lend;** -e Tabletten (↑R 40); *vgl.* Schmerz; **Schmerz|tab|let|te; schmerz‿un|emp|find|lich, ...ver|zerrt** (↑R 40), **...voll**
Schmet|ten, der; -s ⟨tschech.⟩ (*ostmitteld. für* Sahne); **Schmetten|kä|se** *(ostmitteld.)*
Schmet|ter|ball *(Sport)*
Schmet|ter|ling; Schmet|terlings‿blü|te, ...blüt|ler *(Bot.),* **...kas|ten, ...netz, ...samm|lung, ...stil** (der; -[e]s; Schwimmstil)
schmet|tern; ich ...ere (↑R 16)
Schmi|cke, die; -, -n (*nordd. für* Peitsche; Ende der Peitschenschnur)
Schmidt-Rott|luff (dt. Maler u. Grafiker)
Schmied, der; -[e]s, -e; **schmiedbar; Schmied|bar|keit,** die; -; **Schmie|de,** die; -, -n; **Schmiede‿ar|beit, ...ei|sen** (das; -s); **schmie|de|ei|sern; Schmie|de‿feu|er, ...ham|mer, ...handwerk** (das; -[e]s), **...kunst** (die; -); **schmie|den; Schmie|deofen** (↑R 132)
Schmie|ge, die; -, -n (*Technik* Winkelmaß mit beweglichen Schenkeln; *auch landsch. für* zusammenklappbarer Maßstab); **schmie|gen;** sich -; **schmiegsam; Schmieg|sam|keit,** die; -
Schmie|le, die; -, -n (Name verschiedener Grasarten); **Schmielgras**
Schmie|ra|lie [...i̯ə], die; -, -n ⟨*Scherzbildung zu* schmieren⟩ (*ugs. scherzh. für* Schmiererei); **Schmier|dienst** (beim Auto); [1]**Schmie|re,** die; -, -n (*abwertend auch für* schlechtes Theater)
[2]**Schmie|re,** die; - ⟨hebr.-jidd.⟩ (*Gaunerspr.* Wache); - stehen
schmie|ren (*ugs. auch für* bestechen); **Schmie|ren‿ko|mö|diant** *(abwertend),* **...schau|spieler** *(abwertend),* **...stück** *(abwertend);* **Schmie|rer; Schmie|rerei; Schmier‿fett, ...film, ...fink** (der; *Gen.* -en, *auch* -s, *Plur.* -en; *ugs.*), **...geld** *(meist Plur.; ugs.),* **...heft; schmie|rig; Schmie|rigkeit,** die; -; **Schmier‿kä|se, ...mit|tel** (das), **...nip|pel, ...öl, ...pres|se, ...sei|fe; Schmierung; Schmier|zet|tel**
Schmin|ke, die; -, -n; **schminken; Schmink‿stift** (der), **...tisch**
[1]**Schmir|gel,** der; -s, - (*ostmitteld. für* Tabakspfeifensaft)
[2]**Schmir|gel,** der; -s ⟨ital.⟩ (ein Schleifmittel); **schmir|geln;** ich ...[e]le (↑R 16); **Schmir|gel|papier**
Schmiss, der; -es, -e (*nur Sing.: ugs. auch für* mitreißender Schwung); **schmis|sig** *(ugs.);* eine -e Zeichnung, Musik
[1]**Schmitz,** der; -es, -e (*veraltet, noch landsch. für* Fleck, Klecks; *Druckw.* verschwommene Wiedergabe)
[2]**Schmitz,** der; -es, -e (*landsch. für* [leichter] Hieb, Schlag); **Schmitze,** die; -, -n (*landsch. für* Peitsche, Ende der Peitschenschnur); **schmit|zen** (*landsch. für* [mit der Peitsche, Rute] schlagen)
Schmock, der; -[e]s, *Plur.* Schmöcke, *auch* -e *u.* -s ⟨slowen.; nach Freytags „Journalisten"⟩ (gesinnungsloser Zeitungsschreiber)
Schmok, der; -s (*nordd. für* Rauch); **Schmö|ker,** der; -s, - (*nordd. für* Raucher; *ugs. für* anspruchsloses, aber fesselndes Buch); **schmö|kern** (*ugs. für* [viel] lesen); ich ...ere (↑R 16)
Schmol|le, die; -, -n (*bayr., österr. für* Brotkrume)
Schmoll|ecke (↑R 132; *ugs.);* **schmol|len**
schmol|lis! (student. Zuruf beim [Brüderschaft]trinken); **Schmollis,** das; -, - *(Studentenspr.);* mit jmdm. - trinken
Schmoll|mund
Schmölln (Stadt in Ostthüringen)
Schmoll|win|kel *(ugs.)*
Schmon|zes, der; - ⟨jidd.⟩ (*ugs. für* leeres, albernes Gerede; überflüssiger Kram); **Schmon|zet|te,** die; -, -n (*ugs. für* [kitschiges] Machwerk)
Schmor|bra|ten; schmo|ren; jmdn. - lassen *(ugs.);* **Schmorfleisch**
schmor|gen (*westmitteld. für* knausern; geizig sein)
Schmor‿obst, ...pfan|ne, ...topf
Schmu, der; -s (*ugs. für* leichter Betrug); - machen (auf harmlose Weise betrügen)
schmuck; Schmuck, der; -[e]s, -e *Plur. selten;* echter -; **Schmuckblatt|te|le|gramm** (↑R 136); **schmü|cken; Schmuck|kästchen;** diese Wohnung ist ein - (rein u. nett gehalten); **Schmuck‿kas|ten, ...kof|fer; schmucklos; Schmuck|lo|sig|keit,** die; -;

Schmuck‿na|del, ...stein, ...stück, ...te|le|gramm; Schmü|ckung; schmuck|voll *(veraltet);* **Schmuck|wa|ren** *Plur.;* **Schmuck|wa|ren|in|dust|rie**
Schmud|del, der; -s (*ugs. für* Unsauberkeit); **Schmud|de|lei** (*ugs. für* Sudelei); **schmud|de|lig,** schmudd|lig (*ugs. für* unsauber); **schmud|deln** (*ugs. für* sudeln, schmutzen); ich ...[e]le (↑R 16); **Schmud|del|wet|ter** (*ugs. für* nasskaltes, regnerisches Wetter); **schmudd|lig** *vgl.* schmuddelig
Schmug|gel, der; -s; **Schmug|ge|lei; schmug|geln;** ich ...[e]le (↑R 16); **Schmug|gel|wa|re; Schmugg|ler; Schmugg|ler‿ban|de, ...ring, ...schiff**
schmu|len (*landsch. für* verstohlen blicken, schielen)
schmun|zeln; ich ...[e]le (↑R 16)
schmur|geln (*landsch. für* in Fett braten); ich ...[e]le (↑R 16)
Schmus, der; -es ‹hebr.-jidd.› (*ugs. für* leeres Gerede; Schöntun); **Schmu|se‿ka|ter, ...kat|ze** *(fam.);* **schmu|sen** *(ugs.);* du schmust; er schmuste; **Schmu|ser** *(ugs.);* **Schmu|se|rei** *(ugs.)*
Schmutt, der; -es (*nordd. für* feiner Regen)
Schmutz, der; -es (*südwestd. auch für* Fett, Schmalz); ein Schmutz abweisendes Material (↑R 40); **Schmutz‿blatt** *(Druckw.),* **...bürs|te; schmut|zen;** du schmutzt; **Schmutz‿fän|ger, ...fink** (der; *Gen.* -en, *auch* -s, *Plur.* -en; *ugs. für* jmd., der schmutzig ist), **...fleck; Schmut|zi|an,** der; -[e]s, -e (*veraltend für* Schmutzfink; *österr. ugs. für* Geizhals); **schmut|zig;** schmutzig gelb, schmutzig grau usw. (↑R 40); **Schmut|zig|keit; Schmutz‿schicht, ...ti|tel** *(Druckw.),* **...wä|sche, ...was|ser** (*Plur.* ...wässer), **...zu|la|ge**
Schna|bel, der; -s, Schnäbel; **Schnä|bel|chen; Schnä|be|lei** (*ugs. auch für* das Küssen); **Schnä|be|lein,** Schnäb|lein; **Schna|bel|flö|te; schna|bel|för|mig; Schna|bel|hieb; ...schnä|be|lig,** ...schnäb|lig (z. B. langschnäb[e]lig); **Schna|bel|kerf** *(Zool.);* **schnä|beln** (*ugs. auch für* küssen); ich ...[e]le (↑R 16); sich -; **Schna|bel‿schuh, ...tas|se, ...tier; Schnäb|lein** *vgl.* Schnäbelein; **...schnäb|lig** *vgl.* ...schnäbelig; **schna|bu|lie|ren** (*ugs. für* mit Behagen essen)
Schnack, der; -[e]s, *Plur.* -s *u.* Schnäcke (*nordd. ugs. für* Plauderei; Scherzwort; Gerede)
schna|ckeln (*bayr. für* schnalzen); ich ...[e]le (↑R 16); **schna|cken** (*nordd. für* plaudern); Platt -; **Schna|ckerl,** der, *auch* das; -s (*österr. für* Schluckauf)
Schna|der|hüp|fe[r]l, das; -s, -[n] (*bayr. u. österr. für* volkstümlicher satir. Vierzeiler, oft improvisiert zum Tanz gesungen)
schna|dern (*landsch. für* schnattern, viel reden); ich ...ere (↑R 16)
schnaf|te (*berlin. veraltend für* hervorragend, vortrefflich)
[1]**Schna|ke,** die; -, -n (*nordd. veraltet für* Schnurre; Scherz)
[2]**Schna|ke,** die; -, -n (eine langbeinige Mücke; *landsch. für* Stechmücke)
schnä|ken (*landsch. für* naschen)
Schna|ken‿pla|ge, ...stich
schna|kig (*nordd. veraltet für* schnurrig)
schnä|kig (*landsch. für* wählerisch [im Essen])
Schnäll|chen; Schnal|le, die; -, -n (*österr. auch svw.* Klinke); **schnal|len** (*südd. auch für* schnalzen); etwas - (*ugs. für* verstehen); **Schnal|len|schuh**
schnal|zen; du schnalzt; **Schnal|zer; Schnalz|laut**
Schnä|pel, der; -s, - (ein Fisch)
schnapp!; schnipp, schnapp!; **Schnäpp|chen** (*ugs. für* vorteilhafter Kauf); **schnap|pen; Schnap|per; Schnäp|per,** *auch* Schnep|per (ein Vogel; *Sport* [Sprung]bewegung; Nadel zur Blutentnahme; *früher für* Armbrust; *landsch. für* Schnappschloss); **schnäp|pern,** *auch* schnep|pern (*Sport* in Hohlkreuzhaltung springen); ich ...ere (↑R 16); **Schnäp|per|sprung,** *auch* Schnep|per|sprung *(Sport);* **Schnapp‿hahn** (*früher für* Wegelagerer), **...mes|ser** (das), **...schloss, ...schuss; Schnaps,** der; -es, Schnäpse; **Schnaps‿bren|ner, ...bren|ne|rei, ...bu|de** *(ugs. abwertend);* **Schnäps|chen; schnäp|seln** (*ugs. svw.* [1]schnapsen); ich ...[e]le (↑R 16); [1]**schnap|sen** (*ugs. für* Schnaps trinken); du schnapst
[2]**schnap|sen** (*bayr., österr. für* Schnapsen spielen); **Schnap|sen,** das; -s (*bayr., österr.* Kartenspiel)
Schnaps‿fah|ne *(ugs.),* **...flasche, ...glas** (*Plur.* ...gläser), **...idee** (↑R 132; *ugs. für* seltsame, verrückte Idee), **...lei|che** (*ugs. scherzh. für* Betrunkener); **Schnaps‿na|se** *(ugs.),* **...stamperl** (*bayr., österr. für* Schnapsglas), **...zahl** (*ugs. scherzh. für* aus gleichen Ziffern bestehende Zahl)
schnar|chen; Schnar|cher
Schnar|re, die; -, -n; **schnar|ren; Schnarr|werk** (bei der Orgel)
Schnat, Schna|te, die; -, ...ten (*landsch. für* junges abgeschnittenes [3]Reis; Grenze einer Flur); **Schnä|tel,** das; -s, - (*landsch. für* Pfeifchen aus Weidenrinde)
Schnat|te|rer; Schnat|ter|gans (*ugs. für* schwatzhaftes Mädchen); **schnat|te|rig,** schnatt|rig; **Schnat|te|rin; Schnat|ter|lie|se** (*ugs. svw.* Schnattergans); **schnat|tern;** ich ...ere (↑R 16); **schnatt|rig** *vgl.* schnatterig
Schnatz, der; -es, Schnätze (*hess. für* Kopfputz [der Braut, der Taufpatin] mit Haarkrönchen); **schnät|zeln** (*hess.; svw.* schnatzen); ich ...[e]le (↑R 16); sich -; **schnat|zen** (*hess. für* sich putzen, das Haar aufstecken); du schnatzt; sich -
Schnau, die; -, -en (*nordd. für* geschnäbeltes Schiff)
schnau|ben; du schnaubst; du schnaubtest (*veraltend* schnobst); du schnaubtest (*veraltend* schnöbest); geschnaubt (*veraltend* geschnoben); schnaub[e]!; **schnäu|big** (*hess. für* wählerisch [im Essen]); **Schnauf,** der; -[e]s, -e (*landsch. für* [hörbarer] Atemzug); **schnau|fen; Schnau|fer** *(ugs.);* **Schnau|ferl,** das; -s, -[n] (*ugs. scherzh. für* altes Auto)
Schnau|pe, die; -, -n (*südd. für* Ausguss an Kannen u. a.)
Schnauz, der; -es, Schnäuze (*bes. schweiz. für* Schnurrbart); **Schnauz|bart; schnauz|bär|tig; Schnäuz|chen; Schnau|ze,** die; -, -n (*auch derb für* Mund); **schnau|zen** *(ugs.);* du schnauzt; **schnäu|zen;** du schnäuzt; sich -; **Schnau|zer,** der; -s, - (Hund einer bestimmten Rasse; *ugs. kurz für* Schnauzbart); **schnau|zig** (grob [schimpfend]); **...schnau|zig, ...schnäu|zig** (*ugs.;* z. B. großschnauzig, großschnäuzig)
Schneck, der; -s, -en (*bes. südd., österr. für* Schnecke); **Schne|cke,** die; -, -n (*landsch. auch* ein Kosewort für Mädchen); **Schne|cken|boh|rer** (ein Werkzeug); **schne|cken|för|mig; Schne|cken‿fri|sur, ...gang** (der; -[e]s), **...ge|häu|se, ...haus, ...li|nie** (*selten für* Spirale), **...nu|del** (*landsch.* ein Hefegebäck), **...post** (die; -; *scherzh.*), **...tem|po** (das; -s; *ugs.*), **...win|dung; Schne|ckerl,** das; -s, -n (*österr. ugs. für* Locke)
schned|de|reng|teng!, schned|de|reng|teng|teng! (Nachahmung des Trompetenschalles)

Schnee, der; -s; im Jahre, anno - (*österr. für* vor langer Zeit); **Schnee|ball** (Kugel aus Schnee; ein Strauch); **schnee|bal|len;** *fast nur im Infinitiv u. Partizip II gebräuchlich;* geschneeballt; **Schnee|ball|schlacht; Schnee|ball|sys|tem,** das; -s (eine bestimmte, in Deutschland verbotene Form des Warenabsatzes); **schnee|be|deckt** (↑R 40); **Schnee|bee|re** (ein Strauch)

[1]**Schnee|berg** (Stadt im westl. Erzgebirge)

[2]**Schnee|berg,** der; -[e]s (höchster Gipfel des Fichtelgebirges)

Schnee|be|sen (ein Küchengerät); **schnee|blind; Schnee˯blind|heit** (die; -), **...brett** (flach überhängende Schneemassen), **...bril|le, ...bruch** (Baumschaden durch zu große Schneelast; *vgl.* [1]Bruch), **...de|cke; Schnee|ei|fel** (↑R 24); *vgl.* Schneifel; **schnee|er|hellt** (↑R 24); **Schnee|eu|le** (↑R 24); **Schnee˯fall** (der), **...flä|che, ...flo|cke, ...frä|se; schnee|frei; Schnee˯gans, ...ge|stö|ber; schnee|glatt;** auf -er Fahrbahn; **Schnee˯glät|te** (die; -), **...glöck|chen, ...gren|ze, ...ha|se, ...hemd, ...hö|he, ...huhn; schnee|ig; Schnee˯ka|no|ne** (Gerät zur Erzeugung von künstlichem Schnee), **...ket|te** *(meist Plur.),* **...kö|nig** (*ostmitteld. für* Zaunkönig; er freut sich wie ein - [*ugs. für* er freut sich sehr])

Schnee|kop|pe, die; - (höchster Berg des Riesengebirges)

Schnee˯land|schaft, ...le|o|pard, ...mann (*Plur.* ...männer), **...matsch** (*vgl.* [2]Matsch), **...mensch** (Fabelwesen; *vgl. auch* Yeti); **Schnee|mo|nat** *od.* **...mond** (*alte Bez. für* Januar); **Schnee˯pflug, ...räu|mer, ...re|gen, ...ru|te** (*österr. für* Schneebesen), **...schleu|der, ...schmel|ze** (die; -); **Schnee|schuh** (*veraltet auch für* Ski); **schnee|si|cher;** ein -es Skigebiet; **Schnee˯sturm** (*vgl.* [1]Sturm), **...trei|ben, ...ver|hält|nis|se** *(Plur.),* **...ver|we|hung, ...was|ser** (das; -s), **...we|be** (die; -, -n; *veraltet für* Schneewehe), **...wech|te, ...we|he** (die); **schnee|weiß; Schnee|witt|chen,** das; -s ‹„Schneeweißchen“› (dt. Märchengestalt); **Schnee|zaun**

Schne|gel, der; -s, - (*landsch. für* [hauslose] Schnecke)

Schneid, der; -[e]s, *südd., österr.* die; - (*ugs. für* Mut; Tatkraft); **Schneid˯ba|cken** (*Plur.*), **...boh|rer, ...bren|ner; Schnei|de,** die; -, -n; **Schneid|ei|sen; Schnei|del|holz,** das; -es (*Forstw.* abgehauene Nadelholzzweige); **Schnei|de|müh|le** (*selten für* Sägemühle); **schnei|den;** du schnittst; du schnittest; ich habe mir, *auch* mich in den Finger geschnitten; schneid[e]!; **Schnei|der; Schnei|de|rei; Schnei|der˯ge|sel|le, ...hand|werk** (das; -[e]s); **Schnei|de|rin; Schnei|der˯kos|tüm, ...krei|de, ...meis|ter, ...meis|te|rin; schnei|dern;** ich ...ere (↑R 16); **Schnei|der˯pup|pe, ...sitz** (der; -es), **...werk|statt; Schnei|de˯tisch** *(Filmwesen),* **...zahn; schnei|dig** (mutig, forsch); **Schnei|dig|keit,** die; -; **Schneid|klup|pe** (Werkzeug zum Gewindeschneiden)

schnei|en

Schnei|fel, *auch* Schnee|ei|fel (↑R 24; ein Teil der Eifel)

Schnei|se, die; -, -n ([gerader] Durchhieb [Weg] im Wald); **schnei|teln** (*Forstw.* von überflüssigen Ästen, Trieben befreien); ich ...[e]le (↑R 16)

schnell; schnellstens; so - wie (*älter* als) möglich; schneller Brüter (ein Kernreaktor); auf die schnelle Tour *(ugs.);* auf die Schnelle (*ugs. für* rasch, schnell); (↑R 108:) Schnelle Medizinische Hilfe; *Abk.* SMH *(vgl. d.)*; **Schnell˯bahn** (*Abk.* S-Bahn), **...boot, ...damp|fer, ...dienst, ...dru|cker;** [1]**Schnel|le,** die; - (Schnelligkeit); [2]**Schnel|le,** die; -, -n (Stromschnelle); **schnel|len; Schnel|ler** (*landsch. für* knipsendes Geräusch, das durch Schnippen mit zwei Fingern entsteht); **Schnell|feu|er; Schnell|feu|er|ge|wehr; schnell|fü|ßig; Schnell˯gang** (der), **...gast|stät|te, ...ge|richt, ...hef|ter; Schnell|heit,** die; - (*selten für* Schnelligkeit); **Schnel|lig|keit** *Plur. selten;* **Schnell˯im|biss, ...koch|plat|te, ...koch|topf, ...kraft** (die; -), **...kurs; Schnell|las|ter** (↑R 136; schnell fahrender Lastkraftwagen); **Schnell|läu|fer** (↑R 136); **schnell|le|big** (↑R 136); **Schnell|le|big|keit** (↑R 136), die; -; **Schnell˯pa|ket, ...rei|ni|gung, ...schuss** (*ugs. für* schnelle Maßnahme, sofortige Reaktion); **schnells|tens; schnellst|mög|lich,** *dafür besser:* möglichst schnell; **Schnell˯stra|ße, ...trieb|wa|gen, ...ver|fah|ren, ...ver|kehr** (der; -s), **...waa|ge; Schnell|wä|sche|rei** (*svw.* Schnellreinigung); **Schnell|zug** (*svw.* D-Zug)

Schnep|fe, die; -, -n (ein Vogel; *derb auch für* Prostituierte); **Schnep|fen˯jagd, ...vo|gel, ...zug** *(Jägerspr.)*

Schnep|pe, die; -, -n (*mitteld. für* Schnabel [einer Kanne]; schnabelförmige Spitze [eines Kleidungsstückes]; *landsch. auch für* Dirne)

Schnep|per, schnep|pern usw. *vgl.* Schnäpper, schnäppern usw.

schnet|zeln (*bes. schweiz. für* [Fleisch] fein zerschneiden); ich ...[e]le (↑R 16); geschnetzeltes Fleisch

Schneuß, der; -es, -e (*Archit.* Fischblase[nornament])

Schneu|ze, die; -, -n (*früher für* Lichtputzschere)

schneu|zen *frühere Schreibung für* schnäuzen

schni|cken (*landsch. für* schnippen); **Schnick|schnack,** der; -[e]s (*ugs. für* [törichtes] Gerede; nutzloser Kleinkram)

schnie|ben (*mitteld. für* schnauben); *auch mit starker Beugung:* du schnobst; du schnöbest; geschnoben

Schnie|del|wutz, der; -es, -e (*ugs. scherzh. für* Penis)

schnie|fen (*bes. mitteld. für* die Luft hörbar durch die Nase einziehen)

schnie|geln (*ugs. für* übertrieben herausputzen); sich -; ich ...[e]le [mich] (↑R 16); geschniegelt und gebügelt *od.* gestriegelt (fein hergerichtet)

schnie|ke (*berlin. für* fein, schick)

Schnie|pel, der; -s, - (*veraltet für* Angeber, Geck; *Kinderspr.* Penis)

Schnip|fel, der; -s, - (*landsch. für* Schnipsel); **schnip|feln** *(landsch.);* ich ...[e]le (↑R 16); **schnipp!;** schnipp, schnapp!; **Schnipp|chen;** *nur noch in* jmdm. ein - schlagen (*ugs. für* einen Streich spielen); **Schnip|pel,** der *od.* das; -s, - (*ugs. für* Schnipsel); **Schnip|pel|chen; Schnip|pe|lei** *(ugs. abwertend);* **schnip|peln** *(ugs.);* ich ...[e]le (↑R 16); **schnip|pen;** mit den Fingern -

schnip|pisch

schnipp, schnapp!; Schnipp|schnapp[|schnurr], das; -[s] (ein [Karten]spiel); **schnips!; Schnip|sel,** der *od.* das; -s, - (*ugs. für* kleines [abgeschnittenes] Stück); **Schnip|se|lei** *(ugs.);* **schnip|seln;** ich ...[e]le (↑R 16); **schnip|sen** (*svw.* schnippen); du schnipst

Schnitt, der; -[e]s, -e; **Schnitt˯blu|me, ...boh|ne, ...brot** (das;

-[e]s); **Schnit|te,** die; -, -n (*österr. auch für* Waffel); **Schnit|ter** (*veraltend für* Mäher); **Schnit|te|rin; schnitt|fest;** -e Wurst; **Schnitt-fläche, ...holz; schnit|tig** (*auch für* rassig); ein -es Auto; **Schnitt-kä|se, ...lauch** (der; -[e]s), **...li|nie, ...meis|ter** (*svw.* Cutter), **...men|ge** (*Math.*), **...mus-ter; Schnitt|mus|ter|bo|gen; Schnitt-punkt, ...stel|le** (*EDV* Verbindungsstelle zweier Geräte od. Anlagenteile), **...wa|re; schnitt|wei|se; Schnitt|wun-de; Schnitz,** der; -es, -e (*landsch. für* kleines [gedörrtes] Obststück); **Schnitz-ar|beit** (Schnitzerei), **...bank** (*Plur.* ...bänke), **...bild;** [1]**Schnit|zel,** das; -s, - (zarte Fleischscheibe zum Braten); Wiener Schnitzel; [2]**Schnit|zel,** das, *österr. nur so, od.* der; -s, - (*ugs. für* abgeschnittenes Stück); **Schnit|zel|bank** *Plur.* ...bänke (*veraltet für* Bank zum Schnitzen; Bänkelsängerverse mit Bildern); **Schnit|ze|lei** (*landsch.*); **Schnit-zel|jagd; schnit|zeln** (*landsch. auch für* schnitzen); ich ...[e]le (↑R 16); **schnit|zen;** du schnitzt; **Schnit|zer** (*ugs. auch für* Fehler); **Schnit|ze|rei; Schnitz|ler** (*schweiz. für* Schnitzer); **Schnitz-mes|ser** (das), **...werk**

schno|bern (*landsch. für* schnuppern); ich ...ere (↑R 16)

schnöd (*bes. südd., österr. für* schnöde)

Schnod|der, der; -s (*derb für* Nasenschleim); **schnod|de|rig,** schnoddrig (*ugs. für* in respektloser Weise provozierend, unverschämt); -e Bemerkungen; **Schnod|de|rig|keit,** Schnoddrig|keit (*ugs.*); **schnodd|rig** usw. *vgl.* schnodderig usw.

schnö|de; schnöder Gewinn, Mammon; **schnö|den** (*schweiz. für* schnöde reden); **Schnöd-heit,** *häufiger* **Schnö|dig|keit** (*geh. abwertend*)

schno|feln (*österr. ugs. für* schnüffeln; durch die Nase sprechen); ich ...[e]le (↑R 16); **Schno|ferl,** das; -s, -n (*österr. ugs. für* Schnüffler; beleidigte Miene)

Schnor|chel, der; -s, - (Luftrohr für das tauchende U-Boot; Teil eines Sporttauchgerätes); **schnor|cheln** (mit dem Schnorchel tauchen); ich ...[e]le (↑R 16)

Schnör|kel, der; -s, -; **Schnör|ke-lei; schnör|kel|haft; schnör|ke-lig; Schnör|kel|kram** (*ugs.*); **schnör|keln;** ich ...[e]le (↑R 16); **Schnör|kel|schrift; schnörk|lig** *vgl.* schnörkelig

schnor|ren, *landsch.* schnur|ren (*ugs. für* [er]betteln); **Schnor|rer,** *landsch.* Schnur|rer; **Schnor|re-rei,** *landsch.* Schnur|re|rei

Schnö|sel, der; -s, - (*ugs. für* dummfrecher junger Mensch); **schnö|se|lig** (*ugs.*)

Schnu|cke, die; -, -n (*kurz für* Heidschnucke); **Schnu|ckel-chen** (Schäfchen; *auch* Kosewort); **schnu|cke|lig,** schnuck|lig (*ugs. für* nett, süß; lecker, appetitlich); **Schnu|cki,** das; -s, -s (*ugs.; svw.* Schnuckelchen); **Schnu|cki-putz,** der; -es, -e (*ugs.; svw.* Schnuckelchen)

schnud|de|lig, schnudd|lig (*ugs. für* unsauber; *berlin. für* lecker)

Schnüf|fe|lei; schnuf|feln (*landsch. für* schnüffeln); **schnüf-feln** (*auch für* spionieren); ich ...[e]le (↑R 16); **Schnüf|fel|stoff** (*ugs. für* Mittel, das berauschende Dämpfe abgibt); **Schnüff|ler**

schnul|len (*landsch. für* saugen); **Schnul|ler** (Gummisauger für Kleinkinder)

Schnul|ze, die; -,-n (*ugs. für* sentimentales Kino-, Theaterstück, Lied); **Schnul|zen-sän|ger, ...sän|ge|rin; schnul|zig** (*ugs.*)

schnup|fen; Schnup|fen, der; -s, -; **Schnup|fen-mit|tel** (das), **...spray; Schnup|fer; Schnupf-ta|bak; Schnupf|ta|bak[s]|do-se; Schnupf|tuch** *Plur.* ...tücher

schnup|pe (*ugs. für* gleichgültig); es ist mir -; **Schnup|pe,** die; -, -n (*landsch. für* verkohlter Docht)

schnup|pern (stoßweise durch die Nase einatmen); ich ...ere (↑R 16)

[1]**Schnur,** die; -, *Plur.* Schnüre, *seltener* Schnuren (Bindfaden, Kordel)

[2]**Schnur,** die; -, -en (*veraltet für* Schwiegertochter)

schnur|ar|tig; Schnür|bo|den (*Theater*); **Schnür|chen;** das geht wie am Schnürchen (*ugs. für* das geht reibungslos); **schnü|ren** (auch von der Gangart des Fuchses); **schnur|ge|ra|de**[1]; **Schnur-ke|ra|mik,** die; - (Kulturkreis der jüngeren Steinzeit); **Schnür-leib** *od.* **...leib|chen** (*veraltet*); **schnur|los;** ein schnurloses Telefon; **Schnürl-re|gen** (*österr.*), **...samt** (*österr. für* Kord); **Schnür|mie|der**

Schnur|rant, der; -en, -en; ↑R 126 (*veraltet für* [Bettel]musikant); **Schnurr|bart; Schnurr|bart|bin-de; schnurr|bär|tig; Schnur|re,** die; -, -n (scherzh. Erzählung); [1]**schnur|ren** (ein brummendes, summendes Geräusch von sich geben); [2]**schnur|ren** *vgl.* schnorren; **Schnur|rer** *vgl.* Schnorrer; **Schnur|re|rei** *vgl.* Schnorrerei; **Schnurr|haar** (bei Raubtieren, bes. bei Katzen)

Schnür|rie|men (Schnürsenkel)

schnur|rig (*veraltend für* komisch); ein -er Kauz; **Schnur|rig-keit**

Schnur|rock, Schnür|rock (*früher* Männerrock mit Schnüren)

Schnurr|pfei|fe|rei *meist Plur.* (*veraltet für* närrische Idee, Handlung)

Schnür-schuh, ...sen|kel, ...stie-fel; schnur|stracks (*ugs.*); **Schnü|rung** (*selten*)

schnurz (*ugs. für* gleich[gültig], egal); das ist mir -; **schnurz|pie-pe, schnurz|piep|egal** (↑R 132; *ugs.*)

Schnüt|chen; Schnu|te, die; -, -n (*bes. nordd. für* Mund; *ugs. für* [Schmoll]mund, unwilliger Gesichtsausdruck)

Scho|ber, der; -s, - (kleine [Feld]scheune; *südd., österr. für* geschichteter Getreidehaufen); **Schö|berl,** das; -s, -n (*österr. für* eine Suppeneinlage); **scho|bern, schö|bern** (*bes. österr. für* in Schober setzen); ich ...ere (↑R 16)

Scho|chen, der; -s, Schöchen (*südd., schweiz. für* kleinerer Heuhaufen)

[1]**Schock,** das; -[e]s, -e (ein altes Zählmaß = 60 Stück); 3 - Eier (↑R 90)

[2]**Schock,** der; -[e]s, *Plur.* -s, *selten* -e ‹engl.› (plötzliche nervliche od. seelische Erschütterung; akutes Kreislaufversagen); **scho|ckant** ‹franz.› (*veraltend für* anstößig); **Schock|be|hand|lung; scho-cken** ‹engl.› (Nervenkranke mit künstlichem Schock behandeln; *ugs. für* schockieren); **Scho|cker,** der; -s, - (*ugs. für* Schauerroman, -film); **Schock|far|be** (besonders grelle Farbe); **schock|far|ben; schock-ge|fro|ren, ...ge|fros-tet; scho|ckie|ren** ‹franz.› (einen Schock versetzen, in große Entrüstung versetzen); **scho|cking** *vgl.* shocking

Schock|schwe|re|not! (*veraltet*)

Schock|the|ra|pie, die; -

schock|wei|se; dreischockweise

Schock-wir|kung, ...zu|stand

Schof, der; -[e]s, -e (*nordd. für* Strohbündel [zum Dachdecken]; *Jägerspr.* Kette [von Gänsen od. Enten])

scho|fel, scho|fe|lig, schof|lig ‹hebr.-jidd.› (*ugs. für* gemein; geizig); eine schof[e]le *od.* schof[e]li-

[1] *Vgl. die Anmerkung zu* „gerade".

ge Person; er hat ihn schofel behandelt; **Scho|fel,** der; -s, - (*ugs. für* schlechte Ware); **scho|fe|lig** *vgl.* schofel
Schöf|fe, der; -n, -n (↑R 126); **Schöf|fen|bank** *Plur.* ...bänke; **Schöf|fen‿ge|richt, ...stuhl; Schöf|fin**
Schof|för, der; -s, -e (*frühere Eindeutschung für* Chauffeur)
schof|lig *vgl.* schofel
Scho|gun, Sho|gun, der; -s, -e ‹jap.› (*früher* Titel jap. Feldherren)
Scho|ko, die; -, -s (*ugs. kurz für* Schokolade); **Scho|ko|la|de,** die; -, -n ‹mexik.›; **scho|ko|la|den** (aus Schokolade); **scho|ko|la|de[n]|braun; Scho|ko|la|de[n]‿eis, ...fab|rik; scho|ko|la|de[n]|far|ben** *od.* **...far|big; Scho|ko|la|de[n]‿guss, ...os|ter|ha|se, ...pud|ding, ...sei|te** (*ugs. für* die Seite, die am vorteilhaftesten aussieht; jmds. angenehme Wesenszüge), **...streu|sel, ...ta|fel, ...tor|te; Scho|ko|rie|gel**
Scho|lar, der; -en, -en (↑R 126) ‹griech.› ([fahrender] Schüler, Student [im MA.]); **Scho|larch** (↑R 132), der; -en, -en; ↑R 126 (mittelalterl. Schulvorsteher); **Scho|las|tik,** die; - (mittelalterl. Philosophie; engstirnige Schulweisheit); **Scho|las|ti|ker** (Anhänger, Lehrer der Scholastik; *auch für* spitzfindiger Mensch); **scho|las|tisch; Scho|las|ti|zis|mus,** der; - (einseitige Überbewertung der Scholastik; *auch für* Spitzfindigkeit)
Scho|li|ast, der; -en, -en (↑R 126) ‹griech.› (Verfasser von Scholien); **Scho|lie** [...iə], die; -, -n *u.* **Scho|li|on,** das; -s, ...lien [...iən] (Anmerkung [zu griech. u. röm. Schriftstellern], Erklärung)
Schol|le, die; -, -n (flacher [Erd-, Eis]klumpen; [Heimat]boden; ein Fisch); **Schol|len‿bre|cher, ...ge|bir|ge** *(Geol.);* **schol|lern** (dumpf rollen, tönen)
Schol|li; *nur in* mein lieber -! (*ugs.* Ausruf des Erstaunens od. der Ermahnung)
schol|lig ‹*zu* Scholle›
Schöll|kraut
Scho|lo|chow [...xɔf] (russ. Schriftsteller)
Schol|ti|sei, die; -, -en (*nordd. veraltet für* Amt des Gemeindevorstehers)
schon; obschon, wennschon; wennschon – dennschon
schön; I. *Kleinschreibung:* **a)** (↑R 108:) die schöne Literatur; die schönen Künste; das schöne (weibliche) Geschlecht; gib die schöne (*ugs. für* rechte) Hand!; **b)** (↑R 47:) am schönsten. **II.** *Großschreibung:* **a)** (↑R 47:) die Schönste unter ihnen; der Schönste der Schönen; die Welt des Schönen; das Gefühl für das Schöne und Gute; auf das *od.* aufs Schönste, *auch* schönste übereinstimmen; etwas Schönes; nichts Schöneres; **b)** (↑R 93:) Schön Rotraud; Philipp der Schöne. **III.** *In Verbindung mit Verben* (↑R 38 f.): schön, schöner sein, werden, anziehen, färben, machen, singen, schreiben usw.; *aber* schönfärben, schönmachen, schönreden, schönschreiben, schöntun *(vgl. d.)*
Schön|berg (österr. Komponist)
Schön|druck *Plur.* ...drucke (Bedrucken der Vorderseite des Druckbogens); **¹Schö|ne,** die; -n, -n; ↑R 5 ff. (schöne Frau); **²Schö|ne,** die; - (*veraltend* Schönheit)
scho|nen; sich -
schö|nen ([Färbungen] verschönern [*vgl.* avivieren]; [Flüssigkeiten] künstlich klar machen)
Scho|nen (Landsch. im Süden Schwedens)
¹Scho|ner (Schutzdeckchen)
²Scho|ner, der; -s, - ‹engl.› (ein zweimastiges Segelschiff)
schön|fär|ben; ↑R 38 f. ([zu] günstig darstellen); ich färbe schön; schöngefärbt; schönzufärben; *aber* das Kleid wurde [besonders] schön gefärbt; **Schön|fär|ber; Schön|fär|be|rei** ([zu] günstige Darstellung)
Schon‿frist, ...gang *(Technik)*
Schon|gau|er (dt. Maler u. Kupferstecher)
Schon‿ge|biet, ...ge|he|ge
Schön|geist *Plur.* ...geister; **Schön|geis|te|rei,** die; - (einseitige Betonung schöngeistiger Interessen); **schön|geis|tig;** -e Literatur; **Schön|heit; Schön|heits‿chi|rurg, ...farm, ...feh|ler, ...fleck, ...ide|al** (↑R 132), **...kö|ni|gin, ...kur, ...mit|tel** (das), **...ope|ra|ti|on** (↑R 132), **...pfläs|ter|chen, ...pfle|ge** (die; -), **...sinn** (der; -[e]s); **schön|heits|trun|ken** *(geh.);* **Schön|heits|wett|be|werb**
Schon|kost (*für* Diät)
Schön|ling (*abwertend für* [übertrieben gepflegter] gut aussehender Mann); **schön|ma|chen;** ↑R 38 f. (verschönern, herausputzen); sie hat sich schöngemacht; der Hund hat schöngemacht (hat Männchen gemacht); *aber* das hat er [besonders] schön gemacht;
Schon|platz (*regional für* Arbeitsplatz für Wiedergenesende, Schwangere); **schön|re|den;** ↑R 38 f. (schmeicheln); er hat schöngeredet; *aber* der Vortragende hat schön geredet; **Schön‿re|de|rei** (die; -; schmeichelnde Darstellung), **...red|ner** (Schmeichler), **...red|ne|rei** (die; -; Schönrederei); **schön|red|ne|risch; schön|schrei|ben;** ↑R 38 f. (Schönschrift schreiben); sie haben in der Schule schöngeschrieben; *aber* er hat diesen Aufsatz [besonders] schön geschrieben; **Schön|schreib‿heft, ...übung** (↑R 132); **Schön|schrift,** die; -; **schöns|tens; Schön|tu|er; Schön|tu|e|rei; schön|tu|e|risch; schön|tun;** ↑R 38 (*ugs. für* schmeicheln); er hat bei ihr immer schöngetan
Scho|nung (*nur Sing.:* Nachsicht, das Schonen; junger geschützter Baumbestand)
Schö|nung ‹*zu* schönen›
scho|nungs|be|dürf|tig; scho|nungs|los; Scho|nungs|lo|sig|keit, die; -; **scho|nungs|voll;**
Schon|wasch|gang
Schön|wet|ter‿la|ge, ...wol|ke
Schon|zeit *(Jägerspr.)*
Scho|pen|hau|er (dt. Philosoph); **Scho|pen|hau|e|ri|a|ner** (Anhänger Schopenhauers); **scho|pen|hau|e|risch, scho|pen|hau|ersch;** ein schopenhauer[i]sches Werk (ein Werk von Schopenhauer); schopenhauer[i]sches Denken (nach Art von Schopenhauer)
Schopf, der; -[e]s, Schöpfe (Haarbüschel; *kurz für* Haarschopf; *landsch. u. schweiz. auch für* Wetterdach; Nebengebäude, [Wagen]schuppen)
Schopf|bra|ten (*österr. für* gebratener Schweinekamm)
Schöpf|brun|nen
Schöpf|chen (kleiner Schopf)
Schöp|fe, die; -, -n (*veraltend für* Gefäß, Platz zum Schöpfen); **Schöpf|ei|mer; ¹schöp|fen** (Flüssigkeit entnehmen)
²schöp|fen (*veraltet für* erschaffen)
¹Schöp|fer (Schöpfgefäß)
²Schöp|fer (Erschaffer, Urheber; *nur Sing.:* Gott); **Schöp|fer‿geist** (der; -[e]s; *geh.*), **...hand** (die; -; *geh.*); **Schöp|fe|rin; schöp|fe|risch; Schöp|fer|kraft** *(geh.);* **Schöp|fer|tum,** das; -s
Schöpf‿ge|fäß, ...kel|le, ...löf|fel
Schöp|fung; Schöp|fungs‿akt, ...be|richt, ...ge|schich|te, ...tag
Schöpp|chen (kleiner Schoppen)

Schöp|pe, der; -n, -n; ↑R 126 (*nordd. für* Schöffe)
schöp|peln (*landsch. für* gern od. auch gewohnheitsmäßig [einen Schoppen] trinken); ich ...[e]le (↑R 16)
schop|pen (*südd., österr. u. schweiz. mdal. für* hineinstopfen, nudeln, zustecken)
Schop|pen, der; -s, - (altes Flüssigkeitsmaß [für Bier, Wein]; *südd. u. schweiz. auch für* Babyflasche; *landsch. für* Schuppen)
Schöp|pen|stedt (Stadt in Niedersachsen); **Schöp|pen|sted|ter** (↑R 103); **schöp|pen|sted|tisch**
Schop|pen|wein; schop|pen|wei|se
Schöps, der; -es, -e (*ostmitteld. u. österr. für* Hammel); **Schöps|chen; Schöp|sen‿bra|ten, ...fleisch; Schöp|ser|ne,** das; -n (*österr. für* Hammelfleisch)
scho|ren (*landsch. für* umgraben)
Schorf, der; -[e]s, -e; **schorf|ar|tig; schor|fig**
Schörl, der; -[e]s, -e (schwarzer Turmalin)
Schor|le, Schor|le|mor|le, die; -, -n, *selten* das; -s, -s (Getränk aus Wein od. Apfelsaft u. Mineralwasser)
Schorn|stein; Schorn|stein‿fe|ger, ...fe|ge|rin
Scho|se, die; -, -n ‹franz.› (*eindeutschende Schreibung für* Chose)
[1]**Schoß,** der; -es, Schöße (beim Sitzen durch Oberschenkel u. Unterleib gebildeter Winkel; *geh. für* Mutterleib; Teil der Kleidung); [2]**Schoß,** die; -, *Plur.* Schoßen *u.* Schöße (*österr. für* Frauenrock)
[1]**Schoss,** der; -es, *Plur.* -e[n] *u.* Schösse[r] (*veraltet für* Zoll, Steuer, Abgabe); [2]**Schoss,** der; -es, -e (junger Trieb)
Schoss|brett (*bayr. veraltet für* [3]Schütz)
Schöß|chen (an der Taille eines Frauenkleides angesetzter [gekräuselter] Stoffstreifen); **Schö|ßel,** der, *auch* das; -s, - (*österr. für* Schößchen; Frackschoß)
schos|sen (austreiben); die Pflanze schosst, schosste, hat geschosst; **Schos|ser,** der; -s, - (verfrüht blühende Pflanze)
Schoß‿hund, ...hünd|chen, ...kind
Schöss|ling (Ausläufer, Trieb einer Pflanze)
Schos|ta|ko|witsch (russ. Komponist)
Scho|t, die; -, -e[n]; *vgl.* [2]Schote
Schöt|chen (kleine [3]Schote)
[1]**Scho|te,** der; -n, -n (↑R 126) ‹hebr.-jidd.› (*ugs. für* Narr, Einfaltspinsel; witzige Geschichte)
[2]**Scho|te,** die; -, -n (*Seemannsspr.* Segelleine)
[3]**Scho|te,** die; -, -n (Fruchtform); **scho|ten|för|mig; Scho|ten|frucht**
[1]**Schott,** der; -s, -s ‹arab.› (mit Salzschlamm gefülltes Becken [im Atlasgebirge])
[2]**Schott,** das; -[e]s, *Plur.* -en, *auch* -e (*Seemannsspr.* wasserdichte [Quer]wand im Schiff)
[1]**Schot|te,** der; -n, -n; ↑R 126 (Bewohner von Schottland)
[2]**Schot|te,** der; -n, -n; ↑R 126 (*nordd. für* junger Hering)
[3]**Schot|te,** die; - (*südd., schweiz. für* Molke); [1]**Schot|ten,** der; -s (*südd., westösterr. für* Quark)
[2]**Schot|ten,** der; -s, - (ein Gewebe); **Schot|ten‿rock, ...witz**
Schot|ter, der; -s, - (zerkleinerte Steine; *auch für* von Flüssen abgelagerte kleine Steine); **Schot|ter|de|cke; schot|tern** (mit Schotter belegen); ich ...ere (↑R 16); **Schot|ter|stra|ße; Schot|te|rung**
Schot|tin; schot|tisch; Schot|tisch, der; -, - *u.* **Schot|ti|sche,** der; -n, -n; ↑R 5 ff. (ein Tanz); einen Schottischen tanzen; **Schott|land; Schott|län|der; schott|län|disch**
Schraf|fe, die; -, -n *meist Plur.* (Strich einer Schraffur); **schraf|fen, schraf|fie|ren** (mit Schraffen versehen; stricheln); **Schraf|fie|rung, Schraf|fung,** *meist* **Schraf|fur,** die; -, -en (feine parallele Striche, die eine Fläche hervorheben)
schräg; schräg halten, laufen, stehen, stellen, liegen; schräg laufende Linien; schräg gegenüber; schräge Musik (*ugs. bes. für* Jazzmusik); **Schräg|bau,** der; -[e]s (*Bergmannsspr.* ein Abbauverfahren in steil gelagerten Flözen); **Schrä|ge,** die; -, -n; **schra|gen** (*veraltet für* zu Schragen verbinden); **schrä|gen** (schräg abkanten); **Schra|gen,** der; -s, - (*veraltet für* schräg od. kreuzweise zueinander stehende Holzfüße od. Pfähle; *auch für* Sägebock; Totenbahre); **Schräg|heit,** die; -; **schräg|hin; Schräg|la|ge; schräg lau|fend** *vgl.* schräg; **Schräg‿schnitt, ...schrift, ...strei|fen, ...strich; schräg|über** (↑R 132; *selten für* schräg gegenüber); **Schrä|gung** (*selten für* Schräge)
schral (*Seemannsspr.* ungünstig); -er Wind; **schra|len;** der Wind schralt
Schram, der; -[e]s, Schräme (*Bergmannsspr.* horizontaler od. geneigter Einschnitt im Flöz); **Schram|boh|rer, Schräm|boh|rer; schrä|men** (Schräme machen); **Schräm|ma|schi|ne** (Maschine zur Herstellung eines Schrams); **Schram|me,** die; -, -n
Schram|mel|mu|sik (↑R 95), die; - ‹nach den österr. Musikern Johann u. Josef Schrammel›
schram|men; schram|mig
Schrank, der; -[e]s, Schränke; **Schrank|bett; Schränk|chen; Schran|ke,** die; -, -n; **Schränk|ei|sen** (Gerät zum Schränken der Säge); **schrän|ken** (die Zähne eines Sägeblattes wechselweise abbiegen; *Jägerspr.* die Tritte etwas versetzt hintereinander setzen [vom Rothirsch]); **Schran|ken,** der; -s, - (*österr. für* Bahnschranke); **schran|ken|los; Schran|ken|lo|sig|keit,** die; -; **Schran|ken|wär|ter; Schrank|fach; schrank|fer|tig;** -e Wäsche; **Schrank‿kof|fer, ...spie|gel, ...tür, ...wand**
Schran|ne, die; -, -n (*südd. veraltend für* Fleischer-, Bäckerladen; Getreidemarkt[halle]; *bayr., österr. landsch. für* Markt[halle])
Schranz, der; -es, Schränze (*südd., schweiz. mdal. für* Riss); **Schran|ze,** die; -, -n, *seltener* der; -n, -n *meist Plur.* (*abwertend für* Höfling)
Schra|pe, die; -, -n (*nordd. für* Gerät zum Schaben); **schra|pen** (*nordd. für* schrappen)
Schrap|nell, das; -s, *Plur.* -e *u.* -s ‹nach dem engl. Artillerieoffizier H. Shrapnel› (*früher* Sprenggeschoss mit Kugelfüllung; *abwertend für* ältere, hässliche Frau)
Schrapp|ei|sen; schrap|pen (*landsch. für* [ab]kratzen); **Schrap|per** (ein Fördergefäß); **Schrap|sel,** das; -s, - (*nordd. für* das Abgekratzte)
Schrat, Schratt, der; -[e]s, -e, *landsch.* **Schrä|tel,** der; -s, - (zottiger Waldgeist)
Schrat|te, die; -, -n (*Geol.* Rinne, Schlucht in Kalkgestein); *vgl.* [2]Karre; **Schrat|ten|kalk,** der; -[e]s (zerklüftetes Kalkgestein)
Schräub|chen; Schrau|be, die; -, -n; **Schrau|bel,** die; -, -n (*Bot.* schraubenförmiger Blütenstand); **schrau|ben; Schrau|ben‿damp|fer, ...dre|her** (*fachspr. für* Schraubenzieher), **...fe|der, ...flü|gel; schrau|ben|för|mig; Schrau|ben‿ge|win|de, ...kopf,**

...li|nie, ...mut|ter (*Plur.* ...muttern), ...pres|se, ...rad *(Technik),* ...sal|to, ...schlüs|sel, ...zie|her; **Schraub|stock** (*Plur.* ...stöcke); **Schrau|bung; Schraub‿verschluss, ...zwin|ge**

Schrau|fen, der; -s, - (*österr. ugs. für* Schraube; hohe Niederlage im Sport)

Schre|ber|gar|ten (↑R 95) ‹nach dem Leipziger Arzt Schreber› (Kleingarten in Gartenkolonien); **Schre|ber|gärt|ner**

Schreck, der; -[e]s, -e *u.* Schrecken, der; -s, -; Schrecken erregen; (↑R 40:) eine Schrecken erregende Nachricht; **Schreck|bild**

Schre|cke, die; -, -n (*kurz für* Heuschrecke)

[1]**schre|cken** (in Schrecken geraten; *nur noch in* erschrecken [du erschrickst, erschrakst, bist erschrocken] *u. in Zusammensetzungen wie* auf-, hoch-, zurück-, zusammenschrecken; *vgl. d.*); du schrickst, *auch* schreckst; du schrakst, *auch* schrecktest, er schrak, *auch* schreckte; du schräkest, *auch* schrecktest; er hat geschreckt; schrick!, *auch* schreck[e]!; [2]**schre|cken** (in Schrecken [ver]setzen; abschrecken; *Jägerspr.* schreien); du schreckst, er schreckt; du schrecktest; er hat geschreckt; schreck[e]!; **Schre|cken, Schrecken er|re|gend;** *vgl.* Schreck; **Schre|ckens|bi|lanz; schreckens‿blass, ...bleich; Schreckens‿bot|schaft, ...herr|schaft, ...nach|richt, ...nacht, ...tat, ...zeit; schreck|er|füllt; Schreck|ge|spenst; schreck|haft; Schreck|haf|tig|keit,** die; -; **schreck|lich** (*vgl.* schlimm); **Schreck|lich|keit; Schreck|nis,** das; -ses, -se *(geh.);* **Schreck‿schrau|be** (*ugs. für* unangenehme Frau), **...schuss; Schreck|schuss|pis|to|le; Schreck|se|kun|de**

Schred|der, der; -s, - ‹engl.› (technische Anlage zum Verschrotten von Autowracks)

Schrei, der; -[e]s, -e; **Schrei|ad|ler**

Schreib‿au|to|mat, ...be|darf, ...block (*vgl.* Block), **...bü|ro; Schrei|be,** die; - (*ugs. für* Geschriebenes; Schreibgerät; Schreibstil); **schrei|ben;** du schriebst; du schriebest; geschrieben; schreib[e]!; er hat mir sage und schreibe (tatsächlich) zwanzig Mark abgenommen; **Schrei|ben,** das; -s, - (Schriftstück); **Schrei|ber; Schrei|be|rei; Schrei|be|rin; Schrei|ber|ling** ([viel u.] schlecht schreibender Autor); **Schrei|ber|see|le** (bürokratischer, kleinlicher Mensch); **schreib|faul; Schreib‿faul|heit** (die; -), **...fe|der, ...feh|ler; schreib|ge|wandt; Schreib‿heft, ...kraft, ...krampf, ...map|pe, ...ma|schi|ne; Schreib|ma|schi|nen‿pa|pier, ...schrift, ...tisch; Schreib‿pa|pier, ...pult, ...schrank, ...schrift, ...stu|be, ...tisch; Schreib|tisch‿gar|ni|tur, ...tä|ter** (jmd., der den Auftrag zu einem Verbrechen [vom Schreibtisch aus] gibt, in führender Position dafür verantwortlich ist); **Schreib|übung** (↑R 132); **Schrei|bung; Schreib‿un|ter|la|ge, ...un|ter|richt, ...wa|ren** *(Plur.);* **Schreib|wa|ren|ge|schäft; Schreib‿wei|se** (die), **...zeug** (das; -[e]s)

schrei|en; du schriest; geschrien; schrei[e]!; die schreiendsten Farben; **Schrei|er; Schrei|e|rei** *(ugs.);* **Schrei‿hals** *(abwertend),* **...krampf**

Schrein, der; -[e]s, -e ‹lat.› (*veraltend für* Schrank; [Reliquien]behältnis); **Schrei|ner** (*bes. südd., westd. für* Tischler); **Schrei|ne|rei; schrei|nern;** ich ...ere (↑R 16)

Schreit|bag|ger; schrei|ten; du schrittst; du schrittest; geschritten; schreit[e]!; **Schreit‿tanz, ...vo|gel**

Schrenz, der; -es, -e (*veraltend für* minderwertiges Papier, Löschpapier)

Schrieb, der; -s, -e *u.* **Schriebs,** der; -es, -e (*ugs., oft abwertend für* Schreiben, Brief); **Schrift,** die; -, -en; die deutsche, gotische, lateinische, griechische, kyrillische -; **Schrift‿art, ...bild; schrift|deutsch; Schrift|deutsch,** das; -[s]; **Schrift|deut|sche,** das; -n; **Schrif|ten** *Plur.* (*schweiz. für* Ausweispapiere); **Schrif|ten‿rei|he, ...ver|zeich|nis; Schrift‿fäl|scher, ...form, ...füh|rer, ...ge|lehr|te** (im N.T.); **schrift|ge|mäß; Schrift‿gie|ßer, ...gie|ße|rei, ...grad, ...gut, ...hö|he, ...lei|ter** (der), **...lei|tung; schrift|lich;** -e Arbeit; -e Prüfung; -e Überlieferung; (↑R 47:) etwas Schriftliches geben; **Schrift|lich|keit,** die; - (schriftliche Niederlegung); **Schrift‿pro|be, ...rol|le, ...sach|ver|stän|di|ge, ...satz, ...set|zer, ...set|ze|rin, ...spie|gel, ...spra|che; schrift|sprach|lich; Schrift|stel|ler; Schrift|stel|le|rei,** die; -; **Schrift|stel|le|rin; schrift|stel|le|risch; schrift|stel|lern;** ich ...ere (↑R 16); geschriftstellert; **Schrift|stück; Schrift|tum,** das; -s; **Schrift‿typ, ...ver|kehr** (der; -s); **schrift|ver|stän|dig; Schrift‿wech|sel, ...zei|chen, ...zug**

schrill; schril|len; Schrill|heit, die; -

Schrimp *vgl.* Shrimp

schrin|nen (*nordd. für* schmerzen); die Wunde schrinnt

Schrip|pe, die; -, -n (*bes. berlin. für* Brötchen)

Schritt, der; -[e]s, -e; 5 Schritt weit (↑R 90); Schritt für Schritt; auf Schritt und Tritt; Schritt fahren, Schritt halten; **Schritt‿feh|ler** *(Sport),* **...fol|ge** (beim Tanzen), **...ge|schwin|dig|keit** (die; -), **...kom|bi|na|ti|on** *(Sport),* **...län|ge, ...ma|cher; Schritt|ma|cher|ma|schi|ne** *(Radrennen);* **Schritt|mes|ser,** der; **Schritt|tanz** (↑R 136); **Schritt|tem|po** (↑R 136), das; -s; **schritt|wei|se; Schritt‿wei|te** (bei der Hose), **...zäh|ler**

Schro|fen, der; -s, - (*landsch., bes. österr. für* Felsklippe); **schroff; Schroff,** der; *Gen.* -[e]s *u.* -en, *Plur.* -en (↑R 126) *u.* **Schrof|fen,** der; -s, - *vgl.* Schrofen; **Schroff|heit**

schroh (*fränk. u. hess. für* hässlich)

schröp|fen; Schröp|fer (*selten für* Schröpfkopf); **Schröpf|kopf** *(Med.)*

Schropp|ho|bel *vgl.* Schrupp|hobel

Schrot, der *od.* das; -[e]s, -e (grob gemahlene Getreidekörner; kleine Bleikügelchen); mit - schießen; **Schrot‿blatt** (mittelalterl. Kunstblatt in Metallschnitt), **...brot; schro|ten** (grob zerkleinern); geschrotet, *älter* geschroten; **Schrö|ter** (*selten für* Hirschkäfer); **Schrot|flin|te**

Schroth|kur (↑R 95) ‹nach dem österr. Naturheilkundler J. Schroth› ([Abmagerungs]kur mit wasserarmer Diät)

Schrot‿korn, ...ku|gel, ...la|dung; Schröt|ling (Metallstück zum Prägen von Münzen); **Schrot‿mehl, ...müh|le, ...sä|ge, ...schuss; Schrot|schuss|krank|heit,** die; - (eine Pflanzenkrankheit); **Schrott,** der; -[e]s, -e *Plur. selten* (Altmetall); **schrot|ten** (zu Schrott machen); **Schrott‿han|del** (*vgl.* [1]Handel), **...händ|ler, ...hau|fen, ...platz, ...pres|se; schrott|reif; Schrott-**

trans|port (↑R 136); **Schrott-wert,** der; -[e]s
Schrot|waa|ge (Vorrichtung zur Prüfung waagerechter Flächen)
Schrub|be|sen (↑R 136; *landsch.*); **schrub|ben** (mit einer Bürste o. Ä. reinigen); *vgl.* schruppen; **Schrub|ber** ([Stiel]-scheuerbürste)
Schrul|le, die; -, -n (seltsame Laune; *auch ugs. für* eigensinnige alte Frau); **schrul|len|haft; schrul|lig; Schrul|lig|keit,** die; -
schrumm!; schrumm|fi|de-bumm!
Schrum|pel, die; -, -n (*landsch. für* Falte, Runzel; alte Frau); **schrum|pe|lig** *vgl.* schrumplig; **schrum|peln** (*landsch. für* schrumpfen); ich ...[e]le (↑R 16); **schrumpf|be|stän|dig;** -e Stoffe; **schrump|fen; Schrumpf|ger-ma|ne** (*ugs. abwertend für* kleinwüchsiger Mensch); **schrump-fig; Schrumpf‿kopf** (eingeschrumpfter Kopf eines getöteten Feindes [als Trophäe]), **...le|ber, ...nie|re; Schrump-fung; schrump|lig,** schrum|pe|lig (*landsch. für* faltig u. eingetrocknet)
Schrund, der; -[e]s, Schründe (*südd., österr., schweiz. für* Fels-, Gletscherspalte); **Schrun|de,** die; -, -n ([Haut]riss, Spalte); **schrun-dig** (*landsch. für* rissig)
schrup|pen (grob hobeln); *vgl.* schrubben; **Schrupp|fei|le; Schrupp|ho|bel,** Schropp|ho|bel
Schruz, der; -es (*obersächs. für* Minderwertiges, Wertloses)
Schtetl *vgl.* Stetl
Schub, der; -[e]s, Schübe; **Schub-ab|schal|tung** *(Kfz-Technik)*
Schub|be|jack, der; -s, -s (*nordd. für* Schubiack); **schub|ben** (*nordd. für* kratzen)
Schu|ber, der; -s, - (Schutzkarton für Bücher; *österr. auch für* Absperrvorrichtung, Schieber)
Schu|bert (österr. Komponist)
Schub|fach
Schu|bi|ack, der; -s, *Plur.* -s *u.* -e ⟨niederl.⟩ (*ugs. für* Lump, niederträchtiger Mensch)
Schub‿kar|re[n], ...kas|ten, ...kraft, ...la|de; schub|la|di|sie-ren (*schweiz. für* unbearbeitet weglegen); **Schub‿leh|re** (*svw.* Schieblehre), **...leich|ter** (Schiff), **...leis|tung; Schüb|lig** *(schweiz. mdal.) u.* **Schüb|ling** (*südd., schweiz. für* [leicht geräucherte] lange Wurst); **Schub|mo|dul,** der; -s, -n *(Physik);* **Schubs,** der; -es, -e (*ugs. für* Stoß); **Schub-schiff; schub|sen** (*ugs. für* [an]stoßen); du schubst; **Schub-se|rei** *(ugs.);* **Schub|stan|ge; schub|wei|se; Schub|wir|kung**
schüch|tern; Schüch|tern|heit, die; -
schu|ckeln (*landsch. für* schaukeln); ich ...[e]le (↑R 16)
schud|dern (*landsch. für* schauern, frösteln); es schuddert mich
Schuf|fel, die; -, -n (ein Gartengerät)
Schuft, der; -[e]s, -e *(abwertend)*
schuf|ten (*ugs. für* hart arbeiten); **Schuf|te|rei** *(ugs.)*
schuf|tig; Schuf|tig|keit
Schuh, der; -[e]s, -e; 3 - lang (↑R 90); **Schuh‿an|zie|her, ...band** (das; *Plur.* ...bänder; *landsch. für* Schnürsenkel), **...bürs|te; Schuh|chen, Schüh-chen; Schuh‿creme, ...fab|rik, ...ge|schäft, ...grö|ße, ...kar|ton, ...la|den** (*Plur.* ...läden); **Schüh-lein; Schuh‿leis|ten, ...löf|fel, ...ma|cher; Schuh|ma|che|rei; Schuh|ma|che|rin; Schuh|ma-cher|lehr|ling; Schuh‿num-mer, ...platt|ler** (ein Volkstanz), **...put|zer, ...rie|men, ...soh|le, ...span|ner, ...werk, ...wich|se** *(ugs.),* **...zeug** (das; -[e]s; *ugs.*)
Schu|ko ® (*Kurzw. für* Schutzkontakt), *in Verbindungen wie* **Schu|ko|ste|cker** (*Kurzw. für* Stecker mit besonderem Schutzkontakt)
Schul‿ab|gän|ger, ...ab|schluss
Schu|lam|mit *vgl.* [2]Sulamith
Schul‿amt, ...an|fang; ...an|fän-ger, ...ar|beit (*österr. auch svw.* Klassenarbeit), **...arzt, ...ärz|tin; schul|ärzt|lich; Schul‿at|las, ...auf|ga|be, ...auf|satz, ...auf-sicht; Schul|auf|sichts|be|hör-de; Schul‿bank** (*Plur.* ...bänke), **...be|ginn, ...be|hör|de, ...bei-spiel, ...be|such, ...bil|dung, ...bub** (*südd., österr. für* Schuljunge), **...buch, ...bus, ...chor**
Schuld, die; -, -en; es ist meine Schuld; [bei jmdm.] Schulden haben, machen; [an etwas] Schuld *od.* die Schuld haben; jmdm. Schuld *od.* die Schuld geben; an etwas Schuld tragen; *aber* (↑R 46): schuld sein; du hast dir etwas zuschulden, *auch* zu Schulden kommen lassen; **Schuld‿ab-än|de|rung** *(Rechtsw.),* **...an|er-kennt|nis** (das; *Rechtsw.*), **...bei-tritt** *(Rechtsw.),* **...be|kennt|nis; schuld|be|la|den;** *(geh.);* **Schuld|be|weis; schuld|be-wusst; Schuld|be|wusst|sein; Schuld|buch|for|de|rung** *(Wirtsch.);* **schul|den; Schul-den‿berg** *(ugs.),* **...er|lass; schul|den|frei** (ohne Schulden); **Schul|den|haf|tung** *(Rechtsspr.);* **schul|den|hal|ber; Schul|den-last; schuld|fä|hig** *(Rechtsspr.);* **Schuld|frage,** die; -; **schuld|frei** (ohne Schuld); **Schuld|ge|fühl; schuld|haft; Schuld|haft,** die; - *(früher)*
Schul|dienst, der; -[e]s; im - [tätig] sein (als Lehrer unterrichten)
schul|dig; der -e Teil; auf - plädieren (Schuldigsprechung beantragen); eines Verbrechens - sein; jmdn. - sprechen; **Schul|di|ge,** der *u.* die; -n, -n (↑R 5 ff.); **Schul-di|ger** (*bibl. für* jmd., der sich schuldig gemacht hat); **schul|di-ger|ma|ßen; Schul|dig|keit;** seine [Pflicht u.] - tun; **Schul|dig-spre|chung; Schuld|komp|lex** *(Psych.);* **schuld|los; Schuld|lo-sig|keit,** die; -; **Schuld|ner; Schuld|ne|rin; Schuld|ner-‿mehr|heit** *(Rechtsw.),* **...ver-zug** *(Rechtsspr.);* **Schuld‿recht** (das; -[e]s; *Rechtsspr.*), **...schein, ...spruch, ...über|nah|me** (↑R 132), **...um|wand|lung, ...ver|hält|nis, ...ver|schrei-bung; schuld|voll; Schuld-‿wech|sel, ...zins** (*Plur.* ...zinsen), **...zu|wei|sung**
Schu|le, die; -, -n; (↑R 108:) die hohe Schule *(vgl. d.);* die höhere Schule (*vgl.* höher); Schule machen (Nachahmer finden); **schul-ei|gen** (↑R 40); **schu|len; Schul-eng|lisch** (Englischkenntnisse, die jmd. auf der Schule erworben hat); **schul|ent|las|sen** (↑R 40); **Schul|ent|las|sung; schul|ent-wach|sen** (↑R 40); **Schü|ler; Schü|ler‿aus|tausch, ...aus-weis; schü|ler|haft; Schü|le|rin; Schü|ler|lot|se** (Schüler, der als Verkehrshelfer eingesetzt ist); **Schü|ler‿mit|ver|ant|wor|tung, ...mit|ver|wal|tung** (*Abk.* SMV), **...par|la|ment; Schü|ler|schaft; Schü|ler‿spra|che** (die; -), **...wett|be|werb, ...zei|tung; Schul‿fach, ...fe|ri|en** *(Plur.);* **schul|frei;** *vgl.* hitzefrei; **Schul-‿freund, ...freun|din, ...funk, ...gang** (der), **...gar|ten, ...ge-bäu|de, ...geld** (das; -[e]s); **Schul|geld|frei|heit,** die; -; **Schul‿ge|lehr|sam|keit, ...ge-mein|de, ...ge|setz, ...haus, ...heft, ...hof, ...hort, ...hy|gi|e-ne; schu|lisch; Schul‿jahr, ...ju-gend, ...jun|ge** (der), **...ka|me-rad, ...kennt|nis|se** *(Plur.),* **...kind, ...klas|se, ...land|heim, ...leh|rer, ...leh|re|rin, ...lei|ter** (der), **...lei|te|rin, ...lei|tung, ...mäd|chen, ...mann** (*svw.* Leh-

rer); **schul|mä|ßig; Schul‿me|di|zin** (die; -), **...meis|ter; schul|meis|ter|lich; schul|meis|tern;** ich ...ere (↑R 16); geschulmeistert; zu -; **Schul‿mu|sik** (die; -), **...or|ches|ter, ...ord|nung**
Schulp, der; -[e]s, -e (Schale der Tintenfische)
Schul|pflicht, die; -; **schul|pflich|tig;** -es Alter; -es Kind; **Schul|pfor|ta** ([*früher* Fürstenschule] bei Naumburg); **Schul‿po|li|tik, ...psy|cho|lo|ge, ...psy|cho|lo|gin, ...ran|zen, ...rat** (*Plur.* ...räte), **...recht** (das; -[e]s), **...re|form, ...rei|fe, ...sack** (*schweiz. für* Schulranzen; Schulbildung), **...schiff, ...schluss** (der; -es), **...spei|sung** (die; -), **...sport, ...spre|cher, ...spre|che|rin, ...stress, ...stun|de, ...sys|tem, ...tag, ...ta|sche**
Schul|ter, die; -, -n; **Schul|ter|blatt; schul|ter|frei; Schul|ter|ge|lenk; ...schul|te|rig,** ...schultrig (z. B. breitschult[e]rig); **Schul|ter|klap|pe** *meist Plur.*; **schul|ter|lang;** -es Haar; **schul|tern;** ich ...ere (↑R 16); **Schul|ter‿pols|ter, ...rie|men, ...schluss** (der; -es; das Zusammenhalten [von Interessengruppen u. a.]), **...sieg** (beim Ringen)
Schult|heiß, der; -en, -en; ↑R 126 (*früher für* Gemeindevorsteher; *im Kanton Luzern* Präsident des Regierungsrates); **Schult|hei|ßen|amt**
...schult|rig *vgl.* ...schulterig
Schul|tü|te (am ersten Schultag); **Schu|lung; Schu|lungs|kurs; Schul‿un|ter|richt, ...ver|sa|gen, ...ver|wal|tung, ...wart** (der; -[e], -e; *österr. für* Hausmeister einer Schule), **...weg, ...weis|heit** (*veraltet für* angelerntes Wissen), **...we|sen** (das; -s), **...wis|sen**
Schul|ze, der; -n, -n; ↑R 126 (*veraltet für* Gemeindevorsteher)
Schul|zeit
Schul|zen|amt (*veraltet*)
Schul‿zent|rum, ...zeug|nis
Schu|man (franz. Politiker)
Schu|mann (dt. Komponist)
Schum|mel, der; -s (*ugs. für* Schummelei, Betrug); **Schum|me|lei** (*ugs.*); **schum|meln** (*ugs. für* [leicht] betrügen); ich ...[e]le (↑R 16)
Schum|mer, der; -s, - (*landsch. für* Dämmerung); **schum|me|rig,** schumm|rig (*ugs. für* dämmerig, halbdunkel); **schum|mern** (*landsch. für* dämmern; *fachspr. für* [Landkarte] schattieren); ich ...ere (↑R 16); (↑R 50:) im Schummern (*landsch. für* in der Dämmerung); **Schum|mer|stun|de** (*landsch.*); **Schum|me|rung,** die; - (*fachspr. für* Schattierung)
Schumm|ler, der; -s, - (*ugs. für* jmd., der schummelt); **Schumm|le|rin**
schumm|rig *vgl.* schummerig
Schum|per|lied (*obersächs. für* Liebeslied, derbes Volkslied); **schum|pern** (*ostmitteld. für* auf dem Schoße schaukeln); ich ...ere (↑R 16)
Schund, der; -[e]s (Wertloses, Minderwertiges); **Schund‿blatt** (*abwertend für* Zeitschrift, die nur Schund enthält), **...heft** (*svw.* Schundblatt), **...li|te|ra|tur** (die; -), **...ro|man**
schun|keln ([sich] hin u. her wiegen; *landsch. für* schaukeln); ich ...[e]le (↑R 16); **Schun|kel|wal|zer**
Schupf, der; -[e]s, -e (*südd., schweiz. mdal. für* Schubs, Stoß, Schwung); **schup|fen**
Schup|fen, der; -s, - (*südd., österr. für* Schuppen, Wetterdach)
Schup|fer (*österr. ugs. für* Stoß, Schubs)
[1]**Schu|po,** die; - (*Kurzw. für* Schutzpolizei); [2]**Schu|po,** der; -s, -s (*veraltet; Kurzw. für* Schutzpolizist)
Schupp, der; -[e]s, -e (*nordd. für* Schubs, Stoß, Schwung)
Schüpp|chen (kleine Schuppe); **Schup|pe,** die; -, -n (Haut-, Hornplättchen)
Schüp|pe, die; -, -n (*landsch. für* Schippe)
Schüp|pel, der; -s, - (*bayr. u. österr. mdal. für* Büschel)
schüp|peln (*veraltet für* schiebend bewegen); ich ...[e]le (↑R 16); [1]**schup|pen** (*landsch. für* stoßen, stoßend schieben)
[2]**schup|pen** ([Fisch]schuppen entfernen)
schüp|pen (*landsch. für* schippen)
Schup|pen, der; -s, - (Raum für Holz u. a.); *vgl.* Schupfen
Schüp|pen *Plur.* (*landsch. für* Schippen)
schup|pen|ar|tig; Schup|pen‿bil|dung, ...flech|te (*Med.*), **...pan|zer, ...tier; schup|pig**
Schups, der; -es, -e (*südd. für* Schubs); **schup|sen** (*südd. für* schubsen); du schupst
Schur, die; -, -en (Scheren [der Schafe])
Schür|ei|sen; schü|ren; Schü|rer (*landsch. für* Schürhaken)
Schurf, der; -[e]s, Schürfe (*Bergmannsspr.* Suche nach nutzbaren Lagerstätten); **schür|fen; Schür|fer** (*Bergmannsspr.*); **Schürf|kü|bel** (ein Fördergerät); **Schürf‿loch, ...recht; Schür|fung; Schürf|wun|de**
schür|gen (*landsch. für* schieben, stoßen, treiben)
Schür|ha|ken
...schü|rig (z. B. dreischürig, *mit Ziffer* 3-schürig; ↑R 44)
Schu|ri|ge|lei (*ugs.*); **schu|ri|geln** (*ugs. für* schikanieren, quälen); ich ...[e]le (↑R 16)
Schur|ke, der; -n, -n; ↑R 126 (*abwertend*); **Schur|ken|streich** (*veraltend*); **Schur|ke|rei** (*abwertend*); **Schur|kin; schur|kisch**
Schur|re, die; -, -n (*landsch. für* Rutsche); **schur|ren** (*landsch. für* mit knirschendem Geräusch über den Boden gleiten, scharren); **Schurr|murr,** der; -s (*landsch. für* Durcheinander; Gerümpel)
Schur|wol|le; schur|wol|len (aus Schurwolle)
Schurz, der; -es, -e; **Schür|ze,** die; -, -n; **schür|zen;** du schürzt; **Schür|zen‿band** (das; *Plur.* ...bänder), **...jä|ger** (*ugs. für* Mann, der ständig Frauen umwirbt), **...kleid, ...zip|fel**
Schusch|nigg (österr. Politiker)
Schuss, der; -es, Schüsse; 2 - Rum (↑R 90); 2 - (*auch* Schüsse) abgeben; in Schuss (*ugs. für* in Ordnung) halten, haben; **Schuss‿ab|ga|be** (die; -; *Amtsspr.*), **...bein** (*Fußball*), **...be|reich** (der); **schuss|be|reit**
[1]**Schus|sel,** der; -s, - *od.* die; -, -n (*ugs. für* unkonzentrierter, vergesslicher Mensch); [2]**Schus|sel,** die; -, -n (*landsch. für* Schlitterbahn)
Schüs|sel, die; -, -n; **schüs|sel|för|mig**
schus|se|lig, schuss|lig (*ugs. für* unkonzentriert, vergesslich, fahrig); **schus|seln** (*ugs. für* fahrig, unruhig sein; *landsch. für* schlittern); ich schussele *u.* schussle (↑R 16)
Schus|ser (*landsch. für* Spielkügelchen); **schus|sern** (*landsch.*); ich schussere *u.* schussre (↑R 16)
Schuss‿fa|den (*Weberei*), **...fahrt** (*Skisport*), **...feld; schuss|fer|tig; schuss|fest** (kugelsicher; *Jägerspr.* an Schüsse gewöhnt); **Schuss‿garn** (*Weberei*), **...ge|le|gen|heit** (*Sport*); **schuss|ge|recht** (*Jägerspr.*); **Schuss|ge|rin|ne** (*Wasserbau*)
schus|sig (*landsch. für* [über]eilig, hastig); **Schuss|ler** (*landsch. für* mit Schussern Spielender; *ugs. svw.* [1]Schussel)

schuss|lig *vgl.* schusselig
Schuss‿li|nie, ...rich|tung
schuss|schwach (↑R 136; *Sport*); **Schuss|schwä|che** (↑R 136; *bes. Fuß-, Handball*); **schuss-stark** (↑R 136; *Sport*); **Schuss-stär|ke** (↑R 136; *bes. Fuß-, Handball*)
Schuss‿ver|let|zung, ...waf|fe, ...wech|sel, ...wei|te, ...wun|de, ...zahl
Schus|ter; Schus|ter‿ah|le, ...draht; Schus|te|rei *(veraltet);* **Schus|ter|jun|ge,** der (*veraltet für* Schusterlehrling; *berlin. für* Roggenbrötchen); **schus|tern** (*landsch., sonst veraltet für* das Schuhmacherhandwerk ausüben; *abwertend für* Pfuscharbeit machen); ich ...ere (↑R 16); **Schus-ter‿pal|me** (eine Pflanze), **...pech, ...pfriem, ...werk|statt**
Schu|te, die; -, -n (flaches, offenes Wasserfahrzeug; haubenartiger Frauenhut)
Schutt, der; -[e]s; **Schutt|ab|la-de|platz; Schütt‿be|ton, ...bo-den** *(landsch.);* **Schüt|te,** die; -, -n (kleiner Behälter [z. B. für Mehl]; *landsch. für* Bund [Stroh]); eine - Stroh; **Schüt|tel‿frost, ...läh|mung** *(Med.);* **schüt|teln;** ich ...[e]le (↑R 16); **Schüt|tel-‿reim, ...rut|sche** *(Bergmannsspr.);* **schüt|ten**
schüt|ter (spärlich; schwach)
schüt|tern (schütteln); der Wagen schüttert
Schütt|gut (*Wirtsch.;* z. B. Kohle, Sand); **Schutt‿hal|de, ...hau-fen, ...ke|gel** *(Geol.);* **Schütt-ofen** (↑R 132; *Hüttenw.*); **Schutt|platz; Schütt‿stein** (*schweiz. für* Ausguss, Spülbecken), **...stroh; Schüt|tung**
Schutz, der; -es, *Plur. (Technik:)* -e; zu - und Trutz
[1]**Schütz,** der; -en, -en; ↑R 126 (*veraltet für* [1]Schütze)
[2]**Schütz,** das; -es, -e (*Elektrotechnik* ferngesteuerter Schalter);
[3]**Schütz,** das; -es, -e *u.* Schüt|ze, die; -, -n (bewegliches Wehr)
Schutz‿an|strich, ...an|zug, ...be-dürf|nis (das; ...nisses); **schutz-be|dürf|tig; Schutz|be|foh|le-ne,** der *u.* die; -n, -n (↑R 5 ff.); **Schutz‿be|haup|tung, ...blech, ...brett, ...brief, ...bril|le, ...bünd-nis, ...dach**
[1]**Schüt|ze,** der; -n, -n; ↑R 126 (Schießender)
[2]**Schüt|ze,** die; -, -n (*svw.* [3]Schütz)
schüt|zen; du schützt
Schüt|zen, der; -s, - (*Weberei* Gerät zur Aufnahme der Schussspulen, Schiffchen)

Schüt|zen‿bru|der, ...fest
Schutz|en|gel
Schüt|zen‿ge|sell|schaft, ...gil-de, ...gra|ben, ...haus, ...hil|fe *(ugs.),* **...kö|nig, ...lie|sel** (die; -, -; ↑R 97), **...li|nie, ...pan|zer, ...platz**
Schüt|zen|steu|e|rung, Schütz-steu|e|rung ⟨*zu* [2]Schütz⟩ *(Elektrotechnik)*
Schüt|zen‿ver|ein, ...wie|se
Schüt|zer (*kurz für* Knie-, Ohrenschützer); **Schutz‿far|be, ...fär-bung** *(Zool.),* **...film, ...frist, ...ge-biet, ...ge|bühr, ...geist** (*Plur.* ...geister), **...geld; Schutz|geld-er|pres|sung; Schutz‿ge|mein-schaft, ...git|ter, ...glas** (*Plur.* ...gläser), **...ha|fen** (*vgl.* [2]Hafen), **...haft** (die), **...hau|be, ...hei|li|ge** *(kath. Kirche),* **...helm, ...herr, ...herr|schaft, ...hül|le, ...hüt|te; schutz|imp|fen;** ich schutzimpfe; schutzgeimpft; schutzzuimpfen; **Schutz‿imp|fung, ...klau|sel, ...klei|dung; Schütz|ling; schutz|los; Schutz|lo|sig|keit,** die; -; **Schutz‿macht, ...mann** (*Plur.* ...männer *u.* ...leute; *ugs. für* [Schutz]polizei), **...mar|ke, ...mas|ke, ...mit|tel** (das), **...pat-ron** (*svw.* Schutzheilige), **...po|li-zei** (die; -; *Kurzw.* [1]Schupo), **...po|li|zist** (*Kurzw.* [2]Schupo), **...raum, ...schicht, ...schild** (der)
Schütz|steu|e|rung *vgl.* Schützensteuerung
Schutz‿trup|pe, ...um|schlag; Schutz-und-Trutz-Bünd|nis (↑R 28; *veraltend*); **Schutz‿ver-band, ...ver|trag, ...vor|keh-rung, ...vor|rich|tung, ...wall, ...weg** (*österr. für* Fußgängerüberweg), **...wehr** (die; *veraltet, noch fachspr.*), **...zoll; Schutz-zoll|po|li|tik,** die; -
Schw. = Schwester
Schwa|bach (Stadt in Mittelfranken); [1]**Schwa|ba|cher** (↑R 103);
[2]**Schwa|ba|cher,** die; - (*Druckw.* eine Schriftgattung); **Schwa|ba-cher Schrift,** die; - -
Schwab|be|lei (*ugs. für* Wackelei; *landsch. für* Geschwätz); **schwab|be|lig,** schwabb|lig (*ugs. für* schwammig, fett; wackelnd); **schwab|beln** (*ugs. für* wackeln; *landsch. für* schwätzen); ich ...[e]le (↑R 16); **Schwab|ber,** der; -s, - (moppähnlicher Besen auf Schiffen); **schwab|bern;** ich ...ere (↑R 16; *svw.* schwabbeln); **schwabb|lig** *vgl.* schwabbelig
[1]**Schwa|be,** der; -n, -n; ↑R 126 (Bewohner von Schwaben)
[2]**Schwa|be** *vgl.* [1]Schabe
schwä|beln (schwäbisch sprechen); ich ...[e]le (↑R 16);

Schwa|ben; Schwa|ben‿al|ter (das; -s; *scherzh. für* 40. Lebensjahr), **...spie|gel** (der; -s; Rechtssammlung des dt. MA.), **...streich** *(scherzh.);* **Schwä|bin; schwä|bisch,** *aber* (↑R 102): die Schwäbische Alb; **Schwä|bisch Gmünd** (Stadt in Baden-Württemberg); **Schwä|bisch Hall** (Stadt in Baden-Württemberg); **schwä|bisch-häl|lisch**
schwach; schwächer, schwächste; das schwache (*veraltend für* weibliches) Geschlecht; eine schwache Stunde; *Sprachw.:* schwache Deklination; ein -es Verb; (↑R 47:) das Recht des Schwachen; *Getrenntschreibung in Verbindung mit dem Partizip II:* ein [sehr] schwach begabter Schüler; eine schwach betonte, schwächer betonte Silbe; die schwach bevölkerte Gegend, am schwächsten bevölkerte Gegenden; die [nur] schwach bewegte See; **schwach-at|mig; schwach be|gabt** *vgl.* schwach; **Schwach|be|gab|ten-för|de|rung; schwach be|tont** *vgl.* schwach; **schwach be|völ-kert** *vgl.* schwach; **schwach be-wegt** *vgl.* schwach; **schwach-brüs|tig; Schwä|che,** die; -, -n; **Schwä|che‿an|fall, ...ge|fühl; schwä|chen; Schwä|che-‿punkt** (*svw.* Schwachpunkt), **...zu|stand; Schwach|heit; schwach|her|zig; Schwach-kopf** (*abwertend für* dummer Mensch); **schwach|köp|fig; schwäch|lich; Schwäch|lich-keit** *Plur. selten;* **Schwäch|ling; Schwach|ma|ti|kus,** der; -, -se (*scherzh. für* Schwächling); **Schwach|punkt; schwach-sich|tig; Schwach|sich|tig|keit,** die; -; **Schwach|sinn,** der; -[e]s; **schwach|sin|nig; Schwach-‿stel|le, ...strom** (der; -[e]s); **Schwach|strom‿lei|tung, ...tech|nik** (die; -); **Schwä-chung**
Schwa|de, die; -, -n *u.* [1]**Schwa-den,** der; -s, - (Reihe abgemähten Grases od. Getreides)
[2]**Schwa|den,** der; -s, - (Dampf, Dunst; *Bergmannsspr.* schlechte [gefährliche] Grubenluft)
schwa|den|wei|se ⟨*zu* Schwade⟩
schwa|dern (*südd. für* plätschern; schwatzen); ich ...ere (↑R 16)
Schwad|ron (↑R 130), die; -, -en ⟨ital.⟩ (*früher* kleinste Einheit der Kavallerie); **schwad|ro-nen|wei|se,** schwad|rons|wei|se; **Schwad|ro|neur** [...'nøːr], der; -s, -e ⟨franz.⟩ (*veraltend für* jmd., der schwadroniert); **schwad|ro-**

nie|ren (wortreich u. prahlerisch schwatzen); **Schwad|rons|chef** *(früher);* **schwad|rons|wei|se** *vgl.* schwadronenweise

Schwa|fe|lei *(ugs. für* törichtes Gerede); **schwa|feln;** ich ...[e]le (↑R 16; *ugs.)*

Schwa|ger, der; -s, Schwäger *(veraltet auch für* Postkutscher); **Schwä|ge|rin; schwä|ger|lich; Schwä|ger|schaft; Schwä|her,** der; -s, - *(veraltet für* Schwiegervater od. Schwager); **Schwä|herschaft** *(veraltet)*

schwai|en *vgl.* schwoien

Schwai|ge, die; -, -n *(bayr. u. österr. für* Sennhütte); **schwaigen** *(bayr. u. österr. für* eine Schwaige betreiben, Käse bereiten); **Schwai|ger** *(bayr. u. österr. für* Almhirt); **Schwaig|hof**

Schwälb|chen; Schwal|be, die; -, -n *(ugs. auch für* absichtliches Hinfallen im Fußballspiel, um ein gegnerisches Foul vorzutäuschen [bes. im Strafraum]); **Schwalben‿nest, ...schwanz**

schwal|chen *(veraltet für* qualmen); **Schwalk,** der; -[e]s, -e *(nordd. für* Dampf, Qualm; Bö); **schwal|ken** *(nordd. für* herumbummeln)

Schwall, der; -[e]s, -e (Gewoge, Welle, Guss [Wasser])

Schwalm, die; - (Fluss u. Landschaft in Hessen); **Schwäl|mer** (↑R 103); **Schwäl|me|rin**

Schwamm, der; -[e]s, Schwämme *(landsch. u. österr. auch für* Pilz); Schwamm drüber! *(ugs. für* vergessen wir das!); **schwamm|artig; Schwämm|chen; Schwammerl,** der; -s, -[n] *(bayr. u. österr. ugs. für* Pilz); **schwammig; Schwam|mig|keit,** die; -; **Schwamm‿spin|ner** (ein Schmetterling), **...tuch** *(Plur.* ...tücher)

Schwan, der; -[e]s, Schwäne; **Schwän|chen**

schwa|nen *(ugs.);* mir schwant (ich ahne) etwas

Schwa|nen‿ge|sang *(geh. für* letztes Werk eines Künstlers; letztes Aufleben einer zu Ende gehenden Epoche o.Ä.), **...hals; Schwa|nen|jung|frau,** Schwanjung|frau *(Mythol.);* **Schwa|nenteich; schwa|nen|weiß**

Schwang, der; *nur noch in* im -[e] (sehr gebräuchlich) sein

schwan|ger; Schwan|ge|re, die; -n, -n; **Schwan|ge|ren‿be|ratung, ...für|sor|ge, ...geld, ...gym|nas|tik; schwän|gern;** ich ...ere (↑R 16); **Schwan|gerschaft; Schwan|ger|schafts‿ab|bruch, ...gym|nas|tik, ...test** (Test zum Nachweis einer bestehenden Schwangerschaft), **...urlaub, ...ver|hü|tung; Schwänge|rung**

Schwan|jung|frau *vgl.* Schwanenjungfrau

schwank *(geh. für* biegsam, schwankend); -e Gestalten; **Schwank,** der; -[e]s, Schwänke; **schwan|ken; Schwank|fi|gur; Schwan|kung**

Schwanz, der; -es, Schwänze; **Schwänz|chen; Schwän|ze|lei** *(ugs);* **schwän|zeln** *(ugs. iron. für* geziert gehen); ich ...[e]le (↑R 16); **schwän|zen** *(ugs. für* [am Schulunterricht o.Ä.] nicht teilnehmen); du schwänzt; **Schwanzen|de; Schwän|zer** *(ugs.);* **Schwanz‿fe|der, ...flos|se; ...schwän|zig** (z.B. langschwänzig); **schwanz|las|tig** (vom Flugzeug); **Schwanz‿lurch, ...spitze, ...stück, ...wir|bel**

schwapp!, schwaps!; **Schwapp,** der; -[e]s, -e *u.* Schwaps, der; -es, -e *(ugs. für* klatschendes Geräusch; Wasserguss); **schwappen,** schwap|sen *(ugs. für* in schwankender Bewegung sein, klatschend überfließen [von Flüssigkeiten]); **schwaps!,** schwapp!; **Schwaps** *vgl.* Schwapp; **schwap|sen;** du schwapst; *vgl.* schwappen

Schwä|re, die; -, -n *(geh. für* Geschwür); **schwä|ren** *(geh. für* eitern); **schwä|rig** *(geh.)*

Schwarm, der; -[e]s, Schwärme; **schwär|men; Schwär|mer** *(auch* ein Feuerwerkskörper; ein Schmetterling); **Schwär|me|rei; Schwär|me|rin; schwär|merisch; Schwarm|geist** *Plur.* ...geister; **Schwärm|zeit** (bei Bienen)

Schwar|te, die; -, -n (dicke Haut [z.B. des Schweins]; *ugs. für* dickes [altes] Buch; zur Verschalung dienendes rohes Brett); **schwar|ten** *(ugs. für* verprügeln; *selten für* viel lesen); **Schwarten|ma|gen** (eine Wurstart); **schwar|tig**

schwarz; schwärzer, schwärzeste; *vgl.* blau. **I.** *Kleinschreibung:* **a)** (↑R 47:) schwarz in schwarz; schwarz auf weiß; **b)** (↑R 108:) schwarze Pocken; ein schwarzes (verbotenes) Geschäft; eine schwarze Messe; das schwarze Brett (Anschlagbrett); die schwarze Kunst (Zauberei; *veraltet für* Buchdruck); der schwarze Mann (Schornsteinfeger; Schreckgestalt); das schwarze Schaf; die schwarze Liste; die schwarze Rasse; der schwarze Tod (Beulenpest im MA.); ein schwarzer Tag; ein schwarzer Freitag, *vgl. aber* der Schwarze Freitag (II, c); schwarze Magie (böse Zauberei); schwarzer Markt; schwarzer Humor; schwarzer Tee; schwarzer Peter (Kartenspiel). **II.** *Großschreibung:* **a)** (↑R 47:) ein Schwarzer (dunkelhäutiger, -haariger Mensch); das Schwarze; die Farbe Schwarz; aus Schwarz Weiß machen wollen; **b)** (↑R 102:) das Schwarze Meer; **c)** (↑R 108:) der Schwarze Erdteil (Afrika); die Schwarze Hand (ehemaliger serb. Geheimbund); Schwarzer Holunder (Sambucus nigra); Schwarzer September (palästinens. Untergrundorganisation); Schwarze Witwe (eine Spinne); der Schwarze Freitag (Name eines Freitags mit großen Börsenstürzen in den USA); **d)** (↑R 47:) ins Schwarze treffen. **III.** *In Verbindung mit Verben* (↑R 39): z.B. schwarz färben, werden; schwarz sehen *(ugs. für* pessimistisch sein); für die Zukunft sehe ich [sehr] schwarz; schwarz malen *(ugs. für* pessimistisch darstellen); sie hat in ihrem Bericht [sehr] schwarz gemalt; *vgl. aber* schwarzarbeiten, schwarzfahren, schwarzgehen, schwarzhören, schwarzschlachten, schwarzsehen. **IV.** *Getrenntschreibung in Verbindung mit dem Partizip II:* ein schwarz gestreifter Stoff; der Stoff ist schwarz und weiß gestreift; [auffallend] schwarz gefärbtes Haar; schwarz gerändertes Briefpapier (↑R 40); **Schwarz,** das; -[es], - (Farbe); ein Abendkleid in Schwarz; er spielte Schwarz aus *(Kartenspiel);* in Schwarz (Trauerkleidung) gehen; Frankfurter Schwarz; *vgl.* Blau; **Schwar|zach** (↑R 132); **Schwarz|af|ri|ka** (die Staaten Afrikas, die von Schwarzen bewohnt und regiert werden); **Schwarz|af|ri|ka|ner; Schwarzar|beit,** die; -; **schwarz|ar|beiten** (↑R 38; unversteuerte Lohnarbeit verrichten); ich arbeite schwarz; schwarzgearbeitet; schwarzzuarbeiten; **Schwarz‿arbei|ter; ...ar|bei|te|rin; schwarzäu|gig; Schwarz|bee|re** *(südd. und österr. neben* Heidelbeere); **schwarz|braun** (↑R 27); **Schwarz‿bren|ner, ...bren|nerei, ...brot, ...bu|che; schwarzbunt;** eine -e Kuh; **Schwarz‿dorn** *(Plur.* ...dorne), **...dros|sel**

(Amsel); [1]**Schwar|ze,** der *u.* die; -n, -n; ↑R 5ff. (dunkelhäutiger, -haariger Mensch); [2]**Schwar|ze,** der; -n (Teufel); [3]**Schwar|ze,** das; -n; ↑R 5ff. (schwarze Stelle); ins - treffen (↑R 47); [4]**Schwar|ze,** der; -n, -n; ↑R 5ff. (*österr. für* Mokka ohne Milch); **Schwär|ze,** die; -, -n (*nur Sing.*: das Schwarzsein; Farbe zum Schwarzmachen); **schwär|zen** (schwarz färben; *südd., österr. veraltend für* schmuggeln); du schwärzt; **Schwär|zer** (*südd., österr. veraltend für* Schmuggler); **Schwarz|er|de** (dunkler Humusboden); **schwarz|fah|ren** (↑R 38; ohne Berechtigung ein [öffentl.] Verkehrsmittel benutzen); sie ist schwarzgefahren; **Schwarz‿fah|rer, ...fahrt, ...fäu|le** (eine Pflanzenkrankheit), **...fil|ter** *(Fotogr.),* **...fleisch** (*landsch. für* durchwachsener geräucherter Speck); **schwarz|ge|hen** (↑R 38; *ugs. für* wildern; unerlaubt über die Grenze gehen); er ist schwarzgegangen; **schwarz ge|rän|dert, gestreift** *vgl.* schwarz, IV; **schwarz|haa|rig; Schwarz|han|del** (*vgl.* [1]Handel); **Schwarz|han|dels|ge|schäft; Schwarz|händ|ler; schwarz|hö|ren** (↑R 38; *Rundfunk* ohne Genehmigung mithören); er hat schwarzgehört; **Schwarz‿hö|rer, ...kit|tel** (Wildschwein; *abwertend für* kath. Geistlicher), **...kunst** (die; -; *svw.* Schabkunst), **...künst|ler; schwärz|lich;** schwärzlich braun u. a. (↑R 27); **schwarz malen** *vgl.* schwarz. III; **Schwarz|ma|ler** (*ugs. für* Pessimist); **Schwarz|ma|le|rei** (*ugs. für* Pessimismus); **Schwarz|markt; Schwarz|markt|preis; Schwarz|meer‿flot|te** (die; -), **...ge|biet** (das; -[e]s; ↑R 105); **Schwarz‿plätt|chen** (Mönchsgrasmücke), **...pul|ver** (das; -s), **...rock** (*abwertend für* kath. Geistlicher); **schwarz|rot|gol|den,** *auch* schwarz-rot-gol|den; eine schwarzrotgold[e]ne, *auch* schwarz-rot-gold[e]ne Fahne; die Fahne Schwarzrotgold, *auch* Schwarz-Rot-Gold; **Schwarz|sau|er,** das; -s (ein nordd. Gericht aus Fleischragout od. Gänseklein); **schwarz|schlach|ten** (↑R 38; [in Not-, Kriegszeiten] ohne amtliche Genehmigung heimlich schlachten); er hat oft schwarzgeschlachtet; **Schwarz|schlach|tung; schwarz|se|hen** (↑R 38f.; *ugs. für* ohne Anmeldung fernsehen); sie hat schwarzgesehen; *vgl. auch* schwarz, III; **Schwarz|se|her** (*ugs. für* Pessimist; jmd., der ohne Anmeldung fernsieht); **Schwarz|se|he|rei** (*ugs. für* Pessimismus; Fernsehen ohne Anmeldung); **schwarz|se|he|risch** (*ugs.* pessimistisch); **Schwarz‿sen|der, ...specht, ...storch; Schwär|zung; Schwarz|wald,** der; -[e]s (dt. Gebirge); **Schwarz|wald|bahn,** die; -; **Schwarz|wäl|der** (↑R 103); Schwarzwälder Kirschtorte; **Schwarz|wäl|de|rin; schwarz|wäl|de|risch; Schwarz|wald|haus; Schwarz|wald|hoch|stra|ße,** die; - (↑R 105); **Schwarz|was|ser|fie|ber,** das; -s (Malaria); **schwarz|weiß** (↑R 27); ein schwarzweiß, *auch* schwarz-weiß verzierter Rand; schwarzweiß, *auch* schwarz-weiß malen (undifferenziert, einseitig positiv od. negativ darstellen); **Schwarz|weiß‿auf|nah|me, ...fern|se|hen, ...fern|se|her, ...film, ...fo|to|gra|fie, ...kunst** (die; -), **...ma|le|rei, ...zeich|nung; Schwarz|wild** (*Jägerspr.* Wildschweine); **Schwarz|wurz** (eine Heilpflanze); **Schwarz|wur|zel** (eine Gemüsepflanze)

Schwatz, der; -es, -e (*ugs. für* Geplauder, Geschwätz); **Schwatz|ba|se** (*ugs. für* geschwätzige Person); **Schwätz|chen; schwat|zen,** *südd.* **schwät|zen;** du schwatzt, *südd.* du schwätzt; **Schwät|zer; Schwät|ze|rei; Schwät|ze|rin; schwät|ze|risch; schwatz|haft; Schwatz|haf|tig|keit,** die; -; **Schwatz|maul** *(derb)*

Schwaz (österreichische Stadt im Inntal)

Schwe|be, die; -; *nur in* in der - (*auch für* unentschieden, noch offen); **Schwe|be‿bahn, ...bal|ken** (ein Turngerät), **...baum** (im Pferdestall); **schwe|ben; Schwe|be‿stoff** (*svw.* Schwebstoff), **...stütz** *(Turnen),* **...teil|chen, ...zu|stand; Schweb|flie|ge; Schweb|stoff** *(Chemie);* **Schwe|bung** *(Physik)*

Schwe|de, der; -n, -n (↑R 126); **Schwe|den; Schwe|den‿kü|che, ...plat|te, ...punsch, ...schan|ze; Schwe|din; schwe|disch;** (↑R 104:) hinter -en Gardinen (*ugs. für* im Gefängnis); *vgl.* deutsch; **Schwe|disch,** das; -[s] (Sprache); *vgl.* Deutsch; **Schwe|di|sche,** das; -n; *vgl.* Deutsche, das

Schwe|fel, der; -s (chem. Element, Nichtmetall; *Zeichen* S); **schwe|fel|ar|tig; Schwe|fel‿ban|de** (*ugs. für* [2]Bande), **Schwe|fel|blu|me** *od.* **...blü|te,** die; - *(Chemie);* **Schwe|fel‿dio|xid** (↑R 132; *vgl.* Oxid), **...far|be; schwe|fel|far|ben** *od.* **...far|big; schwe|fel|gelb; schwe|fel|hal|tig; Schwe|fel|holz, Schwe|fel|hölz|chen** (*veraltet für* Streich-, Zündholz); **schwe|fe|lig** *vgl.* schweflig; **Schwe|fel|kies** (ein Mineral); **Schwe|fel|koh|len|stoff; Schwe|fel‿kopf** (ein Pilz), **...kur, ...le|ber** (die; -; für medizin. Bäder verwendete Schwefelverbindung); **schwe|feln;** ich ...[e]le (↑R 16); **Schwe|fel‿pu|der, ...quel|le, ...sal|be; schwe|fel|sau|er; Schwe|fel|säu|re,** die; -; **Schwe|fe|lung; Schwe|fel|was|ser|stoff** (ein giftiges Gas); **schwef|lig;** -e Säure

Schwe|gel, Schwie|gel, die; -, -n (mittelalterl. Querpfeife; Flötenwerk an älteren Orgeln); **Schweg|ler** (Schwegelbläser)

Schweif, der; -[e]s, -e; **schwei|fen** (*geh. für* ziellos [durch die Gegend] ziehen; ein Brett - (ihm eine gebogene Gestalt geben); **Schweif‿sä|ge, ...stern** (*veraltet für* Komet; *vgl.* [2]Stern); **Schwei|fung; schweif|we|deln** (*veraltet auch für* kriecherisch schmeicheln); ich ...[e]le (↑R 16); geschweifwedelt; zu -; **Schweif|wed|ler** (*veraltet für* Kriecher)

Schwei|ge‿geld, ...marsch, ...mi|nu|te; schwei|gen (still sein); du schwiegst; du schwiegest; geschwiegen; schweig[e]!; die schweigende Mehrheit; **Schwei|gen,** das; -s; **Schwei|ge|pflicht,** die; -; **Schwei|ger;** (↑R 93:) der Große Schweiger (*Bez. für* Moltke); **schweig|sam; Schweig|sam|keit,** die; -

Schwein, das; -[e]s, -e (*nur Sing.: ugs. auch für* Glück); kein - (*ugs. für* niemand); **Schwei|ne‿ba|cke, ...bauch, ...bra|ten, ...fett, ...fi|let, ...fleisch, ...fraß** (*derb für* minderwertiges Essen); **Schwei|ne|hund** *(ugs. abwertend);* der innere - (*ugs. für* Feigheit, Bequemlichkeit); **Schwei|ne|ko|ben,** *nordd.* **Schwei|ne|ko|fen; Schwei|ne‿ko|te|lett, ...le|ber, ...len|de, ...mast** (die), **...mäs|te|rei, ...pest; Schwei|ne|rei** (*derb für* Unordnung, Schmutz; ärgerliche Sache, Anstößiges); **Schwei|ne|ripp|chen; schwei|nern** (vom Schwein stammend); **Schwei|ner|ne,** das; -n; ↑R 5ff. (*südd., österr. für* Schweinefleisch); **Schwei|ne‿schmalz, ...schnit|zel** (*vgl.* [1]Schnitzel); **...stall, ...zucht**

Schwein|furt (Stadt am Main); **Schwein|fur|ter** (↑R 103); **Schwein|fur|ter Grün,** das; - -s (ein Farbstoff)

Schwein|hund *vgl.* Schweinehund; **Schwein|igel** (↑R 132; *ugs. für* schmutziger od. unflätiger Mensch); **Schwein|ige|lei** (↑R 132; *ugs.*); **schwein|igeln** (↑R 132; *ugs. für* unanständige Witze erzählen); ich ...[e]le (↑R 16); geschweinigelt; zu -; **schwei|nisch; Schweins‿bors|te, ...bra|ten** (*südd., österr. u. schweiz. für* Schweinebraten); **Schweins|ga|lopp;** im - (*ugs. scherzh. für* [aus Zeitmangel] schnell u. nicht besonders sorgfältig); **Schweins‿keu|le, ...kopf, ...le|der; schweins|le|dern; Schweins‿ohr** (*auch* ein Gebäck), **...rü|cken, ...schnit|zel** (*österr. für* Schweineschnitzel), **...stel|ze** (*österr. für* Eisbein)

Schweiß, der; -es, -e (*Jägerspr. auch für* Blut des Wildes); **Schweiß‿ab|son|de|rung, ...ap|pa|rat, ...aus|bruch, ...band; schweiß|be|deckt** (↑R 40); **Schweiß‿bil|dung** (die; -), **...blatt** (*meist Plur.; svw.* Armblatt), **...bren|ner, ...draht, ...drü|se; schwei|ßen** (Metalle durch Hämmern od. Aneinanderschmelzen bei Weißglut verbinden; *Jägerspr.* bluten [vom Wild]); du schweißt; du schweißtest; geschweißt; **Schwei|ßer** (Facharbeiter für Schweißarbeiten); **Schwei|ße|rin; Schweiß|fähr|te** (*Jägerspr.*); **schweiß|feucht; Schweiß‿fleck, ...fuß** (*meist Plur.*); **schweiß|ge|ba|det** (↑R 40); **Schweiß|hund** (*Jägerspr.*); **schwei|ßig; Schweiß‿le|der** (ein ledernes Schweißband), **...naht, ...per|le, ...po|re, ...stahl; schweiß|trei|bend, schweiß|trie|fend** (↑R 40); **Schweiß‿trop|fen, ...tuch** (*Plur.* ...tücher); **schweiß|über|strömt** (↑R 132); **Schwei|ßung; schweiß|ver|klebt**

Schweit|zer (elsäss. Missionsarzt)

Schweiz, die; -; die französische, welsche - (franz. Teil der -), *aber* (↑R 102:) die Holsteinische, die Sächsische -; [1]**Schwei|zer** (Bewohner der Schweiz; *auch für* Melker; *landsch. für* Küster in kath. Kirchen); [2]**Schwei|zer** (↑R 105); - Bürger; - Jura (Gebirge), - Käse, - Kühe, - Land (schweizerisches Gebiet; *vgl. aber* Schweizerland), - Reise; **Schwei|zer|de|gen** (jmd., der sowohl als Schriftsetzer als auch als Drucker ausgebildet ist); **schwei|zer|deutsch;** ↑R 106 (schweizerisch mundartlich); *vgl.* deutschschweizerisch; **Schwei|zer|deutsch,** das; -[s]; ↑R 106 (deutsche Mundart[en] der Schweiz); **Schwei|zer‿gar|de** (päpstl. Garde; ↑R 105), **...häus|chen; Schwei|ze|rin; schwei|ze|risch;** die -en Eisenbahnen; -e Post; *aber* (↑R 108): die Schweizerische Eidgenossenschaft; Schweizerische Bundesbahnen (*Abk.* SBB); Schweizerische Depeschenagentur (*Abk.* SDA); **Schwei|zer|land,** das; -[e]s; ↑R 106 (Land der Schweizer); *vgl. aber* Schweizer Land; **Schweiz|rei|se**

Schwejk [ʃvɛjk] (Held eines Romans des tschech. Schriftstellers J. Hašek [ˈhaʃɛk])

Schwel|brand

Schwelch|malz (an der Luft getrocknetes Malz)

schwe|len (langsam flammenlos [ver]brennen; glimmen); schwelender Hass; **Schwe|le|rei** (*Technik*)

schwel|gen; in Erinnerungen -; **Schwel|ger; Schwel|ge|rei; schwel|ge|risch**

Schwel‿koh|le, ...koks

Schwel|le, die; -, -n

[1]**schwel|len** (größer, stärker werden; sich ausdehnen); du schwillst; er schwillt; du schwollst; du schwöllest; geschwollen; schwill!; ihr Hals ist geschwollen; die Brust schwoll ihm vor Freude; [2]**schwel|len** (größer, stärker machen; ausdehnen); du schwellst; du schwelltest; geschwellt; schwell[e]!; der Wind schwellte die Segel; der Stolz hat seine Brust geschwellt; mit geschwellter Brust

Schwel|len|angst, die; - (*Psych.* Angst vor dem Betreten fremder Räume, vor ungewohnter Umgebung [bes. eines potenziellen Käufers gegenüber bestimmten Geschäften]); **Schwel|len‿land** (*Plur.* ...länder; relativ weit industrialisiertes Entwicklungsland), **...wert** (*Psych.*)

Schwel|ler (Teil der Orgel u. des Harmoniums); **Schwell|kopf,** der; -s, ...köpfe (*landsch. für* überlebensgroßer Maskenkopf); **Schwell|kör|per** (*Med.*); **Schwel|lung; Schwell|werk** (Schweller)

Schwel|teer; Schwe|lung

Schwemm|bo|den; Schwem|me, die; -, -n (flache Stelle eines Gewässers als Badeplatz für das Vieh; zeitl. begrenztes überreichliches Warenangebot; *landsch. für* einfaches [Bier]lokal; *österr. für* Warenhausabteilung mit niedrigen Preisen); **schwem|men** (*österr. auch für* Wäsche spülen); **Schwemm‿land** (das; -[e]s), **...sand; Schwemm|sel,** das; -s (*fachspr. für* Angeschwemmtes); **Schwemm|stein**

Schwen|de, die; -, -n (durch Abbrennen urbar gemachter Wald; Rodung); **schwen|den**

Schwen|gel, der; -s, -; **Schwenk,** der; -[e]s, *Plur.* -s, *selten* -e (*Filmw.* durch Schwenken der Kamera erzielte Einstellung); **schwenk|bar; Schwenk‿be|reich** (der), **...büh|ne** (*Bergmannsspr.*); **schwen|ken;** Fahnen -; **Schwen|ker** (Kognakglas); **Schwenk‿glas** (*Plur.* ...gläser), **...kran, ...seil; Schwen|kung**

schwer; schwerer, am schwersten; (↑R 108:) schwere (ernste, getragene) Musik; schweres (großkalibriges) Geschütz; schweres Wasser (Sauerstoff-Deuterium-Verbindung); ein schwerer Junge (*ugs. für* Gewaltverbrecher); ihr Tod war ein schwerer Schlag (großer Verlust) für die Familie. *Getrenntschreibung in Verbindung mit Verben, mit dem Partizip II oder einem Adjektiv* (↑R 39): er ist auf der Treppe sehr schwer gefallen; diese Aufgabe ist ihr [nicht so] schwer gefallen; es hat schwer gehalten (= es war schwierig) ihn davon zu überzeugen; er hat ihr das Leben schwer gemacht; du darfst den Vorwurf nicht so schwer (= ernst) nehmen; ich habe mich, *selten* mir [allzu] schwer getan (*ugs.*); (↑R 40): schwer behindert (durch gesundheitl. Schädigung nur beschränkt erwerbsfähig); ein schwer beladener Wagen; schwer beschädigt (= schwer behindert); ein schwer bewaffneter Polizist; ein [sehr] schwer erziehbares Kind; schwer krank; schwer kriegsbeschädigt; schwer lösliche Substanzen; [sehr] schwer verdauliche Speisen; schwer verletzt; (↑R 47:) die schwer Verletzten, *auch* Schwerverletzten; eine [überaus] schwer verständliche Sprache; ein schwer verträglicher Wein; schwer verwundet; schwer wiegend, schwerer wiegend, am schwersten wiegend, *vgl. auch* schwerwiegend; **Schwer‿ar|bei|ter, ...ath|let, ...ath|le|tik; schwer be|hin-**

dert *vgl.* schwer; **Schwer|be|hin|der|te,** der *u.* die; -n, -n (↑R 5 ff.); **Schwer|be|hin|der|ten‿aus|weis, ...ge|setz; schwer be|la|den, be|schä|digt, be|waff|net** *vgl.* schwer; **Schwer|be|waff|ne|te,** der *u.* die; -n, -n (↑R 5 ff.); **schwer|blü|tig; Schwer|blü|tig|keit,** die; -; **Schwe|re,** die; - (Gewicht); die - der Schuld; **Schwe|re|feld** *(Physik, Astron.);* **schwe|re|los;** -er Zustand; **Schwe|re|lo|sig|keit,** die; -; **Schwe|re|not,** die; *nur in veralteten Fügungen wie* - [noch einmal]!; dass dich die -!; **Schwe|re|nö|ter** (charmanter, durchtriebener Geselle); **schwer er|zieh|bar** *vgl.* schwer; **Schwer|er|zieh|ba|re,** der *u.* die; -n, -n (↑R 5 ff. *u.* R 47); **schwer fal|len** *vgl.* schwer; **schwer|fäl|lig; Schwer‿fäl|lig|keit** (die; -), **...ge|wicht** (*bes. Sport* eine Körpergewichtsklasse); **schwer|ge|wich|tig; Schwer|ge|wicht|ler; Schwer|ge|wichts‿meis|ter, ...meis|ter|schaft; schwer hal|ten** *vgl.* schwer; **schwer|hö|rig; Schwer|hö|rig|keit,** die; -

Schwe|rin (Hptst. von Mecklenburg-Vorpommern)

Schwer‿in|dust|rie, ...kraft (die; -); **schwer krank** *vgl.* schwer; **Schwer|kran|ke** (↑R 47); **schwer kriegs|be|schä|digt** *vgl.* schwer; **Schwer|kriegs|be|schä|dig|te; Schwer|last|ver|kehr; schwer|lich** (kaum); **schwer lös|lich** *vgl.* schwer; **schwer ma|chen** *vgl.* schwer; **Schwer|me|tall; Schwer|mut,** die; -; **schwer|mü|tig; Schwer|mü|tig|keit,** die; -; **schwer neh|men** *vgl.* schwer; **Schwer|öl; Schwer|punkt; schwer|punkt|mä|ßig; Schwer|punkt‿streik, ...the|ma; schwer|reich** (*ugs. für* sehr reich); ein schwerreicher Mann; er ist schwerreich; **Schwer|spat** (ein Mineral); **Schwerst|ar|bei|ter; schwerst|be|hin|dert; schwerst|be|schä|digt; Schwerst|be|schä|dig|te,** der *u.* die; -n, -n (↑R 5 ff.)

Schwert, das; -[e]s, -er; **Schwer|tel,** der, *österr.* das; -s, - (Zierpflanze); **Schwer|ter|ge|klirr** *od.* Schwert|ge|klirr; **Schwert|fisch; schwert|för|mig; Schwert‿fort|satz** (*Med.* Teil des Brustbeins), **...ge|klirr** (*vgl.* Schwertergeklirr), **...knauf, ...lei|te** (*früher* Ritterschlag), **...li|lie** (*vgl.* [3]Iris), **...schlu|cker, ...tanz, ...trä|ger** (ein Fisch)

schwer tun, sich; *vgl.* schwer; **Schwer|ver|bre|cher;** [1]**schwer|ver|dau|lich, ver|letzt** *vgl.* schwer; **Schwer|ver|letz|te,** der *u.* die; -n, -n (↑R 5 ff.); *vgl.* schwer; **schwer ver|ständ|lich, ver|träg|lich, ver|wun|det** *vgl.* schwer; **schwer|wie|gend,** schwerwiegendere, schwerwiegendste Bedenken; *vgl. auch* schwer

Schwe|ser, der; -s (*nordd. für* Bries, Kalbsmilch)

Schwes|ter, die; -, -n (*Abk.* Schw.); **Schwes|ter‿an|stalt** (gleichartige Anstalt), **...fir|ma, ...kind** *(veraltet);* **schwes|ter|lich; Schwes|ter|lie|be** (Liebe der Schwester [zum Bruder, zur Schwester]); **Schwes|tern‿hau|be, ...haus, ...hel|fe|rin, ...lie|be** (Liebe zwischen Schwestern), **...or|den, ...paar; Schwes|tern|schaft** (alle Schwestern); **Schwes|tern‿schu|le, ...schü|le|rin, ...tracht, ...wohn|heim; Schwes|ter‿par|tei, ...schiff**

Schwet|zin|gen (Stadt südl. von Mannheim); **Schwet|zin|ger** (↑R 103)

Schwib|bo|gen (*Archit.* zwischen zwei Mauerteilen frei stehender Bogen)

Schwie|gel *vgl.* Schwegel

Schwie|ger, die; -, -n (*veraltet für* Schwiegermutter); **Schwie|ger‿el|tern** *(Plur.),* **...mut|ter** (*Plur.* ...mütter), **...sohn, ...toch|ter, ...va|ter**

Schwie|le, die; -, -n; **schwie|lig**

Schwie|mel, der; -s, - (*landsch. für* Rausch; leichtsinniger Mensch, Zechbruder); **Schwie|me|ler,** Schwiem|ler (*landsch. für* leichtsinniger Mensch; Zechbruder); **schwie|me|lig,** schwiem|lig (*landsch. für* schwindlig, taumelig); **Schwie|mel|kopf** (*landsch. für* Zechbruder, Herumtreiber); **schwie|meln** (*landsch. für* taumeln; bummeln, leichtsinnig leben); ich ...[e]le (↑R 16); **Schwiem|ler** usw. *vgl.* Schwiemeler usw.

schwie|rig; Schwie|rig|keit; Schwie|rig|keits|grad

Schwimm‿an|zug, ...bad, ...bag|ger, ...bas|sin, ...be|cken, ...be|we|gung *(meist Plur.),* **...bla|se, ...blatt** (*Bot.* an bestimmten Wasserpflanzen), **...dock; schwim|men;** du schwammst; du schwömmest, *auch* schwämmest; geschwommen; schwimm[e]!; **Schwim|mer; Schwim|me|rin; Schwimm‿flos|se, ...fuß** *(meist Plur.),* **...gür|tel, ...hal|le, ...haut, ...kä|fer, ...kom|pass, ...kran, ...leh|rer; Schwimm|meis|ter** (↑R 136); **Schwimm‿sand, ...sport** (der; -[e]s), **...sta|di|on, ...stil, ...vo|gel, ...wes|te**

Schwin|del, der; -s (*ugs. auch für* Lüge; Täuschung); in Schwindel erregender (↑R 40) Höhe; **Schwin|del|an|fall; Schwin|de|lei; Schwin|del er|re|gend** *vgl.* Schwindel; **schwin|del|frei; Schwin|del|ge|fühl; schwin|del|haft; schwin|de|lig** *vgl.* schwindlig; **schwin|deln;** ich ...[e]le (↑R 16); es schwindelt mir, *seltener* mich; **schwin|den;** du schwandst; du schwändest; geschwunden; schwind[e]!; **Schwind|ler; Schwind|le|rin; schwind|le|risch; schwind|lig;** mir wurde ganz -; **Schwind‿maß** (das; *Technik*), **...span|nung** *(Bauw.),* **...sucht** (die; -; *veraltet für* Lungentuberkulose); **schwind|süch|tig** *(veraltet);* **Schwin|dung,** die; - *(fachspr.)*

Schwing‿ach|se (*[Kfz-]Technik*), **...blatt** (*für* Membran), **...büh|ne** *(Technik);* **Schwin|ge,** die; -, -n

Schwin|gel, der; -s, - (ein Rispengras)

schwin|gen (*schweiz. auch für* in besonderer Weise ringen); hin u. her schwingen; du schwangst; du schwängest; geschwungen; schwing[e]!; **Schwin|gen,** das; -s (*schweiz. für* eine Art des Ringens); **Schwin|ger** (Boxschlag mit gestrecktem Arm; *schweiz. für* jmd., der das Schwingen betreibt); **Schwin|get,** der; -s (*schweiz. für* Schwingveranstaltung, -wettkampf); **Schwing‿fest** *(schweiz.),* **...kreis** *(Elektrotechnik),* **...quarz** *(Technik),* **...tür; Schwin|gung; Schwin|gungs‿dämp|fer, ...dau|er, ...kreis** (*svw.* Schwingkreis), **...zahl**

schwipp!; schwipp, schwapp!; **Schwip|pe,** die; -, -n (*landsch. für* biegsames Ende [einer Gerte, Peitsche]; Peitsche); **schwip|pen** *(landsch.);* **Schwipp‿schwa|ger** (*ugs. für* Schwager des Ehepartners od. des Bruders bzw. der Schwester), **...schwä|ge|rin; schwipp, schwapp!; Schwips,** der; -es, -e (*ugs. für* leichter Rausch)

schwir|be|lig, *auch* schwirb|lig (*landsch. für* schwindlig); **schwir|beln** (*landsch. für* schwindeln; im Kreise drehen); ich ...[e]le (↑R 16); **schwirb|lig** *vgl.* schwirbelig

Schwirl, der; -[e]s, -e (ein Singvogel)

schwir|ren; Schwirr|vo|gel (*veraltet für* Kolibri)

Schwitz|bad; Schwit|ze, die; -, -n (*kurz für* Mehlschwitze); **schwit|zen;** du schwitzt; du schwitztest; geschwitzt; **schwit-zig; Schwitz-kas|ten, ...kur**

Schwof, der; -[e]s, -e (*ugs. für* öffentl. Tanzvergnügen); **schwo-fen** (*ugs. für* tanzen)

schwoi|en, schwo|jen ‹niederl.› (*Seemannsspr.* sich [vor Anker] drehen [von Schiffen]); das Schiff schwoit, schwojet, hat geschwoit, geschwojet

schwö|ren; du schworst, *veraltet* schwurst; du schwürest; geschworen; schwör[e]!; auf jmdn., auf eine Sache -

Schwuch|tel, die; -, -n (*ugs. abwertend für* [femininer] Homosexueller)

schwul (*ugs. für* homosexuell); **schwül; Schwu|le,** der; -n, -n; ↑R 5 ff. (*ugs. für* Homosexueller); **Schwü|le,** die; -; **Schwu|li|bus;** *nur in* in - sein (*ugs. scherzh. für* bedrängt sein); **Schwu|li|tät,** die; -, -en (*ugs. für* Verlegenheit, Klemme); in großen -en sein

Schwulst, der; -[e]s, Schwülste; **schwuls|tig** (aufgeschwollen, aufgeworfen; *österr. für* schwülstig); **schwüls|tig** ([in Gedanken u. Ausdruck] überladen, weitläufig); ein -er Stil; ein -er Ausdruck; **Schwüls|tig|keit**

schwum|me|rig, schwumm|rig (*ugs. für* schwindelig; bange)

Schwum|se, die; - (*landsch. für* Prügel, Hiebe)

Schwund, der; -[e]s; **Schwund-aus|gleich** (*Technik*), **...stu|fe** (*Sprachw.*)

Schwung, der; -[e]s, Schwünge; in Schwung kommen; **Schwung-brett, ...fe|der; schwung-haft; Schwung|kraft,** die; -; **schwung|los; Schwung-rad, ...rie|men, ...stem|me** (*Turnen*); **schwung|voll;** eine -e Rede

schwupp!; Schwupp, der; -[e]s, -e *u.* Schwups, der; -es, Schwüpse (*ugs. für* Stoß); **schwupp|di-wupp!; Schwups** *vgl.* Schwupp; **schwups!**

Schwur, der; -[e]s, Schwüre; **Schwur|ge|richt; Schwur|ge-richts|ver|hand|lung; Schwur-hand**

Schwyz [ʃvi:ts] (Kanton der Schweiz u. dessen Hauptort); **Schwy|zer** (↑R 103); **Schwy-zer|dütsch,** Schwy|zer|tütsch, das; -[s] (*schweiz. mdal. für* Schweizerdeutsch); **schwy|ze-risch**

Sci|ence|fic|tion ['saiəns'fikʃ(ə)n], die; - ‹amerik.› (wissenschaftlich-utopische Literatur); **Sci|ence-fic|tion|ro|man**

scil., sc. = scilicet

sci|li|cet ['stsi:litsɛt] ‹lat.› (nämlich; *Abk.* sc., scil.)

Scil|la ['stsila], die; -, - ‹griech.› (eine [Heil]pflanze, Blaustern)

Sci|pio ['stsi:...] (Name berühmter Römer)

Scoop [sku:p], der; -s, -s ‹engl.› (sensationeller [Presse]bericht)

Scor|da|tu|ra, die; - *u.* Skor|da-tur, die; - ‹ital.› (*Musik* Umstimmen von Saiten der Streich- u. Zupfinstrumente)

Score [skɔ:(r)], der; -s, -s ‹engl.› (*Sport* Spielstand, Spielergebnis); **sco|ren** (*Sport* einen Punkt, ein Tor o. Ä. erzielen)

Scotch [skɔtʃ], der; -s, -s ‹engl.› (schottischer Whisky); **Scotch-ter|ri|er** (schottischer Jagdhund)

Sco|tis|mus [sko...], der; - (philos. Lehre nach dem Scholastiker Duns Scotus); **Sco|tist,** der; -en, -en; ↑R 126

Scot|land Yard ['skɔtlənd 'ja:(r)d], der; - - ‹engl.› (Londoner Polizei[gebäude])

Scott (schottischer Dichter)

Scrab|ble ® ['skrɛb(ə)l], das; -s, -s ‹engl.› (ein Gesellschaftsspiel)

Scrat|ching ['skrɛtʃiŋ], das; -s ‹engl.› (das Hervorbringen bestimmter akustischer Effekte durch Manipulation der laufenden Schallplatte)

Scrip, der; -s, -s ‹engl.› (*Wirtsch.* Gutschein über nicht gezahlte Zinsen)

Scu|do, der; -, ...di ‹ital.› (alte ital. Münze)

Scud|ra|ke|te [*auch* 'skad...] (eine militär. Kurz- u. Mittelstreckenrakete)

sculps., sc. = sculpsit

sculp|sit ‹lat., „hat [es] gestochen"› (Zusatz zum Namen des Stechers auf Kupfer- u. Stahlstichen; *Abk.* sc., sculps.)

Scyl|la ['stsyla] (*lat. Form von* Szylla, griech. Skylla)

s. d. = sieh[e] dort!

S. D., S. Dak. = Süddakota

SDA = Schweizerische Depeschenagentur

SDI [ɛsdi'ai] = strategic defense initiative [strɛ'ti:dʒik di'fɛns i'niʃətiv] (US-amerik. Forschungsprojekt zur Stationierung von [Laser]waffen im Weltraum)

SDR = Süddeutscher Rundfunk

SDS = Societatis Divini Salvatoris [zotsie... di'vi:ni zalva...] („von der Gesellschaft vom Göttlichen Heiland"; Salvatorianer)

Se = *chem. Zeichen für* Selen

Se., S. = Seine (Exzellenz usw.)

Seal [si:l], der *od.* das; -s, -s ‹engl.› (Fell der Pelzrobbe; ein Pelz); **Seal|man|tel**

Seals|field ['si:lsfi:ld] (österr. Schriftsteller)

Seal|skin ['si:l...], der *od.* das; -s, -s ‹engl.› (*svw.* Seal; Plüschgewebe als Nachahmung des Seals)

Sean [ʃɔ:n] (m. Vorn.)

Sé|an|ce [se'ã:s(ə)], die; -, -n ‹franz.› ([spiritistische] Sitzung)

Se|at|tle [si'ɛt(ə)l] (Stadt in den USA)

Se|bald, Se|bal|dus (m. Vorn.)

Se|bas|ti|an (m. Vorn.)

Se|bor|rhö[1], **Se|bor|rhöe** [...'rø:], die; -, ...rrhöen ‹lat.; griech.› (*Med.* krankhaft gesteigerte Absonderung der Talgdrüsen)

[1]**sec** = Sekans; Sekunde (*vgl. d.*)

[2]**sec** [sɛk] ‹franz.› (trocken [von franz. Schaumweinen])

Sec|co|re|zi|ta|tiv ‹ital.› (*Musik* nur von einem Tasteninstrument begleitetes Rezitativ)

Se|cen|tis|mus [setʃɛn...], der; - ‹ital.› (Stilrichtung schwülstiger Barockpoesie im Italien des 17. Jh.s); **Se|cen|tist,** der; -en, -en; ↑R 126 (Dichter, Künstler des Secentos); **Se|cen|to,** das; -[s] (*toskan. Form von* Seicento)

Sech, das; -[e]s, -e (messerartiges Teil am Pflug)

sechs; wir sind zu sechsen *od.* zu sechst, wir sind sechs; *vgl.* acht; **Sechs,** die; -, -en (Zahl); er hat eine Sechs gewürfelt; er hat in Latein eine Sechs geschrieben; *vgl.* Eins *u.* [1]Acht; **Sechs|ach|ser** (Wagen mit sechs Achsen; *mit Ziffer* 6-Achser; ↑R 44); **sechs-ach|sig** (*mit Ziffer* 6-achsig; ↑R 44); **Sechs|ach|tel|takt,** der; -[e]s (*mit Ziffern* $^6/_8$-Takt; ↑R 28); im -; **Sechs|eck; sechs-eckig** (↑R 132); **sechs|ein-halb,** sechs|und|ein|halb; **Sechs-en|der** (*Jägerspr.*); **Sech|ser** (*landsch. ugs. für* Fünfpfennigstück); ich gebe keinen Sechser (nichts) mehr für sein Leben; *vgl.* Achter; **sech|ser|lei;** auf - Art; **Sech|ser-pack** (*Plur.* -s *u.* -e), **...pa|ckung, ...rei|he** (in -n); **sechs|fach; Sechs|fa|che,** das; -n; *vgl.* Achtfache; **Sechs|flach,** das; -[e]s, -e *u.* **Sechs|fläch|ner** (*für* Hexaeder); **sechs|hun|dert; Sechs|kant,** das *od.* der; -[e]s, -e (↑R 44); **Sechs|kant|ei|sen** (↑R 44); **sechs|kan|tig; Sechs-ling; sechs|mal;** *vgl.* achtmal;

[1] *Vgl. die Anm. zu* „Diarrhö, Diarrhöe".

sechs|ma|lig; Sechs|pass, der; -es, -e (Maßwerkfigur in der Hochgotik); **Sechs|spän|ner; sechs|spän|nig; sechs|stel|lig; Sechs|stern** (sechsstrahliger Stern der Volkskunst); *vgl.* [2]Stern; **sechst;** *vgl.* sechs; **Sechs|ta|ge|ren|nen** (↑R 50 *u.* R 28); **sechs|tau|send; sechs|te;** er hat den sechsten Sinn (ein Gespür) dafür; *vgl.* achte; **sechs|tel;** *vgl.* achtel; **Sechs|tel,** das, *schweiz. meist* der; -s, -; *vgl.* Achtel; **sechs|tens; Sechs|und|drei|ßig|flach,** das; -[e]s, -e *u.* **Sechs|und|drei|ßig|fläch|ner** (*für* Triakisdodekaeder); **sechs|und|ein|halb,** sechseinhalb; **Sechs|und|sech|zig,** das; - (ein Kartenspiel); **sechs|und|zwan|zig;** *vgl.* acht; **Sechs|zy|lin|der** (*ugs. für* Sechszylindermotor od. damit ausgerüstetes Kraftfahrzeug); **Sechs|zy|lin|der|mo|tor; sechs|zy|lind|rig** (↑R 130; *mit Ziffer* 6-zylindrig; ↑R 44)

Sech|ter, der; -s, - ‹lat.› (ein altes [Getreide]maß; *österr. für* Eimer, Milchgefäß)

sech|zehn; *vgl.* acht; **sech|zehn|hun|dert; Sech|zehn|me|ter|raum** *(Fußball);* **sech|zig** usw. *vgl.* achtzig usw.; **sech|zig|jäh|rig;** *vgl.* achtjährig

Se|cond|hand|shop ['sɛkənd'hɛndʃɔp], der; -s, -s ‹engl.› (Laden, in dem gebrauchte Kleidung u. a. verkauft wird)

Sec|ret Ser|vice ['si:krit 'sœ:(r)vis] (↑R 130), der; - - ‹engl.› (brit. [polit.] Geheimdienst)

SED = Sozialistische Einheitspartei Deutschlands (Staatspartei der DDR [1946–1989])

Se|da (*Plur. von* Sedum)

se|da|tiv (*Med.* beruhigend, Schmerzen stillend); **Se|da|tiv,** das; -s, -e [...və] *u.* **Se|da|ti|vum** [...vum], das; -s, ...va [...va] (*Med.* Beruhigungsmittel)

Se|dez, das; -es ‹lat.› (Sechzehntelbogengröße [Buchformat]; *Abk.* 16°); **Se|dez|for|mat**

Se|dia ges|ta|to|ria [- dʒɛsta...], die; - - ‹ital.› (Tragsessel des Papstes bei feierl. Aufzügen)

Se|di|ment, das; -[e]s, -e ‹lat.› (Ablagerung, Schicht); **se|di|men|tär** (durch Ablagerung entstanden); **Se|di|men|tär|ge|stein; Se|di|men|ta|ti|on,** die; -, -en (Ablagerung); **Se|di|ment|ge|stein; se|di|men|tie|ren**

Se|dis|va|kanz [...va...], die; -, -en ‹lat.› (Zeitraum, während dessen das Amt des Papstes od. eines Bischofs unbesetzt ist)

Se|dum, das; -s, Seda ‹lat.› (*Bot.* Fetthenne)

[1]**See,** der; -s, -n ['ze:ən]; (stehendes Binnengewässer); [2]**See,** die; -, -n ['ze:ən] (*nur Sing.:* Meer; Seegang; *Seemannsspr.* [Sturz]welle); **See‿aal, ...ad|ler, ...amt; see|ar|tig,** seen|ar|tig; **See‿bad, ...bär, ...be|ben; see|be|schä|digt** (*für* havariert); **See‿blick** (ein Zimmer mit -), **...blo|cka|de, ...büh|ne; See|ele|fant** (↑R 132 *u.* 136), der; -en, -en; ↑R 126 (große Robbe); **see|er|fah|ren** (↑R 136); **See|er|fah|rung** (↑R 136), die; -; **See|er|ze** *Plur.* (↑R 136); **see|fah|rend; See‿fah|rer, ...fahrt; See|fahrt|buch**[1]; **See|fahrt|schu|le**[1]; **see|fest; See|fisch; See|fracht; See|fracht|ge|schäft; See‿funk, ...gang** (der; -[e]s); **See Ge|ne|za|reth,** *ökum.* Gen|ne|sa|ret, der; -s - (bibl. Name für den See von Tiberias); **See|gfrör|ni,** die; -, ...nen (*schweiz. für* Zugefrieren, Zugefrorensein eines Sees); **See|gras; See|gras|mat|rat|ze; See‿gur|ke** (ein [meerbewohnender] Stachelhäuter), **...ha|fen** (*vgl.* [2]Hafen), **...han|del** (*vgl.* [1]Handel), **...heil|bad, ...herr|schaft** (die; -), **...hund; See|hunds‿fän|ger, ...fell; See|igel** (↑R 132); **See|igel|kak|tus** (↑R 132); **See‿jung|fer** (eine Libelle), **...jung|frau** (eine Märchengestalt), **...ka|dett, ...kar|te, ...kas|se** (Versicherung für alle in der Seefahrt beschäftigten Personen); **see|klar;** ein Schiff - machen; **See|kli|ma,** das; -s; **see|krank; See‿krank|heit** (die; -), **...krieg, ...kuh, ...lachs**

See|land (dän. Insel; niederl. Provinz)

Seel|chen; See|le, die; -, -n; meiner Seel! (↑R 13); die unsterbliche Seele; **See|len‿ach|se** (in Feuerwaffen), **...adel** (↑R 132; *geh.*); **...amt** (*kath. Kirche* Totenmesse), **...arzt** *(ugs.),* **...blind|heit** (*Med.; für* Agnosie), **...bräu|ti|gam** (*bes. Mystik* Christus), **...frie|de[n], ...grö|ße** (die; -), **...gü|te** *(geh.),* **...heil, ...hirt** (*veraltend für* Geistlicher), **...kun|de** (die; -; *veraltend für* Psychologie); **see|len|kun|dig; See|len‿le|ben** (das; -; *geh.*), **...leh|re** (die; -; *veraltet*); **see|len|los** *(geh.);* **See|len‿mas|sa|ge** (*ugs. für* Trost, Zuspruch), **...mes|se, ...qual** *(geh.),* **...ru|he; see|len|ru|hig; see|len[s]|gut; see|len|stark; see|len|ver|gnügt** (*ugs. für* heiter); **See|len|ver|käu|fer** (*ugs. für* skrupelloser Mensch; *Seemannsspr.* zum Abwracken reifes Schiff); **see|len|ver|wandt; See|len|ver|wandt|schaft; see|len|voll** *(geh.);* **See|len‿wan|de|rung, ...zu|stand; see|lisch;** das -e Gleichgewicht; die -en Kräfte; **Seel|sor|ge,** die; -; **Seel|sor|ger; Seel|sor|ge|rin; seel|sor|ge|risch; seel|sor|ger|lich, seel|sorg|lich**

See‿luft (die; -), **...macht, ...mann** (*Plur.* ...leute); **see|män|nisch; See|manns‿amt, ...brauch; See|mann|schaft,** die; - (seemännische Kenntnisse); **See|manns‿garn** (das; -[e]s; erfundene Geschichte), **...heim, ...le|ben** (das; -s), **...lied, ...los** (das; -es), **...spra|che** (die; -), **...tod; See‿mei|le** (*Zeichen* sm), **...mi|ne** (*vgl.* [1]Mine); **seen|ar|tig** *vgl.* seeartig; **Seen|kun|de,** die; - (*für* Limnologie); **See|not,** die; -; **See|not‿ret|tungs|dienst, ...ret|tungs|kreu|zer, ...zei|chen; Seen|plat|te**

s. e. e. o., s. e. et o. = salvo errore et omissione ‹lat.› (Irrtum und Auslassung vorbehalten)

See‿pferd|chen, ...po|cke (ein Krebstier), **...räu|ber, ...räu|be|rei** (die; -); **see|räu|be|risch; See‿recht** (das; -[e]s), **...rei|se, ...ro|se, ...sack, ...sand, ...schei|de** (ein Manteltier), **...schlacht, ...schlan|ge, ...sper|re, ...stern** (*vgl.* [2]Stern), **...stra|ße; See|stra|ßen|ord|nung,** die; -; **See‿streit|kräf|te** *(Plur.),* **...stück** (Gemälde mit Seemotiv), **...tang**

s. e. et o. *vgl.* s. e. e. o.

see|tüch|tig; See|ufer (↑R 132); **See‿ver|bren|nung** ([Müll]verbrennung auf [2]See), **...ver|si|che|rung, ...wal|ze** (*vgl.* Seegurke), **...war|te** (die Deutsche - in Hamburg); **see|wärts; See|was|ser|aqua|ri|um** (↑R 132); **See‿weg, ...we|sen** (das; -s), **...wet|ter|dienst, ...wind, ...zei|chen, ...zoll|ha|fen, ...zun|ge** (ein Fisch)

Se|gel, das; -s, -; **Se|gel|boot; se|gel|fer|tig; se|gel|flie|gen** *nur im Infinitiv gebräuchlich;* **Se|gel‿flie|ger, ...flug, ...flug|zeug, ...jacht, ...kurs; se|gel|los; Se|gel|ma|cher; se|geln;** ich ...[e]le (↑R 16); **Se|gel‿oh|ren** (*Plur.; ugs. für* abstehende Ohren), **...re|gat|ta, ...schiff, ...sport** (der; -[e]s), **...sur|fen** (das; -s), **...törn** ([...tœ(r)n]; Fahrt mit einem Segelboot), **...tuch** (*Plur.* ...tuche)

[1] *So die amtl. Schreibung ohne Fugen-s.*

Se|gen, der; -s, -; Segen bringen; ich bringe Segen; Segen gebracht; Segen zu bringen; Segen bringend; Segen spendend; **se|gens|reich; Se|gens|spruch; se|gens|voll; Se|gens|wunsch**
Se|ger (dt. Technologe); **Se|ger-ke|gel** ® (↑R 95; *Zeichen* SK), **...por|zel|lan** (das; -s)
Se|ges|tes (Cheruskerfürst; Vater der Thusnelda)
Seg|ge, die; -, -n (*nordd. für* Riedgras, Sauergras)
Se|ghers (dt. Schriftstellerin)
Seg|ler
Seg|ment, das; -[e]s, -e ⟨lat.⟩ (Abschnitt, Teilstück); **seg|men|tal** (in Form eines Segmentes); **seg|men|tär** (aus Abschnitten gebildet); **seg|men|tie|ren; Seg|men|tie|rung** (Gliederung in Abschnitte)
seg|nen; gesegnete Mahlzeit!; **Seg|nung**
Seg|re|gat (↑R 130), das; -[e]s, -e ⟨lat.⟩ (*veraltet für* Ausgeschiedenes); **¹Seg|re|ga|ti|on,** die; -, -en (*Biol.* Aufspaltung der Erbfaktoren während der Reifeteilung der Geschlechtszellen; *veraltet für* Ausscheidung, Trennung); **²Seg|re|ga|ti|on** [sεgri'ge:ʃ(ə)n], die; -, -s ⟨engl.⟩ (*Soziol.* Absonderung einer Bevölkerungsgruppe [nach Rasse, Sprache, Religion]); **seg|re|gie|ren**
Seh|ach|se; seh|be|hin|dert; Seh|be|hin|der|te, der *u.* die; -n, -n (↑R 5 ff.); **Seh|be|hin|de|rung; se|hen;** du siehst, er sieht; ich sah, du sahst; du sähest; gesehen; sieh!, *bei Verweisen u. als Ausrufewort* sieh[e]!; sieh[e] da!; ich habe es gesehen, *aber* ich habe es kommen sehen, *selten* gesehen; (↑R 50:) ich kenne ihn nur vom Sehen; ihm wird Hören u. Sehen, *auch* hören u. sehen vergehen *(ugs.)*; **se|hens-wert, ...wür|dig; Se|hens|wür|dig|keit,** die; -, -en; **Se|her** (*Jägerspr. auch* Auge des Raubwildes); **Se|her-blick, ...ga|be** (die; -); **Se|he|rin; se|he|risch; Seh|feh|ler; seh|ge|schä|digt; Seh|ge|schä|dig|te,** der *u.* die; -n, -n (↑R 5 ff.); **Seh-hil|fe, ...kraft** (die; -), **...kreis, ...loch** (*für* Pupille)
Seh|ne, die; -, -n
seh|nen, sich; (↑R 50:) stilles Sehnen
Seh|nen-ent|zün|dung, ...ref|lex *(Med.)*, **...riss, ...satz** *(Math.)*, **...schei|de; Seh|nen|schei|den|ent|zün|dung; Seh|nen|zer|rung**
Seh|nerv
seh|nig
sehn|lich; Sehn|sucht, die; -, ...süchte; **sehn|süch|tig; sehn|suchts|voll**
Seh-öff|nung, ...or|gan (Auge), **...pro|be, ...prü|fung**
sehr; so sehr; zu sehr; gar sehr; sehr fein (*Abk.* ff); sehr viel, sehr vieles; sehr bedauerlich; er hat die Note „sehr gut" erhalten; *vgl.* ausreichend
seh|ren (*veraltet, aber noch mdal. für* verletzen)
Seh-rohr (*für* Periskop), **...schär|fe; seh|schwach; Seh|schwä|che; Seh|schwa|chen|schu|le; Seh-stäb|chen** *(Med.)*, **...stö|rung, ...test, ...ver|mö|gen** (das; -s), **...zent|rum** *(Med.)*
Sei|ber, Sei|fer, der; -s (*landsch. für* ausfließender Speichel [bes. bei kleinen Kindern]); **sei|bern, sei|fern;** ich ...ere (↑R 16)
Sei|cen|to [sei'tʃεnto], das; -[s] ⟨ital.⟩ (*Kunst* das 17. Jh. in Italien [als Stilbegriff]); *vgl.* Secento
Seich, der; -[e]s *u.* **Sei|che,** die; - (*landsch. derb für* Urin; seichtes Geschwätz; schales Getränk); **sei|chen** (*derb für* urinieren)
Sei|cherl, das; -s, -n (*österr. ugs. für* weichlicher Mensch, Feigling); *vgl. aber* Seiherl
Seiches [sεʃ] *Plur.* ⟨franz.⟩ (periodische Niveauschwankungen von Seen usw.)
seicht; -es Gewässer; **Seicht|heit,** *seltener* **Seich|tig|keit**
seid (*2. Pers. Plur. Indikativ Präs. von* ²sein); ihr seid; seid vorsichtig!; *vgl. aber* seit
Sei|de, die; -, -n
Sei|del, das; -s, - ⟨lat.⟩ (ein Gefäß; ein Flüssigkeitsmaß); 3 - Bier (↑R 90)
Sei|del|bast, der; -[e]s, -e (ein Strauch)
sei|den (aus Seide); **sei|den|ar|tig; Sei|den-at|las** (*Plur.* -se), **...bau** (der; -[e]s), **...blu|se, ...fa|den, ...glanz, ...kleid, ...ma|le|rei; sei|den|matt; Sei|den-pa|pier, ...rau|pe; Sei|den|rau|pen|zucht; Sei|den-schal, ...spin|ner** (ein Schmetterling); **sei|den|weich; sei|dig**
Sei|en|de, das; -n *(Philos.)*
Sei|fe, die; -, -n (Waschmittel; *Geol.* Ablagerung); grüne -; **sei|fen; sei|fen|ar|tig; Sei|fen-bla|se, ...flo|cke, ...ge|bir|ge** (*Geol.* erz- od. edelsteinhaltiges Gebirge); **Sei|fen|kis|ten|ren|nen; Sei|fen-lap|pen, ...lau|ge, ...napf, ...oper** (↑R 132; *ugs. für* triviale, rührselige Rundfunk- od. Fernsehserie), **...pul|ver, ...scha|le, ...schaum** (der; -[e]s), **...sie|der** (jmdm. geht ein Seifensieder auf [*ugs. für* jmd. begreift etwas]), **...was|ser** (das; -s)
Sei|fer usw. *vgl.* Seiber usw.
Seif|fen, Kur|ort (im Erzgebirge)
sei|fig; Seif|ner (*veraltet für* Erzwäscher)
Sei|ge, die; -, -n (*Bergmannsspr.* vertiefte Rinne, in der das Grubenwasser abläuft); **sei|ger** (*Bergmannsspr.* senkrecht); **Sei|ger,** der; -s, - (*landsch. für* Uhr); **sei|gern** (*veraltet für* seihen, sickern; *Hüttenw.* [sich] ausscheiden; ausschmelzen); ich ...ere (↑R 16); **Sei|ger-riss** (bildl. Durchschnitt eines Bergwerks), **...schacht** (*Bergbau* senkrechter Schacht); **Sei|ge|rung** *(Hüttenw.)*
Seig|neur [sεn'jø:r] (↑R 130), der; -s, -s ⟨franz.⟩ (*veraltet für* vornehmer Weltmann)
Sei|he, die; -, -n *(landsch.)*; **sei|hen** (durch ein Sieb gießen, filtern); **Sei|her** (*landsch. für* Sieb für Flüssigkeiten); **Sei|herl,** das; -s, -n (*österr. für* [Tee]sieb); *vgl. aber* Seicherl; **Seih|tuch** *Plur.* ...tücher *(landsch.)*
Seil, das; -[e]s, -e; auf dem Seil laufen, tanzen (*vgl. aber* seiltanzen); über das Seil springen (*vgl. aber* seilspringen); über das Seil hüpfen (*vgl. aber* seilhüpfen); [am] Seil ziehen; **Seil|bahn; ¹sei|len** (Seile herstellen; *selten für* mit einem Seil binden)
²sei|len (*nordd. für* segeln)
Sei|ler; Sei|le|rei; Sei|le|rin; Sei|ler|meis|ter; seil|hüp|fen; *vorwiegend im Infinitiv u. Partizip II gebr.;* seilgehüpft; *vgl.* Seil; **Seil|hüp|fen,** das; -s; **Seil|schaft** (die durch ein Seil verbundenen Bergsteiger; *übertr. für* Gruppe von Personen, die [in der Politik] eng zusammenarbeiten); **Seil|schwe|be|bahn; seil|sprin|gen;** *vorwiegend im Infinitiv u. Partizip II gebr.;* seilgesprungen; *vgl.* Seil; **Seil-sprin|gen** (das; -s), **...steu|e|rung** *(Bobsport)*; **seil|tan|zen;** *vorwiegend im Infinitiv u. Partizip II gebr.;* seilgetanzt; *vgl.* Seil; **Seil-tän|zer, ...tän|ze|rin, ...trom|mel, ...win|de, ...zie|hen** (das; -s), **...zug**
Seim, der; -[e]s, -e (*veraltend für* dicker [Honig]saft); **sei|mig** (*veraltend für* dickflüssig)
¹sein, sei|ne, sein; *aber* (↑R 53): Seine (*Abk.* S[e].), Seiner (*Abk.* Sr.) Exzellenz; (↑R 48:) jedem das Seine, *auch* seine; er muss das Seine, *auch* seine dazu beitragen, tun; sie ist die Seine, *auch* seine;

er sorgte für die Seinen, *auch* seinen; *vgl.* dein
[2]**sein**; ich bin, du bist, er ist, wir sind, ihr seid, sie sind; ich sei, du seist, er sei, wir seien, ihr seiet, sie seien; ich war, du warst, er war, wir waren, ihr wart, sie waren; ich wäre, du wärst, er wäre, wir wären, ihr wärt, sie wären; seiend; gewesen; sei!; seid!; ich möchte das lieber sein lassen (*ugs. für* nicht tun); er hat es sein lassen; sie wollte ihn Sieger sein lassen;
Sein, das; -s; das - und das Nichtsein; das wahre, vollkommene -
sei|ne, sei|ni|ge; *vgl.* deine, deinige
Sei|ne [ˈsɛ:n(ə)], die; - (franz. Fluss)
sei|ner|seits; sei|ner|zeit; ↑R 41 (damals, dann; *Abk.* s. Z.); **sei|ner|zei|tig; sei|nes|glei|chen;** Leute -; er hat nicht -; **sei|net|hal|ben** *(veraltend);* **sei|net|we|gen; sei|net|wil|len;** *nur in* um -;
sei|ni|ge *vgl.* seine
sein las|sen *vgl.* [2]sein
Sei|sing *vgl.* Zeising
Seis|mik, die; - ‹griech.› (Erdbebenkunde); **seis|misch** (die Seismik bzw. Erdbeben betreffend); **Seis|mo|graf** *eindeutschende Schreibung für* Seismograph; **Seis|mo|gramm**, das; -s, -e (Aufzeichnung der Erdbebenwellen); **Seis|mo|graph** (↑R 33), der; -en, -en; ↑R 126 (Gerät zur Aufzeichnung von Erdbeben); **Seis|mo|lo|ge**, der; -n, -n (↑R 126); **Seis|mo|lo|gie**, die; - (*svw.* Seismik); **Seis|mo|lo|gin; seis|mo|lo|gisch; Seis|mo|me|ter**, das; -s, - (Gerät zur Messung der Erdbebenstärke); **seis|mo|me|t|risch** (↑R 130)
seit; *Präp. mit Dat.:* seit dem Zusammenbruch; seit alters (↑R 46), seit damals, gestern, heute; seit kurzem, langem; *Konjunktion:* seit ich hier bin; *vgl. aber* seid
seit|ab (abseits)
seit|dem; seitdem ist er gesund; seitdem ich hier bin
Sei|te, die; -, -n (*Abk.* S.); die linke, rechte Seite; von allen Seiten; von zuständiger Seite; zur Seite treten, stehen; abseits; allerseits; meinerseits; deutscherseits; mütterlicherseits; (↑R 41:) beiseite; seitens *(vgl. d.);* aufseiten, *auch* auf Seiten; vonseiten, *auch* von Seiten; zuseiten, *auch* zu Seiten; *vgl. aber* Saite; **Sei|ten‿al|tar, ...an|sicht, ...arm, ...auf|prall|schutz** *(Kfz-Technik),* **...aus** *(Sport),* **...aus|gang, ...aus|li|nie** *(Sport),* **...bau** (*Plur.* ...bauten), **...blick, ...ein|gang, ...ein|stei|ger, ...ein|stei|ge|rin, ...flü|gel, ...front, ...füh|rung** (der Reifen), **...gang** (der), **...ge|wehr, ...hal|bie|ren|de** (die; -n, -n; *Math.;* zwei -), **...hieb; sei|ten|lang,** *aber* vier Seiten lang; **Sei|ten‿leit|werk** *(Flugw.),* **...li|nie, ...por|tal, ...ram|pe, ...ru|der** *(Flugw.);* **sei|tens** (↑R 46); *Präp. mit Gen. (Amtsspr.):* - des Angeklagten (*dafür besser* von dem Angeklagten) wurde Folgendes eingewendet; **Sei|ten‿schiff** *(Archit.),* **...schnei|der** (ein Werkzeug), **...schritt, ...schwim|men** (das; -s), **...sprung** (sexuelles Abenteuer außerhalb einer festen Bindung); **sei|ten|stän|dig** (*Bot.* von Blättern); **Sei|ten‿ste|chen** (das; -s), **...stra|ße, ...strei|fen, ...stück, ...ta|sche, ...teil** (das, *auch* der), **...trakt, ...trieb** *(Bot.),* **...tür; sei|ten|ver|kehrt; Sei|ten‿wa|gen, ...wahl** *(Sport),* **...wech|sel, ...wind, ...zahl**
seit|her (*selten für* seitdem); **seit|he|rig** *(selten)*
...sei|tig (z. B. allseitig); **seit|lich; Seit|ling**, der; -s, -e (ein Pilz); **seit|lings** *(veraltet);* **Seit|pferd** *(Turnen);* **seit|wärts;** - gehen
Sei|wal ‹norw.› (eine Walart)
Sejm [sɛjm], der; -s ‹poln.› (oberste poln. Volksvertretung)
sek, Sek. = Sekunde *(vgl. d.)*
Se|kans, der; -, *Plur.* -, *auch* Sekanten ‹lat.› (*Math.* Verhältnis der Hypotenuse zur Ankathete im rechtwinkligen Dreieck; *Zeichen* sec); **Se|kan|te**, die; -, -n (Gerade, die eine Kurve schneidet)
Se|kel, *auch* Sche|kel, der; -s, - ‹hebr.› (altbabylon. u. hebr. Gewichts- u. Münzeinheit)
sek|kant ‹ital.› (*veraltet, noch österr. für* lästig, zudringlich); **Sek|ka|tur**, die; -, -en (*veraltet, noch österr. für* Quälerei, Belästigung); **sek|kie|ren** (*veraltet, noch österr. für* quälen, belästigen)
Se|kond|hieb ‹ital.; dt.› (ein Fechthieb)
sek|ret (↑R 130) ‹lat.› (*veraltet für* geheim; abgesondert); [1]**Sek|ret**, das; -[e]s, -e (*Med.* Absonderung; *veraltet für* vertrauliche Mitteilung); [2]**Sek|ret**, die; - (stilles Gebet des Priesters während der Messe); **Sek|re|tar**, der; -s, -e (*veraltet für* Geschäftsführer, Abteilungsleiter; *selten für* Sekretär); **Sek|re|tär**, der; -s, -e (Beamter des mittleren Dienstes; Funktionär in einer Partei, Gewerkschaft o. Ä.; kaufmännischer Angestellter; Schreibschrank; ein Greifvogel); *vgl.* Sekretar; **Sek|re|ta|ri|at**, das; -[e]s, -e (Kanzlei, Geschäftsstelle); **Sek|re|tä|rin; sek|re|tie|ren** (*Med.* absondern); **Sek|re|ti|on**, die; -, -en (*Med.* Absonderung); **sek|re|to|risch**
Sekt, der; -[e]s, -e ‹ital.› (Schaumwein)
Sek|te, die; -, -n ‹lat.› ([kleinere] Glaubensgemeinschaft); **Sek|ten|we|sen**, das; -s
Sekt‿fla|sche, ...früh|stück, ...glas (*Plur.* ...gläser)
Sek|tie|rer ‹lat.› (jmd., der von einer politischen, religiösen o. ä. Richtung abweicht); **sek|tie|re|risch; Sek|tie|rer|tum**, das; -s
Sek|ti|on, die; -, -en ‹lat.› (Abteilung, Gruppe, Zweig[verein]; *Med.* Leichenöffnung; *ehem. in der DDR* Lehr- u. Forschungsbereich einer Hochschule); **Sek|ti|ons‿be|fund** *(Med.),* **...chef** (Abteilungsvorstand; *in Österr.* höchster Beamtentitel); **sek|ti|ons|wei|se**
Sekt‿kelch, ...kel|le|rei, ...kor|ken, ...kü|bel, ...lau|ne
Sek|tor, der; -s, ...oren ([Sach]gebiet, Bezirk; *Math.* Ausschnitt); **Sek|to|ren|gren|ze**
Sekt‿scha|le, ...steu|er (die)
Se|kund, die; -, -en ‹lat.› (*österr. svw.* Sekunde [in der Musik]); **se|kun|da** (*Kaufmannsspr. veraltet für* zweiter Güte); die Ware ist -; **Se|kun|da**, die; -, ...den (*veraltend für* die 6. u. 7. [*in Österr.* 2.] Klasse eines Gymnasiums); **Se|kund|ak|kord** *(Musik);* **Se|kun|da|ner** (Schüler einer Sekunda); **Se|kun|da|ne|rin; Se|kun|dant**, der; -en, -en; ↑R 126 (Beistand, Zeuge [im Zweikampf]; Berater, Betreuer eines Sportlers); **se|kun|där** ‹franz.› (zweitrangig; untergeordnet; nachträglich hinzukommend; Neben...); **Se|kun|dar|arzt** (*österr. für* Assistenzarzt); **Se|kun|där|elek|t|ron** (↑R 132; *Physik* durch Beschuss mit einer primären Strahlung aus einem festen Stoff ausgelöstes Elektron); **Se|kun|där‿emis|si|on** (↑R 132; *Physik* Emission von Sekundärelektronen), **...ener|gie** (↑R 132; *Technik* aus einer Primärenergie gewonnene Energie); **Se|kun|dar|leh|rer** *(schweiz.);* **Se|kun|där|li|te|ra|tur** (wiss. u. krit. Literatur über Dichter, Dichtungen, Dichtungsepochen; *Ggs.* Primärliteratur); **Se|kun|där|roh|stoff** *meist Plur.* (*regional für* Altmaterial); **Se|kun|dar|schu|le** (*schweiz. für* höhere Volksschule); **Se|kun|där‿sta|tis|tik, ...strom** *(Elektrotechnik);*

Se|kun|dar|stu|fe (ab dem 5. Schuljahr); **Se|kun|där_tu|gend** (z. B. Fleiß), **...wick|lung** *(Elektrotechnik);* **Se|kun|da|wech|sel** *(Bankw.);* **Se|künd|chen; Se|kun|de** ($^1/_{60}$ Minute, *Abk.* Sek. [*Zeichen* s; *veraltet* sec, sek]; *Geom.* $^1/_{60}$ Minute [*Zeichen* "]; *Musik* zweiter Ton der diaton. Tonleiter; Intervall im Abstand von 2 Stufen; *Druckerspr.* die am Fuß der dritten Seite eines Bogens stehende Zahl mit Sternchen); **se|kun|den|lang,** *aber* vier Sekunden lang; **Se|kun|den_schnel|le** (die; -; in -), **...zei|ger; se|kun|die|ren** (beistehen [im Zweikampf]; helfen, schützen); jmdm. -; **se|künd|lich,** *auch* se|kund|lich (in jeder Sekunde); **Se|kun|do|ge|ni|tur,** die; -, -en (*früher* Besitz[recht] des zweitgeborenen Sohnes u. seiner Linie)

Se|ku|rit ® [*auch* ...'rit], das; -s ‹nlat.› (nicht splitterndes Glas); **Se|ku|ri|tät,** die; -, -en ‹lat.› (Sicherheit, Sorglosigkeit)

sel. = selig

se|la! ‹hebr.› (*ugs. für* abgemacht!, Schluss!); **Se|la,** das; -s, -s (Musikzeichen in den Psalmen)

Se|la|chi|er [...xiər], der; -s, - *meist Plur.* ‹griech.› (*Zool.* Haifisch)

Se|la|don [*franz.* sela'dɔ̃:], das; -s, -s ‹wohl nach dem graugrünen Gewand des franz. Romanhelden Céladon› (chin. Porzellan mit grüner Glasur); **Se|la|don|por|zel|lan**

Se|la|gi|nel|le, die; -, -n ‹ital.› (*Bot.* Moosfarn)

Se|lam *vgl.* Salam; **Se|lam|lik,** der; -s, -s ‹arab.-türk.› (Empfangsraum im oriental. Haus)

selb|an|der (*veraltet für* zu zweit); **selb|dritt** (*veraltet für* zu dritt); **sel|be;** zur -en (zu derselben) Zeit; durchs selbe (durch dasselbe); **sel|ber** (*meist alltagssprachl. für* selbst); **Sel|ber|ma|chen,** das; -s; ↑R 50 *(ugs.);* **sel|big** *(veraltet);* zu -er Stunde, zur -en Stunde; **selbst** (*vgl. auch* selber); von selbst; selbst wenn (↑R 88); selbst (sogar) bei Glatteis fährt er schnell. *In Verbindung mit Verben und Partizipien gilt im Allgemeinen Getrenntschreibung:* selbst backen; ein selbst gebackener Kuchen; selbst gebrautes Bier; ein selbst ernannter Experte; selbst verdientes Geld; selbst gedreht, geschneidert usw.; *aber* selbstentzündlich (von selbst entzündlich), selbstklebend (von selbst klebend), selbstredend, selbstvergessen usw.; **Selbst,** das; -; ein Stück meines -; **Selbst_ab|hol|ler, ...ach|tung** (die; -), **...ana|ly|se** (↑R 132; *Psych.*); **selb|stän|dig** *vgl.* selbstständig; **Selb|stän|di|ge** *vgl.* Selbstständige; **Selb|stän|dig|keit** *vgl.* Selbstständigkeit; **Selbst_an|fer|ti|gung, ...an|kla|ge, ...an|schluss** *(veraltet),* **...an|ste|ckung, ...an|zei|ge, ...auf|op|fe|rung, ...aus|lö|ser** *(Fotogr.),* **...be|die|nung** (*Plur. selten; Abk.* SB); **Selbst|be|die|nungs|la|den; Selbst_be|frie|di|gung** (*für* Masturbation), **...be|fruch|tung** *(Bot.),* **...be|halt** (der; -[e]s, -e; *Versicherungsw.* Selbstbeteiligung), **...be|haup|tung** (die; -), **...be|herr|schung** (die; -), **...be|kennt|nis** *(veraltend),* **...be|kös|ti|gung, ...be|schei|dung** *(geh.),* **...be|schrän|kung, ...be|schul|di|gung, ...be|sin|nung, ...be|stä|ti|gung, ...be|stäu|bung** *(Bot.),* **...be|stim|mung** (die; -); **Selbst|be|stim|mungs|recht,** das; -[e]s; **Selbst_be|tei|li|gung** *(Versicherungsw.),* **...be|trug, ...be|weih|räu|che|rung** *(ugs.);* **selbst|be|wusst; Selbst_be|wusst|sein, ...be|zeich|nung, ...be|zich|ti|gung; Selbst|be|zich|ti|gungs|schrei|ben; Selbst_bild|nis, ...bin|der, ...bi|o|gra|phie, ...dar|stel|lung, ...dis|zip|lin** (die; -); **selbst|ei|gen** *(veraltet);* **Selbst_ein|schät|zung, ...ein|tritt** *(Wirtsch.),* **...ent|fal|tung; selbst|ent|zünd|lich;** *vgl.* selbst; **Selbst_ent|zün|dung, ...er|fah|rung** (die; -), **...er|hal|tung** (die; -); **Selbst|er|hal|tungs|trieb; Selbst|er|kennt|nis; selbst er|nannt** *vgl.* selbst; **Selbst_er|nied|ri|gung, ...er|zeu|ger, ...er|zie|hung, ...fah|rer, ...fi|nan|zie|rung, ...fin|dung** *(geh.);* **selbst ge|ba|cken, ge|braut, ge|dreht** *vgl.* selbst; **selbst|ge|fäl|lig; Selbst_ge|fäl|lig|keit** (die; -), **...ge|fühl** (das; -[e]s); **selbst ge|macht** *vgl.* selbst; **selbst|ge|nüg|sam; selbst|ge|recht; selbst ge|schnei|dert, ge|schrie|ben** *vgl.* selbst; **Selbst|ge|spräch; selbst ge|strickt** *vgl.* selbst; **selbst|haf|tend;** selbsthaftende Etiketten; **selbst|herr|lich; Selbst_herr|lich|keit** (die; -), **...hil|fe** (die; -), **...hil|fe|grup|pe, ...in|duk|ti|on** *(Elektrotechnik);* **Selbst|iro|nie** (↑R 132), die; -; **selbs|tisch** (*geh. für* egoistisch); **Selbst|jus|tiz; selbst|kle|bend** *vgl.* selbsthaftend; **Selbst_kon|trol|le, ...kos|ten** *(Plur.),* **...kos|ten|preis, ...kos|ten|rech|nung; Selbst|kri|tik** *Plur. selten;* **selbst|kri|tisch; Selbst|la|de_ge|wehr, ...pis|to|le; Selbst|la|der; Selbst_laut** (*für* Vokal), **...lob; selbst|los;** selbstloser Verzicht; **Selbst|lo|sig|keit,** die; -; **Selbst_me|di|ka|ti|on** *(Med.),* **...mit|leid, ...mord, ...mör|der, ...mör|de|rin; selbst|mör|de|risch; selbst|mord|ge|fähr|det; Selbst|mord_kom|man|do, ...ra|te, ...ver|such; Selbst|port|rät; selbst|quä|le|risch; selbst|re|dend** (selbstverständlich); **Selbst|rei|ni|gung;** biologische -; **Selbst|schuss; Selbst|schuss|an|la|ge; Selbst|schutz,** der; -es; **selbst|si|cher; Selbst|si|cher|heit,** die; -; **selbst|stän|dig,** *auch* selb|stän|dig; sich - machen; **Selbst|stän|di|ge,** *auch* Selb|stän|di|ge, der *u.* die; -n, -n (↑R 5 ff.); **Selbst|stän|dig|keit,** *auch* Selb|stän|dig|keit, die; -; **Selbst_stel|ler** *(Rechtsw.),* **...stu|di|um** (das; -s), **...sucht** (die; -); **selbst_süch|tig, ...tä|tig; Selbst_täu|schung, ...tö|tung** (*Amtsspr.* Selbstmord), **...über|he|bung** (↑R 132), **...über|schät|zung** (↑R 132), **...über|win|dung** (↑R 132), **...un|ter|richt, ...ver|ach|tung** (die; -), **...ver|brau|cher, ...ver|bren|nung; selbst ver|dient** *vgl.* selbst; **selbst|ver|ges|sen; Selbst_ver|lag** (der; -[e]s), **...ver|leug|nung; selbst|ver|liebt; Selbst_ver|liebt|heit, ...ver|mark|tung, ...ver|pfle|gung** (die; -), **...ver|schul|den** *(Amtsspr.),* **...ver|sor|ger; selbst|ver|ständ|lich; Selbst_ver|ständ|lich|keit, ...ver|ständ|nis** (das; -ses), **...ver|stüm|me|lung, ...ver|such** *(Med.),* **...ver|tei|di|gung, ...ver|trau|en, ...ver|wal|tung, ...ver|wirk|li|chung, ...vor|wurf; Selbst|wähl|fern|dienst,** der; -[e]s *(Fernspr.);* **Selbst|wert|ge|fühl** *(Psych.);* **Selbst|zer|flei|schung; selbst|zer|stö|re|risch; Selbst|zer|stö|rung; Selbst|zucht,** die; - *(geh.);* **selbst|zu|frie|den; Selbst_zu|frie|den|heit, ...zün|der, ...zweck** (der; -[e]s), **...zwei|fel**

sel|chen (*bayr. u. österr. für* räuchern); **Sel|cher** (*bayr. u. österr. für* jmd., der mit Geselchtem handelt); **Sel|che|rei** (*bayr. u. österr. für* Fleisch- u. Wursträucherei); **Selch_fleisch** *(bayr. u. österr.),* **...kam|mer, ...kar|ree** (das; -s, -s; *österr. für* Kasseler Rippenspeer)

Seld|schu|ke (↑R 130), der; -n, -n; ↑R 126 (Angehöriger eines türk. Volksstammes)

se|le|gie|ren ‹lat.› (auswählen); **Se|lek|ta,** die; -, ...ten (*früher* Oberklasse, Begabtenklasse); **Se|lek|ta|ner** (*früher* Schüler einer Selekta); **Se|lek|ta|ne|rin** (*früher*); **se|lek|tie|ren** (auswählen [für züchterische Zwecke]); **Se|lek|ti|on,** die; -, -en (Auswahl; *Biol.* Auslese); **se|lek|ti|o|nie|ren** (*svw.* selektieren); **Se|lek|ti|ons‿leh|re, ...the|o|rie; se|lek|tiv** (auswählend; mit Auswahl; *Funkw.* trennscharf); *vgl.* elektiv; **Se|lek|ti|vi|tät** [...v...], die; - (Trennschärfe bei Rundfunkempfängern)

Se|len, das; -s ‹griech.› (chem. Element, Nichtmetall; *Zeichen* Se); **Se|le|nat,** das; -[e]s, -e (Salz der Selensäure); **Se|le|ne** (griech. Mondgöttin); **se|le|nig** (*Chemie* Selen enthaltend); -e Säure; **Se|le|nit** [*auch* ...'nit], das; -s, -e (Salz der selenigen Säure); **Se|le|no|gra|phie,** die; - (Beschreibung u. kartograph. Darstellung der Mondoberfläche); **Se|le|no|lo|gie,** die; - (Mondkunde, bes. Mondgeologie); **se|le|no|lo|gisch; Se|len‿säu|re** (*Chemie*), **...zel|le** (ein elektrotechn. Bauelement)

Se|leu|ki|de, Se|leu|zi|de, der; -n, -n; ↑R 126 (Angehöriger einer makedonischen Dynastie in Syrien)

Self... ‹engl.› (Selbst...); **Self|ak|tor,** der; -s, -s (Spinnmaschine); **Self|made|man** ['sɛlfme:dmən], der; -s, ...men [...mən] (jmd., der sich aus eigener Kraft hochgearbeitet hat)

se|lig (*Abk.* sel.); ein seliges Ende haben; selige Weihnachtszeit; selig machen; selig preisen; selig sein; selig sprechen; selig werden

...se|lig (z. B. armselig)

Se|li|ge, der *u.* die; -n, -n (↑R 5 ff.); **Se|lig|keit; se|lig prei|sen** *vgl.* selig; **Se|lig|prei|sung; se|lig spre|chen** *vgl.* selig; **Se|lig|spre|chung**

Sel|le|rie [*österr.* ...'ri:], der; -s, -[s] *od., österr. nur,* die; -, *Plur.* -, *österr.* ...ien ‹griech.› (eine Gemüsepflanze); **Sel|le|rie|sa|lat**

Sel|ma (w. Vorn.)

Sel|mar (m. Vorn.)

sel|ten; seltener, seltenste; seltene Erden (*Chemie* Oxide der Seltenerdmetalle; *unrichtige Bez. für* die Seltenerdmetalle selbst); - gut (*ugs. für* besonders gut); ein -er Vogel (*ugs. auch für* sonderbarer Mensch); **Sel|ten|erd|me|tall** (*Chemie*); **Sel|ten|heit; Sel|ten|heits|wert,** der; -[e]s

Sel|ters (Name versch. Orte); Selterser Wasser; **Sel|ter[s]|was|ser** *Plur.* ...wässer

selt|sam; selt|sa|mer|wei|se; Selt|sam|keit

[1]**Sem** (bibl. m. Eigenn.)

[2]**Sem,** das; -s, -e ‹griech.› (*Sprachw.* kleinster Bestandteil der Wortbedeutung); **Se|man|tik,** die; - (Lehre von der Bedeutung sprachlicher Zeichen); **se|man|tisch; Se|ma|phor,** das *od., österr. nur,* der; -s, -e (Signalmast; opt. Telegraf); **se|ma|pho|risch; Se|ma|si|o|lo|gie,** die; - (Wortbedeutungslehre); **se|ma|si|o|lo|gisch; Se|mei|o|gra|phie,** die; - (*veraltend für* Lehre von den [musikal.] Zeichen; Notenschrift); **Se|mei|o|tik,** die; - (*seltener für* Semiotik)

Se|mes|ter, das; -s, - ‹lat.› ([Studien]halbjahr); **Se|mes|ter‿an|fang, ...be|ginn, ...en|de, ...fe|ri|en** (*Plur.*), **...zeug|nis; se|mes|tral** (↑R 130; *veraltet für* halbjährig; halbjährlich); **...se|mest|rig** (↑R 130; z. B. sechssemestrig)

se|mi... ‹lat.› (halb...); **Se|mi...** (Halb...); **Se|mi|fi|na|le** (*Sport*); **Se|mi|ko|lon,** das; -s, *Plur.* -s *u.* ...la ‹lat.; griech.› (Strichpunkt); **se|mi|lu|nar** ‹lat.› (halbmondförmig); **Se|mi|lu|nar|klap|pe** (*Med.* eine Herzklappe)

Se|mi|nar, das; -s, *Plur.* -e, *österr. u. schweiz. auch* -ien [...iən] ‹lat.› (Übungskurs an Hochschulen; kirchl. Institut zur Ausbildung von Geistlichen [z. B. Priestern]; *früher, aber noch schweiz. für* Lehrerbildungsanstalt); **Se|mi|nar|ar|beit; Se|mi|na|rist,** der; -en, -en; ↑R 126 (Seminarschüler); **Se|mi|na|ris|tin; se|mi|na|ris|tisch; Se|mi|nar‿schein, ...übung** (↑R 132)

Se|mi|o|lo|gie, die; - *u.* **Se|mi|o|tik,** die; - ‹griech.› (Lehre von den Zeichen, Zeichentheorie; *auch svw.* Symptomatologie)

se|mi|per|me|a|bel ‹lat.› (*Chemie, Biol.* halbdurchlässig); ...ab|le (↑R 130) Membran; **Se|mi|per|me|a|bi|li|tät,** die; -

Se|mi|ra|mis (assyrische Königin)

Se|mit, der; -en, -en (↑R 126) ‹*zu* [1]Sem› (Angehöriger einer eine semitische Sprache sprechenden Völkergruppe); **Se|mi|tin; se|mi|tisch; Se|mi|tist,** der; -en, -en; ↑R 126 (Erforscher der alt- u. der neusemit. Sprachen u. Literaturen); **Se|mi|tis|tik,** die; -; **se|mi|tis|tisch**

Se|mi|vo|kal (*Sprachw.* Halbvokal)

Sem|mel, die; -, -n; (*bes. bayr., österr.*); **sem|mel|blond; Sem|mel‿brö|sel, ...kloß, ...knö|del** (*bayr., österr.*), **...mehl**

Sem|mel|weis (ung. Arzt)

Sem|me|ring, der; -[s] (Alpenpass)

Sem|pach (schweiz. Ortsn.); **Sem|pa|cher See,** der; - -s (See im Schweizer Mittelland)

Sem|per (dt. Baumeister)

sem|pern (*österr. ugs. für* nörgeln, jammern); ich ...ere (↑R 16)

Semst|wo (↑R 132), das; -s, -s ‹russ.› (ehem. russ. Selbstverwaltungsorgan)

Sen, der; -[s], -[s] (kleine, wegen des geringen Wertes der Währung meist nur fiktive Währungseinheit in Japan [100 Sen = 1 Yen], Kambodscha [100 Sen = 10 Kak = 1 Riel], Indonesien [100 Sen = 1 Rupiah] und Malaysia [100 Sen = 1 Ringgit])

sen. = senior

Se|nat, der; -[e]s, -e ‹lat.› (Rat [der Alten] im alten Rom; Teil der Volksvertretung, z. B. in den USA; Regierungsbehörde in Hamburg, Bremen u. Berlin; akadem. Verwaltungsbehörde; Richterkollegium bei Obergerichten); **Se|na|tor,** der; -s, ...oren (Mitglied des Senats; Ratsherr); **Se|na|to|rin; se|na|to|risch; Se|nats‿be|schluss, ...prä|si|dent, ...sit|zung, ...spre|cher, ...vor|la|ge; Se|na|tus Po|pu|lus|que Ro|ma|nus** („Senat und Volk von Rom") (*Abk.* S. P. Q. R.)

Sen|cken|berg (dt. Arzt u. Naturforscher); **sen|cken|ber|gisch;** eine senckenbergische Stiftung; *aber* Senckenbergische Naturforschende Gesellschaft (↑R 108)

Send, der; -[e]s, -e (*früher für* [Kirchen]versammlung; geistl. Gericht)

Send|bo|te (*veraltend*); **Sen|de‿an|la|ge, ...an|stalt, ...be|ginn, ...be|reich** (der), **...ein|rich|tung, ...fol|ge, ...ge|biet, ...haus, ...lei|ter** (der); **sen|den;** du sandtest *u.* sendetest; *selten* du sendetest; gesandt *u.* gesendet; send[e]!; *in der Bedeutung* „[vom Rundfunk] übertragen" *nur* er sendete, hat gesendet; **Sen|de‿pau|se, ...plan** (*vgl.* [2]Plan); **Sen|der;** (↑R 108:) Sender Freies Berlin (*Abk.* SFB); **Sen|der|an|la|ge; Sen|de‿raum, ...rei|he; Sen|der|such|lauf** (*Rundf.*); **Sen|de|schluss** (der; -es), **...sta|ti|on; Sen|de- und Emp|fangs|ge|rät** (↑R 23); **Sen|de‿zei|chen, ...zeit, ...zent|ra|le, ...zent|rum**

Send|ge|richt *(früher)* ‹*zu* Send›
Send|schrei|ben; Sen|dung; Sen|dungs|be|wusst|sein
Se|ne|ca (röm. Dichter und Philosoph)
Se|ne|fel|der (österr. Erfinder des Steindruckes)
¹Se|ne|gal, der; -[s] (afrik. Fluss); **²Se|ne|gal** *meist mit Artikel* der; -[s] (Staat in Afrika); **Se|ne|ga|le|se,** der; -n, -n (↑R 126), *auch* Se|ne|ga|ler, der; -s, -; **se|ne|ga|le|sisch,** *auch* **se|ne|ga|lisch**
Se|ne|ga|wur|zel, die; - ‹indian.; dt.› (ein Arzneimittel)
Se|ne|schall, der; -s, -e ‹franz.› (Oberhofbeamter im merowing. Reich)
Se|nes|zenz, die; - ‹lat.› (*Med.* das Altern; [damit verbundene] Altersschwäche)
Senf, der; -[e]s, -e ‹griech.›; **senf|far|ben** *od.* **...far|big; Senf_gur|ke, ...korn** (*Plur.* ...körner), **...pflas|ter, ...so|ße**
Senf|ten|berg (Stadt südwestl. von Cottbus)
Senf|tun|ke
Sen|ge *Plur.* (*landsch. für* ²Prügel); - beziehen; **sen|gen; sen|ge|rig, seng|rig** (*landsch. für* brenzlig; angebrannt)
Sen|hor [sɛn'joːr] (↑R 132), der; -s, -es ‹port.› (*port. Bez. für* Herr; Besitzer); **Sen|ho|ra,** die; -, -s (*port. Bez. für* Dame, Frau; Besitzerin); **Sen|ho|ri|ta,** die; -, -s (*port. Bez. für* unverheiratete Frau)
se|nil ‹lat.› ([geistig] greisenhaft); **Se|ni|li|tät,** die; - (Greisenhaftigkeit); **se|ni|or** ‹„älter"› (*hinter Namen* der Ältere; *Abk.* sen.); Karl Meyer senior; **Se|ni|or,** der; -s, ...oren (Ältester; Vorsitzender; Altmeister; Sprecher; Sportler etwa zwischen 20 u. 30 Jahren; *meist Plur.:* ältere Menschen); **Se|ni|o|rat,** das; -[e]s, -e (*veraltet für* Ältestenwürde, Amt des Vorsitzenden; *auch für* Majorat, Ältestenrecht); **Se|ni|or|chef; Se|ni|o|ren_heim, ...klas|se** *(Sport),* **...kon|vent** *(Studentenspr.),* **...sport, ...treff; Se|ni|o|rin**
Senk|blei, das *(Bauw.);* **Sen|ke,** die; -, -n; **Sen|kel,** der; -s, - (*kurz für* Schnürsenkel; *schweiz. auch für* Senkblei); etwas, jmdn. in den - stellen (*schweiz. für* etwas zurechtrücken, jmdn. zurechtweisen); **sen|ken; Sen|ker** (ein Werkzeug; *auch für* Steckling); **Senk_fuß, ...gru|be, ...kas|ten, ...lot; senk|recht;** eine -e Wand; - [herunter]fallen, stehen; (↑R 47:) das ist das einzig Senkrechte (*ugs. für* Richtige); **Senk|rech|te,** die; -n, -n; zwei -[n]; **Senk|recht_start, ...star|ter** (ein Flugzeugtyp; *ugs. auch für* jmd., der schnell Karriere macht); **Senk|rü|cken; Sen|kung; Sen|kungs|abs|zess** *(Med.);* **Senk|waa|ge** (*Physik* Gerät zur Bestimmung der Dichte von Flüssigkeiten)
Senn, der; -[e]s, -e, *schweiz.* der; -en, -en, *bayr., österr. auch* Senne, der; -n, -n; ↑R 126 (*bayr., österr. u. schweiz. für* Bewirtschafter einer Sennhütte, Almhirt)
Sen|na, die; - ‹arab.› (Blätter verschiedener Arten der Kassie); *vgl.* Kassie
¹Sen|ne *vgl.* Senn; **²Sen|ne,** die; -, -n (*bayr., österr. für* ²Weide)
³Sen|ne, die; - (südwestl. Vorland des Teutoburger Waldes)
sen|nen (*bayr., österr. für* Käse bereiten); **¹Sen|ner** (*bayr., österr. svw.* Senn)
²Sen|ner (Pferd aus der ³Senne)
Sen|ne|rei (*bayr., österr. für* Sennhütte, Käserei in den Alpen); **Sen|ne|rin** (Bewirtschafterin einer Almhütte)
Sen|nes|blät|ter *Plur.* ‹arab.; dt.› (*svw.* Senna); **Sen|nes|blät|ter|tee** (ein Abführmittel); **Sen|nes_pflan|ze** (Kassie), **...scho|te**
Senn|hüt|te; Sen|nin (*svw.* Sennerin); **Senn|wirt|schaft**
Se|non, das; -s ‹nach dem kelt. Stamm der Senonen› (*Geol.* zweitjüngste Stufe der oberen Kreideformation)
Se|ñor [sɛn'joːr], der; -s, -es [...ɛs] ‹span.› (*span. Bez. für* Herr); **Se|ño|ra,** die; -, -s (*span. Bez. für* Frau); **Se|ño|ri|ta,** die; -, -s (*span. Bez. für* unverheiratete Frau)
Sen|sal, der; -s, -e ‹ital.› (*österr. für* Kursmakler); **Sen|sa|lie, Sen|sa|rie,** die; -, ...ien (*österr. für* Maklergebühr)
Sen|sa|ti|on, die; -, -en ‹franz., „Empfindung"› (Aufsehen erregendes Ereignis); **sen|sa|ti|o|nell** (Aufsehen erregend); **Sen|sa|ti|ons_be|dürf|nis** (das; -ses), **...gier; sen|sa|ti|ons|lüs|tern; Sen|sa|ti|ons_ma|che** *(abwertend),* **...mel|dung, ...nach|richt, ...pres|se** (die; -), **...pro|zess, ...sucht** (die; -)
Sen|se, die; -, -n; [jetzt ist aber] Sense! (*ugs. für* Schluss!, jetzt ist es genug!); **sen|sen** (mit der Sense mähen); **Sen|sen_mann** (der; -[e]s; *veraltet für* Schnitter; *verhüllend für* Tod), **...schmied, ...wurf** (Sensenstiel)
sen|si|bel ‹franz.› (reizempfindlich, empfindsam; feinfühlig); ...ib|le (↑R 130) Nerven; **Sen|si|bi|li|sa|tor,** der; -s, ...oren ‹lat.› (die Lichtempfindlichkeit der fotografischen Schicht verstärkender Farbstoff); **sen|si|bi|li|sie|ren** ([licht]empfindlich[er] machen); **Sen|si|bi|li|sie|rung; Sen|si|bi|li|tät,** die; - ‹franz.› ([Reiz-, Schmerz]empfindlichkeit, Empfindsamkeit; Feinfühligkeit); **sen|si|tiv** ‹lat.(-franz.)› (sehr empfindlich; leicht reizbar; feinnervig); **Sen|si|ti|vi|tät** [...v...], die; - ([Über]empfindlichkeit); **Sen|si|to|me|ter,** das; -s, - ‹lat.; griech.› (*Fotogr.* Lichtempfindlichkeitsmesser); **Sen|si|to|met|rie** (↑R 130), die; - (Lichtempfindlichkeitsmessung); **Sen|sor,** der; -s, Sensoren ‹lat.› (*Technik* Messfühler; Berührungsschalter); **Sen|so|ri|en** [...iən] *Plur.* (*Med.* Gebiete der Großhirnrinde, in denen Sinnesreize bewusst werden); **sen|so|risch** (die Sinne betreffend); **Sen|so|ri|um,** das; -s (Gespür; *Med. veraltet für* Bewusstsein; *vgl.* Sensorien); **Sen|sor|tas|te** *(Elektronik);* **Sen|su|a|lis|mus,** der; - (*Philos.* Lehre, nach der alle Erkenntnis allein auf Sinneswahrnehmung zurückführbar ist); **Sen|su|a|list,** der; -en, -en (↑R 126); **sen|su|a|lis|tisch; Sen|su|a|li|tät,** die; - (*Med.* Empfindungsvermögen); **sen|su|ell** ‹franz.› (die Sinne betreffend, sinnlich wahrnehmbar)
Sen|ta (w. Vorn.)
Sen|te, die; -, -n (*nordd. für* [dünne, biegsame] Latte)
Sen|tenz, die; -, -en ‹lat.› (einprägsamer Ausspruch, Denkspruch; Sinnspruch); **sen|tenz|ar|tig** (einprägsam, in der Art einer Sentenz); **sen|tenz|haft** (*svw.* sentenziös); **sen|ten|zi|ös** ‹franz.› (sentenzartig; sentenzenreich)
Sen|ti|ment [sãti'mãː], das; -s, -s ‹franz.› (Empfindung, Gefühl); **sen|ti|men|tal** [zɛntimɛn'taːl] ‹engl.› (*oft abwertend für* [übertrieben] empfindsam; rührselig); **sen|ti|men|ta|lisch** (*veraltet für* sentimental; *Literaturw.* die verloren gegangene Natürlichkeit durch Reflexion wiederzugewinnen suchend); naive und -e Dichtung; **Sen|ti|men|ta|li|tät,** die; -, -en (*oft abwertend für* Empfindsamkeit, Rührseligkeit)
Se|nus|si, der; -, *Plur.* - *u.* ...ssen (Anhänger eines islam. Ordens)
Se|oul [se'uːl] (Hptst. von Südkorea)

se|pa|rat ‹lat.› (abgesondert; einzeln); **Se|pa|rat‿druck** (*Plur.* ...drucke; Sonderdruck), **...ein|gang, ...frie|de[n]; Se|pa|ra|ti|on,** die; -, -en (*veraltend für* Absonderung; Trennung; *früher für* Flurbereinigung); **Se|pa|ra|tis|mus,** der; - (Streben nach Loslösung eines Gebietes aus dem Staatsganzen); **Se|pa|ra|tist,** der; -en, -en (↑R 126); **se|pa|ra|tis|tisch; Se|pa|ra|tor,** der; -s, ...oren (*fachspr. für* Trennschleuder, Zentrifuge); **Sé|pa|rée,** *eindeutschend* Se|pa|ree [sepa're:] (↑R 33), das; -s, -s ‹franz.› (Sonderraum, Nische in einem Lokal; Chambre séparée); **se|pa|rie|ren** (absondern)

Se|phar|dim [*auch* ...'di:m] *Plur.* (Bez. für die span.-port. u. die oriental. Juden); **se|phar|disch**

se|pia ‹griech.› (graubraunschwarz); *vgl.* beige; **Se|pia,** die; -, ...ien [...i̯ən] (*Zool.* Tintenfisch; *nur Sing.:* ein Farbstoff); **Se|pia‿kno|chen, ...schal|le, ...zeich|nung; Se|pie** [...i̯ə], die; -, -n (Sepia [Tintenfisch])

Sepp, Sep|pel (m. Vorn.); **Sep|pel‿ho|se** (kurze Trachtenlederhose), **...hut** (Trachtenhut)

Sep|sis, die; -, Sepsen ‹griech., „Fäulnis"› (*Med.* Blutvergiftung)

Sept. = September

Sep|ta (*Plur. von* Septum)

Sept|ak|kord *vgl.* Septimenakkord

Sep|ta|rie [...i̯ə], die; -, -n ‹lat.› (*Geol.* Knolle mit radialen Rissen in kalkhaltigen Tonen); **Sep|ta|ri|en|ton,** der; -[e]s

Sep|tem|ber, der; -[s], - ‹lat.› (der neunte Monat des Jahres, Herbstmond, Scheiding; *Abk.* Sept.); **Sep|tem|ber-Ok|to|ber-Heft,** *auch* **Sep|tem|ber/Ok|to|ber-Heft** (↑R 28 *u.* 117); **Sep|tett,** das; -[e]s, -e ‹ital.› (Musikstück für sieben Stimmen od. Instrumente; *auch für* die sieben Ausführenden); **Sep|tim,** die; -, -en ‹lat.› (*österr. svw.* Septime); **Sep|ti|ma,** die; -, ...en (*österr. veraltend für* siebte Klasse des Gymnasiums); **Sep|ti|me,** die; -, -n (*Musik* siebenter Ton der diaton. Tonleiter; ein Intervall im Abstand von 7 Stufen); **Sep|ti|men|ak|kord**

sep|tisch ‹griech.› (die Sepsis betreffend; mit Keimen behaftet)

Sep|tu|a|ge|si|ma, die; *Gen.* -, *bei Gebrauch ohne Artikel auch* ...mä ‹lat.› (neunter Sonntag vor Ostern); Sonntag - *od.* Septuagesimä; **Sep|tu|a|gin|ta,** die; -; ([angeblich] von siebzig Gelehrten angefertigte Übersetzung des A. T. ins Griechische)

Sep|tum, das; -s, *Plur.* ...ta *u.* ...ten ‹lat.› (*Med.* Scheidewand, Zwischenwand in einem Organ)

seq. = sequens; **seqq.** = sequentes

se|quens ‹lat.› (*veraltet für* folgend; *Abk.* seq.); **se|quen|tes** (*veraltet für* die Folgenden; *Abk.* seqq.); **se|quen|ti|ell** *vgl.* sequenziell; **Se|quenz,** die; -, -en ([Aufeinander]folge, Reihe; liturg. Gesang; Wiederholung einer musikal. Figur auf verschiedenen Tonstufen; kleinere filmische Handlungseinheit; Serie aufeinander folgender Spielkarten; *EDV* Folge von Befehlen, Daten); **se|quen|zi|ell,** *auch* se|quen|ti|ell (*EDV* fortlaufend, nacheinander zu verarbeiten)

[1]**Se|ques|ter,** der, *auch* das; -s, - ‹lat.› (*svw.* Sequestration; *Med.* abgestorbenes Knochenstück); [2]**Se|ques|ter,** der; -s, - (*Rechtsw.* [Zwangs]verwalter); **Se|quest|ra|ti|on** (↑R 130), die; -, -en (*Rechtsw.* Beschlagnahme; [Zwangs]verwaltung); **se|quest|rie|ren**

Se|quo|ia [...i̯a], **Se|quo|ie** [...i̯ə], die; -, -n ‹indian.› (ein Nadelbaum, Mammutbaum)

Se|ra (*Plur. von* Serum)

Sé|rac [se'rak], der; -s, -s ‹franz.› (*Geogr.* zacken- od. turmartiges Gebilde an Gletschern)

Se|ra|fim *Plur.* (*ökum. für* Seraphim); *vgl.* Seraph

[1]**Se|rail** [ze'rai(l), *auch* se'ra:j], der; -s, -s ‹pers.› (Wolltuch); [2]**Se|rail,** das; -s, -s (Palast [des Sultans])

Se|ra|pei|on, das; -s, ...eia ‹ägypt.-griech.› (*svw.* Serapeum); **Se|ra|pe|um,** das; -s, ...peen (Serapistempel)

Se|raph, der; -s, *Plur.* -e *u.* -im ‹hebr.› ([Licht]engel des A.T.); *vgl.* Serafim; **se|ra|phisch** (zu den Engeln gehörend, engelgleich; verzückt)

Se|ra|pis (altägypt. Gott)

Ser|be, der; -n, -n; ↑R 126 (Angehöriger eines südslaw. Volkes)

ser|beln (*schweiz. für* kränkeln, welken); ich ...[e]le (↑R 16)

Ser|bi|en [...i̯ən] (Gliedstaat Jugoslawiens); **Ser|bin; ser|bisch; Ser|bisch,** das; -[s]; *vgl.* Deutsch; **Ser|bi|sche,** das; -n; *vgl.* Deutsche, das; **Ser|bo|kro|a|tisch,** das; -[s] (Sprache); *vgl.* Deutsch; **Ser|bo|kro|a|ti|sche,** das; -n; *vgl.* Deutsche, das

Se|ren (*Plur. von* Serum)

Se|re|na|de, die; -, -n ‹franz.› (Abendmusik, -ständchen)

Se|ren|ge|ti-Na|ti|o|nal|park, der; -s (Wildreservat in Tansania)

Se|re|nis|si|mus, der; -, ...mi ‹lat.› (*veraltet für* Durchlaucht; *meist scherzh. für* Fürst eines Kleinstaates); **Se|re|ni|tät,** die; - (*veraltet für* Heiterkeit)

Serge ['sɛrʒ, *auch* 'zɛrʒ], die, *österr. auch* der; -, -n [...ʒ(ə)n] ‹franz.› (ein Gewebe)

Ser|geant [...'ʒant, *engl.* 'sa(r)dʒənt], der; -en, -en, *bei engl. Ausspr.* der; -s, -s; ↑R 126 ‹franz. (-engl.)› (Unteroffizier[sdienstgrad])

Ser|gi|us (m. Vorn.)

Se|rie [...i̯ə], die; -, -n ‹lat.› (Reihe; Folge; Gruppe); **se|ri|ell** (serienmäßig; in Reihen); -e Musik (eine Sonderform der Zwölftonmusik); **Se|ri|en‿an|fer|ti|gung, ...bau** (*Plur.* ...bauten), **...bild, ...ein|bre|cher, ...fab|ri|ka|ti|on, ...fer|ti|gung; se|ri|en|mä|ßig; Se|ri|en|pro|duk|ti|on; se|ri|en|reif; Se|ri|en‿rei|fe, ...schal|ter, ...schal|tung** (*Elektrotechnik* Reihenschaltung), **...tä|ter** (*Kriminalistik*); **se|ri|en|wei|se**

Se|ri|fe, die; -, -n *meist Plur.* ‹engl.› (kleiner Abschlussstrich bei Schrifttypen); **se|ri|fen|los**

Se|ri|gra|phie, die; - ‹griech.› (*Druckw.* Siebdruck)

se|ri|ös ‹franz.› (ernsthaft, [vertrauens]würdig); **Se|ri|o|si|tät,** die; -

Ser|mon, der; -s, -e ‹lat.› (*veraltet für* Predigt; *ugs. für* langweiliges Geschwätz)

Sernf, die (Fluss im Schweizer Kanton Glarus)

Se|ro (*regional kurz für* Sekundärrohstoff[e])

Se|ro|di|ag|nos|tik, die; -, -en ‹lat.; griech.› (*Med.* Erkennen einer Krankheit durch Untersuchung des Serums); **Se|ro|lo|gie,** die; - (Lehre vom Blutserum); **se|ro|lo|gisch; se|rös** ‹lat.› (aus Serum bestehend, Serum absondernd)

Ser|pel, die; -, -n ‹lat.› (Röhren bewohnender Borstenwurm); **Ser|pen|tin,** der; -s, -e (ein Mineral, Schmuckstein); **Ser|pen|ti|ne,** die; -, -n (in Schlangenlinie verlaufender Weg an Berghängen; Windung); **Ser|pen|ti|nen|stra|ße; Ser|pen|tin|ge|stein**

Ser|ra|del|la, Ser|ra|del|le, die; -, ...llen ‹port.› (eine Futterpflanze)

Se|rum, das; -s, *Plur.* ...ren *u.* ...ra ‹lat.› (*Med.* wässriger Bestandteil des Blutes; Impfstoff); **Se|rum-**

‿be|hand|lung, ...kon|ser|ve, ...krank|heit

Ser|val [...val], der; -s, *Plur.* -e *u.* -s ‹franz.› (ein Raubtier)

Ser|va|ti|us [...v...], **Ser|vaz** (m. Vorn.)

Ser|ve|la [...v...], die *od.* der; -, *Plur.* -s, *schweiz.* - ‹franz.› (*landsch. für* Zervelatwurst; *schweiz. neben* Cervelat); **Ser|ve|lat|wurst** *vgl.* Zervelatwurst

[1]**Ser|vice** [...'vi:s], das; *Gen.* - [...'vi:s] *u.* -s [...'vi:səs], *Plur.* - [...'vi:s, *auch* ...'vi:sə] ‹franz.› ([Tafel]geschirr); [2]**Ser|vice** ['sœ:(r)vis], der, *auch* das; -, -s [...vis(is)] ‹engl.› ([Kunden]dienst, Bedienung, Kundenbetreuung; *Tennis* Aufschlag[ball]); **Ser|vice|netz** ['sœ:(r)vis...] (Kundendienstnetz); **ser|vie|ren** [zɛr'vi:...] ‹franz.› (bei Tisch bedienen; auftragen; *Tennis* den Ball aufschlagen; einem Mitspieler den Ball [zum Torschuss] genau vorlegen [bes. beim Fußball]); **Ser|vie|re|rin; Ser|vier‿tisch, ...toch|ter** (*schweiz. für* Serviererin, Kellnerin), **...wa|gen; Ser|vi|et|te,** die; -, -n; **Ser|vi|et|ten‿kloß** *(Gastron.)*, **...ring**

ser|vil [...v...] ‹lat.› (unterwürfig, kriechend, knechtisch); **Ser|vi|lis|mus,** der; -, ...men (*selten für* Servilität); **Ser|vi|li|tät,** die; - (Unterwürfigkeit)

Ser|vis [...'vi:s], der; - ‹franz.› (*veraltet für* Quartier-, Verpflegungsgeld; Wohnungs-, Ortszulage)

Ser|vit [...'vi:t], der; -en, -en (↑R 126) ‹lat.› (Angehöriger eines Bettelordens; *Abk.* OSM); **Ser|vi|tin** ‹lat.› (Angehörige des weibl. Zweiges der Serviten); **Ser|vi|ti|um,** das; -s, ...ien [...iən] (*veraltet für* Dienstbarkeit; Sklaverei); **Ser|vi|tut,** das; -[e]s, -e, *schweiz. noch häufig* die; -, -en (*Rechtsw.* Dienstbarkeit, Grundlast); **Ser|vo‿brem|se** (Bremse mit einer die Bremswirkung verstärkenden Vorrichtung), **...len|kung, ...mo|tor** (Hilfsmotor); **ser|vus!** („[Ihr] Diener") (*bes. südd. u. österr.* freundschaftl. Gruß)

Se|sam, der; -s, -s ‹semit.› (eine Pflanze mit ölhaltigem Samen); Sesam, öffne dich! (Zauberformel [im Märchen]); **Se|sam‿bein** (*Med.* ein Knochen), **...brot, ...bröt|chen, ...öl** (das; -[e]s)

Se|schel|len *vgl.* Seychellen

Se|sel, der; -s, - ‹griech.› (eine Heil- u. Gewürzpflanze)

Ses|sel, der; -s, - ([gepolsterter] Stuhl mit Armlehnen; *österr. für* einfacher Stuhl); **Ses|sel‿bahn, ...leh|ne, ...lift**

sess|haft; ein sesshaftes Volk; **Sess|haf|tig|keit,** die; -

Ses|si|on, die; -, -en ‹lat.› (Sitzung[szeit], Sitzungsperiode)

Ses|ter, der; -s, - ‹lat.› (ein altes Hohlmaß)

Ses|terz, der; -es, -e ‹lat.› (altröm. Münze); **Ses|ter|zi|um,** das; -s, ...ien [...iən] (1000 Sesterze)

Ses|ti|ne, die; -, -n ‹ital.› (eine Lied- u. Strophenform)

[1]**Set** *vgl.* Seth

[2]**Set,** das, *auch* der; -[s], -s ‹engl.› (Satz [= Zusammengehöriges]; Platzdeckchen); [3]**Set,** das; -[s] (*Druckw.* Dickteneinheit bei den Monotypeschriften); 7 - (↑R 90)

Seth, *ökum.* Set (bibl. m. Eigenn.); **Se|thit,** der; -en, -en; ↑R 126 (Abkömmling von Seth)

Set|te|cen|to [sɛtə'tʃɛnto], das; -[s] ‹ital.› (das 18. Jh. in Italien [als Stilbegriff])

Set|ter, der; -s, - ‹engl.› (Hund einer bestimmten Rasse)

Setz‿ar|beit (*Bergmannsspr.* nasse Aufbereitung), **...ei; set|zen** (*Jägerspr. auch* gebären [von Hasen u. einigem Hochwild]); du setzt; sich -; **Set|zer** (Schriftsetzer); **Set|ze|rei; Set|ze|rin; Set|zer‿lehr|ling, ...saal; Setz‿feh|ler** *(Druckw.)*, **...gut** (das; -[e]s; *Landw.*), **...ham|mer** (ein Schmiedehammer), **...ha|se** *(Jägerspr.)*, **...holz** (ein Gartengerät), **...kas|ten, ...kopf** (Nietkopf), **...lat|te** (*Bauw.* Richtscheit); **Setz|ling** (junge Pflanze; Zuchtfisch); **Setz‿li|nie** *(Druckw.)*, **...ma|schi|ne** *(Druckw.)*, **...mei|ßel** (ein Schmiedewerkzeug); **Set|zung; Setz|waa|ge** (*svw.* Wasserwaage)

Seu|che, die; -, -n; **Seu|chen‿be|kämp|fung, ...ge|fahr; seu|chen|haft; Seu|chen|herd**

seuf|zen; du seufzt; **Seuf|zer; Seuf|zer|brü|cke,** die; - (in Venedig)

Seu|rat [sœ'ra] (franz. Maler)

Se|ve|rin [...v...], **Se|ve|ri|nus** (m. Vorn.)

Se|ve|rus [...v...] (röm. Kaiser)

Se|ve|so|gift [...v...], das; -[e]s ‹nach der ital. Stadt› (*für* Dioxin)

Se|vil|la [se'vilja] (span. Stadt)

Sèvres ['sɛ:vr] (Vorort von Paris); **Sèvres|por|zel|lan** (↑R 105)

Se|was|to|pol [*russ.* ...'tɔ...] (Stadt auf der Krim)

Sex, der; -[es] ‹engl.› (*ugs. für* Geschlecht[lichkeit]; Geschlechtsverkehr; *kurz für* Sexappeal)

Se|xa|ge|si|ma, die; *Gen.* -, *bei Gebrauch ohne Artikel auch* ...mä (achter Sonntag vor Ostern); Sonntag - *od.* Sexagesimä; **se|xa|ge|si|mal** (sechzigteilig, auf sechzig als Grundzahl zurückgehend); **Se|xa|ge|si|mal|sys|tem,** das; -s (*Math.* Zahlensystem, das auf der Basis 60 aufgebaut ist)

Sex|ap|peal [...ə'pi:l], der; -s ‹engl.-amerik.› (sexuelle Anziehungskraft); **Sex‿bom|be** (*ugs. für* Frau mit starkem sexuellem Reiz [meist von Filmschauspielerinnen]), **...bou|tique, ...film; Se|xis|mus,** der; - ([Diskriminierung auf Grund der] Vorstellung, nach der eines der beiden Geschlechter dem anderen von Natur aus überlegen sei); **Se|xist,** der; -en, -en; ↑R 126 (Vertreter des Sexismus); **Se|xis|tin; se|xis|tisch; Sex|ma|ga|zin; Se|xo|lo|ge,** der; -n, -n; ↑R 126 (Sexualforscher); **Se|xo|lo|gie,** die; -; **se|xo|lo|gisch; Sex|shop** (*svw.* Sexboutique)

Sext, die; -, -en ‹lat.› (drittes Tagesgebet des Breviers; *österr. svw.* Sexte); **Sex|ta,** die; -, ...ten (*veraltende Bez. für* erste [*in Österr.* sechste] Klasse eines Gymnasiums); **Sext|ak|kord** (*Musik* erste Umkehrung des Dreiklangs mit der Terz im Bass); **Sex|ta|ner** (Schüler der Sexta); **Sex|ta|ner|bla|se** (*ugs. scherzh. für* schwache Blase); **Sex|ta|ne|rin; Sex|tant,** der; -en, -en; ↑R 126 (Winkelmessinstrument); **Sex|te,** die; -, -n (*Musik* sechster Ton der diaton. Tonleiter; Intervall im Abstand von 6 Stufen); **Sex|tett,** das; -[e]s, -e ‹ital.› (Musikstück für sechs Stimmen od. sechs Instrumente; *auch für* die sechs Ausführenden); **Sex|til|li|on,** die; -, -en ‹lat.› (sechste Potenz einer Million); **Sex|to|le,** die; -, -n (*Musik* Figur von 6 Noten gleicher Form mit dem Zeitwert von 4 od. 8 Noten)

Sex|tou|ris|mus; se|xu|al ‹lat.› (*meist in Zusammensetzungen, sonst seltener für* sexuell); **Se|xu|al‿auf|klä|rung, ...de|likt, ...er|zie|hung, ...ethik** (↑R 132, die; -), **...for|scher, ...for|sche|rin, ...for|schung, ...hor|mon, ...hy|gi|e|ne; se|xu|a|li|sie|ren** (die Sexualität [in einem bestimmten Bereich] überbetonen); **Se|xu|a|li|sie|rung; Se|xu|a|li|tät,** die; -; (Geschlechtlichkeit); **Se|xu|al|kun|de,** die; -; **Se|xu|al|kun|de|un|ter|richt; Se|xu|al‿le|ben** (das; -s), **...pä|da|go|gik, ...pa|tho|lo|gie** (die; -), **...psy|cho|lo|gie** (die; -), **...tä|ter, ...trieb** (der; -[e]s), **...ver|bre|chen** (Sittlichkeitsverbrechen), **...ver|kehr**

(der; -s); **se|xu|ell** ‹franz.› (die Sexualität betreffend, geschlechtlich); **Se|xus,** der; -, - ['zɛksu:s] ‹lat.› (Geschlecht); **se|xy** ‹engl.› (*ugs. für* erotisch-attraktiv)
Sey|chel|len [se'ʃɛ...] *Plur.* (Inselgruppe u. Staat im Indischen Ozean); **Sey|chel|len|nuss** (↑R 105; Frucht der Seychellennusspalme)
Seyd|litz (preuß. Reitergeneral)
se|zer|nie|ren ‹lat.› (*Med.* [ein Sekret] absondern); **Se|zer|nie|rung** (*Med.* Absonderung)
Se|zes|si|on, die; -, -en ‹lat.› (Absonderung, Trennung von einer polit. od. Künstlergemeinschaft; Abfall der nordamerik. Südstaaten); **Se|zes|si|o|nist,** der; -en, -en; ↑R 126 (Angehöriger einer Sezession; *früher für* Anhänger der nordamerikan. Südstaaten im Sezessionskrieg); **se|zes|si|o|nis|tisch** (der Sezession angehörend); **Se|zes|si|ons‿krieg** (1861–65), **...stil** (der; -[e]s; *Kunst*)
se|zie|ren ‹lat.› (anatomisch zerlegen); **Se|zier|mes|ser,** das
sf = sforzando, sforzato
SFB = Sender Freies Berlin
s-för|mig, S-för|mig; ↑R 25 (in der Form eines S)
sfor|zan|do, sfor|za|to ‹ital.› (*Musik* verstärkt, stark [hervorgehoben]; *Abk.* sf); **Sfor|zan|do,** das; -s, *Plur.* -s *u.* ...di *u.* **Sfor|za|to,** das; -s, *Plur.* -s *u.* ...ti
sfr, *schweiz. nur* **sFr.;** *vgl.* [2]Franken
sfu|ma|to ‹ital.› (*Kunst* duftig; mit verschwimmenden Umrissen [gemalt])
SG = Sportgemeinschaft
s-Ge|ni|tiv (*Sprachw.*)
Sgraf|fi|to, das; -s, *Plur.* -s *u.* ...ti ‹ital.› (*Kunst* Kratzputz [Wandmalerei])
's-Gra|ven|ha|ge [sxra:vən'ha:xə] (*offz. niederl. Form von* Den Haag)
sh, s = Shilling
Shag [ʃɛk, *engl.* ʃɛg], der; -s, -s ‹engl.› (fein geschnittener Pfeifentabak); **Shag‿pfei|fe, ...ta|bak**
[1]**Shake** [ʃe:k], der; -s, -s ‹engl.› (ein Mischgetränk; Modetanz); [2]**Shake,** das; -s, -s (starkes Vibrato im Jazz); **Shake|hands** ['ʃe:khɛndz], das; -, - *meist Plur.* (Händeschütteln); **Sha|ker** ['ʃe:kə(r)], der; -s, - (Mixbecher)
Shakes|peare ['ʃe:kspi:(r)] (↑R 132; engl. Dichter); **shakes|pearesch** [...pi:rʃ], **shakes|pea|risch;** shakespearesche *od.* shakespearische Dramen, Sonette; shakespearesche *od.* shakespearische Lebensnähe
Sham|poo ['ʃampu, *österr.* ʃam'po:] *u.* **Sham|poon** [ʃɛm'pu:n, *auch, österr. nur* ʃam'po:n], das; -s, -s ‹Hindi-engl.› (flüssiges Haarwaschmittel); **sham|poo|nie|ren** *vgl.* schamponieren
Shang|hai *vgl.* Schanghai
Shan|non ['ʃɛnən], der; -[s] (irländ. Fluss)
Shan|ty ['ʃɛnti, *auch* 'ʃanti], das; -s, *Plur.* -s [...ti:s] ‹engl.› (Seemannslied)
Sha|ping|ma|schi|ne ['ʃe:piŋ...] ‹engl.; griech.› (Metallhobelmaschine, Schnellhobler)
Share ['ʃɛ:(r)], der; -, -s ‹engl.› (*engl. Bez. für* Aktie); **Share|ware** ['ʃɛ:(r)wɛ:(r)], die; -, -s (*EDV* zu Testzwecken kostengünstig angebotene Software)
Shaw [ʃɔ:] (ir.-engl. Dichter)
Shed|bau usw. *vgl.* Schedbau usw.
Shef|field ['ʃɛfi:ld] (engl. Stadt)
Shel|ley ['ʃɛli] (engl. Dichterehepaar)
She|riff ['ʃɛ...], der; -s, -s ‹engl.› (Verwaltungsbeamter in England; höchster Vollzugsbeamter [einer Stadt] in den USA)
Sher|lock Holmes [ˌʃœ:(r)lɔk 'ho:mz, *auch* ˌʃɛr... 'hɔlms] (engl. Romanfigur [Detektiv])
Sher|pa [ʃ...], der; -s, -s ‹tibet.-engl.› (Angehöriger eines tibet. Volksstammes, der als Lastträger bei Expeditionen im Himalajagebiet arbeitet)
Sher|ry ['ʃɛri], der; -s, -s ‹engl.› (span. Wein, Jerez)
's-Her|to|gen|bosch [shɛrto:xə(n)'bɔs] (*offz. niederl. Form von* Herzogenbusch)
Shet|land ['ʃɛtlant, *engl.* 'ʃɛtlənd], der; -[s], -s ‹nach den schott. Inseln› (ein grau melierter Wollstoff); **Shet|land‿in|seln** (*Plur.;* Inselgruppe nordöstl. von Schottland), **...po|ny, ...wol|le** (die; -; ↑R 105)
Shil|ling [ʃ...], der; -s, -s ‹engl.› (frühere Münzeinheit in Großbritannien; 20 Shilling = 1 Pfund Sterling; *Abk.* s *od.* sh); 10 - (↑R 90); *vgl. aber* Schilling
Shim|my, der; -s, -s ‹amerik.› (Gesellschaftstanz der 20er Jahre)
Shirt [ʃœ:(r)t], das; -s, -s ‹engl.› ([kurzärmeliges] Baumwollhemd)
Shit [ʃit], der *u.* das; -s ‹engl.› (*ugs. für* Haschisch)
sho|cking ['ʃɔkiŋ] ‹engl.› (anstößig)
Shod|dy ['ʃɔdi], das, *auch* der; -s, -s ‹engl.› (Reißwolle [aus Trikotagen])
Sho|gun ['ʃo:gun] *vgl.* Schogun
Shoo|ting|star ['ʃu:tiŋsta:(r)], der; -s, -s ‹engl.› (jmd., der schnell an die Spitze [z. B. im Schlagergeschäft] gelangt, Senkrechtstarter; neuer, sehr schnell erfolgreich gewordener Schlager)
Shop [ʃɔp], der; -s, -s ‹engl.› (Laden, Geschäft); **Shop|ping,** das; -s, -s (Einkaufsbummel); **Shop|ping|cen|ter** [...sɛntə(r)], das; -s, - (Einkaufszentrum)
Shorts [ʃo:(r)ts, *engl.* 'ʃɔ:(r)ts] *Plur.* ‹engl.› (kurze sportl. Hose);
Short|sto|ry, die; -, -s, *auch* **Short Sto|ry** ['ʃɔ:(r)t 'stɔ:ri], die; - -, - -s (*angelsächs. Bez. für* Kurzgeschichte, Novelle); **Shor|ty** ['ʃɔ:(r)ti], das, *auch* der; -s, -s (Damenschlafanzug mit kurzer Hose)
Show [ʃo:], die; -, -s ‹engl.› (Schau, Darbietung, Vorführung; buntes, aufwändiges Unterhaltungsprogramm); **Show|block** ['ʃo:...] *Plur.* ...blöcke (Show als Einlage in einer Fernsehsendung); **Show|busi|ness,** das; - ‹„Schaugeschäft“› (Vergnügungsindustrie); **Show-down,** *auch* **Show|down** [...'daun], der; -s, -s (Entscheidungskampf [im Wildwestfilm]); **Show|ge|schäft,** das; -[e]s; **Show|man** [...mən], der; -s, ...men (im Showgeschäft Tätiger; geschickter Propagandist); **Show|mas|ter,** der; -s, - ‹anglisierend› (Unterhaltungskünstler, der eine Show präsentiert); **Show|view** ® [...vju:], das; -s (Videoprogrammierung über in Programmzeitschriften ausgedruckte Ziffernreihen)
Shred|der *engl. Schreibung von* Schredder
Shrimp, *eindeutschend* Schrimp [ʃr...], der; -s, -s *meist Plur.* ‹engl.› (kleine Krabbe)
Shuf|fle|board ['ʃaf(ə)lbɔ:(r)d], das; -s ‹engl.› (ein Spiel)
Shunt [ʃant], der; -s, -s ‹engl.› (*Elektrotechnik* parallel geschalteter Widerstand)
Shut|tle ['ʃat(ə)l], der; -s, -s ‹engl.› ([Fahrzeug im] Pendelverkehr; *kurz für* Spaceshuttle)
Shy|lock ['ʃai...], der; -[s], -s ‹nach der Figur in Shakespeares „Kaufmann von Venedig“› (hartherziger Geldverleiher)
Si = *chem. Zeichen für* Silicium
SI = Système International d'Unités [sis.tɛ:m ɛ̃tɛrnasiɔ.nal dyni'te:] (internationales Einheitensystem)
SIA = Schweizerischer Ingenieur- und Architektenverein
Si|al, das; -[s] (*Geol.* oberer Teil der Erdkruste)
Si|am (alter Name von Thailand);
Si|a|me|se, der; -n, -n (↑R 126); **Si|a|me|sin; si|a|me|sisch;** -e

Zwillinge; **Si|am|kat|ze; Si|a|mo|sen** *Plur.* (Schürzenstoffe)
Si|be|li|us (finn. Komponist)
Si|bi|lant, der; -en, -en (↑R 126) ‹lat.› (*Sprachw.* Zischlaut, Reibelaut, z. B. s)
Si|bi|rer (*svw.* Sibirier); **Si|bi|ri|en; Si|bi|ri|er; si|bi|risch**
Si|biu (rumän. Stadt; *vgl.* Hermannstadt)
Si|byl|la, [1]Si|byl|le [*beide* ...'bi...] (w. Vorn.); **[2]Si|byl|le,** die; -, -n ‹griech.› (weissagende Frau, Wahrsagerin); **si|byl|li|nisch** (wahrsagerisch; geheimnisvoll); die sibyllinischen Bücher (der Sibylle von Cumae ['ku:mɛ])
sic! [zi(:)k] ‹lat.› (so!, wirklich so!)
sich; Sich|aus|wei|nen, das; -s (↑R 50)
Si|chel, die; -, -n; **si|chel|för|mig; si|cheln** (mit der Sichel abschneiden); ich ...[e]le (↑R 16); **Si|chel|wa|gen** (Streitwagen im Altertum)
si|cher; ein sicheres Geleit; sichere Quelle; sicher sein; im Sichern sein (*auch für* geborgen sein); das Sicherste sein; auf Nummer Sicher, *auch* sicher sein; auf Nummer Sicher, *auch* sicher gehen; man kann in diesen Schuhen sicher gehen; er ist in ihnen sicher gegangen; *aber* sie will in dieser Sache sichergehen (*für* Gewissheit haben); sicher wirken; ein [ganz] sicher wirkendes Mittel; *vgl.* sicherstellen; **si|cher|ge|hen** *vgl.* sicher; **Si|cher|heit; Si|cher|heits‿ab|stand, ...au|to, ...be|auf|trag|te, ...be|hör|de, ...bin|dung** *(Sport),* **...fach** (*für* Safe), **...glas** (*Plur.* ...gläser), **...grün|de** (*Plur.;* aus -n), **...gurt; si|cher|heits|hal|ber; Si|cher|heits‿ket|te, ...ko|pie, ...la|ge, ...leis|tung** *(Wirtsch.),* **...maß|nah|me, ...na|del, ...or|ga|ne** (*Plur.;* mit Staatsschutz u. Ä. befasste Dienststellen), **...po|li|tik, ...rat** (der; -[e]s; UNO-Behörde), **...ri|si|ko** (jmd. od. etwas die Sicherheit Gefährdendes), **...schloss, ...schwel|le, ...ven|til** *(Technik),* **...ver|schluss, ...vor|keh|rung, ...vor|schrift; si|cher|lich; si|chern;** ich ...ere (↑R 16); **si|cher|stel|len** (sichern; in [polizeilichen] Gewahrsam geben od. nehmen); ein Beweisstück sicherstellen; **Si|cher|stel|lung; Si|che|rung; Si|che|rungs‿ab|tre|tung** *(Wirtsch.),* **...ge|ber** *(Wirtsch.),* **...grund|schuld** *(Rechtsw.),* **...hy|po|thek** *(Rechtsw.),* **...kas|ten, ...neh|mer** *(Wirtsch.),* **...über|eig|nung** (↑R 132; *Rechtsw.*), **...ver|wah|rung** *(Rechtsw.);* **si|cher wir|kend** *vgl.* sicher
Sich|ge|hen|las|sen, das; -s (↑R 50)
Sich|ler (ein Schreitvogel)
Sicht, die; -; auf, bei - (*Kaufmannsspr. auch für* a vista); nach - *(Kaufmannsspr.);* auf lange -; außer, in - kommen, sein; **sicht|bar;** etwas - machen; **Sicht|bar|keit,** die; -; **sicht|bar|lich** *(veraltet);* **Sicht‿be|ton, ...blen|de, ...ein|la|ge** *(Bankw.)*
[1]sich|ten (auswählen, durchsehen)
[2]sich|ten (erblicken); **Sicht‿flug, ...gren|ze** (*auch für* Horizont); **sich|tig** (*Seemannsspr.* klar); -es Wetter; **Sicht|kar|te** (Zeitkarte im Personenverkehr); **Sicht|kar|ten|in|ha|ber** *(Amtsspr.);* **sicht|lich** (offenkundig); **Sicht|li|nie**
Sicht|ma|schi|ne (Sortiermaschine); **[1]Sich|tung** (Ausscheidung)
[2]Sich|tung, die; - (das Erblicken); **Sicht‿ver|hält|nis|se** *(Plur.),* **...ver|merk; sicht|ver|merk|frei** *(Amtsspr.);* **Sicht‿wech|sel** *(Bankw.),* **...wei|se, ...wei|te, ...wer|bung**
[1]Si|cke, die; -, -n (*Technik* rinnenförmige Biegung, Kehlung; Randverzierung, -versteifung)
[2]Si|cke, Sie|ke, die; -, -n (*Jägerspr.* Vogelweibchen)
si|cken (mit [1]Sicken versehen); gesickt; **Si|cken|ma|schi|ne**
Si|cker|gru|be; si|ckern; das Wasser sickert; **Si|cker|was|ser,** das; -s
sic tran|sit glo|ria mun|di! ‹lat.› (so vergeht die Herrlichkeit der Welt!)
Sid|dhar|tha [zi'darta] ‹sanskr.› (weltl. Name Buddhas)
Side|board ['saidbɔ:(r)d], das; -s, -s ‹engl.› (Anrichte, Büfett)
[1]si|de|risch ‹lat.› (auf die Sterne bezüglich; Stern...); siderisches Jahr (Sternjahr)
[2]si|de|risch ‹griech.› (aus Eisen bestehend, auf Eisen reagierend); -es Pendel (in der Parapsychologie verwendetes Gerät); **Si|de|rit** [*auch* ...'rit], der; -s, -e (gelbbraunes Eisenerz); **Si|de|ro|lith** [*auch* ...'lit], der; *Gen.* -s *u.* -en, *Plur.* -e[n]; ↑R 126 (Eisensteinmeteorit)
Si|don (phöniz. Stadt); **Si|do|nia, Si|do|nie** [...iə] (w. Vorn.); **Si|do|ni|er** (Bewohner von Sidon); **si|do|nisch**
sie; sie kommt, sie kommen; **[1]Sie;** ↑R 53 (*veraltete Anrede an eine Person weibl. Geschlechts:* höre Sie!; *Höflichkeitsanrede an eine Person od. mehrere Personen gleich welchen Geschlechts:*) kommen Sie bitte!; jmdn. mit Sie anreden; (↑R 48:) das steife Sie; **[2]Sie,** die; -, -s (*ugs. für* Mensch od. Tier weibl. Geschlechts); es ist eine Sie; ein Er u. eine Sie
Sieb, das; -[e]s, -e; **sieb|ar|tig; Sieb|bein** (ein Knochen); **Sieb|druck,** der; -[e]s (*Druckw.* Schablonierverfahren); *vgl.* Serigraphie; **[1]sie|ben** (durchsieben)
[2]sie|ben (Zahlwort); **I.** *Kleinschreibung* (↑R 48): wir sind zu sieben *od.* zu siebt (*älter* siebent), wir sind sieben; er kommt mit sieben[en]; die sieben Sakramente; die sieben Todsünden; für jmdn. ein Buch mit sieben Siegeln sein (jmdm. völlig unverständlich sein); die sieben fetten u. die sieben mageren Jahre; die sieben freien Künste (im MA.); die sieben Weltwunder; sieben auf einen Streich; die sieben Raben (im Märchen); um sieben Ecken (*ugs. für* weitläufig) mit jmdm. verwandt sein. **II.** *Großschreibung* (↑R 56): Sieben Berge (Landschaft in Niedersachsen); *vgl.* acht; **Sie|ben,** die; -, *Plur.* -, *auch* -en (Zahl); eine böse -; *vgl.* [1]Acht; **sie|ben|ar|mig;** -er Leuchter; **Sie|ben|bür|gen** (*dt. Name von* Transsilvanien); **Sie|ben|bür|ger** (↑R 103); **sie|ben|bür|gisch; Sie|ben|eck; sie|ben|eckig** (↑R 132); **sie|ben|ein|halb, sie|ben|und|ein|halb; Sie|be|ner;** *vgl.* Achter; **sie|be|ner|lei;** auf - Art; **sie|ben|fach; Sie|ben|fa|che,** das; -n; *vgl.* Achtfache; **Sie|ben|ge|bir|ge,** das; -s; **Sie|ben|ge|stirn,** das; -[e]s (Sterngruppe); **sie|ben|hun|dert; sie|ben|jäh|rig,** *aber* (↑R 108): der Siebenjährige Krieg; **Sie|ben|kampf** (Mehrkampf der Frauen in der Leichtathletik); **sie|ben|köp|fig;** ein -es Gremium; **sie|ben|mal;** *vgl.* achtmal; **sie|ben|ma|lig; Sie|ben|mei|len‿schritt** (*meist Plur.; ugs. scherzh. für* riesiger Schritt), **...stie|fel** *(Plur.);* **Sie|ben|me|ter,** der; -s, - *(Hallenhandball);* **Sie|ben|mo|nats|kind; Sie|ben|punkt** (ein Marienkäfer); **Sie|ben|sa|chen** *Plur.* (*ugs. für* Habseligkeiten); seine - packen; **Sie|ben|schlä|fer** (Nagetier; *volkstüml. für* 27. Juni als Lostag für eine Wetterregel); **Sie|ben|schritt,** der; -[e]s (ein Volkstanz); **sie|ben|stel|lig; Sie|ben|stern** (ein Primelgewächs; *vgl.* [2]Stern); **sie|bent** (*älter für* siebt); **sie|ben|tau|send; sie|ben|te** *vgl.* siebte; **sie|ben|tel** *vgl.* siebtel;

Sie|ben|tel *vgl.* Siebtel; **sie|ben|tens** *vgl.* siebtens; **sie|ben|und|ein|halb,** sie|ben|ein|halb; **sie|ben|und|sieb|zig; sie|ben|und|sieb|zig|mal;** *vgl.* acht
sieb|för|mig; Sieb‿kreis *(Elektrotechnik),* **...ma|cher, ...ma|schi|ne, ...mehl** (gesiebtes Mehl), **...röh|re** *(Bot.),* **...schal|tung** *(Elektrotechnik)*
siebt *vgl.* ²sieben; **sieb|te** *od.* sie|ben|te; *vgl.* achte; **sieb|tel;** *vgl.* achtel; **Sieb|tel,** das, *schweiz. meist* der; -s, -; **sieb|tens** *od.* sie|ben|tens; **sieb|zehn;** *vgl.* acht; **sieb|zehn|hun|dert; sieb|zehn|te;** (↑R 108:) Siebzehnter (17.) Juni (Tag des Gedenkens an den 17. Juni 1953, den Tag des Aufstandes in der DDR); *vgl.* achte; **Sieb|zehn|und|vier,** das; - (ein Kartenglücksspiel); **sieb|zig;** *vgl.* achtzig; **sieb|zig|jäh|rig;** *vgl.* achtjährig
siech *(veraltend für* krank, hinfällig); **sie|chen; Sie|chen|haus** *(veraltet);* **Siech|tum,** das; -s
Sie|de, die; - *(landsch. für* gesottenes Viehfutter); **sie|de|heiß** *(selten für* siedend heiß; *vgl.* sieden); **Sie|de|hit|ze**
sie|deln; ich ...[e]le (↑R 16)
sie|den; du sottest *u.* siedetest; du söttest *u.* siedetest; gesotten *u.* gesiedet; sied[e]!; siedend heiß; **Sie|de|punkt; Sie|der; Sie|de|rei; Sied|fleisch** *(südd., schweiz. für* Suppenfleisch)
Sied|ler; Sied|lung; Sied|lungs‿dich|te, ...form, ...ge|biet, ...ge|o|gra|phie, ...haus, ...kun|de (die; -), **...land** (das; -[e]s), **...po|li|tik** (die; -), **...pro|gramm**
¹Sieg, der; -[e]s, -e
²Sieg, die; - (r. Nebenfluss des Rheins)
Sie|gel, das; -s, - ‹lat.› (Stempelabdruck; [Brief]verschluss); **Sie|gel|be|wah|rer** *(früher);* **Sie|gel|lack; sie|geln;** ich ...[e]le (↑R 16); **Sie|gel|ring; Sie|ge|lung,** Sieg|lung
sie|gen; Sie|ger; Sie|ger|eh|rung; Sie|ge|rin; Sie|ger|kranz, Sie|ges|kranz
Sie|ger|land, das; -[e]s (Landschaft); **Sie|ger|län|der; sie|ger|län|disch**
Sie|ger‿macht, ...mann|schaft, ...mie|ne, ...po|dest, ...po|kal, ...stra|ße *(nur in Wendungen wie* auf der - sein [im Begriff sein zu siegen]); **sie|ges|be|wusst; Sie|ges‿bot|schaft, ...fei|er, ...freu|de; sie|ges|froh; Sie|ges|ge|schrei; sie|ges|ge|wiss; Sie|ges‿ge|wiss|heit** (die; -), **...göt|tin; Sie|ges|kranz** *vgl.* Siegerkranz; **Sie|ges‿lauf** (der; -[e]s; *selten für* Siegeszug), **...preis, ...säu|le, ...se|rie** *(Sport);* **sie|ges|si|cher; Sie|ges‿tor, ...tref|fer** *(Sport);* **sie|ges|trun|ken** *(geh.);* **Sie|ges‿wil|le, ...zug**
Sieg|fried (germ. Sagengestalt; m. Vorn.); ↑R 93: Jung - **sieg|ge|wohnt; sieg|haft** *(geh. für* siegessicher; *veraltet für* siegreich)
Sieg|hard (m. Vorn.); **Sieg|lind, Sieg|lin|de** (w. Vorn.)
sieg|los
Sieg|lung *vgl.* Siegelung
Sieg|mund, Si|gis|mund (m. Vorn.)
Sieg|prä|mie; sieg|reich; Sieg|tref|fer *(svw.* Siegestreffer)
Sieg|wurz (Gladiole)
sie|he! *(Abk.* s.); - da!; **sie|he dort!** *(Abk.* s. d.); **sie|he oben!** *(Abk.* s. o.); **sie|he un|ten!** *(Abk.* s. u.)
SI-Ein|heit (internationale Basiseinheit; *vgl.* SI)
Sie|ke *vgl.* ²Sicke
Siel, der *od.* das; -[e]s, -e *(nordd. u. fachspr. für* Abwasserleitung; kleine Deichschleuse)
Sie|le, die; -, -n (Riemen[werk der Zugtiere]); in den -n sterben
sie|len, sich *(landsch. für* sich mit Behagen hin und her wälzen)
Sie|len|ge|schirr; Sie|len|zeug, Siel|zeug
¹Sie|mens (Familienn.; ®); **²Sie|mens,** das; -, - (elektr. Leitwert; *Zeichen* S); **Sie|mens-Mar|tin-Ofen;** ↑R 95 (zur Stahlerzeugung; *Abk.* SM-Ofen); **Sie|mens|stadt** (Stadtteil von Berlin)
si|e|na ‹ital.› (rotbraun); ein - Muster; *vgl.* blau; *vgl. auch* beige; **Si|e|na** (ital. Stadt); **Si|e|na|er|de,** die; -; ↑R 105 (eine Malerfarbe); **Si|e|ne|se,** der; -n, -n (↑R 126); **Si|e|ne|ser** (↑R 103)
Sien|kie|wicz [ʃçɛŋˈkjɛvjitʃ] (poln. Schriftsteller)
Si|er|ra, die; -, *Plur.* ...rren *u.* -s ‹span.› (Gebirgskette); **Si|er|ra Le|o|ne** (Staat in Afrika); **Si|er|ra-Le|o|ner; Si|er|ra-Le|o|ne|rin; si|er|ra-le|o|nisch; Si|er|ra Ne|va|da** [- ...v...], die; - - („Schneegebirge") (span. u. amerik. Gebirge)
Si|es|ta, die; -, *Plur.* ...sten *u.* -s ‹ital.› ([Mittags]ruhe)
Siet|land, das; -[e]s, ...länder *(nordd. für* tief liegendes Marschland); **Siet|wen|dung** *(nordd. für* Binnendeich)
sie|zen *(ugs. für* mit „Sie" anreden); du siezt
Sif *(nord. Mythol.* Gemahlin Thors)
Sif|flö|te ‹franz.› (eine hohe Orgelstimme)
Si|gel, das; -s, - ‹lat.› *u.* **Sig|le** [ˈsiːg(ə)l] (↑R 130), die; -, -n ‹franz.› (festgelegtes Abkürzungszeichen, Kürzel)
Sight|see|ing [ˈsaitsiːiŋ], das; -[s], -s ‹engl.› (Besichtigung von Sehenswürdigkeiten); **Sight|see|ing|tour** (Besichtigungsfahrt)
Si|gil|la|rie [...iə], die; -, -n (fossile Pflanzengattung)
Si|gis|mund *vgl.* Siegmund
Sig|le (↑R 130) *vgl.* Sigel
Sig|ma, das; -[s], -s (griech. Buchstabe: Σ, σ, ς)
Sig|ma|rin|gen (Stadt a. d. Donau); **Sig|ma|rin|ger** (↑R 103); **sig|ma|rin|ge|risch**
sign. = signatum
Sig|na (↑R 130; *Plur. von* Signum)
Sig|nal [*auch* ziŋˈnal] (↑R 130), das; -s, -e ‹lat.› (Zeichen mit festgelegter Bedeutung; [Warn]zeichen); - geben; **Sig|nal‿an|la|ge, ...buch; Sig|na|le|ment** [...ˈmãː, *schweiz.* ...ˈmɛnt], das; -s, -s, *schweiz.* das; -[e]s, -e ‹franz.› ([Personen]beschreibung; *Landw.* Zusammenstellung der ein bestimmtes Tier kennzeichnenden Angaben); **Sig|nal‿far|be, ...feu|er, ...flag|ge, ...gast** *(Plur.* ...gasten; Matrose), **...glo|cke, ...horn** *(Plur.* ...hörner); **sig|na|li|sie|ren** (Signal[e] übermitteln); **Sig|nal‿knopf, ...lam|pe, ...licht** *(Plur.* ...lichter), **...mast** (der), **...pat|ro|ne, ...pfiff, ...reiz** *(svw.* Schlüsselreiz), **...ring** *(Kfz-Technik),* **...sys|tem** *(Psych.),* **...ver|bin|dung**
Sig|na|tar (↑R 130), der; -s, -e ‹lat.› *(veraltet für* Unterzeichner); **Sig|na|tar|macht** ([einen Vertrag] unterzeichnende Macht); **sig|na|tum** (unterzeichnet; *Abk.* sign.); **Sig|na|tur,** die; -, -en (Namenszeichen, Unterschrift; symbol. Landkartenzeichen; *Druckw.* runde od. eckige Einkerbung an Drucktypen; Nummer eines Druckbogens; [Buch]nummer in einer Bibliothek)
Sig|net [siˈnjeː, *eindeutschend* ziˈgneːt] (↑R 130), das; -s, *Plur.* -s, *bei dt.Ausspr.* -e ‹franz.› (Buchdrucker-, Verleger-, Firmenzeichen; *veraltet für* Petschaft); **sig|nie|ren** [ziˈgniː..., *auch* ziŋˈni...] ‹lat.› (mit einer Signatur versehen); **sig|ni|fi|kant** (bedeutsam, kennzeichnend); **Sig|ni|fi|kanz,** die; - (Bedeutsamkeit); **sig|ni|fi|zie|ren** *(selten für* bezeichnen; anzeigen)

Si̲g|nor [sinˈjoːr] (↑R 130), der; -, ...i ⟨ital.⟩ (Herr *[mit folgendem Namen]*); **Sig|no̲|ra**, die; -, *Plur.* -s *u.* ...re (Frau); **Sig|no̲|re**, der; -, ...ri (Herr *[ohne folgenden Namen]*); **Sig|no|ria** [...ˈriːa], **Sig|no|ri̲e**, die; -, ...i̯en (*früher* die höchste Behörde der ital. Stadtstaaten); **Sig|no|ri̲|na**, die; -, *Plur.* -s, *auch* ...ne (unverheiratete Frau); **Sig|no|ri̲|no**, der; -, *Plur.* -s, *auch* ...ni (junger Herr)

Si̲g|num (↑R 130), das; -s, ...na ⟨lat.⟩ (Zeichen; verkürzte Unterschrift)

Si̲g|rid (w. Vorn.)

Si̲g|rist (↑R 130), der; -en, -en (↑R 126) ⟨lat.⟩ (*schweiz. für* Küster, Mesner)

Si̲g|run (w. Vorn.)

Si̲|gurd (m. Vorn.)

Si̲|ka|hirsch ⟨jap.; dt.⟩ (ein ostasiat. Hirsch)

Si̲kh, der; -[s], -s (Anhänger der Sikhreligion); **Si̲kh|re|li|gi|on**, die; -

Sik|ka|ti̲v, das; -s, -e [...və] ⟨lat.⟩ (Trockenmittel für Ölfarben)

Si̲k|kim (ind. Bundesstaat im Himalaja); **Si̲k|ki|mer; si̲k|ki|misch**

Si|la|ge *vgl.* Ensilage

Si̲l|be, die; -, -n; **Si̲l|ben‿maß** (das), **...rät|sel**, **...ste|cher** (*veraltet für* Wortklauber), **...tren|nung; ...sil|ber** *vgl.* ...silbler

Si̲l|ber, das; -s (chem. Element, Edelmetall; *Zeichen* Ag); *vgl.* Argentum; **Si̲l|ber‿ar|beit**, **...bar|ren**, **...berg|werk**, **...be|steck**, **...blick** (*ugs. scherzh. für* leicht schielender Blick), **...bro|kat**, **...dis|tel**, **...draht**, **...fa|den; si̲l|ber|far|ben**, **si̲l|ber|far|big; Si̲l|ber‿fisch|chen** (ein Insekt), **...fuchs**, **...geld** (das; -[e]s), **...glanz; si̲l|ber‿glän|zend**, **...grau**, **...haa|rig**, **...hal|tig**, **...hell; Si̲l|ber|hoch|zeit; si̲l|be|rig**, si̲lb|rig; **Si̲l|ber|ling** (eine alte Silbermünze); **Si̲l|ber‿lö|we** (Puma), **...me|dail|le**, **...mö|we**, **...mün|ze; si̲l|bern** (aus Silber); silberne Hochzeit, *aber* (↑R 108): Silberner Sonntag (*früher* vorletzter Sonntag vor Weihnachten); Silbernes Lorbeerblatt (eine Auszeichnung für besondere Sportleistungen); **Si̲l|ber‿pa|pier**, **...pap|pel**, **...schmied**, **...schmie|din**, **...stift** (ein Zeichenstift), **...strei|fen** (*meist in* Silberstreifen am Horizont [Zeichen beginnender Besserung]); **Si̲l|ber‿tab|lett**, **...tan|ne; si̲l|ber|ver|gol|det;** ein -er Pokal (ein silberner Pokal, der vergoldet ist); **si̲l|ber|weiß; Si̲l|ber|zeug** (*ugs. für* Silbergerät)

...sil|big (z. B. dreisilbig); **si̲l|bisch** (eine Silbe bildend); **...silb|ler**, ...sil|ber (z. B. Zweisilbler, -silber)

si̲lb|rig *vgl.* silberig

Si̲ld, der; -[e]s, -[e] ⟨skand.⟩ (pikant eingelegter junger Hering)

Si|le̲n, der; -s, -e ⟨griech.⟩ (Fabelwesen der griech. Sage, als älterer Satyr Erzieher des Dionysos)

Si|le̲n|ti|um! ⟨lat.⟩ (Ruhe!)

Si̲l|ge, die; -, -n ⟨griech.⟩ (ein Doldengewächs)

Sil|hou|et|te [ziˈlu̯ɛtə], die; -, -n ⟨franz.⟩ (Umriss; Schattenriss, Scherenschnitt); **sil|hou|et|ti̲e|ren** (*veraltend für* als Schattenriss darstellen)

Si|li|ca̲t usw. *vgl.* Silikat usw.; **Si|li̲|ci|um**, Si|li̲|zi|um, das; -s ⟨lat.⟩ (chem. Element, Nichtmetall; *Zeichen* Si)

si|li̲e|ren ⟨span.⟩ ([Futterpflanzen] im Silo einlagern)

Si|li|fi|ka|ti|o̲n, die; -, -en ⟨lat.⟩ (*Geol.* Verkieselung); **si|li|fi|zi̲e|ren; Si|li|ka̲t**, *fachspr.* Si|li|ca̲t, das; -[e]s, -e (*Chemie* Salz der Kieselsäure); **Si|li|ko̲n**, *fachspr.* Si|li|co̲n, das; -s, -e (Kunststoff von großer Wärme- u. Wasserbeständigkeit); **Si|li|ko̲|se**, die; -, -n (*Med.* Steinstaublunge); **Si|li̲|zi|um** *vgl.* Silicium

Si̲l|ke (w. Vorn.)

Si̲l|len *Plur.* ⟨griech.⟩ (altgriech. parodistische Spottgedichte auf Dichter u. a.)

Si̲|lo, der *od.* das; -s, -s ⟨span.⟩ (Großspeicher [für Getreide, Erz u. a.]; Gärfutterbehälter); **Si̲|lo‿fut|ter** (*vgl.* [1]Futter), **...turm**

Si|lu|mi̲n ®, das; -[s] (eine Leichtmetalllegierung aus Aluminium u. Silicium)

Si|lu̲r, das; -s (*Geol.* eine Formation des Paläozoikums); **Si|lu̲|rer** (Angehöriger eines vorkelt. Volksstammes in Wales); **si|lu̲|risch** (*Geol.* das Silur betreffend; im Silur entstanden)

Sil|va̲n, Sil|va̲|nus [*beide* ...v...] (m. Vorn.)

Sil|va̲|ner [...v...] (eine Reb- u. Weinsorte)

[1]Sil|ve̲s|ter [...v...] (m. Vorn.); **[2]Sil|ve̲s|ter**, der, *auch* das; -s, - *meist ohne Artikel* ⟨nach Papst Silvester I.⟩ (letzter Tag im Jahr); **Sil|ve̲s|ter‿abend** (↑R 132), **...ball** (*vgl.* [2]Ball), **...fei|er**, **...nacht**

Sil|via [...vi̯a] (w. Vorn.)

Silv|re̲t|ta [...vr...], **Silv|re̲t|ta|grup|pe** (↑R 105 *u.* 130), die; - (Gebirgsgruppe der Zentralalpen); **Silv|re̲t|ta-Ho̲ch|al|pen|stra|ße**, die; - (↑R 105)

[1]Si̲|ma, die; -, *Plur.* -s *u.* ...men ⟨griech.⟩ (*Archit.* Traufrinne antiker Tempel)

[2]Si̲|ma, das; -[s] ⟨nlat.⟩ (*Geol.* unterer Teil der Erdkruste)

Si̲|mandl, das; -s, -[n] ⟨*eigtl.* Mann, der durch eine Frau (eine „Sie") beherrscht wird⟩ (*bayr. und österr. ugs. für* Pantoffelheld)

Sim|ba̲b|we (Staat in Afrika); **Sim|ba̲b|wer; sim|ba̲b|wisch**

Si̲|me|on (bibl. m. Eigenn. u. Vorn.)

Si̲|mi|li|stein ⟨lat.; dt.⟩ (unechter Schmuckstein)

Si̲m|men|tal (schweiz. Landschaft); **Si̲m|men|ta|ler** (↑R 103)

Si̲m|mer, das; -s, - (ein altes Getreidemaß)

Si̲m|mer|ring ® (eine Antriebswellendichtung)

Si̲|mon (Apostel; m. Vorn.); **Si|mo̲|ne** (w. Vorn.)

Si|mo̲|ni|des (griech. Lyriker)

Si|mo|ni̲e, die; -, ...i̯en ⟨nach dem Zauberer Simon⟩ (Kauf od. Verkauf von geistl. Ämtern); **si|mo̲|nisch;** ↑R 94 (nach Art Simons)

si̲m|pel ⟨franz.⟩ (einfach, einfältig); simp|le (↑R 130) Frage; **Si̲m|pel**, der; -s, - (*landsch. für* Dummkopf, Einfaltspinsel); **si̲m|pel|haft** (*landsch.*)

Si̲mp|lex (↑R 130), das; -, *Plur.* -e *u.* ...pli̲zia ⟨lat.⟩ (*Sprachw.* einfaches, nicht zusammengesetztes Wort); **Simp|li|cis|si|mus**, *eingedeutscht* Simp|li|zis|si|mus, der; - ⟨nlat.⟩ (Titel[held] eines Romans von Grimmelshausen; frühere polit.-satir. deutsche Wochenschrift); **simp|li̲|ci|ter** [...tsi...] ⟨lat.⟩ (*veraltet für* schlechthin); **Simp|li|fi|ka|ti|o̲n**, die; -, -en (*seltener für* Simplifizierung); **simp|li|fi|zi̲e|ren** (in einfacher Weise darstellen; [stark] vereinfachen); **Simp|li|fi|zi̲e|rung; Simp|li̲|zia** (*Plur. von* Simplex); **Simp|li|zi|a̲|de**, die; -, -n (Abenteuerroman um einen einfältigen Menschen, in Nachahmung des „Simplicissimus" von Grimmelshausen); **Simp|li|zis|si|mus** *vgl.* Simplicissimus; **Simp|li|zi|tä̲t**, die; - (Einfachheit, Schlichtheit)

Si̲mp|lon (↑R 130), der; -[s], *auch* **Si̲mp|lon|pass**, der; -es (↑R 105); **Si̲mp|lon‿stra|ße** (die; -; ↑R 105), **...tun|nel** (der; -s; ↑R 105)

Si̲ms, der *od.* das; -es, -e ⟨lat.⟩ (waagerechter [Wand]vorsprung; Leiste)

Si̲m|sa|la|bi̲m (Zauberwort)

Si̲m|se, die; -, -n (ein Riedgras; *landsch. für* Binse)

Sims|ho|bel
Sim|son (bibl. m. Eigenn.); *vgl.* Samson
Si|mu|lant, der; -en, -en (↑R 126) ‹lat.› (jmd., der eine Krankheit vortäuscht); **Si|mu|lan|tin; Si|mu|la|ti|on,** die; -, -en (Vortäuschung [von Krankheiten]; Nachahmung im Simulator o. Ä.); **Si|mu|la|tor,** der; -s, ...oren (Gerät, in dem bestimmte Bedingungen u. [Lebens]verhältnisse wirklichkeitsgetreu herstellbar sind); **si|mu|lie|ren** (vorgeben; sich verstellen; übungshalber im Simulator o. Ä. nachahmen; *ugs. auch für* nachsinnen, grübeln)
si|mul|tan ‹lat.› (gleichzeitig; gemeinsam); **Si|mul|tan‿büh|ne** *(Theater),* **...dol|met|schen** (das; -s), **...dol|met|scher, ...dol|met|sche|rin; Si|mul|ta|ne|i|tät, Si|mul|ta|ni|tät,** die; -, -en (*fachspr. für* Gemeinsamkeit, Gleichzeitigkeit); **Si|mul|tan‿kir|che** (Kirchengebäude für mehrere Bekenntnisse), **...schu|le** (Gemeinschaftsschule), **...spiel** (Schachspiel gegen mehrere Gegner gleichzeitig)
sin = Sinus
Si|nai ['zi:na|i], der; -[s] (Gebirgsmassiv auf der gleichnamigen ägypt. Halbinsel); **Si|na|i‿ge|bir|ge** (↑R 105; das; -s), **...halb|in|sel** (↑R 105; die; -)
Si|nanth|ro|pus (↑R 132), der; -, ...pi ‹griech.› (*Anthropol.* Pekingmensch)
Si|nau, der; -s, -e (Frauenmantel, eine Pflanze)
si|ne an|no ‹lat., „ohne [Angabe des] Jahr[es]"› (veralteter Hinweis bei Buchtitelangaben; *Abk.* s. a.); **si|ne i|ra et stu|dio** [- - - st...] ‹„ohne Zorn u. Eifer"› (sachlich)
Si|ne|ku|re, die; -, -n ‹lat.› (müheloses Amt; Pfründe)
si|ne lo|co ‹lat., „ohne [Angabe des] Ort[es]"› (veralteter Hinweis bei Angaben von Buchtiteln; *Abk.* s. l.); **si|ne lo|co et an|no** ‹„ohne [Angabe des] Ort[es] u. [des] Jahr[es]"› (veralteter Hinweis bei Angaben von Buchtiteln; *Abk.* s. l. e. a.); **si|ne tem|po|re** [- ...re:] (ohne akadem. Viertel, d. h. pünktlich; *Abk.* s. t.); *vgl.* cum tempore
Sin|fo|nie, Sym|pho|nie [zym...], die; -, ...ien ‹griech.› (groß angelegtes Orchesterwerk in meist vier Sätzen); **Sin|fo|nie|kon|zert,** Sym|pho|nie|kon|zert; **Sin|fo|nie|or|ches|ter,** Sym|pho|nie|or|ches|ter; **Sin|fo|ni|et|ta,** die; -, ...tten ‹ital.› (kleine Sinfonie); **Sin|fo|ni|ker,** Sym|pho|ni|ker (Verfasser von Sinfonien; *nur Plur.:* Mitglieder eines Sinfonieorchesters); **sin|fo|nisch,** sym|pho|nisch (sinfonieartig); -e Dichtung
Sing. = Singular
Sing|aka|de|mie (↑R 132)
Sin|ga|pur ['ziŋga..., *auch* ...'pu:r] (Staat u. Stadt an der Südspitze der Halbinsel Malakka); **Sin|ga|pu|rer** (↑R 103); **Sin|ga|pu|re|rin; sin|ga|pu|risch**
sing|bar; Sing|dros|sel; Sin|ge|grup|pe *(ehem. in der DDR);* **sin|gen;** du sangst; du sängest; gesungen; sing[e]!; die singende Säge (ein Musikinstrument)
Sin|ge|ner (Einwohner von Singen); ↑R 103; **Sin|gen (Ho|hen|twiel)** (Stadt im Hegau)
Sin|ge|rei, die; - *(ugs.)*
Sin|gha|le|se [ziŋga...], der; -n, -n; ↑R 126 (Angehöriger eines ind. Volkes auf Sri Lanka); **Sin|gha|le|sin; sin|gha|le|sisch**
[1]**Sin|gle** ['siŋ(gə)l], das; -[s], -[s] ‹engl.› (Einzelspiel [im Tennis o. Ä.]); [2]**Sin|gle,** die; -, -s (kleine Schallplatte); [3]**Sin|gle,** der; -[s], -s (allein stehender Mensch)
Sin|grün, das; -s (Immergrün)
Sing|sang, der; -[e]s *(ugs.);* **Sing|schwan**
Sing-Sing (Staatsgefängnis von New York bei der Industriestadt Ossining [*früher* Sing Sing])
Sing‿spiel, ...stim|me, ...stun|de
Sin|gu|lar, der; -s, -e ‹lat.› (*Sprachw.* Einzahl; *Abk.* Sing.); **sin|gu|lär** (vereinzelt [vorkommend]; selten); **Sin|gu|la|re|tan|tum,** das; -s, *Plur.* - *u.* Singulariatantum (*Sprachw.* nur in der Einzahl vorkommendes Wort, z. B. „das All"); **Sin|gu|lar|form; sin|gu|la|risch** (in der Einzahl [gebraucht, vorkommend]); **Sin|gu|la|ris|mus,** der; - *(Philos.);* **Sin|gu|la|ri|tät,** die; -, -en *meist Plur.* (vereinzelte Erscheinung; Besonderheit)
Sing‿vo|gel, ...wei|se (die)
si|nis|ter ‹lat.› (*selten für* unheilvoll, unglücklich)
sin|ken; er sinkt; ich sank, du sankst; du sänkest; gesunken; sink[e]!; **Sink‿flug, ...kas|ten** (bei Abwasseranlagen), **...stoff** (Substanz, die sich im Wasser absetzt)
Sinn, der; -[e]s, -e; bei, von -en sein; **sinn|be|tö|rend** *(geh.);* **Sinn|bild; sinn|bild|lich; sin|nen;** du sannst; du sännest, *veraltet* sönnest; gesonnen; sinn[e]!; *vgl.* gesinnt *u.* gesonnen; **sin|nen|froh; Sin|nen‿lust** (die; -), **...mensch, ...rausch** (der; -[e]s), **...reiz** (Reiz auf die Sinne, sinnlicher Reiz); **sinn‿ent|leert, ...ent|stel|lend; Sin|nen|welt,** die; -; **Sinn|er|gän|zung** *(Sprachw.);* **Sin|nes‿än|de|rung, ...art, ...ein|druck, ...or|gan, ...reiz** (Reiz, der auf ein Sinnesorgan einwirkt), **...stö|rung, ...täu|schung, ...wahr|neh|mung, ...wan|del, ...zel|le** *(meist Plur.; Physiol.);* **sinn|fäl|lig; Sinn‿fäl|lig|keit** (die; -), **...ge|bung, ...ge|dicht, ...ge|halt** (der); **sinn|ge|mäß; sin|nie|ren** (*ugs. für* in Nachdenken versunken sein); **Sin|nie|rer; sin|nig** (*meist iron. für* sinnvoll, sinnreich; *veraltet für* nachdenklich); ein -er Brauch; **sin|ni|ger|wei|se; Sin|nig|keit,** die; -; **sinn|lich; Sinn|lich|keit,** die; -; **sinn|los; Sinn|lo|sig|keit; Sinn|pflan|ze** (*svw.* Mimose); **sinn|reich;** eine -e Deutung; **Sinn|spruch; sinn‿ver|wandt, ...ver|wir|rend, ...voll, ...wid|rig; Sinn‿wid|rig|keit, ...zu|sam|men|hang**
Si|no|lo|ge, der; -n, -n (↑R 126) ‹griech.› (Chinakundiger, bes. Lehrer u. Erforscher der chin. Sprache); **Si|no|lo|gie,** die; -; **Si|no|lo|gin; si|no|lo|gisch**
sin|te|mal (*veraltet für* da, weil)
Sin|ter, der; -s, - (mineral. Ablagerung aus Quellen); **Sin|ter|glas,** das; -es; **sin|tern** ([durch]sickern; Sinter bilden; *Technik* [keram. Massen] durch Erhitzen zusammenbacken lassen); **Sin|ter|ter|ras|se**
Sint|flut, die; - ‹„umfassende Flut"› *(A. T.); vgl.* Sündflut; **sint|flut|ar|tig;** -e Regenfälle
Sin|ti|za, die; -, -s ‹Zigeunersprache› (w. Sinto); **Sin|to,** der; -, ...ti *meist Plur.* (deutschstämmiger Zigeuner)
Si|nus, der; -, *Plur.* - [...nu:s] *u.* -se *Plur. selten* ‹lat.› (*Med.* Ausbuchtung, Hohlraum; *Math.* eine Winkelfunktion im rechtwinkligen Dreieck, *Zeichen* sin); **Si|nu|si|tis,** die; -, ...itiden (*Med.* Entzündung der Nasennebenhöhle); **Si|nus‿kur|ve** *(Math.),* **...schwin|gung** *(Physik)*
Si|on *vgl.* Zion
Si|oux ['zi:uks], der; -, - (Angehöriger einer Sprachfamilie der nordamerik. Indianer)
Si|pho ['zi:fo], der; -s, ...onen ‹griech.› (*Zool.* Atemröhre der Schnecken, Muscheln u. Tinten-

fische); **Si|phon** [ˈzifɔŋ, *österr.* ziˈfo:n], der; -s, -s (Geruchsverschluss bei Wasserausgüssen; Getränkegefäß, bei dem die Flüssigkeit durch Kohlensäure herausgedrückt wird; *österr. ugs. für* Sodawasser); **Si|pho|no|pho|re,** die; -, -n *meist Plur.* ⟨griech.⟩ (*Zool.* Staats- od. Röhrenqualle); **Si|phon|ver|schluss** [ˈzifɔŋ..., *österr.* ziˈfo:n...] (Geruchsverschluss)

Sip|pe, die; -, -n; **Sip|pen₋for|schung,** **...haf|tung** (die; -), **...kun|de** (die; -); **sip|pen|kund|lich; Sip|pen|ver|band** (*Völkerk.*); **Sipp|schaft** (*abwertend für* Verwandtschaft; Gesindel)

Sir [sœ:(r)], der; -s, -s ⟨engl.⟩ (*engl. Anrede [ohne Namen]* „Herr"; *vor Vorn.* engl. Adelstitel)

Si|rach (bibl. m. Eigenn.); *vgl.* Jesus Sirach

Sire [si:r] ⟨franz.⟩ (Majestät [franz. Anrede an einen Monarchen])

Si|re|ne, die; -, -n ⟨griech., nach den Fabelwesen der griech. Sage⟩ (Nebelhorn, Warngerät; verführerische Frau; *Zool.* Seekuh); **Si|re|nen₋ge|heul,** **...ge|sang; si|re|nen|haft** (verführerisch); **Si|re|nen|pro|be**

Si|ri|us, der; - ⟨griech.⟩ (ein Stern); **si|ri|us|fern**

Sir|rah, die; - ⟨arab.⟩ (ein Stern)

sir|ren (hell klingen[d surren])

Sir|ta|ki, der; -, -s ⟨griech.⟩ (ein griech. Volkstanz)

Si|rup, der; -s, -e ⟨arab.⟩ (dickflüssiger Zucker[rüben]- od. Obstsaft)

Si|sal, der; -s ⟨nach der mexik. Stadt⟩; **Si|sal₋hanf** (Faser aus Agavenblättern), **...läu|fer**

sis|tie|ren ⟨lat.⟩ ([Verfahren] einstellen; *bes. Rechtsspr.* jmdn. zur Feststellung seiner Personalien auf die Polizeiwache bringen); **Sis|tie|rung**

Sis|trum (↑R 130), das; -s, Sistren ⟨griech.⟩ (altägypt. Rassel)

Si|sy|phos ⟨griech.⟩, **Si|sy|phus** (Gestalt der griech. Sage); **Si|sy|phus|ar|beit;** ↑R 95 (vergebliche Arbeit)

Si|tar, der; -[s], -[s] ⟨iran.⟩ (indische Laute)

Sit-in, das; -[s], -s ⟨amerik.⟩ (Sitzstreik)

Sit|ta (w. Vorn.)

Sit|te, die; -, -n

Sit|ten (Hptst. des Kantons Wallis)

Sit|ten₋de|zer|nat, **...ge|mäl|de,** **...ge|schich|te** (die; -), **...ge|setz,** **...ko|dex,** **...leh|re; sit|ten|los; Sit|ten|lo|sig|keit,** die; -; **Sit|ten₋po|li|zei,** **...rich|ter,** **...ro|man,** **...schil|de|rung; sit|ten|streng** (*veraltend*); **Sit|ten|₋stren|ge,** **...strolch,** **...ver|derb|nis** (*geh. für* Sittenverfall), **...ver|fall; sit|ten|wid|rig; Sit|ten|wid|rig|keit,** die; -

Sit|tich, der; -s, -e (ein Papagei)

sitt|lich; -er Maßstab; -er Wert; **Sitt|lich|keit,** die; -; **Sitt|lich|keits₋de|likt,** **...ver|bre|chen,** **...ver|bre|cher; sitt|sam** (*veraltend*); **Sitt|sam|keit,** die; -

Si|tu|a|ti|on, die; -, -en ⟨lat.⟩ ([Sach]lage, Stellung, Zustand); **si|tu|a|ti|ons|be|dingt; Si|tu|a|ti|ons₋ethik** (die; -; ↑R 132), **...ko|mik,** **...ko|mö|die,** **...plan** (*selten für* Lageplan; *vgl.* [2]Plan), **...stück; si|tu|a|tiv** (durch die Situation bedingt); **si|tu|ie|ren** ⟨franz.⟩ (in einen Zusammenhang stellen; einbetten); **si|tu|iert** (in bestimmten [wirtschaftl.] Verhältnissen lebend); sie ist besser situiert als er

Si|tu|la, die; -, ...ulen ⟨lat.⟩ (bronzezeitl. Eimer)

Si|tus, der; -, - [ˈzi:tu:s] ⟨lat.⟩ (*Med.* Lage [von Organen]); *vgl.* in situ

sit ve|nia ver|bo [- ˈve:nia ˈvɛrbo] ⟨lat.⟩ (man verzeihe das Wort!; *Abk.* s. v. v.)

Sitz, der; -es, -e; **Sitz₋bad,** **...ba|de|wan|ne,** **...blo|cka|de,** **...ecke** (↑R 132); **sit|zen;** du sitzt, er sitzt; du saßest, er saß; du säßest; gesessen; sitz[e]!; ich habe (*südd., österr., schweiz.:* bin) gesessen; einen - haben (*ugs. für* betrunken sein); (↑R 50:) ich bin noch nicht zum Sitzen gekommen; sitzen bleiben (*ugs. auch für* in der Schule nicht versetzt werden; nicht geheiratet werden); auf etwas sitzen bleiben (*ugs. auch für* etwas nicht verkaufen können); sitzen geblieben; sitzen zu bleiben; sitzen lassen (*ugs. auch für* in der Schule nicht versetzen; im Stich lassen); ich habe ihn sitzen lassen, *seltener* sitzen gelassen, als er meine Hilfe brauchte; ich habe den Vorwurf nicht auf mir sitzen lassen (nicht unwidersprochen gelassen); **sit|zen blei|ben** *vgl.* sitzen; **Sit|zen|blei|ber; sit|zend;** -e Tätigkeit; **sit|zen las|sen** *vgl.* sitzen; **...sit|zer** (z. B. Zweisitzer); **Sitz₋fal|te,** **...flä|che,** **...fleisch** (das; -[e]s; *ugs. scherzh. für* Ausdauer), **...ge|le|gen|heit,** **...grup|pe; ...sit|zig** (z. B. viersitzig); **Sitz₋kis|sen,** **...mö|bel,** **...ord|nung,** **...platz,** **...rie|se** (*ugs. scherzh. für* jmd. mit kurzen Beinen u. langem Oberkörper), **...stan|ge,** **...streik; Sit|zung; Sit|zungs₋be|richt,** **...geld** (*Politik*), **...saal,** **...zim|mer**

Si|wa[h], die; - (eine Oase)

Six|ti|na, die; - ⟨nach Papst Sixtus IV.⟩ (Kapelle im Vatikan); **six|ti|nisch;** *aber* (↑R 108): Sixtinische Kapelle, Sixtinische Madonna; **Six|tus** (m. Vorn.)

Si|zi|li|a|ne, die; -, -n ⟨ital.⟩ (eine Versform); **Si|zi|li|a|ner,** Si|zi|li|er (Bewohner von Sizilien); **Si|zi|li|a|ne|rin,** Si|zi|li|e|rin; **si|zi|li|a|nisch,** si|zi|lisch, *aber* (↑R 108): Sizilianische Vesper (Volksaufstand in Palermo während der Ostermontagsvesper 1282); **Si|zi|li|en** (südital. Insel); **Si|zi|li|enne** [...ˈliɛn], die; - ⟨franz.⟩ (*svw.* Eolienne); **Si|zi|li|er** usw. *vgl.* Sizilianer usw.

SJ = Societatis Jesu [zotsi̯e...] ⟨lat., „von der Gesellschaft Jesu"⟩ (Jesuit); *vgl.* Societas Jesu

SK = Segerkegel

Ska|bi|es [...bi̯ɛs], die; - ⟨lat.⟩ (*Med.* Krätze); **ska|bi|ös** (an Skabies erkrankt); **Ska|bi|o|se,** die; -, -n (eine Wiesenblume)

Ska|ger|rak, das *od.* der; -s (Meeresteil zwischen Norwegen u. Jütland)

Skai ®, das; -[s] ⟨Kunstwort⟩ (Kunstleder)

skål! [sko:l] ⟨skand.⟩ (*skand. für* prost!, zum Wohl!)

Ska|la, die; -, *Plur.* ...len *u.* -s ⟨ital., „Treppe"⟩ (Maßeinteilung [an Messgeräten]; Stufenfolge, Reihe); *vgl.* Skale *u.* Scala; **Ska|la|hö|he; ska|lar** (*Math.* durch reelle Zahlen bestimmt); **Ska|lar,** der; -s, -e (*Math.* durch einen reellen Zahlenwert bestimmte Größe; *Zool.* ein Buntbarsch)

Skal|de, der; -n, -n (↑R 126) ⟨altnord.⟩ (altnord. Dichter u. Sänger); **Skal|den|dich|tung; skal|disch**

Ska|le, die; -, -n (*in der Bedeutung* „Maßeinteilung" *bes. fachspr. eindeutschend für* Skala); **Ska|len|zei|ger**

Skalp, der; -s, -e ⟨engl.⟩ (*früher bei den Indianern* abgezogene behaarte Kopfhaut des Gegners als Siegeszeichen)

Skal|pell, das; -s, -e ⟨lat.⟩ ([kleines chirurg.] Messer [mit feststehender Klinge])

skal|pie|ren ⟨engl.⟩ (den Skalp nehmen)

Skan|dal, der; -s, -e ⟨griech.⟩ (Ärgernis; Aufsehen; Lärm); **Skan|dal|ge|schich|te; skan|da|lie|ren** (*veraltet für* lärmen); **skan|da|li|sie|ren** (*veraltend für* Ärgernis geben, Anstoß nehmen); sich

über etwas - (an etwas Ärgernis nehmen); **Skan|da̱l|nu|del** (*ugs. für* Frau, die für Skandale sorgt, Aufsehen erregt); **skan|da|lö̱s** (ärgerlich; anstößig; unerhört); **Skan|da̱l|pres|se; skan|da̱l‿süch|tig, ...um|wit|tert**
skan|die̱|ren ⟨lat.⟩ (taktmäßig nach Versfüßen lesen; rhythmisch sprechen [von Sprechchören])
Skan|di|na̱|vi|en [...vi̯ən]; **Skan|di|na̱|vi|er** [...vi̯ər]; **Skan|di|na̱|vi|e|rin; skan|di|na̱|visch,** *aber* (↑R 102): die Skandinavische Halbinsel; **Skạn|di|um** *vgl.* Scandium
Ska|po|li̱th [*auch* ...'lit], der; *Gen.* -s *od.* -en, *Plur.* -e[n] (↑R 126) ⟨lat.; griech.⟩ (ein Mineral)
Ska|pu|li̱er, das; -s, -e ⟨lat.⟩ (bei der Mönchstracht Überwurf über Brust u. Rücken)
Ska|ra|bä̱|en|gem|me; Ska|ra|bä̱|us, der; -, ...äen ⟨griech.⟩ (Pillendreher, Mistkäfer des Mittelmeergebietes; dessen Nachbildung als Siegel [im alten Ägypten] u. später als Amulett)
Ska|ra|mụz, der; -es, -e ⟨ital.⟩ (Figur des prahlerischen Soldaten im franz. u. ital. Lustspiel)
Skạrn, der; -s, -e ⟨schwed.⟩ (*Geol.* vorwiegend aus Kalk-Eisen-Silikaten bestehendes Gestein)
skar|tie̱|ren ⟨ital.⟩ (*österr. Amtsspr. für* alte Akten u. a. ausscheiden)
Ska̱t, der; -[e]s, *Plur.* -e *u.* -s (*nur Sing.:* ein Kartenspiel; zwei verdeckt liegende Karten beim Skatspiel); **Ska̱t‿abend** (↑R 132), **...bru|der** *(ugs.)*
Skate|board ['ske:tbɔ:(r)d], das; -s, -s ⟨engl.⟩ (Rollerbrett); **Skate|boar|der** (jmd., der Skateboard fährt)
ska̱|ten (*ugs. für* Skat spielen); **Ska̱|ter** (*ugs. für* Skatspieler); **Ska̱t‿ge|richt** (das; -[e]s; in Altenburg), **...kar|te**
Ska|to̱l, das; -s ⟨griech.; lat.⟩ (eine chem. Verbindung); **Ska|to|pha̱|ge** usw. *vgl.* Koprophage usw.
Ska̱t‿par|tie, ...run|de, ...spiel, ...spie|ler, ...tur|nier
Skeet|schie|ßen ['ski:t...], das; -s ⟨engl.; dt.⟩ (Wurftaubenschießen mit Schrotgewehren)
Ske|lẹt ⟨griech.⟩ (*teilweise noch in der Med. gebrauchte Nebenform von* Skelett); **Ske|le|ton** ['skɛlət(ə)n], der; -s, -s ⟨engl.⟩ (niedriger Sportrennschlitten); **Ske|lẹtt,** das; -[e]s, -e ⟨griech.⟩ (Knochengerüst, Gerippe; tragendes Grundgerüst); **Ske|lẹtt‿bau** (*Plur.* ...bauten; Gerüst-, Gerippebau), **...bau|wei|se** (die; -), **...bo|den** *(Geol.),* **...form; ske|let|tie̱|ren** (das Skelett bloßlegen); ein Blatt - (*Biol.* bis auf die Rippen abfressen)
Skẹp|sis, die; - ⟨griech.⟩ (Zweifel, kritisch prüfende Haltung); **Skẹp|ti|ker** (Zweifler; Vertreter des Skeptizismus); **skẹp|tisch** (zweifelnd; misstrauisch; kühl u. streng prüfend); **Skep|ti|zis|mus,** der; - (Zweifel [an der Möglichkeit sicheren Wissens]; skeptische Haltung)
Sketch [skɛtʃ], der; -[es], *Plur.* -e[s] *od.* -s, *eindeutschend* **Skẹtsch,** der; -[e]s, -e ⟨engl., „Skizze"⟩ (kurze, effektvolle Bühnenszene im Kabarett od. Varieté)
Ski [ʃi:], Schi, der; -s, *Plur.* -er, *auch* - ⟨norw.⟩; (↑R 39:) - fahren, - laufen; Ski und Eis laufen; Ski Heil! (Skiläufergruß)
Ski|a|gra|phi̱e, die; -, -i̱en ⟨griech.⟩ (antike Schattenmalerei)
Ski|ak|ro|ba|tik ['ʃi:...], Schi̱|ak|ro|ba|tik
Ski|a|sko|pi̱e, die; -, ...i̱en ⟨griech.⟩ (*Med.* Verfahren zur Feststellung von Brechungsfehlern des Auges)
Ski|bob ['ʃi:...], Schi̱|bob (lenkbarer, einkufiger Schlitten); **Ski|fah|rer,** Schi̱|fah|rer; **Ski|fah|re|rin,** Schi̱|fah|re|rin
Ski̱ff, das; -[e]s, -e ⟨engl.⟩ (*Sport* nord. Einmannruderboot)
Ski|flie|gen ['ʃi:...], Schi̱|flie|gen, das; -s; **Ski|flug,** Schi̱|flug; **Ski|gym|nas|tik,** Schi̱|gym|nas|tik; **Ski|ha|serl,** Schi̱|ha|serl, das; -s, -[n] (*ugs. für* junge Anfängerin im Skilaufen); **Ski|kjöl|ring,** *häufig auch* Ski|jö|ring ['ʃi:jø:riŋ], *auch* Schi̱|jö|ring, das; -s, -s ⟨norw.⟩ (Skilauf mit Pferde- od. Motorradvorspann); **Ski|kurs** ['ʃi:...], Schi̱|kurs; **Ski|lauf,** Schi̱|lauf; **Ski|lau|fen,** Schi̱|lau|fen, das; -s; **Ski|läu|fer,** Schi̱|läu|fer; **Ski|läu|fe|rin,** Schi̱|läu|fe|rin; **Ski|leh|rer,** Schi̱|leh|rer; **Ski|leh|re|rin,** Schi̱|leh|re|rin; **Ski|lift,** Schi̱|lift; **Ski|müt|ze,** Schi̱|müt|ze
Ski̱n, der; -s, -s (*kurz für* Skinhead); **Skin|head** ['skinhɛd], der; -s, -s ⟨engl.⟩ ([zu Gewalttätigkeit neigender] Jugendlicher mit kahl geschorenem Kopf)
Ski̱nk, der; -[e]s, -e ⟨griech.⟩ (Glatt- od. Wühlechse)
Ski|no|i̱d ®, das; -[e]s (ein lederähnlicher Kunststoff)
Ski|pass ['ʃi:...], Schi̱|pass; **Ski|pis|te,** Schi̱|pis|te
Skịp|per ⟨engl.⟩ (Kapitän einer [Segel]jacht)
Ski|sport ['ʃi:...], Schi̱|sport, der; -[e]s; **Ski|sprin|ger,** Schi̱|springer; **Ski|sprin|ge|rin,** Schi̱|sprin|ge|rin; **Ski|sprung,** Schi̱|sprung; **Ski|spur,** Schi̱|spur; **Ski|stie|fel,** Schi̱|stie|fel; **Ski|stock,** Schi̱|stock *Plur.* ...stöcke; **Ski|wachs,** Schi̱|wachs; **Ski|wan|dern,** Schi̱|wan|dern, das; -s; **Ski|was|ser,** Schi̱|was|ser, das; -s (ein Getränk); **Ski|zir|kus,** Schi̱|zir|kus (*Bez. für* alpine Skirennen mit den dazugehörenden Veranstaltungen)
Ski̱z|ze, die; -, -n ⟨ital.⟩ ([erster] Entwurf; flüchtige Zeichnung; kleine Geschichte); **Ski̱z|zen‿block** (*vgl.* Block), **...buch; ski̱z|zen|haft; skiz|zi̱e|ren** (entwerfen; andeuten); **Skiz|zi̱e|rer; Skiz|zi̱er|pa|pier; Skiz|zi̱e|rung**
Skla̱|ve [...v..., *auch* ...f...], der; -n, -n (↑R 126) ⟨slaw.⟩ (unfreier, rechtloser Mensch; *abwertend für* jmd., der von etwas od. jmdm. sehr abhängig ist); **Skla̱|ven|ar|beit; skla̱|ven|ar|tig; Skla̱|ven‿hal|ter, ...han|del** (*vgl.* [1]Handel), **...händ|ler, ...markt; Skla̱|ven|tum,** das; -s; **Skla|ve|re̱i,** die; -; **Skla̱|vin; skla̱|visch;** -er Gehorsam
Skle̱|ra, die; -, ...ren ⟨griech.⟩ (*Med.* Lederhaut des Auges); **Skle|ri̱|tis,** die; -, ...iti̱den (Entzündung der Lederhaut des Auges); **Skle|ro|der|mi̱e,** die; -, ...i̱en (krankhafte Hautverhärtung); **Skle|ro|me̱|ter,** das; -s, - (Härtemesser [bei Kristallen]); **Skle|ro̱|se,** die; -, -n (*Med.* krankhafte Verhärtung von Geweben u. Organen); **skle|ro̱|tisch** (verhärtet)
Sko̱|lex, der; -, ...lizes [...litse:s] ⟨griech.⟩ (*Med.* Bandwurmkopf)
Sko̱|li|on, das; -s, ...ien [...i̯ən] ⟨griech.⟩ (altgriech. Tischlied, Einzelgesang beim Gelage)
Sko|li|o̱|se, die; -, -n ⟨griech.⟩ (*Med.* seitliche Verkrümmung der Wirbelsäule)
Sko|lo|pe̱n|der, der; -s, - ⟨griech.⟩ (trop. Tausendfüßer)
skon|ti̱e|ren ⟨ital.⟩ (*Wirtsch.* Skonto gewähren); **Skọn|to,** der *od.* das; -s, *Plur.* -s, *selten* ...ti ([Zahlungs]abzug, Nachlass [bei Barzahlung])
Skont|ra|ti|o̱n (↑R 130), die; -, -en ⟨ital.⟩ (*Wirtsch.* Fortschreibung, Bestandsermittlung von Waren durch Eintragung der Zu- und Abgänge); **skont|ri̱e|ren; Skọnt|ro,** das; -s, -s (Nebenbuch der Buchhaltung zur tägl. Ermittlung von Bestandsmengen); **Skọnt|ro|buch**
Skoo|ter ['sku:tə(r)], der; -s, -

⟨engl.⟩ ([elektr.] Kleinauto auf Jahrmärkten)
Skop, der; -s, -s ⟨angels.⟩ (*früher* Dichter u. Sänger in der Gefolgschaft angelsächsischer Fürsten)
Sko|pze, der; -n, -n (↑R 126) ⟨russ.⟩ (Angehöriger einer russ. Sekte des 19. Jh.s)
Skor|but, der; -[e]s ⟨mlat.⟩ (*Med.* Krankheit durch Mangel an Vitamin C); **skor|bu|tisch**
Skor|da|tur *vgl.* Scordatura
Skore [skɔ:(r)], das; -s, -s ⟨engl.⟩ (*schweiz. Sportspr. svw.* Score); **sko|ren** ⟨engl.⟩ (*österr. u. schweiz. Sportspr. svw.* scoren)
Skor|pi|on, der; -s, -e ⟨griech.⟩ (ein Spinnentier; *nur Sing.*: ein Sternbild)
Sko|te, der; -n, -n; ↑R 126 (Angehöriger eines alten ir. Volksstammes in Schottland)
Sko|tom, das; -s, -e ⟨griech.⟩ (*Med.* Gesichtsfelddefekt)
skr = schwedische Krone
Skri|bent, der; -en, -en (↑R 126) ⟨lat.⟩ (*veraltend für* Schreiberling; Vielschreiber); **Skri|bi|fax,** der; -[es], -e (*selten für* Skribent); **Skript,** das; -[e]s, *Plur.* -en *u.* (*bes. für* Drehbücher:) -s ⟨engl.⟩ (schriftl. Ausarbeitung; Nachschrift einer Hochschulvorlesung; *auch, österr. nur, für* Drehbuch); **Skript|girl,** das; -s, -s (Mitarbeiterin eines Filmregisseurs, die die Einstellung für jede Aufnahme einträgt); **Skrip|tum,** das; -s, *Plur.* ...ten *u.* ...ta ⟨lat.⟩ (*älter, noch bes. österr. für* Skript); **skrip|tu|ral** (die Schrift betreffend)
skro|fu|lös ⟨lat.⟩ (*Med.* an Skrofulose leidend); **Skro|fu|lo|se,** die; -, -n ([tuberkulöse] Haut- u. Lymphknotenerkrankung bei Kindern)
skro|tal ⟨lat.⟩ (*Med.* zum Skrotum gehörend); **Skro|tal|bruch,** der; **Skro|tum,** das; -s, ...ta (Hodensack)
Skrub|ber ['skrabə(r)], der; -s, - ⟨engl.⟩ (*Technik* Anlage zur Gasreinigung)
Skrubs [skraps] *Plur.* ⟨engl.⟩ (minderwertige Tabakblätter)
[1]**Skru|pel,** das; -s, - ⟨lat.⟩ (altes Apothekergewicht); [2]**Skru|pel,** der; -s, - *meist Plur.* (Zweifel, Bedenken; Gewissensbiss); **skru|pel|los; Skru|pel|lo|sig|keit; skru|pu|lös** (*veraltend für* ängstlich; peinlich genau)
Skuld (*nord. Mythol.* Norne der Zukunft)
Skull, das; -s, -s ⟨engl.⟩ (Ruder); **Skull|boot; skul|len** (rudern); **Skul|ler** (Sportruderer)
Skulp|teur [...'tø:r], der; -s, -e ⟨franz.⟩ (Künstler, der Skulpturen herstellt); **skulp|tie|ren** ⟨lat.⟩ (ausmeißeln); **Skulp|tur,** die; -, -en (plastisches Bildwerk; *nur Sing.*: Bildhauerkunst); **skulp|tu|ral** (in der Art, der Form einer Skulptur); **Skulp|tu|ren|samm|lung**
[1]**Skunk,** der; -s, *Plur.* -e *od.* -s ⟨indian.-engl.⟩ (Stinktier); [2]**Skunk,** der; -s, -s *meist Plur.* (Pelz des Stinktiers)
skur|ril ⟨etrusk.-lat.⟩ (verschroben, eigenwillig; drollig); **Skur|ri|li|tät,** die; -, -en
S-Kur|ve (↑R 25)
Skús, der; -, - ⟨franz.⟩ (Trumpfkarte im Tarockspiel)
Sku|ta|ri (albanische Stadt); **Sku|ta|ri|see,** der; -s
Skye|ter|ri|er ['skai...] ⟨engl.⟩ (Hund einer bestimmten Rasse)
Sky|lab ['skailɛb] ⟨engl.⟩ (Name einer amerik. Raumstation)
Sky|light ['skailait], das; -s, -s ⟨engl.⟩ (*Seemannsspr.* Oberlicht [auf Schiffen]); **Sky|line** [...lain], die; -, -s (Horizont[linie], Silhouette einer Stadt)
Skyl|la (*griech. Form von* Szylla)
Sky|the, der; -n, -n; ↑R 126 (Angehöriger eines alten nordiran. Reitervolkes); **Sky|thi|en** (Land); **sky|thisch**
s. l. = sine loco
Sla|lom, der; -s, -s ⟨norw.⟩ (*Ski- u. Kanusport* Torlauf; *auch übertr. für* Zickzacklauf, -fahrt); - fahren, - laufen; **Sla|lom‿kurs, ...lauf, ...läu|fer, ...läu|fe|rin**
Slang [slɛŋ], der; -s, -s ⟨engl.⟩ (saloppe Umgangssprache; Jargon)
Slap|stick ['slɛpstik], der; -s, -s ⟨engl.⟩ (grotesk-komischer Gag, vor allem im [Stumm]film)
s-Laut (↑R 25)
Sla|we, der; -n, -n (↑R 126) ⟨slaw.⟩; **Sla|wen|tum,** das; -s; **Sla|win; sla|wisch; sla|wi|sie|ren** (slawisch machen); **Sla|wis|mus,** der; -, ...men (slaw. Spracheigentümlichkeit in einer nichtslaw. Sprache); **Sla|wist,** der; -en, -en; ↑R 126; **Sla|wis|tik,** die; - (Wissenschaft von den slaw. Sprachen u. Literaturen); **Sla|wis|tin; sla|wis|tisch; Sla|wo|ni|en** (Gebiet in Kroatien); **Sla|wo|ni|er; sla|wo|nisch; Sla|wo|phi|le,** der *u.* die; -n, -n (↑R 5 ff.) ⟨slaw.; griech.⟩ (Slawenfreund)
s. l. e. a. = sine loco et anno
Sleip|nir ⟨altnord.⟩ (*nord. Mythol.* das achtbeinige Pferd Odins)
Sle|vogt (dt. Maler u. Grafiker)
Sli|bo|witz, Sli|wo|witz, der; -[es], -e ⟨serbokroat.⟩ (ein Pflaumenbranntwein)
Slice [slais], der; -, -s [...siz] ⟨engl.⟩ (bestimmter Schlag beim Golf u. beim Tennis)
Slick, der; -s, -s ⟨engl.⟩ (breiter Rennreifen ohne Profil)
Sli|ding|tack|ling ['slaidiŋ'tɛk...] (↑R 33); *vgl.* Tackling
Sling|pumps, der; -, - ⟨engl.⟩ (Pumps, der über der Ferse mit einem Riemchen gehalten wird)
Slip, der; -s, -s ⟨engl.⟩ (Unterhöschen; schiefe Ebene in einer Werft für den Stapellauf eines Schiffes; *Technik* Vortriebsverlust); **Sli|pon,** der; -s, -s (Herrensportmantel mit Raglanärmeln); **Slip|per,** der; -s, -[s] (Schlupfschuh mit niedrigem Absatz)
Sli|wo|witz *vgl.* Slibowitz
Slo|gan ['slo:gən], der; -s, -s ⟨gälisch-engl.⟩ ([Werbe]schlagwort)
Sloop [slu:p] *vgl.* Slup
Slop, der; -s, -s ⟨engl.-amerik.⟩ (Modetanz der sechziger Jahre)
Slo|wa|ke, der; -n, -n; ↑R 126 (Angehöriger eines westslaw. Volkes); **Slo|wa|kei,** die; - (Staat in Mitteleuropa); **Slo|wa|kin; slo|wa|kisch;** -e Literatur, *aber* (↑R 102): Slowakisches Erzgebirge; **Slo|wa|kisch,** das; -[s] (Sprache); *vgl.* Deutsch; **Slo|wa|ki|sche,** das; -n; *vgl.* Deutsche, das;
Slo|we|ne, der; -n, -n; ↑R 126 (Angehöriger eines südslaw. Volkes; Einwohner von Slowenien); **Slo|we|ni|en** (Staat im Südosten Europas); **Slo|we|ni|er** (Slowene); **Slo|we|ni|e|rin, Slo|we|nin; slo|we|nisch; Slo|we|nisch,** das; -[s] (Sprache); *vgl.* Deutsch; **Slo|we|ni|sche,** das; -n; *vgl.* Deutsche, das
Slow|fox ['slo:...] (↑R 51), der; -[es], -e ⟨engl.⟩ (ein Tanz)
Slum [slam], der; -s, -s *meist Plur.* ⟨engl.⟩ (Elendsviertel); **Slum|be|woh|ner**
Slup, die; -, -s ⟨engl.⟩ (Küstenschiff, Segeljacht)
sm = Seemeile
Sm = *chem. Zeichen für* Samarium
S. M. = Seine Majestät
Small|talk *auch* **Small Talk** ['smɔ:l'tɔ:k] (↑R 33), der, *auch* das; -s, -s ⟨engl.⟩ (beiläufige Konversation)
Smal|te *vgl.* Schmalte
Sma|ragd, der; -[e]s, -e ⟨griech.⟩ (ein Edelstein); **Sma|ragd|ei|dech|se; sma|rag|den** (aus Smaragd; grün wie ein Smaragd); **sma|ragd|grün**

smart [*auch* smart] ‹engl.› (modisch elegant, schneidig; clever)
Smash [smɛʃ], der; -[s], -s ‹engl.› (*Tennis, Badminton* Schmetterschlag)
Sme|ta|na (tschech. Komponist)
SMH = Schnelle Medizinische Hilfe (ehem. in der DDR ärztl. Notdienst)
SM-Ofen = Siemens-Martin-Ofen
Smog, der; -[s], -s ‹engl.› (mit Abgasen, Rauch u. a. gemischter Dunst od. Nebel über Industriestädten); **Smog|alarm** (↑R 132)
Smok|ar|beit; smo|ken (Stoff fälteln u. besticken); eine gesmokte Bluse
Smo|king, der; -s, -s ‹engl.› (Gesellschaftsanzug mit seidenen Revers für Herren); **Smo|king-schlei|fe**
Smo|lensk (russ. Stadt)
Smör|re|bröd, das; -s, -s ‹dän.› (reich belegtes Brot)
smor|zan|do ‹ital.› (*Musik* verlöschend); **Smor|zan|do,** das; -s, *Plur.* -s *u.* ...di
Smut|je, der; -s, -s (*Seemannsspr.* Schiffskoch)
SMV = Schülermitverantwortung, Schülermitverwaltung
Smyr|na (türk. Stadt; *heutiger Name* Izmir); **Smyr|na|er;** ↑R 103 (*auch* ein Teppich); **smyr|na|isch; Smyr|na|tep|pich**
Sn = Stannum (*chem. Zeichen für* Zinn)
Snack [snɛk], der; -s, -s ‹engl.› (Imbiss); **Snack|bar,** die (Imbissstube)
Snee|witt|chen (*nordd. für* Schneewittchen)
snif|fen ‹engl.› (*ugs. für* sich durch das Einatmen von Dämpfen [von Klebstoff u. a.] berauschen)
Snob, der; -s, -s ‹engl.› (vornehm tuender, eingebildeter Mensch, Geck); **Sno|bi|e|ty** [...'baiəti], die; - (vornehm tuende Gesellschaft); **Sno|bis|mus,** der; -, ...men; **sno|bis|tisch**
Snow|board ['sno:bɔ:(r)d], das; -s, -s ‹engl.› (als Sportgerät dienendes Brett zum Gleiten auf Schnee); **snow|boar|den** (mit dem Snowboard gleiten); **Snow-boar|der,** der; -s, - (jmd., der Snowboarding betreibt); **Snow-boar|ding,** das; -s (das Gleiten auf Schnee mit einem Snowboard)
so; so sein, so werden, so bleiben; so ein Mann; so einer, so eine, so ein[e]s; so etwas, *ugs.* so was; so dass (*vgl. auch* sodass); so schnell wie *od.* als möglich; die so genannten schnellen Brüter; die Meisterschaft war so gut wie gewonnen; so gegen acht Uhr; so wahr mir Gott helfe. *Zur Getrennt- od. Zusammenschreibung in* sobald, sofern, sogleich usw. *vgl. die einzelnen Stichwörter*
SO = Südost[en]
So. = Sonntag
s. o. = sieh[e] oben!
So|a|res ['suariʃ] (port. Politiker); *vgl. aber* [2]Suárez
so|a|ve [...və] ‹ital.› (*Musik* lieblich, sanft, angenehm, süß)
so|bald; *Konj.:* sobald er kam, *aber (Adverb):* er kam so bald nicht, wie wir erwartet hatten; komme so bald wie *od.* als möglich
So|ci|e|tas Je|su [zo'tsiːe... -], die; - - (*lat. Gen.* Societatis Jesu) ‹lat., „Gesellschaft Jesu"› (der Orden der Jesuiten; *Abk.* SJ); **So|ci|e-tas Ver|bi Di|vi|ni** [- 'vɛrbi di-'vi:ni], die; - - - ‹„Gesellschaft des Göttlichen Wortes"› (kath. Missionsgesellschaft von Steyl in der niederl. Provinz Limburg; *Abk.* SVD)
Söck|chen; So|cke, die; -, -n; **So-ckel,** der; -s, - (unterer Mauervorsprung; Unterbau, Fußgestell, z. B. für Statuen); **So|ckel‿be-trag** (bei Lohnerhöhungen), **...ge|schoss** (*für* Souterrain); **So|cken,** der; -s, - (*landsch. für* Socke); **So|cken|hal|ter**
Sod, der; -[e]s, -e (*veraltet für* das Sieden; *nur Sing.:* Sodbrennen; *bes. schweiz. für* [Zieh]brunnen)
[1]**So|da,** die; - *u.* das; -s ‹span.› (Natriumkarbonat); [2]**So|da,** das; -s (*kurz für* Sodawasser)
So|da|le, der; -n, -n (↑R 126) ‹lat.› (Mitglied einer Sodalität); **So|da-li|tät,** die; -, -en (kath. Genossenschaft, Bruderschaft)
So|da|lith [*auch* ...'lit], der; *Gen.* -s *od.* -en, *Plur.* -e[n] (↑R 126) ‹span.; griech.› (ein Mineral)
so|dann
so|dass, *auch* so dass; er arbeitete Tag und Nacht, sodass (*auch* so dass) er krank wurde, *aber* er arbeitete so, dass er krank wurde
So|da|was|ser *Plur.* ...wässer (kohlensäurehaltiges Mineralwasser)
Sod|bren|nen, das; -s (brennendes Gefühl im Magen u. in der Speiseröhre); **Sod|brun|nen** (*schweiz. für* Ziehbrunnen)
So|de, die; -, -n (*landsch., bes. nordd. für* Rasenstück; ziegelsteingroßes Stechtorfstück; *veraltet für* Salzsiederei)
So|dom (bibl. Stadt); - u. Gomorrha (Zustand der Lasterhaftigkeit; großes Durcheinander); *vgl.* Gomorrha; **So|do|mie,** die; -, ...ien ‹nlat.› (Geschlechtsverkehr mit Tieren); **So|do|mit,** der; -en, -en; ↑R 126 (Einwohner von Sodom; Sodomie Treibender); **so|do|mi|tisch; So|doms|ap|fel** (Gallapfel, ein Gerbemittel)
so|eben (↑R 132; vor einem Augenblick); sie kam soeben herein; *aber* sie hat es so eben (gerade) noch geschafft
Soest [zo:st] (Stadt in Nordrhein-Westfalen); **Soes|ter** (↑R 103); - Börde (Landstrich)
So|fa, das; -s, -s ‹arab.›; **So|fa-‿ecke** (↑R 132), **...kis|sen**
so|fern (falls); sofern er seine Pflicht getan hat, ..., *aber* die Sache liegt mir so fern, dass ...
Soff, der; -[e]s (*landsch. für* Suff); **Söf|fel, Söf|fer,** der; -s, - (*landsch. für* Trinker)
Sof|fit|te, die; -, -n *meist Plur.* ‹ital.› (Deckendekorationsstück einer Bühne); **Sof|fit|ten|lam|pe**
So|fia (Hptst. Bulgariens); **So|fi|a-er** ['zo:fiaər] *vgl.* Sofioter; **So|fie** [*auch* 'zɔfi] *vgl.* Sophia; **So|fi|o-ter** (↑R 103)
so|fort (in [sehr] kurzer Zeit [erfolgend], auf der Stelle); er soll sofort kommen; *aber* immer so fort (immer so weiter); **So|fort|bild-ka|me|ra; So|fort|hil|fe; so|for-tig;** -e Hilfe; **So|fort‿maß|nah-me, ...wir|kung**
Soft|drink, *auch* **Soft Drink** (↑R 33), der; -s, -s ‹engl.› (alkoholfreies Getränk); **Soft|eis,** das; -es (sahniges, weiches Speiseeis); drei -; **Sof|tie,** der; -s, -s (*ugs. für* Mann von sanftem, zärtlichem Wesen); **Soft|por|no,** der; -s, -s; **Soft|rock,** *auch* **Soft Rock** der; -[s] (leisere, melodischere Form der Rockmusik); **Soft|ware** [...wɛ:r], die; -, -s ‹„weiche Ware"› (*EDV* die nichtapparativen Bestandteile der Anlage; *Ggs.* Hardware)
Sog, der; -[e]s, -e (unter landwärts gerichteten Wellen seewärts ziehender Meeresstrom; saugende Luftströmung)
sog. = so genannt
so|gar (noch darüber hinaus); er kam sogar zu mir nach Hause; *aber* er hat so gar kein Vertrauen zu mir
so ge|nannt (*Abk.* sog.) *vgl.* so
sog|gen (sich in Kristallform niederschlagen [vom Salz in der verdampfenden Sole])
so|gleich (sofort); er soll sogleich kommen; *aber* sie sind sich alle so gleich, dass ...

Sohl|bank *Plur.* ...bänke (*Bauw.* Fensterbank); **Soh|le,** die; -, -n ‹lat.› (Fuß-, Talsohle; *Bergmannsspr.* untere Begrenzungsfläche einer Strecke; *landsch. auch für* Lüge); **soh|len** (*landsch. auch für* lügen); **Soh|len|gän|ger** (*Zool.* eine Gruppe von Säugetieren); **Soh|len|le|der,** Sohl|le|der; **...soh|lig** (z. B. doppelsohlig); **söh|lig** (*Bergmannsspr.* waagerecht); **Sohl|le|der** *vgl.* Sohlenleder

Sohn, der; -[e]s, Söhne; **Söhnchen; Soh|ne|mann** *(fam.);* **Soh|nes‿lie|be, ...pflicht**

sohr (*nordd. für* dürr, welk)

Sohr, der; -s (*nordd. für* Sodbrennen)

[1]**Söh|re,** die; - (Teil des Hessischen Berglandes)

[2]**Söh|re,** die; - (*nordd. für* Dürre); **söh|ren** (*nordd. für* verdorren)

soig|niert [soa'nji:rt] (↑R 130) ‹franz.› (*veraltend für* gepflegt)

Soi|ree [soa're:], die; -, ...reen ‹franz.› (Abendgesellschaft)

So|ja, die; -, ...jen ‹jap.-niederl.› (eiweiß- u. fetthaltige Nutzpflanze); **So|ja‿boh|ne, ...mehl, ...öl, ...so|ße**

So|jus [sɔ'jus] ‹russ., „Bund, Bündnis"› (*Bez. für* eine Raumschiffserie der ehem. UdSSR)

So|kra|tes (↑R 130; griech. Philosoph); **Sok|ra|tik,** die; - ‹griech.› (Lehrart des Sokrates); **Sok|ra|ti|ker** (Schüler des Sokrates; Verfechter der Lehre des Sokrates); **sok|ra|tisch;** -e Lehrart; die sokratische Lehre (Lehre des Sokrates)

[1]**Sol** (röm. Sonnengott); [2]**Sol,** der; -[s], -[s] ‹span.› (peruan. Münzeinheit); 5 - (↑R 90)

[3]**Sol,** das; -s, -e (*Chemie* kolloide Lösung)

so|lang, so|lan|ge (während, währenddessen); solang[e] ich krank war, bist du bei mir geblieben; lies den Brief, ich warte solang[e]; *aber* so lang[e] wie *od.* als möglich; dreimal so lang[e] wie ...; du hast mich so lange warten lassen, dass ...; du musst so lange warten, bis ...

So|la|nin, das; -s ‹lat.› (giftiges Alkaloid verschiedener Nachtschattengewächse, bes. der Kartoffel); **So|la|num,** das; -s, ...nen (*Bot.* Nachtschattengewächs)

so|lar ‹lat.› (auf die Sonne bezüglich, von der Sonne herrührend); **So|lar‿au|to, ...bat|te|rie** (Sonnenbatterie), **...ener|gie** (↑R 132), **...farm; So|la|ri|sa|ti|on,** die; -, -en (*Fotogr.* Erscheinung der Umkehrung der Lichteinwirkung bei starker Überbelichtung des Films); **so|la|risch** *vgl.* solar; **So|la|ri|um,** das; -s, ...ien [...i̯ən] (Anlage für künstliche Sonnenbäder unter UV-Bestrahlung); **So|lar‿jahr** *(Astron.),* **...kol|lek|tor** *(Energietechnik),* **...kon|stan|te** *(Meteor.),* **...kraft|werk, ...öl** (das; -[e]s; ein Mineralöl), **...ple|xus** ([*auch* ...plɛ...]; der; -; *Med.* Nervengeflecht im Oberbauch, Sonnengeflecht), **...tech|nik** (die; -), **...zel|le** (Sonnenzelle)

So|la|wech|sel ‹ital.; dt.› (*Finanzw.* Wechsel, bei dem sich der Aussteller selbst zur Zahlung verpflichtet)

Sol|bad

solch; -er, -e, -es; solch ein Widersinn; ein solcher Widersinn; solch einer, solch eine, solch ein[e]s; solch feiner Stoff *od.* solcher feine Stoff; mit solch schönem Schirm, mit solch einem schönen Schirm, mit einem solch[en] schönen Schirm, in solcher erzieherischen, *seltener* erzieherischer Absicht; solch gute *od.* solche guten, *auch* gute Menschen; das Leben solch frommer Leute *od.* solcher frommen, *auch* frommer Leute; solche Gefangenen, *auch* Gefangene; es gibt immer solche und solche; **sol|cher|art;** solcherart Dinge, *aber* Dinge solcher Art; **sol|cher|ge|stalt** *(veraltend); aber* er war von solcher Gestalt, dass ...; **sol|cher|lei; sol|cher|ma|ßen; sol|cher|wei|se;** *aber* in solcher Weise

Sold, der; -[e]s, -e *(Milit.)* ‹lat.›; **Sol|da|nel|le,** die; -, -n ‹ital.› (Alpenglöckchen); **Sol|dat,** der; -en, -en (↑R 126) ‹lat.›; **Sol|da|ten‿fried|hof, ...le|ben** (das; -s), **...rock** (*vgl.* [1]Rock), **...spra|che** (die; -), **...stand** (der; -[e]s); **Sol|da|ten|tum,** das; -s; **Sol|da|tes|ka,** die; -, ...ken (rücksichtslos u. gewalttätig vorgehendes Militär); **Sol|da|tin; sol|da|tisch; Sold|buch; Söld|ling** *(abwertend);* **Söld|ner; Söld|ner‿füh|rer, ...heer; Sol|do,** der; -s, *Plur.* -s *u.* ...di (frühere ital. Münze)

So|le, die; -, -n (kochsalzhaltiges Wasser); **Sol|ei** (in Salzlake eingelegtes hart gekochtes Ei); **So|len|lei|tung**

so|lenn ‹lat.› (*veraltend für* feierlich, festlich); **So|len|ni|tät,** die; -, -en (*veraltend für* Feierlichkeit)

So|le|no|id, das; -[e]s, -e ‹griech.› (*Physik* zylindrische Metallspule, die bei Stromdurchfluss wie ein Stabmagnet wirkt)

Sol|fa|ta|ra, Sol|fa|ta|re, die; -, ...ren ‹ital.› (Ausdünstung schwefelhaltiger heißer Dämpfe in ehem. Vulkangebieten)

sol|feg|gie|ren [...fɛ'dʒi:...] ‹ital.› (*Musik* Solfeggien singen); **Sol|feg|gio** [...'fɛdʒo], das; -s, ...ggien [...'fɛdʒiən] (auf die Solmisationssilben gesungene Übung)

Sol|fe|ri|no (ital. Dorf)

So|li (*Plur. von* Solo)

so|lid, *österr. nur so, od.* so|li|de ‹lat.› (fest; haltbar, zuverlässig; gediegen); **So|li|dar‿bei|trag, ...ge|mein|schaft, ...haf|tung** (die; -; *Rechtsw., Wirtsch.* Haftung von Gesamtschuldnern); **so|li|da|risch** (gemeinsam, übereinstimmend, eng verbunden); **so|li|da|ri|sie|ren,** sich (sich solidarisch erklären); **So|li|da|ri|sie|rung; So|li|da|ris|mus,** der; - (Richtung der [kath.] Sozialphilosophie); **So|li|da|ri|tät,** die; - (Zusammengehörigkeitsgefühl, Gemeinsinn); **So|li|da|ri|täts‿er|klä|rung, ...ge|fühl, ...spen|de, ...streik; So|li|dar‿pakt** *(Politik),* **...schuld|ner** (*Rechtsw.* Gesamtschuldner); **so|li|de** *vgl.* solid; **so|li|die|ren** (*veraltet für* befestigen, versichern); **So|li|di|tät,** die; - (Festigkeit, Haltbarkeit; Zuverlässigkeit; Mäßigkeit)

So|li|lo|qui|um, das; -s, ...ien [...i̯ən] ‹lat.› (Selbstgespräch in der antiken Bekenntnisliteratur)

So|ling, die; -, *Plur.* -s, *auch* -e; *auch* das *od.* der; -s, -s (ein Rennsegelboot)

So|lin|gen (Stadt in Nordrhein-Westfalen); **So|lin|ger** (↑R 103); - Stahl

So|lip|sis|mus (↑R 132), der; - ‹lat.› (philos. Lehre, nach der die Welt für den Menschen nur in seinen Vorstellungen besteht); **So|lip|sist,** der; -en, -en; ↑R 126 (Vertreter des Solipsismus); **so|lip|sis|tisch**

So|list, der; -en, -en; ↑R 126 (Einzelsänger, -spieler); **So|lis|ten|kon|zert; So|lis|tin; so|lis|tisch; So|li|tär,** der; -s, -e ‹franz.› (einzeln gefasster Edelstein; Brettspiel für eine Person); **So|li|tude** [...'ty:d], **So|li|tü|de,** die; -, -n ‹„Einsamkeit"› (Name von Schlössern u. a.)

Sol|jan|ka, die; -, -s ‹russ.› (eine Fleischsuppe)

[1]**Soll,** das; -s, Sölle ‹*zu* Suhle› (*Geol.* runder See eiszeitl. Herkunft)

[2]**Soll,** das; -[s], -[s] (*Bergmannsspr. auch für* festgelegte Fördermenge); das - und [das] Haben; das -

und das Muss; **Soll|be|stand** (↑R 24); **Soll|be|trag** (↑R 24); **Soll|bruch|stel|le** (↑R 24; *Technik*); **Soll|ein|nah|me** (↑R 24); **sol|len;** ich habe gesollt, *aber* ich hätte das nicht tun -

Söl|ler, der; -s, - ‹lat.› (*Archit.* offene Plattform oberer Stockwerke; *landsch. für* Dachboden)

Sol|ling, der; -s (Teil des Weserberglandes)

Soll-Ist-Ver|gleich; ↑R 28 (*Wirtsch.* Gegenüberstellung von Soll- und Istzahlen); **Soll|kauf|mann** (↑R 24); **Soll|kos|ten** *Plur.* (↑R 24); **Soll|kos|ten|rech|nung** (↑R 24); **Soll|sei|te** (↑R 24); **Soll|stär|ke** (↑R 24), die; -, -n; **Soll|zahl** (↑R 24; *Wirtsch.*); **Soll|zeit** (↑R 24; *Wirtsch.*); **Soll|zin|sen** (↑R 24) *Plur.*

Sol|mi|sa|ti|on, die; - ‹ital.› (*Musik* Tonleitersystem mit den Silben do, re, mi, fa, sol, la, si); **Sol|mi|sa|ti|ons|sil|be; sol|mi|sie|ren**

Soln|ho|fen (Ort in Mittelfranken); **Soln|ho|fe|ner** *od.* **Soln|ho|fer** (↑R 103); Solnhof[en]er Schiefer, Platten

so|lo ‹ital.› (*bes. Musik* als Solist; *ugs. für* allein); ganz -; - tanzen; **So|lo,** das; -s, *Plur.* -s *u.* ...li (Einzelvortrag, -spiel, -tanz); ein - singen, spielen, tanzen; **So|lo‿ge|sang, ...in|stru|ment, ...kan|ta|te, ...ma|schi|ne** *(Motorsport)*

So|lon (griech. Gesetzgeber); **so|lo|nisch** (weise wie Solon); solonische Weisheit; die solonische Gesetzgebung

So|lo‿part, ...sän|ger, ...sän|ge|rin, ...stim|me, ...sze|ne (Einzelauftritt, -spiel), **...tanz, ...tän|zer, ...tän|ze|rin**

So|lo|thurn (Kanton u. Stadt in der Schweiz); **So|lo|thur|ner** (↑R 103); **so|lo|thur|nisch**

So|lö|zis|mus, der; -, ...men ‹griech.› (*Rhet.* grober Sprachfehler)

Sol|per, der; -s („Salpeter") (*westmitteld. für* Salzbrühe); **Sol|per|fleisch** (*westmitteld. für* Pökelfleisch)

Sol‿quel|le, ...salz

Sol|sche|ni|zyn (russ. Schriftsteller)

Sols|ti|ti|um [...st...] (↑R 132), das; -s, ...ien [...i̯ən] ‹lat.› (*Astron.* Sonnenwende)

Sol|ti [ˈʃɔlti], György [djørdç] (ung. Dirigent)

so|lu|bel ‹lat.› (*Chemie* löslich, auflösbar); ...ub|le (↑R 130) Mittel; **So|lu|ti|on,** die; -, -en (Arzneimittellösung); **sol|va|bel** [...v...] (auflösbar; *veraltet für* zahlungsfähig); ...ab|le (↑R 130) Geschäftspartner

Sol|veig [ˈzɔlvai̯g] ‹skand.› (w. Vorn.)

Sol|vens [...v...], das; -, *Plur.* ...ven|zien [...i̯ən] *u.* ...ven|tia ‹lat.› (*Med.* [Schleim] lösendes Mittel); **sol|vent** (*bes. Wirtsch.* zahlungsfähig); **Sol|venz,** die; -, -en (Zahlungsfähigkeit); **sol|vie|ren** (eine Schuld abzahlen; *Chemie* auflösen)

Sol|was|ser *Plur.* ...wässer

So|ma, das; -s, -ta ‹griech.› (*Med.* Körper [im Gegensatz zu Geist, Seele, Gemüt])

So|ma|li, der; -[s], -[s] (Angehöriger eines ostafrik. Volkes); **So|ma|lia** (Staat in Afrika); **So|ma|li|er; So|ma|li|e|rin; So|ma|li|land,** das; -[e]s (nordostafrik. Landschaft); **so|ma|lisch**

so|ma|tisch ‹griech.› (*Med.* das Soma betreffend, körperlich); **so|ma|to|gen** (körperlich bedingt); **So|ma|to|lo|gie,** die; - (Lehre vom menschl. Körper)

Somb|re|ro (↑R 130), der; -s, -s ‹span.› (breitrandiger, leichter Strohhut)

so|mit [*auch* ˈzo:...] (mithin, also); somit bist du der Aufgabe enthoben; *aber* ich nehme es so (in dieser Form, auf diese Weise) mit

Som|me|li|er [...ˈi̯e:], der; -s, -s ‹franz.› (Weinkellner)

Som|mer, der; -s, -; Sommer wie Winter; sommers *(vgl. d.)*; sommersüber *(vgl. d.)*; **Som|mer‿abend** (↑R 132), **...an|fang, ...an|zug, ...auf|ent|halt, ...fahr|plan, ...fe|ri|en** *(Plur.)*, **...fest, ...fri|sche** (die; -, -n; *veraltend*); **Som|mer|frisch|ler** *(veraltend)*; **Som|mer‿gers|te, ...ge|trei|de, ...halb|jahr, ...hit|ze; söm|me|rig** (*landsch. für* einen Sommer alt); -e Karpfen; **Som|mer‿kleid, ...klei|dung, ...kol|lek|ti|on** *(Mode)*, **...kurs; som|mer|lich; Som|mer‿loch** (*ugs.; svw.* Saure-Gurken-Zeit), **...mo|nat; som|mern** (*veraltet für* sommerlich werden); es sommert; **söm|mern** (*landsch. für* sonnen; [Vieh] im Sommer auf der Weide halten); ich ...ere (↑R 16); **Som|mer|nacht; Som|mer|nachts|traum** (Komödie von Shakespeare); **Som|mer‿olym|pi|a|de** (↑R 132), **...pau|se, ...preis, ...re|gen, ...rei|se, ...re|si|denz; som|mers** (↑R 46), *aber* des Sommers; **Som|mer|saat; Som|mers|an|fang** (*svw.* Sommeranfang); **Som|mer‿schluss|ver|kauf, ...schuh, ...se|mes|ter, ...ski|ge|biet, ...smog, ...son|nen|wen|de, ...spie|le** *(Plur.)*, **...spros|se** *(meist Plur.)*; **som|mer|spros|sig; som|mers|über** (↑R 132), *aber* den Sommer über; **Som|mers|zeit,** die; - (Jahreszeit; *vgl.* Sommerzeit); **Som|mer|tag; som|mer|tags** (↑R 46); **Som|mer|the|a|ter,** das; -s (*ugs. auch für* Aktivitäten von Politikern während der Parlamentsferien); **Som|me|rung,** die; -, -en (*Landw.* Sommergetreide); **Söm|me|rung** (*landsch. für* das Sömmern); **Som|mer‿vo|gel** (*landsch., bes. schweiz. mdal. für* Schmetterling), **...weg, ...wet|ter** (das; -s), **...zeit** (die; -; Jahreszeit; Vorverlegung der Stundenzählung während des Sommers; *vgl.* Sommerszeit)

som|nam|bul ‹lat.› (schlafwandelnd, mondsüchtig); **Som|nam|bu|le,** der *u.* die; -n, -n; ↑R 5 ff. (Schlafwandler[in]); **Som|nam|bu|lis|mus,** der; - (Schlafwandeln; Mondsüchtigkeit)

so|nach [*auch* ˈzo:...] (folglich, also), *aber* sprich es so nach, wie ich es dir vorspreche

So|na|gramm, das; -s, -e ‹lat.; griech.› *(Phonetik)*; **So|nant,** der; -en, -en (↑R 126) ‹lat.› (*Sprachw.* Silben bildender Laut); **so|nan|tisch** (*Sprachw.* Silben bildend); **So|na|te,** die; -, -n ‹ital.› (aus drei od. vier Sätzen bestehendes Musikstück für ein od. mehrere Instrumente); **So|na|ti|ne,** die; -, -n (kleinere, leichtere Sonate)

Son|de, die; -, -n ‹franz.› (*Med.* Instrument zum Einführen in Körper- od. Wundkanäle; *Technik* Vorrichtung zur Förderung von Erdöl od. Erdgas; *auch kurz für* Raumsonde)

son|der (*veraltet für* ohne); *Präp. mit Akk.:* sonder allen Zweifel, sonder Furcht; **Son|der‿ab|druck** (*Plur.* ...drucke), **...ab|schrei|bung** *(Wirtsch.)*, **...ab|zug, ...an|fer|ti|gung, ...an|ge|bot, ...aus|füh|rung, ...aus|ga|be; son|der|bar; son|der|ba|rer|wei|se; Son|der|bar|keit; Son|der‿be|auf|trag|te, ...be|hand|lung, ...bei|trag, ...be|wa|cher** *(Sportspr.)*, **...bot|schaf|ter, ...brief|mar|ke, ...bund** (der; z. B. in der Schweiz 1845–47)

Son|der|burg (dän. Stadt)

Son|der‿bus, ...de|po|nie, ...de|zer|nat, ...druck (*Plur.* ...drucke), **...ein|satz, ...fahrt, ...fall** (der), **...form, ...ge|neh|mi|gung; son|der|glei|chen; Son|der|heft; Son|der|heit** *(selten)*; in Sonderheit (*geh. für* besonders, im Besonderen); in Sonderheit[,] wenn (↑R 88); **Son|der‿in|te|res|sen** *(Plur.)*, **...klas|se, ...kom|man|do, ...kom|mis|si|on, ...kon|to, ...kos|ten** *(Plur.)*; **son|der|lich;** (↑R 47:) nichts Sonderliches (Ungewöhnliches); **Son|der|ling; Son|der‿ma|schi|ne, ...mel|dung, ...müll** (gefährliche [Gift]stoffe enthaltender Müll); **[1]son|dern;** *Konj.*: nicht nur der Bruder, sondern auch die Schwester; **[2]son|dern;** ich ...ere (↑R 16); **Son|der‿num|mer, ...preis, ...ra|batt, ...ra|ti|on, ...recht, ...re|ge|lung** *od.* **...reg|lung; son|ders;** samt und -; **Son|der‿schicht, ...schu|le, ...sen|dung**

Son|ders|hau|sen (Stadt südl. von Nordhausen); **Son|ders|häu|ser** (↑R 103)

Son|der‿spra|che *(Sprachw.)*, **...sta|tus, ...stel|lung, ...stem|pel, ...steu|er** (die); **Son|de|rung; Son|der‿ur|laub, ...ver|kauf, ...wunsch, ...zie|hungs|recht** (*meist Plur.; Wirtsch.; Abk.* SZR), **...zug**

son|die|ren ‹franz.› ([mit der Sonde] untersuchen; ausforschen, vorfühlen); **Son|die|rung; Son|die|rungs|ge|spräch**

So|nett, das; -[e]s, -e ‹ital.› (eine Gedichtform)

Song, der; -s, -s ‹engl.› (Sonderform des Liedes, oft mit sozialkrit. Inhalt)

Son|ja (w. Vorn.)

Sonn|abend (↑R 132), der; -s, -e; *Abk.* Sa.; *vgl.* Dienstag; **sonn|abend|lich** (↑R 132); **sonn|abends** (↑R 46 *u.* 132); *vgl.* Dienstag; **Son|ne,** die; -, -n; (↑R 108:) Gasthof „Zur Goldenen Sonne"

Son|ne|berg (Stadt am Südrand des Thüringer Waldes)

son|nen; sich -; **Son|nen‿an|be|ter** (*scherzh. für* jmd., der sich gerne sonnt u. bräunt), **...an|be|te|rin; son|nen|arm;** -e Jahre; **Son|nen‿auf|gang, ...bad; son|nen|ba|den** *meist nur im Infinitiv u. Partizip II gebr.*; sonnengebadet; **Son|nen‿bahn, ...ball** (der; -[e]s), **...bank** (*Plur.* ...bänke; Gerät zum Bräunen), **...bat|te|rie** (Vorrichtung, mit der Sonnenenergie in elektr. Energie umgewandelt wird); **Son|nen‿blen|de, ...blu|me; Son|nen|blu|men|kern; Son|nen‿brand, ...bräu|ne** (die; -), **...bril|le, ...cre|me, ...dach, ...deck; son|nen|durch|flu|tet** *(geh.)*; **Son|nen‿ener|gie** (↑R 132), **...fins|ter|nis, ...fleck** (der; -[e]s, -e[n]); **son|nen|ge|bräunt; Son|nen‿ge|flecht** (*für* Solarplexus), **...glast** *(geh.)*, **...glut** (die; -), **...gott; son|nen|halb** (*schweiz. für* auf der Sonnenseite eines Bergtales); **son|nen‿hell, ...hung|rig; Son|nen‿hut** (der), **...jahr; son|nen|klar** *(ugs.)*; **Son|nen‿kol|lek|tor** (zur Wärmegewinnung aus Sonnenenergie), **...kö|nig** (der; -s; Beiname Ludwigs XIV. von Frankreich), **...kraft|werk** (Anlage zur Nutzung der Sonnenenergie), **...krin|gel, ...kult, ...licht** (das; -[e]s), **...nä|he, ...öl, ...pro|tu|be|ran|zen** *(Plur.)*, **...rad, ...schei|be, ...schein** (der; -[e]s), **...schirm, ...schutz; Son|nen|schutz‿creme, ...mit|tel** (das), **...öl; Son|nen|sei|te; son|nen|se|lig; Son|nen‿stäub|chen, ...stich, ...strahl, ...sturm** *(Astron.)*, **...sys|tem, ...tag, ...tau** (der; eine Pflanze), **...tier|chen** (ein Einzeller), **...uhr, ...un|ter|gang; son|nen|ver|brannt; Son|nen‿wa|gen** *(Mythol.)*, **...wär|me; Son|nen|wär|me|kraft|werk; Son|nen‿war|te** (Observatorium zur Sonnenbeobachtung); **Son|nen|wen|de;** *vgl.* [1]Wende; **Son|nen|wend|fei|er,** Sonn|wend|fei|er; **Son|nen|zel|le** (zur Erzeugung von elektr. Energie aus Sonnenenergie); **son|nig; Sonn|sei|te** (*österr. u. schweiz. neben* Sonnenseite); **sonn|sei|tig** *(österr.)*; **Sonn|tag** (*Abk.* So.); des Sonntags, *aber* (↑R 46): sonntags; (↑R 23:) sonn- und alltags, sonn- und feiertags, sonn- und festtags, sonn- und werktags; *vgl.* Dienstag; **Sonn|tag|abend** (↑R 132); *vgl.* Dienstagabend; am -; **sonn|tä|gig;** *vgl.* ...tägig; **sonn|täg|lich;** *vgl.* ...täglich; **sonn|tags** (↑R 46); *vgl.* Dienstag *u.* Sonntag; **Sonn|tags‿an|zug** *(veraltend)*, **...ar|beit, ...aus|ga|be, ...bei|la|ge, ...bra|ten, ...dienst, ...fah|rer** *(iron.)*, **...jä|ger** *(iron.)*, **...kind, ...ma|ler, ...re|de** (unbedeutende Rede), **...rei|ter** *(iron.)*, **...ru|he, ...schu|le** (*früher für* Kindergottesdienst); **sonn|ver|brannt** (*österr. u. schweiz. für* sonnenverbrannt); **Sonn|wend|fei|er** *vgl.* Sonnenwendfeier

Son|ny|boy ['sani..., *auch* 'zɔni...], der; -s, -s ‹engl.› (sympathischer [junger] Mann mit unbeschwert-fröhlichem Charme)

So|no|graph, der; -en, -en; ↑R 126 ‹lat.; griech.›; **So|no|gra|phie,** die; -, ...ien (*Med.* Untersuchung mit Ultraschall)

so|nor ‹lat.› (klangvoll, volltönend); **So|no|ri|tät,** die; - (Klangfülle)

sonst; hast du sonst (außerdem) noch eine Frage, sonst noch etwas auf dem Herzen?; ist sonst jemand, sonst wer bereit mitzuhelfen?; da könnte ja sonst jemand, sonst wer (*ugs. für* irgendjemand) kommen; ich hätte fast sonst was (*ugs. für* wer weiß was) gesagt; kann ich Ihnen sonst wie helfen?; sie könnte ja sonst wo sein; **sons|tig;** die sonstigen Möglichkeiten; (↑R 47:) alles Sonstige besprechen wir morgen (*vgl.* übrig); **sonst je|mand, sonst was** usw. *vgl.* sonst

Sont|ho|fen (Ort im Allgäu)

so|oft; sooft du zu mir kommst, immer ..., *aber* ich habe es dir so oft gesagt, dass ...

Soon|wald, der; -[e]s (Gebirgszug im südöstl. Hunsrück)

Soor, der; -[e]s, -e (*Med.* Pilzbelag in der Mundhöhle); **Soor|pilz**

So|phia, So|phie [*auch* 'zɔfi], *auch* Sofie (w. Vorn.); **So|phi|en|kir|che** (↑R 95); **So|phis|ma,** das; -s, ...men ‹griech.› *u.* **So|phis|mus,** der; -, ...men (Trugschluss; Spitzfindigkeit); **So|phist,** der; -en, -en; ↑R 126 (jmd., der spitzfindig, haarspalterisch argumentiert, Wortverdreher; *urspr.* griech. Wanderlehrer); **So|phis|te|rei** (spitzfindige Argumentation, Haarspalterei); **So|phis|tik,** die; - (griech. philos. Lehre; sophistische Denkart, Argumentationsweise); **so|phis|tisch** (spitzfindig, haarspalterisch)

so|phok|le|isch (↑R 130); sophokleisches Denken (nach Art des Sophokles), sophokleische (von Sophokles stammende) Tragödien; **So|phok|les** (griech. Tragiker)

Soph|ro|sy|ne (↑R 130), die; - ‹griech.› (antike Tugend der Besonnenheit)

So|por, der; -s ‹lat.› (*Med.* starke Benommenheit); **so|po|rös** (benommen)

So|pot ['sɔ...] (poln. Stadt an der Ostsee; *vgl.* Zoppot)

Sop|ran (↑R 130), der; -s, -e ‹ital.› (höchste Frauen- od. Knabenstimme; Sopransänger[in]); **Sop|ra|nist,** der; -en, -en; ↑R 126 (Knabe mit Sopranstimme); **Sop|ra|nis|tin**

Sop|ra|por|te, *auch* Sup|ra|por|te (↑R 130), die; -, -n ‹ital.› ([reliefartiges] Wandfeld über einer Tür)

Sop|ron ['ʃoprɔn] (↑R 130; ung. Stadt); *vgl.* Ödenburg

So|ra|bist, der; -en, -en; ↑R 126; **So|ra|bis|tik,** die; - (Wissenschaft von der sorbischen Sprache u. Kultur); **so|ra|bis|tisch**
So|ra|ya (w. Vorn.)
Sor|be, der; -n, -n; ↑R 126 (Angehöriger einer westslaw. Volksgruppe); **Sor|ben|sied|lung**
Sor|bet [*auch* sɔr'be], der *od.* das; -s, -s; *vgl.* Sorbett; **Sor|bett** *u.* Scher|bett, der *od.* das; -[e]s, -e ⟨arab.⟩ (eisgekühltes Getränk, Halbgefrorenes)
Sor|bin|säu|re (*Chemie* ein Konservierungsstoff)
sor|bisch; Sor|bisch, das; -[s] (Sprache); *vgl.* Deutsch; **Sor|bi|sche,** das; -n; *vgl.* Deutsche, das
[1]**Sor|bit** [*auch* ...'bit], der; -s ⟨lat.⟩ (*Chemie* ein sechswertiger Alkohol; ein pflanzlicher Wirkstoff)
[2]**Sor|bit,** der; -s ⟨nach dem engl. Forscher Sorby⟩ (Bestandteil der Stähle)
Sor|bonne [sɔr'bɔn], die; - (die älteste Pariser Universität)
Sor|di|ne, die; -, -n *u.* **Sor|di|no,** der; -s, *Plur.* -s *u.* ...ni ⟨ital.⟩ (*Musik* Dämpfer); *vgl.* con sordino; **Sor|dun,** der *od.* das; -s, -e (Schalmei des 16. u. 17. Jh.s; früheres dunkel klingendes Orgelregister)
So|re, die; -, -n ⟨Gaunerspr.⟩ (Diebesgut, Hehlerware)
Sor|ge, die; -, -n; - tragen (↑R 39); **sor|gen;** sich -; **Sor|gen|bre|cher** (*scherzh. für* alkohol. Getränk, bes. Wein); **Sor|gen|fal|te; sor|gen|frei; Sor|gen‿kind, ...last; sor|gen‿los** (ohne Sorgen), **...schwer, ...voll; Sor|ge‿pflicht** (die; -), **...recht** (das; -[e]s; *Rechtsw.*); **Sorg|falt,** die; -; **sorg|fäl|tig; Sorg|fäl|tig|keit,** die; -; **Sorg|falts|pflicht**
Sor|gho [...go], der; -s, -s ⟨ital.⟩ *u.* **Sor|ghum** [...gum], das; -s, -s (eine Getreidepflanze)
sorg|lich *(veraltend);* **sorg|los** (ohne Sorgfalt; unbekümmert); **Sorg|lo|sig|keit,** die; -; **sorg|sam; Sorg|sam|keit,** die; -
Sorp|ti|on, die; -, -en ⟨lat.⟩ (*Chemie* Aufnahme eines Gases od. gelösten Stoffes durch einen anderen festen od. flüssigen Stoff)
Sor|rent (ital. Stadt)
Sor|te, die; -, -n ⟨lat.⟩ (Art, Gattung; Wert, Güte); **Sor|ten** *Plur.* (*Bankw.* ausländ. Geldsorten, Devisen); **Sor|ten‿fer|ti|gung** *(Wirtsch.),* **...ge|schäft, ...han|del** (*Börse; vgl.* [1]Handel), **...kal|ku|la|ti|on** *(Wirtsch.),* **...kurs** *(Börse),* **...markt** *(Börse),* **...pro|duk|ti|on** *(Wirtsch.);* **sor|ten|rein; Sor|ten‿ver|zeich|nis, ...zet|tel; sor|tie|ren** (sondern, auslesen, sichten); **Sor|tie|rer; Sor|tie|re|rin; Sor|tier|ma|schi|ne; sor|tiert** (*auch für* hochwertig); **Sor|tie|rung; Sor|ti|le|gi|um,** das; -s, ...ien [...iən] (Weissagung durch Lose); **Sor|ti|ment,** das; -[e]s, -e ⟨ital.⟩ (Warenangebot, -auswahl eines Kaufmanns; *auch für* Sortimentsbuchhandel); **Sor|ti|men|ter** (Angehöriger des Sortimentsbuchhandels, Ladenbuchhändler); **Sor|ti|ments‿buch|han|del, ...buch|händ|ler**
SOS [ɛsǀo:'ɛs] (internationales Seenotzeichen, *gedeutet als* save our ship ['se:v ‚auə(r) 'ʃip] = Rette[t] unser Schiff! *od.* save our souls ['se:v ‚auə(r) 'so:lz] = Rette[t] unsere Seelen!)
so|sehr; sosehr ich diesen Plan auch billige, ...; *aber* er lief so sehr, dass ...
SOS-Kin|der|dorf; ↑R 26 (Einrichtung zur Betreuung und Erziehung elternloser od. verlassener Kinder in familienähnlichen Gruppen)
so|so (*ugs. für* nicht [gerade] gut; ungünstig); es steht damit soso
SOS-Ruf (↑R 26); *vgl.* SOS
So|ße [*österr.* zo:s], die; -, -n ⟨franz.⟩ (Brühe, Tunke; *in der Tabakbereitung* Beize); *vgl.* Sauce; **so|ßen; So|ßen‿koch, ...löf|fel, ...re|zept, ...schüs|sel**
sost. = sostenuto
sos|te|nu|to ⟨ital.⟩ (*Musik* gehalten, getragen; *Abk.* sost.)
So|ter, der; -, -e ⟨griech.⟩ (Retter, Heiland; Ehrentitel Jesu Christi); **So|te|ri|o|lo|gie,** die; - (*Theol.* Lehre vom Erlösungswerk Jesu Christi, Heilslehre); **so|te|ri|o|lo|gisch**
Sott, der *od.* das; -[e]s (*nordd. für* Ruß)
Sot|ti|se [...'ti:zə], die; -, -n ⟨franz.⟩ (*veraltet, aber noch landsch. für* Dummheit; Grobheit)
sot|to vo|ce [- 'vo:tʃə] ⟨ital.⟩ (*Musik* halblaut, gedämpft)
Sou [su:], der; -, -s [su:] ⟨franz.⟩ (franz. Münze im Wert von 5 Centimes)
Soub|ret|te [zu..., *auch* su...] (↑R 130), die; -, -n ⟨franz.⟩ (Sängerin heiterer Sopranpartien in Oper u. Operette)
Sou|chong ['zu:ʃɔŋ, *auch* 'su:...], der; -[s], -e ⟨chin.-franz.⟩ (chin. Tee mit größeren, breiten Blättern); **Sou|chong|tee**
Souf|flé, *eindeutschend* **Souf|flee** [zu'fle:, *auch* su...] (↑R 33 *u.* 130), das; -s, -s ⟨franz.⟩ (*Gastron.* Eierauflauf); **Souf|fleur,** [zu'flø:r, *auch* su...] der; -s, -e (*Theater* jmd., der souffliert); **Souf|fleur|kas|ten; Souf|fleu|se,** [...'flø:zə] die; -, -n; **souf|flie|ren**
Soul [so:l], der; -s ⟨amerik.⟩ (Jazz od. Popmusik mit starker Betonung des Expressiven)
Sò|ul [sɔ'ul] *u.* **Sö|ul** *vgl.* Seoul
Sound [saunt], der; -s, -s ⟨amerik.⟩ (*Musik* Klang[wirkung]; musikalische Stilrichtung)
so|und|so (*ugs. für* unbestimmt wie ...); soundso breit, groß, viel usw.; Paragraph soundso; *aber* etwas so und so (so und wieder anders) erzählen; (↑R 49:) [der] Herr Soundso; **so|und|so|viel|te;** der - Mai, Abschnitt usw., *aber* (↑R 50): am Soundsovielten des Monats
Sound|track ['saundtrɛk], der; -s, -s ⟨engl.⟩ (Tonspur eines Films; Filmmusik)
Sou|per [zu'pe:, *auch* su'pe:], das; -s, -s ⟨franz.⟩ (festliches Abendessen); **sou|pie|ren**
Sou|sa|phon [zuza...], das; -s, -e ⟨nach dem amerik. Komponisten J. Ph. Sousa⟩ (eine Basstuba)
Sous|chef ['su:ʃɛf], der; -s, -s ⟨franz.⟩ (*schweiz. für* Stellvertreter des [Bahnhofs]vorstandes; *Gastron.* Stellvertreter des Küchenchefs); **Sous|sol** [su'sɔl], das; -s, -s (*schweiz. für* Untergeschoss)
Sou|ta|che [zu'taʃ(ə), *auch* su...], die; -, -n (schmale, geflochtene Schnur für Besatzzwecke); **sou|ta|chie|ren**
Sou|ta|ne [zu..., *auch* su...] (↑R 33), die; -, -n ⟨franz.⟩ (Gewand der kath. Geistlichen); **Sou|ta|nel|le,** die; -, -n (bis ans Knie reichender Gehrock der kath. Geistlichen)
Sou|ter|rain [sutɛ'rɛ̃:, *auch* 'zu... *bzw.* 'su...], das; -s, -s ⟨franz.⟩ (Kellergeschoss); **Sou|ter|rain|woh|nung**
Sou|thamp|ton [sau'θɛmptən] (↑R 132; engl. Stadt)
Sou|ve|nir [zuvə'ni:r, *auch* su...], das; -s, -s ⟨franz.⟩ ([kleines Geschenk als] Andenken, Erinnerungsstück); **Sou|ve|nir|la|den**
sou|ve|rän [zuvə..., *auch* suvə...] ⟨franz.⟩ (unumschränkt; selbstständig; überlegen); **Sou|ve|rän,** der; -s, -e (Herrscher; Landes-, Oberherr; *bes. schweiz. für* Gesamtheit der Wähler); **Sou|ve|rä|ni|tät,** die; - (Unabhängigkeit; Landes-, Oberhoheit); **Sou|ve|rä|ni|täts|an|spruch**
Sove|reign ['sɔvrin], der; -s, -s ⟨engl.⟩ (frühere engl. Goldmünze)

so|viel; soviel ich weiß; *aber* so viel (dieses) für heute; sein Wort bedeutet so viel (dasselbe) wie ein Eid; rede nicht so viel!; du kannst haben, so viel [wie] du willst; du kannst so viel haben, wie du willst; so viel als; so viel wie (*Abk.* svw.); so viel wie (*älter:* als) möglich; noch einmal so viel; er hat halb, doppelt so viel Geld wie (*seltener:* als) du; so viel [Geld] wie du hat er auch; du weißt so viel, dass ...; ich habe so viel Zeit, dass ...; er musste so viel leiden; so viele Gelegenheiten; so vieles Schöne; **so|viel|mal,** *aber* so viele Male

so wahr; so wahr mir Gott helfe

so was (*ugs. für* so etwas)

Sow|chos [sɔf'xɔs, *auch* ...'çɔs], der; -, ...chose *u.* **Sow|cho|se,** die; -, -n, *österr. nur so* ‹russ.› (Staatsgut in der ehem. Sowjetunion)

so|weit; soweit ich es beurteilen kann, wird ...; *aber* es, die Sache ist so weit; es geht ihm so weit gut, nur ...; ich bin [noch nicht] so weit; so weit wie (*od.:*) als möglich will ich nachgeben; wirf den Ball so weit wie möglich; es kommt noch so weit, dass ...; so weit, so gut; ich kann den Weg so weit übersehen, dass ...; eine Sache so weit fördern, dass ...

so|we|nig; sowenig ich einsehen kann, dass ..., sowenig verstehe ich, dass ...; *aber* so wenig du auch gelernt hast, das wirst du doch wissen; ich bin so wenig (ebenso wenig) dazu bereit wie du; tu das so wenig wie *od.* als möglich; ich habe so wenig Geld wie du (wir beide haben gleich wenig oder keins); du hast so wenig gelernt, dass du die Prüfung nicht bestehen wirst

so|wie; sowie (sobald) er kommt, soll er nachsehen; *aber* so, wie ich ihn kenne, kommt er nicht; es kam so, wie ich es erwartet hatte; wissenschaftliche und technische sowie (und, und auch) schöne Literatur

so|wie|so

Sow|jet[1] (↑R 132), der; -s, -s ‹russ., „Rat"› (Form der Volksvertretung [*ehem. in der Sowjetunion*]; *nur Plur.:* Sowjetbürger); **Sow|jet‿ar|mee**[1], **...bür|ger; sow|je|tisch; Sow|jet‿re|pub|lik**[1], **...rus|se; sow|jet|rus|sisch**[1]; **Sow|jet‿russ|land**[1], **...stern, ...uni|on** (↑R 132, die; -; *Abk.* SU; bis 1991), **...volk**

---
[1] [*auch* 'sɔ... bzw. 'zɔ...]

so|wohl; sowohl die Eltern als [auch] *od.* wie [auch] die Kinder; *aber* du siehst so wohl aus, dass ...; **So|wohl-als-auch,** das; -

So|zi, der; -s, -s (*abwertende Kurzform von* Sozialdemokrat); **So|zia,** die; -, -s ‹lat.› (*meist scherzh. für* Beifahrerin auf einem Motorrad od. -roller); **so|zi|a|bel** (gesellschaftlich; gesellig; menschenfreundlich); ...ab|le (↑R 130) Menschen; **So|zi|a|bi|li|tät,** die; -; **so|zi|al** (die Gesellschaft, die Gemeinschaft betreffend, gesellschaftlich; Gemeinschafts..., Gesellschafts...; gemeinnützig, wohltätig); - schwach; der *od.* die - Schwache; (↑R 108:) die soziale Frage; soziale Sicherheit; sozialer Wohnungsbau; soziale Marktwirtschaft; **So|zi|al‿ab|ga|ben** (*Plur.*), **...amt, ...ar|beit** (die; -), **...ar|bei|ter** (Berufsbez.), **...ar|bei|te|rin** (Berufsbez.), **...bei|trä|ge** (*Plur.*), **...be|richt, ...be|ruf, ...de|mo|krat** (Mitglied [od. Anhänger] einer sozialdemokratischen Partei), **...de|mo|kra|tie** (die; -; Sozialdemokratische Partei; Gesamtheit der sozialdemokratischen Parteien), **...de|mo|kra|tin; so|zi|al|de|mo|kra|tisch,** *aber* (↑R 108): die Sozialdemokratische Partei Deutschlands (*Abk.* SPD); **So|zi|al‿ein|kom|men, ...ethik** (↑R 132), **...fall** (der), **...für|sor|ge** (*früher* Sozialhilfe der DDR), **...ge|richt, ...ge|richts|bar|keit** (die; -); **So|zi|al|ge|richts|ge|setz; So|zi|al‿ge|setz|ge|bung, ...hil|fe** (*amtl. für* Fürsorge); **So|zi|al|hil|fe‿emp|fän|ger, ...emp|fän|ge|rin; So|zi|al|hy|gi|e|ne; So|zi|a|li|sa|ti|on,** die; - (Prozess der Einordnung des Individuums in die Gesellschaft); **so|zi|a|li|sie|ren** (vergesellschaften, verstaatlichen; in die Gesellschaft einordnen); **So|zi|a|li|sie|rung; So|zi|a|lis|mus,** der; - (Gesamtheit der Theorien, polit. Bewegungen u. Staatsformen, die auf gemeinschaftlichen od. staatlichen Besitz der Produktionsmittel u. eine gerechte Verteilung der Güter hinzielen); **So|zi|a|list,** der; -en, -en (↑R 126); **So|zi|a|lis|tin; so|zi|a|lis|tisch;** -er Realismus (eine auf dem Marxismus gründende künstler. Richtung in den kommunist. Ländern), *aber* (↑R 108): die Sozialistische Internationale; Sozialistische Einheitspartei Deutschlands (*früher* Staatspartei der DDR; *Abk.* SED); **So|zi|al|kri|tik,** die; -; **so|zi|al|kri|tisch; So|zi|al‿kun|de** (die; -), **...las|ten** (*Plur.*), **...leis|tun|gen** (*Plur.*); **so|zi|al-li|be|ral,** *auch* sozialliberal; **So|zi|al‿lohn, ...neid, ...öko|no|mie** (↑R 132), **...pä|da|go|ge, ...pä|da|go|gik, ...pä|da|go|gin; so|zi|al|pä|da|go|gisch; So|zi|al‿part|ner** (*Politik*), **...plan, ...po|li|tik** (die; -), **...po|li|ti|ker, ...po|li|ti|ke|rin; so|zi|al|po|li|tisch; So|zi|al‿pres|ti|ge, ...pro|dukt** (*Wirtsch.*), **...pro|gramm, ...psy|cho|lo|gie, ...raum, ...recht** (das; -[e]s), **...re|form, ...ren|te, ...rent|ner, ...rent|ne|rin, ...staat** (*Plur.* ...staaten), **...sta|ti|on, ...sta|tis|tik, ...struk|tur, ...ta|rif, ...the|ra|pie, ...tou|ris|mus, ...tou|ris|tik, ...ver|mö|gen** (*Wirtsch.*), **...ver|si|che|rung** (*Abk.* SV); **So|zi|al|ver|si|che|rungs|bei|trag; so|zi|al|ver|träg|lich; So|zi|al‿wis|sen|schaf|ten** (*Plur.*), **...woh|nung, ...zu|la|ge; So|zi|e|tät** [...i|e...], die; -, -en (Gesellschaft; Genossenschaft); **So|zi|o|gra|phie,** die; - (*Soziol.* Darstellung der Formen menschlichen Zusammenlebens innerhalb bestimmter Räume u. Zeiten); **so|zi|o|kul|tu|rell** (die soziale Gruppe u. ihr Wertesystem betreffend); **So|zi|o|lekt,** der; -[e]s, -e (*Sprachw.* Sprachgebrauch von Gruppen, Schichten, Institutionen o. Ä.); **So|zi|o|lin|gu|is|tik** (*Sprachw.* wissenschaftl. Betrachtungsweise des Sprechverhaltens verschiedener Gruppen, Schichten o. Ä.); **so|zi|o|lin|gu|is|tisch; So|zi|o|lo|ge,** der; -n, -n (↑R 126) ‹lat.; griech.› (Erforscher u. Lehrer der Soziologie); **So|zi|o|lo|gie,** die; - (Wissenschaft zur Erforschung komplexer Erscheinungen und Zusammenhänge in der menschlichen Gesellschaft); **So|zi|o|lo|gin; so|zi|o|lo|gisch; So|zi|o|met|rie** (↑R 130), die; - (soziolog. Verfahren zur testmäßigen Erfassung der Gruppenstruktur); **so|zi|o|met|risch; so|zi|o|öko|no|misch** (↑R 132); **So|zi|us,** der; -, *Plur.* -se, *auch* ...zii ‹lat.› (*Wirtsch.* Teilhaber; Beifahrer[sitz]); **So|zi|us|sitz** (Rücksitz auf dem Motorrad)

so|zu|sa|gen (man könnte es so nennen, gewissermaßen), *aber* er versucht, es so zu sagen, dass es verständlich ist

Sp. = Spalte (*Buchw.*)

Spa [spa:] (belg. Stadt)

Space|lab ['spe:slɛb], das; -s, -s ‹engl.› (von ESA und NASA entwickeltes Raumlabor); **Space|shut|tle** ['spe:sʃat(ə)l], der; -s, -s

([wieder verwendbare] Raumfähre)
Spach|tel, der; -s, - *od., österr. nur,* die; -, -n, (ein Werkzeug); *vgl.* Spatel; **Spach|tel₋ma|le|rei, ...mas|se; spach|teln** (*ugs. auch für* [tüchtig] essen); ich ...[e]le (↑R 16)
spack (*landsch. für* dürr; eng)
Spa|da [ʃp..., *auch* sp...], die; -, -s ‹ital.› (*veraltend für* Degen); **Spa|dil|le** [...ˈdiljə], die; -, -n (höchste Trumpfkarte im Lomber)
Spa|er [sp...] ‹*zu* Spa› (↑R 103)
[1]**Spa|gat,** der, *österr. nur so, od.* das; -[e]s, -e ‹ital.› (*Gymnastik* Körperhaltung, bei der die Beine so weit gespreizt sind, dass sie eine Gerade bilden)
[2]**Spa|gat,** der; -[e]s, -e ‹ital.› (*südd., österr. für* Bindfaden)
Spa|gat|pro|fes|sor (*ugs. scherzh. für* Professor, dessen Universitäts- u. Wohnort weit auseinander liegen)
Spa|ghet|ti [...ˈgɛti], *eindeutschend* Spa|get|ti (↑R 33) *Plur.* ‹ital.› (lange, dünne, schnurartige Nudeln)
spä|hen; Spä|her; Spä|he|rei; Spä|he|rin
Spa|hi [sp..., *auch* ʃp...], der; -s, -s ‹pers., „Krieger"› (*früher* [adliger] Reiter im türk. Heer; Angehöriger einer aus nordafrik. Eingeborenen gebildeten franz. Reitertruppe)
Späh|trupp (*für* Patrouille)
Spa|ke, die; -, -n (*nordd. für* Hebel, Hebebaum); **spa|kig** (*nordd. für* schimmelig, stockfleckig)
Spa|la|to (*ital. Form von* Split)
Spa|lett, das; -[e]s, -e ‹ital.› (*österr. für* hölzerner Fensterladen); **Spa|lier,** das; -s, -e (Gitterwand; Doppelreihe von Personen als Ehrengasse); - bilden, stehen; **Spa|lier|baum; Spa|lier|obst**
Spalt, der; -[e]s, -e; **spalt|bar; Spalt|bar|keit,** die; -; **spalt|breit;** eine -e Öffnung; **Spalt|breit,** der; -; *nur in Wendungen wie* die Tür einen - öffnen; **Spält|chen; Spal|te,** die; -, -n (*österr. auch für* Schnitz, Scheibe; *Abk.* [*Buchw.*] Sp.); **spal|ten;** gespalten *u.* gespaltet; *in adjektivischem Gebrauch fast nur* gespalten; gespaltenes Holz, eine gespaltene Zunge; **Spal|ten|brei|te; spal|ten|lang;** ein -er Artikel, *aber* drei Spalten lang; **spal|ten|wei|se; spalt|er|big** (*Biol.*); **Spalt|fuß; ...spal|tig** (z. B. zweispaltig); **Spalt|le|der; Spalt₋pilz, ...pro|dukt** (bei der Atomkernspaltung); **Spal|tung; spal|tungs|ir|re** (*für* schizophren); **Spal|tungs|ir|re|sein,** das; -s
Span, der; -[e]s, Späne; **span|ab|he|bend** (↑R 40; *Technik*); **Spän|chen**
Spand|ril|le (↑R 130), die; -, -n ‹ital.› (*Archit.* Bogenzwickel)
spa|nen (Späne abheben); spanende Werkzeuge; [1]**spä|nen** (mit Metallspänen abreiben)
[2]**spä|nen** (*landsch. für* entwöhnen); **Span|fer|kel** (ein vom Muttertier noch nicht entwöhntes Ferkel)
Spän|gel|chen; Span|ge, die; -, -n; **Span|gen|schuh**
Spa|ni|el [ˈʃpa:ni̯əl, *engl.* ˈspɛni̯əl], der; -s, -s ‹engl.› (ein Jagd- u. Haushund); **Spa|ni|en; Spa|ni|er; Spa|ni|e|rin; Spa|ni|ol,** der; -s, -e ‹span.› (span. Schnupftabak); **Spa|ni|o|le,** der; -n, -n; ↑R 126 (Nachkomme von einst aus Spanien vertriebenen Juden); **spa|nisch;** das kommt mir spanisch (*ugs. für* seltsam) vor; (↑R 104:) spanischer Reiter (*Milit.* ein bestimmtes Hindernis); spanischer Stiefel (ein Folterwerkzeug); spanische Wand (*svw.* Paravent), *aber* (↑R 108): der Spanische Erbfolgekrieg; die Spanische Reitschule (in Wien); Spanische Fliege (ein Insekt); **Spa|nisch,** das; -[s] (Sprache); *vgl.* Deutsch; **Spa|ni|sche,** das; -n; *vgl.* Deutsche, das; **Spa|nisch-Gui|nea** (↑R 105)
Span|korb
Spann, der; -[e]s, -e (oberer Teil, Rist des menschlichen Fußes); **Spann|be|ton; Spann|be|ton₋brü|cke, ...kon|struk|ti|on; Spann|dienst** (*früher für* Frondienst); Hand- und Spanndienst leisten; **Span|ne,** die; -, -n (ein altes Längenmaß); **span|nen; span|nend; span|nen|lang;** *aber* vier Spannen lang; **Span|ner** (*ugs. auch für* Voyeur); **...spän|ner** (z. B. Einspänner); **spann|fä|hig; Spann|gar|di|ne; ...spän|nig** (z. B. zweispännig); **Spann₋kraft** (die; -), **...la|ken, ...rah|men** (*Buchbinderei*); **Span|nung;** (↑R 40:) eine Spannung führende Leitung (*Elektrotechnik*); **Span|nungs₋ab|fall** (*Elektrotechnik*), **...feld; span|nungs|füh|rend;** *vgl. auch* Spannung; **Span|nungs₋ge|biet, ...herd, ...ko|ef|fi|zi|ent** (*Physik*); **span|nungs|los; Span|nungs₋mes|ser** (der), **...mo|ment** (das, -s), **...prü|fer, ...reg|ler, ...ver|hält|nis, ...zeit, ...zu|stand; Spann₋vor|rich|tung, ...wei|te**
Span₋plat|te (*Bauw.*), **...schach|tel**
Spant, das, *in der Luftfahrt auch* der; -[e]s, -en *meist Plur.* (rippenähnl. Bauteil zum Verstärken der Außenwand von Schiffs- und Flugzeugrümpfen); **Span|ten|riss** (eine best. Schiffskonstruktionszeichnung)
Spar₋be|trag, ...bren|ner, ...brief, ...buch, ...büch|se, ...ein|la|ge; spa|ren; Spa|rer; Spa|re|rin; Spar₋flam|me, ...för|de|rung
Spar|gel, der; -s, -, *schweiz. auch* die; -, -n (ein[e] Gemüse[pflanze]); **Spar|gel₋beet, ...ge|mü|se, ...grün, ...kraut** (das; -s), **...spit|ze, ...sup|pe**
Spar|gi|ro|ver|kehr [...ʒi:ro...]; **Spar₋gro|schen, ...gut|ha|ben**
Spark, der; -[e]s (eine Pflanze)
Spar|kas|se; Spar|kas|sen|buch; Spar|kon|to; spär|lich; Spär|lich|keit, die; -; **Spar₋maß|nah|me** (*meist Plur.*), **...pa|ket, ...pfen|nig, ...po|li|tik, ...prä|mie, ...pro|gramm, ...quo|te**
Spar|re, die; -, -n (*für* Sparren)
spar|ren ‹engl.› (*Boxen* mit jmdm. im Training boxen); er hat zwei Runden gesparrt
Spar|ren, der; -s, -; **Spar|ren|dach; spar|rig** (*Bot.* seitwärts abstehend); -e Äste
Spar|ring, das; -s (Boxtraining); **Spar|rings₋kampf** (Übungsboxkampf mit dem Sparringspartner), **...part|ner**
spar|sam; Spar|sam|keit, die; -; **Spar₋schwein, ...strumpf**
Spart, der *od.* das; -[e]s, -e (*svw.* Esparto)
Spar|ta [ʃp..., *auch* sp...] (altgriech. Stadt)
Spar|ta|ki|a|de [ʃp..., *auch* sp...], die; -, -n (Sportveranstaltung in osteurop. Ländern [bis 1990]); **Spar|ta|kist,** der; -en, -en (Angehöriger des Spartakusbundes); **Spar|ta|kus** (Führer eines röm. Sklavenaufstandes); **Spar|ta|kus|bund,** der; -[e]s (kommunist. Kampfbund 1917/18)
Spar|ta|ner [ʃp..., *auch* sp...] (Bewohner von Sparta); **spar|ta|nisch;** -e (strenge, harte) Zucht
Spar|te, die; -, -n (Abteilung, Fach, Gebiet; Geschäfts-, Wissenszweig; Zeitungsspalte)
Spar|te|rie, die; - ‹franz.› (Flechtwerk aus Spänen od. Bast)
Spart|gras (*svw.* Espartogras)
Spar|ti|at [ʃp..., *auch* sp...], der; -en, -en; ↑R 126 (dorischer Vollbürger im alten Sparta)
spar|tie|ren [ʃp..., *auch* sp...] ‹ital.› (*Musik* [ein nur in den einzelnen

Stimmen vorhandenes Werk] in Partitur setzen)
Spar- und Dar|le|hens|kas|se (↑R 23); **Spar-ver|trag, ...ziel, ...zins** (*Plur.* ...zinsen)
spas|misch [ʃp..., *auch* sp...] ‹griech.› (*Med.* krampfhaft, krampfartig); **spas|mo|disch** (*svw.* spasmisch); **spas|mo|gen** (krampferzeugend); **Spas|mo|ly|ti|kum,** das; -s, ...ka (krampflösendes Mittel); **spas|mo|ly|tisch; Spas|mus,** der; -, ...men (Krampf)
Spaß, der; -es, Späße; - machen; **Späß|chen; spa|ßen;** du spaßt; **Spa|ße|rei; spa|ßes|hal|ber; Spa|ßet|teln** *Plur.* (*österr. ugs. für* Witz, Scherz); - machen; **spaß|haft; spa|ßig; Spa|ßig|keit,** die; -; **Spaß-ma|cher, ...ver|der|ber, ...vo|gel** (*scherzh., svw.* Spaßmacher)
Spas|ti|ker [ʃp..., *auch* sp...] ‹griech.› (jmd., der an einer spastischen Krankheit leidet); **Spas|ti|ke|rin; spas|tisch** (mit Erhöhung des Muskeltonus einhergehend)
spat (*veraltet für* spät)
[1]**Spat,** der; -[e]s, *Plur.* -e *u.* Späte (ein Mineral)
[2]**Spat,** der; -[e]s (eine Pferdekrankheit)
spät; -er, -est; -estens; spät sein, werden; zu spät kommen; von [morgens] früh bis [abends] spät; am spätesten (↑R 47); eine spät vollendete Oper; der Komponist hat die Oper spät vollendet; ein spät geborenes Kind; **spät|abends** (↑R 132); *aber* eines Spätabends; **Spät|aus|sied|ler; Spät-ba|rock, ...dienst; Spä|te,** die; - (*veraltet*); *noch in* in der -
Spa|tel, der, *österr. nur so, od.* die (*svw.* Spachtel); **Spa|ten,** der; -s, -; **Spa|ten-for|schung** (die; -; archäologische Forschung durch Ausgrabungen), **...stich**
Spät|ent|wick|ler; spä|ter; spä|ter|hin; spä|tes|tens; Spät-fol|ge, ...ge|bä|ren|de (die; -n, -n; ↑R 5 ff.), **...ge|burt, ...go|tik**
Spa|tha [sp..., *auch* ʃp...], die; -, ...then ‹griech.› (*Bot.* Blütenscheide kolbiger Blütenstände)
spat|hal|tig ‹*zu*[1] Spat›
Spät-heim|keh|rer, ...herbst; spät|herbst|lich
Spa|ti|en [ˈʃpa:tsi̯ən, *auch* sp...] (*Plur. von* Spatium); **Spa|ti|en-brei|te** (*Druckw.*), **...keil** (*Druckw.*)
spa|tig (spatkrank; *vgl.* [2]Spat)
spa|ti|ie|ren [ʃp..., *auch* sp...] ‹lat.› (*seltener für* spationieren); **spa|ti|o|nie|ren** (*Druckw.* [mit Zwischenräumen] durchschießen, sperren); **spa|ti|ös** (weit, geräumig [vom Druck]); **Spa|ti|um,** das; -s, ...ien [...i̯ən] (*Druckw.* schmales Ausschlussstück; Zwischenraum)
Spät-jahr (*für* Herbst), **...la|tein; spät|la|tei|nisch; Spät|le|se; Spät|ling; Spät|mit|tel|al|ter; Spät|nach|mit|tag;** eines -s, *aber* eines späten Nachmittags; **spät|nach|mit|tags;** *aber* eines Spätnachmittags; **Spät-nach|rich|ten** (*Plur.*), **...phase, ...pro|gramm, ...ro|man|tik, ...scha|den, ...schicht, ...som|mer; spät|voll|en|det** *vgl.* spät; **Spät-vor|stel|lung, ...werk**
Spatz, der; *Gen.* -en, *auch* -es, *Plur.* -en; **Spätz|chen; Spatz|en-hirn** (*ugs. abwertend für* geringes Denkvermögen), **...nest; Spät|zin; Spätz|le** *Plur.* (schwäb. Mehlspeise); mit Spätzle; **Spätz|li** (*schweiz. für* Spätzle)
Spät|zün|der (*ugs. für* jmd., der nur sehr langsam begreift); **Spät|zün|dung**
spa|zie|ren ‹lat.›; spazieren fahren, führen, gehen usw.; spazieren gegangen; spazieren zu fahren; **Spa|zie|ren|ge|hen,** das; -s (↑R 50); **spa|zie|ren rei|ten** *vgl.* spazieren; **Spa|zier-fahrt, ...gang** (der), **...gän|ger, ...gän|ge|rin, ...ritt, ...stock** (*Plur.* ...stöcke), **...weg**
SPD = Sozialdemokratische Partei Deutschlands
Specht, der; -[e]s, -e (ein Vogel); **Specht|mei|se** (*svw.* Kleiber)
Speck, der; -[e]s, *Plur. (Sorten:)* -e; **speck|bäu|chig; Speck|hals; spe|ckig; Speck-ku|chen, ...na|cken, ...schwar|te, ...sei|te, ...so|ße, ...stein** (*für* Steatit)
spe|die|ren ‹ital.› ([Güter] versenden, befördern, verfrachten); **Spe|di|teur** [...ˈtø:r], der; -s, -e (Transportunternehmer); **Spe|di|ti|on,** die; -, -en (gewerbsmäßige Verfrachtung, Versendung [von Gütern]; Transportunternehmen; Versand[abteilung]); **Spe|di|ti|ons-fir|ma, ...ge|schäft, ...kauf|frau, ...kauf|mann; spe|di|tiv** (*schweiz. für* rasch, zügig)
Speech [spi:tʃ], der; -es, *Plur.* -e *u.* -es [...is] ‹engl.› (Rede; Ansprache)
[1]**Speed** [spi:d], der; -s, -s ‹engl.› (*Sportspr.* [Steigerung der] Geschwindigkeit, Spurt); [2]**Speed,** das; -s, -s (*Jargon* Aufputsch-, Rauschmittel); **Speed|way** [ˈspi:dwe:], der; -s, -s (*Motorsport* Rennstrecke); **Speed|way|ren|nen** (↑R 24; *Motorsport*)
Speer, der; -[e]s, -e; den - werfen; **Speer-län|ge, ...wer|fen** (das; -s; ↑R 50), **...wer|fer, ...wer|fe|rin, ...wurf**
spei|ben (*bayr. u. österr. mdal. für* erbrechen); er hat gespieben
Spei|che, die; -, -n
Spei|chel, der; -s; **Spei|chel-drü|se, ...fluss** (der; -es), **...le|cker** (*abwertend*), **...le|cke|rei** (*abwertend*); **spei|chel|le|cke|risch; spei|cheln;** ich ...[e]le (↑R 16)
Spei|chen|kranz
Spei|cher, der; -s, - (*landsch. auch für* Dachboden); **spei|cher|bar; Spei|cher-bild** (*svw.* Hologramm), **...ka|pa|zi|tät; spei|chern;** ich ...ere (↑R 16); **Spei|cher|ofen** (↑R 132; *für* Regenerativofen); **Spei|che|rung**
spei|en; du spiest; gespien; spei[e]!
Spei|er|ling (ein Obstbaum mit gerbstoffhaltigen Früchten)
Spei|gat[t] (*Seemannsspr.* rundes Loch in der Schiffswand zum Wasserablauf)
Speik, der; -[e]s, -e ‹lat.› (Name mehrerer Pflanzen)
Speil, der; -s, -e (Holzstäbchen [zum Verschließen des Wurstdarmes]); **spei|len**
[1]**Speis,** der; -es ‹lat.› (*landsch. für* Mörtel); [2]**Speis,** die; -, -en (*bayr. u. österr. ugs. für* Speisekammer); **Spei|se,** die; -, -n (*auch für* Mörtel); [mit] Speis und Trank (↑R 13); **Spei|se-brei, ...eis, ...fett, ...fisch, ...gast|stät|te, ...kam|mer; Spei|se|kar|te,** Spei|sen|kar|te; **spei|sen;** du speist; er speis|te; gespeist; (*schweiz. übertr. od. schweiz. mdal., auch scherzh.* gespiesen); **Spei|sen-auf|zug, ...fol|ge; Spei|sen|kar|te** *vgl.* Speisekarte; **Spei|se-öl, ...op|fer, ...plan, ...rest, ...röh|re, ...saal, ...schrank, ...täub|ling** (ein Pilz), **...wa|gen** (bei der Eisenbahn), **...was|ser** (*Plur.* ...wässer; für Dampfkessel), **...wür|ze, ...zet|tel, ...zim|mer; Speis|ko|balt** (ein Mineral); **Spei|sung**
Spei-täub|ling, *auch* **...teu|fel** (ein Pilz); **spei|übel** (↑R 132)
Spek|ta|bi|li|tät [sp..., *auch* ʃp...], die; -, -en ‹lat.› (*veraltet* an Hochschulen Anrede an den Dekan); Eure (*Abk.* Ew.) -; [1]**Spek|ta|kel** [ʃp...], der; -s, - (*ugs. für* Krach, Lärm); [2]**Spek|ta|kel,** das; -s, - (*veraltet für* Schauspiel); **spek|ta|keln** (*ugs. für* lärmen); ich ...[e]le (↑R 16); **spek|ta|ku|lär** (Aufse-

hen erregend); **Spek|ta|ku|lum,** das; -s, ...la (*scherzh. für* ²Spektakel)

Spekt|ra [ʃp..., *auch* sp...] (↑R 130; *Plur. von* Spektrum); **spekt|ral** ‹lat.› (auf das Spektrum bezüglich od. davon ausgehend); **Spekt|ral‿ana|ly|se** (↑R 132), **...ap|pa|rat, ...far|be** *(meist Plur.),* **...klas|se** *(Astron.),* **...li|nie; Spekt|ren** (*Plur. von* Spektrum); **Spekt|ro|me|ter,** das; -s, - ‹lat.; griech.› (Vorrichtung zum genauen Messen von Spektren); **spekt|ro|me|trisch; Spekt|ro|skop,** das; -s, -e (Vorrichtung zum Bestimmen der Wellenlängen von Spektrallinien); **Spekt|ro|sko|pie,** die; -; **spekt|ro|sko|pisch; Spekt|rum,** das; -s, *Plur.* ...tren *u.* ...tra ‹lat.› (durch Lichtzerlegung entstehendes farbiges Band)

Spe|ku|la (*Plur. von* Spekulum); **Spe|ku|lant,** der; -en, -en (↑R 126) ‹lat.› (jmd., der spekuliert); **Spe|ku|la|ti|on,** die; -, -en (auf Mutmaßungen beruhende Erwartung; auf Gewinne aus Preisveränderungen abzielende Geschäftstätigkeit; *Philos.* Vernunftstreben nach Erkenntnis jenseits der Sinnenwelt); **Spe|ku|la|ti|ons‿ge|schäft, ...ge|winn, ...kauf, ...pa|pier, ...steu|er** (die), **...wert**

Spe|ku|la|ti|us, der; -, - ‹niederl.› (ein Gebäck)

spe|ku|la|tiv ‹lat.› (auf Mutmaßungen beruhend; auf Gewinne aus Preisveränderungen abzielend; *Philos.* in reinen Begriffen denkend); **spe|ku|lie|ren** (Spekulationsgeschäfte machen; mit etwas rechnen); **Spe|ku|lum** [sp..., *auch* ʃp...], das; -s, ...la (*Med.* Spiegel)

Spe|lä|o|lo|ge [ʃp..., *auch* sp...], der; -n, -n (↑R 126) ‹griech.›; **Spe|lä|o|lo|gie,** die; - (Höhlenkunde); **Spe|lä|o|lo|gin; spe|lä|o|lo|gisch**

Spelt, der; -[e]s, -e *u.* Spelz, der; -es, -e (eine Getreideart)

Spe|lun|ke, die; -, -n ‹griech.› (verrufene Kneipe)

Spelz *vgl.* Spelt; **Spel|ze,** die; -, -n (Getreidekornhülse; Teil des Gräserblütenstandes); **spel|zig**

Spen|cer ['spɛnsə(r)] (engl. Philosoph); *vgl. aber* Spenser

spen|da|bel ‹lat.› (*ugs. für* freigebig); ...ab|le (↑R 130) Laune; **Spen|de,** die; -, -n; **spen|den** (für wohltätige o. Ä. Zwecke Geld geben); **Spen|den‿ak|ti|on, ...auf|ruf, ...be|schei|ni|gung, ...kon|to; Spen|der; Spen|de|rin; spen|die|ren** (freigebig für jmdn. bezahlen); **Spen|dier|ho|sen;** *nur in* die - anhaben (*ugs. für* freigebig sein); **Spen|dung**

Speng|ler (*bes. südd., österr., schweiz. für* Klempner); **Speng|le|rin**

Spen|ser ['spɛnsə(r)] (engl. Dichter); *vgl. aber* Spencer

Spen|zer, der; -s, - ‹engl.› (kurzes, eng anliegendes Jäckchen)

Sper|ber, der; -s, - (ein Greifvogel); **sper|bern** (*schweiz. für* scharf blicken); ich ...ere (↑R 16)

Spe|renz|chen, Spe|ren|zi|en *Plur.* ‹lat.› (*ugs. für* Umschweife, Schwierigkeiten); [keine] - machen

Sper|gel *vgl.* Spörgel

Sper|ling, der; -s, -e; *vgl. aber* Sperrling; **Sper|lings|vo|gel**

Sper|ma [ʃp..., *auch* sp...], das; -s, *Plur.* ...men *u.* -ta ‹griech.› (*Biol.* männl. Samenzellen enthaltende Flüssigkeit); **Sper|ma|to|ge|ne|se,** die; - (Samenbildung im Hoden); **Sper|ma|tor|rhö**[1], **Sper|ma|tor|rhöe** [...'rø:], die; -, ...rrhöen (*Med.* Samenfluss ohne geschlechtl. Erregung); **Sper|ma|to|zo|on,** das; -s, ...oen (*svw.* Spermium); **Sper|men** (*Plur. von* Sperma); **Sper|mi|en** (*Plur. von* Spermium); **Sper|mi|o|ge|ne|se,** die; - (*svw.* Spermatogenese); **Sper|mi|um,** das; -s, ...ien [...i̯ən] (Samenfaden, reife männl. Keimzelle)

sperr|an|gel|weit *(ugs.);* **Sperr‿bal|lon, ...bat|te|rie** *(Milit.),* **...baum, ...be|trag; Sper|re,** die; -, -n; **sper|ren** (*südd., österr. auch für* schließen); sich -; **Sperr‿feu|er** *(Milit.),* **...frist** *(Rechtsw.),* **...ge|biet, ...ge|trie|be, ...gür|tel, ...gut, ...gut|ha|ben, ...holz** (das; -es); **Sperr|holz|plat|te; sper|rig; Sperr‿jahr** (das; -es; *Wirtsch.*), **...ket|te, ...klau|sel, ...klin|ke** *(Technik),* **...kon|to, ...kreis** *(Elektrotechnik);* **Sperr|ling** (*veraltet für* Knebel); *vgl. aber* Sperling; **Sperr‿mau|er, ...mi|no|ri|tät** *(Wirtsch.),* **...müll**

Sperr|rad (↑R 136), das; -[e]s, ...räder; **Sperr|rie|gel** (↑R 136), der; -s, -

Sperr‿sitz, ...stun|de; Sper|rung; Sperr‿ver|merk, ...zeit (Polizeistunde), **...zoll** (*Plur.* ...zölle), **...zo|ne**

Spe|sen *Plur.* ‹ital.› ([Un]kosten; Auslagen); **spe|sen|frei; Spe|sen‿platz** *(Bankw.),* **...rech|nung, ...rit|ter** (jmd., der hohe Spesen macht u. sich daran bereichert)

Spes|sart, der; -s (Bergland im Mainviereck)

spet|ten ‹ital.› (*schweiz. für* [im Haushalt, in einem Geschäft] aushelfen); **Spet|te|rin** (*schweiz. für* Stundenhilfe)

Spey|er ['ʃpai̯...] (Stadt am Rhein); **Spey|[e]|rer** (↑R 103); **spey|[e]|risch**

Spe|ze|rei *meist Plur.* ‹ital.› (*veraltend für* Gewürze)

¹**Spe|zi,** der; -s, -[s] ‹lat.› (*südd., österr. kurz für* [Busen]freund); ²**Spe|zi,** das; -s, -[s] (*ugs. für* Mischgetränk aus Limonade u. Cola); **spe|zi|al** (*veraltet für* speziell); **Spe|zi|al...** (Sonder..., Einzel..., Fach...); **Spe|zi|al‿aus|bil|dung, ...aus|füh|rung, ...dis|zi|plin, ...fach, ...fahr|zeug, ...ge|biet, ...ge|schäft; Spe|zi|a|li|en** *Plur.* (*veraltet für* Besonderheiten, Einzelheiten); **Spe|zi|a|li|sa|ti|on,** die; -, -en (*seltener für* Spezialisierung); **spe|zi|a|li|sie|ren;** sich - (sich [beruflich] auf ein Teilgebiet beschränken); **Spe|zi|a|li|sie|rung; Spe|zi|a|list,** der; -en, -en; ↑R 126 (Facharbeiter, Fachmann; bes. Facharzt); **Spe|zi|a|lis|ten|tum,** das; -s; **Spe|zi|a|lis|tin; Spe|zi|a|li|tät,** die; -, -en (Besonderheit; Fachgebiet; Liebhaberei); **Spe|zi|a|li|tä|ten|res|tau|rant; Spe|zi|al‿sla|lom** (Wettbewerbsart im alpinen Skisport), **...sprung|lauf** *(Skispringen),* **...trai|ning; spe|zi|ell** (besonders, eigentümlich; eigens; hauptsächlich); ↑R 47: im Speziellen (im Einzelnen); **Spe|zi|es** ['ʃpe:t͜si̯ɛs, *auch* 'spe:...], die; -, - [...e:s] (besondere Art einer Gattung, Tier- od. Pflanzenart); **Spe|zi|es|ta|ler** (*früher* ein harter Taler im Gegensatz zu Papiergeld); **Spe|zi|fi|ka|ti|on** [ʃp..., *auch* sp...], die; -, -en (Einzelaufstellung, -aufzählung); **Spe|zi|fi|ka|ti|ons|kauf** *(Wirtsch.);* **Spe|zi|fi|kum,** das; -s, ...ka (Besonderes, Entscheidendes; *Med.* gegen eine bestimmte Krankheit wirksames Mittel); **spe|zi|fisch** ([art]eigen; kennzeichnend, eigentümlich); -es Gewicht *(Physik);* -e Wärme[kapazität]; -er Widerstand *(Physik);* **Spe|zi|fi|tät,** die; -, -en (Eigentümlichkeit, Besonderheit); **spe|zi|fi|zie|ren** (einzeln aufführen; zergliedern); **Spe|zi|fi|zie|rung; Spe|zi|men** [*österr.* ...'t͜si:...], das; -s, ...imina (*veraltet für* [Probe]arbeit, Muster)

---

[1] *Vgl. die Anmerkung zu* „Diarrhö, Diarrhöe".

Sphä|re, die; -, -n ‹griech., „Himmel[skugel]"› ([Gesichts-, Wirkungs]kreis; [Macht]bereich); **Sphä|ren‿har|mo|nie** (die; -), **...mu|sik** (die; -); **sphä|risch** (die [Himmels]kugel betreffend); -e Trigonometrie (*Math.* Berechnung von Dreiecken auf der Kugeloberfläche); -es Dreieck *(Math.)*; **Sphä|ro|id,** das; -[e]s, -e (kugelähnl. Figur, Rotationsellipsoid); **sphä|ro|i|disch** (kugelähnlich); **Sphä|ro|lith** [*auch* ...'lit], der; *Gen.* -s *u.* -en, *Plur.* -e[n]; ↑R 126 (kugeliges Mineralgebilde); **Sphä|ro|lo|gie,** die; - (Lehre von der Kugel); **Sphä|ro‿me|ter** (das; -s, -; Kugel-, Dickenmesser), **...si|de|rit** [*auch* ...'rit] (der; -s, -e; ein Mineral)

Sphen, der; -s, -e ‹griech.› (ein Mineral); **Sphe|no|id,** das; -[e]s, -e (eine Kristallform); **sphe|no|i|dal** (keilförmig)

Sphink|ter, der; -s, ...ere ‹griech.› (*Med.* Schließmuskel)

[1]**Sphinx,** die; - (geflügelter Löwe mit Frauenkopf in der griech. Sage; Sinnbild des Rätselhaften); [2]**Sphinx,** die; -, -e, *in der archäolog. Fachspr. meist* der; -, *Plur.* -e *u.* Sphingen (ägypt. Steinbild in Löwengestalt, meist mit Männerkopf; Symbol des Sonnengottes od. des Königs)

Sphra|gis|tik, die; - ‹griech.› (Siegelkunde)

Sphyg|mo|gramm, das; -s, -e ‹griech.› (*Med.* durch den Sphygmographen aufgezeichnete Pulskurve); **Sphyg|mo|graph,** der; -en, -en; ↑R 126 (Pulsschreiber)

Spick, der; -[e]s, -e (*Schülerspr. landsch. svw.* Spickzettel)

Spick|aal (*nordd. für* Räucheraal)

Spi|ckel, der; -s, - (*schweiz. für* Zwickel an Kleidungsstücken)

[1]**spi|cken** (Fleisch zum Braten mit Speckstreifen durchziehen)

[2]**spi|cken** (*Schülerspr.* in der Schule abschreiben); **Spi|cker** (*auch svw.* Spickzettel)

Spick|gans (*nordd. für* geräucherte u. gepökelte Gänsebrust)

Spick|na|del

Spick|zet|tel (*Schülerspr.* zum Spicken vorbereiteter Zettel)

Spi|der ['spaidə(r)], der; -s, - ‹engl.› (offener Sportwagen)

Spie|gel, der; -s, - ‹lat.›; **Spie|gel|bild; spie|gel|bild|lich; spie|gel|blank; Spie|gel‿ei, ...fech|ter; Spie|gel|fech|te|rei; Spie|gel‿flä|che, ...ge|wöl|be** *(Bauw.)*, **...glas** (*Plur.* ...gläser); **spie|gel|glatt; spie|ge|lig** (*veraltet für* spiegelartig, glänzend); **Spie|gel|karp|fen; spie|geln;** ich ...[e]le (↑R 16); sich spiegeln; **Spie|gel|re|flex|ka|me|ra; Spie|gel‿saal, ...schrank, ...schrift, ...strich** (waagerechter Strich vor Unterabsätzen), **...te|le|skop; Spie|ge|lung,** Spieg|lung; **spie|gel|ver|kehrt**

Spie|ker, der; -s, - (*nordd. für* großer [Schiffs]nagel); **spie|kern** *(nordd.)*; ich ...ere (↑R 16)

Spie|ker|oog (eine der Ostfries. Inseln)

Spiel, das; -[e]s, -e; **Spiel‿ab|bruch, ...al|ter** (das; -s), **...an|zug** (für Kinder), **...art, ...au|to|mat, ...ball, ...bank** (*Plur.* ...banken), **...be|ginn, ...bein** (*Sport, bild. Kunst; Ggs.* Standbein), **...be|trieb, ...do|se; spie|len;** - gehen; Schach -; sich mit etwas - (*österr. für* etwas nicht ernsthaft betreiben; etwas spielend leicht bewältigen); **Spie|len|de; spie|l|ent|schei|dend;** das -e Tor; **Spie|ler; Spie|le|rei; Spie|le|rin; spie|le|risch** (ohne Anstrengung); mit -er Leichtigkeit; **Spie|ler|trans|fer; Spiel|feld; Spiel|feld|hälf|te; Spiel‿fi|gur, ...film, ...flä|che, ...fol|ge; spiel|frei; Spiel|freu|de; spiel|freu|dig; Spiel‿füh|rer** *(Sport)*, **...füh|re|rin** *(Sport)*, **...ge|fähr|te, ...ge|fähr|tin, ...geld, ...hahn** (*Jägerspr.* Birkhahn), **...hälf|te, ...hal|le, ...höl|le** *(abwertend)*, **...hös|chen; Spie|li|o|thek** *vgl.* Spielothek; **Spiel‿ka|me|rad, ...ka|me|ra|din, ...kar|te, ...ka|si|no, ...klas|se** *(Sport)*, **...lei|den|schaft, ...lei|ter** (der), **...lei|te|rin, ...lei|tung, ...ma|cher** *(Sport)*, **...ma|che|rin** *(Sport)*, **...mann** (*Plur.* ...leute); **Spiel|manns‿dich|tung** (die; -), **...zug; Spiel‿mar|ke, ...mi|nu|te** *(Sport)*, **...oper** (↑R 132); **Spie|lo|thek,** Spie|li|o|thek, die; -, -en (Einrichtung zum Verleih von Spielen; *auch für* Spielhalle); **Spiel‿pha|se, ...plan** (*vgl.* [2]Plan), **...platz, ...rat|te** (*ugs. für* leidenschaftlich spielendes Kind), **...raum, ...re|gel, ...run|de, ...saal, ...sa|chen** *(Plur.)*, **...schuld, ...schu|le, ...stand; spiel|stark** *(Sport)*; eine besonders -e Mannschaft; **Spiel‿stär|ke** *(Sport)*, **...stra|ße, ...tag, ...teu|fel, ...tisch** (*auch* Teil der Orgel), **...trieb, ...uhr, ...ver|bot** *(Sport)*, **...ver|der|ber, ...ver|der|be|rin, ...ver|ei|ni|gung** (*Abk.* Spvg., Spvgg.); **Spiel|wa|ren** *Plur.*; **Spiel|wa|ren‿ge|schäft, ...händ|ler, ...hand|lung, ...in|dust|rie; Spiel‿wei|se** (die), **...werk, ...wie|se, ...witz** (der; -es), **...zeit, ...zeug; Spiel|zeug‿ei|sen|bahn, ...in|dust|rie; ...pis|to|le; Spiel|zim|mer**

Spier, der *od.* das; -[e]s, -e (*nordd. für* Spitze; Grasspitze); **Spier|chen** (*nordd. für* Grasspitzchen); ein Spierchen (*nordd. für* ein wenig); **Spie|re,** die; -, -n (*Seemannsspr.* Rundholz, Segelstange); **Spier|ling** (ein Fisch); **Spier|strauch**

Spieß, der; -es, -e (Kampf-, Jagdspieß; Bratspieß; Erstlingsform des Geweihs der Hirscharten; *Soldatenspr.* Kompaniefeldwebel; *Druckw.* im Satz zu hoch stehendes, deshalb mitdruckendes Ausschlussstück); **Spieß|bock** (einjähriger Rehbock); **Spieß|bür|ger,** Spie|ßer (*abwertend für* engstirniger Mensch); **spieß|bür|ger|lich; Spieß‿bür|ger|lich|keit, ...bür|ger|tum; spie|ßen;** du spießt; sich - (*österr. für* sich nicht bewegen lassen; *übertr. für* stocken); **Spie|ßer** *vgl.* Spießbürger; **spie|ßer|haft; spie|ße|risch; Spie|ßer|tum,** das; -s; **spieß|för|mig; Spieß‿ge|sel|le** (*abwertend für* Mittäter), **...glanz** (der; -es, -e *meist Plur.*; *Sammelbez. für* verschiedene Minerale); **spie|ßig; Spie|ßig|keit; Spieß|ru|te;** -n laufen (↑R 39); **Spieß|ru|ten|lau|fen,** das; -s (↑R 50)

Spi|ka [*auch* sp...], die; - ‹lat., „Ähre"› (ein Stern)

Spike [spaik], der; -s, -s ‹engl.› (Dorn für Laufschuhe od. Autoreifen; *nur Plur.:* rutschfester Laufschuh, Spike[s]reifen); **Spike[s]|rei|fen**

Spill, das; -[e]s, *Plur.* -e *od.* -s ([Anker]winde); **Spill|la|ge** [...'la:ʒə, *österr.* ...'la:ʒ], die; -, -n [...ʒ(ə)n] (*Wirtsch.* Wertverlust trockener Ware durch Eindringen von Feuchtigkeit); **Spil|le,** die; -, -n (*landsch. für* Spindel); **spil|le|rig** *vgl.* spillrig; **Spill|geld** (*landsch. für* Nadelgeld); **Spil|ling,** der; -s, -e (gelbe Pflaume); **spill|rig,** spil|le|rig (*landsch. für* dürr)

Spin [spin], der; -s, -s ‹engl.› (*Physik* Drehimpuls der Elementarteilchen im Atom; *Sport* Effet, Drall)

spi|nal [ʃp..., *auch* sp...] ‹lat.› (*Med.* die Wirbelsäule, das Rückenmark betreffend); -e Kinderlähmung

Spi|nat, der; -[e]s, *Plur. (Sorten:)* -e ‹pers.-arab.› (ein Gemüse); **Spi|nat|wach|tel** (*ugs. abwertend für* schrullige [alte] Frau)

Spind, der *u.* das; -[e]s, -e (einfacher, schmaler Schrank)

Spin|del, die; -, -n; **Spin|del|baum** (ein Zierstrauch); **spin|del|dürr; Spin|del‿la|ger** (*Plur.* ...lager), **...schne|cke**
Spi|nell, der; -s, -e ‹ital.› (ein Mineral)
Spi|nett, das; -[e]s, -e ‹ital.› (kleines Cembalo)
Spin|na|ker, der; -s, - ‹engl.› (*Seemannsspr.* großes Beisegel)
Spinn|dü|se (bei Textilmaschinen); **Spin|ne**, die; -, -n; **Spin|ne|feind** *(ugs.); nur in* jmdm. - sein; **spin|nen;** du spinnst; du spannst; du spönnest, *auch* spännest; gesponnen; spinn[e]!; **Spin|nen‿ar|me** (*Plur.;* lange, dürre Arme), **...bei|ne** *(Plur.)*, **...fa|den** (*vgl.* Spinnfaden), **...ge|we|be** (*vgl.* Spinngewebe); **Spin|nen|netz; Spin|ner; Spin|ne|rei; Spin|ne|rin; Spin|ner|lied; spin|nert** (*bes. südd. für* leicht verrückt); **Spinn‿fa|den, ...fa|ser, ...ge|we|be** (*od.* Spin|nen|ge|we|be); **Spinn‿ma|schi|ne, ...rad, ...ro|cken, ...stoff, ...stu|be, ...we|be** (die; -, -n; *svw.* Spinngewebe), **...wir|tel**
spi|nös [ʃp..., *auch* sp...] ‹lat.› (*veraltend für* schwierig; heikel, sonderbar)
Spi|no|za [spiˈno:za] (niederl. Philosoph); **spi|no|za|isch;** spinozaische Lehre, spinozaische Schriften; **Spi|no|zis|mus** [...ˈtsis...], der; - (Lehre des Spinoza); **Spi|no|zist**, der; -en, -en (↑R 126); **spi|no|zis|tisch**
Spint, der *od.* das; -[e]s, -e (*landsch. für* Fett; weiches Holz); **spin|tig** (*landsch. für* fettig; weich)
spin|ti|sie|ren (*ugs. für* grübeln); **Spin|ti|sie|rer** (jmd., der spintisiert); **Spin|ti|sie|re|rei**
Spi|on, der; -s, -e ‹ital., „Späher"› (heimlicher Kundschafter; Spiegel außen am Fenster; Beobachtungsglas in der Tür); **Spi|o|na|ge** [...ˈna:ʒə], die; - ‹franz.› (Auskundschaftung von wirtschaftl., polit. u. milit. Geheimnissen, Späh[er]dienst); **Spi|o|na|ge‿ab|wehr, ...af|fä|re, ...ap|pa|rat, ...dienst, ...fall** (der), **...film, ...netz, ...ring; spi|o|nie|ren; Spi|o|nie|re|rei** *(ugs.);* **Spi|o|nin**
Spi|räe [ʃp..., *auch* sp...], die; -, -n ‹griech.› (Spierstrauch)
spi|ral ‹griech.› (*fachspr. für* spiralig); **Spi|ral|boh|rer** (schraubenförmiger Bohrer); **Spi|ra|le**, die; -, -n (Schnecken-, Schraubenlinie; Feder einer Uhr); **Spi|ra|len|an|ord|nung; Spi|ral|fe|der; spi|ral|för|mig; spi|ra|lig** (schrauben-, schneckenförmig); **Spi|ral‿li|nie, ...ne|bel, ...win|dung**
Spi|rans, die; -, ...ranten *u.* **Spi|rant** [*beide* sp...], der; -en, -en (↑R 126) ‹lat.› (*Sprachw.* Reibelaut, Frikativlaut, z. B. f); **spi|ran|tisch**
Spi|ril|le, die; -, -n *meist Plur.* ‹griech.› (Bakterie von gedrehter Form, Schraubenbakterie)
Spi|rit [sp...], der; -s, -s ‹lat.-engl.› (Geist [eines Verstorbenen]); **Spi|ri|tis|mus** [ʃp..., *auch* sp...], der; - ‹lat.› (Glaube an vermeintl. Erscheinungen von Seelen Verstorbener; Geisterlehre); **Spi|ri|tist**, der; -en, -en (↑R 126); **Spi|ri|tis|tin; spi|ri|tis|tisch; spi|ri|tu|al** (geistig; übersinnlich); [1]**Spi|ri|tu|al** [sp...], der; *Gen.* -s *u.* -en, *Plur.* -en; ↑R 126 (Seelsorger, Beichtvater in kath. theol. Anstalten u. Klöstern); [2]**Spi|ri|tu|al** [ˈspiritjuəl], das, *auch* der; -s, -s ‹amerik.› (*kurz für* Negro Spiritual); **Spi|ri|tu|a|li|en** [sp...] *Plur.* ‹lat.› (*Rel.* geistl. Dinge); **spi|ri|tu|a|li|sie|ren** [ʃp..., *auch* sp...] (vergeistigen); **Spi|ri|tu|a|li|sie|rung; Spi|ri|tu|a|lis|mus**, der; - (Lehre von der Wirklichkeit u. Wirksamkeit des Geistes); **Spi|ri|tu|a|list**, der; -en, -en (↑R 126); **spi|ri|tu|a|lis|tisch** (den Spiritualismus betreffend); **Spi|ri|tu|a|li|tät**, die; - (Geistigkeit, geistiges Wesen); **spi|ri|tu|ell** ‹franz.› (geistig; geistlich); **spi|ri|tu|os, spi|ri|tu|ös** (*selten für* Weingeist enthaltend, geistig); -e Getränke; **Spi|ri|tu|o|sen** *Plur.* (geistige, d. h. alkohol. Getränke); [1]**Spi|ri|tus** [sp...], der; -, - [...tu:s] ‹lat.› (Hauch, Atem, [Lebens]geist); [2]**Spi|ri|tus** [ʃp...], der; -, *Plur. (Sorten:)* -se (Weingeist, Alkohol); **Spi|ri|tus as|per** [sp... -], der; - -, - -i (*Sprachw.* für den H-Anlaut im Altgriechischen; *Zeichen* ʽ); **Spi|ri|tus fa|mi|li|a|ris**, der; - - (guter Geist des Hauses; Vertraute[r] der Familie); **Spi|ri|tus‿ko|cher** [ʃp...], **...lack, ...lam|pe; Spi|ri|tus Rec|tor** [sp... -], der; - - (leitende, treibende Kraft)
Spir|kel, der; -s, - (*nordostd. für* Griebe; schmächtiger Mensch)
Spi|ro|chä|te [ʃpiroˈçɛ:tə, *auch* sp...], die; -, -n ‹griech.› (*Med.* ein Krankheitserreger)
Spi|ro|er|go|me|ter [sp..., *auch* ʃp...], das; -s, - ‹lat.; griech.› (*Med.* Gerät zur Messung der körperlichen Leistungsfähigkeit anhand des Sauerstoffverbrauchs); **Spi|ro|er|go|met|rie** (↑R 130), die; - (Messung der körperlichen Leistungsfähigkeit mit dem Spiroergometer); **Spi|ro|me|ter**, das; -s, - (*Med.* Atemmesser); **Spi|ro|met|rie** (↑R 130), die; - (Messung [u. Aufzeichnung] der Atmung)
Spir|re, die; -, -n (*Bot.* ein Blütenstand)
Spis|sen, das; -s (*Jägerspr.* Balz-, Lockruf des Haselhahns)
Spi|tal, das; -s, ...täler ‹lat.› (*landsch., bes. schweiz. für* Krankenhaus; *veraltet für* Altersheim, Armenhaus); **Spi|ta|ler, Spi|tä|ler, Spitt|ler** (*veraltet, noch landsch. für* Insasse eines Spitals); **Spi|tals|arzt** *(österr.)*
Spit|tal an der Drau (Stadt in Kärnten)
Spit|tel, das, *auch* der; -s, - (*landsch. für* Spital)
Spit|te|ler (schweiz. Dichter)
Spitt|ler *vgl.* Spitaler
spitz; eine -e Zunge haben (gehässig reden); ein -er Winkel *(Geom.);* **Spitz**, der; -es, -e (eine Hunderasse; *landsch. für* leichter Rausch); **Spitz‿ahorn** (↑R 132), **...bart; spitz|bär|tig; Spitz‿bauch, ...bein** (*Gastron.* unterstes Teil des Fußes des geschlachteten Schweins); **spitz|be|kom|men** (↑R 38; *ugs. für* merken, durchschauen); ich bekomme etwas spitz; ich habe etwas spitzbekommen; spitzzubekommen
Spitz|ber|gen (Insel in der Inselgruppe Svalbard)
Spitz|bo|gen; Spitz|bo|gen|fens|ter; spitz|bo|gig; Spitz‿boh|rer, ...bu|be; Spitz|bü|be|rei; Spitz|bü|bin; spitz|bü|bisch; Spitz|dach; spit|ze (*ugs. für* hervorragend); ein spitze Auto; er hat spitze gespielt; das finde ich spitze (*auch* Spitze; *vgl. d.*); er ist, das ist spitze (*auch* Spitze; *vgl. d.*); **Spit|ze**, die; -, -n; jmd. *od.* etw. ist Spitze (*auch* spitze; *vgl. d.*); **Spit|zel**, der; -s, - (Aushorcher, Spion); **spit|zeln;** ich ...[e]le (↑R 16); **spit|zen;** du spitzt; **Spit|zen‿blu|se, ...deck|chen, ...er|zeug|nis, ...fah|rer, ...film, ...funk|ti|o|när, ...gar|ni|tur, ...ge|schwin|dig|keit, ...grup|pe, ...hau|be, ...kan|di|dat, ...kan|di|da|tin, ...klas|se, ...klöp|pe|lei, ...klöpp|le|rin, ...kön|ner, ...kraft, ...kra|gen, ...leis|tung, ...lohn, ...mann|schaft, ...or|ga|ni|sa|ti|on, ...po|li|ti|ker, ...po|li|ti|ke|rin, ...po|si|ti|on, ...qua|li|tät, ...rei|ter, ...spiel** *(Sport)*, **...spie|ler, ...spie|le|rin, ...sport, ...sport|ler, ...sport|le|rin, ...tanz, ...tech|no|lo|gie, ...tuch** (*Plur.* ...tücher), **...ver|band, ...ver|kehr** (der; -s),

...wert, ...zeit; **Spit|zer** (*kurz für* Bleistiftspitzer); **spitz|fin|dig; Spitz-fin|dig|keit, ...fuß** *(Med.)*, **...gie|bel, ...ha|cke; spit|zig** (veraltend); **Spitz|keh|re; spitz|krie|gen** (↑R 38; *ugs. für* merken, durchschauen); ich kriege etwas spitz; ich habe etwas spitzgekriegt; spitzzukriegen; **Spitz-küh|ler** (*ugs. svw.* Spitzbauch), **...mar|ke** *(Druckw.)*, **...maus, ...na|me; spitz-na|sig, ...oh|rig; Spitz|pfei|ler** (*für* Obelisk)

Spitz|weg (dt. Maler)

Spitz|we|ge|rich (eine Heilpflanze); **spitz-wink|lig, ...zün|gig; Spitz|zün|gig|keit**

Splanch|no|lo|gie [splanç...], die; - ⟨griech.⟩ (*Med.* Lehre von den Eingeweiden)

Spleen [ʃpli:n, *seltener* spli:n], der; -s, *Plur.* -e *u.* -s ⟨engl.⟩ (seltsamer Einfall; Schrulle, Marotte); **splee|nig; Splee|nig|keit**, die; -, -en (spleeniger Zug; *nur Sing.*: Verschrobenheit)

Spleiß, der; -es, -e (*Seemannsspr.* Verbindung von zwei Seil- od. Tauenden); **Splei|ße**, die; -, -n (*landsch. für* Span, Splitter); **splei|ßen** (*landsch. für* fein spalten; *Seemannsspr.* Tauenden miteinander verflechten); du spleißt; du splissest *od.* spleißtest; er spliss *od.* spleißte; gesplissen *od.* gespleißt; spleiß[e]!

Splen [sple:n, *auch* ʃp...], der; - ⟨griech.⟩ (*Med.* Milz)

splen|did [ʃp..., *auch* sp...] ⟨lat.⟩ (*veraltend für* freigebig; glanzvoll; *Druckw.* weiträumig, aufgelockert); **Splen|did I|so|la|tion** ['splɛndid aisə'le:ʃ(ə)n], die; - - ⟨engl.⟩ (Bündnislosigkeit [eines Landes]); **Splen|di|di|tät** [ʃp..., *auch* sp...], die; - ⟨lat.⟩ (*veraltet für* Freigebigkeit)

Spließ, der; -es, -e (Holzspan unter den Dachziegelfugen; Schindel); **Spließ|dach**

Splint, der; -[e]s, -e (*bei Maschinen u. a.* Vorsteckstift als Sicherung); **Splint|holz** (weiche Holzschicht unter der Rinde)

Spliss, der; -es, -e (*landsch. für* Splitter; kleiner Abschnitt); **splis|sen** (*landsch. für* spleißen); du splisst; du splisstest; gesplisst; splisse! *u.* spliss!

Split [split] (Stadt in Kroatien); *vgl.* Spalato

Splitt, der; -[e]s, -e (zerkleinertes Gestein für den Straßenbau; *nordd. für* Span, Schindel); **split|ten** ⟨engl.⟩ (das Splitting anwenden); gesplittet; **Split|ter**, der; -s, -; **Split|ter-bom|be, ...bruch** (der); **split|ter|fa|ser|nackt** (*ugs. für* völlig nackt); **split|ter|frei**; -es Glas; **Split|ter-gra|ben** *(Milit.)*, **...grup|pe; split|te|rig**, splittrig; **split|tern**; ich ...ere (↑R 16); **split|ter|nackt** (*ugs. für* völlig nackt); **Split|ter|par|tei; split|ter|si|cher; Split|ter|wir|kung; Split|ting** ⟨engl.⟩, **Split|ting|sys|tem** [ʃp..., *auch* sp...], das; -s (Form der Haushaltsbesteuerung, bei der das Einkommen der Ehegatten zusammengezählt und beiden zu gleichen Teilen angerechnet wird; Verteilung der Erst- u. Zweitstimmen auf verschiedene Parteien [bei Wahlen]); **splitt|rig** *vgl.* splitterig

Splü|gen, der; -s, *auch* **Splü|gen|pass**, der; -es (ein Alpenpass an der schweizerisch-italien. Grenze)

SPÖ = Sozialdemokratische Partei Österreichs

Spo|di|um [ʃp..., *auch* sp...], das; -s ⟨griech.⟩ (*Chemie* Knochenkohle); **Spo|du|men**, der; -s, -e (ein Mineral)

Spoerl [ʃpœrl] (dt. Schriftsteller)

Spoi|ler ['ʃpɔylə(r), *auch* 'spɔy...], der; -s, - ⟨amerik.⟩ (Luftleitblech [an Autos])

Spö|ken|kie|ker [sp...] (*nordd. für* Geisterseher, Hellseher); **Spö|ken|kie|ke|rei** (*nordd. svw.* Spintisiererei); **Spö|ken|kie|ke|rin**

Spo|li|en|recht ['spo:li̯ən..., *auch* 'ʃpo:...] ⟨lat.; dt.⟩ (im MA. das Recht, den Nachlass kath. Geistlicher einzuziehen); **Spo|li|um**, das; -s, ...ien [...i̯ən] (Beutestück, erbeutete Waffe [im alten Rom])

Spom|pa|na|de[l]n *Plur.* (*österr. ugs. für* Dummheiten, Abenteuer)

spon|de|isch [sp..., *auch* ʃp...] ⟨griech.⟩ (in, mit Spondeen); **Spon|de|us**, der; -, ...deen (ein Versfuß)

spon|die|ren ⟨lat.⟩ (*österr. für* den Magistertitel verleihen; *vgl.* Sponsion)

Spon|dyl|arth|ri|tis [ʃp..., *auch* sp...] ⟨griech.⟩ (*Med.* Entzündung der Wirbelgelenke); **Spon|dy|li|tis**, die; -, ...itiden (Wirbelentzündung); **Spon|dy|lo|se**, die; -, -n (krankhafte Veränderung an den Wirbelkörpern u. Bandscheiben)

Spon|gia [sp..., *auch* ʃp...], die; -, ...ien [...i̯ən] ⟨griech.⟩ (*Biol.* Schwamm); **Spon|gin**, das; -s (Stoff, aus dem das Skelett der Hornschwämme besteht); **spon|gi|ös** (schwammig; locker)

Spon|sa|li|en [ʃpɔn'za:li̯ən, *auch* sp...] *Plur.* ⟨lat.⟩ (*veraltet für* Verlobungsgeschenke); **spon|sern** [ʃp...] ⟨engl.⟩ (als Sponsor fördern); ich ...ere; **Spon|si|on**, die; -, -en ⟨lat.⟩ (*österr. für* [akad. Feier zur] Verleihung des Magistertitels); **Spon|sor** [*engl.* 'spɔnsə(r)], der; -s, *Plur.* ...oren *und bei engl. Ausspr.* -s ⟨engl.⟩ (Förderer; Geldgeber [im Sport]; Person, Gruppe, die Rundfunk- od. Fernsehsendungen [zu Reklamezwecken] finanziert); **Spon|so|ring** [*engl.* 'spɔnsəriŋ], das; -s (das Sponsern); **Spon|sor|schaft**

spon|tan [ʃp..., *auch* sp...] ⟨lat.⟩ (von selbst; von innen heraus, ohne äußeren Anlass, aus eigenem plötzlichem Antrieb); **Spon|ta|ne|i|tät**, *seltener* **Spon|ta|ni|tät**, die; -, -en (Selbsttätigkeit ohne äußere Anregung; Unwillkürlichkeit; eigener, innerer Antrieb); **Spon|ti**, der; -s, -s (*ugs. für* Angehöriger einer undogmatischen linksgerichteten Gruppe); **Spon|ti|grup|pe**

Spor, der; -[e]s, -e (*landsch. für* Schimmel[pilz])

Spo|ra|den [ʃp..., *auch* sp...] *Plur.* ⟨griech.⟩ (Inseln im Ägäischen Meer); **spo|ra|disch** (vereinzelt [vorkommend], zerstreut, [nur] gelegentlich); **Spo|ran|gi|um** (↑R 132), das; -s, ...ien [...i̯ən] (*Bot.* Sporenbildner u. -behälter)

spor|co [ʃp..., *auch* sp...] ⟨ital.⟩ (mit Verpackung); *vgl.* Sporko

Spo|re, die; -, -n ⟨griech.⟩ (ungeschlechtl. Fortpflanzungszelle bestimmter Pflanzen; Dauerform von Bakterien); eine Sporen bildende, tragende Pflanze

Spo|ren (*Plur. von* Sporn *u.* Spore)

Spo|ren|be|häl|ter; Spo|ren bil|dend *vgl.* Spore; **Spo|ren-blatt, ...kap|sel**

spo|ren|klir|rend

Spo|ren-pflan|ze, ...schlauch, ...tier|chen

Spo|ren tra|gend *vgl.* Spore

Spör|gel, Sper|gel, der; -s, - (eine Futterpflanze)

spo|rig (*landsch. für* schimmelig)

Spor|ko [ʃp..., *auch* sp...], das; -s ⟨ital.⟩ (Bruttogewicht); *vgl.* sporco

Sporn, der; -[e]s, *Plur.* Sporen *u., bes. fachspr.*, -e; einem Pferd die Sporen geben; **spor|nen** *(veraltend)*; **Sporn|räd|chen; sporn|streichs**; ↑R 46 (unverzüglich)

Spo|ro|phyt [ʃp..., *auch* sp...], der; -en, -en; ↑R 126 ⟨griech.⟩ (*Bot.* Sporenpflanze); **Spo|ro|zo|on**, das; -s, ...zoen *meist Plur.* (*Zool.* Sporentierchen)

Sport, der; -[e]s, *Plur.* *(Arten:)* -e ⟨engl.⟩ (Körperübung [im Wettkampf]; Liebhaberei); Sport treibend; **Sport-ab|zei|chen, ...an|geln** (das; -), **...ang|ler, ...an|la|ge, ...an|zug, ...art, ...ar|ti|kel, ...arzt, ...aus|rüs|tung; sport|be|geis|tert; Sport-bei|la|ge** (einer Zeitung), **...be|richt, ...be|richt|er|stat|tung, ...boot, ...cou|pé, ...dress**

Spor|tel, die; -, -n *meist Plur.* ‹griech.› (im MA. Teil des Beamteneinkommens [eingenommene Gebühren]); **Spor|tel|frei|heit,** die; - (Kostenfreiheit)

spor|teln (nebenbei u. nicht ernsthaft Sport treiben); **Sport-er|eig|nis, ...feld, ...fest, ...fi|schen** (das; -s), **...flie|ger, ...flie|ge|rei, ...flug|zeug, ...freund, ...funk|ti|o|när, ...geist** (der; -[e]s), **...ge|mein|schaft** (*Abk.* SG), **...ge|rät; sport|ge|recht; Sport-ge|schäft, ...ge|wehr, ...hal|le, ...hemd, ...herz, ...hoch|schu|le, ...ho|se, ...ho|tel, ...in|va|li|de; spor|tiv** ‹engl.› (sportlich); **Sport-jour|na|list, ...ka|me|rad, ...ka|me|rad|schaft, ...ka|no|ne** *(ugs.),* **...klei|dung, ...klub, ...leh|rer, ...leh|re|rin; Sport|ler; Sport|ler|herz; Sport|le|rin; sport|lich; sport|lich-e|le|gant** (↑R 27); **Sport|lich|keit,** die; -; **Sport|ma|schi|ne** (Sportflugzeug); **sport|mä|ßig** *vgl.* sportsmäßig; **Sport-me|di|zin** (die; -), **...me|di|zi|ner; sport|me|di|zi|nisch; Sport-mel|dung, ...mo|tor, ...müt|ze, ...nach|rich|ten** *(Plur.),* **...platz, ...pres|se, ...re|por|ter, ...re|por|te|rin, ...scha|den, ...schuh, ...sen|dung; Sports-freund** (ugs. Anrede), **...geist** (*svw.* Sportgeist), **...ka|no|ne** (*vgl.* Sportkanone), **...mann** (*Plur.* ...leute, *auch* ...männer); **sports|mä|ßig,** sport|mä|ßig; **Sport-spra|che, ...stät|te, ...strumpf, ...stu|dent, ...stu|den|tin; Sports|wear** [ˈspɔ:(r)tswɛ(r)], der *od.* das; -[s] ‹engl.› (sportliche [Freizeit]kleidung); **Sport-tau|chen** (das; -s), **...tau|cher; Sport trei|bend** *vgl.* Sport; **Sport-un|fall, ...un|ter|richt, ...ver|band, ...ver|ein** (*Abk.* SV; ↑R 23: Turn- und Sportverein; *Abk.* TuS), **...ver|let|zung, ...waf|fe, ...wa|gen, ...wart, ...welt** (die; -), **...wis|sen|schaft** (die; -), **...zei|tung, ...zwei|sit|zer**

Spot [spɔt], der; -s, -s ‹engl.› (kurzer Werbetext, -film; *kurz für* Spotlight); **Spot|ge|schäft** (Geschäft gegen sofortige Lieferung u. Kasse [im internationalen Verkehr]); **Spot|light** [...lait], das; -s, -s (auf einen Punkt gerichtetes Licht); **Spot|markt** (Markt, auf dem Rohöl frei verkauft wird)

Spott, der; -[e]s; **Spott|bild; spott|bil|lig** *(ugs.);* **Spott|dros|sel; Spöt|te|lei; spöt|teln;** ich ...[e]le (↑R 16); **spot|ten; Spöt|ter; Spöt|te|rei; Spöt|te|rin; Spott-ge|burt** *(geh. abwertend),* **...ge|dicht, ...geld** (das; -[e]s; *ugs.*); **spöt|tisch; Spott-lust** (die; -), **...na|me, ...preis** *(ugs.),* **...re|de, ...sucht** (die; -), **...vers, ...vo|gel**

S. P. Q. R. = Senatus Populusque Romanus

Sprach-at|las (Kartenwerk zur Sprachgeographie; *vgl.* [4]Atlas), **...bar|ri|e|re** *(Sprachw.),* **...bau** (der; -[e]s); **sprach|be|gabt; Sprach-be|herr|schung, ...be|ra|tung, ...denk|mal; Spra|che,** die; -, -n; **Sprach|ecke** (↑R 132; in Zeitungen und Zeitschriften); **Sprach|emp|fin|den; Spra|chen-fra|ge** (die; -), **...kampf, ...recht** (das; -[e]s), **...schu|le, ...stu|di|um; Sprach-ent|wick|lung, ...er|werb, ...fä|hig|keit, ...fa|mi|lie, ...feh|ler; sprach|fer|tig; Sprach-fer|tig|keit** (die; -), **...for|scher, ...for|sche|rin, ...for|schung, ...füh|rer, ...ge|biet, ...ge|brauch** (der; -[e]s), **...ge|fühl** (das; -[e]s), **...ge|mein|schaft, ...ge|nie, ...ge|o|gra|phie, ...ge|schich|te; sprach|ge|schicht|lich; Sprach-ge|sell|schaft, ...ge|setz; sprach|ge|stört; Sprach|ge|walt,** die; -; **sprach-ge|wal|tig, ...ge|wandt; Sprach-ge|wandt|heit** (die; -), **...gren|ze, ...gut** (das; -[e]s); **...spra|chig** (z. B. fremdsprachig; *vgl. d.*); **Sprach-in|sel, ...kar|te, ...ken|ner, ...kennt|nis|se** *(Plur.),* **...kom|pe|tenz, ...kri|tik, ...kul|tur** (die; -), **...kun|de** *(veraltend);* **sprach|kun|dig; Sprach|kund|ler** *(veraltet);* **sprach|kund|lich** *(veraltet);* **Sprach-kunst** (die; -), **...kurs, ...la|bor, ...laut, ...leh|re, ...leh|rer, ...leh|re|rin, ...len|kung; sprach|lich; ...sprach|lich** (z. B. fremdsprachlich; *vgl. d.*); **sprach|los; Sprach|lo|sig|keit,** die; -; **Sprach-ma|ni|pu|la|ti|on, ...mitt|ler, ...norm, ...nor|mung, ...pfle|ge, ...phi|lo|so|phie, ...psy|cho|lo|gie, ...raum, ...re|ge|lung, ...rein|heit, ...rei|se; sprach|rich|tig; Sprach-rich|tig|keit, ...rohr, ...schatz** (der; -es), **...schicht, ...schnit|zer, ...schöp|fer; sprach|schöp|fe|risch; Sprach-schwie|rig|keit, ...sil|be, ...so|zi|o|lo|gie, ...stamm, ...sta|tis|tik, ...stil, ...stö|rung, ...stu|di|um, ...sys|tem, ...ta|lent, ...teil|ha|ber; sprach|üb|lich; Sprach-übung** (↑R 132), **...un|ter|richt, ...ver|ein, ...ver|glei|chung, ...ver|stoß, ...ver|wir|rung, ...wan|del; sprach|wid|rig; Sprach-wis|sen|schaft, ...wis|sen|schaft|ler, ...wis|sen|schaft|le|rin; sprach|wis|sen|schaft|lich; Sprach-zent|rum** (Teil des Gehirns), **...zeug|nis**

sprat|zen (*Hüttenw.* Gasblasen auswerfen)

Spray [ʃpre:, *auch* spre:], der *od.* das; -s, -s ‹engl.› (Flüssigkeitszerstäuber; in feinsten Tröpfchen versprühte Flüssigkeit); **Spray|do|se; spray|en;** gesprayt; **Spray|er,** der; -s, - (jmd., der [Grafitti an Wände o. Ä.] sprayt)

Sprech-akt *(Sprachw.),* **...an|la|ge, ...bla|se** (in Comics), **...büh|ne, ...chor** (der); **spre|chen;** du sprichst; du sprachst; du sprächest; gesprochen; sprich!; vor sich hin sprechen; das Kind lernt sprechen; (↑R 50:) das lange Sprechen strengt mich an; **Spre|cher; Spre|che|rin; spre|che|risch; Sprech-er|laub|nis, ...er|zie|hung, ...funk; Sprech|funk|ge|rät; Sprech-ge|sang, ...kun|de** (die; -); **sprech|kund|lich; Sprech-kunst, ...leh|rer, ...mu|schel** (am Telefon), **...pau|se** (*vgl.* [1]Pause), **...plat|te** (Schallplatte mit gesprochenem Text), **...rol|le, ...sil|be, ...stö|rung, ...stun|de; Sprech|stun|den|hil|fe; Sprech-tag, ...tech|nik, ...übung** (↑R 132), **...un|ter|richt, ...ver|bot, ...wei|se** (die; -, -n), **...werk|zeu|ge** *(Plur.),* **...zeit, ...zel|le** *(Telefon),* **...zim|mer**

Spree, die; - (l. Nebenfluss der Havel); **Spree-Athen** (*scherzh. für* Berlin); **Spree|wald,** der; -[e]s (↑R 105); **[1]Spree|wäl|der** (↑R 103); - Tracht; **[2]Spree|wäl|der** (Bewohner des Spreewaldes); **Spree|wäl|de|rin**

Spre|he, die; -, -n (*westmitteld. u. nordwestd. für* [3]Star)

Sprei|ßel, der, *österr.* das; -s, - (*landsch., bes. österr. für* Splitter, Span); **Sprei|ßel|holz,** das; -es (*österr. für* Kleinholz)

Spreit|de|cke *od.* **Sprei|te,** die; -, -n (*landsch. für* Lage [Getreide zum Dreschen]; [Bett]decke); **sprei|ten** (*veraltend für* ausbreiten); **Spreit|la|ge** (*landsch. für* Getreidelage)

spreiz|bei|nig; Spreiz|dü|bel; Sprei|ze, die; -, -n (Strebe, Stütze; eine Turnübung); **spreilzen;** du spreizt; gespreizt; **Spreiz˯fuß,** **...sprung** *(Turnen);* **Spreilzung;** **Spreizlwinldel**

Sprenglbomlbe; Sprenlgel, der; -s, - (Amtsgebiet eines Bischofs, Pfarrers; *veraltend, noch österr. für* Amtsbezirk); **sprenlgen;** **Spreng˯gelschoss** *(vgl.* Geschoss), **...gralnalte, ...kammer, ...kaplsel, ...komlmanldo, ...kopf, ...körlper, ...kraft, ...ladung, ...laut** *(für* Explosiv), **...meislter, ...mitltel** (das), **...patrolne, ...pullver, ...punkt, ...satz;** **Sprenglsel,** der *od.* das; -s, - *(ugs. für* Sprenkel); **Sprengstoff; Sprenglstofflanlschlag;** **sprenglstofflhalltig; Sprengstofflpalket; Sprengltrupp;** **Sprenlgung; Spreng˯walgen, ...werk** *(Bauw.* Träger mit Streben), **...wirlkung**

Sprenlkel, der; -s, - (Fleck, Punkt, Tupfen); **sprenlkellig,** sprenklig; **sprenlkeln;** ich ...[e]le (↑R 16); gesprenkelt (getupft); ein gesprenkeltes Fell, Kleid; **sprenklig** *vgl.* sprenkelig

sprenlzen *(südwestd. für* stark sprengen; regnen); du sprenzt

Spreu, die; -; **spreulig**

Sprichlwort *Plur.* ...wörter; **Sprichlwörlterlsammllung;** **sprichlwörtllich;** -e Redensart

Spielgel, der; -s, - (Bügel für das Wagenverdeck; *landsch. für* Aufhängeholz der Fleischer)

Sprielße, die; -, -n *(Bauw.* Stütze, Quer-, Stützbalken; *landsch. für* Sprosse); **Sprielßel,** das; -s, -[n] *(österr. ugs. für* Sprosse); [1]**sprielßen** *(Bauw.* stützen); du sprießt; du sprießtest; gesprießt; sprieß[e]!; [2]**sprielßen** (hervorwachsen); es sprießt; es spross; es sprösse; gesprossen; sprieß[e]!; **Sprießlholz** *Plur.* ...hölzer *(Bauw.)*

Spriet, das; -[e]s, -e *(Seemannsspr.* dünne Spiere)

[1]**Spring,** der; -[e]s, -e *(landsch. für* das Sprudeln; Quelle); [2]**Spring,** die; -, -e *(Seemannsspr.* zum ausgeworfenen Anker führende Trosse); **Spring˯blenlde** *(Fotogr.),* **...brunlnen; sprinlgen;** du springst; du sprangst; du sprängest; gesprungen; spring[e]!; etwas - lassen *(ugs. für* ausgeben); **Sprinlger; Sprinlgelrin; Springerlle,** das; -s, - *(südd.* ein Gebäck), **Sprinlgerlli** das; -s, - *(schweiz. svw.* Springerle); **Spring˯flut, ...form** (eine Kuchenform); **Springlinslfeld,** der; -[e]s, -e *(scherzh.);* **Spring˯kälfer, ...kraut** (das; -[e]s; eine Pflanzengattung); **springllelbenldig;** **Spring˯maus, ...meslser** (das), **...pferd, ...prülfung, ...reilten,** (das, -s, -), **...reilter; Springseil,** Sprunglseil (ein Spiel- und Gymnastikgerät); **Springltilde** *(svw.* Springflut); **Springlwurz,** **Springlwurlzel**

Sprinkller, der; -s, - ‹engl.› (Berieselungsgerät); **Sprinkllerlanllage** (automat. Feuerlöschanlage)

Sprint, der; -s, -s ‹engl.› *(Sport* Kurzstreckenlauf); **sprinlten;** **Sprinlter,** der; -s, -; **Sprinltelrin;** **Sprinlterlrenlnen** *(Radsport);* **Sprint˯strelcke, ...verlmölgen** (das; -s)

Sprit, der; -[e]s, -e *Plur. selten* *(kurz für* Spiritus; *ugs. für* Treibstoff); **sprilig** (spritähnlich)

Spritz˯aplpalrat, ...arlbeit, ...beton, ...beultel *(Gastron.),* **...düse; Spritlze,** die; -, -n; **spritlzen;** du spritzt; **Spritlzen˯haus** *(veraltend),* **...meislter** *(früher);* **Spritlzer; Spritlzelrei; Spritz˯fahrt** *(ugs.),* **...gelbalckelne** (das; -n; ↑R 5 ff.), **...guss** (der; ...gusses; *Technik*); **spritlzig;** -er Wein; **Spritlziglkeit,** die; -; **Spritz˯kulchen, ...lack, ...lackielrung, ...mallelrei, ...pisltole, ...tour** *(ugs.)*

sprÖd, sprölde; [1]**Sprölde,** die; - *(älter für* Sprödigkeit); [2]**Sprölde,** die; -n, -n; ↑R 5 ff. (sprödes Mädchen); **Sprödlheit,** die; -; **Sprödiglkeit,** die; -

Spross, der; -es, *Plur.* Sprosse *u.* Sprossen (Nachkomme; Pflanzentrieb; *Jägerspr.* Teil des Geweihs); **Sprosslachlse** *(Bot.);* **Sprösslchen; Sproslse,** die; -, -n (Querholz der Leiter; Hautfleck; *auch für* Spross [Geweihteil]); **sproslsen;** du sprosst, er sprosst; du sprosstest; gesprosst; sprosse! *u.* spross!; **Sproslsen˯kohl** (der; -[e]s; *österr. für* Rosenkohl), **...wand** (ein Turngerät)

Sproslser, der; -s, - (ein Vogel)

Sprössling *(scherzh. für* jmds. Kind, bes. Sohn); **Sproslsung** *(veraltend)*

Sprotlte, die; -, -n (ein Fisch); Kieler Sprotten; ↑R 103

Spruch, der; -[e]s, Sprüche; **Spruch˯band** (das; *Plur.* ...bänder), **...buch, ...dichltung; Sprüchelkloplfer** *(ugs. abwertend);* **Sprülchelkloplfelrel; Spruchkamlmer** (frühere Entnazifizierungsbehörde); **Sprüchllein;** **spruchlreif; Spruchlweislheit**

Sprulde, der; -s, -; **Sprudellkopf** *(veraltet für* aufbrausender Mensch); **sprulldeln** *(österr. auch für* quirlen); ich ...[e]le (↑R 16); **Sprulldel˯quellle** *(veraltend),* **...stein** *(für* Aragonit), **...wasser** *(Plur.* ...wässer); **Sprudller** *(österr. für* Quirl)

Sprue [spru:], die; - ‹engl.› *(Med.* fieberhafte Erkrankung [mit Gewebsveränderungen])

Sprühldolse; sprülhen; Sprüh˯flalsche, ...plaslter, ...relgen

Sprung, der; -[e]s, Sprünge; immer auf dem - sein; jmdn. auf einen - besuchen; **Sprung˯anllage, ...ballken** (beim Weitsprung), **...belcken, ...bein; sprunglbereit; Sprung˯brett, ...delckel, ...feldet; Sprunglfelderlmatlratze; sprunglferltig; Sprung˯gelenk, ...grulbe; sprunglhaft;** **Sprunglhafltiglkeit,** die; -; **Sprung˯hölhe, ...hülgel, ...kraft, ...lauf** *(Skisport),* **...pferd** *(Turnen),* **...schanlze** *(Skisport),* **...seil** *(vgl.* Springseil), **...stab** *(Stabhochsprung),* **...tuch** *(Plur.* ...tücher), **...turm, ...wurf** *(Handball, Basketball)*

SPS = Sozialdemokratische Partei der Schweiz

Spulcke, die; - *(ugs. für* Speichel); **spulcken** (speien); **Spucklnapf**

Spuk, der; -[e]s, -e (Gespenst[erscheinung]); **spulken** (gespensterhaftes Unwesen treiben); **Spukelrei** *(ugs.);* **Spuk˯gelschichte, ...gelstalt; spuklhaft**

Spül˯aultolmat, ...belcken

Spulle, die; -, -n

Spülle, die; -, -n

spullen

spüllen

Spuller (an der Nähmaschine)

Spüller; Spüllelrin; Spüllicht, das; -s, -e *(veraltend für* Spülwasser); **Spüllkaslten**

Spullmalschilne

Spül˯malschilne, ...mitltel (das), **...stein** *(landsch. für* Spülbecken), **...tisch; Spüllung; Spüllwaslser** *Plur.* ...wässer

Spullwurm

Spulmanlte [sp...], der; -s, -s ‹ital.› *(ital. Bez. für* Schaumwein)

[1]**Spund,** der; -[e]s, *Plur.* Spünde *u.* -e ‹ital.› (Fassverschluss; *Tischlerei* Feder)

[2]**Spund,** der; -[e]s, -e *(ugs. für* junger Kerl)

Spund˯bohlle *(Bauw.),* **...bohlrer;** **spunlden** *(Tischlerei* mit Spund versehen; [Bretter] durch Feder und Nut verbinden); eine gespundete Tür; **spunldig** *(landsch. für* nicht richtig durchgebacken); **Spundlloch; Spunldung;** **Spund˯wand** (wasserdichte

Bohlen- od. Eisenwand), **...zapfen; Spun|ten,** der; -s, - (*schweiz. für* [1]Spund)

Spur, die; -, -en; **spür|bar; Spurbrei|te; spu|ren** (*Skisport* die erste Spur legen; *ugs. für* sich einordnen, gefügig sein); **spü|ren; Spuren|ele|ment** (↑R 132) *meist Plur.* (Element, das für den Organismus unentbehrlich ist, aber nur in sehr geringen Mengen benötigt wird); **Spu|ren◡le|ger** *(Skisport),* **...nach|weis, ...si|che|rung; Spü|rer; Spür|hund; ...spu|rig** (z. B. schmalspurig); **Spur|kranz** (bei Schienenfahrzeugen); **spurlos; Spür|na|se** *(übertr. ugs.);* **Spur|ril|le** *(Verkehrsw.);* **spur|sicher; Spür|sinn,** der; -[e]s

Spurt, der; -[e]s, *Plur.* -s, *selten* -e ‹engl.› (schneller Lauf [über einen Teil einer Strecke]); **spur|ten; spurt◡schnell, ...stark; Spurtver|mö|gen**

Spur◡wech|sel, ...wei|te

Spu|ta (*Plur. von* Sputum)

spu|ten, sich (sich beeilen)

Sput|nik [ʃp..., *auch* sp...], der; -s, -s ‹russ., „Gefährte"› (Bez. für die ersten sowjet. Erdsatelliten)

Spu|tum [ʃp..., *auch* sp...], das; -s, ...ta ‹lat.› (*Med.* Auswurf)

Spvg., Spvgg. = Spielvereinigung

Square [skwɛ:(r)], der *od.* das; -[s], -s ‹engl.› (*engl. Bez. für* Quadrat; Platz); **Square|dance** [...'da:ns], der; -, -s [...siz] (amerik. Volkstanz)

Squash [skvɔʃ], das; - ‹engl.› (Fruchtsaft mit Fruchtfleisch; dem Tennis ähnl. Ballspiel)

Squat|ter ['skwɔtə(r)], der; -s, - ‹engl.› (*früher* [amerik.] Ansiedler, der ohne Rechtsanspruch auf unbebautem Land siedelt)

Squaw [skwɔ:], die; -, -s ‹indian.-engl.› (nordamerik. Indianerfrau)

Squi|re [skwaiə(r)], der; -[s], -s ‹engl.› (engl. Gutsherr)

sr = Steradiant

Sr = *chem. Zeichen für* Strontium

SR = Saarländischer Rundfunk

Sr. = Seiner (Durchlaucht usw.)

SRG = Schweizerische Radio- und Fernsehgesellschaft

SRl *vgl.* Riyal

Sri Lan|ka ‹singhal.› (Inselstaat im Indischen Ozean); **Sri-Lan|ker; Sri-Lan|ke|rin; sri-lan|kisch**

SS. = Sante, Santi

SSD = Staatssicherheitsdienst (ehem. in der DDR)

SSO = Südsüdost[en]

SSR = Sozialistische Sowjetrepublik (bis 1991) (*vgl.* SSSR)

SSSR ‹*für* russ. CCCP› = Union der Sozialistischen Sowjetrepubliken (bis 1991) (ehem. Sowjetunion)

SSW = Südsüdwest[en]

SS 20 (Mittelstreckenrakete der ehem. Sowjetunion); **SS-20-Rake|te**

st! (Ruf, mit dem man [leise] auf sich aufmerksam machen will; Aufforderung, leise zu sein)

St = [2]Saint; Stratus

St. = Sankt; [1]Saint; Satang; Stück; Stunde

s. t. = sine tempore

S. T. = salvo titulo

Sta. = Santa

[1]**Staat,** der; -[e]s, -en ‹lat.›; von -s wegen; Staaten bildende Insekten; [2]**Staat,** der; -[e]s (*ugs. für* Prunk); - machen (mit etwas prunken); **Staa|ten bil|dend** *vgl.* [1]Staat; **Staa|ten|bund** ‹*zu* [1]Bund›; **staa|ten|los; Staa|tenlo|se,** der *u.* die; -n, -n (↑R 5 ff.); **Staa|ten|lo|sig|keit,** die; -; **staat|lich; staat|li|cher|seits; Staat|lich|keit,** die; - (Status eines Staates); **Staats◡af|fä|re, ...akt, ...ak|ti|on, ...ama|teur** (↑R 132; Amateursportler, der vom Staat so sehr gefördert wird, dass er den Sport wie ein Profi betreiben kann); **Staats◡amt, ...an|ge|hö|ri|ge** (der *u.* die), **...an|ge|hö|rig|keit** (die; -, -en), **...an|lei|he, ...an|walt; Staatsan|walt|schaft; Staats◡ap|parat, ...ar|chiv, ...auf|sicht, ...bank** (*Plur.* ...banken), **...bankett, ...bank|rott, ...be|am|te, ...be|gräb|nis, ...be|such, ...betrieb, ...bib|li|o|thek, ...bür|ger, ...bür|ge|rin; Staats|bür|gerkun|de,** die; - (Unterrichtsfach, bes. ehem. in der DDR); **staatsbür|ger|lich;** -e Rechte; **Staatsbür|ger|schaft; Staats◡bürgschaft, ...die|ner, ...dienst; staats|ei|gen;** -er Wald; **Staatsei|gen|tum; staats|er|hal|tend; Staats◡exa|men** (↑R 132), **...fei|er|tag; staats|feind|lich; Staats◡feind|lich|keit** (die; -), **...fi|nan|zen** *(Plur.),* **...flag|ge, ...form, ...füh|rung, ...ge|biet; staats|ge|fähr|dend;** -e Schriften; **Staats◡ge|fähr|dung, ...gefäng|nis, ...ge|heim|nis, ...gelder** *(Plur.),* **...ge|richts|hof** (der; -[e]s), **...ge|walt** (die; -), **...grenze, ...grün|dung, ...haus|halt, ...ho|heit** (die; -), **...hym|ne** (*svw.* Nationalhymne), **...kanz|lei, ...ka|pi|ta|lis|mus, ...ka|ros|se, ...kas|se, ...kir|che, ...kleid** (*ugs. veraltend für* Festtagskleid), **...kos|ten** (*Plur.;* auf -), **...kunst** (die; -), **...leh|re, ...lot|te|rie, ...mann** (*Plur.* ...männer); **staats|män|nisch; Staats◡minis|ter, ...mo|no|pol; staats|mono|po|lis|tisch; Staats◡notstand, ...ober|haupt** (↑R 132), **...ord|nung, ...or|gan, ...pa|pier, ...par|tei, ...po|li|tik** (die; -); **staats|po|li|tisch; Staats◡präsi|dent, ...prä|si|den|tin, ...prüfung** (die erste, die zweite -), **...qual|le** (ein Nesseltier), **...räson, ...rat** (*Plur.* ...räte); **Staatsrats|vor|sit|zen|de; Staatsrecht,** das; -[e]s; **Staats|rechtler; staats|recht|lich; Staats◡re|li|gi|on, ...sä|ckel, ...schauspie|ler, ...schau|spie|le|rin, ...schrei|ber** (*schweiz. für* Vorsteher der Staatskanzlei), **...schulden** *(Plur.),* **...schutz, ...sek|retär, ...sek|re|tä|rin, ...si|cherheit** (die; -); **Staats|si|cherheits|dienst,** der; -[e]s (*früher* polit. Geheimpolizei in der DDR; *Abk.* SSD); **Staats◡so|zi|a|lismus, ...steu|er** (die), **...streich, ...the|a|ter, ...trau|er, ...ver|brechen, ...ver|dros|sen|heit, ...ver|schul|dung, ...ver|trag, ...volk, ...we|sen, ...wirt|schaft, ...wis|sen|schaft, ...wohl**

Stab, der; -[e]s, Stäbe; 25 - Roheisen (↑R 90); **Stab|an|ten|ne**

Sta|bat Ma|ter [st... -], das; - -, - - ‹lat., „die Mutter [Jesu] stand [am Kreuze]"› ([vertonte] mittelalterl. Sequenz)

Stäb|chen; Stab|ei|sen

Sta|bel|le, die; -, -n ‹roman.› (*schweiz. für* Stuhl, dessen Beine [u. Lehne] einzeln in die Sitzfläche eingelassen sind)

stä|beln (*landsch. für* [Pflanzen] anbinden)

sta|bend (*für* alliterierend)

Sta|berl, der; -s (eine Gestalt der Wiener Posse)

stab|för|mig; Stab|füh|rung (musikal. Leitung); unter der - von ...; **Stab|hoch|sprin|ger; Stabhoch|sprung** *(Sport)*

sta|bil ‹lat.› (beständig, fest, haltbar; [körperlich] kräftig, widerstandsfähig); **Sta|bi|le,** das; -s, -s ‹engl.› (Kunstwerk in Form einer [im Gegensatz zum Mobile] auf dem Boden stehenden metallenen Konstruktion); **Sta|bi|li|sa|ti|on,** die; -, -en ‹lat.›; **Sta|bi|li|sa|tor,** der; -s, ...oren (Vorrichtung zur Verringerung der Kurvenneigung bei Kraftwagen; Zusatz, der die Zersetzung chem. Verbindungen verhindern soll; elektr. Spannungsregler); **sta|bi|li|sie|ren** (stabil machen); **Sta|bi|li|sierung; Sta|bi|li|sie|rungs◡flä|che**

(Flugw.), **...flos|se** (bei [Renn]wagen); **Sta|bi|li|tät,** die; - (Beständigkeit, [Stand]festigkeit); **Sta|bi|li|täts|po|li|tik,** die; -

Stab|lam|pe; Stab|reim (Anlautreim, Alliteration); **stab|rei|mend** (*für* alliterierend); **Stabs-arzt, ...feld|we|bel; stab|sich|tig** (*für* astigmatisch); **Stab|sich|tig|keit,** die; - (*für* Astigmatismus); **Stabs-of|fi|zier, ...stel|le, ...ve|te|ri|när, ...wacht|meis|ter; Stab|ta|schen|lam|pe; Stab-wech|sel** (beim Staffellauf), **...werk** *(got. Archit.)*

stacc. = staccato; **stac|ca|to** [sta'ka:to] ‹ital.› (*Musik* deutlich abgesetzt; *Abk.* stacc.); **Stac|ca|to** *vgl.* Stakkato

Sta|chel, der; -s, -n; **Sta|chel-bee|re, ...draht; Sta|chel|draht|ver|hau; Sta|chel-hals|band, ...häu|ter** *(Zool.)*; **sta|che|lig,** stach|lig; **Sta|che|lig|keit,** Stach|lig|keit, die; -; **sta|cheln;** ich ...[e]le (↑R 16); **Sta|chel-schwein, ...zaun** *(veraltet)*; **stach|lig** usw. *vgl.* stachelig usw.

Stack, das; -[e]s, -e (*Seew.* Buhne); **Stack|deich**

stad (*österr. u. bayr. ugs. für* still, ruhig)

Sta|del, der; -s, *Plur.* -, *schweiz.* Städel (*südd., österr., schweiz. für* Scheune, kleines [offenes] Gebäude)

Sta|den, der; -s, - (*südd. für* Ufer[straße])

sta|di|al ‹griech.-lat.› (stufenweise, abschnittsweise); **Sta|di|on,** das; -s, ...ien [...i̯ən] ‹griech.› (altgriech. Wegmaß; Kampfbahn, Sportfeld); **Sta|di|on-an|sa|ge, ...spre|cher; Sta|di|um,** das; -s, ...ien [...i̯ən] ([Zu]stand, [Entwicklungs]stufe, Abschnitt)

Stadt, die; -, Städte[1]; **Stadt|ar|chiv; stadt|aus|wärts; Stadt-au|to|bahn, ...bahn, ...bau** (*Plur.* ...bauten; städt. Bau), **...bau|amt, ...bau|rat; stadt|be|kannt; Stadt-be|völ|ke|rung, ...be|woh|ner, ...be|zirk, ...bib|li|o|thek, ...bild, ...bü|che|rei, ...bum|mel** *(ugs.)*; **Städt|chen**[1]; **Stadt-chro|nik, ...di|rek|tor; Städ|te|bau**[1], der; -[e]s (Anlage u. Planung von Städten); **städ|te|bau|lich**[1]; **Städ|te-bil|der**[1] *(Plur.)*, **...bund** (der; im MA.); **stadt|ein|wärts; Städ|te-kampf**[1], **...part|ner|schaft; Städ|ter**[1]; **Städ|te|rin**[1]; **Städ|te|tag**[1]; **Stadt-fahrt, ...flucht** (*vgl.* ²Flucht), **...füh|rer, ...gar|ten, ...gas** (das; -es), **...ge|biet, ...ge|spräch, ...gra|ben, ...gue|ril|la, ...haus, ...in|di|a|ner** (*ugs. für* jmd., der seine Ablehnung der bestehenden Gesellschaft durch auffällige Kleidung [u. Gesichtsbemalung] zum Ausdruck bringt); **Städt|in|ne|re; städ|tisch**[1]; -es Leben; -e Verwaltung; **Stadt-käm|me|rer, ...kas|se, ...kern, ...klatsch** *(ugs.)*, **...kreis; stadt|kun|dig;** stadt- und landkundig (↑R 23); **Städt|lein**[1]; **Stadt-mau|er, ...mensch, ...mis|si|on, ...mit|te, ...mu|si|kant** (*früher* Musikant im Dienst einer Stadt), **...park, ...pfei|fer** (*vgl.* Stadtmusikant), **...plan** (*vgl.* ²Plan), **...pla|nung, ...prä|si|dent** (*schweiz. svw.* Oberbürgermeister), **...rand; Stadt|rand-er|ho|lung, ...sied|lung; Stadt-rat** (*Plur.* ...räte), **...rä|tin, ...recht** (das; -[e]s), **...rei|ni|gung, ...rund|fahrt, ...sa|nie|rung, ...schrei|ber, ...schrei|be|rin, ...staat, ...strei|cher, ...strei|che|rin, ...teil** (der), **...the|a|ter, ...tor** (das), **...vä|ter** *(Plur.)*, **...ver|kehr** (der; -s), **...ver|ord|ne|te** (der u. die; -n, -n [↑R 5 ff.]); **Stadt|ver|ord|ne|ten|ver|samm|lung; Stadt-ver|wal|tung, ...vier|tel, ...wald, ...wap|pen, ...wer|ke** *(Plur.)*, **...woh|nung, ...zent|rum**

Staël [sta(:)l], Madame de (franz. Schriftstellerin)

Sta|fel, der; -s, Stäfel ‹roman.› (*schweiz. für* Alpweide mit Hütte[n])

Sta|fet|te, die; -, -n ‹ital.› (*früher für* [reitender] Eilbote, Meldereiter; Gruppe von Personen, die, etappenweise wechselnd, etwas [schnell] übermitteln; *Sport veraltet für* Staffel); **Sta|fet|ten|lauf**

Staf|fa|ge [...'fa:ʒə, *österr.* ...'fa:ʒ], die; -, -n [...ʒ(ə)n] ‹französierende Bildung› (Beiwerk, Belebung [eines Bildes] durch Figuren; Nebensächliches, Ausstattung)

Staf|fel, die; -, -n (↑R 28:) 4 × 100-m-Staffel od. 4-mal-100-Meter-Staffel; **Staf|fel-an|lei|he** *(Wirtsch.)*, **...be|tei|li|gung** *(Wirtsch.)*; **Staf|fe|lei; staf|fel|för|mig; staf|fe|lig,** staff|lig; **Staf|fel|lauf** *(Sport)*; **Staf|fel|mie|te; staf|feln;** ich ...[e]le (↑R 16); **Staf|fel-preis** (*vgl.* ²Preis), **...rech|nung, ...span|ne** *(Wirtsch.)*; **Staf|fe|lung,** Staff|lung; **staf|fel|wei|se; Staf|fel|wett|be|werb** *(Sport)*

staf|fie|ren ‹franz.› (*österr. für* schmücken, putzen; einen Stoff auf einen anderen aufnähen; *veraltet für* ausstaffieren); **Staf|fie|rer; Staf|fie|rung**

staff|lig *vgl.* staffelig; **Staff|lung** *vgl.* Staffelung

Stag, das; -[e]s, -e[n] (*Seemannsspr.* Halte-, Stütztau)

Stage [sta:ʒ], der; -s, -s *u.* die; -, -s ‹franz.› (*schweiz. für* Aufenthalt bei einer Firma o. Ä. zur weiterführenden Ausbildung)

Stag|fla|ti|on [ʃt..., *auch* st...], die; -, -en ‹aus Stagnation *u.* Inflation› (von wirtschaftlichem Stillstand begleitete Inflation)

Sta|gi|aire [sta'ʒi̯ɛ:r], der; -s, -s ‹franz.› (*schweiz. für* jmd., der einen Stage absolviert)

Sta|gio|ne [sta'dʒo:nə], die; -, -n ‹ital.› (Spielzeit ital. Operntheater)

Stag|na|ti|on [ʃt..., *auch* st...] (↑R 130), die; -, -en ‹lat.› (Stockung, Stillstand); **stag|nie|ren; Stag|nie|rung**

Stag|se|gel (*Seemannsspr.* an einem Stag gefahrenes Segel)

Stahl, der; -[e]s, *Plur.* Stähle, *selten* Stahle (schmiedbares Eisen); **Stahl-ar|bei|ter, ...bad, ...band** (das; *Plur.* ...bänder), **...bau** (*Plur.* ...bauten), **...be|ton; stahl|blau; Stahl-blech, ...bürs|te, ...draht; stäh|len; stäh|lern** (aus Stahl); -e Waffe; -er Wille; **Stahl-er|zeu|gung, ...fe|der, ...flach|stra|ße** *(Straßenbau)*, **...fla|sche; stahl-grau, ...hart; Stahl-helm** (*vgl.* ¹Helm), **...in|dust|rie, ...kam|mer, ...ko|cher** (*ugs. für* Stahlarbeiter), **...plat|te, ...rohr; Stahl|rohr|mö|bel; Stahl-ross** (*scherzh. für* Fahrrad), **...skel|lett|bau|wei|se** (die; -), **...ste|cher, ...stich, ...stra|ße** (*kurz für* Stahlflachstraße), **...trä|ger, ...tros|se, ...werk, ...wol|le** (die; -)

Sta|ke, die; -, -n *u.* Sta|ken, der; -s, - (*landsch. für* Stange zum Schieben von Flößen, Kähnen); **sta|ken** (*landsch. für* mit Staken fortbewegen; *selten für* staksen); **Stakes** [ste:ks] *Plur.* ‹engl.› (Einsätze bei Pferderennen; Pferderennen, die aus Einsätzen bestritten werden); **Sta|ket,** das; -[e]s, -e ‹niederl.› (Lattenzaun); **Sta|ke|te,** die; -, -n (*bes. österr. für* Latte); **Sta|ke|ten|zaun**

Stak|ka|to [st..., *auch* ʃt...], das; -s, *Plur.* -s *u.* ...ti ‹ital.› (*Musik* kurz abgestoßener Vortrag); *vgl.* staccato

stak|sen (*ugs. für* mit steifen Schritten gehen); du stakst; **stak|sig**

[1] [*auch* 'ʃtɛ...]

Sta|lag|mi̱t [ʃt..., *auch* st..., *auch* ...'mit], der; *Gen.* -s *u.* -en, *Plur.* -e[n] (↑R 126) ‹griech.› (Tropfstein vom Boden her, Auftropfstein); **sta|lag|mi̱|tisch; Sta|lak|ti̱t** [ʃt..., *auch* st..., *auch* ...'tit], der; *Gen.* -s *u.* -en, *Plur.* -e[n]; ↑R 126 (Tropfstein an Decken, Abtropfstein); **Sta|lak|ti̱|ten|ge|wöl|be** (islam. Baukunst); **sta|lak|ti̱|tisch**

Sta̱|lin [ʃt..., *auch* st...] (sowjet. Politiker); **Sta̱|lin|grad** *vgl.* Wolgograd; **Sta|li|ni̱s|mus**, der; - (von Stalin geprägte Interpretation des Marxismus u. die von ihm danach geprägte Herrschaftsform); **Sta|li|ni̱st**, der; -en, -en (↑R 126); **sta|li|ni̱s|tisch; Sta̱|lin|or|gel** (*früher* sowjet. Raketenwerfer; ↑R 95)

Stạll, der; -[e]s, Ställe; **Stạll|bur|sche; Stặll|chen; Stạll|dün|ger** (natürl. Dünger); **stạl|len; Stạll‿füt|te|rung, ...ge|fähr|te** *(Rennsport)*, **...ge|ruch** (*auch für* Zugehörigkeit zu einem bestimmten Verein), **...ha|se** (Hauskaninchen), **...knecht** *(veraltend)*; **Stạll|la|ter|ne** (↑R 136); **Stạll‿magd** *(veraltend)*, **...meis|ter; Stạl|lung; Stạll|wa|che** (*auch für* Präsenz am Regierungssitz während der Parlamentsferien)

Stạm|bul [ʃt..., *auch* st...] (Stadtteil von Istanbul)

Sta|mi|no̱|di|um [ʃt..., *auch* st...], das; -s, ...ien [...i̯ən] ‹lat.› (*Bot.* unfruchtbares Staubblatt)

Stạmm, der; -[e]s, Stämme; **Stạmm|ak|tie; Stạmm‿baum, ...be|leg|schaft, ...be|set|zung, ...buch, ...burg; stạmm|bür|tig** (*Bot.* am Stamm ansetzend [von Blüten]); **Stặmm|chen; Stạmm|da|ten** *Plur. (EDV)*; **Stạmm|ein|la|ge** *(Wirtsch.)*

stạm|meln; ich ...[e]le (↑R 16)

stạm|men

stạm|mern (*nordd. für* stammeln); ich ...ere (↑R 16)

Stạm|mes‿be|wusst|sein, ...füh|rer, ...fürst, ...ge|schich|te (die; -); **stạm|mes|ge|schicht|lich; Stạm|mes‿häupt|ling, ...kun|de** (die; -), **...na|me, ...sa|ge; Stạmm|es|sen; Stạm|mes‿spra|che, ...ver|band, ...zu|ge|hö|rig|keit; Stạmm‿form, ...gast** (*Plur.* ...gäste), **...ge|richt; stạmm|haft; Stạmm‿hal|ter** (*scherzh. für* erster m. Nachkomme eines Ehepaares), **...haus; stặm|mig; Stặm|mig|keit**, die; -; **Stạmm‿ka|pi|tal, ...knei|pe** *(ugs.)*, **...kun|de** (der), **...kund|schaft, ...land** (*Plur.* ...länder)

Stạmm|ler

Stạmm|lo|kal; Stạmm|mann|schaft (↑R 136); **Stạmm|mie|te** (↑R 136); **Stạmm|mie|ter** (↑R 136); **Stạmm|mut|ter** (↑R 136; *Plur.* ...mütter); **Stạmm‿per|so|nal, ...platz, ...re|gis|ter** *(Bankw.)*, **...rol|le** *(Milit.)*, **...sil|be, ...sitz, ...spie|ler** *(Sport)*, **...spie|le|rin** *(Sport)*, **...ta|fel, ...tisch; Stạmm|tisch|po|li|ti|ker; Stạmm|ton** *Plur.* ...töne *(Musik)*; **Stạmm|va|ter; stạmm|ver|wandt; Stạmm‿ver|wandt|schaft, ...vo|kal, ...wäh|ler, ...wort** (*Plur.* ...wörter), **...wür|ze**

Sta̱|mo|kap, der; -[s] (*Kurzw. für* staatsmonopolistischer Kapitalismus)

Stạm|pe, die; -, -n (*bes. berlin. für* Gaststätte, Kneipe)

Stam|pe̱|de [ʃt..., *auch* st..., *engl.* stɛm'pi:d], die; -, *Plur.* -n, *bei engl. Aussprache* -s ‹engl.› (wilde Flucht einer in Panik geratenen [Rinder]herde)

Stạm|per, der; -s, - (Schnapsglas ohne Fuß); **Stạm|perl**, das; -s, -n (*bayr. u. österr. für* Stamper)

Stạmpf|be|ton; Stạmp|fe, die; -, -n; **stạmp|fen; Stạmp|fer; Stạmpf|kar|tof|feln** *Plur.* (*landsch. für* Kartoffelbrei)

Stam|pig|lie [...'piljə] (↑R 130), die; -, -n ‹ital.› (*österr. für* Gerät zum Stempeln; Stempelaufdruck)

Stan [stɛn] (m. Vorn.)

Stạnd, der; -[e]s, Stände; einen schweren Stand haben; standhalten *(vgl. d.)*; (↑R 41:) außerstande, *auch* außer Stande, imstande, *auch* im Stande sein; er ist gut im Stande (bei guter Gesundheit); instand, *auch* in Stand halten; etwas [gut] im Stande (in gutem Zustand) erhalten; instand, *auch* in Stand setzen (ausbessern, wieder herstellen); jmdn. in den Stand setzen, etwas zu tun; zustande, *auch* zu Stande bringen, kommen

Stạn|dard [ʃt..., *auch* st...], der; -s, -s ‹engl.› (Maßstab, Richtschnur, Norm; Qualitäts- od. Leistungsniveau); **Stạn|dard‿aus|rüs|tung, ...brief, ...far|be, ...form; stan|dar|di|si̱e̱|ren** (normen; vereinheitlichen); **Stan|dar|di|si̱e̱|rung; Stạn|dard‿kal|ku|la|ti|on** *(Wirtsch.)*, **...klas|se** *(Sport)*, **...kos|ten** *(Plur.; Wirtsch.)*; **Stạn|dard|kos|ten|rech|nung; Stạn|dard‿lö|sung, ...mo|dell, ...preis, ...si|tu|a|ti|on** (z. B. Freistoß, Eckstoß im Fußball), **...spra|che** (*Sprachw.* gesprochene u. geschriebene Form der Hochsprache), **...tanz, ...werk** (mustergültiges Sach- od. Fachbuch), **...wert** (Festwert)

Stan|da̱r|te, die; -, -n ‹franz.› (kleine [quadrat.] Fahne [als Hoheitszeichen]; *Jägerspr.* Schwanz des Fuchses u. des Wolfes); **Stan|da̱r|ten|trä|ger**

Stạnd‿bein (*Sport, bild. Kunst; Ggs.* Spielbein), **...bild**

Stand-by ['stɛndba̯i], das; -[s], -s ‹engl.› (Form der Flugreise ohne feste Platzbuchung; *Elektronik* Bereitschaftsschaltung)

Stặnd|chen; Stạn|de, die; -, -n (*landsch. u. schweiz.*) *u.* Stạn|den, der; -, - (*landsch. für* [2]Kufe, Bottich); **Stặn|de** *Plur.* (ständische Volksvertretung); **Stặn|de|kam|mer; Stặn|del, Stặn|del|wurz** *vgl.* Stendel, Stendelwurz; **Stạn|den** *vgl.* Stande; **Stặn|de‿ord|nung, ...or|ga|ni|sa|ti|on; Stạn|der**, der; -s, - (Dienstflagge am Auto z. B. von hohen Regierungsbeamten; *Seemannsspr.* kurze, dreieckige Flagge); **Stặn|der**, der; -s, - (*Jägerspr. auch* Fuß des Federwildes); **Stặn|de‿rat**, (der; -[e]s, ...räte; *in der Schweiz* Vertretung der Kantone in der Bundesversammlung u. deren Mitglied), **...recht; Stặn|der‿lam|pe** (*schweiz. für* Stehlampe), **...pilz; Stạn|des|amt; stạn|des|amt|lich**; -e Trauung; **Stạn|des‿be|am|te, ...be|am|tin; stạn|des|be|wusst; Stạn|des‿be|wusst|sein, ...dün|kel, ...eh|re** *(veraltet)*; **stạn|des|ge|mäß**; -es Auskommen; -e Heirat; **Stạn|des‿herr** *(früher)*, **...herr|schaft, ...per|son, ...pflicht, ...recht, ...re|gis|ter; Stặn|de|staat** *Plur.* ...staaten *(früher)*; **Stạn|des‿un|ter|schied, ...wür|de** (die; -); **stạn|des|wür|dig; Stạn|des|zu|ge|hö|rig|keit; Stặn|de‿tag, ...we|sen** (das; -s; *früher*); **stạnd|fest; Stạnd‿fes|tig|keit** (die; -), **...fo|to** *(Filmw.)*, **...fuß|ball** (der; -[e]s; *ugs.*), **...gas** (das; -es; *Kfz-Technik*), **...geld** (Marktgeld), **...ge|richt** *(Milit.)*, **...glas** (*Plur.* ...gläser; Messzylinder); **stạnd|haft; Stạnd|haf|tig|keit**, die; -; **stạnd|hal|ten** (↑R 38); er hält stand; hat standgehalten; standzuhalten; **Stạnd|hei|zung** *(Kfz-Technik)*; **stặn|dig** (dauernd); -er Aufenthalt; -e Wohnung; -es Mitglied, -e Vertretung, *aber* (↑R 108): Ständiger Internationaler Gerichtshof; Ständige Konferenz der Kultusminister der Länder; **Stan|ding|ova|tions**, *auch* **Standing O|va|tions** ['stɛndiŋ-o:'ve:ʃənz] (↑R 33) *Plur.* ‹engl.›

(Ovationen im Stehen); **stän|disch** (die Stände betreffend; nach Ständen gegliedert); -er Aufbau; **Stạndl,** das; -s, -n (*bayr., österr. ugs. für* Verkaufsstand); **Stạnd|licht,** das; -[e]s (bei Kraftfahrzeugen); **Stạnd|ort,** der; -[e]s, -e (*Milit. auch svw.* Garnison); **Stạnd|ort‿äl|tes|te** (der; ↑R 5 ff.), **...be|stim|mung, ...fak|tor** (*Wirtsch.*), **...leh|re** (*Wirtsch.*), **...ori|en|tie|rung** (↑R 132; *Wirtsch.*), **...wech|sel; Stạnd‿pau|ke** (*ugs. für* Strafrede), **...punkt, ...quar|tier, ...recht** (das; -[e]s; Kriegsstrafrecht); **stạnd|recht|lich;** -e Erschießung; **Stạnd|re|de** (Strafrede); **stạnd|si|cher; Stạnd‿si|cher|heit** (die; -), **...spur, ...uhr, ...vo|gel, ...waa|ge** (*Sport*)

Stạn|ge, die; -, -n (*Jägerspr. auch* Stamm des Hirschgeweihes, Schwanz des Fuchses); von der - kaufen (Konfektionsware kaufen); **Stän|gel,** der; -s, - (Teil der Pflanze); **Stän|gel|blatt; Stän|gel|chen, Stän|gel|lein,** Stänglein (kleine Stange; kleiner Stängel); **...stän|ge|lig,** ...stäng|lig (z. B. kurzstäng[e]lig); **stän|gel|los; stän|geln** ([Pflanzen] mit Stangen versehen, an Stangen anbinden); ich ...[e]le (↑R 16); **Stạn|gen‿boh|ne, ...holz, ...pferd** (an der Deichsel gehendes Pferd eines Gespanns), **...rei|ter** (*früher für* Reiter auf dem Stangenpferd), **...spar|gel, ...wa|re, ...weiß|brot; ...stäng|lig** *vgl.* stängelig

Sta|nis|laus, Sta|nis|law [...laf] (m. Vorn.)

Sta|nit|zel *od.* **Sta|nitzl,** das; -s, - (*bayr. u. österr. für* spitze Tüte)

Stạnk, der; -[e]s (*ugs. für* Zank, Ärger); **Stän|ker** (*ugs. abwertend*); **Stän|ke|rei; Stän|ke|rer** (*svw.* Stänker); **stän|ke|rig,** stänk|rig; **stän|kern** (*ugs. für* Gestank verbreiten; für Ärger, Unruhe sorgen); ich ...ere (↑R 16); **stänk|rig** *vgl.* stänkerig

Stan|ley ['stɛnli] (m. Vorn.)

Stan|ni|ol, das; -s, -e ‹nlat.› (eine silberglänzende Zinnfolie, *ugs. auch für* silberglänzende Aluminiumfolie); **Stan|ni|ol‿blätt|chen, ...pa|pier; Stạn|num** [st..., *auch* ʃt...], das; -s (*lat. Bez. für* Zinn; *chem. Zeichen* Sn)

Stans (Hauptort des Halbkantons Nidwalden)

stạn|te pe|de [st... -] ‹lat., „stehenden Fußes"› (*ugs. scherzh. für* sofort)

[1]**Stạn|ze,** die; -, -n ‹ital.› (*Verslehre* achtzeilige Strophenform)

[2]**Stạn|ze,** die; -, -n (Ausschneidewerkzeug, -maschine für Bleche u. a.; Prägestempel); **stạn|zen;** du stanzt; **Stạnz‿form, ...ma|schi|ne**

Sta|pel, der; -s, - (aufgeschichteter Haufen; Schiffsbaugerüst; Platz od. Gebäude für die Lagerung von Waren; Faserlänge); vom - gehen, lassen, laufen; **Sta|pel‿be|trieb** (*EDV*), **...fa|ser, ...glas** (*Plur.* ...gläser), **...holz** (das, -es)

Sta|pe|lie [...i̯ə], die; -, -n ‹nach dem niederl. Arzt J. B. van Stapel› (Aasblume od. Ordensstern)

...sta|pe|lig (z. B. langstapelig); **Sta|pel|lauf; sta|peln;** ich ...[e]le (↑R 16); **Sta|pel|platz; Sta|pe|lung; Sta|pel|wa|re; sta|pel|wei|se**

Stạp|fe, die; -, -n *u.* Stạp|fen, der; -s, - (Fußspur); **stạp|fen; Stạp|fen** *vgl.* Stapfe

Sta|phy|lo|kok|kus [ʃt..., *auch* st...], der; -, ...kken *meist Plur.* ‹griech.› (*Med.* traubenförmige Bakterie)

Stạp|ler (*kurz für* Gabelstapler); **Stạp|ler|fah|rer**

Stạps, der; -es, -e (*obersächs. für* ungelenker Bursche)

[1]**Star,** der; -[e]s, -e ‹*zu* starr› (Augenkrankheit); (↑R 108:) der graue, grüne, schwarze Star

[2]**Star** [st..., *auch* ʃt...], der; -s, -s ‹engl., „Stern"› (berühmte Persönlichkeit [beim Theater, Film]; *kurz für* Starboot)

[3]**Star,** der; -[e]s, -e (ein Vogel)

Stär, der; -[e]s, -e (*landsch. für* Widder)

Star|al|lü|ren [st..., *auch* ʃt...]; *Plur.*; (eitles, launenhaftes Benehmen, Eigenheiten eines [2]Stars); **Star‿an|walt** (berühmter Anwalt), **...auf|ge|bot, ...be|set|zung**

star|blind

Star|boot [st..., *auch* ʃt...] ‹engl.; dt.› (ein Sportsegelboot)

Star|bril|le

stä|ren (*landsch. für* brünstig sein nach dem Stär)

Sta|ren|kas|ten *vgl.* Starkasten

stạrk; stärker, stärkste; eine starke Natur; er hat -e Nerven; *Sprachw.:* starke Deklination; ein -es Verb; (↑R 47:) das Recht des Starken. *Getrenntschreibung in Verbindung mit Verben und Partizipien,* z. B. stark sein, werden, machen; stark erhitzt; stark gehopftes Bier

Star|kas|ten *vgl.* Starenkasten

Stạrk|bier; Stär|ke, die; -, -n; **Stär|ke‿fab|rik, ...ge|halt** (der), **...mehl; stär|ken**

Star|ken|burg (Südteil des Regierungsbezirks Darmstadt); **star|ken|bur|gisch**

Stär|ke|zu|cker

Star|king ['sta:(r)kiŋ], der; -s, -s ‹Herkunft unbekannt› (eine Apfelsorte)

stạrk‿kno|chig, ...lei|big; Stạrk|strom, der; -[e]s; **Stạrk|strom‿lei|tung, ...tech|nik** (die; -), **...tech|ni|ker**

Star|kult [st..., *auch* ʃt...] ‹*zu* [2]Star›

Stär|kung; Stär|kungs|mit|tel, das

Star|let[t] ['sta:(r)lɛt], das; -s, -s ‹engl., „Sternchen"› (Nachwuchsfilmschauspielerin); **Star|man|ne|quin**

Star|matz (*scherzh. für* Star [als Käfigvogel])

Starn|ber|ger See, der; - -s (↑R 103)

Sta|rost [st..., *auch* ʃt...], der; -en, -en (↑R 126) ‹poln.› (*früher* polnischer Kreishauptmann, Landrat); **Sta|ros|tei** (Amt[sbezirk] eines Starosten)

stạrr; ein -es Gesetz; ein -es Prinzip; **Stạrr|ach|se** (*Kfz-Technik*); **Stạr|re,** die; -; **stạr|ren;** von *od.* vor Schmutz -; **Stạrr|heit,** die; -; **Stạrr|kopf** (*abwertend für* eigensinniger Mensch); **stạrr|köp|fig; Stạrr|krampf,** der; -[e]s (*kurz für* Wundstarrkrampf); **Stạrr|sinn,** der; -[e]s; **stạrr|sin|nig; Stạrr|sucht,** die; - (*für* Katalepsie)

Stars and Stripes ['sta:(r)z ənd 'straịps] *Plur.* (Nationalflagge der USA, Sternenbanner)

Stạrt, der; -[e]s, *Plur.* -s, *selten* -e ‹engl.› (Beginn; Ablauf-, Abfahrt-, Abflug[stelle]); fliegender -; stehender -; **Stạrt‿au|to|ma|tik, ...bahn, ...be|rech|ti|gung; stạrt|be|reit; Stạrt|block** *Plur.* ...blöcke (*Sport*); **stạr|ten** (einen Flug, einen Wettkampf, ein Rennen beginnen; *auch für* etwas beginnen lassen); **Stạr|ter** (*Sport* Person, die das Zeichen zum Start gibt; jmd., der startet; Anlasser eines Motors); **Stạrt‿er|laub|nis, ...flag|ge, ...geld, ...hil|fe; Stạrt|hil|fe|ka|bel; Stạrt|ka|pi|tal; stạrt|klar; Stạrt‿kom|man|do, ...läu|fer** (*Sport*), **...läu|fe|rin** (*Sport*), **...li|nie, ...loch, ...ma|schi|ne** (*Pferdesport*), **...num|mer, ...pass, ...pis|to|le, ...platz, ...ram|pe, ...schuss, ...sig|nal, ...sprung; Stạrt-und-Lan|de-Bahn; Stạrt‿ver|bot, ...zei|chen; Stạrt-Ziel-Sieg**

Sta|se, Sta|sis [*beide* st..., *auch* ʃt...], die; -, Stasen ‹griech.› (*Med.* Stauung)

Sta|si, die, *selten* der; - (*ugs. kurz für* Staatssicherheitsdienst der DDR *[ehem.]*); **Sta|si|ak|te**

Sta|sis *vgl.* Stase

Staß|furt (Stadt südl. von Magdeburg); **Staß|fur|ter** (↑R 103)

State De|part|ment ['ste:t di-ˌpa:(r)tmənt], das; - - ‹engl.› (das Außenministerium der USA)

State|ment ['ste:tmənt], das; -s, -s ‹engl.› (Erklärung, Verlautbarung)

sta|tie|ren ‹lat.› (als Statist tätig sein)

Stä|tig|keit, die; - (Störrigkeit [von Pferden]); *vgl. aber* Stetigkeit

Sta|tik [ʃt..., *auch* st...], die; - ‹griech.› (Lehre von den Kräften im Gleichgewicht); **Sta|ti|ker** (Bauingenieur mit speziellen Kenntnissen in der Statik)

Sta|ti|on, die; -, -en ‹lat.› (Haltestelle; Bahnhof; Aufenthalt; Bereich, Krankenhausabteilung; Ort, an dem sich eine techn. Anlage befindet); **sta|ti|o|när** (an einen festen Standort gebunden; unverändert; die Behandlung, den Aufenthalt in einem Krankenhaus betreffend); -e Behandlung; **sta|ti|o|nie|ren** (an bestimmte Plätze stellen; aufstellen); **Sta|ti|o|nie|rung; Sta|ti|o|nie|rungs|kos|ten** *Plur.*; **Sta|ti|ons‿arzt** (Abteilungsarzt), **...pfle|ger, ...schwes|ter, ...tas|te** (zur automat. Einstellung eines Senders beim Radio), **...vor|stand** (*österr. u. schweiz. für* Stationsvorsteher), **...vor|ste|her** (Bahnhofsvorsteher)

sta|ti|ös ‹lat.› (*veraltet für* prunkend; stattlich)

sta|tisch [ʃt..., *auch* st...] ‹griech.› (die Statik betreffend; stillstehend, ruhend)

stä|tisch (störrisch, widerspenstig [von Pferden])

Sta|tist, der; -en, -en (↑R 126) ‹lat.› (*Theater u. übertr.* stumme Person; Nebenfigur); **Sta|tis|te|rie,** die; -, ...ien (Gesamtheit der Statisten); *vgl.* statieren; **Sta|tis|tik,** die; -, -en ([vergleichende] zahlenmäßige Erfassung, Untersuchung u. Darstellung von Massenerscheinungen); **Sta|tis|ti|ker** (Bearbeiter u. Auswerter von Statistiken); **Sta|tis|tin** (*vgl.* Statist); **sta|tis|tisch** (zahlenmäßig), *aber* (↑R 108): das Statistische Bundesamt (in Wiesbaden); **Sta|tiv,** das; -s, -e [...və] ([dreibeiniges] Gestell für Apparate)

Sta|to|blast [ʃt..., *auch* st...], der; -en, -en (↑R 126) ‹griech.› (*Biol.* ungeschlechtlicher Fortpflanzungskörper der Moostierchen); **Sta|to|lith** [*auch* ...'lit], der; *Gen.* -s *u.* -en, *Plur.* -e[n]; ↑R 126 (*Med.* Steinchen im Gleichgewichtsorgan; *Bot.* Stärkekorn in Pflanzenwurzeln)

Sta|tor [ʃt..., *auch* st...], der; -s, ...oren ‹lat.› (feststehender Teil einer elektr. Maschine)

[1]statt, an|statt; ↑R 46; *Präp. mit Gen.:* statt meiner, statt deren (vgl. deren), statt derer (vgl. derer); der Kanzler, statt dessen ein Minister erschienen war, ließ grüßen (*vgl. aber* stattdessen); statt eines Rates; *veraltet od. ugs. mit Dat.:* statt einem Stein; statt dem Vater; *hochsprachlich mit Dat., wenn der Gen. nicht erkennbar wird:* statt Worten will ich Taten sehen; *Konj.:* statt mit Drohungen versucht er es mit Ermahnungen; statt dass ... (↑R 88); statt zu ... (↑R 75); die Nachricht kam an mich statt an dich; er gab das Geld ihm statt mir; **[2]statt;** an meiner statt; an Eides, an Kindes, an Zahlungs statt; **statt|des|sen;** der Kanzler konnte nicht kommen, stattdessen schickte er einen Minister; *vgl. auch* statt; **Stät|te,** die; -, -n; **statt|fin|den** (↑R 38); es findet statt (↑R 46); es hat stattgefunden; stattzufinden; **statt|ge|ben** (↑R 38); *zur Beugung vgl.* stattfinden; **statt|ha|ben** (↑R 38; *veraltet*); es hat statt (↑R 46); es hat stattgehabt; stattzuhaben; **statt|haft; Statt|haf|tig|keit,** die; -; **Statt|hal|ter** (*früher für* Stellvertreter); **Statt|hal|ter|schaft,** die; -

statt|lich ‹*zu* [2]Staat (Prunk)› (ansehnlich); **Statt|lich|keit,** die; -

sta|tu|a|risch [ʃt..., *auch* st...] ‹lat.› (auf die Bildhauerkunst bezüglich, statuenhaft); **Sta|tue** [...tuə], die; -, -n (Standbild, Bildsäule); **sta|tu|en|haft; Sta|tu|et|te,** die; -, -n ‹franz.› (kleine Statue); **sta|tu|ie|ren** ‹lat.› (aufstellen; festsetzen; bestimmen); ein Exempel - (ein warnendes Beispiel geben); **Sta|tur** [ʃt...], die; -, -en (Gestalt; Wuchs); **Sta|tus** [ʃt..., *auch* st...], der; -, - [...tu:s] (Zustand, Stand; Lage, Stellung); **Sta|tus|den|ken; Sta|tus Nas|cen|di** [st... -], der; - - (Zustand chem. Stoffe im Augenblick ihres Entstehens); *vgl. aber* in statu nascendi; **Sta|tus quo,** der; - - (gegenwärtiger Zustand); **Sta|tus quo an|te,** der; - - - (Zustand vor dem bezeichneten Tatbestand, Ereignis); **Sta|tus|sym|bol** [ʃt..., *auch* st...]; **Sta|tut** [ʃt...], das; -[e]s, -en ([Grund]gesetz; Satzung); **sta|tu|ta|risch** (auf Statut beruhend, satzungs-, ordnungsgemäß); **Sta|tu|ten|än|de|rung; sta|tu|ten‿ge|mäß, ...wid|rig**

Stau, der; -[e]s, *Plur.* -s *od.* -e; **Stau|an|la|ge**

Staub, der; -[e]s, *Plur. (Technik:)* -e *u.* Stäube; Staub saugen *od.* staubsaugen *(vgl. d.);* ein Staub abweisendes Gewebe (↑R 40); **staub|be|deckt;** ein -er Tisch; **Staub‿be|sen, ...beu|tel, ...blatt** *(Bot.);* **Stäub|chen; staub|dicht**

Stau|be|cken

stau|ben (Staub von sich geben); es staubt; **stäu|ben** (zerstieben)

Stau|be|ra|ter (eines Automobilklubs)

stäu|bern (*landsch. für* Staub entfernen); ich ...ere (↑R 16); **Staub‿ex|plo|si|on, ...fa|den, ...fän|ger** *(ugs.);* **staub|frei; staub|ge|bo|ren; Staub|ge|bo|re|ne,** der *u.* die; -n, -n; ↑R 5ff. *(bibl.);* **Staub|ge|fäß; stau|big; Staub‿kamm, ...korn** (*Plur.* ...körner), **...lap|pen, ...la|wi|ne; Stäub|ling** (ein Pilz); **Staub‿lun|ge, ...man|tel, ...pin|sel; staub|sau|gen** (er staubsaugte, hat gestaubsaugt) *od.* Staub sau|gen (er saugte Staub, hat Staub gesaugt); **Staub‿sau|ger, ...schicht; staub|tro|cken** (vom Lack); **Staub‿tuch** (*Plur.* ...tücher), **...we|del, ...wol|ke, ...zu|cker** (der; -s)

Stau|che, die; -, -n *meist Plur.* (*landsch. für* Pulswärmer); **stau|chen; Stau|cher** (*ugs. für* Zurechtweisung); **Stau|chung**

Stau|damm

Stau|de, die; -, -n; **stau|den** (*selten für* krautig wachsen); **stau|den|ar|tig; Stau|den‿ge|wächs, ...sa|lat** (*landsch. für* Kopfsalat); **stau|dig**

stau|en ([fließendes Wasser] hemmen; *Seemannsspr.* [Ladung auf Schiffen] unterbringen); sich -; **Stau|er** (jmd., der Schiffe be- u. entlädt)

Stauf, der; -[e]s, -e (*veraltet für* Humpen; ein Flüssigkeitsmaß)

Stau|fe, der; -n, -n (↑R 126) *u.* **Stau|fer,** der; -s, - (Angehöriger eines schwäb. Fürstengeschlechtes); **Stau|fer|zeit,** die; -

Stauf|fer|büch|se (↑R 95) ‹nach dem Hersteller› (Schmiervorrichtung); **Stauf|fer|fett,** das; -[e]s

stau|fisch ‹*zu* Staufe›

Stau‿ge|fahr *(bes. Verkehrsw.),* **...mau|er**

stau|nen; Stau|nen, das; -s; Stau-

nen erregen, eine Staunen erregende Fingerfertigkeit (↑R 40); **stau|nens|wert**
[1]**Stau|pe,** die; -, -n (eine Hundekrankheit)
[2]**Stau|pe,** die; -, -n (*früher* öffentliche Züchtigung); **stäu|pen** (*früher* [öffentlich] auspeitschen)
Stau‿punkt, ...raum, ...see (der); **Stau|strahl|trieb|werk** *(Flugw.)*; **Stau|stu|fe; Stau|ung; Stau|ungs|be|hand|lung; Stau‿was|ser** (*Plur.* ...wasser), **...wehr** (*vgl.* [2]Wehr), **...werk**
St. Chris|toph und Ne|vis [sənt - -ˈni:vis] (*svw.* St. Kitts und Nevis)
Std. = Stunde
Ste = Sainte
Steak [ste:k], das; -s, -s ⟨engl.⟩ (kurz gebratene Fleischschnitte); **Steak|haus**
Stea|mer [ˈsti:mə(r)], der; -s, - ⟨engl.⟩ (Dampfschiff)
Ste|a|rin [ʃt..., *auch* st...], das; -s, -e ⟨griech.⟩ (festes Gemisch aus Stearin- u. Palmitinsäure; Rohstoff für Kerzen); **Ste|a|rin|ker|ze; Ste|a|tit** [*auch* ...ˈtit], der; -s, -e (ein Talk; Speckstein); **Ste|a|to|py|gie** [st..., *auch* ʃt...], die; - (*Med.* starker Fettansatz am Gesäß); **Ste|a|to|se,** die; - (*Med.* Verfettung)
Stech|ap|fel; Stech|be|cken, Steck|be|cken (*veraltet für* Bettpfanne); **Stech‿bei|tel, ...ei|sen; ste|chen;** du stichst; du stachst; du stächest; gestochen; stich!; er sticht ihn, *auch* ihm ins Bein; **Ste|chen,** das; -s, - *(Sportspr.)*; **Ste|cher; Stech‿flie|ge, ...he|ber, ...kar|te** (Karte für die Stechuhr), **...mü|cke, ...pad|del, ...pal|me, ...rüs|sel, ...schritt** *(Milit.)*, **...uhr** (eine Kontrolluhr), **...vieh** (*österr. für* Kälber u. Schweine)
Steck|be|cken *vgl.* Stechbecken; **Steck|brief; steck|brief|lich;** jmdn. - suchen; **Steck|do|se;**
[1]**ste|cken** (sich irgendwo, in etwas befinden, dort festsitzen, befestigt sein); du steckst; du stecktest, *älter u. geh.* stakst; du stecktest, *älter u. geh.* stäkest; gesteckt; steck[e]!; (↑R 39): stecken bleiben; ich bleibe stecken; stecken geblieben; stecken zu bleiben; der Nagel ist stecken geblieben; er ist während des Vortrags stecken geblieben; stecken lassen (vergessen); er hat den Schlüssel stecken lassen, *seltener* stecken gelassen;
[2]**ste|cken** (etwas in etwas einfügen, hineinbringen, etwas festheften); du stecktest; gesteckt; steck[e]!; **Ste|cken,** der; -s, - ([1]Stock); **Ste|cken|blei|ben,** das; -s; **ste|cken blei|ben, las|sen** *vgl.* [1]stecken; **Ste|cken|pferd; Ste|cker; Steck‿kis|sen, ...kon|takt, ...lei|ter** (die); **Steck|ling** (abgeschnittener Pflanzenteil, der neue Wurzeln bildet); **Steck‿mu|schel, ...na|del; steck|na|del|kopf|groß; Steck‿reis** (das), **...rü|be, ...schach, ...schal|le** *(Blumenbinderei)*, **...schloss** (Sicherung gegen Einbruch), **...schlüs|sel, ...schuss, ...schwamm** *(Blumenbinderei)*, **...tuch** (*österr. für* Kavalierstaschentuch), **...va|se, ...zwie|bel**
Ste|din|gen, *auch* Ste|din|ger Land (Marsch zwischen der Hunte u. der Weser unterhalb von Bremen); **Ste|din|ger** („Gestadebewohner"); **Ste|din|ger Land,** das; - -[e]s *vgl.* Stedingen
Steel|band [ˈsti:lbɛnt], die; -, -s ⟨engl.⟩ ([4]Band, deren Instrumente aus leeren Ölfässern bestehen)
Stee|ple|chase [ˈsti:p(ə)ltʃe:s], die; -, -n [...s(ə)n] ⟨engl.⟩ (Wettrennen mit Hindernissen, Jagdrennen); **Steep|ler** [ˈsti:plə(r)], der; -s, - (Pferd für Hindernisrennen)
Ste|fan *vgl.* Stephan; **Ste|fa|nia, Ste|fa|nie** *vgl.* Stephanie; **Stef|fen** *vgl.* Stephan; **Stef|fi** (w. Vorn.)
Steg, der; -[e]s, -e; *Schreibung in Straßennamen* ↑R 123
Ste|go|don [ʃt..., *auch* st...] (↑R 132), der; -s, ...donten ⟨griech.⟩ (urweltliches Rüsseltier); **Ste|go|sau|ri|er** (urweltliches Kriechtier); **Ste|go|ze|pha|le,** der; -n, -n; ↑R 126 (urweltlicher Panzerlurch)
Steg|reif („Steigbügel"); *vgl.* [2]Reif; aus dem - (unvorbereitet); **Steg|reif‿dich|ter, ...ko|mö|die, ...re|de, ...spiel, ...zwei|zei|ler**
Steh|auf, der; -, - (ein altes Trinkgefäß); **Steh|auf|männ|chen; Steh‿bier|hal|le, ...bünd|chen** (an Blusen od. Kleidern), **...emp|fang; ste|hen;** du stehst; du standst; du stündest, *häufig auch* ständest; gestanden; steh[e]!; ich habe, *südd., österr., schweiz.* bin gestanden; zu Diensten, zu Gebote, zur Verfügung stehen; das wird dich, *auch* dir teuer zu stehen kommen; auf jmdn., auf etwas stehen (*ugs. für* eine besondere Vorliebe für jmdn., für etwas haben); (↑R 50:) sie schläft im Stehen; ihr fällt das Stehen schwer; ein guter Platz zum Stehen; zum Stehen bringen; (↑R 39:) stehen bleiben (*auch für* nicht weitergehen; übrig bleiben); ich bleibe stehen; stehen geblieben; stehen zu bleiben; die Uhr ist stehen geblieben; du sollst bei der Begrüßung stehen bleiben; stehen lassen (*auch für* nicht anrühren; vergessen); sie hat die Suppe stehen lassen; man hat ihn einfach am Bahnhof stehen lassen, *seltener* stehen gelassen; man hat die Angeklagten stehen lassen (sie durften sich nicht hinsetzen); *vgl.* stehend; **Ste|hen|blei|ben,** das; -s; **ste|hen blei|ben** *vgl.* stehen; **ste|hend;** stehenden Fußes; das stehende Heer (*vgl.* Miliz); (↑R 47:) alles in ihrer Macht Stehende; **ste|hen las|sen** *vgl.* stehen; **Ste|her** (Radrennfahrer hinter einem Schrittmacher; Rennpferd für lange Strecken; *österr. für* [Zaun]pfosten); **Ste|her|ren|nen** *(Rad-, Pferdesport)*; **Steh‿gei|ger, ...im|biss, ...kon|vent** (*scherzh. für* Gruppe von Personen, die sich stehend unterhalten), **...kra|gen, ...lam|pe, ...lei|ter** (die)
steh|len; du stiehlst, er stiehlt; du stahlst; du stählest, *selten* stöhlest; gestohlen; stiehl!; **Steh|ler;** *meist in* Hehler und -; **Stehl|trieb,** der; -[e]s
Steh‿platz, ...pult, ...satz (der; -es; *Druckw.*), **...ver|mö|gen** (das; -s)
Stei|er|mark, die; - (österr. Bundesland); **Stei|er|mär|ker; stei|er|mär|kisch**
steif; ein steifer Hals; ein -er Gang; ein -er Grog; ein -er Wind; (↑R 39:) steif sein, werden, machen, kochen, schlagen usw.; die Ohren steif halten (sich nicht entmutigen lassen); sie hat den Nacken steif gehalten (sie hat sich behauptet); du musst das Bein steif halten; **steif|bei|nig; Stei|fe,** die; -, -n (*nur Sing.:* Steifheit; Stütze); **stei|fen; steif hal|ten** *vgl.* steif; **Steif|heit,** die; -; **Stei|fig|keit,** die; -; **steif|lei|nen** (aus steifem Leinen); **Steif‿lei|nen, ...lein|wand; Stei|fung,** die; -
Steig, der; -[e]s, -e (steiler, schmaler Weg); **Steig|bü|gel; Stei|ge,** die; -, -n (steile Fahrstraße; Lattenkistchen [für Obst]); **Steig|ei|sen; stei|gen;** du stiegst; du stiegest; gestiegen; steig[e]!; (↑R 50:) das Steigen der Kurse; **Stei|ger** (Aufsichtsperson im Bergbau); **Stei|ge|rer** (jmd., der bei einer Versteigerung bietet); **stei|gern;** ich ...ere (↑R 16); du steigerst dich; **Stei|ge|rung** (*auch für* Komparation; *schweiz. auch für* Versteigerung); **stei|ge|rungs-**

fä|hig; Stei|ge|rungs|ra|te *(Wirtsch.);* **Stei|ge|rungs|stu|fe;** erste - (*für* Komparativ); zweite - (*für* Superlativ); **Steig‿fä|hig|keit** (bei Kraftfahrzeugen), **...fell** *(Skisport),* **...flug, ...hö|he, ...lei|ter** (die), **...lei|tung, ...rie|men** (am Pferdesattel), **...rohr, ...übung** (↑R 132); **Stei|gung; Stei|gungs‿ta|fel, ...win|kel; Steig|wachs** *(Skisport)*

steil; Steil|ab|fahrt *(Skisport);* **Stei|le,** die; -, -n; **stei|len** (*selten für* steil emporsteigen, -ragen); **Steil|feu|er** (das; -); **Steil|feu|er|ge|schütz; Steil|hang; Steil|heit,** die; -; **Steil‿kur|ve, ...küs|te, ...pass** *(Sport),* **...rand, ...schrift, ...spiel** (das; -[e]s; *Sport*), **...ufer** (↑R 132), **...vor|la|ge** *(Sport),* **...wand; Steil|wand|zelt**

Stein, der; -[e]s, -e; eine zwei - starke Mauer (↑R 90); **Stein|ad|ler; stein|alt** (sehr alt); **Stein‿axt, ...bank** (*Plur.* ...bänke), **...bau** (*Plur.* ...bauten), **...bau|kas|ten, ...bei|ßer** (ein Fisch), **...block** (*vgl.* Block), **...bock, ...bo|den, ...boh|rer, ...brech** (der; -[e]s, -e; eine Pflanze), **...bre|cher** (Maschine, die Gestein zerkleinert), **...bruch** (der), **...butt** (ein Fisch), **...damm, ...druck** (*nur Sing.:* ein Druckverfahren; Erzeugnis dieses Druckverfahrens [*Plur.* ...drucke]), **...ei|che; stei|nen** (*veraltet für* ab-, umgrenzen); **stei|nern** (aus Stein); ein -es Kreuz; ein -es (mitleidsloses) Herz, *aber* (↑R 102): Steinernes Meer; **Stein|er|wei|chen,** das; *nur in* zum - *(ugs.);* **Stein‿flie|se, ...frucht, ...fuß|bo|den, ...gar|ten** (Felsengarten), **...grab, ...gut** (das; -[e]s, *Plur. [Sorten:]* -e), **...ha|gel; stein|hart; Stein|hau|er; Stein|hau|er|lun|ge** *(Med.);* **Stein‿hau|fen, ...holz** (das; -es; ein Fußbodenbelag)

Stein|hu|der Meer, das; - -[e]s (See zwischen Weser u. Leine)

stei|nig; stei|ni|gen; Stei|ni|gung; Stein‿kauz, ...klee (der; -s), **...koh|le; Stein|koh|len‿berg|werk, ...för|de|rung, ...for|ma|ti|on** (die; -; *Geol.* eine Formation des Paläozoikums), **...in|dust|rie, ...la|ger, ...teer, ...ze|che, ...zeit** (die; -; *für* Karbon); **Stein‿la|wi|ne, ...lei|den** *(Med.),* **...mar|der, ...metz** (der; -en, -en; ↑R 126), **...nel|ke, ...obst, ...öl** (das; -[e]s; *veraltet für* Petroleum), **...pilz;** [1]**stein|reich;** -er Boden; [2]**stein|reich;** ein -er Mann; **Stein‿salz** (das; -es), **...sarg, ...schlag; Stein|schlag|ge|fahr,** die; -; **Stein‿schleu|der, ...schmät|zer** (ein Vogel); **Stein|schnei|de|kunst,** die; -; **Stein‿schnei|der** (*svw.* Graveur), **...set|zer** (Pflasterer), **...wein** (ein Frankenwein), **...werk** (Steinbruch[groß]betrieb), **...wild, ...wurf, ...wüs|te, ...zeich|nung, ...zeit** (die; -); **stein|zeit|lich; Stein|zeit|mensch; Stein|zeug**

Stei|per, der; -s, - (*landsch. für* [untergestellte] Stütze)

Stei|rer; ↑R 103 (Bewohner der Steiermark); **Stei|rer|an|zug** (österr. Trachtenanzug); **Stei|re|rin; stei|risch**

Steiß, der; -es, -e; **Steiß‿bein, ...la|ge** *(Med.)*

Stek [st..., *auch* ʃt...], der; -s, -s (*Seemannsspr.* [Schiffer]knoten)

Ste|le [st..., *auch* ʃt...], die; -, -n ‹griech.› (Grabsäule od. -tafel)

Stel|la (w. Vorn.)

Stel|la|ge [...ˈla:ʒə, *österr.* ...ˈla:ʒ], die; -, -n [...ʒ(ə)n] ‹niederl.› (Gestell, Ständer); **Stel|la|ge|ge|schäft** (Börsentermingeschäft)

stel|lar [ʃt..., *auch* st...] ‹lat.› (die Fixsterne betreffend); **Stel|lar|ast|ro|nom** ‹lat.; griech.› (Fixsternforscher); **Stel|lar|ast|ro|no|mie**

Stell|dich|ein, das; -[s], -[s] (*veraltend für* Verabredung); **Stel|le,** die; -, -n; anstelle, *auch* an Stelle von Worten; anstelle, *auch* an Stelle des Vaters; *aber* an die Stelle des Vaters ist der Vormund getreten; zur Stelle sein; an erster, zweiter Stelle; ↑R 41; **stel|len; Stel|len‿an|ge|bot, ...be|set|zung, ...bil|dung, ...dienst|al|ter, ...ge|such; stel|len|los; Stel|len|lo|sig|keit,** die; -; **Stel|len‿markt** (*svw.* Arbeitsmarkt), **...nach|weis, ...plan** (*vgl.* [2]Plan), **...ver|mitt|lung, ...wech|sel; stel|len|wei|se; Stel|len|wert; Stel|ler,** der; -s, - *(Volleyball);* **Stell‿flä|che, ...he|bel; ...stel|lig** (z. B. vierstellig, *mit Ziffer* 4-stellig; ↑R 44); **Stel|ling,** die; -, *Plur.* -e, *auch* -s (*Seemannsspr.* an Seilen hängendes Brettgerüst zum Arbeiten an der Bordwand eines Schiffes); **Stell|ma|cher** (*landsch. für* Wagenbauer); **Stell|ma|che|rei; Stell‿netz, ...platz, ...pro|be** *(Theater),* **...rad, ...schrau|be; Stel|lung;** - nehmen; **Stel|lung|nah|me,** die; -, -n; **Stel|lungs‿be|fehl, ...kampf, ...krieg; stel|lungs|los; Stel|lungs|lo|se,** der *u.* die; -n, -n (↑R 5 ff.); **Stel|lungs|spiel** *(Sport);* **Stel|lung[s]|su|che;** auf - sein; **stel|lung[s]|su|chend; Stel|lung[s]|su|chen|de,** der *u.* die; -n, -n (↑R 5 ff.); **stell|ver|tre|tend;** der -e Vorsitzende; **Stell‿ver|tre|ter, ...ver|tre|te|rin; Stell|ver|tre|ter|krieg; Stell‿ver|tre|tung, ...wand, ...werk** *(Eisenb.);* **Stell|werks|meis|ter**

St.-Elms-Feu|er (↑R 95); *vgl.* Elmsfeuer *u.* Sankt

Stelz|bein *(ugs.);* **Stel|ze,** die; -, -n (*österr. auch für* Eisbein); -n laufen (↑R 39); **stel|zen** *(meist iron.);* du stelzt; **Stel|zen|läu|fer; Stelz‿fuß, ...gang** (der); **stel|zig; Stelz‿vo|gel, ...wur|zel** *(Bot.)*

Stem|ma [ʃt..., *auch* st...], das; -s, -ta (Stammbaum, bes. der verschiedenen Handschriften eines literar. Werks)

Stemm|bo|gen *(Skisport);* **Stem|me,** die; -, -n *(Turnen);* **Stemm|ei|sen; stem|men; Stemm|mei|ßel** (↑R 136), der; -s, -

Stem|pel, der; -s, -; **Stem|pel‿far|be, ...geld** (*ugs. für* Arbeitslosenunterstützung), **...hal|ter, ...kar|te, ...kis|sen, ...mar|ke; stem|peln;** ich ...[e]le (↑R 16); - gehen (*ugs. für* Arbeitslosenunterstützung beziehen); **stem|pel|pflich|tig** (*österr. für* gebührenpflichtig); **Stem|pel‿schnei|der** (Berufsbez.), **...stän|der, ...steu|er** (die); **Stem|pe|lung,** Stemplung; **Stem|pen,** der; -s, - (*bayr. für* kurzer Pfahl, Pflock)

Sten|dal (Stadt in der Altmark)

Sten|del, *auch* **Stän|del,** der; -s, - *u.* **Sten|del|wurz,** *auch* **Stän|del|wurz** (eine Orchideengattung)

Sten|dhal [stɛ̃ˈdal] (franz. Schriftsteller)

Sten|ge, die; -, -n (*Seemannsspr.* Verlängerung des Mastes)

Sten|gel usw. *frühere Schreibung für* Stängel usw.

ste|no... ‹griech.› (eng...); **Ste|no...** (Eng...); [1]**Ste|no,** die; - (*ugs. Kurzw. für* Stenographie); [2]**Ste|no,** das; -s, -s (*ugs. Kurzw. für* Stenogramm); **Ste|no|block** (*vgl.* Block; *ugs. svw.* Stenogrammblock); **Ste|no|graf,** *auch* Ste|no|graph, der; -en -en (↑R 33 u. 126; Kurzschriftler); **Ste|no|gra|fie,** *auch* Ste|no|gra|phie, die; -, ...ien (R 33; Kurzschrift); **ste|no|gra|fie|ren,** *auch* ste|no|gra|phie|ren; **Ste|no|gra|fin,** *auch* Ste|no|gra|phin; **ste|no|gra|fisch,** *auch* ste|no|gra|phisch; **Ste|no|gramm,** das; -s, -e (Text in Stenographie); **Ste|no|gramm‿block** (*vgl.* Block), **...hal|ter; Ste|no|graph,**

Ste|no|gra|phie usw. *vgl.* Stenograf, Stenografie usw.
Ste|no|kar|die [ʃt..., *auch* st...], die; -, ...ien (*Med.* Herzbeklemmung [bei Angina pectoris]); **Ste|no|kon|to|ris|tin** [ʃt...]; **Ste|no|se, Ste|no|sis** [ʃt..., *auch* st...], die; -, ...osen (*Med.* Verengung [der Blutgefäße]); **ste|no|therm** (*Biol.* nur geringe Temperaturschwankungen ertragend [von Pflanzen u. Tieren]); **ste|no|top** (*Biol.* begrenzt verbreitet); **ste|no|ty|pie|ren** [ʃt...] (in Kurzschrift aufnehmen u. danach in Maschinenschrift übertragen); **Ste|no|ty|pist**, der; -en, -en; ↑R 126 (Kurzschriftler u. Maschinenschreiber); **Ste|no|ty|pis|tin**
Sten|tor [ʃt..., *auch* st...] (stimmgewaltiger Held der griech. Sage); **Sten|tor|stim|me** (↑R 95)
Stenz, der; -es, -e (*ugs. für* geckenhafter junger Mann [der gern Damenbekanntschaften macht])
Step *frühere Schreibung für* Stepp
Ste|phan, (↑R 92:) Ste|fan, Steffen (m. Vorn.); **Ste|pha|nia**, Stefa|nia, **Ste|pha|nie**, Ste|fa|nie [*auch* 'ʃtɛfani, *österr.* ...'ni:] (w. Vorn.); **Ste|pha|nit** [*auch* ...'nit], der; -s, -e (ein Mineral); **Ste|pha|ni|tag; Ste|phans⌣dom** (der; -[e]s; in Wien), **...tag**
Ste|phen|son ['sti:vəns(ə)n] (Gründer des engl. Eisenbahnwesens)
Stepp, der; -s, -s ‹engl.› (eine Tanzart); Stepp tanzen
Stepp|de|cke
Step|pe, die; -, -n ‹russ.› (baumlose, wasserarme Ebene)
[1]**step|pen** (Stofflagen zusammennähen)
[2]**step|pen** ‹engl.› (Stepp tanzen)
Step|pen⌣be|woh|ner, ...flo|ra, ...fuchs, ...gras, ...huhn, ...wolf (*svw.* Präriewolf)
Step|per [ʃt..., *auch* st...] (Stepptänzer)
Step|pe|rei ‹*zu* [1]steppen›; [1]**Step|pe|rin**
[2]**Step|pe|rin** [ʃt..., *auch* st...] (Stepptänzerin)
Stepp⌣fut|ter (*zu* [2]Futter), **...jacke**
Stepp|ke, der; -[s], -s (*ugs., bes. berlin. für* kleiner Kerl)
Stepp⌣man|tel, ...ma|schi|ne, ...naht
Stepp|schritt
Stepp⌣sei|de, ...stich
Stepp|tanz; Stepp|tän|zer; Stepp|tän|ze|rin
Ster, der; -s, *Plur.* -e *u.* -s ‹griech.› (ein Raummaß für Holz); 3 Ster (↑R 90)

Ste|ra|di|ant, der; -en, -en (↑R 126) ‹griech.; lat.› (*Math.* Einheit des Raumwinkels; *Zeichen* sr)
Ster|be⌣ab|lass, ...amt *(kath. Kirche),* **...bett, ...buch, ...da|tum, ...fall** (der), **...ge|läut, ...geld** (das; -es), **...glo|cke, ...hil|fe, ...kas|se, ...ker|ze, ...kreuz; ster|ben;** du stirbst; du starbst, du stürbest; gestorben *(vgl. d.);* stirb!; **Ster|ben**, das; -s; im Sterben liegen; das große Sterben (die Pest); es ist zum Sterben langweilig (*ugs. für* sehr langweilig); **Ster|bens|angst; ster|bens⌣elend** (↑R 132), **...krank, ...lang|wei|lig, ...matt; Ster|bens|see|le;** *nur in* keine, nicht eine - (niemand); **Ster|bens|wort, Ster|bens|wört|chen** *(ugs.); nur in* kein -; **Ster|be⌣ort** (*Plur.* ...orte), **...sak|ra|men|te** *(Plur.),* **...stun|de, ...tag, ...ur|kun|de, ...zim|mer; sterb|lich; Sterb|li|che**, der *u.* die; -n, -n (↑R 5 ff.); **Sterb|lich|keit**, die; -; **Sterb|lich|keits|zif|fer**
ste|reo [ʃt..., *auch* st...] ‹griech.› (*kurz für* stereophon); die Schallplatte wurde - aufgenommen; **Ste|reo**, das; -s, -s (*nur Sing.: kurz für* Stereophonie; *auch kurz für* Stereotypplatte); **ste|re|o...** (starr, massiv, unbeweglich; räumlich, körperlich); **Ste|re|o...** (Fest..., Raum..., Körper...); **Ste|re|o⌣an|la|ge** (Anlage für den stereophonen Empfang), **...bild** (Raumbild), **...che|mie** (Lehre von der räuml. Anordnung der Atome im Molekül), **...emp|fang, ...fern|se|hen, ...film** (stereoskop. Film); **ste|re|o|fon, Ste|re|o|fo|nie** usw. *eindeutschende Schreibungen für* stereophon, Stereophonie usw.; **Ste|re|o⌣fo|to|gra|fie** (die; -; Herstellung von Stereoskopbildern), **...ka|me|ra, ...kom|pa|ra|tor** (Instrument zur Ausmessung stereoskopischer Fotografien), **...laut|spre|cher; Ste|re|o|me|ter**, das; -s, - (opt. Gerät zur Messung des Volumens fester Körper); **Ste|re|o|met|rie** (↑R 130), die; - (Geometrie des Raumes; Raumlehre); **ste|re|o|met|risch** (↑R 130; körperlich, Körper...)
ste|re|o|phon, ste|re|o|pho|nisch (↑R 33); **Ste|re|o|pho|nie**, die; - (Technik der räuml. wirkenden Tonübertragung); **ste|re|o|pho|nisch** *vgl.* stereophon
Ste|re|o|pho|to|gra|phie *vgl.* Stereofotografie; **Ste|re|o|plat|te; Ste|re|o|sen|dung; Ste|re|o|skop**, das; -s, -e (Vorrichtung, durch die man Bilder plastisch sieht); **Ste|re|o|sko|pie**, die; - (Raumbildtechnik); **ste|re|o|sko|pisch** (plastisch erscheinend, raumbildlich [von Bildern]); **Ste|re|o|ton**, *Plur.* ...töne (räuml. wirkender [2]Ton); **ste|re|o|typ** ([fest]stehend, unveränderlich; *übertr. für* ständig [wiederkehrend], leer, abgedroschen; mit feststehender Schrift gedruckt); **Ste|re|o|typ**, das; -s, -e (*Psych.* oft vereinfachtes, stereotypes Urteil); **Ste|re|o|typ|druck** (*nur Sing.:* Druck von der Stereotypplatte; Erzeugnis dieses Druckes [*Plur.* ...drucke]); **Ste|re|o|ty|peur** [...'pø:r], der; -s, -e ‹franz.› (*Druckw.* jmd., der Matern herstellt u. ausgießt); **Ste|re|o|ty|pie**, die; -, ...ien ‹griech.› (*Druckw.; nur Sing.:* Herstellung u. Ausgießen von Matern; Arbeitsraum der Stereotypeure); **ste|re|o|ty|pie|ren** *(Druckw.);* **Ste|re|o|typ⌣me|tall, ...plat|te** (feste Druckplatte)
ste|ril [ʃt..., *auch* st...] ‹lat.› (unfruchtbar; keimfrei); **Ste|ri|li|sa|ti|on**, die; -, -en (Unfruchtbarmachung; Entkeimung); **Ste|ri|li|sa|tor**, der; -s, ...oren (Entkeimungsapparat); **Ste|ri|li|sier|ap|pa|rat; ste|ri|li|sie|ren** (haltbar machen [von Nahrungsmitteln]; zeugungsunfähig machen); **Ste|ri|li|sie|rung; Ste|ri|li|tät**, die; - (Unfruchtbarkeit; Keimfreiheit; *übertr. für* geistiges Unvermögen, Unproduktivität)
Ste|rin [ʃt..., *auch* st...], das; -s, -e ‹griech.› (eine organische chemische Verbindung)
Ster|ke, die; -, -n (*nordd. für* Färse)
Ster|let[t], der; -s, -e ‹russ.› (ein Fisch)
Ster|ling ['stɛr..., *auch* 'ʃtɛr..., *engl.* 'stœ:(r)...], der; -s, -e (engl. Währungseinheit); Pfund - (*Zeichen u. Abk.* £, £Stg); 2 Pfund -
[1]**Stern**, der; -s, -e ‹engl.› (*Seemannsspr.* Heck des Schiffes)
[2]**Stern**, der; -[e]s, -e (Himmelskörper); **Stern⌣bild, ...blu|me; Stern|chen|nu|del** *meist Plur.* (eine Suppeneinlage); **Stern|deu|ter** (*für* Astrologe); **Stern|deu|te|rei; Stern|deu|te|rin; Stern|deu|tung**, die; -; **Ster|nen|ban|ner; ster|nen|hell** (*svw.* sternhell); **Ster|nen|him|mel** (*svw.* Sternhimmel); **ster|nen|klar** (*svw.* sternklar); **Ster|nen|licht**, das; -[e]s; **ster|nen⌣los, ...wärts; Ster|nen|zelt**, das; -[e]s

(geh.); **Stern|fahrt** (*für* Rallye); **stern|för|mig; Stern⌣for|scher, ...ge|wöl|be** *(Archit.),* **...gu|cker** *(ugs.)*; **stern|ha|gel|voll** (*ugs. für* sehr betrunken); **Stern|hau|fen** *(Astron.);* **stern|hell; Stern⌣him|mel** (der; -s); **...jahr** (*svw.* siderisches Jahr), **...kar|te; stern|klar; Stern|kun|de,** die; -; **stern|kun|dig; Stern⌣marsch** (der), **...mo|tor, ...na|me, ...ort** (der; -[e]s, ...örter), **...schnup|pe, ...sin|gen** (das; -s; Volksbrauch zur Dreikönigszeit), **...sin|ger, ...stun|de** (glückliche Schicksalsstunde), **...sys|tem, ...war|te, ...wol|ke** *(Astron.),* **...zei|chen, ...zeit**

Stert, der; -[e]s, -e (*nordd. für* ²Sterz [Schwanz usw.])

¹Sterz, der; -es, -e (*südd. u. österr. für* eine [Mehl]speise)

²Sterz, der; -es, -e (Schwanz[ende]; Führungs- u. Haltevorrichtung an Geräten); **ster|zeln** (den Hinterleib aufrichten [von Bienen])

stet *(veraltet);* -e Vorsicht; **Ste|te, Stet|heit,** die; - (*veraltend für* Stetigkeit)

Ste|tho|skop [ʃt..., *auch* st...] (↑R 132), das; -s, -e ‹griech.› (*Med.* Hörrohr)

ste|tig (ständig, fortwährend); **Ste|tig|keit,** die; -; *vgl. aber* Stätigkeit

Stetl, *auch* Schtetl, das; -s, - ‹jidd.› (*früher* überwiegend von Juden bewohnter Ort [in Osteuropa], in dem die Bevölkerung nach jüdischen Traditionen lebte)

stets; stets|fort (*schweiz. für* fortwährend)

Stet|tin (*poln.* Szczecin); **Stet|ti|ner** (↑R 103); **Stet|ti|ner Haff,** das; - -[e]s, *auch* Oderhaff, das; -[e]s

¹Steu|er, das; -s, - (Lenkvorrichtung); **²Steu|er,** die; -, -n (Abgabe); direkte, indirekte, staatliche -; **Steu|er|ab|zug; Steu|er|än|de|rungs|ge|setz; Steu|er|an|ge|le|gen|heit; Steu|er|an|pas|sungs|ge|setz; Steu|er⌣an|spruch, ...auf|kom|men, ...auf|sicht** (die; -); **Steu|er|aus|gleichs|kon|to; Steu|er|aus|schuss; ¹steu|er|bar** (*Amtsspr.* steuerpflichtig); das -e Einkommen; **²steu|er|bar** (sich steuern lassend); **Steu|er|bar|keit; steu|er|be|güns|tigt;** -es Sparen; **Steu|er|be|hör|de; Steu|er|be|mes|sungs|grund|la|ge; Steu|er⌣be|ra|ter, ...be|ra|te|rin, ...be|scheid, ...be|trag, ...be|voll|mäch|tig|te** (der *u.* die), **...bi|lanz; Steu|er|bord,** das; -[e]s, -e (rechte Schiffsseite); **steu|er|bord[s]; Steu|er|ein|nah|me; Steu|e|rer,** Steu|rer; **Steu|er⌣er|hö|hung, ...er|klä|rung, ...er|lass, ...er|leich|te|rung, ...er|mä|ßi|gung, ...er|mitt|lungs|ver|fah|ren, ...er|stat|tung, ...fahn|der, ...fahn|dung, ...flucht** (die; -), **...for|mu|lar; Steu|er|frau** (*w. Form von* Steuermann); **steu|er|frei;** -er Betrag; **Steu|er|frei|be|trag; Steu|er⌣gel|der** *(Plur.),* **...ge|rät** (Teil einer Stereoanlage), **...ge|setz, ...hel|fer, ...hin|ter|zie|hung, ...kar|te, ...klas|se, ...knüp|pel** (im Flugzeug), **...last, ...leh|re; steu|er|lich; steu|er|los;** ein -es Schiff; **Steu|er⌣mann** (*Plur.* ...leute, *auch* ...männer; *Rudern*), **...mar|ke; Steu|er|mess|be|trag; steu|ern;** ich ...ere (↑R 16); ein Boot -; dem Übel - (*geh. für* entgegenwirken); **Steu|er|oa|se** (↑R 132; Land mit bes. günstigen steuerlichen Verhältnissen für Ausländer); **Steu|er⌣pa|ra|dies** *(ugs.),* **...pflicht; steu|er|pflich|tig; Steu|er⌣po|li|tik, ...pro|gres|si|on, ...prü|fer, ...pult, ...rad, ...recht; steu|er|recht|lich; Steu|er⌣re|form, ...ru|der, ...satz, ...säu|le** *(Kfz-Technik),* **...schrau|be** (*nur in Wendungen wie* die - anziehen, an der - drehen), **...schuld, ...sen|kung, ...straf|recht, ...sys|tem, ...ta|bel|le, ...ta|rif, ...trä|ger; Steu|e|rung; Steu|er⌣ven|til, ...ver|an|la|gung, ...ver|ge|hen, ...ver|güns|ti|gung, ...ver|gü|tung, ...vo|raus|zah|lung, ...vor|rich|tung, ...werk** *(EDV),* **...we|sen** (das; -s), **...zah|ler, ...zah|le|rin, ...zet|tel, ...zu|schlag; Steu|rer,** Steu|e|rer

Ste|ven [...v...], der; -s, - (*nordd. für* das Schiff vorn u. hinten begrenzender Balken)

Ste|ward [ˈstju:ə(r)t], der; -s, -s ‹engl.› (Betreuer an Bord von Flugzeugen, Schiffen u. a.); **Ste|war|dess** [ˈstju:ə(r)dɛs, *auch* ...ˈdɛs], die; -, -en (Betreuerin an Bord von Flugzeugen u. a.)

Steyr (oberösterr. Stadt)

Stg., St. = Satang

StGB = Strafgesetzbuch

Sthe|nie [st..., *auch* ʃt...], die; - ‹griech.› (*Med.* Körperkraft); **sthe|nisch** (kraftvoll)

sti|bit|zen (*ugs. für* entwenden, sich listig aneignen); du stibitzt; er hat stibitzt

Sti|bi|um [ʃt..., *auch* st...], das; -s ‹griech.-lat.› (*lat. Bez. für* Antimon; *Zeichen* Sb)

Stich, der; -[e]s, -e; im - lassen; etwas hält Stich (*veraltend für* erweist sich als einwandfrei); **Stich⌣bahn** *(Eisenb.),* **...blatt** (Handschutz bei Fechtwaffen), **...bo|gen** (flacher Rundbogen); **Sti|chel,** der; -s, - (ein Werkzeug); **Sti|che|lei** (*auch für* Neckerei; Boshaftigkeiten); **Sti|chel|haar; sti|chel|haa|rig;** ein -er Hund; **sti|cheln** (*auch für* mit Worten necken, boshafte Bemerkungen machen); ich ...[e]le (↑R 16); (↑R 50:) er kann das Sticheln nicht lassen; **stich|fest;** hieb- und stichfest (↑R 23); **Stich⌣flam|me, ...fra|ge, ...gra|ben; Stich hal|ten** *vgl.* Stich; **stich|hal|tig,** *österr.* **stich|häl|tig; Stich|hal|tig|keit,** *österr.* **Stich|häl|tig|keit,** die; -; **sti|chig** (einen Stich habend, säuerlich); **...sti|chig** (z. B. wurmstichig); **Stich⌣jahr, ...kampf** *(Sport),* **...ka|nal** *(Wasserbau),* **...kap|pe** *(Bauw.);* **Stich|ler** ‹*zu* sticheln›; **Stich|ling** (ein Fisch)

Sti|cho|my|thie [ʃt..., *auch* st...], die; -, -n ‹griech.› (versweise wechselnde Rede u. Gegenrede in einem Versdrama)

Stich|pro|be; stich|pro|ben|wei|se; Stich|punkt; stich|punkt|ar|tig; Stich⌣sä|ge, ...stra|ße (größere Sackgasse [mit Wendeplatz]), **...tag, ...waf|fe, ...wahl; Stich|wort** *Plur.* (*für* Wort, das in einem Wörterbuch, Lexikon o. Ä. behandelt wird:) ...wörter *u.* (*für* Einsatzwort für den Schauspieler *od. für* kurze Aufzeichnung aus einzelnen wichtigen Wörtern:) ...worte; **stich|wort|ar|tig; Stich|wort⌣re|gis|ter, ...ver|zeich|nis; Stich|wun|de**

Sti|ckel, der; -s, - (*südd. u. schweiz. für* Stecken; Stützstange für Erbsen, Reben u. a.)

sti|cken; ¹Sti|cker (jmd., der stickt)

²Sti|cker [st...], der; -s, - ‹engl.› (Aufkleber)

Sti|cke|rei; Sti|cke|rin; Stick|garn; Stick|hus|ten (*veraltet für* Keuchhusten); **sti|ckig; Stick⌣luft** (die; -), **...ma|schi|ne, ...mus|ter; Stick|mus|ter|tuch** *Plur.* ...tücher; **Stick⌣oxid** (↑R 132; *vgl.* Oxid), **...rah|men, ...stoff** (der; -[e]s; chem. Element, Gas; *Zeichen* N; *vgl.* Nitrogenium); **Stick|stoff⌣bak|te|ri|en** *(Plur.),* **...dün|ger; stick|stoff|frei** (↑R 136); **stick|stoff|hal|tig**

stie|ben; du stobst, *auch* stiebtest; du stöbest, *auch* stiebtest; gestoben, *auch* gestiebt; stieb[e]!

Stief|bru|der
Stie|fel, der; -s, - (Fußbekleidung; Trinkglas in Stiefelform); **Stie|fel|chen; Stie|fe|let|te,** die; -, -n (Halbstiefel); **Stie|fel|knecht; stie|feln** (*ugs. für* gehen, stapfen, trotten); ich ...[e]le (↑R 16); **Stie|fel|schaft,** der
Stief₋el|tern (*Plur.*), **...ge|schwis|ter** (*Plur.*), **...kind, ...mut|ter** (*Plur.* ...mütter), **...müt|ter|chen** (eine Zierpflanze); **stief|müt|ter|lich**
Stie|fo₋gra|fie *od.* **...gra|phie,** die; - ⟨nach dem dt. Stenographen H. Stief⟩ (ein Kurzschriftsystem)
Stief₋schwes|ter, ...sohn, ...toch|ter, ...va|ter
Stie|ge, die; -, -n (Verschlag, flache [Latten]kiste; Zählmaß [20 Stück]; enge Holztreppe; *bes. südd., österr. für* Treppe[nflur]); **Stie|gen₋be|leuch|tung, ...ge|län|der, ...haus** (*südd., österr. für* Treppenhaus)
Stieg|litz, der; -es, -e ⟨slaw.⟩ (Distelfink)
stie|kum ⟨hebr.-jidd.⟩ (*ugs. für* heimlich, leise)
Stiel, der; -[e]s, -e (Handhabe; Griff; Stängel); mit Stumpf und -; **Stiel₋au|ge** (*ugs. scherzh. in* -n machen), **...be|sen, ...bril|le** (*veraltet für* Lorgnette), **...bürs|te; stie|len** (*selten für* mit Stiel versehen); *vgl.* gestielt; **Stiel|glas** *Plur.* ...gläser; **...stie|lig** (z. B. kurzstielig); **Stiel|kamm; stiel|los;** *vgl. aber* stillos; **Stiel|mus,** das; -es (*landsch. für* Gemüse aus Rübenstielen u. -blättern); **Stiel|stich** (*Stickerei*)
stie|men (*nordd. für* dicht schneien; qualmen); **Stiem|wet|ter,** das; -s (*nordd. für* Schneesturm)
stier (starr; *österr., schweiz. mdal. auch für* ohne Geld)
Stier, der; -[e]s, -e
[1]**stie|ren** (starr blicken)
[2]**stie|ren** (*svw.* rindern); **stie|rig** (brünstig [von der Kuh]); **Stier|kampf; Stier|kampf|are|na** (↑R 132); **Stier₋kämp|fer, ...na|cken; stier|na|ckig**
Stie|sel, Stie|ßel, der; -s, - (*ugs. für* ungeschickter Mensch, Dummkopf, Flegel); **stie|se|lig, sties|lig, stie|ße|lig, stieß|lig**
[1]**Stift,** der; -[e]s, -e (Bleistift; Nagel); [2]**Stift,** der; -[e]s, -e (*ugs. für* halbwüchsiger Junge, Lehrling)
[3]**Stift,** das; -[e]s, -e, *selten* -er (fromme Stiftung; *veraltet für* Altersheim); [1]**stif|ten** (spenden; gründen; bewirken)
[2]**stif|ten;** *nur in* stiften gehen (*ugs. für* [heimlich] ausreißen, fliehen)

[1]**Stif|ter** (österr. Schriftsteller)
[2]**Stif|ter; Stif|ter|fi|gur** (*bild. Kunst);* **Stif|te|rin; Stif|ter|ver|band;** - für die Deutsche Wissenschaft; **stif|tisch** (*veraltet für* zu einem [3]Stift gehörend); **Stift|ler** (*veraltet für* Stiftsangehöriger); **Stifts₋da|me, ...fräu|lein, ...herr, ...kir|che, ...schu|le; Stif|tung; Stif|tungs₋brief, ...fest, ...rat** (*Plur.* ...räte; *kath. Kirche* dem Pfarrer unterstehender Gemeindeausschuss zur Verwaltung des Kirchenvermögens), **...ur|kun|de**
Stift|zahn
Stig|ma [st..., *auch* ʃt...], das; -s, *Plur.* ...men *u.* -ta ⟨griech., „Stich"⟩ ([Wund-, Brand]mal; *Bot.* Narbe der Blütenpflanzen; *Zool.* äußere Öffnung der Tracheen; Augenfleck der Einzeller); **Stig|ma|ti|sa|ti|on,** die; -, -en (Auftreten der fünf Wundmale Christi bei einem Menschen); **stig|ma|ti|sie|ren** (brandmarken, zeichnen); **Stig|ma|ti|sier|te,** der *u.* die; -n, -n (↑R 5 ff.); **Stig|ma|ti|sie|rung**
Stil [ʃt..., *auch* st...], der; -[e]s, -e ⟨lat.⟩ (Einheit der Ausdrucksformen [eines Kunstwerkes, eines Menschen, einer Zeit]; Darstellungsweise, Art [Bau-, Schreibart usw.]); *Zeitrechnung* alten -s (*Abk.* a. St.), neuen -s (*Abk.* n. St.); **Stil|art**
Stilb [ʃt..., *auch* st...], das; -s, - ⟨griech.⟩ (*Physik* eine veraltete Einheit der Leuchtdichte; *Zeichen* sb); 4 Stilb
stil|bil|dend; - für eine Epoche; **Stil₋blü|te, ...bruch** (der), **...ebe|ne** (↑R 132; *Sprachw.*); **stil|echt;** -e Möbel; etwas - renovieren; **Stil₋ele|ment** (↑R 132), **...emp|fin|den, ...ent|wick|lung**
Sti|lett [ʃt..., *auch* st...], das; -s, -e ⟨ital.⟩ (kleiner Dolch)
Stil₋feh|ler, ...fi|gur
Stilf|ser Joch, das; - -[e]s (ein Alpenpass)
Stil|ge|fühl, das; -[e]s; **stil|ge|recht; sti|li|sie|ren** ⟨lat.⟩ (nur in den wesentlichen Grundstrukturen darstellen); **Sti|li|sie|rung; Sti|list,** der; -en, -en; ↑R 126 (jmd., der guten Stil beherrscht); **Sti|lis|tik,** die; -, -en (Stilkunde); **Sti|lis|tin; sti|lis|tisch; Stil|kun|de,** die; -, -en; **stil|kund|lich**
still; (↑R 108:) *Kaufmannsspr.* stiller Teilhaber, stille Reserven, Rücklagen, stille Beteiligung; *ugs. scherzh.* das stille Örtchen (Toilette); *kath. Kirche* eine stille Messe. *Großschreibung:* im Stillen

(unbemerkt); (↑R 102:) der Stille Ozean; (↑R 108:) der Stille Freitag (Karfreitag); die Stille Woche (Karwoche). *Schreibung in Verbindung mit Verben* (↑R 39): still sein, werden, sitzen, stehen, halten; in der Kirche sollen wir ganz still (ruhig) sitzen; du musst die Lampe ganz still (ruhig) halten; *vgl. aber* stillhalten, stilllegen, stillliegen usw.; **stil|le** (*ugs. für* still); **Stil|le,** die; -; in aller -
Stil|leh|re
stil|len; Still|geld (Unterstützung für stillende Mütter); **still|ge|stan|den!** (milit. Kommando); **Still|hal|te|ab|kom|men; still|hal|ten;** (↑R 38 f.; alles geduldig ertragen); wir haben lange genug stillgehalten; *vgl. aber* still; **Still|le|ben** (↑R 136), das; -s, - (*Malerei* bildl. Darstellung von Gegenständen in künstl. Anordnung); **still|le|gen** (↑R 136 *u.* 38 f.; außer Betrieb setzen); ich lege still; stillgelegt; stillzulegen; die Eisenbahnlinie wurde stillgelegt; **Still|le|gung** (↑R 136); **still|lie|gen** (↑R 136 *u.* 38 f.; außer Betrieb sein); die Fabrik hat stillgelegen; *aber* das Kind hat ganz still (ruhig) gelegen
stil|los; *vgl. aber* stiellos; **Stil|lo|sig|keit**
still|schwei|gen (↑R 38 f.; schweigen, nichts verraten); er hat lange stillgeschwiegen; **Still|schwei|gen;** jmdm. - auferlegen; **still|schwei|gend; still|sit|zen** (↑R 38 f.; nicht beschäftigt sein); *aber* still (ruhig) sitzen; *vgl.* still; **Still|stand,** der; -[e]s; **still|ste|hen** (↑R 38 f.; in der Bewegung aufhören); sein Herz hat stillgestanden; stillgestanden! (*Milit.*); *aber* das Kind hat lange ganz still (ruhig) gestanden; **Stil|lung,** die; -; **still|ver|gnügt; Still|zeit**
Stil₋mit|tel (das), **...mö|bel, ...no|te** (*Sport*), **...rich|tung; Stil₋schicht** (*svw.* Stilebene), **...übung** (↑R 132), **...un|ter|su|chung; stil|voll; Stil|wan|del; stil|wid|rig; Stil|wör|ter|buch**
Stimm₋ab|ga|be, ...auf|wand, ...band (das; *Plur.* ...bänder); **stimm|be|rech|tigt; Stimm|be|rech|tig|te,** der *u.* die; -n, -n (↑R 5 ff.); **Stimm₋be|rech|ti|gung, ...be|zirk; stimm|bil|dend; Stimm₋bil|dung, ...bruch** (der; -[e]s), **...bür|ger** (*schweiz.);* **Stimm|chen; Stim|me,** die; -, -n; **stim|men; Stim|men₋an|teil, ...aus|zäh|lung, ...fang** (der; -[e]s), **...ge|winn, ...ge|wirr, ...gleich|heit** (die; -), **...kauf,**

...mehr|heit; Stim|ment|hal|tung; Stim|men⌣ver|hält|nis, ...ver|lust; Stim|mer (eines Musikinstrumentes); **stimm|fä|hig; Stimm⌣füh|rung** (die; -; *Musik*), **...ga|bel; stimm|ge|wal|tig; stimm|haft** (*Sprachw.* weich auszusprechen); **Stimm|haf|tig|keit,** die; -; **stim|mig** (passend, richtig, [überein]stimmend); **...stim|mig** (z. B. vierstimmig, *mit Ziffer* 4-stimmig); **Stim|mig|keit,** die; -; **Stimm|la|ge; stimm|lich; stimm|los** (*Sprachw.* hart auszusprechen); **Stimm|lo|sig|keit,** die; -; **Stimm|mit|tel** (↑R 136), das; -s, -; **Stimm⌣recht, ...rit|ze, ...schlüs|sel** (Gerät zum Klavierstimmen), **...stock** (in Streichinstrumenten); **Stim|mung; Stim|mungs⌣ba|ro|me|ter** *(ugs.)*, **...bild, ...ka|no|ne** (*ugs. für* jmd., der für Stimmung sorgt, sehr gut unterhält), **...ka|pel|le, ...ma|che, ...mu|sik, ...um|schwung; stim|mungs|voll; Stimm⌣vieh** *(abwertend)*, **...zet|tel**

Sti|mu|lans [st..., *auch* ʃt...], das; -, *Plur.* ...lantia *u.* ...lanzien [...i̯ən] ‹lat.› (*Med.* anregendes Mittel, Reizmittel); **Sti|mu|lanz,** die; -, -en (Anreiz, Antrieb); **Sti|mu|la|ti|on** [ʃt..., *auch* st...], die; -, -en (*seltener für* Stimulierung); **sti|mu|lie|ren; Sti|mu|lie|rung** (Erregung, Anregung, Reizung); **Sti|mu|lus** [st..., *auch* ʃt...], der; -, ...li (Reiz, Antrieb)

Sti|ne (w. Vorn.)

stink|be|sof|fen (*derb für* völlig betrunken); **Stink|bom|be; Stin|ke|fin|ger** (*ugs.;* obszöne Geste); **stin|ken;** du stankst; du stänkest; gestunken; stink[e]!; **Stin|ker** (*ugs. für* unangenehmer Mensch); **stink|faul** (*ugs. für* sehr faul); **stink|fein** *(ugs.)*; **Stink|fritz,** der; -en, -en; ↑R 126 (*ugs. svw.* Stinker); **stin|kig; Stink|käl|fer** (*landsch. für* Mistkäfer); **stink|lang|wei|lig** *(ugs.)*; **Stink|lau|ne** (*ugs. für* sehr schlechte Laune); **Stink⌣mar|der** (*Jägerspr.* Iltis), **...mor|chel; stink|nor|mal** *(ugs.)*; **stink|sau|er** (*ugs. für* sehr verärgert); **Stink⌣stie|fel** (*derb für* übel gelaunter, unangenehmer Mensch), **...tier; stink|vor|nehm** *(ugs.)*; **Stink|wan|ze; Stink|wut** *(ugs.)*

Stint, der; -[e]s, -e (ein Fisch)

Sti|pen|di|at, der; -en, -en (↑R 126) ‹lat.› (jmd., der ein Stipendium erhält); **Sti|pen|di|en|ver|ga|be; Sti|pen|di|um,** das; -s, ...ien [...i̯ən] (Geldbeihilfe für Schüler, Studierende, Gelehrte)

Stipp, der; -[e]s, -e *u.* Stip|pe, die; -, -n (*landsch. für* Kleinigkeit; Punkt; Pustel; Tunke); auf den Stipp (sofort); **Stipp|be|such** (*ugs. für* kurzer Besuch); **Stipp|chen; stip|pen** (*ugs. für* tupfen, tunken); **stip|pig** (*landsch. für* gefleckt; mit Pusteln besetzt); **Stip|pig|keit,** die; - *(landsch.)*; **Stipp|vi|si|te** (*ugs. für* kurzer Besuch)

Sti|pu|la|ti|on [ʃt..., *auch* st...], die; -, -en ‹lat.› (vertragl. Abmachung, Übereinkunft); **sti|pu|lie|ren; Sti|pu|lie|rung**

Stirn, die; -, -en, *geh.* Stir|ne, die; -, -n; **Stirn⌣band** (das; *Plur.* ...bänder), **...bein; Stir|ne** *vgl.* Stirn; **Stirn⌣fal|te, ...flä|che, ...glat|ze, ...höh|le; Stirn|höh|len⌣ent|zün|dung, ...ver|ei|te|rung; ...stir|nig** (z. B. breitstirnig); **Stirn⌣lo|cke, ...reif, ...rie|men, ...run|zeln** (das; -s); **stirn|run|zelnd; Stirn⌣sei|te, ...wand, ...zie|gel**

St. Kitts und Ne|vis [sənt - - 'ni:vis] (Staat im Bereich der Westindischen Inseln)

St. Lu|cia [s(ə)nt -] (Staat im Bereich der Westindischen Inseln); *vgl.* Lucianer

Sto. = Santo

Stoa [st...], die; -, Stoen ‹griech.› (*nur Sing.:* altgriech. Philosophenschule; altgriech. Säulenhalle)

Stö|ber, der; -s, - (*Jägerspr.* Hund, der zum [Auf]stöbern des Wildes gebraucht wird); **Stö|be|rei** (*landsch. auch für* Großreinemachen); **Stö|ber|hund; stö|bern** (*ugs. für* suchen, [wühlend] herumsuchen; *Jägerspr.* aufjagen; flockenartig umherfliegen; *landsch. auch für* sauber machen); ich ...ere (↑R 16); es stöbert (*landsch. für* es schneit)

Sto|chas|tik [sto'xas..., *auch* ʃt...], die; - ‹griech.› (Betrachtungsweise der analytischen Statistik nach der Wahrscheinlichkeitstheorie); **sto|chas|tisch**

Sto|cher, der; -s, - (Werkzeug zum Stochern); **Sto|cher|kahn; sto|chern;** ich ...ere (↑R 16)

[1]**Stock,** der; -[e]s, Stöcke (Stab u. Ä., Baumstumpf); über Stock und Stein; in den - (Fußblock) legen; [2]**Stock,** der; -[e]s, - (Stockwerk); das Haus hat zwei -, ist zwei - hoch; ein Haus von drei -

[3]**Stock** [stɔk], der; -s, -s ‹engl.› (*Wirtsch.* Vorrat, Warenlager; Grundkapital)

Stock|aus|schlag (*Forstw.* Bildung von Sprossen an Baumstümpfen); **stock⌣be|trun|ken** (*ugs. für* völlig betrunken), **...blind** (*ugs. für* völlig blind)

Stock|car ['stɔkka:(r)] (↑R 33), der; -s, -s ‹engl.› (*Motorsport* mit starkem Motor ausgestatteter Serienwagen, mit dem Rennen gefahren werden); **Stock|car|ren|nen**

Stöck|chen; Stock|de|gen; stock⌣dumm (*ugs. für* sehr dumm), **...dun|kel** (*ugs. für* völlig dunkel); **Stock|ei|sen;** [1]**Stö|ckel,** der; -s, - (*ugs. für* hoher Absatz); [2]**Stö|ckel,** das; -s, - (*österr. für* Nebengebäude [von Schlössern od. Bauernhäusern]); **Stö|ckel|ab|satz; stö|ckeln** (*ugs. für* auf [1]Stöckeln laufen); ich ...[e]le (↑R 16); **Stö|ckel|schuh; sto|cken** (nicht vorangehen; *bayr. u. österr. auch für* gerinnen); (↑R 50:) ins Stocken geraten, kommen; gestockte Milch (*bayr. u. österr. für* Dickmilch); **Stock|en|te; Sto|ckerl,** das; -s, -n (*bayr. u. österr. für* Hocker); **Stock⌣fäu|le** *(Forstw.)*, **...feh|ler** *([Eis]hockey)*; **stock|fins|ter** (*ugs. für* völlig finster); **Stock⌣fisch** (*ugs. auch für* wenig gesprächiger Mensch), **Stock⌣fleck** *od.* **...fle|cken; stock|fle|ckig; stock|hei|ser** (*ugs. für* sehr heiser)

Stock|holm [*auch* ...'hɔlm] (Hptst. von Schweden); **Stock|hol|mer** (↑R 103)

sto|ckig (muffig; stockfleckig); **...stö|ckig** (z. B. vierstöckig, *mit Ziffer* 4-stöckig; ↑R 44); **stock|kon|ser|va|tiv** (*ugs. für* sehr konservativ); **Stöck|li,** das; -s, - (*schweiz. für* Nebengebäude eines Bauernhofs; Altenteil); **Stock|na|gel; stock|nüch|tern** (*ugs. für* ganz nüchtern); **Stock⌣punkt** (*Chemie* Temperatur der Zähigkeitszunahme von Ölen), **...ro|se** (Malve); **stock|sau|er** (*ugs. für* sehr verärgert, sehr wütend); **Stock⌣schirm, ...schla|gen** (das; -s; *Eishockey*), **...schnup|fen, ...schwämm|chen** (ein Pilz); **stock⌣steif** (*ugs. für* völlig steif), **...taub** (*ugs. für* völlig taub); **Stock|uhr** (*österr. veraltet für* Standuhr); **Sto|ckung; Stock|werk; Stock|zahn** (*südd., österr., schweiz. für* Backenzahn)

Stoff, der; -[e]s, -e; **Stoff⌣bahn, ...bal|len, ...be|hang**

Stof|fel, der; -s, - (*ugs. für* ungeschickter, unhöflicher Mensch, Tölpel); **stof|fe|lig,** stoff|lig (*ugs. für* tölpisch, unhöflich)

Stoff|far|be (↑R 136); **Stoff|fet|zen** (↑R 136), der; -s, -; **Stoff|fül|le** (↑R 136), die; -; **stoff|hal|tig;**

stoff|lich (materiell); **Stoff|lich|keit,** die; -
stoff|lig *vgl.* stoffelig
Stoff₋rest, ...samm|lung, ...ser|vi|et|te, ...tier; Stoff|wech|sel; Stoff|wech|sel|krank|heit
stöh|nen; (↑R 50:) leises Stöhnen
stoi! [stɔy] ⟨russ.⟩ (halt!)
Sto|i|ker [ʃt..., *auch* st...] ⟨griech.⟩ (Anhänger der Stoa; Vertreter des Stoizismus); **sto|isch** (zur Stoa gehörend; unerschütterlich, gleichmütig); **Sto|i|zis|mus,** der; - (Lehre der Stoiker; Unerschütterlichkeit, Gleichmut)
Sto|la [ʃt..., *auch* st...], die; -, ...len ⟨griech.⟩ (altröm. Ärmelgewand; gottesdienstl. Gewandstück des kath. Geistlichen; langer, schmaler Umhang)
Stol|berg (Harz) (Kurort in Sachsen-Anhalt); **Stol|berg (Rhld.)** (Stadt bei Aachen)
Stol|ge|büh|ren [ʃt..., *auch* st...] *Plur.* (Pfarramtsnebenbezüge)
Stoll|berg (Erzgeb.) (Stadt in Sachsen)
Stol|le, die; -, -n *od.* [1]**Stol|len,** der; -s, - (ein Weihnachtsgebäck); [2]**Stol|len,** der; -s, - (Zapfen am Hufeisen, an [Fußball]schuhen; *Bergmannsspr.* waagerechter Grubenbau; *Verslehre* eine Strophe des Aufgesangs im Meistersang); **Stol|len₋bau** (der; -[e]s), **...gang** (der), **...mund|loch** *(Bergmannsspr.)*
Stol|per|draht; Stol|pe|rer; stol|pern (straucheln); ich ...ere (↑R 16); **Stol|per|stein** (Schwierigkeit, an der etwas, jmd. leicht scheitern kann)
stolz; Stolz, der; -es
Stol|ze (Erfinder eines Kurzschriftsystems); **Stol|ze-Schrey;** das Kurzschriftsystem Stolze-Schrey
stolz|ge|schwellt; mit -er Brust; **stol|zie|ren** (stolz einherschreiten)
Sto|ma [st..., *auch* ʃt...], das; -s, -ta ⟨griech.⟩ (*Med.* Mund-, Spaltöffnung; künstlicher Darmausgang o.Ä.; *Biol.* Spaltöffnung des Pflanzenblattes); **sto|ma|chal** [...x...] (*Med.* durch den Magen gehend, den Magen betreffend); **Sto|ma|ti|tis,** die; -, ...itiden (Entzündung der Mundschleimhaut); **Sto|ma|to|lo|gie,** die; - (Lehre von den Erkrankungen der Mundhöhle); **sto|ma|to|lo|gisch**
Stone|henge [ˈsto:nhɛndʒ] (Kultstätte der Jungsteinzeit u. frühen Bronzezeit in Südengland)
stop! [st..., *auch* ʃt...] ⟨engl.⟩ (*auf Verkehrsschildern* halt!; *im Telegrafenverkehr für* Punkt); *vgl.* stopp!; **Stop** *frühere Schreibung für* **Stopp** *(Tennis);* **Stop-and-go-Ver|kehr** [ˈstɔpəndˈgo:...] (durch langsames Fahren u. häufiges Anhalten der Fahrzeuge gekennzeichneter Verkehr)
Stopf₋buch|se *od.* **...bü|chse** (Maschinenteil), **...ei; stop|fen; Stop|fen,** der; -s, - (*landsch. für* Stöpsel, Kork); **Stop|fer; Stopf₋garn, ...na|del, ...pilz; Stop|fung**
stopp! (halt!); *vgl.* stop!; **Stopp,** der; -s, -s (Halt, Unterbrechung; *bes. Tennis* Stoppball); **Stopp|ball** *(Sport)*
[1]**Stop|pel,** der; -s, - (*österr. für* Stöpsel)
[2]**Stop|pel,** die; -, -n; **Stop|pel|bart** *(ugs.);* **stop|pel|bär|tig; Stop|pel₋feld, ...haar** (das; -[e]s); **stop|pe|lig,** stopp|lig; **Stop|pe|lig|keit,** Stopp|lig|keit, die; -; **stop|peln** (Ähren u. Ä. aufsammeln); ich ...[e]le (↑R 16)
Stop|pel|zie|her (*österr. für* Korkenzieher)
stop|pen (anhalten; mit der Stoppuhr messen); **Stop|per** (*Fußball* Mittelläufer); **Stopp|licht** *Plur.* ...lichter
stopp|lig *vgl.* stoppelig; **Stopp|lig|keit** *vgl.* Stoppeligkeit
Stopp|preis (↑R 136; Höchstpreis); **Stopp₋schild** (das), **...signal, ...stra|ße, ...uhr**
Stöp|sel, der; -s, -; **stöp|seln;** ich ...[e]le (↑R 16)
[1]**Stör,** der; -[e]s, -e (ein Fisch)
[2]**Stör,** die; -, -en (*südd., österr. u. schweiz. für* Arbeit, die ein Gewerbetreibender im Hause des Kunden verrichtet); auf der Stör arbeiten; auf die *od.* in die - gehen
[3]**Stör,** die; - (Fluss in Schleswig-Holstein)
Stör|ak|ti|on; stör|an|fäl|lig; ein -es Gerät; **Stör|an|fäl|lig|keit**
Sto|rax *vgl.* Styrax
Storch, der; -[e]s, Störche; **Storch|bein; storch|bei|nig; stor|chen** (*ugs. für* wie ein Storch einherschreiten); **Stor|chen|nest; Stör|chin; Störch|lein; Storch|nest** (*svw.* Storchennest); **Storch|schna|bel** (eine Pflanze; Gerät zum mechan. Verkleinern od. Vergrößern von Zeichnungen)
[1]**Store** [ʃto:r, *auch* st..., *schweiz.* ˈʃto:rə], der; -s, -s, *schweiz. meist* die; -, -n ⟨franz.⟩ (Fenstervorhang; *schweiz. für* Markise; Sonnenvorhang aus Segeltuch od. aus Kunststofflamellen)
[2]**Store** [stɔ:(r)], der; -s, -s ⟨engl.⟩ (*engl. Bez. für* Vorrat, Lager; Laden)
Sto|ren [ˈʃto:rən], der; -s, - (*schweiz. neben* [1]Store)
[1]**stö|ren** (*südd. u. österr. für* auf der [2]Stör arbeiten, auf die, in die [2]Stör gehen)
[2]**stö|ren** (hindern, belästigen); sich -; ich störte mich an seinem Benehmen; **Stö|ren|fried,** der; -[e]s, -e *(abwertend)*
[1]**Stö|rer** (*südd. u. österr. für* auf der [2]Stör Arbeitender; Landfahrer)
[2]**Stö|rer** (jmd., der [2]stört); **Stö|re|rei; Stö|re|rin; Stör₋fall** (der; Störung, bes. in einem Kernkraftwerk), **...feu|er** *(Milit.);* **stör|frei**
stor|gen (*landsch. für* als Landstreicher umherziehen); **Stor|ger** (*landsch. für* Landstreicher)
Stör|ge|räusch
Storm (dt. Schriftsteller)
Stör|ma|nö|ver
Stor|marn (Gebiet u. Landkreis im südl. Holstein); **Stor|mar|ner** (↑R 103); **stor|marnsch**
stor|nie|ren [ʃt..., *auch* st...] ⟨ital.⟩ (*Kaufmannsspr.* rückgängig machen; Fehler [in der Buchung] berichtigen); **Stor|nie|rung; Stor|no,** der *u.* das; -s, ...ni (Berichtigung; Rückbuchung, Löschung); **Stor|no|bu|chung**
stör|rig (*seltener für* störrisch); **Stör|rig|keit,** die; - (*seltener für* Störrischkeit); **stör|risch; Stör|risch|keit,** die; -
Stör|schnei|de|rin ⟨*zu* [2]Stör⟩
Stör₋schutz (gegen Rundfunkstörungen), **...sen|der, ...stel|le**
Stör|te|be|ker (ein Seeräuber)
Stor|ting [ˈsto:r..., *norw.* ˈstu:r...], das; -s (norw. Volksvertretung)
Stö|rung; Stö|rungs|feu|er (*vgl.* Störfeuer); **stö|rungs|frei** *(bes. Technik);* **Stö|rungs₋front** *(Meteor.),* **...stel|le** (für Störungen im Fernsprechverkehr zuständige Abteilung bei der Telekom), **...su|che**
Sto|ry [ˈstɔ:ri], die; -, -s ⟨engl.⟩ ([Kurz]geschichte)
Stoß, der; -es, Stöße (*Bergmannsspr. auch für* seitl. Begrenzung eines Grubenbaus); **Stoß₋band** (das; *Plur.* ...bänder), **...bor|te** (an der Hose); **Stöß|chen; Stoß₋dämp|fer, ...de|gen; Stö|ßel,** der; -s, - (Stoßgerät); **stoß|emp|find|lich; sto|ßen;** du stößt, er stößt; du stießest; gestoßen; stoß[e]!; er stößt ihn, *auch* ihm in die Seite; **Stö|ßer** (*auch für* Sperber); **Sto|ße|rei; stoß|fest; Stoß₋ge|bet, ...ge|schäft; stö|ßig;** ein -er Zie-

genbock; **Stoß|kraft,** die; -; **stoß|kräf|tig; Stoß_rich|tung, ...seuf|zer; stoß|si|cher; Stoß_stan|ge, ...the|ra|pie** *(Med.),* **...trupp** *(Milit.);* **Stoß|trupp|ler; Stoß_ver|kehr** (der; -s; Verkehr zur Zeit der stärksten Verkehrsdichte), **...waf|fe; stoß|wei|se; Stoß_zahn, ...zeit** *(Verkehrsw.)*

Sto|ti|n|ka [st...], die; -, ...ki ‹bulgar.› (bulgar. Münze; 100 Stotinki = 1 Lew)

Stot|te|rei *(ugs.);* **Stot|te|rer; stot|te|rig,** stott|rig; **Stot|te|rin,** Stott|re|rin; **stot|tern;** ich ...ere (↑R 16); ↑R 50: ins Stottern geraten; etwas auf Stottern *(ugs. für* auf Ratenzahlung) kaufen; **Stott|re|rin** *vgl.* Stotterin; **stott|rig** *vgl.* stotterig

Stotz, der; -es, -e *u., schweiz. nur,* **Stot|zen,** der; -s, - *(landsch. für* Baumstumpf; Bottich; *schweiz. für* Keule eines Schlachttiers); **stot|zig** *(südwestd. u. schweiz. mdal. für* steil)

Stout [staut], der; -s, -s ‹engl.› (dunkles engl. Bier)

Sto|v|chen, Stöv|chen *(nordd. für* Kohlenbecken; Wärmevorrichtung für Tee od. Kaffee); **Sto|ve** [...və], die; -, -n *(nordd. für* Trockenraum); **sto|wen** *(nordd. für* dämpfen, dünsten); gestowtes Obst

StPO = Strafprozessordnung

Str. = Straße

stra|ba|n|zen, stra|wa|n|zen *(bayr. u. österr. mdal. für* sich herumtreiben); **Stra|ba|n|zer,** Stra|wa|n|zer

Stra|bo[n] [st...] (griech. Geograph u. Geschichtsschreiber)

Strac|chi|no [straˈkiːno], der; -[s] ‹ital.› (ein ital. Käse)

[1]**Strac|cia|tel|la** [stratʃa...], das; -[s] ‹ital.› (Speiseeissorte aus Milchspeiseeis mit Schokoladenstückchen); [2]**Strac|cia|tel|la,** die; -, ...le ‹ital.› (ital. [Eier]einlaufsuppe)

strack *(landsch. für* gerade, straff, steif; faul, träge; *auch für* völlig betrunken); **stracks** (geradeaus; sofort)

Strad|dle [ˈstrɛd(ə)l], der; -[s], -s ‹engl.› *(Leichtathletik* ein Sprungstil im Hochsprung)

[1]**Stra|di|va|ri** [stradiˈvaːri] (ital. Meister des Geigenbaues); [2]**Stra|di|va|ri,** die; -, -[s] (Stradivarigeige); **Stra|di|va|ri|gei|ge** (↑R 95)

Straf_ak|ti|on, ...an|dro|hung, ...an|stalt, ...an|trag, ...an|zei|ge, ...ar|beit, ...ar|rest, ...auf|he|bung; Straf|auf|he|bungs|grund; Straf_auf|schub, ...aus|set|zung, ...bank *(Plur.* ...bänke; *Sport*); **straf|bar;** -e Handlung; **Straf|bar|keit,** die; -; **Straf_be|fehl, ...be|fug|nis, ...be|scheid; straf|be|wehrt** *(Rechtsspr.* mit Strafe bedroht); Diebstahl ist strafbewehrt; **Stra|fe,** die; -, -n; **Straf|ecke** (↑R 132; *Sport);* **stra|fen; Straf|ent|las|se|ne,** der *u.* die; -n, -n (↑R 5 ff.); **Straf|er|lass; straf|er|schwe|rend; straf|exer|zie|ren** (↑R 132) *nur im Infinitiv u. Partizip I u. II gebr.;* **Straf|ex|pe|di|ti|on**

straff

straf|fäl|lig; Straf|fäl|lig|keit, die; -

straf|fen (straff machen); sich - (sich recken); **Straff|heit,** die; -

straf|frei; Straf_frei|heit (die; -), **...ge|fan|ge|ne, ...ge|richt, ...ge|richts|bar|keit, ...ge|setz, ...ge|setz|buch** *(Abk.* StGB), **...ge|setz|ge|bung, ...ge|walt** (die; -), **...kam|mer, ...ko|lo|nie, ...kom|pa|nie** *(Milit.),* **...la|ger** *(Plur.* ...lager); **sträf|lich;** -er Leichtsinn; **Sträf|lich|keit,** die; -; **Sträf|ling; Sträf|lings|klei|dung; straf|los; Straf|lo|sig|keit,** die; -; **Straf_man|dat, ...maß** (das); **straf|mil|dernd; Straf_mil|de|rung, ...mi|nu|te** *(Sport);* **straf|mün|dig; Straf_por|to, ...pre|digt, ...pro|zess; Straf|pro|zess|ord|nung** *(Abk.* StPO); **Straf_punkt** *(Sport),* **...raum** *(Sport),* **...recht** (das; -[e]s); **Straf|recht|ler; straf|recht|lich; Straf|rechts|re|form; Straf_re|gis|ter, ...sa|che, ...se|nat, ...stoß** *(Sport),* **...tat, ...tä|ter, ...til|gung; Straf|til|gungs|grund; Straf_um|wand|lung, ...ver|bü|ßung, ...ver|fah|ren, ...ver|fol|gung, ...ver|fü|gung** (Strafmandat); **straf|ver|schär|fend; Straf|ver|schär|fung; straf|ver|set|zen** *nur im Infinitiv u. Partizip II gebr.;* strafversetzt; **Straf_ver|set|zung, ...ver|tei|di|ger, ...ver|tei|di|ge|rin, ...voll|stre|ckung, ...voll|zug; Straf|voll|zugs|an|stalt; straf|wei|se; straf|wür|dig; Straf_zeit** *(Sport),* **...zet|tel, ...zu|mes|sung**

Strahl, der; -[e]s, -en; **Strahl|an|trieb; Strah|le|mann** *Plur.* ...männer *(ugs. für* jmd., der ein [übertrieben] fröhliches Gesicht macht); **strah|len**

sträh|len *(landsch. u. schweiz. für* kämmen)

Strah|len_be|hand|lung, ...be|las|tung, ...bi|o|lo|gie, ...bre|chung, ...bün|del, ...che|mie; strah|lend; Strah|len|do|sis; strah|len|för|mig; Strah|len_krank|heit, ...kranz, ...kun|de (die; -; *svw.* Radiologie), **...pilz, ...schä|di|gung, ...schutz** (der; -es), **...the|ra|pie, ...tier|chen, ...tod; Strah|ler** *(schweiz. auch für* [Berg]kristallsucher); **Sträh|ler** *vgl.* Strehler; **Strahl|flug|zeug** (Düsenflugzeug); **strah|lig; ...strah|lig** (z. B. achtstrahlig, *mit Ziffer* 8-strahlig; ↑R 44); **Strahl_kraft** (die), **...rich|tung, ...rohr, ...stär|ke, ...trieb|werk; Strah|lung; Strah|lungs_ener|gie** (↑R 132), **...gür|tel, ...in|ten|si|tät, ...wär|me**

Strähn, der; -[e]s, -e *(österr. für* Büschel von Wolle od. Garn); **Sträh|ne,** die; -, -n; **sträh|nig; ...sträh|nig** (z. B. dreisträhnig, *mit Ziffer* 3-strähnig; ↑R 44)

Strak, das; -s, -e *(Schiffbau* der Verlauf der Linien eines Bootskörpers); **stra|ken** *(Schiffbau, Technik* vorschriftsmäßig verlaufen [von einer Kurve]; streichen, strecken)

Stral|sund [*auch* ...ˈzunt] (Hafenstadt an der Ostsee); **Stral|sun|der** (↑R 103)

Stral|zie|rung [ʃt..., *auch* st...], *österr.* **Stral|zio,** der; -s, -s ‹ital.› *(Kaufmannsspr. veraltet für* Liquidation)

Stra|min, der; -s, -e ‹niederl.› (Gittergewebe für Kreuzstickerei); **Stra|min|de|cke**

stramm; ein strammer Junge; strammer Max (Spiegelei u. Schinken auf Brot); das Seil stramm ziehen, noch strammer ziehen; ich ziehe ihm den Hosenboden stramm; *vgl.* strammstehen; **stram|men** *(landsch. für* straff anziehen); **Stramm|heit,** die; -; **stramm|ste|hen** (↑R 38 f.); ich stehe stramm; strammgestanden; strammzustehen; **stramm zie|hen** *vgl.* stramm

Stram|pel_an|zug, ...hös|chen; stram|peln; ich ...[e]le (↑R 16); **Stram|pel|sack; stramp|fen** *(südd. u. österr. für* stampfen; strampeln); **Stramp|ler**

Strand, der; -[e]s, Strände; **Strand_an|zug, ...bad, ...burg, ...ca|fé, ...dis|tel; stran|den; Strand_gut** (das; -[e]s), **...ha|fer; Strand|hau|bit|ze;** *nur in Wendungen wie* voll, betrunken, blau wie eine - sein *(ugs. für* völlig betrunken sein); **Strand_kleid, ...korb, ...krab|be, ...läu|fer** (ein Vogel), **...recht** (das; -[e]s); **Stran|dung; Strand|wa|che**

Strang, der; -[e]s, Stränge; über die Stränge schlagen *(ugs.);*

Stran|ge, die; -, -n (*schweiz. für* Strang, Strähne); eine - Garn, Wolle; **strän|gen** (*veraltend für* [ein Zugtier] anspannen)
Stran|gu|la|ti|on, Stran|gu|lie|rung, die; -, -en ‹griech.› (Erdrosselung; *Med.* Abklemmung); **stran|gu|lie|ren**
Strang|u|rie [st..., *auch* ʃt...], die; -, ...ien (*Med.* Harnzwang)
Stra|paz... (*österr. für* Strapazier..., z. B. Strapazhose); **Stra|pa|ze**, die; -, -n ‹ital.› ([große] Anstrengung, Beschwerlichkeit); **stra|paz|fä|hig** (*österr. für* strapazierfähig); **Stra|paz|ho|se** (*österr. für* Strapazierhose); **stra|pa|zier|bar**; **Stra|pa|zier|bar|keit**, die; -; **stra|pa|zie|ren** (übermäßig anstrengen, in Anspruch nehmen; abnutzen); sich - (*ugs. für* sich [ab]mühen); **stra|pa|zier|fä|hig**; **Stra|pa|zier|fä|hig|keit**, die; -; **Stra|pa|zier‿ho|se** (strapazierfähige Hose für den Alltag), **...schuh**, **...wa|re**; **stra|pa|zi|ös** (anstrengend); **Stra|paz|schuh** (*österr. für* Strapazierschuh)
Straps [ʃt..., *auch* st..., *engl.* strɛps], der; -es, -e ‹engl.› (Strumpfhalter)
Stras|bourg [stras'bu:r] (*franz. Schreibung von* Straßburg)
Stras|burg (Stadt in der nördl. Uckermark)
Strass, der; *Gen.* - *u.* -es, *Plur.* -e (nach dem Erfinder Stras) (Edelsteinimitation aus Glas)
straß|auf, **straß|ab** (überall in den Straßen)
Straß|burg (Stadt im Elsass); *vgl.* Strasbourg; **Straß|bur|ger** (↑R 103); - Münster; - Eide; **straß|bur|gisch**
Sträß|chen; **Stra|ße**, die; -, -n (*Abk.* Str.); *Schreibung in Straßennamen* ↑R 123; **Stra|ßen‿an|zug**, **...ar|bei|ten** (*Plur.*), **...ar|bei|ter**, **...bahn**; **Stra|ßen|bah|ner** (*ugs. für* Angestellter der Straßenbahn); **Stra|ßen|bahn‿fah|rer**, **...fah|re|rin**, **...hal|te|stel|le**, **...schaff|ner**, **...schaff|ne|rin**, **...wa|gen**; **Stra|ßen‿ban|kett** (*vgl.* [2]Bankett), **...bau** (der; -[e]s); **Stra|ßen|bau|amt**; **Stra|ßen|be|gren|zungs|grün**; **Stra|ßen‿be|kannt|schaft**, **...be|lag**, **...be|leuch|tung**, **...bild**, **...bö|schung**, **...ca|fé**, **...damm**, **...de|cke**, **...dorf**, **...ecke** (↑R 132), **...fe|ger** (*landsch.*; *ugs. auch für* attraktive Fernsehsendung), **...fest**, **...füh|rung**, **...glät|te**, **...gra|ben**, **...han|del** (*vgl.* [1]Handel), **...händ|ler**, **...händ|le|rin**, **...kar|te**, **...keh|rer** (*landsch.*), **...kreu|zer** (*ugs. für* großer Pkw), **...kreu|zung**, **...la|ge**, **...lärm**, **...la|ter|ne**, **...mäd|chen** (*für* Prostituierte), **...meis|te|rei**, **...mu|si|kant**, **...na|me**, **...netz**, **...pflas|ter**, **...rand**, **...raub**, **...räu|ber**, **...rei|ni|gung**, **...ren|nen** (*Radsport*), **...rol|ler** (*svw.* Culemeyer), **...samm|lung**, **...sän|ger**, **...schild** (das), **...schlacht**, **...schuh**, **...sei|te**, **...sper|re**, **...sper|rung**, **...the|a|ter**, **...tun|nel**, **...über|füh|rung** (↑R 132), **...un|ter|füh|rung**, **...ver|kehr** (der; -s); **Stra|ßen|ver|kehrs|ord|nung**, die; - (*Abk.* StVO); **Stra|ßen|ver|kehrs-Zu|las|sungs-Ord|nung**, die; - (*Abk.* StVZO); **Stra|ßen‿ver|zeich|nis**, **...wal|ze**, **...zoll**, **...zug**, **...zu|stand**; **Stra|ßen|zu|stands|be|richt**; **Stra|ße-Schie|ne-Ver|kehr**, der; -[e]s (↑R 28)
Stra|te|ge [ʃt..., *auch* st...], der; -n, -n (↑R 126) ‹griech.› (jmd., der strategisch vorgeht, Strategie beherrscht); **Stra|te|gie**, die; -, ...ien (Kriegskunst; genau geplantes Vorgehen); **stra|te|gisch**; -e Verteidigung
Stra|ti|fi|ka|ti|on [ʃt..., *auch* st...], die; -, -en ‹lat.› (*Geol.* Schichtung; *Landw.* Schichtung von Saatgut in feuchtem Sand od. Wasser); **stra|ti|fi|zie|ren** (*Geol.* die Reihenfolge der Schichten feststellen; *Landw.* [Saatgut] schichten); **Stra|ti|gra|phie**, die; - ‹lat.; griech.› (*Geol.* Schichtenkunde); **stra|ti|gra|phisch**; **Stra|to|sphä|re**, die; - (Schicht der Erdatmosphäre in einer Höhe von etwa 12 bis 80 km); **Stra|to|sphä|ren|flug**; **stra|to|sphä|risch**; **Stra|tus**, der; -, ...ti ‹lat.› (tiefer hängende, ungegliederte Schichtwolke; *Abk.* St); **Stra|tus|wol|ke**
sträu|ben; sich -; (↑R 50:) da hilft kein Sträuben; **strau|big** (*landsch. für* struppig)
Strau|bin|ger; *nur in* Bruder - (*veraltet scherzh. für* Landstreicher)
Strauch, der; -[e]s, Sträucher; **strauch|ar|tig**; **Strauch|dieb** (*veraltet für* herumstreifender, sich in Gebüschen versteckender Dieb); **strau|cheln**; ich ...[e]le (↑R 16); **strau|chig**; **Sträuch|lein**; **Strauch‿rit|ter** (*veraltet abwertend*), **...werk** (das; -[e]s)
Straus, Oscar (österr. Komponist)
Straus|berg (Stadt östl. von Berlin)
[1]Strauß (Name mehrerer österr. Komponisten)
[2]Strauß, der; -es, -e (ein Vogel); Vogel -; *vgl.* Vogel-Strauß-Politik
[3]Strauß, der; -es, Sträuße (Blumenstrauß; *geh. veraltend für* Kampf)
Strauss, Richard (dt. Komponist)
Sträuß|chen
Strau|ßen‿ei, **...farm**, **...fe|der**
Strauß|wirt|schaft (*landsch. für* durch Zweige [Strauß] kenntlich gemachter Ausschank für eigenen [neuen] Wein)
stra|wan|zen usw. *vgl.* strabanzen usw.
Stra|wins|ky[1] (russ. Komponist)
Straz|za [ʃt..., *auch* st...], die; -, ...zzen ‹ital.› (Abfall bei der Seidenverarbeitung); **Straz|ze**, die; -, -n (*Kaufmannsspr.* Kladde)
Streb, der; -[e]s, -e (*Bergmannsspr.* Kohlenabbaufront zwischen zwei Strecken); **Streb|bau**, der; -[e]s (bergmänn. Gewinnungsverfahren); **Stre|be**, die; -, -n (schräge Stütze); **Stre|be‿bal|ken**, **...bo|gen**; **stre|ben**; (↑R 50:) das Streben nach Geld; **Stre|be|pfei|ler**; **Stre|ber**; **Stre|be|rei**, die; -; **stre|ber|haft**; **stre|be|risch**; **Stre|ber|tum**, das; -s; **Stre|be|werk** (*Bauw.*); **streb|sam**; **Streb|sam|keit**, die; -; **Stre|bung** (*geh.*); sie kannte seine geheimen -en
streck|bar; **Streck|bar|keit**, die; -; **Streck|bett** (*Med.*); **Stre|cke**, die; -, -n (*Bergmannsspr. auch* meist waagerecht vorgetriebener Grubenbau); zur - bringen (*Jägerspr.* erlegen); **stre|cken**; jmdn. zu Boden -; **Stre|cken‿ab|schnitt**, **...ar|bei|ter**, **...fern|spre|cher**, **...flug**, **...füh|rung**, **...netz**, **...re|kord** (*Sport*), **...strich** (*Druckw.*), **...tau|chen**, **...wär|ter**; **stre|cken|wei|se**; **Stre|cker** (*svw.* Streckmuskel); **Streck‿me|tall** (*Technik*), **...mus|kel**; **Stre|ckung**; **Streck‿ver|band**, **...win|kel** (*für* Supplementwinkel)
Street|work ['stri:twœ:(r)k], die; - ‹engl.› (Hilfe u. Beratung für Drogenabhängige u. a. innerhalb ihres Wohnbereichs); **Street|wor|ker** [...wœ:(r)kə(r)], der; -s, - (jmd., der Streetwork durchführt); **Street|wor|ke|rin**
Streh|ler (ein Werkzeug zum Gewindeschneiden)
Streich, der; -[e]s, -e; **Streich-**

[1] *So die eigene Schreibung des Komponisten. Nach dem vom Duden verwendeten russ. Transkriptionssystem müsste Strawinski geschrieben werden.*

bürs|te; Strei|che, die; -, -n (*früher* Flanke einer Festungsanlage); **Strei|chel|ein|heit** (*scherzh. für* freundliche Zuwendung, Lob); **strei|cheln;** ich ...[e]le (↑R 16); **Strei|che|ma|cher; strei|chen;** du strichst; du strichest; gestrichen; streich[e]!; **Strei|chen,** das; -s (ein Gangfehler beim Pferd; *Geol.* Verlauf der Streichlinie); **Strei|cher** (Spieler eines Streichinstrumentes); **Strei|che|rei** *(ugs.)*; **Strei|che|rin; streich|fä|hig; Streich|fä|hig|keit,** die; -; **streich|fer|tig;** -e Farbe; **Streich‿flä|che, ...form, ...garn, ...holz** (Zündholz); **Streich|holz|schach|tel; Streich‿in|stru|ment, ...kä|se, ...kon|zert, ...li|nie** (*Geol.* waagerechte Linie auf der Schichtfläche einer Gebirgsschicht), **...mu|sik, ...or|ches|ter, ...quar|tett, ...quin|tett, ...trio; Strei|chung; Streich|wurst**

Streif, der; -[e]s, -e (*Nebenform von* Streifen); **Streif|band,** das; *Plur.* ...bänder *(Postw.)*; **Streif|band|zei|tung** *(Postw.)*; **Strei|fe,** die; -, -n (zur Kontrolle eingesetzte kleine Militär- od. Polizeieinheit, *auch für* Fahrt, Gang einer solchen Einheit); **strei|fen; Strei|fen,** der; -s, -; **Strei|fen‿be|am|te, ...bil|dung, ...dienst; strei|fen|för|mig; Strei|fen‿füh|rer, ...gang** (der), **...wa|gen; strei|fen|wei|se; Strei|fe|rei** (Streifzug); **strei|fig; Streif|licht** *Plur.* ...lichter; **Streif|ling** (Apfel mit rötl. Streifen); **Streif‿schuss, ...zug**

Streik, der; -[e]s, -s ‹engl.› (Arbeitsniederlegung); **Streik‿ak|ti|on, ...auf|ruf, ...be|we|gung, ...bre|cher, ...bruch** (der); **streik|brü|chig; strei|ken; Strei|ken|de,** der *u.* die; -n, -n (↑R 5 ff.); **Streik‿geld, ...kas|se, ...ko|mi|tee, ...lei|tung, ...lo|kal, ...pos|ten, ...recht** (das; -[e]s), **...wel|le**

Streit, der; -[e]s, -e; **Streit|axt; streit|bar; Streit|bar|keit,** die; -; **strei|ten;** du strittst; du strittest; gestritten; streit[e]!; **Strei|ter; Strei|te|rei; Strei|te|rin; Streit‿fall** (der), **...fra|ge, ...ge|gen|stand, ...ge|spräch, ...hahn** (*ugs. für* streitsüchtiger Mensch), **...ham|mel** (*ugs. svw.* Streithahn), **...han|sel** *od.* **...hansl** (der; -s, -[n]; *österr. ugs. svw.* Streithahn); **strei|tig** *(Rechtsw. nur so) od.* strit|tig; die Sache ist streitig *od.* strittig; *aber nur* jmdm. etwas streitig machen; **Strei|tig|kei|ten** *Plur.*; **Streit‿kräf|te** *(Plur.)*, **...lust** (die; -); **streit|lus|tig; Streit‿macht** (die; -; *veraltend*), **...ob|jekt, ...punkt, ...ross** *(veraltet)*, **...sa|che, ...schrift, ...sucht** (die; -); **streit|süch|tig; Streit‿ver|kün|dung** *(Rechtsspr.)*, **...wa|gen, ...wert**

Stre|mel, der; -s, - (*nordd. für* [langer] Streifen); seinen - wegarbeiten (*ugs. für* zügig arbeiten)

strem|men (*landsch. ugs. für* zu eng, zu straff sein; beengen); es stremmt; sich - (*landsch. für* sich anstrengen)

streng; (↑R 47:) auf das, aufs Strengste (*auch* auf das, aufs strengste); strengstens. *Getrenntschreibung in Verbindung mit Verben und Partizipien* (↑R 39 f.): streng sein, bestrafen, urteilen usw.; streng nehmen, streng genommen (genau genommen); **Stren|ge,** die; -; eine drakonische -; **stren|gen** (*veraltet für* einengen; straff anziehen); **streng ge|nom|men** *vgl.* streng; **streng|gläu|big; Streng|gläu|big|keit,** die; -; **streng neh|men** *vgl.* streng; **strengs|tens**

stren|zen (*südd. ugs. für* stehlen); du strenzt

Strep|to|kok|kus [ʃt..., *auch* st...], der; -, ...kken *meist Plur.* ‹griech.› (Ketten bildende Bakterie); **Strep|to|my|zin** [...ts...], *fachspr. meist* Strep|to|my|cin, das; -s (ein Antibiotikum)

¹Stre|se|mann (dt. Staatsmann); **²Stre|se|mann,** der; -s (ein bestimmter Gesellschaftsanzug)

Stress [ʃt..., *auch* st...], der; -es, -e ‹engl.› (*Med.* starke körperliche u. seelische Belastung, die zu Schädigungen führen kann; Überbeanspruchung, Anspannung); **stres|sen** (*ugs. für* als Stress wirken; überbeanspruchen); der Lärm stresst; gestresst; **stres|sig** (*ugs. für* aufreibend, [sehr] anstrengend); **Stress|si|tu|a|ti|on** (↑R 136)

Stretch [strɛtʃ], der; -[e]s, -es [...is] ‹engl.› (ein elastisches Gewebe); **Stret|ching** [ˈstrɛtʃɪŋ], das; -s (aus Dehnungsübungen bestehende Form der Gymnastik)

Streu, die; -, -en; **Streu‿be|sitz, ...büch|se; Streue,** die; -, -n (*schweiz. neben* Streu); **streu|en; Streu|er** (Streubüchse); **Streu‿fahr|zeug, ...feu|er** *(Milit.)*, **...ge|biet, ...gut** (das; -[e]s), **...ko|lon|ne, ...licht** (das; -[e]s; *Optik*), **...mus|ter**

streu|nen (sich herumtreiben); **Streu|ner** *(ugs.)*; **Streu|ne|rin**

Streu|obst; Streu|obst|wie|se; Streu‿pflicht (die; -), **...salz, ...sand** (der; -[e]s); **Streu|sel,** der *od.* das; -s, - *meist Plur.*; **Streu|sel|ku|chen; Streu|sied|lung; Streu|ung; Streu|ungs‿ko|ef|fi|zi|ent, ...maß** (das; *Statistik*); **Streu‿wa|gen, ...zu|cker**

Strich, der; -[e]s, -e (*südd. u. schweiz. mdal. auch für* Zitze; *ugs. auch für* Straßenprostitution); **Strich‿ät|zung** *(Druckw.)*, **...ein|tei|lung; stri|cheln** (feine Striche machen); ich ...[e]le (↑R 16); **Stri|cher** (*ugs. für* Strichjunge); **Strich|jun|ge; Strich|kode** (Verschlüsselung bestimmter Angaben [auf Waren] in Form paralleler Striche); **strich|lie|ren** (*österr. für* stricheln); **Strich‿mäd|chen** (*für* Prostituierte), **...männ|chen, ...punkt** (*für* Semikolon), **...re|gen, ...vo|gel; strich|wei|se; Strich‿zeich|nung, ...zeit** (der Strichvögel)

Strick, der; -[e]s, -e (*ugs. scherzh. auch für* durchtriebener Bursche, Spitzbube); **Strick‿ap|pa|rat, ...ar|beit, ...beu|tel, ...bünd|chen; stri|cken; Stri|cker; Stri|cke|rei; Stri|cke|rin; Strick‿garn, ...ja|cke, ...kleid, ...lei|ter** (die); **Strick|lei|ter|ner|ven|sys|tem** *(Zool.)*; **Strick‿ma|schi|ne, ...mo|de, ...mus|ter, ...na|del, ...stoff, ...strumpf, ...wa|ren** *(Plur.)*, **...wes|te, ...zeug**

Stri|du|la|ti|ons|or|gan [ʃt..., *auch* st...] ‹lat.; griech.› (*Zool.* Werkzeug mancher Insekten zur Erzeugung zirpender Töne)

Strie|gel, der; -s, - ‹lat.› (Gerät mit Zacken; harte Bürste [zur Pflege des Pferdefells]); **strie|geln** (*ugs. auch für* hart behandeln); ich ...[e]le (↑R 16)

Strie|me, die; -, -n, *häufiger* **Strie|men,** der; -s, -; **strie|mig**

¹Strie|zel, der; -s, - (*landsch. ugs. für* Lausbub)

²Strie|zel, der; -s, - (*landsch. u. österr. für* eine Gebäckart)

strie|zen (*ugs. für* quälen; *nordd. ugs. auch für* stehlen); du striezt

strikt [ʃt..., *auch* st...] ‹lat.› (streng; genau; *auch für* strikte); **strik|te** (streng, genau); etwas - befolgen; **Strik|ti|on,** die; -, -en (*selten für* Zusammenziehung); **Strik|tur,** die; -, -en (*Med.* [krankhafte] Verengung von Körperkanälen)

Strind|berg (schwed. Dichter)

string. = stringendo; **strin|gen|do** [strinˈdʒɛndo] ‹ital.› (*Musik* schneller werdend)

strin|gent [st..., *auch* ʃt...] ‹lat.› (bündig, zwingend); **Strin|genz,** die; -

String|re|gal ['ʃt..., *auch* 'st...], das; -s, -e ⟨engl.; dt.⟩ ([1]Regal, dessen Bretter in ein an der Wand befestigtes Metallgestell eingelegt sind)
Strip [strip], der; -s, -s ⟨engl.-amerik.⟩ (*kurz für* Striptease; [Wundpflaster]streifen)
Strip|pe, die; -, -n (*landsch. für* Bindfaden; Band; *ugs. scherzh. für* Fernsprechleitung)
strip|pen [st...] ⟨engl.-amerik.⟩ (*ugs. für* einen Striptease vorführen; *Druckw.* [Zeilen] im Film montieren); **Strip|pe|rin** (*ugs. für* Stripteasetänzerin); **Strip|tease** ['stripti:s], der *od.* das; - (Entkleidungsvorführung [in Nachtlokalen]); **Strip|tease‿lo|kal, ...tän|ze|rin, ...vor|füh|rung**
Stritt, der; -[e]s (*bayr. für* Streit); **strit|tig** *vgl.* streitig
Stritt|mat|ter (dt. Schriftsteller)
Striz|zi, der; -s, -s (*bes. südd., österr. u. schweiz. mdal. für* Strolch; Zuhälter)
Stro|bel, der; -s, - (*landsch. für* struppiger Haarschopf); **stro|be|lig** usw. (*landsch. für* strubbelig usw.); **stro|beln** (*landsch. für* struppig machen; struppig sein); ich ...[e]le (↑R 16); **strob|lig** *vgl.* strobelig
Stro|bo|skop [st..., *auch* ʃt...] (↑R 132), das; -s, -e ⟨griech.⟩ (ein opt. Gerät zur Messung von Drehzahlen o.Ä.); **stro|bo|sko|pisch; Stro|bo|skop|licht** (schnell aufblitzendes Licht)
Stroh, das; -[e]s; **Stroh|bal|len; stroh|blond; Stroh‿blu|me, ...bund** (das), **...dach; stroh|dumm** (sehr dumm); **stro|hern** (aus Stroh); **stroh‿far|ben** *od.* **...far|big; Stroh‿feim** *od.* **...fei|me** *od.* **...fei|men** (*vgl.* Feim), **...feu|er; stroh|ge|deckt; Stroh‿halm, ...hau|fen, ...hut** (der), **...hüt|te; stro|hig** (*auch für* wie Stroh; saftlos, trocken); **Stroh‿kopf** (*ugs. scherzh. für* Dummkopf), **...mann** (*Plur.* ...männer; vorgeschobene Person), **...mat|te, ...pres|se, ...pup|pe, ...sack, ...schuh; stroh|tro|cken; Stroh‿wisch, ...wit|we** (*ugs. für* Ehefrau, die vorübergehend ohne ihren Mann lebt), **...wit|wer** (*ugs.; vgl.* Strohwitwe)
Strolch, der; -[e]s, -e; **strol|chen; Strol|chen|fahrt** (*schweiz. für* Fahrt mit einem gestohlenen Wagen)
Strom, der; -[e]s, Ströme; elektrische, magnetische Ströme; es regnet in Strömen; ein Strom führendes Kabel (↑R 40); **strom|ab; Strom‿ab|nah|me, ...ab|neh|mer; strom|ab|wärts; strom|an; strom|auf, strom|auf|wärts; Strom‿aus|fall, ...bett** (*svw.* Flussbett)
[1]Strom|bo|li [st...] (eine der Liparischen Inseln); **[2]Strom|bo|li**, der; - (Vulkan auf dieser Insel)
strö|men
Stro|mer (*ugs. für* Herumtreiber, Landstreicher, Strolch); **stro|mern**; ich ...ere (↑R 16)
Strom‿er|zeu|ger, ...er|zeu|gung; Strom füh|rend *vgl.* Strom; **Strom‿ka|bel, ...kreis, ...lei|tung; Ström|ling** (eine Heringsart); **Strom|li|nie; Strom|li|ni|en|form**, die; -; **strom|li|ni|en|för|mig; Strom|li|ni|en|wa|gen; Strom‿men|ge, ...mes|ser** (der), **...netz, ...preis, ...rech|nung, ...re|gu|lie|rung, ...schie|ne, ...schlag, ...schnel|le, ...sper|re, ...stär|ke, ...stoß; Strö|mung; Strö|mungs‿ge|schwin|dig|keit, ...leh|re; Strom‿un|ter|bre|cher, ...ver|brauch, ...ver|sor|gung; strom|wei|se; Strom‿wen|der, ...zäh|ler**
Stron|ti|um [st..., *auch* ʃt...], das; -s ⟨nach dem schott. Dorf Strontian⟩ (chem. Element, Metall; *Zeichen* Sr)
Stro|phan|thin [ʃt..., *auch* st...] (↑R 132), das; -s, -e ⟨griech.⟩ (ein Arzneimittel); **Stro|phan|thus**, der; -, - (Heilpflanze, die das Strophanthin liefert)
Stro|phe, die; -, -n ⟨griech.⟩ (sich in gleicher Form wiederholender Liedteil, Gedichtabschnitt); **Stro|phen‿an|fang, ...bau** (der; -s), **...en|de, ...form, ...ge|dicht, ...lied; ...stro|phig** (z. B. dreistrophig, *mit Ziffer* 3-strophig; ↑R 44); **stro|phisch** (in Strophen geteilt)
Stropp, der; -[e]s, -s (*Seemannsspr.* kurzes Tau mit Ring od. Schlinge; *landsch. für* Aufhänger; *scherzh. für* kleines Kind)
Stros|se, die; -, -n (*Bergmannsspr.* Stufe, Absatz)
strot|zen; du strotzt; er strotzt vor *od.* von Energie
strub; strüber, strübste (*schweiz. mdal. für* struppig; schwierig); **strub|be|lig**, strubb|lig (*ugs.*); *vgl.* strobelig; **Strub|bel|kopf** *vgl.* Struwwelkopf
Stru|del, der; -s, - ([Wasser]wirbel; *bes. südd., österr. für* ein Gebäck); **Stru|del|kopf** (*veraltet für* Wirrkopf); **stru|deln**; das Wasser strudelt; **Stru|del|topf** (Kolk, Gletschermühle)
Struk|tur [ʃt..., *auch* st...], die; -, -en ⟨lat.⟩ ([Sinn]gefüge, Bau; Aufbau, innere Gliederung); **struk|tu|ral** (*seltener für* strukturell); **Struk|tu|ra|lis|mus**, der; - (*Sprachw.* Richtung, die Sprache als ein geschlossenes Zeichensystem versteht u. die Struktur dieses Systems erfassen will); **Struk|tu|ra|list**, der; -en, -en; ↑R 126; **struk|tu|ra|lis|tisch; Struk|tur|ana|ly|se** (↑R 132; die Analyse der Struktur, der einzelnen Strukturelemente von etwas, z. B. in der Chemie, Wirtschafts-, Literaturwissenschaft); **Struk|tur|än|de|rung; struk|tur|be|stim|mend; struk|tu|rell; Struk|tur‿for|mel** (*Chemie*), **...ge|we|be, ...hil|fe; struk|tu|rie|ren** (mit einer Struktur versehen); **Struk|tu|riert|heit**, die; -; **Struk|tu|rie|rung; Struk|tur‿kri|se, ...po|li|tik** (die; -), **...re|form; struk|tur|schwach** (industriell nicht entwickelt); **Struk|tur‿ta|pe|te, ...wan|del**
strul|len (*bes. nordd. ugs. für* urinieren)
Stru|ma [ʃt..., *auch* st...], die; -, *Plur.* ...men *u.* ...mae [...mɛ] ⟨lat.⟩ (*Med.* Kropf); **stru|mös** (kropfartig)
Strumpf, der; -[e]s, Strümpfe; **Strumpf|band;** *vgl.* [3]Band; **Strümpf|chen; Strumpf‿fab|rik, ...hal|ter, ...ho|se ...mas|ke, ...wa|ren** (*Plur.*), **...wir|ker, ...wir|ke|rei**
Strunk, der; -[e]s, Strünke; **Strünk|chen**
Strup|fe, die; -, -n (*südd., österr. veraltet für* Strippe; Schuhlasche); **strup|fen** (*südd. u. schweiz. mdal. für* [ab]streifen)
strup|pig; Strup|pig|keit, die; -
Struw|wel|kopf (*landsch. für* Strubbelkopf); **Struw|wel|pe|ter**, der; -s, - (*fam. für* Kind mit strubbeligem Haar; *nur Sing.:* Gestalt aus einem Kinderbuch)
Strych|nin [ʃt..., *auch* st...], das; -s ⟨griech.⟩ (ein giftiges Alkaloid; ein Arzneimittel)
Stu|art ['ʃtu:art, *engl.* stju'ə(r)t], der; -s, -s (Angehöriger eines schott. Geschlechts); **Stu|art|kra|gen**
Stu|bai, das; -s (ein Tiroler Alpental); **Stu|bai|er Al|pen** *Plur.;* **Stu|bai|tal**
Stub|ben, der; -s, - (*nordd. für* [Baum]stumpf; *auch für* grobschlächtiger Mensch, Flegel)
Stub|ben|kam|mer, die; - (Kreidefelsen auf Rügen)
[1]Stüb|chen, das; -s, - (ein altes Flüssigkeitsmaß)

²Stüb|chen (kleine Stube); **Stu|be,** die; -, -n; **Stu|ben_äl|tes|te, ...ar|rest, ...dienst, ...flie|ge, ...ge|lehr|te, ...ho|cker** (*ugs. für* jmd., der kaum ausgeht, sich meist im Hause aufhält); **Stu|ben|ho|cke|rei** (*ugs.*); **Stu|ben|mäd|chen; stu|ben|rein; Stu|ben|wa|gen** (im Haus verwendeter Korbwagen für Säuglinge)

Stü|ber, der; -s, - ‹niederl.› (ehem. niederrhein. Münze; *auch kurz für* Nasenstüber)

Stuck, der; -[e]s ‹ital.› (aus einer Gipsmischung hergestellte Ornamentik)

Stück, das; -[e]s, -e (*Abk.* St.); ↑R 90 f.: 5 - Zucker; Stücker zehn (*ugs. für* ungefähr zehn)

Stuck|ar|beit

Stück|ar|beit, die; - (Akkordarbeit)

Stu|cka|teur [...'tø:r] (↑R 89), der; -s, -e ‹franz.› (Stuckarbeiter, -künstler); **Stu|cka|tor,** der; -s, ...oren ‹ital.› (Stuckkünstler); **Stu|cka|tur,** die; -, -en (Stuckarbeit); **Stuck|de|cke**

stü|ckeln; ich ...[e]le (↑R 16); **Stü|cke|lung,** Stück|lung

stu|cken (*landsch. u. österr. ugs. für* büffeln, angestrengt lernen)

stü|cken (*selten für* zusammen-, aneinander stücken); **Stü|cker** *vgl.* Stück

stu|cke|rig (*nordd.*); **stu|ckern** (*nordd. für* holpern, rütteln; ruckweise fahren)

Stü|cke|schrei|ber (Schriftsteller, der Theaterstücke, Fernsehspiele o. Ä. verfasst); **Stück_fass** (ein Weinmaß), **...ge|wicht, ...gut** (stückweise verkaufte od. als Frachtgut aufgegebene Ware)

stu|ckie|ren ‹ital.› (*selten für* [Wände] mit Stuck versehen)

Stück_kauf, ...koh|le, ...kos|ten (*Plur.*), **...lis|te, ...lohn; Stück|lung,** Stü|cke|lung; **Stück_no|tie|rung** (*Börse*), **...rech|nung** (*Wirtsch.*); **stück|wei|se; Stück_werk** (*nur in* etwas ist, bleibt -), **...zahl** (*Kaufmannsspr.*), **...zin|sen** (*Plur.; Bankw.* bis zu einem Zwischentermin aufgelaufene Zinsen)

stud. = studiosus [st...], z. B. - medicinae [- ...tsi:nɛ:] ‹lat.› (Student der Medizin; *Abk.* stud. med.); *vgl.* Studiosus; **Stu|dent** [ʃt...], der; -en, -en (↑R 126) ‹lat.› (Hochschüler; *österr. auch für* Schüler einer höheren Schule); *vgl.* Studiosus; **Stu|den|ten_aus|weis, ...be|we|gung, ...blu|me** (Name verschiedener Pflanzen), **...bu|de** (*ugs.*), **...fut|ter** (*vgl.* ¹Futter), **...ge|mein|de, ...heim, ...knei|pe** (*ugs.*), **...lied, ...müt|ze, ...par|la|ment, ...pfar|rer, ...re|vol|te; Stu|den|ten|schaft; Stu|den|ten_spra|che** (die; -), **...un|ru|hen** (*Plur.*), **...ver|bin|dung, ...werk, ...wohn|heim; Stu|den|tin; stu|den|tisch; Stu|die** [...i̯ə], die; -, -n (Entwurf, kurze [skizzenhafte] Darstellung; Vorarbeit [zu einem Werk der Wissenschaft od. Kunst]); **Stu|di|en** (*Plur. von* Studie *u.* Studium); **Stu|di|en_ab|bre|cher, ...as|ses|sor, ...as|ses|so|rin, ...be|wer|ber, ...brief** (*svw.* Lehrbrief), **...buch, ...di|rek|tor, ...di|rek|to|rin, ...fach, ...freund, ...freun|din, ...gang** (der); **stu|di|en|hal|ber; Stu|di|en_kol|leg** (Vorbereitungskurs an einer Hochschule, bes. für ausländische Studenten), **...kol|le|ge, ...kol|le|gin, ...platz, ...pro|fes|sor, ...rat** (*Plur.* ...räte), **...rä|tin, ...re|fe|ren|dar, ...re|fe|ren|da|rin, ...rei|se, ...zeit, ...zweck** (zu -en); **stu|die|ren** ([er]forschen, lernen; die Hochschule [*österr. auch* höhere Schule] besuchen); eine studierte Kollegin; (↑R 50:) Probieren (*auch* probieren) geht über Studieren (*auch* studieren); **Stu|die|ren|de,** der *u.* die; -n, -n (↑R 5 ff.); **Stu|dier|stu|be; Stu|dier|te,** der *u.* die; -n, -n; ↑R 5 ff. (*ugs. für* jmd., der studiert hat); **Stu|dier|zim|mer; Stu|di|ker** (*ugs. scherzh. für* Student); **Stu|dio,** das; -s, -s ‹ital.› (Atelier; *Film- u. Rundfunk* Aufnahmeraum; Versuchsbühne); **Stu|di|o_büh|ne, ...film, ...mu|si|ker; Stu|di|o|sus,** der; -, ...si (*scherzh. für* Studierender; Student); *vgl.* stud.; **Stu|di|um,** das; -s, ...ien [...i̯ən] (wissenschaftl. [Er]forschung; Hochschulbesuch, -ausbildung; [kritisches] Durchlesen, -arbeiten); **Stu|di|um ge|ne|ra|le** [ʃt..., *auch* st...], das; - - (frühe Form der Universität im MA.; Vorlesungen allgemein bildender Art an einer Hochschule)

Stu|fe, die; -, -n; **stu|fen; Stu|fen_abi|tur** (↑R 132), **...bar|ren** (*Turnen*), **...dach, ...fol|ge; stu|fen|för|mig; Stu|fen_füh|rer|schein** (für Motorradfahrer), **...gang** (der), **...ge|bet** (*kath. Kirche früher*), **...heck** (*vgl.* ¹Heck), **...lei|ter** (die); **stu|fen|los; Stu|fen_plan, ...py|ra|mi|de, ...ra|ke|te; stu|fen|wei|se; stu|fig** (mit Stufen versehen); **...stu|fig** (z. B. fünfstufig, *mit Ziffer* 5-stufig; ↑R 44); **Stu|fung**

Stuhl, der; -[e]s, Stühle (*auch kurz für* Stuhlgang); elektrischer -; der Heilige, der Päpstliche - (↑R 108); **Stuhl|bein; Stühl|chen; Stuhl_drang** (der; -[e]s; *Med.*), **...ent|lee|rung** (*Med.*); **Stuhl|fei|er,** die; -; Petri - (kath. Fest); **Stuhl_gang** (der; -[e]s), **...kan|te, ...kis|sen, ...leh|ne, ...un|ter|su|chung**

Stu|ka ['ʃtu(:)ka], der; -s, -s (*kurz für* Sturzkampfflugzeug)

Stuk|ka|teur usw. *frühere Schreibung für* Stuckateur usw.

Stul|le, die; -, -n (*bes. berlin. für* Brotschnitte [mit Belag])

Stulp|är|mel (*svw.* Stulpenärmel); **Stul|pe,** die; -, -n (Aufschlag an Ärmeln u. a.); **stül|pen; Stul|pen_är|mel, ...hand|schuh, ...stie|fel; Stülp|na|se**

stumm; Stum|me, der *u.* die; -n, -n (↑R 5 ff.)

Stum|mel, der; -s, -; **Stum|mel|af|fe; Stum|mel|chen, Stüm|mel|chen; stüm|meln** (*selten für* verstümmeln; *landsch. für* Bäume stark zurückschneiden); ich ...[e]le (↑R 16); **Stum|mel_pfei|fe, ...schwanz**

Stumm|film; Stumm|heit, die; -

Stump, der; -s, -e (*landsch. veraltend für* [Baum]stumpf); **Stümp|chen; Stum|pe,** der; -n, -n *u.* **¹Stum|pen,** der; -s, - (*landsch. für* [Baum]stumpf); **²Stum|pen,** der; -s, - (Grundform des Filzhutes; Zigarre); **Stüm|per** (*abwertend für* Nichtskönner); **Stüm|pe|rei; stüm|per|haft; Stüm|pe|rin; stüm|per|mä|ßig; stüm|pern** (schlecht arbeiten); ich ...ere (↑R 16); **stumpf; Stumpf,** der; -[e]s, Stümpfe; mit Stumpf und Stiel (restlos); **Stümpf|chen; stump|fen** (stumpf machen); **Stumpf|heit; Stumpf_näs|chen** *od.* **...na|se** (*landsch.*); **stumpf|na|sig; Stumpf|sinn,** der; -[e]s; **stumpf|sin|nig; Stumpf|sin|nig|keit; stumpf|wink|lig**

Stünd|chen; Stun|de, die; -, -n (*Abk.* Std., *auch* St.; *Zeichen* h [*Astron.* ʰ]); eine halbe Stunde, eine viertel Stunde (*vgl.* Viertelstunde); von Stund an (*veraltend für* von diesem Augenblick an); *vgl.* null u. stundenlang; **stun|den** (Zeit, Frist zur Zahlung geben); **Stun|den_buch** Gebetbuch des MA.), **...frau** (*landsch. für* Frau, die einige Stunden im Haushalt hilft), **...ge|bet, ...ge|schwin|dig|keit, ...glas** (*Plur.* ...gläser; Sanduhr), **...halt** (*schweiz. für* [stündl.] Marschpause), **...ho|tel; Stun|den|ki|lo|me|ter** (*für* Kilometer je Stunde; *vgl.* km/h); **stun|den-**

lang, *aber* eine Stunde lang, ganze Stunden lang; **Stun|den‿lohn, ...plan** (*vgl.* [2]Plan), **...schlag, ...takt** (im -); **stun|den|wei|se; stun|den|weit,** *aber* drei Stunden weit; **Stun|den|zei|ger** (bei der Uhr); **...stün|dig** (z. B. zweistündig, *mit Ziffer* 2-stündig [zwei Stunden dauernd]; ↑R 44); **Stünd|lein; stünd|lich** (jede Stunde); **...stünd|lich** (z. B. zweistündlich, *mit Ziffer* 2-stündlich [alle zwei Stunden wiederkehrend]; ↑R 44); **Stun|dung** ⟨*zu* stunden⟩

Stunk, der; -s (*ugs. für* Zank, Unfrieden, Nörgelei)

Stunt [stant], der; -s, -s ⟨engl.⟩ (gefährliches, akrobatisches Kunststück [als Filmszene]); **Stunt|girl** [...gœ:(r)l], das; -s, -s *u.* **Stuntman** [...mɛn], der; -s, ...men (*Film* Double für gefährliche, akrobatische o. ä. Szenen)

stu|pend [st..., *auch* ʃt...] ⟨lat.⟩ (erstaunlich); -e Kenntnisse

Stupf, der; -[e]s, -e (*südd., schweiz. mdal. für* Stoß); **stup|feln** *u., schweiz. nur,* **stup|fen** (*südd., österr. ugs., schweiz. mdal. für* stupsen); **Stup|fer** (*südd., österr. ugs., schweiz. mdal. für* Stups)

stu|pid [ʃt..., *auch* st...], *österr. nur so, u.* **stu|pi|de** ⟨lat.⟩ (dumm, stumpfsinnig); **Stu|pi|di|tät,** die; -, -en; **Stu|por,** der; -s (*Med.* Starrheit, Regungslosigkeit)

Stupp, die; - (*österr. für* Streupulver, Puder); **stup|pen** (*österr. für* einpudern)

Stu|prum [ʃt..., *auch* st...] (↑R 130) das; -s, ...pra ⟨lat., „Schändung"⟩ (Vergewaltigung)

Stups, der; -es, -e (*ugs. für* Stoß); **stup|sen** (*ugs. für* stoßen); du stupst; **Stups|na|se** (*ugs.*)

stur (*ugs. für* stier, unbeweglich, hartnäckig); stur Heil (*ugs. für* mit großer Sturheit); **Stur|heit,** die; - (*ugs.*)

sturm (*südwestd. u. schweiz. mdal. für* verworren, schwindelig); **[1]Sturm,** der; -[e]s, Stürme; - laufen; - läuten; **[2]Sturm,** der; -[e]s (*österr. für* in Gärung übergegangener Most); **Sturm‿an|griff, ...ball** (*Seew.*), **...band** (das; *Plur.* ...bänder); **sturm|be|reit; Sturm‿bö, ...bock** (*früher* ein Belagerungsgerät), **...böe** (*svw.* Sturmbö), **...boot** (*Milit.*), **...deich; stür|men; Stür|mer; Stür|me|rei** (*ugs.*); **Stür|me|rin; sturm|er|probt** (*svw.* kampferprobt); **Stür|mer und Drän|ger,** der; -s - -s, - - -; **Stur|mes|brausen,** das; -s (*geh.*); **Sturm‿fah|ne** (*früher*), **...flut; sturm|frei** (*ugs.*); eine -e Bude; **Sturm‿fri|sur** (*scherzh.*), **...ge|päck** (*Milit.*); **sturm|ge|peitscht;** die -e See; **Sturm|glo|cke; Sturm|hau|be;** die Große -, Kleine - (Gipfel im Riesengebirge); **Sturm|hut,** der (*svw.* Eisenhut); **stür|misch; Sturm‿la|ter|ne, ...lauf, ...läuten** (das; -s), **...lei|ter** (die), **...möwe; sturm|reif** (*Milit.*); **Sturm‿rei|he** (*Sport*), **...rie|men, ...schritt** (*meist in* im -); **sturmschwach** (*Sport*); **Sturm‿signal, ...spit|ze** (*Sport*), **...tief** (*Meteor.*); **Sturm und Drang,** der; *Gen.* - - -[e]s *u.* - - -; **Sturm-und-Drang-Zeit,** die; - (↑R 28); **Sturm‿vo|gel, ...war|nung, ...wind, ...zei|chen**

Sturz, der; -es, *Plur.* Stürze, *auch* (*für* Träger:) Sturze (jäher Fall; *Bauw.* waagerechter Träger als oberer Abschluss von Tür- od. Fensteröffnungen); **Sturz‿acker** (↑R 132), **...bach; sturz|be|trunken** (*ugs. für* völlig betrunken); **Stür|ze,** die; -, -n (*landsch. für* Topfdeckel); **Stur|zel, Stür|zel,** der; -s, - (*landsch. für* stumpfes Ende, [Baum]stumpf); **stür|zen;** du stürzt; **Sturz‿flug, ...flut, ...ge|burt** (*Med.*), **...gut** (z. B. Kohle, Schotter), **...helm** (*vgl.* [1]Helm), **...kampf|flug|zeug** (im 2. Weltkrieg; *Abk.* Stuka), **...pflug, ...re|gen, ...see** (die; -, -n)

Stuss, der; -es ⟨hebr.-jidd.⟩ (*ugs. für* Unsinn, Dummheit); - reden

Stut|buch (Stammtafeln der zur Zucht verwendeten Pferde); **Stute,** die; -, -n

Stu|ten, der; -s, - (*landsch. für* [längliches] Weißbrot)

Stu|ten|zucht; Stu|te|rei (*veraltet für* Gestüt); **Stut|foh|len** (weibl. Fohlen)

Stutt|gart (Stadt am Neckar); **Stutt|gart-Bad Cann|statt** (↑R 105); **Stutt|gar|ter** (↑R 103)

Stutz, der; -es, *Plur.* -e *od.* Stütze (*landsch. für* Stoß; verkürztes Ding [Federstutz u. a.]; Wandbrett; *schweiz. mdal. für* steiler Hang, bes. steiles Wegstück); auf den - (*landsch. für* plötzlich; sofort)

Stütz, der; -es, -e (*Turnen*); **Stützbal|ken; Stüt|ze,** die; -, -n

stut|zen (erstaunt sein; verkürzen); du stutzt; **Stut|zen,** der; -s, - (kurzes Gewehr; Wadenstrumpf; Ansatzrohrstück)

stüt|zen; du stützt

Stut|zer (*veraltend für* geckenhaft wirkender, eitler Mann; knielanger Herrenmantel; *schweiz. auch für* Stutzen [Gewehr]); **stut|zerhaft; Stut|zer|haf|tig|keit,** die; -; **stut|zer|mä|ßig; Stut|zer|tum,** das; -s

Stutz|flü|gel (*Musik* kleiner, kurzer Flügel)

Stütz|ge|we|be (*Med.*)

stut|zig; stüt|zig (*südd. für* stutzig; widerspenstig)

Stütz‿keh|re (*Turnen*), **...korsett, ...kurs, ...last, ...mau|er, ...pfei|ler, ...punkt, ...rad, ...sprung** (*Turnen*), **...strumpf**

Stutz|uhr (kleine Standuhr)

Stüt|zung; Stüt|zungs|kauf (*Finanzw.*); **Stütz|ver|band** (*Med.*)

St. Vin|cent und die Gre|na|dinen [s(ə)nt 'vinsənt - - -], - -s und der - (Inselstaat im Bereich der Westindischen Inseln); *vgl.* Vincenter

StVO = Straßenverkehrsordnung

StVZO = Straßenverkehrs-Zulassungs-Ordnung

sty|gisch [st...] (zum Styx gehörend; schauerlich, unheimlich)

sty|len ['stailən] ⟨engl.⟩ (entwerfen, gestalten); gestylt; **Sty|ling** ['stailiŋ], das; -s, -s (Formgebung; äußere Gestaltung); **Sty|list** [stai'list], der; -en, -en; ↑R 126 (Formgestalter; jmd., der das Styling [bes. von Autos] entwirft); **Sty|lis|tin**

Sty|lit [st..., *auch* ʃt...], der; -en, -en (↑R 126) ⟨griech.⟩ (auf einer Säule lebender frühchristl. Eremit)

Stym|pha|li|de [st..., *auch* ʃt...], der; -n, -n *meist Plur.* (↑R 126) ⟨griech.⟩ (Vogelungeheuer in der griech. Sage)

Sty|rax, Sto|rax [*beide* st..., *auch* ʃt...], der; -[es], -e ⟨griech.⟩ (eine Heilpflanze; Balsam)

Sty|rol [ʃt..., *auch* st...], das; -s ⟨griech.; arab.⟩ (eine chem. Verbindung)

Sty|ro|por ® [ʃt..., *auch* st...], das; -s ⟨griech.; lat.⟩ (ein Kunststoff)

Styx [st...], der; - (Fluss der Unterwelt in der griech. Sage)

SU = Sowjetunion

s. u. = sieh[e] unten!

Su|a|da, Su|a|de, die; -, ...den ⟨lat.⟩ (Beredsamkeit; Redeschwall)

[1]Su|a|he|li, Swa|hi|li, der; -[s], -[s]; (Afrikaner, dessen Muttersprache [2]Suaheli ist); **[2]Su|a|he|li,** Swa|hili, das; -[s] (Sprache); *vgl.* Kisuaheli

[1]Su|á|rez [sua(:)rɛθ], Francisco [...'θisko] (span. Theologe, Jesuit)

[2]Su|á|rez [sua(:)rɛθ], Adolfo [a'ðɔlfo] (span. Politiker); *vgl. aber* Soares

su|a|so|risch ‹lat.› (überredend)
sub... ‹lat.› (unter...); **Sub...** (Unter...)
sub|al|pin, *auch* **sub|al|pi|nisch** ‹lat.› (*Geogr.* räumlich an die Alpen anschließend; bis zur Nadelwaldgrenze reichend)
sub|al|tern ‹lat.› (untergeordnet; unselbstständig); **Sub|al|tern|be|am|te; Sub|al|ter|ne,** der *u.* die; -n, -n (↑R 5 ff.)
sub|ant|ark|tisch ‹lat.; griech.› (*Geogr.* zwischen Antarktis u. gemäßigter Klimazone gelegen); **sub|ark|tisch** (zwischen Arktis u. gemäßigter Klimazone gelegen); subarktische Zone
Sub|bot|nik, der; -s, -s ‹russ.› (*ehem. in der DDR* [freiwilliger] unentgeltl. Arbeitseinsatz)
Sub|di|a|kon ‹lat.; griech.› (*kath. Kirche früher* Inhaber der untersten der höheren Weihen)
Sub|do|mi|nan|te [*od.* ...'nantə] ‹lat.› (*Musik* die Quarte vom Grundton aus)
sub|fos|sil ‹lat.› (*Biol.* in geschichtl. Zeit ausgestorben)
sub|gla|zi|al ‹lat.› (*Geol.* unter dem Gletschereis befindlich)
su|bi|to ‹ital.› (*Musik* schnell, sofort anschließend)
Sub|jekt, das; -[e]s, -e ‹lat.› (*Sprachw.* Satzgegenstand; *Philos.* wahrnehmendes, denkendes Wesen; *abwertend für* gemeiner Mensch); **Sub|jek|ti|on,** die; -, -en (*Rhet.* Aufwerfen einer Frage, die man selbst beantwortet); **sub|jek|tiv** [*auch* 'zup...] (dem Subjekt angehörend, in ihm begründet; persönlich; einseitig, parteiisch, unsachlich); **Sub|jek|ti|vis|mus** [...v...], der; - (philos. Denkrichtung, nach der das Subjekt für die Geltung der Erkenntnis entscheidend ist; *auch für* Ichbezogenheit); **sub|jek|ti|vis|tisch; Sub|jek|ti|vi|tät,** die; - (persönl. Auffassung, Eigenart; Einseitigkeit); **Sub|jekt|satz** *(Sprachw.)*
Sub|junk|tiv [*auch* ...'ti:f], der; -s, -e [...və] ‹lat.› (*selten für* Konjunktiv)
Sub|ka|te|go|rie ‹lat.; griech.› (*bes. Sprachw.* Unterordnung, Untergruppe einer Kategorie)
Sub|kon|ti|nent ‹lat.› (geogr. geschlossener Teil eines Kontinents, der aufgrund seiner Größe u. Gestalt eine gewisse Eigenständigkeit hat); der indische -
Sub|kul|tur ‹lat.› (bes. Kulturgruppierung innerhalb eines übergeordneten Kulturbereichs); **sub|kul|tu|rell**
sub|ku|tan ‹lat.› (*Med.* unter der Haut [befindlich], unter die Haut [erfolgend])
sub|lim ‹lat.› (erhaben; fein; nur einem feineren Verständnis od. Empfinden zugänglich); **Sub|li|mat,** das; -[e]s, -e (Ergebnis einer Sublimation; eine Quecksilberverbindung); **Sub|li|ma|ti|on,** die; -, -en (*Chemie* unmittelbarer Übergang eines festen Stoffes in den Gaszustand u. umgekehrt); **sub|li|mie|ren** (erhöhen; läutern, verfeinern; in künstler. Leistung[en] umsetzen; *Chemie* der Sublimation unterwerfen); **Sub|li|mie|rung; Sub|li|mi|tät,** die; - (*selten für* Erhabenheit)
sub|ma|rin ‹lat.› (*Biol.* unterseeisch)
Sub|mer|si|on, die; -, -en ‹lat.› (*Geol.* Untertauchen des Festlandes unter den Meeresspiegel; *veraltet für* Überschwemmung)
Sub|mis|si|on, die; -, -en ‹lat.› (*Wirtsch.* öffentl. Ausschreibung; Vergabe an denjenigen, der das günstigste Angebot macht; *veraltet für* Ehrerbietigkeit, Unterwürfigkeit; Unterwerfung); **Sub|mis|si|ons‿kar|tell** *(Wirtsch.)*, **...weg** (im -[e]); **Sub|mit|tent,** der; -en, -en; ↑R 126 (Bewerber [um einen Auftrag]; [An]bieter); **sub|mit|tie|ren** (sich [um einen Auftrag] bewerben)
Sub|or|di|na|ti|on, die; -, -en ‹lat.› (*Sprachw.* Unterordnung; *veraltend für* Unterordnung, Gehorsam); **sub|or|di|nie|ren;** subordinierende Konjunktion (unterordnendes Bindewort, z. B. „weil")
sub|po|lar ‹lat.› (*Geogr.* zwischen Polarzone u. gemäßigter Klimazone gelegen)
sub|se|quent ‹lat.› (*Geogr.* den weicheren Schichten folgend [von Flüssen])
sub|si|di|är, *älter* **sub|si|di|a|risch** ‹lat.› (helfend, unterstützend); **Sub|si|di|a|ris|mus,** der; - *u.* **Sub|si|di|a|ri|tät,** die; - (gegen den Zentralismus gerichtete Anschauung, die dem Staat nur die helfende Ergänzung der Selbstverantwortung kleiner Gemeinschaften, bes. der Familie, zugestehen will); **Sub|si|di|a|ri|täts|prin|zip,** das; -s; **Sub|si|di|en** *Plur.* (*veraltet für* Hilfsgelder)
Sub|sis|tenz, die; -, -en ‹lat.› (*veraltet für* [Lebens]unterhalt); **Sub|sis|tenz|wirt|schaft** (bäuerl. Produktion nur für den eigenen Bedarf)
Sub|skri|bent, der; -en, -en (↑R 126) ‹lat.› (Vorausbesteller von Büchern); **sub|skri|bie|ren; Sub|skrip|ti|on,** die; -, -en (Vorausbestellung von später erscheinenden Büchern); **Sub|skrip|ti|ons‿ein|la|dung, ...preis**
sub spe|cie ae|ter|ni|ta|tis [- 'spe:tsie ε...] ‹lat.› (unter dem Gesichtspunkt der Ewigkeit); **Sub|spe|zi|es** [...iεs] ‹lat.› (*Biol.* Unterart)
Sub|stan|dard, der; -s ‹engl.› (*Sprachw.* Sprachebene unterhalb der Hochsprache; *bes. österr. für* unterdurchschnittliche Qualität); **Sub|stan|dard|woh|nung** *(bes. österr.)*
Sub|stan|ti|a|li|tät *vgl.* Substanzialität; **sub|stan|ti|ell** *vgl.* substanziell; **sub|stan|ti|ie|ren** *vgl.* substanziieren; **Sub|stan|tiv,** das; -s, -e ‹lat.› (*Sprachw.* Hauptwort, Dingwort, Nomen, z. B. „Haus, Wald, Ehre"); **sub|stan|ti|vie|ren** [...v...] (zum Substantiv machen; als Substantiv gebrauchen); **sub|stan|ti|viert; Sub|stan|ti|vie|rung** (z. B. „das Schöne, das Laufen"); **sub|stan|ti|visch** (in der Art eines Substantivs); **Sub|stanz,** die; -, -en ([körperl.] Masse, Stoff, Bestand[teil]; *nur Sing.: Philos.* das Dauernde, das Wesentliche; *auch für* Materie); **Sub|stan|zi|a|li|tät,** *auch* Sub|stan|ti|a|li|tät, die; - (Wesentlichkeit, Substanzsein); **sub|stan|zi|ell,** *auch* sub|stan|ti|ell (wesenhaft, wesentlich; stofflich; materiell; nahrhaft); **sub|stan|zi|ie|ren,** *auch* sub|stan|ti|ie|ren (mit Substanz erfüllen, begründen, fundieren); **Sub|stanz|ver|lust**
sub|sti|tu|ier|bar; sub|sti|tu|ie|ren ‹lat.› (*Philos.* [einen Begriff] austauschen, ersetzen); **Sub|sti|tu|ie|rung** *(Philos.);* **[1]Sub|sti|tut,** das; -[e]s, -e (*svw.* Surrogat); **[2]Sub|sti|tut,** der; -en, -en; ↑R 126 (Verkaufsleiter); **Sub|sti|tu|tin; Sub|sti|tu|ti|on,** die; -, -en (*fachspr. für* Stellvertretung, Ersetzung); **Sub|sti|tu|ti|ons|pro|be** *(Sprachw.)*
Sub|strat, das; -[e]s, -e ‹lat.› (*fachspr. für* [materielle] Grundlage; Substanz; *Sprachw.* überlagerte sprachliche Grundschicht; *Landw.* Nährboden)
sub|su|mie|ren ‹lat.› (ein-, unterordnen; unter einem Thema zusammenfassen); **Sub|su|mie|rung; Sub|sum|ti|on,** die; -, -en; **sub|sum|tiv** (*Philos.* unterordnend; einbegreifend)
Sub|teen ['sabti:n], der; -s, -s ‹amerik.› (Mädchen od. Junge im Alter von etwa zehn Jahren)
sub|til ‹lat.› (zart, fein, sorgsam;

spitzfindig, schwierig); **Sub|ti|li|tät,** die; -, -en

Sub|tra|hend, der; -en, -en (↑R 126) ⟨lat.⟩ (abzuziehende Zahl); **sub|tra|hie|ren** (*Math.* abziehen); **Sub|trak|ti|on,** die; -, -en (das Abziehen); **Sub|trak|ti|ons|ver|fah|ren; sub|trak|tiv** (auf Subtraktion beruhend)

Sub|tro|pen *Plur.* ⟨lat.; griech.⟩ (*Geogr.* Gebiete des Übergangs von den Tropen zur gemäßigten Klimazone); **sub|tro|pisch**

Su|burb [ˈsabœ:(r)b] (↑R 132), die; -, -s ⟨engl.⟩ (*angloamerikan. Bez. für* Vorstadt); **sub|ur|bi|ka|risch** [zup|ur...] ⟨lat.⟩ (*kath. Kirche* vor Rom gelegen); -es Bistum

Sub|ven|ti|on [...v...], die; -, -en *meist Plur.* ⟨lat.⟩ (*Wirtsch.* zweckgebundene Unterstützung aus öffentl. Mitteln); **sub|ven|ti|o|nie|ren; Sub|ven|ti|ons‿ab|bau, ...be|geh|ren**

Sub|ver|si|on [...v...], die; -, -en ⟨lat.⟩ (Umsturz); **sub|ver|siv** (zerstörend, umstürzlerisch)

sub vo|ce [- ˈvo:tsə] ⟨lat.⟩ (unter dem [Stich]wort; *Abk.* s. v.)

Such‿ak|ti|on, ...an|zei|ge, ...ar|beit, ...au|to|ma|tik, ...bild, ...dienst; Su|che, die; -, *Plur.* (*Jägerspr.:*) -n; auf der - sein; auf die - gehen; **su|chen; Su|cher; Su|che|rei; Such‿flug|zeug, ...hund, ...lauf, ...lis|te, ...mel|dung, ...schein|wer|fer, ...schiff**

Sucht, die; -, *Plur.* Süchte *od.* Suchten (Krankheit; krankhaftes Verlangen [nach Rauschgift]); **Sucht|ge|fahr; süch|tig; Süch|ti|ge,** der *u.* die; -n, -n (↑R 5 ff.); **Süch|tig|keit,** die; -; **sucht|krank; Sucht|kran|ke**

Such|trupp

su|ckeln (*landsch. für* nuckeln); ich ...[e]le (↑R 16)

[1]**Suc|re** [ˈsukrə] (↑R 130; Hptst. von Bolivien)

[2]**Suc|re** [ˈsukrə] (↑R 130), der; -, - ⟨span.⟩ (ecuadorian. Währungseinheit; 1 Sucre = 100 Centavos)

Sud, der; -[e]s, -e (Flüssigkeit, in der etwas gekocht wurde; durch Auskochen erhaltene Lösung)

[1]**Süd** (Himmelsrichtung; *Abk.* S); Nord und Süd; *fachspr.* der Wind kommt aus Süd; Autobahnausfahrt Frankfurt Süd (*auch* Frankfurt-Süd; ↑R 106); *vgl.* Süden; [2]**Süd,** der; -[e]s, -e *Plur. selten* (*geh. für* Südwind); der warme Süd blies um das Haus; **Süd|af|ri|ka;** Republik -; **Süd|af|ri|ka|ner; Süd|af|ri|ka|ne|rin; süd|af|ri|ka|nisch,** *aber* (↑R 102): die Südafrikanische Union (*ehem. Bez. für* Republik Südafrika); **Süd|ame|ri|ka** (↑R 132); **Süd|ame|ri|ka|ner; Süd|ame|ri|ka|ne|rin; süd|ame|ri|ka|nisch**

Su|dan *meist mit Artikel* der; -[s] ⟨arab.⟩ (Staat in Mittelafrika); *vgl.* Irak; **Su|da|ner** *vgl.* Sudanese; **Su|da|ne|se,** der; -n, -n; ↑R 126 (Bewohner des Sudans); **Su|da|ne|sin; su|da|ne|sisch; su|da|nisch** (*svw.* sudanesisch)

süd|asi|a|tisch (↑R 132); **Süd|asi|en**

Su|da|ti|on, die; - ⟨lat.⟩ (*Med.* das Schwitzen)

Süd|aust|ra|li|en; Süd|ba|den; *vgl.* Baden; **Süd|da|ko|ta** (Staat in den USA; *Abk.* S. Dak., S. D.)

Sud|den|death, *auch* **Sud|den Death** [ˈsad(ə)nˈdɛθ] (↑R 33), der; -, - ⟨engl.⟩ (*Sport* Spielentscheidung durch das erste gefallene Tor in einem zusätzlichen Spielabschnitt)

süd|deutsch; *vgl.* deutsch; **Süd|deut|sche,** der *u.* die; **Süd|deutsch|land**

Su|del, der; -s, - (*schweiz. für* flüchtiger Entwurf, Kladde; *landsch. für* Schmutz; Pfütze); **Su|de|lei** *(ugs.);* **Su|de|ler, Sud|ler** *(ugs.);* **su|de|lig, sud|lig** *(ugs.);* **su|deln** (*ugs. für* Schmutz verursachen; schmieren; pfuschen); ich ...[e]le (↑R 16); **Su|del|wet|ter,** das; -s *(landsch.)*

Sü|den, der; -s (Himmelsrichtung; *Abk.* S); der Wind kommt aus -; gen Süden; *vgl.* Süd; **Sü|der|dith|mar|schen** (Teil von Dithmarschen); **Sü|der|oog** (eine Hallig)

Su|de|ten *Plur.* (Gebirge in Mitteleuropa); **su|de|ten|deutsch; Su|de|ten|land,** das; -[e]s; **su|de|tisch** (die Sudeten betreffend)

Süd|eu|ro|pa; süd|eu|ro|pä|isch; Süd|frank|reich; Süd|frucht *meist Plur.;* **Süd|früch|ten‿händ|ler** *(österr.),* **...hand|lung** *(österr.);* **Süd|hang**

Sud|haus (für die Bierherstellung)

Süd|hol|land; Süd|ita|li|en (↑R 132); **Süd|ka|ro|li|na** (Staat in den USA; *Abk.* S. C.); **Süd|ko|rea** (↑R 105; *nichtamtl. Bez. für* Republik Korea); **Süd|küs|te; Süd|län|der,** der; **Süd|län|de|rin; süd|län|disch; s[üdl]. Br.** = südlicher Breite

Sud|ler *vgl.* Sudeler

süd|lich; südlicher Breite (*Abk.* s[üdl]. Br.); südlich des Waldes, südlich vom Wald; südlich von München, *selten* südlich Münchens; südlicher Sternenhimmel, *aber* (↑R 108): das Südliche Kreuz (ein Sternbild)

sud|lig *vgl.* sudelig

Süd|nord|ka|nal, der; -s (Kanal in Nordwestdeutschland); [1]**Süd|ost** (Himmelsrichtung; *Abk.* SO); [2]**Süd|ost,** der; -[e]s, -e *Plur. selten* (Wind); **Süd|ost|asi|en** (↑R 132); **Süd|os|ten,** der; -s (*Abk.* SO); gen Südosten; *vgl.* Südost; **süd|öst|lich; Süd|ost|wind**

Sud|pfan|ne

Süd|pol, der; -s; **Süd|po|lar‿ex|pe|di|ti|on, ...meer** (das; -[e]s)

Süd|rho|de|si|en (*früherer Name von* Simbabwe); **Süd|see,** die; - (Pazifischer Ozean, bes. der südl. Teil); **Süd|see|in|su|la|ner; Süd|sei|te; süd|sei|tig; Süd|staa|ten** *Plur.* (in den USA); **Süd|süd|ost** (Himmelsrichtung; *Abk.* SSO); **Süd|süd|os|ten,** der; -s (*Abk.* SSO); **Süd|süd|west** (Himmelsrichtung; *Abk.* SSW); **Süd|süd|wes|ten,** der; -s (*Abk.* SSW); **Süd|ti|rol** (Gebiet der Provinz Bozen; *früher* der 1919 an Italien gefallene Teil des altösterr. Kronlandes Tirol); **Süd|ti|ro|ler; süd|ti|ro|lisch; süd|wärts; Süd|wein;** [1]**Süd|west** (Himmelsrichtung; *Abk.* SW); [2]**Süd|west,** der; -[e]s, -e *Plur. selten* (Wind); **süd|west|deutsch;** *vgl.* deutsch; **Süd|west|deutsch|land; Süd|wes|ten,** der; -s (*Abk.* SW); gen Südwesten; **Süd|wes|ter,** der; -s, - (wasserdichter Seemannshut); **süd|west|lich; Süd|west‿staat** (der; -[e]s; anfängliche Bez. des Landes Baden-Württemberg), **...wind; Süd|wind**

Su|es (ägypt. Stadt); *vgl.* Suez; **Su|es|ka|nal,** der; -s; ↑R 105 (Kanal zwischen Mittelmeer u. Rotem Meer)

Su|e|ve [...və] usw. *vgl.* Swebe usw.

Su|ez [ˈzu:ɛs, *auch* ˈzu:ɛts] usw. (*franz. Schreibung von* Sues usw.)

Suff, der; -[e]s (*ugs. für* das Betrunkensein; Trunksucht); der stille -; **Süf|fel,** der; -s, - (*landsch. für* Säufer); **süf|feln** (*ugs. für* gern Alkohol trinken); ich ...[e]le (↑R 16); **süf|fig** (*ugs. für* gut trinkbar, angenehm schmeckend); ein -er Wein

Süf|fi|sance [...zã:s], die; - ⟨franz.⟩ (*svw.* Süffisanz); **süf|fi|sant; Süf|fi|sanz,** die; - (Selbstgefälligkeit; Spott)

Suf|fix [*auch* zuˈfiks], das; -es, -e ⟨lat.⟩ (*Sprachw.* Nachsilbe, z. B. „-heit" in „Weisheit"); **Suf|fi|xo|id,** das; -[e]s, -e (einem Suffix ähnliches Wortbildungsmittel; z. B. „-papst" in „Literaturpapst")

suf|fi|zi|ent ⟨lat.⟩ (*bes. Med.* hinlänglich, genügend, ausreichend); **Suf|fi|zi|enz,** die; - (Hinlänglichkeit; *Med.* ausreichende Leistungsfähigkeit [eines Organs])

Süff|ler, Süff|ling (*landsch. für* jmd., der gern u. viel trinkt)

Suff|ra|gan (↑R 130), der; -s, -e ‹lat.› (einem Erzbischof unterstellter Diözesanbischof); **Suff|ra|get|te,** die; -, -n ‹engl.› (engl. Frauenrechtlerin)

Suf|fu|si|on, die; -, -en ‹lat.› (*Med.* Blutaustritt unter die Haut)

Su|fi, der; -[s], -s ‹arab.› (Anhänger des Sufismus); **Su|fis|mus,** der; - (eine asketisch-mystische Richtung im Islam)

Su|gamb|rer (↑R 130), der; -s, - (Angehöriger eines germ. Volkes)

sug|ge|rie|ren ‹lat.› (seelisch beeinflussen; einreden); **sug|ges|ti|bel** (beeinflussbar); ...ib|le (↑R 130) Menschen; **Sug|ges|ti|bi|li|tät,** die; - (Empfänglichkeit für Beeinflussung); **Sug|ges|ti|on,** die; -, -en (seelische Beeinflussung); **sug|ges|tiv** (seelisch beeinflussend; verfänglich); **Sug|ges|tiv|fra|ge** (Frage, die eine bestimmte Antwort suggeriert)

Suhl (Stadt am SW-Rand des Thüringer Waldes)

Suh|le, die; -, -n (Lache; feuchte Bodenstelle); **suh|len,** sich (*Jägerspr.* sich in einer Suhle wälzen [vom Rot- u. Schwarzwild])

Süh|ne, die; -, -n; **Süh|ne‿al|tar, ...geld** *(veraltet),* **...ge|richt, ...maß|nah|me; süh|nen; Süh|ne‿op|fer, ...rich|ter, ...ter|min, ...ver|fah|ren, ...ver|such; Sühn|op|fer; Süh|nung**

sui ge|ne|ris ‹lat.› (nur durch sich selbst eine Klasse bildend, einzig, besonders)

Suit|case [ˈsju:tke:s], das *od.* der; -, *Plur. - u.* -s [...zis] ‹engl.› (*engl. Bez. für* kleiner Handkoffer)

Sui|te [ˈsvi:t(ə)], die; -, -n ‹franz.› (Gefolge [eines Fürsten]; *Musik* Folge von [Tanz]sätzen); *vgl.* à la suite; **Sui|ti|er** [sviˈtie:], der; -s, -s (*veraltet für* lustiger Bursche; Schürzenjäger)

Su|i|zid, der, *auch* das; -[e]s, -e ‹lat.› (Selbstmord); **su|i|zi|dal** (selbstmörderisch); **Su|i|zi|dent,** der; -en, -en; ↑R 126 (Selbstmörder); **Su|i|zid‿ra|te, ...ri|si|ko**

Su|jet [zyˈʒə:], das; -s, -s ‹franz.› (Gegenstand künstlerischer Darstellung; Stoff)

Suk|ka|de, die; -, -n ‹roman.› (kandierte Fruchtschale)

Suk|ku|bus, der; -, ...ku|ben ‹lat.› (weibl. Buhlteufel des mittelalterl. Volksglaubens); *vgl.* Inkubus

suk|ku|lent ‹lat.› (*Bot.* saftvoll, fleischig); **Suk|ku|len|te,** die; -, -n (Pflanze trockener Gebiete); **Suk|ku|lenz,** die; - (*Bot.* Saftfülle)

Suk|kurs, der; -es, -e ‹lat.› (Hilfe, Unterstützung)

Suk|zes|si|on, die; -, -en ‹lat.› ([Rechts]nachfolge; Thronfolge; *Biol.* Entwicklungsreihe); **Suk|zes|si|ons‿krieg** (*svw.* Erbfolgekrieg), **...staat** (*Plur.* ...staaten; Nachfolgestaat); **suk|zes|siv** (allmählich [eintretend]); **suk|zes|si|ve** [...və] *Adverb* (allmählich, nach und nach)

[1]**Su|la|mith** [*auch* ...ˈmi:t] (w. Vorn.); [2]**Su|la|mith,** *ökum.* Schu|lam|mit (bibl. w. Eigenn.)

Sul|lei|ka (w. Vorn.)

Sul|fat, das; -[e]s, -e ‹lat.› (Salz der Schwefelsäure); **Sul|fid,** das; -[e]s, -e (Salz der Schwefelwasserstoffsäure); **sul|fi|disch** (Schwefel enthaltend); **Sul|fit** [*auch* ...ˈfit], das; -s, -e (Salz der schwefligen Säure); **Sul|fit|lau|ge**

Sülf|meis|ter (*veraltet für* Besitzer eines Salzwerkes; *nordd. für* Pfuscher)

Sul|fo|na|mid (↑R 132), das; -[e]s, -e *meist Plur.* (ein chemotherapeutisches Arzneimittel gegen Infektionskrankheiten); **Sul|fur,** das; -s ‹lat.› (*lat. Bez. für* Schwefel; *Zeichen* S)

Sul|ky [*engl.* ˈsalki], das; -s, -s ‹engl.› (zweirädriger Wagen für Trabrennen)

Süll, der *od.* das; -[e]s, -e (*nordd. für* [hohe] Türschwelle; *Seemannsspr.* Lukeneinfassung)

Sul|la (röm. Feldherr u. Staatsmann)

Sul|tan, der; -s, -e ‹arab., „Herrscher"› (Titel islamischer Herrscher); **Sul|ta|nat,** das; -[e]s, -e (Sultansherrschaft); **Sul|ta|nin; Sul|ta|ni|ne,** die; -, -n (große kernlose Rosine)

Sulz, die; -, -en *u.* **Sul|ze,** die; -, -n (*südd., österr., schweiz. für* Sülze); **Sül|ze,** die; -, -n (Fleisch, Fisch u. a. in Gallert); **sul|zen** (*südd., österr., schweiz. für* sülzen); du sulzt; gesulzt; **sül|zen** (zu Sülze verarbeiten; *ugs. auch für* [dummes Zeug] reden, quatschen); du sülzt; gesülzt; **Sülz|ko|te|lett**

Su|mach, der; -s, -e ‹arab.› (ein Gerbstoffe lieferndes Holzgewächs); *vgl.* [1]Schmack

Su|mat|ra [*auch* ˈzu:...] (↑R 130; zweitgrößte der Großen Sundainseln)

Su|mer (das alte Südbabylonien); **Su|me|rer,** der; -s, - (Angehöriger des ältesten Volkes in Südbabylonien); **su|me|risch;** *vgl.* deutsch; **Su|me|risch,** das; -[s] (Sprache); *vgl.* Deutsch; **Su|me|ri|sche,** das; -n; *vgl.* Deutsche, das

summ!; summ, summ!

Sum|ma, die; -, Summen ‹lat.› (in der Scholastik die zusammenfassende Darstellung von Theologie u. Philosophie; *veraltet für* Summe; *Abk.* Sa.); *vgl.* in summa; **sum|ma cum lau|de** ‹„mit höchstem Lob"› (höchstes Prädikat bei Doktorprüfungen); **Sum|mand,** der; -en, -en; ↑R 126 (*Math.* hinzuzuzählende Zahl); **sum|ma|risch** (kurz zusammengefasst); **Sum|ma|ri|um,** das; -s, ...ien [...i̯ən] (*veraltet für* kurze Inhaltsangabe, Inbegriff); **sum|ma sum|ma|rum** (alles in allem); **Sum|ma|ti|on,** die; -, -en (*bes. Math.* Bildung einer Summe; Aufrechnung); **Sümm|chen; Sum|me,** die; -, -n; [1]**sum|men,** sich (*veraltet für* sich summieren)

[2]**sum|men;** eine Melodie -

Sum|men‿bi|lanz *(Wirtsch.),* **...ver|si|che|rung**

Sum|mer (Vorrichtung, die Summtöne erzeugt); **Sum|mer|zei|chen**

sum|mie|ren ‹lat.› (zusammenzählen, vereinigen); sich - (anwachsen); **Sum|mie|rung**

Summ|ton *Plur.* ...töne

Sum|mum Bo|num, das; - - ‹lat.› (*Philos.* höchstes Gut; Gott); **Sum|mus E|pis|co|pus** (↑R 132), der; - - (oberster Bischof, Papst; *früher für* Landesherr als Oberhaupt einer ev. Landeskirche in Deutschland)

Su|mo, das; - ‹jap.› (eine japanische Form des Ringkampfes)

Sum|per, der; -s, - (*österr. ugs. für* Spießer, Banause)

Sumpf, der; -[e]s, Sümpfe; **Sumpf‿bi|ber** (Nutria), **...blü|te** (*abwertend für* moralische Verfallserscheinung; Auswuchs), **...bo|den; Sumpf|dot|ter|blu|me; sump|fen** (*ugs. für* liederlich leben; zechen); **sümp|fen** (*Bergmannsspr.* entwässern; *Töpferei* Ton mit Wasser ansetzen); **Sumpf‿fie|ber** (*für* Malaria), **...gas, ...ge|biet, ...ge|gend, ...huhn** (*auch ugs.* scherzh. für unsolider Mensch); **sump|fig; Sumpf|land,** das; -[e]s; **Sumpf‿ot|ter** (der; Nerz), **...pflan|ze, ...zyp|res|se**

Sums, der; -es (*ugs. svw.* Gesums); [einen] großen - machen

Sund, der; -[e]s, -e (Meerenge [zwischen Ostsee u. Kattegat])

Sun|da|in|seln *Plur.*; ↑R 105 (südostasiat. Inselgruppe); die Großen, die Kleinen -

Sün|de, die; -, -n; **Sün|den_ba|bel** (das; -s; *meist scherzh.*), **...be|kennt|nis, ...bock** *(ugs.)*, **...fall** (der), **...last** (die; -), **...lohn** (der; -[e]s; *geh.*); **sün|den|los,** sündlos; **Sün|den|lo|sig|keit,** Sündlo|sig|keit, die; -; **Sün|den_pfuhl** *(abwertend od. scherzh.)*, **...re|gis|ter** *(ugs.)*, **...ver|ge|bung; Sün|der; Sün|de|rin; Sün|der|mie|ne** *(ugs.)*; **Sünd|flut** (*volksmäßige Umdeutung von* Sintflut; *vgl. d.*); **sünd|haft;** - teuer (*ugs. für* überaus teuer); **Sünd|haf|tig|keit,** die; -; **sün|dig; sün|di|gen; sünd|lich** (*landsch. svw.* sündig); **sünd|los** *vgl.* sündenlos; **Sünd|lo|sig|keit** *vgl.* Sündenlosigkeit; **sünd|teu|er** (*österr. für* überaus teuer)

Sun|nit, der; -en, -en; ↑R 126 (Angehöriger der orthodoxen Hauptrichtung des Islams); **Sun|ni|tin; sun|ni|tisch**

Sün|tel, der; -s (Bergzug im Weserbergland)

[1]Su|o|mi [*finn.* 'suɔmi] (*finn. Name für* Finnland); **[2]Su|o|mi,** das; - (finn. Sprache)

su|per ‹lat.› (*ugs. für* hervorragend, großartig); das war -, eine - Schau; er hat - gespielt; **[1]Su|per,** der; -s, - (*Kurzform von* Superheterodynempfänger); **[2]Su|per,** das; -s *meist ohne Artikel* (*kurz für* Superbenzin); **su|per...** (über...); **Su|per...** (Über...); **su|perb** *(bes. österr.)*, **sü|perb** ‹franz.› (vorzüglich; prächtig); **Su|per_ben|zin, ...cup** *(Fußball)*; **su|per|fein** (*ugs. für* sehr fein); **Su|per|frau; Su|per-G** [...dʒi:], der; -[s], -[s] ‹engl.› (alpiner Skiwettbewerb zw. Abfahrtslauf und Riesenslalom); **Su|per-GAU** (allergrößter GAU; *vgl. d.*); **Su|per|het,** der; -s, -s (*Kurzform von* Superheterodynempfänger); **Su|per|he|te|ro|dyn|emp|fän|ger** ‹lat.; griech.; dt.› (Rundfunkempfänger mit hoher Verstärkung, guter Regelung u. hoher Trennschärfe); **Su|per|in|ten|dent** [*auch* 'zu:...], der; -en, -en (↑R 126) ‹lat.› (höherer ev. Geistlicher); **Su|per|in|ten|den|tur,** die; -, -en (Superintendentenamt, -wohnung); **Su|pe|ri|or,** der; -s, ...oren (Oberer, Vorgesetzter, bes. in Klöstern); **Su|pe|ri|o|rin; Su|pe|ri|o|ri|tät,** die; - (Überlegenheit; Übergewicht); **Su|per|kar|go,** der; -s, -s ‹lat.; span.› (*Seemannsspr., Kaufmannsspr.* bevollmächtigter Frachtbegleiter); **su|per|klug** *(ugs.)*; **Su|per|la|tiv,** der; -s, -e [...və] ‹lat.› (*Sprachw.* 2. Steigerungsstufe, Höchststufe, Meiststufe, z. B. „schönste"; *übertr. für* etwas, was zum Besten gehört); **su|per|la|ti|visch** [*auch* ...'ti:viʃ]; **su|per|leicht** (*ugs. für* sehr leicht); **Su|per|macht; Su|per|mann** *Plur.* ...männer; **Su|per|markt** (großes Warenhaus mit Selbstbedienung u. umfangreichem Sortiment); **su|per|mo|dern** (*ugs. für* sehr modern); **Su|per|na|tu|ra|lis|mus** usw. *vgl.* Supranaturalismus usw.; **Su|per|no|va** [...va] (*Astron.* bes. lichtstarke Nova); *vgl.* [1]Nova; **Su|per|phos|phat** ‹lat.; griech.› (phosphorhaltiger Kunstdünger); **Su|per|preis** (besonders günstiger Preis); **Su|per|re|vi|si|on** [...v...] (*Wirtsch.* Nach-, Überprüfung); **Su|per|rie|sen|sla|lom; su|per|schlau** (*ugs. für* sehr schlau); **su|per|schnell** (*ugs. für* sehr schnell); **Su|per|star** (*ugs. für* bes. großer, berühmter Star); *vgl.* [2]Star; **Su|per|sti|ti|on,** die; - (*veraltet für* Aberglaube); **Su|per|strat,** das; -[e]s, -e (*Sprachw.* bodenständig gewordene Sprache eines Eroberervolkes); *vgl.* Substrat; **Su|per|zei|chen** *(Kybernetik)*

Su|pi|num, das; -s, ...na (lat. Verbform)

Süpp|chen; Sup|pe, die; -, -n

Sup|pé [zu'pe:] (österr. Komponist)

Sup|pen_fleisch, ...grün (das; -s), **...huhn, ...kas|par** (der; -s; Gestalt aus dem Struwwelpeter; ↑R 97), **...kas|per** (*ugs. für* Kind, das seine Suppe nicht essen will), **...kel|le, ...kno|chen, ...kraut, ...löf|fel, ...nu|del, ...schüs|sel, ...tas|se, ...tel|ler, ...ter|ri|ne, ...wür|fel; sup|pig**

Sup|ple|ant, der; -en, -en (↑R 126) ‹franz.› (*schweiz. für* Ersatzmann [in einer Behörde]); **Sup|ple|ment,** das; -[e]s, -e ‹lat.› (*Buchw.* Ergänzung[sband, -teil]; *kurz für* Supplementwinkel); **Sup|ple|ment_band** (der), **...lie|fe|rung, ...win|kel** (*Math.* Ergänzungswinkel); **Sup|plent,** der; -en, -en; ↑R 126 (*österr. veraltet für* Aushilfslehrer); **sup|ple|to|risch** (*veraltet für* ergänzend, stellvertretend, nachträglich)

Sup|pli|kant, der; -en, -en ‹lat.› (*veraltet für* Bittsteller); **sup|pli|zie|ren** (*veraltet für* ein Bittgesuch einreichen)

sup|po|nie|ren ‹lat.› (voraussetzen; unterstellen)

Sup|port, der; -[e]s, -e ‹lat.› (*Technik* schlittenförmiger Werkzeugträger auf dem Bett einer Drehbank); **Sup|port|dreh|bank**

Sup|po|si|ti|on, die; -, -en ‹lat.› (Voraussetzung; Unterstellung); **Sup|po|si|to|ri|um,** das; -s, ...ien [...iən] (*Med.* Arzneizäpfchen); **Sup|po|si|tum,** das; -s, ...ta (*veraltet für* Vorausgesetztes, Annahme)

Sup|pres|si|on, die; -, -en ‹lat.› (*Med.* Unterdrückung; Zurückdrängung); **sup|pres|siv; sup|pri|mie|ren**

sup|ra|lei|tend (↑R 130) ‹lat.; dt.›; -er Draht; **Sup|ra|lei|ter,** der (elektr. Leiter, der bei einer Temperatur nahe dem absoluten Nullpunkt fast unbegrenzt leitfähig wird)

sup|ra|na|ti|o|nal (↑R 130) ‹lat.› (übernational [von Kongressen, Gemeinschaften, Parlamenten u. a.])

Sup|ra|na|tu|ra|lis|mus (↑R 130), Su|per|na|tu|ra|lis|mus, der; - ‹lat.› (Glaube an Übernatürliches); **sup|ra|na|tu|ra|lis|tisch,** su|per|na|tu|ra|lis|tisch

Sup|ra|por|te (↑R 130) *vgl.* Sopraporte

Sup|re|mat, der *od.* das; -[e]s, -e ‹lat.› *u.* **Sup|re|ma|tie** (↑R 130), die; -, ...ien ([päpstl.] Obergewalt; Überordnung); **Sup|re|mat[s]|eid** (*früher* Eid der engl. Beamten u. Geistlichen, mit dem sie den Supremat des engl. Königs anerkannten)

Su|re, die; -, -n ‹arab.› (Kapitel des Korans)

Surf|brett ['sœ:(r)f...] ‹engl.; dt.›; **sur|fen** (auf dem Surfbrett fahren); **Sur|fer; Sur|fe|rin; Sur|fing,** das; -s (Wellenreiten, Brandungsreiten [auf einem Surfbrett]; Windsurfen)

Sur|fleisch (*österr. für* Pökelfleisch)

Surf|ri|ding ['sœ:(r)fraidiŋ] ‹engl.›; *vgl.* Surfing

Su|ri|nam, der; -[s] (Fluss im nördl. Südamerika); **Su|ri|na|me** [syri...] (Republik im nördl. Südamerika); **Su|ri|na|mer; Su|ri|na|me|rin; su|ri|na|misch**

Sur|plus ['sœ:(r)pləs], das; -, - ‹engl.› (*Wirtsch.* Überschuss, Gewinn)

Sur|re|a|lis|mus [*auch* syre...], der; - ‹franz.› (Kunst- u. Literaturrichtung, die das Traumhaft-Unbewusste künstlerisch darstellen will); **Sur|re|a|list,** der; -en, -en (↑R 126); **Sur|re|a|lis|tin; sur|re|a|lis|tisch**

sur|ren
Sur|ro|gat, das; -[e]s, -e ‹lat.› (Ersatz[mittel, -stoff], Behelf; *Rechtsw.* Ersatz für einen Gegenstand, Wert); **Sur|ro|ga|ti|on,** die; -, -en (*Rechtsw.* Austausch eines Vermögensgegenstandes gegen einen anderen, der den gleichen Rechtsverhältnissen unterliegt)
Su|sa (altpers. Stadt)
Su|san ['su:zən] (w. Vorn.); **Su|san|na, Su|san|ne** (w. Vorn.); **Su|se, Su|si** (w. Vorn.)
Su|si|ne, die; -, -n ‹ital.› (eine ital. Pflaume)
sus|pekt (↑R 132) ‹lat.› (verdächtig)
sus|pen|die|ren ‹lat.› (zeitweilig aufheben; [einstweilen] des Dienstes entheben; *Med.* anheben, aufhängen; *Chemie* eine Suspension herbeiführen); **Sus|pen|die|rung; Sus|pen|si|on,** die; -, -en ([einstweilige] Dienstenthebung; zeitweilige Aufhebung; *Med.* Anhebung, Aufhängung; *Chemie* Aufschwemmung feinstverteilter fester Stoffe in einer Flüssigkeit); **sus|pen|siv** (aufhebend, -schiebend); **Sus|pen|so|ri|um,** das; -s, ...ien [...i̯ən] (*Med.* Tragverband, z. B. für den Hodensack; *Sport* Schutz für die männl. Geschlechtsteile)
süß; am süßesten; **Süß,** das; -es (*Druckw.* geleistete, aber noch nicht bezahlte Arbeit); **Sü|ße,** die; -; **sü|ßen;** du süßt; **Süß|holz** (eine Pflanzengattung; Droge); **Süß|holz|rasp|ler** (*ugs. für* jmd., der einer Frau mit schönen Worten schmeichelt); **Sü|ßig|keit; Süß‿kar|tof|fel, ...kir|sche; süß|lich; Süß|lich|keit,** die; -; **Süß|ling** (*veraltet für* fader, süßlich tuender Mensch); **Süß‿most, ...mos|ter** (jmd., der Süßmost o. Ä. herstellt), **...mos|te|rei; Süß|rahm|but|ter; süß|sau|er** (↑R 27); ein süßsaures Bonbon; **Süß‿spei|se, ...stoff, ...wa|ren** *(Plur.)*; **Süß|wa|ren|ge|schäft; Süß|was|ser** *Plur.* ...wasser; **Süß|was|ser‿fisch, ...tier; Süß|wein**
Sust, die; -, -en (*schweiz. früher für* öffentl. Rast- u. Lagerhaus)
Sus|ten, der; -s, *auch* **Sus|ten|pass**
sus|zep|ti|bel ‹lat.› (*veraltet für* empfänglich; reizbar); ...ib|le (↑R 130) Natur; **Sus|zep|ti|bi|li|tät,** die; -; **Sus|zep|ti|on,** die; -, -en (*Bot.* Reizaufnahme der Pflanze); **sus|zi|pie|ren** (einen Reiz aufnehmen [von Pflanzen])
Su|ta|ne *vgl.* Soutane
Su|tasch *vgl.* Soutache
Süt|ter|lin|schrift, die; - (↑R 95) ‹nach dem dt. Pädagogen u. Grafiker› (Grundlage der 1935 eingeführten dt. Schreibschrift)
Su|tur, die; -, -en ‹lat.› (*Med.* [Knochen-, Schädel]naht)
su|um cu|i|que [- ku...] ‹lat., „jedem das Seine"› (preuß. Wahlspruch)
[1]Su|va (Hptst. v. Fidschi)
SUVA, [2]Su|va = Schweizerische Unfallversicherungsanstalt
s. v. = salva venia; sub voce
SV = Sozialversicherung; Sportverein
sva. = so viel als
Sval|bard ['sva:lbar(d)] ‹norw.› (norw. Inselgruppe im Nordpolarmeer)
SVD = Societas Verbi Divini
Sven [svɛn] (m. Vorn.); **Sven|ja** (w. Vorn.)
SVP = Schweizerische Volkspartei
s. v. v. = sit venia verbo
svw. = so viel wie
SW = Südwest[en]
Swa|hi|li *vgl.* [1,2]Suaheli
Swa|mi, der; -s, -s ‹Hindi› (hinduistischer Mönch, Lehrer)
Swap|ge|schäft ['svɔp...] ‹engl.; dt.› (*Börse* Devisenaustauschgeschäft)
SWAPO, die; - = South West African People's Organization ['sau̯θ 'wɛst 'ɛfrikən 'pi:p(ə)lz ɔ:(r)gənai̯'ze:ʃ(ə)n] (südwestafrikanische Befreiungsbewegung)
Swa|si, der; -, - (Bewohner von Swasiland); **Swa|si|land** (in Südafrika); **swa|si|län|disch**
Swas|ti|ka, die; -, ...ken, *auch* der; -[s], -s ‹sanskr.› (altind. Bez. des Hakenkreuzes)
Swea|ter ['sve:tə(r)], der; -s, - ‹engl.› (*veraltend für* Pullover); **Sweat|shirt** ['svɛtʃœ:(r)t] (weit geschnittener Pullover)
Swe|be, der; -n, -n; ↑R 126 (Angehöriger eines Verbandes westgerm. Stämme); **swe|bisch**
Swe|den|borg (schwed. Naturphilosoph); **Swe|den|bor|gi|a|ner** (Anhänger Swedenborgs)
SWF = Südwestfunk
Swift (engl.-ir. Schriftsteller)
Swim|ming|pool ['swimiŋpu:l], der; -s, -s ‹engl.› (Schwimmbecken)
Swi|ne, die; - (Hauptmündungsarm der Oder)
Swin|egel (↑R 132), der; -s, - (*nordd. für* Igel)
Swi|ne|mün|de (Hafenstadt u. Seebad auf Usedom [Polen])
Swing, der; -[s] ‹engl.› (ein Stil des Jazz; *Wirtsch.* Kreditgrenze bei bilateralen Handelsverträgen); **swin|gen;** swingte; geswingt; **Swing|fox**
Swiss|air [...sɛ:(r)], die; - ‹engl.› (schweiz. Luftfahrtgesellschaft)
Sy|ba|ris (antike griech. Stadt in Unteritalien); **Sy|ba|rit,** der; -en, -en; ↑R 126 (Einwohner von Sybaris; *veraltet für* Schlemmer); **sy|ba|ri|tisch** (Sybaris od. den Sybariten betreffend; *veraltet für* genusssüchtig)
Syd|ney ['sidni] (Hptst. von Neusüdwales in Australien)
Sy|e|ne (*alter Name von* Assuan); **Sy|e|nit** [*auch* ...'nit], der; -s, -e ‹griech.› (ein Tiefengestein); **Sy|e|nit‿gneis, ...por|phyr**
Sy|ko|mo|re, die; -, -n ‹griech.› (ägypt. Maulbeerfeigenbaum); **Sy|ko|mo|ren|holz; Sy|ko|phant,** der; -en, -en; ↑R 126 (im alten Athen gewerbsmäßiger Ankläger; *veraltet für* Verräter, Verleumder); **sy|ko|phan|tisch** (*veraltet für* anklägerisch, verräterisch, verleumderisch)
Sy|ko|se, die; -, -n ‹griech.› (*Med.* Bartflechte[nbildung])
syl... ‹griech.› (mit..., zusammen...); **Syl...** (Mit..., Zusammen...)
syl|la|bisch ‹griech.› (*veraltet für* silbenweise); **Syl|la|bus,** der; -, *Plur.* - *u.* ...bi (Zusammenfassung; Verzeichnis [der früher durch den Papst verurteilten Lehren]); **Syl|lep|se, Syl|lep|sis,** die; -, ...epsen (*Rhet.* Zusammenfassung, eine Form der Ellipse); **syl|lep|tisch**
Syl|lo|gis|mus, der; -, ...men ‹griech.› (*Philos.* logischer Schluss vom Allgemeinen auf das Besondere); **syl|lo|gis|tisch**
[1]Syl|phe, der; -n, -n (↑R 126), *auch* die; -, -n ‹lat.› ([männl.] Luftgeist des mittelalterl. Zauberglaubens); **[2]Syl|phe,** die; -, -n (ätherisch zartes weibliches Wesen); **Syl|phi|de,** die; -, -n (weibl. [1]Sylphe; schlankes, anmutiges Mädchen); **syl|phi|den|haft** (zart, schlank)
Sylt (eine der Nordfriesischen Inseln)
Syl|ves|ter *vgl.* [1]Silvester
Syl|vin [...'vi:n], das, *auch* der; -s, -e ‹nach dem Arzt Sylvius› (ein Mineral)
sym... ‹griech.› (mit..., zusammen...); **Sym...** (Mit..., Zusammen...)
Sym|bi|ont, der; -en, -en (↑R 126) ‹griech.› (*Biol.* Partner einer Symbiose); **Sym|bi|o|se,** die; -, -n;

(„Zusammenleben" ungleicher Lebewesen zu gegenseitigem Nutzen); **sym|bi|o|tisch** (in Symbiose lebend)

Sym|bol, das; -s, -e ⟨griech.⟩ ([Wahr]zeichen; Sinnbild; Zeichen für eine [physikal.] Größe); **Sym|bol‿cha|rak|ter** (der; -s), **...fi|gur; sym|bol|haft; Sym|bol|haf|tig|keit,** die; -; **Sym|bo|lik,** die; - (sinnbildl. Bedeutung od. Darstellung; Bildersprache; Verwendung von Symbolen); **sym|bo|lisch** (sinnbildlich); -e Bücher (Bekenntnisschriften); -e Logik (Behandlung log. Gesetze mithilfe von mathemat. Symbolen); **sym|bo|li|sie|ren** (sinnbildlich darstellen); **Sym|bo|li|sie|rung; Sym|bo|lis|mus,** der; - (Strömung in Literatur und bildender Kunst als Reaktion auf Realismus und Naturalismus); **Sym|bo|list,** der; -en, -en (↑R 126); **sym|bo|lis|tisch; Sym|bol‿kraft** (die; -), **...spra|che** *(EDV);* **sym|bol|träch|tig; Sym|bol|träch|tig|keit,** die; -

Sym|ma|chie [...x...], die; -, ...ien ⟨griech.⟩ (Bundesgenossenschaft der altgriech. Stadtstaaten)

Sym|met|rie (↑R 130), die; -, ...ien ⟨griech.⟩ (spiegelbildliche Übereinstimmung); **Sym|met|rie‿ach|se** (*Math.* Spiegelachse), **...ebe|ne** (↑R 132; *Math.*); **sym|me|trisch** (spiegelbildlich übereinstimmend)

sym|pa|the|tisch ⟨griech.⟩ (von geheimnisvoller Wirkung); -e Kur (Wunderkur); -es Mittel (Geheimmittel); -e Tinte (unsichtbare Geheimtinte); **Sym|pa|thie,** die; -, ...ien ([Zu]neigung; Wohlgefallen); **Sym|pa|thie‿be|kun|dung, ...er|klä|rung, ...kund|ge|bung, ...streik, ...trä|ger** (jmd., der die Sympathie anderer auf sich zieht); **Sym|pa|thi|kus,** der; - (*Med.* Teil des vegetativen Nervensystems); **Sym|pa|thi|sant,** der; -en, -en; ↑R 126 (jmd., der einer Gruppe od. einer Anschauung wohlwollend gegenübersteht); **Sym|pa|thi|san|tin; sym|pa|thisch** (anziehend; ansprechend; zusagend); **sym|pa|thi|sie|ren** (gleiche Anschauungen haben); mit jemandem -

Sym|pho|nie usw. *vgl.* Sinfonie usw.

Sym|phy|se, die; -, -n ⟨griech.⟩ (*Med.* Verwachsung; Knochenfuge); **sym|phy|tisch** (zusammengewachsen)

Symp|le|ga|den (↑R 130 *u.* 132); *Plur.* (zwei zusammenschlagende Felsen vor dem Eingang ins Schwarze Meer [in der griech. Sage])

Sym|po|si|on, Sym|po|si|um, das; -s, ...ien [...i̯ən] ⟨griech.⟩ (wissenschaftl. Tagung; Trinkgelage im alten Griechenland)

Symp|tom (↑R 132), das; -s, -e ⟨griech.⟩ (Anzeichen; Merkmal; Krankheitszeichen); **Symp|to|ma|tik,** die; - (*Med.* Gesamtheit von Symptomen); **symp|to|ma|tisch** (anzeigend, warnend; bezeichnend); **Symp|to|ma|to|lo|gie,** die; - (*Med.* Lehre von den Krankheitszeichen)

syn... ⟨griech.⟩ (mit..., zusammen...); **Syn...** (Mit..., Zusammen...)

sy|na|go|gal (↑R 132) ⟨griech.⟩ (den jüd. Gottesdienst od. die Synagoge betreffend); **Sy|na|go|ge,** die; -, -n (gottesdienstl. Versammlungsort der jüd. Gemeinde)

sy|nal|lag|ma|tisch (↑R 132) ⟨griech.⟩ (*Rechtsw.* gegenseitig)

Sy|na|lö|phe (↑R 132), die; -, -n ⟨griech.⟩ (*Verslehre* Verschmelzung zweier Silben)

sy|nand|risch (↑R 130 *u.* 132) ⟨griech.⟩ (*Bot.* mit verwachsenen Staubblättern); -e Blüte

Sy|nap|se (↑R 132), die; -, -n ⟨griech.⟩ (*Biol.* Verbindung zwischen Zellen zur Reizübertragung)

Sy|nä|re|se, Sy|nä|re|sis (↑R 132), die; -, ...resen ⟨griech.⟩ (*Sprachw.* Zusammenziehung zweier Vokale zu einer Silbe)

Syn|äs|the|sie (↑R 132), die; -, ...ien ⟨griech.⟩ (*Med.* Miterregung eines Sinnesorgans bei Reizung eines andern; *Stilk.* sprachliche Verschmelzung mehrerer Sinneseindrücke); **syn|äs|the|tisch**

syn|chron [...k...] ⟨griech.⟩ (gleichzeitig, zeitgleich, gleichlaufend; *auch für* synchronisch); **Syn|chron|ge|trie|be; Syn|chro|nie,** die; - (*Sprachw.* Darstellung des Sprachzustandes eines bestimmten Zeitraums); **Syn|chro|ni|sa|ti|on,** die; -, -en *u.* Syn|chro|ni|sie|rung (Herstellen des Synchronismus; Zusammenstimmung von Bild, Sprechton u. Musik im Film; bild- und bewegungsechte Übertragung fremdsprachiger Partien eines Films); **syn|chro|nisch** (die Synchronie betreffend); **syn|chro|ni|sie|ren** ⟨*zu* Synchronisation⟩; **Syn|chro|ni|sie|rung** *vgl.* Synchronisation; **Syn|chro|nis|mus,** der; -, ...men (Gleichzeitigkeit; Gleichlauf; zeitl. Übereinstimmung); **syn|chro|nis|tisch** (Gleichzeitiges zusammenstellend); -e Tafeln; **Syn|chron‿ma|schi|ne, ...mo|tor, ...spre|cher, ...spre|che|rin, ...uhr; Syn|chrot|ron** (↑R 130), das; -s, *Plur.* -e, *auch* -s (*Kernphysik* Beschleuniger für geladene Elementarteilchen)

Syn|dak|ty|lie, die; -, ...ien ⟨griech.⟩ (*Med.* Verwachsung von Fingern od. Zehen)

syn|de|tisch ⟨griech.⟩ (*Sprachw.* durch Bindewort verbunden)

Syn|di|ka|lis|mus, der; - ⟨griech.⟩ (*Bez. für* sozialrevolutionäre Bestrebungen mit dem Ziel der Übernahme der Produktionsmittel durch autonome Gewerkschaften); **Syn|di|ka|list,** der; -en, -en (↑R 126); **syn|di|ka|lis|tisch; Syn|di|kat,** das; -[e]s, -e (*Wirtsch.* Verkaufskartell; *Bez. für* geschäftlich getarnte Verbrecherorganisation in den USA); **Syn|di|kus,** der; -, *Plur.* -se *u.* ...dizi (*Rechtsspr.* Rechtsbeistand einer Körperschaft)

Syn|drom (↑R 132), das; -s, -e ⟨griech.⟩ (*Med.* Krankheitsbild)

Sy|ne|chie [...ɛ'çi:] (↑R 132), die; -, ...ien ⟨griech.⟩ (*Med.* Verwachsung)

Sy|ned|ri|on (↑R 130 *u.* 132), das; -s, ...ien [...i̯ən] ⟨griech.⟩ (altgriech. Ratsbehörde; *svw.* Synedrium); **Sy|ned|ri|um,** das; -s, ...ien [...i̯ən] (Hoher Rat der Juden in griech. u. röm. Zeit)

Sy|nek|do|che [...dɔxe] (↑R 132), die; -, -n [...'dɔxən] ⟨griech.⟩ (*Rhet., Stilk.* Setzung des engeren Begriffs für den umfassenderen)

Sy|ner|ge|tik (↑R 132), die; - ⟨griech.⟩ (die Lehre vom Zusammenwirken; Selbstorganisation); **sy|ner|ge|tisch** (zusammen-, mitwirkend); **Sy|ner|gie,** die; - (Zusammenwirken); **Sy|ner|gie|ef|fekt** (positive Wirkung, die sich aus dem Zusammenschluss od. der Zusammenarbeit zweier Unternehmen o.Ä. ergibt); **Sy|ner|gis|mus,** der; - (*Theol.* Lehre vom Zusammenwirken des menschl. Willens u. der göttl. Gnade; *Chemie, Med.* Zusammenwirken von Substanzen od. Faktoren); **sy|ner|gis|tisch**

Sy|ne|sis (↑R 132), die; -, ...esen ⟨griech.⟩ (*Sprachw.* singgemäß richtige Wortfügung, die streng genommen nicht den grammatischen Regeln entspricht, z. B. „eine Menge Äpfel fielen vom Baum" statt „...fiel vom Baum")

Syn|kar|pie, die; - ⟨griech.⟩ (*Bot.*

Zusammenwachsen der Fruchtblätter zu einem einzigen Fruchtknoten)
syn|kli|nal ⟨griech.⟩ (*Geol.* muldenförmig [von Lagerstätten]); **Syn|kli|na|le,** *auch* **Syn|kli|ne,** die; -, -n (*Geol.* Mulde)
Syn|ko|pe [ˈzynkope, *Musik nur* ...ˈkoːpə], die; -, ...open ⟨griech.⟩ (*Sprachw.* Ausfall eines unbetonten Vokals zwischen zwei Konsonanten im Wortinnern, z. B. „ich handle" statt „ich handele"; *Verslehre* Ausfall einer Senkung im Vers; *Med.* kurze Bewusstlosigkeit; *Musik* Betonung eines unbetonten Taktwertes); **syn|ko|pie|ren; syn|ko|pisch**
Syn|kre|tis|mus, der; - ⟨griech.⟩ (Verschmelzung, Vermischung [von Lehren od. Religionen]); **Syn|kre|tist,** der; -en, -en (↑R 126); **syn|kre|tis|tisch**
Sy|nod (↑R 132), der; -[e]s, -e ⟨griech.⟩ (*früher* oberste Behörde der russ. Kirche); Heiliger -; **sy|no|dal** (die Synode betreffend); **Sy|no|da|le,** der *u.* die; -n, -n; ↑R 5 ff. (Mitglied einer Synode); **Sy|no|dal‿ver|fas|sung, ...ver|samm|lung; Sy|no|de,** die; -, -n (Kirchenversammlung, bes. die evangelische); **sy|no|disch** (*seltener für* synodal)
sy|no|nym (↑R 132) ⟨griech.⟩ (*Sprachw.* sinnverwandt); -e Wörter; **Sy|no|nym,** das; -s, *Plur.* -e, *auch* Synonyma (*Sprachw.* sinnverwandtes Wort, z. B. „Frühjahr, Lenz, Frühling"); **Sy|no|ny|men|wör|ter|buch** *vgl.* Synonymwörterbuch; **Sy|no|ny|mie,** die; - (Sinnverwandtschaft [von Wörtern u. Wendungen]); **Sy|no|ny|mik,** die; - (Lehre von den sinnverwandten Wörtern); **sy|no|ny|misch** (*älter für* synonym); **Sy|no|nym|wör|ter|buch** (Wörterbuch, in dem Synonyme in Gruppen dargestellt sind)
Sy|nop|se, Sy|nop|sis (↑R 132), die; -, ...opsen ⟨griech.⟩ (knappe Zusammenfassung; vergleichende Übersicht; Nebeneinanderstellung von Texten, bes. der Evangelien des Matthäus, Markus u. Lukas); **Sy|nop|tik,** die; - (*Meteor.* für eine Wettervorhersage notwendige großräumige Wetterbeobachtung); **Sy|nop|ti|ker** (einer der drei Evangelisten Matthäus, Markus u. Lukas); **sy|nop|tisch** ([übersichtlich] zusammengestellt, nebeneinander gereiht); -e Evangelien
Sy|nö|zie (↑R 132), die; -, ...ien ⟨griech.⟩ (*Zool.* Zusammenleben verschiedener Organismen, das den Wirtstieren weder schadet noch nützt; *Bot. auch für* Monözie); **sy|nö|zisch**
Syn|tag|ma, das; -s, *Plur.* ...men *od.* ...ta ⟨griech.⟩ (*Sprachw.* syntaktisch gefügte Wortgruppe, in der jedes Glied seinen Wert erst durch die Fügung bekommt); **syn|tag|ma|tisch** (das Syntagma betreffend); **syn|tak|tisch** (die Syntax betreffend); -er Fehler (Fehler gegen die Syntax); -e Fügung; **Syn|tax,** die; -, -en (*Sprachw.* Lehre vom Satzbau; Satzlehre)
Syn|the|se, die; -, -n ⟨griech.⟩ (Zusammenfügung [einzelner Teile zu einem Ganzen]; *Philos.* Aufhebung des sich in These u. Antithese Widersprechenden in eine höhere Einheit; *Chemie* Aufbau einer Substanz); **Syn|the|se|pro|dukt** (Kunststoff); **Syn|the|si|zer** [ˈzyntəsaizə(r), *engl.* ˈsinθisaizə(r)], der; -s, - ⟨griech.-engl.⟩ (*Musik* Gerät zur elektron. Klangerzeugung); **Syn|the|tics** [zynˈteːtiks] *Plur.* (*Sammelbez. für* synthet. erzeugte Kunstfasern u. Produkte daraus); **Syn|the|tik,** das; -s *meist ohne Artikel* ([Gewebe aus] Kunstfaser); **syn|the|tisch** ⟨griech.⟩ (zusammensetzend; *Chemie* künstlich hergestellt); -es Urteil *(Philos.)*; -e Edelsteine; **syn|the|ti|sie|ren** (*Chemie* aus einfacheren Stoffen herstellen)
Syn|zy|ti|um, das; -s, ...ien [...iən] ⟨griech.⟩ (*Biol.* mehrkernige, durch Zellenfusion entstandene Plasmamasse)
Sy|phi|lis, die; - ⟨nach dem Titel eines lat. Lehrgedichts des 16. Jh.s⟩ (*Med.* eine Geschlechtskrankheit); **sy|phi|lis|krank; Sy|phi|li|ti|ker** (an Syphilis Leidender); **sy|phi|li|tisch** (die Syphilis betreffend)
Sy|ra|kus (Stadt auf Sizilien); **Sy|ra|ku|ser** (↑R 103); **sy|ra|ku|sisch**
Sy|rer, *auch* Sy|ri|er; **Sy|re|rin,** *auch* Sy|ri|e|rin; **Sy|ri|en** (Staat im Vorderen Orient); **Sy|ri|er** usw. *vgl.* Syrer usw.
Sy|rin|ge, die; -, -n ⟨griech.⟩ (Flieder); **[1]Sy|rinx** (griech. Nymphe); **[2]Sy|rinx,** die; -, ...ingen (Hirtenflöte; Stimmorgan der Vögel)
sy|risch (aus Syrien; Syrien betreffend), *aber* (↑R 102): die Syrische Wüste
Syr|jä|ne, der; -n, -n; ↑R 126 (Angehöriger eines finnisch-ugrischen Volkes)
Sy|ro|lo|ge, der; -n, -n (↑R 126) ⟨griech.⟩ (Erforscher der Sprachen, der Geschichte u. der Altertümer Syriens); **Sy|ro|lo|gie,** die; -; **Sy|ro|lo|gin**
Syr|te, die; -, -n ⟨griech.⟩ (*veraltet für* Untiefe, Sandbank); die Große -, die Kleine - (zwei Meeresbuchten an der Küste Nordafrikas)
Sys|tem, das; -s, -e ⟨griech.⟩ (Gliederung, Aufbau; Ordnungsprinzip; einheitlich geordnetes Ganzes; Lehrgebäude; Regierungs-, Staatsform; Einordnung [von Tieren, Pflanzen u. a.] in verwandte od. ähnlich gebaute Gruppen); **Sys|tem‿ana|ly|se** (↑R 132), **...ana|ly|ti|ker** (↑R 132; Fachmann in der EDV); **Sys|te|ma|tik,** die; -, -en (planmäßige Darstellung, einheitl. Gestaltung; *nur Sing.: Biol.* Lehre vom System der Lebewesen); **Sys|te|ma|ti|ker** (jmd., der systematisch vorgeht); **sys|te|ma|tisch** (das System betreffend; in ein System gebracht; planmäßig); **sys|te|ma|ti|sie|ren** (in ein System bringen; in einem System darstellen); **Sys|te|ma|ti|sie|rung; Sys|tem‿bau|wei|se** (die; -), **...cha|rak|ter** (der; -s), **...feh|ler** *(EDV)*; **sys|tem‿feind|lich, ...fremd, ...im|ma|nent, ...kon|form; Sys|tem‿kri|ti|ker, ...leh|re** (die; -; *veraltend für* Systematik); **sys|tem|los** (planlos); **Sys|tem|lo|sig|keit,** die; -; **Sys|tem‿ma|nage|ment** (systematische Unternehmensführung), **...ma|na|ger** *(EDV)*; **sys|te|mo|id** (einem System ähnlich); **Sys|te|mo|id,** das; -[e]s, -e (systemoides Gebilde); **Sys|tem‿pro|gram|mie|rer** *(EDV)*, **...ver|än|de|rer, ...zwang**
Sys|to|le [...le, *auch* ...ˈtoːlə] (↑R 132), die; -, ...olen (*Med.* Zusammenziehung des Herzmuskels); **sys|to|lisch;** -er Blutdruck
Sy|zy|gie, die; -, ...ien ⟨griech.⟩ (*Astron.* Konjunktion u. Opposition von Sonne u. Mond)
s. Z. = seinerzeit
Szcze|cin [ˈʃtʃɛtʃin] (poln. Hafenstadt an der Oder); *vgl.* Stettin
Sze|ged, *auch* **Sze|ge|din** [*beide* ˈsɛ...] (ung. Stadt); **Sze|ge|di|ner** (↑R 103); - Gulasch
Szek|ler [ˈsɛ...], der; -s, - (Angehöriger eines ung. Volksstammes)
Sze|nar, das; -s, -e ⟨lat.⟩ (*seltener für* Szenario, Szenarium); **Sze|na|rio,** das; -s, -s ⟨ital.⟩ ([in Szenen gegliederter] Entwurf eines Films; *auch für* Szenarium); **Sze|na|ri|um,** das; -s, ...ien [...iən]

‹lat.› (Übersicht über Szenenfolge, szenische Ausstattung u. a. eines Theaterstücks); **Sze|ne,** die; -, -n ‹franz.› (Schauplatz; Auftritt als Unterabteilung des Aktes; Vorgang, Anblick; Zank, Vorhaltungen; charakteristischer Bereich für bestimmte Aktivitäten); **Sze|ne|gän|ger; Sze|ne|jar|gon; Sze|nen‿ap|plaus, ...fol|ge, ...wech|sel; Sze|ne|rie,** die; -, ...ien (Bühnen-, Landschaftsbild); **sze|nisch** (bühnenmäßig)

Szep|ter (*veraltend, noch österr. für* Zepter)

szi|en|ti|fisch [stsiɛn...] ‹lat.› (*fachspr. für* wissenschaftlich); **Szi|en|tis|mus,** der; - (die auf Wissen u. Wissenschaft gegründete Haltung; Lehre der Szientisten); **Szi|en|tist,** der; -en, -en; ↑R 126 (Angehöriger einer christl. Sekte); **szi|en|tis|tisch**

Szil|la *vgl.* Scilla

Szin|ti|gramm, das; -s, -e; *Med.* (durch die Einwirkung der Strahlung radioaktiver Stoffe auf eine fluoreszierende Schicht erzeugtes Leuchtbild)

Szin|til|la|ti|on, die; -, -en ‹lat.› (*Astron.* Funkeln [von Sternen]; *Physik* Lichtblitze beim Auftreffen radioaktiver Strahlung auf fluoreszierende Stoffe); **szin|til|lie|ren** (funkeln, flimmern)

SZR = Sonderziehungsrecht

Szyl|la, die; - ‹griech.› (*eindeutschend für lat.* Scylla, *griech.* Skylla; bei Homer Seeungeheuer in einem Felsenriff in der Straße von Messina); zwischen - und Charybdis (in einer ausweglosen Lage)

Szy|ma|nows|ki [ʃima'nɔfski], Ka|rol (poln. Komponist)

Szy|the usw. *vgl.* Skythe usw.

T

T (Buchstabe); das T; des T, die T, *aber* das t in Rate (↑R 60); der Buchstabe T, t

t = Tonne

T, τ = [3]Tau

Θ, ϑ = Theta

T = Tera...; Tesla; *chem. Zeichen für* Tritium

T. = Titus

Ta = *chem. Zeichen für* Tantal

Tab [*engl.* tɛb], der; -[e]s, -e, *bei engl. Ausspr.* der; -s, -s (vorspringender Teil einer Karteikarte zur Kenntlichmachung bestimmter Merkmale)

Ta|bak [*auch* 'ta:... *u., bes. österr.,* ta'bak], der; -s, *Plur. (Sorten:)* -e ‹span.›; **Ta|bak‿bau** (der; -[e]s), **...blatt, ...brü|he, ...in|dust|rie, ...mo|no|pol, ...pflan|ze, ...pflan|zer, ...pflan|zung, ...plan|ta|ge, ...rau|cher; Ta|baks‿beu|tel, ...do|se, ...pfei|fe; Ta|bak‿steu|er** (die), **...strauch; Ta|bak‿tra|fik** (*österr. für* Laden für Tabakwaren, Briefmarken, Zeitungen u. Ä.), **...tra|fi|kant** (*österr. für* Besitzer einer Tabaktrafik); **Ta|bak|wa|ren** *Plur.*

Ta|bas|co ® [...ko], der; -s ‹span.› (eine scharfe Würzsoße); **Ta|bas|co|so|ße**

Ta|ba|ti|e|re, die; -, -n ‹franz.› (*früher für* Schnupftabaksdose; *österr. auch noch für* Zigaretten-, Tabaksdose)

ta|bel|la|risch ‹lat.› (in der Anordnung einer Tabelle; übersichtlich); **ta|bel|la|ri|sie|ren** (übersichtlich in Tabellen [an]ordnen); **Ta|bel|la|ri|sie|rung; Ta|bel|le,** die; -, -n (listenförmige Zusammenstellung, Übersicht); **Ta|bel|len‿en|de, ...ers|te, ...form; ta|bel|len|för|mig; Ta|bel|len‿füh|rer, ...füh|rung, ...letz|te, ...platz, ...spit|ze, ...stand** (der; -[e]s; *Sportspr.*); **ta|bel|lie|ren** (auf maschinellem Wege in Tabellenform darstellen); **Ta|bel|lie|rer; Ta|bel|lier|ma|schi|ne** (*EDV* Lochkartenmaschine, die Tabellen ausdruckt)

Ta|ber|na|kel, das, *auch, bes. in der kath. Kirche,* der; -s, - ‹lat.› (*kath. Kirche* Aufbewahrungsort der Eucharistie [auf dem Altar]; Ziergehäuse in der gotischen Baukunst)

Ta|bes, die; - ‹lat.› (*Med.* Rückenmarksschwindsucht); **Ta|bi|ker** (Tabeskranker); **ta|bisch**

Tab|lar (↑R 130), das; -s, -e ‹franz.› (*schweiz. für* Gestellbrett); **Tab|leau** [ta'blo:], das; -s, -s (wirkungsvoll gruppiertes Bild, bes. im Schauspiel; *veraltet für* Gemälde; *österr. auch für* Übersicht, Tabelle); **Tab|le d'hôte** [ta:blə 'do:t], die; - - (*veraltet für* [gemeinschaftliche] Gasthaustafel); **Tab|lett,** das; -[e]s, *Plur.* -s, *auch* -e (Servierbrett)

Tab|let|te (↑R 130), die; -, -n (als kleines, flaches Stück gepresstes Arzneimittel); **tab|let|ten|ab|hän|gig; Tab|let|ten‿ab|hän|gi|ge** (der *u.* die; -n, -n; ↑R 5 ff.), **...ab|hän|gig|keit** (die; -), **...form** (die; -; in -), **...miss|brauch** (der; -[e]s), **...röhr|chen, ...sucht** (die; -); **tab|let|ten|süch|tig; Tab|let|ten|süch|ti|ge,** der *u.* die; -n, -n (↑R 5 ff.); **tab|let|tie|ren** (in Tablettenform bringen)

Tab|li|num (↑R 130), das; -s, ...na ‹lat.› (getäfelter Hauptraum des altröm. Hauses)

[1]Ta|bor, der; -[s] (Berg in Israel)

[2]Ta|bor (tschech. Stadt); **Ta|bo|rit,** der; -en, -en (↑R 126) ‹nach der Stadt Tabor› (*früher* radikaler Hussit)

Täb|ris (↑R 130), der; -, - ‹nach der iran. Stadt› (ein Perserteppich)

ta|bu ‹polynes., „verboten"› (unverletzlich, unantastbar); *nur prädikativ:* das ist tabu; **Ta|bu,** das; -s, -s (*Völkerk.* Gebot bei [Natur]völkern, bes. geheiligte Personen, Tiere, Pflanzen, Gegenstände zu meiden; *allgem. für* etwas, wovon man nicht sprechen darf); es ist für ihn ein Tabu; **ta|bu|ie|ren** *u.* ta|bu|i|sie|ren (für tabu erklären, als ein Tabu behandeln); **Ta|bu|ie|rung** *u.* Ta|bu|i|sie|rung; **ta|bu|i|sie|ren** usw. *vgl.* tabuieren usw.

Ta|bu|la ra|sa, die; - - ‹lat., „abgeschabte Tafel"› (*meist übertr. für* unbeschriebenes Blatt); Tabula rasa machen (reinen Tisch machen, rücksichtslos Ordnung schaffen); **Ta|bu|la|tor,** der; -s, ...oren (Spaltensteller an der Schreibmaschine)

Ta|bu|rett, das; -[e]s, -e ‹arab.-franz.› (*schweiz., sonst veraltet für* Hocker, Stuhl ohne Lehne)

Ta|bu‿schran|ke, ...schwel|le, ...the|ma, ...wort (*Plur.* ...wörter), **...zo|ne**

Ta|che|les ‹hebr.-jidd.›; *nur in* - reden (*ugs. für* offen miteinander reden, jmdm. seine Meinung sagen)

ta|chi|nie|ren (*österr. ugs. für* faulenzen); **Ta|chi|nie|rer** (*österr. ugs. für* Faulenzer)

Ta|chis|mus [ta'ʃis...], der; - ‹nlat.› (Richtung der abstrakten Malerei, die Empfindungen durch spontanes Auftragen von Farbflecken auszudrücken sucht)

Ta|cho, der; -s, -s (*ugs. kurz für* Tachometer); **Ta|cho|graph,** Ta|chy|graph, der; -en, -en (↑R 126) ‹griech.› (selbst schreibender Tachometer); **Ta|cho|me|ter,** der, *auch* das; -s, - ([Fahr]geschwindigkeitsmesser; Drehzahlmesser); **Ta|chy|graph** *vgl.* Tachograph; **Ta|chy|gra|phie**, die; -, ...ien (aus Zeichen für Silben bestehendes Kurzschriftsystem des Altertums); **ta|chy|gra|phisch**; **Ta|chy|kar|die**, die; -, ...ien (*Med.* beschleunigter Herzschlag); **Ta|chy|me|ter**, das; -s, - (*Geodäsie* Schnellmesser für Geländeaufnahmen); **Ta|chy|on**, das; -s, ...onen *meist Plur.* (*Kernphysik* hypothet. Elementarteilchen, das Überlichtgeschwindigkeit besitzen soll)

ta|ci|te|isch [tatsi...]; die taciteischen Schriften (↑R 94); **Ta|ci|tus** (altröm. Geschichtsschreiber)

Ta|cker, der; -s, - ‹engl.› (Handwerkszeug zum Einschlagen u-förmiger Klammern)

Tack|ling ['tɛk...], das; -s, -s ‹engl., *eigtl.* Slidingtackling ['slaidiŋ...]› (*Fußball* Verteidigungstechnik, bei der der Verteidigende in die Füße des Gegners hineinrutscht)

Täcks, Täks, der; -es, -e ‹engl.› (kleiner keilförmiger Stahlnagel zur Verbindung von Oberleder und Brandsohle beim Schuh)

Tad|dä|us *vgl.* Thaddäus

Ta|del, der; -s, -; **Ta|de|lei**; **ta|del|frei**; **ta|del|haft**; **ta|del|los**; **ta|deln**; ich ...[e]le (↑R 16); **ta|delns‿wert**, **...wür|dig**; **Ta|del|sucht**, die; -; **ta|del|süch|tig**; **Tad|ler**; **Tad|le|rin**

Tad|schi|ke [...'dʒi:kə] (↑R 130), der; -n, -n; ↑R 126 (Angehöriger eines iran. Volkes in Mittelasien); **tad|schi|kisch**; **Tad|schi|kis|tan** (Staat im Südosten Mittelasiens)

Tadsch Ma|hal, der; - -[s] (Mausoleum in Agra in Indien)

Taek|won|do [tɛ...] (↑R 132), das; - ‹korean.› (korean. Abart des Karate)

Tael [tɛ:l, *auch* te:l], das; -s, -s (früheres chin. Gewicht); 5 - (↑R 90)

Taf. = Tafel; **Ta|fel**, die; -, -n; *Abk.* Taf.; **ta|fel|ar|tig**; **Ta|fel‿auf|satz**, **...berg**, **...be|steck**, **...bild**; **Tä|fel|chen**; **Ta|fel|en|te**; **ta|fel‿fer|tig**, **...för|mig**; **Ta|fel‿freu|den** *(Plur.)*, **...ge|bir|ge**, **...ge|schirr**, **...glas** (*Plur.* ...gläser), **...leuch|ter**, **...ma|le|rei**, **...mu|sik**; **ta|feln** (*geh. für* speisen); ich ...[e]le (↑R 16); **tä|feln** (mit Steinplatten, Holztafeln verkleiden); ich ...[e]le (↑R 16); **Ta|fel‿obst**, **...öl**, **...run|de**, **...sche|re** *(Technik)*, **...spitz** (*österr.* äußerstes Ende vom Rinderschwanzstück), **...tuch** (*Plur.* ...tücher); **Tä|fe|lung**; **Ta|fel‿waa|ge**, **...was|ser** (*Plur.* ...wässer), **...wein**, **...werk**; **Tä|fer**, das; -s, - (*schweiz. für* Täfelung); **tä|fern** (*schweiz. für* täfeln); ich ...ere (↑R 16); **Tä|fe|rung** (*schweiz. für* Täfelung); **Täf|lung** (*seltener für* Täfelung)

Taft, der; -[e]s, -e ‹pers.› ([Kunst]seidengewebe in Leinwandbindung); **taf|ten** (aus Taft); **Taft|kleid**

Tag, der; -[e]s, -e. *Großschreibung:* am, bei Tage; heute über acht Tage, in acht Tagen, vor vierzehn Tagen; von Tag zu Tag; Tag für Tag; des Tags; eines [schönen] Tag[e]s; nächsten Tag[e]s, nächster Tage; im Laufe des heutigen Tag[e]s; unter Tags, *österr.* untertags (den Tag über); vor Tag[e], vor Tags; den ganzen Tag; Guten, *auch* guten Tag sagen; Tag und Nacht. *Kleinschreibung:* (↑R 46): tags; tags darauf, tags zuvor; tagsüber; tagaus, tagein; tagtäglich; heutigentags *(vgl. d.)*; heutzutage; tagelang *(vgl. d.)*. *In Fügungen:* über Tag, unter Tage *(Bergmannsspr.)*; zutage, *auch* zu Tage bringen, fördern, kommen, treten; **Tag...** (*südd., österr. u. schweiz. in Zusammensetzungen für* Tage..., z. B. Tagbau, Tagblatt, Tagdieb, Taglohn u. a.); **tag|aus**, **tag|ein**; **Tag|dienst** (*Ggs.* Nachtdienst); **Ta|ge‿ar|beit** (*früher für* Arbeit des Tagelöhners), **...bau** (*Plur.* ...baue; *vgl.* Tag...), **...blatt** (*vgl.* Tag...), **...buch**; **Ta|ge|buch‿auf|zeich|nung**, **...no|tiz**, **...num|mer** (*Abk.* Tgb.-Nr.); **Ta|ge‿dieb** (Nichtstuer, Müßiggänger; *vgl.* Tag...), **...geld**; **ta|ge|lang**, *aber* ganze, mehrere, zwei Tage lang; **Ta|ge‿lied** *(Literaturw.)*, **...lohn** (*vgl.* Tag...), **...löh|ner** (*vgl.* Tag...); **ta|ge|löh|nern** (*vgl.* Tag...); ich ...ere (↑R 16); **Ta|ge|marsch** *vgl.* Tagesmarsch; **ta|gen**; **Ta|ge|rei|se**; **Ta|ges‿ab|lauf**, **...an|bruch**, **...ar|beit** (Arbeit eines Tages), **...aus|flug**, **...be|darf**, **...be|fehl** *(Milit.)*, **...de|cke**, **...dienst** (Dienst an einem bestimmten Tag), **...ein|nah|me**, **...er|eig|nis**, **...form**, **...ge|sche|hen**, **...ge|spräch**; **ta|ges|hell** (*seltener für* taghell); **Ta|ges‿kar|te**, **...kas|se**, **...kurs**, **...lauf**, **...leis|tung**, **...licht** (das; -[e]s); **Ta|ges|licht|pro|jek|tor** (*für* Overheadprojektor); **Ta|ges‿lo|sung**, **...marsch** (der), **...mut|ter** (*Plur.* ...mütter), **...ord|nung**, **...po|li|tik** (die; -), **...pres|se** (die; -), **...ra|ti|on**, **...raum**, **...satz**, **...sieg**, **...sie|ger**, **...stät|te**, **...sup|pe**, **...wan|de|rung**, **...zeit**, **...zei|tung**, **...zug** (*Ggs.* Nachtzug)

Ta|ge|tes, die; -, - ‹lat.› (Studenten- od. Samtblume)

ta|ge|wei|se; **Ta|ge|werk** (altes Feldmaß; *nur Sing.*: *geh. für* tägliche Arbeit, Aufgabe; Arbeit eines Tages); **Tag‿fahrt** (*Bergmannsspr.* Ausfahrt aus dem Schacht), **...fal|ter**, **...ge|bäu|de** (*Bergmannsspr.* Schachtgebäude); **tag|hell**; **...tä|gig** (z. B. sechstägig, *mit Ziffern* 6-tägig [sechs Tage alt, dauernd]; ↑R 44)

Tag|li|a|tel|le [talja...] (↑R 130) *Plur.* ‹ital.› (dünne ital. Bandnudeln)

täg|lich (alle Tage); -es Brot; -e Zinsen; -er Bedarf; **...täg|lich** (z. B. sechstäglich, *mit Ziffer* 6-täglich [alle sechs Tage wiederkehrend]; ↑R 44); **Tag|lohn** *vgl.* Tag...

Ta|go|re [ta'go:r(ə)], Ra|bind|ra|nath (↑R 130; ind. Dichter u. Philosoph)

Tag‿por|ti|er (*Ggs.* Nachtportier), **...raum** (*österr. für* Tagesraum); **tags**; tags darauf, tags zuvor; *vgl.* Tag; **Tag‿sat|zung** (*österr. für* behördlich bestimmter Termin; *schweiz. [früher] für* Tagung der Ständevertreter), **...schicht** (*Ggs.* Nachtschicht), **...sei|te**; **tags|über** (↑R 132); **tag|täg|lich**; **Tag‿traum**, **...träu|mer**, **...träu|me|rin**; **Tag|und|nacht|glei|che**, die; -, -n; Frühjahrs-Tagundnachtgleiche; **Ta|gung**; **Ta|gungs‿bü|ro**, **...ge|bäu|de**, **...map|pe**, **...ort** (*Plur.* ...orte), **...teil|neh|mer**, **...teil|neh|me|rin**; **Tag|wa|che**, *schweiz. auch* **Tag|wacht** (*österr., schweiz. für* Weckruf der Soldaten); **Tag|werk** (*bes. südd., österr. für* Tagewerk)

Ta|hi|ti (die größte der Gesellschaftsinseln)

Tai *vgl.* Thai

Tai|fun, der; -s, -e ‹chin.› (trop. Wirbelsturm in Südostasien)

Tai|ga, die; - ‹russ.› (sibirischer Waldgürtel)

Tail|le ['taljə, *österr.* 'tailjə], die; -, -n ‹franz.› (schmalste Stelle des Rumpfes; Gürtelweite; *veraltet für* Mieder; *Kartenspiel* Aufdecken der Blätter für Gewinn oder Verlust); **tail|len|be|tont**; ein -es Kleid; **Tail|len|wei|te**; [1]**Tail|leur** [ta'jø:r], der; -s, -s (*veraltet für* Schneider); [2]**Tail|leur**, das; -s, -s (*bes. schweiz. für* Schneiderkostüm); **tail|lie|ren** [ta(l)'ji:...]; **tail|liert**; **...tail|lig** [...taljiç] (z. B.

kurztaillig); **Tai|lor|made** ['te:-lə(r)me:d], das; -, -s ⟨engl.⟩ (im konventionellen Stil geschneidertes Kostüm)
Taine [tɛ:n] (franz. Geschichtsschreiber)
Tai|peh [*auch* ...'pe:] (Hptst. Taiwans)
Tai|wan [*auch* ...'va(:)n] (Inselstaat in Ostasien); **Tai|wa|ner; Tai-wa|ne|rin; tai|wa|nisch**
Ta|jo [*span.* 'taxo], der; -[s] (span.-port. Fluss); *vgl.* Tejo
Take [te:k], der *od.* das; -s, -s ⟨engl.⟩ (*Film, Fernsehen* einzelne Szenenaufnahme, Szenenabschnitt)
Ta|kel, das; -s, - (*Seemannsspr.* schwere Talje; Takelage); **Ta|ke-la|ge** [...'la:ʒə, *österr.* ...'la:ʒ], die; -, -n [...'la:ʒ(ə)n] ⟨mit franz. Endung⟩ (Segelausrüstung eines Schiffes); **Ta|ke|ler,** Tak|ler (im Takelwerk Arbeitender); **ta|keln;** ich ...[e]le (↑R 16); **Ta|ke|lung,** Tak|lung; **Ta|kel|werk,** das; -[e]s
Take-off ['te:kɔf], das *od.* der; -s, -s ⟨engl.⟩ (Start eines Flugzeugs o. Ä.; Beginn [einer Show])
Tak|ler *vgl.* Takeler; **Tak|lung** *vgl.* Takelung
Täks *vgl.* Täcks
[1]Takt, der; -[e]s, -e ⟨lat.⟩ (*nur Sing.:* Zeit-, Tonmaß; Zeiteinheit in einem Musikstück; *Technik* einer von mehreren Arbeitsgängen im Motor, Hub; Arbeitsabschnitt in der Fließbandfertigung oder in der Automation); - halten; **[2]Takt,** der; -[e]s ⟨franz.⟩ (Feingefühl; Lebensart; Zurückhaltung); **tak|ten** (*Technik* in Arbeitstakten bearbeiten); **Takt|feh|ler; takt|fest; Takt|ge|fühl,** das; -[e]s; **[1]tak|tie-ren** (den [1]Takt angeben)
[2]tak|tie|ren ⟨*zu* Taktik⟩ (taktisch vorgehen); **Tak|tie|rer** (jmd., der [2]taktiert); **Tak|tik,** die; -, -en ⟨griech.⟩ (geschicktes Vorgehen, kluges Verhalten, planmäßige Ausnutzung einer Lage; *Milit.* Truppenführung); **Tak|ti|ker; tak|tisch**
takt|los; Takt|lo|sig|keit; Takt-maß, das; **takt|mä|ßig; Takt-‿mes|ser** (der), **...stock** (*Plur.* ...stöcke), **...stra|ße** (*Technik*), **...strich** (*Musik* Trennstrich zwischen den Takten); **takt|voll**
Tal, das; -[e]s, Täler; zu -[e] fahren; **tal|ab|wärts**
Ta|lar, der; -s, -e ⟨ital.⟩ (langes Amtskleid); **ta|lar|ar|tig**
tal|auf|wärts; tal|aus; Tal‿bo-den, ...brü|cke, Täl|chen; Tal-en|ge
Ta|lent, das; -[e]s, -e ⟨griech.⟩ (Begabung, Fähigkeit; jmd., der [auf einem bestimmten Gebiet] besonders begabt ist; altgriech. Gewichts- und Geldeinheit); **ta|len-tiert** (begabt); **Ta|len|tiert|heit,** die; -; **ta|lent|los; Ta|lent|lo|sig-keit,** die; -; **Ta|lent‿pro|be, ...schmie|de** (*ugs.*), **...su|che; ta-lent|voll**
Ta|ler, der; -s, - (ehem. Münze), *vgl.* Joachimstaler; **ta|ler|groß; Ta|ler|stück**
Tal|fahrt (Fahrt abwärts auf Flüssen, Bergbahnen o. Ä.)
Talg, der; -[e]s, *Plur.* (*Arten:*) -e ([Rinder-, Hammel]fett); **talg|ar-tig; Talg|drü|se; tal|gen; tal|gig; Talg|licht** *Plur.* ...lichter
Ta|li|on, die; -, -en ⟨lat.⟩ (Vergeltung [durch das gleiche Übel]); **Ta|li|ons|leh|re,** die; - (Rechtslehre von der Wiedervergeltung)
Ta|lis|man, der; -s, -e ⟨griech.⟩ (Gegenstand, dem Glück bringende Kraft zugeschrieben wird)
Tal|je, die; -, -n ⟨niederl.⟩ (*Seemannsspr.* Flaschenzug); **tal|jen** (aufwinden); er taljet, hat getaljet; **Tal|je|reep** (über die Talje laufendes starkes Tau)
[1]Talk, der; -[e]s ⟨arab.⟩ (ein Mineral)
[2]Talk [tɔ:k], der; -s, -s ⟨engl.⟩ (*ugs. für* Unterhaltung, Plauderei, [öffentl.] Gespräch); **tal|ken** ['tɔ:k(ə)n] (*ugs. für* sich unterhalten, eine Talkshow durchführen)
Talk|er|de, die; -
Talk|mas|ter ['tɔ:k...] ⟨*zu* [2]Talk⟩ (Moderator einer Talkshow); **Talk|mas|te|rin**
Talk|pu|der
Talkshow ['tɔ:kʃo:] (↑R 33), die; -, -s ⟨engl.⟩ (Unterhaltungssendung, in der bekannte Persönlichkeiten interviewt werden)
Tal|kum, das; -s ⟨arab.⟩ (feiner weißer [1]Talk als Streupulver); **tal-ku|mie|ren** (Talkum einstreuen)
Tal|ley|rand [talɛ'rã:] (franz. Staatsmann)
Tal|linn (Hptst. von Estland); *vgl.* Reval
tal|mi ⟨franz.⟩ (*österr. für* unecht); *vgl.* talmin; **Tal|mi,** das; -s (vergoldete [Kupfer-Zink-]Legierung; *übertr. für* Unechtes); **Tal-mi‿glanz, ...gold; tal|min** (*selten für* aus Talmi; unecht); *vgl.* talmi; **Tal|mi|wa|re**
Tal|mud, der; -[e]s, -e ⟨hebr., „Lehre"⟩ (Sammlung der Gesetze und religiösen Überlieferungen des nachbibl. Judentums); **tal-mu|disch; Tal|mu|dis|mus,** der; -; **Tal|mu|dist,** der; -en, -en; ↑R 126 (Talmudkenner)
Tal|mul|de
Ta|lon [ta'lɔ̃:, *österr.* ta'lo:n], der; -s, -s ⟨franz.⟩ (Kontrollabschnitt einer Eintrittskarte, Wertmarke o. Ä.; Spielkartenrest [beim Geben], Kartenstamm [bei Glücksspielen]; Kaufsteine [beim Dominospiel]; *Börse* Erneuerungsschein bei Wertpapieren; *Musik* Griffende [„Frosch"] des Bogens)
Tal|schaft (*schweiz. u. westösterr. für* Land und Leute eines Tales; *Geogr.* Gesamtheit eines Tales und seiner Nebentäler); **Tal‿schi** (*vgl.* Talski), **...sen|ke; Tal|ski,** Tal|schi (bei der Fahrt am Hang der untere Ski); **Tal‿soh|le, ...sper|re; Ta|lung** (*Geogr.*); **tal-wärts**
Ta|ma|ra (w. Vorn.)
Ta|ma|rin|de, die; -, -n ⟨arab.⟩ (eine trop. Pflanzengattung)
Ta|ma|ris|ke, die; -, -n ⟨vulgärlat.⟩ (ein Strauch mit kleinen Blättern u. rosafarbenen Blüten)
Tam|bour [...bur, *auch* ...'bu:r], der; -s, *Plur.* -e, *schweiz.* -en ['tambu:rən] ⟨pers.⟩ (*veraltend für* Trommler; *Archit.* Zwischenstück bei Kuppelgewölben; *Technik* Trommel, zylindrischer Behälter [an Maschinen]); **Tam|bour|ma-jor** (Leiter eines Spielmannszuges); **Tam|bur,** der; -s, -e (Stickrahmen; Stichfeld); **tam|bu|rie-ren** (mit Tamburierstichen sticken; Haare zwischen Tüll und Gaze einknoten [bei der Perückenherstellung]); **Tam|bu|rier-stich** (flächendeckender Zierstich); **Tam|bu|rin** [*auch* ...'ri:n], das; -s, -e (kleine Hand-, Schellentrommel; Stickrahmen)
Ta|mil, das; -[s] (Sprache der Tamilen); **Ta|mi|le,** der; -n, -n; ↑R 126 (Angehöriger eines vorderind. Volkes); **Ta|mi|lin; ta|mi-lisch;** -e Sprache
Tamp, der; -s, -e *u.* **Tam|pen,** der; -s, - (*Seemannsspr.* Tau-, Kettenende)
Tam|pon [*auch* ...'pɔ̃:, *österr.* 'po:n], der; -s, -s (*Med.* [Watte-, Mull]bausch; *Druckw.* Ballen, mit denen gestochene Platten für den Druck eingeschwärzt werden); **Tam|po|na|de** [...po'na:də], die; -, -n (*Med.* Aus-, Zustopfung); **Tam|po|na|ge** [...'na:ʒə], die; -, -n (*Technik* Abdichtung eines Bohrlochs); **tam|po|nie|ren** (*Med.* [mit Tampons] ausstopfen)
Tam|tam [*auch* 'tam...], das; -s, -s ⟨Hindi⟩ (chinesisches, mit einem Klöppel geschlagenes Becken; Gong; *nur Sing.: ugs. für* laute,

Aufmerksamkeit erregende Betriebsamkeit)
Ta|mu|le usw. *vgl.* Tamile usw.
tan = Tangens
Ta|nag|ra (↑R 130; altgriech. Stadt); **Ta|nag|ra|fi|gur** (↑R 105; Tonfigur aus Tanagra)
Ta|na|na|ri|vo [...vo] (früherer Name von Antananarivo)
Tand, der; -[e]s ‹lat.› (wertloses Zeug); **Tän|de|lei; Tän|de|ler** *vgl.* Tändler; **Tan|del|markt** (*österr. für* Tändelmarkt); **Tän|del|markt** (*landsch. für* Trödelmarkt); **tän|deln;** ich ...[e]le (↑R 16)
Tan|dem, das; -s, -s ‹lat.-engl.› (zweisitziges Fahrrad; Wagen mit zwei hintereinander gespannten Pferden; *Technik* zwei hintereinander geschaltete Antriebe); **Tan|dem|ach|se** *(Kfz-Technik)*
Tand|ler (*bayr. u. österr. ugs. für* Tänd[e]ler); **Tänd|ler** (Schäker; *landsch. für* Trödler)
Tang, der; -[e]s, -e ‹nord.› (Bezeichnung mehrerer größerer Arten der Braunalgen)
[1]**Tan|ga** ['taŋga], der; -s, -s ‹Tupi› (sehr knapper Bikini od. Slip)
[2]**Tan|ga** ['taŋga] (Stadt in Tanganjika); **Tan|gan|ji|ka** (↑R 132; Teilstaat von Tansania); **Tan|gan|ji|ka|see,** der; -s (↑R 105)
Tan|ga|slip
Tan|gens ['taŋgɛns], der; -, - ‹lat.› (*Math.* eine Winkelfunktion im Dreieck; *Zeichen* tan); **Tan|gens‿kur|ve, ...satz** (der; -es); **Tan|gen|te,** die; -, -n (Gerade, die eine gekrümmte Linie in einem Punkt berührt); **Tan|gen|ten|flä|che; tan|gen|ti|al** (eine gekrümmte Linie od. Fläche berührend)
Tan|ger (marokkan. Hafenstadt)
tan|gie|ren [...ŋg...] (berühren); die Sache tangiert mich nicht
Tan|go ['taŋgo], der; -s, -s ‹span.› (ein Tanz)
Tan|ja (w. Vorn.)
Tank, der; -s, *Plur.* -s, *seltener* -e ‹engl.›; **tan|ken; Tan|ker** (Tankschiff); **Tan|ker|flot|te; Tank‿fahr|zeug, ...fül|lung, ...in|halt, ...la|ger**
Tank|red (m. Vorn.)
Tank‿säu|le, ...schiff, ...schloss, ...stel|le, ...uhr, ...ver|schluss, ...wa|gen, ...wart, ...war|tin
Tann, der; -[e]s, -e (*geh. für* [Tannen]wald); im dunklen -; **Tann|ast** (*schweiz. neben* Tannenast)
Tan|nat, das; -[e]s, -e ‹franz.› (Gerbsäuresalz)
Tänn|chen; Tan|ne, die; -, -n; **tan|nen** (aus Tannenholz); **Tan|nen‿ast, ...baum, ...hä|her, ...harz** (das), **...holz, ...ho|nig, ...mei|se, ...na|del, ...reis** *(geh.),* **...rei|sig, ...wald, ...zap|fen, ...zweig**
Tann|häu|ser (ein Minnesänger)
Tan|nicht, Tän|nicht, das; -[e]s, -e (*veraltet für* Tannenwäldchen)
tan|nie|ren ‹franz.› (mit Tannin behandeln); **Tan|nin,** das; -s, -e (Gerbsäure); **Tan|nin|bei|ze**
Tänn|ling (junge Tanne); **Tann|zap|fen** (*landsch., bes. schweiz.* für Tannenzapfen)
Tan|sa|nia [*auch* ...'za:nia] (Staat in Afrika); **Tan|sa|ni|er; Tan|sa|ni|e|rin; tan|sa|nisch; Tan|sa|nit** [*auch* ...'nit], der; -s, -e (ein Edelstein)
Tan|se, die; -, -n (*schweiz. für* auf dem Rücken zu tragendes Gefäß für Milch, Wein, Trauben u. Ä.)
Tan|tal, das; -s ‹griech.› (chem. Element, Metall; *Zeichen* Ta); **Tan|ta|li|de,** der; -n, -n *meist Plur.;* ↑R 126 (Nachkomme des Tantalus); **Tan|ta|lus** (in der griech. Sage König in Phrygien); **Tan|ta|lus|qua|len** *Plur.* (↑R 95)
Tant|chen; Tan|te, die; -, -n; **Tan|te-Em|ma-La|den; tan|ten|haft** (betulich)
Tan|tes *vgl.* Dantes
Tan|ti|e|me [tã'tie:mə], die; -, -n (*Kaufmannsspr.* Gewinnanteil, Vergütung nach der Höhe des Geschäftsgewinnes)
Tant|ra (↑R 130), das; -[s] (Lehre einer religiösen Strömung in Indien)
Tanz, der; -es, Tänze; **Tanz‿abend** (↑R 132), **...bar** (die), **...bär, ...bein** (*in der Wendung* das - schwingen *[ugs.]*), **...boden** (*Plur.* ...böden), **...ca|fé; Tänz|chen; Tanz|die|le; tän|zeln;** ich ...[e]le (↑R 16); **tan|zen;** du tanzt; **Tän|zer; Tan|ze|rei; Tän|ze|rin; tän|ze|risch; Tanz‿flä|che, ...girl, ...grup|pe, ...ka|pel|le, ...kar|te** *(früher),* **...kunst, ...kurs** *od.* **...kur|sus, ...leh|rer, ...leh|re|rin, ...lied, ...lo|kal; tanz|lus|tig; Tanz‿mu|sik, ...or|ches|ter, ...part|ner, ...part|ne|rin, ...platz** *(veraltend),* **...saal, ...schritt, ...schu|le, ...schü|ler, ...schü|le|rin, ...sport, ...stun|de, ...tee, ...tur|nier, ...un|ter|richt, ...ver|an|stal|tung**
Tao ['ta:o, *auch* tau], das; - ‹chin., „der Weg"› (das All-Eine, das absolute, vollkommene Sein in der chin. Philosophie); **Ta|o|is|mus,** der; - (chin. Volksreligion)
Tape [te:p], das, *auch* der; -, -s ‹engl.› (Band, Tonband); **Tape|deck,** das; -s, -s (Tonbandgerät ohne Verstärker u. Lautsprecher)
Ta|per|greis *(ugs.);* **ta|pe|rig,** taprig (*nordd. für* unbeholfen, gebrechlich); **ta|pern** (*nordd. für* sich unbeholfen bewegen); ich ...ere (↑R 16)
Ta|pet, das ‹griech.›; *nur noch in* etwas aufs - (*ugs. für* zur Sprache) bringen; **Ta|pe|te,** die; -, -n; **Ta|pe|ten‿bahn, ...kleis|ter, ...leim, ...mus|ter, ...rol|le, ...tür, ...wech|sel** *(ugs.);* **Ta|pe|zier,** der; -s, -e ‹ital.› (*südd. für* Tapezierer); **Ta|pe|zier|ar|beit,** Ta|pe|zie|rer|ar|beit; **ta|pe|zie|ren; Ta|pe|zie|rer; Ta|pe|zier|tisch; Ta|pe|zier|werk|statt,** Ta|pe|zie|rer|werk|statt
Tap|fe, die; -, -n *u.* **Tap|fen,** der; -s, - *meist Plur.* (Fußspur)
tap|fer; Tap|fer|keit, die; -; **Tap|fer|keits|me|dail|le**
Ta|pi|o|ka, die; - ‹indian.› (gereinigte Stärke aus Maniokwurzeln); **Ta|pi|o|ka|stär|ke,** die; -
Ta|pir [*österr.* ta'pi:r], der; -s, -e ‹indian.› (südamerik. u. asiat. Tier mit dichtem Fell u. kurzem Rüssel)
Ta|pis|se|rie, die; -, ...ien ‹franz.› (teppichartige Stickerei; Handarbeitsgeschäft)
tapp!; tapp, tapp!
Tapp, das; -s (ein Kartenspiel)
tap|pen; tap|pig *(landsch.);* **täp|pisch; tapp|rig** (*Nebenform von* taperig); **tap|rig** *vgl.* taperig; **Taps,** der; -es, -e (*landsch. für* Schlag; *ugs. für* täppischer Bursche); Hans -; **tap|sen** (*ugs. für* plump auftreten); du tapst; **tap|sig** *(ugs.)*
Ta|ra, die; -, ...ren ‹arab.› (*Kaufmannsspr.* die Verpackung; deren Gewicht)
Ta|ran|tel, die; -, -n ‹ital.› (südeurop. Wolfsspinne); **Ta|ran|tel|la,** die; -, *Plur.* -s *u.* ...llen (südital. Volkstanz)
Tar|busch, der; -[e]s, -e ‹pers.› (*arab. Bez. für* Fes)
tar|dan|do ‹ital.› (*Musik* zögernd, langsam); **Tar|dan|do,** das; -s, *Plur.* -s *u.* ...di
Ta|ren (*Plur. von* Tara)
Ta|rent (ital. Stadt); **Ta|ren|ter, Ta|ren|ti|ner** (↑R 103); **ta|ren|ti|nisch**
Tar|gi, der; -[s], Tuareg (Angehöriger berberischer Volksstämme in der Sahara)
Tar|hon|ya [...ja], die; - ‹ung.› (eine ung. Mehlspeise)
ta|rie|ren ‹arab.› (Gewicht eines Gefäßes od. einer Verpackung

bestimmen od. ausgleichen); **Ta|rier|waa|ge**

Ta|rif, der; -s, -e ⟨arab.-franz.⟩ (planvoll geordnete Zusammenstellung von Güter- od. Leistungspreisen, auch von Steuern u. Gebühren; Preis-, Lohnstaffel; Gebührenordnung); **ta|ri|fa|risch** (*seltener für* tariflich); **Ta|rif‿ab|schluss, ...au|to|no|mie, ...be|reich, ...be|zirk, ...er|hö|hung, ...grup|pe, ...ho|heit; ta|ri|fie|ren** (die Höhe einer Leistung durch Tarif bestimmen; in einen Tarif aufnehmen); **Ta|ri|fie|rung; Ta|rif‿kom|mis|si|on, ...kon|flikt; ta|rif|lich; Ta|rif|lohn; ta|rif|los; ta|rif|mä|ßig; Ta|rif‿ord|nung, ...part|ner, ...po|li|tik; ta|rif|po|li|tisch; Ta|rif‿ren|te, ...run|de, ...satz, ...ver|hand|lung, ...ver|trag; ta|rif|ver|trag|lich**

Tar|la|tan, der; -s, -e ⟨franz.⟩ (feines Baumwoll- od. Zellwollgewebe)

Tarn‿an|strich, ...an|zug; tar|nen; sich -; **Tarn‿far|be, ...kap|pe; Tarn|kap|pen|bom|ber** (ein [mit Radar nicht erkennbares] amerik. Kampfflugzeug); **Tarn‿man|tel, ...na|me, ...netz; Tar|nung**

Ta|ro, der; -s, -s ⟨polynes.⟩ (eine trop. Knollenfrucht)

Ta|rock, das, *österr. nur so, od.* der; -s, -s ⟨ital.⟩ (ein Kartenspiel); **ta|ro|cken, ta|ro|ckie|ren** (Tarock spielen); **Ta|rock|spiel**

Ta|rot [ta'ro:], das *od.* der; -s, -s ⟨franz.-engl.⟩ (dem Tarock ähnliches Kartenspiel, das zu spekulativen Deutungen verwendet wird)

Tar|pan, der; -s, -e ⟨russ.⟩ (ein ausgestorbenes Wildpferd)

Tar|pe|ji|sche Fels, der; -n -en *od.* **Tar|pe|ji|sche Fel|sen,** der; -n -s (Richtstätte im alten Rom)

Tar|quin, Tar|qui|ni|us (in der röm. Sage Name zweier Könige); **Tar|qui|ni|er,** der; -s, - (Angehöriger eines etrusk.-röm. Geschlechtes)

[1]**Tar|ra|go|na** (span. Stadt); [2]**Tar|ra|go|na,** der; -s, -s (ein span. Wein); **Tar|ra|go|ne|se,** der; -n, -n; ↑R 126

Tar|ser; tar|sisch; [1]**Tar|sus** ⟨griech.⟩ (Stadt in Kleinasien)

[2]**Tar|sus,** der; -, ...sen ⟨griech.⟩ (*Med.* Fußwurzel; Lidknorpel; *Zool.* „Fuß" des Insektenbeines)

[1]**Tar|tan** [*engl.* 'tartən], der; -[s], -s ⟨engl.⟩ (Plaid in buntem Karomuster; karierter Umhang der Schotten)

[2]**Tar|tan** ®, der; -s ⟨Kunstwort⟩ (ein wetterfester Kunststoffbelag für Laufbahnen); **Tar|tan‿bahn, ...be|lag**

Tar|ta|ne, die; -, -n ⟨ital.⟩ (Fischerfahrzeug im Mittelmeer)

tar|ta|re|isch ⟨griech.⟩ (zur Unterwelt gehörend, unterweltlich); **Tar|ta|ros** *vgl.* [1]Tartarus; [1]**Tar|ta|rus,** der; - (Unterwelt in der griechischen Mythologie)

[2]**Tar|ta|rus,** der; - ⟨mlat.⟩ (Weinstein); **Tart|rat** (↑R 130), das; -[e]s, -e (Salz der Weinsäure)

Tart|sche, die; -, -n ⟨franz.⟩ (ein mittelalterlicher Schild)

Tar|tu (Stadt in Estland)

Tar|tüff, der; -s, -e ⟨nach einer Gestalt bei Molière⟩ (Heuchler)

Tar|zan (Dschungelheld in Büchern von E. R. Burroughs)

Täsch|chen; Ta|sche, die; -, -n; **Tä|schel|kraut,** das; -[e]s; **Ta|schen‿aus|ga|be, ...buch, ...dieb, ...fahr|plan, ...for|mat, ...geld, ...ka|len|der, ...kamm, ...krebs, ...lam|pe, ...mes|ser** (das), **...rech|ner, ...schirm, ...spie|gel, ...spie|ler, ...spie|le|rei; ta|schen|spie|lern;** ich ...ere (↑R 16); getaschenspielert; zu -; **Ta|schen|spie|ler|trick; Ta|schen‿tuch** (*Plur.* ...tücher), **...uhr, ...wör|ter|buch; Ta|scherl,** das; -s, -n (*bayr. u. österr. ugs. für* kleine Tasche, *auch* eine Süßspeise); **Tasch|ner** (*österr. u. südd. für* Täschner); **Täsch|ner** (Taschenmacher)

Tas|ma|ni|en (austral. Insel); **Tas|ma|ni|er; tas|ma|nisch**

TASS, die; - (Nachrichtenagentur der ehem. Sowjetunion)

Täss|chen; Tas|se, die; -, -n (*österr. auch für* Tablett); **Tas|sen|rand**

Tas|so (ital. Dichter)

Tas|ta|tur, die; -, -en ⟨ital.⟩; **tast|bar; Tas|te,** die; -, -n; **Tast|emp|fin|dung; tas|ten** (*Druckw. auch für* den Taster bedienen); **Tas|ten‿druck** (der; -[e]s), **...in|stru|ment, ...scho|ner, ...te|le|fon; Tas|ter** (ein Abtastgerät; *Zool. svw.* Palpe; *Druckw.* schreibmaschinenähnl. Teil der Setzmaschine; Setzer, der den Taster bedient); **Tast‿or|gan, ...sinn** (der; -[e]s)

Tat, die; -, -en; in der -

[1]**Ta|tar,** der; -en, -en; ↑R 126 (Angehöriger eines Mischvolkes im Wolgagebiet in Südrussland, in der Ukraine u. Westsibirien); [2]**Ta|tar,** das; -s, -[s] ⟨nach den Tataren⟩ (rohes, geschabtes Rindfleisch [mit Ei u. Gewürzen]); **Ta|tar|beef|steak; Ta|ta|rei,** die; - (die innerasiatische Heimat der Tataren); (↑R 102:) die Große, die Kleine -; **Ta|ta|ren|nach|richt** (*veraltend für* unwahrscheinliche Schreckensnachricht); **ta|ta|risch**

ta|tau|ie|ren ⟨tahit.⟩ (*Völkerk.* tätowieren)

Tat‿be|richt, ...be|stand; Tat|ein|heit, die; -; in - mit ... *(Rechtsspr.);* **Ta|ten‿drang** (der; -[e]s), **...durst** *(geh.);* **ta|ten‿durs|tig** *(geh.),* **...froh; ta|ten|los; Ta|ten|lo|sig|keit,** die; -; **Tä|ter; Tä|ter|be|schrei|bung; Tä|te|rin; Tä|ter|schaft,** die; -; **Tat|form,** Tä|tig|keits|form (*für* Aktiv); **Tat‿ge|sche|hen, ...her|gang**

Ta|ti|an (frühchristl. Schriftsteller)

tä|tig; tä|ti|gen *(Kaufmannsspr.)* ein Geschäft, einen Kauf - (*dafür besser:* abschließen); **Tä|tig|keit; Tä|tig|keits‿be|reich, ...be|richt, ...drang** (der; -[e]s), **...feld, ...form** (*vgl.* Tatform); **...wort** (*Plur.* ...wörter; *für* Verb); **Tä|ti|gung** *(Kaufmannsspr.)*

Tat|ja|na (w. Vorn.)

Tat|kraft, die; -; **tat|kräf|tig; tät|lich;** - werden; -er Angriff; **Tät|lich|keit** *meist Plur.;* **Tat‿mensch, ...mo|tiv, ...ort** (der; -[e]s, ...orte)

tä|to|wie|ren ⟨tahit.⟩ (Zeichnungen mit Farbstoffen in die Haut einritzen); **Tä|to|wie|rer; Tä|to|wie|rung** (Hautzeichnung)

Tat|ra (↑R 130), die; - (Gebirgskette der Karpaten); (↑R 102:) die Hohe, die Niedere -

Tat|sa|che; Tat|sa|chen‿be|richt, ...ent|schei|dung (*Sport* vom Schiedsrichter während des Spiels gefällte Entscheidung), **...ma|te|ri|al; tat|säch|lich** [*auch* ...'zεç...]; **Tat|säch|lich|keit** [*auch* ...'zεç...], die; -

Tätsch, der; -[e]s, -e (*südd. für* Brei; ein Backwerk)

Tat|sche, die; -, -n (*landsch. für* Hand; leichter Schlag, Berührung); **tät|scheln;** ich ...[e]le (↑R 16); **tat|schen** (*ugs. für* plump anfassen); du tatschst

Tatsch|kerl (*ostösterr. ugs. svw.* Tascherl [Süßspeise])

Tat|tedl *vgl.* Thaddädl

Tat|ter|greis *(ugs.);* **Tat|te|rich,** der; -[e]s (*ugs. für* [krankhaftes] Zittern); **tat|te|rig,** tatt|rig *(ugs.);* **tat|tern** (*ugs. für* zittern); ich ...ere (↑R 16)

Tat|ter|sall, der; -s, -s ⟨nach dem engl. Stallmeister⟩ (geschäftl. Unternehmen für Reitsport; Reitbahn, -halle)

Tat|too [tɛˈtu:], das; -[s], -s ‹engl.› (Zapfenstreich)
tatt|rig *vgl.* tatterig
ta|tü|ta|ta!; Ta|tü|ta|ta, das; -s, -s *(ugs.)*
Tat|ver|dacht; tat|ver|däch|tig; Tat‿ver|däch|ti|ge, ...waf|fe
Tätz|chen; Tat|ze, die; -, -n (Pfote, Fuß der Raubtiere; *ugs. für* plumpe Hand)
Tat|zeit
Tat|zel|wurm, der; -[e]s (sagenhaftes Kriechtier im Volksglauben einiger Alpengebiete)
Tat‿zeu|ge, ...zeu|gin
[1]**Tau,** der; -[e]s (Niederschlag)
[2]**Tau,** das; -[e]s, -e (starkes [Schiffs]seil)
[3]**Tau,** das; -[s], -s (griech. Buchstabe: *T, τ*)
taub; taube (leere) Nuss; taubes Gestein (*Bergmannsspr.* Gestein ohne Erzgehalt); **taub|blind** (↑R 27); **Taub|blin|de**
Täub|chen; [1]**Tau|be,** die; -, -n
[2]**Tau|be,** der *u.* die; -n, -n (↑R 5 ff.)
tau|ben|blau (blaugrau); **Tau|ben|ei**
tau|be|netzt ‹*zu* [1]Tau›
tau|ben|grau (blaugrau); **Tau|ben‿haus, ...ko|bel** (*südd., österr. für* Taubenschlag), **...nest, ...post, ...schlag, ...stö|ßer** (Wanderfalke), **...zucht, ...züch|ter;** [1]**Tau|ber, Täu|ber,** der; -s, - *u.* Tau|be|rich, Täu|be|rich, der; -s, -e
[2]**Tau|ber,** die; - (linker Nebenfluss des Mains); **Tau|ber|bi|schofs|heim** (Stadt an der [2]Tauber)
Tau|be|rich, Täu|be|rich *vgl.* [1]Tauber
Taub|heit, die; -
Täu|bin
Täub|ling (ein Pilz)
Taub|nes|sel (eine Pflanze); **taub|stumm** (↑R 27); **Taub|stum|me; Taub|stum|men‿leh|rer, ...leh|re|rin, ...spra|che, ...un|ter|richt; Taub|stumm|heit,** die; -
Tauch|boot (Unterseeboot); **tau|chen; Tau|chen,** das; -s; **Tauch|en|te; Tau|cher; Tau|cher‿an|zug, ...aus|rüs|tung, ...bril|le, ...glo|cke, ...helm** (*vgl.* [1]Helm); **Tau|che|rin; Tau|cher‿krank|heit** (*svw.* Caissonkrankheit), **...ku|gel; Tauch|fahrt; tauch|klar** (von U-Booten); **Tauch‿kurs, ...ma|nö|ver, ...sie|der, ...sport, ...sta|ti|on, ...tie|fe**
[1]**tau|en;** es taut
[2]**tau|en** (*nordd. für* mit einem Tau vorwärts ziehen; schleppen); **Tau|en|de**
[1]**Tau|ern,** der; -s, - (*Bez. für* Übergänge in den [2]Tauern); [2]**Tau|ern** *Plur.* (Gruppe der Ostalpen); (↑R 102:) die Hohen -, die Niederen -; **Tau|ern‿bahn** (die; -; ↑R 105), **...ex|press, ...tun|nel**
Tauf‿be|cken, ...be|kennt|nis, ...brun|nen, ...buch (*svw.* Taufregister); **Tau|fe,** die; -, -n; **tau|fen;** getauft *(vgl. d.);* **Täu|fer; Tauf‿for|mel, ...ge|lüb|de; Tauf|ge|sinn|te,** der *u.* die; -n, -n; ↑R 5 ff. (*svw.* Mennonit); **Tauf‿ka|pel|le, ...ker|ze, ...kleid; Täuf|ling; Tauf‿na|me, ...pa|te** (der *u.* die), **...pa|tin, ...re|gis|ter**
tau|frisch ‹*zu* [1]Tau›
Tauf‿schal|le, ...schein, ...stein
tau|gen; das taugt nichts; **Tau|ge|nichts,** der; *Gen.* - *u.* -es, *Plur.* -e; **taug|lich; Taug|lich|keit,** die; -
tau|ig (*geh. für* feucht von [1]Tau)
Tau|mel, der; -s; **tau|me|lig, taum|lig; Tau|mel|lolch** (eine Grasart); **tau|meln;** ich ...[e]le (↑R 16); **taum|lig** *vgl.* taumelig
tau|nass ‹*zu* [1]Tau›
Tau|nus, der; - (Teil des Rheinischen Schiefergebirges)
Tau|punkt, der; -[e]s
Tau|ri|en (früheres russ. Gouvernement); **Tau|ri|er; Tau|ris** (alter Name für die Krim)
Tau|rus, der; - (Gebirge in Kleinasien)
Tau|salz (*svw.* Streusalz)
Tausch, der; -[e]s, -e; **tau|schen;** du tauschst; **täu|schen;** du täuschst; täuschend ähnlich; **Täu|scher; Tau|sche|rei** *(ugs.);* **Tausch‿ge|schäft, ...han|del** (*vgl.* [1]Handel)
tau|schie|ren ‹arab.-franz.› (Edelmetalle in unedle Metalle einhämmern); **Tau|schie|rung**
Tausch|ob|jekt; Täu|schung; Täu|schungs‿ma|nö|ver, ...ver|such; Tausch‿ver|fah|ren, ...ver|trag; tausch|wei|se; Tausch‿wert, ...wirt|schaft (die; -)
tau|send (*als röm. Zahlzeichen* M); *zur Klein- oder Großschreibung vgl.* hundert; Land der tausend Seen (Finnland); tausend und abertausend, *auch* Tausend und Abertausend Sterne; tausende und abertausende, *auch* Tausende und Abertausende bunter Laternen; *vgl.* aber; [1]**Tau|send,** der (*veraltet für* Teufel); *nur noch in* ei der Tausend!, potztausend!; [2]**Tau|send,** die; -, -en (Zahl); *vgl.* [1]Acht; [3]**Tau|send,** das; -s, -e (Maßeinheit; *Abk.* Tsd.); das ist ein Tausend Zigarren (eine Kiste mit einem Tausend Zigarren); [fünf] von Tausend (*Abk.* v.T., p.m.; *Zeichen* ‰); *vgl.* tausend; **Tau|send|blatt,** das; -[e]s (eine Wasserpflanze); **tau|send|ein,** tau|send|und|ein *(vgl. d.);* **tau|send|eins,** tau|send|und|eins; **Tau|sen|der;** *vgl.* Achter; **tau|sen|der|lei; tau|send|fach; Tau|send|fa|che,** das; -n; *vgl.* Achtfache; **tau|send|fäl|tig; Tau|send‿fuß** *(veraltet),* **...fü|ßer, ...füß|ler; Tau|send|gul|den|kraut, Tau|send|gül|den|kraut,** das; -[e]s (eine Heilpflanze); **Tau|send|jahr|fei|er** (*mit Ziffern* 1 000-Jahr-Feier; ↑R 28); **tau|send|jäh|rig,** *aber* (↑R 108): das Tausendjährige Reich *(bibl.), jedoch klein, weil kein Name:* das tausendjährige Reich (*iron. Bez. für* die Zeit der nationalsoz. Herrschaft); *vgl.* achtjährig; **Tau|send|künst|ler; tau|send|mal;** *vgl.* achtmal *u.* hundertmal; **tau|send|ma|lig; Tau|send|mark|schein;** *vgl.* Hundertmarkschein; **tau|send|sa|cker|ment!** *(veraltet);* **Tau|send|sa|sa, Tau|send|sas|sa,** der; -s, -[s] (vielseitig begabter Mensch); **Tau|send|schön,** das; -s, -e *u.* **Tau|send|schön|chen** (eine Pflanze); **tau|send|sei|tig; tau|sends|te;** *vgl.* achte *u.* hundertste; **tau|sends|tel;** *vgl.* achtel; **Tau|sends|tel,** das, *schweiz. meist* der; -s, -; *vgl.* Achtel; **Tau|sends|tel|se|kun|de; tau|sends|tens; tau|send|und|ein,** tau|send|ein; *vgl.* hundert[und]ein; (↑R 109:) ein Märchen aus Tausendundeiner Nacht; **tau|send|und|eins** *vgl.* tausendeins
Tau|to|lo|gie, die; -, ...ien (Fügung, die einen Sachverhalt doppelt wiedergibt, z. B. „immer und ewig", „voll und ganz"; *auch svw.* Pleonasmus); **tau|to|lo|gisch; tau|to|mer** (der Tautomerie unterliegend); **Tau|to|me|rie,** die; -, ...ien (*Chemie* eine Art der chem. Isomerie)
Tau‿trop|fen, ...was|ser (*Plur.* ...wasser; *svw.* Schmelzwasser)
Tau|werk, das; -[e]s
Tau‿wet|ter (das; -s), **...wind**
Tau|zie|hen, das; -s (*übertr. auch für* Hin und Her)
Ta|ver|ne [...v...], die; -, -n ‹ital.› (italienisches Wirtshaus)
Ta|xa|me|ter, das *od.* der ‹lat.; griech.› (Fahrpreisanzeiger in Taxis; *veraltet für* Taxi); **Tax|amt; Ta|xa|ti|on,** die; -, -en ‹lat.› ([Ab]schätzung, Wertermittlung); **Ta|xa|tor,** der; -s, ...oren ([Ab]schätzer, Wertermittler); [1]**Ta|xe,** die; -, -n ([Wert]schät-

zung; [amtlich] festgesetzter Preis; Gebühr); ²**Ta|xe,** die; -, -n (*svw.* Taxi); **tax|frei** (gebührenfrei); **Ta|xi,** das, *schweiz. auch* der; -s, -s (Auto zur Personenbeförderung gegen Bezahlung); **Taxi|chauf|feur; ta|xie|ren** ([ab]schätzen, den Wert ermitteln); **Ta|xie|rung** *vgl.* Taxation; **Ta|xi-fah|rer, ...fah|re|rin, ...fahrt, ...stand; Tax|ler** (*österr. ugs. für* Taxifahrer)

Ta|xo|no|mie, die; - ‹griech.› (Einordnung in ein bestimmtes System); **ta|xo|no|misch**

Tax|preis (geschätzter Preis)

Ta|xus, der; -, - ‹lat.› (*Bot.* Eibe); **Ta|xus|he|cke**

Tax|wert (Schätzwert)

Tay|lor|sys|tem ['te:lə(r)...], das; -s ‹nach dem Amerikaner F. W. Taylor› (System der wissenschaftlichen Betriebsführung mit dem Ziel, einen möglichst wirtschaftlichen Betriebsablauf zu erzielen)

Ta|zet|te, die; -, -n ‹ital.› (eine Narzissenart)

Tb = *chem. Zeichen für* Terbium

Tb, Tbc = Tuberkulose

Tbc-krank, Tb-krank, Tbk-krank; ↑R 26 *u.* 60 (tuberkulosekrank); **Tbc-Kran|ke,** Tb-Kran|ke, Tbk-Kran|ke, der *u.* die; -n, -n (↑R 5 ff. *u.* R 26)

Tbi|lis|si (*georg. Form von* Tiflis)

Tbk = Tuberkulose

Tb-krank, Tbk-krank *vgl.* Tbc-krank usw.

T-Bone-Steak ['ti:bo:n...] ‹engl.› (Steak aus dem Rippenstück des Rinds)

Tc = *chem. Zeichen für* Technetium

TCS = Touring-Club der Schweiz

Te = *chem. Zeichen für* Tellur

Teach-in ['ti:tʃ'|in], das; -[s], -s ‹amerik.› (Protestdiskussion)

Teak [ti:k], das; -s ‹engl.› (*kurz für* Teakholz); **Teak|baum** (ein südostasiat. Baum mit wertvollem Holz); **tea|ken** ['ti:kən] (aus Teakholz); **Teak|holz**

Team [ti:m], das; -s, -s ‹engl.› (Arbeitsgruppe; *Sport* Mannschaft, *österr. auch für* Nationalmannschaft); **Team-ar|beit** (die; -), **...chef, ...geist** (der; -[e]s); **Team|work** ['ti:mwœ:(r)k], das; -s (Gemeinschaftsarbeit)

Tea|room ['ti:ru:m] (↑R 24), der; -s, -s ‹engl.› (Teestube [in Hotels]; *schweiz. für* Café, in dem kein Alkohol ausgeschenkt wird)

Tech|ne|ti|um, das; -s ‹griech.› (chem. Element; *Zeichen* Tc)

tech|ni|fi|zie|ren ‹griech.; lat.› (technisch gestalten); **Tech|ni|fi|zie|rung; Tech|nik,** die; -, -en ‹griech.› (Herstellungsverfahren, Arbeitsweise; Kunstfertigkeit; *österr. Kurzw. für* techn. Hochschule; *nur Sing.:* Gesamtheit der techn. Verfahren; techn. Ausrüstung); **Tech|ni|ker; Tech|ni|ke|rin; Tech|ni|kum,** das; -s, *Plur.* ...ka, *auch* ...ken (technische Fachschule); **tech|nisch** ‹griech.-franz.› (zur Technik gehörend, sie betreffend; kunstgerecht, fachgemäß); technische Atmosphäre (*vgl.* Atmosphäre); technischer Ausdruck (Fachwort); er ist technischer Zeichner; [eine] technische Hochschule, [eine] technische Universität, *aber* (↑R 108): die Technische Hochschule (*Abk.* TH) Darmstadt, die Technische Universität (*Abk.* TU) Berlin; Technisches Hilfswerk (Name einer Hilfsorganisation; *Abk.* THW); Technischer Überwachungs-Verein (*Abk.* TÜV); **tech|ni|sie|ren** (für technischen Betrieb einrichten); **Tech|ni|sie|rung; Tech|ni|zis|mus,** der; -, ...men (techn. Ausdrucksweise)

Tech|no ['tɛkno], das *od.* der; -[s] ‹engl.› (elektronische, von bes. schnellem Rhythmus bestimmte Tanzmusik)

Tech|no|krat, der; -en, -en; ↑R 126 ‹griech.› (Vertreter der Technokratie); **Tech|no|kra|tie,** die; - (vorherrschende Stellung der Technik in Wirtschaft u. Politik); **tech|no|kra|tisch; Tech|no|lo|ge,** der; -n, -n (↑R 126); **Tech|no|lo|gie,** die; -, ...ien (Gesamtheit der techn. Prozesse in einem Fertigungsbereich; techn. Verfahren; *nur Sing.:* Lehre von der Umwandlung von Rohstoffen in Fertigprodukte); **Tech|no|lo|gie|park** (Gelände, auf dem Firmen angesiedelt sind, die moderne Technologien entwickeln); **Tech|no|lo|gie|trans|fer** (Weitergabe technologischer Forschungsergebnisse); **tech|no|lo|gisch**

Tech|tel|mech|tel [*auch* 'tɛç...], das; -s, - (*ugs. für* Liebelei, Flirt)

Te|ckel, der; -s, - (*fachspr. für* Dackel)

TED [tɛd], der; -s ‹*Kurzwort aus* Teledialog› (Computer, der telefonische Stimmabgaben annimmt u. hochrechnet)

Ted|dy, der; -s, -s ‹engl.› (Stoffbär als Kinderspielzeug); **Ted|dy-bär** (der; -en, -en), **...fut|ter** (*vgl.* ²Futter), **...man|tel**

Te|de|um, das; -s, -s ‹lat., *aus* „Te Deum laudamus" = „Dich, Gott, loben wir!"› (*nur Sing.: kath. Kirche* Hymnus der lateinischen Liturgie; musikalisches Werk über diesen Hymnus)

Tee, der; -s, -s ‹chin.›; schwarzer, grüner, russischer Tee

TEE = Trans-Europ-Express

Tee-abend (↑R 132), **...bä|cke|rei** (*österr. für* Teegebäck), **...beu|tel, ...blatt** (*meist Plur.*), **...brett, ...but|ter** (*österr. für* Markenbutter); **Tee|ei** (↑R 136); **Tee|ern|te** (↑R 136); **Tee-ge|bäck, ...ge|sell|schaft, ...glas** (*Plur.* ...gläser), **...haus, ...kan|ne, ...kes|sel** (*auch* ein Ratespiel), **...kü|che, ...licht** (*Plur.* ...lichter *u.* ...lichte), **...löf|fel; tee|löf|fel|wei|se**

Teen [ti:n], der; -s, -s *meist Plur.* ‹amerik.› *u.* **Tee|na|ger** ['ti:ne:dʒə(r)] (↑R 132), der; -s, - (*ugs. für* Junge od. Mädchen im Alter zwischen 13 und 19 Jahren); **Tee|nie, Tee|ny** ['ti:ni], der; -s, -s ([jüngerer, bes. weibl.] Teen)

Teer, der; -[e]s, -e; **Teer-dach|pap|pe, ...de|cke; tee|ren;** - und federn (früher als Strafe); **Teer-far|be, ...farb|stoff, ...fass; teer|hal|tig; tee|rig; Teer|ja|cke** (*scherzh. für* Matrose)

Tee|ro|se (eine Rosensorte)

Teer-pap|pe, ...schwe|le|rei, ...sei|fe, ...stra|ße; Tee|rung

Tee-ser|vice (*vgl.* ¹Service), **...sieb, ...strauch, ...stu|be, ...tas|se, ...tisch, ...wa|gen, ...was|ser** (das; -s), **...wurst**

Te|fil|la, die; - ‹hebr.› (jüd. Gebet[buch]); **Te|fil|lin** *Plur.* (Gebetsriemen der Juden)

Tef|lon ®, das; -s ‹Kunstwort› (hitzefeste Kunststoffbeschichtung in Pfannen o. Ä.); **tef|lon|be|schich|tet; Tef|lon|pfan|ne**

¹**Te|gel,** der; -s (kalkreicher Ton)

²**Te|gel** (Stadtteil u. Flughafen von Berlin); -er Schloss, -er See

¹**Te|gern|see,** der; -s (See in Oberbayern); ²**Te|gern|see** (Stadt am gleichnamigen See); **Te|gern|se|er** [...ze:ər] (↑R 103)

Te|gu|ci|gal|pa [...si...] (Hptst. von Honduras)

Te|he|ran [*auch* ...'ra:n] (Hptst. von Iran)

Teich, der; -[e]s, -e (Gewässer); **Teich-huhn, ...molch, ...mu|schel**

Tei|cho|sko|pie (↑R 132), die; - ‹griech., „Mauerschau"› (Schilderung von Ereignissen durch einen Schauspieler, der diese außerhalb der Bühne zu sehen scheint)

Teich-pflan|ze, ...rohr; Teich|rohr|sän|ger (ein Vogel); **Teich-ro|se, ...schilf**

teig (*landsch. für* überreif, weich); **Teig,** der; -[e]s, -e; den - gehen lassen; **Teig|far|be; tei|gig; Teig‿mas|se, ...men|ge, ...räd|chen, ...schüs|sel, ...wa|ren** *(Plur.)*
Teil, der *od.* das; -[e]s, -e. *Großschreibung:* zum Teil (*Abk.* z. T.); ein großer Teil des Tages; jedes Teil (Stück) prüfen; das (*selten* der) bessere Teil; er hat sein Teil getan; ein gut Teil; sein[en] Teil dazu beitragen; ich für mein[en] Teil. *Kleinschreibung:* (↑R 46:) teils *(vgl. d.)*; einesteils, meinesteils, ander[e]nteils; großen-, größten-, meistenteils; (↑R 41:) zuteil werden; *vgl. auch* teilhaben, teilnehmen; **Teil‿ab|schnitt** (z. B. einer Autobahn), **...an|sicht, ...as|pekt; teil|au|to|ma|ti|siert; Teil|au|to|ma|ti|sie|rung; teil|bar; Teil|bar|keit,** die; -; **Teil‿be|reich** (der), **...be|trag; Teil|chen; Teil|chen‿be|schleu|ni|ger** *(Kernphysik)*, **...strah|lung** *(Physik)*; **tei|len;** geteilt; zehn geteilt durch fünf ist, macht, gibt (*nicht:* sind, machen, geben) zwei; sich -; **Tei|ler;** größter gemeinsamer Teiler (*Abk.* g. g. T., ggT); **Tei|ler|folg; tei|ler|fremd;** -e Zahlen *(Math.)*; **Tei|le|zu|rich|ter** (Anlernberuf); **Teil‿fab|ri|kat, ...ge|biet; Teil|ha|be,** die; -; **teil|ha|ben** (↑R 38); du hast teil (↑R 46), *aber* du hast keinen Teil; teilgehabt; teilzuhaben; **Teil|ha|ber; Teil|ha|be|rin; Teil|ha|ber|schaft,** die; -; **Teil|ha|ber|ver|si|che|rung; teil|haf|tig** [*auch* ...'haf...] *(geh.)*; einer Sache - sein, werden; **...tei|lig** (z. B. zehnteilig, *mit Ziffern* 10-teilig; ↑R 44); **teil|kas|ko|ver|si|chert; Teil|kas|ko|ver|si|che|rung; Teil‿kos|ten|rech|nung, ...leis|tung, ...men|ge** *(Math.)*; **teil|möb|liert; Teil|nah|me,** die; -; **Teil|nah|me|be|din|gung; teil|nah|me|be|rech|tigt; Teil|nah|me|be|rech|tig|te; teil|nahms|los; Teil|nahms|lo|sig|keit,** die; -; **teil|nahms|voll; teil|neh|men** (↑R 38); du nimmst teil (↑R 46); teilgenommen; teilzunehmen; **teil|neh|mend; Teil|neh|mer; Teil|neh|mer|feld; Teil|neh|me|rin; Teil|neh|mer‿lis|te, ...zahl; teils** (↑R 46); teils gut, teils schlecht; **...teils** (z. B. einesteils); *vgl.* Teil; **Teil|schuld; Teil|schuld|ver|schrei|bung** (*für* Partialobligation); **Teil‿stre|cke, ...strich, ...stück; Tei|lung; Tei|lungs|zei|chen** (*für* Trennungsstrich); **Teil|ver|hält|nis** *(Math.)*; **teil|wei|se; Teil|zah|lung; Teil|zah|lungs|kre|dit; Teil|zeit|ar|beit; Teil|zeit ar|bei|ten;** ich arbeite Teilzeit; weil sie Teilzeit arbeitet; du hast Teilzeit gearbeitet; Teilzeit zu arbeiten; Teilzeit arbeitende Frauen; in Teilzeit arbeiten; **Teil|zeit‿be|schäf|tig|te, ...be|schäf|ti|gung**
Te|in *auch* The|in, das; -s ⟨chin.-nlat.⟩ (Alkaloid in Teeblättern, Koffein)
Teint [tɛ̃:], der; -s, -s ⟨franz.⟩ (Gesichtsfarbe; Beschaffenheit der Gesichtshaut)
T-Ei|sen; ↑R 25 (von T-förmigem Querschnitt)
Teis|te, die; -, -n (ein Seevogel)
Te|ja[s] (letzter Ostgotenkönig)
Te|jo ['tɛʒu] (*port. Form von* Tajo)
Tek|to|nik, die; - ⟨griech.⟩ (*Geol.* Lehre vom Bau der Erdkruste); **tek|to|nisch**
Tek|tur, die; -, -en ⟨lat.⟩ (*Buchw.* Deckblatt, Korrekturstreifen)
Tel A|viv-Jaf|fa [tɛl a'vi:f...] (Stadt in Israel)
te|le... ⟨griech.⟩ (fern...); **Te|le...** (Fern...)
Te|le|ban|king [...bɛŋkiŋ], das; -s ⟨engl.⟩ (Abwicklung von Bankgeschäften über Telekommunikation)
Te|le|di|a|log *vgl.* TED
Te|le|fax, das; -, -[e] ⟨Kunstwort⟩ (Fernkopie; Fernkopierer; *nur Sing.:* Fernkopiersystem); **te|le|fa|xen** (fernkopieren); du telefaxt; **Te|le|fax|num|mer**
Te|le|fon, das; -s, -e ⟨griech.⟩; **Te|le|fon‿an|ruf, ...an|schluss, ...ap|pa|rat; Te|le|fo|nat,** das; -[e]s, -e (Ferngespräch, Anruf); **Te|le|fon‿buch, ...dienst, ...ge|bühr, ...ge|spräch, ...hö|rer; te|le|fo|nie|ren; te|le|fo|nisch; Te|le|fo|nist,** der; -en, -en; ↑R 126 (Angestellter im Fernsprechverkehr); **Te|le|fo|nis|tin; Te|le|fon‿ka|bel, ...kar|te, ...lei|tung, ...netz, ...num|mer, ...rech|nung, ...schnur, ...seel|sor|ge, ...sex, ...über|wa|chung** (↑R 132), **...ver|bin|dung, ...zel|le, ...zent|ra|le**
Te|le‿fo|to (*kurz für* Telefotografie), **...fo|to|gra|fie** (fotograf. Fernaufnahme)
te|le|gen ⟨griech.⟩ (für Fernsehaufnahmen geeignet)
Te|le|graf, der; -en, -en; ↑R 33 *u.* 126 ⟨griech., „Fernschreiber"⟩ (Apparat zur Übermittlung von Nachrichten durch vereinbarte Zeichen); **Te|le|gra|fen‿amt, ...bü|ro, ...draht, ...lei|tung, ...mast** (der), **...netz, ...stan|ge; Te|le|gra|fie,** die; - (elektrische Fernübertragung von Nachrichten mit vereinbarten Zeichen); **te|le|gra|fie|ren; te|le|gra|fisch;** -e Antwort; **Te|le|gra|fist,** der; -en, -en; ↑R 126 (Telegrafenbeamter); **Te|le|gra|fis|tin**
Te|le|gramm, das; -s, -e ⟨griech.⟩ (telegrafisch beförderte Nachricht); **Te|le|gramm‿ad|res|se, ...bo|te, ...for|mu|lar, ...ge|bühr, ...stil** (der; -[e]s; im -)
Te|le|graph usw. *vgl.* Telegraf usw.
Te|le|ka|me|ra
Te|le|ki|ne|se, die; - ⟨griech.⟩ (das Bewegtwerden von Gegenständen in der Parapsychologie)
Te|le|kol|leg (unterrichtende Sendereihe im Fernsehen)
Te|le|kom (*kurz für* Deutsche Telekom AG [Unternehmen auf dem Telekommunikationssektor]); **Te|le|kom|mu|ni|ka|ti|on** (Kommunikation mithilfe elektronischer Medien)
te|le|ko|pie|ren; Te|le|ko|pie|rer (Fernkopierer)
Te|le|krat, der; -en, -en; ↑R 126 ⟨griech.⟩ (Vertreter der Telekratie); **Te|le|kra|tie,** die; - (Vorherrschaft der elektronischen Medien); **te|le|kra|tisch**
Te|le|mach (Sohn des Odysseus)
Te|le|mann (dt. Komponist)
[1]Te|le|mark (norw. Verwaltungsgebiet); **[2]Te|le|mark,** der; -s, -s (früher üblicher Bremsschwung im Skilauf); **Te|le|mark‿auf|sprung** (beim Skispringen), **...schwung**
Te|le|me|ter, das; -s, - ⟨griech.⟩ (Entfernungsmesser); **Te|le|met|rie** (↑R 130), die; - (Entfernungsmessung); **te|le|met|risch**
Te|le|ob|jek|tiv (Linsenkombination für Fernaufnahmen)
Te|le|o|lo|gie, die; - ⟨griech.⟩ (Lehre vom Zweck u. von der Zweckmäßigkeit); **te|le|o|lo|gisch** (durch den Zweck bestimmt; aus der Zweckmäßigkeit der Welt; zweckhaft); -er Gottesbeweis
Te|le|path, der; -en, -en (↑R 126) ⟨griech.⟩ (für Telepathie Empfänglicher); **Te|le|pa|thie,** die; - (Fernfühlen ohne körperliche Vermittlung); **te|le|pa|thisch**
Te|le|phon usw. *frühere Schreibung für* Telefon usw.
Te|le|pho|to|gra|phie *vgl.* Telefotografie
Te|le|plas|ma (angeblich von Medien abgesonderter Stoff in der Parapsychologie)
Te|le|skop (↑R 132), das; -s, -e ⟨griech.⟩ (Fernrohr); **Te|le|skop‿an|ten|ne, ...au|ge; te|le|sko|pisch** (das Teleskop betreffend;

[nur] durch das Teleskop sichtbar); **Te|le|sko̱p|mast**, der (ein ausziehbarer Mast)
Te̱|le|spiel (elektron. Spiel, das auf dem Fernsehbildschirm abläuft)
Te|le|vi|si|o̱n [*engl.* 'tɛliviʒən], die; - ‹engl.› (Fernsehen; *Abk.* TV)
Te̱|lex, das, *schweiz.* der; -, -[e] ‹*Kurzw. aus engl.* teleprinter exchange› (Fernschreiben, Fernschreiber; *nur Sing.*: Fernschreibnetz); **te̱|le|xen** (als Fernschreiben übermitteln); du telext
Te̱ll (Schweizer Volksheld)
Te̱l|ler, der; -s, -; **Te̱l|ler‿brett**, **...ei|sen** (Fanggerät für Raubwild); **te̱l|ler|fer|tig; Te̱l|ler-fleisch** (eine Speise); **te̱l|ler|för|mig; Te̱l|ler‿ge|richt** (ein einfaches Gericht), **...mi|ne** *(Milit.)*, **...müt|ze; te̱l|lern** (in Rückenlage mit Handbewegungen schwimmen); ich ...ere (↑R 16); **Te̱l|ler‿rand**, **...tuch** (*Plur.* ...tücher), **...wä|scher**
Te̱lls|ka|pel|le, die; -
Tel|lu̱r, das; -s ‹lat.› (chem. Element, Halbmetall; *Zeichen* Te); **tel|lu|rig** *(Chemie);* -e Säure; **tel|lu̱|risch** (*Geol.* auf die Erde bezüglich, von ihr herrührend); -e Kräfte; **Tel|lu|ri̱t** [*auch* ...'rit], das; -s, -e (Salz der tellurigen Säure); **Tel|lu̱|ri|um**, das; -s, ...ien [...i̯ən] (*Astron.* Gerät zur Veranschaulichung der Bewegung der Erde um die Sonne)
Te|lo|pha̱|se, die; -, -n ‹griech.› (*Biol.* Endstadium der Kernteilung)
[1]Tel|tow ['tɛlto:] (Stadt bei Berlin); **[2]Te̱l|tow**, der; -s (Gebiet südl. von Berlin); **Te̱l|tow|er** [...to:ər] (↑R 103); Teltower Rübchen; **Te̱l|tow|ka|nal**, der; -s (↑R 105)
Te̱m|pel, der; -s, - ‹lat.›; **Te̱m|pel‿bau** (*Plur.* ...bauten), **...ge|sell|schaft** (die; -; eine Sekte), **...herr** (Templer), **...or|den** (der; -s; Templerorden), **...pros|ti|tu|ti|on**, **...rit|ter**
Te̱m|pe|ra‿far|be ‹ital.› (eine Deckfarbe), **...ma|le|rei**
Tem|pe|ra|me̱nt, das; -[e]s, -e ‹lat.› (Wesens-, Gemütsart; *nur Sing.*: lebhafte Wesensart, Schwung, Feuer); **tem|pe|ra|me̱nt|los; Tem|pe|ra|me̱nt|lo|sig|keit**, die; -; **Tem|pe|ra|me̱nts|aus|bruch; tem|pe|ra|me̱nt|voll**
Tem|pe|ra|tu̱r, die; -, -en ‹lat.› (Wärme[grad, -zustand]; [leichtes] Fieber); **tem|pe|ra|tu̱r|ab|hän|gig; Tem|pe|ra|tu̱r‿an|stieg**, **...aus|gleich**, **...er|hö|hung**, **...reg|ler**, **...rück|gang**, **...schwan|kung**, **...sturz**, **...un|ter|schied**, **...wech|sel; Tem|pe|re̱nz**, die; - (*selten für* Mäßigkeit, bes. im Alkoholgenuss); **Tem|pe|re̱nz|ler** (Mitglied des Temperenzvereins); **Tem|pe|re̱nz|ver|ein** (Verein der Gegner des Alkoholmissbrauchs); **Te̱m|per|guss**, der; -es ‹engl.; dt.› (schmiedbares Gusseisen); **tem|pe|ri̱e|r|bar; tem|pe|ri̱e|ren** ‹lat.› (die Temperatur regeln; *veraltend für* mäßigen); **Tem|pe|ri̱e|rung; Te̱m|per|koh|le**, die; - ‹engl.; dt.›; **te̱m|pern** ‹engl.› (*Hüttenw.* Eisenguss durch Glühverfahren schmiedbar machen); ich ...ere (↑R 16)
Tem|pest|boot ['tɛmpist...] ‹engl.; dt.› (ein Sportsegelboot); **tem|pes|to̱|so** ‹ital.› (*Musik* heftig, stürmisch)
Te̱m|pi pas|sa̱|ti *Plur.* ‹ital.› (vergangene Zeiten)
Templ|le̱i|se (↑R 130), der; -n, -n *meist Plur.;* (↑R 126) ‹franz.› (Gralsritter); **Te̱mp|ler** (Angehöriger des Templerordens; Mitglied der Tempelgesellschaft); **Te̱mp|ler|or|den**, der; -s (ein geistl. Ritterorden des Mittelalters)
Te̱m|po, das; -s, *Plur.* -s *u.* ...pi ‹ital.› (Zeit[maß], Takt; *nur Sing.*: Geschwindigkeit, Schnelligkeit); **Te̱m|po|li|mit** (allgemeine Geschwindigkeitsbegrenzung)
Te̱m|po|ra (*Plur. von* Tempus); **tem|po|ra̱l** ‹lat.› (*Sprachw.* zeitlich; *Med.* zu den Schläfen gehörend); -e Bestimmung *(Sprachw.);* **Tem|po|ra̱|li|en** [...i̯ən] *Plur.* (mit der Verwaltung eines kirchl. Amtes verbundene weltl. Rechte und Einkünfte der Geistlichen im MA.); **Tem|po|ra̱l|satz** (*Sprachw.* Umstandssatz der Zeit); **tem|po|rä̱r** ‹franz.› (zeitweilig, vorübergehend); **Te̱m|po‿sün|der**, **...ver|lust** (der; -[e]s); **Te̱m|pus**, das; -, ...pora ‹lat.› (*Sprachw.* Zeitform [des Verbs])
ten. = tenuto
Te|na̱|kel, das; -s, - ‹lat.› (*Druckw.* Gerät zum Halten des Manuskriptes beim Setzen, Blatthalter); **Te|na|zi|tä̱t**, die; - (*Chemie, Physik* Zähigkeit; Ziehbarkeit)
Ten|de̱nz, die; -, -en ‹lat.› (Streben nach einem bestimmten Ziel, Absicht; Neigung, Strömung; Zug, Richtung, Entwicklung[slinie]); **Ten|de̱nz‿be|trieb**, **...dich|tung; ten|den|zi|e̱ll** (der Tendenz nach, entwicklungsmäßig); **ten|den|zi|ö̱s** (etwas bezweckend, beabsichtigend; parteilich zurechtgemacht, gefärbt); **Ten|de̱nz‿stück**, **...wen|de**
Te̱n|der, der; -s, - ‹engl.› (Vorratswagen der Dampflokomotive [für Kohle u. Wasser]; *Seew.* Begleitschiff, Hilfsfahrzeug)
ten|di̱e|ren ‹lat.› ([zu etwas] hinneigen); *vgl. aber* tentieren
Te|ne|rif|fa (eine der Kanarischen Inseln)
Te|ni̱e|rs (niederländ. Malergeschlecht)
Te̱nn, das; -s, -e (*schweiz. Nebenform von* Tenne)
Tenn. = [2]Tennessee
Te̱n|ne, die; -, -n; **Te̱n|nen|raum**
[1]Ten|nes|see [...'si:, *auch* 'tɛ...], der; -[s] (l. Nebenfluss des Ohio); **[2]Ten|nes|see** (Staat in den USA; *Abk.* Tenn.)
Te̱n|nis, das; - ‹engl.› (ein Ballspiel); - spielen (↑R 39); **Te̱n|nis‿arm** (*svw.* Tennisellbogen), **...ball**, **...ell|bo|gen** (*Med.* Entzündung am Ellbogengelenk), **...match**, **...part|ner**, **...part|ne|rin**, **...platz**, **...schlä|ger**, **...schuh**, **...spiel**, **...spie|ler**, **...spie|le|rin**, **...tur|nier**, **...wand**, **...zir|kus** (Tenniswettkämpfe mit den dazugehörigen Veranstaltungen)
Te̱n|no, der; -s, -s ‹jap.› (jap. Kaisertitel); *vgl.* [1]Mikado
Ten|ny|son ['tɛnisən] (engl. Dichter)
[1]Te̱|nor, der; -s ‹lat.› (Haltung; Inhalt, Sinn, Wortlaut); **[2]Te|no̱r**, der; -s, ...nö̱re ‹ital.› (hohe Männerstimme; Tenorsänger); **Te|no̱r‿buf|fo**, **...horn** (*Plur.* ...hörner); **Te|no|ri̱st**, der; -en, -en; ↑R 126 (Tenorsänger); **Te|no̱r|schlüs|sel**
Ten|si̱d, das; -[e]s, -e *meist Plur.* ‹lat.› (aktiver Stoff in Waschmitteln u. Ä.); **Ten|si|o̱n**, die; -, -en (*Physik* Spannung der Gase und Dämpfe; Druck)
Ten|ta̱|kel, der *od.* das; -s, - *meist Plur.* ‹lat.› (Fanghaar Fleisch fressender Pflanzen; Fangarm); **Ten|ta|ku|li̱t** [*auch* ...'lit], der; -en, -en; ↑R 126 (eine fossile Flügelschnecke); **Ten|ta̱|men**, das; -s, ...mina (Vorprüfung [z. B. beim Medizinstudium]; *Med.* Versuch); **ten|ti̱e|ren** (*veraltet, aber noch landsch. für* prüfen; versuchen, unternehmen; *österr. ugs. für* beabsichtigen); *vgl. aber* tendieren
Te|nü *u.* **Te|nue** [tə'ny:], das; -s, -s ‹franz.› (*schweiz. für* vorgeschriebene Art, sich zu kleiden; Anzug)
Te̱|nu|is, die; -, ...ues [...nue:s] ‹lat.› (*Sprachw.* stimmloser Verschlusslaut, z. B. p)

te|nu|to ‹ital.› (*Musik* ausgehalten; *Abk.* ten.); ben - (gut gehalten)

Teo *vgl.* Theo; **Te|o|bald** *vgl.* Theobald; **Te|o|de|rich** *vgl.* Theoderich

Te|pi|da|ri|um, das; -s, ...ien [...i̯ən] ‹lat.› (temperierter Aufenthaltsraum im römischen Bad)

Tep|li|ce [ˈtɛplit͜sɛ] (Kurort in Böhmen); **Tep|litz** (*dt. Form von* Teplice)

Tepp *vgl.* Depp; **tep|pert** *vgl.* deppert

Tep|pich, der; -s, -e; **Tep|pich‿bo|den, ...bürs|te, ...flie|se, ...ge|schäft, ...händ|ler, ...kehr|ma|schi|ne, ...klop|fer, ...mus|ter, ...stan|ge**

Te|qui|la [teˈki:la], der; -[s] ‹span.› (ein mexik. Branntwein)

Ter (span. Fluss)

Te|ra... ‹griech.› (das Billionenfache einer Einheit, z. B. Terameter = 10^{12} Meter; *Zeichen* T)

te|ra|to|gen ‹griech.› (*Med.* Missbildungen bewirkend [bes. von Medikamenten]); **Te|ra|to|lo|ge,** der; -n, -n (↑R 126); **Te|ra|to|lo|gie,** die; - ‹griech.› (Lehre von den Missbildungen der Lebewesen); **Te|ra|to|lo|gin; te|ra|to|lo|gisch**

Ter|bi|um, das; -s ‹nach dem schwed. Ort Ytterby› (chem. Element, Metall; *Zeichen* Tb)

Te|re|bin|the, die; -, -n ‹griech.› (Terpentinbaum)

Te|renz (altröm. Lustspieldichter)

Term, der; -s, -e ‹lat.› (*Math.* Glied einer Formel, bes. einer Summe; *Physik* ein Zahlenwert von Frequenzen od. Wellenzahlen eines Atoms, Ions od. Moleküls; *Sprachw. svw.* Terminus); **Ter|me,** der; -n, -n (*veraltet für* Grenzstein); **Ter|min,** der; -s, -e (für eine Lieferung, Zahlung, Gerichtsverhandlung usw. festgesetzter Tag, Zeitpunkt); **ter|mi|nal** (*veraltet für* die Grenze, das Ende betreffend; *Math.* am Ende stehend); **Ter|mi|nal** [ˈtœ:(r)minəl], der, *auch, EDV nur,* das; -s, -s ‹engl.› (Abfertigungshalle für Fluggäste; Zielbahnhof für Containerzüge; *EDV* Datenendstation, Abfragestation); **Ter|min‿druck** (der; -[e]s), **...ein|la|ge** *(Bankw.);* **ter|min‿ge|mäß, ...ge|recht; Ter|min|ge|schäft** (*Kaufmannsspr.* Lieferungsgeschäft); **Ter|mi|ni** (*Plur. von* Terminus); **ter|mi|nie|ren** ‹lat.› (befristen; zeitlich festlegen); **Ter|mi|nie|rung; Ter|min|ka|len|der; ter|min|lich; Ter|min|not,** die; -; **Ter|mi|no|lo|ge,** der; -n, -n (↑R 126) ‹lat.; griech.›; **Ter|mi|no|lo|gie,** die; -, ...ien (Gesamtheit, Systematik eines Fachwortschatzes); **ter|mi|no|lo|gisch; Ter|mi|nus,** der; -, ...ni ‹lat.› (Fachwort, -ausdruck); **Ter|mi|nus tech|ni|cus,** der; - -, ...ni ...ci (Fachwort, -ausdruck)

Ter|mi|te, die; -, -n *meist Plur.* ‹lat.› (ein Insekt); **Ter|mi|ten‿hü|gel, ...staat** (*Plur.* ...staaten)

ter|när ‹lat.› (*Chemie* dreifach; Dreistoff...); -e Verbindung; **Ter|ne,** die; -, -n ‹ital.› (Reihe von drei gesetzten od. gewonnenen Nummern in der alten Zahlenlotterie); **Ter|no,** der; -s, -s (*österr. svw.* Terne)

Ter|pen, das; -s, -e ‹griech.› (Bestandteil ätherischer Öle); **ter|pen|frei; Ter|pen|tin,** das, *österr. meist* der; -s, -e (ein Harz); **Ter|pen|tin|öl**

Terp|si|cho|re [...çore] (↑R 132; Muse des Tanzes und des Chorgesanges)

Ter|ra di Si|e|na, die; - - - ‹ital.› (Sienaerde, eine braune Farbe)

Ter|rain [tɛˈrɛ̃:], das; -s, -s ‹franz.› (Gebiet; [Bau]gelände, Grundstück); **Ter|rain|be|schrei|bung**

Ter|ra in|co|gni|ta (↑R 130), die; - - ‹lat., „unbekanntes Land"› (unerforschtes Gebiet); **Ter|ra|kot|ta,** die; -, ...tten, *österr. nur so, u.* **Ter|ra|kot|te,** die; -, -n ‹ital.› (*nur Sing.:* gebrannter Ton; Gefäß od. Bildwerk daraus)

Ter|ra|ri|a|ner ‹lat.› (Terrarienliebhaber); **Ter|ra|ri|en|kun|de** [...i̯ən...], die; -; **Ter|ra|ris|tik,** die; - (Terrarienkunde); **Ter|ra|ri|um,** das; -s, ...ien [...i̯ən] (Behälter für die Haltung kleiner Lurche u. Ä.)

Ter|ras|se, die; -, -n ‹franz.›; **ter|ras|sen|ar|tig; Ter|ras|sen|dach; ter|ras|sen|för|mig; Ter|ras|sen‿gar|ten, ...haus; ter|ras|sie|ren** (terrassenförmig anlegen, erhöhen); **Ter|ras|sie|rung; Ter|raz|zo,** der; -[s], ...zzi ‹ital.› (mosaikartiger Fußbodenbelag); **Ter|raz|zo|fuß|bo|den**

ter|rest|risch (↑R 130) ‹lat.› (die Erde betreffend; Erd...); -es Beben (Erdbeben)

ter|ri|bel ‹lat.› (*veraltet für* schrecklich); ...ib|le (↑R 130) Zustände

Ter|ri|er [...i̯ər], der; -s, - ‹engl.› (kleiner bis mittelgroßer engl. Jagdhund)

ter|ri|gen ‹lat.; griech.› (*Biol.* vom Festland stammend)

Ter|ri|ne, die; -, -n ‹franz.› ([Suppen]schüssel)

ter|ri|to|ri|al ‹lat.› (zu einem Gebiet gehörend, ein Gebiet betreffend); **Ter|ri|to|ri|al‿ge|walt** (die; -), **...ge|wäs|ser, ...heer** *(Milit.),* **...ho|heit** (die; -); **Ter|ri|to|ri|a|li|tät,** die; - (Zugehörigkeit zu einem Staatsgebiet); **Ter|ri|to|ri|a|li|täts|prin|zip** (das; -s); **Ter|ri|to|ri|al‿kom|man|do** *(Milit.),* **...staat** (*Plur.* ...staaten), **...ver|tei|di|gung** *(Milit.);* **Ter|ri|to|ri|um,** das; -s, ...ien [...i̯ən] (Grund; Bezirk; [Staats-, Hoheits]gebiet)

Ter|ror, der; -s ‹lat.› (Gewaltherrschaft; rücksichtsloses Vorgehen); **Ter|ror‿akt, ...an|schlag, ...herr|schaft; ter|ro|ri|sie|ren** ‹franz.› (Terror ausüben; ständig belästigen, unter Druck setzen); **Ter|ro|ri|sie|rung; Ter|ro|ris|mus,** der; - (Ausübung von [polit. motivierten] Gewaltakten); **Ter|ro|rist,** der; -en, -en (↑R 126); **Ter|ro|ris|tin; ter|ro|ris|tisch; Ter|ror‿jus|tiz, ...kom|man|do, ...me|tho|de, ...or|ga|ni|sa|ti|on, ...wel|le**

[1]**Ter|tia,** die; -, ...ien [...i̯ən] ‹lat., „dritte"› (*veraltende Bez.* [Unter- u. Obertertia] *für* die 4. u. 5. [*in Österr.* 3.] Klasse eines Gymnasiums); [2]**Ter|tia,** die; - (*Druckw.* ein Schriftgrad); **Ter|ti|al,** das; -s, -e (*veraltet für* Jahresdrittel); **Ter|ti|a|na|fie|ber** (*Med.* Dreitagewechselfieber); **Ter|ti|a|ner** (Schüler der [1]Tertia); **Ter|ti|a|ne|rin; ter|ti|är** ‹franz.› (die dritte Stelle in einer Reihe einnehmend; das Tertiär betreffend); **Ter|ti|är,** das; -s (*Geol.* der ältere Teil der Erdneuzeit); **Ter|ti|är|for|ma|ti|on,** die; -; **Ter|ti|a|ri|er** *vgl.* Terziar; **Ter|ti|um Com|pa|ra|ti|o|nis,** das; - -, ...ia - ‹lat.› (Vergleichspunkt)

Ter|tul|li|an (röm. Kirchenschriftsteller)

Terz, die; -, -en ‹lat.› (ein Fechthieb; *Musik* dritter Ton der diaton. Tonleiter; Intervall im Abstand von 3 Stufen); **Ter|zel,** der; -s, - (*Jägerspr.* männl. Falke); **Ter|ze|rol,** das; -s, -e ‹ital.› (kleine Pistole); **Ter|zett,** das; -[e]s, -e (dreistimmiges Gesangstück; *auch für* Gruppe von drei Personen; dreizeilige Strophe des Sonetts); **Ter|zi|ar,** der; -s, -en ‹lat.› *u.* Ter|ti|a|ri|er [...i̯ər] (Angehöriger eines Dritten Ordens); **Ter|zi|ne,** die; -, -n *meist Plur.* ‹ital.› (Strophe von drei Versen)

Te|sa|film ® (ein Klebeband)

Te|sching, das; -s, *Plur.* -e *u.* -s (eine kleine Handfeuerwaffe)

Tes|la, das; -, - ‹nach dem amerik. Physiker› (Einheit der magnet. Induktion; *Zeichen* T); **Tes|la-**

strom (↑R 95), der; -[e]s (*Elektrotechnik* Hochfrequenzstrom sehr hoher Spannung)

[1]**Tes|sin,** der; -s (schweiz.-ital. Fluss); [2]**Tes|sin,** das; -s (schweiz. Kanton); **Tes|si|ner** (↑R 103); **tes|si|nisch**

Test, der; -[e]s, *Plur.* -s, *auch* -e ‹engl.› (Probe; Prüfung; psycholog. Experiment; Untersuchung)

Tes|ta|ment, das; -[e]s, -e ‹lat.› (letztwillige Verfügung; Bund Gottes mit den Menschen); ↑R 108: Altes - (*Abk.* A. T.), Neues - (*Abk.* N. T.); **tes|ta|men|ta|risch** (durch letztwillige Verfügung, letztwillig); testamentarische Verfügung; **Tes|ta|ments‿er|öff|nung, ...voll|stre|cker; Tes|tat,** das; -[e]s, -e (Zeugnis, Bescheinigung); **Tes|ta|tor,** der; -s, ...oren (Person, die ein Testament errichtet; Erblasser)

Tes|ta|zee, die; -, -n *meist Plur.* ‹lat.› (*Biol.* Schalen tragende Amöbe, Wurzelfüßer)

Test‿bild *(Fernsehen),* **...bo|gen; tes|ten** ‹*zu* Test›; **Tes|ter** (jmd., der testet); **Tes|te|rin; Test‿fah|rer, ...fahrt, ...fall** (der), **...flug, ...fra|ge, ...ge|län|de**

tes|tie|ren ‹lat.› (ein Testat geben, bescheinigen; *Rechtsw.* ein Testament errichten); **Tes|tie|rer** (*svw.* Testator); **Tes|tie|rung**

Tes|ti|kel, der; -s, - ‹lat.› (*Med.* Hoden)

Tes|ti|mo|ni|um, das; -s, *Plur.* ...ien [...iən] *u.* ...ia ‹lat.› (*Rechtsw.* Zeugnis); **Tes|ti|mo|ni|um Pau|per|ta|tis,** das; - -, ...ia - (*Rechtsw.* amtliche Bescheinigung der Mittellosigkeit für Prozessführende; *geh. für* Armutszeugnis)

Test‿kan|di|dat, ...kan|di|da|tin, ...lauf, ...me|tho|de, ...ob|jekt

Tes|tos|te|ron, das; -s ‹lat.› (*Med.* männl. Keimdrüsenhormon)

Test‿per|son, ...pi|lot, ...rei|he, ...sa|tel|lit, ...se|rie, ...spiel, ...stopp (*kurz für* Atomteststopp), **...stre|cke**

Tes|tu|do, die; -, ...dines [...ne:s] ‹lat., „Schildkröte"› (im Altertum Schutzdach [bei Belagerungen]; *Med.* Schildkrötenverband)

Tes|tung; Test|ver|fah|ren

Te|ta|nie, die; -, ...ien ‹griech.› (schmerzhafter Muskelkrampf); **te|ta|nisch; Te|ta|nus** [*auch* 'tɛ...], der; - (*Med.* Wundstarrkrampf); **Te|ta|nus‿imp|fung, ...se|rum**

Te|te ['tɛ:tə], die; -, -n ‹franz., „Kopf"› (*veraltet für* Anfang, Spitze [eines Truppenkörpers]); **tête-à-tête** [tɛ:ta'tɛ:t] (*veraltet für* vertraulich, unter vier Augen); **Tete-a-tete,** *auch* **Tête-à-tête** (↑R 33), das; -, -s (zärtliches Beisammensein)

[1]**Te|thys** (in der altgriech. Mythol. Gattin des Okeanos u. Mutter der Gewässer); *vgl. aber* Thetis; [2]**Te|thys,** die; - (urzeitliches Meer)

Tet|ra (↑R 130), der; -s (*Kurzw. für* Tetrachlorkohlenstoff); **Tet|ra|chlor|koh|len|stoff** ‹griech.; dt.› (ein Lösungsmittel); **Tet|ra|chord** [...k...], der *od.* das; -[e]s, -e (Folge von vier Tönen einer Tonleiter); **Tet|ra|e|der,** das; -s, - (Vierflächner, dreiseitige Pyramide); **Tet|ra|gon,** das; -s, -e (Viereck); **tet|ra|go|nal**

Tet|ra|lin ® (↑R 130), das; -s (ein Lösungsmittel)

Tet|ra|lo|gie (↑R 130), die; -, ...ien ‹griech.› (Folge von vier eine Einheit bildenden Dichtwerken, Kompositionen u. a.); **Tet|ra|me|ter,** der; -s, - (aus vier Einheiten bestehender Vers); **Tet|ra|po|die,** die; - (Vierfüßigkeit [der Verse]); **Tet|rarch,** der; -en, -en; ↑R 126 ‹„Vierfürst"› (im Altertum Herrscher über den vierten Teil eines Landes); **Tet|rar|chie,** die; -, ...ien (Vierfürstentum); **Tet|ro|de,** die; -, -n (elektron. Bauelement; Vierpolröhre)

Tet|zel (Ablassprediger zur Zeit Luthers)

Teu|chel, der; -s, - (*südd. u. schweiz. für* hölzerne Wasserleitungsröhre)

teu|er; teurer, -ste; ein teures Kleid; das kommt mir *od.* mich teuer zu stehen; **Teu|e|rung; Teu|e|rungs‿aus|gleich, ...ra|te, ...wel|le, ...zu|la|ge, ...zu|schlag**

Teu|fe, die; -, -n (*Bergmannsspr.* Tiefe)

Teu|fel, der; -s, -; zum - jagen *(ugs.);* zum -! *(ugs.);* auf - komm raus (*ugs. für* ohne Vorsicht, bedenkenlos); **Teu|fe|lei; Teu|fe|lin; Teu|fels‿aus|trei|ber** (*für* Exorzist), **...aus|trei|bung** (*für* Exorzismus), **...bra|ten** (*ugs. für* Tunichtgut, boshafter Mensch; tollkühner Bursche), **...brut** (die; -; *ugs.*), **...kerl** *(ugs.),* **...kreis, ...kunst, ...weib** *(ugs.),* **...werk, ...zeug** (das; -s; *ugs.*)

teu|fen (*Bergmannsspr.* einen Schacht herstellen)

teuf|lisch; -er Plan

Teu|fung *(Bergmannsspr.)*

Teu|to|bur|ger Wald, der; - -[e]s (Höhenzug des Weserberglandes); **Teu|to|ne,** der; -n, -n; ↑R 126 (Angehöriger eines germ. Volksstammes); **Teu|to|nia** (*lat. Bezeichnung für* Deutschland); **teu|to|nisch** (*auch abwertend für* deutsch)

tex = Tex; **Tex,** das; -, - ‹lat.› (internationales Maß für die längenbezogene Masse textiler Fasern u. Garne; *Zeichen* tex)

Tex. = Texas; **Te|xa|ner; te|xa|nisch; Te|xas** (Staat in den USA; *Abk.* Tex.); **Te|xas|fie|ber,** das; -s; ↑R 105 (Rindermalaria); **Te|xas Ran|gers** [- 'reːndʒə(r)z] *vgl.* Ranger

[1]**Text,** der; -[e]s, -e ‹lat.› (Wortlaut, Beschriftung; [Buch]stelle); [2]**Text,** die; - (*Druckw.* ein Schriftgrad); **Text‿ab|druck** (*Plur.* ...drucke), **...au|to|mat, ...buch, ...dich|ter; tex|ten** (einen [Schlager-, Werbe]text gestalten); **Tex|ter** (Verfasser von [Schlager-, Werbe]texten); **Text|er|fas|ser** (jmd., der [berufsmäßig] Texte in eine EDV-Anlage eingibt); **Text‿er|fas|se|rin, ...er|fas|sung; Tex|te|rin; text|ge|mäß; Text‿ge|stal|ter, ...ge|stal|te|rin; Text|ge|stal|tung; tex|tie|ren** (*selten für* mit einer [Bild]unterschrift versehen); **Tex|tie|rung; tex|til** (die Textiltechnik, die Textilindustrie betreffend; Gewebe...); **Tex|til‿ar|bei|ter, ...ar|bei|te|rin, ...be|trieb, ...fab|rik, ...fab|ri|kant; tex|til|frei** (*scherzh. für* nackt); **Tex|til|ge|wer|be; Tex|til|groß|han|del;** (↑R 23:) Textilgroß- u. -einzelhandel; **Tex|ti|li|en** *Plur.* (Gewebe, Faserstofferzeugnisse [außer Papier]); **Tex|til‿in|dust|rie, ...tech|ni|ker, ...tech|ni|ke|rin, ...ver|ed|ler, ...ver|ed|le|rin, ...wa|ren** *(Plur.);* **Text|kri|tik; text|lich; Text‿lin|gu|is|tik, ...sor|te** *(Sprachw.),* **...stel|le; Tex|tur,** die; -, -en (*Chemie, Technik* Gewebe, Verbindung); **tex|tu|rie|ren** (*Textilw.* ein Höchstmaß an textilen Eigenschaften verleihen); **Text|ver|ar|bei|tung** *(EDV);* **Text|ver|ar|bei|tungs‿ge|rät, ...pro|gramm, ...sys|tem; Text‿ver|gleich, ...wort** (*Plur.* ...worte)

Te|zett [*auch* te'tsɛt], das (Buchstabenverbindung „tz"); *in* bis ins, bis zum - (*ugs. für* vollständig)

T-för|mig; ↑R 25 (in Form eines lat. T)

Tgb.-Nr. = Tagebuchnummer

TGL = Technische Normen, Gütevorschriften und Lieferbedingungen (*ehem. in der DDR* Zeichen für techn. Standards, z. B. TGL 11801)

Th = *chem. Zeichen für* Thorium

TH = technische Hochschule; *vgl.* technisch
Tha|cke|ray ['θɛkəri] (engl. Schriftsteller)
Thad|dädl, der; -s, -[n] (*österr. ugs. für* willensschwacher, einfältiger Mensch); **Thad|dä|us,** *ökum.* Tad|dä|us (Apostel)
[1]**Thai,** der; -[s], -[s] (Bewohner Thailands; Angehöriger einer Völkergruppe in Südostasien); [2]**Thai,** das; - (Sprache der Thai); **Thai|land** (Staat in Hinterindien); **Thai|län|der; Thai|län|de|rin; thai|län|disch**
Tha|is ['ta:is] (altgriech. Hetäre)
Tha|la|mus, der; -,...mi ‹griech.› (*Med.* Hauptteil des Zwischenhirns)
tha|las|so|gen ‹griech.› (*Geogr.* durch das Meer entstanden); **Tha|las|so|me|ter,** das; -s, - (Meerestiefenmesser; Messgerät für Ebbe und Flut); **Tha|lat|ta, Tha|lat|ta!** ‹„das Meer, das Meer!"› (Freudenruf der Griechen nach der Schlacht von Kunaxa, als sie das die Nähe der Heimat anzeigende Meer erblickten)
Tha|le (Harz) (Stadt an der Bode); **Tha|len|ser** (↑R 103)
Tha|les (altgriech. Philosoph)
Tha|lia (Muse der heiteren Dichtkunst u. des Lustspieles; eine der drei Chariten)
Thal|li|um, das; -s ‹griech.› (chem. Element, Metall; *Zeichen* Tl); **Thal|lus,** der; -,...lli (*Bot.* Pflanzenkörper ohne Wurzel, Stängel u. Blätter)
Thäl|mann (dt. kommunist. Politiker)
Tha|na|to|lo|gie, die; - ‹griech.› (*Med., Psych.* Sterbekunde)
Thanks|gi|ving Day ['θɛŋksgiviŋ 'de:], der; - -, - -s (Erntedanktag in den USA [4. Donnerstag im November])
Tha|randt (Stadt südwestl. von Dresden); **Tha|rand|ter** (↑R 103)
That|cher ['θɛtʃə(r)], Margaret ['ma:(r)gərit] (engl. Politikerin); **That|che|ris|mus,** der; - ‹nach der engl. Politikerin› (von ihr geprägte Form der Sozial-, Finanz- u. Wirtschaftspolitik)
Tha|ya, die; - (niederösterr. Fluss)
Thea (w. Vorn.)
The|a|ter, das; -s, - ‹griech.› (Schauspielhaus, Opernhaus; [Schauspiel-, Opern]aufführung; *nur Sing.: ugs. für* Unruhe, Aufregung; Vortäuschung); **The|a|ter‿abon|ne|ment** (↑R 132), **...abon|nent** (↑R 132), **...auf|füh|rung, ...bau** (*Plur.* ...bauten), **...be|such, ...be|su|cher, ...de|ko|ra|ti|on, ...ge|schich|te, ...kar|te, ...kas|se, ...kri|ti|ker, ...pro|be, ...pro|gramm, ...pub|li|kum, ...raum, ...re|gis|seur, ...ring** (Besucherorganisation), **...saal, ...stück, ...vor|stel|lung, ...wis|sen|schaft**
The|a|ti|ner, der; -s, - (Angehöriger eines ital. Ordens)
The|at|ra|lik (↑R 130), die; - ‹griech.› (übertriebenes schauspielerisches Wesen); **the|at|ra|lisch** (bühnenmäßig; gespreizt, pathetisch)
The|ba|is (*altgriech. Bez. für* das Gebiet um die ägypt. Stadt Theben); **The|ba|ner** (Bewohner der griech. Stadt Theben); **the|ba|nisch; The|ben** (Stadt im griech. Böotien; *im Altertum auch* Stadt in Oberägypten)
Thé dan|sant [te dã'sã:], der; - -, -s -s [te dã'sã:] ‹franz., „Tanztee"› (kleiner [Haus]ball); **The|in** *vgl.* Tein
The|is|mus, der; - ‹griech.› (Lehre von einem persönlichen, außerweltlichen Gott)
Theiß, die; - (l. Nebenfluss der Donau)
The|ist, der; -en, -en; ↑R 126 ‹griech.› (Anhänger des Theismus); **the|is|tisch**
The|ke, die; -, -n ‹griech.› (Schanktisch; *auch für* Ladentisch)
The|k|la (↑R 130; w. Vorn.)
The|ma, das; -s, *Plur.* ...men, *auch* -ta ‹griech.› (Aufgabe, Gegenstand; Gesprächsstoff; Leitgedanke [bes. in der Musik]); **The|ma|tik,** die; -, -en (Themenstellung; Ausführung eines Themas); **the|ma|tisch** (dem Thema entsprechend); **the|ma|ti|sie|ren** (zum Thema machen); **The|ma|ti|sie|rung; The|men‿be|reich** (der), **...ka|ta|log, ...kreis, ...stel|lung, ...wahl, ...wech|sel**
The|mis (griech. Göttin des Rechtes)
The|mis|tok|les (↑R 130; athenischer Staatsmann)
Them|se, die; - (Fluss in England)
Theo, Teo (m. Vorn.)
The|o|bald; ↑R 92 (m. Vorn.)
The|o|bro|min, das; -s ‹griech.› (Alkaloid der Kakaobohnen)
The|o|de|rich; ↑R 92 (m. Vorn.)
The|o|di|zee, die; -, ...een ‹griech.› (Rechtfertigung Gottes hinsichtlich des von ihm in der Welt zugelassenen Übels)
The|o|do|lit, der; -[e]s, -e (ein Winkelmessgerät)
The|o|dor (m. Vorn.); **The|o|do|ra, The|o|do|re** (w. Vorn.)
The|o|do|sia (w. Vorn.); **the|o|do|si|a|nisch** (↑R 94); *aber* der Theodosianische Kodex (↑R 56); **The|o|do|si|us** (röm. Kaiser)
The|o|gno|sie *u.* **The|o|gno|sis,** die; - ‹griech.› (Gotteserkenntnis); **The|o|go|nie,** die; -, ...ien (myth. Lehre von Entstehung und Abstammung der Götter); **The|o|krat,** der; -en, -en; ↑R 126 (*selten für* Anhänger der Theokratie); **The|o|kra|tie,** die; -, ...ien („Gottesherrschaft") (Herrschaftsform, bei der die Staatsgewalt allein religiös legitimiert ist); **the|o|kra|tisch**
The|o|krit (altgriech. Idyllendichter); **the|o|kri|tisch;** ein theokritisches Gedicht
The|o|lo|ge, der; -n, -n (↑R 126) ‹griech., „Gottesgelehrter"› (jmd., der Theologie studiert hat, auf dem Gebiet der Theologie beruflich tätig ist); **The|o|lo|gie,** die; -, ...ien (systematische Auslegung u. Erforschung einer Religion); **The|o|lo|gin; the|o|lo|gisch; the|o|lo|gi|sie|ren** (etwas unter theologischem Aspekt erörtern); **The|o|ma|nie,** die; -, ...ien (*veraltet für* religiöser Wahnsinn); **The|o|man|tie,** die; -, ...ien (Weissagung durch göttliche Eingebung); **the|o|morph, the|o|mor|phisch** (in göttlicher Gestalt [auftretend, erscheinend]); **The|o|pha|nie,** die; -, ...ien (Gotteserscheinung); **The|o|phil, The|o|phi|lus** (m. Vorn.)
The|or|be, die; -, -n ‹ital.› (tief gestimmte Laute des 16. bis 18. Jh.s.)
The|o|rem, das; -s, -e ‹griech.› ([mathemat., philos.] Lehrsatz); **The|o|re|ti|ker** (*Ggs.* Praktiker); **the|o|re|tisch;** die theoretische Physik; **the|o|re|ti|sie|ren** (etwas rein theoretisch erwägen); **The|o|rie,** die; -, ...ien; **The|o|ri|en|streit**
The|o|soph, der; -en, -en (↑R 126) ‹griech.› (Anhänger der Theosophie); **The|o|so|phie,** die; -, ...ien ‹„Gottesweisheit"› (Erlösungslehre, die durch Meditation über Gott den Sinn des Weltgeschehens erkennen will); **the|o|so|phisch**
The|ra|peut, der; -en, -en; ↑R 126 ‹griech.› (behandelnder Arzt, Heilkundiger); **The|ra|peu|tik,** die; - (Lehre von der Behandlung der Krankheiten); **The|ra|peu|ti|kum,** das; -s, ...ka (Heilmittel); **The|ra|peu|tin; the|ra|peu|tisch; The|ra|pie,** die; -, ...ien (Heilbehandlung); **The|ra|pie-**

for|schung, ...platz; the|ra|pie|ren (einer Therapie unterziehen); **the|ra|pie|re|sis|tent**

The|re|se, The|re|sia (w. Vorn.); **the|re|si|a|nisch** (↑R 94); die Stiftung Theresianische Akademie (in Wien); **The|re|si|en|stadt** (Stadt in der Tschechischen Republik; Konzentrationslager der Nationalsozialisten)

The|ri|ak, der; -s ‹griech.› (ein Heilmittel des MA.); **The|ri|ak[s]|wur|zel**

therm... ‹griech.› (warm...); **Therm...** (Wärme...); **ther|mal** (auf Wärme, auf warme Quellen bezogen); **Ther|mal‿bad, ...quel|le, ...salz; Ther|me,** die; -, -n (warme Quelle); **Ther|men** *Plur.* (warme Bäder im antiken Rom); **Ther|mi|dor,** der; -[s], -s ‹franz., „Hitzemonat"› (11. Monat des Kalenders der Franz. Revolution: 19. Juli bis 17. Aug.); **Ther|mik,** die; - ‹griech.› (*Meteor.* aufwärts gerichtete Warmluftbewegung); **Ther|mik|se|gel|flug; ther|misch** (die Wärme betreffend, Wärme...); -e Ausdehnung *(Physik);* -er Äquator *(Meteor.);* **Ther|mit** ® [*auch* ...'mit], das; -s, -e (große Hitze entwickelndes Gemisch aus pulverisiertem Aluminium u. Metalloxid); **Ther|mit|schwei|ßen,** das; -s (ein Schweißverfahren); **Ther|mo|che|mie** [*auch* ...'mi:] (Untersuchung der Wärmeumsetzung bei chem. Vorgängen); **ther|mo|che|misch** [*auch* ...'çe:...]; **Ther|mo|chro|mie** [...k...], die; - (*Chemie* Wärmefärbung); **Ther|mo|dy|na|mik** [*auch* ...'na:...] (*Physik* Wärmelehre); **ther|mo|dy|na|misch** [*auch* ...'na:...]; -e Temperaturskala; **ther|mo|elek|trisch** [*auch* ...'lɛk...] (↑R 132); -er Ofen; **Ther|mo|elek|tri|zi|tät** [*auch* ...'tɛ:t] (↑R 132; durch Wärmeunterschied erzeugte Elektrizität); **Ther|mo|ele|ment** (↑R 132; ein Temperaturmessgerät); **Ther|mo|gramm,** das; -s, -e (bei der Thermographie entstehende Aufnahme); **Ther|mo|graph,** der; -en, -en; ↑R 126 (Temperaturschreiber); **Ther|mo|gra|phie,** die; - (Verfahren zur fotografischen Aufnahme von Objekten mittels ihrer unterschiedlichen Wärmestrahlung); **Ther|mo|ho|se; Ther|mo|kau|ter,** der; -s, - (*Med.* Glüheisen, -stift für Operationen); **Ther|mo|man|tel; Ther|mo|me|ter,** das; -s, - (ein Temperaturmessgerät); **ther|mo|nuk|le|ar** [*auch* 'tɛr...] (*Physik* die bei der Kernreaktion auftretende Wärme betreffend); -e Reaktion; **Ther|mo|nuk|le|ar|waf|fe; Ther|mo|pane** ® [...'pe:n], das; - (ein Isolierglas); **Ther|mo|pane|fens|ter; ther|mo|phil** (*Biol.* die Wärme liebend); **Ther|mo|phor,** der; -s, -e (*Med.* Wärmflasche, Heizkissen); **Ther|mo|plast,** der; -[e]s, -e *meist Plur.* (bei höheren Temperaturen formbarer Kunststoff); **Ther|mo|py|len** *Plur.* (Engpass im alten Griechenland); **Ther|mos|fla|sche** ® (Warmhaltegefäß); **Ther|mo|sphä|re,** die; - (*Meteor.* Schicht der Erdatmosphäre in etwa 80 bis 130 km Höhe); **Ther|mos|tat** (↑R 132), der; *Gen.* -[e]s *u.* -en, *Plur.* -e[n]; ↑R 126 (automat. Temperaturregler)

The|ro|phyt, der; -en, -en (↑R 126) ‹griech.› (*Bot.* einjährige Pflanze)

Ther|si|tes (schmäh- u. streitsüchtiger Grieche vor Troja)

the|sau|rie|ren ‹griech.› ([Geld, Wertsachen, Edelmetalle] horten); **The|sau|rie|rung; The|sau|rus,** der; -, *Plur.* ...ren *u.* ...ri ‹„[Wort]schatz"› (Titel wissenschaftlicher Sammelwerke u. umfangreicher Wörterbücher)

The|se, die; -, -n ‹griech.› (aufgestellter [Leit]satz, Behauptung); *vgl. aber* Thesis

The|sei|on, das; -s (Heiligtum des Theseus in Athen)

the|sen|haft (in der Art einer These); **The|sen|pa|pier**

The|seus [...zɔys] (griech. Sagenheld)

The|sis, die; -, ...sen ‹griech.› (*Verslehre* Senkung)

Thes|pis (Begründer der altgriech. Tragödie); **Thes|pis|kar|ren;** ↑R 95 (Wanderbühne)

Thes|sa|li|en [...iən] (Landschaft in Nordgriechenland); **Thes|sa|li|er** [...iər]; **thes|sa|lisch; Thes|sa|lo|ni|cher** (Einwohner von Thessaloniki); **Thes|sa|lo|ni|ki** (*griech. Name für* Saloniki); **thes|sa|lo|nisch**

The|ta, das; -[s], -s (griech. Buchstabe: Θ, ϑ)

The|tis (Meernymphe der griech. Sage, Mutter Achills); *vgl. aber* [1]Tethys

Thid|reks|sa|ga, die; -; ↑R 95 (norw. Sammlung dt. Heldensagen um Dietrich von Bern)

Thig|mo|ta|xis, die; -, ...xen ‹griech.› (*Biol.* durch Berührungsreiz ausgelöste Orientierungsbewegung bei Tieren u. niederen Pflanzen)

Thi|lo *vgl.* Tilo

Thim|bu (Hptst. von Bhutan)

Thi|mig (österr. Schauspielerfamilie)

Thing, das; -[e]s, -e ‹*nord. Form von* Ding› (germ. Volksversammlung); *vgl.* [2]Ding; **Thing‿platz, ...stät|te**

Thi|o|phen, das; -s ‹griech.› (schwefelhaltige Verbindung im Steinkohlenteer)

thi|xo|trop ‹griech.› (Thixotropie aufweisend); **Thi|xo|tro|pie,** die; - (*Chemie* Eigenschaft gewisser Gele, sich durch Rühren, Schütteln u. Ä. zu verflüssigen)

Tho|los, die, *auch* der; -, *Plur.* ...loi [...ɔy] *u.* ...len ‹griech.› (altgriech. Rundbau mit Säulenumgang)

[1]**Tho|ma,** Hans (dt. Maler)

[2]**Tho|ma,** Ludwig (dt. Schriftsteller)

Tho|ma|ner, der; -s, - (Mitglied des Thomanerchors); **Tho|ma|ner|chor,** der; -s (an der Thomaskirche in Leipzig); [1]**Tho|mas** (m. Vorn.); [2]**Tho|mas,** *ökum.* To|mas (Apostel); ungläubiger Thomas, ungläubige Thomasse; **Tho|mas a Kem|pis** (mittelalterl. Theologe); **Tho|mas|kan|tor** (Leiter des Thomanerchores); **Tho|mas|mehl,** das; -[e]s; ↑R 95 (Düngemittel); **Tho|mas|stahl;** ↑R 95 ‹nach dem brit. Metallurgen S. G. Thomas› (nach dem Thomasverfahren hergestellter Stahl); **Tho|mas|ver|fah|ren;** ↑R 95 (ein Eisenverhüttungsverfahren); **Tho|mas von Aquin** (mittelalterl. Kirchenlehrer); **Tho|mis|mus,** der; - (Lehre des Thomas von Aquin); **Tho|mist,** der; -en, -en; ↑R 126 (Vertreter des Thomismus); **tho|mis|tisch**

Thon, der; -s, -s ‹franz.› (*schweiz. für* Thunfisch)

Tho|net|stuhl; ↑R 95 ‹nach dem dt. Industriellen M. Thonet› (aus gebogenem Holz in einer bestimmten Technik hergestellter Stuhl)

Thor (*nord. Mythol.* Sohn Odins); *vgl.* Donar

Tho|ra [*auch, österr. nur,* 'to:ra], die; - ‹hebr., „Lehre"› (die 5 Bücher Mosis, das mosaische Gesetz)

tho|ra|kal ‹griech.› (*Med.* den Brustkorb betreffend); **Tho|ra|ko|plas|tik** (Operation mit Rippenentfernung)

Tho|ra|rol|le (Rolle mit dem Text der Thora)

Tho|rax, der; -[es], -e ‹griech.› (Brustkorb; mittleres Segment bei Gliederfüßern)

Tho|ri|um, das; -s ⟨nach dem Gott Thor⟩ (radioaktives chem. Element, Metall; *Zeichen* Th)
Thorn (*poln.* Toruń)
Thors|ten *vgl.* Torsten
Thor|vald|sen [...valsən], *auch* **Thor|wald|sen** (dän. Bildhauer)
Thot[h] (ägypt. Gott)
Thra|ker (Bewohner von Thrakien); **Thra|ki|en** (Gebiet auf der Balkanhalbinsel); **thra|kisch; Thra|zi|er** usw. *vgl.* Thraker usw.
Thril|ler ['θri...], der; -s, - ⟨amerik.⟩ (ganz auf Spannungseffekte abgestellter Film, Roman u. Ä.)
Thrips, der; -, -e ⟨griech.⟩ (*Zool.* Blasenfüßer)
Throm|bo|se, die; -, -n ⟨griech.⟩ (*Med.* Verstopfung von Blutgefäßen durch Blutgerinnsel); **Throm|bo|se|nei|gung; throm|bo|tisch; Throm|bo|zyt,** der; -en, -en; ↑R 126 (*Med.* Blutplättchen); **Throm|bus,** der; -, ...ben (*Med.* Blutgerinnsel, Blutpfropf)
Thron, der; -[e]s, -e ⟨griech.⟩; **Thron‿an|wär|ter, ...an|wär|te|rin, ...be|stei|gung; thro|nen; Thron‿er|be** (der), **...er|bin, ...fol|ge** (die; -), **...fol|ger, ...fol|ge|rin, ...prä|ten|dent , ...räu|ber, ...re|de, ...saal, ...ses|sel**
thu|cy|di|de|isch usw. *vgl.* thukydideisch usw.
Thu|ja, *österr. auch* **Thu|je,** die; -, ...jen ⟨griech.⟩ (Lebensbaum)
thu|ky|di|de|isch ⟨griech.⟩; die thukydideischen Reden (↑R 94); **Thu|ky|di|des** (altgriech. Geschichtsschreiber)
Thu|le (in der Antike sagenhafte Insel im hohen Norden); **Thu|li|um,** das; -s (chem. Element, Metall; *Zeichen* Tm)
Thun (schweiz. Stadt); **Thu|ner See,** der; - -s
Thun|fisch, *auch* Tun|fisch ⟨griech.; dt.⟩
Thur, die; - (l. Nebenfluss des Hochrheins); **Thur|gau,** der; -s (schweiz. Kanton); **Thur|gau|er** (↑R 103); **thur|gau|isch**
Thü|rin|gen; Thü|rin|ger (↑R 103); - Wald; **Thü|rin|ge|rin; thü|rin|gisch**
Thurn und Ta|xis (ein Adelsgeschlecht); die Thurn-und-Taxis'sche Post (↑R 96)
Thus|nel|da (Gattin des Arminius)
THW = Technisches Hilfswerk
Thy|mi|an, der; -s, -e ⟨griech.⟩ (eine Gewürz- u. Heilpflanze)
Thy|mus, der; -, ...mi ⟨griech.⟩ (hinter dem Brustbein gelegene Drüse, Wachstumsdrüse); **Thy|mus|drü|se** (*svw.* Thymus)

Thy|re|o|i|di|tis, die; -, ...itiden ⟨griech.⟩ (*Med.* Schilddrüsenentzündung)
Thy|ris|tor, der; -s, ...oren ⟨griech.-lat.⟩ (*Elektrotechnik* steuerbares Halbleiterelement)
Thyr|sos, der; -, ...soi [...zɔy] *u.* Thyr|sus, der; -, ...si ⟨griech.⟩ (Bacchantenstab); **Thyr|sos|stab,** Thyr|sus|stab
Ti = *chem. Zeichen für* ²Titan
Ti|a|ra, die; -, ...ren ⟨pers.⟩ (Kopfbedeckung der altpers. Könige; dreifache Krone des Papstes)
Ti|ber, der; -[s] (ital. Fluss)
Ti|be|ri|as (Stadt am See Genezareth)
Ti|be|ri|us (röm. Kaiser)
¹Ti|bet [*auch* ti'be:t] (Hochland in Zentralasien); **²Ti|bet,** der; -[e]s, -e (ein Wollgewebe; eine Reißwollart); **Ti|be|ta|ner** usw. *vgl.* Tibeter usw.; **Ti|be|ter** [*auch* 'ti:...]; **Ti|be|te|rin; ti|be|tisch**
Ti|bor (m. Vorn.)
Tic [tik], der; -s, -s ⟨franz.⟩ (*Med.* krampfartiges Zusammenziehen der Muskeln; Zucken); **Tick,** der; -[e]s, -s (wunderliche Eigenart, Schrulle; *auch für* Tic)
ti|cken (*ugs. auch für* intakt sein, denken u. handeln); du tickst wohl nicht ganz richtig; **Ti|cker** (*ugs. für* Fernschreiber)
Ti|cket, das; -s, -s ⟨engl., „Zettel"⟩ (*engl. Bez. für* Fahrkarte, Eintrittskarte)
tick|tack!; Tick|tack, das; -s
Ti|de, die; -, -n (*nordd. für* die regelmäßig wechselnde Bewegung der See; Flut); **Ti|de|hub** *vgl.* Tidenhub; **Ti|den** *Plur.* (Gezeiten); **Ti|den|hub** (Wasserstandsunterschied bei den Gezeiten)
Tie|break, *auch* **Tie-Break** ['taibre:k] (↑R 33), der *od.* das; -s, -s ⟨engl.⟩ (*Tennis* Satzverkürzung [beim Stand 6 : 6])
Tieck (dt. Dichter)
tief; auf das, aufs Tiefste *od.* auf das, aufs tiefste beklagen (↑R 47); zutiefst; tiefblau usw.; *Schreibung in Verbindung mit Verben* (↑R 38 f.): tief sein, werden, graben, stehen, bohren (*vgl. aber* tiefbohren, tiefstapeln); *Schreibung in Verbindung mit einem Adjektiv oder Partizip* (↑R 40): ein tief ausgeschnittenes Kleid; mit tief bewegter Stimme; tief empfundenes Mitleid; die tief erschütterte Frau; tief gefühlter Schmerz, *vgl. aber* tiefst; eine tief gehende Untersuchung, *vgl. aber* tiefst; eine tief greifende Veränderung, *vgl. aber* tiefst; tief liegende Augen; eine tief schürfende Abhandlung, *vgl. aber* tiefst; ein moralisch tief stehender Mensch; eine tief verschneite Landschaft; **Tief,** das; -s, -s (Fahrrinne; *Meteor.* Gebiet tiefen Luftdrucks); **Tief‿aus|läu|fer** *(Meteor.)*, **...bau** (der; -[e]s); **Tief|bau|amt; tief be|wegt** *vgl.* tief; **tief|blau; tief|boh|ren** ([nach Erdöl] bis in große Tiefe bohren); ↑R 37 f.; **Tief‿boh|rung, ...bun|ker, ...de|cker** (Flugzeugtyp); **Tief|druck,** der; -[e]s, *Plur. (Druckw.:)* -e; **Tief|druck|ge|biet** *(Meteor.)*; **Tie|fe,** die; -, -n; **Tief|ebe|ne** (↑R 132); **tief emp|fun|den** *vgl.* tief; **Tie|fen‿be|strah|lung** *(Med.)*, **...ge|stein, ...in|ter|view, ...li|nie, ...mes|sung, ...psy|cho|lo|gie, ...rausch** (beim Tieftauchen), **...schär|fe** *(Fotogr.)*, **...wir|kung; tief|ernst; tief er|schüt|tert** *vgl.* tief; **Tief|flie|ger** (Flugzeug); **Tief|flie|ger|an|griff; Tief|flug; Tief|flug|ver|bot; Tief|gang,** der; -[e]s *(Schiffbau)*; **Tief|gang|mes|ser,** der; **Tief|ga|ra|ge; tief|ge|frie|ren** (bei tiefer Temperatur schnell einfrieren); ↑R 37 f.; **tief ge|fühlt** *vgl.* tief; **tief ge|hend** *vgl.* tief; **tief|ge|kühlt;** (↑R 40:) tiefgekühltes Gemüse od. Obst; das Obst ist tiefgekühlt; **tief grei|fend** *vgl.* tief; **tief|grün|dig; tief|küh|len** (*svw.* tiefgefrieren); **Tief|kühl‿fach, ...ket|te, ...kost, ...schrank, ...tru|he; Tief|la|der** (*kurz für* Tiefladewagen, Wagen mit tief liegender Ladefläche); **Tief|land** *Plur.* ...lande *u.* ...länder; **Tief|land|bucht; tief lie|gend** *vgl.* tief; **Tief‿punkt, ...schlaf, ...schlag** ([Box]hieb unterhalb der Gürtellinie), **...schnee; Tief|schnee|fah|ren,** das; -s *(Ski)*; **tief schür|fend** *vgl.* tief; **tief|schwarz; Tief|see,** die; -; **Tief|see‿for|schung** (die; -), **...tau|cher; Tief|sinn,** der; -[e]s; **tief|sin|nig; Tief|sin|nig|keit; tiefst...** *in Verbindung mit Partizipien gilt grundsätzlich die Zusammenschreibung, z. B.* tiefstempfunden, tiefstgefühlt, tiefstgehend, tiefstschürfend usw.; *vgl. aber* tief; **Tief|stand,** der; -[e]s; **Tief|sta|pe|lei; tief|sta|peln** (*Ggs.* hochstapeln); tiefgestapelt, tiefzustapeln; **Tief|stap|ler; Tief|start** *(Sportspr.)*; **tief ste|hend** *vgl.* tief; **Tiefst‿kurs, ...preis; Tief|strah|ler; Tiefst‿stand, ...tem|pe|ra|tur, ...wert; tief|tau|chen** (↑R 37) *nur im Infinitiv und Partizip II gebr.*; **tief|trau|rig; tief ver|schneit** *vgl.* **tief**
Tie|gel, der; -s, -; **Tie|gel|druck**

Plur. ...drucke; **Tie|gel|druck|pres|se; Tie|gel⌣guss, ...ofen** (↑R 132)

Tien|gen/Hoch|rhein ['tiŋən...] (Stadt in Baden-Württemberg)

Ti|en|schan [ti̯ɛn..., *auch* 'ti̯ɛn...], der; -[s] (Gebirgssystem Innerasiens)

Ti|ent|sin [ti̯ɛn..., *auch* 'ti̯ɛn...] (↑R 132; chin. Stadt)

Tier, das; -[e]s, -e; **Tier⌣art, ...arzt, ...ärz|tin; tier|ärzt|lich;** [eine] -e Hochschule, *aber* (↑R 108): die Tierärztliche Hochschule Hannover; **Tier⌣asyl** (↑R 132), **...bän|di|ger, ...bild, ...buch, ...fa|bel, ...fän|ger, ...freund, ...gar|ten, ...gärt|ner, ...ge|schich|te, ...ge|stalt** (in -); **tier|haft; Tier⌣hal|ter, ...hal|te|rin, ...hal|tung** (die; -), **...händ|ler, ...hand|lung, ...heil|kun|de** (die; -), **...heim; tie|risch** (*ugs. auch für* sehr, äußerst); **Tier|kör|per|be|sei|ti|gungs|an|stalt** (*Amtsspr. svw.* Abdeckerei); **Tier|kreis,** der; -es *(Astron.);* **Tier|kreis|zei|chen; Tier|kun|de,** die; - (*für* Zoologie); **tier|lieb; Tier|lie|be; tier|lie|bend; Tier⌣me|di|zin** (die; -), **...park, ...pfle|ger, ...pfle|ge|rin, ...pro|duk|ti|on** (die; -; *regional für* Viehzucht), **...quä|ler, ...quä|le|rei, ...reich** (das; -[e]s), **...schau, ...schutz, ...schüt|zer; Tier|schutz|ver|ein; Tier⌣ver|such, ...welt** (die; -), **...zucht** (die; -), **...züch|ter**

Tif|fa|ny|lam|pe ['tifənl...] (↑R 95) ⟨nach dem amerik. Kunsthandwerker⟩ (Lampe mit einem aus bunten Glasstücken zusammengesetzten Schirm)

Tif|lis ['ti(:)...] (Hptst. von Georgien); *vgl. auch* Tbilissi

Ti|fo|so, der; -, ...si *meist Plur.* ⟨ital.⟩ (*italien. Bez. für* [Fußball]fan)

Ti|ger, der; -s, - ⟨griech.-lat.⟩; **Ti|ger⌣au|ge** (Edelstein aus der Quarzgruppe), **...fell, ...hai, ...kat|ze, ...li|lie; ti|gern** (streifig machen; *ugs. für* irgendwohin gehen); ich ...ere (↑R 16)

Tig|ris (↑R 130), der; - (Strom in Vorderasien)

Til|bu|ry [...bəri], der; -s, -s ⟨engl.⟩ (früher üblicher leichter zweirädriger Wagen in Nordamerika)

Til|de, die; -, -n ⟨span.⟩ (span. u. portug. Aussprachezeichen; *Druckw.* Wiederholungszeichen: ~)

tilg|bar; til|gen; Til|gung; Til|gungs⌣an|lei|he *(Wirtsch.),* **...ka|pi|tal, ...ra|te, ...sum|me**

Till (m. Vorn.)

Til|la (w. Vorn.)

Till Eu|len|spie|gel (niederd. Schelmengestalt)

Til|ly (Feldherr im Dreißigjährigen Krieg)

Till|mann (m. Vorn.)

Ti|lo, Thi|lo (m. Vorn.)

Til|sit (Stadt an der Memel); **[1]Til|si|ter** (↑R 103); - Friede[n], - Käse; **[2]Til|si|ter,** der; -s, - (ein Käse)

Tim, Timm (m. Vorn.)

Timb|re ['tɛ̃:br(ə)] (↑R 130), das; -s, -s ⟨franz.⟩ (Klangfarbe der Gesangsstimme); **timb|rie|ren** [tɛ̃...] (Klangfarbe geben); timbriert

Tim|buk|tu (Stadt in [2]Mali)

ti|men ['ta̯imən] ⟨engl.⟩ (*Sport* mit der Stoppuhr messen; zeitlich abstimmen); ein gut getimter Ball;

Time-out ['ta̯im'a̯ut], das; -[s], -s (*Basketball, Volleyball* Auszeit);

Times [ta̯ims, *auch* ta̯imz], die; - ⟨engl. Zeitung⟩; **Time|sha|ring** ['ta̯imʃɛ:riŋ], das; -s, -s ⟨engl.⟩ (*EDV* Zeitzuteilung bei der gleichzeitigen Benutzung eines Großrechners durch viele Benutzer); **Ti|ming** ['ta̯imiŋ], das; -s, -s (zeitl. Abstimmen von Abläufen)

Timm *vgl.* Tim

Ti|mo|kra|tie, die; -, ...ien ⟨griech.⟩ (Herrschaft der Besitzenden); **ti|mo|kra|tisch**

Ti|mon; - von Athen (athen. Philosoph u. Sonderling; Urbild des Menschenhassers); **ti|mo|nisch** (*veraltet für* menschenfeindlich)

Ti|mor (eine Sundainsel)

Ti|mo|the|us [...te|us] (Gehilfe des Paulus)

Ti|mo|the|us|gras [...te|us...], das; -es (ein Futtergras)

Tim|pa|no, der; -s, ...ni ⟨griech.⟩ (*Musik* Pauke)

Ti|mur, Ti|mur-Leng (mittelasiat. Eroberer)

Ti|na, Ti|ne, Ti|ni (w. Vorn.)

tin|geln (*ugs. für* Tingeltangel spielen; [mal hier, mal dort] im Tingeltangel auftreten); ich ...[e]le (↑R 16); **Tin|gel|tan|gel** [*österr.* ...'taŋ(ə)l], der *u., österr. nur,* das; -s, - (*ugs. für* niveaulose Unterhaltungsmusik; Tanzlokal; Varieté)

Ti|ni *vgl.* Tina

Tink|ti|on, die; -, -en ⟨lat.⟩ (*Chemie* Färbung); **Tink|tur,** die; -, -en ([Arznei]auszug)

Tin|nef, der; -s ⟨hebr.-jidd.⟩ (*ugs. für* Schund; dummes Zeug)

Tin|te, die; -, -n; **Tin|ten⌣fass, ...fisch, ...fleck** *od.* **...fle|cken, ...klecks, ...kleck|ser** (*ugs. svw.* Schreiberling), **...ku|li, ...lö|scher, ...pilz, ...stift** (*vgl.* [1]Stift), **...wi|scher; tin|tig; Tint|ling** (Tintenpilz)

Tin|to|ret|to (ital. Maler)

Tip usw. *frühere Schreibung für* Tipp usw.

Ti|pi, das; -s, -s ⟨Indianerspr.⟩ (kegelförmiges Indianerzelt)

Tipp, der; -s, -s ⟨engl.⟩ (nützlicher Hinweis; Vorhersage bei Lotto u. Toto; *ugs. für* ausgefüllter Wettschein)

Tip|pel, der; -s, - (*nordd. für* Punkt; *österr. ugs. für* Beule); *vgl.* Dippel; **Tip|pel|bru|der** (*veraltet für* wandernder Handwerksbursche; *ugs. für* Landstreicher); **Tip|pel|chen** (*landsch. für* Tüpfelchen); bis aufs -; **Tip|pe|lei,** die; - *(ugs.);* **tip|pe|lig,** tipp|lig (*landsch. für* kleinlich); **tip|peln** (*ugs. für* zu Fuß gehen, wandern); ich ...[e]le (↑R 16)

[1]tip|pen (*ugs. für* Maschine schreiben; *nordd., mitteld. für* leicht berühren; Dreiblatt spielen); er hat ihm, *auch* ihn auf die Schulter getippt

[2]tip|pen ⟨engl.⟩ (wetten)

Tip|pen, das; -s (ein Kartenspiel)

Tip|per ⟨*zu* [2]tippen⟩

Tipp-Ex ®, das; - (Korrekturflüssigkeit od. -streifen); **Tipp⌣feh|ler** (*ugs. für* Fehler beim Maschineschreiben), **...fräu|lein** (*veraltet für* Maschinenschreiberin)

Tipp|ge|mein|schaft ⟨*zu* [2]tippen⟩

tipp|lig *vgl.* tippelig

Tipp|se, die; -, -n (*ugs. abwertend für* Maschinenschreiberin)

tipp|topp ⟨engl.⟩ (*ugs. für* hochfein; tadellos)

Tipp|zet|tel (Wettzettel)

Ti|ra|de, die; -, -n ⟨franz.⟩ (Wortschwall; *Musik* tonleiterartige Verzierung)

Ti|ra|mi|su, das; -s, -s ⟨ital.⟩ (Süßspeise aus einer quarkähnlichen Käsesorte u. getränkten Biskuits)

Ti|ra|na (Hptst. von Albanien)

Ti|rass, der; -es, -e ⟨franz.⟩ (*Jägerspr.* Deckgarn, -netz); **ti|ras|sie|ren** ([Vögel] mit dem Tirass fangen)

ti|ri|li!; Ti|ri|li, das; -s; **ti|ri|lie|ren** (pfeifen, singen [von Vögeln])

ti|ro! ⟨franz., „schieße hoch!"⟩ (Zuruf an den Schützen, wenn Federwild vorbeistreicht)

Ti|ro (Freund Ciceros)

Ti|rol (österr. Bundesland); **Ti|ro|ler** (↑R 103); Tiroler Ache (↑R 105); **Ti|ro|le|rin; ti|ro|le|risch** *(österr. nur so);* **Ti|ro|li|enne** [...li̯ɛn], die; -, -n ⟨franz.⟩ (ein ländlerartiger Rundtanz); **ti|ro|lisch**

ti|ro|ni|sche Noten *Plur.* (↑R 94) ⟨*zu* Tiro⟩ (altröm. Kurzschriftsystem)

Ti|ryns (altgriech. Stadt); **Ti|ryn|ther; ti|ryn|thisch**

Tisch, der; -[e]s, -e; bei - (beim Essen) sein; am - sitzen; zu - gehen; Gespräch am runden -; **Tisch‿bein, ...be|sen, ...com|pu|ter, ...da|me, ...de|cke; ti|schen** (*schweiz. für* den Tisch decken); du tischst; **tisch|fer|tig; Tisch‿fuß|ball|spiel, ...ge|bet, ...ge|sell|schaft, ...ge|spräch, ...grill, ...herr, ...kan|te, ...kar|te, ...lam|pe, ...läu|fer; Tisch|lein|deck|dich,** das; -; **Tisch|ler; Tisch|ler|ar|beit; Tisch|le|rei; Tisch|le|rin; tisch|lern;** ich ...ere (↑R 16); **Tisch|ler‿plat|te, ...werk|statt; Tisch‿ma|nie|ren** *(Plur.)*, **...nach|bar, ...nach|ba|rin, ...ord|nung, ...plat|te, ...rand** (*Plur.* ...ränder), **...rech|ner, ...re|de, ...re|ser|vie|rung, ...rü|cken** (das; -s), **...se|gen, ...te|le|fon, ...ten|nis; Tisch|ten|nis‿ball, ...plat|te, ...schlä|ger, ...spiel, ...spie|ler, ...spie|le|rin; Tisch|tuch** *Plur.* ...tücher; **Tisch|tuch|klam|mer; Tisch‿vor|la|ge, ...wein, ...zeit**

Ti|si|pho|ne [...ne] (eine der drei Erinnyen)

Tit. = Titel

[1]**Ti|tan,** Ti|ta|ne, der; ...nen, ...nen *meist Plur.;* ↑R 126 (einer der riesenhaften, von Zeus gestürzten Götter der griech. Sage; *übertr. für* jmd., der durch außergewöhnliche Leistung, Machtfülle o. Ä. beeindruckt); [2]**Ti|tan,** das; -s ‹griech.› (chem. Element, Metall; *Zeichen* Ti); **Ti|ta|ne** *vgl.* [1]Titan; **Ti|tan|ei|sen|erz; ti|ta|nen|haft** (riesenhaft); **Ti|ta|nia** (Feenkönigin, Gemahlin Oberons); **Ti|ta|nic,** die; - (engl. Schnelldampfer, der 1912 nach Zusammenstoß mit einem Eisberg unterging); **Ti|ta|ni|de,** der; -n, -n (↑R 126) ‹griech.› (Nachkomme der Titanen); **ti|ta|nisch** (riesenhaft); **Ti|ta|no|ma|chie** [...'xi:], die; - (Kampf der Titanen gegen Zeus in der griech. Sage); **Ti|tan|ra|ke|te** ‹*zu*[1] Titan›

Ti|tel [*auch* 'ti...], der; -s, - ‹lat.› (Überschrift; Aufschrift; Amts-, Dienstbezeichnung; [Ehren]anrede[form]; *Rechtsw.* Rechtsgrund; Abschnitt; *Abk.* Tit.); **Ti|tel‿am|bi|ti|on** *(meist Plur.)*, **...an|wär|ter** *(Sportspr.)*, **...an|wär|te|rin** *(Sportspr.)*, **...auf|la|ge, ...bild, ...blatt, ...bo|gen; Ti|te|lei** (Gesamtheit der dem Textbeginn vorangehenden Seiten mit den Titelangaben eines Druckwerkes); **Ti|tel‿ge|schich|te** [*auch* 'ti...], **...held, ...hel|din, ...kampf** *(Sportspr.)*, **...kir|che** (Kirche eines Kardinalpriesters in Rom); **ti|tel|los; ti|teln** ([einen Film] mit Titel versehen); ich ...[e]le (↑R 16); **Ti|tel‿rol|le, ...schrift, ...schutz** (der; -es; *Rechtsspr.*), **...sei|te, ...song, ...sucht** (die; -); **ti|tel|süch|tig; Ti|tel‿trä|ger, ...trä|ge|rin, ...ver|tei|di|ger** *(Sportspr.)*, **...ver|tei|di|ge|rin** *(Sportspr.)*, **...zei|le**

Ti|ter, der; -s, - ‹*eindeutschend für* Titre› (Maß für die Feinheit eines Seiden-, Reyonfadens; *Chemie* Gehalt einer Lösung)

Ti|thon, das; -s ‹griech.› (*Geol.* oberste Stufe des Malms)

Ti|ti|ca|ca|see, der; -s (See in Südamerika)

Ti|ti|see, der; -s (See im südl. Schwarzwald)

Ti|to|is|mus, der; - ‹nach dem jugoslaw. Staatspräsidenten Josip Broz Tito› (kommunist. Staatsform im ehem. Jugoslawien); **Ti|to|ist,** der; -en, -en; ↑R 126

Tit|ra|ti|on (↑R 130), die; -, -en ‹lat.› (Bestimmung des Titers, Ausführung einer chem. Maßanalyse); **Tit|re** ['ti:t(ə)r], der; -s, -s (*veraltet für* Titer; *im franz. Münzwesen Bez. für* Feingehalt); **tit|rie|ren** *(Chemie)*

tit|schen (*landsch. für* eintunken); du titschst

Tit|te, die; -, -n *meist Plur.* (*derb für* weibl. Brust)

Ti|tu|lar, der; -s, -e ‹lat.› (*veraltet für* Titelträger); **Ti|tu|lar...** (nur dem Titel nach, ohne das Amt); **Ti|tu|lar‿bi|schof, ...pro|fes|sor, ...rat** (*Plur.* ...räte); **Ti|tu|la|tur,** die; -, -en (Betitelung); **ti|tu|lie|ren** (Titel geben, benennen); **Ti|tu|lie|rung; Ti|tu|lus,** der; -, ...li (mittelalterliche Bildunterschrift [meist in Versform])

Ti|tus (röm. Kaiser; altröm. m. Vorn.; *Abk.* T.)

Tiu (altgerm. Gott); *vgl.* Tyr, Ziu

[1]**Ti|vo|li** [...v...] (ital. Stadt); [2]**Ti|vo|li,** das; -[s], -s (Vergnügungsort; Gartentheater; italienisches Kugelspiel)

Ti|zi|an (ital. Maler); **ti|zi|a|nisch;** tizianische Malweise (↑R 94); **ti|zi|an|rot**

tja! [tja(:)]

Tjalk, die; -, -en ‹niederl.› (ein einmastiges Küstenfahrzeug)

Tjost, die; -, -en *od.* der; -[e]s, -e ‹franz.› (mittelalterl. Reiterzweikampf mit scharfen Waffen)

tkm = Tonnenkilometer

Tl = *Zeichen für* Thallium

TL = [2]Lira

Tm = *Zeichen für* Thulium

Tme|sis, die; -, ...sen ‹griech.› (*Sprachw.* Trennung eigentlich zusammengehörender Wortteile, z. B. „ich *vertraue* dir ein Geheimnis *an*")

TNT = Trinitrotoluol

Toast [to:st], der; -[e]s, *Plur.* -e *u.* -s ‹engl.› (geröstete Weißbrotschnitte; Trinkspruch); **Toast|brot; toas|ten** ([Weißbrot] rösten; einen Trinkspruch ausbringen); **Toas|ter** (elektr. Gerät zum Rösten von Weißbrotscheiben)

To|ba|go *vgl.* Trinidad

To|bak, der; -[e]s, -e (*veraltet für* Tabak); *vgl.* anno

To|bel, der, *österr. nur so, od.* das; -s, - (*südd., österr., schweiz. für* enge [Wald]schlucht)

to|ben; To|be|rei

To|bi|as (m. Vorn.)

To|bog|gan, der; -s, -s ‹indian.› (ein kufenloser [kanad. Indianer]schlitten)

Tob|sucht, die; -; **tob|süch|tig; Tob|suchts|an|fall**

Toc|ca|ta *vgl.* Tokkata

Toch|ter, die; -, Töchter; **Töch|ter|chen; Toch|ter‿fir|ma, ...ge|schwulst** (*für* Metastase), **...ge|sell|schaft** *(Wirtsch.)*; **Toch|ter|kir|che; töch|ter|lich; Töch|ter|schu|le** *(veraltet);* höhere -; **Toch|ter|zel|le** *(Med.)*

Tod, der; -[e]s, -e *Plur. selten;* zu Tode fallen, hetzen, erschrecken; **tod‿bang, ...be|reit; tod|blass** *vgl.* totenblass; **tod|bleich** *vgl.* totenbleich; **tod|brin|gend** (↑R 40)

Tod|dy, der; -[s], -s ‹Hindi-engl.› (Palmwein; grogartiges Getränk)

tod‿elend (↑R 132; *ugs. für* sehr elend), **...ernst** (*ugs. für* sehr ernst); **To|des‿ah|nung, ...angst, ...an|zei|ge, ...art, ...be|reit|schaft** (die; -), **...da|tum, ...fall** (der), **...fol|ge** (die; -; *Rechtsspr.*), **...furcht, ...ge|fahr, ...jahr, ...kampf, ...kan|di|dat, ...mut; to|des|mu|tig; To|des‿nach|richt, ...not** *(geh.)*, **...op|fer, ...qual, ...ritt, ...schuss, ...schüt|ze, ...spi|ra|le** *(Eiskunstlauf)*, **...stoß, ...stra|fe, ...stun|de, ...tag, ...ur|sa|che, ...ur|teil, ...ver|ach|tung; to|des|wür|dig; To|des‿zeit, ...zel|le; Tod|feind;** jmdm. - sein; **Tod‿feind, ...fein|din; tod|ge|weiht** *(geh.)*; **Tod|ge|weih|te,** der *u.* die; -en, -en (↑R 5 ff.); **tod|krank; Tod|kran|ke; tod|lang|wei|lig** *(ugs.)*; **töd|lich; tod‿matt** *(ugs.)*, **...mü|de** *(ugs.)*, **...schick** (*ugs. für* sehr schick), **...si|cher** (*ugs. für* so sicher wie der Tod), **...ster|bens-krank** *(ugs.)*, **...still** (*svw.* totenstill); **Tod|sün|de**

Todt|moos (Ort im Schwarzwald)

tod‿trau|rig, ...un|glück|lich, ...wund *(geh.)*

Toe|loop ['tu:lu:p, *auch* 'to:...], der; -[s], -s ‹engl.› (Drehsprung beim Eiskunstlauf)

töff; töff, töff!; **Töff,** das *u.* der; -s, - (*schweiz. mdal. für* Motorrad)

Tof|fee ['tɔfi, 'tɔfe], das; -s, -s ‹engl.› (eine Weichkaramelle)

Tof|fel, Töf|fel, der; -s, - (dummer Mensch)

töff, töff!; Töff|töff, das; -s, -s (*Kinderspr.* Kraftfahrzeug)

To|fu, der; -[s] ‹jap.› (aus Sojabohnenmilch gewonnenes quarkähnliches Produkt)

To|ga, die; -, ...gen ‹lat.› ([altröm.] Obergewand)

Tog|gen|burg, das; -s (schweiz. Tallandschaft)

To|go (Staat in Westafrika); **To|go|er; To|go|e|rin; to|go|isch; To|go|le|se** usw. *vgl.* Togoer usw.

To|hu|wa|bo|hu, das; -[s], -s ‹hebr., „wüst und leer"› (Wirrwarr, Durcheinander)

Toi|let|te [toa...], die; -, -n ‹franz.› (Frisiertisch; [feine] Kleidung; Ankleideraum; Klosett); - machen (sich [gut] anziehen); **Toi|let|ten‿ar|ti|kel**[1], **...frau, ...mann, ...pa|pier, ...raum, ...sei|fe, ...spie|gel, ...tisch, ...was|ser** (*Plur.* ...wässer)

Toise [toa:s], die; -, -n [toa:z(ə)n] ‹franz.› (altes franz. Längenmaß)

toi, toi, toi! ['tɔy 'tɔy 'tɔy] (*ugs. für* unberufen!)

To|ka|dil|le [...'diljə], das; -s ‹span.› (ein Brettspiel)

To|kai|er, *auch* To|ka|jer ‹nach der ung. Stadt Tokaj› (ung. Natursüßwein); **To|kai|er‿trau|be, ...wein; To|kaj** ['to(:)kai] (ung. Stadt)

To|kio (Hptst. von Japan); **To|ki|o|er, To|ki|o|ter** (↑R 103)

Tok|ka|ta, *auch* Toc|ca|ta, die; -, ...ten ‹ital.› (ein Musikstück)

To|ko|go|nie, die; -, ...ien ‹griech.› (*Biol.* geschlechtl. Fortpflanzung)

Tö|le, die; -, -n (*ugs. für* Hund, Hündin)

To|le|da|ner (↑R 103); - Klinge; **To|le|do** (span. Stadt)

to|le|ra|bel ‹lat.› (erträglich, zulässig); ...ab|le (↑R 130) Werte; **to|le|rant** (duldsam; nachsichtig; weitherzig); **To|le|ranz,** die; -, *Plur.* (Technik:) -en (Duldung, Duldsamkeit; *Technik* zulässige Abweichung vom vorgegebenen Maß); **To|le|ranz‿be|reich** (der; *Technik*), **...do|sis** (für den Menschen zulässige Strahlungsbelastung), **...edikt** (↑R 132, das; -[e]s), **...gren|ze; to|le|rie|ren** (dulden, gewähren lassen); **To|le|rie|rung**

toll; toll|dreist

Tol|le, die; -, -n (*ugs. für* Büschel; Haarschopf)

tol|len; Tol|le|rei; Toll‿haus, ...häus|ler (*früher für* Insasse einer psychiatr. Klinik); **Toll|heit; Tol|li|tät,** die; -, -en (Fastnachtsprinz od. -prinzessin); **Toll|kir|sche; toll|kühn; Toll|kühn|heit**

Toll|patsch, der; -[e]s, -e ‹ung.› (*ugs. für* ungeschickter Mensch); **toll|pat|schig** *(ugs.)*; **Toll|pat|schig|keit,** die; -

Toll|wut; toll|wü|tig

Tol|patsch usw. *frühere Schreibung für* Tollpatsch usw.

Töl|pel, der; -s, -; **Töl|pe|lei; töl|pel|haft; töl|peln** (*selten für* einherstolpern); ich ...[e]le (↑R 16); **töl|pisch**

Tols|toi [...'stɔy] (↑R 132; russ. Dichter)

Tölt, der; -s ‹isländ.› (Gangart des Islandponys zwischen Schritt u. Trab mit sehr rascher Fußfolge)

Tol|te|ke, der; -n, -n; ↑R 126 (Angehöriger eines altmexikan. Kulturvolkes); **tol|te|kisch**

To|lu|bal|sam, der; -s (↑R 105) ‹nach der Hafenstadt Tolú in Kolumbien› (ein Pflanzenbalsam); **To|lu|i|din,** das; -s (eine Farbstoffgrundlage); **To|lu|ol,** das; -s (ein Lösungsmittel)

To|ma|hawk ['tɔmaha:k], der; -s, -s ‹indian.› (Streitaxt der [nordamerik.] Indianer)

To|mas *vgl.* Thomas

To|ma|te, die; -, -n ‹mex.›; **To|ma|ten‿ket|schup,** *auch* **...ket|chup, ...mark** (das), **...saft, ...sa|lat, ...so|ße, ...sup|pe; to|ma|ti|sie|ren** (*Gastron.* mit Tomatenmark versehen)

Tom|bak, der; -s ‹malai.› (eine Legierung, Goldimitation)

Tom|bo|la, die; -, *Plur.* -s, *selten* ...bo|len ‹ital.› (Verlosung bei Festen)

Tom|my ['tɔmi], der; -s, -s ‹engl.› (m. Vorn.; Spitzname des engl. Soldaten)

To|mo|gra|phie, die; - ‹griech.› (schichtweises Röntgen)

Tomsk (westsibir. Stadt)

[1]**Ton,** der; -[e]s, *Plur. (Sorten:)* -e (Verwitterungsrückstand tonerdehaltiger Silikate)

[2]**Ton,** der; -[e]s, Töne ‹griech.› (Laut usw.); den Ton angeben; Ton in Ton gemustert; **Ton|ab|neh|mer; to|nal** (*Musik* auf einen Grundton bezogen); **To|na|li|tät,** die; - (Bezogenheit aller Töne auf einen Grundton); **ton|an|ge|bend** (↑R 40); **Ton|arm;** [1]**Ton|art** *(Musik)*

[2]**Ton|art** ‹*zu* [1]Ton›; **ton|ar|tig**

Ton‿auf|nah|me, ...auf|zeich|nung, ...aus|fall, ...band (das; *Plur.* ...bänder); **Ton|band‿auf|nah|me** (*kurz* Bandaufnahme), **...ge|rät, ...pro|to|koll**

Ton|bank *Plur.* ...bänke (*nordd. für* Ladentisch, Schanktisch)

Ton‿bild, ...blen|de

Tøn|der ['tø(:)nər] (*dän. Form von* Tondern); **Ton|dern** (dän. Stadt)

Ton‿dich|ter, ...dich|tung

Ton|do, das, *fachspr. auch* der; -s, *Plur.* -s *u.* ...di ‹ital.› (Rundbild, bes. in der Florentiner Kunst des 15. u. 16. Jh.s)

to|nen (*Fotogr.* den Farbton verbessern); [1]**tö|nen** (färben)

[2]**tö|nen** (klingen)

To|ner, der; -s, - ‹engl.› (Druckfarbe für Kopiergeräte, Drucker o. Ä.)

Ton|er|de; essigsaure - (↑R 108); **tö|nern** (aus [1]Ton); es klingt - (hohl); -es Geschirr

Ton‿fall (der), **...film, ...fol|ge, ...fre|quenz**

Ton|ga ['tɔŋga] (Inselstaat im Pazifik); **Ton|ga|er** (↑R 103); **Ton|ga|in|seln** (↑R 105) *Plur.*; **ton|ga|isch; Ton|ga|spra|che,** die; -

Ton|ge|bung *(Musik, Sprachw.)*

Ton‿ge|fäß, ...ge|schirr, ...gru|be; ton|hal|tig; -e Erde

Ton|hö|he

[1]**To|ni** (m. u. w. Vorn.); [2]**To|ni,** der; -s, -s (*ehem. ugs. für* Funkstreifenwagen der Volkspolizei in der DDR)

To|nic ['tɔnik], das; -[s], -s ‹engl.› (*kurz für:* Tonicwater); **To|nic|wa|ter** [tɔnik'wɔtə], das; -s, - (Limonade mit Chininzusatz)

to|nig ‹*zu* [1]Ton› (tonartig)

...to|nig (z. B. hochtonig); **...tö|nig** (z. B. eintönig)

To|ni|ka, die; -, ...ken ‹griech.› (*Musik* Grundton eines Tonstücks; der darauf aufgebaute Dreiklang)

To|ni|kum, das; -s, ...ka ‹griech.› (*Med.* stärkendes Mittel)

Ton|in|ge|ni|eur

to|nisch ‹*zu* Tonikum›

Ton|ka|bi|ne

Ton|ka|boh|ne ‹indian.; dt.› (ein Aromatisierungsmittel)

Ton‿ka|me|ra, ...kon|ser|ve,

---

[1] *Die Form* Toiletteartikel [toa'lɛt...] usw. *ist österr. u. kommt sonst nur gelegentlich vor.*

...**kopf**, ...**kunst** (die; -), ...**künstler**, ...**lage**, ...**leiter** (die); **tonlos**; -e Stimme; **Tonlosigkeit**, die; -; **Tonmalerei**; **Ton‿meister** *(Film, Rundfunk)*, ...**meisterin**, ...**möbel**

Tonnage [tɔ'na:ʒə, *österr.* tɔ'na:ʒ], die; -, -n [...ʒ(ə)n] (Rauminhalt eines Schiffes); **Tönnchen**; **Tonne**, die; -, -n ‹mlat.› (*auch* Maßeinheit für Masse = 1 000 kg; *Abk.* t); **Tonnen‿dach**, ...**gehalt** (der; Raumgehalt eines Schiffes), ...**gewölbe**, ...**kilometer** (Maßeinheit für Frachtsätze; *Zeichen* tkm), ...**leger** (Fahrzeug, das Seezeichen [Tonnen] auslegt); **tonnenweise**; ...**tonner** (z. B. Dreitonner [Laster mit 3 t Ladegewicht]; *mit Ziffer* 3-Tonner; ↑R 44)

Tonpfeife ‹*zu* [1]Ton›

Ton‿qualität, ...**schneider** (beim Tonfilm), ...**setzer** (*für* Komponist)

Tonsille, die; -, -n *meist Plur.* ‹lat.› (*Med.* Gaumen-, Rachenmandel); **Tonsillektomie** (↑R 132), die; -, ...ien ‹lat.; griech.› (operative Entfernung der Gaumenmandeln); **Tonsillitis**, die; -, ...itiden (Mandelentzündung)

Ton‿spur *(Film)*, ...**störung**, ...**stück** (Musikstück)

Tonsur, die; -, -en ‹lat.› (*früher* kahl geschorene Stelle auf dem Kopf kath. Geistlicher); **tonsurieren** (die Tonsur schneiden)

Ton‿tafel, ...**taube** (*Sport* Wurftaube); **Tontaubenschießen**, das; -s

Ton‿techniker, ...**technikerin**, ...**träger**

Tönung (Art der Farbgebung)

Tonus, der; -, Toni ‹griech.› (*Med.* Spannungszustand der Gewebe, bes. der Muskeln)

Tonware

Ton‿wert, ...**zeichen**

Top, das; -s, -s ‹engl.› ([ärmelloses] Oberteil)

TOP (*kurz für* Tagesordnungspunkt); TOP 2 [und 3]

Top... ‹engl.› (in Zusammensetzungen = Spitzen..., z. B. Topmodell, Topstar)

Topas [*österr. meist* 'to:...], der; -es, -e ‹griech.› (ein Schmuckstein); **topasfarben** *od.* ...**farbig**

Topf, der; -[e]s, Töpfe; **Topf‿blume**, ...**braten**; **Töpfchen**; **topfen** (in einen Topf pflanzen); getopft; **Topfen**, der; -s (*bayr. u. österr. für* Quark); **Topfen‿knödel** *(bayr. u. österr.)*, ...**kolatsche** *(österr.)*, ...**palatschinke** *(österr.)*, ...**tascherl** *(bayr. u. österr.)*; **Töpfer**; **Töpferei**; **Töpfer‿erde**, ...**handwerk** (das; -[e]s); **Töpferin**; **Töpfer‿markt**, ...**meister**; [1]**töpfern** (irden, tönern); [2]**töpfern** (Töpferwaren machen); ich ...ere (↑R 16); **Töpfer‿scheibe**, ...**ware**; **Topfgucker** *(ugs.)*

topfit ‹engl.› (in bester [körperlicher] Verfassung)

Topf‿kuchen, ...**lappen**, ...**markt**

Topform, die; - (*bes. Sportspr.* Bestform)

Topf‿pflanze, ...**reiniger**, ...**schlagen** (das; -s; ein Spiel)

Topik, die; - ‹griech.› (Lehre von den Topoi; *vgl.* Topos)

Topinambur, der; -s, *Plur.* -s *u.* -e *od.* die; -, -en ‹bras.› (eine Gemüse- u. Futterpflanze)

topisch ‹griech.› (*Med.* örtlich, äußerlich wirkend)

topless ‹engl.-amerik., „oben ohne"› (busenfrei)

Topmanagement (*Wirtsch.* Spitze der Unternehmensleitung); **Topmanager**

Topograf, **Topografie** usw. *eindeutschende Schreibung für* Topograph, Topographie usw.; **Topograph** (↑R 33), der; -en, -en (↑R 126) ‹griech.› (Vermessungsingenieur); **Topographie** (↑R 33), die; -, ...ien (Orts-, Lagebeschreibung, -darstellung); **topographisch** (↑R 33); **Topoi** ['tɔpɔy] (*Plur. von* Topos); **Topologie**, die; - (Lehre von der Lage u. Anordnung geometrischer Gebilde im Raum); **topologisch**; **Toponymie**, **Toponymik** (↑R 132), die; - (Ortsnamenforschung); **Topos**, der; -, ...poi ['tɔpɔy] (*Sprachw.* feste Wendung, immer wieder gebrauchte Formulierung, z. B. „wenn ich nicht irre")

topp! (zustimmender Ausruf)

Topp, der; -s, *Plur.* -e[n] *u.* -s (*Seemannsspr.* oberstes Ende eines Mastes; *ugs. scherzh. für* oberster Rang im Theater)

Töppel, der; -s, - (*landsch. für* Kopffederbüschel [bei Vögeln]); **toppen** (*Seemannsspr.* [die Rahen] zur Mastspitze ziehen; *Chemie* Benzin durch Destillation vom Rohöl scheiden)

Toppflagge

topplastig (*Seew.* zu viel Gewicht in der Takelage habend); **Topplaterne**

Toppsegel; **Toppsgast** *Plur.* ...gasten (Matrose, der das Toppsegel bedient)

topsecret ['tɔpsi:krit] (↑R 130) ‹engl.› (streng geheim)

Topspin (*bes. Golf, [Tisch]tennis* starker Drall des Balls in Flugrichtung); **Topstar** (Spitzenstar); **Topten**, *auch* **Top Ten**, die; -, -s (Hitparade [aus zehn Titeln, Werken u. a.])

Toque [tɔk], die; -, -s ‹span.› (kleiner barettartiger Frauenhut)

[1]**Tor**, das; -[e]s, -e (große Tür; *Sport* Angriffsziel); *Schreibung in Straßennamen:* ↑R 123

[2]**Tor**, der; -en, -en; ↑R 126 (törichter Mensch)

Tor‿aus *(Sport)*, ...**ausbeute** *(Sport)*, ...**bilanz** *(Sport)*, ...**bogen**, ...**chance** *(Sport)*

Tordalk, der; *Gen.* -[e]s *od.* -en, *Plur.* -e[n] (↑R 126) ‹schwed.› (ein arkt. Seevogel)

Tordifferenz *(Sport)*

Torero, der; *Gen.* -s *u.* -en, *Plur.* -e[n] (↑R 126) ‹span.› ([berittener] Stierkämpfer)

Tor‿einfahrt, ...**erfolg** *(Sport)*

Torero, der; -[s], -s ‹span.› (nicht berittener Stierkämpfer)

Torschluss *vgl.* Torschluss

Toreut, der; -en, -en (↑R 126) ‹griech.› (Künstler, der Metalle ziseliert od. „treibt"); **Toreutik**, die; - (Kunst der Metallbearbeitung)

Torf, der; -[e]s, *Plur. (Arten:)* -e (zersetzte Pflanzenreste); - stechen; **Torf‿ballen**, ...**boden**, ...**erde**, ...**feuerung**, ...**gewinnung**; **torfig**; **Torf‿moor**, ...**moos** (*Plur.* ...moose), ...**mull**

Torfrau *(Sport)*

Torf‿stecher, ...**stich**, ...**streu**

Torgau (Stadt a. d. Elbe); **Torgauer** (↑R 103); **torgauisch**

torgefährlich *(Sport)*; **Torgefährlichkeit**

törggelen ‹*zu* [1]Torkel› (*südtirol. für* im Spätherbst den neuen Wein trinken); ich ...[e]le (↑R 16)

Torheit

Tor‿höhe, ...**hüter** *(bes. Sport)*

töricht; **törichterweise**

Tories ['tɔri:s, *engl.* 'tɔ:riz] *Plur.* (*früher* die Konservative Partei in England); *vgl.* Tory

Törin (w. [2]Tor)

Torino (*ital. Form von* Turin)

Tor‿instinkt, ...**jäger** *(Sport)*

[1]**Torkel**, der; -s, - *od.* die; -, -n (*landsch. für* Weinkelter); [2]**Torkel**, der; -s, - (*landsch. für* ungeschickter Mensch; *nur Sing.:* Taumel; unverdientes Glück); **torkeln** (*ugs. für* taumeln); ich ...[e]le (↑R 16)

Törl, das; -s, - (*österr. für* Felsendurchgang; Gebirgsübergang);

Tor₋lauf (*für* Slalom), **...li|nie; tor|los;** ein -es Unentschieden; **Tor|mann** *Plur.* ...männer, *auch* ...leute (*svw.* Torwart, -hüter)
Tor|men|til, der; -s ‹lat.› (Blutwurz, eine Heilpflanze)
Törn, der; -s, -s ‹engl.› (*Seemannsspr.* Fahrt mit einem Segelboot)
Tor|na|do, der; -s, -s ‹engl.› (Wirbelsturm in Nordamerika)
Tor|nis|ter, der; -s, - ‹slaw.› ([Fell-, Segeltuch]ranzen, bes. des Soldaten)
To|ron|to (kanad. Stadt)
tor|pe|die|ren ‹lat.› (mit Torpedo[s] beschießen, versenken; *übertr. für* stören, verhindern); **Tor|pe|die|rung; Tor|pe|do,** der; -s, -s (Unterwassergeschoss); **Tor|pe|do|boot**
Tor₋pfei|ler, ...pfos|ten
Tor|qua|tus (altröm. m. Eigenn. [Ehrenname])
tor|quie|ren ‹lat.› (*Technik* krümmen, drehen)
Torr, das; -s, - ‹nach E. Torricelli; *vgl. d.*› (alte Maßeinheit des Luftdrucks)
Tor|raum *(Fußball, Handball);* **Tor|raum|li|nie** *(Handball);* **torreif** *(bes. Fußball);* eine -e Situation
Tor|ren|te, der; -, -n ‹ital.› (*Geogr.* Gießbach, Regenbach)
Tor|res|stra|ße, die; - (↑R 105) ‹nach dem span. Entdecker› (Meerenge zwischen Australien u. Neuguinea)
Tor|ri|cel|li [...'tʃɛli] (ital. Physiker); **tor|ri|cel|lisch;** die torricellische Leere (im Luftdruckmesser; ↑R 94))
Tor|schluss, To|res|schluss, der; -es; vor -; **Tor|schluss|pa|nik; Tor₋schuss** *(Sport),* **...schüt|ze** *(Sport);* **Tor|schüt|zen|kö|nig**
Tor|si|on, die; -, -en ‹lat.› (*bes. Technik* Verdrehung, Verdrillung, Verwindung); **Tor|si|ons₋elas|ti|zi|tät** (↑R 132), **...fes|tig|keit** (Verdrehungsfestigkeit), **...modul** (Materialkonstante, die bei der Torsion auftritt), **...waa|ge**
Tor|so, der; -s, *Plur.* -s *u.* ...si ‹ital.› (unvollständig erhaltene Statue; Bruchstück; unvollendetes Werk)
Tors|ten, Thors|ten (m. Vorn.)
Tort, der; -[e]s ‹franz.› (*veraltend für* Kränkung, Unbill); jmdm. einen - antun; zum -
Tört|chen; Tor|te, die; -, -n ‹ital.›; **Tor|te|lett,** das; -s, -s *u.* **Tor|te|let|te,** die; -, -n (Törtchen aus Mürbeteigboden)
Tor|tel|li|ni *Plur.* ‹ital.› (gefüllte, ringförmige Nudeln)
Tor|ten₋bo|den, ...guss, ...he|ber, ...schau|fel
Tor|til|la [...'tilja], die; -, -s ‹span.› (Fladenbrot; Omelette)
Tor|tur, die; -, -en ‹lat.› (Folter, Qual)
To|ruń ['tɔrun] (poln. Stadt; *vgl.* Thorn)
Tor₋ver|hält|nis *(Sport),* **...wache** *(früher),* **...wäch|ter, ...wart** *(Sport),* **...wär|ter** *(früher),* **...weg**
To|ry ['tɔri, *engl.* 'tɔ:ri], der; -s, ...ies [*engl.* 'tɔ:riz] (Vertreter der konservativen Politik in Großbritannien); *vgl.* Tories; **To|rys|mus** [...'ris...], der; - *(früher);* **to|rys|tisch**
Tos|be|cken *(Wasserbau)*
Tos|ca|ni|ni (ital. Dirigent)
to|sen; der Bach tos|te
to|si|sche Schloss (↑R 94), das; -n -es, -n Schlösser ‹nach dem ital. Schlosser Tosi› (ein Sicherheitsschloss)
Tos|ka|na, die; - (ital. Landschaft); **Tos|ka|ner** (↑R 103); **tos|ka|nisch**
tot; der tote Punkt; ein totes Gleis; toter Mann (*Bergmannsspr.* abgebaute Teile einer Grube); toter Briefkasten (Agentenversteck für Mitteilungen u. a.); ein tot geborenes Kind. *Großschreibung:* (↑R 47:) etwas Starres und Totes; der, die Tote *(vgl. d.);* (↑R 102:) das Tote Gebirge (in Österr.), das Tote Meer; (↑R 108:) die Tote Hand (öffentlich-rechtliche Körperschaft oder Stiftung, bes. Kirche, Klöster, im Hinblick auf ihr nicht veräußerbares od. vererbbares Vermögen). *Schreibung in Verbindung mit Verben* (↑R 38 f.): tot sein; sich tot stellen; *vgl. aber* totarbeiten, totfahren usw.
to|tal ‹franz.› (gänzlich, völlig; Gesamt...); **To|tal,** das; -s, -e (*schweiz. für* Gesamt, Summe); **To|tal₋an|sicht, ...aus|ver|kauf; To|ta|le,** die; -, -n (*Film* Kameraeinstellung, die das Ganze einer Szene erfasst); **To|ta|li|sa|tor,** der; -s, ...oren (amtliche Wettstelle auf Rennplätzen; *Kurzw.* Toto); **to|ta|li|sie|ren** (*veraltet für* zusammenzählen); **to|ta|li|tär** (diktatorisch, sich alles unterwerfend [vom Staat]; *selten für* ganzheitlich); **To|ta|li|ta|ris|mus,** der; - ‹lat.›; **to|ta|li|ta|ris|tisch; To|ta|li|tät,** die; -, -en ‹franz.› (Gesamtheit, Ganzheit); **To|ta|li|täts|an|spruch; To|tal₋ope|ra|ti|on** (↑R 132; *Med.*), **...scha|den, ...vi|si|on** (*svw.* Cinemascope)
tot|ar|bei|ten, sich; ↑R 38 f. (*ugs. für* sich verausgaben); ich arbeite mich tot; totgearbeitet; totzuarbeiten; **tot|är|gern,** sich; ↑R 38 f. (*ugs. für* sich sehr ärgern); ich habe mich totgeärgert;
To|te, der *u.* die; -n, -n; ↑R 5 ff.
To|tem, das; -s, -s ‹indian.› (*Völkerk.* bei Naturvölkern Ahnentier u. Stammeszeichen der Sippe); **To|tem₋fi|gur, ...glau|be; To|te|mis|mus,** der; - (Glaube an die übernatürliche Kraft des Totems und seine Verehrung); **to|te|mis|tisch; To|tem₋pfahl, ...tier**
tö|ten; To|ten|acker (↑R 132; *veraltet für* Friedhof); **to|ten|ähn|lich; To|ten₋amt** *(kath. Kirche),* **...bah|re, ...be|schwö|rung, ...bett; to|ten|blass,** tod|blass; **To|ten|bläs|se; to|ten|bleich,** tod|bleich; **To|ten₋eh|rung, ...fei|er, ...fest, ...glo|cke, ...grä|ber, ...hemd, ...kla|ge, ...kopf; To|ten|kopf|schwär|mer** (ein Schmetterling); **To|ten₋mas|ke, ...mes|se** (*vgl.* [1]Messe), **...op|fer, ...schä|del, ...schein, ...sonn|tag, ...stadt** (*für* Nekropole), **...star|re; to|ten|still,** tod|still; **To|ten₋stil|le, ...tanz, ...vo|gel, ...wa|che; tot|fah|ren** (↑R 38 f.); er hat ihn totgefahren; **tot|fal|len,** sich (↑R 38 f.; *veraltend*); er hat sich totgefallen; **tot ge|bo|ren** *vgl.* tot; **Tot|ge|burt; Tot|ge|glaub|te,** der *u.* die; -n, -n (↑R 5 ff.); **Tot|ge|sag|te,** der *u.* die; -n, -n (↑R 5 ff.)
To|ti|la (Ostgotenkönig)
tot|krie|gen (↑R 38 f.; *ugs.*); er ist nicht totzukriegen (er hält viel aus); **tot|la|chen,** sich; ↑R 38 f. (*ugs. für* heftig lachen); ich habe mich [fast, halb] totgelacht; (↑R 50:) das ist zum Totlachen; **tot|lau|fen,** sich; ↑R 38 f. (*ugs. für* von selbst zu Ende gehen); es hat sich totgelaufen; **tot|ma|chen** (↑R 38 f.; *ugs. für* töten); er hat den Käfer totgemacht; **Tot|mann|brem|se** *od.* **...knopf** (*Eisenb.* eine Bremsvorrichtung)
To|to, das, *auch* der; -s, -s (*Kurzw. für* Totalisator; Sport-, Fußballtoto); **To|to₋er|geb|nis** *(meist Plur.),* **...ge|winn, ...schein**
Tot|punkt *(Technik);* **Tot|rei|fe** *(Landw.);* **tot|sa|gen** (↑R 38 f.); sie wurde totgesagt; **tot|schie|ßen** (↑R 38 f.); der Hund wurde totgeschossen; **Tot|schlag,** der; -[e]s; **tot|schla|gen** (↑R 38 f.); er wurde [halb] totgeschlagen; er hat seine Zeit totgeschlagen (*ugs. für* nutzlos verbracht); **Tot|schlä|ger; tot|schwei|gen** (↑R 38 f.); sie hat den Vorfall totgeschwie-

gen; **tot stel|len** *vgl.* tot; **totstür|zen,** sich (↑R 38 f.); er hat sich totgestürzt; **tot|tram|peln** (↑R 38); er wurde totgetrampelt; **tot|tre|ten** (↑R 38 f.); er hat den Käfer totgetreten; **Töl|tung;** fahrlässige -; **Töl|tungs‿ab|sicht, ...ver|such; Tot|zeit** *(Technik)*

Touch [tatʃ], der; -s, -s ‹engl.› (Anstrich; Anflug, Hauch); **tou|chie|ren** [tuˈʃi:...] ‹franz.› (*Sport* [nur leicht] berühren)

Tou|lon [tuˈlɔ̃:] (franz. Stadt)

Tou|louse [tuˈlu:s, *auch* tuˈlu:z] (franz. Stadt)

Tou|louse-Laut|rec [tuˈlu:zloˈtrɛk] (↑R 130; franz. Maler u. Grafiker)

Tou|pet [tuˈpe:], das; -s, -s ‹franz.› (Halbperücke; Haarersatz; *schweiz. auch für* Unverfrorenheit); **tou|pie|ren** (dem Haar durch Auflockern ein volleres Aussehen geben); **Tou|pie|rung**

Tour [tu:r], die; -, -en ‹franz.› (Ausflug, Wanderung; [Geschäfts]reise, Fahrt, Strecke; Wendung, Runde, z. B. beim Tanz; *meist Plur.:* Umdrehung[szahl]); in einer Tour (*ugs. für* ohne Unterbrechung); auf Touren kommen (eine hohe Geschwindigkeit erreichen; *übertr. für* in Schwung kommen)

Tou|raine [tuˈrɛ(:)n], die; - (westfranz. Landschaft)

Tour de France [tur də ˈfrã:s], die; - - - ‹franz.› (in Frankreich alljährlich von Berufsradsportlern in Etappen ausgetragenes Radrennen); **Tour de Suisse** [tur də ˈsvis], die; - (schweiz. Radrennen); **Tour d'Ho|ri|zon** [tur dɔriˈzõ], die; - -, -s [tur] - (informativer Überblick); **Tou|ren‿schi** [ˈtu:...], **...ski, ...wa|gen, ...zahl** (*svw.* Drehzahl), **...zäh|ler** (Drehzahlmesser); **Tou|ris|mus,** der; - ‹engl.› (Fremdenverkehr); **Tou|rist,** der; -en, -en; ↑R 126 (Urlaubsreisender); **Tou|ris|ten‿at|trak|ti|on, ...klas|se** (die; -; preiswerte Reiseklasse im See- u. Luftverkehr); **Tou|ris|tik,** die; - (Gesamtheit der touristischen Einrichtungen u. Veranstaltungen); **Tou|ris|tin; tou|ris|tisch**

Tour|nai [turˈnɛ] (belg. Stadt); **Tour|nai|tep|pich** (↑R 105)

Tour|né [turˈne:], das; -s, -s ‹franz.› (*Kartenspiel* aufgedecktes Kartenblatt, dessen Farbe als Trumpffarbe gilt); **Tour|ne|dos** [turnəˈdo:], das; - [...ˈdo:(s)], - [...ˈdo:s] (runde Lendenschnitte); **Tour|nee,** die; -, *Plur.* -s *u.* ...neen (Gastspielreise von Künstlern); **Tour|nee‿lei|ter** (der), **...ver|an|stal|ter**

tour-re|tour [tu:rreˈtu:r] ‹franz.› (*österr. für* hin und zurück)

To|wa|rischtsch, der; -[s], *Plur.* -s, *auch* -i ‹russ.› (*russ. Bez. für* Genosse)

Tow|er [ˈtauə(r)], der; -s, - ‹engl., „Turm"› (*nur Sing.:* ehemalige Königsburg in London; Flughafenkontrollturm); **Tow|er|brü|cke,** die; -

Town|ship [ˈtaunʃip], die; -, -s (von Farbigen bewohnte städtische Siedlung [in Südafrika])

To|xal|bu|min (↑R 132) ‹griech.; lat.› (eiweißartiger Giftstoff); **to|xi|gen** (Giftstoffe erzeugend; durch eine Vergiftung verursacht); **To|xi|ko|lo|ge,** der; -n, -n (↑R 126) ‹griech.›; **To|xi|ko|lo|gie,** die; - (Lehre von den Giften u. ihren Wirkungen); **To|xi|ko|lo|gin; to|xi|ko|lo|gisch; To|xi|kum,** das; -s, ...ka (*Med.* Gift); **To|xin,** das; -s, -e (*Med.* organischer Giftstoff [von Bakterien]); **to|xisch** (giftig; durch Gift verursacht); **To|xi|zi|tät,** die; -

Toyn|bee [ˈtɔynbi] (engl. Historiker)

TP = Triangulationspunkt, trigonometrischer Punkt

Trab, der; -[e]s; - laufen, rennen, reiten (↑R 39)

[1]**Tra|bant,** der; -en, -en; ↑R 126 (*früher für* Begleiter; Diener; *Astron.* Mond; *Technik* künstl. Erdmond, Satellit); [2]**Tra|bant ®** (Kraftfahrzeug aus der ehem. DDR); **Tra|ban|ten|stadt** (selbstständige Randsiedlung einer Großstadt); **Trab|bi, Tra|bi,** der; -s, -s (*kurz für* [2]Trabant)

tra|ben; Tra|ber (Pferd); **Tra|ber|bahn**

Tra|bi *vgl.* Trabbi

Trab‿renn|bahn, ...ren|nen

Trab|zon [...zɔn, *auch* ...ˈzɔn] (türk. Hafenstadt)

Tra|chea [...x..., *auch* ˈtra...], die; -, ...een (*Med.* Luftröhre); **Tra|chee,** die; -, ...een (Atmungsorgan niederer Tiere; *Bot.* Wasser leitendes pflanzl. Gefäß)

Tracht, die; -, -en; eine - Prügel *(ugs.)*

trach|ten; nach etwas -

Trach|ten‿an|zug, ...fest, ...grup|pe (*vgl.* [1]Gruppe), **...ja|cke, ...ka|pel|le, ...kos|tüm; träch|tig; Träch|tig|keit,** die; -; **Tracht|ler** (*landsch. für* Teilnehmer an einem Trachtenfest); **Tracht|le|rin** *(landsch.)*

Tra|chyt [...ˈxy:t], der; -s, -e ‹griech.› (ein Ergussgestein)

Trade|mark [ˈtre:d...], die; -, -s ‹engl.› (*engl. Bez. für* Warenzeichen)

Tra|des|kan|tie, die; -, -n ‹nach dem Engländer Tradescant› (Dreimasterblume, eine Zierpflanze)

Trade U|ni|on [ˈtre:d ju:niən], die; - -, - -s ‹engl.› (*engl. Bez. für* Gewerkschaft)

tra|die|ren ‹lat.› (überliefern); **Tra|di|ti|on,** die; -, -en (Überlieferung; Herkommen; Brauch); **Tra|di|ti|o|na|lis|mus,** der; - (bewusstes Festhalten an der Tradition); **Tra|di|ti|o|na|list,** der; -en, -en (↑R 126); **tra|di|ti|o|na|lis|tisch; tra|di|ti|o|nell** ‹franz.› (überliefert, herkömmlich); **tra|di|ti|ons|be|wusst; Tra|di|ti|ons|be|wusst|sein; tra|di|ti|ons‿ge|bun|den, ...ge|mäß, ...reich**

träf (*schweiz. für* treffend, schlagend)

Tra|fal|gar (Kap an der span. Atlantikküste südöstl. von Cádiz)

Tra|fik, die; -, -en ‹franz.› (*bes. österr. für* [Tabak]laden); **Tra|fi|kant,** der; -en, -en (↑R 126); **Tra|fi|kan|tin;** *vgl.* Tabaktrafik usw.

Tra|fo, der; -[s], -s (*Kurzw. für* Transformator); **Tra|fo|sta|ti|on**

Traft, die; -, -en ‹poln.› (*nordostd. für* großes Floß auf der Weichsel); **Traf|ten|füh|rer**

träg *vgl.* träge

Tra|gant, der; -[e]s, -e ‹griech.› (eine Pflanze; Gummisubstanz als Bindemittel)

Trag‿bah|re, ...band (das; *Plur.* ...bänder); **trag|bar; Trag‿büt|te, ...de|cke; Tra|ge,** die; -, -n

trä|ge, träg

Tra|ge‿gurt, ...korb

Tra|ge|laph (↑R 132), der; -en, -en (↑R 126) ‹griech.› (altgriech. Fabeltier)

tra|gen; du trägst, er trägt; du trugst; du trügest; getragen; trag[e]!; (↑R 50:) zum Tragen kommen; **Trä|ger; Trä|ge|rin; Trä|ger‿kleid, ...kol|lon|ne, ...lohn; trä|ger|los;** ein -es Abendkleid; **Trä|ger‿ra|ke|te, ...rock, ...schür|ze, ...wel|le** *(Funktechnik);* **Tra|ge‿ta|sche, ...tü|te; Tra|ge|zeit,** Trag|zeit (Dauer der Trächtigkeit); **trag|fä|hig; Trag|fä|hig|keit,** die; -; **Trag|flä|che; Trag|flä|chen|boot**

Träg|heit, die; -, -en; **Träg|heits‿ge|setz** (das; -es; *Physik*), **...mo|ment** (das)

Trag‿him|mel (Baldachin), **...holz** (*svw.* Fruchtholz)

tra|gie|ren ⟨griech.⟩ (*veraltend für* eine Rolle [tragisch] spielen); **Tra|gik,** die; - (Kunst des Trauerspiels; schweres, schicksalhaftes Leid); **Tra|gi|ker** (Trauerspieldichter); **Tra|gi|ko|mik; tra|gi|ko|misch** (halb tragisch, halb komisch); **Tra|gi|ko|mö|die** (Schauspiel, in dem Tragisches u. Komisches miteinander verbunden sind); **tra|gisch** (das Trauerspiel betreffend; erschütternd, ergreifend)
Trag‿korb, ...kraft (die; -); **trag|kräf|tig; Trag|last; Trag|luft|hal|le**
Tra|gö|de, der; -n, -n (↑R 126) ⟨griech.⟩ (Heldendarsteller); **Tra|gö|die** [...iə], die; -, -n (Trauerspiel; [großes] Unglück); **Tra|gö|di|en‿dar|stel|ler, ...dich|ter; Tra|gö|din**
Trag‿rie|men, ...seil, ...ses|sel, ...tier, ...wei|te (die; -), **...werk** (*Bauw., Flugzeugbau*); **Trag|zeit** *vgl.* Tragezeit
Traid‿bo|den, ...kas|ten (*österr. mdal. für* Getreidespeicher)
Trai|ler ['tre:...], der; -s, - ⟨engl.⟩ (Anhänger [zum Transport von Booten, Containern u. a.]; als Werbung für einen Film gezeigte Ausschnitte)
Train [trɛ̃:, *auch, österr. nur,* trɛ:n], der; -s, -s ⟨franz.⟩ (*früher für* Tross, Heeresfuhrwesen); **Trai|nee** [tre:'ni:], der; -s, -s ⟨engl.⟩ (jmd., der innerhalb eines Unternehmens für eine bestimmte Aufgabe vorbereitet wird); **Trai|ner** ['trɛ:nə(r), *auch* 'tre:...], der; -s, - (jmd., der Sportler systematisch auf Wettkämpfe vorbereitet; Betreuer von Rennpferden; *schweiz. auch kurz für* Trainingsanzug); **Trai|ner|bank** *Plur.* ...bänke; **Trai|ne|rin; Trai|ner‿li|zenz, ...schein, ...wech|sel; trai|nie|ren** [trɛ..., *auch* tre...]; **Trai|ning** ['trɛ:..., *auch* 'tre:...], das; -s, -s (systematische Vorbereitung [auf Wettkämpfe]); **Trai|nings‿an|zug, ...ein|heit, ...ho|se, ...ja|cke, ...la|ger** (*Plur.* ...lager), **...me|tho|de, ...mög|lich|keit, ...rück|stand, ...zeit**
Trai|teur [trɛ'tø:r], der; -s, -e ⟨franz.⟩ (Leiter einer Großküche; *schweiz. für* Hersteller u. Lieferant von Fertiggerichten)
Tra|jan [*österr.* 'tra:...], Tra|ja|nus (röm. Kaiser); **Tra|jans‿säu|le** (die; -; ↑R 95), **...wall** (der; -[e]s); **Tra|ja|nus** *vgl.* Trajan
Tra|jekt, der *od.* das; -[e]s, -e ⟨lat.⟩ ([Eisenbahn]fährschiff; *veraltet für* Überfahrt); **Tra|jek|to|ri|en** [...iən] *Plur.* (*Math.* Kurven, die sämtliche Kurven einer ebenen Kurvenschar schneiden)
Tra|keh|nen (Ort in Ostpreußen); [1]**Tra|keh|ner** (↑R 103); - Hengst; [2]**Tra|keh|ner** (Pferd)
Trakl (österr. Dichter)
Trakt, der; -[e]s, -e ⟨lat.⟩ (Gebäudeteil; *bes. Med.* Längsausdehnung, z. B. Darmtrakt); **trak|ta|bel** (*veraltet für* leicht zu behandeln, umgänglich); ...ab|ler (↑R 130) Mensch; **Trak|ta|ment,** das; -s, -e (*veraltend, noch landsch. für* Behandlung; Bewirtung); **Trak|tan|den|lis|te** (*schweiz. für* Tagesordnung); **Trak|tan|dum,** das; -s, ...den (*schweiz. für* Tagesordnungspunkt); **Trak|tat,** das *od.* der; -[e]s, -e ([wissenschaftl.] Abhandlung; religiöse Schrift); **Trak|tät|chen** (*abwertend für* kleine Schrift [mit religiösem Inhalt]); **trak|tie|ren** (schlecht behandeln, quälen; *veraltet für* großzügig bewirten); **Trak|tie|rung; Trak|tor,** der; -s, ...oren (Zugmaschine, Schlepper); **Trak|to|rist,** der; -en, -en ⟨lat.-russ.⟩ (*regional für* Traktorfahrer); **Trak|to|ris|tin**
Tral|je, die; -, -n ⟨niederl.⟩ (*nordd. für* Gitter[stab])
tral|la!; tral|la|[la|]la! [*auch* 'tra...]
Träl|le|borg (*frühere Schreibung für* Trelleborg)
träl|lern; ich ...ere (↑R 16)
[1]**Tram,** der; -[e]s, *Plur.* -e *u.* Träme (*österr. svw.* Tramen); [2]**Tram,** die; -, -s, *schweiz.* das; -s, -s ⟨engl.⟩ (*südd. u. österr. veraltend, schweiz. für* Straßenbahn); **Tram|bahn** (*südd. für* Straßenbahn); **Trä|mel,** der; -s, - (*landsch. für* Klotz, Baumstumpf); **Tra|men,** der; -s, - (*südd. für* Balken); *vgl.* [1]Tram
Tra|min (Ort in Südtirol); [1]**Tra|mi|ner** (↑R 103); - Wein; [2]**Tra|mi|ner** (eine Reb- u. Weinsorte)
Tra|mon|ta|na, Tra|mon|ta|ne, die; -, ...nen ⟨ital., „von jenseits des Gebirges"⟩ (ein kalter Nordwind in Italien)
Tramp [trɛmp], der; -s, -s ⟨engl.⟩ (Landstreicher, umherziehender Gelegenheitsarbeiter [bes. in den USA]; Trampschiff); **Tram|pel** ['tram...], der *od.* das; -s, - (*ugs. für* plumper Mensch); **tram|peln** (mit den Füßen stampfen); ich ...[e]le (↑R 16); **Tram|pel‿pfad, ...tier** (zweihöckeriges Kamel; *ugs. für* plumper Mensch); **tram|pen** ['trɛm...] ⟨engl.⟩ (per Anhalter reisen; *veraltend für* als Tramp leben); **Tram|per; Tram|pe|rin; Tramp|fahrt** ['tramp...] (Fahrt eines Trampschiffes); **Tram|po|lin** [*auch* ...'li:n], das; -s, -e ⟨ital.⟩ (ein Sprunggerät); **Tram|po|lin|sprung; Tramp‿schiff, ...schiff|fahrt** (nicht an feste Linien gebundene Frachtschifffahrt); **tramp|sen** (*landsch. für* trampeln); du trampst
Tram|way ['tramvai], die; -, -s ⟨engl.⟩ (*österr. für* Straßenbahn)
Tran, der; -[e]s, *Plur. (Sorten:)* -e (flüssiges Fett von Seesäugetieren, Fischen)
Tran|ce ['trã:s(ə)], die; -, -n [...s(ə)n] ⟨franz.⟩ (schlafähnlicher Zustand [in Hypnose]); **Tran|ce|zu|stand**
Tranche [trã:ʃ], die; -, -n [...ʃ(ə)n] ⟨franz.⟩ (fingerdicke Fleisch- od. Fischschnitte; *Wirtsch.* Teilbetrag einer Wertpapieremission)
Trän|chen (kleine Träne)
tran|chie|ren [trã:'ʃi:...] usw. *vgl.* transchieren usw.
Trä|ne, die; -, -n; **trä|nen; Trä|nen‿bein** (*Med.*), **...drü|se; trä|nen‿er|stickt, ...feucht; Trä|nen‿fluss** (*Plur. selten*), **...gas** (das; -es), **...gru|be** (beim Hirsch); **trä|nen‿nass, ...reich; Trä|nen‿sack, ...schlei|er; trä|nen|über|strömt** (↑R 132)
Tran‿fun|zel, *selten* **...fun|sel** (*ugs. für* schlecht brennende Lampe; [geistig] schwerfälliger Mensch); **tra|nig** (voller Tran; wie Tran)
Trank, der; -[e]s, Tränke; **Tränk|chen; Trän|ke,** die; -, -n (Tränkplatz für Tiere); **trän|ken; Tränk‿op|fer, ...sa|me** (die; -; *schweiz. für* Getränk); **Tränk|stoff; Trän|kung**
Tran|lam|pe
Tran|qui|li|zer ['trɛŋkwilaizə(r)], der; -s, - ⟨engl.⟩ (beruhigendes Medikament); **tran|quil|lo** [tran...] ⟨ital.⟩ (*Musik* ruhig)
trans..., Trans... ⟨lat.⟩ ([nach] jenseits)
Trans|ak|ti|on, die; -, -en ⟨lat.⟩ (größeres finanzielles Unternehmen)
trans‿al|pin, ...al|pi|nisch ⟨lat.⟩ ([von Rom aus] jenseits der Alpen liegend)
trans|at|lan|tisch (überseeisch)
Trans|bai|ka|li|en (Landschaft östl. vom Baikalsee)
tran|schie|ren, *auch* tran|chie|ren [trã:ʃ...] ⟨franz.⟩ ([Fleisch, Geflügel, Braten] zerlegen); **Tran|schier|mes|ser,** *auch* Tran|chier|mes|ser, das
Tran|sept, der *od.* das; -[e]s, -e ⟨mlat.⟩ (*Archit.* Querhaus)
Trans-Eu|rop-Ex|press (*früher*

Fernschnellzug, der nur Wagen erster Klasse führt; *Abk.* TEE)

Trans|fer, der; -s, -s ⟨engl.⟩ (*Wirtsch.* Zahlung ins Ausland in fremder Währung; *Sport* Wechsel eines Berufsspielers zu einem anderen Verein; Weitertransport im Reiseverkehr); **trans|fe|ra|bel** *(Wirtsch.);* eine ...ab|le (↑R 130) Währung; **Trans|fer|ab|kom|men; trans|fe|rie|ren** (Geld in eine fremde Währung umwechseln; *österr. Amtsspr.* [dienstlich] versetzen); **Trans|fe|rie|rung; Trans|fer‿lis|te** *(Fußball),* **...ru|bel, ...stra|ße** *(Technik)*

Trans|fi|gu|ra|ti|on, die; -, -en ⟨lat.⟩ ([Darstellung der] Verklärung Christi)

Trans|for|ma|ti|on, die; -, -en ⟨lat.⟩ (Umformung; Umwandlung; Umgestaltung); **Trans|for|ma|ti|ons|gram|ma|tik,** die; - *(Sprachw.);* **Trans|for|ma|tor,** der; -s, ...oren (elektr. Umspanner; *Kurzw.* Trafo); **Trans|for|ma|tor|an|la|ge; Trans|for|ma|to|ren|häus|chen, Trans|for|ma|tor|häus|chen; trans|for|mie|ren** (umformen, umwandeln; umspannen); **Trans|for|mie|rung**

trans|fun|die|ren ⟨lat.⟩ (*Med.* [Blut] übertragen); **Trans|fu|si|on,** die; -,-en

Tran|sis|tor, der; -s, ...oren ⟨engl.⟩ (*Elektronik* ein Halbleiterbauelement); **Tran|sis|tor|ge|rät; tran|sis|to|rie|ren** *od.* **tran|sis|to|ri|sie|ren; Tran|sis|tor|ra|dio**

Tran|sit [*auch* ...'zit, 'tran...], der; -s, -e ⟨ital.⟩ (*Wirtsch.* Durchfuhr von Waren; Durchreise von Personen); **Tran|sit‿ab|kom|men, ...han|del** (*vgl.* [1]Handel); **tran|si|tie|ren** (*Wirtsch.* durchlaufen, passieren); **tran|si|tiv** ⟨lat.⟩ (*Sprachw.* ein Akkusativobjekt fordernd; zielend); -es Verb; **Tran|si|tiv,** das; -s, -e [...və] (zielendes Verb; z. B. [den Hund] „schlagen"); **Tran|si|ti|vum** [...v...], das; -s, ...va [...va] (*älter für* Transitiv); **tran|si|to|risch** (vorübergehend); **Tran|si|to|ri|um,** das; -s, ...ien [...iən] (*Wirtsch.* vorübergehender Haushaltsposten [für die Dauer eines Ausnahmezustandes]); **Tran|sit‿rei|sen|de, ...ver|bot** (Durchfuhrverbot), **...ver|kehr** (der; -[e]s), **...vi|sum, ...wa|re, ...weg, ...zoll**

Trans|jor|da|ni|en (östlich des Jordans gelegener Teil Jordaniens)

Trans|kau|ka|si|en [...iən] (Landschaft zwischen Schwarzem Meer u. Kaspischem Meer); **trans|kau|ka|sisch**

Trans|kei, die; - ([formal unabhängige] Republik in Südafrika [jenseits des Flusses Kei])

trans|kon|ti|nen|tal ⟨lat.⟩ (einen Erdteil durchquerend); eine -e Eisenbahn

tran|skri|bie|ren ⟨lat.⟩ (*Sprachw.* einen Text in eine andere Schrift, z. B. eine phonet. Umschrift, übertragen; Wörter aus Sprachen, die keine Lateinschrift haben, annähernd lautgerecht in Lateinschrift wiedergeben [*vgl.* Transliteration]; *Musik* umsetzen); **Tran|skrip|ti|on,** die; -, -en

Trans|li|te|ra|ti|on, die; -, -en ⟨lat.⟩ (*Sprachw.* buchstabengetreue Umsetzung eines Textes in eine andere Schrift [bes. aus nichtlateinischer in lat. Schrift] mit zusätzlichen Zeichen); **trans|li|te|rie|ren**

Trans|lo|ka|ti|on, die; -, -en ⟨lat.⟩ (*Biol.* Verlagerung eines Chromosomenbruchstückes in ein anderes Chromosom; *veraltet für* Ortsveränderung, Versetzung); **trans|lo|zie|ren** (*Biol.* sich verlagern; *veraltet für* [an einen anderen Ort] versetzen)

trans‿ma|rin, ...ma|ri|nisch ⟨lat.⟩ (*veraltet für* überseeisch)

Trans|mis|si|on, die; -, -en ⟨lat.⟩ ([Vorrichtung zur] Kraftübertragung von einem Antriebssystem auf mehrere Maschinen); **Trans|mis|si|ons|rie|men** (Treibriemen); **trans|mit|tie|ren** (übertragen, übersenden)

trans|na|ti|o|nal (*Wirtsch.* übernational); -e Monopole

trans|oze|a|nisch (↑R 132; jenseits des Ozeans liegend)

trans|pa|rent ⟨lat.-franz.⟩ (durchscheinend; durchsichtig; durchschaubar); **Trans|pa|rent,** das; -[e]s, -e (Spruchband; durchscheinendes Bild); **Trans|pa|rent|pa|pier** (Pauspapier); **Trans|pa|renz,** die; - (Durchsichtigkeit; Durchschaubarkeit)

Tran|spi|ra|ti|on, die; - ⟨lat.⟩ (Schweißbildung; Hautausdünstung; *Bot.* Abgabe von Wasserdampf, bes. an den Blättern); **tran|spi|rie|ren**

Trans|plan|tat, das; -[e]s, -e ⟨lat.⟩ (überpflanztes Gewebestück); **Trans|plan|ta|ti|on,** die; -, -en (*Med.* Überpflanzung von Organen, Gewebeteilen od. lebenden Zellen; *Bot.* Pfropfung); **trans|plan|tie|ren** *(Med.)*

trans|po|nie|ren ⟨lat.⟩ (*Musik* in eine andere Tonart übertragen); **Trans|po|nie|rung**

Trans|port, der; -[e]s, -e ⟨lat.⟩ (Beförderung); **trans|por|ta|bel** (tragbar, beförderbar); ...ab|ler (↑R 130) Ofen; **Trans|port‿an|la|ge** (Förderanlage), **...ar|bei|ter; Trans|por|ta|ti|on,** die; -, -en (*selten für* Transportierung); **Trans|port‿band** (*Plur.* ...bänder), **...be|häl|ter; Trans|por|ter,** der; -s, - ⟨engl.⟩ (Transportauto, -flugzeug, -schiff); **Trans|por|teur** [...'tø:r], der; -s, -e ⟨franz.⟩ (jmd., der etwas transportiert; *veraltet für* Winkelmesser; Zubringer an der Nähmaschine); **trans|port|fä|hig; Trans|port‿fä|hig|keit** (die; -), **...flug|zeug, ...füh|rer, ...ge|fähr|dung, ...ge|wer|be** (das; -s), **...gut; trans|por|tie|ren** (befördern); **Trans|por|tie|rung; Trans|port‿kas|ten, ...kis|te, ...kos|ten** *(Plur.),* **...mit|tel** (das), **...schiff, ...un|ter|neh|men, ...we|sen** (das; -s)

Trans|po|si|ti|on, die; -, -en ⟨lat.⟩ (Übertragung eines Musikstückes in eine andere Tonart)

Trans|ra|pid ®, der; -[s] (eine Magnetschwebebahn)

Trans|sib [*auch* 'trans...], die; - (*kurz für* Transsibirische Eisenbahn); **trans|si|bi|risch** (Sibirien durchquerend), *aber* (↑R 108): die Transsibirische Eisenbahn

Trans|sil|va|ni|en [...'va:niən] (*alter Name von* Siebenbürgen); **trans|sil|va|nisch,** *aber* (↑R 102): die Transsilvanischen Alpen

Trans|sub|stan|ti|a|ti|on, die; -, -en ⟨lat.⟩ (*kath. Kirche* Verwandlung von Brot und Wein in Leib und Blut Christi); **Trans|sub|stan|ti|a|ti|ons|leh|re,** die; -

Trans|su|dat, das; -[e]s, -e ⟨lat.⟩ (*Med.* abgesonderte Flüssigkeit in Körperhöhlen)

Trans|syl|va|ni|en usw. *vgl.* Transsilvanien usw.

Trans|uran (↑R 132), das; -s, -e *meist Plur.* ⟨lat.; griech.⟩ (künstlich gewonnenes radioaktives Element mit höherem Atomgewicht als Uran)

Tran|su|se, die; -, -n (*ugs. für* langweiliger Mensch)

Trans|vaal [...'va:l] (Provinz der Republik Südafrika)

trans|ver|sal [...v...] ⟨lat.⟩ (quer verlaufend, schräg); **Trans|ver|sa|le,** die; -, -n (Gerade, die eine geometr. Figur durchschneidet); drei -[n]; **Trans|ver|sal|wel|le** *(Physik)*

Trans|ves|tis|mus [...v...] *vgl.* Transvestitismus; **Trans|ves|tit,** der; -en, -en (↑R 126); **Trans-**

ves|ti|tis|mus, der; - ‹lat.› (*Med., Psych.* [sexuelles] Bedürfnis, Kleidung des anderen Geschlechts zu tragen)
trans|zen|dent (↑R 132) ‹lat.› (übersinnlich, -natürlich); **trans|zen|den|tal** (*Philos.* aller Erfahrungserkenntnis zugrunde liegend; *Scholastik svw.* transzendent); -e Logik; **Trans|zen|denz,** die; - (das Überschreiten der Grenzen der Erfahrung, des Bewusstseins); **trans|zen|die|ren**
Trap, der; -s, -s ‹engl.› (Geruchsverschluss)
Tra|pez, das; -es, -e ‹griech.› (Viereck mit zwei parallelen, aber ungleich langen Seiten); **Tra|pez‿akt** (am Trapez ausgeführte Zirkusnummer), **...form; tra|pez|för|mig; Tra|pez‿künst|ler, ...li|nie; Tra|pe|zo|e|der,** das; -s, - (*Geom.* Körper, der von gleichschenkeligen Trapezen begrenzt wird); **Tra|pe|zo|id,** das; -[e]s, -e (Viereck ohne parallele Seiten)
Tra|pe|zunt (*früherer Name von* Trabzon)
trapp!; trapp, trapp!
Trapp, der; -[e]s, -e ‹schwed.› (*Geol.* großflächiger, in mehreren Lagen treppenartig übereinander liegender Basalt)
[1]Trap|pe, die; -, -n, *Jägerspr. auch* der; -n, -n; ↑R 126 ‹slaw.› (ein Steppenvogel)
[2]Trap|pe, die; -, -n (*nordd. für* [schmutzige] Fußspur); **trap|peln** (mit kleinen Schritten rasch gehen); ich ...[e]le (↑R 16); **trap|pen** (schwer auftreten)
Trap|per, der; -s, - ‹engl., „Fallensteller"› (nordamerik. Pelzjäger)
Trap|pist, der; -en, -en (↑R 126) ‹nach der Abtei La Trappe› (Angehöriger des Ordens der reformierten Zisterzienser mit Schweigegelübde); **Trap|pis|ten‿kä|se, ...klos|ter, ...or|den** (der; -s); **Trap|pis|tin** (Angehörige des w. Trappistenordens)
Trap|schie|ßen ‹engl.; dt.› (Wurftaubenschießen mit Schrotgewehren)
trap|sen (*ugs. für* sehr laut auftreten); du trapst
tra|ra!; Tra|ra, das; -s (*ugs. für* Lärm; großartige Aufmachung, hinter der nichts steckt)
Tra|si|me|ni|sche See, der; -n -s (↑R 102; in Italien)
Trass, der; -es, -e ‹niederl.› (vulkanisches Tuffgestein)
Tras|sant, der; -en, -en (↑R 126) ‹ital.› (*Wirtsch.* Aussteller eines gezogenen Wechsels); **Tras|sat,** der; -en, -en; ↑R 126 (Wechselbezogener); **Tras|se,** die; -, -n ‹franz.› ([abgesteckter] Verlauf eines Verkehrsweges, einer Versorgungsleitung usw.; Bahnkörper, Bahn-, Straßendamm); **Tras|see,** das; -s, -s (*schweiz. für* Trasse); **tras|sie|ren** (eine Trasse abstecken, vorzeichnen; *Wirtsch.* einen Wechsel auf jmdn. ziehen oder ausstellen); **Tras|sie|rung**
Tras|te|ve|re [...vere] ‹ital., „jenseits des Tibers"› (röm. Stadtteil); **Tras|te|ve|ri|ner** (↑R 103)
Tratsch, der; -[e]s (*ugs. für* Geschwätz, Klatsch); **trat|schen** (*ugs.);* du tratschst; **Trat|sche|rei** (*ugs.)*
Trat|te, die; -, -n ‹ital.› (*Bankw.* gezogener Wechsel)
Trat|to|ria, die; -, ...ien ‹ital.› (*ital. Bez. für* Wirtshaus)
Trau|al|tar
Träub|chen; Trau|be, die; -, -n; **trau|ben|för|mig; Trau|ben‿ho|lun|der, ...kamm** (Stiel der Weintraube), **...kir|sche, ...kur, ...le|se, ...most, ...saft, ...wick|ler** (ein Schmetterling), **...zu|cker** (der; -s); **trau|big**
Traud|chen, Trau|de[l], Trudchen, Tru|de (w. Vorn.)
trau|en; der Pfarrer traut das Paar; jmdm. - (vertrauen); sich -; ich traue mich nicht (*selten* mir nicht), das zu tun
Trau|er, die; -; **Trau|er‿an|zei|ge, ...ar|beit** (die; -; *Psych.*), **...bin|de, ...bot|schaft, ...brief, ...de|ko|ra|ti|on, ...fall** (der), **...fei|er, ...flor, ...gast** (*Plur.* ...gäste), **...ge|fol|ge, ...ge|leit, ...ge|mein|de, ...got|tes|dienst, ...haus, ...jahr, ...kar|te, ...klei|dung, ...kloß** (*ugs. scherzh. für* langweiliger, energieloser Mensch), **...man|tel** (ein Schmetterling), **...marsch** (der), **...mie|ne; trau|ern;** ich ...ere (↑R 16); **Trau|er‿nach|richt, ...rand, ...schlei|er, ...schwan, ...spiel, ...wei|de, ...zeit, ...zug**
Trau|fe, die; -, -n; **träu|feln;** ich ...[e]le (↑R 16); **träu|fen** (*veraltet für* träufeln)
Trau|gott (m. Vorn.)
trau|lich; ein -es Heim; **Trau|lich|keit,** die; -
Traum, der; -[e]s, Träume
Trau|ma, das; -s, *Plur.* ...men *u.* -ta ‹griech.› (starke seelische Erschütterung; *Med.* Wunde); **trau|ma|tisch** (das Trauma betreffend)
Traum‿au|to, ...be|ruf, ...bild, ...buch, ...deu|ter, ...deu|te|rin, ...deu|tung, ...dich|tung
Trau|men (*Plur. von* Trauma)
träu|men; ich träumte von meinem Bruder; mir träumte von ihm; es träumte mir (*geh.);* das hätte ich mir nicht - lassen (*ugs. für* hätte ich nie geglaubt); **Träu|mer; Träu|me|rei; Traum|er|geb|nis; Träu|me|rin; träu|me|risch; Traum‿fab|rik** (Welt des Films), **...frau, ...ge|bil|de, ...ge|sicht** (*Plur.* ...gesichte); **traum|haft**
Trau|mi|net, der; -s, -s (*österr. ugs. für* Feigling)
Traum‿job (*vgl.* [2]Job), **...mann, ...no|te, ...paar, ...tän|zer** (*abwertend für* wirklichkeitsfremder Mensch), **...tän|ze|rin; traum‿ver|lo|ren, ...ver|sun|ken; traum|wan|deln** usw. *vgl.* schlafwandeln usw.
traun! (*geh. veraltet für* in der Tat!)
Traun, die; - (r. Nebenfluss der Donau); **Trau|ner,** der; -s, - (*österr. für* ein flaches Lastschiff); **Traun|see,** der; -s (oberösterr. See); **Traun|vier|tel,** das; -s (oberösterr. Landschaft)
trau|rig; Trau|rig|keit
Trau‿ring, ...schein
traut; ein -es (den Eindruck von Geborgenheit vermittelndes) Heim; -er (lieber) Freund
Traut|chen *vgl.* Traudchen; **[1]Trau|te** (w. Vorn.); *vgl.* Traude[l]
[2]Trau|te, die; - (*ugs. für* Vertrauen, Mut); keine - haben
Trau|to|ni|um ®, das; -s, ...ien [...iən] ‹nach dem Erfinder F. Trautwein› (elektron. Musikinstrument)
Trau|ung; Trau‿zeu|ge, ...zeu|gin
Tra|vel|ler|scheck [ˈtrɛvələ(r)...] ‹engl.› (Reisescheck)
tra|vers [...ˈvɛrs] ‹franz.› (quer [gestreift]); -e Stoffe; **Tra|vers** [...ˈvɛːr, *auch* ...ˈvɛrs], der; - (Gangart beim Schulreiten); **Tra|ver|se** [...ˈvɛrzə], die; -, -n (*Archit.* Querbalken, Ausleger; *Technik* Querverbinder zweier fester oder parallel beweglicher Maschinenteile; *Wasserbau* Querbau zur Flussregelung; *Bergsteigen* Quergang); **tra|ver|sie|ren** (*Reiten* eine Reitbahn in der Diagonale durchreiten; *Fechten* durch Seitwärtstreten dem gegnerischen Angriff ausweichen; *Bergsteigen* eine Wand od. einen Hang horizontal überqueren); **Tra|ver|sie|rung**
Tra|ver|tin [...v...], der; -s, -e ‹ital.› (mineralischer Kalkabsatz bei Quellen u. Bächen)
Tra|ves|tie [...v...], die; -, ...ien

⟨lat.⟩ ([scherzhafte] Umgestaltung [eines Gedichtes]); **tra|ves|tie|ren** (*auch für* ins Lächerliche ziehen); **Tra|ves|tie|show** ⟨engl.⟩ (Darbietung, bei der vorwiegend Männer in weiblicher Kostümierung auftreten)

Trawl [ˈtrɔ:l], das; -s, -s ⟨engl.⟩ (Grundschleppnetz); **Traw|ler,** der; -s, - (ein Fischdampfer)

Trax, der; -[es], -e ⟨aus amerik. Traxcavator ®⟩ (*schweiz. für* fahrbarer Bagger)

Treat|ment [ˈtri:tmənt], das; -s, -s ⟨engl.⟩ (Vorstufe des Drehbuchs)

Tre|be, die; *nur in* auf [die] - gehen (*ugs. für* sich herumtreiben); **Tre|be|gän|ger** (*ugs. für* jugendlicher Herumtreiber); **Tre|be|gän|ge|rin**

Tre|ber *Plur.* (Rückstände [beim Keltern und Bierbrauen])

Tre|cen|tist [...tʃɛn...], der; -en, -en (↑R 126) ⟨ital.⟩ (Dichter, Künstler des Trecentos); **Tre|cen|to** [...ˈtʃɛnto], das; -[s] (*Kunstw.* das 14. Jh. in Italien [als Stilbegriff])

Treck, der; -s, -s (Zug von Menschen, Flüchtenden [mit Fuhrwerken]); **tre|cken** (ziehen; mit einem Treck wegziehen); **Tre|cker** (Traktor); **Tre|cking** *eindeutschende Schreibung für* Trekking; **Treck|schu|te** (*veraltet für* Zugschiff)

[1]**Treff,** das; -s, -s ⟨franz.⟩ (Kreuz, Eichel [im Kartenspiel])

[2]**Treff,** der; -[e]s, -e (*veraltet für* Schlag, Hieb; Niederlage)

[3]**Treff,** der; -s, -s (*ugs. für* Treffen, Zusammenkunft)

Treff|ass [*auch* ˈtrɛfˈ|as] ⟨*zu* [1]Treff⟩

tref|fen; du triffst; du trafst; du träfest; getroffen; triff!; **Tref|fen,** das; -s, -; **tref|fend; Tref|fer; Tref|fer⌣an|zei|ge, ...quo|te, ...zahl; treff|lich; Treff|lich|keit,** die; -; **Treff|punkt; treff|si|cher; Treff|si|cher|heit,** die; -

Treib⌣an|ker, ...ar|beit, ...ball (der; -[e]s; ein Spiel), **...eis; trei|ben;** du triebst; du triebest; getrieben; treib[e]!; zu Paaren treiben; **Trei|ben,** das; -s, *Plur.* (*für* Treibjagden:) -; **Trei|ber; Trei|be|rei; Trei|be|rin; Treib⌣fäus|tel** (*Bergmannsspr.* schwerer Bergmannshammer), **...gas, ...gut, ...haus; Treib|haus⌣ef|fekt** (der; -[e]s), **...kul|tur, ...luft** (die; -); **Treib⌣holz** (das; -es), **...jagd, ...la|dung, ...mi|ne, ...mit|tel** (das), **...öl, ...rie|men, ...sand, ...satz** *(Technik)*, **...stoff**

Trei|del, der; -s, -n (*früher für* Zugtau zum Treideln); **Trei|de|lei,** die; - (Treidlergewerbe); **Trei|de|ler** *vgl.* Treidler; **trei|deln** (ein Wasserfahrzeug vom Ufer aus stromaufwärts ziehen); ich ...[e]le (↑R 16); **Trei|del⌣pfad, ...weg** (Leinpfad); **Treid|ler** (jmd., der einen Kahn treidelt)

trei|fe ⟨hebr.-jidd.⟩ (nach jüd. Speisegesetzen unrein; *Ggs.* koscher)

Trek|king (↑R 33), das; -s, -s ⟨engl.⟩ (mehrtägige Wanderung od. Fahrt [durch ein unwegsames Gebiet])

Trel|le|borg [*schwed.* ...ˈbɔrj] (schwed. Stadt)

Tre|ma, das; -s, *Plur.* -s *u.* -ta ⟨griech.⟩ (Trennpunkte, Trennungszeichen [über einem von zwei getrennt auszusprechenden Vokalen, z. B. franz. naïf „naiv"]; *Med.* Lücke zwischen den mittleren Schneidezähnen)

Tre|ma|to|de, die; -, -n *meist Plur.* (*Biol.* Saugwurm)

tre|mo|lan|do ⟨ital.⟩ (*Musik* bebend, zitternd); **tre|mo|lie|ren,** *auch* tre|mu|lie|ren (beim Gesang [übersteigert] beben und zittern); **Tre|mo|lo,** das; -s, *Plur.* -s *u.* ...li; **Tre|mor,** der; -s, ...ores [...re:s] ⟨lat.⟩ (*Med.* das Muskelzittern)

Trem|se, die; -, -n (*nordd. für* Kornblume)

Tre|mu|lant, der; -en, -en (↑R126) ⟨lat.⟩ (Orgelhilfsregister); **tre|mu|lie|ren** *vgl.* tremolieren

Trench|coat [ˈtrɛntʃko:t], der; -[s], -s ⟨engl.⟩ (ein Wettermantel)

Trend, der; -s, -s ⟨engl.⟩ (Grundrichtung einer Entwicklung)

tren|deln (*landsch. für* nicht vorankommen); ich ...[e]le (↑R 16)

Trend|mel|dung; Trend|set|ter [...sɛ...], der; -s, - ⟨engl.⟩ (jmd., der den Trend bestimmt; etwas, was einen Trend auslöst); **Trend|wen|de**

trenn|bar; Trenn|bar|keit, die; -; **Trenn|di|ät** (eine Schlankheitsdiät); **tren|nen;** sich -; **Trenn⌣li|nie, ...mes|ser** (das), **...punk|te** (*Plur.; für* Trema); **trenn|scharf** *(Funkw.)*; **Trenn⌣schär|fe** (die; -; *Funkw.*), **...schei|be; Tren|nung; Tren|nungs⌣ent|schä|di|gung, ...geld, ...li|nie, ...schmerz** (der; -es), **...strich, ...zei|chen; Trenn|wand**

Tren|se, die; -, -n ⟨niederl.⟩ (leichter Pferdezaum); **Tren|sen|ring**

Trente-et-qua|rante [trãtekaˈrã:t], das; - ⟨franz., „dreißig und vierzig"⟩ (ein Kartenglücksspiel)

Tren|to (*ital. Form von* Trient)

tren|zen (*Jägerspr.* in besonderer Weise röhren [vom Hirsch])

Tre|pang, der; -s, *Plur.* -e *u.* -s ⟨malai.⟩ (getrocknete Seegurke)

trepp|ab; trepp|auf; -, treppab laufen; **Trepp|chen; Trep|pe,** die; -, -n; -n steigen

Trep|pel|weg (*bayr., österr. für* Treidelweg)

Trep|pen⌣ab|satz, ...be|leuch|tung, ...flur (der), **...ge|län|der, ...gie|bel, ...haus, ...läu|fer, ...po|dest, ...rei|ni|gung, ...stei|gen** (das; -s), **...stu|fe, ...wan|ge** (*Bauw.* Seitenverkleidung einer [Holz]treppe), **...witz**

Tre|sen, der; -s, - (*nordd. u. mitteld. für* Laden-, Schanktisch)

Tre|sor, der; -s, -e ⟨franz.⟩ (Panzerschrank; Stahlkammer); **Tre|sor⌣raum, ...schlüs|sel**

Tres|pe, die; -, -n (ein Gras); **tres|pig** (voller Trespen [vom Korn])

Tres|se, die; -, -n ⟨franz.⟩ (Borte); **Tres|sen⌣rock, ...stern** (*vgl.* [2]Stern), **...win|kel; tres|sie|ren** (*Perückenmacherei* kurze Haare mit Fäden aneinander knüpfen)

Tres|ter, der; -s, - (Tresterbranntwein; *Plur.:* Rückstände beim Keltern); **Tres|ter⌣brannt|wein, ...schnaps**

Tret⌣au|to, ...boot, ...ei|mer; tre|ten; du trittst; du tratst; du trätest; getreten; tritt!; er tritt ihn (*auch* ihm) auf den Fuß; beiseite treten; **Tre|ter** *meist Plur.* (*ugs. für* [sehr bequemer] Schuh); **Tre|te|rei** *(ugs.)*; **Tret⌣mi|ne, ...müh|le** (*ugs. für* gleichförmiger [Berufs]alltag), **...rad, ...rol|ler**

treu; -er, -[e]ste; zu treuen Händen übergeben ([ohne Rechtssicherheit] anvertrauen, vertrauensvoll zur Aufbewahrung übergeben). *Getrenntschreibung in Verbindung mit Verben und Partizipien:* treu sein, bleiben; ein mir treu ergebener Freund; der Freund ist mir treu ergeben; treuer, am treu[e]sten ergeben; eine treu gesinnte Freundin; ein treu sorgender Vater; **Treu|bruch,** der; **treu|brü|chig; treu|deutsch** (*ugs. für* typisch deutsch); **treudoof** (↑R 27; *ugs. für* naiv u. ein wenig dümmlich); **Treue,** die; -; in guten -n (*schweiz. für* im guten Glauben); auf Treu und Glauben (↑R 13); meiner Treu!; **Treu|e|ge|löb|nis; Treu|eid; Treu|e⌣pflicht** (die; -; *Rechtsspr.*), **...prä|mie, ...ra|batt; treu er|ge|ben** *vgl.* treu; **Treu|e|schwur; treu ge|sinnt** *vgl.* treu; **Treu|hand,** die; - (*Rechtsw.* Treuhandgesellschaft); **Treu|hand|an|stalt,** die; -; **Treu|hän|der** (jmd., dem etwas „zu treuen Händen" übertragen wird); **Treu|hän|der|de|pot** *(Bankw.);* **treu|hän|de|risch; Treu|hand‿ge|schäft** *(Rechtsw.),* **...ge|sell|schaft** (Gesellschaft, die fremde Rechte ausübt), **...kon|to; Treu|hand|schaft; treu|her|zig; Treu|her|zig|keit,** die; -; **treu|lich** (*veraltend für* getreulich); **treu|los; Treu|lo|sig|keit,** die; -; **Treu|pflicht** *vgl.* Treuepflicht; **Treu|schwur** *vgl.* Treueschwur; **treu sor|gend** *vgl.* treu

Tre|vi|ra ® [...'vi:ra], das; -[s] (ein Gewebe aus synthetischer Faser)

Tre|vi|sa|ner [...v...] (↑R 103); **Tre|vi|so** (ital. Stadt)

Tri|a|de, die; -, -n ‹griech.› (Dreizahl, Dreiheit; chin. [kriminelle] Geheimorganisation)

Tri|a|ge [tri'a:ʒə], die; -, -n (Ausschuss [bei Kaffeebohnen])

Tri|al ['traiəl], das; -s, -s ‹engl.› (Geschicklichkeitsprüfung von Motorradfahrern)

Tri|an|gel [*österr.* ...'aŋ(ə)l], der, *österr.* das; -s, - ‹lat.› (*Musik* ein Schlaggerät); **tri|an|gu|lär** (dreieckig); **Tri|an|gu|la|ti|on,** die; -, -en (*Geodäsie* Festlegung eines Netzes von trigonometrischen Punkten); **Tri|an|gu|la|ti|ons|punkt** (*Zeichen* TP); **tri|an|gu|lie|ren; Tri|an|gu|lie|rung**

Tri|a|non [...'nɔ̃:], das; -s, -s (Name zweier Versailler Lustschlösser)

Tri|a|ri|er ‹lat.› (altröm. Legionsveteran in der 3. [letzten] Schlachtreihe)

Tri|as, die; -, - ‹griech., „Dreiheit"› (Dreizahl, Dreiheit; *nur Sing.: Geol.* unterste Formation des Mesozoikums); **Tri|as|for|ma|ti|on,** die; -; **tri|as|sisch** (zur Trias gehörend)

Tri|ath|let (jmd., der Triathlon betreibt); **Tri|ath|lon,** das *u.* der; -s, -s ‹griech.› (Mehrkampf aus Schwimmen, Radfahren u. Laufen an einem Tag; *Skisport* Mehrkampf aus Langlauf, Schießen u. Riesenslalom)

Tri|ba|de, die; -, -n ‹griech.› (*veraltet für* Lesbierin); **Tri|ba|die,** die; - (*veraltet für* lesbische Liebe)

Tri|ba|lis|mus, der; - ‹lat.-engl.› (Stammesbewusstsein, Stammesegoismus); **tri|ba|lis|tisch**

Tri|bun, der; *Gen.* -s *u.* -en, *Plur.* -e[n] (↑R 126) ‹lat.› ([altröm.] Volksführer); **Tri|bu|nal,** das; -s, -e ([hoher] Gerichtshof); **Tri|bu|nat,** das; -[e]s, -e (Amt, Würde eines Tribuns); **Tri|bü|ne,** die; -, -n ‹franz.› ([Redner-, Zuhörer-, Zuschauer]bühne; *auch für* Zuhörer-, Zuschauerschaft); **Tri|bü|nen|platz; tri|bu|ni|zisch** ‹lat.› (Tribunen...); -e Gewalt; **Tri|bus,** die; -, - [...bu:s] (Wahlbezirk im alten Rom); **Tri|but,** der; -[e]s, -e (Abgabe, Steuer); etwas fordert einen hohen - (hohe Opfer); einer Sache - zollen (sie anerkennen); **tri|bu|tär** (*veraltet für* tributpflichtig); **Tri|but|last; tri|but|pflich|tig**

Tri|chi|ne, die; -, -n ‹griech.› (schmarotzender Fadenwurm); **tri|chi|nen|hal|tig; Tri|chi|nen‿schau** (die; -), **...schau|er** (*vgl.* [2]Schauer); **tri|chi|nös** (mit Trichinen behaftet); **Tri|chi|no|se,** die; -, -n (Trichinenkrankheit)

Tri|cho|to|mie, die; -, ...ien ‹griech.› (Dreiteilung); **tri|cho|to|misch**

Trich|ter, der; -s, -; **trich|ter|för|mig; Trich|ter|ling** (ein Pilz); **Trich|ter|mün|dung** (*Geogr.* trichterförmige Flussmündung); **trich|tern;** ich ...ere (↑R 16)

Trick, der; -s, -s ‹engl.› (Kunstgriff; Kniff; List); **Trick‿auf|nah|me, ...be|trug, ...be|trü|ger, ...be|trü|ge|rin, ...dieb, ...die|bin, ...dieb|stahl, ...film, ...kis|te** *(ugs.);* **trick|reich; Trick|schi|lau|fen** *vgl.* Trickskilaufen; **trick|sen** (*ugs. für* mit Tricks arbeiten, mit Tricks bewerkstelligen); **Trick|ski|lau|fen,** Trick|schi|laufen, das; -s (Sportart, bei der auf besonderen Skiern artistische Sprünge, Drehungen u. Ä. gemacht werden)

Trick|track, das; -s, -s ‹franz.› (ein Brett- und Würfelspiel)

tri|cky ‹engl.› (*ugs. für* trickreich)

Tri|dent, der; -[e]s, -e ‹lat.› (Dreizack)

Tri|den|ti|ner (↑R 103) ‹*zu* Trient›; - Alpen; **tri|den|ti|nisch,** *aber* (↑R 108): das Tridentinische Konzil; das Tridentinische Glaubensbekenntnis; **Tri|den|ti|num,** das; -s (das Tridentinische Konzil)

Tri|du|um, das; -s, ...duen [...duən] ‹lat.› (Zeitraum von drei Tagen)

Trieb, der; -[e]s, -e; **trieb|ar|tig; Trieb‿be|frie|di|gung, ...fe|der; trieb|haft; Trieb|haf|tig|keit,** die; -; **Trieb‿hand|lung, ...kraft, ...le|ben** (das; -s); **trieb|mä|ßig; Trieb‿mör|der, ...rad, ...sand, ...tä|ter, ...ver|bre|chen, ...ver|bre|cher, ...wa|gen, ...werk**

Trief|au|ge; trief|äu|gig; trie|fen; du triefst; du trieftest, *geh.* troffst; du triefest, *geh.* tröffest; getrieft, *selten noch* getroffen; trief[e]!; **trief|nass**

[1]**Triel,** der; -[e]s, -e (ein Vogel)

[2]**Triel,** der; -[e]s, -e (*südd. für* Wamme; Maul); **trie|len** (*südd. für* sabbern); **Trie|ler** (*südd. für* Sabberlätzchen)

Tri|en|ni|um, das; -s, ...ien [...iən] ‹lat.› (Zeitraum von drei Jahren)

Tri|ent (ital. Stadt); *vgl.* Trento *u.* Tridentiner

Trier (Stadt an der Mosel)

Tri|e|re, die; -, -n ‹griech.› (ein antikes Kriegsschiff)

Trie|rer ‹*zu* Trier› (↑R 103); **trie|risch**

Tri|est (Stadt an der Adria); **Tri|es|ter** (↑R 103)

Tri|eur [...ø:r], der; -s, -e ‹franz.› (Getreidereinigungsmaschine)

trie|zen (*ugs. für* quälen, plagen); du triezt

Tri|fle ['traif(ə)l], das; -s, -s ‹engl.› (eine engl. Süßspeise)

Tri|fo|kal|bril|le ‹lat.; dt.› (Brille mit Trifokalgläsern); **Tri|fo|kal|glas** *Plur.* ...gläser (Brillenglas mit drei verschieden geschliffenen Teilen für drei Entfernungen)

Tri|fo|li|um, das; -s, ...ien [...iən] ‹lat.› (*Bot.* Drei-, Kleeblatt)

Tri|fo|ri|um, das; -s, ...ien [...iən] ‹lat.› (*Archit.* säulengetragene Galerie in Kirchen)

Trift, die; -, -en (Weide; Holzflößung; *auch svw.* Drift); **trif|ten** (loses Holz flößen); [1]**trif|tig** (*svw.* driftig)

[2]**trif|tig** ([zu]treffend); -er Grund; **Trif|tig|keit,** die; -

Tri|ga, die; -, *Plur.* -s *u.* ...gen ‹lat.› (Dreigespann)

Tri|ge|mi|nus, der; -, ...ni ‹lat.› (*Med.* aus drei Ästen bestehender fünfter Hirnnerv); **Tri|ge|mi|nus|neu|ral|gie**

Tri|glyph, der; -s, -e *u.* **Tri|gly|phe,** die; -, -n ‹griech.› (*Archit.* dreiteiliges Feld am Fries des dorischen Tempels)

tri|go|nal ‹griech.› (*Math.* dreieckig); **Tri|go|nal|zahl** (Dreieckszahl); **Tri|go|no|me|trie** (↑R 130), die; - (Dreiecksmessung, -berechnung); **tri|go|no|me|trisch** (↑R 130); -er Punkt (*Zeichen* TP)

tri|klin ‹griech.›; -es System (ein Kristallsystem); **Tri|kli|ni|um,** das; -s, ...ien [...iən] (altröm. Esstisch, an drei Seiten von Speisesofas umgeben)

Tri|ko|li|ne, die; - (ein Gewebe); **tri|ko|lor** ‹lat.› (dreifarbig); **Tri|ko|lo|re,** die; -, -n ‹franz.› (dreifarbige [franz.] Fahne)

[1]**Tri|kot** [...'ko:, *auch* 'triko], der, *selten* das; -s, -s ‹franz.› (maschinengestrickter od. gewirkter

Stoff); **²Tri|kot,** das; -s, -s (eng anliegendes gewirktes, auch gewebtes Kleidungsstück); **Tri|ko|ta|ge** [...'ta:ʒə, *österr.* ...'ta:ʒ], die; -, -n [...ʒ(ə)n] *meist Plur.* (Wirkware); **Tri|kot|wer|bung** [...'ko:..., *auch* 'tri...] (Werbung auf den Trikots von Sportlern)

tri|la|te|ral ‹lat.› (dreiseitig); -e Verträge

Tril|ler ‹ital.›; **tril|lern;** ich ...ere (↑R 16); **Tril|ler|pfei|fe**

Tril|li|ar|de, die; -, -n ‹lat.› (tausend Trillionen); **Tril|li|on,** die; -, -en (eine Million Billionen)

Tri|lo|bit [*auch* ...'bit], der; -en, -en (↑R 126) ‹griech.› (ein urweltliches Krebstier)

Tri|lo|gie, die; -, ...ien ‹griech.› (Folge von drei [zusammengehörenden] Dichtwerken, Kompositionen u. a.)

Tri|ma|ran, der; -s, -e ‹lat.; tamil.-engl.› (Segelboot mit drei Rümpfen)

Tri|mes|ter, das; -s, - ‹lat.› (Zeitraum von drei Monaten; Dritteljahr eines Unterrichtsjahres)

Tri|me|ter, der; -s, - ‹griech.› (aus drei Versfüßen bestehender Vers)

Trimm, der; -[e]s ‹engl.› (*Seemannsspr.* Lage eines Schiffes bezüglich Tiefgang u. Schwerpunkt; ordentlicher u. gepflegter Zustand eines Schiffes); **Trimm|ak|ti|on; Trimm-dich-Pfad; trim|men** (*bes. Seemannsspr.* zweckmäßig verstauen, in die optimale Lage bringen; *Funktechnik* auf die gewünschte Frequenz einstellen; [Hunden] das Fell scheren; *ugs. für* [mit besonderer Anstrengung] in einen gewünschten Zustand bringen); ein auf alt getrimmter Schrank; sich -; trimm dich durch Sport!; **Trim|mer** (Arbeiter, der auf Schiffen die Ladung trimmt, Kohlen vor die Kessel schafft usw.; *Technik* verstellbarer Kleinkondensator; *ugs. für* Person, die sich trimmt); **Trimm|spi|ra|le** (Testkarte der Trimmaktion); **Trimm|trab; Trim|mung** (Längsrichtung eines Schiffes)

tri|morph ‹griech.› (dreigestaltig [z. B. von Pflanzenfrüchten]); **Tri|mor|phie,** die; - *u.* **Tri|mor|phis|mus,** der; -

Tri|ne, die; -, -n (ugs. Schimpfwort); dumme -

Tri|ni|dad (südamerik. Insel); **Tri|ni|dad und To|ba|go** (Staat im Karibischen Meer)

Tri|ni|ta|ri|er [...iər], der; -s, - ‹lat.› (Bekenner der Dreieinigkeit; Angehöriger eines kath. Bettelordens); **Tri|ni|tät,** die; - (*christl. Rel.* Dreieinigkeit, Dreifaltigkeit); **Tri|ni|ta|tis** (Sonntag nach Pfingsten); **Tri|ni|ta|tis|fest**

Tri|nit|ro|to|lu|ol (↑R 130), das; -s (stoßunempfindlicher Sprengstoff; Abk.: TNT); *vgl.* Trotyl

trink|bar; Trink|bar|keit, die; -; **Trink‿be|cher, ...brannt|wein; trin|ken;** du trankst; du tränkest; getrunken; trink[e]!; **Trin|ker; Trin|ke|rei; Trin|ker|heil|an|stalt; Trin|ke|rin; trink|fest; Trink|fes|tig|keit; Trink|fla|sche; trink|freu|dig; Trink|freu|dig|keit; Trink‿ge|fäß, ...ge|la|ge, ...geld, ...glas** (*Plur.* ...gläser), **...hal|le, ...halm, ...horn, ...kur** (*vgl.* [1]Kur), **...lied, ...milch, ...scha|le, ...spruch, ...was|ser** (das; -s); **Trink|was|ser‿auf|be|rei|tung, ...qua|li|tät, ...schutz|ge|biet, ...ver|sor|gung**

Tri|nom, das; -s, -e ‹griech.› (*Math.* dreigliedrige Zahlengröße); **tri|no|misch**

Trio, das; -s, -s ‹ital.› (Musikstück für drei Instrumente, *auch für* die drei Ausführenden; Gruppe von drei Personen); **Tri|o|de,** die; -, -n ‹griech.› (*Elektrotechnik* Verstärkerröhre mit drei Elektroden); **Tri|o|le,** die; -, -n ‹ital.› (*Musik* Figur von 3 Tönen im Taktwert von 2 oder 4 Tönen; *ugs. auch für* Geschlechtsverkehr zu dritt); **Tri|o|lett,** das; -[e]s, -e ‹franz.› (eine Gedichtform)

Trip, der; -s, -s ‹engl.› (Ausflug, Reise; Rauschzustand durch Drogeneinwirkung, *auch für* die dafür benötigte Dosis)

¹Tri|pel, das; -s, - ‹franz.› (die Zusammenfassung dreier Dinge, z. B. Dreieckspunkte); **²Tri|pel,** der; -s, - (*veraltet für* dreifacher Gewinn)

³Tri|pel, der; -s ‹nach Tripolis› (*Geol.* Kieselerde)

Tri|pel|al|li|anz (*Völkerrecht* Allianz von drei Staaten)

Triph|thong (↑R 132), der; -s, -e ‹griech.› (*Sprachw.* Dreilaut, drei eine Silbe bildende Selbstlaute, z. B. ital. miei „meine")

Trip|lé [...'ple:] (↑R 130), das; -s, -s ‹franz.› (*Billard* Zweibandenball); **Trip|lik,** die; -, -en ‹lat.› (*veraltend für* die Antwort des Klägers auf eine Duplik); **Trip|li|kat,** das; -[e]s, -e (*selten für* dritte Ausfertigung); **Trip|li|zi|tät,** die; - (*selten für* dreifaches Auftreten); **trip|lo|id** (einen dreifachen Chromosomensatz enthaltend)

Trip|ma|dam, die; -, -en ‹franz.› (zu den Fetthennen gehörende Pflanze)

Tri|po|den (*Plur. von* Tripus)

Tri|po|lis (Hptst. von Libyen); **Tri|po|li|ta|ni|en** (Gebiet in Libyen); **tri|po|li|ta|nisch**

trip|peln (mit kleinen, schnellen Schritten gehen); ich ...[e]le (↑R 16); **Trip|pel|schritt**

Trip|per, der; -s, - ‹*zu nordd.* drippen = tropfen› (eine Geschlechtskrankheit)

Trip|tik (↑R 132; *eindeutschend für* Triptyk); **Trip|ty|chon,** das; -s, *Plur.* ...chen *u.* ...cha ‹griech.› (dreiteiliger Altaraufsatz); **Trip|tyk,** Trip|tik, das; -s, -s ‹engl.› (dreiteiliger Grenzübertrittsschein für Wohnanhänger und Wasserfahrzeuge); **Tri|pus,** der; -, ...poden ‹griech.› (Dreifuß, altgriech. Gestell für Gefäße)

Tri|re|me, die; -, -n ‹lat.› (*svw.* Triere)

Tris|me|gis|tos, der; - ‹griech., „der Dreimalgrößte"› (Beiname des ägypt. Hermes)

Tris|mus, der; -, ...men ‹griech.› (*Med.* Kiefersperre)

trist ‹franz.› (traurig, öde)

Tris|tan (mittelalterl. Sagengestalt)

Tris|te, die; -, -n (*bayr., österr. u. schweiz. für* um eine Stange aufgehäuftes Heu od. Stroh)

Tris|tesse [...'tɛs], die; -, -n [...s(ə)n] ‹franz.› (Traurigkeit, trübe Stimmung); **Trist|heit,** die; -; **Tris|ti|en** *Plur.* ‹lat.› (Trauergedichte [Ovids])

Tri|ta|go|nist (↑R 132), der; -en, -en (↑R 126) ‹griech.› (dritter Schauspieler auf der altgriech. Bühne)

Tri|ti|um, das; -s ‹griech.› (schweres Wasserstoffisotop; *Zeichen* T); **¹Tri|ton,** das; -s, ...onen (schwerer Wasserstoffkern)

²Tri|ton (griech. fischleibiger Meergott, Sohn Poseidons); **³Tri|ton,** der; ...onen, ...onen; ↑R 126 (Meergott im Gefolge Poseidons)

Tri|to|nus, der; - ‹griech.› (*Musik* übermäßige Quarte)

Tritt, der; -[e]s, -e; - halten; **Tritt|brett; Tritt|brett|fah|rer** (*ugs. für* jmd., der von einer Sache zu profitieren versucht, ohne selbst etwas dafür zu tun); **tritt|fest; Tritt|lei|ter,** die; **tritt|si|cher**

Tri|umph, der; -[e]s, -e ‹lat.› (großer Sieg, Erfolg; *nur Sing.:* Siegesfreude, -jubel); **tri|um|phal** (herrlich, sieghaft); **Tri|um|pha|tor,** der; -s, ...oren (feierlich einziehender Sieger); **Tri|umph|bo|gen; tri|umph|ge|krönt; Tri|umph|ge|schrei; tri|um|phie|ren** (siegen; jubeln); **Tri|umph‿wa|gen, ...zug**

Tri|um|vir [...v...], der; *Gen.* -s *u.* -n, *Plur.* -n (↑R 126) ‹lat.› (Mitglied eines Triumvirats); **Tri|um|vi|rat,** das; -[e]s, -e (Dreimännerherrschaft [im alten Rom])

tri|va|lent [...v...] ‹lat.› (*fachspr. für* dreiwertig)

tri|vi|al [...v...] ‹lat.› (platt, abgedroschen); **Tri|vi|a|li|tät,** die; -, -en; **Tri|vi|al‿li|te|ra|tur, ...ro|man, ...schrft|stel|ler; Tri|vi|um,** das; -s („Dreiweg") (im mittelalterl. Universitätsunterricht die Fächer Grammatik, Dialektik u. Rhetorik)

Tri|zeps, der; -[es], -e ‹lat., „Dreiköpfiger"› (*Med.* Oberarmmuskel)

Tro|as, die; - (im Altertum kleinasiat. Landschaft)

Tro|ca|de|ro [...ka...], der; -[s] (ein Palast in Paris)

tro|chä|isch [...x...] ‹griech.› (aus Trochäen bestehend); **Tro|chä|us,** der; -, ...äen ([antiker] Versfuß)

Tro|chi|lus [...x...], der; -, ...ilen ‹griech.› (*Archit.* Hohlkehle in der Basis ionischer Säulen)

Tro|chit [...x..., *auch* ...xit], der; *Gen.* -s *u.* -en, *Plur.* -en (↑R 126) ‹griech.› (Stängelglied versteinerter Seelilien); **Tro|chi|ten|kalk** (*Geol.;* viele Trochiten enthaltender Kalkstein); **Tro|cho|pho|ra,** die; -, ...phoren (*Biol.* Larve der Ringelwürmer)

tro|cken; *Schreibung in Verbindung mit Verben* (↑R 38 f.): trocken sein, werden; trocken (= in trockenem Zustand, an trockener Stelle) liegen, stehen, sitzen, reiben; trocken sitzen (*auch ugs. für* nichts [mehr] zu trinken haben); *vgl. aber* trockenlegen, trockenreiben, trockenstehen; ↑R 16. *Schreibung in Fügungen* (↑R 47): auf dem Trock[e]nen (auf trockenem Boden) stehen, auf dem Trock[e]nen sein (*ugs. für* festsitzen; nicht weiterkommen); auf dem Trock[e]nen sitzen (*ugs. für* nicht flott, in Verlegenheit sein); im Trock[e]nen sein (auf trockenem Boden) sein; *ugs. auch für* geborgen sein); sein Schäfchen im Trock[e]nen haben, ins Trock[e]ne bringen (*ugs. für* sich wirtschaftlich gesichert haben, sichern); **Tro|cken‿an|la|ge, ...ap|pa|rat; Tro|cken|bee|ren|aus|le|se; Tro|cken‿bi|o|top, ...blu|me, ...bo|den, ...dock, ...ei** (das; -[e]s; Eipulver), **...eis** (feste Kohlensäure), **...ele|ment** (↑R 132), **...far|be, ...fut|ter, ...füt|te|rung, ...ge|mü|se, ...ge|stell, ...hau|be, ...he|fe; Tro|cken|heit; tro|cken|le|gen;** ↑R 38 (entwässern; mit frischen Windeln versehen); einen Sumpf trockenlegen; das Kind wird trockengelegt; *vgl. aber* trocken; **Tro|cken‿le|gung, ...milch, ...ofen** (↑R 132), **...pe|ri|o|de, ...platz, ...ra|sie|rer** (*ugs.*), **...ra|sur, ...raum; tro|cken|rei|ben;** ↑R 38 (durch Reiben trocknen); das Kind wurde nach dem Bad trockengerieben; *vgl. aber* trocken; **Tro|cken|schi|kurs** *vgl.* Trockenskikurs; **Tro|cken|schleu|der; tro|cken|schleu|dern;** ↑R 38 (durch Schleudern trocknen); die Wäsche wurde trockengeschleudert; **tro|cken sit|zen** *vgl.* trocken; **Tro|cken|ski|kurs, Tro|cken|schi|kurs; Tro|cken‿spin|ne, ...spi|ri|tus; tro|cken|ste|hen;** ↑R 38 (keine Milch geben); die Kuh hat mehrere Wochen trockengestanden; *vgl. aber* trocken; **Tro|cken‿übung** (↑R 132; *Sport* vorbereitende Übung beim Erlernen einer sportl. Tätigkeit), **...wä|sche, ...zeit; Tröck|ne,** die; - (*schweiz. für* anhaltende Trockenheit); **trock|nen; Trock|ner; Trock|nung,** die; -

Trod|del, die; -, -n (kleine Quaste); **Trod|del|blu|me; Trod|del|chen, Tröd|del|chen**

Trö|del, der; -s (*ugs. für* alte, wertlose Gegenstände; Kram); **Trö|del|bu|de; Trö|de|lei; Trö|del‿frit|ze** (*ugs. für* m. Person, die ständig trödelt), **...kram, ...la|den, ...lie|se** (*vgl.* Trödelfritze), **...markt; trö|deln** (*ugs. für* beim Arbeiten u. Ä. langsam sein; schlendern); ich ...[e]le (↑R 16); **Tröd|ler; Tröd|le|rin; Tröd|ler|la|den**

Tro|er *vgl.* Trojaner

Trog, der; -[e]s, Tröge

Trog|lo|dyt (↑R 130), der; -en, -en (↑R 126) ‹griech.› (*veraltet für* als Höhlenbewohner lebender Eiszeitmensch)

Troi|er *vgl.* Troyer

Troi|ka ['trɔyka], die; -, -s ‹russ.› (russ. Dreigespann)

tro|isch *vgl.* trojanisch

Trois|dorf ['tro:s...] (Stadt in Nordrhein-Westfalen)

Tro|ja (antike kleinasiat. Stadt); **Tro|ja|ner** (Bewohner von Troja); **tro|ja|nisch;** die trojanischen Helden, *aber* (↑R 108): der Trojanische Krieg; das Trojanische Pferd

trö|len (*schweiz. für* [den Gerichtsgang] leichtfertig od. frevelhaft verzögern); **Trö|le|rei,** die; -

Troll, der; -[e]s, -e (Kobold); **Troll|blu|me; trol|len,** sich (*ugs.*)

Trol|ley|bus ['trɔli...] ‹engl.› (*bes. schweiz. für* Oberleitungsbus)

Trol|lin|ger, der; -s, - (eine Reb- u. Weinsorte)

Trom|be, die; -, -n ‹ital.(-franz.)› (*Meteor.* Wasser-, Sand-, Windhose)

Trom|mel, die; -, -n; **Trom|mel|brem|se; Tröm|mel|chen; Trom|me|lei** (*ugs.*); **Trom|mel‿fell, ...feu|er; trom|meln;** ich ...[e]le (↑R 16); **Trom|mel|re|vol|ver, ...schlag, ...schlä|gel, ...schlä|ger, ...stock** (*Plur.* ...stöcke), **...wasch|ma|schi|ne, ...wir|bel; Tromm|ler; Tromm|le|rin**

Trom|pe|te, die; -, -n ‹franz.›; **trom|pe|ten;** er hat trompetet; **Trom|pe|ten‿baum, ...si|gnal, ...so|lo, ...stoß, ...tier|chen** (ein Wimperntierchen); **Trom|pe|ter; Trom|pe|te|rin; Trom|pe|ter|vo|gel**

Trom|sø ['trɔmzø] (norwegische Stadt)

Trond|heim (*norw. Schreibung von* Drontheim)

Troo|per ['tru:pə(r)] ‹engl.› (Geländefahrzeug)

Tro|pe, die; -, -n *u.* Tro|pus, der; -, ...pen ‹griech., „Wendung"› (Vertauschung des eigentlichen Ausdrucks mit einem bildlichen, z. B. „Bacchus" statt „Wein"); **Tro|pen** *Plur.* (heiße Zone zwischen den Wendekreisen); **Tro|pen‿an|zug, ...fie|ber** (das; -s), **...helm, ...in|sti|tut, ...kli|ma** (das; -s), **...kol|ler** (der; -s), **...krank|heit, ...me|di|zin** (die; -), **...pflan|ze; tro|pen|taug|lich; Tro|pen|taug|lich|keit**

[1]**Tropf,** der; -[e]s, Tröpfe (*ugs. für* einfältiger Mensch); [2]**Tropf,** der; -[e]s, -e (*Med.* Vorrichtung für die Tropfinfusion); **tropf|bar; tropf|bar|flüs|sig; Tröpf|chen; Tröpf|chen|in|fek|ti|on; tröpf|chen|wei|se; tröp|feln;** ich ...[e]le (↑R 16); **trop|fen; Trop|fen,** der; -s, -; **Trop|fen‿fän|ger, ...form** (die; -); **trop|fen‿för|mig, ...wei|se; Tröp|ferl|bad** (*ostösterr. ugs. für* Brausebad); **Tropf‿fla|sche, ...in|fu|si|on; tropf|nass; Tropf‿röhr|chen, ...stein; Tropf|stein|höh|le**

Tro|phäe, die; -, -n ‹griech.› (Siegeszeichen [erbeutete Waffen, Fahnen u. Ä.]; Jagdbeute [z. B. Geweih])

tro|phisch ‹griech.› (*Med.* mit der Ernährung zusammenhängend)

Tro|pi|cal [...k(ə)l], der; -s, -s

⟨griech.-engl., „tropisch"⟩ (luftdurchlässiger Anzugstoff in Leinenbindung); **Tro|pi|ka,** die; - ⟨griech.⟩ (schwere Form der Malaria); **tro|pisch** (zu den Tropen gehörend; südlich, heiß; *Rhet.* bildlich); **Tro|pis|mus,** der; -, ...men (*Bot.* Krümmungsbewegung der Pflanze, die durch äußere Reize hervorgerufen wird); **Tro|po|sphä|re,** die; - (*Meteor.* unterste Schicht der Erdatmosphäre); **¹Tro|pus** *vgl.* Trope; **²Tro|pus,** der; -, Tropen (im gregorianischen Gesang der Kirchenton u. die Gesangsformel für das Schluss-Amen; melodische Ausschmückung von Texten im gregorianischen Choral)

tross! (*landsch. für* schnell!)

Tross, der; -es, -e ⟨franz.⟩ (*Milit. früher* der die Truppe mit Verpflegung u. Munition versorgende Wagenpark; *übertr. für* Gefolge, Haufen);

Tros|se, die; -, -n (starkes Tau; Drahtseil); **Tross‿knecht, ...schiff** (↑R 136)

Trost, der; -es; ein Trost bringender Brief (↑R 40); **trost|be|dürf|tig; Trost brin|gend** *vgl.* Trost; **trös|ten;** sich -; **Trös|ter; Trös|te|rin; tröst|lich; trost|los; Trost|lo|sig|keit,** die; -; **Trost‿pflas|ter, ...preis; trost|reich; Trost|spruch; Trös|tung; Trost|wort** *Plur.* ...worte

Trö|te, die; -, -n (*landsch. für* Blasinstrument, bes. [Kinder]trompete); **trö|ten** (*landsch.*)

Trott, der; -[e]s, -e (lässige Gangart; *ugs. für* langweiliger, routinemäßiger [Geschäfts]gang; eingewurzelte Gewohnheit); **Trott|baum** (Teil der [alten] Weinkelter); **Trot|te,** die; -, -n (*südwestd. u. schweiz. für* [alte] Weinkelter)

Trot|tel, der; -s, - (*ugs. für* einfältiger Mensch, Dummkopf); **Trot|te|lei; trot|tel|haft; Trot|tel|haf|tig|keit; trot|te|lig; Trot|te|lig|keit,** die; -

trot|teln (*ugs. für* langsam [u. unaufmerksam] gehen); ich ...[e]le (↑R 16); **trot|ten** (*ugs. für* schwerfällig gehen); **Trot|teur** [...'tø:r], der; -s, -s ⟨franz.⟩ (Laufschuh mit niedrigem Absatz); **Trot|ti|nett,** das; -s, -e ⟨franz.⟩ (*schweiz. für* Kinderroller); **Trot|toir** [...'to̯a:r], das; -s, *Plur.* -e *u.* -s (*schweiz., sonst veraltet für* Bürgersteig)

Tro|tyl, das; -s (*svw.* Trinitrotoluol)

trotz (↑R 46); *Präp. mit Gen.:* trotz des Regens, trotz vieler Ermahnungen; *auch, bes. südd., schweiz. u. österr., mit Dat.:* trotz dem Regen; *mit Dat. auch, wenn der Artikel fehlt, und immer, wenn der Gen. Plur. nicht erkennbar ist:* trotz nassem Asphalt, trotz Atomkraftwerken; *ebenso in:* trotz all[e]dem, trotz allem; *ein stark gebeugtes Substantiv im Sing. ohne Artikel u. Attribut bleibt oft schon ungebeugt:* trotz Regen [und Kälte], trotz Umbau; **Trotz,** der; -es; aus Trotz; dir zum Trotz; Trotz bieten; **Trotz|al|ter,** das; -s; **trotz|dem;** trotzdem ist es falsch; *auch als Konj.:* trotzdem (*älter* trotzdem dass) du nicht rechtzeitig eingegriffen hast; **trot|zen;** du trotzt; **Trot|zer** (*auch Bot.* zweijährige Pflanze, die im zweiten Jahr keine Blüten bildet); **trot|zig**

Trotz|ki (russ. Revolutionär); **Trotz|kis|mus,** der; - (von Trotzki begründete u. vertretene revolutionäre Theorie); **Trotz|kist,** der; -en, -en; ↑R 126 (Anhänger des Trotzkismus); **trotz|kis|tisch**

Trotz|kopf; trotz|köp|fig; Trotz‿pha|se, ...re|ak|ti|on

Trou|ba|dour ['tru:badu:r, *auch* ...'du:r], der; -s, *Plur.* -e *u.* -s ⟨franz.⟩ (provenzal. Minnesänger des 12. u. 13. Jh.s)

Trou|ble ['trab(ə)l], der; -s ⟨engl.⟩ (*ugs. für* Ärger, Unannehmlichkeiten)

Trou|pi|er [tru'pi̯e:], der; -s, -s ⟨franz.⟩ (*veraltet für* altgedienter Soldat)

Trou|vère [tru'vɛ:r], der; -s, -s ⟨franz.⟩ ([nord]franz. Minnesänger des 12. u. 13. Jh.s)

Troy|er, Troi|er ['trɔyər], der; -s, - (Matrosenunterhemd)

Troyes [tro̯a] (franz. Stadt)

Troy|ge|wicht ['trɔy...] ⟨*zu* Troyes⟩ (Gewicht für Edelmetalle u. a. in England u. in den USA)

Trub, der; -[e]s (*fachspr. für* Bodensatz beim Wein, Bier); **trüb, trü|be;** im Trüben fischen (*ugs.* unklare Zustände zum eigenen Vorteil ausnutzen); **Trü|be,** die; -

Tru|bel, der; -s

trü|ben; sich -; **Trüb|heit,** die; -; **Trüb|nis,** die; -, -se (*veraltet*); **Trüb|sal,** die; -, -e; **trüb|se|lig; Trüb|se|lig|keit,** die; -; **Trüb|sinn,** der; -[e]s; **trüb|sin|nig; Trub|stof|fe** *Plur.*; *vgl.* Trub; **Trü|bung**

Truch|sess, der; *Gen.* -es, *älter* -en, *Plur.* -e (im Mittelalter für Küche u. Tafel zuständiger Hofbeamter)

Truck [trak], der; -s, -s ⟨engl.⟩ (*amerik. u. internat. Bez. für* Lastkraftwagen); **Tru|cker** [trakə], der; -s, - ⟨engl.⟩ (Lastwagenfahrer)

Truck|sys|tem ['trak...], das; -s ⟨engl.⟩ (frühere Form der Lohnzahlung in Waren, Naturalien)

Trud|chen, Tru|de, Tru|di (w. Vorn.)

tru|deln (*Fliegerspr.* drehend niedergehen od. abstürzen; *landsch. für* würfeln); ich ...[e]le (↑R 16)

Tru|di *vgl.* Trude

Trüf|fel, die; -, -n, *ugs. meist* der; -s, - ⟨franz.⟩ (ein Pilz; eine kugelförmige Praline); **Trüf|fel|le|ber|pas|te|te; trüf|feln** (mit Trüffeln anrichten); ich ...[e]le (↑R 16); **Trüf|fel‿schwein, ...wurst**

Trug, der; -[e]s; [mit] Lug und -; **Trug‿bild, ...dol|de; trü|gen;** du trogst; du trögest; getrogen; trüg[e]!; **trü|ge|risch; Trug‿ge|bil|de, ...schluss**

Tru|he, die; -, -n; **Tru|hen|de|ckel**

Trum, der *od.* das; -[e]s, *Plur.* -e *u.* Trümer ⟨Nebenform von ¹Trumm⟩ (*Bergmannsspr.* Abteilung eines Schachtes; kleiner Gang; *Maschinenbau* frei laufender Teil des Förderbandes od. des Treibriemens)

Tru|man ['tru:mən] (Präsident der USA)

¹Trumm, der *od.* das; -[e]s, *Plur.* -e *u.* Trümmer (*svw.* Trum); **²Trumm,** das; -[e]s, Trümmer (*landsch. für* großes Stück, Exemplar); **Trüm|mer** *Plur.* ([Bruch]stücke); etwas in - schlagen; **Trüm|mer‿feld, ...flo|ra, ...frau, ...ge|stein, ...grund|stück; trüm|mer|haft; Trüm|mer‿hau|fen, ...land|schaft**

Trumpf, der; -[e]s, Trümpfe ⟨lat.⟩ (eine der [wahlweise] höchsten Karten beim Kartenspielen, mit denen Karten anderer Farben gestochen werden können); **Trumpf|ass; trump|fen; Trumpf‿far|be, ...kar|te, ...kö|nig**

Trunk, der; -[e]s, Trünke *Plur. selten* (geh.); **trun|ken;** er ist vor Freude -; **Trun|ken|bold,** der; -[e]s, -e (*abwertend*); **Trun|ken|heit,** die; -; **Trunk|sucht,** die; -; **trunk|süch|tig; Trunk|süch|ti|ge,** der *u.* die; -en, -en (↑R 5 ff.)

Trupp, der; -s, -s ⟨franz.⟩; **Trüpp|chen; Trup|pe,** die; -, -n; **Trup|pen** *Plur.*; **Trup|pen‿ab|bau, ...ab|zug, ...arzt, ...auf|marsch, ...be|treu|ung, ...be|we|gung, ...ein|heit, ...füh|rer, ...gat|tung, ...kon|tin|gent, ...kon|zent|ra|ti|on, ...pa|ra|de, ...stär|ke, ...teil**

(der), **...trans|port, ...trans|por|ter, ...übungs|platz** (↑R 132), **...un|ter|kunft, ...ver|pfle|gung; trupp|wei|se**
Trü|sche, die; -, -n (ein Fisch)
Trust [trast], der; -[e]s, *Plur.* -e *u.* -s ‹engl.› (Konzern); **trust|ar|tig; Trus|tee** [tras'ti:], der; -s, -s (*engl. Bez. für* Treuhänder); **trust|frei**
Trut‿hahn, ...hen|ne, ...huhn
Trutz, der; -es *(veraltet);* zu Schutz und -; Schutz-und-Trutz-Bündnis *(vgl. d.);* **Trutz|burg; trut|zen** (*veraltet für* trotzen); du trutzt; **trut|zig** *(veraltet)*
Try|pa|no|so|ma, das; -s, ...men *meist Plur.* ‹griech.› (*Zool.* Geißeltierchen)
Tryp|sin, das; -s ‹griech.› (Ferment der Bauchspeicheldrüse)
Tsat|si|ki (↑R 130) *vgl.* Zaziki
[1]Tschad, der; -[s] (*kurz für* Tschadsee); **[2]Tschad,** der; -[s] *meist mit Artikel* (Staat in Afrika); **Tscha|der; Tscha|de|rin; tschadisch**
Tscha|dor, der; -s, -s ‹pers.› ([von persischen Frauen getragener] langer Schleier)
Tschad|see, der; -s (See in Zentralafrika)
Tschai|kows|ky[1] [...'kɔfski] (russ. Komponist)
Tscha|ko, der; -s, -s ‹ung.› (*früher* Kopfbedeckung bei Militär u. Polizei)
Tschan|du, das; -s ‹Hindi› (zum Rauchen zubereitetes Opium)
Tschap|ka, die; -, -s ‹poln.› (Kopfbedeckung der Ulanen); *vgl. aber* Schapka
Tschap|perl, das; -s, -n (*österr. ugs. für* tapsiger Mensch)
Tschar|dasch *frühere Eindeutschung für* Csárdás
tschau! *vgl.* ciao!
Tsche|che, der; -n, -n; ↑R 126; **Tsche|cherl,** das; -s, -n (*ostösterr. ugs. für* kleines, einfaches Gast-, Kaffeehaus); **Tsche|chi|en** (*kurz für* Tschechische Republik); **Tsche|chin; tsche|chisch;** *aber* (↑R 102 *u.* 108): die Tschechische Republik; **Tsche|chisch,** das; -[s] (Sprache); *vgl.* Deutsch; **Tsche|chi|sche,** das; -n; *vgl.* Deutsche, das; **Tsche|chi|sche Re|pub|lik** (Staat in Mitteleuropa); **Tsche|cho|slo|wa|ke,** der; -n, -n (↑R 126); **Tsche|cho|slo|wa|kei,** die; - (ehem. Staat in Mitteleuropa; *Abk.* ČSFR); **Tsche|cho|slo|wa|kin; tsche|cho|slo|wa|kisch**
Tsche|chow ['tʃɛxɔf] (russ. Schriftsteller)
Tsche|ki|ang (chin. Prov.)
tschen|tschen (*südösterr. für* raunzen, kritisieren); du tschentschst
Tscher|kes|se, der; -n, -n; ↑R 126 (Angehöriger einer Gruppe kaukas. Volksstämme); **Tscher|kes|sin; tscher|kes|sisch**
Tscher|no|byl (Stadt in der Ukraine)
Tscher|no|sem [...'sjɔm] *u.* **Tscher|no|sjom,** das; -s ‹russ., „Schwarzerde" *[vgl. d.]*›
Tsche|ro|ke|se, der; -n, -n; ↑R 126 (Angehöriger eines nordamerik. Indianerstammes)
Tscher|per, der; -s, - (*Bergmannsspr. veraltet* kurzes Messer)
Tscher|wo|nez, der; -, ...wonzen (ehem. russ. Währungseinheit); 3 - (↑R 90)
Tschet|sche|ne (↑R 130), der; -n, -n; ↑R 126 (Angehöriger eines kaukas. Volkes)
Tschi|buk [*österr.* 'tʃi:...], der; -s, -s ‹türk.› (lange türkische Tabakspfeife)
Tschick, der; -s, - ‹ital.› (*österr. ugs. für* Zigarette[nstummel])
Tschi|kosch ['tʃi(:)...] *vgl.* Csikós
tschil|pen (zwitschern [vom Sperling])
Tschi|nel|len *Plur.* ‹ital.› (Becken [messingnes Schlaginstrument])
tsching!; tsching|bum!
Tschis|ma, der; -s, ...men ‹ung.› (niedriger, farbiger ung. Stiefel)
Tschukt|sche (↑R 130), der; -n, -n; ↑R 126 (Angehöriger eines altsibir. Volkes)
tschüs!, *auch* tschüss! (*ugs. für* auf Wiedersehen!)
Tschusch, der; -en, -en ‹slaw.› (*österr. ugs. für* Ausländer, Fremder, bes. Südslawe, Slowene)
tschüss *vgl.* tschüs
Tschu|wa|sche, der; -n, -n; ↑R 126 (Angehöriger eines ostfinn.-turktatar. Mischvolkes)
Tsd. = [3]Tausend
Tse|tse‿flie|ge ‹Bantu; dt.› (Stechfliege, die bes. die Schlafkrankheit überträgt), **...pla|ge**
T-Shirt ['ti:ʃœ:(r)t] ‹engl.› ([kurzärmliges] Oberteil aus Trikot)
Tsi|nan (chin. Stadt)
Tsing|tau (chin. Stadt)
Tsjao, der; -[s], -[s] ‹chin.› (chin. Münze); 10 - (↑R 90)
Tsu|ga, die; -, *Plur.* -s *u.* ...gen ‹jap.› (Schierlings- od. Hemlocktanne)
T-Trä|ger, der; -s, -; ↑R 25 *(Bauw.)*
TU = technische Universität; *vgl.* technisch
Tu|a|reg [*auch* ...'rɛk] (*Plur. von* Targi)
Tu|ba, die; -, ...ben ‹lat.› (Blechblasinstrument; *Med.* Eileiter, Ohrtrompete)
Tüb|bing, der; -s, -s (*Bergmannsspr.* Tunnel-, Schachtring)
Tu|be, die; -, -n ‹lat.› (röhrenförmiger Behälter [für Farben u. a.]; *Med. auch für* Tuba); **Tu|ben** (*Plur. von* Tuba *u.* Tubus); **Tu|ben|schwan|ger|schaft**
Tu|ber|kel, der; -s, -, *österr. auch* die; -, -n ‹lat.› (*Med.* Knötchen); **Tu|ber|kel‿bak|te|rie, ...ba|zil|lus; tu|ber|ku|lar** (knotig); **Tu|ber|ku|lin,** das; -s (Substanz zum Nachweis von Tuberkulose); **tu|ber|ku|lös** (mit Tuberkeln durchsetzt; schwindsüchtig); **Tu|ber|ku|lo|se,** die; -, -n (eine Infektionskrankheit; *Abk.* Tb, Tbc, Tbk); **Tu|ber|ku|lo|se|für|sor|ge; tu|ber|ku|lo|se|krank** (*Abk.* Tbc-krank, Tb-krank, Tbk-krank; ↑R 26 *u.* R 60); **Tu|ber|ku|lo|se|kran|ke**
Tu|be|ro|se, die; -, -n ‹lat.› (eine aus Mexiko stammende stark duftende Zierpflanze)
Tü|bin|gen (Stadt am Neckar); **Tü|bin|ger** (↑R 103)
tu|bu|lär, tu|bu|lös ‹lat.› (*Med* röhrenförmig); -e Drüsen; **Tu|bus,** der; -, *Plur.* ...ben *u.* -se (bei optischen Geräten das linsenfassende Rohr; bei Glasgeräten der Rohransatz)
Tuch, das; -[e]s, *Plur.* Tücher *u.* *(Arten:)* -e; **Tuch‿an|zug, ...art; tuch|ar|tig; Tuch|bahn; Tü|chel|chen; tu|chen** (aus Tuch)
Tu|chent, die; -, -en (*bayr., österr. für* mit Federn gefüllte Bettdecke)
Tuch‿fab|rik, ...fab|ri|kant, ...füh|lung (die; -; *nur in Wendungen wie* [mit jmdm.] - haben), **...han|del** (*vgl.* [1]Handel); **Tüch|lein; Tuch‿ma|cher, ...man|tel**
Tu|chols|ky [...ki] (dt. Journalist u. Schriftsteller)
Tuch|rock; *vgl.* [1]Rock
tüch|tig; Tüch|tig|keit, die; -
Tü|cke, die; -, -n
tu|ckern (vom Motor)
tü|ckisch; eine -e Krankheit; **tück|schen** (*ostmitteld. u. nordd. für* heimlich zürnen); du tückschst
tuck|tuck! (Lockruf für Hühner)
Tü|der, der; -s, - (*nordd. für* Seil zum Anbinden von Tieren auf der Weide); **tü|dern** (*nordd. für* Tiere auf der Weide anbinden; in Un-

[1] *So die eigene Schreibung des Komponisten. Nach dem vom Duden verwendeten Transkriptionssystem müsste* Tschaikowski *geschrieben werden.*

ordnung bringen); ich ...ere (↑R 16)

Tu|dor ['tu:dɔr, *engl.* 'tju:də(r)], der; -[s], -s (Angehöriger eines engl. Herrschergeschlechtes); **Tu|dor‿bo|gen** *(Archit.),* **...stil** (der; -[e]s)

Tu|e|rei (*ugs. für* Sichzieren)

[1]Tuff, der; -s, -s (*landsch. für* Strauß, Büschel [von Blumen o. Ä.])

[2]Tuff, der; -s, -e ‹ital.› (ein Gestein); **Tuff|fels, Tuff|fel|sen** (↑R 136); **tuf|fig; Tuff|stein**

Tüf|tel|ar|beit *(ugs.);* **Tüf|te|lei** *(ugs.);* **Tüf|te|ler** usw. *vgl.* Tüftler usw.; **tüf|teln** (*ugs. für* eine knifflige Aufgabe mit Ausdauer zu lösen suchen); ich ...[e]le (↑R 16)

Tuf|ting... ['taf...] ‹engl.› (*in Zus.* Spezialfertigungsart für Auslegeware u. Teppiche, bei der Schlingen in das Grundgewebe eingenäht werden); **Tuf|ting‿schlin|gen|wa|re, ...tep|pich, ...ver|fah|ren** (das; -s)

Tüft|ler; Tüft|le|rin; tüft|lig

Tu|gend, die; -, -en; **Tu|gend|bold,** der; -[e]s, -e (*iron. für* tugendhafter Mensch); **tu|gend|haft; Tu|gend|haf|tig|keit,** die; -; **Tu|gend‿held** *(auch iron.),* **...hel|din; tu|gend|lich** *(veraltet);* **tu|gend|los; Tu|gend|lo|sig|keit,** die; -; **tu|gend|sam** *(veraltend);* **Tu|gend|sam|keit,** die; -; **Tu|gend‿wäch|ter** *(iron.),* **...wäch|te|rin**

Tui|le|ri|en [tÿilə'ri:ən] *Plur.* ‹„Ziegeleien"› (ehem. Residenzschloss der franz. Könige in Paris)

Tu|is|ko *u.* **Tu|is|to** (germ. Gottheit, Stammvater der Germanen)

Tu|kan [*auch* tu'ka:n], der; -s, -e ‹indian.› (Pfefferfresser [ein mittel- u. südamerik. Vogel])

Tu|la (russ. Stadt); **Tu|la|ar|beit** (↑R 105; Silberarbeit mit Ornamenten)

Tu|la|rä|mie (↑R 132), die; - ‹indian.; griech.; *erster Wortteil nach* der kaliforn. Landschaft Tulare› (Hasenpest, die auf Menschen übertragen werden kann)

Tu|la|sil|ber (*svw.* Tulaarbeit)

Tu|li|pan, der; -[e]s, -e *u.* **Tu|li|pa|ne,** die; -, -n ‹pers.› (*veraltet für* Tulpe)

Tüll, der; -s, *Plur. (Arten:)* -e ‹nach der franz. Stadt Tulle› (netzartiges Gewebe); **Tüll|blu|se**

Tül|le, die; -, -n (*landsch. für* [Ausguss]röhrchen; kurzes Rohrstück zum Einstecken)

Tüll|gar|di|ne

Tul|lia (altröm. w. Eigenn.); **Tul|li|us** (altröm. m. Eigenn.)

Tüll‿schlei|er, ...vor|hang

Tul|pe, die; -, -n ‹pers.›; **Tul|pen‿feld, ...zwie|bel**

...tum (z. B. Besitztum, das[1]; -s, ...tümer)

tumb (*altertümelnd scherzh. für* einfältig)

[1]Tum|ba, die; -, ...ben ‹griech.› (Scheinbahre beim kath. Totengottesdienst; Überbau eines Grabes mit Grabplatte)

[2]Tum|ba, die; -, -s ‹span.› (eine große Trommel)

Tumb|heit, die; - (das Tumbsein)

...tüm|lich (z. B. eigentümlich)

Tum|mel, der; -s, - (*landsch. für* Rausch); **tum|meln** (bewegen); sich - ([sich be]eilen; *auch für* herumtollen); ich ...[e]le [mich] (↑R 16); **Tum|mel|platz; Tumm|ler** („Taumler") (*früher* Trinkgefäß mit abgerundetem Boden, Stehauf); **Tümm|ler** (Delphin; eine Taube)

Tu|mor [*nichtfachsprachl. auch* tu'mo:r], der; -s, *Plur.* ...oren, *nichtfachsprachl. auch* ...ore ‹lat.› (*Med.* Geschwulst); **Tu|mor‿wachs|tum, ...zel|le**

Tüm|pel, der; -s, -

Tu|mu|li (*Plur. von* Tumulus)

Tu|mult, der; -[e]s, -e ‹lat.› (Lärm; Unruhe; Auflauf; Aufruhr); **Tu|mul|tu|ant,** der; -en, -en; ↑R 126 (Unruhestifter; Ruhestörer, Aufrührer); **tu|mul|tu|a|risch** (lärmend, unruhig, erregt); **tu|mul|tu|ös** (*svw.* tumultuarisch)

Tu|mu|lus, der; -, ...li ‹lat.› (vorgeschichtliches Hügelgrab)

tun; ich tue *od.* tu, du tust, er tut, wir tun, ihr tut, sie tun; du tatst (tatest), er tat; du tätest; tuend; getan; tu[e]!, tut!; *vgl.* dick[e]tun, gut tun, schöntun, wohl tun; **Tun,** das; -s; das Tun und Treiben

Tün|che, die; -, -n; **tün|chen; Tün|cher** *(landsch.);* **Tün|cher|meis|ter**

Tund|ra (↑R 130), die; -, ...dren ‹finn.-russ.› (baumlose Kältesteppe jenseits der arktischen Waldgrenze); **Tund|ren|step|pe**

Tu|nell, das; -s, -e (*landsch., vor allem südd. u. österr. svw.* Tunnel)

tu|nen ['tju:nən] ‹engl.› (die Leistung [eines Kfz-Motors] nachträglich steigern); ein getunter Motor, Wagen; **Tu|ner** ['tju:nə(r)], der; -s, - (*Elektronik* Kanalwähler)

Tu|ne|si|en (Staat in Nordafrika); **Tu|ne|si|er; Tu|ne|si|e|rin; tu|ne|sisch**

Tun|fisch *vgl.* Thun|fisch

Tun|gu|se, der; -n, -n; ↑R 126 (*svw.* Ewenke)

Tu|nicht|gut, der; *Gen.* - *u.* -[e]s, *Plur.* -e

Tu|ni|ka, die; -, ...ken ‹lat.› (altröm. Untergewand)

Tu|ning ['tju:...], das; -s ‹engl.› (nachträgliche Erhöhung der Leistung eines Kfz-Motors)

Tu|nis (Hptst. von Tunesien); **Tu|ni|ser** (↑R 103); **tu|ni|sisch**

Tun|ke, die; -, -n; **tun|ken**

tun|lich (*veraltend für* ratsam, angebracht); **Tun|lich|keit,** die; -; **tun|lichst** (*svw.* möglichst)

Tun|nel, der; -s, *Plur.* - *u.* -s ‹engl.›; *vgl. auch* Tunell; **tun|neln** (*ugs., bes. Fußball* den Ball zwischen den Beinen des Gegners hindurchspielen)

Tun|te, die; -, -n (*ugs. für* Frau; Homosexueller mit femininem Gebaren); **tun|ten|haft; tun|tig**

Tun|wort *vgl.* Tuwort

Tu|pa|ma|ro, der; -s, -s *meist Plur.* ‹nach dem Inkakönig Túpac Amaru› (uruguayischer Stadtguerilla)

Tupf, der; -[e]s, -e (*südd., österr. u. schweiz. für* Tupfen); **Tüp|fel,** der *od., österr. nur,* das; -s, - (Pünktchen); **Tüp|fel|chen;** das Tüpfelchen auf dem i (↑R 60); das i-Tüpfelchen (↑R 25); **Tüp|fel|farn; tüp|fe|lig,** tüpflig; **tüp|feln;** ich ...[e]le (↑R 16); **tup|fen; Tup|fen,** der; -s, - (Punkt; [kreisrunder] Fleck); **Tup|fer; tüpf|lig** *vgl.* tüpfelig

[1]Tu|pi, der; -[s], -[s] (Angehöriger einer südamerik. Sprachfamilie); **[2]Tu|pi,** das; - (indian. Verkehrssprache in Südamerika)

Tür, die; -, -en; von - zu -; du kriegst die - nicht zu! (*ugs. für* das ist nicht zu fassen!)

Tu|ran (Tiefland in Mittelasien)

Tu|ran|dot (pers. Märchenprinzessin)

Tür|an|gel

Tu|ras, der; -, -se (*Technik* Kettenstern [bei Baggern])

Tur|ban, der; -s, -e ‹pers.› ([moslem.] Kopfbedeckung); **tur|ban|ar|tig**

Tur|bel|la|rie [...iə], die; -, -n *meist Plur.* ‹lat.› (*Zool.* Strudelwurm); **Tur|bi|ne,** die; -, -n ‹franz.› (*Technik* eine Kraftmaschine); **Tur|bi|nen‿an|trieb, ...flug|zeug, ...haus; Tur|bo,** der; -s, -s (*Kfz-Technik kurz für* Turbolader); **Tur|bo‿ge|ne|ra|tor** ‹lat.›, **...kom|pres|sor** (Kreiselverdichter), **...la|der, ...mo|tor; Tur|bo-Prop-Flug|zeug** (Turbinen-Propeller-Flugzeug); **Tur|bo|ven|ti|la|tor** (Kreisellüfter); **tur|bu|lent** (stürmisch, unge-

stüm); **Tur|bu|lenz,** die; -, -en (turbulentes Geschehen; *Physik* Auftreten von Wirbeln in einem Luft-, Gas- od. Flüssigkeitsstrom)
Tür|chen; Tür|drü|cker; Tü|re, die; -, -n (*landsch. neben* Tür)
Turf, der; -s ⟨engl., „Rasen"⟩ (Pferderennbahn)
Tür‿fal|le (*schweiz. für* Türklinke), **...flü|gel, ...fül|lung**
Tur|gen|jew [...'gɛnjɛf] (russ. Dichter)
Tur|gor, der; -s ⟨lat.⟩ (*Med.* Spannungszustand des Gewebes; *Bot.* Innendruck der Pflanzenzellen)
Tür‿griff, ...he|ber, ...hü|ter; ...tü|rig (z. B. eintürig)
Tu|rin (ital. Stadt); *vgl.* Torino; **Tu|ri|ner** (↑R 103); **tu|ri|nisch**
Tür|ke, der; -n, -n; ↑R 126 (*auch für* [nach]gestellte Szene im Fernsehen); einen -n bauen (*ugs. für* etwas vortäuschen, vorspielen); **Tür|kei,** die; -; **tür|ken** (*ugs. für* vortäuschen, fälschen); **Tür|ken,** der; -s (*österr. ugs. für* Mais); **Tür|ken‿bund** (der; -[e]s, ...bünde; eine Lilienart), **...pfei|fe, ...säbel, ...sitz** (der; -es), **...tau|be; Tur|kes|tan** [*auch* ...s'ta:n] (innerasiat. Gebiet)
Tur|key ['tœ:(r)ki], der; -s, -s ⟨engl.⟩ (unangenehmer Zustand, nachdem die Wirkung eines Rauschgiftes nachgelassen hat)
Tür|kin; tür|kis ⟨franz.⟩ (türkisfarben); ein - Kleid; *vgl. auch* beige; [1]**Tür|kis,** der; -es, -e (ein Schmuckstein); [2]**Tür|kis,** das; - (türkisfarbener Ton); in - (↑R 47); **tür|kisch;** -es Pfund (*Abk.* Ltq); **Tür|kisch,** das; -[s] (Sprache); *vgl.* Deutsch; **Tür|ki|sche,** das; -n; *vgl.* Deutsche, das; **Tür|kisch|rot; tür|kis|far|ben, tür|kis|far|big; tur|ki|sie|ren** (türkisch machen)
Tür‿klin|ke, ...klop|fer
Turk|me|ne, der; -n, -n; ↑R 126 (Angehöriger eines Turkvolkes); **Turk|me|ni|en** [...i̯ən] *vgl.* Turkmenistan; **Turk|me|nin; turk|me|nisch; Turk|me|nis|tan** [*auch* ...s'ta:n], Turk|me|ni|en (Staat in Mittelasien); **Tur|ko|lo|ge,** der; -n, -n (↑R 126) ⟨türk.; griech.⟩ (Wissenschaftler auf dem Gebiet der Turkologie); **Tur|ko|lo|gie,** die; - (Erforschung der Turksprachen u. -kulturen); **Tur|ko|lo|gin; Turk‿spra|che, ...stamm, ...ta|ta|ren** (*Plur.;* Turkvolk der Tataren), **...volk** (Volk mit einer Turksprache)
Turm, der; -[e]s, Türme
Tur|ma|lin, der; -s, -e ⟨singhal.-franz.⟩ (ein Schmuckstein)
Turm|bau *Plur.* ...bauten; **Türm|chen; Turm|dreh|kran;** [1]**tür|men** (aufeinander häufen)
[2]**tür|men** ⟨hebr.⟩ (*ugs. für* weglaufen, ausreißen)
Tür|mer; Turm‿fal|ke, ...hau|be; turm|hoch; ...tür|mig (z. B. zweitürmig); **Turm‿sprin|gen** (das; -s; *Sport*), **...uhr, ...wäch|ter**
Turn [tœ:(r)n], der; -s, -s ⟨engl.⟩ (Kehre im Kunstfliegen); *vgl. aber* Törn
Turn|an|zug; tur|nen; Tur|nen, das; -s; **Tur|ner; Tur|ne|rei,** die; -, -en; **Tur|ne|rin; tur|ne|risch; Tur|ner|schaft; Turn‿fest, ...ge|rät, ...hal|le, ...hemd, ...ho|se**
Tur|nier, das; -s, -e ⟨franz.⟩ (*früher* ritterliches, *jetzt* sportliches Kampfspiel; Wettkampf); **tur|nie|ren** *(veraltet);* **Tur|nier‿pferd, ...rei|ter, ...rei|te|rin, ...tanz, ...tän|zer, ...tän|ze|rin**
Turn‿klei|dung, ...leh|rer, ...leh|re|rin, ...schuh; Turn|schuh|ge|ne|ra|ti|on, die; -; (Generation von Jugendlichen [bes. der 80er Jahre], die lässige Kleidung bevorzugt); **Turn‿stun|de, ...übung** (↑R 132), **...un|ter|richt**
Tur|nus, der; -, -se ⟨griech.⟩ (Reihenfolge; Wechsel; Umlauf; *österr. auch für* Arbeitsschicht, praktische Ausbildungszeit des Arztes); im -; **Tur|nus|arzt** *(österr.);* **tur|nus|ge|mäß; tur|nus|mä|ßig** (*dafür besser* turnusgemäß)
Turn|va|ter, der; -s; - Jahn; **Turn|ver|ein** (*Abk.* TV); (↑R 23:) Turn- und Sportverein (*Abk.* TuS); **Turn‿wart, ...zeug** (das; -[e]s)
Tür|öff|ner (elektr. Anlage)
Tu|ron, das; -s (*Geol.* zweitälteste Stufe der oberen Kreide)
Tür‿pfos|ten, ...rah|men, ...rie|gel, ...schild (das), **...schlie|ßer, ...schloss, ...schnal|le** (*österr. für* Türklinke), **...schwel|le, ...spalt, ...ste|her, ...stock** (*Plur.* ...stöcke; *Bergmannsspr.* senkrecht aufgestellter Holzpfahl, Streckenausbauteil; *österr. für* [Holz]einfassung der Türöffnung); **Tür|sturz** *Plur.* -e *u.* ...stürze *(Bauw.)*
tur|teln (girren); ich ...[e]le (↑R 16); **Tur|tel|tau|be**
TuS = Turn- und Sportverein
Tusch, der; -[e]s, -e (Musikbegleitung bei einem Hochruf); einen - blasen
Tu|sche, die; -, -n ⟨franz.⟩ (Zeichentinte)
Tu|sche|lei; tu|scheln (heimlich [zu]flüstern); ich ...[e]le (↑R 16)
[1]**tu|schen** ⟨franz.⟩ (mit Tusche zeichnen); du tuschst
[2]**tu|schen** (*landsch. für* zum Schweigen bringen); du tuschst
Tusch|far|be; tu|schie|ren (*fachspr. für* ebene Metalloberflächen [nach Markierung mit Tusche] herstellen); **Tusch‿kas|ten, ...ma|le|rei, ...zeich|nung**
Tus|ku|lum, das; -s, ...la ⟨lat.; nach dem altröm. Tusculum⟩ (*veraltet für* [ruhiger] Landsitz)
Tus|nel|da *vgl.* Thusnelda
Tus|si, die; -, -s (*ugs. abwertend für* Mädchen, Frau, Freundin)
tut!; tut, tut!
Tu|tan|cha|mun, *auch* Tu|ten|cha|mun (↑R 132; ägypt. König)
Tüt|chen; Tu|te, die; -, -n (*ugs. für* Signalhorn, Hupe; *landsch. auch für* Tüte); **Tü|te,** die; -, -n
Tu|tel, die; -, -en ⟨lat.⟩ (Vormundschaft); **tu|te|la|risch**
tu|ten; (↑R 50:) von Tuten und Blasen keine Ahnung haben *(ugs.)*
Tu|ten|cha|mun *vgl.* Tutanchamun
Tut|horn *Plur.* ...hörner
Tu|tor, der; -s, ...oren ⟨lat.⟩ (jmd., der Studienanfänger betreut; *im röm. Recht für* Vormund); **Tu|to|rin; Tu|to|ri|um,** das; -s, ...ien [...i̯ən] ([begleitende] Übung an einer Hochschule)
Tüt|tel, der; -s, - (*veraltet, noch landsch. für* Pünktchen); **Tüt|tel|chen** (*ugs. für* ein Geringstes); kein - preisgeben
tut|ti ⟨ital., „alle"⟩ *(Musik);* **Tut|ti,** das; -[s], -[s] (volles Orchester); **Tut|ti|frut|ti,** das; -[s], -[s] ⟨„alle Früchte"⟩ (eine Süßspeise; *veraltet für* Allerlei); **Tut|ti|spie|ler** (Orchestermusiker ohne solistische Aufgaben)
tut, tut!
Tu|tu [ty'ty:], das; -[s], -s ⟨franz.⟩ (Ballettröckchen)
TÜV [tyf] = Technischer Überwachungs-Verein (*vgl.* technisch)
Tu|va|lu [...v...] (Inselstaat im Pazifik); **Tu|va|lu|er; tu|va|lu|isch**
TÜV-ge|prüft (↑R 26)
Tu|wort, Tun|wort (*Plur.* ...wörter; *für* Verb)
TV = Turnverein
TV [te'fau̯, *engl.* ti:'vi:] = Television
Tweed [twi:t], der; -s, *Plur.* -s *u.* -e ⟨engl.⟩ (ein Gewebe)
Twen, der; -[s], -s ⟨anglisierend⟩ (junger Mann, junge Frau um die zwanzig)
Twen|ter, das; -s, - (*nordd. für* zweijähriges Schaf, Rind od. Pferd)
Twie|te, die; -, -n (*nordd. für* Zwischengässchen)
Twill, der; -s, *Plur.* -s *u.* -e ⟨engl.⟩

(Baumwollgewebe [Futterstoff]; Seidengewebe)
Twin|set, das, *auch* der; -[s], -s ‹engl.› (Pullover u. Jacke von gleicher Farbe u. aus gleichem Material)
[1]**Twist,** der; -es, -e ‹engl.› (mehrfädiges Baumwoll[stopf]garn); [2]**Twist,** der; -s, -s ‹amerik.› (ein Tanz); **twis|ten** (Twist tanzen)
Two|stepp ['tu:stɛp], der; -s, -s ‹engl., „Zweischritt"› (ein Tanz)
[1]**Ty|che** ['ty:çe] (griech. Göttin des Glücks u. des Zufalls); [2]**Ty|che,** die; - (Schicksal, Zufall, Glück)
Ty|coon [tai'ku:n], der; -s, -s ‹jap.-amerik.› (mächtiger Geschäftsmann od. Parteiführer)
Tym|pa|non, [1]**Tym|pa|num,** das; -s, ...na ‹griech.› (*Archit.* Giebelfeld über Fenstern u. Türen [oft mit Reliefs geschmückt]); [2]**Tym|pa|num,** das; -s, ...na (altgriech. Handtrommel; trommelartiges Schöpfrad in der Antike; *Med. veraltend* Paukenhöhle [im Ohr])
[1]**Typ,** der; -s, -en ‹griech.› (*nur Sing.: Philos.* Urbild, Beispiel; *Psych.* bestimmte psych. Ausprägung; *Technik* Gattung, Bauart, Muster, Modell); [2]**Typ,** der; *Gen.* -s, *auch* -en, *Plur.* -en; ↑R 126 (*ugs. für* Mensch, Person); **Ty|pe,** die; -, -n ‹franz.› (gegossener Druckbuchstabe, Letter; *ugs. für* komische Figur; *seltener, aber bes. österr., svw.* Typ *[Technik]*); **ty|pen** ([industrielle Artikel] nur in bestimmten notwendigen Größen herstellen); **Ty|pen‿druck** (*Plur.* ...drucke), **...he|bel, ...rad** (für Schreibmaschinen), **...rei|ni|ger, ...setz|ma|schi|ne**
Typh|li|tis (↑R 130), die; -, ...iti̱den ‹griech.› (*Med.* Blinddarmentzündung)
ty|phös ‹griech.› (typhusartig); **Ty|phus,** der; - (eine Infektionskrankheit); **Ty|phus‿epi|de|mie** (↑R 132), **...er|kran|kung**
Ty|pik, die; -, -en ‹griech.› (Lehre vom Typ *[Psych.]*); **ty|pisch** (gattungsmäßig; kenn-, bezeichnend; ausgeprägt; eigentümlich, üblich; *veraltet für* mustergültig, vorbildlich); **ty|pi|sie|ren** (typisch darstellen, gestalten, auffassen; typen); **Ty|pi|sie|rung; Ty|po|graf, Ty|po|gra|fie** usw. *eindeutschend für* Typograph, Typographie usw.; **Ty|po|graph** (↑R 33), der; -en, -en (↑R 126; Schriftsetzer; Zeilensetzmaschine); **Ty|po|gra|phie** (↑R 33), die; -, ...ien (Buchdruckerkunst; typographische Gestaltung); **ty|po|gra|phisch** (↑R 33); typographischer Punkt (*vgl.* Punkt); **Ty|po|lo|gie,** die; -, ...ien (Lehre von den Typen, Einteilung nach Typen); **ty|po|lo|gisch; Ty|po|skript,** das; -[e]s, -e (maschinengeschriebenes Manuskript); **Ty|pung** ‹*zu* typen›; **Ty|pus,** der; -, Typen (*svw.* [1]Typ *[Philos., Psych.]*)
Tyr (altgerm. Gott); *vgl.* Tiu, Ziu
Ty|rann, der; -en, -en (↑R 126) ‹griech.› (Gewaltherrscher; *auch* herrschsüchtiger Mensch); **Ty|ran|nei,** die; -, -en (Gewaltherrschaft; Willkür[herrschaft]); **Ty|ran|nen|herr|schaft; Ty|ran|nen|tum,** das; -s; **Ty|ran|nin; Ty|ran|nis,** die; - (Gewaltherrschaft, bes. im alten Griechenland); **ty|ran|nisch** (gewaltsam, willkürlich); **ty|ran|ni|sie|ren** (gewaltsam, willkürlich behandeln; unterdrücken); **Ty|ran|ni|sie|rung; Ty|ran|no|sau|rus,** der; -, ...rier (riesiger Dinosaurier)
Ty|ras (ein Hundename)
Ty|rer *vgl.* Tyrier; **Ty|ri|er,** *ökum.* Ty|rer (Bewohner von Tyros); **ty|risch; Ty|ros** (phöniz. Stadt)
Ty|ro|sin, das; -s ‹griech.› (*Biochemie* eine Aminosäure)
Tyr|rhe|ner (Bewohner Etruriens); **tyr|rhe|nisch,** *aber* (↑R 102): das Tyrrhenische Meer (Teil des Mittelmeeres)
Ty|rus (*lat. Name von* Tyros)
Tz *vgl.* Tezett

U

U (Buchstabe); das U; des U, die U, *aber* das u in Mut (↑R 60); der Buchstabe U, u
Ü (Buchstabe; Umlaut); das Ü; des Ü, die Ü, *aber* das ü in Mütze (↑R 60); der Buchstabe Ü, ü
U = Unterseeboot; *chem. Zeichen für* Uran
u., *in Firmen auch* & = und
u. a. = und and[e]re, und and[e]res, unter ander[e]m, unter ander[e]n
u. Ä. = und Ähnliche[s] (*vgl.* ähnlich)
u. a. m. = und and[e]re mehr, und and[e]res mehr
u. A. w. g. *od.* **U. A. w. g.** = um [*od.* Um] Antwort wird gebeten
U-Bahn; ↑R 25 (*kurz für* Untergrundbahn); **U-Bahn|hof; U-Bahn-Netz; U-Bahn-Sta|ti|on; U-Bahn-Tun|nel** (↑R 28)
ü|bel; üble Nachrede; übler Ruf; mir ist übel; ich habe nicht übel Lust, das zu tun (ich möchte es tun); jmdm. etwas übel nehmen; Menschen, die uns übel wollen; in übel wollender Neugier; (↑R 39:) ein übel gelaunter Chef; sie wäre übel beraten, wenn sie sich darauf einließe; übel gesinnte Nachbarn; übel riechende Abfälle; (↑R 47:) er hat mir etwas Übles angetan; **Ü|bel,** das; -s, -; das ist von, *geh.* vom -; **ü|bel be|ra|ten, ge|launt, ge|sinnt** *vgl.* übel; **Ü|bel|keit; ü|bel|lau|nig; Ü|bel|lau|nig|keit; ü|bel neh|men** *vgl.* übel; **Ü|bel|neh|me|rei; ü|bel|neh|me|risch; ü|bel rie|chend** *vgl.* übel; **Ü|bel‿sein** (das; -s), **...stand, ...tat** *(geh.),* **...tä|ter, ...tä|te|rin; ü|bel wol|len** *vgl.* übel; **Ü|bel|wol|len,** das; -s; **ü|bel wol|lend** *vgl.* übel
[1]**ü|ben;** ein Klavierstück -; sich -
[2]**ü|ben** (*landsch. für* drüben)
ü|ber; *Präp. mit Dat. u. Akk.:* das Bild hängt über dem Sofa, *aber* das Bild über das Sofa hängen; überm, übers *(vgl. d.);* über Gebühr; über die Maßen; über Nacht; über Tag *(Bergmannsspr.);* über Wunsch, Antrag von ... (*österr. Amtsspr. für* auf Wunsch, Antrag von ...); über kurz oder lang (↑R 47); Kinder über acht Jahre; Gemeinden über 10 000 Einwohner; über dem Lesen ist er eingeschlafen; *Adverb:* über und über (sehr; völlig); die ganze Zeit [über]; es waren über (= mehr als) 100 Gäste; wir mussten über (= mehr als) zwei Stunden warten; Gemeinden von über (= mehr als) 10 000 Einwohnern; die über Siebzigjährigen; er ist mir über (überlegen)
ü|ber... *in Verbindung mit Verben:* **I.** *unfeste Zusammensetzungen* (↑R 38), z. B. überbauen *(vgl. d.),* er baut über, hat übergebaut; überzubauen; **II.** *feste Zusammensetzungen* (↑R 37), z. B. überbauen *(vgl. d.),* er überbaut, hat überbaut; zu überbauen
ü|ber|all [*auch* 'y:...]; **ü|ber|all|her,** *aber* von überall her; **ü|ber|all|hin**
ü|ber|al|tert; Ü|ber|al|te|rung, die; -
Ü|ber|an|ge|bot
ü|ber|ängst|lich
ü|ber|an|stren|gen; sich -; ich

habe mich überanstrengt; **Über|an|stren|gung**

über|ant|wor|ten (*geh. für* übergeben, überlassen); die Gelder wurden ihm überantwortet; **Über|ant|wor|tung**

über|ar|bei|ten (*landsch.*); sie hat einige Stunden übergearbeitet; **über|ar|bei|ten;** sich -; du hast dich völlig überarbeitet; sie hat den Aufsatz überarbeitet (nochmals durchgearbeitet); **Über|ar|bei|tung** (gründliche Durcharbeitung; *nur Sing.:* Erschöpfung)

über|aus

über|ba|cken; das Gemüse wird überbacken

[1]**Über|bau,** der; -[e]s, *Plur.* -e *u.* -ten (vorragender Oberbau, Schutzdach; *Rechtsspr.* Bau über die Grundstücksgrenze hinaus); [2]**Über|bau,** der; -[e]s, -e (nach Marx die auf den wirtschaftl. u. sozialen Grundlagen basierenden Anschauungen einer Gesellschaft u. die entsprechenden Institutionen); **über|bau|en;** er hat übergebaut (über die Baugrenze hinaus); **über|bau|en;** er hat die Einfahrt (mit einem Dach) überbaut; **Über|bau|ung**

über|be|an|spru|chen; du überbeanspruchst den Wagen; er ist überbeansprucht; überzubeanspruchen; **Über|be|an|spru|chung**

über|be|hal|ten (*landsch. für* übrig behalten); wir behalten nichts über, haben nichts überbehalten; überzubehalten

Über|bein (verhärtete Sehnengeschwulst an einem [Hand]gelenk)

über|be|kom|men (*ugs.*); ich bekam das fette Essen bald über, habe es überbekommen; überzubekommen

über|be|las|ten; du überbelastest den Wagen, sie ist überbelastet; überzubelasten; **Über|be|las|tung**

über|be|le|gen; der Raum war überbelegt; überzubelegen; *selten:* er überbelegt den Raum; **Über|be|le|gung**

über|be|lich|ten (*Fotogr.*); du überbelichtest die Aufnahme, sie ist überbelichtet; überzubelichten; **Über|be|lich|tung**

Über|be|schäf|ti|gung, die; -

über|be|to|nen; sie überbetont diese Entwicklung, sie hat sie lange Zeit überbetont; überzubetonen; **Über|be|to|nung**

über|be|trieb|lich; -e Mitbestimmung

über|be|völ|kert (übervölkert); **Über|be|völ|ke|rung,** die; -

über|be|wer|ten; er überbewertet diese Vorgänge; er hat sie überbewertet; überzubewerten; **Über|be|wer|tung**

über|be|zah|len; er ist überbezahlt; überzubezahlen; *selten:* er überbezahlt ihn; **Über|be|zah|lung**

über|biet|bar; über|bie|ten; sich -; der Rekord wurde überboten; **Über|bie|tung**

über|bin|den (*Musik*); diese Töne müssen übergebunden werden; **über|bin|den** (*schweiz. für* [eine Verpflichtung] auferlegen); die Aufgabe wurde ihr überbunden

Über|biss (*ugs. für* das Überstehen der oberen Schneidezähne über die unteren)

über|bla|sen (*Musik* bei Holz- u. Blechblasinstrumenten durch stärkeres Blasen die höheren Töne hervorbringen)

über|blat|ten (Hölzer in bestimmter Weise verbinden); der Schrank wird überblattet; **Über|blat|tung**

über|blei|ben (*landsch. für* übrig bleiben); es bleibt nicht viel über, es ist nicht viel übergeblieben; überzubleiben; **Über|bleib|sel,** das; -s, -

über|blen|den; die Bilder werden überblendet; **Über|blen|dung** (*Film* die Überleitung eines Bildes in ein anderes)

Über|blick; über|bli|cken; sie hat den Vorgang überblickt; **über|blicks|wei|se**

über|bor|den (über die Ufer treten; über das normale Maß hinausgehen, ausarten); der Betrieb ist, *auch* hat überbordet

über|bra|ten; *nur in* jmdm. eins - (*ugs. für* einen Schlag, Hieb versetzen)

über|breit; -es Fahrzeug; **Über|brei|te**

Über|brettl, das; -s, - ([frühere Berliner] Kleinkunstbühne)

über|brin|gen; er hat die Nachricht überbracht; **Über|brin|ger; Über|brin|ge|rin; Über|brin|gung**

über|brück|bar; über|brü|cken; sie hat den Gegensatz klug überbrückt; **Über|brü|ckung; Über|brü|ckungs_[bei]hil|fe, ...kre|dit, ...zah|lung**

über|bür|den (*geh.*); er ist mit Arbeit überbürdet; **Über|bür|dung**

Über|dach; über|da|chen; der Bahnsteig wurde überdacht; **Über|da|chung**

Über|dampf, der; -[e]s (der nicht für den Gang der Maschine notwendige Dampf)

über|dau|ern; die Altertümer haben Jahrhunderte überdauert

Über|de|cke; über|de|cken (*ugs.*); ich habe das Tischtuch übergedeckt; **über|de|cken;** mit Eis überdeckt; **Über|de|ckung**

über|deh|nen ([bis zum Zerreißen] dehnen, auseinander ziehen); der Muskel ist überdehnt; **Über|deh|nung**

über|den|ken; sie hat es lange überdacht

über|deut|lich

über|dies [*auch* 'y:...]

über|di|men|si|o|nal (übermäßig groß); **über|di|men|si|o|niert; Über|di|men|si|o|nie|rung**

über|do|sie|ren; er überdosiert das Medikament, hat es überdosiert; überzudosieren; **Über|do|sie|rung; Über|do|sis;** eine - Schlaftabletten

über|dre|hen; die Uhr ist überdreht; die Kinder waren überdreht (*ugs.*)

[1]**Über|druck,** der; -[e]s, ...drücke (zu starker Druck); [2]**Über|druck,** der; -[e]s, ...drucke (nochmaliger Druck auf Geweben, Papier u. Ä.); **über|dru|cken;** die Briefmarke wurde überdruckt; **Über|druck_ka|bi|ne** (↑R 136), **...tur|bi|ne, ...ven|til**

Über|druss, der; -es; **über|drüs|sig;** *mit Gen.:* des Lebens, des Freundes - sein; seiner - sein, *selten auch mit Akk.:* ich bin ihn -

über|dün|gen; die Felder sind völlig überdüngt; **Über|dün|gung**

über|durch|schnitt|lich

über|eck; - stellen

Über|ei|fer; über|eif|rig

über|eig|nen (überweisen; zu eigen [über]geben); das Haus wurde ihm übereignet; **Über|eig|nung**

Über|ei|le; über|ei|len; sich -; du hast dich übereilt; **über|eilt** (verfrüht); ein übereilter Schritt; **Über|ei|lung**

über|ei|nan|der (↑R 132); *in Verbindung mit Verben immer getrennt:* übereinander reden; übereinander schlagen, werfen usw.; wir haben die Kisten übereinander gestellt; übereinander liegende Decken; sie begann, die Kartons übereinander zu schichten

über|ein|kom|men; ich komme überein; übereingekommen; um übereinzukommen; **Über|ein|kom|men** (Abmachung, Einigung); **Über|ein|kunft,** die; -, ...künfte (Übereinkommen)

über|ein|stim|men; Nachfrage und Angebot stimmen überein, haben übereingestimmt; übereinzustimmen; **Ü|ber|ein|stim|mung**

ü|ber|ein|tref|fen *vgl.* übereinkommen

ü|ber|emp|find|lich; Ü|ber|emp|find|lich|keit

ü|ber|er|fül|len; den Plan - (*ehem. in der DDR);* sie übererfüllt den Plan; sie hat den Plan übererfüllt; überzuerfüllen; **Ü|ber|er|fül|lung**

Ü|ber|er|näh|rung, die; -

ü|ber|er|reg|bar; Ü|ber|er|reg|bar|keit, die; -

ü|ber|es|sen; ich habe mir die Speise übergegessen (ich mag sie nicht mehr); *vgl.* überbekommen; **ü|ber|es|sen,** sich; ich habe mich übergessen (zu viel gegessen)

ü|ber|fach|lich

ü|ber|fah|ren; ich bin übergefahren (über den Fluss); **ü|ber|fah|ren;** das Kind ist - worden; er hätte mich bei den Verhandlungen fast - (*ugs. für* überrumpelt); **Ü|ber|fahrt; Ü|ber|fahrts|zeit**

Ü|ber|fall, der; **ü|ber|fal|len** (*Jägerspr.* ein Hindernis überspringen [vom Schalenwild]); **ü|ber|fal|len;** man hat ihn -; **Ü|ber|fall|ho|se; ü|ber|fäl|lig** (zur erwarteten Zeit noch nicht eingetroffen [bes. von Schiffen u. Flugzeugen]); ein -er (verfallener) Wechsel; **Ü|ber|fall|kom|man|do,** *österr.* **Ü|ber|falls|kom|man|do**

Ü|ber|fang (farbige Glasschicht auf Glasgefäßen); **ü|ber|fan|gen; die Vase ist blau -; Ü|ber|fang|glas** *Plur.* ...gläser

ü|ber|fär|ben (*fachspr. für* abfärben); die Druckschrift hat übergefärbt; **ü|ber|fär|ben;** der Stoff braucht nur überfärbt zu werden

ü|ber|fein; ü|ber|fei|nern; ich ...ere (↑R 16); überfeinert; **Ü|ber|fei|ne|rung**

ü|ber|fir|nis|sen; der Schrank wurde überfirnisst

ü|ber|fi|schen (den Fischbestand durch zu viel Fischerei bedrohen); überfischt; **Ü|ber|fi|schung**

Ü|ber|fleiß; ü|ber|flei|ßig

ü|ber|flie|gen (*ugs. für* nach der anderen Seite fliegen); die Hühner sind übergeflogen; **ü|ber|flie|gen;** er hat die Alpen überflogen; ich habe das Buch überflogen; **Ü|ber|flie|ger** (jmd., der begabter, tüchtiger ist als der Durchschnitt)

ü|ber|flie|ßen; das Wasser ist übergeflossen; er floss über vor Dankbarkeit; **ü|ber|flie|ßen;** das Gelände ist von Wasser überflossen

Ü|ber|flug (das Überfliegen); **ü|ber|flü|geln;** er hat alle überflügelt; **Ü|ber|flü|ge|lung, Ü|ber|flüg|lung**

Ü|ber|fluss, der; -es; **Ü|ber|fluss|ge|sell|schaft,** die; -; **ü|ber|flüs|sig; ü|ber|flüs|si|ger|wei|se**

ü|ber|flu|ten; das Wasser ist übergeflutet; **ü|ber|flu|ten;** der Strom hat die Dämme überflutet; **Ü|ber|flu|tung**

ü|ber|for|dern (mehr fordern, als geleistet werden kann); er hat mich überfordert; **Ü|ber|for|de|rung**

Ü|ber|fracht; ü|ber|frach|ten (*svw.* überladen); **Ü|ber|frach|tung**

ü|ber|fra|gen (Fragen stellen, auf die man nicht antworten kann); **ü|ber|fragt;** ich bin -

ü|ber|frem|den; ein Land ist überfremdet; **Ü|ber|frem|dung**

ü|ber|fres|sen, sich; du hast dich - *(derb)*

ü|ber|frie|ren; die Straße ist überfroren; überfrierende Nässe

Ü|ber|fuhr, die; -, -en (*österr. für* Fähre)

ü|ber|füh|ren, ü|ber|füh|ren (an einen anderen Ort bringen); man überführte ihn in eine Spezialklinik *od.* führte ihn in eine Spezialklinik über; die Leiche wurde nach ... übergeführt *od.* überführt; **ü|ber|füh|ren** (einer Schuld); der Mörder wurde überführt; **Ü|ber|füh|rung;** - der Leiche; - einer Straße; - eines Verbrechers; **Ü|ber|füh|rungs|kos|ten** *Plur.*

Ü|ber|fül|le; ü|ber|fül|len; der Bus ist überfüllt; **Ü|ber|fül|lung**

Ü|ber|funk|ti|on; - der Schilddrüse

ü|ber|füt|tern; eine überfütterte Katze; **Ü|ber|füt|te|rung**

Ü|ber|ga|be; Ü|ber|ga|be|ver|hand|lun|gen *Plur.*

Ü|ber|gang, der; **Ü|ber|gangs|bahn|hof, ...bei|hil|fe, ...be|stim|mung, ...er|schei|nung; ü|ber|gangs|los; Ü|ber|gangs|lö|sung, ...man|tel, ...pe|ri|o|de, ...pha|se, ...re|ge|lung, ...sta|di|um, ...sta|ti|on, ...stel|le, ...stil, ...stu|fe, ...zeit, ...zu|stand**

Ü|ber|gar|di|ne *meist Plur.*

ü|ber|ge|ben; ich habe ihr gegen die Kälte ein Tuch übergegeben *(ugs.);* ich habe ihm eins übergegeben (*ugs. für* einen Schlag, Hieb versetzt); **ü|ber|ge|ben;** er hat die Festung übergeben; ich habe mich übergeben (erbrochen)

Ü|ber|ge|bot (höheres Gebot bei einer Versteigerung)

ü|ber|ge|hen; wir gingen zum nächsten Thema über; das Grundstück ist in andere Hände übergegangen; die Augen gingen ihm über (er war überwältigt; *geh. auch für* er hat geweint); **ü|ber|ge|hen** (unbeachtet lassen); sie überging ihn; sie hat den Einwand übergangen; **Ü|ber|ge|hung,** die; -; mit -

ü|ber|ge|meind|lich

ü|ber|ge|nau

ü|ber|ge|nug; davon gibt es genug und -

Ü|ber|ge|nuss (*österr. Amtsspr.* Überzahlung)

ü|ber|ge|ord|net; einige -e Gesichtspunkte

Ü|ber-ge|päck *(Flugw.),* **...ge|wicht** (das; -[e]s); **ü|ber|ge|wich|tig**

ü|ber|gie|ßen (in ein anderes Gefäß gießen; über einen Gefäßrand hinausgießen); sie hat [die Milch] übergegossen; **ü|ber|gie|ßen** (oberflächlich gießen; oben begießen); sie hat die Blumen nur übergossen; übergossen mit ..., *aber* (↑R 102): die Übergossene Alm (ein Gletscher in den Alpen); **Ü|ber|gie|ßung**

ü|ber|gip|sen; die Wand wurde übergipst; **Ü|ber|gip|sung**

ü|ber|gla|sen (mit Glas decken); du überglast; er überglaste den Balkon; der Balkon ist überglast; **Ü|ber|gla|sung**

ü|ber|glück|lich

ü|ber|gol|den; der Ring wurde übergoldet

ü|ber|grei|fen; das Feuer, die Seuche hat übergegriffen; **Ü|ber|griff**

ü|ber|groß; Ü|ber|grö|ße

ü|ber|grü|nen; das Haus ist [mit Efeu] übergrünt

Ü|ber|guss

ü|ber|ha|ben (*ugs. für* satt haben; angezogen haben; *landsch. für* übrig haben); er hat die ständigen Klagen übergehabt; er hat den Mantel übergehabt

ü|ber|hal|ten (*Forstw.* stehen lassen); eine Kiefer -; **ü|ber|hal|ten** (*österr. veraltend für* [beim Einkauf] übervorteilen); man hat ihn überhalten; **Ü|ber|häl|ter** (*Forstw.* Baum, der beim Abholzen stehen gelassen wird)

ü|ber|hand; überhand nehmen; etwas nimmt überhand; es hat überhand genommen; überhand zu nehmen; **Ü|ber|hand|nah|me,** die; -

Ü|ber|hang; - der Zweige, des Obstes, der Felsen; - der Waren; **[1]ü|ber|hän|gen;** die Felsen hingen über; *vgl.* [1]hängen; **[2]ü|ber|hän|gen;** sie hat den Mantel

übergehängt; *vgl.* ²hängen; **ü|ber|hän|gen;** sie hat den Käfig mit einem Tuch überhängt; *vgl.* ²hängen; **Ü|ber|hang|man|dat** (in Direktwahl gewonnenes Mandat, das über die Zahl der einer Partei nach dem Stimmenverhältnis zustehenden Parlamentssitze hinausgeht); **Ü|ber|hangs|recht,** das; -[e]s
ü|ber|happs (*bayr. u. österr. ugs. für* übereilt; ungefähr)
ü|ber|hart; -er Einsatz
ü|ber|has|ten; das Tempo ist überhastet; **Ü|ber|has|tung**
ü|ber|häu|fen; sie war mit Arbeit überhäuft; der Tisch ist mit Papieren überhäuft; **Ü|ber|häu|fung**
ü|ber|haupt
ü|ber|he|ben; wir sind der Sorge um ihn überhoben (*veraltend für* enthoben); sich überheben; ich habe mich überhoben (*landsch. für* verhoben); **ü|ber|heb|lich** (anmaßend); **Ü|ber|heb|lich|keit; Ü|ber|he|bung** (*veraltend*)
Ü|ber|he|ge (*Forstw.*)
ü|ber|hei|zen (zu stark heizen); das Zimmer ist überheizt
ü|ber|hin (*veraltet für* oberflächlich); etwas - prüfen
ü|ber|hit|zen (zu stark erhitzen); du überhitzt; der Ofen ist überhitzt; **Ü|ber|hit|zung**
ü|ber|hö|hen; die Kurve ist überhöht; **Ü|ber|hö|hung**
ü|ber|ho|len (*Seemannsspr.*); die Segel wurden übergeholt; das Schiff hat übergeholt (sich auf die Seite gelegt); **ü|ber|ho|len** (hinter sich lassen; übertreffen; ausbessern, wieder herstellen); er hat ihn überholt; diese Anschauung ist längst überholt; die Maschine ist überholt worden; **Ü|ber|hol‿ma|nö|ver, ...spur; Ü|ber|ho|lung; ü|ber|ho|lungs|be|dürf|tig; Ü|ber|hol‿ver|bot, ...ver|such, ...vor|gang**
ü|ber|hö|ren (*ugs.*); ich habe mir den Schlager übergehört; **ü|ber|hö|ren;** das möchte ich überhört haben!
Ü|ber|ich; ↑R 24 (*Psychoanalyse*)
ü|ber|in|di|vi|du|ell
ü|ber|ir|disch
ü|ber|jäh|rig (*veraltet*)
ü|ber|kan|di|delt (*ugs. für* überspannt)
Ü|ber|ka|pa|zi|tät *meist Plur.* (*Wirtsch.*)
ü|ber|kip|pen; er ist nach vorn übergekippt
ü|ber|kle|ben; überklebte Plakate
Ü|ber|kleid; ü|ber|klei|den; der Balken wird mit Spanplatten überkleidet (*veraltend*); **Ü|ber|klei|dung** (Überkleider); **Ü|ber|klei|dung** (*veraltend für* Verkleidung [eines Wandschadens])
ü|ber|klet|tern; er hat den Zaun überklettert
ü|ber|klug
ü|ber|ko|chen; die Milch ist übergekocht; **ü|ber|ko|chen** (*landsch.*); die Suppe muss noch einmal überkocht werden
ü|ber|kom|men (*Seemannsspr.* über das Deck spülen, spritzen; *landsch. für* etwas endlich fertig bringen od. sagen); die Brecher kommen über; er ist damit übergekommen; **ü|ber|kom|men;** eine überkommene Verpflichtung; der Ekel überkam ihn, hat ihn überkommen
Ü|ber|kom|pen|sa|ti|on; ü|ber|kom|pen|sie|ren (in übersteigertem Maße ausgleichen)
ü|ber|kon|fes|si|o|nell; eine -e Arbeitsgruppe
Ü|ber|kopf|ball (*Tennis*)
über Kreuz *vgl.* Kreuz; **ü|ber|kreu|zen;** sich -
ü|ber|krie|gen (*ugs.; svw.* überbekommen)
ü|ber|kro|nen; der Zahn wurde überkront
ü|ber|krus|ten; die Nudeln werden überkrustet
ü|ber|küh|len (*österr. für* [langsam] abkühlen); Speisen - lassen
¹ü|ber|la|den; das Schiff war überladen; ich habe mir den Magen überladen; *vgl.* ¹laden; **²ü|ber|la|den;** ein -er Stil; **Ü|ber|la|dung** (übermäßige Beladung)
ü|ber|la|gern; überlagert; sich -; **Ü|ber|la|ge|rung; Ü|ber|la|ge|rungs|emp|fän|ger** (*für* Superheterodynempfänger)
Ü|ber|land‿bahn, ...bus, ...fahrt, ...kraft|werk, ...lei|tung
ü|ber|lang; Ü|ber|län|ge
ü|ber|lap|pen; überlappt; **Ü|ber|lap|pung**
ü|ber|las|sen (*landsch. für* übrig lassen); sie hat ihm etwas übergelassen; **ü|ber|las|sen** (abtreten; anvertrauen); sie hat mir das Haus -; **Ü|ber|las|sung**
ü|ber|las|ten; ü|ber|las|tet; ü|ber|las|tig; Ü|ber|las|tung
Ü|ber|lauf (Ablauf für überschüssiges Wasser); **ü|ber|lau|fen;** das Wasser läuft über; er ist zum Feind übergelaufen; die Galle ist ihm übergelaufen; **ü|ber|lau|fen;** der Arzt wird von Kranken -; es hat mich kalt -; **Ü|ber|läu|fer** (Soldat, der zum Gegner überläuft; *Jägerspr.* Wildschwein im zweiten Jahr)
ü|ber|laut
ü|ber|le|ben; er hat seine Frau überlebt; diese Vorstellungen sind überlebt; **Ü|ber|le|ben|de,** der *u.* die; -n, -n (↑R 5 ff.); **Ü|ber|le|bens|chan|ce** *meist Plur.*; **ü|ber|le|bens|groß;** eine -e Abbildung; **Ü|ber|le|bens|grö|ße,** die; -; **Ü|ber|le|bens|trai|ning**
ü|ber|le|gen (*ugs. für* darüberlegen); sie legte eine Decke über; sie hat ein Tuch übergelegt; du gehörst übergelegt (übers Knie gelegt); **¹ü|ber|le|gen** (bedenken, nachdenken); er überlegte lange; ich habe mir das überlegt; (↑R 50:) nach reiflichem Überlegen; **²ü|ber|le|gen;** sie ist mir -; mit -er Miene; **Ü|ber|le|gen|heit,** die; -; **ü|ber|legt** (*auch für* sorgsam); **Ü|ber|le|gung;** mit -
ü|ber|lei|ten; ein Lied leitete zum zweiten Teil über; **Ü|ber|lei|tung**
ü|ber|le|sen ([schnell] durchlesen; [bei oberflächlichem Lesen] nicht bemerken); er hat den Brief nur -; er hat diesen Druckfehler -
Ü|ber|licht|ge|schwin|dig|keit
ü|ber|lie|fern; diese Bräuche wurden uns überliefert; **Ü|ber|lie|fe|rung;** schriftliche -
ü|ber|lie|gen (länger als vorgesehen in einem Hafen liegen [von Schiffen]); **Ü|ber|lie|ge|zeit**
Ü|ber|lin|gen (Stadt am Bodensee); **Ü|ber|lin|ger See,** der; - -s; ↑R 105 (Teil des Bodensees)
ü|ber|lis|ten; er wurde überlistet; **Ü|ber|lis|tung**
ü|berm; ↑R 13 (*ugs. für* über dem); überm Haus
ü|ber|ma|chen (*veraltend für* vererben, vermachen); er hat ihm sein Vermögen übermacht
Ü|ber|macht, die; -; **ü|ber|mäch|tig**
ü|ber|ma|len (*ugs.*); sie hat [über den Rand] übergemalt; **ü|ber|ma|len;** das Bild war übermalt; **Ü|ber|ma|lung**
ü|ber|man|gan|sau|er; übermangansaures Kali (*alte Bez. für* Kaliumpermanganat)
ü|ber|man|nen; der Schlaf hat sie übermannt; **ü|ber|manns|hoch**
Ü|ber|man|tel
ü|ber|mar|chen (*schweiz., sonst veraltet für* eine festgesetzte Grenze überschreiten)
Ü|ber|maß, das; -es; im -; **ü|ber|mä|ßig**
ü|ber|mäs|ten; übermästete Tiere
Ü|ber|mensch, der; **ü|ber|mensch|lich**
Ü|ber|mi|kro|skop (*für* Elektronen-, Ultramikroskop)
ü|ber|mit|teln (mit-, zuteilen); ich

...[e]le (↑R 16); er hat diese freudige Nachricht übermittelt; **Übermittelung, Übermittlung**
übermorgen; übermorgen Abend (↑R 45)
übermüde; übermüden; übermüdet; - sein; **Übermüdung**
Übermut; übermütig
übern; ↑R 13 (*ugs. für* über den); übern Graben
übernächste; am -n Freitag
übernachten; er hat hier übernachtet; **übernächtig,** *österr. nur so, sonst meist* **übernächtigt** (von zu langem Aufbleiben müde); **Übernächtler** (*schweiz. für* in Stall, Schuppen usw. Übernachtender); **Übernachtung**
Übernahme, die; -, -n; **Übernahmsstelle** (*österr. für* Annahmestelle)
Übername (Spitzname)
übernational
übernatürlich
übernehmen; sie hat die Tasche übergenommen *(ugs.);* **übernehmen;** sie hat das Geschäft übernommen; ich habe mich übernommen; **Übernehmer**
überordnen; er ist ihm übergeordnet; **Überordnung**
Überorganisation, die; - (Übermaß von Organisation); **überorganisiert**
überörtlich
überparteilich
überpflanzen (*Med. selten für* transplantieren); **Überpflanzung**
überpinseln
Überplanbestand *meist Plur.* (in der ehem. sozialist. Wirtschaft)
Überpreis
überprivilegiert
Überproduktion
überproportional
überprüfbar; überprüfen; sein Verhalten wurde überprüft; **Überprüfung; Überprüfungskommission**
überpudern; die Nase -
überquellen (überfließen); der Eimer quoll über; der Teig ist übergequollen; überquellende Freude, Dankbarkeit
überquer (*veraltend für* über Kreuz); **überqueren;** er hat den Platz überquert; **Überquerung**
überragen (hervorstehen); der Balken hat übergeragt; ein überragender Balken; **überragen;** sie hat alle überragt; ein überragender Erfolg
überraschen; du überraschst; er wurde überrascht; **überraschend; überraschenderweise; Überraschung; Überraschungs_effekt, ...erfolg, ...mannschaft** *(Sport),* **...moment** (das), **...sieg**
überreagieren; Überreaktion; eine - der Haut
überrechnen (rechnerisch überschlagen); das Vorhaben wurde überrechnet
überreden; sie hat mich dazu überredet; **Überredung; Überredungskunst**
überregional
überreich
überreichen; überreicht
überreichlich; Nahrungsmittel waren - vorhanden
Überreichung
Überreichweite (von [Rundfunk]sendern)
überreif; Überreife
überreißen; einen Ball - *(Tennis)*
überreiten; jmdn. - (umreiten)
überreizen; seine Augen sind überreizt; **Überreiztheit,** die; -; **Überreizung**
überrennen; er wurde überrannt
Überrepräsentation; überrepräsentiert
Überrest *meist Plur.*
überrieseln *(geh.);* ein Schauer überrieselte sie; **Überrieselung, Überrieslung**
Überrock (*veraltet für* Gehrock, Überzieher); *vgl.* [1]Rock
Überrollbügel (bes. bei Sport- u. Rennwagen); **überrollen;** er wurde überrollt
überrumpeln; der Feind wurde überrumpelt; **Überrumpelung, Überrumplung**
überrunden (im Sport); er wurde überrundet; **Überrundung**
übers; ↑R 13 (*ugs. für* über das); übers Wochenende
übersäen (besäen); übersät (dicht bedeckt); der Himmel ist mit Sternen übersät
übersatt; übersättigen; er ist übersättigt; eine übersättigte Lösung *(Chemie);* **Übersättigung**
übersäuern; Übersäuerung
Überschall_flug, ...flugzeug, ...geschwindigkeit
Überschar, die; -, -en (*Bergmannsspr.* zwischen Bergwerken liegendes, wegen geringen Ausmaßes nicht zur Bebauung geeignetes Land)
überschatten; Überschattung
überschätzen; überschätzt; **Überschätzung**
Überschau, die; - (*svw.* Übersicht); **überschaubar; Überschaubarkeit,** die; -; **überschauen;** überschaut
überschäumen; der Sekt war übergeschäumt; überschäumende Lebenslust
Überschicht (zusätzliche Arbeitsschicht)
überschießen (*landsch. für* überfließen; über ein Maß hinausgehen); der überschießende Betrag
überschlächtig (*fachspr. für* durch Wasser von oben angetrieben); -es [Wasser]rad
überschlafen; das muss ich erst [noch] -
Überschlag, der; -[e]s, ...schläge; **überschlagen;** die Stimme ist übergeschlagen; [1]**überschlagen;** ich habe die Kosten -; er hat sich -; [2]**überschlagen;** das Wasser ist überschlagen (*landsch. für* lauwarm); **überschlägig** (ungefähr); **Überschlaglaken** (Teil der Bettwäsche); **überschläglich** (*svw.* überschlägig); **Überschlagsrechnung**
überschließen *(Druckw.);* einige Wörter wurden übergeschlossen
überschnappen; der Riegel des Schlosses, das Schloss hat *od.* ist übergeschnappt; die Stimme ist übergeschnappt; du bist wohl übergeschnappt (*ugs. für* du hast wohl den Verstand verloren)
überschneiden, sich; ihre Arbeitsgebiete haben sich überschnitten; **Überschneidung**
überschneien; überschneite Dächer
überschnell
überschreiben; das Gedicht ist nicht überschrieben; das Haus ist auf ihn überschrieben; **Überschreibung** (Übereignung [einer Forderung usw.])
überschreien; er hat ihn überschrie[e]n
überschreiten; du hast die Grenze überschritten; (↑R 50:) das Überschreiten der Gleise ist verboten; **Überschreitung**
Überschrift
Überschuh
überschuldet (mit Schulden übermäßig belastet); **Überschuldung**
Überschuss; überschüssig; Überschuss_land, ...produkt, ...produktion
überschütten *(ugs.);* sie hat etwas übergeschüttet; **überschütten;** sie hat mich mit Vorwürfen überschüttet; **Überschüttung**
Überschwang, der; -[e]s; im - der Gefühle; **überschwänglich; Überschwänglichkeit**

ụ̈|ber|schwap|pen (*ugs. für* verschüttet werden, überlaufen); die Suppe ist übergeschwappt
ü|ber|schwẹm|men; die Uferstraße ist überschwemmt; **Ü|ber|schwẹm|mung; Ü|ber|schwẹm|mungs‿ge|biet, ...ka|ta|stro|phe**
ụ̈|ber|schweng|lich *frühere Schreibung für* überschwänglich
ụ̈|ber|schwer; -e Lasten, Transportgüter
Ụ̈|ber|see *ohne Artikel* (die „über See" liegenden Länder); nach - gehen; Waren von -, aus -; Briefe für -; **Ụ̈|ber|see‿brü|cke, ...damp|fer, ...ha|fen** (*vgl.* [2]Hafen); **ụ̈|ber|see|isch;** -er Handel
ü|ber|sẹh|bar; ụ̈|ber|se|hen (*ugs.*); du hast dir dieses Kleid übergesehen; **ü|ber|sẹ|hen;** ich habe den Fehler -; er konnte vom Fenster aus das Tal -
ü|ber|sẹn|den; der Brief wurde ihr übersandt; **Ü|ber|sẹn|dung**
ü|ber|sẹtz|bar; Ü|ber|sẹtz|bar|keit, die; -; **ụ̈|ber|set|zen** (ans andere Ufer bringen od. gelangen); wir setzen über; er hat den Wanderer übergesetzt; **ü|ber|sẹt|zen** (in eine andere Sprache übertragen); wir übersetzen ins Englische; ich habe den Satz übersetzt; **Ü|ber|sẹt|zer; Ü|ber|sẹt|ze|rin; ü|ber|sẹtzt** (*landsch., bes. schweiz. für* überhöht); -e Preise, -e Geschwindigkeit; **Ü|ber|sẹt|zung** ([schriftliche] Übertragung; Kraft-, Bewegungsübertragung); **Ü|ber|sẹt|zungs‿ar|beit, ...bü|ro, ...feh|ler**
Ụ̈|ber|sicht, die; -, -en; **ụ̈|ber|sich|tig** (*veraltend für* weitsichtig); -e Augen; **Ụ̈|ber|sich|tig|keit,** die; - (*veraltend*); **ụ̈|ber|sicht|lich** (leicht zu überschauen); **Ụ̈|ber|sicht|lich|keit,** die; -; **Ụ̈|ber|sichts‿kar|te, ...ta|fel**
ụ̈|ber|sie|deln [*auch* ...ˈziː...] (den Wohnort wechseln); ich sied[e]le über, *auch* ich übersied[e]le; ich bin damals übergesiedelt, *auch* übersiedelt; **Ụ̈|ber|sie|de|lung** [*auch* ...ˈziː...] *vgl.* Übersiedlung
Ụ̈|ber|sied|ler [*auch* ...ˈziː...]; **Ụ̈|ber|sied|lung** [*auch* ...ˈziː...] *vgl.* Ü|ber|sie|de|lung
ụ̈|ber|sinn|lich; Ụ̈|ber|sinn|lich|keit
Ụ̈|ber|soll
ü|ber|sọnnt
ü|ber|spạn|nen; ich habe den Bogen überspannt; **ü|ber|spạnnt** (übertrieben); -e Anforderungen; -es (verschrobenes) Wesen; **Ü|ber|spạnnt|heit; Ụ̈|ber|span|nung** (zu hohe Spannung in einer elektrischen Anlage); **Ü|ber|spạn|nung; Ụ̈|ber|span|nungs|schutz**
ü|ber|spie|len; sie überspielte die peinliche Situation; er hatte die Deckung überspielt (*Sport*); er hat die Platte auf ein Tonband überspielt; **ü|ber|spie̲lt** (*Sportspr.* durch [zu] häufiges Spielen überanstrengt; *österr. für* häufig gespielt, nicht mehr neu [vom Klavier]); **Ü|ber|spie̲|lung**
ü|ber|spịt|zen (übertreiben); **ü|ber|spịtzt** (übermäßig); **Ü|ber|spịtzt|heit; Ü|ber|spịt|zung**
ü|ber|sprẹ|chen (*Rundfunk, Fernsehen* in eine aufgenommene [fremdsprachige] Rede einen anderen Text hineinsprechen)
ü|ber|sprẹn|keln; übersprenkelt
ụ̈|ber|sprin|gen; der Funke ist übergesprungen; **ü|ber|sprịn|gen;** ich habe eine Klasse übersprungen; **Ü|ber|sprịn|gung**
ụ̈|ber|spru|deln; das Wasser ist übergesprudelt
Ụ̈|ber|sprung|hand|lung (*Verhaltensforschung* bestimmte Verhaltensweise in Konfliktsituationen)
ü|ber|spü̲|len; das Ufer ist überspült
ụ̈|ber|staat|lich; eine -e Regelung anstreben
Ụ̈|ber|stän|der (*Forstw.* überalterter, nicht mehr wachsender Baum); **ụ̈|ber|stän|dig;** -e Bäume
ụ̈|ber|stark
ụ̈|ber|ste|chen (im Kartenspiel eine höhere Trumpfkarte ausspielen); er hat übergestochen; **ü|ber|stẹ|chen;** er hat ihn überstochen
ụ̈|ber|ste|hen; der Balken steht über; **ü|ber|stẹ|hen;** sie überstand die Operation; die Gefahr ist überstanden
ü|ber|steig|bar; ụ̈|ber|stei|gen; sie ist übergestiegen; **ü|ber|stei̲|gen;** sie hat den Grat überstiegen; das übersteigt meinen Verstand
ü|ber|stei̲|gern (überhöhen); die Preise sind übersteigert; **Ü|ber|stei̲|ge|rung**
Ü|ber|stei̲|gung
ü|ber|stẹl|len (*Amtsspr.* [weisungsgemäß] einer anderen Stelle übergeben); er wurde überstellt; **Ü|ber|stẹl|lung**
ü|ber|stẹm|peln
Ụ̈|ber|sterb|lich|keit, die; - (höhere Sterblichkeit, als erwartet)
ü|ber|steu̲|ern (*Elektrotechnik* einen Verstärker überlasten, so dass der Ton verzerrt wird; *Kfz-Technik* zu starke Wirkung des Lenkradeinschlags zeigen); **Ü|ber|steu̲|e|rung**
ü|ber|stịm|men; er wurde überstimmt; **Ü|ber|stịm|mung**
ü|ber|stra̲h|len; ihr Charme hat alles überstrahlt
ụ̈|ber|stra|pa|zie|ren (zu häufig gebrauchen); ein überstrapaziertes Schlagwort
ụ̈|ber|strei|chen; die Wand wird nicht tapeziert, sondern nur übergestrichen; **ü|ber|strei̲|chen;** er hat die Täfelung mit Lack überstrichen
ụ̈|ber|strei|fen; sie hat den Handschuh übergestreift
ü|ber|streu̲|en; mit Zucker überstreut
ụ̈|ber|strö|men; er ist von Dankesworten übergeströmt; **ü|ber|strö̲|men;** der Fluss hat die Felder weithin überströmt
Ụ̈|ber|strumpf (*veraltend für* Gamasche)
ụ̈|ber|stül|pen; sie haben ihm den Taucherhelm übergestülpt
Ụ̈|ber|stun|de; -n machen; **Ụ̈|ber|stun|den‿geld, ...zu|schlag**
ü|ber|stụ̈r|zen (übereilen); er hat die Angelegenheit überstürzt; die Ereignisse überstürzten sich; **Ü|ber|stụ̈r|zung** (Übereilung)
ụ̈|ber|ta|rif|lich; -e Bezahlung
ü|ber|täu̲|ben; das hat seinen Schmerz übertäubt; **Ü|ber|täu̲|bung**
ü|ber|tau̲|chen (*österr. ugs. für* [eine Grippe] überstehen)
ü|ber|teu̲|ern; ich ...ere (↑R 16); überteuerte Ware; **Ü|ber|teu̲|e|rung**
ü|ber|tọ̈l|peln; er wurde von ihnen übertölpelt; **Ü|ber|tọ̈l|pe|lung, Ü|ber|tölp|lung**
ü|ber|tö̲|nen; Ü|ber|tö̲|nung
Ụ̈|ber|topf (für einfache, schmucklose Blumentöpfe)
Ụ̈|ber|trag, der; -[e]s, ...träge (Übertragung auf die nächste Seite); **ü|ber|tra̲g|bar; Ü|ber|tra̲g|bar|keit,** die; -; [1]**ü|ber|tra̲|gen** (auftragen; anordnen; übergeben; im Rundfunk wiedergeben); er hat mir das -; ich habe ihm das Amt -; sich - (übergehen) auf ...; die Krankheit hat sich auf mich -; [2]**ü|ber|tra̲|gen;** eine -e Bedeutung; -e (*österr. für* gebrauchte, abgetragene) Kleidung; **Ü|ber|tra̲|ger** (*Fernmeldewesen svw.* Transformator); **Ü|ber|trä̲|ger; Ü|ber|trä̲|ge|rin; Über|tra̲|gung; Ü|ber|tra̲|gungs‿sa|tel|lit, ...ver|merk, ...wa|gen** (*Abk.* Ü-Wagen), **...wei|se** (die)
ụ̈|ber|trai|niert (überanstrengt durch übermäßiges Training)
ü|ber|trẹf|fen; seine Leistungen haben alles übertroffen

ü|ber|trei|ben; er hat die Sache übertrieben; **Ü|ber|trei|bung**
ü|ber|tre|ten; er ist zur evangelischen Kirche übergetreten; sie hat, ist beim Weitsprung übergetreten *(Sport);* **ü|ber|tre|ten;** ich habe das Gesetz -; ich habe mir den Fuß - (*landsch. für* vertreten); **Ü|ber|tre|tung; Ü|ber|tre|tungs|fall,** der; *nur in* im -[e] *(Amtsspr.)*
ü|ber|trie|ben *vgl.* übertreiben; **Ü|ber|trie|ben|heit**
Ü|ber|tritt
ü|ber|trump|fen (überbieten, ausstechen); übertrumpft
ü|ber|tun *(ugs.);* ich habe mir einen Mantel übergetan; **ü|ber|tun,** sich (*landsch. für* sich übernehmen); du hast dich übertan
ü|ber|tün|chen; die Wand wurde übertüncht
ü|ber|über|mor|gen (↑R 132)
Ü|ber|va|ter (Respekt einflößende, beherrschende Figur)
ü|ber|ver|si|chern; ich überversichere (↑R 16); die Schiffsladung war überversichert; **Ü|ber|ver|si|che|rung**
ü|ber|völ|kern; diese Provinz ist über[be]völkert; **Ü|ber|völ|ke|rung,** die; -
ü|ber|voll
ü|ber|vor|sich|tig
ü|ber|vor|tei|len; er wurde übervorteilt; **Ü|ber|vor|tei|lung**
ü|ber|wach (hellwach, angespannt); **ü|ber|wa|chen** (beaufsichtigen); er wurde überwacht
ü|ber|wach|sen; mit Moos -
ü|ber|wäch|tet *frühere Schreibung für* überwechtet
Ü|ber|wa|chung; Ü|ber|wa|chungs‿dienst, ...staat (*Plur.* ...staaten), **...stel|le, ...sys|tem**
ü|ber|wal|len (sprudelnd überfließen); das Wasser ist übergewallt; **ü|ber|wal|len** *(geh.);* von Nebel überwallt
ü|ber|wäl|ti|gen; er wurde überwältigt; **ü|ber|wäl|ti|gend** (ungeheuer groß); **Ü|ber|wäl|ti|gung**
ü|ber|wäl|zen (abwälzen); die Kosten wurden auf die Gemeinden überwälzt
ü|ber|wech|seln (hinübergehen); das Wild ist in das Nachbarrevier übergewechselt
ü|ber|wech|tet (von einem Schneeüberhang bedeckt); -e Gletscherspalten
Ü|ber|weg
ü|ber|wei|sen; sie hat das Geld überwiesen
ü|ber|wei|ßen (hell überstreichen); er hat die Wand überweißt
Ü|ber|wei|sung (Übergabe; [Geld]anweisung); **Ü|ber|wei|sungs‿auf|trag, ...for|mu|lar, ...schein**
ü|ber|weit; Ü|ber|wei|te; Kleider in Überweiten
Ü|ber|welt; ü|ber|welt|lich (übersinnlich, übernatürlich)
ü|ber|wend|lich *(Handarbeit);* - nähen (so nähen, dass die Fäden über die aneinander gelegten Stoffkanten hinweggehen); -e Naht; **ü|ber|wend|lings;** - nähen
ü|ber|wer|fen; er hat den Mantel übergeworfen; **ü|ber|wer|fen,** sich; wir haben uns überworfen (verfeindet); **Ü|ber|wer|fung**
ü|ber|wer|ten (*selten für* überbewerten); **ü|ber|wer|tig** *(Psych.);* **Ü|ber|wer|tig|keit,** die; -; **Ü|ber|wer|tung**
Ü|ber|we|sen
ü|ber|wie|gen (*ugs. für* ein zu hohes Gewicht haben); der Brief wiegt über; **ü|ber|wie|gen** ([an Zahl od. Einfluss] stärker sein); die Laubbäume -; die Mittelmäßigen haben überwogen; **ü|ber|wie|gend** [*auch* 'y:...]
ü|ber|wind|bar; ü|ber|win|den; die Schwierigkeiten wurden überwunden; sich -; **Ü|ber|win|der; Ü|ber|win|dung,** die; -
ü|ber|win|tern; ich ...ere (↑R 16); das Getreide hat gut überwintert; **Ü|ber|win|te|rung**
ü|ber|wöl|ben; der Raum wurde überwölbt; **Ü|ber|wöl|bung**
ü|ber|wu|chern; das Unkraut hat den Weg überwuchert; **Ü|ber|wu|che|rung**
Ü|ber|wurf (Umhang; *Ringen* ein Hebegriff; *österr. u. schweiz. auch für* Zierdecke)
Ü|ber|zahl, die; -; in der - sein; **ü|ber|zah|len** (zu hoch bezahlen); er hat den Gebrauchtwagen überzahlt; **ü|ber|zäh|len** (nachzählen); sie hat den Betrag noch einmal überzählt; **ü|ber|zäh|lig; Ü|ber|zah|lung**
ü|ber|zeich|nen (*ugs. für* über den vorgesehenen Rand zeichnen); übergezeichnete Buchstaben; **ü|ber|zeich|nen;** die Anleihe ist überzeichnet; **Ü|ber|zeich|nung**
Ü|ber|zeit, die; -, -en (*schweiz. für* Überstunden); **Ü|ber|zeit|ar|beit,** die; - *(schweiz.)*
ü|ber|zeu|gen; sie hat ihn überzeugt; sich -; ein überzeugter (unbedingter) Anhänger; **ü|ber|zeu|gend; Ü|ber|zeugt|heit,** die; -; **Ü|ber|zeu|gung; Ü|ber|zeu|gungs‿ar|beit** (die; -; *svw.* Agitation), **...kraft** (die; -), **...tä|ter** (*Rechtsspr.* jmd., der um einer [politischen, religiösen o.ä.] Überzeugung willen straffällig geworden ist); **ü|ber|zeu|gungs|treu**
ü|ber|zie|hen; er zieht eine Jacke über, hat eine Jacke übergezogen; **ü|ber|zie|hen;** sie überzieht den Kuchen mit einem Zuckerguss; überzogen mit Rost; er hat sein Konto überzogen; **Ü|ber|zie|her; Ü|ber|zie|hungs|kre|dit**
ü|ber|züch|tet; der Hund ist überzüchtet
ü|ber|zu|ckern; das Gebäck ist überzuckert
Ü|ber|zug; Ü|ber|zugs|pa|pier
ü|ber|zwerch [*auch* ...'tsvɛrç] (*landsch. für* quer, über Kreuz; verschroben)
U|bi|er ['u:bi̯ər], der; -s, - (Angehöriger eines germ. Volksstammes)
U|bi|quist, der; -en, -en; ↑R 126 ⟨lat.⟩ (*Biol.* auf der gesamten Erdkugel verbreitete Pflanzen- od. Tierart); **u|bi|qui|tär** (überall verbreitet)
üb|lich; (↑R 47:) seine Rede enthielt nur das Übliche; **...üb|lich** (z. B. ortsüblich); **üb|li|cher|wei|se; Üb|lich|keit,** die; -
U-Bo|gen (↑R 25)
U-Boot[1] (↑R 26; Unterseeboot; *Abk.* U); **U-Boot-Krieg** (↑R 28)
üb|rig; übriges Verlorenes; übrige kostbare Gegenstände; (↑R 47:) ein Übriges tun (mehr tun, als nötig ist); im Übrigen (sonst, ferner); das, alles Übrige; die, alle Übrigen; *Schreibung in Verbindung mit Verben immer getrennt:* übrig behalten, bleiben, lassen; mir ist nichts anderes übrig geblieben; nichts zu wünschen übrig lassen; **üb|ri|gens; üb|rig las|sen** *vgl.* übrig
Ü|bung; Ü|bungs‿an|zug, ...ar|beit, ...auf|ga|be, ...buch; ü|bungs|hal|ber; Ü|bungs‿hang, ...platz, ...schie|ßen, ...stück
Ücht|land *vgl.* Üechtland
U|cker|mark, die; - (nordostdt. Landschaft); **U|cker|mär|ker** (↑R 103); **u|cker|mär|kisch**
Ud, die; -, -s ⟨arab.⟩ (Laute mit 4 bis 7 Saitenpaaren)
u. d. Ä. = und dem Ähnliche[s] (*vgl.* ähnlich)
u. desgl. [m.] = und desgleichen [mehr]; **u. dgl. [m.]** = und dergleichen [mehr]
u. d. M. = unter dem Meeresspiegel; **ü. d. M.** = über dem Meeresspiegel
U|do (m. Vorn.)
UdSSR = Union der Sozialisti-

[1] *Bundeswehramtlich* Uboot.

schen Sowjetrepubliken (bis 1991)

u. E. = unseres Erachtens

Ü|echt|land [ˈyːɛçt...], *auch* Ụchtland, das; -[e]s (in der Schweiz); *vgl.* Freiburg im Üechtland

Ue|cker [ˈykər], die; - (nordd. Fluss)

UEFA, die; - (*Kurzw. für* Union Européenne de Football Association [yˈniɔ̃ː ørɔpeˈɛn də futˈboːl asosiaˈsiɔ̃ː]; Europäischer Fußballverband); **UEFA-Po|kal** (↑R 26)

U-Ei|sen; ↑R 25 (Walzeisen von U-förmigem Querschnitt); **U-Eisen-för|mig** (↑R 28)

Uel|zen [ˈyl...] (Stadt in der Lüneburger Heide); **Uel|ze|ner, Uelzer** (↑R 103)

Uer|din|gen [ˈyːr...] (Stadtteil von Krefeld)

U|fa, ® die; - (Universum-Film-AG); **U|fa-Film** (↑R 26); **U|fa-The|a|ter** (↑R 26)

U|fer, das; -s, -; *Schreibung in Straßennamen:* ↑R 123 ff.; **U|ferbau** (*Plur.* ...bauten), **...be|fes|tigung, ...bö|schung, ...geld** (Hafengebühr), **...land|schaft, ...läufer** (ein Vogel); **u|fer|los;** seine Pläne gingen ins Uferlose (allzu weit); **U|ferpro|me|na|de, ...schwal|be, ...stra|ße**

uff!

u. ff. = und folgende [Seiten]

Uf|fi|zi|en [...iən] *Plur.* (Palast mit Gemäldesammlung in Florenz)

Uffz. = Unteroffizier

UFO, U|fo, das; -[s], -s (*Kurzw. für* unbekanntes Flugobjekt [*für engl.* unidentified flying object])

u-för|mig, *auch* **U-för|mig;** ↑R 25 (in Form eines lat. U)

...uf|rig (z. B. linksufrig)

U|gan|da (Staat in Afrika); **U|gander; U|gan|de|rin; u|gan|disch**

ug|risch (↑R 130) *vgl.* finnisch-ugrisch

uh!

U-Haft; ↑R 26 (*kurz für* Untersuchungshaft)

U-Ha|ken (↑R 25)

Uh|land (dt. Dichter)

Uhr, die; -, -en; Punkt, Schlag acht Uhr; es ist zwei Uhr nachts; es ist ein Uhr, *aber* es ist eins; es ist 6.30 [Uhr], 6^{30} [Uhr] (*gesprochen* sechs Uhr dreißig); es schlägt 12 [Uhr]; um fünf [Uhr] (*volkstümlich* um fünfe) aufstehen; ich komme um 20 Uhr; der Zug fährt um halb acht [Uhr] abends; ich wartete bis zwei Uhr nachmittags; Achtuhrzug (*mit Ziffer* 8-Uhr-Zug; ↑R 28); *vgl.* hora; **Uhr|band**, das; *Plur.* ...bänder; **Ühr|chen; Uhrenin|dust|rie, ...kas|ten, ...radio; Uhr|ket|te; Uhr|ma|cher; Uhr|ma|che|rei; Uhr|ma|cherin; Uhrta|sche, ...werk, ...zeiger; Uhr|zei|ger|sinn**, der; -[e]s (Richtung des Uhrzeigers); *nur in* im *u.* entgegen dem -; **Uhr|zeit**

U|hu, der; -s, -s (ein Vogel)

ui! [uj]; **ui je!** (*österr. für* oje!)

UIC = UEFA-Intertotocup (ein europ. Fußballwettbewerb)

U|kas, der; -ses, -se ‹russ.› (Erlass, Verordnung [des Zaren])

U|ke|lei, der; -s, *Plur.* -e *u.* -s ‹slaw.› (ein Karpfenfisch)

Uk|ra|i|ne (↑R 130), die; - (Staat in Osteuropa); **Uk|ra|i|ner; Uk|ra|ine|rin; uk|ra|i|nisch; Uk|ra|inisch**, das; -[s] (Sprache); *vgl.* Deutsch; **Uk|ra|i|ni|sche**, das; -n; *vgl.* Deutsche, das

U|ku|le|le, die *od.* das; -, -n ‹hawaiisch› (kleine, viersaitige Gitarre)

UKW = Ultrakurzwelle; **UKW-Emp|fän|ger** (↑R 26); **UKW-Sen|der** (↑R 26)

Ul, die; -, -en (*nordd. für* Eule; Handbesen)

U|lan, der; -en, -en (↑R 126) ‹türk.-poln.› (*früher* Lanzenreiter)

U|lan Ba|tor (Hptst. der Mongolei)

U|lan|ka, die; -, -s ‹poln.› (Waffenrock der Ulanen)

U|le|ma, der; -s, -s ‹arab., „Stand der Gelehrten"› (islamischer Rechts- u. Religionsgelehrter)

Ul|len|flucht, die; -, -en ‹„Eulenflug"› (*nordd. für* Dachöffnung des westfäl. Bauernhauses; *nur Sing.: veraltet für* Dämmerung); **Ul|len|spie|gel** (*Nebenform von* Eulenspiegel)

Ul|fi|las, Wụl|fi|la (Bischof der Westgoten)

U|li [*auch* ˈuli] (m. Vorn.)

U|li|xes, U|lys|ses (*lat. Name von* Odysseus)

Ulk, der; *Gen.* -s, *seltener* -es, *Plur.* -e (Spaß; Unfug)

Ülk, der; -[e]s, -e (*nordd. für* Iltis)

ul|ken; Ul|ke|rei; ul|kig (*ugs.*); **Ulk|nu|del** (*ugs. scherzh.*)

Ul|kus, das; -, Ulzera ‹lat.› (*Med.* Geschwür)

Ul|la (w. Vorn.)

[1]Ulm (Stadt an der Donau)

[2]Ulm, [1]Ul|me, die; -, ...men (*Bergmannsspr.* seitliche Fläche im Bergwerksgang)

[2]Ul|me, die; -, -n ‹lat.› (ein Laubbaum); **Ul|men|blatt**

Ul|mer; ↑R 103 (aus [1]Ulm); der - Spatz

Ul|rich (m. Vorn.); **Ul|ri|ke** (w. Vorn.)

[1]Uls|ter [*engl.* ˈalstə(r)] ‹engl.› (historische Provinz im Norden der Insel Irland); **[2]Uls|ter**, der; -s, - (weiter [Herren]mantel; schwerer Mantelstoff)

ult. = ultimo

Ul|ti|ma Ra|tio (↑R 33), die; - - ‹lat.› (letztes Mittel); **ul|ti|ma|tiv** (in Form eines Ultimatums; nachdrücklich); **Ul|ti|ma|tum**, das; -s, ...ten (letzte, äußerste Aufforderung); **ul|ti|mo** (am Letzten [des Monats]; *Abk.* ult.); ultimo März; **Ul|ti|mo**, der; -s, -s (letzter Tag [des Monats]); **Ul|timo|ge|schäft**

Ult|ra (↑R 130), der; -s, -s ‹lat.› (polit. Fanatiker, Rechtsextremist)

ult|ra|hart (↑R 130); **ult|ra|kurz; Ult|ra|kurz|wel|le** (↑R 130; *Physik, Rundf.* elektromagnetische Welle unter 10 m Länge; *Abk.* UKW); **Ult|ra|kurz|wel|lenemp|fän|ger, ...sen|der, ...thera|pie; ult|ra|lang** (↑R 130)

Ult|ra|leicht|flug|zeug (↑R 130; besonders leicht u. einfach gebautes [Sport]flugzeug für ein bis zwei Personen)

ult|ra|ma|rin (↑R 130) ‹lat., „übers Meer" [eingeführt]› (kornblumenblau); **Ult|ra|ma|rin**, das; -s

Ult|ra|mik|ro|skop (↑R 130; zur Beobachtung kleinster Teilchen)

ult|ra|mon|tan (↑R 130) ‹lat., „jenseits der Berge [Alpen]"› (streng päpstlich gesinnt); **Ult|ramon|ta|nis|mus**, der; - (streng päpstliche Gesinnung [im ausgehenden 19. Jh.])

ult|ra|rot (↑R 130; *svw.* infrarot)

Ult|ra|schall (↑R 130), der; -[e]s (mit dem menschlichen Gehör nicht mehr wahrnehmbarer Schall); **Ult|ra|schallbe|handlung, ...di|ag|nos|tik, ...schweißung, ...the|ra|pie, ...wel|le** (*meist Plur.*)

Ult|ra|strah|lung (↑R 130; kosmische Höhenstrahlung)

ult|ra|vi|o|lett [...v...] (↑R 130; [im Sonnenspektrum] über dem violetten Licht; *Abk.* UV); -e Strahlen (*kurz* UV-Strahlen; ↑R 26); **Ult|ra|vi|o|lett**, das; -s (*Abk.* UV)

U|lys|ses *vgl.* Ulixes

Ul|ze|ra (*Plur. von* Ulkus); **Ul|zera|ti|on**, die; -, -en ‹lat.› (*Med.* Geschwürbildung); **ul|ze|rie|ren** (geschwürig werden); **ul|ze|rös** (geschwürig); -es Organ

um; I. *Präp. mit Akk.:* um vieles, nichts, ein Mehrfaches größer; um alles in der Welt [nicht]; einen Tag um den anderen; um Rat fragen; ich komme um 20 Uhr (*vgl.* Uhr); ich gehe um Milch (*österr.*

für um Milch zu holen); (↑R 47:) um ein Bedeutendes, ein Beträchtliches, ein Erkleckliches (sehr); um ... willen, *mit Gen.:* um einer Sache willen, um jemandes willen, um Gottes willen, um meinetwillen; umeinander; umsonst; umso größer, umso mehr, umso weniger; ums (um das). **II.** *Adverb:* um sein (*ugs. für* vorüber sein); da die Zeit um ist, um war; die Zeit ist um gewesen; um und um; links um! (*vgl.* links); es waren um [die] (= etwa) zwanzig Mädchen; Gemeinden von um (= etwa) 10 000 Einwohnern. **III.** *Infinitivkonjunktion:* um zu; er kommt[,] um uns zu helfen (↑R 75). **IV.** *Großschreibung* (↑R 49): das Um und Auf (*österr. für* das Ganze, das Wesentliche)

um... *in Verbindung mit Verben:* **a)** *unfeste Zusammensetzungen* (↑R 38), z. B. umbauen *(vgl. d.),* umgebaut; **b)** *feste Zusammensetzungen* (↑R 37), z. B. umbauen *(vgl. d.),* umbaut

um|ackern (↑R 132); umgeackert

um|ad|res|sie|ren; umadressiert

um|än|dern; umgeändert; **Um|än|de|rung**

um Ant|wort wird ge|be|ten *od.* **Um Ant|wort wird ge|be|ten** (*Abk.* u. [*od.* U.] A. w. g.)

um|ar|bei|ten; der Anzug wurde umgearbeitet; **Um|ar|bei|tung**

um|ar|men; er hat sie umarmt; sie umarmten sich; **Um|ar|mung**

Um|bau, der; -[e]s, *Plur.* -e *u.* -ten; **um|bau|en** (anders bauen); das Theater wurde völlig umgebaut; **um|bau|en** (mit Bauten umschließen); er hat seinen Hof mit Ställen umbaut; umbauter Raum

um|be|hal|ten *(ugs.);* sie hat den Schal -

um|be|nen|nen; umbenannt; **Um|be|nen|nung**

[1]**Um|ber** *vgl.* Umbra

[2]**Um|ber,** der; -s, -n ‹lat.› (ein Speisefisch des Mittelmeeres)

Um|ber|to (m. Vorn.)

um|be|schrie|ben *(Math.);* der -e Kreis (Umkreis)

um|be|set|zen; die Rolle wurde umbesetzt (einem anderen Darsteller übertragen); **Um|be|set|zung**

um|be|sin|nen, sich (seine Meinung ändern); ich habe mich umbesonnen

um|bet|ten (in ein anderes Bett, in ein anderes Grab legen); wir haben den Kranken, die Toten umgebettet; **Um|bet|tung**

um|bie|gen; er hat den Draht umgebogen

um|bil|den; die Regierung wurde umgebildet; **Um|bil|dung**

um|bin|den; er hat ein Tuch umgebunden; **um|bin|den;** er hat den Finger mit Leinwand umbunden

um|bla|sen; der Wind hat sie fast umgeblasen; **um|bla|sen;** von Winden -

Um|blatt (inneres Hüllblatt der Zigarre); **um|blät|tern;** umgeblättert

Um|blick; um|bli|cken, sich; du hast dich umgeblickt

Umb|ra (↑R 130), die; - *u.* **Um|ber,** der; -s ‹lat.› (ein brauner Farbstoff)

Umb|ral|glas ® (↑R 130; getöntes Brillenglas)

um|bran|den; von Wellen umbrandet

um|brau|sen; von Beifall umbraust

um|bre|chen; den Acker -; der Zaun ist umgebrochen worden; **um|bre|chen** (*Druckw.* den Drucksatz in Seiten einteilen); er umbricht den Satz; der Satz wird umbrochen, ist noch zu -; **Um|bre|cher** (*Druckw. für* Metteur)

Umb|rer (↑R 130), der; -s, - (Angehöriger eines italischen Volksstamms); **Umb|ri|en** [...i̯ən] (ital. Region)

um|brin|gen; umgebracht; sich -

umb|risch (↑R 130; aus Umbrien)

Um|bruch, der; -[e]s, ...brüche (grundlegende [polit.] Änderung, Umwandlung; *nur Sing.: Druckw.* das Umbrechen); **Um|bruch‿kor|rek|tur, ...re|vi|si|on**

um|bu|chen; einen Betrag -; sie hat die Reise umgebucht; **Um|bu|chung**

um|da|tie|ren; er hat den Brief umdatiert

um|den|ken (die Grundlage seines Denkens ändern); **Um|denk|pro|zess, Um|den|kungs|pro|zess**

um|deu|ten (anders deuten); **Um|deu|tung**

um|di|ri|gie|ren; wir haben den Transport umdirigiert

um|dis|po|nie|ren (seine Pläne ändern); ich habe umdisponiert

um|drän|gen; sie wurde von allen Seiten umdrängt

um|dre|hen; sich -; er dreht jeden Pfennig um (ist sehr sparsam); er hat den Spieß umgedreht (ist seinerseits [mit denselben Mitteln] zum Angriff übergegangen); du hast dich umgedreht; **Um|dre|hung; Um|dre|hungs‿ge|schwin|dig|keit, ...zahl** (*svw.* Drehzahl)

Um|druck *Plur.* ...drucke (*nur Sing.:* ein Vervielfältigungsverfahren; Ergebnis dieses Verfahrens); **Um|druck|ver|fah|ren**

um|düs|tern, sich

um|ei|nan|der (↑R 132); *Schreibung in Verbindung mit Verben immer getrennt:* sich umeinander kümmern; umeinander laufen, herumtanzen

um|er|zie|hen; sie wurden politisch umerzogen; **Um|er|zie|hung**

um|fä|cheln *(geh.);* der Wind hat mich umfächelt

um|fah|ren (fahrend umwerfen; *landsch. für* fahrend einen Umweg machen); er hat das Verkehrsschild umgefahren; ich bin [beinahe eine Stunde] umgefahren; **um|fah|ren** (um etwas herumfahren); er umfuhr das Hindernis; er hat die Insel umfahren; **Um|fahrt; Um|fah|rung** (*österr. u. schweiz. auch svw.* Umgehungsstraße); **Um|fah|rungs|stra|ße** *(österr., schweiz.)*

Um|fall, der; -[e]s (*ugs. für* plötzlicher Gesinnungswandel); **um|fal|len;** er ist tot umgefallen; bei der Abstimmung ist er doch noch umgefallen *(ugs.);* (↑R 50:) sie war zum Umfallen müde *(ugs.)*

Um|fang; um|fan|gen *(geh.);* die Nacht umfing uns; ich halte ihn umfangen; **um|fäng|lich; um|fang|mä|ßig** *vgl.* umfangsmäßig; **um|fang|reich; Um|fangs|be|rech|nung; um|fangs|mä|ßig,** um|fang|mä|ßig

um|fär|ben; der Mantel wurde umgefärbt

um|fas|sen (anders fassen; *landsch. auch für* den Arm um jmdn. legen); der Schmuck wird umgefasst; er fasste das Mädchen um; **um|fas|sen** (umschließen; in sich begreifen); ich habe ihn umfasst; die Sammlung umfasst alles Wesentliche; **um|fas|send; Um|fas|sung; Um|fas|sungs|mau|er**

Um|feld (Umwelt, Umgebung); das soziale -

um|fir|mie|ren (einen anderen Handelsnamen annehmen); wir haben umfirmiert

um|flech|ten; eine umflochtene Weinflasche

um|flie|gen (*landsch. für* fliegend einen Umweg machen; *ugs. für* hinfallen); das Flugzeug war eine weite Strecke umgeflogen; das Schild ist umgeflogen; **um|flie|gen;** die Krähen haben den alten Turm umflogen

um|flie|ßen; umflossen von ...

um|flo|ren *(geh.);* Tränen umflorten seinen Blick; mit von Trauer umflorter Stimme

ụm|for|men; er formt den Satz um; das Leben hat ihn umgeformt; **Ụm|for|mer** *(Elektrotechnik)*

um|for|mu|lie|ren; sie hat den Text umformuliert

Ụm|for|mung

Ụm|fra|ge; - halten; **ụm|fra|gen;** die Meinungsforscher haben wieder umgefragt

um|frie|den, umfriedet, *seltener* **um|frie|di|gen,** umfriedigt (mit einem Zaun umgeben); er hat seinen Garten umfriedet, *seltener* umfriedigt; **Um|frie|di|gung,** *häufiger* **Um|frie|dung**

ụm|fül|len; sie hat den Wein umgefüllt; **Ụm|fül|lung**

ụm|funk|ti|o|nie|ren (die Funktion von etwas ändern; zweckentfremdet einsetzen); die Veranstaltung wurde zu einer Protestversammlung umfunktioniert; **Ụm|funk|ti|o|nie|rung**

Ụm|gang; ụm|gäng|lich (freundlich, erträglich); **Ụm|gäng|lich|keit,** die; -; **Ụm|gangs‿form** *(meist Plur.),* **...spra|che; ụm|gangs|sprach|lich; Ụm|gangs|ton** *Plur.* ...töne

um|gạr|nen; sie hat ihn umgarnt; **Um|gạr|nung**

um|gau|keln; der Schmetterling hat die Blüten umgaukelt; **Um|gau|ke|lung, Um|gauk|lung**

ụm|ge|ben *(landsch.);* er gab mir den Mantel um, hat mir den Mantel umgegeben (umgehängt); **um|ge|ben;** er umgab das Haus mit einer Hecke; sie war von Kindern umgeben; sich umgeben mit ...

Ụm|ge|bin|de|haus *(Bauw.)*

Um|ge|bung

Ụm|ge|gend *(ugs.)*

ụm|ge|hen; ein Gespenst geht dort um; er ist umgegangen (*landsch. für* hat einen Umweg gemacht); ich bin mit ihm nett umgegangen (*veraltend für* habe mit ihm nett verkehrt); **um|ge|hen;** er umgeht alle Fragen; er hat das Gesetz umgangen; **ụm|ge|hend;** mit -er (nächster) Post; **Um|ge|hung; Um|ge|hungs|stra|ße**

ụm|ge|kehrt; es verhält sich -, als du denkst

ụm|ge|stal|ten; sie hat den Park umgestaltet; **Ụm|ge|stal|tung**

ụm|gie|ßen; sie hat den Wein umgegossen

um|git|tern; umgittert; **Um|git|te|rung**

um|glän|zen *(geh.);* von Licht umglänzt

um|gọl|den *(geh.);* umgoldet

ụm|gra|ben; er hat das Beet umgegraben; **Ụm|gra|bung**

ụm|grei|fen (in einen anderen Griff wechseln); er hat bei der Riesenfelge umgegriffen; **um|grei|fen** (*svw.* umfassen); er hatte den Stock fest umgriffen

um|grẹn|zen; sie umgrenzte das Aufgabengebiet; der Garten ist von Steinen umgrenzt; umgrenzte Vollmachten; **Um|grẹn|zung**

ụm|grup|pie|ren; umgruppiert; **Ụm|grup|pie|rung**

ụm|gu|cken, sich (*ugs. für* sich umsehen)

ụm|gür|ten *(früher);* ich habe mir das Schwert umgegürtet; **um|gür|ten** *(früher);* sich -; mit dem Schwert umgürtet

ụm|ha|ben *(ugs.);* sie hat nichts um, sie hat nicht einmal ein Tuch umgehabt

ụm|ha|cken; der Baum wurde umgehackt

um|hä|keln; ein umhäkeltes Taschentuch

um|hạl|sen; sie hat ihn umhalst; **Um|hạl|sung**

Ụm|hang; ụm|hän|gen; ich hängte mir den Mantel um; ich habe die Bilder umgehängt (anders gehängt); *vgl.* ²hängen; **um|hạn|gen** (hängend umgeben); das Bild war mit Flor umhängt; *vgl.* ²hängen; **Ụm|hän|ge|ta|sche,** Ụm|häng|ta|sche; **Ụm|hän|ge|tuch,** Ụm|hang|tuch, Ụm|häng|tuch *Plur.* ...tücher; **Ụm|häng|ta|sche** *vgl.* Umhängetasche; **Ụm|hang|tuch, Ụm|häng|tuch** *vgl.* Umhängetuch

ụm|hau|en (abschlagen, fällen usw.); er haute, *geh.* hieb den Baum um; das hat mich umgehauen (*ugs. für* das hat mich in großes Erstaunen versetzt)

um|he|ben *(Druckw.);* einige Zeilen wurden umhoben

um|he|gen *(geh.);* umhegt; **Um|he|gung**

um|her (im Umkreis); **um|her...** (bald hierhin, bald dorthin ..., z. B. umherlaufen; er läuft umher, ist umhergelaufen); **um|her‿bli|cken, ...fah|ren, ...flie|gen, ...ge|hen, ...geis|tern, ...ir|ren, ...ja|gen, ...lau|fen, ...lie|gen, ...rei|sen, ...schlei|chen, ...schlen|dern, ...schwei|fen, ...schwir|ren, ...strei|fen, ...tra|gen, ...zie|hen**

um|hịn|kom|men (*svw.* umhinkönnen)

um|hịn|kön|nen; *nur verneint:* ich kann nicht umhin, es zu tun; ich habe nicht umhingekonnt; nicht umhinzukönnen

ụm|hö|ren, sich; ich habe mich danach umgehört

um|hül|len; umhüllt mit ...; **Um|hül|lung**

U|mi|ak, der *od.* das; -s, -s ‹eskim.› (Boot der Eskimofrauen)

U/min = Umdrehungen pro Minute

Ụm|in|ter|pre|ta|ti|on; ụm|in|ter|pre|tie|ren (umdeuten)

um|ju|beln; umjubelt

um|kạ̈mp|fen; die Festung war hart umkämpft

Ụm|kar|ton *(fachspr.)*

Ụm|kehr, die; -; **ụm|kehr|bar; Ụm|kehr|bar|keit,** die; -; **ụm|keh|ren;** sich -; sie ist umgekehrt; sie hat die Tasche umgekehrt; **Ụm|kehr|film** (Film, der beim Entwickeln ein Positiv liefert); **Ụm|keh|rung**

ụm|kip|pen; der Stuhl kippte um; er ist bei den Verhandlungen umgekippt (*ugs. für* hat seinen Standpunkt geändert); er ist plötzlich umgekippt (*ugs. für* ohnmächtig geworden); **Ụm|kip|pen,** das; -s (biolog. Absterben eines Gewässers)

um|klạm|mern; er hielt ihre Hände umklammert; **Um|klạm|me|rung**

ụm|klapp|bar; ụm|klap|pen; er hat den Deckel umgeklappt; er ist umgeklappt (*landsch. für* ohnmächtig geworden)

Ụm|klei|de, die; -, -n (*ugs. für* Umkleideraum); **Ụm|klei|de|ka|bi|ne; ụm|klei|den,** sich; ich habe mich umgekleidet (anders gekleidet); **um|klei|den** (umgeben, umhüllen); umkleidet mit, von ...; **Ụm|klei|de|raum; Ụm|klei|dung,** die; -; **Um|klei|dung**

ụm|kni|cken; sie ist [mit dem Fuß] umgeknickt

ụm|kom|men; er ist im Krieg umgekommen; (↑ R 50:) die Hitze ist ja zum Umkommen *(ugs.)*

ụm|ko|pie|ren *(Fototechnik)*

um|krạ̈n|zen; umkränzt; **Um|krạ̈n|zung**

Ụm|kreis, der; -es *Plur. (Geom.:)* -e; **um|krei|sen;** der Storch hat das Nest umkreist; **Um|krei|sung**

ụm|krem|peln (*ugs. auch für* völlig ändern); er hat die Ärmel umgekrempelt

ụm|la|den; die Säcke wurden umgeladen; *vgl.* ¹laden; **Ụm|la|dung**

Ụm|la|ge (Steuer; Beitrag); **ụm|la|gern** (an einen anderen Platz bringen [zum Lagern]); die Waren wurden umgelagert; **um|la|gern** (umgeben, eng umschließen); umlagert von ...; *vgl.* lagern; **Ụm|la|ge|rung; Um|la|ge|rung**

Ụm|land, das; -[e]s (ländliches Gebiet um eine [Groß]stadt)

Ụm|lauf (*auch für* Fruchtfolge; *Med.* eitrige Entzündung an Finger oder Hand); in Umlauf geben, sein (von Zahlungsmitteln); **Ụm|lauf|bahn; ụm|lau|fen** (laufend umwerfen; *landsch. für* einen Umweg machen; weitergegeben werden); wir sind umgelaufen; eine Nachricht ist umgelaufen; **um|lau|fen;** der Mond umläuft die Erde in 28 Tagen; ich habe den Platz umlaufen; **Ụm|lauf|mit|tel** *Plur.* (Geld); **Ụm|lauf[s]‿ge|schwin|dig|keit, ...zeit; Ụm|lauf|ver|mö|gen** *(Wirtsch.)*

Ụm|laut (*Sprachw.* ä, ö, ü); **ụm|lau|ten;** ein umgelautetes U ist ein Ü

Ụm|le|ge‿ka|len|der, ...kra|gen; ụm|le|gen (*derb auch für* erschießen); er legte den Mantel um; er hat die Karten umgelegt (gewendet od. anders gelegt); **um|le|gen;** ein Braten, umlegt mit Gemüse; **Ụm|le|gung** (*auch für* Flurbereinigung); **Um|le|gung**

ụm|lei|ten (anders leiten); der Verkehr wurde umgeleitet; **Ụm|lei|tung; Ụm|lei|tungs|schild,** das

ụm|len|ken; die Fahrzeuge wurden umgelenkt; **Ụm|len|kung**

ụm|ler|nen; sie hat umgelernt

ụm|lie|gend; -e Ortschaften

Ụm|luft, die; - (*Technik* aufbereitete, zurückgeleitete Luft)

um|man|teln *(Technik);* ich ...[e]le (↑R 16); ein ummanteltes Kabel; **Um|man|te|lung**

um|mau|ern (mit Mauerwerk umgeben); das Tiergehege wurde ummauert; **Um|mau|e|rung**

ụm|mel|den; ich habe mich polizeilich umgemeldet; **Ụm|mel|dung**

ụm|mo|deln (ändern, umgestalten); umgemodelt; **Ụm|mo|de|lung, Ụm|mod|lung**

ụm|mün|zen; die Niederlage wurde in einen Sieg umgemünzt (umgedeutet); **Ụm|mün|zung**

um|nach|tet (*geh. für* geisteskrank); **Um|nach|tung** *(geh.)*

ụm|nä|hen; sie hat den Saum umgenäht (eingeschlagen u. festgenäht); **um|nä|hen;** eine umnähte (eingefasste) Kante

um|ne|beln; ich ...[e]le (↑R 16); er hat ihn mit seinem Zigarrenrauch umnebelt; sie war leicht umnebelt (benommen); **Um|ne|be|lung, Um|neb|lung**

ụm|neh|men *(ugs.);* sie hat eine Decke umgenommen

ụm|nie|ten (*derb für* niederschlagen, -schießen); sie haben ihn umgenietet

Ụm|or|ga|ni|sa|ti|on; ụm|or|ga|ni|sie|ren

ụm|pa|cken (anders packen); der Koffer wurde umgepackt

ụm|pflan|zen (verpflanzen); die Blumen wurden umgepflanzt; **um|pflan|zen** (mit Pflanzen umgeben); umpflanzt mit ...; **Ụm|pflan|zung; Um|pflan|zung**

ụm|pflü|gen (mit dem Pflug bearbeiten); er hat den Acker umgepflügt; **Ụm|pflü|gung**

ụm|po|len (*Physik, Elektrotechnik* Plus- u. Minuspol vertauschen); umgepolt

ụm|prä|gen; die Goldstücke wurden umgeprägt; **Ụm|prä|gung**

ụm|pro|gram|mie|ren; Ụm|pro|gram|mie|rung

ụm|pum|pen; die Ladung des Tankers wurde umgepumpt

ụm|quar|tie|ren (in ein anderes Quartier legen); er wurde umquartiert; **Ụm|quar|tie|rung**

ụm|rah|men (mit anderem Rahmen versehen); das Bild muss umgerahmt werden; **um|rah|men** (mit Rahmen versehen, einrahmen); die Vorträge wurden von musikalischen Darbietungen umrahmt; **Ụm|rah|mung; Um|rah|mung**

um|ran|den; er hat den Artikel mit Rotstift umrandet; **um|rän|dert;** seine Augen waren rot umrändert; **Um|ran|dung**

um|ran|gie|ren [...raŋˈʒiː...]; umrangiert

um|ran|ken; von Rosen umrankt; **Um|ran|kung**

Ụm|raum (umgebender Raum); **ụm|räu|men;** wir haben das Zimmer umgeräumt; **Ụm|räu|mung**

ụm|rech|nen; sie hat DM in Schweizer Franken umgerechnet; **Ụm|rech|nung; Ụm|rech|nungs|kurs**

um|rei|sen; er hat die Erde umreist

ụm|rei|ßen (einreißen; zerstören); er hat den Zaun umgerissen; **um|rei|ßen** (im Umriss zeichnen; andeuten); sie hat die Situation kurz umrissen

ụm|rei|ten (reitend umwerfen); er hat den Mann umgeritten; **um|rei|ten;** er hat das Feld umritten

ụm|ren|nen; sie hat das Kind umgerannt

um|rin|gen (umgeben, umstehen); von Kindern umringt

Ụm|riss; Ụm|riss|zeich|nung

Ụm|ritt

ụm|rüh|ren; umgerührt

um|run|den; das Raumschiff hat den Mond umrundet; **Um|run|dung**

um|rüst|bar; um|rüs|ten (für bestimmte Aufgaben technisch verändern); die Maschine wurde umgerüstet; **Ụm|rüs|tung**

ụms; ↑R 13 (um das); es geht ums Ganze; ein Jahr ums *od.* um das andere; *aber* (↑R 13): um's (um des) Himmels willen! *(ugs.); vgl. auch* Himmel

ụm|sä|beln (*ugs. für* zu Fall bringen); er hat den Stürmer umgesäbelt

ụm|sä|gen; er hat den Baum umgesägt

ụm|sat|teln (*ugs. übertr. auch für* einen anderen Beruf ergreifen); er hat das Pferd umgesattelt; der Student hat umgesattelt (ein anderes Studienfach gewählt); **Ụm|sat|te|lung, Ụm|satt|lung**

Ụm|satz; Ụm|satz‿ana|ly|se (↑R 132; *Wirtsch.*), **...an|stieg, ...be|tei|li|gung, ...ein|bu|ße, ...pro|vi|si|on, ...rück|gang, ...stei|ge|rung, ...steu|er** (die), **...ver|gü|tung** (*für* Umsatzprovision)

ụm|säu|men; das Kleid muss noch umgesäumt werden (der Saum muss umgelegt u. genäht werden); **um|säu|men;** das Dorf ist von Bergen umsäumt (umgeben)

ụm|schaf|fen (umformen); sie hat ihren Roman umgeschaffen; *vgl.* [2]schaffen; **Ụm|schaf|fung**

ụm|schal|ten; die Ampel schaltet auf Rot um; er hat den Strom umgeschaltet; **Ụm|schal|ter; Ụm|schalt|he|bel; Ụm|schal|tung**

Um|scha|lung

um|schat|ten; ihre Augen waren umschattet

Ụm|schau, die; -; - halten; **ụm|schau|en,** sich; ich habe mich umgeschaut

Ụm|schicht (*Bergmannsspr.* Wechsel); **ụm|schich|ten;** das Heu wurde umgeschichtet; **ụm|schich|tig** (wechselweise); **Ụm|schich|tung; Ụm|schich|tungs|pro|zess**

ụm|schif|fen (in ein anderes Schiff bringen); die Waren, die Passagiere wurden umgeschifft; **um|schif|fen;** er hat die Klippe umschifft (die Schwierigkeit umgangen); **Ụm|schif|fung; Um|schif|fung**

Ụm|schlag (*auch für* Umladung); **Ụm|schlag|bahn|hof; ụm|schla|gen** (umsetzen; umladen); die Güter wurden umgeschlagen; das Wetter ist, *auch* hat umgeschlagen; **um|schla|gen** (einpacken); die Druckbogen werden - (*Druckw.* gewendet); **Ụm|schlag-**

entǀwurf; Umǀschlaǀgeǀtuch *vgl.* Umschlagtuch; **Umǀschlag‿haǀfen** (*vgl.* [2]Hafen), **...platz; Umǀschlagǀtuch,** Umǀschlaǀgeǀtuch *Plur.* ...tücher; **Umǀschlagǀzeichǀnung**

umǀschleiǀchen; die Katze hat das Futter umschlichen

umǀschlieǀßen; von einer Mauer umschlossen; **Umǀschlieǀßung**

umǀschlinǀgen; ich habe mir das Tuch umgeschlungen; **umǀschlinǀgen;** sie hielt ihn fest umschlungen; **Umǀschlinǀgung; Umǀschlinǀgung**

Umǀschluss (*Amtsspr.* gegenseitiger Besuch od. gemeinsamer Aufenthalt von Häftlingen in einer Zelle)

umǀschmeiǀcheln; sie wird von der Katze umschmeichelt

umǀschmeiǀßen *(ugs.);* er hat den Tisch umgeschmissen

umǀschmelǀzen (durch Schmelzen umformen); das Altmetall wurde umgeschmolzen; **Umǀschmelǀzung**

umǀschnalǀlen; umgeschnallt

umǀschreiǀben (neu, anders schreiben; übertragen); er hat den Aufsatz umgeschrieben; die Hypothek wurde umgeschrieben; **umǀschreiǀben** (mit anderen Worten ausdrücken); sie hat unsere Aufgabe mit wenigen Worten umschrieben; **Umǀschreiǀbung** (Neuschreibung; andere Buchung); **Umǀschreiǀbung** (andere Form des Ausdrucks); **umǀschrieǀben** (*Med. auch für* deutlich abgegrenzt, bestimmt); eine -e Hautflechte; **Umǀschrift**

umǀschubǀsen *(ugs.);* er hat ihn umgeschubst

umǀschulǀden (*Wirtsch.* Kredite umwandeln); umgeschuldet; **Umǀschulǀdung**

umǀschuǀlen; umgeschult; **Umǀschüǀler; Umǀschüǀleǀrin; Umǀschuǀlung**

umǀschütǀten; umgeschüttet

umǀschwärǀmen; umschwärmt

umǀschweǀben; umschwebt

Umǀschweiǀfe *Plur.;* ohne -e (geradeheraus); **umǀschweiǀfen;** umschweift

umǀschwenǀken; er ist plötzlich umgeschwenkt

umǀschwirǀren; von Mücken umschwirrt

Umǀschwung, der; -s, ...schwünge (*nur Sing.: schweiz. auch für* Umgebung des Hauses)

umǀseǀgeln; er hat die Insel umsegelt; **Umǀseǀgeǀlung, Umǀsegǀlung**

umǀseǀhen, sich; ich habe mich danach umgesehen; **Umǀseǀhen,** das; -s; *nur in* im - (*veraltend für* plötzlich, sofort)

um sein *vgl.* um, II

umǀseiǀtig; umǀseits *(Amtsspr.)*

umǀsetzǀbar; umǀsetǀzen (anders setzen; verkaufen); sich -; sie setzte die Pflanzen um; er hat alle Waren umgesetzt; ich habe mich umgesetzt; **Umǀsetǀzung**

Umǀsichǀgreiǀfen, das; -s (↑R 50)

Umǀsicht, die; -; **umǀsichǀtig; Umǀsichǀtigǀkeit,** die; -

umǀsieǀdeln; umgesiedelt; **Umǀsieǀdeǀlung; Umǀsiedǀler; Umǀsiedǀleǀrin; Umǀsiedǀlung**

umǀsinǀken; er ist vor Müdigkeit umgesunken

umǀso; umso besser; umso größer; umso schöner; **umǀso eǀher[,] als** (↑R 88); **umǀso mehr[,] als** (↑R 88)

umǀsonst

umǀsorǀgen; umsorgt

umǀso weǀniǀger[,] als (↑R 88); *vgl.* um

umǀspanǀnen (neu, anders [be]spannen; *auch für* transformieren); der Strom wurde auf 9 Volt umgespannt; **umǀspanǀnen** (umfassen); seine Arbeit hat viele Wissensgebiete umspannt; **Umǀspanǀner** (*für* Transformator); **Umǀspanǀnung; Umǀspanǀnung; Umǀspannǀwerk**

umǀspieǀlen; er hat die Abwehr umspielt *(Sport)*

umǀspinǀnen; umsponnener Draht

umǀsprinǀgen; der Wind ist umgesprungen; er ist übel mit dir umgesprungen; **umǀsprinǀgen** (springend umgeben); umsprungen von Hunden; **Umǀsprung**

umǀspuǀlen; das Tonband wird umgespult

umǀspüǀlen; von Wellen umspült

Umǀstand; unter Umständen (*Abk.* u. U.); in anderen Umständen (*verhüllend für* schwanger) sein; mildernde Umstände *(Rechtsspr.);* keine Umstände machen; gewisser Umstände halber, eines gewissen Umstandes halber, *aber* umständehalber, umstandshalber; **umǀstänǀdeǀhalǀber** *vgl.* Umstand; **umǀständǀlich; Umǀständǀlichǀkeit,** die; -; **Umǀstands‿anǀgaǀbe, ...beǀstimǀmung** *(Sprachw.),* **...erǀgänǀzung, ...fürǀwort; umǀstandsǀhalǀber** *vgl.* Umstand; **Umǀstands‿kleid, ...kleiǀdung, ...kräǀmer** (*ugs. für* umständlicher Mensch), **...satz, ...wort** (*Plur.* ...wörter; *für* Adverb); **umǀstandsǀwörtǀlich** (*für* adverbial)

umǀsteǀchen; wir haben das Beet umgestochen; **umǀsteǀchen** (mit Stichen befestigen); die Stoffkanten werden umstochen

umǀsteǀcken (anders stecken); sie hat die Blumen umgesteckt; *vgl.* [2]stecken; **umǀsteǀcken;** umsteckt mit ...; *vgl.* [2]stecken

umǀsteǀhen (*landsch. für* verenden; verderben); umgestanden (verdorben [von Flüssigkeiten]; verendet [von Tieren]); **umǀsteǀhen;** umstanden von ...; **umǀsteǀhend;** (↑R 47:) im Umstehenden finden sich die näheren Erläuterungen; er soll Umstehendes beachten; das Umstehende (auf der anderen Seite Gesagte), die Umstehenden (die Zuschauer)

Umǀsteiǀge‿fahrǀschein, ...karǀte; umǀsteiǀgen; sie ist umgestiegen; **Umǀsteiǀger; Umǀsteig‿fahrǀschein, ...karǀte**

Umǀstellǀbahnǀhof; umǀstellǀbar; umǀstelǀlen (anders stellen; auf etwas Neues einstellen); er stellte die Mannschaft um; der Schrank wurde umgestellt; sich umstellen; **umǀstelǀlen** (umgeben); sie umstellten das Wild; die Polizei hat das Haus umstellt; **Umǀstelǀlung; Umǀstelǀlung; Umǀstelǀlungsǀproǀzess**

umǀstemǀpeln (neu, anders stempeln); der Pass wurde umgestempelt

umǀsteuǀern (anders ausrichten); der Satellit soll umgesteuert werden; **Umǀsteuǀeǀrung**

umǀstimǀmen; er hat sie umgestimmt; **Umǀstimǀmung**

umǀstoǀßen; er hat den Stuhl umgestoßen

umǀstrahǀlen; umstrahlt von ...

umǀstriǀcken (neu, anders stricken); sie hat den Pullover umgestrickt; **umǀstriǀcken;** umstrickt ([unlösbar] umgeben, umgarnt) von Intrigen; **Umǀstriǀckung; Umǀstriǀckung**

umǀstritǀten

umǀströǀmen; umströmt von ...

umǀstrukǀtuǀrieǀren; umstrukturiert; **Umǀstrukǀtuǀrieǀrung**

umǀstülǀpen; er hat das Fass umgestülpt; **umǀstülǀpen** *(Druckw.);* er hat das Papier umstülpt; **Umǀstülǀpung**

Umǀsturz *Plur.* ...stürze; **Umǀsturzǀbeǀweǀgung; umǀstürǀzen;** das Gerüst ist umgestürzt; **Umǀstürzǀler; Umǀstürzǀleǀrin; umǀstürzǀleǀrisch; Umǀstürǀzung; Umǀsturzǀverǀsuch**

umǀtanǀzen; sie haben das Feuer umtanzt

umǀtauǀfen; er wurde umgetauft

Umǀtausch, der; -[e]s, -e *Plur. sel-*

ten; **ụm|tau|schen;** sie hat das Kleid umgetauscht; **Ụm|tauschrecht**
ụm|tip|pen (*ugs. für* neu, anders tippen); sie hat den Brief umgetippt
ụm|ti|teln; der Film wurde umgetitelt
ụm|top|fen; der Gärtner hat die Pflanze umgetopft
um|to̲|sen *(geh.);* umtost von ...
ụm|trei|ben (planlos herumtreiben); er wurde von Angst umgetrieben; **Ụm|trieb** (*Landw.* Zeit vom Pflanzen eines Baumbestandes bis zum Fällen; Nutzungszeit bei Reben, Geflügel, Vieh; *Bergmannsspr.* Strecke, die an Schächten vorbei- od. um sie herumführt; *meist Plur.: schweiz. für* Aufwand [z. B. an Zeit, Arbeit, Geld]); **Ụm|trie|be** *Plur.* (umstürzlerische Aktivitäten)
Ụm|trunk, der; -[e]s, Umtrünke
ụm|tun *(ugs.);* sich -; ich habe mich danach umgetan
U̲-Mu|sik, die; -; ↑R 26 (*kurz für* Unterhaltungsmusik); *Ggs.* E-Musik
Ụm|ver|pa|ckung (für Verkauf od. Transport einer Ware entbehrliche Verpackung)
ụm|ver|tei|len; die Lasten werden umverteilt; **Ụm|ver|tei|lung**
um|wach|sen; mit Gebüsch -
um|wạl|len *(geh.);* von Nebel umwallt
Um|wạl|lung ⟨*zu* ²Wall⟩
Ụm|wälz|an|la|ge (Anlage für den Abfluss verbrauchten u. den Zustrom frischen Wassers o. Ä.); **ụm|wäl|zen;** er hat den Stein umgewälzt; **Ụm|wälz|pum|pe; Ụm|wäl|zung**
ụm|wan|deln (ändern); sie war wie umgewandelt; **um|wạn|deln** (*geh. für* um etwas herumwandeln); sie hat den Platz umwandelt; **Ụm|wan|de|lung** *vgl.* Umwandlung
um|wạn|dern; sie haben den See umwandert
Ụm|wand|lung, *seltener* Ụm|wan|de|lung (Änderung); **Ụm|wand|lungs|pro|zess**
ụm|wech|seln; er hat das Geld umgewechselt; **Ụm|wechs|lung,** *seltener* Ụm|wech|se|lung
Ụm|weg
ụm|we|hen; das Zelt wurde umgeweht ([vom Wind] umgerissen); **um|we̲|hen;** umweht von ...
Ụm|welt; Ụm|welt|au|to (*ugs. für* umweltfreundlicheres Auto); **ụm|welt|be|dingt; Ụm|welt‿be|din|gun|gen** *(Plur.),* **...be|las|tung, ...ein|fluss, ...fak|tor; ụm|welt|feind|lich; Ụm|welt|for|schung,** die; -; **ụm|welt|freund|lich; Ụm|welt|kri|mi|na|li|tät; ụm|welt|neut|ral; Ụm|welt‿pa|pier** (Recyclingpapier), **...po|li|tik** (die; -), **...schä|den** *(Plur.);* **ụm|welt|schäd|lich; Ụm|welt‿schutz** (der; -es), **...schüt|zer, ...sün|der** *(ugs.),* **...ver|schmut|zung; ụm|welt|ver|träg|lich**
ụm|wen|den; er wandte *od.* wendete die Seite um, hat sie umgewandt *od.* umgewendet; sich -; **Ụm|wen|dung**
um|wẹr|ben; eine viel umworbene Sängerin
ụm|wer|fen; er warf den Tisch um; diese Nachricht hat ihn umgeworfen (*ugs. für* aus der Fassung gebracht, erschüttert); **ụm|wer|fend;** -e Komik
ụm|wer|ten; alle Werte wurden umgewertet; **Ụm|wer|tung**
ụm|wi|ckeln (neu, anders wickeln); er hat die Schnur umgewickelt; **um|wị|ckeln;** umwickelt mit ...; **Ụm|wi|cke|lung,** Ụm|wick|lung; **Um|wị|cke|lung, Um|wịck|lung**
ụm|wid|men (*Amtsspr.* für einen anderen Zweck bestimmen); in Industriegelände umgewidmetes Agrarland; **Ụm|wid|mung**
ụm|win|den; sie hat das Tuch umgewunden; **um|wịn|den;** umwunden mit ...
um|wịt|tern *(geh.);* von Geheimnissen, Gefahren umwittert
um|wo̲|ben *(geh.);* von Sagen -
um|wo̲|gen *(geh.);* umwogt von ...
ụm|woh|nend; (↑R 47:) die Umwohnenden; **Ụm|woh|ner**
um|wọ̈l|ken; seine Stirn war vor Unmut umwölkt; **Um|wọ̈l|kung**
ụm|wüh|len; umgewühlt
um|zäu|nen; der Garten wurde umzäunt; **Um|zäu|nung**
ụm|zeich|nen (anders zeichnen); sie hat das Bild umgezeichnet
ụm|zie|hen; sich -; ich habe mich umgezogen; wir sind [nach Frankfurt] umgezogen; **um|zie|hen;** der Himmel hat sich umzogen; umzogen mit ...
um|zịn|geln; das Lager wurde umzingelt; **Um|zịn|ge|lung, Um|zịng|lung**
ụm zu *vgl.* um, III
Ụm|zug; ụm|zugs|hal|ber; Ụm|zugs‿kos|ten *(Plur.),* **...tag**
um|zün|geln; umzüngelt von Flammen
UN = United Nations [ju'naitid 'ne:ʃ(ə)nz] *Plur.* ⟨engl.⟩ (Vereinte Nationen); *vgl. auch* UNO *u.* VN
un|ab|ạ̈n|der|lich [*auch* 'un...]; **Un|ab|än|der|lich|keit,** die; -
un|ab|dịng|bar [*auch* 'un...]; **Un|ab|ding|bar|keit,** die; -; **un|ab|dịng|lich** [*auch* 'un...]
ụn|ab|hän|gig; Ụn|ab|hän|gig|keit, die; -; **Ụn|ab|hän|gig|keits|er|klä|rung**
ụn|ab|kömm|lich [*auch* ...'kœm...]; **Un|ab|kömm|lich|keit,** die; -
un|ab|läs|sig [*auch* 'un...]
un|ab|se̲h|bar [*auch* 'un...]; unabsehbare Folgen; die Kosten steigen ins Unabsehbare; **Un|ab|seh|bar|keit,** die; -
ụn|ab|setz|bar [*auch* ...'zɛts...]
ụn|ab|sicht|lich
un|ab|we̲is|bar [*auch* 'un...]; **un|ab|we̲is|lich** [*auch* 'un...]
un|ab|wẹnd|bar [*auch* 'un...]; ein -es Verhängnis; **Un|ab|wend|bar|keit,** die; -
ụn|acht|sam; Ụn|acht|sam|keit
ụn|ähn|lich; Ụn|ähn|lich|keit, die; -
ụn|an|bring|lich (*Postw.* unzustellbar)
un|an|fecht|bar [*auch* ...'fɛçt...]; **Un|an|fecht|bar|keit,** die; -
ụn|an|ge|bracht; eine -e Frage
ụn|an|ge|foch|ten
ụn|an|ge|mel|det
ụn|an|ge|mes|sen; Ụn|an|ge|mes|sen|heit, die; -
ụn|an|ge|nehm
ụn|an|ge|passt; Ụn|an|ge|passt|heit, die; -
¹ụn|an|ge|se|hen (nicht angesehen); **²ụn|an|ge|se|hen** (*Amtsspr.* ohne Rücksicht auf); *Präp. mit Gen. od. Akk.:* - der Umstände *od.* - die Umstände
ụn|an|ge|tas|tet; - bleiben
un|an|greif|bar [*auch* ...'grai̯f...]; **Un|an|greif|bar|keit,** die; -
un|an|nehm|bar [*auch* ...'ne:m...]; **Un|an|nehm|bar|keit,** die; -; **Ụn|an|nehm|lich|keit** *meist Plur.* (ärgerliche Schwierigkeit)
ụn|an|sehn|lich; Ụn|an|sehn|lich|keit, die; -
ụn|an|stän|dig; Ụn|an|stän|dig|keit
ụn|an|stö|ßig; Ụn|an|stö|ßig|keit, die; -
un|an|tạst|bar [*auch* 'un...]; **Un|an|tast|bar|keit,** die; -
ụn|ap|pe|tit|lich; Ụn|ap|pe|tit|lich|keit, die; -
¹Ụn|art (Unartigkeit); **²Ụn|art,** der; -[e]s, -e (*veraltet für* unartiges Kind); **ụn|ar|tig; Ụn|ar|tig|keit**
ụn|ar|ti|ku|liert (unverständlich, undeutlich ausgesprochen)
U̲|na Sạnc|ta, die; - - ⟨lat., „die eine heilige [Kirche]"⟩ (Selbstbez. der röm.-kath. Kirche)
ụn|äs|the|tisch (unschön, abstoßend)

un|auf|dring|lich; Un|auf|dring|lich|keit, die; -

un|auf|fäl|lig; Un|auf|fäl|lig|keit, die; -

un|auf|find|bar [*auch* 'un...]

un|auf|ge|for|dert

un|auf|ge|klärt

un|auf|halt|bar [*auch* 'un...]; **un|auf|halt|sam** [*auch* 'un...]; **Un|auf|halt|sam|keit,** die; -

un|auf|hör|lich [*auch* 'un...]

un|auf|lös|bar [*auch* 'un...]; **Un|auf|lös|bar|keit,** die; -; **un|auf|lös|lich** [*auch* 'un...]; **Un|auf|lös|lich|keit,** die; -

un|auf|merk|sam; Un|auf|merk|sam|keit

un|auf|rich|tig; Un|auf|rich|tig|keit

un|auf|schieb|bar [*auch* 'un...]; **Un|auf|schieb|bar|keit,** die; -; **un|auf|schieb|lich** [*auch* 'un...]

un|aus|bleib|lich [*auch* 'un...]

un|aus|denk|bar [*auch* 'un...]

un|aus|führ|bar [*auch* 'un...]; **Un|aus|führ|bar|keit,** die; -

un|aus|ge|bil|det

un|aus|ge|füllt; Un|aus|ge|füllt|sein, das; -s

un|aus|ge|gli|chen; Un|aus|ge|gli|chen|heit, die; -

un|aus|ge|go|ren

un|aus|ge|schla|fen

un|aus|ge|setzt (unaufhörlich)

un|aus|ge|spro|chen

un|aus|lösch|lich [*auch* 'un...]; ein -er Eindruck

un|aus|rott|bar [*auch* 'un...]; ein -es Vorurteil

un|aus|sprech|bar [*auch* 'un...]; **un|aus|sprech|lich** [*auch* 'un...]

un|aus|steh|lich [*auch* 'un...]; **Un|aus|steh|lich|keit,** die; -

un|aus|tilg|bar [*auch* 'un...]

un|aus|weich|lich [*auch* 'un...]

Un|band, der; -[e]s, *Plur.* -e *u.* ...bände (*veraltet, noch landsch. für* Wildfang); **un|bän|dig**

un|bar (bargeldlos)

un|barm|her|zig; Un|barm|her|zig|keit, die; -

un|be|ab|sich|tigt

un|be|ach|tet; un|be|acht|lich *(Rechtsspr.)*

un|be|an|stan|det

un|be|ant|wort|bar [*auch* 'un...]; **un|be|ant|wor|tet**

un|be|ar|bei|tet

un|be|baut

un|be|dacht (unüberlegt, vorschnell); eine -e Äußerung; **un|be|dach|ter|wei|se; Un|be|dacht|heit; un|be|dacht|sam; Un|be|dacht|sam|keit**

un|be|darft (unerfahren; naiv); **Un|be|darft|heit,** die; -

un|be|deckt

un|be|denk|lich; Un|be|denk|lich|keit, die; -; **Un|be|denk|lich|keits|be|schei|ni|gung** *(Finanzw.)*

un|be|deu|tend; Un|be|deu|tend|heit, die; -

un|be|dingt [*auch* ...'diŋt]; -e Reflexe; **Un|be|dingt|heit,** die; -

un|be|ein|druckt

un|be|ein|fluss|bar [*auch* unbə'ain...]; **Un|be|ein|fluss|bar|keit,** die; -; **un|be|ein|flusst**

un|be|fahr|bar [*auch* ...'fa:r...]

un|be|fan|gen; Un|be|fan|gen|heit, die; -

un|be|fleckt, *aber* (↑R 108): die Unbefleckte Empfängnis [Mariens]

un|be|frie|di|gend; seine Arbeit war -; **un|be|frie|digt; Un|be|frie|digt|heit,** die; -

un|be|fris|tet; -es Darlehen

un|be|fugt; Un|be|fug|te, der *u.* die; -n, -n (↑R 5ff.)

un|be|gabt; Un|be|gabt|heit, die; -

un|be|greif|lich [*auch* ...'grajf...]; **un|be|greif|li|cher|wei|se; Un|be|greif|lich|keit** [*auch* ...'grajf...]

un|be|grenzt; -es Vertrauen; **Un|be|grenzt|heit,** die; -

un|be|grün|det; ein -er Verdacht

un|be|haart

Un|be|ha|gen; un|be|hag|lich; Un|be|hag|lich|keit

un|be|hau|en; aus -en Steinen

un|be|haust (*geh. für* kein Zuhause habend)

un|be|hel|ligt [*auch* ...'hɛl...]

un|be|herrscht; Un|be|herrscht|heit

un|be|hilf|lich (*veraltend für* unbeholfen)

un|be|hin|dert

un|be|hol|fen; Un|be|hol|fen|heit, die; -

un|be|irr|bar [*auch* 'un...]; **Un|be|irr|bar|keit,** die; -; **un|be|irrt** [*auch* 'un...]; **Un|be|irrt|heit,** die; -

un|be|kannt; ein unbekannter Mann; [nach] unbekannt verzogen; Anzeige gegen unbekannt erstatten; das Grab des Unbekannten Soldaten; (↑R 47:) der große Unbekannte; eine Gleichung mit mehreren Unbekannten *(Math.)*; **un|be|kann|ter|wei|se; Un|be|kannt|heit,** die; -

un|be|klei|det

un|be|küm|mert [*auch* ...'kym...]; **Un|be|küm|mert|heit,** die; -

un|be|las|tet

un|be|lebt; eine -e Straße

un|be|leckt; von etwas - sein (*ugs. für* von etwas nichts wissen, verstehen)

un|be|lehr|bar [*auch* ...'le:r...]; **Un|be|lehr|bar|keit,** die; -

un|be|leuch|tet

un|be|lich|tet *(Fotogr.)*

un|be|liebt; Un|be|liebt|heit, die; -

un|be|mannt

un|be|merkt

un|be|mit|telt

un|be|nom|men [*auch* 'un...]; es bleibt ihm - (steht ihm frei)

un|be|nutz|bar [*auch* ...'nuts...];

un|be|nutzt

un|be|o|bach|tet (↑R 132)

un|be|quem; Un|be|quem|lich|keit

un|be|re|chen|bar [*auch* 'un...]; **Un|be|re|chen|bar|keit,** die; -

un|be|rech|tigt; un|be|rech|tig|ter|wei|se

un|be|rück|sich|tigt [*auch* unbə'ryk...]

un|be|ru|fen; in -e Hände gelangen; **un|be|ru|fen!** [*auch* 'un...]

un|be|rührt; Un|be|rührt|heit, die; -

un|be|scha|det [*auch* ...'ʃa:...] (ohne Schaden für ...); *Präp. mit Gen.:* - seines Rechtes *od.* seines Rechtes -; **un|be|schä|digt**

un|be|schäf|tigt

un|be|schei|den; Un|be|schei|den|heit, die; -

un|be|schol|ten (untadelig, integer); **Un|be|schol|ten|heit,** die; -; **Un|be|schol|ten|heits|zeug|nis**

un|be|schrankt; -er Bahnübergang; **un|be|schränkt** [*auch* ...'ʃrɛŋkt] (nicht eingeschränkt); *vgl.* eGmuH; **Un|be|schränkt|heit,** die; -

un|be|schreib|lich [*auch* 'un...]; **Un|be|schreib|lich|keit,** die; -; **un|be|schrie|ben;** ein -es Blatt sein (*ugs. für* unbekannt, unerfahren sein)

un|be|schützt

un|be|schwert; Un|be|schwert|heit, die; -

un|be|seelt

un|be|se|hen [*auch* 'un...]; das glaubt man - (ohne Nachprüfung, ohne zu zögern)

un|be|sieg|bar [*auch* 'un...]; **Un|be|sieg|bar|keit,** die; -; **un|be|sieg|lich** [*auch* 'un...]; **Un|be|sieg|lich|keit,** die; -; **un|be|siegt** [*auch* 'un...]

un|be|son|nen; Un|be|son|nen|heit

un|be|sorgt

un|be|spiel|bar [*auch* 'un...]; der Platz war -; **un|be|spielt;** eine -e Kassette

un|be|stän|dig; Un|be|stän|dig|keit, die; -

un|be|stä|tigt [*auch* ...'ʃtɛ:...]; nach -en Meldungen
un|be|stech|lich [*auch* ...'ʃtɛç...]; **Un|be|stech|lich|keit,** die; -
un|be|stimm|bar [*auch* ...'ʃtim...]; **Un|be|stimm|bar|keit,** die; -;
un|be|stimmt; -es Fürwort (*für* Indefinitpronomen); **Un|be|stimmt|heit,** die; -; **Un|be|stimmt|heits|re|la|ti|on** (Begriff der Quantentheorie)
un|be|streit|bar [*auch* 'un...]; **un|be|strit|ten** [*auch* ...'ʃtri...]
un|be|tei|ligt [*auch* ...'tai...]; **Un|be|tei|ligt|heit,** die; -
un|be|tont
un|be|trächt|lich [*auch* ...'trɛçt...]; **Un|be|trächt|lich|keit,** die; -
un|be|tre|ten; -es Gebiet
un|beug|bar [*auch* ...'bɔyk...]; **un|beug|sam** [*auch* ...'bɔyk...]; -er Wille; **Un|beug|sam|keit,** die; -
un|be|wacht
un|be|waff|net
un|be|wäl|tigt [*auch* ...'vɛl...]; die -e Vergangenheit
un|be|weg|lich [*auch* ...'ve:k...]; **Un|be|weg|lich|keit,** die; -; **un|be|wegt**
un|be|weibt (*scherzh. für* ohne [Ehe]frau)
un|be|wie|sen; eine -e Behauptung
un|be|wohn|bar [*auch* 'un...]; **un|be|wohnt**
un|be|wusst; Un|be|wuss|te, das; -n (↑R 5 ff.); **Un|be|wusst|heit,** die; -
un|be|zahl|bar [*auch* 'un...]; **Un|be|zahl|bar|keit,** die; -; **un|be|zahlt;** -er Urlaub
un|be|zähm|bar [*auch* 'un...]; **Un|be|zähm|bar|keit,** die; -
un|be|zwei|fel|bar [*auch* 'un...]
un|be|zwing|bar [*auch* 'un...]; **un|be|zwing|lich** [*auch* 'un...]
Un|bil|den *Plur.* (*geh. für* Unannehmlichkeiten); die - der Witterung; **Un|bil|dung,** die; - (Mangel an Wissen); **Un|bill,** die; - (*geh. für* Unrecht); **un|bil|lig** *(geh.);* -e (nicht angemessene) Härte; **Un|bil|lig|keit** *(geh.)*
un|blu|tig; eine -e Revolution
un|bot|mä|ßig; Un|bot|mä|ßig|keit
un|brauch|bar; Un|brauch|bar|keit, die; -
un|bü|ro|kra|tisch
un|buß|fer|tig *(christl. Rel.);* **Un|buß|fer|tig|keit,** die; -
un|christ|lich; Un|christ|lich|keit, die; -
Un|cle Sam ['aŋk(ə)l 'sɛm] (*scherzh. für* die USA)
und (*Abk.* u., *bei Firmen auch* &); und and[e]re, and[e]res (*Abk.* u. a.); und and[e]re mehr, und and[e]res mehr (*Abk.* u. a. m.); und Ähnliche[s] (*Abk.* u. Ä.); und dem Ähnliche[s] (*Abk.* u. d. Ä.); drei und drei ist, macht, gibt (*nicht* sind, machen, geben) sechs
Un|dank; un|dank|bar; eine -e Aufgabe; **Un|dank|bar|keit,** die; -
un|da|tiert
und der|glei|chen [mehr] (*Abk.* u. dgl. [m.]); **und des|glei|chen [mehr]** (*Abk.* u. desgl. [m.])
un|de|fi|nier|bar [*auch* ...'ni:r...]
un|de|kli|nier|bar [*auch* ...'ni:r...]
un|de|mo|kra|tisch
un|denk|bar; un|denk|lich
Un|der|co|ver|agent ['andə(r)kavə(r)...] (↑R 132) ⟨engl.; lat.⟩ (Geheimagent, der sich in eine heimlich zu überwachende Gruppe einschleust)
Un|der|dog ['andə(r)dɔg], der; -s, -s ⟨engl.⟩ ([sozial] Benachteiligter, Schwächerer)
un|der|dressed ['andə(r)drɛst] ⟨engl.⟩ (zu schlecht angezogen; *Ggs.* overdressed)
Un|der|ground ['andə(r)graund], der; -s ⟨engl., „Untergrund"⟩ (eine avantgardistische künstlerische Protestbewegung)
Un|der|state|ment [andə(r)'ste:tmənt], das; -s, -s ⟨engl.⟩ (Untertreibung)
un|deut|lich; Un|deut|lich|keit, die; -
Un|de|zi|me, die; -, -n ⟨lat.⟩ (*Musik* elfter Ton der diaton. Tonleiter; Intervall im Abstand von 11 Stufen)
un|dicht; Un|dich|tig|keit, die; -
un|dif|fe|ren|ziert; -e Kritik
Un|di|ne, die; -, -n ⟨lat.⟩ (weibl. Wassergeist)
Un|ding, das; -[e]s, -e (Unmögliches; Unsinniges); *meist in* das ist ein -
un|dis|ku|ta|bel [*auch* ...'ta:...]
un|dis|zi|pli|niert; Un|dis|zi|pli|niert|heit, die; -
un|dog|ma|tisch
un|dra|ma|tisch; ein -es Finale
Und|set, Sigrid (norw. Dichterin)
und so fort (*Abk.* usf.); **und so wei|ter** (*Abk.* usw.)
Un|du|la|ti|on, die; -, -en ⟨lat.⟩ (*Physik* Wellenbewegung; *Geol.* Sattel- u. Muldenbildung durch Gebirgsbildung); **Un|du|la|ti|ons|the|o|rie,** die; - (*Physik* Wellentheorie); **un|du|la|to|risch** (*Physik* wellenförmig)
un|duld|sam; Un|duld|sam|keit, die; -
un|du|lie|ren ⟨lat.⟩ (*bes. Med., Biol.* wellenförmig verlaufen)
un|durch|dring|bar [*auch* 'un...]; **un|durch|dring|lich** [*auch* 'un...]; **Un|durch|dring|lich|keit,** die; -
un|durch|führ|bar [*auch* 'un...]; **Un|durch|führ|bar|keit,** die; -
un|durch|läs|sig; Un|durch|läs|sig|keit, die; -
un|durch|schau|bar [*auch* 'un...]; **Un|durch|schau|bar|keit,** die; -
un|durch|sich|tig; Un|durch|sich|tig|keit, die; -
und vie|le[s] an|de|re [mehr] (*Abk.* u. v. a. [m.]); **und zwar** (*Abk.* u. zw.); ↑R 67
un|eben (↑R 132); **Un|eben|heit**
un|echt; -e Brüche *(Math.);* **Un|echt|heit,** die; -
un|edel (↑R 132); uned|le Metalle
un|egal (↑R 132; *landsch. für* uneben)
un|ehe|lich (↑R 132); ein -es Kind; *vgl.* nichtehelich; **Un|ehe|lich|keit,** die; -
Un|eh|re, die; *(geh.);* **un|eh|ren|haft; Un|eh|ren|haf|tig|keit,** die; -; **un|ehr|er|bie|tig; Un|ehr|er|bie|tig|keit,** die; -; **un|ehr|lich; Un|ehr|lich|keit,** die; -
un|eid|lich; eine -e Erklärung
un|ei|gen|nüt|zig; Un|ei|gen|nüt|zig|keit, die; -
un|ei|gent|lich
un|ein|ge|schränkt; Un|ein|ge|schränkt|heit
un|ein|ge|weiht
un|ei|nig; Un|ei|nig|keit
un|ein|nehm|bar [*auch* 'un...]; **Un|ein|nehm|bar|keit,** die; -
un|eins; - sein
un|ein|sich|tig; Un|ein|sich|tig|keit, die; -
un|emp|fäng|lich; Un|emp|fäng|lich|keit, die; -
un|emp|find|lich; Un|emp|find|lich|keit, die; -
un|end|lich; von eins bis unendlich (*Math.; Zeichen* ∞); bis ins Unendliche (unaufhörlich, immerfort); der Weg scheint bis ins Unendliche (bis ans Ende der Welt) zu führen; im, aus dem Unendlichen (im, aus dem unendlichen Raum); unendliche Mal, unendliche Male. *aber* unendlichmal; **Un|end|lich|keit,** die; -; **un|end|lich|mal** *vgl.* unendlich
un|ent|behr|lich [*auch* ...'be:r...]; **Un|ent|behr|lich|keit,** die; -
un|ent|deckt [*auch* ...'dɛkt]
un|ent|gelt|lich [*auch* ...'gɛlt...]
un|ent|rinn|bar [*auch* 'un...]; **Un|ent|rinn|bar|keit,** die; -
un|ent|schie|den; Un|ent|schie|den, das; -s, - *(Sport u. Spiel);* **Un|ent|schie|den|heit,** die; -
un|ent|schlos|sen; Un|ent|schlos|sen|heit, die; -

un|ent|schuld|bar [*auch* 'un...]; **un|ent|schul|digt**
un|ent|wegt [*auch* 'un...]
un|ent|wirr|bar [*auch* 'un...]
un|er|ach|tet [*auch* 'un...] (*veraltet für* ungeachtet); *Präp. mit Gen.:* unerachtet der Bitten
un|er|bitt|lich [*auch* 'un...]; **Un|er|bitt|lich|keit,** die; -
un|er|fah|ren; Un|er|fah|ren|heit, die; -
un|er|find|lich [*auch* ...'fint...] (unbegreiflich)
un|er|forsch|lich [*auch* ...'fɔrʃ...]
un|er|freu|lich
un|er|füll|bar [*auch* 'un...]; **Un|er|füll|bar|keit,** die; -; **un|er|füllt; Un|er|füllt|heit,** die; -
un|er|gie|big; Un|er|gie|big|keit, die; -
un|er|gründ|bar [*auch* 'un...]; **Un|er|gründ|bar|keit,** die; -; **un|er|gründ|lich** [*auch* 'un...] (geheimnisvoll, rätselhaft); **Un|er|gründ|lich|keit,** die; -
un|er|heb|lich (gering, bedeutungslos); **Un|er|heb|lich|keit**
[1]**un|er|hört** (unglaublich); sein Verhalten war -; [2]**un|er|hört;** seine Bitte blieb -
un|er|kannt; un|er|kenn|bar [*auch* 'un...]; **Un|er|kenn|bar|keit,** die; -
un|er|klär|bar [*auch* 'un...]; **Un|er|klär|bar|keit,** die; -; **un|er|klär|lich** [*auch* 'un...]; **Un|er|klär|lich|keit,** die; -
un|er|läss|lich [*auch* 'un...] (unbedingt nötig, geboten)
un|er|laubt; eine -e Handlung
un|er|le|digt
un|er|mess|lich [*auch* 'un...]; (↑R 47:) ins Unermessliche steigen; **Un|er|mess|lich|keit,** die; -
un|er|müd|lich [*auch* 'un...]; **Un|er|müd|lich|keit,** die; -
un|ernst; Un|ernst
un|er|quick|lich (unerfreulich)
un|er|reich|bar [*auch* 'un...]; **Un|er|reich|bar|keit,** die; -; **un|er|reicht**
un|er|sätt|lich [*auch* 'un...]; **Un|er|sätt|lich|keit,** die; -
un|er|schlos|sen
un|er|schöpf|lich [*auch* 'un...]; **Un|er|schöpf|lich|keit,** die; -
un|er|schro|cken; Un|er|schro|cken|heit, die; -
un|er|schüt|ter|lich [*auch* 'un...]; **Un|er|schüt|ter|lich|keit,** die; -
un|er|schwing|lich [*auch* 'un...]; -e Preise
un|er|setz|bar [*auch* 'un...]; **un|er|setz|lich** [*auch* 'un...]; **Un|er|setz|lich|keit,** die; -
un|er|sprieß|lich [*auch* 'un...] (nicht förderlich, nicht nützlich)
un|er|träg|lich [*auch* 'un...]; **Un|er|träg|lich|keit,** die; -
un|er|wähnt; nicht - bleiben
un|er|war|tet [*auch* ...'var...]
un|er|weis|bar [*auch* 'un...]; **un|er|weis|lich** [*auch* 'un...] *(selten)*
un|er|wi|dert
un|er|wünscht
un|er|zo|gen
UNESCO, die; - ‹engl.; *Kurzwort für* United Nations Educational, Scientific and Cultural Organization [ju.naitid 'ne:ʃ(ə)nz ɛdju.ke:ʃ(ə)nəl saiən.tifik ənd .kaltʃərəl ɔ:(r)gənai'ze:ʃ(ə)n]› (Organisation der Vereinten Nationen für Erziehung, Wissenschaft und Kultur)
un|fä|hig; Un|fä|hig|keit, die; -
un|fair ['unfɛ:r] (regelwidrig, unerlaubt; unfein; ohne sportl. Anstand); **Un|fair|ness**
Un|fall, der; **Un|fall‿arzt, ...be|tei|lig|te** (der *u.* die), **...chi|rur|gie; Un|fäl|ler,** der; -s, - (*bes. Psych.* jmd., der häufig in Unfälle verwickelt ist); **Un|fall‿fah|rer, ...flucht** (*vgl.* [2]Flucht), **...fol|gen** *(Plur.);* **un|fall|frei;** -es Fahren; **Un|fall|ge|fahr; un|fall|ge|schä|digt; Un|fall‿ge|schä|dig|te** (der *u.* die), **...her|gang, ...hil|fe** (die; -), **...kli|nik, ...op|fer, ...ort** (*Plur.* ...orte), **...quo|te, ...ra|te, ...schutz** (der; -es), **...sta|ti|on, ...sta|tis|tik, ...stel|le, ...tod** (der; -[e]s), **...to|te** (der *u.* die; *meist Plur.*); **un|fall|träch|tig;** eine -e Kurve; **Un|fall‿ur|sa|che, ...ver|hü|tung** (die; -), **...ver|letz|te** (der *u.* die), **...ver|si|che|rung, ...wa|gen** (Wagen, der einen Unfall hatte; Rettungswagen), **...zeit, ...zeu|ge**
un|fass|bar [*auch* 'un...]; **un|fass|lich**
un|fehl|bar [*auch* 'un...]; **Un|fehl|bar|keit,** die; -; **Un|fehl|bar|keits|glau|be[n]** *(kath. Kirche)*
un|fein; Un|fein|heit, die; -
un|fern; *als Präp. mit Gen.:* - des Hauses
un|fer|tig; Un|fer|tig|keit, die; -
Un|flat, der; -[e]s (*geh. für* widerlicher Schmutz, Dreck); **un|flä|tig; Un|flä|tig|keit**
un|flek|tiert (*Sprachw.* ungebeugt)
un|flott *(ugs.);* nicht - aussehen
un|folg|sam; Un|folg|sam|keit, die; -
Un|form; un|för|mig (ohne schöne Form; sehr groß); **un|förm|lich** (nicht förmlich; *veraltet für* unförmig)
un|fran|kiert (unfrei [Gebühren nicht bezahlt])
un|frei; Un|frei|heit, die; -; **un|frei|wil|lig**
un|freund|lich; ein -er Empfang; er war - zu ihm, *selten* gegen ihn; **Un|freund|lich|keit**
Un|frie|de[n], der; ...dens
un|fri|siert
un|fromm
un|frucht|bar; Un|frucht|bar|keit, die; -; **Un|frucht|bar|ma|chung**
Un|fug, der; -[e]s
...ung (z. B. Prüfung, die; -, -en)
un|gal|lant
un|gang|bar; ein -er (nicht begehbarer) Weg
Un|gar ['uŋgar], der; -n, -n (↑R 126); **Un|ga|rin; un|ga|risch,** *aber* (↑R 108): die Ungarische Rhapsodie [von Liszt]; **Un|ga|risch,** das; -[s] (Sprache); *vgl.* Deutsch; **Un|ga|ri|sche,** das; -n; *vgl.* Deutsche, das; **un|gar|län|disch** *(selten);* **Un|garn**
un|gast|lich; Un|gast|lich|keit, die; -
un|ge|ach|tet [*auch* ...'ax...]; *Präp. mit Gen.:* ungeachtet wiederholter Bitten *od.* wiederholter Bitten ungeachtet; dessen ungeachtet *od.* des ungeachtet; ungeachtet [dessen], dass ...
un|ge|ahn|det [*auch* ...'a:n...] (unbestraft)
un|ge|ahnt [*auch* ...'a:nt] (nicht vorhergesehen)
un|ge|bär|dig (*geh. für* ungezügelt, wild); **Un|ge|bär|dig|keit,** die; -
un|ge|be|ten; -er Gast
un|ge|beugt
un|ge|bil|det
un|ge|bo|ren; -es Leben
un|ge|bräuch|lich; eine -e Methode; **un|ge|braucht**
un|ge|bro|chen
Un|ge|bühr, die; - *(veraltend);* **un|ge|büh|rend; un|ge|bühr|lich;** -es Verhalten; **Un|ge|bühr|lich|keit**
un|ge|bun|den; ein -es Leben; **Un|ge|bun|den|heit,** die; -
un|ge|deckt; -er Scheck
un|ge|dient (*Milit.* ohne gedient zu haben); **Un|ge|dien|te,** der; -n, -n (↑R 5 ff.)
un|ge|druckt
Un|ge|duld; un|ge|dul|dig
un|ge|eig|net
un|ge|fähr [*auch* ...'fɛ:r]; von - (zufällig); **Un|ge|fähr,** das; -s (*veraltend für* Zufall); **un|ge|fähr|det** [*auch* ...'fɛ:r...]; **un|ge|fähr|lich; Un|ge|fähr|lich|keit,** die; -
un|ge|fäl|lig; Un|ge|fäl|lig|keit, die; -
un|ge|färbt
un|ge|fes|tigt; ein -er Charakter
un|ge|formt

un|ge|fragt
un|ge|früh|stückt (*ugs. scherzh. für* ohne gefrühstückt zu haben)
un|ge|fü|ge (*geh. für* unförmig; schwerfällig)
un|ge|ges|sen (nicht gegessen; *ugs. scherzh. für* ohne gegessen zu haben)
un|ge|glie|dert
un|ge|hal|ten (ärgerlich); **Un|ge|hal|ten|heit,** die; -
un|ge|hei|ßen (*geh. für* unaufgefordert)
un|ge|heizt
un|ge|hemmt
un|ge|heu|er [*auch* ...'hɔyər]; ungeheurer, -ste; eine ungeheure Verschwendung; (↑R 47:) die Kosten steigen ins Ungeheure; **Un|ge|heu|er,** das; -s, -; **un|ge|heu|er|lich** [*auch* 'un...]; **Un|ge|heu|er|lich|keit**
un|ge|hin|dert
un|ge|ho|belt [*auch* ...'ho:...] (*auch übertr. für* ungebildet; grob)
un|ge|hö|rig; ein -es Benehmen; **Un|ge|hö|rig|keit**
un|ge|hor|sam; Un|ge|hor|sam
un|ge|hört
Un|geist, der; -[e]s (*geh. für* zerstörerische Ideologie); **un|geis|tig**
un|ge|kämmt
un|ge|klärt
un|ge|kocht
un|ge|krönt; der -e König (*übertr. für* der Beste, Erfolgreichste) der Schwimmer
un|ge|kün|digt; in -er Stellung
un|ge|küns|telt
un|ge|kürzt
Un|geld (mittelalterl. Abgabe, Steuer)
un|ge|le|gen (unbequem); sein Besuch kam mir -; **Un|ge|le|gen|heit**
un|ge|leh|rig; un|ge|lehrt (*veraltend*)
un|ge|lenk, un|ge|len|kig; Un|ge|len|kig|keit, die; -
un|ge|lernt; ein -er Arbeiter; **Un|ge|lern|te,** der *u.* die; -n, -n (↑R 5 ff.)
un|ge|liebt
un|ge|lo|gen
un|ge|löscht; -er Kalk
un|ge|löst; eine -e Aufgabe
Un|ge|mach, das; -[e]s (*veraltend für* Unannehmlichkeit, Ärger)
un|ge|mäß; *nur in* jmdm., einer Sache - (nicht angemessen) sein
un|ge|mein [*auch* ...'main]
un|ge|mes|sen [*auch* ...'mes...]
un|ge|min|dert; mit -er Stärke
un|ge|mischt
un|ge|müt|lich; Un|ge|müt|lich|keit, die; -
un|ge|nannt
un|ge|nau; Un|ge|nau|ig|keit
un|ge|niert [...ʒe...] (zwanglos); **Un|ge|niert|heit,** die; - (Zwanglosigkeit)
un|ge|nieß|bar [*auch* ...'ni:s...]; eine -e Speise; **Un|ge|nieß|bar|keit,** die; -
Un|ge|nü|gen, das; -s (*geh.*); **un|ge|nü|gend** *vgl.* ausreichend
un|ge|nutzt, un|ge|nützt
un|ge|ord|net
un|ge|pflegt; Un|ge|pflegt|heit, die; -
un|ge|prüft
un|ge|rächt
un|ge|ra|de, *ugs.* un|gra|de; - Zahl (*Math.*)
un|ge|ra|ten; ein -es (unerzogenes, missratenes) Kind
un|ge|rech|net; *Präp. mit Gen.:* - des Schadens
un|ge|recht; un|ge|rech|ter|wei|se; un|ge|recht|fer|tigt; un|ge|recht|fer|tig|ter|wei|se; Un|ge|rech|tig|keit
un|ge|re|gelt; ein -es Leben
un|ge|reimt (nicht im Reim gebunden; verworren, sinnlos); **Un|ge|reimt|heit**
un|gern
un|ge|rührt (unbeteiligt, gleichgültig); **Un|ge|rührt|heit,** die; -
un|ge|rupft; er kam - (*ugs. für* ohne Schaden) davon
un|ge|sagt; vieles blieb -
un|ge|sal|zen
un|ge|sät|tigt; -e Lösung
un|ge|säu|ert; -es Brot
[1]**un|ge|säumt** [*auch* ...'zɔymt] (*geh. veraltend für* sofort)
[2]**un|ge|säumt** (ohne Saum)
un|ge|schält; -er Reis
un|ge|sche|hen; etwas - machen
un|ge|scheut (*geh. für* frei, ohne Scheu)
Un|ge|schick, das; -[e]s; **un|ge|schick|lich** (*veraltend für* ungeschickt); **Un|ge|schick|lich|keit; un|ge|schickt; Un|ge|schickt|heit**
un|ge|schlacht (plump, grobschlächtig); ein -er Mensch; **Un|ge|schlacht|heit,** die; -
un|ge|schla|gen (unbesiegt)
un|ge|schlecht|lich; -e Fortpflanzung
un|ge|schlif|fen (*auch für* unerzogen, ohne Manieren); **Un|ge|schlif|fen|heit**
un|ge|schmä|lert (ohne Einbuße)
un|ge|schmei|dig
un|ge|schminkt (*auch für* den Tatsachen entsprechend, unverblümt)
un|ge|scho|ren
un|ge|schrie|ben; ein -es Gesetz
un|ge|schult
un|ge|schützt
un|ge|se|hen; sich - anschleichen
un|ge|sel|lig; Un|ge|sel|lig|keit, die; -
un|ge|setz|lich; Un|ge|setz|lich|keit
un|ge|sit|tet; sich - benehmen
un|ge|stalt (*veraltet für* missgestaltet); -er Mensch; **un|ge|stal|tet** (nicht gestaltet); -e Masse
un|ge|stem|pelt; -e Briefmarken
un|ge|stillt; -e Sehnsucht
un|ge|stört; Un|ge|stört|heit, die; -
un|ge|straft; - davonkommen
un|ge|stüm (*geh. für* schnell, heftig); **Un|ge|stüm,** das; -[e]s; mit -
un|ge|sühnt; ein -er Mord
un|ge|sund; ein -es Aussehen
un|ge|süßt; -er Tee
un|ge|tan; etwas - lassen
un|ge|teilt
un|ge|treu (*geh.*)
un|ge|trübt; -e Freude
Un|ge|tüm, das; -[e]s, -e (*svw.* Monstrum)
un|ge|übt
un|ge|wandt
un|ge|wa|schen; -es Obst
un|ge|wiss; (↑R 47:) im Ungewissen bleiben, lassen, sein; eine Fahrt ins Ungewisse; **Un|ge|wiss|heit**
Un|ge|wit|ter (*veraltet für* Unwetter)
un|ge|wöhn|lich; Un|ge|wöhn|lich|keit, die; -; **un|ge|wohnt**
un|ge|wollt; eine -e Schwangerschaft
un|ge|würzt
un|ge|zählt (*auch für* unzählig; *vgl. d.*)
un|ge|zähmt
un|ge|zeich|net; -e Flugblätter
Un|ge|zie|fer, das; -s
un|ge|zie|mend (*geh.*)
un|ge|zo|gen; Un|ge|zo|gen|heit
un|ge|zu|ckert
un|ge|zü|gelt; -er Hass
un|ge|zwun|gen; -es Benehmen; **Un|ge|zwun|gen|heit,** die; -
un|gif|tig; dieser Pilz ist -
Un|glau|be[n]; un|glaub|haft; un|gläu|big; ein ungläubiger Thomas (*ugs. für* jmd., der an allem zweifelt); **Un|gläu|bi|ge,** der *u.* die; -n, -n (↑R 5 ff.); **un|glaub|lich** [*auch* 'un...]; es geht ins, grenzt ans Unglaubliche (↑R 47); **un|glaub|wür|dig; Un|glaub|wür|dig|keit,** die; -
un|gleich; un|gleich|ar|tig; un|gleich|er|big (*für* heterozygot); **un|gleich|för|mig; un|gleich|ge|schlecht|lich** (*Biol.*); **Un|gleich|ge|wicht; Un|gleich|heit; un-**

gleich|mä|ßig; Un|gleich|mä|ßig|keit; Un|glei|chung *(Math.)*

Un|glück, das; -[e]s, -e; **un|glück|lich; Un|glück|li|che,** der *u.* die; -n, -n (↑R 5 ff.); **un|glück|li|cher|wei|se; Un|glücks-bo|te, ...bot|schaft; un|glück|se|lig; un|glück|se|li|ger|wei|se; Un|glück|se|lig|keit,** die; -; **Un|glücks-fah|rer, ...fall** (der), **...ma|schi|ne, ...mensch** (der; *svw.* Pechvogel), **...nach|richt, ...ort** (*Plur.* ...orte), **...ra|be** *(ugs.)*; **un|glücks|schwan|ger** *(geh.)*; **Un|glücks-stel|le, ...tag, ...wa|gen, ...wurm** (der; *ugs.*)

Un|gna|de, die; -; *nur in Wendungen wie* [bei jmdm.] in - fallen; **un|gnä|dig**

un|grad *(landsch.)*, **un|gra|de** *vgl.* ungerade

un|gra|zi|ös

Un|gu|la|ten *Plur.* ‹lat.› (*Zool.* Huftiere)

un|gül|tig; Un|gül|tig|keit, die; -; **Un|gül|tig|keits|er|klä|rung; Un|gül|tig|ma|chung** *(Amtsspr.)*

Un|gunst; zu seinen, zu seines Freundes Ungunsten; zuungunsten, *auch* zu Ungunsten der Arbeiter; **un|güns|tig; Un|güns|tig|keit,** die; -

un|gus|ti|ös *vgl.* gustiös

un|gut; nichts für ungut (es war nicht böse gemeint)

un|halt|bar [*auch* ...'halt...]; -e Zustände; **Un|halt|bar|keit,** die; -; **un|hal|tig** (*Bergmannsspr.* kein Erz usw. enthaltend)

un|hand|lich; Un|hand|lich|keit, die; -

un|har|mo|nisch

Un|heil; Unheil bringende Veränderungen; ein Unheil [ver]kündendes Zeichen (↑R 40); **un|heil|bar** [*auch* ...'hail...]; **Un|heil|bar|keit,** die; -; **Un|heil brin|gend** *vgl.* Unheil; **un|heil|dro|hend; un|hei|lig; Un|heil kün|dend** *vgl.* Unheil; **un|heil|schwan|ger** *(geh.)*; **Un|heil|stif|ter; Un|heil ver|kün|dend** *vgl.* Unheil; **un|heil|voll**

un|heim|lich [*auch* 'un...] (nicht geheuer; unbehaglich; *ugs. auch für* sehr, überaus); **Un|heim|lich|keit,** die; -

un|his|to|risch

un|höf|lich; Un|höf|lich|keit

un|hold (*veraltet für* abgeneigt; feindselig); *nur in* jmdm., einer Sache unhold sein; **Un|hold,** der; -[e]s, -e (böser Geist; Wüstling, Sittlichkeitsverbrecher)

un|hör|bar [*auch* 'un...]; **Un|hör|bar|keit,** die; -

un|hy|gi|e|nisch

u|ni ['yni, *auch* y'ni:] ‹franz.› (einfarbig, nicht gemustert); ein uni Kleid; uni gefärbte Stoffe; *vgl. auch* beige; **[1]U|ni,** das; -s, -s (einheitliche Farbe); in verschiedenen Unis

[2]U|ni, die; -, -s (*kurz für* Universität)

UNICEF ['unitsɛf], die; - ‹engl.; *Kurzw. für* United Nations International Children's Emergency Fund [ju.naitid 'ne:ʃ(ə)nz intə(r)-.nɛʃ(ə)nəl 'tʃildrənz i.mœ:(r)dʒənsi 'fand]› (Weltkinderhilfswerk der UNO)

u|nie|ren ‹franz.› (vereinigen [bes. von Religionsgemeinschaften]); unierte Kirchen (die mit der röm.-kath. Kirche wieder vereinigten Ostkirchen; die ev. Unionskirchen); **U|ni|fi|ka|ti|on,** die; -, -en *vgl.* Unifizierung; **u|ni|fi|zie|ren** (vereinheitlichen); **U|ni|fi|zie|rung** (Vereinheitlichung, Vereinigung); **u|ni|form** (gleich-, einförmig; gleichmäßig); **U|ni|form** [*auch* 'uni..., *österr.* 'u:ni...], die; -, -en (einheitl. Dienstkleidung); **u|ni|for|mie|ren** (einheitlich [ein]kleiden; gleichförmig machen); **U|ni|for|mie|rung; U|ni|for|mi|tät,** die; -, -en (Einförmigkeit; Gleichmäßigkeit); **U|ni|form|ver|bot; u|ni ge|färbt** ['ynl, *auch* y'ni: ...] *vgl.* uni; **U|ni|kat** [uni...], das; -[e]s, -e ‹lat.› (einzige Ausfertigung [eines Schriftstückes]); **U|ni|kum,** das; -s, *Plur.* (*für* [in seiner Art] Einziges:) ...ka, (*für* Sonderling:) -s, *österr.* ...ka; **u|ni|la|te|ral** (einseitig)

un|in|for|miert; Un|in|for|miert|heit, die; -

un|in|te|res|sant (langweilig, reizlos); **un|in|te|res|siert** (ohne innere Anteilnahme); **Un|in|te|res|siert|heit,** die; -

U|nio mys|ti|ca, die; - - ‹lat.› (geheimnisvolle Vereinigung der Seele mit Gott in der Mystik); **U|ni|on,** die; -, -en (Bund, Vereinigung [bes. von Staaten]); Union der Sozialistischen Sowjetrepubliken (*vgl.* UdSSR); Christlich-Demokratische Union [Deutschlands] (*Abk.* CDU); Christlich-Soziale Union (*Abk.* CSU); Junge Union (*vgl.* jung); **U|ni|o|nist,** der; -en, -en; ↑R 126 (Anhänger einer Union, z. B. der amerikanischen im Unabhängigkeitskrieg 1776/83); **U|ni|on Jack** ['ju:njən 'dʒɛk], der; - -s, - -s ‹engl.› (brit. Nationalflagge); **U|ni|ons-kir|che, ...par|tei|en** (*Plur.; zusammenfassende Bez. für* CDU *u.* CSU)

u|ni|pe|tal ‹lat.; griech.› (*Bot.* einblättrig); **u|ni|po|lar** (*Elektrotechnik* einpolig); -e Leitfähigkeit; **U|ni|po|lar|ma|schi|ne**

un|ir|disch (nicht irdisch)

U|ni|sex ‹engl.› (Verwischung der Unterschiede zwischen den Geschlechtern [im Erscheinungsbild])

u|ni|so|no ‹ital.› (*Musik* auf demselben Ton od. in der Oktave [zu spielen]); **U|ni|so|no,** das; -s, *Plur.* -s *u.* ...ni *(Musik)*

U|ni|ta|ri|er [...i̯ər], der; -s, - ‹lat.› (Anhänger einer protestant. Richtung, die die Einheit Gottes betont u. die Dreifaltigkeit ablehnt); **u|ni|ta|risch** (Einigung bezweckend); **U|ni|ta|ris|mus,** der; - (Streben nach Stärkung der Zentralgewalt; Lehre der Unitarier); **U|ni|tät,** die; -, -en (Einheit, Einzig[artig]keit)

U|ni|ted Na|tions [ju'naitid 'ne:ʃ(ə)nz] usw. *vgl.* UN, UNO, UNESCO, VN; **U|ni|ted Press In|ter|na|tio|nal** [ju'naitid 'prɛs intə(r)'nɛʃ(ə)nəl], die; - - - ‹engl.› (eine US-amerik. Nachrichtenagentur; *Abk.* UPI); **U|ni|ted States [of A|me|ri|ca]** [ju'naitid 'ste:ts (əv ə'mɛrikə)] *Plur.* (Vereinigte Staaten [von Amerika]; *Abk.* US[A])

u|ni|ver|sal [...v...], **u|ni|ver|sell** ‹lat.› (allgemein, gesamt; [die ganze Welt] umfassend); **U|ni|ver|sal-bil|dung, ...er|be** (der), **...ge|nie, ...ge|schich|te** (die; -; Weltgeschichte); **U|ni|ver|sa|li|en** [...i̯ən] *Plur.* (*Philos.* Allgemeinbegriffe, allgemein gültige Aussagen); **U|ni|ver|sa|lis|mus,** der; - (Lehre vom Vorrang des Allgemeinen, Ganzen vor dem Besonderen, Einzelnen; *auch für* Universalität); **u|ni|ver|sa|lis|tisch; U|ni|ver|sa|li|tät,** die; - (Allgemeinheit, Gesamtheit; Allseitigkeit; alles umfassende Bildung); **U|ni|ver|sal|mit|tel,** das (Allerweltsmittel, Allheilmittel); **u|ni|ver|sell** *vgl.* universal; **U|ni|ver|si|a|de,** die; -, -n (Studentenwettkämpfe nach dem Vorbild der Olympischen Spiele); **u|ni|ver|si|tär** (die Universität betreffend); **U|ni|ver|si|tät,** die; -, -en (Hochschule); **U|ni|ver|si|täts-aus|bil|dung, ...bib|li|o|thek, ...buch|hand|lung, ...in|sti|tut, ...kli|nik, ...lauf|bahn, ...pro|fes|sor, ...pro|fes|so|rin, ...stadt, ...stu|di|um, ...we|sen** (das; -s); **U|ni|ver|sum,** das; -s, ...sen ([Welt]all)

un|ka|me|rad|schaft|lich; Un|ka|me|rad|schaft|lich|keit, die; -

Ụn|ke, die; -, -n (ein Froschlurch); **ụn|ken** (*ugs. für* Unglück prophezeien); **Ụn|ken|art**
ụn|kennt|lich; Ụn|kennt|lich|keit, die; -; **Ụn|kennt|nis,** die; -
Ụn|ken|ruf (*auch für* pessimist. Voraussage)
ụn|keusch *(veraltend);* **Ụn|keusch|heit,** die; -
ụn|kind|lich; Ụn|kind|lich|keit, die; -
ụn|kirch|lich
ụn|klar; (↑R 47:) im Unklaren bleiben, lassen, sein; **Ụn|klar|heit**
ụn|kleid|sam
ụn|klug; ein -es Vorgehen; **Ụn|klug|heit**
ụn|kol|le|gi|al; -es Verhalten
ụn|kom|pli|ziert
ụn|kon|trol|lier|bar [*auch* ...'li:r...]; **ụn|kon|trol|liert**
ụn|kon|ven|ti|o|nell [...v...]
ụn|kon|zent|riert
ụn|kör|per|lich
ụn|kor|rekt; Ụn|kor|rekt|heit
Ụn|kos|ten *Plur.;* sich in - stürzen *(ugs.);* **Ụn|kos|ten|bei|trag**
Ụn|kraut
ụn|krie|ge|risch
ụn|kri|tisch; ein -er Leser
Unk|ti|on, die; -, -en ⟨lat.⟩ (*Med.* Einreibung, Einsalbung)
ụn|kul|ti|viert [...v...]; **Ụn|kul|tur,** die; - (Mangel an Kultur)
ụn|künd|bar [*auch* ...'kynt...]; ein -es Darlehen; **Un|künd|bar|keit,** die; -
ụn|kun|dig; des Lesens - sein
ụn|künst|le|risch
Ụn|land, das; -[e]s, Unländer (*Landw. für* nicht nutzbares Land)
ụn|längst (vor Kurzem)
ụn|lau|ter; -er Wettbewerb
ụn|leid|lich; Ụn|leid|lich|keit
ụn|le|ser|lich [*auch* ...'le:...]; **Un|le|ser|lich|keit,** die; -
un|leug|bar [*auch* 'un...]
ụn|lieb; un|lie|bens|wür|dig; ụn|lieb|sam; Ụn|lieb|sam|keit
ụn|li|mi|tiert (unbegrenzt)
ụn|li|niert, *österr. nur so, auch* **ụn|li|ni|iert**
ụn|lo|gisch
ụn|lös|bar [*auch* ...'lø:s...]; **Un|lös|bar|keit,** die; -; **un|lös|lich**
Ụn|lust, die; -; **Ụn|lust|ge|fühl; ụn|lus|tig**
ụn|ma|nier|lich
ụn|männ|lich; -e Eigenschaften
Ụn|maß, das; -es (Unzahl, übergroße Menge)
Ụn|mas|se (sehr große Menge)
ụn|maß|geb|lich [*auch* ...'ge:p...]; **ụn|mä|ßig;** - essen; **Ụn|mä|ßig|keit,** die; -
ụn|me|lo|disch
Ụn|men|ge
Ụn|mensch, der; -en, -en (grausamer Mensch); **ụn|mensch|lich** [*auch* ...'mɛnʃ...]; -e Verhältnisse; **Ụn|mensch|lich|keit**
un|mẹrk|lich [*auch* 'un...]
ụn|me|tho|disch
ụn|mi|li|tä|risch
ụn|miss|ver|ständ|lich [*auch* ...'ʃtɛnt...]
ụn|mit|tel|bar; Ụn|mit|tel|bar|keit, die; -
ụn|möb|liert; ein -es Zimmer
ụn|mo|dern; ụn|mo|disch
ụn|mög|lich [*auch* ...'mø:k...]; nichts Unmögliches (↑R 47) verlangen; **Un|mög|lich|keit**
Ụn|mo|ral; ụn|mo|ra|lisch
ụn|mo|ti|viert [...v...] (unbegründet)
ụn|mün|dig; Ụn|mün|dig|keit, die; -
ụn|mu|si|ka|lisch; ụn|mu|sisch
Ụn|mut, der; -[e]s; **ụn|mu|tig; ụn|muts|voll**
ụn|nach|ahm|lich [*auch* ...'a:m...]
ụn|nach|gie|big; eine -e Haltung; **Ụn|nach|gie|big|keit,** die; -
ụn|nach|sich|tig; Ụn|nach|sich|tig|keit, die; -; **ụn|nach|sicht|lich** (*älter für* unnachsichtig)
un|nah|bar [*auch* 'un...]; **Un|nah|bar|keit,** die; -
Ụn|na|tur, die; -; **ụn|na|tür|lich; Ụn|na|tür|lich|keit,** die; -
un|nenn|bar [*auch* 'un...]
ụn|nor|mal
ụn|no|tiert *(Börse)*
ụn|nö|tig; ụn|nö|ti|ger|wei|se
ụn|nütz; ụn|nüt|zer|wei|se
UNO, *auch* **Ụ|no,** die; - ⟨engl.; *Kurzwort für* United Nations Organization⟩ (Organisation der Vereinten Nationen); *vgl.* UN *u.* VN
ụn|öko|no|misch (↑R 132)
ụn|or|dent|lich; Ụn|or|dent|lich|keit, die; -; **Ụn|ord|nung,** die; -
ụn|or|ga|nisch; ụn|or|ga|ni|siert
ụn|or|tho|dox
ụn|or|tho|gra|phisch (↑R 33)
UNO-Si|cher|heits|rat, der; -[e]s; ↑R 26
ụn|paar; Ụn|paar|hu|fer *(Zool.);* **ụn|paa|rig; Ụn|paar|ze|her** *(Zool.)*
ụn|pä|da|go|gisch
ụn|par|tei|isch (neutral, nicht parteiisch); ein -es Urteil; **Ụn|par|tei|i|sche,** der *u.* die; -n, -n (↑R 5 ff.); **ụn|par|tei|lich** (keiner bestimmten Partei angehörend); **Ụn|par|tei|lich|keit,** die; -
ụn|pass (*veraltend für* unpässlich; *landsch. für* ungelegen, zu unrechter Zeit); sie ist -; das kommt mir -; **ụn|pas|send**
ụn|pas|sier|bar [*auch* ...'si:r...]
ụn|päss|lich ([leicht] krank; unwohl); **Ụn|päss|lich|keit**
ụn|pa|the|tisch
Ụn|per|son ([von den Medien] bewusst ignorierte Person); **ụn|per|sön|lich;** -es Fürwort (*für* Indefinitpronomen); **Ụn|per|sön|lich|keit,** die; -
ụn|pfänd|bar [*auch* ...'pfɛnt...]
ụn|plat|ziert *(Sport);* unplatziert (ungezielt) schießen
un pọ|co ⟨ital.⟩ (*Musik* ein wenig)
ụn|po|e|tisch
ụn|po|liert; -es Holz
ụn|po|li|tisch; er war völlig -
ụn|po|pu|lär; -e Maßnahmen
ụn|prak|tisch; er ist -
ụn|prä|ten|ti|ös
ụn|prä|zis; ụn|prä|zi|se
ụn|prob|le|ma|tisch
ụn|pro|duk|tiv; -e Arbeit; **Ụn|pro|duk|ti|vi|tät,** die; -
ụn|pro|fes|si|o|nell
ụn|pro|por|ti|o|niert; Ụn|pro|por|ti|o|niert|heit, die; -
ụn|pünkt|lich; er ist sehr -; **Ụn|pünkt|lich|keit,** die; -
ụn|qua|li|fi|ziert (*auch für* unangemessen, ohne Sachkenntnis); -e Bemerkungen
ụn|ra|siert
[1]**Ụn|rast,** der; -[e]s, -e (*veraltet für* ruheloser Mensch, bes. Kind); [2]**Ụn|rast,** die; - (Ruhelosigkeit)
Ụn|rat, der; -[e]s (*geh. für* Schmutz); - wittern (Schlimmes ahnen)
ụn|ra|ti|o|nell; ein -er Betrieb
ụn|rat|sam
ụn|re|al; ụn|re|a|lis|tisch
ụn|recht; in unrechte Hände gelangen; am unrechten Platz sein; unrecht sein; jmdm. unrecht tun; ihr habt unrecht daran getan; *Großschreibung* (↑R 47): etwas Unrechtes; an den Unrechten kommen; *vgl.* recht u. Unrecht; **Ụn|recht,** das; -[e]s; besser Unrecht leiden als Unrecht tun; es geschieht ihm Unrecht; ein Unrecht begehen; im Unrecht sein; jmdn. ins Unrecht setzen; jmdm. ein Unrecht [an]tun; zu Unrecht bestehen; Unrecht bekommen, geben, haben; *vgl.* unrecht u. Recht; **ụn|recht|mä|ßig;** -er Besitz; **ụn|recht|mä|ßi|ger|wei|se; Ụn|recht|mä|ßig|keit; Ụn|rechts|be|wusst|sein**
ụn|re|di|giert (vom Herausgeber nicht überarbeitet [von Zeitungsartikeln u. dgl.])
ụn|red|lich; Ụn|red|lich|keit
ụn|re|ell [...re|ɛl]; ein -es Geschäft
ụn|re|flek|tiert (ohne Nachdenken [entstanden]; spontan)

un|re|gel|mä|ßig; -e Verben *(Sprachw.);* **Un|re|gel|mä|ßigkeit**
un|re|gier|bar [*auch* ...'gi:r...]
un|reif; Un|rei|fe
un|rein; ins Unreine schreiben (↑R 47); **Un|rein|heit; un|reinlich; Un|rein|lich|keit,** die; -
un|ren|ta|bel; ein unrentab|ler (↑R 130) Betrieb; **Un|ren|ta|bi|lität,** die; -
un|rett|bar [*auch* 'un...]; sie waren - verloren
un|rich|tig; un|rich|ti|ger|wei|se; Un|rich|tig|keit
un|rit|ter|lich
un|ro|man|tisch
Un|ruh, die; -, -en (Teil der Uhr, des Barometers usw.); **Un|ru|he** (fehlende Ruhe; *ugs. auch für* Unruh); **Un|ru|he|herd** (*svw.* Krisenherd); **Un|ru|he|stif|ter; unru|hig**
un|rühm|lich; Un|rühm|lich|keit, die; -
un|rund *(Technik)*
uns
un|sach|ge|mäß; un|sach|lich; Un|sach|lich|keit
un|sag|bar [*auch* 'un...]; **un|säglich** [*auch* 'un...]
un|sanft; jmdn. - wecken
un|sau|ber; Un|sau|ber|keit
un|schäd|lich; ein -es Mittel; **Unschäd|lich|keit,** die; -; **Unschäd|lich|ma|chung,** die; -
un|scharf; ...schärfer, ...schärfste; **Un|schär|fe; Un|schär|fe‿bereich** (der; *Optik*), **...re|la|ti|on** *(Physik)*
un|schätz|bar [*auch* 'un...]
un|schein|bar; Un|schein|barkeit, die; -
un|schick|lich (*geh. für* unanständig); **Un|schick|lich|keit**
un|schlag|bar [*auch* 'un...]
Un|schlitt, das; -[e]s, -e (*veraltend für* Talg); **Un|schlitt|ker|ze**
un|schlüs|sig; Un|schlüs|sigkeit, die; -
un|schmelz|bar [*auch* 'un...]
un|schön
un|schöp|fe|risch
Un|schuld, die; -; **un|schul|dig;** ein unschuldiges Mädchen; *aber* (↑R 108): Unschuldige Kinder (kath. Fest); **Un|schul|di|ge,** der *u.* die; -n, -n (↑R 5 ff.); **un|schuldi|ger|wei|se; Un|schulds‿beteu|e|rung** *(meist Plur.)*, **...en|gel** *(iron.)*, **...lamm** *(iron.)*, **...mie|ne; un|schulds|voll**
un|schwer (leicht)
Un|se|gen, der; -s *(geh.)*
un|selbst|stän|dig, *auch* un|selbstän|dig; **Un|selbst|stän|digkeit,** *auch* Un|selb|stän|dig|keit

un|se|lig *(geh.);* ein -es Geschick; **un|se|li|ger|wei|se** *(geh.)*
un|sen|ti|men|tal
[1]un|ser, uns[e]re, unser; unser Tisch, unserm, uns[e]rem Tisch; unser von allen unterschriebener Brief (↑R 5); unseres Wissens (*Abk.* u. W.); (↑R 93 *u.* 108:) Unsere Liebe Frau (Maria, Mutter Jesu); Uns[e]rer Lieben Frau[en] Kirche; *vgl.* dein; **[2]un|ser** (*Gen. von* „wir"); unser (*nicht* unserer) sind drei; gedenke, erbarme dich unser (*nicht* unserer); **un|se|re,** uns|re, uns|ri|ge; (↑R 48:) die Unser[e]n, Unsren, Unsrigen *od.* unser[e]n, unsren, unsrigen; das Uns[e]re, Unsrige *od.* uns[e]re, unsrige; *vgl.* deine, deinige; **unser|ei|ner, un|ser|eins; un|serer|seits,** un|ser|seits, uns|rerseits; **un|se|res|glei|chen,** unsers|glei|chen, uns|res|glei|chen; **un|se|res|teils,** uns|res|teils; **unse|ret|hal|ben** usw. *vgl.* unserthalben usw.
un|se|ri|ös; ein -es Angebot
un|ser|seits *vgl.* unsererseits; **unsers|glei|chen** *vgl.* unseresgleichen; **un|sert|hal|ben** *(veraltend);* **un|sert|we|gen; un|sertwil|len;** um -
Un|ser|va|ter, das; -s, - (*landsch., bes. schweiz. für* Vaterunser)
un|si|cher; im Unsichern (zweifelhaft) sein (↑R 47); **Un|si|cherheit; Un|si|cher|heits|fak|tor**
un|sicht|bar; Un|sicht|bar|keit, die; -; **un|sich|tig** (trüb, undurchsichtig); die Luft wird -
un|sink|bar [*auch* ...'ziŋk...]
Un|sinn, der; -[e]s; **un|sin|nig; unsin|ni|ger|wei|se; Un|sin|nigkeit,** die; -; **un|sinn|lich**
Un|sit|te; un|sitt|lich; ein -er Antrag; **Un|sitt|lich|keit**
un|sol|da|tisch
un|so|lid *od.* **un|so|li|de; Un|so|lidi|tät,** die; -
un|so|zi|al; -es Verhalten
un|spek|ta|ku|lär
un|spe|zi|fisch
un|spiel|bar [*auch* 'un...]
un|sport|lich; Un|sport|lich|keit
uns|re *vgl.* unsere; **uns|rer|seits** *vgl.* unsererseits; **uns|res|gleichen** *vgl.* unseresgleichen; **unsres|teils** *vgl.* unseresteils; **uns|rige** *vgl.* unsere
un|sta|bil; Un|sta|bi|li|tät
un|stän|dig *(selten);* - Beschäftigte
Un|stä|te, die; - (*veraltet für* Unruhe); *vgl. aber* unstet
un|statt|haft
un|sterb|lich [*auch* ...'ʃtɛrp...]; die -e Seele; **Un|sterb|lich|keit,** die; -; **Un|sterb|lich|keits|glau|be[n]**

Un|stern, der; -[e]s (*geh. für* Unglück); *meist in* unter einem - stehen
un|stet; ein -es Leben; *vgl. aber* Unstäte; **Un|stet|heit,** die; - (unstete [Wesens]art); **un|ste|tig** (*veraltend für* unstet); **Un|ste|tigkeit,** die; -
un|still|bar [*auch* 'un...]
un|stim|mig; Un|stim|mig|keit
un|sträf|lich [*auch* ...'ʃtrɛ:f...] (*veraltend für* untadelig)
un|strei|tig [*auch* ...'ʃtrai...] (sicher, bestimmt); **un|strit|tig** [*auch* ...'ʃtrit...]
Un|strut, die; - (l. Nebenfluss der Saale)
Un|sum|me (sehr große Summe)
un|sym|met|risch
un|sym|pa|thisch; er ist mir -
un|sys|te|ma|tisch; - vorgehen
un|ta|de|lig, un|tad|lig [*beide auch* ...'ta:...]; ein -es Leben
un|ta|len|tiert
Un|tat (Verbrechen); **Un|tät|chen** (*landsch. für* kleiner Makel); *nur in* es ist kein - an ihm
un|tä|tig; Un|tä|tig|keit, die; -
un|taug|lich; Un|taug|lich|keit, die; -
un|teil|bar [*auch* 'un...]; **Un|teilbar|keit,** die; -; **un|teil|haf|tig;** einer Sache - sein
un|ten; nach, von, bis unten; nach unten hin, zu; von unten her, hinauf; weiter unten; man wusste kaum noch, was unten und was oben war; unten sein, bleiben, liegen, stehen; bei jemandem unten durch sein (*ugs. für* sich jmds. Wohlwollen verscherzt haben); die unten liegenden Schichten; die unten erwähnten, genannten, stehenden Fakten; unten Stehendes *od.* Untenstehendes ist zu beachten; das unten Stehende *od.* Untenstehende gilt auch weiterhin; im unten Stehenden *od.* Untenstehenden heißt es, dass ...; *vgl.* oben; **un|ten|an;** - stehen, - sitzen; **un|ten|drun|ter** *(ugs.);* **unten|durch** *vgl. auch* unten; **unten er|wähnt, genannt** *vgl.* unten; **un|ten|her,** *aber* von unten her; **un|ten|he|rum** (*ugs. für* im unteren Teil; unten am Körper); **un|ten|hin,** *aber* nach unten hin; **un|ten lie|gend** *vgl.* unten; **unten|rum** (*svw.* untenherum); **unten ste|hend** *vgl.* unten
un|ter; *Präp. mit Dat. u. Akk.:* unter dem Tisch stehen, *aber* unter den Tisch stellen; unter der Bedingung, dass ... (↑R 88); Kinder unter zwölf Jahren haben keinen Zutritt; unter ander[e]m, unter ander[e]n (*Abk.* u. a.); unter ei-

nem (*österr. für* zugleich); unter Tage *(Bergmannsspr.);* unter üblichem Vorbehalt (bei Gutschrift von Schecks; *Abk.* u. ü. V.); unter Umständen (*Abk.* u. U.); *Adverb:* es waren unter (= weniger als) 100 Gäste; unter (= noch nicht) zwölf Jahre alte Kinder; Gemeinden von unter (= weniger als) 10 000 Einwohnern
Un|ter, der; -s, - (Spielkarte)
un|ter... *in Verbindung mit Verben:* **I.** *unfeste Zusammensetzungen,* z. B. unterhalten *(vgl. d.),* er hält unter, hat untergehalten; unterzuhalten; **II.** *feste Zusammensetzungen,* z. B. unterhalten *(vgl. d.)*, er unterhält, hat unterhalten; zu unterhalten
Un|ter|ab|tei|lung
Un|ter|arm
Un|ter|bau *Plur.* ...bauten
Un|ter|bauch
un|ter|bau|en; er hat den Sockel unterbaut; **Un|ter|bau|ung**
Un|ter|be|griff
Un|ter|be|klei|dung
un|ter|be|legt; ein -es Hotel; **Un|ter|be|le|gung**
un|ter|be|lich|ten *(Fotogr.);* du unterbelichtest; die Aufnahme ist unterbelichtet; unterzubelichten; **Un|ter|be|lich|tung**
un|ter|be|schäf|tigt; Un|ter|be|schäf|ti|gung
un|ter|be|setzt; die Dienststelle ist - (hat nicht genug Personal)
Un|ter|bett
un|ter|be|wer|ten; er unterbewertet diese Leistung; er hat sie unterbewertet; unterzubewerten; **Un|ter|be|wer|tung**
un|ter|be|wusst; Un|ter|be|wusst|sein
un|ter|be|zah|len; sie ist unterbezahlt; unterzubezahlen; *selten* sie unterbezahlt ihre Angestellten; **Un|ter|be|zah|lung**
un|ter|bie|ten; er hat die Rekorde unterboten; **Un|ter|bie|tung**
Un|ter|bi|lanz (Verlustabschluss)
un|ter|bin|den *(ugs.);* sie hat ein Tuch untergebunden; **un|ter|bin|den;** der Handelsverkehr ist unterbunden; **Un|ter|bin|dung**
un|ter|blei|ben; die Buchung ist leider unterblieben
Un|ter|bo|den‿schutz (der; -es; *Kfz-Technik*), **...wä|sche**
un|ter|bre|chen; sie hat die Reise unterbrochen; jmdn., sich -; **Un|ter|bre|cher** *(Elektrotechnik);* **Un|ter|bre|cher|kon|takt; Un|ter|bre|chung**
un|ter|brei|ten (darlegen; vorschlagen); er hat ihm einen Plan unterbreitet; **Un|ter|brei|tung**
un|ter|brin|gen; er hat das Gepäck im Wagen untergebracht; **Un|ter|brin|gung**
Un|ter|bruch, der; -[e]s, ...brüche (*schweiz. neben* Unterbrechung)
un|ter|bü|geln (*ugs. für* rücksichtslos unterdrücken)
un|ter|but|tern (*ugs. für* rücksichtslos unterdrücken; zusätzlich verbrauchen); das Geld wurde noch mit untergebuttert
un|ter|chlo|rig [...k...] *(Chemie);* -e Säure
Un|ter|deck (ein Schiffsteil)
Un|ter|de|ckung *(Kreditwesen)*
un|ter der Hand (im Stillen, heimlich)
un|ter|des|sen, *älter* un|ter|des
Un|ter|druck, der; -[e]s, ...drücke;
un|ter|drü|cken; er hat seinen Unwillen unterdrückt; **Un|ter|drü|cker; Un|ter|drü|cke|rin; un|ter|drü|cke|risch; Un|ter|druck|kam|mer** *(Technik);* **Un|ter|drü|ckung**
un|ter|du|cken *(landsch.);* sie hat ihn im Bad untergeduckt
un|ter|durch|schnitt|lich
un|te|re; die unter[e]n Klassen, *aber* (↑R 102): Unterer Neckar (Region in Baden-Württemberg); *vgl.* unterste
un|ter|ei|nan|der (↑R 132); *Schreibung in Verbindung mit Verben immer getrennt:* die Zahlen untereinander schreiben; untereinander stehende Wörter
Un|ter|ein|heit
un|ter|ent|wi|ckelt; -e Länder; **Un|ter|ent|wick|lung**
un|ter|er|nährt; -e Kinder; **Un|ter|er|näh|rung,** die; -
un|ter|fah|ren; einen Viadukt -
Un|ter|fa|mi|lie *(Biol.)*
un|ter|fan|gen; du hast dich -, einen Roman zu schreiben; die Mauer wird - (*Bauw.* abgestützt); **Un|ter|fan|gen,** das; -s, - (Vorhaben; Wagnis)
un|ter|fas|sen *(ugs.);* sie gehen untergefasst
un|ter|fer|ti|gen (*Amtsspr.* unterschreiben); unterfertigt; unterfertigtes Protokoll; **Un|ter|fer|tig|te,** der *u.* die; -n, -n (↑R 5 ff.)
Un|ter|feu|e|rung *(Technik)*
un|ter|flie|gen; er hat den Radar unterflogen
un|ter|flur *(fachspr.);* etwas - einbauen; **Un|ter|flur‿ga|ra|ge, ...hyd|rant** (unter der Straßendecke liegende Zapfstelle), **...motor** (unter dem Fahrzeugboden eingebauter Motor), **...stra|ße** (unterirdische Straße)
un|ter|for|dern; Schüler -
Un|ter|fran|ken
un|ter|füh|ren; die Straße wird unterführt; ein Wort -
Un|ter|füh|rer *(Milit.)*
Un|ter|füh|rung; Un|ter|füh|rungs|zei|chen (für gleiche untereinander stehende Wörter; *Zeichen* „)
Un|ter|funk|ti|on *(Med.)*
Un|ter|fut|ter ‹*zu* [2]Futter›; **un|ter|füt|tern**
Un|ter|gang, der; -[e]s, ...gänge;
Un|ter|gangs|stim|mung
un|ter|gä|rig; -es Bier; **Un|ter|gä|rung,** die; -
un|ter|ge|ben; Un|ter|ge|be|ne, der *u.* die; -n, -n (↑R 5 ff.)
un|ter|ge|hen; die Sonne ist untergegangen; (↑R 50:) sein Stern ist im Untergehen [begriffen]
un|ter|ge|ord|net
Un|ter|ge|schoss
Un|ter|ge|stell
Un|ter|ge|wicht, das; -[e]s; **un|ter|ge|wich|tig**
Un|ter|gla|sur|far|be (*svw.* keramische Farbe)
un|ter|glie|dern; Un|ter|glie|de|rung (das Untergliedern)
Un|ter|glie|de|rung (Unterabteilung)
un|ter|gra|ben; sie hat den Dünger untergegraben; **un|ter|gra|ben;** das hat ihre Gesundheit -;
Un|ter|gra|bung, die; -
Un|ter|gren|ze
Un|ter|grund, der; -[e]s, ...gründe *Plur. selten;* **Un|ter|grund‿bahn** (*kurz* U-Bahn; ↑R 26), **...be|we|gung; un|ter|grün|dig; Un|ter|grund‿kämp|fer, ...li|te|ra|tur, ...mu|sik, ...or|ga|ni|sa|ti|on**
Un|ter|grup|pe
un|ter|ha|ben (*ugs. für* etwas unter einem anderen Kleidungsstück tragen); nichts -
un|ter|ha|ken *(ugs.);* sie hatten sich untergehakt
un|ter|halb; *als Präp. mit Gen.:* der Neckar unterhalb Heidelbergs (von Heidelberg aus flussabwärts)
Un|ter|halt, der; -[e]s; **un|ter|hal|ten** *(ugs.);* er hat die Hand untergehalten, z. B. unter den Wasserhahn; **un|ter|hal|ten;** ich habe mich gut -; er wird vom Staat -; **Un|ter|hal|ter; un|ter|halt|sam** (fesselnd); **Un|ter|halt|sam|keit,** die; -; **Un|ter|halts‿an|spruch, ...bei|trag; un|ter|halts|be|rech|tigt; Un|ter|halts‿kla|ge, ...kos|ten** *(Plur.),* **...pflicht; un|ter|halts|pflich|tig, un|ter|halts|ver|pflich|tet; Un|ter|halts|zah|lung; Un|ter|hal|tung; Un|ter|hal|tungs‿bei|la|ge, ...elekt|ro|nik** (↑R 132), **...film, ...in|dust|rie, ...kos|ten** *(Plur.),* **...li|te|ra-**

tur (die; -), **...mu|sik** (die; -; *kurz* U-Musik), **...pro|gramm, ...ro|man, ...sen|dung, ...teil** (der)
un|ter|han|deln; er hat über den Abschluss des Vertrages unterhandelt; **Un|ter|händ|ler; Un|ter|hand|lung**
Un|ter|haus (im Zweikammerparlament); das britische -; **Un|ter|haus₋mit|glied, ...sit|zung**
un|ter|he|ben; dann wird der Eischnee vorsichtig untergehoben
Un|ter|hemd
Un|ter|hit|ze, die; -; bei - backen
un|ter|höh|len; unterhöhlt
Un|ter|holz, das; -es (niedriges Gehölz im Wald)
Un|ter|ho|se
Un|ter|in|stanz
un|ter|ir|disch
Un|ter|ita|li|en (↑R 105 *u.* 132)
Un|ter|ja|cke
un|ter|jo|chen; das Volk wurde unterjocht; **Un|ter|jo|chung**
un|ter|ju|beln; das hat er ihm untergejubelt (*ugs. für* heimlich [mit etwas anderem] zugeschoben)
un|ter|kant *(schweiz.); als Präp. mit Gen.:* unterkant des Fensters, *auch* unterkant Fenster
un|ter|kel|lern; ich ...ere (↑R 16); das Haus wurde nachträglich unterkellert; **Un|ter|kel|le|rung**
Un|ter|kie|fer, der; **Un|ter|kie|fer₋drü|se, ...kno|chen**
Un|ter₋kleid, ...klei|dung
un|ter|kom|men; sie ist gut untergekommen; das ist mir noch nie untergekommen (*landsch., bes. südd., österr. für* vorgekommen); **Un|ter|kom|men,** das; -s, -
Un|ter|kör|per
un|ter|kö|tig (*landsch. für* eitrig entzündet)
un|ter|krie|chen *(ugs.);* er ist bei Freunden untergekrochen
un|ter|krie|gen (*ugs. für* bezwingen; entmutigen); er hat mich nicht untergekriegt
un|ter|küh|len (die Körpertemperatur unter den Normalwert senken; *Technik* unter den Schmelzpunkt abkühlen); unterkühlt; **Un|ter|küh|lung**
Un|ter|kunft, die; -, ...künfte
Un|ter|la|ge
Un|ter|land, das; -[e]s (tiefer gelegenes Land; Ebene); **Un|ter|län|der,** der; -s, - (Bewohner des Unterlandes)
Un|ter|län|ge
Un|ter|lass, der; *nur in* ohne -; **un|ter|las|sen;** sie hat es -; **Un|ter|las|sung; Un|ter|las|sungs₋de|likt, ...kla|ge, ...sün|de**
Un|ter|lauf, der; -[e]s, ...läufe; **un|ter|lau|fen;** er hat ihn unterlaufen *(Ringen);* es sind einige Fehler unterlaufen, *seltener* untergelaufen; **un|ter|läu|fig** (*Technik* [durch Wasser] von unten angetrieben); -e Mahlgänge; **Un|ter|lau|fung** (*auch für* Blutunterlaufung)
Un|ter|le|der
un|ter|le|gen; untergelegter Stoff; er hat etwas untergelegt; diese Absicht hat man mir untergelegt; [1]**un|ter|le|gen;** der Musik wurde ein anderer Text unterlegt; [2]**un|ter|le|gen** (*Partizip II zu* unterliegen; *vgl. d.*); **Un|ter|le|gen|heit,** die; -; **Un|ter|leg|schei|be** *(Technik);* **Un|ter|le|gung** (einer Absicht); **Un|ter|le|gung** (Verstärkung, Vermehrung usw.)
Un|ter|leib; Un|ter|leib|chen (ein Kleidungsstück); **Un|ter|leibs₋krank|heit, ...lei|den, ...ope|ra|ti|on** (↑R 132), **...schmerz**
Un|ter|lid
un|ter|lie|gen *(ugs.);* das Badetuch hat, *südd.* ist untergelegen; **un|ter|lie|gen;** er ist seinem Gegner unterlegen
Un|ter|lip|pe
un|term; ↑R 13 (*ugs. für* unter dem); unterm Dach
un|ter|ma|len; die Szene wurde durch Musik untermalt; **Un|ter|ma|lung,** die; -
Un|ter|mann, der; -[e]s, ...männer (*Sport, Artistik* unterster Mann bei einer akrobatischen Übung)
Un|ter|maß, das (*selten für* nicht ausreichendes Maß)
un|ter|mau|ern; er hat seine Beweisführung gut untermauert; **Un|ter|mau|e|rung**
un|ter|mee|risch (in der Tiefe des Meeres befindlich)
Un|ter|men|ge (*Math.* Teilmenge)
un|ter|men|gen; die schlechte Ware wurde mit untergemengt; **un|ter|men|gen** (vermischen); untermengt mit ...
Un|ter|mensch (nationalsoz. diffamierende Bez. für einen als minderwertig angesehenen Menschen)
Un|ter|mie|te, die; -; zur - wohnen; **Un|ter|mie|ter; Un|ter|mie|te|rin**
un|ter|mi|nie|ren; die Stellung des Ministers war schon lange unterminiert; **Un|ter|mi|nie|rung**
un|ter|mi|schen; sie hat das Wertlose mit untergemischt; **un|ter|mi|schen;** untermischt mit ...; **Un|ter|mi|schung** (von etwas Wertlosem); **Un|ter|mi|schung** (mit etwas)
un|ter|mo|to|ri|siert (*Kfz-Technik* mit einem zu schwachen Motor ausgestattet)
un|tern; ↑R 13 (*ugs. für* unter den); untern Tisch fallen
Un|ter|näch|te *Plur.* (*landsch. für* die Zwölf Nächte)
un|ter|neh|men (*ugs. für* unter den Arm nehmen); er hat den Sack untergenommen; **un|ter|neh|men;** er hat nichts unternommen; **Un|ter|neh|men,** das; -s, -; **un|ter|neh|mend** (aus, mit Unternehmungsgeist); **Un|ter|neh|mens₋be|ra|ter, ...be|ra|te|rin, ...be|ra|tung, ...form, ...for|schung** (die; -), **...füh|rung, ...lei|ter** (der), **...lei|te|rin, ...po|li|tik** (die; -); **...pro|fil; Un|ter|neh|mer; Un|ter|neh|mer₋frei|heit** (die; -), **...geist** (der; -[e]s), **...ge|winn; Un|ter|neh|me|rin; un|ter|neh|me|risch; Un|ter|neh|mer|schaft; Un|ter|neh|mer|tum,** das; -s; **Un|ter|neh|mer|ver|band; Un|ter|neh|mung; Un|ter|neh|mungs₋geist** (der; -[e]s), **...lust** (die; -); **un|ter|neh|mungs|lus|tig**
Un|ter|of|fi|zier (*Abk.* Uffz., *in der Schweiz* Uof); **Un|ter|of|fi|ziers₋an|wär|ter**[1], **...mes|se, ...schu|le**
un|ter|ord|nen; er ist ihm untergeordnet; **un|ter|ord|nend; Un|ter|ord|nung**
Un|ter|pfand
Un|ter|pflas|ter[|stra|ßen]|bahn (*kurz* U-Strab)
un|ter|pflü|gen; untergepflügt
Un|ter|pri|ma [*auch* ...ˈpriːma]
un|ter|pri|vi|le|giert; Un|ter|pri|vi|le|gier|te, der *u.* die (↑R 5 ff.)
Un|ter|punkt
un|ter|que|ren; das Atom-U-Boot hat den Nordpol unterquert
un|ter|re|den, sich; du hast dich mit ihm unterredet; **Un|ter|re|dung**
un|ter|re|prä|sen|tiert; Frauen sind im Parlament -
Un|ter|richt, der; -[e]s, -e *Plur. selten;* **un|ter|rich|ten;** er ist gut unterrichtet; sich -; **un|ter|richt|lich; Un|ter|richts₋auf|ga|be, ...brief, ...ein|heit, ...fach, ...film, ...for|schung; un|ter|richts|frei** *vgl.* hitzefrei; **Un|ter|richts₋ge|gen|stand, ...kun|de** (die; -); **un|ter|richts|kund|lich; Un|ter|richts₋leh|re, ...me|tho|de, ...mit|tel** (das), **...pro|gramm, ...schritt, ...stun|de, ...wei|se** (die), **...ziel; Un|ter|rich|tung**
Un|ter|rock *vgl.* [1]Rock
un|ter|rüh|ren; die Flüssigkeit wird vorsichtig untergerührt

[1] *Vgl. die Anm. zu* „Offiziersanwärter".

un|ters; ↑R 13 (*ugs. für* unter das); unters Bett
Un|ter|saat (*Landw.* eine Art des Zwischenfruchtanbaus)
un|ter|sa|gen; das Rauchen ist untersagt; **Un|ter|sa|gung**
Un|ter|satz; fahrbarer - (*ugs. scherzh. für* Auto)
Un|ters|berg, der; -[e]s (Bergstock der Salzburger Kalkalpen); **Un|ters|ber|ger Kalk|stein,** der; --[e]s
un|ter|schät|zen; unterschätzt
un|ter|schei|bar; un|ter|schei|den; die Bedeutungen müssen unterschieden werden; sich -; **Un|ter|schei|dung; Un|ter|schei|dungs_merk|mal, ...ver|mö|gen** (das; -s)
Un|ter|schen|kel
Un|ter|schicht
[1]un|ter|schie|ben (darunter schieben); er hat ihr ein Kissen untergeschoben; **[2]un|ter|schie|ben** [*auch* ...ˈʃiː...]; er hat ihm eine schlechte Absicht untergeschoben, *auch* unterschoben; ein untergeschobenes Kind
Un|ter|schied, der; -[e]s, -e; zum - von; im - zu; **un|ter|schie|den** (verschieden); **un|ter|schied|lich; Un|ter|schied|lich|keit; Un|ter|schieds|be|trag** (*für* Differenz); **un|ter|schieds|los**
un|ter|schläch|tig (durch Wasser von unten angetrieben); ein -es Mühlrad
Un|ter|schlag, der; -[e]s, Unterschläge (Schneidersitz; *Druckw.* äußerstes [unteres] Ende der Seite); **un|ter|schla|gen;** mit untergeschlagenen Beinen; **un|ter|schla|gen** (veruntreuen); sie hat [die Beitragsgelder] unterschlagen; **Un|ter|schla|gung**
Un|ter|schleif, der; -[e]s, -e (*veraltet für* Unterschlagung)
un|ter|schlie|ßen *(Druckw.);* der Setzer hat hier und da ein Wort untergeschlossen
Un|ter|schlupf; un|ter|schlüp|fen, *südd. ugs.* un|ter|schlup|fen; er ist untergeschlüpft
un|ter|schnei|den; den Ball stark - *([Tisch]tennis);* das Gesims wurde unterschnitten (*Bauw.* an der Unterseite abgeschrägt)
un|ter|schrei|ben; ich habe den Brief unterschrieben
un|ter|schrei|ten; die Einnahmen haben den Voranschlag unterschritten; **Un|ter|schrei|tung**
Un|ter|schrift; Un|ter|schrif|ten_ak|ti|on, ...kam|pag|ne, ...map|pe, ...samm|lung; un|ter|schrift|lich (*Amtsspr.* mit od. durch Unterschrift); **un|ter|schrifts|be|rech|tigt; Un|ter|schrifts_be|rech|ti|gung, ...be|stä|ti|gung, ...pro|be; un|ter|schrifts|reif**
Un|ter|schuss (*veraltet für* Defizit)
Un|ter|schutz|stel|lung; die - eines Biotops, eines historischen Gebäudes
un|ter|schwef|lig *(Chemie);* -e Säure
un|ter|schwel|lig (unterhalb der Bewusstseinsschwelle [liegend])
Un|ter|see, der; -s (Teil des Bodensees)
Un|ter|see|boot (*Abk.* U-Boot, U); **un|ter|see|isch**
Un|ter|sei|te; un|ter|seits (an der Unterseite)
Un|ter|se|kun|da [*auch* ...ˈkunda]
un|ter|set|zen; ich habe den Eimer untergesetzt; **un|ter|set|zen;** untersetzt (gemischt) mit ...; **Un|ter|set|zer** (Schale für Blumentöpfe u. a.); **un|ter|setzt** (von gedrungener Gestalt); **Un|ter|setzt|heit,** die; -; **Un|ter|set|zung** *(Kfz-Technik);* **Un|ter|set|zungs|ge|trie|be**
un|ter|sin|ken; das Schiff ist untergesunken
un|ter|spickt (*österr. für* mit Fett durchzogen); -es Fleisch
un|ter|spie|len (als nicht so wichtig hinstellen); die Sache wurde unterspielt
un|ter|spü|len; die Fluten hatten den Damm unterspült
un|terst *vgl.* unterste
Un|ter|staats|sek|re|tär [*auch* ˈun...] *(früher)*
Un|ter|stand; Un|ter|stän|der (Stützbalken; *Heraldik* unterer Teil des Schildes); **un|ter|stän|dig** *(Bot.);* -er Fruchtknoten; -er Baumwuchs; **un|ter|stands|los** (*österr. neben* obdachlos)
un|ters|te; der unterste Knopf, *aber* (↑R 47): das Unterste zuoberst, das Oberste zuunterst kehren
un|ter|ste|hen (unter einem schützenden Dach stehen); sie hat beim Regen untergestanden; **un|ter|ste|hen;** er unterstand einem strengen Lehrmeister; es hat keinem Zweifel unterstanden (es gab keinen Zweifel); du hast dich unterstanden (gewagt); untersteh dich [nicht], das zu tun!
un|ter|stel|len; ich habe den Wagen untergestellt; sich -; ich habe mich während des Regens untergestellt; **un|ter|stel|len;** er ist meinem Befehl unterstellt; man hat ihr etwas unterstellt ([etwas Falsches] über sie behauptet, [Unbewiesenes] als wahr angenommen); **Un|ter|stel|lung,** die; - (das Unterstellen); **Un|ter|stel|lung** (befehlsmäßige Unterordnung; [falsche] Behauptung)
un|ter|steu|ern (*Kfz-Technik* zu schwache Wirkung des Lenkradeinschlags zeigen); der Wagen hat untersteuert
Un|ter|stock, der; -[e]s; **Un|ter|stock|werk**
un|ter|stop|fen; ein untergestopftes Kissen
un|ter|strei|chen; sie hat mehrere Wörter unterstrichen; sie hat diese Behauptung nachdrücklich unterstrichen (betont); (↑R 50:) etwas durch Unterstreichen hervorheben; **Un|ter|strei|chung**
Un|ter|strö|mung
Un|ter|stu|fe
un|ter|stüt|zen; er hat den Arm [unter das Kinn] untergestützt; **un|ter|stüt|zen;** ich habe ihn mit Geld unterstützt; der zu Unterstützende; **Un|ter|stüt|zung; un|ter|stüt|zungs|be|dürf|tig; Un|ter|stüt|zungs_bei|hil|fe, ...emp|fän|ger, ...geld, ...kas|se, ...satz**
Un|ter|such, der; -s, -e (*schweiz. neben* Untersuchung); **un|ter|su|chen;** der Arzt hat mich untersucht; **Un|ter|su|chung; Un|ter|su|chungs_aus|schuss, ...be|fund, ...ge|fan|ge|ne, ...ge|fäng|nis, ...haft** (die; *kurz* U-Haft), **...häft|ling, ...kom|mis|si|on, ...rich|ter, ...rich|te|rin, ...ver|fah|ren, ...zim|mer** (beim Arzt)
Un|ter|tag|ar|bei|ter, *häufiger* **Un|ter|ta|ge|ar|bei|ter** *(Bergbau);* **Un|ter|ta|ge|bau,** der; -[e]s; **un|ter|tags** (*südd., österr. u. schweiz. für* tagsüber)
un|ter|tan (*veraltend für* ergeben); **Un|ter|tan,** der; *Gen.* -s, *älter* -en, *Plur.* -en (↑R 126); **Un|ter|ta|nen_geist** (der; -[e]s), **...pflicht; un|ter|tä|nig** (ergeben); **Un|ter|tä|nig|keit,** die; -; **Un|ter|ta|nin**
Un|ter|tas|se; fliegende -
un|ter|tau|chen; der Schwimmer ist untergetaucht; der Verbrecher war schnell untergetaucht (verschwunden); **un|ter|tau|chen;** die Robbe hat das Schleppnetz untertaucht
Un|ter|teil, das, *auch* der; **un|ter|tei|len;** die Skala ist in 10 Teile unterteilt; **Un|ter|tei|lung**
Un|ter|tem|pe|ra|tur
Un|ter|ter|tia [*auch* ...ˈtɛr...]
Un|ter|ti|tel; un|ter|ti|teln; ein untertiteltes Foto
Un|ter|ton *Plur.* ...töne

un|ter|tou|rig [...tu:...] (*Technik* mit zu niedriger Drehzahl); der Wagen darf nicht - gefahren werden
un|ter|trei|ben; er hat untertrieben; **Un|ter|trei|bung**
un|ter|tun|neln; ich ...[e]le (↑R 16); der Berg wurde untertunnelt; **Un|ter|tun|ne|lung**
un|ter|ver|mie|ten; sie hat ein Zimmer untervermietet; **Un|ter|ver|mie|tung**
un|ter|ver|si|chern (zu niedrig versichern); die Möbel sind unterversichert; **Un|ter|ver|si|che|rung**
un|ter|ver|sor|gen; unterversorgte Gebiete; **Un|ter|ver|sor|gung**
Un|ter|wal|den nid dem Wald (schweiz. Halbkanton; *Kurzform* Nidwalden); **Un|ter|wal|den ob dem Wald** (schweiz. Halbkanton; *Kurzform* Obwalden); **Un|ter|wald|ner** (↑R 103); **un|ter|wald|ne|risch**
un|ter|wan|dern (sich [als Fremder od. heimlicher Gegner] unter eine Gruppe mischen); die Partei wurde unterwandert; **Un|ter|wan|de|rung**
un|ter|wärts *(ugs.)*
Un|ter|wä|sche, die; -
un|ter|wa|schen; das Ufer ist -; **Un|ter|wa|schung**
Un|ter|was|ser, das; -s (Grundwasser)
Un|ter|was|ser‿ar|chä|o|lo|gie, ...auf|nah|me, ...be|hand|lung, ...ka|me|ra, ...mas|sa|ge, ...sta|ti|on, ...streit|kräf|te *(Plur.)*
un|ter|wegs (auf dem Wege)
un|ter|wei|len (*veraltet für* bisweilen; unterdessen)
un|ter|wei|sen; er hat sie beide unterwiesen; **Un|ter|wei|sung**
Un|ter|welt, die; -; **un|ter|welt|lich**
un|ter|wer|fen; sich -; das Volk wurde unterworfen; du hast dich dem Richterspruch unterworfen; **Un|ter|wer|fung**
Un|ter|werks|bau, der; -[e]s (*Bergmannsspr.* Abbau unterhalb der Fördersohle)
un|ter|wer|tig; Un|ter|wer|tig|keit, die; -
un|ter|win|den *(veraltet);* sich einer Sache - (sie übernehmen, sich daran wagen); unterwunden
un|ter|wür|fig [*auch* 'un...]; **Un|ter|wür|fig|keit,** die; -
un|ter|zeich|nen; sie hat den Brief unterzeichnet; **Un|ter|zeich|ner; Un|ter|zeich|ne|te,** der *u.* die; -n, -n (↑R 5 ff.; *Amtsspr.*); der rechts, links Unterzeichnete *od.* der Rechts-, Linksunterzeichnete (bei Unterschriften); **Un|ter|zeich|nung**
Un|ter|zeug, das; -[e]s *(ugs.)*
un|ter|zie|hen; ich habe eine wollene Jacke untergezogen; **un|ter|zie|hen;** du hast dich diesem Verhör unterzogen
un|tief (seicht); **Un|tie|fe** (große Tiefe; *auch für* seichte Stelle)
Un|tier (Ungeheuer)
un|tilg|bar [*auch* 'un...]
Un|to|te (*svw.* Vampir)
un|trag|bar [*auch* 'un...]; **Un|trag|bar|keit,** die; -
un|trai|niert [...trɛ...]
un|trenn|bar [*auch* 'un...]
un|treu; Un|treue
un|tröst|lich [*auch* 'un...]
un|trüg|lich [*auch* 'un...]; ein -es (absolut sicheres) Zeichen
un|tüch|tig; Un|tüch|tig|keit, die; -
Un|tu|gend
un|tun|lich *(veraltend)*
un|ty|pisch
un|über|biet|bar [*auch* 'un...] (↑R 132)
un|über|brück|bar [*auch* 'un...] (↑R 132)
un|über|hör|bar [*auch* 'un...] (↑R 132)
un|über|legt (↑R 132); **Un|über|legt|heit**
un|über|schau|bar [*auch* 'un...] (↑R 132)
un|über|schreit|bar [*auch* 'un...] (↑R 132)
un|über|seh|bar [*auch* 'un...] (↑R 132)
un|über|setz|bar [*auch* 'un...] (↑R 132)
un|über|sicht|lich (↑R 132); **Un|über|sicht|lich|keit,** die; -
un|über|steig|bar [*auch* 'un...] (↑R 132)
un|über|trag|bar [*auch* 'un...] (↑R 132)
un|über|treff|lich [*auch* 'un...] (↑R 132); **Un|über|treff|lich|keit,** die; -; **un|über|trof|fen** [*auch* 'un...]
un|über|wind|bar [*auch* 'un...] (↑R 132); **un|über|wind|lich** [*auch* 'un...]
un|üb|lich
un|um|gäng|lich [*auch* 'un...]; **Un|um|gäng|lich|keit,** die; -
un|um|schränkt [*auch* 'un...]
un|um|stöß|lich [*auch* 'un...]; **Un|um|stöß|lich|keit,** die; -
un|um|strit|ten [*auch* 'un...]
un|um|wun|den [*auch* ...'vun...] (offen, freiheraus)
un|un|ter|bro|chen [*auch* ...'brɔ...]
un|ver|än|der|lich [*auch* 'un...]; **Un|ver|än|der|lich|keit,** die; -; **un|ver|än|dert** [*auch* ...'ɛn...]
un|ver|ant|wort|lich [*auch* 'un...]; **Un|ver|ant|wort|lich|keit,** die; -
un|ver|ar|bei|tet [*auch* ...'a:r...]; -e Eindrücke
un|ver|äu|ßer|lich [*auch* 'un...]
un|ver|bau|bar [*auch* 'un...]; -er Fernblick
un|ver|bes|ser|lich [*auch* 'un...]; **Un|ver|bes|ser|lich|keit,** die; -
un|ver|bil|det (noch ganz natürlich)
un|ver|bind|lich [*auch* ...'bint...]; **Un|ver|bind|lich|keit**
un|ver|bleit; -es Benzin
un|ver|blümt [*auch* 'un...] (offen; ohne Umschweife)
un|ver|braucht
un|ver|brüch|lich [*auch* 'un...]; -e Treue
un|ver|bürgt [*auch* 'un...]
un|ver|däch|tig [*auch* ...'dɛç...]
un|ver|dau|lich [*auch* ...'dau...]; **Un|ver|dau|lich|keit,** die; -; **un|ver|daut** [*auch* ...'daut]
un|ver|dient [*auch* ...'di:nt]; **un|ver|dien|ter|ma|ßen; un|ver|dien|ter|wei|se**
un|ver|dor|ben; Un|ver|dor|ben|heit, die;
un|ver|dros|sen [*auch* ...'drɔsən]
un|ver|dünnt
un|ver|ehe|licht (↑R 132)
un|ver|ein|bar [*auch* 'un...]; **Un|ver|ein|bar|keit**
un|ver|fälscht [*auch* ...'fɛlʃt]; **Un|ver|fälscht|heit,** die; -
un|ver|fäng|lich [*auch* ...'fɛŋ...]
un|ver|fro|ren [*auch* ...'fro:...] (keck; frech); **Un|ver|fro|ren|heit**
un|ver|gäng|lich [*auch* ...'gɛŋ...]; **Un|ver|gäng|lich|keit,** die; -
un|ver|ges|sen; un|ver|gess|lich [*auch* 'un...]
un|ver|gleich|bar [*auch* 'un...]; **un|ver|gleich|lich** [*auch* 'un...]
un|ver|go|ren; -er Süßmost
un|ver|hält|nis|mä|ßig [*auch* ...'hɛlt...]; - groß
un|ver|hei|ra|tet
un|ver|hofft [*auch* ...'hɔft]
un|ver|hoh|len [*auch* ...'ho:...]
un|ver|hüllt
un|ver|käuf|lich [*auch* ...'kɔyf...]; **Un|ver|käuf|lich|keit,** die; -
un|ver|kenn|bar [*auch* 'un...]
un|ver|langt; -e Manuskripte werden nicht zurückgesandt
un|ver|läss|lich
un|ver|letz|bar [*auch* 'un...]; **un|ver|letz|lich** [*auch* 'un...]; **Un|ver|letz|lich|keit,** die; -; **un|ver|letzt**
un|ver|lier|bar [*auch* 'un...]
un|ver|lösch|lich [*auch* 'un...] *(geh.)*
un|ver|mählt

un|ver|meid|bar [*auch* 'un...]; **un|ver|meid|lich** [*auch* 'un...]
un|ver|merkt (*veraltend für* unbemerkt)
un|ver|min|dert
un|ver|mischt
un|ver|mit|telt (plötzlich, abrupt); **Un|ver|mit|telt|heit,** die; - (*selten*)
Un|ver|mö|gen, das; -s (Mangel an Kraft, Fähigkeit); **un|ver|mö|gend; Un|ver|mö|gend|heit,** die; - (*selten für* Armut); **Un|ver|mö|gen|heit,** die; - (*veraltet für* Unvermögen); **Un|ver|mö|gens|fall,** der; -[e]s (*Amtsspr.*); im -[e]
un|ver|mu|tet
Un|ver|nunft; un|ver|nünf|tig; Un|ver|nünf|tig|keit
un|ver|öf|fent|licht; -e Manuskripte
un|ver|packt
un|ver|putzt; der Neubau ist -
un|ver|rich|tet; un|ver|rich|te|ter Din|ge (ohne etwas erreicht zu haben); **un|ver|rich|te|ter Sa|che**
un|ver|rück|bar [*auch* 'un...]
un|ver|schämt; Un|ver|schämt|heit
un|ver|schlos|sen [*auch* ...'ʃlɔ...]
un|ver|schul|det [*auch* ...'ʃul...]; **un|ver|schul|de|ter|ma|ßen; un|ver|schul|de|ter|wei|se**
un|ver|se|hens [*auch* ...'ze:...] (plötzlich)
un|ver|sehrt; Un|ver|sehrt|heit, die; -
un|ver|sieg|bar [*auch* 'un...]; **un|ver|sieg|lich** [*auch* 'un...]
un|ver|söhn|bar [*auch* ...'zø:n...]; **un|ver|söhn|lich** [*auch* ...'zø:n...]; **Un|ver|söhn|lich|keit,** die; -
un|ver|sorgt
Un|ver|stand (Mangel an Verstand, an Einsicht); **un|ver|stan|den; un|ver|stän|dig** (ohne den nötigen Verstand); **Un|ver|stän|dig|keit,** die; -; **un|ver|ständ|lich** (undeutlich; unbegreiflich); **Un|ver|ständ|lich|keit; Un|ver|ständ|nis**
un|ver|stellt [*auch* ...'ʃtɛlt]
un|ver|steu|ert [*auch* ...'ʃtɔy...]
un|ver|sucht [*auch* ...'zu:xt]; *meist in* nichts - lassen
un|ver|träg|lich [*auch* ...'trɛ:k...]; **Un|ver|träg|lich|keit,** die; -
un|ver|wandt; jmdn. - ansehen
un|ver|wech|sel|bar [*auch* 'un...]; **Un|ver|wech|sel|bar|keit,** die; -
un|ver|wehrt [*auch* ...'ve:rt]; das bleibt dir - (unbenommen)
un|ver|weilt [*auch* ...'vailt] (*veraltend für* unverzüglich)
un|ver|wes|lich [*auch* ...'ve:s...]
un|ver|wisch|bar [*auch* 'un...]
un|ver|wund|bar [*auch* 'un...]; **Un|ver|wund|bar|keit**
un|ver|wüst|lich [*auch* 'un...]; **Un|ver|wüst|lich|keit,** die; -
un|ver|zagt; Un|ver|zagt|heit, die; -
un|ver|zeih|bar [*auch* 'un...]; **un|ver|zeih|lich** [*auch* 'un...]
un|ver|zicht|bar [*auch* 'un...]
un|ver|zins|lich [*auch* 'un...]
un|ver|zollt
un|ver|züg|lich [*auch* 'un...]
un|voll|en|det [*auch* ...'ɛn...]
un|voll|kom|men [*auch* ...'kɔ...]; **Un|voll|kom|men|heit**
un|voll|stän|dig [*auch* ...'ʃtɛn...]; **Un|voll|stän|dig|keit,** die; -
un|vor|be|rei|tet
un|vor|denk|lich; in -en Zeiten (sehr weit zurückliegend)
un|vor|ein|ge|nom|men; Un|vor|ein|ge|nom|men|heit, die; -
un|vor|greif|lich [*auch* 'un...] (*veraltet für* ohne einem anderen vorgreifen zu wollen)
un|vor|her|ge|se|hen
un|vor|schrifts|mä|ßig
un|vor|sich|tig; un|vor|sich|ti|ger|wei|se; Un|vor|sich|tig|keit
un|vor|stell|bar [*auch* 'un...]
un|vor|teil|haft
un|wäg|bar [*auch* 'un...]; -e Risiken; **Un|wäg|bar|keit,** die; -, -en
un|wahr; un|wahr|haf|tig (*geh.*); **Un|wahr|haf|tig|keit; Un|wahr|heit; un|wahr|schein|lich; Un|wahr|schein|lich|keit**
un|wan|del|bar [*auch* 'un...]; **Un|wan|del|bar|keit,** die; -
un|weg|sam; -es Gelände
un|weib|lich; sie wirkt -
un|wei|ger|lich [*auch* 'un...]
un|weit; *als Präp. mit Gen.:* - des Flusses
un|wert (*geh.*); **Un|wert,** der; -[e]s
Un|we|sen, das; -s; er trieb sein -; **un|we|sent|lich**
Un|wet|ter
un|wich|tig; Un|wich|tig|keit
un|wi|der|leg|bar [*auch* 'un...]; **un|wi|der|leg|lich** [*auch* 'un...]
un|wi|der|ruf|lich [*auch* 'un...]; zum letzten Mal
un|wi|der|spro|chen [*auch* 'un...]
un|wi|der|steh|lich [*auch* 'un...]; **Un|wi|der|steh|lich|keit,** die; -
un|wie|der|bring|lich [*auch* 'un...] (verloren, vergangen); **Un|wie|der|bring|lich|keit,** die; -
Un|wil|le[n], der; Unwillens; **un|wil|lent|lich; un|wil|lig; un|will|kom|men; un|will|kür|lich** [*auch* ...'ky:r...]
un|wirk|lich; Un|wirk|lich|keit, die; -
un|wirk|sam; ein -es Mittel; **Un|wirk|sam|keit,** die; -
un|wirsch (unfreundlich)
un|wirt|lich (unbewohnt, einsam; unfruchtbar); eine -e Gegend; **Un|wirt|lich|keit,** die; -
un|wirt|schaft|lich; Un|wirt|schaft|lich|keit, die; -
un|wis|send; Un|wis|sen|heit, die; -; **un|wis|sen|schaft|lich; un|wis|sent|lich**
un|wohl; mir ist unwohl; unwohl sein; **Un|wohl|sein,** das; -s; wegen Unwohlseins
Un|wort (unschönes, unerwünschtes Wort)
Un|wucht, die; -, -en (ungleich verteilte Massen [an einem Rad])
un|wür|dig; Un|wür|dig|keit, die; -
Un|zahl, die; - (sehr große Zahl); **un|zähl|bar** [*auch* 'un...]; **un|zäh|lig** [*auch* 'un...] (sehr viel); unzählige Notleidende; (↑R 47:) es haben sich Unzählige an der Aktion beteiligt; unzählige Mal, unzählige Male
un|zähm|bar [*auch* 'un...]
[1]**Un|ze,** die; -, -n ‹lat.› (Gewicht)
[2]**Un|ze,** die; -, -n ‹griech.› (*selten für* Jaguar)
Un|zeit, die; *nur noch in* zur - (zu unpassender Zeit); **un|zeit|ge|mäß; un|zei|tig** (unreif)
un|zen|siert
un|zen|wei|se
un|zer|brech|lich [*auch* ...'brɛç...]; **Un|zer|brech|lich|keit,** die; -
un|zer|kaut
un|zer|reiß|bar [*auch* 'un...]
un|zer|stör|bar [*auch* 'un...]; **un|zer|stört**
un|zer|trenn|bar [*auch* 'un...]; **un|zer|trenn|lich** [*auch* 'un...]
Un|zi|al|buch|sta|be; Un|zi|a|le, die; -, -n ‹lat.› (zollgroßer Buchstabe); **Un|zi|al|schrift,** die; -
un|zie|mend; un|ziem|lich (*veraltend für* ungehörig)
un|zi|vi|li|siert
Un|zucht, die; -; **un|züch|tig; Un|züch|tig|keit**
un|zu|frie|den; Un|zu|frie|den|heit, die; -
un|zu|gäng|lich; Un|zu|gäng|lich|keit, die; -
un|zu|kömm|lich (*österr. für* nicht ausreichend); eine -e Nahrung; **Un|zu|kömm|lich|keit,** die; -, -en (*österr. für* Missstand; *schweiz. auch für* Unzulänglichkeit)
un|zu|läng|lich; Un|zu|läng|lich|keit
un|zu|läs|sig; Un|zu|läs|sig|keit, die;
un|zu|mut|bar; Un|zu|mut|bar|keit
un|zu|rech|nungs|fä|hig; Un|zu|rech|nungs|fä|hig|keit, die; -

un|zu|rei|chend
un|zu|sam|men|hän|gend
un|zu|stän|dig; Un|zu|stän|dig|keit, die; -
un|zu|stell|bar; -e Sendungen
un|zu|träg|lich; Un|zu|träg|lich|keit, die; -
un|zu|tref|fend; (↑R 47:) Unzutreffendes bitte streichen!
un|zu|ver|läs|sig; Un|zu|ver|läs|sig|keit, die; -
un|zweck|mä|ßig; Un|zweck|mä|ßig|keit, die; -
un|zwei|deu|tig; Un|zwei|deu|tig|keit, die; -
un|zwei|fel|haft [*auch* ...'tsvai...]
U|pa|ni|schad, die; -, ...schaden *meist Plur.* ⟨sanskr.⟩ (Gruppe altind. philosophisch-theologischer Schriften)
Up|date ['apde:t], das; -s, -s ⟨engl.⟩ (*EDV* Aktualisierung; aktualisierte [u. verbesserte] Version eines Programms, einer Datei o. Ä.)
UPI [jupi'ai] = United Press International
Up|per|class ['apə(r)kla:s], die; - ⟨engl.⟩ (Oberschicht)
Up|per|cut ['apə(r)kat], der; -s, -s ⟨engl.⟩ (*Boxen* Aufwärtshaken)
üp|pig; Üp|pig|keit, die; -
Upp|sa|la (schwed. Stadt); **Upp|sa|la|er** (↑R 103)
up to date [ap tu 'de:t] ⟨engl.⟩ (zeitgemäß, auf der Höhe)
Ur, der; -[e]s, -e (Auerochse)
Ur|ab|stim|mung (Abstimmung aller Mitglieder einer Organisation, bes. einer Gewerkschaft, über die Ausrufung eines Streiks)
Ur|adel (↑R 132)
Ur‿ahn, ...ah|ne (der; Urgroßvater; Vorfahr), **...ah|ne** (die; Urgroßmutter)
U|ral, der; -[s] (Gebirge zwischen Asien u. Europa; Fluss); **u|ral|al|ta|isch;** -e Sprachen; **U|ral|ge|biet; u|ra|lisch** (aus der Gegend des Ural)
ur|alt; Ur|al|ter, das; -s; von uralters her (↑R 46)
U|rä|mie (↑R 132), die; - ⟨griech.⟩ (*Med.* Harnvergiftung); **u|rä|misch**
U|ran, das; -s ⟨nach dem Planeten Uranus⟩ (radioaktives chem. Element, Metall; *Zeichen* U); **U|ran‿berg|werk, ...erz**
Ur|an|fang; ur|an|fäng|lich
Ur|angst
u|ran|hal|tig
U|ra|nia (Muse der Sternkunde; Beiname der Aphrodite); **U|ra|nis|mus,** der; - (*selten für* Homosexualität); **U|ra|nist,** der; -en, -en; ↑R 126 (*selten für* Homosexueller); **U|ran|mi|ne; U|ra|nos** *vgl.* [1]Uranus; **U|ran|pech|blen|de** (radiumhaltiges Mineral); **[1]U|ra|nus,** U|ra|nos (griech. Gott des Himmels); **[2]U|ra|nus,** der; - (ein Planet)
u|ras|sen (*österr. ugs. für* verschwenden); du urasst
U|rat, das; -[e]s, -e ⟨griech.⟩ (*Chemie* Harnsäuresalz); **u|ra|tisch**
ur|auf|füh|ren; *meist im Infinitiv u. Partizip II gebr.;* die Oper wurde uraufgeführt; **Ur|auf|füh|rung**
U|rä|us|schlan|ge ⟨griech.; dt.⟩ (afrik. Hutschlange, als Sonnensymbol am Diadem der altägypt. Könige)
ur|ban ⟨lat.⟩ (städtisch; gebildet; weltmännisch); **Ur|ban** (m. Vorn.); **Ur|ba|ni|sa|ti|on,** die; -, -en; **ur|ba|ni|sie|ren** (verstädtern); **Ur|ba|ni|sie|rung; Ur|ba|nis|tik,** die; - (Wissenschaft des Städtebaus); **Ur|ba|ni|tät,** die; - (Bildung, weltmännische Art; städtische Atmosphäre)
ur|bar; - machen; **Ur|bar** [*auch* 'u:r...], das; -s, -e *u.* Ur|ba|ri|um, das; -s, ...ien [...iən] (mittelalterliches Güter- u. Abgabenverzeichnis großer Grundherrschaften; Grundbuch); **ur|ba|ri|sie|ren** (*schweiz. für* urbar machen); **Ur|ba|ri|sie|rung** (*schweiz. für* Urbarmachung); **Ur|ba|ri|um** *vgl.* Urbar; **Ur|bar|ma|chung**
Ur|be|deu|tung
Ur|be|ginn; von - der Welt
Ur|be|stand|teil, der
Ur|be|völ|ke|rung
Ur|be|woh|ner
ur|bi et or|bi ⟨lat., „der Stadt [d. i. Rom] und dem Erdkreis"⟩; etwas - - - (allgemein) verkünden
Ur|bild; ur|bild|lich
ur|chig (*schweiz. für* urwüchsig)
Ur|chris|ten|tum; ur|christ|lich
Urd (*nord. Mythol.* Norne der Vergangenheit)
Ur|darm (*Biol.* einen Hohlraum umschließende Einstülpung mit einer Mündung nach außen); **Ur|darm|tier** (*für* Gasträa)
ur|deutsch (typisch deutsch)
Ur|druck *Plur.* ...drucke (Erstveröffentlichung eines Schachproblems)
Ur|du, das; - (eine neuind. Sprache, Amtssprache in Pakistan)
ur|ei|gen; ur|ei|gen|tüm|lich
Ur|ein|woh|ner
Ur|el|tern *Plur.*
Ur|en|kel; Ur|en|ke|lin
U|re|ter, der; -s, *Plur.* ...teren, *auch* - ⟨griech.⟩ (*Med.* Harnleiter); **U|reth|ra** (↑R 130), die; -, ...thren (Harnröhre); **u|re|tisch** (harntreibend)
Ur|fas|sung
Ur|feh|de (im MA. eidliches Friedensversprechen mit Verzicht auf Rache); - schwören
Ur|form; ur|for|men; *nur im Infinitiv u. Partizip II gebr. (Technik)*
Urft, die; - (r. Nebenfluss der Rur); **Urft|tal|sper|re,** die; - (↑R 105)
Ur|ge|mein|de (urchristliche Gemeinde)
ur|ge|müt|lich
ur|gent ⟨lat.⟩ (*veraltet für* dringend); **Ur|genz,** die; -, -en *(veraltet)*
ur|ger|ma|nisch
Ur|ge|schich|te, die; -; **Ur|ge|schicht|ler; ur|ge|schicht|lich**
Ur|ge|sell|schaft, die; -
Ur|ge|stalt
Ur|ge|stein
Ur|ge|walt
ur|gie|ren ⟨lat.⟩ (*veraltet, noch österr. für* drängen)
Ur‿groß|el|tern *(Plur.),* **...groß|mut|ter; ur|groß|müt|ter|lich; Ur|groß|va|ter; ur|groß|vä|ter|lich**
Ur|grund
Ur|he|ber; Ur|he|be|rin; Ur|he|ber|recht; ur|he|ber|recht|lich; Ur|he|ber|schaft, die; -; **Ur|he|ber|schutz**
Ur|hei|mat
U|ri (schweiz. Kanton)
U|ria, U|ri|as, *ökum.* U|ri|ja (bibl. m. Eigenn.); *vgl.* Uriasbrief
U|ri|an, der; -s, -e (unwillkommener Gast; *nur Sing.:* Teufel)
U|ri|as *vgl.* Uria; **U|ri|as|brief** (Brief, der dem Überbringer Unheil bringt); **U|ri|el** [...e:l, *auch* ...εl] (einer der Erzengel)
u|rig (urtümlich; originell)
U|ri|ja *vgl.* Uria
U|rin, der; -s, -e *Plur. selten* ⟨lat.⟩ (Harn); **U|ri|nal,** das; -s, -e (Harnflasche; Becken zum Urinieren für Männer); **u|ri|nie|ren** (harnen)
Ur|ins|tinkt
U|rin|un|ter|su|chung
Ur|kan|ton (Kanton der Urschweiz)
Ur|kir|che
Ur|knall, der; -[e]s (Explodieren der Materie bei der Entstehung des Weltalls)
ur|ko|misch
Ur|kraft, die
Ur|kun|de, die; -, -n; **ur|kun|den** (*fachspr. für* in Urkunden schreiben, urkundlich erscheinen); **Ur|kun|den‿fäl|schung, ...for|schung, ...leh|re, ...samm|lung; ur|kund|lich; Ur|kunds‿be|am|te, ...re|gis|ter**
Ur|land|schaft

Ur|laub, der; -[e]s, -e; in *od.* im - sein; **ur|lau|ben** *(ugs.)*; **Ur|lau|ber; Ur|lau|be|rin; Ur|lau|ber|zug** ⟨*zu* [1]Zug⟩; **Ur|laubs‿be|kannt|schaft, ...bräu|ne, ...geld, ...ge|such, ...kas|se, ...lis|te; ur|laubs|reif; Ur|laubs‿rei|se, ...schein, ...sper|re, ...tag, ...ver|tre|tung, ...zeit**
Ur|meer
Ur|mensch, der; **ur|mensch|lich**
Ur|me|ter, das; -s (in Paris aufbewahrtes, ursprüngliches Normalmaß des Meters)
Ur|mut|ter *Plur.* ...mütter (Stammmutter)
Ur|ne, die; -, -n ⟨lat.⟩ ([Aschen]gefäß; Behälter für Stimm- und Wahlzettel); **Ur|nen‿fried|hof, ...gang** (der; *svw.* Wahl), **...grab, ...hal|le**
Ur|ner; ↑R 103 (von Uri); - See (Teil des Vierwaldstätter Sees); **ur|ne|risch** (aus Uri)
Ur|ning, der; -s, -e; *vgl.* Uranist
u|ro|ge|ni|tal ⟨griech.; lat.⟩ (zu den Harn- und Geschlechtsorganen gehörend); **U|ro|ge|ni|tal|sys|tem; U|ro|lith** [*auch* ...'lit], der; *Gen.* -s *u.* -en, *Plur.* -e[n] (↑R 126) ⟨griech.⟩ (Harnstein); **U|ro|lo|ge,** der; -n, -n; ↑R 126 (Arzt für Krankheiten der Harnorgane); **U|ro|lo|gie,** die; - (Lehre von den Erkrankungen der Harnorgane); **U|ro|lo|gin; u|ro|lo|gisch**
Ur|oma (↑R 132; *Kinderspr.*); **Ur|opa** (↑R 132; *Kinderspr.*)
U|ro|sko|pie, die; -, ...ien ⟨griech.⟩ (Harnuntersuchung)
Ur|pflan|ze
ur|plötz|lich
Ur|pro|dukt; Ur|pro|duk|ti|on (Gewinnung von Rohstoffen)
Ur|quell, Ur|quel|le
Urs (m. Vorn.)
Ur|sa|che; Ur|sa|chen|for|schung; ur|säch|lich; Ur|säch|lich|keit
Ur|schel, die; -, -n (*landsch. für* törichte [junge] Frau)
ur|schen (*ostmitteld. für* vergeuden); du urschst
Ur|schlamm, der; -[e]s
Ur|schleim, der; -[e]s
Ur|schrift; ur|schrift|lich
Ur|schweiz (Gebiet der ältesten Eidgenossenschaft [Uri, Schwyz, Unterwalden])
Ur|sel (w. Vorn.)
ur|sen|den; *nur im Infinitiv u. Partizip II gebr.*; **Ur|sen|dung** (erstmalige Sendung im Rundfunk od. Fernsehen)
Ur|se|ren|tal, das; -[e]s, *auch* Ur|se|ren (Tal der oberen Reuß im Kanton Uri); **Urs|ner** (↑R 103)
urspr. = ursprünglich
Ur|spra|che
Ur|sprung; ur|sprüng|lich (*Abk.* urspr.); **Ur|sprüng|lich|keit,** die; -; **Ur|sprungs‿ge|biet, ...land, ...nach|weis, ...zeug|nis**
urst (*regional ugs. für* großartig, sehr [schön])
Ur|stand, der; -[e]s, Urstände (*veraltet für* Urzustand); **Ur|ständ,** die; - (*veraltet für* Auferstehung); *nur scherzh. in* fröhliche - feiern (aus der Vergessenheit wieder auftauchen)
Ur|stoff; ur|stoff|lich
Ur|strom|tal
Ur|su|la (w. Vorn.); **Ur|su|li|ne,** die; -, -n *u.* Ur|su|li|ne|rin, die; -, -nen ⟨nach der Märtyrerin Ursula⟩ (Angehörige eines kath. Ordens); **Ur|su|li|nen|schu|le; Ur|su|li|ne|rin** *vgl.* Ursuline
Ur|teil, das; -s, -e
Ur|teil|chen (Elementarteilchen)
ur|tei|len; Ur|teils|be|grün|dung; ur|teils|fä|hig; Ur|teils‿fä|hig|keit (die; -), **...fin|dung, ...kraft,** (die; -); **ur|teils|los; Ur|teils‿schel|te** (öffentliche Kritik an einem gerichtlichen Urteil), **...spruch, ...ver|kün|dung, ...ver|mö|gen, ...voll|stre|ckung, ...voll|zug**
Ur|text
Ur|tier|chen *meist Plur.* (einzelliges tierisches Lebewesen)
Ur|ti|ka|ria, die; - ⟨lat.⟩ (*Med.* Nesselsucht)
Ur|trieb
ur|tüm|lich (ursprünglich; natürlich); **Ur|tüm|lich|keit,** die; -
Ur|typ, Ur|ty|pus
[1]**U|ru|gu|ay** [...'guai, *auch* 'u...], der; -[s] (Fluss in Südamerika); [2]**U|ru|gu|ay** (Staat in Südamerika); **U|ru|gu|ay|er** (↑R 103); **U|ru|gu|ay|e|rin; u|ru|gu|ay|isch**
Ur|ur‿ahn, ...en|kel, ...groß|mut|ter, ...groß|va|ter
Ur|va|ter (Stammvater); **ur|vä|ter|lich; Ur|vä|ter|zeit;** seit -en
ur|ver|wandt; Ur|ver|wandt|schaft
Ur|viech, Ur|vieh (*ugs. scherzh. für* urwüchsiger, etwas komisch wirkender Mensch)
Ur|vo|gel
Ur|volk
Ur‿wahl *(Politik)*, **...wäh|ler**
Ur|wald; Ur|wald|ge|biet
Ur|welt; ur|welt|lich
ur|wüch|sig; Ur|wüch|sig|keit, die; -
Ur|zeit; seit -en; **ur|zeit|lich**
Ur|zel|le
Ur|zeu|gung, die; - (elternlose Entstehung von Lebewesen)
Ur|zi|dil (österr. Schriftsteller)
Ur|zu|stand; ur|zu|ständ|lich
u. s. = ut supra
US[A] = United States [of America] [ju'naitid 'ste:ts (əv ə'mɛrikə)] *Plur.* (Vereinigte Staaten [von Amerika])
U|sam|ba|ra (Gebirgszug in Tanganjika); **U|sam|ba|ra|veil|chen** (↑R 105)
US-A|me|ri|ka|ner [u:'ɛs...]; **US-a|me|ri|ka|nisch** (↑R 26 *u.* R 60)
U|sance [y'zã:s], die; -, -n [...s(ə)n] ⟨franz.⟩ (Brauch, Gepflogenheit im Geschäftsverkehr); **u|sance|mä|ßig; U|san|cen|han|del** (Devisenhandel in fremder Währung); **U|sanz** [u'zants], die; -, -en (*schweiz. für* Usance)
Us|be|ke, der; -n, -n; ↑R 126 (Angehöriger eines Turkvolkes); **us|be|kisch; Us|be|kis|tan** (↑R 132; Staat im nördl. Mittelasien)
U|schi (w. Vorn.)
US-Dol|lar [u:'ɛs...]; ↑R 26; *vgl.* Dollar
U|se|dom (Insel in der Ostsee)
U|ser ['ju:zə(r)], der; -s, - ⟨engl.⟩ (jmd., der Drogen nimmt; *EDV* Benutzer, Anwender eines Systems, Programms)
usf. = und so fort
U|so, der; -s ⟨ital.⟩ ([Handels]brauch, Gewohnheit); *vgl.* Usus
U-Strab, die; -, -s; ↑R 26 (*kurz für* Unterpflaster[straßen]bahn)
u|su|ell ⟨franz.⟩ (gebräuchlich, üblich)
U|sur|pa|ti|on, die; -, -en ⟨lat.⟩ (widerrechtliche Besitz-, Machtergreifung); **U|sur|pa|tor,** der; -s, ...oren (eine Usurpation Erstrebender); **u|sur|pa|to|risch; u|sur|pie|ren; U|sur|pie|rung**
U|sus, der; - ⟨lat.⟩ (Brauch, Gewohnheit, Sitte)
usw. = und so weiter
Ut. = Utah
U|ta, U|te (*dt. Sage* Mutter der Nibelungenkönige; w. Vorn.)
U|tah ['ju:ta] (Staat in den USA; *Abk.* Ut.)
U|ten|sil, das; -s, -ien [...iən] *meist Plur.* ⟨lat.⟩ ([notwendiges] Gerät, Gebrauchsgegenstand)
u|te|rin ⟨lat.⟩ (*Med.* auf die Gebärmutter bezüglich); **U|te|rus,** der; -, ...ri (Gebärmutter)
Ut|gard (*nord. Mythol.* Reich der Dämonen u. Riesen)
u|ti|li|tär ⟨lat.⟩ (auf den Nutzen bezüglich); **U|ti|li|ta|ri|er** [...iər] (*svw.* Utilitarist); **U|ti|li|ta|ris|mus,** der; - (Nützlichkeitslehre, -standpunkt); **U|ti|li|ta|rist,** der;

-en, -en; ↑R 126 (nur auf den Nutzen Bedachter; Vertreter des Utilitarismus); **u|ti|li|ta|ris|tisch; U|ti|li|tät,** die; - (*veraltet für* Nützlichkeit); **U|ti|li|täts|leh|re**

Ut|lan|de *Plur.* ‹„Außenlande"› (Landschaftsbez. für die Nordfries. Inseln, bes. die Halligen mit Pellworm u. Nordstrand)

U|to|pia, U|to|pi|en [...i̯ən], das; -s *meist ohne Artikel* ‹griech.› (erdachtes Land); **U|to|pie,** die; -, ...i̯en (als unausführbar geltender Plan; Zukunftstraum); **U|to|pi|en** *vgl.* Utopia; **u|to|pisch** (schwärmerisch; unerfüllbar); **U|to|pis|mus,** der; -, ...men (Neigung zu Utopien; utopische Vorstellung); **U|to|pist,** der; -en, -en; ↑R 126 (Schwärmer)

Ut|ra|quis|mus (↑R 130), der; - ‹lat.› (Lehre der Utraquisten); **Ut|ra|quist,** der; -en, -en; ↑R 126 (Angehöriger einer hussitischen Richtung, die das Abendmahl in beiderlei Gestalt [Brot u. Wein] forderte); **ut|ra|quis|tisch** (den Utraquismus betreffend)

Ut|recht [*niederl.* 'y:trɛxt] (niederl. Provinz u. Stadt); **Ut|rech|ter** (↑R 103)

Ut|ril|lo [u'trilj̯o] (↑R 130; franz. Maler)

ut sup|ra ‹lat.› (↑R 130; *Musik* wie oben; *Abk.* u. s.)

Utz (m. Vorn.)

u. U. = unter Umständen

u. ü. V. = unter üblichem Vorbehalt

UV = ultraviolett (*in* UV-Strahlen u. a.)

u. v. a. = und viele[s] andere

u. v. a. m. = und viele[s] andere mehr

UV-bestrahlt; ↑R 26; **UV-Fil|ter** [u'fau̯...]; ↑R 26 (*Fotogr.* Filter zur Dämpfung der ultravioletten Strahlen); **UV-Lam|pe;** ↑R 26 (Höhensonne); **UV-Strah|len** *Plur.*; ↑R 26 (*Abk. für* ultraviolette Strahlen); **UV-Strah|lung,** die; -; ↑R 26 (Höhenstrahlung)

U|vu|la ['u:vula], die; -, ...lae [...lɛ:] ‹lat.› (*Med.* Gaumenzäpfchen); **u|vu|lar** (*Sprachw.* mit dem Zäpfchen gebildet)

u. W. = unseres Wissens

Ü-Wa|gen; ↑R 26 (*kurz für* Übertragungswagen)

U|we (m. Vorn.)

u. Z. = unsere[r] Zeitrechnung

Uz, der; -es, -e (*ugs. für* Neckerei); **Uz|bru|der** (*ugs. für* jmd., der gern andere neckt); **u|zen** (*ugs.*); du uzt; **U|ze|rei** (*ugs.*); **Uz|na|me** (*ugs.*)

u. zw. = und zwar

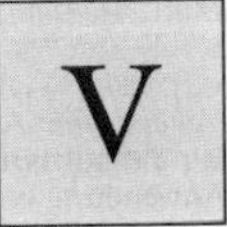

V (Buchstabe); das V; des V, die V, *aber* das v in Steven (↑R 60); der Buchstabe V, v

v = velocitas [v...] ‹lat.› (*Zeichen für* Geschwindigkeit)

V = *chem. Zeichen für* Vanadium

V = Volt; Volumen (Rauminhalt)

V (röm. Zahlzeichen) = 5

V, vert = vertatur

v. = vom; von; vor (*vgl. d.*)

v. = vide; vidi

V. = Vers

VA = Voltampere

Va. = [2]Virginia

v. a. = vor allem

Va|banque, *auch* **va banque** [va 'bã:k] ‹franz., „es gilt die Bank"›; Vabanque, *auch* va banque spielen (alles aufs Spiel setzen); **Va|banque|spiel,** das; -[e]s

va|cat ['va...] ‹lat., „es fehlt"› (nicht vorhanden, leer); *vgl.* Vakat

Va|che|le|der ['vaʃ...], das; -s ‹franz.; dt.› (glaciertes Sohlenleder)

Va|de|me|kum [v...], das; -s, -s ‹lat.› (Taschenbuch; Leitfaden, Ratgeber)

Va|di|um [v...], das; -s, ...ien [...i̯ən] ‹germ.-mlat.› (*im älteren dt. Recht* symbolisches Pfand)

va|dos [v...] ‹lat.› (*Geol. in Bezug auf Grundwasser* von Niederschlägen herrührend)

Va|duz [fa'duts, *auch* va'du:ts] (Hptst. des Fürstentums Liechtenstein)

vae vic|tis! ['vɛ: 'vikti:s] ‹lat., „wehe den Besiegten!"›

vag *vgl.* vage; **Va|ga|bon|da|ge** [vagabɔn'da:ʒə, *österr.* ...'da:ʒ], die; - ‹franz.› (Landstreicherei); **Va|ga|bund** [v...], der; -en, -en; ↑R 126 (Landstreicher); **Va|ga|bun|den|le|ben,** das; -s; **Va|ga|bun|den|tum,** das; -s; **va|ga|bun|die|ren** ([arbeitslos] umherziehen, herumstrolchen); vagabundierende Ströme (*Elektrotechnik*); **Va|gant,** der; -en, -en; ↑R 126 (fahrender Student od. Kleriker im MA.); **Va|gan|ten-dich|tung** (die; -), **...lied; va|ge,** vag (unbestimmt; ungewiss); **Vag|heit** (Unbestimmtheit, Ungewissheit); **va|gie|ren** (*geh. für* umherschweifen, -ziehen)

Va|gi|na [v..., *auch* 'va:...], die; -, ...nen ‹lat.› (*Med.* weibl. Scheide); **va|gi|nal** (die Scheide betreffend); **Va|gi|nis|mus,** der; -, ...men (*Med.* Scheidenkrampf)

Va|gus [v...], der; - ‹lat.› (*Med.* ein Hirnnerv)

va|kant [v...] ‹lat.› (leer; unbesetzt, offen, frei); **Va|kanz,** die; -, -en (freie Stelle; *landsch. für* Ferien); **Va|kat,** das; -[s], -s (*Druckw.* leere Seite); *vgl.* vacat; **Va|ku|o|le,** die; -, -n (*Biol.* mit Flüssigkeit od. Nahrung gefülltes Bläschen im Zellplasma, insbesondere der Einzeller); **Va|ku|um,** das; -s, *Plur.* ...kua *od.* ...kuen ([nahezu] luftleerer Raum); **Va|ku|um-ap|pa|rat, ...brem|se, ...me|ter** (das; -s, -; Unterdruckmesser), **...pum|pe** ([Aus]saugpumpe), **...röh|re; va|ku|um|ver|packt; Va|ku|um|ver|pa|ckung**

Vak|zin [v...], das; -s, -e ‹lat.› (*svw.* Vakzine); **Vak|zi|na|ti|on,** Vakzi|nie|rung, die; -, -en (*Med.* Schutzimpfung); **Vak|zi|ne,** die; -, -n (Impfstoff aus Krankheitserregern); **vak|zi|nie|ren; Vak|zi|nie|rung** *vgl.* Vakzination

Va|land ['fa:...] (*ältere Nebenform von* Voland)

va|le! ['va:le] ‹lat., „leb wohl!"›

Va|len|cia [va'lɛn(t)si̯a] (span. Stadt)

Va|len|ci|ennes|spit|ze [valã'si̯ɛn...] ‹nach der franz. Stadt› (sehr feine Klöppelspitze)

Va|lens ['va:...] (röm. Kaiser); **Va|len|tin** (m. Vorn.); **Va|len|ti|ne** (w. Vorn.); **Va|len|tins|tag** (14. Febr.)

Va|lenz [v...], die; -, -en ‹lat.› (*Chemie* Wertigkeit; *Sprachw.* Eigenschaft des Verbs, im Satz Ergänzungsbestimmungen zu fordern)

Va|le|ri|an, Va|le|ri|a|nus [v...] (m. Vorn.); **Va|le|ri|a|na,** die; -, ...nen (*Bot.* Baldrian); **Va|le|rie** [...i̯ə, *auch* ...'ri:] (w. Vorn.); **Va|le|ri|us** (röm. Kaiser)

Va|lé|ry [vale'ri] (franz. Dichter)

Va|les|ka [v...] (w. Vorn.)

[1]Va|let [va'lɛt, *auch* va'le:t], das; -s, -s ‹lat.› (Lebewohl; veralteter Abschiedsgruß); - sagen

[2]Va|let [va'le:], der; -s, -s ‹franz.› (Bube im franz. Kartenspiel)

Va|leur [va'lø:r], der; -s, -s, *auch* die; -, -s ‹franz.› (*veraltet für* Wert[papier]; *meist Plur.: Malerei* Farbwert, Farbtonabstufung); **Va|li|da|ti|on** [v...], die; -, -en ‹lat.› (Gültigkeitserklärung; *auch svw.* Validierung); **va|li|die|ren** ([rechts]gültig machen); **Va|li|die|rung,** die; -, -en (das Validieren);

Va|li|di|tät, die; - (*veraltet für* Rechtsgültigkeit; *bes. Psych.* Zuverlässigkeit [eines Versuchs])
val|le|ra! [v..., *auch* f...]; **val|le|ri, val|le|ra!**
Val|let|ta [v...] (Hptst. von Malta)
Va|lo|ren [v...] *Plur.* ‹lat.› (*Wirtsch.* Wert-, Schmucksachen, Wertpapiere); **Va|lo|ren|ver|si|che|rung; Va|lo|ri|sa|ti|on,** die; -, -en (staatl. Preisbeeinflussung zugunsten der Produzenten); **va|lo|ri|sie|ren** (Preise durch staatl. Maßnahmen zugunsten der Produzenten anheben); **Va|lo|ri|sie|rung** (*svw.* Valorisation)
Val|pa|rai|so [v...] (↑R 103); **Val|pa|ra|i|so** [*auch* ...'raịzo] (Stadt in Chile)
Va|lu|ta [v...], die; -, ...ten ‹ital.› (Geld in ausländischer Währung; [Gegen]wert; *nur Plur.:* Zinsscheine ausländ. Wertpapiere); **Va|lu|ta‿an|lei|he, ...klau|sel, ...kre|dit** (der); **Va|lu|ta|mark,** die; - (ehem. Rechnungseinheit in der DDR); **va|lu|tie|ren** (ein Datum festsetzen, das für den Zeitpunkt der Leistung maßgebend ist; *selten für* den Wert angeben, bewerten)
Val|va|ti|on [valv...], die; -, -en ‹franz.› (*Wirtsch.* [Ab]schätzung [von Münzen]; Wertbestimmung); **val|vie|ren** (*veraltet für* valutieren)
Vamp [vɛmp], der; -s, -s ‹engl.› (verführerische, kalt berechnende Frau); **Vam|pir** ['vam..., *auch* ...'pi:r], der; -s, -e ‹serbokroat.› (eine Fledermausart; *Volksglauben* Blut saugendes Nachtgespenst; *selten für* Wucherer, Blutsauger)
van [van, *auch* fan] ‹niederl.› (von); z. B. van Dyck
Va|na|di|um [v...], *auch* Va|na|din, das; -s ‹nlat.› (chem. Element, Metall; *Zeichen* V)
Van-Al|len-Gür|tel [vɛn'ɛlin...], der; -s (↑R 95) ‹nach dem amerik. Physiker› (ein Strahlungsgürtel der Erde)
Van|cou|ver [vɛn'ku:və(r)] (Insel u. Stadt in Kanada)
Van|da|le usw. *vgl.* Wandale usw.
Van-Dyck-Braun [van'daịk..., *auch* fan...], das; -s (↑R 95); *vgl.* Dyck
Va|nes|sa [v...] (w. Vorn.)
Va|nil|le [va'nil(j)ə, *schweiz.* 'vanil], die; - ‹franz.› (eine trop. Orchidee; Gewürz); **Va|nil|le‿eis, ...kip|ferl** (das; -s, -n; *österr. für* Gebäck mit Vanille), **...pud|ding, ...scho|te** (*zu* [3]Schote), **...so|ße, ...stan|ge, ...zu|cker; Va|nil|lin,** das; -s (Riech- u. Aromastoff; Vanilleersatz)
Va|nu|a|tu [vɛnu'a:tu:] (Inselstaat im Pazifik)
Va|po|ri|me|ter [v...], das; -s, - ‹lat.; griech.› (*veraltend für* Alkoholmesser); **Va|po|ri|sa|ti|on,** die; - ‹lat.› (*Med.* Anwendung von Wasserdampf zur Blutstillung); **va|po|ri|sie|ren** (*veraltend für* verdampfen; den Alkoholgehalt in Flüssigkeiten bestimmen)
Va|que|ro [va'ke:ro], der; -[s], -s ‹span.› (Cowboy im Südwesten der USA u. in Mexiko)
var. = Varietät (bei naturwiss. Namen)
Va|ra|na|si [v...] (Stadt in Indien); *vgl.* Benares
Va|ran|ger|fjord [v...] (↑R 132), der; -[e]s (der nordöstlichste Fjord in Norwegen)
Va|rel ['fa:...] (Stadt in Niedersachsen)
Va|ria [v...] *Plur.* ‹lat.› (*Buchw.* Vermischtes, Allerlei); **va|ri|a|bel** ‹franz.› (veränderlich, [ab]wandelbar); ...ab|le (↑R 130) Kosten; **Va|ri|a|bi|li|tät,** die; -, -en; (Veränderlichkeit); **Va|ri|a|ble** (↑R 130), die; -n, *Plur.* -n, *ohne Artikel fachspr. auch* - (*Math.* veränderliche Größe; *Ggs.* Konstante); zwei -[n]; **Va|ri|an|te,** die; -, -n (Abweichung, Abwandlung; verschiedene Lesart; Spielart); **va|ri|an|ten|reich; Va|ri|a|ti|on,** die; -, -en (Abwechslung; Abänderung; Abwandlung); **Va|ri|a|ti|ons|brei|te; va|ri|a|ti|ons|fä|hig; Va|ri|a|ti|ons|mög|lich|keit; Va|ri|e|tät** [vari|e...], die; -, -en (geringfügig abweichende Art, Spielart; *Abk.* var.)
Va|ri|e|tee, *auch* Va|ri|e|té, [vari|e'te:] (↑R 33), das; -s, -s ‹franz.› (Theater mit bunt wechselndem, unterhaltsamem Programm); **Va|ri|e|tee|the|a|ter,** *auch* Va|ri|e|té|the|a|ter
va|ri|ie|ren (verschieden sein; abweichen; verändern; [ab]wandeln)
va|ri|kös [v...] ‹lat.› (*Med.* die Krampfadern betreffend); **Va|ri|ko|se,** die; -, -n (Krampfaderleiden); **Va|ri|ko|si|tät,** die; -, -en (Krampfaderbildung); **Va|ri|ko|ze|le,** die; -, -n ‹lat.; griech.› (Krampfaderbruch)
Va|ri|nas [v..., *auch* va'ri:...], der; -, *Plur. (Sorten:)* - ‹nach dem früheren Namen der Stadt Barinas in Venezuela› (südamerik. Tabak)
Va|ri|o|la [v...], die; -, *Plur.* ...lä *u.* ...olen *u.* **Va|ri|o|le,** die; -, -n, *beide meist Plur.* ‹lat.› (*Med.* Pocken)
Va|ri|o|me|ter [v...], das; -s, - ‹lat.; griech.› (Vorrichtung zur Messung von Luftdruck- od. erdmagnetischen Schwankungen)
Va|ris|ki|sche [v...] *od.* **Va|ris|zi|sche Ge|bir|ge,** das; -n -s; ↑R 102 (mitteleurop. Gebirge der Steinkohlenzeit)
Va|ris|tor [v...], der; -s, ...oren ‹engl.› (*Elektrotechnik* spannungsabhängiger Widerstand)
Va|ri|ty|per ['vɛritaịpə(r)], der; -s, - ‹engl.› (auf dem Schreibmaschinenprinzip aufgebaute Setzmaschine)
Va|rix [v...], die; -, Varizen ‹lat.› (*Med.* Krampfader); **Va|ri|ze,** die; -, -n (*svw.* Varix); **Va|ri|zel|le,** die; -, -n *meist Plur.* (Windpocken)
Va|rus [v...] (altrömischer Feldherr)
Va|sa [v...], der; -[s], - (Angehöriger eines schwed. Königsgeschlechts)
Va|sall [v...], der; -en, -en (↑R 126) ‹franz.› (Lehnsmann im MA.); **Va|sal|len|staat** *Plur.* ...staaten; **Va|sal|len|tum,** das; -s
Väs|chen [v...] ‹*zu* Vase›
Vas|co da Ga|ma ['vasko - -] (port. Seefahrer)
Va|se [v...], die; -, -n ‹franz.› ([Zier]gefäß)
Va|sek|to|mie (↑R 132), die; -, ...ien ‹lat.; griech.› (*Med.* operative Entfernung eines Stückes des Samenleiters, Sterilisation)
Va|se|lin [v...], das; -s *u.* **Va|se|li|ne,** die; - ‹Kunstwort› (Salbengrundlage)
va|sen|för|mig [v...]; **Va|sen|ma|le|rei**
Va|so|mo|to|ren *Plur.* ‹lat.› (*Med.* Gefäßnerven); **va|so|mo|to|risch**
Va|ter, der; -s, Väter; **Va|ter‿bild, ...bin|dung; Vä|ter|chen; Va|ter‿fi|gur, ...freu|den** (*Plur.; nur in* - entgegensehen [bald Vater werden]), **...haus, ...land** (*Plur.* ...länder); **va|ter|län|disch; Va|ter|lands|lie|be; va|ter|lands‿lie|bend, ...los; Va|ter|lands‿ver|rä|ter, ...ver|tei|di|ger; vä|ter|lich; vä|ter|li|cher|seits; Vä|ter|lich|keit,** die; -; **va|ter|los; Va|ter|mör|der** (*ugs. auch für* hoher, steifer Kragen); **Va|ter|na|me,** Va|ters|na|me (Familien-, Zuname); **Va|ter|recht,** das; -[e]s *(Völkerk.)*; **Va|ter|schaft,** die; -, -en; die natürliche -; **Va|ter|schafts‿be|stim|mung, ...kla|ge; Va|ters|na|me** *vgl.* Vatername; **Va|ter‿stadt, ...stel|le** (*nur in* - vertreten), **...tag** (*scherzh. für* Him-

melfahrtstag); **Va|ter|un|ser,** das; -s, -; *aber im Gebet:* Vater unser im Himmel ...; **Va|ti,** der; -s, -s (*Koseform von* Vater)

Va|ti|kan [v...], der; -s (Residenz des Papstes in Rom; oberste Behörde der kath. Kirche); **va|ti|ka|nisch,** *aber* (↑R 108): die Vatikanische Bibliothek, das Vatikanische Konzil; **Va|ti|kan|stadt,** die; -

Vau|de|ville [vod(ə)'vi:l], das; -s, -s ‹franz.› (franz. volkstüml. Lied; Singspiel)

Vaughan Wil|li|ams [vɔ:n 'wiljəmz], Ralph [rɛlf] (engl. Komponist)

V-Aus|schnitt (↑R 25)

v. Chr. = vor Christo, vor Christus; **v. Chr. G.** = vor Christi Geburt

v. d. = vor der (*bei Ortsnamen,* z. B. Bad Homburg v. d. H. [vor der Höhe])

VDE = Verband Deutscher Elektrotechniker; **VDE-ge|prüft** (↑R 26 *u.* R 60)

VDI = Verein Deutscher Ingenieure

VdK = Verband der Kriegs- und Wehrdienstopfer, Behinderten und Sozialrentner

VDM = Verbi Divini Minister *od.* Ministra ‹lat.› (*schweiz. für* ordinierter reformierter Theologe *od.* ordinierte reformierte Theologin)

VDS = Verband Deutscher Studentenschaften, *jetzt* Vereinigte Deutsche Studentenschaften

vdt. = vidit

VEB = volkseigener Betrieb *(ehem. in der DDR); vgl.* volkseigen

Vech|ta ['fɛçta] (Stadt bei Oldenburg)

Vech|te ['fɛçtə], die; - (ein Fluss)

Ve|da [v...] *vgl.* Weda

Ve|det|te [v...], die; -, -n ‹franz.› (*svw.* [2]Star)

ve|disch [v...] *vgl.* wedisch

Ve|du|te [v...], die; -, -n ‹ital.› (*Malerei* naturgetreue Darstellung einer Landschaft); **Ve|du|ten‿ma|ler, ...ma|le|rei**

Ve|ga|ner ‹engl.› (Vegetarier, der auch auf Eier und Milchprodukte verzichtet); **ve|ge|ta|bil** [v...] *vgl.* vegetabilisch; **Ve|ge|ta|bi|li|en** [...iən] *Plur.* ‹lat.› (pflanzl. Nahrungsmittel); **ve|ge|ta|bi|lisch** (pflanzlich, Pflanzen...); **Ve|ge|ta|ri|a|ner** (*svw.* Vegetarier); **Ve|ge|ta|ri|er** [...iər] (jmd., der sich vorwiegend von pflanzl. Kost ernährt); **Ve|ge|ta|ri|e|rin** [...riə...]; **ve|ge|ta|risch** (pflanzlich, Pflanzen...); **Ve|ge|ta|ris|mus,** der; - (Ernährung durch pflanzl. Kost); **Ve|ge|ta|ti|on,** die; -, -en (Pflanzenwelt, -wuchs); **Ve|ge|ta|ti|ons‿ge|biet, ...kult, ...or|gan** *(Bot.),* **...pe|ri|o|de, ...punkt** *(Bot.);* **ve|ge|ta|tiv** (zur Vegetation gehörend, pflanzlich; *Biol.* ungeschlechtlich; *Med.* unbewusst); -es Nervensystem (dem Einfluss des Bewusstseins entzogenes Nervensystem); **ve|ge|tie|ren** (kümmerlich [dahin]leben)

ve|he|ment [v...]; ‹lat.› (heftig); **Ve|he|menz,** die; -

Ve|hi|kel [v...], das; -s, - ‹lat.› (schlechtes, altmodisches Fahrzeug; Hilfsmittel)

Vei|ge|lein (*veraltet für* Veilchen); **Vei|gerl,** das; -s, -n (*bayr., österr. für* Veilchen)

Veil [vɛj], Simone (franz. Politikerin)

Veil|chen; veil|chen|blau; Veil|chen‿duft, ...strauß, ...wur|zel

Veit [fait] (m. Vorn.); *vgl.* Vitus; **Veits‿boh|ne, ...tanz** (der; -es; ein Nervenleiden)

Vek|tor [v...], der; -s, ...oren ‹lat.› (physikal. od. math. Größe, die durch Pfeil dargestellt wird u. durch Angriffspunkt, Richtung und Betrag festgelegt ist); **Vek|tor|glei|chung** *(Math.);* **vek|to|ri|ell; Vek|tor‿raum, ...rech|nung**

Ve|la (*Plur. von* Velum); **Ve|lar** [v...], der; -s, -e ‹lat.› (*Sprachw.* Gaumensegellaut, Hintergaumenlaut, z. B. k)

Ve|laz|quez [ve'laskɛs], *span.* **Ve|láz|quez** [be'laθkɛθ] (span. Maler)

Ve|lin [ve..., *auch* ve'lɛ̃:], das; -s ‹franz.› (weiches Pergament; ungeripptes Papier)

Ve|lo [v...], das; -s, -s ‹*verkürzt aus* Veloziped› (*schweiz. für* Fahrrad); Velo fahren (Rad fahren); **Ve|lo|drom,** das; -s, -e ‹franz.› ([geschlossene] Radrennbahn); **Ve|lo|fah|ren,** das; -s *(schweiz.)*

[1]**Ve|lours** [və'lu:r, *auch* ve...], der; - [...lu:rs], - [...lu:rs] (Samt; Gewebe mit gerauter, weicher Oberfläche); [2]**Ve|lours,** das; -, *Plur. (Sorten:)* - (samtartiges Leder); **Ve|lours|le|der**

Ve|lo|zi|ped [v...], das; -[e]s, -e ‹franz.› (*veraltet für* Fahrrad)

Vel|pel ['fɛl...], der; -s, - ‹ital.› (*Nebenform von* Felbel)

Vel|ten [fɛl...] (m. Vorn.)

Velt|lin [v..., *auch, schweiz. nur,* f...], das; -s (Talschaft oberhalb des Comer Sees); [1]**Velt|li|ner** (↑R 103); - Wein; [2]**Velt|li|ner** (Wein)

Ve|lum [v...], das; -s, ...la ‹lat.› (Teil der gottesdienstl. Kleidung kath. Priester; Kelchtuch; *Med.* Gaumensegel); **Ve|lum pa|la|ti|num,** das; - -, ...la ...na (*Med.* Gaumensegel; weicher Gaumen)

Vel|vet ['vɛlvət], der *od.* das; -s, -s ‹engl.› (Baumwollsamt)

Ven|dee [vã'de:], *franz.* **Ven|dée,** die; - (franz. Departement); **Ven|de|er** (↑R 103 *u.* 105); **Ven|de|mi|aire** [vãde'miɛ:r], der; -[s], -s ‹franz., „Weinmonat"› (1. Monat des Kalenders der Franz. Revolution: 22. Sept. bis 21. Okt.)

Ven|det|ta [v...], die; -, ...tten ‹ital.› ([Blut]rache)

Ve|ne [v...], die; -, -n ‹lat.› (Blutgefäß, das zum Herzen führt)

Ve|ne|dig [v...] (ital. Stadt); *vgl.* Venezia; **Ve|ne|di|ger|grup|pe,** die; -; ↑R 105 (Gebirgsgruppe)

Ve|nen|ent|zün|dung [v...]

ve|ne|ra|bel [v...] ‹lat.› (*veraltet für* verehrungswürdig, ehrbar); **Ve|ne|ra|bi|le** [...le], das; -[s] (Allerheiligstes in der kath. Kirche)

ve|ne|risch [v...] ‹*zu* [1]Venus› (*Med.* auf die Geschlechtskrankheiten bezogen); -e Krankheiten

Ve|ne|ter [v...] (Bewohner von Venetien); **Ve|ne|ti|en** (ital. Region); **Ve|ne|zia** (*ital. Form von* Venedig); **Ve|ne|zi|a|ner;** ↑R 103 (Einwohner von Venedig); **Ve|ne|zi|a|ne|rin; ve|ne|zi|a|nisch**

Ve|ne|zo|la|ner [v...], Ve|ne|zu|e|ler (↑R 103); **Ve|ne|zo|la|ne|rin,** Ve|ne|zu|e|le|rin; **ve|ne|zo|la|nisch,** ve|ne|zu|e|lisch; **Ve|ne|zu|e|la** (Staat in Südamerika); **Ve|ne|zu|e|ler** usw. (↑R 103) *vgl.* Venezolaner usw.

Ve|nia Le|gen|di [v... -], die; - - ‹lat.› (Erlaubnis, an Hochschulen zu lehren)

ve|ni, vi|di, vi|ci ['ve:ni: 'vi:di: 'vi:tsi:] ‹lat., „ich kam, ich sah, ich siegte"› (Ausspruch Cäsars)

Venn [fɛn], das; -s; (↑R 102:) Hohes Venn (Teil der Eifel)

Ven|ner [f...], der; -s, - (*schweiz. für* Fähnrich)

ve|nös [v...]; ‹lat.› (*Med.* die Vene[n] betreffend)

Ven|til [v...], das; -s, -e ‹lat.› (Absperrvorrichtung; Luft-, Dampfklappe); **Ven|ti|la|ti|on,** die; -, -en ([Be]lüftung, Luftwechsel); **Ven|ti|la|tor,** der; -s, ...oren; **Ven|til|gum|mi,** der *u.* das; **ven|ti|lie|ren** (lüften; *übertr. für* sorgfältig erwägen); **Ven|ti|lie|rung; Ven|til‿kol|ben, ...spiel, ...steu|e|rung; Ven|tose** [vã'to:s], der; -[s], -s ‹franz., „Windmonat"› (6. Monat des Kalenders der

Franz. Revolution: 19. Febr. bis 20. März)
vent|ral [v...] (↑R 130) ‹lat.› (*Med.* den Bauch betreffend; bauchwärts); **Vent|ri|kel,** der; -s, - (Kammer [in Herz, Hirn usw.]); **vent|ri|ku|lär** (den Ventrikel betreffend); **Vent|ri|lo|quist,** der; -en, -en; ↑R 126 (Bauchredner)
[1]Ve|nus [v...] (röm. Liebesgöttin); **[2]Ve|nus,** die; - (ein Planet); **Ve|nus‿berg** (weiblicher Schamberg), **...flie|gen|fal|le** (eine Fleisch fressende Pflanze), **...hü|gel** (*svw.* Venusberg), **...son|de** (Raumsonde zur Erforschung des Planeten Venus)
ver... (*Vorsilbe von Verben,* z. B. verankern, du verankerst, verankert, zu verankern)
Ve|ra ['ve:ra] (w. Vorn.)
ver|aa|sen (*ugs. für* verschleudern, vergeuden)
ver|ab|fol|gen (*Amtsspr. veraltend* aus-, abgeben)
ver|ab|re|den; sich -; **ver|ab|re|de|ter|ma|ßen; Ver|ab|re|dung**
ver|ab|rei|chen; ein Medikament -; **Ver|ab|rei|chung**
ver|ab|säu|men (*besser nur:* versäumen)
ver|ab|scheu|en; ver|ab|scheu|ens|wert; Ver|ab|scheu|ung, die; -; **ver|ab|scheu|ungs|wür|dig**
ver|ab|schie|den; sich -; **Ver|ab|schie|dung; ver|ab|schie|dungs|reif;** ein -es Gesetz
ver|ab|so|lu|tie|ren; Ver|ab|so|lu|tie|rung
ver|ach|ten; das ist nicht zu - (*ugs. für* das ist gut, schön); **ver|ach|tens|wert; Ver|äch|ter; Ver|äch|te|rin; ver|ächt|lich; Ver|ächt|lich|ma|chung,** die; -; **Ver|ach|tung,** die; -; **ver|ach|tungs|voll; ver|ach|tungs|wür|dig** (*veraltend*)
Ve|ra|cruz, *eindeutschend* **Ve|ra|kruz** [*beide* vera'kru:s] (Staat u. Stadt in Mexiko)
ver|al|bern; Ver|al|be|rung
ver|all|ge|mei|nern; ich ...ere (↑R 16); **Ver|all|ge|mei|ne|rung**
ver|al|ten; veraltend; veraltet
Ve|ran|da [v...], die; -, ...den ‹engl.› (überdachter u. an den Seiten verglaster Anbau); **ve|ran|da|ar|tig; Ve|ran|da|auf|gang**
ver|än|der|bar; ver|än|der|lich; das Barometer steht auf „veränderlich"; **Ver|än|der|li|che,** die; -n, -n; ↑R 5 ff. (eine mathemat. Größe, deren Wert sich ändern kann; *Ggs.* Konstante); zwei -; **Ver|än|der|lich|keit; ver|än|dern;** sich -; **Ver|än|de|rung**

ver|ängs|ti|gen; ver|ängs|tigt; Ver|ängs|ti|gung
ver|an|kern; Ver|an|ke|rung
ver|an|la|gen (einschätzen); **ver|an|lagt;** gut, schlecht, künstlerisch - sein; **Ver|an|la|gung** (Einschätzung; Begabung); **Ver|an|la|gungs|steu|er,** die
ver|an|las|sen; du veranlasst, er veranlasst; du veranlasstest; veranlasst; veranlasse!; sich veranlasst sehen; **Ver|an|las|ser; Ver|an|las|sung;** zur weiteren - (*Amtsspr.; Abk.* z. w. V.); **Ver|an|las|sungs|wort** *Plur.* ...wörter (*für* Kausativ)
ver|an|schau|li|chen; Ver|an|schau|li|chung
ver|an|schla|gen (ansetzen); du veranschlagtest; er hat die Kosten viel zu niedrig veranschlagt; **Ver|an|schla|gung**
ver|an|stal|ten; Ver|an|stal|ter; Ver|an|stal|te|rin; Ver|an|stal|tung; Ver|an|stal|tungs|ka|len|der
ver|ant|wor|ten; ver|ant|wort|lich; eine -e Stellung; **Ver|ant|wort|lich|keit; Ver|ant|wor|tung; ver|ant|wor|tungs|be|wusst; Ver|ant|wor|tungs|be|wusst|sein; ver|ant|wor|tungs|freu|dig; Ver|ant|wor|tungs|ge|fühl,** das; -[e]s; **ver|ant|wor|tungs|los; Ver|ant|wor|tungs|lo|sig|keit,** die; -; **Ver|ant|wor|tungs|trä|ger; ver|ant|wor|tungs|voll**
ver|äp|peln (*ugs. für* veralbern, anführen); ich ...[e]le ihn (↑R 16)
ver|ar|beit|bar; Ver|ar|beit|bar|keit, die; -; **ver|ar|bei|ten; Ver|ar|bei|tung**
ver|ar|gen (*geh.*); jmdm. etwas -
ver|är|gern; Ver|är|ge|rung
ver|ar|men; Ver|ar|mung
ver|ar|schen (*derb für* veralbern)
ver|arz|ten (*ugs. für* [ärztl.] behandeln); **Ver|arz|tung** (*ugs.*)
ver|aschen (↑R 132; *Chemie* ohne Flamme verbrennen); du veraschst
ver|äs|teln, sich; der Baum verästelt sich; **Ver|äs|te|lung, Ver|äst|lung**
ver|ät|zen; Ver|ät|zung
ver|auk|ti|o|nie|ren (versteigern)
ver|aus|ga|ben (ausgeben); sich - (sich bis zur Erschöpfung anstrengen); **Ver|aus|ga|bung**
ver|aus|la|gen; Geld - (auslegen); **Ver|aus|la|gung**
ver|äu|ßer|lich (verkäuflich); **ver|äu|ßer|li|chen** (äußerlich, oberflächlich machen, werden); **Ver|äu|ßer|li|chung; ver|äu|ßern** (verkaufen); **Ver|äu|ße|rung**

Verb [v...], das; -s, -en ‹lat.› (*Sprachw.* Zeitwort, Tätigkeitswort, z. B. „laufen, bauen"); **ver|bal** (als Verb gebraucht; wörtlich; mündlich); -e Klammer; **Ver|ba|le,** das; -s, ...lien [...iən] *meist Plur.* (*Sprachw.* von einem Verb abgeleitetes Wort; *veraltet für* wörtl. Äußerung); **Ver|bal|in|ju|rie,** die; -, -n (Beleidigung mit Worten); **ver|ba|li|sie|ren** (in Worten ausdrücken; *Sprachw.* zu einem Verb umbilden); **Ver|ba|lis|mus,** der; - (Vorherrschaft des Wortes statt der Sache im Unterricht); **Ver|ba|list,** der; -en, -en; ↑R 126 (jemand, der sich zu sehr ans Wort klammert); **ver|ba|lis|tisch; ver|ba|li|ter** (*veraltend für* wörtlich)
ver|bal|lern (*ugs. für* verschießen)
ver|ball|hor|nen ‹nach dem Buchdrucker Bal[l]horn› (verschlimmbessern); **Ver|ball|hor|nung**
Ver|bal|no|te [v...] ‹lat.› (zu mündlicher Mitteilung bestimmte, nicht unterschriebene, vertrauliche diplomatische Note); **Ver|bal|stil,** der; -[e]s (Stil, der das Verb bevorzugt; *Ggs.* Nominalstil); **Ver|bal|sub|stan|tiv** (*Sprachw.* zu einem Verb gebildetes Substantiv, das [zum Zeitpunkt der Bildung] eine Geschehensbezeichnung ist, z. B. „Gabe, Zerrüttung")
Ver|band, der; -[e]s, ...bände; **Ver|band|kas|ten** *vgl.* Verbandskasten; **Ver|bands|kas|se; Ver|bands|kas|ten,** Ver|band|kasten; **Ver|bands|lei|ter,** der; **Ver|band[s]‿ma|te|ri|al, ...päck|chen, ...platz, ...stoff; Ver|bands‿vor|sit|zen|de, ...vor|stand; Ver|band[s]‿wat|te, ...zeug** (das; -[e]s), **...zim|mer**
ver|ban|nen; Ver|ban|nung; Ver|ban|nungs|ort
ver|bar|ri|ka|die|ren; sich -
Ver|bas|kum [v...], das; -s, ...ken ‹lat.› (*Bot.* Königskerze)
ver|bau|en
ver|bau|ern (*ugs. für* [geistig] abstumpfen); ich ...ere (↑R 16); **Ver|bau|e|rung,** die; -
Ver|bau|ung
ver|be|am|ten; Ver|be|am|tung, die; -
ver|bei|ßen; die Hunde hatten sich ineinander verbissen; sich den Schmerz - (sich den Schmerz nicht anmerken lassen); sich in eine Sache - (*ugs. für* hartnäckig an einer Sache festhalten)
ver|bel|len (*Jägerspr.* durch Bellen zum verwundeten od. verendeten Wild führen)
Ver|be|ne [v...], die; -, -n ‹lat.› (*Bot.* Eisenkraut)

ver|ber|gen *vgl.* [2]verborgen; **Ver|ber|gung**
Ver|bes|se|rer, Ver|bess|rer; **ver|bes|sern; Ver|bes|se|rung,** Ver|bess|rung; **ver|bes|se|rungs‿be|dürf|tig, ...fä|hig; Ver|bes|se|rungs‿vor|schlag, ...we|sen** (das; -s)
ver|beu|gen, sich; **Ver|beu|gung**
ver|beu|len
ver|bie|gen; Ver|bie|gung
ver|bies|tern, sich (*landsch. für* sich verirren; sich in etwas verrennen; verwirren, verärgern); ich ...ere mich (↑R 16); **ver|bies|tert** (*landsch. für* verstört, verärgert)
ver|bie|ten; Betreten verboten!; *vgl.* verboten
ver|bil|den; ver|bild|li|chen; Ver|bild|li|chung; Ver|bil|dung
ver|bil|li|gen; Ver|bil|li|gung
ver|bim|sen (*ugs. für* verprügeln)
ver|bin|den; Ver|bin|der *(Sport);* **ver|bind|lich** (höflich, zuvorkommend; bindend, verpflichtend); eine -e Zusage; **Ver|bind|lich|keit; Ver|bind|lich|keits|er|klä|rung; Ver|bin|dung; Ver|bin|dungs‿gra|ben, ...li|nie, ...mann** (*Plur.* ...männer *u.* ...leute; *Abk.* V-Mann), **...of|fi|zier, ...stel|le, ...stra|ße, ...stück, ...tür**
Ver|biss, der; -es, -e (*Jägerspr.* Abbeißen von Knospen, Trieben u. Ä. durch Wild); **ver|bis|sen;** er ist ein -er (zäher) Gegner; ein -es (verkrampftes) Gesicht; **Ver|bis|sen|heit,** die; -
ver|bit|ten; ich habe mir eine solche Antwort verbeten
ver|bit|tern; ich ...ere (↑R 16); verbittert; **Ver|bit|te|rung**
[1]**ver|bla|sen** (*Jägerspr.* erlegtes Wild mit einem Hornsignal anzeigen); den Hirsch, die Strecke -;
[2]**ver|bla|sen** (schwülstig, verschwommen); ein -er Stil; **Ver|bla|sen|heit**
ver|blas|sen; die Farbe verblasst; die Erinnerungen an die Kindheit sind verblasst
ver|blät|tern; eine Seite -
ver|bläu|en (*ugs. für* verprügeln)
Ver|bleib, der; -[e]s; **ver|blei|ben; Ver|blei|ben,** das; -s; dabei muss es sein - haben *(Amtsspr.)*
ver|blei|chen (bleich werden); du verblichst; du verblichest; verblichen; *vgl.* [2]bleichen
ver|blei|en (mit Blei versehen, auslegen; *auch für* plombieren [mit einer Bleiplombe versehen]); **Ver|blei|ung**
ver|blen|den (*Bauw. auch* [Mauerwerk o. Ä. mit besserem Material] verkleiden); **Ver|blen|dung**

ver|bleu|en *frühere Schreibung für* verbläuen
ver|bli|chen; -es Bild; **Ver|bli|che|ne,** der *u.* die; -n, -n; ↑R 5 ff. (*geh. für* Tote)
ver|blö|den *(ugs.);* **Ver|blö|dung,** die; -
ver|blüf|fen; verblüfft sein; **ver|blüf|fend; Ver|blüfft|heit,** die; -; **Ver|blüf|fung**
ver|blü|hen
ver|blümt (andeutend, umschreibend)
ver|blu|ten; sich -; **Ver|blu|tung**
ver|bo|cken (*ugs. für* fehlerhaft ausführen; verderben, verpfuschen)
Ver|bod|mung (*svw.* Bodmerei)
ver|bo|gen; -es Blech
ver|boh|ren, sich (*ugs. für* sich verrennen); **ver|bohrt;** er ist - (*ugs. für* uneinsichtig, starrköpfig); **Ver|bohrt|heit,** die; - *(ugs.)*
[1]**ver|bor|gen** (ausleihen)
[2]**ver|bor|gen;** eine -e Gefahr; (↑R 47): im Verborgenen (unbemerkt) bleiben, blühen; das Verborgene u. das Sichtbare; **Ver|bor|gen|heit,** die; -
ver|bos [v...] ‹lat.› (*geh. für* [allzu] wortreich, weitschweifig)
ver|bö|sern (*scherzh. für* schlimmer machen); ich ...ere (↑R 16)
Ver|bot, das; -[e]s, -e; **ver|bo|ten;** -er Eingang; -e Früchte; **ver|bo|te|ner|wei|se; Ver|bots‿schild** (*Plur.* ...schilder), **...ta|fel; ver|bots|wid|rig; Ver|bots|zei|chen**
ver|brä|men (am Rand verzieren; [eine Aussage] verschleiern, ausschmücken); **Ver|brä|mung**
ver|bra|ten (*ugs. für* verbrauchen); beim Neubau wurden große Summen verbraten
Ver|brauch, der; -[e]s, *Plur. (fachspr.)* ...bräuche; **ver|brau|chen; Ver|brau|cher; Ver|brau|cher‿auf|klä|rung, ...be|ra|tung, ...ge|nos|sen|schaft** (*für* Konsumgenossenschaft); **Ver|brau|che|rin; Ver|brau|cher‿markt, ...preis** (*vgl.* [2]Preis), **...ver|band, ...zent|ra|le; Ver|brauchs‿frist, ...gut** *(meist Plur.),* **...len|kung** (die; -), **...pla|nung; Ver|brauchs|steu|er, Ver|brauch|steu|er,** die (↑R 34)
ver|bre|chen; Ver|bre|chen, das; -s, -; **Ver|bre|chens|be|kämp|fung,** die; -; **Ver|bre|cher; Ver|bre|cher|al|bum** *(veraltend);* **Ver|bre|che|rin; ver|bre|che|risch; Ver|bre|cher|kar|tei; Ver|bre|cher|tum,** das; -s
ver|brei|ten; er hat diese Nachricht verbreitet; sich - (etwas ausführlich darstellen); **Ver|brei|ter;**

Ver|brei|te|rin; ver|brei|tern (breiter machen); ich ...ere (↑R 16); sich - (breiter werden); **Ver|brei|te|rung; Ver|brei|tung,** die; -; **Ver|brei|tungs|ge|biet**
ver|brenn|bar; ver|bren|nen; das Holz ist verbrannt; du hast dir den Mund verbrannt (*ugs. für* dir durch Reden geschadet); **Ver|bren|nung; Ver|bren|nungs‿ma|schi|ne, ...mo|tor**
ver|brie|fen ([urkundlich] sicherstellen); ein verbrieftes Recht
ver|brin|gen (*Amtsspr. auch für* irgendwohin schaffen); jmdn. in eine geschlossene Anstalt -; **Ver|brin|gung**
ver|brü|dern, sich; ich ...ere mich (↑R 16); **Ver|brü|de|rung**
ver|brü|hen; Ver|brü|hung
ver|bu|chen (*Kaufmannsspr.* in das [Geschäfts]buch eintragen); Erfolg - (verzeichnen); **Ver|bu|chung**
ver|bud|deln (*ugs. für* vergraben)
Ver|bum [v...], das; -s, *Plur.* ...ba *u.* ...ben ‹lat.› (*svw.* Verb); - finitum (*Plur.* Verba finita; Personalform des Verbs)
ver|bum|fie|deln (*ugs. für* verschwenden; verlieren); ich ...[e]le (↑R 16)
ver|bum|meln; er hat seine Zeit verbummelt (*ugs. für* nutzlos vertan); **ver|bum|melt** (*ugs. für* heruntergekommen); ein -es Genie
Ver|bund, der; -[e]s, *Plur.* -e *u.* Verbünde (Verbindung); **Ver|bund|bau|wei|se,** die; -; **ver|bün|den,** sich; **Ver|bun|den|heit,** die; -; **Ver|bün|de|te,** der *u.* die; -n, -n (↑R 5 ff.); **ver|bund|fah|ren;** *nur im Infinitiv gebr.* (innerhalb eines Verkehrsverbundes verschiedene öffentl. Verkehrsmittel benutzen); **Ver|bund‿fens|ter, ...glas** (das; -es), **...kar|te** (im Lochkartensystem), **...lam|pe** (*Bergmannsspr.* elektr. Lampe in Verbindung mit einer Wetterlampe), **...ma|schi|ne, ...netz** (die miteinander verbundenen Hochspannungsleitungen), **...pflas|ter|stein, ...ski|pass** (*u.* ...schi|pass), **...sys|tem, ...wirt|schaft** (die; -; Zusammenschluss mehrerer Betriebe [der Energiewirtschaft] zur Steigerung der Wirtschaftlichkeit)
ver|bür|gen; sich -
ver|bür|ger|li|chen; Ver|bür|ger|li|chung, die; -
Ver|bür|gung
ver|bü|ßen; eine Strafe -
ver|bü|xen (*nordd. für* verprügeln); du verbüxt
Verb|zu|satz [v...] (*Sprachw.* der

nichtverbale Bestandteil einer unfesten Zusammensetzung mit einem Verb als Grundwort, z. B. „durch" in „durchführen, führe durch")
ver|char|tern [...'(t)ʃar...] (ein Schiff od. Flugzeug vermieten)
ver|chro|men [...k...] (mit Chrom überziehen); **Ver|chro|mung**
Ver|cin|ge|to|rix [vɛrtsiŋ'ge:toriks] (ein Gallierfürst)
Ver|dacht, der; -[e]s, *Plur.* -e *u.* Verdächte; **ver|däch|tig; Ver|däch|ti|ge,** der *u.* die; -n, -n (↑R 5 ff.); **ver|däch|ti|gen; Ver|däch|ti|gung; Ver|dachts‿grund, ...mo|ment** *(das)*
ver|dam|men; ver|dam|mens|wert; Ver|damm|nis, die; - *(Rel.);* **ver|dammt** (*ugs. auch für* sehr); - schnell; **Ver|dam|mung**
ver|damp|fen; Ver|damp|fer *(Technik);* **Ver|damp|fung; Ver|damp|fungs|an|la|ge**
ver|dan|ken (*schweiz. auch für* für etwas Dank abstatten)
ver|da|ten (*EDV* in Daten umsetzen)
ver|dat|tert (*ugs. für* verwirrt)
ver|dau|en; ver|dau|lich; leicht verdauliche, schwer verdauliche Nahrungsmittel; die Speise ist leicht verdaulich, schwer verdaulich; **Ver|dau|lich|keit,** die; -; **Ver|dau|ung,** die; -; **Ver|dau|ungs‿ap|pa|rat, ...be|schwer|den** *(Plur.),* **...ka|nal, ...or|gan, ...stö|rung, ...trakt**
Ver|deck, das; -[e]s, -e; **ver|decken; ver|deck|ter|wei|se**
Ver|den (Al|ler) ['fe:r...] (Stadt an der Aller); **Ver|de|ner** (↑R 103)
ver|den|ken; jmdm. etwas -
Ver|derb, der; -[e]s; auf Gedeih und -; **ver|der|ben** (schlechter werden; zugrunde richten); du verdirbst; du verdarbst; du verdürbest; verdorben; verdirb!; das Fleisch ist verdorben (schlecht geworden), *aber* er hat mir den ganzen Ausflug verdorben (verleidet); **Ver|der|ben,** das; -s; eine Verderben bringende Politik (↑R 40); **Ver|der|ber; ver|derb|lich;** -e Esswaren; **Ver|derb|lich|keit,** die; -; **Ver|derb|nis,** die; - *(veraltend);* **ver|derbt** (verdorben [von Stellen in alten Handschriften]); **Ver|derbt|heit,** die; -
ver|deut|li|chen; Ver|deut|li|chung
ver|deut|schen; du verdeutschst; **Ver|deut|schung**
Ver|di [v...] (ital. Komponist)
ver|dicht|bar; ver|dich|ten; Ver|dich|ter *(Technik);* **Ver|dich|tung**
ver|di|cken; Ver|di|ckung
ver|die|nen; (↑R 50:) das Verdienen (der Gelderwerb) wird schwerer; **Ver|die|ner;** [1]**Ver|dienst,** der; -[e]s, -e (Lohn, Gewinn); [2]**Ver|dienst,** das; -[e]s, -e (Anspruch auf Dank u. Anerkennung); **Ver|dienst‿aus|fall, ...be|schei|ni|gung, ...gren|ze, ...kreuz** (ein Orden); **ver|dienst|lich; Ver|dienst‿mög|lich|keit, ...or|den, ...span|ne; ver|dienst|voll; ver|dient;** -er Mann, *aber in Titeln* (↑R 56): Verdienter Aktivist *(ehem. in der DDR);* **ver|dien|ter|ma|ßen; ver|dien|ter|wei|se**
ver|die|seln (*Eisenb.* mit Diesellokomotiven ausstatten); ich ...[e]le (↑R 16)
Ver|dikt [v...], das; -[e]s, -e ‹lat.› ([Verdammungs]urteil)
Ver|ding, der; -[e]s, -e (*svw.* Verdingung); **Ver|ding|bub** (*schweiz. für* durch die Waisenbehörde gegen Entschädigung bei Pflegeeltern untergebrachter Junge); **ver|din|gen** *(veraltend);* du verdingst; du verdingtest; verdungen, *auch* verdingt; verding[e]!; sich als Gehilfe -; **ver|ding|lichen; Ver|ding|li|chung; Ver|din|gung** *(veraltet)*
ver|do|len ‹*zu* Dole› (überdecken)
ver|dol|met|schen; sie hat das Gespräch verdolmetscht; **Ver|dol|met|schung**
ver|don|nern (*ugs. für* verurteilen); ich ...ere (↑R 16); **ver|donnert** (*ugs. veraltend für* erschreckt, bestürzt)
ver|dop|peln; Ver|dop|pe|lung, Ver|dopp|lung
ver|dor|ben; Ver|dor|ben|heit, die; -
ver|dor|ren; verdorrt
ver|dö|sen *(ugs.);* die Zeit -; *vgl.* dösen
ver|drah|ten (mit Draht verschließen; *Elektrotechnik* mit Schaltdrähten verbinden)
ver|drän|gen; Ver|drän|gung; Ver|drän|gungs‿me|cha|nis|mus, ...wett|be|werb
ver|dre|cken (*ugs. für* verschmutzen)
ver|dre|hen; Ver|dre|her *(ugs.);* **ver|dreht** (*ugs. für* verwirrt; verschroben); **Ver|dreht|heit** *(ugs.);* **Ver|dre|hung**
ver|drei|fa|chen
ver|dre|schen (*ugs. für* verprügeln)
ver|drie|ßen (missmutig machen, verärgern); du verdrießt, er verdrießt; du verdrossest, er verdross; du verdrössest; verdrossen; verdrieß[e]!; es verdrießt mich; ich lasse es mich nicht -;
ver|drieß|lich; Ver|drieß|lich|keit
ver|dril|len (miteinander verdrehen); **Ver|dril|lung** (*für* Torsion)
ver|dros|sen; Ver|dros|sen|heit, die; -
ver|dru|cken
ver|drü|cken (*ugs. auch für* essen); sich - (*ugs. für* sich heimlich entfernen)
Ver|druss, der; -es, -e
ver|duf|ten; [sich] - (*ugs. für* sich unauffällig entfernen)
ver|dum|men; Ver|dum|mung, die; -
ver|dump|fen; Ver|dump|fung
Ver|dun [vɛr'dœ̃:] (franz. Stadt)
ver|dun|keln; ich ...[e]le (↑R 16); **Ver|dun|ke|lung,** Ver|dunk|lung; **Ver|dun|ke|lungs|ge|fahr** (die; -), **Ver|dunk|lungs|ge|fahr,** die; - *(Rechtsspr.)*
ver|dün|nen; ver|dün|ni|sie|ren, sich (*ugs. für* sich entfernen); **Ver|dün|nung**
ver|duns|ten (zu Dunst werden; langsam verdampfen); **ver|dünsten** (*selten für* zu Dunst machen); **Ver|duns|tung,** die; -; **Ver|düns|tung,** die; -; **Ver|duns|tungs|mes|ser,** der
Ver|du|re [vɛr'dy:rə], die; -, -n ‹franz.› (ein in grünen Farben gehaltener Wandteppich [des MA.])
ver|durs|ten
ver|düs|tern; ich ...ere (↑R 16)
ver|dut|zen (verwundern, irritieren); **ver|dutzt** (verwirrt); **Ver|dutzt|heit,** die; -
ver|eb|ben
ver|edeln (↑R 132); ich ...[e]le (↑R 16); **Ver|ede|lung,** Ver|edlung; **Ver|ede|lungs|ver|fah|ren, Ver|ed|lungs|ver|fah|ren**
ver|ehe|li|chen (↑R 132), sich; **Ver|ehe|li|chung**
ver|eh|ren; Ver|eh|rer; Ver|eh|re|rin; Ver|eh|rung, die; -; **ver|eh|rungs‿voll, ...wür|dig**
ver|ei|di|gen; vereidigte Sachverständige; **Ver|ei|di|gung**
Ver|ein, der; -[e]s, -e; im - mit ...; - Deutscher Ingenieure (*Abk.* VDI); *vgl.* eingetragen; **ver|ein|bar; ver|ein|ba|ren; ver|ein|bar|ter|ma|ßen; Ver|ein|ba|rung; ver|ein|ba|rungs|ge|mäß; ver|ei|nen,** ver|ei|ni|gen; vereint *(vgl. d.);* sich vereinen, vereinigen
ver|ein|fa|chen; ein Verfahren -; **Ver|ein|fa|chung**
ver|ein|heit|li|chen; Ver|ein|heit|li|chung
ver|ei|ni|gen; (↑R 108:) die Vereinigten Staaten [von Amerika]; *vgl.* US[A] *u.* Ver. St. v. A.; Verei-

nigte Arabische Emirate; Vereinigtes Königreich Großbritannien u. Nordirland; **Ver|ei|ni|gung; Ver|ei|ni|gungs‿frei|heit,** (die; -), **...kri|mi|na|li|tät**
ver|ein|nah|men (einnehmen, als Einnahme in Empfang nehmen); **Ver|ein|nah|mung**
ver|ein|sa|men; Ver|ein|sa|mung, die; -
ver|ein|sei|ti|gen (in einseitiger Weise darstellen); **Ver|ein|sei|ti|gung**
Ver|eins‿elf (die; *Fußball*), **...far|be** *(meist Plur.)*, **...haus, ...lei|tung, ...lo|kal** (Vereinsraum, -zimmer), **...mann|schaft, ...mei|er** *(ugs. abwertend)*, **...mei|e|rei** (die; -; *ugs. abwertend*), **...re|gis|ter, ...sat|zung, ...wech|sel, ...we|sen** (das; -s); **ver|eint;** mit -en Kräften, *aber* (↑R 108): die Vereinten Nationen (*Abk.* UN, VN); *vgl. auch* UNO, UNESCO
ver|ein|zeln; ich ...[e]le (↑R 16); **ver|ein|zelt;** -e Niederschläge; Vereinzelte saßen im Freien; **Ver|ein|ze|lung**
ver|ei|sen (von Eis bedeckt werden; *Med.* durch Kälte unempfindlich machen); die Tragflächen ver|eis|ten; **ver|eist;** -e (eisbedeckte) Wege; **Ver|ei|sung**
ver|ei|teln; ich ...[e]le (↑R 16); **Ver|ei|te|lung,** Ver|eit|lung
ver|ei|tern; Ver|ei|te|rung
Ver|eit|lung *vgl.* Vereitelung
ver|ekeln (↑R 132); jmdm. etwas -; **Ver|eke|lung, Ver|ek|lung**
ver|elen|den (↑R 132); **Ver|elen|dung, Ver|elen|dungs|the|o|rie,** die; - (Theorie, nach der sich die Lebensverhältnisse der Arbeiterklasse im Kapitalismus ständig verschlechtern)
Ve|re|na [v...] (w. Vorn.)
ver|en|den
ver|en|gen; ver|en|gern; ich ...ere (↑R 16); **Ver|en|ge|rung; Ver|en|gung**
ver|erb|bar; ver|er|ben; ver|erb|lich; Ver|er|bung; Ver|er|bungs‿gang (der), **...leh|re** (die; -)
ver|es|tern (*Chemie* zu Ester umwandeln); ich ...ere (↑R 16); **Ver|es|te|rung**
ver|ewi|gen (↑R 132); sich -; **Ver|ewig|te,** der *u.* die; -n, -n (↑R 5 ff.); **Ver|ewi|gung**
¹ver|fah|ren (vorgehen, handeln); ich bin so -, dass ...; so darfst du nicht mit ihr - (umgehen); sich - (einen falschen Weg fahren); ich habe mich -; (↑R 50:) ein Verfahren ist auf dieser Strecke kaum möglich; eine Schicht - (*Bergmannsspr.* eine Schicht machen);
²ver|fah|ren (ausweglos scheinend); eine -e Situation; **Ver|fah|ren,** das; -s, -; ein neues -; **Ver|fah|rens‿fra|ge, ...recht** (das; -[e]s); **ver|fah|rens|recht|lich; Ver|fah|rens‿re|gel, ...tech|nik** (die; -), **...wei|se** (die)
Ver|fall, der; -[e]s; in - geraten; **ver|fal|len;** das Haus ist -; er ist dem Alkohol -; **Ver|fall|er|klä|rung** *(Rechtsspr.)*; **Ver|falls‿da|tum, ...er|schei|nung; Ver|fall[s]‿tag, ...zeit**
ver|fäl|schen; er hat den Wein verfälscht; **Ver|fäl|schung**
ver|fan|gen; sich -; du hast dich in Widersprüche -; **ver|fäng|lich;** eine -e Frage, Situation; **Ver|fäng|lich|keit**
ver|fär|ben; sich -; **Ver|fär|bung**
ver|fas|sen; sie hat den Brief verfasst; **Ver|fas|ser; Ver|fas|se|rin; Ver|fas|ser|schaft,** die; -; **Ver|fas|sung; ver|fas|sung|ge|bend; Ver|fas|sungs‿än|de|rung, ...be|schwer|de, ...bruch** (*vgl.* ¹Bruch), **...feind; ver|fas|sungs‿feind|lich, ...ge|mäß; Ver|fas|sungs‿ge|richt, ...kla|ge; ver|fas|sungs|kon|form; ver|fas|sungs|mä|ßig; Ver|fas|sungs‿ord|nung, ...recht** (das; -[e]s), **...schutz** (der; -es); **...schüt|zer** *(ugs.)*, **ver|fas|sungs|treu; Ver|fas|sungs|ur|kun|de; ver|fas|sungs|wid|rig**
ver|fau|len; Ver|fau|lung
ver|fech|ten (verteidigen); er hat sein Recht tatkräftig verfochten; **Ver|fech|ter; Ver|fech|te|rin; Ver|fech|tung,** die; -
ver|feh|len (nicht erreichen, nicht treffen); sich - (*veraltend für* eine Verfehlung begehen); **Ver|feh|lung**
ver|fein|den, sich; sich mit jmdm. -; **Ver|fein|dung**
ver|fei|nern; ich ...ere (↑R 16); **Ver|fei|ne|rung**
ver|fe|men (für vogelfrei erklären; ächten); **Ver|fem|te,** der *u.* die; -n, -n (↑R 5 ff.); **Ver|fe|mung**
ver|fer|ti|gen; Ver|fer|ti|gung
ver|fes|ti|gen; Ver|fes|ti|gung
ver|fet|ten; Ver|fet|tung
ver|feu|ern; ich ...ere (↑R 16)
ver|fil|men; Ver|fil|mung
ver|fil|zen; die Decke ist verfilzt; sich - (sich unentwirrbar verwickeln); **Ver|fil|zung**
ver|fins|tern; sich -; **Ver|fins|te|rung**
ver|fit|zen (*ugs. für* verwirren); sie hat die Wolle verfitzt
ver|fla|chen; Ver|fla|chung
ver|flech|ten; Ver|flech|tung
ver|flie|gen (verschwinden); der Zorn ist verflogen; sich - (mit dem Flugzeug vom Kurs abkommen)
ver|flie|ßen *vgl.* verflossen
ver|flixt (*ugs. für* verflucht; *auch für* unangenehm, ärgerlich)
Ver|floch|ten|heit, die; -
ver|flos|sen; verflossene *od.* verflossne Tage
ver|flu|chen; ver|flucht (verdammt; sehr, äußerst); so ein -er Idiot; es ist - heiß; verflucht u. zugenäht!
ver|flüch|ti|gen (in den gasförmigen Zustand überführen); sich - (in den gasförmigen Zustand übergehen; *ugs. scherzh. für* sich heimlich entfernen); **Ver|flüch|ti|gung**
Ver|flu|chung
ver|flüs|si|gen; Ver|flüs|si|gung
Ver|folg, der; -[e]s (*Amtsspr.* Verlauf); *nur in* im *od.* in - der Sache; **ver|fol|gen; Ver|fol|ger; Ver|fol|ge|rin; Ver|folg|te,** der *u.* die; -n, -n (↑R 5 ff.); **Ver|fol|gung; Ver|fol|gungs‿jagd, ...ren|nen** *(Radsport)*, **...wahn**
ver|form|bar; Ver|form|bar|keit; ver|for|men; Ver|for|mung
ver|frach|ten; Ver|frach|ter; Ver|frach|tung
ver|fran|zen, sich (*Fliegerspr.* sich verfliegen; *ugs. auch für* sich verirren); du verfranzt dich
ver|frem|den; Ver|frem|dung; Ver|frem|dungs|ef|fekt
¹ver|fres|sen (*derb für* für Essen ausgeben); sein ganzes Geld -;
²ver|fres|sen (*derb für* gefräßig); **Ver|fres|sen|heit,** die; - *(derb)*
ver|fro|ren
ver|frü|hen, sich; **ver|früht;** sein Dank kam -; **Ver|frü|hung;** die; -
ver|füg|bar; -es Kapital; **Ver|füg|bar|keit,** die; -
ver|fu|gen; Kacheln -
ver|fü|gen (bestimmen, anordnen; besitzen)
Ver|fu|gung
Ver|fü|gung; (↑R 23:) zur Verfügung u. bereithalten, *aber* bereit- u. zur Verfügung halten; **ver|fü|gungs|be|rech|tigt; Ver|fü|gungs‿ge|walt** (die; -), **...recht**
ver|füh|ren; Ver|füh|rer; Ver|füh|re|rin; ver|füh|re|risch; Ver|füh|rung; Ver|füh|rungs|kunst
ver|fuhr|wer|ken (*schweiz. für* verpfuschen)
ver|füt|tern (als ¹Futter geben)
Ver|ga|be, die; -, -n; - von Arbeiten; **ver|ga|ben** (*schweiz. für* schenken, vermachen); **Ver|ga|bung** (*schweiz. für* Schenkung, Vermächtnis)
ver|gack|ei|ern (*ugs. für* zum Narren halten); ich ...ere (↑R 16)

ver|gaf|fen, sich (*ugs. für* sich verlieben); du hast dich in sie vergafft
ver|gagt [...ˈgɛkt] ⟨dt.; engl.-amerik.⟩ (*ugs. für* voller Gags)
ver|gäl|len (verbittern; *Chemie* ungenießbar machen); er hat ihm die Freude vergällt; vergällter Alkohol; **Ver|gäl|lung**
ver|ga|lop|pie|ren, sich (*ugs. für* [sich] irren, einen Missgriff tun)
ver|gam|meln (*ugs. für* verderben; verwahrlosen); die Zeit - (*ugs. für* vertrödeln)
ver|gan|den (*schweiz. für* verwildern [von Alpweiden])
Ver|gan|gen|heit; Ver|gan|gen|heits|be|wäl|ti|gung, die; -; **ver|gäng|lich; Ver|gäng|lich|keit,** die; -
ver|gan|ten ⟨*zu* Gant⟩ (*südd., österr. mdal. veraltet u. schweiz. für* zwangsversteigern); **Ver|gan|tung**
ver|ga|sen (*Chemie* in gasförmigen Zustand überführen; mit [Gift]gasen verseuchen, töten); **Ver|ga|ser** (Vorrichtung zur Erzeugung des Luft-Kraftstoff-Gemisches für Verbrennungskraftmaschinen); **Ver|ga|sung**
ver|gat|tern (mit einem Gatter versehen; *ugs. für* jmdn. zu etwas verpflichten); ich ...ere (↑R 16); **Ver|gat|te|rung**
ver|ge|ben; eine Chance -; er hat diesen Auftrag -; seine Sünden sind ihm vergeben worden; ich vergebe mir nichts, wenn ...; **ver|ge|bens; Ver|ge|ber; ver|geb|lich; Ver|geb|lich|keit,** die; -; **Ver|ge|bung** *(geh.)*
ver|ge|gen|ständ|li|chen; Ver|ge|gen|ständ|li|chung
ver|ge|gen|wär|ti|gen [*auch* ...ˈvɛr...], sich; **Ver|ge|gen|wär|ti|gung**
ver|ge|hen; die Jahre sind vergangen; sich - (z. B. gegen Gesetze verstoßen); er hat sich an ihr vergangen; **Ver|ge|hen,** das; -s, -
ver|gei|gen (*ugs. für* zu einem Misserfolg machen)
ver|gei|len (*Bot.* durch Lichtmangel aufschießen [von Pflanzen]); **Ver|gei|lung**
ver|geis|ti|gen; Ver|geis|ti|gung
ver|gel|ten; sie hat immer Böses mit Gutem vergolten; vergilt!; einem ein „Vergelt's Gott!" zurufen; **Ver|gel|tung; Ver|gel|tungs‿maß|nah|me, ...schlag, ...waf|fe**
ver|ge|sell|schaf|ten; Ver|ge|sell|schaf|tung
ver|ges|sen; du vergisst, er vergisst; du vergaßest; du vergäßest; vergessen; vergiss!; etwas vergessen; die Arbeit über dem Vergnügen vergessen; auf, an etwas vergessen (*landsch., bes. südd. u. österr. für* an etwas nicht rechtzeitig denken); **Ver|ges|sen|heit,** die; -; in - geraten; **ver|gess|lich; Ver|gess|lich|keit,** die; -
ver|geu|den; ver|geu|de|risch; Ver|geu|dung
ver|ge|wal|ti|gen; Ver|ge|wal|ti|gung
ver|ge|wis|sern, sich; ich vergewissere mich seiner Sympathie; **Ver|ge|wis|se|rung**
ver|gie|ßen
ver|gif|ten; Ver|gif|tung; Ver|gif|tungs‿er|schei|nung, ...ge|fahr
Ver|gil [vɛr...] (altröm. Dichter)
ver|gil|ben; vergilbte Papiere, Gardinen
Ver|gi|li|us [vɛr...] *vgl.* Vergil
ver|gip|sen; du vergipst
Ver|giss|mein|nicht, das; -[e]s, -[e] (eine Blume)
ver|git|tern; ich ...ere (↑R 16)
ver|gla|sen; du verglast; er verglas|te; verglaste (glasige, starre) Augen; **Ver|gla|sung**
Ver|gleich, der; -[e]s, -e; im - mit, zu ..., ein gütlicher -; **ver|gleich|bar; Ver|gleich|bar|keit,** die; -; **ver|glei|chen;** sie hat diese beiden Bilder verglichen; sich -; die Parteien haben sich verglichen; die vergleichende Anatomie; vergleich[e]! (*Abk.* vgl.); **Ver|gleichs‿form** (*svw.* Steigerungsform), **...gläu|bi|ger** *(Rechtsspr.)*, **...grö|ße, ...kampf** *(Sport)*, **...mög|lich|keit, ...ob|jekt, ...par|ti|kel** *(Sprachw.)*, **...schuld|ner** *(Rechtsspr.)*, **...ver|fah|ren; ver|gleichs|wei|se; Ver|gleichs|zahl; Ver|glei|chung**
ver|glet|schern; Ver|glet|sche|rung
ver|glim|men
ver|glü|hen
ver|gnat|zen (*landsch. für* verärgern); ich bin vergnatzt
ver|gnü|gen; sich -; **Ver|gnü|gen,** das; -s, -; viel -!; **ver|gnü|gens|hal|ber; ver|gnüg|lich; ver|gnügt; Ver|gnü|gung** *meist Plur.*; **Ver|gnü|gungs|fahrt; ver|gnü|gungs|hal|ber; Ver|gnü|gungs‿in|dust|rie, ...park, ...rei|se, ...steu|er** (die; ↑R 34), **...sucht** (die; -); **ver|gnü|gungs|süch|tig**
ver|gol|den; Ver|gol|der; Ver|gol|de|rin; Ver|gol|dung
ver|gön|nen ([aus Gunst] gewähren); es ist mir vergönnt
ver|got|ten (*svw.* vergöttlichen); **ver|göt|tern** (wie einen Gott verehren); ich ...ere (↑R 16); **Ver|göt|te|rung; ver|gött|li|chen** (zum Gott machen; als Gott verehren); **Ver|gött|li|chung; Ver|got|tung**
ver|gra|ben; er hat sich -; er ist tief in seine Bücher -; er hat seine Hände in den Hosentaschen -
ver|grä|men (verärgern; *Jägerspr.* [Wild] verscheuchen); **ver|grämt;**
ver|grät|zen (*landsch. für* verärgern); du vergrätzt
ver|grau|en (grau werden); vergraute Wäsche
ver|grau|len (*ugs. für* verärgern [u. dadurch vertreiben])
ver|grei|fen; sich an jmdm., an einer Sache -; du hast dich an fremdem Gut, im Ton vergriffen
ver|grei|sen; du vergreist; er vergreis|te; **Ver|grei|sung,** die; - (das Vergreistsein; das Vergreisen)
ver|grel|len (*landsch. für* zornig machen); man hat ihn vergrellt
ver|grif|fen; das Buch ist - (nicht mehr lieferbar)
ver|grö|bern; ich ...ere (↑R 16); **Ver|grö|be|rung**
Ver|grö|ße|rer *(Optik)*; **ver|grö|ßern;** ich ...ere (↑R 16); **Ver|grö|ße|rung; Ver|grö|ße|rungs‿ap|pa|rat, ...glas** (*Plur.* ...gläser), **...spie|gel**
ver|gu|cken, sich (*ugs. für* sich verlieben)
ver|gül|den (*geh. für* vergolden)
Ver|gunst (*veraltend für* Erlaubnis); *nur noch in* mit - (mit Verlaub); **ver|güns|ti|gen** *(veraltet)*; **Ver|güns|ti|gung**
ver|gü|ten (*auch für* veredeln); **Ver|gü|tung**
verh. (*Zeichen* ⚭) = verheiratet
Ver|hack, der; -[e]s, -e (*veraltet für* Verhau); **Ver|ha|ckert,** das; -s (*österr. für* Brotaufstrich aus Schweinefett u. a.); **ver|hack|stü|cken** (*ugs. für* bis ins Kleinste besprechen u. kritisieren)
Ver|haft, der; -[e]s (*veraltet für* Verhaftung); **ver|haf|ten; ver|haf|tet** (*auch für* eng verbunden); einer Sache - sein; **Ver|haf|te|te,** der *u.* die; -n, -n (↑R 5 ff.); **Ver|haf|tung; Ver|haf|tungs|wel|le**
ver|ha|geln; das Getreide ist verhagelt
ver|ha|ken, sich; die Geweihe verhakten sich ineinander
ver|hal|len; sein Ruf verhallte
Ver|halt, der; -[e]s, -e (*veraltet für* Verhalten; Sachverhalt); [1]**ver|hal|ten** (stehen bleiben; zurückhalten; *österr. u. schweiz. Amtsspr.* zu etwas verpflichten, anhalten); sie verhielt auf der Treppe; er ver-

hält den Harn, den Atem; ich habe mich abwartend -; ²**ver|hal|ten;** ein -er (gedämpfter, unterdrückter) Zorn, Trotz; -er (verzögerter) Schritt; -er (gezügelter) Trab; **Ver|hal|ten,** das; -s; **Ver|hal|ten|heit,** die; -; **ver|hal|tens|auf|fäl|lig** *(Psych., Med.);* **Ver|hal|tens‿auf|fäl|lig|keit, ...for|scher, ...for|sche|rin, ...for|schung** (die; -), **...fra|ge; ver|hal|tens|ge|stört** *(Psych., Med.);* **Ver|hal|tens‿maß|re|gel** *(meist Plur.),* **...mus|ter** *(Psych.),* **...re|gel, ...steu|e|rung, ...stö|rung** *(Med., Psych.),* **...wei|se** (die); **Ver|hält|nis,** das; -ses, -se; geordnete Verhältnisse; ein geometrisches -; **Ver|hält|nis|glei|chung** *(Math.);* **ver|hält|nis|mä|ßig; Ver|hält|nis|mä|ßig|keit** *Plur. selten;* die - der Mittel; **Ver|hält|nis‿wahl, ...wahl|recht** (das; -[e]s), **...wort** (*Plur.* ...wörter; *für* Präposition), **...zahl; Ver|hal|tung; Ver|hal|tungs|maß|re|gel** (*svw.* Verhaltensmaßregel)

ver|han|deln; über, *selten* um etwas -; **Ver|hand|lung; Ver|hand|lungs|ba|sis; ver|hand|lungs|be|reit; Ver|hand|lungs|be|reit|schaft,** die; -; **ver|hand|lungs|fä|hig; Ver|hand|lungs‿grund|la|ge, ...part|ner, ...part|ne|rin, ...spra|che, ...tisch** (*in* sich an den - setzen; an den - zurückkehren), **...weg** (*nur in* auf dem - [durch Verhandeln])

ver|han|gen; ein -er Himmel; **ver|hän|gen** *vgl.* ²hängen; mit verhängten (locker gelassenen) Zügeln; **Ver|häng|nis,** das; -ses, -se; **ver|häng|nis|voll;** ein -er Fehler; **Ver|hän|gung**

ver|harm|lo|sen; du verharmlost; er verharmlos|te; **Ver|harm|lo|sung**

ver|härmt

ver|har|ren *(geh.);* **Ver|har|rung**

ver|har|schen; Ver|har|schung

ver|här|ten; Ver|här|tung

ver|has|peln (verwirren); sich - (*ugs. für* sich beim Sprechen verwirren); **Ver|has|pe|lung, Ver|hasp|lung**

ver|hasst

ver|hät|scheln (*ugs. für* verzärteln); **Ver|hät|sche|lung, Ver|hätsch|lung**

ver|hatscht (*österr. ugs. für* ausgetreten); -e Schuhe

Ver|hau, der *od.* das; -[e]s, -e; ¹**ver|hau|en** (*ugs. für* durchprügeln); er verhaute ihn; sich - (*ugs. für* sich gröblich irren); ²**ver|hau|en** (*ugs. für* unmöglich); der sieht ja - aus

ver|he|ben, sich; ich habe mich verhoben

ver|hed|dern (*ugs. für* verwirren); ich ...ere (↑R 16); sich -

ver|hee|ren (verwüsten, zerstören); **ver|hee|rend;** das ist - (sehr unangenehm; furchtbar); -e Folgen haben; **Ver|hee|rung**

ver|heh|len *(geh.);* er hat uns die Wahrheit verhehlt; *vgl.* verhohlen

ver|hei|len; Ver|hei|lung

ver|heim|li|chen; Ver|heim|li|chung

ver|hei|ra|ten; sich -; **ver|hei|ra|tet** (*Abk.* verh.; *Zeichen* ⚭); **Ver|hei|ra|te|te,** der *u.* die; -n, -n (↑R 5 ff.); **Ver|hei|ra|tung**

ver|hei|ßen; er hat mir das -; *vgl.* ¹heißen; **Ver|hei|ßung; ver|hei|ßungs|voll**

ver|hei|zen; Kohlen -; jmdn. - (*ugs. für* jmdn. rücksichtslos einsetzen [u. opfern])

ver|hel|fen; jmdm. zu etwas -; sie hat mir dazu verholfen

ver|herr|li|chen; Ver|herr|li|chung

ver|het|zen; er hat die Massen verhetzt; **Ver|het|zung**

ver|heu|ern (*Seemannsspr. svw.* heuern); ich ...ere (↑R 16)

ver|heult (*ugs. für* verweint); mit -en Augen

ver|he|xen; das ist wie verhext!; **Ver|he|xung**

Ver|hieb (*Bergmannsspr.* Art u. Richtung, in der der Kohlenstoß abgebaut wird)

ver|him|meln (*ugs. für* vergöttern)

ver|hin|dern; Ver|hin|de|rung; Ver|hin|de|rungs|fall, der; *nur in* im -[e] *(Amtsspr.)*

ver|hoch|deut|schen

ver|hof|fen (sichern [vom Wild])

ver|hoh|len (verborgen); mit kaum -er Schadenfreude

ver|höh|nen; ver|hoh|ne|pi|peln (*ugs. für* verspotten, verulken); ich ...[e]le (↑R 16); **Ver|höh|nung**

ver|hö|kern (*ugs. für* [billig] verkaufen)

Ver|hol|bo|je *(Seemannsspr.);* **ver|ho|len** ([ein Schiff] an eine andere Stelle bringen)

ver|hol|zen; Ver|hol|zung

Ver|hör, das; -[e]s, -e; **ver|hö|ren**

ver|hor|nen; Ver|hor|nung

ver|hu|deln (*landsch. für* durch Hast, Nachlässigkeit verderben)

ver|hül|len; ver|hüllt; eine kaum -e Drohung; **Ver|hül|lung**

ver|hun|dert|fa|chen

ver|hun|gern; (↑R 50:) vor dem Verhungern retten

ver|hun|zen (*ugs. für* verderben; verunstalten; verschlechtern); du verhunzt; **Ver|hun|zung** *(ugs.)*

ver|hu|ren (*derb für* [sein Geld] bei Prostituierten ausgeben); **ver|hurt** (*derb für* sexuell ausschweifend)

ver|huscht (*ugs. für* scheu u. zaghaft)

ver|hü|ten (verhindern)

ver|hüt|ten (Erz auf Hüttenwerken verarbeiten); **Ver|hüt|tung**

Ver|hü|tung; Ver|hü|tungs|mit|tel, das

ver|hut|zelt ([gealtert u.] zusammengeschrumpft); ein -es Männchen

Ve|ri|fi|ka|ti|on [v...], die; -, -en ‹lat.› (das Verifizieren); **ve|ri|fi|zier|bar** (nachprüfbar); **Ve|ri|fi|zier|bar|keit,** die; -; **ve|ri|fi|zie|ren** (durch Überprüfen die Richtigkeit bestätigen)

ver|in|ner|li|chen; Ver|in|ner|li|chung

ver|ir|ren, sich; **Ver|ir|rung**

Ve|ris|mus [v...], der; - ‹lat.› (krass wirklichkeitsgetreue künstlerische Darstellung); **Ve|rist,** der; -en, -en (↑R 126); **ve|ris|tisch**

ve|ri|ta|bel [v...] ‹franz.› (wahrhaft; echt); ...ab|le (↑R 130) Größe

ver|ja|gen

ver|jäh|ren; Ver|jäh|rung; Ver|jäh|rungs|frist

ver|jaz|zen; ein verjazztes Kirchenlied

ver|ju|beln (*ugs. für* [sein Geld] für Vergnügungen ausgeben)

ver|juch|hei|en (*landsch. für* verjubeln)

ver|jün|gen; er hat das Personal verjüngt; sich -; die Säule verjüngt sich (wird [nach oben] dünner); **Ver|jün|gung; Ver|jün|gungs‿kur** (*vgl.* ¹Kur), **...trank**

ver|ju|xen (*ugs. für* vergeuden, verulken); du verjuxt

ver|ka|beln (mit Kabeln anschließen); **Ver|ka|be|lung**

ver|kad|men *vgl.* kadmieren

ver|kal|ben; die Kuh hat verkalbt

ver|kal|ken (*ugs. auch für* alt werden, die geistige Frische verlieren)

ver|kal|ku|lie|ren, sich (sich verrechnen, falsch veranschlagen)

Ver|kal|kung

ver|ka|mi|so|len (*ugs. veraltend für* verprügeln)

ver|kannt; ein -es Genie

ver|kan|ten

ver|kap|pen (unkenntlich machen); **ver|kappt;** ein -er Spion, Betrüger; **Ver|kap|pung**

ver|kap|seln; ich ...[e]le (↑R 16); **Ver|kap|se|lung, Ver|kaps|lung**

ver|kars|ten (zu ²Karst werden); **Ver|kars|tung**

ver|kar|ten (für eine Kartei auf Karten schreiben); **Ver|kar|tung**

ver|ka|se|ma|tu|ckeln (*ugs. für* verkonsumieren; genau erklären); ich ...[e]le (↑R 16)

ver|kä|sen (zu Käse werden)

ver|käs|teln (einschachteln); **ver|käs|ten** (*Bergbau* auszimmern)

Ver|kä|sung

ver|ka|tert (*ugs. für* an den Folgen übermäßigen Alkoholgenusses leidend)

Ver|kauf, der; -[e]s, ...käufe; der - von Textilien, *in der Kaufmannsspr. gelegentl. auch* der - in Textilien; An- und Verkauf (↑R 23); **ver|kau|fen;** du verkaufst; er verkauft, verkaufte, hat verkauft (*nicht korrekt:* du verkäufst; er verkäuft); **Ver|käu|fer; Ver|käu|fe|rin; ver|käuf|lich; Ver|käuf|lich|keit,** die; -; **Ver|kaufs‿ab|tei|lung, ...aus|stel|lung, ...be|din|gung, ...fah|rer, ...flä|che; ver|kaufs|för|dernd; Ver|kaufs‿för|de|rung, ...ge|spräch, ...lei|ter** (der); **ver|kaufs|of|fen;** -er Samstag; **Ver|kaufs‿preis, ...raum, ...schla|ger, ...stand, ...stel|le, ...tisch**

Ver|kehr, der; *Gen.* -s, *seltener* -es, *Plur. (fachspr.)* -e; im - mit ...; in - treten; **ver|keh|ren; Ver|kehrs‿ader** (↑R 132), **...am|pel, ...amt, ...auf|kom|men** (das; -s); **ver|kehrs|be|ru|higt;** eine -e Straße; **Ver|kehrs‿be|ru|hi|gung, ...be|trieb** *(meist Plur.)*, **...bü|ro, ...cha|os, ...de|likt, ...dich|te** (die; -), **...dis|zip|lin** (die; -), **...er|zie|hung, ...fluss** (der; -es); **ver|kehrs|frei; Ver|kehrs‿funk, ...ge|fähr|dung, ...ge|sche|hen; ver|kehrs|güns|tig; Ver|kehrs‿hin|der|nis, ...in|sel, ...kno|ten|punkt, ...kon|trol|le, ...la|ge, ...lärm, ...mel|dung, ...mi|nis|ter, ...mit|tel** (das), **...netz, ...op|fer, ...ord|nung** (die; -), **...plan** (*vgl.* [2]Plan), **...pla|nung, ...po|li|zei, ...recht** (das; -[e]s); **Ver|kehrs|re|ge|lung** *od.* **...reg|lung; ver|kehrs|reich; Ver|kehrs‿schild** (das), **...schrift** (die; -; erster Grad der Kurzschrift), **...schutz|mann; ver|kehrs|si|cher; Ver|kehrs‿si|cher|heit** (die; -), **...sig|nal, ...spra|che, ...stär|ke, ...sta|tis|tik, ...stau, ...steu|er** (die; *Wirtsch.*), **...sto|ckung, ...stö|rung, ...strei|fe, ...sün|der** *(ugs.)*, **...sün|de|rin** *(ugs.)*, **...taug|lich|keit, ...teil|neh|mer, ...teil|neh|me|rin, ...to|te** (*meist Plur.;* ↑R 5 ff.), **...tüch|tig|keit, ...un|fall, ...ver|bin|dung, ...ver|bund, ...ver|ein, ...vor|schrift, ...weg, ...wert** *(Wirtsch.)*, **...we|sen** (das; -s); **ver|kehrs|wid|rig; Ver|kehrs|zei|chen; ver|kehrt;** seine Antwort ist -; - herum; Kaffee - (*ugs. für* mehr Milch als Kaffee); **Ver|kehrt|heit; Ver|keh|rung**

ver|kei|len; die Autos verkeilten sich [ineinander]; jmdn. - (*ugs. für* jmdn. verprügeln)

ver|ken|nen; er wurde von allen verkannt; *vgl.* verkannt; **Ver|ken|nung**

ver|ket|ten; Ver|ket|tung

ver|ket|zern (verurteilen, schmähen); ich ...ere (↑R 16); **Ver|ket|ze|rung**

ver|kie|seln (*fachspr. für* von Kieselsäure durchtränkt werden); **Ver|kie|se|lung**

ver|kip|pen ([Abfallstoffe] auf Deponien ablagern); **Ver|kip|pung**

ver|kit|schen (kitschig gestalten; *landsch. für* [billig] verkaufen)

ver|kit|ten (mit Kitt befestigen)

ver|kla|gen

ver|klam|mern; Ver|klam|me|rung

ver|klap|pen ([Abfallstoffe] ins Meer versenken); **Ver|klap|pung**

ver|kla|ren (*nordd. für* [mühsam] erklären; *Seemannsspr.* über Schiffsunfälle eidlich aussagen)

ver|klä|ren (ins Überirdische erhöhen)

Ver|kla|rung (gerichtliche Feststellung bei Schiffsunfällen)

Ver|klä|rung

ver|klat|schen (*ugs. für* verpetzen, verraten); man hat ihn verklatscht

ver|klau|su|lie|ren (schwer verständlich formulieren; mit vielen Vorbehalten versehen); **Ver|klau|su|lie|rung**

ver|kle|ben; Ver|kle|bung

ver|kle|ckern *(ugs.);* ich ...ere (↑R 16)

ver|klei|den; Ver|klei|dung

ver|klei|nern; ich ...ere (↑R 16); **Ver|klei|ne|rung; Ver|klei|ne|rungs‿form, ...sil|be**

ver|kleis|tern (*ugs. für* verkleben); **Ver|kleis|te|rung** *(ugs.)*

ver|klem|men; ver|klemmt (gehemmt, voller Komplexe)

ver|kli|ckern (*ugs. für* erklären)

ver|klin|gen

ver|klop|pen (*ugs. für* verprügeln; [unter dem Wert] verkaufen); sie haben ihn tüchtig verkloppt; er hat seine Bücher verkloppt

ver|klüf|ten, sich (*Jägerspr.* sich im Bau vergraben)

ver|klum|pen (klumpig werden)

Ver|klum|pung

ver|kna|cken ⟨jidd.⟩ (*ugs. für* [gerichtlich] verurteilen)

ver|knack|sen, sich *(ugs.);* du hast dir den Fuß verknackst (verstaucht)

ver|knal|len (*ugs. für* [sinnlos] verschießen); sich - (*ugs. für* sich heftig verlieben); zu Silvester werden Unsummen verknallt; du hast dich, du bist in sie verknallt

ver|knap|pen; Ver|knap|pung

ver|knas|ten (*ugs. für* zu einer Freiheitsstrafe verurteilen)

ver|knäu|len; sich -

ver|knaut|schen *(ugs.);* du verknautschst

ver|knei|fen *(ugs.);* das Lachen -; sich etwas - (auf etwas verzichten; etwas unterdrücken); **ver|knif|fen** (verbittert, verhärtet); **Ver|knif|fen|heit,** die; -

ver|knit|tern; ich ...ere (↑R 16)

ver|knö|chern; ich ...ere (↑R 16); **ver|knö|chert** (*ugs. auch für* alt, geistig unbeweglich); **Ver|knö|che|rung**

ver|knor|peln; Ver|knor|pe|lung, Ver|knorp|lung

ver|kno|ten

ver|knül|len (*landsch. für* zerknüllen)

ver|knüp|fen; Ver|knüp|fung

ver|knur|ren *(ugs.);* jmdn. zu zehn Tagen Arrest -

ver|knu|sen; *nur noch in* jmdn. nicht verknusen (*ugs. für* nicht ausstehen) können

ver|ko|chen ([zu] lange kochen)

[1]**ver|koh|len** ⟨jidd.⟩ (*ugs. für* veralbern; scherzhaft belügen)

[2]**ver|koh|len** (in Kohle umwandeln); **Ver|koh|lung**

ver|ko|ken (zu [1]Koks machen, werden); **Ver|ko|kung**

ver|kom|men; er verkam im Schmutz; ein -er Mensch; **Ver|kom|men|heit,** die; -

ver|kom|pli|zie|ren ([unnötig] kompliziert machen)

ver|kon|su|mie|ren (*ugs. für* aufessen, verbrauchen)

ver|kop|peln; Ver|kop|pe|lung, Ver|kopp|lung

ver|kor|ken (mit einem Korken verschließen); **ver|kork|sen** (*ugs. für* verderben, verpfuschen); du verkorkst

ver|kör|nen (*Technik* granulieren)

ver|kör|pern; ich ...ere (↑R 16); **Ver|kör|pe|rung**

ver|kos|ten (kostend prüfen); Wein -; **Ver|kos|ter; ver|kös|ti|gen; Ver|kös|ti|gung; Ver|kos|tung**

ver|kra|chen (*ugs. für* zusammenbrechen); sich - (*ugs. für* sich entzweien); **ver|kracht** (*ugs. für* gescheitert); ein -er Student; eine -e Existenz

ver|kraf|ten (*ugs. für* ertragen können)
ver|kral|len; das Eichhörnchen verkrallte sich in der Rinde
ver|kra|men (*ugs. für* verlegen)
ver|kramp|fen, sich; **verkrampft; Ver|kramp|fung**
ver|krat|zen
ver|krau|chen, sich (*landsch. für* sich verkriechen)
ver|krau|ten; der See verkrautet
ver|krie|chen, sich
ver|kröp|fen (*Bauw. svw.* kröpfen); **Ver|kröp|fung**
ver|krü|meln, sich (*ugs. für* sich unauffällig entfernen)
ver|krüm|men; sich -; **Ver|krümmung**
ver|krum|peln (*landsch. für* zerknittern); ich ...[e]le (↑R 16)
ver|krüp|peln; ich ...ele (↑R 16); **Ver|krüp|pe|lung, Ver|krüpplung**
ver|krus|ten; etwas verkrustet; **Ver|krus|tung**
ver|küh|len, sich (*landsch. für* sich erkälten); **Ver|küh|lung** (*landsch.*)
ver|küm|mern; ver|küm|mert; Ver|küm|me|rung
ver|kün|den (*geh.*); **Ver|kün|der; Ver|kün|de|rin; ver|kün|di|gen** (*geh.*); **Ver|kün|di|ger; Ver|kün|di|ge|rin; Ver|kün|di|gung, Ver|kün|dung;** das kath. Fest Mariä Verkündigung, *ugs.* Maria Verkündigung
ver|kup|fern; ich ...ere (↑R 16); **Ver|kup|fe|rung**
ver|kup|peln; Ver|kup|pe|lung, Ver|kupp|lung
ver|kür|zen; verkürzte Arbeitszeit; **Ver|kür|zung**
ver|la|chen (auslachen)
Ver|lad, der; -s (*schweiz. für* Verladung); **Ver|la|de‿bahn|hof, ...brü|cke, ...kran; ver|la|den;** *vgl.* [1]laden; **Ver|la|der; Ver|la|de|ram|pe; Ver|la|dung**
Ver|lag, der; -[e]s, -e (*schweiz. auch für* das Herumliegen [von Gegenständen]); **ver|la|gern; Ver|la|ge|rung; Ver|lags‿an|stalt, ...buch|händ|ler, ...buch|händ|le|rin, ...[buch|]hand|lung, ...haus, ...ka|ta|log, ...kauf|frau, ...kauf|mann, ...pro|gramm, ...pros|pekt, ...recht, ...ver|trag, ...we|sen** (das; -s)
Ver|laine [vɛr'lɛ:n] (franz. Dichter)
ver|lam|men; das Schaf hat verlammt
ver|lan|den (von Seen usw.); **Ver|lan|dung**
ver|lan|gen; Ver|lan|gen, das; -s, -; auf -
ver|län|gern; ich ...ere (↑R 16); **ver|län|gert;** -er Rücken (*ugs. scherzh. für* Gesäß); **Ver|län|ger|te,** der; -n, -n (↑R 5 ff.; *österr. für* dünner Kaffee); **Ver|län|ge|rung; Ver|län|ge|rungs‿ka|bel, ...schnur**
ver|lang|sa|men; Ver|lang|sa|mung
ver|läp|pern (*ugs. für* [Geld] vergeuden); **Ver|läp|pe|rung**
Ver|lass, der; -es; es ist kein - auf ihn; [1]**ver|las|sen;** sich auf eine Sache, einen Menschen -; er hatte sich auf ihn -; [2]**ver|las|sen** (vereinsamt); das Dorf lag - da; **Ver|las|sen|heit,** die; -; **Ver|las|sen|schaft** (*bes. österr. für* Hinterlassenschaft); **ver|läs|sig** (*veraltet für* zuverlässig); **ver|läs|si|gen,** sich (*landsch. für* sich vergewissern); **ver|läss|lich** (zuverlässig); **Ver|läss|lich|keit,** die; -
ver|läs|tern; Ver|läs|te|rung
Ver|laub, der; *nur noch in* mit -
Ver|lauf; im -; **ver|lau|fen;** die Sache ist gut verlaufen; sich -; er hat sich verlaufen; **Ver|laufs|form** (*Sprachw.* sprachl. Fügung, die angibt, dass ein Geschehen gerade abläuft, z. B. „er ist beim Arbeiten")
ver|lau|sen; Ver|lau|sung
ver|laut|ba|ren; es verlautbart, dass ...; **Ver|laut|ba|rung; ver|lau|ten;** wie verlautet
ver|le|ben; ver|le|ben|di|gen (anschaulich, lebendig machen); **Ver|le|ben|di|gung; ver|lebt;** ein -es Gesicht
[1]**ver|le|gen** ⟨*zu* legen⟩ (an einen anderen Platz legen; auf einen anderen Zeitpunkt festlegen; im Verlag herausgeben; *Technik* [Rohre u. a.] legen, zusammenfügen); (↑R 50:) [das] Verlegen von Rohren; [2]**ver|le|gen** ⟨*zu* liegen⟩ (befangen, unsicher); sie war -; **Ver|le|gen|heit; Ver|le|gen|heits‿ge|schenk, ...lö|sung; Ver|le|ger; Ver|le|ge|rin; ver|le|ge|risch; Ver|le|ger|zei|chen; Ver|le|gung**
ver|lei|den (jmdm. die Freude an etwas nehmen); es ist mir alles verleidet; **Ver|lei|der,** der; -s (*schweiz. mdal. für* Überdruss); er hat den - bekommen
Ver|leih, der; -[e]s, -e; **ver|lei|hen;** sie hat das Buch verliehen; (↑R 50:) [das] Verleihen von Geld; **Ver|lei|her; Ver|lei|he|rin; Ver|lei|hung**
ver|lei|men; Ver|lei|mung
ver|lei|ten (verführen)
ver|leit|ge|ben ⟨*zu* Leitgeb⟩ (*landsch. für* Bier od. Wein ausschenken)
Ver|lei|tung
ver|ler|nen
ver|le|sen (ablesen; sondern [z. B. Erbsen]); sie hat den Text verlesen; sich - (falsch lesen); **Ver|le|sung**
ver|letz|bar; Ver|letz|bar|keit, die; -; **ver|let|zen;** er ist verletzt; **ver|let|zend; ver|letz|lich; Ver|letz|lich|keit,** die; -; **ver|letzt; Ver|letz|te,** der *u.* die; -n, -n (↑R 5 ff.); **Ver|let|zung; Ver|let|zungs‿ge|fahr, ...pau|se** (*Sport*)
ver|leug|nen; Ver|leug|nung
ver|leum|den; Ver|leum|der; Ver|leum|de|rin; ver|leum|de|risch; Ver|leum|dung; Ver|leum|dungs|kam|pag|ne
ver|lie|ben, sich; **ver|liebt;** ein -es Paar; **Ver|lieb|te,** der *u.* die; -n, -n (↑R 5 ff.); **Ver|liebt|heit,** die; -
ver|lie|ren; du verlorst; du verlörest; verloren (*vgl. d.*); verlier[e]!; sich verlieren; **Ver|lie|rer; Ver|lie|re|rin; Ver|lies,** das; -es, -e ([unterird.] Gefängnis, Kerker)
ver|lo|ben; sich -; **Ver|löb|nis,** das; -ses, -se; **Ver|lob|te,** der *u.* die; -n, -n (↑R 5 ff.); **Ver|lo|bung; Ver|lo|bungs‿an|zei|ge, ...ring, ...zeit**
ver|lo|cken; Ver|lo|ckung
ver|lo|dern (*geh. für* lodernd verlöschen)
ver|lo|gen (lügenhaft); **Ver|lo|gen|heit**
ver|lo|hen (*geh. für* erlöschen)
ver|loh|nen; sich -; es verlohnt sich zu leben; *vgl.* lohnen
ver|lo|ren; verlorene Eier (in kochendem Wasser ohne Schale gegarte Eier); der verlorene Sohn; auf verlorenem Posten stehen; verloren sein; das Spiel ist längst verloren gewesen; verloren geben; sie haben das Spiel frühzeitig verloren gegeben; verloren gehen; mein Pass ist verloren gegangen; der Krieg, der verloren ging; **Ver|lo|ren|heit,** die; -
[1]**ver|lö|schen;** eine Schrift - (auslöschend verwischen); *vgl.* [1]löschen; [2]**ver|lö|schen;** die Kerze verlischt; *vgl.* [2]löschen
ver|lo|sen; Ver|lo|sung
ver|lö|ten; einen Blechkanister -; einen - (*ugs. für* Alkohol trinken)
ver|lot|tern (*ugs. für* verkommen); **Ver|lot|te|rung** (*ugs.*)
ver|lu|dern (*ugs. für* verkommen)
ver|lum|pen (verkommen)
Ver|lust, der; -[e]s, -e; **ver|lust|arm; Ver|lust‿be|trieb, ...geschäft**
ver|lus|tie|ren, sich (*scherzh. für* sich vergnügen)
ver|lus|tig; *meist in* einer Sache -

gehen (eine Sache verlieren, preisgeben müssen); **Ver|lust|lis|te; ver|lust|reich**

verm. (*Zeichen* ⚭) = vermählt

ver|ma|chen (vererben; *ugs. für* überlassen); **Ver|mächt|nis,** das; -ses, -se; **Ver|mächt|nis|neh|mer** *(Rechtsspr.)*

ver|mah|len (zu Mehl machen); *vgl. aber* vermalen

ver|mäh|len *(geh.);* sich -; **ver|mählt** (*Abk.* verm. [*Zeichen* ⚭]); **Ver|mähl|te,** der *u.* die; -n, -n (↑R 5 ff.); **Ver|mäh|lung; Ver|mäh|lungs|an|zei|ge**

ver|mah|nen (*veraltend für* ernst ermahnen); **Ver|mah|nung**

ver|ma|le|dei|en (*veraltend für* verfluchen, verwünschen); **Ver|ma|le|dei|ung**

ver|ma|len ([Farben] malend verbrauchen); *vgl. aber* vermahlen

ver|männ|li|chen

ver|man|schen (*ugs. für* vermischen)

ver|mar|ken (*fachspr. für* vermessen)

ver|mark|ten (*Wirtsch.* [bedarfsgerecht zubereitet] auf den Markt bringen); **Ver|mark|tung**

Ver|mar|kung (*fachspr. für* Vermessung)

ver|mas|seln ‹*zu* [1]Massel› (*ugs. für* zunichte machen); ich vermassele *u.* vermassle (↑R 16)

ver|mas|sen (etwas zur Massenware machen; in der Masse aufgehen); du vermasst; vermasst; **Ver|mas|sung**

ver|mau|ern

Ver|meer van Delft [vər... fan, *auch* van -], Jan (niederl. Maler)

ver|meh|ren; sich -; **Ver|meh|rung**

ver|meid|bar; ver|mei|den; sie hat diesen Fehler vermieden; **vermeid|lich; Ver|mei|dung**

ver|meil [vɛrˈmɛːj] ‹franz.› (hochrot); **Ver|meil,** das; -s (vergoldetes Silber)

ver|mei|nen ([irrtümlich] glauben); **ver|meint|lich**

ver|mel|den (*veraltend für* mitteilen)

ver|men|gen; Ver|men|gung

ver|mensch|li|chen

Ver|merk, der; -[e]s, -e; **ver|merken;** etwas am Rande -

[1]**ver|mes|sen;** Land -; sich - (sich beim Messen irren; *geh. für* sich unterfangen); er hat sich -, alles zu sagen *(geh.);* [2]**ver|mes|sen;** ein -es (tollkühnes) Unternehmen; **Ver|mes|sen|heit** (Kühnheit); **Ver|mes|sung; Ver|messungs‿in|ge|ni|eur** (*Abk.* Verm.-Ing.), **...schiff, ...ur|kun|de**

Ver|mi|celles [vɛrmisɛl] *Plur.* ‹franz.› (*schweiz.* eine Süßspeise aus Kastanienpüree)

ver|mi|ckert, ver|mie|kert (*ugs. für* klein, schwächlich)

ver|mie|sen (*ugs. für* verleiden); du vermiest; er vermies|te

ver|mie|ten; Ver|mie|ter; Ver|mie|te|rin; Ver|mie|tung

Ver|mil|lon [vɛrmiˈjɔ̃ː], das; -s ‹franz.› (feinster Zinnober)

ver|min|dern; Ver|min|de|rung

ver|mi|nen (Minen legen; durch Minen versperren)

Verm.-Ing. = Vermessungsingenieur

Ver|mi|nung

ver|mi|schen; Ver|mi|schung

ver|mis|sen; als vermisst gemeldet; **Ver|miss|te,** der *u.* die; -n, -n (↑R 5 ff.); **Ver|miss|ten|an|zei|ge**

ver|mit|teln; ich ...[e]le (↑R 16); **ver|mit|tels[t];** *Präp. mit Gen.* vermittels[t] des Eimers (*besser:* mit dem Eimer *od.* mithilfe des Eimers); *vgl.* mittels; **Ver|mitt|ler; Ver|mitt|le|rin; Ver|mitt|ler|rol|le; Ver|mitt|lung; Ver|mitt|lungs‿amt, ...ge|bühr, ...stel|le, ...ver|such**

ver|mö|beln (*ugs. für* verprügeln); ich ...[e]le (↑R 16)

ver|mo|dern; Ver|mo|de|rung, Ver|mod|rung

ver|mö|ge; *Präp. mit Gen. (geh.):* vermöge seines Geldes; **ver|mögen; Ver|mö|gen,** das; -s, -; **vermö|gend; Ver|mö|gens‿ab|gabe, ...be|ra|ter, ...be|ra|te|rin, ...be|steu|e|rung, ...bil|dung, ...er|klä|rung, ...la|ge; ver|mögens|los; Ver|mö|gens|recht,** das; -[e]s; **Ver|mö|gens|steu|er, Ver|mö|gen|steu|er,** die (↑R 34); **Ver|mö|gens‿ver|si|che|rung, ...ver|tei|lung, ...ver|wal|tung; ver|mö|gens|wirk|sam;** -e Leistungen; **Ver|mö|gens|zu|wachs; ver|mög|lich** (*landsch. u. schweiz. für* wohlhabend)

Ver|mont [v...] (Staat in den USA; *Abk.* Vt.)

ver|moo|ren; die Wiesen -

ver|mor|schen; vermorscht

ver|mot|tet

ver|mü|ckert, *auch* **ver|mü|kert** (*landsch. für* klein, schwächlich)

ver|mum|men (fest einhüllen); sich - (durch Verkleidung u. Ä. unkenntlich machen); **Ver|mummung; Ver|mum|mungs|ver|bot**

[1]**ver|mu|ren** ‹*zu* Mure› (*Geol.* durch Schutt verwüsten)

[2]**ver|mu|ren** ‹engl.› (*Seew.* vor zwei Anker legen); *vgl.* muren

ver|murk|sen (*ugs. für* verderben)

ver|mu|ten; ver|mut|lich; Vermu|tung; ver|mu|tungs|wei|se

ver|nach|läs|sig|bar; ver|nachläs|si|gen; Ver|nach|läs|si|gung

ver|na|geln; ver|na|gelt (*ugs. auch für* äußerst begriffsstutzig); **Ver|na|ge|lung, Ver|nag|lung**

ver|nä|hen; eine Wunde -; sie hat das Garn vernäht

ver|nar|ben; Ver|nar|bung

ver|nar|ren, sich -; in jmdn., in etwas vernarrt sein; **Ver|narrt|heit**

ver|na|schen; sein Geld -; ein Mädchen - (*ugs. für* mit ihm schlafen); **ver|nascht** (*svw.* naschhaft)

ver|ne|beln; ich ...[e]le (↑R 16); **Ver|ne|be|lung, Ver|neb|lung**

ver|nehm|bar; ver|neh|men; er hat das Geräusch vernommen; der Angeklagte wurde vernommen; **Ver|neh|men,** das; -s; *meist in* dem - nach; **Ver|nehm|lassung** (*schweiz. für* Stellungnahme, Verlautbarung); **ver|nehmlich; Ver|neh|mung** ([gerichtl.] Befragung); **ver|neh|mungs‿fähig, ...un|fä|hig**

ver|nei|gen, sich; **Ver|nei|gung**

ver|nei|nen; Ver|nei|ner; Verneine|rin; Ver|nei|nung; Ver|nei|nungs‿fall (der; im -[e] *[Amtsspr.]*), **...wort** *(Sprachw.)*

ver|net|zen (miteinander verbinden, verknüpfen); **Ver|net|zung**

ver|nich|ten; eine vernichtende Kritik; **Ver|nich|ter; Ver|nich|te|rin; Ver|nich|tung; Ver|nichtungs‿feld|zug, ...kraft** *(Jargon),* **...krieg, ...la|ger, ...waf|fe, ...werk** (das; -[e]s), **...wut**

ver|ni|ckeln; ich ...[e]le (↑R 16); **Ver|ni|cke|lung; Ver|nick|lung**

ver|nied|li|chen; Ver|nied|lichung

ver|nie|ten (mit Nieten verschließen); **Ver|nie|tung**

Ver|nis|sa|ge [vɛrniˈsaːʒə], die; -, -n ‹franz.› (Ausstellungseröffnung [in kleinerem Rahmen])

Ver|nunft, die; -; **ver|nunft|begabt; Ver|nunft|ehe** (↑R 132); **Ver|nünf|te|lei** *(veraltend);* **vernünf|teln;** ich ...[e]le (↑R 16) *(veraltend);* **ver|nunft|ge|mäß; Vernunft‿glau|be[n], ...hei|rat; vernünf|tig; ver|nünf|ti|ger|wei|se; Ver|nünft|ler** *(veraltend);* **Vernunft|mensch,** der; **ver|nunftwid|rig;** -es Verhalten; **Vernunft|wid|rig|keit**

ver|nu|ten (durch Nut verbinden); **Ver|nu|tung**

ver|öden (↑R 132); **Ver|ödung**

ver|öf|fent|li|chen; Ver|öf|fent|lichung

ver|ölen (↑R 132; ölig werden)
Ve|ro|na [v...] (ital. Stadt); [1]**Ve|ro|ne|se,** der; -n, -n (↑R 126) *u.* Ve|ro|ne|ser; ↑R 103 (Einwohner von Verona); [2]**Ve|ro|ne|se** (ital. Maler); **Ve|ro|ne|ser** *vgl.* [1]Veronese; **Ve|ro|ne|ser Er|de,** die; - - (Farbe); **Ve|ro|ne|ser Gelb,** das; - -s; **ve|ro|ne|sisch**
[1]**Ve|ro|ni|ka** [v...] (w. Vorn.); [2]**Ve|ro|ni|ka,** die; -, ...ken ‹nach der hl. Veronika› (Ehrenpreis [eine Pflanze])
ver|ord|nen; Ver|ord|nung; Ver|ord|nungs|blatt
ver|paa|ren, sich *(Zool.);* **ver|paart**
ver|pach|ten; Ver|päch|ter; Ver|päch|te|rin; Ver|pach|tung
ver|pa|cken; Ver|pa|ckung; Ver|pa|ckungs|ma|te|ri|al
ver|päp|peln (*ugs. für* verzärteln); du verpäppelst dich
[1]**ver|pas|sen** (versäumen); sie hat den Zug verpasst; [2]**ver|pas|sen** (*ugs. für* geben; schlagen); die Uniform wurde ihm verpasst; dem werde ich eins verpassen
ver|pat|zen (*ugs. für* verderben); er hat die Arbeit verpatzt
ver|pen|nen (*ugs. für* verschlafen)
ver|pes|ten; die Luft -; **Ver|pes|tung**
ver|pet|zen (*ugs. für* verraten); er hat ihn verpetzt
ver|pfän|den; Ver|pfän|dung
ver|pfei|fen (*ugs. für* verraten); er hat ihn verpfiffen
ver|pflan|zen; die Blumen wurden verpflanzt; **Ver|pflan|zung**
ver|pfle|gen; Ver|pfle|gung *Plur. selten;* **Ver|pfle|gungs_geld, ...satz**
ver|pflich|ten; sich -; sie ist mir verpflichtet; **Ver|pflich|tung;** eine moralische -; **Ver|pflich|tungs|ge|schäft** *(Rechtsw.)*
ver|pfrün|den (*südd. u. schweiz. für* durch lebenslänglichen Unterhalt versorgen); **Ver|pfrün|dung** *(südd. u. schweiz.)*
ver|pfu|schen (*ugs. für* verderben); er hat die Zeichnung verpfuscht; ein völlig verpfuschtes Leben
ver|pi|chen (mit Pech ausstreichen)
ver|pie|seln, sich (*landsch. für* sich entfernen, davonlaufen); ich ...[e]le mich (↑R 16)
ver|pim|peln (*ugs. für* verzärteln); du verpimpelst dich
ver|pis|sen; sich - (*derb für* sich [heimlich] entfernen)
ver|pla|nen (falsch planen; *auch für* in einen Plan einbauen)
ver|plap|pern, sich (*ugs. für* etwas voreilig u. unüberlegt heraussagen)
ver|plat|ten (mit Platten versehen)
ver|plät|ten (*ugs. für* verprügeln)
Ver|plat|tung
ver|plau|dern ([Zeit] mit Plaudern verbringen); sich -
ver|plem|pern (*ugs. für* vergeuden); Zeit -; du verplemperst dich
ver|plom|ben (mit einer Plombe versiegeln); **Ver|plom|bung**
ver|pö|nen ‹dt.; lat.› (*veraltend für* missbilligen; [bei Strafe] verbieten); **ver|pönt** (verboten, nicht statthaft)
ver|pop|pen; ein verpoppter (mit den Mitteln der Popkunst veränderter) Klassiker
ver|pras|sen; er hat das Geld verprasst
ver|prel|len (verwirren, verärgern; *Jägerspr.* [Wild] verscheuchen)
ver|pro|le|ta|ri|sie|ren; Ver|pro|le|ta|ri|sie|rung, die; -
ver|pro|vi|an|tie|ren [...vi̯an...] (mit Proviant versorgen); **Ver|pro|vi|an|tie|rung,** die; -
ver|prü|geln
ver|puf|fen ([schwach] explodieren; *auch für* ohne Wirkung bleiben); **Ver|puf|fung**
ver|pul|vern (*ugs. für* unnütz verbrauchen)
ver|pum|pen (*ugs. für* verleihen)
ver|pup|pen, sich; **Ver|pup|pung** (Umwandlung der Insektenlarve in die Puppe)
ver|pus|ten; sich - (*ugs. für* Luft schöpfen)
Ver|putz (Mauerbewurf); **ver|put|zen** (*ugs. auch für* [Geld] durchbringen, vergeuden; [schnell] aufessen); jmdn. nicht - (*ugs. für* nicht ausstehen) können; **Ver|put|zer** *(Bauw.)*
ver|qual|men (*ugs. für* mit Rauch, Qualm erfüllen)
ver|quält; -e (von Sorgen gezeichnete) Züge; - aussehen
ver|qua|sen (*nordd. für* vergeuden); du verquast; er verquas|te; **ver|quast** (*landsch. für* verworren)
ver|quat|schen, sich (*ugs. für* sich versprechen; etwas preisgeben, verraten)
ver|quel|len; das Fenster verquillt; *vgl.* verquollen *u.* [1]quellen
ver|quer; mir geht etwas - (*ugs. für* es misslingt mir)
ver|qui|cken (vermischen; in enge Verbindung bringen); **Ver|qui|ckung**
ver|quir|len (mit einem Quirl o. Ä. verrühren)
ver|quis|ten (*nordd. veraltend für* vergeuden)
ver|quol|len; -e Augen; -es Holz
ver|ram|meln, ver|ram|men; **Ver|ram|me|lung, Ver|ramm|lung, Ver|ram|mung**
ver|ram|schen (*ugs. für* zu Schleuderpreisen verkaufen); *vgl.* [1]ramschen
ver|rannt (*ugs. für* vernarrt; festgefahren); in jmdn., in etwas - sein
Ver|rat, der; -[e]s; **ver|ra|ten;** sich -; dadurch hast du dich verraten; **Ver|rä|ter; Ver|rä|te|rei; Ver|rä|te|rin; ver|rä|te|risch**
ver|ratzt; *nur in* - sein (*ugs. für* verloren, in einer schwierigen, ausweglosen Lage sein)
ver|rau|chen; ver|räu|chern
ver|rau|schen; der Beifall verrauschte
ver|rech|nen; sich - (*auch für* sich täuschen); **Ver|rech|nung; Ver|rech|nungs_ein|heit** *(Wirtsch.),* **...kon|to, ...preis, ...scheck**
ver|re|cken (*derb für* verenden; elend zugrunde gehen)
ver|reg|nen; verregnet
ver|rei|ben; Ver|rei|bung
ver|rei|sen (auf die Reise gehen); sie ist verreist
ver|rei|ßen (*landsch. auch für* zerreißen); er hat das Theaterstück verrissen (vernichtend kritisiert)
ver|rei|ten, sich (einen falschen Weg reiten); er hat sich verritten
ver|ren|ken; sich -; die Tänzer verrenkten sich auf der Bühne; ich habe mir den Fuß verrenkt; **Ver|ren|kung**
ver|ren|nen; sich in etwas - (hartnäckig an etwas festhalten)
ver|ren|ten *(Amtsspr.);* **Ver|ren|tung**
ver|rich|ten; Ver|rich|tung
ver|rie|geln; Ver|rie|ge|lung, Ver|rieg|lung
ver|rin|gern; ich ...ere (↑R 16); **Ver|rin|ge|rung,** die; -
ver|rin|nen
Ver|riss, der; -es, -e (vernichtende Kritik); *vgl.* verreißen
ver|ro|hen
ver|roh|ren (*fachspr. für* mit Rohren versehen; Rohre verlegen); **Ver|roh|rung**
ver|roht; Ver|ro|hung, die; -
ver|rol|len; der Donner verrollt in der Ferne
ver|ros|ten
ver|rot|ten (verfaulen, modern; zerfallen); **Ver|rot|tung,** die; -
ver|rucht; Ver|rucht|heit, die; -
ver|rü|cken; ver|rückt; Ver|rück|te, der *u.* die; -n, -n (↑R 5 ff.); **Ver|rückt|heit; Ver|rückt|wer|den,** das; -s; das ist zum - *(ugs.);* **Ver|rü|ckung**

Ver|ruf, der (schlechter Ruf); *nur noch in* in - bringen, geraten, kommen; **ver|ru|fen** (übel, berüchtigt); die Gegend ist -
ver|rüh|ren; zwei Eier -
ver|run|zelt (runzelig)
ver|ru|ßen; der Schornstein ist verrußt; **Ver|ru|ßung**
ver|rut|schen
Vers [*österr. auch* vɛrs], der; -es, -e ‹lat.› (Zeile, Strophe eines Gedichtes; *Abk.* V.); ich kann mir keinen - darauf *od.* daraus machen *(ugs.)*
ver|sach|li|chen; Ver|sach|li|chung, die; -
ver|sa|cken (wegsinken; *ugs. für* liederlich leben)
ver|sa|gen; er hat ihr keinen Wunsch versagt; seine Beine haben versagt; ich versagte mir diesen Genuss; (↑R 50:) das Unglück ist auf menschliches Versagen zurückzuführen; **Ver|sa|ger** (nicht fähige Person; nicht explodierende Patrone usw.); **Ver|sa|gung**
Ver|sail|ler [vɛrˈzajər] (↑R 103); - Vertrag; **Ver|sailles** [vɛrˈzaj] (franz. Stadt)
Ver|sal [v...], der; -s, -ien [...i̯ən] *meist Plur.* ‹lat.› (großer [Anfangs]buchstabe); **Ver|sal|buch|sta|be**
ver|sal|zen (*fachspr. für* mit Salzen durchsetzt werden; *ugs. auch für* verderben, die Freude an etwas nehmen); versalzt *u. (übertr. nur:)* versalzen; die Suppe versalzen; der Fluss versalzt immer mehr; wir haben ihm die Freude versalzen
ver|sam|meln; Ver|samm|lung; Ver|samm|lungs‿frei|heit (die; -), **...lo|kal, ...recht** (das; -[e]s)
Ver|sand, der; -[e]s (Versendung); **Ver|sand|ab|tei|lung; ver|sand|be|reit; Ver|sand|buch|han|del**
ver|san|den (sich mit Sand füllen, vom Sand zugedeckt werden; nachlassen, aufhören)
ver|sand|fer|tig; Ver|sand‿ge|schäft, ...gut, ...han|del (*vgl.* [1]Handel), **...haus; Ver|sand|haus|ka|ta|log; Ver|sand|kos|ten** *Plur.;* **ver|sandt,** ver|sen|det; *vgl.* senden
Ver|san|dung, die; -
Vers‿an|fang, ...art
Ver|satz, der; -es (das Versetzen, Verpfänden; *Bergmannsspr.* Auffüllung von Hohlräumen unter Tage, Gestein dafür); **Ver|satz‿amt** (*bayr. u. österr. für* Leihhaus), **...stück** (bewegliche Bühnendekoration; *österr. auch für* Pfandstück)

ver|sau|beu|teln (*ugs. für* beschmutzen; verlegen, verlieren); **ver|sau|en** *(derb)*
ver|sau|ern (sauer werden; *ugs. auch für* geistig verkümmern); ich ...ere (↑R 16)
ver|sau|fen; sein Geld - *(derb)*
ver|säu|men; Ver|säum|nis, das; -ses, -se, *veraltet* die; -, -se; **Ver|säum|nis|ur|teil** *(Rechtsw.);* **Ver|säu|mung**
Vers|bau, der; -[e]s
ver|scha|chern (*ugs. für* [teuer] verkaufen)
ver|schach|telt; ein -er Satz
ver|schaf|fen; *vgl.* [1]schaffen; du hast dir Genugtuung verschafft
ver|scha|len (mit Brettern verkleiden)
ver|schal|ken (*Seemannsspr.* [Luken] schließen)
Ver|scha|lung (Auskleidung mit Brettern; [Holz]verkleidung)
ver|schämt; - tun; **Ver|schämt|heit,** die; -; **Ver|schämt|tun,** das; -s
ver|schan|deln (*ugs. für* verunzieren); ich ...[e]le (↑R 16); **Ver|schan|de|lung, Ver|schand|lung**
ver|schan|zen; das Lager wurde verschanzt; sich -; du hast dich hinter Ausreden verschanzt; **Ver|schan|zung**
ver|schär|fen; die Lage verschärft sich; **Ver|schär|fung**
ver|schar|ren
ver|schät|zen, sich
ver|schau|en, sich (*österr. ugs. für* sich verlieben)
ver|schau|keln (*ugs. für* betrügen, hintergehen)
ver|schei|den (*geh. für* sterben); er ist verschieden
ver|schei|ßen (*derb für* mit Kot beschmutzen); *vgl.* verschissen; **ver|schei|ßern** (*derb für* zum Narren halten); ich ...ere (↑R 16)
ver|schen|ken
ver|scher|beln (*ugs. für* [billig] verkaufen)
ver|scher|zen ([durch Leichtsinn] verlieren); sich etwas -; du hast dir ihre Liebe verscherzt
ver|scheu|chen
ver|scheu|ern (*ugs. für* verkaufen)
ver|schi|cken; Ver|schi|ckung
ver|schieb|bar; Ver|schie|be|bahn|hof (Rangierbahnhof); **ver|schie|ben; Ver|schie|bung**
[1]**ver|schie|den** (*geh. für* gestorben)
[2]**ver|schie|den;** verschieden lang; verschiedene Mal *od.* Male; (↑R 47:) wenn Verschiedene sagen, dass...; Verschiedenes war mir unklar; etwas Verschiedenes;

ver|schie|den|ar|tig; Ver|schie|den|ar|tig|keit, die; -; **ver|schie|de|ne Mal** *vgl.* verschieden; **ver|schie|de|ner|lei; ver|schie|den‿far|big, ...ge|schlecht|lich, ...ge|stal|tig; Ver|schie|den|heit; ver|schie|dent|lich**
ver|schie|ßen (*auch für* ausbleichen); *vgl.* verschossen
ver|schif|fen; Ver|schif|fung; Ver|schif|fungs|ha|fen *vgl.* [2]Hafen
ver|schil|fen ([mit Schilf] zuwachsen)
ver|schim|meln
ver|schimp|fie|ren (*veraltet für* verunstalten; beschimpfen)
Ver|schiss (*derb für* schlechter Ruf); *nur noch in* in - geraten, kommen; **ver|schis|sen;** es bei jmdm. - haben (*derb für* bei jmdm. in Ungnade gefallen sein)
ver|schla|cken; der Ofen ist verschlackt; **Ver|schla|ckung**
[1]**ver|schla|fen;** ich habe [mich] verschlafen; sie hat den Morgen verschlafen; [2]**ver|schla|fen;** er sieht - aus; **Ver|schla|fen|heit,** die; -
Ver|schlag, der; -[e]s, Verschläge; [1]**ver|schla|gen;** die Kiste wurde mit Brettern -; es verschlägt mir die Sprache; es verschlägt (*landsch. für* nützt) nichts; [2]**ver|schla|gen** ([hinter]listig); ein -er Mensch; **Ver|schla|gen|heit,** die; -
ver|schlam|men; der Fluss ist verschlammt; **ver|schläm|men** (mit Schlamm füllen); die Abfälle haben das Rohr verschlämmt; **Ver|schlam|mung; Ver|schläm|mung**
ver|schlam|pen (*ugs. für* verlegen, verlieren; verkommen [lassen])
ver|schlan|ken (verkleinern, reduzieren); die Produktion -
ver|schlech|tern; ich ...ere (↑R 16); sich -; **Ver|schlech|te|rung**
ver|schlei|ern; ich ...ere (↑R 16); **Ver|schlei|e|rung; Ver|schlei|e|rungs‿tak|tik, ...ver|such**
ver|schlei|fen (durch [1]Schleifen glätten); **Ver|schlei|fung**
ver|schlei|men; ver|schleimt; Ver|schlei|mung
Ver|schleiß, der; -es, -e (Abnutzung; *österr. auch für* Kleinverkauf, Vertrieb); **ver|schlei|ßen;** etwas verschleißen (etwas [stark] abnutzen); Waren verschleißen (*österr. für* verkaufen, vertreiben); du verschlisst, *österr. auch* verschleißtest; verschlissen, *österr. auch* verschleißt; **Ver|schlei|ßer** (*österr. veraltend für*

Kleinhändler); **Ver|schlei|ße|rin** *(österr. veraltend);* **Ver|schleiß-_er|schei|nung, ...fes|tig|keit, ...prü|fung, ...teil** (das)
ver|schlem|men (verprassen)
ver|schlep|pen; einen Prozess -; eine verschleppte Grippe; **Ver|schlep|pung; Ver|schlep-pungs_ma|nö|ver, ...tak|tik**
ver|schleu|dern; Ver|schleu|de-rung
ver|schließ|bar; ver|schlie|ßen *vgl.* verschlossen; **Ver|schlie-ßung**
ver|schlimm|bes|sern; er hat alles nur verschlimmbessert; **Ver|schlimm|bes|se|rung; ver-schlim|mern;** ich ...ere (↑R 16); **Ver|schlim|me|rung**
ver|schlin|gen; Ver|schlin|gung
ver|schlos|sen (zugeschlossen; verschwiegen); **Ver|schlos|sen-heit,** die; -
ver|schlu|cken; sich -
ver|schlu|dern (*ugs. für* verlieren, verlegen; verkommen lassen)
Ver|schluss; Ver|schluss|de-ckel; ver|schlüs|seln; Ver-schlüs|se|lung; Ver|schluss-_kap|pe, ...laut (*für* Explosiv)
Ver|schluss|sa|che (↑R 136); **Ver|schluss|schrau|be; Ver-schluss|strei|fen** (↑R 136)
ver|schmach|ten *(geh.)*
ver|schmä|hen; Ver|schmä-hung, die; -
ver|schmä|lern; sich -
ver|schmau|sen
[1]**ver|schmel|zen** (flüssig werden; ineinander übergehen); *vgl.* [1]schmelzen; [2]**ver|schmel|zen** (zusammenfließen lassen; ineinander übergehen lassen); *vgl.* [2]schmelzen; **Ver|schmel|zung**
ver|schmer|zen
ver|schmie|ren; Ver|schmie-rung
ver|schmitzt (schlau, verschlagen); **Ver|schmitzt|heit,** die; -
ver|schmockt (*ugs. für* vordergründig, effektvoll, ohne wirklichen Gehalt)
ver|schmust (*ugs. für* gern schmusend)
ver|schmut|zen; ver|schmutzt; Ver|schmut|zung
ver|schnap|pen, sich (*landsch. für* sich verplappern)
ver|schnau|fen; sich -; **Ver-schnauf|pau|se**
ver|schnei|den (*auch für* kastrieren); verschnitten; **Ver|schnei-dung**
ver|schneit; -e Wälder
ver|schnip|peln (*landsch. für* verschneiden)
Ver|schnitt, der; -[e]s, -e (*auch für* Mischung alkoholischer Flüssigkeiten); **Ver|schnit|te|ne,** der; -n, -n; ↑R 5 ff. (*für* Kastrat)
ver|schnör|keln; verschnörkelte Ornamente; **Ver|schnör|ke-lung, Ver|schnörk|lung**
ver|schnup|fen (verärgern); mit dieser Bemerkung verschnupfte sie ihn; **ver|schnupft** (einen Schnupfen habend; *auch für* gekränkt); **Ver|schnup|fung**
ver|schnü|ren; Ver|schnü|rung
ver|schol|len (unauffindbar und für tot, verloren gehalten)
ver|scho|nen; jmdn. -
ver|schö|nen; sie hat [mir] das Fest verschönt; **ver|schö|nern;** ich ...ere (↑R 16); **Ver|schö|ne-rung**
Ver|scho|nung
Ver|schö|nung
ver|schor|fen; die Wunde verschorft; **Ver|schor|fung**
ver|schos|sen (ausgebleicht); ein -es Kleid; in jmdn. - (*ugs. für* heftig verliebt) sein
ver|schram|men; verschrammt
ver|schrän|ken; mit verschränkten Armen; **Ver|schrän|kung**
ver|schrau|ben; Ver|schrau-bung
ver|schre|cken (ängstigen, verstört machen); *vgl.* [2]schrecken; **ver|schreckt;** die -e Konkurrenz
ver|schrei|ben (falsch schreiben; gerichtlich übereignen; mit Rezept verordnen); sich -; **Ver-schrei|bung; ver|schrei|bungs-pflich|tig; Ver|schrieb,** der; -s, -e (*schweiz. für* Schreibfehler, falsche Schreibung)
ver|schrie|en, ver|schrien; er ist als Geizhals -
ver|schro|ben (seltsam; wunderlich); **Ver|schro|ben|heit**
ver|schro|ten (zu Schrot machen)
ver|schrot|ten (zu Schrott machen, als Altmetall verwerten); **Ver|schrot|tung**
ver|schrum|peln *(ugs.);* **Ver-schrum|pe|lung,** Ver|schrump-lung; **ver|schrump|fen** (*selten für* verschrumpeln)
ver|schüch|tern; ich ...ere (↑R 16); das Kind war völlig verschüchtert; **Ver|schüch|te|rung**
ver|schul|den; Ver|schul|den, das; -s; ohne [sein] -; **ver|schul-det; ver|schul|de|ter|ma|ßen; Ver|schul|dung**
ver|schu|len (dem Schulunterricht annähern; *Landw.* Sämlinge ins Pflanzbeet umpflanzen); das Studium -; **Ver|schu|lung**
ver|schup|fen (*landsch. für* fort-, verstoßen, stiefmütterlich behandeln)
ver|schus|seln (*ugs. für* verlieren, verlegen, vergessen)
ver|schüt|ten
ver|schütt ge|hen ⟨Gaunerspr.⟩ (*ugs. für* verloren gehen)
Ver|schüt|tung
ver|schwä|gert; Ver|schwä|ge-rung
ver|schwei|gen; Ver|schwei-gung, die; -
ver|schwei|ßen; Ver|schwei-ßung
ver|schwe|len (schwelend verbrennen); **Ver|schwe|lung**
ver|schwen|den; Ver|schwen-der; Ver|schwen|de|rin; ver-schwen|de|risch; Ver|schwen-dung; Ver|schwen|dungs-sucht, die; -; **ver|schwen-dungs|süch|tig**
ver|schwie|gen; Ver|schwie-gen|heit, die; -
ver|schwim|men; die Berge sind im Dunst verschwommen; es verschwimmt [mir] vor den Augen
ver|schwin|den; Ver|schwin-den, das; -s
ver|schwis|tert (*auch für* zusammengehörend); **Ver|schwis|te-rung**
ver|schwit|zen (*ugs. auch für* vergessen); verschwitzt
ver|schwol|len; -e Augen
ver|schwom|men; -e Vorstellungen; **Ver|schwom|men|heit,** die; -
ver|schwö|ren, sich; **Ver|schwo-re|ne,** Ver|schwor|ne, der *u.* die; -n, -n (↑R 5 ff.); **Ver|schwö|rer; Ver|schwö|re|rin; ver|schwö-re|risch; Ver|schwor|ne** *vgl.* Verschworene; **Ver|schwö|rung**
Vers|dra|ma (in Versen abgefasstes Drama)
ver|se|hen; er hat seinen Posten treu -; sich - (sich versorgen; sich irren); ich habe mich mit Nahrungsmitteln -; ich habe mich - (geirrt); ehe du dichs (*vgl.* [2]es) versiehst *(veraltend);* **Ver|se|hen,** das; -s, - (Irrtum); aus -; **ver|se-hent|lich** (aus Versehen); **Ver-seh|gang,** der; -[e]s, ...gänge (Gang des kath. Priesters zur Spendung der Sakramente an Kranke, bes. an Sterbende)
ver|seh|ren (*veraltet für* verletzen, beschädigen); versehrt; **Ver-sehr|te,** der *u.* die; -n, -n; ↑R 5 ff. (Körperbeschädigte[r]); **Ver-sehr|ten|sport,** der; -[e]s; **Ver-sehrt|heit,** die; -
ver|sei|fen; Ver|sei|fung (*fachspr. für* Spaltung der Fette in Glyzerin u. Seifen durch Kochen in Alkalien)
ver|selbst|stän|di|gen, *auch* ver-

selb|stän|di|gen, sich; **Ver|selbst|stän|di|gung,** *auch* Ver|selb|stän|di|gung
Ver|se|ma|cher *(abwertend)*
ver|sen|den; versandt *u.* versendet; *vgl.* senden; **Ver|sen|der; Ver|sen|dung**
ver|sen|gen; die Hitze hat den Rasen versengt; **Ver|sen|gung**
ver|senk|bar; eine -e Nähmaschine; **Ver|senk|büh|ne; ver|sen|ken** (untertauchen, zum Sinken bringen); sich in ein Buch - (vertiefen); **Ver|sen|kung**
Vers|epos (↑R 132; *svw.* Versdrama); **Ver|se|schmied** *(abwertend)*
ver|ses|sen (eifrig bedacht, erpicht); auf etwas - sein; **Ver|ses|sen|heit,** die; -
ver|set|zen; der Schüler wurde versetzt; sich in jmds. Lage -; sie hat ihn versetzt (*ugs. für* vergeblich warten lassen); er hat seine Uhr versetzt (verkauft, ins Leihhaus gebracht); **Ver|set|zung; Ver|set|zungs|zei|chen** (*Musik* Zeichen zur Erhöhung od. Erniedrigung einer Note)
ver|seu|chen; Ver|seu|chung
Vers‿form, ...fuß
Ver|si|che|rer; ver|si|chern; die Versicherung versichert dich gegen Unfall; ich versichere dich meines Vertrauens *(geh.), auch* ich versichere dir mein Vertrauen; ich versichere dir, dass ...; **Ver|si|cher|te,** der *u.* die; -n, -n (↑R 5 ff.); **Ver|si|che|rung; Ver|si|che|rungs‿agent** (↑R 132), **...an|spruch, ...bei|trag, ...be|trug, ...fall** (der), **...ge|ber, ...ge|sell|schaft, ...kar|te, ...kauf|frau, ...kauf|mann, ...leis|tung, ...neh|mer, ...pflicht** (die; -); **ver|si|che|rungs|pflich|tig; Ver|si|che|rungs‿po|li|ce, ...prä|mie, ...recht** (das; -[e]s), **...schein, ...schutz** (der; -es); **Ver|si|che|rungs|steu|er,** Ver|si|che|rung|steu|er, die (↑R 34); **Ver|si|che|rungs|sum|me; Ver|si|che|rung|steu|er** *vgl.* Versicherungssteuer; **Ver|si|che|rungs‿trä|ger, ...ver|tre|ter, ...wert, ...we|sen** (das; -s)
ver|si|ckern; Ver|si|cke|rung
ver|sie|ben (*ugs. für* verderben; verlieren; vergessen); er hat [ihm] alles versiebt
ver|sie|geln; Ver|sie|ge|lung, *seltener* Ver|sieg|lung
ver|sie|gen (austrocknen); versiegte Quelle
Ver|sieg|lung *vgl.* Versiegelung
Ver|sie|gung, die; -
ver|siert [v...] ‹lat.›; in etwas - (erfahren, bewandert) sein; **Ver|siert|heit,** die; -
Ver|si|fex [v...], der; -es, -e ‹lat.› (Verseschmied)
ver|sifft (*ugs. für* verschmutzt)
Ver|si|fi|ka|ti|on, die; -, -en ‹lat.›; **ver|si|fi|zie|ren** (in Verse bringen)
Ver|sil|be|rer; ver|sil|bern (*ugs. auch für* verkaufen); ich ...ere (↑R 16); **Ver|sil|be|rung**
ver|sim|peln (*ugs. für* zu sehr vereinfachen; dumm werden)
ver|sin|ken; versunken
ver|sinn|bild|li|chen; Ver|sinn|bild|li|chung; ver|sinn|li|chen; Ver|sinn|li|chung
Ver|si|on [v...], die; -, -en ‹franz.› (Fassung; Lesart; Ausführung)
ver|sippt (verwandt); **Ver|sip|pung**
ver|sit|zen (*ugs. für* [die Zeit] mit Herumsitzen verbringen; beim Sitzen zerknittern [von Kleidern]); *vgl.* versessen
ver|skla|ven [...vən, *auch* ...fən]; **Ver|skla|vung**
Vers‿kunst (die; -), **...leh|re**
ver|slu|men [...'slamən] ‹dt.; engl.› (zum Slum werden); verslumte Stadtteile
Vers|maß, das
ver|snobt ‹dt.; engl.› (in der Art eines Snobs, um gesellschaftliche Exklusivität bemüht)
Ver|so [v...], das; -s, -s ‹lat.› (*fachspr. für* [Blatt]rückseite)
ver|sof|fen (*derb für* trunksüchtig)
ver|soh|len (*ugs. für* verprügeln)
ver|söh|nen; sich -; **Ver|söh|ner; Ver|söh|ne|rin; Ver|söh|ner** (*veraltend für* jmd., der aus opportunist. Gründen Abweichungen von der Parteilinie o. Ä. nicht entschieden genug bekämpft); **ver|söhn|lich; Ver|söhn|lich|keit,** die; -; **Ver|söh|nung; Ver|söh|nungs‿fest** *(jüd. Rel.),* **...tag**
ver|son|nen (sinnend, träumerisch); **Ver|son|nen|heit,** die; -
ver|sor|gen; Ver|sor|gung, die; -; **Ver|sor|gungs‿amt, ...an|spruch, ...aus|gleich; ver|sor|gungs|be|rech|tigt; Ver|sor|gungs‿be|rech|tig|te** (der *u.* die; -n, -n; ↑R 5 ff.), **...ein|heit** *(Milit.),* **...eng|pass, ...la|ge, ...lei|tung, ...netz, ...schwie|rig|kei|ten** *(Plur.)*
ver|sot|ten (durch sich ablagernde Rauchrückstände verunreinigt werden [von Schornsteinen]); versottet; **Ver|sot|tung**
ver|spach|teln (*ugs. auch für* aufessen)
ver|spakt (*nordd. für* angefault, stockfleckig, verschimmelt)
ver|span|nen; Ver|span|nung
ver|spä|ten, sich; **ver|spä|tet;** sein Dank kam -; **Ver|spä|tung**
ver|spei|sen *(geh.);* er hat den Braten verspeist; **Ver|spei|sung,** die; -
ver|spe|ku|lie|ren
ver|sper|ren; Ver|sper|rung
ver|spie|len; ver|spielt; ein -er Junge; bei jmdm. - haben; **Ver|spielt|heit,** die; -
ver|spie|ßern (zum Spießer werden); ich ...ere (↑R 16)
ver|spil|lern (*Bot.* vergeilen); die Pflanze verspillert; **Ver|spil|le|rung**
ver|spin|nen; versponnen
ver|splei|ßen (*Seemannsspr.* spleißend verbinden); zwei Tauenden [miteinander] -
ver|spot|ten; Ver|spot|tung
ver|spre|chen; er hat ihr die Heirat versprochen; sich - (beim Sprechen einen Fehler machen); ich verspreche mir nichts davon; **Ver|spre|chen,** das; -s, -; **Ver|spre|cher; Ver|spre|chung** *meist Plur.*
ver|spren|gen; Ver|spreng|te, der; -n, -n; ↑R 5 ff. *(Milit.);* **Ver|spren|gung**
ver|sprit|zen
ver|spro|che|ner|ma|ßen
ver|spru|deln (*österr. für* verquirlen)
ver|sprü|hen (zerstäuben)
ver|spun|den, *auch* **ver|spün|den** (mit einem Spund schließen); ein Fass -
ver|spü|ren
ver|staat|li|chen (in Staatseigentum überführen); **Ver|staat|li|chung**
ver|städ|tern [*auch* ...'ʃtɛ...] (städtisch machen, werden); ich ...ere (↑R 16); **Ver|städ|te|rung,** die; -; **Ver|stadt|li|chung** (*selten für* Überführung in städtischen Besitz)
ver|stäh|len (*fachspr. für* mit einer Stahlschicht überziehen); **Ver|stäh|lung**
Ver|stand, der; -[e]s; **Ver|stan|des|kraft; ver|stan|des|mä|ßig; Ver|stan|des‿mensch** (der), **...schär|fe** (die; -); **ver|stän|dig** (besonnen); **ver|stän|di|gen;** sich mit jmdm. -; **Ver|stän|dig|keit,** die; - (Klugheit); **Ver|stän|di|gung; Ver|stän|di|gungs‿be|reit|schaft** (die; -), **...schwie|rig|kei|ten** *(Plur.),* **...ver|such; ver|ständ|lich; ver|ständ|li|cher|wei|se; Ver|ständ|lich|keit,** die; - (Klarheit); **Ver|ständ|nis,** das; -ses, -se *Plur. selten;* **ver|ständ|nis|in|nig; ver|ständ|nis|los;**

Ver|stạ̈nd|nis|lo|sig|keit, die; -; **ver|stạ̈nd|nis|voll**
ver|stạ̈n|kern *(ugs.);* ich ...ere (↑R 16); mit dem Käse verstänkerst du das ganze Zimmer!
ver|stär|ken; in verstärktem Maße; **Ver|stär|ker; Ver|stär|ker|röh|re; Ver|stär|kung; Ver|stär|kungs|pfei|ler**
ver|stä|ten *(schweiz. für* festmachen [bes. das Fadenende])
ver|stạt|ten *(veraltet für* gestatten); **Ver|stạt|tung,** die; -
ver|stau|ben; ver|stäu|ben; Insektizide -; **ver|staubt** *(auch für* altmodisch, überholt)
ver|stau|chen; ich habe mir den Fuß verstaucht; **Ver|stau|chung**
ver|stau|en ([auf relativ engem Raum] unterbringen)
Ver|stẹck, das; -[e]s, -e; Versteck spielen; **ver|stẹ|cken;** *vgl.* ²stecken; sie hatte die Ostereier gut versteckt; sich -; du hattest dich hinter der Mutter versteckt; **Ver|stẹ|cken,** das; -s; Verstecken spielen; **Ver|stẹ|cken|spie|len,** das; -s; **Ver|stẹ|ckerl|spiel,** das; -s *(österr. neben* Versteckenspielen); **Ver|stẹck|spiel,** das; -[e]s; **Ver|stẹckt|heit,** die; -
ver|ste|hen; verstanden; sich zu einer Sache -; jmdm. etwas zu - geben; **Ver|ste|hen,** das; -s
ver|stei|fen *(auch Bauw.* abstützen, unterstützen); sich auf etwas - (auf etwas beharren); **Ver|stei|fung**
ver|stei|gen, sich; er hatte sich in den Bergen verstiegen; du verstiegst dich zu der übertriebenen Forderung *(geh.); vgl.* verstiegen
Ver|stei|ge|rer; ver|stei|gern; Ver|stei|ge|rung
ver|stei|nen *(veraltet für* mit Grenzsteinen versehen); **ver|stei|nern** (zu Stein machen, werden); ich ...ere (↑R 16); wie versteinert; **Ver|stei|ne|rung**
ver|stẹll|bar; Ver|stẹll|bar|keit, die; -; **ver|stẹl|len;** verstellt; sich -; **Ver|stẹl|lung; Ver|stẹl|lungs|kunst**
ver|stẹp|pen (zu Steppe werden); das Land ist versteppt; **Ver|stẹp|pung**
ver|stẹr|ben; *nur noch im Präteritum u. im Partizip II gebr.;* verstarb, verstorben *(vgl. d.)*
ver|ste|ti|gen *(bes. Wirtsch.* gleichmäßig u. beständig machen); **Ver|ste|ti|gung;** - des Wachstums
ver|steu|ern; Ver|steu|e|rung
ver|stie|ben *(veraltet für* in Staub zerfallen; wie Staub verfliegen); der Schnee ist verstoben
ver|stie|gen (überspannt); **Ver|stie|gen|heit**
ver|stịm|men *(auch für* verärgern); **ver|stịmmt; Ver|stịmmt|heit,** die; -; **Ver|stịm|mung**
ver|stọckt (uneinsichtig, störrisch, starrsinnig); **Ver|stọckt|heit,** die; -
ver|stoh|len (heimlich); **ver|stoh|le|ner|wei|se**
ver|stọl|pern *(Sportspr.);* er hat den Ball verstolpert
ver|stọp|fen; Ver|stọp|fung
ver|stọr|ben *(Zeichen* †); **Ver|stọr|be|ne,** der *u.* die; -n, -n (↑R 5 ff.)
ver|stö|ren (verwirren); es verstört mich, dass ...; **ver|stört; Ver|stört|heit,** die; -
Ver|stoß, der; -es, ...stöße; **ver|sto|ßen; Ver|sto|ßung**
ver|stre|ben; Ver|stre|bung
ver|strei|chen *(auch für* vorübergehen; vergehen); verstrichen
ver|streu|en; verstreut
ver|strị|cken; sich [in Widersprüche] -; **Ver|strị|ckung**
ver|strö|men (zur Gewinnung elektrischer Energie verbrauchen); Kohle -
ver|strö|men; einen Duft -
Ver|strö|mung
ver|strub|beln *(ugs.);* jmdm. die Haare -
ver|stüm|meln; ich ...ele (↑R 16); verstümmelt; **Ver|stụ̈m|me|lung,** *seltener* Ver|stụ̈mm|lung
ver|stum|men
Ver|stụ̈mm|lung *vgl.* Verstümmelung
Ver. St. v. A. = Vereinigte Staaten von Amerika
Ver|such, der; -[e]s, -e; **ver|su|chen; Ver|su|cher; Ver|su|che|rin; Ver|suchs‿ab|tei|lung, ...an|la|ge, ...an|ord|nung, ...an|stalt, ...bal|lon, ...ge|län|de, ...ka|nin|chen** *(ugs. für* Versuchstier, Versuchsperson), **...lei|ter** (der), **...per|son** *(Psych.; Abk.* Vp., VP), **...sta|ti|on, ...tier; ver|suchs|wei|se; Ver|su|chung**
ver|süh|nen *(veraltet für* versöhnen)
ver|sụmp|fen *(ugs. auch für* moralisch verkommen); **Ver|sụmp|fung**
ver|sün|di|gen, sich *(geh.);* **Ver|sün|di|gung**
ver|sụn|ken; in etwas - sein; **Ver|sụn|ken|heit,** die; -
vẹr|sus [v...] ‹lat.› (gegen; *Abk.* vs.)
ver|sü|ßen; Ver|sü|ßung
vert. *(Druckw.* V) = vertatur
ver|tä|feln; ich ...[e]le (↑R 16); **Ver|tä|fe|lung, Ver|täf|lung**
ver|ta|gen (aufschieben); **Ver|ta|gung**
ver|tạ̈n|deln (nutzlos [die Zeit] verbringen)
ver|ta|tur! [v...] ‹lat.› (man wende!, man drehe um!; *Abk.* vert. [*Druckw.* V])
ver|tau|ben *(Bergmannsspr.* in taubes Gestein übergehen); **Ver|tau|bung**
ver|täu|en *(Seemannsspr.* durch Taue festmachen); das Schiff ist vertäut
ver|tausch|bar; Ver|tausch|bar|keit, die; -; **ver|tau|schen; Ver|tau|schung**
ver|tau|send|fa|chen
Ver|täu|ung *(Seemannsspr.)*
ver|te! [ˈvɛrtə] ‹lat.› *(Musik* wende um!, wenden!); **ver|te|bral** [v...] *(Med.* zur Wirbelsäule gehörend, auf sie bezüglich); **Ver|te|brat,** der; -en, -en *meist Plur. (Zool.* Wirbeltier)
ver|tei|di|gen *(auch Sport);* **Ver|tei|di|ger; Ver|tei|di|ge|rin; Ver|tei|di|gung; Ver|tei|di|gungs‿aus|ga|ben** *(Plur.),* **...bei|trag, ...be|reit|schaft** (die; -), **...bünd|nis, ...drit|tel** *(Eishockey),* **...fall** (der), **...haus|halt, ...krieg, ...mi|nis|ter, ...mi|nis|te|ri|um, ...pakt, ...schrift, ...stel|lung, ...waf|fe, ...zu|stand**
ver|tei|len; Ver|tei|ler; Ver|tei|ler‿do|se, ...kas|ten, ...netz, ...ring, ...schlüs|sel, ...ta|fel; Ver|tei|lung; Ver|tei|lungs‿stel|le, ...zahl|wort *(für* Distributivzahl)
ver|te|le|fo|nie|ren *(ugs.);* sie hat zwanzig Mark vertelefoniert
ver|te, si pla|cet! [ˈvɛrtə - ...tsɛt] ‹lat.› *(Musik* bitte wenden!; *Abk.* v. s. pl.)
ver|teu|ern; sich -; ich ...ere (↑R 16); **Ver|teu|e|rung**
ver|teu|feln; jmdn., etwas - (als böse, schlecht hinstellen); ich ...[e]le (↑R 16); **ver|teu|felt** *(ugs. für* verzwickt; über die Maßen; verwegen); **Ver|teu|fe|lung, Ver|teuf|lung**
ver|tie|fen; sich in eine Sache -; **Ver|tie|fung**
ver|tie|ren (zum Tier werden, machen); **ver|tiert** (tierisch)
ver|ti|kal [v...] ‹lat.› (senkrecht, lotrecht); **Ver|ti|ka|le,** die; -, -n; vier -[n]; **Ver|ti|kal‿ebe|ne** (↑R 132), **...kreis**
Vẹr|ti|ko [v...], das, *selten* der; -s, -s ‹angeblich nach dem Tischler Vertikow› (kleiner Zierschrank)
ver|ti|ku|tie|ren [v...] ‹lat.› ([Rasen] lüften, entfilzen); **Ver|ti|ku|tie|rer; Ver|ti|ku|tier|ge|rät**

ver|til|gen; Ver|til|gung, die; -, -en; **Ver|til|gungs|mit|tel,** das
ver|tip|pen (*ugs. für* falsch [1]tippen); sich -; vertippt
ver|to|ba|ken (*ugs. veraltend für* verprügeln)
ver|to|nen; das Gedicht wurde vertont; **Ver|to|ner** *(selten);* **[1]Ver|to|nung** (das Vertonen)
[2]Ver|to|nung (Darstellung von Küstenansichten [von See aus])
ver|tor|fen (zu Torf werden); **Ver|tor|fung**
ver|trackt (*ugs. für* verwickelt; unangenehm, ärgerlich); **Ver|trackt|heit** *(ugs.)*
Ver|trag, der; -[e]s, ...träge; **ver|tra|gen;** er hat den Wein gut -; sich -; die Kinder werden sich schon -; Zeitungen - (*schweiz. für* austragen); **Ver|trä|ger** (*schweiz. für* jmd., der Zeitungen u. Ä. austrägt); **ver|trag|lich** (dem Vertrag nach; durch Vertrag); **ver|träg|lich** (friedfertig; bekömmlich); er ist sehr -; die Speise ist leicht, gut -; **Ver|träg|lich|keit,** die; -; **ver|trag|los;** ein -er Zustand; **Ver|trags‿ab|schluss, ...bruch** (der); **ver|trags|brü|chig; Ver|trags|brü|chi|ge,** der *u.* die; -n, -n (↑R 5 ff.); **ver|trag|schlie|ßend;** die -en Parteien; **Ver|trag|schlie|ßen|de,** der *u.* die; -n, -n (↑R 5 ff.); **ver|trags|ge|mäß; Ver|trags|ho|tel; ver|trags|los** *vgl.* vertraglos; **Ver|trags‿part|ner, ...part|ne|rin, ...punkt, ...schluss, ...spie|ler** *(Sport früher),* **...stra|fe, ...text, ...werk|statt; ver|trags|wid|rig; Ver|trags|wid|rig|keit,** die; -
ver|trau|en; Ver|trau|en, das; -s; - erwecken; ein Vertrauen erweckender Verkäufer (↑R 40); **Ver|trau|ens‿an|walt, ...arzt; ver|trau|ens|ärzt|lich;** eine -e Untersuchung; **Ver|trau|ens‿ba|sis, ...be|weis; ver|trau|ens|bil|dend;** -e Maßnahmen; **Ver|trau|ens‿bruch** (der), **...fra|ge, ...frau, ...grund|la|ge, ...kri|se, ...mann** (*Plur.* ...männer *u.* ...leute; *Abk.* V-Mann), **...per|son, ...sa|che; ver|trau|ens|se|lig; Ver|trau|ens‿se|lig|keit** (die; -), **...stel|lung, ...ver|hält|nis; ver|trau|ens|voll; Ver|trau|ens|vo|tum; ver|trau|ens|wür|dig; Ver|trau|ens|wür|dig|keit,** die; -
ver|trau|ern
ver|trau|lich; Ver|trau|lich|keit
ver|träu|men; ver|träumt; Ver|träumt|heit, die; -
ver|traut; jmdn., sich mit etwas - machen; **Ver|trau|te,** der *u.* die; -n, -n (↑R 5 ff.); **Ver|traut|heit**
ver|trei|ben; Ver|trei|ber; Ver|trei|bung
ver|tret|bar; -e Sache *(BGB);* **Ver|tret|bar|keit,** die; -; **ver|tre|ten; Ver|tre|ter; Ver|tre|ter|be|such; Ver|tre|te|rin; Ver|tre|tung;** in - (*Abk.* i. V., I. V.; *vgl. d.*); **Ver|tre|tungs|stun|de; ver|tre|tungs|wei|se**
Ver|trieb, der; -[e]s, -e (Verkauf); **Ver|trie|be|ne,** der *u.* die; -n, -n (↑R 5 ff.); **Ver|triebs‿ab|tei|lung, ...ge|sell|schaft, ...kos|ten** *(Plur.),* **...lei|ter** (der), **...recht**
ver|trim|men (*ugs. für* verprügeln)
ver|trin|ken; sein Geld -
ver|trock|nen
ver|trö|deln (*ugs. für* [seine Zeit] unnütz hinbringen); **Ver|trö|de|lung, Ver|tröd|lung,** die; - *(ugs.)*
ver|trös|ten; Ver|trös|tung
ver|trot|teln *(ugs.);* ich ...[e]le (↑R 16); **ver|trot|telt**
ver|trus|ten [...ˈtrastən] (*Wirtsch.* zu einem Trust vereinigen); die Betriebe sind vertrustet; **Ver|trus|tung**
ver|tü|dern (*nordd. für* verwirren); sich -
Ver|tum|na|li|en [v...] *Plur.* (ein altröm. Fest)
ver|tun (verschwenden); vertan; sich - (*ugs. für* sich irren)
ver|tu|schen (*ugs. für* verheimlichen); du vertuschst; **Ver|tu|schung**
ver|übeln (↑R 132; übel nehmen); ich ...[e]le (↑R 16); jmdm. etwas -
ver|üben (↑R 132); ein Verbrechen -
ver|ul|ken; Ver|ul|kung
ver|un|eh|ren (*veraltet für* im Ansehen schädigen)
ver|un|ei|ni|gen
ver|un|fal|len (*Amtsspr.* verunglücken); **Ver|un|fall|te,** der *u.* die; -n, -n (↑R 5 ff.)
ver|un|glimp|fen (schmähen, beleidigen); **Ver|un|glimp|fung**
ver|un|glü|cken; Ver|un|glück|te, der *u.* die; -n, -n (↑R 5 ff.)
ver|un|krau|ten; der Acker ist verunkrautet
ver|un|mög|li|chen (*bes. schweiz. für* verhindern, vereiteln)
ver|un|rei|ni|gen; Ver|un|rei|ni|gung
ver|un|si|chern (unsicher machen); **Ver|un|si|che|rung**
ver|un|stal|ten (entstellen); **Ver|un|stal|tung**
ver|un|treu|en (unterschlagen); **Ver|un|treu|er; Ver|un|treu|ung**
ver|un|zie|ren (verschandeln); **Ver|un|zie|rung**
ver|ur|sa|chen; Ver|ur|sa|cher; Ver|ur|sa|che|rin; Ver|ur|sa|cher|prin|zip, das; -s *(Rechtsspr.);* **Ver|ur|sa|chung,** die; -
ver|ur|tei|len; Ver|ur|tei|lung
Ver|ve [ˈvɛrvə], die; - ‹franz.› (Begeisterung, Schwung)
ver|viel|fa|chen; Ver|viel|fa|chung; ver|viel|fäl|ti|gen; Ver|viel|fäl|ti|ger; Ver|viel|fäl|ti|gung; Ver|viel|fäl|ti|gungs‿ap|pa|rat, ...zahl|wort (z. B. achtmal, dreifach)
ver|vier|fa|chen
ver|voll|komm|nen; sich -; **Ver|voll|komm|nung; ver|voll|komm|nungs|fä|hig**
ver|voll|stän|di|gen; Ver|voll|stän|di|gung
verw. = verwitwet
[1]ver|wach|sen; die Narbe ist verwachsen; mit etwas - (innig verbunden) sein; sich - ([beim Wachsen] verschwinden); **[2]ver|wach|sen** (schief gewachsen, verkrüppelt); **Ver|wach|sung**
ver|wa|ckeln; die Aufnahme ist verwackelt (unscharf)
ver|wäh|len, sich (beim Telefonieren)
Ver|wahr, der *(veraltet); nur noch in* in - geben, nehmen; **ver|wah|ren** (*veraltet auch für* in Haft nehmen, unterbringen); es ist alles wohl verwahrt (aufbewahrt); sich gegen etwas - (etwas energisch zurückweisen); **Ver|wah|rer; Ver|wah|re|rin; ver|wahr|lo|sen;** du verwahrlost; **Ver|wahr|los|te,** der *u.* die; -n, -n (↑R 5 ff.); **Ver|wahr|lo|sung,** die; -; **Ver|wahr|sam,** der; -s *(veraltet); noch in* in - geben, nehmen; **Ver|wah|rung**
ver|wai|sen (elternlos werden; einsam werden); du verwaist; er verwais|te; **ver|waist;** ein verwais|tes Haus
ver|wal|ken (*ugs. für* verprügeln)
ver|wal|ten; Ver|wal|ter; Ver|wal|te|rin; Ver|wal|tung; Ver|wal|tungs‿akt, ...an|ge|stell|te (der *u.* die), **...ap|pa|rat, ...auf|ga|ben** *(Plur.),* **...be|am|te, ...be|zirk, ...dienst** (der; -[e]s), **...ge|bäu|de, ...ge|richt, ...ge|richts|hof, ...kos|ten** *(Plur.),* **...rat** (*Plur.* ...räte), **...recht** (das; -[e]s), **...re|form; ver|wal|tungs|tech|nisch; Ver|wal|tungs|vor|schrift**
ver|wam|sen (*ugs. für* verprügeln); du verwamst
ver|wan|del|bar; ver|wan|deln; Ver|wand|lung; Ver|wand|lungs|künst|ler; ver|wand|lungs|reich; ver|wandt (zur gleichen Familie, Art gehörend); **Ver|wand|te,** der *u.* die; -n, -n (↑R 5 ff.); **Ver|wandt|schaft;**

ver|wandt|schaft|lich; Ver|wandt|schafts|grad
ver|wanzt (voller Wanzen)
ver|war|nen; Ver|war|nung; Ver|war|nungs|geld *(Amtsspr.)*
ver|wa|schen
ver|wäs|sern; Ver|wäs|se|rung, Ver|wäss|rung
ver|we|ben; *meist schwach gebeugt, wenn es sich um die handwerkliche Tätigkeit handelt:* bei dieser Matte wurden Garne unterschiedlicher Stärke verwebt; *meist stark gebeugt bei übertragener Bedeutung:* zwei Melodien sind miteinander verwoben
ver|wech|sel|bar; ver|wech|seln; (↑R 50:) zum Verwechseln ähnlich; **Ver|wech|se|lung, Ver|wechs|lung**
ver|we|gen; Ver|we|gen|heit
ver|we|hen; vom Winde verweht
ver|weh|ren; jmdm. etwas - (untersagen); **Ver|weh|rung,** die; -
Ver|we|hung
ver|weich|li|chen; Ver|weich|li|chung, die; -
Ver|wei|ge|rer, der; -s, - (*auch kurz für* Kriegsdienstverweigerer); **ver|wei|gern; Ver|wei|ge|rung; Ver|wei|ge|rungs|fall,** der; im -[e] *(Rechtsspr.)*
Ver|weil|dau|er *(fachspr.);* **ver|wei|len** *(geh.);* sich -
ver|weint; -e Augen
Ver|weis, der; -es, -e (ernste Zurechtweisung; Hinweis); **¹ver|wei|sen** (*veraltend für* vorhalten; verbieten; tadeln); jmdm. seine Verhaltensweise -; sie hat dem Jungen seine Frechheit verwiesen; **²ver|wei|sen** (einen Hinweis geben; verbannen); auf eine andere Stelle des Buches -; der Verbrecher wurde des Landes verwiesen; **Ver|wei|sung** (Hinweis, Verweis; Ausweisung)
ver|wel|ken
ver|welt|li|chen (weltlich machen); **Ver|welt|li|chung,** die; -
ver|wend|bar; Ver|wend|bar|keit, die; -; **ver|wen|den;** ich verwandte *od.* verwendete, habe verwandt *od.* verwendet; **Ver|wen|dung;** zur besonderen Verwendung (*Abk.* z.b.V.); **ver|wen|dungs|fä|hig; Ver|wen|dungs‿mög|lich|keit, ...wei|se, ...zweck**
ver|wer|fen; der Plan wurde verworfen; die Arme - (*schweiz. für* heftig gestikulieren); **ver|werf|lich; Ver|werf|lich|keit,** die; -; **Ver|wer|fung** (*auch für* geol. Schichtenstörung)
ver|wert|bar; ver|wer|ten; Ver|wer|ter; Ver|wer|tung

¹ver|we|sen (sich zersetzen, in Fäulnis übergehen)
²ver|we|sen (*veraltet für* stellvertretend verwalten); du verwest; **Ver|we|ser**
ver|wes|lich; Ver|wes|lich|keit, die; -; **Ver|we|sung,** die; -; **Ver|we|sungs|ge|ruch**
ver|wet|ten
ver|wi|chen (*veraltend für* vergangen); im -en Jahre
ver|wich|sen (*ugs. für* verprügeln; [Geld] vergeuden)
ver|wi|ckeln; ver|wi|ckelt; Ver|wi|cke|lung, Ver|wick|lung
ver|wie|gen (*fachspr. für* wiegen); **Ver|wie|ger; Ver|wie|gung**
ver|wil|dern; ver|wil|dert; Ver|wil|de|rung
¹ver|win|den (über etwas hinwegkommen); verwunden; den Schmerz -; **²ver|win|den** (*Technik* verdrehen); **Ver|win|dung; ver|win|dungs|fest** *(Technik)*
ver|win|kelt (winklig)
ver|wir|ken; sein Leben -
ver|wirk|li|chen; sich [selbst] -; **Ver|wirk|li|chung**
Ver|wir|kung, die; - *(Rechtsspr.)*
ver|wir|ren; ich habe das Garn verwirrt; ich bin ganz verwirrt; *vgl.* verworren; **Ver|wirr|spiel; Ver|wirrt|heit,** die; -; **Ver|wir|rung**
ver|wirt|schaf|ten (mit etwas schlecht wirtschaften); **Ver|wirt|schaf|tung,** die; -
ver|wi|schen; die Unterschrift war verwischt; **Ver|wi|schung**
ver|wit|tern (durch den Einfluss der Witterung angegriffen werden); das Gestein ist verwittert; **Ver|wit|te|rung; Ver|wit|te|rungs|pro|dukt**
ver|wit|wet (Witwe[r] geworden; *Abk.* verw.)
ver|wo|ben (eng verknüpft mit ...); *vgl.* verweben
ver|woh|nen (durch Wohnen abnutzen); verwohnte Räume
ver|wöh|nen; ver|wöhnt; Ver|wöhnt|heit, die; -; **Ver|wöh|nung,** die; -
ver|wor|fen (lasterhaft, schlecht); ein verworfenes Geschöpf; **Ver|wor|fen|heit,** die; -
ver|wor|ren; das hört sich ziemlich - an; *vgl.* verwirren; **Ver|wor|ren|heit,** die; -
ver|wund|bar; Ver|wund|bar|keit, die; -; **¹ver|wun|den** (verletzen)
²ver|wun|den *vgl.* verwinden
ver|wun|der|lich; ver|wun|dern; es ist nicht zu -; sich -; **Ver|wun|de|rung,** die; -
ver|wun|det; Ver|wun|de|te, der *u.* die; -n, -n (↑R 5 ff.); **Ver|wun|de|ten|trans|port; Ver|wun|dung**
ver|wun|schen (verzaubert); ein -es Schloss; **ver|wün|schen** (verfluchen; verzaubern); er hat sein Schicksal oft verwünscht; **verwünscht** (verflucht); - sei diese Reise!; **Ver|wün|schung**
Ver|wurf (*svw.* Verwerfung *[Geol.]*)
ver|wursch|teln, ver|wurs|teln (*ugs. für* durcheinander bringen, verwirren)
ver|wur|zeln; Ver|wur|ze|lung, Ver|wurz|lung
ver|wu|scheln (*ugs. für* zerzausen)
ver|wüs|ten; Ver|wüs|tung
Verz. = Verzeichnis
ver|za|gen (ängstlich, wankelmütig werden); **ver|zagt; Ver|zagt|heit,** die; -
ver|zäh|len, sich
ver|zah|nen (an-, ineinander fügen); **Ver|zah|nung**
ver|zan|ken, sich (*ugs. für* in Streit geraten)
ver|zap|fen (durch Zapfen verbinden; *landsch. für* [vom Fass] ausschenken; *ugs. für* etwas [Unsinniges] anstellen, reden); **Ver|zap|fung**
ver|zär|teln; sie verzärtelt das Kind; **Ver|zär|te|lung,** die; -
ver|zau|bern; Ver|zau|be|rung
ver|zäu|nen; Ver|zäu|nung
ver|zehn|fa|chen; ver|zehn|ten (*früher für* den Zehnten von etwas zahlen)
Ver|zehr, der; -[e]s (das Verzehren; das Verzehrte); **Ver|zehr|bon; ver|zeh|ren; Ver|zeh|rer** *(selten);* **Ver|zehr|zwang,** der; -[e]s
ver|zeich|nen (vermerken; falsch zeichnen); **Ver|zeich|nis,** das; -ses, -se (*Abk.* Verz.); **Ver|zeich|nung; ver|zeich|nungs|frei** (*für* orthoskopisch)
ver|zei|gen (*schweiz. für* anzeigen)
ver|zei|hen; er hat ihr verziehen; **ver|zeih|lich; Ver|zei|hung,** die; -
ver|zer|ren; Ver|zer|rung
¹ver|zet|teln (für eine Kartei auf Zettel schreiben)
²ver|zet|teln (vergeuden); sich - (sich mit zu vielen [nebensächlichen] Dingen beschäftigen)
¹Ver|zet|te|lung (Aufnahme auf Zettel für eine Kartei)
²Ver|zet|te|lung (das Sichverzetteln)
¹Ver|zett|lung *vgl.* ¹Verzettelung
²Ver|zett|lung *vgl.* ²Verzettelung
Ver|zicht, der; -[e]s, -e; - leisten;

ver|zich|ten; **Ver|zicht[s]‿er|klä|rung, ...leis|tung, ...po|li|tik**
ver|zie|hen; die Eltern - ihr Kind; er ist nach Frankfurt verzogen; Rüben -; sich -; wir haben uns still verzogen (*ugs. für* sind still verschwunden)
ver|zie|ren; Ver|zie|rung
ver|zim|mern *(Bauw.);* **Ver|zim|me|rung**
[1]**ver|zin|ken** (*Gaunerspr.* verraten, anzeigen)
[2]**ver|zin|ken** (mit Zink überziehen); **Ver|zin|kung**
ver|zin|nen; Ver|zin|nung
ver|zins|bar; ver|zin|sen; ver|zins|lich; Ver|zins|lich|keit, die; -; **Ver|zin|sung**
ver|zo|gen; ein -er Junge
ver|zö|gern; Ver|zö|ge|rung; Ver|zö|ge|rungs|tak|tik
ver|zol|len; Ver|zol|lung
ver|zü|cken
ver|zu|ckern; Ver|zu|cke|rung
ver|zückt; Ver|zückt|heit, die; -; **Ver|zü|ckung;** in - geraten
Ver|zug, der; -[e]s (*Bergmannsspr. auch* gitterartige Verbindung zwischen Ausbaurahmen); im - sein (im Rückstand sein); in - geraten, kommen; in - setzen; ohne - (sofort); **Ver|zugs|zin|sen** *Plur.*
ver|zwat|zeln (*landsch. für* [vor Ungeduld] vergehen, verzweifeln)
ver|zwei|feln; (↑R 50:) es ist zum Verzweifeln; **ver|zwei|felt; Ver|zweif|lung,** die; -; **Ver|zweif|lungs|tat; ver|zweif|lungs|voll**
ver|zwei|gen, sich; **Ver|zwei|gung**
ver|zwickt (*ugs. für* verwickelt, schwierig); eine -e Geschichte; **Ver|zwickt|heit,** die; -
ver|zwir|nen (Garne zusammendrehen)
Ve|si|ka|to|ri|um [v...], das; -s, ...ien [...i̯ən] ‹lat.› (*Med.* Blasen ziehendes Mittel, Zugpflaster)
Ves|pa ® ['vɛspa], die; -, -s ‹ital.› (ein Motorroller)
Ves|pa|si|an, Ves|pa|si|a|nus [*beide* v...] (röm. Kaiser)
Ves|per ['fɛs...], die; -, -n, *südd. für* „Zwischenmahlzeit" *auch* das; -s, - ‹lat.› (Zeit gegen Abend; Abendandacht; Stundengebet; *bes. südd. für* Zwischenmahlzeit, bes. am Nachmittag); **Ves|per‿bild** *(Kunstwiss.),* **...brot; ves|pern** (*bes. südd. für* [Nachmittags-, Abend]imbiss einnehmen); ich ...ere (↑R 16)
Ves|puc|ci [vɛs'putʃi], Amerigo (ital. Seefahrer)
Ves|ta ['vɛsta] (röm. Göttin des häusl. Herdes); **Ves|ta|lin,** die; -, -nen (Priesterin der Vesta)
Ves|te [f...], die; -, -n (*veraltet für* Feste); Veste Coburg
Ves|ti|bül [v...], das; -s, -e ‹franz.› (Vorhalle); **Ves|ti|bu|lum,** das; -s, ...la ‹lat.› (Vorhalle des altröm. Hauses)
Ves|ti|tur [v...], die; -, -en ‹lat.› (*svw.* Investitur)
Ves|ton [vɛs'tõ:], das *auch* der; -s, -s ‹franz.› (*schweiz. für* Herrenjackett)
Ve|suv [ve'zu:f], der; -[s] (Vulkan bei Neapel); **Ve|su|vi|an** [vezu'vi̯a:n], der; -s, -e (ein Mineral); **ve|su|visch** [ve'zu:viʃ]
Ve|te|ran [v...], der; -en, -en (↑R 126) ‹lat.› (altgedienter Soldat; ehem. langjähriger Mitarbeiter; altes [Auto]modell); **Ve|te|ra|nen|klub** (*regional für* Treffpunkt alter Menschen)
ve|te|ri|när [v...] ‹franz.› (tierärztlich); **Ve|te|ri|när,** der; -s, -e (Tierarzt); **ve|te|ri|när|ärzt|lich; Ve|te|ri|nä|rin; Ve|te|ri|när|me|di|zin,** die; - (Tierheilkunde); **ve|te|ri|när|me|di|zi|nisch**
Ve|to [v...], das; -s, -s ‹lat.› (Einspruch[srecht]); **Ve|to|recht**
Vet|tel [f...], die; -, -n (*veraltend für* unordentliche, ungepflegte [alte] Frau)
Vet|ter, der; -s, -n; **Vet|te|rin** *(veraltet);* **vet|ter|lich; Vet|tern|schaft; Vet|tern|wirt|schaft,** die; - *(abwertend);* **Vet|ter|schaft** *vgl.* Vetternschaft
Ve|xier|bild [v...] ‹lat.; dt.›; **ve|xie|ren** ‹lat.› (*veraltet für* irreführen; quälen; necken); **Ve|xier‿rät|sel, ...spie|gel**
v-för|mig, *auch* **V-för|mig** ['fau...]; ↑R 25 (in der Form eines V)
vgl. = vergleich[e]!
v., g., u. = vorgelesen, genehmigt, unterschrieben
v. H., p. c., % = vom Hundert; *vgl.* Prozent, pro centum
VHS = Volkshochschule
via ['vi:a] ‹lat.› ([auf dem Wege] über); - Triest; **Via Ap|pia,** die; - - (Straße bei Rom); **Vi|a|dukt** [v...], der, *auch* das; -[e]s, -e (Talbrücke, Überführung); **Via Ma|la,** die; - - (Schlucht in Graubünden); **Vi|a|ti|kum,** das; -s, *Plur.* ...ka *u.* ...ken (*kath. Kirche* dem Sterbenden gereichte letzte Kommunion)
Vib|ra|phon, *eindeutschend* Vib|ra|fon [v...] (↑R 33 *u.* 130), das; -s, -e ‹lat.; griech.› (ein Musikinstrument); **Vib|ra|pho|nist,** *eindeutschend* Vib|ra|fo|nist, der; -en, -en (↑R 126)
Vib|ra|ti|on (↑R 130), die; -, -en ‹lat.› (Schwingung, Beben, Erschütterung); **Vib|ra|ti|ons|mas|sa|ge; vib|ra|to** ‹ital.› (*Musik* bebend); **Vib|ra|to,** das; -s, *Plur.* -s *u.* ...ti; **Vib|ra|tor,** der; -s, ...oren ‹lat.› (Gerät, das Schwingungen erzeugt; Massagestab); **vib|rie|ren** (schwingen; beben, zittern); **Vib|ro|mas|sa|ge** (*kurz für* Vibrationsmassage)
vi|ce ver|sa ['vi:tsə 'vɛrza] ‹lat.› (umgekehrt; *Abk.* v. v.)
Vi|co [v...] (m. Vorn.)
Vi|comte [vi'kõ:t], der; -s, -s (franz. Adelstitel); **Vi|com|tesse** [vikõ'tɛs], die; -, -n [...s(ə)n] (*weibl. Form von* Vicomte)
[1]**Vic|to|ria** [v...] (Gliedstaat des Australischen Bundes); [2]**Vic|to|ria** (Hptst. der Seychellen); **Vic|to|ri|a|fäl|le,** *Plur.* (große Wasserfälle des Sambesi)
Vic|to|ria re|gia [v... -], die; - -, - -s (eine südamerik. Seerose)
vi|de! [v...] ‹lat.› (*veraltet für* siehe!; *Abk.* v.); **Vi|deo,** das; -s, -s ‹engl.› (*ugs. kurz für* Videoband, -clip, -film; *nur Sing.:* Videotechnik)
Vi|de|o‿auf|zeich|nung, ...band (*vgl.* [3]Band), **...clip** (kurzer Videofilm zu einem Popmusikstück), **...film, ...ge|rät, ...ka|me|ra, ...kas|set|te, ...pro|gramm|sys|tem** (zur automatischen Videoaufzeichnung von Fernsehsendungen; *Abk.* VPS), **...re|kor|der** *od.* **...re|cor|der** (Speichergerät für Fernsehaufnahmen), **...spiel** (*svw.* Telespiel), **...tech|nik** (die; -); **Vi|de|o|text** ([geschriebene] Information, die auf Abruf über den Fernsehbildschirm vermittelt wird); **Vi|de|o|thek,** die; -, -en (Sammlung von Videofilmen od. Fernsehaufzeichnungen); **vi|di** (*veraltet für* ich habe gesehen; *Abk.* v.); **vi|die|ren** (*veraltet, noch österr. für* beglaubigen, unterschreiben); **Vi|di|ma|ti|on,** die; -, -en (Beglaubigung); **vi|dit** (*veraltet für* hat [es] gesehen; *Abk.* vdt.)
Viech, das; -[e]s, -er (*ugs. für* Tier; *auch* Schimpfwort); **Vie|che|rei** (*ugs. für* Gemeinheit, Niedertracht; große Anstrengung); **Vieh,** das; -[e]s; **Vieh‿be|stand, ...fut|ter** (*vgl.* [1]Futter), **...hal|ter, ...hal|tung, ...han|del** (*vgl.* [1]Handel), **...händ|ler, ...her|de; vie|hisch; Vieh‿salz** (das; -es), **...wa|gen, ...wei|de, ...zeug** *(ugs.),* **...zucht** (die; -), **...züch|ter**
viel (↑R 48:) die vielen; viele sagen ...; in vielem, mit vielem, um vieles; wer vieles bringt, ...; ich habe viel[es] erlebt; *aber* das Lob der vielen, *auch* Vielen (der breiten Masse); (↑R 47:) viel Gutes *od.*

vieles Gute; vielen Schlafes; mit viel Gutem *od.* mit vielem Guten; vieler schöner Schnee; mit vieler natürlicher Anmut; vieles milde Nachsehen; mit vielem kalten Wasser; viel[e] gute Nachbildungen; vieler guter, *seltener* guten Nachbildungen; (↑R 6:) viele Begabte, vieler Begabter, *seltener* Begabten; viel[e] Menschen; die vielen Menschen; so viel arbeiten, dass ...; soviel *(vgl. d.);* soviel ich weiß ...; vielmal[s]; vieltausendmal; vielmehr *(vgl. d.);* wir haben gleich viel; gleichviel[,] ob du kommst oder nicht (↑R 89); soundso viel; am soundsovielten Mai; zu viel, zu viele Menschen; viel zu viel; viel zu wenig; viel zu teuer; es gab noch vieles, was (*nicht* das *od.* welches) besprochen werden sollte; allzu viel (*vgl.* allzu). *Getrenntschreibung in Verbindung mit Partizipien* (↑R 40:) ein viel (häufig) besprochener Fall; der Fall wurde viel besprochen; ein viel diskutiertes Buch; ein viel erörtertes Thema; eine viel gereiste Frau; ein viel (sehr) umworbener, viel gepriesener Star usw.; ein viel sagender Blick; ein viel versprechendes Projekt, *aber* ein noch vielversprechenderes Projekt; **Viel**, das; -s; viele Wenig machen ein Viel

viel|ar|mig; eine -e Abwehr *(Sport);* **viel|bän|dig;** ein -es Werk; **viel be|fah|ren, be|schäf|tigt, be|spro|chen** *vgl.* viel; **viel|deu|tig; Viel|deu|tig|keit; viel dis|ku|tiert** *vgl.* viel; **Viel|eck; viel|eckig** (↑R 132); **Viel|ehe** (↑R 132); **vie|ler|lei; viel er|ör|tert** *vgl.* viel; **vie|ler|orts; viel|fach;** (↑R 47:) um ein Vielfaches klüger; **Viel|fa|che,** das; -n (↑R 5ff.); das kleinste gemeinsame - (*Abk.* k.g.V., kgV); *vgl.* Achtfache; **Viel|falt,** die; -; **viel|fäl|tig** (mannigfaltig, häufig); **Viel|fäl|tig|keit,** die; -; **viel|far|big;** ein -es Muster; **Viel|flach,** das; -[e]s, -e *u.* Viel|fläch|ner (*für* Polyeder); **viel|flä|chig; Viel|fläch|ner** *vgl.* Vielflach

Viel|fraß, der; -es, -e (Marderart; *ugs. für* jmd., der unmäßig isst) **viel ge|fragt, ge|kauft, ge|le|sen, ge|prie|sen** usw. *vgl.* viel; **Viel|ge|reis|te,** der *u.* die; -n, -n (↑R 5ff.); **viel ge|schmäht** *vgl.* viel; **viel|ge|stal|tig; Viel|ge|stal|tig|keit,** die; -; **viel|glied|rig; Viel|glied|rig|keit,** die; -; **Viel|göt|te|rei,** die; - (*für* Polytheismus); **Viel|heit,** die; -; **viel|hun|dert|mal,** *aber* viele hundert Male; *vgl.* Mal; **viel|köp|fig; viel|leicht**

Viel|lieb|chen ‹*Umdeutung aus* Valentine *bzw.* Philippine› (doppelter Mandelkern, den zwei Personen gemeinsam essen, wobei sie wetten, wer den andern am nächsten Tag zuerst daran erinnert)

viel|mal (*veraltet für* vielmals); **viel|ma|lig; viel|mals; Viel|män|ne|rei,** die; - (*für* Polyandrie); **viel|mehr** [*auch* 'fi:l...]; er ist nicht dumm, weiß vielmehr gut Bescheid, *aber* er weiß viel mehr als du; **viel sa|gend** *vgl.* viel; **viel|schich|tig; Viel|schich|tig|keit,** die; -; **Viel|schrei|ber** *(abwertend);* **viel|sei|tig; Viel|sei|tig|keit,** die; -; **Viel|sei|tig|keits|prü|fung** *(Reitsport);* **viel-sil|big, ...spra|chig, ...stim|mig, ...stro|phig; viel|tau|send|mal,** *aber* viele tausend Male; *vgl.* Mal; **viel um|wor|ben** *vgl.* viel; **viel ver|spre|chend** *vgl.* viel; **Viel|völ|ker|staat** *Plur.* ...staaten; **Viel|wei|be|rei,** die; - (*für* Polygamie); **Viel|zahl,** die; -; **Viel|zel|ler** *(Biol.);* **viel|zel|lig**

Vi|en|tiane [viɛn'tja(:)n] (Hptst. von Laos)

vier; *Kleinschreibung* (↑R 48): die vier Elemente; die vier Jahreszeiten; die vier Evangelisten; etwas in alle vier Winde [zer]streuen; in seinen vier Wänden (*ugs. für* zu Hause) bleiben; sich auf seine vier Buchstaben setzen (*ugs. scherzh. für* sich hinsetzen); unter vier Augen etwas besprechen; alle viere von sich strecken (um tüchtig zu schlafen *[ugs]; ugs. auch für* tot sein); auf allen vieren; wir sind zu vieren *od.* zu viert; ein Grand mit vier[en]; *vgl.* acht, drei; **Vier,** die; -, -en (Zahl); eine Vier würfeln; er hat in Latein eine Vier geschrieben; *vgl.* [1]Acht *u.* Eins; **Vier|ach|ser** (Wagen mit vier Achsen; *mit Ziffer* 4-Achser; ↑R 44); **vier|ar|mig; Vier|bei|ner; vier|bei|nig; vier|blät|te|rig, vier|blätt|rig; vier|di|men|si|o|nal; Vier-drei-drei-Sys|tem,** das; -s; ↑R 28 (*mit Ziffern* 4-3-3-System; *Fußball* eine bestimmte Art der Mannschaftsaufstellung); **Vier|eck; vier|eckig** (↑R 132); **vier|ein|halb,** vier|und|ein|halb; **Vie|rer;** *vgl.* Achter; **Vie|rer|bob; vie|rer|lei; Vie|rer|rei|he;** in -n; **Vie|rer|zug; vier|fach; Vier|fa|che,** das; -n; *vgl.* Achtfache; **Vier|far|ben|druck** *Plur.* ...drucke; **Vier|far|ben|ku|gel|schrei|ber, Vier|farb|ku|gel|schrei|ber; Vier|flach,** das; -[e]s, -e *u.* **Vier|fläch|ner** (*für* Tetraeder); **Vier|fürst** (*für* Tetrarch); **Vier|fü|ßer; vier|fü|ßig; Vier-füß|ler, ...ge|spann; vier|hän|dig;** - spielen; **vier|hun|dert; Vier|jah|res|plan; vier|kant** (*Seemannsspr.* waagerecht); **Vier|kant,** das *od.* der; -[e]s, -e; **Vier|kant|ei|sen; vier|kan|tig; Vier|lan|de** *Plur.* (hamburgische Landschaft); **Vier|ling; Vier|mäch|te|kon|fe|renz; vier|mal;** *vgl.* achtmal; **vier|ma|lig; Vier|mas|ter; Vier|mast|zelt; vier|mo|to|rig; Vier|pass,** der; -es, -e (*Archit.* Verzierungsform mit vier Bogen); **Vier|plät|zer** (*schweiz. für* Viersitzer); **vier|plät|zig** (*schweiz. für* viersitzig); **Vier|rad-an|trieb, ...brem|se; vier|rä|de|rig, vier|räd|rig; Vier|ru|de|rer** (*für* Quadrireme); **vier|sai|tig;** ein -es Streichinstrument; **vier|schrö|tig** (stämmig); **vier|sei|tig; Vier|sit|zer; vier|sit|zig; Vier|spän|ner; vier|spän|nig; vier|stel|lig; Vier|ster|ne|ho|tel; vier|stim|mig** *(Musik);* ein -er Satz; - singen; **vier|stö|ckig; viert** *vgl.* vier; **Vier|tak|ter** *vgl.* Zweitakter; **Vier|takt|mo|tor; vier|tau|send; vier|te;** - Dimension; der - Stand (*früher für* Arbeiterschaft); *vgl.* achte; **vier|tei|len;** gevierteilt; **vier|tei|lig; vier|tel** ['fir...]; eine viertel Million; *vgl.* achtel; um viertel acht; *vgl.* Viertel; **Vier|tel,** das, *für* „vierter Teil" *schweizer. meist* der; -s, -; es ist [ein] Viertel vor, nach eins; es hat [ein] Viertel eins geschlagen; es ist fünf Minuten vor drei Viertel; *aber* wir treffen uns um viertel acht, um drei viertel acht; drei Viertel der Bevölkerung; *vgl.* Achtel, drei *u.* viertel; **Vier|tel|fi|na|le** *(Sportspr.),* **...ge|viert** *(Druckw.);* **Vier|tel-jahr, ...jahr|hun|dert; vier|tel|jäh|rig** (ein Vierteljahr alt, dauernd); -e Kündigung (mit einer ein Vierteljahr dauernden Frist); **vier|tel|jähr|lich** (alle Vierteljahre wiederkehrend); -e Kündigung (alle Vierteljahre mögliche Kündigung); **Vier|tel|li|ter;** *vgl.* achtel; **vier|teln** (in vier Teile zerlegen); ich ...[e]le (↑R 16); **Vier|tel|no|te; Vier|tel|pfund;** *vgl.* achtel; **Vier|tel|stun|de;** eine Viertelstunde, *auch* eine viertel Stunde; *vgl.* drei *u.* achtel; **vier|tel|stün|dig** ['fir...] (eine Viertelstunde dauernd); **vier|tel|stünd|lich** (alle Viertelstunden wiederkehrend); **Vier|tels|wen|dung; Vier|tel|ton** *Plur.* ...töne; **Vier|tel|zent|ner;** *vgl.* achtel; **vier|tens; viert|letzt;**

vgl. drittletzt; **vier|tü|rig; vier|und|ein|halb;** *vgl.* viereinhalb; **vier|und|zwan|zig;** *vgl.* acht; **Vier|und|zwan|zig|flach,** das; -[e]s, -e *u.* **Vier|und|zwan|zig|fläch|ner** (*für* Ikositetraeder); **Vie|rung** (*Archit.* Geviert; Viereck); **Vie|rungs‿kup|pel, ...pfei|ler; Vier|vier|tel|takt** [...'fir...], der; -[e]s; *vgl.* Achtel; **Vier|wald|stät|ter See,** der; - -s; ↑R 105 (See am Nordrand der Alpen bei Luzern); **vier|wer|tig; vier|zehn** ['fir...]; *vgl.* acht; **Vier|zehn|hei|li|gen** (Wallfahrtskirche südl. von Lichtenfels); **vier|zehn|hun|dert** ['fir...]; **vier|zehn‿tä|gig** (*vgl.* ...tägig), **...täg|lich** (*vgl.* ...täglich); **Vier|zei|ler; vier|zei|lig; vier|zig** ['fir...] usw.; *vgl.* achtzig usw.; **vier|zig|jäh|rig;** *vgl.* achtjährig; **Vier|zig|stun|den|wo|che** (*mit Ziffern* 40-Stunden-Woche; ↑R 28); **Vier|zim|mer|woh|nung** [fi:r...] (*mit Ziffer* 4-Zimmer-Wohnung; ↑R 28); **Vier-zwei-vier-Sys|tem,** das; -s; ↑R 28 (*mit Ziffern* 4-2-4-System; *Fußball* eine bestimmte Art der Mannschaftsaufstellung); **Vier|zy|lin|der** *vgl.* Achtzylinder; **Vier|zy|lin|der|mo|tor; vier|zy|lind|rig** (*mit Ziffer* 4-zylindrig; ↑R 44)

Vi|et|cong [viɛt'kɔŋ], der; -s, -[s] ‹vietnames.› (*nur Sing.:* polit. Bewegung im früheren Südvietnam; Mitglied dieser Bewegung); **Vi|et|nam** [viɛt'na(:)m] (Staat in Indochina); **Vi|et|na|me|se,** der; -n, -n (↑R 126); **Vi|et|na|me|sin; vi|et|na|me|sisch; Vi|et|nam|krieg,** der; -[e]s

vif [vi:f] ‹franz.› (*veraltend für* lebendig, lebhaft)

Vi|gil [v...], die; -, -ien [...i̯ən] ‹lat.› (Vortag hoher kath. Feste); **vi|gi|lant** (*veraltend für* pfiffig, aufgeweckt); **Vi|gi|lie** [...i̯ə], die; -, -n (bei den Römern die Nachtwache des Heeres); **vi|gi|lie|ren** (*veraltet für* wachsam sein)

Vig|net|te [vi'njɛtə] (↑R 130), die; -, -n ‹franz.› (kleine Verzierung [in Büchern]; *Fotogr.* Verdeckung bestimmter Stellen des Negativs beim Kopieren; Gebührenmarke für die Autobahnbenutzung [in der Schweiz])

Vi|gog|ne [vi'gɔnjə] (↑R 130), die; -, -n ‹indian.-franz.› (Mischgarn aus Wolle und Baumwolle)

vi|go|ro|so [v...] ‹ital.› (*Musik* kräftig, stark, energisch)

Vi|kar [v...], der; -s, -e ‹lat.› (*kath. Kirche* Amtsvertreter; *ev. Kirche* Theologe nach dem ersten Examen; *schweiz. auch für* Stellvertreter eines Lehrers); **Vi|ka|ri|at,** das; -[e]s, -e (Amt eines Vikars); **vi|ka|ri|ie|ren** (das Amt eines Vikars versehen); **Vi|ka|rin** (ev. weibl. Vikar)

Vik|tor [v...] ‹lat.› (m. Vorn.); **Vik|tor E|ma|nu|el** (Name mehrerer ital. Könige); [1]**Vik|to|ria** (Sieg [als Ausruf]); - rufen; [2]**Vik|to|ria** *vgl.* Victoria; [3]**Vik|to|ria** (w. Vorn.); **vik|to|ri|a|nisch;** viktorianische Sitten, *aber* (↑R 108:) die Viktorianische Zeit (der engl. Königin Viktoria)

Vik|tu|a|li|en [viktu'a:li̯ən] *Plur.* ‹lat.› (*veraltet für* Lebensmittel [für den täglichen Bedarf]); **Vik|tu|a|li|en‿hand|lung, ...markt**

Vi|kun|ja [v...], das; -s, -s *u.* die; -, ...jen ‹indian.› (höckerloses südamerik. Kamel); **Vi|kun|ja|wol|le**

Vi|la [v...] (Hptst. von Vanuatu)

Vil|la [v...], die; -, ...llen ‹lat.› (vornehmes Einzelwohnhaus)

Vil|lach [f...] (Stadt in Kärnten)

Vil|la|nell [v...], das; -s, -e *u.* **Vil|la|nel|le,** die; -, -n ‹ital.› (ital. Bauern-, Hirtenliedchen, bes. des 16. u. 17. Jh.s)

vil|len|ar|tig [v...]; ein -es Haus; **Vil|len‿ge|gend, ...vier|tel**

Vil|lin|gen-Schwen|nin|gen [f...] (Stadt an der Brigach)

Vil|lon [vi'jõ:] (franz. Lyriker)

Vil|ma [v...] (w. Vorn.)

Vil|ni|us [v...] (*litauische Form von* Wilna)

Vils|ho|fen [f...] (Stadt in Bayern)

Vi|mi|nal [v...], der; -s (Hügel in Rom)

Vi|naig|ret|te [vinɛ'grɛt(ə)] (↑R 130 *u.* 132), die; -, -n ‹franz.› (mit Essig bereitete Soße)

Vin|cen|ter ['vinsən...] (Einwohner des Staates St. Vincent und die Grenadinen); **vin|cen|tisch**

Vin|ci ['vintʃi], Leonardo da (ital. Künstler)

Vin|de|li|zi|er [vinde'li:tsi̯ər], der; -s, - (Angehöriger einer kelt. Volksgruppe); **vin|de|li|zisch;** *aber* (↑R 102:) die Vindelizische Schwelle (*Geol.* Landschwelle des Erdmittelalters im Alpenvorland)

Vin|di|ka|ti|on [v...], die; -, -en ‹lat.› (*Rechtsw.* Herausgabeanspruch des Eigentümers einer Sache gegenüber deren Besitzer); **vin|di|zie|ren; Vin|di|zie|rung** *vgl.* Vindikation

Vi|ne|ta [v...] ‹*verderbt aus* Jumneta› (sagenhafte untergegangene Stadt an der Ostseeküste)

Vingt-et-un [vɛ̃te'œ̃:], **Vingt-un** [vɛ̃'tœ̃:], das; - ‹franz., „einundzwanzig"› (ein Kartenglücksspiel)

Vin|ku|la|ti|on [v...], die; -, -en ‹lat.› (*Bankw.* Bindung des Rechtes der Übertragung eines Wertpapiers an die Genehmigung des Emittenten); **vin|ku|lie|ren; Vin|ku|lie|rung**

Vintsch|gau, Vinsch|gau [f...], der; -[e]s (Talschaft oberhalb von Meran)

Vin|zen|tia [v...] (w. Vorn.); **Vin|zenz** (m. Vorn.)

[1]**Vi|o|la** [v...] *u.* Vi|o|le, die; -, Violen ‹lat.› (*Bot.* Veilchen); [2]**Vi|o|la** (w. Vorn.)

[3]**Vi|o|la** [v...], die; -, ...len ‹ital.› (Bratsche); **Vi|o|la da Brac|cio** [- - 'bratʃo], die; - - -, ...le - - (Bratsche); **Vi|o|la da Gam|ba,** die; - - -, ...le - - (Gambe); **Vi|o|la d'A|mo|re,** die; - -, ...le - (eine Gambenart in Altlage)

Vi|o|le *vgl.* [1]Viola; **Vi|o|len** (*Plur. von* [1, 3]Viola)

vi|o|lent [v...] ‹lat.› (*veraltet für* heftig, gewaltsam); **Vi|o|lenz,** die; - (*veraltet für* Heftigkeit, Gewaltsamkeit)

vi|o|lett [v..., *schweiz. auch* f...] ‹franz.› (veilchenfarbig); *vgl.* blau; **Vi|o|lett,** das; -s, *Plur.* -, *ugs.* -s (violette Farbe); *vgl.* Blau; **Vi|o|let|ta** (w. Vorn.)

Vi|o|lin|bo|gen [v...]; **Vi|o|li|ne,** die; -, -n ‹ital.› (Geige); **Vi|o|li|nist,** der; -en, -en; ↑R 126 (Geiger); **Vi|o|lin‿kon|zert, ...schlüs|sel; Vi|o|lon|cel|list,** der; -en, -en; ↑R 126 (Cellist); **Vi|o|lon|cel|lo,** das; -s, *Plur.* -s *u.* ...celli (Kniegeige); **Vi|o|lo|ne,** der; -[s], *Plur.* -s *u.* ...ni (Vorgänger des Kontrabasses; eine Orgelstimme); **Vi|o|lo|phon,** das; -s, -e (im Jazz gebräuchliche Violine)

VIP *od.* **V. I. P.** = very important person[s] ['vɛri im'pɔ:(r)tənt 'pœ:(r)sən(z)] ‹engl.› (sehr wichtige Person[en], Persönlichkeit[en])

Vi|per [v..., *schweiz. auch* f...], die; -, -n ‹lat.› (Giftschlange)

VIP-Lounge ['vip...] ‹*zu* VIP›

Vi|ra|gi|ni|tät [v...], die; - ‹lat.› (*Med.* männliche Eigenschaften der Frau in körperl. u. psych. Hinsicht); **Vi|ra|go,** die; -, *Plur.* -s *u.* ...gines [...ne:s] (*Med.* Frau mit Anzeichen der Viraginität)

Vir|chow ['virço:, *auch* f...] (dt. Arzt)

Vi|re|ment [vir(ə)'mã:], das; -s, -s ‹franz.› (im Staatshaushalt die Übertragung von Mitteln von einem Titel auf einen anderen oder auf ein anderes Haushaltsjahr)

Vi|ren (*Plur. von* Virus)

Vir|gil [v...] *vgl.* Vergil

[1]**Vir|gi|nia** [v...] (w. Vorn.); [2]**Vir|gi-**

nia [*auch, österr. nur,* ...dʒ..., *engl.* vœ(r)ˈdʒinjə] (Staat in den USA; *Abk.* Va.); **³Vir|gi|nia** [*auch* ...dʒ...], die; -, -s (Zigarre einer bestimmten Sorte); **Vir|gi|ni|a|tabak; Vir|gi|ni|er** [...i̯ər]; **vir|gi|nisch; Vir|gi|ni|tät,** die; - (Jungfräulichkeit; Unberührtheit)

vi|ril [v...] ‹lat.› (*Med.* männlich); **Vi|ri|lis|mus,** der; - (Vermännlichung [einer Frau]); **Vi|ri|li|tät,** die; - (*Med.* männliche Kraft; Mannbarkeit)

Vi|ro|lo|ge [v...], der; -en, -en (↑R 126) ‹lat.; griech.› (Virusforscher); **Vi|ro|lo|gie,** die; - (Lehre von den Viren); **Vi|ro|lo|gin; vi|ro|lo|gisch; vi|rös** (durch Viren hervorgerufen

Vir|tu|a|li|tät, die; -, -en ‹franz.› (innewohnende Kraft od. Möglichkeit); **vir|tu|a|li|ter** ‹lat.› (als Möglichkeit); **vir|tu|ell** ‹franz.› (der Kraft od. Möglichkeit nach vorhanden, scheinbar); -es Bild (*Optik*)

vir|tu|os [v...] ‹ital.› (meisterhaft, technisch vollkommen); **Vir|tu|o|se,** der; -n, -n; ↑R 126 ([techn.] hervorragender Meister, bes. Musiker); **Vir|tu|o|sen|tum,** das; -s; **Vir|tu|o|sin; Vir|tu|o|si|tät,** die; - (Kunstfertigkeit; Meisterschaft, bes. als Musiker); **Vir|tus,** die; - ‹lat.› (*Ethik* Tüchtigkeit, Tapferkeit; Tugend)

vi|ru|lent [v...] ‹lat.› (krankheitserregend, aktiv, ansteckend [von Krankheitserregern]); **Vi|ru|lenz,** die; - (Ansteckungsfähigkeit [von Bakterien]); **Vi|rus,** das, *außerhalb der Fachspr. auch* der; -, ...ren (kleinster Krankheitserreger); **Vi|rus‿grip|pe, ...in|fek|ti|on, ...krank|heit**

Vi|sa (*Plur. von* Visum)

Vi|sa|ge [viˈza:ʒə, *österr.* ...ˈza:ʒ], die; -, -n [...ʒ(ə)n] ‹franz.› (*ugs. abwertend für* Gesicht); **Vi|sa|gist** [...ˈʒist], der; -en, -en; ↑R 126 (Kosmetiker, Maskenbildner); **Vi|sa|gis|tin; vis-a-vis,** *auch* **vis-à-vis** [vizaˈvi:] (gegenüber); **Vi|sa|vis,** das; - [...ˈvi:(s)], - [...ˈvi:s] (Gegenüber)

Vis|count [ˈvai̯kau̯nt], der; -s, -s ‹engl.› (engl. Adelstitel); **Vis|coun|tess** [...tis], die; -, -es [...tisiz] (*weibliche Form von* Viscount)

Vi|sen (*Plur. von* Visum); **Vi|sier** [v...], das; -s, -e ‹franz.› (beweglicher, das Gesicht deckender Teil des Helmes; Zielvorrichtung); **vi|sie|ren** (auf etwas zielen); **Vi|sier‿fern|rohr, ...li|nie**

Vi|si|on [v...], die; -, -en ‹lat.› (Erscheinung; Traumbild; Zukunftsentwurf); **vi|si|o|när** (traumhaft; seherisch); **Vi|si|o|när,** der; -s, -e (visionär begabter Mensch); **Vi|si|ons|ra|di|us** (*Optik* Sehachse)

Vi|si|ta|ti|on [v...], die; -, -en ‹lat.› (Durchsuchung, z. B. des Gepäcks; [Kontroll]besuch des vorgesetzten Geistlichen in den ihm unterstellten Gemeinden); **Vi|si|te,** die; -, -n ‹franz.› (Krankenbesuch des Arztes im Krankenhaus; *veraltet, noch scherzh. für* Besuch); **Vi|si|ten|kar|te** (Besuchskarte); **vi|si|tie|ren** (durch-, untersuchen; besichtigen); **Vi|sit|kar|te** (*österr. neben* Visitenkarte)

vis|kos, *selten* **vis|kös** [*beide* v...] ‹lat.› (zäh[flüssig], leimartig); -e Körper; **Vis|ko|se,** die; - (*Chemie* Zelluloseverbindung); **Vis|ko|si|me|ter,** das; -s, - ‹lat.; griech.› (Zähflüssigkeitsmesser); **Vis|ko|si|tät,** die; - ‹lat.› (Zähflüssigkeit)

Vis ma|jor [vi:s -], die; - - ‹lat.› (*Rechtsspr.* höhere Gewalt)

Vis|ta [v...], die; - ‹ital.› (*Bankw.* Sicht, Vorzeigen eines Wechsels); *vgl.* a vista *u.* a prima vista; **Vis|ta|wech|sel** (Sichtwechsel)

vi|su|a|li|sie|ren [v...] ‹lat.› (optisch darstellen); **Vi|su|a|li|sie|rung; Vi|su|a|li|zer** [ˈvizju̯əlai̯zə(r)], der; -s, - ‹engl.› (Fachmann für die grafische Gestaltung von Werbeideen); **vi|su|ell** [vizu...] ‹franz.› (das Sehen betreffend); -er Typ (jmd., der Gesehenes besonders leicht in Erinnerung behält); **Vi|sum,** das; -s, *Plur.* ...sa *u.* ...sen ‹lat.› (Ein- od. Ausreiseerlaubnis; Sichtvermerk im Pass; *schweiz. auch für* Namenszeichen, Abzeichnung); **Vi|sum|an|trag; vi|sum|frei; Vi|sum|zwang,** der; -[e]s

vis|ze|ral [v...] ‹lat.› (*Med.* Eingeweide...)

Vi|ta [v...], die; -, *Plur.* Viten *u.* Vitae [ˈvi:tɛ:] ‹lat.› (Leben, Lebensbeschreibung); **vi|tal** (lebenskräftig, -wichtig; frisch, munter); **Vi|tal|fär|bung** (*Mikroskopie* Färbung lebender Zellen u. Gewebe)

Vi|ta|li|a|ner [v...] *Plur.* ‹lat.; *zu* Viktualien› (*selten für* Vitalienbrüder); **Vi|ta|li|en|brü|der** *Plur.* (Seeräuber in der Nord- u. Ostsee im 14. u. 15. Jh.)

vi|ta|li|sie|ren [v...] ‹lat.› (beleben, anregen); **Vi|ta|lis|mus,** der; - (philos. Lehre von der „Lebenskraft"); **Vi|ta|list,** der; -en, -en; ↑R 126 (Anhänger des Vitalismus); **vi|ta|lis|tisch; Vi|ta|li|tät,** die; - (Lebendigkeit, Lebensfülle, -kraft); **Vi|ta|min** (↑R 132), das; -s, -e ([lebenswichtiger] Wirkstoff); - C; des Vitamin[s] C; **vi|ta|min|arm; Vi|ta|min-B-hal|tig** [...ˈbe:...] (↑R 28); **Vi|ta|min-B-Man|gel,** der; -s (↑R 28); **Vi|ta|min-B-Man|gel-Krank|heit,** die; -, -en (↑R 28); **vi|ta|mi|nie|ren, vi|ta|mi|ni|sie|ren** (mit Vitaminen anreichern); **Vi|ta|min‿man|gel** (der), **...prä|pa|rat; vi|ta|min|reich;** -e Kost; **Vi|ta|min|stoß** (Zufuhr von großen Vitaminmengen auf einmal)

vite [vit] ‹franz.› (*Musik* schnell, rasch)

Vi|tel|li|us [v...] (röm. Kaiser)

vi|te|ment [vit(ə)ˈmã:] (*Musik* schnell, rasch)

Vi|ti|um [v...], das; -s, ...tia ‹lat.› (*Med.* Fehler, Defekt)

Vit|ri|ne [v...] (↑R 130), die; -, -n ‹franz.› (gläserner Schaukasten, Schauschrank); **Vit|ri|ol,** das; -s, -e ‹lat.› (*veraltet für* kristallisiertes, kristallwasserhaltiges Sulfat von Zink, Eisen od. Kupfer); **vit|ri|ol|hal|tig; Vit|ri|ol|lö|sung**

Vit|ruv [v...], **Vit|ru|vi|us** [...vi̯us] (↑R 130; altröm. Baumeister)

Vi|tus [v...] (m. Vorn.)

Vitz|li|putz|li [v...], der; -[s] ‹aus „Huitzilopochtli", einem Stammesgott der Azteken› (Schreckgestalt, Kinderschreck; *volkstümlich auch für* Teufel)

vi|va|ce [viˈva:tʃə] ‹ital.› (*Musik* munter, lebhaft); **Vi|va|ce,** das; -, -; **vi|va|cis|si|mo** [...ˈtʃi...] (sehr lebhaft); **Vi|va|cis|si|mo,** das; -s, *Plur.* -s *u.* ...mi

Vi|val|di [viˈvaldi] (ital. Komponist)

vi|vant! [ˈvi:vant] ‹lat.› (sie sollen leben!); **Vi|va|ris|tik,** die; - (das Halten kleiner Tiere im Vivarium); **Vi|va|ri|um,** das; -s, ...ien [...i̯ən] (Aquarium mit Terrarium; *auch für* Gebäude hierfür); **vi|vat!** [ˈvi:vat] (er [sie, es] lebe!); **Vi|vat,** das; -s, -s (Hochruf); ein - ausbringen, rufen; **vi|vat, cres|cat, flo|re|at!** [- ...kat -] (er [sie, es] lebe, blühe und gedeihe!); **vi|vi|par** [vivi...] (*Biol.* lebend gebärend); **Vi|vi|sek|ti|on,** die; -, -en (Eingriff am lebenden Tier zu wissenschaftl. Versuchszwecken); **vi|vi|se|zie|ren**

Vi|ze... [ˈfi:tsə, *seltener* v...] ‹lat.› (stellvertretend); **Vi|ze‿kanz|ler, ...kö|nig, ...kon|sul, ...meis|ter** (*Sportspr.*), **...prä|si|dent**

Viz|tum [ˈfits..., *auch* ˈvi:ts...], der; -s, -e ‹lat.› (im MA. Verwalter weltl. Güter von Geistlichen u. Klöstern)

v. J. = vorigen Jahres

Vla|me ['fla:mə] usw. *vgl.* Flame usw.
Vlies [f...], das; -es, -e ‹niederl.› ([Schaf]fell; Rohwolle; *Spinnerei* breite Faserschicht); (↑R 108:) das Goldene Vlies *(griech. Sage)*
Vlie|se|li|ne ® [f...], die; - (Einlage z. B. zum Verstärken von Kragen und Manschetten)
Vlis|sin|gen [f...] (niederl. Stadt)
vm. *vgl.* ²vorm.
v. M. = vorigen Monats
V-Mann = Vertrauensmann, Verbindungsmann
VN = Vereinte Nationen *Plur.; vgl.* UN *u.* UNO
v. o. = von oben
Vöck|la|bruck [f...] (oberösterr. Stadt)
Vo|gel, der; -s, Vögel; **Vo|gel‿art, ...bad, ...bau|er** (das, *seltener* der; -s, -; Käfig); **Vo|gel|beer|baum** (Eberesche); **Vo|gel|bee|re; Vö|gel|chen; Vo|gel‿dreck, ...dunst** (der; -es; *Jägerspr.* feinster Schrot); **Vö|ge|lein; Vo|ge|ler** *vgl.* Vogler; **Vo|gel‿fän|ger, ...flug; Vo|gel|flug|li|nie,** die; - (kürzeste Verkehrsverbindung zwischen Hamburg u. Kopenhagen); **vo|gel|frei** (rechtlos); **Vo|gel‿fut|ter** (*vgl.* ¹Futter), **...häus|chen, ...herd** (*früher für* Vogelfangplatz), **...kir|sche, ...kun|de** (die; -; *für* Ornithologie), **...mie|re** (eine Pflanze); **vö|geln** (*derb für* Geschlechtsverkehr ausüben); ich ...[e]le (↑R 16); **Vo|gel‿nest, ...per|spek|ti|ve** (die; -; Vogelschau); **Vo|gels|berg,** der; -[e]s (Teil des Hessischen Berglandes); **Vo|gel‿schau** (die; -), **...scheu|che, ...schutz** (der; -[e]s); **Vo|gel|schutz‿ge|biet, ...war|te; Vo|gel‿schwarm, ...spin|ne, ...stel|ler** (*veraltet für* Vogelfänger), **...stim|me; Vo|gel-Strauß-Po|li|tik,** die; - (↑R 28); **Vo|gel‿war|te, ...welt** (die; -), **...züch|ter, ...zug; Vo|gerl|sa|lat** (*österr. für* Feldsalat)
Vo|ge|sen [v...] *Plur.* (Gebirgszug westl. des Oberrheins)
Vög|lein; Vog|ler (*veraltet für* Vogelfänger)
Vogt, der; -[e]s, Vögte (*früher für* Schirmherr; Richter; Verwalter); **Vog|tei** (*früher für* Amtsbezirk, Sitz eines Vogtes); **vog|tei|lich; Vög|tin; Vogtl.** = Vogtland; **Vogt|land,** das; -[e]s (Bergland zwischen Frankenwald, Fichtelgebirge u. Erzgebirge; *Abk.* Vogtl.); **Vogt|län|der** (↑R 103); **vogt|län|disch; Vogt|schaft**
voi|là! [voa'la] ‹franz., „sieh da!"› (da haben wir es!)
Voile [voa:l], der; -, -s ‹franz.› (ein durchsichtiger Stoff); **Voile|kleid**
Vo|ka|bel [v...], die; -, -n, *österr. auch* das; -s, - ‹lat.› ([einzelnes] Wort einer Fremdsprache); **Vo|ka|bel‿heft, ...schatz** (der; -es); **Vo|ka|bu|lar,** das; -s, -e *u. älter* **Vo|ka|bu|la|ri|um,** das; -s, ...ien [...iən] (Wortschatz; Wörterverzeichnis)
vo|kal [v...] ‹lat.› (*Musik* die Singstimme betreffend, gesangsmäßig); **Vo|kal,** der; -s, -e (*Sprachw.* Selbstlaut, z. B. a, e); **Vo|ka|li|sa|ti|on,** die; -, -en (Aussprache eines Konsonanten in der Art eines Vokals; die Aussprache der Vokale, bes. beim Gesang); **vo|ka|lisch** (den Vokal betreffend); **Vo|ka|li|se,** die; -, -n ‹franz.› (*Musik* Gesangsübung, -stück auf einen oder mehrere Vokale); **vo|ka|li|sie|ren** (einen Konsonanten wie einen Vokal sprechen; beim Singen die Vokale bilden u. aussprechen); **Vo|ka|li|sie|rung; Vo|ka|lis|mus,** der; - (Vokalbestand einer Sprache); **Vo|ka|list,** der; -en, -en; ↑R 126 (Sänger); **Vo|ka|lis|tin; Vo|kal‿mu|sik** (die; -; Gesang), **...stück** (*svw.* Vokalmusik); **Vo|ka|ti|on,** die; -, -en (Berufung in ein Amt); **Vo|ka|tiv** [v..., *auch* ...'ti:f], der; -s, -e [...və] (*Sprachw.* Anredefall)
vol. = Volumen (Schriftrolle, ¹Band)
Vol.-% = Volumprozent
Vo|land [f...], der; -[e]s (*alte Bez. für* Teufel); Junker -
Vo|lant [vo'laŋ, *auch* vɔ'lã:], der, *schweiz. meist* das; -s, -s ‹franz.› (Besatz an Kleidungsstücken, Falbel; *veraltend für* Lenkrad, Steuer [am Kraftwagen])
Vo|la|pük [v...], das; -s (eine künstliche Weltsprache)
Vo|li|e|re [v...], die; -, -n ‹franz.› (Vogelhaus)
Volk, das; -[e]s, Völker
Vol|kard *vgl.* Volkhard
volk|arm; Völk|chen
Vol|ker (Spielmann im Nibelungenlied; m. Vorn.)
Völ|ker‿ball (der; -[e]s; Ballspiel), **...bund** (der; -[e]s; *früher*), **...fa|mi|lie** (die; -), **...freund|schaft** (die; -), **...ge|misch, ...kun|de** (die; -); **Völ|ker|kund|ler; völ|ker|kund|lich; Völ|ker‿mord, ...recht** (das; -[e]s), **...recht|ler; völ|ker|recht|lich; Völ|ker|schaft**
Vol|kert *vgl.* Volkhard
völ|ker|ver|bin|dend; Völ|ker‿ver|stän|di|gung, ...wan|de|rung
Volk|hard, Vol|kard, Vol|kert (m. Vorn.)
völ|kisch; volk|lich
Volk|mar (m. Vorn.)
volk|reich; Volks‿ab|stim|mung, ...ak|tie, ...ak|ti|o|när, ...ar|mee (die; -; *ehem. in der DDR*), **...ar|mist** (der; -en, -en; ↑R 126; *ehem. in der DDR*), **...auf|stand, ...aus|ga|be, ...bank** (*Plur.* ...banken), **...be|fra|gung, ...be|geh|ren, ...be|lus|ti|gung, ...bib|li|o|thek; volks|bil|dend; Volks‿bil|dung** (die; -), **...brauch, ...buch, ...bü|che|rei, ...de|mo|kra|tie** (Staatsform kommunist. Länder, bei der die gesamte Staatsmacht in den Händen der Partei liegt), **...deut|sche** (der *u.* die; -n, -n; ↑R 5 ff.), **...dich|tung; volks|ei|gen** *(ehem. in der DDR);* ein -es Gut, ein -er Betrieb, *aber* (↑R 108): „Volkseigener Betrieb Buntgarnwerke Leipzig"; (*Abk.* VEB ...); **Volks‿ei|gen|tum, ...ein|kom|men, ...emp|fin|den** (das; -s), **...ent|scheid, ...ety|mo|lo|gie** (↑R 132; Bez. für die naive Verdeutlichung eines unbekannten Wortes durch dessen Anlehnung an bekannte, klangähnliche Wörter, z. B. „Hängematte" an „hängen" u. „Matte" statt an indianisch „hamaca"); **volks|ety|mo|lo|gisch** (↑R 132); **Volks|feind; volks|feind|lich; Volks‿fest, ...front** (Bündnis der linken bürgerlichen Parteien mit den Kommunisten), **...ge|mur|mel, ...ge|sund|heit** (die; -), **...glau|be[n], ...held, ...herr|schaft** (die; -), **...hoch|schu|le** (*Abk.* VHS), **...kam|mer** (die; -; *ehem. in der DDR* höchstes staatl. Machtorgan), **...kir|che, ...kor|res|pon|dent** *(ehem. in der DDR),* **...kun|de** (die; -); **Volks|kund|ler; volks|kund|lich; Volks‿kunst** (die; -), **...lauf** *(Sport),* **...le|ben** (das; -s), **...lied, ...mär|chen; Volks|ma|ri|ne** *(ehem. in der DDR);* **Volks‿men|ge, ...mund** (der; -[e]s), **...mu|sik, ...nah|rungs|mit|tel, ...po|li|zei** (die; -; *ehem. in der DDR; Abk.* VP), **...po|li|zist** *(ehem. in der DDR),* **...red|ner, ...re|pub|lik** (*Abk.* VR), **...schau|spie|ler, ...schau|spie|le|rin, ...schicht, ...schu|le, ...schü|ler, ...schü|le|rin; Volks|schul‿leh|rer, ...leh|re|rin; Volks‿see|le** (die; -), **...so|li|da|ri|tät** (Organisation für solidar. Hilfe, bes. in der DDR), **...sport** (der; -[e]s), **...spra|che; volks|sprach|lich; Volks‿stamm, ...stück, ...tanz, ...tracht, ...trau-**

er|tag, ...tri|bun; Vọlks|tum, das; -s; **vọlks|tüm|lich; Vọlks|tüm|lich|keit,** die; -; **vọlks|ver|bun|den; Vọlks‿ver|bun|den|heit** (die; -), **...ver|mö|gen, ...ver|tre|ter, ...ver|tre|tung, ...wa|gen ®** (*Abk.* VW); **Vọlks|wa|gen|werk; Vọlks‿wei|se** (die), **...weis|heit, ...wirt, ...wirt|schaft; Vọlks|wirt|schaf|ter** (*schweiz. überwiegend für* Volkswirtschaftler); **Vọlks|wirt|schaft|ler; vọlks|wirt|schaft|lich; Vọlks‿wirt|schafts|leh|re, ...wohl, ...zäh|lung**

vọll; voll Wein[es], voll [des] süßen Weines; voll[er] Angst; ein Fass voll[er] Öl; der Saal war voll[er] Menschen, voll von Menschen; voll heiligem Ernst; zehn Minuten nach voll (*ugs. für* nach der vollen Stunde); voll verantwortlich sein; ein Arm voll, eine Hand voll, ein Mund voll (*vgl.* Arm, Hand, Mund); (↑R 47:) aus dem Vollen schöpfen; im Vollen leben; ein Wurf in die Vollen (auf 9 Kegel); in die Vollen gehen (*ugs. für* etwas mit Nachdruck betreiben); ins Volle greifen. *Schreibung in Verbindung mit Verben* (↑R 37 ff.): voll sein, werden; [ganz] voll füllen, gießen, kotzen, laden, laufen, machen, packen, pfropfen, pumpen, schenken, schreiben, tanken, zeichnen; voll scheißen *(derb);* voll schmieren, spritzen, stopfen *(ugs.);* sich voll essen, fressen, saufen *(ugs.);* ich habe mich [ziemlich] voll gegessen; er hat sich den Bauch voll geschlagen (*ugs. für* sehr viel gegessen); jmdm. die Hucke voll hauen (*ugs. für* jmdn. verprügeln); jmdm. die Hucke voll lügen (*ugs. für* jmdn. sehr belügen); jmdn. nicht für voll nehmen (*ugs. für* nicht ernst nehmen); den Mund recht voll nehmen (*ugs. für* prahlen); etwas voll (ganz) begreifen; *vgl. aber* vollbringen, vollenden, vollführen, vollstrecken, vollziehen

Vọll|aka|de|mi|ker (↑R 132)

vọll|auf [*auch* ...'auf]; - genug

vọll|au|to|ma|tisch; vọll|au|to|ma|ti|siert

Vọll|bad

Vọll|bart; vọll|bär|tig

vọll|be|schäf|tigt; Vọll|be|schäf|ti|gung, die; -

Vọll|be|sitz; im - seiner Kräfte

Vọll|blut, das; -[e]s (reinrassiges Pferd); **Vọll|blü|ter; vọll|blü|tig; Vọll|blü|tig|keit,** die; -; **Vọll|blut|pferd**

Vọll|brem|sung

voll|brịn|gen; ↑R 37 (ausführen; vollenden); ich vollbringe; vollbracht; zu -; **Vọll|brịn|gung**

vọll|bu|sig

Vọll|dampf, der; -[e]s

Vọ̈l|le|ge|fühl, das; -s

vọll|elas|tisch (↑R 132)

vọll|elekt|ro|nisch (↑R 132)

voll|ẹn|den (↑R 37); ich vollende; vollendet; zu -; **Voll|ẹn|der; Voll|ẹn|de|rin; vol|lends** (↑R 132); **Voll|ẹn|dung**

vọl|ler *vgl.* voll

Völ|le|rei (unmäßiges Essen u. Trinken); **vọ̈l|lern**

vọll es|sen, sich; *vgl.* voll

vol|ley ['vɔli] ‹engl.›; einen Ball - (aus der Luft) nehmen; **Vọl|ley,** der; -s, -s (*Tennis* Flugball); **Vol|ley|ball** ['vɔli..., *auch* 'vɔle...], der; -[e]s (ein Ballspiel)

vọll fres|sen *vgl.* voll

voll|füh|ren (↑R 37); ich vollführe; vollführt; zu vollführen; **Voll|füh|rung**

vọll fül|len *vgl.* voll

Vọll|gas, das; -es; - geben

Vọll|gat|ter (*Technik* eine Säge)

Vọll|ge|fühl, das; -[e]s; im - seiner Macht

vọll ge|pfropft, ge|stopft *vgl.* voll

vọll gie|ßen *vgl.* voll

vọll|gül|tig

Vọll|gum|mi|rei|fen

Vọll|idi|ot (↑R 132; *ugs.*)

vọ̈l|lig

vọll|in|halt|lich

vọll|jäh|rig; Vọll|jäh|rig|keit, die; -; **Vọll|jäh|rig|keits|er|klä|rung**

Vọll|ju|rist

vọll|kas|ko|ver|si|chert; Vọll|kas|ko|ver|si|che|rung

Vọll|kauf|mann

vọll|kli|ma|ti|siert (↑R 40)

voll|kọm|men [*auch* 'fɔl...]; **Voll|kọm|men|heit,** die; -

Vọll|korn|brot

vọll kot|zen *vgl.* voll

Vọll|kraft, die; -

vọll la|den *vgl.* voll *u.* [1]laden

Vọll|last (↑R 136; *Technik*)

vọll lau|fen *vgl.* voll *u.* laufen

vọll|lei|big (↑R 136)

vọll ma|chen *vgl.* voll

Vọll|macht, die; -, -en; **Vọll|macht|ge|ber; Vọll|machts|ur|kun|de**

vọll|mast *(Seemannsspr.);* - flaggen; auf - stehen

Vọll|mat|ro|se

Vọll|milch; Vọll|milch|scho|ko|la|de

Vọll|mit|glied; Vọll|mit|glied|schaft

Vọll|mond, der; -[e]s; **Vọll|mond|ge|sicht** *Plur.* ...gesichter *(ugs.)*

vọll|mun|dig (voll im Geschmack; *auch für* großsprecherisch)

Vọll|nar|ko|se

vọll pa|cken *vgl.* voll

Vọll|pap|pe (massive Pappe)

Vọll|pen|si|on, die; -

vọll pfrop|fen, pumpen *vgl.* voll

Vọll|rausch

vọll|reif; Vọll|rei|fe

vọll sau|fen, schei|ßen, schen|ken, schlagen *vgl.* voll

vọll|schlank

vọll schmie|ren, schreiben *vgl.* voll

Vọll|sinn; im - des Wortes

vọll sprit|zen *vgl.* voll

Vọll|spur, die; - *(Eisenb.);* **vọll|spu|rig**

vọll|stän|dig; Vọll|stän|dig|keit, die; -

vọll|stock *(Seemannsspr.);* - flaggen; auf - stehen

vọll stop|fen *vgl.* voll

voll|strẹck|bar *(Rechtsw.);* **Voll|strẹck|bar|keit,** die; -; **voll|strẹ|cken** (↑R 37); ich vollstrecke; vollstreckt; zu vollstrecken; **Voll|strẹ|cker; Voll|strẹ|ckung; Voll|strẹ|ckungs‿be|am|te, ...be|scheid**

vọll tan|ken *vgl.* voll

vọll|tö|nend (↑R 40); **vọll|tö|nig**

Vọll|tref|fer

vọll|trun|ken; Vọll|trun|ken|heit, die; -

vọll|um|fäng|lich (*bes. schweiz.* in vollem Umfang)

Vọll|verb *(Sprachw.)*

Vọll|ver|pfle|gung

Vọll|ver|samm|lung

Vọll|wai|se

Vọll|wasch|mit|tel

vọll|wer|tig; Vọll|wer|tig|keit, die; -; **Vọll|wert|kost,** die; -

vọll|wich|tig (volles Gewicht habend)

vọll|zäh|lig; Vọll|zäh|lig|keit, die; -

vọll zeich|nen *vgl.* voll

Vọll|zeit ar|bei|ten *vgl.* Teilzeit arbeiten; **Vọll|zeit|schu|le**

voll|zie|h|bar; Voll|zieh|bar|keit, die; -; **voll|zie|hen** (↑R 37); ich vollziehe; vollzogen; zu vollziehen; **Voll|zie|her; Voll|zie|hung; Voll|zie|hungs|be|am|te; Voll|zug,** der; -[e]s (Vollziehung); **Voll|zugs‿an|stalt** (Gefängnis), **...be|am|te, ...ge|walt** (die; -), **...we|sen** (das; -s)

Vo|lon|tär [v..., *auch* volɔŋ...], der; -s, -e ‹franz.› (ohne od. nur gegen eine kleine Vergütung zur berufl. Ausbildung Arbeitender); **Vo|lon|ta|ri|at,** das; -[e]s, -e (Ausbildungszeit, Stelle eines Volontärs); **Vo|lon|tä|rin; vo|lon|tie|ren** (als Volontär[in] arbeiten)

Vọls|ker [v...], der; -s, - (Angehöriger eines ehem. Volksstammes in Mittelitalien); **vols|kisch**

Volt [v...], das; *Gen.* - *u.* -[e]s, *Plur.* - ⟨nach dem ital. Physiker Volta⟩ (Einheit der elektr. Spannung; *Zeichen* V); 220 - (↑R 90); **Vol|ta|ele|ment** (↑R 95 *u.* 132)

Vol|taire [vɔlˈtɛːr] (franz. Schriftsteller); **Vol|tai|ri|a|ner** (Anhänger Voltaires)

vol|ta|isch *od.* vol|tasch [v...] (nach Volta benannt; galvanisch); voltaische *od.* voltasche Säule; **Vol|ta|me|ter**, das; -s, - (Stromstärkemesser); *vgl. aber* Voltmeter; **Volt|am|pere** (Einheit der elektr. Leistung; *Zeichen* VA); **vol|tasch** *vgl.* voltaisch

Vol|te [v...], die; -, -n ⟨franz.⟩ (Reitfigur; Kunstgriff beim Kartenmischen; Verteidigungsart beim Fechtsport); die - schlagen; **Vol|ten|schlä|ger; Vol|te|schlagen**, das; -s; **vol|tie|ren** (*svw.* voltigieren); **Vol|ti|ge** [...ˈtiːʒə], die; -, -n (Sprung eines Kunstreiters auf das Pferd); **Vol|ti|geur** [...ˈʒøːr], der; -s, -e (Kunstspringer); **vol|ti|gie|ren** [...ˈʒiː...] (eine Volte ausführen; Luft-, Kunstsprünge, Turnübungen auf dem [galoppierenden] Pferd ausführen)

Volt|me|ter [v...], das; -s, - (*Elektrotechnik* Spannungsmesser); *vgl. aber* Voltameter; **Volt|se|kun|de** (Einheit des magnetischen Flusses; *Zeichen* Vs)

Vo|lu|men [v...], das; -s, *Plur.* - *u.* ...mina ⟨lat.⟩ (Rauminhalt [*Zeichen* V]; Schriftrolle, Band [*Abk.* vol.]; Stromstärke einer Fernsprech- od. Rundfunkübertragung; Umfang, Gesamtmenge von etwas); **Vo|lu|men|ge|wicht** *vgl.* Volumgewicht; **Vo|lu|men|pro|zent** *vgl.* Volumprozent; **Vo|lu|met|rie** (↑R 130), die; - (Messung von Rauminhalten); **Vo|lum|ge|wicht** (spezifisches Gewicht, Raumgewicht); **vo|lu|mi|nös** ⟨franz.⟩ (umfangreich, massig); **Vo|lum|pro|zent** (Hundertsatz vom Rauminhalt; *Abk.* Vol.-%)

Vo|lun|ta|ris|mus [v...], der; - ⟨lat.⟩ (philos. Lehre, die allein den Willen als maßgebend betrachtet); **Vo|lun|ta|rist**, der; -en, -en (↑R 126); **vo|lun|ta|ris|tisch; Vo|lun|ta|tiv**, der; -s (*Sprachw.* Form des Verbs, die einen Wunsch o. Ä. ausdrückt)

Völ|us|pa [v...] (↑R 132), die; - ⟨altnord.⟩ (Eddalied vom Ursprung u. vom Untergang der Welt)

Vo|lu|te [v...], die; -, -n ⟨lat.⟩ (*Kunstw.* spiralförmige Einrollung am Kapitell ionischer Säulen)

Vol|vu|lus [ˈvɔlvu...], der; -, ...li ⟨lat.⟩ (*Med.* Darmverschlingung)

vom (von dem; *Abk.* v.)

Vom|hun|dert|satz *vgl.* Hundertsatz

vo|mie|ren [v...] ⟨lat.⟩ (*Med.* sich erbrechen)

Vom|tau|send|satz (*für* Promillesatz)

von (*Abk.* v.); *Präp. mit Dat.*: von dem Haus; von der Art; von [ganzem] Herzen; von [großem] Nutzen, Vorteil sein; von Gottes Gnaden; von Hand zu Hand; von Sinnen; vonseiten, *auch* von Seiten *(vgl. d.);* von neuem; von nah u. fern; eine Frau von heute; von links, von rechts; von oben (*Abk.* v. o.); von unten (*Abk.* v. u.); von ungefähr; von vorn[e]; von vornherein; von jetzt an (*ugs.* ab); von klein auf; von Grund auf *od.* aus; von mir aus; von Haus[e] aus; von Amts wegen; von Rechts wegen; mit Grüßen von Haus zu Haus; von weit her; von alters her; von dorther; von jeher; von dannen, hinnen gehen; von wegen! (*ugs. für* auf keinen Fall!); **von|ei|n|an|der** (↑R 132); etwas voneinander haben, voneinander gehen, wissen, scheiden usw.; *vgl.* aneinander

von|nö|ten; ↑R 41 ([dringend] nötig); - sein

von oben (*Abk.* v. o.)

von Rechts we|gen (*Abk.* v. R. w.)

von|sei|ten, *auch* **von Sei|ten;** *mit Gen.*: vonseiten, *auch* von Seiten seines Vaters

von|stat|ten (↑R 41); *in* - gehen

von un|ten (*Abk.* v. u.)

von we|gen! (*ugs. für* auf keinen Fall!)

[1]**Vo|po**, der; -s, -s (*ugs. kurz für* Volkspolizist); [2]**Vo|po**, die; - (*ugs. kurz für* Volkspolizei)

vor (*Abk.* v.); *Präp. mit Dat. u. Akk.*: vor dem Zaun stehen, *aber* sich vor den Zaun stellen; vor allem *(vgl. d.);* vor diesem; vor alters *(vgl. d.);* vor der Zeit; Gnade vor Recht ergehen lassen; vor sich gehen; vor sich hin brummen usw.; vor Christi Geburt (*Abk.* v. Chr. G.); vor Christo *od.* Christus (*Abk.* v. Chr.); vor allem[,] wenn/weil *(vgl. d.)*

vor... (*in Zus. mit Verben,* z. B. vorsingen, du singst vor, vorgesungen, vorzusingen)

vor|ab (zunächst, zuerst)

Vor|ab|druck *Plur.* ...drucke

Vor|abend (↑R 132)

Vor|ab|in|for|ma|ti|on

Vor‿ah|nung, ...alarm (↑R 132)

vor al|lem (*Abk.* v. a.); vor allem[,] wenn/weil ... (↑R 88)

Vor|al|pen *Plur.*

vor al|ters; ↑R 46 (*veraltet für* in alter Zeit)

vo|ran (↑R 132); der Sohn voran, der Vater hinterdrein; **vo|ran...** (z. B. vorangehen); **vo|ran|ge|hen;** ich gehe voran; vorangegangen; voranzugehen; **vo|ran|ge|hend;** die vorangehenden Ausführungen; *aber* (↑R 47:) Vorangehendes; im Vorangehenden (weiter oben); der, die, das Vorangehende; *vgl.* folgend; **vo|ran|kom|men**

Vor|an|kün|di|gung

vo|ran|ma|chen (*ugs. für* sich beeilen)

vor|an|mel|den *nur im Infinitiv u. Partizip II gebr.;* vorangemeldet; **Vor‿an|mel|dung, ...an|schlag** *(Wirtsch.)*

vo|ran‿stel|len, ...trei|ben

Vor‿an|zei|ge, ...ar|beit; vor|ar|bei|ten; Vor|ar|bei|ter; Vor|ar|bei|te|rin

Vor|arl|berg[1] (österr. Bundesland); **Vor|arl|ber|ger**[1] (↑R 103); **vor|arl|ber|gisch**[1]

vo|rauf (↑R 132; *selten für* voran *u.* voraus); **vo|rauf|ge|hen** *(geh.);* ich gehe vorauf; voraufgegangen; voraufzugehen

vo|raus (↑R 132); er war allen voraus; *aber* im, *landsch.* zum Voraus [*auch* ˈfoː...]; **Vo|raus,** der; - (*Rechtsw.* besonderer Erbanspruch eines überlebenden Ehegatten); **vo|raus...** (z. B. vorausgehen); **Vo|raus|ab|tei|lung** *(Milit.);* **vo|raus|be|din|gen** *(veraltet);* ich bedinge voraus; vorausbedungen; vorauszubedingen; **Vo|raus|be|din|gung; vo|raus|be|re|chen|bar; vo|raus|be|rech|nen; vo|raus|be|stim|men; vo|raus|be|zah|len; Vo|raus|be|zah|lung; vo|raus|da|tie|ren** (mit einem späteren Datum versehen); **vo|raus|ei|len; Vo|raus|exemp|lar** (↑R 132); **vo|raus|fah|ren; vo|raus|ge|hen; vo|raus|ge|hend;** die vorausgehenden Verhandlungen; *aber* (↑R 47:) Vorausgehendes; im Vorausgehenden (weiter oben); der, die, das Vorausgehende; *vgl.* folgend; **vo|raus|ge|setzt**[,] **dass** (↑R 88); **vo|raus|ha|ben;** jmdm. etwas -; **Vo|raus‿kas|se, ...kor|rek|tur; vo|raus|lau|fen;**

---

[1] [*auch* ...ˈarl...]

vo|raus|sag|bar; Vo|raus|sa|ge; vo|raus|sa|gen; Vo|raus|schau; vo|raus|schau|en
Vor|aus|schei|dung *(Sport)*
vo|raus|schi|cken; vo|raus|seh|bar; vo|raus|se|hen; vo|raus|set|zen; Vo|raus|set|zung; vo|raus|set|zungs|los; Vo|raus|sicht, die; -; aller - nach; in der -, dass ...; **vo|raus|sicht|lich**
Vor|aus|wahl (vorläufige Auswahl)
vo|raus|wis|sen; vo|raus|zah|len; Vo|raus|zah|lung
Vor|bau *Plur.* ...bauten; **vor|bau|en** *(auch für* vorbeugen); der kluge Mann baut vor
vor|be|dacht; nach einem vorbedachten Ziel; - sein; **Vor|be|dacht,** der; *nur in* mit, ohne - [handeln]
Vor|be|deu|tung
Vor|be|din|gung
Vor|be|halt, der; -[e]s, -e (Bedingung); mit, unter, ohne -; **vor|be|hal|ten;** ich behalte es mir vor; ich habe es mir -; vorzubehalten; **vor|be|halt|lich,** *schweiz.* **vor|be|hält|lich;** *Präp. mit Gen. (Amtsspr.):* - unserer Rechte; **vor|be|halt|los; Vor|be|halts‿gut, ...klau|sel, ...ur|teil**
vor|be|han|deln; Vor|be|hand|lung
vor|bei; vorbei (vorüber) sein; als er kam, war bereits alles vorbei; **vor|bei...** (z. B. vorbeigehen); **vor|bei|be|neh|men,** sich *(ugs. für* sich unpassend, ungehörig benehmen); **vor|bei|brin|gen; vor|bei|dür|fen** *(ugs. für* vorbeigehen dürfen); **vor|bei|fah|ren; vor|bei|flie|gen; vor|bei|flie|ßen; vor|bei|füh|ren; vor|bei|ge|hen; vor|bei|kom|men;** bei jmdm. - *(ugs. für* jmdn. kurz besuchen); **vor|bei|kön|nen** *(ugs.);* **vor|bei|las|sen** *(ugs.);* **vor|bei|lau|fen; Vor|bei|marsch,** der; **vor|bei|mar|schie|ren; vor|bei|müs|sen** *(ugs.);* **vor|bei|pla|nen;** am Verbraucher -; **vor|bei|re|den;** am Thema -; **vor|bei|rei|ten; vor|bei|schau|en;** der Arzt will noch einmal -; **vor|bei|schie|ßen; vor|bei|zie|hen**
vor|be|las|tet; erblich - sein; **Vor|be|las|tung**
Vor|be|mer|kung
Vor|be|ra|tung
vor|be|rei|ten; Vor|be|rei|tung; Vor|be|rei|tungs|dienst; Vor|be|rei|tungs|kurs *od.* **...kur|sus**
Vor|be|richt
vor|be|sagt *(veraltend für* eben genannt)
Vor|be|scheid
Vor|be|sit|zer; Vor|be|sit|ze|rin
Vor|be|spre|chung
vor|be|stel|len; Vor|be|stel|lung
vor|be|stim|men *(svw.* vorherbestimmen); **Vor|be|stim|mung**
vor|be|straft; Vor|be|straf|te, der *u.* die; -n, -n (↑R 5 ff.)
vor|be|ten; Vor|be|ter; Vor|be|te|rin
Vor|beu|ge|haft, die *(Rechtsw.);* **vor|beu|gen;** (↑R 50:) Vorbeugen, *auch* vorbeugen ist besser als Heilen, *auch* heilen; **Vor|beu|gung; Vor|beu|gungs|maß|nah|me**
vor|be|zeich|net *(veraltend für* eben genannt, eben aufgeführt)
Vor|bild; vor|bil|den; vor|bild|haft; vor|bild|lich; Vor|bild|lich|keit, die; -; **Vor|bil|dung,** die; -
vor|bin|den; eine Schürze -
vor|bla|sen *(ugs. für* vorsagen)
Vor|blick
vor|boh|ren
Vor|bör|se, die; - (der eigtl. Börsenzeit vorausgehende Börsengeschäfte); **vor|börs|lich**
Vor|bo|te; Vor|bo|tin
vor|brin|gen
Vor|büh|ne
vor Chris|ti Ge|burt *(Abk.* v. Chr. G.); **vor|christ|lich; vor Chris|to, vor Chris|tus** *(Abk.* v. Chr.)
Vor|dach
vor|da|tie|ren (mit einem späteren Datum versehen [*vgl.* vorausdatieren]; *auch für* mit einem früheren Datum versehen [*vgl.* zurückdatieren]); **Vor|da|tie|rung**
Vor|deck *(svw.* Vorderdeck)
vor|dem [*auch* ˈfoːr...] *(veraltend für* früher)
Vor|den|ker (jmd., der kommende Entwicklungen erkennt, auf sie hinweist); **Vor|den|ke|rin**
Vor|der‿ach|se, ...an|sicht; vor|der|asi|a|tisch (↑R 132); **Vor|der‿asi|en** (↑R 132), **...aus|gang, ...bein, ...deck; vor|de|re,** *aber:* der Vordere Orient; *vgl.* vorderst; **Vor|der‿front, ...fuß, ...gau|men; Vor|der|gau|men|laut** *(für* Palatal); **Vor|der|grund; vor|der|grün|dig**
vor|der|hand [*auch* ...ˈhant] (↑R 41) ‹*zu* vor› (einstweilen)
Vor|der|hand, die; - ‹*zu* vordere›
Vor|der‿haus, ...hirn
Vor|der|in|di|en (↑R 105)
Vor|der‿kip|per *(Kfz-Technik),* **...la|der** (eine alte Feuerwaffe), **...mann** *(Plur.* ...männer), **...pfo|te, ...rad; Vor|der|rad‿an|trieb, ...brem|se; Vor|der‿rei|fen, ...satz** *(Sprachw.),* **...schiff, ...schin|ken, ...sei|te, ...sitz**
vor|derst; zuvorderst; der vorderste Mann, *aber* (↑R 47): die Vordersten sollen sich setzen
Vor|der‿ste|ven, ...teil (das *od.* der), **...tür, ...zim|mer**
vor|drän|geln, sich; ich dräng[e]le mich vor (↑R 16); **vor|drän|gen;** sich -
vor|drin|gen; vor|dring|lich (besonders dringlich); **Vor|dring|lich|keit,** die; -
Vor|druck *Plur.* ...drucke
vor|ehe|lich (↑R 132)
vor|ei|lig; Vor|ei|lig|keit
vor|ei|nan|der (↑R 132 *u.* 39); sich voreinander fürchten, sich voreinander hüten, sich voreinander hinstellen usw.; *vgl.* aneinander
vor|ein|ge|nom|men; Vor|ein|ge|nom|men|heit, die; -
Vor|ein|sen|dung; gegen - des Betrages in Briefmarken
vor|eis|zeit|lich
Vor|el|tern *Plur.* (Vorfahren, Ahnen)
vor|ent|hal|ten; ich enthalte vor; ich habe vorenthalten; vorzuenthalten; **Vor|ent|hal|tung**
Vor|ent|scheid; Vor|ent|schei|dung; Vor|ent|schei|dungs|kampf
[1]Vor|er|be, der; **[2]Vor|er|be,** das
vor|erst
vor|er|wähnt *(Amtsspr.)*
vor|er|zäh|len *(ugs. für* jmdn. etwas glauben machen wollen, was nicht wahr ist)
Vor|es|sen *(schweiz. für* Ragout)
Vor|exa|men (↑R 132)
vor|exer|zie|ren (↑R 132; *ugs.)*
Vor|fab|ri|ka|ti|on; vor|fab|ri|zie|ren
Vor|fahr, der; -en, -en (↑R 126) *u.* **Vor|fah|re,** der; -n, -n (↑R 126); **vor|fah|ren; Vor|fah|rin; Vor|fahrt,** die; -; [die] - haben, beachten; **vor|fahrt[s]|be|rech|tigt; Vor|fahrt[s]‿recht** (das; -[e]s), **...re|gel, ...schild** (das), **...stra|ße, ...zei|chen**
Vor|fall, der; **vor|fal|len**
Vor|fei|er
Vor|feld; im - der Wahlen
Vor|film
vor|fi|nan|zie|ren; Vor|fi|nan|zie|rung
vor|fin|den
Vor|flu|ter (Abzugsgraben; Entwässerungsgraben)
Vor|form; vor|for|men; vor|for|mu|lie|ren
Vor|fra|ge
Vor|freu|de
vor|fris|tig; etwas - liefern
Vor|früh|ling
vor|füh|len (vorsichtig zu erkunden suchen)

Vor|führ|da|me; vor|füh|ren; Vor|füh|rer; Vor|füh|re|rin; Vor|führ‿ge|rät, ...raum; Vor|füh|rung; Vor|füh|rungs|raum; Vor|führ|wa|gen

Vor|ga|be (Richtlinie; *Sport* Vergünstigung für Schwächere; *Bergmannsspr.* das, was an festem Gestein [od. Kohle] durch Sprengung gelöst werden soll); **Vor|ga|be|zeit** *(Wirtsch.)*

Vor|gang; Vor|gän|ger; Vor|gän|ge|rin; vor|gän|gig (*schweiz. für* zuvor); **Vor|gangs|wei|se,** die (*österr. für* Vorgehensweise)

Vor|gar|ten

vor|gau|keln; ich gauk[e]le dir etwas vor (↑R 16)

vor|ge|ben

Vor|ge|bir|ge

vor|geb|lich (*veraltend für* angeblich)

vor|ge|fasst; -e Meinung

Vor|ge|fecht

vor|ge|fer|tigt; -e Bauteile

Vor|ge|fühl; im - seines Glücks

Vor|ge|gen|wart (*svw.* Perfekt)

vor|ge|hen; Vor|ge|hen, das; -s; **Vor|ge|hens|wei|se,** die

vor|ge|la|gert; -e Inseln

Vor|ge|län|de

Vor|ge|le|ge (*Technik* eine Übertragungsvorrichtung)

vor|ge|le|sen, ge|neh|migt, un|ter|schrie|ben (gerichtl. Formel; *Abk.* v., g., u.)

vor|ge|nannt *(Amtsspr.)*

vor|ge|ord|net (*veraltet für* übergeordnet)

Vor|ge|plän|kel

Vor|ge|richt (Vorspeise)

vor|ger|ma|nisch

Vor|ge|schich|te, die; -; **Vor|ge|schicht|ler; vor|ge|schicht|lich; Vor|ge|schichts|for|schung**

Vor|ge|schmack, der; -[e]s

vor|ge|schrit|ten; in -em Alter

Vor|ge|setz|te, der *u.* die; -n, -n (↑R 5 ff.); **Vor|ge|setz|ten|ver|hält|nis**

Vor|ge|spräch

vor|ges|tern; vorgestern Abend (↑R 45); **vor|gest|rig**

vor|glü|hen (beim Dieselmotor)

vor|grei|fen; vor|greif|lich *(veraltet); vgl.* unvorgreiflich; **Vor|griff**

vor|gu|cken *(ugs.)*

vor|ha|ben; etwas -; **Vor|ha|ben,** das; -s, - (Plan, Absicht)

Vor|hal|le

Vor|halt (*Musik* ein dissonanter Ton, der an Stelle eines benachbarten Akkordtones steht, in den er sich auflöst; *schweiz. neben* Vorhaltung); **vor|hal|ten; Vor|hal|tung** *meist Plur.* (ernste Ermahnung)

Vor|hand, die; - (*bes. [Tisch]tennis* ein bestimmter Schlag; *beim Pferd* auf den Vorderbeinen ruhender Rumpfteil; Kartenspieler, der beim Austeilen die erste Karte erhält); in [der] - sein, sitzen; die - haben

vor|han|den; - sein; **Vor|han|den|sein,** das; -s (↑R 50)

Vor|hang, der; -[e]s, ...hänge; [1]**vor|hän|gen;** das Kleid hing unter dem Mantel vor; *vgl.* [1]hängen; [2]**vor|hän|gen;** sie hat das Bild vorgehängt; *vgl.* [2]hängen; **Vor|hän|ge|schloss; Vor|hang‿stan|ge, ...stoff**

Vor‿haus (*landsch. für* Hauseinfahrt, -flur), **...haut** (*für* Präputium); **Vor|haut|ver|en|gung** (*für* Phimose)

vor|hei|zen

vor|her [*auch* ...'he:r]; vorher (früher) war es besser; einige Tage vorher. *Schreibung in Verbindung mit Verben* (↑R 38 f.): **a)** *Getrenntschreibung, wenn* „vorher" *im Sinne von* „früher" *gebraucht wird, z. B.* vorher (früher) gehen; **b)** *Zusammenschreibung, wenn* „vorher" *im Sinne von* „voraus" *verwendet wird; vgl.* vorherbestimmen, vorhergehen, vorhersagen, vorhersehen; **vor|her|be|stim|men;** ↑R 38 (vorausbestimmen); er bestimmt vorher; vorherbestimmt; vorherzubestimmen; *aber* er hat den Zeitpunkt vorher (früher, im Voraus) bestimmt; **Vor|her|be|stim|mung,** die; -; **vor|her|ge|hen;** ↑R 38 (voraus-, vorangehen); es geht vorher; vorhergegangen; vorherzugehen; *vgl.* vorher a; **vor|her|ge|hend;** die vorhergehenden Ereignisse; *aber* (↑R 47:) Vorhergehendes; im Vorhergehenden (weiter oben); der, die, das Vorhergehende; *vgl.* folgend; **vor|he|rig** [*auch* 'fo:r...]

Vor|herr|schaft, die; -; **vor|herr|schen**

vor|her|sag|bar; Vor|her|sa|ge, die; -, -n; **vor|her|sa|gen;** ↑R 38 (voraussagen); ich sage vorher; vorhergesagt; vorherzusagen; (↑R 47:) das Vorhergesagte; *vgl. aber* vorher a: das vorher Gesagte

vor|her|seh|bar; vor|her|se|hen; ↑R 38 (im Voraus erkennen); ich sehe vorher; vorhergesehen; vorherzusehen; *vgl.* vorher a

vor|heu|len (*ugs. für* laut klagen); du heulst mir etwas vor

vor|hin [*auch* ...'hin]

Vor|hi|nein; *nur in der Fügung* im Vorhinein (*bes. österr. für* im Voraus)

Vor‿hof, ...höl|le, ...hut (die; -, -en)

vo|rig; vorigen Jahres (*Abk.* v. J.); vorigen Monats (*Abk.* v. M.); (↑R 47:) der, die, das Vorige; im Vorigen (weiter vorher); die Vorigen (Personen des Theaterstückes), das Vorige (die vorigen Ausführungen; die Vergangenheit); *vgl.* folgend

vor|in|do|ger|ma|nisch

Vor|in|for|ma|ti|on; vor|in|for|mie|ren

Vor|jahr; Vor|jah|res|sie|ger; vor|jäh|rig

vor|jam|mern (*ugs. svw.* vorheulen); du jammerst mir etwas vor

Vor‿kal|ku|la|ti|on *(Kaufmannsspr.),* **...kam|mer, ...kämp|fer, ...kämp|fe|rin, ...kas|se** (*svw.* Vorauskasse)

vor|kau|en (*ugs. auch für* in allen Einzelheiten erklären)

Vor|kauf; Vor|käu|fer; Vor|kaufs|recht

Vor|kehr, die; -, -en (*schweiz. für* Vorkehrung); **vor|keh|ren** (*schweiz. für* vorsorglich anordnen); **Vor|keh|rung** ([sichernde] Maßnahme); -[en] treffen

Vor|keim *(Bot.)*

Vor|kennt|nis *meist Plur.*

vor|kli|nisch; die -en Semester

vor|knöp|fen *(ugs.);* ich habe ihn mir vorgeknöpft (zurechtgewiesen)

vor|koh|len (*ugs. für* vorlügen); *vgl.* [2]kohlen

vor|kom|men; Vor|kom|men, das; -s, -; **vor|kom|men|den|falls** *(Amtsspr.); vgl.* Fall, der; **Vor|komm|nis,** das; -ses, -se

Vor|kost (Vorspeise); **Vor|kos|ter**

vor|kra|gen (*Bauw.* herausragen; *seltener für* herausragen lassen)

Vor|kriegs‿er|schei|nung, ...ge|ne|ra|ti|on, ...wa|re, ...zeit

vor|la|den *vgl.* [2]laden; **Vor|la|dung**

Vor|la|ge

Vor|land, das; -[e]s

vor|las|sen

Vor|lauf (zeitl. Vorsprung; *Chemie* erstes Destillat; *Sport* Ausscheidungslauf); **Vor|läu|fer; Vor|läu|fe|rin; vor|läu|fig; Vor|läu|fig|keit,** die; -

vor|laut

vor|le|ben; der Jugend Toleranz -; **Vor|le|ben,** das; -s (früheres Leben)

Vor|le|ge‿be|steck, ...ga|bel; vor|le|gen; Vor|le|ger (kleiner Teppich); **Vor|le|ge|schloss; Vor|le|gung**

vor|leh|nen, sich

Vor|leis|tung

vor|le|sen; Vor|le|se|pult; Vor|le|ser; Vor|le|se|wett|be|werb; Vor|le|sung; vor|le|sungs|frei; Vor|le|sungs‿ge|bühr, ...ver|zeich|nis
vor|letzt; zu vorletzt; der vorletzte Mann, *aber* (↑R 48): er ist der Vorletzte [der Klasse]
Vor|lie|be, die; -, -n; **vor|lieb neh|men;** ich nehme vorlieb; vorlieb genommen; vorlieb zu nehmen; *vgl.* fürlieb nehmen
vor|lie|gen; vor|lie|gend; -er Fall; (↑R 47:) Vorliegendes; im Vorliegenden (*Amtsspr.* hier); das Vorliegende; *vgl.* folgend
vor|lings (*Sportspr.* dem Gerät [mit der Vorderseite des Körpers] zugewandt)
vor|lü|gen
vorm; ↑R 13 (*ugs. für* vor dem); vorm Haus[e]
[1]**vorm.** = vormals
[2]**vorm.,** *bei Raummangel* vm. = vormittags
vor|ma|chen *(ugs.);* jmdm. etwas - (vorlügen; jmdn. täuschen)
Vor|macht, die; -; **Vor|macht|stel|lung,** die; -
Vor|ma|gen (*svw.* Pansen)
vor|ma|lig; vor|mals (*Abk.* vorm.)
Vor|mann *Plur.* ...männer
Vor|marsch, der
Vor|märz, der; -[e]s (Periode von 1815 bis zur Märzrevolution von 1848); **vor|märz|lich**
Vor|mast, der (vorderer Schiffsmast)
Vor|mau|er
Vor|mensch, der (*Bez. für* Vorläufer des Urmenschen)
Vor|merk|buch; vor|mer|ken; Vor|mer|kung (*auch für* vorläufige Eintragung ins Grundbuch)
Vor|mie|ter; Vor|mie|te|rin
Vor|milch, die; - (*für* Kolostrum)
Vor|mit|tag; vormittags; ↑R 46 (*Abk.* vorm., *bei Raummangel* vm.), *aber* des Vormittags; heute Vormittag (↑R 45); *vgl.* [1]Mittag; **vor|mit|tä|gig** *vgl.* ...tägig; **vor|mit|täg|lich** *vgl.* ...täglich; **vor|mit|tags** *vgl.* Vormittag; **Vor|mit|tags‿stun|de, ...vor|stel|lung**
Vor|mo|nat
Vor|mund, der; -[e]s, *Plur.* -e *u.* ...münder; **Vor|mund|schaft; Vor|mund|schafts|ge|richt**
[1]**vorn,** *ugs.* vor|ne; noch einmal von - beginnen
[2]**vorn;** ↑R 13 (*ugs. für* vor den); vorn Kopf
Vor|nah|me, die; -, -n (Ausführung)
Vor|na|me
vorn|an[1] [*auch* 'fɔrn|an]; **vor|ne** *vgl.* [1]vorn
vor|nehm; vornehm tun
vor|neh|men; sich etwas -
Vor|nehm|heit, die; -; **vor|nehm|lich** (*geh. für* vor allem, besonders); **Vor|nehm|tu|e|rei,** die; - *(abwertend)*
vor|nei|gen; sich -
vor|ne|weg [*auch* ...'vɛk], vornweg [*auch* ...'vɛk]
vorn|he|rein[1] [*auch* ...'rain]; von vornherein
vorn|über[1] (↑R 132); **vorn|über...** (z. B. vornüberstürzen; er ist vornübergestürzt); **vorn|über‿beu|gen, ...fal|len, ...kip|pen, ...stür|zen**
vorn|weg *vgl.* vorneweg
Vor|ort, der; -[e]s, ...orte; *vgl. aber* vor Ort sein; Vor-Ort-Begehung; **Vor|ort[s]‿ver|kehr** (der; -s), **...zug**
vor|pla|nen; Vor|pla|nung
Vor|platz
Vor|pom|mern (Teil des Bundeslandes Mecklenburg-Vorpommern)
Vor|pos|ten
vor|prel|len (nach vorn eilen; übereilt handeln)
vor|pre|schen
Vor|pro|gramm; vor|pro|gram|mie|ren; vor|pro|gram|miert
Vor|prü|fung
vor|quel|len
Vor|rang, der; -[e]s; **vor|ran|gig; Vor|ran|gig|keit,** die; -; **Vor|rang|stel|lung**
Vor|rat, der; -[e]s, ...räte; **vor|rä|tig;** etw. - haben; **Vor|rats‿hal|tung, ...kam|mer, ...kel|ler, ...raum, ...schrank**
Vor|raum
vor|rech|nen; jmdm. etwas -
Vor‿recht, ...re|de, ...red|ner, ...rei|ter
vor|ren|nen; Vor|ren|nen *(Sport)*
vor|re|vo|lu|ti|o|när
vor|rich|ten (*landsch. für* herrichten); **Vor|rich|tung**
vor|rü|cken
Vor|ru|he|stand (freiwilliger vorzeitiger Ruhestand); **Vor|ru|he|stands‿geld, ...re|ge|lung**
Vor|run|de *(Sport);* **Vor|run|den|spiel**
vors; ↑R 13 (*ugs. für* vor das); - Haus
Vors. = Vorsitzende[r], Vorsitzer
Vor|saal (*landsch. für* Diele)
vor|sa|gen; Vor|sa|ger
Vor‿sai|son, ...sän|ger, ...sän|ge|rin
Vor|satz, der, *Druckw.* das; -es, Vorsätze; **Vor|satz|blatt** (*svw.* Vorsatzpapier); **vor|sätz|lich; Vor|sätz|lich|keit,** die; -; **Vor|satz|pa|pier** *(Druckw.)*
Vor|schalt‿ge|setz (vorläufige gesetzliche Regelung), **...wi|der|stand** *(Elektrotechnik)*
Vor|schau
Vor|schein; *nur noch in* zum - kommen, bringen
vor|schi|cken
vor|schie|ben
vor|schie|ßen *(ugs.);* jmdm. hundert Mark -
Vor|schiff
vor|schla|fen *(ugs.)*
Vor|schlag; auf - von ...; **vor|schla|gen; Vor|schlag|ham|mer; Vor|schlags‿recht** (das; -[e]s), **...we|sen** (das; -s)
Vor|schluss|run|de *(Sport)*
vor|schme|cken
vor|schnell; - urteilen
Vor|schot|mann *Plur.* ...männer *u.* ...leute *(Seemannsspr.)*
vor|schrei|ben; Vor|schrift; Dienst nach -; **vor|schrifts‿ge|mäß, ...mä|ßig, ...wid|rig**
[1]**Vor|schub;** *nur noch in* jmdm. *od.* einer Sache - leisten (begünstigen, fördern); [2]**Vor|schub** (*Technik* Maß der Vorwärtsbewegung eines Werkzeuges); **Vor|schub|lei|s|tung**
Vor|schul|al|ter; Vor|schu|le; Vor|schul|er|zie|hung; vor|schu|lisch; Vor|schu|lung
Vor|schuss; Vor|schuss|lor|bee|ren *Plur.* (im Vorhinein erteiltes Lob); **vor|schuss|wei|se; Vor|schuss|zah|lung**
vor|schüt|zen (als Vorwand angeben); keine Müdigkeit -
vor|schwär|men; jmdm. etwas -
vor|schwe|ben; mir schwebt etwas Bestimmtes vor
vor|se|hen; Vor|se|hung, die; -
vor|set|zen
vor sich ... *vgl.* vor
Vor|sicht, die; -; **vor|sich|tig; Vor|sich|tig|keit,** die; -; **vor|sichts|hal|ber; Vor|sichts‿maß|nah|me, ...maß|re|gel**
Vor|sig|nal *(Eisenb.)*
Vor|sil|be
vor|sin|gen
vor|sint|flut|lich (*ugs. für* längst veraltet, unmodern); *vgl.* Sintflut
Vor|sitz, der; -es; **vor|sit|zen;** einem Ausschuss -; **Vor|sit|zen|de,** der *u.* die; -n, -n; ↑R 5 ff. (*Abk.* Vors.); **Vor|sit|zer** (Vorsitzender; *Abk.* Vors.); **Vor|sit|ze|rin**
Vor|som|mer
Vor|sor|ge, die; -; - treffen; **vor|sor|gen; Vor|sor|ge|un|ter|su|chung; vor|sorg|lich**

[1] *Ugs.* vorne...

Vọr|spann, der; -[e]s, -e (zusätzliches Zugtier od. -fahrzeug; Titel, Darsteller- u. Herstellerverzeichnis beim Film, Fernsehen; Einleitung eines Presseartikels o.Ä.); *vgl.* Nachspann; **vọr|span|nen; Vọr|spann|mu|sik** *(Film o.Ä.)*
Vọr|spei|se
vọr|spie|geln; ich spieg[e]le (↑R 16) vor; **Vọr|spie|ge|lung, Vọr|spieg|lung;** das ist - falscher Tatsachen
Vọr|spiel; vọr|spie|len; Vọr|spie|ler
Vọr|spinn|ma|schi|ne (Flyer)
Vọr|spra|che (das Vorsprechen); **vọr|spre|chen**
vọr|sprin|gen; Vọr|sprin|ger (beim Skispringen)
Vọr|spruch
Vọr|sprung
Vọr|sta|di|um
Vọr‿stadt, ...städ|ter; vọr|städ|tisch; Vọr|stadt‿ki|no, ...the|a|ter
Vọr|stand, der; -[e]s, Vorstände (*österr. auch svw.* Vorsteher); **Vọr|stands‿mit|glied, ...sit|zung, ...vor|sit|zen|de**
Vọr|ste|cker (Splint, Vorsteckkeil); **Vọr|steck‿keil, ...na|del**
vọr|ste|hen; vọr|ste|hend; (↑R 47:) Vorstehendes, im Vorstehenden (*Amtsspr.* weiter oben); das Vorstehende; *vgl.* folgend; **Vọr|ste|her; Vọr|ste|her|drü|se** (*für* Prostata); **Vọr|ste|he|rin; Vọr|steh|hund**
vọr|stell|bar; das ist kaum -; **vọr|stel|len;** sich etwas -; **vọr|stel|lig;** - werden; **Vọr|stel|lung; Vọr|stel|lungs‿ga|be** (die; -), **...ge|spräch, ...kraft** (die; -), **...ver|mö|gen** (das; -s), **...welt**
Vọr|ste|ven *(Seew.)*
Vọr|stop|per *(Fußball)*
Vọr|stoß; vọr|sto|ßen
Vọr|stra|fe; Vọr|stra|fen|re|gis|ter
vọr|stre|cken; kannst du mir das Geld -?
vọr|strei|chen; Vọr|streich|far|be
Vọr‿stu|die, ...stu|fe
vọr|sünd|flut|lich *vgl.* Sündflut
Vọr|tag
vọr|tan|zen; Vọr|tän|zer; Vọr|tän|ze|rin
vọr|täu|schen; Vọr|täu|schung
Vọr|teil, der; -s, -e; von -; im - sein; **vọr|teil|haft;**
Vọr|trab, der; -[e]s, -e (*veraltet für* Vorhut einer Reiterabteilung)
Vọr|trag, der; -[e]s, ...träge; **vọr|tra|gen; Vọr|tra|gen|de,** der *u.* die; -n, -n (↑R 5ff.); **Vọr|trags‿be|zeich|nung** *(Musik),* **...fol|ge, ...kunst** (die; -), **...künst|ler, ...rei|he**
vor|tręff|lich; Vor|tręff|lich|keit, die; -
vọr|trei|ben
vọr|tre|ten
Vọr|trieb *(Physik, Technik, Bergmannsspr.);* **Vọr|triebs|ver|lust**
Vọr|tritt, der; -[e]s (*schweiz. auch für* Vorfahrt); jmdm. den - lassen
Vọr|trupp
Vọr|tuch, das; -[e]s, ...tücher (*landsch. für* Schürze)
vọr|tur|nen; Vọr|tur|ner; Vọr|tur|ner|rie|ge
vo|rü|ber (↑R 132); - sein; es ist alles -; **vo|rü|ber|ge|hen;** ich gehe vorüber; vorübergegangen; vorüberzugehen; im Vorübergehen (↑R 50); **vo|rü|ber|ge|hend**
Vọr|über|le|gung (↑R 132)
vo|rü|ber|zie|hen (↑R 132)
Vọr|übung (↑R 132)
Vọr|un|ter|su|chung
Vọr|ur|teil; keine -e haben; **vọr|ur|teils‿frei, ...los; Vọr|ur|teils|lo|sig|keit,** die; -
Vọr|vä|ter *Plur.* (geh.); zur Zeit unserer -
vọr|ver|gan|gen *(veraltet);* **Vọr|ver|gan|gen|heit,** die; - (*für* Plusquamperfekt)
Vọr|ver|hand|lung *meist Plur.;* die -en führen
Vọr|ver|kauf, der; -[e]s; **Vọr|ver|kaufs|stel|le**
vọr|ver|le|gen; Vọr|ver|le|gung
vọr|ver|öf|fent|li|chen; Vọr|ver|öf|fent|li|chung
Vọr|ver|stär|ker *(Elektrotechnik)*
Vọr|ver|trag
vọr|ver|ur|tei|len; Vọr|ver|ur|tei|lung
vọr|vor|ges|tern; vọr|vo|rig (vorletzt); -e Woche; **vọr|vor|letzt;** auf der -en Seite
vọr|wa|gen, sich
Vọr|wahl (*auch für* Vorwahlnummer); **vọr|wäh|len; Vọr|wahl|num|mer, Vọr|wähl|num|mer**
vọr|wal|ten *(veraltend);* unter den vorwaltenden Umständen
Vọr|wand, der; -[e]s, ...wände
vọr|wär|men; Vọr|wär|mer
vọr|war|nen; Vọr|war|nung
vọr|wärts; vor- und rückwärts (↑R 23); vorwärts bringen (*auch für* fördern), vorwärts gehen (*auch für* besser werden), vorwärts kommen (*auch für* Karriere machen) usw.; er ist vorwärts gekommen; vorwärts zu kommen; eine vorwärts weisende Entwicklung; **Vọr|wärts|gang,** der; **vọr|wärts ge|hen, kom|men** *vgl.* vorwärts; **Vọr|wärts|ver|tei|di|gung** (offensiv geführte Verteidigung); **vọr|wärts wei|send** *vgl.* vorwärts
Vọr|wä|sche; vọr|wa|schen; Vọr|wasch|gang
vor|węg
Vọr|weg; *nur in der Fügung* im Vorweg[e] (vorsorglich)
Vor|węg|leis|tung (*svw.* Vorleistung); **Vor|węg|nah|me,** die; -; **vor|węg|neh|men;** ich nehme vorweg; vorweggenommen; vorwegzunehmen; **vor|węg|sa|gen; vor|węg|schi|cken**
Vọr|weg|wei|ser *(Verkehrsw.)*
Vọr|we|he ‹*zu* [1]Wehe›
vọr|weih|nacht|lich; Vọr|weih|nachts|zeit, die; -
Vọr|weis, der; -es, -e *(veraltet);* **vọr|wei|sen; Vọr|wei|sung**
Vọr|welt, die; -; **vọr|welt|lich**
vọr|werf|bar *(Amtsspr.);* eine -e Handlung; **vọr|wer|fen**
Vọr|werk
vọr|wie|gen; diese Themen wiegen in der Diskussion vor; **vọr|wie|gend**
Vọr|win|ter
Vọr|wis|sen; ohne mein -; **vọr|wis|sen|schaft|lich**
Vọr|witz (Neugierde; vorlaute Art); *vgl.* Fürwitz; **vọr|wit|zig** *vgl.* fürwitzig
Vọr|wo|che; vọr|wö|chig
vọr|wöl|ben; Vọr|wöl|bung
[1]Vọr|wort, das; -[e]s, -e (Vorrede in einem Buch); **[2]Vọr|wort,** das; -[e]s, ...wörter (*österr., sonst veraltet für* Verhältniswort)
Vọr|wurf; vọr|wurfs‿frei, ...voll
vọr|zäh|len
vọr|zau|bern; er zauberte ihnen etwas vor
Vọr|zei|chen; vọr|zeich|nen; Vọr|zeich|nung
vọr|zeig|bar; Vọr|zei|ge|frau; vọr|zei|gen; Vọr|zei|ge‿sport|ler *(ugs.),* **...ver|merk**
Vọr|zeit; vor|zei|ten, *aber* vor langen Zeiten; **vọr|zei|tig; Vọr|zei|tig|keit** *(Sprachw.);* **vọr|zeit|lich** (der Vorzeit angehörend); **Vọr|zeit|mensch,** der
Vọr|zen|sur
vọr|zie|hen; etwas, jmdn. -
Vọr|zim|mer (*österr. auch für* Hausflur, Diele, Vorraum); **Vọr|zim|mer‿da|me** *(ugs.),* **...wand** (*österr. für* Kleiderablage)
Vọr|zin|sen *Plur.* (*für* Diskont)
vor|zu (*schweiz. für* jeweils, im Augenblick)
Vọr|zug; vor|züg|lich [*auch* 'fo:r...]; **Vor|züg|lich|keit,** die; -; **Vọr|zugs‿ak|tie, ...milch** (die; -), **...preis, ...schü|ler** (*österr. für* Schüler mit sehr guten Noten), **...stel|lung; vọr|zugs|wei|se**

Vor|zu|kunft, die; - (*für* Futurum exaktum)
Voß (dt. Schriftsteller); Voß' Nachdichtungen (↑R 98)
Vo|ta (*Plur. von* Votum); **Vo|tant** [v...], der; -en, -en (↑R 126) ⟨lat.⟩ (*veraltet für* der Votierende); **Vo-ten** (*Plur. von* Votum); **vo|tie|ren** (sich entscheiden, stimmen für; abstimmen); **Vo|tiv˯bild** (einem od. einer Heiligen als Dank geweihtes Bild), **...ga|be, ...ka|pel-le, ...ker|ze, ...kir|che, ...mes|se** (*vgl.* [1]Messe), **...ta|fel; Vo|tum,** das; -s, *Plur.* ...ten *u.* ...ta (Gelübde; Urteil; Stimme; Entscheid[ung])
Vou|cher [ˈvautʃə(r)], das *od.* der; -s, -[s] ⟨engl.⟩ (*Touristik* Gutschein für im Voraus bezahlte Leistungen)
Vou|te [ˈvuːtə], die; -, -n ⟨franz.⟩ (*Bauw.* Verstärkungsteil; Hohlkehle zwischen Wand u. Decke)
vox po|pu|li vox Dei [vɔks - vɔks -] ⟨lat., „Volkes Stimme [ist] Gottes Stimme"⟩ (die öffentl. Meinung [hat großes Gewicht])
Vo|yeur [voaˈjøːr], der; -s, -e ⟨franz.⟩ (jmd., der als Zuschauer bei sexuellen Betätigungen anderer Befriedigung erfährt); **Vo-yeu|ris|mus; vo|yeu|ris|tisch**
Vp., VP = Versuchsperson
VP = Volkspolizei *(in der ehem. DDR)*
VPS = Videoprogrammsystem
VR = Volksrepublik
Vra|nitz|ky [f...] (österr. Politiker)
Vre|ni [f..., *auch* v...] (w. Vorn.)
Vro|ni [f..., *auch* v...] (w. Vorn.)
v. R. w. = von Rechts wegen
Vs = Voltsekunde
vs. = versus
V. S. O. P. = very special old pale [ˈveri ˈspɛʃ(ə)l ˈoːld ˈpeːl] ⟨engl., „ganz besonders alt und blass"⟩ (Gütekennzeichen für Cognac od. Weinbrand)
v. s. pl. = verte, si placet! (bitte wenden!)
v. T., p. m., ‰ = vom Tausend; *vgl.* pro mille
Vt. = Vermont
v. u. = von unten
vul|gär [v...] ⟨lat.⟩ (gewöhnlich; gemein; niedrig); **vul|ga|ri|sie|ren; Vul|ga|ri|sie|rung; Vul|ga|ris-mus,** der; -, ...men (*bes. Sprachw.* vulgäres Wort, vulgäre Wendung); **Vul|ga|ri|tät,** die; -, -en; **Vul|gär˯la|tein** (Volkslatein), **...spra|che; Vul|ga|ta,** die; - (vom Konzil zu Trient für authentisch erklärte lat. Bibelübersetzung des hl. Hieronymus); **Vul|gi-va|ga** [...vaga], die; - ⟨„Umherschweifende"⟩ (herabsetzender Beiname der Liebesgöttin Venus); Venus -; **vul|go** (gemeinhin [so genannt])
[1]**Vul|kan** [vul...] (röm. Gott des Feuers); [2]**Vul|kan,** der; -s, -e ⟨lat.⟩ (Feuer speiender Berg); **Vul|kan-aus|bruch; Vul|kan|fi|ber,** die; - (lederartiger Kunststoff aus Zellulose); **Vul|ka|ni|sa|ti|on,** die; -, -en, Vul|ka|ni|sie|rung (Verarbeitung von Rohkautschuk zu Gummi); **vul|ka|nisch** (durch Vulkanismus entstanden, von Vulkanen herrührend); **Vul|ka|ni|seur** [...ˈzøːr], der; -s, -e (Facharbeiter in der Gummiherstellung); **Vul-ka|ni|sier|an|stalt; vul|ka|ni|sie-ren** (Rohkautschuk zu Gummi verarbeiten); **Vul|ka|ni|sie|rung** *vgl.* Vulkanisation; **Vul|ka|nis-mus,** der; - (Gesamtheit der vulkan. Erscheinungen)
Vul|va [ˈvulva], die; -, Vulven ⟨lat.⟩ (*Med.* die äußeren weibl. Geschlechtsorgane)
v. u. Z. = vor unserer Zeitrechnung
v. v. = vice versa
VVN = Vereinigung der Verfolgten des Naziregimes
VW ®, der; -[s], -s (Volkswagen)
VWD = Vereinigte Wirtschaftsdienste
VW-Fah|rer (↑R 26; *vgl.* VW)

W (Buchstabe); das W; des W, die W, *aber* das w in Löwe (↑R 60); der Buchstabe W, w
W = Watt; Werst; West[en]; *chem. Zeichen für* Wolfram
Waadt [va(ː)t], die; - (schweiz. Kanton); **Waadt|land,** das; -[e]s (*svw.* Waadt); **Waadt|län|der** (↑R 103); **waadt|län|disch**
[1]**Waag,** die; - (*bayr. für* Flut, Wasser)
[2]**Waag,** die; - (l. Nebenfluss der Donau in der Slowakei)
Waa|ge, die; -, -n; **Waa|ge˯amt, ...bal|ken, ...geld, ...meis|ter; Waa|gen|fab|rik; waa|ge|recht,** waag|recht; **Waa|ge|rech|te,** Waag|rech|te, die; -n, -n; vier -[n]; **waag|recht** usw. *vgl.* waagerecht usw.; **Waag|scha|le**
Waal, die; - (Mündungsarm des Rheins)
wab|be|lig, wabb|lig (*ugs. für* gallertartig wackelnd; unangenehm weich); **wab|beln** (*ugs. für* hin u. her wackeln); der Pudding wabbelt; **wabb|lig** *vgl.* wabbelig
Wa|be, die; -, -n (Zellenbau des Bienenstockes); **Wa|ben|ho|nig**
Wa|ber|lo|he (*altnord. Dichtung* flackernde, leuchtende Flamme, Glut); **wa|bern** (*veraltet, aber noch landsch. für* sich hin u. her bewegen, flackern)
wach; wach sein, bleiben, werden; sich wach halten; die Erinnerung an etwas wach halten (↑R 39); *vgl. aber* wachrufen, wachrütteln; **Wach|ab|lö|sung**
Wa|chau (↑R 132), die; - (Engtal der Donau zwischen Krems u. Melk)
Wach˯ba|tail|lon *(Milit.)*, **...boot, ...buch, ...dienst; Wa|che,** die; -, -n; Wache halten, stehen; ein Wache stehender Soldat; **Wa|che-be|am|te** (*österr. Amtsspr. für* Polizist); **wa|chen;** über jmdn. -; **Wa|che|ste|hen,** das; -s; **Wa-che ste|hend** *vgl.* Wache; **Wach|feu|er; wach|ha|bend;** der -e Offizier; **Wach|ha|ben|de,** der *u.* die; -n, -n (↑R 5 ff.); **wach hal|ten** *vgl.* wach; **Wach|heit,** die; -; **Wach|hund**
Wach|ler (*südd. für* Gamsbart)
Wach˯lo|kal, ...mann (*Plur.* ...leute *u.* ...männer), **...mann|schaft**
Wa|chol|der, der; -s, - (eine Pflanze; ein Branntwein); **Wa|chol-der˯baum, ...bee|re, ...dros|sel** (ein Singvogel), **...schnaps, ...strauch**
Wach|pos|ten, *auch* Wacht|posten
wach|ru|fen (↑R 38; hervorrufen; wecken); das hat ihren Ehrgeiz wachgerufen; das hat längst Vergessenes in ihr wachgerufen; **wach|rüt|teln** (↑R 38; aufrütteln; *auch für* wecken); diese Nachricht hat ihn wachgerüttelt; wir haben ihn wachgerüttelt
Wachs, das; -es, -e; **Wachs|ab-guss**
wach|sam; Wach|sam|keit, die; -
Wachs|bild; wachs|bleich; Wachs˯blu|me, ...boh|ne
Wach|schiff
wach|seln (*österr. für* [Skier] wachsen); ich ...[e]le (↑R 16)
[1]**wach|sen** (größer werden, im Wachsen sein); du wächst, er

wächst; du wuchsest, er wuchs; du wüchsest; gewachsen; wachs[e]!
[2]**wach|sen** (mit Wachs glätten); du wachst, er wachst; du wachstest; gewachst; wachs[e]!; **wäch|sern** (aus Wachs); **Wachs‿far|be, ...fi|gur; Wachs|fi|gu|ren|ka|bi|nett; Wachs‿ker|ze, ...lein|wand** (*österr. für* Wachstuch), **...licht** (*Plur.* ...lichter), **...ma|le|rei, ...mal|krei|de, ...mal|stift, ...mo|dell, ...pa|pier, ...plat|te, ...stock** (*Plur.* ...stöcke), **...ta|fel**
Wach‿sta|ti|on (im Krankenhaus), **...stu|be**
Wachs|tuch
Wachs|tum, das; -s; **wachs|tums‿för|dernd, ...hem|mend** (↑R 40); **Wachs|tums‿hor|mon, ...ra|te** *(Wirtsch.),* **...stö|rung**
wachs|weich; Wachs‿zel|le, ...zie|her
Wacht, die; -, -en (*geh. für* Wache); - halten
Wäch|te *frühere Schreibung für* Wechte
Wach|tel, die; -, -n (ein Vogel); **Wach|tel‿ei, ...hund, ...kö|nig** (ein Vogel), **...ruf, ...schlag**
Wäch|ter; Wäch|ter‿lied, ...ruf; Wacht‿meis|ter, ...pa|ra|de; Wacht|pos|ten *vgl.* Wachposten; **Wach|traum; Wacht|turm,** *häufiger* **Wach|turm; Wach- und Schließ|ge|sell|schaft** (↑R 23); **Wach‿zim|mer** (*österr. für* Polizeibüro), **...zu|stand**
Wa|cke, die; -, -n (*veraltet, noch landsch. für* bröckeliges Gestein)
Wa|cke|lei, die; -; **wa|cke|lig,** wacklig; - stehen (*ugs. auch für* dem Bankrott nahe sein); **Wa|ckel|kon|takt; wa|ckeln;** ich ...[e]le (↑R 16); **Wa|ckel‿pe|ter** (*scherzh. für* Wackelpudding), **...pud|ding** *(ugs.)*
wa|cker (*veraltend für* redlich; tapfer)
Wa|cker|stein (*südd. für* Gesteinsbrocken)
wack|lig *vgl.* wackelig
Wad, das; -s ‹engl.› (ein Mineral)
Wa|dai (afrik. Landschaft)
Wad|di|ke, die; - (*nordd. für* Molke, Käsewasser)
Wa|de, die; -, -n; **Wa|den‿bein, ...krampf; wa|den|lang; Wa|den|wi|ckel**
Wa|di, das; -s, -s ‹arab.› (wasserloses Flusstal in Nordafrika u. im Vorderen Orient)
Wa|di-Qum|ran *vgl.* Kumran
Wäd|li, das; -s, - (*schweiz. für* Eisbein)
Wa|fer ['we:fə(r)], der; -s, -[s] ‹engl.› (dünne Scheibe aus Halbleitermaterial für die Herstellung von Mikrochips)
Waf|fe, die; -, -n; atomare, biologische, chemische, konventionelle, nukleare Waffen
Waf|fel, die; -, -n ‹niederl.› (ein Gebäck); **Waf|fel|ei|sen**
Waf|fen‿ar|se|nal, ...be|sitz; Waf|fen|be|sitz|kar|te *(Amtsspr.);* **Waf|fen‿bru|der, ...brü|der|schaft, ...em|bar|go; waf|fen|fä|hig** *(veraltend);* **Waf|fen‿gang** (der; *veraltend*), **...gat|tung, ...ge|walt** (die; -), **...han|del** (*vgl.* [1]Handel), **...händ|ler, ...kun|de** (die; -), **...la|ger, ...lie|fe|rung; waf|fen|los; Waf|fen‿platz** (*schweiz. für* Truppenausbildungsplatz), **...ru|he, ...schein, ...schmied, ...schmie|de; waf|fen|star|rend; Waf|fen|still|stand; Waf|fen|still|stands‿ab|kom|men, ...li|nie; Waf|fen‿sys|tem, ...tanz** *(Völkerk.),* **...tech|nik; waff|nen** *(veraltet);* sich -
Wa|ga|du|gu (eingedeutschte Schreibung von Ouagadougou)
wäg|bar; Wäg|bar|keit
Wa|ge|hals *(veraltend);* **wa|ge|hal|sig** usw. *vgl.* waghalsig usw.
Wä|gel|chen (kleiner Wagen)
Wa|ge|mut; wa|ge|mu|tig; wa|gen; du wagtest; gewagt; sich -
Wa|gen, der; -s, *Plur.* -, *südd. auch* Wägen
wä|gen (*fachspr., sonst veraltet für* das Gewicht bestimmen; *geh. für* prüfend bedenken, nach der Bedeutung einschätzen); du wägst; du wogst; du wögest; gewogen; wäg[e]!; *selten schwache Beugung* du wägtest; gewägt; *vgl.* [2]wiegen
Wa|gen‿bau|er (der; -s, -), **...burg** *(früher),* **...dach, ...füh|rer, ...he|ber, ...ko|lon|ne, ...la|dung, ...pa|pie|re** *(Plur.),* **...park, ...pla|ne, ...rad, ...ren|nen, ...schlag** *(veraltend),* **...schmie|re, ...tür, ...typ, ...wä|sche**
Wa|ge|stück *(geh.)*
Wag|gerl (österr. Erzähler)
Wag|gon, *auch* **Wa|gon** [va'gõ:, *auch* va'gɔŋ, *österr.* va'go:n], der; -s, *Plur.* -s, *österr. auch* -e ‹engl.› ([Eisenbahn]wagen); **wag|gon|wei|se,** *auch* **wa|gon|wei|se**
wag|hal|sig, wa|ge|hal|sig; **Wag|hal|sig|keit,** Wa|ge|hal|sig|keit
[1]**Wag|ner,** der; -s, - (*südd., österr. u. schweiz. für* Wagenbauer, Stellmacher)
[2]**Wag|ner** (dt. Komponist); **Wag|ne|ri|a|ner** (Anhänger Wagners); **Wag|ner|oper,** die; -, -n (↑R 95 *u.* 132)
Wag|nis, das; -ses, -se
Wa|gon *vgl.* Waggon
Wä|gung
Wä|he, die; -, -n (*südwestd., schweiz. für* flacher Kuchen mit süßem od. salzigem Belag)
Wah|ha|bit [vaha...], der; -en, -en (↑R 126) ‹arab.› (Angehöriger einer Reformsekte des Islams)
Wahl, die; -, -en; **Wahl‿abend** (↑R 132), **...al|ter, ...an|zei|ge, ...auf|ruf, ...aus|gang, ...aus|schuss; wähl|bar; Wähl|bar|keit,** die; -; **Wahl‿be|ein|flus|sung, ...be|nach|rich|ti|gung; wahl|be|rech|tigt; Wahl‿be|rech|tig|te, ...be|rech|ti|gung, ...be|tei|li|gung, ...be|zirk, ...el|tern** (*Plur.; österr. neben* Adoptiveltern); **wäh|len; Wäh|ler; Wäh|ler|auf|trag; Wahl‿er|folg, ...er|geb|nis; Wäh|le|rin; Wäh|ler|ini|ti|a|ti|ve** (↑R 132); **wäh|le|risch; Wäh|ler|lis|te; Wäh|ler|schaft; Wäh|ler‿stim|me, ...ver|zeich|nis, ...wil|le; Wahl|fach; wahl|frei; Wahl‿frei|heit** (die; -), **...gang** (der), **...ge|heim|nis** (das; -ses), **...ge|schenk, ...ge|setz, ...hei|mat, ...hel|fer**
wäh|lig (*nordd. für* wohlig; munter, übermütig)
Wahl‿jahr, ...ka|bi|ne, ...kampf, ...kind (*österr. neben* Adoptivkind), **...kreis, ...lei|ter** (der), **...lis|te, ...lo|kal, ...lo|ko|mo|ti|ve** (als zugkräftig angesehener Kandidat einer Partei); **wahl|los; Wahl‿lü|ge, ...mann** (*Plur.* ...männer), **...mo|dus, ...mög|lich|keit, ...nacht, ...nie|der|la|ge, ...pa|ro|le, ...par|ty, ...pe|ri|o|de, ...pflicht** (die; -), **...pla|kat, ...pro|gramm, ...pro|pa|gan|da, ...recht** (das; -[e]s), **...re|de; Wähl|schei|be** (am Telefon); **Wahl‿schein, ...sieg, ...spruch**
Wahl|statt (Ort in Schlesien); Fürst von - (Blücher)
Wahl‿sys|tem, ...tag; Wähl|ton (beim Telefon); *vgl.* [2]Ton; **Wahl‿ur|ne, ...ver|samm|lung, ...ver|spre|chen, ...ver|tei|di|ger** *(Rechtsw.);* **wahl|ver|wandt; Wahl|ver|wandt|schaft; wahl|wei|se; Wahl‿wer|ber** (*österr. für* Wahlkandidat), **...wie|der|ho|lung** (beim Telefon), **...zu|ckerl** (*österr. ugs. für* politisches Zugeständnis vor einer Wahl)
Wahn, der; -[e]s; **Wahn|bild; wäh|nen; Wahn|fried** (Wagners Haus in Bayreuth); **Wahn‿idee** (↑R 132), **...kan|te** (schiefe Kante am Bauholz); **wahn|schaf|fen** (*nordd. für* hässlich, missgestaltet); **Wahn|sinn,** der; -[e]s; **wahn|sin|nig; Wahn|sin|ni|ge,**

der *u.* die; -n, -n (↑R 5 ff.); **Wahn|sin|nig|wer|den,** das; -s; *in* das ist zum -; **Wahn|sinns‿ar|beit** (*ugs. für* unsinnig schwere Arbeit), **...hit|ze** (*ugs. für* unerträgliche Hitze), **...tat; Wahn‿vor|stel|lung, ...witz** (der; -es); **wahn|wit|zig**

wahr (wirklich); nicht wahr?; sein wahres Gesicht zeigen; der wahre Jakob (*ugs. für* der rechte Mann); wahr sein, bleiben, werden; etwas für wahr halten; seine Drohungen wahr machen; *vgl.* wahrhaben, wahrnehmen, wahrsagen

wah|ren (bewahren); er hat den Anschein gewahrt

wäh|ren (*geh. für* dauern); **während;** *Konj.:* sie las, während er Radio hörte; *Präp. mit Gen.:* während des Krieges; der Zeitraum, während dessen das geschah (*vgl. aber* währenddessen); die Tage, während deren ...; *ugs. auch mit Dat.:* während dem Schießen; *hochspr. mit Dat., wenn der Gen. im Plural nicht erkennbar ist:* während fünf Jahren, elf Monaten, *aber* während zweier, dreier Jahre; **wäh|rend|dem; wäh|rend|des, wäh|rend|des|sen;** sie hatte währenddessen geschlafen (*vgl.* während)

wahr|ha|ben; er will es nicht wahrhaben (nicht gelten lassen); **wahr|haft** (wahrheitsliebend; wirklich); **wahr|haf|tig; Wahr|haf|tig|keit,** die; -; **Wahr|heit; Wahr|heits‿be|weis** (*bes. Rechtsspr.*), **...fin|dung** (*bes. Rechtsspr.*), **...ge|halt** (der; -[e]s); **wahr|heits‿ge|mäß, ...ge|treu; Wahr|heits|lie|be,** die; -; **wahr|heits|lie|bend; Wahr|heits‿sinn** (der; -[e]s), **...su|cher; wahr|heits|wid|rig; wahr|lich** (*veraltend für* in der Tat, wirklich)

wahr|nehm|bar; Wahr|nehm|bar|keit, die; -; **wahr|neh|men** (↑R 38); ich nehme wahr; wahrgenommen; wahrzunehmen; **Wahr|neh|mung; Wahr|neh|mungs|ver|mö|gen,** das; -s

Wahr|sa|ge|kunst, die; -; **wahr|sa|gen** (↑R 38; prophezeien); du sagtest wahr *od.* du wahrsagtest; sie hat wahrgesagt *od.* gewahrsagt; **Wahr|sa|ger; Wahr|sa|ge|rei; Wahr|sa|ge|rin; wahr|sa|ge|risch; Wahr|sa|gung**

währ|schaft (*schweiz. für* Gewähr bietend; dauerhaft, echt)

Wahr|schau, die; - (*Seemannsspr.* Warnung); Wahrschau! (Vorsicht!); **wahr|schau|en** (↑R 37; warnen); ich wahrschaue; gewahrschaut; **Wahr|schau|er**

wahr|schein|lich [*auch* 'va:r...]; **Wahr|schein|lich|keit; Wahr|schein|lich|keits‿grad, ...rech|nung** (die; -), **...the|o|rie** (die; -)

Wah|rung, die; - (Aufrechterhaltung, Bewahrung)

Wäh|rung (staatl. Ordnung des Geldwesens; gesetzl. Zahlungsmittel); **Wäh|rungs‿aus|gleich, ...aus|gleichs|fonds, ...block** (*Plur.* ...blöcke, *selten* ...blocks), **...ein|heit, ...kri|se, ...kurs, ...po|li|tik** (die; -), **...re|form, ...re|ser|ve** (*meist Plur.*), **...schlan|ge** (der Verbund der Währungen der EG-Staaten zur Begrenzung der Wechselkursschwankungen [bis 1979]); **Wäh|rungs|sys|tem;** Europäisches - (↑R 56; *Abk.* EWS); **Wäh|rungs|uni|on** (↑R 132); Währungs-, Wirtschafts- und Sozialunion (↑R 23)

Wahr|zei|chen

Waib|lin|gen (Stadt nordöstl. von Stuttgart); **Waib|lin|ger,** der; -s, - (Beiname der Hohenstaufen)

waid..., Waid... *in der Bedeutung* „Jagd" *vgl.* weid..., Weid...

Waid, der; -[e]s, -e (eine [Färber]pflanze; blauer Farbstoff)

Wai|se, die; -, -n (elternloses Kind; *Verslehre* einzelne reimlose Gedichtzeile); **Wai|sen‿geld, ...haus** (*früher*), **...kind, ...kna|be** (*meist nur noch in Wendungen wie* gegen jmdn. der reinste - sein), **...ren|te**

Wa|ke, die; -, -n (*nordd. für* Öffnung in der Eisdecke)

Wake|field ['we:kfi:ld] (engl. Stadt)

Wal, der; -[e]s, -e (ein Meeressäugetier)

Wa|la, die; -, Walen (altnord. Weissagerin)

Wa|la|che, der; -n, -n; ↑R 126 (Bewohner der Walachei); **Wa|la|chei,** die; - (rumän. Landschaft); (↑R 102:) die Große -, die Kleine -; **wa|la|chisch**

Wal|burg, Wal|bur|ga (w. Vorn.)

[1]**Wal|chen|see** (Ort am gleichnamigen See); [2]**Wal|chen|see,** der; -s (See in den bayer. Voralpen)

Wald, der; -[e]s, Wälder; **Wald‿amei|se** (↑R 132), **...ar|bei|ter, ...bo|den, ...brand; Wäld|chen**

Wal|deck (Gebiet des ehem. dt. Fürstentums Waldeck in Hessen; Landkreis in Hessen; Stadt am Edersee); **Wal|de|cker** (↑R 103); **wal|de|ckisch**

Wald|ein|sam|keit (*geh.*)

Wal|de|mar (m. Vorn.)

Wal|den|ser ‹nach dem Lyoner Kaufmann Petrus Waldes› (Angehöriger einer ev. Kirche in Oberitalien, die auf eine südfranz. vorreformator. Bewegung zurückgeht)

Wald|erd|bee|re; Wal|des‿dun|kel (*geh.*), **...rand** (*geh. für* Waldrand), **...rau|schen** (das; -s; *geh.*); **Wald‿farn, ...fre|vel, ...geist** (*Plur.* ...geister), **...horn** (*Plur.* ...hörner), **...hu|fen|dorf** (*vgl.* Hufe), **...hü|ter; wal|dig; Wald‿kauz, ...lauf, ...läu|fer, ...lehr|pfad; Wald|lich|tung; Wald|meis|ter,** der; -s (eine Pflanze); **Wald|meis|ter|bow|le**

Wal|do (m. Vorn.)

Wald|ohr|eu|le

Wal|dorf|sa|lat (*Gastron.*); **Waldorf|schu|le** (Privatschule mit besonderem Unterrichtssystem)

Wald‿rand, ...re|be (eine Pflanze); **wald|reich; Wald‿schrat[t]** (Waldgeist), **...spa|zier|gang, ...sport|pfad; Wald|städ|te** *Plur.* (vier Städte am Rhein: Rheinfelden, Säckingen, Laufenburg u. Waldshut); **Wald|statt,** die; -, ...stätte *meist Plur.* (einer der drei Urkantone [Uri, Schwyz, Unterwalden], *auch* Luzern); **Wald‿ster|ben** (das; -s), **...tau|be; Wal|dung; Wald|vier|tel,** das; -s (eine niederösterr. Landschaft); **Wald|vö|gel|lein** (eine Orchidee); **wald|wärts; Wald|weg**

Wa|len|see, der; -s (in der Schweiz)

Wales ['we:ls, *auch* 'we:lz] (Halbinsel im Westen der Insel Großbritannien)

Wal|fang; die Walfang treibenden Nationen; **Wal|fän|ger; Wal|fang‿flot|te, ...schiff; Wal|fang trei|bend** *vgl.* Walfang; **Wal|fisch** *vgl.* Wal

Wäl|ger|holz (*landsch.*); **wäl|gern** (*landsch. für* [Teig] glatt rollen); ich ...ere (↑R 16)

Wal|hall [*auch* ...'hal], das; -s ‹altnord.›, [1]**Wal|hal|la,** das; -[s] *u.* die; - (*nord. Mythol.* Halle Odins, Aufenthalt der im Kampf Gefallenen); [2]**Wal|hal|la,** die; - (Ruhmeshalle bei Regensburg)

Wa|li|ser (Bewohner von Wales); **wa|li|sisch**

Wal|ke, die; -, -n (Verfilzmaschine; Vorgang des Verfilzens); **walken** (*Textiltechnik* verfilzen; *ugs. für* kneten; prügeln); **Wal|ker**

Wal|kie-Tal|kie ['wɔ:ki'tɔ:ki], das; -[s], -s ‹engl.› (tragbares Funksprechgerät); **Walk|man** ® ['wɔ:kmən], der; -s, -s u. ...men [...mən] (kleiner Kassettenrecorder mit Kopfhörern)

Walk|müh|le (*früher*)

Wal|kü|re [*auch* 'val...], die; -, -n

⟨altnord.⟩ (*nord. Mythol.* eine der Botinnen Odins, die die Gefallenen nach Walhall geleiten)
[1]**Wall,** der; -[e]s, *Plur.* - *u.* -e (altes Stückmaß [bes. für Fische]; 80 Stück); 2 Wall (↑R 90)
[2]**Wall,** der; -[e]s, Wälle ⟨lat.⟩ (Erdaufschüttung, Mauerwerk usw.)
Wal|la|by ['wɔləbi], das; -s, -s ⟨engl.⟩ (eine Känguruart)
Wal|lace ['wɔləs], Edgar (engl. Schriftsteller)
Wal|lach, der; -[e]s, -e (kastrierter Hengst)
[1]**wal|len** (sprudeln, bewegt fließen; sich [wogend] bewegen)
[2]**wal|len** (*veraltet für* pilgern)
wäl|len (*landsch. für* wallen lassen); gewällte Kartoffeln
Wal|len|stein (Heerführer im Dreißigjährigen Krieg)
[1]**Wal|ler** *vgl.* [1]Wels
[2]**Wal|ler** (*veraltet für* Wallfahrer); **wall|fah|ren;** du wallfahrst; du wallfahrtest; gewallfahrt; zu -; *vgl.* wallfahrten; **Wall|fah|rer; Wall|fah|re|rin; Wall|fahrt; wall|fahr|ten** (*veraltend für* wallfahren); ich wallfahrtete; gewallfahrtet; zu -; **Wall|fahrts‿kir|che, ...ort** (der; -[e]s, -e)
Wall|gra|ben
Wall|holz (*schweiz. für* Nudelholz)
Wal|li (w. Vorn.)
Wal|lis, das; - (schweiz. Kanton); **Wal|li|ser** (↑R 103); **Wal|li|ser Al|pen** *Plur.*; **wal|li|se|risch**
Wal|lo|ne, der; -n, -n; ↑R 126 (Nachkomme romanisierter Kelten in Belgien u. Nordfrankreich); **Wal|lo|ni|en** [...i̯ən]; **wal|lo|nisch;** -e Sprache; **Wal|lo|nisch,** das; -[s] (Sprache); *vgl.* Deutsch; **Wal|lo|ni|sche,** das; -n; *vgl.* Deutsche, das
Wall|street *u.* **Wall Street** [*beide* 'wɔ:lstri:t], die; - ⟨amerik.⟩ (Geschäftsstraße in New York [Bankzentrum]; *übertr. für* Geld- u. Kapitalmarkt der USA)
Wal|lung
Wal|ly (w. Vorn.)
[1]**Walm,** der; -[e]s (*landsch. für* [Wasser]wirbel, das Wallen)
[2]**Walm,** der; -[e]s, -e (dreieckige Dachfläche); **Walm|dach**
Wal|nuss (ein Baum; dessen Frucht); **Wal|nuss|baum**
Wal|lo|ne, die; -, -n ⟨ital.⟩ (*Bot.* Gerbstoff enthaltender Fruchtbecher der Eiche)
Wal|per|tin|ger *vgl.* Wolpertinger
Wal|platz ['va(:)l...] (*veraltet für* Kampfplatz)
Wal|pur|ga, Wal|pur|gis (w. Vorn.); **Wal|pur|gis|nacht**
Wal|rat, der *od.* das; -[e]s ([aus dem Kopf von Pottwalen gewonnene] fettartige Masse); **Wal|rat|öl,** das; -[e]s; **Wal|ross,** das; -es, -e (eine Robbe)
[1]**Wal|ser,** Martin (dt. Schriftsteller)
[2]**Wal|ser,** Robert (schweiz. Lyriker u. Erzähler)
Wal|ser|tal, das; -[e]s ⟨nach den im 13. Jh. eingewanderten Wallisern⟩ (Tal in Vorarlberg); (↑R 102:) das Große -; das Kleine -
Wal|statt ['va(:)l...], die; -, ...stätten (*veraltet für* Kampfplatz; Schlachtfeld)
wal|ten (*geh. für* gebieten; sich sorgend einer Sache annehmen); Gnade - lassen; (↑R 50:) das Walten der Naturgesetze
Wal|ter, *auch* Wal|ther; ↑R 92 (m. Vorn.)
Wal|tha|ri|lied [*auch* ...'ta:...], das; -[e]s; ↑R 95 (ein Heldenepos)
Wal|ther *vgl.* Walter
Wal|ther von der Vo|gel|wei|de (dt. Dichter des MA.)
Wal|traud, Wal|traut, Wal|trud (w. Vorn.)
Walt|run (w. Vorn.)
Wal|va|ter ['va(:)l...] (*Bez. für* Odin)
Walz|blech; Wal|ze, die; -, -n (*veraltet auch für* Wanderschaft eines Handwerksburschen); **walzen;** du walzt; **wäl|zen;** du wälzt; sich -; **Wal|zen|bruch,** der; -[e]s, ...brüche; **wal|zen|för|mig; Walzen‿müh|le, ...spin|ne, ...stra|ße** (*vgl.* Walzstraße); **Wal|zer** (ein Tanz); **Wäl|zer** (*ugs. für* großes, schweres Buch); **Wal|zer‿mu|sik, ...takt** (*vgl.* [1]Takt), **...tän|zer; wal|zig** (walzenförmig); **Wälz‿la|ger, ...sprung** (*für* Straddle); **Walz‿stahl, ...stra|ße** (*od.* Wal|zen|stra|ße), **...werk; Walz|werk|er|zeug|nis**
Wam|me, die; -, -n (vom Hals herabhängende Hautfalte [des Rindes]); **Wam|pe,** die; -, -n (*svw.* Wamme; *ugs. auch für* dicker Bauch); **wam|pert** (*österr. ugs. für* dickbäuchig)
Wam|pum [*auch* ...'pum], der; -s, -e ⟨indian.⟩ (bei nordamerik. Indianern Gürtel aus Muscheln u. Schnecken, als Zahlungsmittel u. Ä. dienend)
Wams, das; -es, Wämser (*früher, aber noch landsch. für* Jacke); **Wäms|chen; wam|sen** (*landsch. für* verprügeln); du wamst; **Wäms|lein**
Wand, die; -, Wände
Wan|da (w. Vorn.)
Wan|da|le, Van|da|le, der; -n, -n; ↑R 126 (Angehöriger eines germ. Volksstammes; *übertr. für* zerstörungswütiger Mensch); **wan|da|lisch,** van|da|lisch (*auch für* zerstörungswütig); **Wan|da|lis|mus,** Van|da|lis|mus, der; - (Zerstörungswut)
Wand‿be|hang, ...be|span|nung, ...bord (*vgl.* [1]Bord), **...brett**
Wan|del, der; -s; **Wan|del|an|lei|he** (*Bankw.*); **wan|del|bar; Wan|del|bar|keit,** die; -; **Wan|del‿gang** (der), **...hal|le, ...mo|nat** *od.* **...mond** (*alte Bez. für* April); **wan|deln;** ich ...[e]le (↑R 16); sich -; **Wan|del‿ob|li|ga|ti|on** (*Bankw.*), **...schuld|ver|schrei|bung** (*Bankw.*), **...stern** (*veraltet für* Planet); **Wan|de|lung** (*bes. Rechtsspr.*)
Wan|der‿amei|se (↑R 132), **...ar|bei|ter, ...aus|stel|lung, ...büh|ne, ...bur|sche** (*früher*), **...dü|ne; Wan|de|rer,** Wand|rer; **Wan|der‿fahrt, ...fal|ke, ...ge|sel|le** (*früher*), **...ge|wer|be** (*für* ambulantes Gewerbe), **...heu|schre|cke; Wan|de|rin,** Wand|re|rin; **Wan|der‿jahr** (*meist Plur.*), **...kar|te, ...le|ber, ...lied, ...lust** (die; -); **wan|der|lus|tig; wan|dern;** ich ...ere (↑R 16); (↑R 50:) das Wandern ist des Müllers Lust; **Wan|der‿nie|re, ...po|kal, ...pre|di|ger, ...preis, ...rat|te; Wan|der|schaft; Wan|der|schuh; Wan|ders|mann** *Plur.* ...leute; **Wan|der‿stab, ...tag; Wan|de|rung; Wan|der‿vo|gel, ...weg, ...zir|kus**
Wand‿fach, ...ge|mäl|de; ...wan|dig (z. B. dünnwandig); **Wand‿kal|len|der, ...kar|te**
Wand|ler (*Technik*); **Wand|lung** *vgl.* Wandelung; **wand|lungs|fä|hig; Wand|lungs|fä|hig|keit,** die; -; **Wand|lungs|pro|zess;** einen - durchmachen
Wand|ma|le|rei
Wand|rer *vgl.* Wanderer; **Wand|re|rin** *vgl.* Wanderin
Wands|be|cker[1] **Bo|te,** der; - -n (ehem. Zeitung); **Wands|bek** (Stadtteil von Hamburg)
Wand‿schirm, ...schrank, ...spie|gel, ...spruch, ...ta|fel, ...tel|ler, ...tep|pich, ...uhr; Wan|dung; Wand‿ver|klei|dung, ...zei|tung
Wa|ne, der; -n, -n *meist Plur.*; ↑R 126 (*nord. Mythol.* Angehöriger eines Göttergeschlechts)
Wan|ge, die; -, -n; **Wan|gen‿kno|chen, ...mus|kel**

[1] *In alter Schreibung des Stadtnamens.*

Wan|ger|oog [...'o:k, *auch* 'va...], *früher neben* **Wan|ger|oo|ge** [...'o:gə, *auch* 'va...] (eine der Ostfriesischen Inseln)
...wan|gig (z. B. rotwangig); **Wäng|lein**
Wank, der; -[e]s *(veraltet); nur noch in* keinen - tun *(schweiz. mdal. für* sich nicht bewegen, keinen Finger rühren)
Wan|kel (dt. Ingenieur u. Erfinder; *als* ® *für* einen Motor); **Wan|kel|mo|tor** (↑R 95)
Wan|kel|mut; wan|kel|mü|tig; Wan|kel|mü|tig|keit, die; -; **wan|ken;** (↑R 50:) ins Wanken geraten
wann; dann und wann
Wänn|chen; Wan|ne, die; -, -n
Wan|ne-Ei|ckel; ↑R 106 (Stadt im Ruhrgebiet)
wan|nen; *nur noch in* von wannen *(veraltet für* woher)
Wan|nen|bad
Wann|see, der; -s (in Berlin)
[1]**Wanst,** der; -es, Wänste (Tierbauch; *ugs. für* dicker Bauch); [2]**Wanst,** das *od.* der; -es, Wänster *(landsch. svw.* [2]Balg); **Wänstchen, Wänst|lein**
Want, die; -, -en *meist Plur. (Seemannsspr.* starkes [Stahl]tau zum Verspannen des Mastes)
Wan|ze, die; -, -n *(auch übertr. für* Abhörgerät); **wan|zen** *(volkstüml. für* von Wanzen reinigen); du wanzt; **Wan|zen|ver|til|gungs|mit|tel,** das
Wa|pi|ti, der; -[s], -s ‹indian.› (eine nordamerik. Hirschart)
Wap|pen, das; -s, -; **Wap|pen⌣brief, ...feld, ...kun|de** (die; -), **...schild** (der *od.* das), **...spruch, ...tier; wapp|nen** *(geh.);* sich - (sich vorbereiten); ich wappne mich mit Geduld (gedulde mich)
Wa|rä|ger, der; -s, - ‹schwed.› (Wikinger)
Wa|ran, der; -s, -e ‹arab.› (eine trop. Echse)
War|deln, der; -[e]s, -e ‹niederl.› *(früher für* [Münz]prüfer); **war|die|ren** *(früher für* [den Wert der Münzen] prüfen)
Wa|re, die; -, -n; **Wa|ren⌣an|gebot, ...an|nah|me, ...aus|fuhr, ...aus|ga|be, ...aus|tausch, ...begleit|schein, ...be|stand, ...einfuhr, ...ex|port, ...han|del** *(vgl.* [1]Handel), **...haus, ...im|port, ...korb** *(Statistik),* **...kre|dit; Waren|kre|dit|brief** *(Bankw.);* **Waren⌣kun|de** (die; -), **...la|ger, ...pro|be, ...re|gal, ...rück|ver|gütung, ...sen|dung, ...sor|ti|ment, ...stem|pel, ...test, ...um|schlag** (der; -[e]s), **...um|schlie|ßung** (Verpackung[sgewicht]), **...zeichen, ...zoll**
Warf, der *od.* das; -[e]s, -e *(Weberei* Aufzug)
Warf[t], die; -, -en (Wurt in Nordfriesland)
War|hol ['wɔ:(r)ho:l], Andy ['ɛndi] (amerik. Maler u. Grafiker)
warm; wärmer, wärmste; warme Miete *(ugs. für* Miete mit Heizung); auf kalt und warm reagieren; das Essen warm machen, stellen, halten; sich einen Geschäftsfreund [besonders] warm halten *(ugs. für* sich seine Gunst erhalten); sich warm machen, laufen (beim Sport); den Motor warm laufen lassen (auf günstige Betriebstemperatur bringen); **Warm⌣bier** (das; -[e]s), **...blut** (das; -[e]s; Pferd einer bestimmten Rasse), **...blü|ter; warm|blü|tig; Wär|me,** die; -, -n *Plur. selten;* **Wär|me⌣aus|tausch** *(Technik),* **...be|hand|lung; wär|me|däm|mend** (↑R 40); **Wär|me⌣däm|mung, ...deh|nung, ...ein|heit, ...ener|gie** (↑R 132), **...ge|wit|ter, ...grad; wär|me|hal|tig; wär|me|iso|lie|rend** (↑R 132 *u.* 40); **Wär|me⌣iso|lie|rung** (↑R 132), **...ka|pa|zi|tät, ...leh|re** (die; -), **...lei|ter** (der), **...leit|zahl, ...mes|ser** (der); **wär|men;** sich -; **Wär|me⌣pum|pe, ...quel|le, ...reg|ler, ...schutz** (der; -es), **...spei|cher, ...strah|len** *(Plur.),* **...tech|nik** (die; -); **wär|me|tech|nisch; Wär|me⌣ver|lust, ...zäh|ler; Wärm|fla|sche; Warm|front** *(Meteor.);* **warm hal|ten** *vgl.* warm; **Warm|hal|te|plat|te; Warm|haus** (Gewächshaus für Pflanzen mit hohen Wärmeansprüchen); **warm|her|zig; Warm|her|zig|keit,** die; -; **warm lau|fen** *vgl.* warm; **Warm⌣laufen** (das; -s), **...luft** (die; -); **Warm|luft|hei|zung; Warm|mie|te** (Miete mit Heizung)
Warm-up ['wɔ:map], das; -s, -s ‹engl.› (das Aufwärmen; das Einstimmen von Zuschauern, Zuhörern auf ein Thema)
Warm|was|ser, das; -s; **Warm|was|ser⌣be|rei|ter, ...hei|zung, ...ver|sor|gung**
War|na (bulg. Stadt)
Warn|an|la|ge; Warn|blink⌣an|la|ge, ...leuch|te; Warn|drei|eck
Warndt, der; -s (Berg- u. Hügelland westl. der Saar)
war|nen; War|ner; Warn⌣kreuz, ...leuch|te, ...licht *(Plur.* ...lichter), **...ruf, ...schild** (das), **...schuss, ...sig|nal, ...streik; War|nung; Warn|zei|chen**
[1]**Warp,** der *od.* das; -s, -e ‹engl.› *(Weberei* Kettgarn)
[2]**Warp,** der; -[e]s, -e ‹niederl.› *(Seemannsspr.* Schleppanker); **Warp|an|ker; war|pen** (durch Schleppanker fortbewegen); **Warp|schiff|fahrt,** die; -
Warp|we|ber; *vgl.* [1]Warp
War|rant *[engl.* 'vɔrənt], der; -s, -s ‹engl.› *(Wirtsch.* Lager[pfand]schein)
War|schau (Hptst. Polens); **War|schau|er** (↑R 103); **War|schau|er Pakt** *(früher);* **War|schau|er-Pakt-Staa|ten** (↑R 28); **war|schau|isch; War|sza|wa** [var'ʃa(:)va] *(poln. Form von* Warschau)
Wart|burg, die; -; **Wart|burg|fest,** das; -[e]s (1817)
War|te, die; -, -n (Beobachtungsort); *übertr. in Wendungen wie* von meiner - (meinem Standpunkt) aus; **War|te⌣frau, ...hal|le, ...lis|te; war|ten;** auf sich warten lassen; eine Maschine warten (pflegen, bedienen); (↑R 50:) das Warten auf ihn hat ein Ende; **Wär|ter; War|te|raum; War|te|rei** *(ugs.);* **Wär|te|rin; War|te⌣saal, ...schlan|ge, ...schlei|fe** *(auch übertr.),* **...stand** (der; -[e]s), **...zeit, ...zim|mer**
War|the, die; - (r. Nebenfluss der unteren Oder)
...wärts (z. B. anderwärts)
Wart|saal *(schweiz. neben* Wartesaal); **Wart|turm; War|tung; war|tungs⌣arm, ...frei, ...freund|lich**
wa|rum (↑R 132); warum nicht?; nach dem Warum fragen (↑R 49)
Wärz|chen; War|ze, die; -, -n; **war|zen|för|mig; War|zen⌣hof, ...schwein; war|zig**
was; was ist los?; er will wissen, was los ist; was für ein; was für einer; *(ugs. auch für* etwas:) was Neues (↑R 47), irgendwas; das ist das Schönste, was ich je erlebt habe; all das Schöne, das Gute, etwas anderes, Erschütterndes, was wir erlebt haben; nichts, vieles, allerlei, manches, sonstiges usw., was ..., *aber* das Werkzeug, das ...; das Kind, das sie im Arm hielt
Wa|sa, der; -[s], - *(eindeutschend für* Vasa)
wasch|ak|tiv; -e Substanzen; **Wasch⌣an|la|ge, ...an|lei|tung, ...an|stalt** *(veraltend),* **...au|tomat; wasch|bar; Wasch⌣bär, ...be|cken, ...ben|zin, ...ber|ge** *(Plur.; Bergmannsspr.* Steine, die bei der Aufbereitung der Kohle anfallen), **...be|ton** (der; -s),

...brett, ...büt|te; Wạ̈|sche, die; -, -n; **Wạ̈|sche|beu|tel; wạsch|echt;** -e Farben; **Wạ̈|sche‿ge|schäft, ...klam|mer, ...knopf, ...korb** (*od.* Wạsch|korb), **...lei|ne, ...man|gel** (die); **wạ|schen;** du wäschst, er wäscht; du wu̲|schest; du wü̲schest; gewaschen; wasch[e]!; sich -; **Wä|sche|re̲i; Wạ̈|sche|rin; Wạ̈|sche‿schleu|der, ...schrank, ...spin|ne** (zum Wäscheaufhängen), **...stän|der, ...tin|te, ...trock|ner, ...zei|chen; Wạsch‿frau, ...gang** (der), **...ge|le|gen|heit, ...haus, ...kes|sel, ...korb** (*vgl.* Wäschekorb), **...kraft** *(Werbespr.),* **...kü|che, ...lap|pen** (*ugs. auch für* Feigling, Schwächling), **...lau|ge, ...le|der; wạsch|le|dern** (aus Waschleder); **Wạsch|ma|schi|ne; wạsch|ma|schi|nen|fest; Wạsch‿mit|tel** (das), **...pro|gramm, ...pul|ver, ...raum, ...rum|pel** (*landsch. für* Waschbrett), **...sa|lon, ...schüs|sel, ...sei|de, ...stra|ße, ...tag, ...tisch, ...trog; Wạ|schung; Wạsch‿was|ser** (das; -s), **...weib** (*ugs. für* geschwätzige Frau), **...zet|tel** (vom Verlag selbst stammende Bücherempfehlung), **...zeug** (das; -s), **...zu|ber, ...zwang** (der; -[e]s)

[1]**Wa̲|sen,** der; -s, - (*svw.* Wrasen)

[2]**Wa̲|sen,** der; -s, - (*landsch. für* Rasen; *meist Plur.: nordd. für* Reisigbündel)

Wa̲|serl, das; -s, -n (*österr. ugs. für* unbeholfener Mensch)

Wạs|gau, der; -[e]s; **Wạs|gen|wald,** der; -[e]s (*veraltete Bez. für* Vogesen)

Wash. = Washington (Staat in den USA)

wash and wear ['wɔʃ ənd 'wɛ:(r)] ⟨engl., „waschen und tragen"⟩ (Bez. von Textilien, die nach dem Waschen [fast] ohne Bügeln wieder getragen werden können)

[1]**Wa|shing|ton** ['wɔʃiŋtən] (erster Präsident der USA); [2]**Wa|shing|ton** (Staat in den USA [*Abk.* Wash.]; Bundeshauptstadt der USA)

Wạs|ser, das; -s, *Plur.* - *u.* (*für* Mineral-, Spül-, Speise-, Abwasser u. a.:) Wässer; leichtes, schweres Wasser *(Chemie);* zu Wasser und zu Land[e]; eine Wasser abstoßende, abweisende Imprägnierung (↑R 40); **wạs|ser|arm; Wạs|ser‿auf|be|rei|tung, ...bad, ...ball** (*vgl.* [1]Ball), **...bau** (der; -[e]s), **...bett, ...bom|be, ...büf|fel, ...burg; Wạ̈s|ser|chen; Wạs|ser|dampf; wạs|ser|dicht; Wạs|ser‿ei|mer, ...fahr|zeug, ...fall** (der), **...far|be; wạs|ser|fest; Wạs|ser‿flä|che, ...fla|sche, ...floh, ...flug|zeug; wạs|ser|ge|kühlt;** ein -er Motor (↑R 40); **Wạs|ser‿glas** (*Plur.* ...gläser; Trinkglas; *nur Sing.:* Kalium- od. Natriumsilikat), **...glät|te** (*für* Aquaplaning), **...gra|ben, ...hahn, ...här|te, ...haus|halt, ...heil|ver|fah|ren, ...ho|se** (Wasser mitführender Wirbelsturm), **...huhn; wạ̈s|se|rig** usw. *vgl.* wässrig usw.; **Wạs|ser‿jung|fer** (Libelle), **...ka|nis|ter, ...kan|te** (die; -; *selten für* Waterkant), **...kes|sel, ...klo|sett** (*Abk.* WC; *vgl. d.*), **...kopf** *(Med.),* **...kraft** (die), **...kraft|werk, ...kunst**

Wạs|ser|kup|pe, die; - (Berg in der Rhön); **Wạs|ser‿la|che, ...lauf, ...läu|fer; wạs|ser|le|bend** (*Zool.;* ↑R 40); **Wạs|ser|lei|che; Wạ̈s|ser|lein; Wạs|ser‿lei|tung, ...lin|se; wạs|ser|lös|lich; Wạs|ser‿man|gel** (der; -s), **...mann** (der; -[e]s; ein Sternbild), **...me|lo|ne, ...müh|le; wạs|sern** (auf dem Wasser niedergehen [z. B. von Flugzeugen]); ich wassere *u.* wassre (↑R 16); **wạ̈s|sern** (in Wasser legen; mit Wasser versorgen; Wasser absondern); ich wässere *u.* wässre (↑R 16); **Wạs|ser‿ni|xe, ...not** (die; -; *veraltet für* Mangel an Wasser; *vgl. aber* Wassersnot), **...ober|flä|che** (↑R 132), **...pest** (die; -; eine Wasserpflanze), **...pfei|fe, ...pflan|ze, ...pis|to|le, ...po|li|zei, ...pum|pe, ...rad, ...rat|te** (*ugs. scherzh. auch für* jmd., der sehr gern schwimmt), **...recht** (das; -[e]s); **wạs|ser|reich; Wạs|ser‿re|ser|voir, ...rohr, ...säu|le** *(Physik),* **...scha|den, ...schei|de** *(Geogr.);* **wạs|ser|scheu; Wạs|ser‿scheu, ...schi** (*vgl.* Wasserski), **...schlan|ge, ...schlauch, ...schloss, ...schutz|ge|biet, ...schutz|po|li|zei, ...schwall; Wạs|ser|ski,** Wạs|ser|schi, der; -[s], *Plur.* -er *od.* -, *als Sportart* das; -[s]; **Wạs|sers|not** (*veraltet für* Überschwemmung; *vgl. aber* Wassernot); **Wạs|ser‿spei|er, ...spie|gel, ...spiel** *(meist Plur.),* **...sport** (der; -[e]s), **...sport|ler; wạs|ser|sport|lich; Wạs|ser‿spü|lung, ...stand; Wạs|ser|stands‿an|zei|ger, ...mel|dung** *(meist Plur.),* **...reg|ler; Wạs|ser|stoff,** der; -[e]s (chem. Element, Gas; *Zeichen* H); **wạs|ser|stoff|blond; Wạs|ser|stoff|bom|be** (H-Bombe); **Wạs|ser|stoff|flam|me** (↑R 136); **Wạs|ser|stoff|pe̲r|oxid** (↑R 132), das; -[e]s; *vgl.* Oxid; **Wạs|ser‿strahl, ...stra|ße, ...sucht** (die; -; *für* Hydropsie); **wạs|ser|süch|tig; Wạs|ser‿tank, ...tem|pe|ra|tur, ...tie|fe, ...trä|ger** (*ugs. auch für* jmd., der einem anderen Hilfsdienste leistet), **...tre|ten** (das; -s), **...trop|fen, ...turm, ...uhr; Wạs|se|rung** ⟨*zu* wassern⟩; **Wạ̈s|se|rung; Wạs|ser‿ver|brauch, ...ver|drän|gung, ...ver|schmut|zung, ...vo|gel, ...waa|ge, ...weg, ...wer|fer, ...werk, ...zäh|ler, ...zei|chen** (im Papier); **wạ̈ss|rig,** wäs|se|rig; **Wạ̈ss|rig|keit,** Wäs|se|rig|keit

wa̲|ten; gewatet

Wa̲|ter|kant, die; - (*scherzh. für* nordd. Küstengebiet)

Wa̲|ter|loo (Ort in Belgien)

Wa|ter|proof ['wɔ:tə(r)pru:f], der; -s, -s ⟨engl.⟩ (wasserdichter Stoff; Regenmantel)

Wa̲t|sche [*auch* 'vat...], die; -, -n *u.* Wa̲t|schen, die; -, - (*bayr., österr. ugs. für* Ohrfeige)

wa̲t|sche|lig, wa̲tsch|lig [*auch* 'vat...] *(ugs.);* **wa̲t|scheln** [*auch* 'vat...] (*ugs. für* wackelnd gehen); ich ...[e]le (↑R 16)

wa̲t|schen [*auch* 'vat...] (*bayr., österr. ugs. für* ohrfeigen); **Wa̲t|schen** [*auch* 'vat...] *vgl.* Watsche; **Wa̲t|schen|mann** [*auch* 'vat...] (Figur im Wiener Prater; *übertr. für* Zielscheibe der Kritik)

wa̲tsch|lig [*auch* 'vat...] *vgl.* watschelig

[1]**Watt** [wɔt] (Erfinder der verbesserten Dampfmaschine); [2]**Watt** [vat], das; -s, - (Einheit der physikal. Leistung; *Zeichen* W); 40 -

[3]**Wạtt,** das; -[e]s, -en (seichter Streifen der Nordsee zwischen Küste u. vorgelagerten Inseln)

Wạt|te, die; -, -n ⟨niederl.⟩

Wat|teau [va'to:] (franz. Maler)

Wạt|te|bausch

Wạt|ten, das; -s (*österr.* ein Kartenspiel)

Wạt|ten|meer ⟨*zu* [3]Watt⟩

Wạt|ten|scheid (Stadt im Ruhrgebiet)

Wạt|te|pfrop|fen

wat|ti̲e̲|ren (mit Watte füttern); **Wat|ti̲e̲|rung; wạt|tig**

Wạtt‿me|ter (das; -s, -; elektr. Messgerät), **...se|kun|de** (Einheit der Energie u. Leistung; *Abk.* Ws)

Wạtt|wan|de|rung ⟨*zu* [3]Watt⟩

Wa̲t|vo|gel (am Wasser, im Moor o. Ä. lebender Vogel)

Wa̲u̲, der; -[e]s, -e (eine Färberpflanze)

wa̲u̲, wa̲u̲!; Wa̲u̲|wau, der; -s, -s (*Kinderspr.* Hund)

WC [veˈtseː] = water closet [ˈwɔːtə(r) ˈklɔzit], das; -[s], -[s] ‹engl.› (Wasserklosett)
WDR = Westdeutscher Rundfunk
We|be, die; -, -n (*österr. für* Gewebe [für Bettzeug]); **We|be|lei|ne** (*Seemannsspr.* gewebte Sprosse der Wanten); **we|ben;** du webtest, *schweiz., sonst geh. u. übertr.* wobst; du webtest, *geh. u. übertr.* wöbest; gewebt, *schweiz., sonst geh. u. übertr.* gewoben; web[e]!
[1]**We|ber,** Carl Maria von (dt. Komponist)
[2]**We|ber; We|be|rei; We|be|rin; We|ber‿kamm, ...knecht** (ein Spinnentier), **...kno|ten**
We|bern, Anton von (österr. Komponist)
We|ber‿schiff|chen (*od.* Webschiff|chen), **...vo|gel; Web‿feh|ler, ...garn, ...kan|te, ...pelz; Web|schiff|chen** *vgl.* Weberschiffchen; **Web‿stuhl, ...wa|ren** *(Plur.)*
Wech|sel, der; -s, -; **Wech|sel‿bad, ...balg** (der; missgebildetes untergeschobenes Kind), **...bank** (*Plur.* ...banken), **...be|zie|hung; wech|sel|be|züg|lich;** -e Verfügung *(Rechtsw.);* **Wech|sel‿bür|ge, ...bürg|schaft, ...fäl|le** *(Plur.),* **...fäl|schung, ...fie|ber** (das; -s; *für* Malaria), **...geld, ...ge|sang; wech|sel|haft; Wech|sel|haf|tig|keit,** die; -; **Wech|sel‿jah|re** *(Plur.),* **...kas|se, ...kre|dit, ...kurs; wech|seln;** ich ...[e]le (↑R 16); Wäsche zum Wechseln (↑R 50); **Wech|sel‿rah|men, ...re|de** (*auch für* Diskussion), **...re|gress** *(Bankw.);* **Wech|sel|rei|te|rei** (unlautere Wechselausstellung); **Wech|sel‿schal|ter, ...schicht, ...schritt; wech|sel|sei|tig; Wech|sel|sei|tig|keit,** die; -; **Wech|sel‿steu|er** (die), **...strom, ...stu|be, ...sum|me; Wech|se|lung,** Wechs|lung; **Wech|sel|ver|kehr,** der; -s *(Verkehrsw.);* **wech|sel|voll; Wech|sel|wäh|ler; wech|sel|warm** *(Zool.);* **Wech|sel|warm|blü|ter** *(Zool.);* **wech|sel|wei|se; Wech|sel|wir|kung; Wechs|ler; Wechs|lung** *vgl.* Wechselung
Wech|te, die; -, -n (überhängende Schneemasse; *schweiz. auch für* Schneewehe); **Wech|ten|bil|dung**
[1]**Weck** (Familienn.; *als* ® *für* Einkochgeräte)
[2]**Weck,** der; -[e]s, -e *u.* We|cke, die; -, -n *u.* We|cken, der; -s, - (*südd., österr. für* Weizenbrötchen; Brot in länglicher Form)
We|cka|min (↑R 132), das; -s, -e (ein stimulierendes Kreislaufmittel)
Weck|ap|pa|rat ® (↑R 95)
Weck‿au|to|ma|tik, ...dienst (per Telefon)
We|cke *vgl.* [2]Weck
we|cken; [1]**We|cken,** das; -s
[2]**We|cken** *vgl.* [2]Weck
We|cker
We|ckerl, das; -s, -n (*bayr., österr. für* längliches Weizenbrötchen); *vgl.* [2]Weck
Weck|glas ® *Plur.* ...gläser; ↑R 95; *vgl.* [1]Weck
Weck|ruf
We|da, der; -[s], *Plur.* ...den *u.* -s ‹sanskr.› (die heiligen Schriften der alten Inder)
We|de|kind (dt. Dramatiker)
We|del, der; -s, -; **We|del|kurs** *(Skisport);* **we|deln;** ich ...[e]le (↑R 16)
We|den (*Plur. von* Weda)
we|der; weder er noch sie haben, *auch* hat davon gewusst
Wedg|wood [ˈwɛdʒwud], das; -[s] ‹nach dem engl. Erfinder› (berühmtes engl. Steingut); **Wedg|wood|wa|re** (↑R 95)
we|disch (die Weden betreffend); die wedische Religion
Week|end [ˈwiːkɛnd], das; -[s], -s ‹engl.› (Wochenende)
Weft, das; -[e]s, -e ‹engl.› (*Weberei* hart gedrehtes Kammgarn)
weg; weg da! (fort!); sie ist ganz weg (*ugs. für* begeistert, verliebt); frisch von der Leber weg (*ugs. für* ganz offen, ungehemmt) reden; sie ist längst darüber weg (hinweg); sie wird schon weg sein, wenn ...
Weg, der; -[e]s, -e; *Schreibung in Straßennamen* ↑R 123; im Weg[e] stehen; wohin des Weg[e]s?; halbwegs; gerade[n]wegs; keineswegs; alle[r]wege, allerwegen; unterwegs; zuwege, *auch* zu Wege bringen
weg... (*in Zus. mit Verben,* z. B. weglaufen, du läufst weg, weggelaufen, wegzulaufen)
We|ga, die; - ‹arab.› (ein Stern)
weg|ar|bei|ten *(ugs.);* sie hat alles weggearbeitet; **weg|be|kom|men;** die Regel hatte er - (*ugs. für* verstanden); er hat einen Schlag - (*ugs. für* erhalten)
Weg‿be|rei|ter, ...be|rei|te|rin, ...bie|gung
weg|bla|sen; er hat den Zigarrenrauch weggeblasen; er war wie weggeblasen (*ugs. für* er war spurlos verschwunden); **weg|blei|ben** *(ugs.);* sie ist auf einmal weggeblieben; **weg|brin|gen** *(ugs.);* **weg|dis|ku|tie|ren** *(ugs.);* **weg|drän|gen; weg|drü|cken**
We|ge|bau *Plur.* ...bauten; **We|ge|geld,** Weg|geld; **We|ge|la|ge|rer; we|ge|la|gern;** ich ...ere (↑R 16); gewegelagert; zu -; **We|ge|la|ge|rung**
we|gen (↑R 46); *Präp. mit Gen.:* wegen Diebstahls, wegen des Vaters *od.* des Vaters wegen; wegen der hohen Preise; wegen der Leute *od.* der Leute wegen; wegen meiner *(noch landsch.); ein allein stehendes, stark gebeugtes Substantiv steht im Sing. oft schon ungebeugt:* wegen Umbau, wegen Diebstahl; *ugs. mit Dat.:* wegen dem Kind, wegen mir; *hochspr. mit Dat. in bestimmten Verbindungen u. wenn bei Pluralformen der Gen. nicht erkennbar ist:* wegen etwas anderem, wegen manchem, wegen Vergangenem; wegen Geschäften; *Abk.* wg.; *Zusammensetzungen u. Fügungen:* des- *od.* dessentwegen; meinet-, deinet-, seinet-, ihret-, unsert-, euret- *od.* euertwegen; von Amts, Rechts, Staats wegen; von wegen! (*ugs. für* auf keinen Fall!)
Weg|en|ge
We|ger, der; -s, - (Schiffsplanke)
We|ge|recht, das; -[e]s
We|ge|rich, der; -s, -e (eine Pflanze)
we|gern (*Schiffbau* die Innenseite der Spanten mit Wegern belegen); ich ...ere (↑R 16); **We|ge|rung**
weg|es|sen; du hast mir alles weggegessen; **weg|fah|ren; Weg|fahr|sper|re** *(Kfz-Wesen);* **Weg|fall,** der; -[e]s; in - kommen (*dafür besser:* wegfallen); **weg|fal|len** (nicht mehr in Betracht kommen); **weg|fe|gen; weg|fi|schen** (*ugs. auch für* vor der Nase wegnehmen); sie hat ihm die besten Bissen weggefischt; **weg|flie|gen; weg|fres|sen; weg|füh|ren**
Weg|ga|be|lung, Weg|gab|lung
Weg|gang, der; -[e]s; **weg|ge|ben**
Weg|ge|fähr|te
weg|ge|hen
Weg|geld *vgl.* Wegegeld
Weg|gen, der; -s, - (*schweiz. für* [2]Wecken)
Weg|ge|nos|se
Wegg|li, das; -s, - (*schweiz. für* eine Art Brötchen)
weg|gu|cken *(ugs.);* **weg|ha|ben;** er hat einen weggehabt (*ugs. für* er war betrunken, nicht ganz bei Verstand); sie hat das weggehabt (*ugs. für* gründlich beherrscht); die Ruhe - (*ugs. für* sich nicht aus der Fassung bringen lassen);

weg|hän|gen; *vgl.* ²hängen; **weg|ho|len; weg|hö|ren** *(ugs.);* **weg|ja|gen; weg|keh|ren; weg|kom|men** *(ugs. auch für* verschwinden); gut dabei -; **weg|krat|zen**
Weg‿kreuz, ...kreu|zung
weg|krie|gen
weg|kun|dig
weg|las|sen; weg|lau|fen; er ist weggelaufen; **weg|le|gen**
Weg|lei|tung (*schweiz. für* Anweisung); **weg|los**
weg|ma|chen (*ugs. für* entfernen)
Weg|mar|ke; weg|mü|de *(geh.)*
weg|müs|sen (*ugs. für* weggehen müssen, nicht mehr bleiben können); weggemusst; **Weg|nah|me,** die; -, -n *(Amtsspr.);* **weg|neh|men;** weggenommen; **weg|pa|cken; weg|put|zen** (*ugs. auch für* aufessen); er hat das ganze Fleisch weggeputzt; **weg|ra|die|ren**
Weg‿rain, ...rand
weg|ra|ti|o|na|li|sie|ren; weg|räu|men; weg|rei|ßen; weg|ren|nen; weg|rol|len
weg|sam *(veraltet)*
weg|sa|nie|ren *(iron.);* **weg|schaf|fen;** *vgl.* ¹schaffen
Weg|scheid, der; -[e]s, -e, *österr.* die; -, -en, *häufiger* **Weg|schei|de,** die; -, -n (Straßengabelung)
weg|sche|ren, sich (*ugs. für* weggehen); scher dich weg!; **weg|scheu|chen; weg|schi|cken; weg|schlei|chen;** er ist weggeschlichen; sich -; du hast dich weggeschlichen; **weg|schlie|ßen; weg|schmei|ßen** *(ugs.);* **weg|schnap|pen** *(ugs.);* **weg|schnei|den; weg|schüt|ten; weg|set|zen;** das Geschirr -; sich -; du hast dich über den Ärger weggesetzt *(ugs.);* **weg|ste|cken** *(ugs.);* er hat das Geld weggesteckt; so einen Schicksalsschlag kann man nicht einfach - (verkraften); **weg|steh|len;** sich -; du hast dich weggestohlen (heimlich entfernt); **weg|stel|len; weg|ster|ben** *(ugs.);* **weg|sto|ßen**
Weg|stre|cke
weg|strei|chen; weg|tra|gen; weg|trei|ben; weg|tre|ten; weggetreten! (milit. Kommando); **weg|trin|ken; weg|tun**
Weg‿über|füh|rung (↑R 132), **...un|ter|füh|rung, ...war|te** (eine Pflanze); **weg|wei|send; Weg|wei|ser**
weg|wer|fen; alles wurde weggeworfen; sich wegwerfen; **weg|wer|fend;** eine wegwerfende Handbewegung; **Weg|werf‿fla|sche, ...ge|sell|schaft, ...men|ta|li|tät** (die; -), **...win|del; weg|wi|schen; weg|wol|len** *(ugs.);* **weg|zau|bern**
Weg‿zeh|rung, ...zei|chen
weg|zie|hen; Weg|zug
¹**weh;** er hat einen wehen Finger; es war ihm weh ums Herz; *vgl.* wehe, wehtun; ²**weh** *vgl.* wehe; **Weh,** das; -[e]s, -e; (↑R 49:) mit Ach und Weh; Ach und Weh schreien, ein „Wehe!" ausrufen; *vgl.* ²Wehe; **we|he, weh;** weh[e] dir!; o weh!; ¹**We|he,** die; -, -n *meist Plur.* (das Zusammenziehen der Gebärmutter bei der Geburt); ²**We|he,** das; -s (*Nebenform von* Weh)
³**We|he,** die; -, -n (zusammengewehte Anhäufung von Schnee od. Sand); **we|hen**
Weh‿ge|schrei, ...kla|ge *(geh.);* **weh|kla|gen** *(geh.);* ich wehklage; gewehklagt; zu -
Wehl, das; -[e]s, -e *u.* **Weh|le,** die; -, -n (*nordd. für* an der Binnenseite eines Deiches gelegener Teich)
weh|lei|dig; Weh|lei|dig|keit, die; -; **Weh|mut,** die; -; **weh|mü|tig; Weh|mü|tig|keit,** die; -; **weh|muts|voll; Weh|mut|ter** *Plur.* ...mütter (*veraltet für* Hebamme)
¹**Wehr,** die; -, -en (Befestigung, Verteidigung, Abwehr; *kurz für* Feuerwehr); sich zur - setzen; ²**Wehr,** das; -[e]s, -e (Stauwerk); **wehr|bar; Wehr‿be|auf|trag|te, ...be|reich** (der); **Wehr|be|reichs|kom|man|do; Wehr|dienst** (der; -[e]s); **wehr|dienst|taug|lich; Wehr|dienst|taug|lich|keit,** die; -; **wehr|dienst|un|taug|lich; Wehr|dienst|un|taug|lich|keit,** die; -; **Wehr|dienst‿ver|wei|ge|rer, ...ver|wei|ge|rung; weh|ren;** sich -; **Wehr|er|satz|dienst,** der; -[e]s; (*svw.* Zivildienst); **wehr|fä|hig; Wehr‿fä|hig|keit** (die; -), **...gang** (der), **...ge|hän|ge, ...ge|henk** *(veraltet),* **...ge|rech|tig|keit** (die; -), **...ge|setz; wehr|haft; Wehr|haf|tig|keit,** die; -; **Wehr‿kir|che** (burgartig gebaute Kirche), **...kun|de** (die; -); **wehr|los; Wehr|lo|sig|keit,** die; -; **Wehr|macht,** die; - (*früher für* Gesamtheit der [deutschen] Streitkräfte); **Wehr|macht[s]|an|ge|hö|ri|ge,** der *u.* die; **Wehr‿mann** (*Plur.* ...männer; *schweiz. für* Soldat), **...pass, ...pflicht** (die; -; die allgemeine -); **wehr|pflich|tig; Wehr|pflich|ti|ge,** der; -n, -n (↑R 5ff.); **Wehr|turm; Wehr|übung** (↑R 132)
weh|tun (↑R 38f.); ich habe mir wehgetan; das braucht nicht wehzutun; **Weh|weh** [*auch* veːˈveː], das; -s, -s (*Kinderspr.* Schmerz; kleine Verletzung, Wunde); **Weh|weh|chen,** das; -s, -
Weib, das; -[e]s, -er; **Weib|chen**
Wei|bel, der; -s, - (*früher u. schweiz. für* Amtsbote); **wei|beln** (*schweiz. für* werbend umhergehen); ich ...b|le (↑R 16)
Wei|ber‿fas[t]|nacht (*vgl.* Altweiberfas[t]nacht), **...feind, ...ge|schich|ten** *(Plur.),* **...held** *(abwertend);* **wei|bisch; Weib|lein;** Männlein und Weiblein; **weib|lich;** -es Geschlecht; **Weib|lich|keit,** die; -; **Weibs|bild** (*ugs. abwertend für* weibl. Person); **Weib|sen,** das; -s, - (*ugs. abwertend für* Frau); **Weibs‿leu|te** (*Plur.; ugs. abwertend für* Frauen), **...per|son** *u.* **...stück** (*ugs. abwertend für* Frau)
weich; weich sein, werden, klopfen, kochen, machen; weich gedünstetes Gemüse; ein weich gekochtes Ei; weich geklopftes Fleisch; er hat mich mit seinen Fragen [richtig] weich gemacht (*ugs. für* zermürbt); schließlich ist er weich geworden *(ugs.)* und hat zugestimmt; *vgl. aber* weichlöten
Weich|bild (Randbezirke; Ortsgebiet; *früher* Bezirk, wo das Ortsrecht gilt)
¹**Wei|che,** die; -, -n (Umstellvorrichtung bei Gleisen)
²**Wei|che,** die; -, -n (*nur Sing.:* Weichheit; Körperteil)
¹**wei|chen** (einweichen, weich machen, weich werden); du weichtest; geweicht; weich[e]!
²**wei|chen** (zurückgehen; nachgeben); du wichst; du wichest; gewichen; weich[e]!
Wei|chen‿stel|ler, ...wär|ter
weich ge|düns|tet, ge|klopft, ge|kocht *vgl.* weich; **Weich|heit; weich|her|zig; Weich|her|zig|keit,** die; -; **Weich‿holz, ...kä|se; weich|lich; Weich|lich|keit,** die; -; **Weich|ling** (*abwertend* weichlicher Mann, Schwächling); **weich|lö|ten** *(Technik); nur im Infinitiv u. im Partizip II gebr.;* weichgelötet; **weich ma|chen** *vgl.* weich; **Weich|ma|cher** *(Chemie);* **weich|mü|tig** *(veraltend);* **Weich|mü|tig|keit,** die; - *(veraltend);* **weich|scha|lig**
¹**Weich|sel,** die; - (osteurop. Strom)
²**Weich|sel,** die; -, -n (*landsch. u. schweiz. kurz für* Weichselkirsche); **Weich|sel‿kir|sche** (ein Obstbaum; dessen Frucht),

...**rohr** (Pfeifenrohr aus Weichselholz)
Weich|spü|ler *(Werbespr.);* **Weich|spül|mit|tel; Weich₋tei|le** *(Plur.),* ...**tier** (*meist Plur.; für* Molluske), ...**wer|den** (das; -s), ...**zeich|ner** (fotograf. Vorsatzlinse)
[1]**Wei|de,** die; -, -n (ein Baum)
[2]**Wei|de,** die; -, -n (Grasland); **Wei|de|land** *Plur.* ...länder; **Wei|del|gras,** das; -es (*auch für* Raigras); **Wei|de|mo|nat** (*alte dt. Bez., meist für* Mai); **wei|den;** sich an etwas -
Wei|den₋baum, ...**busch,** ...**ger|te,** ...**kätz|chen,** ...**rös|chen**
Wei|de|platz
Wei|de|rich, der; -s, -e (Name verschiedener Pflanzen)
Wei|de₋rind, ...**wirt|schaft** (die; -)
weid|ge|recht[1]; **weid|lich** (jagdgerecht; gehörig, tüchtig); **Weid|ling,** der; -s, -e (*südwestd. u. schweiz. für* Fischerkahn); **Weid₋loch**[1] (After beim Wild), ...**mann** (*Plur.* ...männer); **weid|män|nisch**[1]; **Weid|manns|dank!**[1]; **Weid|manns|heil!**[1]; **Weid₋mes|ser**[1] (das), ...**sack** (*Jägerspr.* Pansen [vom Wild]), ...**spruch** (alte Redensart der Jäger), ...**werk** (das; -[e]s); **weid|wund**[1] (verwundet durch Schuss in die Eingeweide)
Wei|fe, die; -, -n (*Textiltechnik* Garnwinde); **wei|fen** ([Garn] haspeln)
Wei|gand, der; -[e]s, -e (*veraltet für* Kämpfer, Held)
wei|gern; sich -; ich ...ere [mich] (↑R 16); **Wei|ge|rung; Wei|ge|rungs|fall,** der; im -[e] *(Amtsspr.)*
Weih *vgl.* [1]Weihe
Weih|bi|schof
[1]**Wei|he,** die; -, -n *u.* Weih, der; -[e]s, -e (ein Greifvogel)
[2]**Wei|he,** die; -, -n (*Rel.* Weihung; *nur Sing.: geh. für* feierl. Stimmung); **Wei|he|akt; wei|hen**
Wei|hen|ste|phan (Stadtteil von Freising)
Wei|her, der; -s, - ‹lat.› (Teich)
Wei|he₋re|de, ...**stun|de; wei|he|voll; Weih₋ga|be,** ...**kes|sel** (Weihwasserkessel); **Weih|ling** (Person, die geweiht wird)
Weih|nacht, die; -; **weih|nach|ten;** es weihnachtet; geweihnachtet; **Weih|nach|ten,** das; -, - (Weihnachtsfest); Weihnachten ist bald vorbei, war dieses Jahr sehr kalt; *landsch., bes. österr. u. schweiz. als Plur.:* die[se] Weihnachten waren verschneit; nach [den] Weihnachten; *in Wunschformeln auch allg. als Plur.:* fröhliche Weihnachten!; zu *(bes. nordd.),* an *(bes. südd.)* Weihnachten; **weih|nacht|lich,** *schweiz. auch* **weih|nächt|lich; Weih|nachts₋abend** (↑R 132), ...**bä|cke|rei,** ...**baum,** ...**ein|kauf,** ...**en|gel,** ...**fei|er,** ...**fei|er|tag,** ...**fe|ri|en** *(Plur.),* ...**fest,** ...**gans,** ...**ge|bäck,** ...**geld,** ...**ge|schäft,** ...**ge|schenk,** ...**ge|schich|te** (die; -), ...**gra|ti|fi|ka|ti|on,** ...**kak|tus,** ...**krip|pe,** ...**lied,** ...**mann** (*Plur.* ...männer), ...**markt,** ...**pa|pier,** ...**spiel,** ...**stern,** ...**stol|le** *od.* ...**stol|len** (*vgl.* Stolle; Backwerk), ...**tag,** ...**tel|ler,** ...**tisch,** ...**ver|kehr** (der; -s), ...**zeit** (die; -)
Weih|rauch (duftendes Harz); **weih|räu|chern;** ich ...ere (↑R 16); **Wei|hung; Weih|was|ser,** das; -s; **Weih|was|ser₋be|cken,** ...**kes|sel; Weih|we|del**
weil; [all]dieweil *(veraltet)*
wei|land (*veraltet, noch scherzh. für* vormals)
Weil|chen; warte ein -!; ein - ruhen; **Wei|le,** die; -; Lang[e]weile; Kurzweil; alleweil[e], bisweilen, zuweilen; [all]dieweil; einstweilen; mittlerweile; **wei|len** (*geh. für* sich aufhalten, bleiben)
Wei|ler, der; -s, - ‹lat.› (mehrere beieinander liegende Gehöfte; kleine Gemeinde)
Wei|mar (Stadt a. d. Ilm); **Wei|ma|rer** (↑R 103); **wei|ma|risch**
Wei|muts|kie|fer *vgl.* Weymouthskiefer
Wein, der; -[e]s, -e ‹lat.›; **Wein₋an|bau** (der; -[e]s), ...**bau,** (der; -[e]s); **wein|bau|end; Wein₋bau|er** (der; *Gen.* -n, *selten* -s, *Plur.* -n), ...**bee|re,** ...**bei|ßer** (*österr. für* eine Lebkuchenart; Weinkenner), ...**berg; Wein|berg[s]|be|sit|zer; Wein|berg|schne|cke; Wein|brand,** der; -s, ...brände (ein Branntwein); **Wein|brand|boh|ne**
wei|nen; (↑R 50:) in Weinen ausbrechen; ihr war das Weinen näher als das Lachen; das ist zum Weinen!; **wei|ner|lich; Wei|ner|lich|keit,** die; -
Wein₋es|sig, ...**fass,** ...**fla|sche,** ...**gar|ten** (*landsch. für* Weinberg), ...**gärt|ner** (*landsch. für* Winzer), ...**geist** (*Plur. [Sorten:]* ...geiste), ...**glas** (*Plur.* ...gläser), ...**gut,** ...**händ|ler,** ...**hand|lung,** ...**hau|er** (*österr. für* Winzer), ...**haus,** ...**he|fe; wei|nig** (weinhaltig; weinartig); **Wein₋kar|te,** ...**kauf** (Trunk bei Besiegelung eines Geschäftes; Draufgabe), ...**kel|ler,** ...**kel|le|rei,** ...**kell|ner,** ...**kel|ter,** ...**ken|ner,** ...**kö|ni|gin**
Wein|krampf
Wein₋la|ge, ...**le|se,** ...**lo|kal,** ...**mo|nat** *od.* ...**mond** (*alte dt. Bez. für* Oktober), ...**pan|scher** *(abwertend),* ...**pro|be,** ...**ran|ke,** ...**re|be; wein|rot; Wein|schaum** *(Gastron.);* **Wein|schaum|creme; wein|se|lig; Wein₋stein** (der; -[e]s; kaliumsaures Salz der Weinsäure), ...**steu|er** (die), ...**stock** (*Plur.* ...stöcke), ...**stra|ße** (die Deutsche Weinstraße; ↑R 108), ...**stu|be,** ...**trau|be,** ...**zierl** (der; -s, -n; *bayr., österr. mdal. für* Winzer, Weinbauer), ...**zwang** (der; -[e]s; Verpflichtung, in einem Lokal Wein zu bestellen)
wei|se (klug); [1]**Wei|se,** der *u.* die; -n, -n; ↑R 5 ff. (kluger Mensch); die Sieben Weisen (↑R 108)
[2]**Wei|se,** die; -, -n (Art; Singweise); auf diese Weise
...**wei|se;** *Zusammensetzungen* **a)** *aus Adjektiv u.* ...weise (z. B. klugerweise) *werden nur adverbiell gebraucht:* klugerweise sagte er nichts dazu, *aber* in kluger Weise; **b)** *aus Substantiv u.* ...weise (z. B. probeweise) *als Adverb:* er wurde probeweise eingestellt; *auch als Adjektiv bei Bezug auf ein Substantiv, das ein Geschehen ausdrückt:* eine probeweise Einstellung
Wei|sel, der; -s, -, *auch* die; -, -n (Bienenkönigin); **wei|sen** (zeigen; anordnen); du weist, er weist; du wiesest, er wies; gewiesen; weis[e]!; **Wei|ser** (*veraltet für* Uhrzeiger); **Weis|heit; weis|heits|voll; Weis|heits|zahn; weis|lich** (*veraltend für* wohlerwogen); **weis|ma|chen** (*ugs. für* vormachen, belügen, einreden usw.); ich mache weis; weisgemacht; weiszumachen; jmdm. etwas -
weiß (Farbe); *vgl.* blau. **I.** *Kleinschreibung:* **a)** (↑R 47:) etwas schwarz auf weiß (schriftlich) haben, nach Hause tragen; **b)** (↑R 108:) die weiße Fahne hissen (als Zeichen des Sichergebens); ein weißer Fleck auf der Landkarte (unerforschtes Gebiet); weiße Kohle (Wasserkraft); der weiße Sport (Tennis; Skisport); der weiße Tod (Erfrieren); ein weißer Rabe (*für* eine Seltenheit); eine weiße Weste haben (*ugs. für* unschuldig sein); weiße Mäuse sehen (*ugs. für* [im Rausch] Wahn-

[1] *Besonders fachsprachlich oft mit „ai" geschrieben.*

vorstellungen haben); weiße Maus (*ugs. auch für* Verkehrspolizist). **II.** *Großschreibung:* **a)** (↑R 47:) ein Weißer (weißer Mensch); eine Weiße (Berliner Bier); das Weiße; die Farbe Weiß; aus Schwarz Weiß, aus Weiß Schwarz machen; **b)** (↑R 102:) das Weiße Meer; der Weiße Berg; **c)** (↑R 108:) die Weiße Frau (Unglück kündende Spukgestalt in Schlössern); das Weiße Haus (Amtssitz des Präsidenten der USA in Washington); die Weiße Rose (Name einer Widerstandsgruppe während der Zeit des Nationalsozialismus); der Weiße Sonntag (Sonntag nach Ostern). **III.** *Schreibung in Verbindung mit Verben u. Partizipien:* weiß färben, kleiden, machen, werden; die Wäsche weiß waschen, *vgl. aber* weißbluten, weißwaschen *u.* weißnähen; weiß glühendes Metall; weiß gekleidete Kinder (*vgl.* Weiß); weiß gefärbte Stoffe; [1]**Weiß,** das; -[es], - (weiße Farbe); in Weiß [gekleidet]; mit Weiß [bemalt]; Stoffe in Weiß

[2]**Weiß,** Ernst (österr. Schriftsteller)

[3]**Weiß,** Konrad (dt. Lyriker, Dramatiker u. Essayist)

Weiss, Peter (dt. Schriftsteller)

weis|sa|gen; ich weissage; geweissagt; zu -; **Weis|sa|ger; Weis|sa|ge|rin; Weis|sa|gung**

Weiß‿bier, ...bin|der (*landsch. für* Böttcher, Anstreicher), **...blech; weiß|blond; weiß|blu|ten** (sich völlig verausgaben); (↑R 50:) bis zum Weißbluten (*ugs. für* sehr, in hohem Maße); **Weiß‿brot, ...buch** (Dokumentensammlung der dt. Regierung zu einer bestimmten Frage); **Weiß‿bu|che** (Hainbuche), **...dorn** (*Plur.* ...dorne); [1]**Wei|ße,** die; -, -n; ↑R 5 ff. (Bierart; *auch für* ein Glas Weißbier); [2]**Wei|ße,** der *u.* die; -n, -n; ↑R 5 ff. (Mensch mit heller Hautfarbe); [3]**Wei|ße,** die; - (Weißsein); **Wei|ße-Kra|gen-Kri|mi|na|li|tät,** die; -; ↑R 28 (z. B. Steuerhinterziehung); **wei|ßeln** (*südd. u. schweiz. für* weißen); ich ...[e]le (↑R 16); **wei|ßen** (weiß färben, machen; tünchen); du weißt, er weißt; du weißtest; geweißt; weiß[e]!

Wei|ßen|fels (Stadt an der Saale)

Wei|ße|ritz, die; - (l. Nebenfluss der mittleren Elbe)

Weiß‿fisch, ...fluss (der; -es; *Med.* weißlicher Ausfluss aus der Scheide), **...gar|dist** *(früher);* **weiß ge|klei|det** *vgl.* weiß; **Weiß|ger|ber; Weiß|ger|be|rei; weiß glü|hend** *vgl.* weiß; **Weiß‿glut** (die; -), **...gold**

weiß Gott!; für weiß Gott was halten *(ugs.)*

weiß|grau (↑R 27); **weiß|haa|rig; Weiß‿herbst** (hell gekelterter Wein aus blauen Trauben), **...käse** (Quark), **...kohl** (der; -[e]s), **...kraut** (das; -[e]s); **Weiß|la|cker** (eine Käsesorte); **weiß|lich; Weiß|lie|gen|de,** das; -n; ↑R 5 ff. (*Geol.* oberste Schicht des Rotliegenden); **Weiß|ling** (ein Schmetterling); **Weiß|ma|cher** (*Werbespr.* optischer Aufheller in einem Waschmittel); **weiß|nä|hen** (↑R 38 f.; Wäsche nähen); ich nähe weiß; weißgenäht; weißzunähen; **Weiß‿nä|he|rin, ...pap|pel**

Weiß|rus|se; Weiß|rus|sin; weiß|rus|sisch; *vgl.* belarussisch; **Weiß|russ|land** (Staat in Osteuropa)

Weiß‿sucht (die; -; *für* Albinismus), **...tan|ne; Wei|ßung** (Weißfärbung, Tünchung); **Weiß|wand|rei|fen; Weiß‿waren** *(Plur.),* **...wä|sche** (weiße [Koch]wäsche); **weiß|wa|schen** (↑R 38 f.); sich, jmdn. weißwaschen (*ugs. für* sich *od.* jmdn. von einem Verdacht od. Vorwurf befreien); *meist nur im Infinitiv u. Partizip II* (weißgewaschen) *gebr.; aber* Wäsche weiß waschen; **Weiß‿wein, ...wurst, ...zeug** (das; -[e]s; *veraltend für* Weißwaren)

Weis|tum, das; -s, ...tümer (Aufzeichnung von Rechtsgewohnheiten u. Rechtsbelehrungen im MA.); **Wei|sung** (Auftrag, Befehl); **Wei|sungs|be|fug|nis; wei|sungs‿be|rech|tigt, ...gebun|den, ...ge|mäß; Wei|sungsrecht**

weit; *vgl. auch* weiter. **I.** *Groß- u. Kleinschreibung:* (↑R 47:) am weitesten; bei, von weitem; weit und breit; so weit, so gut; das Weite suchen (sich [rasch] fortbegeben); sich ins Weite verlieren. **II. 1.** *In Verbindung mit Verben meist getrennt:* weit fahren, springen, bringen usw.; sie hat es weit gebracht; zu weit gehen; ..., was entschieden zu weit geht; *vgl. aber* weitspringen; **2.** *In Verbindung mit Partizipien* (↑R 40): eine weit geöffnete Tür; weit hergeholte Vermutungen; eine weit gereiste Forscherin; weit, weiter, am weitesten blickend, *auch* weitblickend, weitblickender, am weitblickendsten; er stellte weiter gehende, *auch* weitgehendere Forderungen; der Fall ist weitgehend gelöst; weit, weiter greifende, *auch* weitgreifende, weitgreifendere Pläne; [zu] weit reichende, *auch* weitreichende Vollmachten; weit, weiter tragende, *auch* weittragendere Konsequenzen; hierbei handelt es sich um weit verbreitete, *auch* weitverbreitete Pflanzen; ein weit verzweigtes, *auch* weitverzweigtes Unternehmen; **III.** *Zusammensetzungen:* insoweit *(vgl. d.);* inwieweit *(vgl. d.);* meilenweit *(vgl. d.);* soweit *(vgl. d.);* weither *(vgl. d.);* weithin *(vgl. d.);* **Weit,** das; -[e]s, -e (*fachspr. für* größte Weite [eines Schiffes]); **weit|ab; weit|aus;** - größer; **Weit|blick,** der; -[e]s; **weit|bli|ckend** *vgl.* weit, II 2; **Wei|te,** die; -, -n; **wei|ten** (weit machen, erweitern); sich -; **wei|ter;** weitere neue Bücher; weiteres Wichtiges; **I.** *Groß- u. Kleinschreibung* (↑R 47): bis auf weiteres; ohne weiteres (*österr. auch* ohneweiters); das Weitere hierüber folgt alsbald; [ein] Weiteres findet sich im nächsten Abschnitt; als Weiteres erhalten Sie ...; des Weiteren wurde berichtet ...; des Weiter[e]n enthoben sein; alles, einiges Weitere demnächst; wie im Weiteren dargestellt ... **II.** *In Verbindung mit Verben* (↑R 38 f.): **1.** *Getrenntschreibung:* **a)** *wenn* „weiter" *im Sinne von* „weiter als" *gebraucht wird;* weiter gehen; er kann weiter gehen als ich; **b)** *wenn* „weiter" *betont im Sinne von* „weiterhin" *gebraucht wird;* weiter helfen; er hat dir weiter (weiterhin) geholfen; die Probleme werden weiter bestehen; **2.** *Zusammenschreibung:* **a)** *wenn* „weiter" *in der Bedeutung von* „vorwärts", „voran" *(auch im übertragenen Sinne) gebraucht wird, z. B.* weiterbefördern; weiterhelfen; **b)** *wenn die Fortdauer eines Geschehens ausgedrückt wird, z. B.* weiterspielen

Wei|ter|ar|beit, die; -; **wei|ter|ar|bei|ten;** *vgl.* weiter, II

wei|ter|be|för|dern; ich befördere weiter; der Spediteur hat die Kiste nach Berlin weiterbefördert; *aber* der Kraftverkehr kann Stückgüter weiter befördern als die Eisenbahn; *vgl.* weiter, II; **Wei|ter|be|för|de|rung,** die; -

wei|ter be|ste|hen *vgl.* weiter, II

wei|ter|bil|den (fortbilden); *vgl.* weiter, II; **Wei|ter|bil|dung,** die; -

wei|ter|brin|gen; *vgl.* weiter, II

wei|ter|emp|feh|len; *vgl.* weiter, II

wei|ter|ent|wi|ckeln; *vgl.* weiter, II; **Wei|ter|ent|wick|lung**
wei|ter|er|zäh|len; *vgl.* weiter, II
wei|ter|fah|ren; *vgl.* weiter, II; **Wei|ter|fahrt,** die; -
wei|ter|flie|gen; *vgl.* weiter, II; **Wei|ter|flug,** der; -[e]s
wei|ter|füh|ren; *vgl.* weiter, II; **wei|ter|füh|rend;** die -en Schulen
Wei|ter|ga|be, die; -
Wei|ter|gang, der; -[e]s (Fortgang, Entwicklung)
wei|ter|ge|ben; *vgl.* weiter, II
wei|ter|ge|hen (vorangehen); die Arbeiten sind gut weitergegangen; bitte weitergehen!; *aber* ich kann weiter gehen als du; *vgl.* weiter, II
wei|ter|hel|fen; *vgl.* weiter, II
wei|ter|hin
wei|ter|kom|men; *vgl.* weiter, II
wei|ter|kön|nen (*ugs. für* weitergehen, weiterarbeiten können); *vgl.* weiter, II
wei|ter|lau|fen; *vgl.* weiter, II *u.* weitergehen
wei|ter|le|ben; *vgl.* weiter, II
wei|ter|lei|ten; *vgl.* weiter, II; **Wei|ter|lei|tung,** die; -
wei|ter|ma|chen; *vgl.* weiter, II
wei|tern (*selten für* erweitern); ich ...ere (↑R 16)
Wei|ter|rei|se, die; -; **wei|ter|rei|sen;** *vgl.* weiter, II
wei|ters (*österr. für* weiterhin)
wei|ter|sa|gen; *vgl.* weiter, II
wei|ter|schla|fen; *vgl.* weiter, II
wei|ter|se|hen; *vgl.* weiter, II
wei|ter|spie|len; *vgl.* weiter, II
wei|ter|trat|schen (*ugs. für* weitererzählen); *vgl.* weiter, II
wei|ter|trei|ben; *vgl.* weiter, II
Wei|te|rung *meist Plur.* (Schwierigkeit, Verwicklung)
wei|ter|ver|ar|bei|ten; *vgl.* weiter, II
wei|ter|ver|brei|ten; er hat das Gerücht weiterverbreitet; *aber* diese Krankheit ist heute weiter verbreitet als früher; *vgl.* weiter, II; **Wei|ter|ver|brei|tung**
wei|ter|ver|er|ben; *vgl.* weiter, II
wei|ter|ver|fol|gen; sein Ziel unbeirrt weiterverfolgen; *vgl.* weiter, II
Wei|ter|ver|kauf; wei|ter|ver|kau|fen; *vgl.* weiter, II
wei|ter|ver|mie|ten (in Untermiete geben); *vgl.* weiter, II
wei|ter|ver|mit|teln; *vgl.* weiter, II
wei|ter|ver|wen|den; *vgl.* weiter, II; **Wei|ter|ver|wen|dung**
wei|ter|wis|sen; *vgl.* weiter, II
wei|ter|wol|len (*ugs. für* weitergehen wollen); *vgl.* weiter, II
wei|ter|zah|len; *vgl.* weiter, II
wei|ter|zie|hen; *vgl.* weiter, II
weit|ge|hend *vgl.* weit, II 2
weit ge|reist *vgl.* weit, II 2
weit grei|fend *vgl.* weit, II 2
weit|her (aus großer Ferne), *aber* von weit her; damit ist es nicht weit her (das ist nicht bedeutend)
weit|her|zig; Weit|her|zig|keit, die; -
weit|hin; weithin zu hören sein; **weit|hi|naus** (↑R 132)
weit|läu|fig; Weit|läu|fig|keit
Weit|ling, der; -s, -e (*bayr., österr. für* große Schüssel)
weit|ma|schig
weit|räu|mig
weit rei|chend *vgl.* weit, II 2
weit schau|end *vgl.* weit, II 2
weit|schich|tig
Weit|schuss *(Sport)*
weit|schwei|fig; Weit|schwei|fig|keit
Weit|sicht, die; -; **weit|sich|tig; Weit|sich|tig|keit,** die; -
weit|sprin|gen *nur im Infinitiv gebr.;* **Weit|sprin|gen,** das; -s; **Weit|sprung**
weit tra|gend *vgl.* weit, II 2
Wei|tung
weit ver|brei|tet *vgl.* weit, II 2
weit ver|zweigt *vgl.* weit, II 2
Weit|win|kel|ob|jek|tiv
Wei|zen, der; -s, *Plur. (Sorten:)* -; **Wei|zen‿bier, ...brot, ...bröt|chen, ...ern|te, ...feld, ...keim** *(meist Plur.);* **Wei|zen|keim|öl; Wei|zen‿kleie, ...korn, ...mehl, ...preis**
Weiz|mann, Chaim [xaim] (israel. Staatsmann)
[1]**Weiz|sä|cker,** Carl Friedrich Freiherr von (dt. Physiker u. Philosoph); [2]**Weiz|sä|cker,** Richard Freiherr von (sechster dt. Bundespräsident)
welch; -er, -e, -es; welch ein Held; welch Wunder; welch große Männer; welches reizende Mädchen; welche großen, *seltener* große Frauen; welche Stimmberechtigten; welchen, *seltener* welches Staates?; **wel|che** (*ugs. für* etliche, einige); es sind - hier; **wel|cher|art;** wir wissen nicht, welcherart (was für ein) Interesse sie veranlasst ..., *aber* wir wissen nicht, welcher Art (Sorte, Gattung) diese Bücher sind; **wel|cher|ge|stalt; wel|cher|lei; wel|ches** (*ugs. auch für* etwas); Hat noch jemand Brot? Ich habe -
Welf, der; -[e]s, -e *od.* das; -[e]s, -er (*Nebenform von* Welpe)
Wel|fe, der; -n, -n; ↑R 126 (Angehöriger eines dt. Fürstengeschlechtes); **wel|fisch**
welk; -e Blätter; **wel|ken; Welk|heit,** die; -
Well‿baum (um seine Achse beweglicher Balken [am Mühlrad u. a.]), **...blech; Well|blech|dach;**
Wel|le, die; -, -n; grüne -; **wel|len;** gewelltes Blech, Haar; **wel|len|ar|tig; Wel|len‿bad, ...berg, ...bre|cher; wel|len|för|mig; Wel|len‿gang** (der; -[e]s), **...kamm, ...län|ge, ...li|nie, ...rei|ten** (das; -s; *Wassersport*), **...rei|ter, ...sa|lat** (der; -[e]s; *ugs. für* ein Nebeneinander sich gegenseitig störender Sender), **...schlag** (der; -[e]s), **...sit|tich** (ein Vogel), **...strah|len** *(Plur.; Physik),* **...strah|lung, ...tal; Wel|ler,** der; -s, - (mit Stroh vermischter Lehm zur Ausfüllung von Fachwerk); **wel|lern** (Weller herstellen, [Fachwerk] mit Weller ausfüllen); ich ...ere (↑R 16); **Wel|ler|wand** (Fachwerkwand); **Well|fleisch; Well|horn|schne|cke; wel|lig** (wellenartig, gewellt); **Wel|lig|keit,** die; -; **Wel|li|né** [...'ne:], der; -[s], -s (ein Gewebe)
Wel|ling|ton [*engl.* 'wɛliŋtən] (brit. Feldmarschall; Hptst. von Neuseeland); **Wel|ling|to|nia,** die; -, ...ien [...iən] (*svw.* Sequoie)
Well‿pap|pe, ...rad; Wel|lung
Wel|pe, der; -n, -n; ↑R 126 (das Junge von Hund, Fuchs, Wolf)
[1]**Wels,** der; -es, -e (ein Fisch)
[2]**Wels** (oberösterr. Stadt)
welsch ⟨kelt.⟩ (*urspr. für* keltisch, *später für* romanisch, französisch, italienisch; *veraltet für* fremdländisch; *schweiz. svw.* welschschweizerisch); **Wel|sche,** der *u.* die; -n, -n; ↑R 5 ff. *(veraltet);* **wel|schen** (*veraltet für* viele entbehrliche Fremdwörter gebrauchen); du welschst; **Welsch‿kraut** (das; -[e]s; *landsch. für* Wirsing), **...land** (das; -[e]s; *schweiz. für* franz. Schweiz), **...schwei|zer** (Schweizer mit franz. Muttersprache); **welsch|schwei|ze|risch** (die franz. Schweiz betreffend)
Welt, die; -, -en; die Dritte - (die Entwicklungsländer); Welten umspannend (*geh. für* weltumspannend); **welt|ab|ge|wandt; Welt‿ab|ge|wandt|heit** (die; -), **...all; welt|an|schau|lich; Welt‿an|schau|ung, ...at|las, ...aus|stel|lung, ...bank** (die; -); **welt‿be|kannt, ...be|rühmt; Welt|be|rühmt|heit; welt|bes|te;** die -n Sprinter; **Welt|best‿leis|tung** *(Sport),* **...zeit** *(Sport);* **welt|be|we|gend** (↑R 40); **Welt‿bild, ...bumm|ler** (*vgl.* Weltenbumm-

ler), **...bund, ...bür|ger; welt|bür|ger|lich; Welt‿bür|ger|tum** (das Weltbürgersein), **...chro|nik, ...cup** *(Sport);* **Welt|cup‿punkt, ...ren|nen; Welt|eli|te** (↑R 132; *bes. Sport);* **Wel|ten‿bumm|ler** (*od.* Welt|bumm|ler), **...raum** (*geh. für* Weltraum); **welt|ent|rückt** *(geh.);* **Wel|ten um|span|nend** *vgl.* Welt; **Welt|er|folg**

Wel|ter|ge|wicht ⟨engl.; dt.⟩ (eine Körpergewichtsklasse in der Schwerathletik); **Wel|ter|ge|wicht|ler**

wel|ter|schüt|ternd (↑R 40); **Welt|esche** (↑R 132), die; -; *vgl.* Yggdrasil; **welt|fern; Welt|flucht,** die; -; **welt|fremd; Welt‿fremd|heit, ...frie|de[n]** (der; ...ns), **...geist** (der; -[e]s), **...geist|li|che** (der), **...gel|tung, ...ge|richt** (das; -[e]s), **...ge|sche|hen, ...ge|schich|te** (die; -); **welt|ge|schicht|lich; Welt|ge|sund|heits|or|ga|ni|sa|ti|on,** die; -; (*vgl.* WHO); **welt|ge|wandt; Welt|ge|wandt|heit; Welt‿ge|werk|schafts|bund** (der; -[e]s; *Abk.* WGB), **...han|del** (*vgl.* [1]Handel), **...herr|schaft** (die; -), **...hilfs|spra|che; Welt|jah|res‿best|leis|tung** *(Sport),* **...best|zeit** *(Sport);* **Welt‿kar|te, ...kir|chen|kon|fe|renz, ...klas|se** (die; -; *Sport*); **Welt|klas|se‿sport|ler, ...sport|le|rin; welt|klug; Welt|klug|heit,** die; -; **Welt|krieg;** (↑R 56:) der Erste Weltkrieg (1914–1918); der Zweite Weltkrieg (1939–1945); **Welt‿ku|gel, ...kul|tur|er|be, ...lauf** (der; -[e]s; *selten*); **welt|läu|fig; Welt|läu|fig|keit,** die; -; **welt|lich; Welt|lich|keit,** die; -; **Welt‿li|te|ra|tur** (die; -), **...macht, ...mann** (*Plur.* ...männer); **welt|män|nisch; Welt‿mar|ke, ...markt, ...meer, ...meis|ter, ...meis|te|rin, ...meis|ter|schaft** (*Abk.* WM); **welt|of|fen; Welt|of|fen|heit,** die; -; **Welt‿öf|fent|lich|keit** (die; -), **...ord|nung, ...po|li|tik** (die; -); **welt|po|li|tisch; Welt|post|ver|ein,** der; -s; **Welt‿pre|mi|e|re, ...pres|se, ...pries|ter, ...rang; Welt|rang|lis|te** *(Sport);* **Welt|raum** (der; -[e]s); **Welt|raum‿fah|rer, ...fahrt, ...fahr|zeug, ...flug, ...for|schung** (die; -), **...la|bor, ...son|de, ...sta|ti|on; Welt‿reich, ...rei|se, ...rei|sen|de, ...re|kord, ...re|li|gi|on, ...re|vo|lu|ti|on** (die; -), **...ruf** (der; -[e]s; Berühmtheit), **...ruhm, ...schmerz** (der; -es), **...si|cher|heits|rat** (der; -[e]s), **...spar|tag, ...spit|ze, ...spra|che, ...stadt, ...star** (*vgl.* [2]Star), **...um|se|ge|lung, ...um|seg|ler, ...um|seg|lung; welt|um|span|nend; Welt‿un|ter|gang, ...ver|bes|se|rer, ...wäh|rungs|kon|fe|renz; welt|weit; Welt|wirt|schaft,** die; -; **Welt|wirt|schafts|kri|se; Welt‿wun|der, ...zeit|uhr**

wem; Wem|fall, der (*für* Dativ)

wen

Wen|cke (w. Vorn.)

[1]**Wen|de,** die; -, -n (Drehung, Wendung; Turnübung)

[2]**Wen|de,** der; -n, -n; ↑R 126 (Sorbe; *nur Plur.: frühere dt. Bez. für* die Slawen)

Wen|de‿hals (ein Vogel; *ugs. abwertend für* jmd., der sich polit. Änderungen schnell anpasst), **...ham|mer** (am Ende einer Sackgasse), **...kreis; Wen|del,** die; -, -n (schraubenförmige Wicklung [z. B. eines Lampenglühdrahtes]);

Wen|del|boh|rer

Wen|de|lin (m. Vorn.)

Wen|del‿rut|sche (*Bergmannsspr.* Rutschenspirale zum Abwärtsfördern von Kohlen u. Steinen), **...trep|pe; Wen|de‿ma|nö|ver, ...mar|ke** *(Sport);* **wen|den;** du wandtest *u.* wendetest; du wendetest; gewandt *u.* gewendet; wend[e]!; *in der Bed.* „die Richtung während der Fortbewegung ändern" [z. B. mit dem Auto] *u.* „umkehren, umdrehen [u. die andere Seite zeigen]", z. B. „einen Mantel usw., Heu wenden", *nur:* er wendete, hat gewendet; ein gewendeter Rock; *sonst:* sie wandte, *seltener* wendete sich zu ihm, hat sich zu ihm gewandt, *seltener* gewendet; ein gewandter (geschickter) Mann; sich wenden; bitte wenden! (*Abk.* b. w.); **Wen|de‿platz, ...punkt, ...schal|tung** *(Elektrotechnik);* **wen|dig** (sich leicht lenken, steuern lassend; geschickt, geistig regsam, sich schnell anpassend); **Wen|dig|keit,** die; -

Wen|din ⟨*zu* [2]Wende⟩; **wen|disch**

Wen|dung

Wen|fall, der (*für* Akkusativ)

we|nig; (↑R 48:) ein wenig (etwas, ein bisschen); ein weniges; mit ein wenig Geduld; ein klein wenig; einiges wenige; das, dies, dieses wenige; dieses Kleine u. wenige; weniges genügt; die wenigen; wenige glauben; einige wenige; mit wenig[em] auskommen; in dem wenigen, was erhalten ist; fünf weniger drei ist, macht, gibt (*nicht:* sind, machen, geben) zwei; umso weniger; nichts weniger als; nicht[s] mehr u. nicht[s] weniger; nichtsdestoweniger; du weißt nicht, wie wenig ich habe; wie wenig gehört dazu!; ein wenig gelesenes Buch; (↑R 47:) wenig Gutes *od.* weniges Gutes, wenig Neues; (↑R 48:) es ist das wenigste; das wenigste, was du tun kannst, ist ...; am, zum wenigsten; er beschränkt sich auf das wenigste; die wenigsten; wenigstens; du hast für dieses Amt zu wenig Erfahrung; ein Zuwenig an Fleiß. *Beugung der Adjektive in Verbindung mit* „wenige": mit weniger geballter Energie; mit wenigem guten Getränk; wenige gute Nachbildungen; weniger guter Menschen; wenige Gute gleichen viel[e] Schlechte aus; das Leiden weniger Guter; **We|nig,** das; -s, -; viele Wenig machen ein Viel; **We|nig|keit,** die; -; eine - an Mühe; meine - (*ugs. scherzh. für* ich); **we|nigs|tens**

wenn; wenn auch; wenngleich (*doch auch durch ein Wort getrennt,* z. B. wenn ich gleich Hans heiße); wennschon; wennschon – dennschon; *aber* wenn schon das nicht geht; (↑R 81:) komme doch [,] wenn möglich [,] schon um 17 Uhr; **Wenn,** das; -s, - (↑R 49); das Wenn und das Aber; ohne Wenn und Aber; viele Wenn und Aber; **wenn|gleich;** *vgl.* wenn; **wenn|schon;** *vgl.* wenn

[1]**Wen|zel** (m. Vorn.); [2]**Wen|zel,** der; -s, - (*Kartenspiel* Bube, Unter); **Wen|zels|kro|ne,** die; - (böhm. Königskrone); **Wen|zes|laus** (m. Vorn.)

wer *fragendes, bezügliches u. (ugs.) unbestimmtes Pronomen;* Halt! Wer da? (*vgl.* Werda); wer (derjenige, welcher) das tut, [der] ...; ist wer (*ugs. für* jemand) gekommen?; wer alles; irgendwer (*vgl.* irgend); wes *(vgl. d.)*

We|ra (w. Vorn.)

Wer|be‿ab|tei|lung, ...agen|tur (↑R132), **...an|teil** (*für* Provision), **...bran|che, ...etat** (↑R 132), **...fach|mann, ...feld|zug, ...fern|se|hen, ...film, ...funk, ...ge|schenk, ...gra|fi|ker** (↑R 33), **...gra|fi|ke|rin, ...kam|pag|ne, ...kauf|frau, ...kauf|mann, ...kos|ten** *(Plur.);* **wer|be|kräf|tig; Wer|be‿lei|ter** (der), **...mit|tel** (das); **wer|ben;** du wirbst; du warbst; du würbest; geworben; wirb!; **Wer|ber; Wer|be|rin; wer|be|risch; Wer|be‿slo|gan, ...spot, ...spruch, ...text, ...tex|ter** (jmd., der Werbetexte ver-

fasst), **...tex|te|rin, ...trä|ger, ...trom|mel** (*in* die - rühren [*ugs. für* Reklame machen]); **wer|be|wirk|sam; Wer|be_wirk|sam|keit, ...zweck** (*meist in* zu -en); **werb|lich** (die Werbung betreffend); **Wer|bung; Wer|bungs|kos|ten** *Plur.*
Wer|da, das; -[s], -s (*Milit.* Postenanruf)
Wer|dan|di (*nord. Mythol.* Norne der Gegenwart)
Wer|da|ruf
Wer|de|gang, der; **wer|den;** du wirst, er wird; du wurdest, *geh. noch* wardst, er wurde, *geh. noch* ward, wir wurden; du würdest; *als Vollverb:* geworden; er ist groß geworden; *als Hilfsverb:* worden; er ist gelobt worden; werd[e]!; (↑R 50:) das ist noch im Werden; **wer|dend;** eine werdende Mutter
Wer|der, der, *selten* das; -s, - (Flussinsel; Landstrich zwischen Fluss u. stehenden Gewässern)
Wer|der (Ha|vel) (Stadt westl. von Potsdam)
Wer|fall, der (*für* Nominativ)
Wer|fel (österr. Schriftsteller)
wer|fen (*von Tieren auch für* gebären); du wirfst; du warfst; du würfest; geworfen; wirf!; sich werfen; **Wer|fer; Wer|fe|rin**
Werft, die; -, -en ‹niederl.› (Anlage zum Bauen u. Ausbessern von Schiffen); **Werft|ar|bei|ter**
Werg, das; -[e]s (Flachs-, Hanfabfall)
Wer|geld (Sühnegeld für Totschlag im germ. Recht)
wer|gen (aus Werg); wergene Stricke
Werk, das; -[e]s, -e; ans Werk!; ans Werk, zu Werke gehen; ins Werk setzen; **Werk_an|ge|hö|ri|ge**[1], **...an|la|ge**[1], **...ar|beit, ...arzt**[1], **...bank** (*Plur.* ...bänke), **...bü|che|rei**[1], **...bund** (der; Deutscher -), **...bus**[1]; **werk|el|gen**[1]; **Wer|kel**, das; -s, -[n] (*österr. ugs. für* Leierkasten, Drehorgel); **Wer|kel|mann** *Plur.* ...männer (*österr. für* Drehorgelspieler); **wer|keln** (*landsch. für* [angestrengt] werken); ich ...[e]le (↑R 16); **wer|ken** (tätig sein; [be]arbeiten); **...wer|ker** (z.B. Handwerker, Heimwerker); **Werk_fah|rer**[1], **...ga|ran|tie**[1], **...ge|rech|tig|keit** (*Theol.*); **werk|ge|treu; Werk_hal|le**[1], **...kin|der|gar|ten**[1], **...kü|che**[1], **...leh|rer**[1], **...lei|ter**[1] (der), **...lei|tung**[1]; **werk|lich** (*veraltet*);

[1] *Auch, österr. nur,* werks..., Werks...

Werk_meis|ter, ...schu|le, ...schutz; werk|sei|tig[1] (vonseiten des Werks); **Werk|spi|o|na|ge**[1]; **Werk|statt**, Werk|stät|te, die; -, ...stätten; **Werk|stät|te** *vgl.* Werkstatt; **werk|statt|ge|pflegt;** ein -es Auto; **Werk|statt|ta|ge** (↑R 136) *Plur.*; - der Kunst und Kultur; **Werk|stoff; Werk|stoff|for|schung** (↑R 136), die; -; **werk|stoff|ge|recht; Werk|stoff_in|ge|ni|eur, ...kun|de** (die; -); **Werk|stoff_prü|fung; Werk_stück, ...stu|dent; Werk|tag** (Arbeitstag); des Werktags, *aber* (↑R 46): werktags; **werk|täg|lich; werk|tags;** *vgl.* Werktag; **Werk|tags|ar|beit; werk|tä|tig; Werk|tä|ti|ge**, der *u.* die; -n, -n (↑R 5 ff.); **Werk_ti|tel, ...treue, ...un|ter|richt, ...ver|zeich|nis** (*Musik, bild. Kunst*), **...woh|nung**[1], **...zeit|schrift**[1], **...zeug; Werk|zeug_kas|ten, ...ma|cher, ...ma|che|rin, ...ma|schi|ne, ...stahl** (*vgl.* [1]Stahl)
Wer|mut, der; -[e]s, -s (eine Pflanze; Wermutwein); **Wer|mut|bru|der** (*ugs. für* [betrunkener] Stadtstreicher); **Wer|mut[s]|trop|fen; Wer|mut|wein**
Wer|ner, *älter* Wern|her (m. Vorn.)
Wern|hard (m. Vorn.)
Wer|ra, die; - (Quellfluss der Weser)
Wer|re, die; -, -n (*südd., österr. u. schweiz. mdal. für* Maulwurfsgrille; Gerstenkorn)
Werst, die; -, -en ‹russ.› (altes russ. Längenmaß; *Zeichen* W); 5 - (↑R 90)
wert; wert sein; du bist keinen Schuss Pulver (*ugs. für* nichts) wert; das ist keinen Heller (*ugs. für* nichts) wert; *in der Bedeutung* „würdig" *mit Gen.:* das ist höchster Bewunderung wert; es ist nicht der Rede wert; jmdn. des Vertrauens [für] wert achten, halten; *vgl. aber* wertschätzen; **Wert**, der; -[e]s, -e (Bedeutung, Geltung); auf etwas - legen; von - sein; **Wert_ach|tung** (*veraltet*), **...an|ga|be, ...ar|beit** (die; -); **wert|be|stän|dig; Wert|be|stän|dig|keit**, die; -; **Wert|brief; wer|ten; Wert|er|mitt|lung** (*für* Taxation); **Wer|te|ska|la**, Wertska|la; **wert|frei;** -es Urteil; **Wert|ge|gen|stand**
Wer|ther (Titelgestalt eines Romans von Goethe)
...wer|tig (z.B. minderwertig);

[1] *Auch, österr. nur,* werks..., Werks...

Wer|tig|keit; Wert|leh|re (*Philos.*); **wert|los; Wert|lo|sig|keit**, die; -; **Wert_mar|ke, ...maß** (das); **wert|mä|ßig; Wert_mes|ser** (der), **...min|de|rung, ...pa|ket, ...pa|pier; Wert|pa|pier|bör|se; Wert|sa|che** *meist Plur.*; **wert|schät|zen** (*veraltend;* ↑R 37 f.); du schätzt wert *od.* wertschätzt; wertgeschätzt; wertzuschätzen; **Wert_schät|zung, ...schrift** (*schweiz. für* Wertpapier), **...sen|dung, ...ska|la** (*vgl.* Werteskala), **...stei|ge|rung, ...stel|lung** (*Bankw.*), **...stoff; Wert|stoff_samm|lung, ...ton|ne; Wer|tung; Wer|tungs|lauf** (*Motorsport*); **Wert|ur|teil; wert|voll; Wert_vor|stel|lung** (*meist Plur.*), **...zei|chen, ...zu|wachs; Wert|zu|wachs|steu|er**, die
wer|wei|ßen (*schweiz. für* hin u. her raten); du werweißt; gewerweißt
Wer|wolf, der (im Volksglauben Mensch, der sich zeitweise in einen Wolf verwandelt)
wes (*ältere Form von* wessen); wes das Herz voll ist, des geht der Mund über; wes Brot ich ess, des Lied ich sing!; weshalb (*vgl. d.*); weswegen (*vgl. d.*)
We|sel (Stadt am Niederrhein)
we|sen (*veraltet für* als lebende Kraft vorhanden sein); du west; er wes|te; **We|sen**, das; -s, -; viel Wesen[s] machen; sein Wesen treiben; **we|sen|haft** (*geh.*); **We|sen|heit**, die; - (*geh.*); **we|sen|los; We|sen|lo|sig|keit**, die; -; **We|sens|art; we|sens_ei|gen, ...fremd, ...ge|mäß, ...gleich, ...ver|wandt; We|sens|zug; we|sent|lich;** (↑R 47): das Wesentliche; etwas, nichts Wesentliches; im Wesentlichen
We|ser, die; - (dt. Strom); **We|ser|berg|land**, das; -[e]s (↑R 105); **We|ser|ge|bir|ge**, das; -s; ↑R 105 (Höhenzug im Weserbergland)
Wes|fall, der (*für* Genitiv); **wes|halb** [*auch* 'vɛs...]
We|sir, der; -s, -e ‹arab.› (*früher* Minister islam. Herrscher)
Wes|ley ['wɛsli] (engl. Stifter des Methodismus); **Wes|ley|a|ner**
Wes|pe, die; -, -n; **Wes|pen_nest, ...stich, ...tail|le** (sehr schlanke Taille)
Wes|sel|bu|ren (Stadt in Schleswig-Holstein)
Wes|se|ly (österr. Schauspielerin)
wes|sen; *vgl.* wes; **wes|sent|we|gen** (*veraltet für* weswegen); **wes|sent|wil|len;** *nur in* um - (*veraltend*)

Wẹs|si, der; -s, -s (*ugs. für* Bewohner der alten Bundesländer, Westdeutscher)
Wes|so|brụnn (Ort in Oberbayern); **Wes|so|brụn|ner** (↑R 103); das - Gebet
[1]**Wẹst** (Himmelsrichtung; *Abk.* W); Ost u. West; *fachspr.*: der Wind kommt aus West; Autobahnausfahrt Frankfurt West (↑R 106); *vgl.* Westen; [2]**Wẹst**, der; -[e]s, -e *Plur. selten* (*geh. für* Westwind); der kühle West blies um das Haus; **Wẹst‿a̱f|ri|ka, ...aust|ra̱|li|en; Wẹst|ber|lin** (↑R 105); **Wẹst|ber|li|ner; wẹstdeutsch,** *aber* (↑R 108): Westdeutsche Rektorenkonferenz; **Wẹst|deutsch|land**
Wẹs|te, die; -, -n ‹franz.›
Wẹs|ten, der; -s (Himmelsrichtung; *Abk.* W); gen Westen; *vgl.* [1]West; Wilder Westen (↑R 108)
Wẹst|end, das; -s, -s ‹engl.› (vornehmer Stadtteil [Londons])
Wẹs|ten|ta|sche; Wẹs|ten|taschen|for|mat; im - (*scherzh. für* klein; unbedeutend)
Wẹs|tern, der; -[s], - ‹amerik.› (Film, der im sog. Wilden Westen [Amerikas] spielt)
Wẹs|ter|wald, der; -[e]s (Teil des Rheinischen Schiefergebirges); **Wẹs|ter|wäl|der**, der; **wẹs|terwäl|disch;** -e Mundarten
Wẹst|eu|ro̱|pa; wẹst|eu|ro|pä̱isch; -e Zeit (*Abk.* WEZ); *aber* (↑R 108): die Westeuropäische Union (*Abk.* WEU)
West|fa̱|le, der; -n, -n (↑R 126); **West|fa̱|len; West|fä̱|lin; westfä̱|lisch;** (↑R 104 *u.* R 108:) westfälischer Schinken, *aber* (↑R 102): die Westfälische Pforte (*vgl.* [1]Porta Westfalica); (↑R 108:) der Westfälische Friede[n]
Wẹst|flan|dern (belg. Provinz)
Wẹst|geld (*in der ehem. DDR ugs. für* frei konvertierbare Währung als zweites Zahlungsmittel)
wẹst|ger|ma|nisch
Wẹst|ịn|di|en; wẹst|ịn|disch, *aber* (↑R 102): die Westindischen Inseln
Wes|ting|house|brem|se ® ['wɛstiŋha̱us...] (↑R 95; *Eisenb.*)
Wẹst|küs|te; Wẹst|ler (*ugs. für* Bewohner der Bundesrepublik aus der Sicht der ehem. DDR); **wẹst|le|risch** ([betont] westlich [westeuropäisch] eingestellt); **wẹst|lich;** westlich des Waldes, westlich vom Wald; westlicher Länge (*Abk.* w[estl]. L.); die westliche Hemisphäre; **Wẹst|li|che Dwi̱|na**, die; -n -; ↑R 102 (russ.-lett. Strom; *vgl.* Dwina)
Wẹst|mäch|te *Plur.*
Wẹst|mark, die; -, - (*ugs. für* Mark der Bundesrepublik Deutschland bis zur Währungsunion 1990)
Wẹst|mins|ter|ab|tei, die; - (in London)
[1]**West|nord|wẹst**, der; -s (Himmelsrichtung; *Abk.* WNW); [2]**West|nord|wẹst**, der; -[e]s, -e *Plur. selten* (Wind; *Abk.* WNW); **West|nord|wẹs|ten**, der; -s (*Abk.* WNW)
wẹst|ọ̈st|lich; ein westöstlicher Wind, *aber* (↑R 108): der Westöstliche Diwan (Gedichtsammlung Goethes); **Wẹst-Ọst-Verkehr** (↑R 28)
Wes|to̱|ver [...vər] (↑R 132), der; -s, - ‹engl.› (ärmelloser Pullover mit [spitzem] Ausschnitt)
Wẹst|rom; wẹst|rö|misch, *aber* das Weströmische Reich
West|sa|mo̱a (Inselstaat im Pazifischen Ozean); **West|sa|mo|a̱ner; west|sa|mo|a̱|nisch**
[1]**West|süd|wẹst** (Himmelsrichtung; *Abk.* WSW); [2]**West|südwẹst**, der; -[e]s, -e *Plur. selten* (Wind; *Abk.* WSW); **West|südwẹs|ten**, der; -s (*Abk.* WSW)
Wẹst Vir|gi|nia [- vir'gi:..., *auch, österr. nur,* vir'd͜ʒi:..., *engl.* 'wɛst vœ(r)'d͜ʒinjə] (Staat in den USA; *Abk.* W. Va.)
wẹst|wärts; Wẹst|wind
wes|we̱|gen
wẹtt (*selten für* quitt); wett sein; *vgl. aber* wetteifern, wettlaufen, wettmachen, wettrennen, wettstreiten, wettturnen; **Wẹtt‿annah|me, ...be|werb** (der; -[e]s, -e), **...be|wer|ber; wẹtt|bewerb|lich; Wẹtt|be|werbs‿bedin|gung, ...be|schrän|kung; wẹtt|be|werbs|fä|hig; Wẹtt|bewerbs‿teil|neh|mer, ...ver|zerrung, ...wirt|schaft** (die; -); **Wẹtt|bü|ro; Wẹt|te**, die; -, -n; um die - laufen; **Wẹtt‿ei|fer, ...ei|fe|rer; wẹtt|ei|fern** (↑R 37) ich wetteifere (↑R 16); gewetteifert; zu wetteifern; **wẹt|ten;** [1]**Wẹt|ter**, der (jmd., der wettet)
[2]**Wẹt|ter**, das; -s, - (*Bergmannsspr auch für* alle in der Grube vorkommenden Gase); schlagende, böse, matte - *(Bergmannsspr.)*; **Wẹt|ter‿amt, ...an|sa|ge**
Wẹt|te|rau, die; - (Senke zwischen dem Vogelsberg u. dem Taunus)
Wẹt|ter‿aus|sicht *(meist Plur.)*, **...be|richt, ...be|ru|hi|gung, ...bes|se|rung; wẹt|ter‿bestän|dig, ...be|stim|mend; Wẹtter‿dach, ...dienst, ...fah|ne; wẹt|ter|fest; Wẹt|ter‿fleck** (*österr. für* Lodencape), **...frosch; wẹt|ter|füh|lig; Wẹt|ter|füh|ligkeit**, die; -; **Wẹt|ter‿füh|rung** *(Bergmannsspr.)*, **...glas** (*Plur.* ...gläser; *veraltet für* Barometer), **...gott, ...hahn, ...häus|chen, ...kar|te, ...kun|de** (die; -; *für* Meteorologie); **wẹt|ter|kun|dig; wẹt|ter|kund|lich** (*für* meteorologisch); **Wẹt|ter|la|ge; wẹt|terleuch|ten** (↑R 37); es wetterleuchtet; gewetterleuchtet; zu wetterleuchten; **Wẹt|ter|leuchten**, das; -s; **wẹt|tern** (gewittern; *ugs. für* laut schelten); ich ...ere (↑R 16); es wettert; **Wẹtter‿prog|no|se, ...pro|phet** (*scherzh. für* Meteorologe), **...regel, ...sa|tel|lit, ...schei|de, ...seite, ...sta|ti|on, ...sturz, ...umschlag, ...um|schwung, ...vorher|sa|ge, ...war|te, ...wech|sel; wẹt|ter|wen|disch**
Wẹtt‿fah|rer, ...fahrt
Wet|ti̱n (Stadt a. d. Saale); Haus - (ein dt. Fürstengeschlecht); **Wetti̱|ner**, der; -s, - (↑R 103); **wet|ti̱nisch,** *aber* (↑R 108): die Wettinischen Erblande
Wẹtt‿kampf *(bes. Sport)*, **...kämp|fer, ...kämp|fe|rin; wẹtt|kampf|mä|ßig; Wẹtt|lauf; wẹtt|lau|fen** *nur im Infinitiv gebr.*; **Wẹtt|lau|fen**, das; -s; **Wẹtt‿läu|fer, ...läu|fe|rin; wẹttma|chen** (↑R 38; ausgleichen); ich mache wett; wettgemacht; wettzumachen; **wẹtt|ren|nen;** *vgl.* wettlaufen; **Wẹtt‿ren|nen, ...ru|dern** (das; -s), **...rüs|ten** (das; -s), **...schwim|men** (das; -s), **...spiel, ...streit; wẹtt|streiten;** *vgl.* wettlaufen; **Wẹtt|tauchen** (↑R 136), das; -s; **Wẹttteu|fel** (↑R 136); **wẹtt|tur|nen** (↑R 136); *vgl.* wettlaufen; **Wẹtttur|nen** (↑R 136), das; -s, -
wẹt|zen; du wetzt
Wẹtz|lar (Stadt an der Lahn)
Wẹtz‿stahl (*vgl.* [1]Stahl), **...stein**
WEU = Westeuropäische Union
Wey|mouths|kie|fer ['va̱imu:t͜s...], *auch* **We̱i|muts|kie|fer** ‹nach Lord Weymouth› (nordamerik. Kiefer)
WEZ = westeuropäische Zeit
WG = Wohngemeinschaft
wg. = wegen
WGB = Weltgewerkschaftsbund
Whig [wig], der; -s, -s ‹engl.› (Angehöriger der brit. liberalen Partei); *vgl.* Tory
Whip|cord ['wip...], der; -s, -s ‹engl.› (ein Anzugstoff mit Schrägrippen)
Whirl|pool ® ['wœ:(r)lpu:l], der; -s, -s ‹engl.› (Bassin mit sprudelndem Wasser)

Whis|key ['wiski], der; -s, -s ‹gälisch-engl.› (amerik. od. irischer Whisky); **Whis|ky** ['wiski], der; -s, -s ([schott.] Branntwein aus Getreide od. Mais); - pur
Whist [wist], das; -[e]s ‹engl.› (ein Kartenspiel); **Whist|spiel**
Whit|man ['witmən], Walt [wɔ:lt] (amerik. Lyriker)
Whit|worth|ge|win|de ['witwœ(r)θ...]; ↑R 95 (einheitliches Gewindesystem des engl. Ingenieurs Whitworth)
WHO = World Health Organization ['wœ:(r)ld 'hɛlθ ɔ:(r)gənaj'ze:ʃ(ə)n] (Weltgesundheitsorganisation)
Who's who ['hu:z 'hu:] ‹engl., „Wer ist wer?"› (Titel biograph. Lexika)
wib|be|lig (*landsch. für* nervös)
Wib|ke *vgl.* Wiebke
Wichs, der; -es, -e, *österr.* die; -, -en (Festkleidung der Korpsstudenten); in vollem -; sich in - werfen; **Wichs|bürs|te** (*ugs. für* Schuhbürste); **Wich|se,** die; -, -n (*ugs. für* Schuhwichse; *nur Sing.:* Prügel); **wich|sen** (*auch derb für* onanieren); du wichst; **Wich|ser** (derbes Schimpfwort); **Wichs|lein|wand** (*österr. ugs. für* Wachstuch)
Wicht, der; -[e]s, -e (Wesen; Kobold; *abwertend für* elender Kerl)
Wich|te, die; -, -n (*Physik veraltet für* Dichte)
Wich|tel, der; -s, -, **Wich|tel|männ|chen** (Heinzelmännchen)
wich|tig; am wichtigsten; (↑R 47:) alles Wichtige, etwas, nichts Wichtiges, Wichtigeres; sich wichtig machen; etwas, sich wichtig nehmen; [sich] wichtig tun; irgendwelche wichtig tuende Leute; **Wich|tig|keit; Wich|tig|macher** (*österr. für* Wichtigtuer); **wich|tig tu|end** *vgl.* wichtig; **Wich|tig|tu|er; Wich|tig|tu|e|rei; wich|tig|tu|e|risch**
Wi|cke, die; -, -n ‹lat.› (eine Pflanze); in die -n gehen (*ugs. für* verloren gehen)
Wi|ckel, der; -s, -; **Wi|ckel‿ga|ma|sche, ...kind, ...kom|mo|de; wi|ckeln;** ich ...[e]le (↑R 16); **Wi|ckel‿rock, ...tisch, ...tuch** (*Plur.* ...tücher); **Wi|cke|lung,** Wicklung
Wi|cken‿blü|te, ...duft
Wick|ler; Wick|lung *vgl.* Wickelung
Wi|dah, die; -, -s ‹nach dem Ort Ouidah in Afrika› (ein afrikan. Vogel); **Wi|dah|vo|gel**
Wid|der, der; -s, - (männl. Zuchtschaf; *nur Sing.:* ein Sternbild)
wi|der (*meist geh. für* [ent]gegen); *Präp. mit Akk.:* das war wider meinen ausdrücklichen Wunsch; wider [alles] Erwarten; wider Willen; *vgl. aber* wieder; das Für und [das] Wider
wi|der... *in Verbindung mit Verben:* **a)** *in unfesten Zusammensetzungen* (↑R 38), z. B. widerhallen *(vgl. d.),* widergehallt; **b)** *in festen Zusammensetzungen* (↑R 37), z. B. widersprechen *(vgl. d.),* widersprochen
wi|der|bors|tig (*ugs. für* hartnäckig widerstrebend)
Wi|der|christ, der; -[s] (*Rel.* der Teufel) *u.* der; -en, -en; ↑R 126 (Gegner des Christentums)
Wi|der|druck, der; -[e]s, ...drucke (*Druckw.* Bedrucken der Rückseite des Druckbogens [*vgl.* Schöndruck]); *vgl. aber* Wiederdruck
wi|der|ei|nan|der (*veraltend für* gegeneinander); *in Verbindung mit Verben immer getrennt:* widereinander arbeiten, kämpfen; widereinander stoßen usw.
wi|der|fah|ren; mir ist ein großes Unglück -
Wi|der|ha|ken
Wi|der|hall, der; -[e]s, -e (Echo); **wi|der|hal|len;** das Echo hat widergehallt
Wi|der|halt, der; -[e]s (Gegenkraft, Stütze)
Wi|der|hand|lung (*schweiz. für* Zuwiderhandlung)
Wi|der‿kla|ge (Gegenklage), **...klä|ger** (Gegenkläger)
Wi|der|klang; wi|der|klin|gen; der Schall hat widergeklungen
Wi|der|la|ger (*Technik* Verankerung, Auflagefläche für Bogen, Gewölbe, Träger); **wi|der|leg|bar; wi|der|le|gen;** er hat diesen Irrtum widerlegt; **Wi|der|le|gung**
wi|der|lich; Wi|der|lich|keit; Wi|der|ling (widerlicher Mensch)
wi|der|na|tür|lich; Wi|der|na|tür|lich|keit
Wi|der|part, der; -[e]s, -e (Gegner[schaft]); - geben, bieten
wi|der|ra|ten (*veraltend für* abraten); ich habe [es] ihm -
wi|der|recht|lich; Wi|der|recht|lich|keit
Wi|der|re|de; keine -!; **wi|der|re|den** (*selten für* widersprechen); sie hat widerredet
Wi|der|rist (erhöhter Teil des Rückens bei Vierfüßern)
Wi|der|ruf; bis auf -; **wi|der|ru|fen** (zurücknehmen); er hat sein Geständnis -; **wi|der|ruf|lich** [*auch* ...'ru:f...] *(Rechtsspr.);* **Wi|der|ruf|lich|keit,** die; -; **Wi|der|ru|fung**
Wi|der|sa|cher, der; -s, -
wi|der|schal|len (*veraltend für* widerhallen); der Ruf hat widergeschallt
Wi|der|schein (Gegenschein); **wi|der|schei|nen;** das Licht hat widergeschienen
Wi|der|see, die (*Seemannsspr.* rücklaufende Brandung)
wi|der|set|zen, sich; ich habe mich dem Plan widersetzt; **wi|der|setz|lich; Wi|der|setz|lich|keit**
Wi|der|sinn, der; -[e]s (Unsinn; logische Verkehrtheit); **wi|der|sin|nig; Wi|der|sin|nig|keit**
wi|der|spens|tig; Wi|der|spens|tig|keit
wi|der|spie|geln; die Sonne hat sich im Wasser widergespiegelt; **Wi|der|spie|ge|lung, Wi|der|spieg|lung**
Wi|der|spiel, das; -[e]s (*geh. für* das Gegeneinanderwirken)
wi|der|spre|chen; mir wird widersprochen; sich -; du widersprichst dir; **Wi|der|spruch; wi|der|sprüch|lich; Wi|der|sprüch|lich|keit; wi|der|spruchs|frei; Wi|der|spruchs‿geist** (der; -[e]s, ...geister; *nur Sing.:* Neigung, zu widersprechen; *ugs. für* jmd., der widerspricht), **...kla|ge** *(Rechtsw.);* **wi|der|spruchs|los; wi|der|spruchs|voll**
Wi|der|stand; Wi|der|stands|be|we|gung; wi|der|stands|fä|hig; Wi|der|stands‿fä|hig|keit (die; -), **...kampf** (der; -[e]s), **...kämp|fer, ...kraft** (die), **...li|nie; wi|der|stands|los; Wi|der|stands|lo|sig|keit,** die; -; **Wi|der|stands‿mes|ser** (der; *Elektrotechnik*), **...nest** *(Milit.),* **...pflicht** (die; -), **...recht** (das; -[e]s), **...wil|le; wi|der|ste|hen;** sie hat der Versuchung widerstanden
Wi|der|strahl; wi|der|strah|len; das Licht hat widergestrahlt
wi|der|stre|ben (entgegenwirken); es hat ihm widerstrebt; **Wi|der|stre|ben,** das; -s; **wi|der|stre|bend** (ungern)
Wi|der|streit; im - der Meinungen; **wi|der|strei|ten;** er hat ihm widerstritten
wi|der|wär|tig; Wi|der|wär|tig|keit
Wi|der|wil|le, *seltener* **Wi|der|wil|len; wi|der|wil|lig; Wi|der|wil|lig|keit**
Wi|der|wort *Plur.* ...worte; Widerworte geben
wid|men; sie hat ihm ihr letztes Buch gewidmet; ich habe mich der Kunst gewidmet; **Wid|mung; Wid|mungs|ta|fel**

Wi|do (m. Vorn.)
wid|rig (zuwider; *übertr. für* unangenehm); ein -es Geschick; **wid|ri|gen|falls** *(Amtsspr.); vgl.* Fall, der; **Wid|rig|keit**
Wi|du|kind, Wit|te|kind (ein Sachsenherzog)
Wi|dum, das; -s, -e (*österr. veraltet für* Pfarrgut)
wie; wie geht es dir?; sie ist so schön wie ihre Freundin, *aber bei Ungleichheit:* sie ist schöner als ihre Freundin; (↑R 72:) er ist so stark wie Ludwig; so schnell wie, *älter* als möglich; im Krieg wie [auch] (und [auch]) im Frieden; die Auslagen[,] wie [z. B.] Post- und Fernsprechgebühren sowie Eintrittsgelder[,] ersetzen wir; ich begreife nicht, wie so etwas möglich ist; komm so schnell, wie du kannst; (↑R 81:) er legte sich[,] wie üblich[,] ins Bett; wieso; wiewohl *(vgl. d.)*; wie sehr; wie lange; wie oft; wie viel *(vgl. d.);* wie [auch] immer; (↑R 49:) es kommt auf das Wie an
Wie|bel, der; -s, - (*landsch. für* Kornwurm, -käfer); **wie|beln** (*landsch. für* sich lebhaft bewegen; *ostmitteld. für* sorgfältig flicken, stopfen); ich ...[e]le (↑R 16); *vgl.* wiefeln
Wieb|ke, Wib|ke (w. Vorn.)
Wie|chert (dt. Schriftsteller)
[1]Wied, die; - (r. Nebenfluss des Mittelrheins); **[2]Wied** (mittelrhein. Adelsgeschlecht)
Wie|de, die; -, -n (*südd., südwestd. für* Weidenband, Flechtband)
Wie|de|hopf, der; -[e]s, -e (Vogel)
wie|der (nochmals, erneut; zurück); um, für nichts und wieder nichts; hin und wieder (zuweilen); wieder einmal; *vgl. aber* wider. **I.** *In Verbindung mit Verben gilt Zusammenschreibung vor allem dann, wenn* „wieder" *im Sinne von* „zurück" *verstanden wird:* ich kann dir das Geld erst morgen wiedergeben; der Restbetrag wurde ihr wiedererstattet; er hat alle geliehenen Bücher wiedergebracht; kann ich bitte meinen Kugelschreiber wiederhaben?; wenn du jetzt gehst, brauchst du nicht mehr wiederzukommen! *Zusammen schreibt man außerdem, wenn das Verb allein im gegebenen Zusammenhang unüblich wäre:* wiederkäuen ([von bestimmten Tieren:] nochmals kauen; *auch übertr. für* ständig wiederholen); Festtage, die jährlich wiederkehren (sich wiederholen); sie hat den Text wörtlich wiedergegeben (wiederholt); er wollte den Vorfall wahrheitsgetreu wiedergeben (schildern, darstellen); würden Sie den letzten Satz bitte wiederholen; das Fernsehspiel ist schon mehrfach wiederholt worden; eine Klasse, den Lehrstoff wiederholen; das Gebäude wird wiederhergestellt (renoviert); die Kranke ist noch nicht ganz wiederhergestellt (gesundet), *vgl. aber* wieder II. **II.** *Dagegen schreibt man in den anderen Fällen meist getrennt, vor allem wenn* „wieder" *im Sinne von* „nochmals, erneut" *verstanden wird:* dieses Modell wird jetzt wieder hergestellt (erneut produziert); wieder geboren (nochmals auf die Welt gekommen) sein; wir werden die Firma wieder aufbauen; sie wollen das Theaterstück wieder aufführen; sie haben sich sofort wieder erkannt; ich verspreche, alle Fehler wieder gutzumachen; eine Verordnung wieder aufheben; sie hat ihre Arbeit wieder aufgenommen; wir versuchen, den Unglücklichen wieder aufzurichten (zu trösten); du musst den Mast wieder aufrichten; der Vermisste ist wieder aufgetaucht; dies hat die Wirtschaft wieder belebt; das Geschäft hat gestern wieder eröffnet; wir haben uns erst nach Jahren wieder gesehen; sie hat so etwas nie wieder getan; das Land wurde wieder vereinigt; die Materialien können wieder verwendet, wieder verwertet werden; die Vorsitzende wurde wieder gewählt; *vgl. aber* wieder I
Wie|der|ab|druck *Plur.* ...drucke
Wie|der|an|pfiff (der; -[e]s; *Sportspr.*), **...an|spiel** (das; -[e]s), **...an|stoß** (der; -es)
Wie|der|auf|bau, der; -[e]s; **Wie|der|auf|bau|ar|beit;** **wie|der auf|bau|en** *vgl.* wieder, II
wie|der auf|be|rei|ten *vgl.* wieder, II; **Wie|der|auf|be|rei|tung;** **Wie|der|auf|be|rei|tungs|an|la|ge**
wie|der auf|füh|ren *vgl.* wieder, II; **Wie|der|auf|füh|rung**
wie|der auf|he|ben *vgl.* wieder, II
Wie|der|auf|nah|me; **Wie|der|auf|nah|me|ver|fah|ren** *(Rechtsspr.);* **wie|der auf|neh|men** *vgl.* wieder, II
wie|der auf|rich|ten *vgl.* wieder, II; **Wie|der|auf|rich|tung**
wie|der auf|su|chen, auf|tau|chen *vgl.* wieder, II
Wie|der|be|ginn
wie|der|be|kom|men (zurückbekommen); ich habe das Buch wiederbekommen; *aber* (*vgl.* wieder, II): er wird diesen Ausschlag nicht wieder (nicht ein zweites Mal) bekommen
wie|der be|le|ben *vgl.* wieder, II; **Wie|der|be|le|bung;** **Wie|der|be|le|bungs|ver|such**
wie|der|brin|gen (zurückbringen); sie hat das Buch wiedergebracht; *aber* (*vgl.* wieder, II): wenn er dasselbe Argument schon wieder bringt ...
Wie|der|druck, der; -[e]s, -e (Neudruck); *vgl. aber* Widerdruck
wie|der ein|fal|len *vgl.* wieder, II
Wie|der|ein|glie|de|rung
wie|der ein|set|zen *vgl.* wieder, II; **Wie|der|ein|set|zung;** - in den vorigen Stand *(Rechtsw.)*
Wie|der|ein|tritt
wie|der ent|de|cken *vgl.* wieder, II; **Wie|der|ent|de|ckung**
wie|der er|ken|nen *vgl.* wieder, II
wie|der|er|lan|gen (zurückbekommen); *vgl.* wieder, I; **Wie|der|er|lan|gung**
wie|der|er|o|bern (zurückerobern); der Verein hat seine führende Stellung wiedererobert; *vgl.* wieder, I; **Wie|der|er|o|be|rung**
wie|der er|öff|nen *vgl.* wieder, II; **Wie|der|er|öff|nung**
wie|der|er|stat|ten (zurückerstatten); die Bank hat das Geld wiedererstattet; *vgl.* wieder, I; **Wie|der|er|stat|tung**
wie|der er|we|cken *vgl.* wieder, II; **Wie|der|er|we|ckung**
wie|der fin|den *vgl.* wieder, II
wie|der|for|dern (zurückfordern); ich fordere wieder; er hat das Geld wiedergefordert; *vgl.* wieder, I; *aber* wir wurden vom Gegner wieder (erneut) gefordert
Wie|der|ga|be; die - eines Konzertes auf Tonband
Wie|der|gän|ger (ruheloser Geist eines Toten)
wie|der|ge|ben (zurückgeben; darbieten); ich gebe wieder; die Freiheit wurde ihm wiedergegeben; sie hat das Gedicht vollendet wiedergegeben; *vgl.* wieder, I; *aber* sie hat ihm die Schlüssel schon wieder (nochmals) gegeben
wie|der ge|bo|ren *vgl.* wieder, II; **Wie|der|ge|burt**
wie|der|ge|win|nen (zurückgewinnen); er hat sein verlorenes Geld wiedergewonnen; *vgl.* wieder, I; *aber* wieder gewinnen (nochmals gewinnen)
wie|der gut|ma|chen *vgl.* wieder, II; **Wie|der|gut|ma|chung**
wie|der|ha|ben (*ugs. für* zurückbekommen); ich habe das Buch wieder; er hat es wiedergehabt; *vgl.* wieder, I

wie|der her|rich|ten *vgl.* wieder, II

wie|der|her|stel|len *vgl.* wieder, I *u.* II; **Wie|der|her|stel|lung; Wie|der|her|stel|lungs|kos|ten** *Plur.*

wie|der|hol|bar; wie|der|ho|len (zurückholen); ich hole wieder; er hat seine Bücher wiedergeholt; *aber* wieder holen (nochmals holen); *vgl.* wieder, I, II; **wie|der|ho|len;** ich wiederhole; sie hat ihre Forderungen wiederholt; *vgl.* wieder, I; **wie|der|holt** (noch-, mehrmals); **Wie|der|ho|lung; Wie|der|ho|lungs‿fall** (der; im -[e]; *Amtsspr.*), **...kurs** (*schweiz. für* jährl. Militärübung; *Abk.* WK), **...spiel** *(Sport),* **...tä|ter** *(Rechtsw.),* **...zei|chen** *(Musik)*

Wie|der|hö|ren, das; -s; auf -! (Grußformel im Fernsprechverkehr u. im Rundfunk)

Wie|der|in|be|sitz|nah|me

Wie|der|in|stand|set|zung

wie|der|käu|en; die Kuh käut wieder; *vgl.* wieder, I; **Wie|der|käu|er**

Wie|der|kauf (Rückkauf); **wie|der|kau|fen** (zurückkaufen, einlösen); *vgl.* wieder, I; **Wie|der|käu|fer; Wie|der|kaufs|recht** *(Rechtsspr.)*

Wie|der|kehr, die; -; **wie|der|keh|ren** (zurückkehren; sich wiederholen); *vgl.* wieder, I

wie|der|kom|men (zurückkommen); ich komme wieder; sie ist heute wiedergekommen; *vgl.* wieder, I; *aber* wieder kommen (nochmals kommen); **Wie|der|kunft,** die; - (*veraltend für* Rückkehr)

Wie|der|schau|en, das; -s *(landsch.);* auf -!

wie|der|schen|ken (zurückgeben); *vgl.* wieder, I

wie|der se|hen *vgl.* wieder, II; **Wie|der|se|hen,** das; -s, -; auf -!; jmdm. Auf, *auch* auf - sagen; **Wie|der|se|hens|freu|de,** die; -

Wie|der‿tau|fe (die; -; *Rel.*), **...täu|fer**

wie|der tun *vgl.* wieder, II

wie|de|rum (↑R 132)

wie|der ver|ei|ni|gen *vgl.* wieder, II; **Wie|der|ver|ei|ni|gung**

Wie|der|ver|hei|ra|tung

Wie|der|ver|käu|fer (Händler)

wie|der ver|wen|den *vgl.* wieder, II; **Wie|der|ver|wen|dung;** zur - (*Abk.* z. Wv.)

wie|der ver|wer|ten *vgl.* wieder, II; **Wie|der|ver|wer|tung**

Wie|der|vor|la|ge, die; -; zur Wiedervorlage (*Amtsspr.; Abk.* z. Wv.)

Wie|der|wahl; wie|der wäh|len *vgl.* wieder, II

Wie|de|wit|te, die; -, -n (*nordd. für* Champignon)

wie|feln (*landsch. u. schweiz. für* vernähen, stopfen); ich ...[e]le (↑R 16); *vgl.* wiebeln

wie|fern (*veraltet für* inwiefern)

Wie|ge, die; -, -n; **wie|geln** (*landsch. für* leise wiegen; *selten für* aufwiegeln); ich ...[e]le (↑R 16); **Wie|ge|mes|ser,** das;

[1]**wie|gen** (schaukeln; zerkleinern); du wiegst; du wiegtest; gewiegt; sich -

[2]**wie|gen** (das Gewicht feststellen; *fachspr. nur für* Gewicht haben); du wiegst; du wogst; du wögest; gewogen; wieg[e]!; ich wiege das Brot; das Brot wiegt (hat ein Gewicht von) zwei Kilo; *vgl.* wägen

Wie|gen‿druck (*Plur.* ...drucke), **...fest** (*geh. für* Geburtstag), **...lied**

wie|hern; ich ...ere (↑R 16)

Wiek, die; -, -en (*nordd. für* [kleine] Bucht an der Ostsee)

[1]**Wie|land** (Gestalt der germ. Sage)

[2]**Wie|land** (dt. Schriftsteller); **wie|lan|disch, wie|landsch;** wielandd[i]sche Übersetzungen

Wie|lands|lied, das; -[e]s

wie lang, wie lan|ge; - - ist das her?; - - ist das her!

Wie|ling, die; -, -e (*Seemannsspr.* Fender für Boote)

Wie|men, der; -s, - (*nordd., westd. für* Latte, Lattengerüst zum Trocknen u. Räuchern; Schlafstange der Hühner)

Wien (Hptst. Österreichs); **Wie|ner** (↑R 103); - Kalk; - Schnitzel; - Würstchen; **wie|ne|risch; Wie|ner|le,** das; -s, - *(landsch.),* **Wie|ner|li,** das; -s, - (*schweiz. für* Wiener Würstchen); **wie|nern** (*ugs. für* blank putzen); ich ...ere (↑R 16); **Wie|ner Neu|stadt;** ↑R 103 (österr. Stadt); **Wie|ner|stadt,** die; - (volkstüml. Bez. Wiens); **Wie|ner|wald,** der; -[e]s; ↑R 105 (nordöstl. Ausläufer der Alpen)

Wie|pe, die; -, -n (*nordd. für* Strohwisch)

Wies|ba|den (Hptst. von Hessen); **Wies|ba|de|ner,** Wies|bad|ner (↑R 103); **wies|ba|densch,** wiesba|disch; **Wies|ba|den Süd** (↑R 106); **wies|ba|disch** *vgl.* wiesbadensch; **Wies|bad|ner** *vgl.* Wiesbadener

Wies|baum, Wie|se|baum (Stange über dem beladenen [Heu]wagen, Heubaum); **Wie|se,** die; -, -n; **Wie|se|baum** *vgl.* Wiesbaum

wie sehr

Wie|sel, das; -s, - (ein Marder); **wie|sel|flink; wie|seln** (sich [wie ein Wiesel] eilig, schnell bewegen); ich ...[e]le (↑R 16)

Wie|sen‿blu|me, ...cham|pig|non, ...grund *(veraltend),* **...schaum|kraut, ...tal; Wie|sen|wachs** *od.* Wies|wachs, der; -es (*veraltet, noch landsch. für* Grasertrag der Wiesen); **Wies|land,** das; -[e]s *(schweiz.);* **Wies|lein**

wie|so

Wies|wachs *vgl.* Wiesenwachs

wie|ten (*landsch. für* jäten)

wie viel [*auch* 'vi:...]; wie viel[e] Personen; wievielmal [*auch* ...'fi:l...], *aber* wie viele Male; ich weiß nicht, wie viel er hat; wenn du wüsstest, wie viel ich verloren habe; [um] wie viel mehr; **wie|vie|ler|lei** [*auch* 'vi: -]; **wie|viel|mal** [*auch* 'vi:...], *aber* wie viele Male; *vgl.* Mal *u.* wie viel; **wie|viel|te** [*auch* 'vi: -]; zum wievielten Male ich das schon gesagt habe; (↑R 48): der Wievielte ist heute?

wie|weit (inwieweit); ich bin im Zweifel, wieweit ich mich darauf verlassen kann, *aber* wie weit ist es von hier bis ...?

wie we|nig *vgl.* wenig

wie|wohl *(veraltend);* die einzige, wiewohl wertvolle Belohnung, *aber* wie wohl du aussiehst!

Wight [wait] (engl. Insel)

Wig|wam, der; -s, -s ‹indian.-engl.› (Zelt, Hütte nordamerikanischer Indianer)

Wi|king, der; -s, -er *u.* **Wi|kin|ger** ['vi(:)...] ‹altnord.› (Normanne); **Wi|kin|ger‿sa|ge** (die; -), **...schiff; wi|kin|gisch**

Wik|lif (↑R 130) *vgl.* Wyclif; **Wik|li|fit,** der; -en, -en; ↑R 126 (Anhänger Wyclifs)

Wil|la|jet, das; -[e]s, -s ‹arab.-türk.› (Verwaltungsbezirk im Osman. Reich)

wild; wild wachsen; wild wachsende Pflanzen; wilde Ehe; wilder Streik; wildes Tier; wilder Wein; er spielt den wilden Mann *(ugs.);* die wild lebenden Tiere; ein wild gewordener (*ugs. abwertend für* unbeherrschter) Kontrolleur; (↑R 108:) Wilder Westen; die Wilde Jagd (Geisterheer); der Wilde Jäger (eine Geistergestalt); (↑R 102:) Wilder Kaiser; Wilde Kreuzspitze; (↑R 47:) sich wie ein Wilder gebärden (*ugs.; vgl.* [2]Wilde); **Wild,** das; -[e]s; **Wild‿bach, ...bahn** (*meist in* in freier -), **...bestand; Wild|bret,** das; -s (Fleisch des geschossenen Wildes)

Wild|card ['waild ka:(r)d], die; -, -s ⟨engl.⟩ (*Tennis* vom Veranstalter vergebene freie Platzierung bei einem Turnier)
Wild|dieb; wild|die|ben; ich wilddiebe; gewilddiebt; zu -; **Wild-die|be|rei**
[1]**Wilde** [waild], Oscar (engl. Dichter)
[2]**Wil|de,** der *u.* die; -n, -n (↑R 5 ff.); **Wild⌣eber** (↑R 132), **...en|te; wil|den|zen** (*landsch. für* stark nach Wild riechen); **Wil|de|rei; Wil|de|rer** (Wilddieb); **wil|dern** (unbefugt jagen); ich ...ere (↑R 16); **Wild|fang** (ausgelassenes Kind); **wild|fremd** (*ugs. für* völlig fremd); **Wild⌣gans, ...gatter, ...he|ger; Wild|heit; Wild⌣heu|er** (der; jmd., der an gefährlichen Hängen in den Alpen Heu macht), **...hund, ...hü|ter, ...ka-nin|chen, ...kat|ze, ...kraut; wild le|bend** *vgl.* wild; **Wild|le|der; Wild|ling** (Unterlage für die Veredelung von Obst u. Ziergehölzen; *Forstw.* wild gewachsenes Bäumchen; ungezähmtes Tier; *veraltend für* sich wild gebärdender Mensch); **Wild|nis,** die; -, -se; **Wild⌣park, ...pferd, ...pflan|ze; wild|reich; Wild|reich|tum,** der; -s; **Wild|rind; wild|ro|man-tisch; Wild⌣sau, ...scha|den; Wild|schütz,** der (*veraltend für* Wilddieb); **Wild⌣schwein, ...tau|be; wild wach|send** *vgl.* wild; **Wild|was|ser,** das; -s, - (Wildbach); **Wild|was|ser|fahrt; Wild|wech|sel; Wild|west** *ohne Artikel;* **Wild|west|film; Wild-wuchs; wild|wüch|sig; Wild-zaun**
Wil|fried (m. Vorn.)
Wil|helm (m. Vorn.); **Wil|hel|mi-ne** (w. Vorn.); **wil|hel|mi|nisch;** *aber* (↑R 56:) das Wilhelminische Zeitalter (Kaiser Wilhelms II.); **Wil|helms|ha|ven** [...'ha:f(ə)n] (Hafenstadt an der Nordsee); **Wil|helms|ha|ve|ner** (↑R 103)
Will (m. Vorn.)
Wil|le, der; -ns, -n *Plur. selten;* der letzte Wille (↑R 108); wider Willen; jmdm. zu Willen sein; voll guten Willens; willens sein *(vgl. d.)*
Wil|le|gis (m. Vorn.)
wil|len; (↑R 46:) um ... willen, um Gottes willen, um seiner selbst willen, um meinet-, deinet-, dessent-, derent-, seinet-, ihret-, unsert-, euretwillen; **Wil|len,** der; -s, - *Plur. selten* (*Nebenform von* Wille); **wil|len|los; Wil|len|lo|sig-keit,** die; -; **Wil|lens⌣akt, ...äu-ße|rung, ...bil|dung, ...er|klä-rung, ...frei|heit** (die; -), **...kraft** (die; -); **wil|lens|schwach;** ...schwächer, ...schwächste; **Wil-lens|schwä|che,** die; -; **wil|lens sein;** ↑R 46 (beabsichtigen); **wil-lens|stark;** ...stärker, ...stärkste; **Wil|lens|stär|ke,** die; -; **wil|lent-lich** (mit voller Absicht)
will|fah|ren, *auch* will|fah|ren; du willfahrst; du willfahrtest; (*zu* willfahren:) willfahrt *od.* (*zu* willfahren:) gewillfahrt; zu -; **will-fäh|rig** [*auch* ...'fɛ:...]; **Will|fäh-rig|keit** [*auch* ...'fɛ:...], die; -
Wil|li (m. Vorn.); **Wil|liam** ['wil-jəm] (m. Vorn.); **Wil|liams Christ|bir|ne** (eine Tafelbirne); **Wil|li|bald, Wil|li|brord** (m. Vorn.)
wil|lig (bereit); **wil|li|gen** *(geh.);* er willigte in die Heirat
Wil|li|gis *vgl.* Willegis
Wil|li|ram (m. Vorn.)
Will|komm, der; -s, -e, *häufiger* **Will|kom|men,** das, *österr. nur so, selten* der; -s, -; einen Willkomm zurufen; ein fröhliches Willkommen!; **will|kom|men;** jmdn. willkommen heißen; herzlich willkommen! **Will|kom-mens⌣gruß, ...trunk**
Will|kür, die; -; **Will|kür⌣akt, ...herr|schaft; will|kür|lich; Will-kür|maß|nah|me** *meist Plur.*
Wil|ly, Wilm (m. Vorn.); **Wil|ma** (w. Vorn.); **Wil|mar** (m. Vorn.)
Wil|na (Hptst. von Litauen; *vgl.* Vilnius)
Wil|pert, das; -[e]s (*thüring. für* Wildbret)
Wil|son ['wils(ə)n] (Präsident der USA)
Wils|ter (Ortsn.); **Wils|ter-marsch,** die; - ([2]Marsch nördl. der Niederelbe)
Wil|traud, Wil|trud (w. Vorn.)
Wim (m. Vorn.)
Wim|ble|don ['wimb(ə)ldən] (Vorort von London; Austragungsort eines berühmten Tennisturniers)
wim|meln; es wimmelt von Ameisen
wim|men, wüm|men ⟨lat.⟩ (*schweiz. mdal. für* Trauben lesen); gewimmt
[1]**Wim|mer,** der; -s, - (Knorren; Maser[holz]; *auch, bes. südd. für* Schwiele, kleine Warze)
[2]**Wim|mer,** die; -, -n ⟨lat.⟩ (*landsch. für* Weinlese); [3]**Wim|mer,** der; -s, - (*landsch. für* Winzer)
Wim|mer|holz (*ugs. scherzh. für* Geige, Laute); **wim|me|rig**
Wim|merl, das; -s, -n (*bayr. u. österr. ugs. für* Hitze- od. Eiterbläschen)
wim|mern; ich ...ere (↑R 16); (↑R 50:) das ist zum Wimmern (*ugs. für* das ist furchtbar, *auch für* das ist zum Lachen)
Wim|met, Wüm|met, der; -s ⟨lat.⟩ (*schweiz. mdal. für* Weinlese)
Wim|pel, der; -s, - ([kleine] dreieckige Flagge)
Wim|per, die; -, -n
Wim|perg, der; -[e]s, -e *u.* **Wim-per|ge,** die; -, -n (*Bauw.* got. Spitzgiebel)
Wim|pern|tu|sche; Wim|per-tier|chen (einzelliges Lebewesen)
Win|ckel|mann (dt. Altertumsforscher)
wind *(veraltet); nur noch in* - u. weh (*südwestd. u. schweiz. für* höchst unbehaglich, elend)
Wind, der; -[e]s, -e; - bekommen (*ugs. für* heimlich, zufällig erfahren); **Wind|ab|wei|ser** (am Autofenster od. -dach); **Wind|bä-cke|rei** (*österr. für* Schaumgebäck); **Wind|beu|tel** (ein Gebäck; *ugs. auch für* leichtfertiger Mensch); **Wind|beu|te|lei** *(ugs.);* **Wind⌣bö,** *auch* **Wind⌣böe, ...bruch** (der), **...büch|se** (Luftgewehr); **Wind|chill** [...tʃil], der; -s ⟨engl.⟩ (durch Wind verursachte verstärkte Kälteempfindung)
Win|de, die; -, -n (eine Hebevorrichtung; eine Pflanze)
Wind|ei (*Zool.* Vogelei mit weicher Schale; *Med.* abgestorbene Leibesfrucht)
Win|del, die; -, -n; **win|deln;** ich ...[e]le (↑R 16); **win|del|weich**
[1]**win|den** (drehen); du wandest; du wändest; gewunden; wind[e]!; sich -
[2]**win|den** (windig sein; *Jägerspr.* wittern); es windet; das Wild windet; **Wind⌣ener|gie** (die; -; ↑R 132), **...er|hit|zer** *(Hüttenw.);* **Win|des|ei|le;** in, mit -; **Wind-⌣fang, ...flüch|ter** (vom Wind verformter Baum, Strauch); **wind|ge|schützt; Wind⌣har|fe** (*für* Äolsharfe), **...hauch, ...ho|se** (Wirbelsturm)
Wind|huk (Hptst. von Namibia)
Wind|hund (*ugs. auch für* leichtfertiger Mensch)
win|dig (winderfüllt; *ugs. auch für* nicht solide, zweifelhaft); **Wind⌣ja|cke, ...jam|mer** (der; -s, -; großes Segelschiff), **...ka-nal, ...kraft; Wind|kraft|werk; Wind⌣licht** (*Plur.* ...lichter), **...ma|cher** (*ugs. für* Wichtigtuer), **...ma|che|rei** *(ugs.),* **...ma|schi-ne, ...mo|tor, ...müh|le; Wind-müh|len|flü|gel** *meist Plur.;* **Wind⌣po|cken** (*Plur.;* eine Kinderkrankheit), **...rad, ...rich|tung, ...rös|chen** (*für* Anemone), **...ro-**

se (Windrichtungs-, Kompassscheibe), ...sack (an einer Stange aufgehängter Beutel, der Richtung u. Stärke des Windes anzeigt); Winds|braut, die; - (veraltend für heftiger Wind); Wind|schat|ten, der; -s (Leeseite eines Berges; geschützter Bereich hinter einem fahrenden Fahrzeug)

wind|schief (ugs. für krumm)

windˬschlüp|fig, ...schnit|tig (für aerodynamisch); Wind|schutzˬschei|be, ...strei|fen (Landw.)

Wind|sor ['wintsə(r)] (engl. Stadt; Name des engl. Königshauses)

Wind|spiel (kleiner Windhund)

Wind|stär|ke; wind|still; Windˬstil|le, ...stoß; wind|sur|fen [...sœ:(r)fən] nur im Infinitiv gebr.; Wind|sur|fer ‹dt.; engl.›; Wind|sur|fing, das; -s (Segeln auf einem Surfbrett)

Win|dung

Wind|zug, der; -[e]s

Win|fried (m. Vorn.)

Win|gert, der; -s, -e (südd., westd. u. schweiz. für Weingarten, Weinberg)

Win|golf, der; -s, -e („Freundeshalle" der nord. Mythol.)

Wink, der; -[e]s, -e; win|ke; nur in winke, winke machen (Kinderspr.)

Win|kel, der; -s, -; Win|kelˬad|vo|kat (abwertend), ...ei|sen, ...funk|ti|on (Math.), ...ha|ken (Druckw.), ...hal|bie|ren|de (die; -n, -n; ↑R 5 ff.); win|ke|lig vgl. winklig; Win|kelˬklam|mer, ...maß (das), ...mes|ser (der); win|keln; ich ...[e]le den Arm (↑R 16)

Win|kel|ried (schweiz. Held)

Win|kel|zug meist Plur.

win|ken; gewinkt (nicht korrekt: gewunken); Win|ker; Win|kerˬflag|ge (Seew.), ...krab|be; win|ke, win|ke vgl. winke

wink|lig, win|ke|lig

Win|ne|tou [...tu] (idealisierte Indianergestalt bei Karl May)

Win|ni|peg ['wini...] (kanad. Stadt); Win|ni|peg|see, der; -s

Winsch, die; -, -en ‹engl.› (Seemannsspr. Winde zum Heben schwerer Lasten)

Win|se|lei (ugs. für das Winseln); win|seln; ich ...[e]le (↑R 16)

Win|ter, der; -s, -; Sommer wie -; winters (vgl. d.); wintersüber (vgl. d.); Win|terˬabend (↑R 132), ...an|fang, ...ap|fel, ...bau (der; -[e]s; das Bauen im Winter), ...cam|ping, ...ein|bruch, ...fahr|plan; win|ter|fest; -e Kleidung; Win|terˬfri|sche (die; -, -n; veraltet), ...frucht, ...gar|ten, ...gers|te, ...ge|trei|de, ...ha|fen (vgl. [2]Hafen), ...halb|jahr; win|ter|hart; -e Pflanzen; Win|terˬkar|tof|fel, ...kleid, ...klei|dung, ...kohl (der; -[e]s), ...kol|lek|ti|on (Mode), ...land|schaft; win|ter|lich; Win|ter|ling (eine Pflanze); Win|ter|man|tel; [1]Win|ter|mo|nat (in die Winterzeit fallender Monat); [2]Win|terˬmo|nat od. ...mond (alte dt. Bez. für Dezember; schweiz. [früher] für November); win|tern; es wintert; Win|terˬnacht, ...obst; win|ter|of|fen; -e Pässe; Win|terˬolym|pi|a|de (↑R 132), ...pau|se, ...quar|tier, ...rei|fen, ...rei|se; win|ters (↑R 46), aber des Winters; Win|terˬsaat, ...sa|chen (Plur.; Kleidung für den Winter), ...sai|son; Win|ters|an|fang (svw. Winteranfang); Win|terˬschlaf (Zool.), ...schluss|ver|kauf, ...schuh, ...se|mes|ter, ...son|nen|wen|de, ...spie|le (Plur.; die Olympischen -), ...sport, ...sport|ler, ...star|re; win|ters|über; aber den Winter über; Win|ters|zeit, die; - (Jahreszeit); vgl. auch Winterzeit; Win|ter|tag; win|ter|taug|lich; Win|ter|taug|lich|keit, die; -

Win|ter|thur (schweiz. Stadt)

Win|ter|zeit, die; - (Jahreszeit; Rückverlegung der Stundenzählung während des Winters)

Win|zer, der; -s, -; Win|zer|ge|nos|sen|schaft; Win|ze|rin; Win|zer|mes|ser, das

win|zig; Win|zig|keit; Winz|ling (ugs.)

Wip|fel, der; -s, -; wip|fe|lig, wipf|lig

Wip|pe, die; -, -n (Schaukel); wip|pen; Wip|per; vgl. [1]Kipper; wip|pern (landsch. für wackeln, schwanken); ich ...ere (↑R 16); Wipp|sterz (landsch. für Bachstelze)

wir (von Herrschern: Wir); wir alle, wir beide; (↑R 5:) wir bescheidenen Leute; wir Armen; wir Deutschen, auch wir Deutsche

Wir|bel, der; -s, -; wir|be|lig, wirb|lig; Wir|bel|kno|chen; wir|bel|los; Wir|bel|lo|se Plur. (Zool. zusammenfassende Bez. für alle Vielzeller außer den Wirbeltieren); wir|beln; ich ...[e]le (↑R 16); Wir|belˬsäu|le; Wir|bel|säu|len|ver|krüm|mung; Wir|belˬsturm (vgl. [1]Sturm), ...tier, ...wind; wirb|lig vgl. wirbelig

wir|ken; (↑R 50:) sein segensreiches Wirken; Wir|ker; Wir|ke|rei; Wir|ke|rin; Wirkˬkraft (Wirkungskraft), ...leis|tung (Elektrotechnik); Wirkl. Geh. Rat = Wirklicher Geheimer Rat; wirk|lich; Wirk|li|che Ge|hei|me Rat, der; -n -n -[e]s, -n -n Räte (früher; Abk. Wirkl. Geh. Rat); Wirk|lich|keit; wirk|lich|keits|fern; Wirk|lich|keits|form (für Indikativ); wirk|lich|keitsˬfremd, ...ge|treu; Wirk|lich|keits|mensch (für Realist); wirk|lich|keits|nah; Wirk|lich|keitsˬsinn (der; -[e]s; er hat viel -), ...treue; wirk|sam; Wirk|sam|keit, die; -; Wirk|stoff; Wir|kung; Wir|kungsˬbe|reich (der), ...feld, ...ge|schich|te; wir|kungs|ge|schicht|lich; Wir|kungsˬgrad, ...kraft (die), ...kreis; wir|kungs|los; Wir|kungs|lo|sig|keit, die; -; Wir|kungs|me|cha|nis|mus; wir|kungs|reich; Wir|kungs|stät|te; wir|kungs|voll; Wir|kungs|wei|se, die; Wirk|wa|ren Plur. (gewirkte Waren)

wirr; Wir|ren Plur.; Wirr|heit; wir|rig (landsch. für verworren; zornig); Wirr|kopf (abwertend); Wirr|nis, die; -, -se; Wirr|sal, das; -[e]s, -e u. die; -, -e (geh.); Wir|rung; Irrungen u. Wirrungen; Wirr|warr, der; -s; wirsch (landsch. für aufgeregt; ärgerlich)

Wir|sing, der; -s ‹ital.› u. Wir|sing|kohl, der; -[e]s

Wirt, der; -[e]s, -e

Wir|tel, der; -s, - (Schwunggewicht an der Spindel; Bot. Aststellung in Form eines Quirls); wir|tel|för|mig; wir|te|lig, wirt|lig (quirlförmig)

wir|ten (schweiz. für eine Gastwirtschaft führen); Wir|tin; wirt|lich (gastlich); Wirt|lich|keit, die; -

wirt|lig vgl. wirtelig

Wirt|schaft; wirt|schaf|ten; gewirtschaftet; Wirt|schaf|ter (Verwalter); Wirt|schaf|te|rin; Wirt|schaft|ler (Wirtschaftskundler; Unternehmer, leitende Persönlichkeit in Handel u. Industrie); Wirt|schaft|le|rin; wirt|schaft|lich; Wirt|schaft|lich|keit, die; -; Wirt|schaftsˬab|kom|men, ...asy|lant (↑R 132; jmd., der aus wirtschaftl. Gründen Asyl sucht, aber vorgibt, politisch verfolgt zu sein), ...auf|schwung, ...aus|schuss, ...be|ra|ter, ...be|zie|hun|gen (Plur.), ...block (Plur. ...blöcke, selten ...blocks), ...de|likt, ...em|bar|go, ...flücht|ling, ...ge|bäu|de, ...geld, ...ge|mein|schaft (Europäische -; Abk. EWG), ...ge|o|gra|phie, ...ge|schich|te (die; -); wirt|schafts|ge|schicht|lich; Wirt|schaftsˬgip|fel, ...gym|nasi|um, ...hil|fe, ...hoch|schu|le, ...in|ge|ni|eur, ...in|ge|ni|eu|rin, ...jahr, ...jour|na|list, ...jour|na|lis|tin, ...kam|mer, ...kraft, ...krieg, ...kri|mi|na|li|tät, ...kri|se, ...la|ge, ...le|ben (das; -s), ...leh|re, ...len|kung, ...mi|nis|ter, ...mi|nis|te|rin, ...mi|nis|te|ri|um, ...ord|nung, ...po|li|tik; **wirt|schafts|po|li|tisch; Wirt|schafts‿pres|se** (die; -), **...prü|fer, ...prü|fe|rin, ...prü|fung, ...raum, ...re|form, ...sank|ti|o|nen** (*Plur.*), **...spi|o|na|ge, ...stand|ort, ...sys|tem, ...teil** (der; Teil einer Zeitung), **...the|o|rie, ...ver|band, ...wachs|tum, ...wis|sen|schaft, ...wis|sen|schaft|ler, ...wis|sen|schaft|le|rin; wirt|schafts|wis|sen|schaft|lich; Wirt|schafts‿wun|der** *(ugs.)*, **...zweig**

Wirts|haus; Wirts‿leu|te *(Plur.)*, **...or|ga|nis|mus** *(Biol.)*, **...pflan|ze, ...stu|be, ...tier**

Wirz, der; -es (*schweiz. für* Wirsing)

Wis. = [2]Wisconsin

Wisch, der; -[e]s, -e; **Wisch|arm** (am Scheibenwischer); **wi|schen;** du wischst; **Wi|scher** (*ugs. auch für* Tadel); **Wi|scher|blatt** (am Scheibenwischer); **wisch|fest; wi|schig** (*nordd. für* zerstreut, kopflos); **Wi|schi|wa|schi,** das; -s (*ugs. für* unpräzise Darstellung); **Wisch|lap|pen**

Wisch|nu (einer der Hauptgötter des Hinduismus)

Wisch|tuch *Plur.* ...tücher

[1]**Wis|con|sin** [wis'kɔnsin], der; -[s] (l. Nebenfluss des Mississippis); [2]**Wis|con|sin** (Staat in den USA; *Abk.* Wis.)

Wi|sent, der; -s, -e (ein Wildrind)

Wis|mut, *chem. fachspr. auch* Bismut, das; -[e]s (chem. Element, Metall; *Zeichen* Bi)

wis|peln (*landsch. für* wispern); ich ...[e]le (↑R 16); **wis|pern** (flüstern); ich ...ere (↑R 16)

Wiss|be|gier[|de], die; -; **wiss|be|gie|rig; wis|sen;** du weißt, er weiß, ihr wisst; du wusstest; du wüsstest; gewusst; wisse!; jmdm. etwas kund und zu wissen tun *(altertümelnd)*; jmdn. etwas wissen lassen; wer weiß!; **Wis|sen,** das; -s; meines Wissens (*Abk.* m.W.) ist es so; wider besseres Wissen; **Wis|sen|de,** der *u.* die; -n, -n; ↑R 5ff. (Eingeweihte[r]); **Wis|sen|schaft; Wis|sen|schaf|ter** (*schweiz., österr. auch, sonst veraltet für* Wissenschaftler); **Wis|sen|schaft|ler; Wis|sen|schaft|le|rin; wis|sen|schaft|lich;** (↑R 56:) Wissenschaftlicher Rat (Titel); **Wis|sen|schaft|lich|keit,** die; -; **Wis|sen|schafts‿be|griff, ...be|trieb** (der; -[e]s); **wis|sen|schafts|gläu|big; Wis|sen|schafts‿the|o|rie** (die; -), **...zweig; Wis|sens‿drang** (der; -[e]s), **...durst; wis|sens|dur|stig; Wis|sens‿ge|biet, ...lü|cke, ...stand, ...stoff** (der; -[e]s), **...vor|sprung** (der; -[e]s); **wis|sens|wert; wis|sent|lich**

Wiss|mann (dt. Afrikaforscher)

wist! (*Fuhrmannsruf* links!)

Wis|ta|rie [...i̯ə], die; -, -n (*svw.* Glyzine)

Wit|frau *(schweiz., sonst veraltet)*; **Wi|tib,** *österr.* Wit|tib, die; -, -e (*veraltet für* Witwe); **Wit|mann** *Plur.* ...männer, *österr.* Wit|ti|ber (*veraltet für* Witwer)

Wi|told (m. Vorn.)

wit|schen (*ugs. für* schlüpfen, huschen); du witschst

Wit|te|kind *vgl.* Widukind

Wit|tels|bach (oberbayr. Stammburg); Haus - (Herrschergeschlecht); **Wit|tels|ba|cher,** der; -s, - (Angehöriger eines dt. Herrschergeschlechtes)

Wit|ten|berg, Lu|ther|stadt (Stadt an der mittleren Elbe); **Wit|ten|ber|ge** (Stadt an der unteren Elbe); **Wit|ten|ber|ger** (von Wittenberg od. Wittenberge) ↑R 103; **wit|ten|ber|gisch** (von Wittenberg od. Wittenberge), *aber* (↑R 108): die Wittenbergische Nachtigall (*Bez. für* Luther)

wit|tern ([mit dem Geruch] wahrnehmen); ich ...ere (↑R 16); **Wit|te|rung** (*auch Jägerspr.* das Wittern u. der vom Wild wahrzunehmende Geruch); **wit|te|rungs|be|dingt; Wit|te|rungs‿ein|fluss, ...um|schlag, ...ver|hält|nis|se** *(Plur.)*

Witt|gen|stein (österr. Philosoph)

Wit|tib *vgl.* Witib; **Wit|ti|ber** *vgl.* Witmann

Witt|ling (ein Seefisch)

Wit|tum, das; -[e]s, ...tümer (*veraltet* der Witwe zustehender Besitz)

Wit|we, die; -, -n (*Abk.* Wwe.); **Wit|wen‿geld, ...ren|te; Wit|wen|schaft,** die; -; **Wit|wen|schlei|er; Wit|wen|tum,** das; -s; **Wit|wer** (*Abk.* Wwr.); **Wit|wer|schaft,** die; -; **Wit|wer|tum,** das; -s

Witz, der; -es, -e; **Witz|blatt; Witz|blatt|fi|gur; Witz|bold,** der; -[e]s, -e; **Wit|ze|lei; wit|zeln;** ich ...[e]le (↑R 16); **Witz|fi|gur** *(abwertend)*; **wit|zig; Wit|zig|keit,** die; -; **witz|los; Witz|wort** *Plur.* ...worte

WK = Wiederholungskurs

w. L. = westlicher Länge

Wla|di|mir [*auch* 'vla:...] (m. Vorn.); **Wla|dis|laus, Wla|dis|law** (m. Vorn.); **Wla|di|wos|tok** [*auch* ...'vɔs...] (russ. Stadt)

WM = Weltmeisterschaft

WNW = Westnordwest[en]

wo; wo ist er?; wo immer er auch sein mag; er geht wieder hin, wo er hergekommen ist; der Tag, wo (an dem) er sie das erste Mal sah; (↑R 49:) das Wo spielt keine Rolle; *vgl.* woanders, woher, wohin, wohinaus, womöglich, wo nicht

w. o. = wie oben

wo|an|ders (irgendwo sonst; an einem anderen Ort); ich werde ihn woanders suchen, *aber* wo anders (wo sonst) als hier sollte ich ihn suchen?; **wo|an|ders|hin**

wob|beln (*Funktechnik* Frequenzen verschieben); die Welle wobbelt; **Wob|bel|span|nung**

wo|bei

Wo|che, die; -, -n; **Wo|chen‿ar|beits|zeit, ...bett, ...blatt, ...en|de; Wo|chen|end‿ehe** (↑R 132), **...flug, ...haus; Wo|chen|end|ler; Wo|chen|kar|te; wo|chen|lang; Wo|chen‿lohn, ...markt, ...schau, ...spiel|plan, ...stun|de, ...tag; wo|chen|tags** (↑R 46), *aber* des Wochentags; **wö|chent|lich** (jede Woche); **...wö|chent|lich** (z. B. dreiwöchentlich [alle drei Wochen wiederkehrend]; *mit Ziffer* 3-wöchentlich; ↑R 44); **wo|chen|wei|se; Wo|chen|zei|tung; ...wo|chig** (*seltener für* ...wöchig); **...wö|chig** (z. B. dreiwöchig [drei Wochen alt, dauernd]; *mit Ziffer* 3-wöchig; ↑R 44); **Wöch|ne|rin**

Wo|cken, der; -s, - (*nordd. für* Rocken)

Wo|dan (höchster germ. Gott); *vgl.* Odin *u.* Wotan

Wod|ka, der; -s, -s ⟨russ., „Wässerchen"⟩ (ein Branntwein)

Wo|du, der; - ⟨kreol.⟩ (Geheimkult auf Haiti)

wo|durch; wo|fern (*veraltet für* sofern); **wo|für**

Wo|ge, die; -, -n

wo|ge|gen

wo|gen

wo|her; woher es kommt, weiß ich nicht; er geht wieder hin, woher er gekommen ist, *aber* er geht wieder hin, wo er hergekommen ist; **wo|he|rum; wo|hin;** ich weiß nicht, wohin er geht; sieh, wohin er geht, *aber* sieh, wo er hingeht; **wo|hi|nauf; wo|hi|naus;** ich weiß nicht, wohinaus du willst, *aber* ich weiß nicht, wo du hinauswillst; **wo|hi|nein; wo|hin|ge|gen; wo|hin|ter; wo|hi|nun|ter**

wohl; besser, beste *u.* wohler, wohlste; wohl ihm!; wohl oder übel (ob er wollte oder nicht) musste er zuhören; das ist wohl das Beste; leben Sie wohl!; wohl bekomms! (↑R 13); ich bin wohl; mir ist wohl, wohler, am wohlsten; wohl sein; lass es dir wohl sein; (↑R 38 ff.:) sich wohl fühlen; es ist mir immer wohl ergangen; sie wird es wohl (wahrscheinlich) tun; es wird dir wohl tun (gut tun); sie wird es wohl (wahrscheinlich) wollen; sie hat ihm stets wohl gewollt; wohl bekannt, besser bekannt, am besten bekannt; bestbekannt; wohl beraten, durchdacht, erhalten usw.; ein wohl unterrichteter, besser unterrichteter, bestunterrichteter Mann usw.; gleichwohl; obwohl; sowohl; wiewohl; **Wohl,** das; -[e]s; auf dein -!; zum -!

wohl|an! *(veraltend)*

wohl|an|stän|dig (↑R 40); **Wohl|an|stän|dig|keit,** die; -

wohl|auf *(geh.);* - sein

wohl aus|ge|wo|gen *vgl.* wohl

wohl be|dacht *vgl.* wohl; **Wohl-be|fin|den, ...be|ha|gen**

wohl|be|hal|ten; er kam - an

wohl be|hü|tet, be|kannt, be|ra|ten *vgl.* wohl

wohl|be|stallt *(veraltend);* ein -er Beamter

wohl durch|dacht *vgl.* wohl

Wohl|er|ge|hen, das; -s

wohl er|hal|ten *vgl.* wohl

wohl|er|wo|gen; ein -er Plan

wohl|er|wor|ben; -e Rechte

wohl|er|zo|gen; ein wohlerzogenes Kind; wohlerzogenere Kinder; **Wohl|er|zo|gen|heit,** die; -

Wohl|fahrt, die; -; **Wohl|fahrts-mar|ke, ...pfle|ge** (die; -), **...staat**

wohl|feil *(veraltend);* -er, -ste; eine -e Ware

wohl|ge|bo|ren *(veraltet);* Euer Wohlgeboren (Anrede)

Wohl|ge|fal|len, das; -s; **wohl|ge|fäl|lig;** etwas - betrachten

wohl|ge|formt; wohlgeformtere Sätze

Wohl|ge|fühl, das; -[e]s

wohl|ge|lit|ten; wohlgelittener, wohlgelittenste

wohl ge|meint *vgl.* wohl

wohl|ge|merkt

wohl|ge|mut; sie ist stets -

wohl|ge|nährt

wohl ge|ord|net *vgl.* wohl

wohl|ge|ra|ten; wohlgeratener, wohlgeratenste; ein -es Werk

Wohl-ge|ruch, ...ge|schmack (der; -[e]s)

wohl|ge|setzt; in wohlgesetzten, wohlgesetzteren Worten

wohl|ge|sinnt; sie ist mir wohlgesinnt, wieder wohlgesinnter

wohl|ge|stalt *(veraltet für* wohlgestaltet); **wohl|ge|stal|tet;** eine wohlgestaltetere Form

wohl|ge|tan *(veraltet);* die Arbeit ist wohlgetan; *vgl. aber* wohl

wohl|ha|bend; die wohlhabenderen Bürger; **Wohl|ha|ben|heit,** die; -

wohl|lig; ein -es Gefühl; **Wohl|lig|keit,** die; -

Wohl|klang; wohl|klin|gend; wohlklingendere Töne

Wohl|laut; wohl|lau|tend; wohllautendere Instrumente

Wohl|le|ben, das; -s

wohl|mei|nend; die wohlmeinenderen Freunde rieten ihr ab

wohl|pro|por|ti|o|niert

wohl|rie|chend; noch wohlriechendere Blumen

wohl|schme|ckend; die wohlschmeckendsten Speisen

wohl sein *vgl.* wohl; **Wohl|sein,** das; -s; zum -!

wohl si|tu|iert *vgl.* wohl

Wohl|stand, der; -[e]s; im - leben; **Wohl|stands-bür|ger, ...den|ken, ...ge|sell|schaft, ...kri|mi|na|li|tät, ...müll**

Wohl-tat, ...tä|ter, ...tä|te|rin; wohl|tä|tig; -er, -ste; ein -er Mann; **Wohl|tä|tig|keit,** die; -; **Wohl|tä|tig|keits-ball** (*vgl.* [2]Ball), **...ba|sar, ...kon|zert, ...ver|an|stal|tung, ...ver|ein**

wohl tem|pe|riert *vgl.* wohl; **Wohl|tem|pe|rier|te Kla|vier,** das; -n -s (Sammlung von Präludien u. Fugen von J. S. Bach)

wohl|tu|end (angenehm); die Ruhe ist wohltuend, wohltuender (↑R 40); **wohl tun** *vgl.* wohl

wohl über|legt *vgl.* wohl

wohl un|ter|rich|tet *vgl.* wohl

wohl|ver|dient; ein -er Urlaub

Wohl|ver|hal|ten

Wohl|ver|leih, der; -[e]s, -[e] (Arnika)

wohl ver|sorgt *vgl.* wohl

wohl|ver|stan|den; er war[,] wohlverstanden[,] kein schlechter Mensch

wohl ver|wahrt *vgl.* wohl

wohl|weis|lich; sie hat sich - gehütet

wohl wol|len *vgl.* wohl; **Wohl|wol|len,** das; -s; **wohl|wol|lend;** ein wohlwollenderes Urteil

Wohn-an|hän|ger, ...bau (*Plur.* ...bauten), **...be|reich, ...block** (*vgl.* Block), **...die|le, ...ein|heit; woh|nen; Wohn-flä|che, ...ge|bäu|de, ...ge|biet, ...geld; Wohn|geld|ge|setz; Wohn|ge|mein|schaft** (*Abk.* WG); **wohn|haft** (*Amtsspr.* wohnend); **Wohn-haus, ...heim, ...kom|plex** (*regional für* größeres Wohngebiet), **...kü|che, ...kul|tur** (die; -), **...la|ge; wohn|lich; Wohn|lich|keit,** die; -; **Wohn-mo|bil, ...ort** (*Plur.* ...orte), **...raum; Wohn|raum|len|kung** (*ehem. in der DDR* administrative Wohnungsvergabe); **Wohn-sitz, ...stu|be; Woh|nung; Woh|nungs-amt, ...bau** (der; -[e]s), **...bau|ge|nos|sen|schaft, ...ei|gen|tum, ...ei|gen|tü|mer, ...ei|gen|tü|me|rin, ...ein|rich|tung, ...geld; woh|nungs|los; Woh|nungs-mak|ler, ...markt, ...not, ...schlüs|sel, ...su|che; woh|nungs|su|chend; Woh|nungs|su|chen|de,** der *u.* die; -n, -n (↑R 5 ff.); **Woh|nungs-tausch, ...tür; woh|nung|su|chend** (*svw.* wohnungssuchend); **Woh|nung|su|chen|de** (*svw.* Wohnungssuchende); **Woh|nungs-wech|sel, ...zwangs|wirt|schaft; Wohn-vier|tel, ...wa|gen, ...zim|mer**

Wöhr|de, die; -, -n (*nordd. für* um das Wohnhaus gelegenes Ackerland)

Woi|lach ['wɔy...], der; -s, -e ⟨russ.⟩ (wollene [Pferde]decke)

Woi|wod, Woi|wo|de [*beide* wɔy...], der; ...den, ...den; ↑R 126 ⟨poln.⟩ (*früher* Fürst, *heute* oberster Beamter eines poln. Bezirks); **Woi|wod|schaft** (Amt u. Amtsbezirk eines Woiwoden)

Wok, der; -, -s ⟨chin.⟩ (flacher Kochtopf mit rundem Boden)

wöl|ben; sich -; **Wöl|bung**

Wol|de|mar (m. Vorn.)

[1]Wolf (m. Vorn.)

[2]Wolf, Hugo (österr. Komponist)

[3]Wolf, der; -[e]s, Wölfe (ein Raubtier); **Wölf|chen**

Wolf|diet|rich [*auch* 'vɔlf...] (m. Vorn.)

wöl|fen (gebären [von Wolf u. Hund])

Wolf|gang (m. Vorn.); **Wolf|gang|see** *vgl.* Sankt-Wolfgang-See; **Wolf|hard** (m. Vorn.)

Wöl|fin; wöl|fisch; Wölf|ling (junger Pfadfinder)

[1]Wolf|ram (m. Vorn.)

[2]Wolf|ram, das; -s (chem. Element, Metall; *Zeichen* W); **Wolf|ra|mit** [*auch* ...'mit], das; -s (Wolframerz)

Wolf|ram von E|schen|bach; (dt. Dichter des MA.); Wolfram von Eschenbachs Lieder, *aber* die Lieder Wolframs von Eschenbach; eine Wolfram-von-Eschenbach-Ausgabe (↑R 95)

Wolfs‿an|gel (ein Fanggerät), **...gru|be** (überdeckte Grube zum Fangen von Wölfen), **...hund** (einem Wolf ähnlicher dt. Schäferhund), **...hun|ger** (*ugs. für* großer Hunger), **...milch** (eine Pflanze), **...ra|chen** (angeborene Gaumenspalte), **...schlucht**, **...spin|ne**, **...spitz** (eine Hunderasse)

Wol|ga, die; - (Strom in Osteuropa); **Wol|go|grad** (russ. Stadt; *früher* Stalingrad)

Wo|lhy|ni|en usw. *vgl.* Wolynien usw.

Wölk|chen; Wol|ke, die; -, -n; **wöl|ken;** sich -; **Wol|ken‿bruch** (der), **...de|cke** (die; -), **...krat|zer** (Hochhaus); **Wol|ken|ku|ckucks|heim**, das; -[e]s (Luftgebilde, Hirngespinst); **wol|ken|los; Wol|ken|wand**, die; -; **wol|kig**

Woll|de|cke; Wol|le, die; -, *Plur. (Arten:)* -n; [1]**wol|len** (aus Wolle)

[2]**wol|len;** ich will, du willst; du wolltest *(Indikativ);* du wolltest *(Konjunktiv);* gewollt; wolle!; ich habe das nicht gewollt, *aber* ich habe helfen wollen

wöl|len (*Jägerspr.* das Gewölle auswerfen)

Woll‿fa|den, ...garn, ...ge|we|be, ...gras, ...han|del (*vgl.* [1]Handel); **Woll|hand|krab|be; wol|lig**

Wol|lin (eine Ostseeinsel)

Woll‿kamm, ...käm|mer, ...käm|me|rei, ...kleid, ...knäu|el; Woll|lap|pen (↑R 136); **Woll|laus** (↑R 136); **Woll‿maus** (*ugs. für* größere Staubflocke auf dem Fußboden), **...sa|chen** *(Plur.)*, **...sie|gel, ...spin|ne|rei, ...stoff**

Wol|lust, die; -, Wollüste; **wol|lüs|tig; Wol|lüst|ling**

Woll|wa|ren *Plur.*

Wol|per|tin|ger, der; -s, - (ein bayr. Fabeltier)

Wo|ly|ni|en [...i̯ən] (ukrain. Landschaft); **wo|ly|nisch;** -es Fieber (Fünftagefieber)

Wol|zo|gen (ein Adelsgeschlecht)

Wom|bat, der; -s, -s ‹austral.› (ein austral. Beuteltier)

wo|mit; wo|mög|lich; womöglich (vielleicht) kommt sie, *aber* wo möglich (wenn es irgendwie möglich ist)[,] kommt sie; **wo|nach; wo|ne|ben** *(selten);* **wo nicht;** er will ihn erreichen, wo nicht übertreffen

Won|ne, die; -, -n; **Won|ne‿ge|fühl, ...mo|nat** *od.* **...mond** (*alte Bez. für* Mai), **...prop|pen** (der; -s, -; *landsch. für* niedliches, wohlgenährtes [Klein]kind); **won|ne|trun|ken** *(geh.);* **won|ne|voll** *(geh.);* **won|nig; won|nig|lich** *(veraltend)*

Woog, der; -[e]s, -e (*landsch. für* Teich; tiefe Stelle im Fluss)

wo|ran (↑R 132); **wo|rauf; wo|rauf|hin; wo|raus**

[1]**Worb**, der; -[e]s, Wörbe *u.* [2]**Worb, Wor|be**, die; -, ...ben (*landsch. für* Griff am Sensenstiel)

Worces|ter|so|ße [ˈwustə(r)...]; ↑R 105 ‹nach der engl. Stadt Worcester› (scharfe Würztunke)

Words|worth [ˈwœ:(r)dzwœ:(r)θ] (engl. Dichter)

wo|rein (↑R 132)

wor|feln (*früher für* Getreide reinigen); ich ...[e]le (↑R 16)

Wörgl (österr. Stadt)

wo|rin (↑R 132)

Wö|ris|ho|fen, Bad (Stadt in Bayern)

Wor|ka|ho|lic [wœ:(r)kəˈhɔlik] (↑R 132), der; -s, -s ‹engl.› (*Psych.* jmd., der zwanghaft ständig arbeitet); **Work|shop** [ˈwœ:(r)kʃɔp], der; -s, -s (Seminar, Arbeitsgruppe)

World|cup [ˈwœ:(r)ldkap], der; -s, -s ‹engl.› ([Welt]meisterschaft [in verschiedenen sportlichen Disziplinen]); **World Wide Fund for Nature** [ˈwœ:(r)ld ˈwaid ˈfand ˈfə(r) ˈne:tʃə(r)], der; - - -s - - (internationale Naturschutzorganisation; *Abk.* WWF)

Wör|litz (Stadt östl. von Dessau); Wörlitzer Park

Worms (Stadt am Rhein); **Wormser** (↑R 103); - Konkordat (1122); **worm|sisch**

Worps|we|de (Ort im Teufelsmoor, nördl. von Bremen)

Wort, das; -[e]s, *Plur.* Wörter *u.* Worte; *Plur.* Wörter *für Einzelwort od. vereinzelte Wörter ohne Rücksicht auf den Zusammenhang,* z. B. Fürwörter; dieses Verzeichnis enthält 100 000 Wörter; *Plur.* Worte *für Äußerung, Ausspruch, Beteuerung, Erklärung, Begriff, Zusammenhängendes,* z. B. Begrüßungsworte; *auch für bedeutsame einzelne Wörter,* z. B. drei Worte nenn ich euch, inhaltsschwer; mit ander[e]n -en (*Abk.* m. a. W.); mit guten, mit wenigen -en; dies waren seine [letzten] -e; ich will nicht viel[e] -e machen; geflügelte, goldene -e; aufs -; - für -; von - zu -; - halten; beim - nehmen; zu -[e] kommen; **Wort‿ak|zent** *(Sprachw.)*, **...art** *(Sprachw.)*, **...aus|wahl, ...be|deu|tung; Wort|be|deu|tungs|leh|re**, die; - (*für* Semantik); **Wort‿bil|dung** *(Sprachw.)*, **...bruch** (der); **wort|brü|chig; Wört|chen; Wor|te|ma|che|rei** *(abwertend);* **Wör|ter‿buch, ...ver|zeich|nis; Wort‿fa|mi|lie** *(Sprachw.)*, **...feld** *(Sprachw.)*, **...fet|zen, ...fol|ge, ...for|schung, ...füh|rer, ...füh|re|rin, ...ge|fecht, ...ge|klin|gel** *(abwertend)*, **...ge|o|gra|phie, ...ge|plän|kel, ...ge|schich|te; wort‿ge|schicht|lich, ...ge|treu, ...ge|wal|tig, ...ge|wandt; Wort‿ge|wandt|heit, ...got|tes|dienst, ...grup|pe** *(Sprachw.)*

Wör|ther See, der; - -s, *auch* **Wör|ther|see**, der; -s (See in Kärnten)

Wörth|see, der; -s (See im oberbayr. Alpenvorland)

wort|karg; Wort‿karg|heit (die; -), **...klas|se** (*svw.* Wortart), **...klau|ber** *(abwertend)*, **...klau|be|rei** *(abwertend)*, **...kreu|zung** (*für* Kontamination), **...laut** (der; -[e]s), **...leh|re** (die; -); **wört|lich;** -e Rede; **wort|los; Wort‿mel|dung, ...re|gis|ter; wort|reich; Wort‿reich|tum** (der; -s), **...schatz** (*Plur.* ...schätze), **...schöp|fung, ...schwall** (der; -[e]s), **...sinn** (der; -[e]s), **...spiel, ...stamm** *(Sprachw.)*, **...streit, ...ver|dre|her, ...wahl** (die; -), **...wech|sel; wort|wört|lich; Wort|zei|chen** (als Warenzeichen schützbares Emblem)

wo|rü|ber (↑R 132); **wo|rum;** ich weiß nicht, - es geht; **wo|run|ter; wo|selbst** *(veraltet)*

Wo|tan (*Nebenform von* Wodan)

Wot|ru|ba (↑R 130; österr. Bildhauer)

wo|von; wo|vor

Woy|zeck [ˈvɔy...] (Titel[held] eines Dramenfragments von G. Büchner)

wo|zu; wo|zwi|schen *(selten)*

Woz|zeck (Titel[held] einer Oper von A. Berg)

wrack (*Seemannsspr.* völlig defekt, beschädigt; *Kaufmannsspr.* schlecht [von der Ware]); - werden; **Wrack**, das; -[e]s, *Plur.* -s, *selten* -e (gestrandetes od. stark beschädigtes, *auch* altes Schiff; *übertr. für* jmd., dessen körperliche Kräfte völlig verbraucht sind)

Wra|sen, der; -s, - (*nordd. für* Dampf, Dunst); **Wra|sen|ab|zug** (über dem Küchenherd)

wri|cken *u.* **wrig|gen** (*nordd. für* ein Boot durch einen am Heck hin u. her bewegten Riemen fortbewegen)

wrin|gen (nasse Wäsche auswinden); du wrangst; du wrängest; gewrungen; wring[e]!

Wroc|ław ['vrɔtswaf] (poln. Stadt an der Oder; *vgl.* Breslau)
Wru|ke, die; -, -n (*nordostd. für* Kohlrübe)
Ws = Wattsekunde
WSW = Westsüdwest[en]
Wu|cher, der; -s; **Wu|cher|blu|me** (Margerite); **Wu|che|rei; Wu|che|rer; Wu|che|rin; wu|che|risch; wu|chern;** ich ...ere (↑R 16); **Wu|cher|preis; Wu|cher|tum,** das; -s; **Wu|che|rung; Wu|cher|zin|sen** *Plur.*
Wuchs, der; -es, *Plur. (fachspr.)* Wüchse; **...wüch|sig** (z. B. urwüchsig); **Wuchs|stoff** (hormonartiger, das Wachstum der Zellen fördernder Stoff)
Wucht, die; -; **Wucht|baum** (*landsch. für* Hebebaum); **wuch|ten** (*ugs. für* schwer heben); **wuch|tig; Wuch|tig|keit,** die; -
Wühl|ar|beit; wüh|len; Wüh|ler; Wüh|le|rei (*ugs. für* ständiges Wühlen, Aufhetzen); **wüh|le|risch; Wühl‿maus, ...tisch** (*ugs.;* bes. in Kaufhäusern)
Wu|hne *vgl.* Wune
Wuhr, das; -[e]s, -e *u.* Wuh|re, die; -, -n (*bayr., südwestd. u. schweiz. für* [2]Wehr; Buhne); **Wuhr|baum; Wuh|re** *vgl.* Wuhr
Wul|fe|nit [*auch* ...'nit], das; -s (ein Mineral)
Wul|fi|la *vgl.* Ulfilas
Wulst, der; -es, *Plur.* Wülste, *fachspr. auch* -e *od.* die; -, Wülste; **Wülst|chen; wuls|tig; Wulst|ling** (ein Pilz)
wumm!
wum|men *vgl.* wimmen
wum|mern (*ugs. für* dumpf dröhnen); es wummert
Wüm|met *vgl.* Wimmet
wund; wund sein, werden; sich wund laufen, reiben; sich den Mund reden; sich wund liegen; sie hat sich wund gelegen; **Wund‿arzt** *(veraltend),* **...be|hand|lung, ...brand** (der; -[e]s); **Wun|de,** die; -, -n
Wun|der, das; -s, -; Wunder tun, wirken; kein Wunder; was Wunder, wenn ...; du wirst dein blaues Wunder erleben; er glaubt, Wunder was getan zu haben *(ugs.);* er glaubt, Wunder *od.* (↑R 46:) wunders wie geschickt er sei *(ugs.); vgl.* wundernehmen; **wun|der|bar; wun|der|ba|rer|wei|se; Wun|der‿blu|me, ...dok|tor, ...glau|be; wun|der|gläu|big; Wun|der‿hei|ler, ...hei|lung; wun|der|hübsch; Wun|der‿ker|ze, ...kind, ...kna|be, ...kraft** (die), **...kur** (*vgl.* [1]Kur); **Wun|der|lam|pe** (in Märchen); **wun|der|lich** (eigenartig); **Wun|der|lich|keit; wun|der|mild** *(veraltet);* **Wun|der|mit|tel,** das; **wun|dern;** es wundert mich, dass ...; mich wundert, dass ...; sich -; ich ...ere mich (↑R 16); **wun|der|neh|men** (↑R 46); es nimmt mich wunder (*schweiz. auch für* ich möchte wissen); es hat dich wundergenommen, braucht dich nicht wunderzunehmen; **wun|ders** *vgl.* Wunder; **wun|der|sam** *(geh.);* **wun|der|schön; Wun|der‿tat, ...tä|ter, ...tä|te|rin; wun|der|tä|tig; Wun|der‿tier** *(auch ugs. scherzh.),* **...tü|te; wun|der|voll; Wun|der|werk**
Wund‿fie|ber, ...in|fek|ti|on; wund lie|gen *vgl.* wund; **Wund‿mal** (*Plur.* ...male), **...pflas|ter, ...sal|be, ...starr|krampf** (der; -[e]s; *für* Tetanus)
Wundt (dt. Psychologe u. Philosoph)
Wund|ver|band
Wu|ne, Wuh|ne, die; -, -n (ins Eis gehauenes Loch)
Wunsch, der; -[e]s, Wünsche; **wünsch|bar** (*schweiz. für* wünschenswert); **Wunsch‿bild, ...den|ken** (das; -s); **Wün|schel|ru|te; Wün|schel|ru|ten|gän|ger; wün|schen;** du wünschst; **wün|schens|wert; Wunsch‿form** (*für* Optativ), **...geg|ner; wunsch|ge|mäß; Wunsch‿kan|di|dat, ...kan|di|da|tin, ...kind, ...kon|zert, ...lis|te; wunsch|los;** wunschlos glücklich; **Wunsch‿traum, ...vor|stel|lung, ...zet|tel**
wupp|dich!; Wupp|dich, der; *nur in* mit einem - (*ugs. für* schnell, gewandt); ↑R 49
Wup|per, die; - (r. Nebenfluss des Rheins); [1]**Wup|per|tal,** das; -[e]s; [2]**Wup|per|tal** (Stadt an der Wupper)
Wür|de, die; -, -n; **wür|de|los; Wür|de|lo|sig|keit,** die; -; **Wür|den|trä|ger; wür|de|voll; wür|dig; wür|di|gen; Wür|dig|keit,** die; -; **Wür|di|gung**
Wurf, der; -[e]s, Würfe; **Wurf|bahn; Würf|chen; Wür|fel,** der; -s, -; **Wür|fel|be|cher; Wür|fel|ohen; wür|fe|lig,** würf|lig; **wür|feln;** ich ...[e]le (↑R 16); gewürfeltes Muster; **Wür|fel‿spiel, ...zu|cker; Wurf‿ge|schoss, ...kreis** *(Handball);* **würf|lig** *vgl.* würfelig; **Wurf‿pfeil, ...sen|dung, ...tau|be** *(Sport);* **Wurf|tau|ben|schie|ßen**
Wür|ge‿griff, ...mal (*Plur.* ...male, *seltener* ...mäler); **wür|gen;** (↑R 50:) mit Hängen und Würgen (*ugs. für* mit großer Mühe, gerade noch); **Würg|en|gel** *(A. T.);* **Wür|ger** (Würgender; ein Vogel)
Wurm, der (*für* „hilfloses Kind" *ugs. auch* das); -[e]s, Würmer; **Würm|chen; Wurm|ei; wur|men** *(ugs.);* es wurmt (ärgert) mich; **Wurm‿farn, ...fort|satz** (am Blinddarm), **...fraß; wur|mig; Wurm|krank|heit; Wurm‿loch, ...mit|tel** (das)
Würm|see, der; -s (*früher für* Starnberger See)
wurm|sti|chig
Wurst, die; -, Würste; das ist mir -, *auch* Wurscht (*ugs. für* ganz gleichgültig); - wider -! (*ugs. für* wie du mir, so ich dir!); es geht um die - (*ugs. für* um die Entscheidung); mit der - nach der Speckseite werfen (*ugs. für* mit Kleinem Großes erreichen wollen); **Wurst‿brot, ...brü|he; Würst|chen; Würst|chen‿bu|de, ...stand; Wurs|tel,** der; -s, - (*bayr. u. österr. für* Hanswurst); **Würs|tel,** das; -s, - (*österr. für* Würstchen); **Wurs|te|lei** *(ugs.);* **wurs|teln** (*ugs. für* ohne Überlegung u. Ziel arbeiten); ich ...[e]le (↑R 16); **Wurs|tel|pra|ter,** der; -s (Vergnügungspark im Wiener Prater); **wurs|ten** (Wurst machen); **Wurs|ter,** Wurst|ler (*landsch. für* Fleischer, der besonders Wurst herstellt); **Wurs|te|rei,** Wurst|le|rei *(landsch.);* **Wurst|fin|ger** *(ugs.);* **wurs|tig** (*ugs. für* gleichgültig); **Wurs|tig|keit,** die; - *(ugs.);* **Wurst|kü|che; Wurst|ler** *vgl.* Wurster; **Wurst|le|rei** *vgl.* Wursterei; **Wurst‿sa|lat, ...sup|pe, ...wa|ren** *(Plur.),* **...zip|fel**
Wurt, die; -, -en, *auch* **Wur|te,** die; -, -n (*nordd. für* aufgeschütteter Erdhügel als Wohnplatz [zum Schutz vor Sturmfluten]); *vgl.* Warf[t]
Würt|tem|berg; Würt|tem|ber|ger (↑R 103); **würt|tem|ber|gisch**
Wurt|zit [*auch* ...'tsit], der; -s, -e ⟨nach dem franz. Chemiker Wurtz⟩ (ein Mineral)
Wurz, die; -, -en (*landsch. für* Wurzel)
Würz|burg (Stadt am Main); **Würz|bur|ger** (↑R 103); **würz|bur|gisch**
Wür|ze, die; -, -n; **Wur|zel,** die; -, -n (*Math. auch* Grundzahl einer Potenz); **Wur|zel‿bal|len, ...be|hand|lung** *(Zahnmed.),* **...bürs|te; Wür|zel|chen; wur|zel|echt;** -e Pflanze (Pflanze mit eigenen Wurzeln); **Wür|ze|lein; Wur|zel-**

‿fa|ser, ...fü|ßer (ein Urtierchen), **...haut; Wur|zel|haut|ent|zün|dung; wur|ze|lig,** wurz|lig; **Wur|zel|knol|le; wur|zel|los; Wur|zel|lo|sig|keit,** die; -; **wur|zeln;** die Eiche wurzelt tief [im Boden]; **Wur|zel‿sil|be** *(Sprachw.),* **...stock** *(Plur.* ...stöcke), **...werk** (das; -[e]s), **...zei|chen** *(Math.),* **...zie|hen** (das; -s; *Math.*); **wur|zen** *(bayr. u. österr. ugs. für* ausbeuten); du wurzt; **wür|zen** (mit Würze versehen); du würzt; **Würz|fleisch; wür|zig; Würz|lein; wurz|lig** *vgl.* wurzelig; **Würz|mi|schung; Wür|zung**

Wu|schel|haar *(ugs. für* lockiges od. unordentliches Haar); **wu|sche|lig** *(ugs.);* **Wu|schel|kopf**

wu|se|lig *(landsch.);* **wu|seln** *(landsch. für* sich schnell bewegen; geschäftig hin und her eilen; wimmeln); ich ...[e]le (↑R 16)

WUSt, Wust = Warenumsatzsteuer (in der Schweiz)

Wust, der; -[e]s (Durcheinander, ungeordnete Menge); **wüst; Wüs|te,** die; -, -n; **wüs|ten** (verschwenderisch umgehen); **Wüs|te|nei; Wüs|ten‿fuchs, ...kli|ma, ...kö|nig** *(geh. für* Löwe), **...sand, ...schiff** *(scherzh. für* Kamel), **...tier; Wüst|ling** (zügelloser Mensch); **Wüs|tung** (verlassene Siedlung und Flur; *Bergw.* verlassene Lagerstätte)

Wut, die; -; **Wut‿an|fall, ...aus|bruch; wü|ten; wü|tend; wut|ent|brannt; Wü|ter; Wü|te|rich,** der; -s, -e; **Wut|ge|heul; wut|schäu|mend** (↑R 40); *aber* vor Wut schäumend

wut|schen *(ugs. für* schnell, eilig sein); du wutschst

wut|schnau|bend (↑R 40)

Wutz, die; -, -en, *auch* der; -en, -en; ↑R 126 *(landsch. für* Schwein); **Wutz|chen**

wu|zeln *(bayr. u. österr. ugs. für* drehen, wickeln; sich drängen)

W. Va. = West Virginia

Wwe. = Witwe

WWF = World Wide Fund for Nature

Wwr. = Witwer

Wy. = Wyoming

Wy|an|dot ['wa̱iəndɔt], der; -, -s (Angehöriger eines nordamerik. Indianerstammes); **Wy|an|dot|te,** das; -, -s *od.* die; -, -n (eine amerik. Haushuhnrasse)

Wyc|lif ['wiklif] (↑R 130; engl. Reformator)

Wyk auf Föhr ['vi:k - -] (Stadt auf der Nordseeinsel Föhr)

Wy|o|ming [wa̱i'o:miŋ] (Staat in den USA; *Abk.* Wy.)

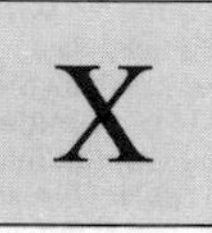

X [iks] (Buchstabe); das X; des X, die X, *aber* das x in Faxe (↑R 60); der Buchstabe X, x; jmdm. ein X für ein U vormachen

X (röm. Zahlzeichen) = 10

X, das; -, - (unbekannte Größe; unbekannter Name); ein Herr, eine Frau X; der Tag, die Stunde X; *in math. Formeln usw. kleingeschrieben:* 3x = 15

X, χ = Chi

Ξ, ξ = Xi

x-Ach|se ['iks...]; ↑R 25 *(Math.* Abszissenachse im [rechtwinkligen] Koordinatensystem)

Xan|ten (Stadt im Niederrhein. Tiefland); **Xan|te|ner** (↑R 103)

Xan|thin, das; -s ‹griech.› (eine Stoffwechselverbindung)

[1]**Xan|thip|pe** (Gattin des Sokrates); [2]**Xan|thip|pe,** die; -, -n *(ugs. für* zanksüchtige Frau)

Xan|tho|phyll, das; -s ‹griech.› *(Bot.* gelber Pflanzenfarbstoff)

Xa|ver ['ksa:vər] (m. Vorn.); **Xa|ve|ria** (w. Vorn.)

X-Bei|ne ['iks...] *Plur.* (↑R 25); **x-bei|nig,** *auch* **X-bei|nig** (↑R 25)

x-be|lie|big ['iks...] (↑R 25); jeder x-Beliebige (↑R 47); *vgl.* beliebig

X-Chro|mo|som ['iks...]; ↑R 25 *(Biol.* eines der beiden Geschlechtschromosomen)

Xe = *chem. Zeichen für* Xenon

X-Ein|heit ['iks...]; ↑R 25 (Längeneinheit für Röntgenstrahlen)

Xe|nia (w. Vorn.)

Xe|nie [...i̯ə], die; -, -n ‹griech.› *u.* **Xe|ni|on,** das; -s, ...ien [...i̯ən] (kurzes Sinngedicht); **Xe|no|kra|tie,** die; -, ...ien *(selten für* Fremdherrschaft); **Xe|non,** das; -s (chem. Element, Edelgas; *Zeichen* Xe); **Xe|non|lam|pe**

Xe|no|pha|nes (altgriech. Philosoph)

Xe|no|phon (altgriech. Schriftsteller); **xe|no|phon|tisch** (↑R 94); die xenophontischen Schriften

Xe|res ['çe:rɛs] usw. *vgl.* Jerez usw.

Xe|ro|gra|phie (↑R 33), die; -, ...ien ‹griech.› *(Druckw.* ein Vervielfältigungsverfahren); **xe|ro|gra|phie|ren; xe|ro|gra|phisch; Xe|ro|ko|pie,** die; -, ...ien (xerographisch hergestellte Kopie); **xe|ro|ko|pie|ren; xe|ro|phil** (die Trockenheit liebend [von Pflanzen]); **Xe|ro|phyt,** der; -en, -en; ↑R 126 (an trockene Standorte angepasste Pflanze)

Xer|xes (Perserkönig)

x-fach ['iks...] *(Math.* x-mal so viel); ↑R 25; **x-fa|che,** das; -n; ↑R 5 ff. *u.* R 25; *vgl.* Achtfache

x-för|mig, *auch* **X-för|mig** ['iks...] (↑R 25)

X-Ha|ken ['iks...]; ↑R 25 (Aufhängehaken für Bilder)

Xi, das; -[s], -s (griech. Buchstabe: *Ξ, ξ*)

x-mal ['iks...] (↑R 25)

X-Strah|len ['iks...] *Plur.;* ↑R 25 (Röntgenstrahlen)

x-te ['iks...] (↑R 25); x-te Potenz; zum x-ten Mal[e]; *vgl.* Mal

Xy|len, das; -s *(svw.* Xylol); **Xy|lo|graph** (↑R 33), der; -en, -en (↑R 126) ‹griech.› (Holzschneider); **Xy|lo|gra|phie,** die; -, ...ien *(nur Sing.:* Holzschneidekunst; Holzschnitt); **xy|lo|gra|phisch** (in Holz geschnitten); **Xy|lol,** das; -s ‹griech.; arab.› (ein Lösungsmittel); **Xy|lo|me|ter,** das; -s, - (Gerät zur Bestimmung des Rauminhalts unregelmäßig geformter Hölzer); **Xy|lo|phon,** das; -s, -e (ein Musikinstrument); **Xy|lo|se,** die; - (Holzzucker)

Y ['ypsilɔn, *österr. oft* y'psi:...] (Buchstabe); das Y; des Y, die Y, *aber* das y in Doyen (↑R 60); der Buchstabe Y, y

Y, das; -, - (Bez. für eine unbekannte Größe); *in math. Formeln usw. kleingeschrieben:* $y = 2x^2$

Y = *chem. Zeichen für* Yttrium

¥ = Yen

Y, υ = [2]Ypsilon

y., yd. = Yard

y-Ach|se ['ypsilɔn...]; ↑R 25 *(Math.* Ordinatenachse im [rechtwinkligen] Koordinatensystem)

Yacht [jaxt] *vgl.* Jacht

Yak [jak] *vgl.* Jak

Ya|ma|shi|ta [jama'ʃi:ta], der; -[s], -s ‹nach dem jap. Kunstturner Yamashita› (ein bestimmter Sprung am Langpferd)

Ya|mous|souk|ro [jamusu'kro] (↑R 130; Hptst. der ²Elfenbeinküste)
Yams|wur|zel ['jams...] *vgl.* Jamswurzel
Yang [jaŋ], das; -[s] ‹chin.› (männl., schöpferisches Prinzip in der chin. Philosophie)
Yan|kee ['jɛŋki], der; -s, -s ‹amerik.› (Spitzname für den US-Amerikaner); **Yan|kee Doo|dle** [- du:d(ə)l], der; - -[s] ([früheres] Nationallied der US-Amerikaner); **Yan|kee|tum,** das; -s
Yard [ja:(r)t], das; -s, -s ‹engl.› (angelsächs. Längenmaß; *Abk.* y. *od.* yd., *Plur.* yds.); 5 Yard[s] (↑R 90)
Ya|rẹn [ja...] (Hptst. von Nauru)
Yawl [jɔ:l], die; -, *Plur.* -e *u.* -s ‹engl.› (ein zweimastiges Segelboot)
Yb = *chem. Zeichen für* Ytterbium
¹Ybbs [ips], die; - (r. Nebenfluss der Donau); **²Ybbs an der Donau** (österr. Stadt)
Y-Chro|mo|som ['ypsilɔn...] (↑R 25; *Biol.* eines der beiden Geschlechtschromosomen)
yd., y. = Yard; **yds.** = Yards
Yel|low|stone-Na|ti|o|nal|park ['jɛlosto:n...], der; -[e]s (ein Naturschutzgebiet in den USA)
Yen [jɛn], der; -[s], -[s] ‹jap.› (Währungseinheit in Japan; 1 Yen = 100 Sen; *Abk.* ¥); 5 - (↑R 90)
Ye|ti ['je:ti], der; -s, -s ‹nepal.› (legendärer Schneemensch im Himalajagebiet)
Ygg|dra|sil ['yk...] (*nord. Mythol.* Weltesche, Weltbaum)
Yin [jin], das; -[s] ‹chin.› (weibl., empfangendes Prinzip in der chin. Philosophie)
Yip|pie ['jipi], der; -s, -s ‹amerik.› (aktionistischer, ideologisch radikalisierter Hippie)
Y|lang-Y|lang-Baum ['i:laŋ-'i:laŋ...] ‹malai.; dt.› (ein trop. Baum); **Y|lang-Y|lang-Öl** (Öl des Ylang-Ylang-Baumes)
Y-Li|nie ['ypsilɔn...] (↑R 25)
YMCA [waiɛmsi:'e:] = Young Men's Christian Association ['jaŋ 'mens 'kristjən əso:'sie:ʃ(ə)n] (Christlicher Verein Junger Männer)
Y|mir ['y:...] (*nord. Mythol.* Urriese, aus dessen Körper die Welt geschaffen wurde)
Yo|ga ['jo:ga], Jo|ga, der *u.* das; -[s] ‹sanskr.› (ind. philos. System [mit körperlichen u. geistigen Übungen]); **Yo|ga|übung** (↑R 132)
Yo|gi ['jo:...], Jo|gi *u.* **Yo|gin,** Jogin, der; -s, -s ‹sanskr.› (Anhänger des Yoga)
Yo|him|bin [jo...], das; -s ‹Bantuspr.› (*Biochemie* Alkaloid aus der Rinde eines westafrik. Baumes)
Yo|ko|ha|ma [jo...] (Stadt in Japan)
Yonne [jɔn] (l. Nebenfluss der Seine)
Yorck von War|ten|burg [jɔrk - -] (preuß. Feldmarschall)
York [jɔrk] (engl. Stadt); **York|shire|ter|ri|er** ['jɔrkʃi:(r)...]
Young|plan ['jaŋ...] ‹nach dem amerik. Finanzmann Owen Young›; ↑R 95 (Plan zur Regelung der dt. Reparationen 1930 bis 1932)
Youngs|ter ['jaŋstə(r)], der; -s, -[s] ‹engl.› (junger Sportler)
Yo-Yo [jo'jo:] *vgl.* Jo-Jo
Y|pern ['y:...] (belg. Stadt)
¹ Yp|si|lon ['ypsilɔn] *vgl.* Y (Buchstabe); **²Yp|si|lon,** das; -[s], -s (griech. Buchstabe: *Y, υ*); **³Yp|si|lon,** das; -s, -s *u.* **Yp|si|lon|eu|le,** die; -, -n (ein Nachtfalter)
Y|sop ['i:zɔp], der; -s, -e ‹semit.› (eine Heil- u. Gewürzpflanze)
Y|tong ® ['y:...], der; -s, -s (dampfgehärteter Leichtkalkbeton)
Yt|ter|bi|um [y'tɛr...], das; -s ‹nach dem schwed. Ort Ytterby›(chem. Element, Seltenerdmetall; *Zeichen* Yb); **Yt|ter|er|den** [y'tər...] *Plur.* (Seltenerdmetalle, die hauptsächlich in den Erdmineralien von Ytterby vorkommen); **Ytt|ri|um** (↑R 130), das; -s (chem. Element, Seltenerdmetall; *Zeichen* Y)
Yu|an ['ju:an], der; -[s], -[s] ‹chin.› (Währungseinheit in China); 5 Yuan (↑R 90)
Yu|ca|tán *vgl.* Yukatan
Yuc|ca ['juka], die; -, -s ‹span.› (Palmlilie)
Yu|ka|tan, *offz.* Yu|ca|tán [*beide* juka'tan] (mexikan. Halbinsel u. Staat)
¹Yu|kon ['ju:...], der; - (nordamerik. Fluss); **²Yu|kon** (kanad. Territorium); **Yu|kon|ter|ri|to|ri|um** (↑R 105), das; -s
Yun [jun], Isang (korean. Komponist)
Yup|pie ['jupi, *engl.* 'japi], der; -s, -s ‹amerik.› (junger karrierebewusster, großstädtischer Mensch)
Y|ver|don [ivɛr'dõ:] (schweiz. Stadt)
Y|vonne [i'vɔn] (w. Vorn.)
YWCA [waidablju:si:'e:] = Young Women's Christian Association ['jang 'wiminz 'kristjən əso:'sie:ʃ(ə)n] (Christlicher Verein Junger Mädchen)

Z (Buchstabe); das Z; des Z, die Z, *aber* das z in Gazelle (↑R 60); der Buchstabe Z, z; von A bis Z)
Z, ζ = Zeta
Z. = Zahl; Zeile
Za|bag|li|o|ne [...bal'jo:nə] (↑R 130), **Za|ba|io|ne** [...ba'jo:nə], die; -, -s ‹ital.› (Weinschaumcreme)
zạch (*landsch. für* geizig; zaghaft; zäh)
Za|cha|ri|as (m. Vorn.); *vgl.* Sacharja
Za|chä|us (bibl. Eigenn.)
zạck!; zạck, zạck!; **Zạck,** der; *in der Wendung* auf Zack sein (*ugs. für* schnell, aufgeweckt, fähig sein); **Zäck|chen; Zạ|cke,** die; -, -n (Spitze); **zạ|cken** (mit Zacken versehen); gezackt; **Zạ|cken,** der; -s, - (*bes. südd., österr. Nebenform von* Zacke); **zạ|cken|ar|tig; Zạ|cken‿kro|ne, ...li|nie**
zạ|ckern (*südwestd., westmitteld. für* pflügen); ich ...ere (↑R 16)
zạ|ckig (*ugs. auch für* schneidig); **Zạ|ckig|keit,** die; -; **zạck, zạck!**
zag (*geh. für* scheu)
Za|gel, der; -s, - (*landsch. für* Schwanz; Büschel)
za|gen (*geh.*); **zag|haft; Zag|haf|tig|keit,** die; -; **Zag|heit,** die; -
Zag|reb ['za:...] (↑R 130; Hptst. Kroatiens)
zäh; zäher, am zäh[e]sten; **Zä|heit** *frühere Schreibung für* Zähheit; **zäh|flüs|sig; Zäh|flüs|sig|keit,** die; -; **Zäh|heit,** die; -; **Zä|hig|keit,** die;
Zahl, die; -, -en (*Abk.* Z.); natürliche Zahlen *(Math.)*; **Zahl|ad|jek|tiv; Zähl|ap|pa|rat; zahl|bar** (zu [be]zahlen); **zähl|bar** (was gezählt werden kann); **Zahl|bar|keit,** die; -; **Zähl|bar|keit,** die; -; **Zähl|brett**
zäh|le|big
zah|len; er hat pünktlich gezahlt, *häufig auch* bezahlt; Lehrgeld zahlen; **zäh|len; Zah|len‿an|ga|be, ...fol|ge, ...ge|dächt|nis** (das; -ses), **...kom|bi|na|ti|on, ...lot|te|rie, ...lot|to; zah|len|mä|ßig; Zah|len‿ma|te|ri|al** (das; -s), **...mys|tik, ...rei|he, ...schloss, ...ska|la, ...sym|bo|lik; Zah|ler; Zäh|ler; Zahl|gren|ze; Zähl-**

kam|mer (*Med., Biol.* Glasplatte mit Netzeinteilung zum Zählen von Zellen); **Zähl|kan|di|dat** (*Polit.* aussichtsloser Kandidat, dessen Kandidatur lediglich die Zahl seiner Anhänger zeigen soll); **Zahl⌣kar|te, ...kell|ner; zahl|los;** *aber* (↑R 47 f.): sie gehört zu den Zahllosen, die ...; **Zähl|maß** (*Kaufmannsspr.* Maßeinheit für zählbare Mengen, z. B. Dutzend); **Zahl|meis|ter; zahl|reich;** *vgl.* zahllos; **Zähl|rohr** (Gerät zum Nachweis radioaktiver Strahlen); **Zahl⌣stel|le, ...tag; Zah|lung;** Zahlung leisten (*Kaufmannsspr.* zahlen); an Zahlungs statt; **Zäh|lung; Zah|lungs⌣an|wei|sung, ...auf|for|de|rung, ...auf|schub, ...be|din|gun|gen** *(Plur.)*, **...be|fehl** (*vgl.* Mahnbescheid), **...bi|lanz, ...er|leich|te|rung; zah|lungs|fä|hig; Zah|lungs⌣fä|hig|keit** (die; -), **...frist; zah|lungs|kräf|tig** *(ugs.)*; **Zah|lungs⌣mit|tel** (das), **...ter|min** (Zahlungsfrist); **zah|lungs|un|fä|hig; Zah|lungs⌣un|fä|hig|keit** (die; -), **...ver|kehr** (der; -[e]s), **...ver|pflich|tung, ...wei|se** (die); **Zähl|werk; Zahl⌣wort** (*Plur.* ...wör|ter), **...zei|chen**

zahm; ein zahmes Tier; **zähm|bar; Zähm|bar|keit,** die; -; **zäh|men; Zahm|heit,** die; -; **Zäh|mung**

Zahn, der; -[e]s, Zähne; ein hohler -; künstliche Zähne; **Zahn|arzt; Zahn|arzt|hel|fe|rin; Zahn|ärz|tin; zahn|ärzt|lich; Zahn|arzt|stuhl; Zahn⌣be|hand|lung, ...bein** (das; -[e]s; *für* Dentin), **...be|lag, ...bett, ...bürs|te; Zähn|chen; Zahn⌣creme, ...durch|bruch** (*für* Dentition); **zäh|ne|ble|ckend; zäh|ne|flet|schend;** ein -er Hund (↑R 40); **Zäh|ne|klap|pern,** das; -s; **zäh|ne⌣klap|pernd** (↑R 40), **...knir|schend** (↑R 40); **zäh|neln** (*selten für* zähnen); ich ...[e]le (↑R 16); **zah|nen** (Zähne bekommen); **zäh|nen** (mit Zähnen versehen); **Zahn⌣er|satz, ...fäu|le** (*für* Karies), **...fis|tel; Zahn|fleisch; Zahn|fleisch⌣blu|ten** (das; -s), **...ent|zün|dung; Zahn⌣fül|lung, ...hals, ...heil|kun|de** (die; -); **zah|nig** (*veraltet für* mit Zähnen versehen); **...zah|nig, ...zäh|nig** (z. B. scharfzahnig; scharfzähnig); **Zahn|klemp|ner** (*ugs. scherzh. für* Zahnarzt); **zahn|krank; Zahn⌣krank|heit, ...laut** (*Sprachw. für* Dental); **zahn|los; Zahn|lo|sig|keit,** die; -; **Zahn|lü|cke; zahn|lü|ckig; Zahn|me|di|zin,** die; -; **zahn|me|di|zi|nisch; Zahn⌣pas|ta,** *auch* **...pas|te, ...pfle|ge, ...pul|ver, ...rad; Zahn|rad|bahn; Zahn⌣schmelz** (der; -es), **...schmerz** *(meist Plur.)*, **...sei|de, ...span|ge, ...stein** (der; -[e]s), **...sto|cher, ...tech|nik** (die; -), **...tech|ni|ker, ...tech|ni|ke|rin; Zäh|nung** *(Philatelie)*; **Zahn⌣wal, ...weh** (das; -s), **...wur|zel**

Zäh|re, die; -, -n (*veraltet* Träne)

Zäh|rin|ger, der; -s, - (Angehöriger eines südd. Fürstengeschlechtes)

Zähr|te (*fachspr. für* [1]Zärte)

Zain, der; -[e]s, -e (*landsch. für* Zweig, Weidengerte; Metallstab; Rute; *Jägerspr.* Schwanz des Dachses); **Zai|ne,** die; -, -n (*veraltet, noch landsch. für* Flechtwerk, Korb); *vgl.* Zeine; **zai|nen** (*veraltet, noch landsch. für* flechten)

Za|i|re [za'i:r(ə)] (Staat in Afrika); **Za|i|rer; Za|i|re|rin; za|i|risch**

Za|ko|pa|ne [za...] (poln. Wintersportplatz, Luftkurort)

Zam|ba ['samba], die; -, -s ‹span.› (weiblicher Nachkomme eines schwarzen u. eines indian. Elternteils); **Zam|bo** ['sambo], der; -s, -s (männlicher Nachkomme eines schwarzen u. eines indian. Elternteils)

Zam|pa|no, der; -s, -s ‹nach einer Figur des ital. Films „La Strada"› (prahlerischer Mann)

Zam|perl, der; -s, -[n] (*bayr. für* [kleiner] nicht reinrassiger Hund)

Zan|der, der; -s, - ‹slaw.› (ein Fisch)

Za|nel|la, der; -s, *Plur. (Sorten:)* -s ‹ital.› (ein Gewebe)

Zan|ge, die; -, -n; **Zän|gel|chen; Zan|gen|be|we|gung; zan|gen|för|mig; Zan|gen|ge|burt**

Zank, der; -[e]s; **Zank|ap|fel,** der; -s (Gegenstand eines Streites); **zan|ken;** sich -; **Zän|ker; Zan|ke|rei** (*ugs. für* wiederholtes Zanken); **Zän|ke|rei** *meist Plur.* (kleinlicher Streit); **zän|kisch; Zank|sucht,** die; -; **zank|süch|tig**

Zä|no|ge|ne|se, die; -, -n ‹griech.› (Auftreten von Besonderheiten während der stammesgeschichtl. Entwicklung der Tiere); **zä|no|ge|ne|tisch**

Zapf, der; -[e]s, Zäpfe (*seltene Nebenform von* Zapfen; *südd. selten für* Ausschank); [1]**Zäpf|chen** (Teil des weichen Gaumens); [2]**Zäpf|chen** (kleiner Zapfen); **Zäpf|chen-R,** *auch* **Zäpf|chen-r,** das; -; ↑R 25 *(Sprachw.)*; **zap|fen; Zap|fen,** der; -s, -; **zap|fen|för|mig; Zap|fen|streich** (*Milit.* Abendsignal zur Rückkehr in die Unterkunft); der Große - (↑R 108); **Zap|fen|zie|her** (*südwestd. u. schweiz. für* Korkenzieher); **Zap|fer; Zapf|hahn; Zäpf|lein** *vgl.* [2]Zäpfchen; **Zapf⌣säu|le** (bei Tankstellen), **...stel|le, ...wel|le** *(Technik)*

za|po|nie|ren (mit Zaponlack überziehen); **Za|pon|lack** (farbloser Lack [als Metallschutz])

Zap|pe|ler, Zapp|ler; **zap|pe|lig,** zapp|lig; **zap|peln;** ich ...[e]le (↑R 16); **Zap|pel|phi|lipp,** der; -s, *Plur.* -e *u.* -s ‹nach einer Figur aus einem Kinderbuch› (zappeliges, unruhiges Kind)

zap|pen [*engl.* 'zɛpn̩] ‹engl.› (*ugs. für* mit der Fernbedienung ständig das Fernsehprogramm wechseln)

zap|pen|dus|ter (*ugs. für* sehr dunkel; aussichtslos)

Zapp|ler *vgl.* Zappeler; **Zapp|le|rin; zapp|lig** *vgl.* zappelig

Zar, der; -en, -en (↑R 126) ‹lat.› (ehem. Herrschertitel bei Russen, Serben, Bulgaren)

Za|ra|go|za [sara'gɔsa] (span. Stadt); *vgl.* Saragossa

Za|ra|thus|tra (↑R 130; Neugestalter der altiran. Religion); *vgl.* Zoroaster

Za|ren⌣fa|mi|lie, ...herr|schaft (die; -), **...reich; Za|ren|tum,** das; -s; **Za|re|witsch,** der; -[e]s, -e (Sohn eines russ. Zaren; russ. Kronprinz); **Za|rew|na,** die; -, -s (Tochter eines russ. Zaren)

Zar|ge, die; -, -n (*fachspr. für* Einfassung; Seitenwand)

Za|rin; Za|ris|mus, der; - (Zarenherrschaft); **za|ris|tisch; Za|ri|za,** die; -, *Plur.* -s *u.* ...zen (Frau od. Witwe eines Zaren)

zart; zart besaitet, zarter besaitet, am zartesten besaitet (*auch* zartbesaitet, zartbesaiteter, zartestbesaitet *od.* zartbesaitetste); *ebenso:* zart fühlend, *auch* zartfühlend; *in anderen Zusammensetzungen:* zartbitter, zartblau usw.; **zart|be|sai|tet** *vgl.* zart; **zart|bit|ter;** zartbittere Schokolade

[1]**Zär|te,** die; -, -n ‹slaw.› (ein Fisch); *vgl.* Zährte

[2]**Zär|te,** die; - (*veraltet für* Zartheit); **Zär|te|lei; zär|teln** (*selten für* Zärtlichkeiten austauschen); ich ...[e]le (↑R 16); **zart|füh|lend;** *vgl.* zart; **Zart|ge|fühl,** das; -[e]s; **Zart|heit; zärt|lich; Zärt|lich|keit; zart|ro|sa**

Za|sel, Za|ser, die; -, -n (*veraltet, noch landsch. für* Faser); **Za|ser** *vgl.* Zasel; **Zä|ser|chen; za|se|rig** *(veraltet)*; **za|sern** (*veraltet für* fasern); ich ...ere (↑R 16)

Zä|si|um, *chem. fachspr.* Cae|si|um ['tsɛ:...], das; -s ‹lat.› (chem. Element, Metall; *Zeichen* Cs)
Zas|pel, die; -, -n (altes Garnmaß)
Zas|ter, der; -s ‹sanskr.-zigeun.› (*ugs. für* Geld)
Zä|sur, die; -, -en ‹lat.› (Einschnitt [in einer Entwicklung]; *Verslehre* Einschnitt im Vers; *Musik* Ruhepunkt)
Zat|tel|tracht, die; - (eine mittelalterl. Kleidermode)
Zau|ber, der; -s, -; **Zau|ber‿bann, ...buch; Zau|be|rei; Zau|be|rer,** Zaub|rer; **Zau|ber‿flö|te, ...formel; zau|ber|haft; Zau|ber|hand;** *nur in* wie von *od.* durch Zauberhand; **Zau|be|rin,** Zaub|re|rin; **zau|be|risch; Zau|ber‿kas|ten, ...kraft** (die); **zau|ber|kräf|tig; Zau|ber‿kunst, ...künst|ler, ...kunst|stück, ...lehr|ling; zau|bern;** ich ...ere (↑R 16); **Zau|ber‿nuss** (die; -; *svw.* Hamamelis), **...spruch, ...stab, ...trank, ...trick, ...wort** (*Plur.* ...worte); **Zaub|rer** *vgl.* Zauberer; **Zaub|re|rin** *vgl.* Zauberin
Zau|che, die; -, -n (*veraltet, noch landsch. für* Hündin; liederliche Frau)
Zau|de|rei; Zau|de|rer, Zaud|rer; **Zau|de|rin,** Zaud|re|rin; **zau|dern;** ich ...ere (↑R 16); (↑R 50:) da hilft kein Zaudern; **Zaud|rer** *vgl.* Zauderer; **Zaud|re|rin** *vgl.* Zauderin
Zaum, der; -[e]s, Zäume (über den Kopf und ins Maul von Zug- u. Reittieren gelegte Vorrichtung aus Riemen u. Metallteilen [zum Lenken u. Führen]); im Zaum halten; **zäu|men; Zäu|mung; Zaum|zeug**
Zaun, der; -[e]s, Zäune; **Zäun|chen; zaun|dürr** (*österr. ugs. für* sehr mager); **Zaun|ei|dech|se; zäu|nen** (einzäunen); **Zaun‿gast** (*Plur.* ...gäste), **...kö|nig** (ein Vogel); **Zaun|pfahl;** ein Wink mit dem Zaunpfahl (*ugs. für* deutlicher Hinweis); **Zaun‿re|be** (Name einiger Pflanzen, bes. des Waldnachtschattens), **...schlüp|fer** (*landsch. für* Zaunkönig)
Zau|pe, die; -, -n (*landsch. für* Hündin; liederliche Frau)
zau|sen; du zaust; er zaus|te; **zau|sig** (*österr. für* zerzaust); -e Haare
Za|zi|ki *u.* Tsa|tsi|ki, der *u.* das; -s, -s ‹ngriech.› (Joghurt mit Knoblauch u. Salatgurkenstückchen)
Zä|zi|lie *vgl.* Cäcilie
z. B. = zum Beispiel
z. b. V. = zur besonderen Verwendung
z. D. = zur Disposition
z. d. A. = zu den Akten (erledigt)
ZDF = Zweites Deutsches Fernsehen
z. E. = zum Exempel
Zea, die; - ‹griech.› (*Bot.* Mais)
Ze|ba|oth, *ökum.* Ze|ba|ot *Plur.* ‹hebr., „himmlische Heerscharen"›; der Herr Zebaot[h] (alttest. Bez. Gottes)
Ze|be|dä|us (bibl. Eigenn.)
Ze|bra (↑R 130), das; -s, -s ‹afrik.› (gestreiftes südafrik. Wildpferd); **ze|bra|ar|tig; Ze|bra|strei|fen** (Kennzeichen von Fußgängerüberwegen); **Ze|bro|id,** das; -[e]s, -e ‹afrik.; griech.› (Kreuzung aus Zebra und Pferd)
Ze|bu, der *od.* das; -s, -s ‹tibet.› (ein asiat. Buckelrind)
Zech|bru|der *(ugs.);* **Ze|che,** die; -, -n (Rechnung für genossene Speisen u. Getränke; Bergwerk); die Zeche prellen; **ze|chen** (große Mengen Alkohol trinken); **Ze|chen‿ster|ben, ...still|le|gung; Ze|cher; Ze|che|rei; Ze|che|rin; Zech|ge|la|ge**
Ze|chi|ne, die; -, -n ‹ital.› (eine alte venezian. Goldmünze)
Zech‿kum|pan, ...prel|ler; Zech|prel|le|rei; Zech|prel|le|rin
Zech|stein, der; -[e]s (*Geol.* Abteilung des Perms)
Zech|tour
[1]Zeck, der *od.* das; -[e]s (*landsch. für* ein Kinderspiel [Haschen])
[2]Zeck, der; -[e]s, -e (*südd. u. österr. neben* Zecke); **Ze|cke,** die; -, -n (eine parasitisch lebende Milbe)
ze|cken (*landsch. für* [1]Zeck spielen; necken, reizen); necken und zecken; **Zeck|spiel,** das; -[e]s
Ze|de|kia, *ökum.* Zid|ki|ja (bibl. Eigenn.)
Ze|dent, der; -en, -en (↑R 126) ‹lat.› (*Rechtsw.* Gläubiger, der seine Forderung an einen Dritten abtritt)
Ze|der, die; -, -n ‹griech.› (immergrüner Nadelbaum); **ze|dern** (aus Zedernholz); **Ze|dern|holz**
ze|die|ren ‹lat.› (*Rechtsw.* eine Forderung an einen Dritten abtreten)
Zed|re|la‿baum (↑R 130; span.; dt.; *svw.* Zedrele), **...holz; Zed|re|le,** die; -, -n ‹lat.› (ein trop. Baum)
Zee|se, die; -, -n (Schleppnetz [der Ostseefischer]); **Zee|sen|boot**
Ze|fan|ja *vgl.* Zephanja
Zeh *vgl.* Zehe; **Ze|he,** die; -, -n, *auch* Zeh, der; -s, -en; die kleine, große Zehe, der kleine, große Zeh; **Ze|hen‿gän|ger** (*Zool.* eine Gruppe der Säugetiere), **...na|gel, ...spit|ze, ...stand; ...ze|her** (z. B. Paarzeher); **...ze|hig** (z. B. fünfzehig; *mit Ziffer* 5-zehig; ↑R 44)
zehn; wir sind zu zehnen *od.* zu zehnt; sich alle zehn Finger nach etwas lecken (*ugs. für* sehr begierig auf etwas sein); ↑R 108: die Zehn Gebote; *vgl.* acht; **Zehn,** die; -, -en (Zahl); *vgl.* [1]Acht; **Zehn|eck; zehn|eckig** (↑R 132); **zehn|ein|halb,** zehn|und|ein|halb; **Zehn|en|der** *(Jägerspr.);* **Zeh|ner** (*ugs. auch für* Zehnpfennigstück); *vgl.* Achter; **Zeh|ner|bruch,** der (*für* Dezimalbruch); **Zeh|ner|jau|se** (*ostösterr. ugs. veraltet für* Gabelfrühstück); **Zeh|ner|kar|te** (↑R 44); **zeh|ner|lei;** auf zehnerlei Art; **Zeh|ner‿pa|ckung ...stel|le** *(Math.);* **zehn|fach;** die -e Menge; *vgl.* achtfach; **Zehn|fa|che,** das; -n; *vgl.* Achtfache; **Zehn|fin|ger-Blind‿schrei|be|me|tho|de** *od.* **...schreib|me|tho|de** (die; -); **Zehn|fin|ger|sys|tem,** das; -s; **Zehn|flach,** das; -[e]s, -e, **Zehn|fläch|ner** (*für* Dekaeder); **Zehn|fuß|krebs** (*für* Dekapode); **Zehn|jah|res|fei|er** *od.* ...jahr|feier; **Zehn|jah|res|plan** (*mit Ziffern* 10-Jahres-Plan); ↑R 28; **Zehn|jahr|fei|er** *vgl.* Zehnjahresfeier; **zehn|jäh|rig;** *vgl.* achtjährig; **Zehn‿kampf** *(Sport),* **...kämp|fer; Zehn|klas|sen|schu|le** (bes. ehem. in der DDR); **zehn|mal;** *vgl.* achtmal; **zehn|ma|lig; Zehn|mark|schein** (↑R 28); **Zehn|me|ter|brett** (*mit Ziffern* 10-Meter-Brett *od.* 10-m-Brett); ↑R 28; **Zehn|pfen|nig‿brief|mar|ke, ...stück** (↑R 28); **zehnt;** *vgl.* zehn; **Zehnt,** Zehn|te, der; ...ten, ...ten (*früher* [Steuer]abgabe); den Zehnten fordern, geben; **zehn|tau|send;** die oberen zehntausend (↑R 48); **zehn|te;** *vgl.* achte *u.* Muse; **Zehn|te** *vgl.* Zehnt; **zehn|tel;** *vgl.* achtel; **Zehn|tel,** das, *schweiz. meist* der; -s, -; *vgl.* Achtel; **Zehn|tel‿gramm, ...se|kun|de; zehn|tens; Zehn|ton|ner** (*mit Ziffer* 10-Tonner; ↑R 44); **Zehnt|recht,** das; -[e]s; **zehn|und|ein|halb** *vgl.* zehneinhalb
zeh|ren; Zehr‿geld *(veraltet),* **...pfen|nig** *(veraltet);* **Zeh|rung** *(veraltet)*
Zei|chen, das; -s, -; - setzen; **Zei|chen‿block** (*vgl.* Block), **...brett, ...drei|eck, ...er|klä|rung, ...feder, ...film, ...heft, ...leh|rer, ...leh|re|rin, ...pa|pier, ...saal, ...schutz** (*svw.* Warenzeichen), **...set|zung** (die; -; *für* Interpunktion), **...spra|che, ...stift** (der),

...stun|de, ...trick|film, ...un|ter|richt, ...vor|la|ge; zeich|nen; Zeich|nen, das; -s; Zeich|ner; Zeich|ne|rin; zeich|ne|risch; Zeich|nung; zeich|nungs|be|rech|tigt; Zeich|nungs|be|rech|ti|gung

Zei|del|meis|ter (*veraltet für* Bienenzüchter); zei|deln (*veraltet für* Honigwaben ausschneiden); ich ...[e]le (↑R 16); Zeid|ler (*veraltet für* Bienenzüchter); Zeid|le|rei (*veraltet für* Bienenzucht)

Zei|ge|fin|ger, *schweiz. auch* Zeig|fin|ger; zei|gen; etwas zeigen; sich [großzügig] zeigen; Zei|ger; Zei|ge|stock *Plur.* ...stöcke; Zeig|fin|ger *vgl.* Zeigefinger

zei|hen *(geh. veraltend);* du ziehst; du ziehest; geziehen; zeih[e]!

Zei|le, die; -, -n (*Abk.* Z.); Zei|len‿ab|stand, ...dorf, ...gieß|ma|schi|ne *od.* ...guss|ma|schi|ne, ...ho|no|rar, ...län|ge, ...maß (das), ...schal|ter (an der Schreibmaschine), ...sprung *(Verslehre);* zei|len|wei|se; ...zei|ler (z. B. Zweizeiler, *mit Ziffer* 2-Zeiler; ↑R 44); ...zei|lig (z. B. sechszeilig, *mit Ziffer* 6-zeilig; ↑R 44)

Zei|ne, die; -, -n (*schweiz. für* großer Korb mit zwei Griffen, z. B. für Wäsche); *vgl.* Zaine

Zeis|chen (kleiner Zeisig)

Zei|sel|bär (*landsch. für* Tanzbär); [1]zei|seln (*landsch. für* eilen, geschäftig sein); ich ...[e]le (↑R 16) [2]zei|seln (*schwäb. für* anlocken); ich ...[e]le (↑R 16)

Zei|sel|wa|gen ‹*zu* [1]zeiseln› (*landsch. für* Leiterwagen)

zei|sen (*bayr. für* Verworrenes auseinander zupfen); du zeist; er zeis|te

Zei|sig, der; -s, -e ‹tschech.› (ein Vogel); Zei|sig|fut|ter; *vgl.* [1]Futter; zei|sig|grün

Zei|sing, der; -s, -e (*Seemannsspr. für* Segeltuchstreifen, Tauende)

Zeiß, Carl (dt. Mechaniker); Zeiss (®: opt. u. fotogr. Erzeugnisse); Zeisssche Erzeugnisse; Zeiss|glas *Plur.* ...gläser; ↑R 95

zeit; *Präp. mit Gen.:* zeit meines Lebens, *aber* zeitlebens; Zeit, die; -, -en; zu meiner, seiner, uns[e]rer Zeit; zu aller Zeit, *aber* all[e]zeit; auf Zeit (*Abk.* a. Z.); eine Zeit lang; einige, eine kurze Zeit lang; es ist an der Zeit; von Zeit zu Zeit; Zeit haben; beizeiten; vorzeiten; zurzeit (gerade jetzt), zuzeiten (bisweilen), *aber* zur Zeit, zu der Zeit, zu Zeiten (*Abk.* z. Z., z. Zt.) Karls d. Gr.; jederzeit, *aber* zu jeder Zeit; derzeit; seinerzeit (*Abk.* s. Z.), *aber* alles zu seiner Zeit; zeitlebens; auf Zeit spielen *(Sportspr.);* eine [viel] Zeit sparende Lösung, *aber* eine zeitsparende, zeitsparendere Lösung; Zeit‿ab|schnitt, ...ab|stand, ...ach|se, ...al|ter, ...an|ga|be (*Sprachw.* Umstandsangabe der Zeit), ...an|sa|ge *(Rundf.),* ...ar|beit, ...auf|nah|me *(Fotogr.),* ...auf|wand; zeit|auf|wen|dig; Zeit‿bom|be, ...dau|er, ...do|ku|ment, ...druck (der; -[e]s), ...ein|heit, ...ein|tei|lung; Zei|ten‿fol|ge (die; -; *für* Consecutio Temporum), ...wen|de (*od.* Zeitwende); Zeit|er|fas|sung; Zeit|er|fas|sungs|ge|rät; Zeit‿er|schei|nung, ...er|spar|nis, ...fah|ren (das; -s; *Radsport*), ...fak|tor (der; -s), ...feh|ler *(Reiten),* ...form (*für* Tempus), ...fra|ge; zeit|fremd; zeit|ge|bun|den; Zeit‿ge|fühl (das; -[e]s), ...geist (der; -[e]s); zeit|ge|mäß; Zeit‿ge|nos|se, ...ge|nos|sin; zeit|ge|nös|sisch; zeit|ge|recht (*österr. neben* rechtzeitig); Zeit‿ge|schäft *(Kaufmannsspr.),* ...ge|sche|hen, ...ge|schich|te (die; -), ...ge|schmack, ...ge|winn; zeit|gleich; zeit|her (*veraltet, noch landsch. für* seither, bisher); zeit|he|rig *(veraltet, noch landsch.);* zei|tig; zei|ti|gen (hervorbringen); Erfolge zeitigen; Zeit‿kar|te, ...kri|tik (die; -); zeit|kri|tisch; Zeit lang *vgl.* Zeit; Zeit|lauf, der; -[e]s, *Plur.* ...läufte, *seltener* ...läufe *meist Plur.;* zeit|le|bens; zeit|lich (*österr. ugs. auch für* zeitig, früh); das Zeitliche (↑R 47) segnen (*veraltend für* sterben; *ugs. scherzh. für* entzwei gehen); Zeit|lich|keit, die; - (Leben auf Erden, irdische Vergänglichkeit); Zeit|lohn; zeit|los; Zeit|lo|se, die; -, -n (Pflanze [*meist für* Herbstzeitlose]); Zeit|lo|sig|keit, die; -; Zeit|lu|pe, die; -; Zeit|lu|pen|tem|po, das; -s; Zeit‿man|gel (der; -s), ...maß (das), ...mes|ser (der; *für* Chronometer); Zeit|mes|sung; zeit‿nah, ...na|he; Zeit|nah|me, die; - *(Sport);* Zeit‿neh|mer *(Sport),* ...not (die; -), ...per|so|nal, ...plan, ...punkt, ...raf|fer *(Film);* zeit|rau|bend; ein zeitraubendes (viel Zeit kostendes) Verfahren; *vgl.* Zeit; Zeit‿raum, ...rech|nung; zeit|schnell *(Sport);* die -sten Läufer; Zeit|schrift (*Abk.* Zs., Zschr.); Zeit|schrif|ten‿auf|satz, ...ver|lag, ...ver|le|ger; Zeit‿sinn (der; -[e]s), ...sol|dat, ...span|ne; zeit|spa|rend *vgl.* Zeit; Zeit‿sprin|gen (das; -s, -; *Reitsport*), ...stra|fe *(Sport),* ...ta|fel, ...takt *(Fernsprechwesen);* Zei|tung; Zei|tung|le|sen, das; -s; Zei|tungs‿ab|la|ge, ...an|non|ce, ...an|zei|ge, ...ar|ti|kel, ...aus|schnitt, ...be|richt, ...en|te *(ugs.),* ...frau, ...in|se|rat, ...ki|osk, ...kor|res|pon|dent, ...le|ser, ...mann (*Plur.* ...männer *od.* ...leute), ...mel|dung, ...no|tiz, ...pa|pier, ...ro|man, ...trä|ger, ...ver|käu|fer, ...ver|käu|fe|rin, ...ver|lag, ...ver|le|ger, ...we|sen (das; -s), ...wis|sen|schaft (die; -); Zeit‿ver|geu|dung, ...ver|lust, ...ver|schie|bung, ...ver|schwen|dung; zeit|ver|setzt; eine -e Fernsehübertragung; Zeit‿ver|trag, ...ver|treib (der; -[e]s, -e); zeit|wei|lig; zeit|wei|se; Zeit‿wen|de (*vgl.* Zeitenwende), ...wert, ...wort (*Plur.* ...wörter); Zeit|wort|form; zeit|wört|lich

Zeitz (Stadt an der Weißen Elster)

Zeit|zei|chen *(Rundf., Funkw.)*

Zeit|zer (↑R 103)

Zeit‿zeu|ge, ...zeu|gin, ...zo|ne, ...zün|der

Ze|leb|rant (↑R 130), der; -en, -en (↑R 126) ‹lat.› (die Messe lesender Priester); Ze|leb|ra|ti|on, die; -, -en (Feier [des Messopfers]); ze|leb|rie|ren (feierlich begehen; die Messe lesen); Ze|leb|ri|tät, die; -, -en (*selten für* Berühmtheit)

Zel|ge, die; -, -n (*südd. für* [bestelltes] Feld, Flurstück)

Zell (Name mehrerer Städte)

Zel|la-Meh|lis; ↑R 106 (Stadt im Thüringer Wald)

Zell|at|mung, die; -; Zel|le, die; -, -n ‹lat.›; Zel|len|bil|dung; zel|len|för|mig; Zel|len|ge|we|be, Zell|ge|we|be; Zel|len‿leh|re (die; -; *für* Zytologie), ...schmelz (*für* Cloisonné)

Zel|ler, der; -s (*österr. ugs. für* Sellerie)

Zell‿for|schung (die; -), ...ge|we|be (*vgl.* Zellengewebe); Zell|ge|webs|ent|zün|dung; Zell|glas, das; -es (eine Folie); zel|lig; Zell|kern; Zell|leh|re (↑R 136) *vgl.* Zellenlehre; Zell|memb|ran; Zel|lo|i|din|pa|pier [...o|i...] ‹lat.; griech.› (Kollodiumschichtträger für Bromsilber bei fotogr. Filmen); Zel|lo|phan usw. *vgl.* Cellophan usw.; Zell|stoff (Produkt aus Zellulose); Zell|stoff|fab|rik (↑R 136), die; -, -en; Zell|tei|lung; zel|lu|lar, zel|lu|lär ‹lat.› (aus Zellen gebildet); Zel|lu|lar|pa|tho|lo|gie, die; - (*Med.* Lehre, nach der krankhafte Veränderungen in den Zellveränderungen zu suchen sind); Zel|lu|li|tis, die; -, ...iti|den (Entzündung des Zellge-

webes); **Zel|lu|lo̱id,** *fachspr.* Cel|lu|lo̱id, das; -[e]s ‹lat.; griech.› (Kunststoff, Zellhorn); **Zel|lu|lo̱|se,** *fachspr.* Cel|lu|lo̱|se, die; -, *Plur. (Sorten:)* -n ‹lat.› (Hauptbestandteil der pflanzlichen Zellwände; Zellstoff); **Zẹll‿ver|meh|rung, ...wand, ...wol|le** (die; -)
Ze|lo̱t, der; -en, -en (↑R 126) ‹griech.› ([Glaubens]eiferer); **ze|lo̱|tisch; Ze|lo|tịs|mus,** der; -
[1]**Zẹlt,** der; -[e]s (wiegende Gangart von Pferden)
[2]**Zẹlt,** das; -[e]s, -e; **Zẹlt|bahn; Zẹlt|bla|che** (*schweiz. für* Zeltbahn); **Zẹlt|blatt** (*österr. für* Zeltbahn); **Zẹl|te,** der; -n, -n (↑R 126) *u.* **Zẹl|ten,** der; -s, - (*südd., österr. für* kleiner, flacher [Leb]kuchen); **zẹl|ten** (in Zelten übernachten, wohnen); gezeltet; [1]**Zẹl|ter** (*selten für* Zeltler)
[2]**Zẹl|ter,** der; -s, - (auf Passgang abgerichtetes Damenreitpferd); **Zẹlt|gang,** der (Passgang)
Zẹlt‿he|ring, ...la|ger (*Plur.* ...lager), **...lein|wand** (die; -); **Zẹlt|ler** (jmd., der zeltet)
Zẹlt|li, das; -s, - (*schweiz. mdal. für* Bonbon)
Zẹlt‿mast (der), **...mis|si|on** (die; -; *ev. Kirche*), **...pflock, ...pla|ne, ...platz, ...stadt, ...stock** (*Plur.* ...stöcke), **...wand**
Ze|mẹnt, der, (*für* Zahnbestandteil:) das; -[e]s, -e ‹lat.› (Bindemittel; Baustoff; Bestandteil der Zähne); **Ze|men|ta|ti|o̱n,** die; -, -en (Härtung der Stahloberfläche; Abscheidung von Metallen aus Lösungen); **Ze|mẹnt‿bo|den, ...dach; ze|men|ti̱e|ren** (mit Zement ausfüllen, verputzen; eine Zementation durchführen; *übertr. auch für* [einen Zustand, Standpunkt u. dgl.] starr u. unverrückbar festlegen); **Ze|men|ti̱e|rung; Ze|mẹnt‿röh|re, ...sack, ...si|lo**
Zen [zɛn, *auch* tsɛn], das; -[s] (jap. Richtung des Buddhismus)
Ze̱|ner|di|o|de (↑R 95) ‹nach dem Physiker› (eine Halbleiterdiode)
Ze|ni̱t [*auch* ...'nit], der; -[e]s ‹arab.› (Scheitelpunkt [des Himmels]); **Ze|ni̱t|hö|he**
Ze̱|no[n] (Name zweier altgriech. Philosophen; byzant. Kaiser)
Ze|no|ta̱ph *vgl.* Kenotaph
zen|si̱e|ren ‹lat.› (benoten; [auf unerlaubte Inhalte] prüfen); **Zen|si̱e|rung; Zẹn|sor,** der; -s, ...o̱ren (altröm. Beamter; Beurteiler, Prüfer); **zen|so̱|risch** (den Zensor betreffend); **Zen|su̱r,** die; -, -en (*nur Sing.:* behördl. Prüfung [und Verbot] von Druckschriften u. a.; [Schul]note); **zen|su|ri̱e|ren** (*österr., schweiz. für* prüfen, beurteilen); **Zẹn|sus,** der; -, - (Schätzung; Volkszählung)
Zẹnt, die; -, -en ‹lat., „Hundertschaft"› (germ. Gerichtsverband)
Zen|ta̱ur, Ken|ta̱ur, der; -en, -en (↑R 126) ‹griech.› (Wesen der griech. Sage mit menschlichem Oberkörper u. Pferdeleib)
Zen|te|na̱r, der; -s, -e ‹lat.› (*selten für* Hundertjähriger); **Zen|te|na̱r‿aus|ga|be, ...fei|er; Zen|te|na̱|ri|um,** das; -s, ...ien [...i̯ən] (Hundertjahrfeier); **zen|te|si|ma̱l** (hundertteilig); **Zen|te|si|ma̱l|waa|ge; zẹnt|frei** (*früher* dem Zentgericht nicht unterworfen); **Zẹnt‿ge|richt** (*früher*), **...graf** (*früher*); **Zen|ti...** (Hundertstel...; ein Hundertstel einer Einheit, z. B. Zentimeter = 10^{-2} Meter; *Zeichen* c); **Zen|ti|fo̱|lie** [...i̯ə], die; -, -n (eine Rosenart); **Zen|ti‿grạmm**[1] (1/100 g; *Zeichen* cg), **...li̱|ter**[1] (1/100 l; *Zeichen* cl), **...me̱|ter**[1] (*Zeichen* cm); **Zen|ti|me̱|ter|maß,** das; **Zẹnt|ner,** der; -s, - (100 Pfund od. 50 kg; *Abk.* Ztr.; *Österreich u. Schweiz* 100 kg [Meterzentner], *Zeichen* q); **Zẹnt|ner‿ge|wicht, ...last; zẹnt|ner|schwer; zẹnt|ner|wei|se**
zent|ra̱l (↑R 130) ‹griech.› (in der Mitte; im Mittelpunkt befindlich, von ihm ausgehend; Mittel..., Haupt..., Gesamt...); **Zent|ra̱l|af|ri|ka; Zent|ra̱l|af|ri|ka|ner; zent|ra̱l|af|ri|ka|nisch,** *aber* (↑R 108): die Zentralafrikanische Republik; **Zent|ra̱l|ame|ri|ka** (↑R 132; festländischer Teil Mittelamerikas)
Zent|ra̱l‿bank (↑R 130; *Plur.* ...banken), **...bau** (*Plur.* ...bauten; *Archit.*); **zent|ra̱l|be|heizt; Zent|ra̱l|be|hör|de** (oberste Behörde); **Zent|ra̱|le,** die; -, -n (zentrale Stelle; Hauptort, -geschäft, -stelle; Fernsprechvermittlung [in einem Großbetrieb]; *Geom.* Mittelpunktslinie); **Zent|ra̱l‿fi|gur, ...flug|ha|fen** (Flughafen, der nach allen Flugrichtungen offen ist und allen Fluggesellschaften dient); **zent|ra̱l|ge|heizt** (*svw.* zentralbeheizt); **Zent|ra̱l‿ge|walt, ...hei|zung** (Sammelheizung)
Zent|ra|li|sa|ti|o̱n (↑R 130), die; -, -en ‹franz.› (Zentralisierung); **zent|ra|li|si̱e|ren** (zusammenziehen, in einem [Mittel]punkt vereinigen); **Zent|ra|li|si̱e|rung** (Zusammenziehung, Vereinigung in einem [Mittel]punkt); **Zent|ra|lịs|mus,** der; - ‹griech.› (Streben nach Zusammenziehung [der Verwaltung u. a.]); **zent|ra|lis|tisch; Zent|ra|li|tä̱t,** die; - (Mittelpunktslage von Orten); **Zent|ra̱l‿ko|mi|tee** (oberstes Organ der kommunist. u. mancher sozialist. Parteien; *Abk.* ZK), **...kraft** (die; *Physik*), **...mas|siv** (das; -s; in Frankreich), **...ner|ven|sys|tem, ...or|gan, ...per|spek|ti|ve** (*fachspr.*), **...prob|lem, ...stel|le, ...ver|band, ...ver|wal|tung**
zent|ri̱e|ren (↑R 130; auf die Mitte einstellen); sich -; **Zent|ri̱e|rung; Zent|ri̱er|vor|rich|tung; zent|ri|fu|ga̱l** ‹griech.; lat.› (vom Mittelpunkt wegstrebend); **Zent|ri|fu|ga̱l‿kraft** (die), **...pum|pe** (Schleuderpumpe); **Zent|ri|fu̱|ge,** die; -, -n (Schleudergerät zur Trennung von Flüssigkeiten); **zent|ri|fu|gi̱e|ren** (mithilfe der Zentrifuge zerlegen); **zent|ri|pe|ta̱l** (zum Mittelpunkt hinstrebend); **Zent|ri|pe|ta̱l|kraft,** die; **zẹnt|risch** ‹griech.› (im Mittelpunkt befindlich, mittig); **Zẹnt|ri|win|kel** (Mittelpunktswinkel)
Zẹnt|rum (↑R 130), das; -s, ...tren (Mittelpunkt; Innenstadt; Haupt-, Sammelstelle; *nur Sing.:* Partei des politischen Katholizismus 1870-1933); **Zẹnt|rums|par|tei,** die; -
Zen|tu̱|rie [...i̯ə], die; -, -n ‹lat.› (altröm. Soldatenabteilung von 100 Mann); **Zen|tu̱|rio,** der; -s, ...o̱nen (Befehlshaber einer Zenturie)
Zẹn|zi (w. Vorn.)
Ze|o|li̱th [*auch* ...'lit], der; *Gen.* -s *u.* -en, *Plur.* -e[n] (↑R 126) ‹griech.› (ein Mineral)
Ze|pha̱n|ja, *ökum.* Ze|fan|ja (bibl. Prophet)
Ze̱|phir, *auch* Ze̱|phyr, der; -s, *Plur.* -e, *österr.* ...i̱re ‹griech.› (ein Baumwollgewebe; *nur Sing.: geh. für* milder Wind); **ze|phi̱|risch,** *auch* ze|phy̱|risch (*geh. für* säuselnd, lieblich, sanft); **Ze̱|phir|wol|le,** Ze̱|phyr|wol|le; **Ze̱|phyr** usw. *vgl.* Zephir usw.
[1]**Zẹp|pe|lin** (Familienn.); [2]**Zẹp|pe|lin,** der; -s, -e (Luftschiff); **Zẹp|pe|lin|luft|schiff**
Zẹp|ter, das, *seltener* der; -s, - ‹griech.› (Herrscherstab); das Zepter führen
zer... (*Vorsilbe von Verben,* z. B. zerbröckeln, du zerbröckelst, zerbröckelt, zu zerbröckeln)
Zer *vgl.* Cer
Ze|ra̱t, das; -[e]s, -e ‹lat.› (Wachssalbe)
Zẹr|be *vgl.* Zirbe
zer|bei̱|ßen

[1] [*auch* 'tsɛn]

zer|bers|ten
Zer|be|rus, der; -, -se (*griech. Sage* der den Eingang der Unterwelt bewachende Hund; *scherzh. für* grimmiger Wächter)
zer|beu|len
zer|bom|ben
zer|bre|chen; zer|brech|lich; Zer|brech|lich|keit, die; -
zer|brö|ckeln; Zer|brö|cke|lung, Zer|bröck|lung
Zerbst (Stadt in Sachsen-Anhalt); **Zerbs|ter** (↑R 103)
zer|deh|nen
zer|dep|pern (*ugs. für* [durch Werfen] zerstören); ich ...ere (↑R 16)
zer|drü|cken
Ze|re|a|lie [...i̯ə], die; -, ...ien [...i̯ən] *meist Plur.* ⟨lat.⟩ (Getreide; Feldfrucht)
Ze|re|bel|lum, *med. fachspr.* Ce|re|bel|lum [tse...], das; -s, ...bella ⟨lat.⟩ (*Med.* Kleinhirn)
ze|reb|ral (↑R 130; das Zerebrum betreffend); **Ze|reb|ral,** der; -s, -e *od.* **Ze|reb|ral|laut,** der; -[e]s, -e (*Sprachw.* mit der Zungenspitze am Gaumen gebildeter Laut); **ze|reb|ro|spi|nal** (*Med.* Hirn u. Rückenmark betreffend); **Ze|reb|rum,** *med. fachspr.* Ce|reb|rum, das; -s, ...bra (Großhirn, Gehirn)
Ze|re|mo|nie [*auch, österr. nur,* ...'mo:ni̯ə], die; -, ...i̯en [*auch* ...'mo:ni̯ən] ⟨lat.⟩ (feierl. Handlung; Förmlichkeit); **ze|re|mo|ni|ell** (feierlich; förmlich, gemessen; steif, umständlich); **Ze|re|mo|ni|ell,** das; -s, -e ([Vorschrift für] feierliche Handlungen); **Ze|re|mo|ni|en|meis|ter; ze|re|mo|ni|ös** (steif, förmlich)
Ze|re|sin, *fachspr.* Ce|re|sin, das; -s ⟨lat.⟩ (gebleichtes Erdwachs aus hochmolekularen Kohlenwasserstoffen)
Ze|re|vis [...'vi:s], das; -, - ⟨kelt.⟩ (*Studentenspr. veraltet für* Bier; Käppchen der Verbindungsstudenten)
¹zer|fah|ren; die Wege sind -; **²zer|fah|ren** (verwirrt; gedankenlos); **Zer|fah|ren|heit,** die; -
Zer|fall, der; -[e]s, ...fälle (*nur Sing.:* Zusammenbruch, Zerstörung; *Kernphysik* spontane Spaltung des Atomkerns); **zer|fal|len;** die Mauer ist zerfallen; er ist mit der ganzen Welt zerfallen (nichts ist ihm recht); **Zer|falls_er|schei|nung, ...pro|dukt, ...stoff**
zer|fa|sern
zer|fet|zen; Zer|fet|zung
zer|flat|tern
zer|fled|dern *vgl.* zerfledern; **zer|fle|dern** (*ugs. für* durch häufigen Gebrauch [an den Rändern] abnutzen, zerfetzen [von Büchern, Zeitungen o. Ä.]); ich ...ere (↑R 16)
zer|flei|schen (zerreißen); du zerfleischst; **Zer|flei|schung**
zer|flie|ßen
zer|fran|sen
zer|fres|sen
zer|fur|chen; zer|furcht; eine zerfurchte Stirn
zer|ge|hen
zer|gen (*landsch. für* necken)
zer|glie|dern; Zer|glie|de|rung
zer|grü|beln; ich zergrübelte mir den Kopf
zer|ha|cken
zer|hau|en
zer|kau|en
zer|klei|nern; ich ...ere (↑R 16); **Zer|klei|ne|rung,** die; -; **Zer|klei|ne|rungs|ma|schi|ne**
zer|klüf|tet; zerklüftetes Gestein; **Zer|klüf|tung**
zer|knal|len
zer|knäu|len *(landsch.)*
zer|knaut|schen *(ugs.)*
zer|knirscht; ein zerknirschter Sünder; **Zer|knirscht|heit,** die; -; **Zer|knir|schung,** die; -
zer|knit|tern; zer|knit|tert; nach der Strafpredigt war er ganz zerknittert (*ugs. für* gedrückt)
zer|knül|len
zer|ko|chen
zer|kör|nen (*für* granulieren)
zer|krat|zen
zer|krü|meln
zer|las|sen; zerlassene Butter
zer|lau|fen (*svw.* zerfließen)
zer|leg|bar; Zer|leg|bar|keit, die; -; **zer|le|gen; Zer|leg|spiel; Zer|le|gung**
zer|le|sen; ein zerlesenes Buch
zer|lö|chern
zer|lumpt *(ugs.)*
zer|mah|len
zer|mal|men; Zer|mal|mung
zer|man|schen (*ugs. für* völlig zerdrücken, zerquetschen)
zer|mar|tern, sich; ich habe mir den Kopf zermartert
Zer|matt (schweiz. Kurort)
zer|mür|ben; zer|mürbt; Zer|mür|bung
zer|na|gen
zer|nepft (*ostösterr. ugs. für* zerzaust, verwahrlost)
zer|nich|ten (*veraltet für* vernichten)
Ze|ro ['ze:ro], die; -, -s *od.* das; -s, -s ⟨arab.⟩ (Null, Nichts; *im Roulett* Gewinnfeld des Bankhalters)
Ze|ro|graph, der; -en, -en (↑R 126) ⟨griech.⟩ (die Zerographie Ausübender); **Ze|ro|gra|phie,** die; -, ...i̯en (Wachsgravierung); **Ze|ro|plas|tik** (Wachsbildnerei); **Ze|ro|tin|säu|re,** die; - (Bestandteil des Bienenwachses)
zer|pflü|cken
zer|plat|zen
zer|pul|vern (*für* pulverisieren)
zer|quält; ein zerquältes Gesicht
zer|quet|schen
zer|rau|fen; sich die Haare -
Zerr|bild
zer|re|den
zer|reib|bar; zer|rei|ben; Zer|rei|bung
zer|rei|ßen; sich -; **zer|reiß|fest; Zer|reiß|fes|tig|keit,** die; -; **Zer|reiß|pro|be; Zer|rei|ßung**
zer|ren; Zer|re|rei
zer|rin|nen
zer|ris|sen; Zer|ris|sen|heit, die; -
Zerr|spie|gel; Zer|rung
zer|rup|fen
zer|rüt|ten (zerstören); **zer|rüt|tet;** eine zerrüttete Ehe; **Zer|rüt|tung**
zer|sä|gen
zer|schel|len (zerbrechen); zerschellt
zer|schie|ßen
zer|schla|gen; die Pläne haben sich -; alle Glieder sind mir wie -; **Zer|schla|gen|heit,** die; -; **Zer|schla|gung**
zer|schlei|ßen
zer|schlit|zen
zer|schmei|ßen *(ugs.)*
zer|schmet|tern; zer|schmet|tert; -e Glieder; **Zer|schmet|te|rung**
zer|schnei|den; Zer|schnei|dung
zer|schrammt; -e Hände
zer|schrün|det ([völlig] von Schrunden, Rissen zerfurcht); ein -es Gletscherfeld
zer|schun|den; seine Haut war ganz -
zer|set|zen; der Kompost zersetzt sich; zersetzende Propaganda; **Zer|set|zung; Zer|set|zungs_er|schei|nung, ...pro|dukt, ...pro|zess**
zer|sie|deln ([die Natur] durch Siedlungen zerstören); **Zer|sie|de|lung**
zer|sin|gen (den ursprüngl. Wortlaut eines Volksliedes durch ungenaue Überlieferung ändern)
zer|spal|ten; zerspalten *u.* zerspaltet; *vgl.* spalten; **Zer|spal|tung**
zer|spa|nen; Zer|spa|nung
zer|spel|len (*veraltet für* [völlig] spalten)
zer|splei|ßen (*veraltet für* [völlig] [auf]spalten)
zer|split|tern (in Splitter zerschlagen; in Splitter zerfallen); sich - (sich verzetteln); **Zer|split|te|rung**

zer|sprat|zen (*Geol.* sich aufblähen u. zerbersten [von glühenden Gesteinen])
zer|spren|gen; Zer|spren|gung
zer|sprin|gen
zer|stamp|fen
zer|stäu|ben; Zer|stäu|ber (Gerät zum Versprühen von Flüssigkeiten); **Zer|stäu|bung**
zer|ste|chen
zer|stie|ben
zer|stör|bar; zer|stö|ren; Zer|stö|rer; zer|stö|re|risch; Zer|stö|rung; Zer|stö|rungs‿trieb (der; -[e]s), **...wut; zer|stö|rungs|wü|tig**
zer|sto|ßen
zer|strah|len (*Kernphysik*); **Zer|strah|lung**
zer|strei|ten, sich
zer|streu|en; sich - (sich leicht unterhalten, ablenken, erholen); **zer|streut;** ein -er Professor; -es (diffuses) Licht; **Zer|streut|heit,** die; -; **Zer|streu|ung; Zer|streu|ungs|lin|se** (*Optik*)
zer|stü|ckeln; Zer|stü|cke|lung, Zer|stück|lung
zer|talt (*Geogr.* durch Täler stark gegliedert); ein -es Gelände
zer|tei|len; Zer|tei|lung
zer|tep|pern *vgl.* zerdeppern
Zer|ti|fi|kat, das; -[e]s, -e ⟨lat.⟩ ([amtl.] Bescheinigung, Zeugnis, Schein); **Zer|ti|fi|ka|ti|on,** die; -, -en (das Ausstellen eines Zertifikats); **zer|ti|fi|zie|ren;** zertifiziert; **Zer|ti|fi|zie|rung**
zer|tram|peln
zer|tren|nen; Zer|tren|nung
zer|tre|ten; Zer|tre|tung
zer|trüm|mern; ich ...ere (↑R 16); **Zer|trüm|me|rung**
Zer|ve|lat|wurst [zɛrvə..., *auch* tsɛr...], *auch* Ser|ve|lat|wurst ⟨ital.; dt.⟩ (eine Dauerwurst)
zer|wer|fen, sich (sich entzweien, verfeinden)
zer|wir|ken; das Wild - (*Jägerspr.* die Haut des Wildes abziehen u. das Wild zerlegen)
zer|wüh|len
Zer|würf|nis, das; -ses, -se
zer|zau|sen; Zer|zau|sung
zer|zup|fen
zes|si|bel ⟨lat.⟩ (*Rechtsw.* abtretbar); **Zes|si|on,** die; -, -en (Übertragung eines Anspruchs von dem bisherigen Gläubiger auf einen Dritten); *vgl.* zedieren; **Zes|si|o|nar,** der; -s, -e; (jmd., an den eine Forderung abgetreten wird)
Ze|ta, das; -[s], -s (griech. Buchstabe: Z, ζ)
Ze|ter, das; *nur noch in* Zeter u. Mord[io] schreien (*ugs.*); **Ze|ter|ge|schrei** (*ugs.*); **ze|ter|mor|dio!;** *nur noch in* zetermordio schreien (*ugs.*); **Ze|ter|mor|dio,** das; -s (*ugs.*); **ze|tern** (*ugs. für* wehklagend schreien); ich ...ere (↑R 16)
Zett; *vgl.* Z (Buchstabe)
[1]**Zet|tel,** der; -s, - (*Weberei* Kette; Reihenfolge der Kettfäden)
[2]**Zet|tel,** der; -s, - ⟨lat.⟩ (Streifen, kleines Blatt Papier); **Zet|te|lei** (Aufnahme in Zettelform, karteimäßige Bearbeitung; *auch für* Zettelkram; unübersichtliches Arbeiten); **Zet|tel‿kar|tei, ...kas|ten, ...kram; zet|teln** (*landsch. für* verstreuen, weithin ausbreiten); ich ...[e]le (↑R 16); *vgl.* [2]verzetteln; **Zet|tel|wirt|schaft** (*ugs.*)
zeuch!, zeuchst, zeucht (*veraltet geh. für* zieh[e]!, ziehst, zieht)
Zeug, das; -[e]s, -e; jmdm. etwas am Zeug flicken (*ugs. für* an jmdm. kleinliche Kritik üben); **Zeug‿amt** (*Milit. früher* das Zeughaus verwaltende Behörde), **...druck** (*Plur.* ...drucke; gefärbter Stoff); **Zeu|ge,** der; -n, -n (↑R 126); [1]**zeu|gen** (hervorbringen; erzeugen); [2]**zeu|gen** (bezeugen); es zeugt von Fleiß; **Zeu|gen‿aus|sa|ge, ...bank** (*Plur.* ...bänke), **...be|ein|flus|sung, ...be|fra|gung; Zeu|gen|schaft,** die; -; **Zeu|gen‿stand** (der; -[e]s), **...ver|neh|mung; Zeug|haus** (*Milit. früher* Lager für Waffen u. Vorräte); **Zeu|gin**
Zeug|ma, das; -s, *Plur.* -s *u.* -ta ⟨griech.⟩ (*Sprachw.* unpassende Beziehung eines Satzgliedes auf andere Satzglieder [z. B. er schlug die Stühl' und Vögel tot])
Zeug|nis, das; -ses, -se; **Zeug|nis‿ab|schrift, ...aus|ga|be, ...ver|wei|ge|rung**
Zeugs, das; - (*ugs. für* Gegenstand, Sache); so ein -
Zeu|gung; Zeu|gungs|akt; zeu|gungs|fä|hig; Zeu|gungs‿fä|hig|keit (die; -), **...glied** (*für* Penis); **zeu|gungs|un|fä|hig; Zeu|gungs|un|fä|hig|keit,** die; -
Zeus (höchster griech. Gott); **Zeus|tem|pel** (↑R 95)
Zeu|te, die; -, -n (*rhein., hess. für* Zotte [Schnauze])
Zeu|xis (altgriech. Maler)
ZGB (in der Schweiz) = Zivilgesetzbuch
z. H., z. Hd. = zu Händen, zuhanden
Zib|be, die; -, -n (*nordd., mitteld. für* Mutterschaf, -kaninchen; *abwertend für* Frau, Mädchen)
Zi|be|be, die; -, -n ⟨arab.-ital.⟩ (*südd., österr. für* große Rosine)
Zi|be|li|ne, die; - ⟨slaw.⟩ (ein Wollgarn, -gewebe)
Zi|bet, der; -s ⟨arab.⟩ (als Duftstoff verwendete Drüsenabsonderung der Zibetkatze); **Zi|bet|kat|ze**
Zi|bo|ri|um, das; -s, ...ien [...i̯ən] ⟨griech.⟩ (in der röm.-kath. Kirche Aufbewahrungsgefäß für Hostien; Altarbaldachin)
Zi|cho|rie [...i̯ə], die; -, -n ⟨griech.⟩ (Pflanzengattung der Korbblütler mit zahlreichen Arten [z. B. Wegwarte]; ein Kaffeezusatz); **Zi|cho|ri|en|kaf|fee,** der; -s
Zi|cke, die; -, -n (weibl. Ziege); *vgl.* Zicken; **Zi|ckel,** das; -s, -[n]; **Zi|ckel|chen; zi|ckeln** (Junge werfen [von der Ziege]); **Zi|cken** *Plur.* (*ugs. für* Dummheiten); mach keine -!; **zi|ckig** (*ugs. für* überspannt, launisch, eigensinnig; ziemlich prüde und verklemmt)
Zick|zack, der; -[e]s, -e; im Zickzack laufen, *aber* zickzack den Berg hinunterlaufen; **zick|za|cken;** gezickzackt; **Zick|zack‿kurs, ...kur|ve, ...li|nie**
Zi|der *vgl.* Cidre
Zid|ki|ja *vgl.* Zedekia
Zie|che, die; -, -n (*südd. u. österr. für* Bettbezug u. a.); *vgl.* Züchen
Ziech|ling (Ziehklinge, Schaber des Tischlers)
Zie|fer, das; -s, - (*südwestd. für* Federvieh)
zie|fern (*mitteld. für* wehleidig sein; frösteln; vor Schmerz zittern; *bayr. für* leise regnen); ich ...ere (↑R 16)
Zie|ge, die; -, -n
Zie|gel, der; -s, -; **Zie|gel‿bren|ner, ...bren|ne|rei, ...dach; Zie|ge|lei; zie|geln** (*veraltet für* Ziegel machen); ich ...ele (↑R 16); **Zie|gel|ofen** (↑R 132); **zie|gel|rot; Zie|gel‿stein, ...strei|cher**
Zie|gen‿bart (*auch* ein Pilz), **...bock, ...her|de, ...kä|se, ...le|der, ...lip|pe** (ein Pilz), **...mel|ker** (ein Vogel), **...milch; Zie|gen|pe|ter,** der; -s, - (Mumps)
Zie|ger, der; -s, - (*südd., österr. für* Quark, Kräuterkäse)
Zieg|ler (*veraltet für* Ziegelbrenner)
Zieh|brun|nen; Zie|he, die; - (*landsch. für* Pflege u. Erziehung); ein Kind in - geben; **Zieh|el|tern** *Plur.* (*landsch.*); **zie|hen;** du zogst; du zögest; gezogen; zieh[e]!; *vgl.* zeuch! usw.; nach sich -; **Zieh‿har|mo|ni|ka, ...kind** (*landsch.*), **...mut|ter** (*Plur.* ...mütter; *landsch.*), **...pflas|ter** (*svw.* Zugpflaster); **Zie|hung; Zieh|va|ter** (*landsch.*)
Ziel, das; -[e]s, -e; **Ziel‿bahn|hof, ...band** (das *Plur.* ...bänder); **ziel-**

be|wusst; **Ziel‿be|wusst|heit, ...ein|rich|tung; zie|len; zie|lend;** -es Verb (*für* Transitiv); **Ziel‿fahn|dung** (gezielte Fahndung), **...fahrt** (*Motorsport* kleinere Sternfahrt), **...fern|rohr, ...fo|to|gra|fie, ...ge|biet** *(Milit.)*, **...ge|ra|de** (*Sport* letztes gerades Bahnstück vor dem Ziel); **ziel|ge|rich|tet; Ziel‿grup|pe, ...ha|fen** (*vgl.* [2]Hafen), **...ka|me|ra, ...kauf** *(Wirtsch.)*, **...kur|ve** (*Sport* Kurve vor der Zielgeraden), **...li|nie; ziel|los; Ziel|lo|sig|keit,** die; -; **Ziel‿rich|ter, ...schei|be, ...set|zung; ziel|si|cher; Ziel‿si|cher|heit** (die; -), **...spra|che** *(Sprachw.)*, **...stel|lung** (*regional für* Zielsetzung); **ziel|stre|big; Ziel|stre|big|keit,** die; -; **Ziel‿vor|ga|be, ...vor|rich|tung, ...vor|stel|lung**

Ziem, der; -[e]s, -e (*veraltet für* oberes Keulenstück [des Rindes])

zie|men *(geh.)*; es ziemt sich, es ziemt mir

Zie|mer, der; -s, - (Rückenbraten [vom Wild]; Ochsenziemer)

ziem|lich (fast, annähernd)

Ziep|chen, Zie|pel|chen (*landsch. für* Küken, Hühnchen); **zie|pen** (*landsch., bes. nordd. für* zupfend ziehen; einen Pfeifton von sich geben)

Zier, die; -; **Zie|rat** *frühere Schreibung für* Zierrat; **Zier|de,** die; -, -n; **zie|ren;** sich -; **Zie|re|rei; Zier‿fisch, ...gar|ten, ...gras, ...kür|bis, ...leis|te; zier|lich; Zier|lich|keit,** die; -; **Zier‿pflan|ze, ...pup|pe, ...rand; Zier|rat,** der; -[e]s, -e; **Zier‿stich, ...strauch, ...stück, ...vo|gel**

Zie|sel, der, *österr.* das; -s, - ‹slaw.› (ein Nagetier)

Ziest, der; -[e]s, -e ‹slaw.› (eine Heilpflanze)

Zie|t[h]en (preuß. Reitergeneral)

Ziff. = Ziffer

Zif|fer, die; -, -n ‹arab.› (Zahlzeichen; *Abk.* Ziff.); arabische, römische -n; **Zif|fer|blatt; ...zif|fe|rig,** ...ziff|rig (z. B. zweiziff[e]rig, *mit Ziffer* 2-ziff[e]rig; ↑R 44); **Zif|fer[n]|kas|ten** *(Druckw.)*; **zif|fern|mä|ßig; Zif|fer|schrift; ...ziff|rig** *vgl.* ...zifferig

zig *(ugs.)*; zig Mark; mit zig Sachen in die Kurve; *in Zusammensetzungen:* zigfach, zigmal, ein Zigfaches; zigtausend, *auch* Zigtausend Menschen; Zigtausende, *auch* zigtausende von Menschen

Zi|ga|ret|te, die; -, -n ‹franz.›; **Zi|ga|ret|ten‿asche, ...au|to|mat, ...etui, ...fab|rik, ...kip|pe, ...län|ge** (*nur in* auf eine - *[ugs.]*), **...pa|pier, ...pau|se, ...rauch, ...rau|cher, ...schach|tel, ...spit|ze, ...stum|mel; Zi|ga|ril|lo** [*selten auch* ...'riljo], der, *auch* das; -s, -s, *ugs. auch* die; -, -s ‹span.› (kleine Zigarre); **Zi|gärr|chen; Zi|gar|re,** die; -, -n; **Zi|gar|ren‿ab|schnei|der, ...asche** (↑R 132), **...fab|rik, ...kis|te, ...rauch, ...rau|cher, ...spit|ze, ...stum|mel**

Zi|ger, der; -s, - (*schweiz. Schreibweise für* Zieger)

Zi|geu|ner[1], der; -s, -; **zi|geu|ner|haft; Zi|geu|ne|rin; zi|geu|ne|risch; Zi|geu|ner‿ka|pel|le, ...le|ben** (das; -s), **...mu|sik; zi|geu|nern** (*ugs. für* sich herumtreiben); ich ...ere (↑R 16); **Zi|geu|ner‿pri|mas, ...schnit|zel** *(Gastron.)*, **...spra|che**

zig|fach; zig|hun|dert; zig|mal; zig|tau|send; *vgl.* zig

Zi|ka|de, die; -, -n ‹lat.› (ein Insekt); **Zi|ka|den|männ|chen**

zi|li|ar ‹lat.› (*Med.* die Wimpern betreffend); **Zi|li|ar‿kör|per** (ein Abschnitt der mittleren Hautschicht des Auges), **...mus|kel, ...neu|ral|gie** (Schmerzen in Augapfel u. Augenhöhle); **Zi|li|a|te,** die; -, -n *meist Plur.* (*Biol.* Wimpertierchen [Einzeller]); **Zi|lie** [...i̯ə], die; -, -n (*Med.* feines Haar; Wimper)

Zi|li|zi|en usw. *vgl.* Kilikien usw.

[1]**Zil|le** (dt. Zeichner)

[2]**Zil|le,** die; -, -n ‹slaw.› (*ostmd., österr. für* leichter, flacher [Fracht]kahn); **Zil|len|schlep|per** (Schleppschiff)

Zil|ler|tal, das; -[e]s; **Zil|ler|ta|ler** (↑R 103); Zillertaler Alpen

Zil|li (w. Vorn.)

Zim|bab|we (*engl. Schreibung von* Simbabwe)

Zim|bal, das; -s, *Plur.* -e *u.* -s ‹griech.› (mit Hämmerchen geschlagenes Hackbrett); **Zim|bel,** die; -, -n (gemischte Orgelstimme; kleines Becken)

Zim|ber, Kim|ber, der; -s, -n (Angehöriger eines germ. Volksstammes); **zimb|risch,** kimb|risch (↑R 130), *aber nur* die zimbrischen Sprachinseln *u.* (↑R 102): die Zimbrische Halbinsel (Jütland)

Zi|ment, das; -[e]s, -e ‹lat.› (*bayr. u. österr. veraltet für* metallenes zylindrisches Maßgefäß [der Wirte])

Zi|mier, das; -s, -e ‹griech.› (Helmschmuck)

---

[1] *Vom Zentralrat Deutscher Sinti und Roma als diskriminierend abgelehnte Bezeichnung.*

Zim|mer, das; -s, -; **Zim|mer|an|ten|ne; Zim|mer|ar|beit,** Zim|me|rer|ar|beit; **Zim|mer‿brand, ...de|cke, ...ecke** (↑R 132); **Zim|me|rei; Zim|mer|ein|rich|tung; Zim|me|rer; Zim|me|rer|ar|beit** *vgl.* Zimmerarbeit; **Zim|me|rer|hand|werk** (*seltener für* Zimmerhandwerk); **Zim|mer‿flucht** (zusammenhängende Reihe von Zimmern; *vgl.* [1]Flucht), **...hand|werk, ...herr** (*veraltet für* Untermieter); **...zim|me|rig,** ...zimm|rig (z. B. zweizimm[e]rig, *mit Ziffer* 2-zimm[e]rig; ↑R 44); **Zim|mer‿kell|ner, ...laut|stär|ke, ...lin|de; Zim|mer|ling** (*Bergmannsspr.* Zimmermann); **Zim|mer‿mäd|chen, ...mann** (*Plur.* ...leute), **...mie|te; zim|mern;** ich ...ere (↑R 16); **Zim|mer‿num|mer, ...pflan|ze, ...su|che, ...tan|ne, ...tem|pe|ra|tur, ...the|a|ter; Zim|me|rung; Zim|mer|ver|mitt|lung; ...zimm|rig** *vgl.* ...zimmerig

zim|per|lich; Zim|per|lich|keit; Zim|per|lie|se, die; -, -n (*ugs. für* zimperliches Mädchen); **zim|pern** (*landsch. für* zimperlich sein, tun); ich ...ere (↑R 16)

Zimt, der; -[e]s, *Plur. (Sorten:)* -e (ein Gewürz); **Zimt|baum; zimt‿far|ben** *od.* **...far|big; Zimt‿stan|ge, ...stern; Zimt|zi|cke, Zimt|zie|ge** (Schimpfwort)

Zin|cke|nit [*auch* ...'nit], der; -s ‹nach dem dt. Bergdirektor Zincken› (ein Mineral)

Zin|cum, das; -s (*latinisierte Nebenform von* Zink)

Zin|del|taft ‹griech.; pers.› (ein Gewebe)

Zin|der, der; -s, - *meist Plur.* ‹engl.› (ausgeglühte Steinkohle)

Zi|ne|ra|ria, Zi|ne|ra|rie [...i̯ə], die; -, ...ien [...i̯ən] ‹lat.› (Zierpflanze)

[1]**Zin|gel,** der; -s, -[n] (ein Fisch)

[2]**Zin|gel,** der; -s, - ‹lat.› (*veraltet für* Ringmauer); **Zin|gu|lum,** das; -s, *Plur.* -s *u.* ...la (Gürtel[schnur] der Albe)

[1]**Zink,** das; -[e]s (chem. Element, Metall; *Zeichen* Zn); *vgl.* Zincum

[2]**Zink,** der; -[e]s, -en; ↑R 128 (ein hist. Blasinstrument)

Zink‿ät|zung, ...blech, ...blen|de

Zin|ke, die; -, -n (Zacke); [1]**zin|ken** (mit Zinken, Zeichen versehen)

[2]**zin|ken** (von, aus [1]Zink)

Zin|ken, der; -s, - ([Gauner]zeichen; *ugs. für* große Nase)

Zin|ken|blä|ser; Zin|ke|nist, der; -en, -en; ↑R 126 (*schwäb., sonst veraltet für* Zinkenbläser, Stadtmusikant); **Zin|ker** (*ugs. für* Falschspieler, Spitzel); **...zin|kig**

(z. B. dreizinkig; *mit Ziffer* 3-zinkig; ↑R 44)
Zink|leim|ver|band *(Med.)*; **Zin|ko|gra|phie**, die; -, ...ien ‹dt.; griech.› (Zinkflachdruck); **Zin|ko|ty|pie**, die; -, ...ien (Zinkhochätzung); **Zink_oxid** (↑R 132; *vgl.* Oxid), **...sal|be, ...sarg, ...sul|fat, ...wan|ne, ...weiß** (eine Malerfarbe)
Zinn, das; -[e]s (chem. Element, Metall; *Zeichen* Sn); *vgl.* Stannum; **Zinn|be|cher**
Zin|ne, die; -, -n (zahnartiger Mauerabschluss)
zin|nern (von, aus Zinn); **Zinn_fi|gur, ...fo|lie** (Blattzinn), **...gie|ßer**
Zin|nie [...iə], die; -, -n ‹nach dem dt. Botaniker Zinn› (eine Gartenblume)
Zinn_kraut (das; -[e]s; Ackerschachtelhalm), **...krug**
[1]**Zin|no|ber**, der; -s, - ‹pers.› (ein Mineral); [2]**Zin|no|ber**, der, *auch, österr. nur,* das; -s (eine rote Farbe); [3]**Zin|no|ber**, der; -s (*ugs. für* Blödsinn, wertloses Zeug); **zin|no|ber|rot; Zin|no|ber|rot**, das; -s
Zinn_sol|dat, ...tel|ler
Zinn|wal|dit [*auch* ...'dit], der; -s ‹nach dem Ort Zinnwald› (ein Mineral)
[1]**Zins**, der; -es, -en ‹lat.› (Ertrag); [2]**Zins**, der; -es, -e (*früher* Abgabe; *landsch., bes. südd., österr. u. schweiz. für* Miete); **zins|bar; zin|sen** (*schweiz., sonst veraltet für* Zins[en] zahlen); du zinst; **Zin|sen|dienst; Zins_er|hö|hung, ...er|trag; Zin|ses|zins** *Plur.* ...zinsen; **Zin|ses|zins|rech|nung; Zins_fuß** (*Plur.* ...füße), **...gro|schen** *(früher)*; **zins|güns|tig; Zins_haus** (*bes. südd., österr. für* Mietshaus), **...herr|schaft** (die; -), **...knecht|schaft** (im MA.); **zins|los; Zins|pflicht**, die; - (im MA.); **zins|pflich|tig; Zins|po|li|tik**, die; - ; **zins|po|li|tisch; Zins_satz, ...sen|kung, ...ter|min** (Zinszahlungstag); **zins|ver|bil|ligt; Zins|ver|bil|li|gung; Zins_wu|cher, ...zahl** (*Abk.* Zz.)
Zin|zen|dorf (Stifter der Herrnhuter Brüdergemeine)
Zi|on, der; -[s] ‹hebr.› (Tempelberg in Jerusalem; *ohne Artikel auch für* Jerusalem); **Zio|nis|mus**, der; - (Bewegung zur Gründung u. Sicherung eines nationalen jüdischen Staates); **Zio|nist**, der; -en, -en; ↑R 126 (Anhänger des Zionismus); **zio|nis|tisch; Zi|o|nit**, der; -en, -en; ↑R 126 (Angehöriger einer schwärmerischen christl. Sekte des 18. Jh.s)

[1]**Zipf**, der; -[e]s (*südd. u. ostmitteld. für* Pips)
[2]**Zipf**, der; -[e]s, -e (*österr. ugs. für* Zipfel; fader Kerl)
Zip|fel, der; -s, -; **zip|fe|lig; Zip|fel|müt|ze; zipf|lig**
Zi|pol|le, die; -, -n ‹lat.› (*nordd., auch mitteld. für* Zwiebel)
Zipp ®, der; -s, -s (*österr. für* Reißverschluss)
Zipp|dros|sel, Zip|pe, die; -, -n (*landsch. für* Singdrossel)
Zip|per|lein, das; -s (*veraltet für* [Fuß]gicht)
Zip|pus, der; -, *Plur.* Zippen *u.* Zippi ‹lat.› (antiker Gedenk-, Grenzstein)
Zipp|ver|schluss ‹engl.; dt.› (*österr. für* Reißverschluss); *vgl.* Zipp ®
Zips, die; - (Gebiet in der Slowakei); **Zip|ser** (↑R 103)
Zir|be, Zir|bel, die; -, -n (*landsch. für* eine Kiefer); **Zir|bel_drü|se** *(Med.)*, **...kie|fer** (die; *vgl.* Arve), **...nuss**
Zir|co|ni|um *vgl.* Zirkonium
zir|ka, *auch* cir|ca (ungefähr, etwa; *Abk.* ca. [*für* lat. circa]); **Zir|ka|auf|trag** (Börsenauftrag, bei dem der Kommissionär um ¼ od. ½% vom gesetzten Limit abweichen darf)
Zir|kel, der; -s, - ‹griech.› (Gerät zum Kreiszeichnen u. Strecken[ab]messen; [gesellschaftlicher] Kreis); **Zir|kel|kas|ten; zir|keln** (Kreis ziehen; genau einteilen, [ab]messen); ich ...[e]le (↑R 16); **zir|kel|rund; Zir|kel|schluss**
Zir|kon, der; -s, -e ‹nlat.› (ein Mineral); **Zir|ko|ni|um**, *chem. fachspr.* Zir|co|ni|um, das; -s (chem. Element; *Zeichen* Zr)
zir|ku|lar, zir|ku|lär ‹griech.› (kreisförmig); **Zir|ku|lar**, das; -s, -e (*schweiz., sonst veraltet für* Rundschreiben); **Zir|ku|lar|no|te** (*Völkerrecht* eine mehreren Staaten gleichzeitig zugestellte Note gleichen Inhalts); **Zir|ku|la|ti|on**, die; -, -en (Kreislauf, Umlauf); **zir|ku|lie|ren**
zir|kum... ‹griech.› (um..., herum...); **Zir|kum...** (Um..., Herum...); **zir|kum|flek|tie|ren** (mit Zirkumflex versehen); **Zir|kum|flex**, der; -es, -e (*Sprachw.* ein Dehnungszeichen; *Zeichen* ˆ, z. B. â); **Zir|kum|po|lar|stern** (Stern, der für den Beobachtungsort nie untergeht); *vgl.* [2]Stern; **zir|kum|skript** (*Med.* umschrieben, [scharf] abgegrenzt); **Zir|kum|skrip|ti|on**, die; -, -en (Abgrenzung kirchlicher Gebiete); **zir|kum|ter|res|trisch** (im Umkreis der Erde); **Zir|kum|zi|si|on** (*Med.* Beschneidung); **Zir|kus**, *auch* Cir|cus, der; -, -se (großes Zelt od. Gebäude, in dem Tierdressuren u. a. gezeigt werden; *nur Sing.: ugs. für* Durcheinander, Trubel); **Zir|kus_clown, ...di|rek|tor, ...pferd, ...rei|ter, ...rei|te|rin, ...vor|stel|lung, ...zelt**
Zir|pe, die; -, -n (*landsch. für* Grille, Zikade); **zir|pen**
Zir|ren (*Plur. von* Zirrus)
Zir|rho|se, die; -, -n ‹griech.› (*Med.* chronische Wucherung von Bindegewebe mit nachfolgender Verhärtung u. Schrumpfung)
Zir|ro|ku|mu|lus ‹lat.› (*Meteor.* Schäfchenwolke); **Zir|ro|stra|tus** (ungegliederte Streifenwolke in höheren Luftschichten); **Zir|rus**, der; -, *Plur.* - *u.* Zirren (Federwolke); **Zir|rus|wol|ke**
zir|zen|sisch ‹griech.› (den Zirkus betreffend, in ihm abgehalten)
zis|al|pin, zis|al|pi|nisch ‹lat.› ([von Rom aus] diesseits der Alpen liegend)
Zi|schel|lei; zi|scheln; ich ...[e]le (↑R 16); **zi|schen**; du zischst; **Zisch|laut**
Zi|se|leur [...'lø:r], der; -s, -e ‹franz.› *u.* Zi|se|lie|rer (Metallstecher); **zi|se|lie|ren** ([in Metall] mit Punze, Ziselierhammer [kunstvoll] einarbeiten); **Zi|se|lie|rer** *vgl.* Ziseleur; **Zi|se|lie|rung**
[1]**Zis|ka** (*dt. Form von* Žižka)
[2]**Zis|ka** (w. Vorn.)
Zis|la|weng, der ‹franz.›; *in der Fügung* mit einem - (*ugs. für* mit Schwung)
zis|pa|da|nisch ([von Rom aus] diesseits des Pos liegend)
Zis|sa|li|en [...iən] *Plur.* ‹lat.› (fehlerhafte Münzen, die wieder eingeschmolzen werden)
Zis|so|i|de, die; -, -n ‹griech.› (*Math.* Efeublattkurve; ebene Kurve dritter Ordnung)
Zis|ta, Zis|te, die; -, Zisten ‹griech.› (altgriech. zylinderförmiger Korb; frühgeschichtl. Urne)
Zis|ter|ne, die; -, -n ‹griech.› (Behälter für Regenwasser); **Zis|ter|nen|was|ser**, das; -s
Zis|ter|zi|en|ser, der; -s, - (Angehöriger eines kath. Ordens); **Zis|ter|zi|en|se|rin** (Angehörige des Ordens der Zisterzienserinnen); **Zis|ter|zi|en|ser|or|den**, der; -s
Zist|rös|chen, Zist|ro|se ‹griech.; dt.› (eine Pflanze)
Zi|ta (w. Vorn.)
Zi|ta|del|le, die; -, -n ‹franz.› (Befestigungsanlage innerhalb einer Stadt od. einer Festung)

Zi|tat, das; -[e]s, -e ‹lat.› (wörtlich angeführte Belegstelle; *auch für* bekannter Ausspruch); **Zi|ta|ten‿le|xi|kon, ...schatz; Zi|ta|ti|on,** die; -, -en (*veraltet für* [Vor]ladung vor Gericht; *auch für* Zitierung)

Zi|ther, die; -, -n ‹griech.› (ein Saiteninstrument); **Zi|ther|spiel,** das; -[e]s

zi|tie|ren ‹lat.› ([eine Textstelle] wörtlich anführen; vorladen); **Zi|tie|rung**

Zit|rat, *fachspr.* Cit|rat [tsi...] (↑R 130), das; -[e]s, -e ‹lat.› (Salz der Zitronensäure); [1]**Zit|rin,** der; -s, -e (gelber Bergkristall); [2]**Zit|rin,** das; -s (Bestandteil eines gelben Farbstoffs); **Zit|ro|nat** das; -[e]s, *Plur.(Sorten:)* -e ‹franz.› (kandierte Fruchtschale einer Zitronenart)

Zit|ro|ne (↑R 130), die; -, -n ‹ital.›; **Zit|ro|nen‿baum, ...fal|ter; zit|ro|nen‿far|ben** *od.* **...far|big, ...gelb; Zit|ro|nen‿li|mo|na|de, ...me|lis|se, ...pres|se, ...saft** (der; -[e]s); **zit|ro|nen|sau|er** *(Chemie);* **Zit|ro|nen‿säu|re** (die; -), **...scha|le, ...was|ser**

Zit|rul|le (↑R 130), die; -, -n ‹franz.› (*veraltet für* Wassermelone); **Zi|t|rus‿frucht** ‹lat.; dt.› (Zitrone, Apfelsine, Mandarine u. a.), **...öl, ...pflan|ze**

Zit|scher|ling (*veraltet für* Birkenzeisig)

Zit|ter‿aal, ...gras; zit|te|rig, zittrig; **zit|tern;** ich ...ere (↑R 16); ↑R 50: er hat das Zittern *(ugs.);* **Zit|ter‿pap|pel, ...par|tie** (*bes. für* Spiel, bei dem eine Mannschaft bis zuletzt um den Sieg fürchten muss); **Zit|ter|ro|chen** (ein Fisch); **zitt|rig** *vgl.* zitterig

Zit|wer, der; -s, - ‹pers.› (ein Korbblütler, dessen Samen als Wurmmittel verwendet werden)

Zit|ze, die; -, -n (Organ zum Säugen bei weibl. Säugetieren)

Ziu (altgerm. Gott); *vgl.* Tiu, Tyr

Zi|vi [...v...], der; -s, -s (*ugs. kurz für* Zivildienstleistender); **zi|vil** ‹lat.› (bürgerlich); zivile (niedrige) Preise; ziviler Bevölkerungsschutz, Ersatzdienst; **Zi|vil,** das; -s (bürgerl. Kleidung); **Zi|vil‿an|zug, ...be|ruf, ...be|schä|dig|te** (der *u.* die; -n, -n; ↑R 5 ff.), **...be|völ|ke|rung, ...cou|ra|ge, ...dienst** (der; -[e]s); **Zi|vil|dienst‿be|auf|trag|te** (der; -n, -n; ↑R 5 ff.), **...leis|ten|de** (der; -n, -n; ↑R 5 ff.); **Zi|vil‿ehe** (↑R 132; standesamtl. geschlossene Ehe), **...fahn|der, ...fahn|dung, ...ge|setz|buch** (*Abk. [in der Schweiz]* ZGB); **Zi|vi|li|sa|ti|on,** die; -, -en (die durch den Fortschritt der Wissenschaft u. der Technik verbesserten sozialen u. materiellen Lebensbedingungen); **Zi|vi|li|sa|ti|ons|krank|heit** *meist Plur.;* **zi|vi|li|sa|ti|ons|mü|de; Zi|vi|li|sa|ti|ons‿mü|dig|keit, ...müll; zi|vi|li|sa|to|risch; zi|vi|li|sie|ren** (der Zivilisation zuführen); **zi|vi|li|siert; Zi|vi|li|siert|heit,** die; -; **Zi|vi|li|sie|rung,** die; -; **Zi|vi|list,** der; -en, -en; ↑R 126 (Bürger, Nichtsoldat); **zi|vi|lis|tisch; Zi|vil‿kam|mer** (Spruchabteilung für privatrechtl. Streitigkeiten bei den Landgerichten), **...kla|ge, ...klei|dung, ...le|ben, ...lis|te** (für den Monarchen bestimmter Betrag im Staatshaushalt), **...per|son, ...pro|zess** (Gerichtsverfahren, dem die Bestimmungen des Privatrechts zugrunde liegen); **Zi|vil|pro|zess‿ord|nung** (*Abk.* ZPO), **...recht** (das; -[e]s); **Zi|vil|recht,** das; -[e]s; **zi|vil|recht|lich; Zi|vil|schutz,** der; -es; **Zi|vil|stand** (*schweiz. für* Familien-, Personenstand); **Zi|vil|stands|amt** (*schweiz. für* Standesamt); **Zi|vil‿trau|ung, ...ver|tei|di|gung**

zi|zerl|weis (*bayr., österr. ugs. für* nach und nach, ratenweise)

Žiž|ka [ˈʒiʃka] (Hussitenführer); *vgl.* [1]Ziska

ZK = Zentralkomitee

Zl, Zł Zloty, Złoty

Zlo|ty [ˈsloti], *poln.* **Zło|ty** [ˈzwɔti], der; -s, -s ‹poln.› (poln. Währungseinheit; 1 Zloty = 100 Groszy; *Abk.* Zl, Zł); 5 - (↑R 90)

Zn = *chem. Zeichen für* Zink

Znü|ni, der *od.* das; -s, - (*schweiz. mdal. für* Vormittagsimbiss)

Zo|bel, der; -s, - ‹slaw.› (Marder; Pelz); **Zo|bel|pelz**

Zo|ber, der; -s, - (*landsch. für* Zuber)

Zoc|co|li *Plur.* ‹ital.› (*schweiz. für* Holzsandalen)

zo|ckeln (*svw.* zuckeln); ich ...[e]le (↑R 16)

zo|cken ‹jidd.› (*ugs. für* Glücksspiele machen); **Zo|cker,** der; -s, - (Glücksspieler)

zo|di|a|kal ‹griech.› (den Zodiakus betreffend); **Zo|di|a|kal|licht,** das; -[e]s, -er (*Astron.* Tierkreislicht, pyramidenförmiger Lichtschein in der Richtung des Tierkreises); **Zo|di|a|kus,** der; - (Tierkreis)

Zoe (Name byzant. Kaiserinnen)

Zo|fe, die; -, -n; **Zo|fen|dienst**

Zoff, der; -s (*ugs. für* Ärger, Streit, Unfrieden)

zö|ger|lich (zögernd); **zö|gern;** ich ...ere (↑R 16); ↑R 50: nach anfänglichem Zögern; ohne Zögern einspringen

Zög|ling

Zo|he, die; -, -n (*südwestd. für* Hündin)

Zo|la [zɔˈla] (franz. Schriftsteller)

[1]**Zö|les|tin,** der; -s, -e ‹lat.› (ein Mineral); [2]**Zö|les|tin,** Zö|les|ti|nus (m. Vorn.); **Zö|les|ti|ne** (w. Vorn.); **Zö|les|ti|ner,** der; -s, - (Angehöriger eines ehem. kath. Ordens); **Zö|les|ti|nus** *vgl.* [2]Zölestin; **zö|les|tisch** (*veraltet für* himmlisch)

Zö|li|bat, das, *Theol.* der; -[e]s ‹lat.› (pflichtmäßige Ehelosigkeit aus religiösen Gründen, bes. bei kath. Geistlichen); **zö|li|ba|tär; Zö|li|ba|tär,** der; -s, -e (jmd., der im Zölibat lebt); **Zö|li|bats|zwang,** der; -[e]s

[1]**Zoll,** der; -[e]s, Zölle ‹griech.› (Abgabe)

[2]**Zoll,** der; -[e]s, - (altes Längenmaß; *Zeichen* "); 3 Zoll (↑R 90) breit

Zoll‿ab|fer|ti|gung, ...amt; zoll|amt|lich; Zoll|an|mel|dung; zoll|bar (zollpflichtig); **Zoll‿be|am|te, ...be|am|tin, ...be|hör|de**

zoll|breit; ein zollbreites Brett, *aber* das Brett ist einen Zoll breit; **Zoll|breit,** der; -, -; keinen Zollbreit zurückweichen

Zoll‿bürg|schaft, ...dek|la|ra|ti|on, ...ein|neh|mer *(früher)*

zol|len; jmdm. Bewunderung zollen *(geh.)*

...zöl|ler (z. B. Achtzöller)

Zoll‿er|klä|rung, ...fahn|der, ...fahn|dung; Zoll|fahn|dungs|stel|le; Zoll|for|ma|li|tät *meist Plur.;* **zoll|frei; Zoll|frei|heit,** die; -; **Zoll‿ge|biet, ...grenz|be|zirk, ...gren|ze**

zoll|hoch, *aber* einen Zoll hoch; **...zol|lig** *u.* **...zöl|lig,** *österr. nur so* (z. B. vierzollig, vierzöllig, *mit Ziffer* 4-zollig, 4-zöllig; ↑R 44)

Zoll|in|halts|er|klä|rung; Zoll|kon|trol|le; zoll|lang (↑R 136), *aber* einen Zoll lang; **Zoll|li|nie** (↑R 136), die; -, -n ; **Zöll|ner** (*früher* Zoll-, Steuereinnehmer; *veraltend für* Zollbeamter); **Zoll|ord|nung; zoll|pflich|tig; Zoll‿recht** (das; -[e]s), **...schran|ke, ...sta|ti|on, ...stel|le**

Zoll|stock *Plur.* ...stöcke

Zoll‿ta|rif, ...uni|on (↑R 132), **...ver|trag**

Zö|lom, das; -s, -e ‹griech.› (*Biol.* Leibeshöhle [der Säugetiere])

Zom|bie, der; -[s], -s ‹afrikan. Wort› (Toter, der durch Zauberei wieder zum Leben erweckt wurde [und willenloses Werkzeug des Zauberers ist])

Zö|me|te|ri|um, das; -s, ...ien [...iən] ‹griech.› (Ruhestätte, Friedhof, *auch für* Katakombe)

zo|nal, zo|nar ‹griech.-lat.› (zu einer Zone gehörend, eine Zone betreffend); **Zo|ne,** die; -, -n (abgegrenztes Gebiet; Besatzungszone); **Zo|nen‿ta|rif, ...zeit**

Zö|no|bit, der; -en, -en (↑R 126) ‹griech.› (im Kloster lebender Mönch); **Zö|no|bi|um,** das; -s, ...ien [...iən] (Kloster; *Biol.* kolonieartiger Zusammenschluss von Einzellern)

Zoo [tso:], der; -s, -s ‹griech.› (*kurz für* zoologischer Garten); **zo|o|gen** [tso|o...] (aus tierischen Resten gebildet [von Gesteinen]); **Zo|o|gra|phie,** die; -, ...ien (Benennung u. Einordnung der Tierarten); **Zoo|hand|lung** ['tso:...]; **Zo|o|lat|rie** [tso|o...] (↑R 130), die; -, ...ien (Tierkult); **Zo|o|lith** [*auch* ...'lit], der; *Gen.* -s *od.* -en, *Plur.* -e[n]; ↑R 126 (Tierversteinerung); **Zo|o|lo|ge,** der; -n, -n; ↑R 126 (Tierforscher); **Zo|o|lo|gie,** die; - (Tierkunde); **Zo|o|lo|gin; zo|o|lo|gisch** (tierkundlich); ein zoologischer Garten, *aber* (↑R 108): der Zoologische Garten Frankfurt

Zoom [zu:m], das; -s, -s ‹engl.› (Objektiv mit veränderlicher Brennweite; Vorgang, durch den der Aufnahmegegenstand näher an den Betrachter herangeholt oder weiter von ihm entfernt wird); **zoo|men** ['zu:mən]; gezoomt

Zo|on po|li|ti|kon, das; - - ‹griech.› (der Mensch als Gemeinschaftswesen [bei Aristoteles]); **Zoo|or|ches|ter,** *auch* **Zoo-Or|ches|ter** ['tso:...] (↑R 24); **zo|o|phag** [tso|o...] (Fleisch fressend [von Pflanzen]); **Zo|o|pha|ge,** der; -n, -n; ↑R 126 (Fleisch fressende Pflanze); **Zo|o|phyt,** der *od.* das; -en, -en; ↑R 126 (*veraltete Bez. für* Hohltier od. Schwamm); **Zoo|tech|ni|ker** ['tso:...] (*regional für* [Zoo]tierpfleger); **Zo|o|to|mie** [tso|o...], die; - (Tieranatomie)

Zopf, der; -[e]s, Zöpfe; ein alter - (*ugs. für* überlebter Brauch); **Zöpf|chen; zop|fig; Zopf‿mus|ter, ...stil** (der; -[e]s; *Kunstw.*), **...zeit** (die; -)

Zop|pot (*poln.* Sopot)

Zo|res, der; - ‹hebr.-jidd.› (*landsch. für* Ärger; Gesindel)

Zo|ril|la, der; -s, -s, *auch* die; -, -s ‹span.› (eine afrik. Marderart)

Zorn, der; -[e]s; **Zorn‿ader** (↑R 132; *vgl.* Zornesader), **...ausbruch** (*vgl.* Zornesausbruch), **...bin|kel** (der; -s, -[n]; *österr. ugs. für* jähzorniger Mensch); **zornent|brannt** (↑R 40); **Zor|nes‿ader** (↑R 132), **...aus|bruch, ...rö|te; zor|nig; zorn|mü|tig** (*geh. für* zu Zorn neigend); **Zornrö|te** *vgl.* Zornesröte; **zornschnau|bend** (↑R 40)

Zo|ro|as|ter (*Nebenform von* Zarathustra); **zo|ro|ast|risch** (↑R 130); die zoroastrische Lehre (↑R 94)

Zos|se, der; -n, -n *u.* **Zos|sen,** der; -, - ‹hebr.-jidd.› (*landsch. für* Pferd)

Zos|ter, der; -[s], - ‹griech.› (*Med.* Gürtelrose)

Zo|te, die; -, -n (unanständiger Ausdruck; unanständiger Witz); **zo|ten; Zo|ten|rei|ßer; zo|tig; Zo|tig|keit**

Zot|te, die; -, -n (*südwestd. u. mitteld. für* Schnauze, Ausgießer)

Zot|tel, die; -, -n (Haarbüschel; Quaste, Troddel u. a.); **Zot|tel‿bär, ...haar; zot|te|lig,** zott|lig; **zot|teln** (*ugs. für* langsam gehen); ich ...[e]le (↑R 16); **zot|tig; zottlig** *vgl.* zottelig

ZPO = Zivilprozessordnung

Zr = *chem. Zeichen für* Zirkonium

Zs. = Zeitschrift

Zschok|ke (schweiz. Schriftsteller)

[1]Zscho|pau (Stadt südöstlich von Chemnitz); **[2]Zscho|pau,** die; - (Fluss in Sachsen)

Zschr. = Zeitschrift

Z-Sol|dat; ↑R 26 (*kurz für* Zeitsoldat)

z. T. = zum Teil

Ztr. = Zentner (50 kg)

zu; *Präp. mit Dat.:* zu dem Garten; zum Bahnhof; zu zwei[e]n, zu zweit; vier zu eins (4 : 1); zu viel, zu wenig, zu weit, zu spät; jmdm. etwas zu Eigen geben; zuletzt, *aber* zu guter Letzt; zuäußerst; zuoberst; zutiefst; zuunterst; zulasten, *auch* zu Lasten; zugunsten, *auch* zu Gunsten; zuungunsten, *auch* zu Ungunsten; zuseiten (*vgl. d.*); sich etwas zunutze, *auch* zu Nutze machen; zuzeiten (bisweilen), *aber* zu Großmutters Zeiten; zu Zeiten Goethes; zugrunde, *auch* zu Grunde gehen; jmdm. etw. zuleide, *auch* zu Leide tun; mir ist fröhlich zumute, *auch* zu Mute; mit etwas zurande, *auch* zu Rande kommen; jmdn. zurate, *auch* zu Rate ziehen; zuschanden, *auch* zu Schanden werden; sich etw. zuschulden, *auch* zu Schulden kommen lassen; zustande, *auch* zu Stande kommen; zutage, *auch* zu Tage fördern, treten; zuwege, *auch* zu Wege bringen; zu Berge stehen; sich jmdn. zu Dank verpflichten; zu herzlichstem Dank verpflichtet; zu Ende gehen; zu Haus[e] (*österr., schweiz. auch* zuhause) sein; zu Herzen gehen; jmdm. zu Ohren kommen; zu Recht bestehen; zu Werke gehen; zu Willen sein; zum (zu dem; *vgl.* zum); zur (zu der; *vgl.* zur); *bilden* „zu", „zum", „zur" *den ersten Bestandteil eines Gebäudenamens, so sind sie großzuschreiben* (↑R 108), z. B. Zum Löwen (Gasthaus), Zur Alten Post (Gasthaus), das Gasthaus [mit dem Namen] „Zum Löwen", „Zur Alten Post", *aber* das „Gasthaus zum Löwen"; *bei Familiennamen schwankt die Schreibung,* z. B. Familie Zur Nieden, *auch* Familie zur Nieden; der zu versichernde Angestellte, *aber* der zu Versichernde, *entsprechend:* der aufzunehmende Fremde, der Aufzunehmende; „zu" *als „Vorwort" des Verbs:* der Hund ist mir zugelaufen, der Vogel ist mir zugeflogen, *aber* „zu" *als Adverb:* sie sind der Stadt zu (= stadtwärts) gegangen; zu sein (*ugs. für* geschlossen sein); alle Läden sind zu gewesen; *zum Komma* ↑R 75 ff.: er hofft[,] pünktlich zu kommen

zu... (*in Zus. mit Verben,* z. B. zunehmen, du nimmst zu, zugenommen, zuzunehmen)

zu|al|ler|al|ler|letzt; zu|al|lererst; zu|al|ler|letzt; zu|al|lermeist

Zu|ar|beit; zu|ar|bei|ten; sie haben ihm fleißig zugearbeitet

zu|äu|ßerst

zu|bal|lern; er hat die Tür zugeballert (*ugs. für* heftig ins Schloss geworfen)

Zu|bau, der; -[e]s, -ten (*österr. für* Anbau); **zu|bau|en;** zugebaut

Zu|be|hör, das, *seltener* der; -[e]s, *Plur.* -e, *schweiz. auch* -den; *vgl.* Zugehör; **Zu|be|hör|in|dust|rie; Zu|be|hör|teil,** das

zu|bei|ßen; zugebissen

zu|be|kom|men (*ugs. für* dazu bekommen; *ugs. für* schließen können); zubekommen

Zu|ber, der; -s, - (*landsch. für* [Holz]bottich)

zu|be|rei|ten; zubereitet; **Zu|berei|ter; Zu|be|rei|tung**

zu|be|to|nie|ren; zubetoniert

Zu|bett|ge|hen, das; -s; vor dem -

zu|bil|li|gen; zugebilligt; **Zu|bil|ligung**

zu|bin|den

Zu|biss
zu|blei|ben (*ugs. für* geschlossen bleiben); zugeblieben
zu|blin|zeln; zugeblinzelt
zu|brin|gen; zugebracht; **Zu|brin|ger; Zu|brin|ger‿bus, ...dienst, ...stra|ße**
Zu|brot, das; -[e]s (*landsch. auch für* zusätzlicher Verdienst)
Zu|bu|ße (*veraltet für* Geldzuschuss)
zu|but|tern (*ugs. für* [Geld] zusetzen); zugebuttert
Zuc|chet|to [tsuk...], der; -s, ...tti *meist Plur.* ‹ital.› (*schweiz. für* Zucchini); **Zuc|chi|ni,** die; -, -, *seltener* **Zuc|chi|no,** der; -, ...ni *meist Plur.* (ein gurkenähnl. Gemüse)
Zü|chen, der; -s, - (*landsch. svw.* Zieche)
Zucht, die; -, *Plur. (Landw.:)* -en; **Zucht‿buch, ...bul|le, ...eber** (↑R 132); **züch|ten;** Rosen, Schafe -; **Züch|ter; Zucht|er|folg; Züch|te|rin; züch|te|risch; Zucht‿haus, ...häus|ler; Zucht|haus|stra|fe; Zucht|hengst; züch|tig** (*veraltet für* sittsam); **züch|ti|gen** *(geh.);* **Züch|tig|keit,** die; - *(veraltet);* **Züch|ti|gung; zucht|los; Zucht|lo|sig|keit; Zucht‿mit|tel** (das; *Rechtsspr.*), **...per|le, ...stier, ...tier; Züch|tung; Zucht‿vieh, ...wahl**
zuck!; Zuck, der; -[e]s, -e; in einem -; **zu|ckeln** (*ugs. für* langsam u. ohne Hast trotten, fahren); ich ...[e]le (↑R 16); *vgl. auch* zockeln; **Zu|ckel|trab** *(ugs.);* im -; **zucken;** der Blitz zuckt; **zü|cken** (rasch [heraus]ziehen); das Portemonnaie zücken
Zu|cker, der; -s, *Plur.(Sorten:)* -; **Zu|cker|bä|cker** (*südd. u. österr., sonst veraltet für* Konditor); **Zu|cker|bä|cker|stil** (*abwertend für* [sowjet.] Baustil nach dem 2. Weltkrieg); **Zu|cker|brot; Zu|cker|chen** (*landsch. für* Bonbon); **Zu|cker‿cou|leur** (die; -; gebrannter Zucker zum Färben von Lebensmitteln), **...do|se, ...erb|se, ...fab|rik, ...ge|halt** (der), **...guss; zu|cker|hal|tig; Zu|cker|harn|ruhr** (*für* Diabetes mellitus); **Zu|cker|hut,** der; **zu|cke|rig,** zuck|rig; **Zu|cker|kand,** der; -[e]s *u.* **Zu|cker|kan|dis,** der; - (*ugs. für* Kandiszucker); **Zu|cker|kandl,** das; -s, -[n] (*österr. veraltend für* Kandiszucker); **zu|cker|krank; Zu|cker|krank|heit; Zu|ckerl,** das; -s, -n (*österr. für* Bonbon); **Zu|cker|le|cken,** das; *nur in* kein - sein (unangenehm, anstrengend sein); **zu|ckern** (mit Zucker süßen); ich ...ere (↑R 16); **Zu|cker‿raf|fi|na|de, ...raf|fi|ne|rie, ...rohr, ...rü|be, ...schle|cken** (*vgl.* Zuckerlecken), **...stan|ge, ...streu|er; zu|cker|süß; Zu|cker‿tü|te, ...was|ser** (das; -s), **...wat|te, ...zan|ge**
Zuck|fuß, der; -es (fehlerhafter Gang des Pferdes)
Zuck|may|er, Carl (dt. Schriftsteller u. Dramatiker)
Zuck|mü|cke
zuck|rig *vgl.* zuckerig
Zu|ckung
Zu|de|cke (*ugs. für* Bettdecke); **zu|de|cken;** zugedeckt
zu|dem (außerdem)
zu|die|nen (*schweiz. für* Handreichung tun); zugedient
zu|dik|tie|ren; zudiktiert
zu|dre|hen; zugedreht
zu drei|en, zu dritt
zu|dring|lich; Zu|dring|lich|keit
zu dritt *vgl.* zu dreien
zu|drü|cken; zugedrückt
zu Ei|gen; jmdm. etwas zu Eigen geben *(geh.);* sich etwas zu Eigen machen (↑R 47); **zu|eig|nen** (*geh. für* widmen; schenken); zugeeignet; **Zu|eig|nung**
zu|ei|nan|der *in Verbindung mit Verben immer getrennt* (↑R 39): zueinander finden; zueinander sprechen, passen usw.
zu En|de *vgl.* Ende
zu|er|ken|nen; man erkannte mir die Berechtigung zu; zuerkannt; **Zu|er|ken|nung**
zu|erst; der zuerst genannte Verfasser ist nicht mit dem zuletzt genannten zu verwechseln; zuerst einmal; *aber* zu zweit
zu|er|tei|len *(selten);* zuerteilt; **Zu|er|tei|lung**
Zu|er|werb, der; -[e]s (*svw.* Nebenerwerb); **Zu|er|werbs|be|trieb** *(Landw.)*
zu|fä|cheln; zugefächelt
zu|fah|ren; zugefahren; **Zu|fahrt; Zu|fahrts‿stra|ße, ...weg**
Zu|fall, der; **zu|fal|len;** zugefallen; **zu|fäl|lig; zu|fäl|li|ger|wei|se; Zu|fäl|lig|keit; Zu|falls‿aus|wahl** *(Statistik),* **...be|kannt|schaft, ...er|geb|nis, ...grö|ße** *(Math.),* **...streu|be|reich** *(Statistik),* **...streu|ung** *(Statistik),* **...tref|fer**
zu|fas|sen; zugefasst
zu|fli|cken *(ugs.);* zugeflickt
zu|flie|gen; zugeflogen
zu|flie|ßen; zugeflossen
Zu|flucht, die; -; **Zu|flucht|nah|me,** die; -; **Zu|fluchts‿ort** (der; -[e]s, -e), **...stät|te**
Zu|fluss
zu|flüs|tern; zugeflüstert
zu|fol|ge (↑R 41) *Präp., bei Nachstellung mit Dat.:* dem Gerücht zufolge, demzufolge *(vgl. d.), aber bei Voranstellung mit Gen.:* zufolge des Gerüchtes
zu|frie|den; zufrieden mit dem Ergebnis; zufrieden machen, sein, werden; sich zufrieden geben; zufrieden gegeben; zufrieden zu geben; jmdn. zufrieden lassen; jmdn. zufrieden stellen; ein zufrieden stellendes (*aber* zufriedenstellenderes) Ergebnis; unsere zufrieden gestellten Kunden; **Zu|frie|den|heit,** die; -; **Zu|frie|den|stel|lung,** die; -
zu|frie|ren; zugefroren
zu|fü|gen; zugefügt; **Zu|fü|gung**
Zu|fuhr, die; -, -en (Herbeischaffen); **zu|füh|ren** (*bes. ehem. in der DDR auch für* [vorläufig] verhaften); zugeführt; **Zu|füh|rung; Zu|füh|rungs‿lei|tung, ...rohr**
[1]Zug, der; -[e]s, Züge; im Zuge des Wiederaufbaus; Zug um Zug; Dreiuhrzug (*mit Ziffer* 3-Uhr-Zug; ↑R 28)
[2]Zug (Kanton u. Stadt in der Schweiz)
Zu|ga|be
Zug|ab|teil; *vgl. auch* Zugsabteil
Zu|gang; zu|gan|ge (↑R 41); - sein *(ugs.);* **zu|gän|gig** (*seltener für* zugänglich); **zu|gäng|lich** (leicht Zugang gewährend); **Zu|gäng|lich|keit,** die; -
Zug‿be|glei|ter, ...brü|cke
zu|ge|ben; zugegeben *(vgl. d.)*
zu|ge|dacht *(geh.);* diese Auszeichnung war eigentlich ihm -
Zu|ge|führ|te, der *u.* die; -n, -n; ↑R 5 ff. (*Amtsspr., bes. ehem. in der DDR* [vorläufig] Verhaftete[r])
zu|ge|ge|ben; zugegeben, dass dein Freund Recht hat; **zu|ge|ge|be|ner|ma|ßen**
zu|ge|gen *(geh.);* [bei etwas] zugegen sein
zu|ge|hen; auf jmdn. zugehen; auf dem Fest ist es lustig zugegangen; der Koffer geht nicht zu *(ugs.);* **Zu|ge|he|rin, Zu|geh|frau** (*südd., westösterr. für* Aufwartefrau)
Zu|ge|hör, das; -[e]s, *schweiz.* die; - (*österr. u. schweiz. Rechtsspr., sonst veraltet für* Zubehör); **zu|ge|hö|ren** *(geh.);* zugehört; **zu|ge|hö|rig; Zu|ge|hö|rig|keit,** die; -; **Zu|ge|hö|rig|keits|ge|fühl,** das; -[e]s
zu|ge|knöpft; sie war sehr zugeknöpft (*ugs. für* verschlossen); **Zu|ge|knöpft|heit,** die; -
Zü|gel, der; -s, -; **Zü|gel‿hand** (linke Hand des Reiters), **...hil|fe; zü|gel|los; Zü|gel|lo|sig|keit; zü-**

geln (*schweiz. mdal. auch für* umziehen); ich ...[e]le (↑R 16); **Zü|gel|lung,** Züg|lung

Zu|ge|mü|se (*veraltet für* Gemüsebeilage)

Zü|gen|glöck|lein (*österr. für* Totenglocke)

Zu|ger (von, aus ²Zug; ↑R 103)

Zu|ge|reis|te, der *u.* die; -n, -n (↑R 5 ff.)

zu|ge|risch; Zu|ger See, der; - -s

zu|ge|sel|len; zugesellt; sich -

zu|ge|stan|den; zugestanden, dass dich keine Schuld trifft; **zu|ge|stan|de|ner|ma|ßen; Zu|ge|ständ|nis; zu|ge|ste|hen;** zugestanden

zu|ge|tan (*auch für* wohlwollend, freundlich gesinnt); er ist ihr von Herzen zugetan

zu|ge|wandt *u.* **zu|ge|wen|det** *vgl.* zuwenden

Zu|ge|winn; Zu|ge|winn|ge|mein|schaft (Form des Güterrechts)

zug|fest; Zug‿fes|tig|keit (die; -), **...fol|ge, ...füh|rer** (*vgl. auch* Zugsführer); **Zug|hub,** der; -[e]s, -e (*Bergmannsspr.* ein Hebegerät)

zu|gie|ßen; zugegossen

zu|gig (windig); **zü|gig** (in einem Zuge; *schweiz. auch für* zugkräftig); **...zü|gig** (z. B. zweizügig [von Schulen]); **Zü|gig|keit,** die; - (das Zügigsein); **Zug‿kon|trol|le, ...kraft** (die); **zug|kräf|tig; Zug|last**

zu|gleich

Zug|lei|ne; Züg|le|te, die; -, -n (*schweiz. mdal. für* Umzug, Wohnungswechsel); **Zug|luft,** die; -

Züg|lung *vgl.* Zügelung

Zug‿ma|schi|ne, ...num|mer, ...per|so|nal, ...pferd, ...pflas|ter

zu|grei|fen; greifen Sie zu!; zugegriffen; **Zu|griff,** der; -[e]s, -e; **zu|grif|fig** (*schweiz. für* zugreifend, tatkräftig); **zu|griffs|be|rech|tigt** (*bes. EDV*); **Zu|griffs‿be|rech|ti|gung, ...mög|lich|keit, ...zeit** (*bes. EDV*)

zu|grun|de, *auch* **zu Grun|de;** zugrunde, *auch* zu Grunde gehen, legen, liegen, richten; es scheint etwas anderes zugrunde, *auch* zu Grunde zu liegen; zugrunde liegend, *auch* zu Grunde liegend; **Zu|grun|de‿ge|hen** (das; -s), **...le|gung** (unter - von ...)

Zugs|ab|teil (*österr.*); **Zug|sal|be; Zug|scheit** *Plur.* ...scheite (*landsch. für* Ortscheit); **Zug|seil; Zugs|füh|rer** (*österr.*)

Zug|spitz|bahn; Zug|spit|ze, die; - (höchster Berg Deutschlands); **Zug|spitz|platt,** das; -s

Zug‿stan|ge, ...stück; Zugs‿ver|kehr (*österr., auch schweiz.*), **...ver|spä|tung** (*österr.*); **Zug|te|le|fon; Zug|tier**

zu|gu|cken (*ugs.*); zugeguckt

Zug-um-Zug-Leis|tung; ↑R 28 (*Rechtsw.*)

Zug|un|glück

zu|guns|ten, *auch* **zu Guns|ten;** *Präp., bei Voranstellung mit Gen.:* zugunsten, *auch* zu Gunsten bedürftiger Kinder, *aber bei (seltener) Nachstellung mit Dat.:* dem Freund zugunsten, *auch* zu Gunsten; *vgl.* Gunst

zu|gut; zugut haben (*schweiz. für* guthaben); **zu|gu|te** (↑R 41); zugute halten, kommen, tun

zu gu|ter Letzt *vgl.* Letzt

Zug‿ver|bin|dung, ...ver|kehr (*vgl. auch* Zugsverkehr), **...ver|spä|tung, ...vieh, ...vo|gel, ...vor|rich|tung; zug|wei|se; Zug‿wind, ...zwang** (unter - stehen)

zu|ha|ben (*ugs. für* geschlossen haben); zugehabt

zu|ha|cken; zugehackt

zu|ha|ken; zugehakt

zu|hal|ten; zugehalten; **Zu|häl|ter; Zu|häl|te|rei,** die; -; **zu|häl|te|risch**

¹zu|han|den (↑R 41); zuhanden kommen, sein; **²zu|han|den, zu Hän|den** ↑R 41; (*Abk.* z. H., z. Hd.); zuhanden *od.* zu Händen des Herrn ..., *meist* zuhanden *od.* zu Händen von Herrn ..., *auch* zuhanden *od.* zu Händen Herrn ...

zu|hän|gen *vgl.* ²hängen

zu|hau|en; *zur Beugung vgl.* hauen

zu|hauf; ↑R 41 (*geh. für* in großer Anzahl); es gab Kartoffeln zuhauf; kommet zuhauf!

zu Hau|s, zu Hau|se, *österr., schweiz. auch* zu|hau|se; sich wie zu Hause fühlen; etwas für zu Hause mitnehmen; ich freue mich auf zu Hause, *aber nur* auf mein Zuhause; **Zu|hau|se,** das; -[s]; er hat kein Zuhause mehr; **Zu|hau|se|ge|blie|be|ne,** der *u.* die; -n, -n (↑R 5 ff.)

zu|hef|ten; zugeheftet

zu|hei|len; zugeheilt

Zu|hil|fe|nah|me, die; -; unter Zuhilfenahme von ...

zu|hin|terst

zu|höchst

zu|hor|chen (*landsch. für* zuhören); zugehorcht

zu|hö|ren; zugehört; **Zu|hö|rer; Zu|hö|rer|bank** *Plur.* ...bänke; **Zu|hö|re|rin; Zu|hö|rer|schaft**

Zui|der|see ['zɔy...], die; - *od.* der; -s; *vgl.* Ijsselmeer

zu|in|nerst (*geh.*)

zu|ju|beln; zugejubelt

Zu|kauf (*bes. Finanzw.*); **zu|kau|fen;** wir haben weitere Bezugsrechte zugekauft

zu|keh|ren; sie hat mir den Rücken zugekehrt

zu|klap|pen; zugeklappt

zu|kle|ben; zugeklebt

zu|knal|len (*ugs.*); zugeknallt

zu|knei|fen; zugekniffen

zu|knöp|fen; zugeknöpft (*vgl. d.*)

zu|kno|ten; zugeknotet

zu|kom|men; zugekommen; er ist auf mich zugekommen; er hat ihm das Geschenk zukommen lassen, *seltener* gelassen; ihm etwas zukommen zu lassen

zu|kor|ken; zugekorkt

Zu|kost

Zu|kunft, die; -, Zukünfte *Plur. selten;* **zu|künf|tig; Zu|künf|ti|ge,** der *u.* die; -n, -n; ↑R 5 ff. (Verlobte[r]); **Zu|kunfts‿angst, ...aus|sich|ten** (*Plur.*), **...for|scher, ...for|schung, ...glau|be[n]; zu|kunfts|gläu|big; Zu|kunfts|mu|sik** (*ugs.*); **zu|kunfts|ori|en|tiert** (↑R 132); **Zu|kunfts‿per|spek|ti|ve, ...plan** (*meist Plur.*); **zu|kunfts|reich; Zu|kunfts‿ro|man, ...staat** (*Plur.* ...staaten); **zu|kunfts‿träch|tig, ...voll; zu|kunft[s]|wei|send**

zu|lä|cheln; zugelächelt

zu|la|chen; zugelacht

Zu|la|ge

zu Lan|de; bei uns zu Lande; hier zu Lande, *auch* hierzulande (↑R 41); zu Wasser u. zu Lande

zu|lan|gen; zugelangt; **zu|läng|lich** (hinreichend); **Zu|läng|lich|keit**

zu|las|sen; zugelassen; **zu|läs|sig** (erlaubt); **Zu|läs|sig|keit,** die; -; **Zu|las|sung; Zu|las|sungs‿be|gren|zung, ...num|mer, ...stel|le**

zu|las|ten, *auch* **zu Las|ten;** zulasten, *auch* zu Lasten des ... *od.* von ...

Zu|lauf; zu|lau|fen; zugelaufen

zu|le|gen; zugelegt

zu|leid, zu|lei|de, *auch* zu Leid, zu Lei|de (↑R 41); *nur in* jmdm. etwas zuleid[e], *auch* zu Leid[e] tun

zu|lei|ten; zugeleitet; **Zu|lei|tung; Zu|lei|tungs|rohr**

zu|ler|nen (*ugs.*); zugelernt

zu|letzt, *aber* zu guter Letzt

zu|lie|be, *österr. auch* zu|lieb (↑R 41); *Präp. mit vorangestelltem Dat.:* mir, dir usw. zuliebe

Zu|lie|fe|rant, der; -en, -en; **Zu|lie|fe|rer** (*Wirtsch.*); **Zu|lie|fe|rer|in|dust|rie, Zu|lie|fer|in|dust|rie; Zu|lie|fe|rung**

zul|len (*landsch. für* lutschend saugen); **Zulp,** der; -[e]s, -e (*ostmitteld. für* Schnuller); **zul|pen** (*ostmitteld. für* saugen)

Zu|lu, der; -[s], -[s] (Angehöriger eines Bantustammes in Südafrika)
Zu|luft, die; - (*Technik* zugeleitete Luft)
zum; ↑R 13 (zu dem); zum einen ..., zum anderen ...; (↑R 47:) zum Ersten, zum Zweiten, zum Dritten; zum Höchsten, Mindesten, Wenigsten; zum ersten Mal[e]; zum letzten Mal[e]; zum Teil (*Abk.* z. T.); etwas zum Besten geben, haben, halten; es steht nicht zum Besten (nicht gut); zum Besten der Armen; sich zum Besten kehren, lenken, wenden; (↑R 50:) das ist zum Weinen, zum Totlachen. *Zur Schreibung von „zum" als Teil von Eigennamen vgl.* zu
zu|ma|chen (*ugs. für* schließen); zugemacht; auf- und zumachen (↑R 23), *aber* es ist nichts zu machen
zu|mal (↑R 41; besonders); - [da, wenn]
zu|mau|ern; zugemauert
zum Bei|spiel (*Abk.* z. B.); ↑R 67
zu|meist
zu|mes|sen; zugemessen
zum E|xem|pel (*veraltend für* zum Beispiel; *Abk.* z. E.)
zu|min|dest, *aber* zum Mindesten
zum Teil (*Abk.* z. T.)
zu|mut|bar; Zu|mut|bar|keit
zu|mu|te *auch* **zu Mu|te;** mir ist gut, schlecht zumute, *auch* zu Mute
zu|mu|ten; zugemutet; **Zu|mu|tung**
zum Vo|raus (↑R 49 u. 132; *landsch. für* im Voraus)
zu|nächst; zunächst ging er nach Hause; zunächst dem Hause *od.* dem Hause zunächst; **Zu|nächst|lie|gen|de,** das; -n (↑R 5 ff.)
zu|na|geln; zugenagelt
zu|nä|hen; zugenäht
Zu|nah|me, die; -, -n (Vermehrung)
Zu|na|me, der; -ns, -n (Familienname; *veraltend für* Beiname)
zünd|bar; Zünd|blätt|chen; Zun|del, der; -s (*veraltet für* Zunder); **zün|deln** (*südd., österr. für* mit dem Feuer spielen); ich ...[e]le (↑R 16); **zün|den; zün|dend; Zun|der,** der; -s, - (ein altes Zündmittel; *Technik* Oxidschicht); **Zün|der** ([Gas-, Feuer]anzünder; Zündvorrichtung in Sprengkörpern; *österr. auch svw.* Zündhölzer); **Zun|der|schwamm** (ein Pilz); **Zünd‿flam|me, ...fun|ke[n]** (*Kfz-Technik*), **...holz, ...hölz|chen; Zünd|holz|schach|tel; Zünd‿hüt|chen, ...ka|bel, ...ker|ze, ...la|dung, ...na|del; Zünd|na|del|ge|wehr** (*früher*); **Zünd‿plätt|chen** (*svw.* Zündblättchen), **...schloss, ...schlüs|sel, ...schnur, ...stoff; Zün|dung; Zünd‿ver|tei|ler, ...vor|rich|tung, ...zeit|punkt** (*Kfz-Technik*)
zu|neh|men; zugenommen; *vgl.* ab
zu|nei|gen; zugeneigt; **Zu|nei|gung**
Zunft, die; -, Zünfte; **Zunft‿ge|nos|se, ...haus; zünf|tig** (*ugs. auch für* ordentlich, tüchtig); **Zünft|ler** (*früher* Angehöriger einer Zunft); **Zunft‿meis|ter, ...ord|nung, ...recht, ...wap|pen, ...zwang** (der; -[e]s)
Zun|ge, die; -, -n; **Zün|gel|chen; zün|geln; Zun|gen|bre|cher; zun|gen|fer|tig; Zun|gen‿fer|tig|keit** (die; -), **...kuss, ...laut** (*für* Lingual); **Zun|gen-R,** *auch* **Zun|gen-r,** das; -, - (↑R 25; *Sprachw.*); **Zun|gen‿schlag, ...spit|ze, ...wurst**
zu|nich|te (↑R 41); zunichte machen, werden
zu|ni|cken; zugenickt
zu|nie|derst (*landsch. für* zuunterst)
Züns|ler, der; -s, - (ein Kleinschmetterling)
zu|nut|ze, *auch* **zu Nut|ze;** sich etwas zunutze, *auch* zu Nutze machen; *aber* zu Nutz u. Frommen
zu|oberst (↑R 132)
zu|or|den|bar; zu|ord|nen; zugeordnet; **Zu|ord|nung**
zu|pa|cken; zugepackt
zu|par|ken; ein zugeparkter Hof
zu|pass, zu|pas|se (↑R 41); zupass *od.* zupasse kommen
zu|pas|sen (*bes. Fußball*); zugepasst; dem Mitspieler den Ball -
zup|fen; Zupf|gei|ge (*ugs. veraltet für* Gitarre); **Zupf|gei|gen|hansl,** der; -s, - (eine Liedersammlung); **Zupf|in|stru|ment**
zu|pflas|tern; zugepflastert
zu|pres|sen; zugepresst
zu|pros|ten; zugeprostet
zur; ↑R 13 (zu der); zur Folge haben; sich zur Ruhe setzen; zur Schau stellen; zurzeit, zur Zeit (*Abk.* z. Z., z. Zt.; *vgl. d.*). *Zur Schreibung von „zur" als Teil eines Eigennamens vgl.* zu
zu|ran|de, *auch* **zu Ran|de;** mit etwas zurande, *auch* zu Rande kommen; *vgl.* [1]Rand
zu|ra|te, *auch* **zu Ra|te;** jmdn. zurate, *auch* zu Rate ziehen
zu|ra|ten; zugeraten
zu|rau|nen (*geh.*); zugeraunt
Zür|cher; ↑R 103 (*schweiz. Form von* Züricher); **zür|che|risch**
zur Dis|po|si|ti|on (zur Verfügung; *Abk.* z. D.); zur Disposition stellen; **Zur|dis|po|si|ti|on|stel|lung**
zu|re|chen|bar; Zu|re|chen|bar|keit, die; -; **zu|rech|nen;** zugerechnet; **Zu|rech|nung; zu|rech|nungs|fä|hig; Zu|rech|nungs|fä|hig|keit,** die; -
zu|recht... *nur in Zus. mit Verben,* z. B. zurechtkommen usw., *aber* zu Recht bestehen; **zu|recht‿bas|teln, ...bie|gen, ...fei|len, ...fin|den** (sich), **...fli|cken, ...kom|men, ...le|gen, ...ma|chen** (*ugs.*), **...rü|cken, ...schnei|den, ...schus|tern** (*ugs.*), **...set|zen, ...stel|len, ...stut|zen, ...wei|sen; Zu|recht|wei|sung; zu|recht|zim|mern**
zu|re|den; zugeredet; **Zu|re|den,** das; -s; auf vieles Zureden; trotz allem Zureden, trotz allen *od.* alles Zuredens
zu|rei|chen; zugereicht; **zu|rei|chend;** zureichende Gründe
zu|rei|ten; zugeritten
Zü|rich [*schweiz.* 'tsyriç] (Kanton u. Stadt in der Schweiz); **Zü|ri[ch]|biet,** das; -s (*svw.* Kanton Zürich); **Zü|ri[ch]|bie|ter** (↑R 103); **Zü|ri|cher,** *in der Schweiz nur* Zür|cher (↑R 103); **zü|ri|che|risch,** *in der Schweiz nur* zür|che|risch; **Zü|rich|see,** der; -s
Zu|rich|te|bo|gen (*Druckw.*); **zu|rich|ten;** zugerichtet; **Zu|rich|ten,** das; -s; **Zu|rich|ter; Zu|rich|te|rei; Zu|rich|te|rin; Zu|rich|tung**
zu|rie|geln; zugeriegelt
zür|nen (*geh.*)
zu|rol|len; zugerollt
zur|ren ⟨niederl.⟩ (*Seemannsspr.* festbinden); **Zur|ring,** der; -s, *Plur.* -s *u.* -e (*Seemannsspr.* Leine zum Zurren)
Zur|schau|stel|lung
zu|rück; zurück sein; (↑R 49:) es gibt kein Zurück mehr
zu|rück... (*in Zus. mit Verben,* z. B. zurücklegen, du legst zurück, wenn du zurücklegst, zurückgelegt, zurückzulegen)
zu|rück|be|hal|ten; er hat es zurückbehalten; **Zu|rück|be|hal|tung; Zu|rück|be|hal|tungs|recht,** das; -[e]s (*Rechtsw.*)
zu|rück|be|kom|men; sie hat es zurückbekommen
zu|rück|be|ru|fen; man hat ihn zurückberufen
zu|rück|beu|gen; zurückgebeugt
zu|rück|be|we|gen; zurückbewegt
zu|rück|be|zah|len; zurückbezahlt

zu|rück|bil|den; zurückgebildet; sich -; **Zu|rück|bil|dung**
zu|rück|blei|ben; zurückgeblieben
zu|rück|blen|den *(Film);* zurückgeblendet
zu|rück|bli|cken; zurückgeblickt
zu|rück|brin|gen; zurückgebracht
zu|rück|däm|men; wir haben die Inflation zurückgedämmt
zu|rück|da|tie|ren (mit einem früheren Datum versehen); zurückdatiert
zu|rück|den|ken; zurückgedacht
zu|rück|drän|gen; sie hat zurückgedrängt; **Zu|rück|drän|gung**
zu|rück|dre|hen; zurückgedreht
zu|rück|dür|fen; zurückgedurft
zu|rück|ei|len; zurückgeeilt
zu|rück|er|bit|ten; zurückerbeten
zu|rück|er|hal|ten; wir haben alles zurückerhalten
zu|rück|er|o|bern; zurückerobert; **Zu|rück|er|o|be|rung**
zu|rück|er|stat|ten; zurückerstattet; **Zu|rück|er|stat|tung**
zu|rück|fah|ren; zurückgefahren
zu|rück|fal|len; zurückgefallen
zu|rück|fin|den; zurückgefunden
zu|rück|flie|gen; zurückgeflogen
zu|rück|for|dern; zurückgefordert
zu|rück|fra|gen; zurückgefragt
zu|rück|füh|ren; zurückgeführt; **Zu|rück|füh|rung**
zu|rück|ge|ben; zurückgegeben
zu|rück|ge|hen; zurückgegangen
zu|rück|ge|win|nen; zurückgewonnen
zu|rück|ge|zo|gen; **Zu|rück|ge|zo|gen|heit,** die; -
zu|rück|grei|fen; zurückgegriffen
zu|rück|ha|ben; etwas - wollen
zu|rück|hal|ten; zurückgehalten; sich -; **zu|rück|hal|tend; Zu|rück|hal|tung,** die; -
zu|rück|ho|len; zurückgeholt
zu|rück|käm|men; zurückgekämmt
zu|rück|keh|ren; zurückgekehrt
zu|rück|klap|pen; zurückgeklappt
zu|rück|kom|men; zurückgekommen
zu|rück|kön|nen *(ugs.);* zurückgekonnt
zu|rück|krie|chen; zurückgekrochen
zu|rück|krie|gen *(ugs.);* zurückgekriegt
zu|rück|las|sen; zurückgelassen; **Zu|rück|las|sung;** unter -
zu|rück|le|gen; (*österr. auch für* [ein Amt] niederlegen); zurückgelegt; sich -
zu|rück|leh|nen, sich; zurückgelehnt
zu|rück|lie|gen; zurückgelegen
zu|rück|müs|sen *(ugs.);* zurückgemusst
Zu|rück|nah|me, die; -, -n; **zu|rück|neh|men;** zurückgenommen
zu|rück|pral|len; zurückgeprallt
zu|rück|rol|len; zurückgerollt
zu|rück|ru|fen; zurückgerufen; rufen Sie bitte zurück!
zu|rück|schaf|fen; *vgl.* [1]schaffen
zu|rück|schal|ten; zurückgeschaltet
zu|rück|schau|dern; sie ist zurückgeschaudert
zu|rück|schau|en; wir haben gern zurückgeschaut
zu|rück|scheu|en; das Pferd hat zurückgescheut
zu|rück|schi|cken; der Brief wurde zurückgeschickt
zu|rück|schla|gen; die Angreifer wurden zurückgeschlagen
zu|rück|schnei|den; die Rosen wurden zurückgeschnitten
[1]**zu|rück|schre|cken;** er schrak zurück; er ist zurückgeschreckt, *selten* er ist zurückgeschrocken; *vgl.* [1]schrecken; *aber übertr.:* vor etwas zurückschrecken (etwas nicht wagen); er schreckte vor etwas zurück, ist vor etwas zurückgeschreckt; [2]**zu|rück|schre|cken;** das schreckte ihn zurück; *vgl.* [2]schrecken
zu|rück|seh|nen, sich; zurückgesehnt
zu|rück sein; *vgl.* zurück
zu|rück|sen|den; zurückgesandt *u.* zurückgesendet
zu|rück|set|zen; zurückgesetzt; **Zu|rück|set|zung**
zu|rück|spie|len; er hat den Ball zurückgespielt
zu|rück|ste|cken; zurückgesteckt
zu|rück|ste|hen; zurückgestanden
zu|rück|stel|len (*österr. auch für* zurückgeben, -senden); zurückgestellt; **Zu|rück|stel|lung**
zu|rück|sto|ßen; zurückgestoßen
zu|rück|strah|len; zurückgestrahlt; **Zu|rück|strah|lung**
zu|rück|stu|fen; zurückgestuft; **Zu|rück|stu|fung**
zu|rück|stut|zen; zurückgestutzt
zu|rück|trei|ben; zurückgetrieben
zu|rück|tre|ten; zurückgetreten
zu|rück|tun *(ugs.);* zurückgetan; einen Schritt zurücktun
zu|rück|ver|fol|gen; zurückverfolgt
zu|rück|ver|lan|gen; zurückverlangt
zu|rück|ver|set|zen; zurückversetzt; sich -
zu|rück|ver|wei|sen; zurückverwiesen
zu|rück|wei|chen; zurückgewichen
zu|rück|wei|sen; ein Angebot, einen Vorwurf zurückweisen; zurückgewiesen; **Zu|rück|wei|sung**
zu|rück|wen|den; zurückgewandt
zu|rück|wer|fen; zurückgeworfen
zu|rück|wir|ken; zurückgewirkt
zu|rück|wol|len *(ugs.);* zurückgewollt
zu|rück|zah|len; zurückgezahlt; **Zu|rück|zah|lung**
zu|rück|zie|hen; zurückgezogen; sich -; **Zu|rück|zie|her** (*seltener für* Rückzieher)
zu|rück|zu|cken; zurückgezuckt
Zu|ruf; zu|ru|fen; zugerufen
zur|zeit (*Abk.* zz., zzt.); sie ist zurzeit krank, *aber* sie lebte zur Zeit Karls des Großen
Zu|sa|ge, die; -, -n; **zu|sa|gen;** es sagt mir zu; zugesagt; **zu|sa|gend** (passend, willkommen)
zu|sam|men; zusammen mit; (↑R 38 f.): zusammenarbeiten, zusammenballen, zusammenbeißen, zusammenbinden usw.; ich binde zusammen, habe zusammengebunden, um zusammenzubinden; *aber Getrenntschreibung, wenn* „zusammen" *svw.* „gemeinsam, gleichzeitig" *bedeutet,* z. B. sie können nicht zusammen [in einem Raum] arbeiten; wir sind zusammen angekommen; jetzt sollen alle zusammen singen; *nur getrennt:* zusammen sein; wenn er mit uns zusammen ist; sie waren zusammen gewesen (*aber* das Zusammensein)
Zu|sam|men|ar|beit, die; -; **zu|sam|men|ar|bei|ten** (Tätigkeiten auf ein Ziel hin vereinigen); die beiden Firmen sind übereingekommen zusammenzuarbeiten; (*vgl.* zusammen)
zu|sam|men|bal|len (verdichten); sich -; die Wolken haben sich, das Verhängnis hat sich zusammengeballt (*vgl.* zusammen); **Zu|sam|men|bal|lung**
Zu|sam|men|bau *Plur.* -e (*für* Montage); **zu|sam|men|bau|en;** er hat das Modellschiff zusammengebaut; sie wollen zusammen (gemeinsam) bauen (*vgl.* zusammen)
zu|sam|men|bei|ßen; sie hat die Zähne zusammengebissen (*vgl.* zusammen)
zu|sam|men|bin|den (in eins binden); er hat die Blumen zusammengebunden (*vgl.* zusammen)
zu|sam|men|blei|ben (sich nicht wieder trennen); wir lieben uns und wollen zusammenbleiben (*vgl.* zusammen)
zu|sam|men|brau|en (*ugs. für* aus verschiedenen Dingen mischen); was für ein Zeug hast du da zu-

sammengebraut! (*vgl.* zusammen); sich zusammenbrauen

zu|sạm|men|bre|chen (einstürzen; schwach werden); die Brücke ist zusammengebrochen; sein Vater ist völlig zusammengebrochen (*vgl.* zusammen)

zu|sạm|men|brin|gen (vereinigen); er hat die Gegner zusammengebracht; *aber* sie werden das Gepäck zusammen (gemeinsam) bringen (*vgl.* zusammen)

Zu|sạm|men|bruch, der; -[e]s, ...brüche

zu|sạm|men|drän|gen (auf engem Raum vereinigen); die Menge wurde von der Polizei zusammengedrängt (*vgl.* zusammen); sich zusammendrängen

zu|sạm|men|drück|bar; zu|sạm|men|drü|cken (durch Drücken verkleinern); sie hat die Schachtel zusammengedrückt; *aber* sie haben die Schulbank zusammen (gemeinsam) gedrückt (*vgl.* zusammen)

zu|sạm|men|fah|ren (aufeinander stoßen; erschrecken); die Radfahrer sind zusammengefahren; er ist bei dem Knall zusammengefahren; *aber* sie sind zusammen (gemeinsam) gefahren (*vgl.* zusammen)

Zu|sạm|men|fall, der; -[e]s; **zu|sạm|men|fal|len** (einstürzen; gleichzeitig erfolgen); das Haus ist zusammengefallen; Sonn- und Feiertag sind zusammengefallen; *aber* die Kinder sind zusammen gefallen (*vgl.* zusammen)

zu|sạm|men|fal|ten; hast du das Papier zusammengefaltet? (*vgl.* zusammen)

zu|sạm|men|fas|sen (raffen); er hat den Inhalt der Rede zusammengefasst; *aber* sie haben den Verbrecher zusammen (gemeinsam) gefasst (*vgl.* zusammen); **Zu|sạm|men|fas|sung**

zu|sạm|men|fe|gen; *vgl.* zusammenkehren

zu|sạm|men|fin|den, sich (sich treffen); sie haben sich zu gemeinsamer Arbeit zusammengefunden (*vgl.* zusammen)

zu|sạm|men|fli|cken (*ugs. für* notdürftig flicken; kunstlos zusammenfügen); *auch übertr.:* der Arzt hat ihn wieder zusammengeflickt (*vgl.* zusammen)

zu|sạm|men|flie|ßen (sich vereinen); wo Fulda und Werra zusammenfließen (*vgl.* zusammen); **Zu|sạm|men|fluss**

zu|sạm|men|fü|gen (vereinigen); er hat alles schön zusammengefügt (*vgl.* zusammen); sich zusammenfügen; **Zu|sạm|men|fü|gung**

zu|sạm|men|füh|ren (zueinander hinführen); die Flüchtlinge wurden zusammengeführt; *aber* wir werden den Blinden zusammen (gemeinsam) führen (*vgl.* zusammen); **Zu|sạm|men|füh|rung**

zu|sạm|men|ge|hö|ren (eng verbunden sein); wir beide haben immer zusammengehört; *aber* das Auto wird uns zusammen (gemeinsam) gehören (*vgl.* zusammen); **zu|sạm|men|ge|hö|rig; Zu|sạm|men|ge|hö|rig|keit,** die; -; **Zu|sạm|men|ge|hö|rig|keits|ge|fühl,** das; -[e]s

zu|sạm|men|ge|setzt; zusammengesetztes Wort (*für* Kompositum)

zu|sạm|men|ge|wür|felt

zu|sạm|men|ha|ben (*ugs. für* gesammelt haben); ich bin froh, dass wir jetzt das Geld dafür zusammenhaben (*vgl.* zusammen)

Zu|sạm|men|halt, der; -[e]s; **zu|sạm|men|hal|ten** (sich nicht trennen lassen; verbinden); die beiden Freunde haben immer zusammengehalten; er hat die beiden Stoffe [vergleichend] zusammengehalten; *aber* sie werden die Leiter zusammen (gemeinsam) halten (*vgl.* zusammen)

Zu|sạm|men|hang; im *od.* in Zusammenhang stehen; [1]**zu|sạm|men|hän|gen;** er weiß, dass Ursache und Wirkung zusammenhängen; *vgl.* [1]hängen; [2]**zu|sạm|men|hän|gen;** er wollte die beiden Bilder zusammenhängen; *vgl.* [2]hängen (*vgl.* zusammen); **zu|sạm|men|hän|gend; zu|sạm|men|hang[s]|los; Zu|sạm|men|hang[s]|lo|sig|keit,** die; -

zu|sạm|men|hau|en (*ugs. für* schwer verprügeln; grob, unsachgemäß anfertigen); sie haben ihn zusammengehauen; er hatte den Tisch in fünf Minuten zusammengehauen (*vgl.* zusammen)

zu|sạm|men|hef|ten (durch Heften vereinigen); sie hat die Stoffreste zusammengeheftet (*vgl.* zusammen)

zu|sạm|men|keh|ren (auf einen Haufen kehren); hast du die Scherben zusammengekehrt?; *aber* wir können den Hof zusammen (gemeinsam) kehren (*vgl.* zusammen)

zu|sạm|men|klap|pen (falten; *ugs. für* zusammenbrechen); sie hat den Fächer zusammengeklappt; er ist vor Erschöpfung zusammengeklappt (*vgl.* zusammen)

zu|sạm|men|kle|ben; er hat das Modellschiff zusammengeklebt (*vgl.* zusammen)

zu|sạm|men|knei|fen (zusammenpressen); er hat die Lippen zusammengekniffen (*vgl.* zusammen)

zu|sạm|men|knül|len (zu einer Kugel o. Ä. knüllen); sie knüllte die Zeitung zusammen (*vgl.* zusammen)

zu|sạm|men|kom|men (sich begegnen); die Mitglieder sind alle zusammengekommen; *aber* wenn möglich, wollen wir zusammen (gemeinsam) kommen (*vgl.* zusammen)

zu|sạm|men|kra|chen (*ugs.*); der Stuhl ist zusammengekracht; zwei Autos sind auf der Kreuzung zusammengekracht (*vgl.* zusammen)

zu|sạm|men|krat|zen (*ugs.*); er hat sein Geld zusammengekratzt (*vgl.* zusammen)

Zu|sạm|men|kunft, die; -, ...künfte

zu|sạm|men|läp|pern, sich (*ugs. für* sich aus kleinen Mengen ansammeln); die Ausgaben haben sich ganz schön zusammengeläppert (*vgl.* zusammen)

zu|sạm|men|lau|fen (sich treffen; ineinander fließen); die Menschen sind zusammengelaufen; die Farben sind zusammengelaufen; *aber* wir wollen ein Stück zusammen (gemeinsam) laufen (*vgl.* zusammen)

zu|sạm|men|le|ben; sie haben lange zusammengelebt (einen gemeinsamen Haushalt geführt); sie haben sich gut zusammengelebt (sich aufeinander eingestellt); *vgl.* zusammen; **Zu|sạm|men|le|ben,** das; -s

zu|sạm|men|leg|bar; zu|sạm|men|le|gen (vereinigen; falten); die Grundstücke wurden zusammengelegt; das Tischtuch wurde zusammengelegt (*vgl.* zusammen); **Zu|sạm|men|le|gung**

zu|sạm|men|le|sen (sammeln); er hat die Früchte zusammengelesen; *aber* wir wollen das Buch zusammen (gemeinsam) lesen (*vgl.* zusammen)

zu|sạm|men|nä|hen; sie hat die Stoffbahnen zusammengenäht; *aber* morgen wollen sie zusammen (gemeinsam) nähen (*vgl.* zusammen)

zu|sạm|men|neh|men; sich - (sich beherrschen); du hast dich heute sehr zusammengenommen (*vgl.* zusammen)

zu|sạm|men|pa|cken; du kannst

deine Sachen zusammenpacken; *aber* wir wollten doch zusammen (gemeinsam) packen (*vgl.* zusammen)

zu|sạm|men|pas|sen; das hat gut zusammengepasst (*vgl.* zusammen)

zu|sạm|men|pfer|chen; wir wurden in einem kleinen Raum zusammengepfercht (*vgl.* zusammen)

Zu|sạm|men|prall; zu|sạm|men|pral|len (mit Wucht aneinander stoßen); zwei Autos sind auf der Kreuzung zusammengeprallt (*vgl.* zusammen)

zu|sạm|men|pres|sen (mit Kraft zusammendrücken); sie hatte die Hände zusammengepresst (*vgl.* zusammen)

zu|sạm|men|raf|fen (gierig an sich bringen); er hat ein großes Vermögen zusammengerafft *vgl.* zusammen

zu|sạm|men|rau|fen, sich (*ugs. für* sich einigen); man hatte sich schließlich zusammengerauft (*vgl.* zusammen)

zu|sạm|men|rech|nen; sie haben die Kosten zusammengerechnet (addiert); *vgl.* zusammen

zu|sạm|men|rei|men; ich kann mir das nicht zusammenreimen; wie reimt sich das zusammen?; zusammengereimt (*vgl.* zusammen)

zu|sạm|men|rei|ßen, sich (*ugs. für* sich zusammennehmen); ich habe mich zusammengerissen (*vgl.* zusammen)

zu|sạm|men|rol|len; sich -; sie haben den Teppich zusammengerollt (*vgl.* zusammen)

zu|sạm|men|rot|ten, sich; die Meuterer hatten sich zusammengerottet (*vgl.* zusammen); **Zu|sạm|men|rot|tung**

zu|sạm|men|ru|fen; die Schüler wurden in den Hof zusammengerufen; das Parlament wurde zusammengerufen (*vgl.* zusammen)

zu|sạm|men|sa|cken (*ugs. für* zusammenbrechen); er ist unter der Last zusammengesackt (*vgl.* zusammen)

Zu|sạm|men|schau, die; -

zu|sạm|men|schei|ßen (*derb für* scharf abkanzeln); er wurde von seinem Chef zusammengeschissen (*vgl.* zusammen)

zu|sạm|men|schla|gen (*ugs. für* schwer verprügeln); er hat ihn brutal zusammengeschlagen (*vgl.* zusammen)

zu|sạm|men|schlie|ßen, sich (sich vereinigen); verschiedene Firmen haben sich zusammengeschlossen (*vgl.* zusammen); **Zu|sạm|men|schluss**

zu|sạm|men|schmel|zen (in eins schmelzen; kleiner werden); die Metalle wurden zusammengeschmolzen; ihr Vermögen ist zusammengeschmolzen (*vgl.* zusammen)

zu|sạm|men|schnü|ren (miteinander verbinden; einengen); sie hat die Kleidungsstücke zusammengeschnürt; die Angst hat seine Kehle zusammengeschnürt (*vgl.* zusammen)

zu|sạm|men|schre|cken; *vgl.* [1]schrecken

zu|sạm|men|schrei|ben (in eins schreiben; aus anderen Texten zusammenstellen); die beiden Wörter werden zusammengeschrieben; dieses Buch ist aus anderen Büchern zusammengeschrieben; *aber* wir wollen dieses Buch zusammen (gemeinsam) schreiben (*vgl.* zusammen); **Zu|sạm|men|schrei|bung**

zu|sạm|men|schrump|fen; der Vorrat ist zusammengeschrumpft (*vgl.* zusammen)

zu|sạm|men|schus|tern (*ugs. für* notdürftig herstellen); er hat die Liste zusammengeschustert (*vgl.* zusammen)

zu|sạm|men|schwei|ßen (durch Schweißen verbinden; eng vereinigen); die Schienen wurden zusammengeschweißt; die Gefahr hat die Gruppe noch mehr zusammengeschweißt (*vgl.* zusammen)

zu|sạm|men sein *vgl.* zusammen; **Zu|sạm|men|sein,** das; -s

zu|sạm|men|set|zen (nebeneinander setzen, zueinander fügen); sie haben das Puzzle zusammengesetzt; sich - (*vgl.* zusammen); **Zu|sạm|men|set|zung** (*auch für* Kompositum)

zu|sạm|men|sit|zen; sie haben den ganzen Abend zusammengesessen (*vgl.* zusammen)

Zu|sạm|men|spiel, das; -[e]s; **zu|sạm|men|spie|len** (aufeinander abgestimmt spielen); die Mannschaft hat gut zusammengespielt; *aber* die Kinder haben schön zusammen (gemeinsam) gespielt (*vgl.* zusammen)

zu|sạm|men|stau|chen (*ugs. für* zurechtweisen); er hat ihn richtig zusammengestaucht (*vgl.* zusammen)

zu|sạm|men|ste|hen; sie haben im Hof zusammengestanden; sie haben immer zusammengestanden (zusammengehalten); *vgl.* zusammen

zu|sạm|men|stel|len (nebeneinander stellen; zueinander fügen); die Kinder haben sich zusammengestellt; das Menü wurde zusammengestellt (*vgl.* zusammen); **Zu|sạm|men|stel|lung**

zu|sạm|men|stim|men (übereinstimmen, harmonieren); seine Angaben, die Instrumente haben nicht zusammengestimmt (*vgl.* zusammen)

Zu|sạm|men|stoß; zu|sạm|men|sto|ßen (aufeinander prallen); zwei Autos sind zusammengestoßen (*vgl.* zusammen)

zu|sạm|men|strei|chen (*ugs.*); der Etat wurde rigoros zusammengestrichen (gekürzt)

zu|sạm|men|strö|men (sich in großer Zahl vereinigen); die Menschen sind zusammengeströmt (*vgl.* zusammen)

Zu|sạm|men|sturz; zu|sạm|men|stür|zen (einstürzen); das Gerüst ist zusammengestürzt (*vgl.* zusammen)

zu|sạm|men|su|chen (von überall her suchend zusammentragen); ich musste das Werkzeug erst zusammensuchen; *aber* lasst uns zusammen (gemeinsam) suchen! (*vgl.* zusammen)

zu|sạm|men|tra|gen (sammeln); sie haben das Holz zusammengetragen; *aber* ihr sollt den Sack zusammen (gemeinsam) tragen (*vgl.* zusammen)

zu|sạm|men|tref|fen (begegnen); sie sind im Theater zusammengetroffen (*vgl.* zusammen); **Zu|sạm|men|tref|fen**

zu|sạm|men|trei|ben (auf einen Haufen treiben); sie haben die Herde zusammengetrieben; *aber* sie haben die Herde zusammen (gemeinsam) auf die Weide getrieben (*vgl.* zusammen)

zu|sạm|men|tre|ten; die Schläger haben ihn brutal zusammengetreten; das Parlament ist zusammengetreten (hat sich versammelt); *vgl.* zusammen

zu|sạm|men|trom|meln (*ugs. für* herbeirufen); er hat alle Freunde zusammengetrommelt (*vgl.* zusammen)

zu|sạm|men|tun (*ugs. für* vereinigen); sie haben sich zusammengetan; *aber* wir wollen das zusammen (gemeinsam) tun (*vgl.* zusammen)

zu|sạm|men|wach|sen (in eins wachsen); der Knochen ist wieder zusammengewachsen (*vgl.* zusammen)

zu|sạm|men|wir|ken (vereint wirken); hier haben alle Kräfte zusammengewirkt (*vgl.* zusammen); **Zu|sạm|men|wir|ken,** das; -s

zu|sạm|men|zäh|len (addieren); sie hat die Zahlen zusammengezählt; *aber* lasst uns zusammen (gemeinsam) zählen! (*vgl.* zusammen); **Zu|sạm|men|zäh|lung**

zu|sạm|men|zie|hen (verengern; vereinigen; addieren); sie hat das Loch im Strumpf zusammengezogen; die Truppen wurden zusammengezogen; er hat die Zahlen zusammengezogen; sich -; *aber* sie haben den Wagen zusammen (gemeinsam) gezogen (*vgl.* zusammen); **zu|sạm|men|zie|hend;** ein zusammenziehendes Mittel; **Zu|sạm|men|zie|hung**

zu|sạm|men|zu|cken (eine zuckende Bewegung machen); ich bin bei dem Knall zusammengezuckt (*vgl.* zusammen)

zu|sạmt *(veraltet); Präp. mit Dat.:* zusamt den Rindern

Zu̲|satz; Zu̲|satz‿ab|kom|men, ...aus|bil|dung, ...be|stim|mung, ...brems|leuch|te *(Kfz-Technik),* **...ge|rät; zu̲|sätz|lich; Zu̲|satz‿steu|er** (die), **...ta|rif, ...ver|si|che|rung, ...zahl** (beim Lotto)

zu Scha̲|den *vgl.* Schaden

zu|schạn|den, *auch* **zu Schạn|den;** zuschanden, *auch* zu Schanden machen, werden

zu̲|schan|zen (*ugs. für* zu etwas verhelfen); er hat ihm den Posten zugeschanzt

zu̲|schar|ren; zugescharrt

zu̲|schau|en; alle haben dabei zugeschaut; **Zu̲|schau|er; Zu̲|schau|e|rin; Zu̲|schau|er‿ku|lis|se, ...rang, ...raum, ...tri|bü|ne, ...zahl**

zu̲|schau|feln; zugeschaufelt

zu̲|schi|cken; zugeschickt

zu̲|schie|ben (*ugs. auch für* [heimlich] zukommen lassen); er hat ihm diesen Vorteil zugeschoben

zu̲|schie|ßen (beisteuern); sie hat schon eine Menge Geld zugeschossen

Zu̲|schlag; zu̲|schla|gen ([sich] laut schließen; [bei einer Versteigerung] zuerteilen; losschlagen; zusetzen); zugeschlagen; **zu̲|schlag|frei** *(bes. Eisenb.);* **Zu̲|schlag‿kal|ku|la|ti|on** (*vgl.* Zuschlagskalkulation), **...kar|te** *(Eisenb.);* **zu̲|schlag|pflich|tig** *(bes. Eisenb.);* **Zu̲|schlag|satz,** Zu|schlags|satz; **Zu̲|schlags|kal|ku|la|ti|on,** Zu̲|schlag|kal|ku|la|ti|on; **Zu̲|schlags|satz** *vgl.* Zuschlagsatz; **Zu̲|schlag|stoff** *(Technik)*

zu̲|schlie|ßen; zugeschlossen

zu̲|schnap|pen; zugeschnappt

Zu̲|schnei|de|ma|schi|ne; zu̲|schnei|den; zugeschnitten; **Zu̲|schnei|der; Zu̲|schnei|de|rin**

zu̲|schnei|en; zugeschneit

Zu̲|schnitt

zu̲|schnü|ren; zugeschnürt

zu̲|schrau|ben; zugeschraubt

zu̲|schrei|ben; die Schuld an diesem Unglück wird ihm zugeschrieben; **Zu̲|schrift**

zu|schụl|den, *auch* **zu Schụl|den;** du hast dir etwas zuschulden, *auch* zu Schulden kommen lassen

Zu̲|schuss; Zu̲|schuss‿be|trieb, ...bo|gen *(Druckw.),* **...wirt|schaft** (die; -)

zu̲|schus|tern (*ugs. für* heimlich zukommen lassen; zusetzen); er hat ihm den Posten zugeschustert

zu̲|schüt|ten; zugeschüttet

zu̲|se|hen; zugesehen; (↑R 50:) bei genauerem Zusehen; **zu̲|se|hends** (rasch; offenkundig); **Zu̲|se|her** (*österr. neben* Zuschauer)

zu̲ sein *vgl.* zu

zu|sei̲|ten, *auch* **zu Sei̲|ten** (↑R 41); *Präp. mit Gen.:* zuseiten, *auch* zu Seiten des Festzuges

zu̲|sen|den; *vgl.* senden; **Zu̲|sen|dung**

zu̲|set|zen; er hat mir tüchtig zugesetzt

zu̲|si|chern; zugesichert; **Zu̲|si|che|rung**

Zu|spä̲t|kom|men|de, der *u.* die; -n, -n (↑R 5 ff.)

Zu̲|spei|se *(österr., sonst veraltet)*

zu̲|sper|ren (*südd., österr. für* abschließen); zugesperrt

Zu̲|spiel, das; -[e]s *(Sport);* **zu̲|spie|len;** zugespielt

zu̲|spit|zen; die Lage hat sich zugespitzt; **Zu̲|spit|zung**

zu̲|spre|chen; zugesprochen; **Zu̲|spre|chung; Zu̲|spruch,** der; -[e]s (Anklang, Zulauf; Trost); großen -, viel - haben

Zu̲|stand; zu|stạn|de, *auch* **zu Stạn|de;** zustande, *auch* zu Stande bringen, kommen; **Zu|stạn|de|brin|gen,** das; -s; **Zu|stạn|de|kom|men,** das; -s; **zu̲|stän|dig** (Maß gebend); - sein nach (*österr. für* ansässig sein in); **zu̲|stän|di|gen|ọrts; Zu̲|stän|dig|keit; Zu̲|stän|dig|keits|be|reich,** der; **zu̲|stän|dig|keits|hal|ber; zu̲|ständ|lich** (*selten für* einen Zustand betreffend, darin verharrend); **Zu̲|stands‿än|de|rung, ...glei|chung** *(Physik),* **...pas|siv** *(Sprachw.),* **...verb** *(Sprachw.)*

zu|stạt|ten; *nur in* zustatten kommen

zu̲|ste|chen; zugestochen

zu̲|ste|cken; zugesteckt

zu̲|ste|hen; zugestanden

zu̲|stei|gen; zugestiegen

zu̲|stel|len; zugestellt; **Zu̲|stel|ler** *(Amtsspr.);* **Zu̲|stell|ge|bühr** *(Postw.);* **Zu̲|stel|lung; Zu̲|stel|lungs|ur|kun|de** *(Amtsspr.);* **Zu̲|stell|ver|merk** *(Postw.)*

zu̲|steu|ern; zugesteuert

zu̲|stim|men; zugestimmt; **Zu̲|stim|mung**

zu̲|stop|fen; zugestopft

zu̲|stöp|seln; zugestöpselt

zu̲|sto|ßen; es ist ihm ein Unglück zugestoßen

zu̲|stre|ben; zugestrebt

Zu̲|strom, der; -[e]s; **zu̲|strö|men;** zugeströmt

Zu̲|stupf, der; -[e], *Plur.* -e *u.* ...stüpfe (*schweiz. für* Zuschuss, Zuverdienst)

zu̲|stut|zen; zugestutzt

zu|ta̲|ge, *auch* **zu Ta̲|ge;** *nur in* zutage, *auch* zu Tage bringen, fördern, kommen, treten

Zu̲|tat *meist Plur.*

zu|tei̲l (↑R 41); *nur in* zuteil werden; **zu̲|tei|len;** zugeteilt; **Zu̲|tei|lung**

zu|tie̲fst (völlig; im Innersten)

zu̲|tra|gen (heimlich berichten); zugetragen; sich zutragen (geschehen); **Zu̲|trä|ger; Zu|trä|ge|rei̲; zu̲|träg|lich** (nützlich); **Zu̲|träg|lich|keit,** die; -

zu̲|trau|en; sie hat es mir zugetraut; **Zu̲|trau|en,** das; -s; **zu̲|trau|lich; Zu̲|trau|lich|keit**

zu̲|tref|fen; zugetroffen; **zu̲|tref|fend; Zu̲|tref|fen|de,** das; -n (↑R 5 ff.); Zutreffendes ankreuzen; **zu̲|tref|fen|den|fạlls;** *vgl.* Fall, der

zu̲|trei|ben; zugetrieben

zu̲|trin|ken; zugetrunken

Zu̲|tritt, der; -[e]s

zut|schen (*landsch. für* lutschen, saugen); du zutschst; er zutschte

zu̲|tu|lich, zu̲|tun|lich (zutraulich, anschmiegend); **zu̲|tun** (*ugs. für* hinzufügen; schließen); ich habe kein Auge zugetan; **Zu̲|tun,** das; -s (Hilfe, Unterstützung); *noch in* ohne mein Zutun; **zu̲|tun|lich** *vgl.* zutulich

zu|ụn|guns|ten, *auch* **zu Ụn|guns|ten** (zum Nachteil); *Präp., bei Voranstellung mit Gen.:* zuungunsten, *auch* zu Ungunsten vieler Antragsteller, *bei (seltener) Nachstellung mit Dat.:* dem Antragsteller zuungunsten, *auch* zu Ungunsten; *vgl.* Gunst

zu|ụn|terst; das Oberste zuunterst kehren

zu̲|ver|die|nen (*ugs. für* dazuverdienen); **Zu̲|ver|dienst,** der

zu̲|ver|läs|sig; Zu̲|ver|läs|sig|keit, die; -; **Zu̲|ver|läs|sig|keits‿fahrt, ...prü|fung, ...test**

Zu|ver|sicht, die; -; **zu|ver|sicht|lich; Zu|ver|sicht|lich|keit,** die; -
zu viel; zu viel des Guten; es sind zu viele Menschen; er weiß zu viel; du hast viel zu viel gesagt; besser zu viel als zu wenig; **Zu|viel,** das; -s (↑R 49); ein Zuviel ist besser als ein Zuwenig
zu vie|ren, zu viert
zu|vor (vorher); meinen herzlichen Glückwunsch zuvor!; *vgl.* zuvorkommen, zuvortun
zu|vor|derst (ganz vorn); **zu|vör|derst** (*veraltend für* zuerst)
zu|vor|kom|men (schneller sein); ich komme ihm zuvor; zuvorgekommen; zuvorzukommen; *aber* alles, was zuvor (vorher) gekommen war; **zu|vor|kom|mend** (liebenswürdig); **Zu|vor|kom|men|heit,** die; -
zu|vor|tun (besser tun); ich tue es ihm zuvor; zuvorgetan; zuvorzutun; *aber* was zuvor (vorher) zu tun ist
Zu|waa|ge, die; - (*bayr., österr. für* Knochen[zugabe] zum Fleisch)
Zu|wachs, der; -es, *Plur. (fachspr.)* Zuwächse (Vermehrung, Erhöhung); **zu|wach|sen** (größer werden); es ist ständig Vermögen zugewachsen; **Zu|wachs|ra|te**
Zu|wan|de|rer, Zu|wand|rer; **zu|wan|dern;** zugewandert; **Zu|wan|de|rung; Zu|wand|rer** *vgl.* Zuwanderer
zu|war|ten (untätig warten); zugewartet; **Zu|war|ten,** das; -s
zu|we|ge, *auch* **zu We|ge;** *nur in Wendungen wie* zuwege, *auch* zu Wege bringen; [gut] zuwege, *auch* zu Wege sein (*ugs. für* wohlauf sein)
zu|we|hen; zugeweht
zu|wei|len
zu|wei|sen; zugewiesen; **Zu|wei|sung**
zu|wen|den; ich wandte *od.* wendete mich ihr zu; er hat sich ihr zugewandt *od.* zugewendet; **Zu|wen|dung**
zu we|nig; du weißt [viel] zu wenig; du weißt auch zu wenig!; es gab zu wenig[e] Parkplätze; **Zu|we|nig,** das; -s (↑R 49); ein Zuviel ist besser als ein Zuwenig
zu|wer|fen; zugeworfen
zu|wi|der; zuwider sein, werden; dem Gebot zuwider; das, er ist mir zuwider; *aber* (↑R 38): **zu|wi|der|han|deln** (Verbotenes tun); ich hand[e]le zuwider; zuwidergehandelt; zuwiderzuhandeln; **zu|wi|der|han|delnd; Zu|wi|der|han|deln|de,** der *u.* die; -n, -n (↑R 5ff.); **Zu|wi|der|hand|lung; zu|wi|der|lau|fen;** ↑R 38 (entgegenstehen); sein Verhalten läuft meinen Absichten zuwider; zuwidergelaufen; zuwiderzulaufen
zu|win|ken; zugewinkt
zu|zah|len; zugezahlt; **zu|zäh|len;** zugezählt; **Zu|zah|lung; Zu|zäh|lung**
zu|zei|ten; ↑R 41 (bisweilen), *aber* zu Zeiten Karls d. Gr.
zu|zeln (*bayr. u. österr. ugs. für* lutschen; lispeln); ich ...[e]le (↑R 16)
zu|zie|hen; du hast dir eine Krankheit zugezogen; **Zu|zie|hung,** die; -; **Zu|zug** (Zuziehen); **Zu|zü|ger** (*schweiz. für* Zuzügler); **Zu|züg|ler; zu|züg|lich** (*Kaufmannsspr.* unter Hinzurechnung); *Präp. mit Gen.:* zuzüglich der Transportkosten; *ein allein stehendes, stark gebeugtes Substantiv steht im Sing. ungebeugt:* zuzüglich Porto;
Zu|zugs|ge|neh|mi|gung
zu zwei|en, zu zweit
zu|zwin|kern; zugezwinkert
Zvie|ri ['tsfiəri], der *od.* das; -s, - (*bes. schweiz. mdal. für* Nachmittagsimbiss)
ZVS = Zentralstelle für die Vergabe von Studienplätzen
zwa|cken (*ugs. für* kneifen)
Zwang, der; -[e]s, Zwänge; **zwän|gen** (bedrängen; klemmen; einpressen); sich -; **zwang|haft; Zwang|huf,** der; -[e]s (eine Hufkrankheit); **zwang|läu|fig** (*Technik* nicht gewünschte Bewegungen ausschließend); vgl. *aber* zwangsläufig; **Zwang|läu|fig|keit,** die; - *(Technik); vgl. aber* Zwangsläufigkeit; **zwang|los;** ein -es Fest; **Zwang|lo|sig|keit,** die; -; **Zwangs‿an|lei|he, ...ar|beit** (die; -), **...ar|bei|ter, ...ar|bei|te|rin, ...auf|ent|halt, ...be|wirt|schaf|tung; Zwang|schie|ne** (bei Gleiskrümmungen, Weichen u. a.); **Zwangs‿ein|wei|sung, ...er|näh|rung, ...geld** *(Rechtsw.),* **...hand|lung, ...herr|schaft, ...hy|po|thek, ...ja|cke, ...kurs** *(Bankw.),* **...la|ge; zwangs|läu|fig** (automatisch, anders nicht möglich); *vgl. aber* zwangläufig; **Zwangs|läu|fig|keit;** *vgl. aber* Zwangläufigkeit; **Zwangs|li|zenz; zwangs|mä|ßig; Zwangs‿maß|nah|me, ...mit|tel** (das), **...neu|ro|se, ...räu|mung, ...re|gu|lie|rung** *(Börse),* **...spa|ren** (das; -s); **zwangs|um|sie|deln;** zwangsumgesiedelt; *nur im Infinitiv u. Partizip II gebr.;* **Zwangs‿um|sied|lung, ...ur|laub, ...ver|fah|ren** *(Rechtsw.),* **...ver|gleich; zwangs|ver|schi|cken** (*für* deportieren); *vgl.* zwangsumsiedeln; **Zwangs‿ver|schi|ckung, ...ver|set|zung, ...ver|si|che|rung; zwangs|ver|stei|gern;** *vgl.* zwangsumsiedeln; **Zwangs‿ver|stei|ge|rung, ...ver|wal|tung, ...voll|stre|ckung; zwangs|vor|füh|ren;** zwangsvorgeführt; **Zwangs‿vor|füh|rung, ...vor|stel|lung** *(Psych.);* **zwangs|wei|se; Zwangs|wirt|schaft**
zwan|zig usw. *vgl.* achtzig usw.; **zwan|zi|ger;** die goldenen Zwanzigerjahre, *auch* zwanziger Jahre; die goldenen Zwanziger; **Zwan|zig|flach,** das; -[e]s, -e, **Zwan|zig|fläch|ner** (*für* Ikosaeder); **zwan|zig|jäh|rig;** *vgl.* achtjährig; **Zwan|zig|mark|schein** (*mit Ziffern* 20-Mark-Schein; ↑R 28); **Zwan|zig|pfen|nig|mar|ke** (*mit Ziffern* 20-Pfennig-Marke, 20-Pf-Marke; ↑R 28); **zwan|zigs|te;** (↑R 108:) Zwanzigster Juli (20. Juli 1944, der Tag des Attentats auf Hitler); *vgl.* achte; **zwan|zig|tau|send; Zwan|zig|uhr|nach|rich|ten** *Plur.;* **Zwan|zig|uhr|vor|stel|lung**
zwar; er ist zwar alt, aber rüstig; viele Sorten, und zwar ...
zwat|ze|lig (*landsch. für* zappelig); **zwat|zeln** (*landsch. für* zappeln, unruhig sein); ich ...[e]le (↑R 16)
Zweck, der; -[e]s, -e (Ziel[punkt]; Absicht; Sinn); zwecks *(vgl. d.);* zum Zweck[e]; **Zweck‿auf|wand** *(Finanzw.),* **...bau** (*Plur.* ...bauten), **...be|haup|tung** (nur dem Erreichen eines bestimmten Ziels dienende Behauptung), **...be|stim|mung** (die; -), **...bin|dung** *(Finanzw.);* **zweck|dien|lich; Zweck|dien|lich|keit,** die; -; **Zwe|cke,** die; -, -n (*landsch. für* kurzer Nagel mit breitem Kopf); **zwe|cken** (*landsch. für* anzwecken); **zweck|ent|frem|den;** zweckentfremdet; *meist nur im Infinitiv u. Partizip II gebr.;* **Zweck|ent|frem|dung; zweck‿ent|spre|chend, ...frei, ...ge|bun|den; Zweck|ge|bun|den|heit,** die; -; **zweck|ge|mäß; zweck|haft; zweck|los; Zweck|lo|sig|keit,** die; -; **Zweck|lü|ge; zweck|mä|ßig; zweck|mä|ßi|ger|wei|se; Zweck|mä|ßig|keit,** die; -; **Zweck|mä|ßig|keits|er|wä|gung; Zweck‿op|ti|mis|mus, ...pes|si|mis|mus, ...pro|pa|gan|da; zwecks;** ↑R 46 (*Amtsspr.* zum Zweck von); *Präp. mit Gen.:* zwecks eines Handels (*dafür besser die Präp.* „zu" *od. Nebensatz*); **Zweck‿satz** (*für* Finalsatz), **...spa|ren** (das; -s), **...steu|er** (die), **...stil, ...ver|band** (Vereinigung von [wirtschaftli-

chen] Unternehmungen), **...ver|mö|gen** *(Rechtsw.)*; **zweck-voll, ...wid|rig**

zween *vgl.* zwei

Zweh|le, die; -, -n (*westmitteld. für* Tisch-, Handtuch)

zwei[1]; *Gen.* zweier, *Dat.* zweien, zwei; wir sind zu zweien *od.* zu zweit; herzliche Grüße von uns zweien (↑R 48); (↑R 6:) zweier guter, *selten* guten Menschen; zweier Liebenden, *seltener* Liebender; *vgl.* acht, drei; **Zwei,** die; -, -en (Zahl); eine Zwei würfeln; er hat in Latein eine Zwei geschrieben; *vgl.* [1]Acht *u.* Eins; **Zwei|ach|ser** (Wagen mit zwei Achsen; *mit Ziffer* 2-Achser; ↑R 44); **zwei|ach|sig; Zwei|ak|ter;** *vgl.* Einakter; **zwei|ak|tig; zwei|ar|mig; Zwei|bei|ner** (*scherzh. für* Mensch); **zwei|bei|nig; Zwei|bett|zim|mer** (*mit Ziffer* 2-Bett-Zimmer; ↑R 28)

Zwei|brü|cken (Stadt in Rheinland-Pfalz); **Zwei|brü|cke|ner, Zwei|brü|cker** (↑R 103)

Zwei-bund (der; -[e]s; *früher*), **...de|cker** (Flugzeug); **zwei|deu|tig; Zwei|deu|tig|keit; zwei|di|men|si|o|nal; Zwei|drit|tel|mehr|heit; zwei|ei|ig;** zweieiige Zwillinge; **zwei|ein|halb,** zwei|und|ein|halb; **Zwei|er;** *vgl.* Achter; **Zwei|er-be|zie|hung, ...bob, ...ka|jak; zwei|er|lei; Zwei|er|rei|he; zwei|fach;** *vgl.* zwiefach; **Zwei|fa|che,** das; -n; *vgl.* Achtfache; **Zwei|fa|mi|li|en|haus; Zwei|far|ben|druck** *Plur.* ...drucke; **zwei|far|big**

Zwei|fel, der; -s, -; **zwei|fel|haft; zwei|fel|los; zwei|feln;** ich ...[e]le (↑R 16); **Zwei|fels|fall,** der; im -[e]; **Zwei|fels|fra|ge; zwei|fels|frei; zwei|fels|oh|ne; Zwei|fel|sucht,** die; -; **Zweif|ler; Zweif|le|rin; zweif|le|risch**

zwei|flü|ge|lig *vgl.* zweiflüglig; **Zwei|flüg|ler,** der; -s, - *(Zool.)*; **zwei|flüg|lig,** zwei|flü|ge|lig; **Zwei|fran|ken|stück** (*mit Ziffer* 2-Franken-Stück; ↑R 28); **Zwei|fränk|ler** *(schweiz.)*; **Zwei|fron|ten|krieg; Zwei|fü|ßer** (*svw.* Zweibeiner)

[1]**Zweig,** Arnold (dt. Schriftsteller)

[2]**Zweig,** Stefan (österr. Schriftsteller)

[3]**Zweig,** der; -[e]s, -e; **Zweig|bahn**

zwei|ge|schlech|tig *(Bot.)*; **Zwei-ge|schlech|tig|keit** (die; -), **...ge|spann, ...ge|spräch** (*veraltet für* Zwiegespräch); **zwei|ge|stri|chen** *(Musik)*; -e Note

Zweig|ge|schäft

zwei-glei|sig, ...glie|de|rig *od.* **...glied|rig**

Zweig-li|nie, ...nie|der|las|sung, ...post|amt, ...stel|le, ...werk

Zwei|hän|der (Schwert, das mit beiden Händen geführt wird); **zwei|hän|dig; zwei|häu|sig** (*Bot.* entweder mit männl. oder weibl. Blüten auf einer Pflanze); **Zwei|häu|sig|keit,** die; -; **Zwei|heit,** die; - (*für* Dualismus); **zwei|hun|dert; Zwei|hun|dert|mark|schein** (*mit Ziffer* 200-Mark-Schein; ↑R 28); **Zwei-jah|res|plan, ...kam|mer|sys|tem; Zwei|kampf; Zwei|ka|nal|ton** *(Fernsehen)*; **zwei|keim|blät|te|rig, zwei|keim|blätt|rig** *(Bot.)*; -e Pflanzen (Pflanzen mit zwei Keimblättern); **zwei|köp|fig; Zwei|kreis-brem|se** *(Kfz-Technik)*, **...sys|tem** *(Finanzw.)*; **Zwei|li|ter|fla|sche** (*mit Ziffer* 2-Liter-Flasche; ↑R 28); **zwei|mäh|dig** (*svw.* zweischürig); **zwei|mal;** (↑R 23:) ein- bis zweimal (1- bis 2-mal); *vgl.* achtmal; **zwei|ma|lig; Zwei|mann|boot** (*mit Ziffer* 2-Mann-Boot; ↑R 28); **Zwei|mark|stück** (*mit Ziffer* 2-Mark-Stück; ↑R 28); **Zwei|mas|ter** (Segelschiff); **zwei|mo|to|rig; Zwei|par|tei|en|sys|tem; Zwei|pfen|nig|stück** (*mit Ziffer* 2-Pfennig-Stück; **Zwei|pfün|der** (*mit Ziffer* 2-Pfünder); **Zwei|pha|sen|strom; 2π-fach** [...'pi...] (↑R 25); **Zwei|rad; zwei-rä|de|rig, ...räd|rig; Zwei|rei|her; zwei|rei|hig; Zwei|ru|de|rer** (*für* Bireme); **zwei|sam; Zwei|sam|keit; zwei|schlä|fe|rig, zwei|schlä|fig, zwei|schläf|rig;** *vgl.* einschläfig; **zwei|schnei|dig; zwei|schü|rig** (zwei Ernten liefernd [von der Wiese]); **zwei|sei|tig; zwei|sil|big; Zwei|sit|zer** (Wagen, Motorrad u. a. mit zwei Sitzen); **zwei|sit|zig; zwei|spal|tig; Zwei|spän|ner** (Wagen mit Zweigespann); **zwei|spän|nig; zwei|spra|chig; Zwei|spra|chig|keit,** die; -; **zwei|spu|rig; zwei|stel|lig;** -e Zahlen; **zwei|stim|mig; zwei|stö|ckig; zwei|strah|lig; Zwei|strom|land; zwei|stück|wei|se** (↑R 28); **Zwei|stu|fen|ra|ke|te; zwei|stu|fig; zwei|stün|dig** (zwei Stunden dauernd); -e Fahrt; **zwei|stünd|lich** (alle zwei Stunden [wiederkehrend]); - einen Esslöffel voll; **zweit;** *vgl.* zwei; **Zwei|tak|ter** (*ugs. für* Zweitaktmotor od. damit ausgerüstetes Kraftfahrzeug); **Zwei|takt|mo|tor; zwei|tau|send; Zwei|tau|sen|der** ([über] 2 000 m hoher Berg); **Zweit|aus|fer|ti|gung; zweit|bes|te;** sie ist die zweitbeste Schülerin, *aber* sie ist die Zweitbeste in der Klasse (↑R 47); **Zweit|druck** *Plur.* ...drucke; **zwei|te**[1]; **I.** *Kleinschreibung:* die zweite Geige spielen; er ist zweiter Geiger; das zweite Gesicht (Gabe, Zukünftiges vorauszusehen); etwas aus zweiter Hand kaufen; er ist sein zweites Ich (bester Freund); in zweiter Linie; das ist ihr zur zweiten Natur geworden; der zweite Rang; sie singt die zweite Stimme; der zweite Stock eines Hauses; der zweite Bildungsweg. **II.** *Großschreibung:* **a)** (↑R 48:) er hat wie kein Zweiter gearbeitet; jeder Zweite; zum Ersten, zum Zweiten, zum Dritten; es ist noch ein Zweites zu erwähnen; **b)** (↑R 108:) Zweites Deutsches Fernsehen (*Abk.* ZDF); das Zweite Programm (ZDF); die Zweite Bundesliga; die Zweite Republik (Staatsform Österreichs nach 1945); der Zweite Weltkrieg; *vgl.* achte *u.* erste; **Zwei|tei|ler; zwei|tei|lig; Zwei|tei|lung; zwei|tens; Zwei|te[r]-Klas|se-Ab|teil** (↑R 28); **Zweit-fahr|zeug, ...fri|sur** (Perücke), **...ge|rät; zweit-größ|te, ...höchs|te; zweit|klas|sig; Zweit|kläss|ler;** *vgl.* Erstklässler; **Zweit|klass|wa|gen** *(schweiz.)*; **zweit|letz|te;** die zweitletzte Teilnehmerin, *aber* sie war die Zweitletzte im Weitsprung (↑R 47); **zwei|tou|rig; zweit|ran|gig; Zweit|schlag** *(Milit.)*; **zweit|schlech|tes|te; Zweit-schlüs|sel, ...schrift, ...stim|me; zwei|tü|rig; Zweit-wa|gen, ...woh|nung; zwei|und|ein|halb** *vgl.* zweieinhalb; **zwei|und|zwan|zig;** *vgl.* acht; **zwei|wer|tig; Zwei|zei|ler; zwei|zei|lig; Zwei|zim|mer|woh|nung** (*mit Ziffer* 2-Zimmer-Wohnung; ↑R 28); **Zwei|zü|ger,** der; -s, - (mit zwei Zügen zu lösende Schachauf-

---

[1] *Die Formen* „zween" *für das männliche,* „zwo" *für das weibliche Geschlecht sind veraltet. Wegen der leichteren Unterscheidbarkeit von* „drei" *ist* „zwo" *(ohne Unterschied des Geschlechtes) in neuerer Zeit im Fernsprechverkehr üblich geworden und von da in die Umgangssprache gedrungen. Die veraltete Form* „zwote" *für die Ordnungszahl* „zweite" *ist gleichfalls sehr verbreitet.*

[1] *Zur veralteten Form* „zwote" *vgl. Fußnote zu* „zwei".

gabe); **Zwei|zy|lin|der** (*ugs. für* Zweizylindermotor od. damit ausgerüstetes Kraftfahrzeug); **Zwei|zy|lin|der|mo|tor; zwei|zy|lind|rig** (*mit Ziffer* 2-zylindrig; ↑R 44)

Zwen|ke, die; -, -n (ein Süßgras)

zwerch (*landsch. für* quer); **Zwerch|fell; Zwerch|fell|at|mung,** die; -; **zwerch|fell|er|schüt|ternd;** -es Lachen

Zwerg, der; -[e]s, -e; **zwerg|ar|tig; Zwerg|baum; zwer|gen|haft; Zwer|gen|kö|nig** (*Märchen*); **Zwer|gen|volk** (*Märchen*); **zwerg|haft; Zwerg|haf|tig|keit,** die; -; **Zwerg|huhn; zwer|gig; Zwer|gin; Zwerg‿kie|fer** (die), **...obst, ...pin|scher, ...pu|del, ...staat** (*Plur.* ...staaten), **...volk** (z. B. Pygmäen), **...wuchs; zwerg|wüch|sig**

Zwet|sche, die; -, -n; **Zwet|schen‿baum, ...kern, ...ku|chen, ...mus, ...schnaps; Zwetsch|ge** (*südd., schweiz. u. fachspr. für* Zwetsche); **Zwetsch|ke** (*bes. österr. für* Zwetsche); **Zwetsch|ken‿knö|del** (*österr.*), **...rös|ter** (*österr. für* gedünstete Pflaumen)

Zwi|ckau (Stadt in Sachsen); **Zwi|ckau|er** (↑R 103)

Zwi|cke, die; -, -n (*landsch. für* Beißzange; *auch für* als Zwilling mit einem männl. Kalb geborenes Kuhkalb; *veraltet für* Zwecke); **Zwi|ckel,** der; -s, - (keilförmiger Stoffeinsatz; *Bauw.* dreieckiges Verbindungsstück); **zwi|cken** (*ugs. für* kneifen); er zwickt ihn, *auch* ihm ins Bein; **Zwi|cker** (Klemmer, Kneifer); **Zwick|müh|le** (Stellung im Mühlespiel); in der - (*ugs. für* in einer misslichen Lage) sein

Zwie|back, der; -[e]s, *Plur.* ...bäcke *u.* -e

Zwie|bel, die; -, -n ‹lat.›; **Zwie|bel|fisch** *meist Plur.* (*Druckw.* fälschlich aus anderen Schriften gesetzte Buchstaben od. durcheinander liegende Buchstaben verschiedener Schrifttypen); **Zwie|bel‿ge|wächs, ...hau|be** (Turmdachform), **...ku|chen, ...mus|ter** (das; -s; beliebtes Muster der Meißner Porzellanmanufaktur); **zwie|beln** (*ugs. für* quälen; übertriebene Anforderungen stellen); ich ...[e]le (↑R 16); **Zwie|bel‿ring, ...scha|le, ...sup|pe, ...turm**

Zwie|bra|che, die; -, -n (*veraltet für* zweites Pflügen des Brachackers im Herbst); **zwie|bra|chen; zwie|fach** (*veraltend für* zwei|fach); **zwie|fäl|tig** (*veraltend*); **Zwie|ge|sang; Zwie|ge|spräch; Zwie|laut** (*für* Diphthong); **Zwie|licht,** das; -[e]s; **zwie|lich|tig;** eine -e Gestalt; **Zwie|na|tur**

[1]**Zwie|sel** (Stadt in Bayern)

[2]**Zwie|sel,** die; -, -n, *auch* der; -s, - (*landsch. für* Gabelzweig; Gabelung); **Zwie|sel‿bee|re** (*landsch. für* Vogelkirsche), **...dorn** (*Plur.* ...dörner; Stechpalme); **zwie|se|lig,** zwies|lig (gespalten); **zwie|seln,** sich (sich gabeln, spalten); **zwies|lig** *vgl.* zwieselig

Zwie|spalt, der; -[e]s, *Plur.* -e *u.* ...spälte; **zwie|späl|tig; Zwie|späl|tig|keit,** die; -; **Zwie|spra|che; Zwie|tracht,** die; - (*geh.*); **zwie|träch|tig**

Zwilch, der; -[e]s, -e (*svw.* Zwillich); **zwil|chen** (aus Zwillich)

Zwil|le, die; -, -n (*nordd. für* Holzgabel; kleine Schleuder)

Zwil|lich, der; -s, -e (Gewebe); **Zwil|lich|ho|se**

Zwil|ling, der; -s, -e; siamesische Zwillinge; **Zwil|lings‿bru|der, ...for|mel** (*Sprachw.*), **...for|scher, ...for|schung, ...frucht, ...ge|burt, ...paar, ...rei|fen, ...schwes|ter**

Zwing|burg (*früher*); **Zwin|ge,** die; -, -n (ein Werkzeug); **zwin|gen;** du zwangst; du zwängest; gezwungen; zwing[e]!; **zwin|gend; Zwin|ger** (Gang, Platz zwischen innerer u. äußerer Burgmauer; fester Turm; Käfig für wilde Tiere; umzäunter Auslauf für Hunde); Dresdener Zwinger (Barockbauwerk in Dresden); **Zwing‿herr** (*früher*), **...herr|schaft**

Zwing|li (schweiz. Reformator); **Zwing|li|a|ner** (Anhänger der Lehre Zwinglis)

zwin|ken (*veraltet für* zwinkern); **zwin|kern;** ich ...ere (↑R 16)

zwir|beln; ich ...[e]le (↑R 16)

Zwirn, der; -[e]s, *Plur.* (*Sorten:*) -e; [1]**zwir|nen** (von, aus Zwirn); [2]**zwir|nen** (Garne zusammendrehen); **Zwir|ne|rei** (Zwirnarbeit; Zwirnfabrik); **Zwirns|fa|den** *Plur.* ...fäden

zwi|schen; *Präp. mit Dat. od. Akk.:* zwischen den Tischen stehen, *aber* zwischen die Tische stellen; inzwischen; die Gegensätze zwischen den Arbeitgebern und den Arbeitnehmern (= zwischen der Arbeitgeberschaft u. der Arbeitnehmerschaft), *aber* die Gegensätze zwischen den Arbeitgebern (= innerhalb der Arbeitgeberschaft) und zwischen den Arbeitnehmern (= innerhalb der Arbeitnehmerschaft); **Zwi|schen|akt; Zwi|schen|akt|mu|sik; Zwi|schen‿ap|plaus, ...be|mer|kung, ...be|richt, ...be|scheid, ...bi|lanz; zwi|schen|blen|den** (*Film*); *nur im Infinitiv u. Partizip II gebr.*; zwischengeblendet; **Zwi|schen‿buch|han|del, ...deck, ...ding** (*vgl.* [1]Ding); **zwi|schen|drein** (*ugs.; Frage* wohin?); - legen; **zwi|schen|drin** (*ugs.; Frage* wo?); - liegen; **zwi|schen|durch** (*ugs.*); - fallen; **Zwi|schen‿er|geb|nis, ...fall** (der); **zwi|schen|fi|nan|zie|ren; Zwi|schen‿fi|nan|zie|rung, ...fra|ge, ...gas** (*Kfz-Technik*), **...ge|richt** (*Gastron.*), **...ge|schoss, ...glied, ...grö|ße, ...han|del** (*vgl.* [1]Handel), **...händ|ler; zwi|schen|hi|nein** (*schweiz., sonst veraltet*); **Zwi|schen‿hirn, ...hoch** (*Meteor.*); **zwi|schen|in|ne** (*landsch.*); **Zwi|schen|kie|fer; Zwi|schen|kie|fer|kno|chen; Zwi|schen‿knor|pel, ...la|ger; zwi|schen|la|gern; Zwi|schen|la|ge|rung; zwi|schen|lan|den** *meist im Infinitiv u. Partizip II gebr.*; zwischengelandet; *seltener:* das Flugzeug landet in Rom zwischen; **Zwi|schen‿lan|dung, ...lauf** (*Sport*), **...lö|sung, ...mahl|zeit; zwi|schen|mensch|lich;** -e Beziehungen; **Zwi|schen‿prü|fung, ...raum, ...reich** (*veraltet*), **...ruf, ...ru|fer, ...run|de, ...satz** (*Sprachw.*), **...spiel, ...spurt; zwi|schen|staat|lich** (*auch für* international); **Zwi|schen‿sta|ti|on, ...stock[|werk]** (*svw.* Zwischengeschoss), **...stu|fe, ...trä|ger, ...tür, ...wand, ...wirt** (*Biol.*), **...zeit; zwi|schen|zeit|lich; Zwi|schen‿zeug|nis, ...zins|sen** (*Plur.*)

Zwist, der; -[e]s, -e; **zwis|tig** (*veraltet*); **Zwis|tig|keit**

zwit|schern; ich ...ere (↑R 16)

Zwit|ter, der; -s, - (Wesen mit männl. u. weibl. Geschlechtsmerkmalen); **Zwit|ter‿bil|dung, ...blü|te, ...form; zwit|ter|haft; Zwit|ter|haf|tig|keit,** die; -; **zwit|te|rig,** zwitt|rig; **Zwit|ter‿stel|lung, ...we|sen** (das; -s); **zwitt|rig** *vgl.* zwitterig; **Zwitt|rig|keit,** die; -

zwo *vgl.* zwei

zwölf; wir sind zu zwölfen *od.* zu zwölft; es ist fünf [Minuten] vor zwölf (*ugs. übertr. auch für* es ist allerhöchste Zeit); die zwölf Apostel; (↑R 108:) die Zwölf Nächte (nach Weihnachten), auch „Zwölften" genannt; *vgl.*

acht; **Zwölf,** die; -, -en (Zahl); er hat eine Zwölf geschossen; *vgl.* ¹Acht; **Zwölf|ach|ser** (Wagen mit zwölf Achsen; *mit Ziffern* 12-Achser; ↑R 44); **zwölf|ach|sig** (*mit Ziffern* 12-achsig; ↑R 44); **Zwölf|eck;** **zwölf|eckig** (↑R 132); **zwölf|ein|halb,** zwölf|und|ein|halb; **Zwölf|en|der** *(Jägerspr.);* **Zwöl|fer;** *vgl.* Achter; **zwöl|fer|lei;** **zwölf|fach;** **Zwölf|fa|che,** das; -n; *vgl.* Achtfache; **Zwölf|fin|ger|darm;** **Zwölf|flach,** das; -[e]s, -e, **Zwölf|fläch|ner** (*für* Dodekaeder); **Zwölf|kampf** *(Turnen);* **Zwölf|kämp|fer;** **zwölf|mal;** *vgl.* achtmal; **zwölf|ma|lig;** **Zwölf|mei|len|zo|ne;** **zwölft;** *vgl.* zwölf; **Zwölf|ta|fel|ge|set|ze** *Plur.;* **zwölf|tau|send;** **zwölf|te;** *vgl.* achte; **zwölf|tel;** *vgl.* achtel; **Zwölf|tel,** das, *schweiz. meist* der; -s, -; *vgl.* Achtel; **Zwölf|ten** *Plur.* (*landsch. für* die „Zwölf Nächte"; *vgl.* zwölf); **zwölf|tens;** **Zwölf|tö|ner** (Vertreter der Zwölftonmusik); **Zwölf|ton|mu|sik,** die; - (Kompositionsstil); **Zwölf|ton|ner** (*mit Ziffern* 12-Tonner; ↑R 44); **zwölf|und|ein|halb** *vgl.* zwölfeinhalb; **Zwölf|zy|lin|der** (*ugs. für* Zwölfzylindermotor od. damit ausgerüstetes Kraftfahrzeug); **Zwölf|zy|lin|der|mo|tor;** **zwölf|zy|lind|rig** (*mit Ziffern* 12-zylindrig; ↑R 44)

zwo|te *vgl.* zwei

z. Wv. = zur Wiederverwendung; zur Wiedervorlage

z. w. V. = zur weiteren Veranlassung

Zy|an, *chem. fachspr.* Cy|an [tsy'a:n], das; -s ‹griech.› (chem. Verbindung aus Kohlenstoff u. Stickstoff); **Zy|a|ne,** die; -, -n (Kornblume); **Zy|a|nid,** das; -s, -e (Salz der Blausäure); **Zy|an|ka|li,** *älter* **Zy|an|ka|li|um,** das; -s (stark giftiges Kaliumsalz der Blausäure); **Zy|a|no|se,** die; -, -n (*Med.* bläuliche Verfärbung der Haut); **Zy|a|no|ty|pie,** die; -, ...ien (*nur Sing.:* spez. Lichtpausverfahren; Kopie nach diesem Verfahren)

Zy|a|thus *vgl.* Kyathos

Zy|go|ma [*auch* tsy'go:ma], das; -s, ...omata ‹griech.› (*Med.* Jochbogen); **zy|go|morph** (*Bot.* mit nur einer Symmetrieebene [von Blüten]); **Zy|go|te,** die; -, -n (*Biol.* die befruchtete Eizelle nach der Verschmelzung der beiden Geschlechtskerne)

Zyk|la|den (↑R 130); *vgl.* Kykladen; **Zyk|la|me,** die; -, -n ‹griech.› (*österr. u. schweiz. für* Zyklamen); **Zyk|la|men,** das; -s, - (Alpenveilchen); **Zyk|len** (*Plur. von* Zyklus); **Zyk|li|ker** [*auch* 'tsy...] (altgriech. Dichter von Epen, die später zu einem Zyklus mit Ilias und Odyssee als Mittelpunkt gestaltet wurden); **zyk|lisch** [*auch* 'tsy...], *chem. fachspr.* cyc|lisch (↑R 130; kreisläufig, -förmig; sich auf einen Zyklus beziehend; regelmäßig wiederkehrend); **Zyk|lo|i|de,** die; -, -n (math. Kurve); **Zyk|lo|id|schup|pe** (dünne Fischschuppe mit hinten abgerundetem Rand); **Zyk|lon,** der; -s, -e ‹engl.› (Wirbelsturm; *als* ®: Fliehkraftabscheider [für Staub]); **Zyk|lo|ne,** die; -, -n (*Meteor.* Tiefdruckgebiet); **Zyk|lop,** der; -en, -en; ↑R 126 (einäugiger Riese der griech. Sage); **Zyk|lo|pen|mau|er** (frühgeschichtl. Mauer aus unbehauenen Bruchsteinen); **Zyk|lo|pie,** die; - (*Med.* eine Gesichtsmissbildung); **zyk|lo|pisch** (riesenhaft); **zyk|lo|thym** (*Psych.* [seelisch] aufgeschlossen, gesellig mit wechselnder Stimmung); **Zyk|lo|thy|me,** der *u.* die; -n, -n; ↑R 5 ff. (jmd., der ein zyklothymes Temperament besitzt); **Zyk|lo|thy|mie,** die; - (Wesensart des Zyklothymen); **Zyk|lot|ron** [*auch* 'tsy...] (↑R 130), das; -s, *Plur.* -s, *auch* ...one (Beschleuniger für positiv geladene Elementarteilchen); **Zyk|lus** [*auch* 'tsy...], der; -, Zyklen (Kreis[lauf]; Folge; Reihe)

Zy|lin|der [tsi..., *auch* tsy...], der; -s, - ‹griech.› (Walze; röhrenförmiger Hohlkörper; Stiefel [bei Pumpen]; hoher Herrenhut); **...zy|lin|der** (z. B. Achtzylinder); **Zy|lin|der‿block** (*Plur.* ...blöcke), **...bü|ro** (Schreibsekretär mit Rollverschluss), **...glas** (*Plur.* ...gläser; nur in einer Richtung gekrümmtes Brillenglas), **...hut** (der), **...kopf** *(Kfz-Technik);* **Zy|lin|der|kopf|dich|tung;** **Zy|lin|der|pro|jek|ti|on** (Kartendarstellung besonderer Art); **...zy|lind|rig** (↑R 130; z. B. achtzylindrig); **zy|lind|risch** (walzenförmig)

Zy|ma|se, die; - ‹griech.› (die alkoholische Gärung bewirkendes Gemisch von Enzymen); **Zy|mo|lo|gie,** die; - (Gärungslehre); **Zy|mo|tech|nik,** die; - (Gärungstechnik); **zy|mo|tisch** (Gärung bewirkend)

Zy|ni|ker ‹griech.› (zynischer Mensch); *vgl. aber* Kyniker; **zy|nisch** (auf grausame, beleidigende Weise spöttisch); **Zy|nis|mus,** der; -, ...men (*nur Sing.:* philos. Richtung der Kyniker; *nur Sing.:* zynische Einstellung; zynische Äußerung)

Zy|per‿gras (einjähriges Riedgras), **...kat|ze;** **Zy|pern** (Inselstaat im Mittelmeer); **Zy|per|wein;** **Zyp|rer** (↑R 130; Bewohner von Zypern)

Zyp|res|se (↑R 130), die; -, -n ‹griech.› (bes. im Mittelmeerraum wachsender Nadelbaum); **zyp|res|sen** (aus Zypressenholz); **Zyp|res|sen‿hain, ...holz, ...kraut**

Zyp|ri|an, Zyp|ri|a|nus (↑R 130; ein Heiliger)

Zyp|ri|er, Zyp|ri|ot (↑R 130), der; -en, -en; *vgl.* Zyprer; **zyp|ri|o|tisch, zyp|risch** (von Zypern)

Zy|ri|a|kus (ein Heiliger)

zy|ril|lisch *vgl.* kyrillisch

Zys|tal|gie (↑R 132), die; -, ...ien ‹griech.› (*Med.* Blasenschmerz); **Zys|te,** die; -, -n (mit Flüssigkeit gefüllte Geschwulst); **Zys|tek|to|mie** (↑R 132), die; -, -n [...iən] (operative Entfernung einer Zyste); **zys|tisch** (blasenartig; auf die Zyste bezüglich); **Zys|ti|tis,** die; -, ...titiden (Entzündung der Harnblase); **Zys|to|skop,** das; -s, -e (Blasenspiegel)

Zy|to|de, die; -, -n ‹griech.› (kernloses Protoplasmaklümpchen); **zy|to|gen** (von der Zelle gebildet); **Zy|to|lo|ge** (Zellforscher); **Zy|to|lo|gie,** die; - (Zellenlehre); **Zy|to|lo|gin;** **zy|to|lo|gisch;** **Zy|to|plas|ma** (Zellplasma); **Zy|to|sta|ti|kum,** das; -s, ...ka (*Med.* das Zellwachstum hemmende Substanz); **zy|to|sta|tisch;** **Zy|to|stom,** das; -s, -e *u.* **Zy|to|sto|ma,** das; -s, -ta (*Biol.* Zellmund der Einzeller); **Zy|to|to|xin** (Zellgift); **zy|to|to|xisch** (*Med., Biol.* [die Zelle] schädigend, vergiftend); **Zy|to|to|xi|zi|tät** (Fähigkeit, Gewebszellen zu schädigen)

zz., zzt. = zurzeit

Zz. = Zinszahl

z. Z., z. Zt. = zur Zeit

Die amtliche Regelung der deutschen Rechtschreibung

Der folgende Text gibt den unveränderten und vollständigen „Teil I: Regeln" der amtlichen Neuregelung wieder. Mit dem darin erwähnten „Wörterverzeichnis" ist der Teil II (die Wortliste des Regelwerks) gemeint, der hier nicht abgedruckt ist.

A Laut-Buchstaben-Zuordnungen

0 Vorbemerkungen

(1) Die Schreibung des Deutschen beruht auf einer Buchstabenschrift. Jeder Buchstabe existiert als Kleinbuchstabe und als Großbuchstabe (Ausnahme *ß*):

a b c d e f g h i j k l m n o p q r s t u v w x y z ä ö ü ß

A B C D E F G H I J K L M N O P Q R S T U V W X Y Z Ä Ö Ü

Die Umlautbuchstaben *ä, ö, ü* werden im Folgenden mit den Buchstaben *a, o, u* zusammen eingeordnet; *ß* nach *ss*. Zum Ersatz von *ß* durch *ss* oder *SS* siehe § 25 E_2 und E_3.

In Fremdwörtern und fremdsprachigen Eigennamen kommen außerdem Buchstaben mit zusätzlichen Zeichen sowie Ligaturen vor (zum Beispiel *ç, é, â, œ*).

(2) Für die Schreibung des Deutschen gilt:

(2.1) Buchstaben und Sprachlaute sind einander zugeordnet. Die folgende Darstellung bezieht sich auf die Standardaussprache, die allerdings regionale Varianten aufweist.

(2.2) Die Schreibung der Wortstämme, Präfixe, Suffixe und Endungen bleibt bei der Flexion der Wörter, in Zusammensetzungen und Ableitungen weitgehend konstant (zum Beispiel *Kind, die Kinder, des Kindes, Kindbett, Kinderbuch, Kindesalter, kindisch, kindlich; Differenz, Differenzial, differenzieren;* aber *säen, Saat; nähen, Nadel*). Dies macht es in vielen Fällen möglich, die Schreibung eines Wortes aus verwandten Wörtern zu erschließen.

Dabei ist zu beachten, dass Wortstämme sich verändern können, so vor allem durch Umlaut (zum Beispiel *Hand – Hände, Not – nötig, Kunst – Künstler, rauben – Räuber*), durch Ablaut (zum Beispiel *schwimmen – er schwamm – geschwommen*) oder durch *e/i*-Wechsel (zum Beispiel *geben – du gibst – er gibt*).

In manchen Fällen werden durch verschiedene Laut-Buchstaben-Zuordnungen gleich lautende Wörter unterschieden (zum Beispiel *malen ≠ mahlen, leeren ≠ lehren*).

(3) Der folgenden Darstellung liegt die deutsche Standardsprache zugrunde.

Besonderheiten sind bei Fremdwörtern und Eigennamen zu beachten.

(3.1) Fremdwörter unterliegen oft fremdsprachigen Schreibgewohnheiten (zum Beispiel *Chaiselongue, Sympathie, Lady*). Ihre Schreibung kann jedoch – und Ähnliches gilt für die Aussprache – je nach Häufigkeit und Art der Verwendung integriert, das heißt dem Deutschen angeglichen werden (zum Beispiel *Scharnier* aus französisch *charnière, Streik* aus englisch *strike*). Manche Fremdwörter werden sowohl in einer integrierten als auch in einer fremdsprachigen Schreibung verwendet (zum Beispiel *Fotograf / Photograph*).

Nicht integriert sind üblicherweise

a) zitierte fremdsprachige Wörter und Wortgruppen (zum Beispiel: *Die Engländer nennen dies „one way mind"*);

b) Wörter in international gebräuchlicher oder festgelegter – vor allem fachsprachlicher – Schreibung (zum Beispiel *City;* medizinisch *Phlegmone*).

Für die nicht oder nur teilweise integrierten Fremdwörter lassen sich wegen der Vielgestaltigkeit fremdsprachiger Schreibgewohnheiten keine handhabbaren Regeln aufstellen. In Zweifelsfällen siehe das Wörterverzeichnis.

(3.2) Für Eigennamen (Vornamen, Familiennamen, geographische Eigennamen und dergleichen) gelten im Allgemeinen amtliche Schreibungen. Diese entsprechen nicht immer den folgenden Regeln.

Eigennamen aus Sprachen mit nicht lateinischem Alphabet können unterschiedliche Schreibungen haben, die auf die Verwendung verschiedener Umschriftsysteme zurückgehen (zum Beispiel *Schanghai, Shanghai*).

(4) Beim Aufbau der folgenden Darstellung sind zunächst Vokale (siehe Abschnitt 1) und Konsonanten (siehe Abschnitt 2) zu unterscheiden.

Unterschieden sind des Weiteren in beiden Gruppen grundlegende Zuordnungen (siehe Abschnitt 1.1 und 2.1), besondere Zuordnungen (siehe Abschnitte 1.2 bis 1.7 und 2.2 bis 2.7) sowie spezielle Zuordnungen in Fremdwörtern (siehe Abschnitt 1.8 und 2.8).

Laute werden im Folgenden durch die phonetische Umschrift wiedergegeben (zum Beispiel das lange *a* durch [aː]). Sind die Buchstaben gemeint, so ist dies durch kursiven Druck gekennzeichnet (zum Beispiel der Buchstabe *h* oder *H*).

1 Vokale

1.1 Grundlegende Laut-Buchstaben-Zuordnungen

§ 1 Als grundlegend im Sinne dieser orthographischen Regelung gelten die folgenden Laut-Buchstaben-Zuordnungen.

Besondere Zuordnungen werden in den sich anschließenden Abschnitten behandelt.

(1) Kurze einfache Vokale

Laute	Buchstaben	Beispiele
[a]	*a*	*ab, Alter, warm, Bilanz*
[ɛ], [e]	*e*	*enorm, Endung, helfen, fett, penetrant, Prozent*
[ə]	*e*	*Atem, Ballade, gering, nobel*
[ɪ], [i]	*i*	*immer, Iltis, List, indiskret, Pilot*
[ɔ], [o]	*o*	*ob, Ort, folgen, Konzern, Logis, Obelisk, Organ*
[œ], [ø]	*ö*	*öfter, Öffnung, wölben, Ökonomie*
[ʊ], [u]	*u*	*unten, Ulme, bunt, Museum*
[ʏ], [y]	*ü*	*Küste, wünschen, Püree*

(2) Lange einfache Vokale

Laute	Buchstaben	Beispiele
[aː]	*a*	*artig, Abend, Basis*
[eː]	*e*	*edel, Efeu, Weg, Planet*
[ɛː]	*ä*	*äsen, Ära, Sekretär*
[iː]	*ie*	(in einheimischen Wörtern:) *Liebe, Dieb*
	i	(in Fremdwörtern:) *Diva, Iris, Krise, Ventil*
[oː]	*o*	*oben, Ofen, vor, Chor*
[øː]	*ö*	*öde, Öfen, schön*
[uː]	*u*	*Ufer, Bluse, Muse, Natur*
[yː]	*ü*	*üben, Übel, fügen, Menü, Molekül*

(3) Diphthonge

Laute	Buchstaben	Beispiele
[aɪ]	*ei*	*eigen, Eile, beiseite, Kaleidoskop*
[aʊ]	*au*	*auf, Auge, Haus, Audienz*
[ɔʏ]	*eu*	*euch, Eule, Zeuge, Euphorie*

1.2 Besondere Kennzeichnung der kurzen Vokale

Folgen auf einen betonten Vokal innerhalb des Wortstammes – bei Fremdwörtern betrifft dies auch den betonten Wortausgang – zwei verschiedene Konsonanten, so ist der Vokal in der Regel kurz; folgt kein Konsonant, so ist der Vokal in der Regel lang; folgt nur ein Konsonant, so ist der Vokal kurz oder lang. Deshalb beschränkt sich die besondere grafische Kennzeichnung des kurzen Vokals auf den Fall, dass nur ein einzelner Konsonant folgt.

§ 2 Folgt im Wortstamm auf einen betonten kurzen Vokal nur ein einzelner Konsonant, so kennzeichnet man die Kürze des Vokals durch Verdopplung des Konsonantenbuchstabens.

Das betrifft Wörter wie:

Ebbe; Paddel; schlaff, Affe; Egge; generell, Kontrolle; schlimm, immer; denn, wann, gönnen; Galopp, üppig; starr, knurren; Hass, dass (Konjunktion), *bisschen, wessen, Prämisse; statt (≠ Stadt), Hütte, Manschette*

§ 3 Für k und z gilt eine besondere Regelung:
(1) Statt kk schreibt man ck.
(2) Statt zz schreibt man tz.

Das betrifft Wörter wie:

Acker, locken, Reck; Katze, Matratze, Schutz

Ausnahmen: Fremdwörter wie *Mokka, Sakko; Pizza, Razzia, Skizze*

E zu § 2 und § 3: Die Verdopplung des Buchstabens für den einzelnen Konsonanten bleibt üblicherweise in Wörtern, die sich aufeinander beziehen lassen, auch dann erhalten, wenn sich die Betonung ändert, zum Beispiel:

Galopp – galoppieren, Horror – horrend, Kontrolle – kontrollieren, Nummer – nummerieren, spinnen – Spinnerei, Stuck – Stuckatur, Stuckateur

§ 4 In acht Fallgruppen verdoppelt man den Buchstaben für den einzelnen Konsonanten nicht, obwohl dieser einem betonten kurzen Vokal folgt.

Dies betrifft

(1) eine Reihe einsilbiger Wörter (besonders aus dem Englischen), zum Beispiel:

Bus, Chip, fit, Gag, Grog, Jet, Job, Kap, Klub, Mob, Pop, Slip, top, Twen

E_1: Ableitungen schreibt man entsprechend § 2 mit doppeltem Konsonantenbuchstaben:

jobben – du jobbst – er jobbt; jetten, poppig, Slipper; außerdem: *die Busse* (zu *Bus*)

(2) die fremdsprachigen Suffixe *-ik* und *-it,* die mit kurzem, aber auch mit langem Vokal gesprochen werden können, zum Beispiel:

Kritik, Politik; Kredit, Profit

(3) einige Wörter mit unklarem Wortaufbau oder mit Bestandteilen, die nicht selbständig vorkommen, zum Beispiel:

Brombeere, Damwild, Himbeere, Imbiss, Imker (aber *Imme*), *Sperling, Walnuss;* aber: *Bollwerk*

(4) eine Reihe von Fremdwörtern, zum Beispiel:

Ananas, April, City, Hotel, Kamera, Kapitel, Limit, Mini, Relief, Roboter

(5) Wörter mit den nicht mehr produktiven Suffixen *-d, -st* und *-t,* zum Beispiel:

Brand (trotz *brennen*), *Spindel* (trotz *spinnen*); *Geschwulst* (trotz *schwellen*), *Gespinst* (trotz *spinnen*), *Gunst* (trotz *gönnen*); *beschäftigen, Geschäft* (trotz *schaffen*), *(ins)gesamt, sämtlich* (trotz *zusammen*)

(6) eine Reihe einsilbiger Wörter mit grammatischer Funktion, zum Beispiel:

ab, an, dran, bis, das (Artikel, Pronomen), *des* (aber *dessen*), *in, drin* (aber *innen, drinnen*), *man, mit, ob, plus, um, was, wes* (aber *wessen*)

E_2: Aber entsprechend § 2:

dann, denn, wann, wenn; dass (Konjunktion)

(7) die folgenden Verbformen:

ich bin, er hat; aber nach der Grundregel (§ 2): *er hatte, sie tritt, nimm!*

(8) die folgenden Ausnahmen:

Drittel, Mittag, dennoch

§ 5 In vier Fallgruppen verdoppelt man den Buchstaben für den einzelnen Konsonanten, obwohl der vorausgehende kurze Vokal nicht betont ist.

Dies betrifft

(1) das scharfe (stimmlose) *s* in Fremdwörtern, zum Beispiel:

Fassade, Karussell, Kassette, passieren, Rezession

(2) die Suffixe *-in* und *-nis* sowie die Wortausgänge *-as, -is, -os* und *-us*, wenn in erweiterten Formen dem Konsonanten ein Vokal folgt, zum Beispiel:

-in: *Ärztin – Ärztinnen, Königin – Königinnen*
-nis: *Beschwernis – Beschwernisse, Kenntnis – Kenntnisse*
-as: *Ananas – Ananasse, Ukas – Ukasse*
-is: *Iltis – Iltisse, Kürbis – Kürbisse*
-os: *Albatros – Albatrosse, Rhinozeros – Rhinozerosse*
-us: *Diskus – Diskusse, Globus – Globusse*

(3) eine Reihe von Fremdwörtern, zum Beispiel:

Allee, Batterie, Billion, Buffet, Effekt, frappant, Grammatik, Kannibale, Karriere, kompromittieren, Konkurrenz, Konstellation, Lotterie, Porzellan, raffiniert, Renommee, skurril, Stanniol

E: In Zusammensetzungen mit fremdsprachigen Präfixen wie *ad-, dis-, in-, kon-/con-, ob-, sub-* und *syn-* ist deren auslautender Konsonant in manchen Fällen an den Konsonanten des folgenden Wortes angeglichen, zum Beispiel:

Affekt, akkurat, Attraktion (vgl. aber *Advokat, addieren*); ebenso: *Differenz, Illusion, korrekt, Opposition, suggerieren, Symmetrie*

(4) wenige Wörter mit *tz* (siehe § 3 (2)), zum Beispiel:

Kiebitz, Stieglitz

1.3 Besondere Kennzeichnung der langen Vokale

Folgt im Wortstamm auf einen betonten Vokal kein Konsonant, ist er lang. Die regelmäßige Kennzeichnung mit *h* hat auch die Aufgabe, die Silbenfuge zu markieren, zum Beispiel *Kü|he;* vgl. § 6. Folgt nur ein Konsonant, so kann der Vokal kurz oder lang sein. Die Länge wird jedoch nur bei einheimischen Wörtern mit [i:] regelmäßig durch *ie* bezeichnet; vgl. § 1. Ansonsten erfolgt die Kennzeichnung nur ausnahmsweise:

a) in manchen Wörtern vor *l, m, n, r* mit *h;* vgl. § 8;
b) mit Doppelvokal *aa, ee, oo;* vgl. § 9;
c) mit *ih, ieh;* vgl. § 12.

Zum *ß* (statt *s*) nach langem Vokal und Diphthong siehe § 25.

§ 6 Wenn einem betonten einfachen langen Vokal ein unbetonter kurzer Vokal unmittelbar folgt oder in erweiterten Formen eines Wortes folgen kann, so steht nach dem Buchstaben für den langen Vokal stets der Buchstabe *h*.

Dies betrifft Wörter wie:

ah: *nahen, bejahen* (aber *ja*)
eh: *Darlehen, drehen*
oh: *drohen, Floh* (wegen *Flöhe*)
uh: *Kuh* (wegen *Kühe*), *Ruhe, Schuhe*
äh: *fähig, Krähe, zäh* (Ausnahme *säen*)
öh: *Höhe* (Ausnahme *Bö*, trotz *Böe, Böen*)
üh: *früh* (wegen *früher*)

Zu *ieh* siehe § 12 (2).
Zu *See* u.a. siehe § 9.

§ 7 Das *h* steht ausnahmsweise auch nach dem Diphthong [aɪ].

Das betrifft Wörter wie:
gedeihen, Geweih, leihen (≠ Laien), Reihe, Reiher, seihen, verzeihen, weihen, Weiher; aber sonst: *Blei, drei, schreien*

§ 8 Wenn einem betonten langen Vokal einer der Konsonanten [l], [m], [n] oder [r] folgt, so wird in vielen, jedoch nicht in der Mehrzahl der Wörter nach dem Buchstaben für den Vokal ein *h* eingefügt.

Dies betrifft

(1) Wörter, in denen auf [l], [m], [n] oder [r] kein weiterer Konsonant folgt, zum Beispiel:

ah: *Dahlie, lahm, ahnen, Bahre*
eh: *Befehl, benehmen, ablehnen, begehren*
oh: *hohl, Sohn, bohren*
uh: *Pfuhl, Ruhm, Huhn, Uhr*
äh: *ähneln, Ähre*
öh: *Höhle, stöhnen, Möhre*
üh: *fühlen, Bühne, führen*

Zu *ih* siehe § 12 (1).

(2) die folgenden Einzelfälle: *ahnden, fahnden*

E_1: Zu unterscheiden sind gleich lautende, aber unterschiedlich geschriebene Wortstämme wie:
Mahl ≠ Mal, mahlen ≠ malen, Sohle ≠ Sole; dehnen ≠ denen; Bahre ≠ Bar, wahr ≠ er war, lehren ≠ leeren, mehr ≠ Meer, Mohr ≠ Moor, Uhr ≠ Ur, währen ≠ sie wären

E_2 zu § 6 bis 8: Das *h* bleibt auch bei Flexion, Stammveränderung und in Ableitungen erhalten, zum Beispiel:
befehlen – befiehl – er befahl – befohlen, drehen – gedreht – Draht, empfehlen – empfiehl – er empfahl – empfohlen, gedeihen – es gedieh – gediehen, fliehen – er floh – geflohen, leihen – er lieh – geliehen, mähen – Mahd, nähen – Naht, nehmen – er nahm, sehen – er sieht – er sah – gesehen, stehlen – er stiehlt – er stahl – gestohlen, verzeihen – er verzieh – verziehen, weihen – geweiht – Weihnachten

Ausnahmen, zum Beispiel: *Blüte, Blume* (trotz *blühen*), *Glut* (trotz *glühen*), *Nadel* (trotz *nähen*)

E_3: In Fremdwörtern steht bis auf wenige Ausnahmen wie *Allah, Schah* kein *h*

§ 9 Die Länge von [a:], [e:] und [o:] kennzeichnet man in einer kleinen Gruppe von Wörtern durch die Verdopplung *aa, ee* bzw. *oo*.

Dies betrifft Wörter wie:

aa: *Aal, Aas, Haar, paar, Paar, Saal, Saat, Staat, Waage*
ee: *Beere, Beet, Fee, Klee, scheel, Schnee, See, Speer, Tee, Teer,* außerdem eine Reihe von Fremdwörtern mit *ee* im Wortausgang wie: *Armee, Idee, Kaffee, Klischee, Tournee, Varietee*
oo: *Boot, Moor, Moos, Zoo*

Zu *die Feen, Seen* siehe § 19.

E_1: Zu unterscheiden sind gleich lautende, aber unterschiedlich geschriebene Wortstämme wie: *Waage ≠ Wagen; Heer ≠ her, hehr; leeren ≠ lehren; Meer ≠ mehr; Reede ≠ Rede; Seele, seelisch ≠ selig; Moor ≠ Mohr*

E_2: Bei Umlaut schreibt man nur *ä* bzw. *ö*, zum Beispiel:
Härchen – aber *Haar; Pärchen* – aber *Paar; Säle* – aber *Saal; Bötchen* – aber *Boot*

§ 10 Wenige einheimische Wörter und eingebürgerte Entlehnungen mit dem langen Vokal [i:] schreibt man ausnahmsweise mit *i*.

Dies betrifft Wörter wie:
dir, mir, wir; gib, du gibst, er gibt (aber *ergiebig*); *Bibel, Biber, Brise, Fibel, Igel, Liter, Nische, Primel, Tiger, Wisent*

E: Zu unterscheiden sind gleich lautende, aber unterschiedlich geschriebene Wörter wie:
Lid ≠ Lied; Mine ≠ Miene; Stil ≠ Stiel; wider ≠ wieder

§ 11

> Für langes [i:] schreibt man *ie* in den fremdsprachigen Suffixen und Wortausgängen *-ie, -ier* und *-ieren.*

Dies betrifft Wörter wie:

Batterie, Lotterie; Manier, Scharnier; marschieren, probieren

Ausnahmen, zum Beispiel: *Geysir, Saphir, Souvenir, Vampir, Wesir*

§ 12

> In Einzelfällen kennzeichnet man die Länge des Vokals [i:] zusätzlich mit dem Buchstaben *h* und schreibt *ih* oder *ieh.*

Im Einzelnen gilt:

(1) *ih* steht nur in den folgenden Wörtern (vgl. § 8):

ihm, ihn, ihnen; ihr (Personal- und Possessivpronomen), außerdem *Ihle*

(2) *ieh* steht nur in den folgenden Wörtern (vgl. § 6):

fliehen, Vieh, wiehern, ziehen

Zu *ieh* in Flexionsformen wie *befiehl* (zu *befehlen*) siehe § 8 E_2.

1.4 Umlautschreibung bei [ɛ]

§ 13

> Für kurzes [ɛ] schreibt man *ä* statt *e,* wenn es eine Grundform mit *a* gibt.

Dies betrifft flektierte und abgeleitete Wörter wie:

Bänder, Bändel (wegen *Band*); *Hälse* (wegen *Hals*); *Kälte, kälter* (wegen *kalt*); *überschwänglich* (wegen *Überschwang*)

E_1: Man schreibt *e* oder *ä* in *Schenke/Schänke* (wegen *ausschenken/Ausschank*), *aufwendig/aufwändig* (wegen *aufwenden/Aufwand*).

E_2: Für langes [e:] und langes [ɛ:], die in der Aussprache oft nicht unterschieden werden, schreibt man *ä,* sofern es eine Grundform mit *a* gibt, zum Beispiel: *quälen* (wegen *Qual*). Wörter wie *sägen, Ähre (≠ Ehre), Bär* sind Ausnahmen.

§ 14

> In wenigen Wörtern schreibt man ausnahmsweise *ä.*

Dies betrifft Wörter wie:

ätzen, dämmern, Geländer, Lärm, März, Schärpe

E: Zu unterscheiden sind gleich lautende, aber unterschiedlich geschriebene Wörter wie:
Äsche ≠ Esche; Färse ≠ Ferse; Lärche ≠ Lerche

§ 15

> In wenigen Wörtern schreibt man ausnahmsweise *e.*

Das betrifft Wörter wie:

Eltern (trotz *alt*); *schwenken* (trotz *schwanken*)

1.5 Umlautschreibung bei [ɔʏ]

§ 16

> Für den Diphthong [ɔʏ] schreibt man *äu* statt *eu,* wenn es eine Grundform mit *au* gibt.

Dies betrifft flektierte und abgeleitete Wörter wie:

Häuser (wegen *Haus*), *er läuft* (wegen *laufen*), *Mäuse, Mäuschen* (wegen *Maus*); *Gebäude* (wegen *Bau*), *Geräusch* (wegen *rauschen*), *sich schnäuzen* (wegen *Schnauze*), *verbläuen* (wegen *blau*)

§ 17

> In wenigen Wörtern schreibt man ausnahmsweise *äu.*

Das betrifft Wörter wie:

Knäuel, Räude, sich räuspern, Säule, sich sträuben, täuschen

1.6 Ausnahmen beim Diphthong [aɪ]

§ 18 In wenigen Wörtern schreibt man den Diphthong [aɪ] ausnahmsweise *ai*.

Das betrifft Wörter wie:
Hai, Kaiser, Mai

E: Zu unterscheiden sind gleich lautende, aber unterschiedlich geschriebene Wortstämme wie:
Bai ≠ bei; Laib ≠ Leib; Laich ≠ Leiche; Laie, Laien ≠ leihen; Saite ≠ Seite; Waise ≠ Weise, weisen

1.7 Besonderheiten beim *e*

§ 19 Folgen auf *-ee* oder *-ie* die Flexionsendungen oder Ableitungssuffixe *-e, -en, -er, -es, -ell,* so lässt man ein *e* weg.

Das betrifft Wörter wie:
die Feen; die Ideen; die Mondseer, des Sees; die Knie, knien; die Fantasien; sie schrien, geschrien; ideell; industriell

1.8 Spezielle Laut-Buchstaben-Zuordnungen in Fremdwörtern

§ 20 Über die bisher dargestellten Laut-Buchstaben-Zuordnungen hinaus treten in Fremdwörtern auch fremdsprachige Zuordnungen auf. In den folgenden Listen sind nur die wichtigeren angeführt.

Dabei ist zu beachten, dass Kürze und Länge der Vokale von der Betonung abhängen. Vokale, die in betonten Silben lang sind, werden in unbetonten Silben kurz gesprochen, zum Beispiel *Analyse* mit langem Vokal [y:] – *analysieren* mit kurzem Vokal [y].

(1) Fremdsprachige Laut-Buchstaben-Zuordnungen

Laute	Buchstaben	Beispiele
[a], [a:]	*u*	*Butler, Cup, Make-up, Slum*
	at	*Eklat, Etat*
[ɛ], [ɛ:]	*a*	*Action, Camping, Fan, Gag*
	ai	*Airbus, Chaiselongue, fair, Flair, Saison*
[e], [e:]	*é*	*Abbé, Attaché, Lamé*
	er	*Atelier, Bankier, Premier*
	et	*Budget, Couplet, Filet*
	ai	*Cocktail, Container*
[i], [i:]	*y*	*Baby, City, Lady, sexy*
	ea	*Beat, Dealer, Hearing, Jeans, Team*
	ee	*Evergreen, Spleen, Teenager*
[o], [o:]	*au*	*Chaussee, Chauvinismus*
	eau	*Niveau, Plateau, Tableau*
	ot	*Depot, Trikot*
[ø:]	*eu*	*adieu, Milieu;* häufig in den Suffixen *-eur, -euse: Ingenieur, Souffleuse*
[ʊ], [u], [u:]	*oo*	*Boom, Swimmingpool*
	ou	*Journalist, Rouge, Route, souverän*
[ʏ], [y], [y:]	*y*	*Analyse, Hymne, Physik, System, Typ;* auch in den Präfixen *dys-(≠ dis-), hyper-, hypo-, syl-, sym-, syn-: dysfunktional, hyperkorrekt, Hypozentrum, Syllogismus, Symbiose, synchron*
[ã], [ã:]	*an*	*Branche, Chance, Orange, Renaissance, Revanche*
	ant	*Avantgarde, Pendant, Restaurant*
	en	*engagiert, Ensemble, Entree, Pendant, Rendezvous*
	ent	*Abonnement, Engagement*

[ɛ̃], [ɛ:]	*ain*	*Refrain, Souterrain, Terrain*
	eint	*Teint*
	in	*Bulletin, Dessin, Mannequin*
[ɔ̃], [ɔ̃:]	*on*	*Annonce, Chanson, Pardon*
[œ̃], [œ̃:]	*um*	*Parfum*
[aʊ]	*ou*	*Couch, Count-down, Foul, Sound*
	ow	*Clown, Count-down, Cowboy, Power(play)*
[aɪ]	*i*	*Lifetime, Pipeline*
	igh	*Copyright, high, Starfighter*
	y	*Nylon, Recycling*
[ɔʏ]	*oy*	*Boy, Boykott*
[oa]	*oi*	*Memoiren, Repertoire, Reservoir, Toilette*

(2) Doppelschreibungen

Im Prozess der Integration entlehnter Wörter können fremdsprachige und integrierte Schreibung nebeneinander stehen. (Zu Haupt- und Nebenform siehe das Wörterverzeichnis.)

Laute	Buchstaben	Beispiele
[ɛ], [ɛ:]	*ai – ä*	*Drainage – Dränage, Mayonnaise – Majonäse, Mohair – Mohär, Polonaise – Polonäse*
[e], [e:]	*é – ee*	*Bouclé – Buklee, Doublé – Dublee, Exposé – Exposee*
		Café – Kaffee (mit Bedeutungsdifferenzierung), *Kommuniqué – Kommunikee, Varieté – Varietee*
[o], [o:]	*au – o*	*Sauce – Soße*
[ʊ],[u],[u:]	*ou – u*	*Bravour – Bravur, Bouquet – Buket(t), Doublé – Dublee, Coupon – Kupon, Nougat – Nugat*

§ 21 Fremdwörter aus dem Englischen, die auf *-y* enden und im Englischen den Plural *-ies* haben, erhalten im Plural ein *-s*.

Das betrifft Wörter wie:
Baby – Babys, Lady – Ladys, Party – Partys

E: Bei Zitatwörtern gilt die englische Schreibung, zum Beispiel: *Grand Old Ladies*.

2 Konsonanten

2.1 Grundlegende Laut-Buchstaben-Zuordnungen

§ 22 Als grundlegend im Sinne dieser orthographischen Regelung gelten die folgenden Laut-Buchstaben-Zuordnungen.

Besondere Zuordnungen werden in den sich anschließenden Abschnitten behandelt.

(1) Einfache Konsonanten

Laute	Buchstaben	Beispiele
[b]	*b*	*backen, Baum, Obolus, Parabel*
[ç], [x]	*ch*	*ich, Bücher, lynchen; ach, Rauch*
[d]	*d*	*danken, Druck, leiden, Mansarde*
[f]	*f*	*fertig, Falke, Hafen, Fusion*
[g]	*g*	*gehen, Gas, sägen, Organ, Eleganz*
[h]	*h*	*hinterher, Haus, Hektik, Ahorn, vehement*
[j]	*j*	*ja, Jagd, Boje, Objekt*
[k]	*k*	*Kiste, Haken, Flanke, Majuskel, Konkurs*
[l]	*l*	*laufen, Laut, Schale, lamentieren*
[m]	*m*	*machen, Mund, Lampe, Maximum*
[n]	*n*	*nur, Nagel, Ton, Natur, nuklear*

[ŋ]	*ng*	*Gang, Länge, singen, Zange*
[p]	*p*	*packen, Paste, Raupe, Problem*
[r], [ʀ], [ʁ]	*r*	*rauben, Rampe, hören, Zitrone*
[s]	*s*	*skurril, Skandal, Hast, hopsen*
[z]	*s*	*sagen, Seife, lesen, Laser*
[ʃ]	*sch*	*scharf, Schaufel, rauschen*
[t]	*t*	*tragen, Tür, fort, Optimum*
[v]	*w*	*wann, Wagen, Möwe*

(2) Konsonantenverbindungen (innerhalb des Stammes)

Laute	Buchstaben	Beispiele
[kv]	*qu*	*quälen, Quelle, liquid, Qualität*
[ks]	*x*	*xylographisch, Xenophobie, boxen, toxisch*
[ts]	*z*	*zart, Zaum, tanzen, speziell, Zenit*

2.2 Auslautverhärtung und Wortausgang *-ig*

§ 23 Die in großen Teilen des deutschen Sprachgebiets auftretende Verhärtung der Konsonanten [b], [d], [g], [v] und [z] am Silbenende sowie vor anderen Konsonanten innerhalb der Silbe wird in der Schreibung nicht berücksichtigt.

E_1: Bei vielen Wörtern kann die Schreibung aus der Aussprache erweiterter Formen oder verwandter Wörter abgeleitet werden, in denen der betreffende Konsonant am Silbenanfang steht, zum Beispiel:

Konsonant am Silbenende usw.	Konsonant am Silbenanfang
Lob, löblich, du lobst	*Lobes, belobigen* (aber *Isotop – Isotope*)
trüb, trübselig, eingetrübt	*trübe, eintrüben* (aber *Typ – Typen*)
Rad, Radumfang	*Rades, rädern* (aber *Rat – Rates*)
absurd	*absurde, Absurdität* (aber *Gurt – Gurte*)
Sieg, siegreich, er siegt	*siegen* (aber *Musik – musikalisch*)
Trug, er betrog, Betrug	*betrügen* (aber *Spuk – spuken*)
gläubig	*gläubige* (aber *Plastik – Plastiken*)
Möwchen	*Möwe* (aber *Öfchen – Ofen*)
naiv, Naivling, Naivheit	*Naive, Naivität* (aber *er rief – rufen*)
Preis, preislich, preiswert	*Preise* (aber *Fleiß – fleißig*)
Haus, häuslich, behaust	*Häuser* (aber *Strauß – Sträuße*)

E_2: Bei einer kleinen Gruppe von Wörtern ist es nicht oder nur schwer möglich, eine solche Erweiterung durchzuführen oder eine Beziehung zu verwandten Wörtern herzustellen. Man schreibt sie trotzdem mit *b, d, g* bzw. *s*, zum Beispiel:

ab, Eisbein (Eis – Eises), flugs (Flug), Herbst, hübsch, jeglich, Jugend, Kies (Kiesel), Lebkuchen, morgendlich, ob, Obst, Plebs (Plebejer), preisgeben, Rebhuhn, redlich (Rede), Reis (Reisig), Reis (= Korn; *Reise* fachsprachlich = Reissorten; aber *Grieß), ihr seid (≠ seit), sie sind, und, Vogt, weg (Weges), weissagen (weise)*

§ 24 Für den Laut [ç] schreibt man regelmäßig *g*, wenn erweiterte Formen am Silbenanfang mit dem Laut [g] gesprochen werden.

Das betrifft Wörter wie:

ewig, Ewigkeit (wegen *ewige*), *gläubig* (wegen *gläubige*); aber: *unglaublich* (wegen *unglaubliche*); *heilig, Käfig, ruhig*

E: In einigen Sprachlandschaften wird *-ig* mit [k] gesprochen; dann gilt § 23.

2.3 Besonderheiten bei [s]

§ 25 Für das scharfe (stimmlose) [s] nach langem Vokal oder Diphthong schreibt man *ß*, wenn im Wortstamm kein weiterer Konsonant folgt.

Das betrifft Wörter wie:

Maß, Straße, Grieß, Spieß, groß, grüßen; außen, außer, draußen, Strauß, beißen, Fleiß, heißen

Ausnahme: *aus*

Zur Schreibung von [s] in Wörtern mit Auslautverhärtung wie *Haus, graziös, Maus, Preis* siehe § 23.

E_1: In manchen Wortstämmen wechselt bei Flexion und in Ableitungen die Länge und Kürze des Vokals vor [s]; entsprechend wechselt die Schreibung *ß* mit *ss*. Beispiele:

fließen – er floss – Fluss – das Floß
genießen – er genoss – Genuss
wissen – er weiß – er wusste

E_2: Steht der Buchstabe *ß* nicht zur Verfügung, so schreibt man *ss*. In der Schweiz kann man immer *ss* schreiben. Beispiel:

Straße – Strasse

E_3: Bei Schreibung mit Großbuchstaben schreibt man *SS*, zum Beispiel:

Straße – STRASSE

§ 26 Folgt auf das *s, ss, ß, x* oder *z* eines Verb- oder Adjektivstammes die Endung *-st* der 2. Person Singular bzw. die Endung *-st(e)* des Superlativs, so lässt man das *s* der Endung weg.

Das betrifft Wörter wie:

du reist (zu *reisen*), *du hasst* (zu *hassen*), *du reißt* (zu *reißen*), *du mixt* (zu mixen), *du sitzt* (zu *sitzen*); *(groß – größer –) größte*

2.4 Besonderheiten bei [ʃ]

§ 27 Für den Laut [ʃ] am Anfang des Wortstammes vor folgendem [p] oder [t] schreibt man *s* statt *sch*.

Das betrifft Wörter wie:

spielen, verspotten; starren, Stelle, Stunde

2.5 Besonderheiten bei [ŋ]

§ 28 Für den Laut [ŋ] vor [k] oder [g] im Wortstamm schreibt man *n* statt *ng*.

Das betrifft Wörter wie:

Bank, dünken, Enkel, Schranke, trinken; Mangan, Singular

2.6 Besonderheiten bei [f] und [v]

§ 29 Für den Laut [f] schreibt man *v* statt *f* in *ver-* (wie in *verlaufen*) sowie am Anfang einiger weiterer Wörter.

Das betrifft Wörter wie:

Vater, Veilchen, Vettel, Vetter, Vieh, viel, vielleicht, vier, Vlies, Vogel, Vogt, Volk, voll (aber *füllen*), *von, vor, vordere, vorn*

Dazu kommen *Frevel, Nerv (Nerven)*

§ 30 Für den Laut [v] schreibt man in Fremdwörtern regelmäßig und in wenigen eingebürgerten Entlehnungen *v* statt *w*.

Das betrifft Wörter wie:

privat, Revolution, Universität, Virus, zivil, Malve, Vase; Suffix bzw. Endung *-iv, -ive: Aktivität, die Detektive, Motivation; Initiative, Perspektive*

E: Bei einigen Wörtern schwankt die Aussprache von *v* zwischen [v] und [f] wie bei *Initiative, Larve, Pulver, evangelisch, Vers, Vesper, November, brave*.

2.7 Besonderheiten bei [ks]

§ 31 Für die Lautverbindung [ks] schreibt man in einigen Wortstämmen ausnahmsweise *chs* bzw. *ks* statt *x*.

Das betrifft Wörter wie:

Achse, Achsel, Büchse, Dachs, drechseln, Echse, Flachs, Fuchs, Lachs, Luchs, Ochse, sechs, Wachs, wachsen, Wechsel, Weichsel(kirsche), wichsen

Keks, schlaksig

E: Die bei Flexion und in Ableitungen entstehende Lautverbindung [ks] wird je nach dem zugrunde liegenden Wort *gs, ks* oder *cks* geschrieben, zum Beispiel:

du hegst (wegen *hegen*), *du hinkst* (wegen *hinken*), *Streiks* (wegen *Streik*), *Häcksel* (wegen *hacken*)

2.8 Spezielle Laut-Buchstaben-Zuordnungen in Fremdwörtern

§ 32 Über die bisher dargestellten Laut-Buchstaben-Zuordnungen hinaus treten in Fremdwörtern auch fremdsprachige Zuordnungen auf.

In den folgenden Listen sind nur die wichtigeren angeführt.

(1) Fremdsprachige Laut-Buchstaben-Zuordnungen

(1.1) Einfache Konsonanten

Laute	Buchstaben	Beispiele
[f]	*ph*	*Atmosphäre, Metapher, Philosophie, Physik*
[k]	*c*	*Clown, Container, Crew*
	ch	*Chaos, Charakter, Chlor, christlich*
	qu	*Mannequin, Queue*
[r]	*rh*	*Rhapsodie, Rhesusfaktor*
	rt	*Dessert, Kuvert, Ressort*
[s]	*c, ce*	*Annonce, Chance, City, Renaissance, Service*
[ʃ]	*ch*	*Champignon, Chance, charmant, Chef*
	sh	*Geisha, Sheriff, Shop, Shorts*
[ʒ]	*g*	*Genie, Ingenieur, Loge, Passagier, Regime;* auch im Suffix *-age: Blamage, Garage*
	j	*Jalousie, Jargon, jonglieren, Journalist*
[t]	*th*	*Ethos, Mathematik, Theater, These*
[v]	*v*	*Virus, zivil* (vgl. § 30)

(1.2) Konsonantenverbindungen

Laute	Buchstaben	Beispiele
[dʒ]	*g*	*Gentleman, Gin, Manager, Teenager*
	j	*Jazz, Jeans, Jeep, Job, Pyjama*
[lj] / [j]	*ll*	*Billard, Bouillon, brillant, Guerilla, Medaille, Pavillon, Taille*
[nj]	*gn*	*Champagner, Kampagne, Lasagne*
[ts]	*c*	*Aceton, Celsius, Cellophan*
	t (vor [i] + Vokal)	sehr häufig im Suffix *-tion;* außerdem häufig in Fällen wie *-tie, -tiell, -tiös: Funktion, Nation, Produktion; Aktie, partiell, infektiös*
[tʃ]	*c*	*Cello, Cembalo*
	ch	*Chip, Coach, Ranch*
	ge, dge	*College, Bridge*

(2) Doppelschreibungen

Im Prozess der Integration entlehnter Wörter können fremdsprachige und integrierte Schreibung nebeneinander stehen. (Zu Haupt- und Nebenformen siehe das Wörterverzeichnis.)

Laute	Buchstaben	Beispiele
[f]	*ph – f*	*-photo- – -foto-*, zum Beispiel *Photographie – Fotografie* *-graph- – -graf-*, zum Beispiel *Graphik – Grafik* *-phon- – -fon-*, zum Beispiel *Mikrophon – Mikrofon* *Delphin – Delfin, phantastisch – fantastisch*
[g]	*gh – g*	*Ghetto – Getto, Joghurt – Jogurt,* *Spaghetti – Spagetti*
[j]	*y – j*	*Yacht – Jacht, Yoga – Joga,* *Mayonnaise – Majonäse*
[k]	*c – k*	*Calcit – Kalzit, Caritas – Karitas,* *Code – Kode, codieren – kodieren, circa – zirka*
	qu – k	*Bouquet – Buket(t), Kommuniqué – Kommunikee*
[r]	*rh – r*	*Katarrh – Katarr, Myrrhe – Myrre*
[s]	*c– ss, ß*	*Facette – Fassette, Necessaire – Nessessär,* *Sauce – Soße*
[ʃ]	*ch – sch*	*Anchovis – Anschovis, Chicorée – Schikoree,* *Sketch Sketsch*
[t]	*th – t*	*Kathode – Katode, Panther – Panter,* *Thunfisch – Tunfisch*
[ts]	*c – z*	*Acetat – Azetat, Calcit – Kalzit,* *Penicillin – Penizillin, circa – zirka*
	t – z (vor [i] + Vokal)	*pretiös – preziös, Pretiosen – Preziosen;* *potentiell – potenziell* (wegen *Potenz*), *substantiell – substanziell* (wegen *Substanz*)

B Getrennt- und Zusammenschreibung

0 Vorbemerkungen

(1) Die Getrennt- und Zusammenschreibung betrifft die Schreibung von Wörtern, die im Text unmittelbar benachbart und aufeinander bezogen sind. Handelt es sich um die Bestandteile von Wortgruppen, so schreibt man sie voneinander getrennt. Handelt es sich um die Bestandteile von Zusammensetzungen, so schreibt man sie zusammen. Manchmal können dieselben Bestandteile sowohl eine Wortgruppe als auch eine Zusammensetzung bilden. Die Verwendung als Wortgruppe oder als Zusammensetzung kann dabei von der Aussageabsicht des Schreibenden abhängen.

(2) Bei der Regelung der Getrennt- und Zusammenschreibung wird davon ausgegangen, dass die getrennte Schreibung der Wörter der Normalfall und daher allein die Zusammenschreibung regelungsbedürftig ist.

(3) Soweit dies möglich ist, werden zu den Regeln formale Kriterien aufgeführt, mit deren Hilfe sich entscheiden lässt, ob man im betreffenden Fall getrennt oder ob man zusammenschreibt. So wird zum Beispiel stets zusammengeschrieben, wenn der erste oder der zweite Bestandteil in dieser Form als selbständiges Wort nicht vorkommt (wie bei *wissbegierig, zuinnerst*). So wird zum Beispiel stets getrennt geschrieben, wenn der erste oder der zweite Bestandteil erweitert ist (wie bei *viele Kilometer weit*, aber *kilometerweit; irgend so ein*, aber *irgendein*).

(4) Bei den verschiedenen Wortarten sind – auch in Abhängigkeit von sprachlichen Entwicklungsprozessen – spezielle Bedingungen zu beachten. Daher ist die folgende Darstellung nach der Wortart der Zusammensetzung gegliedert:

1 Verb (§ 33 bis § 35)
2 Adjektiv und Partizip (§ 36)
3 Substantiv (§ 37 bis § 38)
4 Andere Wortarten (§ 39)

1 Verb

Zusätzlich zu der generellen Einteilung in Wortgruppen (wie *in die Ferne sehen*) und Zusammensetzungen (wie *fernsehen*) sind bei Verben zu unterscheiden:

a) untrennbare Zusammensetzungen wie *maßregeln, langweilen*

Untrennbare Zusammensetzungen erkennt man daran, dass die Reihenfolge der Bestandteile stets unverändert bleibt.

maß + regeln: Wer jemanden *maßregelt* ... Man *maßregelte* ihn. Niemand wagte, ihn zu *maßregeln*. Er wurde offiziell *gemaßregelt*.

Siehe im Einzelnen § 33.

b) trennbare Zusammensetzungen wie *hinzukommen, fehlgehen, bereithalten, wundernehmen*

Trennbare Zusammensetzungen erkennt man daran, dass die Reihenfolge der Bestandteile in Abhängigkeit von ihrer Stellung im Satz wechselt.

hinzu + kommen: Wenn dieses Argument *hinzukommt* ... Dieses Argument scheint *hinzuzukommen*. Dieses Argument ist *hinzugekommen*.

Dieses Argument *kommt hinzu*. Dieses Argument *kommt* erschwerend *hinzu*.

Siehe im Einzelnen § 34.

§ 33 Substantive, Adjektive oder Partikeln können mit Verben untrennbare Zusammensetzungen bilden. Man schreibt sie stets zusammen.

Dies betrifft

(1) Zusammensetzungen aus Substantiv + Verb, zum Beispiel:

brandmarken (gebrandmarkt, zu brandmarken), handhaben, lobpreisen, maßregeln, nachtwandeln, schlafwandeln, schlussfolgern, wehklagen, wetteifern

E_1: In einzelnen Fällen stehen Zusammensetzung und Wortgruppe nebeneinander, zum Beispiel:

danksagen (er danksagt) oder *Dank sagen (er sagt Dank); gewährleisten (sie gewährleistet)* oder *Gewähr leisten (sie leistet Gewähr)*

E_2: Eine Reihe untrennbarer Zusammensetzungen wird fast nur im Infinitiv oder substantivisch, in Einzelfällen auch im Partizip I und im Partizip II gebraucht, zum Beispiel:

bauchreden, bergsteigen, bruchlanden, bruchrechnen, brustschwimmen, kopfrechnen, notlanden, punktschweißen, sandstrahlen, schutzimpfen, segelfliegen, seiltanzen, seitenschwimmen, sonnenbaden, wettlaufen, wettrennen, zwangsräumen

(2) Zusammensetzungen aus Adjektiv + Verb, zum Beispiel:

frohlocken (frohlockt, zu frohlocken), langweilen, liebäugeln, liebkosen, vollbringen, vollenden, weissagen

(3) Zusammensetzungen mit den Partikeln *durch-, hinter-, über-, um-, unter-, wider-, wieder-* + Verb (mit Ton auf dem zweiten Bestandteil), zum Beispiel:

durchbrechen (er durchbricht die Regel, zu durchbrechen), hintergehen, übersetzen (er übersetzt das Buch), umfahren, unterstellen, widersprechen, wiederholen

§ 34 Partikeln, Adjektive oder Substantive können mit Verben trennbare Zusammensetzungen bilden. Man schreibt sie nur im Infinitiv, im Partizip I und im Partizip II sowie im Nebensatz bei Endstellung des Verbs zusammen.

Zu Verbindungen mit dem Verb *sein* siehe § 35.

Dies betrifft

(1) Zusammensetzungen aus Partikel + Verb mit den folgenden ersten Bestandteilen:

ab- (Beispiele: *abändern, abbauen, abbeißen, abbestellen, abbiegen*), *an-, auf-, aus-, bei-, beisammen-, da-, dabei-, dafür-, dagegen-, daher-, dahin-, daneben-, dar-, d(a)ran-, d(a)rein-, da(r)nieder-, darum-, davon-, dawider-, dazu-, dazwischen-, drauf-, drauflos-, drin-, durch-, ein-, einher-, empor-, entgegen-, entlang-, entzwei-, fort-, gegen-, gegenüber-, her-, herab-, heran-, herauf-, heraus-, herbei-, herein-, hernieder-, herüber-, herum-, herunter-, hervor-, herzu-, hin-, hinab-, hinan-, hinauf-, hinaus-, hindurch-, hinein-, hintan-, hintenüber-, hinterher-, hinüber-, hinunter-, hinweg-, hinzu-, inne-, los-, mit-, nach-, nieder-, über-, überein-, um-, umher-, umhin-, unter-, vor-, voran-, vorauf-, voraus-, vorbei-, vorher-, vorüber-, vorweg-, weg-, weiter-, wider-, wieder-, zu-, zurecht-, zurück-, zusammen-, zuvor-, zuwider-, zwischen-*

Auch: *auf- und abspringen, ein- und ausführen, hin- und hergehen* usw.

E_1: Aber als Wortgruppe: *dabei* (bei der genannten Tätigkeit) *sitzen, daher* (aus dem genannten Grund) *kommen, wieder* (erneut, nochmals) *gewinnen, zusammen* (gemeinsam) *spielen* usw.

E_2: Zu den trennbaren Zusammensetzungen gehören auch Zusammensetzungen mit *haben* und *werden* wie: *innehaben, vorhaben, voraushaben; innewerden*. Zu Verbindungen mit dem Verb *sein* siehe § 35.

(2) Zusammensetzungen aus Adverb oder Adjektiv + Verb, bei denen

(2.1) der erste, einfache Bestandteil in dieser Form als selbständiges Wort nicht vorkommt, zum Beispiel:

fehlgehen, fehlschlagen, feilbieten, kundgeben, kundtun, weismachen

(2.2) der erste Bestandteil in dieser Verbindung weder erweiterbar noch steigerbar ist, wobei die Negation *nicht* nicht als Erweiterung gilt, zum Beispiel:

bereithalten, bloßstellen, fernsehen, festsetzen (= bestimmen), freisprechen (= für nicht schuldig erklären), gutschreiben (= anrechnen), hochrechnen, schwarzarbeiten, totschlagen, wahrsagen (= prophezeien)

Zu Zweifelsfällen siehe § 34 E_3.

(3) Zusammensetzungen aus (teilweise auch verblasstem) Substantiv + Verb mit den folgenden ersten Bestandteilen:

heim-	zum Beispiel: *heimbringen, heimfahren, heimführen, heimgehen, heimkehren, heimleuchten, heimreisen, heimsuchen, heimzahlen*
irre-	*irreführen, irreleiten;* außerdem: *irrewerden*
preis-	*preisgeben*
stand-	*standhalten*
statt-	*stattfinden, stattgeben, statthaben*
teil-	*teilhaben, teilnehmen*
wett-	*wettmachen*
wunder-	*wundernehmen*

E_3: In den Fällen, die nicht durch § 34 (1) bis (3) geregelt sind, schreibt man getrennt. Siehe auch § 34 E_4.
Dies betrifft

(1) Partikel, Adverb, Adjektiv oder Substantiv + Verb in finiter Form am Satzanfang, zum Beispiel:

Hinzu kommt, dass ...
Fehl ging er in der Annahme, dass ...
Bereit hält er sich für den Fall, dass ...
Wunder nimmt nur, dass ...

(2) (zusammengesetztes) Adverb + Verb, zum Beispiel:

abhanden kommen, anheim fallen (geben, stellen), beiseite legen (stellen, schieben), fürlieb nehmen, überhand nehmen, vonstatten gehen, vorlieb nehmen, zugute halten (kommen, tun), zunichte machen, zupass kommen, zustatten kommen, zuteil werden

Zu Fällen wie *zu Hilfe (kommen)* siehe § 39 E_2 (2.1); zu Fällen wie *infrage (stellen)/in Frage (stellen)* siehe § 39 E_3 (1).

aneinander denken (grenzen, legen), aufeinander achten (hören, stapeln), auseinander gehen (laufen, setzen), beieinander bleiben (sein, stehen), durcheinander bringen (reden, sein)

auswendig lernen, barfuß laufen, daheim bleiben; auch: *allein stehen, (sich) quer stellen*

abseits stehen, diesseits/jenseits liegen; abwärts gehen, aufwärts streben, rückwärts fallen, seitwärts treten, vorwärts blicken

(3) Adjektiv + Verb, wenn das Adjektiv in dieser Verbindung erweiterbar oder steigerbar ist, wenigstens durch *sehr* oder *ganz*, zum Beispiel:

bekannt machen (etwas noch bekannter machen, etwas ganz bekannt machen), fern liegen (ferner liegen, sehr fern liegen), fest halten, frei sprechen (= ohne Manuskript sprechen), genau nehmen, gut gehen, gut schreiben (= lesbar, verständlich schreiben), hell strahlen, kurz treten, langsam arbeiten, laut reden, leicht fallen, locker sitzen, nahe bringen, sauber schreiben, schlecht gehen, schnell laufen, schwer nehmen, zufrieden stellen

Fälle, in denen der erste Bestandteil eine Ableitung auf *-ig, -isch, -lich* ist, zum Beispiel:

lästig fallen, übrig bleiben; kritisch denken, spöttisch reden; freundlich grüßen, gründlich säubern

(4) Partizip + Verb, zum Beispiel:

gefangen nehmen (halten), geschenkt bekommen, getrennt schreiben, verloren gehen

(5) Substantiv + Verb, zum Beispiel:

Angst haben, Auto fahren, Diät halten, Eis laufen, Feuer fangen, Fuß fassen, Kopf stehen, Leid tun, Maß halten, Not leiden, Not tun, Pleite gehen, Posten stehen, Rad fahren, Rat suchen, Schlange stehen, Schuld tragen, Ski laufen, Walzer tanzen

(6) Verb (Infinitiv) + Verb, zum Beispiel:
kennen lernen, liegen lassen, sitzen bleiben, spazieren gehen

E_4: Lässt sich in einzelnen Fällen der Gruppe aus Adjektiv + Verb zwischen § 34 (2.2) und § 34 E_3 (3) keine klare Entscheidung für Getrennt- oder Zusammenschreibung treffen, so bleibt es dem Schreibenden überlassen, ob er sie als Wortgruppe oder als Zusammensetzung verstanden wissen will.

Zu den Wortgruppen mit einem Partizip als letztem Bestandteil wie *abhanden gekommen, sitzen geblieben* siehe § 36 E_1 (1).

Zu den Substantivierungen wie *das Abhandenkommen, das Autofahren, das Sitzenbleiben* siehe § 37 (2).

§ 35 Verbindungen mit *sein* gelten nicht als Zusammensetzung. Dementsprechend schreibt man stets getrennt.

Beispiele:
außerstande sein (auch: *außer Stande sein;* § 39 E_3 (1)), *beisammen sein (wenn sie beisammen sind), da sein, fertig sein, inne sein, los sein, pleite sein* (siehe auch § 56 (1)), *vonnöten sein, vorbei sein, vorhanden sein, vorüber sein, zufrieden sein, zuhanden sein, zumute sein* (auch: *zu Mute sein;* § 39 E_3 (1)), *zurück sein, zusammen sein*

2 Adjektiv und Partizip

Für Partizipien gelten dieselben Regeln wie für Adjektive; zu diesen werden hier auch die Kardinal- und die Ordinalzahlen gerechnet.

Bei den Adjektiven/Partizipien sind zu unterscheiden

(1) Zusammensetzungen wie: *angsterfüllt, altersschwach, schwerstbehindert, wehklagend, blaugrau, bitterböse, dreizehn, siebzehnte*

(2) Wortgruppen wie: *abhanden gekommen, Rat suchend, sitzen geblieben, riesig groß, blendend weiß, mehrere Jahre lang; zwei Milliarden*

Siehe im Einzelnen § 36.

Zu Fällen wie *nicht öffentlich/nichtöffentlich* siehe § 36 E_2.

§ 36 Substantive, Adjektive, Verbstämme, Adverbien oder Pronomen können mit Adjektiven oder Partizipien Zusammensetzungen bilden. Man schreibt sie zusammen.

Dies betrifft

(1) Zusammensetzungen, bei denen der erste Bestandteil für eine Wortgruppe steht, zum Beispiel:

angsterfüllt (= von Angst erfüllt), bahnbrechend (= sich eine Bahn brechend), butterweich (= weich wie Butter), fingerbreit (= einen Finger breit), freudestrahlend (= vor Freude strahlend), herzerquickend (= das Herz erquickend), hitzebeständig (= gegen Hitze beständig), jahrelang (= mehrere Jahre lang), knielang (= lang bis zum Knie), meterhoch (= einen oder mehrere Meter hoch), milieubedingt (= durch das Milieu bedingt)

denkfaul, fernsehmüde, lernbegierig, röstfrisch, schreibgewandt, tropfnass; selbstbewusst, selbstsicher

Mit Fugenelement, zum Beispiel: *altersschwach, anlehnungsbedürftig, geschlechtsreif, lebensfremd, sonnenarm, werbewirksam*

(2) Zusammensetzungen, bei denen der erste oder der zweite Bestandteil in dieser Form nicht selbständig vorkommt, zum Beispiel:

einfach, zweifach; letztmalig, redselig, saumselig, schwerstbehindert, schwindsüchtig; blauäugig, großspurig, kleinmütig, vieldeutig

(3) Zusammensetzungen, bei denen das dem Partizip zugrunde liegende Verb entsprechend § 33 bzw. § 34 mit dem ersten Bestandteil zusammengeschrieben wird, zum Beispiel:

wehklagend (wegen *wehklagen*); *herunterfallend, heruntergefallen; irreführend, irregeführt; teilnehmend, teilgenommen*

(4) Zusammensetzungen aus gleichrangigen (nebengeordneten) Adjektiven, zum Beispiel:

blaugrau, dummdreist, feuchtwarm, grünblau, nasskalt, taubstumm

Zur Schreibung mit Bindestrich siehe § 45 (2).

(5) Zusammensetzungen mit bedeutungsverstärkenden oder bedeutungsmindernden ersten Bestandteilen, die zum Teil lange Reihen bilden, zum Beispiel:

bitter- (bitterböse, bitterernst, bitterkalt), brand-, dunkel-, erz-, extra-, gemein-, grund-, hyper-, lau-, minder-, stock-, super-, tod-, ultra-, ur-, voll-

(6) mehrteilige Kardinalzahlen unter einer Million sowie alle mehrteiligen Ordinalzahlen, zum Beispiel:

dreizehn, siebenhundert, neunzehnhundertneunundachtzig; der siebzehnte Oktober, der einhundertste Geburtstag, der fünfhunderttausendste Fall, der zweimillionste Besucher

Beachte aber Substantive wie *Dutzend, Million, Milliarde, Billion,* zum Beispiel: *zwei Dutzend Hühner, eine Million Teilnehmer, zwei Milliarden fünfhunderttausend Menschen*

E_1: In den Fällen, die nicht durch § 36 (1) bis (6) geregelt sind, schreibt man getrennt. Siehe auch § 36 E_2.

Dies betrifft

(1) Fälle, bei denen das dem Partizip zugrunde liegende Verb vom ersten Bestandteil getrennt geschrieben wird, und zwar

(1.1) entsprechend § 35, zum Beispiel:

beisammen gewesen (wegen *beisammen sein*), *zurück gewesen*

(1.2) entsprechend § 34 E_3 (2) bis (6), zum Beispiel:

abhanden gekommen (abhanden kommen), auseinander laufend, auswendig gelernt, vorwärts blickend
hell strahlend (hell strahlen), laut redend
gefangen genommen (gefangen nehmen), verloren gegangen
Rat suchend (Rat suchen), Not leidend, Rad fahrend
kennen gelernt (kennen lernen), sitzen geblieben

(2) Fälle, bei denen der erste Bestandteil eine Ableitung auf *-ig, -isch, -lich* ist, zum Beispiel:

riesig groß, mikroskopisch klein, schrecklich nervös

Zur Schreibung mit Bindestrich in Fällen wie *wissenschaftlich-technisch* siehe § 45 (2).

(3) Fälle, bei denen der erste Bestandteil ein (adjektivisches) Partizip ist, zum Beispiel:

abschreckend hässlich, blendend weiß, gestochen scharf, kochend heiß, leuchtend rot, strahlend hell

(4) Fälle, bei denen der erste Bestandteil erweitert oder gesteigert ist bzw. erweitert oder gesteigert werden kann, zum Beispiel:

vor Freude strahlend, gegen Hitze beständig, zwei Finger breit, drei Meter hoch, mehrere Jahre lang, seiner selbst bewusst; sehr ernst gemeint, leichter verdaulich

dicht behaart, dünn bewachsen, schwach bevölkert

E_2: Lässt sich in einzelnen Fällen der Gruppen aus Adjektiv, Adverb oder Pronomen + Adjektiv/Partizip zwischen § 36 und § 36 E_1 keine klare Entscheidung für Getrennt- oder Zusammenschreibung treffen, so bleibt es dem Schreibenden überlassen, ob er sie als Wortgruppe oder als Zusammensetzung verstanden wissen will, zum Beispiel *nicht öffentlich* (Wortgruppe)/*nichtöffentlich* (Zusammensetzung).

3 Substantiv

Bei den Substantiven sind zu unterscheiden

(1) Zusammensetzungen, bei denen der letzte Bestandteil ein Substantiv ist, zum Beispiel: *Feuerstein, Fünfkampf, Achtelliter*

(2) substantivisch gebrauchte Zusammensetzungen, bei denen der letzte Bestandteil kein Substantiv ist, zum Beispiel: *das Autofahren, das Stelldichein*

(3) Zusammensetzungen mit einem Eigennamen oder einer Einwohnerbezeichnung als erstem Bestandteil, zum Beispiel *Goethegedicht, Danaergeschenk*

(4) Zusammensetzungen, die als Ganzes einen Eigennamen bilden, zum Beispiel: *Bahnhofstraße*.

§ 37 Substantive, Adjektive, Verbstämme, Pronomen oder Partikeln können mit Substantiven Zusammensetzungen bilden. Man schreibt sie ebenso wie mehrteilige Substantivierungen zusammen.

Dies betrifft

(1) Zusammensetzungen, bei denen der letzte Bestandteil ein Substantiv ist, zum Beispiel:

Feuerstein, Lebenswerk, Kirschbaum, Kohlenwasserstoff, Wochenlohn, Dienstagabend

Airbag, Bandleader, Football, Ghostwriter, Mountainbike, Nightclub, Streetwork, Weekend, Worldcup

Zweierbob, Fünfkampf, Selbstsucht, Leerlauf, Faultier, Außenpolitik, Rastplatz, Nichtraucher, Ichsucht, Achtzigerjahre (auch *achtziger Jahre*), *Vierachteltakt, Dreiviertelliterflasche*

Background, Bestseller, Bluejeans, Bypassoperation, Clearingstelle, Hardware, Secondhandshop, Selfmademan, Swimmingpool, Upperclass; Bigband, Blackbox, Softdrink

E_1: Bei Verbindungen aus Adjektiv und Substantiv wie in *Bigband, Blackbox, Softdrink* ist in Anlehnung an die Herkunftssprache auch Getrenntschreibung möglich: *Big Band, Black Box, Soft Drink*. Zur Groß- und Kleinschreibung siehe § 55 (3); zur Schreibung mit Bindestrich siehe § 45 (2).

ein Viertelkilogramm, drei Achtelliter, fünf Hundertstelsekunden

E_2: In Verbindung mit einer unmittelbar folgenden Maßbezeichnung kann die Bruchzahl auch als Zahladjektiv aufgefasst werden, zum Beispiel:
ein viertel Kilogramm, drei achtel Liter, fünf hundertstel Sekunden

(2) Substantivisch gebrauchte Zusammensetzungen, bei denen der letzte Bestandteil kein Substantiv ist, zum Beispiel:
das Autofahren (aber *Auto fahren*), *das Ratholen, das Abhandenkommen, das Unrechttun, das Aufrechtgehen, das Bekanntmachen, das Sitzenbleiben, das Liegenlassen, das Infragestellen; das Suppengrün; das Stelldichein, das Vergissmeinnicht*

(3) Zusammensetzungen mit einem Eigennamen oder einer Einwohnerbezeichnung als erstem Bestandteil, zum Beispiel:
Goethegedicht, Europabrücke, Jakobsplan, Brennerpass, Glocknergruppe; Schweizergarde, Römerbrief, Danaergeschenk

(4) Zusammensetzungen, die als Ganzes einen Eigennamen bilden, insbesondere Straßennamen, zum Beispiel:
Bahnhofstraße, Drosselgasse, Neugraben

§ 38 Ableitungen auf *-er* von geographischen Eigennamen, die sich auf die geographische Lage beziehen, schreibt man von dem folgenden Substantiv getrennt.

Beispiele:
Allgäuer Alpen, Brandenburger Tor, Naumburger Dom, Potsdamer Abkommen, Thüringer Wald, Wiener Straße

4 Andere Wortarten

Manche mehrteilige Adverbien, Konjunktionen, Präpositionen und Pronomen sind aus Elementen verschiedener Wortarten entstanden. Zum Teil sind sie als Wortgruppe erhalten geblieben, zum Teil haben sie sich zu einer Zusammensetzung entwickelt.

In Zweifelsfällen siehe das Wörterverzeichnis.

§ 39 Mehrteilige Adverbien, Konjunktionen, Präpositionen und Pronomen schreibt man zusammen, wenn die Wortart, die Wortform oder die Bedeutung der einzelnen Bestandteile nicht mehr deutlich erkennbar sind.

Dies betrifft

(1) Adverbien, zum Beispiel:
bergab, bergauf; kopfüber; landaus, landein; stromabwärts, stromaufwärts; tagsüber; zweifelsohne

-dessen	*indessen, infolgedessen, unterdessen*
-dings	*allerdings, neuerdings, schlechterdings*
-falls	*allenfalls, ander(e)nfalls, keinesfalls, schlimmstenfalls*
-halber	*ehrenhalber, umständehalber*
-mal	*diesmal, einmal, zweimal, keinmal, manchmal*
-mals	*erstmals, letztmals, vielmals*
-maßen	*dermaßen, einigermaßen, gleichermaßen, solchermaßen, zugegebenermaßen*
-orten	*allerorten, mancherorten*
-orts	*allerorts, ander(e)norts, mancherorts*
-seits	*allseits, allerseits, and(e)rerseits, einerseits, meinerseits*
-so	*ebenso, genauso, geradeso, sowieso, umso, wieso*
-teils	*einesteils, großenteils, meistenteils*

-wärts	*himmelwärts, meerwärts, seitwärts*
-wegen	*deinetwegen, deswegen, meinetwegen*
-wegs	*geradewegs, keineswegs, unterwegs*
-weil	*alldieweil, alleweil, derweil*
-weilen	*bisweilen, derweilen, zuweilen*
-weise	*probeweise, klugerweise, schlauerweise*
-zeit	*all(e)zeit, derzeit, jederzeit, seinerzeit, zurzeit*
-zeiten	*beizeiten, vorzeiten, zuzeiten*
-zu	*allzu, geradezu, hierzu, immerzu*
bei-	*beileibe, beinahe, beisammen, beizeiten*
der-	*derart, dereinst, dergestalt, dermaßen, derweil(en), derzeit*
irgend-	*irgendeinmal, irgendwann, irgendwie, irgendwo, irgendwohin*
nichts-	*nichtsdestominder, nichtsdestoweniger*
zu-	*zuallererst, zuallerletzt, zuallermeist, zuerst, zuhauf, zuhinterst, zuhöchst, zuletzt, zumal, zumeist, zumindest, zunächst, zuoberst, zutiefst, zuunterst, zuweilen, zuzeiten*

E_1: Zu Fällen wie *abhanden kommen, anheim fallen* siehe § 34 E_3 (2); zu Fällen wie *außerstand setzen/außer Stand setzen, imstande sein/im Stande sein* siehe unten E_3 (1).

(2) Konjunktionen, zum Beispiel:

anstatt (dass/zu), indem, inwiefern, sobald, sofern, solange, sooft, soviel, soweit

(3) Präpositionen, zum Beispiel:

anhand, anstatt (des/der), infolge, inmitten, zufolge, zuliebe

(4) Pronomen, zum Beispiel:

irgend-: irgendein, irgendetwas, irgendjemand, irgendwas, irgendwelcher, irgendwer

E_2: In anderen Fällen schreibt man getrennt. Siehe auch § 39 E_3 (1).

Dies betrifft

(1) Fälle, bei denen ein Bestandteil erweitert ist, zum Beispiel:

dies eine Mal (aber *diesmal*), *den Strom abwärts* (aber *stromabwärts*)

der Ehre halber (aber *ehrenhalber*), *in keinem Fall, das erste Mal, ein einziges Mal, in bekannter Weise, zu jeder Zeit, eine Zeit lang*

irgend so ein/eine/einer (aber *irgendein*), *irgend so etwas*

(2) Fälle, bei denen die Wortart, die Wortform oder die Bedeutung der einzelnen Bestandteile deutlich erkennbar sind, und zwar

(2.1) Fügungen in adverbialer Verwendung, zum Beispiel:

zu Ende (gehen, kommen), zu Fuß (gehen), zu Hause (bleiben, sein) (österreichisch und schweizerisch auch: *zuhause bleiben, sein*), *zu Hilfe (kommen), zu Lande, zu Wasser und zu Lande, zu Schaden (kommen) darüber hinaus, nach wie vor, vor allem*

(2.2) mehrteilige Konjunktionen, zum Beispiel:

ohne dass, statt dass, außer dass

(2.3) Fügungen in präpositionaler Verwendung, zum Beispiel:

zur Zeit (Goethes), zu Zeiten (Goethes)

(2.4) *so, wie* oder *zu* + Adjektiv, Adverb oder Pronomen, zum Beispiel:

so (wie, zu) hohe Häuser; er hat das schon so (wie, zu) oft gesagt; so (wie, zu) viel Geld; so (wie, zu) viele Leute; so (wie, zu) weit

(2.5) *gar kein, gar nicht, gar nichts, gar sehr, gar wohl*

E_3: In den folgenden Fällen bleibt es dem Schreibenden überlassen, ob er sie als Zusammensetzung oder als Wortgruppe verstanden wissen will:

(1) Fügungen in adverbialer Verwendung, zum Beispiel:

außerstand setzen/außer Stand setzen; außerstande sein/außer Stande sein; imstande sein/im Stande sein; infrage stellen/in Frage stellen; instand setzen/in Stand setzen; zugrunde gehen/zu Grunde gehen; zuleide tun/zu Leide tun; zumute sein/zu Mute sein; zurande kommen/zu Rande kommen; zuschanden machen, werden/zu Schanden machen, werden; zuschulden kommen lassen/zu Schulden kommen lassen; zustande bringen/zu Stande bringen; zutage fördern, treten/zu Tage fördern, treten; zuwege bringen/zu Wege bringen

(2) die Konjunktion

sodass/so dass

(3) Fügungen in präpositionaler Verwendung, zum Beispiel:

anstelle/an Stelle; aufgrund/auf Grund; aufseiten/auf Seiten; mithilfe/mit Hilfe; vonseiten/von Seiten; zugunsten/zu Gunsten; zulasten/zu Lasten; zuungunsten/zu Ungunsten

C Schreibung mit Bindestrich

0 Vorbemerkungen

(1) Der Bindestrich bietet dem Schreibenden die Möglichkeit, anstelle der sonst bei Zusammensetzungen und Ableitungen üblichen Zusammenschreibung die einzelnen Bestandteile als solche zu kennzeichnen, sie gegeneinander abzusetzen und sie dadurch für den Lesenden hervorzuheben.

(2) Die Schreibung mit Bindestrich bei Fremdwörtern (zum Beispiel bei *7-Bit-Code, Stand-by-System*) folgt den für das Deutsche geltenden Regeln.

Die Schreibung mit Bindestrich bei Eigennamen entspricht nicht immer den folgenden Regeln, so dass nur allgemeine Hinweise gegeben werden können. Zusammensetzungen aus Eigennamen und Substantiv zur Benennung von Schulen, Universitäten, Betrieben, Firmen und ähnlichen Institutionen werden so geschrieben, wie sie amtlich festgelegt sind. In Zweifelsfällen sollte man nach § 46 bis § 52 schreiben.

Steht ein Bindestrich am Zeilenende, so gilt er zugleich als Trennungsstrich.

(3) Zu unterscheiden sind:

- Zusammensetzungen und Ableitungen, die keine Eigennamen als Bestandteile enthalten (§ 40 bis § 45)
- Zusammensetzungen und Ableitungen, die Eigennamen als Bestandteile enthalten (§ 46 bis § 52)
- Gruppen, in denen man den Bindestrich setzen muss (§ 40 bis § 44; § 46 und § 48 bis § 50), und solche, in denen der Gebrauch des Bindestrichs dem Schreibenden freigestellt ist (§ 45, § 51 bis § 52).

Zum Ergänzungsstrich (zum Beispiel in *Haupt- und Nebeneingang*) siehe § 98.

1 Zusammensetzungen und Ableitungen, die keine Eigennamen als Bestandteile enthalten

§ 40 Man setzt einen Bindestrich in Zusammensetzungen mit Einzelbuchstaben, Abkürzungen oder Ziffern.

Dies betrifft

(1) Zusammensetzungen mit Einzelbuchstaben, zum Beispiel:

A-Dur (ebenso *Cis-Dur*), *b-Moll, β-Strahlen, i-Punkt, n-Eck, S-Kurve, s-Laut, s-förmig, T-Shirt, T-Träger, x-beliebig, x-beinig, x-mal, y-Achse; Dativ-e, Zungenspitzen-r, Fugen-s*

(2) Zusammensetzungen mit Abkürzungen und Initialwörtern, zum Beispiel:

dpa-Meldung, D-Zug, Kfz-Schlosser, km-Bereich, UNO-Sicherheitsrat, VIP-Lounge; Fußball-WM, Lungen-Tbc; H_2O*-gesättigt, DGB-eigen, Na-haltig, UV-bestrahlt; Abt.-Leiter, Inf.-Büro*

Abt.-Ltr. (= Abteilungsleiter), Dipl.-Ing. (= Diplomingenieur), Tgb.-Nr. (= Tagebuchnummer), Telegr.-Adr. (= Telegrammadresse)

E: Aber ohne Bindestrich bei Kurzformen von Wörtern (Kürzeln), zum Beispiel: *Busfahrt, Akkubehälter*

(3) Zusammensetzungen mit Ziffern, zum Beispiel:

3-Tonner, 2-Pfünder, 8-Zylinder; 5-mal, 4-silbig, 100-prozentig, 1-zeilig, 17-jährig, der 17-Jährige

8:6-Sieg, 2:3-Niederlage, der 5:3-[2:1-]Sieg (auch *5:3[2:1]-Sieg*)

$^2/_3$*-Mehrheit,* $^3/_4$*-Takt,* 2^n*-Eck*

§ 41 Vor Suffixen setzt man nur dann einen Bindestrich, wenn sie mit einem Einzelbuchstaben verbunden werden.

Beispiele:

der x-te, zum x-ten Mal, die n-te Potenz

E: Aber: *abclich, ÖVPler; der 68er, ein 32stel, 100%ig, 25fach, das 25fache*

§ 42 Bilden Verbindungen aus Ziffern und Suffixen den vorderen Teil einer Zusammensetzung, so setzt man nach dem Suffix einen Bindestrich.

Beispiele:

ein 100stel-Millimeter, die 61er-Bildröhre, eine 25er-Gruppe, in den 80er-Jahren (auch *in den 80er Jahren*)

E: Aber ausgeschrieben: *die Zweierbeziehung, die Zehnergruppe, die Achtzigerjahre* (auch *die achtziger Jahre*)

§ 43 Man setzt Bindestriche in substantivisch gebrauchten Zusammensetzungen (Aneinanderreihungen), insbesondere bei substantivisch gebrauchten Infinitiven mit mehr als zwei Bestandteilen.

Beispiele:

das Entweder-oder, das Teils-teils, das Als-ob, das Sowohl-als-auch; der Boogie-Woogie, das Walkie-Talkie; das Make-up, das Rooming-in

das Auf-die-lange-Bank-Schieben, das An-den-Haaren-Herbeiziehen, das In-den-Tag-Hineinträumen, das Von-der-Hand-in-den-Mund-Leben

E: Dies gilt nicht für einfache Zusammensetzungen mit Infinitiv, zum Beispiel:

das Autofahren, das Ballspielen, beim Walzertanzen

Zur Groß- und Kleinschreibung siehe § 57 E_3.

§ 44 Man setzt einen Bindestrich zwischen allen Bestandteilen mehrteiliger Zusammensetzungen, in denen eine Wortgruppe oder eine Zusammensetzung mit Bindestrich auftritt.

Beispiele:

A-Dur-Tonleiter, D-Zug-Wagen, S-Kurven-reich (aber *kurvenreich*), *Vitamin-B-haltig* (aber *vitaminhaltig*), *K.-o.-Schlag, UV-Strahlen-gefährdet* (aber *strahlengefährdet*), *Dipl.-Ing.-Ök.*

2-Mark-Stück, 800-Jahr-Feier, 35-Stunden-Woche, 10-Pfennig-Briefmarke, 8-Zylinder-Motor, 400-m-Lauf, 2-kg-Büchse, 3-Zimmer-Wohnung, $^1/_2$-kg-Packung

Berg-und-Tal-Bahn, Frage-und-Antwort-Spiel; Kopf-an-Kopf-Rennen, Mund-zu-Mund-Beatmung, Wort-für-Wort-Übersetzung

Arzt-Patient-Verhältnis, Grund-Folge-Beziehung, Links-rechts-Kombination, Hals-Nasen-Ohren-Klinik, Ost-West-Gespräche, September-Oktober-Heft (auch *September/Oktober-Heft;* siehe § 106 (1))

Ad-hoc-Bildung, Als-ob-Philosophie, De-facto-Anerkennung, Do-it-yourself-Bewegung, Erste-Hilfe-Lehrgang, Go-go-Girl, Rooming-in-System; Make-up-freie Haut, Ruhe-vor-dem-Sturm-artig, Fata-Morgana-ähnlich; Trimm-dich-Pfad

Abend-Make-up, Wasch-Eau-de-Cologne

§ 45 Man kann einen Bindestrich setzen zur Hervorhebung einzelner Bestandteile, zur Gliederung unübersichtlicher Zusammensetzungen, zur Vermeidung von Missverständnissen, in Zusammensetzungen aus gleichrangigen (nebengeordneten) Adjektiven oder beim Zusammentreffen von drei gleichen Buchstaben.

Dies betrifft

(1) Hervorhebung einzelner Bestandteile, zum Beispiel:

der dass-Satz, die Ich-Erzählung, das Ist-Aufkommen, die Kann-Bestimmung, die Soll-Stärke; die Hoch-Zeit, das Nach-Denken, Vor-Sätze, be-greifen

(2) Unübersichtliche Zusammensetzungen, auch mit Fremdwörtern, zum Beispiel:

Arbeiter-Unfallversicherungsgesetz, Haushalt-Mehrzweckküchenmaschine, Lotto-Annahmestelle, Mosel-Winzergenossenschaft, Software-Angebotsmesse, Ultraschall-Messgerät; Desktop-Publishing, Midlife-Crisis

der wissenschaftlich-technische Fortschritt, ein lateinisch-deutsches Wörterbuch, deutsch-österreichische Angelegenheiten; physikalisch-chemisch-biologische Prozesse

Zu Verbindungen wie *Blackbox/Black Box* siehe § 37 E_1.

(3) Vermeidung von Missverständnissen, zum Beispiel:

Drucker-Zeugnis und *Druck-Erzeugnis, Musiker-Leben* und *Musik-Erleben; re-integrieren*

(4) Zusammentreffen von drei gleichen Buchstaben in Zusammensetzungen, zum Beispiel: *Hawaii-Inseln, Kaffee-Ersatz, See-Elefant, Zoo-Orchester; Bett-Tuch, Schiff-Fahrt, Schrott-Transport*

2 Zusammensetzungen und Ableitungen, die Eigennamen als Bestandteile enthalten

§ 46 Man setzt einen Bindestrich in Zusammensetzungen, die als zweiten Bestandteil einen Eigennamen enthalten oder die aus zwei Eigennamen bestehen.

Dies betrifft

(1) Zusammensetzungen mit Personennamen, zum Beispiel:
Frau Müller-Weber, Herr Schmidt-Wilpert; Eva-Maria (auch *Eva Maria, Evamaria*), *Karl-Heinz* (auch *Karl Heinz, Karlheinz)*

die Bäcker-Anna, der Schneider-Karl; Blumen-Richter, Foto-Müller, Möbel-Schmidt; Müller-Lüdenscheid, Schneider-Partenkirchen

E_1: Die standesamtliche Schreibung mehrteiliger Personennamen kann von dieser Regelung abweichen.

(2) geographische Eigennamen, zum Beispiel:
Annaberg-Buchholz, Baden-Württemberg, Flughafen Köln-Bonn, Neu-Bamberg, Rheinland-Pfalz, Sachsen-Anhalt

E_2: Die amtliche Schreibung von Zusammensetzungen mit einem geographischen Eigennamen, die ihrerseits zu einem geographischen Eigennamen geworden sind, kann von dieser Regelung abweichen.

Adjektiv + Eigenname, zum Beispiel:
Neu Seehagen, Neubrandenburg

Immer Getrenntschreibung bei *Sankt*, zum Beispiel: *Sankt Georgen (St. Georgen)*

Substantiv + Eigenname, zum Beispiel:
Nordkorea, Königs Wusterhausen, Marktredwitz, Markt Indersdorf, Stadtlauringen, Stadt Rottenmann

Immer Getrenntschreibung bei *Bad*, zum Beispiel: *Bad Säckingen*

Zwei Eigennamen, zum Beispiel:
Grindelwald Grund, Rostock Lütten Klein; Berlin Schönefeld (auch *Berlin-Schönefeld*)

§ 47 Werden Zusammensetzungen mit einem ursprünglichen Personennamen als Gattungsbezeichnung gebraucht, so schreibt man ohne Bindestrich zusammen.

Beispiele:
Gänseliesel, Heulsuse, Meckerfritze

§ 48 Bei Ableitungen von Verbindungen mit einem Eigennamen als zweitem Bestandteil bleibt der Bindestrich erhalten.

Beispiele:
baden-württembergisch (Baden-Württemberg), rheinland-pfälzisch, alt-wienerische/Alt-Wiener Kaffeehäuser, Spree-Athener

§ 49 Bei Ableitungen von mehreren Eigennamen, von Titeln und Eigennamen oder von einem mehrteiligen Eigennamen setzt man einen Bindestrich.

Beispiele:
die sankt-gallischen/st.-gallischen Klosterschätze (St. Gallen), die gräflich-rieneckische Güterverwaltung (Graf Rieneck)

die kant-laplacesche Theorie (Kant und Laplace), der de-costersche Roman (de Coster), die gräflich-rienecksche Güterverwaltung (Graf Rieneck)

die Kant-Laplace'sche Theorie (Kant und Laplace), der de Coster'sche Roman (de Coster), die Gräflich-Rieneck'sche Güterverwaltung (Graf Rieneck)

Zur Groß- und Kleinschreibung und zur Schreibung mit Apostroph siehe § 62.

E: Bei Ableitungen auf *-er* kann man den Bindestrich weglassen, zum Beispiel:
die Bad-Schandauer (Bad Schandau)/Bad Schandauer, die Sankt-Galler/Sankt Galler, die New-Yorker/New Yorker

§ 50 Man setzt einen Bindestrich zwischen allen Bestandteilen mehrteiliger Zusammensetzungen, deren erste Bestandteile aus Eigennamen bestehen.

Beispiele:
Albrecht-Dürer-Allee, Heinrich-Heine-Platz, Kaiser-Karl-Ring, Ernst-Ludwig-Kirchner-Straße, Rainer-Maria-Rilke-Promenade, Thomas-Müntzer-Gasse

Elbe-Havel-Kanal, Oder-Neiße-Grenze, La-Plata-Mündung

Albert-Einstein-Gedenkstätte, Georg-Büchner-Preis, Jacob-und-Wilhelm-Grimm-Preis, Goethe-Schiller-Archiv, Johann-Sebastian-Bach-Gymnasium, Van-Gogh-Ausstellung

am Lago-di-Como-seitigen Abhang, Fidel-Castro-freundlich

§ 51 Man kann einen Bindestrich in Zusammensetzungen setzen, die als ersten Bestandteil einen Eigennamen haben, der besonders hervorgehoben werden soll, oder wenn der zweite Bestandteil bereits eine Zusammensetzung ist.

Beispiele:
Goethe-Ausgabe, Johannes-Passion, Richelieu-freundlich, Kafka-Kolloquium; Goethe-Geburtshaus, Brecht-Jubiläumsausgabe

Ganges-Ebene, Krim-Treffen, Mekong-Delta; Elbe-Wasserstandsmeldung, Helsinki-Nachfolgekonferenz

§ 52 Wird ein geographischer Eigenname von einem nachgestellten Substantiv näher bestimmt, so kann man einen Bindestrich setzen.

Beispiele:
Frankfurt Hauptbahnhof/Frankfurt-Hauptbahnhof, München Ost/München-Ost

D Groß- und Kleinschreibung

0 Vorbemerkungen

(1) Die Großschreibung, das heißt die Schreibung mit einem großen Anfangsbuchstaben, dient dem Schreibenden dazu, den Anfang bestimmter Texteinheiten sowie Wörter bestimmter Gruppen zu kennzeichnen und sie dadurch für den Lesenden hervorzuheben.

(2) Die Großschreibung wird im Deutschen verwendet zur Kennzeichnung von

- Überschriften, Werktiteln und dergleichen
- Satzanfängen
- Substantiven und Substantivierungen
- Eigennamen mit ihren nichtsubstantivischen Bestandteilen
- bestimmten festen nominalen Wortgruppen mit nichtsubstantivischen Bestandteilen
- Anredepronomen und Anreden

(3) Die Abgrenzung von Groß- und Kleinschreibung, wie sie sich in der Tradition der deutschen Orthographie herausgebildet hat, macht es erforderlich, neben den Regeln für die Großschreibung auch Regeln für die Kleinschreibung zu formulieren. Diese werden in den einzelnen Teilabschnitten jeweils im Anschluss an die Großschreibungsregeln angegeben. In einigen Fallgruppen ist eine eindeutige Zuweisung zur Groß- oder Kleinschreibung fragwürdig. Hier sind beide Schreibungen zulässig.

(4) Entsprechend gliedert sich die folgende Darstellung in die Abschnitte:

1 Kennzeichnung des Anfangs bestimmter Texteinheiten durch Großschreibung (§ 53: Überschriften, Werktitel und dergleichen; § 54: Ganzsätze)
2 Anwendung von Groß- oder Kleinschreibung bei bestimmten Wörtern und Wortgruppen
2.1 Substantive und Desubstantivierungen (§ 55 bis § 56)
2.2 Substantivierungen (§ 57 bis § 58)

1 Kennzeichnung des Anfangs bestimmter Texteinheiten durch Großschreibung

§ 53 Das erste Wort einer Überschrift, eines Werktitels, einer Anschrift und dergleichen schreibt man groß.

Dies betrifft unter anderem

(1) Überschriften und Werktitel (etwa von Büchern und Theaterstücken, Werken der bildenden Kunst und der Musik, Rundfunk- und Fernsehproduktionen), zum Beispiel:

Allmähliche Normalisierung im Erdbebengebiet
Hohe Schneeverwehungen behindern Autoverkehr
Keine Chance für eine diplomatische Lösung!
Kleines Wörterbuch der Stilkunde
Wo warst du, Adam?
Der kaukasische Kreidekreis
Der grüne Heinrich
Hundert Jahre Einsamkeit
Ungarische Rhapsodie
Unter den Dächern von Paris
Ein Fall für zwei

(2) Titel von Gesetzen, Verträgen, Deklarationen und dergleichen sowie Bezeichnungen für Veranstaltungen, zum Beispiel:

Bayerisches Hochschulgesetz
Potsdamer Abkommen
Internationaler Ärzte- und Ärztinnenkongress
Grüne Woche (in Berlin)

E_1: Die Großschreibung des ersten Wortes bleibt auch dann erhalten, wenn eine Überschrift, ein Werktitel und dergleichen innerhalb eines Textes gebraucht wird, zum Beispiel:

Das Theaterstück „Der kaukasische Kreidekreis" steht auf dem Programm. Sie lesen Kellers Roman „Der grüne Heinrich".

Wird dabei am Anfang ein Titel und dergleichen verkürzt oder sein Artikel verändert, so schreibt man das nächstfolgende Wort des Titels groß, zum Beispiel:

Wir haben im Theater Brechts „Kaukasischen Kreidekreis" gesehen. Sie lesen den „Grünen Heinrich".

Zur Schreibung nach Gliederungsangaben oder nach Auslassungszeichen und Zahlen siehe § 54 (5) und (6). Zum Gebrauch der Anführungszeichen siehe § 94 (1).

(3) Anschriften, Datumszeilen und Anreden sowie Grußformeln etwa in Briefen, zum Beispiel:

Donnerstag, 15. Februar 1996

Frau
Ulla Schröder
Rüdesheimer Str. 29
D-65197 Wiesbaden

Sehr geehrte Frau Schröder,

entsprechend unserer telefonischen Vereinbarung ...
... erwarten wir Ihre Antwort.

Mit freundlichen Grüßen

Werner Meier

E_2: Wenn man nach der Anrede – wie in der Schweiz üblich – auf ein Satzzeichen verzichtet, schreibt man das erste Wort des folgenden Abschnitts groß.

Siehe auch § 69 E_3.

§ 54

> Das erste Wort eines Ganzsatzes schreibt man groß.

Beispiele:

Gestern hat es geregnet. Du kommst bitte morgen! Hat er das wirklich gesagt?

Nachdem sie von der Reise zurückgekehrt war, hatte sie den dringenden Wunsch, ein Bad zu nehmen. Im Hausflur war es still, ich drückte erwartungsvoll auf die Klingel. Meine Freundin hatte den Zug versäumt, deshalb kam sie eine halbe Stunde zu spät. Wir sehen nach, was Paul macht. Sehen Sie nur, wie schön die Aussicht ist. Haben Sie ihn aufgefordert, die Wohnung zu verlassen?

Kommt doch schnell! Bitte die Türen schließen und Vorsicht bei der Abfahrt des Zuges!

Ob sie heute kommt? Nein, morgen. Warum nicht? Gute Reise!

Vorwärts! Vgl. Anlage 3, Ziffer 7.

Alles war zerstört: das Haus, der Stall, die Scheune. Die Teeküche kann zu folgenden Zeiten benutzt werden: morgens von 7 bis 8 Uhr, abends von 18 bis 19 Uhr.

Im Einzelnen ist zu beachten:

(1) Wird die nach dem Doppelpunkt folgende Ausführung als Ganzsatz verstanden, so schreibt man das erste Wort groß, zum Beispiel:

Beachten Sie bitte folgenden Hinweis: Alle Bänke sind frisch gestrichen. Die Regel lautet: Würfelt man eine Sechs, dann ...

(2) Das erste Wort der wörtlichen Rede schreibt man groß, zum Beispiel:

Sie fragte: „Kommt er heute?" Er sagte: „Wir wissen es nicht." Alle baten: „Bleib!"

(3) Folgt dem wörtlich Wiedergegebenen der Begleitsatz oder ein Teil von ihm, so schreibt man das erste Wort nach dem abschließenden Anführungszeichen klein, zum Beispiel:

„Hörst du?", fragte sie. „Ich verstehe dich gut", antwortete er. „Mit welchem Recht", fragte er, „willst du das tun?" Sie rief mir zu: „Wir treffen uns auf dem Schulhof!", und lief weiter.

(4) Das erste Wort von Parenthesen schreibt man klein, wenn es nicht nach einer anderen Regel großzuschreiben ist, zum Beispiel:

Eines Tages, es war mitten im Sommer, hagelte es. Er behauptete – so eine Frechheit! –, dass er im Kino gewesen sei. Sie hat das (erinnerst du dich?) gestern gesagt.

Zu den Satzzeichen siehe § 77 (1), § 84 (1), § 86 (1).

(5) Gliederungsangaben wie Ziffern, Paragraphen, Buchstaben gehören nicht zum nachfolgenden Ganzsatz; entsprechend schreibt man das folgende Wort groß. Dies gilt auch für Überschriften, Werktitel und dergleichen. Beispiele:

3. Die Besitzer und Besitzerinnen von Haustieren sollten ...
§ 13 Die Behandlung sollte sofort einsetzen.
c) Vgl. Anlage 3, Ziffer 7.
2 Die Säugetiere

(6) Auslassungspunkte, Apostroph oder Zahlen zu Beginn eines Ganzsatzes gelten als Satzanfang; entsprechend bleibt die Schreibung des folgenden Wortes unverändert. Dies gilt auch für Überschriften, Werktitel und dergleichen. Beispiele:

... und gab keine Antwort.
's ist schade um sie.
52 volle Wochen hat das Jahr.

2 Anwendung von Groß- oder Kleinschreibung bei bestimmten Wörtern und Wortgruppen

2.1 Substantive und Desubstantivierungen

§ 55

> Substantive schreibt man groß.

Beispiele:

Tisch, Wald, Milch, Mond, Genie, Team, Ladung, Feuer, Wasser, Luft, Sandkasten

Verständnis, Verantwortung, Freiheit, Aktion

Gabriela, Markus, Europa, Wien, Alpen

Substantive dienen der Bezeichnung von Gegenständen, Lebewesen und abstrakten Begriffen. Sie besitzen in der Regel ein festes Genus (Maskulinum, Femininum, Neutrum) und sind im Numerus (Singular, Plural) und im Kasus (Nominativ, Genitiv, Dativ, Akkusativ) bestimmt.

Die Großschreibung gilt auch

(1) für nichtsubstantivische Wörter, wenn sie am Anfang einer Zusammensetzung mit Bindestrich stehen, die als Ganzes die Eigenschaften eines Substantivs hat, zum Beispiel:

die Ad-hoc-Entscheidung, der A-cappella-Chor (vgl. auch § 55 E_2), *das In-den-Tag-hinein-Leben* (vgl. auch § 57 (2)), *der Trimm-dich-Pfad, die X-Beine, die S-Kurve*

Abkürzungen sowie zitierte Wortformen und Einzelbuchstaben und dergleichen bleiben allerdings unverändert, zum Beispiel:

die km-Zahl, die pH-Wert-Bestimmung, der dass-Satz, die x-Achse, der i-Punkt (der Punkt auf dem kleinen *i*)

(2) für Substantive – auch Initialwörter (§ 102 (2)) und Einzelbuchstaben, sofern sie nicht als Kleinbuchstaben zitiert sind – als Teile von Zusammensetzungen mit Bindestrich, zum Beispiel:

die Natrium-Chlor-Verbindung, der 400-Meter-Lauf, zum Aus-der-Haut-Fahren (vgl. auch § 57 (2))

pH-Wert-neutral, Napoleon-freundlich, S-Kurven-reich, Formel-1-tauglich

UV-empfindlich, T-förmig (in der Form eines großen *T*), *S-förmig* oder *s-förmig* (in der Form eines großen *S* bzw. eines kleinen *s*), *x-beliebig*

(3) für Substantive aus anderen Sprachen, wenn sie nicht als Zitatwörter gemeint sind. Sind sie mehrteilig, wird der erste Teil großgeschrieben. Beispiele:

das Crescendo, der Drink, das Center, die Ratio; die Conditio sine qua non, das Cordon bleu, eine Terra incognita; das Know-how, das Make-up

Substantivische Bestandteile werden auch im Innern mehrteiliger Fügungen großgeschrieben, die als Ganzes die Funktion eines Substantivs haben, zum Beispiel:

die Alma Mater, die Ultima Ratio, das Desktop-Publishing, der Full-Time-Job, der Soft Drink, der Sex-Appeal, der Cash-Flow, das Corned Beef, der Chewing-Gum

E_1: Teilweise wird auch zusammengeschrieben, siehe Getrennt- und Zusammenschreibung, § 37 (1), und Schreibung mit Bindestrich, § 44 und § 45.

Beispiele: *der Fulltimejob, der Softdrink, der Sexappeal, das Cornedbeef, der Chewinggum*

(4) für Substantive, die Bestandteile fester Gefüge sind und nicht mit anderen Bestandteilen des Gefüges zusammengeschrieben werden (siehe dazu auch Teil B, Getrennt- und Zusammenschreibung, § 34 (3) und § 39), zum Beispiel:

auf Abruf, in Bälde, in/mit Bezug auf, im Grunde, auf Grund (auch *aufgrund*); *zu Grunde gehen* (auch *zugrunde gehen*), *zu Händen von* (aber *zuhanden von; abhanden kommen*), *in Hinsicht auf* (aber *infolge*), *zur Not* (aber *vonnöten*), *zur Seite, von Seiten, auf Seiten* (auch *aufseiten, vonseiten;* aber nur *beiseite*)

etwas außer Acht lassen, die Haare stehen jemandem zu Berge, in Betracht kommen, zu Hilfe kommen, in Kauf nehmen

Auto fahren, Rad fahren, Maschine schreiben, Kegel schieben, Diät leben, Folge leisten, Maß halten, Hof halten, Kopf stehen, Leid tun, Not leiden, Not tun, Pleite gehen (aber nach § 56 (1): *pleite sein*), *Eis laufen* (aber nach § 34 (3): *irreführen, preisgeben, stattfinden, teilnehmen, wundernehmen*)

Recht haben/behalten/bekommen, Unrecht haben/behalten/bekommen, Ernst machen mit etwas, Wert legen auf etwas, Angst haben, jemandem Angst (und Bange) machen, (keine) Schuld tragen (vgl. aber Fügungen mit Adjektiven: *recht sein, unrecht sein, ernst sein/werden, etwas ernst nehmen, wert sein, angst (und bange) sein* (§ 56 (1)), *schuld sein* (§ 56 (1))

zum ersten Mal (aber nach § 39 (1): *einmal, diesmal, nochmal*)

eines Abends, des Nachts, letzten Endes, guten Mutes, schlechter Laune (aber nach § 56 (3): *abends, nachts;* aber nach § 39 (1): *keinesfalls, andernorts)*

E_2: In festen adverbialen Fügungen, die als Ganzes aus einer fremden Sprache entlehnt worden sind, gilt Kleinschreibung, zum Beispiel:

a cappella, in flagranti, à discrétion, de jure, de facto, in nuce, pro domo, ex cathedra, coram publico

Zu Schreibungen wie *A-cappella-Chor, De-facto-Anerkennung* siehe oben Absatz (1).

(5) für Zahlsubstantive, zum Beispiel:

ein Dutzend, das Schock (= 60 Stück), *das Paar* (aber *ein paar = einige*), *das Hundert* (zum Beispiel: *das erste Hundert Schrauben*), *das Tausend, eine Million, eine Milliarde, eine Billion*

Zu *Dutzend, Hundert* und *Tausend* siehe auch § 58 E_5.

(6) für Ausdrücke, die als Bezeichnung von Tageszeiten nach den Adverbien *vorgestern, gestern, heute, morgen, übermorgen* auftreten, zum Beispiel:

Wir treffen uns heute Mittag. Die Frist läuft übermorgen Mitternacht ab. Sie rief gestern Abend an.

Zu Verbindungen wie *(am) Dienstagabend* siehe § 37 (1).

§ 56 Klein schreibt man Wörter, die ihre substantivischen Merkmale eingebüßt und die Funktion anderer Wortarten übernommen haben (= Desubstantivierungen).

Dies betrifft

(1) folgende Wörter, die in Verbindung mit den Verben *sein, bleiben, werden* als Adjektive gebraucht werden:

angst, bange, gram, leid, pleite, schuld

Beispiele:

Mir wird angst. Uns ist angst und bange. Wir sind ihr gram. Mir ist das alles leid. Die Firma ist pleite. Er ist schuld daran.

E_1: Zu Wörtern wie *recht, unrecht, ernst* vgl. § 55 (4).

(2) den ersten Bestandteil unfest zusammengesetzter Verben auch in getrennter Stellung (siehe auch § 34 (3)), zum Beispiel:

Ich nehme daran teil (teilnehmen). Die Besprechung findet am Freitag statt (stattfinden). Er führt uns irre (irreführen). Wir geben unser Ziel nicht preis (preisgeben). Es nimmt mich wunder (wundernehmen).

E_2: Wird ein Substantiv mit dem Infinitiv nicht zusammengeschrieben, so schreibt man es entsprechend § 55 (4) groß, zum Beispiel:

Ich nehme daran Anteil (Anteil nehmen). Du fährst Auto, und ich fahre Rad (Auto fahren, Rad fahren). Sie leistete der Aufforderung nicht Folge (Folge leisten). Meine Schwester läuft Eis (Eis laufen).

(3) Adverbien, Präpositionen, Konjunktionen auf *-s* und *-ens*, zum Beispiel:

abends, anfangs, donnerstags, schlechterdings, morgens, hungers (hungers sterben), willens, rechtens (rechtens sein, etwas rechtens machen); abseits, angesichts, mangels, mittels, namens, seitens; falls, teils ... teils

(4) die folgenden Präpositionen:

dank, kraft (kraft ihres Amtes), laut, statt, an ... statt (an Kindes statt, an seiner statt), trotz, wegen, von ... wegen (von Amts wegen), um ... willen, zeit (zeit seines Lebens)

(5) die folgenden unbestimmten Zahlwörter:

ein bisschen (= ein wenig), ein paar (= einige)

Beispiele:

ein bisschen Leim, dieses kleine bisschen Leim; ein paar Steine, diese paar Steine (aber nach § 55 (5): *ein Paar Schuhe*)

(6) Bruchzahlen auf *-tel* und *-stel*

(6.1) vor Maßangaben (siehe auch § 37 E_2), zum Beispiel:

ein zehntel Millimeter, ein viertel Kilogramm, in fünf hundertstel Sekunden, nach drei viertel Stunden

E_3: Hier ist auch Zusammenschreibung nach § 37 (1) möglich, zum Beispiel:

ein Zehntelmillimeter, ein Viertelkilogramm, in fünf Hundertstelsekunden, nach drei Viertelstunden

(6.2) in Uhrzeitangaben unmittelbar vor Kardinalzahlen, zum Beispiel:

um viertel fünf, gegen drei viertel acht

E_4: In allen übrigen Fällen schreibt man Bruchzahlen auf *-tel* und *-stel* entsprechend § 55 groß, zum Beispiel:

ein Drittel, das erste Fünftel, neun Zehntel des Umsatzes, um drei Viertel größer, um (ein) Viertel vor fünf

2.2 Substantivierungen

§ 57 Wörter anderer Wortarten schreibt man groß, wenn sie als Substantive gebraucht werden (= Substantivierungen).

Substantivierte Wörter nehmen die Eigenschaften von Substantiven an (vgl. § 55). Man erkennt sie im Text an zumindest einem der folgenden Merkmale:

a) an einem vorausgehenden Artikel *(der, die, das; ein, eine, ein)*, Pronomen *(dieser, jener, welcher, mein, kein, etwas, nichts, alle, einige ...)* oder unbestimmten Zahlwort *(ein paar, genug, viel, wenig ...)*, die sich auf das substantivierte Wort beziehen;

b) an einem vorangestellten adjektivischen Attribut oder einem nachgestellten Attribut, das sich auf das substantivierte Wort bezieht;

c) an ihrer Funktion als kasusbestimmtes Satzglied oder kasusbestimmtes Attribut.

Siehe dazu folgende Beispiele:

Das In-Kraft-Treten (a, b, c) *des Gesetzes verzögert sich. Er übersah alles Kleingedruckte* (a, c). *Das Ausschlaggebende* (a, b, c) *für ihre Einstellung war ihr sicheres Auftreten* (a, b, c). *Nichts Menschliches* (a, c) *war ihr fremd. Das Deutsche* (a, c) *gilt als schwere Sprache. Sie bot ihr das Du* (a, c) *an. Der Beschluss fiel nach langem Hin und Her* (b, c). *Bananen kosten jetzt das Zweifache* (a, b, c) *des früheren Preises. Lesen und Schreiben* (c) *sind Kulturtechniken. Sie brachte eine Platte mit Gebratenem* (c). *Du sollst Gleiches* (c) *nicht mit Gleichem* (c) *vergelten. Man sagt, Liebende* (c) *seien blind.*

E_1: Zahlreiche Substantivierungen sind ein fester Bestandteil des Substantivwortschatzes geworden, zum Beispiel:

das Essen, das Herzklopfen, das Leben, das Deutsche, die Grünen, die Studierenden, der/die Angestellte, das Durcheinander, das Jenseits, das Vergissmeinnicht

Die folgende Aufgliederung der Großschreibung von Substantivierungen ist nach Wortarten geordnet.

(1) Substantivierte Adjektive und adjektivisch gebrauchte Partizipien, besonders auch in Verbindung mit Wörtern wie *alles, allerlei, etwas, genug, nichts, viel, wenig*, zum Beispiel:

Wir wünschen alles Gute. Zum Aperitif gab es Süßes und Salziges. Geh nicht mit Unbekannten! Das Ausschlaggebende für die Einstellung war ihre Erfahrung. Er hat nichts/wenig/etwas/viel Bedeutendes geschrieben. Das nie Erwartete trat ein. Sie hatte nur Angenehmes erlebt. Der Umsatz war dieses Jahr um das Dreifache höher. Das andere Gebäude war um ein Beträchtliches höher. Das ist das einzig Richtige, was du tun kannst. Es wäre wohl das Richtige, wenn wir noch einmal darüber reden. Bitte lesen Sie das unten Stehende/unten Stehendes genau durch. Wir haben das Folgende/Folgendes verabredet. Wir werden das im Folgenden noch genauer darstellen. Des Näheren vermag ich mich nicht zu entsinnen. Sie hat mir die Sache des Näheren erläutert. Wir haben alles des Langen und Breiten diskutiert. Wir wohnen im Grünen. Beim Umweltschutz liegen noch viele Dinge im Argen. Wir sind uns im Großen und Ganzen einig. Die Arbeiten sind im Allgemeinen nicht schlecht geraten. Das ist im Wesentlichen richtig. Im Einzelnen sind aber noch Verbesserungen möglich. Plötzlich ertönte eine Stimme aus dem Dunkeln. Die Polizei tappt im Dunkeln. Die Direktorin war auf dem Laufenden.

Sie war unsere Jüngste. Das Beste, was dieser Ferienort bietet, ist die Ruhe. Es ist das Beste, wenn du kommst. Es änderte sich nicht das Geringste. Dies geschieht zum Besten unserer Kinder. Er gab wieder einmal eine seiner Geschichten zum Besten. Sie konnte uns vor dem Ärgsten bewahren. Daran haben wir nicht im Entferntesten gedacht. Sie war bis ins Kleinste vorbereitet. Sie war aufs Schrecklichste/auf das Schrecklichste gefasst. Sie hat uns aufs Herzlichste/auf das Herzlichste begrüßt (siehe auch § 58 E_1).

Die Pest traf Hohe und Niedrige/Hoch und Niedrig. Diese Musik gefällt Jungen und Alten/Jung und Alt. Die Teilnehmenden diskutierten über den Konflikt zwischen Jungen und Alten/zwischen Jung und Alt. Das ist ein Fest für Junge und Alte/für Jung und Alt.

Sie trug das kleine Schwarze. Der Zeitungsbericht traf ins Schwarze. Wenn man Schwarz mit Weiß mischt, entsteht Grau. Die Ampel schaltete auf Rot. Wir liefern das Gerät in Grau oder Schwarz.

Das Englische ist eine Weltsprache. Ihr Englisch hatte einen südamerikanischen Akzent. Mit Englisch kommt man überall durch. In Ostafrika verständigt man sich am besten auf Swahili oder auf Englisch.

E_2: Gelegentlich ist Groß- oder Kleinschreibung möglich, zum Beispiel:

Sie spricht Englisch (was? – die englische Sprache)/englisch (wie?).

Ordnungszahladjektive sowie sinnverwandte Adjektive, zum Beispiel:

Die Miete ist am Ersten jedes Monats zu bezahlen. Er ist schon der Zweite, der den Rekord des vergangenen Jahres überboten hat. Jeder Fünfte lehnte das Projekt ab. Endlich war sie die Erste im Staat. Dieses Vorgehen verletzte die Rechte Dritter. Er kam als Dritter an die Reihe. Er kam vom Hundertsten ins Tausendste. Fürs Erste wollen wir nicht mehr darüber reden. Die Nächste bitte! Liebe deinen Nächsten wie dich selbst! Trotz ihrer Verletzung wurde sie noch Viertletzte. Als Letztes muss der Deckel angeschraubt werden. Arthur und Armin gingen unterschiedliche Wege: der Erste/Ersterer wurde Beamter, der Zweite/der Letzte/Letzterer hatte als Schauspieler Erfolg.

Unbestimmte Zahladjektive (siehe aber auch § 58 (5)), zum Beispiel:

Den Kometen haben Unzählige (Ungezählte, Zahllose) gesehen. Ich muss noch Verschiedenes erledigen. Er hatte das Ganze rasch wieder vergessen. Der Kongress war als Ganzes ein Erfolg. Das muss jeder Einzelne mit sich selbst ausmachen. Anita war die Einzige, die alles wusste. Alles Übrige besprechen wir morgen. Er gab sein Geld für alles Mögliche aus.

(2) Substantivierte Verben, zum Beispiel:

Das Lesen fällt mir schwer. Sie hörten ein starkes Klopfen. Wer erledigt das Fensterputzen? Viele waren am Zustandekommen des Vertrages beteiligt. Die Sache kam ins Stocken. Das ist zum Lachen. Euer Fernbleiben fiel uns auf. Uns half nur noch lautes Rufen. Die Mitbewohner begnügten sich mit Wegsehen und Schweigen.

Sie wollte auf Biegen und Brechen gewinnen. Er klopfte mit Zittern und Zagen an. Ich nehme die Tabletten auf Anraten meiner Ärztin.

Sie hat ihr Soll erfüllt. Dies ist ein absolutes Muss.

Bei mehrteiligen Fügungen, deren Bestandteile mit einem Bindestrich verbunden werden, schreibt man das erste Wort, den Infinitiv und die anderen substantivischen Bestandteile groß (siehe auch § 55 (1) und (2)), zum Beispiel:

es ist zum Auf-und-davon-Laufen, das Hand-in-Hand-Arbeiten, das In-den-Tag-hinein-Leben

E_3: Gelegentlich ist bei einfachen Infinitiven Groß- oder Kleinschreibung möglich, zum Beispiel: *Der Gehörgeschädigte lernt Sprechen.* (Wie: *Der Gehörgeschädigte lernt das Sprechen/das deutliche Sprechen.*) Oder: *Der Gehörgeschädigte lernt sprechen.* (Wie: *Der Gehörgeschädigte lernt deutlich sprechen.*) (Ebenso:) *Bekanntlich ist Umlernen/umlernen schwieriger als Dazulernen/dazulernen. Doch geht Probieren/probieren über Studieren/studieren.*

(3) Substantivierte Pronomen (vgl. aber auch § 58 (4)), zum Beispiel:

Sie hatte ein gewisses Etwas. Er bot ihm das Du an. Das ist ein Er, keine Sie. Wir standen vor dem Nichts. Er konnte Mein und Dein nicht unterscheiden.

(4) Substantivierte Grundzahlen als Bezeichnung von Ziffern, zum Beispiel:

Er setzte alles auf die Vier. Sie fürchtete sich vor der Dreizehn. Der Zeiger nähert sich der Elf. Sie hat lauter Einsen im Zeugnis. Er würfelt eine Sechs.

(5) Substantivierte Adverbien, Präpositionen, Konjunktionen, Interjektionen, zum Beispiel:

Es gab ein großes Durcheinander. Mich störte das ewige Hin und Her. Ich will das noch im Diesseits erleben. Auf das Hier und Jetzt kommt es an. Das Danach war ihr egal. Es gibt kein Übermorgen. Sie hatte so viel wie möglich im Voraus erledigt. Im Nachhinein wussten wir es besser. Er stand im Aus. Sie überlegte sich das Für und Wider genau. Sein ständiges Aber stört mich. Es kommt nicht nur auf das Dass an, sondern auch auf das Wie. Er erledigte es mit Ach und Krach. Ein vielstimmiges Ah ertönte. Ihr freudiges Oh freute ihre Kolleginnen. Das Nein fällt ihm schwer.

E_4: Bei mehrteiligen substantivierten Konjunktionen, die mit einem Bindestrich verbunden werden (siehe § 43), schreibt man nur das erste Wort groß, zum Beispiel:

ein Entweder-oder, das Als-ob, das Sowohl-als-auch

§ 58 In folgenden Fällen schreibt man Adjektive, Partizipien und Pronomen klein, obwohl sie formale Merkmale der Substantivierung aufweisen.

(1) Adjektive, Partizipien und Pronomen, die sich auf ein vorhergehendes oder nachstehendes Substantiv beziehen, zum Beispiel:

Sie war die aufmerksamste und klügste meiner Zuhörerinnen. Der Verkäufer zeigte mir seine Auswahl an Krawatten, die gestreiften und gepunkteten gefielen mir am besten. Vor dem Haus spielten viele Kinder, einige kleine im Sandkasten, die größeren am Klettergerüst. Es waren neun Teilnehmer erschienen, auf den zehnten wartete man vergebens. Alte Schuhe sind meist bequemer als neue. Dünne Bücher lese ich in der Freizeit, dicke im Urlaub. Zwei Männer betraten den Raum; der erste trug einen Anzug, der zweite Jeans und Pullover. Leih mir bitte deine Farbstifte, ich habe meine/die meinen/die meinigen vergessen.

(2) Superlative mit „am“, nach denen mit „Wie?“ gefragt werden kann, zum Beispiel:

Dieser Weg ist am steilsten. (Frage: Wie ist der Weg?) *Dieser Stift schreibt am feinsten.* (Frage: Wie schreibt dieser Stift?) *Der ICE fährt am schnellsten.*

E_1: Superlative mit „am“ gehören zur regulären Flexion des Adjektivs; „am“ ist in diesen Fügungen nicht in „an dem“ auflösbar. Beispiele: *Dieser Weg ist steil – steiler – am steilsten. Dieser Stift schreibt fein – feiner – am feinsten.*

In Anlehnung an diese Fügungen kann man auch feste adverbiale Wendungen mit „aufs“ oder „auf das“, die mit „Wie?“ erfragt werden können, kleinschreiben, zum Beispiel:

Sie hat uns aufs/auf das herzlichste begrüßt. (Frage: Wie hat sie uns begrüßt?) *Der Fall ließ sich aufs/auf das einfachste lösen.*

Superlative, nach denen mit „Woran?“ („An was?“) oder „Worauf?“ („Auf was?“) gefragt werden kann, schreibt man nach § 57 (1) groß, zum Beispiel:

Es fehlt ihnen am/an dem Nötigsten. (Frage: Woran fehlt es ihnen?) *Wir sind aufs/auf das Beste angewiesen.* (Frage: Worauf sind wir angewiesen?)

(3) bestimmte feste Verbindungen aus Präposition und nichtdekliniertem oder dekliniertem Adjektiv ohne vorangehenden Artikel, zum Beispiel:

Ich hörte von fern ein dumpfes Grollen. Die Pilger kamen von nah und fern. Die Ware wird nur gegen bar ausgeliefert. Die Mädchen hielten durch dick und dünn zusammen. Das wird sich über kurz oder lang herausstellen. Damit habe ich mich von klein auf beschäftigt.

Das werde ich dir schwarz auf weiß beweisen. Die Stimmung war grau in grau.

Aus der Brandruine stieg von neuem Rauch auf. Wir konnten das Feuer nur von weitem betrachten. Der Fahrplan bleibt bis auf weiteres in Kraft. Unsere Pressesprecherin gibt Ihnen ohne weiteres Auskunft. Der Termin stand seit längerem fest.

E_2: Substantivierungen, die auch ohne Präposition üblich sind, werden nach § 57 (1) auch dann großgeschrieben, wenn sie mit einer Präposition verbunden werden, zum Beispiel:

Die Historikerin beschäftigt sich mit dem Konflikt zwischen Arm und Reich. Das ist ein Fest für Jung und Alt. (Vgl.: *Die Königin lud Arm und Reich ein. Das Fest gefiel Jung und Alt.*)

Die Ampel schaltete auf Rot. Wir liefern das Gerät in Grau (= in grauer Farbe). (Vgl.: *Das ist ein grelles Rot. Sie hasst Grau.*)

Mit Englisch kommst du überall durch. In Ostafrika verständigt man sich am besten auf Swahili oder Englisch. (Vgl.: *Bekanntlich ist Englisch eine Weltsprache. Sein Englisch war gut verständlich.*)

(4) Pronomen, auch wenn sie als Stellvertreter von Substantiven gebraucht werden, zum Beispiel:

In diesem Wald hat sich schon mancher verirrt. Ich habe mich mit diesen und jenen unterhalten. Wenn einer eine Reise tut, so kann er was erzählen. Das muss (ein) jeder mit sich selbst ausmachen. Wir haben alles mitgebracht. Sie hatten beides mitgebracht. Man muss mit (den) beiden reden.

Zur Großschreibung der Anredepronomen siehe § 65, § 66.

E_3: In Verbindung mit dem bestimmten Artikel oder dergleichen lassen sich Possessivpronomen auch als substantivische possessive Adjektive bestimmen, entsprechend kann man hier nach § 57 (1) auch großschreiben, zum Beispiel:

Grüß mir die deinen/Deinen (die deinigen/Deinigen)! Sie trug das ihre/Ihre (das ihrige/Ihrige) zum Gelingen bei. Jedem das seine/Seine!

(5) die folgenden Zahladjektive mit allen ihren Flexionsformen:

viel, wenig; (der, die, das) eine, (der, die, das) andere

Beispiele:

Das haben schon viele erlebt. Zum Erfolg trugen auch die vielen bei, die ohne Entgelt mitgearbeitet haben. Nach dem Brand war nur noch weniges zu gebrauchen. Sie hat das wenige, was noch da war, in eine Kiste versorgt. Die meisten haben diesen Film schon einmal gesehen. Die einen kommen, die anderen gehen. Was der eine nicht tut, soll der andere nicht lassen. Die anderen kommen später. Das können auch andere bestätigen. Alles andere erzähle ich dir später. Sie hatte noch anderes zu tun. Unter anderem wurde auch über finanzielle Angelegenheiten gesprochen.

E_4: Wenn hervorgehoben werden soll, dass das Adjektiv nicht als unbestimmtes Zahlwort zu verstehen ist, kann nach § 57 (1) auch großgeschrieben werden, zum Beispiel:

Sie strebte etwas ganz Anderes (= völlig Neues) an.

(6) Kardinalzahlen unter einer Million, zum Beispiel:

Was drei wissen, wissen bald dreißig. Diese drei kommen mir bekannt vor. Sie rief um fünf an. Wir waren an die zwanzig. Er sollte die Summe durch acht teilen. Dieser Kandidat konnte nicht bis drei zählen. Wir fünf gehören zusammen. Der Abschnitt sieben fehlt im Text. Der Mensch über achtzig schätzt die Gesundheit besonders.

E_5: Wenn *hundert* und *tausend* eine unbestimmte (nicht in Ziffern schreibbare) Menge angeben, können sie auch auf die Zahlsubstantive *Hundert* und *Tausend* bezogen werden (vgl. § 55 (5)); entsprechend kann man sie dann klein- oder großschreiben, zum Beispiel:

Es kamen viele tausende/Tausende von Zuschauern. Sie strömten zu aberhunderten/Aberhunderten herein. Mehrere tausend/Tausend Menschen füllten das Stadion. Der Beifall zigtausender/Zigtausender von Zuschauern war ihr gewiss.

Entsprechend auch: *Der Stoff wird in einigen Dutzend/dutzend Farben angeboten. Der Fall war angesichts Dutzender/dutzender von Augenzeugen klar.*

2.3 Eigennamen mit ihren nichtsubstantivischen Bestandteilen sowie Ableitungen von Eigennamen

§ 59 Eigennamen schreibt man groß.

Eigennamen sind Bezeichnungen zur Identifizierung bestimmter einzelner Gegebenheiten (eine Person, ein Ort, ein Land, eine Institution usw.). Viele sind einfache, zusammengesetzte oder abgeleitete Substantive, zum Beispiel *Peter, Wien, Deutschland, Europa, Südamerika, Bahnhofstraße, Sigmaringen. Albrecht-Dürer-Allee, Ostsee-Zeitung*. Sie werden nach § 55 großgeschrieben. Daneben gibt es mehrteilige Eigennamen, die häufig auch nichtsubstantivische Bestandteile enthalten, zum Beispiel *Kap der Guten Hoffnung, Norddeutsche Neueste Nachrichten, Vereinigte Staaten von Amerika*. Im Folgenden wird die Groß- und Kleinschreibung dieser Gruppe von Eigennamen dargestellt.

§ 60 In mehrteiligen Eigennamen mit nichtsubstantivischen Bestandteilen schreibt man das erste Wort und alle weiteren Wörter außer Artikeln, Präpositionen und Konjunktionen groß.

E_1: Ein vorangestellter Artikel ist in der Regel nicht Bestandteil des Eigennamens und wird darum kleingeschrieben. Zu Ausnahmen siehe unten, Absatz (4.4).

Als Eigennamen im Sinne dieser orthographischen Regelung gelten:

(1) Personennamen, Eigennamen aus Religion, Mythologie sowie Beinamen, Spitznamen und dergleichen, zum Beispiel:

Johann Wolfgang von Goethe, Gertrud von Le Fort, Charles de Coster, Ludwig van Beethoven, der Apokalyptische Reiter, Walther von der Vogelweide, Holbein der Jüngere, der Alte Fritz, Katharina die Große, Heinrich der Achte, Elisabeth die Zweite; Klein Erna

Präpositionen wie *von, van, de, ten, zu(r)* in Personennamen schreibt man im Satzinnern auch dann klein, wenn ihnen kein Vorname vorausgeht, zum Beispiel:

Der Autor dieses Buches heißt von Ossietzky.

(2) Geographische und geographisch-politische Eigennamen, so

(2.1) von Erdteilen, Ländern, Staaten, Verwaltungsgebieten und dergleichen, zum Beispiel:

Vereinigte Staaten von Amerika, Freie und Hansestadt Hamburg (als Bundesland), *Tschechische Republik*

(2.2) von Städten, Dörfern, Straßen, Plätzen und dergleichen, zum Beispiel:

Neu Lübbenau, Groß Flatow, Rostock-Lütten Klein, Unter den Linden, Lange Straße, In der Mittleren Holdergasse, Am Tiefen Graben, An den Drei Pfählen, Hamburger Straße, Neuer Markt

(2.3) von Landschaften, Gebirgen, Wäldern, Wüsten, Fluren und dergleichen, zum Beispiel:

Kahler Asten, Hohe Tatra, Holsteinische Schweiz, Schwäbische Alb, Bayerischer Wald, Libysche Wüste, Goldene Aue, Thüringer Wald

(2.4) von Meeren, Meeresteilen und -straßen, Flüssen, Inseln und Küsten und dergleichen, zum Beispiel:

Stiller Ozean, Indischer Ozean, Rotes Meer, Kleine Antillen, Großer Belt, Schweriner See, Straße von Gibraltar, Kapverdische Inseln, Kap der Guten Hoffnung

(3) Eigennamen von Objekten unterschiedlicher Klassen, so

(3.1) von Sternen, Sternbildern und anderen Himmelskörpern, zum Beispiel:

Kleiner Bär, Großer Wagen, Halleyscher Komet (auch: *Halley'scher Komet;* § 62)

(3.2) von Fahrzeugen, bestimmten Bauwerken und Örtlichkeiten, zum Beispiel:
die Vorwärts (Schiff), *der Blaue Enzian* (Eisenbahnzug), *der Fliegende Hamburger* (Eisenbahnzug), *die Blaue Moschee* (in Istanbul), *das Alte Rathaus* (in Leipzig), *der Französische Dom* (in Berlin), *die Große Mauer* (in China), *der Schiefe Turm* (in Pisa)

(3.3) von einzeln benannten Tieren, Pflanzen und gelegentlich auch von Einzelobjekten weiterer Klassen, zum Beispiel:
der Fliegende Pfeil (ein bestimmtes Pferd), *die Alte Eiche* (ein bestimmter Baum)

(3.4) von Orden und Auszeichnungen, zum Beispiel:
das Blaue Band des Ozeans, Großer Österreichischer Staatspreis für Literatur

(4) Eigennamen von Institutionen, Organisationen, Einrichtungen, so

(4.1) von staatlichen bzw. öffentlichen Dienststellen, Behörden und Gremien, von Bildungs- und Kulturinstitutionen und dergleichen, zum Beispiel:
Deutscher Bundestag, Statistisches Bundesamt, Mecklenburgisches Staatstheater Schwerin, Museum für Deutsche Geschichte (in Berlin), *Naturhistorisches Museum* (in Wien), *Grünes Gewölbe* (in Dresden), *Klinik für Innere Medizin der Universität Rostock, Akademie für Alte Musik Berlin, Zweites Deutsches Fernsehen, Eidgenössische Technische Hochschule* (in Zürich)

(4.2) von Organisationen, Parteien, Verbänden, Vereinen und dergleichen, zum Beispiel:
Vereinte Nationen, Internationales Olympisches Komitee, Deutscher Gewerkschaftsbund, Sozialdemokratische Partei Deutschlands, Christlich-Demokratische Union, Allgemeiner Deutscher Automobilclub, Börsenverein des Deutschen Buchhandels, Österreichisches Rotes Kreuz

(4.3) von Betrieben, Firmen, Genossenschaften, Gaststätten, Geschäften und dergleichen, zum Beispiel:
Deutsche Bank, Österreichischer Raiffeisenverband, Bibliographisches Institut (in Mannheim), *Deutsche Bahn, Weiße Flotte, Städtisches Klinikum Berlin-Buch, Hotel Vier Jahreszeiten, Gasthaus zur Neuen Post, Zum Goldenen Anker* (Gaststätte), *Salzburger Dombuchhandlung, Rheinisch-Westfälisches Elektrizitätswerk AG*

(4.4) von Zeitungen und Zeitschriften und dergleichen, zum Beispiel:
Berliner Zeitung, Sächsische Neueste Nachrichten, Deutsch als Fremdsprache, Dermatologische Monatsschrift, Die Zeit

Wird der Artikel am Anfang verändert, so schreibt man ihn klein, zum Beispiel:
Sie hat das in der Zeit gelesen.

(5) inoffizielle Eigennamen, Kurzformen sowie Abkürzungen von Eigennamen, zum Beispiel:
Schwarzer Kontinent, Ferner Osten, Naher Osten, Vereinigte Staaten
A. Müller, Astrid M., A. M. (= Astrid Müller), J. W. v. Goethe; SPD (= Sozialdemokratische Partei Deutschlands), DGB (= Deutscher Gewerkschaftsbund), EU (= Europäische Union), SBB (= Schweizerische Bundesbahnen), ORF (= Österreichischer Rundfunk)

E_2: In einigen der oben genannten Namengruppen kann die Schreibung im Einzelfall abweichend festgelegt sein, zum Beispiel:
neue deutsche literatur, profil, konkret (Zeitschriften); *Institut für deutsche Sprache, Akademie für Musik und darstellende Kunst „Mozarteum"; Zur letzten Instanz* (Gaststätte)

Zur Kennzeichnung der Namen von Zeitungen und Zeitschriften mit Anführungszeichen siehe § 94 (1).

§ 61 Ableitungen von geographischen Eigennamen auf *-er* schreibt man groß.

Beispiele:
die Berliner Bevölkerung, die Mecklenburger Landschaft, der Schweizer Käse, das St. Galler/Sankt Galler Kloster, das Bad Krozinger Kurgebiet, die New Yorker Kunstszene

Zur Schreibung mit oder ohne Bindestrich siehe § 49 E.

§ 62 Kleingeschrieben werden adjektivische Ableitungen von Eigennamen auf *-(i)sch*, außer wenn die Grundform eines Personennamens durch einen Apostroph verdeutlicht wird, ferner alle adjektivischen Ableitungen mit anderen Suffixen.

Beispiele:
die darwinsche/die Darwin'sche Evolutionstheorie, das wackernagelsche/Wackernagel'sche Gesetz, die goethischen/goetheschen/Goethe'schen Dramen, die bernoullischen/Bernoulli'schen Gleichungen

die homerischen Epen, das kopernikanische Weltsystem, die darwinistische Evolutionstheorie, tschechisches Bier, indischer Tee, englischer Stoff

mit eulenspiegelhaftem Schalk, eine kafkaeske Stimmung

Zur Schreibung mit Apostroph siehe auch Zeichensetzung, § 97 E.

Zur Schreibung mehrteiliger Ableitungen mit Bindestrich siehe § 49 E.

2.4 Feste Verbindungen aus Adjektiv und Substantiv

§ 63 In substantivischen Wortgruppen, die zu festen Verbindungen geworden, aber keine Eigennamen sind, schreibt man Adjektive klein.

Beispiele:

der italienische Salat, der blaue Brief, das autogene Training, das neue Jahr, die gelbe Karte, das gelbe Trikot, der goldene Schnitt, die goldene Hochzeit, das große Los, die höhere Mathematik, die innere Medizin, die künstliche Intelligenz, die grüne Lunge, das olympische Feuer, der schnelle Brüter, das schwarze Brett, das schwarze Schaf, die schwedischen Gardinen, der weiße Tod, das zweite Gesicht, die graue Eminenz

§ 64 In bestimmten substantivischen Wortgruppen werden Adjektive großgeschrieben, obwohl keine Eigennamen vorliegen.

Dies betrifft

(1) Titel, Ehrenbezeichnungen, bestimmte Amts- und Funktionsbezeichnungen, zum Beispiel:
der Heilige Vater, die Königliche Hoheit, der Erste Bürgermeister, der Regierende Bürgermeister, der Technische Direktor

(2) fachsprachliche Bezeichnungen bestimmter Klassifizierungseinheiten, so von Arten, Unterarten oder Rassen in der Botanik und Zoologie, zum Beispiel:
die Schwarze Witwe, das Fleißige Lieschen, der Rote Milan, die Gemeine Stubenfliege

(3) besondere Kalendertage, zum Beispiel:
der Heilige Abend, der Weiße Sonntag, der Internationale Frauentag, der Erste Mai

(4) bestimmte historische Ereignisse und Epochen, zum Beispiel:
der Westfälische Friede, der Deutsch-Französische Krieg 1870/1871, der Zweite Weltkrieg, die Goldenen Zwanziger, die Jüngere Steinzeit

2.5 Anredepronomen und Anreden

§ 65 Das Anredepronomen *Sie* und das entsprechende Possessivpronomen *Ihr* sowie die zugehörigen flektierten Formen schreibt man groß.

Beispiele:

Würden Sie mir helfen? Wie geht es Ihnen? Ist das Ihr Mantel? Bestehen Ihrerseits Bedenken gegen den Vorschlag?

E_1: Großschreibung gilt auch für ältere Anredeformen wie: *Habt Ihr es Euch überlegt, Fürst von Gallenstein? Johann, führe Er die Gäste herein.*

E_2: In Anreden wie *Seine Majestät, Eure Exzellenz, Eure Magnifizenz* schreibt man das Pronomen ebenfalls groß.

§ 66 Die Anredepronomen *du* und *ihr,* die entsprechenden Possessivpronomen *dein* und *euer* sowie das Reflexivpronomen *sich* schreibt man klein.

Beispiele:

Würdest du mir helfen? Hast du dich gut erholt? Haben Sie sich schon angemeldet?

Lieber Freund,
ich schreibe dir diesen Brief und schicke dir eure Bilder …

E Zeichensetzung

0 Vorbemerkungen

(1) Die Satzzeichen sind Grenz- und Gliederungszeichen. Sie dienen insbesondere dazu, einen geschriebenen Text übersichtlich zu gestalten und ihn dadurch für den Lesenden überschaubar zu machen. Zudem kann der Schreibende mit den Satzzeichen besondere Aussageabsichten oder Einstellungen zum Ausdruck bringen oder stilistische Wirkungen anstreben.

Zu unterscheiden sind Satzzeichen

- zur Kennzeichnung des Schlusses von Ganzsätzen: Punkt, Ausrufezeichen, Fragezeichen
- zur Gliederung innerhalb von Ganzsätzen: Komma, Semikolon, Doppelpunkt, Gedankenstrich, Klammern
- zur Anführung von Äußerungen oder Textstellen bzw. zur Hervorhebung von Wörtern oder Textteilen: Anführungszeichen

(2) Daneben dienen bestimmte Zeichen

- zur Markierung von Auslassungen: Apostroph, Ergänzungsstrich, Auslassungspunkte
- zur Kennzeichnung der Wörter bestimmter Gruppen: Punkt nach Abkürzungen bzw. Ordinalzahlen, Schrägstrich

1 Kennzeichnung des Schlusses von Ganzsätzen

Der Kennzeichnung des Schlusses von Ganzsätzen dienen:

- der Punkt
- das Ausrufezeichen
- das Fragezeichen

Ganzsätze im Sinne dieser orthographischen Regelung zeigen Beispiele wie:

Gestern hat es geregnet. Du kommst bitte morgen! Hat er das wirklich gesagt? Im Hausflur war es still, ich drückte erwartungsvoll auf die Klingel. Ich hoffe, dass wir uns bald wiedersehen. Meine Freundin hatte den Zug versäumt; deshalb kam sie eine halbe Stunde zu spät.

Niemand kannte ihn. Auch der Gärtner nicht. Bitte die Türen schließen und Vorsicht bei der Abfahrt des Zuges! Ob er heute kommt? Nein, morgen. Warum nicht? Gute Reise! Hilfe!

Zu den Zeichen in Verbindung mit Gedankenstrich oder Klammern siehe § 85 bzw. § 88.

Zu den Zeichen bei wörtlich Wiedergegebenem siehe § 90.

Zum Gedankenstrich zwischen zwei Ganzsätzen siehe § 83.

§ 67 Mit dem Punkt kennzeichnet man den Schluss eines Ganzsatzes.

Ich habe ihn gestern gesehen. Sie kommt morgen. Das Kind weinte, weil es seinen Schlüssel verloren hatte.

Wir sehen nach, was Paul macht. Sie habe ihn gestern gesehen, behauptete sie. Sie forderte ihn auf die Wohnung sofort zu verlassen. Ich wünschte, die Prüfung wäre vorbei. Sie fragte ungeduldig, ob er endlich komme. Der Redner stellte die Frage, wie es nach diesen Umweltschäden weitergehen solle.

Im Hausflur war es still. Ich drückte erwartungsvoll auf die Klingel.

E_1: Wenn aber als mehrteiliger Ganzsatz verstanden, entsprechend § 71 (1) bzw. § 80 (1) mit Komma oder Semikolon:

Im Hausflur war es still, ich drückte erwartungsvoll auf die Klingel.
Im Hausflur war es still; ich drückte erwartungsvoll auf die Klingel.

E_2: Bei Aufforderungen, denen man keinen besonderen Nachdruck geben will, setzt man einen Punkt und kein Ausrufezeichen (hierzu siehe § 69):

Rufen Sie bitte später noch einmal an. Nehmen Sie doch Platz. Vgl. S. 25 seiner letzten Veröffentlichung.

E_3: In den folgenden Fällen setzt man keinen Punkt:
- am Ende von frei stehenden Zeilen (siehe § 68)
- am Ende einer kolumnenartigen Aufzählung ohne schließende Satzzeichen (siehe § 71 E_2)
- am Ende von Parenthesen (mit Gedankenstrich siehe § 85, mit Klammern siehe § 88)
- bei wörtlich Wiedergegebenem am Anfang oder im Inneren von Ganzsätzen (siehe § 92)
- nach Auslassungspunkten (siehe § 100)
- nach Punkt zur Kennzeichnung von Abkürzungen (siehe §103) und Ordinalzahlen (siehe §105)

§ 68

Nach frei stehenden Zeilen setzt man keinen Punkt.

Dies betrifft unter anderem

(1) Überschriften und Werktitel (etwa von Büchern und Theaterstücken, Werken der bildenden Kunst und der Musik, Rundfunk- und Fernsehproduktionen):

Allmähliche Normalisierung im Erdbebengebiet
Schneeverwehungen behindern Autoverkehr
Chance für eine diplomatische Lösung
Einführung in die höhere Mathematik
Der kaukasische Kreidekreis
Die Zauberflöte

Zum Ausrufezeichen siehe § 69 E_2 (1); zum Fragezeichen siehe § 70 E_2.

(2) Titel von Gesetzen, Verträgen, Deklarationen und dergleichen sowie Bezeichnungen für Veranstaltungen:

Bundesgesetz über den Straßenverkehr
Konferenz über Sicherheit und Zusammenarbeit in Europa
Internationaler Ärztekongress

(3) Anschriften und Datumszeilen sowie Grußformeln und Unterschriften etwa in Briefen:

Werner Meier — *Donnerstag, 15. Februar 1996*
Gerichtsweg 12
04103 Leipzig

Herrn Rudolf Schröder
Rüdesheimer Str. 29
62123 Wiesbaden

Sehr geehrter Herr Schröder,
entsprechend unserer telefonischen Vereinbarung ...
...
Mit freundlichen Grüßen
Ihr Werner Meier

Zur Zeichensetzung bei der Anrede etwa in Briefen siehe § 69 E_3.

§ 69

Mit dem Ausrufezeichen gibt man dem Inhalt des Ganzsatzes einen besonderen Nachdruck wie etwa bei nachdrücklichen Behauptungen, Aufforderungen, Grüßen, Wünschen oder Ausrufen.

Ich habe ihn gestern bestimmt gesehen! Komm bitte morgen! Du kommst morgen! Lasst uns keine Zeit verlieren! Du musst die Arbeit abgeben, weil morgen der letzte Termin ist!

Seht nach, was Paul macht! Sehen Sie nur, wie schön die Aussicht ist! Bitte fordern Sie ihn auf die Wohnung sofort zu verlassen! Frag ihn, ob er kommt!

Ruhe! Bitte nicht stören! Zurücktreten! Bitte die Türen schließen und Vorsicht bei der Abfahrt des Zuges! Guten Morgen! Hoffentlich sehen wir uns bald wieder! Wäre nur die Prüfung erst einmal vorbei! Wenn ich dich noch einmal erwische, kannst du was erleben! Das ist ja großartig! Welch ein Glück! Au! Das tut weh! Nein! Nein!

Zum Punkt nach Aufforderungen ohne besonderen Nachdruck siehe § 67 E_2.

E_1: Wenn aber als mehrteiliger Ganzsatz oder als Teile einer Aufzählung verstanden, entsprechend § 71 mit Komma (siehe auch § 79 (2) und (3)):

Das ist ja großartig, welch ein Glück! Au, das tut weh! Nein, nein!

E_2: Zur Kennzeichnung eines besonderen Nachdrucks setzt man auch nach frei stehenden Zeilen ein Ausrufezeichen.

Dies betrifft

(1) Überschriften und Werktitel:

Chance für eine diplomatische Lösung!
Kämpft für den Frieden!
Endlich!

Zum Punkt siehe § 68 (1); zum Fragezeichen siehe § 70 E_2.

(2) die Anrede:

Sehr geehrter Herr Präsident! Meine Damen und Herren!

E_3: Nach der Anrede etwa in Briefen kann man ein Ausrufezeichen oder entsprechend § 79 (1) ein Komma setzen:

Sehr geehrter Herr Schröder!
Entsprechend unserer telefonischen Vereinbarung ...

Sehr geehrter Herr Schröder,
entsprechend unserer telefonischen Vereinbarung ...

In der Schweiz auch ohne Zeichen am Ende:

Sehr geehrter Herr Schröder
Entsprechend unserer telefonischen Vereinbarung ...

§ 70 Mit dem Fragezeichen kennzeichnet man den Ganzsatz als Frage.

Hast du ihn gestern gesehen? Wann kommst du? Kommst du wirklich morgen? Ob er morgen kommt? Soll er ihm einen Brief schreiben oder ist es besser, dass er ihn anruft?

Habt ihr nachgesehen, was Paul macht? Sehen Sie, wie schön die Aussicht ist? Haben Sie ihn aufgefordert die Wohnung sofort zu verlassen? Hat er gefragt, ob Fritz kommt?

Warst du im Kino? In welchem Film? Dein Freund war auch mit? Was möchtet ihr trinken: Bier, Wein oder Apfelmost? Ist das nicht großartig? Ist das nicht ein Glück? Warum? Weshalb? Weswegen?

E_1: Wenn aber als mehrteiliger Ganzsatz oder als Teile einer Aufzählung verstanden, entsprechend § 71 mit Komma:

Ist das nicht großartig, ist das nicht ein Glück? Warum, weshalb, weswegen?

E_2: Zur Kennzeichnung einer Frage setzt man auch nach frei stehenden Zeilen, zum Beispiel nach Überschriften und Werktiteln, ein Fragezeichen:

Chance für eine diplomatische Lösung?
Wo warst du, Adam?
Quo vadis?

Zum Punkt siehe § 68 (1); zum Ausrufezeichen siehe § 69 E_2.

2 Gliederung innerhalb von Ganzsätzen

(1) Der Gliederung des Ganzsatzes dienen die folgenden Satzzeichen:

- das Komma
- das Semikolon
- der Doppelpunkt
- der Gedankenstrich
- die Klammern

Zu den Auslassungspunkten siehe § 99 bis § 100.

(2) Das Komma wird sowohl einfach als auch paarig gebraucht:

Er trug einen schwarzen, breitkrempigen Hut. Seine Kopfbedeckung, ein schwarzer und breitkrempiger Hut, lag auf dem Tisch.

Dasselbe gilt für den Gedankenstrich.

Nur paarig werden die Klammern gebraucht, nur einfach das Semikolon und der Doppelpunkt.

(3) Manchmal kann man zwischen verschiedenen Zeichen wählen:

Im Hausflur war es still, ich drückte erwartungsvoll auf die Klingel.
Im Hausflur war es still; ich drückte erwartungsvoll auf die Klingel.
Im Hausflur war es still – ich drückte erwartungsvoll auf die Klingel.

Zur stärkeren Abgrenzung kann man entsprechend § 67 auch einen Punkt setzen:

Im Hausflur war es still. Ich drückte erwartungsvoll auf die Klingel.

Eines Tages, es war mitten im Sommer, hagelte es. Eines Tages – es war mitten im Sommer – hagelte es. Eines Tages (es war mitten im Sommer) hagelte es.

2.1 Komma

§ 71

> Gleichrangige (nebengeordnete) Teilsätze, Wortgruppen oder Wörter grenzt man mit Komma voneinander ab.

Dies betrifft (siehe aber § 72)

(1) gleichrangige Teilsätze

Im Hausflur war es still, ich drückte erwartungsvoll auf die Klingel. Die Musik wird leiser, der Vorhang hebt sich, das Spiel beginnt. Er dachte angestrengt nach, aber ihr Name fiel ihm nicht ein. Ich wollte ihm helfen, doch er ließ es nicht zu. Ich wollte ihm helfen, er ließ es jedoch nicht zu. Das ist ja großartig, welch ein Glück! Ist das nicht großartig, ist das nicht ein Glück?

Zur Möglichkeit der Wahl zwischen Komma, Semikolon oder Punkt siehe § 80 (1).

Er log beharrlich, er wisse von nichts, er sei es nicht gewesen. Wenn das wahr ist, wenn du ihn wirklich nicht gesehen hast, brauchst du dir keine Vorwürfe zu machen. Er erkundigte sich, was es Neues gebe, ob Post gekommen sei. Dass sie ihn nicht nur übersah, sondern dass sie auch noch mit anderen flirtete, kränkte ihn sehr.

(2) gleichrangige Wortgruppen oder Wörter in Aufzählungen:

Der Nachbar hatte versprochen den Briefkasten zu leeren, die Blumen zu gießen, hin und wieder zu lüften. Völlig erschöpft, hungrig und frierend, vom Regen durchnässt kamen sie nach Hause. Er hat nicht behauptet in Berlin gewesen zu sein, sondern in Mainz seinen Onkel besucht zu haben. Sie ärgerte sich ständig über ihren Mann, über die Kinder, über die Hausbewohner.

Er trug einen schwarzen, breitkrempigen Hut. Das ist ein ausgesprochen süßes, widerlich klebriges Getränk. (Siehe aber unten E_1.)

Zu Fällen wie den folgenden siehe § 77 (4): *Auf der Ausstellung waren viele ausländische, insbesondere holländische Firmen vertreten. Als er sein Herz ausgeschüttet, das heißt alles erzählt hatte, fühlte er sich besser.*

Die Buchstaben x, y, z bilden den Schluss des Alphabets. Frühling, Sommer, Herbst, Winter.

Er fährt nicht mit dem Auto, sondern mit dem Zug. Er ist klug, (dabei) aber faul. Einerseits ist er klug, andererseits faul. Der März war teils freundlich, teils regnerisch, aber im Ganzen zu kalt. Sie lächelte halb verlegen, halb belustigt.

Nein, nein! Warum, weshalb, weswegen?

Zum Ausrufe- oder Fragezeichen siehe § 69 bzw. § 70.
Zum Komma bei mehrteiligen Orts-, Wohnungs-, Zeit- und Literaturangaben siehe § 77 (3).

E_1: Sind zwei Adjektive nicht gleichrangig, so setzt man kein Komma.

die letzten großen Ferien, eine neue blaue Bluse, dunkles bayerisches Bier, die allgemeine wirtschaftliche Lage, zahlreiche wertende Stellungnahmen

Gelegentlich kann der Schreibende dadurch, dass er ein Komma setzt oder nicht, deutlich machen, ob er die Adjektive als gleichrangig verstanden wissen will oder nicht.

Gleichrangig: *neue, umweltfreundliche Verfahren* (neben den bisherigen Verfahren, die nicht umweltfreundlich sind, gibt es nunmehr neue und umweltfreundliche Verfahren)

Nicht gleichrangig: *neue umweltfreundliche Verfahren* (zusätzlich zu den bisherigen umweltfreundlichen Verfahren gibt es weitere umweltfreundliche Verfahren)

E_2: Das Komma und der Schlusspunkt können in kolumnenartigen Aufzählungen fehlen, zum Beispiel:

Unser Sonderangebot:
- *Äpfel*
- *Birnen*
- *Orangen*

§ 72

> Sind die gleichrangigen Teilsätze, Wortgruppen oder Wörter durch *und, oder, beziehungsweise/bzw., sowie (= und), wie (= und), entweder ... oder, nicht ... noch, sowohl ... als (auch), sowohl ... wie (auch)* oder durch *weder ... noch* verbunden, so setzt man kein Komma.

Dies betrifft

(1) gleichrangige Teilsätze (siehe aber § 73):

Die Musik wird leiser und der Vorhang hebt sich und das Spiel beginnt. Ich habe sie oft besucht und wir saßen bis spät in die Nacht zusammen. Seid ihr mit meinem Vorschlag einverstanden oder habt ihr Einwände vorzubringen?

Sie wisse Bescheid und der Vorgang sei ihr völlig klar, sagte sie. Er erkundigte sich, was es Neues gebe und ob Post gekommen sei. Alle wollten wissen, wie es gewesen sei und warum es so lange gedauert habe. Ich hoffe, dass es dir gefällt und dass du zufrieden bist.

(2) gleichrangige Wortgruppen oder Wörter in Aufzählungen:

Der Nachbar hatte versprochen den Briefkasten zu leeren und die Blumen zu gießen und hin und wieder zu lüften. Völlig erschöpft und vom Regen durchnässt kamen sie nach Hause.

Sie fährt sowohl bei gutem als auch bei schlechtem Wetter. Der März war kalt und unfreundlich. Das ist ein ausgesprochen süßes sowie widerlich klebriges Getränk. Feuer, Wasser, Luft und Erde

Sie fährt entweder mit dem Auto oder mit dem Zug. Er ist klug und dabei faul. Nein und abermals nein! Wie und warum und wozu?

E_1: Ein Komma vor *und* usw. kann dadurch begründet sein, dass mit ihm entsprechend § 74 ein Nebensatz, entsprechend § 77 ein Zusatz oder Nachtrag bzw. entsprechend § 93 ein wörtlich wiedergegebener Satz abgeschlossen wird:

Er sagte, dass er morgen komme, und verabschiedete sich. Mein Onkel, ein großer Tierfreund, und seine Katzen leben in einer alten Mühle. Sie fragte: „Brauchen Sie die Unterlagen?", und öffnete die Schublade.

E_2: Bei entgegenstellenden Konjunktionen wie *aber, doch, jedoch, sondern* steht nach der Grundregel (§ 71) ein Komma, wenn sie zwischen gleichrangigen Wörtern oder Wortgruppen stehen:

Sie fährt nicht nur bei gutem, sondern auch bei schlechtem Wetter. Der März war sonnig, aber kalt. Er hat mir ein süßes, jedoch wohlschmeckendes Getränk eingeschenkt.

§ 73 Bei gleichrangigen Teilsätzen, die durch *und, oder* usw. verbunden sind, kann man ein Komma setzen, um die Gliederung des Ganzsatzes deutlich zu machen.

Ich habe sie oft besucht(,) und wir saßen bis spät in die Nacht zusammen, wenn sie in guter Stimmung war. Es war nicht selten, dass er sie besuchte(,) und dass sie bis spät in die Nacht zusammensaßen, wenn sie in guter Stimmung war.

Er traf sich mit meiner Schwester(,) und deren Freundin war auch mitgekommen. Wir warten auf euch(,) oder die Kinder gehen schon voraus. Ich fotografierte die Berge(,) und meine Frau lag in der Sonne.

§ 74 Nebensätze grenzt man mit Komma ab; sind sie eingeschoben, so schließt man sie mit paarigem Komma ein.

Am Anfang des Ganzsatzes:

Was ich anfangen soll, weiß ich nicht. Als wir nach Hause kamen, war es schon spät. Dass es dir wieder besser geht, freut mich sehr. Obwohl schlechtes Wetter war, suchten wir die Ostereier im Garten. Ist dir der Weg zu weit, kannst du mit dem Bus fahren. Er komme morgen, sagte er. Als er sich niederbeugte, weil er ihre Tasche aufheben wollte, stießen sie mit den Köpfen zusammen.

Eingeschoben:

Das Buch, das ich dir mitgebracht habe, liegt auf dem Tisch. Seine Annahme, dass Peter käme, erfüllte sich nicht. Sie konnte, wenn sie wollte, äußerst liebenswürdig sein. Er sagte, dass er morgen komme, und verabschiedete sich. Er sagte, er komme morgen, und verabschiedete sich.

Am Ende des Ganzsatzes:

Ich weiß nicht, was ich anfangen soll. Sie beobachtete die Kinder, die auf der Wiese ihre Drachen steigen ließen. Gestern traf ich eine Freundin, von der ich lange nichts mehr gehört hatte. Das Kind weinte, weil es seinen Schlüssel verloren hatte. Ich hätte nie gedacht, dass du mich so enttäuschen würdest. Sie sah gesünder aus, als sie sich fühlte. Seine Tochter war ebenso rothaarig, wie er es als Kind gewesen war. Sie sagte, sie komme morgen. Er war zu klug, als dass er in die Falle gegangen wäre, die man ihm gestellt hatte.

E_1: Besteht die Einleitung eines Nebensatzes aus einem Einleitewort und weiteren Wörtern, so gilt:

(1) Man setzt das Komma vor die ganze Wortgruppe:

Ich habe sie selten besucht, aber wenn ich bei ihr war, saßen wir bis spät in die Nacht zusammen. Er rannte, als ob es um sein Leben ginge, über die Straße. Sie rannte, wie wenn es um ihr Leben ginge. Ein Passant hatte bereits Risse in den Pfeilern der Brücke bemerkt, zwei Tage bevor sie zusammenbrach.

(2) In einigen Fällen kann der Schreibende zusätzlich ein Komma zwischen den Bestandteilen der Wortgruppe setzen:

Morgen wird es regnen, angenommen(,) dass der Wetterbericht stimmt. Wir fahren morgen, ausgenommen(,) wenn es regnet. Ich glaube nicht, dass er anruft, geschweige(,) dass er vorbeikommt. Ich glaube nicht, dass er anruft, geschweige denn(,) dass er vorbeikommt. Ich komme morgen, gleichviel(,) ob er es will oder nicht. Ich werde ihnen gegenüber abweisend oder entgegenkommend sein, je nachdem(,) ob sie hartnäckig oder sachlich sind.

(3) Der Schreibende kann durch das Komma deutlich machen, ob er Wörter als Bestandteil der Nebensatzeinleitung verstanden wissen will oder nicht:

Ich freue mich, auch wenn du mir nur eine Karte schreibst. Ich freue mich auch, wenn du mir nur eine Karte schreibst. Die Rehe bemerkten ihn, gleich als er sein Versteck verließ. Die Rehe bemerkten ihn gleich, als er sein Versteck verließ. Er ärgerte sich zeitlebens, so dass er schon früh graue Haare bekam. Er ärgerte sich zeitlebens so, dass er schon früh graue Haare bekam. Sie sorgt sich um ihn, vor allem(,) wenn er nachts unterwegs ist. Sie sorgt sich um ihn vor allem, wenn er nachts unterwegs ist.

E_2: Wenn eine beiordnende Konjunktion wie *und, oder* (§ 72) Satzglieder oder Teile von Satzgliedern mit Nebensätzen verbindet, so steht zwischen den Bestandteilen einer solchen Reihung kein Komma. Gegenüber dem übergeordneten Satz sind die Teile der Reihung nur dann mit Komma abgetrennt, wenn der Nebensatz anschließt, nicht aber, wenn das Satzglied bzw. ein Teil eines Satzgliedes anschließt:

Außerordentlich bedauert hat er diesen Vorfall und dass das hier geschehen konnte.

Bei großer Dürre oder wenn der Föhn weht, ist das Rauchen hier streng verboten.
Wenn der Föhn weht oder bei großer Dürre ist das Rauchen hier streng verboten.
Das Rauchen ist hier streng verboten bei großer Dürre oder wenn der Föhn weht.
Das Rauchen ist hier streng verboten, wenn der Föhn weht oder bei großer Dürre.

E_3: Vergleiche mit *als* oder *wie* in Verbindung mit einer Wortgruppe oder einem Wort sind keine Nebensätze; entsprechend setzt man kein Komma (zu *wie* siehe auch § 78 (2)):

Früher als gewöhnlich kam er von der Arbeit nach Hause. Wie im letzten Jahr hatten wir auch diesmal einen schönen Herbst. Er kam früher als gewöhnlich von der Arbeit nach Hause. Er kam wie am Vortage auch heute zu spät. Peter ist größer als sein Vater. Heute war er früher da als gestern. Das ging schneller als erwartet. Er ist genauso groß wie sie.

§ 75 Bei formelhaften Nebensätzen kann man das Komma weglassen.

Wie bereits gesagt(,) verhält sich die Sache anders. Ich komme(,) wenn nötig(,) bei dir noch vorbei.

§ 76 Bei Infinitiv-, Partizip- oder Adjektivgruppen oder bei entsprechenden Wortgruppen kann man ein (gegebenenfalls paariges) Komma setzen, um die Gliederung des Ganzsatzes deutlich zu machen bzw. um Missverständnisse auszuschließen.

Sie ist bereit(,) zu diesem Unternehmen ihren Beitrag zu leisten. Etwas Schöneres(,) als bei dir zu sein(,) gibt es nicht. Durch eine Tasse Kaffee gestärkt(,) werden wir die Arbeit fortsetzen. Darauf aufmerksam gemacht(,) haben wir den Fehler beseitigt. Er sah sich(,) ihn laut und wütend beschimpfend(,) nach einem Fluchtweg um. Sie suchte(,) den etwas ungenauen Stadtplan in der Hand(,) ein Straßenschild.

Ich hoffe(,) jeden Tag(,) in die Stadt gehen zu können. Ich rate(,) ihm(,) zu helfen. Die Kranke versuchte(,) täglich(,) etwas länger aufzubleiben. Sabine versprach(,) ihrem Vater(,) einen Brief zu schreiben(,) und verabschiedete sich. Er ging(,) gestern(,) von allen wütend beschimpft(,) zur Polizei.

Zum Komma bei Infinitivgruppen usw. in Verbindung mit einem hinweisenden Wort siehe § 77 (5).

Zum Komma bei nachgetragenen Infinitivgruppen oder entsprechenden Wortgruppen siehe § 77 (6), bei nachgetragenen Partizip-, Adjektivgruppen oder entsprechenden Wortgruppen auch am Ende des Ganzsatzes siehe § 77 (7).

Zur Möglichkeit der Wahl, Infinitivgruppen usw. mit Komma als Zusatz oder Nachtrag zu kennzeichnen, siehe § 78 (3).

§ 77 Zusätze oder Nachträge grenzt man mit Komma ab; sind sie eingeschoben, so schließt man sie mit paarigem Komma ein.

Möglich sind in bestimmten Fällen auch Gedankenstrich (siehe § 84) oder Klammern (siehe § 86); mit diesen Zeichen kennzeichnet man stärker, dass man etwas als Zusatz oder Nachtrag verstanden wissen will.

Dies betrifft (1) Parenthesen, (2) Substantivgruppen als Nachträge (Appositionen), (3) Orts-, Wohnungs-, Zeit- und Literaturangaben ohne Präposition, (4) Erläuterungen, (5) angekündigte Wörter oder Wortgruppen, (6) Infinitivgruppen und (7) Partizip- oder Adjektivgruppen.

(1) Parenthesen:

Eines Tages, es war mitten im Sommer, hagelte es. Dieses Bild, es ist das letzte und bekannteste des Künstlers, wurde nach Amerika verkauft. Ihre Forderung, um das noch einmal zu sagen, halten wir für wenig angemessen.

Zum Gedankenstrich oder zu Klammern siehe § 84 (1) bzw. § 86 (1).

(2) Substantivgruppen als Nachträge (Appositionen), insbesondere auch Titel, Berufsbezeichnungen und dergleichen in Verbindung mit Eigennamen:

Mein Onkel, ein großer Tierfreund, und seine Katzen leben in einer alten Mühle. Wir gingen in die Hütte, einen kalten Raum mit kleinen Fenstern. Wir gingen in die Hütte, einen kalten Raum mit kleinen Fenstern, und zündeten ein Feuer an. Walter Gerber, Mannheim, und Anita Busch, Berlin, verlobten sich letzte Woche.

Mainz ist die Geburtsstadt Johannes Gutenbergs, des Erfinders der Buchdruckerkunst. Johannes Gutenberg, der Erfinder der Buchdruckerkunst, wurde in Mainz geboren. Professor Dr. med. Max Müller, Direktor der Kinderklinik, war unser Gesprächspartner. Franz Meier, der Angeklagte, verweigerte die Aussage. Gertrud Patzke, Hebamme des Dorfes, wurde 60 Jahre alt.

Zum Gedankenstrich oder zu Klammern siehe § 84 (2) bzw. § 86 (2).

E_1: Folgt der Eigenname einem Titel, einer Berufsbezeichnung und dergleichen, so kann man nach § 78 (4) das Komma weglassen:

Der Erfinder der Buchdruckerkunst(,) Johannes Gutenberg(,) wurde in Mainz geboren.

E_2: Bestandteile von mehrteiligen Eigennamen und vorangestellte Titel ohne Artikel sind keine Zusätze oder Nachträge; entsprechend setzt man kein Komma.

Wilhelm der Eroberer unterwarf ganz England. Direktor Professor Dr. med. Max Müller führte uns durch die Klinik.

Frau Schmidt geb. Kühn hat dies mitgeteilt.

Nach der Grundregel (§ 77) auch mit Komma: *Frau Schmidt, geb. Kühn, hat dies mitgeteilt.*

(3) Mehrteilige Orts-, Wohnungs-, Zeit- und Literaturangaben ohne Präposition (das schließende Komma kann hier auch weggelassen werden):

Orts-, Wohnungs- und Zeitangaben:

Gustav Meier, Wiesbaden, Wilhelmstr. 24, 1. Stock(,) hat diese Annonce aufgegeben. Gabi Schmid, Berlin, Landsberger Allee 209, 3. Stock(,) gewann eine Reise in den Harz. Aber: *Gabi hat lange in Köln am Kirchplatz 4 gewohnt.*

Die Tagung soll Mittwoch, (den) 14. November(,) beginnen. Die Tagung soll am Mittwoch, dem 14. November(,) beginnen. Die Tagung soll am Mittwoch, dem 14. November, (um) 9.00 Uhr(,) im Rosengarten beginnen.

Mehrteilige Hinweise auf Stellen aus Büchern, Zeitschriften und dergleichen:

Die Zeitschrift Spektrum, Jahrgang 29, Heft 2, S. 134(,) hat darüber berichtet. In der Zeitschrift Spektrum, Jahrgang 29, Heft 2, S. 134(,) findet sich ein entsprechendes Zitat.

Ausnahme: In mehrteiligen Hinweisen auf Gesetze, Verordnungen und dergleichen setzt man kein Komma:

§ 6 Abs. 2 Satz 3 der Verordnung

(4) Nachgestellte Erläuterungen, die häufig mit *also, besonders, das heißt (d.h.), das ist (d.i.), genauer, insbesondere, nämlich, und das, und zwar, vor allem, zum Beispiel (z.B.)* oder dergleichen eingeleitet werden:

Sie isst gern Obst, besonders Apfelsinen und Bananen. Obst, besonders Apfelsinen und Bananen, isst sie gern. Wir erwarten dich nächste Woche, und zwar am Dienstag. Nachmittags kommt Gewitterneigung auf, vor allem im Süden. Mit einem Scheck über 2000 DM, in Worten: zweitausend Mark, hat er die Rechnung bezahlt. Sie bezahlte mit einem Scheck über 2000 DM, in Worten: zweitausend Mark.

Auf der Ausstellung waren viele ausländische Firmen, insbesondere holländische [Maschinenhersteller/Firmen], vertreten. Wir erwarten dich nächste Woche, das heißt vielleicht auch übernächste [Woche], zu einem Gespräch. Als sie ihr Herz ausgeschüttet hatte, das heißt alles erzählt hatte, fühlte sie sich besser.

Wird – im Unterschied zu den letztgenannten Beispielen – die Erläuterung in die substantivische oder verbale Fügung einbezogen, so grenzt man sie mit einfachem Komma ab:

Auf der Ausstellung waren viele ausländische, insbesondere holländische Firmen vertreten. Wir erwarten dich nächste, das heißt vielleicht auch übernächste Woche zu einem Gespräch. Er wird sein Herz ausgeschüttet, das heißt alles erzählt haben.

Zum Gedankenstrich oder zu Klammern siehe § 84 (3) bzw. § 86 (3).

(5) Wörter oder Wortgruppen, die durch ein hinweisendes Wort oder eine hinweisende Wortgruppe angekündigt werden:

Sie, die Gärtnerin, weiß das ganz genau. Wir beide, du und ich, wissen es genau.

Daran, den Job länger zu behalten, dachte sie nicht. Sie dachte nicht daran, den Job länger zu behalten, und kündigte. Sein größter Wunsch ist es, eine Familie zu gründen. Dies, eine Familie zu gründen, ist sein größter Wunsch.

So, aus vollem Halse lachend, kam sie auf mich zu. So, mit dem Rucksack bepackt, standen wir vor dem Tor. So bepackt, den Rucksack auf dem Rücken, standen wir vor dem Tor.

Werden Wörter oder Wortgruppen durch ein hinweisendes Wort oder eine hinweisende Wortgruppe wieder aufgenommen, so grenzt man sie mit einfachem Komma ab:

Denn die Gärtnerin, die weiß das ganz genau. Und du und ich, wir beide wissen das genau. Wie im letzten Jahr, so hatten wir auch diesmal einen schönen Herbst.

... und den Job länger zu behalten, daran dachte sie nicht und kündigte. Eine Familie zu gründen, das ist sein größter Wunsch.

Aus vollem Halse lachend, so kam sie auf mich zu. Mit dem Rucksack bepackt, so standen wir vor dem Tor. Den Rucksack auf dem Rücken, so bepackt standen wir vor dem Tor.

Zum Gedankenstrich siehe § 84 (4).

(6) nachgetragene Infinitivgruppen oder entsprechende Wortgruppen (siehe dazu auch § 78 (3)):

Er, ohne den Vertrag vorher gelesen zu haben, hatte ihn sofort unterschrieben. Er, ohne jede Kenntnis des Vertragsinhalts, hatte sofort unterschrieben. Er, statt ihm zu Hilfe zu kommen, sah tatenlos zu.

(7) nachgetragene Partizip- oder Adjektivgruppen oder entsprechende Wortgruppen auch am Ende des Ganzsatzes (siehe auch § 78 (3)):

Sie, aus vollem Halse lachend, kam auf mich zu. Er, außer sich vor Freude, lief auf sie zu und umarmte sie. Sie, ganz in Decken verpackt, saß auf der Terrasse. Er kam auf mich zu, aus vollem Halse lachend. Er lief auf sie zu und umarmte sie, außer sich vor Freude. Sie saß auf der Terrasse, ganz in Decken verpackt. Die Klasse, zum Ausflug bereit, war auf dem Schulhof versammelt. Wir, den Rucksack auf dem Rücken, standen vor dem Tor. Die Klasse war auf dem Schulhof versammelt, zum Ausflug bereit. Wir standen vor dem Tor, den Rucksack auf dem Rücken.

Suchen Mitarbeiter, sprachkundig und schreibgewandt. Mehrere Mitarbeiter, sprachkundig und schreibgewandt, werden gesucht. Der November, kalt und nass, löste eine Grippe aus.

E_3: In einer festen Verbindung mit einem nachgestellten Adjektiv setzt man kein Komma.

Hänschen klein, Forelle blau, Whisky pur

§ 78

Oft liegt es im Ermessen des Schreibenden, ob er etwas mit Komma als Zusatz oder Nachtrag kennzeichnen will oder nicht.

Dies betrifft

(1) Gefüge mit Präpositionen, entsprechende Wortgruppen oder Wörter:

Die Fahrtkosten(,) einschließlich D-Zug-Zuschlag(,) betragen 25,00 Mark. Die Fahrtkosten betragen 25,00 Mark(,) einschließlich D-Zug-Zuschlag. Sie hatte(,) trotz aller guten Vorsätze(,) wieder zu rauchen angefangen. Sie hatte(,) bedauerlicherweise(,) wieder zu rauchen angefangen. Der Kranke hatte(,) entgegen ärztlichem Verbot(,) das Bett verlassen. Das war(,) nach allgemeinem Urteil(,) eine Fehlleistung. Er hatte sich(,) den ganzen Tag über(,) mit diesem Problem beschäftigt. Die ganze Familie(,) samt Kindern und Enkeln(,) besuchte die Großeltern.

(2) Gefüge mit *wie* (zu *wie* in Vergleichen siehe § 74 E_3):

Ihre Ausgaben(,) wie Fahrt- und Übernachtungskosten(,) werden Ihnen ersetzt.

(3) Infinitiv-, Partizip- oder Adjektivgruppen oder entsprechende Wortgruppen (siehe auch § 77 (6) und (7)):

Er hatte den Vertrag(,) ohne ihn vorher gelesen zu haben(,) sofort unterschrieben. Er hatte(,) ohne jede Kenntnis des Vertragsinhalts(,) sofort unterschrieben. Er hatte den Vertrag sofort unterschrieben(,) ohne ihn vorher gelesen zu haben. Er hatte sofort unterschrieben(,) ohne jede Kenntnis des Vertragsinhalts. Er sah(,) statt ihm zu Hilfe zu kommen(,) tatenlos zu. Er sah tatenlos zu(,) statt ihm zu Hilfe zu kommen. Sie hatte(,) um nicht zu spät zu kommen(,) ein Taxi genommen. Sie hatte ein Taxi genommen(,) um nicht zu spät zu kommen. Sein Wunsch(,) eine Familie zu gründen(,) war groß. Unfähig(,) einen Kompromiss zu schließen(,) beendete er die Verhandlung.

Sie kam(,) aus vollem Halse lachend(,) auf mich zu. Er lief(,) außer sich vor Freude(,) auf sie zu und umarmte sie. Sie saß(,) ganz in Decken verpackt(,) auf der Terrasse. Die Klasse war(,) zum Ausflug bereit(,) auf dem Schulhof versammelt. Wir standen(,) den Rucksack auf dem Rücken(,) vor dem Tor. Er sah(,) den Spazierstock in der Hand(,) tatenlos zu.

(4) Eigennamen, die einem Titel, einer Berufsbezeichnung und dergleichen folgen (siehe auch § 77 (2)):

Der Erfinder der Buchdruckerkunst(,) Johannes Gutenberg(,) wurde in Mainz geboren. Der Direktor der Kinderklinik(,) Professor Dr. med. Max Müller(,) war der Gesprächspartner. Der Angeklagte(,) Franz Meier(,) verweigerte die Aussage. Die Hebamme des Dorfes(,) Gertrud Patzke(,) wurde 60 Jahre alt.

§ 79 Anreden, Ausrufe oder Ausdrücke einer Stellungnahme, die besonders hervorgehoben werden sollen, grenzt man mit Komma ab; sind sie eingeschoben, so schließt man sie mit paarigem Komma ein.

Dies betrifft

(1) Anreden:

Kinder, hört doch mal zu. Hört doch mal zu, Kinder. Hört, Kinder, doch mal zu. Du, stell dir vor, was mir passiert ist! Kommst du mit ins Kino, Klaus-Dieter? Für heute sende ich dir, liebe Ruth, die herzlichsten Grüße.

Zur Möglichkeit der Wahl zwischen Komma oder Ausrufezeichen nach der Anrede etwa in Briefen siehe § 69 E_3.

(2) Ausrufe:

Oh, wie kalt das ist! Au, das tut weh! He, was machen Sie da? Was, du bist umgezogen? Du bist umgezogen, was? So ist es, ach, nun einmal. So ist es nun einmal, ach ja. Ach ja, so ist es nun einmal.

Aber ohne Hervorhebung:

Oh wenn sie doch käme! Ach lass mich doch in Ruhe!

(3) Ausdrücke einer Stellungnahme wie etwa einer Bejahung, Verneinung, Bekräftigung oder Bitte:

Ja, daran ist nicht zu zweifeln. Nein, das sollten Sie nicht tun, nein! Tatsächlich, das ist es. Das ist es, tatsächlich. Leider, das hat er gesagt. Das hat er gesagt, leider. Sie hat uns angerufen, eine gute Idee. Er hat, eine Unverschämtheit, uns auch noch angerufen.

Bitte, komm doch morgen pünktlich. Komm doch, bitte, morgen pünktlich. Komm doch morgen pünktlich, bitte. Danke, ich habe schon gegessen. Ich habe schon gegessen, danke.

Aber ohne Hervorhebung:

Bitte komm doch morgen pünktlich!

Zum Ausrufezeichen siehe § 69.
Zur Möglichkeit der Wahl zwischen Komma, Gedankenstrich oder Doppelpunkt siehe § 82.

2.2 Semikolon

§ 80 Mit dem Semikolon kann man gleichrangige (nebengeordnete) Teilsätze oder Wortgruppen voneinander abgrenzen. Mit dem Semikolon drückt man einen höheren Grad der Abgrenzung aus als mit dem Komma und einen geringeren Grad der Abgrenzung als mit dem Punkt.

Zur Abgrenzung mit Punkt siehe § 67; zur Abgrenzung mit Komma siehe § 71.

Dies betrifft

(1) gleichrangige, vor allem auch längere Hauptsätze (mit Nebensatz):

Im Hausflur war es still; ich drückte erwartungsvoll auf die Klingel. Meine Freundin hatte den Zug versäumt; deshalb kam sie eine halbe Stunde zu spät. Steffen wünscht sich schon lange einen Hund; aber seine Eltern dulden keine Tiere in der Wohnung. Die Angelegenheit ist erledigt; darum wollen wir nicht länger streiten. Wir müssen uns überlegen, mit welchem Zug wir fahren wollen; wenn wir den früheren Zug nehmen, müssen wir uns beeilen.

Möglich sind hier auch das schwächer abgrenzende Komma oder der stärker abgrenzende Punkt:

Im Hausflur war es still, ich drückte erwartungsvoll auf die Klingel.
Im Hausflur war es still. Ich drückte erwartungsvoll auf die Klingel.

Zum hier ebenfalls möglichen Gedankenstrich siehe § 82.

(2) gleichrangige Wortgruppen gleicher Struktur in Aufzählungen:

Unser Proviant bestand aus gedörrtem Fleisch, Speck und Rauchschinken; Ei- und Milchpulver; Reis, Nudeln und Grieß.

Möglich ist hier auch das schwächer abgrenzende, nicht untergliedernde Komma:

Unser Proviant bestand aus gedörrtem Fleisch, Speck und Rauchschinken, Ei- und Milchpulver, Reis, Nudeln und Grieß.

2.3 Doppelpunkt

§ 81 Mit dem Doppelpunkt kündigt man an, dass etwas Weiterführendes folgt.

Zur Schreibung des ersten Wortes nach Doppelpunkt siehe § 54 (1) und (2).

Dies betrifft

(1) wörtlich wiedergegebene Äußerungen oder Textstellen, wenn der Begleitsatz oder ein Teil von ihm vorausgeht:

Er sagte: „Ich komme morgen." Er sagte zu ihr: „Komm bitte morgen!" Er fragte: „Kommst du morgen?" Sie sagte: „Brauchen Sie die Unterlagen?", und öffnete die Schublade. Die Zeitung schrieb, dass die Bahn erklären ließ: „Wir haben die feste Absicht die Strecke stillzulegen."

Zu den Anführungszeichen siehe § 89.

(2) Aufzählungen, spezielle Angaben, Erklärungen oder dergleichen:

Er hat schon mehrere Länder besucht: Frankreich, Spanien, Rumänien, Polen. Die Namen der Monate sind folgende: Januar, Februar, März usw. Er hatte alles verloren: seine Frau, seine Kinder und sein ganzes Vermögen.

Wir stellen ein: Maschinenschlosser
Reinigungskräfte
Kraftfahrer

Nächste Arbeitsberatung: 30. 09. 1997

Familienstand: ledig

Latein: befriedigend

Robert Musil: Der Mann ohne Eigenschaften

Gebrauchsanweisung: Man nehme jede zweite Stunde eine Tablette.

Beachten Sie bitte folgenden Hinweis: Infolge der anhaltenden Trockenheit besteht Waldbrandgefahr.

(3) Zusammenfassungen des vorher Gesagten oder Schlussfolgerungen aus diesem:

Haus und Hof, Geld und Gut: alles ist verloren.

Wer immer nur an sich selbst denkt, wer nur danach trachtet, andere zu übervorteilen, wer sich nicht in die Gemeinschaft einfügen kann: der kann von uns keine Hilfe erwarten.

Möglich ist hier auch ein Gedankenstrich:

Haus und Hof, Geld und Gut – alles ist verloren.

Zur Möglichkeit der Wahl zwischen Doppelpunkt, Gedankenstrich und Komma siehe § 82.

2.4 Gedankenstrich

§ 82 Mit dem Gedankenstrich kündigt man an, dass etwas Weiterführendes folgt oder dass man das Folgende als etwas Unerwartetes verstanden wissen will.

Sie trat in das Zimmer und sah – ihren Mann. Im Hausflur war es still – ich drückte erwartungsvoll auf die Klingel. Zuletzt tat er etwas, woran niemand gedacht hatte – er beging Selbstmord. Plötzlich – ein vielstimmiger Schreckensruf!

Möglich sind hier teilweise auch Doppelpunkt oder Komma:

Plötzlich: ein vielstimmiger Schreckensruf!
Plötzlich, ein vielstimmiger Schreckensruf!

Zur Möglichkeit der Wahl zwischen Gedankenstrich und Doppelpunkt siehe § 81 (3).

§ 83 Zwischen zwei Ganzsätzen kann man zusätzlich zum Schlusszeichen einen Gedankenstrich setzen, um – ohne einen neuen Absatz zu beginnen – einen Wechsel deutlich zu machen.

Dies betrifft

(1) den Wechsel des Themas oder des Gedankens:

Wir sind nicht in der Lage diesen Wunsch zu erfüllen. – Nunmehr ist der nächste Punkt der Tagesordnung zu besprechen.

(2) den Wechsel des Sprechers:

Komm bitte einmal her! – Ja, ich komme sofort.

§ 84 Mit dem Gedankenstrich grenzt man Zusätze oder Nachträge ab; sind sie eingeschoben, so schließt man sie mit paarigem Gedankenstrich ein.

Möglich sind auch Kommas (siehe § 77) oder Klammern (siehe § 86).

Dies betrifft

(1) Parenthesen:

Eines Tages – es war mitten im Sommer – hagelte es. Eines Tages – es war mitten im Sommer! – hagelte es. Eines Tages – war es mitten im Sommer? – hagelte es. Dieses Bild – es ist das letzte und bekannteste des Künstlers – wurde nach Amerika verkauft. Ihre Forderung – um das noch einmal zu sagen – halten wir für wenig angemessen.

Zum Komma oder zu Klammern siehe § 77 (1) bzw. § 86 (1).

(2) Substantivgruppen als Nachträge (Appositionen):

Mein Onkel – ein großer Tierfreund – und seine Katzen leben in einer alten Mühle. Wir gingen in die Hütte – einen kalten Raum mit kleinen Fenstern. Wir gingen in die Hütte – einen kalten Raum mit kleinen Fenstern – und zündeten ein Feuer an. Johannes Gutenberg – der Erfinder der Buchdruckerkunst – wurde in Mainz geboren.

Zum Komma oder zu Klammern siehe § 77 (2) bzw. § 86 (2).

(3) nachgestellte Erläuterungen, die häufig mit *also, besonders, das heißt (d.h.), das ist (d.i.), genauer, insbesondere, nämlich, und das, und zwar, vor allem, zum Beispiel (z.B.)* oder dergleichen eingeleitet werden:

Sie isst gern Obst – besonders Apfelsinen und Bananen. Obst – besonders Apfelsinen und Bananen – isst sie gern. Wir erwarten dich nächste Woche – und zwar am Dienstag. Mit einem Scheck über 2 000 DM – in Worten: zweitausend Mark – hat er die Rechnung bezahlt. Er bezahlte mit einem Scheck über 2 000 DM – in Worten: zweitausend Mark.

Auf der Ausstellung waren viele ausländische Maschinenhersteller – insbesondere holländische – vertreten. Auf der Ausstellung waren viele ausländische Maschinenhersteller – vor allem holländische Firmen – vertreten. Auf der Ausstellung waren viele ausländische – insbesondere holländische – Maschinenhersteller vertreten.

Zum Komma oder zu Klammern siehe § 77 (4) bzw. § 86 (3).

(4) Wörter oder Wortgruppen, die durch ein hinweisendes Wort oder eine hinweisende Wortgruppe angekündigt werden:

Sie – die Gärtnerin – weiß es ganz genau. Wir beide – du und ich – wissen das genau. Das – eine Familie zu gründen – ist sein größter Wunsch.

Werden Wörter oder Wortgruppen durch ein hinweisendes Wort oder eine hinweisende Wortgruppe wieder aufgenommen, so grenzt man sie mit einfachem Gedankenstrich ab.

Denn die Gärtnerin – die weiß das ganz genau. Und du und ich – wir beide wissen das genau. Eine Familie zu gründen – das ist sein größter Wunsch.

Zum Komma siehe § 77 (5).

§ 85 Ausrufe- oder Fragezeichen, die zum Zusatz oder Nachtrag im paarigen Gedankenstrich gehören, setzt man vor den abschließenden Gedankenstrich; ein Schlusspunkt wird weggelassen.
Satzzeichen, die zum einschließenden Satz gehören und daher auch bei Weglassen des Zusatzes oder Nachtrags stehen müssten, dürfen nicht weggelassen werden.

Er behauptete – so eine Frechheit! –, dass er im Kino gewesen sei. Sie hat das – erinnerst du dich nicht? – gestern gesagt.

Sie betonte – ich weiß es noch ganz genau –, dass sie für einen Erfolg nicht garantieren könne. Vgl.: *Sie betonte, dass sie für einen Erfolg nicht garantieren könne.*

2.5 Klammern

§ 86

> Mit Klammern schließt man Zusätze oder Nachträge ein.

Möglich sind auch Komma (siehe § 77) oder Gedankenstrich (siehe § 84).

Dies betrifft

(1) Parenthesen:

Eines Tages (es war mitten im Sommer) hagelte es. Eines Tages (es war mitten im Sommer!) hagelte es. Eines Tages (war es mitten im Sommer?) hagelte es. Dieses Bild (es ist das letzte und bekannteste des Künstlers) wurde nach Amerika verkauft. Ihre Forderung (um das noch einmal zu sagen) halten wir für wenig angemessen.

Zum Komma oder zum Gedankenstrich siehe § 77 (1) bzw. § 84 (1).

(2) Substantivgruppen als Nachträge (Appositionen):

Mein Onkel (ein großer Tierfreund) und seine Katzen leben in einer alten Mühle. Wir gingen in die Hütte (einen kalten Raum mit kleinen Fenstern). Wir gingen in die Hütte (einen kalten Raum mit kleinen Fenstern) und zündeten ein Feuer an. Johannes Gutenberg (der Erfinder der Buchdruckerkunst) wurde in Mainz geboren.

Zum Komma oder zum Gedankenstrich siehe § 77 (2) bzw. § 84 (2).

(3) nachgestellte Erläuterungen, die häufig mit *also, besonders, das heißt (d.h.), das ist (d.i.), genauer, insbesondere, nämlich, und das, und zwar, vor allem, zum Beispiel (z.B.)* oder dergleichen eingeleitet werden:

Sie isst gern Obst (besonders Apfelsinen und Bananen). Obst (besonders Apfelsinen und Bananen) isst sie gern. Wir erwarten dich nächste Woche (und zwar am Dienstag). Mit einem Scheck über 2000 DM (in Worten: zweitausend Mark) hat er die Rechnung bezahlt. Er bezahlte mit einem Scheck über 2000 DM (in Worten: zweitausend Mark).

Auf der Ausstellung waren viele ausländische Maschinenhersteller (insbesondere holländische) vertreten. Auf der Ausstellung waren viele ausländische Maschinenhersteller (vor allem holländische Firmen) vertreten. Auf der Ausstellung waren viele ausländische (insbesondere holländische) Maschinenhersteller vertreten.

Zum Komma oder zum Gedankenstrich siehe § 77 (4) bzw. § 84 (3).

(4) Worterläuterungen, geographische, systematische, chronologische, biografische Zusätze und dergleichen:

Frankenthal (Pfalz)

Grille (Insekt) – Grille (Laune)

Als Hauptwerke Matthias Grünewalds gelten die Gemälde des Isenheimer Altars (vollendet 1511 oder 1515).

§ 87

> Mit Klammern kann man neben einzelnen Ganzsätzen insbesondere auch größere Textteile einschließen und auf diese Weise als selbständige Texteinheit kennzeichnen.

Sie betonte, dass sie für den Erfolg garantieren könne. (Ich weiß es noch ganz genau, da ich mir das notiert hatte. Und ich habe ihr diese Notiz auch gezeigt.)
Aber heute will sie nichts mehr davon wissen.

§ 88

> Ausrufe- oder Fragezeichen, die zum Zusatz oder Nachtrag in Klammern gehören, setzt man vor die abschließende Klammer.
> Ist der Zusatz oder Nachtrag in einen anderen Satz einbezogen, so lässt man seinen Schlusspunkt weg; wird er als Ganzsatz oder als selbständige Texteinheit verstanden, so setzt man den Schlusspunkt.
> Satzzeichen, die zum einschließenden Satz gehören und daher auch bei Weglassen des Zusatzes oder Nachtrags stehen müssten, dürfen nicht weggelassen werden.

Das geliehene Buch (du hast es schon drei Wochen!) hast du mir noch nicht zurückgegeben. Er hat das (erinnerst du dich nicht?) gestern gesagt.

Damit wäre dieses Thema vorerst erledigt (weitere Angaben siehe Seite 145). Damit wäre dieses Thema vorerst erledigt. (Weitere Angaben siehe Seite 145.)

Er sagte (dabei senkte er seine Stimme), dass das nicht alle wissen müssten.

„Der Staat bin ich" (Ludwig der Vierzehnte).

3 Anführung von Äußerungen oder Textstellen bzw. Hervorhebung von Wörtern oder Textstellen

3.1 Anführungszeichen

§ 89 Mit Anführungszeichen schließt man etwas wörtlich Wiedergegebenes ein.

Dies betrifft

(1) wörtlich wiedergegebene Äußerungen (direkte Rede):

„Es ist unbegreiflich, wie ich das hatte vergessen können", sagte sie. „Immer muss ich arbeiten!", seufzte sie. „Dass ich immer arbeiten muss!", seufzte sie. Er fragte: „Kommst du morgen?" „Kommst du morgen?", fragte er. Er fragte: „Kommst du morgen?", und verabschiedete sich. „Du siehst", sagte die Mutter, „recht gut aus." „Wir haben die feste Absicht die Strecke stillzulegen", erklärte der Vertreter der Bahn, „aber die Entscheidung der Regierung steht noch aus."

Dies gilt auch für Beispiele wie:

„Das war also Paris!", dachte Frank. „Du hast schon Recht", lächelte sie.

(2) wörtlich wiedergegebene Textstellen (Zitate):

Über das Ausscheidungsspiel berichtete ein Journalist: „Das Stadion glich einem Hexenkessel. Das Publikum stürmte auf das Spielfeld und bedrohte den Schiedsrichter."

Zum Doppelpunkt siehe § 81 (1)

§ 90 Satzzeichen, die zum wörtlich Wiedergegebenen gehören, setzt man vor das abschließende Anführungszeichen; Satzzeichen, die zum Begleitsatz gehören, setzt man nach dem abschließenden Anführungszeichen.

Im Einzelnen gilt:

§ 91 Sowohl der angeführte Satz als auch der Begleitsatz behalten ihr Ausrufe- oder Fragezeichen.

„Du kommst jetzt!", rief sie. „Kommst du morgen?", fragte er. Du solltest ihm sagen: „Ich kann das auf keinen Fall akzeptieren"! Hast du gesagt: „Ich kann das auf keinen Fall akzeptieren"? Sag ihm: „Ich habe keine Zeit!"! Fragtest du: „Wann beginnt der Film?"?

§ 92 Beim angeführten Satz lässt man den Schlusspunkt weg, wenn er am Anfang oder im Innern des Ganzsatzes steht.
Beim Begleitsatz lässt man den Schlusspunkt weg, wenn der angeführte Satz oder ein Teil von ihm am Ende des Ganzsatzes steht.

„Ich komme morgen", versicherte sie. Sie sagte: „Ich komme gleich wieder", und holte die Unterlagen.

Die Bahn erklärte: „Wir haben die feste Absicht die Strecke stillzulegen." Sie versicherte: „Ich komme morgen!" Er rief: „Du kommst jetzt!" Er fragte: „Kommst du?" „Komm bitte", sagte er, „morgen pünktlich."

§ 93 Folgt nach dem angeführten Satz der Begleitsatz oder ein Teil von ihm, so setzt man nach dem abschließenden Anführungszeichen ein Komma.
Ist der Begleitsatz in den angeführten Satz eingeschoben, so schließt man ihn mit paarigem Komma ein.

„Ich komme gleich wieder", versicherte sie. „Komm bald wieder!", rief sie. „Wann kommst du wieder?", rief sie. Sie sagte: „Ich komme gleich wieder", und holte die Unterlagen. Sie fragte: „Brauchen Sie die Unterlagen?", und öffnete die Schublade.

„Ich werde", versicherte sie, „bald wiederkommen." „Kommst du wirklich", fragte sie, „erst morgen Abend?"

§ 94 Mit Anführungszeichen kann man Wörter oder Teile innerhalb eines Textes hervorheben und in bestimmten Fällen deutlich machen, dass man zu ihrer Verwendung Stellung nimmt, sich auf sie bezieht.

Dies betrifft

(1) Überschriften, Werktitel (etwa von Büchern und Theaterstücken), Namen von Zeitungen und dergleichen:

Sie las den Artikel „Chance für eine diplomatische Lösung" in der „Wochenpost". Sie liest Heinrich Bölls Roman „Wo warst du, Adam?". Kennst du den Roman „Wo warst du, Adam?"? Wir lesen gerade den „Kaukasischen Kreidekreis" von Brecht.

Zur Groß- und Kleinschreibung siehe § 53 E_2.

(2) Sprichwörter, Äußerungen und dergleichen, zu denen man kommentierend Stellung nehmen will:

Das Sprichwort „Eile mit Weile" hört man oft. „Aller Anfang ist schwer" ist nicht immer ein hilfreicher Spruch.

Sein kritisches „Der Wein schmeckt nach Essig" ärgerte den Kellner. Ihr bittendes „Kommst du morgen?" stimmte mich um. Seine ständige Entschuldigung „Ich habe keine Zeit!" ist wenig glaubhaft. Mich nervt sein dauerndes „Ich kann nicht mehr!".

Textteile dieser Art werden nicht mit Komma abgegrenzt. Im Übrigen gilt § 90 bis § 92.

(3) Wörter oder Wortgruppen, über die man eine Aussage machen will:

Das Wort „fälisch" ist gebildet in Anlehnung an West„falen". Der Begriff „Existenzialismus" wird heute vielfältig verwendet. Alle seine Freunde nannten ihn „Dickerchen". Die Präposition „ohne" verlangt den Akkusativ.

(4) Wörter oder Wortgruppen, die man anders als sonst – etwa ironisch oder übertragen – verstanden wissen will:

Und du willst ein „treuer Freund" sein? Für diesen „Liebesdienst" bedanke ich mich. Er bekam wieder einmal seine „Grippe". Sie sprang diesmal „nur" 6,60 Meter.

§ 95 Steht in einem Text mit Anführungszeichen etwas ebenfalls Angeführtes, so kennzeichnet man dies durch die so genannten halben Anführungszeichen.

Die Zeitung schrieb: „Die Bahn hat bereits im Frühjahr erklärt: ‚Wir haben die feste Absicht die Strecke stillzulegen', und sie hat das auf Anfrage gestern noch einmal bestätigt." „Das war ein Satz aus Bölls ‚Wo warst du, Adam?', den viele nicht kennen", sagte er.

4 Markierung von Auslassungen

4.1 Apostroph

Mit dem Apostroph zeigt man an, dass man in einem Wort einen Buchstaben oder mehrere ausgelassen hat.

Zu unterscheiden sind:

a) Gruppen, bei denen man den Apostroph setzen muss (siehe § 96),

b) Gruppen, bei denen der Gebrauch des Apostrophs dem Schreibenden freigestellt ist (siehe § 97).

§ 96 Man setzt den Apostroph in drei Gruppen von Fällen.

Dies betrifft

(1) Eigennamen, deren Grundform (Nominativform) auf einen s-Laut (geschrieben: *-s, -ss, -ß, -tz, -z, -x, -ce*) endet, bekommen im Genitiv den Apostroph, wenn sie nicht einen Artikel, ein Possessivpronomen oder dergleichen bei sich haben:

Aristoteles' Schriften, Carlos' Schwester, Ines' gute Ideen, Felix' Vorschlag, Heinz' Geburtstag, Alice' neue Wohnung

E_1: Aber ohne Apostroph:

die Schriften des Aristoteles, die Schwester des Carlos, der Geburtstag unseres kleinen Heinz

E_2: Der Apostroph steht auch, wenn *-s, -z, -x* usw. in der Grundform stumm sind:
Cannes' Filmfestspiele, Boulez' bedeutender Beitrag, Giraudoux' Werke

(2) Wörter mit Auslassungen, die ohne Kennzeichnung schwer lesbar oder missverständlich sind:
In wen'gen Augenblicken ... 's ist schade um ihn. Das Wasser rauscht', das Wasser schwoll.

(3) Wörter mit Auslassungen im Wortinneren wie:
D'dorf (= Düsseldorf), M'gladbach (= Mönchengladbach), Ku'damm (= Kurfürstendamm)

§ 97 Man kann den Apostroph setzen, wenn Wörter gesprochener Sprache mit Auslassungen bei schriftlicher Wiedergabe undurchsichtig sind.

der Käpt'n, mit'm Fahrrad
Bitte, nehmen S' (= Sie) doch Platz! Das war 'n (= ein) Bombenerfolg!

E: Von dem Apostroph als Auslassungszeichen zu unterscheiden ist der gelegentliche Gebrauch dieses Zeichens zur Verdeutlichung der Grundform eines Personennamens vor der Genitivendung *-s* oder vor dem Adjektivsuffix *-sch:*
Carlo's Taverne, Einstein'sche Relativitätstheorie

Zur Schreibung der adjektivischen Ableitungen von Personennamen auf *-sch* siehe auch § 49 und § 62.

4.2 Ergänzungsstrich

§ 98 Mit dem Ergänzungsstrich zeigt man an, dass in Zusammensetzungen oder Ableitungen einer Aufzählung ein gleicher Bestandteil ausgelassen wurde, der sinngemäß zu ergänzen ist.

Zum Bindestrich wie in *A-Dur* siehe § 40 ff.

Dies betrifft

(1) den letzten Bestandteil:
Haupt- und Nebeneingang (= Haupteingang und Nebeneingang); Eisenbahn-, Straßen-, Luft- und Schiffsverkehr; vitamin- und eiweißhaltig, saft- und kraftlos, ein- und ausladen

Natur- und synthetische Gewebe, Standard- und individuelle Lösungen; zurück-, voraus- oder abwärts fahren; (in umgekehrter Abfolge:) *synthetische und Naturgewebe, individuelle und Standardlösungen; abwärts, voraus- oder zurückfahren*

(2) den ersten Bestandteil:
Verkehrslenkung und -überwachung (= Verkehrslenkung und Verkehrsüberwachung); Schulbücher, -hefte, -mappen und -utensilien; heranführen oder -schleppen, bergauf und -ab

Mozart-Symphonien und -Sonaten (= Mozart-Symphonien und Mozart-Sonaten)

(3) den letzten und den ersten Bestandteil:
Textilgroß- und -einzelhandel (= Textilgroßhandel und Textileinzelhandel), Eisenbahnunter- und -überführungen

Werkzeugmaschinen-Import- und -Exportgeschäfte

4.3 Auslassungspunkte

§ 99 Mit drei Punkten (Auslassungspunkten) zeigt man an, dass in einem Wort, Satz oder Text Teile ausgelassen worden sind.

Du bist ein E...! Scher dich zum ...!

„... ihm nicht weitersagen“, hörte er ihn gerade noch sagen. Der Horcher an der Wand ...

Vollständiger Text: *In einem Buch heißt es: „Die zahlreichen Übungen sind konkret auf das abgestellt, was vorher behandelt worden ist. Sie liefern in der Regel Material, mit dem selbst gearbeitet und an dem geprüft werden kann, ob das, was vorher dargestellt wurde, verstanden worden ist oder nicht. Die im Anhang zusammengestellten Lösungen machen eine unmittelbare Kontrolle der eigenen Lösungen möglich.“*

Mit Auslassung: *In einem Buch heißt es: „Die ... Übungen ... liefern ... Material, mit dem selbst gearbeitet ... werden kann ... Die ... Lösungen machen eine ... Kontrolle ... möglich."*

§ 100 Stehen die Auslassungspunkte am Ende eines Ganzsatzes, so setzt man keinen Satzschlusspunkt.

Ich habe die Nase voll und ...
Diese Szene stammt doch aus dem Film „Die Wüste lebt" ...
Mit „Es war einmal ..." beginnen viele Märchen.
Viele Märchen beginnen mit den Worten: „Es war einmal ..."
Aber: *Verflixt! Ich habe die Nase voll und ...!*

5 Kennzeichnung der Wörter bestimmter Gruppen

5.1 Punkt

§ 101 Mit dem Punkt kennzeichnet man bestimmte Abkürzungen (abgekürzte Wörter)

Dies betrifft Fälle wie:

Tel. (= Telefon), Pf. (= Pfennig), Ztr. (= Zentner), v. (= von), Bd. (= Band), Bde. (= Bände), Ms. (= Manuskript), Jg. (= Jahrgang), Jh. (= Jahrhundert), Jh.s (= des Jahrhunderts), f. (= folgende Seite), ff. (= folgende Seiten); lfd. Nr. (= laufende Nummer), z. B. (= zum Beispiel), u. A. w. g. (= um Antwort wird gebeten); Weißenburg i. Bay. (= Weißenburg in Bayern), Bad Homburg v. d. H. (= Bad Homburg vor der Höhe); Reg.-Rat (= Regierungsrat), Masch.-Schr. (= Maschinenschreiben); Abt.-Leiter (= Abteilungsleiter), Rechnungs-Nr. (= Rechnungsnummer); Tsd. (= Tausend), Mio. (= Million(en)), Mrd. (= Milliarde(n))

Dr. med., stud. med., stud. phil., a. D., h. c.

§ 102 Bestimmte Abkürzungen, Kurzwörter und dergleichen stehen üblicherweise ohne Punkt.

Dies betrifft

(1) Abkürzungen, die national oder international festgelegt sind, wie etwa Abkürzungen

(1.1) für Maße in Naturwissenschaft und Technik nach dem internationalen Einheitssystem:
m (= Meter), g (= Gramm), km/h (= Kilometer pro Stunde), s (= Sekunde), A (= Ampere), Hz (= Hertz)

(1.2) für Himmelsrichtungen:
NO (= Nordost), SSW (= Südsüdwest)

(1.3) für bestimmte Währungsbezeichnungen:
DM (= Deutsche Mark)

(2) sogenannte Initialwörter und Kürzel:
BGB (= Bürgerliches Gesetzbuch), TÜV (= Technischer Überwachungsverein), Na (= Natrium; so alle chemischen Grundstoffe);

des PKW(s), die EKG(s), KFZ-Papiere, FKKler, U-Bahn

E_1: Ohne Punkt stehen teilweise auch fachsprachliche Abkürzungen wie:

RücklVO (= Rücklagenverordnung), LArbA (= Landesarbeitsamt)

E_2: In einigen Fällen gibt es Doppelformen.

Co./Co (ko) (= Companie), M.d.B./MdB (= Mitglied des Bundestages), G.m.b.H./GmbH (= Gesellschaft mit beschränkter Haftung); WW/Wirk. Wort (= Wirkendes Wort; Titel einer Zeitschrift), AA/Ausw. Amt (= Auswärtiges Amt)

§ 103 Am Ende eines Ganzsatzes setzt man nach Abkürzungen nur *einen* Punkt.

Sein Vater ist Regierungsrat a. D.
Aber: *Ist sein Vater Regierungsrat a. D.?*

§ 104 Mit dem Punkt kennzeichnet man Zahlen, die in Ziffern geschrieben sind, als Ordinalzahlen.

der 2. Weltkrieg, der II. Weltkrieg; Sonntag, den 20. November; Friedrich II., König von Preußen; die Regierung Friedrich Wilhelms III. (des Dritten)

§ 105 Am Ende eines Ganzsatzes setzt man nach Ordinalzahlen, die in Ziffern geschrieben sind, nur *einen* Punkt.

Der König von Preußen hieß Friedrich II.
Aber: *Wann regierte Friedrich II.?*

5.2 Schrägstrich

§ 106 Mit dem Schrägstrich kennzeichnet man, dass Wörter (Namen, Abkürzungen), Zahlen oder dergleichen zusammengehören.

Dies betrifft

(1) die Angaben mehrerer (alternativer) Möglichkeiten im Sinne einer Verbindung mit *und, oder, bzw., bis* oder dergleichen:

die Schüler/Schülerinnen der Realschule, das Semikolon/der Strichpunkt als stilistisches Zeichen, Männer/Frauen/Kinder; Abfahrt vom Dienstort/Wohnort, die Rundfunkgebühren für Januar/Februar/März, Montag/Dienstag, Wien/Heidelberg 1967, September/Oktober-Heft (auch *September-Oktober-Heft;* siehe § 44)

die Koalition CDU/FDP, die SPÖ/ÖVP-Koalition

das Wintersemester 1996/97, am 9./10. Dezember 1997

(2) die Gliederung von Adressen, Telefonnummern, Aktenzeichen, Rechnungsnummern, Diktatzeichen und dergleichen:

Linzer Straße 67/I/5-6, 0621/1581-0, Az III/345/5, Re-Nr 732/24, me/la

(3) die Angabe des Verhältnisses von Zahlen oder Größen im Sinne einer Verbindung mit *je/pro:*

im Durchschnitt 80 km/h, 1 000 Einwohner/km²

F Worttrennung am Zeilenende

0 Vorbemerkungen

(1) Wörter mit mehr als einer Silbe kann man am Ende einer Zeile trennen.

(2) Steht am Zeilenende ein Bindestrich, so gilt er zugleich als Trennungsstrich.

§ 107 Geschriebene Wörter trennt man am Zeilenende so, wie sie sich bei langsamem Sprechen in Silben zerlegen lassen.

Beispiele:

Bau-er, Ei-er, steu-ern, na-iv, Mu-se-um, in-di-vi-du-ell; eu-ro-pä-i-sche, Ru-i-ne, na-ti-o-nal, Fami-li-en; Haus-tür, Be-fund, ehr-lich

E: Die Abtrennung eines einzelnen Vokals am Ende ist überflüssig, da der Trennungsstrich den gleichen Raum in Anspruch nimmt, zum Beispiel:

Kleie, laue (nicht: *Klei-e, lau-e*)

Dabei gilt im Einzelnen:

§ 108 Steht in einfachen Wörtern zwischen Vokalbuchstaben ein einzelner Konsonantenbuchstabe, so kommt er bei der Trennung auf die neue Zeile. Stehen mehrere Konsonantenbuchstaben dazwischen, so kommt nur der letzte auf die neue Zeile.

Beispiele:

Au-ge, A-bend, Bre-zel, He-xe, bei-ßen, Rei-he, Wei-mar; Trai-ning, ba-nal, trau-rig, nei-disch, Hei-mat

El-tern, Gar-be, Hop-fen, Lud-wig, ros-ten, leug-nen, sin-gen, sin-ken, sit-zen, Städ-te; Bag-ger, Wel-le, Kom-ma, ren-nen, Pap-pe, müs-sen, beis-sen (wenn *ss* statt *ß*, vgl. § 25 E_2 und E_3), *Drit-tel; zän-kisch, Ach-tel, Rech-ner, ber-gig, wid-rig, Ar-mut, freund-lich, frucht-bar, ernst-lich, sechs-te; imp-fen, Karp-fen, kühns-te, knusp-rig, dunk-le*

§ 109 Stehen Buchstabenverbindungen wie *ch, sch; ph, rh, sh* oder *th* für *einen* Konsonanten, so trennt man sie nicht. Dasselbe gilt für *ck*.

Beispiele;

la-chen, wa-schen, Deut-sche; Sa-phir, Ste-phan, Myr-rhe, Bu-shel, Zi-ther, Goe-the; bli-cken, Zu-cker

§ 110 In Fremdwörtern können die Verbindungen aus Buchstaben für einen Konsonanten + *l*, *n* oder *r* entweder entsprechend § 108 getrennt werden, oder sie kommen ungetrennt auf die neue Zeile.

Beispiele:

nob-le/no-ble, Zyk-lus/Zy-klus, Mag-net/Ma-gnet, Feb-ruar/Fe-bruar, Hyd-rant/Hy-drant, Arth-ritis/Ar-thritis

§ 111 Zusammensetzungen und Wörter mit Präfix trennt man zwischen den einzelnen Bestandteilen.

Beispiele:

Heim-weg, Schul-hof, Week-end; Ent-wurf, Er-trag, Ver-lust, syn-chron, Pro-gramm, At-traktion, kom-plett, In-stanz

E_1: Die Bestandteile selbst trennt man entsprechend §108 bis § 110 wie einfache Wörter, zum Beispiel: *Papp-pla-kat, Schwimm-meis-ter, Po-ly-tech-nik, Kon-zert-di-rek-tor, Lud-wigs-ha-fen, ab-fah-ren, be-rich-ten, emp-fan-gen, a-ty-pisch, Des-il-lu-si-on, in-of-fi-zi-ell, ir-re-al*

E_2: Irreführende Trennungen sollte man vermeiden, zum Beispiel:
Altbau-erhaltung (nicht *Altbauer-haltung*)
Sprech-erziehung (nicht *Sprecher-ziehung*)
See-ufer (nicht *Seeu-fer*)

Zum Bindestrich zur Vermeidung von Missverständnissen siehe § 45 (3).

§ 112 Wörter, die sprachhistorisch oder von der Herkunftssprache her gesehen Zusammensetzungen sind, aber oft nicht mehr als solche empfunden oder erkannt werden, kann man entweder nach § 108 bis §110 oder nach § 111 trennen.

Beispiele:

hi-nauf/hin-auf, he-ran/her-an, da-rum/dar-um, wa-rum/war-um

ei-nan-der/ein-an-der, vol-len-den/voll-en-den, Klei-nod/Klein-od, Lie-be-nau /Lie-ben-au

Chry-san-the-me/Chrys-an-the-me, Hek-tar/Hekt-ar, He-li-kop-ter/He-li-ko-pter, in-te-res-sant/in-ter-es-sant, Li-no-le-um/Lin-ole-um, Pä-da-go-gik/Päd-a-go-gik

Notizen

Notizen

Notizen

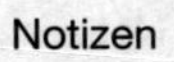
Notizen

Notizen